CHILTON'S TRUCK and VAN REPAIR MANUAL 1975-82

Pick-Ups, Vans, RV's and 4-Wheel Drives through 1 ton models

Editorial Director	Alan F. Turner
Managing Editor	Kerry A. Freeman, S.A.E.
Senior Editor	Richard J. Rivele, S.A.E.
Technical Editors	Martin A. Gunther
	Rob Webb
	Mark F. Devlin
	Lindsay Brooke
	Dean Morgantini
Production Manager	Warren Owens
Assistant Production Manager	Timothy Frelick
Production Assistant	Nancy A. Hassler
Mechanical Pasteup	Dru Brown
	Donna P. Fisher
	Robin Miller
	Margaret A. Stoner
	Geraldine M. Basso

OFFICERS

President	William A. Barbour
Executive Vice President	James Miades
Vice President & General Manager	John P. Kushnerick

CHILTON BOOK COMPANY
Chilton Way, Radnor, PA l9089

Manufactured in USA
© 1982 by Chilton Book Company
ISBN 0-8019-7150-0
Library of Congress Card No. 81-70221

234567890   098765432

CONTENTS

AMERICAN TRUCK SERVICE

IMPORT TRUCK SERVICE

AMERICAN TRUCK
UNIT REPAIR SECTIONS

AMERICAN TRUCK SECTION

Chevrolet and GMC

INDEX

BEFORE SERVICING, SEE THE SAFETY NOTICE AT THE FRONT OF THE BOOK

GENERAL ENGINE SPECIFICATIONS

Year	Engine No. Cyl Displacement Cu In.	Carburetor Type	Advertised Horsepower @ rpm ■	Advertised Torque @ rpm (ft lbs) ■	Bore and Stroke (in.)	Advertised Compression Ratio	Oil Pressure @ 2000 rpm
'75	6-250	1bbl	105 @ 3800	185 @ 1200	3.875 × 3.530	8.25:1	40
	6-292	1 bbl	120 @ 3600	213 @ 2000	3.875 × 4.120	8.0:1	40
	8-350	4 bbl	160 @ 3800	250 @ 2400	4.000 × 3.480	8.5:1	40
	8-350	4 bbl	160 @ 3800	250 @ 2400	4.000 × 3.480	8.5:1	40
	8-400	4 bbl	175 @ 3600	290 @ 2800	4.125 × 3.750	8.5:1	40
	8-454	4 bbl	245 @ 4000	355 @ 3000①	4.125 × 4.000	8.25:1	40
'76	6-250	1 bbl	105 @ 3800	185 @ 1200	3.875 × 3.530	8.25:1	40–60
	6-250 HD	1 bbl	100 @ 3600	175 @ 1800	3.875 × 3.530	8.25:1	40–60
	6-292	1 bbl	120 @ 3600	215 @ 2000	3.870 × 4.120	8.0:1	40–60
	8-350	2 bbl	145 @ 3800	250 @ 2200	4.000 × 3.480	8.5:1	40
	8-350	4 bbl	165 @ 3800	260 @ 2400②	4.000 × 3.480	8.5:1	40
	8-400	4 bbl	175 @ 3600	290 @ 2800	4.125 × 3.750	8.5:1	40
	8-454	4 bbl	245 @ 3800	365 @ 2800	4.251 × 4.000	8.25:1	40
	8-454 HD	4 bbl	240 @ 3800③	370 @ 2800④	4.251 × 4.000	8.15:1	40
'77	6-250	1 bbl	110 @ 3800	195 @ 1600	3.875 × 3.530	8.3:1	40–60
	6-250 HD	1 bbl	100 @ 3600	175 @ 1800	3.875 × 3.530	8.0:1	40–60
	6-292	1 bbl	120 @ 3600	215 @ 2000	3.870 × 4.120	8.0:1	40–60
	8-305⑤	2 bbl	145 @ 3800	245 @ 2200	3.740 × 3.480	8.5:1	40
	8-305 HD⑤	2 bbl	140 @ 3800	235 @ 2000	3.740 × 3.480	8.5:1	40
	8-350	4 bbl	165 @ 3800	260 @ 2400	4.000 × 3.480	8.5:1	40
	8-400	4 bbl	175 @ 3600	290 @ 2800	4.125 × 3.750	8.5:1	40
	8-454	4 bbl	245 @ 3800	365 @ 2800	4.251 × 4.000	8.25:1	40
	8-454 HD	4 bbl	240 @ 3800③	370 @ 2800④	4.251 × 4.000	8.15:1	40
'78	6-250 LD	1 bbl	115 @ 3800	195 @ 1600	3.870 × 3.530	8.0:1	40–60
	6-250 Calif	1 bbl	100 @ 3800	185 @ 1600	3.870 × 3.530	8.1:1	40–60
	6-250 HD	1 bbl	100 @ 3600	175 @ 1800	3.870 × 3.530	8.1:1	40–60
	6-292	1 bbl	120 @ 3600	215 @ 2000	3.870 × 4.120	8.0:1	40–60
	8-305	2 bbl	145 @ 3800	245 @ 2400	3.740 × 3.480	8.4:1	45
	8-350 LD	4 bbl	165 @ 3800	260 @ 2400	4.000 × 3.480	8.2:1	45
	8-350 HD	4 bbl	165 @ 3800	255 @ 2800	4.000 × 3.480	8.3:1	45
	8-350 Diesel	FI	120 @ 3600	220 @ 1600	4.057 × 3.385	22.5:1	35
	8-400	4 bbl	175 @ 3600	290 @ 2800	4.125 × 3.750	8.3:1	40
	8-400 Calif	4 bbl	165 @ 3600	290 @ 2000	4.125 × 3.750	8.2:1	40
	8-454 LD	4 bbl	205 @ 3600	335 @ 2800	4.250 × 4.000	8.0:1	40
	8-454 HD	4 bbl	240 @ 3800	370 @ 2800	4.250 × 4.000	7.9:1	40
	8-454 HD Calif	4 bbl	250 @ 3800	385 @ 2800	4.250 × 4.000	7.9:1	40

GENERAL ENGINE SPECIFICATIONS

Year	Engine No. Cyl Displacement Cu In.	Carburetor Type	Advertised Horsepower @ rpm ■	Advertised Torque @ rpm (ft lbs) ■	Bore and Stroke (in.)	Advertised Compression Ratio	Oil Pressure @ 2000 rpm
'79	6-250 LD	2 bbl	130 @ 3800	210 @ 2400	3.870 × 3.530	8.3:1	40–60
	6-250 Calif	2 bbl	125 @ 4000	205 @ 2000	3.870 × 3.530	8.3:1	40–60
	6-250 HD	2 bbl	130 @ 4000	205 @ 2000	3.870 × 3.530	8.3:1	40–60
	6-292	1 bbl	115 @ 3400	215 @ 1600	3.870 × 4.120	7.8:1	40–60
	8-305	2 bbl	140 @ 4000	240 @ 2000	3.740 × 3.480	8.4:1	45
	8-350 LD	4 bbl	165 @ 3600	270 @ 2000	4.000 × 3.480	8.2:1	45
	8-350 Hi Alt	4 bbl	155 @ 3600	260 @ 2000	4.000 × 3.480	8.2:1	45
	8-350 HD	4 bbl	165 @ 3800	255 @ 2800	4.000 × 3.480	8.3:1	45
	8-350	Diesel	120 @ 3600	220 @ 1600	4.057 × 3.385	22.5:1	35
	8-400 HD	4 bbl	180 @ 3600	310 @ 2400	4.125 × 3.750	8.2:1	40
	8-454 LD	4 bbl	205 @ 3600	335 @ 2800	4.250 × 4.000	8.0:1	40
	8-454 HD	4 bbl	210 @ 3800	340 @ 2800	4.250 × 4.000	7.9:1	40
'80	6-250	2 bbl	130 @ 4000	210 @ 2000	3.870 × 3.530	8.3:1	40–60
	6-250 Calif	2 bbl	130 @ 4000	205 @ 2000	3.870 × 3.530	8.3:1	40–60
	6-292	1 bbl	115 @ 3400	215 @ 1600	3.870 × 4.120	7.8:1	40–60
	8-305	2 bbl	135 @ 4200	235 @ 2400	3.740 × 3.480	8.5:1	45
	8-350 LD	4 bbl	175 @ 4000	275 @ 2400	4.000 × 3.480	8.2:1	45
	8-350 LD Calif	4 bbl	170 @ 4000	275 @ 2000	4.000 × 3.480	8.2:1	45
	8-350 HD	4 bbl	165 @ 3800	255 @ 2800	4.000 × 3.480	8.3:1	45
	8-350	Diesel	125 @ 3600	225 @ 1600	4.057 × 3.385	22.5:1	35
	8-400 HD	4 bbl	180 @ 3600	310 @ 2400	4.125 × 3.750	8.3:1	40
	8-454 HD	4 bbl	210 @ 3800	340 @ 2800	4.250 × 4.000	7.9:1	40
'81	6-250	2 bbl	130 @ 4000	210 @ 2000	3.870 × 3.530	8.3:1	40–60
	6-250 Calif	2 bbl	130 @ 4000	205 @ 2000	3.870 × 3.530	8.3:1	40–60
	6-292	1 bbl	115 @ 3400	215 @ 1600	3.870 × 4.120	7.8:1	40–60
	8-305	2 bbl	135 @ 4200	235 @ 2400	3.740 × 3.480	8.5:1	45
	8-305	4 bbl	155 @ 4400	252 @ 2400	3.740 × 3.480	9.2:1	45
	8-350 LD	4 bbl	175 @ 4000	275 @ 2000	4.000 × 3.480	8.2:1	45
	8-350 HD	4 bbl	165 @ 3800	255 @ 2800	4.000 × 3.480	8.3:1	45
	8-350	Diesel	125 @ 3600	225 @ 1600	4.057 × 3.385	22.5:1	35
	8-454	4 bbl	210 @ 3800	340 @ 2800	4.250 × 4.000	7.9:1	40
'82	6-250	2 bbl	130 @ 4000	210 @ 2000	3.870 × 3.530	8.3:1	40–60
	6-292	1 bbl	115 @ 3400	215 @ 1600	3.870 × 4.120	7.8:1	40–60
	8-305	4 bbl	140 @ 4200	240 @ 2400	3.740 × 3.480	8.5:1	45
	8-305	4 bbl	155 @ 4400	252 @ 2100	3.740 × 3.480	9.2:1	45
	8-350 LD	4 bbl	175 @ 4000	275 @ 2000	4.000 × 3.480	8.2:1	45

CHEVROLET/GMC
PICK-UPS, VANS, BLAZER, JIMMY, SUBURBAN

GENERAL ENGINE SPECIFICATIONS

Year	Engine No. Cyl Displacement Cu In.	Carburetor Type	Advertised Horsepower @ rpm ∎	Advertised Torque @ rpm (ft lbs) ∎	Bore and Stroke (in.)	Advertised Compression Ratio	Oil Pressure @ 2000 rpm
	8-350 HD	4 bbl	165 @ 3800	255 @ 2800	4.000 × 3.480	8.3:1	45
	8-379	Diesel	130 @ 3600	240 @ 2000	3.980 × 3.800	21.5:1	45
	8-454	4 bbl	210 @ 3800	340 @ 2800	4.250 × 4.000	7.9:1	40

∎Starting 1972, horsepower and torque are SAE net figures. They are measured at the rear of the transmission with all accessories installed and operating. Since the figures vary when a given engine is installed in different models, some are representative rather than exact.

① 375 @ 2800—Calif.
② 255 @ 2800 HD
③ 250 @ 3800—Calif.
④ 385 @ 2800—Calif.
⑤ Not available in California
FI—Fuel Injection

CAPACITIES
Blazer and Jimmy

Year	Engine No. Cyl. Displacement (cu in.)	Engine Crankcase (qts) incl. Filter	Transmission Pts To Refill After Draining 3-Speed	4-Speed	Automatic	Transfer Case (Pts)	Drive Axle (pts) Front/ Rear	Gasoline Tank (gals) Std/ Opt	Cooling System ∎ (qts) With Heater	A/C	With HD Cooling
'75	6-250	5	3	8	5	—	—/3½	25/30	14.8	15.6	14.8
	8-350 2 bbl	5	3	—	5	—	—/3½	25/30	17.6	18	18
	8-350 4 bbl	5	—	8	5	5④	5/3½	25/30	17.6	18	18
	8-400	5	—	—	5	5④	5/3½	25/30	19.6	20.4	20.4
'76	6-250	5	3③	8	5	5④	5/3½	25/31	14.8	15.6	14.8
	8-350	5	3③	8	5	5④	5/3½	25/31	17.6	18	18
	8-400	5	—	—	5	5④	5/3½	25/31	19.6	20.4	20.4
'77	6-250	5	3.5	8.3	5	5④	5/3½	25/31	14.8	15.6	14.8
	8-305	5	3.5	8.3	5	5④	5/3½	25/31	17.6	18	18
	8-350	5	3.5	8.3	5	5④	5/3½	25/31	17.6	18	18
	8-400	5	—	—	5	5④	5/3½	25/31	19.6	20.4	20.4
'78	6-250	5	3	8	5	5④	5/3.5⑤	25/31	15	15.6	15.6
	8-305	5	3	8	5	5④	5/3.5⑤	25/31	17.5	18	18.4
	8-350	5	3.0	8.0	5.0	5.0④	5/3.5⑤	25/31	17.6	17.6	17.6
	8-400	5	—	—	5.0	5.0④	5/3.5⑤	25/31	19.7	20.4	20.4
'79	6-250	5	3.0	8.0	5.0	5.0④	5/3.5⑤	25//31	15	15.5	15.5
	8-305	5	3.0	8.0	5.0	5.0④	5/3.5⑤	25/31	17.5	17.5	17.5
	8-350	5	3.0	8.0	5.0	5.0④	5/3.5⑤	25/31	17.5	18	18
	8-400	5	—	—	5.0	5.0④	5/3.5⑤	25/31	18	19	19
'80–'81	6-250	5	3.0	8.0	5.0	5.0	5/3.5⑤	25/31	15	15.5	15.5
	8-305	5	3.0	8.0	5.0	5.0	5/3.5⑤	25/31	17.5	17.5	17.5
	8-350	5	3.0	8.0	5.0	5.0	5/3.5⑤	25/31	17.5	18	18

CAPACITIES
Blazer and Jimmy

| Year | Engine No. Cyl. Displacement (cu in.) | Engine Crankcase (qts) incl. Filter | Transmission Pts To Refill After Draining | | | Transfer Case (Pts) | Drive Axle (pts) Front/ Rear | Gasoline Tank (gals) Std/ Opt | Cooling System■ (qts) | | |
| | | | Manual | | Automatic | | | | With Heater | A/C | With HD Cooling |
			3-Speed	4-Speed							
'82	6-250	5	2.0	8.0	6.0	5.0	5/⑦	25/31	15.0	15.5	—
	8-305	5	2.0	8.0	6.0	5.0	5/⑦	25/31	17.5	18.0	—
	8-350	5	2.0	8.0	6.0⑥	5.0	5/⑦	25/31	17.5	18.0	—
	8-379	7	—	8.0	6.0⑥	5.0	5/⑦	27/32	24.8	24.8	—

■ Automatic transmission models have either
the A/C or HD radiator; capacity may be
increased on trucks with 4.11:1 axle ratios;
when two figures are separated by a slash,
the first is for 2 wheel drive
① 5 with automatic transmission
② 5 with automatic or 4-speed transmission
③ 3½ with top-cover Tremec three-speed
④ 8¼ with full-time 4 wheel drive

⑤ 8.5 ring gear—4.2
⑥ with TH-M 400: 7.0
with TH-M 700-R4: 10.0
⑦ 8½" ring gear: 4.25
8⅞" ring gear: 3.5
9¾" ring gear (Dana): 6.0
10½" ring gear (Dana): 7.2
(Chev.): 6.5

CAPACITIES
Pick-Ups and Suburban

| Year | Engine Displacement (cu. in.) | Engine Crankcase (qts) With Filter | Transmission (pts) | | Auto (Refill) | Drive Axle (pts) | | Transfer Case (pts) | Fuel Tank (gals) | Cooling System (qts) | | |
| | | | Manual | | | Front | Rear | | | w/o A/C | w/A/C | HD |
			3-spd	4-spd								
'75	6-250	5	3.2⑦	8.3	②	5	⑥	20⑩	5⑤	14.8	15.4	14.8
	6-292	6	3.2⑦	8.3	②	5	⑥	20⑩	5⑤	14.8	15.6	14.8
	8-350	5	3.2⑦	8.3	②	5	⑥	20⑩	5⑤	17.6	18.0	18.0
	8-400	5	3.2⑦	8.3	②	5	⑥	20⑩	5⑤	19.6	20.4	20.4
	8-454	5	3.2⑦	8.3	②	5	⑥	20⑩	5⑤	24.8	24.8	24.8
'76–'81	6-250	5	3.2⑦	8.0	②	5⑧	⑥	20⑩	5⑤	15.0	15.6	15.0
	6-292	6	3.2⑦	8.0	②	5⑧	⑥	20⑩	5⑤	14.8	15.4	14.8
	8-305	5	3.2⑦	8.0	②	5⑧	⑥	20⑩	5⑤	17.6	18.0	18.0
	8-350	5	3.2⑦	8.0	②	5⑧	⑥	20⑩	5⑤	17.6	18.0	18.0
	8-350 Diesel	7	—	—	5.0	—	⑥	20⑩	—	18.0	18.0	18.0
	8-400	5	3.2⑦	8.0	②	5⑧	⑥	20⑩	5⑤	20.4	20.4	20.4
	8-454	5⑪	3.2⑦	8.0	②	5⑧	⑥	20⑩	5⑤	24.4⑨	24.7	24.7
'82	6-250	5	3.0	8.0	6.0	5.0	⑯	5.0⑬	⑭	15.0	15.5	—
	6-292	6	3.0	8.0	6.0	5.0	⑯	5.0⑬	⑭	15.0	15.5	—
	8-305	5	3.0	8.0	6.0	5.0	⑯	5.0⑬	⑭	17.5	18.0	—
	8-350	5	3.0	8.0	⑮	5.0	⑯	5.0⑬	⑭	17.5	18.0	—

CAPACITIES
Pick-Ups and Suburban

Year	Engine Displacement (cu. in.)	Engine Crankcase (qts) With Filter	Transmission (pts)			Drive Axle (pts)		Transfer Case (pts)	Fuel Tank (gals)	Cooling System (qts)		
			Manual		Auto (Refill)							
			3-spd	4-spd		Front	Rear			w/o A/C	w/A/C	HD
	8-379	7	—	8.0	⑮	5.0	⑯	5.0⑬	⑭	23.0	24.5	—
	8-454	7	—	8.0	⑮	5.0	⑯	5.0⑬	⑭	23.0	24.5	—

① Heavy-duty 3-speed—3.5 pts
② Turbo Hydra-Matic 350—5.0 pts
  Turbo Hydra-Matic 400—7.5 pts
③ 3,300 and 3,500 lb Chevrolet axles—4.5 pts
  5,200 and 7,200 lb Chevrolet axles—6.5 pts
  5,500 lb Dana axles—6.0 pts
  11,000 lb Chevrolet axles—14.0 pts
④ 20 Series—21.0 gals
⑤ Full-time 4 wd—8.25 pts
⑥ 8½ in. ring gear—4.2 pts
  8⅞ in. ring gear (Chevrolet)—4.5 pts (3.5 pts '77–'78)
  10½ in. ring gear (Chevrolet)—5.4 pts

10½ in. ring gear (Dana)—7.2 pts
12½ in. ring gear (Chevrolet)—26.8 pts
⑦ Tremec 3-spd—4.0 pts
  Muncie 3-spd—3.0 pts
⑧ 8½ in. ring gear—4.25 pts ('77–'81)
⑨ 22.8—'79–'81
⑩ 16.0 gal—short wheelbase models
⑪ 6 qts with filter, 5 qts without filter, '78–'81
⑫ OPT.: 20 gal
⑬ All 1-ton models: 10.0
⑭ Short bed w/single tank: 16 gal.
  Short bed w/dual tanks: 32 gal.
  Longbed w/single tank: 20 gal.
  Long bed gasoline models w/dual tanks, under 8600 lb GVWR: 32 gal

Long bed gasoline models with dual tanks over 8600 lb GVWR, and all diesel models w/dual tanks: 40 gal.
⑮ TH-M 350: 6.0
  TH-M 400: 7.0
  TH-M 700-R4:10.0
⑯ Ring gear / Capacity
  8½" — 4.25
  8⅞" — 3.5
  9¾" (Dana) — 6.0
  10½" (Dana) — 7.2
  10½" (Chev) — 6.5
  12¼" (Dana) — 26.8

CAPACITIES
Vans

Year	Model	Engine Displacement (cu in.)	Engine Crankcase (qts) With Filter	Transmission (pts)			Drive Axle (pts)	Gasoline Tank (gals)	Cooling System (qts)	
				Manual		Automatic			wo/AC	w/AC
				3-spd	4-spd					
'75	All	6-250	5	3.2	—	5	4.3	21/36	15	16.5
	20, 2500	6-292	6	3.2	—	5	3.5	21/36	14.8	15.7
	30, 3500	6-292	6	3.2	—	5	5.4	21/36	14.8	15.7
	All	8-350 2 bbl	5	3.2	—	5	4.3	21/36	17.5	19.0
'75	10, 1500	8-350 4 bbl	5	3.2	—	5	4.3	21/36	18	19.5
	20, 2500	8-350 4 bbl	5	4.6	—	5	3.5	21/36	18	19.5
	30, 3500	8-350 4 bbl	5	4.6	—	5	5.4	21/36	18	19.5
	20, 2500	8-400	5	—	—	5	3.5	21/36	19.9	21.0
	30, 2500	8-400	5	—	—	5	5.4	21/36	19.9	21.0
'76	All	6-250	5	3.2	—	5	4.3	21/36	15	16.5
	20, 2500	6-292	6	3.2	—	5	3.5	21/36	14.8	15.7
	30, 3500	6-292	6	3.2	—	5	5.4	21/36	14.8	15.7
	10, 1500	8-350	5	4.6	—	5	4.3	21/36	18	19.5
	20, 2500	8-350	5	4.6	—	5	3.5	21/36	18	19.5
	30, 3500	8-350	5	4.6	—	5	5.4	21/36	18	19.5

CAPACITIES
Vans

Year	Model	Engine Displacement (cu in.)	Engine Crankcase (qts) With Filter	Transmission (pts) Manual 3-spd	4-spd	Automatic	Drive Axle (pts)	Gasoline Tank (gals)	Cooling System (qts) wo/AC	w/AC
	20, 2500	8-400	5	—	—	5	3.5	21/36	19.9	21.0
	30, 3500	8-400	5	—	—	5	5.4	21/36	19.9	21.0
'77–'78	All	6-250	5	3.2	—	5	3.5	22/33	15	16.5
	20, 2500	6-292	6	3.2	—	5	3.5	22/33	14.8	15.7
	30, 3500	6-292	6	3.2	—	5	5.4	22/33	14.8	15.7
	All	8-305	5	3.2	—	5	3.5	22/33	18	19.5
	10, 20, 1500, 2500	8-350	5	4.6①	—	5	3.5	22/33	18	19.5
	30, 3500	8-350	5	4.6①	—	5②	5.4	22/33	18	19.5
	20, 2500	8-400	5	—	—	5	3.5	22/33	19.9	21.0
	30, 3500	8-400	5	—	—	5②	5.4	22/33	19.9	21.0
'79–'82	All	6-250	5	3.2	—	5③	3.5④	22/33	17	18.5
	All	8-305	5	3.2①	—	5③	3.5④	22/33	19.5	21.0
	10, 20, 1500, 2500	8-350	5	3.2①	—	5③	3.5④	22/33	20	21.5
	30, 3500	8-350	5	3.2①	—	5③	3.5④	22/33	20	21.5
	All	8-400	5	3.2①	—	5③	3.5④	22/33	20	21.5

① 4 pts with top-cover Tremec three-speed and Saginaw three-speed
② 7 pts with 10,000 lb or higher GVW.
③ '82 TH-M 350: 6.0
  TH-M 400: 7.0
  TH-M 700-R4: 10.0
④ 9¾" ring gear: 6.0
  10½" ring gear (Dana): 7.2
  10½" ring gear (Chev): 6.5
  12½" ring gear (Dana): 26.8

TUNE-UP SPECIFICATIONS
Pick-ups and Suburban

Year	Engine Displacement (cu in.)	Spark Plugs Type	Gap (in.)	Distributor Point Dwell (deg)	Point Gap (in.)	Ignition Timing (deg) MT	AT	Fuel Pump Pressure (psi)	Compression Pressure (psi) ●	Idle Speed (rpm)* MT	AT	Valve Clearance (in.) Ex	In
'75	6-250	R46TX	0.060	—	—	10B	10B	3.5–4.5	130	900	550	Hyd	Hyd
	6-292 (HD)	R44TX	0.060	—	—	8B	8B	3.5–4.5	130	600	600	Hyd	Hyd
	8-350 (2 bbl)	R44TX	0.060	—	—	—	6B	7.0–8.5	150	—	600	Hyd	Hyd
	8-350 (4 bbl)	R44TX	0.060	—	—	6B	6B	7.0–8.5	150	800	600	Hyd	Hyd
	8-350 (HD, Fed)	R44TX	0.060	—	—	8B	8B	7.0–8.5	150	600	600	Hyd	Hyd
	8-350 (HD, Calif)	R44TX	0.060	—	—	2B	2B	7.0–8.5	150	700	700	Hyd	Hyd
	8-400 (HD, Fed)	R44TX	0.060	—	—	4B	4B	7.0–8.5	150	700	700	Hyd	Hyd
	8-400 (HD, Calif)	R44TX	0.060	—	—	2B	2B	7.0–8.5	150	700	700	Hyd	Hyd
	8-454 (LD)	R44TX	0.060	—	—	—	16B	7.0–8.5	150	—	650	Hyd	Hyd
	8-454 (HD, Fed)	R44TX	0.060	—	—	8B	8B	7.0–8.5	150	700	700	Hyd	Hyd
	8-454 (HD, Calif)	R44TX	0.060	—	—	8B	8B	7.0–8.5	150	600	600	Hyd	Hyd

CHEVROLET/GMC
PICK-UPS, VANS, BLAZER, JIMMY, SUBURBAN

TUNE-UP SPECIFICATIONS
Pick-ups and Suburban

Year	Engine Displacement (cu in.)	Spark Plugs Type	Gap (in.)	Distributor Point Dwell (deg)	Point Gap (in.)	Ignition Timing (deg) MT	AT	Fuel Pump Pressure (psi)	Compression Pressure (psi) ●	Idle Speed (rpm)* MT	AT	Valve Clearance (in.) Ex	In
'76	6-250	R46TS	0.035	—	—	10B	10B	3.5–4.5	130	900	550	Hyd	Hyd
	6-250 (Calif)	R46TS	0.035	—	—	6B	10B	3.5–4.5	130	1000	600	Hyd	Hyd
	6-250 (HD)	R46T	0.035	—	—	6B	6B	3.5–4.5	130	600	600(N)	Hyd	Hyd
	6-292 (HD)	R44T	0.035	—	—	8B	8B	3.5–4.5	130	600	600(N)	Hyd	Hyd
	8-350	R45TS	0.045	—	—	2B	6B	7–8.5	150	800	600	Hyd	Hyd
	8-350 (4 bbl)	R45TS	0.045	—	—	8B	8B	7–8.5	150	800	600	Hyd	Hyd
	8-350 (4 bbl Calif)	R45TS	0.045	—	—	6B	6B	7–8.5	150	800	600	Hyd	Hyd
	8-350 (HD)	R44TX	0.060	—	—	8B	8B	7–8.5	150	600	600(N)	Hyd	Hyd
	8-350 (HD Calif)	R44TX	0.060	—	—	2B	2B	7–8.5	150	700	700(N)	Hyd	Hyd
	8-400 (HD)	R44TX	0.060	—	—	4B	4B	7–8.5	150	—	700(N)	Hyd	Hyd
	8-400 (HD Calif)	R44TX	0.060	—	—	2B	2B	7–8.5	150	—	700(N)	Hyd	Hyd
	8-454 (w/cat)	R45TS	0.045	—	—	12B	12B	7–8.5	150	—	600	Hyd	Hyd
	8-454 (w/o cat)	R45TS	0.045	—	—	8B	8B	7–8.5	150	—	600	Hyd	Hyd
	8-454 (HD)	R44T	0.045	—	—	8B	8B	7–8.5	150	700	700(N)	Hyd	Hyd
'77	6-250	R46TS	0.035	—	—	8B	12B	3.5–4.5	130	750	550	Hyd	Hyd
	6-250 (High Alt)	R46TS	0.035	—	—	8B	12B	3.5–4.5	130	750	600	Hyd	Hyd
	6-250 (Calif)	R46TS	0.035	—	—	6B	10B	3.5–4.5	130	850	600	Hyd	Hyd
	6-250 (HD)	R46T	0.035	—	—	6B	6B	3.5–4.5	130	600	600(N)	Hyd	Hyd
	6-292	R44T	0.035	—	—	8B	8B	3.5–4.5	130	600	600(N)	Hyd	Hyd
	8-305	R45TS	0.045	—	—	8B	8B	7–8.5	150	600	500	Hyd	Hyd
	8-305 (HD)	R44T	0.045	—	—	6B	6B	7–8.5	150	700	700(N)	Hyd	Hyd
	8-350	R45TS	0.045	—	—	8B	8B	7–8.5	150	700	500	Hyd	Hyd
	8-350 (High Alt)	R45TS	0.045	—	—	—	6B	7–8.5	150	—	600	Hyd	Hyd
	8-350 (Calif)	R45TS	0.045	—	—	6B	6B	7–8.5	150	700	500	Hyd	Hyd
	8-350 (HD)	R44T	0.045	—	—	8B	8B	7–8.5	150	700	700(N)	Hyd	Hyd
	8-350 (HD Calif)	R44TX	0.060	—	—	2B	2B	7–8.5	150	700	700(N)	Hyd	Hyd
	8-400 (HD)	R44T	0.045	—	—	—	4B	7–8.5	150	—	700(N)	Hyd	Hyd
	8-400 (HD Calif)	R44T	0.045	—	—	—	2B	7–8.5	150	—	700(N)	Hyd	Hyd
	8-454	R45TS	0.045	—	—	—	4B	7–8.5	150	—	600	Hyd	Hyd
	8-454 (HD)	R44T	0.045	—	—	8B	8B	7–8.5	150	700	700(N)	Hyd	Hyd
'78	6-250 (LD Fed)	R46TS	0.035	—	—	8B	8B	4.5–6.0	130	750	550	Hyd	Hyd
	6-250 (LD Calif)	R46TS	0.035	—	—	8B	8B	4.5–6.0	130	750	750	Hyd	Hyd
	6-250 (LD High Alt)	R46TS	0.035	—	—	8B	12B	4.5–6.0	130	750	600	Hyd	Hyd
	6-250 (HD)	R46T	0.035	—	—	6B	6B	4.5–6.0	130	600	600(N)	Hyd	Hyd
	6-292 (HD)	R44T	0.035	—	—	8B	8B	4.5–6.0	130	600	600(N)	Hyd	Hyd
	8-305 (LD)	R45TS	0.045	—	—	4B	4B	7.5–9.0	150	600	500	Hyd	Hyd

TUNE-UP SPECIFICATIONS
Pick-ups and Suburban

Year	Engine Displacement (cu in.)	Spark Plugs Type	Gap (in.)	Distributor Point Dwell (deg)	Point Gap (in.)	Ignition Timing (deg) MT	AT	Fuel Pump Pressure (psi)	Compression Pressure (psi) ●	Idle Speed (rpm)* MT	AT	Valve Clearance (in.) Ex	In
	8-305 (HD)	R44T	0.045	—	—	6B	6B	7.5–9.0	150	700	700(N)	Hyd	Hyd
	8-350 (LD)	R45TS	0.045	—	—	8B	8B	7.5–9.0	150	600①	500	Hyd	Hyd
	8-350 (HD Fed)	R44T	0.045	—	—	8B	8B	7.5–9.0	150	700	700(N)	Hyd	Hyd
	8-350 (HD Calif)	R44TX	0.060	—	—	2B	2B	7.5–9.0	150	700	700(N)	Hyd	Hyd
	8-400 (LD)	R45TS	0.045	—	—	—	4B	7.5–9.0	150	—	500	Hyd	Hyd
	8-400 (HD Fed)	R44T	0.045	—	—	—	4B	7.5–9.0	150	—	700(N)	Hyd	Hyd
	8-400 (HD Calif)	R44T	0.045	—	—	—	2B	7.5–9.0	150	—	700(N)	Hyd	Hyd
	8-454 (LD Fed)	R45TS	0.045	—	—	—	8B	7.5–9.0②	150	—	550	Hyd	Hyd
	8-454 (LD Calif)	R45TS	0.045	—	—	—	8B	7.5–9.0②	150	—	700(N)	Hyd	Hyd
	8-454 (HD)	R44T	0.045	—	—	8B	8B	7.5–9.0②	150	700	700(N)	Hyd	Hyd
'79	6-250 (LD Fed)	R46TS	0.035	—	—	10B	10B	4.5–6.0	130	750	600	Hyd	Hyd
	6-250③	R46TS	0.035	—	—	6B	8B	4.5–6.0	130	750	600	Hyd	Hyd
	6-292	R44T	0.035	—	—	8B	8B	4.5–6.0	130	700	700	Hyd	Hyd
	8-305	R45TS	0.045	—	—	6B	6B	7.5–9.0	150	600	500	Hyd	Hyd
	8-350 (LD)	R45TS	0.045	—	—	8B	8B	7.5–9.0	150	700	500	Hyd	Hyd
	8-350 (HD)	R44T	0.045	—	—	4B	4B	7.5–9.0	150	700	700(N)	Hyd	Hyd
	8-400	R45TS	0.045	—	—	—	4B	7.5–9.0	150	—	500	Hyd	Hyd
	8-454 (LD)	R45TS	0.045	—	—	8B	8B	7.5–9.0②	150	700	500	Hyd	Hyd
	8-454 (HD)	R44T	0.045	—	—	—	4B	7.5–9.0②	150	—	700(N)	Hyd	Hyd
'80	6-250 (LD Fed)	R46TS	0.035	—	—	10B	10B	4.5–6.0	130	750	650	Hyd	Hyd
	6-250 (LD Calif)	R46TS	0.035	—	—	10B	10B	4.5–6.0	130	750	600	Hyd	Hyd
	6-250③	R46TS	0.035	—	—	—	8B	4.5–6.0	130	—	600	Hyd	Hyd
	6-292	R44T	0.035	—	—	8B	8B	4.5–6.0	130	700	700(N)	Hyd	Hyd
	8-305	R45TS	0.045	—	—	8B	8B	7.5–9.0	150	600	500	Hyd	Hyd
	8-350 (LD)	R45TS	0.045	—	—	8B	8B	7.5–9.0	150	700	500	Hyd	Hyd
	8-350 (HD Fed)	R44T	0.045	—	—	4B	4B	7.5–9.0	150	700	700(N)	Hyd	Hyd
	8-350 (HD Calif)	R44T	0.045	—	—	6B	6B	7.5–9.0	150	700	700(N)	Hyd	Hyd
	8-400 (HD Fed)	R44T	0.045	—	—	—	4B	7.5–9.0	150	—	700(N)	Hyd	Hyd
	8-400 (HD Calif)	R44T	0.045	—	—	—	6B	7.5–9.0	150	—	700(N)	Hyd	Hyd
	8-454	R44T	0.045	—	—	4B	4B	7.5–9.0②	150	700	700(N)	Hyd	Hyd
'81	6-250 (Fed)	R45TS	0.035	—	—	10B	10B	4.5–6.0	130	750	650(D)	—	—
	6-250 (Calif)	R46TS	0.035	—	—	10B	10B	4.5–6.0	130	750	650(D)	—	—
	6-292	R44T	0.035	—	—	8B	8B	4.5–6.0	130	700	700(N)	—	—
	8-305 2 bbl	R45TS	0.045	—	—	8B	8B	7.5–9.0	150	600	500(D)	—	—
	8-305 4 bbl	R45TS	0.045	—	—	4B	4B④	7.5–9.0	150	700	500(D)	—	—
	8-350 (LD)	R45TS	0.045	—	—	8B	8B⑤	7.5–9.0	150	700	500(D)	—	—
	8-350 (HD Fed)	R44T	0.045	—	—	4B	4B	7.5–9.0	150	700	700(N)	—	—
	8-350 (HD Calif)	R44T	0.045	—	—	6B	6B	7.5–9.0	150	700	700(N)	—	—

TUNE-UP SPECIFICATIONS
Pick-ups and Suburban

Year	Engine Displacement (cu in.)	Spark Plugs Type	Gap (in.)	Point Dwell (deg)	Point Gap (in.)	Ignition Timing (deg) MT	AT	Fuel Pump Pressure (psi)	Compression Pressure (psi) ●	Idle Speed (rpm)* MT	AT	Valve Clearance (in.) Ex	In
	8-350 Diesel	—	—	—	—	—	8B⑥		450	—	575(D)⑦	—	—
	8-454	R44T	0.045	—	—	4B	4B	7.5–9.0	150	700	700(N)	—	—
'82	See underhood specifications sticker												

NOTE: Part numbers in this chart are not recommendations by Chilton for any product by brand name.

● Maximum variation among cylinders—20 psi
B Before Top Dead Center
LD Light-duty
HD Heavy-duty
Fed Federal (49 states)
Calif California only
MT Manual transmission
AT Automatic transmission
N Neutral

* Automatic transmission idle speed set in Drive unless otherwise indicated
NA Not available
— Not applicable
Hyd Hydraulic
① 700 rpm—California
② 5.5–7.0 with vapor return line
③ California C-20, C-2500 only

④ Calif.: 8B
   High Alt.: 2B
   Emission Label Code AAN: 6B
⑤ Calif.: 6B
   Calif. w/Emission Label Code AAD: 8B
⑥ Calif.: 5B
⑦ Calif.: 600(D)

TUNE-UP SPECIFICATIONS
Vans

When analyzing compression results, look for uniformity among cylinders rather than specific pressures.

Year	Engine Cu In. Displacement	Spark Plugs Orig Type	Gap (in.)	Point Dwell (deg)	Point Gap (in.)	Ignition Timing (deg)▲ MT	AT	Intake Valve Opens (deg)	Fuel Pump Pressure (psi)	Curb Idle Speed (rpm)● MT	AT
'75	6-250	R46TX	.060	Electronic		10B	10B	16	3.5–4.5	900	550
	6-292	R44TX	.060	Electronic		8B	8B	33	3.5–4.5	600	600
	8-350 (2-bbl)	R44TX	.060	Electronic		①	6B	28	7–8.5	①	600
	8-350 (4-bbl) LD	R44TX	.060	Electronic		6B	6B	28	7–8.5	800	600
	8-350 (4-bbl) HD	R44TX	060	Electronic		8B(2B)	8B(2B)	28	7–8.5	600(700)	600(700)
	8-400	R44TX	.060	Electronic		—	4B(8B)	28	7–8.5	—	700
'76	6-250	R46TS	.035	Electronic		6B	10B	16	3.5–4.5	900(1000)②	550(600)②
	6-292	R44T	.035	Electronic		8B	8B	33	3.5–4.5	600	600N
	8-350 (2-bbl)	R45TS	.045	Electronic		2B	6B	28	7–8.5	800	600
	8-350 (4-bbl) LD	R45TS	.045	Electronic		8B(6B)	8B(6B)	28	7–8.5	800	600
	8-350 (4-bbl) HD	R44TX	.060	Electronic		8B(2B)	8B(2B)	28	7–8.5	600(700)	600(700) N
	8-400	R44TX	.060	Electronic		—	4B	28	7–8.5	—	700N
'77	6-250	R46TS	.035	Electronic		8B(6B)	12B (10B)	16	3.5–4.5	750(850)②	600②
	6-292	R44T	.035	Electronic		8B	8B	33	3.5–4.5	600	600 N
	8-305	R45TS	.045	Electronic		8B	8B	28	7–8.5	600	500
	8-350 LD	R45TS	.045	Electronic		8B(6B)	8B(6B)	28	7–8.5	700	500
	8-350 HD	R44T (R44TX)	.045 (.060)	Electronic		8B(2B)	8B(2B)	28	7–8.5	700	700N
	8-400	R44T	.045	Electronic		—	4B(2B)	28	7–8.5	—	700N

TUNE-UP SPECIFICATIONS
Vans

When analyzing compression results, look for uniformity among cylinders rather than specific pressures.

Year	Engine Cu In. Displacement	Spark Plugs Orig Type	Spark Plugs Gap (in.)	Distributor Point Dwell (deg)	Distributor Point Gap (in.)	Ignition Timing (deg)▲ MT	Ignition Timing (deg)▲ AT	Intake Valve Opens (deg)	Fuel Pump Pressure (psi)	Curb Idle Speed (rpm)● MT	Curb Idle Speed (rpm)● AT
'78	6-250	R46TS	.035	Electronic		8B	8B (10B) ④	16	4.5–6	750	600③
	6-292	R44T	.035	Electronic		8B	8B	33	4.5–6	600	600
	8-305	R45TS	.045	Electronic		4B	4B	28	7.5–9	600	500
	8-350 LD	R45TS	.045	Electronic		8B	8B	28	7.5–9	600(700)	500
	8-350 HD	R44T (R44TX)	.045 (.060)	Electronic		8B(2B)	8B(2B)	28	7.5–9	700	700
	8-400 LD⑤	R45TS	.045	Electronic		—	4B	28	7.5–9	—	500
	8-400 HD	R44T	.045	Electronic		—	4B(2B)	28	7.5–9	—	700
'79	6-250	R46TS	.035	Electronic		10B⑥	10B⑦	16	4.5–6	750	600
	8-305	R45TS	.045	Electronic		6B	6B	28	7.5–9	700	600
'79	8–350⑧	R45TS	.045	Electronic		8B	8B	28	7.5–9	700	500
	8-400⑧	R45TS	.045	Electronic		—	4B	28	7.5–9	—	500
'80–'81	6-250	R46TS	.035	Electronic		10B	8B⑨	16	4–6	750	650(D)
	8-305 (2-bbl)	R45TS	.045	Electronic		8B	8B	28	7–9	700	600(D)
	8-305 (4-bbl)	R45TS	.045	Electronic		6B	4B	28	7–9	700	500(D)
	8-350	R45TS	.045	Electronic		8B⑩	8B⑪	28	7–9	700	500(D)⑫
'82	see the underhood specifications sticker										

NOTE: The underhood specifications sticker often reflects tune-up specifications changes made in production. Sticker figures must be used if they disagree with those in this chart.

NOTE: Part numbers in this chart are not recommendations by Chilton for any product by brand name.

● Figures in parentheses are for California, and are given only if they differ from the 49 state specification. Automatic transmission idle speeds are set in Drive, unless specified otherwise.

▲ At idle speed with vacuum advance hose disconnected and plugged, unless specified otherwise in the text.

N—Transmission in Neutral
D—Transmission in Drive

HD Heavy Duty
LD Light Duty
① See the underhood specifications sticker
② Air conditioner on
③ 49 state without A/C—550
④ High alt.—12B
⑤ California only
⑥ G-20, G-30, 2500, 3500 series in Calif.—6B
⑦ G-20, G-30, 2500, 3500 series in Calif.—8B

⑧ Some G-30/3500 series vans differ. Check the underhood emission sticker.
⑨ High Alt.—10B
⑩ Fed 1 ton models—4B
   Calif ¾ and 1 ton models—6B
⑪ 1 ton models—6B
⑫ 1 ton models—700(N)
   Calif. ½ and ¾ ton models—550 (D)

TUNE-UP SPECIFICATIONS
Blazer/Jimmy

When analyzing compression test results, look for uniformity among cylinders rather than specific pressures.

Year	Engine No. Cyl Displacement	Spark Plugs Orig Type	Spark Plugs ● Gap (in.)	Distributor Point Dwell (deg)	Distributor Point Gap (in.)	Ignition Timing (deg) Man Trans	Ignition Timing (deg) ● Auto Trans	Fuel Pump Pressure (psi)	Idle Speed (rpm) Man Trans	Idle Speed (rpm) ● Auto Trans ▲
'75	6-250	R46TX	.060	Electronic		10B	10B	3½–4½	900/425①	550(600)/425①
	8-350 2bbl	R44TX	.060	Electronic		6B	6B	7–8½	600/700①	600
	8-350 4 bbl, 2WD	R44TX	.060	Electronic		6B	6B	7–8½	800/450	600/450

TUNE-UP SPECIFICATIONS
Blazer/Jimmy

When analyzing compression test results, look for uniformity among cylinders rather than specific pressures.

Year	Engine No. Cyl Displacement	Spark Plugs Orig Type	● Gap (in.)	Distributor Point Dwell (deg)	Point Gap (in.)	Ignition Timing (deg) Man Trans	● Auto Trans	Fuel Pump Pressure (psi)	Idle Speed (rpm) Man Trans	● Auto Trans ▲
	8-350 4 bbl, 4WD	R44TX	.060	Electronic		8B(2B)	8B(2B)	7–8½	600(700)①	600(700)①
	8-400	R44TX	.060	Electronic		—	4B(2B)	7–8½	—	700①
'76	6-250	R46T	.035	Electronic		6B	6B	3½–4½	600①	600①N
	8-350	R44TX	.060	Electronic		8B(2B)	8B(2B)	7–8½	600(700)	600(700)N
	8-400	R44TX	.060	Electronic		—	4B	7–8½	—	700N
'77–'78	6-250	R46T	.035	Electronic		6B	6B	3½–4½	600/450	600/450
	8-305	R44T	.045	Electronic		6B	6B	7–8½	700	700
	8-350	R44T (R44TX)	.045 (.060)	Electronic		8B(2B)	8B(2B)	7–8½	700	700
	8-400	R44T	.045	Electronic		—	4B(2B)	7–8½	—	700
'79	6-250	R46TS	.035	Electronic		10B	10B	4½–6	750	600
	8-305	R45TS	.045	Electronic		6B	6B	7–9	600	500
	8-350	R45TS	.045	Electronic		8B	8B	7–9	700	500
	8-400	R45TS	.060	Electronic		—	4B	7–9	—	500
'80–'81	6-250	R46TS	.035	Electronic		10B	10B	3.5–4.5	750	650(D)
	8-305	R45TS	.045	Electronic		4B	2B	7.0–8.5	700	500(D)
	8-350	R45TS	.045	Electronic		8B	8B	7.0–8.5	700	500(D)
'82				See underhood specifications sticker						

NOTE: The underhood specifications sticker often reflects tuneup specification changes made in production. Sticker figures must be used if they disagree with those in this chart. Part numbers in this chart are not recommendations by Chilton for any product name.

● Figures in parentheses are for California, and are given only when they differ from the 49 State models. When two idle speeds separated by a slash are given, the lower figure is with the solenoid disconnected.

▲ Automatic transmission idle speed set in Drive unless otherwise indicated

B Before Top Dead Center
N Neutral
TDC Top Dead Center
2WD Two wheel drive
4WD 4 wheel drive
① Air conditioning on

Firing Orders

To avoid confusion, replace spark plug wires one at a time.

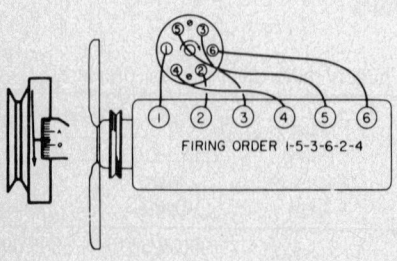

Six cylinder

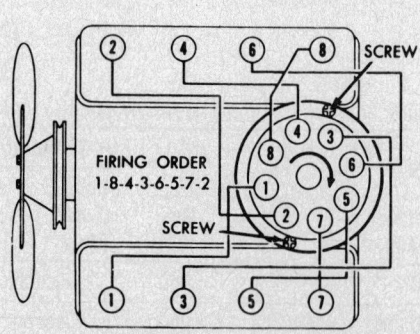

V8

PISTON AND RING SPECIFICATIONS

Engine	Year	Piston to Bore Clearance	Ring Side Clearance			Ring Gap		
			Top Compression	Bottom Compression	Oil Control	Top Compression	Bottom Compression	Oil Control
6-250	'75–'82	0.0005–0.0015①	0.0012–0.0027	0.0012–0.0032	.005 max	0.010–0.020	0.010–0.020	0.015–0.055
6-292	'75–'82	0.0026–0.0036	0.0020–0.0040	0.0020–0.0040	.005 max	0.010–0.020	0.010–0.020	0.015–0.055
8-305	'77–'82	0.0007–0.0017	0.0012–0.0032	0.0012–0.0032	0.002–0.007	0.010–0.020	0.010–0.025	0.015–0.055
8-350	'75–'82	0.0007–0.0017②	0.0012–0.0032	0.0012–0.0032	0.002–0.007	0.010–0.020	0.010–0.025③	0.015–0.055
8-350 Diesel	'78–'81	0.0050–0.0060	0.0040–0.0060	0.0018–0.0038	0.001–0.005	0.015–0.025	0.015–0.025	0.015–0.055
8-379 Diesel	'82	0.0040–0.0050	0.0030–0.0070	0.0015–0.0031	0.0016–0.0038	0.012–0.021	0.030–0.039	0.0098–0.020
8-400	'75–'81	0.0014–0.0024	0.0012–0.0032	0.0012–0.0032	0.002–0.007	0.010–0.020	0.010–0.025	0.010–0.055④
8-454	'75–'82	0.0014–0.0024⑤	0.0017–0.0032	0.0017–0.0032	0.002–0.007	0.010–0.020	0.010–0.020	0.010–0.055⑥

① '78–'82: 0.0010–0.0020
② '75–'76: 0.0007–0.0013
③ '75–'76: 0.013–0.025
④ '75–'76: 0.010–0.035
⑤ '75–'76: 0.0018–0.0028
⑥ '75–'76: 0.010–0.0030

CRANKSHAFT AND CONNECTING ROD SPECIFICATIONS

All measurements are given in in.

Year	Engine No. Cyl Displacement (cu in.)	Crankshaft				Connecting Rod		
		Main Brg Journal Dia	Main Brg Oil Clearance	Shaft End-Play	Thrust on No.	Journal Diameter	Oil Clearance	Side Clearance
'75–'77	6-250	2.2983–2.2993	.0003–.0029	.002–.006	7	1.999–2.000	.0007–.0027	.006–.017
	6-292	2.2983–2.2993	.0008–.0034	.002–.006	7	2.099–2.100	.0007–.0027	.006–.017
	8-305, 307 350, 400	2.4484–2.4493①⑤	.0008–.0020②	.002–.006	5	2.199–2.200	.0013–.0035	.008–.014
	8-454	③	④	.006–.010	5	2.1985–2.1995	.0009–.0025	.013–.023
'78–'81	6-250	2.2979–2.2994	Nos. 1–6 .0010–.0024 No. 7 .0016–.0035	.002–.006	7	1.999–2.000	.0010–.0026	.006–.017
	6-292	2.2979–2.2994	Nos. 1–6 .0010–.0024 No. 7 .0016–.0035	.002–.006	7	2.099–2.100	.0010–.0026	.006–.017
	8-305, 350, 400	⑤	.0008–.0020②	.002–.006	5	2.199–2.200①②	.0013–.0035	.008–.014
	8-454	③	④	.006–.010	5	2.1985–2.1995	.0009–.0025	.013–.023
	8-350 Diesel	2.9993–3.0003	Nos. 1–4 .0005–.0021 No. 5 .0015–.0031	.0035–.0135	5	2.1238–2.1248	.0005–.0026	.006–.020
'82	6-250	2.2979–2.2994	Nos. 1–6 0.0010–0.0024 No. 7 0.0016–0.0025	0.002–0.006	7	1.999–2.000	0.0010–0.0026	0.006–0.017

CRANKSHAFT AND CONNECTING ROD SPECIFICATIONS

All measurements are given in in.

Year	Engine No. Cyl Displacement (cu in.)	Crankshaft				Connecting Rod		
		Main Brg Journal Dia	Main Brg Oil Clearance	Shaft End-Play	Thrust on No.	Journal Diameter	Oil Clearance	Side Clearance
	6-292	2.2979–2.2994	Nos. 1–6 0.0010–0.0024 No. 7 0.0016–0.0025	0.002–0.006	7	2.099–2.100	0.0010–0.0026	0.006–0.017
	8-305	⑤	0.0008–0.0020②	0.002–0.006	5	2.0988–2.0998	0.0013–0.0035	0.008–0.014
	8-350	⑤	0.0008–0.0020②	0.002–0.006	5	2.0988–2.0998	0.0013–0.0035	0.008–0.014
	8-379 Diesel	⑧	⑨	0.002–0.007	5	2.3981–2.3991	0.0018–0.0039	0.007–0.025
	8-454	⑦	④	0.006–0.010	5	2.2000–2.1990	0.0009–0.0025	0.013–0.023

① No. 5—2.4479–2.4488
② Nos. 2–4—.0011–.0023
No. 5—.0017–.0033
③ No. 1—2.7485–2.7494
Nos. 2–4—2.7481–2.7490
No. 5—2.7478–2.7488
④ Nos. 1–4—.0013–.0025

No. 5—.0024–.0040
⑤ '77–'82 only: 305,
350—No. 1—2.4484–2.4493
Nos. 2–4—2.4481–2.4490
No. 5—2.4479–2.4488
400—Nos. 1–4—2.6484–2.6493
No. 5—2.6479–2.6488

⑥ '79–'81: 2.0988–2.0998
⑦ Nos. 1–4—2.7481–2.7490
No. 5—2.7476–2.7486
⑧ Nos. 1–4—2.9495–2.9504
No. 5—2.9492–2.9502
⑨ Nos. 1–4—0.0018–0.0033
No. 5—0.0022–0.0037

VALVE SPECIFICATIONS

Engine No. Cyl Displacement (cu in.)	Seat Angle (deg)	Face Angle (deg)	Spring Test Pressure (lbs @ in.)	Spring Installed Height (in.) ①	Stem to Guide Clearance (in.)		Stem Diameter (in.)	
					Intake	Exhaust	Intake	Exhaust
6-250	46	45	60 @ 1.66	1²¹⁄₃₂	0.0010–0.0027	0.0015–0.0032	0.3414	0.3414
6-292	46	45⑤	89 @ 1.69⑥	1⁵⁄₈⑦	0.0010–0.0027	0.0015–0.0032	0.3414	0.3414
8-305	46	45	80 @ 1.70②	③	0.0010–0.0027	0.0010–0.0027	0.3414	0.3414
8-350	46	45	80 @ 1.70②	③	0.0010–0.0027	0.0010–0.0027	0.3414	0.3414
8-379 Diesel	46	45	230 @ 1.39	1.81	0.0010–0.0027	0.0010–0.0027	0.3414	0.3414
8-400	46	45	80 @ 1.70②	③	0.0010–0.0027	0.0012–0.0029	0.3414	0.3414
8-454	46	45	80 @ 1.88	1⁷⁄₈	0.0010–0.0027	0.0012–0.0029	0.3719	0.3719
8-350 Diesel	⑧	④	80 @ 1.67	1⁴³⁄₆₄	0.0010–0.0027	0.0015–0.0032	0.3429	0.3424

① ± ¹⁄₃₂ in.
② Exhaust—80 @ 1.61
③ Intake—1²³⁄₃₂
Exhaust—1¹⁹⁄₃₂
④ Intake—44°
Exhaust—30°

⑤ '78–'82: 46°
⑥ '78–'82: 82 @ 1.66
⑦ '78–'82: 1²⁵⁄₃₂
⑧ Intake—45°
Exhaust—31°

TORQUE SPECIFICATIONS
(ft. lb.)

Engine	Cylinder Head Bolts	Rod Bearing Bolts	Main Bearing Bolts	Crank-shaft Damper Bolt	Fly-wheel Bolts	Manifold	
						Intake	Exhaust
6-250	95	35	65	—	60	—	30①
6-292	95	35	65	—	110	35	30
8-305	65	45	70	60	60	30	20
8-350	65	45	70	60	60	30	30①
8-350 Diesel	130②	42	120	200–310	60	40②	25
8-379 Diesel	88–103	44–52	④	140–162	60	25–37	18–25
8-400	65	45	70	60	60	30	30
8-454	80	50③	110	65	65	30	20

① End bolts: 20
② Dip in oil
③ 7/16 in. bolts: 70
④ inner: 105–117
　 outer: 94–105

BATTERY AND STARTER SPECIFICATIONS

Year	Battery			Starter ③			
	Amp Hour Capacity	Volts	Ground Terminal	Identification	No Load Test		
					Volts	Amps ①	rpm
'75	60	12	Neg	1108744 1108788②	9	50–80	5500–10,500
	80	12	Neg	1108747 1108780②	9	50–80	3500–6000
				1108748 1108781②	9	65–90	7500–10,500
	125	12	Neg	1108748 1108781②	9	65–90	7500–10,500
'76	60	12	Neg	1108778②	9	50–80	5500–10,500
	80	12	Neg	1108780②	9	50–80	3500–6000
				1108781②	9	65–90	7500–10,500
	125	12	Neg	1108781②	9	65–90	7500–10,500
'77–'82	60	12	Neg	1108778②	9	50–80	5500–10,500
	80	12	Neg	1187780②	9	50–80	3500–6000
				1109056②	9	50–80	5500–10,500
				1109052②	9	65–95	7500–10,500
				1108776②	9	65–95	7500–10,500
	125	12	Neg	1108776②	9	65–95	7500–10,500

① Solenoid included
② "R" terminal removed
③ Brush spring tension is 35 oz. for all
　 starters. Lock test is not recommended.

ALTERNATOR AND REGULATOR SPECIFICATIONS

| | Alternator | | | Regulator | | | | | | | |
| | | | | | Field Relay | | | Regulator | | | |
Year	Part No. or Manufacturer	Field Current @ 12 V	Output (amps)	Part No.. or Manufacturer	Air Gap (in.)	Point Gap (in.)	Volts to Close	Air Gap (in.)	Point Gap (in.)	Volts at 75° F
'75–'77	1100497	4.4–4.9	37	Integral with the alternator						
	1100934	4.4–4.5	37	Integral with the alternator						
	1102394 1102483, 91 1102889	4.0–4.5	37	Integral with the alternator						
	1102346, 49, 82 1102485 1102841, 87 1100573	4.0–4.5	42	Integral with the alternator						
	1100560, 75 1102478, 79, 93	4.0–4.5	55	Integral with the alternator						
	1100597 1102347, 50, 83 1102480, 86, 90 1102886, 88	4.0–4.5	61	Integral with the alternator						
'78–'82	1102394 1102491 1102889	4.0–4.5	37	Integral with the alternator						
	1102485 1102841, 87	4.0–4.5	42	Integral with the alternator						
	1102480, 86 1102886, 88	4.0–4.5	61	Integral with the alternator						
	1101016, 28	4.0–4.5	80	Integral with the alternator						

—Not available
NA Not applicable

WHEEL ALIGNMENT SPECIFICATIONS
Vans

| | | Caster (deg) | | Camber (deg) | | Toe-In (in.) | Steering Axis Inclination (deg) |
Year	Model	Range	Preferred Setting	Range	Preferred Setting		
'75–'80	All	①	①	0–½P	¼P	³⁄₁₆	8½
'81–'82	G10,20	②	②	0–1P	½P	³⁄₁₆	8½
'81–'82	G30	②	②	⅘N– 1⅕P	⅕P	³⁄₁₆	8½

Measure the distance from the pump stop bracket to the frame. Read the caster angle from the chart below.

① Bumper stop bracket-to-frame (in.)	2½	2¾	3	3¼	3½	3¾	4	4¼	4½	4¾	5
Caster	2¼P	2P	1½P	1¼P	1P	¾P	½P	¼P	0	¼N	½N

WHEEL ALIGNMENT SPECIFICATIONS
Vans

Year	Model	Caster (deg)		Camber (deg)		Toe-In (in.)	Steering Axis Inclination (deg)
		Range	Preferred Setting	Range	Preferred Setting		

② Bumper stop bracket-to-frame (in.)		1½	1¾	2	2¼	2½	3	3¼	3½	3¾	4	4¼
Caster	G10,G20	3½P	3½P	3¹⁄₁₀P	2⁹⁄₁₀P	2⁷⁄₁₀P	2⁴⁄₁₀P	2²⁄₁₀P	2¹⁄₁₀P	1⁹⁄₁₀P	1⁸⁄₁₀P	1⁶⁄₁₀P
	G30	2⁸⁄₁₀P	2½P	2²⁄₁₀P	1⁹⁄₁₀P	1⁶⁄₁₀P	1P	⁷⁄₁₀P	½P	²⁄₁₀P	0	²⁄₁₀N

WHEEL ALIGNMENT SPECIFICATIONS
Pick-ups and Suburban

Year	Model	Caster (deg.)		Camber (deg.)		Toe-in (in.)	Steering Axis inclination (deg.)
		Range	Preferred Setting	Range	Preferred Setting		
'75–'82	All	①	①	—	¼P	¹⁄₁₆	8½

Measure the distance from the bumper stop to the frame. Read the caster angle in the chart below.

① Bumper stop-to-frame (in.)	2½	2¾	3	3¼	3½	3¾	4	4¼	4½	4¾	5
Caster '75–'76 C10 (deg)			2P	1½P	1¼P	1P	¾P	½P	¼P	0	½P
'75–'76 C20,30	1½P	1¼P	1P	¾P	½P	¼P	0	¼N	½N	¾N	1N
'78–'82 C10	2²⁄₅P	2¹⁄₁₀P	1⅘P	1½P	1⅕P	1P	⁷⁄₁₀P	½P	⅕P	¹⁄₁₀P	³⁄₁₀
'78–'82 C20,30	1½P	1⅕P	⁹⁄₁₀P	⅗P	³⁄₁₀P	¹⁄₁₀P	0	¹⁄₁₀N	⁷⁄₁₀N	1N	1⅕N

FRONT END ALIGNMENT SPECIFICATIONS
Blazer and Jimmy

Year	Model	Caster (deg)②	Camber (deg)②	Toe-In (in.)
'75–'80	2WD	①	¼	⅛–¼
'75	4WD	4	1½	0
'76 thru mid-Jan.	4WD	4	1½	0
'76 from mid-Jan.	4WD	8	1½	0
'77–'78	4WD	8	1½	0
'79–'82	4WD	8	1	0

① Specifications not given. See text for explanation.
② All caster and camber figures are positive (+).

TUNE-UP

High Energy Ignition (HEI) System

The General Motors HEI system is a pulse-triggered, transistored-controlled, inductive discharge ignition system. Except on early inline six-cylinder models, the entire HEI system is contained within the distributor cap. Inline six-cylinder engines through 1977 have an external coil. Otherwise, the systems are the same.

The distributor, in addition to housing the mechanical and vacuum advance mechanisms, contains the ignition coil (except on 1975–77 inline six engines), the electronic control module, and the magnetic triggering device. The magnetic pick-up assembly contains a permanent magnet, a pole piece with internal ''teeth,'' and a pick-up coil (not to be confused with the ignition coil).

In the HEI system, as in other electronic ignition systems, the breaker points have been replaced with an electronic switch—a transistor—which is located *within* the control module. This switching transistor performs the same function the points did in a conventional ignition system; it simply turns coil primary current on and off at the correct time. Essentially then, electronic and conventional ignition systems operate on the same principle.

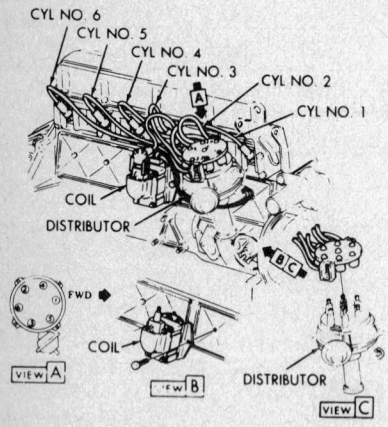

Six cylinder HEI wiring with non-integral coil

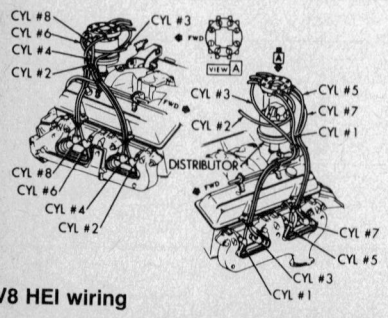

V8 HEI wiring

The module which houses the switching transistor is controlled (turned on and off) by a magnetically generated impulse induced in the pick-up coil. When the teeth of the rotating timer align with the teeth of the pole piece, the induced voltage in the pick-up coil signals the electronic module to open the coil primary circuit. The primary current then decreases, and a high voltage is induced in the ignition coil secondary windings which is then directed through the rotor and high voltage leads (spark plug wires) to fire the spark plugs.

In essence then, the pick-up coil module system simply replaces the conventional breaker points and condenser. The condenser found within the distributor is for radio suppression purposes only and has nothing to do with the ignition process. The module automatically controls the dwell period, increasing it with increasing engine speed. Since dwell is automatically controlled, it cannot be adjusted. The module itself is non-adjustable and non-repairable and must be replaced if found defective.

HEI SYSTEM PRECAUTIONS

Before going on to troubleshooting, it might be a good idea to take note of the following precautions.

Timing Light Use

Inductive pick-up timing lights are the best kind to use if your truck is equipped with HEI. Timing lights which connect between the spark plug and the spark plug wire occasionally (not always) give false readings.

Spark Plug Wires

The plug wires used with HEI systems are of a different construction than conventional wires. When replacing them, make sure you get the correct wires, since conventional wires won't carry the voltage. Also, handle them carefully to avoid cracking or splitting them and *never* pierce them.

Tachometer Use

Not all tachometers will operate or indicate correctly when used on a HEI system. While some tachometers may give a reading, this does not necessarily mean the reading is correct. In addition, some tachometers hook up differently from others. If you can't figure out whether or not your tachometer will work on your car, check with the tachometer manufacturer. Dwell readings, of course, have no significance at all.

HEI System Testers

Instruments designed specifically for testing HEI systems are available from several tool manufacturers. Some of these will even test the module itself. However, the tests given in the following section will require only an ohmmeter and a voltmeter.

Ignition Timing

Timing should be checked at each tune-up. It isn't likely to change much with HEI. The timing marks consist of a notch on the rim of the crankshaft pulley or vibration damper and a graduated scale attached to the engine front (timing) cover. A stroboscopic flash (dynamic) timing light must be used, as a static light is too inaccurate for emission controlled engines.

There are three basic types of timing light available. The first is a simple neon bulb with two wire connections. One wire connects to the spark plug terminal and the other plugs into the end of the spark plug wire for the no. 1 cylinder, thus connecting the light in series with the spark plug. This type of light is pretty dim and must be held very closely to the timing marks to be seen. Sometimes a dark corner has to be sought out to see the flash at all. This type of light is very inexpensive. The second type operates from the vehicle battery—two alligator clips connect to the battery terminals, while an adapter enables a third clip to be connected between the no. 1 spark plug and wire. This type is a bit more expensive, but it provides a nice bright flash that you can see even in bright sunlight. It is the type most often seen in professional shops. The third type replaces the battery power source with 110 volt current.

To check and adjust the timing:

1. Warm up the engine to normal operating temperature. Stop the engine and connect the timing light to the no. 1 (left front on V8, front on six) spark plug wire, either at the plug or at the distributor cap. You can also use the No. 6 wire, if it is more convenient. No. 6 is the rear cylinder on a six, and the third cylinder back on the right bank of a V8.

NOTE: Do not pierce the plug wire insulation with HEI; it will cause a miss. The best method is an inductive pickup timing light.

Clean off the timing marks and mark the pulley or damper notch and timing scale with white chalk.

2. Disconnect and plug the vacuum line at the distributor. This is done to prevent any distributor vacuum advance. Check the underhood emission sticker for any other hoses or wires which may need to be disconnected.

3. Start the engine and adjust the idle speed to that specified in the ''Tune-Up Specifications'' chart. With automatic transmission, set the specified idle speed in Park. It will be too high, since it is normally (in most cases) adjusted in Drive. You can disconnect the idle solenoid, if any, to get the speed down. Otherwise, adjust the idle speed screw. This is done to prevent any centrifugal (mechanical) advance. The tachometer connects to the TACH terminal on the distributor or on the coil (sixes through 1977) and to a ground. Some tachometers must connect to the TACH terminal and to

the positive battery terminal. Some tachometers won't work with HEI.

4. Aim the timing light at the pointer marks. Be careful not to touch the fan, because it may appear to be standing still. If the pulley or damper notch isn't aligned with the proper timing mark (see the "Tune-Up Specifications" chart), the timing will have to be adjusted.

NOTE: TDC or top dead center corresponds to 0 degrees. B, BTDC or before top dead center may be shown as BEFORE. A, ATDC or after top dead center may be shown as AFTER.

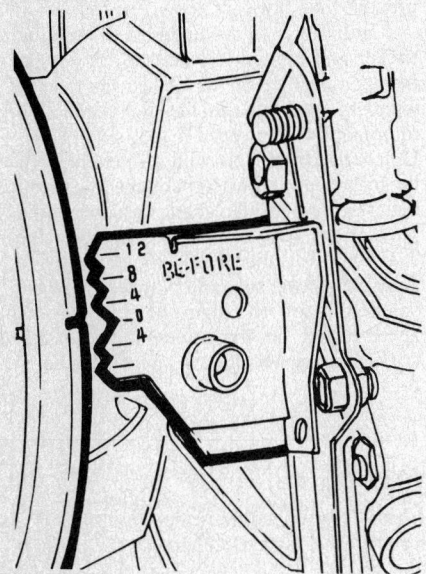

Typical timing marks

5. Loosen the distributor base clamp locknut. You can buy trick wrenches which make this task a lot easier on V8s. Turn the distributor slowly to adjust the timing, holding it by the body and not the cap. Turn the distributor in the direction of rotor rotation to retard, and against the direction of rotation to advance.

6. Tighten the locknut. Check the timing again, in case the distributor moved slightly as you tightened it.

7. Replace the distributor vacuum line. Correct the idle speed.

8. Stop the engine and disconnect the timing light.

Carburetor

IDLE SPEED AND MIXTURE ADJUSTMENT

These procedures require the use of a tachometer. Tachometer hookup was explained

earlier under Ignition Timing, Step 3. In some cases, the degree of accuracy required is greater than that available on a hand-held unit; a shop tachometer would be required to follow the instructions exactly. If the idle speed screws have plastic limiter caps, it is not recommended that they be removed unless a satisfactory idle cannot be obtained with them in place. If the caps are removed, exhaust emissions may go beyond the specified legal limits. This can be checked on an exhaust gas analyzer.

NOTE: Most four barrel carburetors have an internal fuel passage restriction; beyond a certain limited point, turning the idle mixture screws out has no further richening effect.

Idle speed and mixture are set with the engine at normal running temperature. The automatic transmission should be in Drive, except when specified otherwise. The air conditioner should be off for adjusting mixture and off unless otherwise specified in the text or specifications chart for setting idle speed.

1975

Six cylinder: Do not disconnect the distributor vacuum line. Disconnect the vapor canister "FUEL TANK" hose. With automatic transmission in Drive and manual in Neutral, adjust the solenoid to get the specified idle speed. Use a 1/8 in. Allen wrench in the end of the solenoid body to set the low idle speed to 450 rpm with the solenoid wire disconnected. Reset the idle speed with the air conditioning on, except on the 250 engine.

V8 with two barrel carburetor: Disconnect the vapor canister "FUEL TANK" hose. Leave the distributor vacuum advance hose in place. Adjust the idle speed screw to get the specified idle speed with automatic in Drive and manual in Neutral.

Light duty V8 with four barrel carburetor: Disconnect the vapor canister "FUEL TANK" hose. Leave the distributor vacuum advance hose in place. Disconnect the solenoid wire. Place automatic in Drive and manual in Neutral. Turn the low idle speed screw on the carburetor to get about 450 rpm. Connect the solenoid wire and open the throttle slightly, so that the solenoid plunger can extend. Turn the plunger screw to get the specified idle speed.

Heavy duty V8 with four barrel carburetor: This adjustment is the same as for 1976. Reset the idle speed with the air conditioner on.

1976

Six cylinder: Disconnect and plug the "CARBURETOR" and "PCV" vapor canister hoses on the 250. Disconnect the canister "FUEL TANK" hose on the 292. If the engine has a vacuum advance hose running directly from the vacuum source to the distributor vacuum advance unit, disconnect and plug it. Turn the air conditioner on, only on the 292. Set the manual transmission in Neutral. Set the 250 automatic in Drive and the 292 in Neutral. Turn the solenoid to get the specified idle speed. Disconnect the solenoid wire and turn off the air conditioner. Use a 1/8 in. Allen wrench in the end of the solenoid body to set the low idle speed to 450 rpm.

V8 with two barrel carburetor: This procedure is the same as 1975, except that the canister hose can be left in place.

Light duty V8 with four barrel carburetor: Place the automatic in Drive and manual in Neutral. Set the idle speed screw on the carburetor to obtain the specified rpm.

Heavy duty V8 with four barrel carburetor: Disconnect the vapor canister "FUEL TANK" hose on California models. Leave the vacuum advance hose in place. Turn the air conditioner on. Set the automatic in Park and manual in Neutral. Set the idle speed screw on the carburetor to obtain the specified rpm.

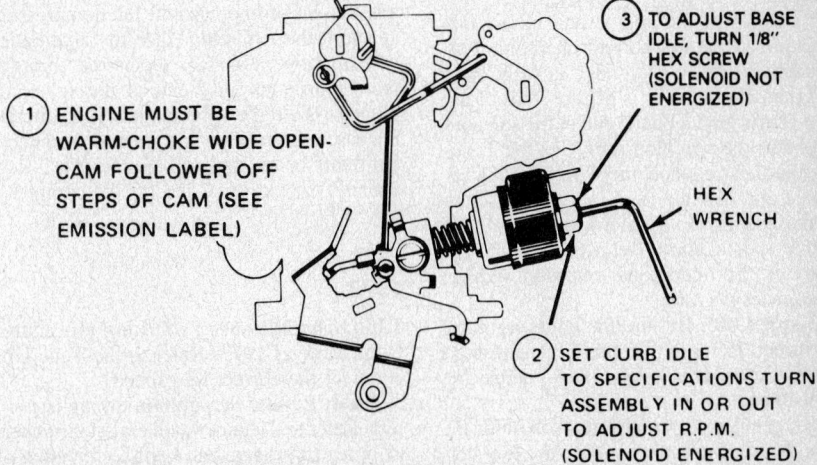

① ENGINE MUST BE WARM-CHOKE WIDE OPEN-CAM FOLLOWER OFF STEPS OF CAM (SEE EMISSION LABEL)

② SET CURB IDLE TO SPECIFICATIONS TURN ASSEMBLY IN OR OUT TO ADJUST R.P.M. (SOLENOID ENERGIZED)

③ TO ADJUST BASE IDLE, TURN 1/8" HEX SCREW (SOLENOID NOT ENERGIZED)

HEX WRENCH

Idle speed adjustment for 250 and 292 sixes 1976–78, and 292 sixes 1979–82

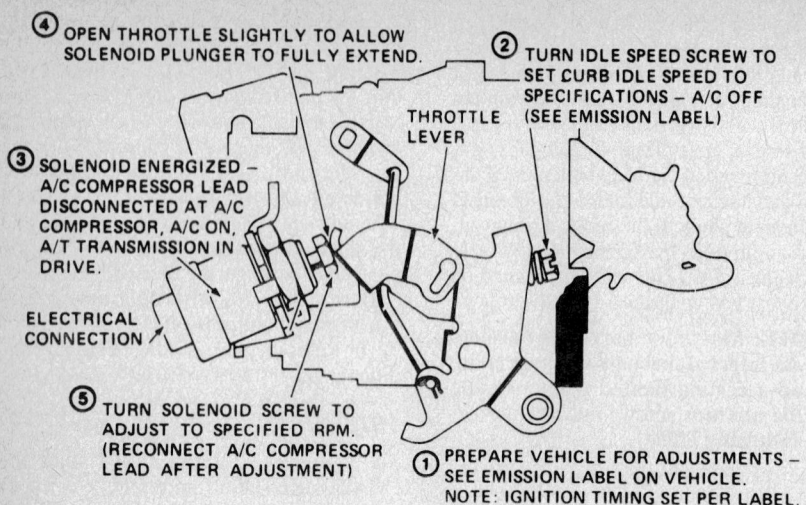

④ OPEN THROTTLE SLIGHTLY TO ALLOW SOLENOID PLUNGER TO FULLY EXTEND.

② TURN IDLE SPEED SCREW TO SET CURB IDLE SPEED TO SPECIFICATIONS – A/C OFF (SEE EMISSION LABEL)

THROTTLE LEVER

③ SOLENOID ENERGIZED – A/C COMPRESSOR LEAD DISCONNECTED AT A/C COMPRESSOR, A/C ON, A/T TRANSMISSION IN DRIVE.

ELECTRICAL CONNECTION

⑤ TURN SOLENOID SCREW TO ADJUST TO SPECIFIED RPM. (RECONNECT A/C COMPRESSOR LEAD AFTER ADJUSTMENT)

① PREPARE VEHICLE FOR ADJUSTMENTS – SEE EMISSION LABEL ON VEHICLE. NOTE: IGNITION TIMING SET PER LABEL.

1977–78 2-bbl idle speed adjustment with solenoid

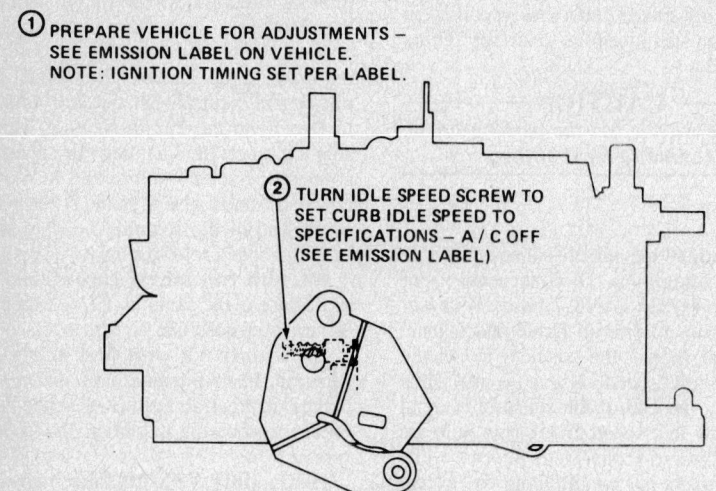

① PREPARE VEHICLE FOR ADJUSTMENTS – SEE EMISSION LABEL ON VEHICLE. NOTE: IGNITION TIMING SET PER LABEL.

② TURN IDLE SPEED SCREW TO SET CURB IDLE SPEED TO SPECIFICATIONS – A/C OFF (SEE EMISSION LABEL)

1977 and later 4-bbl idle speed adjustment without solenoid

1977

See the underhood emission sticker for any hoses or wires that may need to be disconnected.

1 bbl: Start the engine and allow it to run until it reaches normal operating temperature. Be sure the choke is fully open and the cam follower is off the steps of the cam. Turn the nut on the end of the solenoid to obtain the specified rpm. See the Tune-Up chart. Disconnect the wire from the solenoid and turn the 1/8 in. allen head screw in the end of the solenoid to set the base idle to specification. Refer to the Tune-Up chart or the underhood emission sticker. Reconnect the wire.

2 and 4 bbl: Be sure the ignition timing is correct. Refer to the underhood emission sticker in order to prepare the vehicle for adjustment.

On carburetors without a solenoid: Be sure the idle speed screw is on the low step of the fast idle cam. Turn the screw to obtain the idle specified in the Tune-Up chart.

On carburetors with a solenoid: Turn the idle screw to obtain the idle speed specified in the Tune-Up chart. Disconnect the electrical lead from between the solenoid and the A/C compressor at the compressor and turn the A/C On. Place the automatic transmission in Drive. Open the throttle momentarily to fully extend the solenoid plunger. Turn the solenoid screw to obtain the base idle speed as specified in the Tune-Up chart or on the emission sticker. Reconnect the electrical lead at the compressor.

1978

1 bbl: The idle speed adjusting procedure is the same as 1977. Refer to the Tune-Up chart for the correct idle speed.

2 bbl: Be sure the ignition timing is correct. Refer to the underhood emission sticker in order to prepare the vehicle for adjustment.

On carburetors without a solenoid: This procedure is the same as 1977. See the Tune-Up chart for the correct idle speed.

On models with a solenoid and without air conditioning: Rev the engine momentarily to fully extend the solenoid plunger. Turn the solenoid screw to obtain the curb idle speed listed in the Tune-Up chart. Disconnect the wire from the solenoid. Turn the idle speed screw to obtain the solenoid idle speed listed on the underhood emission sticker. Reconnect the wire at the solenoid.

On models with air conditioning: Turn the idle speed screw to obtain the idle speed listed in the Tune-Up chart. Disconnect the wire at the A/C compressor and turn the A/C On. Rev the engine momentarily to fully extend the solenoid plunger. Turn the solenoid screw to obtain the solenoid idle speed listed on the underhood emission sticker. Reconnect the wire at the compressor.

4 bbl: Refer to the underhood emission sticker and prepare the vehicle for adjustment as specified on the sticker. On models without a solenoid, turn the idle speed screw to obtain the idle speed listed in the Tune-Up chart. On models with a solenoid, turn the idle speed screw to obtain the idle speed listed in the Tune-Up chart. Disconnect the wire at the A/C compressor and turn the A/C On. Rev the engine momentarily to fully extend the solenoid plunger. Turn the solenoid screw to obtain the solenoid idle speed listed on the underhood emission sticker. Reconnect the A/C wire at the compressor.

1979–82

1 bbl: This procedure is the same as 1977. Refer to the Tune-Up chart for the correct idle speed.

2 bbl (six cylinder): Be sure the ignition timing is correct. Refer to the underhood emission sticker and prepare the engine for adjustment as specified on the sticker. Rev the engine momentarily to fully extend the solenoid plunger. Turn the solenoid screw to obtain the curb idle speed as listed in the Tune-Up chart. Disconnect the wire at the solenoid and turn the idle speed screw to adjust the base idle. Refer to the Tune-Up chart or the underhood emission sticker. Reconnect the wire at the solenoid.

2 bbl (V8): Be sure the engine timing is correct. Refer to the underhood emission label in order to prepare the vehicle for adjustment. Turn the idle speed screw to adjust the curb idle speed. Disconnect the wire from the solenoid to the A/C compressor at the compressor and turn the A/C On. Open the throttle momentarily to fully extend the solenoid plunger. Turn the A/C On. Open the throttle momentarily to fully extend the solenoid plunger. Turn the solenoid screw to obtain the base idle speed. Refer to the Tune-Up chart or the underhood emission sticker for the correct speeds.

4 bbl: This procedure is the same as for 1977.

ENGINE ELECTRICAL

Distributor

REMOVAL AND INSTALLATION

1. Disconnect the wiring harness connectors at the side of the distributor cap.

2. Remove the distributor cap and lay it aside.

3. Disconnect the vacuum advance line.

4. Scribe a mark on the engine in line with the rotor and note the approximate position of the vacuum advance unit in relation to the engine.

5. Remove the distributor hold-down clamp and nut.

6. Lift the distributor from the engine.
To install the distributor with the engine undisturbed:

7. Reinsert the distributor into its opening, aligning the previously-made marks on the housing and the engine block.

8. The rotor may have to be turned either way a slight amount to align the rotor-to-housing marks.

9. Install the retaining clamp and bolt. Install the distributor cap, primary wire, and the vacuum hose.

10. Start the engine and check the ignition timing.
To install the distributor with the engine disturbed:

11. Turn the engine so the no. 1 piston is at the top of its compression stroke. This may be determined by covering the no. 1 spark plug hole with your thumb and slowly turning the engine over. When the timing mark on the crankshaft pulley aligns with the 0 on the timing scale and your thumb is pushed out by compression, no. 1 piston is at top-dead-center (TDC).

12. Install the distributor to the engine block so that the vacuum advance unit points in the correct direction.

13. Turn the rotor so that it will point to the no. 1 terminal in the cap.

14. Install the distributor into the engine block. It may be necessary to turn the rotor a little in either direction in order to engage the gears.

15. Tap the starter a few times to ensure that the oil pump shaft is mated to the distributor shaft.

16. Bring the engine to no. 1 TDC again and check to see that the rotor is indeed pointing toward the no. 1 terminal of the cap.

17. After correct positioning is assured, turn the distributor housing so that the points are just opening. Tighten the retaining clamp. Install the cap and hoses. Check the timing.

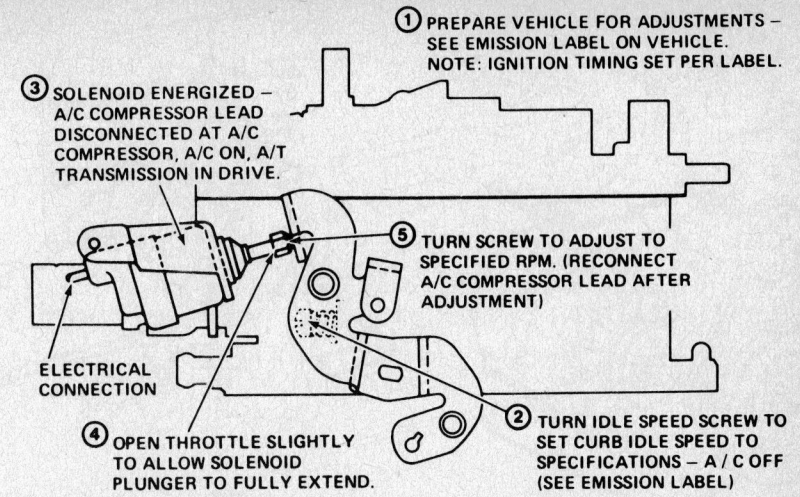

① PREPARE VEHICLE FOR ADJUSTMENTS — SEE EMISSION LABEL ON VEHICLE. NOTE: IGNITION TIMING SET PER LABEL.

③ SOLENOID ENERGIZED — A/C COMPRESSOR LEAD DISCONNECTED AT A/C COMPRESSOR, A/C ON, A/T TRANSMISSION IN DRIVE.

⑤ TURN SCREW TO ADJUST TO SPECIFIED RPM. (RECONNECT A/C COMPRESSOR LEAD AFTER ADJUSTMENT)

ELECTRICAL CONNECTION

④ OPEN THROTTLE SLIGHTLY TO ALLOW SOLENOID PLUNGER TO FULLY EXTEND.

② TURN IDLE SPEED SCREW TO SET CURB IDLE SPEED TO SPECIFICATIONS — A/C OFF (SEE EMISSION LABEL)

1977 and later 4-bbl and 1979 and later 2-bbl (V8 only) idle speed adjustment with solenoid

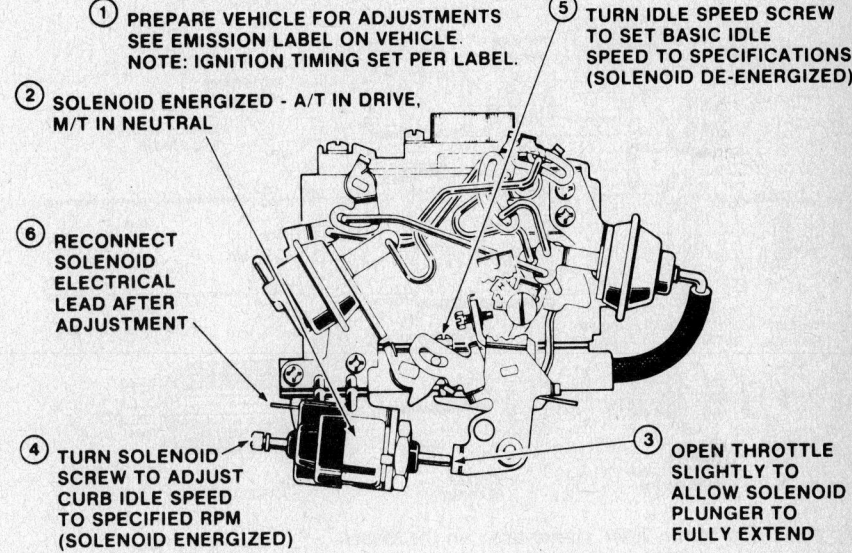

① PREPARE VEHICLE FOR ADJUSTMENTS SEE EMISSION LABEL ON VEHICLE. NOTE: IGNITION TIMING SET PER LABEL.

② SOLENOID ENERGIZED - A/T IN DRIVE, M/T IN NEUTRAL

⑥ RECONNECT SOLENOID ELECTRICAL LEAD AFTER ADJUSTMENT

④ TURN SOLENOID SCREW TO ADJUST CURB IDLE SPEED TO SPECIFIED RPM (SOLENOID ENERGIZED)

⑤ TURN IDLE SPEED SCREW TO SET BASIC IDLE SPEED TO SPECIFICATIONS (SOLENOID DE-ENERGIZED)

③ OPEN THROTTLE SLIGHTLY TO ALLOW SOLENOID PLUNGER TO FULLY EXTEND

1979–82 250 six idle speed adjustment

Alternator

ALTERNATOR PRECAUTIONS

1. When installing a battery, ensure that the ground polarity of the battery and the ground polarity of the alternator and the regulator are the same.

2. When connecting a jumper battery, be certain that the correct terminals are connected.

3. When charging, connect the correct charger leads to the battery terminals.

4. Never operate the alternator on an open circuit. Be sure that all connections in the charging circuit are tight.

5. Do not short across or ground any of the terminals on the alternator or regulator.

6. Never polarize an AC system.

PRELIMINARY CHARGING SYSTEM TESTS

1. If you suspect a defect in your charging system, first perform these general checks before going on to more specific tests.

2. Check the condition of the alternator belt and tighten it if necessary.

3. Clean the battery cable connections at the battery. Make sure the connections between the battery wires and the battery clamps are good. Reconnect the negative terminal only and proceed to the next step.

4. With the key off, insert a test light between the positive terminal on the battery and the disconnected positive battery terminal clamp. If the test light comes on, there is a short in the electrical system of the van. The short must be repaired before proceeding. If the light does not come on, proceed to the next step.

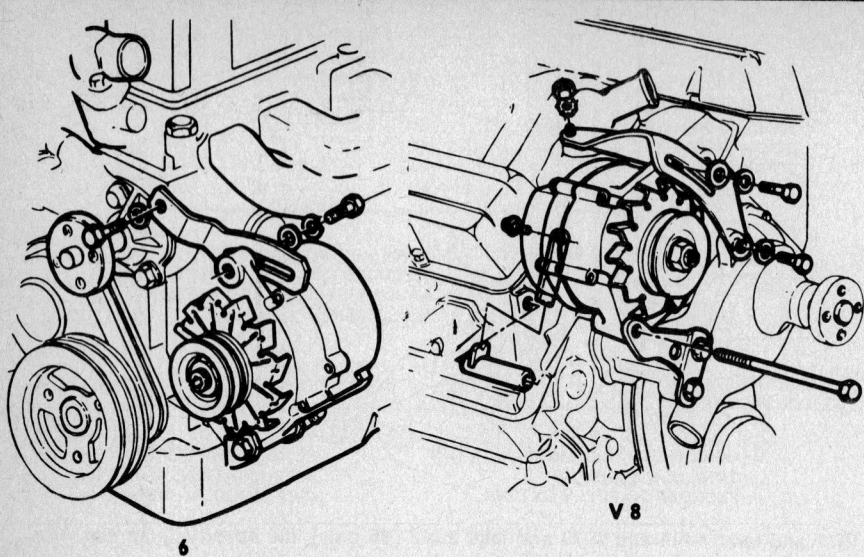

V 8

6

Typical alternator mounting

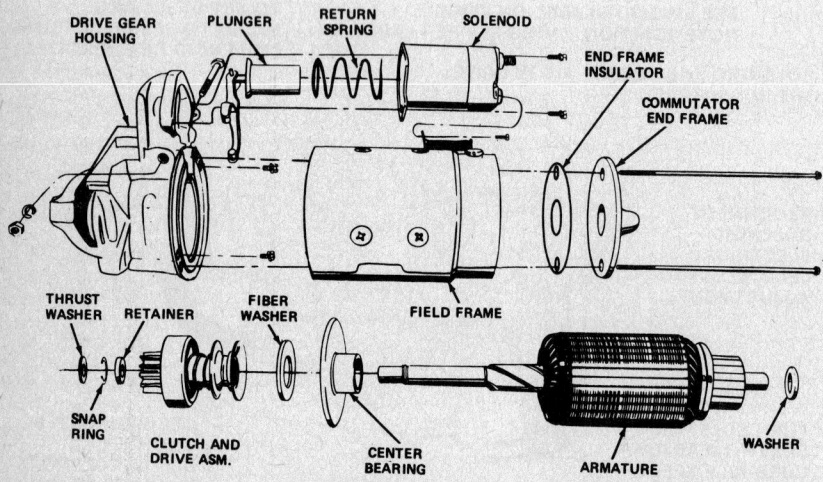

Exploded view of the 20MT starter used on the diesel.

NOTE: If the truck is equipped with an electric clock, the clock must be disconnected.

5. Check the charging system wiring for any obvious breaks or shorts.

6. Check the battery to make sure it is fully charged and in good condition.

CHARGING SYSTEM OPERATIONAL TEST

NOTE: You will need a current indicator to perform this test. If the current indicator is to give an accurate reading, the battery cables must be the same gauge and length as the original equipment.

1. With the engine running and all electrical systems turned off, place a current indicator over the positive battery cable.

2. If a charge of roughly five amps is recorded, the charging system is working.

If a draw of about five amps is recorded, the system is not working. The needle moves toward the battery when a charge condition is indicated, and away from the battery when a draw condition is indicated.

3. If a draw is indicated, proceed with further testing. If an excessive charge (10–15 amps) is indicated, the regulator may be at fault.

OUTPUT TEST

1. You will need an ammeter for this test.

2. Disconnect the battery ground cable.

3. Disconnect the wire from the battery terminal on the alternator.

4. Connect the ammeter negative lead to the battery terminal wire removed in step three, and connect the ammeter positive lead to the battery terminal on the alternator.

5. Reconnect the battery ground cable

and turn on all electrical accessories. If the battery is fully charged, disconnect the coil wire and bump the starter a few times to partially discharge it.

6. Start the engine and run it until you obtain a maximum current reading on the ammeter.

7. If the current is within ten amps of the rated output of the alternator, the alternator is working properly. If the current is not within ten amps, insert a screwdriver in the test hole in the end frame of the alternator and ground the tab in the test hole against the side of the hole.

8. If the current is now within ten amps of the rated output, remove the alternator and have the voltage regulator replaced. If it is still below ten amps of rated output, have the alternator repaired.

REMOVAL AND INSTALLATION

1. Disconnect the battery ground cable to prevent diode damage.

2. Disconnect and tag all wiring to the alternator.

3. Remove the alternator brace bolt.

4. Remove the drive belt.

5. Support the alternator and remove the mounting bolts. Remove the alternator.

6. Install the unit using the reverse procedure of removal. Adjust the belt to have ½ in. depression under thumb pressure on its longest run.

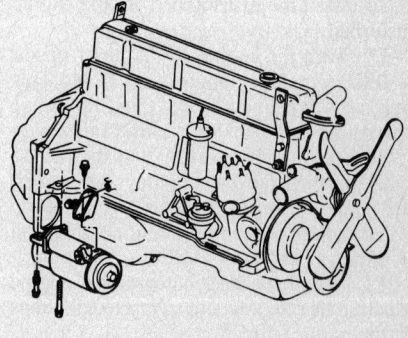

6

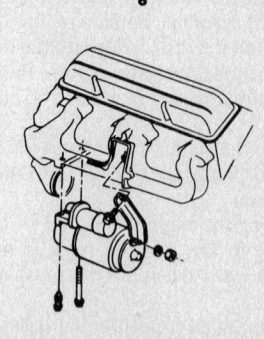

V 8

Typical starter mountings

22

Regulator

REMOVAL AND INSTALLATION

The regulator on these models is an integral part of the alternator. Alternator disassembly is required to replace it.

VOLTAGE ADJUSTMENT

The 10 SI Delcotron is used which is equipped with an integral regulator that cannot be adjusted.

Starter

REMOVAL AND INSTALLATION

The following is a general procedure for all trucks, and may vary slightly depending on model and series.

1. Disconnect the battery ground cable at the battery.
2. Raise and support the vehicle.
3. Disconnect and tag all wires at the solenoid terminal.

NOTE: 1975 and later starters do not require the "R" terminal. The High Energy Ignition System does not need a cable from solenoid to ignition coil.

4. Reinstall all nuts as soon as they are removed, since the thread sizes are different.
5. Remove the front bracket from the starter and the two mounting bolts. On engines with a solenoid heat shield, remove the front bracket upper bolt and detach the bracket from the starter.
6. Remove the front bracket bolt or nut. Lower the starter front end first, and then remove the unit from the truck.
7. Reverse the removal procedures to install the starter. Torque the two mounting bolts to 25–35 ft. lbs.

BRUSH REPLACEMENT

1. Disconnect the field coil connectors from the starter motor solenoid terminal.
2. Remove the through bolts.
3. Remove the end frame and the field frame from the drive housing.
4. Disassemble the brush assembly from the field frame by releasing the spring and removing the supporting pin. Pull the brushes and the brush holders out and disconnect the wiring.
5. Install the new brushes into the holders.
6. Assemble the brush holder using the spring and position the unit on the supporting pin.
7. Install the unit in the starter motor and attach the wiring.
8. Position the field frame over the armature.

9. Install the through bolts.
10. Connect the field coil connectors to the solenoid.

STARTER DRIVE REPLACEMENT

1. Remove the starter motor as previously outlined.
2. Disconnect the field coil connections from the solenoid terminal.
3. Remove the through bolts.
4. Remove the commutator end frame, the field frame assembly and the armature assembly from the housing.
5. Remove the armature assembly from the housing. On some models it may be necessary to remove the solenoid and the shift lever assembly from the housing first.
6. Remove the thrust collar from the shaft.
7. Slide a small piece of ½ in. pipe over the end of the shaft so the end of the pipe butts against the edge of the retainer. Carefully tap the end of the pipe with a hammer, driving the retainer towards the armature end of the snap-ring.
8. Remove the snap-ring from the groove.
9. Slide the retainer and clutch off the shaft.
To assemble the drive mechanism:
10. Slide the drive assembly onto the armature shaft after lubricating it with silicone.
11. Position the retainer on the shaft with the cupped surface facing away from the pinion.
12. Place the snap-ring over the end of the shaft and slide it into the groove.
13. Place the thrust collar on the shaft with its shoulder next to the snap-ring.
14. Using two sets of pliers, one on either side, force the snap-ring into the retainer.
15. Lubricate the drive housing bushing and slide the armature shaft into the housing.
16. Lubricate the commutator bushing with silicone.
17. Place the leather brake washer in position and assemble the commutator end of the starter.

SOLENOID REPLACEMENT

1. Remove the screw and washer from the motor connector strap terminal.
2. Remove the two solenoid retaining screws.
3. Twist the housing clockwise to remove the flange key from the keyway in the housing. Then remove the housing.
4. To install the unit, place the return spring on the plunger and place the solenoid body on the drive housing. Turn counterclockwise to engage the flange key. Place the two retaining screws in position and install the screw and washer which secures the strap terminal. Install the unit on the starter.

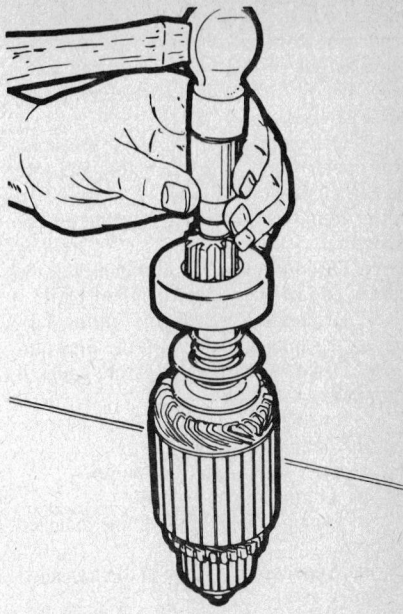

Use a piece of pipe to drive the retainer toward the snap-ring

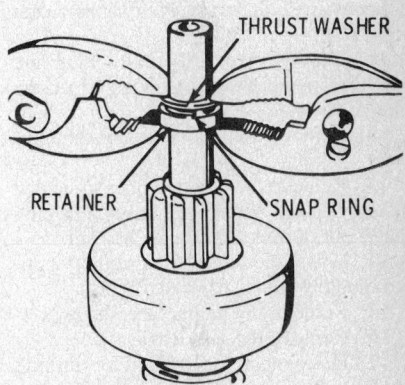

Snap-ring installation

ENGINE MECHANICAL

Engine Removal and Installation

VANS

1975–76

The engines on these vehicles are removed through the front of the vehicle. A portable boom type hoist is necessary for this job.

1. Remove the grille. It is attached with screws.
2. Drain the cooling system and disconnect the heater hoses at the engine. Disconnect the radiator hoses at the engine.
3. Disconnect the A/C compressor mounting bracket and position the com-

pressor out of the way. Also remove the condenser from in front of the radiator. Position it out of the way. DO NOT DISCONNECT ANY OF THE REFRIGERANT LINES.

4. Disconnect the automatic transmission cooler lines at the radiator. Remove the fan guard and radiator.

5. Remove the radiator upper tie bar and radiator support.

6. Disconnect the battery cables at the battery and at the radiator support baffle.

7. Disconnect the engine wiring harness at the junction block on the firewall.

8. Disconnect the oil pressure gauge if equipped.

9. Raise and support the van. Disconnect the following items:
   a. Fuel line at the fuel pump
   b. Engine ground straps
   c. Battery cables at the frame mounted clip
   d. Speedometer cable at the transmission
   e. Exhaust pipes from the manifolds, remove the exhaust system
   f. Transmission at the crossmember.

10. Disconnect the clutch linkage or the transmission linkage and remove the clutch cross-shaft.

11. Remove the driveshaft. Plug the opening in the extension housing of the transmission.

12. Remove the engine mount through-bolts.

13. Remove the crossmember-to-engine mount-bracket (right-side only) attaching bolts, but do not remove the bracket.

14. Lower the vehicle and support it approximately 12 in. from the floor.

15. Remove the engine access cover.

16. Remove the air cleaner.

17. Disconnect the carburetor throttle linkage. Disconnect and plug the fuel line from the carburetor and remove the carburetor.

18. Disconnect the power brake vacuum line from the intake manifold.

19. Disconnect the spark plug wires from the spark plugs and position them out of the way.

20. Remove the ignition coil and rear lifting bracket.

21. Securely attach a boom hoist to the engine.

22. With the aid of an assistant, slowly raise the engine to take the weight off the engine mounts. Remove the right mount frame bracket and mount.

23. Continue raising the engine and move it forward out of the van. Check often to be sure that all necessary components are disconnected.

24. Remove the transmission.

25. Installation is the reverse of removal. Check all fluid levels and check for leaks.

1977–78

1. Scribe matchmarks on the hood hinges for reassembly and remove the hood

and the grille. Remove the grille cross brace.

2. Disconnect the negative battery cable, then the positive battery cable, at the battery.

3. Remove the air cleaner.

4. Drain the cooling system and disconnect the heater hoses and radiator hoses at the radiator.

5. Disconnect the A/C compressor mounting bracket and position the compressor out of the way. Also remove the condenser from in front of the radiator. Position it out of the way. DO NOT DISCONNECT ANY OF THE REFRIGERANT LINES.

6. Remove the radiator and the fan shroud.

7. Disconnect and label the wiring at the starter solenoid, alternator, temperature sending switch, oil pressure switch and the coil. Disconnect the engine ground strap.

8. Disconnect:
   a. the accelerator at the intake manifold
   b. the fuel line from the tank at the fuel pump (plug the line)
   c. the hoses at the fuel vapor storage canister (if so equipped)
   d. the vacuum line to the power brake booster at the manifold (if so equipped)

9. Remove the power steering pump mounting bolts and lay the pump aside. Do not disconnect any of the lines.

10. Raise the van on a hoist and drain the crankcase.

11. Disconnect the exhaust pipe at the manifold. If equipped with a catalytic converter, disconnect the converter bracket at the rear transmission mount.

12. Remove the starter motor.

13. Remove the flywheel splash shield or the converter cover, as applicable.

14. On vans with automatic transmissions, remove the converter-to-flywheel attaching bolts.

15. Remove the engine mount through bolts.

16. Remove the bellhousing bolts.

17. Lower the van.

18. Using a floor jack, raise the transmission.

19. Attach a boom hoist to the engine and raise the engine slightly.

20. Remove the engine mount-to-engine brackets.

21. Remove the engine.

22. Reverse the removal procedure to install.

1979–82

1. Disconnect the negative battery cable, then the positive battery cable, at the battery.

2. Drain the cooling system.

3. Remove the engine cover.

4. Remove the air cleaner. On the V8 remove the air stove pipe.

5. Remove the grille. On the six cylinder, remove the grille cross brace. On the V8, remove the upper radiator support and the lower grille valance.

6. Disconnect the radiator hoses at the radiator.

7. On the V8, remove the radiator coolant reservoir bottle.

8. If the van is equipped with an automatic transmission, remove the fluid cooler lines from the radiator.

─────── **CAUTION** ───────

Discharging the air conditioning refrigerant should only be attempted by those who have the proper tools and training to do so, as serious personal injury may result. The refrigerant will instantly freeze any surface it comes in contact with, including your eyes.

─────────────────────────

9. Discharge the air conditioning system and remove the A/C vacuum reservoir. On the V8, remove the A/C condenser from in front of the radiator. On the six cylinder, remove the A/C compressor.

10. Remove the windshield washer jar and bracket.

11. Disconnect the accelerator linkage at the carburetor and remove the carburetor.

12. Remove the radiator support bracket and remove the radiator and the shroud.

13. On the six cylinder, remove the A/C compressor mounting bracket and position the compressor out of the way.

14. On the V8, disconnect the engine wiring harness from the firewall connection. On the six cylinder, disconnect the wiring at the alternator, distributor, oil pressure and temperature sending switches and the starter motor.

15. On the V8:
   a. Disconnect the heater hoses at the engine.
   b. Remove the thermostat housing.
   c. Remove the oil filler pipe.
   d. Remove the cruise control servo, servo bracket and transducer.

16. Raise the vehicle and drain the engine oil.

17. Remove the fuel line from the fuel tank at the fuel pump.

18. Disconnect the exhaust pipe at the manifold.

19. Remove the driveshaft and plug the end of the transmission.

20. Disconnect the transmission shift linkage and the speedometer cable.

21. Remove the transmission mounting bolts.

22. On the six cylinder with manual transmission, disconnect the clutch linkage and remove the clutch cross shaft.

23. On the V8, remove the engine mount bracket-to-frame bolts.

24. Remove the engine mount through bolts.

25. On the six cylinder:
   a. Lower the van and attach a lifting device to the engine.
   b. Raise the engine slightly and remove the right hand mount from the engine.

26. On the V8:
   a. Raise the engine slightly and re-

move the engine mounts. Support the engine with wood between the oil pan and the crossmember.

27. Remove the engine and transmission as one unit.

28. Reverse the removal procedure to install.

PICK-UPS AND SUBURBAN

The factory recommended procedure for engine removal is to remove the engine/transmission as a unit on two wheel drive models, except for the diesel. Only the engine should be removed on diesels and four wheel drive models.

1. Disconnect and remove the battery, negative cable first. On diesels, disconnect the negative cables at the batteries and ground wires at the inner fender panel.

2. Drain the cooling system.

3. Drain the engine oil.

4. Remove the air cleaner and ducts.

5. Scribe alignment marks around the hood hinges, and remove the hood.

6. Remove the radiator and hoses, and the fan shroud if so equipped.

7. Disconnect and label the wires at:

   a. Starter solenoid

   b. Alternator

   c. Temperature switch

   d. Oil pressure switch

   e. Transmission controlled spark solenoid

   f. CEC solenoid

   g. Coil

   h. Neutral safety switch

8. Disconnect:

   a. Accelerator linkage (hairpin at bellcrank, throttle and T.V. cables at intake manifold brackets on diesels. Position away from the engine.)

   b. Choke cable at carburetor (if so equipped)

   c. Fuel line to fuel pump

   d. Heater hoses at engine

   e. Air conditioning compressor with hoses attached. Do not remove the hoses from the air conditioning compressor. Remove it as a unit and set it aside. Its contents are under pressure, and can freeze body tissue on contact.

   f. Transmission dipstick and tube on automatic transmission models, except for diesel. Plug the tube hole.

   g. Oil dipstick and tube. Plug the hole.

   h. Vacuum lines

   i. Oil pressure line to gauge, if so equipped

   j. Parking brake cable

   k. Power steering pump. This can be removed as a unit and set aside, without removing any of the hoses.

   l. Engine ground straps

   m. Exhaust pipe (support if necessary)

9. Loosen and remove the fan belt, remove the fan blades and pulley. If you have the finned aluminum viscous drive fan clutch, keep it upright in its normal position. If the fluid leaks out, the unit will have to be

replaced.

10. Remove the clutch cross-shaft.

11. Attach a chain or lifting device to the engine. If your engine doesn't have any lifting eyes, the usual locations are under the intake manifold bolts on V8s, or under the cylinder head bolts at either end on the sixes. You may have to remove the carburetor. Take the engine weight off the engine mounts, and unbolt the mounts. On all models except the gas-engined C-10, 1500, C-20, and 2500, support and disconnect the transmission. With automatic transmission, remove the torque converter underpan and starter, unbolt the converter from the flywheel, detach the throttle linkage and vacuum modulator line, and unbolt the engine from the transmission. Be certain that the converter does not fall out. With manual transmission, unbolt the clutch housing from the engine.

12. On two wheel drive models, remove the driveshaft. Either drain the transmission or plug the driveshaft opening. Disconnect the speedometer cable at the transmission. Disconnect the TCS switch wire, if so equipped. Disconnect the shift linkage or lever, or the clutch linkage. Disconnect the transmission cooler lines, if so equipped. If you have an automatic or a four speed transmission, the rear crossmember must be removed. With the three speed, unbolt the transmission from the crossmember. Raise the engine/transmission assembly and pull it forward.

13. On diesels, remove the three bolts, transmission, right side; disconnect the wires to the starter and remove the starter.

14. On four wheel drive, raise and pull the engine forward until it is free of the transmission. On diesels, slightly raise the transmission, remove the three left transmission to engine bolts, and remove the engine.

15. On all trucks, lift the engine out slowly, making certain as you go that all lines between the engine and the truck have been disconnected.

Installation is as follows:

1. On four wheel drive and diesels, lower the engine into place and align it with the transmission. Push the engine back gently and turn the crankshaft until the manual transmission shaft and clutch engage. Bolt the transmission to the engine. With automatic transmission, align the converter with the flywheel, bolt the transmission to the engine, bolt the converter to the flywheel, replace the underpan and starter, and connect the throttle linkage and vacuum modulator line.

2. On two wheel drive, lower the engine/transmission unit into place. Replace the rear crossmember if removed. Bolt the three speed transmission back to the crossmember. Replace the driveshaft.

3. Install the engine mounts.

4. Replace all transmission connections and the clutch cross-shaft. Replace the fan, pulley, and belts.

5. Replace all the items removed from

the engine earlier. Connect all the wires which were detached.

6. Replace the radiator and fan shroud, air cleaner, and battery or battery cables. Fill the cooling system and check the automatic transmission fuel level. Fill the crankcase with oil. Check for leaks.

BLAZER AND JIMMY

1975–76

1. Disconnect the negative battery cable, then the positive battery cable.

2. Drain the cooling system.

3. Remove the air cleaner.

4. Scribe matchmarks on the hood hinges for reassembly and remove the hood.

5. Remove the radiator and fan shroud as outlined later in this chapter.

6. Disconnect and label (to avoid confusion) the wires at the following locations:

   a. Starter solenoid

   b. Alternator

   c. Temperature sending switch

   d. Oil pressure sending switch

   e. Coil

   f. Vacuum advance solenoid and/or the CEC solenoid

   g. TCS solenoid (V8, if so equipped)

7. Disconnect the:

   a. Accelerator linkage at the manifold

   b. Fuel line from the tank at the fuel pump

   c. Heater hoses at the engine block

   d. Oil pressure gauge and the vacuum lines at the engine

   e. Evaporative emission system lines at the carburetor (on 1978 and later models, the hose at the fuel vapor storage canister)

   f. Power steering pump at the mounting bracket (lay the pump aside without disconnecting any of the lines)

   g. Ground straps at the engine block

   h. Exhaust pipe at the manifold (hang the pipe from the frame with a wire)

   i. TCS switch at the transmission (V8, if so equipped)

   j. Vacuum line to the power brake unit at the manifold

8. If equipped with air conditioning, unbolt the compressor at the bracket and lay it aside.

——— CAUTION ———

Do not disconnect any of the refrigerant lines. Evacuation of the air conditioning system should only be performed by someone who has the proper skill and training to do so, as the refrigerant will instantly freeze anything it contacts, including your eyes.

9. Unbolt the engine fan and remove the fan and pulley.

10. On manual transmission models:

   a. Disconnect the clutch fork return spring at the fork.

   b. Disconnect the clutch pedal pushrod at the cross shaft lever. Let the pushrod hang from the lower lever.

c. At the frame end of the cross shaft, remove the ball stud and retaining nut.

d. Slide the shaft toward the engine, lift it up to clear the bracket and remove the shaft from the engine ball stud.

11. On the six cylinder, remove the rocker arm cover.

12. Attach a chain or lifting device to the brackets on the engine. If your engine doesn't have lifting eyes, good locations are under the intake manifold bolts on V8s or under the cylinder head bolts at either end on the sixes. You may need to remove the carburetor for clearance. Lift the engine slightly, just enough to take the weight off the motor mounts.

13. On four wheel drive models, support the transmission using a floor jack and disconnect it from the engine. Remove the engine mount bolts.

14. On two wheel drive models:

a. Remove the driveshaft.

b. Disconnect the TCS switch at the transmission.

c. Disconnect the speedometer cable at the transmission.

d. Disconnect the shift linkage.

e. On manual transmission models, disconnect the clutch linkage.

f. Remove the engine mount bolts.

g. Remove the transmission cooler lines, if so equipped.

h. Remove the rear mount crossmember.

i. Raise the engine and transmission slightly and check that everything is disconnected and ready for removal.

j. Pull the engine/transmission assembly forward and remove it from the vehicle.

15. On four wheel drive models:

a. Raise the engine slightly and pull it forward until it is disconnected from the transmission.

b. Raise the engine and remove it from the vehicle.

16. Reverse the removal procedure to install.

1977 and Later

1. Refer to steps 1–8 of the 1975–76 procedure.

2. Raise the vehicle on a hoist and drain the engine oil.

3. Disconnect the exhaust pipe at the manifold.

4. Remove the flywheel splash shield or the converter housing cover, as applicable.

5. Remove the starter motor as outlined earlier in this chapter.

6. On automatic transmission models remove the converter-to-flywheel attaching bolts.

7. Remove the engine mount through bolts.

8. On 1979 and later four wheel drive models, remove the strut rods at the engine mount.

9. Remove the engine-to-bellhousing attaching bolts.

10. Lower the vehicle from the hoist.

11. Using a floor jack, raise the transmission slightly.

12. Attach a lifting device to the engine and raise it slightly, taking the weight off the engine mounts.

13. Remove the engine mount-to-engine brackets.

14. Remove the engine.

15. Reverse the removal procedure to install.

Cylinder Head

REMOVAL AND INSTALLATION

Six Cylinder

1. Drain the cooling system and remove the air cleaner. Disconnect the PCV hose. If equipped, disconnect the air injection hose.

2. Disconnect the accelerator pedal rod at the bellcrank on the manifold, and the fuel and vacuum lines at the carburetor.

3. Disconnect the exhaust pipe at the manifold flange, then remove the manifold bolts and clamps and remove the manifolds and carburetor as an assembly.

4. Remove the fuel and vacuum line retaining clip from the water outlet. Then disconnect the wire harness from the heat sending unit and coil, leaving the harness clear of clips on the rocker arm cover.

5. Disconnect the radiator hose at the water outlet housing and the battery ground strap at the cylinder head.

6. Disconnect the wires and remove the spark plugs. Disconnect the coil-to-distributor primary wire lead at the coil and remove the coil on models without HEI.

7. Remove the rocker arm cover. Back off the rocker arm nuts, pivot the rocker arms to clear the pushrods and remove the pushrods.

8. Remove the cylinder head bolts, cylinder head and gasket.

To install:

1. Place a new cylinder head gasket over the dowel pins in the cylinder block with the bead up. Do not use sealer on composition steel/asbestos gaskets.

2. Guide and lower the cylinder head into place over the dowels and gasket.

3. Use sealant on the cylinder head bolts, install and tighten them down snugly.

4. Tighten the cylinder head bolts a little at a time with a torque wrench in the correct sequence. Final torque should be as specified.

5. Install the valve pushrods down through the cylinder head openings and seat them in their lifter sockets.

6. Install the rocker arms, balls and nuts and tighten the rocker arm nuts until all pushrod play is taken up.

7. Install the thermostat, the thermostat housing and the water outlet using new gaskets. Then connect the radiator hose.

8. Install the temperature sending switch.

9. Install the spark plugs.

10. Use new plug gaskets (if required) and torque to specifications.

11. Install the coil, then connect the heat sending unit and coil primary wires, and the battery ground cable at the cylinder head.

12. Clean the surfaces and install a new gasket over the manifold studs. Install the manifold. Install the bolts and clamps and torque as specified.

13. Connect the throttle linkage.

14. Connect the PCV fuel and vacuum lines and secure the lines in the clip at the water outlet. Connect the air injection line.

15. Fill the cooling system and check for leaks.

16. Adjust the valve lash as explained later.

17. Install the rocker arm cover and position the wiring harness in the clips.

18. Clean and install the air cleaner.

V8 Gasoline Engines

1. Remove the intake manifold as described later.

2. Remove the exhaust manifolds as described later and tie out of the way.

3. If the truck is equipped with air conditioning, remove the A/C compressor and the forward mounting bracket and lay the compressor aside. Do not disconnect any of the refrigerant lines.

4. Back off the rocker arm nuts and pivot the rocker arms out of the way so that the pushrods can be removed. Identify the pushrods so that they can be installed in their original positions.

5. Remove the cylinder head bolts and remove the heads.

6. Install the cylinder heads using new gaskets. Install the gaskets with the head up.

NOTE: Coat a steel gasket on both sides with sealer. If a composition gasket is used, do not use sealer.

7. Clean the bolts, apply sealer to the threads, and install them hand tight.

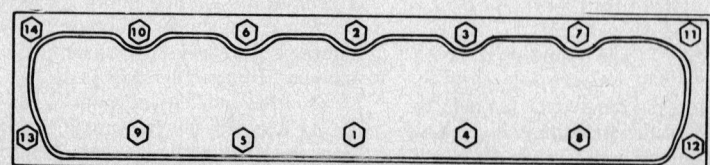

6-250, 292 head bolt torque sequence

8. Tighten the head bolts a little at a time in the sequence shown. Head bolt torque is listed in the Torque Specifications chart.

9. Install the intake and exhaust manifolds.

10. Adjust the rocker arms as explained later.

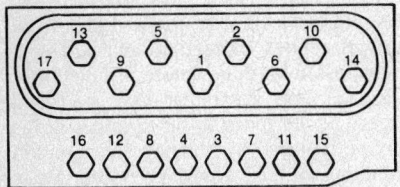

Small block V8 head bolt tightening sequence

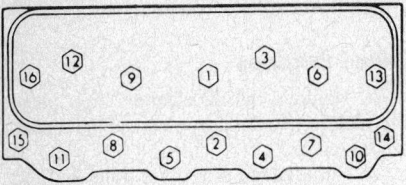

8-454 head bolt torque sequence

Diesel

It is strongly recommended that the cylinder heads not be removed on diesels. The procedure requires that the intake manifold and rocker arms be removed, which, in turn, requires removal of the valve lifters, disassembly, and reassembly while submerged in kerosene or diesel fuel. The valve lifters must then be bled down using a specially weighted press. In addition, removal of the intake manifold requires re-timing of the injection pump, which involves grinding off the old timing marks and using a special timing tool to scribe new marks while the pump is torqued to specification. It is advised that any work of this nature be performed by a qualified dealer or mechanic, as the tools involved are expensive and not generally available.

However, if the necessary tools are available, the cylinder heads may be removed and installed as follows:

1. Remove the intake manifold, using the procedure outlined later in this chapter.

2. Remove the rocker arm cover(s), after removing any accessory brackets which interfere with cover removal.

3. Disconnect and label the glow plug wiring.

4. If the right cylinder head is being removed, remove the ground strap from the head.

5. Remove the rocker arm bolts, the bridge pivots, the rocker arms, and the pushrods, keeping all the parts in order so that they can be returned to their original positions. It is a good practice to number or mark the parts to avoid interchanging them.

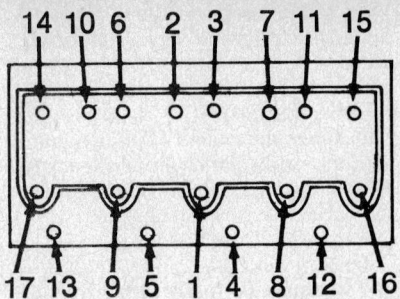

8-379 (6.2L) diesel head bolt torque sequence

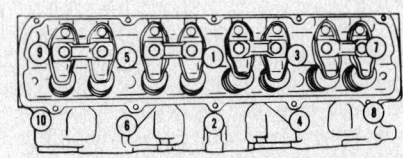

8-350 (5.7L) diesel head bolt torque sequence

6. Remove the fuel return lines from the nozzles.

7. Remove the exhaust manifold(s), using the procedure outlined later in this chapter.

8. Remove the engine block drain plug on the side of the engine from which the cylinder head is being removed.

9. Remove the head bolts. On the 379 cid (6.2 L), the rear left head bolt may have to remain in the head. Remove the cylinder head.

10. To install, first clean the mating surfaces thoroughly. Install new head gaskets on the engine block. Do NOT coat the gaskets with any sealer. The gaskets have a special coating that eliminates the need for sealer. The use of sealer will interfere with this coating and cause leaks. Install the cylinder head onto the block. On the 379 cid, install the left rear head bolt before installing the head.

11. Clean the head bolts thoroughly. On the 350 (5.7 L), dip the bolts in clean engine oil and install into the cylinder block until the heads of the bolts lightly contact the cylinder head. On the 379 cid, coat the bolt threads with GM sealer.

12. Tighten the bolts, in the sequence illustrated, to 100 ft. lbs. for the 350, and 60 ft. lbs. for the 379 (6.2 L). When all bolts have been tightened to this figure, begin the tightening sequence again, and torque all bolts to 130 ft. lbs. for the 350, and 95 ft. lbs. for the 379 (6.2 L).

13. Install the engine block drain plug(s), the exhaust manifold(s), the fuel return lines, the glow plug wiring, and the ground strap for the right cylinder head.

14. After disassembling, cleaning, and reassembling the valve lifters, bleed them down using the appropriate procedure outlined later in this section, and install them into the engine. Install the pushrods, rocker

arms, and pivots into their original locations.

15. Install the intake manifold.

16. Install the rocker cover(s). The covers do not use gaskets, but are sealed with a bead of RTV (room temperature vulcanizing) silicone sealer instead. Apply a $\frac{3}{32}$ inch bead of RTV sealer, G.M. #1052289 or the equivalent, to the clean and dry mating surface of the rocker arm cover. Run the bead of sealer to the inside of the bolt holes. Install the cover to the head within 10 minutes (while the sealer is still wet).

Rocker Arm Cover

REMOVAL AND INSTALLATION

1. Disconnect the negative battery cable.

2. Remove the air cleaner.

3. Disconnect the crankcase ventilation hose at the rocker arm covers.

4. Disconnect the wiring from the rocker arm clips.

5. Remove the carburetor heat stove pipe, on models so equipped. On diesels, remove the injection lines.

6. If the truck is equipped with A/C, remove the compressor rear brace. Do not disconnect any of the refrigerant lines.

7. Remove the rocker arm attaching bolts and remove the cover. If the cover is difficult to remove, gently tap the front of the cover rearward with your hand or a rubber mallet. If this still does not work, CAREFULLY pry the cover off. Be very careful not to distort the sealing surface or you'll be buying a new cover.

8. On installation, apply a $\frac{3}{16}$ in. bead of sealer to the mating surface after removing all the old loose sealer.

9. Reverse the removal procedure to install.

10. Install the fuel lines, and, with the protective covers, J-29664-1 installed, start the engine.

Valve System

VALVE LASH ADJUSTMENT

All engines described in this book use hydraulic lifters, which require no periodic adjustment. In the event of cylinder head removal or any operation that requires disturbing the rocker arms, the rocker arms will have to be adjusted.

Gasoline Engines

1. Remove the rocker covers and gaskets.

2. Adjust the valves on six cylinder engines as follows:

   a. Mark the distributor housing with a piece of chalk at No. 1 and 6 plug wire positions. Remove the distributor cap with the plug wires attached.

b. Crank the engine until the distributor rotor points to no. 1 cylinder and the points are open. At this point, adjust the following valves:

No. 1—exhaust and intake
No. 2—intake
No. 3—exhaust
No. 4—intake
No. 5—exhaust

c. Back out the adjusting nut until lash is felt at the pushrod, then turn the adjusting nut in until all lash is removed. This can be determined by checking pushrod end-play while turning the adjusting nut. When all play has been removed, turn the adjusting nut in 1 full turn.

d. Crank the engine until the distributor rotor points to no. 6 cylinder and the points are open. The following valves can be adjusted:

No. 2—exhaust
No. 3—intake
No. 4—exhaust
No. 5—intake

Six cylinder valve arrangement

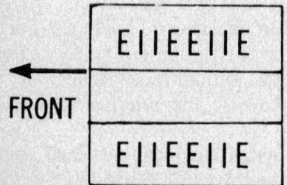

V8 valve arrangement

No. 6—intake and exhaust

3. Adjust the valves on V8 engines as follows:

a. Crank the engine until the mark on the damper aligns with the TDC or 0° mark on the timing tab and the engine is in no. 1 firing position. This can be determined by placing the fingers on the no. 1 cylinder valves as the marks align. If the valves do not move, it is in no. 1 firing position. If the valves move, it is in no. 6 firing position and the crankshaft should be rotated one more revolution to the no. 1 firing position.

b. The adjustment is made in the same manner as 6 cylinder engines.

c. With the engine in no. 1 firing position, the following valves can be adjusted:

Exhaust—1,3,4,8
Intake—1,2,5,7

d. Crank the engine 1 full revolution until the marks are again in alignment. This is no. 6 firing position. The following valves can now be adjusted:

Exhaust—2,5,6,7
Intake—3,4,6,8

4. Reinstall the rocker arm covers using new gaskets.

5. Install the distributor cap and wire assembly.

Diesel

Valve lash adjustment in diesel engines is controlled by the valve lifters, rather than through adjustments to the rocker arms. If the intake manifold has been removed, or if the heads have been removed, it will be necessary to remove those valve lifters affected, disassemble, reassemble, and bleed them down under pressure from a specially weighted testing press. It is for this reason that removal of the valve lifters, intake manifold, or cylinder heads is specifically not recommended. The procedure is complicated and requires expensive tools not generally available.

If the intake manifold has not been removed but rocker arms have been loosened or removed, valve lifters can be bled down by the following procedure:

1. For cylinders no. 3,5,7,2,4 and 8, turn the crankshaft so the saw slot on the harmonic balancer is at 0° on the timing indicator. For cylinders no. 1,3,7,2,4 and 6, turn the crankshaft so that the saw slot on the harmonic balancer is at 4 o'clock.

2. Tighten the rocker arm pivot bolts to 25 ft. lbs.

NOTE: It will take up to 45 minutes at each position for the valve lifters to be completely bled down.

————— CAUTION —————
Do not rotate the engine until the valve lifters have been bled down, or damage to the valve train could occur.

3. If any additional lifters need to be bled, rotate the crankshaft to the second position. Again, you must wait at least 45 minutes before rotating the crankshaft.

4. Finish reassembling the engine as the lifters are being bled.

VALVE GUIDES

Valve guides are integral with the cylinder head on all engines. Valve guide bores may be reamed to accommodate oversize valves. If wear permits, valve guides can be knurled to allow the retention of standard valves. Maximum allowable valve stem-to-guide bore clearances are listed under Valve Specifications.

Rocker Arms
REMOVAL AND INSTALLATION
Gasoline Engines

Rocker arms are removed by removing the adjusting nut. Be sure to adjust the valve lash after replacing the rocker arms. Coat the replacement rocker arm and ball with engine assembly lube before installation.

Rocker arm studs that have damaged threads or are loose in the cylinder heads may be replaced by reaming the bore and installing oversize studs. Oversizes available are .003 and .013 in. The bores may also be tapped and screw-in studs installed. Several aftermarket companies produce complete rocker arm stud kits with installation tools.

Diesel Engines

1. Remove the air cleaner, high pressure fuel lines to the injectors, and the rocker arm cover.

2. Remove the arm pivot bolts and the pivot(s). Remove the rocker arms. The use of bridged pivots requires that the rocker arms be removed in pairs.

3. To install, position the set of rocker arms in the original locations.

4. Lubricate the pivot contact surfaces and install the pivot(s).

5. Install the pivot bolts. Tighten the bolts alternately and evenly to 25 ft. lbs., following the bleed down procedure outlined previously under Valve Lash Adjustment for diesel engines.

6. Install the rocker arm cover as outlined in step 16 of the diesel engine cylinder head removal and installation procedure. Install the fuel lines and the air cleaner.

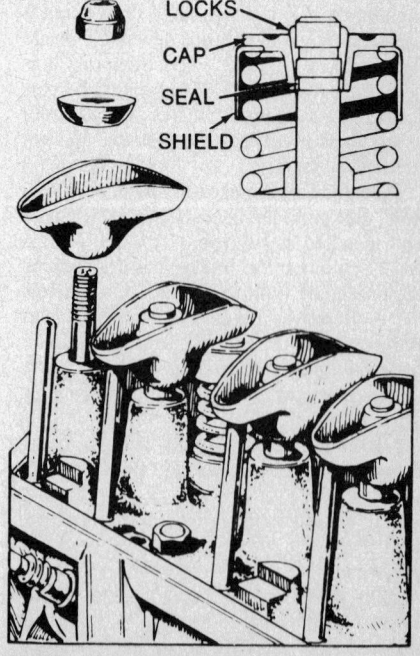

Rocker arm components

Valve Lifter Removal, Installation, Disassembly, and Bleed Down

DIESEL ENGINES

Whenever the rocker arms have been removed and the intake manifold removed, the valve lifters must be removed, disassembled, assembled while submerged in diesel fuel or kerosene, and bled down using a specially-weighted press. The lifters also must be disassembled, reassembled while submerged, and bled down on the press whenever they are removed. Note that if the rocker arms have been removed but the intake manifold has not been disturbed, the lifters can be bled down as outlined in the ''Valve Lash Adjustment'' procedure for diesel engines. The following procedure is to be used for lifter removal and installation, or whenever both the rocker arms and the intake manifold have been disturbed.

1. Remove the intake manifold.
2. Remove the rocker covers, the rocker arms, and the pushrods. Keep all the parts in order so that they may be installed in their original locations.
3. Remove the valve lifters.

To disassemble the lifters:

4. Remove the retainer ring with a small screwdriver.
5. Remove the pushrod seat. Remove the oil metering valve. Remove the plunger and plunger spring. Remove the check valve retainer from the plunger, and remove the valve and its spring.
6. Clean all parts in a safe solvent. Check for burrs, nicks, scoring, or excessive wear, and replace as necessary.
7. Check for lifter foot for excessive wear:
    a. Place a straightedge across the lifter foot.
    b. Hold the lifter at eye level. Check for light appearing between the lifter foot and the straightedge.
    c. If light is visible, indicating a concave surface, the lifter should be replaced and the camshaft inspected. If the cam lobe is worn across the full width of the cam base circle (opposite the high lobe of the cam), the camshaft should be replaced. Wear at the center of the cam base circle is normal. Wear across the full width of the nose of the lobe is also normal.
8. After the lifter parts have been cleaned, assemble the valve disc spring and retainer into the plunger. Be sure the retainer flange is pressed tightly against the bottom of the recess in the plunger.
9. Install the plunger spring over the check retainer.
10. Hold the plunger with the spring up. Insert into the lifter body. Hold the plunger

vertically while doing this to avoid cocking the spring.

11. Fill the reservoir of G.M. tool no. J-5790 with kerosene to within ½ inch of the top of the reservoir. This tool is a specially weighted press with provision for reservoir rotation.
12. Place the valve lifter assembly into the reservoir. Position the oil control valve and the pushrod seat onto the plunger.
13. Install a ¼ inch steel ball onto the pushrod seat. Lower the tester ram until it contacts the steel ball. Do not press on the ram. Allow the ram to move downward by its own weight, until the air bubbles expelled from the lifter assembly disappear.
14. Raise the ram, then allow it to lower by its own weight. Repeat this operation until all air is expelled from the lifter. Do not attempt to hasten the process by pumping the ram up and down.
15. After all air has been expelled, allow the ram to descend, bleeding the lifter, until the retaining ring groove is exposed. Install the retaining ring.
16. Adjust the ram screw so that it contacts the steel ball in the pushrod seat at the same time as the pointer is at the start line.
17. Raise the arm of the tester, then start the bleed down test by resting the ram on the steel ball and starting a timer. Rotate the reservoir one revolution every two seconds, and time the indicator from the start line to the stop line. Acceptable leak down time is 6 seconds minimum for used lifters, and from 9 to 60 seconds for a new lifter.
18. If the lifter leak down rate falls within the specified limit, the lifter may be reused. If not, new lifters should be installed in the engine.
19. If new lifters are to be installed, they must first be filled with kerosene or diesel fuel. Install the lifter in the tester. Fill the reservoir to within ½ inch of the top, and fill the lifter as outlined in steps 13, 14, and 15 of this procedure.

To install the lifters:

20. Coat the foot of the lifter with G.M. lubricant #562458 or the equivalent.
21. Install the lifters into their original positions. Install the pushrods into their original positions.
22. Install the intake manifold.
23. Install the rocker arms and pivots.
24. Bleed down the lifters as outlined under Valve Lash Adjustment for the diesel engine.
25. Install the rocker covers.

Intake Manifold

REMOVAL AND INSTALLATION

Six Cylinder with Combination Manifold

The intake and exhaust manifolds are removed as an assembly.
1. Remove the air cleaner.

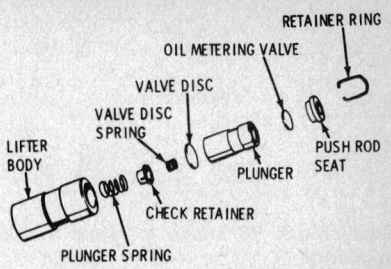

Exploded view of the 5.7L diesel valve lifter

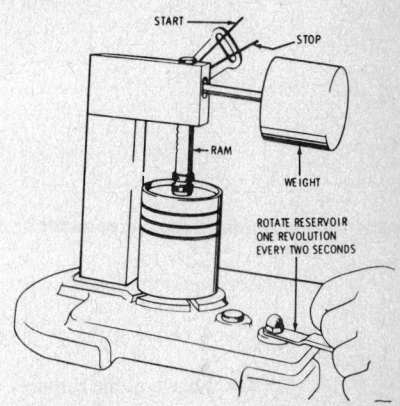

A specially weighted hand press must be used to assemble the diesel valve lifters

2. Disconnect the throttle rods at the bellcrank and remove the throttle return spring.
3. Disconnect the fuel and vacuum lines at the carburetor. Plug the fuel line. Disconnect the choke cable at the carburetor.
4. Disconnect the crankcase ventilation hose at the carburetor. Disconnect the vapor hose at the evaporative canister, if so equipped.
5. Disconnect the exhaust pipe at the manifold flange and discard the packing.
6. Disconnect the EGR valve hose (if equipped).
7. Remove the manifold attaching bolts and clamps and remove the manifold assembly. Discard the gaskets.
8. The manifold assembly can be separated by removing 1 bolt and 2 nuts at the center. Don't tighten these down all the way until the manifold assembly is installed on the engine.
9. Check the manifold for straightness along the exhaust port faces. If it is distorted more than 0.015 in. it should be replaced. Clean all mounting faces.
10. Installation is the reverse of removal. Use all new gaskets. Bolt torques are given in the Torque Specifications.

V8 Except Diesel

1. Remove the air cleaner.
2. Drain the radiator.
3. Disconnect:
    a. Battery cables at the battery.
    b. Upper radiator and heater hoses at the manifolds.

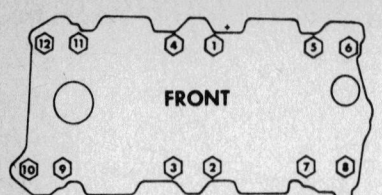

Small block V8 intake manifold torque sequence

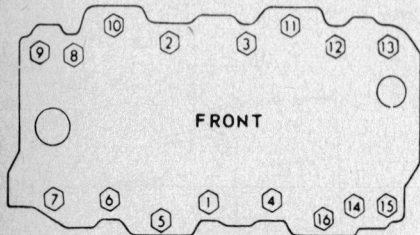

8-454 intake manifold torque sequence

c. Crankcase ventilation hoses as required.

d. Fuel line and choke cable at the carburetor.

e. Accelerator linkage at the carburetor.

f. Vacuum hose at the distributor.

g. Power brake hose at the carburetor base or manifold, if applicable.

h. Temperature sending switch wires.

i. Water pump by-pass at the water pump (Mark IV only).

4. Remove the distributor cap and scribe the rotor position relative to the distributor body.

5. Remove the distributor.

6. As required, remove the oil filler bracket, air cleaner bracket, air compressor and bracket and accelerator bellcrank.

7. Remove the manifold-to-head attaching bolts then remove the manifold and carburetor as an assembly.

8. If the manifold is to be replaced, transfer the carburetor (and mounting studs), water outlet and thermostat (use a new gasket) heater hose adapter, EGR valve (use new gasket) and, if applicable, TVS switch and the choke coil. All engines use a carburetor heat choke tube which must be transferred to a new manifold.

9. Before installing the manifold, thoroughly clean the gasket and seal surfaces of the cylinder heads and manifold.

10. Install the manifold end seals, folding the tabs if applicable, and the manifold/head gaskets, using a sealing compound around the water passages. 1978 and later models use RTV (Room Temperature Vulcanizing) silicone seal at the front and rear ridges of the cylinder block, instead of seals. On these models, remove any loose RTV from the sealing surfaces. Apply a 3/16 inch bead of RTV sealer, G.M. #1052366 or the equivalent, on the front and rear ridges, extending the bead up 1/2 inch on the cylinder heads to seal and retain the intake manifold side gaskets.

NOTE: 1975 350 V8 engines require a new intake manifold side gasket on 4-bbl engines. The new gasket has restricted cross-over ports. The 350 2-bbl uses a restricted cross-over gasket on the right-hand side and an open gasket on the left. The 350 4-bbl uses restricted cross-over gaskets on both sides.

11. When installing the manifold, care should be taken not to dislocate the end seals. It is helpful to use a pilot in the distributor opening. Tighten the manifold bolts to 30 ft. lbs. in the sequence illustrated.

12. Install the ignition coil (point-type ignitions).

13. Install the distributor with the rotor in its original location as indicated by the scribe line. If the engine has been disturbed, refer to Distributor Removal and Installation.

14. If applicable, install the alternator upper bracket and adjust the belt tension.

15. Connect all components disconnected in steps 3 and 6.

16. Fill the cooling system, start the engine, check for leaks and adjust the ignition timing and carburetor idle speed and mixture.

Diesel

It is not recommended that the intake manifold be removed on diesel engines. The procedure requires re-timing of the injection pump. This involves grinding off the old timing mark and scribing a new mark with a special timing tool while re-torquing the pump to specification. It is strongly advised that any work of this nature be performed only be a qualified mechanic or dealer.

If the necessary tools are available, the intake manifold can be removed and installed using the following procedure.

1. Remove the air cleaner.

2. Drain the radiator. Loosen the upper bypass hose clamp, remove the thermostat housing bolts, and remove the housing and the thermostat from the intake manifold.

3. Remove the breather pipes from the rocker covers and the air crossover. Re-

move the air crossover. It is a good idea to cover the air intakes in the manifold to prevent nuts and bolts from falling down into the engine, if dropped. The intake passages can simply be taped over.

4. Disconnect the throttle rod and the return spring. If equipped with cruise control, remove the servo.

5. Remove the hairpin clip at the bellcrank and disconnect the cables. Remove the throttle cable from the bracket on the manifold; position the cable away from the engine. Disconnect and label any wiring as necessary.

6. Remove the alternator bracket as necessary. If the truck is equipped with air conditioning, remove the compressor mounting bolts and move the compressor aside, without disconnecting any of the hoses. Remove the compressor mounting bracket from the intake manifold.

7. Disconnect the fuel line from the pump and the fuel filter. Remove the fuel filter and bracket.

8. Disconnect the fuel return line from the injection pump. Using two wrenches to prevent the lines from being twisted, disconnect the injection pump lines at the nozzles.

CAUTION
Do not bend the injection pump lines!

9. Remove the three nuts retaining the injection pump, using G.M. special tool no. J-26987 or the equivalent. Remove the pump and cap all open lines and nozzles.

10. Disconnect the vacuum lines at the vacuum pump. Remove the bolt and the bracket holding the pump to the block and remove the pump.

11. Remove the intake manifold drain tube clamp and remove the drain tube.

12. Remove the intake manifold bolts and remove the manifold. Remove the adapter seal. Remove the injection pump adapter.

13. Clean the mating surfaces of the cylinder heads and the intake manifold using a putty knife. Be extremely careful not to scratch or gouge the surfaces. Clean and dry the surfaces with solvent.

To install the manifold:

NOTE: If the rocker arms have been removed, the valve lifters must be re-

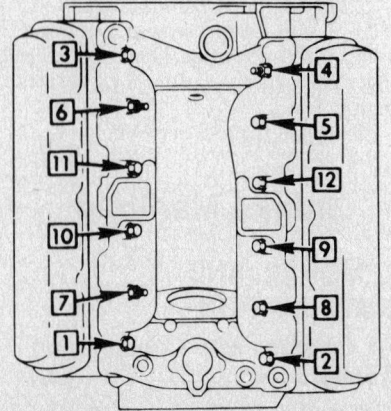

8-350 diesel intake manifold torque sequence

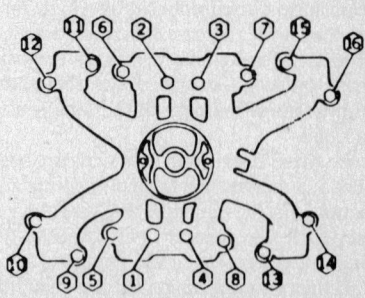

8-379 diesel intake manifold torque sequence

moved, disassembled, then reassembled while submerged in kerosene or diesel fuel, then bled down using the specially weighted press. See the procedure earlier in this chapter. Do not install the manifold until the affected lifters have been serviced.

14. Coat both sides of the gasket surface that seal the intake manifold to the cylinder heads with G.M. sealer #1050805 or the equivalent. Position the intake manifold gaskets on the cylinder heads. Install the end seals, making sure that the ends are positioned under the cylinder heads.

15. Carefully lower the intake manifold into place on the engine.

16. Clean the intake manifold bolts thoroughly, then dip them in clean engine oil. Install the bolts and tighten to 15 ft. lbs. in the sequence shown. Next, tighten all the bolts to 30 ft. lbs., in sequence, and finally tighten to 40 ft. lbs. in sequence.

17. Install the intake manifold drain tube and clamp.

18. File the mark from the injection pump adapter.

CAUTION

Do not file the mark from the injection pump.

---

19. Place the engine on TDC for the No. 1 cylinder. The mark on the harmonic balancer on the crankshaft will be aligned with the zero mark on the timing tab, and both valves for no. 1 cylinder will be closed. The index mark on the injection pump driven gear should be offset to the right when no. 1 is at TDC. Check that all these conditions are met before continuing.

20. Apply chassis grease to the seal area on the adapter, the tapered edge and the seal area on the intake manifold. Install the adapter but leave the bolts loose.

21. Apply chassis grease to the inside and outside diameters of the adapter seal, and to the seal installing tool, G.M. no. J-28425. Install the seal onto the tool.

22. Push the seal onto the injection pump adapter, using the tool (no. J-28425 or the equivalent). Remove the tool and inspect the seal to see if it is properly positioned.

23. Tighten the adapter bolts to 25 ft. lbs.

24. Install a timing tool, G.M. no. J-26896 or the equivalent, into the injection pump adapter. Tighten the tool toward No. 1 cylinder to 50 ft. lbs. While holding the tool and adapter at this torque, mark the injection pump adapter by striking the marking pin with a hammer. Remove the tool.

25. Remove the protective caps from the lines. Line up the offset tang on the injection pump driveshaft with the pump driven gear. Install the pump.

26. Install the three retaining nuts and lockwashers for the injection pump but do not tighten the nuts. Connect the injection pump lines to the nozzles. Use two wrenches to tighten the lines (25 ft. lbs.).

CAUTION

Do not bend or twist the injection pump lines.

---

27. Connect the fuel return lines to the pump.

28. Align the injection pump mark with the adapter mark and tighten the nuts. Use a ¾ inch open end wrench on the boss at the front of the injection pump to aid in rotating the pump to align the marks. Tighten the nuts to 18 ft. lbs.

29. Adjust the throttle rod and return spring.

30. Install the fuel filter and bracket and install the fuel line to the pump and the filter.

31. Install the vacuum pump and the vacuum lines. Do not operate the engine without the vacuum pump installed—it is the drive for the engine oil pump.

32. Connect the wiring.

33. Install the alternator and air conditioning compressor brackets.

34. Install the cable in the bracket and bellcrank, then install the bellcrank.

35. Connect the throttle rod and the return spring.

36. Remove the tape from the air intakes and install the air crossover. Install the breather tubes and the flow control valve at the air crossover. Connect the upper radiator hose and the heater hose, install thermostat and thermostat housing, fill the cooling system, start the engine and check for leaks.

Exhaust Manifold

REMOVAL AND INSTALLATION

Six Cylinder, Non-Integral Head

See the ''Intake Manifold Removal and Installation'' section.

Six Cylinder With Integral Head

1. Remove the air cleaner. Disconnect negative battery terminal.

2. Remove the power steering pump and, if equipped, the AIR pump.

3. Remove the EFE (early fuel evaporation) valve bracket.

4. Disconnect the throttle controls and the throttle return spring.

5. Disconnect the exhaust pipe at the manifold flange. Disconnect the converter bracket at the transmission mount, if so equipped. If equipped with manifold converter, disconnect the exhaust pipe from the converter, and remove the converter.

6. Remove the manifold attaching bolts and remove the manifold. Discard the gasket.

7. Check for cracks in the manifold before it is replaced.

8. Install a new gasket on the exhaust manifold.

9. Clean and oil the bolts and install

the bolts, torquing them to specifications.

10. Connect the exhaust pipe, throttle controls, and return spring. Install the air cleaner, start the engine, and check for leaks.

V8 Except Diesel

1. If equipped with AIR, remove the

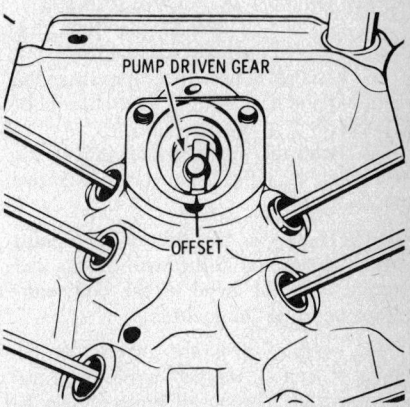

The index mark on the injection pump driven gear will be offset to the right when the no. 1 cylinder is at TDC

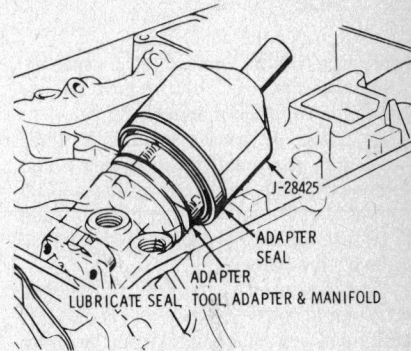

Adapter seal installation

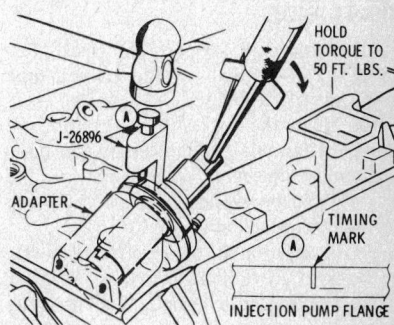

Injection pump timing mark application

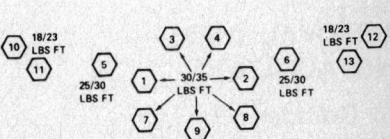

Six cylinder integral manifold torque sequence

air injector assembly. The ¼ in. pipe threads in the manifold are straight cut threads. Do not use a ¼ in. tapered pipe tap to clean the threads.

2. Disconnect the battery.

3. If equipped, remove the carburetor heat stove pipe.

4. Remove the spark plug wire heat shields. On Mark IV, remove spark plugs.

5. On the left exhaust manifold, disconnect and remove the alternator.

6. Disconnect the exhaust pipe from the manifold and hang it from the frame out of the way.

7. Bend the locktabs and remove the end bolts, then the center bolts. Remove the manifold.

NOTE: A ⁹⁄₁₆ in. thin wall 6-point socket, sharpened at the leading edge and tapped onto the head of the bolt, simplifies bending the locktabs.

8. Installation is the reverse of removal. Clean all mating surfaces and use new gaskets. Torque all bolts to specifications from the inside working out.

Diesel

LEFT SIDE

1. Remove the air cleaner.

2. Remove the lower alternator bracket.

3. Raise the truck and remove the exhaust pipe from the manifold flange.

4. Lower the truck. Bend the locktabs away from the manifold mounting bolts. Remove the bolts and remove the manifold from above. Do not lose the locktabs, and do not use the washers for the bolts, which go under the locktabs.

5. Installation is the reverse. Tighten the manifold bolts to 25 ft. lbs. in two stages, working in a circular pattern from the center to the ends. Then tighten the front bolt to 30 ft. lbs.

RIGHT SIDE

1. Raise and support the truck. Remove the bolts retaining the exhaust pipe to the manifold flange.

2. Bend the locktabs away from the manifold mounting bolts. Remove the bolts and remove the manifold. Do not lose the locktabs and the washers for the bolts, which go under the locktabs.

3. Installation is the reverse. Tighten the bolts to 25 ft. lbs. in two progressive steps, working in a circular pattern from the center to the ends.

Timing Gear Cover

REMOVAL AND INSTALLATION

Six Cylinder

1. Remove the radiator after draining it.

2. Remove the fan, pulley, and belt.

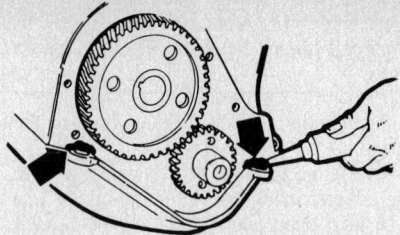

Apply sealer to the six cylinder timing cover at the areas shown

Remove any power steering and/or AIR pump drive belts. Remove any braces for the above pumps which will interfere with cover removal and position the pumps out of the way.

3. Remove the crankshaft pulley and damper. Use a puller to remove the damper. Do not attempt to pry or hammer the damper off, or it will be damaged.

4. On all 1975–78 models, and on all 1979–82 250 sixes, pull the cover forward slightly and cut the oil pan front seal off flush with the block. Remove the cover. 1979–82 292 sixes have RTV (room temperature vulcanizing) silicone seal at the oil pan to front cover junction; no front rubber seal is used.

5. Cut the tabs from a new oil pan front seal and install the seal to the front cover, pressing the tips into the holes provided in the cover. On 1979–82 models using no rubber seal, apply a ³⁄₁₆ inch bead of RTV silicone seal on the cover sealing surface.

6. On all models, coat the front cover gasket with sealer and use a ⅛ in. bead of silicone sealer at the oil pan to cylinder block joint. Replace the damper before tightening the cover bolts down, so that the cover seal will align. The damper must be drawn into place. Hammering it will destroy it.

7. Replace the oil pan if it was removed, and fill the crankcase with oil.

REMOVAL

Small Block V8

1. Drain the oil.

2. Drain and remove the radiator.

3. Remove the fan, pulley and belt. Remove any power steering and/or AIR pump drive belts. Remove any braces for these pumps which will interfere with cover removal and position the pumps out of the way.

4. Remove the water pump.

5. Remove the crankshaft pulley and damper. Use a puller on the damper. Do not attempt to pry or hammer the damper off.

6. Rotate the retaining bolts, and remove the timing cover.

INSTALLATION

1975–76 Small Block V8

1. Clean the gasket mating surfaces.

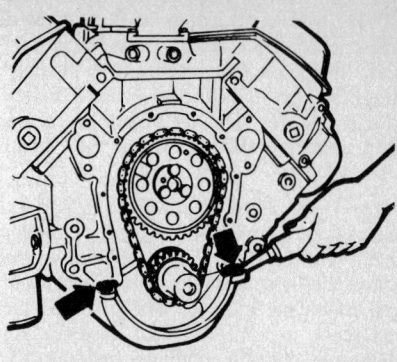

Apply sealer to the V8 cover pads at the areas shown

2. Remove any oil pan gasket material that may still be adhering to the oil pan-engine block joint face.

3. Apply a ⅛ in. bead of silicone sealant (part no. 1051435) or the equivalent to the joint formed by the oil pan and cylinder block, as well as to the entire oil pan front lip.

4. Coat the cover gasket with gasket sealer and place it in position on the front cover.

5. Apply a bead of sealant to the bottom of the lower seal and install it on the cover. Loosely install the front cover on the block. Install the 4 top bolts loosely (about 3 turns). Install two ¼-20 × ½ in. screws in the hole at each side of the front cover.

6. Tighten the screws evenly while aligning the dowel pins and holes in the front cover.

7. Remove the ¼-20 × ½ in. screws and install the rest of the cover screws.

8. Further installation is the reverse of removal. Refill the engine with oil.

INSTALLATION

1977–82 Small Block V8

1. Clean the gasket surfaces on the block and the front cover.

2. Use a sharp knife to trim any excess oil pan gasket material which protrudes from the oil pan-to-engine block junction.

3. Apply a ⅛ inch bead of RTV silicone sealer, G.M. #1052366 or the equivalent, to the joint of the oil pan and cylinder block.

4. Coat the front cover gasket with sealer and install the gasket onto the cover.

5. Install the front cover-to-oil pan seal. Lightly coat the bottom of the seal with clean engine oil and position over the crankshaft end.

6. Loosely install the front cover upper attaching bolts.

7. Press downward on the cover so that the dowels in the block are aligned with the holes in the cover. While holding the cover in position, tighten the upper attaching bolts alternately and evenly.

8. Install the remaining bolts and tighten all the bolts to specification.

9. Install the torsional damper and the water pump.

REMOVAL AND INSTALLATION

Mark IV V8

1. Remove the torsional damper and water pump.

2. Remove the two oil pan-to-front cover attaching screws.

3. Remove the front cover-to-block attaching screws.

4. Pull the cover slightly forward to permit cutting the oil pan front seal.

5. Using a sharp knife, cut the oil pan front seal flush with the cylinder block at both sides of the cover.

6. Remove the front cover and the portion of the oil pan front seal. Remove the front cover gasket.

7. Clean the gasket mating surfaces.

8. Cut the tabs from a new oil pan front seal, using a sharp knife to get a clean cut.

9. Install the seal on the front cover pressing the tips into the holes in the front cover.

10. Coat a new gasket with gasket sealer and install the gasket on the cover.

11. Apply a ⅛ in. bead of sealant to the joint formed at the junction of the oil pan and cylinder block.

12. Place the front cover in position.

13. Align the cover over the dowel pins in the block.

14. Further installation is the reverse of removal.

REMOVAL AND INSTALLATION

Diesel

1. Drain cooling system. Disconnect radiator hoses and bypass hose.

2. Remove all belts, fan and fan pulley, crankshaft pulley and harmonic balancer, and accessory brackets. The harmonic balancer must be removed with a puller which pulls from the rear center of the balancer. Any other type of puller, such as a universal claw type which pulls on the outside of the hub, can destroy the balancer. The outside ring of the balancer is bonded in rubber to the hub; by pulling on the outside, it is possible to break that bond.

3. Remove cover-to-block attaching bolts and remove the cover, timing indicator and water pump assembly.

4. Remove the front cover and dowel pins. It may be necessary to grind a flat on the pins to get a rough surface for gripping.

To install:

5. Grind a chamfer on one end of each dowel pin.

6. Cut excess material from front end of oil pan gasket on each side of engine block.

7. Clean block, oil pan, and front cover mating surfaces with solvent.

8. Trim about ⅛ in. from each end of a new front pan seal, using a sharp knife to insure a straight cut.

9. Install new front cover gasket on engine block and new front seal on front cover. Apply sealer to gasket around coolant holes and place on block.

10. Apply silicone sealer at junction of block, pan, and front cover.

11. Place cover on block and press downward to compress the seal. Rotate cover left and right and guide pan seal into cavity using a small screwdriver.

12. Apply engine oil to bolts (threads and heads). Install two bolts finger tight to hold cover in place.

13. Install two dowel pins chamfered end first.

14. Install timing indicator and water pump assembly. Torque bolts evenly to 13 ft. lbs. for the water pump bolts, and 35 ft. lbs. for cover bolts.

15. Apply lubricant to balancer seal surface. Install balancer, and balancer bolt. Torque to approximately 250 ft. lbs.

16. Install brackets. Connect bypass hose and radiator hoses. Install crankshaft pulley and four attaching bolts. Torque to 20 ft. lbs.

17. Install fan pulley, fan, and four attaching bolts. Torque to 20 ft. lbs. Install belts and adjust tension. Fill radiator. Road test and check for leaks.

Timing Gear Cover Oil Seal

REPLACEMENT

All Engines

The seal may be replaced with the cover either on or off the engine. With the cover removed:

1. Pry the old seal from the cover using a wooden or plastic pick to prevent damage to the sealing lip. A plastic knitting needle makes a good removal tool.

2. Oil the lip of the new seal. Place a support under the cover so that it is not damaged when the seal is installed.

3. Install the seal so that the open side of the seal is toward the inside of the cover. Drive the seal into place with a tool made for the purpose (G.M. tool no. J-23042 or the equivalent).

The seal can also be replaced with the cover in place on the engine:

1. Remove the torsional damper. Pry the old seal from the cover, as outlined in step 1 of the removal procedure with the cover removed.

2. Oil the lip of the new seal and place it into position, with the open side of the seal toward the engine. Drive the seal into position with a tool designed for the purpose (G.M. tool no. J-23042 or the equivalent).

3. Install the damper.

Timing Chain or Gear

REMOVAL AND INSTALLATION

Six Cylinder

The six-cylinder camshaft is gear driven. To remove the camshaft gear, remove the camshaft and press the gear off.

--- **CAUTION** ---

The thrust plate must be positioned so that the Woodruff key in the shaft does not damage it when the shaft is pressed out of the gear. Support the hub of the gear or the gear will be seriously damaged.

Installing the front cover oil seal (cover off)

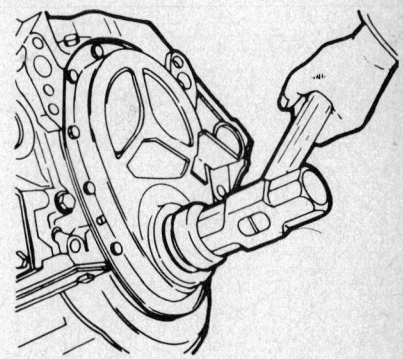

Installing the front cover oil seal (cover installed)

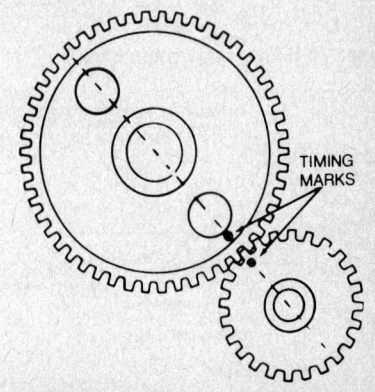

Six cylinder timing gear alignment

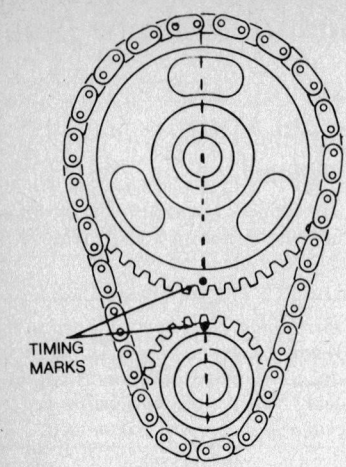

V8 timing mark alignment

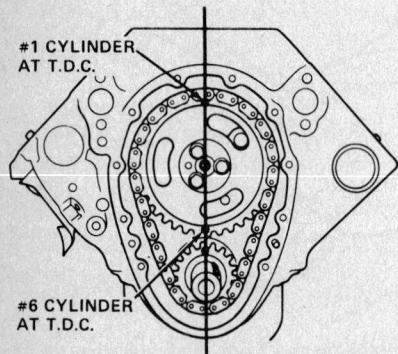

1979–82 V8 timing sprocket alignment

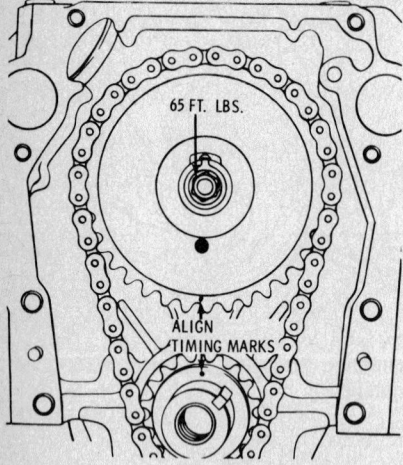

Diesel V8 timing mark alignment

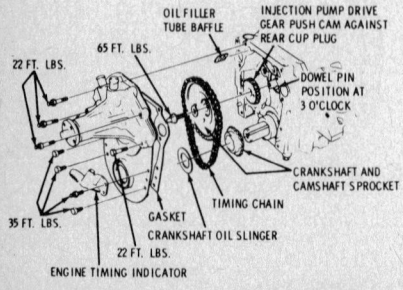

Injection pump drive gear installation

The crankshaft gear may be removed with a gear puller while in place in the block.

V8 Except Diesel

V8 models are equipped with a timing chain. To replace the chain, remove the radiator core, water pump harmonic balancer, and the crankcase front cover. This will allow access to the timing chain. Crank the engine until the zero marks punched on both sprockets are closest to one another and in line between the shaft centers. Then, take out the three bolts that hold the camshaft gear to the camshaft. This gear is a light press fit on the camshaft and will come off readily. It is located by a dowel.

The chain comes off with the camshaft gear.

A gear puller will be required to remove the crankshaft gear.

Without disturbing the position of the engine, mount the new crank gear on the shaft, then mount the chain over the camshaft gear. Arrange the camshaft gear in such a way that the timing marks will line up between the shaft centers and the camshaft locating dowel will enter the dowel hole in the cam sprocket.

Place the cam sprocket, with its chain mounted over it, in position on the front of the camshaft and pull up with the three bolts that hold it to the camshaft.

After the gears are in place, turn the engine two full revolutions to make certain that the timing marks are in correct alignment between the shaft centers.

Diesel

It is not recommended that the timing chain and gears be removed or replaced, because this requires that the engine be retimed. Retiming of the engine requires removal of the injection pump and fuel lines, and the injection pump adapter. The timing mark must be filed off the injection pump adapter, and a new mark must be scribed with a special timing tool. It is recommended that all such work be left to a qualified dealer or mechanic who has access to such equipment.

If the necessary tools are available, the timing chain and gears may be replaced as follows:

1. Remove the crankshaft pulley, harmonic balancer and front cover, using the procedure outlined earlier in this section. Be certain to use the correct tool for balancer removal, to avoid damaging the part.

2. Align the timing marks on the crankshaft and camshaft sprockets by rotating the crankshaft in the direction of normal engine rotation. The marks should be closest to one another and in line between the shaft centers, as shown in the accompanying diagram. Do not disturb the position of the engine.

3. Remove the oil slinger from the crankshaft. Remove the camshaft sprocket retaining nut.

4. Remove the crankshaft sprocket. The sprocket-to-crankshaft fit is such that a puller may be necessary. If possible, the crankshaft key should be removed before using the puller. If this is not possible, align the puller so that the fingers of the tool do not overlap the end of the key when the sprocket is removed. The keyway is machined only partway in the crankshaft sprocket, and breakage can occur if the sprocket is improperly removed.

5. Remove the timing chain and camshaft sprocket.

6. The fuel pump eccentric is behind the crankshaft sprocket, and may be removed if necessary.

7. Install the key in the crankshaft, if removed. Install the fuel pump eccentric, if removed.

8. Install the camshaft sprocket, crankshaft sprocket, and the timing chain together, with the timing marks aligned. Tighten the camshaft sprocket retaining bolt to 65 ft. lbs.

NOTE: When the two timing marks are in alignment and closest together, the No. 6 cylinder is at TDC. To obtain TDC for No. 1 cylinder, slowly rotate the crankshaft one full revolution. This will move the camshaft sprocket timing mark to the top. No. 1 cylinder will then be at TDC.

9. Install the oil slinger.

10. The injection pump must be retimed. Follow steps 1, 2, 3, 4, 5, 7, 8 and 9 of the intake manifold removal and installation procedure. Remove the injection pump adapter and the seal from the injection pump adapter.

11. Follow steps 18, 19, 20, 21, 22, 23, 24, 25, 26, 27, 28, 29, 30, 32, 34, 35 and 36 of the intake manifold removal and installation procedure.

12. Install the front cover, harmonic balancer, and the crankshaft pulley.

Camshaft

REMOVAL AND INSTALLATION

NOTE: Whenever a new camshaft is installed, it is recommended that all valve lifters be replaced, to insure the durability of the camshaft lobes and the valve lifter feet.

Six Cylinder

1. In addition to removing the timing gear cover, remove the grille and radiator. If the truck has air conditioning, the condenser must be moved to provide room for camshaft removal. It may be possible to unbolt the condenser and move it aside, far enough for clearance. Otherwise, the air conditioning system must be discharged and the condenser removed. Do not disconnect any of the air conditioning lines unless you are thoroughly familiar with A/C

systems and the hazards involved. It is recommended that you have the system discharged by a professional.

---------------- CAUTION ----------------

Compressed refrigerant expands (boils) into the atmosphere at a temperature of −21°F or less. It will freeze any surface it contacts, including your skin or eyes.

---

2. Remove the valve cover and gasket, loosen all the valve rocker arm nuts and pivot the arms clear of the pushrods.

3. Remove the distributor and fuel pump.

4. Remove the coil (through 1977), side covers and gaskets. Remove the pushrods and valve lifters.

5. Align the timing gear marks and remove the two camshaft thrust plate retaining screws by working through the holes in the camshaft gear.

6. Remove the camshaft and gear assembly by pulling it out through the front of the block. Be careful not to dislodge the camshaft bearings.

NOTE: If renewing either camshaft or camshaft gear, the gear must be pressed off the camshaft. Install press plates under the camshaft gear and press the camshaft from the gear. The thrust plate must be positioned so that the Woodruff key in the camshaft does not damage the shaft when the camshaft is pressed from the gear. Support the hub of the gear to prevent damage to the part. The replacement parts must be assembled in the same manner (under pressure). In placing the gear on the camshaft, press the gear onto the shaft until it bottoms against the gear spacer ring. The end clearance of the thrust plate should be .001 to .005 in.

7. Install the camshaft assembly in the engine.

NOTE: Pre-lube the cam lobes with E.O.S. or SAE 90 gear lubricant. Do not dislodge the cam bearings when inserting the camshaft.

8. Turn the crankshaft and camshaft to align and bring the timing marks together. Push the camshaft into this aligned position.

9. Runout on either crankshaft or camshaft gear should not exceed .003 in.

10. Backlash between the two gears should be between .004 and .006 in.

11. Install the timing gear cover and gasket.

12. Install the oil pan and gaskets.

13. Install the harmonic balancer.

14. Line up the keyway in the balancer with the key on the crankshaft and drive the balancer onto the shaft until it bottoms against the crankshaft gear.

15. Install the valve lifters and pushrods. Install the side covers with new gaskets. Later models use RTV sealer instead of gaskets. Attach the coil wires; install the fuel pump.

16. Install the distributor and set the tim-

ing as described under the Distributor Removal and Installation section at the beginning of the chapter.

17. Pivot the rocker arms over the pushrods and adjust the valves.

18. Add oil to the engine. Install and adjust the fan belt.

19. Install the radiator or shroud.

20. Install the grille assembly.

21. Fill the cooling system, start the engine and check for leaks.

22. Check and adjust the timing.

V8 Except Diesel

1. Remove the intake manifold, valve lifters and timing chain cover as previously described.

2. Remove the grille and radiator. If the truck has air conditioning, the condenser must be moved to provide room for camshaft removal. It may be possible to unbolt the condenser and move it aside, far enough for clearance. Otherwise, the air conditioning system must be discharged and the condenser removed. Do not disconnect any of the air conditioning lines unless you are thoroughly familiar with A/C systems and the hazards involved. It is recommended that you have the system discharged by a professional.

---------------- CAUTION ----------------

Compressed refrigerant expands (boils) into the atmosphere at a temperature of −21°F or less. It will freeze any surface it contacts, including your skin or eyes.

---

3. Remove the fuel pump and pump pushrod.

4. Remove the camshaft sprocket bolts, sprocket and timing chain. A light blow to the lower edge of a tight sprocket should free it (use a plastic mallet).

5. Install two $1/16$-18 × 14 in. bolts in the cam bolt holes and pull the cam from the block.

6. To install, reverse the removal procedure aligning the timing marks.

NOTE: Pre-lube the cam lobes with E.O.S. or SAE 90 gear lubricant. Do not dislodge the cam bearings when installing the camshaft.

350 (5.7L) Diesel

Removal of the camshaft also requires removal of the injection pump drive and driven gears, removal of the intake manifold, disassembly of the valve lifters, and re-timing of the injection pump.

1. Disconnect the negative battery cables. Drain the coolant. Remove the radiator.

2. Remove the intake manifold and gasket and the front and rear intake manifold seals. Refer to the intake manifold removal and installation procedure.

3. Remove the balancer pulley and the balancer. Refer to the procedure earlier in this chapter. Remove the engine front cover using the appropriate procedure.

4. Remove the valve covers. Remove the rocker arms, pushrods and valve lifters; see the procedures earlier in this chapter. Be sure to keep the parts in order so that they may be returned to their original positions.

5. If the truck has air conditioning, the condenser must be moved to provide room for camshaft removal. It may be possible to unbolt the condenser and move it aside far enough for clearance. Otherwise, the air conditioning system must be discharged and the condenser removed. Do not disconnect any of the air conditioning lines unless you are thoroughly familiar with A/C systems and the hazards involved. It is recommended that you have the system discharged by a professional.

---------------- CAUTION ----------------

Compressed refrigerant expands (boils) into the atmosphere at a temperature of −21°F or less. It will freeze any surface it contacts, including your skin or eyes.

---

6. Remove the camshaft sprocket retaining bolt, and remove the timing chain and sprockets, using the procedure outlined earlier in this chapter.

7. Position the camshaft dowel pin at the 3 o'clock position.

8. Push the camshaft rearward and hold it there, being careful not to dislodge the oil gallery plug at the rear of the engine. Remove the pump drive gear by sliding it from the camshaft while rocking the pump driven gear.

9. To remove the pump driven gear, remove the injection pump adapter, remove the snap-ring, and remove the selective washer. Remove the driven gear and spring.

10. Remove the camshaft by sliding it out the front of the engine. Be extremely careful not to allow the cam lobes to contact any of the bearings, or the journals to dislodge the bearings during camshaft removal. Do not force the camshaft, or bearing damage will result.

11. Coat the camshaft and the cam bearings with G.M. lubricant #562458 or the equivalent.

12. Carefully slide the camshaft into position in the engine.

13. Install the timing chain and sprockets, aligning the marks as shown in the procedure earlier in the section.

14. Check the injection pump driven gear bushing and replace as necessary.

15. Install the injection pump driven gear, spring, shim, and snap-ring. Check the gear end-play. If the end-play is not within 0.002–0.005 in., replace the shim to obtain the specified clearance. Shims are available in 0.003 in. increments, from 0.080 to 0.115 in.

16. Position the camshaft dowel pin at the 3 o'clock position. Align the zero marks on the pump drive gear and pump driven gear. Hold the camshaft in the rearward position and slide the pump drive gear onto the camshaft.

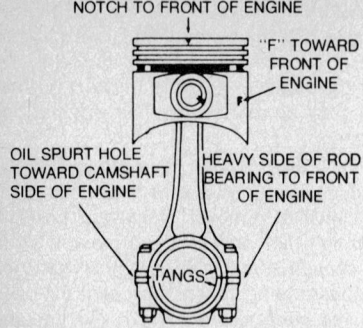

6-250 and 292 piston/rod assembly

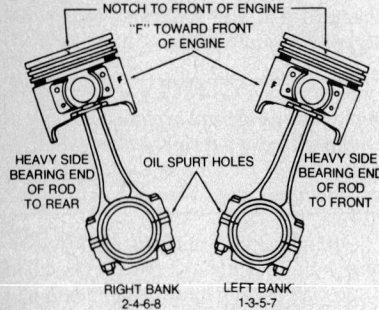

Small block V8 piston/rod assembly

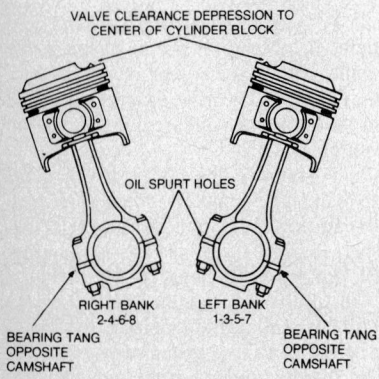

8-454 piston/rod assembly

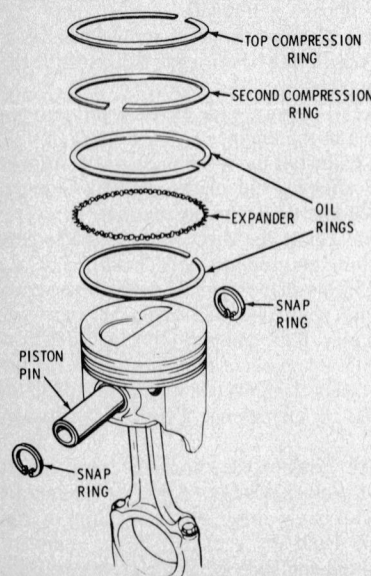

Diesel piston assembly

17. Disassemble, assemble, and bleed the valve lifters as outlined earlier. Install the lifters, pushrods, rocker arms, and pivots. Install the injection pump adapter and injection pump, re-timing the engine as outlined in the intake manifold removal and installation procedure.

18. Install the intake manifold, as outlined earlier. Install the rocker covers.

19. Install the engine front cover, balancer and pulley.

20. Install the radiator. Install the air conditioning condenser, if equipped. Fill the cooling system. Check the automatic transmission fluid level. Connect the negative battery cables.

379 (6.2L) Diesel

1. Disconnect the battery.
2. Raise the vehicle.
3. Drain the radiator and block.
4. Disconnect the exhaust pipe at the exhaust manifolds.
5. Remove the fan shroud lower attaching bolts.
6. Lower the vehicle.
7. Remove the fan shroud upper attaching bolts.
8. Remove the radiator.
9. Remove the fan.
10. Remove the vaccum pump.
11. Remove the intake manifold as previously outlined.
12. Remove the injection pump lines at the pump and nozzles. Cap the injection nozzles to prevent dirt from entering fuel. (Tag injection lines for reinstallation).
13. Remove the water pump.
14. Remove the injection pump gear.
15. Scribe a mark on the front cover aligning the line on the injection pump flange to the front cover.
16. Remove the injection pump from the cover.
17. Remove the power steering pump and the generator and lay aside.
18. If equipped with A/C remove the compressor and lay aside.
19. Remove the rocker arm covers as previously outlined.
20. Remove the rocker arm shaft assembly and pushrods. Place the parts in a rack so they may be reinstalled in the same location.
21. Remove the thermostat housing/crossover from the cylinder heads.
22. Remove the cylinder head as previously outlined with the exhaust manifolds attached.
23. Remove the valve lifter clamps, guide plates and valve lifters. Place the parts in a rack so they may be reinstalled in the same location.
24. Remove the front cover.
25. Remove the timing chain.
26. Remove the fuel pump.
27. Remove the cam retainer plate.
28. If equipped with A/C remove the A/C condensor mounting bolts, and with the aid of an assistant, lift the condenser.
29. Remove the camshaft.

NOTE: Whenever a new camshaft is installed, replacement of all valve lifters, oil filter, and new oil is recommended to insure durability of the camshaft lobes and lifters. Whenever a new camshaft is installed coat the camshaft lobes with Molycote or its equivalent.

30. Lubricate the camshaft journals with engine oil and install the camshaft.
31. Install the retainer plate (20 ft. lbs.).
32. Install the fuel pump.
33. Install the timing chain.
34. Install the front cover.
35. Install the valve lifters, guide plates and clamps, rotate the crankshaft as outlined in Valve Lifter Installation to insure the valve lifters are free to travel.
36. Install the cylinder head as previously outlined.
37. Install the rocker arm shaft assembly and pushrods as outlined. Care must be taken to insure the pushrods are installed properly.
38. Install the rocker arm covers.
39. Install the injection pump to the front cover, making sure the lines on the pump and the scribe line on the front cover are aligned.
40. Install the injection pump driven gear, making sure the gears are aligned. Any time the timing chain, gears, or sprockets are replaced, it will be necessary to retime the engine.
41. Install the water pump.
42. Install the injection lines.
43. Install the generator, power steering and A/C.
44. Install the crank pulley.
45. Install the fan.
46. Install the drive belts and adjust as necessary.
47. Install the fan shroud.
48. Install the radiator, and fill with coolant.
49. Connect the necessary wires and hoses.
50. Raise the vehicle.
51. Connect the exhaust pipes to the exhaust manifold.
52. Lower the vehicle.
53. Install the vacuum pump.
54. Connect the secondary fuel filter lines (with adapter).
55. Install the cylinder head covers J-29664-1.
56. Connect the battery.
57. Start the engine and check for leaks.
58. Stop the engine.
59. Remove the protective covers.
60. Loosen the vacuum pump hold-down and disconnect the secondary filter (with adapter) from the fuel lines.
61. Install the intake manifold as previously outlined.

Piston and Connecting Rods

Piston and connecting rod removal, installation and piston ring removal/installation are detailed in the Engine Rebuilding section.

ENGINE LUBRICATION

Oil Pan

PICK-UPS AND SUBURBAN

Removal and Installation

SIX CYLINDER

1. Disconnect the battery ground cable.
2. Raise and support the vehicle. Disconnect the starter leaving the wires attached and swing it out of the way.
3. If there is not enough clearance, remove the bolts securing the engine mounts to the crossmember and raise the engine high enough to insert a 2 in. × 4 in. piece of wood between the engine mounts and the crossmember brackets.
4. Drain the engine oil.
5. Remove the flywheel or converter cover.
6. Remove the oil pan.
7. Clean all gasket surfaces and install a new seal in the rear main bearing groove and a new seal in the crankcase front cover. Installation is the reverse of removal. Install new side gaskets on the block, but do not use sealer. Fill the engine with oil and run the engine, checking for leaks.

V8 EXCEPT DIESEL

1. Drain the engine oil.
2. Remove the oil dipstick and tube.
3. If necessary, remove the exhaust crossover. On 454s, remove the air cleaner, fan shroud, and distributor cap.
4. Remove the flywheel or converter cover. Remove the starter. On 454s, remove the oil pressure line from the block. On four wheel drive models with automatic transmission, remove the strut rods at the motor mounts.
5. On 454s only, remove the engine mount through bolts and raise the engine.
6. Remove the oil pan and discard the gaskets.
7. Installation is the reverse of removal. Clean all gasket surfaces and use new gaskets to assemble. Use gasket sealer to retain the side gaskets to the cylinder block. Install a new oil pan rear seal in the rear main bearing cap slot with the ends butting the side gaskets. Install a new front seal in the crankcase front cover with the ends butting the side gaskets. Fill the engine with oil and check for leaks.

DIESEL

1. Remove the drive and vacuum pump.
2. Disconnect the battery cables.
3. Remove the fan shroud attaching screws and pull the shroud up from the clips.
4. Block the rear wheels and jack up the front of the truck. Drain the oil.
5. Remove the flywheel cover.
6. Remove the starter and solenoid.
7. Remove both of the engine mount through bolts and raise the engine. Loosen the right hand mount and remove the left hand mount.
8. Unbolt and remove the oil pan.

NOTE: If extended work is to be done, the mounts should be reinstalled and the engine lowered to the frame brackets.

To install:
1. After cleaning the mounting surfaces thoroughly, apply sealer to both sides of the pan gaskets and install the gaskets on the block.
2. Install the front and rear rubber seals.
3. Apply a thin coat of all purpose grease on the seals, and install the oil pan. Torque the bolts to 10 ft. lbs. in a circular sequence, starting in the middle and working out.
4. Further installation is the reverse of removal. Fill the engine with oil and check for leaks.

VANS

Removal and Installation

1975 SIX CYLINDER

1. Disconnect the battery ground cable.
2. Raise and support the vehicle. Disconnect the starter leaving the wires attached and swing it out of the way.
3. If there is not enough clearance, remove the bolts securing the engine mounts to the crossmember and raise the engine high enough to insert a 2 in. × 4 in. piece of wood between the engine mounts and the crossmember brackets.
4. Drain the engine oil.
5. Remove the flywheel or converter cover.
6. Remove the oil pan.
7. Clean all gasket surfaces and install a new seal in the rear main bearing groove and a new seal in the crankcase front cover. Installation is the reverse of removal. Install new side gaskets on the block, but do not use sealer. Fill the engine with oil and run the engine, checking for leaks.

1976–77 SIX CYLINDER

1. Disconnect the battery ground cable.
2. Drain the oil.
3. Remove the starter.
4. Remove the manual transmission flywheel splash shield or the automatic transmission converter housing underpan.
5. Support the front of the engine. Re-

move the engine mount through-bolts.
6. Raise the front of the engine enough to replace the through-bolts in the engine half of the mounts.
7. Lower the engine and remove the pan bolts.
8. Clean all gasket surfaces and install a new seal in the rear main bearing cap and on the crankcase front cover. Install new side gaskets to the block, using sealer.
9. Replace the pan.
10. Raise the engine and replace the mount through-bolts. Fill the engine with oil and run it, watching for leaks.

1978 AND LATER SIX CYLINDER

1. Disconnect the negative battery cable and remove the engine cover.
2. Remove the air cleaner and studs.
3. Remove the fan finger guard.
4. Remove the radiator upper supporting brackets.
5. Raise the van on a hoist.
6. On vans with manual transmissions:
   a. Disconnect the clutch cross shaft from the left front mounting bracket.
   b. Remove the transmission-to-bellhousing upper bolt.
   c. Remove the transmission rear mounting bolts and install two 7/16 × 3 in. bolts.
   d. Raise the transmission and place a small piece of 2 × 4 wood in between the mount and the crossmember.
7. Remove the starter motor.
8. Drain the engine oil.
9. Remove the engine mount through bolts.
10. Raise the engine slightly and place small 2 × 4 wooden blocks in between mount and the block.
11. Remove the flywheel splash shield or the converter cover, as applicable.
12. Remove the oil pan attaching bolts and remove the oil pan.
13. Clean the gasket surface thoroughly and use a new gasket on installation.
14. Reverse to install.

V8

1. Drain the engine oil.
2. Remove the oil dipstick and tube.
3. If necessary, remove the exhaust pipe crossover.
4. If equipped with automatic transmission, remove the converter housing pan.
5. Remove the starter brace and bolt and swing the starter aside.
6. Remove the oil pan and discard the gaskets.
7. Installation is the reverse of removal. Clean all gasket surfaces and use new gaskets to assemble. Use gasket sealer to retain the side gaskets to the cylinder block. Install a new oil pan rear seal in the rear main bearing cap slot with the ends butting the side gaskets. Install a new front seal in the crankcase front cover with the ends butting the side gaskets. Fill the engine with oil and check for leaks.

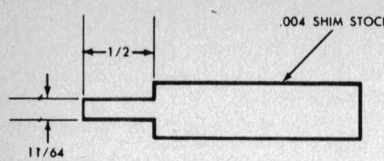

Fabricated oil seal installation tool

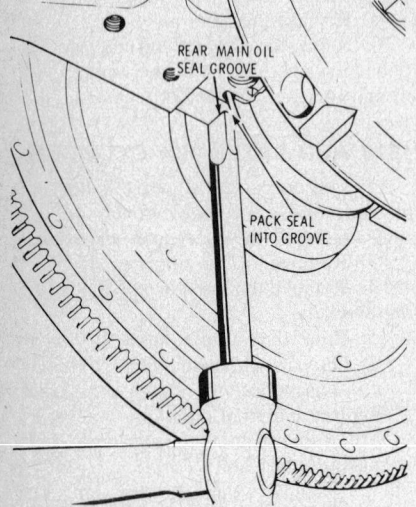

Pack the old seal into the groove

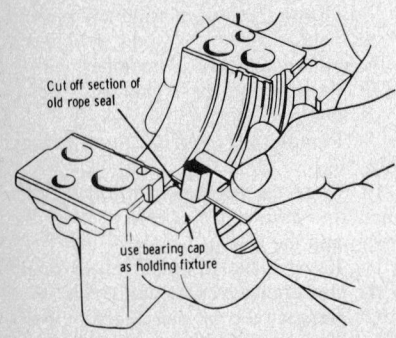

Use the bearing cap as a holding fixture for cutting the old rope seal

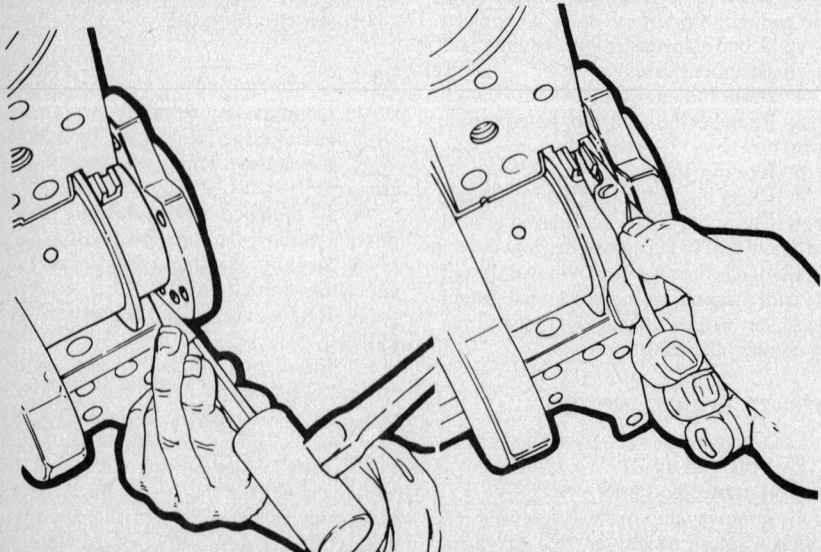

Removing the upper half of the oil seal

BLAZER AND JIMMY

Removal and Installation

SIX CYLINDER

1. Disconnect the battery ground cable.

2. Raise and support the vehicle. Disconnect the starter leaving the wires attached and swing it out of the way. Leave the starter in place on 1976 automatic transmission models.

3. Remove the flywheel or converter cover.

4. Drain the engine oil.

5. On models through 1975, there may be enough clearance to remove the oil pan without raising the engine. If there isn't, remove the bolts securing the engine mounts to the crossmember and raise the engine high enough to insert a 2 in. × 4 in. piece of wood between the engine mounts and the crossmember brackets.

6. On 1976 and later models:

  a. Remove the front engine mount through bolts.

  b. Using a floor jack, raise the engine about three inches.

  c. Install the through bolts and tighten them just enough to hold them in place.

  d. Lower the engine so it rests on the engine mounts, in a slightly raised position. This should provide enough clearance.

7. Remove the oil pan attaching screws.

8. Remove the oil pan.

9. Clean all gasket surfaces and install a new seal in the rear main bearing groove and a new seal in the crankcase front cover. Installation is the reverse of removal. Install new side gaskets on the block, but do not use sealer. Fill the engine with oil and run the engine, checking for leaks.

V8 EXCEPT DIESEL

NOTE: For diesel engine pan removal and installation, see the Pick-up instructions above.

1. Drain the engine oil.

2. On models through 1978, remove the oil dipstick and tube.

3. If necessary, remove the exhaust pipe crossover.

4. If equipped with automatic transmission, remove the converter housing pan.

5. On models through 1978, remove the starter brace and bolt and swing the starter aside.

6. On 1979 and later four wheel drive models equipped with automatic transmission, remove the strut rods at the engine mounts.

7. Remove the oil pan and discard the gaskets.

8. Installation is the reverse of removal. Clean all gasket surfaces and use new gaskets to assemble. Use gasket sealer to retain the side gaskets to the cylinder block. Install a new oil pan rear seal in the rear main bearing cap slot with the ends butting the side gaskets. Install a new front seal in the crankcase front cover with the ends butting the side gaskets. Reassemble, fill the engine with oil and check for leaks.

Oil Pump

REMOVAL AND INSTALLATION

NOTE: Before installing an oil pump, fill it with clean oil.

Six Cylinder

1. Drain the oil and remove the oil pan.

2. Remove the 2 flanged mounting bolts and remove the pickup pipe bolt.

3. Remove the pump and screen as an assembly.

4. To install, align the oil pump driveshafts with the distributor tang and install the oil pump. Position the flange over the distributor lower bushing, using no gasket. The oil pump should slide easily into place. If not, remove it and reposition the slot to align with the distributor tang.

5. Reinstall the oil pan and fill the engine with oil.

V8 and Diesel

1. Drain the oil and remove the oil pan.

2. Remove the bolt (two bolts on diesels) holding the pump to the rear main bearing cap. Remove the pump and extension shaft.

3. To install, assemble the pump and extension shaft to the rear main bearing cap aligning the slot on the top of the extension shaft with the drive tang on the distributor driveshaft. The installed position of the oil pump screen is with the bottom edge parallel to the oil pan rails. Further installation is the reverse of removal.

Rear Main Oil Seal

REPLACEMENT

All Engines Except Diesel

Both halves of the rear main oil seal can be replaced without removing the crankshaft. Always replace the upper and lower seal together. The lip should face the front of the engine. Be very careful that you do not break the sealing bead in the channel on the outside portion of the seal while installing it. An installation tool can be fabricated to protect the seal bead.

1. Remove the oil pan, oil pump and rear main bearing cap.
2. Remove the oil seal from the bearing cap by prying it out with a small screwdriver.
3. Remove the upper half of the seal with a small punch. Drive it around far enough to be gripped with pliers.
4. Clean the crankshaft and bearing cap.
5. Coat the lips and bead of the seal with light engine oil, keeping oil from the ends of the seal.
6. Position the fabricated tool between the crankshaft and seal seat.
7. Position the seal between the crankshaft and tip of the tool so that the seal bead contacts the tip of the tool. The oil seal lip should face forward.
8. Roll the seal around the crankshaft using the tool to protect the seal bead from the sharp corners of the crankcase.
9. The installation tool should be left installed until the seal is properly positioned with both ends flush with the block.
10. Remove the tool.
11. Install the other half of the seal in the bearing cap using the tool in the same manner as before. Light thumb pressure should install the seal.
12. Install the bearing cap with sealant applied to the mating areas of the cap and block. Keep sealant from the ends of the seal.
13. Torque the main bearing cap retaining bolts to 10–12 ft.lbs. Tap the end of the crankshaft first rearward, then forward with a lead hammer. This will line up the rear main bearing and the crankshaft thrust surfaces. Tighten the main bearing cap to specification.
14. Further installation is the reverse of removal.

Diesel

It is not necessary to remove the crankshaft to correct seal leaks at the rear main bearing.

1. Drain oil and remove oil pan as previously outlined. Remove rear main bearing cap.
2. Insert a packing tool such as a screwdriver or a punch against one end of the seal in the cylinder block and drive the old seal gently into the groove until it is packed tight. This varies from ¼ in. to ¾ in., depending on the pack required. Be careful not to nick the main bearing when packing the seal.
3. Repeat this procedure on the other end of the cylinder block seal.
4. Measure the amount the seal was driven up on one side. Add ¹⁄₁₆ in., then use a razor blade to cut this length from the old seal removed from the bearing cap. Repeat for the other side.
5. Place a drop of sealer on each end of the cut pieces of seal.
6. Work these two pieces of seal into the cylinder block with two small screwdrivers. Pack them into the block firmly. Trim the ends of the seal flush with the block.

NOTE: Place a piece of shim stock or strip of metal between the seal and the crankshaft to protect the bearing surface before trimming.

7. Clean the bearing cap and seal grooves.
8. Install a new seal into the bearing cap, packing by hand.
9. Using a seal installer, pack the seal firmly into the groove. These tools are generally available in automotive parts stores.
10. Cut the seal flush with the mating surface of the bearing cap. Pack the seal end fibers away from the edges, toward the center with a screwdriver.
11. Clean the bearing insert and install in the bearing cap.
12. Clean the crankshaft bearing journal, and the mating surface of the bearing cap. Place a dab of sealer, such as Loctite® 496, on the mating surface of the cap. Lay a piece of Plastigage® on the bearing surface.
13. Install the bearing cap, lubricate the bolt threads with engine oil, and install. Torque the bolts to 120 ft. lbs. on the 350 and 70 ft. lbs. on the 379. Check the bearing clearance. If clearance is excessive, check for frayed seal edges. When the clearance is correct, retorque the cap.
14. Install the oil pan as previously outlined.

ENGINE COOLING

Radiator

REMOVAL AND INSTALLATION

1. Drain the radiator.

――――― CAUTION ―――――
Do not attempt to start the siphoning process with your mouth. The coolant is poisonous and can cause death.

2. Disconnect the hoses and automatic transmission cooler line (if equipped). Plug the cooler lines. Diesels have transmission cooler and oil cooler lines.
3. Disconnect the coolant recovery system hose.
4. If the vehicle is equipped with a fan shroud, detach the shroud and hang it over the fan to provide clearance.
5. On six cylinder engines, remove the finger guard.
6. Remove the mounting panel from the radiator support and remove the upper mounting pads.
7. Lift the radiator up and out of the truck. Lift the shroud out if necessary.
8. Installation is the reverse of removal. Fill the cooling system and check the automatic transmission fluid level, and run the engine, checking for leaks.

Water Pump

REMOVAL AND INSTALLATION

1. Drain the radiator and loosen the fan pulley bolts.
2. Disconnect the heater hose and radiator. Disconnect the lower radiator hose at the water pump.
3. Loosen the alternator swivel bolt and remove the fan belt. Remove the fan bolts, fan and pulley.
4. Remove the water pump attaching bolts and remove the pump and gasket from the engine. On inline engines, remove the water pump straight out of the block to avoid damaging the impeller.

NOTE: Do not store viscous drive (thermostatic) fan clutches in any other position than the normal installed position. They should be supported so that the clutch disc remains vertical; otherwise, silicone fluid may leak out.

5. Installation is the reverse of removal. Clean the gasket surfaces and install new gaskets. Coat the gasket with sealer. A ⁵⁄₁₆ in. × 24 × 1 in. guide stud installed in one hole of the fan will make installing the fan onto the hub easier. It can be removed after the other 3 bolts are started. Fill the cooling system and adjust the fan belt tension.

Thermostat

The factory installed thermostat is a 195°F unit.

NOTE: Poor heater output and slow warmup is often caused by a thermostat stuck in the open position; occasionally one sticks shut causing immediate overheating. Do not attempt to correct a chronic overheating condition by permanently removing the thermostat. Thermostat flow restriction is designed

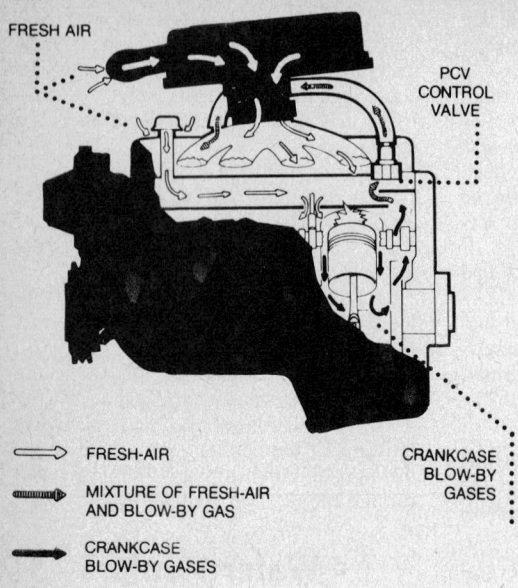

FRESH AIR

PCV CONTROL VALVE

⇒ FRESH-AIR

▭▭▭▭▷ MIXTURE OF FRESH-AIR AND BLOW-BY GAS

➡ CRANKCASE BLOW-BY GASES

CRANKCASE BLOW-BY GASES

PCV system

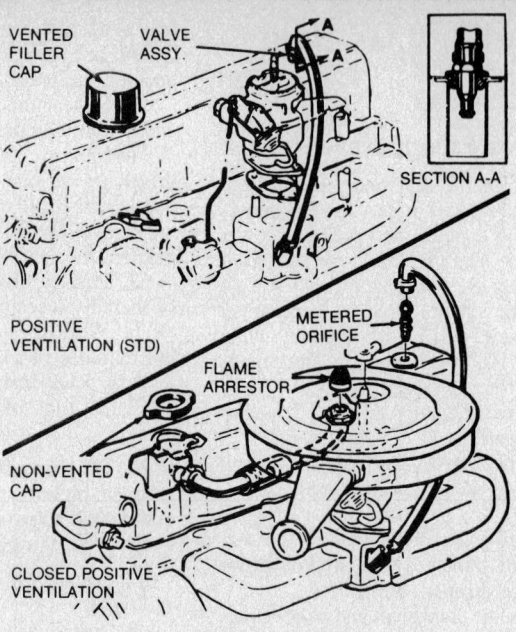

VENTED FILLER CAP

VALVE ASSY.

SECTION A-A

POSITIVE VENTILATION (STD)

METERED ORIFICE

FLAME ARRESTOR

NON-VENTED CAP

CLOSED POSITIVE VENTILATION

Closed and positive PCV systems

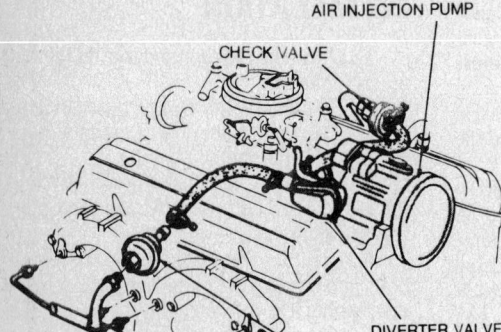

AIR INJECTION PUMP

CHECK VALVE

DIVERTER VALVE

CHECK VALVE

A.I.R. system

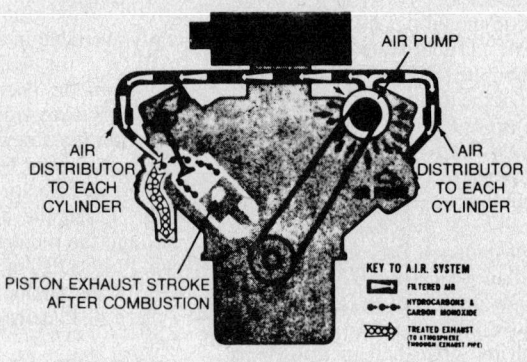

AIR PUMP

AIR DISTRIBUTOR TO EACH CYLINDER

AIR DISTRIBUTOR TO EACH CYLINDER

PISTON EXHAUST STROKE AFTER COMBUSTION

KEY TO A.I.R. SYSTEM
FILTERED AIR
HYDROCARBONS & CARBON MONOXIDE
TREATED EXHAUST (TO ATMOSPHERE THROUGH EXHAUST PIPE)

A.I.R. schematic

into the system; without it, localized overheating due to turbulence may occur.

REMOVAL AND INSTALLATION

1. Drain approximately ⅓ of the coolant. This will reduce the coolant level to below the level of the thermostat housing.
2. It is not necessary to remove the upper radiator hose from the thermostat housing. Remove the 2 retaining bolts from the thermostat housing (located on the front top of V8 intake manifolds and directly in front of the valve cover on six cylinder engines) and remove the thermostat.
3. To test the thermostat, place it in hot water or a solution of 33% glycol, 25° above the temperature stamped on the valve. Submerge the valve and agitate the solution. The valve should open fully. Remove the thermostat and place it in the same solution 10° below the temperature stamped on the valve. The valve should close completely.
4. Installation is the reverse of re-

moval. Use a new gasket and sealer. Refill the cooling system and run the engine, checking for leaks.

EMISSION CONTROLS

Positive Crankcase Ventilation

PCV is the earliest form of emission control. Prior to its use, crankcase vapors were vented into the atmosphere through a road draft tube or crankcase breather.

This system draws crankcase vapors that are formed through normal combustion into the intake manifold and subsequently into the combustion chambers to be burned. Fresh air is introduced to the crankcase by way of a hose connected to the carburetor air cleaner or a vented oil filler cap on older models. Manifold vacuum is used to draw

the vapors from the crankcase through a PCV valve and into the intake manifold.

SERVICE

Other than checking and replacing the PCV valve and associated hoses, there is no service required. Engine operating conditions that would direct suspicion to the PCV system are rough idle, oil present in the air cleaner, oil leaks and excessive oil sludging or dilution. If any of the above conditions exist, remove the PCV valve and shake it. A clicking sound indicates that the valve is free. If no clicking sound is heard, replace the valve. Inspect the PCV breather in the air cleaner. Replace the breather if it is so dirty that it will not allow gases to pass through. Check all the PCV hoses for condition and tight connections. Replace any hoses that have deteriorated.

Air Injector Reactor (Air Pump)

The AIR system injects compressed air into

the exhaust system, near enough to the exhaust valves to continue the burning of the normally unburned segment of the exhaust gases. To do this it employs an air injection pump and a system of hoses, valves, tubes, etc., necessary to carry the compressed air from the pump to the exhaust manifolds.

A diverter valve is used to prevent backfiring. The valve senses sudden increases in manifold vacuum and ceases the injection of air during fuel-rich periods. During coasting, this valve diverts the entire flow through a muffler and during high engine speeds, expels it through a relief valve. Check valves in the system prevent exhaust gases from entering the pump.

TESTING

Check Valve

To test the check valve, disconnect the hose at the diverter valve. Blow into the hose and suck on it. Air should flow only into the engine.

Diverter Valve

Pull off the vacuum line to the top of the valve with the engine running. There should be vacuum in the line. Replace the line. No air should be escaping with the engine running at a steady idle. Open and quickly close the throttle. A blast of air should come out of the valve muffler for at least one second.

Air Pump

Disconnect the hose from the diverter valve. Start the engine and accelerate it to about 1,500 rpm. The air flow should increase as the engine is accelerated. If no air flow is noted or it remains constant, check the following:

1. Drive belt tension.
2. Listen for a leaking pressure relief valve. If it is defective, replace the whole relief/diverter valve.
3. Foreign matter in pump filter openings. If the pump is defective or excessively noisy, it must be replaced.

SERVICE

All hoses and fittings should be inspected for condition and tightness of connections. Check the drive belt for wear and tension periodically.

NOTE: The AIR system is not completely silent under normal conditions. Noises will rise in pitch as engine speed increases. If the noise is excessive, eliminate the air pump itself by disconnecting the drive belt. If the noise disappears, the air pump is at fault.

AIR PUMP REMOVAL AND INSTALLATION

1. Disconnect the output hose.

2. Hold the pump from turning by squeezing the drive belt.
3. Loosen the pulley bolts.
4. Loosen the alternator so the belt can be removed.
5. Remove the pulley.
6. Remove the pump mounting bolts and the pump.
7. Install the pump with the mounting bolts loose.
8. Install the pulley and tighten the bolts finger-tight.
9. Install and adjust the drive belt.
10. Squeeze the drive belt to prevent the pump from turning.
11. Torque the pulley bolts to 25 ft. lbs. Tighten the pump mountings.
12. Check and adjust the belt tension again, if necessary.
13. Connect the hose.
14. If any hose leaks are suspected, pour soapy water over the suspected area with the engine running. Bubbles will form wherever air is escaping.

FILTER REPLACEMENT

1. Disconnect the air and vacuum hoses from the diverter valve.
2. Loosen the pump pivot and adjusting bolts and remove the drive belt.
3. Remove the pivot and adjusting bolts from the pump. Remove the pump and the diverter valve as an assembly.

-------- CAUTION --------
Do not clamp the pump in a vise or use a hammer or pry bar on the pump housing.

4. To change the filter, break the plastic fan from the hub. It is seldom possible to remove the fan without breaking it.
5. Remove the remaining portion of the fan filter from the pump hub. Be careful that filter fragments do not enter the air intake hole.
6. Position the new centrifugal fan filter on the pump hub. Place the pump pulley against the fan filter and install the securing screws. Torque the screws alternately to 95 in. lbs. and the fan filter will be pressed onto the pump hub.
7. Install the pump on the engine and adjust its drive belt.

Controlled Combustion System

The CCS system is a combination of systems and calibrations. Many of these are not visible or serviceable, but are designed into the engine.

The various systems, CHA, TCS, CEC and EGR are all part of the Controlled Combustion System.

Carburetor Heated Air

This system is designed to warm the air

entering the carburetor when underhood temperatures are low. This allows more precise calibration of the carburetor.

The thermostatically-controlled air cleaner is composed of the air-cleaner body, a filter, sensor unit, vacuum diaphragm, damper door and associated hoses and connections. Heat radiating from the exhaust manifold is trapped by a heat stove and is ducted to the air cleaner to supply heated air to the carburetor. A movable door in the air cleaner snorkel allows air to be drawn in from the heat stove (cold operation) or from the underhood air (warm operation). Periods of extended idling, climbing a grade or high-speed operation are followed by a considerable increase in engine compartment temperature. Excessive fuel vapors enter the

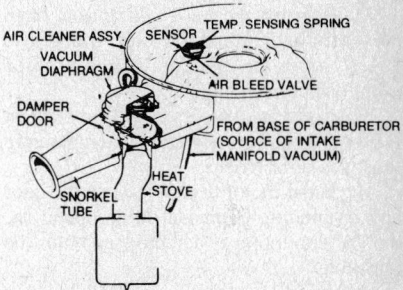

Thermostatically controlled air cleaner

intake manifold causing an over-rich mixture, resulting in a rough idle. To overcome this, some engines may be equipped with a hot idle compensator.

SERVICE

1. Either start with a cold engine or remove the air cleaner from the engine for at least half an hour. While cooling the air cleaner, leave the engine compartment hood open.
2. Tape a thermometer, of known accuracy, to the inside of the air cleaner so that it is near the temperature sensor unit. Install the air cleaner on the engine but do not fasten its securing nut.
3. Start the engine. With the engine cold and the outside temperature less than 90°F., the door should be in the "heat on" position (closed to outside air).

NOTE: Due to the position of the air cleaner on some trucks, a mirror may be necessary when observing the position of the air door.

4. Operate the throttle lever rapidly to ½–¾ of its opening and release it. The air door should open to allow outside air to enter and then close again.
5. Allow the engine to warm up to normal temperature. Watch the door. When it opens to the outside air, remove the cover from the air cleaner. The temperature should be over 90°F and no more than 130°F; 115°F is about normal. If the door does not work within these temperature ranges, or fails to

work at all, check for linkage or door binding.

If binding is not present and the air door is not working, proceed with the vacuum tests, given below. If these indicate no faults in the vacuum motor and the door is not working, the temperature sensor is defective and must be replaced.

Vacuum Motor Test

NOTE: Be sure that the vacuum hose which runs between the temperature switch and the vacuum motor is not pinched by the retaining clip under the air cleaner. This could prevent the air door from closing.

1. Check all of the vacuum lines and fittings for leaks. Correct any leaks. If none are found, proceed with the test.
2. Remove the hose which runs from the sensor to the vacuum motor. Run a hose directly from the manifold vacuum source to the vacuum motor.
3. If the motor closes the air door, it is functioning properly and the temperature sensor is defective.
4. If the motor does *not* close the door and no binding is present in its operation, the vacuum motor is defective and must be replaced.

NOTE: If an alternate vacuum source is applied to the motor, insert a vacuum gauge in the line by using a T-fitting. Apply at least 9 in. Hg of vacuum in order to operate the motor.

Exhaust Gas Recirculation

The EGR system and valve were introduced in 1973. Its purpose is to control oxides of nitrogen which are formed during the peak combustion temperatures. The end products of combustion are relatively inert gases derived from the exhaust gases which are directed into the EGR valve to help lower peak combustion temperatures.

The EGR valve contains a vacuum dia-

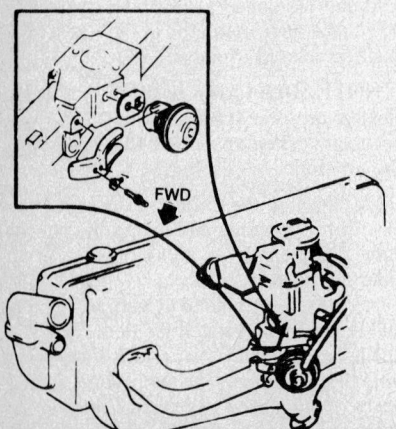

Six cylinder EGR system

phragm operated by manifold vacuum. The vacuum signal port is located in the carburetor body and is exposed to engine vacuum in the off-idle and part-throttle operation. A thermo-delay switch was added to delay operation of the valve during engine warmup, when NO_x levels are already at a minimum.

On sixes, the EGR valve is located on the intake manifold adjacent to the carburetor. On V engines, the valve is located on the right rear side of the intake manifold adjacent to the rocker arm cover.

SERVICE

The EGR valve is not serviceable, except for replacement. To check the valve, proceed as follows:

1. Connect a tachometer to the engine.
2. With the engine running at normal operating temperature, with the choke valve fully open, set the engine rpm at 2000. The transmission should be in Park (automatic) or Neutral (manual) with the parking brake On and the wheels blocked.
3. Disconnect the vacuum hose at the valve. Make sure that vacuum is available at the valve and look at the tachometer to see if the engine speed increases. If it does, a malfunction of the valve is indicated.
4. If necessary, replace the valve.

Evaporation Control System

This system reduces the amount of escaping gasoline vapors. Float bowl emissions are controlled by internal carburetor modifications. Redesigned bowl vents, reduced bowl capacity, heat shields, and improved intake manifold-to-carburetor insulation serve to reduce vapor loss into the atmosphere. The venting of fuel tank vapors into the air has been stopped. Fuel vapors are now directed through lines to a canister containing an activated charcoal filter. Unburned vapors are trapped here until the engine is started. When the engine is running, the canister is purged by air drawn in by manifold vacuum. The air and fuel vapors are directed into the engine to be burned.

Early Fuel Evaporation System

This system is used on all light duty models. The six cylinder system consists of an EFE valve mounted at the flange of the exhaust manifold, an actuator, a thermal vacuum switch (TVS), and a vacuum solenoid. The TVS is on the right side of the engine forward of the oil pressure switch. The TVS is normally closed and sensitive to oil temperature.

The V8 EFE system consists of an EFE valve at the flange of the exhaust manifold, an actuator, and a thermal vacuum switch. The TVS is located in the coolant outlet housing and directly controls vacuum.

In both systems, manifold vacuum is applied to the actuator, which in turn, closes the EFE valve. This routes hot exhaust gases to the base of the carburetor. When coolant (V8) or oil (six cylinder) temperatures reach a set limit, vacuum is denied to the actuator allowing an internal spring to return the actuator to its normal position, opening the EFE valve.

Throttle Return Control System

A throttle return control system (TRC) is used on some California truck engines. When the truck is coasting against the engine, the control valve is open to allow vacuum to operate the throttle lever actuator. The throttle lever actuator then pushes the throttle lever slightly open reducing the HC (hydrocarbon) emission level during coasting. When manifold vacuum drops below a predetermined level, the control valve closes, the throttle lever retracts, and the throttle lever closes to the idle position.

SERVICE

Control Valve Check and Adjustment

1. Disconnect the valve-to-carburetor hose and connect it to an external vacuum source and a vacuum gauge.
2. Disconnect the valve-to-actuator hose at the connector and connect it to a vacuum gauge.
3. Place a finger firmly over the end of the bleed fitting.
4. Apply a minimum of 23 in. Hg vacuum to the control valve and seal off the vacuum source. The gauge on the actuator side should read the same as the gauge on the source side. If not, the valve needs adjustment. If vacuum drops off on either side (with the finger still on the bleed fitting), the valve is defective and should be replaced.
5. With a minimum of 23 in. Hg vacuum in the valve, remove the finger from the bleed fitting. The vacuum level in the actuator side will drop to zero and the reading on the source side will drop to a value that will be the valve set point of 21.5 in. Hg. If the valve is not within ½ in. Hg vacuum of the specified valve set point, adjust the valve.
6. Gently pry off the conical plastic cover.
7. Turn the adjusting screw in (clockwise) to raise the set point or out (counterclockwise) to lower the set point.
8. Recheck the valve set point.
9. If necessary, repeat the adjustment.

Throttle Valve Check and Adjustment

1. Disconnect the valve-to-actuator hose at the valve and connect it to an external vacuum source.

2. Apply 20 in. Hg vacuum to the actuator and seal the vacuum source. If the vacuum gauge reading drops, the valve is leaking and should be replaced.

3. Check the throttle lever, shaft, and linkage for freedom of operation.

4. Start the engine and warm it to operating temperature.

5. Note the idle rpm.

6. Apply 20 in. Hg vacuum to the actuator and manually operate the throttle. Allow it to close against the extended actuator plunger. Note the engine rpm.

7. Release and reapply 20 in. Hg vacuum to the actuator and note the rpm at which the engine speed increases (do not assist the actuator).

8. If the engine speed obtained in step 7 is not within 150 rpm of that obtained in step 6, then the actuator may be binding. If the binding cannot be corrected, replace the actuator.

9. Release the vacuum from the actuator and the engine speed should return to within 50 rpm of the speed noted in steps 4 and 5.

To adjust the actuator:

10. Turn the screw on the actuator plunger until the specified TRC speed range (1475–1525 rpm) is obtained.

Oxidizing Catalytic Converter

An underfloor oxidizing catalytic converter is used to control hydrocarbon and carbon monoxide emissions on many 1975 and later models. Control is accomplished by placing a catalyst in the exhaust system to enable all exhaust gas flow to pass through it and undergo a chemical reaction before passing into the atmosphere. The chemical reaction involved is the oxidizing of hydrocarbons and carbon monoxide into water vapor and carbon dioxide.

REMOVAL AND INSTALLATION

---- CAUTION ----

Catalytic converter operating temperatures are extremely high. Outside converter temperatures can go well over 1,000°F. Use extreme care when working on or around the catalytic converter.

1. Raise and support the truck.

2. Remove the clamps at the front and rear of the converter.

3. Cut the converter pipes at the front and rear of the converter and remove it.

4. Remove the support from the transmission.

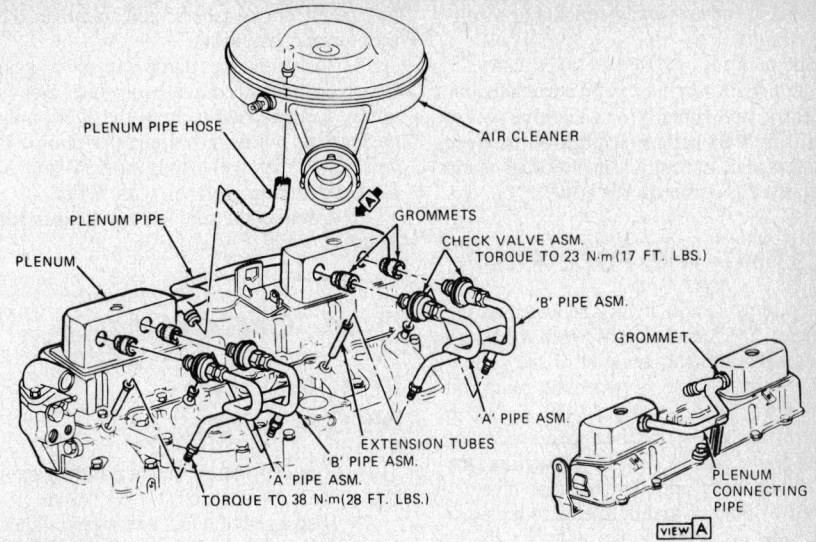

PAIR system

5. Remove the converter pipe-to-exhaust pipe and the converter pipe-to-tailpipe.

To install the converter:

6. Install the exhaust pipe and tailpipe into the converter with sealer.

7. Loosely install the support on the transmission.

8. Install new U-bolts and clamps, check all clearances and tighten the clamps.

9. Lower the truck.

NOTE: Dealers have equipment to remove and replace the converter contents (pellets) without removing the converter from the exhaust system.

Pulse Air Injection Reactor System

This system consists of four air valves which inject fresh air into the exhaust system in order to further the combustion process of the exhaust gases. The firing of the engine creates a pulsating flow of exhaust gases, which are of either positive or negative pressure. Negative pressure at the pulse air valve will result in air being injected into the exhaust system. Positive pressure will force the check valve closed and no exhaust gases will flow into the fresh air supply.

Regularly inspect the pulse air valves, pipes, grommets and hose for cracks and leaks. Replace the necessary part if any are found. If a check valve fails, exhaust gases will get into the carburetor through the air cleaner and cause the engine to surge and perform poorly.

If exhaust gases pass through a pulse air valve, the paint will be burned off the rocker arm cover plenum as a result of the excessive heat. The rubber grommets and hose will also deteriorate. Failure of the pulse air valve can also be indicated by a hissing sound.

REMOVAL AND INSTALLATION

1. Remove the air cleaner. Disconnect the rubber hose from the plenum connecting pipe. (See the illustration.)

2. Disconnect the four check valve fittings at the cylinder head and remove the check valve pipes from the plenum grommets.

3. Disconnect the check valve from the check valve pipe.

4. Assemble the replacement check valve to the check valve pipe.

5. Attach the check valve assembly to the cylinder head as illustrated. Hand tighten the fittings.

6. Using a 1 inch open end wrench as a lever, align the check valve on pipe "A" with the plenum grommet. Using the palm of your left hand, press the check valve into the grommet. Using a silicone lubricant on the grommet will make things a little easier. Repeat this procedure for pipe "B" using your left hand for the tool and your right hand for installing the valve in the grommet.

GASOLINE FUEL SYSTEM

Fuel Pump

The fuel pump is a single action AC diaphragm type, All fuel pumps used on inline and V8 engines in vans are diaphragm type and because of design are serviced by replacement only. No adjustments or repairs are possible.

The pump is operated by an eccentric on the camshaft. On six cylinder engines, the eccentric acts directly on the pump rocker arm. On V8 engines, a pushrod between the camshaft eccentric and the fuel pump operates the pump rocker arm.

TESTING THE FUEL PUMP

Fuel pumps should always be tested on the vehicle. The larger line between the pump and tank is the suction side of the system and the smaller line, between the pump and carburetor, is the pressure side. A leak in the pressure side would be apparent because of dripping fuel. A leak in the suction side is usually only apparent because of a reduced volume of fuel delivered to the pressure side.

1. Tighten any loose line connections and look for any kinks or restrictions.

2. Disconnect the fuel line at the carburetor. Disconnect the distributor-to-coil primary wire. Place a container at the end of the fuel line and crank the engine a few revolutions. If little or no gasoline flows from the line, either the fuel pump is inoperative or the line is plugged. Disconnect the line at the pump and the tank; blow through the line with compressed air and try again. Reconnect the line. If the problem is traced to the tank, the tank and gauge unit must be removed to check the condition of the inlet filter screen.

3. If fuel flows in good volume, check the fuel pump pressure to be sure.

4. Attach a pressure gauge to the pressure side of the fuel line.

5. Run the engine and note the reading on the gauge. Stop the engine and compare the reading with the specifications listed in the Tune-Up Specifications. If the pump is operating properly, the pressure will be as specified and will be constant at idle speed. If pressure varies or is too high or low, the pump should be replaced.

6. Remove the pressure gauge.

REMOVAL AND INSTALLATION

NOTE: When you connect the fuel pump outlet fitting, always use 2 wrenches to avoid damaging the pump.

1. Disconnect the fuel intake and outlet lines at the pump and plug the pump intake line.

2. On V8 engines, you can remove the upper bolt from the right front engine mounting boss (on the front of the block) and insert a long bolt ⅜-16 × 2 in.) to hold the fuel pump pushrod.

3. Remove the two pump mounting bolts and lockwashers; remove the pump and its gasket.

4. If the rocker arm pushrod is to be removed from V8s, remove the two adapter bolts and lockwashers and remove the adapter and its gasket.

5. Install the fuel pump with a new gasket reversing the removal procedure. Heavy grease can be used to hold the fuel pump pushrod up while installing the pump, if you didn't install the long bolt in step 2. Coat the mating surfaces with sealer.

6. Connect the fuel lines and check for leaks.

Carburetor

REMOVAL AND INSTALLATION

1. Remove the air cleaner and its gasket.

2. Disconnect the fuel and vacuum lines from the carburetor.

3. Disconnect the choke coil rod or heated air line tube.

4. Disconnect the throttle linkage.

5. On automatic transmission cars, disconnect the throttle valve linkage.

6. Remove the CEC valve vacuum hose and electrical connector.

7. Remove the idle stop electrical wiring from the idle stop solenoid, if so equipped.

8. Remove the carburetor attaching nuts and/or bolts, gasket or insulator, and remove the carburetor.

9. Install the carburetor using a reverse of the removal procedure. Use a new gasket and fill the float bowl with gasoline to ease starting the engine.

For carburetor overhaul and adjustments, see the Unit Repair Section of this book.

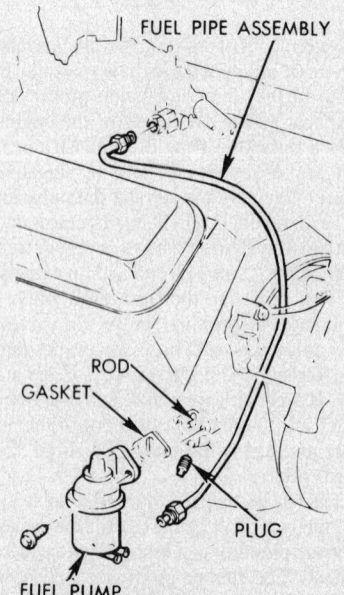

Typical gasoline fuel pump

DIESEL FUEL SYSTEM

Fuel Supply Pump

REMOVAL AND INSTALLATION

The fuel supply pump is serviced in the same manner as the fuel pump on the gasoline engine.

Fuel Filter

REMOVAL AND INSTALLATION

The fuel filter is a square assembly located at the back of the engine above the intake manifold. Disconnect the fuel lines and remove the filter. Install the lines to the new filter. Start the engine and check for leaks.

Fuel Injection Pump and Lines

REMOVAL AND INSTALLATION

NOTE: This procedure contains throttle rod and transmission cable adjustments.

1. Remove the air cleaner.

2. Remove the filters and pipes from the valve covers and air crossover.

3. Remove the air crossover and cap the intake manifold with screened covers (tool J-26996-1) or tape.

4. Disconnect the throttle rod and return spring.

5. Remove the bellcrank.

6. Remove the throttle and transmission cables from the intake manifold brackets.

7. Disconnect the fuel lines from the filter and remove the filter.

8. Disconnect the fuel inlet line at the pump.

9. Remove the rear A/C compressor brace and remove the fuel line.

10. Disconnect the fuel return line from the injection pump.

11. Remove the clamps and pull the fuel return lines from each injection nozzle.

12. Using two wrenches, disconnect the high pressure lines at the nozzles.

13. Remove the three injection pump retaining nuts with tool J-26987 or its equivalent.

14. Remove the pump and cap all lines and nozzles.

To install:

15. Remove the protective caps from all lines and nozzles. Place the engine on TDC for the no. 1 cylinder. The mark on the harmonic balancer on the crankshaft will be aligned with the zero mark on the timing tab, and both valves for no. 1 cylinder will be closed. The index mark on the injection pump driven gear should be offset to the right when no. 1 is at TDC. Check that all of these conditions are met before continuing.

16. Line up the offset tang on the pump driveshaft with the pump driven gear and install the pump.

17. Install, but do not tighten the pump retaining nuts.

18. Connect the high pressure lines at the nozzles.

19. Using two wrenches, torque the high pressure line nuts to 25 ft. lbs.

20. Connect the fuel return lines to the nozzles and pump.

21. Align the timing mark on the injection pump with the line on the timing mark adapter and torque the mounting nuts to 35 ft. lbs.

NOTE: A ¾ in. open end wrench on the boss at the front of the injection pump will aid in rotating the pump to align the marks.

22. Adjust the throttle rod:
   a. Remove the clip from the cruise control rod and remove the rod from the bellcrank.
   b. Loosen the locknut on the throttle rod a few turns, then shorten the rod several turns.
   c. Rotate the bellcrank to the full throttle stop, then lengthen the throttle rod until the injection pump lever contacts the injection pump full throttle stop, then release the bellcrank.
   d. Tighten the throttle rod locknut.

23. Install the fuel inlet line between the transfer pump and the filter.

24. Install the rear A/C compressor brace.

25. Install the bellcrank and clip.

26. Connect the throttle rod and return spring.

27. Adjust the transmission cable:
   a. Push the snap-lock to the disengaged position.
   b. Rotate the injection pump lever to the full throttle stop and hold it there.
   c. Push in the snap-lock until it is flush.
   d. Release the injection pump lever.

28. Start the engine and check for fuel leaks.

29. Remove the screened covers or tape and install the air crossover.

30. Install the tubes in the air flow control valve in the air crossover and install the ventilation filters in the valve covers.

31. Install the air cleaner.

32. Start the engine and allow it to run for two minutes. Stop the engine, let it stand for two minutes, then restart. This permits the air to bleed off within the pump.

SLOW IDLE SPEED ADJUSTMENT

1. Run the engine to normal operating temperature.

2. Insert the probe of a magnetic pickup tachometer into the timing indicator hole.

3. Set the parking brake and block the drive wheels.

4. Place the transmission in Drive and turn the A/C Off.

5. Turn the slow idle screw on the injection pump to obtain the idle specification on the emission control label.

FAST IDLE SOLENOID ADJUSTMENT

1978–79

1. Set the parking brake and block the drive wheels.

2. Run the engine to normal operating temperature.

3. Place the transmission in Drive and disconnect the compressor clutch wire. Turn the A/C On. On cars without A/C, disconnect the solenoid wire, and connect jumper wires to the solenoid terminals. Ground one of the wires and connect the other to a 12 volt battery to activate the solenoid.

4. Adjust the fast idle solenoid plunger to obtain 650 rpm.

1980 and Later

1. With the ignition off, disconnect the single green wire from the fast idle relay located on the front of the firewall.

2. Set the parking brake and block the drive wheels.

3. Start the engine and adjust the solenoid (energized) to the specifications on the underhood emission control label.

4. Turn off the engine and reconnect the green wire.

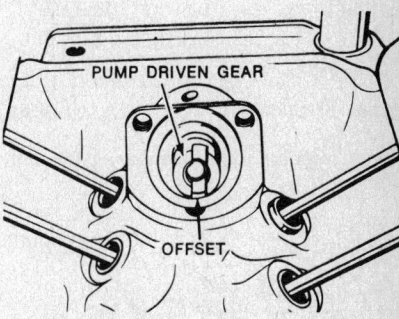

Offset on the diesel fuel pump driven gear

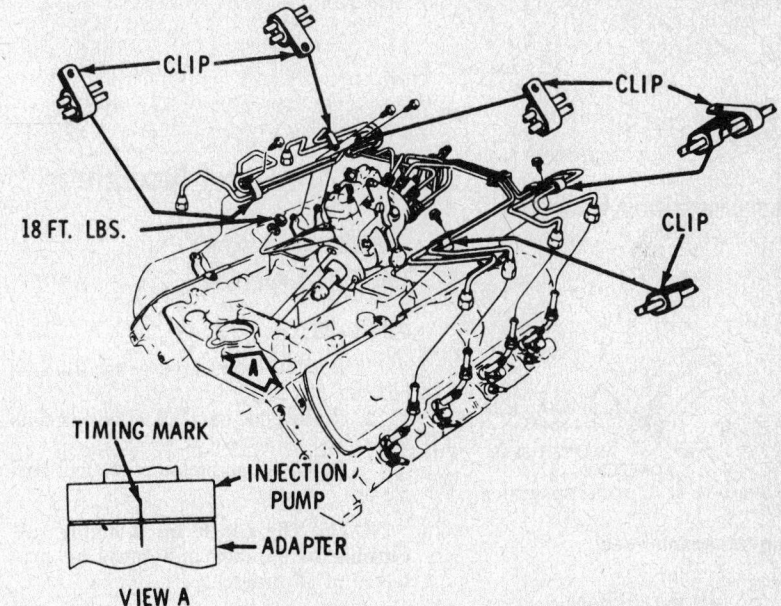

Diesel injection pump timing marks

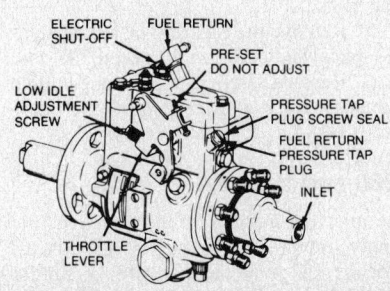

Injection pump

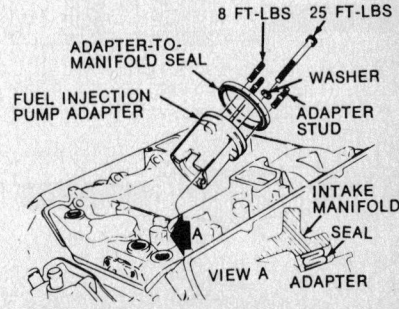

Injection pump adapter bolts

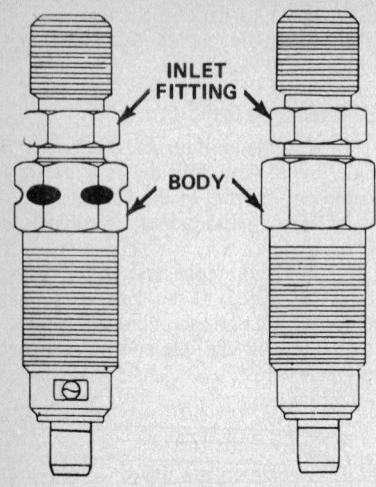

DIESEL EQUIPMENT   C.A.V. LUCAS

Diesel injector identification—1980 and later

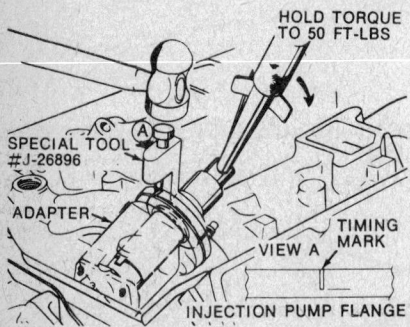

Marking the injection pump adapter

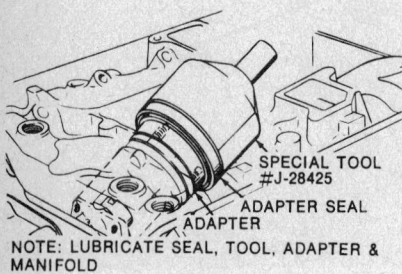

NOTE: LUBRICATE SEAL, TOOL, ADAPTER & MANIFOLD

Installing the adapter seal

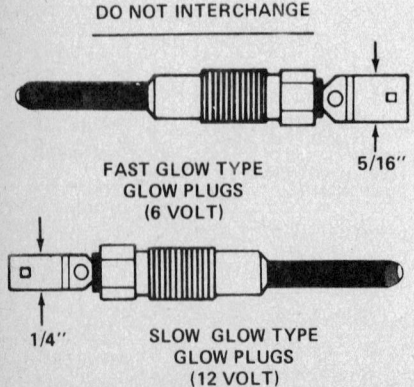

DO NOT INTERCHANGE

FAST GLOW TYPE GLOW PLUGS (6 VOLT)   5/16"

SLOW GLOW TYPE GLOW PLUGS (12 VOLT)   1/4"

Glow plug identification

CRUISE CONTROL SERVO RELAY ROD ADJUSTMENT

1. Turn the engine Off.
2. Adjust the rod to minimum slack then put the clip in the first free hole closest to the bellcrank, but within the servo ball.

INJECTION TIMING ADJUSTMENT

For the engine to be properly timed, the lines on the top of the injection pump adapter and the flange of the injection pump must be aligned.

1. The engine must be off for resetting the timing.
2. Loosen the three pump retaining nuts with J-26987, an injection pump intake manifold wrench, or its equivalent.
3. Align the timing marks and torque the pump retaining nuts to 35 ft. lbs.

NOTE: The use of a ¾ in. open end wrench on the boss at the front of the pump will aid in rotating the pump to align the marks.

4. Adjust the throttle rod. (See Fuel Injection Pump Removal and Installation, step 22.)

Injection Nozzle

REMOVAL AND INSTALLATION

1978–79

1. Remove the fuel return line from the nozzle.
2. Remove the nozzle hold-down clamp and spacer using tool J-26952.
3. Cap the high pressure line and nozzle tip.

NOTE: The nozzle tip is highly susceptible to damage and must be protected at all times.

4. If an old nozzle is to be reinstalled, a new compression seal and carbon stop seal must be installed after removal of the used seals.
5. Remove the caps and install the nozzle, spacer and clamp. Torque to 25 ft. lbs.
6. Replace return line, start the engine and check for leaks.

1980 and Later

The injection nozzles on these engines are simply unbolted from the cylinder head, after the fuel lines are removed, in similar fashion to a spark plug. Be careful not to damage the nozzle end and make sure you

remove the copper nozzle gasket from the cylinder head if it does not come off with the nozzle.

Clean the carbon off the tip of the nozzle with a soft brass wire brush and install the nozzles, with gaskets.

NOTE: 1981 and later models use two type of injectors, CAV Lucas and Diesel Equipment. When installing the inlet fittings, torque the Diesel Equipment injector fitting to 45 ft. lbs. and the CAV Lucas to 25 ft. lbs.

Injection Pump Adapter, Adapter Seal, and New Adapter Timing Mark

REMOVAL AND INSTALLATION

NOTE: Skip steps 4 and 9 if a new adapter is not being installed.

1. Remove injection pump and lines as described earlier.
2. Remove the injection pump adapter.
3. Remove the seal from the adapter.
4. File the timing mark from the adapter. Do not file the mark off the pump.
5. Position the engine at TDC of No. 1 cylinder. Align the mark on the balancer with the zero mark on the indicator. The index is offset to the right when No. 1 is at TDC.
6. Apply chassis lube to the seal areas. Install, but do not tighten the injection pump.
7. Install the new seal on the adapter using tool J-28425, or its equivalent.
8. Torque the adapter bolts to 25 ft. lbs.
9. Install timing tool J-26896 into the injection pump adapter. Torque the tool, toward No. 1 cylinder, to 50 ft. lbs. Mark the injection pump adapter. Remove the tool.
10. Install the injection pump.

GLOW PLUGS

There are two types of glow plugs used on General Motors Corp. diesels: the "fast glow" type and the "slow glow" type. The fast glow type use pulsing current applied to 6 volt glow plugs while the slow glow type use continuous current applied to 12 volt glow plugs.

An easy way to tell the plugs apart is that the fast glow (6 volt) plugs have a 5/16 in. wide electrical connector plug while the slow glow (12 volt) connector plug is ¼ in. wide. Do not attempt to interchange any parts of these two glow plug systems.

Linkage Adjustments

EXCEPT VANS

3-Speed Column Shift

1. Place the column lever in the neutral position.
2. Under the truck, loosen the shift rod clamps. These are at the transmission end.
3. Make sure that the two levers on the transmission are in their center, neutral positions.
4. Install a 3/16 to 7/32 in. pin or drill bit through the alignment holes in the levers at the bottom of the steering column. This holds these levers in the neutral position.
5. Tighten the shift rod clamps.
6. Remove the pin and check the shifting operation.

VANS

The gearshift linkage should be adjusted each time it is disturbed or removed.

1. Install the control rods to both of the levers and set both shifter levers in the Neutral position.
2. Align both shifter tube levers on the mast jacket in Neutral. Install a 3/16–7/16 in. gauge to hold them in place. The gauge is inserted in the holes of the levers.
3. Connect the control rods to the tube levers, making sure that the clamps and tube levers are properly positioned in Neutral.
4. Remove the gauge and move the gearshift lever through all positions to be sure that the adjustment is correct in all positions.

CLUTCH

LINKAGE ADJUSTMENT

This adjustment is for the amount of clutch pedal free travel before the throwout bearing contacts the clutch release fingers. It is required periodically to compensate for clutch lining wear. Incorrect adjustment will cause gear grinding and clutch slippage or wear.

NOTE: If you have a problem with grinding when shifting into gear, shorten the pedal stop bumper to 3/8 in. and readjust the linkage.

1. Disconnect the clutch fork return spring at the fork on the clutch housing.
2. Loosen the outer adjusting nut (A) and back it off approximately 1/2 in. from the swivel.
3. Hold the clutch fork pushrod against the fork to move the throwout bearing against the clutch fingers. The pushrod will slide through the swivel at the cross-shaft.

4. Adjust the inner adjusting nut (B) to obtain 1/4 in. clearance between nut (B) and the swivel.
5. Release the pushrod, connect the return spring and tighten the outer nut (A) to lock the swivel against the inner nut (B).
6. Check the free travel at the pedal and readjust as necessary. It should be 1 1/4– 1 1/2 in.

REMOVAL AND INSTALLATION

There are two types of clutch pressure plates used, diaphragm and coil spring. In general, the larger heavy duty clutches are usually of the coil spring pressure plate type. Most removal and installation details are similar for both types.

Diaphragm Spring Pressure Plate

1. Remove the transmission as previously outlined.
2. Disconnect the fork pushrod and remove the flywheel housing. Remove the clutch throwout bearing from the fork.
3. Remove the clutch fork by pressing it away from the ball mounting with a screwdriver until the fork snaps loose from the ball or remove the ball stud from the clutch housing.
4. Install a pilot tool (an old mainshaft makes a good pilot tool) to hold the clutch while you are removing it.

NOTE: Before removing the clutch from the flywheel, matchmark the flywheel, the clutch cover and one of the pressure plate lugs. These parts must be reassembled in their original positions as they are a balanced assembly.

5. Loosen the clutch attaching bolts one turn at a time to prevent distortion of the clutch cover until the tension is released.
6. Remove the clutch pilot tool and the clutch from the vehicle.
Inspect the flywheel and pressure plate for discoloration, scoring or wear marks. The flywheel can be refaced if necessary, otherwise replace the parts. Also inspect the clutch fork and throwout bearing for looseness or wear. Replace if either is evident.
To install:
7. Install the pressure plate in the cover assembly, aligning the notch in the pressure plate with the notch in the cover flange.
8. Install the pressure plate retracting springs, lockwashers and the drive strap to the pressure plate bolts. Torque to 11 ft. lbs.
9. Turn the flywheel until the X mark is at the bottom.
10. Install the clutch disc, pressure plate and cover, using an old mainshaft as an aligning tool.
11. Turn the clutch until the X mark on the clutch cover aligns with the X mark on the flywheel.

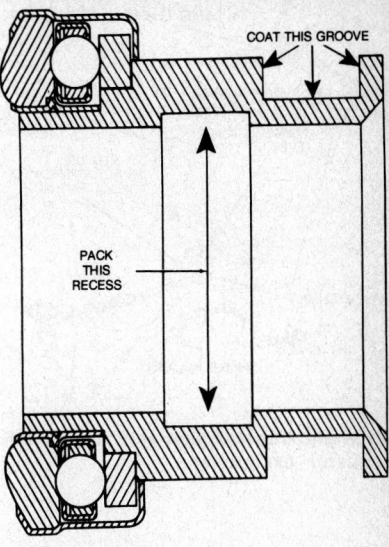

Throwout bearing lube points

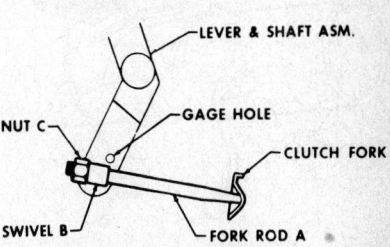

Clutch linkage adjustment

12. Install the attaching bolts and tighten them a little at a time in a crisscross pattern until the spring pressure is taken up.
13 Remove the aligning tool.
14 Pack the clutch ball fork seat with a small amount of high temperature grease. Too much grease will cause slippage.. Install a new retainer in the groove of the clutch fork, if necessary. Install the retainer with the high side up and the open end on the horizontal.
15. If the clutch fork ball was removed, reinstall it in the clutch housing and snap the clutch fork onto the ball.
16. Lubricate the inside of the throwout bearing collar and the throwout fork groove with a small amount of graphite grease.
17. Install the throwout bearing.
18. Install the flywheel housing and transmission.
19. Further installation is the reverse of removal. Adjust the clutch linkage.

Coil Spring Pressure Plate

Basically, the same procedures apply to diaphragm clutch removal as to coil spring clutch removal.

When loosening the clutch holding bolts, loosen them only a turn or two at a time in order to avoid bending the rim of the cover. It will be helpful to place wood or metal

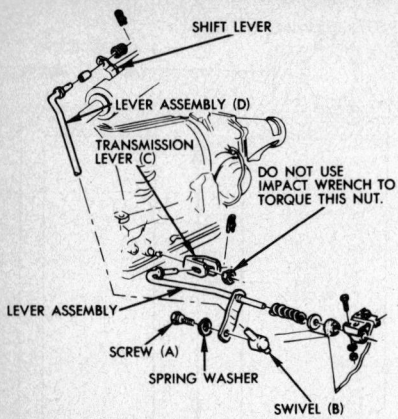

Automatic transmission shift linkage adjustment—except vans

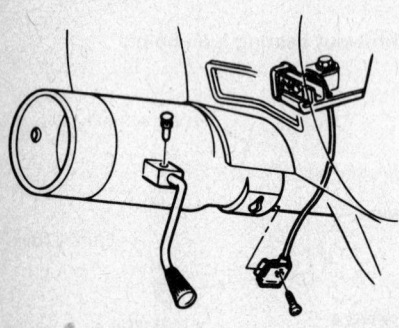

The adjustment point for the transmission shift position indicator is accessible after removing the lower column cover

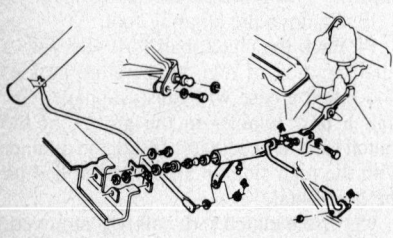

Automatic transmission shift linkage adjustment—vans through 1976

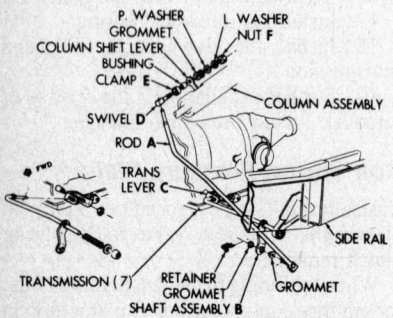

1977 and later shift linkage adjustment—vans

spacers, about ⅜ in. thick, between the clutch levers and the cover to hold the levers down as the holding bolts are being removed or when the clutch is being removed from the engine.

AUTOMATIC TRANSMISSION

Adjustments

SHIFT LINKAGE ADJUSTMENT

Except Vans

1. The shift tube and lever assembly must be free in the mast jacket.
2. Lift the selector lever toward the steering wheel and allow the selector lever to be positioned in Drive by the detent. Do not use the selector lever pointer as a reference.
3. Release the selector lever. The lever should not be able to go into Low unless the lever is lifted.
4. Lift the selector lever toward the steering wheel and allow the lever to be positioned in Neutral by the transmission detent.
5. Release the selector lever. The lever should not be able to engage reverse unless the lever is lifted. A properly adjusted linkage will prevent the lever from moving beyond both the Neutral and Drive detents unless the lever is lifted.
6. If adjustment is required, remove the screw (A) and spring washer from the swivel clamp (B).
7. Set the transmission lever (C) in Neutral by moving it to L_1 and then three detents clockwise.
8. Put the transmission selector lever in Neutral as determined by the mechanical stop in the steering column. Do not use the indicator pointer as a reference. The pointer is the last thing to be adjusted.
9. Assemble the swivel spring and washer to the lever (D) and tighten.
10. Readjust the Neutral safety switch if necessary.
11. To adjust the shift position indicator, remove the column cover at the bottom of the instrument panel and loosen the screw to move the pointer.
12. Check the operation. With the switch in RUN, and the transmission in Reverse, be sure that the key cannot be removed and that the steering wheel is locked. With the key in LOCK and the shift lever in PARK, be sure that the key can be removed, the steering wheel is locked, and that the transmission remains in PARK when the steering column is locked.

Vans

1975–76

1. Lift the selector lever toward the steering wheel and allow the selector lever to be positioned in Drive by the detent. Do not use the selector lever pointer as a reference.
2. Release the selector lever. The lever should not be able to go into Low unless the lever is lifted.
3. Lift the selector lever toward the steering wheel and allow the lever to be positioned in Neutral by the transmission detent.
4. Release the selector lever. The lever should not be able to engage reverse unless the lever is lifted. A properly adjusted linkage will prevent the lever from moving beyond both the Neutral and Drive detents unless the lever is lifted.
5. If adjustment is required, remove the screw and spring washer from the swivel clamp.
6. Set the transmission lever in Neutral by moving it counter-clockwise to 1 and then three detents clockwise.
7. Put the transmission selector lever in Neutral as determined by the mechanical stop in the steering column.
8. Assemble the swivel spring and washer to the lever and tighten.
9. Readjust the Neutral safety switch if necesary.
10. If the indicator pointer fails to line up properly with the gear symbol, adjust the position of the pointer and scale.

1977 AND LATER

———— CAUTION ————

Any inaccuracies in this procedure may lead to premature transmission failure due to operation without the controls in the full detent position. Such operation will result in reduced oil pressure, and therefore only partial engagement of the drive clutches. Partial engagement of the clutches with sufficient pressure to cause apparent normal operation will result in transmission failure after only a few miles of operation.

1. Remove the nut (F) and slide off the washers, grommet, bushing, and clamp (E). Remove swivel (D).
2. Remove the retainer, grommets and the transmission lever (C) from the shaft assembly.
3. Set the transmission lever (C) in the Neutral position either by moving the lever (C) counterclockwise to the L1 position, then clockwise three steps to the Neutral position, or by moving the lever (C) clockwise to the Park position, then counterclockwise two steps to the Neutral position.
4. Set the column shift lever in the Neutral position by rotating the shift lever until it locks into the stop in the column. Do not use the gear select pointer as a reference to position the column shift lever.
5. Attach rod (A) to the shaft assembly

(B) as shown.

6. Slide the swivel (D) and the clamp (E) onto rod (A). Align the column shift lever and loosely attach the assembly.

7. Hold the column shift lever against the Neutral stop, on the Park position side.

8. Tighten the nut (F) to 18 ft. lbs.

9. Adjust the indicator needle if necessary. It may also be necessary to adjust the neutral start switch.

THROTTLE VALVE LINKAGE ADJUSTMENT

Six Cylinder Engines

1. With the accelerator depressed, the bellcrank on the engine must be in the wide-open throttle position.

2. The dash lever must be $1/64$–$1/16$ in. off the lever stop and the transmission lever must be against the transmission internal stop.

V8 Engines

1. Remove the air cleaner.

2. Disconnect the accelerator linkage at the carburetor.

3. Disconnect the accelerator return spring and throttle valve rod return springs.

4. Pull the throttle valve rod forward until the transmission is through the detent. Open the carburetor to the wide-open throttle position. The carburetor must reach the wide-open throttle position at the same time that the ball stud contacts the end of the slot in the upper throttle valve rod.

5. Adjust the swivel on the end of the upper throttle valve rod as per Step 4. The allowable tolerance is approximately $1/32$ in.

6. Connect and adjust the accelerator linkage.

7. Check for freedom of operation. Install the air cleaner.

NEUTRAL START SWITCH ADJUSTMENT

This switch prevents the engine from being started unless the transmission is in Neutral or Park. It is located on the shift linkage

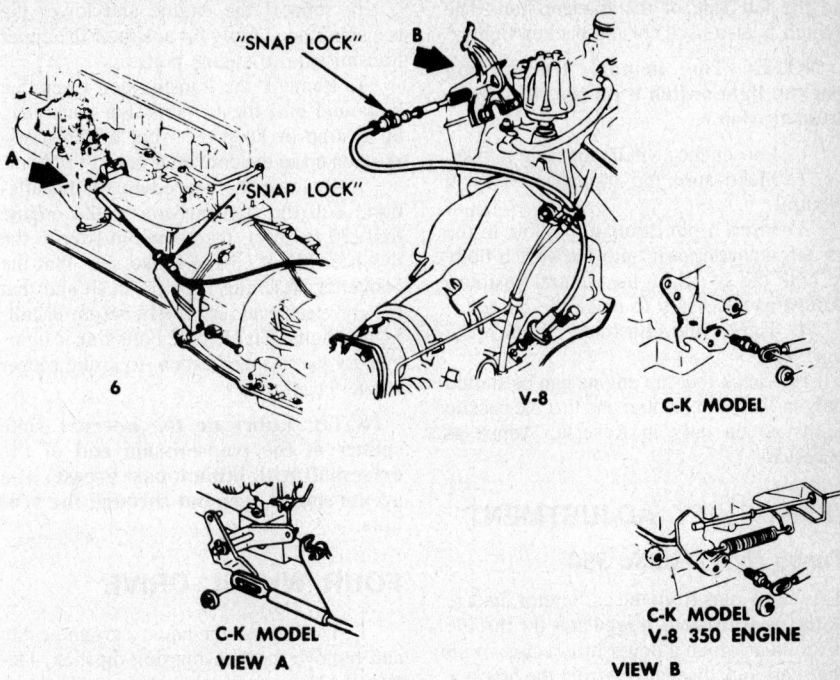

Detent cable adjustment—except diesel

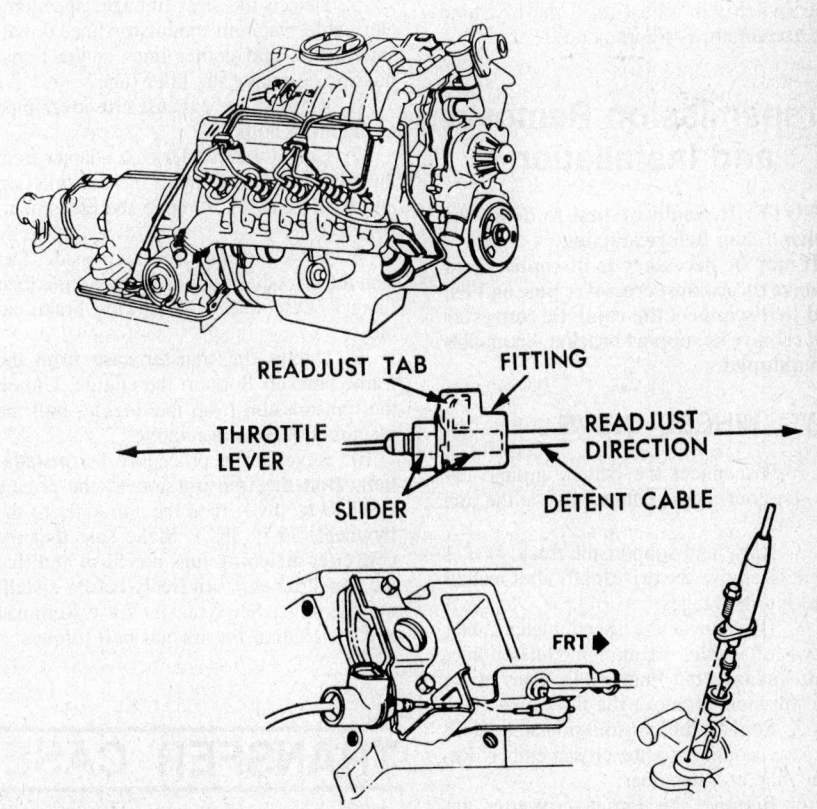

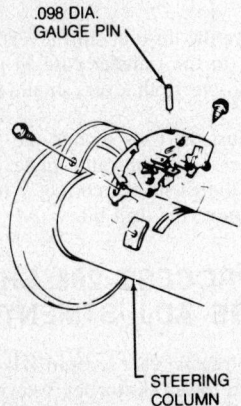

Neutral start switch adjustment

Throttle valve/detent cable adjustment—diesel

on the left side of the transmission. The switch is also used for the backup lights.

NOTE: The manual transmission backup light switch is on the rear of the transmission.

1. Loosen the switch mounting screws.
2. Make sure the transmission is in Neutral.
3. Insert a pin through the hole in the switch actuating arm into the switch body to hold the switch in the Neutral position. Adjust as necessary to make the pin fit.
4. Tighten the adjustment. Remove the pin.
5. Check that the engine can be started only in Park and Neutral and that the backup lights go on only in Reverse. Adjust as necessary.

DOWNSHIFT ADJUSTMENT

Turbo Hydra-Matic 350

This cable runs from the carburetor linkage to the transmission. It regulates the throttle position at which a downshift occurs. With the snap-lock disengaged from the bracket, position the carburetor at the wide open throttle position. Push the snap-lock downward until the top is flush with the rest of the cable.

Turbo Hydra-Matic 400 and 700-R4

When installing a new downshift switch, press the plunger as far forward as possible. The switch will adjust itself the first time the accelerator is floorboarded.

Transmission Removal and Installation

NOTE: It would be best to drain the transmission before starting.
It may be necessary to disconnect and remove the exhaust crossover pipe on V8s, and to disconnect the catalytic converter and remove its support bracket, on models so equipped.

TWO WHEEL DRIVE

1. Disconnect the battery ground cable. Disconnect the detent cable at the carburetor.
2. Raise and support the truck.
3. Remove the driveshaft, after matchmarking its flanges.
4. Disconnect the speedometer cable, downshift cable, vacuum modulator line, shift linkage, and fluid cooler lines at the transmission. Remove the filler tube.
5. Support the transmission and unbolt the rear mount from the crossmember. Remove the crossmember.
6. Remove the torque converter underpan, matchmark the flywheel and converter, and remove the converter bolts.

7. Support the engine and lower the transmission slightly for access to the upper transmission to engine bolts.
8. Remove the transmission to engine bolts and pull the transmission back. Rig up a strap or keep the front of the transmission up so the converter doesn't fall out.
9. Reverse the procedure for installation. Bolt the transmission to the engine first (30 ft. lbs.), then the converter to the flywheel (35 ft. lbs.). Make sure that the converter attaching lugs are flush and that the converter can turn freely before installing the bolts. Tighten the bolts finger tight, then torque to specification, to insure proper converter alignment.

NOTE: Lubricate the internal yoke splines at the transmission end of the driveshaft with lithium base grease. The grease should seep out through the vent hole.

FOUR WHEEL DRIVE

1. Disconnect the battery ground cable and remove the transmission dipstick. Detach the downshift cable at the carburetor. Remove the transfer case shift lever knob and boot.
2. Raise and support the truck.
3. Remove the skid plate, if any. Remove the flywheel cover.
4. Matchmark the flywheel and torque converter, remove the bolts, and secure the converter so it doesn't fall out of the transmission.
5. Detach the shift linkage, speedometer cable, vacuum modulator line, downshift cable, and cooler lines at the transmission. Remove the filler tube.
6. Remove the exhaust crossover pipe to manifold bolts.
7. Unbolt the transfer case adapter from the crossmember. Support the transmission and transfer case. Remove the crossmember.
8. Move the exhaust system aside. Detach the driveshafts after matchmarking their flanges. Disconnect the parking brake cable.
9. Unbolt the transfer case from the frame bracket. Support the engine. Unbolt the transmission from the engine, pull the assembly back, and remove.
10. Reverse the procedure for installation. Bolt the transmission to the engine first (30 ft. lbs.), then the converter to the flywheel (35 ft. lbs.). Make sure that the converter attaching lugs are flush and that the converter can turn freely before installing the bolts. See Transfer Case Removal and Installation for adapter bolt torques.

TRANSFER CASE

There are three transfer cases used. The New Process 205 is used in part time systems with all transmissions in 1975, and in 1980, and with manual transmissions only 1976–79. It has a large New Process emblem on the back of the case. The full time New Process 203 is used with all transmissions in early 1975, and only with automatics from mid-1975 to 1979. It can be identified by the H LOC and L LOC positions on the shifter.

The aluminum case New Process 208 was introduced in 1981 on K-10 and 20 models.

NOTE: Models with the New Process 203 full time four wheel drive transfer case, especially with manual transmissions, may give a front wheel "chatter" or vibration on sharp turns. This is a normal characteristic of this drivetrain combination. If it occurs shortly after shifting out of a LOC position, the transfer case is probably still locked up. This should correct itself after about a mile of driving, or can be alleviated by backing up for a short distance.

--------- CAUTION ---------
Owners of full time four wheel drive trucks (New Process 203 transfer case) often consider either removing the front driveshaft, or installing locking front hubs and operating in a LOC position, as a means of improving gas mileage. This practice will submit the transfer case to stresses beyond its design limits and will void all warranties. Use of any lubricant additive in the transfer case is also not recommended.

NEW PROCESS 203 SHIFT LINKAGE ADJUSTMENT

The full time four wheel drive transfer case is the only one on which linkage adjustment is possible.
1. Place the selector lever in the cab in the Neutral position.
2. Detach the adjustable rod ends from the transfer case levers.
3. Insert an $^{11}/_{64}$ in. drill bit through the alignment holes in the shifter levers. This will lock the shifter in the neutral position with both levers vertical.
4. Place the range shift lever (the outer lever) on the transfer case in the Neutral position.
5. Place the lockout shift lever (the inner lever) on the transfer case in the unlocked position. Both levers should now be vertical.
6. Adjust the rods so that the linkage fits together. The indicator plate can be moved to align with the correct symbol.
7. Remove the drill bit.

NEW PROCESS 208 SHIFT LINKAGE ADJUSTMENT

1. Put transfer case lever in 4HI detent.
2. Push lower shifter lever forward to 4HI stop.
3. Install rod swivel in shift lever hole.

4. Hang .200 thick gauge cover rod behind swivel.

5. Run rear rod nut A against gauge with shifter against 4HI stop.

6. Remove gauge and push swivel rearward against nut A.

7. Run front rod nut B against swivel and tighten.

REMOVAL AND INSTALLATION

NP 203 and 205

1. Raise and support the truck.
2. Drain the transfer case.
3. Disconnect the speedometer cable, back-up light switch, and the TCS switch.
4. If necessary, remove the skid plate and crossmember support.
5. Disconnect the front and rear driveshafts and support them out of the way.

On New Process 205 models, disconnect the shift lever rod from the shift rail link.

On New Process 203 models, disconnect the shift levers at the transfer case.

Adapter to Transfer Case Bolt Torque

Model	Year	Torque (ft. lbs.)
NP 205	'75–'82	25
NP 203	'75–'79	38

Adapter to Transmission Bolt Torque

Model	Torque (ft. lbs.)
NP 205	22 manual
	35 automatic
NP 203	40

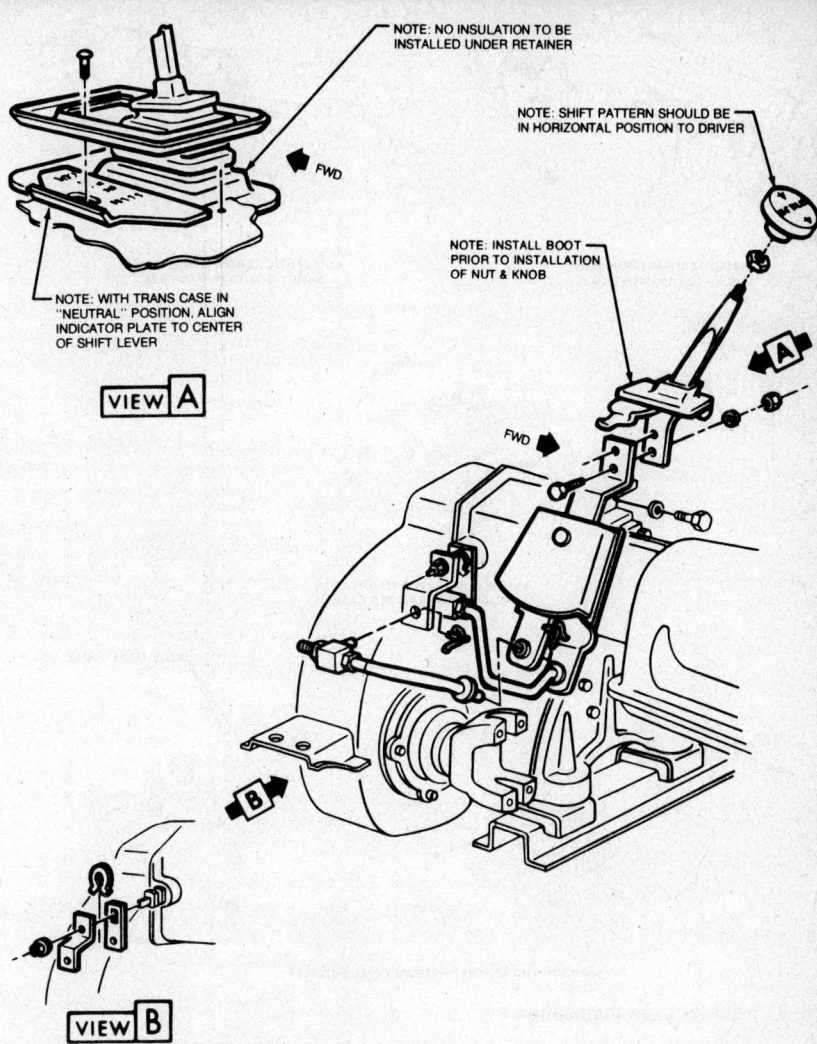

VIEW A

NOTE: NO INSULATION TO BE INSTALLED UNDER RETAINER

NOTE: SHIFT PATTERN SHOULD BE IN HORIZONTAL POSITION TO DRIVER

NOTE: INSTALL BOOT PRIOR TO INSTALLATION OF NUT & KNOB

NOTE: WITH TRANS CASE IN "NEUTRAL" POSITION, ALIGN INDICATOR PLATE TO CENTER OF SHIFT LEVER

VIEW B

NP 203 shift linkage

Adapter to Frame Bolt Torque

Model	Torque (ft. lbs.)
NP 205	130
NP 203 (bracket to frame)	50 upper
	65 lower

6. Remove the transfer case-to-frame mounting bolts.
7. Support the transfer case and remove the bolts attaching the transfer case to transmission adaptor.
8. Move the transfer case to the rear until the input shaft clears the adaptor and lower the transfer case from the truck.

To install the transfer case:

9. Lifting the transfer case on a transmission jack, attach the case to the adapter using through bolts. Torque to specification.
10. Remove the transmission jack and install the transfer case-to-frame rail bolts.

Make certain to bend the locking tabs after installation.

11. Connect the shift linkage.
12. Connect the front driveshaft to the front transfer case output shaft and the rear drive shaft to the rear output shaft.
13. Install the crossmember and skid plate, if equipped.

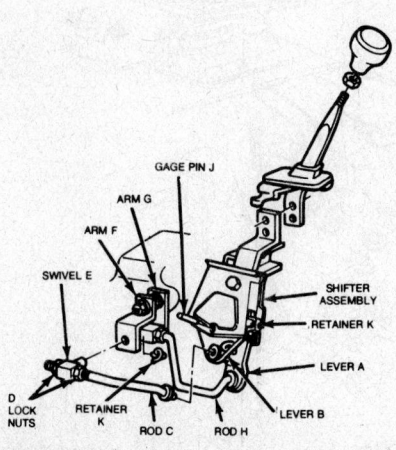

NP 203 linkage adjustment

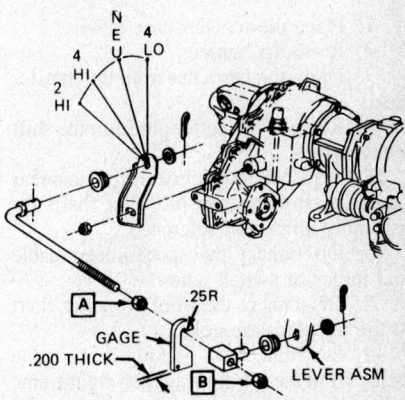

NP 208 linkage adjustment

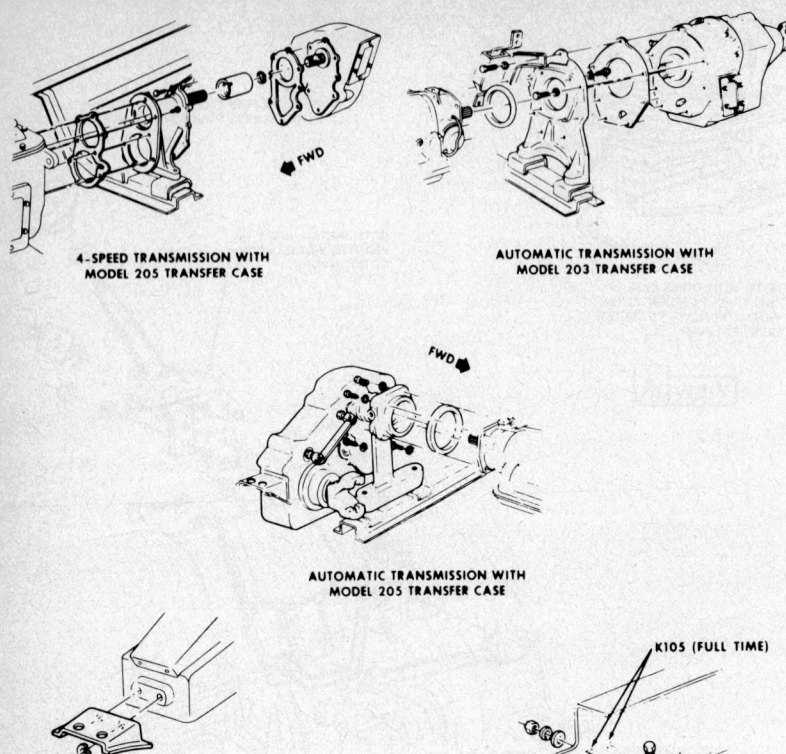

4-SPEED TRANSMISSION WITH
MODEL 205 TRANSFER CASE

AUTOMATIC TRANSMISSION WITH
MODEL 203 TRANSFER CASE

AUTOMATIC TRANSMISSION WITH
MODEL 205 TRANSFER CASE

K105 (FULL TIME)

K10+20

FWD

SUPPORT AND BRACKET ASSEMBLY (ALL MODELS)

1975–81 transfer case installation

the transfer case on automatic transmission models.

10. Place a support under the transfer case and remove the transfer case-to-transmission adapter bolts.

11. Move the transfer case assembly rearward until free of the transmission output shaft and remove the assembly.

12. Remove all gasket material from the rear of the transmission adapter housing.

13. Install the transmission-to-transfer case gasket on the transmission.

14. Shift the transfer case to 4H position if not done previously.

15. Rotate the transfer case output shaft (by turning yoke) until the transmission output shaft gear engages the transfer case input shaft. Move the transfer case forward until the case seats against the transmission. Be sure the transfer case is flush against the transmission. Severe damage to the transfer case will result if the attaching bolts are tightened while the transfer case is cocked or in a bind.

16. Install the transfer case attaching bolts. Tighten the bolts to 30 ft. lbs.

17. Connect the speedometer driven gear to the transfer case.

18. Connect the front and rear propeller shafts to the transfer case. Be sure to align the shafts-to-yokes using the reference marks made during removal. Tighten the shaft-to-yoke clamp strap nuts to 15 ft. lbs.

19. Remove the support stand from under the transfer case.

20. Connect the parking brake cable if disconnected.

21. Attach the cotter pin to the shift lever swivel.

14. Connect the speedometer cable, back-up light, and TCS switches.

15. Fill the transfer case to the proper level with lubricant.

16. Lower the vehicle.

NOTE: Recheck all bolt torques. When attaching the driveshafts, make sure that the flange locknuts are torqued to specifications.

NP 208

1. Place the transfer case in 4H.

2. Raise the vehicle.

3. Drain the lubricant from the transfer case.

4. Remove the cotter pin from the shift lever swivel.

5. Mark the transfer case front and rear output shaft yokes and propeller shafts for assembly alignment reference.

6. Disconnect the speedometer cable and indicator switch wires.

7. Disconnect the front propeller shaft at the transfer case yoke.

8. Disconnect the parking brake cable guide from the pivot located on right frame rail, if necessary.

9. Remove the engine strut rod from

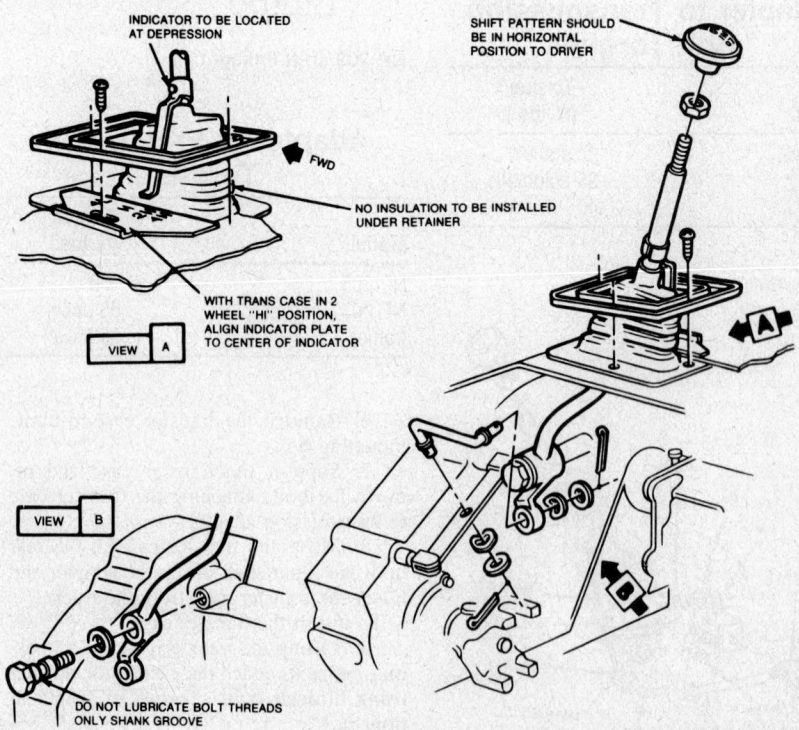

INDICATOR TO BE LOCATED
AT DEPRESSION

FWD

NO INSULATION TO BE INSTALLED
UNDER RETAINER

WITH TRANS CASE IN 2
WHEEL "HI" POSITION,
ALIGN INDICATOR PLATE
TO CENTER OF INDICATOR

VIEW A

SHIFT PATTERN SHOULD
BE IN HORIZONTAL
POSITION TO DRIVER

A

VIEW B

DO NOT LUBRICATE BOLT THREADS
ONLY SHANK GROOVE

NP 205 linkage

22. Connect the engine strut to the transfer case on automatic models.

23. Fill the transfer case with Dexron® II.

24. Lower the vehicle.

DRIVELINE

Front Driveshaft (4 WD Only)

REMOVAL AND INSTALLATION

Chevrolet and GMC use U-bolts or straps to secure the driveshaft to the pinion flange.

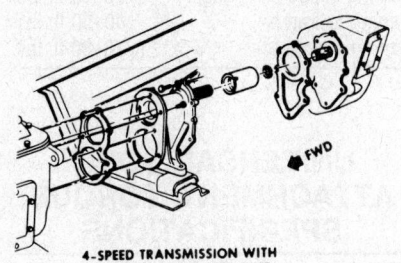

4-SPEED TRANSMISSION WITH MODEL 205 TRANSFER CASE

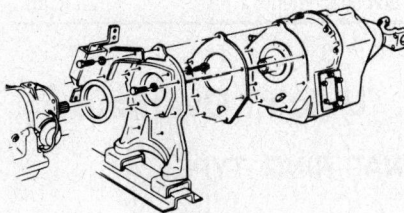

AUTOMATIC TRANSMISSION WITH MODEL 203 TRANSFER CASE

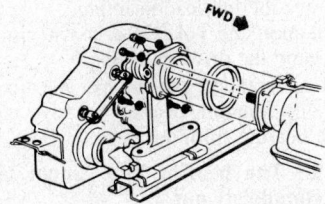

AUTOMATIC TRANSMISSION WITH MODEL 205 TRANSFER CASE

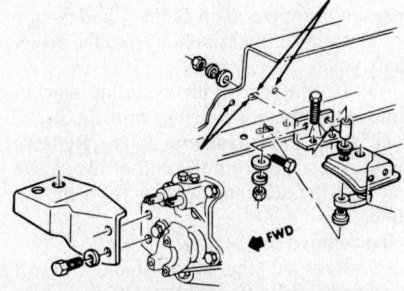

SUPPORT AND BRACKET ASSEMBLY (ALL MODELS)

Transfer case adapters

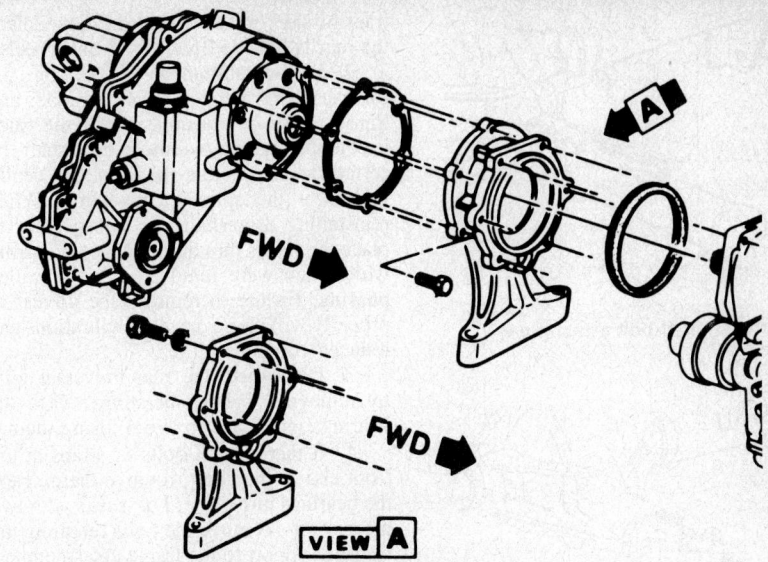

VIEW **A**

WITH AUTOMATIC TRANSMISSION

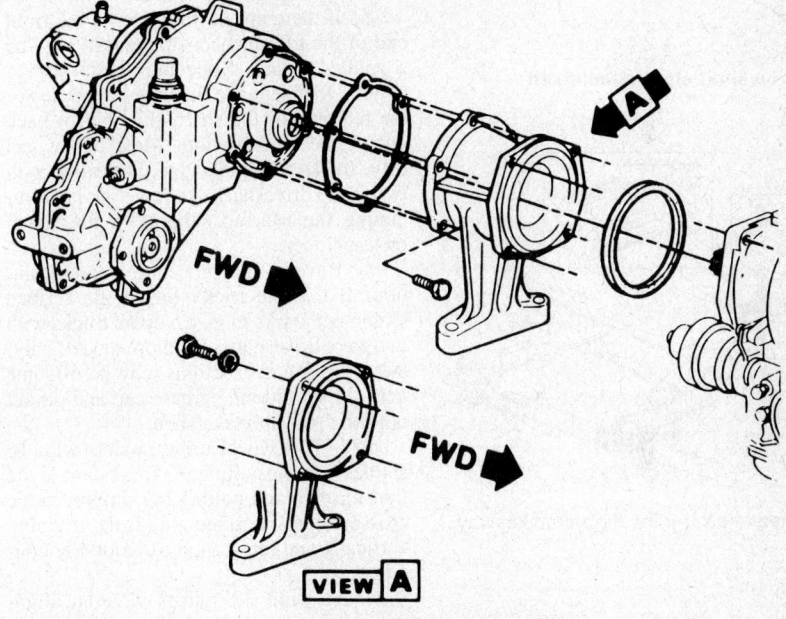

VIEW **A**

WITH MANUAL TRANSMISSION

NP 208 installation

Use the following procedure to remove the driveshaft.

1. Jack the front of the vehicle so that the front wheels are off the ground. Block the rear wheels and safely support the truck on stands.

2. Scribe aligning marks on the driveshaft and the pinion flange to aid in reassembly.

3. Remove the U-bolts or straps at the axle end of the shaft. Compress the shaft slightly and tape the bearings into place to avoid losing them.

4. Remove the U-bolts or straps at the transfer case end of the shaft. Tape the bearings into place.

5. Remove the driveshaft.

6. Reverse the procedure for installa-

tion. Make certain that the marks made earlier line up correctly to prevent possible imbalances. Be sure that the constant velocity joint (the big double one) is at the transfer case end.

Rear Driveshaft (All Models)

REMOVAL AND INSTALLATION

1. Raise and safely support the rear of the truck as necessary. There is less chance of lubricant leakage from the rear of the

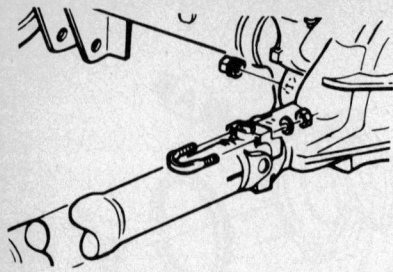

Rear driveshaft U-bolt attachment

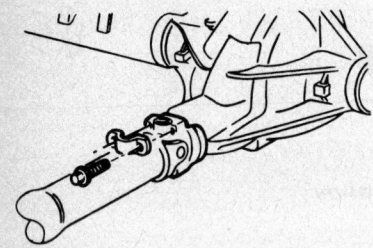

Rear driveshaft strap attachment

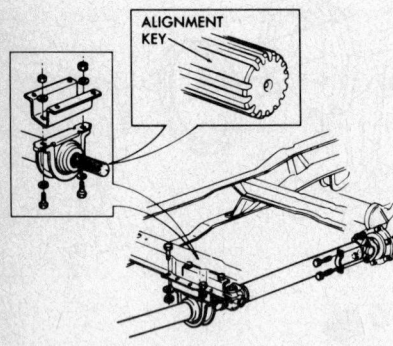

32 splined shaft U-joint alignment keyway

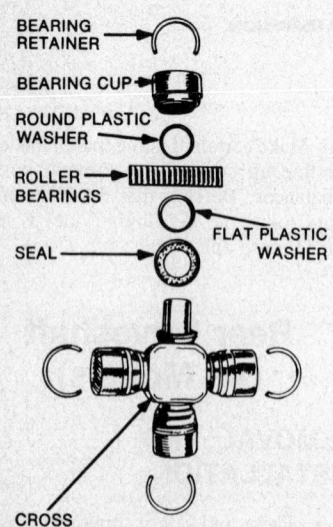

Injection molded retainer U-joint repair kit

transmission on two wheel drive models if the rear is raised. Block the front wheels.

2. Scribe alignment marks on the driveshaft and flange of the rear axle, and transfer case or transmission. If the truck is equipped with a two piece driveshaft, be certain to also scribe marks at the center joint near the splined connection. When reinstalling driveshafts, it is necessary to place the shafts into the same position from which they were removed. This is called phasing. Failure to reinstall the driveshaft properly will cause driveline vibrations and reduced component life.

3. Disconnect the rear universal joint by removing U-bolts or straps. Tape the bearings into place to avoid losing them.

4. If there are U-bolts or straps at the front end of the shaft, remove them. Tape the bearings into place. For trucks with two piece shafts, remove the bolts retaining the bearing support to the frame crossmember. Compress the shaft slightly and remove it. All four wheel drive trucks are of this type.

5. If there are no fasteners at the front end of the transmission, there will only be a splined fitting. Slide the shaft forward slightly to disengage the axle flange, lower the rear end of the shaft, then pull it back out of the transmission. Most two wheel drive trucks are of this type. For trucks with two piece driveshafts, remove the bolts retaining the bearing support to the frame crossmember.

6. Reverse the procedure for installation. It may be tricky to get the scribed alignment marks to match up on trucks with two piece driveshafts. For those models only, the following instructions may be of some help. First, slide the grease cap and gasket onto the rear splines. Then:

1977–82 4-wheel drive models with 16 splines, after installing the front shaft to the transmission and bolting the support to the crossmember, arrange the front trunnion vertically and the second trunnion horizontally.

Models with 32 splines have an alignment key. The driveshaft cannot be replaced incorrectly. Simply match up the key with the keyway.

1975–76 4-wheel drive models with 16 splines, align the trunnions vertically. The shafts should not be rotated before installing the rear shaft to the front shaft.

1975–76 4-wheel drive models with 16 splines, after installing the front shaft to the transmission or transfer case, must align the trunnions vertically, then the rear shaft must be rotated four splines (90°) to the left (driver's) side before installing the rear shaft to the front shaft.

7. On two-wheel drive automatic transmission models, lubricate the internal yoke splines at the transmission end of the shaft with lithium base grease. The grease should seep out through the vent hole.

NOTE: A thump in the rear driveshaft sometimes occurs when releasing the brakes after braking to a stop, especially on a downgrade. This is most common with automatic transmission. It is often caused by the driveshaft splines binding and can be cured by removing the driveshaft, inspecting the splines for rough edges, and carefully lubricating. A similar thump may be caused by the clutch plates in Positraction limited slip rear axles binding. If this isn't caused by wear, it can be cured by draining and refilling the rear axle with the special lubricant and adding Positraction additive, both of which are available from dealers.

DRIVESHAFT ATTACHMENT TORQUE SPECIFICATIONS

To rear axle (strap)	12–17 ft. lbs.
To rear axle (U-bolt)	18–22 ft. lbs.
Bearing support to hanger	20–30 ft. lbs.
Hanger to frame	40–50 ft. lbs.
To transfer case	70–80 ft. lbs.

UNIVERSAL JOINT ATTACHMENT TORQUE SPECIFICATIONS

Strap attachments	15 ft. lbs.
U-bolt attachments	20 ft. lbs.

U-Joint Overhaul

SNAP-RING TYPE

1. Remove the driveshaft(s) from the truck.

2. Remove the lockrings from the yoke and remove the lubrication fitting.

3. Support the yoke in a bench vise. Never clamp the driveshaft tube.

4. Use a soft drift and hammer and drive against one trunnion bearing to drive the opposite bearing from the yoke.

NOTE: The bearing cap cannot be driven completely out.

5. Grasp the cap and work it out.

6. Support the other side of the yoke and drive the other bearing cap from the yoke and remove as in Steps 4 and 5.

7. Remove the trunnion from the driveshaft yoke.

8. If equipped with a sliding sleeve, remove the trunnion bearings from the sleeve yoke in the same manner as above. Remove the seal retainer from the end of the sleeve and pull the seal and washer from the retainer.

To remove the bearing support:

9. Remove the dust shield, or, if equipped with a flange, remove the cotter pin and nut and pull the flange and deflector assembly from the shaft.

10. Remove the support bracket from the rubber cushion and pull the cushion away from the bearing.

11. Pull the bearing assembly from the shaft. If equipped, remove the grease retainers and slingers from the bearing.

Assemble the bearing support as follows:

12. Install the inner deflector on the driveshaft and punch the deflector on 2 opposite sides to be sure that it is tight.

13. Pack the retainers with special high melting grease.

Insert a slinger (if used) inside one retainer and press this retainer over the bearing outer race.

14. Start the bearing and slinger on the shaft journal. Support the driveshaft and press the bearing and inner slinger against the shoulder of the shaft with a suitable pipe.

15. Install the second slinger on the shaft and press the second retainer on the shaft.

16. Install the dust shield over the shaft (small diameter first) and depress it into position against the outer slinger or, if equipped with a flange, install the flange and deflector. Align the centerline of the flange yoke with the centerline of the driveshaft yoke and start the flange straight on the splines of the shaft with the end of the flange against the slinger.

17. Force the rubber cushion onto the bearing and coat the outside diameter of the cushion with clean brake fluid.

18. Force the bracket onto the cushion. Assemble the trunnion bearings:

19. Repack the bearings with grease and replace the trunnion dust seals after any operation that requires disassembly of the U-joint. Be sure that the lubricant reservoir at the end of the trunnion is full of lubricant. Fill the reservoirs with lubricant from the bottom.

20. Install the trunnion into the driveshaft yoke and press the bearings into the yoke over the trunnion hubs as far as it will go.

21. Install the lockrings.

22. Hold the trunnion in one hand and tap the yoke slightly to seat the bearings against the lockrings.

23. On the rear driveshafts, install the sleeve yoke over the trunnion hubs and install the bearings in the same manner as above.

Molded Retainer Type

An injection molded plastic retainer is used on some models. A service repair kit is available for overhaul.

1. Remove the driveshaft.

2. Support the driveshaft in a horizontal position. Place the U-joint so that the lower ear of the shaft yoke is supported by a 1 1/8 in. socket. Press the lower bearing cup out of the yoke ear. This will shear the plastic retaining the lower bearing cup.

NOTE: Never clamp the driveshaft tubing in a vise.

3. If the bearing cup is not completely

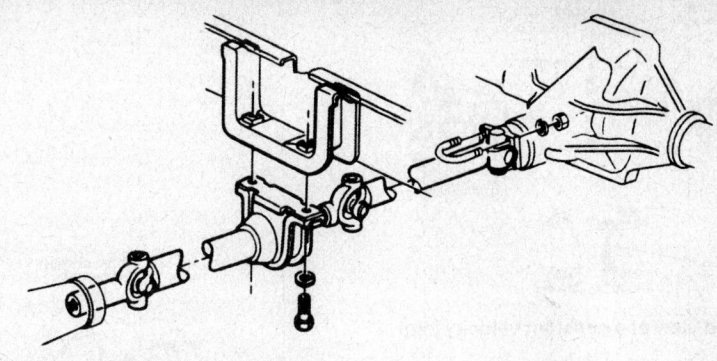

Two-piece driveshaft center bearing

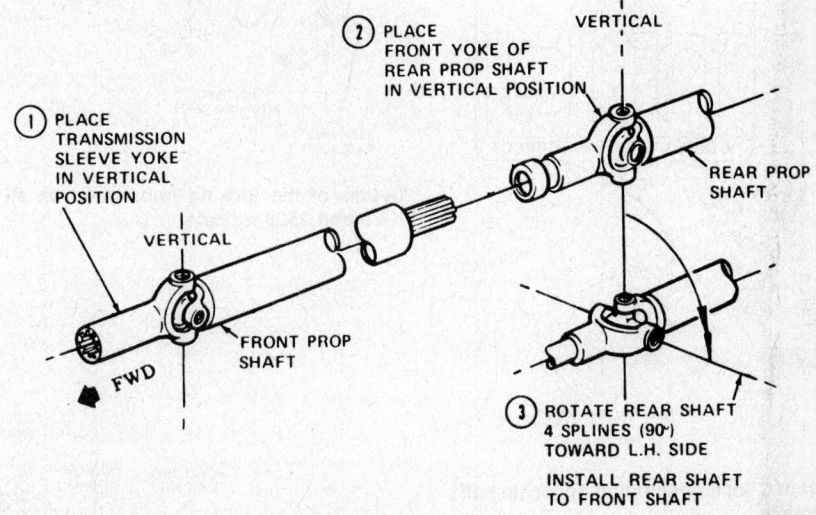

U-joint alignment, 1975–76 C models with 16 splines; 1975–76 K models, use point 1 and 2 only

removed, lift the cross, insert a spacer and press the cup completely out.

4. Rotate the driveshaft, shear the opposite plastic retainer, and press the other bearing cup out in the same manner.

5. Remove the cross from the yoke. Production U-joints cannot be reassembled. There are no bearing retainer grooves in the cups. Discard all parts that were removed and substitute those in the overhaul kit.

6. Remove the sheared plastic bearing retainer. Drive a small pin or punch through the injection holes to aid in removal.

7. If the front U-joint is serviced, remove the bearing cups from the slip yoke in the manner previously described.

8. Be sure that the seals are installed on the service bearing cups to hold the needle bearings in place for handling. Grease the bearings if they aren't pregreased.

9. Install one bearing cup partway into one side of the yoke and turn this ear to the bottom.

10. Insert the cross into the yoke so that the trunnion seats freely in the bearing cup.

11. Install the opposite bearing cup partway. Be sure that both trunnions are started straight into the bearing cup.

12. Press against opposite bearing cups,

working the cross constantly to be sure that it is free in the cups. If binding occurs, check the needle rollers to be sure that one needle has not become lodged under an end of the trunnion.

13. As soon as one bearing retainer groove is exposed, stop pressing and install the bearing retainer snap-ring.

14. Continue to press until the opposite bearing retainer can be installed. If difficulty installing the snap-rings is encountered, rap the yoke with a hammer to spring the yoke ears slightly.

15. Assemble the other half of the U-joint in the same manner.

16. Check that the cross is free in the cups. If it is too tight, smack the yoke ears again to help seat the bearing retainers.

Constant Velocity Joint Overhaul

1. Remove the front driveshaft from the truck.

2. Remove the rear trunnion snap-ring from the center yoke.

3. Remove the grease fitting, if

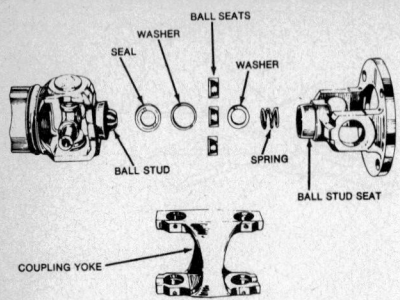

Exploded view of a constant velocity joint

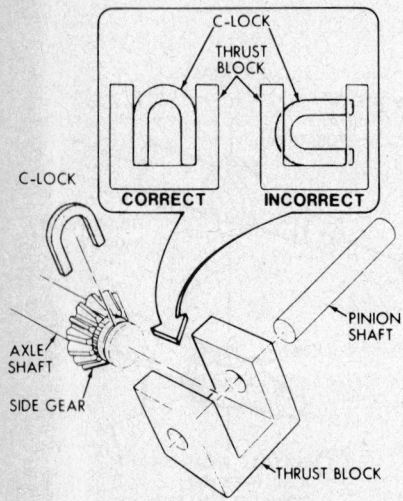

Correct C-lock positioning on locking differentials

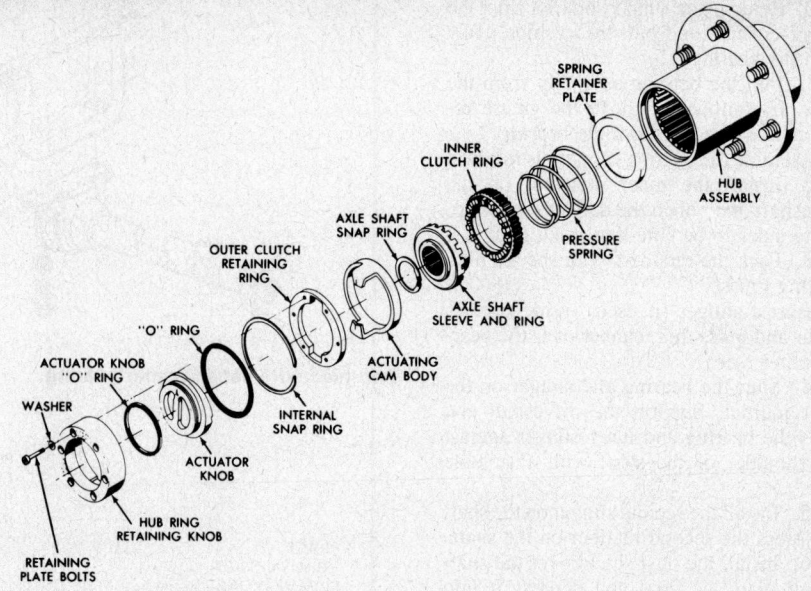

Details of the locking hubs used on all K-10 and 1500 models and 1977 and later K-20 and 2500 models

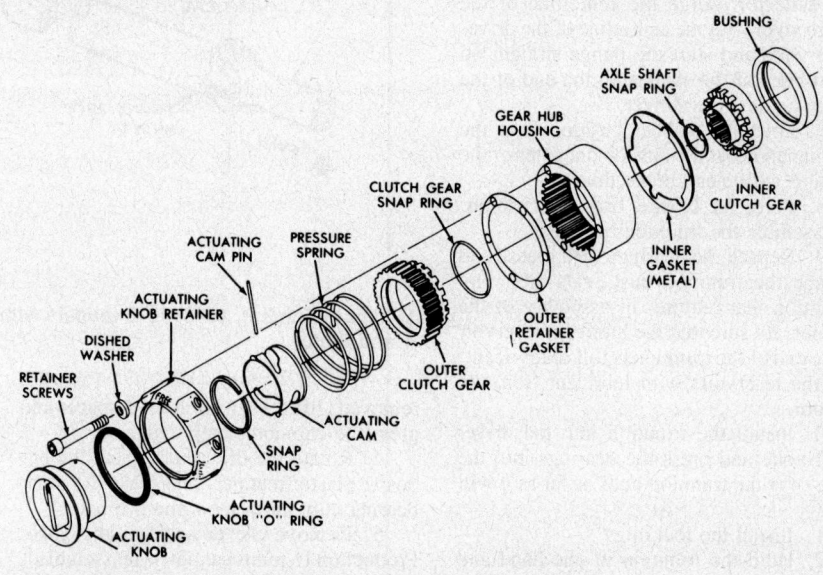

Details of the locking hubs used on 1975–76 K-20 and 2500 models

equipped.

4. Place the driveshaft in a vise as shown.

5. Drive one rear trunnion bearing cap from the center yoke until it protrudes approximately ⅜ in.

6. Release the vise and grasp the protruding portion of the cup in a vise and strike the center yoke until the cup is removed. Remove the cup seal with a thin screwdriver.

7. Repeat Steps 4, 5, and 6 for the remaining bearing cup.

8. When the center yoke cups have been removed, remove the rear yoke half bearing cups.

9. Remove the rear trunnion.

10. Remove the rear yoke half from the driveshaft by gently pulling it off. Remove all loose needle bearings and the spring seal.

11. Remove the front trunnion from the center yoke and the front yoke in the manner previously described. Remove all four bearing cups before the trunnions are removed.

12. Clean and inspect all needle bearings, cups, seals, trunnions, fitting, and yokes.

13. Assemble the needle bearings in the cups. Assemble the needle bearings in the front yoke. Use heavy grease to retain the bearing rollers. Install the seals in the bearing cups.

14. Install the front trunnion in the driveshaft, and install the center yoke in the front trunnion.

15. Install one bearing cup and seal assembly in the front yoke. Drive it into position so that the snap-ring can be installed. Install the snap-ring and the remaining cup and seal in the front yoke. Install the other snap-ring.

16. Install the front trunnion bearing cups in the center yoke in the same manner.

17. With the front trunnion completely installed, install the seal on the driveshaft with the large face first. Gently slip the rear yoke half on the driveshaft using care not to distrub the rollers. Insert the rear trunnion into the center yoke.

18. Install the rear yoke half bearing caps on the rear trunnion. Install one rear trunnion bearing cap in the center yoke and press it into the yoke until the snap-ring can be installed. Install the remaining cap and snap-ring.

19. Grease the U-joint at the two conventional "zerk" fittings (if equipped) and the one in the rear yoke half which requires a needlenose grease gun adapter.

20. Install the driveshaft with the constant velocity joint next to the transfer case.

FRONT DRIVE AXLE

Locking Hub

REMOVAL AND INSTALLATION

NOTE: Locking hubs may not be used with full time four wheel drive. Locking hubs should be run in the lock position for at least 10 miles each month to assure proper differential lubrication.

This procedure requires snap-ring pliers and a special hub nut wrench. It isn't very easy without them. You will have to modify this procedure if you have non-factory installed hubs.

1. Set the hub in the Lock position.
2. Remove the outer retaining plate allen head bolts and take off the plate, O-ring, and knob.
3. Take out the large snap-ring inside the hub and remove the outer clutch retaining ring and actuating cam body.
4. Relieve pressure on the axle shaft snap-ring and remove it.
5. Take out the axle shaft sleeve and clutch ring assembly and the inner clutch ring and bushing assembly. Remove the spring and retainer plate.
6. Clean all the hub components in a safe solvent and dry them. Lubricate everything with a high temperature grease.
7. Install the spring retainer plate with the flange side to the bearing and seat it against the outer bearing cup.
8. Install the spring with the large end against the retainer plate.

NOTE: When the spring is properly installed and seated it will extend past the spindle nuts about 7/8 in.

9. Place the inner clutch ring and bushing assembly into the axle shaft sleeve and clutch ring assembly. Install these components, push in, and install the axle shaft snap-ring. If there are two axle shaft snap-ring grooves, use the inner one.

NOTE: You can install a 7/16 in. bolt in the axle and pull outward on it to aid in seating the snap-ring.

10. Install the actuating cam body with the cams out. Replace the outer clutch retaining ring and then the internal snap-ring.
11. Install a new O-ring, then install the actuating knob and retaining plate in the lock position. The grooves in the knob must fit into the actuator cam body. Install the cover bolts and seals.

Axle Shaft

REMOVAL AND INSTALLATION

NOTE: This procedure requires snapring pliers and a special hub nut wrench. It is not very easy without them.

1. Remove the wheel and tire.
2. For K-10 or K-1500 models and K-20 or K-2500 models 1977–82 with locking front hubs: Lock the hubs. Remove the outer retaining plate Allen head bolts and take off the plate, O-ring, and knob. Take out the large snap-ring inside the hub and remove the outer clutch retaining ring and actuating cam body. This is a lot easier with snap-ring pliers. Relieve pressure on the axle shaft snap-ring and remove it. Take out the axle shaft sleeve and clutch ring assembly and the inner clutch ring and bushing assembly. Remove the spring and retainer plate.
3. For K-20 and K-2500 models 1975–76, with locking front hubs, turn the hub key to the Free position. Remove the Allen head bolts securing the retainer cap assembly to the wheel hub. Pull off the hub cap assembly and gasket, and the exterior sleeve extension housing and its gasket.

NOTE: You will have to modify this procedure for either of the models mentioned above if you have non-factory installed locking hubs.

4. If you don't have locking front hubs, remove the hub cap and snap-ring. Next, remove the drive gear and pressure spring. To prevent the spring from popping out, place a hand over the drive gear and use a screwdriver to pry the gear out. Remove the spring.
5. Remove the wheel bearing outer lock nut, lock ring, and wheel bearing inner adjusting nut. A special wrench is required.
6. Remove the brake disc assembly and outer wheel bearing. Remove the spring retainer plate if you don't have locking hubs. Pull out the axle shaft and universal assembly. When installing the shaft, turn it slowly to mesh the splines.
7. Remove the oil seal and inner bearing cone from the hub using a brass drift and hammer. Discard the oil seal. Use the drift to remove the inner and outer bearing cups.
8. Check the condition of the spindle bearing. If you have drum brakes, remove the grease retainer, gasket, and backing plate after removing the bolts. Unbolt the spindle and tap it with a soft hammer to break it loose. Remove the spindle and check the condition of the thrust washer, replacing it if worn. Now you can remove the oil seal and spindle roller bearing.

NOTE: The spindle bearings must be greased each time the wheel bearings are serviced.

9. Clean all parts in solvent, dry, and

check for wear or damage.

10. Pack both wheel bearings (and the spindle bearing) using wheel bearing grease. Place a healthy glob of grease in the palm of one hand and force the edge of the bearing into it so that grease fills the bearing. Do this until the whole bearing is packed. Grease packing tools are available to make this job a lot less messy.
11. To reassemble the spindle: drive the repacked bearing into the spindle and install the grease seal onto the slinger with the lip toward the spindle. It would be best to replace the axle shaft slinger when the spindle seal is replaced. If you are using the improved seals, fill the seal end of the spindle with grease. If not, apply grease only to the lip of the seal. Install the thrust washer over the axle shaft. The chamfered side of the thrust washer should be toward the slinger. Replace the spindle and torque the nuts to 45 ft. lbs. through 1976, 25 ft. lbs., 1977–78, and 33 ft. lbs., 1979–82.
12. To reassemble the wheel bearings: drive the outer bearing cup into the hub, replace the inner bearing cup, and insert the repacked bearing.
13. Install the disc or drum and outer wheel bearing to the spindle.
14. Adjust the bearings by rotating the hub and torquing the inner adjusting nut to 50 ft. lbs. then loosening it and retorquing to 35 ft. lb. Next, back the nut off 3/8 turn or less. Turn the nut to the nearest hole in the lockwasher. Install the outer locknut and torque to a minimum of 50 ft. lbs. through 1978, or 80 ft. lbs., 1979–82. There should be 0.001–0.010 in. bearing end-play. This can be measured with a dial indicator.
15. Replace the brake components.
16. Lubricate the locking hub components with high temperature grease. Lubrication must be applied to prevent component failure. For K-10 or K-1500 models, and K-20 and K-2500 models, 1977–82, install the spring retainer plate with the flange side facing the bearing over the spindle nuts and seat it against the bearing outer cup. Install the pressure spring with the large end against the spring retaining plate. The spring is an interference fit; when seated, its end extends past the spindle nuts by approximately 7/8 in. Place the inner clutch ring and bushing assembly into the axle shaft sleeve and clutch ring assembly and install that as an assembly onto the axle shaft. Press in on this assembly and install the axle shaft ring. If there are two axle shaft snap-ring grooves (1976–79), use the inner one.

NOTE: You can install a 7/16 in. bolt in the axle shaft end and pull outward on it to aid in seating the snap-ring.

Install the actuating cam body in the cams facing outward, the outer clutch retaining ring, and the internal snap-ring. Install a new O-ring on the retaining plate, and then install the actuating knob in the Lock position. Install the retaining plate. The grooves in the knob must fit into the actuator cam body. Install the seals and six cover bolts and torque them to 30 ft. lbs. Turn the knob to the Free position and check for proper operation.

17. For K-20 or K-2500 models, 1975–76, apply grease generously to the axle splines and teeth of the inner and outer clutch gears.

NOTE: Remove the head from a 5 in. long ⅜ in. bolt and use this to align the hub assembly.

Install the headless bolt into one of the hub housing bolt holes. Install a new exterior sleeve extension housing gasket, the housing, and a new hub retainer cap assembly gasket, and the cap assembly. Install the six Allen head bolts and their washers, and torque them to 30 ft. lbs. Turn the knob to Lock and check engagement.

18. Without locking hubs, replace the snap-ring and hub cap. If there are two axle shaft snap-ring grooves (1976–79), use the inner one.

Axle Shaft U-Joint

OVERHAUL

1. Remove the axle shaft.
2. Squeeze the ends of the trunnion bearings in a vise to relieve the load on the snap-rings. Remove the snap-rings.
3. Support the yoke in a vise and drive on one end of the trunnion bearing with a brass drift enough to drive the opposite bearing from the yoke.
4. Support the other side of the yoke and drive the other bearing out.
5. Remove the trunnion.
6. Clean and check all parts. You can buy U-joint repair kits to replace all the wearing parts.

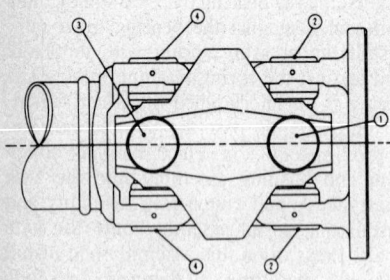

CV joint disassembly sequence

7. Lubricate the bearings with wheel bearing grease.
8. Replace the trunnion and press the bearings into the yoke and over the trunnion hubs far enough to install the lock rings.
9. Hold the trunnion in one hand and tap the yoke lightly to seat the bearings against the lock rings.
10. The axle slingers can be pressed off the shafts.

NOTE: Always replace the slingers if the spindle seals are replaced.

You can use the spindle to start the slinger on the shaft.

11. Replace the shaft.

Ball Joint

REPLACEMENT

The steering knuckle pivot ball joints may need replacement when there is excessive steering play, hard steering, irregular tire wear (especially on the inner edge), or persistent tie rod loosening.

This procedure requires a shop press. Your best bet would be to remove the steering knuckle and take it to the machine shop with the new parts.

1. Remove the hub assembly as previously outlined.
2. Remove the spindle attaching bolts.
3. Tap on the end of the spindle lightly with a wooden mallet (not a metal hammer) to break it loose from the steering knuckle.
4. Remove the spindle and the bronze washer. Replace the washer if it was distorted during removal or if it appears worn.
5. Remove the cotter pin from the tie rod nut.
6. Loosen the tie rod nut and tap on the nut with a wooden mallet in order to break the studs loose from the knuckle arm.
7. Remove the nuts and disconnect the tie rod.
8. Remove the steering arm attaching nuts. Use new, self-locking nuts on installation.
9. Remove the cotter pin from the upper ball joint socket nut.
10. Remove the retaining nuts from the upper and lower ball joint sockets.
11. Remove the knuckle by forcing a wedge between the lower ball stud and the yoke, then between the upper ball stud and the yoke.

NOTE: If you have to loosen the upper ball stud adjusting sleeve to remove the knuckle, don't loosen it more than two turns. The soft threads on the yoke are easily damaged.

12. Remove the lower ball joint snap-ring.
13. Remove the lower ball joint as illustrated using special tool no. J-9519-10 (or a similar C-clamp), J-23454-1 (a solid metal punch), and J-6382-3 (or a piece of 2 ½ in. outer diameter steel pipe with a ³⁄₁₆ in. wall thickness cut to a length of 2 ½ ins.). The lower ball joint must be removed before the upper ball joint can be serviced.
14. Press the new lower ball joint into the knuckle and install the snap-ring. The lower joint doesn't have a cotter pin hole.
15. Press the upper ball joint into the knuckle.
16. Position the knuckle to the yoke. Install new stud nuts finger tight.

17. Push up on the knuckle and tighten the lower nut to 70 ft. lbs.
18. Using a spanner wrench, install and torque the upper ball stud adjusting sleeve to 50 ft. lbs. Torque the upper stud nut to 100 ft. lbs. and install the cotter pin. Don't loosen the nut, but make it tighter to line up the cotter pin hole.
19. Replace the steering arm, using new nuts and torquing to 90 ft. lbs.
20. Attach the tie rod to the steering arm. Tighten the nuts to 45 ft. lbs.
21. Check the knuckle turning torque with a spring scale hooked to the tie rod hole in the steering arm. With the knuckle straight ahead, measure the right angle pull to keep the knuckle turning after initial breakaway, in both directions. The pull should be 25 lbs. or less for axles assembled after Feb. 10, 1976, and 33 lbs. for earlier models.
22. Replace the axle shaft and other components. Tighten the steering linkage nuts to 45 ft. lbs.

REAR AXLE

Some models are equipped with a locking differential rear axle. If you're not sure which one is in your truck, block the front wheels and jack up the rear of the truck. With the transmission in Neutral, spin one of the rear wheels in a forward motion with your hands. If the other wheel travels in the same direction, it is a locking differential.

Axle Shaft, Bearing, and Seal

REMOVAL AND INSTALLATION

All Axles Except Floating and Locking Differentials

This procedure applies to all standard rear axles.

1. Support the axle on jackstands.
2. Remove the wheels and brake drums.
3. Clean off the differential cover area, loosen the cover to drain the lubricant, and remove the cover.
4. Turn the differential until you can reach the differential pinion shaft lockscrew. Remove the lockscrew and the pinion shaft.
5. Push in on the axle end. Remove the C-lock from the inner (button) end of the shaft.
6. Remove the shaft, being careful of the oil seal.
7. You can pry the oil seal out of the housing by placing the inner end of the axle shaft behind the steel case of the seal, then prying it out carefully.
8. A puller or a slide hammer is re-

quired to remove the bearing from the housing.

9. Pack the new or reused bearing with wheel bearing grease and lubricate the cavity between the seal lips with the same grease.

10. The bearing has to be driven into the housing. Don't use a drift, you might cock the bearing in its bore. Use a piece of pipe or a large socket instead. Drive only on the outer bearing race. In a smiliar manner, drive the seal in flush with the end of the tube.

11. Slide the shaft into place, turning it slowly until the splines are engaged with the differential. Be careful of the oil seal.

12. Install the C-lock on the inner axle end. Pull the shaft out so that the C-lock seats in the counterbore of the differential side gear.

13. Position the differential pinion shaft through the case and the pinion gears, aligning the lockscrew hole. Install the lockscrew.

14. Install the cover with a new gasket and tighten the bolts evenly in a criss-cross pattern.

15. Fill the axle with lubricant.

16. Replace the brake drums and wheels.

Locking Differential Axles

This axle uses a thrust block on the differential pinion shaft.

1. Follow Steps 1–3 of the preceding procedure.

2. Rotate the differential case so that you can remove the lockscrew and support the pinion shaft so it can't fall into the housing. Remove the differential pinion shaft lockscrew.

3. Carefully pull the pinion shaft partway out and rotate the differential case until the shaft touches the housing at the top.

4. Use a screwdriver to position the C-lock with its open end directly inward. You can't push in the axle shaft till you do this. Do not force the axle shaft in.

5. Push the axle shaft in and remove the C-lock. Remove the axle shaft and repeat steps 4 and 5 for the other shaft.

6. Follow Steps 7–11 of the preceding procedure.

7. Keep the pinion shaft partway out of the differential case while installing the C-lock on the axle shaft. Put the C-lock on the axle shaft and carefully pull out on the axle shaft until the C-lock is clear of the thrust block.

8. Follow Steps 13–16 of the previous procedure.

Floating Differentials

Some 20, 2500 and all 30 and 3500 models use axles of full floating design. The procedures are the same for locking and non-locking axles.

The best way to remove the bearings from the wheel hub is with an arbor press. Use of a press reduces the chances of damaging the bearing races, cocking the bearing in its bore, or scoring the hub walls. A local machine shop is probably equipped with the tools to remove and install bearings and seals. However, if one is not available, the hammer and drift method outlined can be used.

1. Support the axle on jackstands.

2. Remove the wheels.

3. Remove the bolts and lock washers that attach the axle shaft flange to the hub.

4. Rap on the flange with a soft faced hammer to loosen the shaft. Grip the rib on the end of the flange with a pair of locking pliers and twist to start shaft removal. Remove the shaft from the axle tube.

5. The hub and drum assembly must be removed to remove the bearings and oil seals. You will need a large socket to remove and later adjust the bearing adjustment nut. There are also tools available which resemble the four wheel drive front wheel bearing adjusting tool.

6. Disengage the tang of the locknut retainer from the slot or flat of the locknut, then remove the locknut from the housing tube, using the earlier mentioned tool.

7. Disengage the tang of the retainer from the slot or flat of the adjusting nut and remove the retainer from the housing tube.

8. Remove the adjusting nut from the housing tube with the tool mentioned earlier.

9. Remove the thrust washer from the housing tube.

10. Pull the hub and drum straight off the axle housing.

11. Remove the oil seal and discard.

12. Use a hammer and a long drift to knock the inner bearing, cup, and oil seal from the hub assembly.

13. Remove the outer bearing snap-ring with a pair of pliers. It may be necessary to tap the bearing outer race away from the retaining ring slightly by tapping on the ring to remove the ring.

14. Drive the outer bearing from the hub with a hammer and drift.

15. To reinstall the bearings, place the outer bearing into the hub. The larger outside diameter of the bearing should face the outer end of the hub. Drive the bearing into the hub using a washer that will cover both the inner and outer races of the bearing. Place a socket on the top of this washer, then drive the bearing into place with a series of light taps. If available, an arbor press should be used for this job.

16. Drive the bearing past the snap-ring groove, and install the snap-ring. Then, turning the hub assembly over, drive the bearing back against the snap-ring. Again, protect the bearing by placing a washer on top of it. You can use the thrust washer that fits between the bearing and the adjusting nut for this job.

17. Place the inner bearing into the hub. The thick edge should be toward the shoulder in the hub. Press the bearing into the hub until it seats against the shoulder, using a washer and socket as outlined earlier. Make certain that the bearing is not cocked and that it is fully seated on the shoulder.

18. Pack the cavity between the oil seal lips with front wheel bearing grease, and position it in the hub bore. Carefully press it into place on top of the inner bearing.

19. Pack the wheel bearings with the grease, and lightly coat the inside diameter of the hub bearing contact surface and the outside diameter of the axle housing tube.

20. Make sure that the inner bearing, oil seal, axle housing oil deflector, and outer bearing are properly positioned. Install the hub and drum assembly on the axle housing, exercising care so as not to damage the oil seal or dislocate other internal components.

21. Install the thrust washer so that the tang on the inside diameter of the washer is in the keyway on the axle housing.

22. Install the adjusting nut. Tighten to 50 ft. lbs., at the same time rotating the hub to make sure that all the bearing surfaces are in contact. Back off the nut and retighten to 35 ft. lbs., then back off ¼ of a turn.

23. Install the tanged retainer against the inner adjusting nut. Align the adjusting nut so that the short tang of the retainer will engage the nearest slot on the adjusting nut.

24. Install the outer locknut and tighten to 65 ft. lbs. Bend the long tang of the retainer into the slot of the outer nut. This method of adjustment should provide .001 to .010 in. of end play.

25. Place a new gasket over the axle shaft and position the axle shaft in the housing so that the shaft splines enter the differential side gear. Position the gasket so that the holes are in alignment, and install the flange-to-hub attaching bolts. Torque to 90 ft. lbs. through 1975, 115 ft. lbs. 1976–82.

NOTE: To prevent lubricant from leaking through the flange holes, apply a non-hardening sealer to the bolt threads. Use the sealer sparingly.

27. Replace the wheels.

FRONT SUSPENSION

Two wheel drive models use coil spring independent front suspension. A stabilizer (sway) bar is optional to minimize body lean and sway in curves. Four wheel drive models have a non-independent leaf spring front suspension. A stabilizer bar is standard. A steering linkage damper is standard on late models. Heavy duty shock absorbers, springs, and stabilizer bars have been optional for most models.

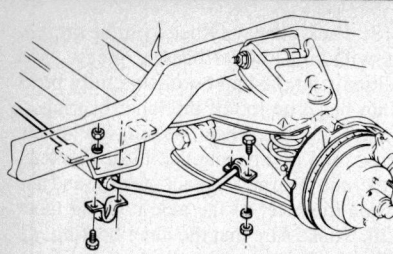

Two wheel drive coil spring and stabilizer

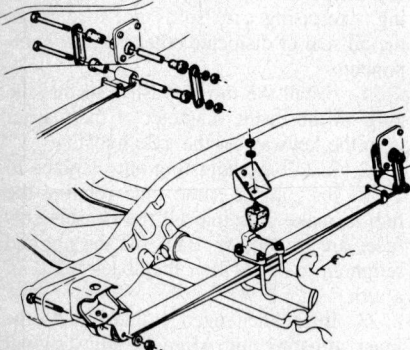

Four wheel drive front leaf spring

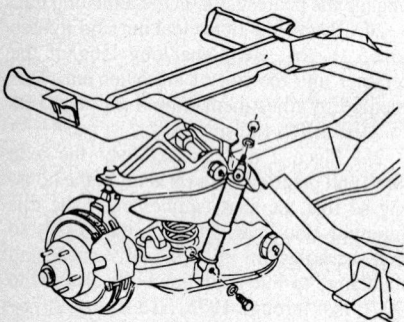

Two wheel drive front shock absorber

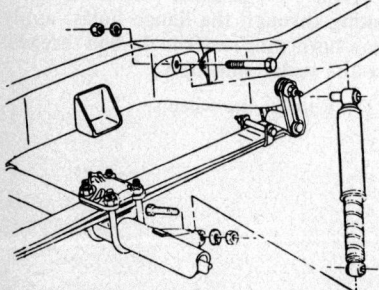

Four wheel drive front shock absorber

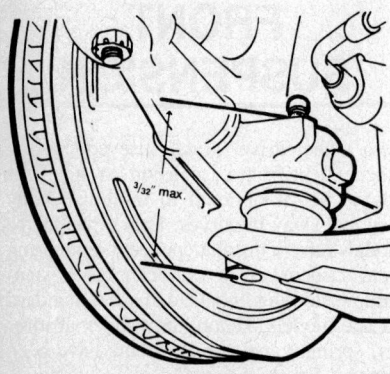

Lower ball joint inspection

Springs

REMOVAL AND INSTALLATION

NOTE: Springs, particularly coil springs, are under considerable tension. Be very careful when removing and installing them; they can exert enough force to cause very serious injuries.

Two Wheel Drive

1. Raise the vehicle and support it under the frame so that the control arms will hang free.

2. Remove the lower shock absorber mounting bolt. Detach the stabilizer bar from the lower control arm.

3. Place a floor jack under the lower control arm crossshaft.

NOTE: As a safety precaution, install a chain through the spring and the lower control arm.

4. Raise the jack. This will remove the tension on the lower control arm so that the two U-bolts which secure the cross-shaft can be removed.

5. Lower the control arm *slowly* by releasing the floor jack to the point where the spring can be removed.

6. Remove the spring.

7. Place the spring on the control arm and then, using a jack, slowly raise the control arm. Use the safety chain as described in Step 3.

8. Place the control arm cross-shaft onto the crossmember and then install the U-bolts and the attaching nuts. Make certain that the indexing hole in the cross-shaft is lined up with the crossmember stud.

9. Torque the U-bolt nuts to 45 ft. lbs. for 1975, 85 ft. lbs. for 1976 and later models. Remove the safety chain.

10. Install the lower part of the shock absorber and the stablizer bar.

11. Lower the vehicle.

Four Wheel Drive

1. Raise and support the truck under the front axle and frame so that the tension on the springs is relieved.

2. Remove the shackle upper retaining bolt and the front spring eye bolt.

3. Remove the spring-to-axle U-bolt nuts. Pull off the spring, the lower plate, and the spring pads.

4. Remove the shackle-to-spring bolt, bushings, and shackle.

To replace the bushing, place the spring onto a press or vise and press out the bushing. Press in the new busing. The new bushing should protrude evenly on both sides of the spring.

5. Install the spring shackle bushings into the spring and then attach the shackle. Do not tighten the bolt.

6. Place the upper spring cushion onto the spring.

7. Place the front of the spring into the frame and install the bolt but do not tighten it.

8. Position the shackle bushing into the frame and attach the rear shackle but do not tighten it.

9. Install the lower spring pad and the spring retainer plate. Tighten the U-bolts to 150 ft. lbs.

10. Torque the rear spring shackle bolts and the rear eye bolts to 50 ft. lbs. and the front eye bolts to 90 ft. lbs.

11. Lower the vehicle.

Shock Absorbers

The usual procedure for testing shock absorbers is to stand on the bumper at the end nearest the shock being tested and start the vehicle bouncing up and down. Step off; the vehicle should come to rest within one bounce cycle. Another good test is to drive the vehicle over a bumpy road. Bouncing over bumps is normal, but the shock absorbers should stop the bouncing, after the bump is passed, within one or two cycles.

REMOVAL AND INSTALLATION

The usual procedure is to replace shock absorbers in axle pairs, to provide equal damping. Heavy duty replacements are available for firmer control

1. Raise and support the front axle as necessary.

2. Remove the bolt and nut from the lower shock end.

3. On two wheel drive original equipment shocks, remove the upper stud nut from inside the frame. Most aftermarket replacement two wheel drive shocks replace the original stud fixed to the top of the shock with a double ended stud; if you have these, you can just remove the outer nut. On four wheel drive shocks, remove the upper bolt and nut.

4. Purge the new shock of air by extending it in its normal position and compressing it while inverted. Do this several times. It is normal for there to be more resistance to extension than to compression.

5. Install the shock absorber. Tighten the two wheel drive upper stud nut (inside the frame) to 140 ft. lbs. and the four wheel drive upper bolt to 65 ft. lbs. Tighten the two wheel drive lower bolt to 60 ft. lbs. Tighten the four wheel drive lower bolt to 65 ft. lbs. You can tighten the two wheel drive outer top stud nut mentioned in step 3 to about 60 ft. lbs.

Ball Joints

Service procedures for the four wheel drive front drive axle are found earlier.

INSPECTION

Excessive ball joint wear will usually show up as wear on the inside of the front tires. Don't jump to conclusions; front end misalignment can give the same symptom.

Upper Ball Joint

1. Raise and support the truck; let the control arms hang freely.
2. The upper ball joint is spring-loaded in its socket. If it has any perceptible lateral shake or can be twisted in its socket, it should be replaced.

Lower Ball Joint

The lower ball joint gets the most wear due to the distribution of suspension load.

1. Support the weight of the control arm at the bottom of the tire.
2. Measure the distance between the tip of the ball joint stud and the tip of the grease fitting below the ball joint.
3. Move the support to the control arm and allow the wheel and tire to hang free. Measure the distance again. If the variation between the two measurements exceeds 3/32 in. the ball joint should be replaced.

NOTE: This is the manufacturer's recommended wear limit. Your state inspection regulations may disagree.

REMOVAL AND INSTALLATION

NOTE: Observe the Caution under Front Spring Removal and Installation when working with ball joints.

Lower Ball Joint

1. Raise and support the truck. Support the lower control arm with a floor jack.
2. Remove the tire and wheel.
3. Remove the lower stud cotter pin and loosen, but do not remove, the stud nut.
4. Loosen the ball joint stud with a ball joint stud removal tool. It may be necessary to remove the brake caliper and wire it to the frame to gain enough clearance. Do not let the caliper hang by the hose.
5. When the stud is loose, remove the tool and ball stud nut.
6. Pull the brake disc and knuckle assembly up and off the ball stud and support the upper arm with a block of wood.
7. Remove the ball joint from the control arm with a ball joint removal tool. It must be pressed out.
To install:
8. Start the new ball joint into the control arm. Position the bleed vent in the rubber boot facing inward.
9. Seat the ball joint in the control arm. It must be pressed in.
10. Lower the upper arm and match the steering knuckle to the lower ball stud.
11. Install the brake caliper, if removed.

12. Install the ball stud nut and torque it to 90 ft. lbs. plus the additional torque necessary to align the cotter pin hole. Do not exceed 130 ft. lbs. or back the nut off to align the holes with the pin.
13. Install a new lube fitting and lubricate the new joint.
14. Install the tire and wheel.
15. Lower the truck.

Upper Ball Joint

1. Raise and support the truck.
2. Support the lower control arm with a floor jack.
3. Remove the cotter pin from the upper ball stud and loosen, but do not remove, the stud nut.
4. Using a ball joint stud removal tool, loosen the ball stud in the steering knuckle. When the stud is loose, remove the tool and the stud nut. It will be necessary to remove the brake caliper and wire it to the frame to gain clearance. Do not allow the caliper to hang by the hose.
5. Drill out the rivets. Remove the ball joint assembly.
To install:
6. Install the service ball joint, using the nuts supplied. Tighten the nuts to 45 ft. lbs.
7. Torque the ball stud nut to 50 ft. lbs. plus the additional torque required to align the cotter pin. Do not exceed 90 ft. lbs. and never back the nut off to align the pin.
8. Install a new cotter pin.
9. Install a new lube fitting and lubricate the new joint.
10. If removed, install the brake caliper.
11. Install the wheel and tire and lower the truck.

Upper Control Arm

REMOVAL AND INSTALLATION

1. Raise and support the truck on jackstands.
2. Support the lower control arm with a floor jack.
3. Remove the wheel and tire.
4. Remove the cotter pin from the upper control arm ball stud and loosen the stud nut one turn.
5. Loosen the upper control arm ball stud in the steering knuckle using a ball joint stud removal tool. Remove the nut from the ball stud and raise the upper arm to clear the steering knuckle. It will be necessary to remove the brake caliper and wire it to the frame to gain clearance.
6. Remove the nuts securing the control arm shaft to the frame and remove the control arm. Tape the shims and spacers together and tag for proper reassembly.
7. Installation is the reverse of removal. Place the control arm in position and install the nuts. Before tightening the nuts to 70 ft. lbs., insert the caster and

camber shims in the same order as when removed. Have the front end alignment checked, and as necessary, adjusted.

Lower Control Arm

REMOVAL AND INSTALLATION

1. Raise and support the truck on jackstands.
2. Remove the spring. See Spring Removal and Installation.
3. Support the inboard end of the control arm after spring removal.
4. Remove the cotter pin from the lower ball stud and loosen the nut one turn.
5. Loosen the lower ball stud in the steering knuckle using a ball joint stud removal tool. When the stud is loose, remove the nut from the stud. It will be necessary to remove the brake caliper and wire it to the frame to gain clearance.
6. Remove the lower control arm.
7. Installation is the reverse of removal.

REAR SUSPENSION

Springs

REMOVAL AND INSTALLATION

1. Raise the vehicle and support it so that there is no tension on the leaf spring assembly.
2. Loosen the spring-to-shackle retaining bolts. (Do not remove these bolts.).
3. Remove the securing bolts which attach the shackle to the spring hanger.
4. Remove the nut and bolt which attach the spring to the front hanger.
5. Remove the U-bolt nuts and remove the spring plate.
6. Pull the spring from the vehicle.

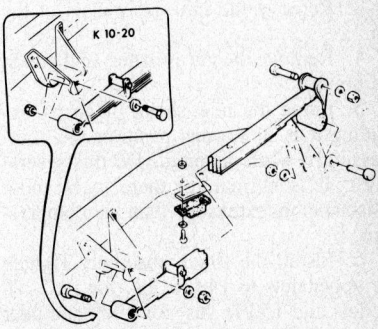

Typical leaf spring installation

7. If the bushings need to be replaced, they must be pressed in and out.

8. Place the spring assembly onto the axle housing.

NOTE: The shackle assembly must be attached to the rear spring eye before the rear shackle is installed.

9. Position the spring retaining plate and the U-bolts (loosely).

10. Install the rear shackle bolt and nut, then the front eye bolt and nut. Tighten the bolts to 110 ft. lbs.

NOTE: Aftermarket kits, consisting of longer axle U-bolts and blocks to be placed between the spring and axle, are available to adjust the rear ride height. If this modification is carried to extremes, the front end caster angle and rear end stability will be affected.

Shock Absorbers

REMOVAL AND INSTALLATION

The usual procedure is to replace shock absorbers in axle pairs, to provide equal damping. Heavy duty replacements are available for firmer control. Air adjustable shock absorbers can be used to maintain a level ride with heavy loads or when towing.

1. Raise and support the rear axle as necessary.

2. If air shocks are installed, bleed the air and detach the lines.

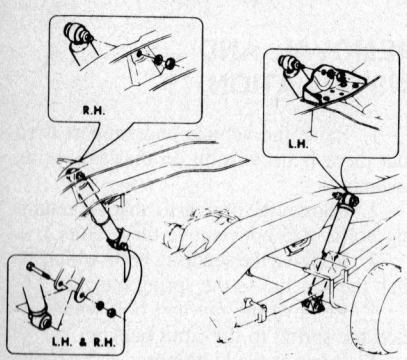

Staggered rear shock absorber details

3. Remove the nut and washer at the top.

4. Remove the nut, washer, and bolt at the bottom.

5. Purge the new shock of air by extending it in its normal position and compressing it while inverted. Do this several times. It is normal for there to be more resistance to extension than to compression.

6. Install the shock absorber. Tighten the upper nuts to 140 ft. lbs. for 1975–78 models and 150 ft. lbs. for 1979 and later models. Tighten the lower nuts to 115 ft. lbs. for all models.

STEERING

A common cause of excessive steering play on these trucks is the steering gear box coming loose from the frame. The torque for these bolts is 65 ft. lbs.

Steering Wheel

REMOVAL AND INSTALLATION

1. Disconnect the battery ground cable.

2. Remove the horn button. Remove the receiving cup, belleville washer, and bushing (if equipped).

3. Mark the steering wheel-to-steering shaft relationship.

4. Remove the snap-ring from the steering shaft.

5. Remove the nut and washer from the steering shaft.

6. Remove the steering wheel with a puller.

CAUTION
Don't hammer on the steering shaft.

---

7. Installation is the reverse of removal. The turn signal control assembly must be in the neutral position to prevent damaging the cancelling cam and control assembly. Tighten the nut to 30 ft. lbs.

NOTE: A steering wheel puller can be made by drilling two holes in a piece of steel the same distance apart as the two threaded holes in the steering wheel. Sometimes an old spring shackle will have the right dimensions. Drill another hole in the center. Place a center bolt with the head against the steering shaft and a nut against the bottom of the homemade puller bar. Thread the two outer bolts into the holes in the wheel. Unscrew the nut on the center bolt to draw the wheel off the shaft.

Turn Signal Switch

REPLACEMENT

1. Remove the steering wheel as previously outlined.

2. Remove the column to instrument panel trim cover. Loosen the three cover screws and lift the cover off the shaft. On 1976 and later models, place a screwdriver in the cover slot and pry out to free the cover.

3. The round lockplate must be pushed down to remove the wire snap-ring from the shaft. A special tool is available to do this. The tool is an inverted U-shape with a hole for the shaft. The shaft nut is used to force it down. Pry the wire snap-ring out of the shaft groove.

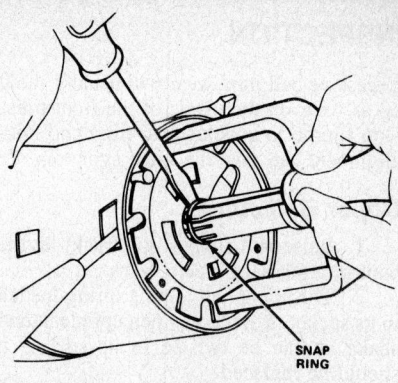

Removing the lockplate retaining ring

4. Remove the tool and lift the lockplate off the shaft.

5. Slip the cancelling cam, upper bearing preload spring, and thrust washer off the shaft.

6. Remove the turn signal lever screw and the lever. Push the flasher knob in and unscrew it.

7. Pull the switch connector out of the mast jacket and tape the upper part to facilitate switch removal. On tilt wheels, place the turn signal and shifter housing in the low position and remove the harness cover.

8. Remove the three switch mounting screws. Remove the switch by pulling it straight up while guiding the wiring harness cover through the column.

9. Install the replacement switch by working the connector and cover down through the housing and under the bracket. On tilt models, the connector is worked down through the housing, under the bracket, and then the cover is installed on the harness.

10. Install the switch mounting screws and the connector on the mast jacket bracket. Install the column to instrument panel trim plate.

11. Install the flasher knob and the turn signal lever.

12. With the turn signal lever in neutral and the flasher knob out, slide the thrust washer, upper bearing pre-load spring, and cancelling cam onto the shaft.

13. Position the lockplate on the shaft and press it down until a new snap-ring can be inserted in the shaft groove.

14. Install the cover and the steering wheel.

Ignition Switch and Lock Cylinder

1975–78 LOCK CYLINDER REMOVAL AND INSTALLATION

The key and lock code numbers are kept in the records of the original selling dealer. This number enables a dealer to supply a new lock cylinder that will operate with the old key.

1. Remove steering wheel and turn signal switch as previously outlined.

NOTE: It is not necessary to completely remove the turn signal switch. Pull the switch over the end of the shaft—no farther.

2. Place lock cylinder in the Run position.

3. Insert a small screwdriver into the rectangular column housing slot. Keeping the screwdriver to the right-side of the slot, break the housing flash loose and depress the spring latch at the lower end of the lock cylinder. Remove the lock cylinder.

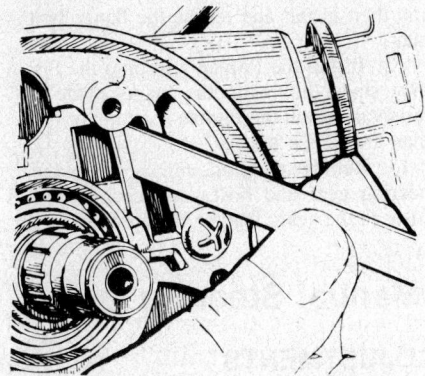

1975–78 ignition lock cylinder removal

NOTE: When ordering a new lock cylinder, specify a cylinder assembly. This will save assembling the cylinder, washer, sleeve and adapter.

4. To install, hold the lock cylinder sleeve and rotate the knob clockwise against the stop. Insert the cylinder into the housing, aligning the key and keyway. Hold a 0.070 in. drill bit between the lock bezel and housing. Rotate the cylinder counterclockwise, maintaining a light pressure until the drive section of the cylinder mates with the sector. Push in until the snap-ring pops into the grooves. Remove the bit. Check cylinder operation.

———— **CAUTION** ————

The drill prevents forcing the lock cylinder inward beyond its normal position. The buzzer switch and spring latch can hold the lock cylinder in too far. Complete disassembly of the upper bearing housing is necessary to release an improperly installed lock cylinder.

1979–82 LOCK CYLINDER REMOVAL AND INSTALLATION

1. Remove the steering wheel and the turn signal switch as previously outlined. It is not necessary to completely remove the turn signal switch. Just pull the switch

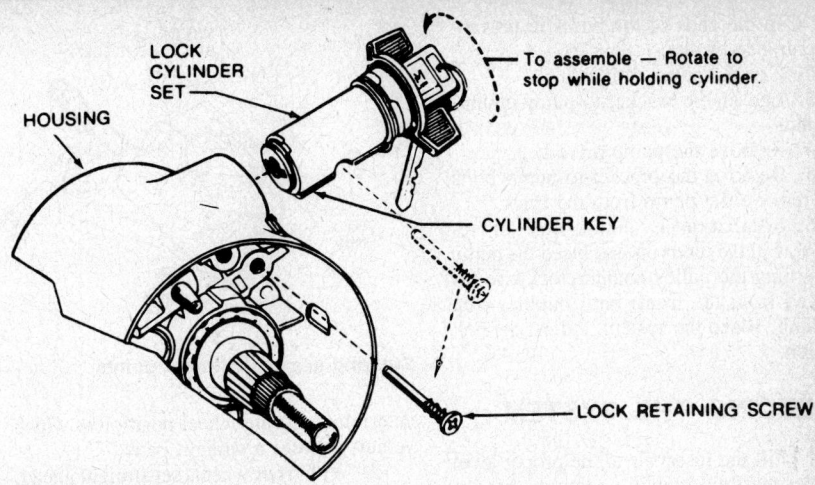

1979–82 ignition lock cylinder removal

out far enough so it can hang out of the steering column shaft. Do not disconnect the wiring harness.

2. With the lock cylinder in the Run position, remove the lock cylinder attaching screw and the cylinder.

3. To install, align the cylinder key with the keyway in the housing and rotate the key all the way clockwise while holding the cylinder body.

4. Insert the cylinder into the housing and install the attaching screw.

5. Install the turn signal switch and the steering wheel as previously outlined.

IGNITION SWITCH REMOVAL AND INSTALLATION

The switch is on the steering column, behind the instrument panel.

1. Lower the steering column, making sure that it is supported.

———— **CAUTION** ————

Extreme care is necessary to prevent damage to the collapsible column.

2. Make sure the switch is in the Lock position. If the lock cylinder is out, pull the switch rod up to the stop, then go down one detent.

3. Remove the two screws and the switch.

4. Before installation, make sure the switch is in the Lock position. The switch can be moved to the Lock position using a screwdriver inserted into the locking rod slot.

5. Install the switch using the original screws.

———— **CAUTION** ————

Use of screws that are too long could prevent the column from collapsing on impact.

6. Replace the column.

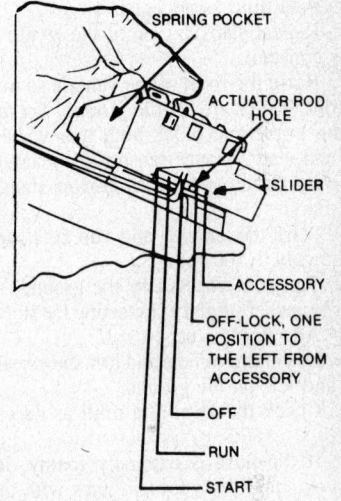

Ignition switch details

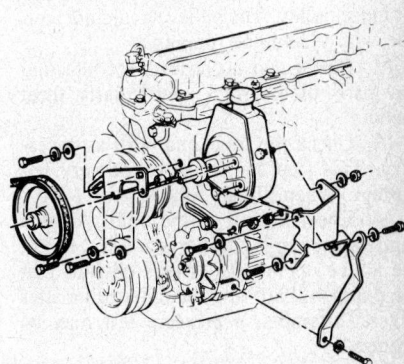

6-250 power steering pump mounting

Power Steering Pump

REMOVAL AND INSTALLATION

1. Disconnect the hoses at the pump. When the hoses are disconnected, secure the ends in a raised position to prevent leak-

age. Cap the ends of the hoses to prevent the entrance of dirt.

2. Cap the pump fittings.

3. Loosen the bracket-to-pump mounting nuts.

4. Remove the pump drive belt.

5. Remove the bracket-to-pump bolts and remove the pump from the truck.

6. Installation is the reverse of removal. Fill the reservoir and bleed the pump by turning the pulley counterclockwise (as viewed from the front) until bubbles stop forming. Bleed the system. Adjust the belt tension.

BLEEDING THE SYSTEM

1. Fill the reservoir to the proper level and let the fluid remain undisturbed for at least 2 minutes.

2. Start the engine and run it for only about 2 seconds.

3. Add fluid as necessary.

4. Repeat steps 1–3 until the level remains constant.

5. Raise the front of the vehicle so that the front wheels are off the ground. Set the parking brake and block both rear wheels front and rear. Manual transmissions should be in Neutral; automatic transmissions should be in Park.

6. Start the engine and run it at approximately 1,500 rpm.

7. Turn the wheels (off the ground) to the right and left, lightly contacting the stops.

8. Add fluid as necessary.

9. Lower the vehicle and turn the wheels right and left on the ground.

10. Check the level and refill as necessary.

11. If the fluid is extemely foamy, let the truck stand for a few minutes with the engine off and repeat the above procedure. Check the belt tension and check for a bent or loose pulley. The pulley should not wobble with the engine running.

12. Check that no hoses are contacting any parts of the truck, particularly sheet metal.

13. Check the level and refill as necessary. This step and the next are very important. When filling, follow steps 1–10.

14. Check for air in the fluid. Aerated fluid appears milky. If air is present, repeat the above operations. If it is obvious that the pump will not respond to bleeding after several attempts, a pressure test may be required.

Power Steering Gear

STEERING GEAR HIGH POINT CENTERING

1. Set front wheels in straight ahead position. This can be checked by driving vehicle a short distance on a **flat** surface to

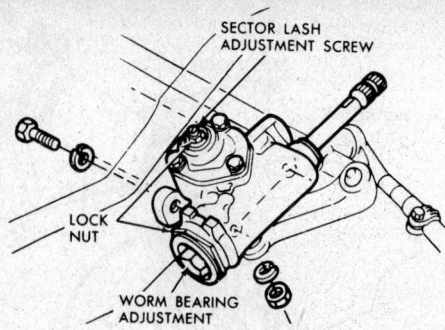

Steering gear adjustment points

determine steering wheel position at which vehicle follows a straight path.

2. With front wheels set straight ahead, check position of mark on wormshaft designating steering gear high point. This mark should be at the top side of the shaft at 12 o'clock position and lined up with the mark in the coupling lower clamp.

3. On C and G series, if gear has been moved off high point when setting wheel in straight ahead position, loosen the adjusting sleeve clamps on both left and right hand tie rods. Then turn both sleeves an equal number of turns in the same direction to bring gear back on high point. Turning the sleeves an unequal number of turns or in different directions will disturb the toe-in setting of the wheels.

4. On K series, if the gear has been moved off high point when setting wheels in straight ahead position, loosen the adjusting sleeve clamps on the connecting rod.Then turn sleeve to bring gear back on high point.

5. Readjust toe-in.

6. Be sure to properly orient sleeve and clamps.

REMOVAL AND INSTALLATION

1. Disconnect hoses at gear. When hoses are disconnected, secure ends in raised position to prevent drainage of oil. Cap or tape the ends of the hoses to prevent entrance of dirt.

2. Install two plugs in gear fittings to prevent entrance of dirt.

3. Remove the flexible coupling to steering shaft flange bolts. Mark the relationship of the universal yoke to the stub shaft.

4. Mark the relationship of the Pitman arm to the Pitman shaft. Remove the Pitman shaft nut or Pitman arm pinch bolt and then remove the Pitman arm from the Pitman shaft using puller J-6632.

5. Remove the steering gear to frame bolts and remove the gear assembly.

6. On G, C and K models, remove the flexible coupling pinch bolt and remove the coupling from the steering gear stub shaft.

7. Install the flexible coupling onto the steering gear stub shaft, aligning the flat in the coupling with the flat on the shaft. Push

the coupling onto the shaft until the stub shaft bottoms on the coupling reinforcement. Install the pinch bolt.

NOTE: The coupling bolt must pass through the shaft undercut, or damage to the components could occur.

8. Place the steering gear in position, guiding the coupling bolt into the steering shaft flange.

9. Install the steering gear to frame bolts.

10. If flexible coupling alignment pin plastic spacers were used, make sure they are buttomed on the pins, tighten the flange bolt nuts and then remove the plastic spacers.

11. If flexible coupling alignment pin plastic spacers were not used, center the pins in the slots in the steering shaft flange and then install and torque the flange bolt nuts.

12. Install the Pitman arm onto the Pitman shaft, lining up the marks made at removal. Install the Pitman shaft nut or Pitman arm pinch bolt.

13. Remove the plugs and caps from the steering gear and hoses and connect the hoses to the gear. Tighten the hose fittings.

Manual Steering Gear

ADJUSTMENTS

Correct adjustment of steering gear is very important. While there are only two adjustments to be made, the following procedure must be followed step-by-step in the order given.

1. Disconnect the battery ground cable.

2. Raise the vehicle.

3. Remove the Pitman arm nut. Mark the relationship of the Pitman arm to the pitman shaft. Remove the Pitman arm with tool J-6632 or J-5504.

4. Loosen the steering gear adjuster plug locknut and back the adjuster plug off ¼ turn.

5. Remove the horn shroud or button cap.

6. Turn the steering wheel gently in one direction until stopped by the gear; then turn back one-half turn.

NOTE: Do not turn the steering wheel hard against the stops when the steering linkage is disconnected from the gear as damage to the ball guides could result.

7. Measure and record "bearing drag" by applying a torque wrench with a socket on the steering wheel nut and rotating through a 90° arc. Do not use a torque wrench having a maximum torque reading of more than 50 inch pounds.

8. Adjust "thrust bearing preload" by tightening the adjuster plug until the proper "thurst loading preload" of 5-8 in. lb. is obtained. When the proper preload has been obtained, tighten the adjuster plug locknut to specifications and recheck torque. If the gear feels "lumpy" after adjustment, there

is probably damage in the bearings due to severe impact or improper adjustment; the gear must be disassembled and inspected for replacement of damaged parts.

9. Adjust "over-center preload" as follows:

a. Turn the steering wheel gently from one stop all the way to the other carefully counting the total number of turns. Turn the wheel back exactly half-way, to center position.

b. Turn the lash adjuster screw clockwise to take out all lash between the ball nut and Pitman shaft sector teeth and then tighten the locknut.

c. Check the torque at the steering wheel, taking the highest reading as the wheel is turned through center position. Preload should be 4-10 in. lb.

d. If necessary, loosen locknut and readjust lash adjuster screw to obtain proper torque. Tighten the locknut to specifications and again check torque reading through center of travel. If maximum specification is exceeded, turn lash adjuster screw counterclockwise, then come up on adjustment by turning the adjuster in a clockwise motion.

10. Reassemble the Pitman arm to the Pitman shaft, lining up the marks made during disassembly. Torque the Pitman shaft nut to 70 ft. lbs.

If a clamp type Pitman arm is used, spread the Pitman arm just enough, with a wedge, to slip the arm onto the Pitman shaft. Do not spread the clamp more than required to slip over Pitman shaft with hand pressure. Do not hammer the Pitman arm onto the Pitman shaft. Be sure to install the hardened steel washer before installing the nut.

11. Install the horn button cap or shroud and connect the battery ground cable.

12. Lower the vehicle to the floor.

Steering Gear High Point Centering

1. Set front wheels in straight ahead position. This can be checked by driving vehicle a short distance on a **flat** surface to determine steering wheel position at which vehicle follows a straight path.

2. With front wheels set straight ahead, check position of mark on wormshaft designating steering gear high point. This mark should be at the top side of the shaft at 12 o'clock position and lined up with the mark in the coupling lower clamp.

3. On C and G series, if the gear has been moved off high point when setting wheel in straight ahead position, loosen adjusting sleeve clamps on both left and right hand tie rods. Then turn both sleeves an equal number of turns in the same direction to bring gear back on high point.

Turning the sleeves an unequal number of turns or in different directions will disturb the toe-in setting of the wheels.

4. On K series, if the gear has been moved off high point when setting wheels in straight ahead position, loosen adjusting

CLAMPING INSTRUCTIONS FOR ALL LIGHT TRUCKS.

A. All bolts must be installed in direction shown.
B. Rotate both inner and outer tie rod sockets rearward to limit of ball stud travel.
C. Position clamps within angles shown.
D. Tighten clamps.
E. With this same rearward rotation, all bolt centerlines must be between angles shown.

CAUTION: CLAMPS MUST BE BETWEEN AND CLEAR OF DIMPLES BEFORE TORQUING NUT.

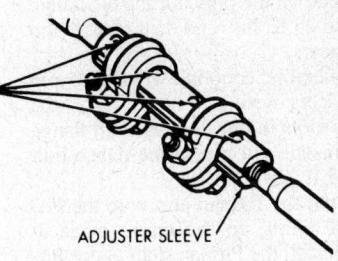

ADJUSTER SLEEVE

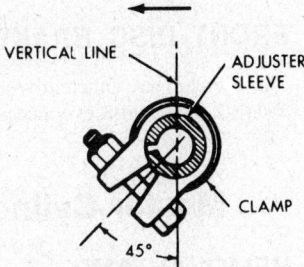

CAUTION: CENTERLINE OF SLOT IN CLAMP MUST BE IN THIS RANGE OF ADJUSTMENT.

NOTE: IMPORTANT - SLOT IN ADJUSTER SLEEVE MUST NOT BE WITHIN OPEN AREA OF CLAMP JAWS OR CLOSER THAN .10 TO THE EDGE OF CLAMP JAW OPENING. ROTATE CLAMP TO MEET REQUIREMENTS WITHIN PROPER POSITION AS SHOWN.

Tie rod sleeve clamp installation

sleeve clamps on the connecting rod. Then turn sleeve to bring gear back on high point.

5. Readjust toe-in.

6. Be sure to properly orient sleeves and clamps when fastening and torqueing clamps.

REMOVAL AND INSTALLATION

1. Set the front wheels in straight ahead position by driving vehicle a short distance on a flat surface.

2. Remove the flexible coupling to steering shaft flange bolts. Mark the relationship of the universal yoke to the wormshaft.

3. Mark the relationship of the Pitman arm to the Pitman shaft. Remove the Pitman shaft nut or Pitman arm pinch bolt and then remove the Pitman arm from the Pitman shaft using puller J-6632.

4. Remove the steering gear to frame bolts and remove the gear assembly.

5. Remove the flexible coupling pinch bolt and remove the coupling from the steering gear wormshaft.

6. Install the flexible coupling onto the steering gear wormshaft, aligning the flat in the coupling with the flat on the shaft. Push the coupling onto the shaft until the wormshaft bottoms on the coupling reinforcement. Install the pinch bolt and torque to 25 ft. lbs. The coupling bolt must pass through the shaft undercut.

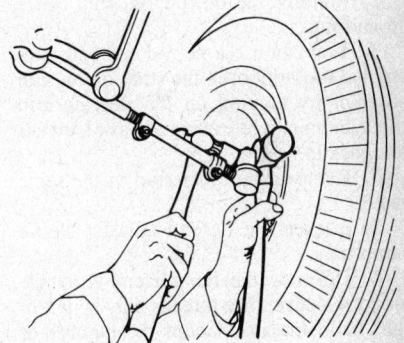

Freeing the tie rod end

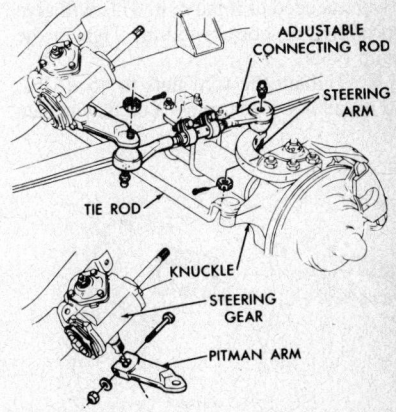

Four wheel drive steering linkage

7. Place the steering gear in position, guiding the coupling bolt into the steering shaft flange.

8. Install the steering gear to frame bolts and torque to 70 ft. lbs.

9. If flexible coupling alignment pin plastic spacers were used, make sure they are bottomed on the pins, torque the flange bolt nuts to 25 ft. lbs. and then remove the plastic spacers.

10. If flexible coupling alignment pin plastic spacers were not used, center the pins in the slots in the steering shaft flange and then install and torque the flange bolt nuts. to 25 ft. lbs.

11. Install the Pitman arm onto the Pitman shaft, lining up the marks made at removal. Install the Pitman shaft nut or Pitman arm pinch bolt and torque to 30 ft. lb.

If a clamp type Pitman arm is used, spread the Pitman arm just enough, with a wedge, to slip the arm onto the Pitman shaft. Do not spread the clamp more than required to slip over Pitman arm onto the Pitman shaft. Be sure to install the hardened steel washer before installing the nut.

Tie Rod Ends

REMOVAL AND INSTALLATION

1. Raise the front of the truck and support it safely on jack stands.

2. Remove the tie rod end stud cotter pin and nut.

3. You can use a tie rod end ball joint removal tool to loosen the stud, or you can loosen it by tapping on the steering arm with a hammer while using a heavy hammer as a backup.

4. Remove the inner stud in the same way.

5. Loosen the tie rod adjuster sleeve clamp nuts.

6. Unscrew the tie rod end from the threaded sleeve. The threads may be left or right hand threads. Count the number of turns required to remove it.

7. To install, grease the threads and turn the new tie rod end in as many turns as were needed to remove it. This will give approximately correct toe-in. Tighten the clamp bolts.

8. Tighten the stud nuts to 45 ft. lbs. and install new cotter pins. You may tighten

the nut to align the cotter pin, but don't loosen it.

9. Adjust the toe-in.

BRAKE SYSTEM

Adjustment

REAR DRUM BRAKES

These brakes are equipped with self-adjusters and no manual adjustment is necessary, except when brake linings are replaced.

FRONT DISC BRAKES

These brakes are inherently self-adjusting and no adjustment is ever necessary or possible.

Master Cylinder

REMOVAL AND INSTALLATION

NOTE: Clean any master cylinder parts in alcohol or brake fluid. Never use mineral-based cleaning solvents such as gasoline, kerosene, carbon-tetrachloride, acetone, or paint thinner as these will destroy rubber parts.

1. Using a clean cloth, wipe the master cylinder and its lines to remove excess dirt and then place cloths under the unit to absorb spilled fluid.

2. Remove the hydraulic lines from the master cylinder and plug the outlets to prevent the entrance of foreign material.

3. Disconnect the brake pushrod from the brake pedal on non-power brakes.

4. Remove the attaching bolts and remove the master cylinder from the firewall or the brake booster.

To install:

5. Connect the pushrod to the brake pedal with the pin and retainer.

6. Connect the brake lines and fill the master cylinder reservoirs to the proper levels.

7. Bleed the brake system as outlined in this Section.

OVERHAUL

In most years, there are 2 sources for master cylinders, Delco-Moraine and Bendix. The Bendix unit can readily be identified by the secondary stop bolt on the bottom, which is not present on the Delco-Moraine unit. Some early models use a Wagner unit which has the cover secured by a bolt. Master cylinders bearing identifying code letters should only be replaced with cylinders bearing the same code letters. Secondary pistons are also coded by rings or grooves on the shank or center section of the piston, and should only be replaced with pistons having the same code. The primary pistons also are of 2 types. One has a deep socket for the pushrod and the other has a very shallow socket. Be sure to replace pistons with identical parts. Failure to do this could result in a malfunction.

NOTE: This procedure applies to all Delco master cylinders, but not to the Bendix unit used on 1976 and later 30 and 3500 motorhome models with the Hydro-Boost brake system.

1. Remove the secondary piston stop screw at the bottom of the master cylinder front reservoir.

2. Position the master cylinder in a vise covering the jaws with cloth to prevent damage. (Do not tighten the vise too tightly.)

3. Remove the lockring from the inside of the piston bore. Once this is done, the primary piston assembly may be removed.

4. The secondary piston, piston spring, and the retainer may be removed by blowing compressed air through the stop screw hole. If compressed air is not available, the piston may be removed with a small piece of wire. Bend the wire ¼ in. from the end into a right angle. Hook this end to the edge of the secondary piston and pull it from the bore. The brass insert should not be removed unless it is being replaced.

5. Inspect the piston bore for corrosion or other obstructions. Make certain that the outer ports are clean and the fluid reservoirs are free of foreign matter. Check the bypass and the compensating ports to see if they are clogged.

6. Remove the primary seal, seal protector, and secondary seals from the secondary piston.

Clean all parts in denatured alcohol or brake fluid. Use a soft brush to clean metal parts and compressed air to dry all parts. If corrosion is found inside the housing, either a crocus cloth or fine emery paper can be used to remove these deposits. Remember to wash all parts after this cleaning. Be sure to keep the parts clean until assembly. If there is any doubt of cleanliness, wash the part again. All rubber parts

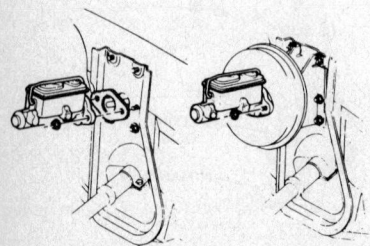

Typical master cylinder installations

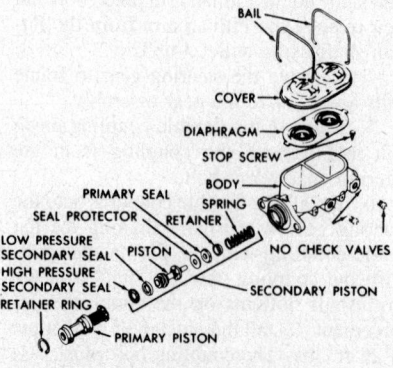

Exploded view of a master cylinder

should be clean and free of fluid. Check each rubber part for cuts, nicks, or other damage. If there is any doubt as to the condition of any rubber part, it is best to replace it.

NOTE: Since there are differences between master cylinders, it is important that the assemblies are identified correctly. There is a two-letter metal stamp located at the end of the master cylinder. The stamp indicates the displacement capabilities of the particular master cylinder. If the master cylinder is replaced, it must be replaced with a cylinder with the same markings.

7. Install the new secondary piston assembly.

NOTE: The seal which is nearest the flat end has its lips facing toward the flat end. On Delco units, the seal in the second groove has its lips facing toward the compensating holes of the secondary piston. On Bendix units, the seal is an O-ring.

8. Install the new primary seal and seal protector over the end of the secondary piston opposite the secondary seals. It should be positioned so that the flat side of the seal seats against the flange of the piston with the compensating holes.

NOTE: The seal protector isn't used on 1977, and later models.

9. Install the complete primary piston assembly included in every repair kit.
10. Coat the master cylinder bore and the primary and secondary seals with brake fluid. Position the secondary seal spring retainer into the secondary piston spring.
11. Place the retainer and spring over the end of the secondary piston so that the retainer is placed inside the lips of the primary seal.
12. Seat the secondary piston. It may be necessary to manipulate the piston to get it to seat.
13. Position the master cylinder with the open end up and coat the primary and secondary seals on the primary piston with brake fluid. Push the primary piston into the bore of the master cylinder. Hold the piston and position the lockring.
14. Still holding the piston down, install and tighten the stop screw to a torque of 25 to 40 in. lbs.
15. Install the reservoir cover and also the cover on the master cylinder and its retaining clip.
16. Bleed the master cylinder of air by positioning it with the front slightly down, filling it with brake fluid, and working the primary piston until all the bubbles are gone.

Combination Valve

This valve is used on all models with disc brakes. It is non-adjustable and non-serviceable. It can be found by following the lines from the master cylinder. The combination valve itself contains a metering valve that restricts flow to the front brakes until the rear brakes overcome the force of their retracting springs to prevent front brake lockup, a pressure differential warning switch which activates a warning light if either the front or rear hydraulic circuit is losing pressure, and a proportioning valve which limits hydraulic pressure to the rear brakes to prevent rear wheel lockup.

The pressure differential warning switch will reset itself automatically when the brakes are used after a malfunction causing the warning light to go on has been corrected.

When the brake hydraulic system is bled of air, the metering valve pin on the end of the combination valve must be held in a slight amount to allow fluid flow to the front brakes.

Bleeding the Brakes

The purpose of bleeding the brakes is to expel air trapped in the hydraulic system. The system must be bled whenever the pedal feels spongy, indicating that compressible air has entered the system. It must also be bled whenever the system has been opened or leaking. You will need a helper for this job.

NOTE: There are gadgets on the market to make it possible for one man to do this job. Usually they are a bleeder hose with a oneway check valve.

Start with the wheel closest to the master cylinder and work out. With disc brakes, the metering valve pin on the end of the combination valve must be held in slightly to allow fluid flow to the front brakes.
1. Clean the bleeder screw at each wheel.
2. Attach a length of hose to the bleeder screw on the right rear brake and submerge the end in a container of clean brake fluid.
3. Fill the master cylinder with brake fluid.

NOTE: Brake fluid picks up moisture from the air. Don't leave the master cylinder or the fluid container uncovered any longer than necessary. Also, be very careful not to spill brake fluid on the paint as damage to the paint will occur.

Check the level often during bleeding.
4. Pump up the pedal and hold it.
5. Open the bleeder screw about ¾ turn. Have your helper press down on the pedal. Close the bleeder screw before the pedal reaches the end of its travel. Have your helper slowly release the pedal. Continue until no more air bubbles are forced out on application of the pedal.
6. Repeat the procedure on the remaining three brakes, starting at the left rear, moving to the right front, then to the left front.

NOTE: It sometimes helps to tap the disc brake caliper with a soft hammer while fluid is flowing when bleeding the front disc brakes.

Front Brake Pads
INSPECTION

Support the front suspension or axle on jack stands and remove the wheels. Look in at the ends of the caliper to check the lining thickness of the outer pad. Look through the inspection hole in the top of the caliper to check the thickness of the inner pad. Minimum acceptable pad thickness is 1/32 in. from the rivet heads on original equipment riveted linings and 1/32 in. lining thickness on bonded linings.

NOTE: These manufacturer's specifications may not agree with your state inspection law.

All original equipment pads are the riveted type; unless you want to remove the pads to measure the actual thickness from the rivet heads, you will have to make the limit for visual inspection 1/16 in. or more. The same applies if you don't know what kind of lining you have. Original equipment pads and GM replacement pads have an integral wear sensor. This is a spring steel tab on the rear edge of the inner pad which produces a squeal by rubbing against the rotor to warn that the pads have reached their wear limit. They do not squeal when the brakes are applied.

— **CAUTION** —
The squeal will eventually stop if the worn pads aren't replaced. Should this happen, replace the pads immediately to prevent expensive rotor (disc) damage.

REPLACEMENT

The caliper has to be removed to replace the pads, so go on to that procedure. Skip steps 8–10, as there is no need to detach the brake line.

Caliper
REMOVAL AND INSTALLATION

1. Remove the cover on the master cylinder and siphon enough fluid out of the reservoirs to bring the level to ⅓ full. This step prevents spilling fluid when the piston is pushed back.
2. Raise and support the vehicle. Remove the front wheels and tires.
3. Push the brake piston back into its bore using a C-clamp to pull the caliper outward.
4. Remove the two bolts which hold the caliper and then lift the caliper off the disc.

CAUTION
Do not let the caliper assembly hang by the brake hose.

5. Remove the inboard and outboard shoe.

NOTE: If the pads are to be reinstalled, mark them inside and outside.

6. Remove the pad support spring from the piston.

7. Remove the two sleeves from the inside ears of the caliper and the 4 rubber bushings from the grooves in the caliper ears.

8. Remove the hose from the steel brake line and tape the fittings to prevent foreign material from entering the line or the hoses.

9. Remove the retainer from the hose fitting.

10. Remove the hose from the frame bracket and pull off the caliper with the hose attached.

NOTE: Check the inside of the caliper for fluid leakage; if so, the caliper should be overhauled.

CAUTION
Do not use compressed air to clean the inside of the caliper as this may unseat the dust boot.

11. Connect the brake line to start reinstallation. Lubricate the sleeves, rubber bushings, bushing grooves, and the end of the mounting bolts using silicone lubricant.

12. Install new bushings in the caliper ears along with new sleeves. The sleeve should be replaced so that the end toward the shoe is flush with the machined surface of the ear.

13. Position the support spring and the inner pad into the center cavity of the piston. The outboard pad has ears which are bent over to keep the pad in position while the inboard pad has ears on the top end which fit over the caliper retaining bolts. A spring which is inside the brake piston holds the bottom edge of the inboard pad.

14. Push down on the inner pad until it lays flat against the caliper. It is important to push the piston all the way into the caliper if new linings are installed or the caliper will not fit over the rotor.

15. Position the outboard pad with the ears of the pad over the caliper ears and the tab at the bottom engaged in the caliper cutout.

16. With the two pads in position, place the caliper over the brake disc and align the holes in the caliper with those of the mounting bracket.

CAUTION
Make certain that the brake hose is not twisted or kinked.

17. Install the mounting bracket bolts through the sleeves in the inboard caliper ears and through the mounting bracket, making sure that the ends of the bolts pass under the retaining ears on the inboard pad.

18. Tighten the mounting bolts to 35 ft. lbs. Pump the brake pedal to seat the pads against the rotor. Don't do this unless both calipers are in place. Use a pair of channel lock pliers to bend over the upper ears of the outer pad so it isn't loose.

19. Install the front wheel and lower the truck.

20. Add fluid to the master cylinder reservoirs so that they are ¼ in. from the top.

21. Test the brake pedal by pumping it to obtain a "hard" pedal. Check the fluid level again and add fluid as necessary. Do not move the vehicle until a "hard" pedal is obtained.

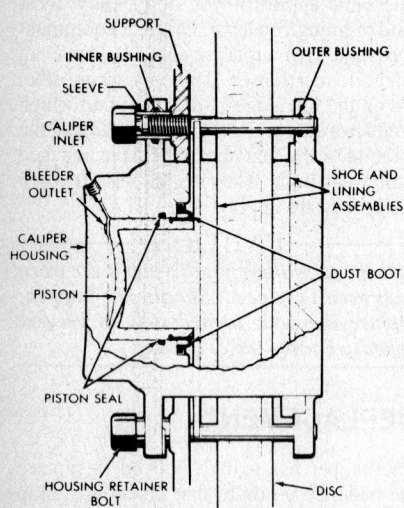

Front disc brake

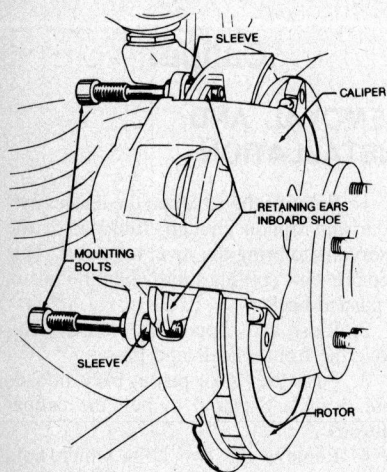

Caliper mounting

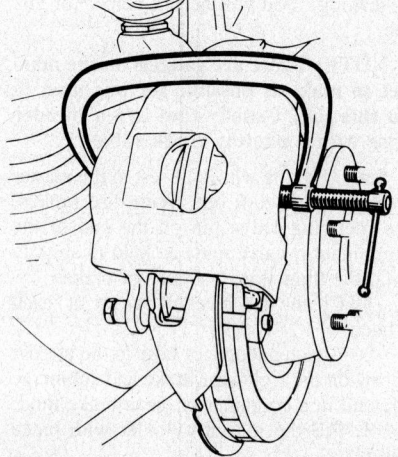

Using a 7 inch C-clamp to push back the piston

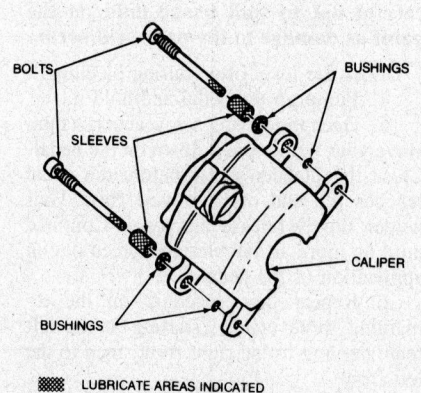

Caliper lubrication points

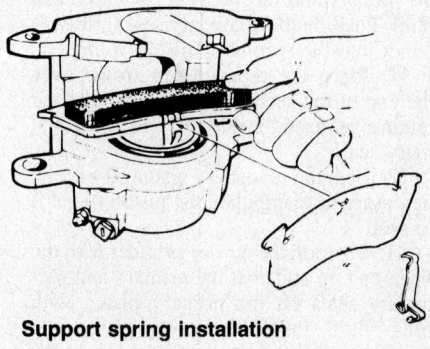

Support spring installation

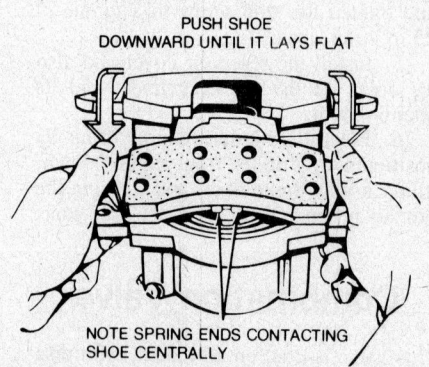

Inner brake pad installation

OVERHAUL

1. Remove the caliper, clean it and place it on a clean and level work surface.
2. Remove the brake hose from the caliper and discard the copper gasket. Check the brake hose for cracks or deterioration. Replace the hose as necessary.
3. Drain the brake fluid from the caliper.
4. Pad the interior of the caliper with cloth and then apply compressed air to the caliper inlet hose.

5. Remove the piston dust boot by prying it out with a screwdriver. Use caution when performing this procedure.
6. Remove the piston seal from the caliper piston bore using a small piece of wood or plastic. DO NOT use any type of metal tool for this procedure.
7. Remove the bleeder valve from the caliper.

NOTE: Dust boot, piston seal, rubber bushings and sleeves are included in every rebuilding kit. These should be replaced at every caliper rebuild.

8. Clean all parts in the recommended solvent and dry them completely using compressed air if possible.

NOTE: The use of shop air hoses may inject oil film into the assembly; use caution when using such hoses.

9. Examine the mounting bolts for rust or corrosion. Replace them as necessary.
10. Examine the piston for scoring, nicks, or worn plating. If any of these conditions are present, replace the piston.

11. Check the piston bore. Small defects can be removed with crocus cloth. If the bore cannot be cleaned in this manner, replace the caliper.
12. Lubricate the piston bore and the new piston seal with brake fluid. Place the seal in the caliper bore groove.
13. Lubricate the piston in the same manner and position the new boot into the groove in the piston so that the fold faces the open end of the piston.
14. Place the piston into the caliper bore using caution not to unseat the seal. Force the piston to the bottom of the bore.

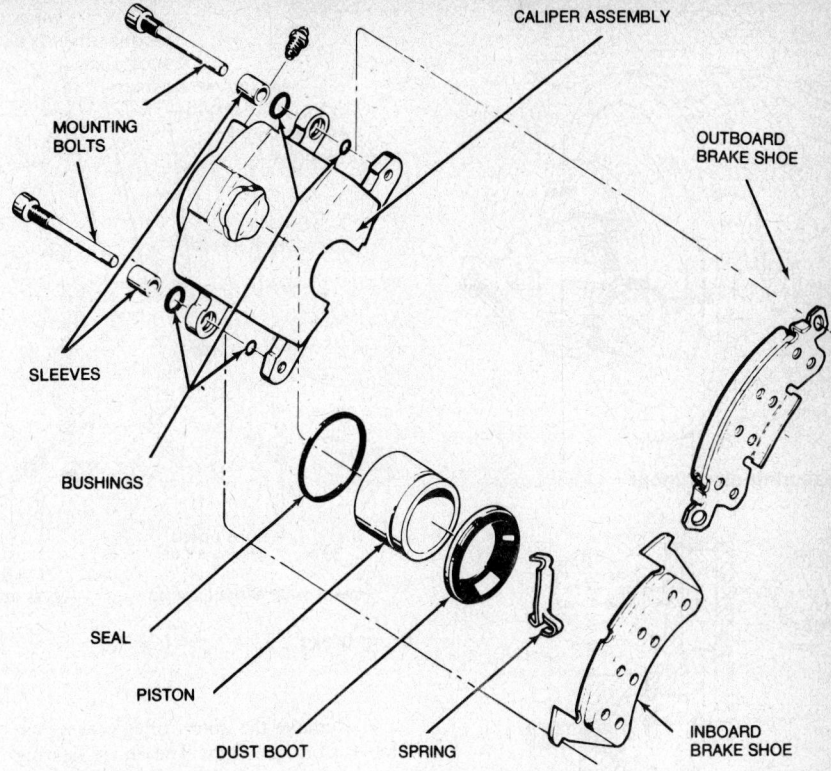

Exploded view of caliper

15. Place the dust boot in the caliper counterbore and seat the boot. Make sure that the boot is positioned correctly and evenly.
16. Install the brake hose in the caliper inlet using a new copper gasket.

NOTE: The hose must be positioned in the caliper locating gate to assure proper positioning of the caliper.

17. Replace the bleeder screw.
18. Bleed the system.

Disc (Rotor)

REMOVAL AND INSTALLATION

1. Follow the procedures outlined for removing the caliper assembly.
2. Remove the bearing dust cap, cotter pin, center nut, and outer bearings.
3. Pull the rotor off the spindle and service it, as necessary.
To install the unit, reverse the removal procedure. Check the rotor before installing it. Pack the inner and outer bearing to the proper specifications. (See "Wheel Bearings.")
4. The minimum wear thickness, 1.215 in., is cast into each disc hub. This is a minimum wear dimension and not a refinish dimension. If the thickness of the disc after refinishing will be 1.230 in. or less, it must be replaced. Refinishing is required when-

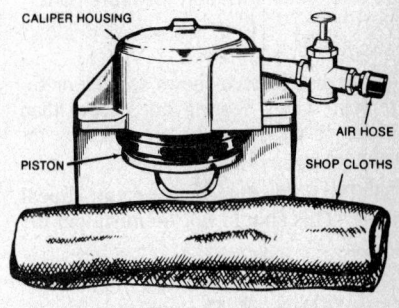

Removing the piston with compressed air

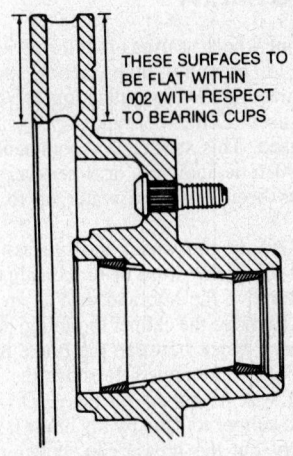

Surface flatness measurement

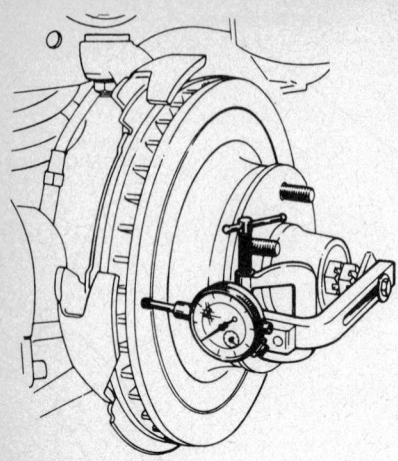

Measuring disc runout

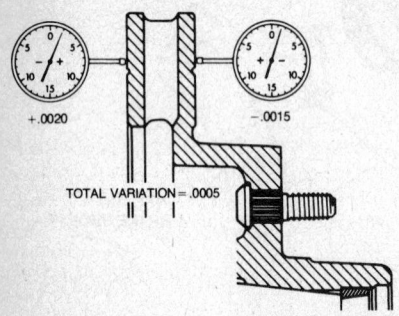

Disc thickness variation measurement

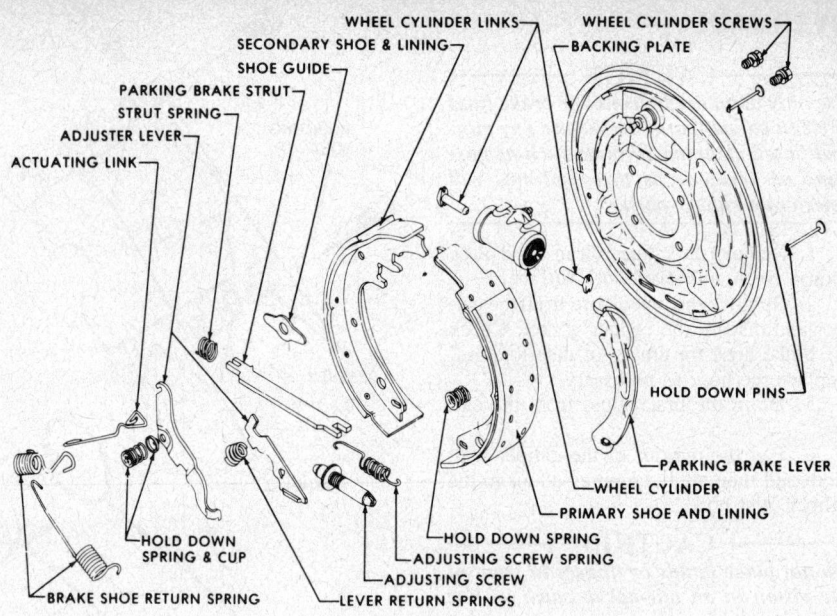

Drum brake

ever the disc surface shows scoring or severe rust scale. Scoring not deeper than .015 in. in depth can be corrected by refinishing.

NOTE: Some discs have an anti-squeal groove. This should not be mistaken for scoring.

Wheel Bearing

LUBRICATION AND ADJUSTMENT

Only front wheel bearings require periodic service. A premium high melting point grease meeting GM specification 6031-M must be used. Long fiber type greases must not be used. This service is recommended at 20,000 mile intervals or whenever the truck has been driven in water up to the hubs.

1. Remove the wheel and tire assembly, and the brake drum or brake caliper.

2. Remove the hub and disc as an assembly. Remove the caliper mounting bolts and insert a block between the brake pads as the caliper is removed. Remove the caliper and wire it out of the way. Do not allow the caliper to hang by the brake hose.

3. Pry out the grease cap, cotter pin, spindle nut, and washer, then remove the hub. Do not drop the wheel bearings.

4. Remove the outer roller bearing assembly from the hub. The inner bearing assembly will remain in the hub and may be removed after prying out the inner seal. Discard the seal.

5. Clean all parts in solvent (air dry) and check for excessive wear or damage.

6. Using a hammer and drift, remove the bearing caps from the hub. When installing new cups, make sure that they are not cocked and that they are fully seated against the hub shoulder.

7. Pack both wheel bearings using high melting point wheel bearing grease made for disc brakes. Ordinary grease will melt and ooze out, ruining the pads. Place a healthy globe of grease in the palm of one hand and force the edge of the bearing into it so that the grease fills the bearing. Do this until the whole bearing is packed. Grease packing tools are available to make this job a lot less messy. There are also tools which make it possible to grease the inner bearing without removing it or the disc from the spindle.

8. Place the inner bearing in the hub and install a new inner seal, making sure that the seal flange faces the bearing cup.

9. Carefully install the wheel hub over the spindle.

10. Using your hands, firmly press the outer bearing into the hub. Install the spindle washer and nut.

11. To adjust the bearings, spin the wheel hub by hand and tighten the nut till it is just snug (12 ft. lbs.). Back off the nut till it is loose, then tighten it finger tight. Loosen the nut until either hole in the spindle lines up with a slot in the nut and insert a new cotter pin. There should be 0.001–0.005 in. end-play. This can be measured with a dial indicator, if you wish.

12. Replace the dust cap, wheel and tire.

Brake Drum

REMOVAL AND INSTALLATION

Drums can be removed by raising the vehicle, removing the wheel lugs and the tire, and pulling the drum from the brake assembly. If the brake drums have been scored from worn linings, the brake adjuster must be backed off so that the brake shoes will retract from the drum. To remove the drums from full-floating rear axles, use Steps 1–11 of the Axle Shaft Removal and Installation procedure. Full-floating rear axles can readily be identified by the bearing housing protruding through the center of the wheel.

The adjuster can be backed off by inserting a brake adjusting tool through the access hole provided. In some cases the access hole is provided in the brake drum. A metal cover plate is over the hole. This may be removed by using a hammer and chisel.

NOTE: Make sure all metal particles are removed from the brake drum before reassembly.

To install, reverse the removal procedure.

——— CAUTION ———
Do not blow the brake dust out of the drums with compressed air. Powdered asbestos has been found to be a cancer-producing agent.

INSPECTION

Lining

Remove the drum and inspect the lining

thickness on both brake shoes. A front brake lining should be replaced if it is less than ⅛ in. thick at the lowest point on the brake shoe. The wear limit for rear brake linings is ¹⁄₁₆.

NOTE: Brake shoes should always be replaced in axle sets. The wear specifications given may disagree with your state inspection rules.

Drum

When a drum is removed, it should be inspected for cracks, scores, or other imperfections. These must be corrected before the drum is replaced.

——— CAUTION ———
If the drum is found to be cracked, replace it. Do not attempt to service a cracked drum.

Minor drum score marks can be removed with fine emery cloth. Heavy score marks must be removed by "turning the drum." This is removing metal from the entire inner surface of the drum on a lathe in order to level the surface. Automotive machine shops and some large parts stores are equipped to perform this operation.

If the drum is not scored, it should be polished with fine emery cloth before replacement. If the drum is resurfaced, it should not be enlarged more than 0.060 in.

NOTE: Your state inspection law may disagree with this specification.

It is advisable, while the drums are off, to check them for out-of-round. An inside micrometer is necessary for an exact measurement, therefore, unless this tool is available the drums should be taken to a machine shop to be checked. Any drum which is more than 0.006 in. out-of-round will result in an inaccurate brake adjustment and other problems, and should be refinished or replaced.

NOTE: Make all measurements at right angles to each other and at the open and closed edges of the drum machined surface.

Brake Shoes

REMOVAL AND INSTALLATION

1. Jack up and securely support the vehicle.
2. Loosen the parking brake equalizer enough to remove all tension on the brake cable (rear brakes only).
3. Remove the brake drums.

——— CAUTION ———
The brake pedal must not be depressed while the drums are removed.

4. Using a brake tool, remove the shoe springs. You can do this with ordinary tools,

but it isn't easy.
5. Remove the self-adjuster actuator spring.
6. Remove the link from the secondary shoe by pulling it from the anchor pin.
7. Remove the hold-down pins. These are the brackets which run through the backing plate. They can be removed with a pair of pliers. Reach around the rear of the backing plate and hold the back of the pin. Turn the top of the pin retainer 45° with the pliers. This will align the elongated tang with the slot in the retainer. Be careful, as the pin is spring-loaded and may fly off when released. Use the same procedure for the other pin assembly.
8. Remove the adjuster actuator assembly.

NOTE: Since the actuator, pivot, and override spring are considered an assembly it is not recommended that they be disassembled.

9. Remove the shoes from the backing plate. Make sure that you have a secure grip on the assembly as the bottom spring will still exert pressure on the shoes. Slowly let the tops of the shoes come together and the tension will decrease and the adjuster and spring may be removed.

NOTE: If the linings are to be reused, mark them for identification.

10. Remove the rear parking brake lever from the secondary shoe. Using a pair of pliers, pull back on the spring which surrounds the cable. At the same time, remove the cable from the notch in the shoe bracket. Make sure that the spring does not snap back or injury may result.
11. Use a cloth to remove dirt from the brake drum. Check the drums for scoring and cracks. Have the drums checked for out-of-round and service the drums as necessary.
12. Check the wheel cylinders by carefully pulling the lower edges of the wheel cylinder boots away from the cylinders. If there is excessive leakage, the inside of the cylinder will be moist with fluid. If there is any leakage at all, a cylinder overhaul is in order. DO NOT delay, as a brake failure could result.

NOTE: A small amount of fluid will be present to act as a lubricant for the wheel cylinder pistons.

13. Check the flange plate, which is located around the axle, for leakage of differential lubricant. This condition cannot be overlooked as the lubricant will be absorbed into the brake linings and brake failure will result. Replace the seals as necessary.

NOTE: If new linings are being installed, check them against the old units for length and type.

14. Check the new linings for imperfections.

——— CAUTION ———
It is important to keep your hands free of

dirt and grease when handling the brake shoes. Foreign matter will be absorbed into the linings and result in unpredictable braking.

15. Lightly lubricate the parking brake and cable and the end of the parking brake lever where it enters the shoe. Use high temperature, waterproof, grease or special brake lube.
16. Install the parking brake lever into the secondary shoe with the attaching bolt, spring washer, lockwasher, and nut. It is important that the lever move freely before the shoe is attached. Move the assembly and check for proper action.
17. Lubricate the adjusting screw and make sure that it works freely. Sometimes the adjusting screw will not move due to lack of lubricant or dirt contamination and the brakes will not adjust. In this case, the adjuster should be disassembled, thoroughly cleaned, and lubricated before installation.
18. Connect the brake shoe spring to the bottom portion of both shoes. Make certain that the brake linings are installed in the correct manner, the primary and secondary shoe in the correct position. If you are not sure remove the other brake drum and check it.
19. Install the adjusting mechanism below the spring and separate the top of the shoes.

NOTE: Make the following checks before installation:

  a. Be certain that the right-hand thread adjusting screw is on the left-hand side of the vehicle and the left-hand screw is on the right-hand side of the vehicle;
  b. Make sure that the star adjuster is aligned with the adjusting hole;
  c. The adjuster should be installed with the starwheel nearest the secondary shoe and the tension spring away from the adjusting mechanism;
  d. If the original linings are being reused, put them back in their original locations.

20. Install the parking brake cable.
21. Position the primary shoe (the shoe with the short lining) first. Secure it with the hold-down pin and with its spring by pushing the pin through the back of the backing plate and, while holding it with one hand, install the spring and the retainer using a pair of needlenose pliers. Install the adjuster actuator assembly.
22. Install the parking brake strut and the strut spring by pulling back the spring with pliers and engaging the end of the cable onto the brake strut and then releasing the spring.
23. Place the small metal guide plate over the anchor pin and position the self-adjuster wire cable eye.

——— CAUTION ———
The wire should not be positioned with the conventional brake installation tool or

damage will result. It should be positioned on the actuator assembly first and then placed over the anchor pin stud by hand with the adjuster assembly in full downward position.

24. Install the actuator return spring. DO NOT pry the actuator lever to install the return spring. Position it using the end of a screwdriver or another suitable tool.

NOTE: If the return springs are bent or in any way distorted, they should be replaced.

25. Using the brake installation tool, place the brake return springs in position. Install the primary spring first over the anchor pin and then place the spring from the secondary shoe over the wire link end.

26. Pull the brake shoes away from the backing plate and apply a *thin* coat of high temperature, waterproof, grease or special brake lube to the brake shoe contact points.

— CAUTION —

Only a small amount is necessary. Keep the lubricant away from the brake linings.

27. Once the complete assembly has been installed, check the operation of the self-adjuster mechanism by moving the actuating lever by hand.

28. Adjust the brakes.

a. Turn the star adjuster until the drum slides over the brake shoes with only a slight drag. Remove the drum;

b. Turn the adjuster back 1¼ turns.

c. Install the drum and wheel and lower the vehicle:

NOTE: If the adjusting hole in the drum has been punched out, make certain that the insert has been removed from the inside of the drum. Install a rubber hole cover to keep dirt out of the brake assembly. Also, be sure that the drums are installed in the same position as they were when removed—with the locating tang in line with the location hole in the axle shaft flange.

d. Make the final adjustment by backing the vehicle and pumping the brakes until the self-adjusting mechanisms adjust to the proper level and the brake pedal reaches satisfactory height.

29. Adjust the parking brake. Details are given later.

Wheel Cylinders

REMOVAL

1. Raise and support the axle.
2. Remove the wheel and tire.
3. Back off the brake adjustment if necessary and remove the drum.
4. Disconnect and plug the brake line.
5. Remove the brake shoe pull-back springs.
6. Remove the screws securing the wheel cylinder to the backing plate.

7. Disengage the wheel cylinder pushrods from the brake shoes and remove the wheel cylinder.

OVERHAUL

As with master cylinders, overhaul kits for wheel cylinders are readily available. When rebuilding and installing wheel cylinders, avoid getting any contaminants into the system. Always install clean, new high-quality brake fluid. If dirty or improper fluid has been used, it will be necessary to drain the entire system, flush the system with proper brake fluid, replace all rubber components, refill, and bleed the system.

1. Remove the rubber boots from the cylinder ends with pliers. Discard the boots.
2. Remove and discard the pistons and cups.
3. Wash the cylinder and metal parts in denatured alcohol or clean brake fluid.

— CAUTION —

Never use a mineral-based solvent such as gasoline, kerosene, or paint thinner for cleaning purposes. These solvents will swell rubber components and quickly deteriorate them.

4. Allow the parts to air dry or use compressed air. Do not use rags for cleaning since lint will remain in the cylinder bore.
5. Inspect the piston and replace it if it shows scratches.
6. Lubricate the cylinder bore and counterbore with clean brake fluid.
7. Install the rubber cups (flat side out) and then the pistons (flat side in).
8. Insert new boots into the counterbores by hand. Do not lubricate the boots.

INSTALLATION

1. Installation is the reverse of removal.
2. Adjust the brakes and bleed the system.

Parking Brakes

ADJUSTMENT

Before attempting parking brake adjustment, make sure that the rear brakes are fully adjusted by making several stops in reverse.

1. Raise and support the rear axle. Release the parking brake.
2. On 1975 models, apply the pedal one click. On 1976 and later models, apply the pedal four clicks.
3. Adjust the cable equalizer nut under the truck until a moderate drag can be felt when the rear wheels are turned forward.
4. Release the parking brake and check that there is no drag when the wheels are turned forward.

NOTE: If the parking brake cable is replaced, prestretch it by applying the parking brake hard about three times before attempting adjustment.

CHASSIS ELECTRICAL

Blower—Except Vans

REMOVAL AND INSTALLATION

1. Disconnect the battery leads, open the hood, and securely support it.
2. Mark the position of the blower motor in relation to its case. Remove the electrical connection at the motor.
3. Remove the blower attaching screws and remove the assembly. Pry gently on the flange if the sealer sticks.

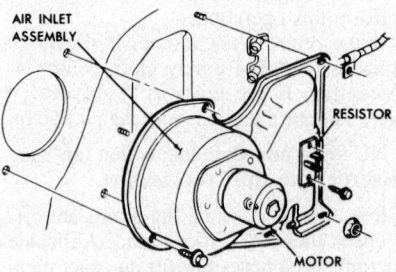

Heater blower assembly—except vans

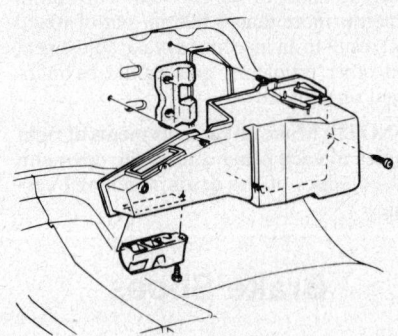

Heater distributor—except vans

4. The blower wheel can be removed from the motor shaft by removing the nut at the center.

To assemble the unit:

5. Assemble the blower wheel to the motor with the open end of the wheel away from the motor and install the unit into the blower case. Connect the ground strap and the electrical connection.
6. Position the hood hinge using the scribe marks and check the hood alignment.
7. Connect the battery.

Core—Except Vans

REMOVAL AND INSTALLATION

Without Air Conditioning

1. Disconnect the battery ground cable.

2. Disconnect the heater hoses at the core tubes and drain the engine coolant. Plug the core tubes to prevent spillage.

3. Remove the nuts from the distributor air ducts in the engine compartment.

4. Remove the glove compartment and door.

5. Disconnect the "Air-Defrost" and "Temperature" door cables.

6. Remove the floor outlet and remove the defroster duct-to-heater distributor screw.

7. Remove the heater distributor-to-instrument panel screws. Pull the assembly rearward to gain access to the wiring harness and disconnect the wires attached to the unit.

8. Remove the heater distributor from the truck.

9. Remove the heater core retaining straps and remove the core from the truck.

10. Installation is the reverse of removal. Be sure that the core-to-case and case-to-dash panel sealer is intact. Fill the cooling system and check for leaks.

With Air Conditioning

1. Disconnect the battery ground cable.

2. Drain the coolant.

3. Remove the heater hoses from the core tubes. Plug the tubes to prevent spillage.

4. Remove the glove box and door.

5. Remove the screws holding the center duct to the selector duct and to the instrument panel. Remove the center upper and lower ducts.

6. Disconnect the control cable at the temperature door.

7. Remove the three stud nuts from the firewall. Remove the selector duct to firewall screw inside the truck.

8. Pull the selector duct assembly back until the core tubes clear the firewall, then lower it to disconnect the vacuum and electrical connections.

9. Remove the selector duct assembly and remove the core mounting straps.

10. Reverse the procedure for installation.

Blower—Vans

REMOVAL AND INSTALLATION

1. Disconnect the battery cables. Remove the battery.

2. Unclip the blower motor lead wire.

3. Remove the blower attaching screws.

4. Remove the blower assembly. It may be necessary to pry gently on the blower flange. Sometimes the sealer acts as an adhesive.

5. If the motor is being replaced, remove the nut attaching the blower wheel to the blower motor shaft and separate the two.

6. Assemble the blower wheel to the motor with the open end away from the motor.

7. If the sealer has hardened or is otherwise useless, apply a new bead of sealer to the mounting flange.

8. Installation of the blower motor and wheel is the reverse of removal. Connect the lead wires and the battery cables and check the operation of the motor.

Core—Vans

REMOVAL AND INSTALLATION

1975–77 Without Air Conditioning

This procedure applies to models without air conditioning and to those with the floor mounted air conditioner.

1. Disconnect the battery ground cable.

2. Place a pan under the van and disconnect the heater intake and outlet hoses. Quickly, remove and plug the heater hoses and support them in an upright position. Drain the coolant from the heater core into the pan.

3. Disconnect the right-hand air distributor hose from the heater case and put it aside.

4. Pry the eyelet clip from the temperature door cable and remove the Bowden cable attaching screw.

5. Remove the distributor duct and pull it rearward from the retainer.

6. Remove the heater case and core as an assembly.

7. Remove the core from the case. To install a new core, reverse the above steps.

1978 Without Air Conditioning

1. Disconnect the negative battery cable.

2. Place a pan under the van and disconnect the heater intake and outlet hoses. Quickly remove and plug the hoses and support them in an upright position. Drain the coolant from the heater core into the pan.

3. Remove the heater distributor duct-to-case attaching screws and the duct-to-engine cover screw. Remove the duct.

4. Remove the screw attaching the defroster duct to the distributor case.

5. Disconnect the temperature door cable. Carefully fold the cable back and out of the way.

6. Remove the three nuts from the engine compartment side of the distributor case and the screw from the passenger compartment side.

7. Remove the heater case and core assembly.

8. Remove the core retaining straps and remove the core.

9. Reverse to install.

1979–82 Without Air Conditioning

1. Refer to steps 1–3 of the 1978 procedure.

2. Remove the engine cover.

3. Remove all the instrument panel attaching screws.

4. Carefully lower the steering column. Raise and support the right side of the instrument panel.

5. Remove the defroster duct-to-case attaching screws and the two screws attaching the distributor to the heater case.

6. Refer to steps 5–9 of the 1978 procedure.

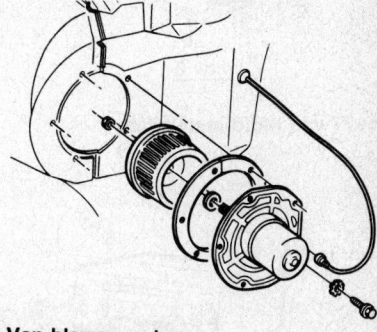

Van blower motor

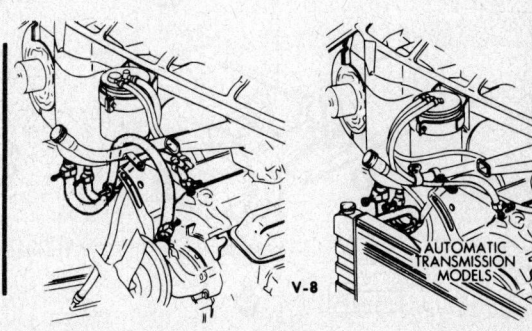

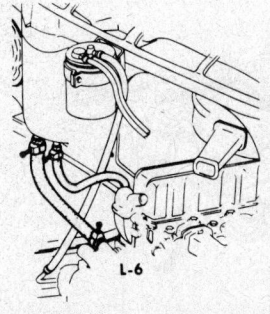

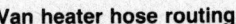

Van heater hose routing

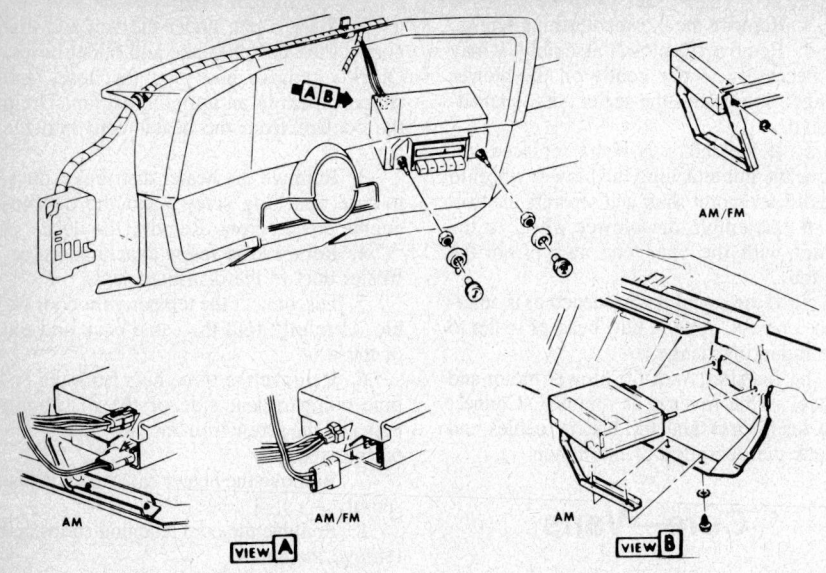

Radio installation, except vans

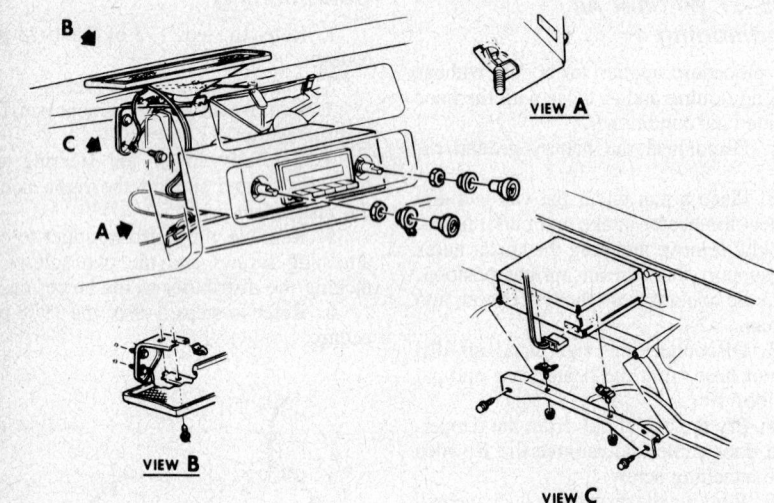

1975–77 van radio installation

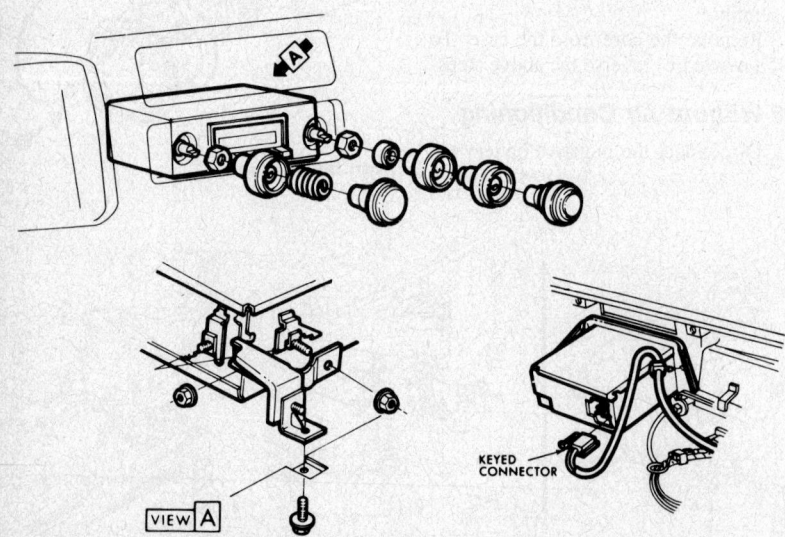

1978–82 van radio installation

1975–77 With Air Conditioning

These models have the air conditioning equipment mounted under the right side of the instrument panel.

1. Remove the battery.

2. Remove the engine cover.

3. Remove the evaporator-blower shield and bracket.

4. Remove the left floor outlet deflector and bracket.

5. Loosen the steering column to instrument panel reinforcement screws. Remove one screw.

6. Disconnect the speedometer cable at the instrument.

7. Remove the instrument panel to lower reinforcement screws. Move the instrument panel back and detach the radio antenna and wires. Disconnect the brake switch electrical connector.

8. Detach the blower-evaporator support bracket from the door pillar and the engine housing. Move it back for access.

9. Detach the heater hoses at the core (from under the hood). Plug the hoses to prevent spillage.

10. Remove the air inlet valve assembly from the kick panel. Remove the temperature door control cable at the heater case.

11. Remove the heater assembly. Remove the core from the assembly.

12. Reverse the procedure for installation. Tighten the column screws to 22 ft. lbs. Refill the cooling system as necessary.

1978–82 With Air Conditioning

1. Disconnect the battery ground cable.

2. Remove the engine cover.

3. Remove the steering column to instrument panel bolts. Lower the column carefully.

4. Remove the upper and lower instrument panel attaching screws. Remove the radio support bracket screw.

5. Raise and support the right side of the instrument panel.

6. Remove the lower right instrument panel bracket.

7. Remove the vacuum actuator from the kick panel.

8. Disconnect the temperature cable and vacuum hoses at the case. Remove the heater distributor duct from over the engine hump.

9. Remove the two defroster duct to firewall attaching screws below the windshield.

10. Under the hood, disconnect and plug the heater hoses at the firewall.

11. Remove the three nuts and one screw (inside) holding the heater case to the firewall.

12. Remove the case from the truck. Remove the gasket for access to the screws holding the case together. Remove the temperature cable support bracket. Remove the screws and separate the case. Remove the heater core.

13. Reverse the procedure for installation. Refill the cooling system as necessary.

Radio

REMOVAL AND INSTALLATION

Except Vans

1. Remove the negative battery cable and the control knobs and the bezels from the radio control shafts.
2. On AM radios, remove the support bracket stud nut and its lockwasher.
3. On AM/FM radios, remove the support bracket-to-instrument panel screws.
4. Lifting the rear edge of the radio, push the radio forward until the control shafts clear the instrument panel. Then lower the radio far enough so that the electrical connections can be disconnected.
5. Remove the power lead, speaker, and antenna wires and then pull out the unit.
6. To install the radio, reverse the above procedure.

Vans

1. Disconnect the ground cable from the battery.
2. Remove the engine cover.
3. Remove the air cleaner from the carburetor.
4. On models through 1977, remove the stud in the carburetor which holds the air cleaner.
5. Cover the carburetor with a clean rag.
6. Remove the knobs, washers and nuts from the front of the radio.
7. Remove the rear bracket screw and bracket from the radio.
8. Remove the radio through the engine access area. Lower the radio far enough to detach the wiring.
9. Remove the radio.
10. Installation is the reverse of removal.

Windshield Wiper Motor

REMOVAL AND INSTALLATION

Except Vans

1. Make sure the wipers are in the park position.
2. Disconnect the battery ground cable.
3. Disconnect the wiring and hoses at the windshield washer pump.
4. Remove the plastic air intake cover screen and reach in to loosen the wiper drive rod attaching screws. There is a small access hole provided. Remove the drive rod from the motor crank arm.
5. Unbolt and remove the motor.
6. Reverse the procedure for installation, making sure to lubricate the motor crank arm pivot.

NOTE: Failure of the washers to operate or to shut off is often caused by grease or dirt on the electromagnetic contacts. Simply unplug the wire and pull off the plastic cover for access. Likewise, failure of the wipers to park is often caused by grease or dirt on the park switch contacts. The park switch is under the cover behind the pump.

Vans

1. Be sure that the wiper motor is in PARK position. The wiper arms should be in their normal OFF position.
2. Open the hood and disconnect the battery ground cable.
3. Remove the exposed cowl cover screws with the hood up.
4. Remove the wiper arms. This can be done by pulling the wiper arms away from the glass to release the clip underneath. The wiper arms are splined to the shafts and can be pulled off.
5. Remove the remaining screws securing the cowl panel and remove it.
6. Loosen the nuts holding the transmission linkage to the wiper motor crank arm.
7. Disconnect the power feed to the wiper arm at the connector next to the radio.
8. Remove the flex hose from the left defroster outlet to gain access to the wiper motor screws.
9. Remove the one screw holding the left-hand heater duct to the engine shroud and move the heater duct down and out.
10. Remove the windshield washer hoses from the pump.
11. Remove the 3 screws holding the wiper motor to the cowl and lift the wiper motor out from under the dash.
12. Installation is the reverse of removal. Install the wiper motor in the PARK position.

Instrument Cluster

REMOVAL AND INSTALLATION

Except Vans

1975–76

1. Remove the negative battery cable.
2. Remove the steering column cover and the cluster bezel.
3. Remove the knob from the clock (if equipped).
4. Remove the lens retaining screws and the lens.
5. Remove the transmission gear indicator (PRNDL) and the cluster retainer.
6. Disconnect the speedometer cable by depressing the spring clip and pulling the cable out of the speedometer head. Disconnect and plug the oil pressure line, if so equipped.
7. Disconnect the cluster wiring harness and remove the cluster retaining screws and pull out the cluster.
8. To install the cluster, reverse the removal procedure.

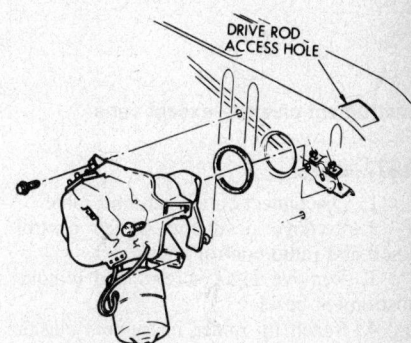

Wiper motor installation—except vans

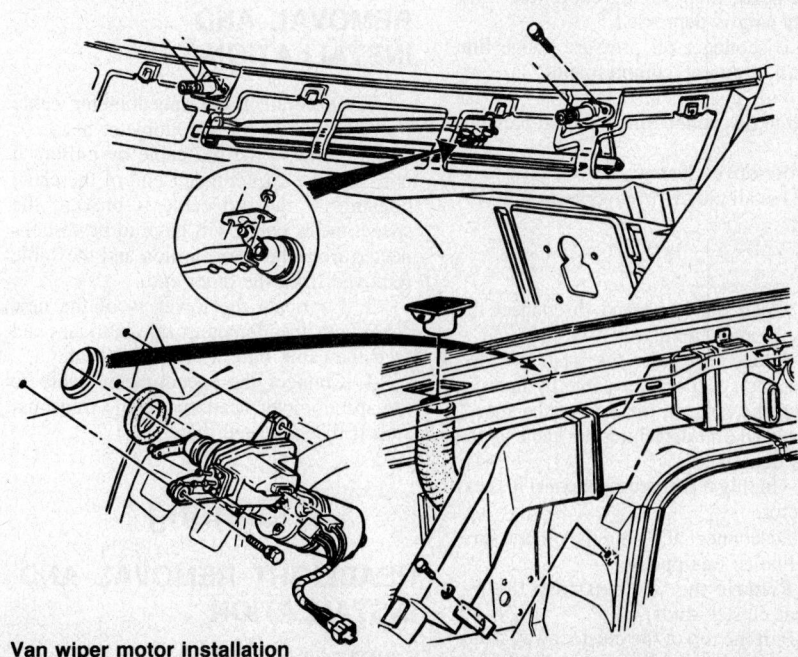

Van wiper motor installation

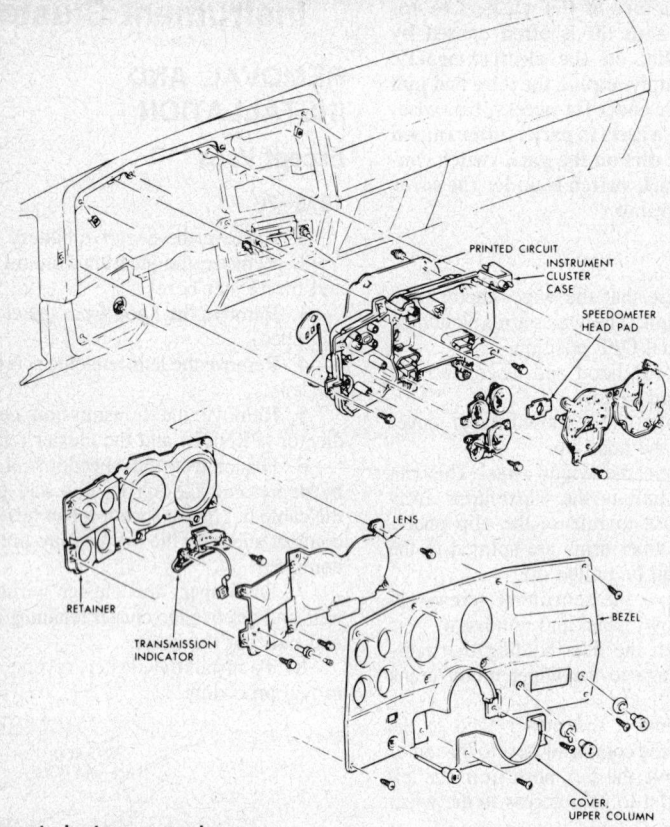

PRINTED CIRCUIT

INSTRUMENT CLUSTER CASE

SPEEDOMETER HEAD PAD

LENS

RETAINER

TRANSMISSION INDICATOR

BEZEL

COVER, UPPER COLUMN

Instrument cluster—except vans

1977–82

1. Disconnect battery ground cable.
2. Remove headlamp switch control knob and radio control knobs.
3. Remove eight screws and remove instrument bezel.
4. Reach up under instrument cluster and disconnect speedometer by first depressing the tang on the rear of the speedometer head, then pulling cable free from head as tang is depressed.
5. Disconnect oil pressure gauge line at fitting in engine compartment.
6. Pull instrument cluster out just far enough to disconnect line from oil pressure gauge.
7. Remove cluster.
8. Install cluster in reverse order of removal.

Vans

1. Open the hood and disconnect the battery ground cable.
2. Reach up under the dash and disconnect the speedometer cable by first depressing the tang on the rear of the speedometer head and detaching the cable as the tang is depressed.
3. Unplug the instrument panel harness connector.
4. Disconnect and plug the oil pressure gauge line (if equipped).
5. Remove the two nuts from the instrument cluster studs.
6. Pull the top of the cluster away from instrument panel and lift out the bottom of

the cluster.
7. Remove the cluster.
8. Installation is the reverse of removal. The clips at the top of the cluster slip into the openings in the instrument panel after the bottom of the cluster is installed.

Speedometer Cable

REMOVAL AND INSTALLATION

1. Disconnect the speedometer cable from the rear of the speedometer head.
2. Remove the old cable by pulling it out from the speedometer end of the cable housing. If the old cable is broken, the speedometer cable will have to be disconnected from the transmission and the cable removed from the other end.
3. Lubricate the lower ¾ of the new cable with speedometer cable lubricant and feed the cable into the cable housing.
4. Connect the speedometer cable to the speedometer head and to the transmission if disconnected there.

Lighting

HEADLIGHT REMOVAL AND INSTALLATION

NOTE: Some 1978 and later models

have rectangular headlights. Otherwise the following removal and installation procedures apply.

1. Remove the headlight bezel by releasing the attaching screws.
2. Remove the spring (if any) from the retaining ring and turn the unit to disengage it from the headlamp adjusting screws.
3. Disconnect the wiring harness connector.

NOTE: Do not disturb the adjusting screws.

4. Remove the retaining ring and the headlamp.
5. Position the new sealed beam unit in the retaining ring.

NOTE: The number which is moulded into the lens must be at the top.

6. Attach the wiring connector.
7. Install the headlamp assembly, twisting the ring slightly to engage the adjusting screws.
8. Install the retaining ring spring and check the operation of the unit. Install the bezel.

Fusible Links

Fusible links are sections of wire, with special insulation, designed to melt under electrical overload. Replacements are simply spliced into the wire in most cases. Circuits protected by fusible links are: high beam indicator, air conditioning hi-blower, horn, and ignition.

Circuit Breakers

A circuit breaker is an electrical switch which breaks the circuit in case of an overload. All models have a circuit breaker in the headlight switch to protect the headlight and parking light systems. An overload may cause the lights to flash on and off. 1975 wiper motors have a circuit breaker at the motor. 1975–82 rear mounted air conditioners have a circuit breaker at the firewall.

Fuses and Flashers

The fuse block is mounted to the firewall, inside the truck, to the left of the steering column. The turn signal flasher and hazard warning flasher plug into the fuse block. Each fuse receptacle is marked as to the circuits it protects and the correct amperage. In-line fuses are also used to protect some circuits. These are: ammeter, and auxiliary heater.

NOTE: A special heavy duty turn signal flasher is required to properly operate the turn signals when a trailer's lights are connected to the system.

Dodge and Plymouth

INDEX

DODGE/PLYMOUTH
PICK-UPS, VANS, RAMCHARGER, TRAIL DUSTER, RAMPAGE

GENERAL ENGINE SPECIFICATIONS

Year	Engine Displacement (cu in.)	Estimated Horsepower (@ rpm)	Estimated Torque@ rpm (ft lbs)	Bore and Stroke (in.)	Compression Ratio	Oil Pressure (psi @ rpm)
'75	6-225	90 @ 3600	170 @ 1600	3.40 × 4.12	8:4 : 1	30–70 @ 2000
	8-318	150 @ 4000	230 @ 2400	3.91 × 3.31	8.6 : 1	30–80 @ 2000
	8-360	175 @ 4000	285 @ 2400	4.00 × 3.58	8.4 : 1	30–80 @ 2000
'76–'77	6-225	95 @ 3600①	170 @ 1600	3.40 × 4.12	8.4 : 1	30–70 @ 2000
	8-318	150 @ 4000	225 @ 1600	3.91 × 3.31	8.6 : 1	30–80 @ 2000
	8-360	170 @ 4000	285 @ 2400	4.00 × 3.58	8.4 : 1	30–80 @ 2000
	8-400	180 @ 3600	315 @ 2400	4.34 × 3.38	8.2 : 1	30–80 @ 2000
	8-440	195 @ 3600	320 @ 2000	4.32 × 3.75	8.2 : 1	30–80 @ 2000
'78	6-225	90 @ 3600①	160 @ 1600	3.40 × 4.12	8.4 : 1	30–70 @ 2000
	6-243 Diesel	100 @ 3700	163 @ 2200	3.62 × 3.94	20 : 1	43 @ 1000
	8-318	140 @ 4000	245 @ 1600	3.91 × 3.31	8.5 : 1	30–80 @ 2000
	8-360	155 @ 3600	270 @ 2400	4.00 × 3.58	8.4 : 1	30–80 @ 2000
	8-400	190 @ 3600	305 @ 3200	4.34 × 3.38	8.2 : 1	30–80 @ 2000
	8-440	225 @ 4400	360 @ 3200	4.32 × 3.75	8.2 : 1	30–80 @ 2000
'79	6-225	90 @ 3600	160 @ 1600	3.40 × 4.12	8.4 : 1	30–70 @ 2000
	6-243 Diesel	100 @ 3700	163 @ 2200	3.62 × 3.94	20 : 1	43 @ 1000
	8-318	140 @ 4000	245 @ 1600	3.91 × 3.31	8.6 : 1	30–80 @ 2000
	8-360	155 @ 3600	270 @ 2400	4.00 × 3.58	8.5 : 1	30–80 @ 2000
'80–'81④	6-225	90 @ 3600	160 @ 1600	3.40 × 4.12	8.4 : 1	35–65 @ 2000
	8-318②	120 @ 3600	245 @ 1600	3.91 × 3.31	8.5 : 1	35–65 @ 2000
	8-318③	155 @ 4000	240 @ 2000	3.91 × 3.31	8.5 : 1	35–65 @ 2000
	8-360②	130 @ 3200	255 @ 2000	4.00 × 3.58	8.4 : 1	35–65 @ 2000
	8-360③	185 @ 4000	275 @ 2000	4.00 × 3.58	8.0 : 1	35–65 @ 2000
'82④	4-135	84 @ 4800	111 @ 2400	3.44 × 3.62	8.5 : 1	50 @ 2000
	6-225	90 @ 3600	160 @ 1600	3.40 × 4.12	8.4 : 1	35–65 @ 2000
	8-318②	120 @ 3600	245 @ 1600	3.91 × 3.31	8.5 : 1	35–65 @ 2000
	8-318③	155 @ 4000	240 @ 2000	3.91 × 3.31	8.5 : 1	35–65 @ 2000
	8-360②	130 @ 3200	255 @ 2000	4.00 × 3.58	8.4 : 1	35–65 @ 2000
	8-360③	185 @ 4000	275 @ 2000	4.00 × 3.58	8.0 : 1	35–65 @ 2000

① 10 more hp with two barrel carburetor
② 2 barrel carb
③ 4 barrel carb
④ Horsepower and torque are SAE net figures. They are measured at the rear of the transmission with all accessories installed and operating. Since the figures vary when a given engine is installed in different models, some ratings are representative rather than exact

TUNE-UP SPECIFICATIONS

Year	Engine No. Cyl. Displacement (cu in.)	Spark Plugs Original Type	Gap (in.)	Point Dwell (deg)	Point Gap (in.)	Ignition Timing (±2°) (deg)▲ MT	AT	Intake Valve Opens (deg)	Fuel Pump Pressure (psi)	Compression Pressure (psi)	Idle Speed (rpm) MT	●AT	Valve Clearance (in.) In	Ex
'75	6-225 LD	BL11Y	.035	Elec.	Elec.	TDC	TDC	16B	3.5–5.0	100 (Min.)	800	750	.012	.024
	6-225 LD Calif.	BL11Y	.035	Elec.	Elec.	2A	2A	16B	3.5–5.0	100 (Min.)	800	750	.012	.024
	6-225 HD-All	BL11Y	.035	Elec.	Elec.	TDC	TDC	16B	3.5–5.0	100 (Min.)	700	700	.012	.024
	V8-318 LD	N11Y	.035	Elec.	Elec.	2B	2B	10B	5.0–7.0	100 (Min.)	750⑥	750	Hyd.	Hyd.
	V8-318 LD Calif.	N11Y	.035	Elec.	Elec.	TDC	TDC	10B	5.0–7.0	100 (Min.)	750	750	Hyd.	Hyd.
	V8-318 HD	N11Y	.035	Elec.	Elec.	2A	2A	10B	5.0–7.0	100 (Min.)	750	750	Hyd.	Hyd.
	V8-318 HD Calif.	N11Y	.035	Elec.	Elec.	TDC	TDC	10B	5.0–7.0	100 (Min.)	700	700	Hyd.	Hyd.
	V8-360 HD	N12Y	.035	Elec.	Elec.	TDC	TDC	16B	5.0–7.0	100 (Min.)	750	750	Hyd.	Hyd.
	V8-360 HD Calif.	N12Y	.035	Elec.	Elec.	4B	4B	16B	5.0–7.0	100 (Min.)	700	700	Hyd.	Hyd.

TUNE-UP SPECIFICATIONS

Year	Engine No. Cyl. Displacement (cu in.)	Spark Plugs Original Type	Gap (in.)	Distributor Point Dwell (deg)	Point Gap (in.)	Ignition Timing (±2°)(deg)▲ MT	AT	Intake Valve Opens (deg)	Fuel Pump Pressure (psi)	Compression Pressure (psi)	Idle Speed (rpm) MT	●AT	Valve Clearance (in.) In	Ex
'76	6-225 LD	BL11Y	.035	Elec.	Elec.	2B[12]	2B[12]	16B	3.5–5.0	100 (Min.)	750	750	.012	.024
	6-225 LD Calif.	BL11Y	.035	Elec.	Elec.	TDC	TDC	16B	3.5–5.0	100 (Min.)	750	750	.012	.024
	6-225 HD	BL11Y	.035	Elec.	Elec.	TDC	TDC	16B	3.5–5.0	100 (Min.)	700[13]	700[13]	.012	.024
	6-225 HD Calif.	BL11Y	.035	Elec.	Elec.	TDC	TDC	16B	3.5–5.0	100 (Min.)	750	750	.012	.024
	V8-318 LD	N11Y	.035	Elec.	Elec.	2B	2B	10B	5.0–7.0	100 (Min.)	750	750	Hyd.	Hyd.
	V8-318 LD Calif.	N11Y	.035	Elec.	Elec.	TDC	TDC	10B	5.0–7.0	100 (Min.)	750	750	Hyd.	Hyd.
	V8-318 HD-All	N11Y	.035	Elec.	Elec.	2A[14]	2A[14]	10B	5.0–7.0	100 (Min.)	750	750	Hyd.	Hyd.
	V8-360 LD	N12Y	.035	Elec.	Elec.	—	6B	18B	5.0–7.0	100 (Min.)	—	700	Hyd.	Hyd.
	V8-360 LD Calif.	N12Y	.035	Elec.	Elec.	—	4B	18B	5.0–7.0	100 (Min.)	—	700	Hyd.	Hyd.
	V8-360 HD	N12Y	.035	Elec.	Elec.	TDC[14]	TDC[14]	18B	5.0–7.0	100 (Min.)	700	700	Hyd.	Hyd.
	V8-360 HD Calif.	N12Y	.035	Elec.	Elec.	4B	4B	18B	5.0–7.0	100 (Min.)	700	700	Hyd.	Hyd.
'77	6-225 LD	RBL15Y	.035	Elec.	Elec.	2B	2B	16B	3.5–5.0	100 (Min.)	750	750	.010	.020
	6-225 LD Calif.	RBL15Y	.035	Elec.	Elec.	TDC	2A	16B	3.5–5.0	100 (Min.)	750	750	.010	.020
	6-225 HD	RBL15Y	.035	Elec.	Elec.	TDC	TDC	16B	3.5–5.0	100 (Min.)	700	700	.010	.020
	V8-318 LD	RN11Y	.035	Elec.	Elec.	2B[15]	2B[15]	10B	5.0–7.0	100 (Min.)	750	750	Hyd.	Hyd.
	V8-318 LD Calif.	RN11Y	.035	Elec.	Elec.	2B	2B	10B	5.0–7.0	100 (Min.)	750	750	Hyd.	Hyd.
	V8-318 HD	RN11Y	.035	Elec.	Elec.	2A	2A	10B	5.0–7.0	100 (Min.)	750	750	Hyd.	Hyd.
	V8-318 HD Calif.	RN11Y	.035	Elec.	Elec.	TDC	TDC	10B	5.0–7.0	100 (Min.)	700	700	Hyd.	Hyd.
	V8-360 LD	RN12Y	.035	Elec.	Elec.	—	6B	18B	5.0–7.0	100 (Min.)	—	700	Hyd.	Hyd.
	V8-360 HD	RN12Y	.035	Elec.	Elec.	2A	TDC	18B	5.0–7.0	100 (Min.)	750	700	Hyd.	Hyd.
	V8-360 HD Calif.	RN12Y	.035	Elec.	Elec.	4B	4B	18B	5.0–7.0	100 (Min.)	700	700	Hyd.	Hyd.
	V8-400 HD	RJ11Y	.035	Elec.	Elec.	2B	2B	18B	5.0–7.0	100 (Min.)	700	700	Hyd.	Hyd.
	V8-440 HD	RJ11Y	.035	Elec.	Elec.	8B	8B	18B	5.0–7.0	100 (Min.)	700	700	Hyd.	Hyd.
	V8-440 HD Calif.	RJ11Y	.035	Elec.	Elec.	8B	8B	18B	5.0–7.0	100 (Min.)	700	700	Hyd.	Hyd.
'78	6-225 LD	RBL16Y	.035	Elec.	Elec.	12B	12B	16B	3.5–5.0	100 (Min.)	750	750	.010	.020
	6-225 LD Calif.	RBL16Y	.035	Elec.	Elec.	8B	8B	16B	3.5–5.0	100 (Min.)	750	750	.010	.020
	6-225 HD	RBL11Y	.035	Elec.	Elec.	TDC	TDC	16B	3.5–5.0	100 (Min.)	700	700	.010	.020
	6-225 HD Calif.	RBL16Y	.035	Elec.	Elec.	8B	8B	16B	3.5–5.0	100 (Min.)	750	750	.010	.020
	6-243 Diesel	—	—	—	—	—	18B[22]	32B	1800[21]	426	—	650	.012	.012
	V8-318 LD	RN11Y	.035	Elec.	Elec.	12B	12B	10B	5.0–7.0	100 (Min.)	750	750	Hyd.	Hyd.
	V8-318 LD Calif.	RN11Y	.035	Elec.	Elec.	12B	12B	10B	5.0–7.0	100 (Min.)	750	750	Hyd.	Hyd.
	V8-318 HD	RN11Y	.035	Elec.	Elec.	2A	2A	10B	5.0–7.0	100 (Min.)	750	750	Hyd.	Hyd.
	V8-318 HD Calif.	RN11Y	.035	Elec.	Elec.	12B	12B	10B	5.0–7.0	100 (Min.)	750	750	Hyd.	Hyd.
	V8-360 LD	RN12Y	.035	Elec.	Elec.	—	6B	18B	5.0–7.0	100 (Min.)	—	750	Hyd.	Hyd.
	V8-360 LD Calif.	RN12Y	.035	Elec.	Elec.	6B	6B	18B	5.0–7.0	100 (Min.)	750	750	Hyd.	Hyd.
	V8-360 HD	RN12Y	.035	Elec.	Elec.	4B	4B	18B	5.0–7.0	100 (Min.)	750	750	Hyd.	Hyd.
	V8-360 HD Calif.	RN12Y	.035	Elec.	Elec.	6B[16]	6B[16]	18B	5.0–7.0	100 (Min.)	750[16]	750[16]	Hyd.	Hyd.
	V8-400 LD	OJ11Y	.035	Elec.	Elec.	—	10B	18B	5.0–7.0	100 (Min.)	—	700	Hyd.	Hyd.
	V8-400 HD	OJ11Y	.035	Elec.	Elec.	2B	2B	18B	5.0–7.0	100 (Min.)	700	700	Hyd.	Hyd.
	V8-440 HD	OJ11Y	.035	Elec.	Elec.	—	8B	18B	5.0–7.0	100 (Min.)	—	700	Hyd.	Hyd.
	V8-440 HD Calif.	OJ11Y	.035	Elec.	Elec.	—	8B	18B	5.0–7.0	100 (Min.)	—	750[17]	Hyd.	Hyd.
'79	6-225 LD	P-560PR	.035	Elec.	Elec.	12B	12B	16B	3.5–5.0	100 (Min.)	675	675	.010	.020
	6-225 LD Calif.	P-560PR	.035	Elec.	Elec.	8B	8B	16B	3.5–5.0	100 (Min.)	800	800	.010	.020
	6-225 HD	P-560PR	.035	Elec.	Elec.	12B	12B	16B	3.5–5.0	100 (Min.)	675	675	.010	.020
	6-243 Diesel	—	—	—	—	—	18B[22]	32B	1800[21]	426	—	650	.012	.012
	V8-318 LD	P-64PR	.035	Elec.	Elec.	12B	12B	10B	5.0–7.0	100 (Min.)	680	680	Hyd.	Hyd.
	V8-318 LD Calif.	P-64PR	.035	Elec.	Elec.	6B	6B[19]	10B	5.0–7.0	100 (Min.)	750	750	Hyd.	Hyd.
	V8-318 HD	P-64PR	.035	Elec.	Elec.	2A	2A[18]	10B	5.0–7.0	100 (Min.)	750	750	Hyd.	Hyd.
	V8-360 LD	P-65PR	.035	Elec.	Elec.	10B[20]	10B[20]	18B	5.0–7.0	100 (Min.)	750[20]	750[20]	Hyd.	Hyd.
	V8-360 LD Calif.	P-65PR	.035	Elec.	Elec.	10B	10B	18B	5.0–7.0	100 (Min.)	750	750	Hyd.	Hyd.
	V8-360 HD	P-65PR	.035	Elec.	Elec.	4B	4B	18B	5.0–7.0	100 (Min.)	750	750	Hyd.	Hyd.
	V8-360 HD Calif.	P-65PR	.035	Elec.	Elec.	—	4B	18B	5.0–7.0		—	750	Hyd.	Hyd.
'80	6-225 LD	560PR	.035	Elec.	Elec.	12B	12B	16B	3.5–5.0	100 (Min.)	600[23]	600[23]	.010	.020
	6-225 MD Calif.	560PR	.035	Elec.	Elec.	12B	12B	16B	3.5–5.0	100 (Min.)	800	800	.010	.020
	6-225 HD Canada	560PR	.035	Elec.	Elec.	12B	12B	16B	3.5–5.0	100 (Min.)	675	675	.010	.020
	V8-318 LD[24]	64PR	.035	Elec.	Elec.	12B	12B	10B	5.0–7.0	100 (Min.)	600	600	Hyd.	Hyd.
	V8-318 LD[25]	64PR	.035	Elec.	Elec.	10B	10B	10B	5.0–7.0	100 (Min.)	750	750	Hyd.	Hyd.

DODGE/PLYMOUTH
PICK-UPS, VANS, RAMCHARGER, TRAIL DUSTER, RAMPAGE

TUNE-UP SPECIFICATIONS

Year	Engine No. Cyl. Displacement (cu in.)	Spark Plugs Original Type	Gap (in.)	Distributor Point Dwell (deg)	Point Gap (in.)	Ignition Timing (±2°)▲ (deg) MT	AT	Intake Valve Opens (deg)	Fuel Pump Pressure (psi)	Compression Pressure (psi)	Idle Speed (rpm) MT	●AT	Valve Clearance (in.) In	Ex
	V8-318 MD Calif.	64PR	.035	Elec.	Elec.	10B	10B	10B	5.0–7.0	100 (Min.)	750	750	Hyd.	Hyd.
	V8-318 HD	64PR	.035	Elec.	Elec.	8B㉖	8B㉖	10B	5.0–7.0	100 (Min.)	750	750	Hyd.	Hyd.
	V8-360 Canada	65PR	.035	Elec.	Elec.	—	4B㉔	18B	5.0–7.0	100 (Min.)	—	750	Hyd.	Hyd.
	V8-360 Canada	65PR	.035	Elec.	Elec.	12B	12B㉗	18B	5.0–7.0	100 (Min.)	650	650	Hyd.	Hyd.
	V8-360 LD㉘	65PR	.035	Elec.	Elec.	12B	12B	18B	5.0–7.0	100 (Min.)	650	650	Hyd.	Hyd.
	V8-360 LD㉙	65PR	.035	Elec.	Elec.	—	10B	18B	5.0–7.0	100 (Min.)	—	750	Hyd.	Hyd.
	V8-360 MD㉚	65PR	.035	Elec.	Elec.	10B	10B	18B	5.0–7.0	100 (Min.)	750	750	Hyd.	Hyd.
	V8-360 HD㉚	65PR	.035	Elec.	Elec.	10B	10B	18B	5.0–7.0	100 (Min.)	750	750	Hyd.	Hyd.
	V8-360 HD	65PR	.035	Elec.	Elec.	4B	4B	18B	5.0–7.0	100 (Min.)	700	700	Hyd.	Hyd.
'81	6-225 LD	560PR	.035	Elec.	Elec.	12B	16B	6B	3.5–5.0	100 (Min.)	㉛	㉛	Hyd.	Hyd.
	6-225 HD	560PR	.035	Elec.	Elec.	12B	16B	6B	3.5–5.0	100 (Min.)	725	750	Hyd.	Hyd.
	V8-318 LD㉔	64PR	.035	Elec.	Elec.	10B	16B	10B	5.0–7.0	100 (Min.)	650	650	Hyd.	Hyd.
	V8-318 HD Canada㉔	64PR	.035	Elec.	Elec.	2A	2A	10B	5.0–7.0	100 (Min.)	750	750	Hyd.	Hyd.
	V8-318 LD㉕	64PR	.035	Elec.	Elec.	12B	16B	10B	5.0–7.0	100 (Min.)	750	750	Hyd.	Hyd.
	V8-318 HD㉕	64PR	.035	Elec.	Elec.	12B	12B	10B	5.0–7.0	100 (Min.)	750	750	Hyd.	Hyd.
	V8-360-1 LD㉕	64PR	.035	Elec.	Elec.	12B	16B	18B	5.0–7.0	100 (Min.)	600㉞	625㉞	Hyd.	Hyd.
	V8-360-1 HD㉔	64PR	.035	Elec.	Elec.	—	4B	18B	5.0–7.0	100 (Min.)	—	750	Hyd.	Hyd.
	V8-360-1 HD㉕	64PR	.035	Elec.	Elec.	—	4B	18B	5.0–7.0	100 (Min.)	—	700	Hyd.	Hyd.
	V8-360-3 HD	73SR	.035	Elec.	Elec.	—	4B㉟	18B	5.0–7.0	100 (Min.)	—	700	Hyd.	Hyd.
	V8-360-3 HD	73SR	.035	Elec.	Elec.	—	10B	18B	5.0–7.0	100 (Min.)	—	750	Hyd.	Hyd.
'82	4-135.0(2.2)	65PR	.035	Elec.	Elec.	12B	12B	14B	4.5–6.0	100 (Min.)	850	900	Hyd.	Hyd.
	6-225-1	560PR	.035	Elec.	Elec.	12B	16B	6B	3.5–5.0	100 (Min.)	600㊲	600㊳	Hyd.	Hyd.
	V8-318㉔	64PR	.035	Elec.	Elec.	12B	12B	10B	4.75–6.25	100 (Min.)	750	750	Hyd.	Hyd.
	V8-318㉕	64PR	.035	Elec.	Elec.	12B	16B	10B	4.75–6.25	100 (Min.)	750	750	Hyd.	Hyd.
	V8-360㉔	65PR	.035	Elec.	Elec.	4B	4B	18B	5.0–7.0	100 (Min.)	—	700	Hyd.	Hyd.
	V8-360㉕	65PR	.035	Elec.	Elec.	—	4B㊴	18B	5.0–7.0	100 (Min.)	—	700㊵	Hyd.	Hyd.

NOTE: The underhood specifications sticker often reflects tune-up specifications changes made in production. Sticker figures must be used if they disagree with those in this chart.

NOTE: All Canadian specifications are the same as Federal specifications unless noted otherwise.

● Manual in neutral, automatic in park.
— Not Applicable
▲ With vacuum advance disconnected and plugged.
B Before Top Dead Center
A After Top Dead Center
TDC Top Dead Center
CAP Cleaner Air Package
Fed. All states except California
(Min.) Minimum
Hyd. Hydraulic valve lifters; no service adjustment
LD Light Duty emissions
MD Medium Duty emissions
HD Heavy Duty emissions
Elec. Electronic ignition
① Without CAP—5B
② Without CAP—5B
③ Without CAP—10B
④ Automatic transmission—110–140
⑤ Without CAP—700 rpm
⑥ 800 for Canada
⑦ With ECS (Electronically Controlled Spark)—700 rpm
⑧ Can be advanced or retarded 2.5° if conditions warrant
⑨ California vehicles only—700 rpm
⑩ California vehicles only—TDC

⑪ 15 Passenger only—800 rpm
⑫ TDC for Canada
⑬ 750 for Canada
⑭ 2B for Canada
⑮ 6B for High Altitude w/auto trans.
⑯ Over 8501 GVWR—TDC @ 700 rpm
⑰ Over 8501 GVWR—700
⑱ 4 bbl for Canada—8B
⑲ For GVWR under 6,000 lbs.—8B
⑳ With 4 bbl for Canada—4B @ 700
㉑ Injector pressure
㉒ Static
㉓ Canada: MT & AT: 675
㉔ 2 barrel carb.
㉕ 4 barrel carb.
㉖ Canada HD engine w/2 bbl.: 2A
㉗ Canada w/4 bbl. and distributor 4111487: 10B
㉘ Distributor 4111947
㉙ Distributor 4111487
㉚ California
㉛ Federal: 600
    California: 800
    Canada: 725

㉜ Canada: 750
㉝ Canada: 10B
㉞ California: 750
㉟ Distributor 4091661
㊱ Distributor 4111950
㊲ Canada: M/T 725
㊳ Canada: A/T 750
㊴ California: 10B
㊵ California: 750

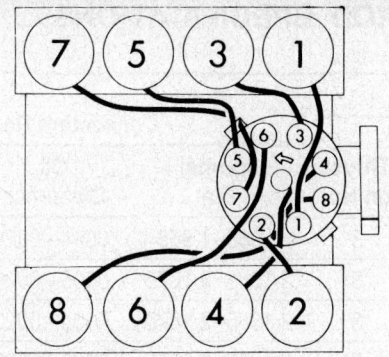

400, 440 V8 engines

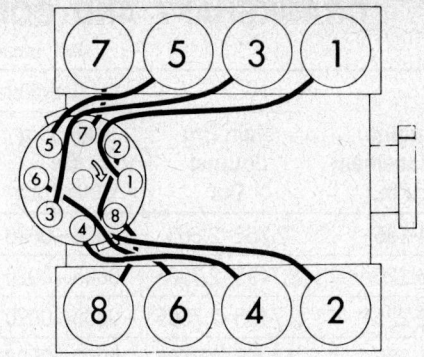

318, 360 V8 engines

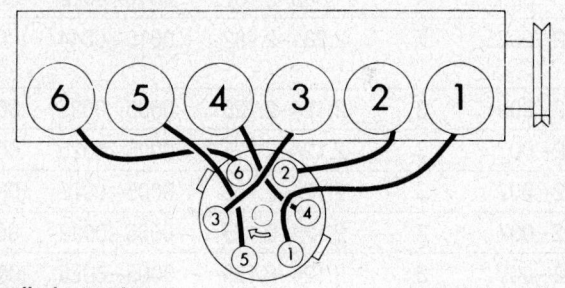

6 cylinder engines

4 cylinder engines

VALVE SPECIFICATIONS

Year	Engine Displacement (cu in.)	Seat Angle (deg)	Face Angle (deg)	Spring Test Pressure (lbs @ in.)	Spring Installed Height (in.)	Stem to Guide Clearance (in.)		Stem Diameter (in.)	
						Intake	Exhaust	Intake	Exhaust
'82	4-135.0	45	45	175 @ 1.22	1.65	.001–.003	.002–.004	.312–.313	.311–.312
'75–'82	6-225	45	④	137–150 @ 1⁵⁄₁₆	1¹¹⁄₁₆	.001–.003	.002–.004	.372–.373	.371–.372
'78–'79	6-243 Diesel	45	45	NA	1⁴⁹⁄₆₄	.002–.003	.003–.004	.314	.314
'75–'78	8-318	45	④	170–184 @1⁵⁄₁₆	1¹¹⁄₁₆	.001–.003	.002–.004	.372–.373	.371–.372
'79–'81	8-318	45	45	⑤	⑥	.001–.003	.002–.004	.372–.373	.371–.372
'82	8-318	45	45	⑨	⑨	.001–.003	.002–.004	.372–.373	.371–.372
'75	8-360	45	④	201–215 @1⁵⁄₁₆	1¹¹⁄₁₆	.001–.003	.002–.004	.372–.373	.371–.372
'76–'77	8-360	45	④	177–188 @1⁵⁄₁₆	1¹¹⁄₁₆	.001–.003	.002–.004	.372–.373	.371–.372
'78–'81	8-360	45	45	⑤	⑥	.001–.003	.002–.004	.372–.373	.371–.372
'82	8-360	45	45	⑤	⑤	.001–.003	.002–.004	.372–.373	.371–.372
'75–'78	8-400 8-440	45	45	192–208 @ 1⁷⁄₁₆	1⁵⁵⁄₆₄	.001–.003	.002–.004⑦	.372–.373	.371–.372⑧

NA—Not available
① Intake; 45°33'
   Exhaust; 43°33'
② Outer; 101 @ .878
   Inner; 49 @ .720
③ Outer; 1.28

Inner; 1.13
④ Intake; 45°
   Exhaust; 43°
⑤ Intake; 170–184 @ 1⁵⁄₁₆
   Exhaust; 181–197 @ 1¹⁄₁₆
⑥ Intake; 1¹¹⁄₁₆

Exhaust; 1³³⁄₆₄
⑦ At hot end; .001–.003 at cold end
⑧ At hot end; .372–.373 at cold end
⑨ Intake; 170–184 @ 1⁵⁄₁₆
   Exhaust; 180–194 @ 1⁵⁄₆₄

CRANKSHAFT AND CONNECTING ROD SPECIFICATIONS

(All measurements given in in.)

| Year | Engine Displacement (cu in.) | Crankshaft | | | | Connecting Rod | | |
		Main Brg Journal Dia	Main Brg Oil Clearance	Shaft End Play	Thrust on No.	Journal Dia	Oil Clearance	Side Clearance
'82	4-135	2.362–2.363	.0004–.0026	.002–.007	3	1.968–1.969	.0004–.0026	.005–.015
'75–'76	6-225	2.7495–2.7505	.0005–.0020	.002–.009	3	2.1865–2.1875	.0005–.0020	.006–.012
'77–'78	6-225	2.7495–2.7505	.0005–.0020	.002–.009	3	2.1865–2.1875	.0005–.0020	.006–.025
'79–'80	6-225	2.7495–2.7505	.0002–.0022	.002–.009	3	2.1865–2.1875	.0002–.0022	.006–.025
'81	6-225	2.7495–2.7505	.0010–.0025	.0035–.0095	3	2.1865–2.1875	.0010–.0022	.007–.013
'82	6-225	2.7495–2.7505	.0010–.0025	.0035–.0095	3	2.1865–2.1875	.0010–.0022	.007–.013
'78–'79	6-243 Diesel	2.754–2.755	.0012–.0035	.0012–.0035	7	2.281–2.282	.0015–.0044	.006–.018
'75–'76	8-318	2.4995–2.5005	.0005–.0020	.002–.009	3	2.124–2.125	.0005–.0025	.006–.014
'77–'80	8-318	2.4995–2.5005	.0005–.0020	.002–.007	3	2.124–2.125	.0005–.0025	.006–.014
'81	8-318	2.4995–2.5005	.0005–.0020	.002–.007	3	2.124–2.125	.0005–.0022	.006–.014
'82	8-318	2.4995–2.5005	.0005–.0020	.002–.007	3	2.124–2.125	.0005–.0022	.006–.014
'75–'80	8-360	2.8095–2.8105	.0005–.0020	.002–.009	3	2.124–2.125	.0005–.0025	.006–.014
'81	8-360	2.8095–2.8105	.0005–.0020	.002–.009	3	2.124–2.125	.0005–.0022	.006–.014
'82	8-360	2.8095–2.8105	.0005–.0020	.002–.009	3	2.124–2.125	.0005–.0022	.006–.014
'75–'78	8-400	2.6245–2.6255	.0005–.0020	.002–.009	3	2.3750–2.3760	.0005–.0025	.009–.017
'75–'78	8-440	2.7495–2.7505	.0005–.0020	.002–.009	3	2.3750–2.3760	.0005–.0030	.009–.017

RING GAP

| Year | Engine Displacement (cu in.) | Top Compression (in.) | | Bottom Compression (in.) | | Oil Control (in.) Steel | |
		Min	Max	Min	Max	Min	Max
'75–'82	4-135.0	.011	.021	.011	.021	—	—
	6-225	.010	.020	.010	.020	.015	.055
	8-318	.010	.020	.010	.020	.015	.055
	8-360	.010	.020	.010	.020	.015	.055
	8-400	.013	.023	0.13	.023	.015	.055
	8-440	.013	.023	.013	.023	.015	.055

NOTE: Gap on all rings in the diesel engine is .012–.020

RING SIDE CLEARANCE

Year	Engine Displacement (cu in.)	Top Compression (in.)		Bottom Compression (in.)		Oil Control (in.) Steel	
		Min	Max	Min	Max	Min	Max
'75–'82	4-135.0	.0015	.0031	.0015	.0037	.0008	.0020
	6-225	.0015	.0030	.0015	.0030	.0002	.0050
	8-318	.0015	.0030	.0015	.0030	.0002	.0050
	8-360	.0015	.0030	.0015	.0030	.0002	.0050
	8-400	.0015	.0030	.0015	.0030	.0000	.0050
	8-440	.0015	.0030	.0015	.0030	.0000	.0050

NOTE: Side clearance for all rings in the diesel engine is .001–.002

PISTON CLEARANCE

Year	Engine Displacement (cu in.)	Measured at top of Skirt (in.)
'75–'82	225	.0005–.0015
	318	.0005–.0015
	360	.0005–.0015
'82	135.0	.0005–.0240
'75–'78	400	.0003–.0013
	440	.0003–.0013
'78–'79	243 Diesel	.0008–.0020

TORQUE SPECIFICATIONS

Year	Engine Displacement (cu in.)	Cylinder Head Bolts	Rod Bearing Bolts	Main Bearing Bolts	Crankshaft Bolt	Flywheel-to Crankshaft Bolts	Manifold	
							Intake	Exhaust
'82	4-135	30⑤	40⑤	30⑤	50	55	15	15
'75–'82	6-225	70	45	85	Press fit	55	20②	10
'78–'79	Diesel	90③	65③	69③④	289	80	—	—
'75–'77	8-318 8-360	95	45	85	100	55	40	20①
'78–'82	8-318 8-360	105	45	85	100	55	40	20①
'75–'78	8-400 8-440	70	45	85	135	55	45	30

① 15 ft lbs for nuts
② 1976 and later—stud-30; nut-20
③ Bolts must be oiled
④ 80 ft lbs with "H" mark
⑤ plus ¼ turn more
⑥ 50 with auto. trans.

DODGE/PLYMOUTH
PICK-UPS, VANS, RAMCHARGER, TRAIL DUSTER, RAMPAGE

CAPACITIES

Year	Engine Displacement Cu In. No. of Cyls	Engine Crankcase (qts) With Filter	Engine Crankcase (qts) Without Filter	Transmission (pts) Manual	Transmission (pts) Automatic	Drive Axle (pts)	Gasoline Tank (gals)	Cooling System (qts)
'75	6-225	6	5	4½	19	⑤	23/36⑨	13②
	V8-318	6	5	4¼	19	⑤	23/36⑨	17
	V8-360	6	5	4¼	19	⑤	23/36⑨	16②
'76–'77	6-225	6	5	⑥	19⑦	⑤	22/36⑨	13②
	V8-318	6	5	⑥	19⑦	⑤	22/36⑨	17
	V8-360	6	5	⑥	19⑦	⑤	22/36⑨	16②
	V8-400,440	6	5	⑥	19⑦	⑤	22/36⑨	15½②
'78	6-225	6	5	⑥	19	⑤	22/36⑨	13
	243 Diesel	8	7	⑥	19	⑤	18/20⑨	13
	V8-318	6	5	⑥	19	⑤	22/36⑨	17
	V8-360	6	5	⑥	19	⑤	22/36⑨	16
	V8-400,440	6	5	⑥	19	⑤	22/36⑨	14½
'79–'80	6-225	6	5	⑥	16⅔	⑤	22/36⑨	12⑧
	V8-318	6	5	⑥	16⅔	⑤	22/36⑨	16⑧
	V8-360	6	5	⑥	16⅔	⑤	22/36⑨	14½⑧
'81	6-225	6	5	⑥	⑩	⑤	20/30⑨	12②
	V8-318	6	5	⑥	⑩	⑤	20/30⑨	16②
	V8-360	6	5	⑥	⑩	⑤	20/30⑨	14½②
'82	4cyl-2.2	4	3.5	4	15⑪	⑪	13	7
	6-225	6	5	⑥	⑩	⑤	22/36⑨	12②
	V8-318	6	5	⑥	⑩	⑤	22/36⑨	16②
	V8-360	6	5	⑥	⑩	⑤	22/36⑨	14½②

① A-903 3 spd (Std)—6 pts
   A-745 3 spd (Opt)—3¼ pts
② Add 1 qt for auxiliary rear heater, air conditioning, or Heavy Duty cooling; add 2 qts for A/C with 400 or 440 V8
③ 100 and 200 (Chrysler)—4¼ pts
   300 (Spicer)—6 pts
④ 100 and 200 (Chrysler)—4¼ pts
   300 (Spicer)—5½ pts
⑤ See Rear Axle Identification Chart
⑥ 4¼ with A-230 heavy duty three speed, 3½ with A-390 top-cover three speed, 7 with 1976 Overdrive-4, 7.5 with 1977 and later Overdrive-4: NP435, 4 speed, 7.5
⑦ 1977—16⅔ pts
⑧ Add 2 qts. with A/C or increased cooling
⑨ Models vary: 1981 Sports models: 35
⑩ A904T/A999: 17.1—A727:7.7 without converter drain
⑪ Auto Transaxle differential; 2.4 pts.

WHEEL ALIGNMENT SPECIFICATIONS

Year	Model	Caster (Deg.)*	Camber (Deg.)	Toe-in (in.)	King Pin Inclination (Deg.)
'75–'81	D100	0 to +½	0 to +½	⅟16-⅛	—
'75–'78	AW, PW, W100	3	1½	0-⅛	7½
'75–'81	200/300/250/350	½	+¼	⅟16-⅛	—
'75–'81	D200/250	0 to +½	0 to +½	⅟16-⅛	—
'75–'81	W200①	3	1½	0-⅛	7½
'75–'81	D300/350	0 to +½	0 to +½	⅟16-⅛	—
'75–'81	W300①	3	½	0-⅛	8½
'82	Rampage	—	−¼ to +¾	⅟16-⅛	—
'82	B15/B350 PB150/PB350	+1¼ to +3¼	0 to +1	0 to +¼	—
'82	150/350	+¼	+½	⅛	—

① Use W300 figures for W200 with Spicer 60 or 70F front axle.

NOTE: Rampage, Ramcharger and Trailduster service procedures are the same as those for conventional trucks, except where specific and separate procedures are given.

TUNE UP

Spark Plugs

The spark plugs should be checked frequently, especially when the truck is operated under constant load conditions. Rough idle, hard starting, frequent engine miss at high speed or physical deterioration of the plug are all indications that the plugs should be replaced.

REMOVAL AND INSTALLATION

1. Raise the hood. Thoroughly clean the area around each spark plug.

NOTE: Label each plug wire to avoid location confusion.

2. Remove the plug wire by twisting and pulling on the boot. DO NOT pull on the wire itself.

3. Use a spark plug socket, extension (if necessary) and a ratchet to remove the spark plug.

4. Compare the spark plugs removed with the illustrations in the ignition repair unit section to help spot any mechanical problems.

5. If the old spark plugs are judged reusable, clean them with a stiff brush or sandblast them on a plug cleaning machine.

6. Check the gap on both used and new plugs before installation. The ground (side) electrode must be parallel to the center electrode. If the center or ground electrodes have worn unevenly, level them with a file.

7. Install the spark plug into the engine and tighten it finger tight. Take care not to crossthread.

NOTE: Some engines do not use gaskets on the spark plugs. The plugs are provided with a tapered seat to seal the cylinder head.

8. Tighten the spark plugs to the required torque; 30 ft. lbs. for plugs that use gaskets. 10 ft. lbs. for plugs with tapered seats.

9. Connect each spark plug wire, make sure the wire and boot are firmly seated.

10. While you are checking or replacing the spark plugs, examine the plug wires. Replace any that have cracked or cut insulation or are in any way damaged.

Electronic Ignition

An electronic ignition system is installed as standard equipment. The distributor housing, cap, rotor and advance unit are the same used on point type systems. A magnetic pickup and control (reluctor) have replaced the points and distributor cam. A condenser is no longer necessary. The only maintenance required with electronic ignition is inspection of the wiring, cap, rotor and periodic cleaning and changing of the spark plugs.

In later model years, depending on the model, the distributor might have two pickups. One controls the start mode; the other, the run mode. If the distributor needs parts

replacement or servicing, maintaining the proper air gap between the pickup and reluctor is necessary.

The electronic ignition system eliminates the contact points and the need to set dwell. Hence, the dwell is non-adjustable and cannot be altered in any way.

AIR GAP-EXCEPT 4 CYL ENGINES

The air gap adjustment is not a regular maintenance item. However, if the gap is too wide a no start condition can exist.

NOTE: When checking the pickup air gap use a non-magnetic feeler gauge. If a non-magnetic feeler-gauge is not available, use brass shim stock of the proper thickness.

NOTE: The reluctor teeth may appear ragged at the edges, but no attempt should be made to clean them. A sharp edge is necessary to quickly decrease the magnetic field and induce negative voltage in the pickup coil. If the teeth are rounded, the voltage signal to the control unit may be erratic.

--- CAUTION ---

Do not touch the round transistor mounted on the control unit when the ignition switch is "On", it can produce a nasty electrical shock.

AIR GAP ADJUSTMENT

On 1975 and 1976 trucks, the air gap is adjusted to .008 inch. 1977 and later models with a single pickup require .006 inch adjustment. Dual pickup equipped dis-

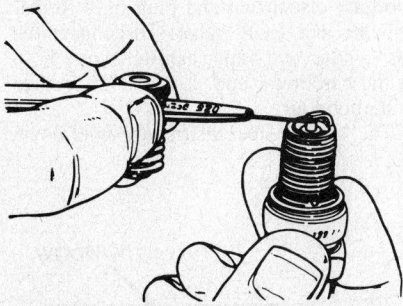

Check the spark plug gap with a wire gauge

Adjust the spark plug with a bending tool

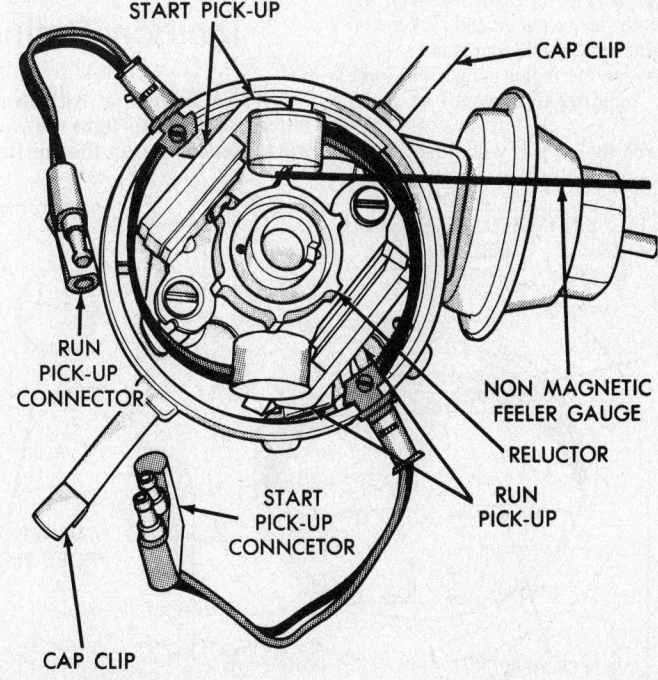

Dual pickup distributor

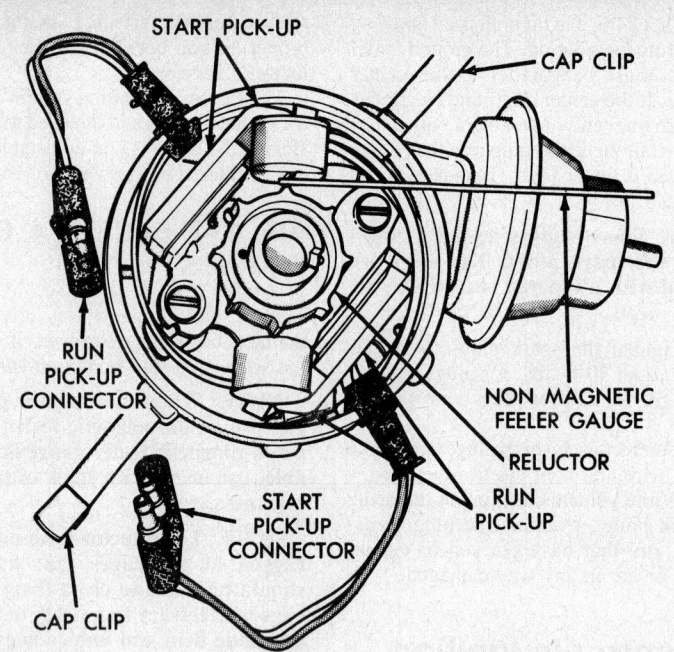

Air gap adjustment

tributors require; Start pickup (identified by a two male prong distributor connector) .006 inch: Run pickup (identified by a male and female connector) .012 inch.

SINGLE PICKUP DISTRIBUTOR

1. Align a reluctor tooth with the pickup coil tooth. Loosen the pickup coil holddown screw.

2. Insert a non-magnetic feeler gauge of the proper size between the reluctor tooth and the pickup coil tooth. Adjust the air gap so that contact is made between the reluctor tooth, feeler gauge and pickup coil tooth. Tighten the holddown screw.

3. Remove the feeler gauge. No force should be required to remove the feeler gauge.

4. Check the air gap with a larger size

(about .002 inch larger) feeler gauge. It should not fit into the air gap so do not try to force it.

DUAL PICKUP DISTRIBUTOR

The procedure is the same as for the single pickup distributor. Adjust the start pickup first and then the run pickup. Test each adjustment with a larger feeler gauge as mentioned in the single pickup distributor air gap adjustment.

Ignition Timing

NOTE: On engines with electronic ignition, your timing light may or may not work, depending on the construction of

the light. Consult the manufacturer of the light if in doubt.

ADJUSTMENT

4-Cylinder Engines

The ignition is timed on No. 1 cylinder, the left-hand side, facing the truck.

1. Connect a timing light according to the manufacturer's instructions.

2. Run the engine to normal operating temperature.

3. Make sure the idle speed is correct.

4. Loosen the distributor holddown screw just enough so that the distributor can be rotated.

5. Ground the carburetor switch (if equipped). Disconnect and plug the vacuum line(s) to the distributor control.

6. Remove the timing hole access cover and aim the timing light at the hole in the clutch housing. Carefully rotate the distributor until the timing marks are aligned.

7. Tighten the distributor and recheck the timing.

8. Check, and if necessary adjust, the idle speed.

6 and 8 Cylinder Engines

1. Connect a timing light and a tachometer. Never puncture the spark plug wires or boots with a probe. Always use the proper adapters.

2. Start the engine and allow it to reach normal operating temperature.

3. Set the idle speed.

4. Put the transmission in Neutral; Park for automatic.

5. Disconnect and plug the vacuum line(s) at the distributor. **1981 and later models;** disconnect and plug lines to distributor and EGR valve. Disconnect the PCV valve and vapor canister purge hose at the carburetor end. Leave both open to underhood air.

6. Loosen the distributor hold-down

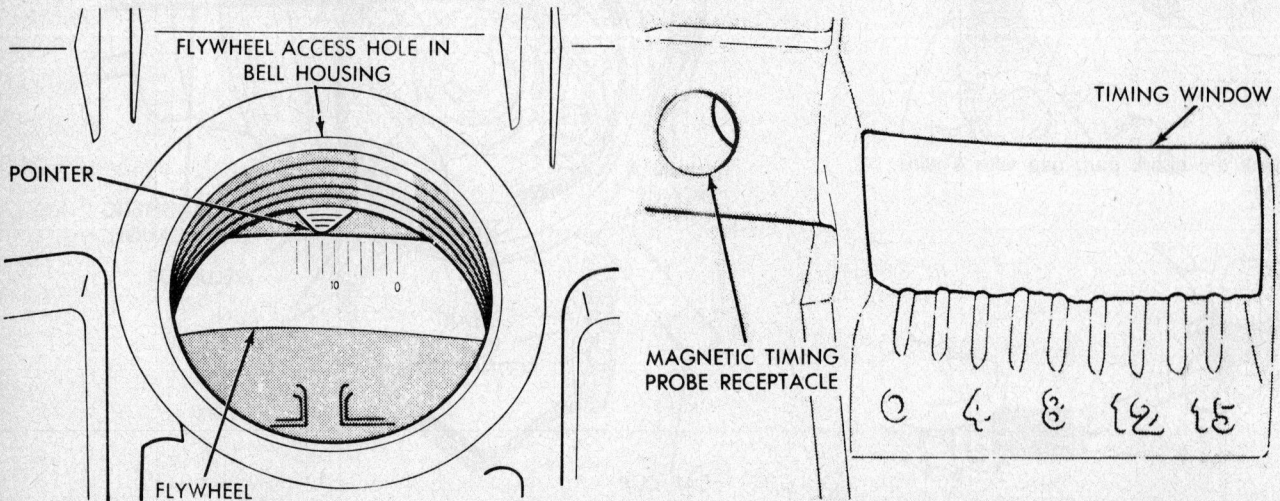

4 cylinder timing mark variations

Typical ignition timing marks—6 cylinder engine

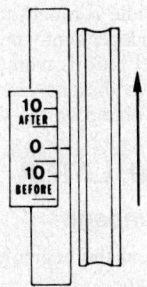

Typical timing marks—V8 engine

screw just enough to permit the distributor to be turned.

7. Aim the timing light at the timing marks on the case cover. Slowly turn the distributor to align the marks to the proper setting.

8. Turn the engine off and tighten the distributor hold-down bolt. Be careful not to move the distributor while you are tightening.

9. Start the engine and recheck the timing.

10. When the timing is correct, reconnect the vacuum line to the distributor.

11. If the engine idle speed has changed, readjust the carburetor. Do not reset the timing.

12. Remove the timing light from the engine.

MOTOR HOME CHASSIS

On some models there is a hole in the torque converter housing to see the timing marks that are located on the converter. The corresponding timing marks are located on the housing. Timing light hook up is the same as on crankshaft pulley timing.

Valve Lash
GASOLINE ENGINES

Valve lash adjustment is necessary on the 6 cylinder 225 engine through 1980.

The 6 cylinder 225 engine (through 1980) requires adjustment at least every 20,000 miles, or when there is excessive valve train noise.

No valve lash adjustment is necessary or possible on any other Chrysler-built engine. Hydraulic valve lifters automatically maintain zero clearance. After engine reassembly these lifters adjust themselves as soon as engine oil pressure builds up.

CAUTION

Do not set the valve lash closer than specified in an attempt to quiet the valve mechanism. This will result in burned valves.

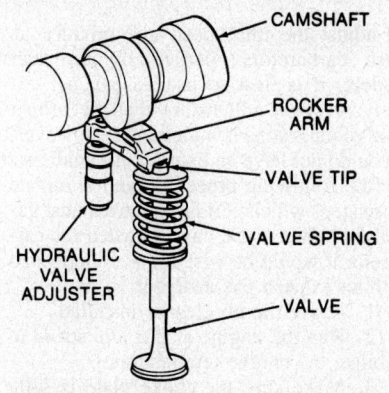

Hydraulic valve adjuster used on (2.2) 4 cylinder engine

6 CYLINDER-225 (THROUGH 1980)

1. The engine must be at normal operating temperature. Mark the crankshaft pulley into three equal 120° segments, starting at the TDC mark.

2. Remove the valve (rocker) cover and the distributor cap.

3. Set the engine at TDC on the no. 1 cylinder by aligning the mark on the crank-

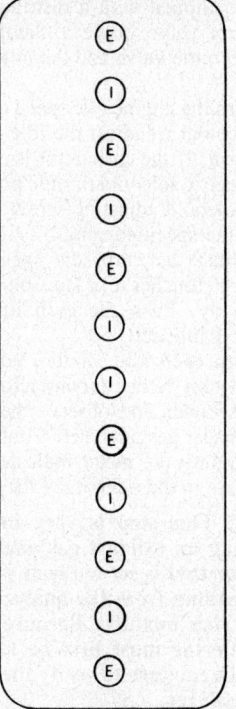

FRONT OF ENGINE

E = EXHAUST
I = INTAKE

Valve location—6 cylinder engine

shaft pulley with the "0" mark on the timing cover pointer. The distributor rotor should point at the position of the no. 1 spark plug wire in the distributor cap. Both rocker arms on the no. 1 cylinder should be free to move slightly.

4. The cylinders are numbered from the front to rear.

5. The lash is measured between the rocker arm and the end of the valve. To check the lash, insert the correct size feeler gauge between the rocker arm and the valve. Press down lightly on the other end of the rocker arm. If the gauge cannot be inserted, loosen the self-locking adjustment nut on the top of the rocker arm. Tighten the nut until the gauge can just be inserted and withdrawn without buckling.

6. After both valves for the no. 1 cylinder are adjusted, turn the engine so that the pulley turns 120° in the normal direction of rotation (clockwise). The distributor rotor will turn 60°, since it turns at half engine speed.

7. Check that the rocker arms are free and adjust the valves for the next cylinder in the firing order, 5. The firing order is 1-5-3-6-2-4.

8. Turn the engine 120° to adjust each of the remaining cylinders in the firing order. When you are done the crankshaft will have made two complete revolutions (720°) and the distributor rotor one complete revolution (360°).

9. Replace the rocker cover with a new gasket. Replace the distributor cap. Start the engine and check for leaks.

DIESEL ENGINE

Valve adjustment is required on the diesel engine every 36,000 miles.

CAUTION

Do not set the valve lash closer than specified in an attempt to quiet the lifters. This will only result in burned valves.

1. The engine must be cold for this adjustment. Mark the crankshaft pulley into three equal 120° sections, starting at the TDC or "0" mark.

2. Remove the valve cover.

3. Disconnect the fuel line from the injector on cylinder no. 1. Be very careful not to kink the line.

4. Using a socket and a breaker bar on the crankshaft bolt, turn the engine in the same direction as it normally runs until the "0" mark on the crankshaft damper rear face is aligned with the pointer on the bottom of the timing gear case. As you are turning, keep an eye on the fuel line that was disconnected. Fuel will squirt out of the line a few degrees before you reach the "0" mark. If it doesn't squirt out, you've got the wrong cylinder at TDC. Turn the engine another 360° (one revolution) and you will have no. 1 at TDC.

5. The cylinders are numbered from front to rear.

6. The lash is measured between the rocker arm and the end of the valve. To check the lash, insert a .012 in. feeler gauge between the rocker arm and the valve. Adjust the proper clearance by loosening the locknut on the rocker arm and turning the adjusting screw. After the adjustment is made, tighten the locknut and recheck the clearance to be sure it did not change as the locknut was being tightened.

7. After both valves for the no. 1 cylinder are adjusted, turn the engine so that the pulley turns 120° in the normal direction of rotation (clockwise). The distributor rotor will turn 60°, since it turns at half engine speed.

8. Check that the rocker arms are free and adjust the valves for the next cylinder in the firing order, 5. The firing order is 1-5-3-6-2-4.

9. Turn the engine 120° to adjust each of the remaining cylinders in the firing order. When you are done the crankshaft will have made two complete revolutions (720°).

10. Replace the rocker cover with a new gasket. Attach the fuel line to the injector. Start the engine and check for leaks.

Carburetor

IDLE SPEED AND MIXTURE ADJUSTMENT

Before suspecting the carburetor as the cause of poor performance or rough idle, check the ignition system thoroughly, including the distributor, timing, spark plugs and wires. Also check the air cleaner, evaporative emission system, PCV system, EGR valve and engine compression. Check the intake manifold, vacuum hoses and other vacuum connections for leaks and cracks.

Mixture, on today's carburetors, is preset at the factory and tampering with the mixture screw will produce little change. Some carburetors have hidden mixture screws which makes adjustment impossible unless special equipment is used.

When performing a tune-up, adjust the idle speed to the specified rpm (tachometer connected), using the idle speed screw or the solenoid adjustment.

NOTE: Beginning in 1977 for 49 state models and in 1978 for California models, the use of a propane enrichment system is necessary to adjust the idle speed and mixture. Since it is not feasible to buy a tank of propane and the necessary attachments for one or two carburetor adjustments, the idle speed and mixture adjustments for trucks requiring propane are not covered here.

1975–76 (THROUGH 1977 IN CALIFORNIA)—WITH CAP (CLEANER AIR PACKAGE) OR CAS (CLEANER AIR SYSTEM)

To adjust the idle speed and mixture on these carburetors, particularly on later models, it is best to use an exhaust gas analyzer. This will insure that the proper level of emissions is maintained. However, if you do not have an exhaust gas analyzer, use the following procedure and eliminate those steps which pertain to the exhaust gas analyzer. When you have adjusted the carburetor it would be wise to have it checked with an exhaust gas analyzer.

1. Leave the air cleaner installed.
2. Run the engine at fast idle speed to stabilize the engine temperature.
3. Make sure the choke plate is fully opened.
4. Connect a tachometer to the engine, following the manufacturer's instructions.
5. Connect an exhaust gas analyzer and insert the probe as far into the tailpipe as possible. On vehicles with dual exhaust, insert the probe into the left side pipe, since this is the side with the heat riser.
6. Check the ignition timing and set it to specification if necessary.
7. If equipped with air conditioning, turn the air conditioner off. On 6-cylinder engines, turn the high beam lights on.
8. Put the transmission in Neutral, Park for automatic. Make sure the hot idle compensator valve is fully seated.
9. If equipped with a distributor vacuum control valve, place a clamp on the line between the valve and the intake manifold.
10. Turn the engine idle speed adjusting screw in or out to adjust the idle speed to specification. If the carburetor is equipped with an electric solenoid throttle positioner, turn the solenoid adjusting screw in or out to obtain the specified rpm.
11. Adjust the curb idle speed screw until it just touches the stop on the carburetor body. Back the curb idle speed screw out 1 full turn.
12. Turn each idle mixture adjustment screw 1/16 turn richer (counterclockwise). Wait 10 seconds and observe the reading on the exhaust gas analyzer. Continue this procedure until the meter indicates a definite increase in the richness of the mixture.

NOTE: This step is very important when using an exhaust gas analyzer. A carburetor that is set too lean will cause a false reading from the analyzer, indicating a rich mixture. Because of this, the carburetor must first be known to have a rich mixture to verify the reading on the analyzer.

13. After verifying the reading on the meter, adjust the mixture screws to obtain an air/fuel ratio of 14.2:1. Turn the mixture screws clockwise (leaner) to raise the meter reading or counterclockwise (richer) to lower the meter reading.

NOTE: On 1975–77 models, adjust to get the air/fuel ratio and percentage of CO indicated on the engine compartment sticker.

14. If the idle speed changes as the mixture screws are adjusted, adjust the speed to specification (see step 10) and readjust the mixture so that the specified air/fuel ratio is maintained at the specified idle speed. If the idle is rough, the screws may be adjusted independently provided that the 14.2:1 air/fuel ratio is maintained.

15. Remove the analyzer, the tachometer, and the clamp on the vacuum line.

1977 AND LATER
Except Rampage

See the Note at the beginning of the Carburetor section.

Rampage

2.2 ENGINE

Chrysler recommends the use of a propane enrichment procedure to adjust the mixture. The equipment needed for this procedure is not readily available to the general public. An alternate method recommended by Chrysler is with the use of an exhaust gas analyzer. If this equipment is not available, and a mixture adjustment must be performed, follow this procedure:

1. Run engine to normal operating temperature.
2. Place the transmission in neutral (Park, if automatic), turn off the lights and air conditioning and make certain that the electric cooling fan is operating.
3. Disconnect the EGR vacuum line, and ground the carburetor idle stop switch (if equipped) with a jumper wire.
4. Connect tachometer according to the manufacturer's specifications.
5. Adjust the idle screw to achieve the curb idle figure listed on the underhood sticker.
6. Back out the mixture screw to achieve the fastest possible idle.
7. Adjust the idle screw to the specified curb idle speed.

FAST IDLE ADJUSTMENT
2.2 Engine

1. Remove the top of the air cleaner.
2. Disconnect and plug the EGR vacuum line.
3. Plug any open vacuum lines, which were connected to the air cleaner.
4. Do not disconnect the vacuum line to the spark control computer. Instead, use a jumper wire to ground the idle stop switch. The air conditioning should be off.

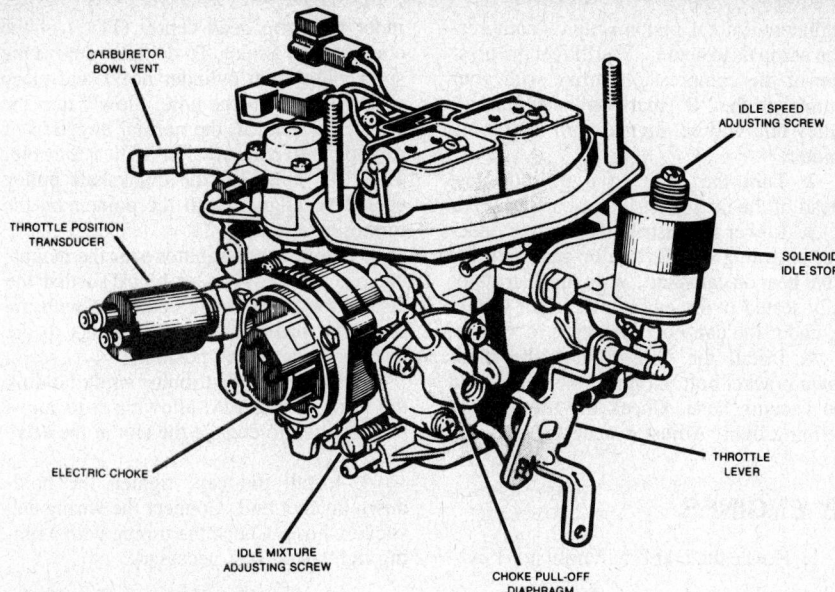

Typical 4 cylinder carburetor

4. Test the above procedure by disconnecting the solenoid wire at the connector. Be sure not to let the lead short to the engine. The solenoid should de-energize and idle speed should drop down below normal. Now reconnect the wire. After you reconnect the solenoid, move the throttle linkage by hand since the solenoid isn't strong enough to move it.

ENGINE ELECTRICAL

Distributor

REMOVAL AND INSTALLATION

1. Remove splash shield (if equipped).

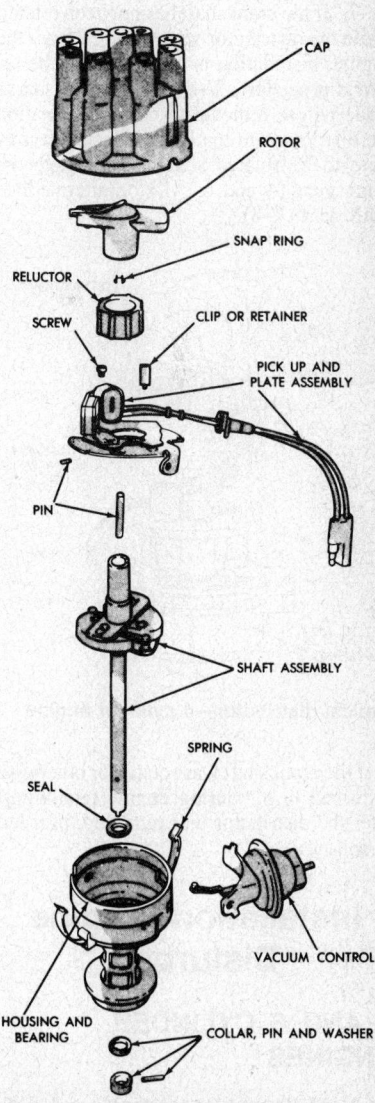

Typical single pickup distributor

5. Disconnect the engine cooling fan at the radiator and complete the circuit at the plug with a jumper wire to energize the fan.

6. Set the brake, place the transmission in neutral and position the first step of the fast idle cam under the adjusting screw.

7. Connect a tachometer according to the manufacturer's specifications.

8. Start the engine and observe the idle speed. With the choke fully open, the speed should remain steady. If it gradually increases, the idle stop switch is not properly grounded.

9. Turn the adjusting screw to give 1100 rpm.

10. Operate the throttle linkage a few times and return the screw to the first cam step to recheck rpm.

THROTTLE POSITION TRANSDUCER ADJUSTMENT

2.2 Engine

1. Disconnect the wiring from transducer.

2. Loosen the locknut and turn the transducer until a gap of $35/64$ inch is obtained between the transducer and the mounting bracket.

3. Tighten the locknut.

IDLE SPEED SOLENOID ADJUSTMENT

This solenoid is energized whenever the ignition circuit is on. Its function is to allow the throttle plates to close farther when the ignition is switched off, thereby preventing engine over-running.

1. Bring the engine to operating temperature and attach a tachometer.

2. With the engine running, adjust the solenoid screw to the proper rpm.

3. Adjust the slow curb idle screw until the screw end just contacts the stop on the carburetor body. Back the screw off one full turn.

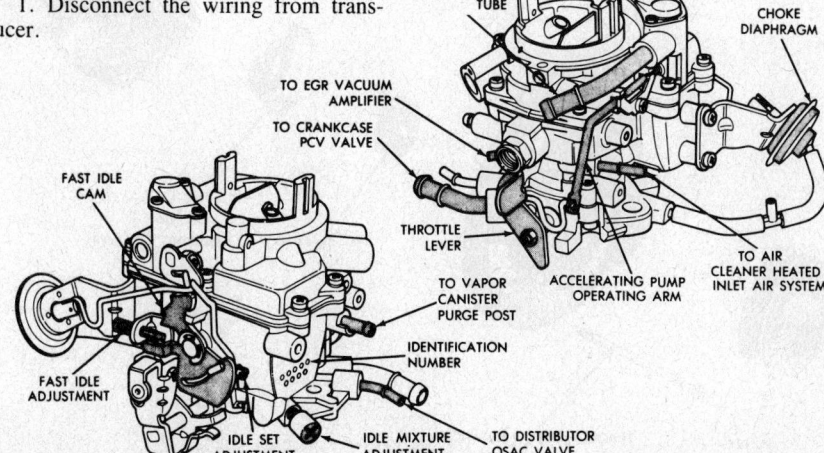

Typical Holley 2 barrel carburetor

Disconnect the vacuum line(s) at the distributor.

2. Disconnect the pickup lead wire connector or connectors from the wiring harness.

3. Unfasten the clips or screws that retain the distributor cap and lift off the cap.

4. Bump the engine around until the rotor is pointing at no. 1 cylinder firing position and the timing marks on the front case and crank pulley are aligned. Disconnect the negative battery cable from the battery.

5. Mark the distributor body and the engine block to indicate the position of the distributor in the block. Mark the distributor body to indicate the rotor position. These marks are used as guides when installing the distributor.

6. Remove the distributor holddown bolt and bracket. Carefully lift the distributor from the engine. The shaft may rotate slightly as the distributor is removed. Make a note of where the movement stops. That point is where the rotor must point when the distributor is reinstalled into the block.

7. If the crankshaft has not been rotated while the distributor was removed from the engine, installation is the reverse of the removal procedure. Use the reference marks made before removal to correctly position the distributor in the block. The shaft may have to be rotated slightly to engage the came gear (4 and 6 cyl.) or intermediate shaft gear (V-8).

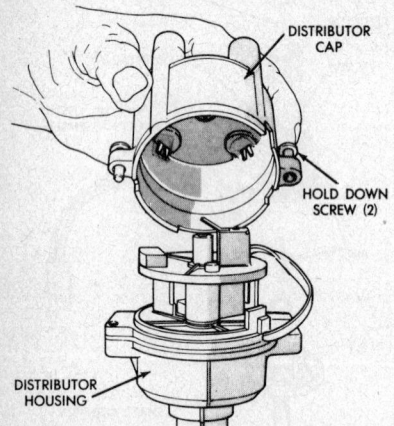

Typical distributor—4 cylinder engine

If the crankshaft was rotated or otherwise disturbed (e.g., during engine rebuilding) after the distributor was removed, proceed as follows.

Installation—Engine Disturbed

4 AND 6 CYLINDER ENGINES

1. Remove no. 1 spark plug and, with your thumb plugging the hole, rotate the engine until no. 1 piston is up on compression at top dead center. You'll feel the pressure of the compression stroke with your thumb and the "0" mark on the crankshaft pulley hub will be aligned with the timing pointer.

2. Turn the rotor to a position just ahead of the no. 1 distributor cap terminal.

3. Lower the distributor into the opening, engaging the distributor gear with the drive gear on camshaft. With the distributor fully seated in the engine, the rotor should be under the cap no. 1 tower.

4. Install the cap, tighten the holddown bracket bolt. Connect the wiring and the vacuum hose. Check the timing with a timing light. Adjust if necessary.

V8 ENGINES

1. Rotate the crankshaft until no. 1 cylinder is at top dead center (TDC) of the compression stroke. To do this, remove the spark plug from cylinder no. 1 and place your thumb over the hole. Slowly turn the engine by hand in the normal direction of rotation until compression is felt at the hole. The "0" mark on the crankshaft pulley should be aligned with the pointer on the timing case cover.

2. Hold the distributor over the mounting pad on the cylinder block so that the distributor body flange coincides with the mounting pad and the rotor points to the no. 1 cylinder firing position.

3. Install the distributor while holding the rotor in position, allowing it to move only enough to engage the slot in the drive gear.

4. Install the cap, tighten the holddown bracket bolt. Connect the wiring and vacuum hose. Check the timing with a timing light. Adjust if necessary.

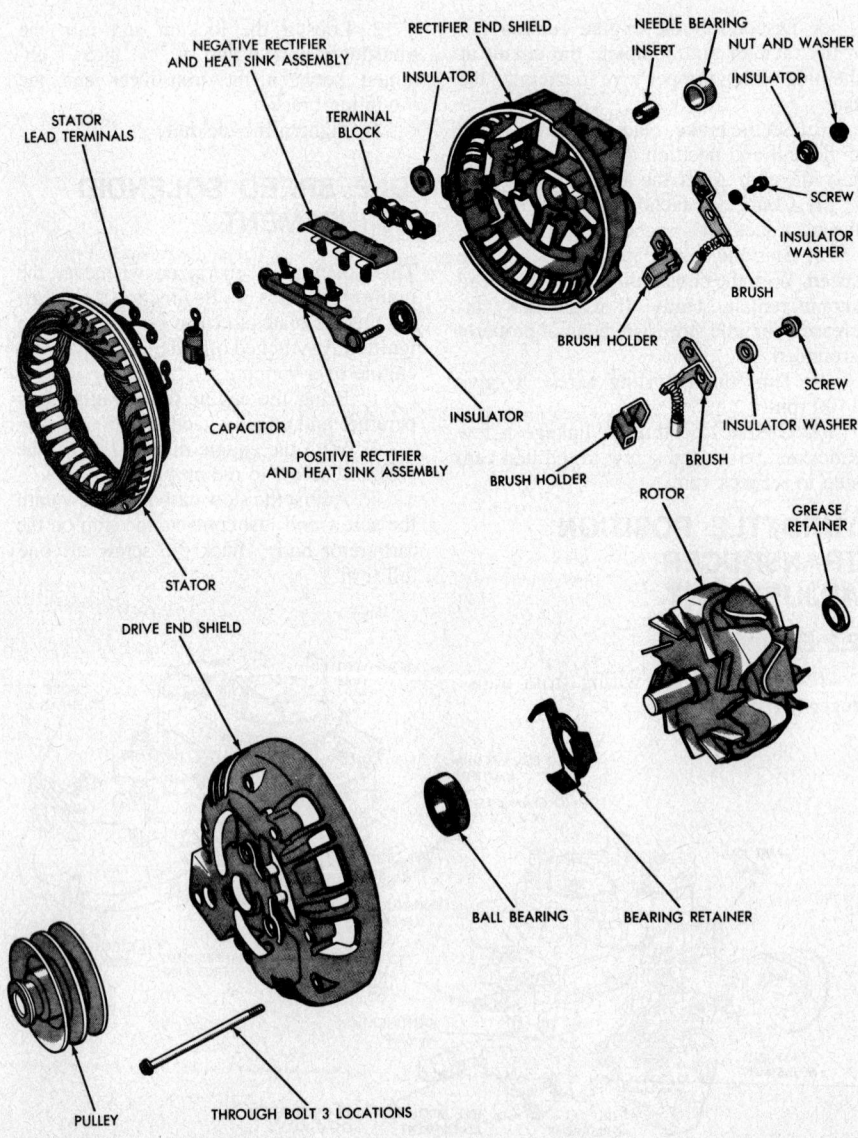

Exploded view of conventional alternator

Alternator

ALTERNATOR PRECAUTIONS

The following are a few precautions to observe when servicing the alternator.
1. Never switch battery polarity.
2. When installing a battery, always connect the non-grounded (positive) terminal first.
3. Never disconnect the battery while the engine is running.
4. If the molded connector is disconnected from the alternator, do not ground the hot wire.
5. Never run the alternator with the main output cable disconnected.
6. Never electric weld around the truck without disconnecting the alternator.
7. Never apply any voltage in excess of battery voltage during testing.
8. Never "jump" a battery for starting purposes with more than 12 volts.

REMOVAL AND INSTALLATION

1. Disconnect the battery ground cable at the battery.
2. Disconnect and label the alternator output (BATT) and field (FLD) leads and disconnect the ground wire.
3. Loosen the alternator adjusting bolt and swing the alternator in toward the engine. Disengage the alternator drive belt.
4. Remove the alternator mounting bolts and remove the alternator from the vehicle.
5. Installation is the reverse of removal. Be sure to connect all ground wires and leads securely.

6. Adjust the belt tension.

Belt Tension Adjustment

NOTE: On some models it may be necessary to remove the lower splash shield to gain clearance when installing a new drive belt.

Belt tension should be checked with a gauge made for the purpose. If a gauge is not available, tension can be checked with moderate thumb pressure applied to the belt

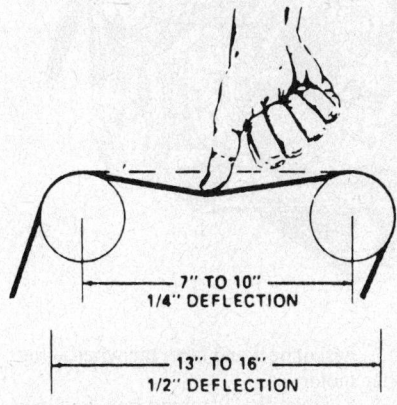

Checking drive belt deflection

at its longest span midway between pulleys. If the belt has a free span less than twelve inches, it should deflect approximately $\frac{1}{4}$ inch. If the span is longer than twelve inches, deflection can range between $\frac{1}{4}$ and $\frac{3}{8}$ inches.

To adjust or replace belts:
1. Loosen the driven accessory's pivot and mounting bolts.

2. Move the accessory toward or away from the engine until the tension is correct. You can use a wooden hammer handle or broomstick as a lever, but do not use anything metallic.
3. Tighten the bolts and recheck the tension. If new belts have been installed, run the engine for a few minutes, then recheck and readjust as necessary.

NOTE: If the driven component has two drive belts, the belts should be replaced in pairs to maintain proper tension.

It is better to have belts too loose than too tight, because overtight belts will lead to bearing failure, particularly in the water pump and alternator. However, loose belts place an extremely high impact load on the driven component due to the whipping action of the belt.

Regulator

REMOVAL AND INSTALLATION

1. Release the spring clips and pull off the regulator wiring plug.
2. Unbolt and remove the regulator.
3. Installation is the reverse of removal. Be sure that the spring clips engage the wiring plug.

ADJUSTMENTS

The electronic voltage regulator has no moving parts and requires no adjustment after it leaves the factory. Any repairs are accomplished by replacement with a new regulator.

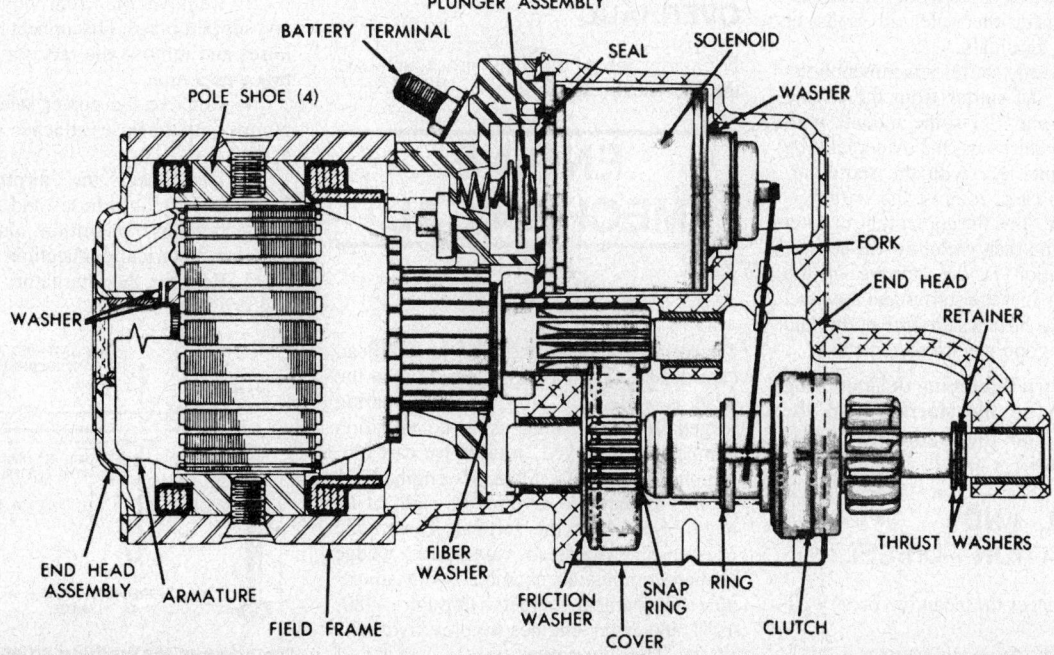

Conventional gear reduction starter

Cutaway view of 6 cylinder engine

Starter

Almost all models are equipped with a reduction gear type starter motor. The only exception being a direct drive type starter used on the Rampage.

REMOVAL AND INSTALLATION—EXCEPT DIESEL

1. Disconnect the ground cable at the battery.
2. Remove the cable from the starter.
3. Disconnect the solenoid leads at their solenoid terminals.
4. Remove the starter attachment bolts and withdraw the starter from the engine flywheel housing. On some models with automatic transmissions, the oil cooler tube bracket will interfere with the starter removal. In this case, remove the starter attachment bolts, slide the cooler tube bracket off the stud, and then withdraw the starter.
5. Installation is the reverse of the above. Be sure that the starter and flywheel housing mating surfaces are free of dirt and oil to make a good electrical contact.

NOTE: When tightening the mounting bolt and nut on the starter, hold the starter away from the engine for the correct alignment.

REMOVAL AND INSTALLATION—DIESEL

1. Disconnect the negative battery cable.
2. Raise the truck and support it safely on jackstands.

3. Disconnect and label the wires at the starter motor.
4. Remove the attaching bolt, nut and washer and lift the starter and solenoid assembly from the engine.
5. Before installing the starter motor, be sure the mounting surface on the drive end housing and the flywheel housing are clean, to ensure good electrical contact. When tightening the attaching bolt and nut, hold the starter away from the engine to ensure the proper alignment.
6. Attach the wiring at the starter.
7. Attach the negative battery cable.

OVERHAUL

For starter motor overhaul procedures see the Electrical section.

ENGINE MECHANICAL

Design

The four cylinder engine is of the overhead cam design. The block is cast iron and the head is aluminum. A five main bearing forged steel crankshaft using no vibration damper is employed, rotated by cast aluminum pistons. The Slant-Six engine (225 cu in.) is inclined toward the right at an angle of 30° from the vertical. The engine uses in-line overhead valves and wedge shaped combustion chambers with adjustable mechanical tappets through 1980. 1981 and latter engines employ hydraulic lifters. The lubrication system consists of an externally mounted rotor type oil pump

on the lower right-hand side of the block. The semi-series flow cooling system contains an aluminum water pump body with a pressed-in ball bearing and seal assembly.

The diesel engine is an in-line six cylinder with overhead valves. The diesel engine is entirely metric, therefore requiring the use of metric tools.

All V8 engines used are valve-in-head type engines with wedge shaped combustion chambers. All are equipped with hydraulic tappets. The 318 and 360 lubrication system is a rotor type oil pump mounted on the rear main bearing cap and a full-flow, throwaway element filter located on the lower right-hand side of the block. The 400 and 440 oil pump and filter are on the outside of the block at the front of the engine.

Engine Removal and Installation

VANS AND PICK-UPS

Except Front Wheel Drive and Diesel

NOTE: Engine removal is a complicated operation. A floor jack is a necessity and you will probably have to fabricate several stands and attaching apparatus. On vehicles equipped with air conditioning, before removing the engine, have an air conditioning expert evacuate the system.

1. Disconnect the battery and drain the coolant from the radiator and engine block. Drain the engine oil. On V8s, remove the oil filter.
2. Remove the engine cover (vans), air cleaner, and starter.
3. Remove the front bumper, grille, and support brace. Disconnect both radiator hoses and remove the radiator and support brace as a unit.
4. Remove the power steering and air pumps with the hoses attached and lay them aside.
5. Disconnect the throttle linkage, heater and vacuum hoses and all electrical connections to the ignition, alternator, and all other electrical connections.
6. Remove the alternator, fan, pulley, and drive belts.

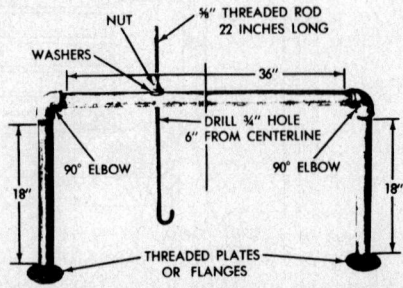

Dimensions for building an engine lift for vans

7. Remove the heater blower motor.

8. Remove and plug the inlet line to the fuel pump.

9. Remove the oil dipstick tube. On V8s, remove the intake manifold and left exhaust manifold. If equipped with air conditioning, remove the right side valve cover.

10. To provide clearance (vans) for engine removal, the oil pan and transmission must be removed. (See 15a.)

11. Raise the engine slightly in preparation for transmission removal. Support it with an engine lifting fixture. This tool can be fabricated from galvanized pipe fittings obtained locally. Use only galvanized parts with an inside diameter of 1½ in. or larger. Be sure they are firmly threaded together to assure maximum strength.

12. Raise the vehicle and support it on jackstands. Remove the starter and distributor.

13. Remove the driveshaft and engine rear support. Remove the rear support by removing the rear mount through-bolt and the U-shaped bracket from the cross-member. Remove the insulator from the bottom face of the transmission housing.

14. If equipped with an automatic transmission, remove the transmission intact with the filler tube and the torque converter separated from the drive plate.

15. Raise the rear of the engine approximately 2 in. and remove the clutch or drive plate and the flywheel.

15a. On vans equipped with V8 engines, to gain necessary clearance, position the cut-out in the crankshaft flange at 3 o'clock. Remove the oil pan screws and lower the oil pan far enough to reach inside and turn the oil pump pick-up tube slightly to the right to clear the pan. Remove the oil pan.

16. Lower the vehicle.

17. Using a boom hoist attached to the engine with the shortest hook-up possible, take up all tension and support the engine. The boom hoist is the ideal tool to use. If one is not available, it may be possible to support the engine on a stationary hoist and roll the vehicle out from under the engine.

18. Remove the engine front mounts and insulators.

19. Carefully remove the engine from the vehicle.

20. Installation is the reverse of removal. Check all fluid levels and perform all tune-up adjustments if the engine was rebuilt.

NOTE: If the engine was rebuilt or new camshaft or lifters installed, add 1 quart of engine oil supplement to aid break-in. This should be left in the engine for at least 500 miles.

DIESEL ENGINE

NOTE: If the truck is equipped with air conditioning, have the system evacuated by a qualified technician. Refer to the air conditioning caution note at the beginning of this section.

1. Disconnect the battery cables and remove the battery.

2. Remove the air cleaner.

3. Scribe matchmarks on the hood hinges and remove the hood.

4. Drain the cooling system.

5. Remove the upper and lower radiator hoses.

6. Remove the coolant reserve tank.

7. Raise the truck and safely support on jackstands. Disconnect and remove the transmission oil cooler lines from the radiator. Remove the lower radiator and fan shroud mounting screws.

8. Lower the truck and remove the upper radiator and fan shroud mounting screws and remove the radiator and the fan shroud.

9. Disconnect the heater hoses from the engine and push them aside.

10. Disconnect the speedometer cable housing from the engine.

11. Disconnect the electrical connections at the alternator, temperature sending unit, starter relay-to-solenoid wires, the oil gauge sending unit and the injection pump control motor. Set the wiring harness aside.

12. Disconnect and plug the fuel line at the transfer pump inlet. Disconnect and cap return line at the injector lines bleed-back connection.

13. Disconnect and remove the injection pump linkage. Disconnect and remove the accelerator and throttle cable linkage.

14. Disconnect the starter motor wire from the solenoid. Remove the starter motor.

15. Remove the battery ground cable from the engine block.

16. Disconnect and plug the power steering hoses at the power steering gear.

17. Raise the truck and disconnect the exhaust pipe from the exhaust manifold.

18. Drain the engine oil and remove the dipstick tube from the oil pan. Remove the transmission cooler line and road draft tube bracket from the oil pan.

19. Remove the oil pan bolts from the oil pan.

20. Remove the transmission inspection plate. Remove the oil pan on vans to gain clearance if necessary. Use a new gasket on installation.

21. Remove the four flex plate-to-torque converter cover bolts.

22. Remove the exhaust pipe bracket and the lower bell housing bolts.

23. Remove any other brackets that can interfere with removal.

24. Support the transmission with a floor jack.

25. Remove the cylinder head (valve) cover and the gasket.

26. Attach a boom hoist to the engine, wrapping the chain as tight and close as possible.

27. Remove the four bolts and six nuts from the engine mounts.

28. Remove the two upper bell housing bolts.

29. Roll the boom hoist back, removing the engine from the van or truck.

30. Installation is the reverse of removal.

RAMCHARGER AND TRAIL DUSTER

1. Drain the coolant from the radiator and cylinder block.

2. Disconnect the battery ground cable. Remove the battery on V8 models.

3. Scribe the outline of the hood hinges and remove the hood.

4. If equipped with air conditioning, remove the compressor with lines attached and lay it aside.

--- CAUTION ---
Do not disconnect any refrigerant lines. Bodily injury could result.

5. Disconnect the electrical connections at the alternator, ignition coil, temperature and oil pressure sending units, starter-to-solenoid, and engine/body ground.

6. Remove the air cleaner and carburetor. Install an engine lifting fixture.

7. Remove the distributor cap and rotor.

8. Disconnect and plug the fuel pump line.

9. Disconnect the radiator and heater hoses. Disconnect and plug the oil cooler lines.

10. Remove the fan, spacer, fluid drive, and radiator. Do not store the fan drive unit with the shaft pointing downward. Fluid will leak out.

11. Raise the truck and support the rear of the engine.

12. Disconnect the exhaust pipes at the manifolds.

13. Remove the starter on V8 models.

14. Remove the automatic transmission dust cover and attach a C-clamp to the front bottom of the torque converter housing to prevent the converter from falling out. Remove the drive plate bolts from the torque converter. On manual transmission models, remove the rear crossmember, transmission, transfer case and adapter. You can leave the transfer case in place on six-cylinder models.

15. Support the transmission and remove the transmission attaching bolts.

16. Lower the truck and attach a hoist to the engine.

17. Remove the front motor mount bolt stud nuts and washers.

18. Carefully remove the engine.

19. Installation is the reverse of removal. Fill the engine with coolant and fresh oil. Adjust the transmission linkage, carburetor, and ignition timing.

RAMPAGE

1. Disconnect the battery.
2. Mark the hood hinge outline and remove the hood.
3. Drain the cooling system.
4. Remove the radiator hoses and remove the radiator and shroud assembly.
5. Remove the air cleaner and hoses.
6. The air conditioning compressor does not have to be disconnected. Remove it from its bracket and position it out of the way. Securing it with wire is the best method.
7. Disconnect and label all wiring from the engine, alternator and carburetor.
8. Disconnect the fuel line, heater hoses and accelerator linkage.
9. Disconnect the air pump lines.
10. Remove the alternator.
11. Disconnect the clutch and speedometer cables.
12. Raise the vehicle and support it on jackstands.
13. Disconnect the driveshafts from the transmission and support them with wires.
14. Disconnect the exhaust pipe.
15. Remove the air pump.
16. Disconnect the transmission linkage.
17. Lower the vehicle.
18. Attach a lifting fixture and a shop crane to the engine. Raise the engine slightly to take up the weight and disconnect the engine mounts in this order: front, right, left. Lift the engine from the car.

To install:

1. Lower the engine into place and loosely install all mounting bolts. When all mounts have been hand tightened, torque each to 40 ft. lbs.
2. Remove the lifting fixture and raise the vehicle, supporting it on jackstands.
3. Connect the driveshafts. Torque the bolts to 35 ft. lbs.
4. Connect the transmission linkage, install the air pump, connect the exhaust pipe and lower the vehicle.
5. Connect the clutch and speedometer cables.
6. Install the alternator.
7. Install the air pump lines.
8. Connect the fuel line, heater hoses and accelerator linkage.
9. Connect all wiring.
10. Mount the air conditioning compressor.
11. Install the air cleaner.
12. Install the radiator and hoses.
13. Fill the cooling system.
14. Install the hood.
15. Connect the battery.
16. Start the engine and run it to normal operating temperature.
17. Check the timing and adjust if necessary. Adjust the carburetor idle speed and mixture, and the transmission linkage.

Cylinder Head

REMOVAL AND INSTALLATION

4 Cylinder Engines

The cylinder head should be cold before it is removed.

1. Disconnect the battery.
2. Drain the cooling system.
3. Remove the air cleaner assembly.
4. Disconnect all lines, hoses and wires from the head, manifold and carburetor.
5. Disconnect the accelerator linkage.
6. Remove the distributor cap.
7. Disconnect the exhaust pipe.
8. Remove the carburetor.
9. Remove the intake and exhaust manifolds.
10. Remove the upper portion of the front cover.
11. Turn the engine by hand until all gear timing marks are aligned.
12. Loosen the drive belt tensioner and slip the belt off the camshaft gear.
13. If equipped with air conditioning, remove the compressor from the mounting brackets and support it out of the way with wires. Remove the mounting brackets from the head.
14. Remove the valve cover, gaskets and seals.
15. Remove head bolts by starting at the ends and working toward the middle.
16. Lift off the head and discard the gasket.
17. Installation is the reverse of removal. Make certain all gasket surfaces are thoroughly cleaned and are free of deep nicks or scratches. Always use new gaskets and seals. Never reuse a gasket or seal, even if it looks good. Tighten bolts from the center of the head working evenly to each end. Make sure all timing marks are aligned before installing the drive belt. The drive belt is correctly tensioned when it can be twisted 90° with the thumb and index finger midway between the camshaft and the intermediate shaft.

6-Cylinder (Except Diesel)

1. Drain the cooling system and disconnect the battery.
2. Remove the air cleaner and the fuel line from the carburetor.
3. Disconnect the accelerator linkage.
4. Remove the vacuum advance line from between the carburetor and the distributor.
5. Disconnect the cables from the spark plugs.
6. Disconnect the heater hose and the clamp which secures the by-pass hose.
7. Disconnect the water temperature sending unit.
8. Disconnect the exhaust pipe at the exhaust manifold flange. Disconnect the diverter valve line (if equipped) from the

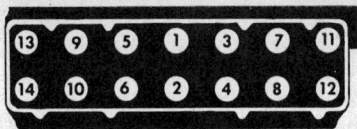

Cylinder head torque sequence—6 cylinder

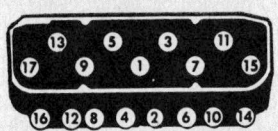

Cylinder head torque sequence—400, 440-V8

intake manifold and remove the air tube assembly from the cylinder head.
9. Remove the intake and exhaust manifolds and the carburetor as an assembly.
10. Remove the closed ventilation system, the evaporative control system (if so equipped), and the valve cover.
11. Remove the rocker arm and shaft assembly.
12. Remove the pushrods and keep them in order to ensure installation in their original locations.
13. Remove the head bolts and remove the cylinder head.
14. Clean all of the gasket surfaces of the engine block and the cylinder head, and install the spark plugs.
15. Inspect all surfaces with a straightedge. If warpage is indicated, measure the amount. This amount must not exceed 0.00075 times the span length in any direction. For example, if a 12 in. span is 0.004 warped, the maximum allowable is $12 \times 0.00075 = 0.009$ in. In this case, the head is within limits. If warpage exceeds the specified limits, either replace the head or lightly machine the head gasket surface.
16. Coat a new cylinder head gasket with sealer, install the gasket, and install the cylinder head.
17. Install the cylinder head bolts. Torque the cylinder head bolts to 50 ft. lbs. in the sequence indicated in the illustration. Repeat this sequence to retorque all the head bolts to specifications.
18. Reverse the removal procedure, Steps 1–12, to complete the installation. When installing the intake and exhaust manifold assembly, loosen the 3 bolts which secure the intake manifold to the exhaust manifold to maintain proper alignment. After installation, torque the 3 bolts in this sequence: inner bolts, then outer bolts. Refer to the manifold section, later in this chapter, for the proper tightening sequence. Check the valve adjustment.

V8

1. Drain the cooling system and disconnect the battery ground cable.
2. Remove the alternator, air cleaner, and fuel line.

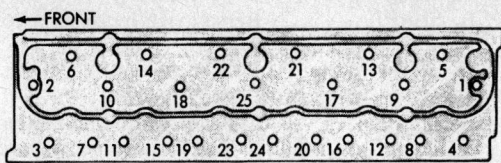

Diesel cylinder head bolt loosening sequence

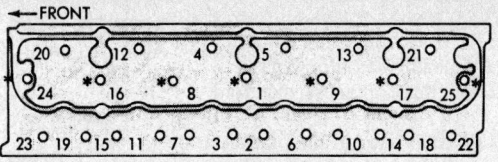

*BOLTS TO BE TIGHTENED TOGETHER WITH THE ROCKER SHAFT BRACKETS.

Diesel cylinder head bolt tightening sequence

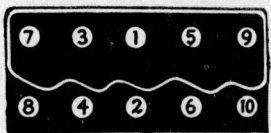

Cylinder head torque sequence—318, 360-V8

3. Disconnect the accelerator linkage.

4. Remove the vacuum advance line from between the carburetor and the distributor.

5. Remove the distributor cap and wires as an assembly.

6. Disconnect the coil wires, water temperature sending unit, heater hoses, and by-pass hose.

7. Remove the closed ventilation system, the evaporative control system (if so equipped), and the valve covers.

8. Remove the intake manifold, ignition coil, and carburetor as an assembly.

9. Remove the exhaust manifolds.

10. Remove the rocker and shaft assemblies.

11. Remove the pushrods and keep them in order to ensure installation in their original locations.

12. Remove the head bolts from each cylinder head and remove the cylinder heads.

13. Clean all the gasket surfaces of the engine block and the cylinder heads. Install the spark plugs.

14. Inspect all surfaces with a straightedge. If warpage is indicated, measure the amount. This amount must not exceed 0.00075 times the span length in any direction. For example, if a 12 in. span is 0.004 in. warped, the maximum allowable difference is $12 \times 0.00075 = 0.009$ in. In this case, the head is within limits. If the warpage exceeds the specified limits, either replace the head or lightly machine the head gasket surface.

15. Coat new cylinder head gaskets with sealer, install the gaskets, and install the cylinder heads.

NOTE: The number and size of the cooling passages in the 318 heads were changed during the 1976 model year. The new type gasket can be used with the old heads, but the old type gasket can't be used with the new heads.

16. Install the cylinder head bolts. Torque the cylinder head bolts to 50 ft. lbs. in the sequence indicated. Repeat this sequence to retorque all the cylinder head bolts to specifications.

17. Reverse the removal procedure Steps 1–12 to complete the installation.

Diesel Engine

1. Drain the cooling system.

2. Disconnect the negative battery cable.

3. Remove the air cleaner.

4. Disconnect the hoses from the fuel filter at the transfer pump and the injection pump. Drain the filter and remove it from the manifold.

5. Remove the manifold nuts and air cleaner mounting bracket attaching nuts.

6. Disconnect the injection lines for cylinders 3 and 6 from the injection pump.

7. Remove the intake manifold and gaskets from the head.

8. Push the exhaust manifold shield to one side.

9. Remove the heater hose and the by-pass hose.

10. Remove the thermostat housing and the upper radiator hose from the water manifold. Remove the spray gasket.

11. Disconnect the temperature sending unit wire.

12. Disconnect the fuel line mounting brackets from the cylinder head and push the fuel lines aside.

13. Remove the three exhaust manifold bridges.

14. Remove the water manifold and gasket from the cylinder head.

15. Raise the truck and support with jackstands.

16. Disconnect the exhaust pipe from the exhaust manifold.

17. Lower the truck. Remove the exhaust manifold, heat shield and gasket.

18. Disconnect and remove the wire from the glow plug buss bar.

19. Remove the injection lines from the injection pump.

20. Disconnect the fuel injection line from the head. Remove the bracket and the ground strap.

21. Disconnect the alternator bracket and the engine lifting fixture. Push them aside.

22. Remove the cylinder head cover and the gasket.

23. Loosen and remove the cylinder head bolts in the sequence illustrated.

24. Lift out the rocker arm and shaft assembly.

25. Remove the push rods, keeping them in order. The push rods MUST be installed in their original location.

26. Remove the injector tubes, injector holders and the injectors.

27. Disconnect and remove the glow plug buss bar.

28. Remove the six glow plugs from the cylinder head.

29. Remove the cylinder head. Check the head for cracks, damage or evidence of water leaks. Clean all the oil, grease, scale, sealant and carbon from the head. Thoroughly clean the gasket surfaces. Also check each combustion chamber jet for cracks or melting. If a jet is cracked or melted, remove it with a push rod inserted through a glow plug bore.

Inspect all cylinder head surfaces with a straightedge. Out-of-flatness must not exceed .010 in. If it does, a surface grinder must be used to bring the head to an out-of-flatness of less than .006 in.

30. Install the glow plugs in the head. Tighten them firmly.

31. Install the glow plug buss bar. Be sure the connections are good.

32. Install the injectors, injector tubes and the injector holders in the head. Tighten the nozzle holder attaching nuts to 37 ft. lbs.

33. Coat the new gasket lightly with sealer. Place the gasket on the block and place the cylinder head over the dowels.

34. Install the cylinder head bolts and tighten them in the sequence illustrated to 90.4 ft. lbs. Do not install the head bolts which retain the rocker shaft assembly.

35. Install the push rods in their original locations.

36. Install the rocker arm and shaft assembly. Tighten the mounting bolts, the same as the cylinder head bolts, to 90.4 ft. lbs.

37. Adjust the valve clearance to .012 in. at top dead center of each compression stroke.

38. Install the cylinder head cover and gasket.

39. Install the alternator bracket and the engine lifting fixture.

40. Connect the fuel lines to the injection pump (except nos. 3 and 6). Install the bracket and the ground strap.

41. Install the fuel line to the transfer pump.

42. Install the exhaust manifold and the heat shield assembly, using a new gasket.

43. Raise the truck and support it safely. Attach the exhaust pipe to the exhaust man-

ifold.

44. Lower the truck and install the water manifold on the head using a new gasket.

45. Install the three exhaust manifold bridges.

46. Install the fuel lines in the bracket.

47. Connect the temperature sending unit wire.

48. Using a new gasket, install the thermostat housing. Attach the upper radiator hose to the thermostat housing.

49. Install the bypass and heater hoses.

50. Install the exhaust manifold heat shield and the exhaust manifold.

51. Using a new gasket and spray shield, install the air intake manifold.

52. Connect the injection lines from cylinders 3 and 6 to the injection pump.

53. Install the fuel filter to the back of the manifold.

54. Connect the fuel hoses.

55. Install the air cleaner bracket and install the air cleaner.

56. Fill the cooling system and connect the battery cables.

Rocker Shafts

REMOVAL AND INSTALLATION

6-Cylinder (Except Diesel)

The rocker arm shaft has 12 straight steel rocker arms arranged on it with hardened steel spacers fitted between each pair of rocker arms. The shaft is secured by bolts and steel retainers which are attached to the 7 cylinder head brackets. To remove the rocker arm and shaft:

1. Remove the closed ventilation system.

2. Remove the evaporative control system (if so equipped).

3. Remove the valve cover and its gasket.

4. Remove the rocker shaft bolts and retainers.

5. Remove the rocker arm and shaft assembly.

6. Reverse the above for installation. The oil hole on the end of the shaft must be on top and point toward the front of the engine to provide proper lubrication to the rocker arms. The special bolt goes to the rear.

7. Torque all bolts to 25 ft. lbs.

8. Temporarily set the intake valve tappet at .015 in. and the exhaust valve at .025 in.

9. Run the engine at 550 rpm until it is fully warmed up and adjust the valves.

V8

The stamped steel rocker arms are arranged on one rocker arm shaft per cylinder head. Because the angle of the pushrods tends to force the rocker arm pairs toward each other, oilite spacers are fitted to absorb the side thrust at each rocker arm. The shaft

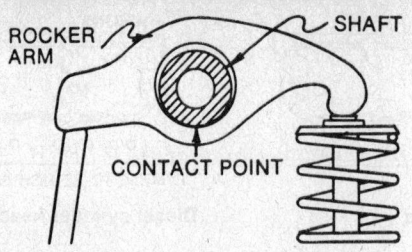

Inspect the rocker-arm-to-rocker shaft contact area

is secured by bolts and steel retainers attached to the brackets on the cylinder head. To remove the arm and shaft from each cylinder head:

1. Disconnect the spark plug wires.

2. Disconnect the closed ventilation system and evaporative control system (if so equipped) from the valve cover.

3. Remove each valve cover and gasket.

4. Remove the rocker shaft bolts and retainer.

5. Remove each rocker arm and shaft assembly. Keep everything in order for installation in the original position.

6. Reverse the above for installation. The notch on the end of both 318 and 360 rocker shafts should point to the engine centerline and toward the front of the engine on the left cylinder head and toward the rear on the right side. On the 400 and 440, the rocker arm lubrication holes must point down and toward the valves. Torque the rocker shaft bolts to 17 ft. lbs. on the 318 and 360, and 25 ft. lbs. on the others.

Diesel Engine

1. Remove the valve cover and the gasket.

2. Remove the nozzle holders and the glow plugs.

3. Remove the rocker shaft retaining bolts.

4. Remove the rocker arm and shaft assembly. Keep everything in order so the rocker assembly can be installed in the original position.

5. To install, position the rocker arm and shaft assembly so the bracket with the oil hole is at the front of the engine.

6. Install the rocker shaft retaining bolts and tighten them to 90.4 ft. lbs.

7. Install the nozzle holders and the glow plugs.

8. Install and tighten the injection lines. Tighten the nozzle holder retaining nuts to between 43.4 and 57.9 ft. lbs.

9. Adjust the valves.

VALVE STEM OIL SEAL REPLACEMENT

If valve stem oil seals are found to be the cause of excessive oil consumption, they may be replaced without removing the cylinder heads.

1. Remove the air cleaner.

2. Remove the rocker arm covers and spark plugs.

3. Detach the coil wire from the distributor.

4. Turn the engine so that no. 1 cylinder is at Top Dead Center on the compression stroke. Both valves for no. 1 cylinder should be fully closed and the crankshaft damper timing mark at TDC. The distributor rotor will point at the no. 1 spark plug wire location in the cap.

5. Remove the rocker shaft and install a dummy shaft.

6. Apply 90-100 psi air pressure to no. 1 cylinder, using a spark plug hole air hose adaptor.

7. Use a valve spring compressor to compress each no. 1 cylinder valve spring and remove the retainer locks and the spring. Remove the old seals.

8. Install a cup shield on the exhaust valve stem. Position it down against the valve guide.

9. Push the intake valve stem seal firmly and squarely over the valve guide.

10. Compress the valve spring only enough to install the lock.

11. Repeat the operation on each successive cylinder in the firing order, making sure that the crankshaft is exactly on TDC for each cylinder. See the Firing Order and Distributor Rotation illustrations in the Specifications section of this chapter for cylinder numbering.

12. Replace the rocker arms, covers, spark plugs, and coil wire.

Manifolds

REMOVAL AND INSTALLATION

4 Cylinder Intake Manifold

1. Drain the cooling system.

2. Remove the air cleaner and hoses.

3. Remove all wiring and any hoses connected to the carburetor and manifold.

4. Disconnect the accelerator linkage and shift linkage (if equipped).

5. Remove the intake-to-exhaust manifold bolts.

6. Remove the manifold-to-head bolts and lift out the intake manifold.

7. Clean all gasket surfaces and install the intake manifold using new gaskets.

8. Connect all hoses and wires, and install the air cleaner.

9. Connect the accelerator linkage and shift linkage (if equipped).

4 Cylinder Exhaust Manifold

1. Follow the intake manifold removal procedure above.

2. Disconnect the exhaust pipe.

3. Unbolt and remove the exhaust manifold.

4. Clean the gasket surfaces, and using a new gasket, install the manifold.

V-8 Intake Manifold

1. Drain cooling system and disconnect battery.
2. Remove alternator, carburetor air cleaner, and fuel line.
3. Disconnect accelerator linkage.

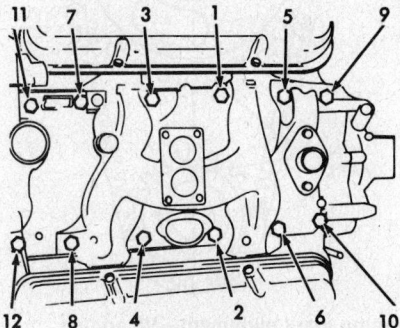

V8 intake manifold tightening sequence

4. Remove vacuum control between carburetor and distributor.
5. Remove the distributor cap and wires.
6. Disconnect coil wires, temperature sending unit wire, heater hoses and bypass hose.
7. Remove intake manifold, ignition coil and carburetor as an assembly.
8. Installation is the reverse of the above procedure. Tighten the intake manifold to head bolts in the sequence illustrated, from center alternating out.
9. Tighten the exhaust manifold mounting nuts to the required torque which is listed in the specifications chart of this section.

V-8 Exhaust Manifold

1. Disconnect the exhaust manifold at the flange where it mates to the exhaust pipe.
2. If the vehicle is equipped with air injection and/or a carburetor-heated air stove, remove them.
3. Remove the exhaust manifold by removing the securing bolts and washers. To reach these bolts, it may be necessary to jack the engine slightly off its front mounts. When the exhaust manifold is removed, sometimes the securing studs will screw out with the nuts. If this occurs, the studs must be replaced with the aid of sealing compound on the coarse thread ends. If this is not done, water leaks may develop at the studs.
4. To install, reverse the removal procedures. On the center branch of the 318 and the 360 exhaust manifold, no conical washers are used.

6-Cylinder Combination Manifold

1. Remove the air cleaner, lines and tubes to the carburetor.
2. Disconnect all the linkages to the

carburetor and remove the carburetor from the manifold.
3. Disconnect the exhaust pipe from the manifold, remove the manifold attaching washers and retaining nuts, and remove the manifold from the cylinder head.
4. Separate the exhaust manifold from the intake manifold, if necessary, and install a new gasket between the two upon reassembly.
NOTE: Do not tighten the three securing bolts until the manifold assembly has been installed on the cylinder head.
5. Position the manifold on the cylinder head using a new gasket, and install the conical and triangular washers, the retaining nuts, and torque the retaining nuts and the three securing bolts to the specified torque.
6. Attach the exhaust pipe to the exhaust manifold flange.
7. Install the carburetor and attach all the lines, tubes, and linkages. Install the air cleaner assembly.

Timing Cover and Belt
4 CYLINDER ENGINES

Timing Cover Removal and Installation

1. Loosen the alternator lock screw and adjusting screw. Remove the drive belt.
2. Remove the power steering pump lock screw. Remove the pivot bolt and nut. Remove the drive belt. Remove the power steering pump and mounting bracket. The hoses need not be disconnected, locate the pump out of the way.
3. Loosen and remove the water pump pulley mounting screws and remove the pulley.
4. From under the vehicle remove the right inner splash shield.
5. Remove the crankshaft pulley.
6. The upper part of the timing cover is retained by nuts, the lower part is retained with screws. Remove the fasteners and the two halves of the timing cover.
7. Reverse the removal order for installation.

Timing Belt Removal and Installation

1. Follow steps 1–6 of the Timing Cover Removal and Installation section.
2. Place a jack under the engine with a piece of wood separating it from the jacking point.
3. Remove the right engine mounting bolt and raise the engine slightly. Be sure the engine is supported securely.
4. Loosen the belt tensioner and remove the timing belt.
5. Turn the crankshaft until the dot mark on the sprocket is at about two o'clock. Turn the intermediate shaft sprocket until the dot mark is at about eight o'clock. Line up the crankshaft and intermediate sprocket marks.

6. Turn the camshaft until the arrows on the mounting hub are in line with the front (no. 1) camshaft retaining cap flat spots. The small hole in the camshaft sprocket must be at the top and be in a vertical center line with the engine.
7. Install the timing belt. Adjust and tighten the belt tensioner.
8. Adjust the tensioner by turning the large tensioner hex to the right. Tension should be correct when the belt can be twisted 90° with the thumb and the forefinger, midway between the camshaft and the intermediate sprocket.
9. Complete the belt installation by reversing the removal steps.

NOTE: After applying the belt tensioner, rotate the engine two complete revolutions and recheck the timing marks for alignment.

Timing Gears

REMOVAL AND INSTALLATION
4 Cylinder

The camshaft, intermediate shaft, and crankshaft pulleys are located by keys on their respective shafts and each is retained by a bolt. To remove any or all of the pulleys, first remove the timing belt cover and belt and then use the following procedure.

NOTE: When removing the crankshaft pulley, don't remove the four socket head bolts which retain the outer belt pulley to the timing belt pulley.

1. Remove the center bolt.
2. Gently pry the pulley off the shaft.
3. If the pulley is stubborn in coming off, use a gear puller. Don't hammer on the pulley.
4. Remove the pulley and key.
5. Install the pulley in the reverse order of removal.
6. Tighten the center bolt to 58 ft. lbs.
7. Install the timing belt, check valve timing, tension belt, and install the cover.

Timing Cover and Chain

REMOVAL AND INSTALLATION
6-Cylinder Engines

1. Drain the cooling system and disconnect the battery.
2. Remove the radiator and fan.
3. With a puller, remove the vibration damper.
4. Loosen the oil pan bolts to allow clearance, and remove the timing case cover and gasket.
5. Slide the crankshaft oil slinger off the front of the crankshaft.
6. Remove the camshaft sprocket bolt.

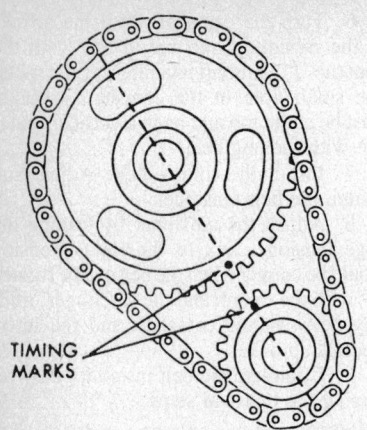

Timing mark alignment—6 cylinder engine

7. Remove the timing chain with the camshaft sprocket.

8. On installation: Turn the crankshaft to line up the timing mark on the crankshaft sprocket with the centerline of the camshaft (without the chain).

9. Install the camshaft sprocket and chain. Align the timing marks.

10. Torque the camshaft sprocket bolt to 35 ft. lbs.

11. Replace the oil slinger.

12. Reinstall the timing case cover with a new gasket and torque the bolts to 17 ft. lbs. Retighten the engine oil pan to 17 ft. lbs.

13. Press the vibration damper back on.

14. Replace the radiator and hoses.

15. Refill the cooling system.

V8 Engines

1. Disconnect the battery and drain the cooling system. Remove the radiator.

2. Remove the vibration damper pulley. Unbolt and remove the vibration damper with a puller. On 318 and 360 engines, remove the fuel lines and fuel pump, then loosen the oil pan bolts and remove the front bolt on each side.

3. Remove the timing gear cover and the crankshaft oil slinger.

4. On 318 and 360 engines, remove the camshaft sprocket lockbolt, securing cup washer, and fuel pump eccentric. Remove the timing chain with both sprockets. On 400 and 440 engines, remove the camshaft sprocket lockbolt and remove the timing chain with the camshaft and crankshaft sprockets.

5. To begin the installation procedure, place the camshaft and crankshaft sprockets on a flat surface with the timing indicators on an imaginary centerline through both sprocket bores. Place the timing chain around both sprockets. Be sure that the timing marks are in alignment.

--- CAUTION ---

When installing the timing chain, have an assistant support the camshaft with a suitable tool to prevent it from contacting the plug in the rear of the engine block. Re-

move the distributor and the oil pump/distributor drive gear. Position the suitable tool against the rear side of the cam gear and be careful not to damage the cam lobes.

6. Turn the crankshaft and camshaft to align them with the keyway location in the crankshaft sprocket and the keyway or dowel hole in the camshaft sprocket.

7. Lift the sprockets and timing chain while keeping the sprockets tight against the chain in the correct position. Slide both sprockets evenly onto their respective shafts.

8. Use a straightedge to measure the alignment of the sprocket timing marks. They must be perfectly aligned.

9. On 318 and 360 engines, install the fuel pump eccentric, cup washer, and camshaft sprocket lockbolt and torque to 35 ft. lbs. If camshaft end play exceeds 0.010 in., install a new thrust plate. It should be 0.002–0.006 in. with the new plate.

On 400 and 440 V8s, install the washer and camshaft sprocket lockbolt(s) and then torque the lockbolt to 35–40 ft. lbs. Check to make sure that the rear face of the camshaft sprocket is flush with the camshaft end.

CHECKING TIMING CHAIN SLACK

1. Position a scale (ruler or straightedge) next to the timing chain to detect any movement in the chain.

2. Place a torque wrench and socket on the camshaft sprocket attaching bolt. Apply either 30 ft. lbs. (if the cylinder heads are installed on the engine) or 15 ft. lbs. (cylinder heads removed) of force to the bolt and rotate the bolt in the direction of crankshaft rotation in order to remove all slack from the chain.

3. While applying torque to the camshaft sprocket bolt, the crankshaft should not be allowed to rotate. It may be necessary to block the crankshaft to prevent rotation.

4. Position the scale over the edge of a timing chain link and apply an equal amount of torque in the opposite direction. If the movement of the chain exceeds ⅛ in., replace the chain.

TIMING GEAR COVER SEAL REPLACEMENT

NOTE: A seal remover and installer tool is required to prevent seal damage.

1. Using a seal puller, separate the seal from the retainer.

2. Pull the seal from the case.

3. To install the seal place it face down in the case with the seal lips downward.

4. Seat the seal tightly against the cover face. There should be a maximum clearance of .0014 in. between the seal and the cover. Be careful not to over-compress the seal.

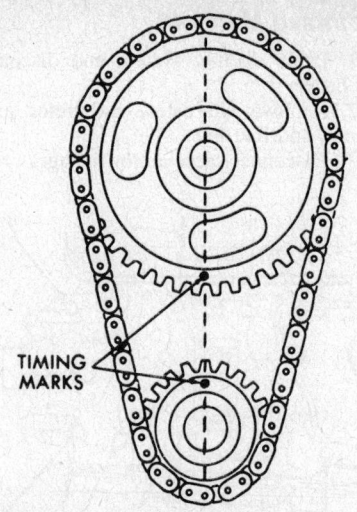

Timing mark alignment—V8 engine

VALVE TIMING OPERATION

6-Cylinder

1. Rotate the crankshaft until no. 6 exhaust valve is closing and no. 6 intake valve is opening.

2. Install a dial indicator so that the indicator pointer contacts the valve spring retainer on the no. 1 intake valve parallel to the axis of the valve stem.

3. Turn the no. 1 intake adjusting screw *in* one complete turn to remove the lash. Adjust the dial indicator to zero.

4. Rotate the crankshaft clockwise normal running direction until the valve has lifted .029 inch.

5. The timing of the crankshaft pulley should now read from 12 degrees BTDC to DC. Readjust lash.

NOTE: If the reading is not within specified limits, inspect the sprocket index marks, inspect the timing chain for wear, and inspect the accuracy of the "DC" mark on the timing indicator.

318, 360, 400 and 440 Cu. In. Engine

1. Turn the crankshaft until the no. 6 exhaust valve is closing and no. 6 intake valve is opening.

2. Insert a ¼ inch spacer between the rocker arm pad and the stem tip of the no. 1 intake valve. Allow the spring load to bleed the tappet down giving, in effect, a solid tappet.

3. Install a dial indicator so that the plunger contacts the valve spring retainer as nearly perpendicular as possible. Zero the indicator.

4. Rotate the crankshaft clockwise (normal running direction) until the valve has lifted .010 inch for 318 cu. in. engines, .020 inch for 1975–1977 360 cu. in. engines, .034 inch for 1978–1982 360 cu. in. engines, and .025 inch with 260–268 degrees camshaft for 400 and 440 cu. in. engines.

NOTE: Do not turn the crankshaft any further clockwise as the valve spring might bottom and result in serious damage.

5. The timing of the crankshaft pulley should now read from 10 degrees BTDC to 2 degrees ATDC. Remove the spacer.

NOTE: If the reading is not within the specified limits, check the sprocket index marks, inspect the timing chain for wear, and check the accuracy of the "DC" mark on the timing indicator.

Timing Gear (Diesel)

REMOVAL AND INSTALLATION

1. Remove the timing gear cover, the gasket and the front oil seal. Remove the idler pulley bracket.

2. Align the timing marks.

3. Using a puller, remove the camshaft drive gear.

4. Turn the injection pump to allow the notch in the drive gear to pass by the idler gear teeth.

5. Loosen the idler gear mounting bolt. Remove the thrust plate and remove the idler gear.
To install:

1. Be sure that the crankshaft is set with no. 1 cylinder at TDC.

2. Install the idler gear on the shaft so the marks on the camshaft drive gear match up with the marks on the idler gear.

3. Install the thrust plate and the hold down bolt.

4. Install the camshaft gear and the thrust plate on the camshaft. Be sure all the marks line up with the marks on the idler gear. Tighten the hold down bolt.

5. Put the injection pump in position and mesh the pump drive gear with the idler gear so the marks on the drive gear match up properly with the marks on the idler gear. Be sure the pump mounting flange scale is set at the proper injection point.

6. Install the mounting nuts to the timing gear case and tighten them.

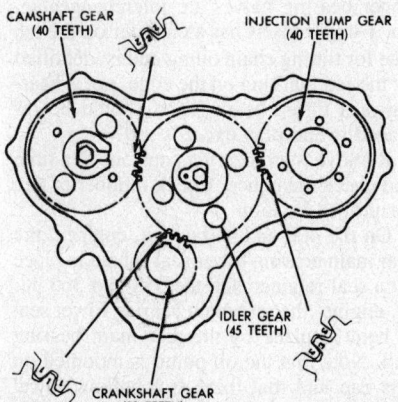

Timing gear alignment—diesel engine

7. Connect the fuel feed line and the filter hoses to the pump.

8. Bleed the air from the fuel system.

9. Connect the injector pipes.

10. Check the idler gear for end play using a feeler gauge between the gear and the thrust plate. It should be between .002 and .006 in. If it exceeds .014 in., replace the thrust plate.

11. Install a new front oil seal (using a new gasket), the timing gear cover and the crankshaft drive pulley.

Camshaft

REMOVAL AND INSTALLATION

4 Cylinder

1. Remove the timing belt cover.

2. Remove the timing belt.

3. Remove the air cleaner assembly.

4. Remove the valve cover.

5. Remove the nos. 1, 3, and 5 camshaft bearing caps.

6. Loosen caps 2 and 4 diagonally and in increments.

7. Lift the camshaft out.

8. Lubricate the camshaft journals and lobes with engine assembly lubricant and position it in the head.

9. Install a new oil seal.

10. Install the nos. 1, 3, 5 bearing caps and torque the nuts to 14 ft. lbs.

11. Install the nos. 2 and 4 caps and diagonally torque the nuts to 14 ft. lbs.

─────── CAUTION ───────
All bearing caps are slightly offset. They should be installed so the numbers on the cap read right side up from the driver's seat.

12. Position a dial indicator so that the feeler touches the front end of the camshaft. Check for end play. Play should not exceed .006 in.

13. Place a new seal on the no. 1 bearing cap. If necessary, replace the end plug in the head.

14. Follow the procedures under Timing Belt Removal and Installation for belt installation and timing.

15. Check the valve clearance and ignition timing.

6-Cylinder Engines—Except Diesel

1. Remove the cylinder head, timing gear cover, camshaft sprocket, and timing chain.

2. Remove the valve tappets, keeping them in order to ensure installation in their original locations.

3. Remove the crankshaft sprocket.

4. Remove the distributor and oil pump.

5. Remove the fuel pump.

6. Install a long bolt into the front of the camshaft to facilitate its removal.

7. Remove the camshaft, being careful not to damage the cam bearings with the cam lobes.

8. Prior to installation, lubricate the camshaft lobes and bearing journals. It is recommended that 1 pt. of crankcase conditioner be added to the initial crankcase oil fill.

9. Install the camshaft in the engine block. From this point, reverse the removal procedure.

V8 Engines

1. Remove the intake manifold, cylinder head covers, rocker arm assemblies, push rods, and valve tappets, keeping them in order to insure the installation in their original locations.

2. Remove the timing gear cover, the camshaft and crankshaft sprockets, and timing chain.

3. Remove the distributor and lift out the oil pump and distributor driveshaft. On 400 and 440 cu. in. engines, remove the fuel pump to allow the push rod to drop away from the cam eccentric.

4. Remove the camshaft thrust plate (on 318 and 360).

5. Install a long bolt into the front of the camshaft and remove the camshaft, being careful not to damage the cam bearings with the cam lobes.

6. Prior to installation, lubricate the camshaft lobes and bearing journals. It is recommended that 1 pt. of Crankcase Conditioner be added to the initial crankcase oil fill. Insert the camshaft into the engine block within 2 in. of its final position in the block.

7. Have an assistant support the camshaft with a suitable tool to prevent the camshaft from contacting the plug in the rear of the engine block. Position the suitable tool against the rear side of the cam gear and be careful not to damage the cam lobes.

8. Replace the camshaft thrust plate. If camshaft end play exceeds 0.010 in., install a new thrust plate. It should be 0.002–0.006 in. with the new plate.

9. Install the timing chain and sprockets, timing gear cover, and pulley.

10. Install the tappets, pushrods, rocker arms, and cylinder head covers. Install fuel pump, if removed.

11. Install the distributor and oil pump driveshaft. Install the distributor.

12. After starting the engine, adjust the ignition timing.

Pistons and Connecting Rods

4 Cylinder

The piston crown is marked with an arrow which must point toward the drive belt end of the engine when installed. The connecting rod and cap are marked with rectangular forge marks which must be mated when assembled and which must be on the intermediate shaft side of the engine when installed.

6 and 8 Cylinder

The notch on the top of each piston must face the front of the engine.

To position the connecting rod correctly, the oil squirt hole should point to the right-side on all six-cylinder engines. On all V8 engines, the larger chamfer of the lower connecting rod bore must face to the rear on the right bank and to the front on the left bank.

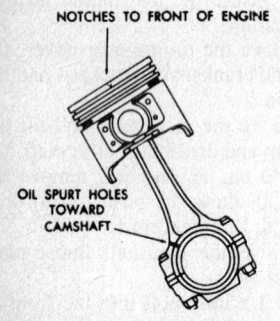

Relation of the piston and connecting rod—6 cylinder

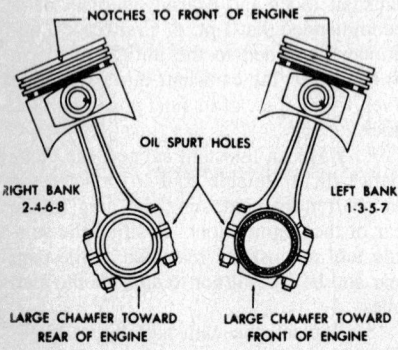

Relation of the piston and connecting rod—V8

REMOVAL AND INSTALLATION

All Engines

1. Follow the instructions under Cylinder Head Removal and Timing Belt, Timing Chain Removal and Oil Pan Removal.

2. Pistons should be removed following the firing order of the engine. Turn the crankshaft until the piston to be removed is at the bottom of its stroke.

3. Place a cloth on the head of the piston to be removed and, using a ridge reamer, remove the deposits from the upper end of the cylinder bore.

NOTE: Never remove more than $^1/_{32}$

in. from the ring travel area when removing the ridges.

4. Mark all connecting rod bearing caps so that they may be returned to their original locations in the engine. The connecting rod caps are usually marked. The marks must be matched when reassembling the engine. Mark all pistons so they can be returned to their original cylinders.

NOTE: After removing the connecting rod cap and bearing, place a short length of rubber hose over the rod bolts to prevent cylinder wall and crank journal scoring when removing or installing the piston and rod assembly.

5. Using an internal micrometer, measure the bores across the thrust faces of the cylinder and parallel to the axis of the crankshaft at a minimum of four equally spaced locations. The bore must not be out-of-round by more than 0.005 in. and it must not taper more than 0.010 in. Taper is the difference in wear between two bore measurements in any cylinder. See the Engine Rebuilding section for complete details.

6. If the cylinder bore is in satisfactory condition, place each ring in the bore in turn and square it in the bore with the head of the piston. Measure the ring gap. If the ring gap is greater than the limit, get a new ring. If the ring gap is less than the limit, file the end of the ring to obtain the correct gap.

7. Check the ring side clearance by installing rings on the piston, and inserting a feeler gauge of the correct dimension between the ring and the lower land. The gauge should slide freely around the ring circumference without binding. Any wear will form a step on the lower land. Remove any pistons having high steps. Before checking the ring side clearance, be sure that the ring grooves are clean and free of carbon, sludge, or grit.

8. Piston rings should be installed so that their ends are at three equal spacings. Avoid installing the rings with their ends in line with the piston pin bosses and the thrust direction.

9. Install the pistons in their original bores, if you are reusing the same pistons. Install short lengths of rubber hose over the connecting rod bolts to prevent damage to the cylinder walls or rod journal.

10. Install a ring compressor over the rings on the piston. Lower the piston and rod assembly into the bore until the ring compressor contacts the block. Using a wooden hammer handle, push the piston into the bore while guiding the rod onto the journal.

Main Bearings

4 Cylinder Engines

The maximum wear limit is .005". A new main bearing should check between .0008"–.003" clearance using PlastiGage. Main bearing shells without lubrication grooves are installed in the bearing caps.

The main bearing shells with lubrication grooves, must be installed into the engine block. Maximum end play is .015". Replace no. 3 (thrust) bearing if end play exceeds that limit.

6 Cylinder Engine

The maximum allowable bearing clearance is .001". no. 1, no. 2 and no. 4 lower inserts are interchangeable. no. 2 and no. 4 upper inserts are interchangeable. no. 1 upper insert has a chamfer on the tab side for timing chain oiling and is identified by the red mark on the edge of the insert. no. 3 upper and lower inserts are flanged. Bearing caps are not interchangeable and are numbered for correct installation. Maximum end play is .0085". Replace no. 3 (thrust) bearing if end play exceeds that amount.

V8 Engine

A Maltese Cross stamped on the engine (except on the 318 and 360) numbering pad indicates that the engine is equipped with a crankshaft which has one or more connecting rods and/or main bearing journal finished .001" undersize. The position of the underside journal(s) is stamped on a machine surface of the no. 3 counterweight. The letter "R" or "M" signifies whether the undersize journal is a rod or main, and the number following the letter indicates which one it is. A Maltese Cross with an "X" indicates that all those journals are .010" undersize. On the 318 and 360 engines, .001 in. undersize journals are indicated by marks on the no. 8 crankshaft counterweight. If the "R" or "M" is followed by "X", all those journals are .010 in. undersize.

Upper and lower bearing inserts are not interchangeable on any of the V8 engines due to oil hole and V-groove in the uppers. On the 318 and 360 cu. in. engine lower bearing halves no. 1, no. 2 and no. 4 are interchangeable; no. 1, no. 2 and no. 4 upper bearing halves are interchangeable. no. 3 bearing is the thrust bearing and no. 5 is the wider rear main bearing. On 400 and 440 cu. in. engines the no. 1, no. 2, no. 4 and no. 5 lower bearing halves are interchangeable; no. 2, no. 4 and no. 5 upper bearing halves are interchangeable. no. 1 upper insert has a chamfer on the tab side for timing chain oiling and is identified by the red marking on the edge. no. 3 bearing is a thrust bearing and should be replaced if end play exceeds .007".

Remove main bearing caps one at a time and check clearance. Check number of cap for proper location.

On the 400 and 440 cu. in. engines, the rear main bearing lower seal is held in place by a seal retainer. On the 318 and 360 cu. in. engine, the rear main bearing lower seal is held in place by the rear main bearing cap. Note that the oil pump is mounted on this cap and that there is a hollow dowel which must be in place when the cap is installed.

Crankshaft Main Bearing

REMOVAL AND INSTALLATION

All Engines

1. Drain the engine oil and remove the oil pan.

2. Mark the bearing caps before removing them.

3. Remove the bearing caps one at a time. Remove the upper half of the bearing by inserting a suitable tool into the oil hole of the crankshaft.

4. Slowly rotate the crankshaft clockwise forcing out the upper half of the bearing shell.

NOTE: Only one main bearing should be selectively fitted while all other main bearing caps are properly torqued. When installing a new upper bearing shell, slightly chamfer the sharp edges from the plain side.

5. To install, start the bearing in place, and insert a suitable tool into the oil hole of the crankshaft. Slowly rotate the crankshaft counter-clockwise sliding the bearing into position. Remove the tool.

6. Continue the installation in the reverse order of the removal.

7. Fill the engine with the proper grade engine oil. Start the engine and check for leaks.

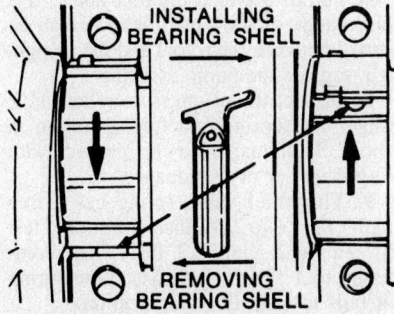

Remove and install the upper main bearing insert using a roll-out pin

Engine Lubrication

4 Cylinder

Lubrication is conventional with a gear type pump. A pressure relief valve prevents extreme pressure from building up in the system.

6 Cylinder—Except Diesel

The engine lubrication system consists of an externally mounted, cam-driven, rotor-type oil pump which is located on the lower right side of the block.

A full-flow disposable oil filter is mounted on the rear of the pump body. Oil is forced from the pump, through the filter, and into a series of internal passages in the engine.

Diesel

The engine oiling system is a full pressure type with a trochoid gear pump and two throwaway oil filters. Oil from the cam driven oil pump is forced into a series of oil passages in the engine. If the oil filter elements become clogged, the pressure difference between the oil filter inlet and outlet will increase and open the pressure relief valve, allowing oil to flow directly into the oil passages bypassing the clogged filter(s).

NOTE: Changing engine oil and filters at the recommended intervals is extremely important to prevent damage in diesel engines.

V8 Engines

The lubrication system for the V8 engines is similar to that of the six-cylinder engines. The major difference is in the location of the rotor-type oil pump. It is internally mounted on the rear main bearing cap on 318 and 360 engines. On 400 and 440 engines, the pump is mounted outside the block on the front of the engine.

Oil Pan

REMOVAL AND INSTALLATION

4 Cylinder

1. Drain the oil pan.

2. Support the pan and remove the attaching bolts.

3. Lower the pan and discard the gaskets.

4. Clean all gasket surfaces thoroughly and install the pan using gasket sealer and a new gasket.

5. Torque the pan bolts to 7 ft. lbs.

6. Refill the pan, start the engine, and check for leaks.

6 Cylinder Vans and Pick-ups

1. Disconnect the battery and remove the dipstick.

2. Remove the engine cover and remove the starter and air cleaner.

3. Raise the van on a hoist and drain the crankcase oil.

4. Install an engine support as described under "Engine Removal."

5. Disconnect and tie out of the way: driveshaft, transmission linkage, and exhaust pipe at the manifold.

6. Remove the clutch torque shaft (if equipped) and the oil cooler lines (if equipped).

7. Disconnect the speedometer cable

and electrical connections to the transmission.

8. Remove the support bracket, inspection plate, and drive plate-to-converter attaching screws if equipped.

9. Remove the bolts which attach the transmission to the clutch housing. Carefully work the transmission and converter rearward off the engine dowels and disengage the converter hub from the end of the crankshaft. Remove the transmission.

10. Support the rear of the engine and raise it two inches.

11. Remove the oil pan attaching bolts. Positioning the crankshaft so that the counterweights will clear the pan, rotate the pan to the steering gear side and remove it. You may have to turn the pump pickup tube for clearance.

12. Installation is the reverse of removal. Make sure that the pickup screen contacts the bottom of the pan. Fill the engine with oil and check for leaks.

11. Remove the oil pan attaching screws and position the crankshaft so that the pan will clear the counterweights. Remove the pan.

12. Installation is the reverse of removal. Check all fluid levels and be sure that there are no leaks.

318 and 360 V8 Vans and Pick-ups

1. Disconnect the battery ground cable. Remove the dipstick and tube, engine cover, and air cleaner.

2. Disconnect the throttle linkage at the rear of the engine and the clutch or automatic transmission linkage.

3. Raise the engine slightly and support it with the device described under "Engine Removal".

4. Raise the vehicle and drain the oil. Remove the starter.

5. Remove the driveshaft and engine rear support.

6. Remove the transmission from the van. Remove the automatic transmission with the filler tube installed and the torque converter separated from the drive plate.

7. Remove the clutch assembly and flywheel (or driveplate) from the crankshaft.

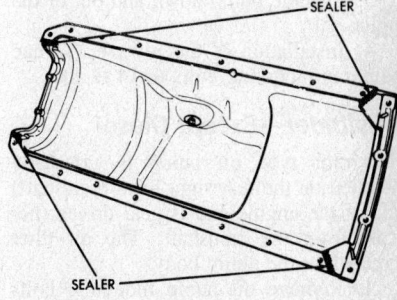

Apply ⅛ inch beads of silicone sealer to the corners of the oil pan—6 cylinder shown

8. Raise the engine about 2 in.

9. Rotate the crankshaft so that the counterweights will clear the oil pan. Maximum clearance is with the notch in the crankshaft flange at the 3 o'clock position. Remove the oil pan. It will be necessary to reach inside the oil pan and turn the oil pick-up tube and strainer slightly to the right to clear the pan.

10. Installation is the reverse of removal. Be sure to check all fluid levels and be sure that there are no leaks.

Two-Wheel Drive Ramcharger and Trail Duster

1. Disconnect the battery cable and remove the dipstick.

2. Raise and support the truck.

3. Drain the oil.

4. Remove the torque converter or clutch housing brace.

5. If necessary, remove the exhaust pipe.

6. Remove the oil pan bolts and remove the pan.

7. Installation is the reverse of removal.

Four-Wheel Drive Ramcharger and Trail Duster

1. Raise vehicle on a hoist.

2. Remove the two front engine mounting bolts.

3. Remove the left-side support, connecting the converter housing and cylinder block.

4. Raise the engine approximately 2 in.

5. Drain oil.

6. Remove the oil pan bolts, lower pan down and to the rear. (Do not turn oil pickup out of position)

Oil Pump

REMOVAL AND INSTALLATION

4 Cylinder

1. Remove the oil pan.

2. Remove the two pump mounting bolts.

3. Pull the pump down and out of the engine.

4. Installation is the reverse. Torque the pump mounting bolts to 14 ft. lbs.

6-Cylinder—Except Diesel

The rotor type oil pump is externally mounted on the rear right-hand (camshaft) side of the engine and is gear driven (helical) from the camshaft. The oil filter screws into the pump body.

1. Remove oil pump mounting bolts and remove pump and filter assembly from engine.

2. Disassemble the oil pump (drive gear must be pressed off) and inspect the

following clearances: maximum cover wear is .0015"; outer rotor to body maximum clearance is .014"; maximum clearance between rotors is .010". Inspect the pressure relief valve for scoring and free operation. Relief valve spring should have a free length of 2¼ in.

3. Install new oil seal rings between cover and body, tightening cover attaching bolts to 95 in. lbs.

4. Install oil pump to engine block using a new gasket and tightening mounting bolts to 200 in. lbs.

Diesel

1. Remove the oil pan, oil pickup tube, strainer and all old gaskets.

2. Remove the oil pump joint bolt, filter assembly to pump tube and the oil pump.

3. Clean all gasket surfaces.

4. Remove the oil pump cover. Remove the inner rotor and shaft assembly and lift out the outer rotor.

5. Clean all parts thoroughly. Mating surfaces of the pump should be smooth. Replace the cover if it is scratched or grooved.

6. Install the outer rotor into the pump body. Install the inner rotor onto the outer rotor and seat it into the pump body. Place a straight edge across the pump face. Insert a feeler gauge between the straight edge and the rotors. Clearance should be between .0014" and .004". If clearance exceeds .006" replace both the inner and outer rotors. Check the clearance between the inner and outer rotor. Clearance should be .007" or less. If clearance exceeds .01" replace both the inner and outer rotors. Measure the clearance between the outer rotor and the pump body. Clearance should be between .008" and .01". If clearance exceeds .02" replace the outer rotor. Measure the rotor chaft OD and the pump body ID. The clearance between the shaft and the body should be between .001" and .003". If clearance exceeds .006" replace the inner rotor and shaft and/or the pump body.

7. Replace all parts that show signs of wear.

8. Installation is in the reverse order of removal. Always use new gaskets.

NOTE: It is necessary to remove the oil pan, and to remove the oil pump from the rear main bearing cap to service the oil pump.

1. Drain the engine oil and remove the oil pan.

2. Remove the oil pump mounting bolts and remove the oil pump from the rear main bearing cap.

3. To remove the relief valve, drill a ⅛ inch hole into the relief valve retainer cap and insert a self-threading sheet metal screw into the cap. Clamp the screw into a vise and while supporting the oil pump, remove the cap by tapping the pump body using a soft hammer. Discard the retainer

cap and remove the spring and the relief valve.

4. Remove the oil pump cover and lockwashers, and lift off the cover. Discard the oil ring seal. Remove the pump rotor and shaft, and lift out the outer rotor.

NOTE: Wash all parts in solvent and inspect for damage or wear. The mating surfaces of the oil pump cover should be smooth. Replace the pump assembly if this is not the case.

5. Lay a straight edge across the pump cover surface and if a .0015 inch feeler gauge can be inserted between the cover and the straight edge, the pump assembly should be replaced. Measure the thickness and the diameter of the outer rotor. If the outer rotor thickness measures .825 inch or less, (.943 inch or less on 360 cu. in. engines 1977–82) or if the diameter is 2.469 inches or less, replace the outer rotor. If the inner rotor measures .825 inch or less, (.943 inch or less on 360 cu. in. engines 1977–82) then the inner rotor and shaft assembly must be replaced.

6. Slide the outer rotor into the pump body, do this by pressing it to one side with your fingers and measure the clearance between the rotor and the pump body. If the measurement is .014 inch or more, replace the oil pump assembly. Install the inner rotor and shaft into the pump body. If the clearance between the inner and outer rotors is .010 inch or more, replace the shaft and both rotors.

7. Place a straight edge across the face of the pump, between the bolt holes. If a feeler gauge of .004 inch or more can be inserted between the rotors and the straight edge, replace the pump assembly.

8. Inspect the oil pressure relief valve plunger for scoring and free operation in its bore. Small marks may be removed with 400-grit wet or dry sandpaper.

9. The relief valve spring has a free length of 2 1/32 to 2 3/64 inch and should test between 16.2 and 17.2 lbs. when compressed to 1 11/32 inch. Replace the spring if it fails to meet this specification.

10. To install, assemble the oil pump, using new parts as required. Tighten the cover bolts to 95 in. lbs.

11. Prime the oil pump before installation by filling the rotor cavity with engine oil. Install the oil pump on the engine and tighten attaching bolts to 30 ft. lbs.

12. Continue the installation in the reverse order of the removal.

13. Fill the engine with the proper grade motor oil. Start the engine and check for leaks.

400, 440 V8 Engines

The rotor type oil pump is externally mounted and gear driven from the camshaft. The oil filter screws into the pump body.

1. Drain engine oil.

2. Remove oil pump and filter assem-

bly.

3. Disassemble and inspect pump components for wear. If 0.0015" feeler gauge can be inserted between cover and straight edge, replace cover. Install outer rotor in pump body and holding against one side of body measure clearance between rotor and body. If clearance is greater than 0.014", replace oil pump body. Install inner rotor into pump body and place straight edge across pump body between bolt holes. If feeler gauge greater than 0.004" can be inserted between rotors and body, replace oil pump body. Measure clearance between tips of inner and outer rotor where they are opposed. If clearance exceeds 0.010", replace inner and outer rotors. Use new oil seal rings between filter base and body. Tighten bolts to 10 ft. lbs. Use a new O-ring seal on pilot of oil pump before attaching pump to engine block.

4. Install oil pump on engine using new gasket and tightening bolts to 30 ft. lbs. The distributor drive gear slot should parallel the crankshaft with no. 1 cylinder on TDC.

5. Install oil filter and fill crankcase with oil.

Rear Main Bearing Oil Seal

REMOVAL AND INSTALLATION

4 Cylinder Engines

The rear main seal is located in a housing on the rear of the block. To replace the seal it is necessary to remove the engine.

1. Remove the transmission and flywheel.

—————— CAUTION ——————

Before removing the transmission, align the dimple on the flywheel with the pointer on the flywheel housing. The transmission will not mate with the engine during installation unless this alignment is observed.

2. Very carefully, pry the old seal out of the support ring.

3. Coat the new seal with clean engine oil and press it into place with a flat piece of metal. Take great care not to scratch the seal or crankshaft.

4. Install the flywheel and transmission.

6 and 8 Cylinder Engines (Except Diesel)

Service replacement seals are of the split rubber type composition. This type of seal makes it possible to replace the upper rear seal without removing the crankshaft. The seal must be used as an upper and lower set and cannot be used with the rope type seal.

NOTE: Rope type seals are included in overhaul gasket sets, for use when the crankshaft has been removed, on all engines, except the 360 V-8, which uses only the composition seal.

The following procedure is for removing the rope type rear main seal and replacing it with the rubber type seal.

1. Remove the oil pan, and both the rear seal retainer and the rear main bearing cap, if separate.

2. Remove the lower rope seal from the cap or retainer by prying the seal out of the groove.

3. With the use of suitable tools, either pull or push the seal from its seat, while rotating the crankshaft, being careful not to damage the surface of the journal. If necessary, loosen all the main bearing caps slightly, to lower the crankshaft, which will aid in the removal and replacement of the seal.

4. Clean and lubricate the crankshaft journal. Hold the seal tight against the crankshaft with the painted stripe to the rear, and install the seal into the block groove.

5. Rotate the crankshaft while pushing the seal into the groove. Be careful that the sharp edges of the block groove, *do not cut or nick the rear of the seal*.

6. Install the lower half of the seal into the lower seal retainer or the main bearing cap, if separate, with the paint stripe facing to the rear.

7. Install the lower seal retainer and/or the rear main bearing cap. Torque all main bearing caps to specifications.

8. Install the oil pan, add oil and check for oil leaks.

Diesel Engine

The rear main oil seal is a one piece design mounted with a sleeve. Two side seals are also used in grooves located on no. 7 main bearing cap.

1. Oil pan and flywheel are removed.

2. Rear seal retainer bolts, retainer and no. 7 main bearing cap are removed.

3. The two side seals are installed after no. 7 main bearing cap has been mounted and torqued to specs. Apply gasket sealer to the seals. Slide the seals into place, do not "drive" them in. When properly installed, the seal should conform to the corners of the mounting grooves.

4. The rear main seal is retained by a sleeve and plate. Remove the old seal from the retainer, clean the retainer, mount a new seal, lubricate the lips of the seal and install seal sleeve and retainer. Torque the mounting bolts to 2.2 ft. lbs. Install the flywheel, oil pan etc.

ENGINE COOLING

Radiator

REMOVAL AND INSTALLATION

4 Cylinder Engines

1. Move the temperature selector to full on.

2. Disconnect negative battery cable. Open the radiator drain cock.

3. When the coolant reserve tank (if equipped) is empty, remove the radiator cap.

4. Remove the hoses.

5. If equipped with automatic transmission, disconnect and plug the fluid cooler lines.

6. Remove the upper and lower mounting brackets.

7. Remove the shroud.

8. Remove the fan motor attaching bolts.

9. Remove the top radiator attaching bolts.

10. Remove the bottom radiator attaching bolts.

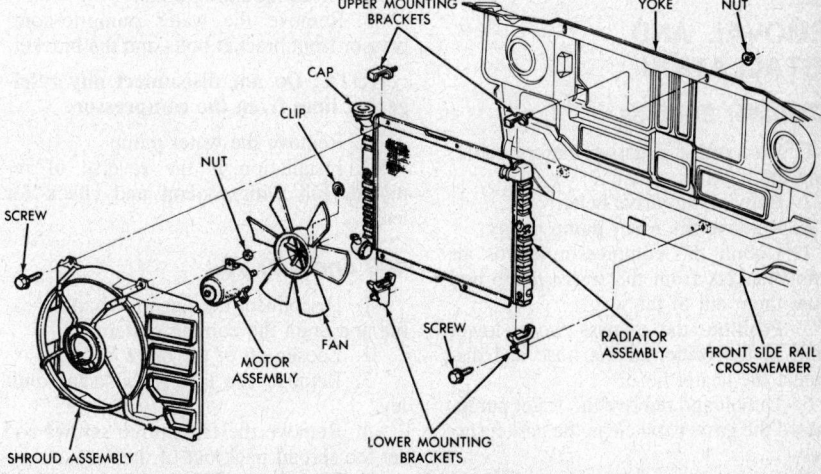

Typical 4 cylinder engine cooling system components

11. Lift radiator from engine compartment.

12. Installation is the reverse of removal.

6 and 8 Cylinder Engines

1. Drain the cooling system.
2. Disconnect the battery ground cable.
3. Detach the upper hose from the radiator.
4. Remove the shroud mounting nuts and position it out of the way.
5. Remove the radiator top mounting screws. If equipped with air conditioning, remove the condenser attaching screws, accessible through the grille. Do not disconnect any air conditioning lines.
6. Raise the vehicle and support it. Disconnect and plug the automatic transmission cooler lines and cap the openings in the cooler.
7. Hold the radiator in place and remove the lower mounting screws. Carefully lower the radiator out of the van or lift it up and out if a pickup truck.
8. Installation is the reverse of removal. Check all fluid levels and run the engine, making sure that there are no leaks.

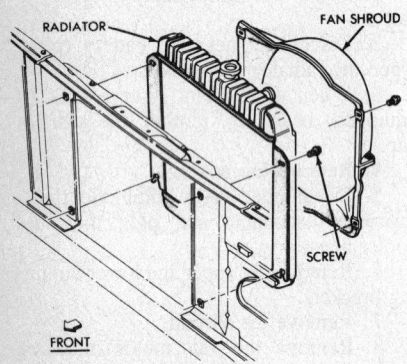

Typical radiator and fan shroud mounting—6 and V8 engines

Water Pump

REMOVAL AND INSTALLATION

4 Cylinder Engines

1. Disconnect negative battery cable. Drain the cooling system.
2. Remove the drive belts.
3. Remove the water pump pulley.
4. Unbolt the compressor and/or air pump brackets from the water pump and secure them out of the way.
5. Position the bypass hose lower clamp in the center of the hose and disconnect the heater hose.
6. Unbolt and remove the water pump. Discard the gasket and clean the gasket surfaces.
7. Installation is the reverse of removal. Torque the water pump bolts to 25

ft. lbs., the alternator adjusting bolt to 30–50 ft. lbs.; the pulley bolts to 85–125 in. lbs.

6 Cylinder—Except Diesel

NOTE: This job can sometimes be done without removing the radiator on models without air-conditioning, if there is enough room to get at the water pump bolts.

1. Remove the radiator.
2. Remove all drive belts.
3. Remove the fan, spacer, pulley, and bolts as an assembly.
4. If equipped with an air pump, remove the pump brackets with the hoses attached and tie it out of the way.
5. Disconnect the heater hose and all other hoses from the pump.
6. Remove the pump from the block.
7. Installation is the reverse of removal. Fill the cooling system and adjust the tension of the drive belts.

318 and 360 V8

1. Remove the radiator.
2. Loosen all accessories that are belt driven and remove all the drive belts.
3. On engines without air conditioning, remove the alternator bracket attaching bolts and tie the alternator and bracket out of the way.
4. On engines with air conditioning, remove the idler pulley assembly, alternator, and adjusting bracket.
5. Remove the fan blade, spacer (or fluid unit), pulley, and bolts as an assembly.

NOTE: To prevent silicone fluid from draining into the drive bearing and ruining the lubricant, do not place the thermostatic fan drive unit with the shaft pointing downward.

6. Disconnect all hoses from the water pump.
7. Remove the air conditioning compressor front mounting bolts.
8. Remove the water pump-to-compressor front bracket bolts and the bracket.

NOTE: Do not disconnect any refrigerant lines from the compressor.

9. Remove the water pump.
10. Installation is the reverse of removal. Fill with coolant and check for leaks.

400 and 440 V8

1. Disconnect the negative battery cable and drain the cooling system.
2. Loosen all of the drive belts.
3. Remove the lower crankshaft pulley.
4. Remove the fan shroud screws and set the shroud back out of the way.
5. Remove the fluid fan drive bolts and set the fluid fan and the fan assembly aside.

6. Remove the water pump and the gasket.
7. Reverse to install. Rotate the pump by hand before attaching any of the drive belts to be sure it rotates freely.

Diesel Engine

1. Drain the cooling system and remove the heater hoses and the bypass hose.
2. Loosen the alternator mounting bolts and remove the belt.
3. Remove the cooling fan, the spacer and the drive pulley.
4. Remove the water pump mounting bolts and remove the pump.
5. Reverse to install.

Thermostat

REMOVAL AND INSTALLATION

4 Cylinder Engines

1. Drain the cooling system to a level below the thermostat.
2. Remove the hoses from the thermostat housing.
3. Remove the thermostat housing.
4. Remove the thermostat and discard the gasket. Clean the gasket surfaces thoroughly.
5. Using a new gasket, position the thermostat and install the housing and bolts. Make sure that the thermostat is seated properly.
6. Refill the cooling system.

6 and 8 Cylinder Engines

1. Drain the cooling system to below the level of the thermostat.
2. Remove the upper radiator hose from the thermostat housing. Note the positioning of the thermostat. It is important that the thermostat is correctly installed.
3. Withdraw the housing bolts and remove the housing and the thermostat.
4. Check to make sure that the thermostat valve closes tightly. If the valve does not close completely due to foreign material, carefully clean the sealing edge of the valve while being careful not to damage the sealing edge. If the valve does not close tightly after it has been cleaned, a new thermostat must be installed.
5. Immerse the thermostat in a container of warm water so that its pellet is completely covered and does not touch the bottom or sides of the container.
6. Heat the water and, while stirring the water continuously (to ensure uniform temperature), check the water temperature with a thermometer at the point when a 0.001 in. feeler gauge can be inserted in the valve opening at a water temperature with ±5 degrees of the standard thermostat opening temperature. If the thermostat does not open within the temperature range, replace it with a new thermostat.

7. Continue heating the water to a temperature of approximately 20 degrees higher than the standard thermostat opening temperature. At this point, the thermostat should be fully open. If it is not, install a new thermostat.

8. To install, use a new gasket and position the thermostat so that its pellet end (the part with the spring) is toward the engine block. On the six, the vent hole must be up. Refit the thermostat housing and tighten its securing bolts.

9. Refit the upper radiator hose.

10. Fill the cooling system to 1.25 in. below the filler neck with the correct water and antifreeze mixture. Warm the engine and inspect the upper radiator hose and the thermostat housing for leaks.

NOTE: Poor heater output and slow engine warm-up is often caused by a thermostat stuck in the open position; occasionally one sticks shut causing immediate overheating. Do not attempt to correct an overheating condition by permanently removing the thermostat. Thermostat flow restriction is designed into the system; without it, localized overheating due to turbulence may occur.

EMISSION CONTROLS

Description

Two basic approaches to emission control have been used on Dodge engines. The first is engine design modifications, which apply to some extent to all engines. The second is a group of specific emission control systems, the application of which varies with model and power train. Those models rated under a specific GVW are subject to stricter light-duty emission regulations, and therefore use more of these systems.

The design modifications and emission control systems are listed here; tests and adjustments for the systems will be found in the General Repair Section on Emission Controls.

Engine Design Modifications

Engine design modifications have been made from model year to model year, to aid in the reduction of harmful emissions.

The intake manifold has been modified to aid in the rapid vaporization of the fuel, and modification of the combustion chamber design allows better combustion of the fuel.

Compression ratios were reduced on most engines, to allow the use of a lower octane fuel, and the cam shaft design was changed to allow greater valve overlap to reduce engine emissions.

Carburetors have continually been modified to aid in fuel distribution and the electronic ignition system is used to reduce the need for continual adjustment of the ignition system and also provides for better and more precise spark.

Electric Assist Choke System

Two types of electric choke controls are used to shorten the choke duration during both winter and summer operation.

The single stage choke control operates a slower choke opening at temperatures of 58° or below, and a rapid choke opening at temperatures of 68° and higher.

The dual stage choke control provides partial power to the choke coil at temperatures of 58° and below, and full power to the choke coil at temperatures of 68° and above, and will stop the current to the choke coil at temperatures of approximately 130° and higher.

Engines started in the winter will experience three levels of current to the choke coil from the dual choke control: LOW during the engine warmup, HIGH after the engine warm-up, and NONE after the engine reaches normal operating temperatures. Engines started in summer weather, will not have the LOW system in operation, nor will an engine that is restarted when hot, have a HIGH.

NOTE: All temperature readings are in Fahrenheit.

SINGLE STAGE CONTROL SWITCH TEST

1. Remove the BAT connector from the control unit.

2. Connect a test lamp to the small terminal of the control to ground.

3. Start the engine and warm it up to normal operating temperature.

4. Reconnect the BAT terminal wire to its post on the control and observe the test lamp.

5. The test lamp should light. It may remain on for a few seconds or for a longer duration, but must not remain on for over five minutes. If so, replace the control switch.

DUAL STAGE CONTROL SWITCH TEST

1. The test procedure is the same for the dual stage control switch as for the single stage switch, except the brightness or intensity of the test lamp should match that of battery current during the test. If the intensity is less, or the light remains on for over five minutes, the control switch is defective and should be replaced.

CHOKE HEATING ELEMENT TEST

1. Disconnect the electric heating element wire at the control switch.

2. Connect an ohmmeter lead to the crimped junction of the element wire at the choke end, avoiding connection with the heater casing. Ground the other lead of the ohmmeter.

3. Resistance of twelve ohms is acceptable. Replace the unit if resistance is outside this range.

4. Make sure choke linkage moves freely when hot and when cold.

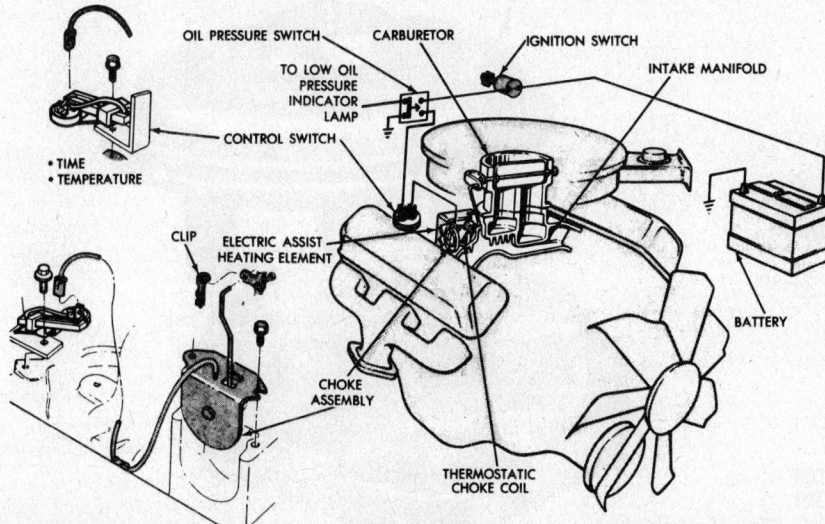

Typical electric choke system components

Heated Air Intake System

The carburetor air preheater is a device which is part of the air cleaner and which keeps the air entering the carburetor at about 100° when underhood temperatures are less than 100°. By using this device, the carburetor can be calibrated much leaner to improve engine warm-up characteristics.

The heated air intake system is basically a two circuit airflow system. When underhood temperatures are less than 100°, the air will flow into the stove, through a flexible connector, into the adaptor on the bottom of the snorkel, and then into the carburetor. When the underhood temperature is above 100°, the airflow will be through the snorkel.

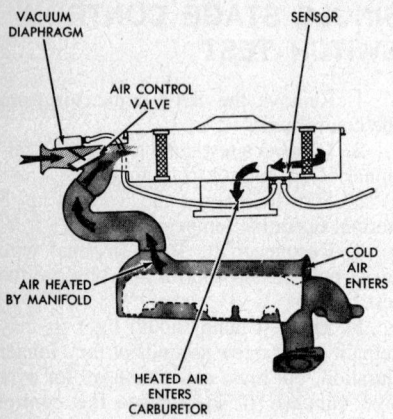

Heated air inlet system

Modulation of the induction air is performed through the use of intake manifold vacuum, a temperature sensor, and a vacuum diaphragm which operates the heat control door in the snorkel.

Orific Spark Advance Control (OSAC)

The OSAC system is used to control NOx. The system controls the amount of vacuum supplied to the vacuum advance mechanism of the distributor.

Exhaust Gas Recirculation (EGR)

EGR is used in conjunction with the vacuum spark advance control to limit peak flame temperatures and thus retard the formation of NOx. Two alternate systems are used.

Ported Vacuum Control System

This system uses a slot type port in the carburetor throttle body which is exposed to an increasing percentage of manifold vacuum by the opening movement of the throttle plate. The throttle bore port is directly connected to the EGR valve through an external nipple. The flow rate of exhaust gases is determined by manifold vacuum, throttle position, and exhaust gas backpressure. Wide open throttle recycling of exhaust gases is prevented by calibrating the valve opening point above manifold vacuum available at wide open throttle, since port vacuum cannot exceed manifold vacuum.

Venturi Vacuum Control System

This system uses a vacuum tap at the throat of the carburetor venturi to provide a control signal. Because the signal is so low however, a vacuum amplifier is used to increase the strength of the signal. The amplifier uses stored manifold vacuum to provide the source for amplification. Elimination of EGR at wide open throttle is accomplished by a "dump" diaphragm which compares venturi and manifold vacuum to determine when wide open throttle is achieved. At wide open throttle, the internal reservoir is "dumped", limiting the output of the EGR valve to manifold vacuum. As with the ported vacuum control system, the valve opening point is set above the manifold vacuum available at wide open throttle, permitting the valve to be closed at wide open throttle.

Coolant Control Exhaust Gas Recirculation Valve

Trucks with EGR are equipped with a CCEGR valve located in the top of the radiator tank. When coolant in the top radiator tank reaches 65°, the valve opens to apply vacuum to the EGR valve to recirculate exhaust gases.

EGR Delay System

Some trucks are equipped with an EGR delay system, which is an electrical timer on the dash to control an engine mounted solenoid. The timer prevents exhaust gas recirculation for about 35 seconds after the ignition is turned on.

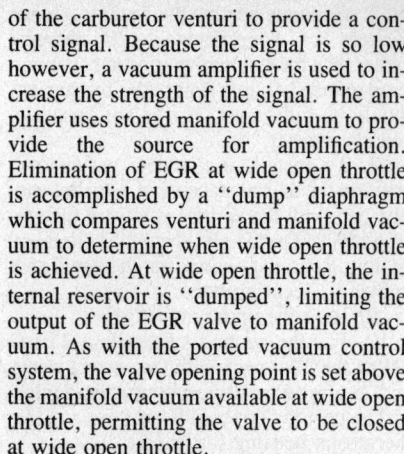

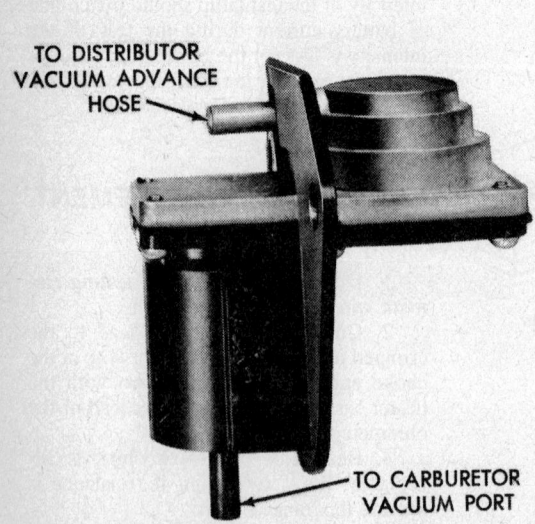

OSAC valve

EGR control valve

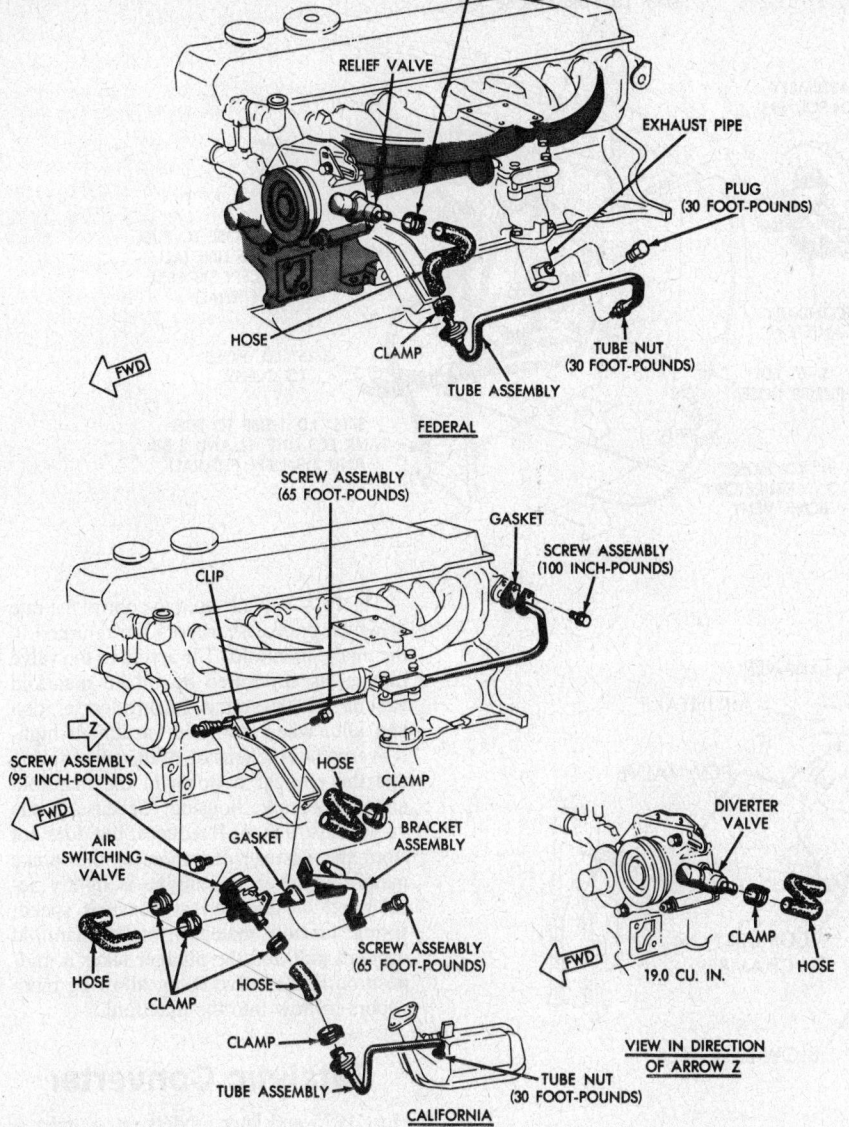

Air injection system—typical 6 cylinder

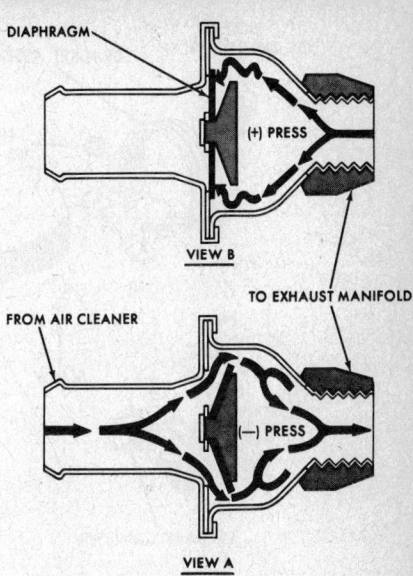

Aspirator valve

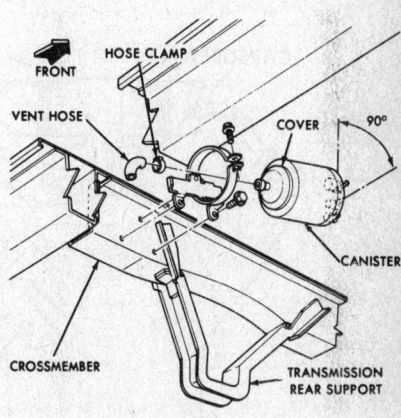

Typical single canister mounting

Air Injection System

This system adds a controlled amount of air through special passages in the cylinder head, to exhaust gases in the exhaust ports, causing oxidation of the gases and thereby reducing carbon monoxide and hydrocarbon emissions to the required levels.

The air injection system consists of a belt-driven air pump, rubber hose, a check valve to protect the hoses and pump from hot gases, injection tubes, and a combination diverter/pressure relief valve assembly.

Aspirator Air System

This valve utilizes exhaust pressure pulsation to draw clean air from the inside of the air cleaner into the exhaust system. The function is to reduce HC (hydrocarbon) emissions. It is located in a tube between the exhaust manifold and the air cleaner.

Evaporative Control System

The function of the evaporative control system is to prevent the emission of raw gasoline vapors from the fuel tank and carburetor into the atmosphere. When fuel evaporates in the tank or float bowl, the vapors pass through lines and into the charcoal canister where they are temporarily stored until they can be drawn into the intake manifold and burned. A vacuum port located in the base of the carburetor governs vapor flow from the canister to the engine.

Closed Crankcase Ventilation System

The closed PCV system operates as follows:

1. In place of a vented oil filler cap, an air intake line is installed between the carburetor air filter and a crankcase opening in the valve cover.

2. A sealed oil filler cap and dipstick are used.

3. A separate PCV air filter is used. The filter is located where the intake air line connects to the valve cover.

Under normal engine operation, air enters through the intake line from the air filter. Under heavy acceleration, any excess vapors back up through the air intake line and are forced to mix with incoming air into the carburetor and are burned in the combustion chamber. Back-up fumes cannot escape into the atmosphere, creating a closed system.

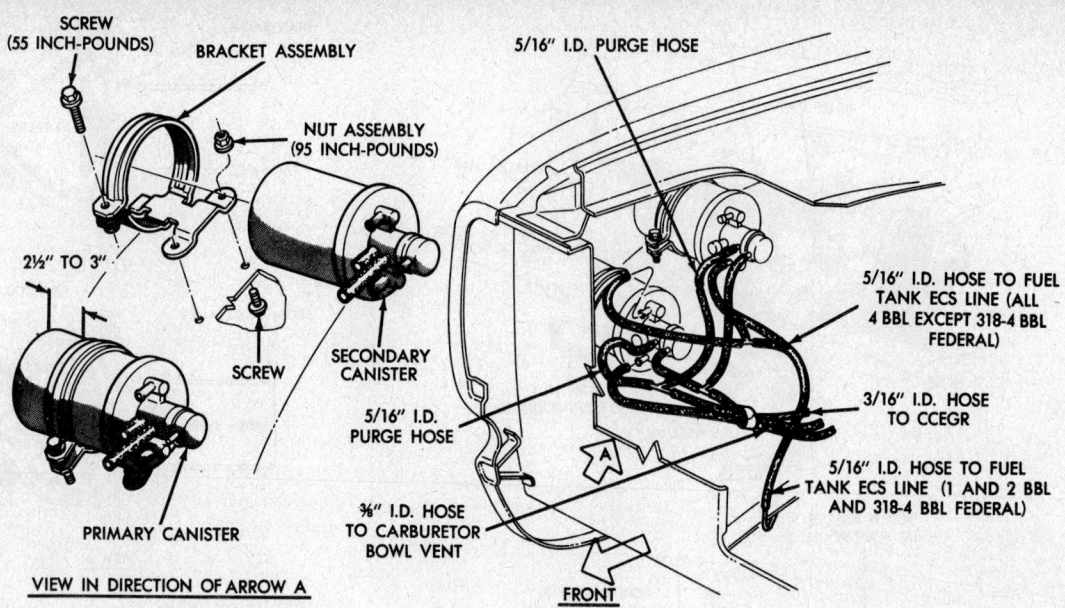

SCREW
(55 INCH-POUNDS)

BRACKET ASSEMBLY

5/16" I.D. PURGE HOSE

NUT ASSEMBLY
(95 INCH-POUNDS)

2½" TO 3"

SCREW

SECONDARY
CANISTER

5/16" I.D.
PURGE HOSE

⅜" I.D. HOSE
TO CARBURETOR
BOWL VENT

PRIMARY CANISTER

5/16" I.D. HOSE TO FUEL
TANK ECS LINE (ALL
4 BBL EXCEPT 318-4 BBL
FEDERAL)

3/16" I.D. HOSE
TO CCEGR

5/16" I.D. HOSE TO FUEL
TANK ECS LINE (1 AND 2 BBL
AND 318-4 BBL FEDERAL)

VIEW IN DIRECTION OF ARROW A

FRONT

Typical dual canister mounting

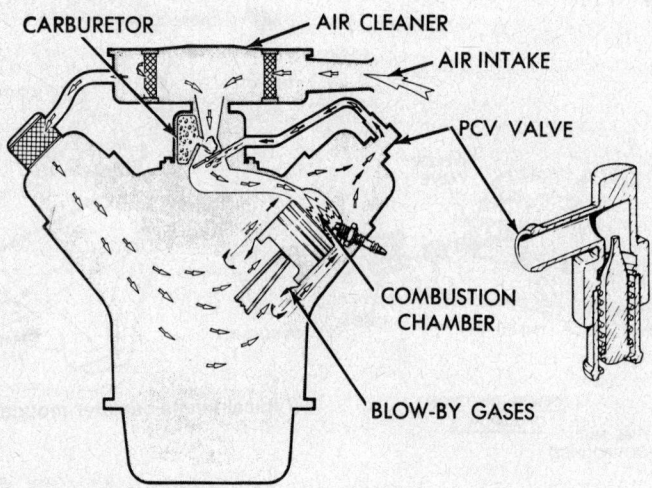

CARBURETOR

AIR CLEANER

AIR INTAKE

PCV VALVE

COMBUSTION
CHAMBER

BLOW-BY GASES

Closed crankcase ventilation system

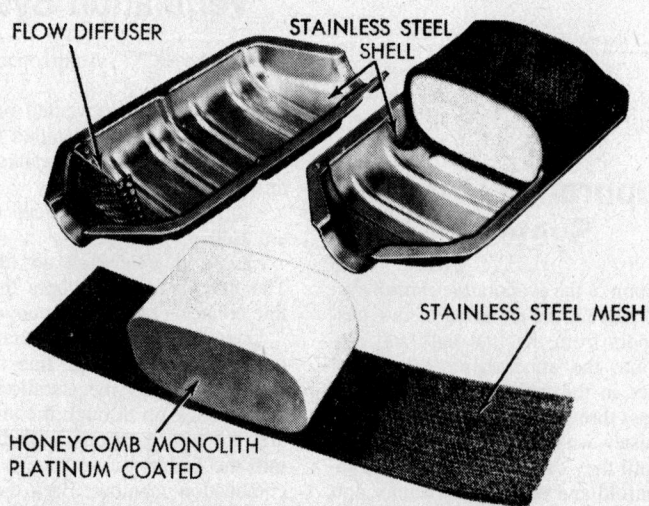

FLOW DIFFUSER

STAINLESS STEEL
SHELL

STAINLESS STEEL MESH

HONEYCOMB MONOLITH
PLATINUM COATED

Typical catalytic converter

The PCV valve is used to control the rate at which crankcase vapors are returned to the intake manifold. The action of the valve plunger is controlled by intake manifold vacuum and the spring. During deceleration and idle, when manifold vacuum is high, it overcomes the tension of the valve spring and the plunger bottoms in the manifold end of the valve housing. Because of the valve construction, it reduces, but does not stop, the passage of vapors to the intake manifold. When the engine is lightly accelerated or operated at constant speed, spring tension matches intake manifold vacuum pull and the plunger takes a mid-position in the valve body, allowing more vapors to flow into the manifold.

Catalytic Converter

Most 1975 and later models rated under a specific GVW, are equipped with catalytic converters. These devices are used to oxidize excess carbon monoxide (CO), hydrocarbons (HC) and, on later models, to help control oxides of nitrogen (NOx) in the exhaust system before they can escape out the tailpipe and into the atmosphere. The converter is installed in front of the mufflers, underneath the truck, and protected by a heat shield.

The expected catalyst life is 50,000 miles, provided that the engine is kept in tune and unleaded fuel is used.

To keep the catalyst from being overheated by an overly rich mixture during deceleration, a catalyst protection system (CPS) is sometimes used. The system consists of a throttle positioner solenoid (not to be confused with the idle stop solenoid), a control box, and an engine rpm sensor.

Any time that the engine speed is more than 2,000 rpm, the solenoid is energized and keeps the throttle butterfly from fully closing, thus preventing the deceleration mixture from becoming too rich.

Vacuum Throttle Positioner

Some 1975 and later models have a throttle positioner to hold the throttle slightly open on deceleration above 2000 rpm. This prevents excessive emission of unburned hydrocarbons. The system consists of an electronic speed switch, a vacuum solenoid valve, and a vacuum actuated throttle positioner. Adjust this device as follows:

1. Run the engine at about 2500 rpm.
2. Loosen the vacuum unit locknut and turn it until it just contacts the throttle lever.
3. Release the throttle. Adjust the unit to decrease engine speed until speed suddenly drops 1000 rpm or more. Back off the adjuster ¼ turn more and tighten the locknut.
4. Check the adjustment by accelerating the engine to about 2500 rpm and releasing the throttle. The engine should return to normal idle speed.

FUEL SYSTEM

Fuel Pump

REMOVAL AND INSTALLATION

1. Disconnect the fuel lines from the inlet and output sides of the fuel pump.
2. Plug these lines to prevent gasoline from leaking out.
3. Unbolt the retaining bolts from the fuel pump and remove the fuel pump from the engine.
4. Remove the old gasket from the engine and/or fuel pump.
5. Clean all mounting surfaces.
6. Using a new gasket, install the fuel pump. Installation is the reverse of removal.

TESTING (ON THE VEHICLE)

1. If leakage is not apparent, the following pressure test should be performed.
2. Insert a "Tee" fitting into the fuel line at the carburetor.
3. Connect a 6 in. piece of hose between the "Tee" fitting and a pressure gauge.
4. Vent the pump for a few seconds to allow the pump to operate at maximum capacity.
5. Connect a tachometer and start the engine. Allow the engine to run at idle speed. The fuel pump pressure should be 3.5–5.0 (6-cylinder) or 5.0–7.0 psi (V8's). When the engine is stopped, the pressure should return to zero very slowly. If it rapidly or instantly drops to zero, a leaky outlet valve is indicated.

VOLUME TEST (ON THE VEHICLE)

1. Disconnect the fuel line from the carburetor. Place the end of the line in a container holding at least 1 quart.
2. The fuel pump should pump out 1 quart in 1 minute or less at 500 rpm.

CARBURETORS

NOTE: Carburetor specifications, exploded views, and basic adjustments are found in the General Repair section under Carburetor Repairs.

REMOVAL AND INSTALLATION

The following is a general removal procedure for all carburetors.
1. Disconnect the battery ground cable.

2. Remove the air cleaner.
3. Remove the fuel tank pressure-vacuum filler cap. The tank could be under a small amount of pressure.
4. Disconnect and plug the fuel lines. Use two wrenches to avoid twisting the fuel line. A container is also useful to catch any fuel which spills from the lines.
5. Disconnect the throttle and choke linkage.
6. Disconnect any vacuum lines.
7. Remove the mounting bolts.
8. Carefully remove the carburetor from the engine and carry it in a level position to a clean work place.
9. Installation is the reverse of removal. Adjust the curb idle speed.

Diesel Injection Pump

TESTING (ON THE VEHICLE)

1. With the engine running, loosen the cap on the fuel injection line at the injection pump outlet. This will relieve pressure and prevent fuel injection into the cylinder.
2. If a cylinder is misfiring, uneven combustion will stop when the fuel is cut off.
3. Proceed from cylinder to cylinder until the faulty cylinder is located.
4. Perform a compression test on the cylinder in question. If the cylinder in question meets the compression specifications, replace the injection pump.

REMOVAL AND INSTALLATION

1. Disconnect the batteries.
2. Disconnect the fuel shutoff rod at the stop lever.
3. Remove the power steering pump and the mounting bracket from the engine and set it aside.

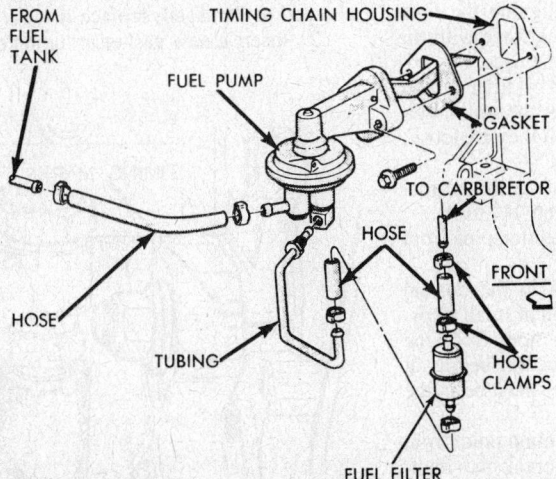

318 and 360 V8 engine fuel pump details

Fuel pump—6 cylinder

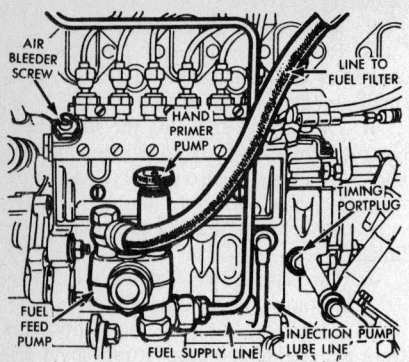

Diesel injection pump details

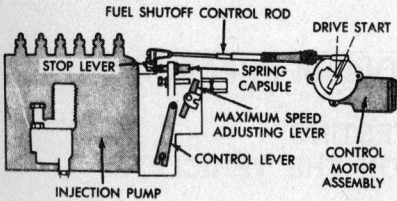

Diesel injection pump linkage components

4. Thoroughly clean the area around the hose fittings and the injection pipes.

5. Drain the engine oil and remove the dipstick and the dipstick tube.

6. Disconnect the throttle cable and the linkage from the injection pump control lever.

7. Remove the throttle control bracket assembly from the crankcase, injection pump and the control bracket and set it aside.

8. Disconnect the fuel supply line to the fuel feed pump and set it aside, loosening the anchoring clamps as necessary.

9. Disconnect the fuel hoses leading to the filter from the feed pump and the injection pump. Replace the screws and seals to prevent dirt from getting into the pump.

10. Rotate the engine so piston no. 1 is approximately 7° before top dead center on the compression stroke.

11. Disconnect the injection pipes from the delivery valves and set them aside. Cap the ends of the valves to prevent the entry of dirt.

12. Disconnect the injection pump lube lines.

13. Remove the five screws and one bolt attaching the pump.

14. Pull the pump to the rear and disengage it from the front plate and timing gear case. Rotate the pump toward the crankcase and continue pulling it to the rear until the automatic timer is freed.

To install:

1. Loosen the four nuts attaching the pump to the mounting flange plate and align the center timing mark on the pump flange with the pointer on the plate. Tighten the four nuts.

2. Be sure that the O-ring is in place on the forward face of the pump mounting flange.

3. Remove the threaded timing port plug on the governor housing behind the control lever to expose the camshaft bushing timing mark. Rotate the pump drive gear to align the timing mark on the camshaft bushing with the pointer on the governor. The guide plate notch will be at approximately the 8 o'clock position as viewed from the front. Be sure the engine is positioned as described in step 10 of the removal procedure.

4. Insert the automatic timer into the timing gear case and with the injection pump rotated against the crankshaft, rotate the pump driver gear to mesh the drive and idler gears. *Do not force the pump into position.*

5. Push the pump forward into the case. Rotate it away from the crankcase to align the attachment holes.

6. Attach the pump to the timing gear case.

7. Rotate the engine crankshaft in the opposite direction of normal operation until the crankshaft reaches the 18° before TDC mark on the crankshaft pulley. The governor pointer and the injection pump camshaft bushing timing marks should now be aligned. If they are not aligned, the pump has been installed incorrectly and must be removed and reinstalled.

8. Install the governor housing timing port plug and proceed with the pump installation by reversing the remainder of the removal procedure. Do not connect the no. 1 injecting pipe, fuel control rod or the batteries.

9. Bleed the air from the fuel filter and the injection pump by removing the air bleeder screws.

10. Time the injection pump.

INJECTION PUMP TIMING

1. Disconnect the batteries and the fuel shut off rod at the stop lever.

2. Rotate the crankshaft in the direction of normal operation until no. 1 cylinder reaches top dead center of the compression stroke. This is done by aligning the lines on the crankshaft pulley rear face with the pointer on the bottom of the case.

3. Remove the forward oil filler cap on the rocker cover and check the no. 1 cylinder valves for looseness. If they are loose, you are at TDC.

4. Rotate the crankshaft in the normal direction of engine operation 1¾ turns.

5. Disconnect no. 1 injection pipe from the delivery valve holder.

6. Turn the crankshaft in the normal direction of engine operation in small steps. Stop when fuel begins to flow from the delivery valve holder. Injection begins at this point. The control lever must be in the idle position.

7. Read the injection timing point from the scale on the back of the crankshaft damper. If the timing is correct, the timing mark should be at the value shown on the Vehicle Emission Control Information label on the rocker cover minus 2 degrees.

8. If the timing point determined differs from the standard value, minus 2 degrees, loosen the four pump-to-flange plate nuts and rotate the pump (toward the crankcase to advance the timing, away from the crankcase to retard it) to correct the difference. Each mark on the injection pump timing scale represents 6 degrees. Tighten the flange plate nuts and repeat the timing procedure to be sure the timing is correct.

FUEL TANK

Vans and Pick-Ups

REMOVAL

1. Disconnect the battery ground cable.

2. Remove the fuel tank filler cap.

3. Raise the vehicle on a lift. Pump all fuel from the tank into an approved holding tank, and raise the vehicle.

4. Disconnect the fuel line and wire lead to the gauge unit. Remove the ground strap.

5. Remove the vent hose shield and the hose clamps from the hoses running to the vapor vent tube.

6. Remove the filler tube hose clamps and disconnect the hose from the tank.

7. Place a transmission jack under the center of the tank and apply sufficient pressure to support the tank.

8. Disconnect the two J-bolts and remove the retaining straps at the rear of the tank. Lower the tank from the vehicle. Feed the two vent tube hoses and filler tube vent hose through the grommets in the frame as the tank is being lowered. Remove the tank gauge unit.

INSTALLATION

1. Inspect the fuel filter, and if it is clogged or damaged, replace it.

2. Insert a new gasket in the recess of

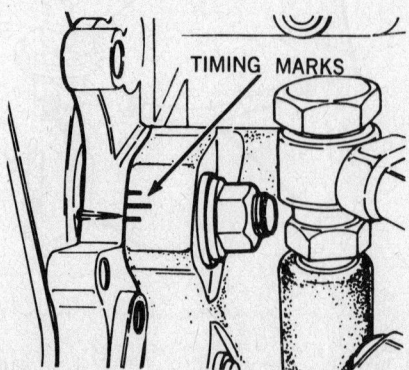

Injection pump timing marks

the fuel gauge opening and slide the gauge into the tank. Align the positioning tangs on the gauge with those on the tank. Install the lock ring, and tighten securely.

3. Position the tank on a transmission jack and hoist it into place, feeding the vent hoses through the grommets on the way up.

4. Connect the J-bolts and retaining straps, and tighten to 40 in. lbs. Remove the jack.

5. Connect the filler tube and all vent hoses.

6. Connect the fuel supply line, ground strap, and gauge unit wire lead.

7. Refill the tank and inspect it for leaks. Connect the battery ground cable.

Ramcharger and Trail Duster

REMOVAL

1. If there is a tank skid plate, remove it.

2. Disconnect the battery ground cable.

3. Remove the tank filler cap.

4. Pump or siphon the contents of the tank into a safe container.

——— CAUTION ———

Siphoning should not be started by mouth. Only fuel-safe pumps should be used.

5. Raise the vehicle on a hoist and disconnect the fuel line and tank sending unit wire. Remove the ground strap or wire.

6. Remove the hose clamps from the vent dome hose.

7. Remove the filler tube hose clamps. Detach the hoses from the tank.

8. Support the tank with a padded transmission jack.

9. Disconnect the two J-bolts and remove the straps at the rear of the tank.

10. Remove the tank gauge sending unit.

INSTALLATION

1. Use a new tank gauge sending unit gasket. Check the filter on the end of the fuel suction tube.

2. Use a new or undamaged tank to frame insulator. Raise the tank into position.

3. Connect the J-bolts and retaining straps. Tighten the bolts until about .97 in. of threads protrude.

4. Connect the filler tube and all hoses. Tighten the clamps.

5. Connect the fuel line, ground strap or wire, and tank sending unit wire. Make sure that all fuel line heat shields are in place.

6. Reconnect the battery ground cable and replace the skid plate.

MANUAL TRANSMISSION

REMOVAL AND INSTALLATION

Manual Transaxle

NOTE: Anytime the differential cover is removed, a new gasket should be formed using RTV sealant.

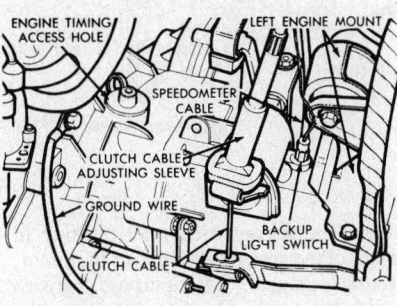

Transaxle connections in the engine compartment

1. Remove the engine timing mark access plug.

2. Rotate the engine to align the drilled mark on the flywheel with the pointer on the engine.

3. Disconnect the battery ground.

4. Disconnect the shift linkage rods.

5. Disconnect the starter and ground wires.

6. Disconnect the backup light switch wire.

7. Remove the starter.

8. Disconnect the clutch cable.

9. Disconnect the speedometer cable.

10. Support the weight of the engine from above, preferably with a shop hoist or the fabricated holding fixture.

11. Raise and support the vehicle.

12. Disconnect the driveshafts and support them out of the way.

13. Remove the left splash shield.

14. Drain the transaxle.

15. Unbolt the left engine mount.

16. Remove the transaxle-to-engine bolts.

17. Slide the transaxle to the left until the mainshaft clears, then, carefully lower it from the car.

18. Installation is the reverse of removal.

19. Adjust the clutch cable.

20. Adjust the shift linkage.

21. Fill the transaxle.

3-Speed 2WD Models

1. Drain lubricant.

2. Disconnect and match-mark the driveshaft. On the sliding spline type, disconnect driveshaft at the rear universal joint, then carefully pull the shaft yoke out of the transmission extension housing. Do not nick or scratch splines.

3. Disconnect gearshift control rods and speedometer cable.

4. Remove backup light switch if so equipped.

5. Support engine.

6. Remove crossmember and rubber insulator on 1975 and later models with A-390 transmission. On all other models, unbolt the insulator or mount from the crossmember. Support the transmission with a jack.

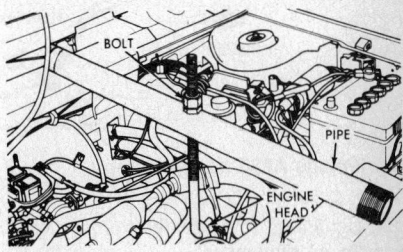

Fabricated engine support fixture

7. Remove transmission to clutch housing bolts.

8. Slide transmission rearward until pinion shaft clears clutch completely, then lower transmission from vehicle.

9. Installation is the reverse order of the above procedure. Before inserting transmission drive shaft into clutch, make sure clutch housing bore, disc and face are aligned. Tighten clutch housing to transmission bolts to 50 ft. lbs. torque.

10. Fill with lubricant.

11. Adjust shift linkage.

12. Road test.

4-Speed 2WD Models

1. Shift transmission into any gear.

2. Disconnect universal joint and loosen yoke retaining nut. Drain lubricant.

3. Disconnect parking brake (if so equipped) and speedometer cables at transmission.

4. Remove lever retainer by pressing down, rotating retainer counter-clockwise slightly, then releasing.

5. Remove lever and its springs and washers.

6. Support the rear of the engine and remove the crossmember. Remove transmission to clutch bell housing retaining bolts and pull transmission rearward until drive pinion clears clutch, then remove transmission.

7. To install, place ½ teaspoon of short fibre grease in pinion shaft pilot bushing, taking care not to get any grease on flywheel face.

8. Align clutch disc and backing plate with a spare drive pinion shaft or clutch aligning tool, then carefully install transmission.

9. Install transmission to bell housing

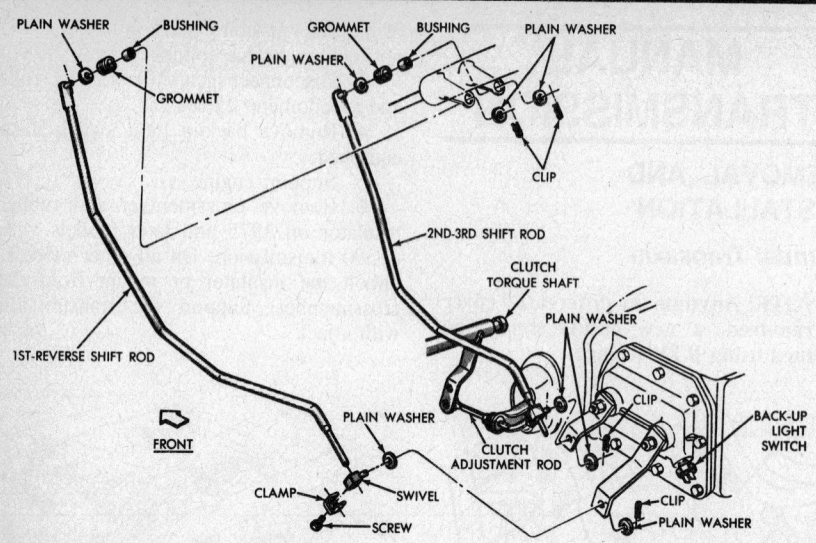

Shift linkage A230 transmission

bolts, tightening to 50 ft. lbs. torque. Replace the crossmember.

10. Install gear shift lever, shift into any gear and tighten yoke nut to 95–105 ft. lbs. torque.

11. Install universal joint, speedometer cable and brake cable.

12. Adjust clutch.

13. Install transmission drain plug and fill transmission with lubricant.

14. Road test.

3- and 4-Speed 4WD Models

1. Raise and support the truck.

2. Remove the skid plate, if any. Drain lubricant from transmission and transfer case.

3. Disconnect the speedometer cable.

4. Disconnect and match-mark the front and rear driveshafts. Suspend each shaft from a convenient place; do not allow them to hang free.

5. Disconnect the shift rods at the transfer case. On 4-speed transmissions, remove the shift lever retainer by pressing down and turning it counterclockwise. Remove the shift lever springs and washers.

6. Remove the rear driveshaft. Match-mark the driveshaft and rear U-joints before removing the driveshaft.

7. Support the transfer case.

8. Remove the extension-to-transfer case mounting bolts.

9. Move the transfer case rearward to disengage the front input shaft spline.

10. Lower and remove the transfer case.

11. Disconnect the back-up light switch.

12. Support the engine.

13. Support the transmission.

14. Remove the transmission crossmember.

15. Remove the transmission-to-clutch housing bolts.

16. Slide the transmission rearward until the mainshaft clears the clutch disc.

17. Lower and remove the transmission.

18. Installation is the reverse of re-

moval. The transmission pilot bushing in the end of the crankshaft requires high-temperature grease. Multipurpose grease should be used. Do not lubricate the end of the mainshaft, clutch splines, or clutch release levers. Adjust the gearshift linkage on 3-speed transmissions.

Transfer Case

REMOVAL AND INSTALLATION

1. Raise and support the truck.

2. Remove the skid plate, if any.

3. Drain the transfer case by removing the bottom bolt from the front output rear cover.

4. Disconnect the speedometer cable.

5. Disconnect the front and rear output shafts. Suspend these from a convenient location; do not allow them to hang free.

6. Disconnect the shift rods at the transfer case.

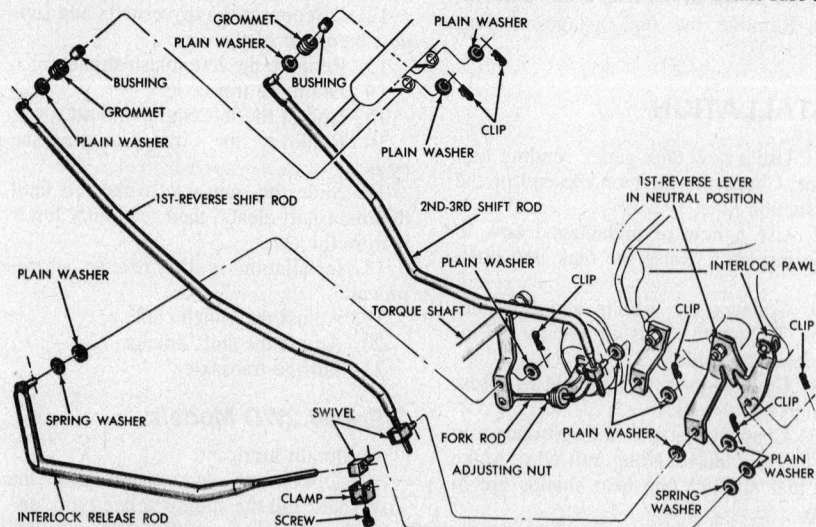

Shift linkage A250 transmission

7. Support the transfer case.

8. Remove the adaptor-to-transfer case mounting bolts and move the transfer case rearward to disengage the front input splines.

9. Lower and remove the transfer case.

10. Installation is the reverse of removal. Adjust the linkage.

Shift Linkage Adjustment

VANS AND PICK-UPS

A-230, A-250

1. Adjust the length of the 2-3 shift rod so the position of the shift lever on the steering column will be correct.

2. Assemble the 1st-reverse and 2-3 shift rods, and place each in its normal position, secured with a clip. Loosen both swivel clamp bolts.

3. Move the 2-3 shift lever into 3rd position (this means moving the forward lever forward). Move the steering column lever until it is about five degrees above the horizontal. Tighten the shift rod swivel clamp bolt.

4. Shift the transmission to neutral. Place a suitable tool between the crossover blade and the 2-3 lever at the steering column so that both lever pins are engaged by the crossover blade.

5. Set the 1st-reverse lever in neutral. Tighten the swivel clamp bolt.

6. Remove the tool from the cross over blade, and check all shifts for smoothness.

RAMCHARGER AND TRAIL DUSTER

A-230

1. Remove both shift rod swivels from the transmission shift levers. Make sure that

the transmission shift levers are in the neutral position (middle detent).

2. Move the shift lever to line up the locating slots in the bottom of the steering column shift housing and bearing housing.

3. Place a suitable tool between the crossover blade and the 2nd and 3rd lever at the steering column, so that both lever pins are engaged by the crossover blade.

4. Set the 1st-reverse lever on the transmission to the reverse position (rotate clockwise).

5. Adjust the 1st-reverse rod swivel by loosening the clamp bolt and sliding the swivel along the rod so it will enter the 1st-reverse lever at the transmission. Install the washers and the clip. Tighten the swivel bolt.

6. Remove the gearshift housing locating tool, and shift the transmission into the neutral position.

7. Adjust the 2nd-3rd rod swivel by loosening the clamp bolt and sliding the swivel along the rod so it will enter the 2nd-3rd lever at the transmission. Install the washers and the clip. Tighten the swivel bolt.

8. Remove the tool from the cross-over blade at the steering column and shift the transmission through all the gears to check the adjustment and the crossover smoothness.

ALL MODELS

A-390

1. Loosen both shift rod swivels. Make sure that the transmission shift levers are in the neutral position (middle detent).

2. Move the shift lever to line up the locating slots in the bottom of the steering column shift housing and bearing housing. Install a suitable tool in the slot.

3. Place a suitable tool between the crossover blade and the 2nd-3rd lever at the steering column so that both lever pins are

engaged by the crossover blade.

4. Tighten both rod swivel bolts. Remove the gearshift housing locating tool.

5. Remove the tool from the crossover blade at the steering column and shift the transmission through all gears to check adjustment and crossover smoothness.

6. Check for proper operation of the steering column lock in reverse. With the proper linkage adjustment, the ignition should lock in reverse only, with hands off the gearshift lever.

TRANSAXLE SHIFT ADJUSTMENT

A double ended pin that is used to lock the linkage in place prior to adjustment.

1. Remove the screw from the top and reinsert the other end, locking the linkage in place.

2. The linkage is locked in the Neutral detent between 1st and 2nd gears.

3. Align the marks on the linkage.

4. Remove the pin and replace it in its original location. Check the operation of the shift linkage.

OVERDRIVE-4

1. Place the floorshift lever in Neutral. Insert a ¼ in. drill bit through the bottom of the shifter to hold the levers in place.

2. Detach the shift rods. Make sure that the three transmission levers are in their Neutral detents.

3. Adjust the shift rods to make the length exactly right to fit into the transmission levers. Start with the 1st-2nd shift rod. It may be necessary to remove the clip at the shifter end of the rod to rotate this rod.

4. Replace the washers and the clips.

5. Remove the drill bit and check the shifting action.

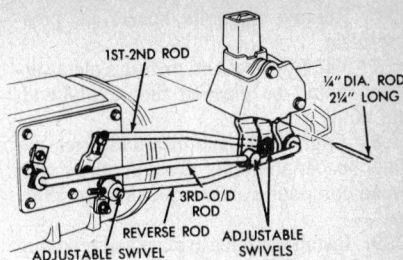

Shift linkage Overdrive 4 adjustment

Clutch Interlock

ADJUSTMENT

A-250 3-Speed

This adjustment is required only on the A-250 3-speed transmission. This is a top cover unit used only as base equipment on light duty six cylinder models. It has synchromesh only on second and third gears.

1. Disconnect the clutch rod swivel from the interlock pawl. Adjust the clutch pedal free play.

2. Shift the transmission to neutral. Loosen swivel clamp bolt and slide the swivel onto the rod until the pawl is positioned fully within the slot in the first-reverse lever. Install the washers and clip.

3. Hold the interlock pawl forward and tighten the swivel clamp bolt. The clutch pedal must be in fully returned position during the adjustment.

NOTE: Do not pull the clutch rod rearward to engage the swivel in the pawl.

4. Shift the transmission into first and reverse and release the clutch pedal while in either gear to check for normal clutch action. Then, shift halfway between neutral and either gear and release clutch. The interlock should hold it to within one or two inches of the floor.

CLUTCH

REMOVAL AND INSTALLATION

4 Cylinder Engines

1. Remove the transaxle.

2. Loosen the flywheel-to-pressure plate bolts diagonally, one or two turns at a time to avoid warpage.

3. Remove the flywheel and clutch disc from the pressure plate.

4. Remove the retaining ring and release plate.

5. Diagonally loosen the pressure plate-to-crankshaft bolts. Mark all parts for reassembly.

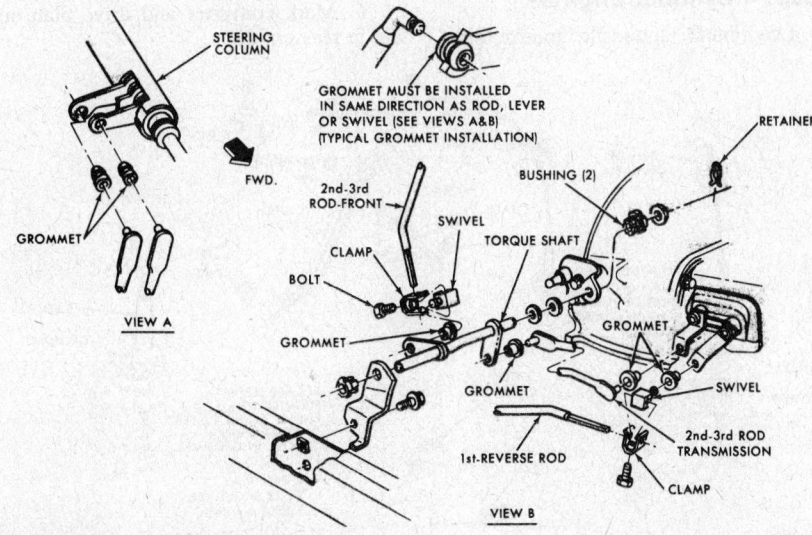

Shift linkage A390 transmission

6. Remove the bolts, spacer and pressure plate.

7. The flywheel and pressure plate surfaces should be cleaned thoroughly with fine sandpaper.

8. Align marks and install the pressure plate, spacer and bolts. Coat the bolts with thread compound and torque them to 55 ft. lbs.

9. Install the release plate and retaining ring.

10. Using special tool L-4533 or its equivalent, install the clutch disc and flywheel on the pressure plate.

CAUTION

Make certain that the drilled mark on the flywheel is at the top, so that the two dowels on the flywheel align with the proper holes in the pressure plate.

11. Install the six flywheel bolts and tighten them to 14.5 ft. lbs.

12. Remove the aligning tool.

13. Install the transmission.

14. Adjust the freeplay.

6 and 8 Cylinder Engines

1. Support the engine on a suitable jack.

2. Remove crossmember.

3. Remove transmission. Remove transfer case, if equipped.

4. Remove clutch housing pan if so equipped.

5. Remove clutch fork, clutch bearing and sleeve assembly if not removed with transmission.

6. Mark clutch cover and flywheel, with a suitable tool to assure correct reassembly.

7. Remove clutch cover retaining bolts, loosening them evenly so clutch cover will not be distorted.

8. Pull pressure plate assembly clear of flywheel and, while supporting pressure plate, slide clutch disc from between flywheel and pressure plate.

9. To install, thoroughly clean all working surfaces of the flywheel and the pressure plate.

10. Grease radius at back of bushing.

11. Rotate clutch cover and pressure plate assembly for maximum clearance between flywheel and frame crossmember if crossmember was not removed during clutch removal.

12. Tilt top edge of clutch cover and pressure plate assembly back and move it up into the clutch housing. Support clutch cover and pressure plate assembly and slide clutch disc into position.

13. Position clutch disc and plate against flywheel and insert spare transmission main drive gear shaft or clutch installing tool through clutch disc hub and into main drive pilot bearing.

14. Rotate clutch cover until the punch marks on cover and flywheel line up.

15. Bolt cover loosely to flywheel. Tighten cover bolts a few turns at a time, in progression, until tight. Then tighten bolts to 20 ft. lbs. torque.

16. Install transmission.

17. Install frame crossmembers and insulator, tighten all bolts.

Mechanical Clutch Linkage Adjustment

4 Cylinder Engines

1. Pull up on the clutch cable.

2. While holding the cable up, rotate the adjusting sleeve downward until a snug contact is made against the grommet.

3. Rotate the sleeve slightly to allow the end of the sleeve to seat in the rectangular hole in the grommet.

6 and 8 Cylinder Engines

The only adjustment required is pedal freeplay. Adjust the clutch actuating fork rod by turning the self-locking adjusting nut to provide ⅛ in. (3/32 in. on vans and wagons) free movement at the end of the fork. This will provide the recommended 1½ in. (1 in. on Vans, Wagons, Ramcharger, and Trailduster) freeplay at the pedal.

AUTOMATIC TRANSMISSION

Except 4 Cylinder Engines

The LoadFlite® automatic transmission consists of a torque converter and a fully automatic three-speed gear system, housed in an integral aluminum casing. The transmission uses two multiple disc clutches, an overrunning clutch, two servos, two bands, and two planetary gearsets to provide three forward, and one reverse speed. The transmission hydraulic system is composed of a fluid pump and a single valve body that contains all of the control valves, except for the governor valve. The torque converter is a sealed unit and cannot be disassembled.

The transmission fluid is filtered through an internal dacron filter which is attached to the lower side of the valve body. The fluid is cooled by circulating it through a cooler in the lower radiator tank.

REMOVAL

1. Remove the transmission and converter as an assembly; otherwise the converter drive plate pump bushing, and oil seal will be damaged. The drive plate will not support a load. Therefore, none of the weight of transmission should be allowed to rest on the plate during removal. Remove the transfer case, as necessary.

2. Attach a remote control starter switch to the starter solenoid so the engine can be rotated from under the vehicle.

3. Disconnect high tension cable from the ignition coil.

4. Remove cover plate from in front of converter assembly to provide access to the converter drain plug and mounting bolts.

5. Rotate engine to bring drain plug to the 6 o'clock position. Drain the converter and transmission.

NOTE: A running production change was made in January 1977 which eliminated the converter drain plug. This means that the transmission must be removed in order to drain the converter on models manufactured after this date.

6. Mark converter and drive plate to aid in reassembly.

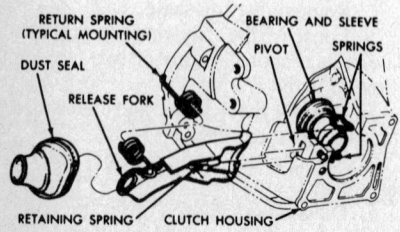

Clutch release fork, bearing and sleeve

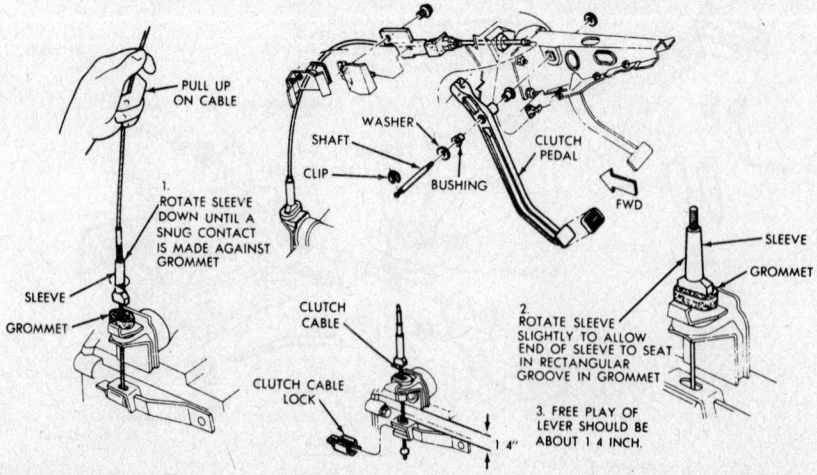

Clutch freeplay adjustment—4 cylinder

7. Rotate the engine with the remote control switch to locate two converter to drive plate bolts at 5 and 7 o'clock positions. Remove the two bolts, rotate engine again and remove the other two bolts.

CAUTION

Do not rotate converter on drive plate by prying with a screwdriver or similar tool as drive plate might become distorted. Also the starter should never be engaged if drive plate is not attached to converter with at least one bolt or if transmission case to engine block bolts have been loosened.

8. Disconnect battery ground cable. Remove engine to transmission struts, if necessary. You may have to drop the exhaust system on some models.
9. Remove the starter.
10. Remove wire from the neutral starting switch.
11. Remove gearshift cable or rod from the transmission and the lever.
12. Disconnect the throttle rod from left side of transmission.
13. Disconnect the oil cooler lines at transmission and remove the oil filler tube. Disconnect the speedometer cable.
14. Disconnect the driveshaft.
15. Install engine support fixture to hold up the rear of the engine.
16. Raise transmission slightly with jack to relieve load and remove support bracket or crossmember. Remove all bell housing bolts and carefully work transmission and converter rearward off engine dowels and disengage converter hub from end of crankshaft.

CAUTION

Attach a small C-clamp to edge of bell housing to hold converter in place during transmission removal; otherwise the front pump bushing might be damaged.

INSTALLATION

NOTE: Install transmission and converter as an assembly. The drive plate will not support a load. Do not allow weight of transmission to rest on the plate during installation.

1. Rotate pump rotors until the rotor lugs are vertical.
2. Carefully slide converter assembly over input shaft and reaction shaft. Make sure converter impeller shaft slots are also vertical and fully engage front pump inner rotor lugs.
3. Use a "C" clamp on edge of converter housing to hold converter in place during transmission installation.
4. Converter drive plate should be free of distortion and drive plate to crankshaft bolts tightened to 55 ft. lbs. torque.
5. Using a jack, position transmission and converter assembly in alignment with engine.
6. Rotate converter so mark on converter (made during removal) will align with mark on drive plate. The offset holes in plate are located next to the 1/8" hole in inner circle of the plate. A stamped "V" mark identifies the offset hole in converter front cover. Carefully work transmission assembly forward over engine block dowels with converter hub entering the crankshaft opening.

7. Install converter housing to engine bolts and tighten to 28 ft. lbs.
8. Install the two lower drive plate to converter bolts and tighten to 270 in. lbs. torque.
9. Install engine to transmission struts, if required. Install starting motor and connect battery ground cable.
10. Rotate engine and install two remaining drive plate to converter bolts.
11. Install crossmember and tighten attaching bolts to 90 ft. lbs. torque. Lower transmission so that extension housing is aligned and rests on the rear mount. Install bolts and tighten to 40 ft. lbs. torque.
12. Remove transmission jack and engine support fixture, then install tie-bars under the transmission.
13. Replace the driveshaft.
14. Connect oil cooler lines, install oil filler tube and connect the speedometer cable.
15. Connect gearshift cable or rod and torqueshaft assembly to the transmission case and to the lever.
16. Connect throttle rod to the lever at left side of transmission bell housing.
17. Connect wire to back-up and neutral starting switch.
18. Install cover plate in front of the converter assembly.
19. Refill transmission with fluid.
20. Adjust throttle and shift linkage.

Pan and Filter Service

NOTE: A running production change was made in January, 1977, which eliminated the converter drain plug. This means that the transmission must be removed in order to drain the converter on models manufactured after this date. (except Rampage).

With Converter Drain Plug

NOTE: To drain only the transmission (not the converter), use steps 1, 2, 4, 6, 7, 8, 9 and 11–15.

1. Jack up the front of the vehicle and support it on jackstands.
2. Remove the converter access plate and turn the converter using the starter, until the converter drain plug is accessible.
3. Remove the converter drain plug and allow the converter to drain completely. 1976–77 models use a 5/16 in. hex head bolt. A six-point socket must be used on the 5/16 in. head.
4. Remove the bolts securing the transmission pan and carefully remove the pan to drain the fluid.

5. Reinstall the drain plug.
6. Clean the transmission pan thoroughly.
7. Remove the three screws from the fluid filter in the bottom of the valve body; remove the filter and discard it.
8. Install a new filter using three screws.
9. Install the pan using a new gasket. Tighten the pan screws to 150 in. lbs. of torque in a criss-cross pattern.
10. Install the torque converter access plate.
11. Pour 6 quarts of Dexron® automatic transmission fluid through the filler tube. If the converter was not drained, use 4 quarts.
12. Start the engine.
13. Let the engine idle for 2 minutes and move the gear selector through all the drive positions, pausing momentarily in each position.
14. Leave the gear selector in Neutral and check the fluid level. If necessary, add enough fluid to bring the level to the "ADD ONE PINT" mark on the dipstick.

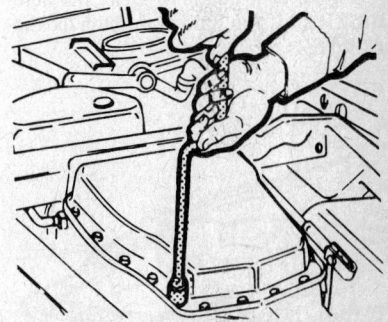

Removing the transmission oil pan bolts

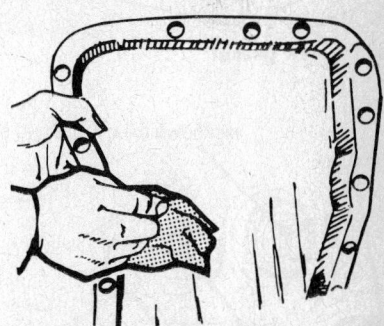

Clean pan with safe solvent and a rag

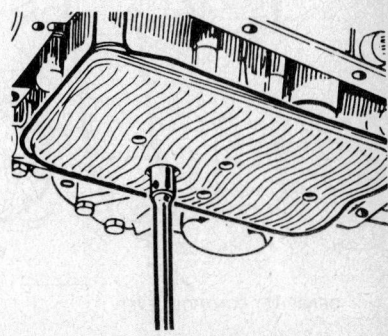

Remove filter attaching screws

——— **CAUTION** ———
Do not overfill the transmission.

15. Make sure the dipstick is fully seated and lower the vehicle.

Without Drain Plug

1. Raise the front of the truck and support it on jackstands. Place a large drain pan under the transmission.

2. Loosen the pan attaching bolts and tap the pan at one corner to break it loose.

3. Allow the fluid to drain into the drain pan.

4. After most of the fluid has drained, carefully remove the attaching bolts, lower the pan and drain the rest of the fluid.

5. Remove the filter attaching screws and remove the filter.

6. Install a new filter. Tighten the screws to 35 in. lbs.

7. Thoroughly clean the fluid pan with safe solvent and allow it to dry.

8. Using a new gasket, install the pan to the transmission. Tighten the attaching bolts to 150 in. lbs.

9. Pour four quarts of Dexron® automatic transmission fluid in through the dipstick tube.

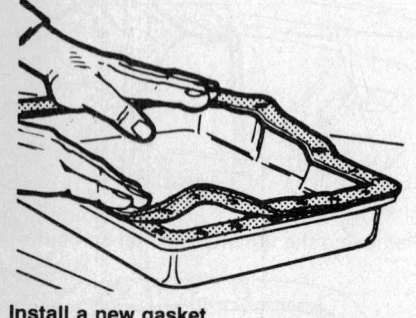

Install a new gasket

10. Start the engine and allow it to run for a few minutes. With the parking brake set, slowly move the gear selector to each position. Return it to the Neutral position.

11. Check the fluid level. Add more fluid as necessary to bring it up to the "ADD ONE PINT" level.

12. Drive the truck to bring the transmission up to normal operating temperature. Check the level again. It should be between the "ADD" and "FULL" marks.

Band Adjustments

Kickdown Band

The kickdown band adjusting screw is located on the left-hand side of the transmission case near the throttle lever shaft.

1. Loosen the locknut and back if off about five turns. Be sure that the adjusting screw turns freely in the case.

2. Torque the adjusting screw to 72 ft. lbs.

3. Back off the adjusting screw 2½ turns on all models except those using a 440 V8 engine. If equipped with the 440 engine back off the adjusting screw 2 turns. Keep the adjusting screw from turning, tighten and torque the locknut to 35 ft. lbs.

Low and Reverse Band

The pan must be removed from the transmission to gain access to the low and reverse band adjusting screw.

1. Remove the skid plate, if any. Drain the transmission fluid and remove the pan.

2. Loosen the band adjusting screw locknut and back if off about five turns. Be sure that the adjusting screw turns freely in the lever.

3. Torque the adjusting screw to 72 ft. lbs.

4. Back off the adjusting screw: All

LoadFlite through 1980; 2 turns. 1981 and later A904T and A999 (wide ratio); 4 turns. 1981 and later A727; 2 turns. Keep the adjusting screw from turning, tighten and torque the locknut to 30 ft. lbs.

5. Use a new gasket and install the transmission pan. Torque the pan bolts to 150 in. lbs. Refill the transmission with Dexron® II fluid.

Shift Linkage Adjustment

NOTE: To insure proper adjustment, it is suggested that new linkage grommets be installed.

1. Place the gearshift lever in the Park position.

2. Move the shift control lever on the transmission all the way to the rear (in the Park detent).

3. Set the adjustable rod to the proper length and install it with no load in either direction. Tighten the swivel bolt.

4. The shift linkage must be free of binding and be positive in all positions. Make sure that the engine can start only when the gearshift lever is in the Park or Neutral position. Be sure that the gearshift lever will not jump into an unwanted gear.

Throttle Adjustment

1. Warm the engine to operating temperature.

2. Block the choke plate fully open.

3. Remove the throttle return spring from the carburetor.

4. Remove the clip, washer and slotted throttle rod from the carburetor pin.

5. Rotate the threaded end of the rod

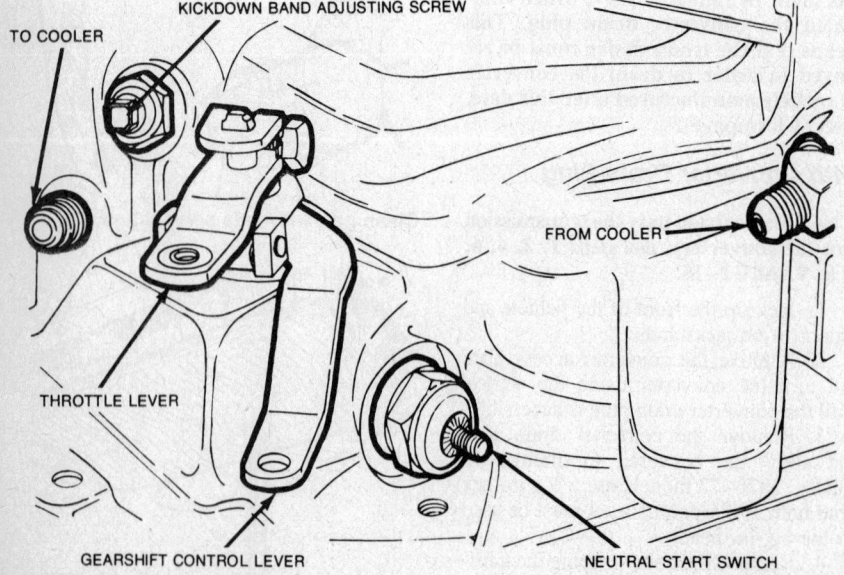

Loadflite adjusting points

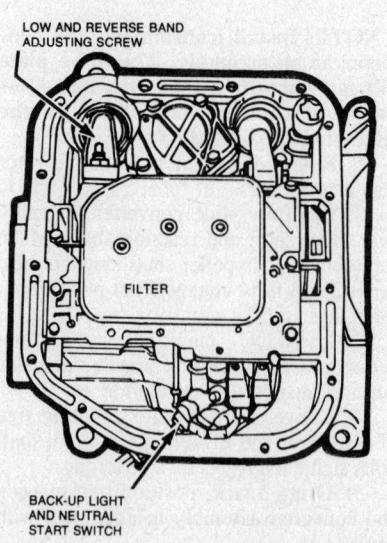

Low and reverse band adjusting screw location

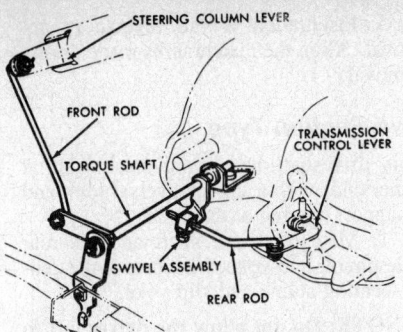

1975–78 gearshift linkage—typical

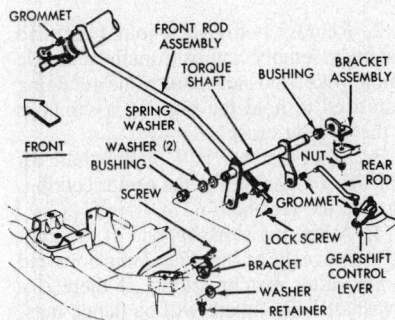

1979 and later gearshift linkage—typical

so that the rear edge of the slot in the rod contacts the carburetor pin when the transmission throttle lever is held forward against its stop.

6. Install the washer and clip to retain the throttle rod to the carburetor.

7. Install the throttle rod return spring.

8. Check the transmission linkage for freedom of operation and unblock the choke plate.

Neutral Start Switch Adjustment

The neutral safety switch is thread mounted into the transmission case. When the gearshift lever is placed in either the Park or Neutral position, a cam, which is attached to the transmission throttle lever inside the transmission, contacts the neutral safety switch and provides a ground to complete the starter solenoid circuit.

The back-up light switch is incorporated into the neutral safety switch. The center terminal is for the neutral safety switch and the two outer terminals are for the backup lamps.

There is no adjustment for the switch. If a malfunction occurs, the switch must be removed and replaced.

To remove the switch, disconnect the electrical leads and unscrew the switch. Use a drain pan to catch the transmission fluid. Using a new seal, install the new switch and torque it to 24 ft. lbs. Refill the transmission.

AUTOMATIC TRANSAXLE

REMOVAL AND INSTALLATION

The automatic transaxle can be removed by itself with the engine still mounted in the truck, but the transaxle and converter must be removed as an assembly. The drive plate, oil pump seal and pump bushing will not support weight such as the converter. If the converter is not removed with the transaxle, damage may occur.

1. Disconnect the negative battery cable.

2. Disconnect the throttle and shift linkage from the transaxle.

3. Raise and support the truck safely on jackstands.

4. Remove the front wheels. Remove the inner fender splash shields.

5. Drain the fluid from the transaxle. Remove the speedometer adapter, cable and drive pinion as an assembly.

6. Remove the sway bar. Remove the lower ball joint to steering knuckle bolts. Pry the lower ball joint from the steering knuckle.

7. Remove the drive axles from the front wheel hubs. See shaft removal in following section.

8. Matchmark the torque converter and drive plate. Remove the torque converter mounting bolts. On some models, the right front splash shield may be removed to provide access to rotate the engine.

9. Remove the lower oil cooler tube, if equipped. Disconnect any wire harness (neutral safety switch, etc.)

10. Install a portable engine support, or devise a method of supporting the engine from the top.

11. Remove the upper bell housing bolts. Remove the engine mount bracket from the front crossmember. Support the transmission.

12. Remove the front mount insulator "through" bolts and the bell housing mount.

13. Remove the long "through" bolt from the left hand engine mount.

14. Raise the transaxle, remove any remaining mounting bolts and separate from the engine. Slowly lower the transaxle to the ground.

15. Installation is in the reverse order of removal. Fill the transaxle with the correct amount of Dexron II. Check for leaks.

NOTE: Pan gaskets are formed with RTV sealant, follow the directions on the tube when applying.

SHIFT LINKAGE ADJUSTMENT

NOTE: When it is necessary to disconnect the linkage cable from the lever,

which uses plastic grommets as retainers, the grommets should be replaced.

1. Make sure that the adjustable swivel block is free to slide on the shift cable.

2. Place the shift lever in Park.

3. With the linkage assembled, and the swivel lock bolt loose, move the shift on the transaxle all the way to the rear detent.

4. Tighten the adjuster swivel lock bolt to 8 ft. lb.

5. Check the linkage action.

NOTE: The automatic transmission gear selector release button may pop up in the knob when shifting from PARK to DRIVE. This is caused by inadequate retention of the selector release knob retaining tab. The release button will always work but the loose button can be annoying. A sleeve and washers are available to cure this condition. If these are unavailable, do the following:

1. Remove the release button.

2. Cut and fold a standard paper match stem as shown.

3. Using tweezers, insert the folded match as far as possible into the clearance slot as shown. The match should be below the knob surface.

4. Insert the button, taking care not to break the button stem.

THROTTLE CABLE ADJUSTMENT

1. Adjust the idle speed as previously described.

2. Run the engine to normal operating temperature.

3. Loosen the adjustment bracket lock screw.

4. Make sure the adjustment bracket is free to slide in its slot.

5. Hold the transmission lever firmly rearward against its internal stop and tighten the adjustment bracket lock screw to 9 ft. lbs.

6. Test the cable operation.

BAND ADJUSTMENTS

Front (Kickdown) Band

Chrysler recommends that the band be adjusted at each fluid change. The adjustment screw is located on the left side of the case.

1. Loosen the locknut and back off the nut about five full turns.

2. Tighten the band adjusting screw to 72 in. lbs.

3. Back off the adjusting screw exactly 2.5 turns.

4. Hold the adjusting screw and tighten the locknut to 35 ft. lbs.

NEUTRAL START SWITCH ADJUSTMENT

The neutral start circuit is the center contact of the three-terminal switch located in the transmission case.

1. Remove the wiring connector and

test for continuity between the center pin and the case. Continuity should exist only in Park and Neutral.

2. Remove the switch and check that the operating lever fingers are centered in the switch opening.

3. Install the switch and a new seal and tighten to 24 ft. lbs. Retest with a lamp.

4. Replace the lost transmission fluid.

5. If shift linkage adjustment is correct and the switch still malfunctions, replace the switch.

PAN REMOVAL AND INSTALLATION, FLUID AND FILTER CHANGE

NOTE: RTV silicone sealer is used in place of a pan gasket.

Chrysler recommends no fluid or filter changes during the normal service life. Severe usage requires a fluid and filter change every 15,000 miles. Severe usage is defined as:

1. More than 50% heavy city traffic during 90°F weather.

2. Commercial operation or trailer towing.

When changing the fluid, only Dexron® II fluid should be used. A filter change should be performed at every fluid change.

1. Raise the vehicle and support it on jackstands.

2. Place a large container under the pan, loosen the pan bolts and tap at one corner to break it loose. Drain the fluid.

3. When the fluid is drained remove the pan bolts.

4. Remove the retaining screws and replace the filter. Tighten the screws to 35 in. lbs.

5. Clean the fluid pan, peel off the old RTV silicone sealer and install the pan, using a ⅛ inch bead of new RTV sealer.

Always run the sealer bead inside the bolt holes. Tighten the pan bolts to 10–12 ft. lbs.

6. Pour four quarts of Dexron® II fluid through the filler tube.

7. Start the engine and idle it for at least 2 minutes. Set the parking brake and move the selector through each position, ending in Park.

8. Add sufficient fluid to bring the level to the FULL mark on the dipstick. The level should be checked in Park, with the engine idling at normal operating temperature.

DRIVE TRAIN

Driveshaft

REMOVAL AND INSTALLATION

Single Section Type

This driveshaft has a universal joint at either end and no external supports.

1. Raise and support the truck with the rear higher.

2. Matchmark the shaft and pinion flange to assure proper balance at installation.

3. Remove both rear U-joint roller and bushing clamps from the rear axle pinion flange. Do not disturb the retaining strap which holds the bushing assemblies on the U-joint cross.

NOTE: Do not allow the driveshaft to hang during removal. Suspend it from the frame with a piece of wire. Before removing the driveshaft, raise the rear end of the truck to prevent loss of transmission fluid.

4. Slide the driveshaft, with the front sliding yoke, off the transmission output shaft.

5. Installation is the reverse of removal. Align the matchmarks made during removal.

Two-Section Type

This driveshaft has a universal joint at either end, with a third universal joint and a support bearing at the center.

1. Matchmark the shaft and the rear axle pinion hub yoke. Matchmark the center bearing spline and slip yoke.

NOTE: Do not allow the driveshaft to hang down during removal. Suspend it from the frame. Raise the rear of the truck to prevent loss of transmission fluid.

2. Remove both rear U-joint roller and bushing assembly clamps from the rear axle pinion yoke. Do not disturb the retaining strap used to hold the bushing assemblies on the U-joint cross.

3. Slide the rear half of the shaft off the front shaft splines at the center bearing. Remove the rear half.

4. At the transmission end of the front half, remove the bushing retaining bolts and clamps, after matchmarking. If there is a driveshaft brake, there will be flange nuts.

5. Unbolt the center bearing mounting nuts and bolts and remove the front half of the shaft.

6. On installation, align the matchmarks at the transmission and start all the bolts and nuts at the front U-joint and the center support bearing.

7. Tighten ¼ in. clamp bolts to 170 in. lbs, and ⁵⁄₁₆ in. bolts to 300 in. lbs. Tighten driveshaft brake flange nuts to 35 ft. lbs. Leave the center bearing bolts just snug.

8. Align the rear shaft matchmarks and slide the yoke onto the front shaft splines.

9. Align the rear U-joint matchmarks and install the bushing clamps and bolts. Tighten the bolts to the torque given in step 7. Grease the joints and splines.

10. Jack up the rear wheels and let the engine drive the shaft. The center support bearing will align itself.

11. Tighten the center bearing bolts to 50 ft. lbs.

Four-Wheel Drive Front Driveshaft

1. Remove the four flange retaining bolts and lockwashers from the constant velocity U-joint at the transfer case. Mark the parts to reinstall them in the same position. To prevent the constant velocity joint from turning while removing the nuts, use a press bar.

2. Remove the nuts and lockwashers from the U-bolts at the differential flange and remove the U-bolts.

3. Support the driveshaft and separate the U-joint at the front the driveshaft yoke, pulling backward to clear the flange. The driveshaft should never be allowed to hang by either universal joint.

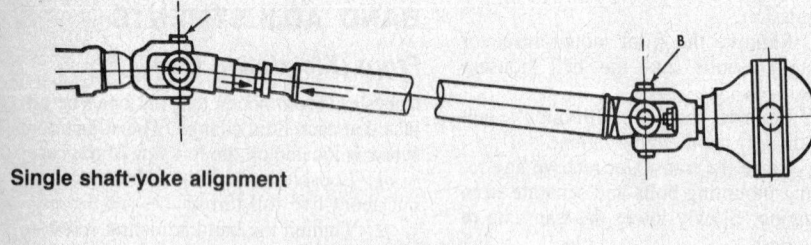

Single shaft-yoke alignment

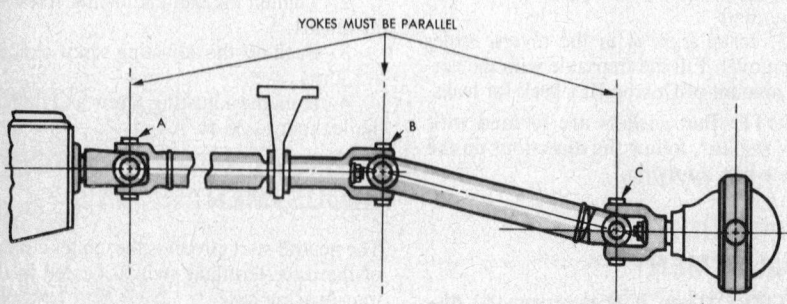

Two-piece shaft-yoke vertical alignment

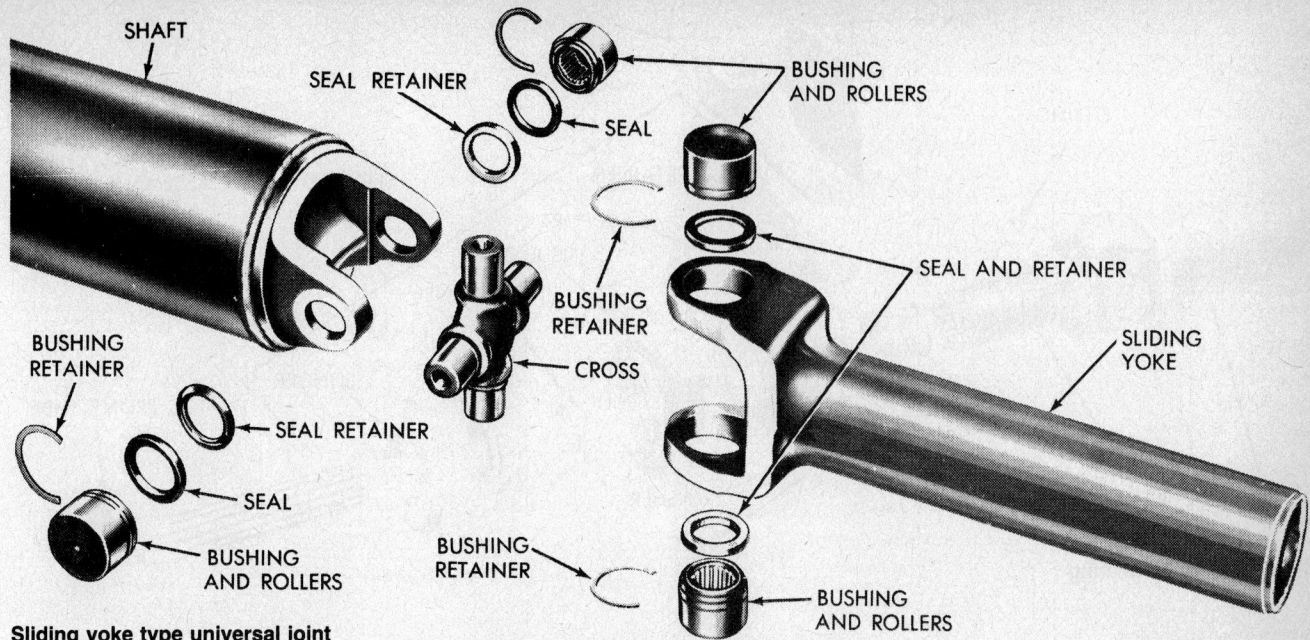

Sliding yoke type universal joint

4. Remove the driveshaft.

5. Installation is the reverse of removal.

Universal Joint Replacement

THE LOCK RING AND THE SNAP RING TYPE

The lock-ring type and the snap-ring type universal joints are basically the same, except for the locations of the retainers. The lock-ring retainers hold the bearing cups in the yoke by being installed in a machined groove on the bearing cup, which is located on the inner side of the yoke when the joint is assembled.

The snap-ring type retainer holds the bearing cup in the yoke by being installed in a machined groove in the upper area of the bearing bore of the yoke.

Disassembly and Assembly

1. Hammer the bushings (roller cups) slightly inward to relieve pressure on the retainers. Remove the retainers.

2. Place the yoke in a vise with a socket bigger than the bushing on one side and one smaller than the bushing on the other side.

3. Apply pressure, forcing one bushing out into the larger socket.

4. Reverse the vise and socket arrange-

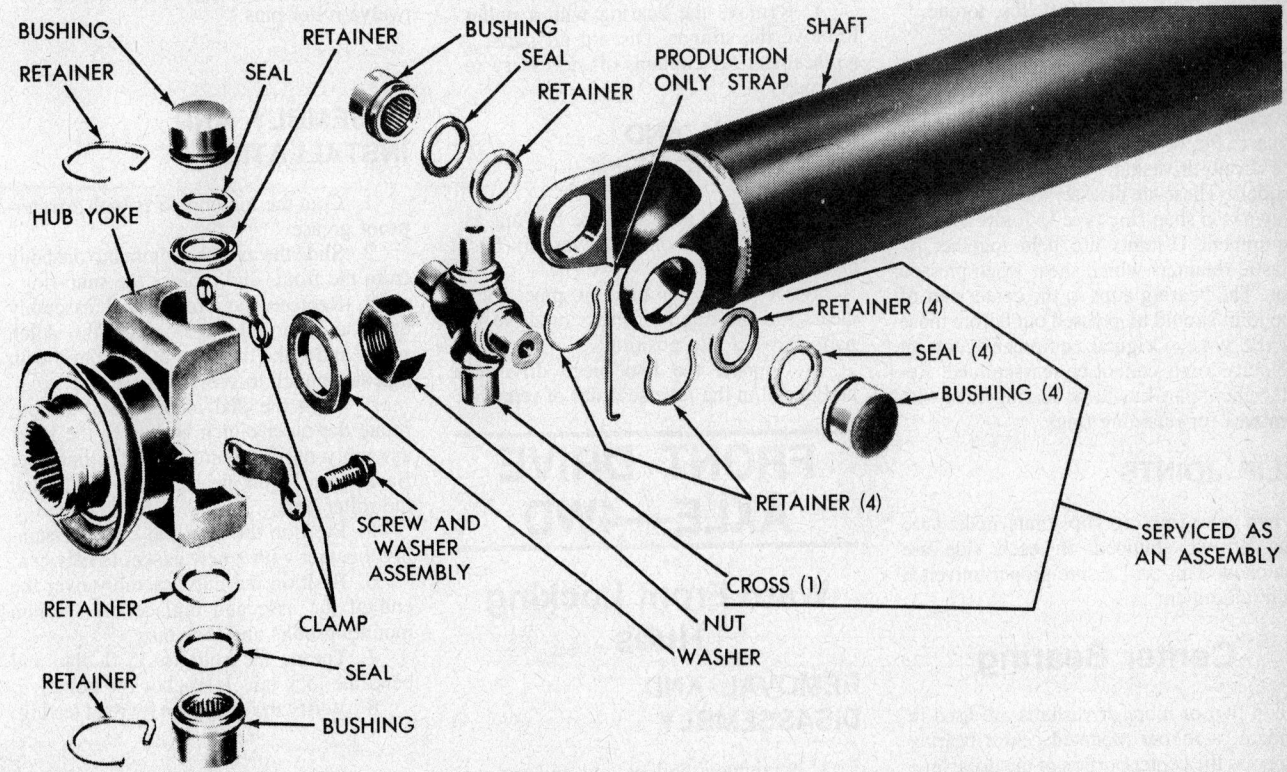

Hub yoke type universal joint

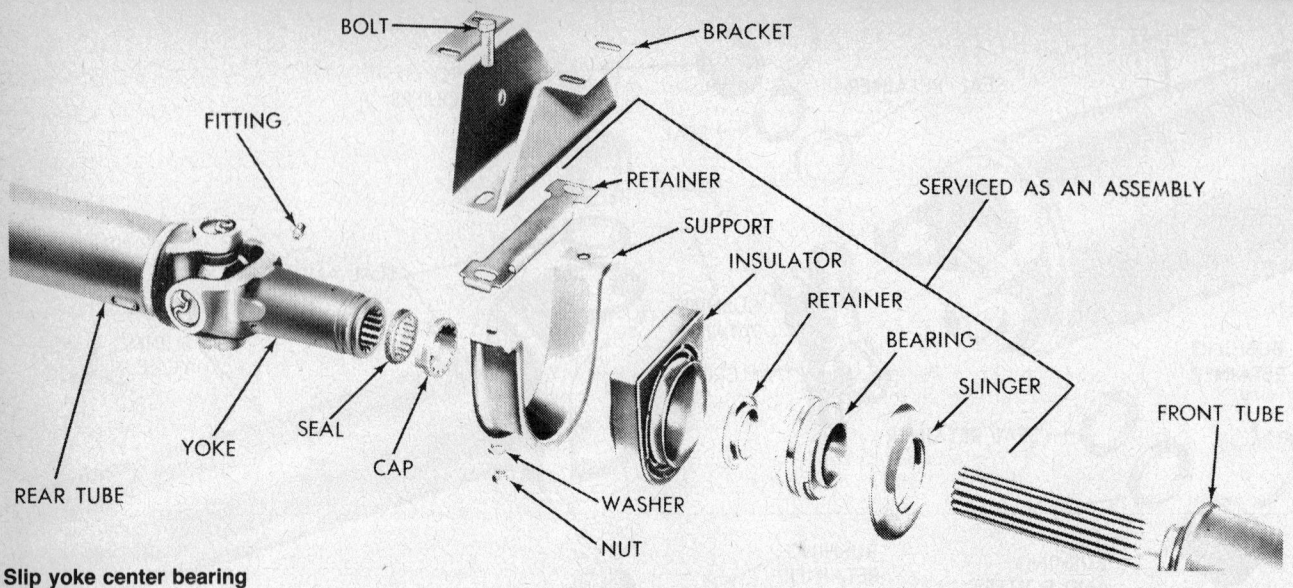

Slip yoke center bearing

ment to remove the other bushing and the cross.

5. On installation, press the new bushings in just far enough to install the retainers.

STRAP CLAMP TYPE (REAR AXLE YOKE)

Unbolt strap bolts and remove straps, bushings, seals and washer retainers. Install new components as required. When assembling, grease bearings. Install with grease fitting parallel to other fittings in drive train. Tighten strap bolts to 20 ft. lbs. torque.

CONSTANT VELOCITY U-JOINT

This is the double universal joint used in the front driveshaft on four-wheel drive models. These are disassembled in the same way as the snap-ring type U-Joint. Original equipment U-joints are held together by plastic retainers which shear when pressed out. The bearing cups in the center part of the joint should be pressed out before those in the yoke. Original equipment constant velocity joints cannot be reassembled. Replacement part kits have bearing cups with grooves for retaining rings.

SLIP JOINTS

When reassembling slip joints make sure that arrows stamped on each side are matched. This will assure proper universal joint alignment.

Center Bearing

When two or more driveshafts are used in tandem, a rubber mounted center bearing supports the center portion of the drive line. The center bearing is mounted in rubber in

a bracket which is bolted to the frame crossmember.

REMOVAL AND DISASSEMBLY

1. Mark parts for reassembly and remove driveshafts as described earlier.
2. Place the front shaft in a vise and pull the bearing support and insulator away from the bearing.
3. Bend the slinger away from the bearing with a hammer to obtain clearance to install a bearing puller.
4. Remove the bearing with a puller. Remove the slinger. Discard all parts. A replacement kit contains all necessary repair parts.

ASSEMBLY AND INSTALLATION

1. Place the new slinger, bearing assembly and retainer on the driveshaft. Each part is a press fit.
2. Use a strong tube or pipe which clears the shaft spline. Press or drive the parts forward into position.
3. Connect the two piece driveshaft and install in the reverse order of removal.

FRONT DRIVE AXLE—4WD

Warn Front Locking Hubs

REMOVAL AND DISASSEMBLY

1. Straighten the lock tabs and remove the six hub mounting bolts.

2. Tap the hub gently with a mallet to remove.
3. Separate the clutch assembly from the body assembly.
4. Remove the snap ring from the rear of the body assembly, using snap-ring pliers. Slip the axle shaft hub out of the body from the front.
5. Remove the Allen screw from the inner side of the clutch, and remove the bronze dial assembly from the front side of the clutch housing assembly.
6. Remove the clutch assembly from the rear of the housing, complete with the twelve roller pins.

ASSEMBLY AND INSTALLATION

1. Coat the moving parts with a waterproof grease.
2. Slide the axle shaft hub into the body from the front, and replace the snap-ring.
3. Replace the bronze dial assembly and the inner clutch. Tighten the Allen screw and stake the edge of the screw with a center punch to prevent loosening.
4. With the dial in the free position, rotate the outer clutch body into the inner assembly until it bottoms in the housing. Back it up to the nearest hole and install the roller pins.
5. Position the hub and clutch assembly together with a new gasket in between.
6. Position the hub assembly over the end of the axle and replace the six hub mounting bolts and lock tabs.
7. Torque the bolts to 35 ft. lbs. and bend the lock tabs to anchor the bolts.
8. Verify the operation by road testing.

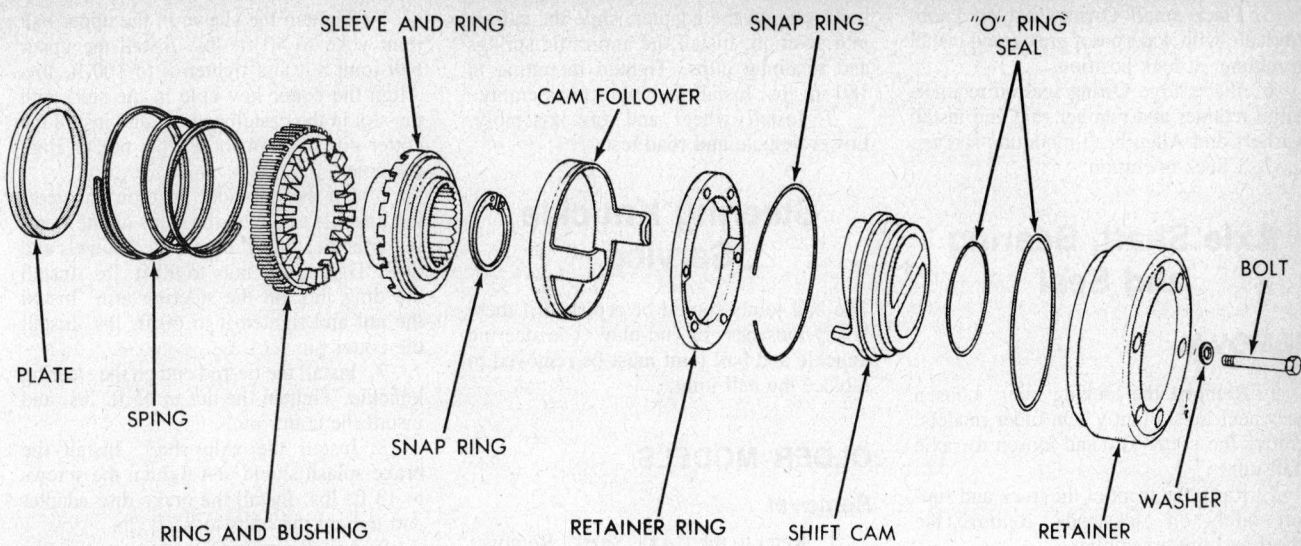

Locking hub component parts

Dana and "Dualmatic" Front Locking Hubs

REMOVAL AND DISASSEMBLY

1. Place hub in lock position. Remove Allen head mounting bolts and washers.

2. Carefully remove retainer, O-ring seal and knob. Separate knob from retainer.

3. Remove large internal snap-ring. Slide retainer ring and cam from hub.

4. While pressing against sleeve and ring assembly, remove axle shaft snap-ring. Relieve pressure and remove sleeve and ring, ring and bushing, spring and plate.

5. Inspect all parts for wear, nicks and burrs. Replace all parts which appear questionable.

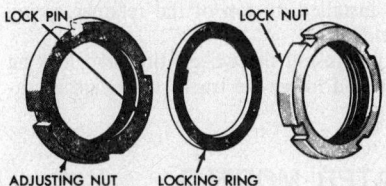

Late model wheel bearing adjusting nut, lock nut and ring—4WD

ASSEMBLY AND INSTALLATION

1. Slide plate and spring (large coils first) into wheel hub housing.

2. Assemble ring and bushing, sleeve and bushing. Slide complete assembly into housing.

3. Compress spring and install axle shaft snap-ring.

4. Position cam and retainer in housing and install large internal snap-ring.

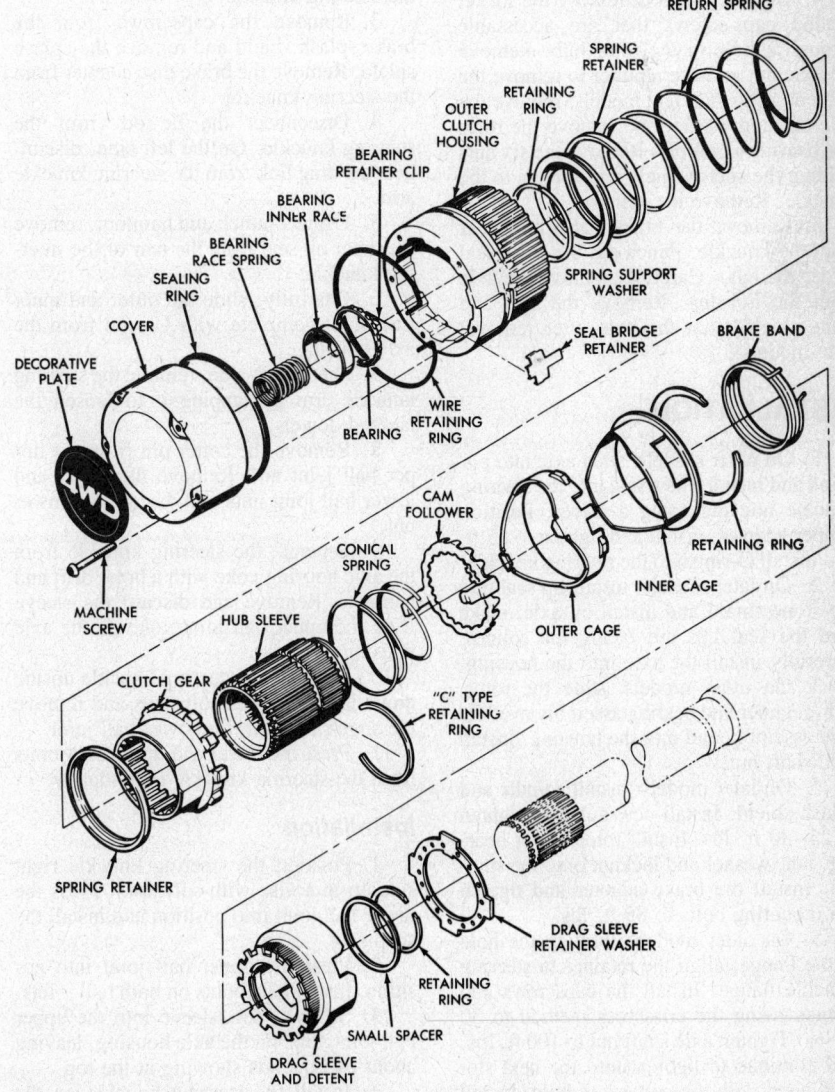

Automatic locking hub—disassembled

123

5. Place small O-ring seal on knob, lubricate with waterproof grease and install in retainer at lock position.

6. Place large O-ring seal on retainer. Align retainer and retainer ring and install washers and Allen head mounting screws.

7. Check operation.

Axle Shaft, Bearing and Seal

REMOVAL

1. Remove the locking hubs. Loosen the wheel lugs slightly. On older models, remove the cotter key and loosen the axle shaft nut.

2. Raise the front of the truck and support safely on jackstands. Remove the wheel and tire assemblies.

3. Remove the caliper and hang it out of the way with wire. Remove the inner brake pad.

4. On older models: remove the socket headed cap screws that are accessible through a hole in the rotor hub. Remove the axle nut and use a puller to remove the hub end rotor. On late models: remove the axle nut and washer and remove the rotor and bearing assembly. Remove the six nuts holding the splash shield and spindle to the knuckle. Remove the spindle.

5. Remove the brake caliper adapter from the knuckle. Punch out the inner seal (older models). Carefully remove the axle from the housing. Remove the seal and stone shield from the axle after removal (late models).

INSTALLATION

1. On older models: slide axle into position and install a new seal into the steering knuckle housing using a driver. Position caliper adapter, install and tighten to 85 ft. lbs. Install O-ring into the steering knuckle.

2. On later models: install lip seal into the stone shield and install on axle, make sure the seal lips are facing the splines. Carefully install the axle into the housing.

3. On older models: slide the rotor, hub, retainer and bearing assembly over the axle assembly and into the housing. Install axle shaft nut.

4. On later models: install spindle and splash shield. Install new nuts and tighten to 25–30 ft. lbs. Install rotor, outer bearing, nut, washer and locknut onto the spindle. Install the brake adapter and tighten the mounting bolts to 85 ft. lbs.

5. On older models: through the hole in the flange, align the retainer to steering knuckle flange. Install the capscrews and tighten using the crisscross method to 30 ft. lbs. Tighten axle shaft nut to 100 ft. lbs. and continue to tighten until the next slot is aligned with the cotter key hole. Install the cotter key.

6. On all models: Locate the inboard brake pad on the adapter, slide the caliper into position. Install the anti-rattle springs and retaining clips. Tighten mounting to 180 in. lbs. Install locking hub assembly.

7. Install wheel and tire assembly. Lower vehicle and road test.

Steering Knuckle Service

The ball joints should be replaced if there is any looseness or end-play. The steering knuckle and ball joint must be removed to replace the ball joint.

OLDER MODELS

Removal

1. Refer to the "Axle Shaft" Removal and Replacement, for the detailed removal of the rotor, hub and bearings.

2. Remove and discard the O-ring from the steering knuckle.

3. Remove the capscrews from the brake splash shield and remove the splash shield. Remove the brake disc adapter from the steering knuckle.

4. Disconnect the tie-rod from the steering knuckle. On the left side, disconnect the drag link from the steering knuckle arm.

5. Using a punch and hammer, remove the inner oil seal from the rear of the steering knuckle.

6. Carefully, slide the outer and inner axle shaft complete with U-joint from the axle housing.

7. On the left-side, remove the steering knuckle arm by tapping it to loosen the tapered dowels.

8. Remove the cotter pin from the upper ball joint nut. Remove the upper and lower ball joint nuts and discard the lower nut.

9. Separate the steering knuckle from the axle housing yoke with a brass drift and hammer. Remove and discard the sleeve from the upper ball joint yoke on the axle housing.

10. Position the steering knuckle upside down in a vise with soft jaws and remove the snap-ring from the lower ball joint.

11. Press the lower and upper ball joints from the steering knuckle individually.

Installation

1. Position the steering knuckle right side up in a vise with soft jaws. Press the lower ball joint into position and install the snap-ring.

2. Press the upper ball joint into position. Install new boots on both ball joints.

3. Screw a new sleeve into the upper ball joint yoke on the axle housing, leaving about two threads showing at the top.

4. Install the steering knuckle on the axle housing yoke and install a new lower ball joint nut, tightening it to 80 ft. lbs.

5. Tighten the sleeve in the upper ball joint yoke to 40 ft. lbs. Install the upper ball joint nut and tighten it to 100 ft. lbs. Align the cotter key hole in the stud with the slot in the castellated nut and install the cotter pin. Do not loosen the nut to align the holes.

6. On the left-side, position the steering knuckle arm over the studs on the steering knuckle. Install the tapered dowels and nuts. Tighten the nuts to 90 ft. lbs. Install the drag link on the steering arm. Install the nut and tighten it to 60 ft. lbs. Install the cotter pin.

7. Install the tie-rod end on the steering knuckle. Tighten the nut to 45 ft. lbs. and install the cotter pin.

8. Install the axle shaft. Install the brake splash shield and tighten the screws to 13 ft. lbs. Install the brake disc adapter and tighten the bolts to 85 ft. lbs.

9. Install a new O-ring in the steering knuckle.

10. Clean any rust from the axle shaft splines.

11. Carefully, slide the hub, rotor and retainer, and bearing onto the axle shaft and start it into the housing. Install the axle shaft nut.

12. Align the retainer with the steering knuckle flange. Install the retainer screws and tighten them in a criss-cross pattern to 30 ft. lbs.

13. Tighten the axle shaft nut to 100 ft. lbs. Tighten the nut until the next slot in the nut aligns with the hole in the axle shaft. Install the cotter pin.

14. Install the inboard brake shoe on the adapter with the shoe flanges in the adapter ways. Install the caliper in the adapter and over the disc. Align the caliper on the machined ways of the adapter. Be careful not to pull the dust boot from its grooves as the piston and boot slide over the inboard shoe.

15. Install the anti-rattle springs and retaining clips. Torque to 16–17 ft. lbs. The inboard shoe anti-rattle spring must always be installed on top of the retainer spring plate.

16. Install the wheel, tire, and locking hub and lower the truck. Lubricate all fittings.

LATER MODELS

The ball joints should be replaced if there is any looseness or end-play. The steering knuckle and ball joint must be removed to replace the ball joint.

Removal

1. Refer to Front Drive Axle Removal and Replacement, for the detailed removal of the rotor hub and bearings. Also refer to Locking Hub section.

2. After removing all necessary brake parts, remove the caliper adapter from the steering knuckle. Remove the six nuts and washers from the spindle to steering knuckle. Remove the splash shield. Take a soft

hammer, hit the spindle lightly to break it free from the steering knuckle. Examine the bronze spacer and needle bearing. Replace any worn parts.

3. Remove the axle shaft assembly.

4. Disconnect the tie rod ends from the steering knuckles. On the left side, disconnect the drag link from the steering knuckle arm.

5. On the left side, remove the nuts and washers from the steering knuckle arm. Tap the steering arm to loosen it from the knuckle. Remove the arm.

6. Remove the cotter key from the upper ball joint nut. Remove the upper and lower ball joint nuts. Use a brass drift and hammer to separate the knuckle from the axle yoke. Remove and discard the sleeve from the upper ball joint yoke.

7. Position the steering knuckle upside down in a vise. Remove the snap-ring from the lower ball joint with a pair of snap-ring pliers. Press the lower ball joint first, then the upper from the steering knuckle.

8. Clean all parts and examine for wear. Replace any worn parts.

Installation

1. Press the lower ball joint into position and install the snap ring. Press in the upper ball joint. Install new boots on both ball joints.

2. Position the steering knuckle into position on the axle housing yoke. Install the lower ball joint nut and tighten to 80 ft. lbs.

3. Install the sleeve into the upper ball joint yoke and tighten to 40 ft. lbs. Install the upper ball joint nut, tighten to 100 ft. lbs. Align the nut with the hole in the ball joint stud and insert a new cotter pin.

4. Position and install the steering arm on the left knuckle, tighten to 90 ft. lbs. Install drag link, tighten to 60 ft. lbs. Install the tie rod ends, tighten to 45 ft. lbs. Align and install new cotter pins.

5. Refer to Front Axle Removal and Installation. Install the axle.

Steering Knuckle—Front Wheel Drive

REMOVAL AND INSTALLATION

Service or repair to the bearing, hub, brake dust shield or the steering knuckle itself will require removal of the knuckle. Before attempting this operation, be aware that to reassemble the components it is necessary to torque the front hub nut to at least 180 ft. lbs. You will need a large torque wrench to read that high and a great deal of strength to attain that much torque on the nut.

1. Remove the cotter pin and nut-lock.

2. Loosen the hub nut while the car is resting on the wheels with the brakes applied.

NOTE: The hub and driveshaft are splined together through the knuckle and retained by the hub nut.

3. Raise and support the car.

4. Remove the wheel and tire.

5. Remove the hub nut. Be sure the splined driveshaft is free to separate from the spline in hub when the knuckle is removed.

6. Disconnect the tie rod end from the steering arm.

7. Disconnect the brake hose retainer from the strut.

8. Remove the slamp bolt holding the ball joint stud in the steering knuckle.

9. Remove the brake caliper adapter screw and washers.

10. Support the caliper on a wire hook.

11. Remove the brake disc.

12. Matchmark the camber adjusting cams and loosen both bolts.

13. Support the steering knuckle and remove the cam adjusting and through-bolts. Remove the upper knuckle leg out of the strut bracket and lift the knuckle from the ball joint stud.

NOTE: Do not allow the driveshaft to hang during this procedure.

14. Service procedures requiring hub removal also require that a new bearing be installed.

15. Installation is the reverse of removal. A new hub nut is required. When the car is resting on the wheels, with the brakes applied, tighten the hub nut to 180 ft. lbs.

Front Drive Axle Assembly

REMOVAL, OVERHAUL

Refer to the Unit Repair section.

Driveshaft—Front Wheel Drive

REMOVAL AND INSTALLATION

Manual Transmission Models

NOTE: Anytime the differential cover is removed, a new gasket should be formed from RTV sealant.

1. With the vehicle on the floor and the brakes applied, loosen the hub nut.

NOTE: The hub and driveshafts are splined together and retained by the hub nut which is torqued to at least 180 ft. lbs.

2. Raise and support the vehicle and remove the hub nut and washer.

NOTE: Always support both ends of the driveshaft during removal to prevent damage to the boots.

3. Disconnect the lower control arm ball joint stud nut from the steering knuckle.

4. Remove the Allenhead screws which secure the CV joint to the transmission flange.

5. Holding the CV housing, push the outer joint and knuckle assembly outward while disengaging the inner housing from the flange face.

NOTE: The outer joint and shaft must be supported during disengagement of the inner joint.

Quickly turn the open end of the joint upward to retain as much lubricant as possible, then carefully pull the outer joint spline out of the hub. Cover the joint with a clean towel to prevent dirt contamination.

6. Before installation, make sure that any lost lubricant is replaced.

7. Clean the joint body and mating flange face.

8. Install the outer joint splined shaft into the hub. Do not secure with the nut and washer.

9. Position the inner joint in the transmission drive flange and secure it with *new* screws. Torque the screws to 37–40 ft. lbs.

10. Connect the lower control arm to the knuckle.

11. Install the outer joint and secure it with a *new* nut and washer. Torque the nut with the car on the ground and the brake set. Torque is 180 ft. lbs.

12. After attaching the driveshaft, if the inboard boot appears to be collapsed or deformed, vent the inner boot by inserting a round-tipped, small diameter rod between the boot and the shaft. As venting occurs, boot will return to its original shape.

Automatic Transaxle Models

The inboard CV joints on early product models may be retained by circlips in the differential side gears. On later production

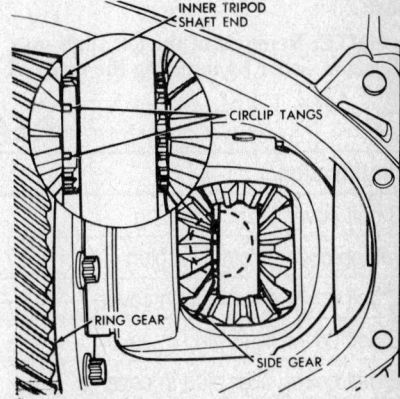

Rotate the driveshaft (axle) to expose the circlip tangs

models, the shafts incorporate the use of a spring within the right and left inboard tripod joint assemblies and do not use a circlip.

To determine whether a spring loaded shaft is installed, place a pry bar between the transaxle extension housing (right shaft) and the face of the tripod joint housing, pry towards the outside of the truck taking care not to damage the seal in the extension housing. If the joint can be moved at least ½ inch from the extension housing, the driveshaft is spring loaded and does not have a circlip retainer.

If complete removal of these driveshafts is required, the splines on the transaxle ends of both shafts can be easily pulled out without having to enter the transaxle.

NOTE: On trucks equipped with spring loaded shafts, exclude steps 2, 4 and 5.

1. With the car on the ground, loosen the hub nut, which has been torqued to 200 ft. lbs.

2. Drain the transaxle differential and remove the cover. See preceding NOTE.

NOTE: Anytime the transaxle differential cover is removed, a new gasket should be formed from RTV sealant.

3. To remove the right-hand driveshaft, disconnect the speedometer cable and remove the cable and gear before removing the driveshaft.

4. Rotate the driveshaft to expose the circlip tangs. See NOTE.

5. Compress the circlip with needle nose pliers and push the shaft into the side gear cavity. See NOTE above.

6. Remove the clamp bolt from the ball stud and steering knuckle.

7. Separate the ball joint stud from the steering knuckle, by prying against the knuckle leg and control arm.

8. Separate the outer CV joint splined shaft from the hub by holding the CV housing and moving the hub away. Do not pry on the slinger or outer CV joint.

9. Support the shaft at the CV joints, remove the six allen head screws (if equipped) from the transaxle drive flange and remove the shaft. Do not pull on the shaft.

NOTE: Removal of the left shaft may be made easier by inserting the blade of

a thin prybar between the differential pinion shaft and prying against the end face of the shaft.

10. Installation is the reverse of removal. Be sure the circlip tangs are positioned against the flattened end of the shaft before installing the shaft. A quick thrust will lock the circlip in the groove. Tighten the hub nut with the wheels to the ground to 180 ft. lbs.

REAR AXLE

Axle Shafts and Bearings

EXCEPT FRONT WHEEL DRIVE

Before servicing any axle shafts, be sure to jack and support the truck so that both rear wheels are off the ground. This will ensure that the vehicle will not roll off the supports if the vehicle is equipped with a limited slip rear axle and one wheel is turned inadvertently.

8⅜ in. and 9¼ in.

NOTE: There is no provision for axle shaft end-play adjustment on these axles.

REMOVAL

1. Jack up the vehicle and remove the rear wheels.

2. Clean all dirt from the housing cover and remove the housing cover to drain the lubricant.

3. Remove the brake drum.

4. Rotate the differential case until the differential pinion shaft lockscrew can be removed. Remove the lockscrew and pinion shaft.

5. Push the axle shafts toward the center of the vehicle and remove the C-locks from the grooves on the axle shafts.

6. Pull the axle shafts from the hous-

ing, being careful not to damage the bearing which remains in the housing.

7. Inspect the axle shaft bearings and replace any doubtful parts. Whenever the axle shaft is replaced, the bearings should also be replaced.

8. Remove the axle shaft seal from the bore in the housing, using the button end of the axle shaft.

9. Remove the axle shaft bearing from the housing. Do not reuse the bearing or the seal.

10. Check the bearing shoulder in the axle housing for imperfections. These should be corrected with a file.

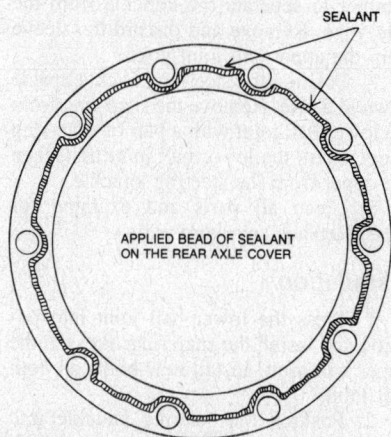

SEALANT

APPLIED BEAD OF SEALANT ON THE REAR AXLE COVER

Rear axle cover sealant application

INSTALLATION

1. Clean the axle shaft bearing cavity.

2. Grease and install the axle shaft bearing in the cavity. Be sure that the bearing is not cocked and that it is seated firmly against the shoulder.

3. Install the axle shaft bearing seal. It should be seated beyond the end of the flange face.

4. Insert the axle shaft, making sure that the splines do not damage the seal. Be sure that the splines are properly engaged with the differential side gear splines.

5. Install the C-locks in the grooves on the axle shafts. Pull the shafts outward so that the C-locks seat in the counterbore of the differential side gears.

6. Install the differential pinion shaft

REAR AXLE IDENTIFICATION CHART

Identification	Ring Gear Size (in.)	Maker and Model	Approximately Capacity (pts) ①
10 bolt cover, front filler plug	8⅜	Chrysler	4.4
Welded cover, front filler plug	8¾	Chrysler	4.0 thru 1969, 4.4 later
12 bolt cover, filler plug in cover	9¼	Chrysler	4.5
10 bolt cover, filler plug in cover	9¾	Spicer 60	6.0
10 bolt cover, filler plug in cover	10½	Spicer 70	7.0 thru 1976, 6.5 for 1977 and later

① These are design capacities and may differ slightly from those given in the Capacities Chart.

through the case and pinions. Install the lockscrew and secure it in position.

7. Clean the housing and gasket surfaces. Install the cover and a new gasket. Refill the axle with the specified lubricant.

NOTE: Replacement differential cover gaskets may not be available. The use of gel type nonsticking sealant is recommended.

8. Install the brake drum and wheel.

9¾ in. (Spicer 60) and 10½ in. (Spicer 70)

REMOVAL AND INSTALLATION

1. Remove the axle shaft flange nuts and washers.
2. Rap the axle shafts sharply in the center of the flange with a hammer to free the dowels.
3. Remove the tapered dowels and axle shafts. Some models are equipped with bolts rather than dowels.
4. Clean the gasket area with solvent and install a new flange gasket.
5. Install the axle shaft into the housing.
6. If the axle has an outer wheel bearing seal, install new gaskets on each side of the seal mounting flange.
7. Install the tapered dowels, lockwashers, and nuts. Torque the nuts to 40–70 ft. lbs. with ⁷⁄₁₆ in. studs and 65–105 with ½ in. Some axles have bolts instead of studs and tapered dowels. Bolt torque is 45–75 ft. lbs.

WHEEL BEARING ADJUSTMENT

1. Raise and support the rear axle.
2. Remove the axle shaft, outer nut, and lockring.
3. Rotate the wheel and tire and tighten the adjusting nut until a slight binding is felt. Back the nut off ⅙ turn.
4. Install the lockring and jamnut. Don't overtighten the jamnut or you will change the adjustment.
5. Install a new gasket and the axle shaft. Lower the vehicle.

FRONT WHEEL DRIVE MODELS

Rear Wheel Bearings

The rear wheel bearings should be inspected and relubricated whenever the rear brakes are serviced or at least every 30,000 miles. Repack the bearings with high temperature multi-purpose grease.

Check the lubricant to see if it is contaminated. If it contains dirt or has a milky appearance indicating the presence of water, the bearings should be cleaned and repacked.

Clean the bearings in kerosene, mineral spirits or other suitable cleaning fluid. Do not dry them by spinning the bearings. Allow them to air dry.

1. Raise and support the truck with the rear wheels off the floor.
2. Remove the wheel grease cap, cotter pin, nut-lock and bearing adjusting nut.
3. Remove the thrust washer and bearing.
4. Remove the drum from the spindle.
5. Thoroughly clean the old lubricant from the bearings and hub cavity. Inspect the bearing rollers for pitting or other signs of wear. Light discoloration is normal.
6. Repack the bearings with high temperature multi-purpose EP grease and add a small amount of new grease to the hub cavity. Be sure to force the lubricant between all rollers in the bearing.
7. Install the drum on the spindle after coating the polished spindle surfaces with wheel bearing lubricant.
8. Install the outer bearing cone, thrust washer and adjusting nut.
9. Tighten the adjusting nut to 20–25 ft. lbs. while rotating the wheel.
10. Back off the adjusting nut to completely release the preload from the bearing.
11. Tighten the adjusting nut finger-tight.
12. Position the nut-lock with one pair of slots in line with the cotter pin hole. Install the cotter pin.
13. Clean and install the grease cap and wheel.
14. Lower the truck.

Differential

Servicing procedures are found in the Unit Repair Section.

STEERING

Steering Wheel

REMOVAL AND INSTALLATION

Except Rampage

1. Remove the horn button from the retainer by rotating it to the left, or remove the horn pad from the retainer by removing the two screws from underneath.
2. Disconnect the horn wire from the horn switch terminal.
3. Remove three screws and lift out the horn switch and button or pad retainer assembly.
4. Back the steering wheel retaining nut off to the top of the shaft.
5. Install a steering wheel puller and

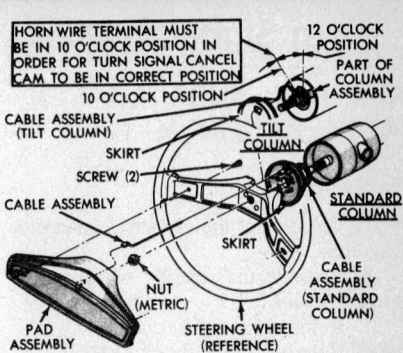

1978 and later steering wheel—typical

draw the steering wheel from the steering shaft splines.

6. Remove the steering wheel nut and pull the steering wheel off of the steering shaft.
7. Installation is the reverse of removal. Tighten the nut to 24 ft. lbs. through 1977, 60 ft. lbs. for 1978 and later models.

Rampage

1. Remove the horn button and horn switch.
2. Remove the steering wheel nut.
3. Using a steering wheel puller, remove the steering wheel.
4. Align the master serration in the wheel hub with the missing tooth on the shaft. Torque the shaft nut to 60 ft. lbs.

———— **CAUTION** ————
Do not torque the nut against the steering column lock or damage will occur.

5. Replace the horn switch and button.

Turn Signal/Hazard Warning Flasher Switch

REMOVAL AND INSTALLATION

Except Rampage

1. Disconnect the battery ground cable. Remove the steering wheel.
2. Remove the turn signal lever screw and the lever. Don't remove the speed control, just let it hang.
3. Remove the switch retainer screws.
4. Lift the automatic transmission selector light out.
5. Remove the retainer plate.
6. Remove the wire cover extension, if any, below the column clamp. Remove the steering column mounting clamp. Remove the column wire cover.
7. Detach the switch wiring connector under the instrument panel.
8. Remove the switch.
9. Reverse the procedure for installation. Tighten the column clamp bolts to 30 ft. lbs.

Turn Signal Switch

REMOVAL AND INSTALLATION

Rampage

1. Disconnect the electrical connector at column.
2. Remove the steering wheel as described earlier.
3. Remove the lower column cover.
4. Remove the wash/wipe switch.
5. Remove the wiring clip and the three screws securing the turn signal switch.
6. Installation is the reverse of removal.

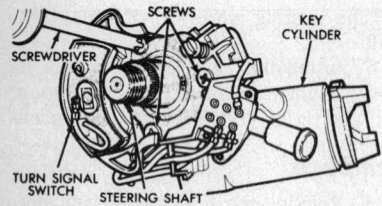

Turn signal switch—typical of Rampage

Ignition and Steering Lock

REMOVAL AND INSTALLATION

Rampage

1. Remove the steering wheel.
2. Remove the upper and lower column covers.
3. Using a hacksaw blade, cut the upper ¼ inch from the key cylinder retainer pin boss.
4. Using a drift, drive the roll pin from the housing and remove the key cylinder.
5. Insert the new cylinder into the housing, making sure that it engages the lug on the ignition switch driver. Install the roll pin.

Ignition Switch

REMOVAL AND INSTALLATION

Rampage

1. Remove the connector from the switch.
2. Place the key in the LOCK position.
3. Remove the key.
4. Remove the two mounting screws from the switch and pushrod to drop below the jacket.
5. Rotate the switch 90 degrees to permit removal of the switch from the pushrod.
6. To install the switch, position the

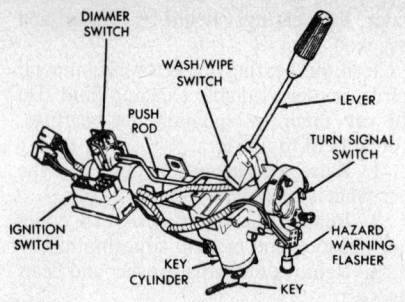

Steering column switch components—Rampage

switch in LOCK (second detent from the top).
7. Place the switch at right angles to the column and insert the pushrod.
8. Align the switch on the bracket and install the screws.
9. With a light rearward load on the switch, tighten the screws. Check for proper operation.

STEERING GEAR

Reference

Refer to the Steering Unit Repair section for the overhaul of the manual and power steering gears and the power steering pump.

Rampage

The manual steering system consists of a tube which contains the toothed rack, a pinion, the rack slipper, and the rack slipper spring. Steering effort is transmitted to the steering arms by the tie rods which are coupled to the ends of the rack, and the tie rod ends. The connection between the ends of the rack and the tie rod is protected by a bellows type oil seal which retains the gear lubricant.

The power steering system consists of four major parts: the power gear, power steering pump, pressure hose and the return hose. As with the manual system, the turning of the steering wheel is converted into linear travel through the meshing of the helical pinion teeth with the rack teeth. Power assist is provided by an open center, rotary type, three-way control valve which directs fluid to either side of the rack control piston.

REMOVAL AND INSTALLATION

Ramcharger and Trail Duster

1. Remove the two bolts from the wormshaft coupling.
2. Remove the steering arm from the steering gear using a suitable tool.
3. Remove the steering gear-to-frame bolts and remove the unit from the vehicle.
4. To install, position the steering gear to the frame and install the mounting bolts.
5. Install the steering arm and place the front wheels in the straight ahead position.
6. Place the steering wheel in the straight ahead position.
7. Install the wormshaft-to-column coupling bolts.

Vans and Pick-Ups

1. Disconnect the battery.
2. Raise the vehicle on a hoist and disconnect "rubber and fabric" coupling (leaving the lower half of the coupling on the wormshaft.
3. Disconnect the shift linkage at the steering column.
4. Remove the steering arm retaining nut and washer. With a suitable tool remove the steering arm from the sector shaft.
5. Remove the three gear mounting bolts. Lower the vehicle from the hoist and remove the toe plate and column support bolts.

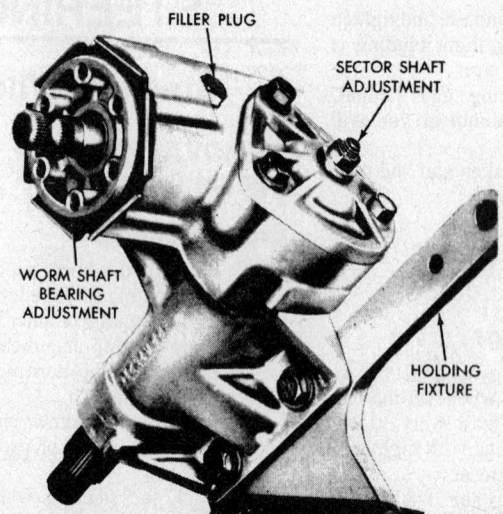

Manual steering gear adjustment points—typical

6. Disconnect the wiring and remove the column assembly.

7. Raise the vehicle on the hoist and remove the steering gear through the opening on the inboard side of the frame. (It may be helpful to remove the three bolts from the left idle arm bracket and move the bracket out of the way to provide additional clearance.)

NOTE: If the lower half of the steering coupling was removed from the gear, reinstall it on the wormshaft and secure it with a roll pin before installing the gear into the vehicle.

8. From underneath the vehicle, place the steering gear in position and install the three mounting bolts.

9. Reinstall the idler arm bracket, if it was removed.

10. Install the steering arm on the sector shaft. Install the washer and retaining nut.

11. Install the steering column assembly. Connect the steering column wiring. Install the shift linkage at the steering column.

12. Connect the steering shaft coupling at the wormshaft.

13. Connect the battery.

Adjustments

Except Rampage

There are two adjustments, the worm bearing preload and the ball nut rack and sector mesh, that can be made. The worm bearing preload must be adjusted first.

WORM BEARING PRELOAD ADJUSTMENT

1. Detach the steering gear arm from the cross-shaft with a suitable puller, after removing the nut.

2. Remove the horn button, ring, or pad from the steering wheel.

3. Loosen the sector shaft screw locknut several turns. Then loosen the adjusting screw two turns. This will remove any friction load present between the ball nut rack and the sector gear teeth.

4. Rotate the steering wheel two *full* turns from straight-ahead. Attach a torque wrench on the steering shaft nut.

5. Turn the steering shaft at least one full turn toward straight-ahead. As the shaft is being rotated, check the torque reading on the wrench. The torque necessary to keep the wheel moving should fall between 1½ to 4½ in. lbs. for 1975 or between 1 and 1½ in. lbs. for 1976 and later. If the reading does not fall within specifications, adjustment is required. The adjuster is threaded into the housing on the upper end of the wormshaft.

6. To adjust, loosen the adjuster locknut. Turn the adjuster clockwise to increase the preload, or counterclockwise to decrease the preload.

7. Tighten the locknut while keeping the adjuster from turning. Retest the preload to see if it falls within specifications.

BALL NUT RACK AND SECTOR MESH ADJUSTMENT

1. Complete the worm bearing preload adjustment first.

2. Turn the steering wheel gently from one lock to the other. Count the number of turns. Turn the wheel back *exactly* to the midpoint of its travel.

3. Turn the sector shaft adjusting screw, which is located on the housing cover, clockwise until there is no lash present between ball nut and sector teeth. Tighten the locknut to 35 ft. lbs.

4. Rotate the steering wheel one-quarter turn away from the center "high spot." Use a torque wrench, attached to the steering wheel nut, to measure the torque force required to turn the wheel through the "high spot." The reading should fall between 8–11 in. lbs. Rotate the sector shaft adjustment screw, if required, to obtain the correct preload.

5. Once the adjustments are completed, straighten the front wheels and install the steering arm on the cross-shaft.

NOTE: Not only should the front wheels be straight-ahead, but both the steering gear and the steering wheel should be centered as well.

6. Tighten the steering arm securing nut to 175 ft. lbs.

7. Install the horn button, ring, or trim pad on the steering wheel.

Power Steering Gear

REMOVAL AND INSTALLATION

Except Rampage

1. Raise the hood and remove the battery.

2. Disconnect the wires from the windshield washer pump. Remove the windshield washer reservoir mounting screws and position the reservoir out of the way.

3. Disconnect the power steering hoses at the steering gear. Cap the fittings at the steering gear and tie the hoses above the fluid level in the pump reservoir to prevent oil leakage.

4. Raise the vehicle on a hoist and disconnect the "rubber and fabric" coupling at the steering gear (leaving the lower half of the coupling on the wormshaft).

5. Disconnect the shift linkage at the steering column.

6. Remove the steering arm shield if so equipped. Remove the nut and washer, then with a suitable tool, remove the steering arm from the sector shaft.

7. Remove the mounting bolt on the left side of the gear.

8. Lower the vehicle and remove one of the two remaining steering gear mounting bolts.

9. Remove the toe plate and column support bolts.

10. Disconnect the steering column wiring and remove the assembly.

11. Raise the vehicle on the hoist. Remove the three bolts from the left idler arm bracket and swing the bracket out of the way.

12. Remove the remaining bolt and the steering gear from underneath of the vehicle, through the opening on the inboard side of the frame.

NOTE: Before installing the steering gear into the vehicle, install the coupling half on the wormshaft and secure it with the roll pin.

13. From the underside of the vehicle, place the steering gear into position on the mounting bracket and install the three mounting bolts.

14. Continue the installation in the reverse order of the removal.

15. Lower the vehicle, start the engine and turn the steering wheel several times from stop to stop to bleed the system of air.

16. Stop the engine and check the fluid level, correct if necessary. Inspect for leaks.

SECTOR ADJUSTMENT

1. Disconnect the center link from the steering gear arm.

2. Start the engine and allow it to run at normal idle speed.

3. Rotate the steering wheel from lock to lock. Carefully count the number of turns required, then rotate the wheel back, exactly to the midpoint of its travel.

4. Loosen the adjusting screw until backlash in the steering gear arm becomes apparent.

NOTE: Backlash is felt by holding the end of the steering gear arm lightly between your thumb and forefinger.

5. Tighten the adjusting screw just enough so that the backlash disappears. Continue to tighten the screw for another ⅜ to ½ turn from this point. Tighten the locknut to 28 ft. lbs.

6. Attach the center link to the steering gear arm.

Power Steering Pump

REMOVAL AND INSTALLATION

Except Rampage

1. Loosen the pump mounting and locking bolts and remove the drive belt.

2. Disconnect and plug both hoses.

3. Remove the mounting and locking bolts and remove the pump.

4. Install the pump on the engine and install the mounting and locking bolts.

5. Install and adjust the drive belt. Tighten the mounting bolts to 30 ft. lbs.

6. Connect the pressure and return hoses. Route the hoses in the same manner as they were routed prior to removal. They should be routed smoothly with no sharp bends. Tighten the pump end hose fitting to 30 ft. lbs. (35 ft. lbs. for 1975 and later) and the gear end fitting to 19 ft. lbs. (25 ft. lbs. for 1975 and later). The hoses should remain at least 1 in. away from pulleys, battery case, and brake lines and at least 2 in. away from exhaust manifolds. If equipped, the protective sponge sleeves should be used to protect the hoses from contact with other parts.

7. Fill the pump with the specified power steering fluid or the equivalent.

8. Start the engine and turn the steering wheel lock-to-lock several times to bleed the system. Check for leaks and recheck the fluid level.

Rampage

1. Disconnect the power steering hoses from the pump.

2. Remove the adjusting bolt and slip off the belt.

3. Support the pump, remove the mounting bolts and lift out the pump.

4. Installation is the reverse of removal. Adjust the belt to specifications.

STEERING LINKAGE

Tie Rods

REMOVAL AND INSTALLATION

Except Rampage

1. Raise the front of the truck and support it safely on jackstands.

2. Remove the cotter pin and the nut from the end of the tie rod.

3. Install a puller and apply sufficient pressure to release the tie rod end from the knuckle. Measure or count the number of exposed threads.

4. Loosen the tie rod sleeve clamping bolt and unscrew the tie rod end.
To install:

1. Screw the new tie rod end into the sleeve.

2. Connect the tie rod end to the knuckle and tighten the nut as follows: ½ in. nut—45 ft. lbs.; ⁹⁄₁₆ in. nut—55 ft. lbs.; ⅝ in. nut—75 ft. lbs. Install the cotter pin.

3. Lower the truck and adjust the toe-in.

4. Tighten the clamping bolt.

Rampage

1. Raise the front of the truck and safely support it on jackstands.

2. Remove the cotter pin and the nut from the end of the tie rod.

3. Install a puller and apply sufficient pressure to release the tie rod from the knuckle arm.

4. Loosen the jam nut and unscrew the tie rod end.

5. Installation is in the reverse order of removal. Have the toe adjustment checked.

FRONT SUSPENSION

Coil Spring

REMOVAL AND INSTALLATION

Except 4WD and Rampage

1. Raise the vehicle and support it with jackstands under the front ends of the frame rails.

2. Remove the wheel.

3. Remove the shock absorber and upper shock absorber bushing and sleeve.

4. If equipped, remove the sway bar.

5. Remove the strut.

6. Install a spring compressor and tighten finger-tight.

7. Remove the cotter pins and ball joint nuts.

8. Install a ball joint breaker tool and turn the threaded portion of the tool to lock it against the lower stud.

9. Spread the tool to place the lower stud under pressure, then strike the steering knuckle sharply with a hammer to free the stud. Do not attempt to force the stud out of the steering knuckle with the tool.

10. Remove the tool. Slowly release the spring compressor until all tension is relieved from the spring.

11. Remove the spring compressor and spring.

12. Installation is the reverse of removal. Compress the spring until the ball joint can be properly positioned in the steering knuckle.

Shock Absorber

REMOVAL AND INSTALLATION

Except 4WD and Rampage

1. Raise and support the vehicle with jackstands positioned at the extreme front ends of the frame rails.

2. Remove the wheel.

3. Remove the upper nut and retainer.

4. Remove the two lower mounting bolts.

5. Remove the shock absorber.

6. Installation is the reverse of removal.

Upper Control Arm

REMOVAL AND INSTALLATION

Except 4WD and Rampage

NOTE: Any time the control arm is removed, it is necessary to align the front end.

1. Raise and support the vehicle with jackstands under the frame rails.

2. Remove the wheel.

3. Remove the shock absorber and shock absorber upper bushing and sleeve.

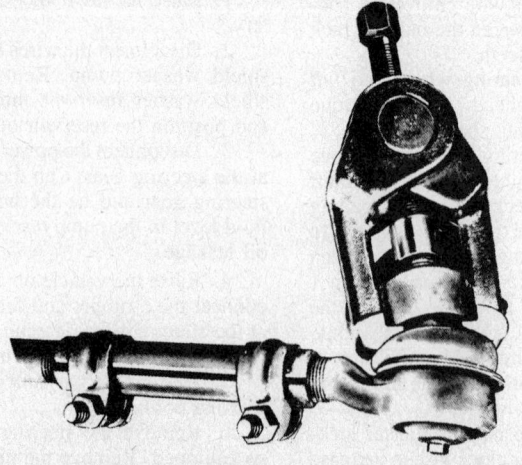

Removing the tie-rod end with a puller

4. Install a spring compressor and tighten it finger-tight.

5. Remove the cotter pins and ball joint nuts.

6. Install a ball joint breaker and turn the threaded portion of the tool, locking it securely against the upper stud. Spread the tool enough to place the upper ball joint under pressure and strike the steering knuckle sharply to loosen the stud. Do not attempt to remove the stud from the steering knuckle with the tool.

7. Remove the tool.

8. Remove the eccentric pivot bolts, after making their relative positions in the control arm.

9. Remove the upper control arm.

10. Installation is the reverse of removal. Tighten the ball joint nuts to 135 ft. lbs. Tighten the eccentric pivot bolts to 70 ft. lbs.

11. Adjust the caster and camber.

Lower Control Arm

REMOVAL AND INSTALLATION

Except 4WD and Rampage

1. Follow the procedure outlined under Coil Spring Removal and Installation.

2. Remove the mounting bolt from the crossmember.

3. Remove the lower control arm from the vehicle.

4. Installation is the reverse of removal. After the vehicle has been lowered to the ground, tighten the mounting bolt to 210 ft. lbs.

Lower Ball Joint

REMOVAL AND INSTALLATION

Except 4WD and Rampage

1. Remove the lower control arm.

2. Remove the ball joint seal.

3. Using an arbor press and a sleeve, press the ball joint from the control arm.

4. Installation is the reverse of removal. Be sure that the ball joint is fully seated. Install a new ball joint seal.

5. Install the lower control arm. Be sure to install the ball joint cotter pins.

Upper Ball Joint

REMOVAL AND INSTALLATION

Except 4WD and Rampage

1. Install a jack under the outer end of the lower control arm and raise the vehicle.

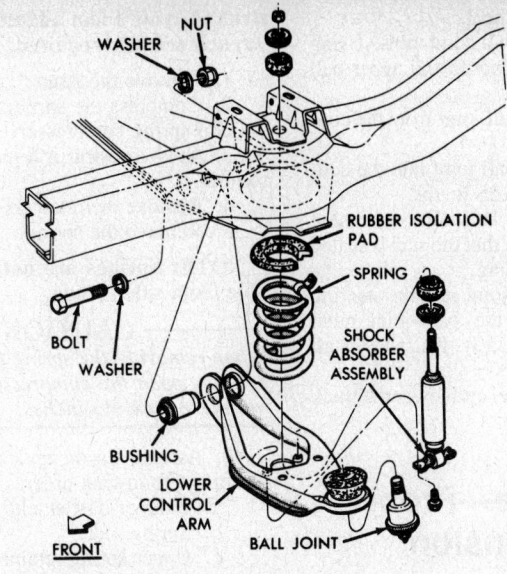

1979 and later coil spring and control arm components

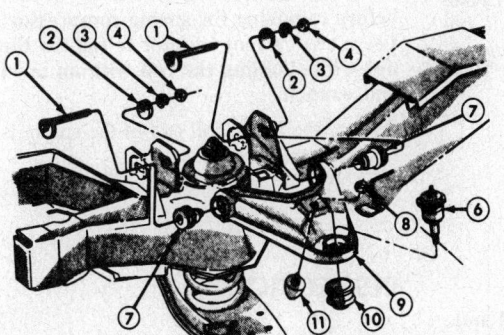

1. Cam and bolt assembly
2. Cam
3. Lock washer
4. Nut
6. Ball joint assembly
7. Bushing assembly
8. Lock nut
9. Upper control arm
10. Upper ball joint assembly
11. Bumper assembly

1975–78 upper control arm

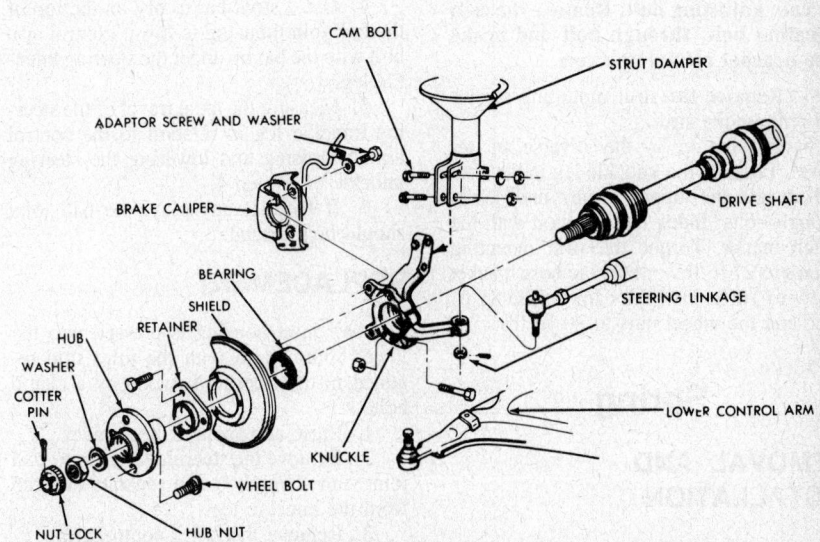

Exploded view front suspension—Rampage

2. Remove the wheel.

3. Remove the ball joint nuts. Using a ball joint breaker, loosen the upper ball joint.

4. Unscrew the ball joint from the control arm.

5. Screw a new ball joint into the control arm and tighten 125 ft. lbs.

6. Install the new ball joint seal, using a 2 in. socket. Be sure that the seal is seated on the ball joint housing.

7. Insert the ball joint into the steering knuckle and install the ball joint nuts. Tighten the nuts to 135 ft. lbs. and install the cotter pins.

8. Install the wheel and lower the truck to the ground.

Rampage—Front Suspension

A MacPherson type front suspension, with vertical shock absorbers attached to the upper fender reinforcement and the steering knuckle, is used. Lower control arms, attached inboard to a cross-member and outboard to the steering knuckle through a ball joint, provide lower steering knuckle position. During steering maneuvers, the upper strut and steering knuckle turn as an assembly.

Strut

REMOVAL AND INSTALLATION

NOTE: To remove the welded nut, grind the hex flats for proper wrench fit.

1. Raise and support the vehicle.
2. Remove the wheel.

NOTE: If the original strut is to be assembled to the original knuckle, mark the cam adjusting bolt. Remove the cam adjusting bolt, through bolt and brake hose bracket retaining screw.

4. Remove the strut mounting screws and remove the strut.

5. Installation is the reverse of removal. Position the knuckle leg in the strut and install the upper (cam) and lower through-bolts. Index the cam bolt with the match marks. Torque the strut mounting screws to 27 ft. lbs.; the brake hose bracket screw to 10 ft. lbs.; the cam bolt to 85 ft. lbs., and the wheel nuts to 80 ft. lbs.

Spring

REMOVAL AND INSTALLATION

NOTE: A spring compressor is required to remove the spring from the

strut. A crow's foot adaptor and torque wrench are also required.

1. Remove the struts.
2. Compress the spring, using a reliable coil spring compressor.
3. Hold the strut rod and remove the rod nut.
4. Remove the retainers and bushings.
5. Remove the spring.

NOTE: Springs are not interchangeable from side to side.

——————— CAUTION ———————
When removing the spring from the compressor, open the compressor evenly and not more than 9¼ inches.

6. Assembly is the reverse of disassembly in the following order:
   a. Bumper dust shield
   b. Spring seat
   c. Upper spring retainer
   d. Bearing and spacer
   e. Mount assembly
   f. Rebound bumper
   g. Retainer
   h. Rod nut

NOTE: Torque rod nut to 55 ft. lbs. before removing the spring compressor. Use a crow's foot adaptor to tighten the nut while holding the rod with an open end wrench.

Be sure the lower coil end of the spring is seated in the seat recess.

Ball Joints

INSPECTION

1. Raise and support the vehicle.
2. With the suspension fully extended (at full travel) clamp a dial indicator to the lower control arm with the plunger indexed against the steering knuckle leg.
3. Zero the dial indicator.
4. Use a stout bar to pry on the top of the ball joint housing-to-lower control arm bolt with the bar tip under the steering knuckle leg.
5. Measure the axial travel of the steering knuckle leg in relation to the control arm by raising and lowering the steering knuckle as in step 4.
6. If there is any play, the ball joint should be replaced.

REPLACEMENT

The ball joint housing is pressed into the lower control arm with the joint stud retained in the steering knuckle by a clamp bolt.

1. Raise and support the vehicle.
2. Remove the steering knuckle-to-ball joint stud clamp bolt and separate the stud from the knuckle leg.
3. Remove the lower control arm.
4. Press the ball joint out of the control arm.

5. Install a new ball joint to the control arm.

6. Install the control arm and connect the ball joint stud to the steering knuckle.

7. Lower the vehicle.

Lower Control Arm

REMOVAL AND INSTALLATION

1. Raise and support the vehicle.
2. Remove the front inner pivot through bolt, the rear stub strut nut, retainer and bushing, and the ball joint-to-steering knuckle clamp bolt.
3. Separate the ball joint stud from the steering knuckle by prying between the ball stud retainer on the knuckle and the lower control arm.

——————— CAUTION ———————
Pulling the steering knuckle out from the vehicle after releasing it from the ball joint can separate the inner C/V joint.

4. Remove the sway bar-to-control arm nut and reinforcement and rotate the control arm over the sway bar. Remove the rear stub strut bushing, sleeve and retainer.

NOTE: The substitution of fasteners other than those of the grade originally used is not recommended.

5. Install the retainer, bushing and sleeve on the stub strut.
6. Position the control arm over the sway bar and install the rear stub strut and front pivot into the crossmember.
7. Install the front pivot bolt and loosely install the nut.
8. Install the stub strut bushing and retainer and loosely assemble the nut.
9. Position the sway bar bracket and stud through the control arm and install the retainer and nut. Tighten the nut to 10 ft. lbs.
10. Install the ball joint stud into the steering knuckle and install the clamp bolt. Torque the clamp bolt to 50 ft. lbs.

Sway Bar

REMOVAL AND INSTALLATION

1. Raise and support the vehicle.
2. Remove the nut from the control arm end bushing and reinforcement plates.
3. Remove the nut, retainers and insulator holding the sway bar to the crossmember linkage.
4. Remove the sway bar.
5. Inspect the sway bar for distortion or fatigue cracks in the metal. Replace any damaged or distorted bushings.
6. Installation is the reverse of removal.

Steering Knuckle

REMOVAL AND INSTALLATION

Service or repair to the bearing, hub, brake dust shield or the steering knuckle itself will require removal of the knuckle. Before attempting this operation, be aware that to reassemble the components it is necessary to torque the front hub nut to at least 180 ft. lbs. You will need a large torque wrench to read that high and a great deal of strength to attain that much torque on the nut.

1. Remove the cotter pin and nut-lock.
2. Loosen the hub nut while the truck is resting on the wheels with the brakes applied.

NOTE: The hub and driveshaft are splined together through the knuckle and retained by the hub nut.

3. Raise and support the vehicle.
4. Remove the wheel and tire.
5. Remove the hub nut. Be sure the splined driveshaft is free to separate from the spline in hub when the knuckle is removed.
6. Disconnect the tie rod end from the steering arm.
7. Disconnect the brake hose retainer from the strut.
8. Remove the slamp bolt holding the ball joint stud in the steering knuckle.
9. Remove the brake caliper adaptor screw and washers.
10. Support the caliper on a wire hook.
11. Remove the brake disc.
12. Matchmark the camber adjusting cams and loosen both bolts.
13. Support the steering knuckle and remove the cam adjusting and through-bolts. Remove the upper knuckle leg out of the strut bracket and lift the knuckle from the ball joint stud.

NOTE: Do not allow the driveshaft to hang during this procedure.

14. Service procedures requiring hub removal also require that a new bearing be installed.
15. Installation is the reverse of removal. A new hub nut is required. When the car is resting in the wheels, with the brakes applied, tighten the hub nut to 180 ft. lbs.

Front End Alignment

STEERING AXIS INCLINATION

Independent Front Suspension Only

Steering axis inclination is the number of degrees that the spindle support centerline is tilted from the true vertical as viewed from the front. It has a fixed relationship with camber and does not change except in the event of damage to a spindle or ball joint. The angle is not adjustable and damaged parts must be replaced.

CAMBER

Camber is expressed as the number of degrees that the top of the wheel is tilted outward or inward from the true vertical when viewed from the front. Inward tilt is negative camber and outward tilt is positive camber. Excessive camber causes premature tire wear; negative camber causes wear on the inside of the tire and positive camber causes the tire to wear on the outside edge.

Camber is adjusted by means of eccentrics at the inner end of the upper control arms or on the strut mount (Rampage). Camber cannot be accurately measured without professional equipment.

CASTER

Caster is the backward or forward tilt from the vertical of the steering knuckle centerline at the top, measured in degrees. A steering knuckle centerline tilted backward has positive ($+$) caster, while one tilted forward has negative ($-$) caster. Positive caster produces greater directional stability and requires greater steering effort, since it increases the self-centering effect at the steering wheel.

Caster is adjusted, except on the Rampage, by means of eccentrics at the inner end of the upper control arms. Caster cannot be measured accurately without professional equipment.

TOE-IN

Toe-in is the amount, measured in inches, that the centerlines of the wheels are closer together at the front than at the rear. Toe-in must be checked after caster and camber have been adjusted, but it can be adjusted without disturbing the other two settings.

You can make this adjustment without special equipment, if you make careful measurements. The adjustment is made at the tie-rod sleeves. The wheels must be straight ahead.

1. Toe-in can be determined by measuring the distance between the centers of the tire treads, front and rear. If the tread pattern makes this impossible, you can measure between the edges of the wheel rims, but make sure to move the van forward and measure in a couple of places to avoid errors caused by bent rims and wheel runout.
2. Loosen the clamp bolts on the tie-rod sleeves (except Rampage).
3. Rotate the sleeves equally (in opposite directions) to obtain the correct measurement. If the sleeves are not adjusted equally, the steering wheel will be crooked. If the steering wheel is already crooked, it can be straightened by turning the sleeves equally in the same direction.
4. When the adjustment is complete, tighten the clamps.

REAR SUSPENSION

Springs

REMOVAL AND INSTALLATION

Except Rampage

1. Raise the truck and support the rear with jackstands under the bumper brackets. Be sure that the front wheels are chocked and that the parking brake is set. Support the axle with a jack.
2. Remove the U-bolts and the U-bolt plate that holds the axle to the springs.
3. Remove the front pivot bolt.

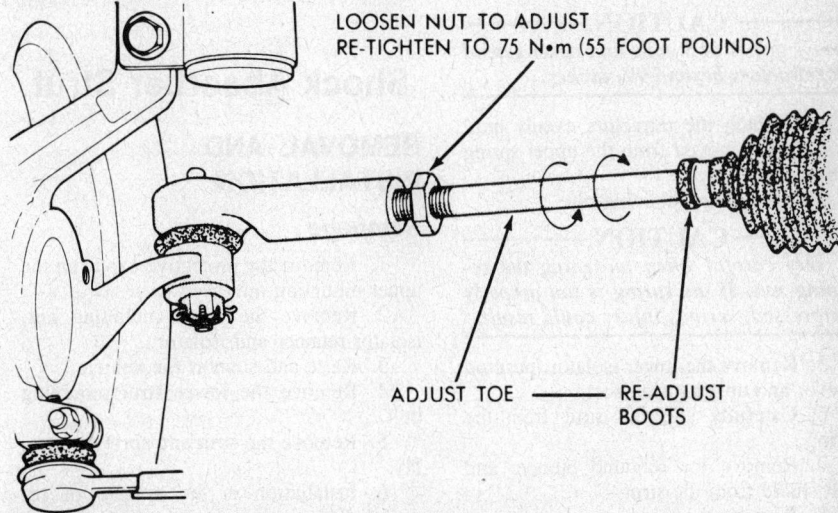

LOOSEN NUT TO ADJUST
RE-TIGHTEN TO 75 N•m (55 FOOT POUNDS)

ADJUST TOE ——— RE-ADJUST BOOTS

Toe adjustment—Rampage

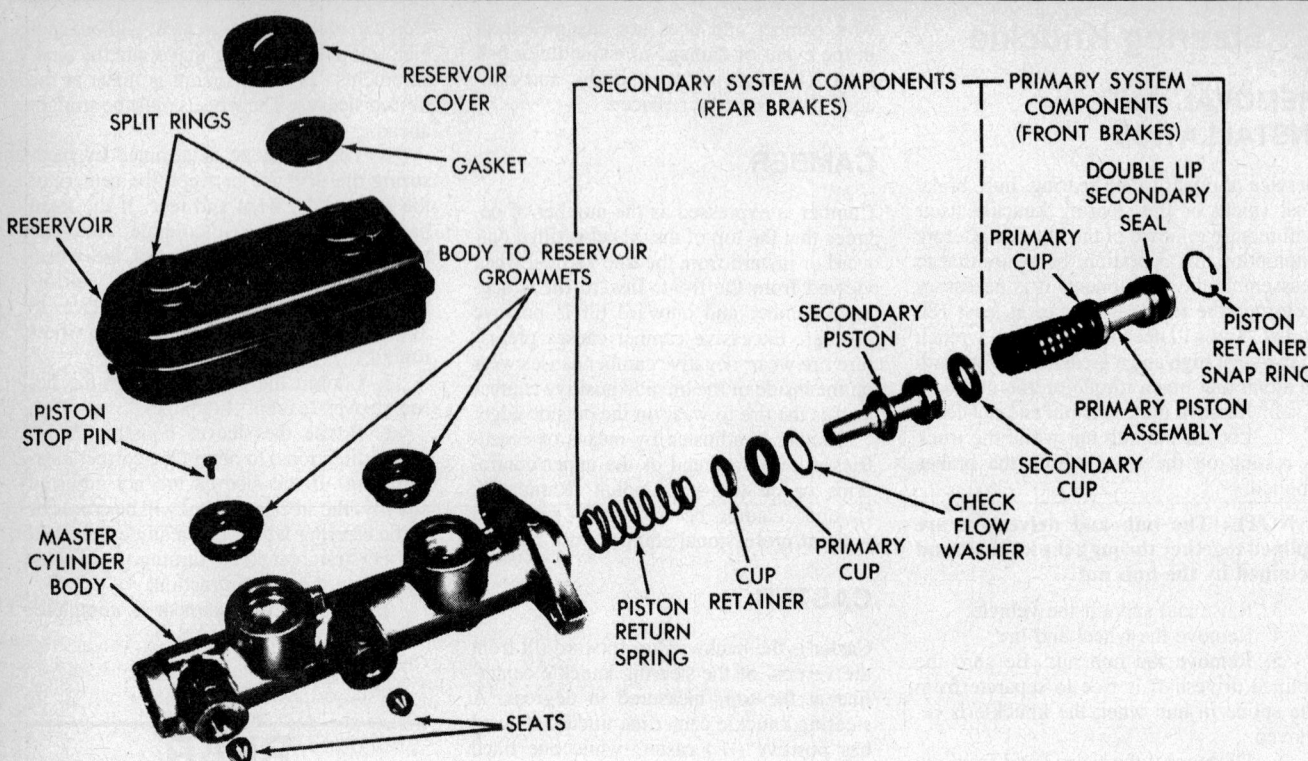

Aluminum master cylinder components

4. Remove the rear shackle bolt nuts and the rear shackle plate.

5. Remove the outer shackle and bolt assembly from the hanger and remove the spring.

6. Installation is the reverse of removal. Be sure that the shackled end of the spring is above the shackle bracket pivot.

Rampage

The use of a coil spring compressor is necessary.

1. Remove the strut and spring assembly.

2. Install the spring compressor on the spring and place it in a vise.

— CAUTION —
Always grip 4 or 5 coils and never extend the retractors beyond 9¼ inches.

3. Tighten the retractors evenly until pressure is removed from the upper spring seat.

4. Loosen the retaining nut.

— CAUTION —
Be very careful when loosening the retaining nut. If the spring is not properly compressed, serious injury could result.

5. Remove the lower isolator, pushrod sleeve, and upper spring seat.

6. Carefully slip the strut from the spring.

7. Remove the rebound bumper and dust shield from the strut.

8. Remove the lower spring seat.

9. Carefully and evenly, remove the compressor from the spring.

10. Install the compressor on the spring, gripping four or five coils.

11. Compress the spring.

12. Install the lower spring seat, dust shield and rebound bumper on the strut.

13. Slip the unit inside the coil spring and install the upper spring seat.

14. Make sure that the level surfaces on the seats are in position with the spring.

15. Install the sleeve on the pushrod and install the retaining nut. Torque the nut to 20 ft. lbs.

16. Install the lower isolator.

17. Install the strut and spring assembly.

Shock Absorber Strut

REMOVAL AND INSTALLATION

Rampage

1. Remove the protective cap from the upper mounting nut.

2. Remove the upper mounting nut, isolator retainer and isolator.

3. Raise and support the vehicle.

4. Remove the lower strut mounting bolt.

5. Remove the strut and spring assembly.

6. Installation is the reverse of removal. Torque the lower mounting bolt to 40 ft. lbs. and the upper nut to 20 ft. lbs.

Shock Absorbers

REMOVAL AND INSTALLATION

Except Rampage

1. Jack and support the truck. Remove the wheel.

2. Remove the nut from the stud or bolt at the upper end. Remove the stud or bolt from the upper end.

3. Remove the lower nut at the bushing end.

4. Pivot the shock absorber and washers from the lower stud.

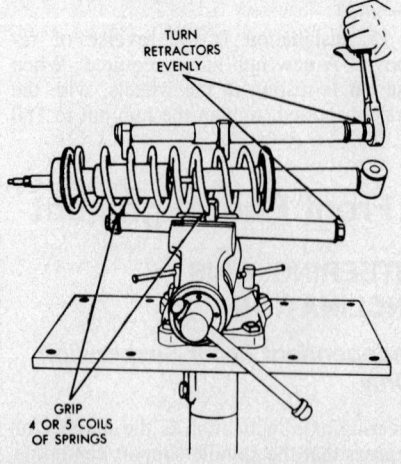

Removing coil spring from rear shock absorber

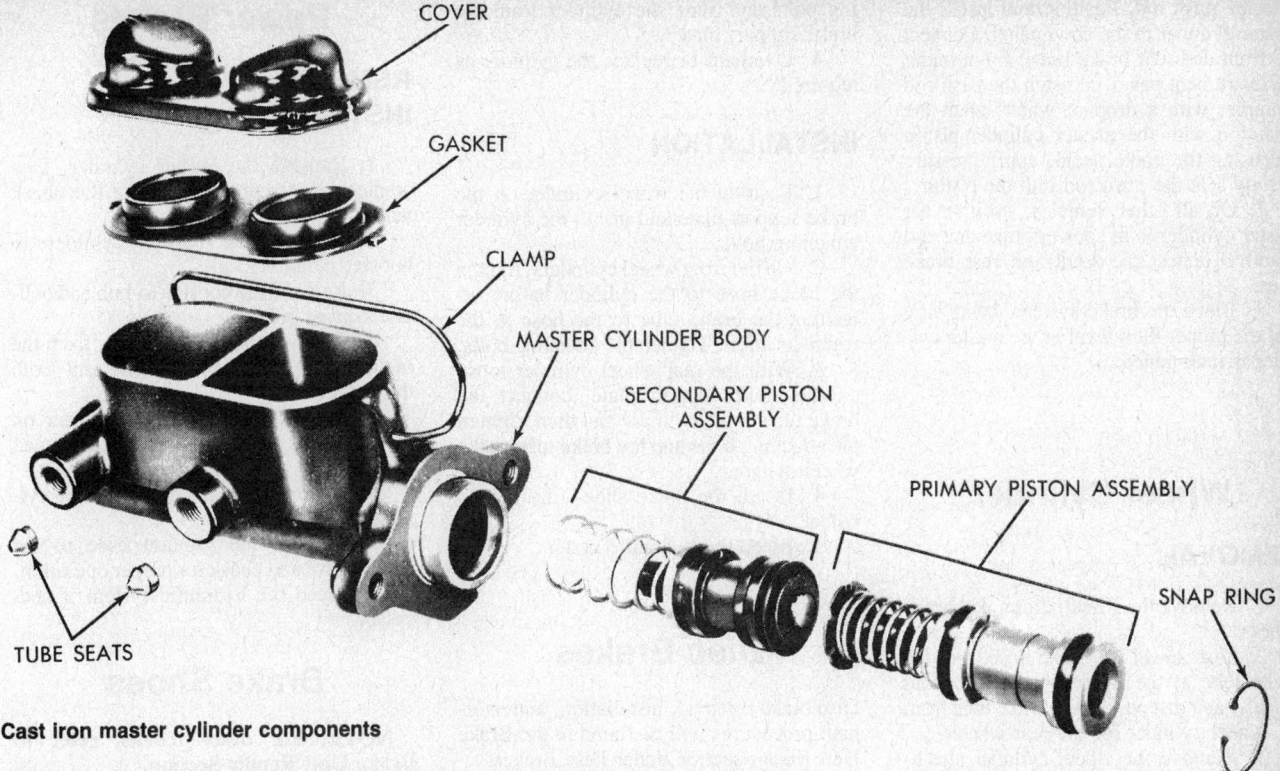

COVER

GASKET

CLAMP

MASTER CYLINDER BODY

SECONDARY PISTON ASSEMBLY

PRIMARY PISTON ASSEMBLY

SNAP RING

TUBE SEATS

Cast iron master cylinder components

5. Remove the shock absorber and washers from the lower stud.

6. Installation is the reverse of removal. Purge the new shock of air by extending it in its normal position and compressing it while inverted. Do this several times. It is normal for there to be more resistance to extension than to compression.

Rear Wheel Alignment

Rampage

Due to the design of the rear suspension, it is possible to adjust both the camber and toe-in of the rear wheels. Alignment is controlled by inserting 0.010 in. shim stock between the spindle mounting surface and the spindle mounting plate. Each 0.010 in. shim stock changes wheel alignment by approximately 0° 18'. Be sure to adjust the rear wheel bearings.

HYDRAULIC BRAKE SYSTEM

Reference

For master, wheel and disc brake caliper overhaul, brake shoe and pad replacement and service procedures, bleeding of the hydraulic system, dual master cylinder,

vacuum-hydraulic booster system and the Bendix hydro-boost booster system refer to the Brake Unit Repair section.

A tandem master cylinder is used on all models which provides partial braking in the event of a failure in half of the system.

All drum brakes, with the exception of the Rampage, are self adjusting. Front disc brakes are inherently self adjusting and there is no provision for manually adjusting these.

Adjustment

Normally, self adjusting drum brakes do not require manual adjustment. In the event of self adjuster failure or in the event of a brake reline, it may be advisable to make the initial adjustment manually. Naturally, this is not necessary for the front wheels equipped with disc brakes.

1. Jack and support the vehicle so that all of the wheels are free to turn.

2. Remove the rear adjusting hole cover from the backing plate.

3. Be sure that the parking brake lever is fully released.

4. Insert the brake adjusting spoon into the star wheel of the adjusting screw. Move the handle of the tool upward until light drag is felt when the wheel is rotated.

5. Insert a thin bladed screwdriver into the brake adjusting hole and push the adjusting lever out of engagement with the star wheel.

6. While holding the adjusting lever out of engagement with the star wheel, back off the star wheel 10–12 notches to ensure a free running wheel with no drag. A large

screwdriver can be used in place of the brake adjusting tool.

7. Repeat the above procedure for each drum brake.

8. Install the plugs in the access holes and lower the truck.

9. Road test the vehicle.

Master Cylinder

REMOVAL AND INSTALLATION

1. Disconnect the primary and secondary brake lines from the master cylinder. Install plugs in the outlets of the master cylinder.

2. On vehicles equipped with manual brakes, disconnect the stop lamp switch mounting bracket from under the instrument panel. Grasp the brake pedal and pull backward to disengage the push rod from the master cylinder piston. This will destroy the push rod retention grommet.

3. Remove the nuts that attach the master cylinder to the cowl panel or the brake booster unit.

4. Remove the master cylinder from the vehicle.

NOTE: On vehicles equipped with manual brakes be sure to remove all traces of the old grommet from the push rod groove and piston socket.

5. To install, bleed the master cylinder before installing it on the vehicle.

6. On vehicles equipped with manual brakes, install a new push rod grommet

onto the push rod. Position and install the master cylinder to the cowl panel. Connect the front and rear brake lines. From under the instrument panel, moisten the push rod grommet with a drop of water, align the push rod with the master cylinder piston and using the brake pedal, apply pressure to fully seat the push rod into the piston.

7. On all other vehicles, position the master cylinder to the power brake unit and install. Connect the front and rear brake lines.

8. Bleed the brake system, being sure that the proper fluid level in the master cylinder is maintained.

Wheel Cylinder

REMOVAL

1. Remove the wheel, drum, and brake shoes.

2. Disconnect the brake hose from the brake tube at the frame bracket for front wheels, and disconnect the brake tube from the wheel cylinder for the rear wheels.

3. Remove the wheel cylinder attach-ing bolts and slide the cylinder from the brake support plate.

4. Overhaul or replace the cylinder as required.

INSTALLATION

1. Position the wheel cylinder on the brake support plate and install the cylinder attaching bolts.

2. On the front wheel cylinders, tighten the brake hose to the cylinder before attaching the brake tube to the hose at the frame location. Tighten the attaching bolts.

3. With the rear wheel cylinder loose on the brake support plate, connect the brake tube to the cylinder and then, tighten the attaching bolts and the brake tube to the wheel cylinder.

4. Install the brake shoes, drum, and wheel.

5. Bleed the hydraulic system.

Disc Brakes

Disc brake removal, installation, and overhaul procedures will be found in the Brake Unit Repair section under Disc Brakes.

Power Brakes

REMOVAL AND INSTALLATION

1. Remove the master cylinder. Disconnect the vacuum hose from the check valve.

2. Remove the master cylinder to booster mounting nuts.

3. Remove the booster-to-hub and bell-crank pivot bolt.

4. Remove the mounting nuts from the mounting plate and remove the unit from the vehicle.

5. To install, position the booster on the mounting plate and install the coned washers and nuts. Install the pivot bolt.

6. Position and install the master cylinder.

7. Connect the vacuum hose to the check valve and check for proper operation.

8. Bleed the hydraulic system if necessary.

Brake Shoes

NOTE: For other trucks, refer to Brake Unit Repair Section.

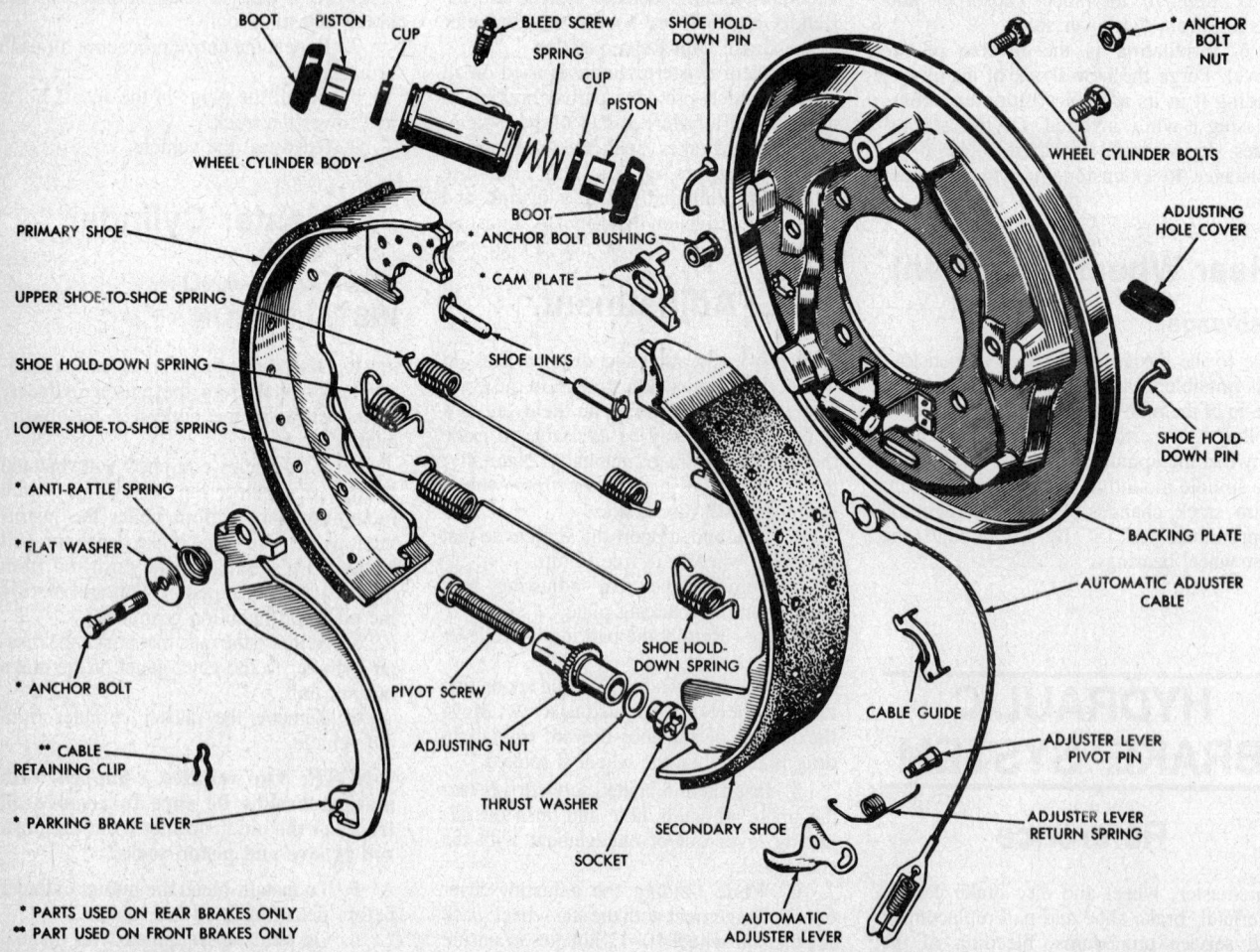

* PARTS USED ON REAR BRAKES ONLY
** PART USED ON FRONT BRAKES ONLY

Typical rear drum brakes and wheel cylinder

REMOVAL AND INSTALLATION

Rampage

NOTE: If you are not thoroughly familiar with the procedures involved in brake replacement, disassemble and assemble one side at a time, leaving the other wheel intact, as a reference.

1. Remove the brake drum.
2. Unhook the parking brake cable from the secondary (trailing) shoe.
3. Remove the shoe-to-anchor springs (retracting springs). They can be gripped and unhooked with a pair of pliers.
4. Remove the shoe hold down springs: compress them slightly and slide them off of the hold down pins.
5. Remove the adjuster screw assembly by spreading the shoes apart. The adjuster nut must be fully backed off.
6. Raise the parking brake lever. Pull the secondary (trailing) shoe away from the backing plate so pull-back spring tension is released.
7. Remove the secondary (trailing) shoe and disengage the spring end from the backing plate.
8. Raise the primary (leading) shoe to release spring tension. Remove the shoe and disengage the spring end from the backing plate.
9. Inspect the brakes (see procedures under Brake Drum Inspection).
10. Lubricate the six shoe contact areas on the brake backing plate and the web end of the brake shoe which contacts the anchor plate. Use a multi-purpose lubricant or a high temperature brake grease made for the purpose.
11. Chrysler recommends that the rear wheel bearings be cleaned and repacked whenever the brakes are renewed. Be sure to install a new bearing seal.
12. With the leading shoe return spring in position on the shoe, install the shoe at the same time as you engage the return spring in the end support.
13. Position the end of the shoe under the anchor.
14. With the trailing shoe return spring in position, install the shoe at the same time as you engage the spring in the support (backing plate).
15. Position the end of the shoe under the anchor.
16. Spread the shoes and install the adjuster screw assembly making sure that the forked end that enters the shoe is curved down.
17. Insert the shoe hold down spring pins and install the hold down springs.
18. Install the shoe-to-anchor springs.
19. Install the parking brake cable onto the parking brake lever.
20. Replace the brake drum and tighten the nut to 240–300 in. lbs. while rotating the wheel.
21. Back off the nut enough to release the bearing preload and position the locknut with one pair of slots aligned with the cotter pin hole.
22. Install the cotter pin. The end play should be 0.001–0.003 in.
23. Install the grease cap.

Control Valves

All vehicles have some type of hydraulic system control valve or switch in the brake system.

Some valves combine the warning switch with a hold-off valve, a proportioning valve, or both. The valve(s) is usually located near the master cylinder.

Hold-off valves are used to momentarily "hold off" front disc brake hydraulic pressure until the rear drum brakes begin to apply.

Proportioning valves control rear braking by restricting, at a given ratio, rear system hydraulic pressure. Under light pedal application, the valve allows full hydraulic pressure to the rear brakes.

The hydraulic brake warning switch is used to warn the operator of hydraulic system failure. A failure in one part of the brake system does not result in failure of the entire system. The warning switch will indicate that one or more parts of the system need attention.

Parking Brake

FRONT PARKING BRAKE CABLE

Removal and Installation Except Rampage

1. Raise and support the vehicle.
2. Unscrew and remove the adjusting nut.
3. Remove the cable retaining clips.
4. From inside the truck, remove the handle assembly from the mounting bracket.
5. Loosen the screw on the cable retaining clamps, push the ball end of the cable out of the handle, and then slide the cable out.
6. Carefully route the cable into position.
7. Slide the cable through the retaining slot and position the ball in the slot.
8. Tighten the hex screw.
9. Install the handle on the mounting bracket.
10. Route the cable underneath the vehicle and install the retaining clips.
11. Install the adjustment nut.
12. Adjust the handbrake.

Rampage

1. Raise and support the vehicle.
2. Disconnect the brake cable from the connector.
3. Force the cable housing and attaching clip forward out of the body crossmember.
4. Fold back the left front edge of the floor covering and pry the rubber grommet out of the hole in the dash or from the floor pan.
5. Remove the cable-to-floor pan clip.
6. Engage the parking brake and work the cable out of the clevis linkage.
7. Force the upper end of the cable housing out of the pedal bracket.
8. Work the cable and housing assembly out of the floor pan.
9. Installation is the reverse of removal. Adjust the parking and service brakes and test the operation of both.

Intermediate Cable

REMOVAL AND INSTALLATION

1. Raise and support the vehicle.

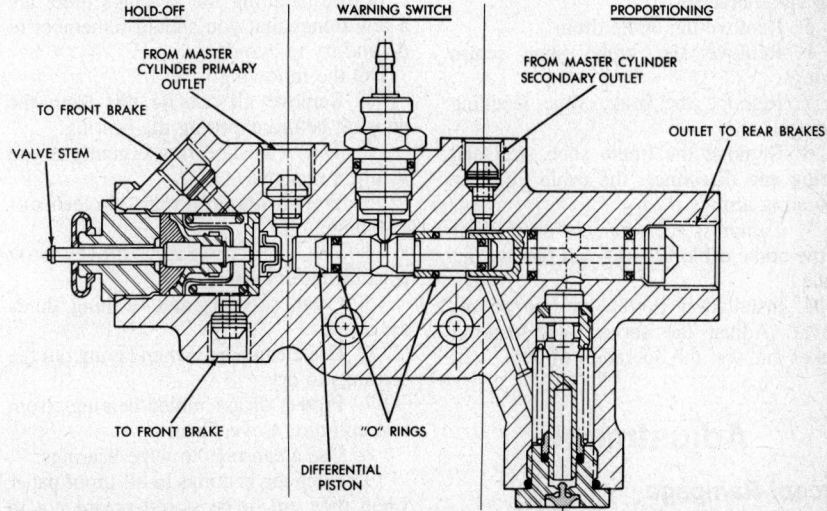

Typical combination switch

2. Release the handbrake.

3. Remove the adjusting nut.

4. Disconnect the cable from the links and the cable guide.

5. Connect the cable guides and cable links.

6. Position the equalizing bar and install the adjusting nut.

7. Adjust the handbrake.

Rear Handbrake Cable

REMOVAL AND INSTALLATION

Except Rampage

1. Raise and support the vehicle.

2. Release the brake and remove the rear wheels.

3. Remove the brake drum.

4. Remove the brake shoe return springs.

5. Remove the brake shoe retaining springs.

6. Remove the brake shoe strut and spring from the support plate.

7. Disconnect the brake cable from the operating arm.

8. Compress the retainers on the end of the brake cable housing and remove the cables from the brake support plate.

9. Remove the retaining bolt and nut from the brake cable bracket and clips at the front bracket.

10. Disconnect the brake cable at the equalizer bar.

11. Remove the cable assembly.

12. Installation is the reverse of removal. Adjust the brakes and the handbrake.

Rampage

1. Raise and support the car.

2. Remove the rear wheels.

3. Disconnect the brake cable from the connector.

4. Remove the retaining clip from the rear cable bracket.

5. Remove the brake drum.

6. Remove the brake shoe return springs.

7. Remove the brake shoe retaining springs.

8. Remove the brake shoe strut and spring and disconnect the cable from the operating arm.

9. Compress the retainers on the end of the brake cable housing and remove the cable.

10. Installation is the reverse of removal. Adjust the service and parking brakes and test the operation of both.

Adjustment

Except Rampage

1. Raise and support the vehicle.

2. Release the handbrake.

3. Loosen the adjustment nut until there is slack in the cables.

4. Adjust the rear brakes by making a few stops in reverse.

5. Tighten the cable adjusting nut at the equalizer bar until the effort required to apply the parking brake handle is between 55 and 65 lbs.

Rampage

The cable operated parking brake is adjusted at the equalizer (connector) under the truck.

1. Adjust the service brakes.

2. Release the parking brake lever and back off the parking brake cable until there is slack in the cable.

3. Clean and lubricate the adjuster threads.

4. Use a brake spoon to turn the starwheel adjuster until there is light shoe-to-drum contact. Back off the starwheel until the wheel rotates freely with no brake drag.

5. Tighten the parking brake adjustment until a slight drag is felt while rotating the wheels.

6. Loosen the cable adjusting nut until both rear wheels can be rotated freely, then back the cable adjuster nut off 2 full turns.

7. Test the parking brake. The rear wheels should rotate freely without dragging.

Wheel Bearings (Front)

It is recommended that the front wheel bearings be cleaned, inspected and repacked periodically and as soon as possible after the front hubs have been submerged in water.

NOTE: Sodium based grease is not compatible with lithium based grease. Be careful not to mix the two types. The best way to prevent this is to completely clean all of the old grease from the hub assembly before installing any new grease.

Before handling the bearings there are a few things that you should remember to do and try to avoid.

DO the following:

1. Remove all outside dirt from the housing before exposing the bearing.

2. Treat a used bearing as gently as you would a new one.

3. Work with clean tools in clean surroundings.

4. Use clean, dry canvas gloves, or at least clean, dry hands.

5. Clean solvents and flushing fluids are a must.

6. Use clean paper when laying out the bearings to dry.

7. Protect disassembled bearings from rust and dirt. Cover them up.

8. Use clean rags to wipe bearings.

9. Keep the bearings in oil-proof paper when they are to be stored or are not in use.

10. Clean the inside of the housing before replacing the bearing.

Do NOT do the following:

1. Don't work in dirty surroundings.

2. Don't use dirty, chipped, or damaged tools.

3. Try not to work on wooden work benches or use wooden mallets.

4. Don't handle bearings with dirty or moist hands.

5. Do not use gasoline for cleaning; use a safe solvent.

6. Do not spin-dry bearings with compressed air. They will be damaged.

7. Do not spin unclean bearings.

8. Avoid using cotton waste or dirty cloths to wipe bearings.

9. Try not to scratch or nick bearing surfaces.

10. Do not allow the bearing to come in contact with dirt or rust at any time.

REPACKING WHEEL BEARINGS

NOTE: Sodium based grease is not compatible with lithium based grease. Be careful not to mix the two types. The best way to prevent this is to completely clean all of the old grease from the hub assembly before installing any new grease.

1. Raise the front of the vehicle and place jackstands under the vehicle. Remove the wheel.

2. Remove the front hub grease cap and driving hub snap-ring.

3. Remove the splined driving hub and the pressure spring. This may require slight prying with a pry bar.

4. Remove the wheel bearing locknut, lockring, and adjusting nut.

5. See the brake section, removal brake caliper suspend on wire out of the way.

6. Carefully drive out the inner bearing cone and grease seal from the hub.

7. Inspect the bearing cups (races) for cracks and pits. If the cups are excessively worn or there are pits or cracks visible, replace them along with the cones. The cups are removed from the hub by driving them out with a drift pin. They are installed in the same manner.

8. If it is determined that the cups are in satisfactory condition and are to remain in the hub, clean and inspect the cones (bearings). Refer to the bearing diagnosis chart. Replace the bearings if necessary. If it is necessary to replace either the cone or the cup, both parts should be replaced as a unit.

9. Thoroughly clean all components in a suitable solvent and blow them dry with compressed air or allow them to dry while resting on clean paper.

NOTE: Do not spin the bearings with compressed air while drying them.

10. Cover the spindle with a cloth and brush all loose dust and dirt from the brake assembly. Remove the cloth and thor-

oughly clean the inside of the hub and the spindle.

11. Pack the inside of the hub with wheel bearing grease. Add grease to the hub until the grease is flush with the inside diameter of the bearing cup.

12. Pack the bearing cone and roller assemblies with wheel bearing grease. A bearing packer is desirable for this operation. If a packer is not available, place a large portion of grease into the palm of your hand and sliding the edge of the roller cage through the grease with your other hand, work as much grease in between the rollers as possible.

13. Position the inner bearing into the inner bearing cup and install the new grease seal.

14. Carefully position the hub assembly onto the spindle. Be careful not to damage the new seal. Install the drum or caliper.

15. Place the outer bearing into position on the spindle and into the bearing cup.

16. Install the bearing adjusting nut and tighten it while rotating the hub back and forth to seat the bearings.

17. Back off the adjusting nut about ¼ turn.

18. Assemble the lockring by turning the nut to the nearest notch where the dowel pin will enter. Install the outer locknut.

19. Install the pressure spring retainer, spring, the driving hub and driving hub snap-ring. This is for vehicles without free-running hubs.

20. Install the grease cap and adjust the brakes, if they were backed off to remove the hub assembly. Remove the jackstands and lower the vehicle.

CHASSIS ELECTRICAL

Heater Core

REMOVAL AND INSTALLATION

Without Air Conditioning— Except Rampage

1. Disconnect the battery ground cable.

2. Drain the radiator.

NOTE: Remove the radiator and grille for clearance, if necessary.

3. Cover the alternator with a waterproof cover.

4. Disconnect the blower motor resistor and ground wires from the heater.

5. Disconnect and plug the heater core hoses.

6. Disconnect the control cables and underdash braces.

7. Remove the retaining screws from the water valve. Do not disconnect the hoses from the water valve; place the water valve with hoses attached to one side.

8. Remove the blower motor cooler tube.

9. Remove the nuts holding the housing to the mounting studs and tip the complete unit for removal.
To remove the heater core:

10. Remove the retaining nuts and lift the blower assembly out of the housing.

11. Remove the cover retaining nuts and lift the cover off the housing.

12. Remove the core retaining screws and lift the core out of the housing.

13. Installation is the reverse of removal. Fill the cooling system.

14. Let the engine warm up with the heater on, then check the coolant level.

With Air Conditioning—Vans and Pick-ups Except Rampage

————— CAUTION —————
The air conditioning system must be discharged to remove the heater core. Do not attempt if you are not familiar with air conditioning service, have a professional discharge the system.

1. Disconnect the battery ground cable and drain the coolant.

2. Remove the grille, condenser, and radiator, if necessary.

3. Place a waterproof cover over the alternator.

4. Disconnect the heater hoses at the water valve and remove the valve and bracket. Disconnect and cap the refrigerant lines.

5. Remove the glovebox, spot cooler bezel, and appearance shield.

6. Working through the glovebox opening, remove the evaporator housing to firewall screws and nuts.

7. Remove the wiper motor. Detach all evaporator housing vacuum and electrical connections. Detach the blower motor cooling hose and the drain hoses.

8. Remove the two 2¼ in. bolts from the crossbar and the four screws from the sealplate on the front of the housing. Separate the evaporator and blower motor housings, remove the evaporator housing.

9. Remove the receiver drier and cap all the openings. Carefully pry the heater core out, leaving the air seal at the front intact.

10. On installation, connect the hoses to the core. Position the evaporator housing on top of the blower housing. Install the mounting screws and nuts.

11. Position the crossbar under the lip on the blower housing opening and install the two 2¼ in. bolts. Install the four seal plate screws at the front of the housing.

12. Replace the wiper motor and connect the vacuum and electrical lines. Connect the blower motor cooler hose and the drain hoses.

13. Connect the heater hoses to the water valve.

14. Install the receiver drier and connect the refrigerant lines.

15. Install the radiator, condenser, and grille.

16. Replace the glovebox, spot cooler bezel, and appearance shield.

17. Install the battery ground cable and fill the cooling system. Let the engine warm up with the *heater on,* then check the coolant. Have the air conditioner charged.

Heater Assembly

REMOVAL AND INSTALLATION

Rampage—Without Air Conditioning

1. Disconnect the battery and drain the cooling system.

2. Remove the center outside air floor vent housing.

3. Remove the ash tray.

4. Remove the two defroster duct adapter screws. The left one is reached through the ash tray opening.

5. Remove the defrost duct adapter and push the flexible hose up out of the way.

6. Disconnect the temperature control cable.

7. Disconnect the blower motor wiring connector.

8. Disconnect the hoses from the heater core and plug the core openings.

9. Remove the two nuts retaining the heater unit to the firewall.

10. Remove the glove compartment and door.

11. Remove the screw attaching the heater brace bracket to the instrument panel.

12. Remove the heater assembly support strap nut. Disconnect the strap from the plenum stud and lower the heater from the instrument panel.

13. Disconnect the control cable and remove the unit from the car.

14. Connect the control cable and raise the unit into position so that the core tubes and mounting studs fit through their holes in the firewall.

15. Install the support strap and hand tighten the nut.

16. Install and tighten the two heater-to-firewall nuts.

17. Unplug and connect the core tubes.

18. Install the defroster duct adaptor.

19. Install the ash tray.

20. Install the center outside air floor vent housing.

21. Install the glove compartment.

22. Refill the cooling system.

Blower Motor

REMOVAL AND INSTALLATION

Rampage—Without Air Conditioning

The blower motor is located under the instrument panel on the left side of the heater assembly.

1. Disconnect the motor wiring.
2. Remove the left outlet duct.
3. Remove the four motor retaining screws and remove the motor.
4. Installation is the reverse of removal.

Rampage—With Air Conditioning

1. Disconnect the battery ground.
2. Remove the three screws securing the glovebox to the instrument panel.
3. Disconnect the wiring from the blower and case.
4. Remove the blower vent tube from the case.
5. Loosen the recirculating door from its bracket and remove the actuator from the housing. Leave the vacuum lines attached.
6. Remove the seven screws attaching the recirculating housing to the A/C unit and remove the housing.
7. Remove the three mounting flange nuts and washers.
8. Remove the blower motor from the unit.
9. Installation is the reverse of removal. Replace any damaged sealer.

Heater Core

REMOVAL AND INSTALLATION

NOTE: Removal of the Heater-Evaporator Unit is required for core removal. Two people will be required to perform the operation. Discharge, evacuation and recharge and leak testing of the refrigerant system is necessary.

—————— CAUTION ——————
This work should be performed only by a trained technician. Have the system discharged before attempting removal.

Rampage—Without Air Conditioning

1. Remove the heater assembly as described earlier.
2. Remove the left outlet duct.
3. Remove the blower motor.
4. Remove the defroster duct adapter.
5. Remove the outside air and defroster door cover.
6. Remove the defroster door.
7. Remove the defroster door control rod.
8. Remove the core cover.
9. Lift the core from the unit.
10. Installation is the reverse of removal.

Rampage—With Air Conditioning

NOTE: During installation, a small can of refrigerant oil will be necessary.

1. Disconnect the battery ground.
2. Drain the coolant.
3. Disconnect the temperature door cable from the heater-evaporator unit.
4. Disconnect the temperature door cable from the retaining clips.
5. Remove the glovebox.
6. Disconnect the vacuum harness from the control head.
7. Disconnect the blower motor lead and anti-diesel relay wire.
8. Remove the seven screws fastening the right trim bezel to the instrument panel. Starting at the right side, swing the bezel clear and remove it.
9. Remove the three screws on the bottom of the center distribution duct cover and slide the cover rearward and remove it.
10. Remove the center distribution duct.
11. Remove the defroster duct adaptor.
12. Remove the H-type expansion valve, located on the right side of the firewall:
    a. remove the $\frac{5}{16}$ in. bolt in the center of the plumbing sealing plate.
    b. carefully pull the refrigerant lines toward the front of the car, taking care to avoid scratching the valve sealing surfaces.
    c. remove the two $\frac{1}{4}$–20 Allen head cap screws and remove the valve.
13. Cap the pipe openings at once. Wrap the valve in a plastic bag.
14. Disconnect the hoses from the core tubes.
15. Disconnect the vacuum lines at the intake manifold and water valve.
16. Remove the unit-to-firewall retaining nuts.
17. Remove the panel support bracket.
18. Remove the right cowl lower panel.
19. Remove the instrument panel pivot bracket screw from the right side.
20. Remove the screws securing the lower instrument panel at the steering column.
21. Pull back the carpet from under the unit as far as possible.
22. Remove the nut from the evaporator-heater unit-to-plenum mounting brace and blower motor ground cable. While supporting the unit, remove the brace from its stud.
23. Lift the unit, pulling it rearward to allow clearance. These operations may require two people.
24. Slowly lower the unit taking care to keep the studs from hanging-up on the insulation.
25. When the unit reaches the floor, slide it rearward until it is out from under the instrument panel.
26. Remove the unit.
27. Place the unit on a workbench. On the inside side, remove the $\frac{1}{4}$-20 nut from the mode door actuator on the top cover and the two retaining clips from the front edge of the cover. To remove the mode door actuator, remove the two screws securing it to the cover.
28. Remove the fifteen screws attaching the cover to the assembly and lift off the cover. Lift the mode door out of the unit.
29. Remove the screw from the core retaining bracket and lift out the core.
To install:
30. Place the core in the unit and install the bracket.
31. Install the actuator arm.

—————— CAUTION ——————
When installing the unit, care must be taken that the vacuum lines to the engine compartment do not hang-up on the accelerator or become trapped between the unit and the firewall. If this happens, kinked lines will result and the unit will have to be removed to free them. Proper routing of these lines will require two people. The portion of the vacuum harness which is routed through the steering column support MUST be positioned BEFORE the distribution housing is installed. The harness MUST be routed ABOVE the temperature control cable.

32. Place the unit on the floor as far under the panel as possible.
33. Raise the unit carefully, at the same time pull the lower instrument panel rearward as far as possible.
34. Position the unit in place and attach the brace to the stud.
35. Install the lower ground cable and attach the nut.
36. Install and tighten the unit-to-firewall nuts.
37. Reposition the carpet and install, but do not tighten the right instrument panel pivot bracket screw.
38. Place a piece of sheet metal or thin cardboard against the evaporator-heater assembly to center the assembly duct seal.
39. Position the center distributor duct in place making sure that the upper left tab comes in through the left center A/C outlet opening and that each air take-off is properly inserted in its respective outlet.

NOTE: Make sure that the radio wiring connector does not interfere with the duct.

40. Install and tighten the screw securing the upper left tab of the center air distribution duct to the instrument panel.
41. Remove the sheet metal or cardboard from between the unit and the duct.

NOTE: Make sure that the unit seal

is properly aligned with the duct opening.

42. Install and tighten the two lower screws fastening the center distribution duct to the instrument panel.

43. Install and tighten the screws securing the lower instrument panel at the steering column.

44. Install and tighten the nut securing the instrument panel to the support bracket.

45. Make sure that the seal on the unit is properly aligned and seated against the distribution duct assembly.

46. Tighten the instrument panel pivot bracket screw and install the right cowl lower trim.

47. Slide the distributor duct cover assembly onto the center distribution duct so that the notches lock into the tabs and the tabs slide over the rear and side ledges of the center duct assembly.

48. Install the three screws securing the ducting.

49. Install the right trim bezel.

50. Connect the vacuum harness to the control head.

51. Connect the blower lead and the anti-diesel wire.

52. Install the glovebox.

53. Connect the temperature door cable.

54. Install new O-rings on the evaporator plate and the plumbing plate. Coat the new O-rings with clean refrigerant oil.

55. Place the H-valve against the evaporator sealing plate surface and install the two ¼-20NC throughbolts. Torque to 6–10 ft. lbs.

56. Carefully hold the refrigerant line connector against the valve and install the 5/16-18-NC bolt. Torque to 14–20 ft. lbs.

57. Install the heater hoses at the core tubes.

58. Connect the vacuum lines at the manifold and water valve.

59. Install the condensate drain tube.

60. Have the system evacuated, charged and leak tested by a trained technician.

Auxiliary Heater, Core and Blower

The auxiliary heater, in some vans, is a rear mounted recirculating heater, temperature controlled by a Bowden cable.

REMOVAL AND INSTALLATION

1. Drain the radiator.
2. Disconnect the negative battery cable.
3. From under the vehicle, disconnect the intake and outlet hoses from the heater. On 1970 and later models, or if so equipped, remove the water valve with hoses attached.
4. Remove the screws that mount the heater to the floor pan and disconnect the wiring to the heater.

To remove the auxiliary heater core:

5. Remove the heater cover attaching screws. The heater core is attached to the heater cover and will come out with the cover.
6. Remove the core from the cover.

To remove the auxiliary heater blower:

7. Remove the screws attaching the blower motor to the heater and remove the blower motor.
8. Installation is the reverse of removal. Be sure to fill the cooling system and check for leaks. Check the operation of the auxiliary heater.

Radio

REMOVAL AND INSTALLATION

1975–77

1. Disconnect the negative battery cable.
2. Remove the mounting strap on the glove box door.
3. Remove the hinge screws and remove the glove box door.
4. Remove the glove box mounting screws and pull the box out of the instrument panel.
5. Remove the radio bezel mounting nuts and remove the bezel.
6. Remove the radio-to-instrument panel attaching bolts and push the radio in to release the mounting tabs.
7. Working through the glove box opening, disconnect the antenna wire from the radio. Remove the right defroster distribution duct on trucks equipped with A/C. Remove the radio rear support bracket nut, tilt the unit up and pull it out to release it from the support bracket. Disconnect the electrical and speaker wires.
8. Remove the radio through the glove box door. If the truck is equipped with A/C, remove the radio through the duct opening.
9. Reverse to install.

1978 and Later—Except Rampage

1. Disconnect the negative battery cable.
2. Remove the seven instrument panel and bezel attaching screws. Pull the bezel off the retaining clips.
3. Remove the five instrument cluster screws.
4. Pull the cluster out far enough to gain access to the speedometer cable. Push the cable spring clip toward the cluster and disconnect the cable.
5. Remove the right and left printed circuit board multiple connectors.
6. Remove the instrument cluster.
7. Remove the radio mounting screws.
8. Remove the ground strap screw.
9. Pull the radio out of the instrument

panel and disconnect the wiring.
10. Reverse to install.

Rampage

1. Remove the seven bezel attaching screws and open the glove compartment.
2. Remove the bezel, guiding the right end around the glove compartment and away from the panel.
3. Disconnect the radio ground strap and remove the two radio mounting screws.
4. Pull the radio from the panel and disconnect the wiring and antenna lead.
5. Installation is the reverse of removal.

TRIMMING THE ANTENNA

All radios are trimmed at the factory and should require no further trimmer adjustment unless the radio is being installed after repair, or if trimmer adjustment is desired because of poor performance.

1. Extend the antenna to full length or to 31–33 in. for best FM reception.
2. Tune the radio to a weak signal between 1400 and 1600 kilocycles on the AM band.
3. Increase the radio volume and set the tone control to maximum treble.
4. The trimmer screw on most radios is located lower rear right-hand corner of the radio and can be reached by inserting a screwdriver into the recess hole.
5. Adjust the trimmer by turning it back and forth until the peak response in volume is obtained.

Wiper Motor

REMOVAL AND INSTALLATION

Except Rampage

The wiper motor is removed from under the hood. It is not necessary to remove the cowl grille.

1. Unplug the electrical wiring at the motor.
2. Remove the 3 mounting bolts from the wiper motor flange.
3. Lower the motor down far enough to gain access to the crank arm to drive link bushing. Pry the bushing from the crank arm.
4. Remove the motor.
5. Hold the drive crank with a wrench while removing the crank nut. Remove the drive crank from the motor.
6. Installation is the reverse of removal. Check and adjust (if necessary) the wiper arm park position.

Rampage

1. Disconnect the linkage from the motor crank arm.
2. Remove the wiper motor plastic cover.

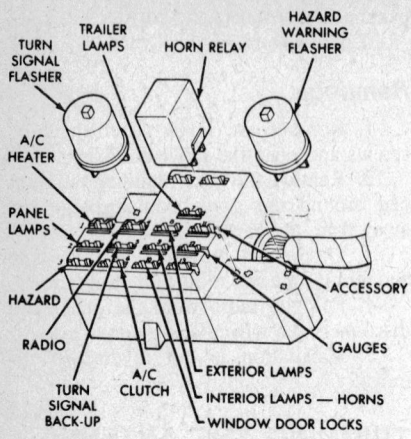

Typical fuse block-1981 shown

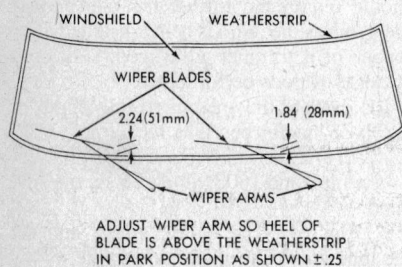

ADJUST WIPER ARM SO HEEL OF
BLADE IS ABOVE THE WEATHERSTRIP
IN PARK POSITION AS SHOWN ±.25

Adjusting wiper arms

3. Disconnect the wiring harness from the motor.

4. Remove the three mounting bolts from the motor bracket and remove the motor.

5. Installation is the reverse of removal.

Linkage

DRIVE LINK

Except Rampage

1. Remove the wiper arms.
2. Remove the cowl grille cover.
3. Reach through the access hole and remove the drive link from the connecting arm and the crank arm. Remove the connecting link pins by prying.
4. Remove the drive link through the access hole.
5. Reverse to install. Use slip joint pliers to snap the links and pins together.

CONNECTING LINK

Except Rampage

1. Remove the cowl grille cover.
2. Reach through the access hole and remove the connecting link from the drive link and the pivot pins by prying the bushings apart.
3. Remove the connecting link through the access hole.
4. Reverse to install. Use slip joint pliers to snap the links and pins together.

Wiper Arm Adjustment

Except Rampage

To determine if an adjustment is required, apply a downward force of 25 oz parallel to the windshield glass at the tip of the wiper arm (where the blade is attached to the arm). With this force applied, pull the wiper blade away from the glass several times to prevent glass friction from affecting downward movement. The clearance between the tip of the wiper blade and the windshield molding should be as specified in the illustration. If the clearance is not as specified, reposition the wiper arm.

To remove the arm, lift it and look for a spring retainer at the bottom. Hold the retainer out of the way, wiggle the arm, and pull it off. To replace it, just push it on, making sure that the latch is out of the way.

Instrument Cluster

REMOVAL AND INSTALLATION

Except Rampage

For instrument cluster removal and installation procedures, refer to steps 1–6 of the 1978 and Later Radio Removal and Installation procedure.

Rampage

1. Remove the two lens assembly lower attaching retaining springs by pulling rearward with a pliers.
2. Allow the lens assembly to drop as it is pulled rearward.
3. Remove the speedometer assembly (two screws).

4. Remove the two wiring harness connectors.
5. Remove the two cluster attaching screws.
6. Pull the two upper spring retainers away from the panel.
7. If equipped with a clock, reach behind the panel and disconnect the wires.
8. Remove the cluster assembly.
9. Installation is the reverse of removal.

Headlights

REMOVAL AND INSTALLATION

1. Remove the headlight bezel attaching screws and remove the bezel. On some models it may not be necessary to remove the bezel, depending on whether the headlight retaining ring is accessible.
2. Remove the headlight ring attaching screws and remove the ring. Do not touch the headlight aiming screws.
3. Pull the sealed beam out slightly and unplug the connector.
4. Reverse to install. As long as the adjusting screws were not moved, the headlight will be held in proper adjustment by the retaining ring.

Fuses and Fusible Links

The fuse panel is usually located on the left side of the steering column, either on the kick panel, steering column or firewall.

Always replace a blown fuse with one of the same rating. If the same fuses continues to blow out, check the circuit for overload or short circuit.

When a fusible link blows it is very important to find out why it blew. They are placed in vehicles electrical system for protection against dead shorts to ground which can be caused by electrical component failure or various wiring failure. Do not just replace a fusible link to correct a problem, find out what caused the problem. For fusible link repair, refer to the Electrical Unit Repair Section.

Ford

INDEX

BEFORE SERVICING, SEE THE SAFETY NOTICE AT THE FRONT OF THE BOOK

GENERAL ENGINE SPECIFICATIONS

Year	Engine Displacement Cu In. (cc)	Carburetor Type	Horsepower (@ rpm)	Torque @ rpm (ft. lbs.)	Bore x Stroke (in.)	Compression Ratio	Oil Pressure @ rpm (psi)
'75	6-300 (4917)	1 bbl	120 @ 3400	229 @ 1400	4.00 × 3.98	8.0 : 1	40-60
	8-302 (4950)	2 bbl	140 @ 3800	230 @ 2600	4.000 × 3.000	8.0 : 1	40-60
	8-351W (5753)	2 bbl	150 @ 3400	290 @ 1800	4.00 × 3.50	8.3 : 1	40-60
	8-360 (5900)	2 bbl	189 @ 3600	287 @ 2400	4.05 × 3.50	8.0 : 1	35-60
	8-390 (6392)	2 bbl	195 @ 4400	319 @ 2400	4.05 × 3.78	8.2 : 1	35-50
	8-460 (7539)	4 bbl	245 @ 4000	380 @ 2600	4.36 × 3.85	8.0 : 1	40-60
'76	6-300 (3934)	1 bbl	120 @ 3400①	229 @ 1400②	4.00 × 3.98	8.0 : 1③	40-60
	8-302 (4950)	2 bbl	134 @ 3600	242 @ 2000	4.000 × 3.000	8.0 : 1	40-60
	8-351W (5753)	2 bbl	147 @ 3400④	276 @ 1800⑤	4.00 × 3.50	8.3 : 1	40-60
	8-360 (5900)	2 bbl	189 @ 3600	287 @ 2400	4.05 × 3.50	8.0 : 1	35-60
	8-390 (6392)	2 bbl	195 @ 4400	319 @ 2400	4.05 × 3.78	8.2 : 1	35-50
	8-460 (7539)	4 bbl	237 @ 4000⑥	365 @ 2600⑦	4.36 × 3.85	8.0 : 1	40-60
'77	6-300 (3934)	1 bbl	120 @ 3400①	229 @ 1400②	4.00 × 3.98	8.0 : 1③	40-60
	8-302 (4950)	2 bbl	134 @ 3600	242 @ 2000	4.000 × 3.000	8.0 : 1	40-60
	8-351M (5753)	2 bbl	132 @ 3600	242 @ 1600	4.00 × 3.50	8.0 : 1	50-75
	8-351W (5753)	2 bbl	147 @ 3400④	276 @ 1800⑤	4.00 × 3.50	8.3 : 1	40-60
	8-400 (6600)	2 bbl	149 @ 3200	300 @ 1400	4.00 × 4.00	8.0 : 1	50-75
	8-460 (7539)	4 bbl	237 @ 4000⑥	365 @ 2600⑦	4.36 × 3.85	8.0 : 1	40-60
'78	6-300 (3934)	1 bbl	132 @ 3600	241 @ 1800	4.00 × 3.98	8.0 : 1③	40-60
	8-302 (4950)	2 bbl	134 @ 3600	242 @ 2000	4.00 × 3.00	8.0 : 1	40-60
	8-351W (5753)	2 bbl	147 @ 3400④	276 @ 1800⑤	4.00 × 3.50	8.3 : 1	40-60
	8-351M (5753)	2 bbl	132 @ 3600①	242 @ 1600②	4.00 × 3.50	8.0 : 1	50-75

GENERAL ENGINE SPECIFICATIONS

Year	Engine Displacement Cu In. (cc)	Carburetor Type	Horsepower (@ rpm)	Torque @ rpm (ft. lbs.)	Bore x Stroke (in.)	Compression Ratio	Oil Pressure @ rpm (psi)
	8–400 (6600)	2 bbl	149 @ 3200	300 @ 1400	4.00 × 4.00	8.0 : 1	50–75
	8–460 (7539)	4 bbl	237 @ 4000⑥	365 @ 2600⑦	4.36 × 3.85	8.0 : 1	40–60
'79	6–300 (3934)	1 bbl	⑧	⑨	4.00 × 3.98	⑩	40–60
	8–302 (4950)	2 bbl	⑪	⑫	4.00 × 3.00	8.4 : 1	40–60
	8–351W (5753)	2 bbl	⑬	⑭	4.00 × 3.50	8.3 : 1	40–60
	8–351M (5753)	2 bbl	132 @ 3600①	242 @ 1600②	4.00 × 3.50	8.0 : 1	50–75
	8–400 (6600)	2 bbl	149 @ 3200	300 @ 1400	4.00 × 4.00	8.0 : 1	50–75
	8–460 (7539)	4 bbl	⑮	⑯	4.36 × 3.85	8.0 : 1	40–60
'80	6–300 (3934)	1 bbl	⑱	⑲	4.00 × 3.98	⑩	40–60
	8–302 (4950)	2 bbl	⑳	㉑	4.00 × 3.98	8.4 : 1	40–60
	8–351W (5753)	2 bbl	㉒	㉓	4.00 × 3.50	8.3 : 1	40–60
	8–400 (6600)	2 bbl	㉔	㉕	4.00 × 4.00	8.0 : 1	55–75
	8–460 (7539)	4 bbl	212 @ 4000	339 @ 2400	4.36 × 3.85	8.0 : 1	40–65
'81	6–300 (4917)	1 bbl	⑱	⑲	4.00 × 3.98	8.9 : 1	40–60
	8–302 (4950)	2 bbl	⑳	㉑	4.00 × 3.00	8.4 : 1	40–60
	8–351W (5753)	2 bbl	㉒	㉓	4.00 × 3.50	8.0 : 1	40–65
	8–400 (6600)	2 bbl	㉔	㉕	4.00 × 4.00	8.0 : 1	50–75
	8–460 (7539)	4 bbl	212 @ 4000	339 @ 2400	4.36 × 3.85	8.0 : 1	40–65
'82	6-232 (3868)	2 bbl	112 @ 4000	175 @ 2600	3.81 × 3.39	8.65:1	40–60
	6–300 (4917)	1 bbl	⑳	㉑	4.00 × 3.98	8.9 : 1⑰	40–60
	8–255 (4179)	2 bbl	115 @ 3400	195 @ 2200	3.68 × 3.00	8.2 : 1	40–60
	8–302 (4950)	2 bbl	130 @ 3400	247 @ 2400	4.00 × 3.00	8.4 : 1	40–60

GENERAL ENGINE SPECIFICATIONS

Year	Engine Displacement Cu In. (cc)	Carburetor Type	Horsepower (@ rpm)	Torque @ rpm (ft. lbs.)	Bore x Stroke (in.)	Compression Ratio	Oil Pressure @ rpm (psi)
	8-351W (5753)	2 bbl	145 @ 3400	265 @ 2000	4.00 × 3.50	8.3 : 1	40–65
	8-400 (6600)	2 bbl	㉔	㉕	4.00 × 4.00	8.0 : 1	50–75
	8-460 (7539)	4 bbl	212 @ 4000	339 @ 2400	4.36 × 3.85	8.0 : 1	40–60

① F & E-100 49 states: 122 @ 3200
F & E-100 Calif.: 123 @ 3200
② F & E-100 49 states: 252 @ 1600
F & E-100 Calif.: 253 @ 1600
③ F & E-100 8.9 : 1
④ F & E-100 49 states: 141 @ 3200
F&E-100 Calif.:
Man Trans., 152 @ 3200
Auto Trans., 143 @ 3200
⑤ Engines subject to noise legislation:
275 @ 1800
F & E-100 49 states: 286 @ 1400
F & E-100 Calif.,
with Man Trans.: 286 @ 2000
with Auto Trans.: 287 @ 1600
⑥ Engines subject to noise legislation:
230 @ 4000
⑦ Engines subject to noise legislation:
359 @ 2600
⑧ F & E-100 exc Calif.; all E-150: 117 @ 3000
F & E-250 Manual trans.: 114 @ 3000
F & E-250 Automatic trans.: 116 @ 3200
F & E-350: 114 @ 3000
⑨ F & E-100, 150: 243 @ 1600
F & E-250 Manual trans.: 234 @ 1600
F & E-250 Automatic trans.: 247 @ 1000
F & E-350: 247 @ 1000
⑩ F & E-100, 150, 250: 8.9:1
F & E-350: 8.0:1
⑪ F & E-100, 150 exc Calif.: 135 @ 3400
F & E-100 Calif.: 129 @ 3200
F & E-150 Calif.: 137 @ 3400
F & E-250: 136 @ 3400

⑫ F & E-100, 150 exc Calif.: 243 @ 2000
F & E-100 Calif.: 238 @ 2400
F & E-150 Calif.: 245 @ 2000
F & E-250: 235 @ 2400
⑬ F & E-100: 135 @ 2800
F & E-150 Manual trans.: 130 @ 3000
F & E-150 Automatic trans, except Calif.: 135 @ 2800
F & E-150 Automatic trans, Calif.: 139 @ 3200
F & E-250 Manual trans.: 130 @ 3000
F & E-250 Automatic trans.: 126 @ 2800
F & E-350: 143 @ 3200
⑭ F & E-100: 274 @ 1400
F & E-150 Manual trans, except Calif.: 267 @ 1800
F & E-150 Automatic trans, except Calif.: 274 @ 1400
F & E-150 Automatic trans, Calif.: 269 @ 1200
F & E-250 Manual trans, 267 @ 1800
F & E-250 Automatic trans, 270 @ 1400
F & E-350: 272 @ 2000
⑮ F & E-250: 214 @ 3600
F & E-350: 217 @ 4000
⑯ F & E-250: 362 @ 1800
F & E-350: 358 @ 2600
⑰ F-250 over 8500 lb GVWR and E&F-350: 8.0:1
⑱ Bronco, F-100, 250 49 states: 119 @ 3200
E-100, 250 49 states: 115 @ 3200
All Calif.: 116 @ 3200

⑲ Bronco, F-100, 250 49 states: 243 @ 1200
E-100, 250 49 states: 241 @ 1200
All Calif.: 244 @ 1200
⑳ Bronco, F-100, 250 49 states: 137 @ 3600
E-100, 250 49 states: 138 @ 3600
Bronco, F-150 (4×4), 250, E-100, 250 Calif.: 136 @ 3600
F-100, 150 (4×2) Calif.: 133 @ 3400
㉑ Bronco, F-100, 250 49 states: 239 @ 1800
E-100, 250 49 states: 242 @ 1800
Bronco, F-150 (4×4), 250, E-100, 250 Calif.: 235 @ 1800
F-100, 150 (4×2) Calif.: 235 @ 2000
㉒ Bronco, F-150, 250 49 states: 138 @ 3400
E-250: 133 @ 3200
Bronco, F-150, E-250 Calif.: 135 @ 3200
F-350, E-350: 142 @ 3400
㉓ Bronco, F-150, 250 49 states: 263 @ 2000
E-250: 265 @ 1600
Bronco, F-150, E-250 Calif.: 259 @ 1600
F-350, E-350: 251 @ 2400
㉔ F-250 (4×4): 136 @ 2800
E-250: 133 @ 2600
F-350, E-350: 153 @ 3200
㉕ F-250 (4×4): 310 @ 1200
E-250: 309 @ 1200
F-350, E-350: 296 @ 1600

TUNE UP SPECIFICATIONS
Pick-Ups

When analyzing compression test results, look for uniformity among cylinders rather than specific pressures.

Year	Engine No. Cyl. Displacement (cu In.)	Spark Plugs Orig Type	Spark Plugs Gap (in.)	Distributor Point Dwell (deg)	Distributor Point Gap (in.)	Ignition Timing (deg) Man	Ignition Timing (deg) Auto	Intake Valve Opens (deg)	Fuel Pump Pressure (psi)	Idle Speed (rpm) ▲ Man	Idle Speed (rpm) ▲ Auto
'75–'76	6—300	BTRF-42B	0.044	Electronic		①	①	12B	4–6	①	①

TUNE UP SPECIFICATIONS
Pick-Ups

When analyzing compression test results, look for uniformity among cylinders rather than specific pressures.

Year	Engine No. Cyl. Displacement (cu In.)	Spark Plugs Orig Type	Gap (in.)	Distributor Point Dwell (deg)	Point Gap (in.)	Ignition Timing (deg) Man	Auto	Intake Valve Opens (deg)	Fuel Pump Pressure (psi)	Idle Speed (rpm) ▲ Man	Auto
	8—302	ARF-42B	0.044	Electronic		12B	6B	16B	4–6	850/550	650
	8—360	BRF-42B	①	Electronic		①	①	13B	4–6	①	①
	8—390	BRF-42B	①	Electronic		①	①	13B	4–6	①	①
	8—460	ARF-52B	①	Electronic		—	12B	—	4–6	—	650
'77	6—300	BSF-42B	0.044②	Electronic		①	①	12B	5–7	①	①
	8—302	ASF-42B	0.044	Electronic		①	①	16B	6–8	①	①
	8—351	ASF-42B	0.044	Electronic		①	①	—	6–8	①	①
	8—400	ASF-42B	0.044	Electronic		①	①	—	6–8	①	①
	8—460	ASF-42B	0.044	Electronic		①	①	—	5–7	①	①
'78–'80	All			See Underhood Specifications Sticker							

① See underhood specifications sticker
② Engines built after 11/15/76: 0.054
▲ Where two figures are separated by a slash, the lower of the two is the rpm with the idle solenoid disconnected.

TUNE-UP SPECIFICATIONS
Bronco

Year	Engine No. Cyl Displacement	Spark Plugs Type	Gap (in.)	Distributor Point Dwell (deg)	Point Gap (in.)	Ignition Timing (deg) Manual Trans	Auto Trans	Intake Valve Opens (deg)	Fuel Pump Pressure (psi)	Compression Pressure (psi)	Idle Speed Manual Trans	Auto Trans	Clearance (in) Intake	Exhaust
'75	8–302	ARF42	.044	Electronic		②	②	20	5–6	①	900	650	Hyd.	Hyd.
'76	8–302	ARF42	.044	Electronic		②	②	20	5–6	①	750	650	Hyd.	Hyd.
'77	8–302	ARF42	.044	Electronic		②	②	20	5–6	①	②	②	Hyd.	Hyd.
'78	8–351M	ASF42	.042–.046	Electronic		6B	14B	—	6–8	①	650	500	Hyd.	Hyd.
	8–400	ASF42	.042–.046	Electronic		12B	12B	—	6–8	①	650	500	Hyd.	Hyd.
'79	8–351M	ASF42	.042–.046	Electronic		②	②	—	6–8	①	②	②	Hyd.	Hyd.
	8–400	ASF42	.042–.046	Electronic		②	②	—	6–8	①	②	②	Hyd.	Hyd.
'80–'82	6–300	BSF42	.042–.046	Electronic		②	②	—	6–8	①	②	②	Hyd.	Hyd.
	8–302	ASF42	.042–.046	Electronic		②	②	—	6–8	①	②	②	Hyd.	Hyd.
	8–351W	ASF42	.042–.046	Electronic		②	②	—	6–8	①	②	②	Hyd.	Hyd.

① Lowest compression ratio should be within 75% of the highest
② See underhood specifications sticker
 Should the figures given on the underhood specifications sticker disagree with those given above, use the sticker figures.

TUNE-UP SPECIFICATIONS
Vans

When analyzing compression test results, look for uniformity among cylinders, rather than specific pressures.

Year	Engine Displacement (Cu In.)	Spark Plugs Type	Gap (in.)	Distributor Point Dwell (deg)	Point Gap (in.)	Ignition Timing (deg) MT	AT	Intake Valve Opens (deg)	Fuel Pump Pressure (psi)	Idle Speed (rpm) MT/AT●	Valve Clear (in.) In	Ex
'75	300	BTRF-42	.044	Electronic		12B	12B	12B	4–6	700/550	Hyd.	Hyd.
	351W	ARF-42	.044	Electronic		14B	14B	16B	5–7	900/650	Hyd.	Hyd.
	460	ARF-42	.044	Electronic		—	12B	8B	5–7	—/650	Hyd.	Hyd.
'76	300	BTRF-42	.044	Electronic		12B	12B①	12B	4-6	700/550	Hyd.	Hyd.
	351W	ARF-32②	.044	Electronic		8B	8B③	16B	5–7	650/650	Hyd.	Hyd.
	460	ARF-42	.044	Electronic		—	12B	8B	5–7	—/650	Hyd.	Hyd.
'77	300	BSF-42	.044	Electronic		10B⑤	10B⑤	12B	4–6	600/600⑥	Hyd.	Hyd.
	351W	ASF-34④	.044	Electronic		8B⑦	8B⑦	16B	5–7	650/550⑧	Hyd.	Hyd.
	460	ASF-42	.044	Electronic		—	12B	8B	5–7	—/650	Hyd.	Hyd.
'78	300	BSF-42	.054⑨	Electronic		⑩	⑩	12B	4–6	⑩	Hyd.	Hyd.
	351W	ASF-42	.044	Electronic		—	⑩	16B	5–7	⑩	Hyd.	Hyd.
	460	ASF-42	.044	Electronic		—	⑩	8B	5–7	⑩	Hyd.	Hyd.
'79	300	BSF-42	.044	Electronic		⑩	⑩	12B	4–6	⑩	Hyd.	Hyd.
	302	ASF-42	.044	Electronic		⑩	⑩	16B	5–7	⑩	Hyd.	Hyd.
	351W	ASF-42	.044	Electronic		—	⑩	16B	5–7	⑩	Hyd.	Hyd.
	460	ASF-42	.044	Electronic		—	⑩	8B	5–7	⑩	Hyd.	Hyd.
'80–'82				See Underhood Sticker								

Part numbers in this chart are not recommendations by Chilton for any product by brand name.
① Calif.: 6B
② E-100: ARF-42
③ Calif.: 12B
④ E-100: ASF-42
⑤ E-100:6B
⑥ E-100: MT 700, AT 550
⑦ E-100 High Altitude: 12B
   E-100 Calif.: MT 8B, AT 14B

All other E-100: see underhood sticker
⑧ E-100 High Altitude: 550
   E-100 Calif.: MT 900, AT 700
   E-100 49 states: MT 800, AT 650
⑨ Calif., and all E-100: .044
⑩ See underhood sticker
● AT in Drive; brake on

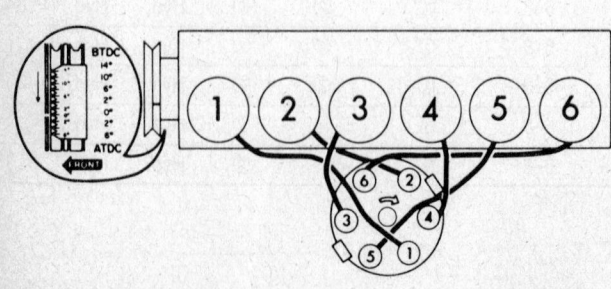

300 6-cylinder

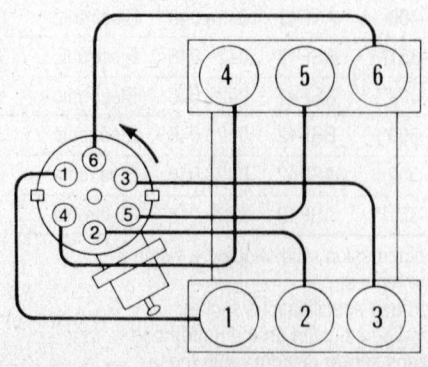

V6-232

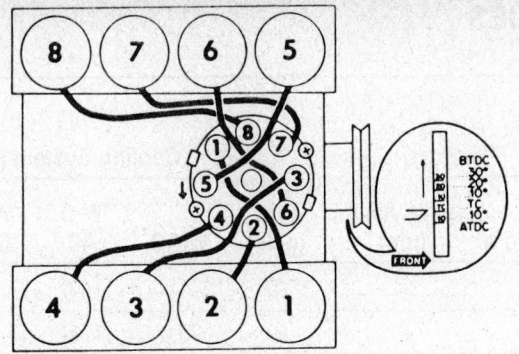

255, 302, 360, 390, 460 V8

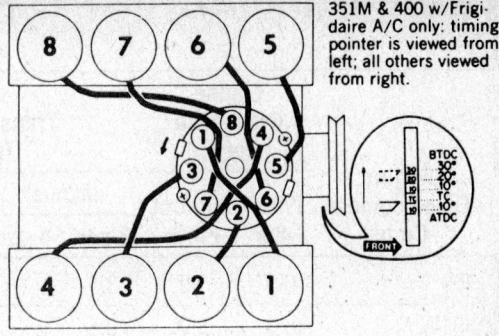

351M & 400 w/Frigidaire A/C only: timing pointer is viewed from left; all others viewed from right.

351W, 351M, 400 V8

CAPACITIES
Bronco

Year	Engine	Crankcase With Filter (qts)	Transmission (pts) Manual	Transmission (pts) Automatic ③	Transfer Case (pts)	Axle (pts) Front	Axle (pts) Rear	Gasoline Tank (gals) Main	Gasoline Tank (gals) Auxilliary	Cooling System (qts)
'75	8-302	6	3.5	17.5	2.75	3.5①	9.0	12.25	7.50	16.0②
'76	8-302	6	3.5	22.0	2.75	3.5	9.0	14.0	7.50	16.0②
'77	8-302	6	3.5	22.0	2.75	3.5	9.0	14.0	7.50	16.0②
'78–'79	8-351M	6	7.0	26.4	4.0④	5.8	6.5⑪	25.0⑤	—	20.0⑥
	8-400	6	7.0	26.4	4.0④	5.8	6.5⑪	25.0⑤	—	22.0⑦
'80–'82	6-300	6	7.0⑫	26.8	6.5	4.0	6.5⑪	25.0⑤	—	13.0⑧
	8-302	6	7.0⑫	26.8	6.5	4.0	6.5⑪	25.0⑤	—	13.0⑨
	8-351W	6	7.0⑫	26.8	6.5	4.0	6.5⑪	25.0⑤	—	15.0⑩

① With locking differential, add 2 oz of friction modifier—Ford part #EST-M2C118-A or equivalent
② With automatic transmission—17.0
③ Includes torque converter
④ Full-time unit: 9.0
⑤ Optional tank: 32.0

⑥ Extra cooling package, air conditioning, automatic transmission or trailer towing package: 22.0
Super Cooling package: 24.0
⑦ Super Cooling package: 24.0
⑧ Air conditioning or Super Cooling package: 14.0

⑨ Extra Cooling package with auto trans; air conditioning; Super Cooling package: 14.0
⑩ Air conditioning or Super Cooling package: 16.0
⑪ With locking differential, use Lubricant Ford part #ESW-M2C6119-A or equivalent
⑫ 4-speed overdrive available in 1981: 4.5

CAPACITIES
Vans

Year	Engine Displacement Cu In.	Engine Crankcase (qts) With Filter	Engine Crankcase (qts) Without Filter	Transmission (pts) Manual 3-spd	Transmission (pts) Manual 4-spd	Transmission (pts) Automatic ■	Drive Axle° (pts)	Gasoline Tank (gals)	Cooling System (qts) W/AC	Cooling System (qts) W/O AC	Cooling System (qts) W/Extra Cooling
'75	300	6.0	5.0	3.5	—	20.5②	①	③	—	14.5④	—
	351W	6.0	5.0	3.5	—	20.5②	①	③	24.0	20.0	24.0
	460	6.0	5.0	—	—	20.5②	①	③	28.0	28.0	—
'76	300	6.0	5.0	3.5	—	20.0	⑤	③	—	14.5	—
	351W	6.0	5.0	3.5	—	20.0②	⑤	③	24.0	20.0	24.0
	460	6.0	5.0	—	—	20.0②	⑤	③	28.0	28.0	—

CAPACITIES
Vans

Year	Engine Displacement Cu In.	Engine Crankcase (qts)		Transmission (pts)			Drive Axle° (pts)	Gasoline Tank (gals)	Cooling System (qts)		
		With Filter	Without Filter	Manual		Automatic ■			W/AC	W/O AC	W/Extra Cooling
				3-spd	4-spd						
'77	300	6.0	5.0	3.5	—	20.0	⑥	③	—	14.5	—
	351W	6.0	5.0	3.5	—	20.0②	⑥	③	20.0	17.0	20.0
	460	6.0	5.0	—	—	20.0②	⑥	③	28.0	28.0	—
'78	300	6.0	5.0	3.5	5.0	20.5	⑥	③	—	14.5	—
	351W	6.0	5.0	—	—	20.0②	⑥	③	20.0	17.0	20.0
	460	6.0	5.0	—	—	20.0②	⑥	③	28.0	28.0	—
'79–'82	300	6.0	5.0	3.5	5.0	20.0	⑦	⑧	20.0	15.0	—
	302	6.0	5.0	3.5	5.0	20.0	⑦	⑧	17.5	15.0⑨	17.5
	351W	6.0	5.0	—	—	23.5	⑦	⑧	20.0	20.0	—
	460	6.0	5.0	—	—	23.5	⑦	⑧	28.0	28.0	—

① Ford axles: 5.0
Dana axles: 6.0
② C-6: 24.5
③ E-100 van and club wagon with evaporative emission controls: 18.0
E-150: 18.0
All others: 22.1
Optional auxiliary: 18.0

④ With auto trans.: 16.6
⑤ Ford axles: 6.5
Dana axles: 6.0
⑥ Ford axles: 6.5
Dana model 61-1: 5.0
Dana model 70: 5.5
⑦
⑧ E-100, 150 with 124 inch wheel base: 18.0

All others: 22.1
Optional auxiliary: 18.0 except E-350 cutaway chassis: 40.0
⑨ With auto trans.: 17.5
*For limited slip units, add 1 oz of limited slip additive
■ Includes torque converter

CRANKCASE AND COOLING SYSTEM (QTS) CAPACITIES
Pick-Up

Year	Engine and Model	Crankcase Oil and Filter Change	Cooling System					
			Standard System		Extra Cooling		With A/C	Super Cooling
			Man Trans	Auto Trans	Man Trans	Auto Trans		
'75	300 eng., F-100 4×2	6.0	14.4	14.4	16.3	16.3	—	—
	F-100/250 4×4	6.0	14.4	—	16.3	—	—	—
	F-150/250 4×2	6.0	14.4	14.4	16.7	16.7	—	—
	F-350	6.0	14.4	16.7	16.7	18.3	—	—
	302 eng., F-100 4×2	6.0	14.8	14.8	14.8	17.5	—	—
	360 eng., F-100 4×2	6.0	19.6	21.9	21.9	22.3	22.3	23.9
	F-150/250 4×2	6.0	19.6	19.6	21.9	22.9	22.3	23.9
	F-100/250 4×4	6.0	22.3	22.3	22.3	22.3	23.9	23.9
	F-350	6.0	22.3	22.3	23.9	23.9	23.9	23.9

CRANKCASE AND COOLING SYSTEM (QTS) CAPACITIES
Pick-Up

Year	Engine and Model	Crankcase Oil and Filter Change	Cooling System					
			Standard System		Extra Cooling			
			Man Trans	Auto Trans	Man Trans	Auto Trans	With A/C	Super Cooling
	390 eng., F-100/150/250 4×2	6.0	22.3	22.3	22.3	22.3	23.9	24.6
	F-350	6.0	22.3	22.3	24.6	23.9	24.6	24.6
	460 eng., F-150/250	6.0	—	22.5	—	22.5	22.5	23.2
	F-350	6.0	—	22.5	—	22.5	23.2	—
'76	300 eng., F-100 4×2	6.0	12.5	14.5	14.5	14.5	—	—
	F-150/250 4×4	6.0	14.5	14.5	16.5	16.5	—	—
	F-150/250 4×2	6.0	12.5	12.5	14.5	14.5	—	—
	F-350	6.0	14.5	14.5	14.5	14.5	14.5	—
	302 eng., F-100 4×2	6.0	15.0	15.0	17.5	17.5	17.5	—
	360 eng., F-100 4×2	6.0	19.5	22.0	22.5	22.5	24.0	24.0
	F-150/250 4×2	6.0	19.5	19.5	22.0	22.5	24.0	24.0
	F-100/150 4×4	6.0	16.5	16.5	16.5	16.5	16.5	—
	F-250 4×4	6.0	16.5	16.5	16.5	16.5	16.5	18.5
	F-350	6.0	22.5	22.5	24.0	24.0	24.0	—
'77	300 eng., F-100/150/250 4×2	6.0	12.5	14.5	14.5	14.5	—	—
	F-150/250 4×4	6.0	14.5	14.5	14.5	14.5	—	—
	F-350	6.0	14.5	14.5	14.5	14.5	—	—
	302 eng., F-100 4×2	6.0	15.5	17.5	15.5	17.5	17.5	—
	351 eng., F-100 4×2	6.0	19.5	22.0	19.5	19.5	22.0	24.0
	F-150/250 4×2	6.0	19.5	19.5	19.5	19.5	22.0	24.0
	F-150/250 4×4	6.0	22.0	22.0	22.0	22.0	22.0	24.0
	F-350	6.0	22.0	22.0	22.0	22.0	22.0	—
	400 eng., F-100/150/250/350	6.0	22.0	22.0	22.0	22.0	22.0	24.0
	460 eng., F-150/250/350	6.0	22.5	22.5	22.5	22.5	22.5	—
'78–'82	300 eng., F-100/250/350	7.0	13.0	14.0	13.0	14.0	17.0	—
	255, 302 eng., F-100/150	6.0	15.0	15.0	15.0	18.0	18.0	—
	351 eng., F-100	6.0	17.0	—	17.0	—	—	24.0
	F-150/350	6.0	15.0	17.0	17.0	17.0	18.0	24.0

CRANKCASE AND COOLING SYSTEM (QTS) CAPACITIES
Pick-Up

Year	Engine and Model	Crankcase Oil and Filter Change	Cooling System					
			Standard System		Extra Cooling			
			Man Trans	Auto Trans	Man Trans	Auto Trans	With A/C	Super Cooling
	400 eng., F/250/350	6.0	18.0	—	18.0	—	18.0	24.0
	F-100/350	6.0	—	18.0	—	18.0	18.0	24.0
	460 eng., 150/350	6.0	24.0	24.0	24.0	24.0	24.0	24.0

SRW—Single rear wheels
DRW—Dual rear wheels

TRANSMISSION AND TRANSFER CASE CAPACITIES
Pick-up

Year	Model	Type	Capacity (pints)
'75–'76	F-100/150/250	Ford 3.03, 3-sp	3.5
	F-100/250/350 4 × 2	Warner T-18, 4-sp	7.0
	F-100/150/250/350	New Process 435 4-sp	
		with extension	7.0
		without extension	6.5
	F-100/150/250	C-4 w/300 cid eng	20.5
		w/302 cid eng	17.5
	F-100	FMX	22.0
	F-100/150/250/350	C-6 4 × 2 w/360, 390 cid eng	24.5
		4 × 2 w/460 cid eng	27.5
		4 × 4	27.5
	F-100 4 × 4	Dana 21 1-sp Transfer Case	1.25
	F-100/250	New Process 205 2-sp Transfer Case	4.5
	F-100/150/250	New Process 203 Full Time Transfer Case	9.0
'77–'78	F-100/150/250	Ford 3.03, 3-sp	3.5
	F-100/150/250 4 × 2 F-250 4 × 4 F-350	Warner T-18 4-sp	6.5
	F-100/150/250/350	New Process 435, 4-sp	
		with extension	7.0
		without extension	6.5
	F-100/150/250	C-4 w/300 cid eng	20.0
		w/302 cid eng	17.5
	F-100/150/250/350	C-6 4 × 2	24.5
		4 × 4	27.5
	F-150/250 4 × 4	New Process 205, 2-sp Transfer Case	4.0
	F-150/250 4 × 4	New Process 203 Full Time Transfer Case	9.0

TRANSMISSION AND TRANSFER CASE CAPACITIES
Pick-up

Year	Model	Type	Capacity (pints)
'79–'82	F-100/250	Ford 3.03, 3-sp	3.5
	F-150/250/350	Warner T-18 4-sp	7.0
	F-100/150/250/350	New Process 435 4-sp with extension without extension	7.0 6.5
	All F Series	Clark 4-sp Overdrive	5.0
	F-100/150 F-150/350	C-4 Automatic	20.0
	F-250 4 × 4	C-6 Automatic 351, 400, 460 engs. All others	26.75 23.5
	F-150/250 4 × 4	New Process, 205, 2-sp Transfer Case	4.5
	F-150/250/350 4 × 4	New Process, 203 Full Time Transfer Case	9.0
	F-150/250 F-250/350	New Process, 208 Transfer Case Borg Warner, 1345 Transfer Case	6.0 6.0

DRIVE AXLES CAPACITIES
Pick-up

Year	Model	Type	Capacity (pints)
'75	F-100	Ford 3300	6.5
	F-100	Ford 3600, 3750	6.5
	F-250	Dana 60, 61	6.0
	F-350	Dana 70	6.0
	F-100	Dana 44-7F Front axle	4.75
	F-250	Dana 44-6CF Front axle	4.6
	F-250	Dana 44-6CF HD Front axle	5.9
	F-250	Dana 60F Front axle	6.0
'76–'78	F-100/150	Ford 3300, 3750	6.5
	F-250	Dana 60, 61	6.0
	F-250	Dana 61-2	5.0
	F-350	Dana-70	6.0
	F-150	Dana 44-7F Front axle	4.75
	F-250	Dana 44-6CF HD Front axle	4.0
	F-250	Dana 60F Front axle	5.5
'79–'82	F-100/150	Ford C4	6.5
	F-250, 4 × 2, F-250/350 4 × 4	Dana 60-2	7.0

DRIVE AXLES CAPACITIES
Pick-up

Year	Model	Type	Capacity (pints)
	F-250	Dana 61-2	6.0
	F-350	Dana 70	7.0
	F-150/250 4 × 4	Dana 44-9F Front axle	3.5*
	F-250/350 4 × 4	Dana 60-7F Front axle	6.0

*4.0—with New Process 205 2-sp Transfer Case

FUEL TANK CAPACITIES
Pick-up

Year	Model	Standard	Optional
'75–'76	F-100	19.2	20.2 4 × 2 frame mount 17.5 in-cab
	F-150/250 4 × 2	19.2	22.5 frame mount exc Calif. 20.2 frame mount Calif. 19.3 in-cab exc Calif. 17.5 in-cab Calif.
	F-250 4 × 4	19.3 exc. Calif. 17.5	—
	F-350	19.3	22.5 midship
	All Supercab	19.2	19.0 frame mount
'77–'78	F-100	19.2	20.2 frame mount
	F-150 4 × 2, 4 × 4, F-250 4 × 2	19.2 exc. Calif. 20.2 Calif.	22.5 frame mount 19.3 in-cab 17.5 in-cab
	F-250 4 × 4 and Crew Cab	22.5 exc. Calif. 20.2 Calif.	—
	F-350	20.2	21.0 Aft./Axle
	All Supercab	19.5 frame mount	—
'79–'82	F-100/250/350 4 × 2 (Reg Cab)	19.2	20.2
	F-250 4 × 4 (Reg Cab)	19.2	—
	F-250/350 4 × 2, (Crew Cab)	20.2	—
	Super Cab	19.2	19.5
	F-350 4 × 2 (Reg Cab)	20.2	19.0
	F-250/350 4 × 4, (Reg Cab)	26.0	19.2

VALVE SPECIFICATIONS

Year	Engine Displacement Cu In.	Seat Angle (deg)	Face Angle (deg)	Spring Test Pressure (lbs @ in.)	Spring Installed Height (in.)	Steam to Guide Clearance (in.)		Stem Diameter (in.)	
						Intake	Exhaust	Intake	Exhaust
'82	6-232	45	44	202 @ 1.28	1.70	.0010–.0025	.0015–.0032	.3422	.3415
'75–'82	6-300	45	44	①	②	.0010–.0027	.0010–.0027	.3420	.3420
'82	8-255	45	46	③	④	.0010–.0027	.0010–.0027	.3420	.3415
'75–'76	8-302	45	46	200 @ 1.22	1.70	.0010–.0027	.0015–.0032	.3420	.3415
'77–'78	8-302	45	44	200 @ 1.31 ⑤	1.70	.0010–.0027	.0015–.0032	.3420	.3415
'79–'82	8-302	45	44	⑥	④	.0010–.0027	.0015–.0032	.3420	.3415
'77–'80	8-351M	45	44	226 @ 1.39	1.81	.0010–.0027	.0015–.0032	.3420	.3415
'75–'76	8-351W	45	44	200 @ 1.34	1.79	.0010–.0027	.0015–.0032	.3420	.3415
'77–'82	8-351W	45	44	⑦	1.80	.0010–.0027	.0015–.0032	.3420	.3415 ⑨
'75–'76	8-360	45	44	220 @ 1.38	1.83 ⑩	.0010–.0027	.0015–.0032	.3714	.3709
'75–'76	8-390	45	44	220 @ 1.38 ⑧	1.83 ⑩	.0010–.0027	.0015–.0032	.3714	.3709
'77–'81	8-400	45	44	229 @ 1.39 ⑪	1.82	.0010–.0027	.0015–.0032	.3420	.3415 ⑫
'75–'76	8-460	45	44	252 @ 1.33	1.82	.0010–.0027	.0010–.0027	.3420	.3420
'77–'82	8-460	45	44	229 @ 1.33	1.82	.0010–.0027	.0010–.0027	.3420	.3420

① 1975–81 intake: 190 @ 1.30
  1982 intake: 197 @ 1.30
  All exhaust: 192 @ 1.18
② All intake: 1.70
  1975–81 exhaust: 1.69
  1982 exhaust: 1.58
③ Intake: 204 @ 1.36

Exhaust: 200 @ 1.20
④ Intake: 1.78
  Exhaust: 1.60
⑤ 1977 exhaust: 1.20
⑥ Intake: 202 @ 1.36
  Exhaust: 200 @ 1.20
⑦ Intake: 200 @ 1.36

Exhaust: 200 @ 1.20
⑧ F-and E-100 intake: 90 @ 1.82
  F- and E-100 exhaust: 183 @ 1.24
⑨ 1982: .3420
⑩ F- and E-100 exhaust: 1.70
⑪ 1982: 226 @ 1.39
⑫ 1982: .3420

CRANKSHAFT AND CONNECTING ROD SPECIFICATIONS

Year	Engine No. Cyl Displacement (cu in.)	Crankshaft				Connecting Rod		
		Main Brg Jounal Dia	Main Brg Oil Clearance	Shaft End-Play	Thrust on No.	Journal Diameter	Oil Clearance	Side Clearance
'82	6-232	2.5190	.0009–.0027	.004–.008	3	2.3107	.0009–.0027	.004–.011
'75–'82	6-300	2.3986	.0008–.0015	.004–.008	5	2.1230	.0008–.0015	.0060–.0130
'82	8-255	2.2490	.0005–.0024 ④	.004–.008	3	2.1232	.0008–.0025	.010–.020

CRANKSHAFT AND CONNECTING ROD SPECIFICATIONS

Year	Engine No. Cyl Displacement (cu in.)	Crankshaft				Connecting Rod		
		Main Brg Jounal Dia	Main Brg Oil Clearance	Shaft End-Play	Thrust on No.	Journal Diameter	Oil Clearance	Side Clearance
'75–'77	8-302	2.2486	.0005–.0024②	.004–.008	3	2.1232	.0008–.0026	.010– .020
'78–'82	8-302	2.2486	.0005–.0015①	.004–.008	3	2.1232	.0008–.0026	.010– .020
'77–'80	8-351M	2.9998	.0008–.0015	.004–.008	3	2.3107	.0008–.0015	.010– .020
'75–'76	8-351W	2.9998	.0008–.0015③	.004–.008	3	2.3107	.0008–.0015	.010– .020
'77–'82	8-351W	2.9998	.0008–.0015	.004–.008	3	2.3107	.0008–.0015	.010– .020
'75–'76	8-360	2.7488	.0005–.0015	.004–.010	3	2.4384	.0008–.0015	.008– .025
'75–'76	8-390	2.7488	.0005–.0015	.004–.010	3	2.4384	.0008–.0015	.010– .020
'77–'82	8-400	2.9998	.0008–.0015	.004–.008	3	2.3107	.0008–.0015	.010– .020
'75–'82	8-460	2.9998	.0008–.0015	.004–.008	3	2.4995	.0008–.0015	.010– .020

① # 1: .0001–.0015
② # 1: .0001–.0015
  '75 only: All bearings .0005–.0015
③ # 1: .0005–.0015
④ # 1: .0001–.0020

PISTON AND RING SPECIFICATIONS

All measurements given in inches

Year	Engine	Piston to Bore Clearance	Ring Side Clearance			Ring Gap		
			Top Compression	Bottom Compression	Oil Control	Top Compression	Bottom Compression	Oil Control
'82	6-232	.0014–.0022	.0020–.0040	.0020–.0040	snug	.0100–.0200	.0100–.0200	.015–.055
'75–'76	6-300	.0014–.0022	.0024–.0041	.0025–.0045	snug	.0100–.0200	.0100–.0200	.015–.055
'77	6-300	.0014–.0022	.0019–.0036	.0020–.0040	snug	.0100–.0200	.0100–.0200	.010–.035
'78	6-300	.0002–.0004①	.0019–.0036	.0020–.0040	snug	.0100–.0200	.0100–.0200	.015–.055
'79–'82	6-300	.0014–.0022	.0019–.0036	.0020–.0040	snug	.0100–.0200	.0100–.0200	.010–.035
'82	8-255	.0014–.0024	.0020–.0040	.0020–.0040	snug	.0100–.0200	.0100–.0200	.015–.055
'75–'77	8-302	.0018–.0026	.0020–.0040	.0020–.0040	snug	.0010–.0020	.0010–.0020	.015–.055
'78–'82	8-302	.0018–.0026	.0020–.0040	.0020–.0040	snug	.0010–.0020	.0010–.0020	.015–.035
'77–'80	8-351M	.0014–.0022	.0019–.0036	.0020–.0040	snug	.0010–.0020	.0010–.0020	.010–.035
'75–'76	8-351W	.0018–.0026	.0020–.0040	.0020–.0040	snug	.0010–.0020	.0010–.0020	.015–.055
'77–'82	8-351W	.0022–.0030	.0019–.0036	.0020–.0040	snug	.0010–.0020	.0010–.0020	.015–.035②
'75–'76	8-360	.0015–.0023	.0020–.0040	.0020–.0040	snug	.0100–.0200	.0100–.0200	.015–.035
'75–'76	8-390	.0015–.0023	.0020–.0040	.0020–.0040	snug	.0100–.0200	.0100–.0200	.015–.035
'77–'80	8-400	.0014–.0022	.0019–.0036	.0020–.0040	snug	.0100–.0200	.0100–.0200	.015–.035
'75–'76	8-460	.0022–.0030	.0020–.0040	.0020–.0040	snug	.0100–.0200	.0100–.0200	.015–.055
'77	8-460	.0014–.0022	.0025–.0045	.0025–.0045	snug	.0100–.0200	.0100–.0200	.010–.030
'78	8-460	.0022–.0030	.0025–.0045	.0025–.0045	snug	.0100–.0200	.0100–.0200	.010–.030
'79–'82	8-460	.0022–.0300	.0019–.0036	.0020–.0040	snug	.0100–.0200	.0100–.0200	.010–.035

① over 6,000 lb GVW: .0003–.0005
② 1978: .015–.055

TORQUE SPECIFICATIONS
(All readings in ft. lbs.)

Year	Engine	Cylinder Head Bolts	Rod Bearing Bolts	Main Bearing Bolts	Crank-shaft Pulley Bolt	Flywheel-to-Crankshaft Bolts	Manifold Intake	Manifold Exhaust
'82	6-232	65–81	30–36	62–81	85–100	75–85	18	15–22
'75–'76	6-300	70–75	40–45	60–70	130–150	75–85	23–28	23–28
'77–'82	6-300	70–75	40–45	60–70	130–150	75–85	22–32	28–33
'82	8-255	65–72	19–24	60–70	70–90	75–85	18–20	18–24
'75–'82	8-302	65–70	19–24	60–70	70–90①	75–85	②	12–16③
'77–'80	8-351M	95–105	40–45	④	70–90	75–85	⑤	18–24
'75–'76	8-351W	65–70	19–24	60–70	70–90	75–85	23–25	18–24
'77–'82	8-351W	105–112	40–45	95–105	70–90	75–85	23–25	18–24
'75–'76	8-360	80–90	40–45	95–105	130–150	75–85	40–45	12–18
'75–'76	8-390	80–90	40–45	95–105	130–150	75–85	40–45	12–18
'77	8-400	95–105	40–45	35–45	70–90	75–85	⑤	18–24
'78–'80	8-400	95–105	40–45	95–105	70–90	75–85	⑤	18–24
'75–'82	8-460	130–140	40–45	95–105	70–90	75–85	25–30	28–33

① '75–'77: 35–50
② '75–'77: 19–27
   '78–'82: 23–25
③ '80–'82: 18–24
④ '77: 35–45
   '78–'80: 95–105
⑤ 3/8": 22–32
   5/16": 17–25

ALTERNATOR SPECIFICATIONS

Year	Color Code	Output Amps	Output Watts	Field Current Amps	Cut-In rpm	Brush Length Inches New	Brush Length Inches Limit
'75	Purple	38	570	2.5	400	1/2	5/16
	Orange	42	630	2.9	400	1/2	5/16
	Red	55	825	2.9	400	1/2	5/16
	Green	61	915	2.9	400	1/2	5/16
'76–'81	Orange	40	600	2.9	400	1/2	5/16
	Green	60	900	2.9	400	1/2	5/16
	Green①	60	900	4.0	400	1/2	3/16
'82	Orange	40	600	2.9	900	1/2	3/16
	Green	60	900	6.0	1025	1/2	3/16
	Green	70	1050	6.0	780	1/2	3/16
	Red	100	1500	6.0	930	1/2	3/16

① Blue ink on pulley face

BATTERY AND STARTER SPECIFICATIONS

Year	Engine	Battery			Starter						Brush Spring Tension (oz)
		Ampere/Hour Capacity	Volts	Ground	Lock Test			No Load Test			
					Amps	Volts	Torque (ft lbs)	Amps	Volts	rpm	
'75–'77	All	45	12	Neg	670	5	15.5	70	12	9500	40
		55	12	Neg	670	5	15.5	70	12	9500	40
		70	12	Neg	670	5	15.5	70	12	9500	40
		80	12	Neg	670	5	15.5	70	12	9500	40
'78	All	41	12	Neg	460	5	9.0	70	12	9500	40
		68	12	Neg	670	5	15.5	80	12	9500	80
					525①	5	17.2	80	11	10,000	50
'79	All	41	12	Neg	460	5	9.0	70	12	9500	40
		53	12	Neg	670	5	15.5	80	12	9500	80
		68	12	Neg							
'80–'81	All	36	12	Neg	460	5	9.0	70	12	9500	40
		45	12	Neg	670	5	15.5	80	12	9500	80
		63	12	Neg							
		81	12	Neg							

① Prestolite model with 400 cid engine

BRAKE SPECIFICATIONS
Pickups and Vans

Year	Model	Master Cylinder Bore	Caliper Bore	Wheel Cylinder Bore		Rotor Diameter	Rotor Minimum Thickness	Rotor Maximum Run-out	Brake Drum Diameter		Machined Oversize	
				Front	Rear				Front	Rear	Front	Rear
'75	F&E-100,150	1.00	2.875	—	.8125	11.72	.940	.003	—	10.0	—	10.06
	F&E-250	1.062	2.180	—	.8125	12.55	1.120	.003	—	11.03	—	11.09
	F&E-350	1.062	2.180	—	.8750	12.55	1.120	.003	—	12.0	—	12.06
'76	F&E-100, 150	1.00	2.875	—	.9375	11.54	1.180	.003	—	11.03	—	11.09
	F&E-250	1.062	2.180	—	1.000	12.50	1.120	.003	—	12.0	—	12.06
	F&E-350	1.062	2.180	—	1.060	12.50	1.120	.003	—	12.0	—	12.06
'77	F&E-100, 150	1.00	2.875	—	.9375	11.54	1.180	.003	—	11.03	—	11.09
	F&E-250	1.062	2.180	—	1.000	12.50	1.120	.003	—	12.0	—	12.06
	F&E-350	1.062	2.180	—	1.062	12.50	1.120	.003	—	12.0	—	12.06
'78	F&E-100, 150	1.00	2.875	—	.9375	11.54	1.180	.003	—	11.03	—	11.09
	F&E-250	1.062	2.180	—	1.000	12.50	1.120	.003	—	12.0	—	12.06
	F&E-350	1.062	2.180	—	1.062	12.50	1.120	.003	—	12.0	—	12.06

BRAKE SPECIFICATIONS
Pickups and Vans

Year	Model	Master Cylinder Bore	Caliper Bore	Wheel Cylinder Bore Front	Wheel Cylinder Bore Rear	Rotor Diameter	Rotor Minimum Thickness	Rotor Maximum Run-out	Brake Drum Diameter Front	Brake Drum Diameter Rear	Machined Oversize Front	Machined Oversize Rear
'79–'80	F&E-100, 150	1.00	2.875	—	.9375	11.54	1.180	.003	—	11.03	—	11.09
	F&E-250	1.062	2.180	—	1.000	12.50	1.120	.003	—	12.0	—	12.06
	F&E-350	1.062	2.180	—	1.062	12.50	1.120	.003	—	12.0	—	12.06
'81–'82	F-100①	1.00	2.599	—	.9375	10.97	1.120⑧	.003	—	10.0	—	10.09
	F-100②, F-150 4×2, E-100, E-150③	1.00④	2.875	—	.9375	11.65	1.120	.003	—	11.03	—	11.09
	F-150 4×4, E-150⑤	1.00④	2.875	—	.9375	11.65	1.120	.003	—	11.03	—	11.09
	F-250 4×2⑥	1.00	2.875	—	.9375	12.59	1.120	.003	—	12.0	—	12.06
	F-250 Super cab, F-200⑦ 4×2, E-250, E-350	1.062	2.180	—	1.062	12.56	1.180	.003	—	12.0	—	12.06
	F-350 4×4, F-350 4×4	1.062	2.180	—	1.062	12.48	1.180	.003	—	12.0	—	12.06

① w/std payload package
② exc. std payload package
③ w/GVWR under 6350 lb.
④ E-150: 1.062
⑤ w/GVWR over 6350 lb.
⑥ Regular cab w/payload under 8500 lb.
⑦ Regular cab w/payload over 8500 lb.
⑧ 1982: .810 or LD models

BRAKE SPECIFICATIONS
Bronco
(All measurements in inches)

Year	Master Cylinder Bore	Caliper Bore	Wheel Cylinder Bore Front	Wheel Cylinder Bore Rear	Rotor Diameter	Rotor Minimum Thickness	Rotor Maximum Run-out	Brake Drum Diameter Front	Brake Drum Diameter Rear	Machined Oversize Front	Machined Oversize Rear
'75–'77	1.00	2.875	—	.9375	11.54	1.180	.003	—	11.03	—	11.09
'78–'81	1.00	2.875	—	.9375	11.72	1.120	.003	—	11.03	—	11.09
'82	1.00	2.875	—	.9375	11.65	1.120	.003	—	11.03	—	11.09

WHEEL ALIGNMENT SPECIFICATIONS
Bronco 1975–79

Year	Caster Range (deg)	Caster Preferred (deg)	Camber Range	Camber Preferred (deg)	Toe-in (in.)	Steering Axis Inclination (deg)
'75–'77	2¾P to 4¼P	3½P	1P to 2P	½P	1/16-¼	—
'78–'79	6½P to 9½P	8P	1P to 3P	1½P	3/32	8½

WHEEL ALIGNMENT SPECIFICATIONS
Bronco 1980–82

Ride Height (in.)	Camber (deg)	Caster (deg)	Toe-in (in.)	King Pin Angle (deg)
2¾-3¼	2½N to ¼N	6P to 9P	1/32 out-5/32 in	13
3¼-3½	1¾N to 1½P	5P to 8P	1/32 out-5/32 in	13
3½-4	¾N to 1½P	4P to 7P	1/32 out-5/32 in	13
4-4¼	0 to 2¼P	3P to 6P	1/32 out-5/32 in	13
4¼-4¾	1P to 3¼P	2P to 5P	1/32 out-5/32 in	13
4¾-5	1¾P to 4P	1P to 4P	1/32 out-5/32 in	13

① 1978–79 caster measured at 3½ inches ride height. Subtract 2° each inch increase in ride height.

WHEEL ALIGNMENT SPECIFICATIONS
Van 1975–77

Year	Model	Caster Range (deg.)	Caster Preferred Setting (deg)	Camber Range (deg)	Camber Preferred Setting (deg)	Toe-in (in.)	Steering Axis Inclination (deg)
'75–'76	E-100, 200	½P to 8½P	4½P	½P to 3½P	2P	3/32 out to 5/32 in	4
	E-300	2½P to 7½P	5P	½P to 3½P	2P	3/32 out to 5/32 in	4
'77	E-100, 150	2P to 5¾P	3⅞P	¾N to 1¾P	½P	3/32 out to 5/32 in	4
	E-250, 350	4P to 8¼P	6⅛P	½N to 2¼P	⅞P	3/32 out to 5/32 in	4

WHEEL ALIGNMENT SPECIFICATIONS
Van 1978–82

Year	Ride Height (inches)	E-100, 150 Caster (deg)	E-100, 150 Camber (deg)	E-250, 350 Caster (deg)	E-250, 350 Camber (deg)
'78①	4.00 to 4.25	3¾P to 6½P	¾N to ½P	6¼P to 9P	1N to ¾P
	4.25 to 4.50	3¼P to 5¾P	½N to ¾P	5¾P to 8¼P	½N to 1¼P
	4.50 to 4.75	2½P to 5¼P	0 to 1¼P	5¼P to 7¾P	0 to 1¾P
	4.75 to 5.00	2P to 4½P	½P to 1¾P	4½P to 7¼P	½P to 2¼P
	5.00 to 5.25	1¼P to 4P	1¼P to 2½P	4P to 6½P	1P to 2¾P
	5.25 to 5.50	¾P to 3¼P	1¾P to 3¼P	3¼P to 6P	1½P to 3¼P
	5.50 to 5.75	0 to 2¾P	1½P to 3¾P	—	—
'79–'82②	3.25 to 3.50	6¼P to 8P	1¾N to ¼N	9P to 10½P	1¾N to ¼N
	3.50 to 3.75	5¾P to 7¼P	1½N to ¼P	8½P to 9¾P	1½N to ¼P
	3.75 to 4.00	5P to 6¾P	1N to ¾P	7⅞P to 9P	1N to ¾P
	4.00 to 4.25	4½P to 5¾P	½N to 1¼P	7⅛P to 8½P	½N to 1¼P

WHEEL ALIGNMENT SPECIFICATIONS
Van 1978–82

Year	Ride Height (inches)	E-100, 150 Caster (deg)	E-100, 150 Camber (deg)	E-250, 350 Caster (deg)	E-250, 350 Camber (deg)
	4.25 to 4.50	4P to 5¼P	0 to 1¾P	6½P to 7¾P	0 to 1¾P
	4.50 to 4.75	3¼P to 4½P	½P to 2¼P	5¾P to 7P	½P to 2¼P
	4.75 to 5.00	2½P to 4P	1P to 2¾P	5¼P to 6½P	1P to 2¾P
	5.00 to 5.25	2P to 3¼P	1½P to 3¼P	4⅝P to 6P	1½P to 3¼P
	5.25 to 5.50	1½P to 2¾P	2P to 3¾P	4P to 5½P	2P to 3¾P

NOTE: Ford states that no adjustments by bending or any other means may be made to effect changes in the caster or camber of its twin I-beam front axles. Adjustment is by replacement of parts, only. 1977 was the last year Ford furnished general specifications for checking caster and camber on these vehicles. Use the following charts to determine the proper caster and camber for a specific vehicle, beginning with the 1978 model year.
① Toe-in: E-100, 150—0 to ¼ inch
   E-250, 350—³⁄₃₂ inch out to ⁵⁄₃₂ inch in
② Toe-in: all models—¹⁄₃₂ inch
P: Positive   N: Negative

WHEEL ALIGNMENT SPECIFICATIONS
Pick-up

Year	Model	Caster Range (deg)	Caster Preferred Setting (deg)	Camber Range (deg)	Camber Preferred Setting (deg)	Toe-in (in.)	Steering Axis Inclination (deg)
'75	F-100, 250 2WD	½ to 8½	4½	½ to 2½	1	³⁄₃₂	7½
	F-250 4WD	3½ to 4½	4	1 to 2	1½	⅛	7½
	F-100, 150 4WD	2¾ to 4½	3½	1 to 2	1½	⁵⁄₃₂	8½
	F-350	½ to 8½	—	0 to 3	—	³⁄₃₂	—
'76	F-100, 250 2WD	½ to 8½	4½	½ to 2½	1	³⁄₃₂	7½
	F-250 4WD	3½ to 4½	4	1 to 2	1½	⅛	7½
	F-100, 150 4WD	2¾ to 4½	3½	1 to 2	1½	⁵⁄₃₂	8½
	F-350	½ to 8½	—	0 to 3	—	⅛	—
'77	F-100, 150, 250 2WD, 6200–6900 GVW	4 to 9	6½	1 to 3	1	³⁄₃₂	—
	F-250 Supercab 2WD; F-250 7800–8000 GVW	3¼ to 8½	5⅞	0 to 3¼	1⅝	³⁄₃₂	—
	F-250 Crewcab 2WD; F-250 Supercab 2WD 8100 GVW	3¼ to 9	6⅛	0 to 3¾	1⅞	³⁄₃₂	—
	F-150 4WD	2¾ to 4¼	3½	1 to 2	1½	⁵⁄₃₂	8½
	F-250 4WD	3 to 5	4	½ to 1½	1	⁵⁄₃₂	7½
	F-350	3¼ to 9	—	0 to 3¾	—	⅛	—
'78	F-150 4WD	4¼ to 5½	3½	1 to 2	1½	³⁄₃₂	8½
	F-250 4 WD	2⅛ to 5	4	½ to 1½	1	⁵⁄₃₂	8½
'79	F-150 4WD	6½ to 9½	3½	1 to 3	1½	³⁄₃₂	8½
	F-150 Supercab 4WD F-250, 350 4WD	2½ to 5½	4	0 to 3	1½	³⁄₃₂	8½

WHEEL ALIGNMENT SPECIFICATIONS
1980-82 F-100 to F-350 Two Wheel Drive

Ride Height (in.)		F-100, 150				F-250, 350			
		Camber (deg)		Caster		Camber (deg)		Caster (deg)	
At Least	Not More Than	Min	Max	Min	Max	Min	Max	Min	Max
2¼	2¾	−3	−½	+6	+10	−1½	+1	+4¾	+8
2¾	3¼	−2	+½	+5	+9	−¾	+1¾	+3¾	+7
3¼	3½	−1¼	+1¼	+4	+8	+¼	+2¾	+2¾	+6
3½	4	−¼	+2¼	+3	+7	+1	+3½	+1¾	+5
4	4¼	+½	+3	+2	+6	+2	+4½	+¾	+4
4¼	4¾	+1½	+4	+1	+5	—	—	—	—

WHEEL ALIGNMENT SPECIFICATIONS
1980-82 F-150, 250, 350 Four Wheel Drive

Ride Height(in.)		F-150				F-250, 350			
		Camber (deg)		Caster (deg)		Camber (deg)		Caster (deg)	
At Least	Not More Than	Min	Max	Min	Max	Min	Max	Min	Max
2¾	3¼	−2½	−¼	+6	+9	—	—	—	—
3¼	3½	−1¾	+½	+5	+8	—	—	—	—
3½	4	−¾	+1½	+4	+7	—	—	—	—
4	4¼	0	+2¼	+3	+6	—	—	—	—
4¼	4¾	+1	+3¼	+2	+5	—	—	—	—
4¾	5	+1¾	+4	+1	+4	−2¾	−¼	+3	+5
5	5½	—	—	—	—	−1¾	+¾	+3⅛	+5⅛
5½	6	—	—	—	—	−¾	+1¾	+3⅛	+5⅛
6	6¼	—	—	—	—	+¼	+2¾	+3¼	+5¼
6¼	6¾	—	—	—	—	+1¼	+4	+3⅜	+5⅜
6¾	7	—	—	—	—	+2½	+5	+3½	+5½

WHEEL ALIGNMENT SPECIFICATIONS
1978 F-100 to F-350 Two Wheel Drive

Ride Height (in.)		F-100/150/250 6200-6900 GVW② Regular Cab				F-250 7800-8000 GVW Regular Cab② 6350-7800 Super Cab				F-350 (All)② F-250 8100 GVW Super Cab F-250 Super Cab w/RPO Suspension			
		Camber (deg)		Caster (deg)		Camber (deg)		Caster (deg)		Camber (deg)		Caster (deg)	
At Least	Not More Than	Min①	Max	Min①	Max	Min①	Max	Min①	Max	Min①	Max	Min①	Max
2.75	3.00	−1°	+½°	8¼°	9⅝°	−½°	+1°	7⅝°	8⅞°	−⅜°	−¼°	9¾°	10⅞°
3.00	3.25	−½°	+1°	7¾°	9°	−¼°	+1½°	6⅞°	8⅜°	−1°	+⅝°	9°	10¼°
3.25	3.50	−¼°	+1½°	7°	8⅜°	0°	+1¾°	5⅜°	7¾°	−½°	+1°	8¼°	9⅝°
3.50	3.75	0°	+1¾°	6¼°	7⅜°	+½°	+2¼°	5¾°	7°	−¼°	+1½°	7⅝°	8⅝°
3.75	4.00	+½°	+2¼°	5¾°	7°	+¾°	+2½°	5°	6½°	0°	+1¾°	6⅞°	8⅜°
4.00	4.25	+¾°	+2½°	5°	6½°	+1¼°	+3°	4½°	5⅞°	+½	+2¼°	6⅜°	7¼°

WHEEL ALIGNMENT SPECIFICATIONS
1979 F-100 to F-350 Two Wheel Drive

Ride Height (in.)		F-100 / F-250 R/C (7700-7900) / F-250 S/C (6300-7800) ①②								F-350 All② / F-250 S/C (3100) / F-250 S/C RPO Suspension ①②			
		Camber (deg)		Caster (deg)		Camber (deg)		Caster (deg)		Camber (deg)		Caster (deg)	
At Least	Note More Than	Min①	Max	Min①	Max	Min①	Max	Min①	Max	Min①	Max	Min①	Max
4.25	4.50	+1¼°	+3°	4½°	5⅞°	+1¾°	+3¼°	3⅞°	5⅛°	+¾°	+2½°	5¾°	7°
4.50	4.75	+1⅝°	+3¼°	3¾°	5	+2°	+3½°	3⅛°	4½°	+1¼°	+3°	5⅛°	6½°
4.75	5.00	+2°	+3¾°	3⅛°	4½°	+2⅜°	+4⅛°	2½°	4°	+1¾°	+3¼°	4½°	5⅞°
5.00	5.25	+2⅜°	+4⅛°	2½°	4°	+2¾°	+4½°	2°	3¼°	+2°	+3¼°	3⅞°	5⅛°

NOTE: Ford states that no adjustments by bending or any other means may be made to effect changes in the caster to camber of its twin I-beam front axles. Adjustment is by replacement of parts, only. 1977 was the last year Ford furnished general specifications for checking caster and camber on these vehicles. Use the following charts to determine the proper caster and camber for a specific vehicle, beginning with the 1978 model year.

NOTE: Toe-in should be checked using a trammel bar with frictionless plates

① All vehicles with normal operating attitudes.
② Toe-in range for these vehicles is 1/32" out to 7/32" in (3/32" nominal).
③ To range for these vehicles is 3/32" out to 5/32" in (1/32" nominal).

WHEEL ALIGNMENT SPECIFICATIONS
1979 F-100 to F-350 Two Wheel Drive

Ride Height (in.)		F-100 / F-250 R/C (7700-7900) / F-250 S/C (6300-7800) ①②				F-350 All② / F-250 S/C (3100) / F-250 S/C RPO Suspension ①②			
		Camber (deg)		Caster (deg)		Camber (deg)		Caster (deg)	
At Least	Note More Than	Min①	Max	Min①	Max	Min①	Max	Min①	Max
2.75	3.00	−1⅞	−¼	7¾	9	−2⅛	−⅝	9⅝	11
3.00	3.25	−1½	+⅛	7	8⅜	−1¾	−¼	8⅞	10⅜
3.25	3.50	−1⅛	+½	6⅜	7¾	−1⅜	+⅛	8⅜	9¾
3.50	3.75	−¾	+⅞	5⅞	7⅛	−1⅛	+½	7¾	9
3.75	4.00	−⅜	+1¼	5⅛	6½	−¾	+¾	7	8⅜
4.00	4.25	0	+1⅝	4½	5⅞	−¼	+1¼	6⅜	7¾
4.25	4.50	⅜	+2	3⅞	5¼	0	+1⅝	5¾	7⅛
4.50	4.75	⅞	2½	3¼	4⅝	+⅜	+2	5⅛	6½
4.75	5.00	1¼	2¾	2⅝	4	+¾	+2⅜	4½	5⅞
5.00	5.25	1⅝	3⅛	2	3⅜	+1¼	+2¾	3⅞	5¼
5.25	5.50	—	—	—	—				

① All vehicles with normal operating attitudes.
② Toe setting is 3/32 inch in.
③ Toe setting is 3/32 inc in.

TUNE-UP

Breakerless Distributor (Solid State)

All 1975 and later engines are equipped with the breakerless electronic ignition system. The conventional contact breaker points and condenser in the distributor are replaced by a permanent magnet low-voltage generator. The generator consists of an armature with four or six teeth mounted on the top of the distributor shaft, and a permanent magnet inside a small coil. The coil is riveted in place to provide a preset air gap with the armature. The distributor base, cap, rotor and vacuum and centrifugal spark advance are about the same as the conventional system.

The distributor is wired to a solid state module in the engine compartment. Inside the module is an electronic circuit board which consists of inner connecting resistors, capacitors, transistors and diodes. The module senses a signal from the magnetic generator to perform the switching function of conventional points and it senses and controls dwell.

Unless a malfunction occurs, or the distributor is moved or replaced, the initial ignition timing remains constant. Because the low voltage coil in the distributor is riveted in position, gap adjustment is not possible.

MODULE TEST

If the electronic module is suspected of being defective, proceed as follows:

1. Without removing the existing module from the vehicle, unplug the connectors from the electronic module. Connect a known good module. The substitute module does not have to be fastened to the vehicle to operate properly.

2. Attempt to start the engine. If the engine starts and accelerates properly, proceed to step three. If the engine will still not start, the fault is in the wiring or other vehicle systems. Inspect and repair as necessary.

3. Reconnect the original module. Again attempt to start and run the engine. If the engine once again will not start, remove the original module and replace with a new one. If, however, the engine will now start and run on the original module, the module is not defective.

4. With the engine operating, check all connections in the primary wiring of the ignition system for such faults as poor wire crimp to terminal or improper engagement. The faulty connection will be observed when the engine misfires or stops. Correct as necessary.

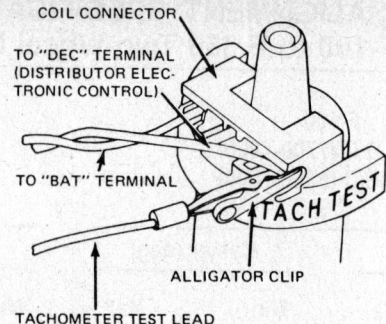

COIL CONNECTOR
TO "DEC" TERMINAL (DISTRIBUTOR ELEC-TRONIC CONTROL)
TO "BAT" TERMINAL
TACH TEST
ALLIGATOR CLIP
TACHOMETER TEST LEAD

Attaching a tachometer lead to the coil connector

TACHOMETER-TO-COIL CONNECTION-ELECTRONIC IGNITION

The new solid state ignition coil connector allows a tachometer test lead with an alligator-type clip to be connected to the DEC (Distributor Electronic Control) terminal without removing the connector.

When engine rpm must be checked, install the tachometer alligator clip into the "TACH TEST" cavity as shown. If the coil connector must be removed, grasp the wires and pull horizontally until it disconnects from the terminals.

Ignition Timing

Ignition timing is the measurement, in degrees of crankshaft rotation, of the point at which the spark plugs fire in each of the cylinders. It is measured in degrees before or after Top Dead Center (TDC) of the compression stroke. Ignition timing is controlled by turning the distributor body in the engine.

Ideally, the air/fuel mixture in the cylinder will be ignited by the spark plug just as the piston passes TDC of the compression stroke. If this happens, the piston will be beginning the power stroke just as the compressed and ignited air/fuel mixture starts to expand. The expansion of the air/fuel mixture then forces the piston down

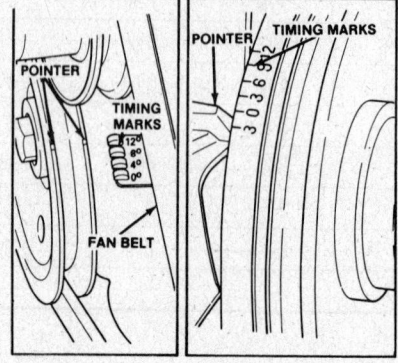

POINTER
TIMING MARKS
FAN BELT
POINTER
TIMING MARKS

Typical timing marks: left, block mounted; right, pulley mounted

on the power stroke and turns the crankshaft.

Because it takes a fraction of a second for the spark plug to ignite the mixture in the cylinder, the spark plug must fire a little before the piston reaches TDC. Otherwise, the mixture will not be completely ignited as the piston passes TDC and the full power of the explosion will not be used by the engine.

The timing measurement is given in degrees of crankshaft rotation before the piston reaches TDC (BTDC). If the setting for the ignition timing is 5° BTDC, each spark plug must fire 5° before each piston reaches TDC. This only holds true, however, when the engine is at idle speed.

As the engine speed increases, the pistons go faster. The spark plugs have to ignite the fuel even sooner if it is to be completely ignited when the piston reaches TDC. To do this, the distributor has a means to advance the timing of the spark as the engine speed increases. This is accomplished by centrifugal weights within the distributor and a vacuum diaphragm mounted on the side of the distributor. It is necessary to disconnect the vacuum lines from the diaphragm when the ignition timing is being set.

If the ignition is set too far advanced (BTDC), the ignition and expansion of the fuel in the cylinder will occur too soon and tend to force the piston down while it is still traveling up. This causes engine ping. If the ignition spark is set too far retarded after TDC (ATDC), the piston will have already passed TDC and started on its way down when the fuel is ignited. This will cause the piston to be forced down for only a portion of its travel. This will result in poor engine performance and lack of power.

The timing is best checked with a timing light. This device is connected in series with the no. 1 spark plug. The current that fires the spark plug also causes the timing light to flash.

There is a notch on the crankshaft pulley on all 6 cyl. engines. A scale of degrees of crankshaft rotation is attached to the engine block in such a position that the notch will pass close by the scale. On the V8 engines, the scale is located on the crankshaft pulley and a pointer is attached to the engine block so that the scale will pass close by. When the engine is running, the timing light is aimed at the mark on the crankshaft pulley and the scale.

IGNITION TIMING ADJUSTMENT

1. Locate the timing marks on the crankshaft pulley and the front of the engine.

2. Clean the timing marks so that you can see them.

3. Mark the timing marks with a piece of chalk or with paint. Color the mark on

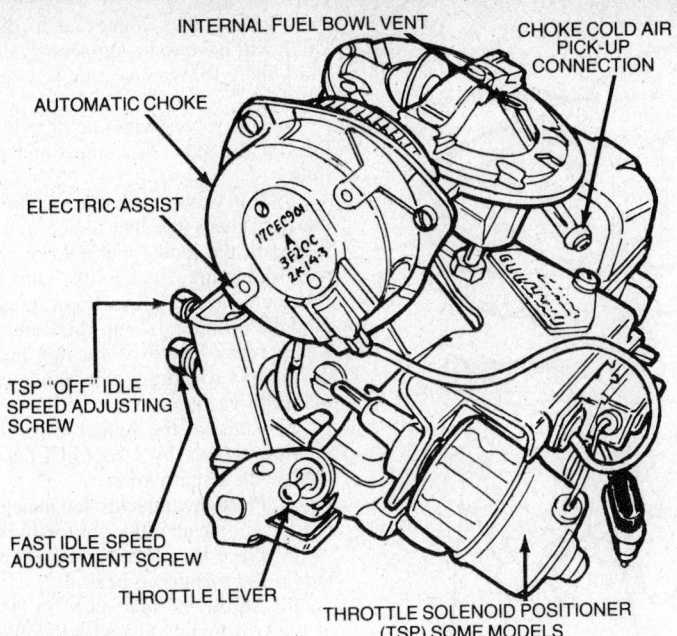

INTERNAL FUEL BOWL VENT

CHOKE COLD AIR PICK-UP CONNECTION

AUTOMATIC CHOKE

ELECTRIC ASSIST

TSP "OFF" IDLE SPEED ADJUSTING SCREW

FAST IDLE SPEED ADJUSTMENT SCREW

THROTTLE LEVER

THROTTLE SOLENOID POSITIONER (TSP) SOME MODELS

Carter YFA carburetor

the scale that will indicate the correct timing when it is aligned with the mark on the pulley or the pointer. It is also helpful to mark the notch in the pulley or the tip of the pointer with a small dab of color.

4. Attach a tachometer to the engine.

5. Attach a timing light according to the manufacturer's instructions. If the timing light has three wires, one is attached to the no. 1 spark plug with an adapter. The other wires are connected to the battery. The red wire goes to the positive side of the battery and the black wire is connected to the negative terminal of the battery.

6. Disconnect the vacuum line to the distributor at the distributor and plug the vacuum line. A golf tee does a fine job.

7. Check to make sure that all of the wires clear the fan and then start the engine.

8. Adjust the idle to the correct setting.

9. Aim the timing light at the timing marks. If the marks that you put on the flywheel or pulley and the engine are aligned when the light flashes, the timing is correct. Turn off the engine and remove the tachometer and the timing light. If the marks are not in alignment, proceed with the following steps.

10. Turn off the engine.

11. Loosen the distributor lockbolt just enough so that the distributor can be turned with a little effort.

12. Start the engine. Keep the wires of the timing light clear of the fan.

13. With the timing light aimed at the pulley and the marks on the engine, turn the distributor in the direction of rotor rotation to retard the spark, and in the opposite direction of rotor rotation to advance the spark. Align the marks on the pulley and the engine with the flashes of the timing light.

14. When the marks are aligned, tighten the distributor lockbolt and recheck the timing with the timing light to make sure that the distributor did not move when you tightened the lockbolt.

15. Turn off the engine and remove the timing light.

Carburetor

IDLE SPEED ADJUSTMENT

1975–76

1. Remove the air cleaner and plug the vacuum lines.

2. Set the parking brake and block the wheels.

3. Connect a tachometer according to the manufacturer's instructions.

4. Run the engine to normalize underhood temperatures.

5. Check, and if necessary, reset the ignition timing.

6. Make certain that the choke plate is fully open.

7. Place the manual transmission in neutral; the automatic in Drive. Block the wheels.

8. Turn the solenoid adjusting screw in or out to obtain the specified idle speed. The idle speed is the higher of the two rpm figures on the underhood specifications sticker.

9. Disconnect the solenoid lead wire. Place the automatic transmission in neutral.

10. Turn the solenoid-off adjusting screw to obtain the solenoid off rpm. This is the lower of the two rpm figures on the underhood specifications sticker.

11. Connect the solenoid lead wire and open the throttle slightly to allow the solenoid plunger to extend.

12. Stop the engine, replace the air cleaner and connect the vacuum lines. Check the idle speed. Readjust if necessary with the air cleaner installed.

1977–82

1. Remove the air cleaner and disconnect and plug the vacuum lines.

2. Block the wheels, apply the parking brake, turn off all accessories, start the engine and run it to normalize underhood temperatures.

3. Check that the choke plate is fully open and connect a tachometer according to the manufacturer's instructions.

Motorcraft 2150 carburetor without solenoid

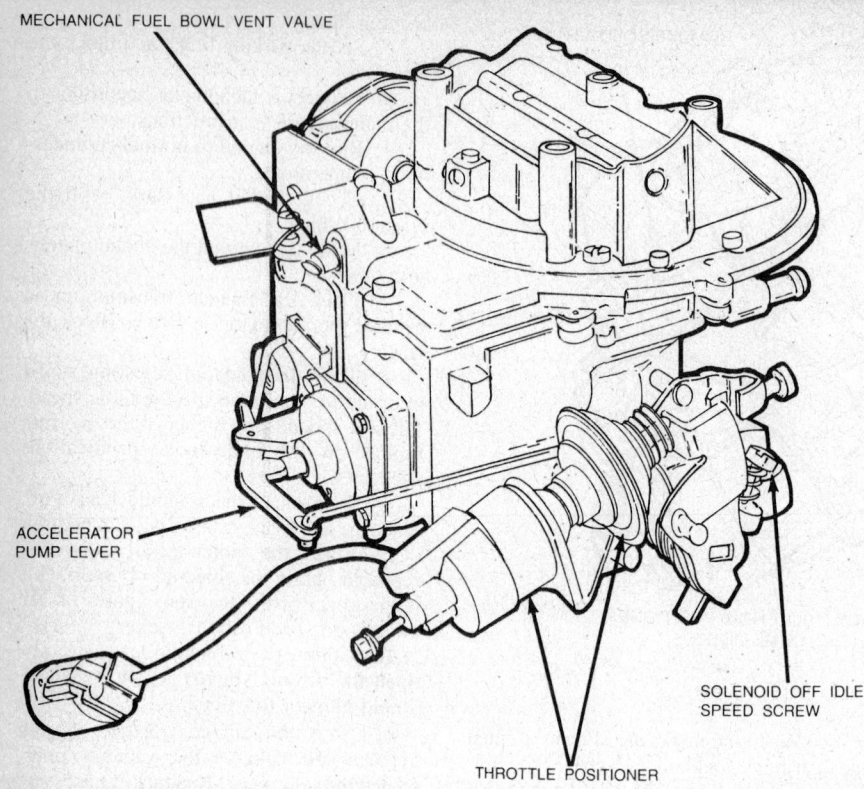

MECHANICAL FUEL BOWL VENT VALVE

ACCELERATOR PUMP LEVER

THROTTLE POSITIONER

SOLENOID OFF IDLE SPEED SCREW

Motorcraft 2150 carburetor with solenoid

4. Check the throttle stop positioner (TSP)-off speed as follows:

a. Collapse the plunger by forcing the throttle lever against it.

b. Place the transmission in neutral and check the engine speed. If necessary, adjust to specified TSP-Off speed with the throttle adjusting screw. See the underhood sticker.

5. Place the manual transmission in neutral; the automatic in Drive and make certain the TSP plunger is extended.

6. Turn the TSP until the specified idle speed is obtained.

7. Install the air cleaner and connect the vacuum lines. Check the idle speed. Adjust, if necessary, with the air cleaner on.

IDLE MIXTURE ADJUSTMENT

NOTE: For this procedure, Ford recommends a propane enrichment procedure. This requires special equipment not available to the general public. In lieu of this equipment the following procedure may be followed to obtain a satisfactory idle mixture.

1. Block the wheels, set the parking brake and run the engine to bring it to normal operating temperature.

2. Disconnect the hose between the emission canister and the air cleaner.

3. On engines equipped with the Thermactor air injection system, the routing of the vacuum lines connected to the dump valve will have to be temporarily changed. Mark them for reconnection before switching them.

4. For valves with one or two vacuum lines at the side, disconnect and plug the lines.

5. For valves with one vacuum line at the top, check the line to see if it is connected to the intake manifold or an intake manifold source such as the carburetor or distributor vacuum line. If not, remove and plug the line at the dump valve and connect a temporary length of vacuum hose from the dump valve fitting to a source of intake manifold vacuum.

6. Remove the limiter caps from the mixture screws by CAREFULLY cutting them with a sharp knife.

7. Place the transmission in neutral and run the engine at 2500 rpm for 15 seconds.

8. Place the automatic transmission in Drive; the manual in neutral.

9. Adjust the idle speed to the higher of the two figures given on the underhood sticker.

10. Turn the idle mixture screws to obtain the highest possible rpm, leaving the screws in the leanest position that will maintain this rpm.

11. Repeat steps 7 thru 10 until further adjustment of the mixture screws does not increase the rpm.

12. Turn the screws in until the lower of the two idle speed figures is reached. Turn the screws in ¼ turn increments each to insure a balance.

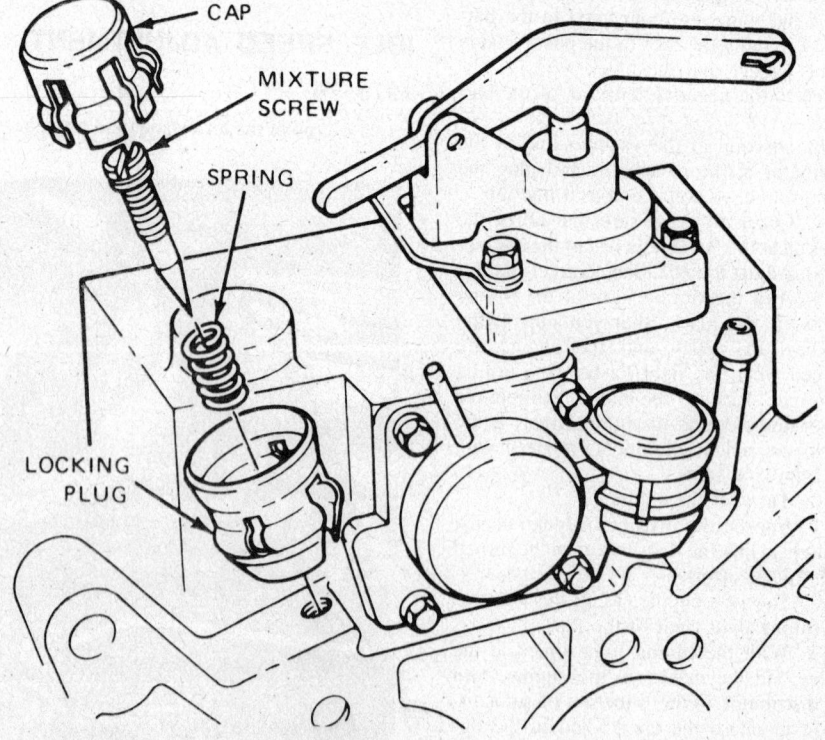

CAP

MIXTURE SCREW

SPRING

LOCKING PLUG

Some 1980 and later models have 2-piece metal plugs in place of the plastic limiter caps on the idle mixture adjusting screws. These caps should be carefully removed before attempting any adjustments.

13. Turn the engine off and remove the tachometer. Reinstall all equipment.

NOTE: Rough idle, that cannot be corrected by normal service procedures on 1977 and later models, may be caused by leakage between the EGR valve body and diaphragm. To determine if this is the cause,

1. Tighten the EGR bolts to 15 ft. lbs. Connect a vacuum gauge to the intake manifold.

2. Lift to exert a sideways pressure on the diaphragm housing. If the idle changes or the reading on the vacuum gauge varies, replace the EGR valve.

ENGINE ELECTRICAL

Distributor

REMOVAL

1. Remove the coil wire from the distributor cap terminal.
2. Remove the distributor cap.
3. Disconnect the vacuum advance line at the distributor.
4. Note the position of the rotor and scribe a mark on the distributor body, indicating its position. Scribe two more marks, one on the body of the distributor and another on the engine block, indicating the position of the distributor body in relation to the engine block. All of the scribe marks should be made in line with each other, starting with the metal tip of the rotor and ending with the mark on the engine block. These marks will be used as guides when installing the distributor in the correctly timed engine (not disturbed).
5. Remove the retaining bolt and lockwasher which hold the distributor in the engine.
6. Lift the distributor out of the engine block. Note that the rotor will turn slightly as it is removed. This is due to the curvature of the distributor drive gear. Take this into consideration in aligning the scribe marks, when installing the distributor.

INSTALLATION (ENGINE NOT DISTURBED)

1. Insert the distributor shaft into the engine. Align the marks on the distributor body with the metal tip of the rotor and the mark made on the engine block. Make sure that the vacuum advance diaphragm is pointed in the same direction as it was pointed originally. This will be done au-

tomatically if the marks on the engine and the distributor are aligned properly.

2. Install the distributor lockbolt and clamp. Leave the screw loose enough that you can turn the distributor with your hand.

3. Connect the distributor primary wire and install the distributor cap. Secure the distributor cap with the spring clips.

4. Install the spark plug wires. Make certain that the wires are pressed all the way into the top of the distributor cap and firmly onto the spark plugs.

INSTALLATION (ENGINE DISTURBED)

If the engine has been disturbed, (i.e., crankshaft turned) while the distributor has been removed or the alignment marks were not drawn, it will be necessary to initially time the engine. Follow the procedure given below:

1. Place the No. 1 piston at TDC of the compression stroke. To determine this, remove the spark plug from the No. 1 cylinder and the high-tension coil wire from the distributor cap. Place your thumb over the spark plug hole while the engine is cranked. You will feel air being forced out of the cylinder as the piston comes up on its compression stroke. As soon as you feel this, stop cranking the engine. The final positioning adjustment for the No. 1 piston is to align the TDC timing mark with the pointer or notch in the crankshaft pulley.

2. Lightly oil the distributor housing, where the distributor mounts on the cylinder block.

3. Install the distributor so that the rotor, which is mounted on the shaft, points toward the No. 1 spark plug terminal of the distributor cap. To facilitate this operation, place the distributor cap on the distributor body in its normal position and make a mark on the body of the distributor just below the No. 1 spark plug terminal tower. Make sure that the metal tip of the rotor is pointing toward the mark when the distributor is installed.

4. When the distributor shaft has reached the bottom of the hole, move the rotor back and forth slightly until the drive gears of the distributor shaft and the camshaft mesh and the distributor assembly slides down into place.

5. When the distributor is correctly installed, the breaker point contacts should be in such a position that they are just ready to break contact with each other. This is accomplished by rotating the distributor body after it has been installed in the engine.

6. Install the distributor retaining plate and lockbolt.

7. Install the spark plug into the No. 1 cylinder spark plug hole and continue from Step 3 of the distributor installation procedure for engines that have not been disturbed.

Alternator

ALTERNATOR PRECAUTIONS

To prevent damage to the alternator and regulator, the following precautions should be taken when working with the electrical system.

1. Never reverse the battery connections.

2. Booster batteries for starting must be connected properly—positive-to-positive and negative-to-negative.

3. Disconnect the battery cables before using a fast charger; the charger has a tendency to force current through the diodes in the opposite direction for which they were designed. This burns out the diodes.

4. Never use a fast charger as a booster for starting the vehicle.

5. Never disconnect the voltage regulator while the engine is running.

6. Avoid long soldering times when replacing diodes or transistors. Prolonged heat is damaging to AC generators.

7. Do not use test lamps of more than 12 volts (V) for checking diode continuity.

8. Do not short across or ground any of the terminals on the AC generator.

9. The polarity of the battery, generator, and regulator must be matched and considered before making any electrical connections within the system.

10. Never operate the alternator on an open circuit. Make sure that all connections within the circuit are clean and tight.

11. Disconnect the battery terminals when performing any service on the electrical system. This will eliminate the possibility of accidental reversal of polarity.

12. Disconnect the battery ground cable if arc welding is to be done on any part of the car.

REMOVAL AND INSTALLATION

While internal alternator repairs are possible, they require specialized tools and training. Therefore, it is advisable to replace a defective alternator, or have it repaired by a qualified shop.

1. Open the hood and disconnect the battery ground cable.

2. Remove the adjusting arm bolt.

3. Remove the alternator through-bolt. Remove the drive belt from the alternator pulley and lower the alternator.

4. Label all of the leads to the alternator so that you can install them correctly and disconnect the leads from the alternator.

5. Remove the alternator from the vehicle.

6. To install, reverse the above procedure.

Belt Tension Adjustment

The fan belt drives the alternator and water

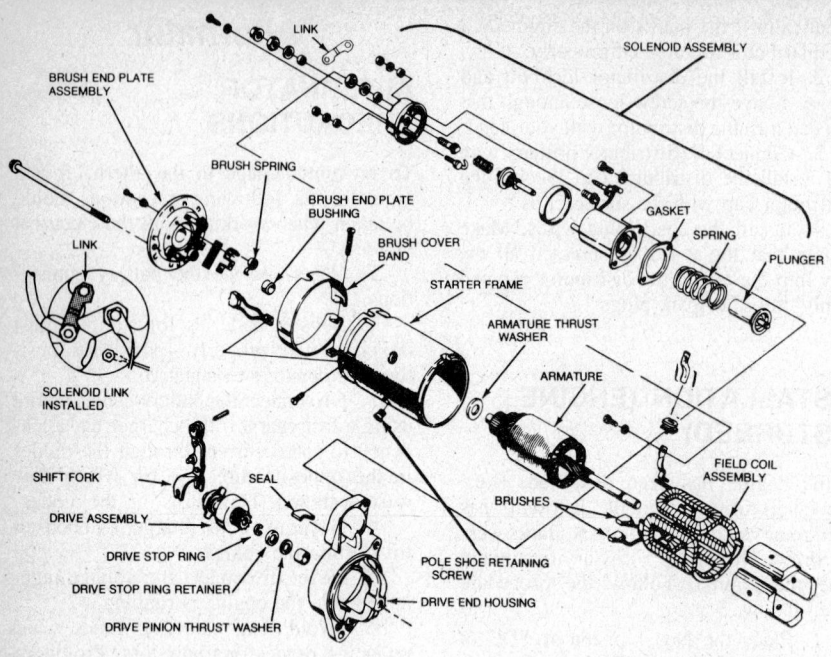

Solenoid actuated starter

pump. If the belt is too loose, it will slip and the alternator will not be able to produce its rated current. Also, the water pump will not operate efficiently and the engine could overheat.

Check the tension of the belt by pushing your thumb down on the longest span of the belt, midway between the pulleys. Belt deflection should be approximately ½ in.

To adjust belt tension, proceed as follows:

1. Loosen the alternator mounting bolt and the adjusting arm bolts.
2. Apply pressure on the alternator front housing only, moving the alternator away from the engine to tighten the belt. Do not apply pressure to the rear of the cast aluminum housing of an alternator; damage to the housing could result.
3. Tighten the alternator mounting bolt and the adjusting arm bolts when the correct tension is reached.

Regulator

The alternator regulator has been designed to control the charging system's rate of charge. The electromechanical regulator is calibrated at the factory and is not adjustable.

REMOVAL AND INSTALLATION

1. Disconnect the positive terminal of the battery. On some models it may be necessary to move the battery.
2. Disconnect all of the electrical leads at the regulator. Label them as removed, so that you can replace them in the correct order on the replacement unit.

3. Remove all of the hold-down screws, then remove the unit from the vehicle.
4. Install the new voltage regulator using the hold-down screws from the old one, or new ones if they are provided with the replacement regulator. Tighten the hold-down screws.
5. Connect all the leads to the new regulator.

Starter Motor

REMOVAL

Positive Engagement Type

1. Disconnect the positive battery terminal.
2. Raise the vehicle and disconnect the starter cable at the starter terminal.
3. Remove all of the starter attaching bolts that attach the starter to the bellhousing.
4. Remove the starter from the engine.
5. Install the starter in the reverse order of removal.

Solenoid Actuated Type—1976–77 With 460 Eng.

1. Disconnect the battery ground cable.
2. Raise the vehicle and disconnect the cables and wires at the starter solenoid.
3. Turn the front wheels to the right and remove the two bolts attaching the steering idler arm to the frame.
4. Remove the starter mounting bolts and remove the starter.
5. Install in the reverse order of removal.

STARTER DRIVE REPLACEMENT

1. Remove the cover of the starter drive's plunger lever arm, and the brush cover band. Remove the through-bolts, starter drive gear housing, and the return spring of the driver gear's actuating lever.
2. Remove the pivot pin which retains the starter gear plunger lever and remove the lever.
3. Remove the stop-ring retainer. Remove and discard the stop-ring which holds the drive gear to the armature shaft and then remove the drive gear assembly.

To install the drive gear assembly:
4. Lightly Lubriplate® the armature shaft splines and install the starter drive gear assembly on the shaft. Install a new stop-ring and stop-ring retainer.
5. Position the starter drive gear plunger lever to the frame and starter drive assembly.
6. Install the pivot pin.
7. Position the drive plunger lever return spring and the drive gear housing to the frame, then install and tighten the through-bolts. Be sure that the stop-ring retainer is properly seated in the drive housing.
8. Position the starter drive plunger lever cover and the brush cover band on the starter. Tighten the brush cover band retaining screw.

BRUSH REPLACEMENT

Replace the starter brushes when they are worn to ¼ in. Always install a complete set of new brushes.
1. Remove the starter from the truck.
2. Loosen and remove the brush cover band, gasket, and starter drive plunger lever cover. Remove the commutator brushes from their holders.
3. Remove the two through-bolts from the starter frame.
4. Remove the drive end housing and the plunger lever return spring.
5. Remove the starter drive plunger lever pivot pin and lever, and remove the armature.
6. Remove the brush end plate.
7. Remove the ground brush attaching screws from the frame and remove the brushes.
8. Cut the insulated brush leads from the field coils as close to the field connection as possible.
9. Clean and inspect the starter motor. Use a brush or air to clean the field coils, armature, commutator, armature shaft, brush end plate, and drive end housing. Wash all of the other parts in solvent and dry them.

Inspect the armature windings for broken or burned insulation and unsoldered connections.
10. Replace the brush end plate if the insulator between the field brush holder and

the end plate is cracked or broken.

11. Position the new insulated field brushes lead on the field coil connection. Position and crimp the clip provided with the brushes to hold the brush lead to the connection. Solder the lead, clip, and connection together.

12. Install the ground brush leads to the frame with the attaching screws.

13. Clean the commutator with 00 to 000 sandpaper.

14. Position the brush end plate to the starter frame, with the end plate boss in the frame slot.

15. Install the armature in the starter frame.

16. Install the starter drive gear plunger lever to the frame and starter drive assembly, and install the pivot pin.

17. Fill and drive end housing bearing bore about ¼ full with grease. Position the return spring on the plunger lever, and the drive end housing to the starter frame. Install the through-bolts and tighten them to 55–75 in. lbs. Be sure that the stop ring retainer is seated properly in the drive end housing.

18. Install the commutator brushes in the brush holders. Center the brush springs on the brushes.

19. Position the plunger lever cover and the brush cover band, with its gasket on the starter. Tighten the band attaching screw.

20. Connect the starter to the battery to check its operation. If it works, install it in the engine.

STARTER RELAY REPLACEMENT

The starter relay is mounted on the inside of the right wheel well. To replace it, disconnect the positive battery cable from the battery, disconnect all of the electrical leads from the relay and remove the relay from the fender well. Replace in the reverse order of removal.

ENGINE MECHANICAL

Engine Removal and Installation

Pick-ups

6-300

1. Drain the cooling system and the crankcase. Remove the hood and the air cleaner. Disconnect the positive battery cable.

2. Disconnect the heater hose from the water pump and coolant outlet housing. Disconnect the flexible fuel line from the fuel pump.

3. Remove the radiator.

4. Remove the fan, water pump pulley, and fan belt.

5. Disconnect the accelerator cable at the carburetor. Remove the throttle return spring. On trucks equipped with power brakes, disconnect the brake booster vacuum hose at the intake manifold. On trucks with automatic transmissions, disconnect the transmission kickdown rod at the bell-crank assembly.

6. Disconnect the exhaust pipe from the exhaust manifold.

7. Disconnect the body ground strap and the battery ground cable from the engine.

8. Disconnect the engine wiring harness at the ignition coil, the coolant temperature sending unit, and the oil pressure sending unit. Position the wiring harness out of the way.

9. Remove the alternator mounting bolts and position the alternator out of the way.

10. On a truck equipped with power steering, remove the power steering pump from the mounting brackets and move it to one side, leaving the lines attached.

11. Raise the truck on a hoist and remove the starter and automatic transmission filler tube bracket, if so equipped. Also, remove the rear engine plate upper right bolt.

12. On manual transmission equipped trucks, remove the flywheel housing lower attaching bolts and disconnect the clutch return spring.

13. On automatic transmission equipped trucks, remove the converter housing access cover assembly and remove the fly-wheel-to-converter attaching nuts. Secure the converter in the housing. Remove the transmission oil cooler lines from the retaining clip at the engine. Remove the lower converter housing-to-engine attaching bolts.

14. Remove the nut from each of the two front engine mounts.

15. Lower the vehicle and position a jack under the transmission and support it. Remove the remaining bellhousing-to-engine attaching bolts.

16. Attach the engine lifting device and raise the engine slightly and carefully pull it from the transmission. Lift the engine out of the vehicle.

To install the engine:

17. Place a new gasket on the muffler inlet pipe.

18. Carefully lower the engine into the truck. Make sure that the dowels in the engine block engage the holes in the bell-housing.

19. On manual transmission equipped trucks, start the transmission input shaft into the clutch disc. It may be necessary to adjust the position of the engine or transmission in order for the input shaft to enter the clutch disc. If necessary, turn the crankshaft until the input shaft splines mesh with the clutch disc splines.

20. On automatic transmission equipped trucks, start the converter pilot into the crankshaft. Unsecure the converter in the housing.

21. Install the bellhousing upper attaching bolts. Remove the jack supporting the transmission.

22. Lower the engine until it rests on the engine mounts. Remove the lifting device.

23. Install the engine mount nuts and tighten them to 45–55 ft. lbs.

24. Install the automatic transmission coil cooler lines bracket, if so equipped.

25. Install the remaining bellhousing attaching bolts.

26. Connect the clutch return spring, if so equipped.

27. Install the starter and connect the starter cable. Attach the automatic transmission fluid filler tube bracket, if so equipped.

28. On trucks with automatic transmissions, install the transmission oil cooler lines in the bracket at the cylinder block.

29. Connect the exhaust pipe to the exhaust manifold. Tighten the nuts to 25–35 ft. lbs.

30. Connect the engine ground strap and negative battery cable.

31. On a truck with an automatic transmission, connect the kick-down rod to the bellcrank assembly on the intake manifold.

32. Connect the accelerator linkage to the carburetor and install the return spring.

33. On a truck with power brakes, connect the brake booster vacuum line to the intake manifold.

34. Connect the coil primary wire, oil pressure and coolant temperature sending unit wires, fuel line, heater hoses, and the battery positive cable.

35. Install the alternator to its mounting bracket. Install the power steering pump to its bracket, if so equipped.

36. Install the water pump pulley, spacer, fan, and fan belt. Adjust the belt tension.

37. Install the radiator and connect the upper and lower radiator hoses to the radiator and engine. Connect the automatic transmission oil cooler lines, if so equipped.

38. Install and adjust the hood.

39. Fill the cooling system. Fill the crankcase.

40. Start the engine and check for leaks. Bleed the cooling system. Adjust the clutch pedal free-play or the automatic transmission control linkage. Install the air cleaner.

V6 and V8 Except 460

1. Drain the cooling system and crankcase. Remove the hood.

2. Disconnect the battery and alternator cables from the cylinder block.

3. Remove the air cleaner and intake duct assembly, plus the crankcase venti-

lation hose.

4. Disconnect the upper and lower radiator hoses, and, if so equipped, the automatic transmission oil cooler lines.

5. Remove the fan shroud and lay it over the fan. Remove the radiator and fan, shroud, fan, spacer, pulley, and belt.

6. Disconnect the alternator leads and the alternator adjusting bolts. Allow the alternator to swing down out of the way.

7. Disconnect the oil pressure sending unit lead from the sending unit.

8. Disconnect the fuel tank-to-pump fuel line at the fuel pump and plug the line.

9. Disconnect the accelerator linkage at the carburetor. Disconnect the automatic transmission kick-down rod and remove the return spring, if so equipped.

10. Disconnect the heater hoses from the water pump and intake manifold. Disconnect the temperature sending unit wire from the sending unit.

11. Remove the upper bellhousing-to-engine attaching bolts.

12. Disconnect the primary wire from the coil. Remove the wiring harness from the left rocker arm cover and position the wires out of the way. Disconnect the ground strap from the cylinder block.

13. Raise the front of the truck and disconnect the starter cable from the starter. Remove the starter.

14. Disconnect the exhaust pipe from the exhaust manifolds.

15. Disconnect the engine mounts from the brackets on the frame.

16. On trucks with automatic transmissions, remove the converter inspection plate and remove the torque converter-to-flywheel attaching bolts.

17. Remove the remaining bellhousing-to-engine attaching bolts.

18. Lower the vehicle and support the transmission with a jack.

19. Install an engine lifting device.

NOTE: On the V6, the intake manifold is aluminum. If a lifting device is attached to the manifold, all manifold bolts must be installed.

20. Raise the engine slightly and carefully pull it out from the transmission. Lift the engine out of the engine compartment.

21. Install the engine in the reverse order of removal. Make sure that the dowels in the engine block engage the holes in the bellhousing through the rear cover plate. If the engine hangs up after the transmission input shaft enters the clutch disc (manual transmission only), turn the crankshaft with the transmission in gear until the input shaft splines mesh with the clutch disc splines.

Tighten the exhaust pipe-to-exhaust manifold nuts to 25–35 ft. lbs., and all others as follows:

¼ in. 20—6–9 ft. lbs.
⁵⁄₁₆ in. 18—12–18 ft. lbs.
⅜ in. 16—22–32 ft. lbs.
⁷⁄₁₆ in. 14—45–57 ft. lbs.
½ in. 13—55–80 ft. lbs.
⁹⁄₁₆ in.—85–120 ft. lbs

460 V8

1. Remove the hood.

2. Drain the cooling system, the radiator and the cylinder block.

3. Disconnect the negative battery cable and remove the air cleaner assembly.

4. Disconnect the upper and lower radiator hoses and the transmission oil cooler lines from the radiator.

5. Remove the fan shroud from the radiator and remove the fan from the water pump. Remove the fan and shroud from the engine compartment.

6. Remove the upper support and remove the radiator.

7. If the truck is equipped with air conditioning, remove the compressor from the engine and position it out of the way. If the compressor must be removed completely, loosen the air conditioning service valves (disconnect) carefully to discharge the air conditioning system. Remove the compressor.

8. Disconnect the power steering pump from the engine, if so equipped, and position it to one side. Do not disconnect the fluid lines.

9. Disconnect the fuel pump inlet line from the pump and plug the line.

10. Remove the alternator drive belts and disconnect the alternator from the engine, positioning it aside.

11. Disconnect the ground cable from the right front corner of the engine.

12. Disconnect the heater hoses.

13. Remove the transmission fluid filler tube attaching bolt from the right-side valve cover and position the tube out of the way.

14. Disconnect all vacuum lines at the rear of the intake manifold.

15. Disconnect the speed control cable at the carburetor, if so equipped. Disconnect the accelerator rod and the transmission kickdown rod and secure them out of the way.

16. Disconnect the engine wiring harness at the connector on the fire wall.

17. Raise the vehicle and disconnect the exhaust pipes at the exhaust manifolds.

18. Disconnect the starter cable and remove the starter. Bring the starter forward and rotate the solenoid outward to remove the assembly.

19. Remove the access cover from the converter housing and remove the flywheel-to-converter attaching nuts. Remove the lower converter housing-to-engine attaching bolts.

20. Remove the engine mount through-bolts attaching the rubber insulators to the frame brackets.

21. Lower the vehicle and place a jack under the transmission to support it.

22. Remove the converter housing-to-engine block attaching bolts (left-side).

23. Disconnect the coil wire and remove the coil and bracket assembly from the intake manifold.

24. Attach the engine lifting device and carefully lift the engine from the engine compartment.

25. Install the engine in the reverse order of removal.

Tighten the alternator pivot bolt to 45–57 ft. lbs and all the rest of the nuts and bolts as is outlined in step 21 of the preceding "V8 except 460 Removal and Installation" procedure.

VANS

1975–82 300 Six-Cylinder

1. Take off the engine cover, drain the coolant, remove the air cleaner, and disconnect the battery.

2. Remove the bumper, grille, and gravel deflector.

3. Detach the upper radiator hose at the engine. Remove the alternator splash shield and detach the lower hose at the radiator. Remove the radiator and shroud, if any.

4. Disconnect the engine heater hoses and the alternator wires. Remove the power steering pump and support.

5. Disconnect and plug the fuel line at the pump.

6. Detach from the engine: distributor and gauge sending unit wires, brake booster hose, accelerator cable and bracket.

7. Disconnect the automatic transmission kickdown linkage at the bellcrank.

8. Remove the exhaust manifold heat deflector and unbolt the pipe from the manifold.

9. Disconnect the automatic transmission vacuum line from the intake manifold and from the junction. Remove the transmission dipstick tube support bolt at the intake manifold.

10. Remove the upper engine-to-transmission bolts.

11. Remove the starter. Remove the flywheel inspection cover. Remove the four automatic transmission torque converter nuts, then remove the front engine support nuts. Take off the oil filter.

12. Remove the rest of the transmission-to-engine fasteners, then lift the engine out from the engine compartment with a floor crane.

13. To replace the engine, lower it into place and start the mounting bolts. Install the upper transmission bolts, the converter nuts, and the lower transmission bolts. Tighten the mounting bolts. Replace all the items removed in the previous steps.

351W, 400, 460 V8 and 1979–82 302 V8

1. Take off the engine cover, drain the coolant, remove the air cleaner, and disconnect the battery. Remove the bumper, grille, and gravel deflector. Remove the upper grille support bracket, hood lock support, and air conditioning condenser upper mounting brackets.

2. With air conditioning, the system must be discharged to remove the condenser. Do not attempt to do this yourself, unless you are trained in air conditioning. Disconnect the lines at the compressor.

3. Remove the accelerator cable bracket and the heater hoses. Detach the radiator hoses and the automatic transmission cooler lines, if any. Remove the fan shroud, fan, and radiator.

4. Pivot the alternator in and detach the wires.

5. Remove the air cleaner, duct and valve, exhaust manifold shroud, and flex tube.

6. Disconnect the automatic transmission shift rod.

7. Disconnect the fuel and choke lines, detach the vacuum lines, and remove the carburetor and spacer.

8. Remove the oil filter. Detach the exhaust pipe from the manifold. Unbolt the automatic transmission tube bracket from the cylinder head. Remove the starter.

9. Remove the engine mount bolts. With automatic, remove the converter inspection cover and unbolt the converter from the flex plate.

10. Unbolt the engine ground cable and support the transmission.

11. Remove the power steering front bracket. Detach only one vacuum line at the rear of the intake manifold. Disconnect the engine wiring loom. Remove the speed control servo from the manifold. Detach the compressor clutch wire.

12. Install a lifting bracket to the intake manifold and attach a floor crane. Remove the transmission-to-engine bolts, making sure the transmission is supported. Remove the engine.

13. To install the engine, align the converter to the flex plate and the engine dowels to the transmission. With manual transmission, start the transmission shaft into the clutch disc. You may have to turn the crankshaft slowly with the transmission in gear. Install the transmission bolts, then the mounting bolts. Replace all the items removed in the previous steps.

BRONCO

302 V8 through 1977

REMOVAL

1. Drain the cooling system and the crankcase.

2. Disconnect the battery and alternator ground cables from the cylinder block

3. Remove the air cleaner and intake duct assembly including the crankcase ventilation hose.

4. Disconnect the radiator lower and upper hose at the radiator. If equipped with an automatic transmission disconnect the transmission oil cooler lines.

5. Remove the fan shroud and position it over the fan. Remove the radiator. Remove the fan shroud, fan spacer, belts and pulley.

6. Disconnect the wires at the alternator adjusting bolts and allow the alternator to swing down and out of the way.

7. Disconnect the oil pressure sending unit wire from the sending unit, and the flexible fuel line at the fuel tank line. Plug the fuel tank line. Disconnect the windshield wiper vacuum line at the fuel pump.

8. Disconnect the accelerator rod from the carburetor.

Disconnect the transmission shift rod and remove the retracting spring if so equipped.

9. Disconnect the heater hoses from the water pump and intake manifold. Disconnect the water temperature sending unit wire from the sending unit.

10. Remove the flywheel housing to engine upper bolts.

11. Disconnect the primary wire from the igniton coil. Remove the wire harness from the left rocker arm cover and position the wires out of the way. Disconnect the ground strap from the block.

12. Raise the front of the vehicle. Disconnect the starter cable from the starter.

Remove the starter and dust seal.

13. Disconnect the muffler inlet pipes from the exhaust manifolds. Disconnect the engine support insulators from the brackets on the frame underbody.

On a vehicle with automatic transmission remove the converter inspection plate. Remove the torque converter-to-flywheel attaching bolts.

Remove the remaining flywheel housing to engine bolts.

14. Lower the vehicle, and then support the transmission. Install the engine left lifting bracket on the front of the left cylinder head, and install the engine right lifting bracket at the rear of the right cylinder head. Then attach an engine lifting sling.

15. Raise the engine slightly and carefully pull it from the transmission. Carefully lift the engine out of the engine compartment so that the rear cover plate is not bent or other components damaged. Install the engine on a work stand.

INSTALLATION

1. Attach the engine lifting brackets and sling. Remove the engine from the work stand.

2. Lower the engine carefully into the engine compartment. Make sure the exhaust manifolds are properly aligned with the muffler inlet pipes and the dowels in the block are through the holes in the flywheel housing.

On a vehicle with manual transmission start the transmission main drive gear into the clutch disc. It may be necessary to adjust the position of the transmission in relation to the engine if the input shaft will not enter the clutch disc. If the engine hangs up after the shaft enters, turn the crankshaft slowly (transmission in gear) until the shaft splines mesh with the clutch disc splines.

3. Install the flywheel housing upper bolts.

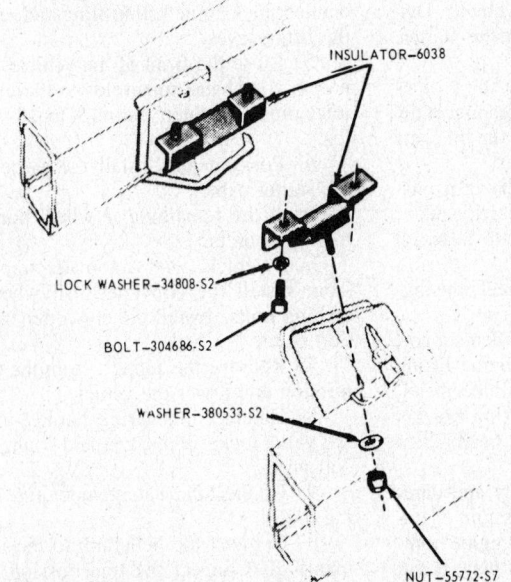

Engine front supports for the 1975–77 8-302

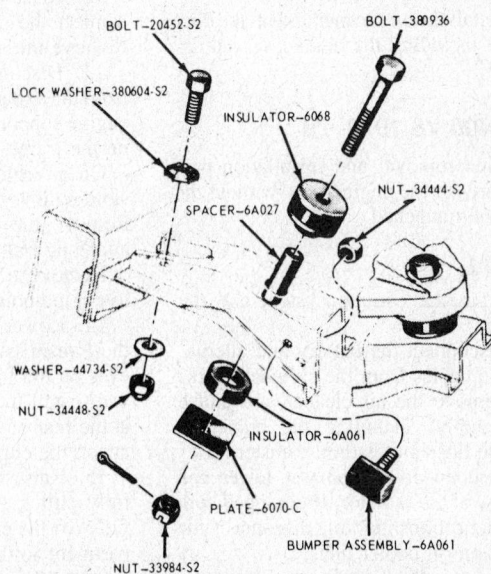

Engine rear supports for the 1975–77 8-302

4. Install the engine support insulator to bracket attaching nuts. Disconnect the engine lifting sling and remove the lifting brackets.

5. Raise the front of the vehicle. Connect both exhaust manifolds to the muffler inlet pipes. Tighten the nuts to 18–22 ft. lbs.

6. Position the dust seal and install the starter and the starter cable.

Install the remaining flywheel housing to engine bolts.

On a vehicle with automatic transmission install the converter to flywheel attaching bolts. Install the converter inspection plate.

7. Remove the support from the transmission and lower the vehicle.

8. Connect the wiring harness to the left valve rocker arm cover and connect the coil wire.

9. Connect the water temperature sending unit wire.

10. Connect the bellcrank to the intake manifold.

Connect the transmission shift rod and install the retracting spring.

Connect the accelerator rod.

11. Remove the plug from the fuel tank line and connect the fuel line and the oil pressure sending unit wire.

12. Install the pulley, belt, spacer and fan. Position the fan shroud over the fan.

13. Position the alternator and install the alternator bolts. Connect the alternator and the battery ground cables. Adjust the belt tension.

14. Install the radiator. Connect the radiator upper and lower hoses. Connect the transmission oil cooler lines if so equipped. Install the fan shroud.

15. Connect the heater hose at the water pump. Fill and bleed the cooling system. Fill the crankcase with the proper grade and quantity of oil.

16. Operate the engine at fast idle and check all gaskets and hose connections for leaks.

17. Install the air cleaner and intake duct assembly including the crankcase ventilation hose.

351M, 400 V8 1978–79

The engine removal and installation procedures are for the engine only without the transmission attached.

REMOVAL

1. Drain the cooling system and the crankcase.

2. Disconnect the battery and alternator ground cables from the cylinder block.

3. Remove the air cleaner and intake duct assembly, including the crankcase ventilation hose and carbon canister hose.

4. Disconnect the radiator lower and upper hose at the radiator. If equipped with an automatic transmission, disconnect the transmission oil cooler lines.

5. Remove the fan shroud and position it over the fan. Remove the radiator. Re-

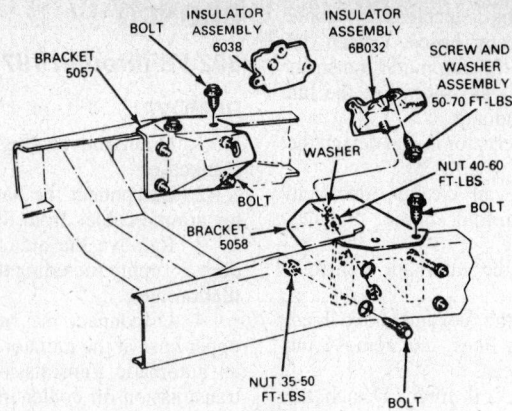

Engine front supports for the 1975–79 8-351M, 400

move the fan shroud, fan spacer, belts and pulley.

6. Disconnect the wires at the alternator adjusting bolts and allow the alternator to swing down and out of the way.

7. Disconnect the oil pressure sending unit wire from the sending unit, and the flexible fuel line at the fuel tank line. Plug the fuel tank line.

8. Disconnect the accelerator cable from the carburetor. Disconnect the transmission kickdown rod and remove the retracting spring if so equipped.

9. Disconnect the heater hoses from the water pump and intake manifold. Disconnect the water temperature sending unit wire from the sending unit.

10. Remove the flywheel housing-to-engine upper bolts.

11. Disconnect the primary wire from the ignition coil. Remove the wire harness from the left rocker arm cover and position the wires out of the way. Disconnect the ground strap from the cylinder block.

12. Raise the front of the vehicle. Disconnect the starter cable from the starter. Remove the starter.

13. Disconnect the muffler inlet pipes from the exhaust manifolds. Disconnect the engine support insulators from the brackets on the frame underbody.

On a vehicle with automatic transmission, remove the converter inspection plate. Remove the torque converter-to-flywheel attaching bolts.

Remove the remaining flywheel housing-to-engine bolts.

14. Lower the vehicle, and then support the transmission. Install the engine lifting eyes on the front of the left cylinder head, and install the engine right lifting bracket at the rear of the right cylinder head. Then attach the engine lifting sling.

15. Raise the engine slightly and carefully pull it from the transmission. Carefully lift the engine out of the engine compartment so that the rear cover plate is not bent or other components damaged. Install the engine on a workstand.

INSTALLATION

1. Attach the engine lifting brackets and sling. Remove the engine from the workstand.

2. Lower the engine carefully into the engine compartment. Make sure the dowels in the block are through the rear cover plate, then engage the holes in the flywheel housing.

On a vehicle with manual transmission, start the transmission main driveshaft into the clutch disc. It may be necessary to adjust the position of the transmission in relation to the engine if the input shaft will not enter the clutch disc. **If the engine hangs up after the shaft enters, turn the crankshaft slowly (transmission in gear) until the shaft splines mesh with the clutch disc splines.**

3. Install the flywheel housing upper bolts.

4. Install the engine support insulator-to-bracket washers and attaching nuts. Disconnect the engine lifting sling and remove the lifting eyes.

5. Raise the front of the vehicle. Connect both exhaust manifolds to the muffler inlet pipes. Tighten the nuts to 18–24 ft. lbs.

6. Position and install the starter and the starter cable.

Install the remaining flywheel housing-to-engine bolts.

On a vehicle with automatic transmission, install the converter-to-flywheel attaching bolts. Install the converter inspection plate.

7. Remove the support from the transmission and lower the vehicle.

8. Connect the wiring harness to the left valve rocker arm cover and connect the coil wire.

9. Connect the water temperature sending unit wire.

10. Connect the bellcrank to the intake manifold. Connect the transmission kickdown rod and install the retracting spring. Connect the accelerator cable.

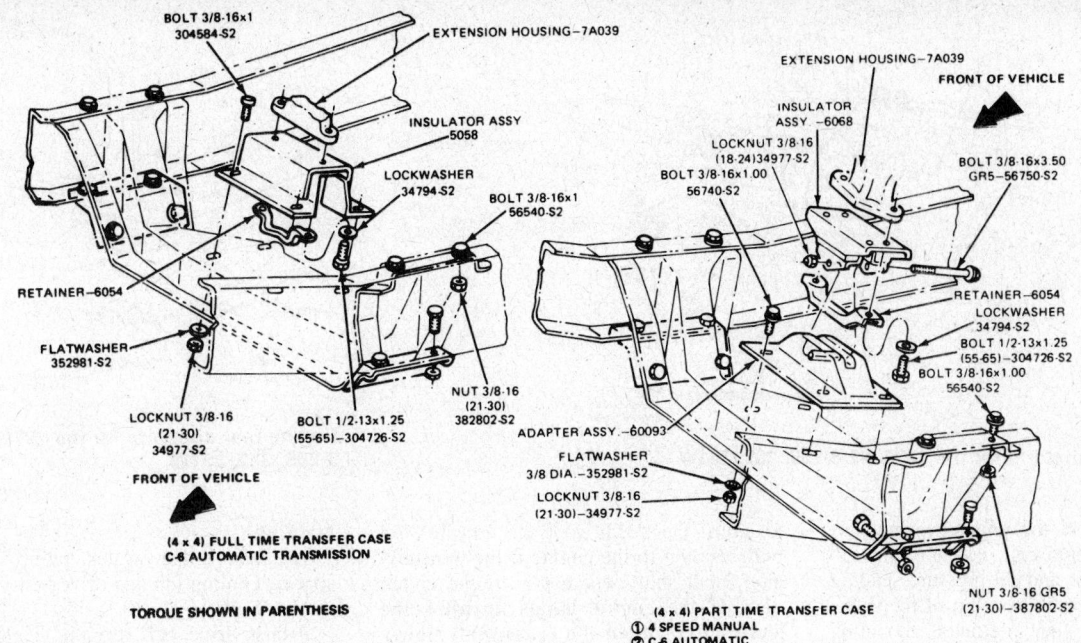

Engine rear supports for the 1975–79 8-351M, 400

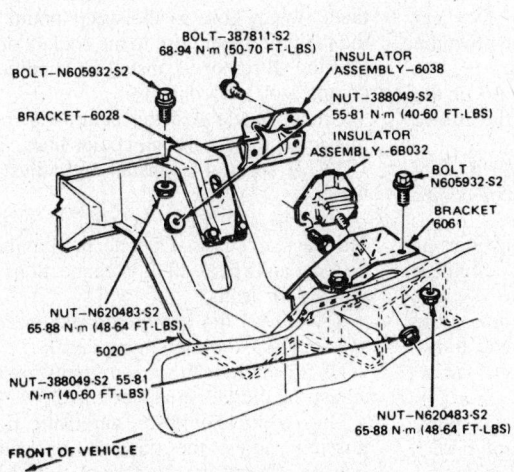

Engine front supports for the 1980–82 6-300

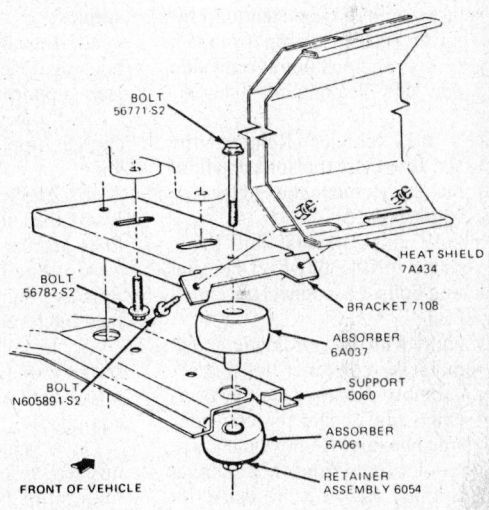

Engine rear supports for the 1980–82 6-300

11. Remove the plug from the fuel tank line and connect the fuel line and the oil pressure sending unit wire.

12. Install the pulley, belt, spacer and fan. Position the fan shroud over the fan.

13. Position the alternator and install the alternator bolts. Connect the alternator and the battery ground cables. Adjust the belt tension.

14. Install the radiator. Connect the radiator upper and lower hoses. Connect the transmission oil cooler lines if so equipped. Install the fan shroud.

15. Connect the heater hose at the water pump. Fill and bleed the cooling system. Fill the crankcase with the proper grade and quantity of oil.

16. Operate the engine at fast idle and check all gaskets and hose connections for leaks.

17. Install the air cleaner and intake duct assembly including the crankcase ventilation hose and carbon canister hose.

6-300 1980–82

The engine removal and installation procedures are for the engine only without the transmission attached.

— **CAUTION** —

Engine removal requires discharge of the air conditioning system. This job should be left to a professional mechanic!

REMOVAL

1. Drain the cooling system and the crankcase. Remove the hood. Remove the air cleaner. Remove air conditioner compressor and condenser.

2. Disconnect the battery ground cable. Disconnect the heater hose from the water pump and coolant outlet housing. Disconnect the flexible fuel line from the fuel pump.

3. Remove the radiator.

4. Remove the cooling fan, spacer, water pump pulley and fan drive belt.

5. Disconnect the accelerator cable and the choke cable at the carburetor. Remove the cable retracting spring.

On a vehicle with power brakes, disconnect the vacuum line at the intake manifold.

On a vehicle with an automatic transmission, disconnect the transmission kickdown rod at the bellcrank assembly.

6. Disconnect the exhaust manifold from the muffler inlet pipe. Disconnect the body ground stop and the battery ground cable at the engine.

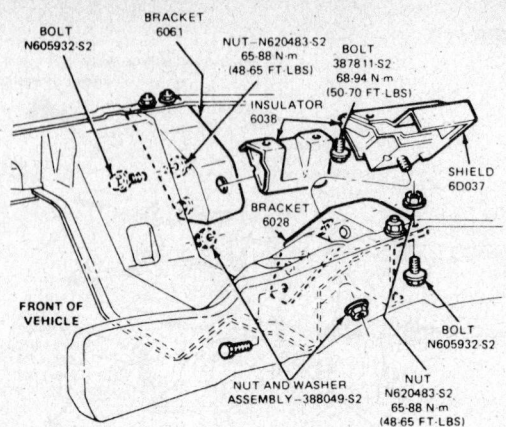

Engine front supports for the 1978–82 8-255, 302, 351W

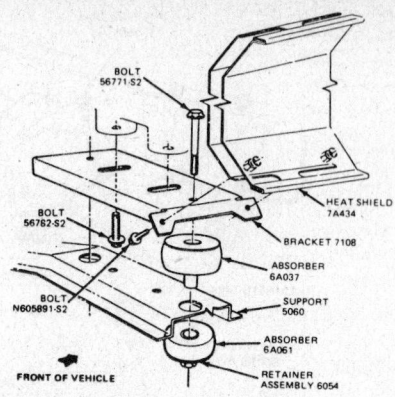

Engine rear supports for the 1978–82 8-255, 302, 351W

7. Disconnect the engine wiring harness at the ignition coil, coolant temperature sending unit and oil pressure sending unit. Position the harness out of the way.

8. Remove the alternator mounting bolts and position the alternator out of the way, leaving the wires attached.

On a vehicle with power steering, remove the power steering pump from the mounting brackets and position it right side up and to one side, leaving the lines attached.

9. Raise the vehicle. Remove the starter (and the automatic transmission fluid filler tube bracket). Remove the engine rear plate upper right bolt.

On a vehicle with a manual shift transmission, remove all the flywheel housing lower attaching bolts. Disconnect the clutch retracting spring.

On a vehicle with an automatic transmission, remove the converter housing access cover assembly. Remove the flywheel-to-converter nuts and secure the converter assembly in the housing. Remove the transmission oil cooler lines from the retaining clip at the engine. Remove the converter housing-to-engine lower attaching bolts.

10. Lower the vehicle and position a transmission jack under the transmission to support it. Remove the remaining flywheel or converter housing-to-engine bolts.

11. Attach the engine lifting sling. Raise the engine slightly and carefully pull it from the transmission. Lift the engine out of the chassis.

INSTALLATION

1. Place a new gasket on the muffler inlet pipe.

2. Lower the engine carefully into the chassis. Make sure the dowels in the block engage the holes in the flywheel or converter housing.

On a vehicle with an automatic transmission, start the converter pilot into the crankshaft. Remove the retainer securing the converter in the housing.

On a vehicle with a manual-shift transmission, start the transmission input shaft into the clutch disc. It may be necessary to adjust the position of the transmission with relation to the engine if the transmission input shaft will not enter the clutch disc. **If the engine hangs up after the shaft enters, turn the crankshaft slowly (with the transmission in gear) until the shaft splines mesh with the clutch disc splines.**

3. Install the converter or flywheel housing upper attaching bolts. Remove the jack supporting the transmission.

4. Lower the engine until it rests on the engine support(s) and remove the lifting sling.

5. Tighten the nuts to 40–60 ft. lbs. Install the automatic transmission oil cooler lines bracket.

6. Install the remaining converter or flywheel housing attaching bolts. Connect the clutch return spring.

7. Install the starter and connect the starter cable. Attach the automatic transmission fluid filler tube bracket, (if so equipped).

On a vehicle with an automatic transmission, install the transmission oil cooler lines in the bracket at the cylinder block.

8. Install the exhaust manifold to muffler inlet pipe lockwashers and nuts. Tighten the nuts to 25–38 ft. lbs.

9. Connect the engine ground strap and the battery ground cable.

10. On a vehicle with an automatic transmission, connect the kickdown rod to the bellcrank assembly on the intake manifold.

Connect the accelerator linkage to the carburetor and install the retracting spring. Connect the choke cable to the carburetor and hand throttle, if so equipped.

On a vehicle with power brakes, connect the brake vacuum line to the intake manifold.

11. Connect the coil primary wire, oil pressure and coolant temperature sending unit wires, flexible fuel line, heater hoses and the battery positive cable.

12. Install the alternator on the mounting bracket.

On a vehicle with power steering, install the power steering pump on the mounting brackets.

13. Install the water pump pulley, spacer, cooling fan and drive belt. Tighten the fan bolts to 12–18 ft. lbs.

Adjust drive belt tension. Tighten the alternator, power steering pump and air compressor mounting bolts.

14. Install the radiator. Connect the radiator lower hose to the water pump and the radiator upper hose to the coolant outlet housing. If removed, install air conditioner compressor and condenser.

On a vehicle with an automatic transmission, connect the oil cooler lines.

15. If applicable, install and adjust the hood.

16. Fill and bleed the cooling system. Fill the crankcase. Operate the engine at fast idle and check all hose connections and gaskets for leaks.

17. Adjust the carburetor idle speed to specifications on the engine decal.

On a vehicle with standard transmission, adjust the clutch pedal free travel.

On a vehicle with an automatic transmission, adjust the transmission control linkage. Check the fluid level and add as required to bring it to the proper level on the oil indicator.

18. Install the air cleaner.

302, 351W 1980–82

The engine removal and installation procedures are for the engine only without the transmission attached.

CAUTION

This procedure requires discharge of the air conditioning system. This job is best left to a professional mechanic!

REMOVAL

1. Drain the cooling system and the crankcase. Remove hood.

2. Disconnect the battery and alternator ground cables from the cylinder block.

3. Remove the air cleaner and intake duct assembly, including the crankcase ventilation hose and carbon cannister hose.

4. Disconnect the radiator lower and

upper hose at the radiator. If equipped with an automatic transmission, disconnect the transmission oil cooler lines.

5. If so equipped, discharge the A/C system and remove the A/C condenser. Disconnect A/C lines at the compressor.

6. Remove the fan shroud and position it over the fan. Remove the radiator. Remove the fan shroud, fan spacer, belts and pulley.

7. Remove the alternator bolts and allow the alternator to swing down and out of the way.

8. Disconnect the oil pressure sending unit wire from the sending unit, and the flexible fuel line at the fuel tank line. Plug the fuel tank line. Disconnect evaporative emission hoses at the evaporative canister.

9. Disconnect the accelerator cable from the carburetor. Disconnect speed control linkages if so equipped. Disconnect the transmission kickdown rod and remove the retracting spring if so equipped. Disconnect power brake booster vacuum hose, if so equipped.

10. Disconnect the heater hoses from the water pump and intake manifold. Disconnect the water temperature sending unit wire from the sending unit.

11. Remove the flywheel housing-to-engine upper bolts.

12. Disconnect the primary wire from the ignition coil. Remove the wire harness from the left rocker arm cover and position the wires out of the way. Disconnect the ground strap from the cylinder block.

13. Raise the front of the vehicle. Disconnect the starter cable from the starter. Remove the starter.

14. Disconnect the muffler inlet pipes from the exhaust manifolds. Disconnect the engine support insulators from the brackets on the frame underbody.

On a vehicle with automatic transmission, remove the converter inspection plate. Remove the torque converter-to-flywheel attaching bolts.

Remove the remaining flywheel housing-to-engine bolts.

15. If so equipped, disconnect A/C compressor magnetic clutch load wire.

16. Lower the vehicle, and then support the transmission. Install the engine lifting brackets on the front of the left cylinder head, and install the engine right lifting bracket at the rear of the right cylinder head. Then attach an engine lifting sling.

17. Raise the engine slightly and carefully pull it from the transmission. Carefully lift the engine out of the engine compartment so that the rear cover plate is not bent or other components damaged. Install the engine on a workstand.

INSTALLATION

1. Attach the engine lifting brackets and sling. Remove the engine from the workstand.

2. Lower the engine carefully into the engine compartment. Make sure the dowels in the block are through the rear cover plate,

then engage the holes in the flywheel housing.

On a vehicle with manual transmission, start the transmission main driveshaft into the clutch disc. It may be necessary to adjust the position of the transmission in relation to the engine if the input shaft will not enter the clutch disc. **If the engine hangs up after the shaft enters, turn the crankshaft slowly (transmission in gear) until the shaft splines mesh with the clutch disc splines.**

3. Install the flywheel housing upper bolts.

4. Install the engine support insulator-to-bracket washers and attaching nuts. Disconnect the engine lifting sling and remove the lifting eyes.

5. Raise the front of the vehicle. Connect both exhaust manifolds to the muffler inlet pipes. Tighten the nuts to 18–24 ft. lbs.

6. Position and install the starter and the starter cable.

7. Install the remaining flywheel housing-to-engine bolts.

8. On a vehicle with automatic transmission, install the converter-to-flywheel attaching bolts. Install the converter inspection plate.

9. Remove the support from the transmission and lower the vehicle.

10. If so equipped, connect the A/C compressor magnetic clutch lead.

11. Connect the wiring harness to the left valve rocker arm cover and connect the coil wire.

12. Connect the water temperature sending unit wire.

13. Connect the bellcrank to the intake manifold. Connect the transmission shift rod and install the retracting spring. Connect the accelerator rod and speed control linkage, if so equipped.

14. Remove the plug from the fuel tank line and connect the fuel line and the oil pressure sending unit wire. Reconnect evaporative emission hoses at the evaporative canister.

15. Install the pulley, belt, spacer and fan. Position the fan shroud over the fan.

16. Position the alternator and install the alternator bolts. Connect the alternator and the battery ground cables. Adjust the belt tension.

17. If so equipped, connect two A/C lines to the A/C compressor.

18. Install the radiator. Connect the radiator upper and lower hoses. Connect the transmission oil cooler lines if so equipped. Install the fan shroud.

19. If so equipped, install the A/C condenser to the radiator.

20. Connect the heater hose at the water pump. Fill and bleed the cooling system. Fill the crankcase with the proper grade and quantity of oil. Connect the power brake booster vacuum hose, if so equipped.

21. Operate the engine at fast idle and check all gaskets and hose connections for leaks.

22. Install the air cleaner and intake duct assembly including the crankcase ventilation hose and carbon canister hose.

23. Adjust idle speed and mixture to specifications on engine decal.

24. Evacuate and charge the A/C System (if so equipped).

25. Install hood.

Cylinder Head

REMOVAL AND INSTALLATION

6-300

1. Drain the cooling system. Remove the air cleaner. Remove the oil filler tube. Disconnect the battery cable at the cylinder head.

2. Disconnect the muffler inlet pipe at the exhaust manifold. Pull the muffler inlet pipe down. Remove the gasket.

3. Disconnect the accelerator rod or cable retracting spring. Disconnect the choke control cable if applicable and the accelerator rod at the carburetor.

4. Disconnect the transmission kickdown rod. Disconnect the accelerator linkage at the bellcrank assembly.

5. Disconnect the fuel inlet line at the fuel filter hose, and the distributor vacuum line at the carburetor. Disconnect other vacuum lines as necessary for accessibility and identify them for proper connection.

6. Remove the radiator upper hose at the coolant outlet housing.

7. Disconnect the distributor vacuum line at the distributor. Disconnect the carburetor fuel inlet line at the fuel pump. Remove the lines as an assembly.

8. Disconnect the spark plug wires at the spark plugs and the temperature sending unit wire at the sending unit.

9. Grasp the PCV vent hose near the PCV valve and pull the valve out of the grommet in the valve rocker arm cover. Disconnect the PCV vent hose at the hose fitting in the intake manifold spacer and remove the vent hose and PCV valve.

10. Disconnect the carburetor air vent tube and remove the valve rocker arm cover.

11. Remove the valve rocker arm shaft assembly. Remove the pushrods in sequence so that they can be identified and reinstalled in their original positions.

12. Remove the cylinder head bolts and remove the cylinder head. Do not pry between the cylinder head and the block as the gasket surfaces may be damaged.

To install the cylinder head:

1. Clean the head and block gasket surfaces. If the cylinder head was removed for a gasket change, check the flatness of the cylinder head and block.

2. Apply sealer to both sides of the new cylinder head gasket. Position the gasket on the cylinder block.

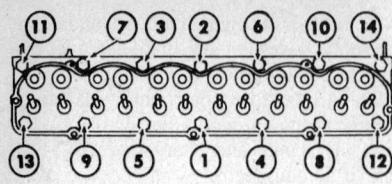

6-300 cylinder head bolt torque sequence

3. Install a new gasket on the flange of the muffler inlet pipe.

4. Lift the cylinder head above the cylinder block and lower it into position using two head bolts installed through the head as guides.

5. Coat the threads of the No. 1 and 6 bolts for the right-side of the cylinder head with a small amount of water-resistant sealer. Oil the threads of the remaining bolts. Install, but do not tighten, two bolts at the opposite ends of the head to hold the head and gasket in position.

6. The cylinder head bolts are tightened in 3 progressive steps. Torque them (in the proper sequence) to 55 ft. lbs., then 65 ft. lbs., and finally to 75 ft. lbs.

7. Apply Lubriplate® to both ends of the pushrods and install them in their original positions.

8. Install the valve rocker arm shaft assembly.

9. Adjust the valves, as necessary.

10. Install the muffler inlet pipe lockwashers and attaching nuts.

11. Connect the radiator upper hose at the coolant outlet housing.

12. Position the distributor vacuum line and the carburetor fuel inlet line on the engine. Connect the fuel line at the fuel filter hose and install a new clamp. Install the distributor vacuum line at the carburetor. Connect the accelerator linkage at the bellcrank assembly. Connect the transmission kickdown rod.

13. Connect the accelerator rod retracting spring. Connect the choke control cable (if applicable) and the accelerator rod at the carburetor.

14. Connect the distributor vacuum line at the distributor. Connect the carburetor fuel inlet line at the fuel pump. Connect all the vacuum lines using their previous identification for proper connection.

15. Connect the temperature sending unit wire at the sending unit. Connect the spark plug wires. Connect the battery cable at the cylinder head.

16. Fill the cooling system.

17. Install the valve rocker cover. Connect the carburetor air vent tube.

18. Connect the PCV vent hose at the carburetor spacer fitting. Insert the PCV valve with the vent hose attached, into the valve rocker arm cover grommet. Install the air cleaner, start the engine and check for leaks.

V6

1. Drain the cooling system.

2. Disconnect the cable from the battery negative terminal.

3. Remove the air cleaner assembly including air intake duct and heat tube.

4. Loosen the accessory drive belt idler. Remove the drive belt.

5. If the left cylinder head is being removed:

   a. If equipped with power steering, remove the pump mounting brackets' attaching bolts, leaving the hoses connected, place the pump/bracket assembly aside in a position to prevent the fluid from leaking out.

   b. If equipped with air conditioning, remove the mounting brackets' attaching bolts, leaving the hoses connected, position the compressor aside.

6. If the right cylinder head is being removed:

   a. Disconnect the thermactor diverter valve and hose assembly at the by-pass valve and downstream air tube.

   b. Remove the assembly.

   c. Remove the accessory drive idler.

   d. Remove the alternator.

   e. Remove the thermactor pump pulley. Remove the thermactor pump.

   f. Remove the alternator bracket.

   g. Remove the PCV valve.

7. Remove the intake manifold.

8. Remove the valve rocker arm cover attaching screws. Loosen the silicone rubber gasketing material by inserting a putty knife under the cover flange. Work the cover loose and remove.

— CAUTION —

The plastic rocker arm covers will break if excessive prying is applied.

9. Remove the exhaust manifold(s).

10. Loosen the rocker arm fulcrum attaching bolts enough to allow the rocker arm to be lifted off the pushrod and rotated to one side.

11. Remove the pushrods. The position of each rod should be installed in the original position during assembly.

12. Remove the cylinder head attaching bolts. Remove the cylinder head(s).

13. Remove and discard the old cylinder head gasket(s). Discard the cylinder head bolts.

14. Lightly oil all bolt and stud bolt threads before installation except those specifying special sealant.

15. Clean the cylinder head, intake manifold, valve rocker arm cover and cylinder head gasket surfaces. If the cylinder head was removed for a cylinder head gasket replacement, check the flatness of the cylinder head and block gasket surfaces.

16. Position new head gasket(s) on the cylinder block using the dowels for alignment.

17. Position the cylinder heads to the block.

18. Apply a thin coating of pipe sealant or equivalent to the threads of the short cylinder head bolts (nearest to the exhaust manifold). Do not apply sealant to the long

bolts. Lightly oil the cylinder head bolt flat washers. Install the flat washers and cylinder head bolts (Eight each side).

— CAUTION —

Always use new cylinder head bolts to assure a leak tight assembly. Torque retention with used bolts can vary, which may result in coolant or compression leakage at the cylinder head mating surface area.

19. Tighten the attaching bolts in sequence as follows:
bolts marked A, 47 ft. lbs.;
bolts marked B, 55 ft. lbs.;
bolts marked C, 63 ft. lbs.;
bolts marked D, 74 ft. lbs.
Back-off the attaching bolts 2–3 turns. Repeat tightening sequence.

NOTE: When the cylinder head attaching bolts have been tightened using the above sequential procedure, it is not necessary to retighten the bolts after extended engine operation. However, the bolts can be checked for tightness if desired.

20. Dip each pushrod end in heavy engine oil. Install the pushrods in their original position. For each valve rotate the crankshaft until the tappet rests on the heel (base circle) of the camshaft lobe.

21. Position the rocker arms over the pushrods, install the fulcrums, and tighten the fulcrum attaching bolts to 61–132 in. lbs.

— CAUTION —

Fulcrums must be fully seated in cylinder head and pushrods must be seated in rocker arm sockets prior to final tightening.

22. Lubricate all rocker arm assemblies with heavy engine oil. Finally tighten the fulcrum bolts to 19–25 ft. lbs. For final tightening, the camshaft may be in any position.

NOTE: If the original valve train components are being installed, a valve clearance check is not required. If a component has been replaced, perform a valve clearance check.

23. Install the exhaust manifold(s).

24. Apply a 1/8–3/16 inch bead of RTV silicone sealant to the rocker arm cover flange. Make sure the sealer fills the channel in the cover flange. The rocker arm cover must be installed within 15 minutes after the silicone sealer application. After this time, the sealer may start to set-up, and its sealing effectiveness may be reduced.

25. Position the cover on the cylinder head and install the attaching bolts. Note the location of the wiring harness routing clips and spark plug wire routing clip stud bolts. Tighten the attaching bolts to 36–60 in. lbs. torque.

26. Install the intake manifold.

27. Install the spark plugs, if necessary.

28. Connect the secondary wires to the

spark plugs.

29. Install the oil fill cap. If equipped with air conditioning, install the compressor mounting and support brackets.

30. On the right cylinder head:

a. Install the PCV valve.

b. Install the alternator bracket. Tighten attaching nuts to 30–40 ft. lbs.

c. Install the thermactor pump and pump pulley.

d. Install the alternator.

e. Install the accessory drive idler.

f. Install the thermactor diverter valve and hose assembly. Tighten the clamps securely.

31. Install the accessory drive belt and tighten to the specified tension.

32. Connect the cable to the battery negative terminal.

33. Fill the cooling system with the specified coolant.

------ CAUTION ------

This engine has an aluminum cylinder head and requires a special unique corrosion inhibited coolant formulation to avoid radiator damage.

34. Start the engine and check for coolant, fuel, and oil leaks.

35. Check and, if necessary, adjust the curb idle speed.

36. Install the air cleaner assembly including the air intake duct and heat tube.

V8 Except 460

1. Remove the intake manifolds and the carburetor as an assembly.

2. Remove the rocker arm cover(s).

3. If the right cylinder head is to be removed, loosen the alternator adjusting arm bolt and remove the alternator mounting bracket bolt and spacer. Swing the alternator down and out of the way. Remove the air cleaner inlet duct from the right cylinder head assembly. Remove the ignition coil on 360 and 390 V8s. On 351 and 400 remove the ground strap at the rear of the head.

If the left cylinder head is being removed, remove the bolts fastening the accelerator shaft assembly at the front of the cylinder head. On vehicles equipped with air conditioning, the system must be discharged and the compressor removed. The procedure is best left to an air conditioning specialist. Persons not familiar with A/C systems can be easily injured when working on the systems.

4. Disconnect the exhaust manifold(s) from the muffler inlet pipe(s).

5. Loosen the rocker arm stud nuts so that the rocker arms can be rotated to the side. Remove the pushrods and identify them so that they can be reinstalled in their original positions.

6. Remove the cylinder head bolts and lift the cylinder head from the block.

To install the cylinder head(s):

1. Clean the cylinder head, intake manifold, and the valve cover and head gasket

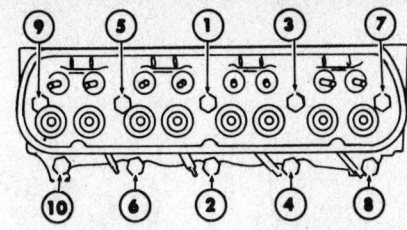

Cylinder head bolt torque sequence, all V8's

surfaces.

2. A specially treated composition head gasket is used. Do not apply sealer to a composition gasket. Position the new gasket over the locating dowels on the cylinder block. Then, position the cylinder head on the block and install the attaching bolts.

3. The cylinder head bolts are tightened in 3 progressive steps. Tighten all the bolts in the proper sequence to 50 ft. lbs., 60 ft. lbs., and finally to 70 ft. lbs. of torque on the 302 V8. On all V8s except the 302, 351M and 400 tighten to 70 ft. lbs., 80 ft. lbs., and finally to 90 ft. lbs. On 351M and 400 V8s, tighten to 70, 80 then 95–105 ft. lbs.

4. Clean the pushrods. Blow out the oil passage in the rods with compressed air. Check the pushrods for straightness. Never try to straighten a pushrod; always replace it.

5. Apply Lubriplate® to the ends of the pushrods and install them in their original positions.

6. Apply Lubriplate® to the rocker arms and their fulcrum seats and install the rocker arms. Adjust the valves.

7. Position a new gasket(s) on the muffler inlet pipe(s) as necessary. Connect the exhaust manifold(s) at the muffler inlet pipe(s).

8. If the right cylinder head was removed, install the alternator, ignition coil and air cleaner duct on the right cylinder head. Adjust the drive belt.

If the left cylinder head was removed, install the accelerator shaft assembly at the front of the cylinder head.

9. Clean the valve rocker arm cover and the cylinder head gasket surfaces. Place the new gaskets in the covers, making sure that the tabs of the gasket engage the notches provided in the cover. Install the compressor, evacuate, charge and leak test the system. Let an expert do this.

10. Install the intake manifold and related parts.

460 V8

1. Remove the intake manifold and carburetor as an assembly.

2. Disconnect the exhaust pipe from the exhaust manifold.

3. Loosen the air conditioning compressor drive belt, if so equipped.

4. Loosen the alternator attaching bolts and remove the bolt attaching the alternator

bracket to the right cylinder head.

5. Disconnect the air conditioning compressor from the engine and move it aside, out of the way. Do not discharge the air conditioning system, if possible.

6. Remove the bolts securing the power steering reservoir bracket to the left cylinder head. Position the reservoir and bracket out of the way.

7. Remove the valve rocker arm covers. Remove the rocker arm bolts, rocker arms, oil deflectors, fulcrums and pushrods in sequence so that they can be reinstalled in their original positions.

8. Remove the cylinder head bolts and lift the head and exhaust manifold off the engine. If necessary, pry at the forward corners of the cylinder head against the casting bosses provided on the cylinder block. Do not damage the gasket mating surfaces of the cylinder head and block by prying against them.

9. Remove all gasket material from the cylinder head and block. Clean all gasket material from the mating surfaces of the intake manifold. If the exhaust manifold was removed, clean the mating surfaces of the cylinder head and exhaust manifold. Apply a thin coat of graphite grease to the cylinder head exhaust port areas and install the exhaust manifold.

10. Position two long cylinder head bolts in the two rear lower bolt holes of the left cylinder head. Place a long cylinder head bolt in the rear lower bolt hole of the right cylinder head. Use rubber bands to keep the bolts in position until the cylinder heads are installed on the cylinder block.

11. Position new cylinder head gaskets on the cylinder block dowels. Do not apply sealer to the gaskets, heads, or block.

12. Place the cylinder heads on the block, guiding the exhaust manifold studs into the exhaust pipe connections. Install the remaining cylinder head bolts. The longer bolts go in the lower row of holes.

13. Tighten all the cylinder head attaching bolts in the proper sequence in three stages: 75 ft. lbs., 105 ft. lbs., and finally, to 135 ft. lbs. When this procedure is used, it is not necessary to retorque the heads after extended use.

14. Make sure that the oil holes in the pushrods are open and install the pushrods in their original positions. Place a dab of Lubriplate® to the ends of the pushrods before installing them.

15. Lubricate and install the valve rockers. Make sure that the pushrods remain seated in their lifters.

16. Connect the exhaust pipes to the exhaust manifolds.

17. Install the intake manifold and carburetor assembly. Tighten the intake manifold attaching bolts in the proper sequence to 25–30 ft. lbs.

18. Install the air conditioning compressor to the engine.

19. Install the power steering reservoir to the engine.

20. Apply oil-resistant sealer to one side

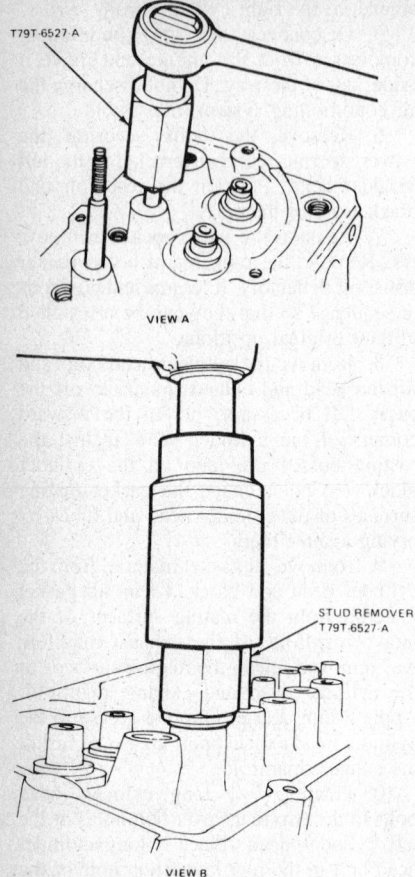

Removing the rocker arm stud on the 6-300

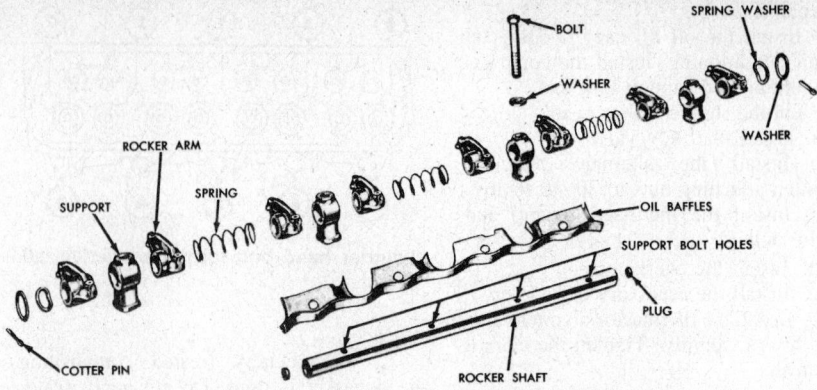

8-360, 390 valve rocker arm shaft

of the new valve cover gaskets and lay the cemented side in place in the valve covers. Install the covers.

21. Install the alternator on the right cylinder head and adjust the alternator drive belt tension.

22. Adjust the air conditioning compressor drive belt tension.

23. Fill the radiator with coolant.

24. Start the engine and check for leaks.

Rocker Studs

REMOVAL AND INSTALLATION

6-300, 8-255 and 8-302

Rocker arm studs which are broken or have damaged threads may be replaced with standard studs. Studs which are loose in the cylinder head must be replaced with oversize studs which are available for service. The amount of oversize and diameter of the studs are as follows:

0.006 in. oversize—0.3774–0.7781 in.
0.010 in. oversize—0.3814–0.3821 in.
0.015 in. oversize—0.3864–0.3871 in.

A tool kit for replacing the rocker studs is available and contains a stud remover and two oversize reamers: one for 0.006

in. and one for 0.015 in. oversize studs. For 0.010 in. oversize studs, use reamer tool T66P-6A527-B. To press the replacement studs into the cylinder head, use the stud replacer tool T69P-6049-D. Use the smaller reamer tool first when boring the hole for oversize studs.

1. Position the sleeve of the rocker arm stud remover over the stud with the bearing end down. When working on a 302 V8, cut the threaded part of the stud off with a hacksaw. Thread the puller into the sleeve and over the stud until it is fully bottomed. Hold the sleeve with a wrench and rotate the puller clockwise to remove the stud.

An alternate method of removing the rocker studs without the special tool is to put spacers over the stud until just enough threads are left showing at the top so a nut can be screwed onto the top of the rocker arm stud and get a full bite. Turn the nut clockwise until the stud is removed, adding spacers under the nut as necessary.

NOTE: If the rocker stud was broken off flush with the stud boss, use an easy-out tool to remove the broken off part of the stud from the cylinder head.

2. If a loose rocker arm stud is being replaced, ream the stud bore for the selected oversize stud.

NOTE: Keep all metal particles away from the valves.

3. Coat the end of the new stud with Lubriplate®. Align the stud and installer with the stud bore and tap the sliding driver until it bottoms. When the installer contacts the stud boss, the stud is installed to its correct height.

Valve Rocker Arm Shaft Assembly

REMOVAL AND INSTALLATION

360 390 Cu. In. Engine

1. Remove air cleaner, disconnect spark plug leads and remove leads from

bracket on the valve rocker cover.

2. Remove crankcase ventilation hose from rocker cover, then remove rocker cover. On left rocker cover the wiring harness must be removed.

3. On right side, start at No. 4 cylinder (rearmost) and loosen the support bolts in sequence, two turns at a time. Remove the shaft assembly and baffle plate after all the bolts have been loosened. The same procedure is followed on the left bank, except that the bolt-loosening sequence starts with the No. 5 cylinder (foremost).

--- CAUTION ---

The above bolt-loosening procedure must be followed to avoid damage to the rocker arm shaft.

4. To install, apply Lubriplate® to the pad end of the rocker arms, to the tip of the valve stems and to both ends of the pushrods.

5. Rotate engine to 45 degrees *past* No. 1 cylinder TDC.

6. With the pushrods in place, position rocker arm shaft assembly and baffle plate on the cylinder head such that *oil holes are on the bottom and identification notch is down and toward the front on the right bank and toward the rear on the left bank.* Tighten support bolts finger tight.

7. On the right bank, start at No. 4 cylinder and tighten the support bolts two turns at a time in sequence (4-3-2-1) until the supports are fully in contact with the cylinder head. Then tighten the support bolts to 40–45 ft. lbs. torque. The same procedure is followed by the left valve rocker arm shaft support bolts, starting with the No. 5 cylinder. This procedure allows time for the hydraulic lifter leakdown and thus prevents damage to pushrods, valves and rocker arms.

8. Check valve clearances and adjust if necessary.

9. Install rocker cover, using new gaskets and sealer.

10. Tighten cover retaining bolts to 10–12 ft. lbs., wait two minutes, then tighten to the same torque again.

11. Install crankcase ventilation regulator valve and hose(s), connect spark plug

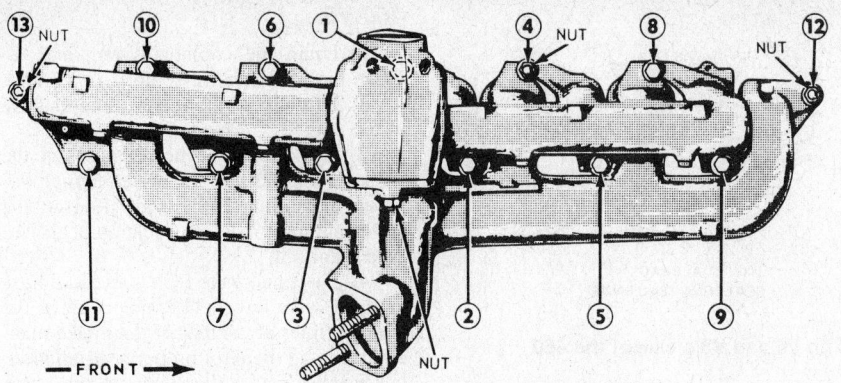

6-300 manifold bolt tightening sequence

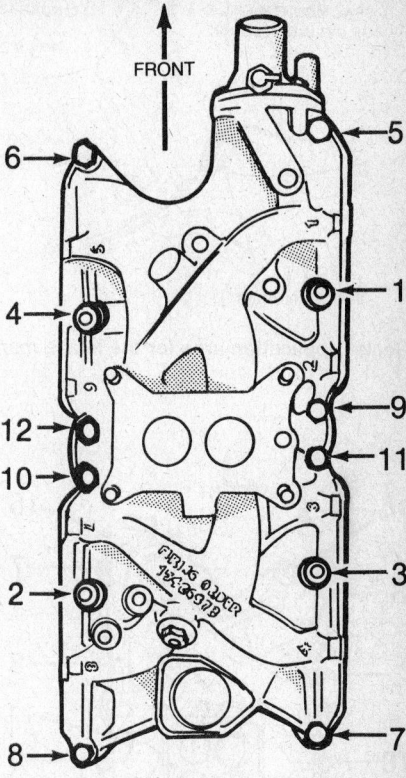

8-255, 302, 351W intake manifold bolt tightening sequence

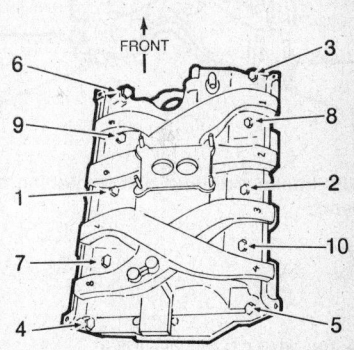

8-360, 390 intake manifold bolt tightening sequence

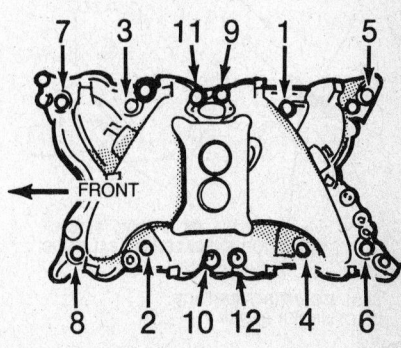

8-351M, 400 intake manifold bolt tightening sequence

wires and crankcase vent hose, and install air cleaner.

Intake Manifold

REMOVAL AND INSTALLATION

6-300

The intake and exhaust manifolds on these engines are known as combination manifolds and are serviced as a unit.

1. Remove the air cleaner. Disconnect the choke cable at the carburetor. Disconnect the accelerator cable or rod at the carburetor. Remove the accelerator retracting spring.

2. On a vehicle with automatic transmission, remove the kick-down rod-retracting spring. Remove the accelerator rod bellcrank assembly.

3. Disconnect the fuel inlet line and the distributor vacuum line from the carburetor.

4. Disconnect the muffler inlet pipe from the exhaust manifold.

5. Disconnect the power brake vacuum line, if so equipped.

6. Remove the bolts and nuts attaching the manifolds to the cylinder head. Lift the manifold assemblies from the engine. Remove and discard the gaskets.

7. To separate the manifolds, remove the nuts joining the intake and exhaust manifolds.

8. Clean the mating surfaces of the cylinder head and the manifolds.

9. If the intake and exhaust manifolds have been separated, coat the mating surfaces lightly with graphite grease and place the exhaust manifold over the studs on the intake manifold. Install the lockwashers and nuts. Tighten them finger tight.

10. Install a new intake manifold gasket.

11. Coat the mating surfaces lightly with graphite grease. Place the manifold assemblies in position against the cylinder head. Make sure that the gaskets have not become dislodged. Install the attaching washers, bolts and nuts. Tighten the attaching nuts

and bolts in the proper sequence to 26 ft. lbs. If the intake and exhaust manifolds were separated, tighten the nuts joining them.

12. Position a new gasket on the muffler inlet pipe and connect the inlet pipe to the exhaust manifold.

13. Connect the crankcase vent hose to the intake manifold inlet tube and position the hose clamp.

14. Connect the fuel inlet line and the distributor vacuum line to the carburetor.

15. Connect the accelerator cable to the carburetor and install the retracting spring. Connect the choke cable to the carburetor.

16. On a vehicle with an automatic transmission, install the bellcrank assembly and the kick-down rod retracting spring. Adjust the transmission control linkage.

17. Install the air cleaner.

V8 Except 460

1. Drain the cooling system, remove the air cleaner and the intake duct assembly.

2. Disconnect the accelerator rod from the carburetor and remove the accelerator retracting spring. Disconnect the automatic transmission kick-down rod at the carburetor, if so equipped.

3. Disconnect the high-tension lead and all other wires from the ignition coil.

4. Disconnect the spark plug wires from the spark plugs by grasping the rubber boots and twisting and pulling at the same time. Remove the wires from the brackets on the rocker covers. Remove the distributor cap and spark plug wire assembly.

5. Remove the carburetor fuel inlet line and the distributor vacuum line from the carburetor.

6. Remove the distributor lockbolt and remove the distributor and vacuum line. See "Distributor Removal and Installation."

7. Disconnect the upper radiator hose from the coolant outlet housing and the water temperature sending unit wire at the sending unit. Remove the heater hose from the intake manifold.

8. Loosen the clamp on the water pump bypass hose at the coolant outlet housing

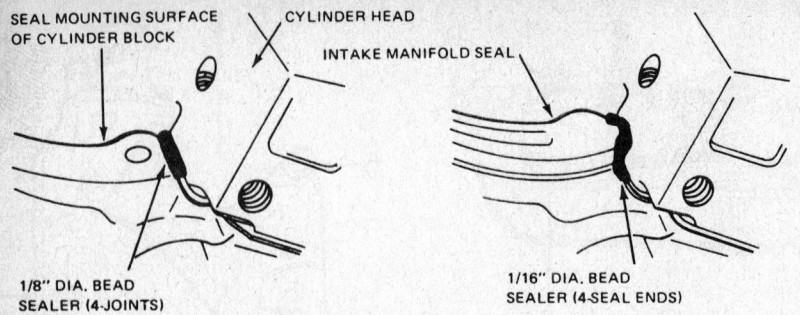

Sealer application area for the intake manifold on V6 and V8's except the 460

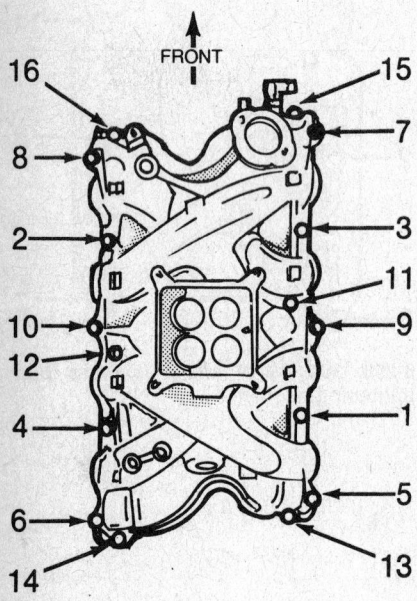

8-460 intake manifold bolt tightening sequence

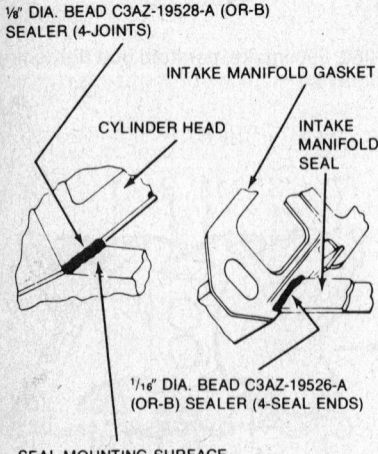

RTV sealer application area for the intake manifold on the 8-460

and slide the hose off the outlet housing.

9. Disconnect the PCV hose at the rocker cover.

10. If the engine is equipped with the Thermactor exhaust emission control system, remove the air pump to cylinder head air hose at the air pump and position it out of the way. Also remove the air hose at the backfire suppressor valve. Remove the air hose bracket from the valve rocker arm cover and position the air hose out of the way.

11. On the 360, 390, V8s, remove the rocker arm shafts and pushrods. The pushrods must be reinstalled in their original positions.

12. Remove the intake manifold and carburetor as an assembly. It may be necessary to pry the intake manifold from the cylinder head. Remove all traces of the intake manifold-to-cylinder head gaskets and the two end seals from both the manifold and the other mating surfaces of the engine.

Installation is as follows:

1. Clean the mating surfaces of the intake manifold, cylinder heads and block with laquer thinner or similar solvent. Apply a ⅛ in. bead of silicone-rubber RTV sealant at the points shown in the accompanying diagram.

─────── CAUTION ───────

Do not apply sealer to the waffle portions of the seals as the sealer will rupture the end seal material.

─────────────────────

2. Position new seals on the block and press the seal locating extensions into the holes in the mating surfaces.

3. Apply a 1/16 in. bead of sealer to the outer end of each manifold seal for the full length of the seal (4 places). As before, do not apply sealer to the waffle portion of the end seals.

NOTE: This sealer sets in about 15 minutes, depending on brand, so work quickly but carefully. DO NOT DROP ANY SEALER INTO THE MANIFOLD CAVITY. IT WILL FORM AND SET AND PLUG THE OIL GALLERY.

4. Position the manifold gasket onto the block and heads with the alignment notches under the dowels in the heads. Be sure gasket holes align with head holes.

5. Install the manifold and related equipment in reverse order of removal.

460 V8

1. Drain the cooling system and remove the air cleaner assembly.

2. Disconnect the upper radiator hose at the engine.

3. Disconnect the heater hoses at the intake manifold and the water pump. Position them out of the way. Loosen the water pump by-pass hose clamp at the intake manifold.

4. Disconnect the PCV valve and hose at right valve cover. Disconnect all of the vacuum lines at the rear of the intake manifold and tag them for proper reinstallation.

5. Disconnect the wires at the spark plugs, and remove the wires from the brackets on the valve covers. Disconnect the high-tension wire from the coil and remove the distributor cap and wires as an assembly.

6. Disconnect all of the distributor vacuum lines at the carburetor and vacuum control valve and tag them for proper installation. Remove the distributor and vacuum lines as an assembly.

7. Disconnect the accelerator linkage at the carburetor. Remove the speed control linkage bracket, if so equipped, from the manifold and carburetor.

8. Remove the bolts holding the accelerator linkage bellcrank and position the linkage and return springs out of the way.

9. Disconnect the fuel line at the carburetor.

10. Disconnect the wiring harness at the coil battery terminal, engine temperature sending unit, oil pressure sending unit, and other connections as necessary. Disconnect the wiring harness from the clips at the left valve cover and position the harness out of the way.

11. Remove the coil and bracket assembly.

12. Remove the intake manifold attaching bolts and lift the manifold and carburetor from the engine as an assembly. It may be necessary to pry the manifold away from the cylinder heads. Do not damage the gasket sealing surfaces.

Installation is as follows:

1. Clean the mating surfaces of the intake manifold, cylinder heads and block with laquer, thinner or similar solvent. Apply a ⅛ in. bead of silicone-rubber RTV sealant at the points shown in the accompanying diagram.

─────── CAUTION ───────

Do not apply sealer to the waffle portions of the seals as the sealer will rupture the end seal material.

─────────────────────

2. Position new seals on the block and press the seal locating extensions into the holes in the mating surfaces.

3. Apply a 1/16 in. bead of sealer to the outer end of each manifold seal for the full length of the seal (4 places). As before, do not apply sealer to the waffle portion of the end seals.

NOTE: This sealer sets in about 15

minutes, depending on brand, so work quickly but carefully. **DO NOT DROP ANY SEALER INTO THE MANIFOLD CAVITY. IT WILL FORM AND SET AND PLUG THE OIL GALLERY.**

4. Position the manifold gasket onto the block and heads with the alignment notches under the dowels in the heads. Be sure gasket holes align with head holes.

5. Install the manifold and related equipment in reverse order of removal.

Exhaust Manifold

REMOVAL AND INSTALLATION

6-300

The intake and exhaust manifold on these engines are known as combination manifolds and are serviced as a unit. See "Intake Manifold Removal and Installation."

V6 and V8

1. Remove the air cleaner if the manifold being removed has the carburetor heat stove attached to it. On 351 and 400 remove the oil filter.

2. Remove the dipstick tube assembly on the 360 and 390 V8s. On the 302 V8, just remove the bracket. On 351 and 400 V8 vehicles with a column mounted automatic transmission lever, disconnect the selector lever cross-shaft for clearance. On 1981–82 models, disconnect the EGO sensor.

3. Disconnect the power steering pump bracket from the cylinder block and move it out of the way on 360, and 390, V8s.

4. Disconnect the exhaust pipe or catalytic converter from the exhaust manifold. Remove and discard the donut gasket.

5. Remove the exhaust manifold attaching screws and remove the manifold from the cylinder head.

6. Disconnect the EGR downtube.

7. Install the exhaust manifold in the reverse order of removal. Apply a light coat of graphite grease to the mating surface of the manifold. Install and tighten the attaching bolts, starting from the center and working to both ends alternately. Tighten to the proper specifications.

Timing Gear Cover

REMOVAL AND INSTALLATION

6-300

1. Drain the cooling system and disconnect the radiator upper hose at the coolant outlet elbow and remove the two upper radiator retaining bolts.

2. Raise the vehicle and drain the crankcase.

3. Remove the splash shield and the automatic transmission oil cooling lines, if so equipped, then remove the radiator.

4. Loosen and remove the fan belt, fan and pulley.

5. Use a gear puller to remove the crankshaft pulley damper.

6. Remove the cylinder front cover retaining bolts and gently pry the cover away from the block. Remove the gasket.

7. Drive out the old seal with a pin punch from the rear of the cover. Clean out the recess in the cover.

8. Coat the new seal with grease and drive it into the cover until it is fully seated. Check the seal to make sure that the spring around the seal is in the proper position.

9. Clean the cylinder front cover and the gasket surface of the cylinder block. Apply an oil-resistant sealer to the new front cover gasket and install the gasket onto the cover.

10. Install the cylinder front cover onto the engine.

NOTE: Trim away the exposed portion of the old oil pan gasket flush with the front of the engine block. Cut and position the required portion of a new gasket to the oil pan and apply sealer to both sides.

11. Lubricate the hub of the crankshaft damper pulley with Lubriplate to prevent damage to the seal during installation or on initial starting of the engine.

12. Install and assemble the remaining components in the reverse order of removal, starting from Step 4. Start the engine and check for leaks.

V6 and V8 Except 460

1. Drain the cooling system and the crankcase.

2. Disconnect the upper and lower radiator hoses from the water pump, transmission oil cooler lines from the radiator, and remove the radiator.

3. Disconnect the heater hose from the water pump. Slide the water pump by-pass hose clamp toward the water pump.

4. Loosen the alternator pivot bolt and the bolt which secures the alternator adjusting arm to the water pump. Position the alternator out of the way.

5. Remove the power steering pump and air conditioning compressor from their mounting brackets, if so equipped.

6. Remove the bolts holding the fan shroud to the radiator, if so equipped. Remove the fan, spacer, pulley and drive belts.

7. Remove the crankshaft pulley from the crankshaft damper. Remove the damper attaching bolt and washer and remove the damper with a puller. On the 360 and 390 V8, remove the crankshaft sleeve with a puller.

8. Disconnect the fuel pump outlet line at the fuel pump. Disconnect the vacuum inlet and outlet lines from the fuel pump. Remove the fuel pump attaching bolts and

lay the pump to one side with the fuel inlet line still attached.

9. Remove the oil level dipstick and the bolt holding the dipstick tube to the exhaust manifold on the 302 V8.

10. Remove the oil pan-to-cylinder front cover attaching bolts. Use a sharp, thin cutting blade to cut the oil pan gasket flush with the cylinder block. Remove the front cover and water pump as an assembly.

11. Discard the front cover gasket.

12. See Steps 7 and 8 of the front cover oil seal replacement procedure for 6 cylinder engines.

13. Assemble the engine in the reverse order of disassembly, referring to steps 9, 10 and 12 of the procedure for six-cylinder engines. It may be necessary to force the cover downward slightly to compress the pan gasket and align the attaching bolt holes in the cover and the cylinder block. This operation can be accomplished by inserting a dowel or drift in the holes and aligning the cover with the block.

460 V8

1. Drain the cooling system and crankcase.

2. Remove the radiator shroud and fan.

3. Disconnect the upper and lower radiator hoses, and the automatic transmission oil cooler lines from the radiator.

4. Remove the radiator upper support and remove the radiator.

5. Loosen the alternator attaching bolts and air conditioning compresser idler pulley and remove the drive belts with the water pump pulley. Remove the bolts attaching the compressor support to the water pump and remove the bracket (support), if so equipped.

6. Remove the crankshaft pulley from the vibration damper. Remove the bolt and washer attaching the crankshaft damper and remove the damper with a puller. Remove the Woodruff key from the crankshaft.

7. Loosen the by-pass hose at the water pump, and disconnect the heater return tube at the water pump.

8. Disconnect and plug the fuel inlet and outlet lines at the fuel pump, and remove the fuel pump.

9. Remove the bolts attaching the front cover to the cylinder block. Cut the oil pan seal flush with the cylinder block face with a thin knife blade prior to separating the cover from the cylinder block. Remove the cover and water pump as an assembly. Discard the front cover gasket and oil pan seal.

10. Transfer the water pump if a new cover is going to be installed. Clean all of the gasket sealing surfaces on both the front cover and the cylinder block.

11. Coat the gasket surface of the oil pan with sealer. Cut and position the required sections of a new seal on the oil pan. Apply sealer to the corners.

12. Coat the gasket surfaces of the cylinder block and cover with sealer and position the new gasket on the block.

13. Position the front cover on the cylinder block. Use care not to damage the seal and gasket or mislocate them.

14. Coat the front cover attaching screws with sealer and install them.

NOTE: It may be necessary to force the front cover downward to compress the oil pan seal in order to install the front cover attaching bolts. Use a screw-

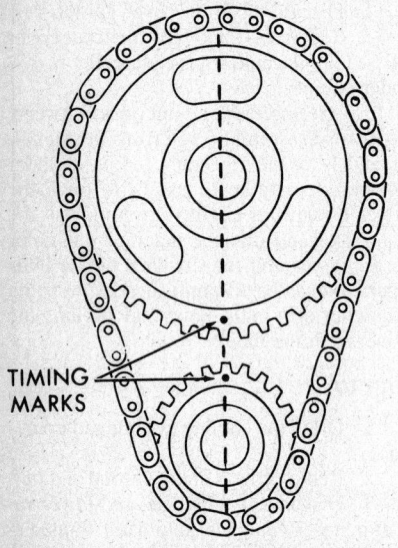

V6 and V8 valve timing mark alignment

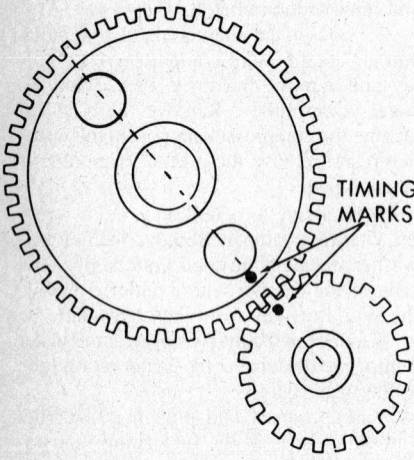

6-300 valve timing mark alignment

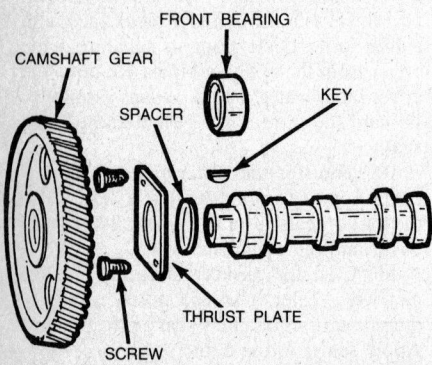

Front end of the camshaft and related components

driver or drift to engage the cover screw holes through the cover and pry downward.

15. Assemble and install the remaining components in the reverse order of removal. Tighten the front cover bolts to 15–20 ft. lbs., the water pump attaching screws to 12–15 ft. lbs., the crankshaft damper to 70–90 ft. lbs., the crankshaft pulley to 35–50 ft. lbs., fuel pump to 19–27 ft. lbs., the oil pan bolts to 9–11 ft. lbs. for the ⁵⁄₁₆ in. screws and to 7–9 ft. lbs. for the ¼ in. screws, and the alternator pivot bolt to 45–57 ft. lbs.

TIMING CHAIN OR GEAR COVER OIL SEAL REPLACEMENT

1. Remove the front cover (timing chain cover) from the engine.
2. Drive the seal out of the front cover from the front with small drift.
3. Clean the seal recess in the cover.
4. Coat the new seal with grease and drive it into place gently with a block of wood and a hammer until it is fully seated.
5. Install the front cover.

Timing Chain

REMOVAL AND INSTALLATION

V6 and V8

1. Remove the front cover.
2. Rotate the crankshaft counterclockwise to take up the slack on the left-side of the chain.
3. Establish a reference point on the cylinder block and measure from this point to the chain.
4. Rotate the crankshaft in the opposite direction to take up the slack on the right-side of the chain.
5. Force the left-side of the chain out with your fingers and measure the distance between the reference point and the chain. The timing chain deflection is the difference between the two measurements. If the deflection exceeds ½ in., replace the timing chain and sprockets.

To replace the timing chain and sprockets:

6. Turn the crankshaft until the timing marks on the sprockets are aligned vertically.
7. Remove the camshaft sprocket retaining screw and remove the fuel pump eccentric and washers.
8. Alternately slide both of the sprockets and timing chain off the crankshaft and camshaft until free of the engine.
9. Position the timing chain on the sprockets so that the timing marks on the sprockets are aligned vertically. Alternately slide the sprockets and chain onto the crankshaft and camshaft sprockets.

10. Install the fuel pump eccentric washers and attaching bolt on the camshaft sprocket. Tighten to 40–45 ft. lbs.
11. Install the front cover.

Timing Gears

REMOVAL AND INSTALLATION

6-300

1. Drain the cooling system and remove the front cover.
2. Crank the engine until the timing marks on the camshaft and crankshaft gears are aligned.
3. Use a gear puller to remove both of the timing gears.
4. Before installing the timing gears, be sure that the key and spacer are properly installed. Align the gear key way with the key and install the gear on the camshaft. Be sure that the timing marks line up on the camshaft and the crankshaft gears and install the crankshaft gear.
5. Install the front cover, and assemble the rest of the engine in the reverse order of disassembly. Fill the cooling system.

Camshaft

REMOVAL AND INSTALLATION

6-300

1. Remove the front cover, align the timing marks, and remove the timing gears, timing chain and related parts as stated before.
2. Remove the cylinder head as previously outlined.

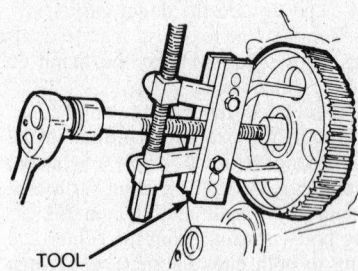

6-300 camshaft removal

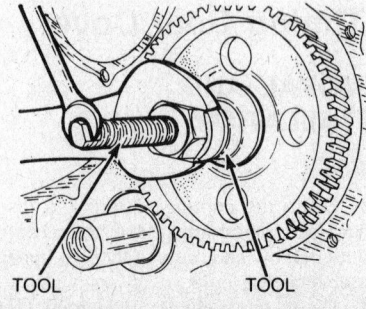

6-300 camshaft sprocket installation

3. Disconnect the distributor primary wire at the ignition coil. Loosen the distributor lockbolt and remove the distributor.

4. Disconnect and plug the fuel inlet line at the fuel pump. Remove the fuel pump and gasket.

5. Remove the valve tappets with a magnet. Note that the tappets must be replaced in the same positions from which they are removed.

6. Remove the oil level dipstick.

7. Remove the headlight doors and disconnect the light ground wires and the screws. Disconnect the headlights and parking lights.

8. Remove the grille and hood lock as an assembly.

9. Remove the camshaft thrust plate.

10. Carefully withdraw the camshaft from the engine.

11. In preparation for installing the camshaft, clean the passage that feeds the rocker arm shaft by blowing compressed air into the opening in the block. Oil the camshaft journals and apply Lubriplate to all of the camshaft lobes. If a new camshaft is being installed, the spacer and dowel from the old camshaft must be used. Carefully slide the camshaft through the bearings.

12. Assemble the engine in the reverse order of disassembly.

V6 and V8

1. Remove the intake manifold and valley pan, if so equipped.

2. Remove the rocker covers, and either remove the rocker arm shafts or loosen the rockers on their pivots and remove the pushrods. The pushrods must be reinstalled in their original positions.

3. Remove the valve lifters in sequence with a magnet. They must be replaced in their original positions.

4. Remove the timing gear cover and timing chain and sprockets.

5. In addition to the radiator and air conditioning condenser, if so equipped, it may be necessary to remove the front grille assembly and the hood lock assembly to gain the necessary clearance to slide the camshaft out the front of the engine.

6. Remove the camshaft thrust plate attaching screws and carefully slide the camshaft out of its bearing bores. Use extra caution not to scratch the bearing journals with the camshaft lobes.

7. Install the camshaft in the reverse order of removal. Coat the camshaft with engine oil liberally before installing it. Slide the camshaft into the engine very carefully so as not to scratch the bearing bores with the camshaft lobes. Install the camshaft thrust plate and tighten the attaching screws to 9–12 ft. lbs. Measure the camshaft end-play. If the end-play is more than 0.009 in., replace the thrust plate. Assemble the remaining components in reverse order of removal.

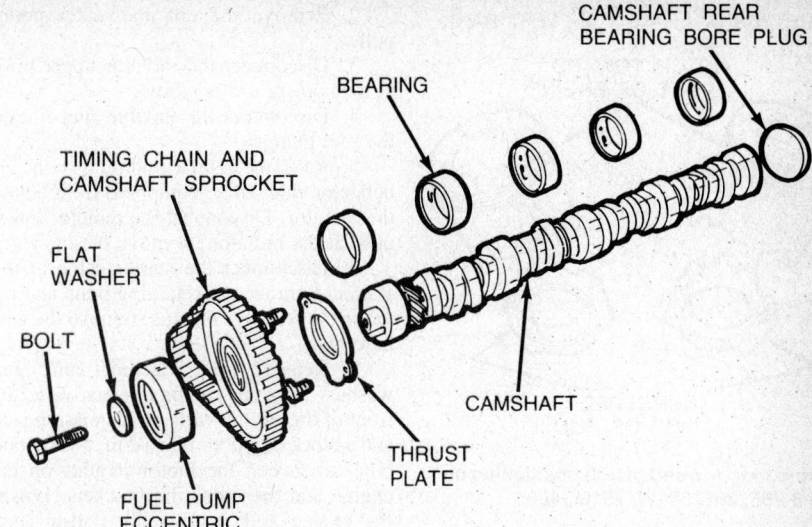

V8 camshaft and related parts

Pistons and Connecting Rods

All Models

1. Drain cooling system and crankcase.

2. Remove the cylinder head.

3. Remove oil pan, oil pump pick-up tube and screen assembly and oil pump.

4. Turning crankshaft so that piston is at the bottom of its stroke, then ridge ream the top of the cylinder. *Never cut into the ring travel area in excess of 1/32" when removing ridges.*

5. Mark each rod bearing cap before removal so that it can be installed in its original location, then remove cap. Caps and rods are numbered on some models.

6. Push connecting rod and piston assembly out the top of the cylinder.

7. Make sure piston is assembled in correct relation to the connecting rod, that is, that the notch on the top of the piston and the oil hole in the rod are positioned as illustrated. Align ring gaps as illustrated and oil the piston rings, pistons and cylinder walls.

8. Install a ring compressor and push the piston and rod assembly into the cylinder (if reinstalling an old piston, make sure it is in the same cylinder). On all but the 360 and 390 cu. in. V-8 engines the piston is installed with the notch on the crown toward the front of the engine. On the 360 and 390 cu. in. engines the notch faces in (toward "V").

9. Fit rod bearings, apply oil to journals and bearings, then install bearings and cap, tightening cap bolts to specified torque (see Specifications at the beginning of this section).

10. Check rod bearing side clearance.

11. Thoroughly clean oil pump assembly, then prime it by filling and rotating

shaft until pump is full. Install pump assembly.

12. Install oil pan, cylinder head and intake manifold (V8 engines).

13. Fill and bleed cooling system.

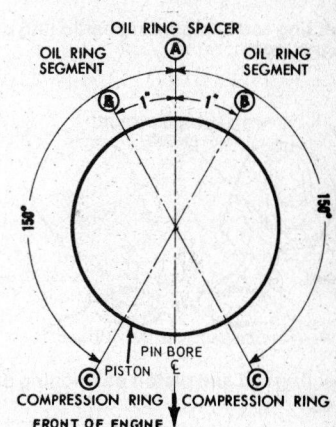

Proper spacing of the piston ring gaps around the piston

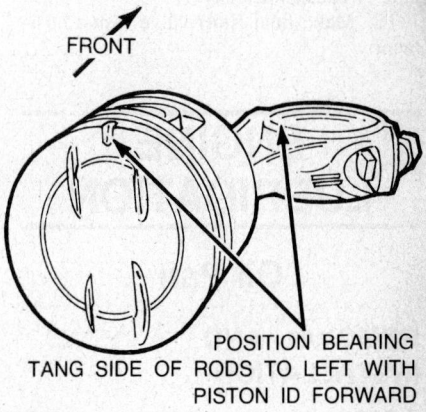

POSITION BEARING TANG SIDE OF RODS TO LEFT WITH PISTON ID FORWARD

Connecting rod and piston positioning on the 6-300

RIGHT BANK   LEFT BANK

NOTCH TOWARD
FRONT OF ENGINE

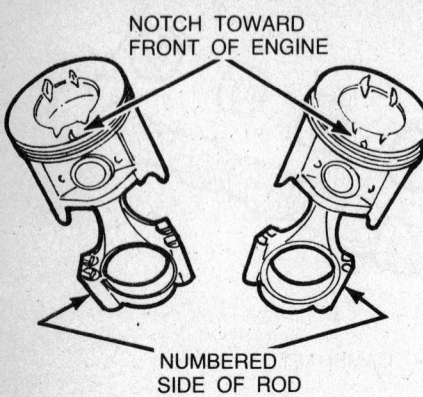

NUMBERED
SIDE OF ROD

Connecting rod and piston positioning on the 8-255, 302, 351W, 351M, 400

LEFT BANK   RIGHT BANK

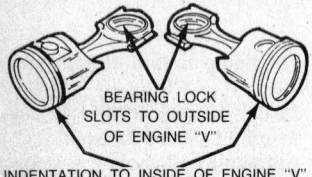

BEARING LOCK
SLOTS TO OUTSIDE
OF ENGINE "V"

INDENTATION TO INSIDE OF ENGINE "V"

Connecting rod and piston positioning on the 8-360, 390

NOTCH TOWARD FRONT
OF ENGINE

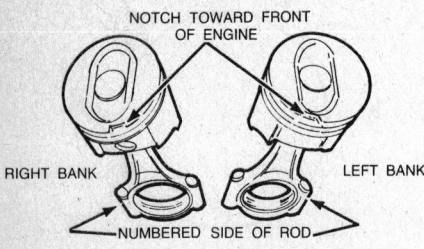

RIGHT BANK   LEFT BANK

NUMBERED SIDE OF ROD

Connecting rod and piston positioning on the 8-460

14. Fill crankcase.

15. Set ignition timing and operate engine to check for leaks.

16. Make final (hot) valve lash adjustment.

ENGINE LUBRICATION

Oil Pan

REMOVAL AND INSTALLATION

6-300

1. Drain the crankcase and cooling system. Remove the oil level dipstick.

2. Remove the fan and water pump pulley.

3. Disconnect the radiator upper hose at the coolant outlet elbow.

4. Disconnect the flexible fuel line at the fuel pump.

5. Raise the vehicle and remove the air deflector chief (if so equipped) from below the radiator. Disconnect the radiator lower hose at the radiator. Remove the radiator.

6. Disconnect the starter cable at the starter. Remove the retaining bolts and remove the starter. On vans, remove the carburetor.

7. Remove the attaching nuts and washers from the motor mounts, raise the front of the engine with a transmission jack and a block of wood. Place 2 in. thick wood blocks between the motor mounts on the engine and the mounting brackets. Lower the engine and remove the transmission jack.

REAR MAIN   APPLY BEAD OF
BEARING CAP   SEALER AS SHOWN

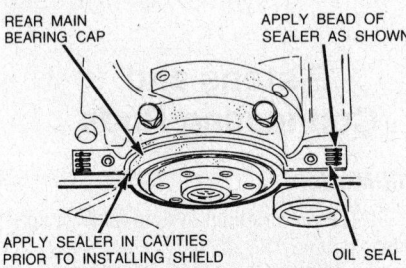

APPLY SEALER IN CAVITIES   OIL SEAL
PRIOR TO INSTALLING SHIELD

6-300 oil pan rear seal installation

SEAL   FRONT
SURFACE

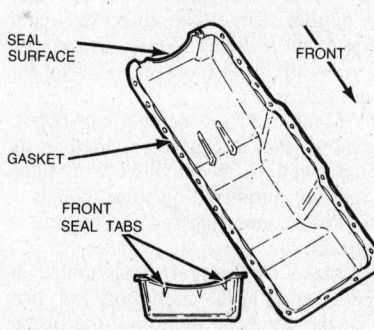

GASKET

FRONT
SEAL TABS

6-300 oil pan front seal installation

8. Remove the oil pan retaining bolts. Remove the oil pump inlet tube retaining bolts, and remove the inlet tube and screen assembly from the oil pump. Leave it in the bottom of the oil pan. Remove the oil pan and gaskets. Remove the inlet tube and screen from the oil pan.

9. In preparation for installation, clean the gasket surfaces of the oil pump, oil pan and cylinder block. Remove the rear main bearing cap-to-oil pan seal and engine front cover-to-oil pan seal. Clean the seal grooves.

10. Position the oil pan front and rear seal on the engine front cover and the rear main bearing cap, respectively. Be sure that the tabs on the seals are over the oil pan gasket.

11. Clean the inlet tube and screen assembly and place it in the oil pan.

12. Position the oil pan under the engine and install the inlet tube and screen assembly on the oil pump with a new gasket. Position the oil pan against the cylinder block and install the retaining bolts.

13. Assemble the rest of the engine in the reverse order of disassembly, starting with step 7.

V6 and V8 All Models except Vans

1. Raise and support the truck on jackstands. Remove the oil dipstick.

2. Remove the bolts attaching the fan shroud and position it over the fan.

3. Remove the engine support insulators-to-chassis bracket attaching nuts and washers. Disconnect the exhaust pipe at the manifolds.

4. If the vehicle is equipped with an automatic transmission, disconnect the oil cooler line at the left-side of the radiator.

5. Raise the engine with a jack placed under the crankshaft damper and a block of wood to act as a cushion. Place wood blocks under the engine supports.

6. Drain the crankcase. Remove the oil filter on the 460 V8.

7. Remove the oil pan attaching screws and lower the oil pan onto the crossmember. Remove the two bolts attaching the oil pump pick-up tube to the oil pump. Lower the pick-up tube and screen into the oil pan, then remove the pan.

NOTE: It may be necessary to turn the crankshaft to provide clearance between the crankshaft counterweights and the oil pan.

REAR SEAL

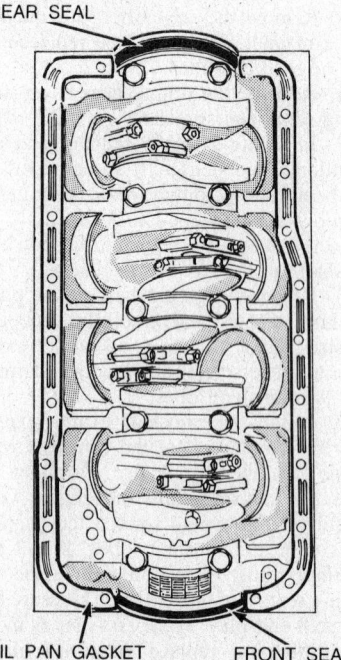

OIL PAN GASKET   FRONT SEAL

8-302 oil pan gasket and seals

8. Clean the oil pan and remove all gasket material from the mating surfaces. Repair and straighten any damage due to overtightening the retaining bolts.

9. Place the new oil pan gasket and end seals on the cylinder block. Use sealer to hold them in place.

10. Position the oil pick-up tube and screen to the oil pump, and install the lower attaching bolt and gasket loosely.

11. Place the oil pan on the crossmember. Install the upper pick-up tube bolt.

12. Position the oil pan to the engine and install the attaching screws. Tighten them to 7–9 ft. lbs. for the ¼ in. screws, and 9–11 ft. lbs. for the 5⁄16 in. screws.

13. Raise the engine and remove the wooden blocks. Lower the engine and install insulator-to-chassis bracket nuts and washers.

14. Connect the transmission oil cooler lines to the radiator, if so equipped. Install the fan shroud.

15. Fill the crankcase with oil, install the dipstick, and operate the engine until it reaches normal operating temperature and check for leaks.

302 V8—Vans Only

1. Raise the vehicle on a hoist.

2. Remove the bolts fastening the oil dipstick tube to the exhaust manifold and the oil pan. Position it to one side.

3. Drain the crankcase and remove the oil filter.

4. Disconnect the steering rod end at the idler arm.

5. Remove the nuts and washers attaching the engine front supports to the engine support crossmember.

6. Position a support jack under the damper and raise the engine as required.

7. Remove the nuts attaching the engine support crossmember to the side rails and frame. Remove the engine support crossmember.

8. Lower the support jack and remove the oil pan attaching bolts and the oil pan with the inlet tube.

9. Clean the oil pan, inlet tube and gasket surfaces.

10. Position a new oil pan gasket and end seals to the cylinder block, then install the oil pump inlet tube.

11. Position the oil pan to the cylinder block and install the attaching bolts and tighten them.

12. Position a support jack under the damper and raise the engine as required.

13. Position the engine support crossmember of the side rails and frame. Install the attaching bolts and nuts and tighten them.

14. Lower the engine and remove the jack.

15. Install the washers and nuts attaching the engine supports and tighten.

16. Connect the steering rod end at the idler arm.

17. Connect the oil dipstick tube to the oil pan and exhaust manifold.

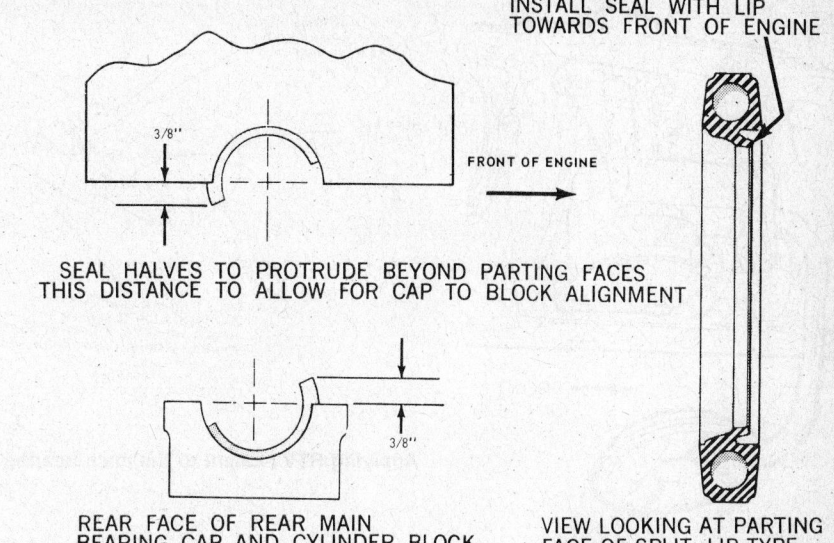

V8 rear main oil seal positioning

18. Install the oil filter.

19. Lower the vehicle and fill the crankcase. Start the engine and check for leaks.

351W, 400 and 460 V8—Vans Only

1. Remove the engine cover. Remove the air cleaner. Disconnect the battery. Remove or set aside the power steering pump, air conditioning compressor, fan shroud, dipstick tube, fuel line, fan and pulleys, transmission cooler lines, exhaust pipe, shift linkage, and driveshaft. The engine is going to be raised about 4 in. so virtually everything will have to be disconnected from the engine and transmission to prevent damage.

2. Unbolt the engine mounts and carefully raise the engine with a padded transmission jack about 4 in. off the mounts. Block it up for safety.

3. The oil pan may now be unbolted and removed.

Rear Main Oil Seal

REPLACEMENT

V6 and V8

1. Drain the crankcase and remove the oil pan, and as necessary, the oil pump.

2. Remove the lower half of the rear main bearing cap and, after removing the oil seal from the cap, drive out the pin in the bottom of the seal groove with a punch.

3. Loosen all the main bearing caps and allow the crankshaft to lower slightly.

NOTE: Do not allow the crankshaft to drop more that 1⁄32 in.

4. Install a small sheet metal screw in one end of the seal, and pull on the screw

to remove the seal. Be careful not to scratch or damage the crankshaft seal surfaces.

5. After removing both halves of the old original rope seal and the retaining pin (which is not used with the replacement seal) from the lower half of the bearing cap, carefully clean the seal grooves in the cap and block with solvent.

6. Soak the new rubber replacement seals in clean engine oil.

7. Install the upper half of the seal in the block with the undercut side of the seal toward the front of the engine. Slide the seal around the crankshaft journal until ⅜ in. protrudes beyond the base of the block.

8. Repeat the above procedure for the lower seal, allowing an equal amount of the seal to protrude beyond the opposite end of the bearing cap.

9. Install the rear bearing cap and torque all the main bearings to the proper specification. Apply sealer only to the rear of the seals.

10. Dip the bearing cap side seals in oil, then immediately install them. Do not use any sealer on the side seals. Tap the seals into place and do not clip the protruding ends.

11. Install the oil pump and oil pan. Fill the crankcase with oil, start the engine and check for leaks.

6-300

1. Remove the starter.

2. Remove the transmission.

3. On trucks with manual transmissions, remove the pressure plate, cover assembly, and clutch disc.

4. Remove the flywheel and the engine rear cover plate.

5. Punch two holes in the crankshaft rear oil seal with an awl. Punch the holes on opposite sides of the crankshaft, just

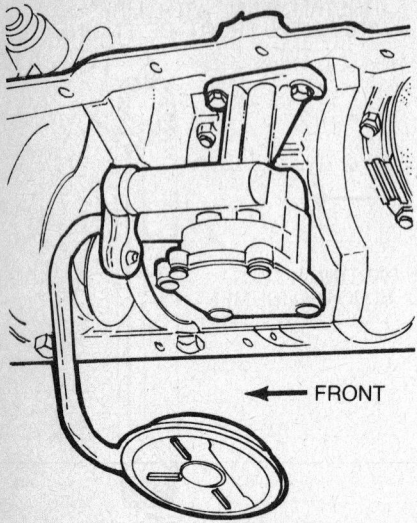

Typical oil pump installation

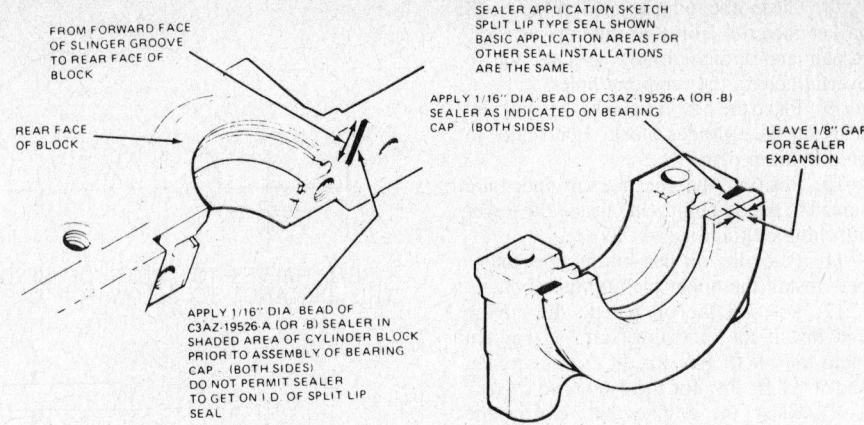

APPLY 1/16" DIA. BEAD OF C3AZ-19526-A (OR -B) SEALER IN SHADED AREA OF CYLINDER BLOCK PRIOR TO ASSEMBLY OF BEARING CAP. (BOTH SIDES) DO NOT PERMIT SEALER TO GET ON I.D. OF SPLIT LIP SEAL

FROM FORWARD FACE OF SLINGER GROOVE TO REAR FACE OF BLOCK

REAR FACE OF BLOCK

SEALER APPLICATION SKETCH SPLIT LIP TYPE SEAL SHOWN BASIC APPLICATION AREAS FOR OTHER SEAL INSTALLATIONS ARE THE SAME.

APPLY 1/16" DIA. BEAD OF C3AZ-19526-A (OR -B) SEALER AS INDICATED ON BEARING CAP (BOTH SIDES)

LEAVE 1/8" GAP FOR SEALER EXPANSION

Applying RTV sealant to the main bearing cap on all V8's

above the bearing cap-to-cylinder block split line. Install a sheet metal screw in each hole.

6. Use two large screwdrivers to pry against both screws at the same time to remove the crankshaft rear oil seal. It may be helpful to place small blocks of wood against the cylinder block to act as fulcrums against which to pry. Be careful not to scratch or damage the crankshaft oil seal surfaces.

7. Clean the oil seal recess in the cylinder block and main bearing cap.

8. Coat the new oil seal and crankshaft with a light film of engine oil. Start the seal in the recess with the seal lip facing forward and install it by tapping it into place with a hammer and a block of wood.

9. Assemble the remaining components in the reverse order of removal.

Oil Pump

REMOVAL AND INSTALLATION

Except V6

1. Remove the oil pan.
2. Remove the oil pump inlet tube and screen assembly.
3. Remove the oil pump attaching bolts and remove the oil pump gasket and intermediate driveshaft.
4. Before installing the oil pump, prime it by filling the inlet and outlet port with engine oil and rotating the shaft of the pump to distribute it.
5. Position the intermediate driveshaft into the distributor socket.
6. Position the new gasket on the pump body and insert the intermediate driveshaft into the pump body.
7. Install the pump and intermediate driveshaft as an assembly. Do not force the

pump if it does not seal readily. The driveshaft may be misaligned with the distributor shaft. To align it, rotate the intermediate driveshaft into a new position.

8. Install the oil pump attaching bolts and torque them to 12–15 ft. lbs. on the 6 cylinder engines and to 20–25 ft. lbs. on the V8 engines.

9. Install the oil pan.

V6

1. If necessary remove the oil filter.
2. Remove the oil pump cover attaching bolts and remove the cover.
3. Lift the pump gears of the pocket in the front cover.
4. Remove the cover gasket. Discard the gasket.
5. If necessary, remove the pump gears from the cover.
6. Pack the gear pocket with petroleum jelly.
DO NOT USE CHASSIS LUBRICANTS.
7. Install the gears in the cover pocket making sure the petroleum jelly fills all voids between the gears and the pocket.

CAUTION
Failure to properly pack the oil pump gears with petroleum jelly may result in failure of the pump to prime when the engine is started.

8. Position the cover gasket and install the pump cover.
9. Tighten the pump cover attaching bolts to 18–22 ft. lbs.

ENGINE COOLING

The satisfactory performance of any engine

is controlled to a great extent by the proper operation of the cooling system. The engine block is fully waterjacketed to prevent distortion of the cylinder walls. Directed cooling and water holes in the cylinder head causes water to flow past the valve seats, which are one of the hottest parts of any engine, to carry heat away from the valves and seats.

The minimum temperature of the coolant is controlled by the thermostat, mounted in the coolant outlet passage of the engine. When the coolant temperature is below the temperature rating of the thermostat, the thermostat remains closed and the coolant is directed through the radiator by-pass hose to the water pump and back into the engine. When the coolant temperature reaches the temperature rating of the thermostat, the thermostat opens and allows coolant to flow past it and into the top of the radiator. The radiator dissipates the excess engine heat before the coolant is recirculated through the engine.

The cooling system is pressurized and operating pressure is regulated by the rating of the radiator cap which contains a relief valve. The reason for a pressurized cooling system is to allow for higher engine operating temperatures with a higher coolant boiling point.

Radiator

REMOVAL AND INSTALLATION

1. Drain the cooling system.
2. Disconnect the transmission cooling lines from the bottom of the radiator, if so equipped.
3. Remove the retaining bolts at each of the four corners of the shroud, if so equipped, and position the shroud over the fan, clear the radiator.
4. Disconnect the upper and lower hoses from the radiator.

5. Remove the radiator retaining bolts or the upper supports and lift the radiator from the vehicle. On some 300 cu in. sixes only, remove the right hood lock bracket and bolts from the radiator grille before removing the radiator.

6. Install the radiator in the reverse order of removal. Fill the cooling system and check for leaks.

Water Pump

REMOVAL AND INSTALLATION

6-300

1. Drain the cooling system.
2. Disconnect the lower radiator hose from the water pump.
3. Remove the drive belt, fan and water

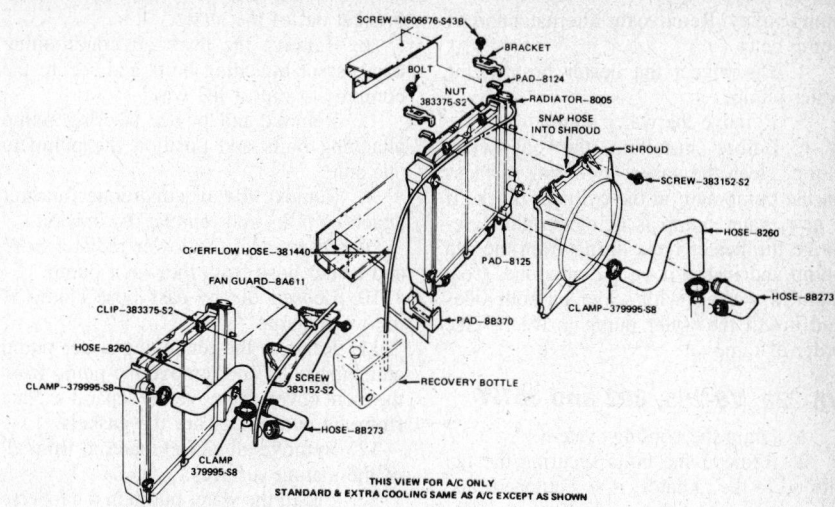

Typical 6-300 radiator installation

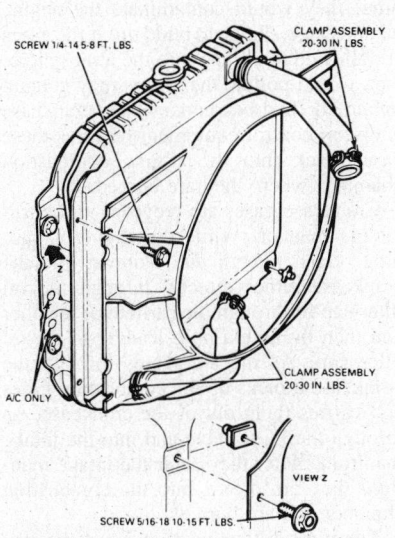

8-400 radiator installation in 1978–79 Bronco

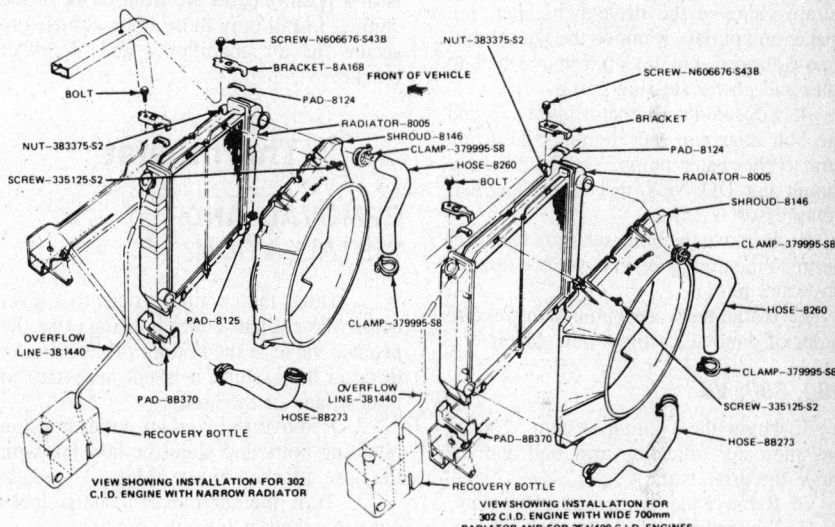

V8 radiator installation typical of Bronco and pick-ups

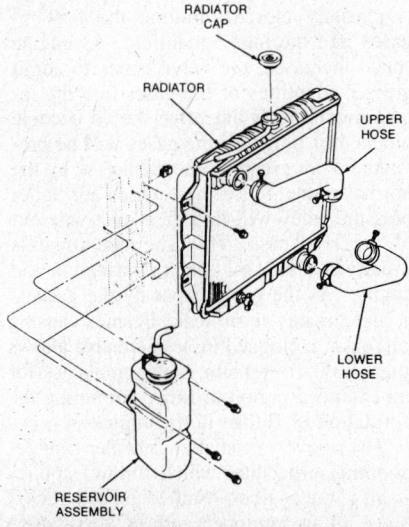

Typical coolant recovery system

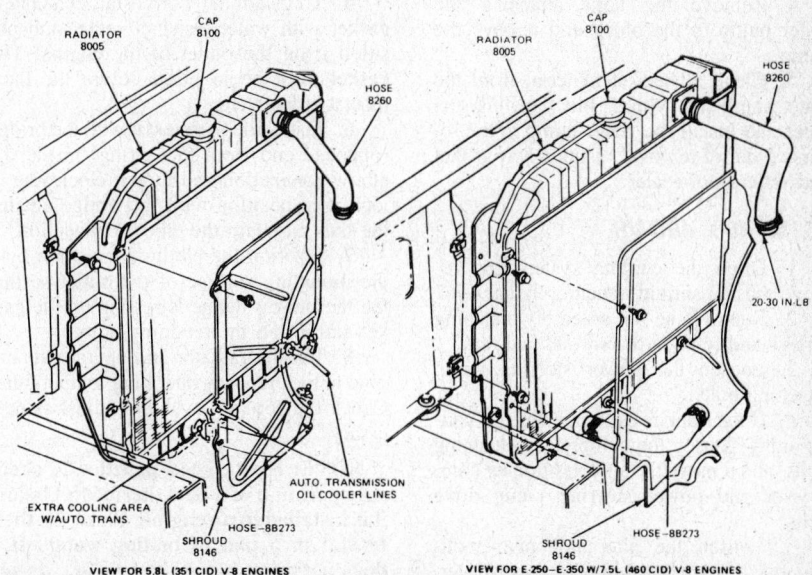

Typical V8 van radiator installation

pump pulley. Remove the alternator and air pump belts.

4. Disconnect the heater hose at the water pump.

5. Remove the water pump.

6. Before installing the old water pump, clean the gasket mounting surfaces on the pump and on the cylinder block. If a new water pump is being installed, remove the heater hose fitting from the old pump and install it on the new one. Coat the new gaskets with sealer on both sides and install the water pump in the reverse order of removal.

V6-232, V8-255, 302 and 351W

1. Drain the cooling system.

2. Remove the bolts securing the fan shroud to the radiator, if so equipped, and position the shroud over the fan.

3. Disconnect the lower radiator hose, heater hose and by-pass hose at the water pump. Remove the drive belts, fan, fan spacer and pulley. Remove the fan shroud, if so equipped. On the V6, remove the belt idler and power steering pump.

4. Loosen the alternator pivot bolt and the bolt attaching the alternator adjusting arm to the water pump. On the V6, dismount but DO NOT disconnect the A/C compressor.

5. Remove the bolts securing the water pump to the timing chain cover and remove the water pump.

6. Install the water pump in the reverse order of removal, using a new gasket.

360, 390, V8

1. Drain the cooling system. Loosen the alternator adjusting arm bolt and remove the drive belt(s).

2. Remove the fan, spacer, and pulley.

3. Disconnect the radiator lower hose, heater hose, and the water pump by-pass hose at the water pump.

4. Remove the bolts attaching the water pump to the block and remove the pump.

5. Clean all gasket material from the water pump and cylinder block mating surfaces and install the water pump in the reverse order of removal, using a new gasket and waterproof sealer.

351M, 400, 460 V8

1. Drain the cooling system and remove the fan shroud attaching bolts.

2. Remove the fan assembly attaching screws and remove the shroud and fan.

3. Loosen the power steering pump attaching bolts.

4. If the truck is equipped with air conditioning, loosen the compressor attaching bolts, and remove the air conditioning compressor and power steering pump drive belts.

5. Loosen the alternator pivot bolt. Remove the two attaching bolts and spacer. Remove the drive belt, then rotate the

bracket out of the way.

6. Remove the three air conditioning compressor attaching bolts and secure the compressor out of the way.

7. Remove the power steering pump attaching bolts and position the pump to one side.

8. Remove the air conditioner bracket attaching bolts and remove the bracket.

9. Disconnect the lower radiator hose and heater hose from the water pump.

10. Loosen the by-pass hose clamp at the water pump.

11. Remove the remaining water pump attaching bolts and remove the pump from the front cover. Remove the separator plate from the pump. Discard the gaskets.

12. Remove all gasket material from all of the mating surfaces.

13. Install the water pump in the reverse order of removal, using a new gasket and waterproof sealer. When the water pump is first positioned to the front cover of the engine, install only those bolts not used to secure the air conditioner and alternator brackets.

Thermostat

REMOVAL AND INSTALLATION

1. Drain the cooling system to a level below the coolant outlet housing. Use the petcock valve at the bottom of the radiator to drain the system; it is not necessary to remove any of the hoses.

2. Remove the coolant outlet housing retaining bolts and slide the housing with the hose attached to one side.

3. Turn the thermostat counterclockwise to unlock it from the outlet.

4. Remove the gasket from the engine block and clean both mating surfaces.

5. To install the thermostat, coat a new gasket with water-resistant sealer and position it on the outlet of the engine. The gasket must be in place before the thermostat is installed.

6. Install the thermostat with the bridge (opposite end from the spring) inside the elbow connection and turn it clockwise to lock it in position with the bridge against the flats cast into the elbow connection.

7. Position the elbow connection onto the mounting surface of the outlet so that the thermostat flange is resting on the gasket and install the retaining bolts.

8. Fill the radiator and operate the engine until it reaches operating temperature. Check the coolant level and adjust as necessary.

NOTE: It is a good practice to check the operation of a new thermostat before it is installed in an engine. Place the thermostat in a pan of boiling water. If it does not open more than ¼ in., do not install it in the engine.

EMISSION CONTROLS

Crankcase Emission Controls

The crankcase emission control equipment consists of a positive crankcase ventilation (PCV) valve, a closed or open oil filler cap and the hoses that connect this equipment.

When the engine is running, a small portion of the gases which are formed in the combustion chamber leak by the piston rings and enter the crankcase. Since these gases are under pressure they tend to escape from the crankcase and enter into the atmosphere. If these gases were allowed to remain in the crankcase for any length of time, they would contaminate the engine oil and cause sludge to build up. If the gases are allowed to escape into the atmosphere, they would pollute the air, as they contain unburned hydrocarbons. The crankcase emission control equipment recycles these gases back into the engine combustion chamber, where they are burned.

Crankcase gases are recycled in the following manner. While the engine is running, clean filtered air is drawn into the crankcase either directly through the oil filler cap or through the carburetor air filter and then through a hose leading to the oil filler cap. As the air passes through the crankcase it picks up the combustion gases and carries them out of the crankcase, up through the PCV valve and into the intake manifold. After they enter the intake manifold they are drawn into the combustion chamber and are burned.

The most critical component of the system is the PCV valve. This vacuum-controlled valve regulates the amount of gases which are recycled into the combustion chamber. At low engine speeds the valve is partially closed, limiting the flow of gases into the intake manifold. As engine speed increases, the valve opens to admit greater quantities of the gases into the intake manifold. If the valve should become blocked or plugged, the gases will be prevented from escaping the crankcase by the normal route. Since these gases are under pressure, they will find their own way out of the crankcase. This alternate route is usually a weak oil seal or gasket in the engine. As the gas escapes by the gasket, it also creates an oil leak. Besides causing oil leaks, a clogged PCV valve also allows these gases to remain in the crankcase for an extended period of time, promoting the formation of sludge in the engine.

The above explanation and the troubleshooting procedure which follows applies to all of the engines installed in Ford trucks, since all are equipped with PCV systems.

TROUBLESHOOTING

With the engine running, pull the PCV valve and hose from the valve rocker cover rubber grommet.

A hissing noise should be heard as air passes through the valve and a strong vacuum should be felt when you place a finger over the valve inlet if the valve is working properly. While you have your finger over the PCV valve inlet, check for vacuum leaks in the hose and at the connections.

When the PCV valve is removed from the engine, a metallic clicking noise should be heard when it is shaken. This indicates that the metal check ball inside the valve is still free and is not gummed up.

REMOVAL

1. Pull the PCV valve and hose from the rubber grommet in the rocker cover.
2. Remove the PCV valve from the hose. Inspect the inside of the PCV valve. If it is dirty, disconnect it from the intake manifold and clean it in a suitable, safe solvent.

To install, proceed as follows:
1. If the PCV valve hose was removed, connect it to the intake manifold.
2. Connect the PCV valve to its hose.
3. Install the PCV valve into the rubber grommet in the valve rocker cover.

Evaporative Emission Controls

Beginning 1970, F-100 pick-ups produced for sale in California were equipped with evaporative emission controls on the fuel system. For 1971, the system was modified somewhat and used on all F-100 pick-ups as standard equipment.

After 1974, F-250 pick-ups sold in California were equipped with the evaporative emission system.

Changes in atmospheric temperature cause fuel tanks to "breathe"; that is, the air within the tank expands and contracts with outside temperature changes. As the temperature rises, air escapes through the tank vent tube or the vent in the tank cap. The air which escapes contains gasoline vapors. In a similar manner, the gasoline which fills the carburetor float bowl expands when the engine is stopped. Engine heat causes this expansion. The vapors escape through the carburetor and air cleaner.

The Evaporative Emission Control System provides a sealed fuel system with the capability to store and condense fuel vapors. The system has three parts: a fill control vent system; a vapor vent and storage system; and a pressure and vacuum relief system (special fill cap).

The fill control vent system is a modification to the fuel tank. It uses a dome air space within the tank which is 10–12% of the tank's volume. The air space is sufficient to provide for the thermal expansion of the fuel. The space also serves as part of the in-tank vapor vent system.

The in-tank vent system consists of the dome air space previously described and a vapor separator assembly. The separator assembly is mounted to the top of the fuel tank and is secured by a cam-lock-ring, similar to the one which secures the fuel sending unit. Foam material fills the vapor separator assembly. The foam material separates raw fuel and vapors, thus retarding the entrance of fuel into the vapor line.

From 1971 and later, the vapor separator is an orifice valve located in the dome of the tank. The restricted size of the orifice (0.050 in.) tends to allow only vapor to pass out of the tank. The orifice valve is connected to the vent line which runs forward to the carbon-filled canister in the engine compartment.

The sealed filler cap has a pressure-vacuum relief valve. Under normal operating conditions, the filler cap operates as a check valve, allowing air to enter the tank to replace the fuel consumed. At the same time, it prevents vapors from escaping through the cap. In case of excessive pressure within the tank, the filler cap valve opens to relieve the pressure.

Because the filler cap is sealed, fuel vapors have only one place through which they may escape—the vapor separator assembly at the top of the fuel tank. The vapors pass through the foam material and continue through a single vapor line which leads to a canister in the engine compartment. The canister is filled with activated charcoal.

Another vapor line runs from the top of the carburetor float chamber to the charcoal canister.

As the fuel vapors (hydrocarbons), enter the charcoal canister, they are absorbed by the charcoal. The air is dispelled through the open bottom of the charcoal canister, leaving the hydrocarbons trapped within the charcoal. When the engine is started, vacuum causes fresh air to be drawn into the canister from its open bottom. The fresh air passes through the charcoal picking up the hydrocarbons which are trapped there and feeding them into the carburetor for burning with the fuel mixture.

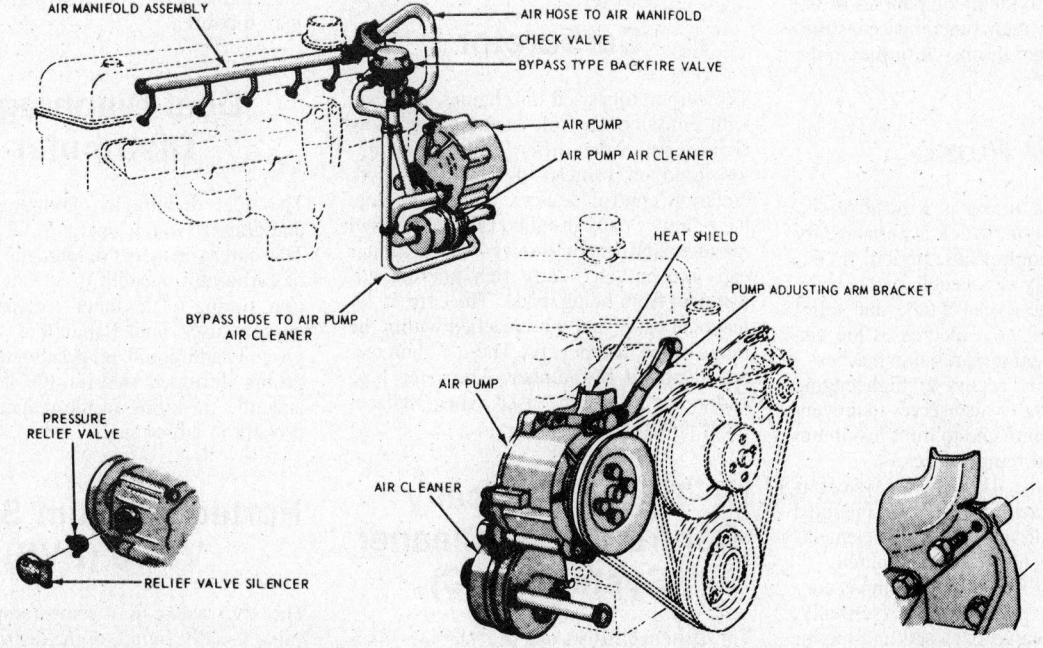

6-300 thermactor exhaust emission system

Exhaust Emission Controls

There are many devices used on the engines installed in Ford pick-ups to control emission of exhaust gases into the atmosphere.

All of the engines may use the air injection reactor system, the Ford terminology for which is the "Thermactor" exhaust emission control system. This system is used on all engines, from 1970 to the present.

The exhaust emission control air injection system consists of a belt-driven air pump, which directs compressed air through connecting hoses to an air manifold and through air nozzles in the exhaust ports adjacent to each exhaust valve. The air, with its normal oxygen content, reacts with the hot, but incompletely burned exhaust gases and permits further combustion in the exhaust port or manifold.

Another emission control system common to all of the engines since 1974 is the Exhaust Gas Recirculation (EGR) system. This system is designed to reduce the amount of oxides of nitrogen (NOx) emitted into the atmosphere by re-introducing small amounts of exhaust gas into the combustion cycle. The amount of recycled exhaust gas depends chiefly on engine vacuum and temperature.

New for 1975 models is the catalytic converter. The converter is a muffler-type device installed in the vehicle's exhaust system containing a chemical catalyst. When exhaust gases pass over and through the catalyst, further chemical reaction occurs and the pollutants are broken down into harmless elements.

The above paragraphs are just a brief summary of the main exhaust emission control systems. Individual components of the various systems, their functions, construction, and repair are discussed further in the following sections.

Air Pump

The air injection pump is a positive-displacement vane type which is permanently lubricated and requires little periodic maintenance. The only serviceable parts on the air pump are the exhaust tube and relief valve. The relief valve decreases the airflow when the pump pressure reaches a preset level. This occurs at high engine rpm. The relief valve also serves to prevent damage to the pump and to limit maximum exhaust manifold temperatures.

Inlet air for the Thermactor system is cleaned by a centrifugal filter fan mounted on the air pump driveshaft, thus an element-type air cleaner (filter) is not required.

The air supply from the air pump is controlled by the air by-pass valve. Normally, the air by-pass valve is closed and the air is directed to the check valve(s) and air manifold(s) for distribution to the cylinder

head exhaust ports. During engine deceleration, the air by-pass valve opens and air delivery to the cylinder head exhaust ports is momentarily diverted to the atmosphere.

A check valve is used in the inlet air side of the air manifold(s) to prevent exhaust gases from flowing back into the air pump and air by-pass valve during the air by-pass cycle or during air pump and/or drive belt failure.

Air Delivery Manifold

The air delivery manifold distributes the air from the pump to each of the air delivery tubes in a uniform manner. This applies only to the 6 cylinder engines, as the air delivery manifold is integral with the cylinder head on the V8 engines.

Air By-Pass Valve

The air by-pass valve prevents engine backfire by briefly interrupting the air being injected into the exhaust manifold during periods of deceleration or rapid throttle closure. The valve opens when a sudden increase in manifold vacuum overcomes the diaphragm spring tension. With the valve in the open position, the airflow is vented to the atmosphere. In addition to preventing backfiring in the exhaust manifold as previously mentioned, the valve also prevents possible damage to the engine by not allowing the overly rich fuel mixture from being burned in the exhaust manifold. A rich mixture in the exhaust manifold is the result of deceleration or rapid throttle closure and to promote its further combustion by injecting air would cause backfiring.

Carburetor

The carburetors used on engines equipped with emission controls have specific flow characteristics that differ from the carburetors used on vehicles not equipped with emission control devices. All carburetors have limiter caps installed on the idle fuel mixture adjustment screws. These limiter caps prevent an overly rich mixture adjustment from being made. The correct adjustment can usually be reached within the range of the limiter caps. These carburetors are identified by number. The same type carburetor should be used when replacement is necessary.

Thermostatically Controlled Air Cleaner System (TAC)

This system consists of a heat shroud which is integral with the right-side exhaust manifold, a hot air hose and a special air cleaner

assembly equipped with a thermal sensor and vacuum motor and air valve assembly.

The temperature of the carburetor intake air is thermostatically controlled by means of a valve plate and a vacuum override built into a duct assembly attached to the air cleaner. The exhaust manifold shroud tube is attached to the shroud over the exhaust manifold for the source of heated air.

The thermal sensor is attached to the air valve actuating lever, along with the vacuum motor lever, both of which control the position of the air valve to supply either heated air from the exhaust manifold or cooler air from the engine compartment.

During the warm-up period, when the under-the-hood temperatures are low, the thermal sensor doesn't exert enough tension on the air valve actuating lever to close (heat off) the air valve. Thus, the carburetor receives heated air from around the exhaust manifold.

As the temperature of the air entering the air cleaner approaches approximately 100°F, the thermal sensor begins to push on the air valve actuating lever and overcome the spring tension which holds the air valve in the open (heat on) position. The air valve begins to move to the closed (heat off) position, allowing only under-the-hood air to enter the air cleaner.

The air valve in the air cleaner will also open, regardless of the air temperature, during heavy acceleration to obtain maximum airflow through the air cleaner. The extreme decrease in intake manifold vacuum during heavy acceleration permits the vacuum motor to override the thermostatic control. This opens the system to both heated air and air from the engine compartment.

The purpose of TAC is to get hot air into the carburetor as soon as possible because the engine will emit less pollutants on a lean mixture.

Dual Diaphragm Distributor

The dual diaphragm distributor has two diaphragms which operate independently. The outer (primary) diaphragm makes use of carburetor vacuum to advance the ignition timing. The inner (secondary) diaphragm uses intake manifold vacuum to provide additional retardation of ignition timing during closed-throttle deceleration and idle, resulting in the reduction of hydrocarbon emissions.

Ported Vacuum Switch Valve (PVS)

The PVS valve is a temperature sensing valve usually found on the distributor vacuum advance line, and is installed in the coolant outlet elbow. During prolonged periods of idle, or any other situation which causes engine operating temperatures to be higher than normal, the valve, which under normal conditions simply connects the vacuum advance diaphragm to its vacuum source within the carburetor, closes the normal source vacuum port and engages an alternate source vacuum port. This alternate source is from the intake manifold which, under idle conditions, maintains a high vacuum. This increase in vacuum supply to the distributor diaphragm advances the timing, increasing the idle speed. The increase in idle speed causes a directly proportional increase in the operation of the cooling sys-

tem. When the engine has cooled sufficiently, the vacuum supply is returned to its normal source, the carburetor.

These switches are used in several places in the emission systems. They can have anywhere from two to four ports and can be used to turn vacuum on and off, or to switch between two vacuum sources for a third delivery point.

When cold, a typical three-port PVS provides a path through the center and top holes. When hot, the top port is closed off and the center and bottom ports are open. The vacuum sources would be connected to the top and bottom ports.

Deceleration Valve

Some engines were equipped with a distributor vacuum advance control valve (deceleration valve) which is used with dual diaphragm distributors to further aid in controlling ignition timing. The deceleration valve is in the vacuum line which runs from the outer (advance) diaphragm to the carburetor, the normal vacuum supply for the distributor. During deceleration, the intake manifold vacuum rises causing the deceleration valve to close off the carburetor vacuum source and connect the intake man-

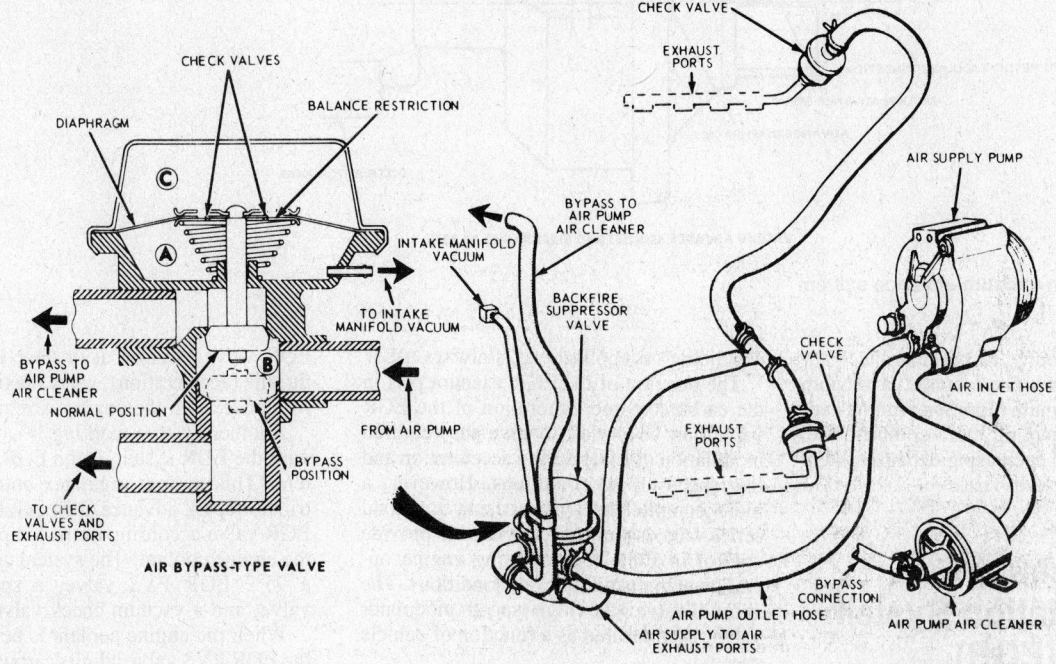

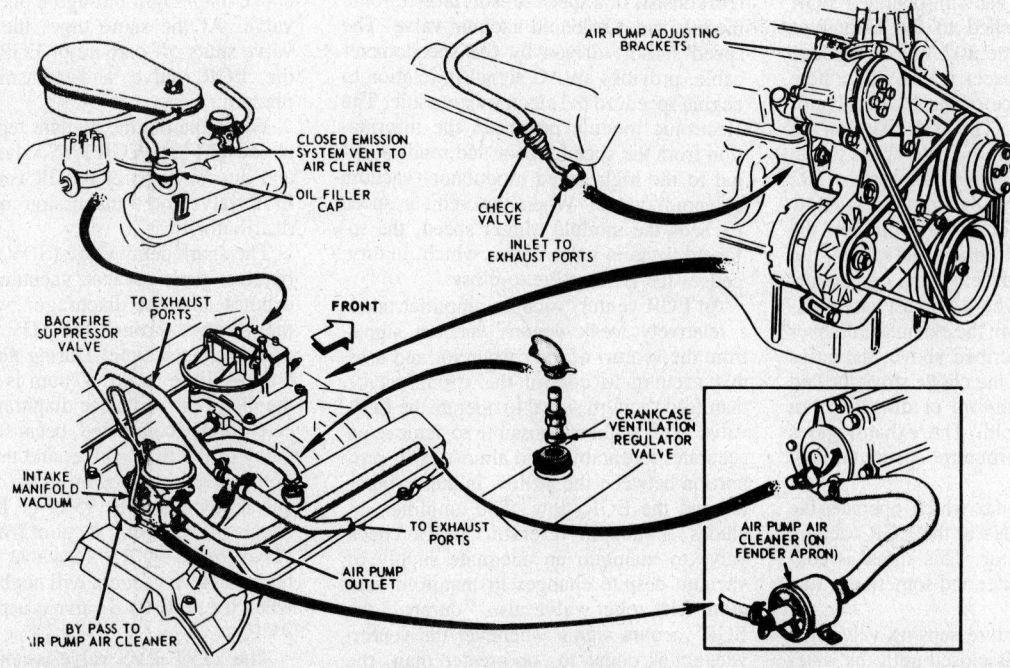

V8 thermactor exhaust emission system

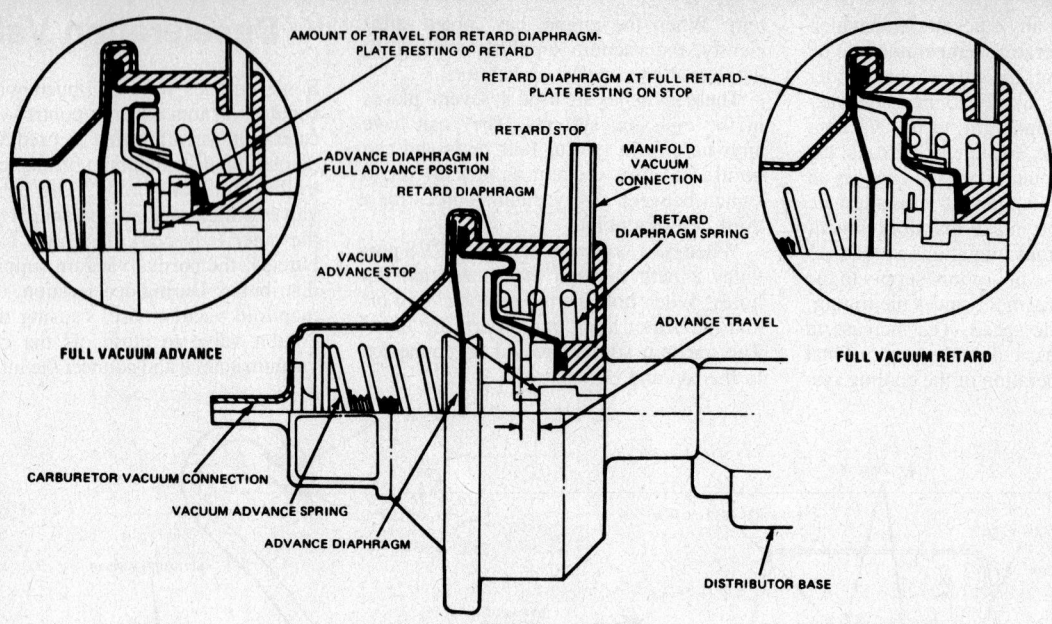

AMOUNT OF TRAVEL FOR RETARD DIAPHRAGM-
PLATE RESTING 0° RETARD

RETARD DIAPHRAGM AT FULL RETARD-
PLATE RESTING ON STOP

RETARD STOP

ADVANCE DIAPHRAGM IN
FULL ADVANCE POSITION

MANIFOLD
VACUUM
CONNECTION

RETARD DIAPHRAGM

RETARD
DIAPHRAGM SPRING

VACUUM
ADVANCE STOP

FULL VACUUM ADVANCE

ADVANCE TRAVEL

FULL VACUUM RETARD

CARBURETOR VACUUM CONNECTION

VACUUM ADVANCE SPRING

ADVANCE DIAPHRAGM

DISTRIBUTOR BASE

VACUUM ADVANCE AND RETARD DIAPHRAGMS AT REST

Dual diaphragm vacuum advance system

ifold vacuum source to the distributor advance diaphragm. The increase in vacuum provides maximum ignition timing advance, thus providing more complete fuel combustion and decreasing exhaust system backfiring.

Exhaust Gas Recirculation System (EGR)

In this system, a vacuum-operated EGR flow valve is attached to the carburetor spacer (except on the 302 V8). A passage in the carburetor spacer mates with a hole in the mounting face of the EGR valve or the intake manifold. The EGR valve on the 302 V8 is located on the rear of the intake manifold. On all engines except the 302 V8, the system allows exhaust gases to flow from the exhaust crossover, through the control valve and through the spacer into the intake manifold below the carburetor. For those engines where exhaust gases cannot be picked up from the exhaust crossover (6 cylinder) as described above, the gases are picked up from the choke stove located on the exhaust manifold or directly from the exhaust manifold. The exhaust gases are routed to the carburetor spacer through steel tubing.

The vacuum signal which operates the EGR valve originates at the EGR vacuum port in the carburetor. This signal is controlled by at least one, and sometimes, two series of valves.

A water temperature sensing valve (the EGR PVS) which is closed until the water temperature reaches either 60°F or 125°F,

depending on application, is always used.

The position of the EGR vacuum port in the carburetor and calibration of the EGR valve can be varied to give the required modulation of EGR during acceleration and low speed cruise conditions. However, a more complicated system using a second series valve is sometimes needed to provide control of EGR for accepting engine operation at high speed cruise conditions. The second valve: the high speed modulator valve, is controlled as a function of vehicle speed.

The high speed EGR modulator subsystem consists of a speed sensor, an electronic module and a solenoid vacuum valve. The speed sensor, driven by the speedometer cable, provides an AC signal in relation to engine speed, to the electronic module. The electronic module processes the information from the speed sensor and sends a signal to the high speed modulator (vacuum solenoid) valve. When the vehicle speed exceeds the module trigger speed, the solenoid vacuum valve closes which, in turn, causes the EGR valve to close.

An EGR venturi vacuum amplifier takes a relatively weak venturi vacuum signal from the venturi of the carburetor and uses this vacuum to control the strong intake manifold vacuum signal to operate the EGR valve. This makes it possible to achieve an accurate, repeatable, and almost exact proportion between the airflow in the carburetor and the EGR flow. The amplifier includes a vacuum reservoir and a check valve to maintain an adequate supply of vacuum despite changes in manifold vacuum. The relief valve also "dumps" the EGR vacuum signal whenever the venturi vacuum is equal to, or greater than, the intake manifold vacuum. This allows the

EGR valve to close at or near wide open throttle (acceleration), when maximum performance from the engine is required.

Another system working in conjunction with the EGR system is the EGR/CSC system. This system regulates both the distributor spark advance and operation of the EGR valve according to the temperature of the engine coolant. The system consists of: a 95°F EGR PVS valve, a spark delay valve, and a vacuum check valve.

When the engine coolant is below 82°F, the EGR PVS valve admits carburetor EGR port vacuum directly to the distributor advance diaphragm through a one-way check valve. At the same time, the EGR PVS valve shuts off carburetor EGR vacuum to the EGR valve and transmission diaphragm.

When the engine coolant temperature is above 95°F, the EGR PVS valve is actuated and directs carburetor EGR vacuum to the EGR valve and transmission instead of the distributor.

The spark delay valve (SDV) delays carburetor spark advance vacuum to the distributor advance diaphragm by restricting the vacuum through the SDV valve for a predetermined time. During normal acceleration, little or no vacuum is admitted to the distributor advance diaphragm until acceleration is completed, because of the time delay of the SDV valve, and the re-routing of the EGR port vacuum, if the engine coolant temperature is 95°F or higher. The check valve blocks vacuum from the SDV valve to the EGR PVS valve so that carburetor spark vacuum will not be dissipated when the EGR PVS valve is actuated above 95°F.

The 235°F PVS valve is not part of the EGR/CSC system, but is connected to the distributor vacuum advance to prevent engine overheating while idling. At idle speeds, no vacuum is generated at the carburetor spark port or the EGR port and the ignition timing is fully retarded. When the engine coolant reaches 235°F, the valve is actuated to admit intake manifold vacuum to the distributor advance diaphragm which advances the ignition timing. The result is the engine speed increases and the increase in coolant circulation and fan speed cools the engine.

Cold Temperature Activated Vacuum System

The cold temperature activated vacuum (CTAV) system was first used in 1974 on 460 V8 engines in F-100 trucks built for sale in California.

The CTAV system more accurately matches spark advance to the engine requirements under cold ambient temperature conditions. The system can select from two vacuum sources for spark advance depending on the ambient temperature: below 49°F—carburetor spark port vacuum; above 65°F—EGR vacuum. In between these two temperature ranges the system will select either source of vacuum, depending on the cycle it is in.

The CTAV system consists of an ambient temperature switch, a three-way vacuum switch, inline vacuum bleed, and a latching relay.

The vacuum from both the spark port of the carburetor and the EGR port is supplied to the three-way solenoid valve. The ambient temperature switch provides the signal that determines which of the sources will be selected. The latching relay provides for only one cycle each time the ignition switch is turned on.

Vacuum and Spring Controlled Heat Control Valve

The heat control valve, commonly known as the heat riser, is mounted between the exhaust pipe and the exhaust manifold. The purpose of the device is to provide a quick warm-up of the carburetor and the rest of the induction system.

Fuel will condense on the cold surfaces of the induction system, which causes air/fuel ratios to fluctuate. These variations can cause uneven acceleration and increased emissions. The exhaust control valve, which is thermostatically-controlled, is closed when the engine is cold and routes hot exhaust gases through a passage under the carburetor and over to the opposite ex-

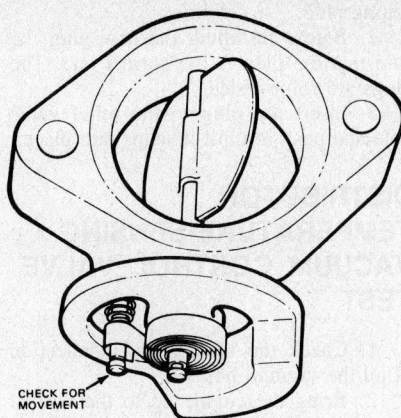

Spring operated exhaust heat riser valve

haust manifold which has no heat control valve and thus no restriction to block the flow of exhaust gases. This quickly warms the air/fuel mixture delivery passages and provides improved mixture control and driveability. As the engine warms up, the valve opens and reduces the flow of exhaust gases through the warm-up passage.

The valve is either operated by a bi-metal temperature sensitive spring or a vacuum motor operated by intake manifold vacuum routed through a PVS switch.

Electrically-Assisted Choke

Some pick-ups use an electrically heated choke thermostatic spring housing as an aid to fast choke release and better emission characteristics during engine warm-up. The heater operates from a lead off the alternator only when the engine is actually running.

The heater element operates only when ambient temperatures are above 60°F (when long periods of choke operation are not necessary for engine driveability). When temperatures are below 60°F, the choke thermostatic spring is heated in the normal manner; via a tube running from an exhaust manifold heat stove.

Thermactor System

AIR BY-PASS VALVE REPLACEMENT

1. Disconnect the air and vacuum hoses at the air by-pass valve body.
2. Position the air by-pass valve and connect the respective hoses.

CHECK VALVE REPLACEMENT

1. Disconnect the air supply hose at the

valve. Use a 1¼ in. crowfoot wrench. The valve has a standard, right-hand pipe thread.
2. Clean the threads on the air manifold adapter (air supply tube on the V8 engines) with a wire brush. Do not blow compressed air through the check valve in either direction.
3. Install the check valve and tighten.
4. Connect the air supply hose.

AIR MANIFOLD REPLACEMENT

Six-Cylinder Engines

1. Disconnect the air supply hose at the check valve, position the hose out of the way and remove the valve.
2. Loosen all of the air manifold-to-cylinder head tube coupling nuts (compression fittings). Inspect the air manifold for damaged threads and fittings and for leaking connections. Repair or replace as required. Clean the manifold and associated parts with kerosene. Do not dry the parts with compressed air.
3. Position the air manifold on the cylinder head. Be sure that all of the tube coupling nuts are aligned with the cylinder head.
4. Screw each coupling nut into the cylinder head, one or two threads. Tighten the tube coupling nuts.
5. Install the check valve and tighten it.
6. Connect the air supply hose to the check valve.

AIR SUPPLY TUBE REPLACEMENT

V8 Engines Only

1. Disconnect the air supply hose at the check valve and position the hose out of the way.
2. Remove the check valve.
3. Remove the air supply tube bolt and seal washer.
4. Carefully remove the air supply tube and seal washer from the cylinder head. Inspect the air supply tube for evidence of leaking threads or seal surfaces. Examine the attaching bolt head, seal washers, and supply tube surface for leaks. Inspect the attaching bolt and cylinder head threads for damage. Clean the air supply tube, seal washers, and bolt with kerosene. Do not dry the parts with compressed air.
5. Install the seal washer and air supply tube on the cylinder head. Be sure that it is positioned in the same manner as before removal.
6. Install the seal washer and mounting bolt. Tighten the bolt.
7. Install the check valve and tighten it.
8. Connect the air supply hose to the check valve.

AIR NOZZLE REPLACEMENT

Six-Cylinder Engines Only

Normally, air nozzles should be replaced during cylinder head reconditioning. A nozzle may be replaced, however, without removing the cylinder head, by removing the air manifold and using a hooked tool.

Clean the nozzle with kerosene and a stiff brush. Inspect the air nozzles for eroded tips.

AIR PUMP AND FILTER FAN REPLACEMENT

1. Loosen the air pump attaching bolts.
2. Remove the drive pulley attaching bolts and pull the pulley off the air pump shaft.
3. Pry the outer disc loose, then remove the centrifugal filter fan. Care must be used to prevent foreign matter from entering the air intake hole, especially if the fan breaks during removal. Do not attempt to remove the metal drive hub.
4. Install the new filter fan by drawing it into position with the pulley bolts.

AIR PUMP REPLACEMENT

1. Disconnect the air outlet hose at the air pump.
2. Loosen the pump belt tension adjuster.
3. Disengage the drive belt.
4. Remove the mounting bolt and air pump.
5. Position the air pump on the mounting bracket and install the mounting bolt.
6. Place the drive belt in the pulley and attach the adjusting arm to the air pump.
7. Adjust the drive belt tension and tighten the adjusting arm and mounting bolts.
8. Connect the air outlet hose to the air pump.

RELIEF VALVE REPLACEMENT

Do not disassemble the air pump on the car to replace the relief valve; remove the pump from the engine.
1. Remove the relief valve with the aid of a slide hammer.
2. Position the relief valve on the pump housing and hold it in position with a block of wood.
3. Use a hammer to lightly tap the wood block until the relief valve is seated.

RELIEF VALVE PRESSURE-SETTING PLUG REPLACEMENT

1. Compress the locking tabs inward (together) and remove the plastic pressure-setting plug.
2. Before installing the new plug, be sure that the plug is the correct one. The plugs are color-coded.
3. Insert the plug in the relief valve hole and push in until it snaps into place.

DISTRIBUTOR TEMPERATURE-SENSING VACUUM CONTROL VALVE TEST

1. Check the routing and connection of all the vacuum hoses.
2. Bring the engine up to the normal operating temperature. The engine must not be overheated.
3. Note the engine rpm, with the transmission in Neutral, and the throttle at curb idle.
4. Disconnect the vacuum hose from the intake manifold at the temperature-sensing valve. Plug or clamp the hose.
5. Note the idle rpm with the hose disconnected. If there is no change in rpm, the valve is good. If there is a drop of 100 or more rpm, the valve should be replaced. Replace the vacuum line.
6. Check to make sure that the all-season coolant mixture meets specifications and that the correct radiator cap is in place and functioning.
7. Block the radiator airflow to induce a higher-than-normal temperature condition.
8. Continue to operate the engine until the temperature or heat indicator shows above normal.

If the engine speed, by this time, has increased 100 or more rpm, the temperature-sensing valve is satisfactory. If not, it should be replaced.

DISTRIBUTOR DECELERATION VACUUM CONTROL VALVE TEST

1. Connect a tachometer to the engine and bring the engine to the normal operating temperature.
2. Check the idle speed and set it to specifications with the headlights on high beam, as necessary.
3. Turn off the headlights and note the idle rpm.
4. Remove the plastic cover from the valve. Slowly turn the adjusting screw counterclockwise without pressing in. After 5, and no more than 6 turns, the idle speed should suddenly increase to about 1000 rpm. If the speed does not increase after six turns, push inward on the valve spring retainer and release. Speed should now increase.
5. Slowly turn the adjusting screw clockwise until the idle speed drops to the speed noted in step 3. Make one more turn clockwise.
6. Increase the engine speed to 2000

rpm, hold for 5 seconds, and release the throttle. The engine speed should return to idle speed within 4 seconds. If idle is not resumed in 4 seconds, back off the dashpot adjustment and repeat the check. If the idle is not resumed in 3 seconds with the dashpot backed off, turn the deceleration valve adjustment screw an additional quarter turn clockwise and repeat the check. Repeat the quarter turn adjustment and idle return checks until the engine returns to idle within the required time.
7. If it takes more than one complete turn from Step 5 to meet the idle return time specification, replace the valve.

DUAL DIAPHRAGM VACUUM ADVANCE AND VACUUM RETARD FUNCTIONAL CHECK

1. To check vacuum advance, disconnect the vacuum lines from both the advance (outer) and retard (inner) diaphragms. Plug the line removed from the retard diaphragm.

Connect a tachometer and timing light to the engine. Increase the idle speed by setting the screw on the first step of the fast idle cam. Note the ignition timing setting, using a timing light.

Connect the carburetor vacuum line to the advance diaphragm. If the timing advances immediately, the advance unit is functioning properly. Adjust the idle speed to 550–600 rpm.
2. Check the vacuum retardation as follows: using a timing light, note the ignition timing. Remove the plug from the manifold vacuum line and connect the line to the inner diaphragm. Timing should retard immediately.
3. If vacuum retardation is not to specifications, replace the dual diaphragm advance unit. If the advance (vacuum) does not function properly, calibrate the unit on a distributor test stand. If the advance part of the unit cannot be calibrated, or if either diaphragm is leaking, replace the dual diaphragm vacuum advance unit.

EVAPORATIVE EMISSION CONTROL SYSTEM CHECK

Other than a visual check to determine that none of the vapor lines are broken, there is no test for this equipment.

ELECTRONIC SPARK CONTROL SYSTEM OPERATION TEST

1. Raise the rear of the vehicle until the rear wheels are clear of the ground by at least 4 in. Support the rear of the vehicle with jackstands.

CAUTION

The rear of the vehicle must be firmly supported during this test. If one of the rear wheels should come in contact with the ground while it is turning, the vehicle will move forward very rapidly and unexpectedly. As an extra precaution, chock the front wheels and do not stand in front of the vehicle while the wheels are turning.

---

2. Disconnect the vacuum hose from the distributor vacuum advance chamber. This is the outer hose on cars with dual diaphragm vacuum advance units.

3. Connect the hose to a vacuum gauge.

4. Pour hot water on the temperature-sensing switch to make sure that it is above 65°F.

5. Start the engine and apply the foot brake. Depress the clutch and shift the transmission into High gear. Release the hand brake and slowly engage the clutch.

6. Have an assistant observe the vacuum gauge while you raise the speed of the engine until the speedometer reads 35 mph, at which time the vacuum gauge should show a reading.

7. If the vacuum gauge shows a reading below 35 mph, a component in the electronic spark control system is defective. If the vacuum gauge does not show a reading, even above 35 mph, there is either a defective component in the electronic spark control system, or there is a broken or clogged vacuum passage between the carburetor and the distributor.

HEATED AIR INTAKE TEST

1. With the engine completely cold, look inside the cold air duct and make sure that the valve plate is fully in the up position (closing the cold air duct).

2. Start the engine and bring it to operating temperature.

3. Stop the engine and look inside the cold air duct again. The valve plate should be down, allowing an opening from the cold air duct into the air cleaner.

4. If the unit appears to be malfunctioning, remove it and examine it to make sure that the springs are not broken or disconnected, and replace the thermostat if all other parts appear intact and properly connected.

TRANSMISSION-REGULATED SPARK

Transmission Valve Test

1. Attach a test light to the wire which connects the transmission valve to the distributor modulator valve.

2. Jack up and support the vehicle, so that the rear wheels are free to turn.

3. Start the engine and engage the transmission in Low gear. Observe the test light, which should be lighted at this time.

4. On standard transmissions, engage High gear and check to see that the light goes out.

5. On automatic transmissions, place the vehicle in Drive and allow it to upshift. Upon the shift into High gear, the test light should go out.

6. If the test lamp fails to function properly, replace the transmission valve.

EGR System

EGR VALVE OPERATION TEST

1. Disconnect the EGR valve vacuum supply line and plug the source side of the line.

2. Start the engine and allow it to reach operating temperature.

3. Supply vacuum to the EGR valve vacuum supply line. The stem of the EGR valve should visibly move. As more vacuum is applied to the valve, it should open fully and the engine idle should roughen, rpm drop, and/or the engine stop completely.

4. If the idle quality doesn't change, there is no EGR taking place. Remove the EGR valve and either replace it or try to clean it. After cleaning, repeat the above test. If the valve still does not perform satisfactorily, replace it.

5. If the valve opens when vacuum is applied and disrupts the engine idle, but the engine doesn't return to a smooth idle when no vacuum is applied to the valve, then the valve may not be closing and sealing properly. Remove the valve and/or clean or replace it. Recheck the operation of the valve if it is cleaned or replaced.

EGR CARBURETOR PORT CHECK

1. Disconnect the vacuum line from the EGR carburetor vacuum port.

2. Open and release the throttle very quickly at least to the ½ open position. Be careful not to overrev the engine. Have a finger placed over the port at the same time the throttle is blipped.

3. Vacuum should be present when the throttle is opened. If no vacuum can be detected, the port is blocked and should be cleaned.

PVS OPERATION CHECK

On PVS units with two or three outlets, vacuum should pass through the PVS when the engine is started and allowed to reach normal operating temperature.

On PVS units with four outlets, vacuum should be routed between the two outlets marked ''D'' and ''M'' when the engine is started and allowed to reach normal operating temperature.

EGR VALVE CLEANING

1. Remove the EGR valve from the engine.

2. Use a small hand drill to clean the orifice hole in the EGR valve body if it is blocked or restricted by deposits. Use EXTREME care not to enlarge the hole or damage the surface.

3. Separate the diaphragm section from the main mounting body.

4. Clean the valve plate, stem, and the mounting plate with a small rotary type wire brush powered by an electric drill. Take care not to damage any parts.

5. Remove deposits between the stem and the valve disc with a steel blade or shim stock. The poppet must be free to wobble and move axially before reassembly.

6. Clean the cavity and passages in the main body section with the rotary type wire brush.

7. Remove all debris with compressed air.

8. Reassemble the diaphragm to the main body using a new gasket between them. Tighten the attaching screws to 28 in. lbs.

9. Clean the orifice plate and the counterbore in the valve body and reinstall the orifice by using a small amount of cement to retain the plate in place while assembling the valve to the engine. Apply cement only to the outer edges of the orifice plate to avoid restricting the orifice.

NOTE: Some EGR valves are riveted together and cannot be taken apart for cleaning. These must be discarded if they cannot be cleaned enough to perform satisfactorily.

EXHAUST HEAT CONTROL VALVE (HEAT RISER) CHECK

Check and make sure that the valve is free to operate and not frozen or restricted from moving by rust. When the engine is first started (cold) the valve should remain closed. As the engine heats up, the valve should gradually open until the engine reaches normal operating temperature when the valve should be completely open. Check the PVS, if the valve is vacuum-operated, in the manner previously described. Make sure that the vacuum line is in good condition and is not restricted in any way.

COLD TEMPERATURE ACTUATED VACUUM SYSTEM (CTAV) DIAGNOSES

1. Connect a tachometer to the engine. Connect a vacuum gauge to the vacuum line leading to the distributor vacuum advance diaphragm. Make sure that the tem-

perature sensing switch is above 65°F. Disconnect the electrical lead from the 3-way solenoid vacuum valve.

2. Start the engine and rev it to 1,500 rpm. There should be about 15 in. Hg. of vacuum present at the distributor advance diaphragm. If no vacuum reading is observed, check the vacuum source back to the carburetor spark port.

3. Connect the electrical lead to the 3-way solenoid vacuum valve. No or low vacuum should be present at the distributor. If the vacuum is substantial, check the vacuum valve ground and electrical source back to the ignition switch.

4. Rev the engine at 3,000 rpm. The vacuum present at the distributor should be about 9 in. Hg. If no vacuum is present, check the vacuum source back to the carburetor.

5. If steps 2 through 4 are positive, the vacuum system is normal and the engine can be shut off.

6. Attach a grounded test light to the 3-way solenoid vacuum valve. Disconnect the electrical connector at the temperature switch located in the air cleaner. Turn the ignition to On.

7. If the test light glows, replace the latching relay.

8. If the test light does not glow, reconnect the electrical connector at the temperature switch in the carburetor air cleaner. The light should come on.

9. If the test light does not glow, check the temperature switch and electrical source back to the ignition switch.

10. If the test light came on in step 8, disconnect the connector at the temperature sensing switch in the air cleaner. The light should remain on. If the light goes out, replace the latching relay.

11. Connect the test light to the temperature switch terminal and cool the switch to below 49°F. The light should go out when the switch is cooled. If the light remains on, replace the temperature switch.

FUEL SYSTEM

Fuel Pump

The mechanical fuel pump used on all of the engines is camshaft eccentric-actuated and located on the lower left center of the engine block on six-cylinder engines and on the left-side of the front cover on V8 engines.

REMOVAL

1. Disconnect the fuel inlet and outlet lines at the fuel pump. Discard the fuel inlet retaining clamp.

2. Remove the pump retaining bolts then remove the pump assembly and gasket from the engine. Discard the gasket.

INSTALLATION

1. If a new pump is to be installed, remove the fuel line connector fitting from the old pump and install it in the new pump.

2. Remove all gasket material from the mounting pad and pump flange. Apply oil-resistant sealer to both sides of a new gasket.

3. Position the new gasket on the pump flange and hold tbe pump in position against the mounting pad. Make sure that the rocker arm is riding on the camshaft eccentric.

4. Press the pump tight against the pad, install the retaining bolts and alternately torque them to 12–15 ft. lbs. on 6 cylinder engines and 20–24 ft. lbs. on the 302; 14–20 on 351 and 400; 19–27 on 360, and 390 engines. Connect the fuel lines. Use a new clamp on the fuel inlet lines.

5. Operate the engine and check for leaks.

TESTING

Incorrect fuel pump pressure and low volume (flow rate) are the two most likely fuel pump troubles that will affect engine performance. Low pressure will cause a lean mixture and fuel starvation at high speeds and excessive pressure will cause high fuel consumption and carburetor flooding.

To determine that the fuel pump is in satisfactory operating condition, tests for both fuel pump pressure and volume should be performed.

The tests are performed with the fuel pump installed on the engine and the engine at normal operating temperature and at idle speed.

Before the test, make sure that the replaceable fuel filter has been changed at the proper mileage interval. If in doubt, install a new filter.

Pressure Test

1. Remove the air cleaner assembly. Disconnect the fuel inlet line of the fuel filter at the carburetor. Use care to prevent fire, due to fuel spillage. Place an absorbent cloth under the connection before removing the line to catch any fuel that might flow out of the line.

2. Connect a pressure gauge, a restrictor and a flexible hose between the fuel filter and the carburetor.

3. Position the flexible hose and the restrictor so that the fuel can be discharged into a suitable, graduated container.

4. Before taking a pressure reading, operate the engine at the specified idle rpm and vent the system into the container by opening the hose restrictor momentarily.

5. Close the hose restrictor, allow the pressure to stabilize and note the reading. The pressure should be 5 psi.

If the pump pressure is not within 4–6 psi and the fuel lines and filter are in satisfactory condition, the pump is defective

and should be replaced.

If the pump pressure is within the proper range, perform the test for fuel volume.

Volume Test

1. Operate the engine at the specified idle rpm.

2. Open the hose restrictor and catch the fuel in the container while observing the time it takes to pump 1 pint. 1 pint should be pumped in 20 seconds. If the pump does not pump to specifications, check for proper fuel tank venting or a restriction in the fuel line leading from the fuel tank to the carburetor before replacing the fuel pump.

Carburetors

REMOVAL AND INSTALLATION

1. Remove the air cleaner.

2. Remove the throttle cable or rod from the throttle lever. Disconnect the distributor vacuum line, EGR vacuum line, if so equipped, the inline fuel filter, and the choke heat tube at the carburetor.

3. Disconnect the choke clean air tube from the air horn. Disconnect the choke actuating cable, if so equipped.

4. Remove the carburetor retaining nuts then remove the carburetor. Remove the carburetor mounting gasket, spacer (if so equipped), and the lower gasket from the intake manifold.

5. Before installing the carburetor, clean the gasket mounting surfaces of the spacer and carburetor. Place the spacer between two new gaskets and position the spacer and gaskets on the intake manifold. Position the carburetor body flange, snug the nuts, then alternately tighten each nut in a criss-cross pattern.

6. Connect the inline fuel filter, throttle cable, choke heat tube, distributor vacuum line, EGR vacuum line, and choke cable.

7. Connect the choke clean air line to the air horn.

8. Adjust the engine idle speed, the idle fuel mixture and anti-stall dashpot (if so equipped). Install the air cleaner.

Fuel Tank

REMOVAL AND INSTALLATION

In-Cab Fuel Tank

1. Siphon the fuel from the tank into a suitable container through the filler neck.

2. Move the seat to the full forward position and tilt the seat forward.

3. Disconnect the fuel gauge sending unit wire and fuel line from the tank. Disconnect the vapor vent chamber and vapor lines of the fuel evaporative emission control system.

4. Loosen the filler neck hose clamp at the tank end of the hose, and pull the filler neck away from the tank.

5. Remove the fuel tank retaining nuts and bolts and lift the tank out of the cab. If the tank is being replaced, remove the fuel gauge sending unit and install it in the new tank.

6. Install the fuel tank in the reverse order of removal.

In-Frame Fuel Tank

1. Drain the fuel from the tank into a suitable container by either removing the drain plug, if so equipped, or siphoning through the filler cap opening.

2. Disconnect the fuel gauge sending unit wire and fuel outlet line.

3. Disconnect the air relief tube from the filler neck and fuel tank.

4. Loosen the filler neck hose clamp at the fuel tank and pull the filler neck away from the tank.

5. Remove the retaining strap mounting nuts and bolts and lower the tank to the floor.

6. If a new tank is being installed, change over the fuel gauge sending unit to the new tank.

7. Install the fuel tank in the reverse order of removal.

Behind-The-Axle Fuel Tank

1. Raise the rear of the truck.

2. Disconnect the negative battery cable.

3. Disconnect the fuel gauge sending unit wire at the fuel tank.

4. Remove the fuel drain plug or siphon the fuel from the tank into a suitable container.

5. Loosen the fuel line hose clamps, slide the clamps forward and disconnect the fuel line at the fuel gauge sending unit.

6. If the sending unit is to be removed, turn the unit retaining ring counterclockwise and remove the sending unit, retaining ring and gasket. Discard the gasket.

7. Loosen the clamps on the fuel filler pipe and vent hose as necessary and disconnect the filler pipe hose and vent hose from the tank.

8. If the tank is the metal type, support the tank and remove the bolts attaching the tank supports to the frame. Carefully lower the tank and disconnect the vent tube from the vapor emisson control valve in the top of the tank. Finish removing the filler pipe and filler pipe vent hose if not possible previously. Remove the tank from under the vehicle.

9. If the tank is the plastic type, support the tank and remove the bolts attaching the combination skid plate and tank support to the frame. Carefully lower the tank and disconnect the vent tube from the vapor emission control valve in the top of the tank. Finish removing the filler pipe and filler pipe vent hose if it was not possible previously. Remove the skid plate and tank

from under the vehicle. Remove the skid plate from the tank.

10. Install the tank in the reverse order of removal.

MANUAL TRANSMISSION

LINKAGE ADJUSTMENT— EXCEPT VANS

Ford 3.03 and Warner T-85N, T-87, T-89

1. Place the shifter in the Neutral position and insert a gauge pin (3/16 in. diameter) through the steering column shift levers and the locating hole in the spacer.

2. If the shift rods at the transmission are equipped with threaded sleeves, adjust the sleeves so that they enter the shift levers on the transmission easily with the shift levers in the Neutral position. Now lengthen the rods seven turns of the sleeves and insert them into the shift levers.

3. If the shift rods are slotted, loosen the attaching nut, make sure that the transmission shift levers are in the Neutral position, then retighten the attaching nuts.

4. Remove the gauge pin and check the operation of the shift linkage.

Ford Four-Speed Overdrive

1. Attach the shift rods to the levers.

2. Rotate the output shaft to determine that the transmission is in neutral.

3. Insert an alignment pin into the shift control assembly alignment hole.

4. Attach the slotted end of the shift rods over the flats of the studs in the shift control assembly.

5. Install the locknuts and remove the alignment pin.

LINKAGE ADJUSTMENT—VANS

3-Speed

1. Place the gearshift lever in the Neutral position.

2. Loosen the adjustment nuts on the transmission shift levers sufficiently to allow the shift rods to slide freely on the transmission shift levers.

3. Insert a 1/4 in. rod (3/16 in. for '76–'82) through the pilot hole in the shift tube mounting bracket (1975 only) until it enters the adjustment hole of both the upper and lower shift lever.

4. Place the transmission shift levers in the Neutral position and tighten the adjustment nuts on the transmission shift levers.

5. Remove the 1/4 in. rod from the pilot hole, and check the operation of the gearshift lever in all gear positions.

4-Speed Overdrive

1. Disconnect the 3 shift rods from the shifter assembly.

2. Insert a .25″ diameter pin through the alignment hole in the shifter assembly. Make sure the levers are in the neutral position.

3. Align the 3 transmission levers as follows: forward lever (3rd–4th lever) in the mid-position (neutral), rearward lever (1st–2nd lever) in the mid-position (neutral), and middle lever (reverse lever) rotate counterclockwise to the neutral position.

4. Rotate the output shaft to assure that the transmission is in neutral.

5. Attach the slotted end of the shift rods over the slots of the studs in the shifter assembly. Install and tighten the locknuts to 15–20 ft. lbs.

6. Remove the alignment pin. Check for proper operation.

Pick-Ups

REMOVAL AND INSTALLATION

Ford 3.03 and Warner T-85N, T-87, T-89

1. Raise the vehicle and support it with jackstands. Support the engine with a jack and a block of wood placed under the oil pan.

2. Drain the lubricant out of the transmission by removing the drain plug if so equipped, or removing the lower extension housing-to-transmission bolt.

3. Position a transmission jack under the transmission.

4. Disconnect the gearshift linkage at the transmission.

5. On the Warner T-85N model, disconnect the solenoid and governor wires at the connectors near the solenoid. Remove the overdrive wiring harness from its clip on the transmission. Disconnect the overdrive cable.

6. If the vehicle has 4WD, remove the transfer case shift lever bracket from the transmission.

7. Disconnect the speedometer cable.

8. Disconnect the driveshaft from the differential and transmission and remove it from the vehicle.

9. Raise the transmission if necessary and remove the rear support.

10. Remove the transmission-to-flywheel housing attaching bolts.

11. Move the transmission to the rear until the input shaft clears the flywheel housing and lower the transmission out and from under the vehicle.

NOTE: Do not depress the clutch pedal while the transmission is removed.

12. Before installing the transmission, apply a light film of grease to the release bearing inner hub surface, the release lever fulcrum and fork, and the front bearing re-

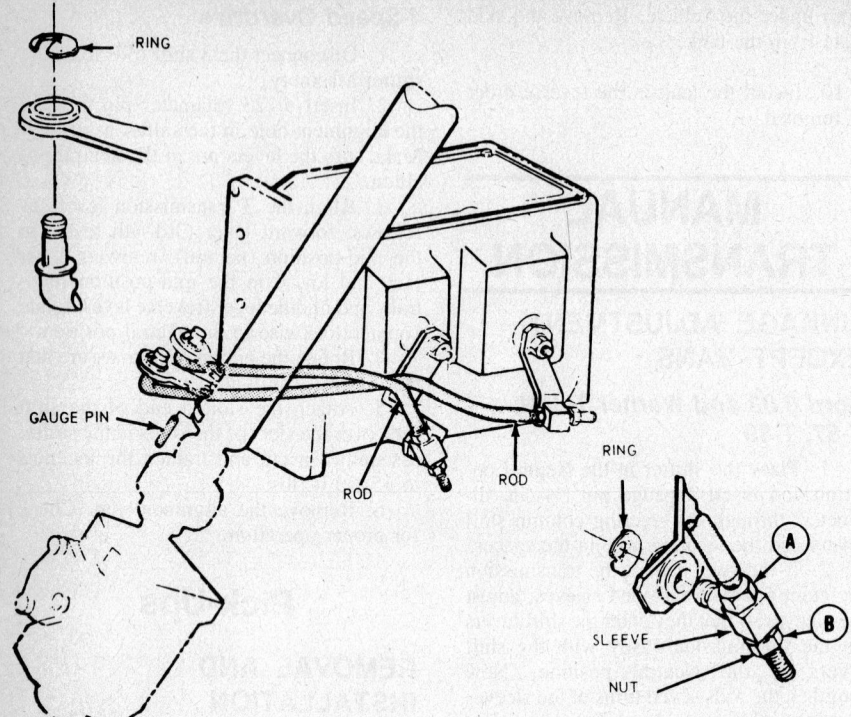

3-speed manual transmission shift linkage adjustment on pick-ups using threaded sleeves

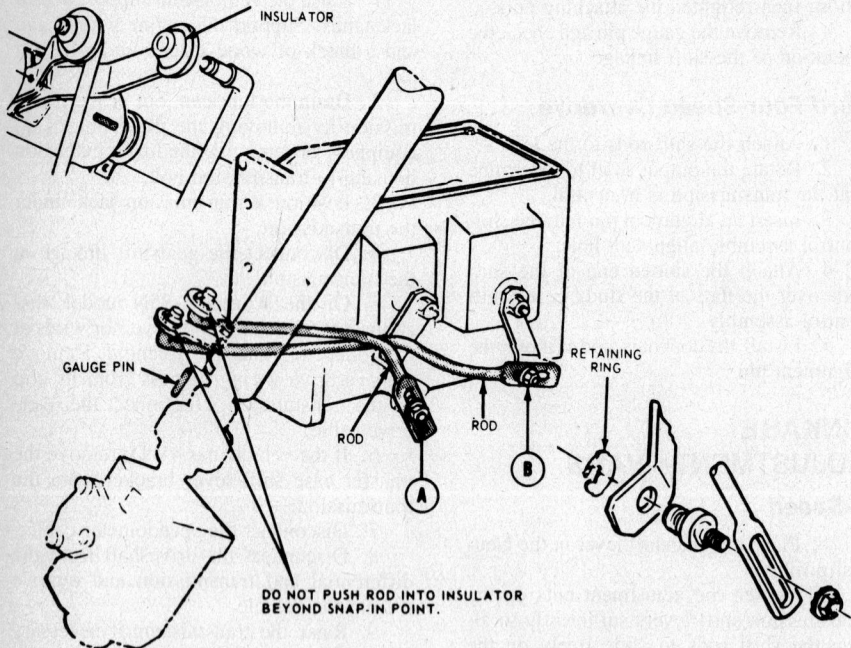

3-speed manual transmission shift linkage adjustment on pick-ups using slotted rods

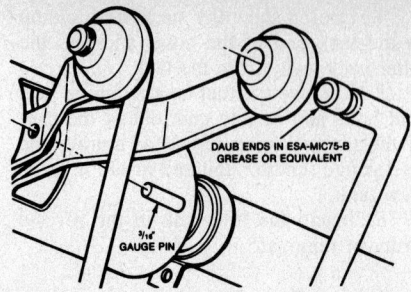

1976 and later van shift linkage adjustment

tainer of the transmission. Do not apply excessive grease because it will fly off due to centrifugal force and contaminate the clutch disc.

13. Install the transmission in the reverse order of removal. It may be necessary to turn the output shaft with the transmission in gear to align the input shaft splines with the splines in the clutch disc. Fill the

transmission with lubricant and adjust the shift linkage.

Warner T-18 4-Speed

1. Disconnect the back-up light switch at the rear of the gearshift housing cover.
2. Remove the rubber boot, floor mat, and the body floor pan cover. Remove the

gearshift lever. Remove the weatherpad.
3. Raise the vehicle and support it with jackstands. Position a transmission jack under the transmission and disconnect the speedometer cable.
4. Disconnect the driveshaft from the transmission and wire it up to one side.
5. Remove the rear transmission support.
6. Remove the transmission attaching bolts.
7. Move the transmission to the rear until the input shaft clears the flywheel housing and lower the transmission.
8. Before installing the transmission, apply a light film of grease to the inner hub surface of the clutch release bearing, the release lever fulcrum and the front bearing retainer of the transmission. Do not apply excessive grease because it will fly off onto the clutch disc.
9. Install the transmission in the reverse order of removal. It may be necessary to turn the output shaft with the transmission in gear to align the input shaft splines with the splines in the clutch disc. Fill the transmission with lubricant if it was drained.

New Process 435 4-Speed

1. Remove the rubber boot and floor mat.
2. Remove the floor pan, transmission cover plate, and weather pad. It may be necessary to remove the seat assembly.
3. Disconnect the back-up light switch located in the rear of the gearshift housing cover.
4. Raise the vehicle and place jackstands under the frame to support it. Place a transmission jack under the transmission and disconnect the speedometer cable.
5. Disconnect the parking brake lever from its linkage and remove the gearshift housing.
6. Disconnect the driveshaft.
7. Remove the transmission rear support.
8. Remove the transmission-to-flywheel housing attaching bolts, slide the transmission rearward until the input shaft clears the flywheel housing and lower it out from under the truck.
9. Before installing the transmission, apply a light film of grease to the inner hub

surface of the clutch release bearing, release lever fulcrum and fork, and the front bearing retainer of the transmission. Do not apply excessive grease because it will fly off and contaminate the clutch disc.

10. Install the transmission in the reverse order of removal. It may be necessary to turn the output shaft with the transmission in gear to align the input shaft splines with the splines in the clutch disc. The front bearing retainer is installed through the clutch release bearing.

Ford Four-Speed Overdrive

1. Raise the truck and support it on jackstands.
2. Mark the driveshaft so that it can be installed in the same position.
3. Disconnect the driveshaft at the rear U-joint and slide it off the transmission output shaft.
4. Disconnect the speedometer cable from the transmission.
5. Remove the shift rods from the levers and the shift control from the extension housing.
6. Support the engine and remove the extension housing-to-crossmember bolts.
7. Support the transmission on a jack and unbolt it from the engine.
8. Move the transmission and jack rearward until clear. If necessary, lower the engine enough for clearance.
9. Installation is the reverse of removal. It is a good idea to install and snug-down the upper transmission-to-engine bolts first, then the lower. For linkage adjustment, see the beginning of this chapter. Check the fluid level.

Single Rail Four-Speed Overdrive

1. Raise the vehicle on a hoist and remove the lubricant.
2. Mark the driveshaft so that it can be installed in the same position then disconnect the driveshaft from the rear U-joint flange. Slide the driveshaft off the transmission output shaft.
3. Disconnect the speedometer cable from the extension housing.
4. Remove the three screws securing the shift tower to the turret assembly.
5. Remove the shift tower from the turret assembly.
6. Support the engine with a transmission jack and remove the bolts which attach the rear extension housing to the engine.
7. Raise the rear of the engine high enough to remove the weight from the crossmember.
8. Remove the bolts retaining the crossmember to the frame side supports and remove the crossmember.
9. Support the transmission on a jack and remove the bolts that attach the transmission to the flywheel housing.
10. Move the transmission and jack rearward until the transmission input shaft clears the flywheel housing.

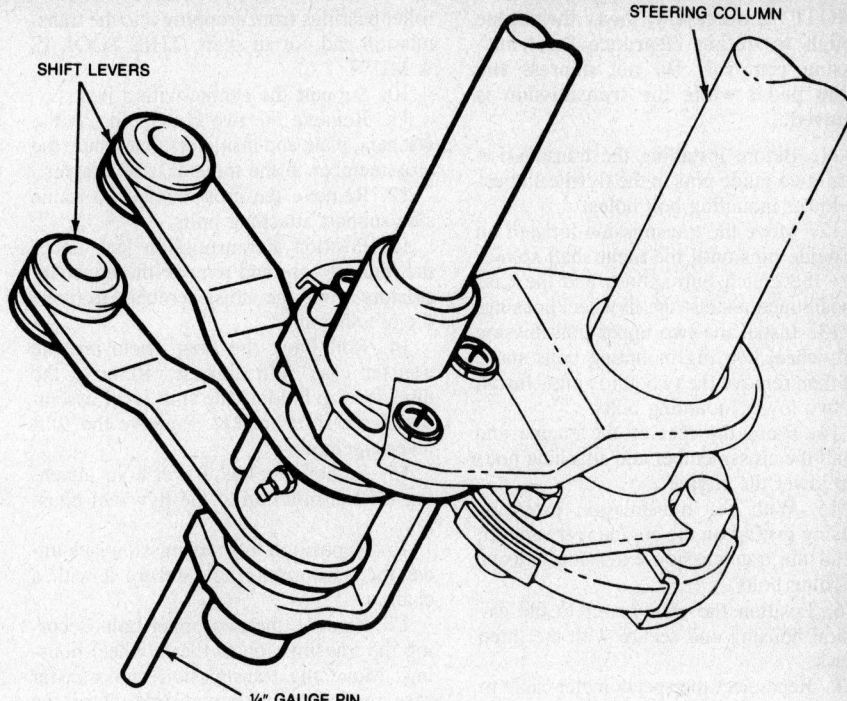

1975 van shift linkage adjustment, 3 speed

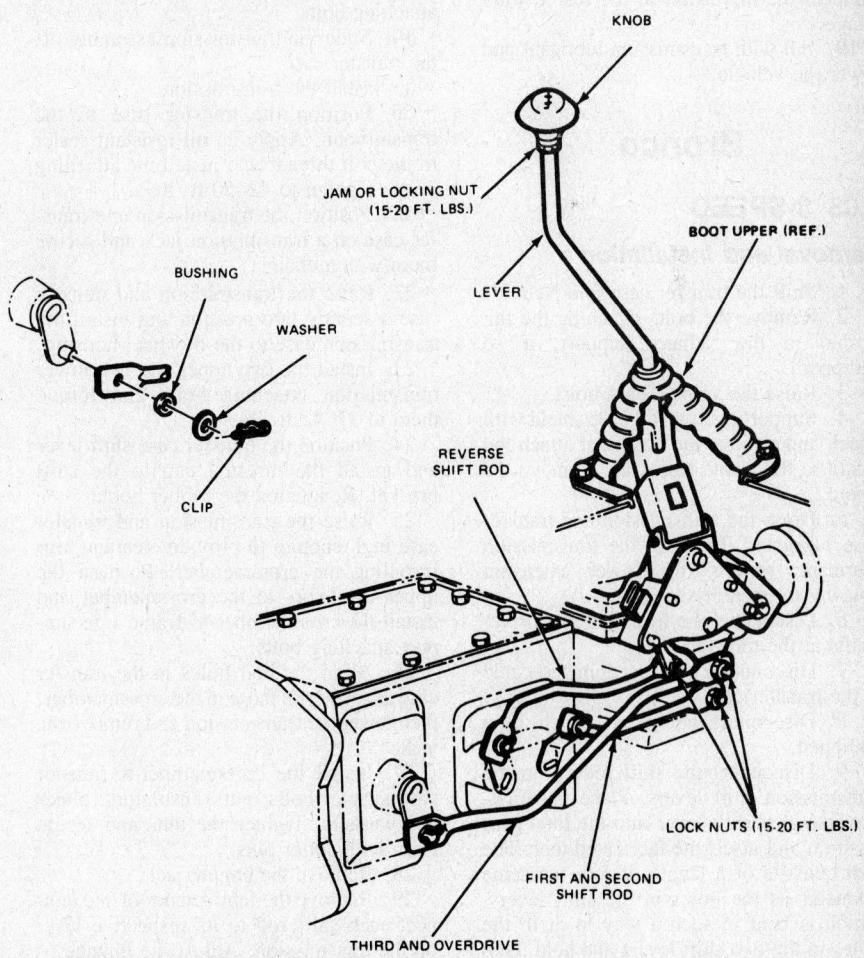

4-speed overdrive shift linkage adjustment

NOTE: If necessary, lower the engine enough to obtain clearance for transmission removal. Do not depress the clutch pedal while the transmission is removed.

11. Before installing the transmission install two guide pins in the flywheel housing lower mounting bolt holes.

12. Move the transmission forward on the guide pins until the input shaft splines enter the clutch hub splines and the case is positioned against the flywheel housing.

13. Install the two upper transmission to flywheel housing mounting bolts snug, and then remove the two guide pins. Install the two lower mounting bolts.

14. Raise the rear of the engine and install the crossmember and attaching bolts then lower the engine.

15. With the transmission extension housing resting on the engine rear support, install the transmission extension housing attaching bolts.

16. Position the shift tower to the extension housing and secure with the three screws.

17. Reconnect the speedometer cable to the extension housing.

18. Slide the forward end of the driveshaft over the transmission output shaft. Connect the driveshaft to the rear U-joint flange.

19. Fill with transmission lubricant and lower the vehicle.

Bronco

3.03 3-SPEED

Removal and Installation

1. Shift the transfer case into Neutral.
2. Remove the bolts attaching the fan shroud to the radiator support, if so equipped.
3. Raise the vehicle on a hoist.
4. Support the transfer case shield with a jack and remove the bolts that attach the shield to the frame side rails. Remove the shield.
5. Drain the transmission and transfer case lubricant. To drain the transmission lubricant, remove the lower extension housing-to-transmission bolt.
6. Disconnect the front and rear driveshafts at the transfer case.
7. Disconnect the speedometer cable at the transfer case.
8. Disconnect the T.R.S. switch, if so equipped.
9. Disconnect the shift rods from the transmission shift levers. Place the First-Reverse gear shift lever into the First gear position and insert the fabricated tool. The tool consists of a length of rod, the same diameter as the holes in the shift levers, which is bent in such a way to fit in the holes in the two shift levers and hold them in the position stated above. More important, this tool will prevent the input shaft

roller bearings from dropping into the transmission and output shaft. THIS TOOL IS A MUST.

10. Support the engine with a jack.
11. Remove the two cotter pins, bolts, washers, plate and insulators that secure the crossmember to the transfer case adapter.
12. Remove the crossmember-to-frame side support attaching bolts.
13. Position a transmission jack under the transfer case and remove the upper insulators from the crossmember. Remove the crossmember.
14. Roll back the boot enclosing the transfer case shift linkage. Remove the threaded cap holding the shift lever assembly to the shift bracket. Remove the shift lever assembly.
15. Remove the two lower bolts attaching the transmission to the flywheel housing.
16. Reposition the transmission jack under the transmission and secure it with a chain.
17. Remove the two upper bolts securing the transmission to the flywheel housing. Move the transmission and transfer case rearward and downward out of the vehicle.
18. Move the assembly to a bench and remove the transfer case-to-transmission attaching bolts.
19. Slide the transmission assembly off the transfer case.

To install the transmission:

20. Position the transfer case to the transmission. Apply an oil-resistant sealer to the bolt threads and install the attaching bolts. Tighten to 42–50 ft. lbs.
21. Position the transmission and transfer case on a transmission jack and secure them with a chain.
22. Raise the transmission and transfer case assembly into position and install the transmission case to the flywheel housing.
23. Install the two upper and two lower transmission attaching bolts and torque them to 37–42 ft. lbs.
24. Position the transfer case shift lever and install the threaded cap to the shift bracket. Reposition the rubber boot.
25. Raise the transmission and transfer case high enough to provide clearance for installing the crossmember. Position the upper insulators to the crossmember and install the crossmember-to-frame side support attaching bolts.
26. Align the bolt holes in the transfer case adapter with those in the crossmember, then lower the transmission and remove the jack.
27. Install the crossmember-to-transfer case adapter bolts, nuts, insulators, plates and washers. Tighten the nuts and secure them with cotter pins.
28. Remove the engine jack.
29. Remove the fabricated tool and connect each shift rod to its respective lever on the transmission. Adjust the linkage.
30. Connect the speedometer cable.
31. Connect the T.R.S. switch, if so

equipped.
32. Install the front and rear driveshafts to the transfer case.
33. Fill the transmission and transfer case to the bottom of the filler hole with the recommended lubricant.
34. Position the transfer case shield to the frame side rails and install the attaching bolts.
35. Lower the vehicle.
36. Install the fan shroud, if so equipped.
37. Check the operation of the transfer case and the transmission shift linkage.

1978–81 NP435

Removal

1. Remove the rubber boot and floor mat.
2. Remove the weather pad. It may be necessary first to remove the seat assembly.
3. Disconnect the back-up light switch located in the rear of the gearshift housing cover.
4. Raise the vehicle and position safety stands. Position a transmission jack under the transmission, and disconnect the speedometer cable.
5. Disconnect the parking brake lever from its linkage, and remove the gearshift housing.
6. Disconnect the driveshaft or coupling shaft. Remove the bolts that attach the coupling shaft center support to the crossmember and wire the coupling shaft and driveshaft to one side. Remove the transfer case.
7. Remove the transmission attaching bolts at the clutch housing, and remove the transmission.

Installation

Before installing the transmission apply a light film of chassis lubricant to the release lever fulcrum and fork. Do not apply a thick coat of grease to these parts, as it will work out and contaminate the clutch disc.

1. Place the transmission on a transmission jack, and raise the transmission until the input shaft splines are aligned with the clutch disc splines. The clutch release bearing and hub must be properly positioned in the release lever fork.
2. Install guide studs in the clutch housing and slide the transmission forward on the guide studs until it is in position on the clutch housing. Install the attaching bolts or nuts, and tighten them to the following torques:

$\frac{7}{16}$–14: 40–50 ft. lbs.
$\frac{5}{8}$–11: 120–150 ft. lbs.
$\frac{9}{16}$–12: 90–115 ft. lbs.
$\frac{5}{8}$–18C: 120–150 ft. lbs.
$\frac{9}{16}$–18C: 90–115 ft. lbs.

Remove the guide studs and install the two lower attaching bolts.

3. Install the bolts attaching the coupling shaft center support to the crossmember. Tighten the bolts to 40–50 ft. lbs.

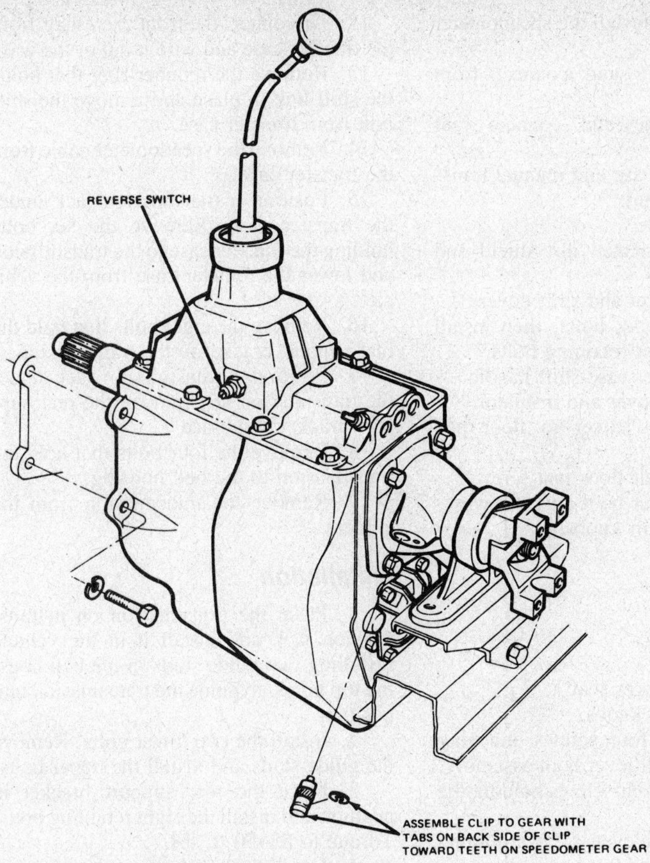

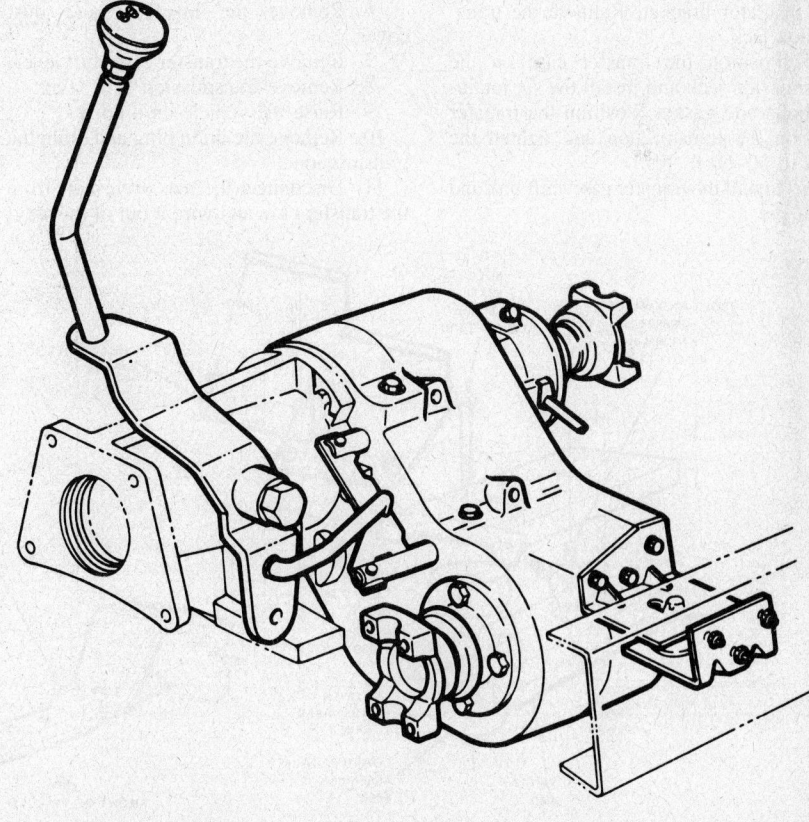

REVERSE SWITCH

ASSEMBLE CLIP TO GEAR WITH
TABS ON BACK SIDE OF CLIP
TOWARD TEETH ON SPEEDOMETER GEAR

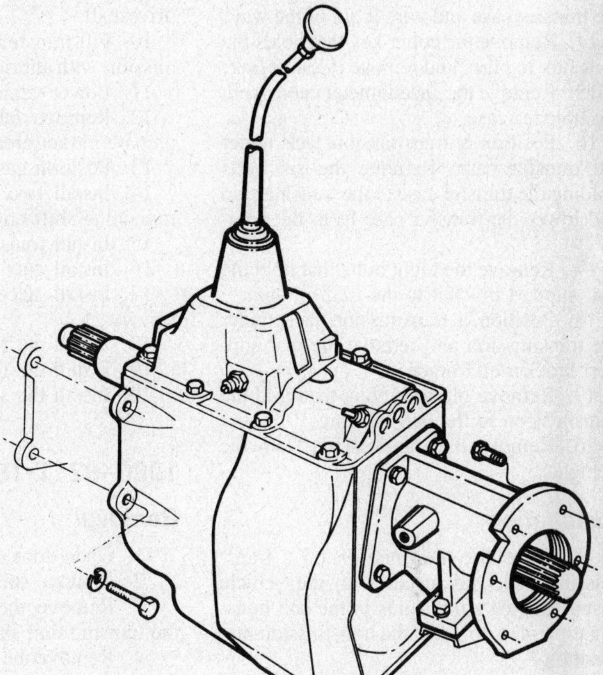

1978 and later NP435 4-speed installation

4. Connect the driveshaft or coupling shaft and the speedometer cable. Tighten the U-joint nuts.

5. Connect the back-up light switch wire.

6. Install the transmission cover plate. Install the seat assembly if it was removed.

7. Install weather pad, pad retainer, floor mat, and rubber boot.

1979 T-18

Removal

1. Open door cover seat.

2. Remove shift knobs.

3. Remove the four screws attaching the transmission shift lever boot assembly.

4. Remove the four screws holding the floor mat.

5. Remove the eleven screws holding the access cover to the floor pan. Place the shift lever in the reverse position and remove the cover.

6. Remove the insulator and dust cover.

7. Remove the transfer case shift lever.

8. Remove the eight bolts holding the shift cover and gasket.

9. Use cardboard or heavy paper to fabricate a suitable cover for the shift cover opening to protect the transmission from dirt during removal.

10. Raise the vehicle on a hoist.

1978 and later NP435 transmission-to-transfer case mounting

11. Remove the drain pan and drain the transmission.

12. Disconnect the rear driveshaft from the transfer case and wire it out of the way.

13. Disconnect the front driveshaft from the transfer case and wire it out of the way.

14. Remove the cotter key that holds the shift link in place and remove the shift link.

15. Remove the speedometer cable from the transfer case.

16. Position a transmission jack under the transfer case. Remove the six bolts holding the transfer case to the transmission and lower the transfer case from the vehicle.

17. Remove the eight bolts that hold the rear support bracket to the transmission.

18. Position a transmission jack under the transmission and remove the rear support bracket and brace.

19. Remove the four bolts that hold the transmission to the bell housing.

20. Remove the transmission from the vehicle.

Installation

1. Place the transmission on a transmission jack and install it in the vehicle installing two guide studs in the bell housing top holes, to guide the transmission into position.

2. Install the two lower bolts. Remove the guide studs and install the upper bolts.

3. Place the rear support bracket in position and install the eight retaining bolts.

4. Install the two bolts at the rear support insulator bracket. Remove the transmission jack.

5. Position the transfer case on the transmission jack and install the six retaining bolts and gasket. Position the transfer case on the transmission and tighten the bolts to 50–60 ft. lbs.

6. Install the transfer case shift link and cotter pin.

7. Position and install the speedometer cable.

8. Remove wire and connect front driveshaft.

9. Remove wire and connect rear driveshaft.

10. Fill transfer case and manual transmission with lubricant.

11. Lower vehicle.

12. Remove fabricated dirt shield and prepare gasket area.

13. Position gasket and shift cover.

14. Install two pilot bolts, then install remaining shift cover retaining bolts.

15. Install transfer case shift handle.

16. Install dust cover and insulator.

17. Install access cover to floor pan screws.

18. Install the four floor mat screws.

19. Install the four boot area screws.

20. Install the shift knobs.

1980–82 T-18

Removal

1. Open door cover seat.

2. Remove shift knobs.

3. Remove the four screws attaching the transmission shift lever boot assembly.

4. Remove the four screws holding the floor mat.

5. Remove the eleven screws holding the access cover to the floor pan. Place the shift lever in the reverse position and remove the cover.

6. Remove the insulator and dust cover.

7. Remove the transfer case shift lever.

8. Remove transmission shift lever.

9. Raise the vehicle on a hoist.

10. Remove the drain plug and drain the transmission.

11. Disconnect the rear driveshaft from the transfer case and wire it out of the way.

12. Disconnect the front driveshaft from the transfer case and wire it out of the way.

13. Remove the retainer ring that holds the shift link in place and remove the shift link from transfer case.

14. Remove the speedometer cable from the transfer case.

15. Position a transmission jack under the transfer case. Remove the six bolts holding the transfer case to the transmission and lower the transfer case from the vehicle.

16. Remove the eight bolts that hold the rear support bracket to the transmission.

17. Position a transmission jack under the transmission and remove the rear support bracket and brace.

18. Remove the four bolts that hold the transmission to the bell housing.

19. Remove the transmission from the vehicle.

Installation

1. Place the transmission on a transmission jack and install it in the vehicle installing two guide studs in the bell housing top holes, to guide the transmission into position.

2. Install the two lower bolts. Remove the guide studs and install the upper bolts.

3. Place the rear support bracket in position and install the eight retaining bolts. Torque to 35–50 ft. lbs.

4. Install the two bolts at the rear support insulator bracket. Remove the transmission jack.

5. Position the transfer case on the transmission jack and install the six retaining bolts and gasket. Position the transfer case on the transmission and tighten the bolts to 28–33 ft. lbs.

6. Install the transfer case shift link and retainer ring.

7. Position and install the speedometer cable.

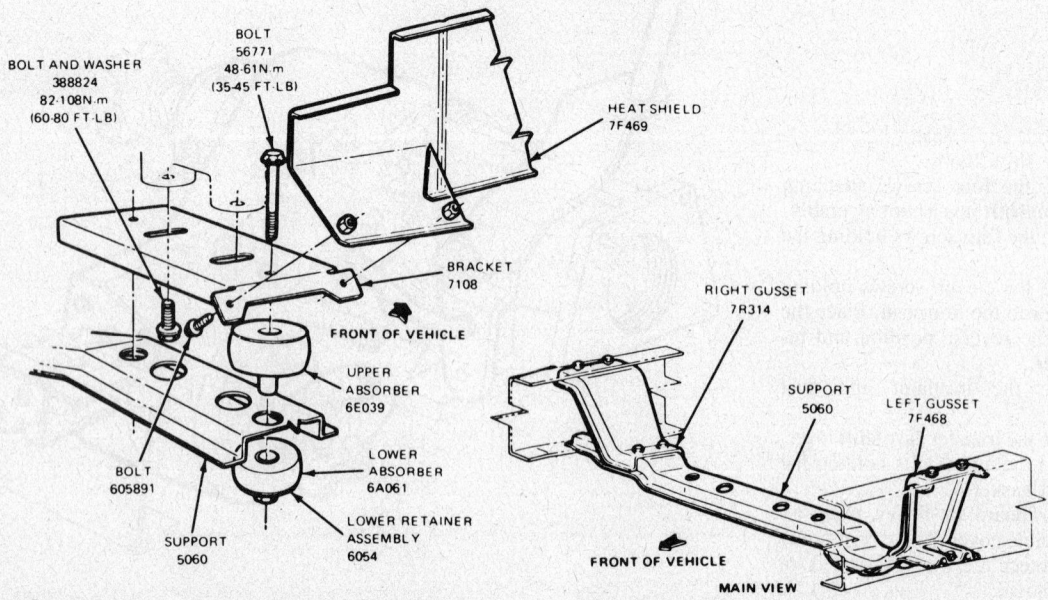

1980 and later T-18 crossmember installation

8. Remove wire and connect front driveshaft.

9. Remove wire and connect rear driveshaft.

10. Fill transfer case and transmission.

11. Lower vehicle.

12. Remove fabricated dirt shield and prepare gasket area.

13. Position gasket and shift cover.

14. Install two pilot bolts, then install remaining shift cover retaining bolts.

15. Install transfer case shift handle and transmission shift lever.

16. Install dust cover and insulator.

17. Install access cover to floor pan screws.

18. Install the four floor mat screws.

19. Install the four boot area screws.

20. Install the shift knobs.

FORD SINGLE RAIL OVERDRIVE

Removal

1. Raise the vehicle and support it on jackstands.

2. Mark the driveshaft so that it may be installed in the same relative position. Disconnect the driveshaft from the rear U-joint flange. Slide the driveshaft off the transmission output shaft and install an extension housing seal installation tool, or rags into the extension housing to prevent lubricant leakage.

3. Disconnect the speedometer cable from the extension housing.

4. Remove three screws securing shift lever to turret assembly.

5. Remove shift lever from turret assembly.

6. Support the engine with a transmission jack and remove the extension housing-to-engine rear support attaching bolts.

7. Raise the rear of the engine high enough to remove the weight from the crossmember. Remove the bolts retaining the crossmember to the frame side supports and remove the crossmember.

8. Support the transmission on a jack and remove the bolts that attach the transmission to the flywheel housing.

9. Move the transmission and jack rearward until the transmission input shaft clears the flywheel housing. If necessary, lower the engine enough to obtain clearance for transmission removal.

—————— CAUTION ——————

Do not depress the clutch pedal while the transmission is removed.

Installation

1. Make sure that the mounting surface of the transmission and the flywheel housing are free of dirt, paint, and burrs. Install two guide pins in the flywheel housing lower mounting bolt holes. Move the transmission forward on the guide pins until the input shaft splines enter the clutch hub

splines and the case is positioned against the flywheel housing.

2. Install the two upper transmission to flywheel housing mounting bolts snug, and then remove the two guide pins. Install the two lower mounting bolts. Torque all mounting bolts to specifications.

3. Raise the rear of the engine and install the crossmember. Install and torque the crossmember attaching bolts to specifications, then lower the engine.

4. With the transmission extension housing resting on the engine rear support, install the transmission extension housing attaching bolts. Torque the bolts to specifications.

5. Position shift tower to extension housing and secure with three screws.

6. Connect the speedometer cable to the extension housing.

7. Remove the extension housing installation tool and slide the forward end of the driveshaft over the transmission output shaft. Connect the driveshaft to the rear U-joint flange.

8. Fill the transmission to the proper level with the specified lubricant.

9. Lower the truck. Check the shift and crossover motion for full shift engagement and smooth crossover operation.

Vans

3-SPEED

Removal and Installation

1. Raise the vehicle on a hoist and drain the lubricant from the transmission by removing the lower extension housing-to-transmission bolt.

2. Disconnect the driveshaft from the flange at the transmission. Secure the front end of the driveshaft out of the way by tying it up with a length of wire.

3. Disconnect the speedometer cable from the extension housing and disconnect the gearshift rods from the transmission. Disconnect the transmission regulated spark switch, if so equipped.

4. Position a transmission jack under the transmission. Chain the transmission to the jack.

5. Raise the transmission slightly and remove the 4 bolts which retain the transmission support crossmember to the frame side rails. Remove the bolt which retains the transmission extension housing to the crossmember.

6. Remove the 4 transmission-to-flywheel housing bolts.

7. Position a bar under the rear of the engine to support it.

8. Remove the transmission from the vehicle by lowering the jack.

To install the transmission:

9. Make sure that the machined surfaces of the transmission case and the flywheel housing are free of dirt, paint, and burrs.

10. Install a guide pin in each lower mounting bolt hole.

11. Start the input shaft through the release bearing. Align the splines on the input shaft with the splines in the clutch disc. Move the transmission forward on the guide pins until the input shaft pilot enters the bearing or bushing in the crankshaft. If the transmission front bearing retainer binds up on the clutch release bearing hub, work the release bearing lever until the hub slides onto the transmission front bearing retainer. Install the two upper mounting bolts and lockwashers which attach the flywheel housing to the transmission. Remove the two guide pins and install the lower mounting bolts and lockwashers.

12. Raise the jack slightly and remove the engine support bar. Position the support crossmember on the frame side rails and install the retaining bolts. Install the extension housing-to-crossmember retaining bolt.

13. Connect the gearshift rods and the speedometer cable. Connect the transmission regulated spark switch lead, if so equipped.

14. Install the driveshaft.

15. Fill the transmission to the bottom of the filler hole with the proper lubricant.

16. Adjust the clutch pedal free-play and the shift linkage as required.

4-SPEED OVERDRIVE

Removal and Installation

1. Raise the vehicle on a hoist.

2. Mark the driveshaft so that it may be installed in the same relative position. Disconnect the driveshaft from the rear U-joint flange. Slide the driveshaft off the transmission output shaft and install the extension housing seal installation tool into the extension housing to prevent lubricant leakage.

3. Disconnect the speedometer cable from the extension housing.

4. Remove the retaining clips, flat washers, and spring washers that secure the shift rods to the shift levers. Remove the bolts connecting the shift control to the transmission extension housing. Remove the nut connecting the shift control to the transmission case.

NOTE: A '6' and '8' is stamped on transmission extension housing by the shift control plate bolt holes. The '6' and '8' refer to either a 6 or 8 cylinder engine application. The shift control plate bolts must be placed in the right holes for proper plate positioning dependent upon engine application.

5. Remove the rear transmission support connecting bolts attaching the support on the crossmember to the transmission extension housing.

6. Support the engine with a transmission jack and remove the extension hous-

ing-to-engine rear support attaching bolts.

7. Raise the rear of the engine high enough to remove the weight from the crossmember. Remove the bolts retaining the crossmember to the frame side supports and remove the crossmember.

8. Support the transmission on a jack and remove the bolts that attach the transmission to the flywheel housing.

9. Move the transmission and jack rearward until the transmission input shaft clears the flywheel housing. If necessary, lower the engine enough to obtain clearance for transmission removal. **Do not depress the clutch pedal while the transmission is removed.**

10. Make sure that the mounting surfaces of the transmission and the flywheel housing are free of dirt, paint, and burrs. Install two guide pins in the flywheel housing lower mounting bolt holes. Move the transmission forward on the guide pins until the input shaft splines enter the clutch hub splines and the case is positioned against the flywheel housing.

11. Install the two upper transmission to flywheel housing mounting bolts snug, and then remove the two guide pins. Install the two lower mounting bolts. Tighten all mounting bolts to 40–45 ft. lbs.

12. Raise the rear of the engine and install the crossmember. Install and torque the crossmember attaching bolts to 20–30 ft. lbs. then lower the engine.

13. With the transmission extension housing resting on the engine rear support, install the transmission extension housing attaching bolts. Tighten the bolts to 42–50 ft. lbs.

14. Install the transmission support bolts and tighten to 40–50 ft. lbs.

15. Position the shift control bracket on the stud on the transmission case and on the bolt attaching holes (holes marked either '6' or '8' dependent upon 6 or 8 cylinder engine application) on the transmission extension housing. Install and hand tighten connecting bolts.

NOTE: The bracket must be placed in the proper position for correct shift control operation.

Tighten the nut connecting the bracket to the transmission case to 22–30 ft. lbs. Tighten the bolts to 22–30 ft. lbs.

16. Secure each shift rod to its respective lever with the spring washer, flat washer, and retaining pin.

17. Connect the speedometer cable to the extension housing.

18. Remove the extension housing installation tool and slide the forward end of the driveshaft over the transmission output shaft. Connect the driveshaft to the rear U-joint flange. Adjust the linkage.

19. Fill the transmission to the proper level with the specified lubricant.

20. Lower the vehicle. Check the shift and crossover motion for full shift engagement and smooth crossover operation.

CLUTCH

Pick-up

PEDAL AND LINKAGE ADJUSTMENT

1. Measure the clutch pedal free-play by depressing the pedal slowly until the free-play between the release bearing assembly and the pressure plate is removed. Note this measurement. The difference between this measurement and when the pedal is not depressed is the free-play measurement.

2. If the free-play measurement is less than ¾ in., the clutch linkage must be adjusted.

3. Loosen the two jam nuts on the release rod under the truck and back off both nuts several turns.

4. Loosen or tighten the first jam nut (nearest the release lever) against the bullet (rod extension) until a free-play measurement of ¾–1½ in. is obtained. A free-play measurement closer to 1½ in. is more desirable.

5. When the correct free-play measurement is obtained, hold the first jam nut in position and securely tighten the other nut against the first.

6. Recheck the free-play adjustment.

NOTE: Total pedal travel is fixed and is not adjustable.

REMOVAL AND INSTALLATION

1. Disconnect the release lever retracting spring and pushrod assembly.

2. Remove the transmission.

3. If the clutch housing does not have a dust cover, remove the starter. Remove the flywheel housing attaching bolts and remove the housing.

4. If the flywheel housing does have a dust cover, remove the cover and then remove the release lever and bearing from the clutch housing.

5. Mark the pressure plate and cover assembly and the flywheel so that they can be reinstalled in the same relative position.

6. Loosen the pressure plate and cover attaching bolts evenly in a staggered sequence a turn at a time until the pressure plate springs are relieved of their tension. Remove the attaching bolts.

7. Remove the pressure plate and cover assembly and the clutch disc from the flywheel.

8. Position the clutch disc on the flywheel so that an aligning tool or spare transmission mainshaft can enter the clutch pilot bearing and align the disc.

9. When reinstalling the original pressure plate and cover assembly, align the

assembly and flywheel according to the marks made during removal. Position the pressure plate and cover assembly on the flywheel, align the pressure plate and disc, and install the retaining bolts. Tighten the bolts in an alternating sequence a few turns at a time until 15–20 ft. lbs. is reached.

10. Remove the tool used to align the clutch disc.

11. With the clutch fully released, apply a light coat of grease on the sides of the driving lugs.

12. Position the clutch release bearing and the bearing hub on the release lever. Install the release lever on the fulcrum in the flywheel housing. Apply a light coating of grease to the release lever fingers and the fulcrum. Fill the groove of the release bearing hub with grease.

13. If the flywheel housing has been removed, position it against the rear engine cover plate and install the attaching bolts and tighten them to 40–50 ft. lbs.

14. Install the starter motor.

15. Install the transmission.

16. Connect the release lever retracting spring and install the dust cover, if so equipped.

17. Adjust the clutch linkage.

Bronco

PEDAL HEIGHT ADJUSTMENT

1975–77

1. Measure the total travel of the pedal.

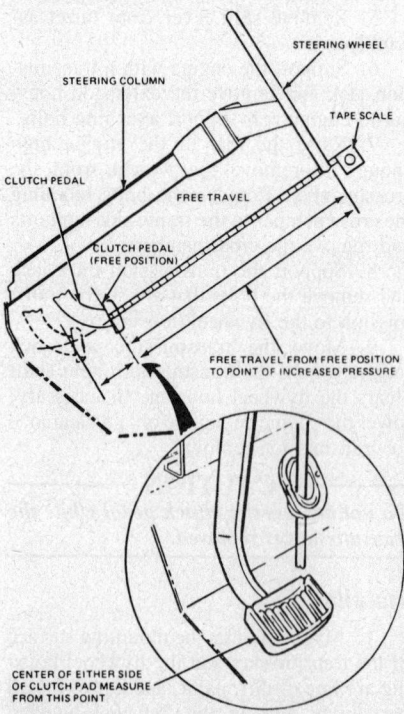

1978 and later Bronco and pick-up clutch pedal free play measurement

If the total travel is less than 6¾ in. or more than 6¼ in., move the clutch pedal bumper and bracket up or down until the travel is within these limits.

2. To check and adjust the pedal free travel, slowly apply the clutch pedal until the clutch fingers contact the clutch release bearing. The distance the clutch pedal moves is the free travel dimension. The free travel should be 1¼ to 1⁷⁄₁₆ in. If it is not within these limits, loosen the nut at the bullet on the clutch release rod and adjust the bullet until the free travel is within the specified range.

3. Tighten the nut at the turnbuckle.

1978–79

1. Measure the clutch pedal free travel using a steel tape. Measure the distance from the clutch pedal pad to the steering wheel rim. Depress the pedal slowly until the free travel between the release bearing assembly and the pressure plate assembly is taken up. Note this measurement. The difference between the two measurements is the free travel.

2. If the free-travel measurement is less than ½ in. 1978; ¾ in. 1979 or greater than 2 inches 1978; 1½ inches 1979, the clutch linkage must be adjusted.

3. With retracting spring removed, hold the release rod firmly against release lever, eliminating lever free play.

4. Position first jam nut .062 inches from the bar while holding needle firmly against release lever.

5. Position second jam nut finger tight against the first nut, while holding second nut. Lock the first nut with 15–20 ft. lbs. torque. This gives ¾ to 1½ inch at pedal pad with 1½ inches prefered.

6. Check adjustment with retracting spring in place.

1980–82

1. Measure the clutch pedal free travel using a steel tape. Measure the distance from the clutch pedal pad to the steering wheel rim. Depress the pedal slowly until the free travel between the release bearing assembly and the pressure plate assembly is taken up. Note this measurement. The difference between the two measurements is the free travel.

2. If the free travel measurement is less than ½ inch or more than 2 inches, the clutch linkage must be adjusted.

3. Remove the retracting spring.

4. Loosen the two jam nuts on the release rod assembly and back off both nuts several turns.

5. Slide the release rod extension (bullet) firmly against the release lever. Push the release rod forward against the equalizer bar lever to eliminate all freeplay from the linkage system.

6. Insert 0.135 inch thick gauge between the jam nut and bullet. Tighten the first jam nut finger tight against the gauge

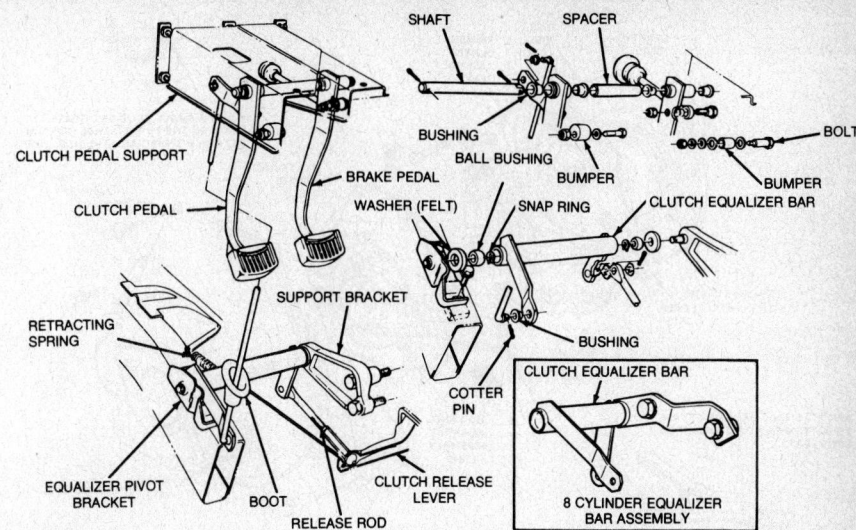

1975–77 clutch linkage

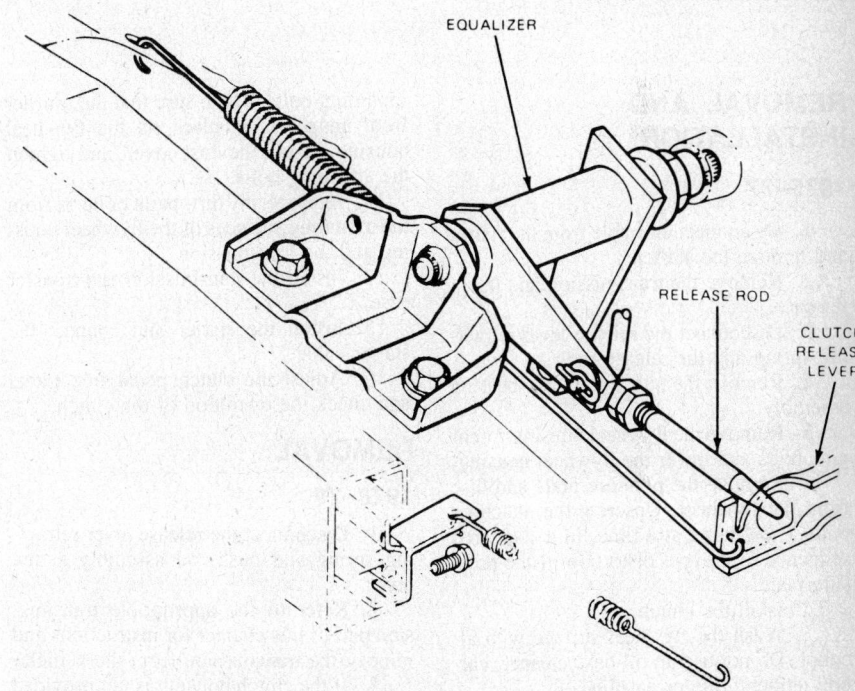

1978–79 van clutch pedal free travel adjustment

with all freeplay eliminated.

7. Tighten the second jam nut finger tight against the first jam nut. Hold the first nut and tighten the second jam nut to 15–20 ft. lbs. Freeplay should measure ¾–1½ inches at the pedal.

8. With the recommended free travel obtained, and holding the first jam nut, position and securely tighten the second jam nut against the first jam nut.

9. Re-check the pedal free travel.

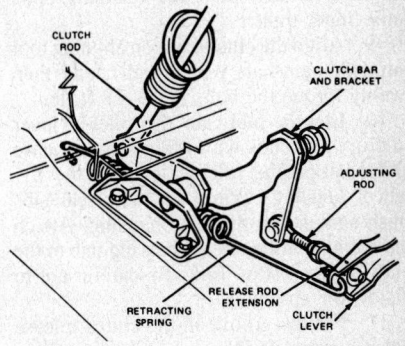

1980 and later van clutch pedal free travel adjustment

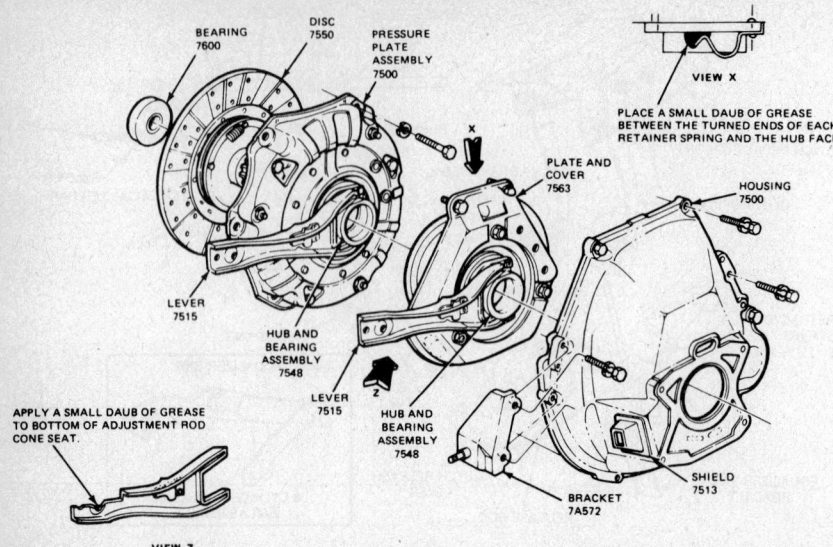

8-351, 400 clutch installation

BEARING 7600 · DISC 7550 · PRESSURE PLATE ASSEMBLY 7500 · LEVER 7515 · HUB AND BEARING ASSEMBLY 7548 · APPLY A SMALL DAUB OF GREASE TO BOTTOM OF ADJUSTMENT ROD CONE SEAT. · VIEW Z · PLATE AND COVER 7563 · LEVER 7515 · HUB AND BEARING ASSEMBLY 7548 · BRACKET 7A572 · HOUSING 7500 · SHIELD 7513 · VIEW X · PLACE A SMALL DAUB OF GREASE BETWEEN THE TURNED ENDS OF EACH RETAINER SPRING AND THE HUB FACE

REMOVAL AND INSTALLATION

1975–77

1. Disconnect the cable from the starter and remove the starter.

2. Remove the transmission and transfer case.

3. Disconnect the release lever retracting spring and the release rod.

4. Remove the hub and release bearing assembly.

5. Remove the flywheel housing-to-engine bolts and lower the flywheel housing.

6. Remove the pressure plate and disc from the flywheel. Unscrew the attaching bolts a few turns at a time, in a staggered sequence to prevent distortion of the pressure plate.

To install the clutch:

7. Wash the flywheel surface with alcohol. Do not use an oil-base cleaner, carbon tetrachloride or gasoline.

8. Place the clutch disc and the pressure plate and cover assembly in position on the flywheel. Start the retaining bolts until finger-tight.

9. Align the clutch disc on aligning tool (an old mainshaft works well), and then evenly torque the bolts to 23–28 ft. lbs.

10. Lightly lubricate the release lever fulcrum and ends with lithium base grease and position the release lever in the flywheel housing. Crimp the dust seal tabs flush against the flywheel housing. Attach the springs of the release bearing hub to the ends of the release fork. Be careful not to distort the springs.

11. Fill the groove in the clutch release bearing hub with lithium base grease. Wipe the excess grease from the hub.

12. Position the flywheel housing and release lever assembly, and install the mounting bolts. Make sure that the muffler front hanger is in place on the flywheel housing. Install the dust cover, and tighten the attaching bolts.

13. Remove any dirt, paint or burrs from the mounting surfaces of the flywheel housing and the transmission.

14. Install the transmission and transfer case.

15. Install the starter and connect the starter cable.

16. Adjust the clutch pedal free travel and check the operation of the clutch.

REMOVAL

1978–79

1. Disconnect the release lever retracting spring and push rod assembly at the lever.

2. Refer to the appropriate transmission part of this chapter for instructions and remove the transmission from the vehicle.

3. If the clutch housing is not provided with a dust cover, remove the starting motor. Remove the flywheel housing attaching bolts and remove the housing.

4. If the flywheel housing is provided with a dust cover, remove it from the housing. Remove the release lever and release bearing from the clutch housing.

5. Mark the pressure plate and cover assembly and the flywheel, so that the parts can be reinstalled in the same relative position.

6. Loosen the pressure plate and cover attaching bolts evenly until the pressure plate springs are expanded, and remove the bolts.

7. Remove the pressure plate and cover assembly and the clutch disc from the flywheel or through the opening in the bottom of the clutch housing. Remove the pilot bearing only for replacement.

INSTALLATION

1978–79

1. Position the clutch disc on the flywheel so that the pilot tool can enter the clutch pilot bearing and align the disc.

2. When re-installing the original pressure plate and cover assembly, align the assembly and flywheel according to the marks made during the removal operations. Position the pressure plate and cover assembly on the flywheel, align the pressure plate and disc, and install the retaining bolts that fasten the assembly to the flywheel. Tighten the bolts to 20–30 ft. lbs., and remove the clutch disc pilot tool.

3. With the clutch fully released, apply a light film of lithium-base grease ESA-M1C75-B or equivalent on the sides of the driving lugs.

4. Position the clutch release bearing and the bearing hub on the release lever. Install the release lever on the trunnion in the flywheel housing. Apply a light film of lithium-base grease ESA-M1C75-B or equivalent to the release lever fingers and to the lever trunnion or fulcrum. Fill the annular groove of the release bearing hub with grease.

5. If the flywheel housing has been removed, position it against the engine rear cover plate and install the attaching bolts. Tighten the bolts to 40–50 ft. lbs.

6. Install the starter motor. Install the transmission assembly on the clutch housing. Tighten the bolts to 50–60 ft. lbs.

7. Install the slave cylinder on vehicles so equipped, and tighten the bolts.

8. Adjust the release lever push rod assembly. Connect the release lever retracting spring.

9. Install the clutch housing dust cover if so equipped.

REMOVAL

1980–82

1. Disconnect the release lever retracting spring and push rod assembly at the lever. Remove starter.

2. Refer to the appropriate transmission part of this chapter for instructions and remove the transmission from the vehicle.

3. If the clutch housing is not provided with a dust cover, remove the starting motor. Remove the flywheel housing attaching bolts and remove the housing.

4. If the flywheel housing is provided with a dust cover, remove it from the housing. Remove the release lever and release bearing from the clutch housing.

5. Loosen the pressure plate and cover attaching bolts evenly until the pressure plate springs are expanded, and remove the bolts.

6. Remove the pressure plate and cover assembly and the clutch disc from the flywheel or through the opening in the bottom of the clutch housing. Remove the pilot bearing only for replacement.

INSTALLATION

1980–82

1. Position the clutch disc on the flywheel so that the pilot tool can enter the clutch pilot bearing and align the disc.

2. When re-installing the original pressure plate and cover assembly, align the assembly and flywheel according to the marks made during the removal operations. Position the pressure plate and cover assembly on the flywheel, align the pressure plate and disc, and install the retaining bolts that fasten the assembly to the flywheel. Tighten the bolts to 20–30 ft. lbs., and remove the clutch disc pilot tool.

3. Position the clutch release bearing and the bearing hub on the release lever. Install the release lever on the pivot bar pedestal in the flywheel housing. Apply a light film of lithium-base grease ESA-M1C75-B or equivalent to the release lever fingers and to the lever pivot ball. Fill the annular groove of the release bearing hub with grease.

4. If the flywheel housing has been removed, position it against the engine rear cover plate and install the attaching bolts. Tighten the bolts to 40–50 ft. lbs.

5. Install the starter motor. Install the transmission assembly on the clutch housing. Tighten the bolts.

6. Adjust the release lever push rod assembly. Connect the release lever retracting spring.

7. Install the clutch housing dust cover if so equipped.

Vans

REMOVAL AND INSTALLATION

1. Disconnect the cable from the starter and remove the starter.

2. Remove the transmission.

3. Disconnect the release lever retracting spring and release the rod.

4. Remove the hub and release bearing assembly.

5. Remove the flywheel housing-to-engine bolts, and lower the flywheel housing.

6. Remove the pressure plate and the disc from the flywheel. Unscrew the attaching bolts a few turns at a time, in a staggered sequence to prevent distortion of the pressure plate.

7. Wash the flywheel surface with alcohol. Do not use an oil-base cleaner, carbon tetrachloride or gasoline.

To install the clutch:

8. Place the clutch disc and the pressure plate and cover assembly in position on the flywheel. Start the retaining bolts until finger-tight.

9. Align the clutch disc with a clutch arbor (an old mainshaft works well) and then evenly torque the bolts to 23–28 ft. lbs.

10. Do not grease the release lever pivot assembly. Crimp the dust seal tabs flush against the flywheel housing. Attach the springs of the release bearing hub to the ends of the release fork. Be careful not to distort the springs.

11. Fill the groove in the clutch release bearing hub with lithium-base grease. Wipe the excess grease from the hub.

12. Position the flywheel housing and release lever assembly, and install the mounting bolts. Make sure that the muffler front hanger is in place on the flywheel housing. Install the dust cover, and tighten the attaching bolts.

13. Remove any dirt, paint, or burrs from the mounting surfaces of the flywheel housing and the transmission.

14. Install the transmission.

15. Install the starter and connect the starter cable.

16. Adjust the clutch pedal free-play and check the operation of the clutch.

CLUTCH PEDAL ADJUSTMENT

To check and adjust the pedal free travel, measure and note the distance from the floor pan to the top of the pedal; then depress the pedal slowly until the clutch release fingers contact the clutch release bearing. Measure and record the distance. The difference between the reading with the pedal in the depressed position and the reading with the pedal in the fully released position is the pedal free travel. The free travel should be as specified.

The pedal height is not adjustable. Pedal height is adjusted by loosening the nut securing the clutch pedal eccentric bumper and rotating the bumper until the clutch pedal height is within 1¼–1½ in.

AUTOMATIC TRANSMISSION

Transmission identification may be made by referring to the Vehicle Certification Label on the driver's side door post. The C4 code is G, C5 code is W, FMX code is J, and C6 code is P and the Automatic Overdrive code is T.

REMOVAL AND INSTALLATION—C4, C5

F-100 thru 250, 1975–77 E-100 thru 250

REMOVAL

1. Raise the vehicle on a hoist.

2. Place the drain pan under the transmission fluid pan. Remove the fluid filler tube from the pan and drain the transmission fluid.

3. Remove the converter drain plug access cover from the lower end of the converter housing.

4. Remove the converter-to-flywheel attaching nuts. Place a wrench on the crankshaft pulley attaching bolt to turn the converter to gain access to the nuts.

5. With the wrench on the crankshaft pulley attaching bolt, turn the converter to gain access to the converter drain plug and remove the plug. Place a drain pan under the converter to catch the fluid. With fluid drained, reinstall the plug.

6. Remove the driveshaft.

7. Disconnect the oil cooler lines from the transmission.

8. Disconnect the manual and downshift linkage rods from the transmission control levers.

9. Remove the speedometer gear from the extension housing.

10. Disconnect the back-up switch wires from the retaining clips and retainer.

11. Disconnect the starter cable. Remove the three starter-to-converter housing attaching bolts and remove the starter.

12. Remove the vacuum line hose from the transmission vacuum unit. Disconnect the vacuum line from the retaining clip.

13. Position the transmission jack to support the transmission. Install the safety chain to hold the transmission on the jack.

14. Remove the two engine rear support crossmember-to-frame attaching bolts.

15. Remove the two engine rear support-to-extension housing attaching bolts.

16. Raise the transmission and remove the rear support. Remove the six converter housing-to-engine attaching bolts.

17. Move the converter and transmission assembly away from the engine. Lower the transmission and remove it from under the vehicle.

INSTALLATION

1. Tighten the converter drain plug to 15-28 ft. lbs.

2. Position the converter on the transmission making sure the converter drive flats are fully engaged in the pump gear.

3. With the converter properly installed, place the transmission on the jack. Secure the transmission to the jack with the safety chain.

4. Rotate the converter until the studs and drain plug are in alignment with their holes in the flywheel.

5. Move the converter and transmission assembly forward into position, using care not to damage the flywheel and the converter pilot. **The converter must rest squarely against the flywheel. This indicates that the converter pilot is not binding in the engine crankshaft.**

6. Install the six converter housing-to-engine attaching bolts. Tighten the bolts to 40–50 ft. lbs.

7. Install the converter-to-flywheel attaching nuts. Tighten the nuts to 20–34 ft. lbs. Remove the safety chain from the transmission.

8. Install the rear support. Install the rear support-to-extension housing attaching bolts. Tighten the bolts.

9. Position the starter into the converter housing and install the three attaching bolts. Tighten the bolts to 20–30 ft. lbs. Install the starter cable.

10. Remove the transmission jack.

11. Connect the transmission filler tube to the transmission pan. Connect the oil cooler lines to the transmission.

12. Attach the back-up switch wires to the connector clip.

13. Install the speedometer driven gear in the extension housing. Tighten the attaching bolt.

14. Connect the transmission linkage rods to the transmission control levers.

NOTE: When making transmission control attachments, new retaining rings and grommets should always be used.

Attach the shift rod to the steering column shift lever. Align the flats of the adjusting stud with the flats of the rod slot and insert the stud through the rod. Assemble the adjusting stud nut and washer to a loose fit. Perform a linkage adjustment.

15. Install the driveshaft.

16. Install the vacuum line in the retaining clip. Connect the vacuum line to the diaphragm unit.

17. At the front lower area of the converter housing, install the lower cover and the control lever dust shield. Install the attaching bolts. Tighten the bolts.

18. Secure the fluid filler tube to the pan. Tighten the fitting to 32–42 ft. lbs.

19. Lower the vehicle.

20. Fill the transmission to the proper level.

21. Raise the vehicle and check for transmission fluid leakage. Lower the vehicle and adjust the throttle and manual linkage.

Bronco 1975–77

1. Disconnect the fan shroud from the radiator.

2. Raise and support the vehicle on jack stands.

3. Remove the transfer case skid plate.

4. Remove the transmission filler tube and drain the fluid.

5. Drain the transfer case.

6. Remove the converter drain plug access cover from the lower end of the converter housing.

7. Remove the converter-to-flywheel attaching nuts. Place a wrench on the crankshaft pulley attaching bolt to turn the converter, thereby giving access to the nuts.

8. Turn the converter to gain access to the drain plug and remove it.

9. When the fluid has drained, replace the plug.

10. Disconnect the rear driveshaft.

11. Remove the front driveshaft.

12. Remove the complete exhaust system.

13. Remove the speedometer cable.

14. Disconnect the transmission oil cooler lines.

15. Disconnect the transmission linkage.

16. Remove the starter.

17. Disconnect the vacuum lines from the transmission.

18. Disconnect the transfer case adapter from the crossmember.

19. Remove the crossmember-to-frame side support attaching bolts.

20. Support the transmisson and transfer case on a jack.

21. Raise the jack slightly, to take up the weight and remove the four bolts securing the left side support bracket, crossmember and upper crossmember insulators.

22. Disconnect the shift rod from the transfer case shift lever bracket.

23. Remove the bolts that attach the shift lever bracket to the transfer case adapter and allow the assembly to hang by the shift lever.

24. Make sure the transmission is secure on the jack and remove the six converter housing-to-engine bolts.

25. Remove the transmission assembly from the engine by rolling the jack backwards and letting it down slowly.

26. When installing the transmisson, turn the converter so that the studs and drain plug are aligned with their holes in the flywheel.

27. Roll the assembly forward into position.

--- CAUTION ---

Make certain that the converter rests squarely against the flywheel. This ensures that the converter pilot is not binding in the engine crankshaft.

28. Install the six mounting bolts and torque to 30 ft. lbs.

29. Install the shift lever bracket.

30. Install the shift rod, spring washer, flat washer and cotter pin.

31. Install the crossmember and insulators.

32. Lower the transmission assembly onto the crossmember and remove the jack.

33. Bolt the transfer case to the crossmember.

34. Install the flywheel-to-converter nuts and torque to 30 ft. lbs.

35. Install the starter and torque the bolts to 30 ft. lbs.

36. Connect the filler tube and oil cooler lines.

37. Install the vacuum lines.

38. Install the speedometer cable.

39. Connect the transmission linkage rods to the levers.

40. Adjust the linkage.

41. Install the exhaust system.

42. Connect the rear driveshaft.

43. Connect the front axle driveshaft.

44. Install the converter drain plug access cover.

45. Fill the transfer case with lubricant as outlined in the first chapter and install the skid plate.

46. Lower the vehicle, install the fan shroud and fill the transmission with type "F" fluid.

47. Adjust the manual and downshift linkage.

REMOVAL AND INSTALLATION—C6 AND FMX

Bronco, F-150-350

REMOVAL

1. Drive the vehicle on a hoist, but do not raise at this time.

2. Remove the two upper converter housing-to-engine bolts.

3. Remove the bolt securing the fluid filler tube to the engine cylinder head.

4. Raise the vehicle on a hoist or stands.

5. Place the drain pan under the transmission fluid pan. Starting at the rear of the pan and working toward the front, loosen the attaching bolts and allow the fluid to drain. Finally remove all of the pan attaching bolts except two at the front, to allow the fluid to further drain. With fluid drained, install two bolts on the rear side of the pan to temporarily hold it in place.

6. Remove the converter drain plug access cover from the lower end of the converter housing.

7. Remove the converter-to-flywheel attaching nuts. Place a wrench on the crankshaft pulley attaching bolt to turn the converter to gain access to the nuts.

8. With the wrench on the crankshaft pulley attaching bolt, turn the converter to gain access to the converter drain plug. Place a drain pan under the converter to catch the fluid and remove the plug. After the fluid has been drained, re-install the plug.

9. Disconnect the driveshaft from the rear axle and slide shaft rearward from the transmission. Install a seal installation tool in the extension housing to prevent fluid leakage.

10. Disconnect the speedometer cable from the extension housing.

11. Disconnect the downshift and manual linkage rods from the levers at the transmission.

12. Disconnect the oil cooler lines from the transmission.

13. Remove the vacuum hose from the vacuum diaphragm unit. Remove the vacuum line retaining clip.

14. Disconnect the cable from the terminal on the starter motor. Remove the three attaching bolts and remove the starter motor.

15. On F-150—F-350 (4 × 4) and Bronco vehicles, remove the transfer case.

16. Remove the two engine rear support and insulator assembly-to-attaching bolts.

17. Remove the two engine rear support and insulator assembly-to-extension housing attaching bolts.

18. Remove the six bolts securing the No. 2 crossmember to the frame side rails.

19. Raise the transmission with a transmission jack and remove both crossmembers.

20. Secure the transmission to the jack with the safety chain.

21. Remove the remaining converter housing-to-engine attaching bolts.

22. Move the transmission away from the engine. Lower the jack and remove the converter and transmission assembly from under the vehicle.

INSTALLATION

1. Tighten the converter drain plug.

2. Position the converter on the transmission making sure the converter drive flats are fully engaged in the pump gear.

3. With the converter properly installed, place the transmission on the jack. Secure the transmission to the jack with the chain.

4. Rotate the converter until the studs and drain plug are in alignment with their holes in the flywheel.

5. Move the converter and transmission assembly forward into position, using care not to damage the flywheel and the converter pilot. **The converter must rest squarely against the flywheel. This indicates that the converter pilot is not binding in the engine crankshaft.**

6. Install and tighten the converter housing-to-engine attaching bolts.

7. Remove the transmission jack safety chain from around the transmission.

8. Position the No. 2 crossmember to the frame side rails. Install and tighten the attaching bolts.

9. Install transfer case on F-150–F-350 (4 × 4) and Bronco.

10. Positon the engine rear support and insulator assembly above the crossmember. Install the rear suport and insulator assembly-to-extension housing mounting bolts and tighten the bolts.

11. Lower the transmission and remove the jack.

12. Secure the engine rear support and insualtor assembly to the crossmember with the attaching bolts and tighten them.

13. Connect the vacuum line to the vacuum diaphragm making sure that the line is in the retaining clip.

14. Connect the oil cooler lines to the transmission.

15. Connect the downshift and manual linkage rods to their respective levers on the transmission.

16. Connect the speedometer cable to the extension housing.

17. Secure the starter motor in place with the attaching bolts. Connect the cable to the terminal on the starter.

18. Install a new O-ring on the lower end of the transmission filler tube and insert the tube in the case.

19. Secure the converter-to-flywheel attaching nuts and tighten them.

20. Install the converter housing access

cover and secure it with the attaching bolts.

21. Connect the drive shaft.

22. Adjust the shift linkage as required.

23. Lower the vehicle. Then install the two upper converter housing-to-engine bolts and tighten them.

24. Position the transmission fluid filler tube to the cylinder head and secure with the attaching bolt.

25. Make sure the drain pan is securely attached, and fill the transmission to the correct level with the specified fluid.

E-100—E-350

REMOVAL

1. Working from inside the vehicle, remove the engine compartment cover.

2. Disconnect the neutral start switch wires at the plug connector.

3. If the vehicle is equipped with a V-8 engine, remove the flexhose from the air cleaner heat tube.

4. Remove the upper converter housing-to-engine attaching bolts (three bolts on 6-cylinder engines; four bolts on 8-cylinder engines).

5. Raise the vehicle on a hoist.

6. Place the drain pan under the transmission fluid pan. Starting at the rear of the pan and working toward the front, loosen the attaching bolts and allow the fluid to drain. Finally remove all of the pan attaching bolts except two at the front, to allow the fluid to further drain. With fluid drained, install two bolts on the rear side of the pan to temporarily hold it in place.

7. Remove the converter drain plug access cover from the lower end of the converter housing.

8. Remove the converter-to-flywheel attaching nuts. Place a wrench on the crankshaft pulley attaching bolt to turn the converter to gain access to the nuts.

9. With the wrench on the crankshaft pulley attaching bolt, turn the converter to gain access to the converter drain plug. Place a drain pan under the converter to catch the fluid. Then, remove the plug. With fluid drained, re-install the plug.

10. Disconnect the drive shaft.

11. Remove fluid filler tube.

12. Disconnect the starter cable at the starter. Remove the starter-to-converter housing attaching bolts and remove the starter.

13. Position the engine support bar (tool T65E-6000-JO) to the frame and engine oil pan flanges.

14. Disconnect the cooler lines from the transmission. Disconnect the vacuum line from the vacuum diaphragm unit. Remove the vacuum line from the retaining clip at the transmission.

15. Remove the speedometer driven gear from the extension housing.

16. Disconnect the manual and downshift linkage rods from the transmission control levers.

17. Position a transmission jack to support the transmission. Install the safety

chain to hold the transmission.

18. Remove the bolts and nuts securing the rear support and insulator assembly to the crossmember. Remove the six bolts retaining the crossmember to the side rails and remove the two support gussets. Raise the transmission with the jack and remove the crossmember.

19. Remove the bolt that retains the transmission filler tube to the cylinder block. Lift the filler tube and dipstick from the transmission.

20. Remove the remaining converter housing-to-engine attaching bolts. Lower the jack and remove the converter and transmission assembly from under the vehicle.

21. Remove the converter and mount the transmission in a holding fixture.

INSTALLATION

1. Tighten the converter drain plug.

2. Position the converter on the transmission making sure the converter drive flats are fully engaged in the pump gear.

3. With the converter properly installed, place the transmission on the jack. Secure the transmission to the jack with the safety chain.

4. Rotate the converter until the studs and drain plug are in alignment with their holes in the flywheel.

5. Move the converter and transmission assembly forward into position, using care not to damage the flywheel and the converter pilot.

The converter must rest squarely against the flywheel. This indicates that the converter pilot is not binding in the engine crankshaft.

6. Install the lower converter housing-to-engine attaching bolts. Tighten the bolts. Install the converter-to-flywheel attaching nuts. Tighten the nuts.

7. Install the crossmember. Install the rear support and insulator assembly-to-crossmember attaching bolts and nuts. Tighten the bolts.

8. Remove the safety chain and remove the jack from under the vehicle. Remove the engine support bar.

9. Install a new O-ring on the lower end of the transmission filler tube and insert the tube and dipstick in the case.

10. Connect the vacuum line to the vacuum diaphragm making sure the line is secured in the retaining clip.

11. Connect the cooler lines to the transmission.

12. Install the speedometer driven gear into the extension housing. Tighten the attaching bolt.

13. Connect the transmission linkage rods to the transmission control levers. When making transmission control attachments new retaining ring and grommet should always be used. Attach the shift rod to the steering column shift lever. Align the flats of the adjusting stud with the flats of the rod slot and insert the stud through the rod. Assemble the adjusting stud nut and

washer to a loose fit. Perform a linkage adjustment.

14. Install the converter housing access cover and tighten the attaching bolts.

15. Position the starter into the converter housing and install the attaching bolts. Tighten the bolts. Install the starter cable.

16. Install the driveshaft.

17. Lower the vehicle.

18. Install the upper converter housing-to-engine attaching bolts. Tighten the bolts.

19. On V8 engines, install the flex hose to the air cleaner heat tube. Install the bolt that retains the filler tube to the cylinder block.

20. Connect the neutral start switch wires at the plug connector.

21. Make sure the transmission fluid pan is securely attached, and fill the transmission to the proper level with the specified fluid.

22. Raise the vehicle and check for transmission fluid leakage. Lower the vehicle and adjust the downshift and manual linkage.

23. Install the engine compartment cover.

REMOVAL AND INSTALLATION—AUTOMATIC OVERDRIVE

F-100 and 150

REMOVAL

1. Raise the vehicle on a hoist or stands.

2. Place the drain pan under the transmission fluid pan. Starting at the rear of the pan and working toward the front, loosen the attaching bolts and allow the fluid to drain. Finally remove all of the pan attaching bolts except two at the front, to allow the fluid to further drain. With fluid drained, install two bolts on the rear side of the pan to temporarily hold it in place.

3. Remove the converter drain plug access cover from the lower end of the converter housing.

4. Remove the converter-to-flywheel attaching nuts. Place a wrench on the crankshaft pulley attaching bolt to turn the converter to gain access to the nuts.

5. Place a drain pan under the converter to catch the fluid. With the wrench on the crankshaft pulley attaching bolt, turn the converter to gain access to the converter drain plug and remove the plug. After the fluid has been drained, reinstall the plug.

6. Disconnect the driveshaft from the rear axle and slide shaft rearward from the transmission. Install a seal installation tool in the extension housing to prevent fluid leakage.

7. Disconnect the cable from the terminal on the starter motor. Remove the three attaching bolts and remove the starter motor. Disconnect the neutral start switch wires at the plug connector.

8. Remove the rear mount-to-cross-member attaching bolts and the two cross-member-to-frame attaching bolts.

9. Remove the two engine rear support-to-extension housing attaching bolts.

10. Disconnect the TV linkage rod from the transmission TV lever. Disconnect the manual rod from the transmission manual lever at the transmission.

11. Remove the two bolts securing the bellcrank bracket to the converter housing.

12. Raise the transmission with a transmission jack to provide clearance to remove the crossmember. Remove the rear mount from the crossmember and remove the crossmember from the side supports.

13. Lower the transmission to gain access to the oil cooler lines.

14. Disconnect each oil line from the fittings on the transmission.

15. Disconnect the speedometer cable from the extension housing.

16. Remove the bolt that secures the transmission fluid filler tube to the cylinder block. Lift the filler tube and the dipstick from the transmission.

17. Secure the transmission to the jack with the chain.

18. Remove the converter housing-to-cylinder block attaching bolts.

19. Carefully move the transmission and converter assembly away from the engine and, at the same time, lower the jack to clear the underside of the vehicle.

20. Remove the converter and mount transmission in a holding fixture.

INSTALLATION

1. Tighten the converter drain plug.

2. Position the converter on the transmission, making sure the converter drive flats are fully engaged in the pump gear by rotating the converter.

3. With the converter properly installed, place the transmission on the jack. Secure the transmission to the jack with a chain.

4. Rotate the converter until the studs and drain plug are in alignment with the holes in the flywheel.

5. Move the converter and transmission assembly forward into position, using care not to damage the flywheel and the converter pilot. The converter must rest squarely against the flywheel. This indicates that the converter pilot is not binding in the engine crankshaft.

6. Install and tighten the converter housing-to-engine attaching bolts to 40–50 ft. lbs.

7. Remove the safety chain from around the transmission.

8. Install a new O-ring on the lower end of the transmission filler tube. Insert the tube in the transmission case and secure the tube to the engine with the attaching bolt.

9. Connect the speedometer cable to the extension housing.

10. Connect the oil cooler lines to the right side of transmission case.

11. Position the crossmember on the side supports. Position the rear mount on the crossmember and install the attaching bolt and nut.

12. Secure the engine rear support to the extension housing and tighten the bolts to 16–20 ft. lbs.

13. Lower the transmission and remove the jack.

PAN REMOVAL AND INSTALLATION

C4, C5

NOTE: The torque converter on all of the transmissions has a drain plug. If the converter is drained, refill the C4 with 5 qts. of fluid and the C6 and FMX models with 8 qts. of fluid.

1. Raise the vehicle so that the transmission oil pan is readily accessible.

2. Disconnect the fluid filler tube from the pan and allow the fluid to drain into an appropriate container.

NOTE: It is not recommended that the drained fluid be used over again; refill the transmission with new fluid. However, in an emergency situation, the hold fluid can be reused. The old fluid should be strained through a #100 screen or a fine mesh cloth before being reinstalled.

3. Remove the transmission oil pan attaching bolts, pan and gasket.

To install the transmission oil pan:

4. Clean the transmission oil pan and transmission mating surfaces.

5. Install the transmission oil pan in the reverse order of removal, torquing the attaching bolts to 12–16 ft. lbs. and using a new gasket. Fill the transmission with 3 qts. of the correct type fluid, check the operation of the transmission and check for leakage.

NOTE: The C4 automatic transmission uses Type F automatic transmission fluid only. The C5 uses Dexron® II. When starting the engine after the transmission fluid has been drained, do not race the engine and move the gearshift selector through all of the ranges before moving the vehicle.

C6, FMX, Automatic Overdrive

1. Raise the truck on a hoist or jackstands.

2. Place a drain pan under the transmission.

3. Loosen the pan attaching bolts and drain the fluid from the transmission.

4. When the fluid has drained to the level of the pan flange, remove the remaining pan bolts working from the rear and both sides of the pan to allow it to drop and drain slowly.

5. When all of the fluid has drained, remove the pan and clean it thoroughly. Discard the pan gasket.

6. Place a new gasket on the pan, and install the pan on the transmission. Tighten

the attaching bolts to 12–16 ft. lbs.

7. Add three quarts of fluid to the transmission through the filler tube.

NOTE: Use only Type F automatic transmission fluid for 1975–76 C6 models. 1977–82 C6 models and the automatic overdrive models require type CJ fluid. Do not race the engine after it is started. Move the gearshift selector through all of the gears before moving the truck.

FILTER SERVICE

1. Remove the transmission oil pan and gasket.

2. Remove the screws holding the fine mesh screen to the lower valve body.

NOTE: Be careful not to lose the throttle pressure limit valve and spring when separating the oil screen from the valve body on a C4.

3. Install the new filter screen and transmission oil pan gasket in the reverse order of removal.

FRONT BAND ADJUSTMENT

FMX

1. Remove the transmission oil pan.

2. Loosen the front servo adjusting screw locknut.

3. Pull back on the actuating rod, and insert a ¼ in. spacer between the adjusting screw and the servo piston stem.

4. Tighten the adjusting screw to 10 in. lbs.

5. Remove the spacer and tighten the adjusting screw an additional ¾ turn.

6. Hold the adjusting screw stationary and tighten the locknut. Tighten the locknut to 20–25 ft. lbs.

7. Install the oil pan and a new gasket in the reverse order of removal.

INTERMEDIATE BAND ADJUSTMENT

C4, C5 and C6

1. Raise the truck on a hoist or jackstands.

2. Clean all dirt away from the band adjusting screw. Remove and discard the locknut.

3. Install a new locknut and tighten the adjusting screw to 10 ft. lbs.

4. On the C4 transmission, back off the adjusting screw *exactly 1¾ turns*. On the C5 back off the adjusting screw exactly 4¼ turns. On a C6 transmission, back off the adjusting screw *exactly 1½ turns*.

5. Hold the adjusting screw from turning and tighten the locknut to 35–45 ft. lbs.

6. Remove the jackstands and lower the vehicle.

LOW-REVERSE BAND ADJUSTMENT

C4, C5

1. Clean all dirt from around the band adjusting screw and remove and discard the locknut.

2. Install a new locknut on the adjusting screw. Using a torque wrench, tighten the adjusting screw to 10 ft. lbs.

3. Back off the adjusting screw *exactly 3 full turns*.

4. Hold the adjusting screw steady and tighten the locknut to 35–45 ft. lbs.

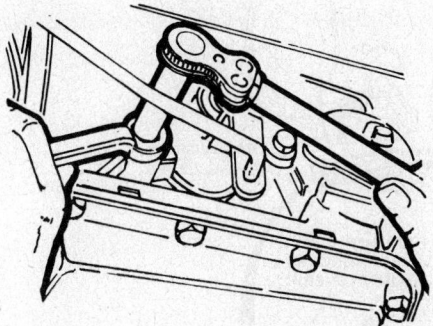

C4 intermediate band adjustment

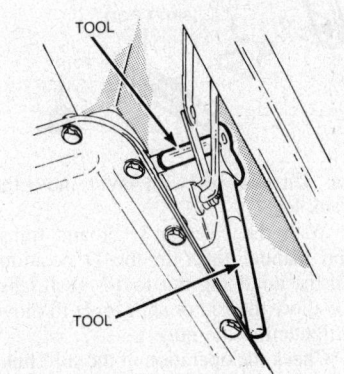

C6 intermediate band adjustment

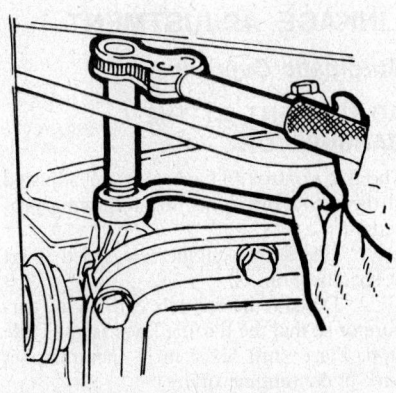

Low-reverse band adjustment

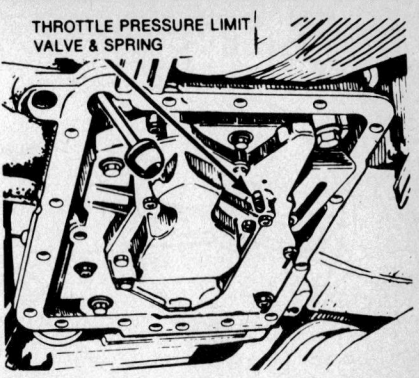

C4 throttle pressure limiter valve which is held in place in the valve body by the filter. The valve is installed with the larger end toward the valve body. The spring fits over the valve stem.

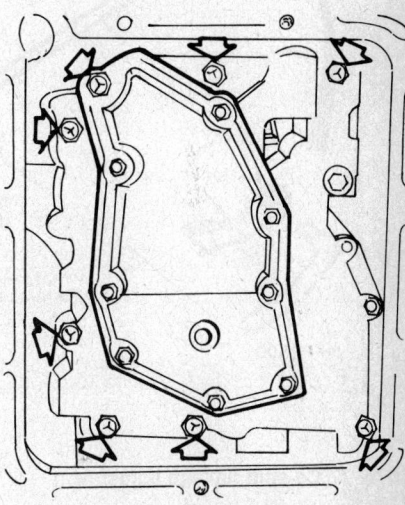

View showing the filter screen which is attached to the lower valve body. Bolts indicated by arrows hold the valve body. If the screen only is being serviced, do not remove these bolts

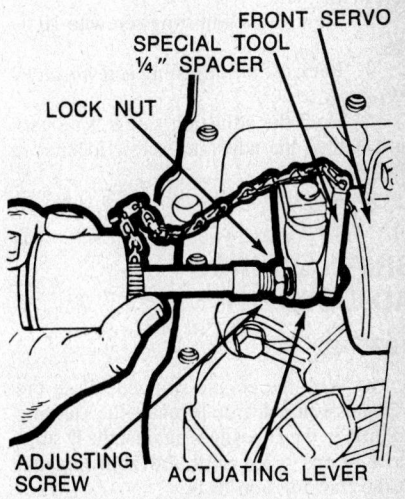

FMX front band adjustment

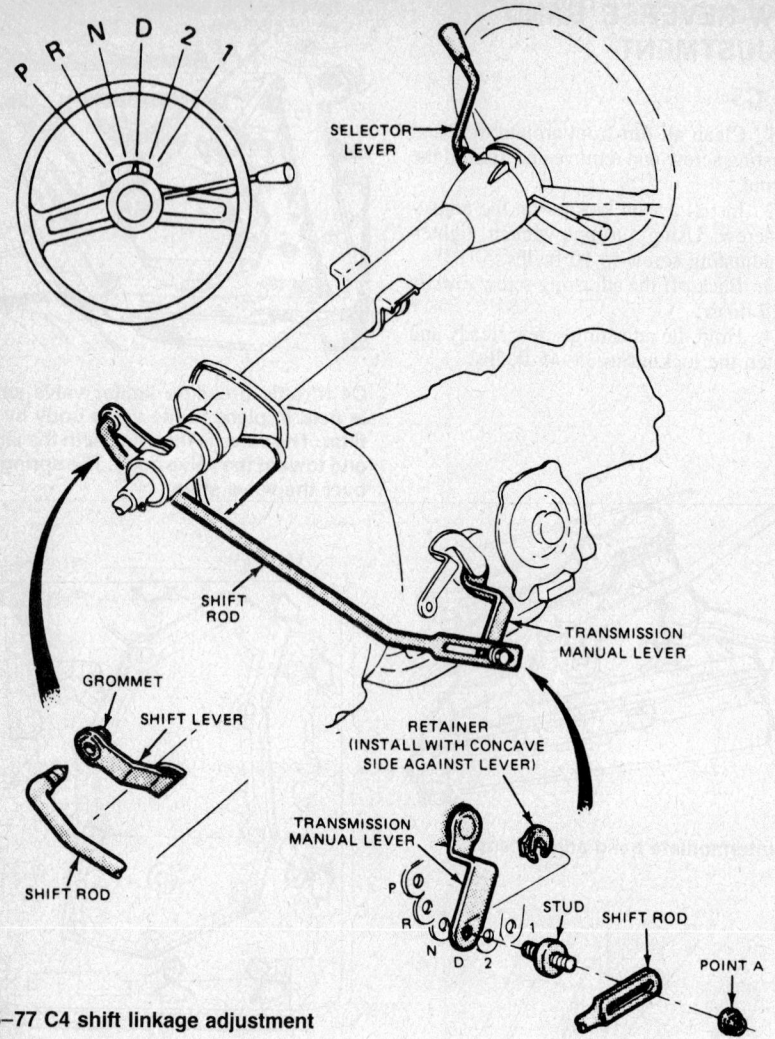

1975–77 C4 shift linkage adjustment

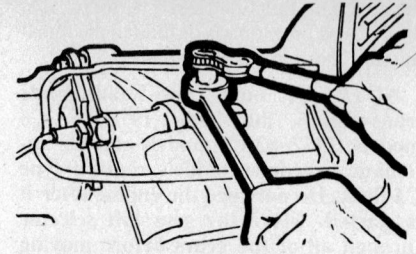

FMX rear band adjustment

REAR BAND ADJUSTMENT

FMX

1. Remove all dirt away from the adjusting screw threads then oil the threads.
2. Loosen the rear band adjusting screw locknut.
3. Tighten the adjusting screw to 10 ft. lbs.
4. Back off the adjusting screw *exactly 1½ turns*.
5. Hold the adjusting screw stationary and tighten the adjusting screw locknut to 35–40 ft. lbs.
6. Reinstall the oil pan and a new gasket.

SHIFT LINKAGE ADJUSTMENT

1975–82

1. With the engine stopped, place the transmission selector lever at the steering column in the D position against the D stop.
2. Loosen the shift rod adjusting nut at the transmission lever.
3. Shift the manual lever at the transmission to the D position, two detents from the rear. On an F-100 with 4WD, move the bellcrank lever.
4. With the selector lever and transmission manual lever in the D position, tighten the adjusting nut to 12–18 ft. lbs. Do not allow the rod or shift lever to move while tightening the nut.
5. Check the operation of the shift linkage.

THROTTLE VALVE LINKAGE ADJUSTMENT

Automatic Overdrive

ADJUSTMENT AT THE CARBURETOR

The TV control linkage may be adjusted at the carburetor using the following procedure:

1. Check that engine idle speed is set at specification.
2. De-cam the fast idle cam on the carburetor so that the throttle lever is at its idle stop. Place shift lever in N (neutral), set park brake (engine off).
3. Backout linkage lever adjusting screw all the way (screw end is flush with lever face).
4. Turn in adjusting screw until a thin shim (.005 inch max.) or piece of writing paper fits snugly between end of screw and Throttle Lever. **To eliminate effect of friction, push linkage lever forward (tending to close gap) and release before checking clearance between end of screw and throttle lever. Do not apply any load on levers with tools or hands while checking gap.**
5. Turn in adjusting screw an additional four turns. (Four turns are preferred. Two turns minimum is permissible if screw travel is limited).
6. If it is not possible to turn in adjusting screw at least two additional turns or if there was insufficient screw adjusting capacity to obtain an initial gap in Step 2 above, refer to Linkage Adjustment at Transmission.

Whenever it is required to adjust idle speed by more than 50 rpm, the adjustment screw on the linkage lever at the carburetor should also be readjusted as shown in following chart:

Idle Speed Change	Turns on Linkage Lever Adjustment Screw
Less than 50 rpm	No change required
50 to 100 rpm increase	1½ turns out
50 to 100 rpm decrease	1½ turns in
100 to 150 rpm increase	2½ turns out
100 to 150 rpm decrease	2½ turns in

After making any idle speed adjustments, always verify the linkage lever and throttle lever are in contact with the throttle lever at its idle stop and the shift lever is in N (neutral).

ADJUSTMENT AT TRANSMISSION

The linkage lever adjustment screw has limited adjustment capability. If it is not possible to adjust the TV linkage using this screw, the length of the TV control rod assembly must be readjusted using the following procedure. This procedure must also be followed whenever a new TV control rod asssembly is installed.

This procedure requires placing the vehicle on jackstands to give access to the linkage components at the transmission TV control lever.

1. Set the engine curb idle speed to specification.

2. With engine off, de-cam the fast idle cam on the carburetor so that the throttle lever is against the idle stop. Place shift lever in Neutral and set park brake (engine off).

3. Set the linkage lever adjustment screw at its approximately mid-range.

4. If a new TV control rod assembly is being installed, connect the rod to the linkage lever at the carburetor.

—————— CAUTION ——————
The following steps involve working in proximity to the exhaust system. Allow the exhaust system to cool before proceeding.

5. Raise the vehicle on the hoist.

6. Using a 13 mm box end wrench, loosen the bolt on the sliding trunnion block on the TV control rod assembly. Remove any corrosion from the control rod and free-up the trunnion block so that it slides freely on the control rod. Insert pin into transmission lever grommet.

7. Push up on the lower end of the control rod to insure that the linkage lever at carburetor is firmly against the throttle lever. Release force on rod. Rod must stay up.

8. Push the TV control lever on the transmission up against its internal stop with a firm force (approximately 5 pounds) and tighten the bolt on the trunnion block. Do not relax force on lever until nut is tightened.

9. Lower the vehicle and verify that the throttle lever is still against the idle stop. If not, repeat steps 2 through 9.

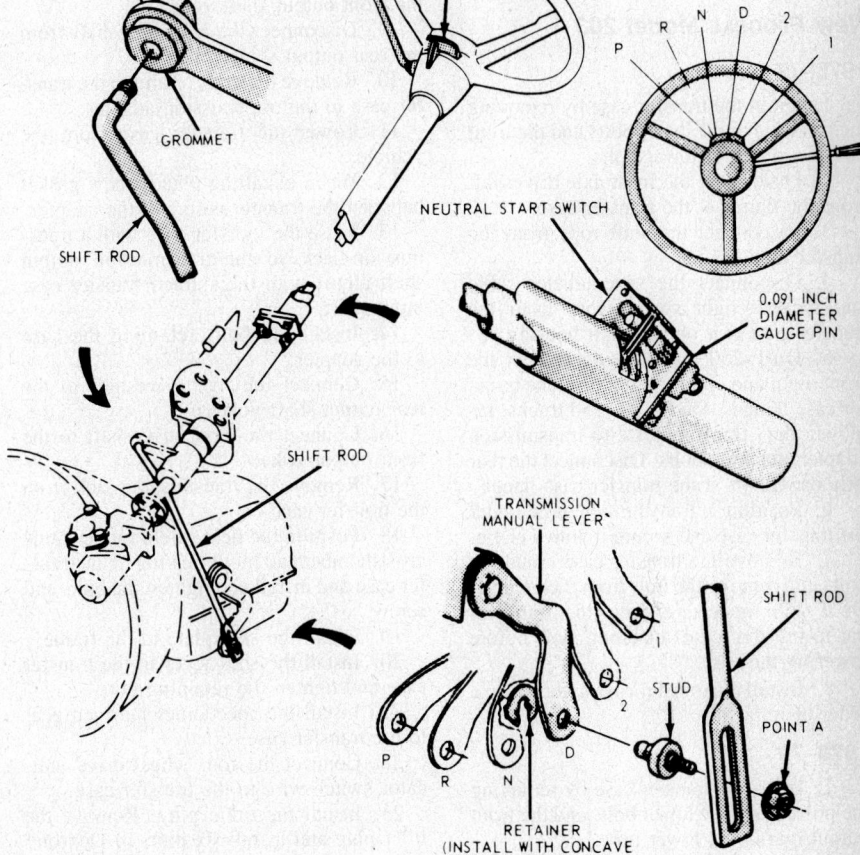

1975 and later C6 shift linkage adjustment

NEUTRAL SAFETY SWITCH ADJUSTMENT

1. Hold the steering column transmission selector lever against the Neutral stop.

2. Move the sliding block assembly on the neutral switch to the neutral position and insert a 0.091 in. gauge pin in the alignment hole on the terminal side of the switch.

3. Move the switch assembly housing so that the sliding block contacts the actuating pin lever. Secure the switch to the outer tube of the steering column and remove the gauge pin.

4. Check the operation of the switch. The engine should only start in Neutral and Park.

THROTTLE KICK-DOWN LINKAGE ADJUSTMENT

1. Move the carburetor throttle linkage to the wide open position.

2. Insert a 0.060 in. thick spacer between the throttle lever and the kickdown adjusting screw.

3. Rotate the transmission kick-down lever until the lever engages the transmission internal stop. Do not use the kickdown rod to turn the transmission lever.

4. Turn the adjusting screw until it contacts the 0.060 in. spacer.

5. Remove the spacer.

TRANSFER CASE

Pick-up

REMOVAL AND INSTALLATION

Dana Model 21

1. Raise the vehicle on a hoist.

2. Disconnect the front and rear driveshafts at the transfer case.

3. Disconnect the shift rod from the transfer case shift lever arm.

4. Remove the bolts and nuts which attach the transfer case to the transmission extension housing and remove the transfer case from under the truck.

5. Install the transfer case in the reverse order of removal, using a new gasket between the transfer case and the transmission extension housing.

New Process Model 205

1. Drain the transfer case and disconnect the rear axle driveshaft from the flange at the transfer case.

2. Disconnect the front wheel driveshaft and the transmission output shaft at the transfer case if on an F-250. On an F-100, disconnect the front wheel driveshaft and remove the bolts attaching the transmission adapter to the transfer case.

3. Disconnect the shift selector rod and the speedometer cable at the transfer case.

4. Place a transmission jack under the transfer case and secure it with a chain.

5. Remove the transfer case mounting bolts and remove the unit from under the vehicle.

6. Install the transfer case in the reverse order of removal.

New Process Model 203

1975–77

1. Drain the transfer case by removing the power take-off lower bolts and the front output rear cover lower bolts.

2. Disconnect the front axle driveshaft from the flange at the transfer case.

3. Disconnect the shift rods from the transfer case.

4. Disconnect the speedometer cable and lockout light switch wire from the transfer case rear output shaft housing.

5. On F-250 pick-ups, disconnect the front input and output shafts from the transfer case flanges. On F-100, 150 trucks, remove the transfer case-to-transmission adapter attaching bolts. Disconnect the rear axle driveshaft at the transfer case flange.

6. Position a transmission jack under the transfer case and secure it with a chain.

7. Remove the transfer case mounting bolts and remove the unit from the vehicle. On F-250 models, remove the stabilizer bar-to-transfer case attaching bolt before lowering the case.

8. Install the transfer case in the reverse order of removal.

1978–79

1. Drain the transfer case by removing the power take-off lower bolts and the front output rear cover lower bolts.

2. Disconnect the front axle drive shaft from the flange of the transfer case.

3. Disconnect the shift rods from the transfer case.

4. Disconnect the speedometer cable and lockout lamp switch wire from the transfer case rear output shaft housing.

5. Remove the bolts which attach the transfer case to the transmission adapter. Disconnect the rear axle drive shaft at the transfer case flange.

6. Position a transmission jack under the transfer case and secure it to the jack.

7. Remove the transfer case mounting bolts and remove the transfer case.

8. Install the transfer case in the reverse order of removal.

New Process Model 208

1. Raise the vehicle on a hoist and drain the fluid from the transfer case.

2. Disconnect the four wheel drive indicator switch wire connector at the transfer case.

3. Disconnect the speedometer driven gear from the transfer case rear bearing retainer.

4. Remove the nut retaining the transmission shift lever assembly to the transfer case.

5. Remove the skid plate from the frame, if so equipped.

6. Remove the heat shield from the frame.

7. Support the transfer case with a transmission jack or equivalent.

8. Disconnect the front driveshaft from the front output shaft yoke.

9. Disconnect the rear driveshaft from the rear output shaft yoke.

10. Remove the bolts retaining the transfer case to the transmission adapter.

11. Lower the transfer case from the vehicle.

12. When installing place a new gasket between the transfer case and the adapter.

13. Raise the transfer case with a transmission jack so the transmission output shaft aligns with the splined transfer case input shaft.

14. Install the bolts retaining the case to the adapter.

15. Connect the rear driveshaft to the rear output shaft yoke.

16. Connect the front driveshaft to the front output yoke.

17. Remove the transmission jack from the transfer case.

18. Position the heat shield to the frame crossmember and mounting lug to the transfer case and install and tighten the bolts and screw.

19. Install the skid plate to the frame.

20. Install the shift lever to the transfer case and tighten the retaining nut.

21. Install the speedometer driven gear to the transfer case.

22. Connect the four wheel drive indicator switch wire to the transfer case.

23. Install the drain plug. Remove the filler plug and install six pints of Dexron® II or equivalent type transmission fluid.

24. Lower the vehicle.

Borg-Warner Model 1345

1. Raise the vehicle on a hoist.

2. Drain the fluid from the transfer case.

3. Disconnect the four wheel drive indicator switch wire connector at the transfer case.

4. Remove the skid plate from the frame, if so equipped.

5. Disconnect the front driveshaft from the front output yoke.

6. Disconnect the rear driveshaft from the rear output shaft yoke.

7. Disconnect the speedometer driven gear from the transfer case rear bearing retainer.

8. Remove the retaining rings and shift rod from the transfer case shift lever.

9. Disconnect the vent hose from the transfer case.

10. Remove the heat shield from the frame.

11. Support the transfer case with a transmission jack.

12. Remove the bolts retaining the transfer case to the transmission adapter.

13. Lower the transfer case from the vehicle.

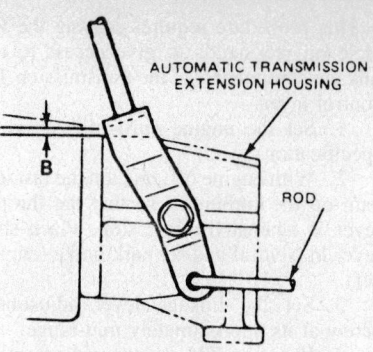

VIEW IN DIRECTION OF ARROW

ADJUSTMENT (AUTOMATIC TRANSMISSION)

TRANSFER CASE MUST BE IN 4 WHEEL LOW (CROSS LINK ASSEMBLY ALL THE WAY IN)

DIMENSION "B" MUST BE .64
.60

ADJUST ROD (7B051) TO CORRECT LENGTH AND TIGHTEN LOCK NUT AT CLEVIS

NP205 transfer case installation showing the adjustment of the shift linkage with automatic transmission

14. When installing place a new gasket between the transfer case and the adapter.

15. Raise the transfer case with the transmission jack so that the transmission output shaft aligns with the splined transfer case input shaft. Install the bolts retaining the transfer case to the adapter.

16. Remove the transmission jack from the transfer case.

17. Connect the rear driveshaft to the rear output shaft yoke.

18. Install the shift lever to the transfer case and install the retaining nut.

19. Connect the speedometer driven gear to the transfer case.

20. Connect the four wheel drive indicator switch wire connector at the transfer case.

21. Connect the front driveshaft to the front output yoke.

22. Position the heat shield to the frame crossmember and the mounting lug on the transfer case. Install and tighten the retaining bolts.

23. Install the skid plate to the frame.

24. Install the drain plug. Remove the filler plug and install six pints of Dexron® II type transmission fluid or equivalent.

25. Lower the vehicle.

TRANSFER CASE SHIFT LINKAGE ADJUSTMENT

New Process Model 205

MANUAL TRANSMISSION

Adjust the length of the shift rod between the transfer case and the shift lever with the lever in 4WD-Low so that the distance between the rear face of the transmission and the shift lever-to-rod clevis pin is 3.94 to 3.82 in.

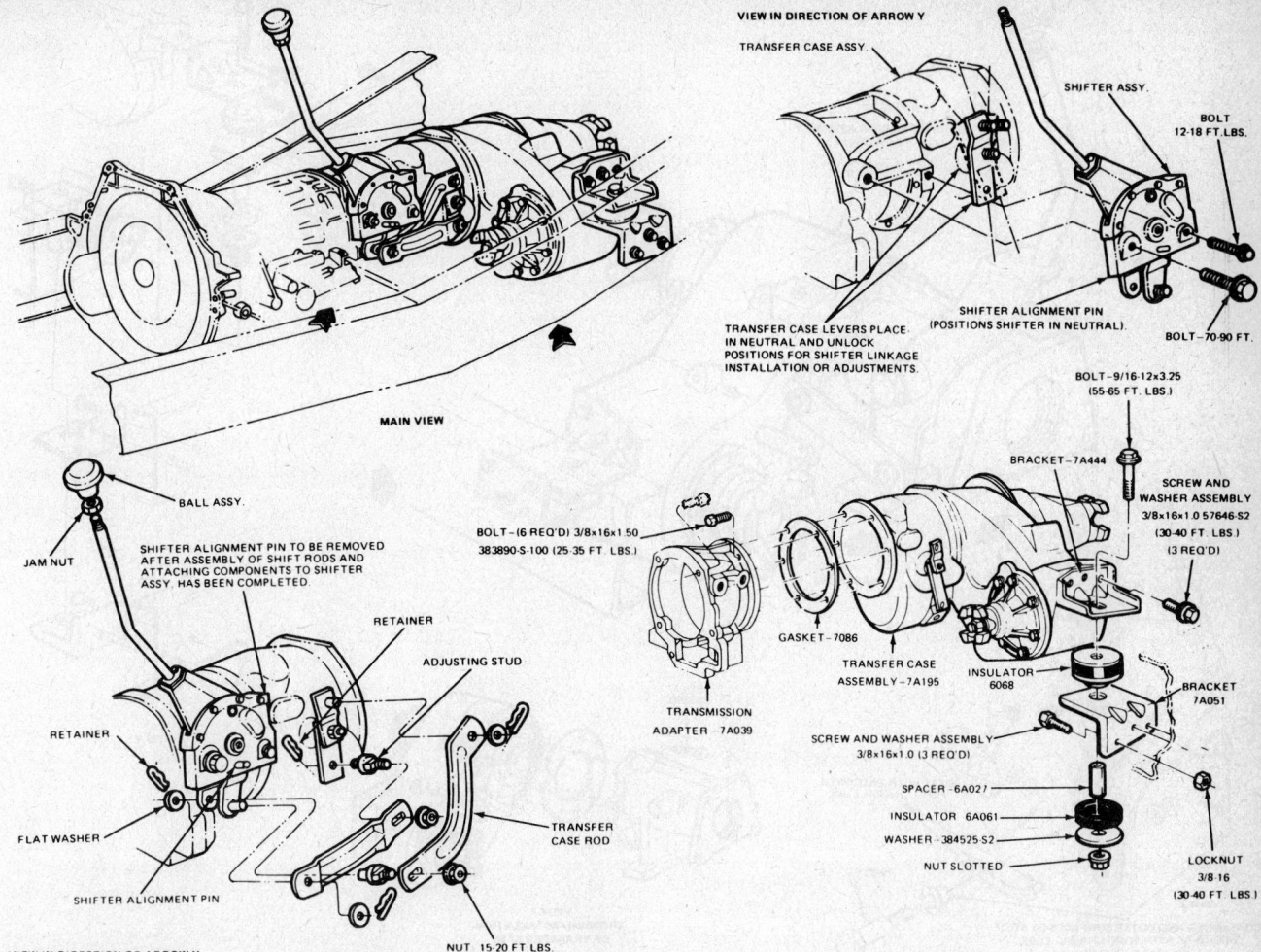

VIEW IN DIRECTION OF ARROW X

NP203 transfer case installation on 1978 and later F-150, 250

AUTOMATIC TRANSMISSION

Adjust the length of the shift rod between the transfer case and the shift lever with the lever in 4WD-Low so that the distance between the upper surface of the automatic transmission extension housing and the upper horizontal edge of the shift lever is 0.640 to 0.600 in.

New Process 203 Full-Time 4WD

1975–76 F-100, F-150

1. Place the shift lever in the Low position.

2. Remove the adjusting stud nuts from the shift rods under the truck.

3 Disconnect the front driveshaft at the transfer case.

4. Remove the transfer case shifter.

5. Unsnap the top snap of the splash boot, peel the boot back and install a new adjustment pin in the rear of the shifter bracket. The pin is 1.5 in. long, ¼ in. in diameter and must be of breakable material. The pin cannot be reached once the shifter is installed.

6. Reinstall the shifter, tightening the rear bolt to 12–17 ft. lbs. and the front bolt

to 70–90 ft. lbs.

7. Move the lower lever on the transfer case completely forward and the upper lever completely rearward.

8. Install new adjusting stud nuts and tighten them to 20–25 ft. lbs.

9. Connect the front driveshaft.

1975–76 F-250

1. Move the transfer case shifter to the Low position.

2. Loosen the adjusting stud nuts.

3. Unsnap the top splash boot snap and peel the boot back. Install a new adjustment pin in the rear of the shifter bracket. The pin is the same size as previously mentioned for the F-100 and F-150. If the pin is made of steel, it must be removed after tightening the adjusting studs.

4. Move the lower lever on the transfer case completely forward and the upper lever completely rearward.

5. Install new adjusting nuts and tighten them to 15–20 ft. lbs.

1977–82

1. Place the shift in the neutral position.

2. Remove the two adjusting stud nuts.

3. Install a 0.025 inch diameter alignment pin (1.25 inches long through the shifter assembly.

4. Align the bottom transfer case lever (Lock lever) by rotating clockwise to the forward position.

5. Align the top transfer case lever (range lever) by placing in the middle or neutral position.

6. Re-position the two shift rods and tighten the adjusting stud nuts to 15–20 ft. lbs.

7. Remove the alignment pin from the shifter assembly.

Bronco

DANA 20

Removal and Installation

1. Shift the transfer case into Neutral.

2. Remove the bolts attaching the fan shroud to the radiator support.

3. Raise the vehicle on a hoist.

4. Support the transfer case shield with a jack and remove the bolts that attach the

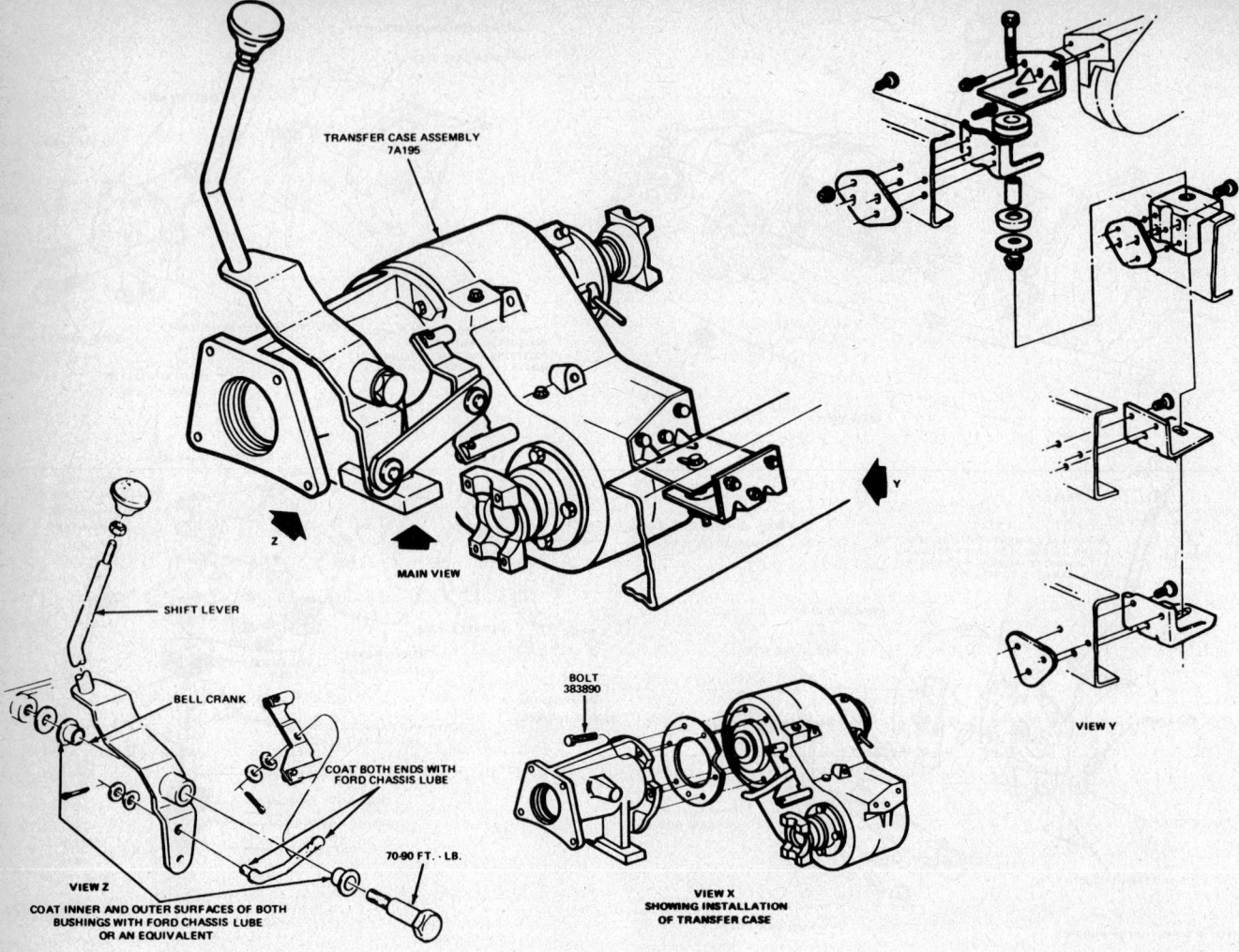

TRANSFER CASE ASSEMBLY
7A195

MAIN VIEW

SHIFT LEVER

BELL CRANK

COAT BOTH ENDS WITH
FORD CHASSIS LUBE

70-90 FT. - LB.

VIEW Z

COAT INNER AND OUTER SURFACES OF BOTH
BUSHINGS WITH FORD CHASSIS LUBE
OR AN EQUIVALENT

BOLT
383890

VIEW X
SHOWING INSTALLATION
OF TRANSFER CASE

VIEW Y

NP205 transfer case installation

shield to the frame side rails. Remove the shield.

5. Drain the transmission and transfer case lubricant.

6. Disconnect the front and rear driveshafts at the transfer case.

7. Disconnect the speedometer cable at the transfer case.

8. If equipped with a manual transmission, disconnect the shift rods from the transmission shift levers. Then, place the First-Reverse gear shift lever in to the First gear position and insert the fabricated tool. (See transmission removal and installation). This tool will prevent the input shaft roller bearings from dropping into the transmission case when separating the transfer case from the transmission and output shaft.

9. Support the engine with a jack.

10. Remove the two cotter pins, bolts, washers, plates and insulators that secure the crossmember to the transfer case adapter.

11. Remove the crossmember to frame side support attaching bolts.

12. Raise the transmission and remove

the upper insulators from the crossmember. Remove the crossmember.

NOTE: For vehicles built before Nov. 1, 1974 use step 13. For those built on or after Nov. 1, 1974 use 13A.

13. Roll back the boot enclosing the transfer case shift linkage. Remove the threaded cap holding the shift lever assembly to the shift bracket. Remove the shift lever assembly.

13A. Remove the carpet from around the shift levers. Remove the bolts holding the shifter to the transmission adapter. Remove the lower spring from the shifter. Remove the boot from the bottom of the shifter. Bend up the left side of the floor opening as required to remove the shifter assembly.

14. Secure the transfer case to a transmission jack and remove the transfer case adapter-to-transmission attaching bolts.

15. Move the transfer case and jack rearward until it clears the transmission output shaft. Lower the transfer case.

16. Installation is the reverse of the removal procedure.

NEW PROCESS 205

Removal

1. Drain the transfer case. Disconnect the rear axle driveshaft and front driveshaft from the flange at the transfer case.

2. Disconnect the shift selector rod steady rest and the speedometer cable at the transfer case.

3. Secure the transfer case to a transmission jack, and remove the mounting bolts.

4. Remove transfer case, and place it on a floor stand or work bench.

Installation

1. Remove the transfer case from the floor stand or bench and place it on the transmission jack.

2. Raise the transfer case into position and attach the mounting bolts. Tighten the bolts and nuts to 20–40 ft. lbs.

3. Connect the shift selector rod, the speedometer cable, and steady rest.

4. Connect the front and rear axle drive

shafts and tighten the universal joint U-bolt nuts.

5. Fill the transfer case to filler plug level with SAE 80W/90 oil. Tighten drain plug to 25–35 ft. lbs.

NEW PROCESS 203

Removal

1. Drain the transfer case by removing the power take-off lower bolts and the front output rear cover lower bolts.

2. Disconnect the front axle drive shaft from the flange at the transfer case.

3. Disconnect the shift rods from the transfer case.

4. Disconnect the speedometer cable and lockout lamp switch wire from the transfer case rear output shaft housing.

5. Remove the transfer case-to-transmission adapter attaching bolts. Disconnect the rear axle driveshaft at the transfer case flange.

6. Position a transmission jack under the transfer case and secure it to the jack.

7. Remove the transfer case mounting bracket support to frame crossmember nuts, bolts, spacers and upper absorbers and remove the transfer case.

8. Using a chain fall, place the transfer case on a suitable work bench.

Installation

1. Using a chain fall, secure the transfer case on a transmission jack.

2. Position the transfer case in the truck, aligning the mounting bracket supports with the lower absorbers. Align the transfer case-to-transmission attaching bolts.

3. Install the transfer case mounting bracket support to frame crossmember bolts with upper absorbers and spacers. Tighten all mounting bolts to 40–50 ft. lbs.

4. Remove the transmission jack.

5. Connect the speedometer cable and the lockout switch wire to the transfer case.

6. Connect the rear axle driveshaft to the transfer case rear output flange.

7. Install the shift rods on the transfer case and adjust the shift linkage.

8. Connect the front axle driveshaft to the transfer case flange.

9. Fill the transfer case with SAE 80W/90 oil. Tighten the filler plug to 25–35 ft. lbs.

NEW PROCESS 208

Removal

1. Raise vehicle on a hoist.

2. Place a drain pan under transfer case, remove drain plug and drain fluid from transfer case.

3. Disconnect four wheel drive indicator switch wire connector at transfer case.

4. Disconnect speedometer driven gear from transfer case rear bearing retainer.

5. Remove nut retaining transmission

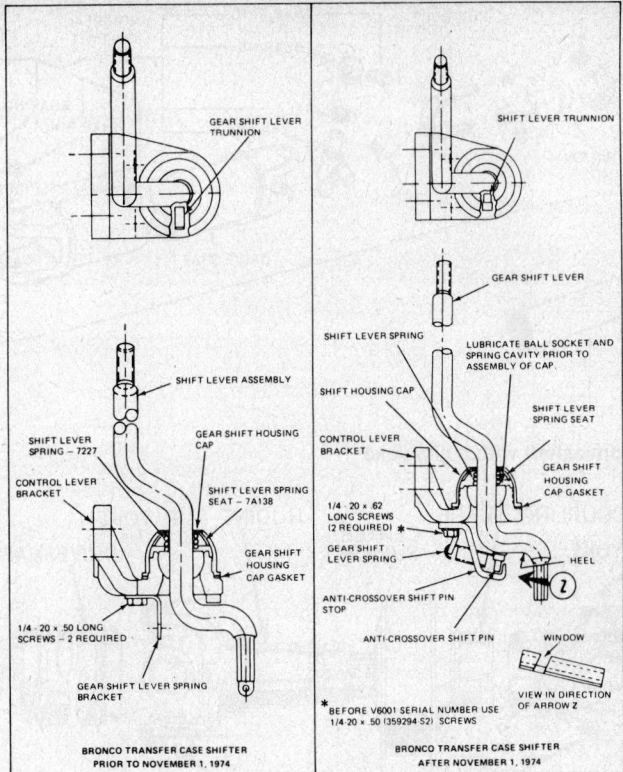

Differences in the Dana 20 transfer case shifter in 1975 Bronco

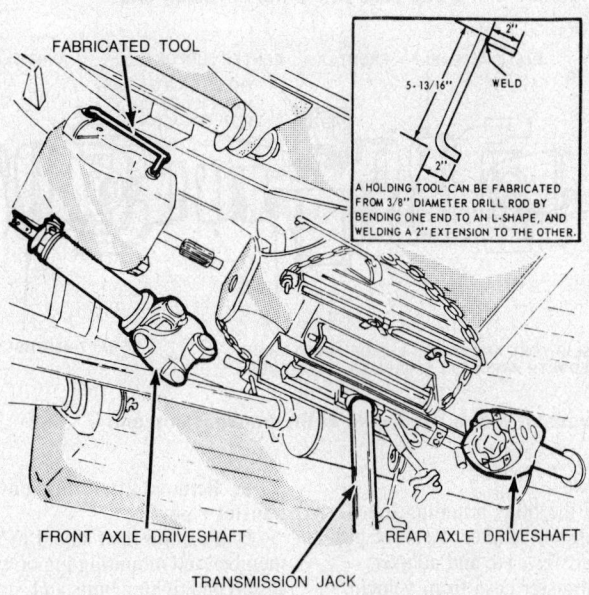

Removal or installation of the Dana 20 transfer case and the dimensions of the holding tool which must be used

shift lever assembly to transfer case.

6. If so equipped, remove skid plate from frame.

7. Remove heat shield from frame.

———— CAUTION ————
Catalytic converter is located beside the heat shield. Be careful when working around catalytic converter because of the extremely high temperatures generated by the converter.

8. Support transfer case with transmission jack.

9. Disconnect fron driveshaft from front output shaft yoke.

10. Disconnect rear driveshaft from rear

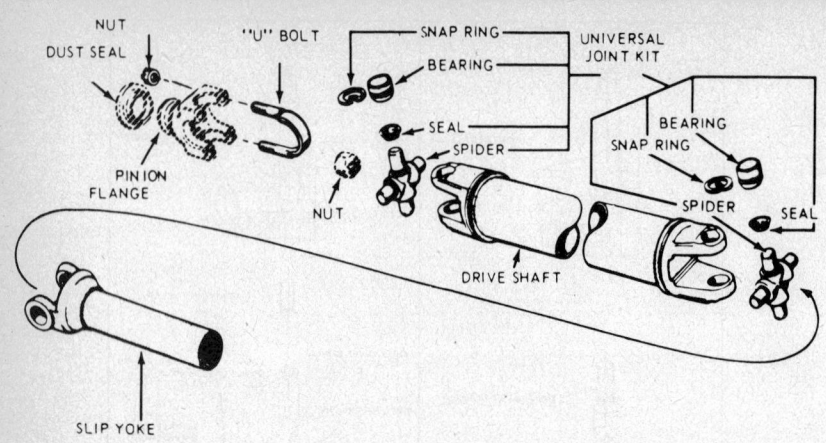

One-piece driveshaft with a slip yoke

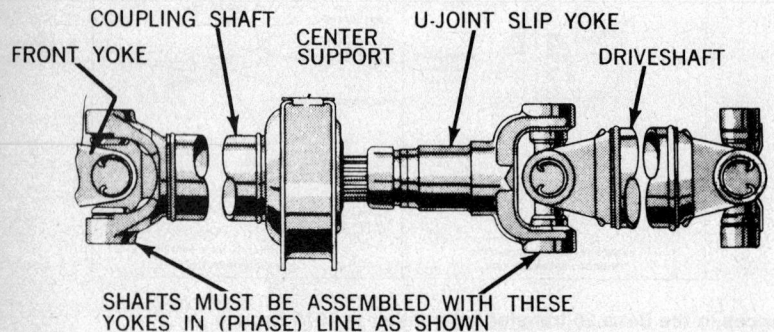

Two-piece driveshaft with a slip yoke at the transmission end

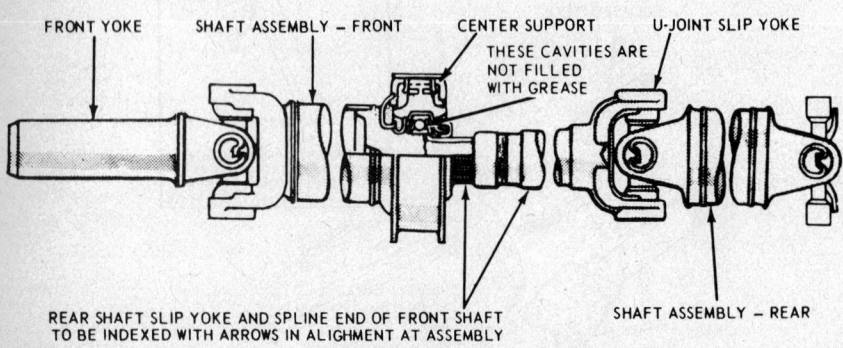

Two-piece driveshaft with a fixed yoke at the transmission end

output shaft yoke.

11. Remove the bolts retaining transfer case to transmission adapter. Remove gasket between transfer case and adapter.

12. Lower transfer case from vehicle.

Installation

1. Place a new gasket between transfer case and adapter.

2. Raise transfer case with transmission jack so transmission output shaft aligns with splined transfer case input shaft. Install bolts retaining transfer case to adapter. Tighten bolts to 30–40 ft. lbs.

3. Connect rear driveshaft to rear output shaft yoke.

4. Connect front driveshaft to front output yoke.

5. Remove transmission jack from transfer case.

6. Position heat shield to frame crossmember and mounting lug on transfer case. Install and tighten bolts and screw to 11–16 ft. lbs.

7. Install skid plate to frame. Tighten nuts and bolts.

8. Install shift lever to transfer case. Install retaining nut.

9. Connect speedometer driven gear to transfer case.

10. Connect four-wheel drive indicator switch wire connector at transfer case.

11. Install drain plug. Remove filler plug and install 2.8 liters (six pints) of automatic transmission fluid Ford type CJ or Dexron® II, Series D or equivalent. Install filler plug.

12. Lower vehicle.

Shift Lever Adjustment

NOTE: The NP 205 and 208 do not require adjustment.

NP 203

1. Place shift lever in neutral position.

2. Remove two adjusting stud nuts.

3. Install 0.25 inch diameter alignment pin (1.25 inches long) through shifter assembly.

4. Align the two transfer case levers as follows:

   a. Bottom lever, (lock lever)—Rotate clockwise to the forward position.

   b. Top lever, (range lever)—Place in the Mid-position or Neutral position.

5. Re-position the two shift rods and tighten new adjusting stud nuts to 15–20 ft. lbs.

6. Remove alignment pin from shifter assembly.

DRIVELINE

Driveshaft

REMOVAL AND INSTALLATION

4WD

1. To remove the rear driveshaft, disconnect the double Cardan joint from the flange at the transfer case and the single U-joint from the flange at the rear axle. Remove the driveshaft.

2. To remove the front driveshaft, disconnect the double Cardan joint from the flange at the transfer case and the single U-joint from the front axle. Remove the driveshaft.

3. Installation is the reverse of removal. Torque driveshaft-to-transfer case bolts to 20–25 ft. lbs.; driveshaft to axle bolts to 8–15 ft. lbs.

2WD

1. Unscrew the nuts attaching the U-bolts to the flange at the rear axle. Remove the U-bolts and allow the rear of the driveshaft to drop down. Slide the front of the driveshaft out of the rear of the transmission, transfer case, or the center support bearing. Remove the driveshaft from the vehicle.

2. On those vehicles equipped with two driveshafts and a center support bearing, unscrew the attaching bolts holding the center support bearing to the frame. If equipped with a sliding yoke at the trans-

mission, slide the coupling shaft out of the rear of the extension housing. Otherwise, remove the nuts from the U-bolts holding the front of the coupling shaft to the flange on the rear of the transmission while supporting the center bearing. Remove the U-bolts from the front flange and remove the coupling shaft assembly together with the center support bearing.

3. Install the driveshaft(s) in the reverse order of removal.

NOTE: All U-joints on two-piece driveshafts must be on the same horizontal plane when installed.

U-JOINT OVERHAUL

1. Remove the driveshaft from the vehicle and place it in a vise, being careful not to damage it.

2. Remove the snap-rings which retain the bearings in the flange and in the driveshaft.

3. Remove the driveshaft tube from the vise and position the U-joint in the vise with a socket smaller than the bearing cap on one side and a socket larger than the bearing cap on the other side.

4. Slowly tighten the jaws of the vise so that the smaller socket forces the U-joint spider and the opposite bearing into the larger socket.

5. Remove the other side of the spider in the same manner (if applicable) and remove the spider assembly from the driveshaft. Discard the spider assemblies.

6. Clean all foreign matter from the yoke areas at the end of the driveshaft(s).

7. Start the new spider and one of the bearing cap assemblies into a yoke by positioning the yoke in a vise with the spider positioned in place with one of the bearing cap assemblies positioned over one of the holes in the yoke. Slowly close the vise, pressing the bearing cap assembly in the yoke. Press the cap in far enough so that the retaining snap-ring can be installed. Use the smaller socket to recess the bearing cap.

8. Open the vise and position the opposite bearing cap assembly over the proper hole in the yoke with the socket that is smaller than the diameter of the bearing cap located on the cap. Slowly close the vise, pressing the bearing cap into the hole in the yoke with the socket. Make sure that the spider assembly is in line with the bearing cap as it is pressed in. Press the bearing cap in far enough so that the retaining snap-ring can be installed.

9. Install all remaining U-joints in the same manner.

10. Install the driveshaft and grease the new U-joints.

CENTER BEARING REMOVAL AND INSTALLATION

1. Remove the driveshafts.

2. Remove the two center support bearing attaching bolts and remove the assembly from the vehicle.

3. Do not immerse the sealed bearing in any type of cleaning fluid. Wipe the bearing and cushion clean with a cloth dampened with cleaning fluid.

4. Check the bearing for wear or rough action by rotating the inner race while holding the outer race. If wear or roughness is evident, replace the bearing.

Examine the rubber cushion for evidence of hardening, cracking, or deterioration. Replace it if it is damaged in any way.

5. Place the bearing in the rubber support and the rubber support in the U-shaped support and install the bearing in the reverse order of removal.

Wheel Bearings

The wheel bearings should be serviced (cleaned, inspected, repacked or replaced) every 20,000 miles, or whenever operated in deep water.

Before handling the bearings there are a few things that you should remember to do and try to avoid.

DO the following:

1. Remove all outside dirt from the housing before exposing the bearing.

2. Treat a used bearing as gently as you would a new one.

3. Work with clean tools in clean surroundings.

4. Use clean, dry canvas gloves, or at least clean, dry hands.

5. Clean solvents and flushing fluids are a must.

6. Use clean paper when laying out the bearings to dry.

7. Protect disassembled bearings from rust and dirt. Cover them up.

8. Use clean rags to wipe bearings.

9. Keep the bearings in oil-proof paper when they are to be stored or are not in use.

10. Clean the inside of the housing before replacing the bearing.

Do NOT do the following:

1. Don't work in dirty surroundings.

2. Don't use dirty, chipped, or damaged tools.

3. Try not to work on wooden work benches or use wooden mallets.

4. Don't handle bearings with dirty or moist hands.

5. Do not use gasoline for cleaning; use a safe solvent.

6. Do not spin-dry bearings with compressed air. They will be damaged.

7. Do not spin unclean bearings.

8. Avoid using cotton waste or dirty cloths to wipe bearings.

9. Try not to scratch or nick bearing surfaces.

10. Do not allow the bearing to come in contact with dirt or rust at any time.

SERVICE

2WD Front

1. Jack the truck up until the wheel to be serviced is off the ground and can spin freely. It is easier to check all the bearings at the same time. If the equipment needed is available, raise the front end of the truck so that both front wheels are off the ground. Use jackstands or suitable blocks to support the vehicle. Make sure that the truck is completely stable before proceeding any further.

2. Remove the lug nuts and remove the wheel/tire assembly from the hub. On models with drum brakes it is possible to remove the hub assembly from the spindle with the wheel/tire assembly still attached, but the added weight makes handling of the entire assembly a little clumsy which could result in possible damage to the bearings or spindle.

On trucks with disc brakes, it is necessary to remove the caliper assembly from the rotor and caliper support. Do not disconnect the brake line from the caliper. Simply hang the caliper with a length of heavy wire above the hub. Be careful not to strain the flexible brake tube.

3. Remove the grease cap with a screwdriver or pliers.

4. Remove the cotter pin and discard it. Cotter pins should never be reused.

5. Remove the nut lock, adjusting nut, and washer from the spindle.

6. Wiggle the hub so that the outer wheel bearing comes loose and can be removed. Remove the outer bearing.

7. Remove the hub from the spindle and place it on a work surface, supported by two blocks of wood under the brake drum or hub.

NOTE: On drum brake equipped models, if the hub will not come off easily, back off the brake shoe adjustment screw so that the shoes do not contact the brake drum.

8. Place a block of wood or drift pin through the spindle hole and tap out the inner grease seal. Tap lightly so not to damage the bearing. When the seal falls out, so will the inner bearing. Discard the seal.

Perform the above procedures to all the wheels that are going to be serviced.

9. Place all of the bearings, nuts, nut locks, washers and grease caps in a container of solvent. Use a light soft brush to thoroughly clean each part. Make sure that every bit of dirt and grease is rinsed off, then place each cleaned part on an absorbent cloth or paper and allow them to dry completely.

10. Clean the inside of the hub, including the bearing races, and the spindle. Remove all traces of old lubricant from these components.

11. Inspect the bearings for pitting, flat spots, rust, and rough areas. Check the races in the hub and the spindle for the same defects and rub them clean with a

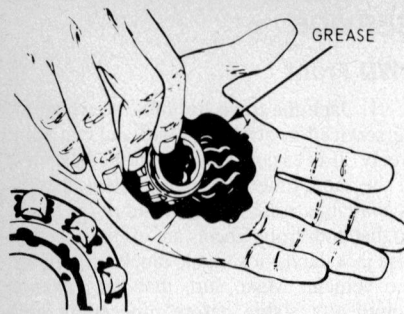

Hand-packing the wheel bearings

cloth that has been soaked in solvent. If the races show hair line cracks or worn shiny areas, they must be replaced. The races are installed in the hub with a press fit and are removed by driving them out with a suitable punch or drift. Place the new races squarely onto the hub and place a block of wood over them. Drive the race into place with a hammer, striking the block of wood. Never hit the race with any metal object.

Replacement seals, bearings, and other required parts can be bought at an auto parts store. The old parts should be taken along to be compared with the replacement parts to ensure a perfect match.

12. Pack the wheel bearings with grease. There are special devices made for the specific purpose of greasing bearings, but if one is not available, pack the wheel bearings by hand. Put a large dab of grease in the palm of your hand and push the bearing through it with a sliding motion. The grease must be forced through the side of the bearing and in between each roller. Continue until the grease begins to ooze out the other side and through the gaps between the rollers; the bearing must be completely packed with grease.

NOTE: Sodium based grease is not compatible with lithium based grease. Be careful not to mix the two types. The best way to prevent this is to completely clean all of the old grease from the hub and spindle before installing any new grease.

13. Turn the hub assembly over so that the inner side faces up, making sure that the race and inner area are clean, and drop the inner wheel bearing into place. Using a hammer and a block of wood, tap the new grease seal in place. Never hit the seal with the hammer directly. Move the block of wood around the circumference until it is properly seated.

14. Slide the hub assembly onto the spindle and push it as far as it will go, making sure that it has completely covered the brake shoes. Keep the hub centered on the spindle to prevent damage to the grease seal and the spindle threads.

15. Place the outer wheel bearing in place over the spindle. Press it in until it is snug. Place the washer on the spindle after the bearing. Screw on the spindle nut and turn it down until a slight binding is felt.

16. With a torque wrench, tighten the nut to 17–25 ft. lbs. to seat the bearings. Install the nut lock over the nut so that the cotter pin hole in the spindle is aligned with a slot in the nut lock. Back off the adjusting nut and the nut lock two slots of the nut lock and install the cotter pin.

17. Bend the longer of the two ends opposite the looped end out and over the end of the spindle. Trim both ends of the cotter pin just enough so that the grease cap will fit, leaving the bent end shaped over the end of the spindle.

18. Install the grease cap, brake caliper if so equipped, and the wheel/tire assembly. The wheel should rotate freely with no noise or noticeable end-play.

19. Adjust the brakes on drum brake equipped trucks.

4WD Front Without Free-Running Hubs

NOTE: Sodium based grease is not compatible with lithium based grease. Be careful not to mix the two types. The best way to prevent this is to completely clean all of the old grease from the hub assembly before installing any new grease.

1. Raise the front of the vehicle and place jackstands under the vehicle. Remove the wheel.

2. Remove the front hub grease cap and driving hub snap-ring. On models equipped with free-running hubs, remove the retainer knob hub ring, actuator knob, snap-ring, outer clutch retaining ring, and actuating cam body.

3. Remove the splined driving hub and the pressure spring. This may require slight prying with a screwdriver.

4. Remove the wheel bearing locknut, lockring, and adjusting nut.

5. Drum Brakes: Remove the hub and drum assembly. This may require that the brake adjusting screw be backed off to move the brake shoes away from the brake drum. The outer wheel bearing and spring retainer will slide out as the hub is removed.

Disc Brakes: See the Brake section for caliper removal. Suspend the caliper out of the way and remove the hub and rotor assembly.

6. Carefully drive out the inner bearing cone and grease seal from the hub.

7. Inspect the bearing cups (races) for cracks and pits. If the cups are excessively worn or there are pits or cracks visible, replace them along with the cones. The cups are removed from the hub by driving them out with a drift pin. They are installed in the same manner.

8. If it is determined that the cups are in satisfactory condition and are to remain in the hub, clean and inspect the cones (bearings). Refer to the bearing diagnosis chart. Replace the bearings if necessary. If it is necessary to replace either the cone or the cup, both parts should be replaced as a unit.

9. Thoroughly clean all components in a suitable solvent and blow them dry with compressed air or allow them to dry while resting on clean paper.

NOTE: Do not spin the bearings with compressed air while drying them.

10. Cover the spindle with a cloth and brush all loose dust and dirt from the brake assembly. Remove the cloth and thoroughly clean the inside of the hub and the spindle.

11. Pack the inside of the hub with wheel bearing grease. Add grease to the hub until the grease is flush with the inside diameter of the bearing cup.

12. Pack the bearing cone and roller assemblies with wheel bearing grease. A bearing packer is desirable for this operation. If a packer is not available, place a large portion of grease into the palm of your hand and sliding the edge of the roller cage through the grease with your other hand, work as much grease in between the rollers as possible.

13. Position the inner bearing into the inner bearing cup and install the new grease seal.

14. Carefully position the hub assembly onto the spindle. Be careful not to damage

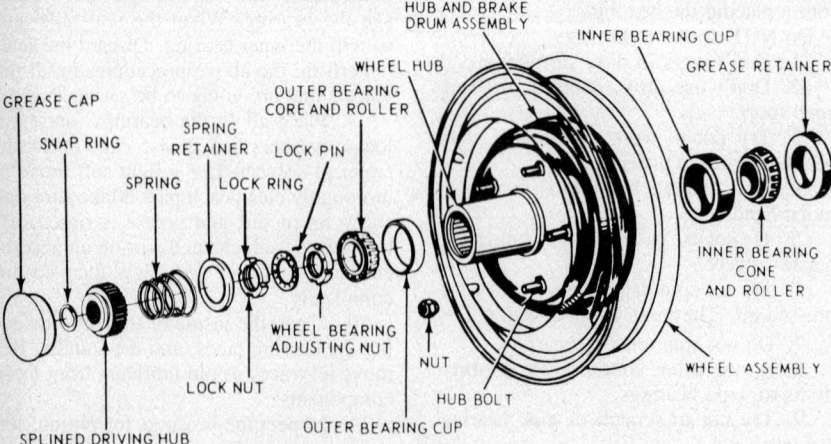

4WD front hub without free-running (locking) hubs

the new seal. Install the drum or caliper.

15. Place the outer bearing into position on the spindle and into the bearing cup.

16. Install the bearing adjusting nut and tighten it to 50 ft. lbs. while rotating the hub back and forth to seat the bearings.

17. Back off the adjusting nut about 90°.

18. Assemble the lockring by turning the nut to the nearest notch where the dowel pin will enter.

19. Install the outer locknut and torque to 80–100 ft. lbs. The final end-play of the wheel on the spindle should be 0.001–0.010 in.

20. Install the pressure spring retainer, spring, the driving hub and driving hub snap-ring. This is for vehicles without free-running hubs.

21. Install the grease cap and adjust the brakes, if they were backed off to remove the hub assembly. Remove the jackstands and lower the vehicle.

Free-Running Hub

1975–79

Removal

1. Remove the free-running hub bolts and washers.

2. Remove the hub ring and the knob. Wipe the parts clean.

3. Remove the internal snap-ring from the groove in the hub.

4. Remove the cam body ring and clutch retainer (as an assembly) from the hub. Disassemble the parts.

5. Remove the axle shaft snap-ring. For easier snap-ring removal, push inward on the axle shaft sleeve ring and, at the same time, pull out on the axle with a bolt.

6. Remove the axle shaft sleeve ring and inner clutch ring. A slight rocking of the hub may make them slide out easier.

7. Remove the pressure spring.

8. Remove the spring retainer ring.

Installation

1. Grease the hub inner spline with Moly grease or equivalent.

2. Install the spring retainer ring, positioned as shown with recessed undercut area going in first. Be sure ring seats against the bearing.

3. Install the coil spring with large end entering first.

4. Grease with Moly grease or equivalent and install the axle shaft sleeve and ring and the inner clutch ring. Be sure that the teeth are meshed together in a locked position for easy assembly. It may be necessary to rock the hub back and forth for spline alignment. Keep the two gears in locked position.

5. Install the axle shaft snap-ring. Push inward on gear and, if necessary, pull out axle shaft with bolt to allow groove clearance on shaft for the snap-ring. Be sure snap-ring is fully seated in the snap-ring

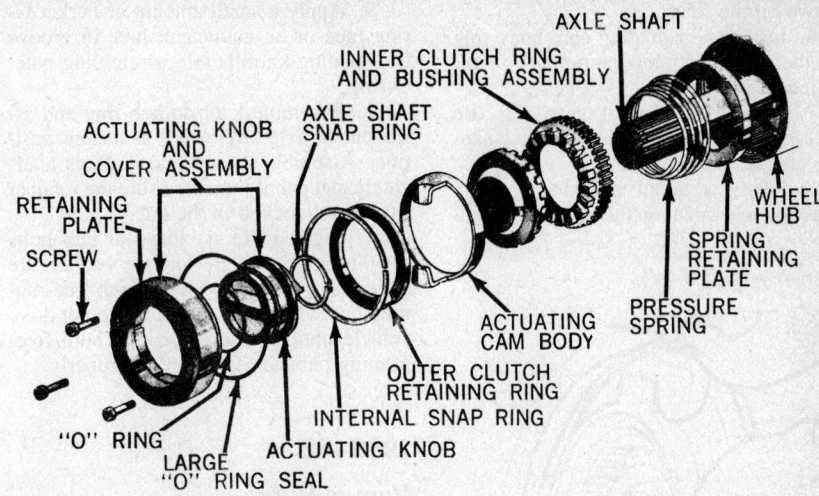

Typical internal locking hub used on 1975–79 models

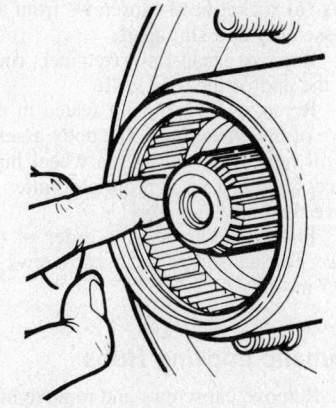

Grease application

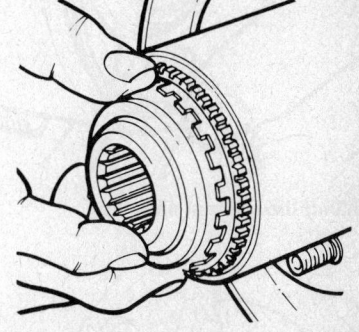

Axle shaft sleeve and ring, and inner clutch ring installation

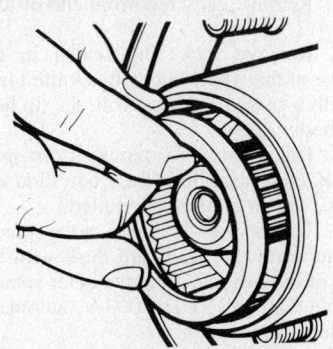

Spring retainer ring installation

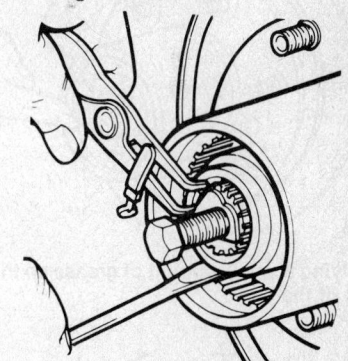

Installing the axle shaft snap-ring

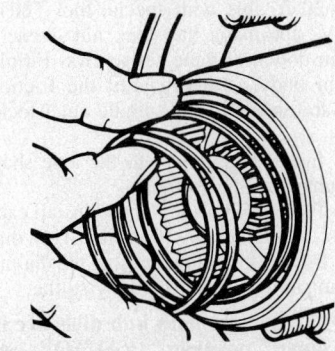

Coil spring installation

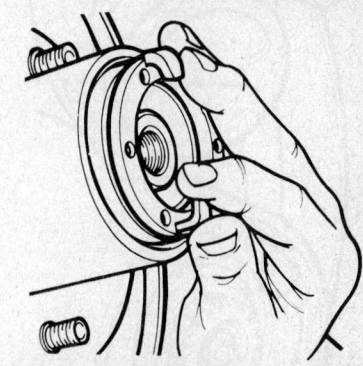

Installing the cam body ring into the clutch retaining ring

groove on the shaft.

6. Install the actuating cam body ring into the outer clutch retaining ring. Assemble into hub.

7. Install the internal snap-ring. Be sure snap-ring is fully seated in the snap-ring groove of the hub.

8. Apply a small amount of Moly grease or equivalent on the ears of the cam.

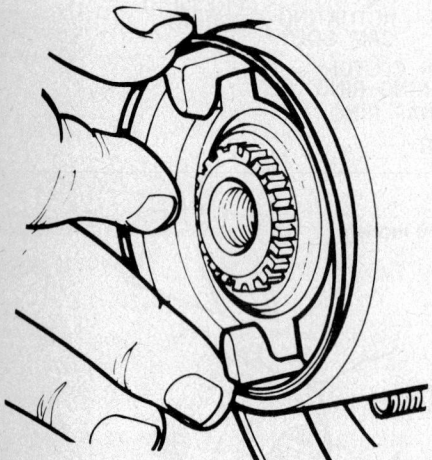

Installing the internal snap-ring

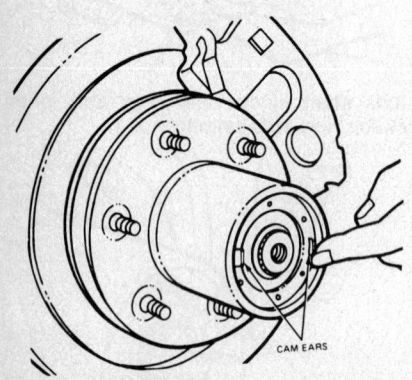

Applying a small amount of grease on the ears of the cam

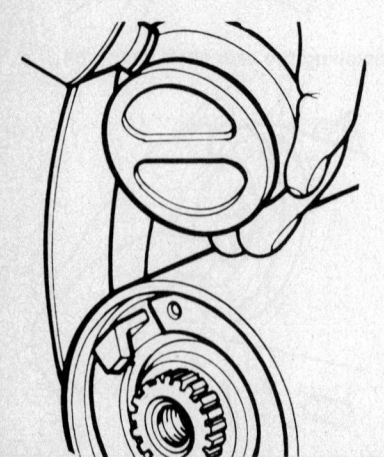

Lubricating the selector knob

9. Apply a small amount of Parker O-ring lube or an equivalent lube in groove of actuating knob before assembling outer O-ring.

10. Assemble knob in hub ring and assemble to axle with knob in locked position. Assemble screws and washers alternately and evenly, making sure the retainer ring is not cocked in the hub.

11. Tighten the six lock-out hub bolts to 30 to 35 in. lbs. Be sure the washers are under each retaining screw. Each free-running hub will fit either wheel. Do not drive vehicle until you are sure that both free-running hubs are functioning properly.

1980–82

Manual Hubs

1. To remove hub, first separate cap assembly from body assembly by removing the six (6) socket head capscrews from the cap assembly and slip apart.

2. Remove snap-ring (retainer ring) from the end of the axle shaft.

3. Remove the lock ring seated in the groove of the wheel hub. The body assembly will now slide out of the wheel hub. If necessary, use an appropriate puller to remove the body assembly.

4. Install hub in reverse order of removal. Torque socket head capscrews to 30–35 in. lbs.

Automatic Locking Hubs

1. Remove capscrews and remove hub cap assembly from spindle.

2. Remove capscrew from end of axle shaft.

3. Remove lock ring seated in the groove of the wheel hub with a knife blade or with a small sharp awl with the tip bent in a hook.

4. Remove body assembly from spindle. If body assembly does not slide out easily, use an appropriate puller.

5. Unscrew all three sets in the spindle locknut until the heads are flush with the edge of the locknut. Remove outer spindle locknut with tool T80T-4000-V, automatic hub lock nut wrench.

6. Reinstall in reverse order of removal. Tighten the outer spindle locknut to 15–20 ft. lbs. with special tool T80T-4000-V, automatic hub lock nut wrench. Tighten down all three set screws. Firmly push in body assembly until the friction shoes are on top of the spindle outer locknut.

7. Install capscrew into the axle shaft and tighten to 35–50 ft. lbs.

8. Place cap on spindle and install capscrews. Tighten to 35–50 in. lbs. Turn dial firmly from stop to stop, causing the dialing mechanism to engage the body spline.

NOTE: Be sure both hub dials are in the same position; "AUTO" or "LOCK."

BEARING REPLACEMENT OR REPACKING

1975–82

1. Raise the vehicle and install safety stands.

2. If equipped with free-running hubs refer to Free-Running Hub Removal and Installation.

3. Remove the front hub grease cap and driving hub snap-ring.

4. Remove the splined driving hub and the pressure spring. This may require a slight prying assist.

5. Remove the wheel bearing lock nut, lock ring, and adjusting nut using tool T59T-1197-B, or equivalent.

6. Remove the hub and disc assembly. The outer wheel bearing and spring retainer will slide out as the hub is removed.

7. Remove the spindle retaining nuts, then carefully remove the spindle from the knuckle studs and axle shaft.

8. Clean all old grease from the needle bearings and wipe clean the spindle face that mates with the spindle bore seal.

9. Remove the spindle bore seal, V-seal, and thrust washer from the outer axle shaft. Clean any old grease or dirt from these parts and replace those that show signs of excessive wear.

10. Using Multi-Purpose Lubricant, Ford Specification ESA-M1C75-B or equivalent, thoroughly lubricate the needle bearing and pack the spindle face that mates with the spindle bore seal.

11. Assemble the V-seal in the spindle bore next to the needle bearing. Assemble the spindle bore seal on the axle shaft.

12. Assemble the spindle with the axle shaft on the knuckle studs. Adjust the retaining nuts to 50–60 ft. lbs.

13. Carefully drive the inner bearing cone and grease seal out of the hub using Tool T69L-1102-A.

14. Inspect the bearing cups for pits or cracks. If necessary, remove them with a drift. If new cups are installed, install new bearings.

15. Lubricate the bearings with Multi-Purpose Lubricant Ford Specification, ESA-M1C7-B or equivalent. Clean all old grease from the hub. Pack the cones and rollers. If a bearing packer is not available, work as much lubricant as possible between the rollers and the cages.

16. Position the inner bearing cone and roller in the inner cup and install the grease retainer.

17. Carefully position the hub and disc assembly on the spindle.

18. Install the outer bearing cone and roller, and the adjusting nut.

19. Using tool T59T-1197-B and a torque wrench, tighten the bearing adjusting nut to 50 ft. lbs., while rotating the wheel back and forth to seat the bearings.

20. Back off the adjusting nut approximately 90 degrees.

21. Assemble the lock ring by turning

the nut to the nearest hole and inserting the dowel pin. Note: The dowel pin must seat in a lock ring hole for proper bearing adjustment and wheel retention.

22. Install the outer lock nut and tighten to 50–80 ft. lbs. Final end play of the wheel on the spindle should be 0.001 to 0.010 inch.

23. Install the pressure spring and driving hub snap-ring.

24. Apply non-hardening sealer to the seating edge of the grease cap, and install the grease cap.

25. Adjust the brake if it was backed off.

26. Remove the safety stands and lower the vehicle.

REAR WHEEL BEARINGS

F-250, 350, E-250, E-300, E-350 Rear

The wheel bearings on the full floating rear axle are packed with wheel bearing grease. Axle lubricant can also flow into the wheel hubs and bearings, however, wheel bearing grease is the primary lubricant. The wheel bearing grease provides lubrication until the axle lubricant reaches the bearings during normal operation.

1. Set the parking brake and loosen the axle shaft bolts.

2. Raise the rear wheels off the floor and place jackstands under the rear axle housing so that the axle is parallel with the floor.

3. Remove the axle shaft bolts.

4. Remove the axle shaft and gaskets.

5. With the axle shaft removed, remove the gasket from the axle shaft flange studs.

6. Bend the lockwasher tab away from the locknut, and then remove the locknut, lockwasher, and the adjusting nut.

7. Remove the outer bearing cone and pull the wheel straight off the axle.

8. With a piece of hardwood which will just clear the outer bearing cup, drive the inner bearing cone and inner seal out of the wheel hub.

9. Wash all the old grease or axle lubricant out of the wheel hub, using a suitable solvent.

10. Wash the bearing cups and rollers and inspect them for pitting, galling, and uneven wear patterns. Inspect the roller for end wear.

11. If the bearing cups are to be replaced, drive them out with a drift. Install the new cups with a block of wood and hammer or press them in.

12. If the bearing cups are properly seated, a 0.0015 in. feeler gauge will not fit between the cup and the wheel hub.

13. Pack each bearing cone and roller with a bearing packer or in the manner previously outlined for the front wheel bearings on 2WD trucks.

14. Place the inner bearing cone and roller assembly in the wheel hub. Install a

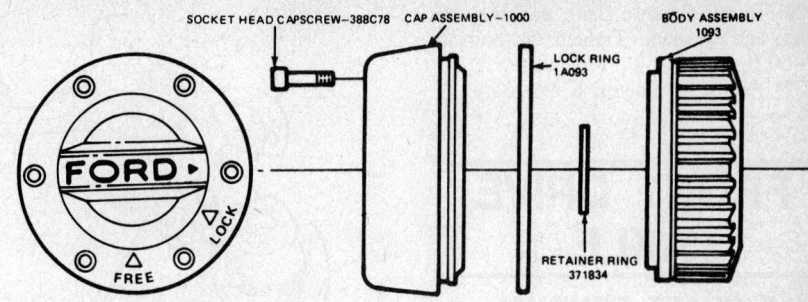

1980 and later manual locking hubs

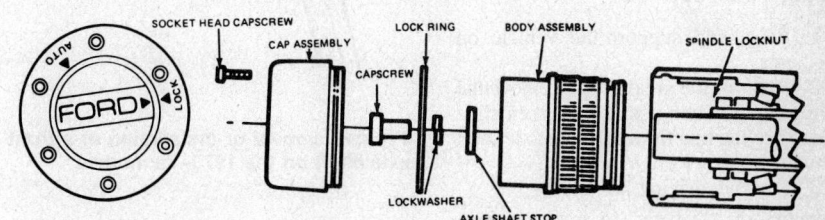

1980 and later automatic locking hubs

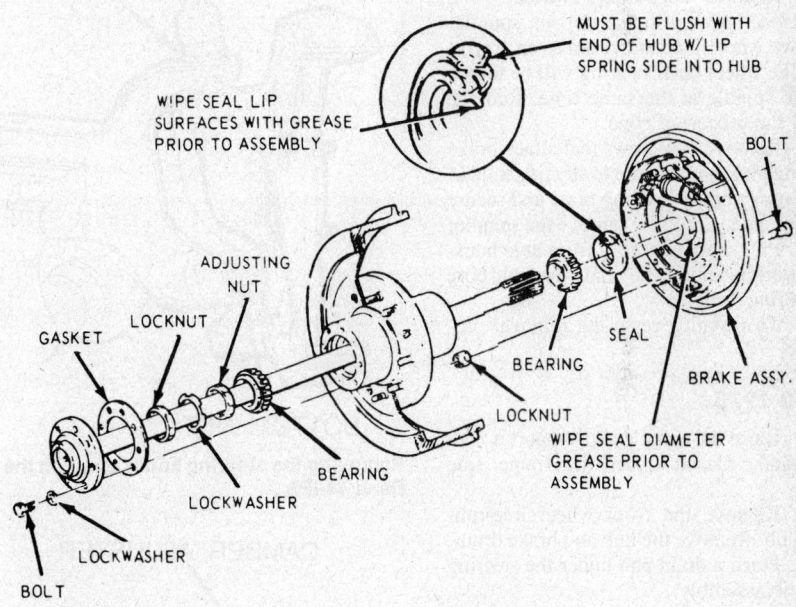

F-250, 350 rear wheel hub assembly with full-floating axles

new inner seal in the hub.

15. Install the wheel.

16. Install and tighten the bearing adjusting nut to 50–80 ft. lbs. while rotating the wheel.

17. Back off (loosen) the adjusting nut ⅛ of a turn.

18. Apply axle lube to a new lockwasher and install it with the smooth side out.

19. Install the locknut and tighten it to 90–110 ft. lbs. The wheel must rotate freely after the locknut is tightened. The wheel end-play should be within 0.001–0.010 in.

20. Bend two lockwasher tabs inward over an adjusting nut flat and two lockwasher tabs outward over the locknut flat.

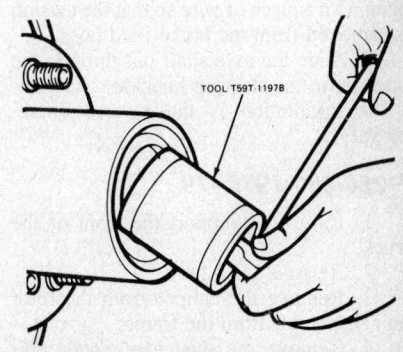

Lock nut, lock ring and adjusting nut removal

21. Install the axle shaft, gasket, lockbolts, and washers. Tighten the bolts to 40–50 ft. lbs.

22. Adjust the brakes, if necessary.

FRONT DRIVE AXLE

AXLE SHAFT REMOVAL AND INSTALLATION

F-100, 150 1975–79

1. Raise and support the vehicle on jackstands.

2. Remove the grease cap. Remove the driving hub retaining snap-ring, then slide splined driving hub from between axle shaft and wheel hub.

3. Remove driving hub spring.

NOTE: If equipped with free-wheeling hubs, see hub removal.

4. Remove lock nut, washer, and wheel bearing adjusting nut from spindle. Remove wheel, hub and drum as an assembly. The wheel outer bearing will be forced off the spindle at the same time. Remove wheel inner bearing cone.

5. Remove capscrews that attach brake backing plate and spindle to steering knuckle. Remove brake backing plate and secure it to one side. Carefully remove the spindle.

6. Pull shaft assembly from axle housing, working universal joint through bore in steering knuckle.

7. To install reverse the removal procedure.

F-250 1975

1. Raise the vehicle and support it with jackstands placed under the frame side rails.

2. Remove the front wheel free-running hub. Remove the hub and brake drum.

3. Place a drain pan under the steering knuckle assembly.

4. Remove the capscrews which hold the brake backing plate and spindle to the steering knuckle. Remove the backing plate and spindle. Support the brake backing plate with a piece of wire so that the tension is removed from the brake fluid hose.

5. Slide the axle shaft out through the opening in the steering knuckle.

6. Installation is the reverse of removal.

F-250-350 1976–79

1. Raise and support the front of the truck.

2. Remove the wheel.

3. Remove the caliper from the rotor and suspend it from the frame.

4. Remove the dust cap, cotter pin, nut, washer and outer bearing and remove the rotor from the spindle.

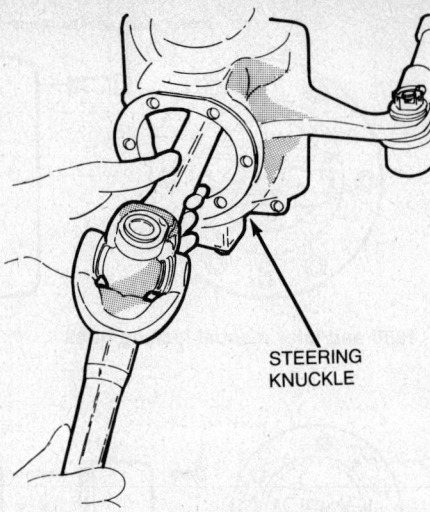

Typical removal or installation of a front axle shaft on the 1975–79 models

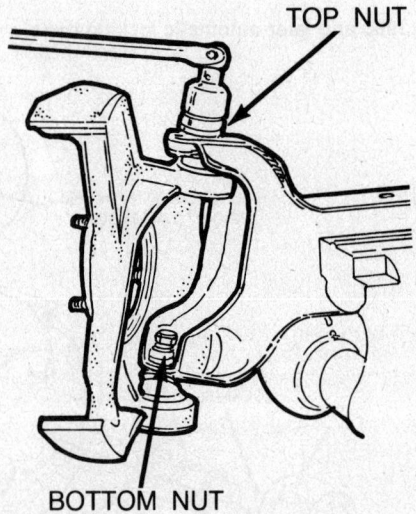

TOP NUT

BOTTOM NUT

Removing the steering knuckle nut on the Dana 44-IFS

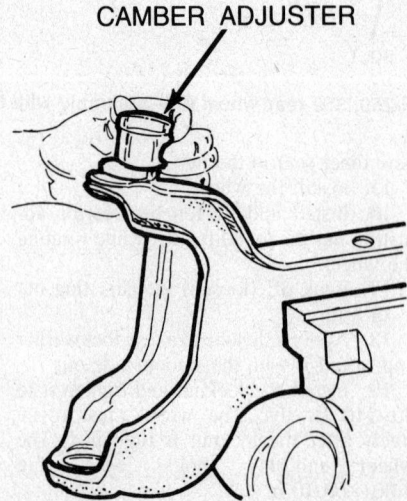

CAMBER ADJUSTER

Removing the camber bushing on the Dana 44-IFS

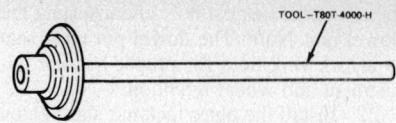

TOOL-T80T-4000-H

Inner axle seal installation tool for the Dana 44-IFS

5. Remove the inner bearing cone and seal.

6. Remove the axle shaft, working the U-joint through the bore of the steering knuckle. Be careful not to damage the seal.

7. Installation is the reverse of removal.

F-150, F-250, F-350 1980–82

1. Remove the axle shaft assembly. Remove the axle bearing as follows:

2. Remove the stub assembly by removing the three bolts attaching the retainer plate to the carrier housing.

3. Place the axle shaft in a vise and drill a ½″ hole in the outside of the bearing retaining ring to a depth of ¾ of the thickness of the ring.

4. Place a chisel across the hole and strike sharply with a hammer to remove the retaining ring. Replace the bearing retaining ring upon assembly.

5. Press the bearing from the axle shaft using special tools axle bearing remover no. T80T-4000M and sleeve no. T80T-4000L.

6. Remove the steal and retainer plate from the stub shaft.

7. To install place the new seal and retainer plate on the shaft.

8. Place the bearing on the shaft with the large radius on the inner race facing the yoke end of the shaft.

9. Press the bearing onto the shaft using an axle bearing replacer no. T80T-4000-N and a pinion bearing cone remover no. T71P-4621-B. A 0.0015 inch feeler gauge should not fit between the bearing seat and the bearing.

10. Using the same special tools in step 9 press the bearing retainer ring onto the stub shaft. A 0.0015 inch feeler gauge should not fit between the ring and the bearing. There must be one point between the bearing and the ring where the feeler gauge cannot enter. If the feeler gauge enters completely around the circumference press the retainer further onto the shaft.

11. Push the seal and retainer plate away from the bearing to form a space between the seal and the bearing. Fill the space with the proper bearing grease and wrap tape around the space.

12. Pull the seal towards the bearing until it contacts the inner race and forces the grease between the rollers and cup. Remove the tape.

13. Install the stub shaft in the carrier and install the three retainer bolts. Tighten to 35 ft. lbs.

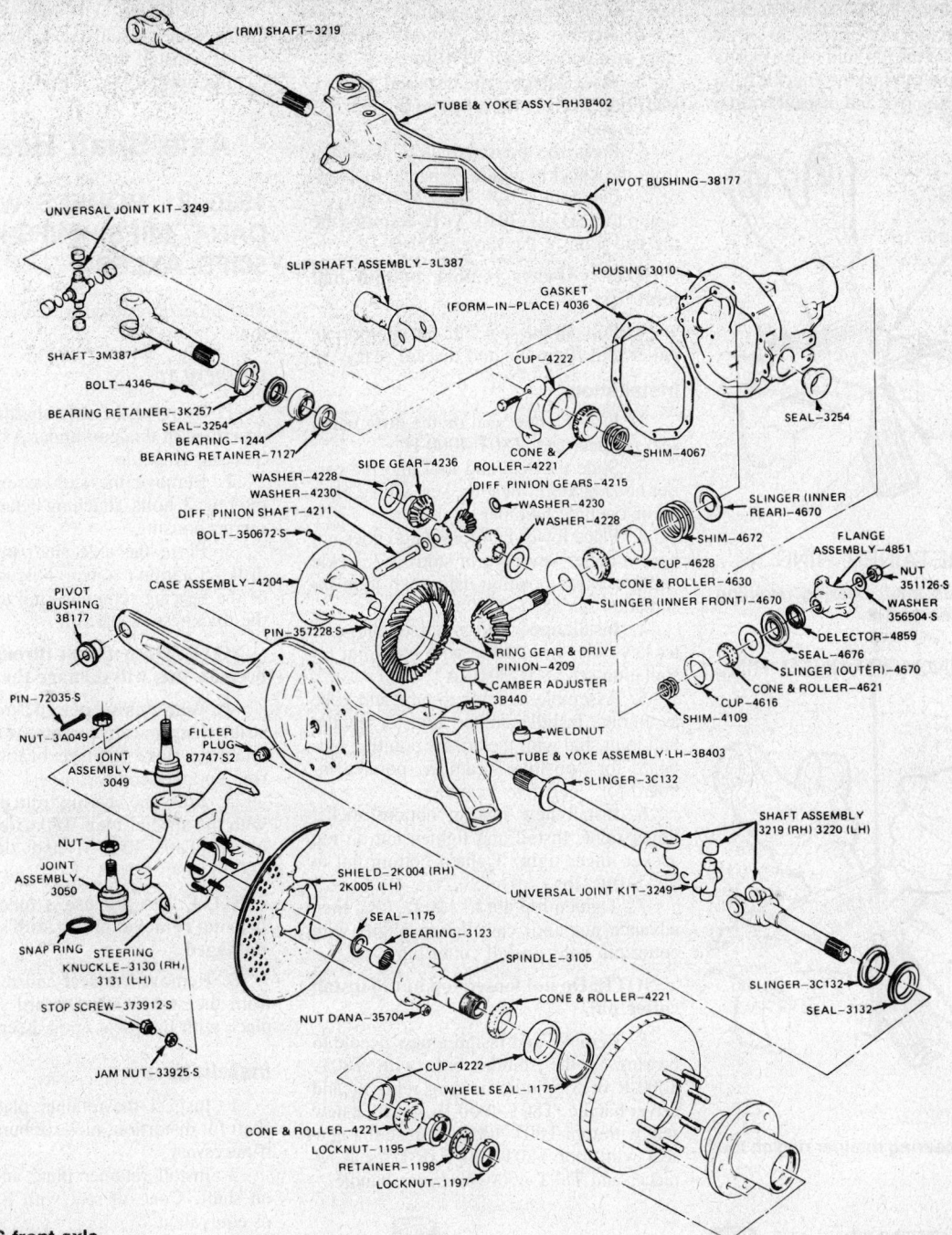

Dana 44-IFS front axle

14. Install the right hand axle shaft assembly into the slip yoke.

15. Install the spindle.

1975–79 Bronco

1. Raise the vehicle and support it on jack stands.

2. Remove the front wheels.

3. On drum brake models, remove the hub, brake drum, backing plate and spindle. Tie the backing plate up to avoid damage to the hose.

4. On disc brake models, remove the hubs, calipers and rotors. Tie up the calipers to avoid damage to the hoses. Remove

the nuts that attach the brake support bracket, dust shield and spindle.

5. Pull the axle shaft from the housing, carefully working the U-joint through the steering knuckle.

6. Install the shaft in reverse order of removal.

1980–82 Bronco

REMOVAL

NOTE: This procedure requires the use of special tools.

1. Remove spindle nuts and remove spindle. It may be necessary to tap the spin-

dle with a rawhide or plastic hammer to break the spindle loose. Remove spindle, splash shield and axle shaft assembly.

2. Place the spindle in a vise with a shop towel around the spindle to protect the spindle from damage. Using a slide hammer T50-T-100-A and seal remover, tool 1175-AC remove the axle shaft seal and then the needle bearing from the spindle bar.

3. If the tie rod has not been removed, then remove cotter key from the tie rod nut and then remove nut. Tap on the tie rod stud to free it from the steering arm.

4. Remove the cotter pin from the top ball joint stud. Loosen the nut on the top

stud and the bottom nut inside the knuckle. Remove the top nut.

5. Sharply hit the top stud with a plastic or rawhide hammer to free the knuckle from the tube yoke. Remove and discard bottom

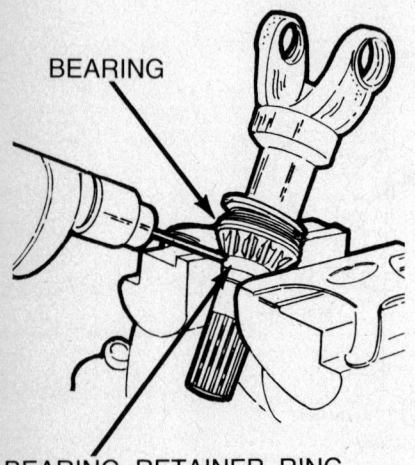

BEARING

BEARING RETAINER RING

Drilling the stub shaft bearing retaining ring on the Dana 44-IFS

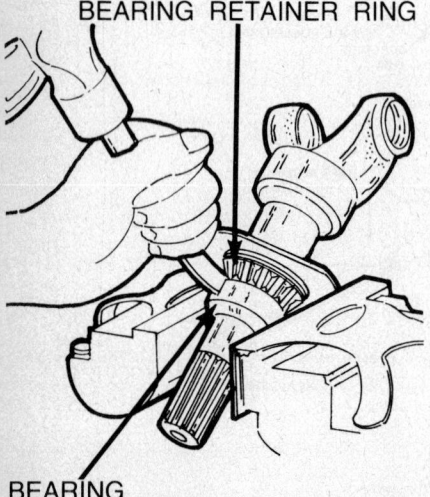

BEARING RETAINER RING

BEARING

Removing the bearing retainer ring on the Dana 44-IFS

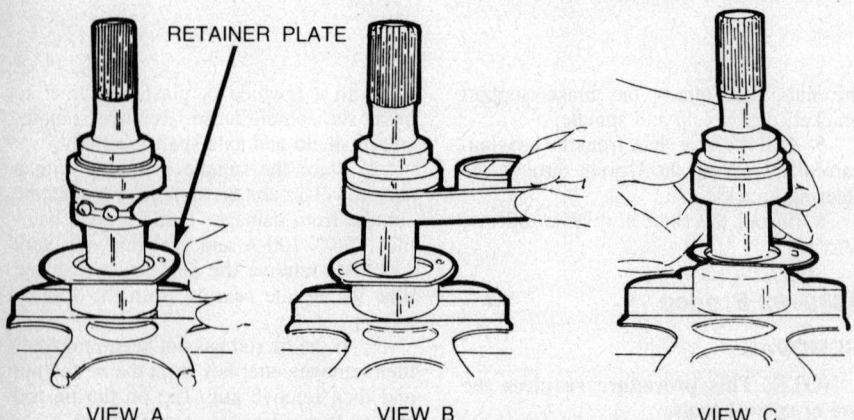

VIEW A   VIEW B   VIEW C

RETAINER PLATE

Lubricating the axle bearing on the Dana 44-IFS

nut. Use new nut upon assembly.

6. Remove camber adjuster with Pitman arm puller T64P-3590-F.

7. Place knuckle in vise and remove snap ring from bottom ball joint socket if so equipped.

8. Press the bottom ball joint socket from the knuckle with the special tools receiver cup tool (P79P-3010-AG) and C1 clamp tool (D79T-3010-A)-B. Remove the top ball joint in the same manner.

NOTE: Always remove bottom ball joint first.

9. Pull out the seal with the appropriate puller tool. Remove and discard seal.

Installation

1. Install a new seal on the differential seal replacer tool T80T-4000-H.

2. Slide the seal and tool into the carrier housing bore. Seat the seal with a plastic or rawhide hammer.

3. Place lower ball joint (stud does not have a cotter key hole in stud) in knuckle and press into position using ball joint installation set T80T-3010-A.

4. Install upper ball joint (stud has cotter key hole) in knuckle with ball joint installation set T80T-3010-A.

5. Assemble knuckle to tube and yoke assembly. Install camber adjuster on top ball joint stud with the arrrow pointing outboard for ''positive'' camber, pointed inboard for ''negative'' camber.

6. Install new nut on bottom socket finger tight. Install and tighten nut on top socket finger tight. Tighten bottom nut to 90–110 ft. lbs.

7. Tighten top nut to 100 ft. lbs., then advance nut until castellation aligns with cotter pin hole. Install cotter pin.

NOTE: Do not loosen top nut to install cotter pin.

8. Remove and install a new needle to bearing in the spindle bare with T80T-4000-R or S spindle bearing replacer and driver handle, T80T-4000-W. Install a new seal with tool T80T-4000-W. Install a new seal with tool T80T-400-T or U, seal replacer and T80T-4000-W driven handle.

9. Install the axle shaft assembly into the housing. Install the splash shield and spindle. Install and tighten the spindle attaching nuts.

Axle Shaft Bearing

1980–81 MODELS WITH DANA 44IFS, 44IFS-HD OR 50IFS AXLES

This procedure requires the use of special tools.

REMOVAL

1. Remove the axle shaft assembly as described in this part under Axle Shaft and Steering Knuckle.

2. Remove the stub assembly by removing 3 bolts attaching retainer plate to carrier housing.

3. Place the axle shaft in a vise and drill a 6.35mm (¼ inch) hole in the outside of the bearing retaining ring to a depth ¾ the thickness of the ring.

NOTE: Do not drill through the ring because this will damage the axle shaft.

4. With a chisel placed across the hole, strike sharply with a hammer to remove the retaining ring. Replace bearing retaining ring upon assembly.

5. Press the bearing from the axle shaft with the special tools T80 axle bearing remover T80T-4000-M and sleeve T80T-4000-L.

NOTE: Do not use a torch to aid in bearing removal or the stub shaft will be damaged.

6. Remove the seal and retainer plate from the stub shaft. Discard seal and replace with new seal upon assembly.

Installation

1. Inspect the retainer plate and stub shaft for distortion, nicks or burns. Replace if necessary.

2. Install retainer plate and new seal on shaft. Coat oil seal with ESA-M175B or equivalent.

3. Place the bearing on the shaft. The large radius on the inner race must face the yoke end of the shaft.

4. Use axle bearing replacer T80T-4000-N and pinion bearing cone remover T71P-4621-B to press the bearing onto the shaft until completely seated. A 0.038mm (0.0015 inch) feeler gauge should not fit between the bearing seat and bearing.

5. Use axle bearing replacer T80T-4000-N and pinion bearing cone remover T71P-4621-B to press the bearing retainer ring onto the stub shaft. Press the bearing retainer ring until completely seated. A 0.038mm (0.0015 inch) feeler gauge should not fit between the ring and bearing. There must be one point between the bearing and ring where the feeler gauge cannot

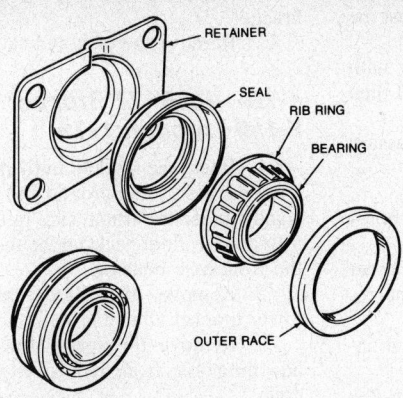

Tapered roller bearings used on some E-100, 150 and 200 axle shafts

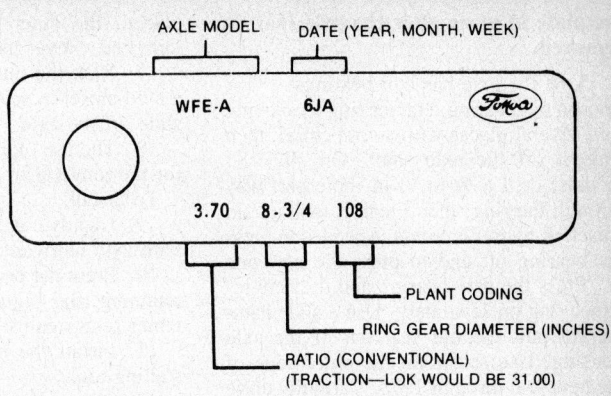

Ford axle identification tag

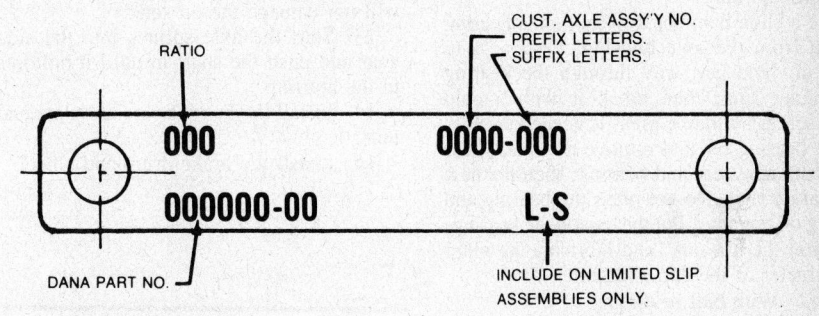

Dana axle identification tag

enter. If feeler gauge enters completely around the circumference press the retainer further onto the shaft.

6. Push the seal and retainer plate away from the bearing to form a space between the seal and bearing. Fill the space with wheel bearing grease meeting Ford specification ESA-MIC75B or equivalent.

7. With the space filled with grease, wrap tape around the space.

8. Pull the seal towards the bearing until it contacts the inner race. This will force grease between the rollers and cup. Remove tape.

NOTE: If grease is not visible on the small end of the rollers, repeat steps 6 through 8 until grease is visible. Install the slip yoke and U-joint to stub shaft.

9. Install the stub shaft in the carrier and install 3 retainer bolts. Torque to 30–40 ft. lbs. Install right hand axle shaft assembly into slip yoke.

10. Install splash shield and spindle.

Axle Shaft U-Joint Overhaul

Follow the procedures outlined under Axle Shaft Removal and Installation to gain access to the U-joints. Overhaul them as described under U-joints.

REAR AXLE

Axle Shaft

REMOVAL AND INSTALLATION

Pick-up

FORD REMOVABLE CARRIER TYPE

1. Raise and support the vehicle and

remove the wheel/tire assembly from the brake drum.

2. Remove the nuts which secure the brake drum to the axle flange, then remove the drum from the flange.

3. Working through the hole provided in each axle shaft flange, remove the nuts which secure the wheel bearing retainer plate.

4. Using an axle puller, pull the axle shaft assembly out of the axle housing.

NOTE: The brake backing plate must not be dislodged. Install one nut to hold the plate in place after the axle shaft is removed.

To replace the axle shaft:

5. Remove the one nut which holds the brake backing plate and carefully slide the axle shaft into the housing, so that the rough forgings on the shaft will not damage the oil seal.

6. Start the axle splines into the side gear and push the shaft in until the bearing bottoms in the housing.

7. Install the bearing retainer plate and the nuts which secure it.

8. Install the brake drum and the drum attaching nuts.

9. Install the wheel/tire assembly and lower the vehicle.

DANA INTEGRAL CARRIER TYPE

1. Remove the lockbolts and lockwashers which hold the axle flange to the hub and drum assembly.

NOTE: It is not necessary to raise the vehicle to remove the axle shafts.

2. Carefully slide the axle shaft out of the axle housing.

3. Clean the mating surfaces of the axle flange and the hub and drum assembly.

4. Position a new gasket on the axle flange and carefully slide the axle shaft into the axle housing. When the splined end of the axle shaft reaches the side gear, gently rotate the shaft until it is inserted into the side gear.

5. Position the gasket between the axle flange and the hub and drum and install the lockbolts and lockwashers.

Van

E-100, E-150, and E-200

1. Raise and support the vehicle and remove the wheel/tire assembly from the brake drum.

2. Remove the clips which secure the brake drum to the axle flange, then remove the drum from the flange.

3. Working through the hole provided in each axle shaft flange, remove the nuts which secure the wheel bearing retainer plate.

4. Pull the axle shaft assembly out of the axle housing. You may need a slide hammer.

NOTE: The brake backing plate must not be dislodged. Install one nut to hold

the plate in place after the axle shaft is removed.

5. If the axle has ball bearings: Loosen the bearing retainer ring by nicking it in several places with a cold chisel, then slide it off the axle shaft. On 1977–80 models, drill a ¼ to ½ in. hole part way through the ring, then break it with a cold chisel. A hydraulic press is needed to press the bearing off and to press the new one on. Press the new bearing and the new retainer ring separately. Use a slide hammer to pull the old seal out of the axle housing. Use sealer on the outer edge of the new seal through 1975. Carefully drive the new seal evenly into the axle housing, preferably with a seal driver tool.

6. If the axle has tapered roller bearings (1975–80 only): Use a slide hammer to remove the bearing cup from the axle housing. Drill a ¼ to ½ in. hole part way through the bearing retainer ring, then break it with a cold chisel. A hydraulic press is needed to press the bearing off and remove the seal. Press on the new seal and bearing, then the new retainer ring. Do not press the bearing and ring on together. Put the cup on the bearing, not in the housing, and lubricate the outer diameter of the cup and seal.

7. With ball bearings: Place a new gasket between the housing flange and backing plate. Carefully slide the axle shaft into place. Turn the shaft to start the splines into the side gear and push it in.

8. With tapered roller bearings: Move the seal out toward the axle shaft flange so there is at least 3/32 between the edge of the outer seal and the bearing cup, to prevent snagging on installation. Carefully slide the axle shaft into place. Turn the shaft to start the splines into the side gear and push it in.

9. Install the bearing retainer plate.

10. Replace the brake drum and the wheel and tire.

E-250, E-300, AND E-350

These procedures are thoroughly covered under Rear Wheel Bearing.

Bronco

NOTE: The following procedure requires the use of special tools, including a shop press.

1. Jack up the vehicle and support it on jackstands.

2. Remove the wheel.

3. Working through the hole in the flange, remove the nuts that secure the wheel bearing retainer.

4. Pull the axle assembly out of the axle housing.

5. Whenever an axle shaft is removed the oil seal should be replaced. Install one nut to hold the brake backing plate in place and remove the oil seal with a slide hammer and adapter.

6. If the wheel bearing is to be re-

placed, the inner retaining ring must be loosened. Never use heat to do this.

7. Nick the retaining ring deeply with a cold chisel in several places. It will then slide off the axle.

8. The use of a shop press is necessary for the removal of the bearing.

To install:

9. Lightly coat the wheel bearing bores with axle lubricant.

10. Press the bearing and then the inner retaining ring onto the shaft until the retainer seats against the bearing.

11. Install the oil seal with a seal installing tool.

12. Place a new gasket between the housing flange and the backing plate, then carefully slide the axle shaft into the housing so that the rough forging of the shaft will not damage the oil seal.

13. Start the axle splines into the side gear and push the shaft in until it bottoms in the housing.

14. Install the bearing retainer plate and nuts.

15. Install the brake drum and wheel.

FRONT SUSPENSION

Springs

REMOVAL AND INSTALLATION

2WD

1. Raise the front of the vehicle and place jackstands under the frame and a jack under the axle.

2. Disconnect the shock absorber from the lower bracket.

3. Remove one bolt and nut and remove the rebound bracket.

4. Remove the two spring upper retainer attaching bolts from the top of the spring upper seat and remove the retainer.

5. Remove the nut attaching the spring lower retainer to the lower seat and axle and remove the retainer.

6. Lower the axle and remove the spring.

7. Place the spring in position and raise the front axle.

8. Position the spring lower retainer over the stud and lower seat, and install the two attaching bolts.

9. Position the upper retainer over the spring coil and against the spring upper seat, and install the two attaching bolts.

10. Tighten the upper and lower retainer attaching nuts and bolts to 15–25 ft. lbs.

11. Connect the shock absorber to the lower bracket and install the rebound

bracket.

12. Remove the jack and safety stands.

4WD—1975–77 Bronco; F-100, F-150 Through 1979

1. Raise the vehicle until the tires are a few inches off the ground and place jack-stands under the frame side rails. Position a hydraulic floor jack under the center of the front axle housing.

2. Remove the shock absorber-to-lower bracket attaching bolt and nut.

3. Remove the spring lower retainer attaching bolts from the inside of the spring coil.

4. Lower the axle enough to relieve tension from the spring.

5. Remove the spring upper retainer attaching bolts and nuts and remove the upper retainer.

6. Remove the spring, lower retainer and the lower seat from the front spring.

7. Position the upper retainer over the spring coil and loosely install the attaching bolts and nuts.

8. Position the spring lower seat, and the lower retainer to the frame spring pocket and the radius arm.

9. Raise the axle up into position and install the two lower retainer attaching bolts and tighten them.

10. Tighten the upper retainer attaching bolts.

11. Position the shock absorber to the lower bracket and install the attaching bolt and nut.

12. Remove the jack stands and lower the vehicle.

1978–79 Bronco

1. Raise the vehicle and remove the shock absorber-to-lower bracket attaching bolt and nut.

2. Remove two spring lower retainer attaching bolts from inside of the spring coil.

3. Remove two spring upper retainer attaching bolts and nuts and remove the upper retainer.

4. Position safety stands under the frame side rails and lower the axle enough to relieve tension from the spring. Remove the spring, lower retainer, and lower the spring from the vehicle.

5. Position the spring, spring lower seat, and lower retainer to the frame spring pocket and the radius arm. Position the spring seat and the lower retainer.

6. Position the upper retainer over the spring coil and loosely install the two attaching bolts and nuts.

7. Install the two lower retainer attaching bolts and tighten to 80–120 ft. lbs.

8. Tighten the upper retainer attaching bolts to 20–30 ft. lbs.

9. Position the shock absorber to the lower bracket and install the attaching bolt and nut. Tighten the bolt and nut to 40–60 ft. lbs. Remove safety stands and lower the vehicle.

4WD—F-250–F-350 Through 1979

1. Raise the vehicle until the weight is off the front spring with the wheels still touching the floor.

2. Disconnect the lower end of the shock absorber from the axle. Remove the U-bolts and spacer.

3. Remove the nut from the shackle bolt retaining spring at the front and drive the shackle bolt out with a drift.

4. Remove the nuts and shackle bar at the rear shackle bracket. Drive out the two shackle bolts and remove the spring.

5. Position the spring on the spring seat cap and install the shackle bolts through the shackle bracket and spring.

6. Install the shackle bar and nuts on the shackle bolts and tighten them to 90–130 ft. lbs.

7. Position the front of the spring to allow the front shackle bolts to be installed. Tighten the nut to 90–130 ft. lbs.

8. Position the U-bolt spacer and place the U-bolts in position through the holes in the spring seat cap. Install the U-bolt nuts, but do not tighten them yet.

9. Connect the lower end of the shock absorber to the axle.

10. Lower the vehicle and tighten the U-bolt nuts to 100–135 ft. lbs.

4WD—Bronco, F-150-1980–82

1. Raise and vehicle and remove the shock absorber lower attaching bolt and nut.

2. Remove the spring lower retainer nuts from inside of the spring coil.

3. Remove the upper spring retainer by removing the attaching screw.

4. Position safety stands under the frame side rails and lower the axle enough to relieve tension from the spring.

NOTE: The axle must be supported on the jack throughout spring removal, and must not be permitted to hang from the brake hose. If the length of the brake hose does not provide sufficient clearance it may be necessary to remove and support the brake caliper.

5. Remove the spring lower retainer and lower the spring from the vehicle.

6. To install place the spring in position and slowly raise the front axle. Make sure the springs are positioned correctly in the upper spring seats.

7. Install the lower spring retainer and torque the nut to 50 ft. lbs.

8. Position the upper retainer over the spring coil and install the attaching screws.

9. Position the shock absorber to the lower bracket and torque the attaching bolt and nut to 53 ft. lbs.

10. Remove the safety stands and lower the vehicle.

4WD—F-250, F-350—1980–82

1. Raise the vehicle frame until the weight is off the front spring with the

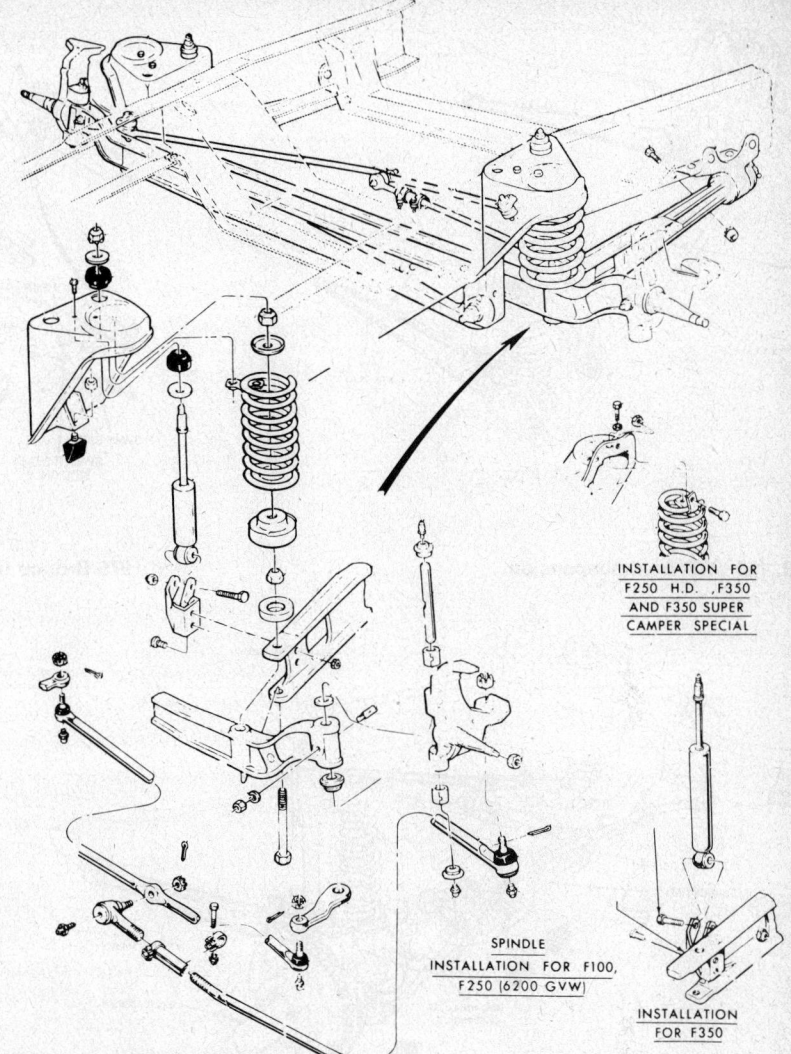

2WD twin I-beam front suspension

wheels still touching the floor. Support the axle to prevent rotation.

2. Disconnect the lower end of the shock absorber from the U-bolt spacer. Remove the U-bolts, U-bolt cap and spacer.

3. Remove the nut from the hanger bolt retaining the spring at the rear and drive out the hanger bolt.

4. Remove the nut connecting the front shackle and spring eye and drive out the shackle bolt and remove the spring.

5. To install position the spring on the spring seat. Install the shackle bolt through the shackle and spring. Torque the nuts to 135 ft. lbs.

6. Position the rear of the spring and install the hanger bolt. Torque the nut to 175 ft. lbs.

7. Position the U-bolt spacer and place the U-bolts in position through the holes in the spring seat cap. Install but do not tighten the U-bolt nuts.

8. Connect the lower end of the shock absorber to the U-bolt spacer.

9. Lower the vehicle and tighten the U-bolt nuts to 100 ft. lbs.

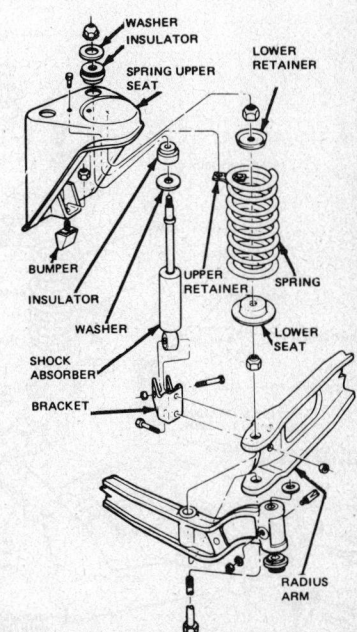

Exploded view of the front spring assembly and shock absorber on 2WD pick-ups

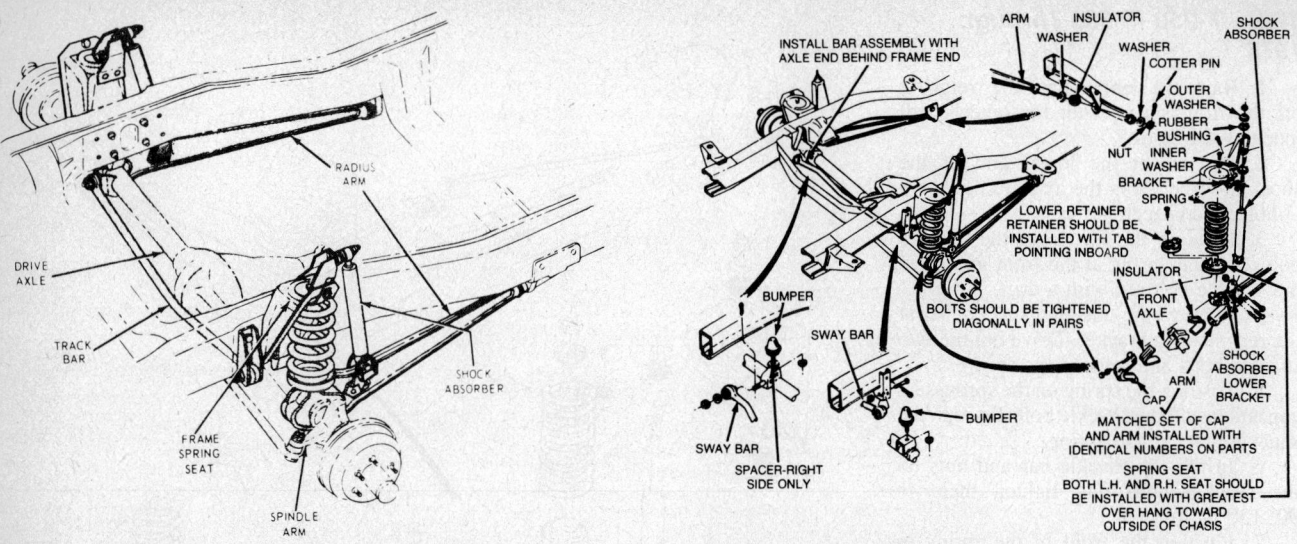

F-100, 150 4WD front suspension

1975 Bronco front suspension

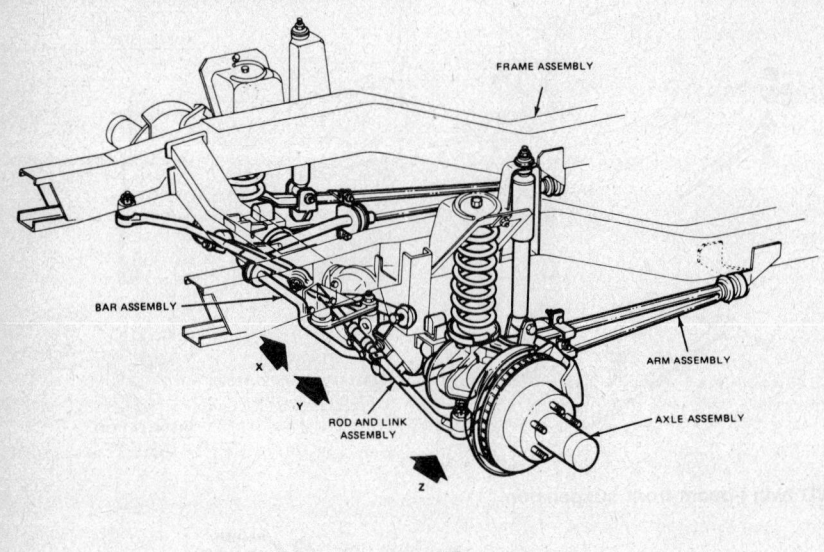

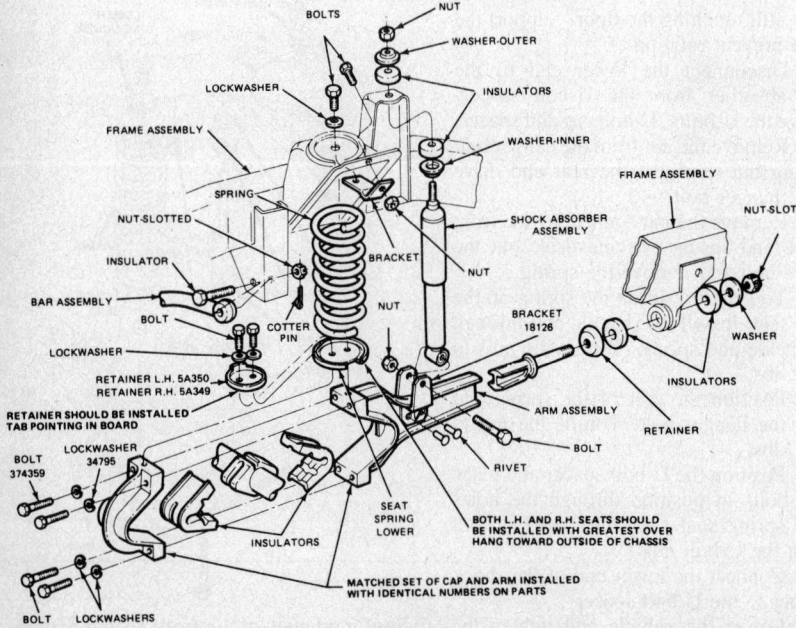

1976–77 Bronco front suspension

Shock Absorbers

REMOVAL AND INSTALLATION

2WD

1. Insert a wrench from the rear side of the upper spring seat to hold the upper shock retaining nut. Loosen the stud by using another wrench on the hex on the shaft.

2. Remove the bolt and nut at the lower end.

3. On installation, make sure to get the washers and insulators in the right place. Tighten the upper nut by turning the hex on the shaft. Replace the lower bolt. It is recommended that new rubber insulators be used.

4WD

1. Raise the vehicle to provide additional access and remove the bolt and nut attaching the shock absorber to the lower bracket on the radius arm.

2. Remove the nut, washer and insulator from the shock absorber at the frame bracket and remove the shock absorber.

To install the front shock absorber:

3. Position the washer and insulator on the shock absorber rod and position the shock absorber to the frame bracket.

4. Position the insulator and washer on the shock absorber rod and install the attaching nut loosely.

5. Position the shock absorber to the lower bracket and install the attaching bolt and nut loosely.

6. Tighten the lower attaching bolts to 40–60 ft. lbs., and the upper attaching bolts to 15–25 ft. lbs.

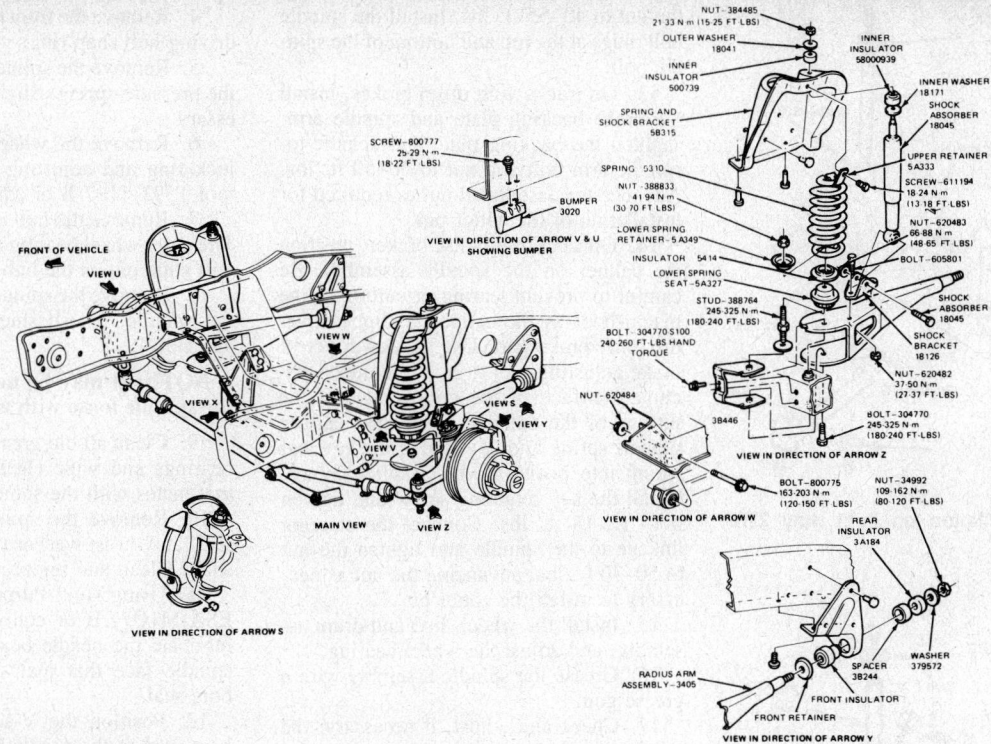

1980 F-150 4WD front suspension

Front Wheel Spindle and King Pin 2WD

REMOVAL AND INSTALLATION

1. Raise the front of the truck until the front wheel clears the ground and place jackstands under the frame.

2. Remove the wheel and tire, and remove the hub, brake drum, and wheel bearings as an assembly. Back off the brake adjustment, if necessary.

3. On a truck with drum brakes, remove the brake backing plate and spindle-to-spindle arm attaching bolt. Remove the spindle arm and the brake backing plate from the spindle. Support the brake backing plate so as not to damage the hose.

4. On a truck with disc brakes, remove the caliper key retaining screw. Drive out the caliper support key and spring with brass drift and hammer. Remove the caliper from the spindle by pushing the caliper downward against the spindle assembly and rotating the upper end of the caliper upward and out of the spindle assembly. It is not necessary to disconnect the brake fluid hose. Wire the caliper to a suspension part to remove the weight of the caliper from the hose. Disconnect the steering linkage from the spindle arm.

5. Disconnect the steering linkage from the integral spindle and spindle arm.

6. Remove the nut and lockwasher from the locking pin, and remove the locking pin.

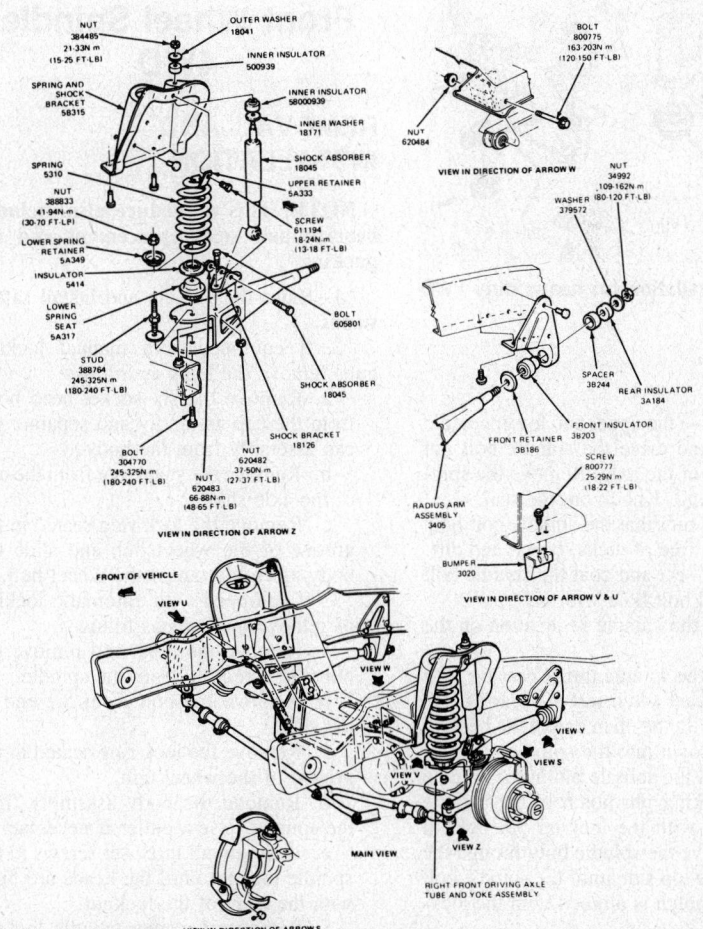

1981–82 4WD pick-up and Bronco front suspension

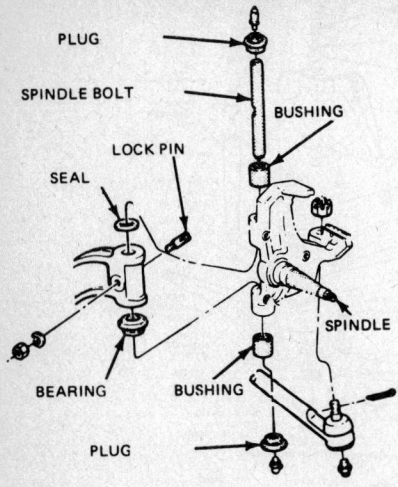

Spindle installation on light duty 2WD pick-ups

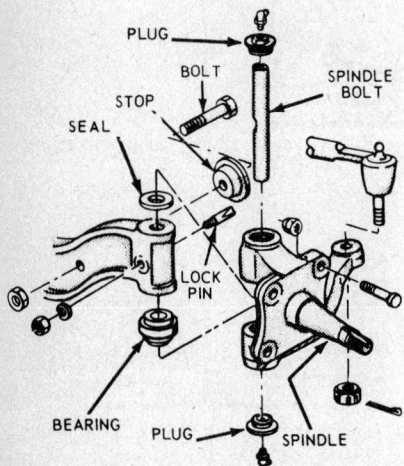

Spindle installation on heavy duty 2WD pick-ups

7. Remove the upper and lower spindle bolt plugs, and drive the spindle bolt out from the top of the axle. Remove the spindle and bearing. Knock out the seal.

8. Make sure that the spindle bolt hole in the axle is free of nicks, burrs, and dirt. Install a new seal and coat the spindle bolt bushings and bolt hole with oil.

9. Place the spindle in position on the axle.

10. Pack the spindle thrust bearing with chassis lubricant and insert the bearing into the spindle with the open end of the bearing seal facing down into the spindle.

11. Install the spindle pin in the spindle with the locking pin notch in the spindle bolt aligned with the locking pin hole in the axle. Drive the spindle bolt through the axle from the top side until the spindle bolt locking pin notch is aligned with the locking pin hole.

12. Install a new locking pin. Install the locking pin lockwasher and nut. Tighten

the nut to 40–55 ft. lbs. Install the spindle bolt plugs at the top and bottom of the spindle bolt.

13. On trucks with drum brakes, install the brake backing plate and spindle arm. Tighten the backing plate and spindle-to-spindle arm bolt and nut to 30–50 ft. lbs. Advance the castellated nut as required for installation of the cotter pin.

14. On trucks with disc brakes, position the caliper on the spindle assembly. Be careful to prevent tearing or cutting of the piston boot as the caliper is slipped over the inner brake pad. Use a screwdriver or brake adjusting tool to hold the upper machined surface of the caliper against the surface of the spindle. Install the caliper support spring and key. Drive the key and spring into position with a soft hammer. Install the key retaining screw and tighten it to 12–18 ft. lbs. Connect the steering linkage to the spindle and tighten the nut to 50–70 ft. lbs. advancing the nut as necessary to install the cotter pin.

15. Install the wheel, hub and drum assembly, and adjust the wheel bearing.

16. Grease the spindle assembly with a grease gun.

17. Check and adjust, if necessary, the toe-in adjustment.

Front Wheel Spindle 4WD

REMOVAL AND INSTALLATION

NOTE: This procedure also includes bearing and seal replacement and repacking.

1. Raise the vehicle and install safety stands.

2. If equipped with manual locking hubs remove the hubs as follows:

   a. Remove the six socket head bolts from the cap assembly and separate the cap assembly from the body.

   b. Remove the snap-ring from the end of the axle shaft.

   c. Remove the lock ring seated in the groove of the wheel hub and slide the body assembly out of the wheel hub.

3. If equipped with automatic locking hubs remove the hubs as follows:

   a. Remove the bolts and remove the hub cap assembly from the spindle.

   b. Remove the bolt from the end of the shaft.

   c. Remove the lock ring seated in the groove of the wheel hub.

   d. Remove the body assembly from the spindle. Use a puller if necessary.

   e. Unscrew all three set screws in the spindle locknut until the heads are flush with the edge of the locknut.

   f. Remove the outer spindle locknut with tool T80T-4000-V, automatic hub locknut wrench.

4. Remove the front hub grease cap and driving hub snap-ring.

5. Remove the splined driving hub and the pressure spring. Slightly pry off if necessary.

6. Remove the wheel bearing locknut, lock ring and adjusting nut using special tool T59T-1197-B or equivalent.

7. Remove the hub and disc assembly. The outer wheel bearing and spring retainer will slide out as the hub is removed.

8. Remove the spindle nuts and remove the spindle, splash shield and axle shaft assembly.

NOTE: It may be necessary to break the spindle loose with a plastic hammer.

9. Clean all old grease from the needle bearings and wipe clean the spindle face that mates with the spindle bore seal.

10. Remove the spindle bore seal, V-seal, and thrust washer from the outer axle shaft. Clean and replace if necessary.

11. Using Multi-Purpose Lubricant Ford ESA-M1C75-B or equivalent, thoroughly lubricate the needle bearing and pack the spindle face that mates with the spindle bore seal.

12. Position the V-seal in the spindle bore next to the needle bearing. Assemble the spindle bore seal on the axle shaft.

13. Assemble the spindle with the axle shaft on the knuckle studs and tighten the retaining nuts to 75 ft. lbs.

14. Carefully drive the inner bearing cone and grease seal out of the hub using tool T77F-1102-A or equivalent.

15. Inspect the inner bearing cups and if necessary remove with a drift.

NOTE: If new cups are installed, install new bearings.

16. Lubricate the bearings with the lubricant specified earlier and clean all old grease from the hub. Pack the cones and rollers with lubricant. Try to pack as much as possible between the rollers and the cages.

17. Position the inner bearing cone and roller in the inner cup and install the grease retainer.

18. Install the hub and disc assembly on the spindle.

19. Install the outer bearing cone and roller, and the adjusting nut.

20. Using tool T59T-1197-B or equivalent and a torque wrench tighten the bearing adjusting nut to 50 ft. lbs. while rotating the wheel back and forth. Back off the adjusting nut no more than 90 degrees.

21. Assemble the lock ring by turning the nut to the nearest hole and inserting the dowel pin.

NOTE: The dowel pin must seat in the lock ring hole for proper bearing adjustment and wheel retention.

22. Install the outer lock nut and tighten to 65 ft. lbs. Final end play on the wheel and spindle should be 0.001–0.006 inch.

23. Adjust the brake if necessary and lower the vehicle.

Knuckle and Ball Joint—4-WD

REPLACEMENT

NOTE: A combination ball joint puller/press and a special spanner wrench are needed for this job. If these aren't available the job should not be attempted.

1. Follow the procedures under Axle Shaft Removal.
2. Disconnect the connecting rod end from the knuckle.
3. Remove the cotter pin from the upper ball socket and loosen the upper and lower ball socket nuts. Discard the nut from the lower ball socket after the knuckle breaks loose from the yoke.
4. Remove the knuckle from the yoke. If the upper socket remains in the yoke, remove it by hitting the top of the stud with a soft-faced hammer. Discard the socket and adjusting sleeve.
5. Remove the bottom socket with a ball joint puller (available at most auto parts stores) after first removing the snap ring.

For installation:

6. Place the knuckle in a vise and assemble the bottom socket. Place the new socket into the knuckle making sure it isn't cocked, place the driver over the socket, place the forcing screw into the socket and force the socket into the knuckle.
7. Make sure that the socket shoulder is seated against the knuckle. Use a .0015 in. feeler gauge between the socket seat and the knuckle.
8. The gauge should not enter the area of minimum contact. Install the snap ring.
9. Assemble the top socket into the knuckle. Assemble the holding plate onto the backing plate screw. Tighten the nuts snugly. Place a new socket into the knuckle. Be sure it is not cocked. Place a driver over the socket and force the socket assembly into the knuckle. Using a .0015 in. gauge, check the fit at the shoulder. The gauge should not enter the area of minimum wrench.
10. Install a new adjusting sleeve into the top of the yoke leaving about two threads exposed.
11. Assemble the knuckle and yoke. Install a new nut on the bottom socket and make it finger tight.
12. Place a wrench and step plate over the adjusting sleeve and install the puller so that it grasps the step plate. Tighten the forcing screw to pull the knuckle assembly into the yoke. With torque still applied, tighten the nut to 70–90 ft. lbs. If the bottom stud should turn with the nut, add more torque to the puller forcing screw. Remove the puller, step plate and holding plate.
13. Tighten the adjusting sleeve to 40 ft. lbs. and remove the wrench.
14. Install the top socket nut and torque it to 100 ft. lbs. Line up the cotter pin hole

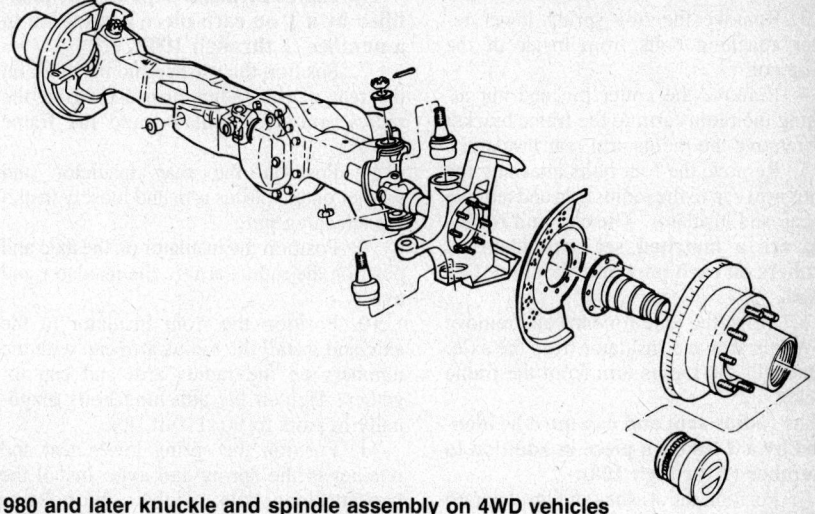

1980 and later knuckle and spindle assembly on 4WD vehicles

by tightening, *not loosening*, the nut. Install the cotter pin and test the steering effort with a spring scale attached to the knuckle. Pull should not exceed 26 ft. lbs. If it does, the ball joints will have to be replaced.

15. Connect the steering linkage to the knuckle. Torque it to 40 ft. lbs.
16. Install the axle shaft as described in the Axle Shaft Removal and Installation procedure.

Radius Arm

REMOVAL AND INSTALLATION

All Except Bronco and 1980–82 F-150 with 4WD

1. Raise the front of the vehicle and place safety stands under the frame and a jack under the wheel or axle.
2. Disconnect the shock absorber from the radius arm bracket.
3. Remove the two spring upper retainer attaching bolts from the top of the spring upper seat and remove the retainer.
4. Remove the nut which attaches the spring lower retainer to the lower seat and axle and remove the retainer.
5. Lower the axle and remove the spring.
6. Disconnect the steering rod from the spindle arm.
7. Remove the spring lower seat and shim from the radius arm. Then, remove the bolt and nut which attach the radius arm to the axle.
8. Remove the cotter pin, nut and washer from the radius arm rear attachment.
9. Remove the bushing from the radius arm and remove the radius arm from the vehicle.
10. Remove the inner bushing from the radius arm.
11. Position the radius arm to the axle and install the bolt and nut finger-tight.

12. Install the inner bushing on the radius arm and position the arm to the frame bracket.
13. Install the bushing, washer, and attaching nut. Tighten the nut and install the cotter pin.
14. Connect the steering rod to the spindle arm and install the attaching nut. Tighten the radius arm-to-axle attaching bolt and nut.

F-150 4WD—1980–82

1. Raise the vehicle and position safety stands under the frame side rails.
2. Remove the shock absorber lower attaching bolt and nut and pull the shock abosrber free of the radius arm.
3. Remove the lower spring retaining bolt from the inside of the spring coil.
4. Remove the nut attaching the radius arm to the frame bracket and remove the radius arm rear insulator. Lower the axle and allow the axle to move forward.

NOTE: The axle must be supported on the jack throughout spring removal, and must not be permitted to hang from the brake hose. If the length of the brake hose does not provide sufficient clearance it may be necessary to remove and support the brake caliper.

5. Remove the bolt and stud attaching the radius arm to the axle.
6. Move the axle forward and remove the radius arm from the axle. Then, pull the radius arm from the frame bracket.
7. Installation is the reverse of removal. Install new bolts and the stud type bolt which attach the radius arm to the axle and tighten to 210 ft. lbs. Tighten the radius arm rear attaching nut to 100 ft. lbs.

1975–77 Bronco

1. Raise the vehicle and position safety stands under the frame side rails.
2. Remove the shock absorber-to-lower bracket attaching bolt and nut and pull the shock absorber free of the radius

arm.

3. Remove the two spring lower retainer attaching bolts from inside of the spring coil.

4. Remove the cotter pin and nut attaching the radius arm to the frame bracket and remove the radius arm rear insulator.

5. Remove the four bolts attaching the radius arm cap to the radius arm and remove the cap and insulator. **The cap and radius arm are a matched set with identical numbers on each part and should not be mixed.**

6. Move the axle forward and remove the radius arm and insulator from the axle. Then, pull the radius arm from the frame bracket.

The radius arm and cap must be identified by a T on each piece in addition to a number (1 through 100).

7. Position the washer and insulator on the rear of the radius arm and insert the radius arm and insulator into the frame bracket.

8. Position the rear insulator and washer on the radius arm and loosely install the attaching nut.

9. Position the insulator on the axle and position the radius arm to the insulator and axle.

10. Position the front insulator to the axle and install the radius arm cap with the numbers on the radius arm and cap together. Torque the attaching bolts diagonally in pairs to 90–10 ft. lbs.

11. Position the spring lower seat and retainer to the spring and axle. Install the two attaching bolts. Torque the bolts to 45–55 ft. lbs.

12. Torque the radius rod rear attaching nut to 80–120 ft. lbs. Advance the nut as required and install the cotter pin.

13. Position the shock absorber to the lower bracket and install the attaching bolt and nut. Torque the nut to 40–60 ft. lbs. Remove safety stands and lower the vehicle.

1978–79 Bronco

1. Raise the vehicle and position safety stands under the frame side rails.

2. Remove the shock absorber-to-lower bracket attaching bolt and nut and pull the shock absorber free of the radius arm.

3. Remove two spring lower retainer attaching bolts from inside of the spring coil.

4. Remove the nut attaching the radius arm to the frame bracket and remove the radius arm rear insulator.

5. Remove four bolts attaching the radius arm cap to the radius arm and remove the cap and insulator. **The cap and radius arm are a matched set with identical numbers on each part and should not be mixed.**

6. Move the axle forward and remove the radius arm and insulator from the axle. Then, pull the radius arm from the frame bracket.

The radius arm and cap must be identified by a T on each piece in addition to a number (1 through 100).

7. Position the washer and insulator on the rear of the radius arm and insert the radius arm and insulator into the frame bracket.

8. Position the rear insulator and washer on the radius arm and loosely install the attaching nut.

9. Position the insulator on the axle and position the radius arm to the insulator and axle.

10. Position the front insulator to the axle and install the radius arm cap with the numbers on the radius arm and cap together. Tighten the attaching bolts diagonally in pairs to 90–110 ft. lbs.

11. Position the spring lower seat and retainer to the spring and axle. Install the two attaching bolts. Tighten the bolts to 45–55 ft. lbs.

12. Tighten the radius rod rear attaching nut to 80–120 ft. lbs.

13. Position the shock absorber to the lower bracket and install the attaching bolt and nut. Tighten the nut to 40–60 ft. lbs. Remove safety stands and lower the vehicle.

1980–82 Bronco

1. Raise the vehicle and position safety stands under the frame side rails.

2. Remove the shock absorber-to-lower bracket attaching bolt and nut and pull the shock absorber free of the radius arm.

3. Remove spring lower retainer attaching bolt from inside of the spring coil.

4. Remove the nut attaching the radius arm to the frame bracket and remove the radius arm rear insulator. Lower the axle and allow axle to move forward.

NOTE: The axle must be supported on the jack throughout spring removal and installation, and must not be permitted to hang by the brake hose. If the length of the brake hose is not sufficient to provide adequate clearance for removal and installation of the spring, the disc brake caliper must be removed from the spindle. After removal, the caliper must be placed on the frame or otherwise supported to prevent suspending the caliper from the caliper hose. These precautions are absolutely necessary to prevent serious damage to the tube portion of the caliper hose assembly.

5. Remove the bolt and stud attaching radius arm to axle.

6. Move the axle forward and remove the radius arm from the axle. Then, pull the radius arm from the frame bracket.

7. Position the washer and insulator on the rear of the radius arm and insert the radius arm into the frame bracket.

8. Position the rear insulator and washer on the radius arm and loosely install the attaching nut.

9. Position the radius arm to the axle.

10. Install new bolts and study-type bolt attaching radius arm to axle. Tighten to 180–240 ft. lbs.

11. Position the spring lower seat, spring insulator and retainer to the spring and axle. Install the two attaching bolts. Tighten the nuts to 30–70 ft. lbs.

12. Tighten the radius rod rear attaching nut to 80–120 ft. lbs.

13. Position the shock absorber to the lower bracket and install the attaching bolt and nut. Tighten the nut to 40–60 ft. lbs. Remove safety stands and lower the vehicle.

Stabilizer Bar

REMOVAL AND INSTALLATION

Bronco and 4-WD Pickups

1978–79

1. Remove locknut, washers, and insulator to remove link assemblies from stabilizer bar. Remove nuts, bolts, and washers connecting link assemblies to frame.

2. Remove nuts on U-bolts to remove stabilizer bar from retainers. Remove stabilizer bar. Remove U-bolts, brackets and retainers.

3. Place bracket assemblies on axle aligning holes in brackets with alignment pins on axles.

4. Install U-bolts through bracket assembly. Position stabilizer bar on brackets. Install retainer and tighten nuts to 35–55 ft. lbs.

5. Install link assemblies on frame. Connect link assemblies to stabilizer bar. Tighten link to stabilizer bar nuts to 18–25 ft. lbs. Tighten link to frame nuts to 40–60 ft. lbs.

1980–82

1. Remove nuts, bolts and washers connecting the stabilizer bar to connecting links. Remove nuts and bolts of the stabilizer bar retainer.

2. Remove stabilizer bar insulator assembly.

3. To remove the stabilizer bar mounting bracket, the coil spring must be removed as described above under spring removal. Remove the lower spring seat. The bracket attaching stud and bracket can now be removed.

4. To install the stabilizer bar mounting brackets, locate the brackets so that the locating tang is positioned in the radius arm notch (or quad shock bracket notch if vehicle has quad shocks). Install a new stud. Torque to 180–220 ft. lbs.

NOTE: A new stud is required because of the adhesive on the threads.

Reposition the spring lower seat and reinstall the spring and retainers.

5. To reinstall the stabilizer bar insulator assembly, assemble all nuts, bolts and

washers to the bar, brackets, retainers and links loosely. With the bar positioned correctly, torque retainer nuts to 32–35 ft. lbs. with retainer around the insulator. Then torque all remaining nuts at the link assemblies to 41–50 ft. lbs.

REAR SUSPENSION

Springs

REMOVAL AND INSTALLATION

2WD Pick-Ups

1. Raise the vehicle by the frame until the weight is off the rear spring with the tires still on the floor.

2. Remove the nuts from the spring U-bolts and drive the U-bolts from the U-bolt plate. Remove the auxiliary spring and spacer, if so equipped.

3. Remove the spring-to-bracket nut and bolt at the front of the spring.

4. Remove the upper and lower shackle nuts and bolts at the rear of the spring and remove the spring and shackle assembly from the rear shackle bracket.

5. Remove the bushings in the spring or shackle, if they are worn or damaged, and install new ones.

6. Position the spring in the shackle and install the upper shackle-to-spring nut and bolt with the bolt head facing outward.

7. Position the front end of the spring in the bracket and install the nut and bolt.

8. Position the shackle in the rear bracket and install the nut and bolt.

9. Position the spring on top of the axle with the spring center bolt centered in the hole provided in the seat. Install the auxiliary spring and spacer, if so equipped.

10. Install the spring U-bolts, plate, and nuts.

11. Lower the vehicle and tighten the attaching hardware as follows: U-bolt nuts, ½ in.—45–70 ft. lbs.; ⁹⁄₁₆ in.—85–115 ft. lbs.; front spring hanger, ⁹⁄₁₆ in.—75–105 ft. lbs.; ⁵⁄₈ in.—150–190 ft. lbs.; rear spring hanger—75–105 ft. lbs.

4WD Pick-ups

1. Raise the truck by the frame until the weight is off the rear springs and the wheels are still touching the ground.

2. Remove the nuts from the spring U-bolts and drive the U-bolts out of the spring seat cap. Remove the spring cap. Remove the auxiliary spring and spacer, if so equipped.

3. Remove the shackle pin lockbolts from each end of the spring. Insert a drift in the hole provided in the frame from the inner side and drive the shackle pin out of

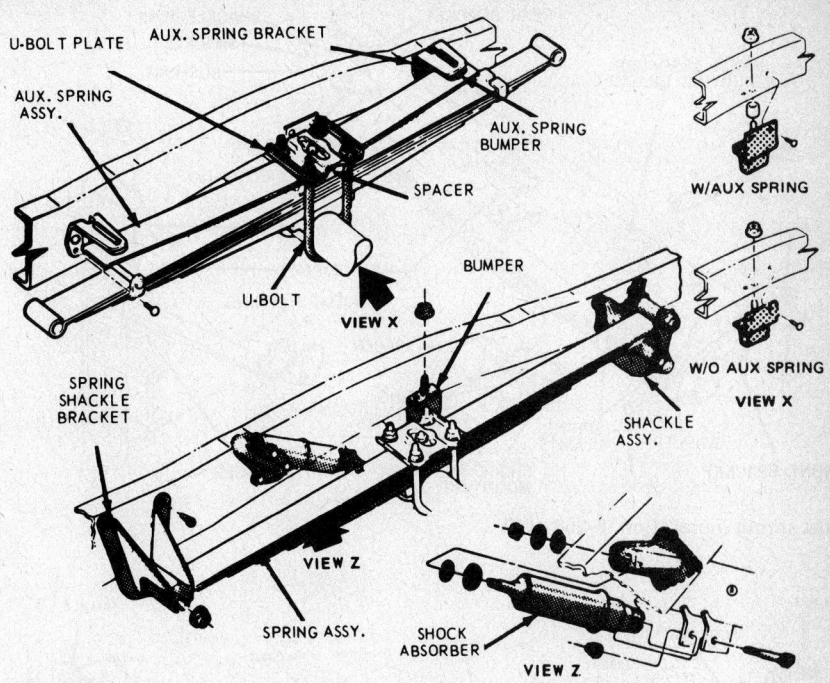

Rear spring installation, F-100, 150 2WD and 4WD, and F-250 2WD

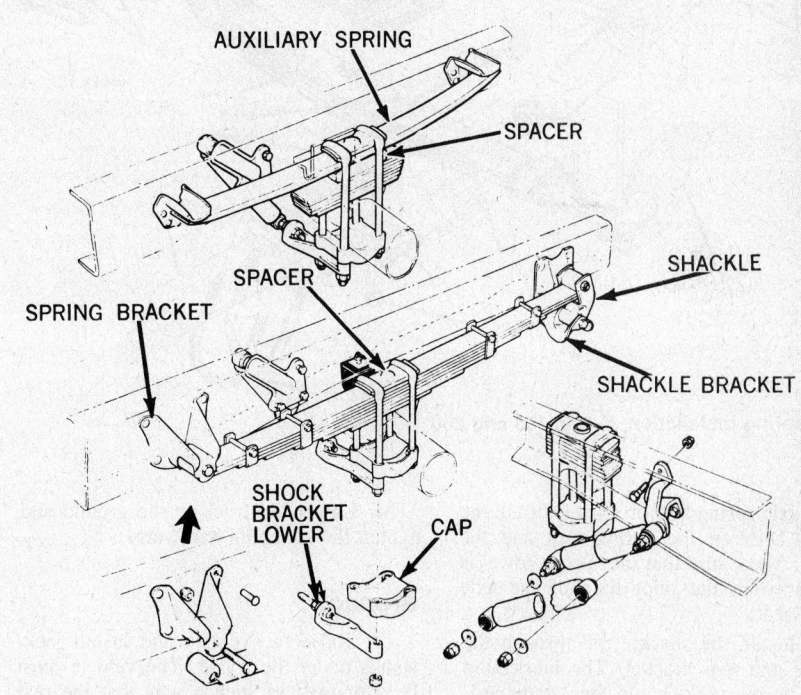

Rear spring installation, F-350

each spring bracket.

4. Remove the spring and shackle from the truck. Remove the spring-to-axle spacer.

5. Drive the remaining shackle pin out of the rear spring eye and remove the shackle from the spring.

6. After checking and replacing worn or damaged bushings, nuts and bolts, and broken or weak springs, position the

shackle to the rear spring eye.

7. Install the shackle pin through the shackle and spring eye with the lubrication fitting on the shackle pin facing outboard.

8. Align the shackle pin lockbolt groove with the lockbolt hole in the shackle, and install the lockbolt, washer, and nut.

9. Position the spring on the axle with the spring center bolt in the hole provided

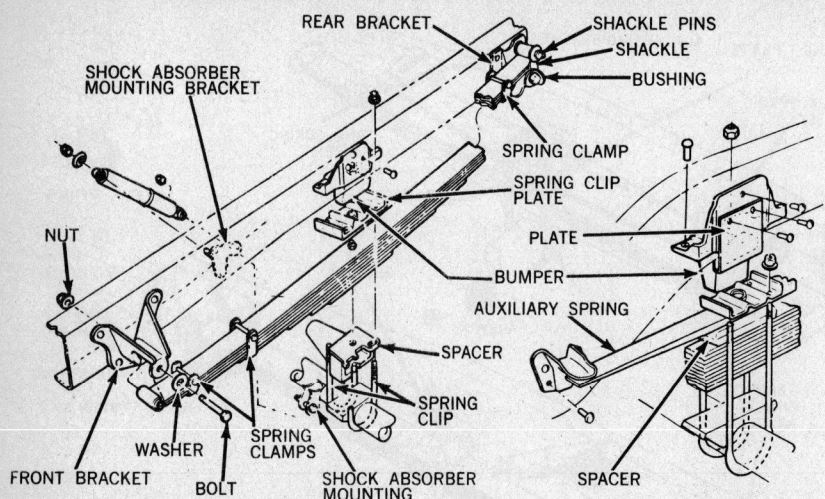

Rear spring installation, F-250 4WD

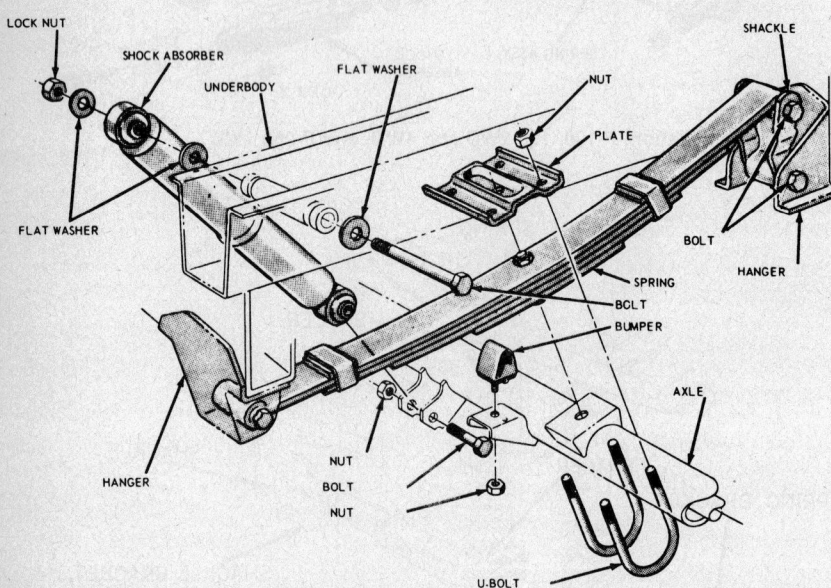

Rear spring installation, E-100, 150 and 200

6. Remove the nut from the shackle-to-hanger attaching bolt and drive the bolt from the shackle and hanger with a drift and remove the spring from the vehicle.

7. Remove the nut from the spring rear attaching bolt. Drive the bolt out of the spring and shackle with a drift.

To install the rear spring:

8. Position the shackle (closed section facing toward the front of the vehicle) to the spring rear eye and install the bolt and nut.

9. Position the spring front eye and bushing to the spring front hanger, and install the attaching bolt and nut.

10. Position the spring rear eye and bushing to the shackle, and install the attaching bolt and nut.

11. Raise the axle to the spring and install the U-bolts and spring clip plate.

12. Torque the U-bolt nuts and spring front and rear attaching bolt nuts to 45–60 ft. lbs.

13. Remove the jackstands and lower the vehicle.

NOTE: Squeaky rear springs can be corrected by tightening the front and rear eye bolts to 150–204 ft. lbs., then raising and supporting the rear of the vehicle so that the rear springs hang, spreading the leaves. Apply a silicone based lubricant for a distance of three inches in from each leaf tip.

E-100, E-150, and E-200

1. Raise the rear of the vehicle and support the chassis with jackstands. Support the rear axle with a floor jack or hoist.

2. Disconnect the lower end of the shock absorber from the bracket on the axle housing.

3. Remove the two U-bolts and plate.

4. Lower the axle and remove the upper and lower rear shackle bolts.

5. Pull the rear shackle assembly and rubber bushings from the bracket and spring.

6. Remove the nut and mounting bolt which secure the front end of the spring. Remove the spring assembly from the front shackle bracket.

7. Install new rubber bushings in the rear shackle bracket and in the rear eye of the replacement spring.

8. Assemble the front eye of the spring to the front shackle bracket with the front mounting bolt and nut. Do not tighten the nut.

9. Mount the rear end of the spring with the upper bolt of the rear shackle assembly passing through the eye of the spring. Insert the lower bolt through the rear spring hanger.

10. Assemble the spring center bolt in the pilot hole in the axle and install the plate. Install the U-bolts through the plate. Do not tighten the attaching nuts at this time.

11. Raise the axle with a floor jack or hoist until the vehicle is free of the jack-

in the axle spring seat or spacer. Install the spacer between the spring seat and the spring. Make sure that the spacer dowel is positioned in the pilot hole of the axle spring seat.

10. Install the shackle pin through the shackle and rear bracket. The lubrication fitting on the shackle pin faces outboard. Align the pin groove with the lock bolt hole in the bracket and install the lockbolt, washer, and nut.

11. Install the shackle pin at the front bracket and spring eye in the same manner as above.

12. Install the auxiliary spring and spacer, if so equipped. Place the spring cap on top of the spring at the center bolt and place the spring U-bolts over the spring assembly and axle.

13. Position the spring seat cap, and install the nuts on the spring U-bolts.

14. Lower the truck to the ground and tighten the attaching hardware.

Bronco

1. Raise the vehicle and install jackstands under the frame. The vehicle must be supported in such a way that the rear axle hangs free with the tire a few inches off the ground. Place a hydraulic floor jack under the center of the axle housing.

2. Disconnect the shock absorber from the axle.

3. Remove the U-bolt attaching nuts and remove the two U-bolts and the spring clip plate.

4. Lower the axle to relieve the spring tension and remove the nut from the spring front attaching bolt.

5. Remove the spring front attaching bolt from the spring and hanger with a drift.

stands. Connect the lower end of the shock absorber to the bracket on the axle housing.

12. Tighten the spring front mounting bolt and nut, the rear shackle nuts and the U-bolt nuts.

13. Remove the jackstands and lower the vehicle.

E-250, E-300, and E-350

1. Raise the rear of the vehicle and support the chassis with jackstands. Support the rear axle with a floor jack or hoist.

2. Disconnect the lower end of the shock absorber from the bracket on the axle housing.

3. Remove the two spring U-bolts and the spring cap.

4. Lower the axle and remove the spring front bolt from the hanger.

5. Remove the two attaching bolts from the rear of the spring. Remove the spring and shackle.

6. Assemble the upper end of the shackle to the spring with the attaching bolt.

7. Connect the front of the spring to the front bracket with the attaching bolt.

8. Assemble the spring and shackle to the rear bracket with the attaching bolt.

9. Place the spring plate over the head of the center bolt.

10. Raise the axle with a jack. Install the center bolt through the pilot hole in the pad on the axle housing.

11. Install the spring U-bolts, cap and attaching nuts. Tighten the nuts snugly.

12. Connect the lower end of the shock absorber to the lower bracket.

13. Tighten the spring front mounting bolt and nut, the rear shackle nuts and the spring U-bolt nuts.

14. Remove the jackstands and lower the vehicle.

Shock Absorbers

REMOVAL AND INSTALLATION

1. Raise the vehicle and place jackstands under the frame.

2. Remove the shock absorber-to-upper bracket attaching nut and washers, and bushing from the shock absorber rod.

3. Remove the shock absorber-to-axle attaching bolt. Drive the bolts from the axle bracket and shock absorber with a brass drift and remove the shock absorber.

4. Position the washers and bushing on the shock absorber rod and position the shock absorber at the upper bracket.

5. Position the bushing and washers on the shock absorber rod and install the attaching nut loosely.

6. Position the shock absorber at the axle housing bracket and install the attaching bolt and nut. Tighten the lower nut to 40–60 ft. lbs. and the upper nut to 15–25 ft. lbs.

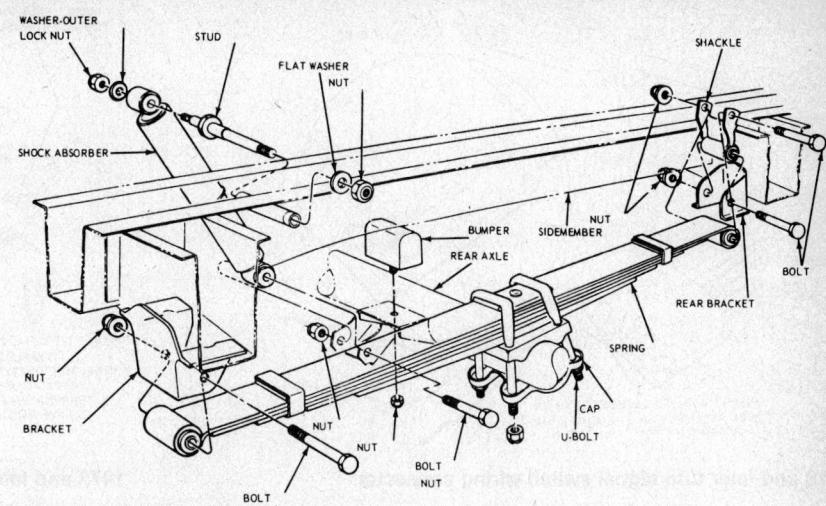

Rear spring installation, E-250, 300 and 350

FRONT END ALIGNMENT

CASTER

1975–77 F-250 (4WD)

The caster angle is controlled by the angle of the front spring pads. The caster angle can be adjusted by installing tapered wedges between the springs and the spring pads. Only one wedge per side should be used.

1975–77 All Models Exc. F-250 (4WD)
1978–82 All Models

The caster angles are designed into the front axle and cannot be adjusted.

CAMBER

The camber angles are designed into the front axle and cannot be adjusted.

TOE-IN ADJUSTMENT

All Models

Toe-in can be measured by either a front end alignment machine or by the following method:

With the front wheels in the straight-ahead position, measure the distance between the extreme front and the extreme rear of the front wheels. In other words, measure the distance across the undercarriage of the vehicle between the two front edges and the two rear edges of the two front wheels. Both of these measurements (front and rear of the two wheels) must be taken at an equal distance from the floor and at the approximate centerline of the spindle. The difference between these two distances is the amount that the wheels toe-in or toe-out. The wheels should always be adjusted to toe-in according to specifications.

1. Loosen the clamp bolts at each end of the left tie-rod, seen from the front of the vehicle. Rotate the connecting rod tube until the correct toe-in is obtained, then tighten the clamp bolts.

2. Recheck the toe-in to make sure that no changes occurred when the bolts were tightened.

NOTE: The clamps should be positioned ³⁄₁₆ in. fron the end of the rod with the clamp bolts in a vertical position in front of the tube, with the nut down.

STEERING

Steering Wheel

REMOVAL AND INSTALLATION

1975–82

1. Disconnect the battery ground and mark the steering wheel-to-column alignment.

2. Remove one screw from the underside of each spoke and lift the horn assembly from the wheel. On vehicles with a sport wheel option, pry the button cover off with a screwdriver.

3. Disconnect the horn switch wires by pulling the spade terminal from the blade connector. Squeeze or pinch the J-clip ground wire terminal fully and pull it out of the hole in the steering wheel. Do not pull the ground terminal out of the threaded hole without squeezing the clip to remove the spring tension.

4. Remove the horn switch assembly.

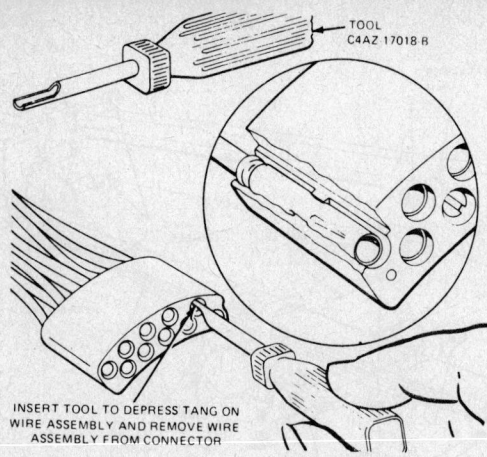

1978 and later turn signal switch wiring connector

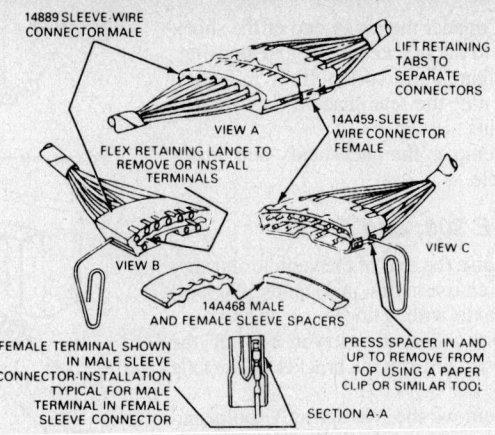

1978 and later turn signal switch terminal removal

5. Remove the steering wheel retaining nut.

6. Using a steering wheel puller, remove the wheel.

To install:

7. Position the steering wheel in alignment with the marks.

8. Tighten the retaining nut to 50 ft. lbs.

9. Connect the wires, install the horn assembly and connect the battery ground.

Turn Signal Switch

REPLACEMENT

1975–77

1. Disconnect the horn and turn signal wires at the connectors located behind the instrument panel. Remove the steering column wires and terminals from the connectors by inserting a small screwdriver or similar tool in the opposite end from which the wire is inserted and depress the tang on the wire. The wire can then be removed from the connector.

NOTE: Be sure to record the color code and location of each wire before removing it from the connector plug. Tape a pull-through wire or cord to one of the wire ends.

2. Remove the steering wheel.

3. Turn the signal switch lever counterclockwise to remove it. Remove the screws and retainer which hold the turn signal switch and wire assembly to the steering column, and pull the assembly from the column. Disconnect the pull-through wire or cord from the end of the wire to which it was taped.

To install the switch:

4. Tape the loose ends of the new turn signal switch wires to the pull-through wire or cord. Carefully pull the wires through the steering column, while guiding the turn

signal switch into position. Install the switch retainer screws.

5. Assemble the rest of the steering column in the reverse order of disassembly.

1978–82

1. Disconnect the battery ground cable.

2. Remove the horn switch.

3. Remove the steering wheel retaining nut and using tool 3600AA or equivalent, remove the steering wheel from the shaft.

4. Remove the turn signal switch lever by unscrewing it from the steering column.

5. Disconnect the turn indicator switch wiring connector plug by lifting up on the tabs and separating and remove the screws that secure the switch assembly to the column.

6. Remove the wires and terminals from the steering column wiring connector plug. Record the color code and location of each wire before removing it from the connector plug.

7. Connect pull through wire to end of wiring harness with tape.

8. Remove the protective wire cover from the wiring harness and remove the switch and wires through the top of the column.

9. Tape the loose ends of the new turn signal switch wires to the pull-through wire or cord. Carefully pull the wires through the steering column while guiding the turn signal switch into position.

10. Install switch assembly retaining screws to column.

11. Install wires into steering column wire connector terminal and connect terminals.

12. Install turn signal lever. Hand-tighten the lever (on flat side) to 10–20 in. lbs. Test turn signal operation, hazard signal operation and PRND21 dial-lamp (if so equipped).

13. Install steering wheel.

14. Install horn switch.

15. Connect battery ground cable.

Power Steering Pump

REMOVAL AND INSTALLATION

1. Position a drain pan under the power steering pump.

2. Disconnect the pressure and return lines at the pump. Disconnect the cooler hoses over the pump.

NOTE: If the power steering pump is being removed from the engine in order to facilitate the removal of some other component, and it is not necessary for the pump to be completely removed from the vehicle, it is not necessary and is not recommended that the pressure and return hoses be disconnected from the pump.

3. Loosen the one pivot bolt and one adjustment bolt. Remove the drive belt.

4. Remove the two water pump bolts from the adjusting bracket attached to the front cover.

5. While holding the pump, use a jam nut and remove the through-bolt from the cylinder head. Remove the pump with both brackets from the vehicle.

To install the power steering pump:

6. If installing a new pump, transfer the pump support brackets to the new unit.

7. Insert the through-bolt from the rear of the pump bracket. Install the pump in the vehicle without the adjusting bracket, inserting the through-bolt into the block.

8. Position the adjusting bracket to the water pump and torque the two retaining bolts to 11–16 ft. lbs.

9. Install the bolt. Install and torque the bolts, retaining the support bracket to the pump and block, to 30–40 ft. lbs. Check the belt tension.

10. Connect the cooler hoses over the pump and tighten the hose clamp to 10–18 in. lbs. Connect the pressure and return lines to the pump.

11. Fill the power steering system with the proper type power steering fluid. Perform the system bleeding operation.

12. Remove the drain pan.

SYSTEM BLEEDING

1. Disconnect the coil wire.

2. Crank the engine and continue adding fluid until the level stabilizes.

3. Continue to crank the engine and rotate the steering wheel about 30° to either side of center.

4. Check the fluid level and add as required.

5. Connect the coil wire and start the engine. Allow it to run for several minutes.

6. Rotate the steering wheel from stop to stop.

7. Shut off the engine and check the fluid level. Add fluid as necessary.

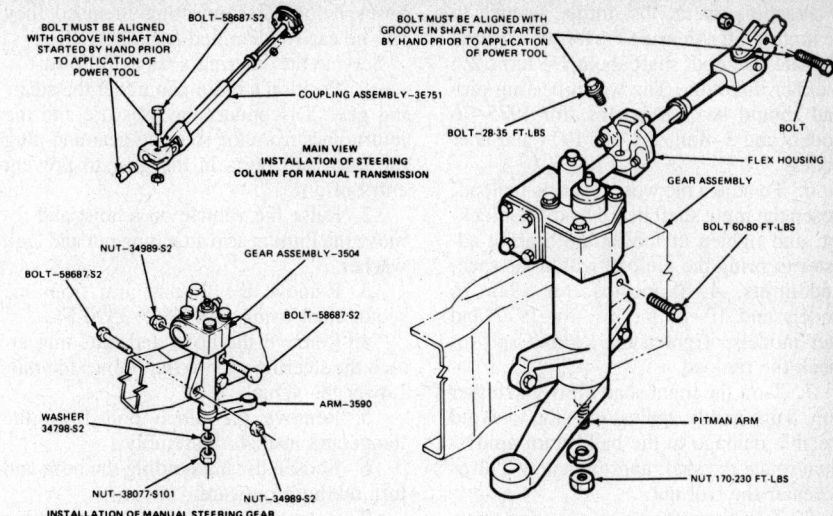

1975–79 steering gear installation

Manual Steering Gear

1975–79

Removal

1. Raise the vehicle on a hoist and remove the Pitman arm attaching nut and lockwasher.

2. Remove the Pitman arm from the sector shaft using tool T64P-3590-F.

3. Remove bolts, nuts and flat washers that attach the steering gear to the frame side rail, and lower the vehicle.

4. Remove the flex coupling bolt and nut from the coupling clamp. Loosen the clamp from the coupling at the end of the steering column and separate the coupling from the steering gear input shaft by pushing the steering shaft toward the steering column. Discard the clamp, bolt, and nut.

5. Remove and discard the flex coupling clamp from the steering gear input shaft, and remove the steering gear from the frame side rail.

Installation

1. Place the steering gear on the frame side rail and install the attaching bolts, nuts, and flat washers.

2. Place the flex coupling and a new clamp on the steering gear input shaft and install the clamp bolt and nut. Tighten the bolt and nut to 28–35 ft. lbs.

3. Install a new steering shaft clamp at the end of the steering column and tighten the bolt and nut to 20–30 ft. lbs.

4. Raise the vehicle and tighten the steering gear attaching bolts and nuts to 60–80 ft. lbs.

5. Place the Pitman arm on the sector shaft and install the washer and attaching nut. Tighten the nut to 170–230 ft. lbs. lower the vehicle, and fill the gear with lubricant SAE-90EP oil.

1980–82

Removal

1. Raise the vehicle on a hoist.

2. Disconnect the flex coupling from the steering shaft flange by removing the two attaching nuts.

3. Disconnect the drag link from the sector shaft (Pitman) arm, using tool 3290-C.

4. Remove the Pitman arm-to-sector shaft attaching nut and washer. Remove the Pitman arm from the gear sector shaft using tool T64P-3590-F. (Do not hammer on end of sector shaft.)

5. While supporting the steering gear, remove the bolts and washers that attach the steering gear assembly to the frame side rail. Lower the steering gear assembly from the vehicle.

6. Remove the coupling to gear attaching bolt from the lower half of the flex coupling and remove the coupling from the steering gear assembly.

Installation

1. Install the flex coupling on the worm (input) shaft of the gear assembly. Install a new coupling-to-gear attaching bolt and tighten to 11–21 ft. lbs.

2. Center the input shaft (the center position is approximately three turns from either stop).

3. Position the steering gear assembly so that the stud bolts on the flex coupling enter the bolt holes in the steering shaft flange, and the holes in the mounting bosses of the gear match the bolt holes in the frame side rail.

4. While supporting the gear in proper position, install the gear-to-frame side rail attaching bolts and washers and tighten to 70 ft. lbs.

If new gear-to-frame bolts and washers are required, use only Grade 9 bolts.

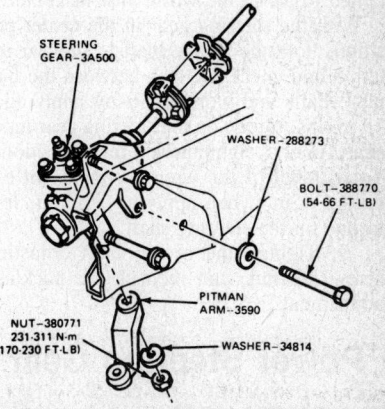

1980–82 steering gear installation

5. Connect the drag link to the Pitman arm, install the drag link ball stud nut, and tighten to 50–75 ft. lbs. Then install the cotter pin.

6. Assemble the Pitman arm on the sector shaft pointing downward. Install the attaching nut and washer, and tighten to 170–230 ft. lbs.

7. Secure the flex coupling to the steering shaft flange with the two attaching nuts and tighten to 28–35 ft. lbs.

MANUAL STEERING GEAR ADJUSTMENTS

1. Be sure that the steering column is properly aligned and is not causing excessive turning effort.

2. The steering gear must be removed from the truck.

3. Be sure that the ball nut assembly and the sector gear are properly adjusted as follows to maintain minimum steering shaft endplay and backlash between the sector gear and ball nut (preload adjustment).

4. Loosen the sector shaft adjusting screw locknut and turn the adjusting screw counterclockwise approximately 3 times.

5. Measure the worm bearing preload

by attaching an in. lbs. torque wrench to the input shaft. Measure the torque required to rotate the input shaft about 1½ turns 2½ in either direction. The worm bearing preload should be 5–8 in. lbs. for 1975–76 models and 3–8 in. lbs. for 1977 and later models.

6. To adjust the worm bearing preload, loosen the input shaft bearing adjuster locknut, and tighten or loosen the bearing adjuster to bring the preload within the specified limits, 4–10 in. lbs. for 1975–76 models and 10–16 in. lbs. for 1977 and later models. Tighten the locknut and recheck the preload.

7. Turn the input shaft slowly to either stop. Turn gently against the stop to avoid possible damage to the ball return guides. Then rotate the shaft approximately 3 turns to center the ball nut.

8. Turn the sector shaft adjusting screw clockwise until the specified pull is obtained to rotate the worm past its center.

With the steering gear in the center position, hold the sector shaft to prevent rotation and check the lash between the ball nuts, balls and worm shaft by applying a 15 in. lbs. torque on the steering gear input shaft, in both right and left turn directions. Total travel of the wrench should not exceed 1¼ in. when applying a 15 in. lbs. torque on the steering shaft.

9. Tighten the sector shaft adjusting screw locknut, and recheck the backlash adjustment.

Power Steering Gear

THROUGH 1977
Removal

When servicing the steering gear, label hoses before disconnecting them so they can be easily identified for reassembly.

Service the steering gear as follows:

1. Position a drain pan under the steering gear. Disconnect the pressure and the return lines from the steering gear and plug the lines and ports in the gear to prevent entry of dirt.

2. Raise the vehicle on a hoist and remove the Pitman arm attaching nut and lock washer.

3. Remove the Pitman arm from the sector shaft using tool T64P-3590-F.

4. Remove the bolts and nuts that attach the steering gear to the frame side rail. Lower the vehicle.

5. Remove the pinch bolt from the flange and insulator assembly.

6. Loosen the nut holding the horn and turn the horn outward.

7. Remove the steering gear attaching bolts and remove the steering gear, shaft, and joint assemblies as a unit.

8. Remove the pinch bolt and nut from the shaft and joint assembly.

9. Remove the shaft and joint assembly from the steering gear.

Installation

1. Before installing the gear in the vehicle, attach the shaft and joint assembly to the steering gear. Install the pinch bolt and torque the nut to 45 to 60 ft. lbs.

2. Raise the vehicle on a hoist. Place the steering gear on the frame side rail and loosely attach the forward attaching bolt and nut.

3. Center the steering gear input shaft.

4. Insert the shaft end of the shaft and joint assembly into the flange and insulator assembly while supporting the rear of the steering gear.

5. Install the remaining steering gear attaching bolts through the steering gear flange, through the frame side rail.

6. Install the remaining steering gear attaching nuts and torque all three attaching nuts to 52 to 90 ft. lbs.

7. Make sure the wheels are in the straight ahead position and install the Pitman arm, lock washer and nut. Torque the nut to 170–230 ft. lbs. Lower the vehicle.

8. Install the pinch bolt in the flange and insulator assembly, and torque to 28 to 35 ft. lbs.

9. Remove the plugs from the pressure and return lines and ports to the steering gear. Connect the lines to gear and torque to 16 to 25 ft. lbs.

10. Turn the horn inward and tighten the retaining nut. Disconnect the coil wire. Fill the power steering pump reservoir. Turn on the ignition and turn the steering wheel to distribute the fluid. Check the fluid level and add fluid, if necessary. Connect the coil wire, start the engine and turn the steering wheel from side to side. Check for fluid leaks.

1978–82
Removal

Service the steering gear as follows:

1. Disconnect the pressure and return lines from the steering gear. Plug the lines and the ports in the gear to prevent entry of dirt. Disconnect brake lines from the steering gear bracket.

2. Remove the bolts that secure the flex coupling to the steering gear and to the column steering shaft assembly.

3. Raise the vehicle and remove the Pitman arm attaching nut, and washer.

4. Remove the Pitman arm from the sector shaft using tool T64P-3590-F. Remove the tool from the Pitman arm. Do not damage the seals.

5. On vehicles with standard transmission remove the clutch release lever retracting spring to provide clearance for removing the steering gear.

6. Support the steering gear, and remove the steering gear attaching bolts.

7. Work the steering gear free of the flex coupling. Remove the steering gear from the vehicle.

Installation

1. Slide the flex coupling into place on the steering shaft assembly. Turn the steering wheel so the spokes are in the horizontal position.

2. Center the steering gear input shaft.

3. Slide the steering gear input shaft into the flex coupling and into place on the frame side rail. Install the attaching bolts and tighten to 60–80 ft. lbs.

4. Be sure the wheels are in the straight ahead position, then install the Pitman arm on the sector shaft. Install the Pitman arm attaching washer and nut. Tighten nut to 170–230 ft. lbs.

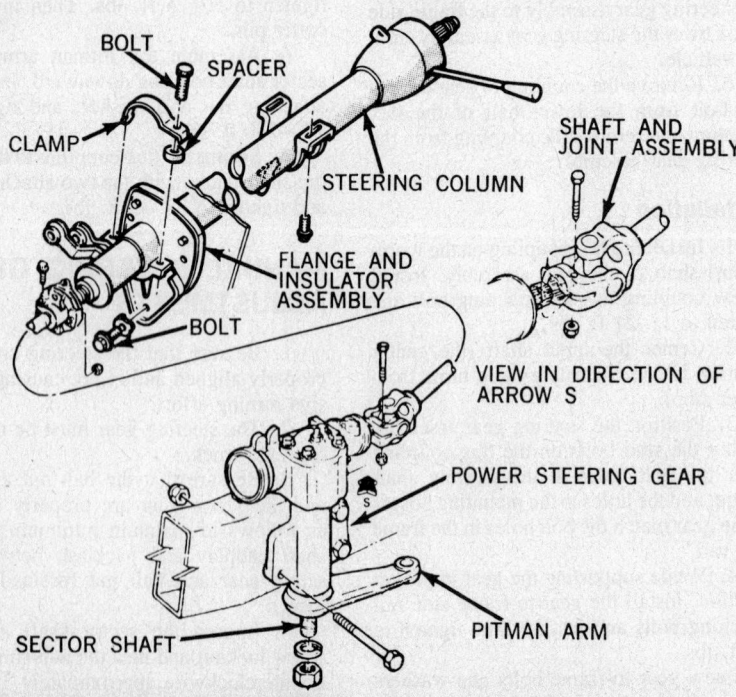

1975–77 power steering gear installation

5. Connect and tighten the pressure and the return lines to the steering gear. Reinstall the brake lines on the steering gear bracket.

6. Disconnect the coil wire. Fill the reservoir. Turn on the ignition and turn the steering wheel from left to right to distribute the fluid.

7. Re-check fluid level and add fluid, if necessary. Connect the coil wire, start the engine and turn the steering wheel from side to side. Inspect for fluid leaks.

POWER STEERING GEAR ADJUSTMENTS

Steering Gear Meshload

1. Make sure that the steering column is correctly aligned.

2. Disconnect the steering linkage from the Pitman arm on the steering gear. Remove the horn pad as explained under Steering Wheel Removal and Installation.

3. Disconnect the fluid reservoir return line and cap the reservoir return line tube. Place the end of the return line in a clean container and turn the steering wheel back and forth several times to empty the steering gear.

4. Turn the steering wheel nut with an inch pound torque wrench slowly. Find the torque required at ½ turn off right and left stops, ½ turn off center both right and left, and over-center (full turn). The over-center torque should be 4–6 in. lbs. more than the end readings, but the total over-center torque must not exceed 14 in. lbs.

5. To correct, back off the Pitman shaft adjuster all the way, then back in ½ turn. Recheck the over-center torque. Loosen the locknut and tighten the sector shaft adjusting screw until the over-center torque reads 4–6 in. lbs. higher, but doesn't exceed 14 in. lbs. Tighten the adjusting screw locknut and recheck.

6. Refill the system with the fluid specified. Bleed the system of air by turning the steering wheel all the way to the right and left several times with the engine warmed up. Do not hold the steering against the stops or pump damage will result.

Steering Linkage Connecting Rods

Replace the drag link if a ball stud is excessively loose or if the drag link is bent. Do not attempt to straighten a drag link. Replace the connecting rod if the ball stud is excessively loose, if the connecting rod is bent or if the threads are stripped. Do not attempt to straighten connecting rod. Always check to insure that the adjustment sleeve and clamp stops are correctly installed on the Bronco.

REMOVAL AND INSTALLATION

Vans and 2-WD Pick-ups

Replace the drag link if a ball stud is excessively loose or if the drag link is bent. **Do not attempt to straighten a drag link.**

Replace the connecting rod if the ball stud is excessively loose, if the connecting rod is bent or if the threads are stripped. Do not attempt to straighten connecting rod.

After installing a connecting rod or adjusting toe-in check to insure that the adjustment sleeve clamps are correctly positioned on the F and E-100 and F and E-150 and to insure that the clamp stop is correctly installed on the F and E-250 and F and E-350.

1. Remove the cotter pins and nuts from the drag link, ball studs and from the right connecting rod ball stud.

2. Remove the right connecting rod ball stud from the drag link.

3. Remove the drag link ball studs from the spindle and the Pitman arm.

4. Position the new drag link, ball studs in the spindle, and Pitman arm and install nuts.

5. Position the right connecting rod ball stud in the drag link and install nut.

6. Tighten the nuts to 50–75 ft. lbs. and install the cotter pins.

7. Remove the cotter pin and nut from the connecting rod.

8. Remove the ball stud from the mating part.

9. Loosen the clamp bolt and turn the rod out of the adjustment sleeve.

10. Lubricate the threads of the new connecting rod, and turn it into the adjustment sleeve to about the same distance the old rods were installed. This will provide an approximate toe-in setting. Position the connecting rod ball studs in the spindle arms.

11. Install the nuts on to the connecting rod ball studs, tighten the nut to 50–75 ft. lbs. and install the cotter pin.

12. Check the toe-in and adjust, if necessary. After checking or adjusting toe-in, center the adjustment sleeve clamps between the locating nibs, position the clamps and tighten the nuts to 29–41 ft. lbs.

4-WD Pick-ups

1. Raise the vehicle on a hoist and disconnect the drag link from the spindle connecting rod end.

2. Disconnect the right spindle connecting rod end from the right spindle arm.

3. Disconnect the left spindle connecting rod ends from the left spindle arm and remove the spindle connecting rod ends from the truck.

4. Place the connecting rod ends in a vise and loosen the connecting rod tube clamps.

5. Remove the short (right) rod end from the connecting rod tube and remove the tube from the long (left) connecting rod end.

6. Clean and oil the threads on all the parts to be reused.

7. Install the connecting rod tube and clamps on the left spindle connecting rod end. Don't tighten the clamps yet.

8. Install the right connecting rod end in the tube and remove the assembly from the vise.

9. Install new dust seals on the left spindle connecting rod end and position the end on the left spindle arm.

10. Install the connecting rod end attaching nut, tighten it, and install the cotter pin.

11. Install new dust seals on the right spindle connecting rod end and position the end on the right spindle arm. Install the attaching nut, tighten it, and install the cotter pin.

12. Install new seals on the drag link ball stud and position the drag link on the spindle connecting rod end. Install the attaching nut, tighten it, and install the cotter pin.

13. Lubricate the spindle connecting rod ends and drag link.

14. Lower the vehicle and check and adjust the toe-in setting. Tighten the connecting rod clamps after adjusting the toe-in.

1975 Bronco

1. Disconnect the connecting rods from the spindles and drag link.

2. Place the connecting rods in a vise and loosen the tube clamps. Disassemble the rods. The right one is shorter than the left one.

3. Clean and oil all threads on components to be reused.

4. Install the left tube and clamps on the left spindle rod end. Do not tighten clamps.

5. Install the right end in the tube and remove the assembly from the vise.

6. Install new dust seal and attach the assembly to the spindles. Torque the nuts to 40 ft. lbs. aligning the cotter pin holes as the nut is tightened.

7. Install new seals on the drag link stud and attach it to the connecting rod. Torque the nut to 40 ft. lbs.

8. Check and adjust toe in and tighten the tube clamps.

1976–77 Bronco

1. Raise vehicle and support on jackstands.

2. Disconnect connecting rod ends from spindles.

3. Remove U-bolts securing left connecting rod to brace.

4. Disconnect right connecting rod end from steering arm.

5. Mount the assembly in a vise and disconnect the right and left rod assemblies.

6. Mark the position of the clamp on the left connecting halves.

7. Clean and oil all threaded parts.

8. Assemble left connecting rod halves in clamp at about the same position marked.

9. Attach right and left connecting rods, but do not tighten nut.

10. Attach connecting rods to the spindles. Torque the nuts to 40 ft. lbs.

11. Check and adjust toe-in by turning the left connecting rod halves. Tighten clamp bolts.

12. Attach the left connecting rod to the brace by tightening the two U-bolts evenly to 20 ft. lbs.

1978–79 Bronco

1. Remove the cotter pins and nuts

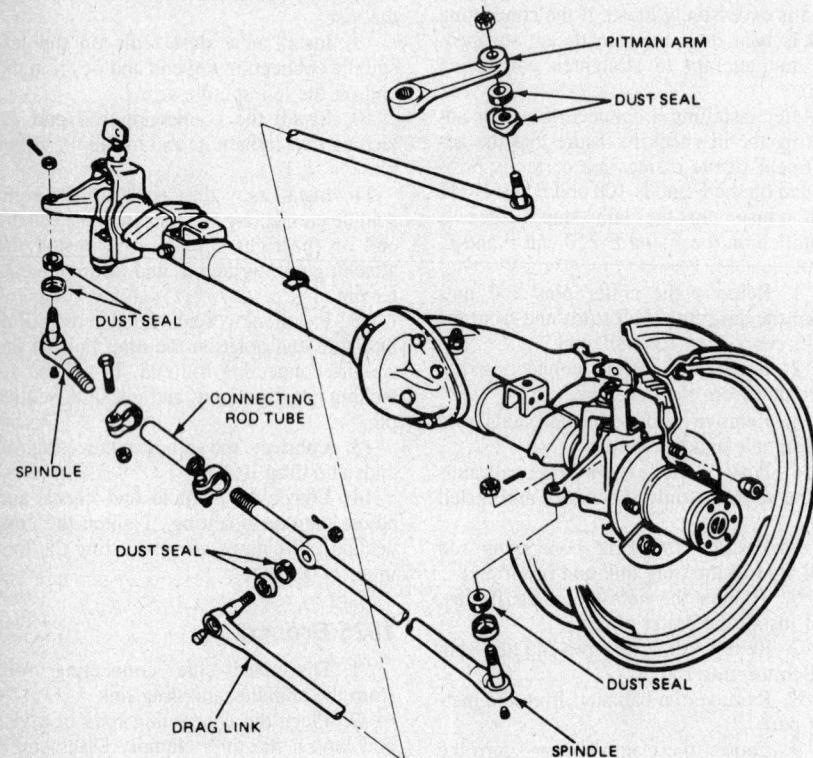

1975 Bronco steering linkage

from the drag link, ball studs and from the right connecting rod ball stud.

2. Remove the right connecting rod ball stud from the drag link.

3. Remove the drag link ball studs from the spindle and the Pitman arm.

4. Position the new drag link, ball studs in the spindle, and Pitman arm and install nuts.

5. Position the right connecting rod ball stud in the drag link and install nut.

6. Tighten the nuts as follows and install the cotter pins: Drag link studs, 50–75 ft. lbs. Ball studs, 50–60 ft. lbs. Connecting rod studs, 35–45 ft. lbs.

7. Remove the cotter pin and nut from the connecting rod.

8. Remove the ball stud from the mating part.

9. Loosen the clamp bolt and turn the rod out of the adjustment sleeve.

10. Lubricate the threads of the new connecting rod, and turn it into the adjustment sleeve to about the same distance the old rods were installed. This will provide an approximate toe-in setting. Position the connecting rod ball studs in the spindle arms.

11. Install the nuts on to the connecting rod ball studs, tighten the nut to specification and install the cotter pin.

12. Check the toe-in and adjust, if necessary. After checking or adjusting toe-in, center the adjustment sleeve clamps between the locating nibbs, position the clamps and tighten the nuts to 35–45 ft. lbs.

1980–82 Bronco

1. Remove the cotter pins and nuts from the drag link, ball studs and from the right connecting rod ball studs.

2. Remove the right connecting rod ball stud from the right spindle assembly and Pitman arm.

3. Remove the drag link ball studs from the spindle and the connecting rod assembly.

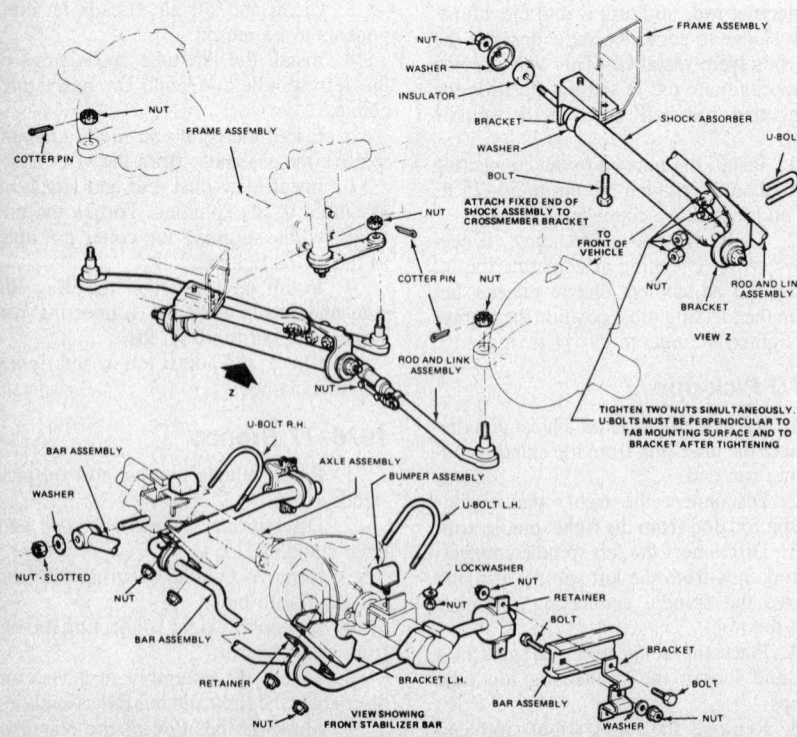

1976–77 Bronco steering linkage

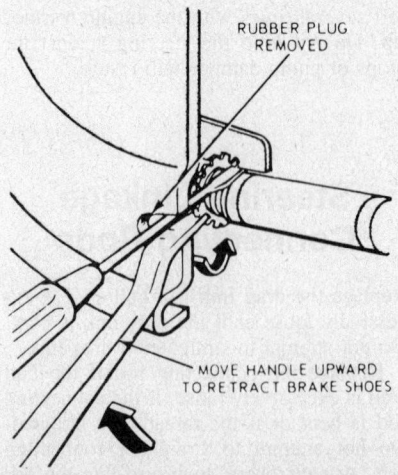

Position and operation of the brake adjusting tools on Bronco, E-100, 150 and 200

4. Loosen the clamp bolt and turn the rod out of the adjustment sleeve.

5. Lubricate the threads of the new connecting rod, and turn it into the adjustment sleeve to about the same distance the old rods were installed. This will provide an approximate toe-in setting. Position the connecting rod ball studs in the spindle arms.

6. Position the new drag link, ball studs in the spindle, and connecting rod assembly and install nuts.

7. Position the right connecting rod ball stud in the drag link and install nut.

8. Tighten all the nuts to 50–75 ft. lbs. and install the cotter pins.

9. Remove the cotter pin and nut from the left connecting rod.

10. Install the nuts on the connecting rod ball studs, tighten the nut to 50–75 ft. lbs. and install the cotter pin.

11. Check the toe-in and adjust, if necessary. After checking or adjusting toe-in, center the adjustment sleeve clamps between the locating nibbs, position the clamps and tighten the nuts to 29–41 ft. lbs.

BRAKE SYSTEM

ADJUSTMENT

The drum brakes are self-adjusting and require a manual adjustment only after the brake shoes have been relined, replaced, or when the length of the adjusting screw has been changed while performing some other service operation, as i.e., taking off the self-adjusters and putting on manual ones.

To adjust the brakes, follow the procedure given below:

1. Raise the vehicle and support it with safety stands.

2. Remove the rubber plug from the adjusting slot on the backing plate.

3. Insert a brake adjusting spoon into the slot and engage the lowest possible tooth on the starwheel. Move the end of the brake spoon downward to move the

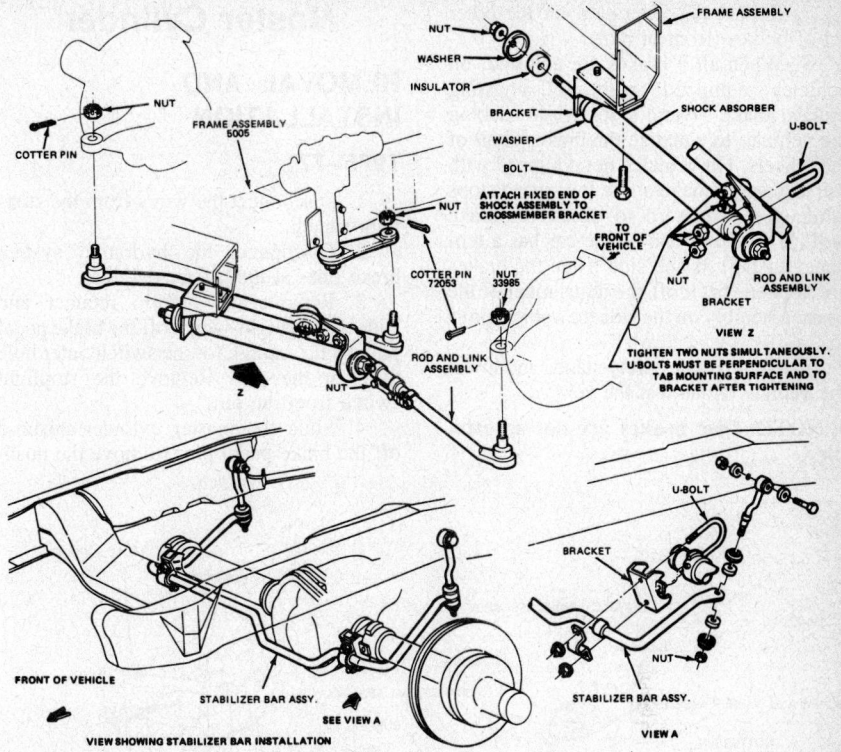

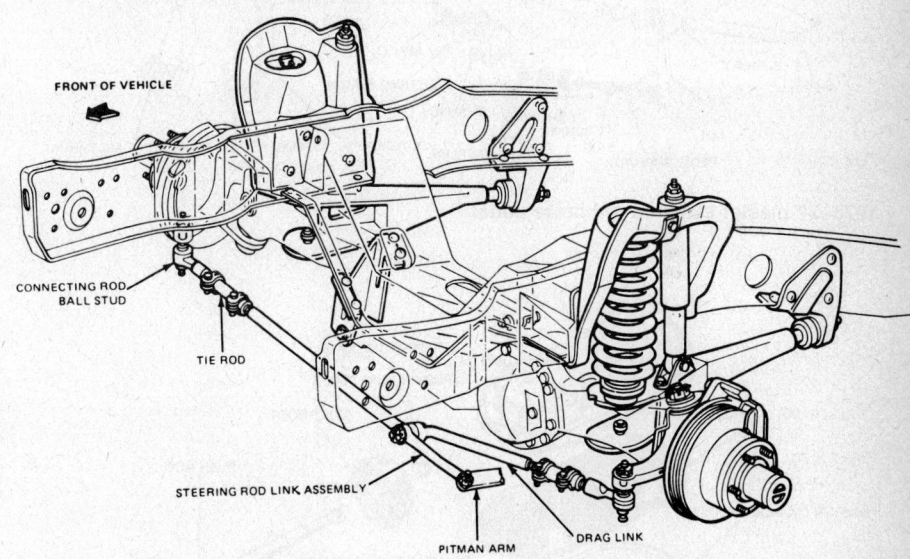

1978–79 Bronco steering linkage

1980–82 Bronco steering linkage

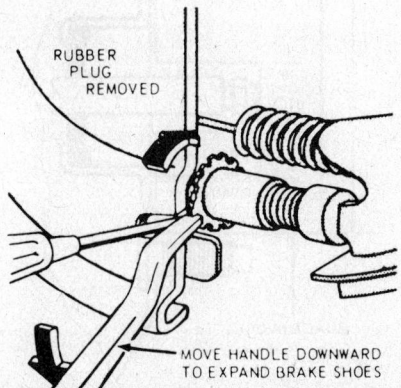

Position and operation of the brake adjusting tools on E&F-250, 300 and 350

starwheel upward and expand the adjusting screw. Repeat this operation until the brakes lock the wheel.

NOTE: Step 4 applies only to vehicles equipped with self-adjusters.

4. Insert a small screwdriver or piece of firm wire (coathanger wire) into the adjusting slot and push the automatic adjusting lever out and free of the starwheel on the adjusting screw and hold it there.

5. Engage the topmost tooth possible on the starwheel with the brake adjusting spoon. Move the end of the adjusting spoon

upward to move the adjusting screw starwheel downward and contract the adjusting screw. Back off the adjusting screw starwheel until the wheel spins freely with a minimum of drag. Keep track of the number of turns that the starwheel is backed off, or the number of strokes taken with the brake adjusting spoon.

6. Repeat this operation for the other side. When backing off the brakes on the other side, the starwheel adjuster must be backed off the same number of turns to prevent side-to-side brake pull.

7. Repeat this operation on the other set of brakes (front or rear).

8. When all 4 brakes are adjusted, on vehicles equipped with self-adjusting brakes, make several stops while backing the vehicle, to equalize the brakes at all of the wheels. On vehicles not equipped with self-adjusters, make a few low-speed stops while going forward to check for brake pull. If the front end of the car has a tendency to pull to one side when the brakes are applied, back off the adjustment of the brake assembly on the side the vehicle pulls to.

9. Remove the safety stands and lower the vehicle. Road test the vehicle.

NOTE: Disc brakes are not adjustable.

Master Cylinder

REMOVAL AND INSTALLATION

1975–77

1. Disconnect the wires from the stoplight switch.

2. Disconnect the hydraulic system brake lines at the master cylinder.

3. Remove the hairpin retainer and slide the stoplight switch off the brake pedal pin just far enough for the switch outer hole to clear the pin. Remove the stoplight switch from the pin.

4. Slide the master cylinder pushrod off the brake pedal pin. Remove the bush-

ings and washers.

5. Remove the master cylinder retaining bolts and remove the master cylinder.

To install the master cylinder:

6. Position the master cylinder assembly on the firewall and install the retaining bolts.

7. Connect the hydraulic system brake lines to the master cylinder.

8. Lubricate the pushrod bushing with clean motor oil. Insert the bushing in the pushrod. Coat the washers with the lubricant, and position the pushrod and bushing, washers and stoplight switch on the brake pedal pin. Install the hairpin-type retainer.

9. Connect the stoplight switch wires to the switch.

10. Bleed the hydraulic brake system.

1978–82

1. With the engine turned off, push the brake pedal down to expel vacuum from the brake booster system.

2. Disconnect the hydraulic lines from the brake master cylinder.

3. Remove the brake booster-to-master cylinder retaining nuts and lock washers. Remove the master cylinder from the brake booster.

4. Before installing the master cylinder, check the distance from the outer end of the booster assembly push rod to the front face of the brake booster assembly. Turn the push rod adjusting screw in or out as required to obtain .880–.895 in. for all 1975–76 trucks; .931–.946 in. for Bronco, E-100-250 and F-100-250; .980–.995 in. for E & F-350.

5. Position the master cylinder assembly over the booster push rod and onto the two studs on the booster assembly. Install the attaching nuts and lockwashers and tighten to 20–30 ft. lbs.

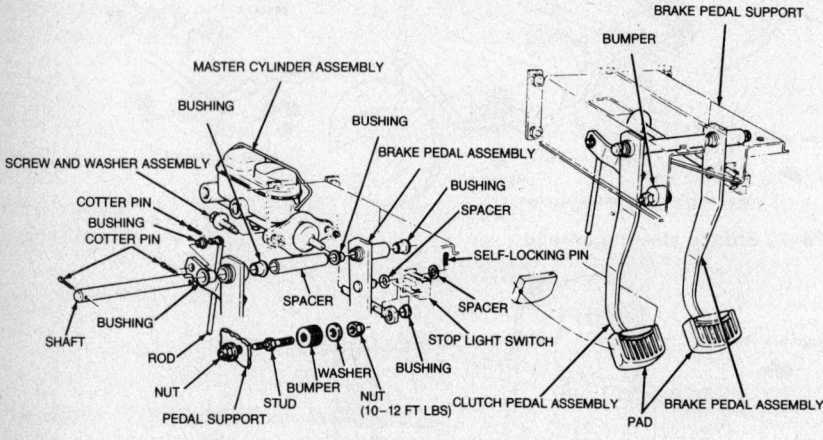

1975–77 master cylinder and brake pedal

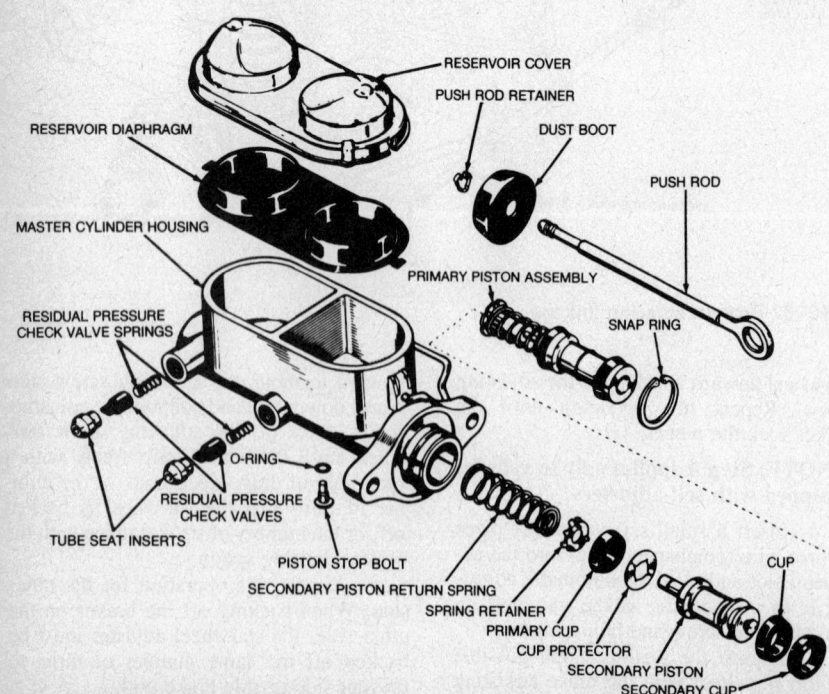

Exploded view of the master cylinder

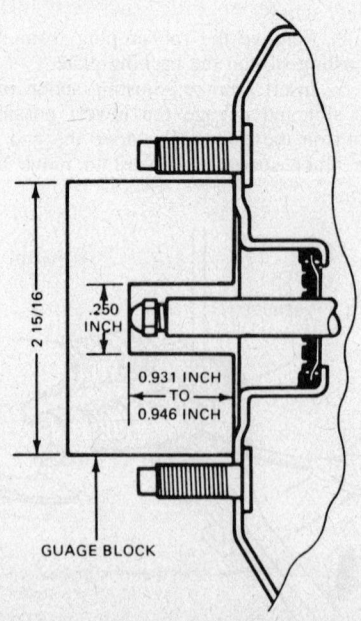

1978 and later Bendix booster pushrod gauge dimensions and adjustment

6. Loosely connect the hydraulic brake system lines to the master cylinder.

7. Bleed the hydraulic brake system. Centralize the differential valve. Then, fill the dual master cylinder reservoirs with DOT 3 brake fluid to within ¼ inch of the top. Install the gasket and reservoir cover.

OVERHAUL

The most important thing to remember when rebuilding the master cylinder is cleanliness. Work in clean surroundings with clean tools and clean cloths or paper for drying purposes. Have plenty of clean alcohol and brake fluid on hand to clean and lubricate the internal components. There are service repair kits available for overhauling the master cylinder.

1. Clean the outside of the master cylinder and remove the filler cap and gasket (diaphragm). Pour out any fluid that remains in the cylinder reservoir. Do not use any fluids other than brake fluid or alcohol to clean the master cylinder.

2. Unscrew the piston stop from the bottom of the cylinder body. Remove the O-ring seal from the piston stop. Discard the seal.

3. Remove the pushrod boot, if so equipped, from the groove at the rear of the master cylinder and slide the boot away from the rear of the master cylinder.

4. Remove the snap-ring retaining the primary and secondary piston assemblies within the cylinder body.

5. Remove the pushrod (if so equipped) and primary piston assembly from the master cylinder. Discard the piston assembly, including the boot (if so equipped).

6. Apply an air hose to the rear brake outlet port of the cylinder body and carefully blow the secondary piston out of the cylinder body.

7. Remove the return spring, spring retainer, cup protector, and cups from the secondary piston. Discard the cup protector and cups.

8. Clean all of the reamaining parts in clean isopropyl alcohol and inspect the parts for chipping, excessive wear or damage. Replace them as required.

NOTE: When using a master cylinder repair kit, install all the parts supplied in the kit.

9. Check all recesses, openings and internal passages to be sure they are open and free from foreign matter. Use compressed air to blow out dirt and cleaning solvent remaining after the parts have been cleaned in the alcohol. Place all the parts on a clean pan, lint-free cloth, or paper to dry.

10. Dip all the parts, except the cylinder body, in clean brake fluid.

11. Assemble the two secondary cups, back-to-back, in the grooves near the end of the secondary piston.

12. Install the secondary piston assembly in the master cylinder.

13. Install a new O-ring on the piston stop, and start the stop into the cylinder body.

14. Position the boot, snap-ring and pushrod retainer on the pushrod. Make sure the pushrod retainer is seated securely on the ball end of the rod. Seat the pushrod in the primary piston assembly.

15. Install the primary piston assembly in the master cylinder. Push the primary piston inward and tighten the secondary piston stop to retain the secondary piston in the bore.

16. Press the pushrod and pistons inward and install the snap-ring in the cylinder body.

17. Before the master cylinder is installed on the vehicle, the unit must be bled: support the master cylinder body in a vise, and fill both fluid reservoirs with brake fluid.

18. Loosely install plugs in the front and rear brake outlet bores. Depress the primary piston several times until air bubbles cease to appear in the brake fluid.

19. Tighten the plugs and attempt to depress the piston. The piston travel should be restricted after all air is expelled.

20. Remove the plugs. Install the cover and gasket (diaphragm) assembly, and make sure the cover retainer is tightened securely.

21. Install the master cylinder in the vehicle and bleed the hydraulic system.

BLEEDING THE BRAKES

When any part of the hydraulic system has been disconnected for repair or replacement, air may get into the lines and cause spongy pedal action (because air can be compressed and brake fluid cannot). To correct this condition, it is necessary to bleed the hydraulic system after it has been properly connected to be sure all air is expelled from the brake cylinders and lines.

When bleeding the brake system, bleed one brake cylinder at a time, beginning at the cylinder with the longest hydraulic line (farthest from the master cylinder) first. Keep the master cylinder reservoir filled with brake fluid during the bleeding operation. Never use brake fluid that has been drained from the hydraulic system, no matter how clean it is.

It will be necessary to centralize the pressure differential valve after a brake system failure has been corrected and the hydraulic system has been bled.

On the Bronco, the primary and secondary hydraulic brake systems are individual systems and are bled separately. During the entire bleeding operation, do not allow the reservoir to run dry. Keep the master cylinder reservoir filled with brake fluid.

1. Clean all dirt from around the master cylinder fill cap, remove the cap and fill the master cylinder with brake fluid until the level is within ¼ in. of the top edge of the reservoir.

2. Clean off the bleeder screws at all 4 wheel cylinders. The bleeder screws are located on the inside of the brake backing plate, on the backside of the wheel cylinders.

3. Attach a length of rubber hose over the nozzle of the bleeder screw at the wheel to be done first. Place the other end of the hose in a glass jar, submerged in brake fluid.

4. Open the bleeder screw valve ½–¾ turn.

5. Have an assistant slowly depress the brake pedal. Close the bleeder screw valve and tell your assistant to allow the brake pedal to return slowly. Continue this pumping action to force any air out of the system. When bubbles cease to appear at the end of the bleeder hose, close the bleeder valve and remove the hose.

6. Check the master cylinder fluid level and add fluid accordingly. Do this after bleeding each wheel.

7. Repeat the bleeding operation at the remaining 3 wheels, ending with the one closest to the master cylinder. Fill the master cylinder reservoir.

Centralizing the Pressure Differential Valve

After any repair or bleeding of the primary (front brake) or secondary (rear brake) system, the dual-brake system warning light will usually remain illuminated due to the pressure differential valve remaining in the off-center position.

To centralize the pressure differential valve and turn off the warning light after the systems have been bled, follow the procedure below.

1. Turn the ignition switch to the ACC or ON position.

2. Check the fluid level in the master cylinder reservoirs and fill them to within ¼ in. of the top with brake fluid, if necessary.

3. Depress the brake pedal and the piston should center itself causing the brake warning light to go out.

4. Turn the ignition switch to the OFF position.

5. Before driving the vehicle, check the operation of the brakes and be sure that a firm pedal is obtained.

Disc Brake Pads

To determine whether your truck has floating or sliding caliper disc brakes, remove the front wheel. The floating caliper unit is operated by two pistons per caliper. The caliper is mounted on a support, and the support and shield are mounted directly to the spindle. There are two types of sliding calipers, the LD sliding caliper and the HD

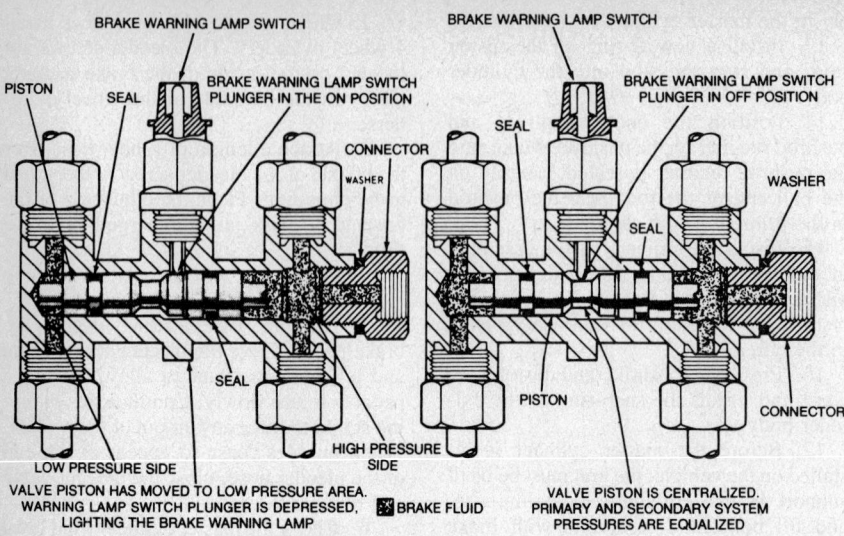

Cutaway view of a typical pressure differential valve

Labels in the left diagram: BRAKE WARNING LAMP SWITCH; PISTON; SEAL; BRAKE WARNING LAMP SWITCH PLUNGER IN THE ON POSITION; CONNECTOR; WASHER; SEAL; LOW PRESSURE SIDE; HIGH PRESSURE SIDE; VALVE PISTON HAS MOVED TO LOW PRESSURE AREA. WARNING LAMP SWITCH PLUNGER IS DEPRESSED, LIGHTING THE BRAKE WARNING LAMP

Labels in the right diagram: BRAKE WARNING LAMP SWITCH; BRAKE WARNING LAMP SWITCH PLUNGER IN OFF POSITION; SEAL; WASHER; SEAL; PISTON; CONNECTOR; VALVE PISTON IS CENTRALIZED. PRIMARY AND SECONDARY SYSTEM PRESSURES ARE EQUALIZED; ▓ BRAKE FLUID

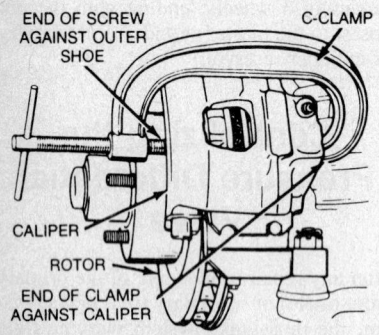

Labels: END OF SCREW AGAINST OUTER SHOE; C-CLAMP; CALIPER; ROTOR; END OF CLAMP AGAINST CALIPER

Bottoming the caliper piston

rail slider caliper. The LD sliding caliper unit is operated by one piston per caliper. The caliper and steering arm are cast as one piece and combined with the spindle stem to form an integral spindle assembly. The HD slider caliper unit contains two pistons on the same side of the rotor. The caliper slides on the support assembly and is retained by a key and spring.

INSPECTION

Remove the brake pads as described below and measure the thickness of the lining. If the lining at any point on the pad assembly is less that 0.210 in. thick (above the backing plate or rivets), or there is evidence of the lining being contaminted by brake fluid or oil, replace the brake pads.

REMOVAL AND INSTALLATION

Floating Caliper

1. Remove the tire and wheel assembly.
2. Remove the brake pad mounting pins, anti-rattle springs, and then lift out the brake pads.

3. Before installing the new brake pads, remove the master cylinder cover, and loosen the piston housing-to-caliper mounting bolts enough to allow installation of the new (thicker) brake pads. Do not move the pistons.
4. Install the new pads. Install the mounting pins and anti-rattle spring.

NOTE: Make sure that the spring tangs engage the holes in the brake pad plates.

5. Tighten the brake pad mounting pins to 17–23 ft. lbs.
6. Tighten the piston-to-housing mounting bolts to reset the pistons in the cylinders.

NOTE: Make sure that you keep the cylinder housing square with the caliper.

7. Tighten the piston housing-to-caliper mounting bolts to 155–185 ft. lbs.
8. Install the wheel and tire assembly.
9. Check the level in the master cylinder. It is normal for the brake fluid level to rise with the replacement of worn front brake pads with new ones. If the fluid level was added to before the old pads were replaced, the master cylinder may overflow. Adjust the level of the brake fluid in the master cylinder reservoir to within ¼ in. from the top of the filler neck as necessary.

LD Sliding Caliper (Single Piston)

1. To avoid overflowing of the master cylinder when the caliper pistons are pressed into the caliper cylinder bores, siphon or dip some brake fluid out of the larger reservoir.
2. Jack up the front of the truck and remove the wheels.
3. Place an 8 in. C-clamp on the caliper and tighten the clamp to bottom the caliper piston in the cylinder bore. Remove the C-clamp.

4. Remove the caliper support key retaining screw.
5. Drive out the caliper support key and support spring with a drift and hammer.
6. Remove the caliper from the spindle assembly by pushing it downward against the spindle assembly, and rotating the upper end upward and out of the spindle assembly. Lay the caliper on the tie-rod.

NOTE: Do not allow the caliper to hang by the brake hose.

7. Remove the outer brake pad from the caliper. It may be necessary to tap the pad loose from the caliper.
8. Remove the inner pad from the spindle assembly. Remove the brake pad anti-rattle clip from the lower pad abutment surface of the spindle assembly.
9. Thoroughly clean the areas of the caliper and spindle assembly which contact each other during the sliding action of the caliper.
10. Place a new anti-rattle clip in the lower pad abutment in the spindle assembly. Make sure that the tabs on the clip are positioned correctly and the loop-type spring is away from the rotor.
11. Place the lower end of the inner brake pad in the spindle assembly pad abutment, against the anti-rattle clip, and slide the upper end of the pad into position. Be sure that the clip is still in position.
12. Check and make sure that the caliper piston is fully bottomed in the cylinder bore. Use a large C-clamp to bottom the piston, if necessary.

NOTE: The replacement outer brake pads differ slightly from the oroginal equipment. The replacement brake pads have tabs on the flange at the lower edge of the pad plate and the distance between the upper tabs and the lower flange is reduced to provide a slip-on interference fit.

13. Position the outer brake pad on the caliper, and press the pad tabs into place with your fingers. If the pad cannot be pressed into place by hand, use a C-clamp. Be careful not to damage the lining with the clamp.
14. Position the caliper on the spindle assembly by pivoting the caliper around the spindle upper mounting surface. Be careful not to tear or cut the piston boot as it slips over the inner brake pad.
15. Hold the upper machined surface of the caliper against the surface of the spindle assembly with a brake adjusting tool or screwdriver and install a new caliper support spring and key. Drive the key and spring assembly into position and install the key retaining screw. Tighten the screw to 12–20 ft. lbs.
16. After the new brake pads and wheel assemblies have been installed on both front wheels, lower the truck, and check the master cylinder reservoirs. Adjust the level of brake fluid in the master cylinder as necessary.

17. Depress the brake pedal firmly several times to seat the brake pad linings against the rotors. Do not move the truck until the pedal is firm.

Rail Slider Sliding Caliper (Two Piston)

1. Raise and secure the vehicle. Remove the wheel and tire assembly.

2. Disconnect the brake hose from the caliper and plug the hose and inlet port.

3. Remove the key retaining screw.

4. Using a brass rod and light hammer drive out the key and spring.

5. Remove the caliper from its support assembly by rotating the key and spring end out and away from the rotor. Slide the opposite end of the caliper clear of the slide in the support and off the rotor. Lay the caliper on the tie rod or axle.

6. Remove the caliper brake shoe anti-rattle spring and the inner and outer shoe and lining assemblies.

7. Thoroughly clean the areas of the caliper and support that contact during the sliding action of the caliper.

8. Place a C-clamp on the caliper housing midway between the piston bores, and using the old inner shoe and lining over the pistons, tighten the clamp to bottom of the caliper pistons in the cylinder bores. Remove the clamp and inner shoe lining assembly.

9. Before installation check to be sure

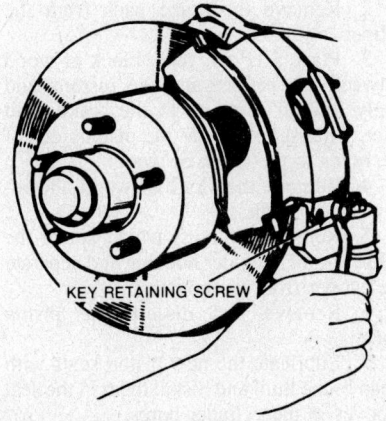

Removing the key retaining screw

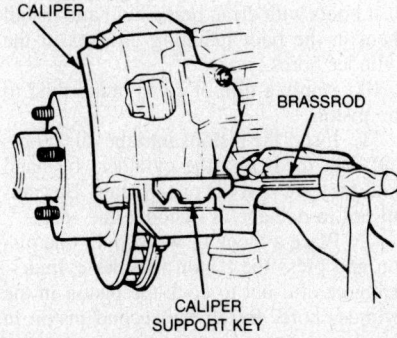

Removing the caliper support spring and key

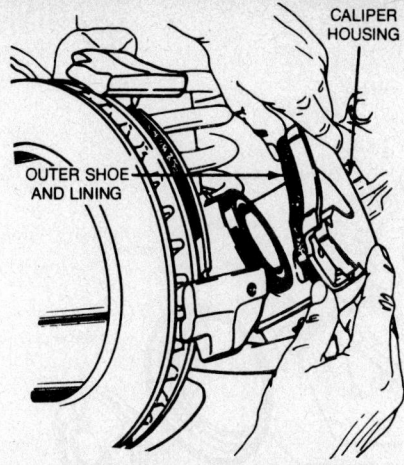

Removing the outer pad and lining

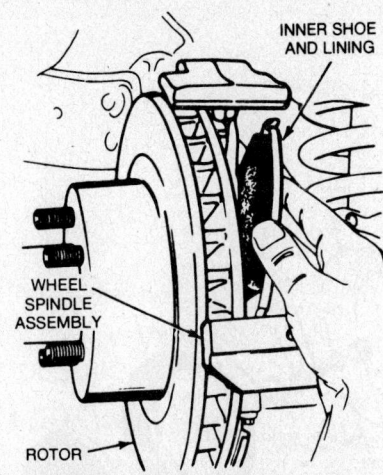

Removing the inner pad and lining

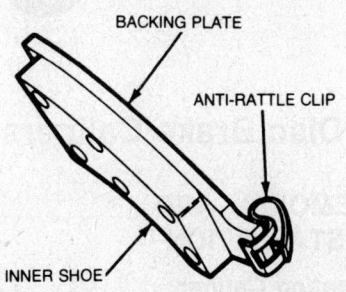

Installing the anti-rattle clip in the inner lining

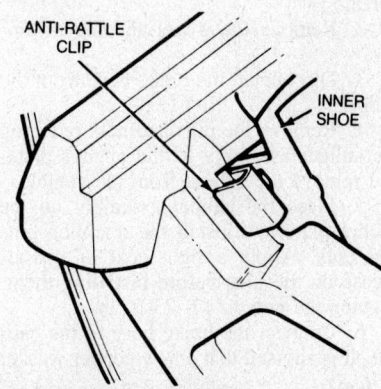

Installing the inner pad

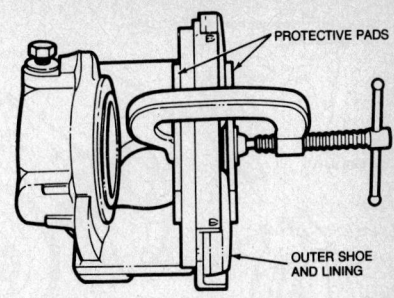

Installing the outer pad

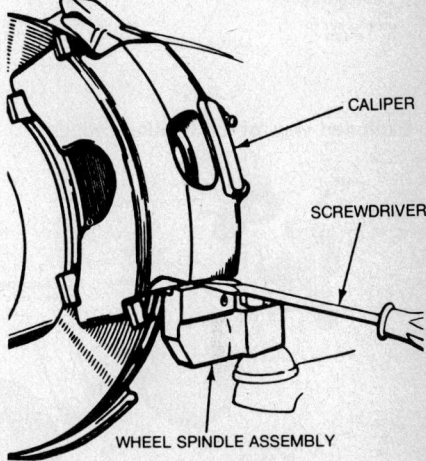

Installing the caliper

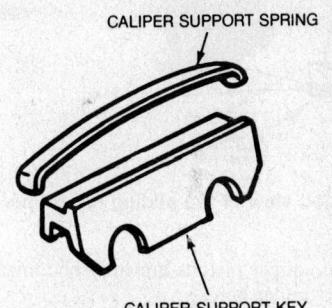

Caliper support spring and key

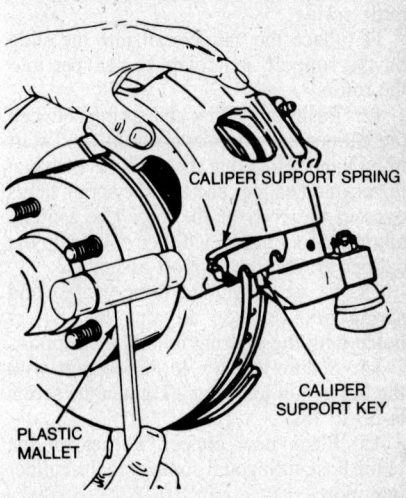

Installing the caliper support spring and key

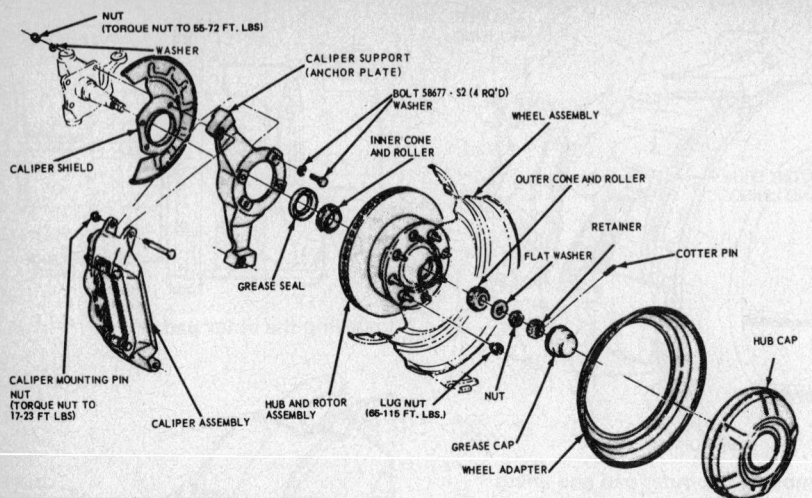

Exploded view of the floating caliper

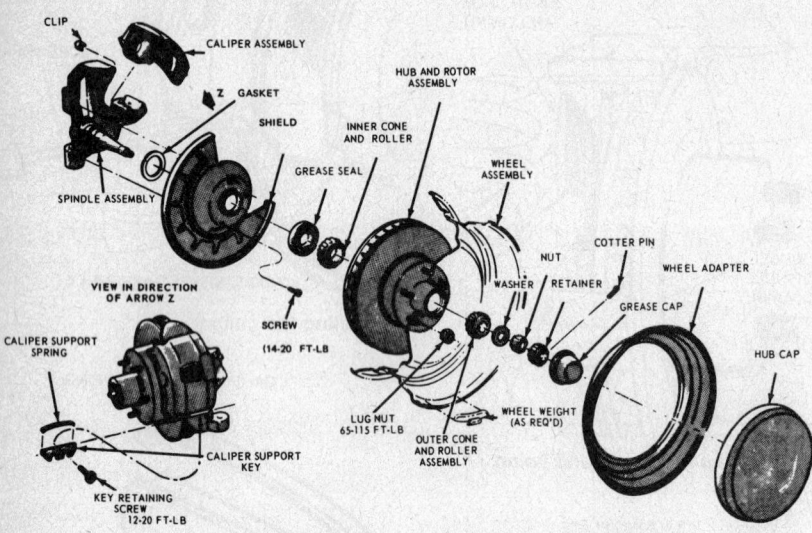

Exploded view of the sliding rail caliper

that the caliper pistons are fully bottomed in the cylinder bores.

10. Install a new inner and outer shoe and lining assemblies and install the anti-rattle spring.

11. Place the caliper rail into the slide on the support and rotate the caliper into the rotor.

12. Position the key and spring between the caliper and support assembly and start in by hand. Note that the spring is between the key and caliper and that the spring tangs overlap the ends of the key. Use a break adjusting tool or screwdriver to hold up the caliper against the support assembly.

13. Using a hammer, drive the key and spring into position aligning the correct notch with the existing hole in the support.

14. Secure the key to the support with the key retaining screw. Tighten the screw to 20 ft. lbs.

15. Place new copper washer on the brake hose fitting and connect to the caliper inlet port.

16. Bleed the system, lower the vehicle, and refill the master cylinder if necessary.

Disc Brake Calipers

REMOVAL AND INSTALLATION

Floating Caliper

1. Raise the front on the truck and support it.

2. Remove the wheel and tire assembly.

3. Disconnect the brake hose from the caliper.

4. Remove the pins and nuts retaining the caliper assembly to the anchor plate, and remove the caliper from the vehicle.

5. Place the caliper assembly on the anchor plate and install the retaining pins and nuts. Apply a light coat of chassis grease on the pins before installing them. Tighten the nuts to 17–23 ft. lbs.

6. Connect the brake hose to the caliper. It is advised that a new copper washer be used.

7. Install the wheel and tire assembly.

8. Bleed the brake hydraulic system and lower the vehicle.

Sliding Caliper

1. Raise the front of the truck and support it. Remove the wheel and tire assembly.

2. Disconnect the brake hose from the caliper.

3. Remove and install the caliper and the brake pads as outlined under Disc Brake Pad Removal and Installation.

4. Connect the brake fluid hose to the caliper. It is recommended that a new copper washer be used at the connection of the brake hose and caliper.

5. Bleed the brake system and install the wheel and tire assembly. Lower the truck.

OVERHAUL

Floating Caliper

NOTE: If the caliper assembly is leaking brake fluid, replace the piston assemblies. If the cylinder bores are scored, corroded or excessively worn, and the leaking cannot be stopped by replacing the pistons, replace the piston housing. Do not hone the cylinder bores. There are no oversize pistons available for oversize bores.

1. Remove the caliper assembly from the truck and secure it in a vise.

2. Remove the brake pads from the caliper.

3. Place a 1⅛ in. thick block of wood between the caliper and the pistons and apply low air pressure to the brake fluid inlet. This should force the pistons out of the bores to the block of wood.

4. Remove the block of wood and remove the pistons.

5. Remove the bolts which attach the caliper to the cylinder housing and separate the caliper from the housing.

6. Remove and discard the piston seals.

7. Lubricate the new piston seals with clean brake fluid and install them in the seal grooves in the cylinder bores.

8. Apply a film of clean brake fluid to the cylinder bores.

9. Lubricate the retaining lips of the dust boots with clean brake fluid and install them in the boot retaining grooves in the cylinder bores.

10. Apply a film of clean brake fluid to the piston.

11. Insert the pistons into the dust boots and start them into the cylinders by hand until they are past the piston seals. Be careful not to damage or dislodge the seal.

12. Place a block of wood over one piston and press the piston into the cylinder, being careful not to cock the piston in the cylinder bore. Install the second piston in the same manner.

13. Install the brake pads.

14. Place the piston housing on the cal-

iper and install the piston housing-to-caliper mounting bolts and washers. Tighten them to 155–185 ft. lbs.

15. Position the caliper assembly on the support and install all the retaining pins and nuts.

16. Install the brake fluid hose, bleed the brake hydraulic system, and center the pressure differential valve. Do not drive the truck until a firm brake pedal is obtained.

LD Sliding Caliper (Single Piston)

1. Clean the outside of the caliper in alcohol after removing it from the vehicle and removing the brake pads.

2. Roll some thick shop cloths or rags and place them between the piston and the outer legs of the caliper.

3. Apply compressed air to the caliper inlet port until the piston comes out of the caliper bore. Use low air pressure to avoid having the piston pop out too rapidly and possibly causing injury.

4. If the piston becomes cocked in the cylinder bore and will not come out, remove the air pressure and tap the piston with a soft hammer to try and straighten it. Do not use a sharp tool or pry the piston out of the bore. Reapply the air pressure.

5. Remove the boot from the piston and seal from the caliper cylinder bore.

6. Clean the piston and caliper in alcohol.

7. Lubricate the piston seal with clean brake fluid, and position the seal in the groove, in the cylinder bore.

8. Coat the outside of the piston and both of the beads of the dust boot with clean brake fluid. Insert the piston through the dust boot until the boot is around the bottom (closed end) of the piston.

9. Hold the piston and dust boot directly above the caliper cylinder bore, and use your fingers to work the bead of the dust boot into the groove near the top of the cylinder bore.

10. After the bead is seated in the groove, press straight down on the piston until it bottoms in the bore. Be careful not to cock the piston in the bore. Use a C-clamp with a block of wood inserted between the clamp and the piston to bottom the piston, if necessary.

11. Install the brake pads and install the caliper. Bleed the brake hydraulic system and recenter the pressure differential valve. Do not drive the vehicle until a firm brake pedal is obtained.

HD Rail Slider Sliding Caliper (Two Piston)

1. Disconnect and plug the flexible brake hose.

2. Remove the front shoe and lining assemblies.

3. Drain the fluid from the cylinders.

4. Secure the caliper in a vise and place a block of wood between the caliper bridge and the cylinders.

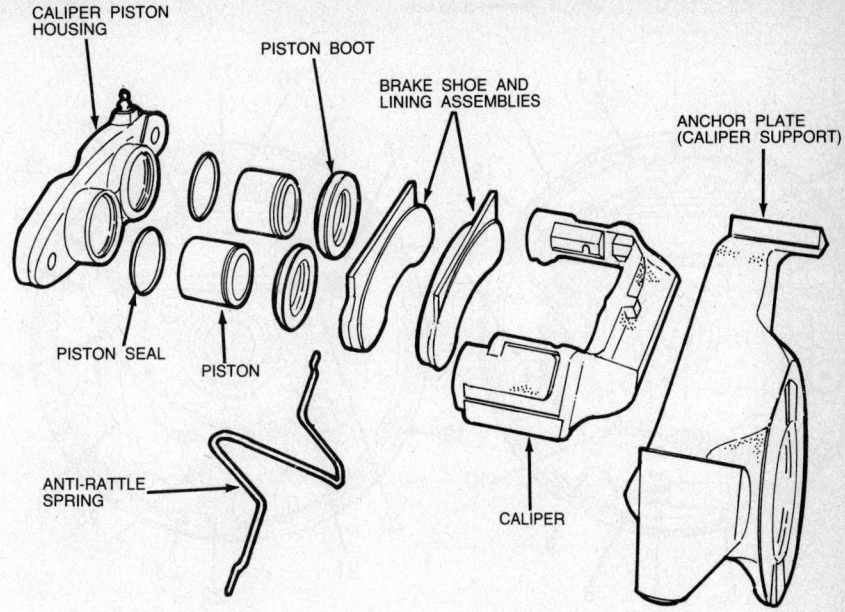

Sliding caliper dual piston brake used on heavy duty models

5. Apply low pressure air to the brake hose inlet and the pistons will be forced out to the wood block.

6. Remove the block of wood and remove the pistons.

7. Remove the bolts and washers that attach the caliper to the cylinder housing and separate the caliper from the housing.

8. Remove the piston seals.

9. Lubricate the new piston seals with clean brake fluid and install them in the seal grooves in the cylinder bores.

10. Lubricate the retaining lips of the dust boots with clean brake fluid and install them in the grooves of the cylinder bores.

11. Apply a film of clean brake fluid to the pistons.

12. Insert the pistons into the dust boots and start them into the cylinders by hand until they are beyond the piston seals. Be careful not to dislodge or damage the piston seal.

13. Place a block of wood over one piston and press the piston into the cylinder. Be careful not to cock the piston in the cylinder bore.

14. Install the second piston in the same manner.

15. Attach the piston housing to the caliper and tighten the mounting bolts to 155–185 ft. lbs.

16. Install the brake shoe assemblies and anti-rattle clip in the caliper assembly. Place the caliper assembly on the support and install the caliper support spring, key and key retaining screw. Tighten the screw to 12–20 ft. lbs.

17. Install the brake hose and bleed the system.

Brake Disc (Rotor)

REMOVAL AND INSTALLATION

1. Jack up the front of the truck and support it with jackstands. Remove the front wheel and tire assembly.

2. Remove the caliper assembly and support it to the frame with a piece of wire without disconnecting the brake fluid hose.

3. Remove the dust cap, cotter pin, nut, washer, and the outer bearing. Remove the rotor/hub from the spindle.

4. If necessary, remove the inner grease seal and inner bearing. Replace the grease seal with a new one.

5. Install the rotor in the reverse order of removal, and adjust the wheel bearing.

INSPECTION

If the rotor is deeply scarred or has shallow cracks, it may be refinished on a disc brake rotor lathe. Also, if the lateral run-out exceeds 0.010 in. within a 6 in. radius when measured with a dial indicator, with the stylus 1 in. in from the edge of the rotor, the rotor should be refinished or replaced.

A maximum of 0.020 in. of material may be removed equally from each friction surface of the rotor. If the damage cannot be corrected when the rotor has been machined to the minimum thickness shown on the rotor (0.940 in.—floating caliper; 1.20 in.—sliding caliper), it should be replaced.

The finished braking surfaces of the rotor must be parallel within 0.007 in. and lateral

The labels on the diagram:
CALIPER PISTON HOUSING
PISTON BOOT
BRAKE SHOE AND LINING ASSEMBLIES
ANCHOR PLATE (CALIPER SUPPORT)
PISTON SEAL
PISTON
ANTI-RATTLE SPRING
CALIPER

← FORWARD

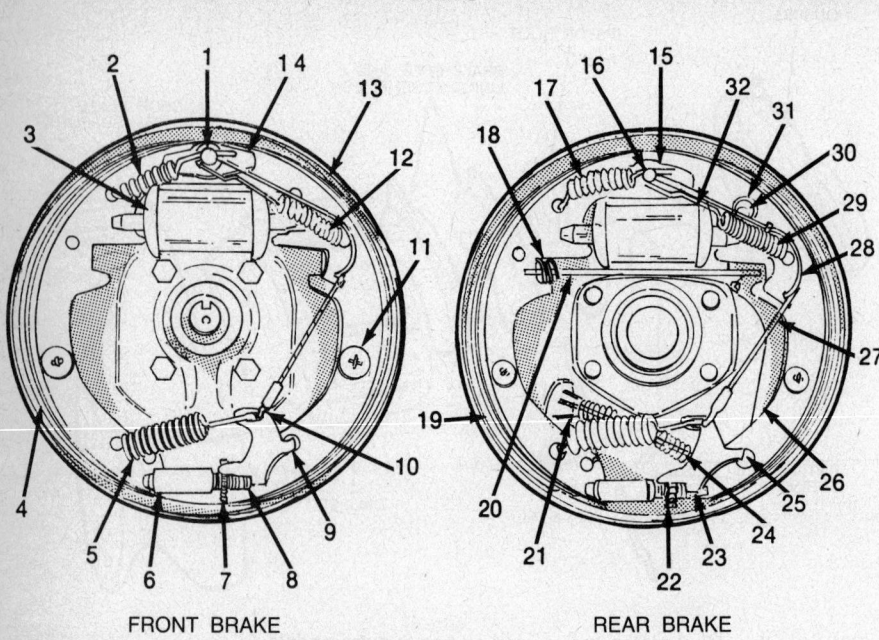

1. Anchor pin
2. Retracting spring
3. Brake cylinder
4. Primary shoe and lining
5. Automatic adjusting spring
6. Pivot nut
7. Adjusting screw
8. Socket
9. Pivot hook
10. Cable hook
11. Brake shoe hold-down spring
12. Retracting spring
13. Secondary shoe and lining
14. Anchor pin plate
15. Anchor pin plate
16. Anchor pin
17. Retracting spring
18. Parking brake link spring
19. Primary shoe and lining
20. Parking brake link
21. Parking brake cable housing retainer
22. Adjusting screw
23. Adjusting lever
24. Parking brake cable
25. Pivot hook
26. Parking brake lever
27. Cable
28. Cable guide
29. Retracting spring
30. Washer
31. Parking brake lever retaining clip
32. Brake cylinder

FRONT BRAKE   REAR BRAKE

Front and rear drum brake assemblies

run-out must not be more than 0.003 in. on the inboard surface in a 5 in. radius.

Brake Drums

REMOVAL AND INSTALLATION

Front—1975–77 Bronco

1. Raise the vehicle and install jackstands.

2. Back off the brake shoe adjustment. Remove the hub dust cap. Remove the hub retaining snap-ring, and slide the splined driving hub from between the axle shaft and the wheel hub. Remove the driving hub spacer and spring.

3. Remove the locknut, nut lock, and the wheel bearing adjusting nut from the spindle. Remove the wheel, hub and drum as an assembly. The wheel outer bearing will be forced off the spindle at the same time, so be prepared to catch it to prevent it from becoming dirty. Remove the wheel inner bearing cone.

NOTE: If the Bronco is equipped with locking-type hubs, refer to "Front Hub Assembly—Wheel Bearings" for the removal and installation procedure.

4. Remove the front wheel-to-hub retaining nuts. Remove the wheel and tire from the hub and drum.

5. Remove the brake drum retaining bolts and nuts.

6. Remove the brake drum from the hub.

To install the brake drum on the vehicle:

7. Place the brake drum to the hub and install the retaining bolts and nuts.

8. Install the wheel and tire to the hub and start the retaining nuts.

9. Install the wheel hub and drum assembly on the spindle. Install the driving hub spacer and then the wheel outer bearing cone and the adjusting nut with the dowel outboard.

10. Rotate the wheel in either direction and, at the same time, tighten the inner locknut to 50 ft. lbs. with a torque wrench.

11. Adjust the front wheel bearings.

12. Slide the driving hub onto the axle shaft and install the snap-ring.

13. Adjust the brake and then tighten the wheel nuts.

14. Install the hub dust cap.

15. Remove the jackstands and lower the vehicle.

Rear—Light Duty

1. Raise the vehicle so that the wheel to be worked on is clear of the floor and install jackstands under the vehicle.

2. Remove the hub cap and the wheel/tire assembly. Remove the 3 retaining nuts and remove the brake drum. It may be necessary to back off the brake shoe adjustment in order to remove the brake drum. This is because the drum might be grooved or worn from being in service for an extended period of time.

3. Before installing a new brake drum, be sure and remove any protective coating with carburetor degreaser.

4. Install the brake drum in the reverse order of removal and adjust the brakes.

F-250, F-350 Heavy-Duty
E-250, E-350 Heavy-Duty

1. Raise the vehicle and install jackstands.

2. Remove the wheel/tire assembly. Loosen the rear brake shoe adjustment.

3. Remove the rear axle retaining bolts and lockwashers, axle shaft, and gasket.

4. Remove the wheel bearing locknut, lockwasher, and adjusting nut.

5. Remove the hub and drum assembly from the axle.

6. Remove the brake drum-to-hub retaining screws, bolts, or bolts and nuts. Remove the brake drum from the hub.

To install the rear brake drum:

7. Place the drum on the hub and attach it to the hub with the attaching nuts and bolts.

8. Place the hub and drum assembly on the axle and start the adjusting nut.

9. Adjust the wheel bearing nut and install the wheel bearing lockwasher and locknut.

10. Install the axle shaft with a new gasket and install the axle retaining bolts and lockwashers.

11. Install the wheel/tire assembly and adjust the brake shoes. Remove the jackstands and lower the vehicle.

INSPECTION

After the brake drum has been removed from the vehicle, it should be inspected for runout, severe scoring, cracks, and the proper inside diameter.

Minor scores on a brake drum can be

removed with fine emery cloth, provided that all grit is removed from the drum before it is installed on the vehicle.

A badly scored, rough, or out-of-round (runout) drum can be ground or turned on a brake drum lathe. Do not remove any more material from the drum than is necessary to provide a smooth surface for the brake shoe to contact. The maximum diameter of the braking surface is shown on the inside of each brake drum. Brake drums that exceed the maximum braking surface diameter shown on the brake drum, either through wear or refinishing, must be replaced. This is because after the outside wall of the brake drum reaches a certain thickness (thinner than the original thickness) the drum loses its ability to dissipate the heat created by the friction between the brake drum and the brake shoes, when the brakes are applied. Also, the brake drum will have more tendency to warp and/or crack.

The maximum braking surface diameter specification, which is shown on each drum, allows for a 0.060 in. machining cut over the original nominal drum diameter plus 0.030 in. additional wear before reaching the diameter where the drum must be discarded. Use a brake drum micrometer to measure the inside diameter of the brake drums.

Brake Shoes

INSPECTION

Remove the brake drum and inspect the brake drum linings for wear or damage which could affect brake operation, i.e., severely cracked or chipped lining, grease or brake fluid soaked lining, or brake lining which is severely gouged or grooved due to the entrance of dirt or sand. Replace any brake lining observed as above or that is worn to within 1/32 in. of any rivet head or brake shoe.

REMOVAL AND INSTALLATION

F-100, F-150, F-250 Light-Duty E-100, E-150, E-250 Light-Duty Bronco

1. Raise and support the vehicle and remove the wheel and brake drum from the wheel to be worked on.

NOTE: If you have never replaced the brakes on a car before and you are not too familiar with the procedures involved, only disassemble and assemble one side at a time, leaving the other side intact as a reference during reassembly.

2. Install a clamp over the ends of the wheel cylinder to prevent the pistons of the wheel cylinder from coming out, causing loss of fluid and much grief.

3. Contract the brake shoes by pulling

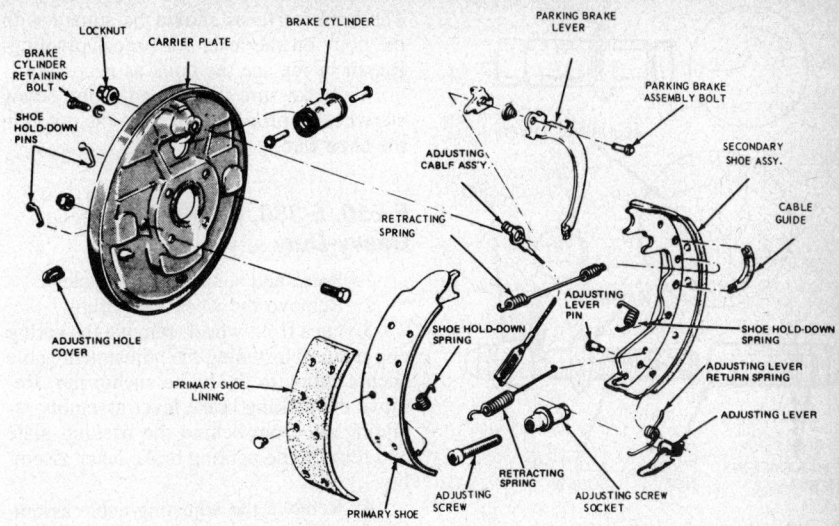

Pick-up and van heavy duty rear brake

the self-adjusting lever away from the starwheel adjustment screw and turn the starwheel up and back until the pivot nut is drawn onto the starwheel as far as it will come.

4. Pull the adjusting lever, cable and automatic adjuster spring down and toward the rear to unhook the pivot hook from the large hole in the secondary shoe web. Do not attempt to pry the pivot hook from the hole.

5. Remove the automatic adjuster spring and the adjusting lever.

6. Remove the secondary shoe-to-anchor spring with a brake tool. Brake tools are very common implements and are available at auto parts stores. Remove the primary shoe-to-anchor spring and unhook the cable anchor. Remove the anchor pin plate.

7. Remove the cable guide from the secondary shoe.

8. Remove the shoe hold-down springs, shoes, adjusting screw, pivot nut, and socket. Note the color of each hold-down spring for assembly. To remove the hold-down springs, reach behind the brake backing plate and place one finger on the end of one of the brake hold-down spring mounting pins. Using a pair of pliers, grasp the washer-type retainer on top of the hold-down spring that corresponds to the pin which you are holding. Push down on the pliers and turn them 90° to align the slot in the washer with the head on the spring mounting pin. Remove the spring and washer retainer and repeat this operation on the holddown spring on the other shoe.

9. Remove the parking brake link and spring. Disconnect the parking brake cable from the parking brake lever.

10. After removing the rear brake secondary shoe, disassemble the parking brake lever from the shoe by removing the retaining clip and spring washer.

To assemble and install the brake shoes:

11. On rear brakes, assemble the parking brake lever to the secondary shoe and

secure it with the spring washer and retaining clip.

12. Apply a *light* coating of Lubriplate® at the points where the brake shoes contact the backing plate.

13. Position the brake shoes on the backing plate, and install the hold-down spring pins, springs, and spring washer-type retainers. On the rear brake, install the parking brake link, spring and washer. Connect the parking brake cable to the parking brake lever.

14. Install the anchor pin plate, and place the cable anchor over the anchor pin with the crimped side toward the backing plate.

15. Install the primary shoe-to-anchor spring with the brake tool.

16. Install the cable guide on the secondary shoe web with the flanged holes fitted into the hole in the secondary shoe web. Thread the cable around the cable guide groove.

17. Install the secondary shoe-to-anchor (long) spring. Be sure that the cable end is not cocked or binding on the anchor pin when installed. All of the parts should be flat on the anchor pin. Remove the wheel cylinder piston clamp.

18. Apply Lubriplate® to the threads and the socket end of the adjusting starwheel screw. Turn the adjusting screw into the adjusting pivot nut to the limit of the threads and then back off 1/2 turn.

NOTE: Interchanging the brake shoe adjusting screw assemblies from one side of the vehicle to the other would cause the brake shoes to retract rather than expand each time the automatic adjusting mechanism operated. To prevent this, the socket end of the adjusting screw is stamped with an "R" or an "L" for RIGHT or LEFT. The adjusting pivot nuts can be distinguished by the number of lines machined around the body of the nut; one line indicates left-

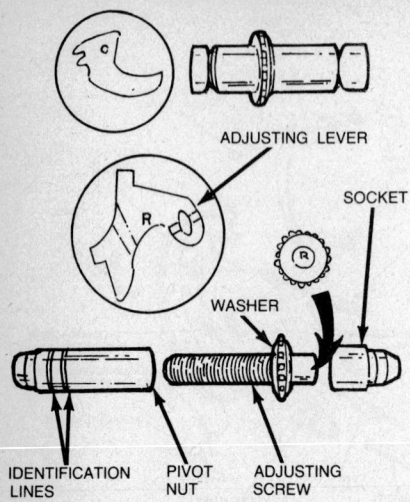

Identification of the adjusting screws and self-adjusting lever

hand nut and two lines indicates a right-hand nut.

19. Place the adjusting socket on the screw and install this assembly between the shoe ends with the adjusting screw nearest to the secondary shoe.

20. Place the cable hook into the hole in the adjusting lever from the backing plate side. The adjusting levers are stamped with an "R" (right) or an "L" (left) to indicate their installation on the right or left-hand brake assembly.

21. Position the hooked end of the adjuster spring in the primary shoe web and connect the loop end of the spring to the adjuster lever hole.

22. Pull the adjuster lever, cable and automatic adjuster spring down toward the rear to engage the pivot hook in the large hole in the secondary shoe web.

23. After installation, check the action of the adjuster by pulling the section of the cable between the cable guide and the adjusting lever toward the secondary shoe web far enough to lift the lever past a tooth on the adjusting screw starwheel. The lever should snap into position behind the next tooth, and release of the cable should cause the adjuster spring to return the lever to its original position. This return action of the lever will turn the adjusting screw starwheel one tooth. The lever should contact the adjusting screw starwheel one tooth above the centerline of the adjusting screw.

If the automatic adjusting mechanism does not perform properly, check the following:

1. Check the cable and fittings. The cable ends should fill or extend slightly beyond the crimped section of the fittings. If this is not the case, replace the cable.

2. Check the cable guide for damage. The cable groove should be parallel to the shoe web, and the body of the guide should lie flat against the web. Replace the cable guide if this is not so.

3. Check the pivot hook on the lever.

The hook surfaces should be square with the body on the lever for proper pivoting. Repair or replace the hook as necessary.

4. Make sure that the adjusting screw starwheel is properly seated in the notch in the shoe web.

E-250, E-350, F-250, F-350 Heavy-Duty

1. Raise and support the vehicle.
2. Remove the wheel and drum.
3. On a front wheel, remove the spring clip retainer fastening the adjustment cable anchor fitting to the brake anchor pin. Remove the parking brake lever assembly retaining nut from behind the backing plate and remove the parking brake lever assembly.
4. Remove the adjusting cable assembly from the anchor pin, cable guide, and adjusting lever.
5. Remove the brake shoe retracting springs.
6. Remove the brake shoe hold-down spring from each shoe.
7. Remove the brake shoes and adjusting screw assembly.
8. Disassemble the adjusting screw assembly.

To install the brake shoes:

9. Clean the ledge pads on the backing plate. Apply a light coat of Lubriplate® to the ledge pads (where the brake shoes rub the backing plate).
10. Apply Lubriplate® to the adjusting screw assembly and the hold-down and retracting spring contacts on the brake shoes.
11. Install the upper retracting spring on the primary and secondary shoes and position the shoe assembly on the backing plate with the wheel cylinder pushrods in the shoe slots.
12. Install the brake shoe hold-down springs.
13. Install the brake shoe adjustment screw assembly with the slot in the head of the adjusting screw toward the primary shoe, lower retracting spring, adjusting lever spring, adjusting lever assembly, and connect the adjusting cable to the adjusting lever. Position the cable in the cable guide and install the cable anchor fitting on the anchor pin.
14. Install the adjusting screw assemblies in the same locations from which they were removed. Interchanging the brake shoe adjusting screws from one side of the vehicle to the other will cause the brake shoes to retract rather than expand each time the automatic adjusting mechanism is operated. To prevent incorrect installation, the socket end of each adjusting screw is stamped with an R or an L to indicate their installation on the right or left-side of the vehicle. The adjusting pivot nuts can be distinguished by the number of lines machined around the body of the nut. Two lines indicate a right-hand nut; one line indicates a left-hand nut.
15. On a rear wheel, install the parking

brake assembly in the anchor pin and secure with the retaining nut behind the backing plate.

16. Adjust the brakes before installing the brake drums and wheels. Install the brake drums and wheels.

17. Lower the vehicle and road test the brakes. New brakes may pull to one side or the other before they are seated. Continued pulling or erratic braking should not occur.

Wheel Cylinders

OVERHAUL

Wheel cylinder rebuilding kits are available for reconditioning wheel cylinders. The kits usually contain new cup springs, cylinder cups, and in some, new boots. The most important factor to keep in mind when rebuilding wheel cylinders is cleanliness. Keep all dirt away from the wheel cylinders when you are reassembling them.

1. To remove the wheel cylinder, jack up the vehicle and remove the wheel, hub, and drum.
2. Disconnect the brake line at the fitting on the brake backing plate.
3. Remove the brake assemblies.
4. Remove the screws that hold the wheel cylinder to the backing plate and remove the wheel cylinder from the vehicle.
5. Remove the rubber dust covers on the ends of the cylinder. Remove the pistons and piston cups and the spring. Remove the bleeder screw and make sure that it is not plugged.
6. Discard all of the parts that the rebuilding kit will replace.
7. Examine the inside of the cylinder. If it is severely rusted, pitted or scratched, then the cylinder must be replaced as the piston cups won't be able to seal against the walls of the cylinder.
8. Using a wheel cylinder hone or emery cloth and crocus cloth, polish the inside of the cylinder. The purpose of this is to put a new surface on the inside of the cylinder. Keep the inside of the cylinder coated with brake fluid while honing.
9. Wash out the cylinder with clean brake fluid after honing.
10. When reassembling the cylinder, dip all of the parts in clean brake fluid. Assemble the wheel cylinder in the reverse order of removal and disassembly.

Parking Brake

ADJUSTMENT

1975–77

1. Raise the rear of the vehicle and support it on jackstands.
2. Depress the parking brake pedal 2 clicks.
3. Tighten the equalizer nut until both

rear wheels are firmly locked. The equalizer nut is the single nut at the yoke where the two rear cables attach.

4. Release the pedal. The rear wheels must turn freely.

5. Lower the vehicle.

1978–79

PRE-TENSION PROCEDURE

NOTE: These procedures require a special tool available at most good auto supply dealers or your Ford dealer. If the special tool is not available, the 1975–77 procedure will be good enough.

1. Depress the parking brake pedal until the parking brake control is in the second tooth (two notches or clicks).

2. Attach a Burroughs gauge, service tool no. BT-33-75 W2-25, or equivalent, to the LH rear cable and adjust the cable tension, registered on the gauge to 250 pounds, by tightening the equalizer nut. Hold for 5 minutes and release pedal.

3. Back off the equalizer nut until zero pounds of tension is registered on the gauge.

FINAL ADJUSTMENT

1. Position the parking brake pedal as outlined under pre-tension procedure.

2. Adjust the final tension to the mean 70 lbs. tension (50–90 lbs. specs) as registered on the Burroughs gauge by tightening the equalizer nut.

3. Remove the gauge and release the parking brake.

4. Check the clearance between the parking brake lever and the cam plate. The clearance should be 0.015 inch with the brakes fully released. If the clearance is not within specifications, readjust the parking brake cable.

5. Place the parking brake pedal in the fully released position, then check the slack in the parking brake two rear cables. The cables should be tight enough to provide full application of the rear brake shoes, when the parking brake lever or foot pedal is placed in the fully applied position, yet loose enough to ensure complete release of the brake shoes when the lever is in the released position.

1980–82

1. Make sure the brake drums are cold for correct adjustment.

2. Depress the parking brake pedal until the parking brake control is in the second tooth (two notches or two clicks).

3. Attach a Rotunda cable tension gauge (model 210018) or equivalent behind the equalizer assembly (either toward the right or left rear drum assembly).

4. Turn the equalizer adjusting nut until the tension reads 250 ft. lbs. as read on the cable tension gauge.

5. Back off the equalizer adjusting nut until the tension reads 50 ft. lbs. on the cable tension gauge.

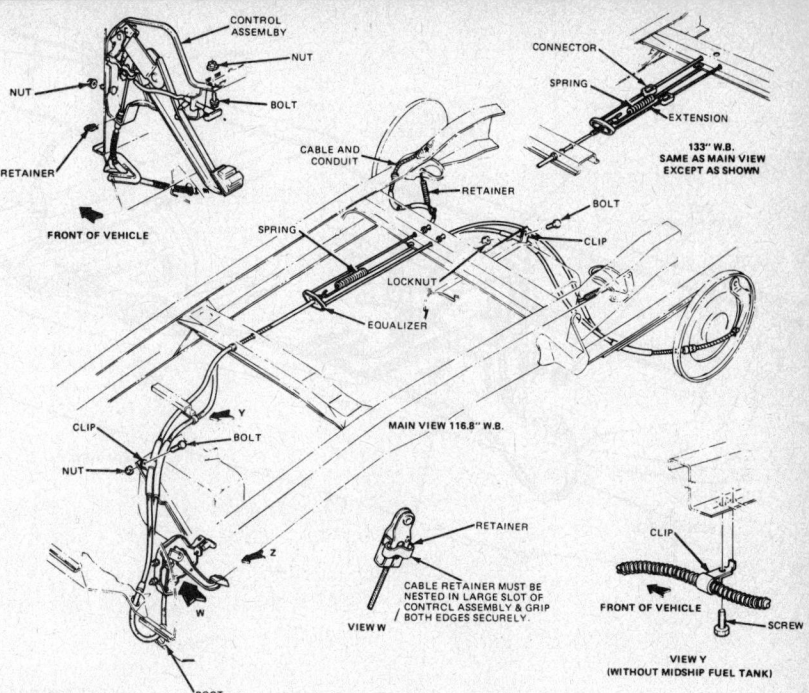

F-100, 150 2WD and 4WD parking brake cable routing

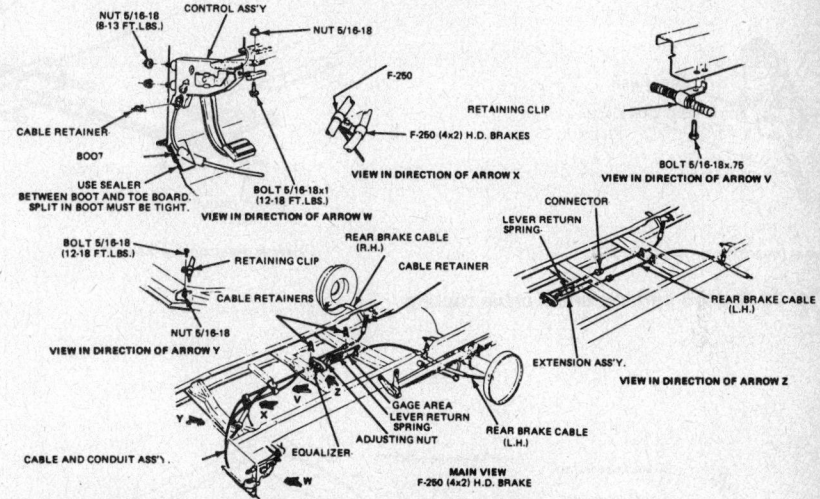

F-250, 350 2WD heavy duty parking brake cable routing

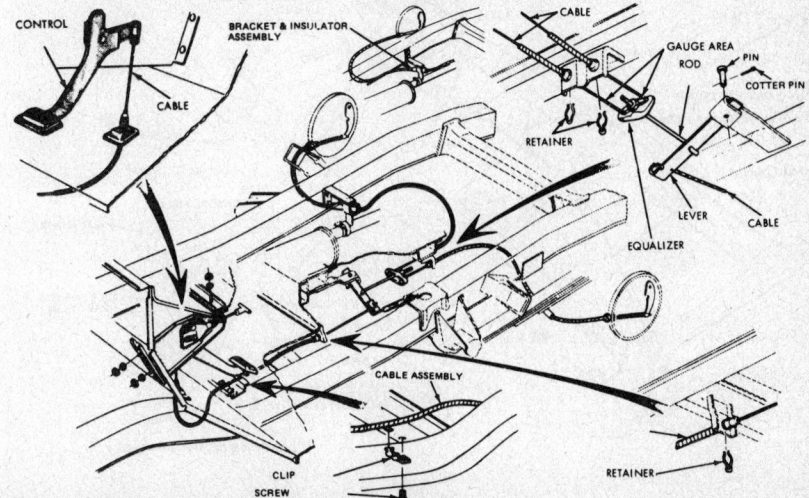

1975–77 Bronco parking brake cable routing

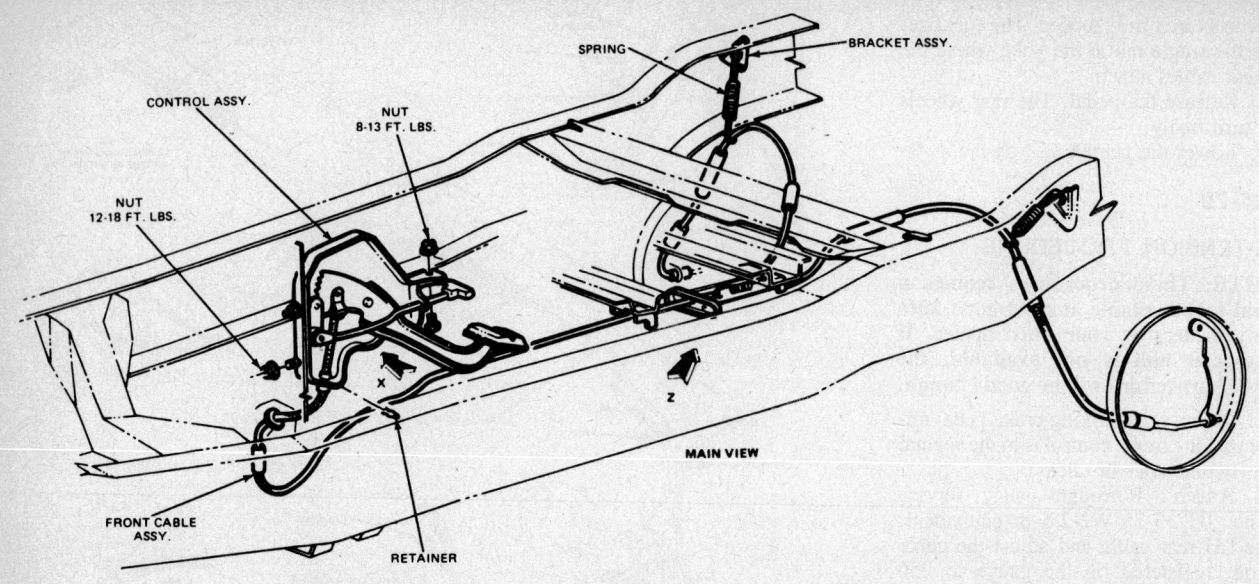

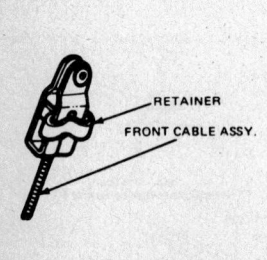

VIEW IN DIRECTION OF ARROW X

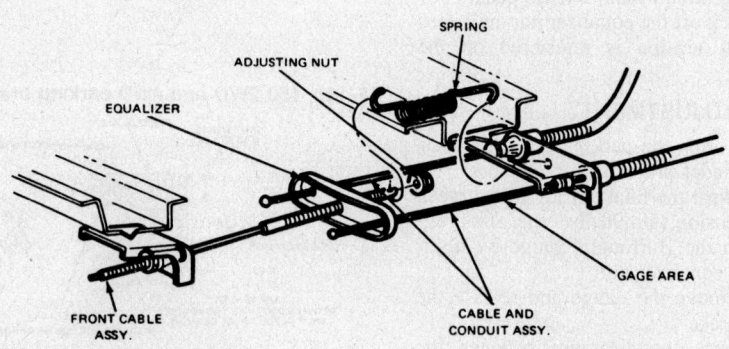

VIEW IN DIRECTION OF ARROW Z

1978–79 Bronco parking brake cable routing

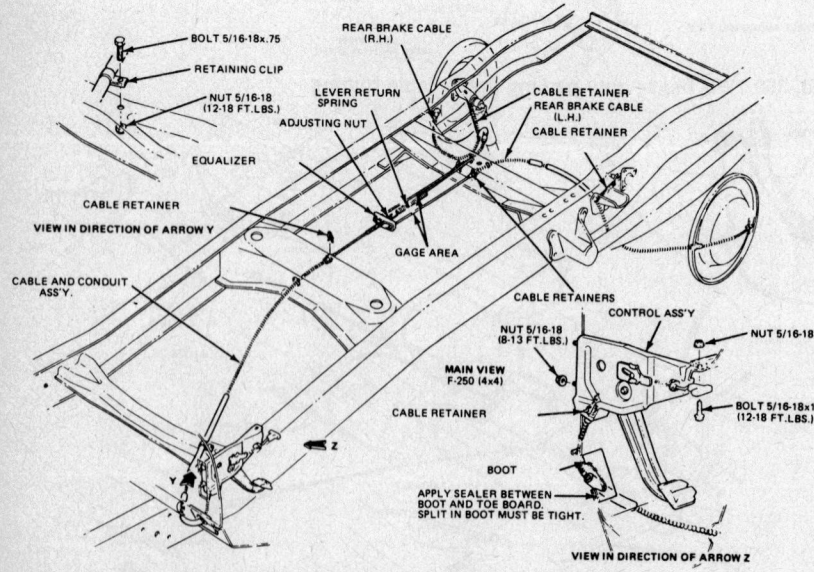

F-250 4WD parking brake cable routing

6. For the final adjustment, retighten the equalizer adjusting nut until the tension reads between 60–100 ft. lbs. as read on the cable tension gauge.

HEATER

Blower

REMOVAL AND INSTALLATION

1975–77 Bronco

1. Disconnect the electrical connectors and the ground wire from the top of the heater.

2. Remove the screws retaining the motor to the plenum chamber and remove the motor assembly.

3. Loosen the blower wheel allen screw and remove the wheel.

4. Remove the motor from the mounting plate.

5. Install the motor to the mounting plate.

6. Install the blower wheel.

7. Position the motor to the plenum

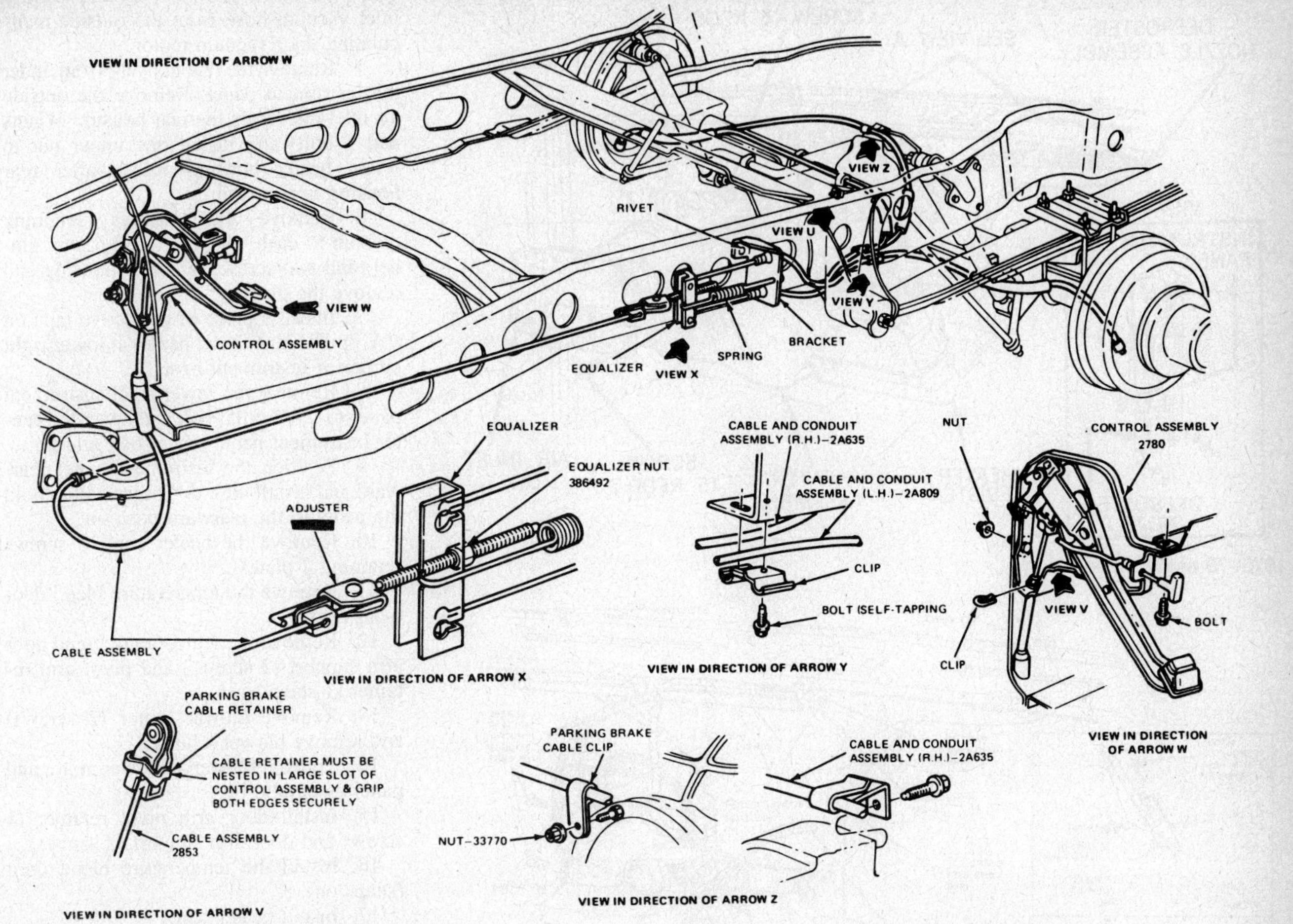

VIEW IN DIRECTION OF ARROW W
VIEW Z
RIVET
VIEW U
VIEW W
VIEW Y
CONTROL ASSEMBLY
BRACKET
SPRING
EQUALIZER
VIEW X
EQUALIZER
EQUALIZER NUT
386492
ADJUSTER
CABLE ASSEMBLY
VIEW IN DIRECTION OF ARROW X
CABLE AND CONDUIT
ASSEMBLY (R.H.)–2A635
CABLE AND CONDUIT
ASSEMBLY (L.H.)–2A809
CLIP
BOLT (SELF-TAPPING
VIEW IN DIRECTION OF ARROW Y
NUT
CONTROL ASSEMBLY
2780
VIEW V
BOLT
CLIP
VIEW IN DIRECTION
OF ARROW W
PARKING BRAKE
CABLE RETAINER
CABLE RETAINER MUST BE
NESTED IN LARGE SLOT OF
CONTROL ASSEMBLY & GRIP
BOTH EDGES SECURELY
CABLE ASSEMBLY
2853
VIEW IN DIRECTION OF ARROW V
PARKING BRAKE
CABLE CLIP
NUT–33770
CABLE AND CONDUIT
ASSEMBLY (R.H.)–2A635
VIEW IN DIRECTION OF ARROW Z

1980–82 Bronco parking brake cable routing

chamber. Install the retaining screws.

8. Connect the electrical lead and the ground wire.

9. Check the operation of the blower motor.

1975–82 Vans w/o Air Conditioning

1. Disconnect the orange motor lead wire. Remove the ground wire screw from the firewall.

2. Disconnect the blower motor cooling tube.

3. Remove the four mounting plate screws and the motor assembly.

4. Reverse the procedure for installation.

1975–82 Vans w/Air Conditioning

1. Disconnect the resistor electrical leads on the front of the blower cover inside the truck.

2. Remove the blower cover.

3. Push the wiring grommet forward out of the housing hole.

4. Remove the blower motor mounting plate. Remove the blower motor.

5. Reverse the procedure for installation.

WELD NUT
CONTROL ASSEMBLY
BOLT 1/4-20
NUT 5/16-18
VIEW A
CABLE
CLIP
SCREW 1/4-20
VIEW C
CONTROL ASSEMBLY
CABLE ASSEMBLY
NUT 5/16-18
CLIP
CABLE ASSEMBLY (R.H.)
CABLE
ASSEMBLY (L.H.)
RETAINER
SPRING
MAIN VIEW
138" AND 158"
WHEELBASE
EQUALIZER
SCREW 1/4-14
CABLE ASSEMBLY (R.H.)
NUT 5/16-24
VIEW B

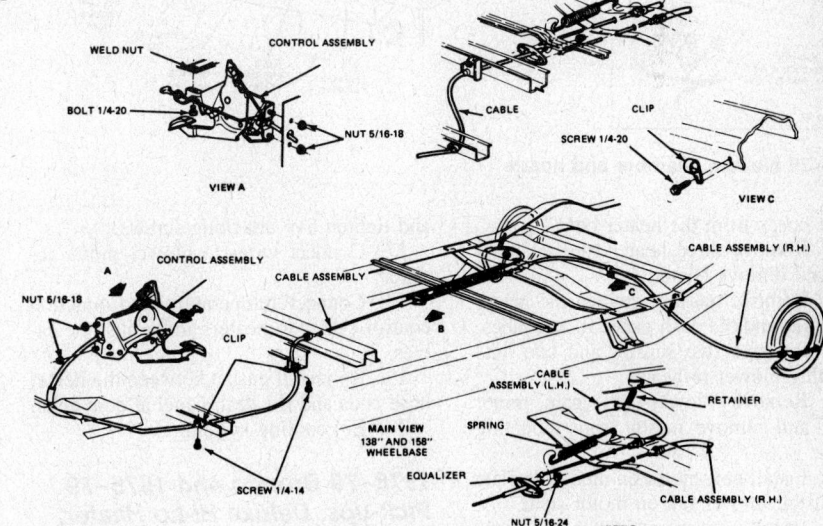

E-100 through 350 pedal operated parking brake cable routing

1978–79 Bronco and 1975–79 Pick-ups, Standard Heater, Without Air Conditioning

1. Disconnect the temperature and function control Bowden cables from the heater housing. This must be done to prevent damage to the cables.

2. Disconnect the wires from the blower resistor.

3. Remove five screws attaching the air inlet (vent) duct to the heater housing.

4. Disconnect the blower wires.

5. Drain the radiator and remove the

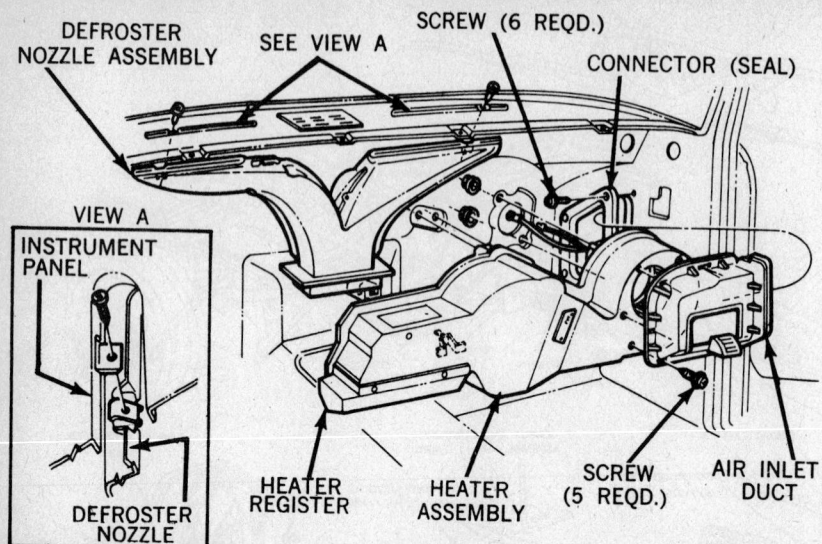

1975–79 heater installation

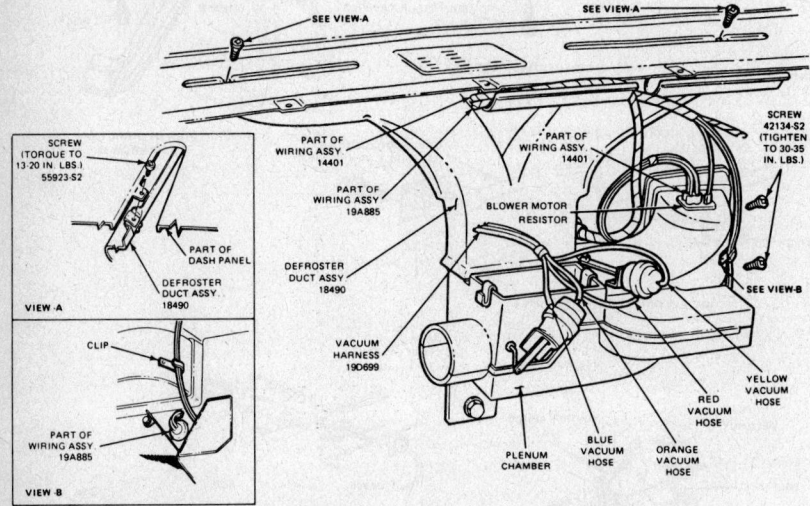

1978–79 plenum chamber and nozzle

heater hoses from the heater core.

6. Remove three heater stud retaining nuts and remove heater.

7. Remove gasket between the heater hose ends and the dash panel at core tubes.

8. Remove two screws and two nuts attaching blower to heater.

9. Remove blower fan from motor shaft, and remove motor from mounting plate.

10. Install new motor on mounting plate and install blower fan on motor shaft.

11. Install blower and motor in heater.

12. Position heater assembly in vehicle and install three stud retaining nuts.

13. Connect heater hoses to heater core and fill radiator.

14. Connect blower motor wires.

15. Place defroster nozzle on heater so that the defroster and heater openings are in the up position and there is no air leak around the seal.

16. Install air inlet (vent) duct to heater. Push duct firmly against seal on side cowl

and tighten five attaching screws.

17. Connect wires to blower motor resistor.

18. Connect temperature and function control cables to heater, and adjust the cables.

19. Re-install gasket between the heater hose ends and the dash panel at core ends.

20. Fill cooling system.

1978–79 Bronco and 1975–79 Pick-ups, Deluxe Hi-Lo Heater, Without Air Conditioning

1. Disconnect the battery cable, remove the carburetor air cleaner and partially drain the coolant system.

2. Remove the heater hoses from the heater core.

3. Remove the glove box liner and remove the register duct by pulling from the instrument panel register and releasing the clip at the plenum.

4. Disconnect the right cowl outside air

inlet vacuum hose from the outside-recirculating door vacuum motor.

5. Remove the rear housing from under the instrument panel. Remove the outside air inlet duct from the rear housing (4 nuts and 1 bolt) and install one upper nut to retain heater housing-to-dash after rear housing is removed.

6. Remove two screws retaining plenum-to-dash (above transmission tunnel) and two screws to heater housing and remove the plenum.

7. Install a piece of protective tape on ''A'' pillar inner cowl panel, at lower right corner of instrument panel.

8. Remove the lower right instrument panel-to-''A'' pillar bolt and lower the center instrument panel brace, bolt and nut.

9. Position the instrument panel rearward and install the ''A'' pillar bolt to hold the panel in the rearward position.

10. Remove the heater core (3 screws retaining 2 plates).

11. Remove the temperature blend door (snaps off).

12. Remove the temperature blend door arm support (2 screws) and pivot arm retainer (1 screw).

13. Remove blower motor (2 screws) and remove blower wheel.

14. Transfer blower to blower motor and panel assembly.

15. Install door arm pivot retainer (1 screw) and door arm support (2 screws).

16. Install the temperature blend door (snaps on).

17. Install heater core.

18. Install the plenum (4 screws).

19. Connect blower wires.

20. Remove heater housing upper retaining nut and install the heater outlet (4 nuts and 1 bolt). Position the air inlet duct.

21. Connect the white vacuum hose to the outside-recirculating door vacuum motor.

22. Reposition the instrument panel, install the retaining bolts and remove the protective tape at the ''A'' pillar inner cowl panel, lower right corner of instrument panel.

23. Install the right register duct assembly and install the glove box liner.

24. Connect heater hoses to the heater core assembly.

25. Fill cooling system, install the air cleaner and connect the battery cable to the battery.

26. Check blower motor operation.

1978–79 Bronco and 1975–79 Pick-ups With Air Conditioning

REMOVAL (WITHOUT DISCHARGING THE A/C SYSTEM)

1. Disconnect the battery cable, remove the carburetor air cleaner and partially drain the coolant system.

2. Remove the heater hoses from the heater core.

3. From under the hood, remove A/C hose support bracket from the cowl (one

screw).

4. Remove the insulation tape from the expansion valve and sensing bulb. Then remove the cover plate and seal from the evaporator housing at the expansion valve (two screws).

5. Remove the glove box liner and remove the A/C duct by pulling from the instrument panel register and releasing the clip at the plenum.

6. Disconnect the right cowl fresh air inlet vacuum hose from the fresh air door vacuum motor.

7. Remove the evaporator rear housing from under the instrument panel. Then, remove the fresh air inlet tube from the evaporator rear housing (4 nuts and 1 bolt) and install one upper nut to retain evaporator housing-to-dash after rear housing is removed.

8. Disconnect wires from the de-icing switch and pull capillary tube out of evaporator core. Remove the de-icing switch mounting plate (four screws).

9. Remove two screws retaining plenum-to-dash (above transmission tunnel) and two screws to evaporator case and remove the plenum.

10. Install a piece of protective tape on "A" pillar inner cowl panel, at lower right corner of instrument panel.

11. Then, remove the lower right instrument panel-to-"A" pillar bolt and lower the center instrument panel brace, bolt and nut.

12. Position the instrument panel rearward and install the "A" pillar bolt to hold the panel in the rearward position.

13. Remove four evaporator retaining screws.

14. Position the evaporator away from the case and secure it rearward and upward. Remove evaporator sealing grommet.

15. Remove heater core (3 screws retaining 2 plates).

16. Remove A/C-heat door (snaps off).

17. Remove A/C-heat door arm support (2 screws) and pivot arm retainer (1 screw).

18. Remove blower motor (2 screws) and remove blower wheel.

INSTALLATION

1. Transfer blower wheel to blower motor and panel assembly.

2. Install door arm pivot retainer (1 screw) and door arm support (2 screws).

3. Install A/C-heat door (snaps on).

4. Install heater core.

5. Remove the retainer that held the evaporator away from the case, install evaporator and tube sealing grommet.

6. Install the plenum (4 screws).

7. Install the de-icing switch mounting plate, install de-icing switch capillary tube back into evaporator core and position blower wire grommet.

8. Connect blower and de-icing switch wires.

9. Remove upper evaporator case retaining nut and install the evaporator outlet (4 nuts and 1 bolt). Then, position the air

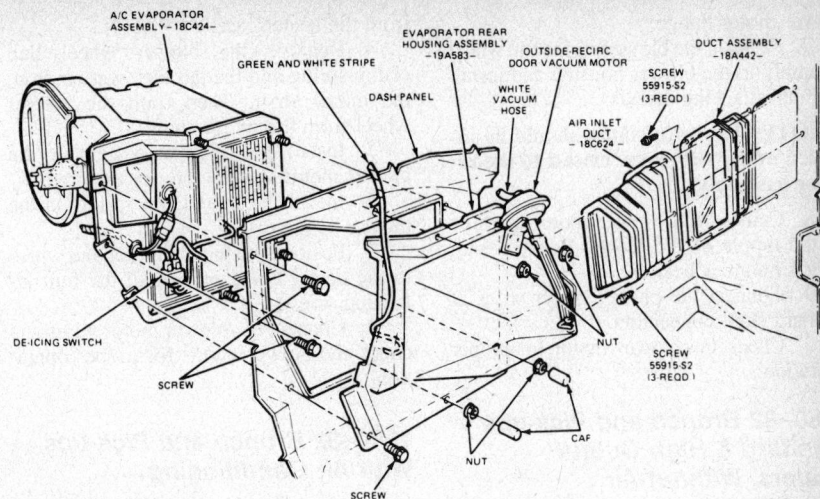

1978–79 evaporator rear housing

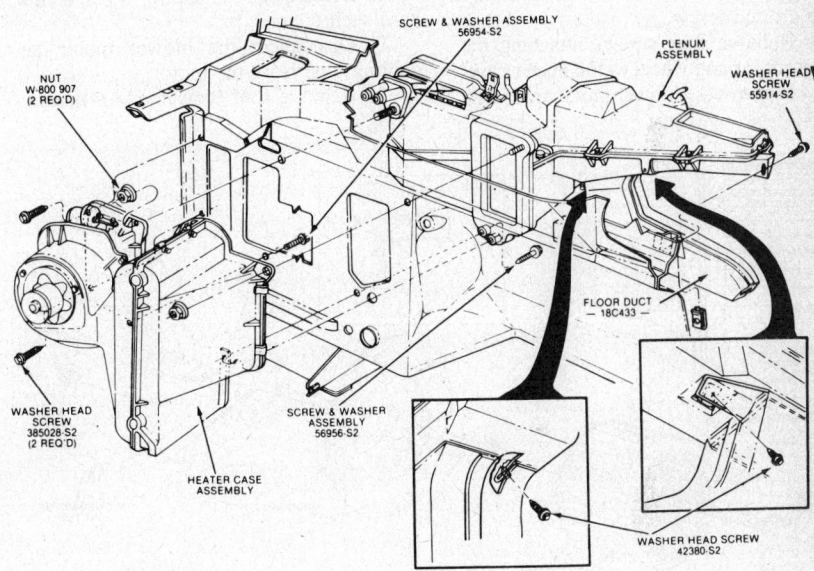

1980–82 heater case and plenum

inlet bellows.

10. Connect the right cowl fresh air inlet vacuum hose to the fresh air door vacuum motor.

11. Reposition the instrument panel, install the retaining bolts and remove the protective tape at the "A" pillar inner cowl panel, lower right corner of instrument panel.

12. Install the right A/C duct assembly and install the glove box liner.

13. Install seal and cover plate to the evaporator case at the expansion valve.

14. Install insulation tape over the expansion valve and sensing bulb.

15. Install the A/C hose support bracket-to-cowl.

16. Connect heater hoses to the heater core assembly.

17. Fill cooling system, install the carburetor air cleaner and connect the battery cable to the battery.

18. Check blower motor operation.

1980–82 Bronco and Pick-ups, Comfort Vent Heaters, Without Air Conditioning

1. Disconnect the motor wires at the hard shell connectors.

2. Disconnect the blower motor air cooling tube from the motor.

3. Remove four blower motor mounting plate attaching screws and remove the motor and wheel assembly from the blower housing.

4. Remove the hub clamp spring from the blower wheel hub and the retainer from the motor shaft. Then, remove the blower wheel from the motor shaft.

5. Position the blower wheel on the blower motor shaft. Then, install a new hub clamp spring on the blower hub as shown. The hub clamp spring is included with a new blower wheel but not with the blower motor.

6. Install a new flange gasket on the

blower motor flange.

7. Position the blower motor and wheel assembly in the blower housing and install the four attaching screws.

NOTE: The wire clamp should be installed under the screw closest to the resistor assembly.

8. Cement the blower motor air tube on the nipple of the blower housing with RTV silicone adhesive.

9. Connect the blower motor wires at the hard shell connectors.

10. Check the blower motor for proper operation.

1980–82 Bronco and Pick-ups Standard & High Output Heaters, Without Air Conditioning

1. Disconnect the motor wire at the hard shell connector and the ground wire at the ground screw.

2. Remove four screws attaching the blower motor and wheel to the heater case.

3. Remove the blower motor and wheel

from the heater case.

4. Remove the blower wheel hub clamp spring and the tab lock washer from the motor shaft. Then, pull the blower wheel from the motor shaft.

5. Install the blower wheel on the blower motor shaft.

6. Install the hub clamp spring on the blower hub.

7. Position the blower motor and wheel to the heater case, and install the four attaching screws.

8. Connect the blower motor wires and check the blower motor for proper operation.

1980–82 Bronco and Pick-ups With Air Conditioning

REMOVAL (WITHOUT DISCHARGING THE A/C SYSTEM)

1. Disconnect the motor wires at the hard shell connectors.

2. Disconnect the blower motor air cooling tube from the motor.

3. Remove four blower motor mount-

ing plate attaching screws and remove the motor and wheel assembly from the blower housing.

4. Remove the hub clamp spring from the blower wheel hub and the retainer from the motor shaft. Then, remove the blower wheel from the motor shaft.

INSTALLATION

1. Position the blower wheel on the blower motor shaft to the dimension shown. Then, install a new hub clamp spring on the blower hub as shown. The hub clamp spring is included with a new blower wheel but not with the blower motor.

2. Install a new flange gasket on the blower motor flange.

3. Position the blower motor and wheel assembly in the blower housing and install the four attaching screws.

NOTE: The wire clamp should be installed under the screw closest to the resistor assembly.

4. Cement the blower motor air tube on the nipple of the blower housing with RTV silicone adhesive.

5. Connect the blower motor wires at the hard shell connectors.

6. Check the blower motor for proper operation.

Heater Core

REMOVAL AND INSTALLATION

1975–77 Bronco

1. Drain the cooling system.

2. Disconnect the two heater hoses at the heater and remove the rubber pads from the core.

3. Remove the nuts and star washers retaining the heater assembly to the dash panel.

4. Disconnect the right and left defroster hoses at the plenum.

5. Disconnect the fresh air inlet at the cowl. Rest the heater on the floor.

6. Disconnect the heat/defrost door cable at the door crank arm.

7. Disconnect the outside air door cable at the crank arm.

8. Disconnect the electrical wires at the connector.

9. Remove the heater assembly from the vehicle.

10. Remove the screws retaining the rear cover. Remove the clip retaining the core in the case and remove the core.

11. Transfer the seals from the old heater core to the new heater core.

12. Position the core in the case. Install the retaining clip. Position the cover and install the retaining screws.

13. Position the heater assembly on the floor in the vehicle. Connect the wire connectors.

14. Connect and adjust the outside air door control cable.

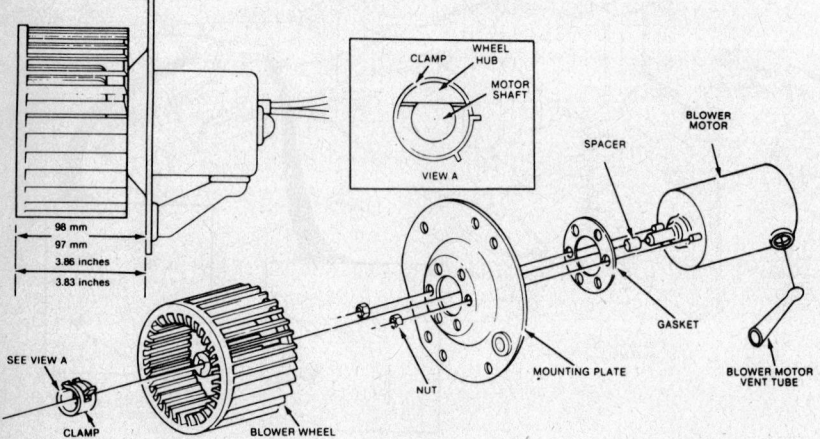

1980–82 blower motor and wheel without A/C

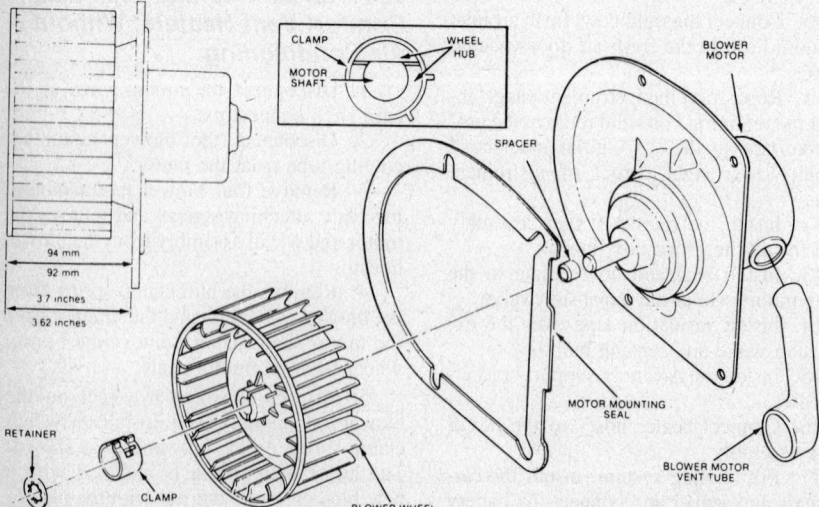

1980–82 blower motor and wheel with A/C

15. Connect and adjust the heat/defrost door control cable.

16. Position the heater assembly to the dash and install the nuts and washers.

17. Position the heater core pads over the core and connect both hoses.

18. Connect the defroster hoses and fresh air intake.

19. Fill the cooling system with the proper coolant mixture.

20. Check the heater operation and check for leaks.

1975–82 Vans Without Air Conditioning

1. Drain the coolant; remove the battery.

2. Disconnect the resistor wiring harness and the orange blower motor lead. Remove the ground wire screw from the firewall.

3. Detach the heater hoses and the plastic hose retaining strap.

4. Remove the five mounting screws inside the truck.

5. Remove the heater assembly.

6. Cut the seal at the top and bottom edge of the core retainer. Remove the two screws and the retainer. Slide the core and seal out of the case.

7. Reverse the procedure for installation.

1975–82 Vans With Air Conditioning

1. Disconnect the resistor electrical leads on the front of the blower cover inside the truck. Detach the vacuum line from the vacuum motor. Remove the blower cover.

2. Remove the nut and push washer from the air door shaft. Remove the control cable from the bracket and the air door shaft.

3. Remove the blower motor housing and the air door housing.

4. Drain the coolant and detach the heater hoses.

5. Remove the heater core retaining brackets. Remove the core and seal assembly.

6. Reverse the procedure for installation.

1978–79 Bronco and 1975–79 Pick-ups Without Air Conditioning

1. Disconnect the temperature and function control Bowden cables from the heater housing. This must be done to prevent damage to the cables.

2. Disconnect the wires from the blower resistor.

3. Remove five screws attaching the air inlet (vent) duct to the heater housing.

4. Disconnect the blower wires.

5. Drain the radiator and remove the heater hoses from the heater core.

6. Remove three heater stud retaining nuts and remove heater.

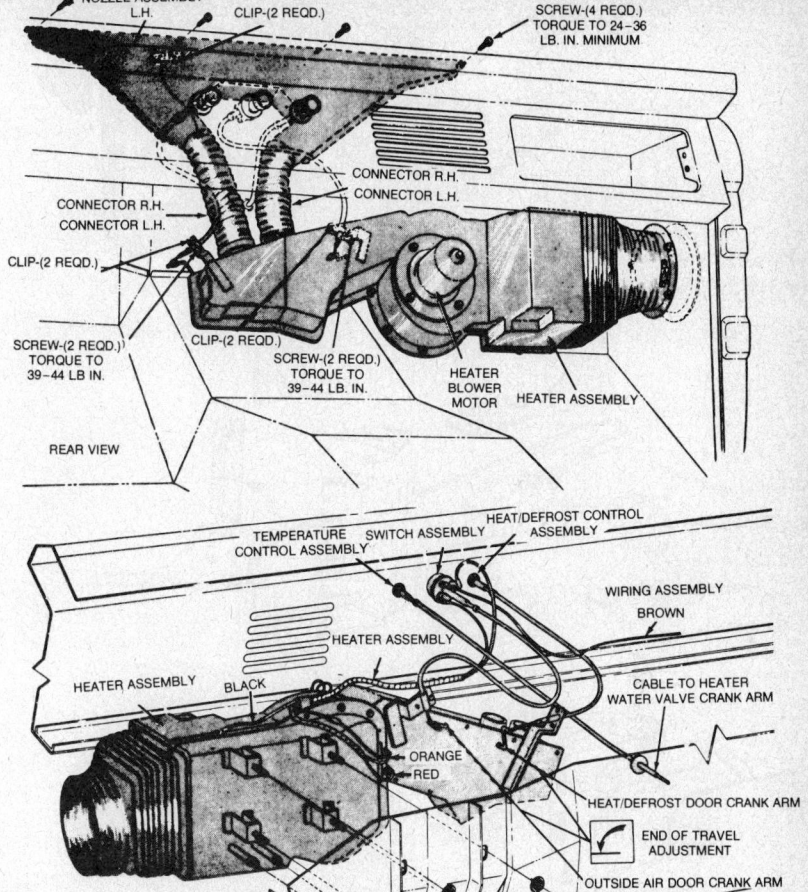

1975–77 Bronco heater

7. Remove gasket between the heater hose ends and the dash panel at core tubes.

8. Remove heater core cover and gasket (four screws).

9. Pull heater core and lower support from heater.

10. Install foam gaskets on heater core and install in heater assembly.

11. Install the core seal and cover plate.

12. Position heater assembly in vehicle and install three stud retaining nuts.

13. Connect heater hoses to heater core and fill radiator.

14. Connect blower motor wires.

15. Place defroster nozzle on heater so that the defroster and heater openings are in the up position and there is no air leak around the seal.

16. Install air inlet (vent) duct to heater. Push duct firmly against seal on side cowl and tighten five attaching screws.

17. Connect wires to blower motor resistor.

18. Connect temperature and function control cables to heater, and adjust the cables.

19. Re-install gasket between the heater

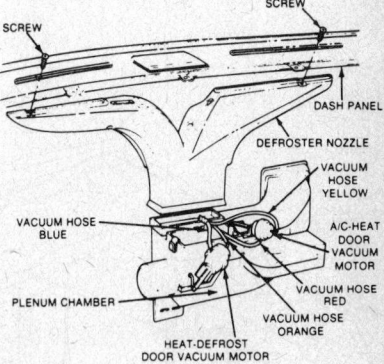

1978–79 A/C-heater control connections

hose ends and the dash panel at core ends.

20. Fill Cooling System.

1978–79 Bronco and 1975–79 Pick-Ups, Deluxe Hi-Lo Heater, Without Air Conditioning

1. Disconnect the battery cable, remove the carburetor air cleaner and partially drain the coolant system.

2. Remove the heater hoses from the

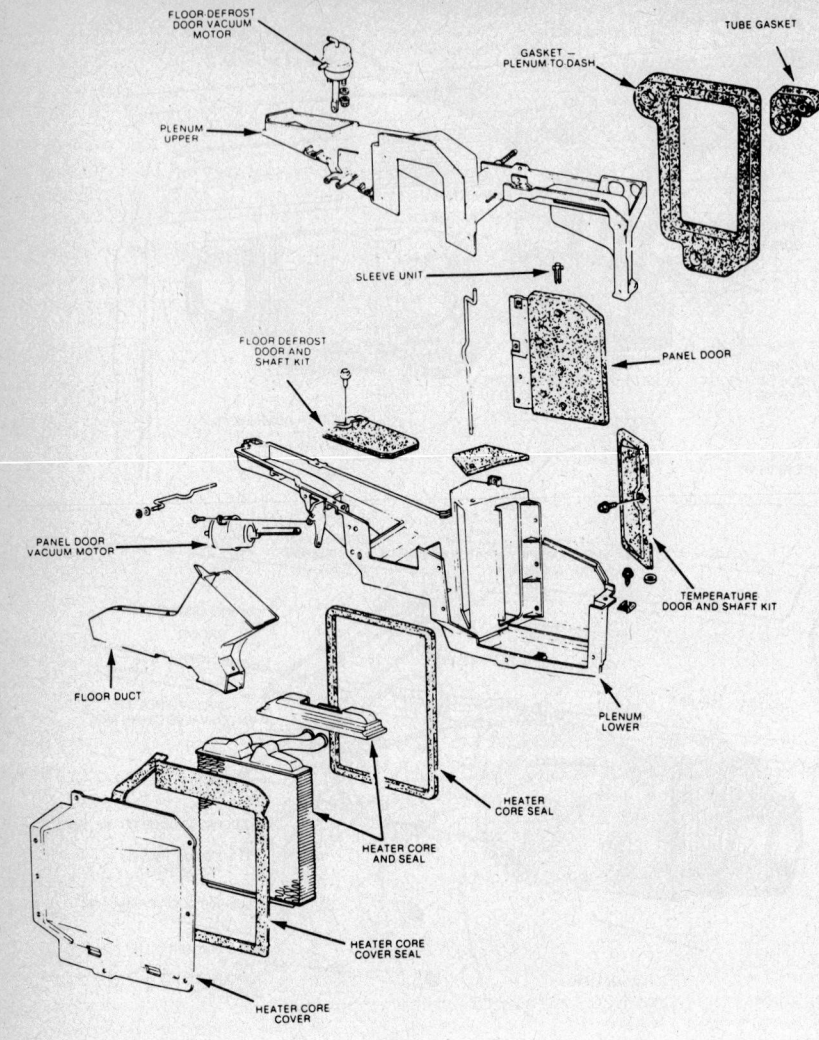

1980–82 comfort control heater plenum

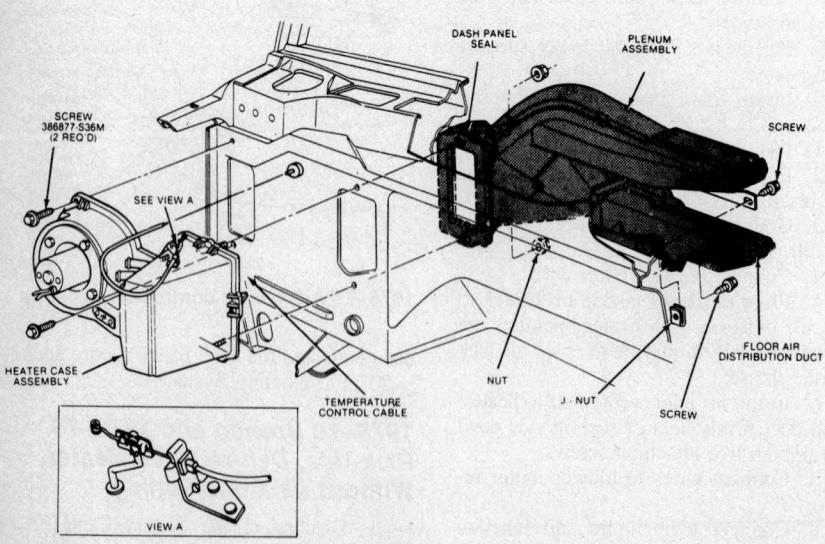

Heater case and plenum assemblies on 1980 and later standard and high output units without A/C

heater core.

3. Remove the glove box liner and re-move the register duct by pulling from the instrument panel register and releasing the clip at the plenum.

4. Disconnect the right cowl outside air inlet vacuum hose from the outside-recir-culating door vacuum motor.

5. Remove the rear housing from under the instrument panel. Remove the outside air inlet duct from the rear housing (4 nuts and 1 bolt) and install one upper nut to retain heater housing-to-dash after rear housing is removed.

6. Remove two screws retaining plenum-to-dash (above transmission tun-nel) and two screws to heater housing and remove the plenum.

7. Install a piece of protective tape on "A" pillar inner cowl panel, at lower right corner of instrument panel.

8. Remove the lower right instrument panel-to-"A" pillar bolt and lower the cen-ter instrument panel brace, bolt and nut.

9. Position the instrument panel rear-ward and install the "A" pillar bolt to hold the panel in the rearward position.

10. Remove heater core (3 screws re-taining 2 plates).

11. Remove the temperature blend door (snaps off).

12. Remove the temperature blend door arm support (2 screws) and pivot arm re-tainer (1 screw).

13. Remove blower motor (2 screws) and remove blower wheel.

14. Transfer blower wheel to blower motor and panel assembly.

15. Install door arm pivot retainer (1 screw) and door arm support (2 screws).

16. Install the temperature blend door (snaps on).

17. Install heater core.

18. Install the plenum (4 screws).

19. Connect blower wires.

20. Remove heater housing upper re-taining nut and install the heater outlet (4 nuts and 1 bolt). Position the air inlet duct.

21. Connect the white vacuum hose to the outside-recirculating door vacuum mo-tor.

22. Reposition the instrument panel, in-stall the retaining bolts and remove the pro-tective tape at the "A" pillar inner cowl panel, lower right corner of instrument panel.

23. Install the right register duct assem-bly and install the glove box liner.

24. Connect heater hoses to the heater core assembly.

25. Fill cooling system, install the air cleaner and connect the battery cable to the battery.

26. Check bower motor operation.

1978–79 Bronco and 1975–79 Pick-ups With Air Conditioning

REMOVAL (WITHOUT DISCHARGING A/C SYSTEM)

1. Disconnect the battery cable, re-

move the carburetor air cleaner and partially drain the coolant system.

2. Remove the heater hoses from the heater core.

3. From under the hood, remove A/C hose support bracket from the cowl (one screw).

4. Remove the insulation tape from the expansion valve and sensing bulb. Then remove the cover plate and seal from the evaporator housing at the expansion valve (two screws).

5. Remove the glove box liner and remove the A/C duct by pulling from the instrument panel register and releasing the clip at the plenum.

6. Disconnect the right cowl fresh air inlet vacuum hose from the fresh air door vacuum motor.

7. Remove the evaporator rear housing from under the instrument panel. Then, remove the fresh air inlet tube from the evaporator rear housing (4 nuts and 1 bolt) and install one upper nut to retain evaporator housing-to-dash after rear housing is removed.

8. Disconnect wires from the de-icing switch and pull capillary tube out of evaporator core. Remove the de-icing switch mounting plate (four screws).

9. Remove two screws retaining plenum-to-dash (above transmission tunnel) and two screws to evaporator case and remove the plenum.

10. Install a piece of protective tape on "A" pillar inner cowl panel, at lower right corner of instrument panel.

11. Then, remove the lower right instrument panel-to-"A" pillar bolt and lower the center instrument panel brace, bolt and nut.

12. Position the instrument panel and rearward and install the "A" pillar bolt to hold the panel in the rearward position.

13. Remove four evaporator retaining screws.

14. Position the evaporator away from the case and secure it rearward and upward. Remove evaporator sealing grommet.

15. Remove heater core (3 screws retaining 2 plates).

16. Remove A/C-heat door (snaps off).

17. Remove A/C-heat door arm support (2 screws) and pivot arm retainer (1 screw).

INSTALLATION

1. Install door arm pivot retainer (1 screw) and door arm support (2 screws).

2. Install A/C-heat door (snaps on).

3. Install heater core.

4. Remove the retainer that held the evaporator away from the case, install evaporator and tube sealing grommet.

5. Install the plenum (4 screws).

6. Install the de-icing switch mounting plate, install de-icing switch capillary tube back into evaporator core and position blower wire grommet.

7. Connect blower and de-icing switch wires.

8. Remove upper evaporator case re-

taining nut and install the evaporator outlet (4 nuts and 1 bolt). Then, position the air inlet bellows.

9. Connect the right cowl fresh air inlet vacuum hose to the fresh air door vacuum motor.

10. Reposition the instrument panel, install the retaining bolts and remove the protective tape at the "A" pillar inner cowl panel, lower right corner of instrument panel.

11. Install the right A/C duct assembly and install the glove box liner.

12. Install seal and cover plate to the evaporator case at the expansion valve.

13. Install insulation tape over the expansion valve and sensing bulb.

14. Install the A/C hose support bracket-to-cowl.

15. Connect heater hoses to the heater core assembly.

16. Fill cooling system, install the carburetor air cleaner and connect the battery cable to the battery.

17. Check blower motor operation.

1980–82 Bronco and Pick-ups, Comfort Vent Heaters, Without Air Conditioning

1. Disconnect the heater hoses from the heater core tubes and plug the hoses with suitable ⅝ inch plugs.

2. Remove the glove compartment liner.

3. Remove two spring clips attaching the heater core cover to the plenum along the top edge of the heater core cover.

4. Remove eight screws attaching the heater core cover to the penum and remove the cover.

5. Remove the heater core from the plenum taking care not to spill coolant from the core.

6. Install the heater core in the planum.

7. Install the heater core cover (eight (8) screws and two spring clips along the top edge of the cover).

8. Install the glove compartment liner.

9. Connect the heater hoses to the heater core. Tighten the hose clamps.

10. Add coolant to raise the coolant level to specification.

11. Check the system for proper operation and for coolant leaks.

1980–82 Bronco and Pick-ups, Standard & High Output Heaters, Without Air Conditioning

1. Disconnect the temperature cable from the temperature blend door and the mounting bracket on top of the heater case.

2. Disconnect the wires from the blower motor resistor and the blower motor.

3. Disconnect the heater hoses from the heater core and plug the hoses with suitable ⅝ inch plugs.

4. Working under the instrument panel, remove two nuts retaining the left

end of the heater case and the right end of the plenum to the dash panel.

5. In the engine compartment, remove one screw attaching the top center of the heater case to the dash panel.

6. Remove two screws attaching the right end of the heater case to the dash panel, and remove the heater case from the vehicle.

7. Remove nine screws and one (1) bolt and nut attaching the heater housing plate to the heater case, and remove the heater housing plate.

8. Remove three screws attaching the heater core frame to the heater case and remove the frame.

9. Remove the heater core and seal from the heater case.

10. Position the heater core and seal in the heater case.

11. Install the heater core frame (3 screws).

12. Position the heater housing plate on the heater case and install the nine screws and one bolt and nut.

13. Position the heater case to the dash panel and install the three attaching screws.

14. Working in the passenger compartment, install two nuts to retain the heater case and plenum right end to the dash panel.

15. Connect the heater hoses to the heater core. Tighten the hose clamps.

16. Connect the wires to the blower motor resistor assembly.

17. Connect the blower motor wires.

18. Position (slide) the self-adjusting clip on the temperature cable to a position approximately one inch from the cable end loop.

19. Snap the temperature cable on the cable mounting bracket of the heater case. Then, position the self-adjusting clip on the door crank arm.

20. Adjust the temperature cable.

21. Check the system for proper operation.

1980–82 Bronco and Pick-ups With Air Conditioning

REMOVAL (WITHOUT DISCHARGING THE A/C SYSTEM)

1. Disconnect the heater hoses from the heater core tubes and plug the hoses with suitable ⅝ inch plugs.

2. Remove the glove compartment liner.

3. Remove eight screws attaching the heater core cover to the plenum and remove the cover.

4. Remove the heater core from the plenum taking care not to spill coolant from the core.

INSTALLATION

1. Install the heater core in the plenum.

2. Install the heater core cover (eight screws).

3. Install the glove compartment liner.

4. Connect the heater hoses to the heater core. Tighten the hose clamps.

5. Add coolant to raise the coolant level to specification.

Auxiliary Heater Case (With or Without A/C)

1975–82 VANS

Removal and Installation

1. Remove the first bench seat (if so equipped).

2. Remove the auxiliary heater and/or air conditioning cover assembly attaching screws and remove the cover.

3. Position the cover assembly to the body side panel and install the attaching screws.

4. Install the bench seat (if removed) and tighten the retaining bolts 25–45 ft. lbs.

Auxiliary Heater Core and Seal Assembly

1975–82 VANS

Removal and Installation

1. Remove the first bench seat (if so equipped).

2. Remove auxiliary heater and/or air conditioning cover attaching screws (15) and remove the cover.

3. Partially drain the engine coolant from the coolant system.

4. Remove the heater hoses from the auxiliary heater core assembly (2 clamps).

5. Pull the wiring assembly away from the heater core seal.

6. Slide the heater core and seal assembly out of the housing slot.

7. Slide the heater core and seal assembly into the housing slot (position the wiring to one side).

8. Install the heater hoses to the heater core assembly (2 clamps).

9. Fill the cooling system to specification.

10. Position the cover assembly to the body side panel and install the attaching screws (15).

11. Install the bench seat (if removed) and tighten the retaining bolts 25–45 ft. lbs.

RADIO

REMOVAL AND INSTALLATION

1975–77 Bronco

1. Disconnect the radio lead wire at the receptacle on the fuse panel.

2. Disconnect the speaker leads at the receptacle on the underside of the radio chassis.

3. Disconnect the antenna lead at the receptacle on the right side of the radio chassis.

4. Remove (pull) the volume control and the manual tuning control knobs from the shafts.

5. Remove the screws that retain the dial assembly to the instrument panel and remove the dial assembly.

6. Remove the retaining nuts and the retaining plate that secure the radio to the instrument panel.

7. Remove the radio bottom support bracket retaining screw and remove the radio assembly from the instrument panel.

To install the radio:

8. Position the radio to the inner side of the instrument panel, and install the right and left support bracket to the radio retaining nuts.

9. Position the retaining plate to the outer side of the instrument panel over the pilot light and control shafts, and install the retaining nuts.

10. Position the dial assembly, install the retaining screw and seat the knobs on the control shafts.

11. Connect the speaker leads, the antenna lead, and the radio power lead wire at the fuse panel.

12. Calibrate the dial pointer with the tuner by rotating the tuning knob until the dial pointer reaches the end of its travel at the right side of the dial.

13. Check the operation of the radio and adjust the antenna trimmer.

1975–82 Vans

1. Detach the battery ground cable.

2. Remove the heater and A/C control knobs. Remove the lighter.

3. Remove the radio knobs and discs.

4. If the truck has a lighter, snap out the name plate at the right side to remove the panel attaching screw.

5. Remove the five finish panel screws.

6. Very carefully pry out the cluster panel in two places.

7. Detach the antenna lead and speaker wires.

8. Remove the two nuts and washers and the mounting plate.

9. Remove the four front radio attaching screws. Remove the rear support nut and washer, and remove the radio.

10. Reverse the procedure for installation.

1978–82 Bronco, 1975–82 Pick-ups

1. Disconnect the battery ground cable.

2. On 1975–79 models, remove the ash tray and bracket.

3. Disconnect the antenna, speakers and radio lead.

4. Remove the bolt attaching the radio rear support to the lower edge of the instrument panel.

5. On 1975–78 models equipped with air conditioning, disconnect the left A/C duct hose from the A/C plenum.

6. Remove the knobs and discs from the radio control shafts.

7. Remove the retaining nuts from the control shafts and remove the bezel.

8. Remove the nuts and washers from the control shafts and remove the radio from the panel.

9. Installation is the reverse of removal.

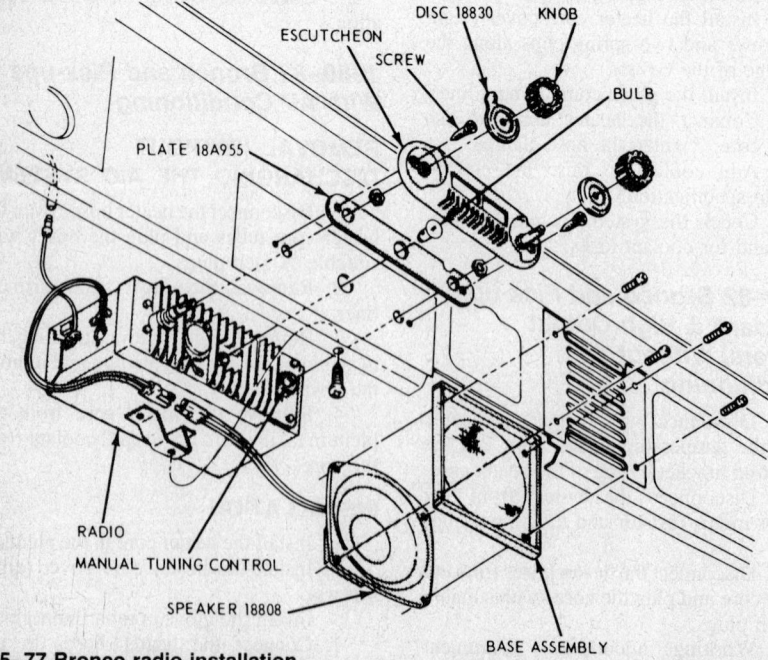

DISC 18830   KNOB
ESCUTCHEON
SCREW
BULB
PLATE 18A955
RADIO
MANUAL TUNING CONTROL
SPEAKER 18808
BASE ASSEMBLY

1975–77 Bronco radio installation

WINDSHIELD WIPERS

Motor

REMOVAL AND INSTALLATION

1975–77 Bronco

1. The motor is mounted on the left side of the windshield header. To remove the motor it will be necessary to first remove the cover and disconnect the linkage arm and pivot shaft assembly from the motor driving arm by removing the retaining clip.

2. Disconnect the motor electrical leads at the multiple connector. Remove the two bolts and nuts that attach the motor mounting bracket to the windshield header, and remove the bracket and motor assembly.

3. Install the windshield wiper motor in the reverse order of removal. When installing the motor, tighten the motor bracket-to-windshield header bolts to 48–72 in. lbs. and the nuts to 20–30 in. lbs.

1978–79 Bronco, 1975–79 Pick-ups

1. Disconnect the battery ground cable.

2. Remove the radio.

3. Remove the engine components attached to the lower wiper bracket bolt, if so equipped.

4. Remove the wiper motor bracket attaching bolts.

5. Disconnect the wiper motor wires. Then, disconnect the wiper arm linkage from the motor shaft.

6. Connect the linkage to motor and install motor bracket attaching bolts. Tighten bolts to 8–12 ft. lbs. and install engine components to lower bracket bolts.

7. Connect wiper motor wires.

8. Install radio.

9. Connect battery cable and check wiper motor operation.

1980–82 Bronco, Pick-ups

1. Disconnect the battery ground cable.

2. Remove the cowl grille attaching screws and lift the cowl grille slightly.

3. Disconnect the washer nozzle hose and remove the cowl grille assembly.

4. Remove the wiper linkage clip from the motor output arm.

5. Disconnect the wiper motor's wiring connector.

6. Remove the wiper motor's three attaching screws and remove the motor.

7. Install the motor and attach the three

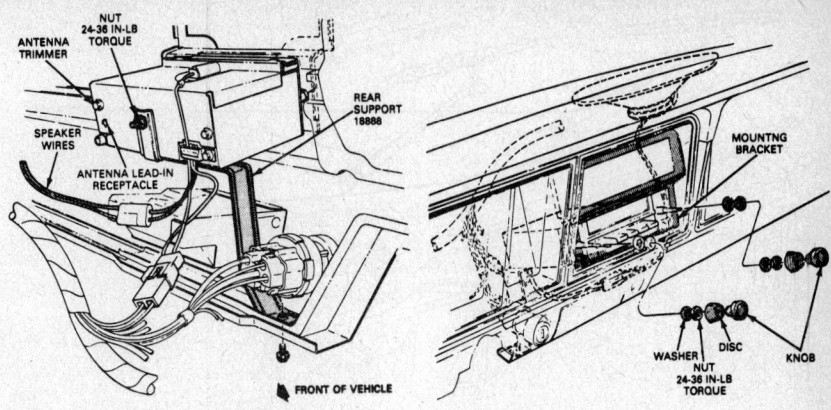

Typical van radio installation

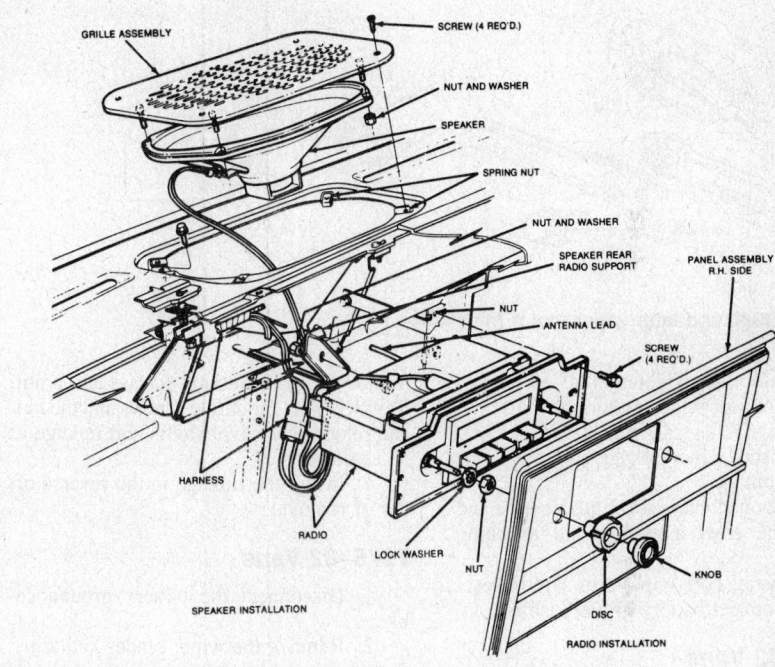

Typical pick-up and 1978–82 Bronco radio installation

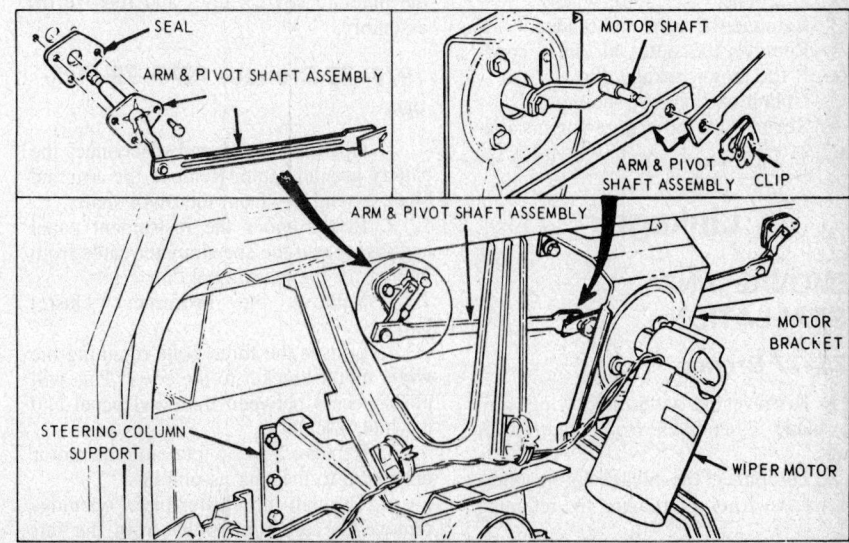

Typical 1975–79 wiper motor installation, except 1975–77 Bronco

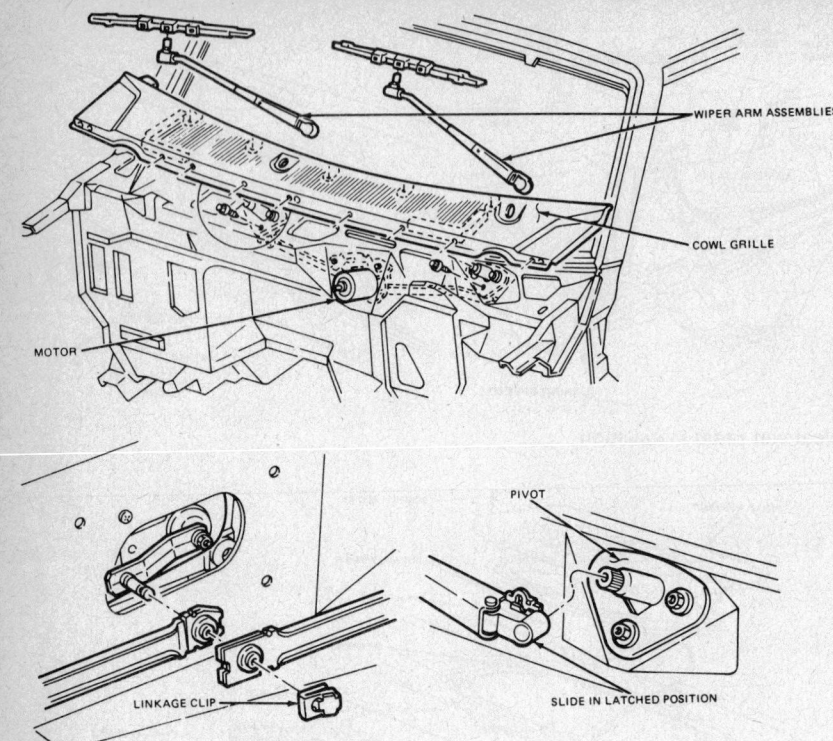

Typical 1980 and later wiper motor installation

attaching screws. Tighten to 60–85 in. lbs.

8. Connect wiper motor's wiring connector.

9. Install wiper linkage clip to the motor's output arm.

10. Connect the washer nozzle hose and install the cowl assembly and attaching screws.

11. Install both wiper arm assemblies.

12. Connect battery ground cable.

1975–82 Vans

1. Disconnect the battery ground cable. Remove the fuse panel and bracket.

2. Disconnect the motor wires.

3. Remove the arms and blades.

4. Remove the outer air inlet cowl. Take off the motor linkage clip.

5. Unbolt and remove the motor.

6. Reverse the procedure for installation.

Linkage

REMOVAL AND INSTALLATION

1975–77 Bronco

1. Remove the windshield wiper arm and blade assemblies from their pivot shafts.

2. Disconnect the linkage arm from the motor drive arm by removing the retaining clip.

3. The right and left pivot shaft assemblies are each retained to the windshield header by two mounting screws and a nut. Remove these mounting screws and the nut, and remove the pivot shafts and linkage as an assembly.

4. Install the linkage in the reverse order of removal.

1975–82 Vans

1. Disconnect the battery ground cable.

2. Remove the wiper blades and arms. Detach the washer hoses.

3. Remove the cowl grille.

4. Remove the linkage clips. Remove the pivot to cowl screws and remove the assembly.

1978–79 Bronco, 1975–79 Pick-ups

1. Open the hood and disconnect the battery ground cable. Remove the arm and blade assemblies from the pivot shafts.

2. Reach under the instrument panel and disconnect the speedometer cable from the rear of the instrument cluster.

3. Remove the instrument cluster bezel.

4. Loosen the three bolts retaining the wiper motor bracket to the cowl. This will allow access between the cowl panel and the link assembly.

5. Remove the clip retaining the motor drive arm to the link assemblies.

6. Through the cluster bezel opening, remove the retaining bolts from the left pivot assembly. Remove the left pivot and link assembly from under the instrument

panel.

7. Remove the glove box assembly.

8. Remove the three bolts retaining the right pivot and link assembly to the cowl panel.

9. Disconnect the right link assembly from the drive arm and remove the right pivot and link assembly.

10. Place gaskets on the pivot shafts and position the shafts to the cowl panel and install the retaining bolts.

11. Install the glove box assembly.

12. Position the link assemblies to the motor drive arm and install the retaining clip.

13. Tighten the bolts retaining the motor bracket to the cowl and then re-install engine components to lower bracket bolt.

14. Install the wiper arm and blade assemblies.

15. Position and install the instrument cluster bezel.

16. Connect the speedometer cable.

17. Connect the battery ground cable and close the hood and check the operation of the wipers.

1980–82 Bronco, Pick-ups

1. Disconnect the battery ground cable.

2. Remove both wiper arm assemblies.

3. Remove the cowl grille attaching screws and lift the cowl grille slightly.

4. Disconnect the washer nozzle hose and remove the cowl grille assembly.

5. Remove the wiper linkage clip from the motor output arm and pull the linkage from the output arm.

6. Remove the pivot body to cowl screws and remove the linkage and pivot shaft assembly (three screws on each side). The left and right pivots and linkage are independent and can be serviced separately.

7. Attach the linkage and pivot shaft assembly to cowl with attaching screws.

8. Replace the linkage to the output arm and attach the linkage clip.

9. Connect the washer nozzle hose and cowl grills assembly.

10. Attach cowl grille attaching screws.

11. Replace both wiper arm assemblies.

12. Connect battery ground cable.

Wiper Arm Assembly

REPLACEMENT

1975–79

Bend the arm backwards at the joint next to the pivot. Now, pull the arm straight off the splined pivot shaft. To replace the arm, hold it in the bent position and slide it on the pivot.

1980–82

Raise the blade end of the arm off of the windshield and move the slide latch away from the pivot shaft. This will unlock the wiper arm from the pivot shaft and hold the blade end of the arm off of the glass at the same time. The wiper arm can now be pulled off of the pivot shaft without the aid of any tools.

Blade Assembly to Wiper Arm

REPLACEMENT

1975–79

Wiper blades are used from two different manufacturers.

Trico and Anco blades come in two types. With a bayonet type, the blade saddle slides over the end of the arm and is engaged by a locking stud. With the bottom type, a screw and nut is used to retain the blade on the arm.

BAYONET TYPE

To remove a Trico type blade, press down on the arm to unlatch the top stud. Depress the tab on the saddle and pull the blade from the arm.

To remove an Anco type blade, press inward on the tab and pull the blade from the arm.

To install a new blade assembly, slide the blade saddle over the end of the wiper arm so that the locking stud snaps into place.

SIDE SADDLE PIN TYPE

To remove a pin type Trico-type blade, insert an appropriate tool into the spring release opening of the blade saddle, depress the spring clip and pull the blade from the arm.

To install, push the blade saddle on to the pin, so that the spring clip engages the pin. Be sure the blade is securely attached to the arm.

1980–82

1. Cycle arm and blade assembly to a position on the windshield where removal of blade assembly can be performed without difficulty. Turn ignition key off at desired position.

2. With blade assembly resting on windshield, grasp either end of the wiper blade frame and pull away from windshield, then pull blade assembly from pin.

NOTE: Rubber element extends past frame. To prevent damage to the blade element, be sure to grasp blade frame and not the end of the blade element.

3. To install, push blade assembly onto pin until fully seated. Be sure blade is securely attached to the wiper arm.

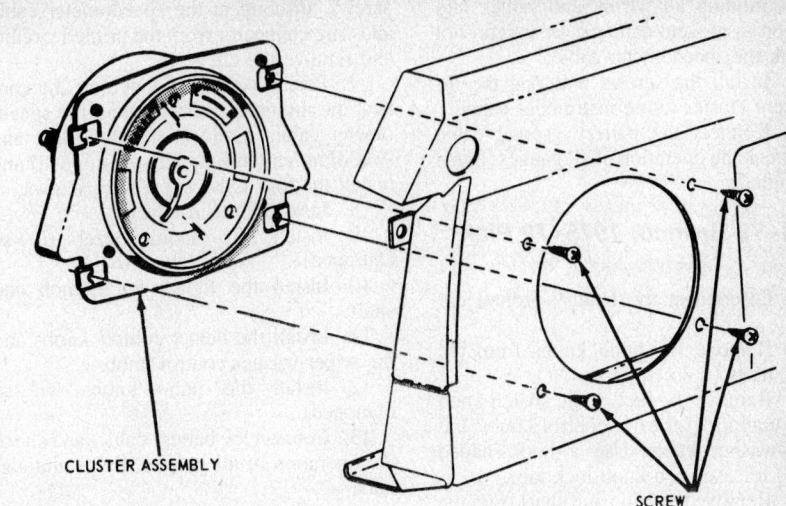

1975–77 Bronco instrument cluster

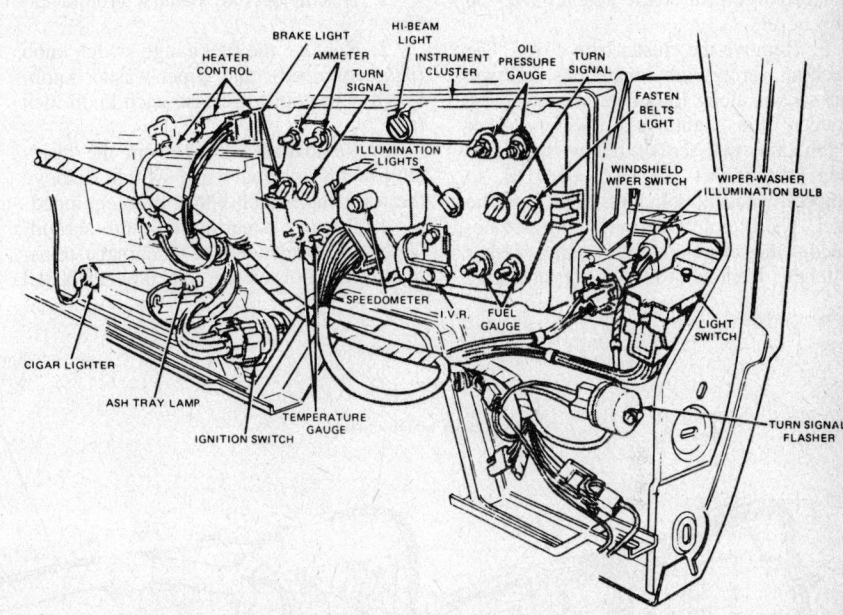

1975–79 pick-up and 1978–79 Bronco instrument panel rear view

INSTRUMENT CLUSTER

REMOVAL AND INSTALLATION

1975–77 Bronco

1. Disconnect the battery ground cable and disconnect the speedometer cable from the speedometer head.

2. Remove the screws retaining the instrument cluster assembly to the instrument panel.

3. Remove the cluster from behind the instrument panel.

4. Disconnect the feed wires to the instruments and the instrument voltage reg-

ulator and remove the light sockets from the cluster back, noting their positions. Remove the two clips that retain the wiring harness to the cluster back and pull the harness away from the cluster. Remove the instrument cluster assembly.

To install the instrument cluster:

5. Mount the wiring harness to the lower edge of the cluster back by installing the two retaining clips.

6. Connect the instrument voltage regulator and the instrument wires to the cluster assembly and install the light sockets. Be sure that the ammeter wire is routed through the ammeter loop of the charge indicator correctly to prevent reverse gauge indications.

7. Connect the speedometer cable and tighten the nut.

8. Carefully move the instrument cluster into position from behind the instrument

panel, guiding all wiring and cables into position to prevent damage. Be careful not to kink the speedometer cable.

9. Install the screws retaining the instrument cluster to the instrument panel.

10. Connect the battery ground cable and check the operation of all gauges, lights and signals.

1978–79 Bronco, 1975–79 Pick-ups

1. Disconnect the battery ground cable.

2. Remove the radio knobs from the radio shafts (if so equipped).

3. Remove the fuel gauge switch knob (if so equipped), heater control knobs and wiper-washer knob. Use a hook-shaped tool to release each knob lock tab.

4. Remove the knob and shaft from the light switch.

5. Remove one nut and washer from each radio control shaft, and remove the radio bezel.

6. Remove the cluster trim cover. The attaching screws are located as follows: four screws along top of bezel; one screw between the lights and wiper-washer switch, and two screws below the radio. Then, disconnect the A/C duct (if so equipped), and illumination light from the bezel. The illumination light is located between the lights and wiper-washer switches. Remove four cluster attaching

screws, disconnect the speedometer cable and wire connector from the printed circuit, and remove the cluster.

7. Position cluster to opening and connect the multiple connector and the speedometer cable. Connect the A/C duct and A/C illumination light (if so equipped) and install the four cluster retaining screws.

8. Install the trim cover.

9. Install the radio bezel (if so equipped).

10. Install the light switch knob and shaft.

11. Install the heater control knobs and the wiper-washer control knobs.

12. Install the radio knobs, (if so equipped).

13. Connect the battery cable, and check the operation of all gauges, lights and signals.

1980–82 Bronco, Pick-ups

1. Disconnect the battery ground cable.

2. Remove the fuel gauge switch knob (if so equipped), and wiper-washer knob. Use a hook tool to release each knob lock tab.

3. Remove the knob from the headlamp and windshield wiper switch. Remove the fog lamp switch knob, if so equipped.

4. Remove steering column shroud. Care must be taken not to damage transmission control selector indicator (PRNDL)

cable on vehicles equipped with automatic transmission.

5. On vehicles equipped with automatic transmission, remove loop on indicator cable assembly from retainer pin. Remove bracket screw from cable bracket and slide bracket out of slot in tube.

6. Remove the cluster trim cover. Remove four cluster attaching screws, disconnect the speedometer cable, wire connector from the printed circuit, 4 × 4 indicator light and remove the cluster.

7. Position cluster to opening and connect the multiple connector, the speedometer cable and 4 × 4 indicator light. Install the four cluster retaining screws.

8. If so equipped, place loop on transmission indicator cable assembly over retainer on column.

9. Position the tab on steering column bracket into slot on column. Align and attach screw.

10. Place transmission selector lever on steering column into "D" position.

11. Adjust slotted bracket so the pin is within the letter band.

12. Install the trim cover.

13. Install the headlamp switch knob. If so equipped, install the fog lamp switch.

14. Install the wiper-washer control knobs.

15. Connect the battery cable, and check the operation of all gauges, lights and signals.

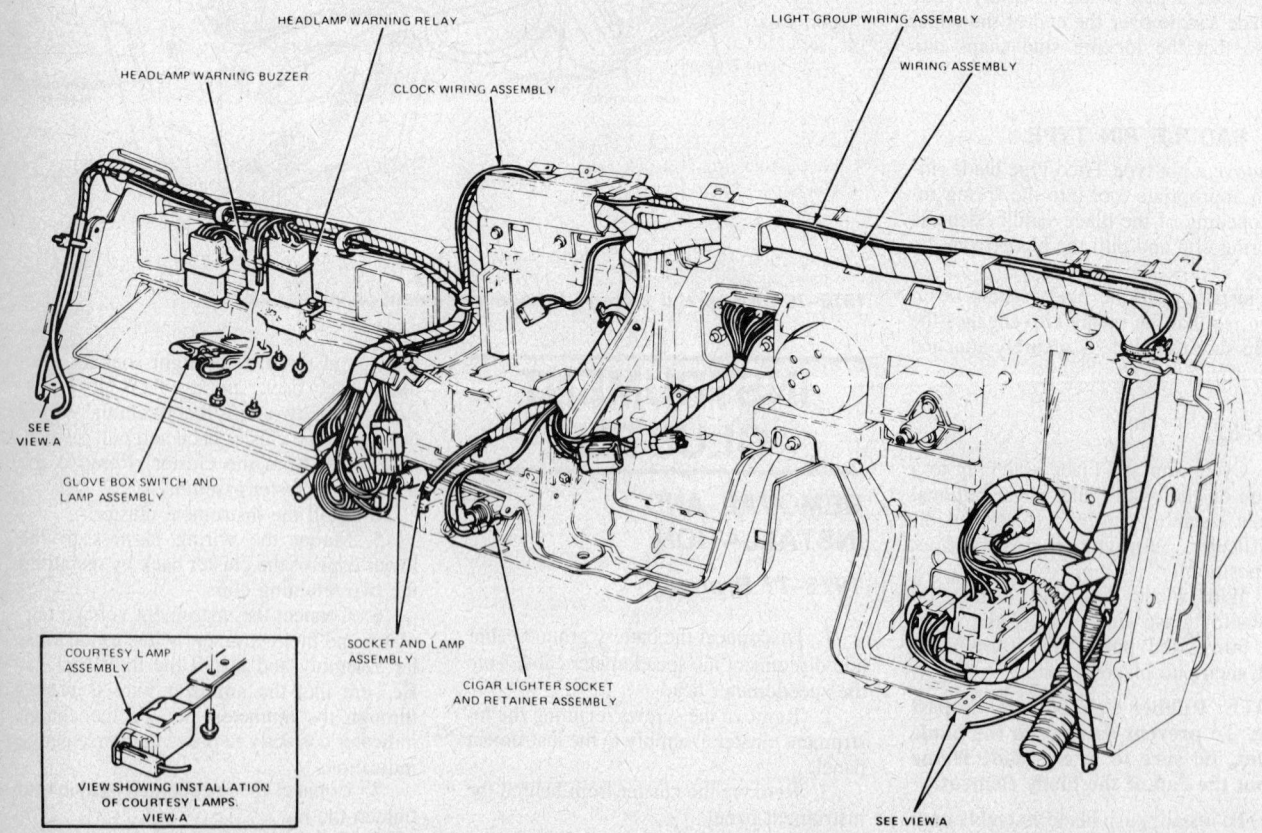

1980–82 pick-up and Bronco instrument cluster rear view

1975–77 Vans

1. Disconnect the battery ground cable.

2. Remove seven instrument cluster-to-panel retaining screws.

3. Position cluster part away from the panel for access to the back of the cluster to disconnect the speedometer cable.

If there is not sufficient access to disengage the speedometer cable from the speedometer, it may be necessary to remove the speedometer cable at the transmission and pull cable through cowl, to allow room to reach the speedometer quick disconnect.

4. Disconnect the harness connector plug from the printed circuit board and remove the cluster assembly from the instrument panel.

5. Remove the cluster.

6. Apply approximately ³⁄₁₆ inch diameter ball of silicone lubricant or equivalent in the drive hole of the speedometer head.

7. Position the cluster near its opening in the instrument panel.

8. Connect the harness connector plug to the printed circuit board.

9. Connect the speedometer cable (quick disconnect) to the speedometer head.

Connect the speedometer cable and housing assembly to the transmission (if removed).

10. Install the seven instrument cluster-to-panel retaining screws and connect the battery ground cable.

11. Check operation of all gauges, lights, and signals.

1978–82 Vans

1. Disconnect the battery ground cable.

2. Remove two steering column shroud to panel retaining screws and remove shroud.

3. Loosen bolts which attach the column to the B and C Support to provide sufficient clearance for cluster removal. (Required for tilt steering column vehicles only).

4. Remove seven instrument cluster to panel retaining screws.

5. Position cluster part away from the panel for access to the back of the cluster to disconnect the speedometer.

If there is not sufficient access to disengage the speedometer cable from the speedometer, it may be necessary to remove the speedometer cable at the transmission and pull cable through cowl, to allow room to reach the speedometer quick disconnect.

6. Disconnect the harness connector plug from the printed circuit board and remove the cluster assembly from the instrument panel.

7. Apply approximately ³⁄₁₆ inch diameter ball of silicone lubricant or equiv-

alent in the drive hole of the speedometer head.

8. Position the cluster near its opening in the instrument panel.

9. Connect the harness connector plug to the printed circuit board.

10. Connect the speedometer cable (quick disconnect) to the speedometer head.

Connect the speedometer cable and housing assembly to the transmission (if removed).

11. Install the seven instrument cluster-to-panel retaining screws and connect the battery ground cable.

12. Check operation of all gauges, lights, and signals.

13. Reinstall the steering column.

14. Position steering column shroud to instrument panel and install two screws.

Speedometer Cable Core

REMOVAL AND INSTALLATION

1. Reach up behind the cluster and disconnect the cable by depressing the quick disconnect tab and pulling the cable away.

2. Remove the cable from the casing. If the cable is broken, raise the vehicle on a hoist and disconnect the cable from the transmission.

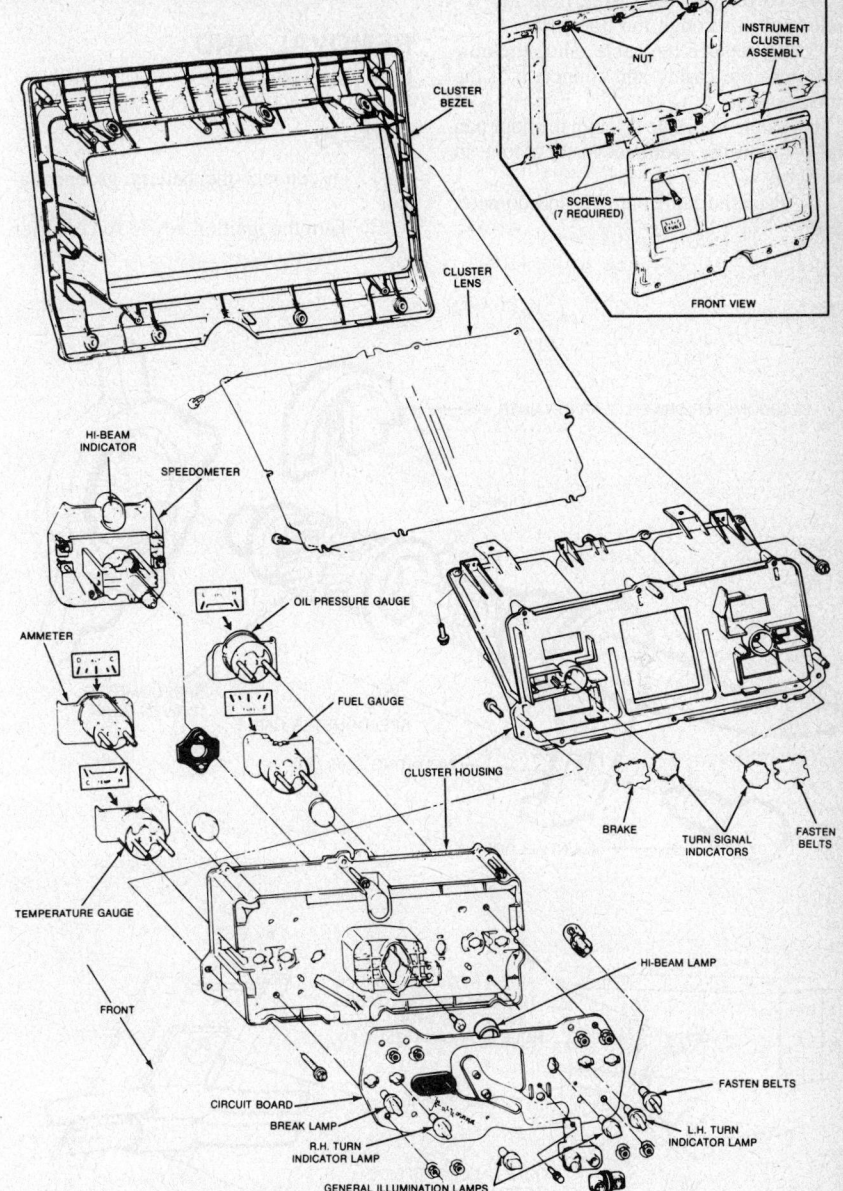

1975–82 van instrument cluster rear view

3. Remove the cable from the casing.

4. To remove the casing from the vehicle, pull it through the floor pan.

5. To replace the cable, slide the new cable into the casing and connect it at the transmission.

6. Route the cable through the floor pan and position the grommet in its groove in the floor.

7. Push the cable onto the speedometer head.

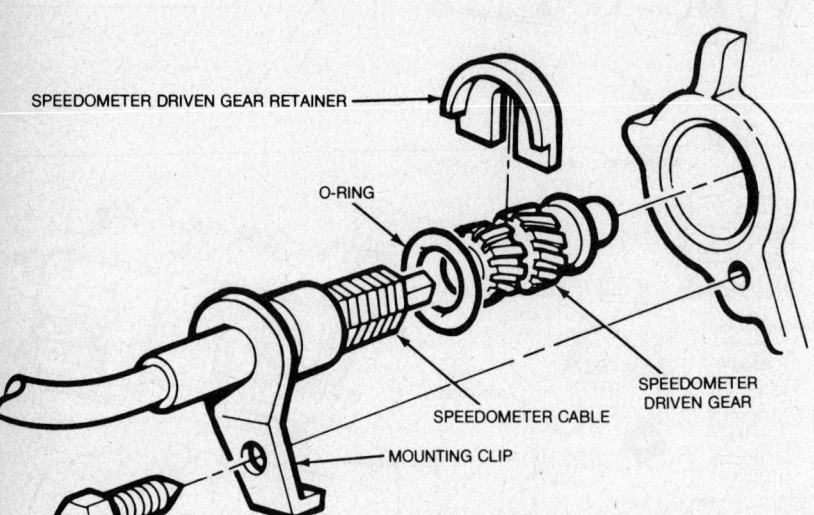

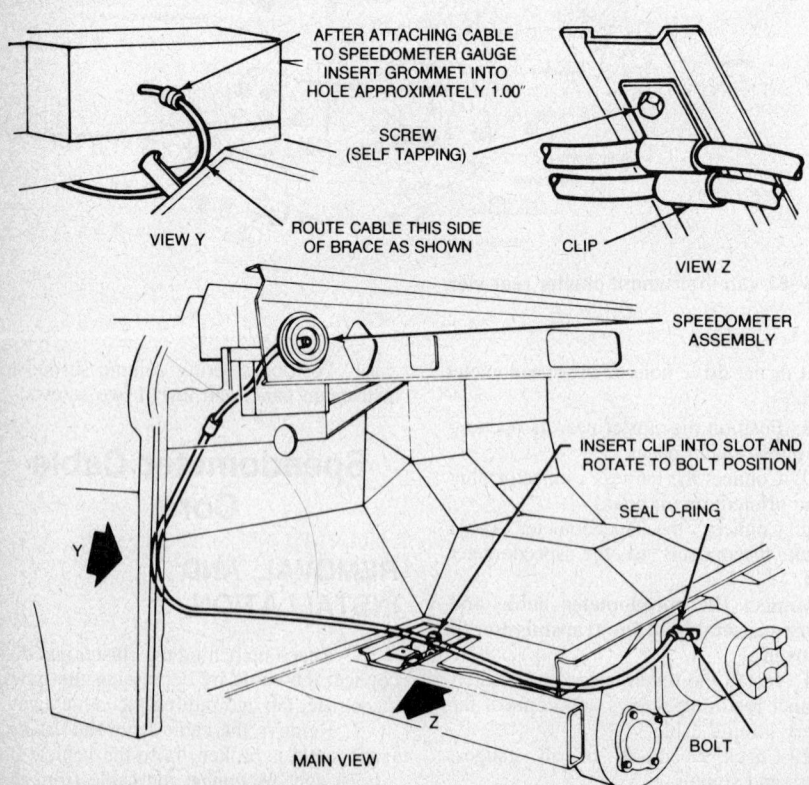

Speedometer cable installation, typical

Ignition Switch

REMOVAL AND INSTALLATION

1975–79

1. Disconnect the battery ground cable.

2. Turn the ignition key to Accessories and slightly depress the release pin in the face of the lock cylinder.

3. Turn the key counterclockwise and pull the key and lock assembly out of the switch.

4. From under the instrument panel, press in on the rear of the switch ⅛ turn counterclockwise.

5. Remove the bezel and switch. Remove the retainer and spring.

6. Remove the nut from the back of the switch.

7. Remove the accessory and gauge feed wires from the accessory terminal of the switch. Pull the insulated plug from the rear of the switch.

8. To install: insert a screwdriver into the lock opening of the switch and turn the slot in the switch to the full counterclockwise position.

9. Connect the insulated plug and wires to the back of the switch. Connect the accessory and gauge wires to the switch and install the retaining nut.

10. Place the bezel and switch in the switch opening, press the switch toward the instrument panel and rotate it ⅛ turn to lock it.

11. Position the spring and retainer on the switch with the open face of the retainer away from the switch. Place the switch in the opening.

12. Press the switch toward the instrument panel and install the bezel.

13. Place the key in the cylinder and turn the key to the accessory position. Place the lock and key in the switch, depress the release pin slightly, and turn the key counterclockwise. Push the new lock cylinder into the switch. Turn the key to check the operation.

14. Connect the battery.

1980–82

1. Disconnect the battery ground cable.

2. Remove steering column shroud and lower the steering column.

3. Disconnect the switch wiring at the multiple plug.

4. Remove the two nuts that retain the switch to the steering column.

5. Lift the switch vertically upward to disengage the actuator rod from the switch and remove switch.

6. When installing the ignition switch, both the locking mechanism at the top of the column and the switch itself must be in LOCK position for correct adjustment. To hold the mechanical parts of the column in LOCK position, move the shift lever into PARK (with automatic transmissions) or REVERSE (with manual transmissions), turn the key to LOCK position, and remove the key. New replacement switches, when received, are already pinned in LOCK position by a metal shipping pin inserted in a locking hole on the side of the switch.

7. Engage the actuator rod in the switch.

8. Position the switch on the column and install the retaining nuts, but do not tighten them.

9. Move the switch up and down along the column to locate the mid-position of rod lash, and then tighten the retaining nuts.

10. Remove the locking pin, connect the battery cable, and check for proper start in PARK or NEUTRAL.

Also check to make certain that the start circuit cannot be actuated in the DRIVE and REVERSE position.

11. Raise the steering column into position at instrument panel. Install steering column shroud.

HEADLIGHTS

REMOVAL AND INSTALLATION

1975–82 Vans, 1975–77 Bronco, 1975–77 Pick-ups, 1978 Pick-ups and Bronco Except Ranger and XLT Options

1. Remove the screws retaining the headlight trim ring and remove the trim ring.

2. Loosen the headlight retaining ring screws, rotate the ring counterclockwise and remove it. Do not disturb the adjusting screw settings.

3. Pull the headlight bulb forward and disconnect the wiring assembly plug from the hub.

4. Connect the wiring assembly plug to the new bulb. Place the bulb in position, making sure that the locating tabs of the bulb are fitted in the positioning slots.

5. Install the headlight retaining ring, slipping the ring tabs over the screws and rotating the ring clockwise as far as possible. Tighten the screws.

6. Place the headlight trim ring into position, and install the retaining screws.

7. Check the operation of the headlight.

1978 Pick-ups and Bronco with Ranger and XLT Option and All 1979–82 Pick-up and Bronco Models

1. Remove the attaching screws and remove the headlamp door attaching screws and remove the headlamp door.

2. Remove the headlight retaining ring screws, and remove the retaining ring. Do not disturb the adjusting screw settings.

3. Pull the headlight bulb forward and disconnect the wiring assembly plug from the bulb.

4. Connect the wiring assembly plug to the new bulb. Place the bulb in position, making sure that the locating tabs of the bulb are fitted in the positioning slots.

5. Install the headlight retaining ring.

6. Place the headlight trim ring or door

into position, and install the retaining screws.

FUSE LINK

The fuse link is a short length of special, Hypalon (high temperature) insulated wire, integral with the engine compartment wiring harness and should not be confused with standard wire. It is several wire gauges smaller than the circuit which it protects. Under no circumstances should a fuse link replacement repair be made using a length of standard wire cut from bulk stock or from another wiring harness.

To repair any blown fuse link use the following procedure:

1. Determine which circuit is damaged, its location and the cause of the open fuse link. If the damaged fuse link is one of three fed by a common No. 10 or 12 gauge feed wire, determine the specific affected circuit.

2. Disconnect the negative battery cable.

3. Cut the damaged fuse link from the wiring harness and discard it. If the fuse link is one of three circuits fed by a single feed wire, cut it out of the harness at each splice end and discard it.

4. Identify and procure the proper fuse link and butt connectors for attaching the fuse link to the harness.

5. To repair any fuse link in a 3-link group with one feed:

   a. After cutting the open link out of the harness, cut each of the remaining

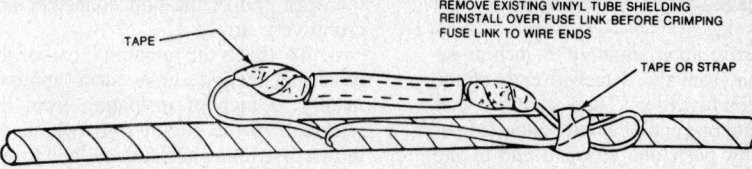

TYPICAL REPAIR USING THE SPECIAL #17 GA. (9.00" LONG-YELLOW) FUSE LINK REQUIRED FOR THE AIR/COND. CIRCUITS (2) #687E and #261A LOCATED IN THE ENGINE COMPARTMENT

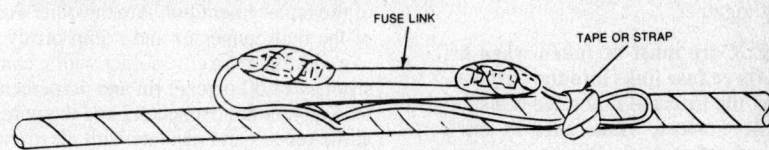

TYPICAL REPAIR FOR ANY IN-LINE FUSE LINK USING THE SPECIFIED GAUGE FUSE LINK FOR THE SPECIFIC CIRCUIT

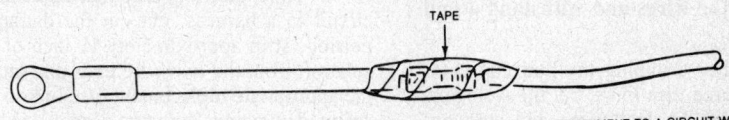

TYPICAL REPAIR USING THE EYELET TERMINAL FUSE LINK OF THE SPECIFIED GAUGE FOR ATTACHMENT TO A CIRCUIT WIRE END

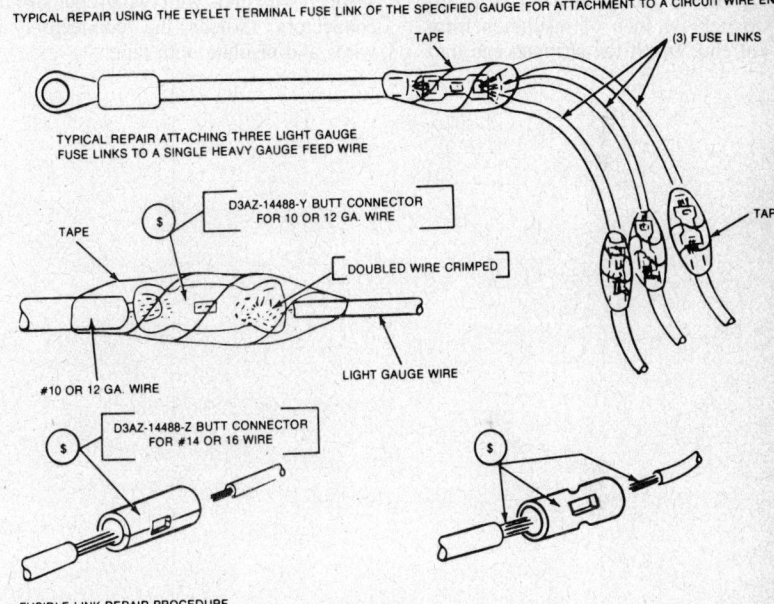

TYPICAL REPAIR ATTACHING THREE LIGHT GAUGE FUSE LINKS TO A SINGLE HEAVY GAUGE FEED WIRE

FUSIBLE LINK REPAIR PROCEDURE

General fuse link repair procedure

undamaged fuse links close to the feed wire weld.

b. Strip approximately ½ inch of insulation from the detached ends of the two good fuse links. Then insert two wire ends into one end of a butt connector and carefully push one stripped end of the replacement fuse link into the same end of the butt connector and crimp all three firmly together.

NOTE: Care must be taken when fitting the three fuse links into the butt connector as the internal diameter is a snug fit for three wires. Make sure to use a proper crimping tool. Pliers, side cutters, etc. will not apply the proper crimp to retain the wires and withstand a pull test.

c. After crimping the butt connector to the three fuse links, cut the weld portion from the feed wire and strip approximately ½ inch of insulation from the cut end. Insert the stripped end into the open end of the butt connector and crimp very firmly.

d. To attach the remaining end of the replacement fuse link, strip approximately ½ inch of insulation from the wire end of the circuit from which the blown fuse link was removed, and firmly crimp a butt connector or equivalent to the stripped wire. Then, insert the end of the replacement link into the other end of the butt connector and crimp firmly.

e. Using rosin core solder with a consistency of 60 percent tin and 40 percent lead, solder the connectors and the wires at the repairs and insulate with electrical tape.

6. To replace any fuse link on a single circuit in a harness, cut out the damaged portion, strip approximately ½ inch of insulation from the two wire ends and attach the appropriate replacement fuse link to the stripped wire ends with two proper size butt connectors. Solder the connectors and wires and insulate with tape.

7. To repair any fuse link which has an eyelet terminal on one end such as the charging circuit, cut off the open fuse link behind the weld, strip approximately ½ inch of insulation from the cut end and attach the appropriate new eyelet fuse link to the cut stripped wire with an appropriate size butt connector. Solder the connectors and wires at the repair and insulate with tape.

8. Connect the negative battery cable to the battery and test the system for proper operation.

NOTE: Do not mistake a resistor wire for a fuse link. The resistor wire is generally longer and has print stating, "Resistor-don't cut or splice."

NOTE: When attaching a single No. 16, 17, 18 or 20 gauge fuse link to a heavy gauge wire, always double the stripped wire end of the fuse link before inserting and crimping it into the butt connector for positive wire retention.

International Harvester

INDEX

General Engine Specifications

Year	Engine No. Cyl Displacement (cu. in.)	Carburetor Type	Horsepower @ rpm	Torque @rpm (ft lbs)	Bore × Stroke (in.)	Compression Ratio	Oil Pressure @2000 rpm (psi)
'75–80	4–196	1V	111 @ 4400	180 @ 2000	4.125 × 3.656	8.1:1	50
'80	6–198 (Turbo)	Diesel	101 @ 3800	175 @ 2200	3.27 × 3.94	20.8:1	—
'76–79	6–198	Diesel	73 @ 3200	133 @ 1600	3.27 × 3.94	22.0:1	—
'75–80	8–304	2V	147 @ 3900	240 @ 2400	3.875 × 3.218	8.2:1	45
'75–80	8–345	2V	157 @ 3800	266 @ 2400	3.875 × 3.656	8.1:1	45
'75	8–392	4V	194 @ 3600	308 @ 2800	4.125 × 3.656	8.0:1	45

TUNE-UP SPECIFICATIONS

Year	Engine No. Cyl Displacement (cu. in.)	Spark Plugs Gap (in.)	Distributor	Ignition Timing (deg) Man	Ignition Timing (deg) Auto	Fuel Pump Pressure (psi)	Idle Speed (rpm) Man	Idle Speed (rpm) Auto
'75–80	4-196	.035	Electronic	TDC	5B	5	575	600
'75–80	8-304	.030	Electronic	TDC	TDC	5	575	600
'75–80	8-345	.035	Electronic	TDC	5B	5	650	700
'75	8-392	.035	Electronic	TDC	5B	5	650	700

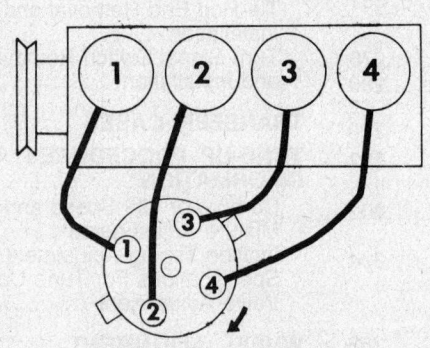

4 cylinder: 1-3-4-2

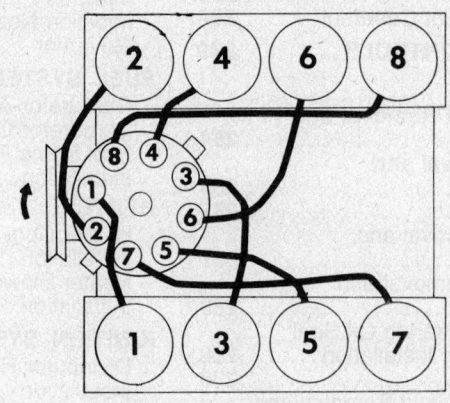

8 cylinder: 1-8-4-3-6-5-7-2

Valve Specifications

Year	Engine No. Cyl Displacement (cu in.)	Seat Angle (deg)	Face Angle (deg)	Spring Test Pressure (lbs @ in.)	Spring Free Height	Stem-to-Guide Clearance (in.) Intake	Stem-to-Guide Clearance (in.) Exhaust	Stem Diameter (in.) Intake	Stem Diameter (in.) Exhaust
'75–80	4–196	①	①	188 @ 1.428	2.065	.001–.0035	.0015–.004	.372	.415
'80	6–198	45	45	57 @ 1.57	1.89	.0006–.0018	.0016–.0028	.314	.314
'76–79	6–198	45	45	33 @ 1.634	1.929	.0006–.0018	.0016–.0028	.314	.314
'75–80	8–304	45	45	180–195 @ 1.429	2.065	.001–.0035	.0015–.004	.372	.371
'75–80	8–345	45	45	180–195 @ 1.429	2.065	.001–.0035	.0015–.004	.372	.371
'75	8–392	①	①	180–195 @ 1.429	2.065	.001–.0035	.0015–.004	.372	.414

① Intake 30°; Exhaust 45°

Crankshaft and Connecting Rod Specifications

(All measurements given in inches)

Year	Engine No Cyl Displacement (cu in.)	Crankshaft Main Brg Journal Dia	Main Brg Oil Clearance	Shaft End-play	Thrust on No	Connecting Rod Journal Diameter	Oil Clearance	Side Clearance
'75–80	4–196	2.7484–2.7494	.001–.004	.003–.008	3	2.373–2.374	.0011–.0036	.004–.011
'80	6–198	2.795	.0016–.0036	.0024–.0055	3	2.087	.0012–.0036	.0039–.0079
'76–79	6–198	2.7918–2.7988	.0013–.0038	.0024–.0094	3	2.0840–2.0906	.0013–.0038	.0039–.0079
'75–80	8–304	2.7484–2.7494	.001–.004	.003–.008	3	2.373–2.374	.0011–.0036	.008–.0016
'75–80	8–345	2.7484–2.7494	.001–.004	.003–.008	3	2.373–2.374	.0011–.0036	.008–.0016
'75	8–392	2.7484–2.7494	.001–.004	.003–.008	3	2.373–2.374	.0011–.0036	.008–.0016

Camshaft Specifications

(All measurements in inches)

Engine	Journal Diameter 1	2	3	4	5	Bearing Clearance	Valve Lift Intake	Exhaust	Camshaft End Play
4–196	2.099–2.100	2.089–2.090	2.079–2.080	2.069–2.070	2.059–2.060	.0015–.0035	.440	.395	.006–.014
6–198①	2.024	2.016	2.008	2.000	—	.0063–.0079	.358	.358	.0032–.0111
6–198②	1.774–1.789	1.714–1.729	1.714–1.729	1.608–1.624	—	.0059–.0079③	.248	.248	.0032–.0102
8–304	2.099–2.100	2.089–2.090	2.079–2.080	2.069–2.070	2.059–2.060	.0015–.0035	.440	.395	.006–.014
8-345	2.099–2.100	2.089–2.090	2.079–2.080	2.069–2.070	2.059–2.060	.0015–.0035	.440	.395	.006–.014
8–392	2.099–2.100	2.089–2.090	2.079–2.080	2.069–2.070	2.059–2.060	.0015–.0035	.440	.395	.006–.014

① 1980
② 1976–79
③ No. 4 bearing

Piston and Ring Specifications

(All measurements given in inches)

Year	Engine	Piston to Bore Clearance	Ring Side Clearance Top Compression	Bottom Compression	Oil Control	Ring Gap Top Compression	Bottom Compression	Oil Control
'75–80	4–196	.0035	.0015–.003	.0015–.003	.002–.0035	.013–.023	.013–.023	.013–.028
'80	6–198	.0047–.0075	.0024–.0039	.0016–.0032①	.0008–.0024	.0059–.0197	.0059–.0197①	.0059–.0197
'76–79	6–198	.0047–.0067	.0024–.0039	.0016–.0032①	.0008–.0024	.0118–.0197	.0118–.0197①	.0118–.0197
'75–80	8–304	.0035	.0015–.003	.0015–.003	.000–.0084	.010–.020	.010–.020	.015–.055
'75–80	8–345	.0035	.0015–.003	.0015–.003	.000–.0084	.010–.020	.010–.020	.015–.055
'75	8–392	.0035	.0015–.003	.0015–.003	.002–.0035	.013–.023	.013–.023	.013–.028

① 2nd and 3rd compression rings

Torque Specifications

(All readings in ft. lbs.)

Year	Engine	Cylinder Head Bolts	Rod Bearing Bolts	Main Bearing Bolts	In.-Ex. Manifold Bolts	Crankshaft Damper Bolt	Flywheel	Injector Nozzle Holder	Injection Pump
'80	6–198	94 large 36 small	37–41	108–116	11–13	217–239	33–36	50–65	15–18
'76–'79	6–198	94 large 36 small	36–40	109–116	11–13	217–239	33–36	50–65	15–18

Torque Specifications
(All readings in ft. lbs.)

Year	Engine	Cylinder Head Bolts	Rod Bearing Bolts	Main Bearing Bolts	Crankshaft Pulley Bolt	Flywheel-to-Crankshaft Bolts	Manifold	
							Intake	Exhaust
'75–'80	4–196	90–100	40–45	75–80	100–110	45–55	40–45	40–45
'75–'80	8–304	90–100	45–55	75–85	100–110	45–55	40–45	40–45
	8–345	90–100	45–55	75–85	100–110	45–55	40–45	40–45
	8–392	90–100	45–55	75–85	100–110	45–55	40–45	40–45

Wheel Alignment Specifications

Year	Model	Preferred Caster (deg.)	Preferred Camber (deg.)	Toe-in (in.)	Steering Axis Inclination (deg.)
'75–'79	2WD	0	1	3/32 to 5/16	8½
'75–'79	FA44	0	1	3/32 to 5/16	8½
'80	FA44	2°30'	30'	.00–.20	9

TUNE-UP

Periodic tune-ups are necessary to keep a vehicle in good running condition. Some owners disregard service until something breaks or until the vehicle will not run. It is important to keep some type of service schedule which lists the date and mileage when the vehicle was last tuned.

Spark Plugs

Before servicing the spark plugs (about every 12,000 miles is suggested), clean any foreign material away from the spark plug ports. This material could fall into the combustion chamber when the plug is removed. Remove the spark plug wires from the plugs, one at a time, by pulling the slip-on connector from the top of the plug. Do not handle or pull on the wire itself. The inner portion breaks easily or could get kinked. This will cause the plug to misfire or not fire at all.

Remove the spark plug with a spark plug socket and examine the condition of the plug electrode. (See the Unit Repair Section for examples of sparkplug wear and problems.) Although sand blasting and cleaning is an acceptable means of servicing spark plugs, it will not provide the benefits of installing new ones.

Install the plugs and replace the plug wires making certain that they fit snugly over the top of the plug. If there is a loose fit, apply light pressure to the end of the wire with a pair of spark plug pliers. Run the wires through the looms making certain that none are touching the exhaust manifolds.

Electronic Ignition System

1975 THROUGH EARLY 1978

The electronic ignition system consists of three major component units: a distributor, an ignition coil and an electronic control unit.

The distributor is conventional except that a sensor and trigger wheel replace the usual contact points, condenser and distributor cam. A standard type ignition coil is used. The electronic ignition control is a completely solid state unit designed for trouble-free service. The control unit electronically makes and breaks the ignition primary circuit in response to triggering signals from the sensor in the distributor. The high voltage is directed in the conventional way, to the rotor, distributor cap, spark plug cables, and to the spark plugs.

Dwell angle is determined by the angle between the adjacent teeth of the trigger wheel and by the air gap between the ends of the wheel teeth and the center line of the sensor. Since no wearing surfaces exist on the trigger wheel and sensor, dwell remains constant and no adjustment is required after the initial sensor air gap is made.

Adjusting Air Gap

The air gap should be adjusted with the use of a brass (non-metallic) feeler gauge, placed between the center line of the sensor and a aligned tooth of the trigger wheel. Loosen the sensor hold down screw and

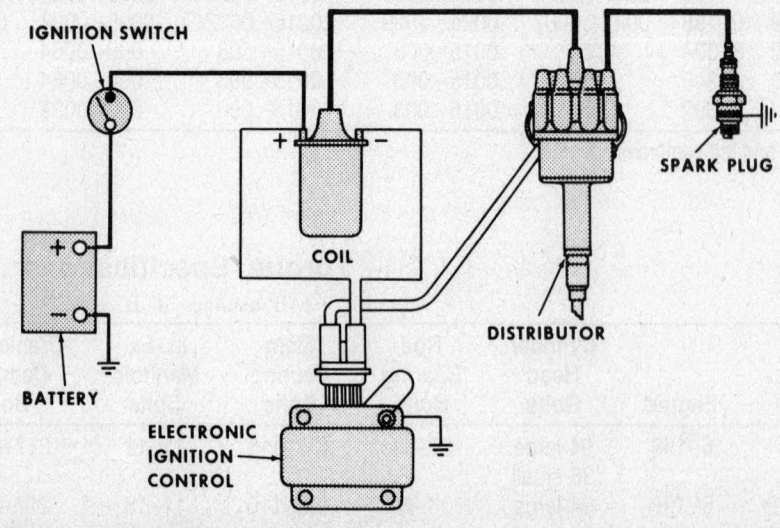

Electronic ignition with external control unit

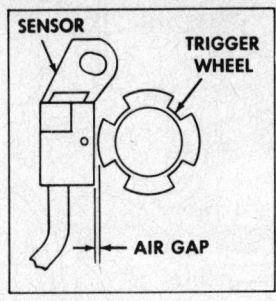

Air gap—4 cylinder

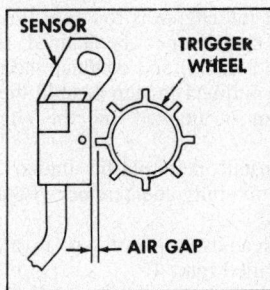

Air gap—V8

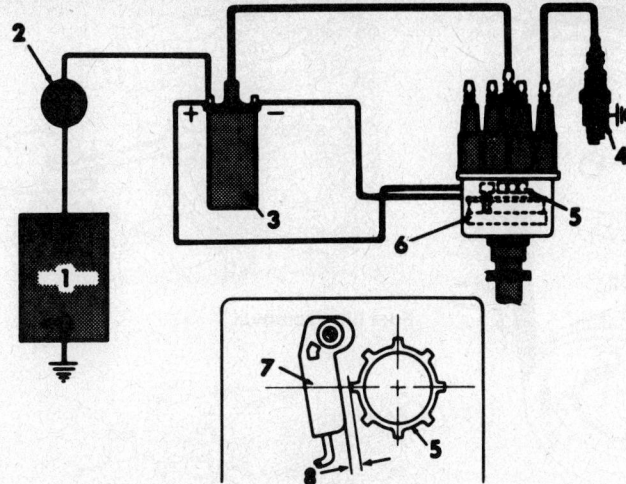

Electronic ignition with built-in control unit

1. Battery
2. Ignition switch
3. Ignition coil
4. Spark plug
5. Trigger wheel
6. Electronic control
7. Sensor
8. Air gap

move the sensor until the gauge will pass through with a slight drag. Tighten the hold down screw.

Engine Misfiring/No Start Condition

In the event of engine misfire or surging, other possible sources of trouble should be checked first, such as carburetion and the fuel supply, before checking the ignition. Check for breaks in the wiring and for corroded or loose connections.

If the engine will not run at all, remove a lead from one of the spark plugs and hold it ½ inch from the engine block while cranking the engine. If there is no spark, check wiring and connections.

CAUTION

Never disconnect the high voltage lead between the coil and the distributor and never disconnect more than three spark plugs at a time unless the ignition switch is off.

To make compression tests; disconnect the harness plug at the control box or disconnect the lead at the negative terminal of the coil.

NOTE: Further ignition testing can be found in the Electrical Unit Section.

1978 AND LATER

The electronic control unit is built into the distributor body instead of being a separate unit. Distributor wiring has been changed and a new design distributor cap is used. The red wire from the distributor connects to the coil positive terminal. The brown wire from the distributor connects to the coil negative terminal and the third wire from the distributor, white in color, con-

nects to the deceleration throttle modulator when used. Because primary voltage (low voltage) current is regulated within the electronic control unit, a ballast resistor or resistance wire is not required in the primary circuit.

NOTE: Refer to the 1975 through '77 section for air gap adjustment instructions.

Ignition Timing

NOTE: The timing light is connected to the No. 1 spark plug wire on 4 cylinder engines: No. 8 plug wire on V8 engines (304, 345 and 392).

Ignition timing is the measurement in degrees of crankshaft rotation at the instant the spark plugs in the cylinders fire, in relation to the location of the piston, while the piston is on the compression stroke.

1. Remove and plug the vacuum line(s) from the distributor advance/retard mechanism. Be sure there is no vacuum leak at the line(s).
2. Connect the timing light.
3. Mark the crank pulley and timing

quadrant lines with chalk or paint to make them easier to see.

4. Start the engine and aim the timing light at the timing quadrant.
5. The timing is adjusted by loosening the distributor hold-down nut and turning the distributor either clockwise or counterclockwise as required until the mark on the pulley aligns with the correct degree marking on the quadrant.
6. Tighten the hold-down nut and recheck the timing, readjust if necessary.
7. Stop the engine, remove the timing light and reconnect the vacuum line(s).

Valve Lash

ADJUSTMENT (GASOLINE ENGINES)

The valve lash is not adjustable since hydraulic valve lifters are employed. If a lifter should become noisy; dirt, grit or metal chips may have becomed lodged in the lifter body. This problem may be alleviated by frequently changing the engine oil and filter. Remove the lifter, clean or replace it

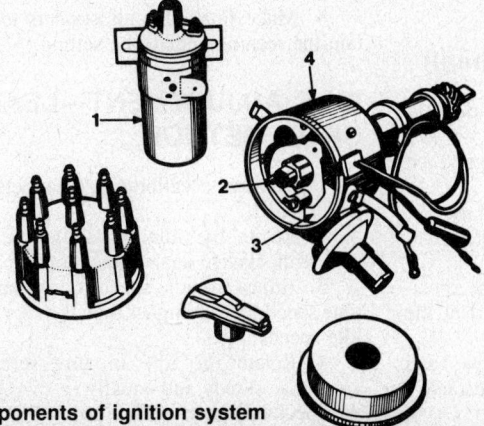

1. Ignition coil
2. Trigger wheel
3. Electronic control
4. Distributor

Components of ignition system

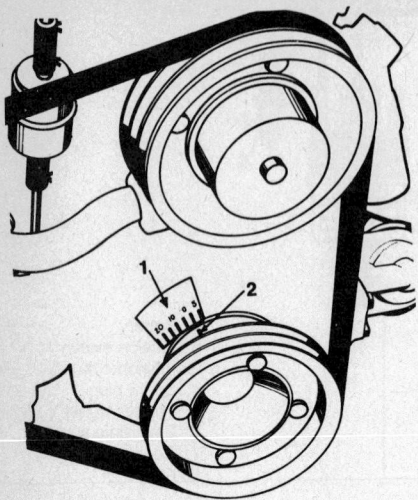

Typical timing marks

Fuel filter removal

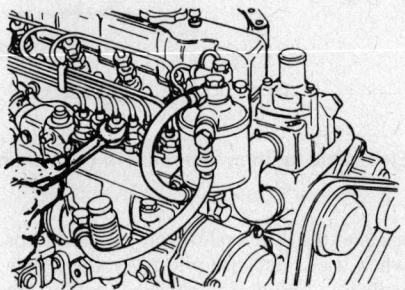

Injection line removal

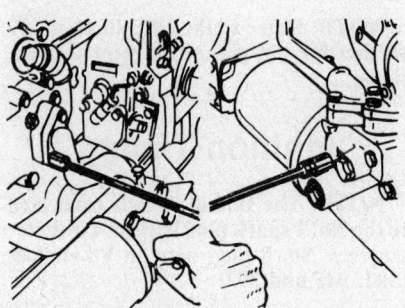

Water passage removal

if the noise persists. Check the other valve train components for wear, replace as necessary.

Idle Mixture and Speed Adjustment

To comply with the mandated emission control requirements, certain procedures must be followed when adjusting the air/fuel mixture and speed. The engine must be at normal operating temperature, choke open, air cleaner installed, dwell and ignition timing correct, and the parking brake applied. The following procedures apply to all carburetors, with minor deviations possible, depending upon the carburetor used.

Observe the following precautions when adjusting the idle mixture and speed.

1. Do not idle the engine for longer than three minutes at a time.

2. After each three minute interval, increase the engine speed to 2,000 rpm for one minute.

3. Continue with the idle adjustment and repeat step 2 as necessary.

PRELIMINARY IDLE SETTING
(After Carburetor Overhaul)

1. Connect a calibrated tachometer to the engine.

2. Connect a test vacuum gauge to the engine intake manifold.

3. Operate the engine at a fast idle speed to bring the operating temperature to normal.

4. Adjust the carburetor to the specified idle speed. Refer to the chart at the beginning of this section.

5. Adjust the idle mixture screw(s) and idle speed screw to obtain "Lean best idle" at the specified speed.

NOTE: "Lean best idle" is the point at which intake manifold vacuum starts to drop due to leanness.

6. Install the colored (service) plastic cap(s) with the tab fully turned counterclockwise against the stop.

7. Adjust the idle speed to specifications.

8. Make final idle adjustments to obtain the recommended idle setting.

IDLE ADJUSTMENT—LEAN DROP METHOD

1. Connect a calibrated tachometer to the engine.

2. Rotate the idle adjusting screw(s) counterclockwise against the stops.

3. Adjust the idle speed to give an engine speed 25 rpm higher than the specified idle speed.

4. Rotate the idle mixture screw(s) clockwise slowly and equally (if two) until the specified speed is obtained.

5. If the engine is rough or the specified idle speed cannot be attained, remove the limiter cap(s) and continue the adjustment as outlined in step 4, until the specified rpm is attained and the engine is smooth.

6. Install new plastic limiter cap(s) with the tab fully counterclockwise against the stop.

7. Readjust as necessary to maintain the specified rpm.

IDLE ADJUSTMENT— EXHAUST ANALYZER METHOD

When exhaust analyzer equipment is used, the following procedure is recommended to be used to adjust the idle mixture and speed. The test equipment must give accurate readings in the 0–5% carbon monoxide (CO) range.

1. Connect a calibrated tachometer to the engine and insert the exhaust analyzer into the exhaust pipe.

NOTE: Refer to the manufacturers instructions for complete connection procedures.

2. Operate the engine for fifteen minutes at fast idle speed (approximately 1000–1200 rpm), to bring engine to normal operating temperature and to stabilize the temperature of the exhaust analyzer.

4. Calibrate the test equipment as per the manufacturers instructions.

NOTE: If the combustion analyzer does not respond to changes in the mixture quality, check for leaks or restrictions in the sample lines. The thermal conductivity instruments used in the analyzer are both temperature and pressure sensitive, and require a definite sample flow. Refer to the manufacturer's instructions as necessary.

5. Adjust the idle mixture screw(s) counterclockwise against the tab stop.

6. Adjust the idle speed screw to obtain the specified idle speed.

7. Observe the analyzer dial and adjust the idle mixture screw(s) clockwise by $\frac{1}{16}$ turn increments to obtain the specified idle mixture setting and readjust the idle speed as necessary.

8. If the idle speed and mixture cannot be obtained, remove the idle limiter cap(s).

NOTE: To prevent damage to the mixture screw(s) or seat, file or grind the side of the plastic cap. Do not pry cap off.

9. With the engine operating, adjust the mixture screw(s) to obtain the "lean best idle" at the specified idle speed.

NOTE: "Lean best idle" is the point at which maximum manifold vacuum begins to drop due to leanness.

10. Install new plastic limiter cap(s) with the tab fully counterclockwise against the stop.

11. Readjust the idle mixture screw(s) to obtain the recommended CO setting.

NOTE: After completing the idle adjustment procedure, if unsatisfactory idle operation still exists, a recheck of the ignition system, crankcase ventilation system, timing advance system, air induction system, exhaust gas recirculation system, or hot idle compensation system should be made.

Diesel Fuel Systems

INJECTION PUMP

Removal and Installation

NOTE: In some applications, this procedure is best done with the engine removed from the vehicle.

1. Remove the inlet and outlet lines from the oil cooler.

2. Remove the bolts (4) and separate the oil filter and lines from the cooler.

3. Remove the coolant hose between the oil cooler and the head.

4. Remove the bolts (10) and separate the cooler from the block.

5. Disconnect the fuel lines and remove the fuel filter from the bracket.

6. Remove the injection lines from the nozzles and pump. Cover all openings immediately.

7. Remove the fan, spacer and pulley from the water pump.

8. Remove the bypass hose from the pump and thermostat housing.

9. Remove the three bolts and lift off the water pump and gasket.

10. Remove the inspection cover and pointer from the flywheel housing and lock the flywheel in place with a locking tool.

11. Flatten the lockwasher and remove the crankshaft pulley nut.

12. Tap evenly around the edge of the pulley using a brass drift, until the cone protrudes from the pulley. Remove the cone.

13. Drive the pulley and damper from the crankshaft with a soft mallet.

14. Remove the inner cover from the timing gear case.

15. Pry out the oil seal.

16. Remove the mounting bolts and tap the case loose with a soft mallet.

Timing cover removal

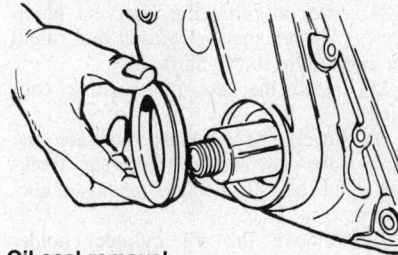

Oil seal removal

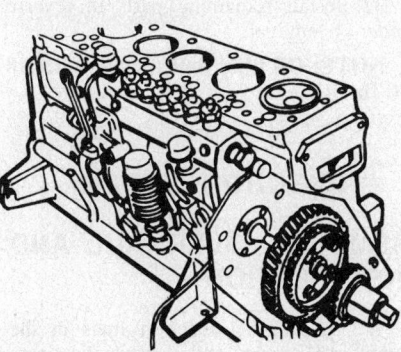

Removing timer round nut

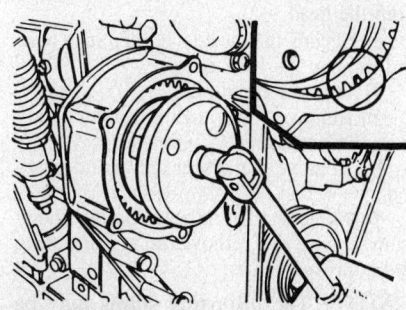

Injection pump and endplate assembly

Timer installation

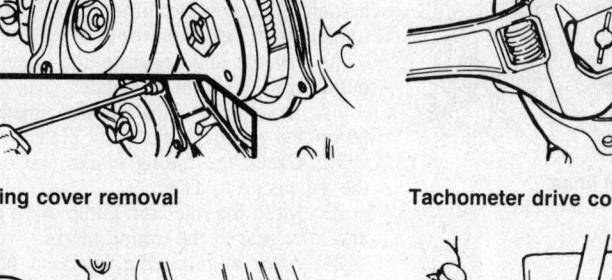

Tachometer drive coupling installation

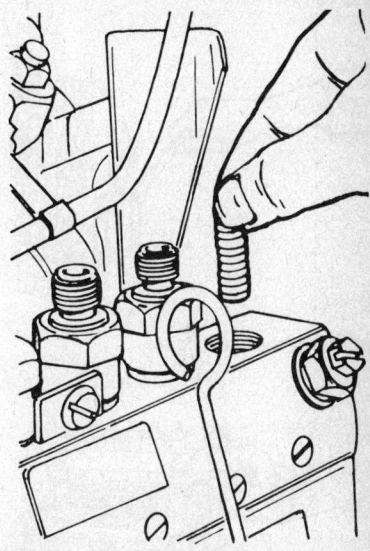

Delivery valve spring removal

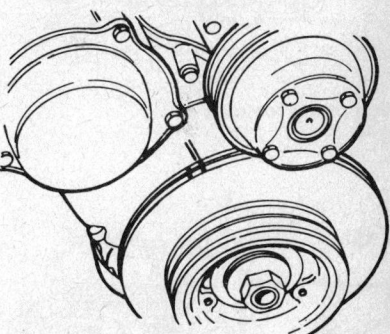

#1 piston at 20° BTDC

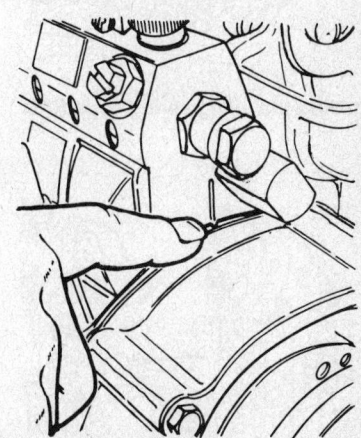

Lock the pump at this point, which is the beginning of injection

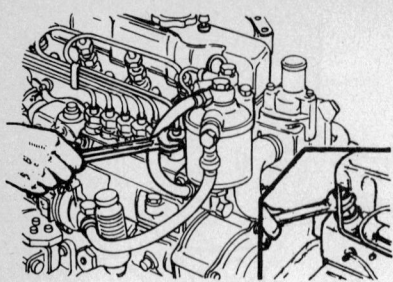

Connecting injection lines

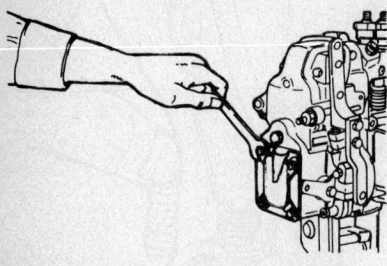

Removing the cam cover

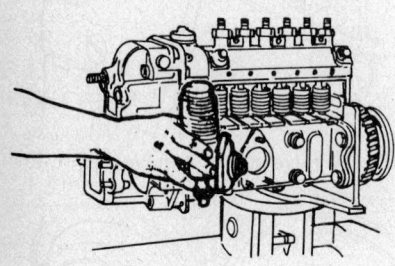

Feed pump removal

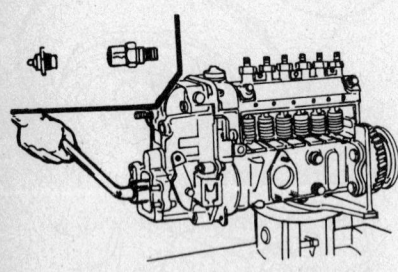

Removing the idling spring, type RAD

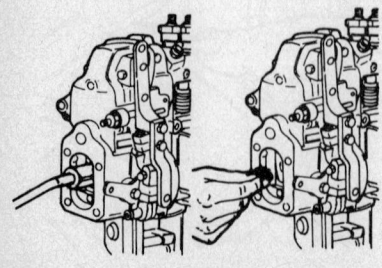

Removing the idling spring, type RSV

17. Remove the tachometer drive support nuts.

18. Remove the timer round nut.

19. Thread the timer extractor, special tool #57926-581 into the timer weight holder. Remove the timer assembly by tightening the extractor bolt.

20. Unbolt and separate the injection pump from the front end plate.

21. Temporarily install the injection pump and gasket on the front plate.

22. Check the timing marks and bring the #1 piston to TDC.

23. Mesh the injection pump drive gear and idler gear at the timing marks.

24. After aligning the injection pump keyway, install the lockwasher and round nut and torque to 50–58 ft. lbs.

25. Install the tachometer drive coupling.

26. Check the backlash between the pump drive gear and the idler gear. Backlash should be .0028–.0079″. Adjust if necessary.

27. Remove the #1 cylinder holder clamp, loosen the delivery valve and pull out the delivery spring. Tighten the valve holder to 22–25 ft. lbs.

28. Connect the fuel supply lines.

29. Bring the #1 piston to 20° BTDC. This can be done by aligning the first mark, in normal rotation, on the crankshaft pulley with the raised line on the gear case.

30. Hand prime the pump. Push the pump in all the way toward the block. Move the pump slowly away from the block until the fuel just stops flowing from the valve holder. Lock the pump in place.

31. Remove the delivery holder and assemble the spring. Torque the holder to 22–25 ft. lbs.

32. Install remaining parts in reverse order of removal.

NOTE: Oil filter bolt torque is 15–18 ft. lbs.

Injection Nozzle

REMOVAL, OVERHAUL AND INSTALLATION

1. Loosen the injection lines at the pump and nozzles and remove the lines. Cap the openings immediately.

2. Unscrew the injector and holder from the head.

3. Secure the nozzle holder in a vise and remove the lock nut.

4. Remove the nipple.

5. Remove the nozzle holder body from the nozzle nut.

6. Remove the spacer collar and pushrod.

7. Remove the nozzle holder body from the vise and remove the nozzle spring and adjusting shims.

NOTE: The adjusting shims may be removed with a piece of wire, but great

care must be taken to avoid damage to the nozzle tip.

8. Clean fuel oil may be used to clean all parts. Inspect all parts for damage and good fit.

9. Assemble the nozzle in reverse order of disassembly.

10. Install the nozzle in a tester.

11. Operate the tester lever at 1 stroke per second and read the pressure at injection. The pointer will oscillate slightly during injection.

12. Increase or decrease the thickness of the nozzle spring adjusting shims until opening pressure is 1,422.3 psi. A total of 31 different shims are available. A shim thickness of .05mm equals a difference of 85.338 psi.

13. Install the nozzles and lines. Torque the nozzles to 50–65 ft. lbs.

Governor

RSV MECHANICAL TYPE REMOVAL

1. Remove the injection pump and place it in a holding fixture.

2. Install the timer.

3. Drain the cam and governor chambers.

4. Remove the supply pump.

5. Remove the cam cover.

6. Using a special wrench, ST-57916-432, on the timer, turn the camshaft until all the tappets are raised to TDC. Place a tappet holder, 57931-210, between the tappet adjusting bolt and nut for each cylinder.

7. Remove the rear cover and dipstick.

8. Loosen the balance idler spring and the auxiliary idler spring lock nut.

9. Loosen the governor cover lock screw.

10. Unbolt and remove the governor cover from the governor body. Remove the link from the control rack.

11. Remove the start spring from the spring eye.

12. Remove the counterweights from the camshaft.

13. Hold the timer and remove the slotted nuts and lockwashers.

14. Using a puller, ST57926-512, remove the flyweight assembly.

15. Remove the timer.

16. Unbolt and remove the governor body.

MZ PNEUMATIC TYPE REMOVAL

1. Follow steps 1 through 6 of RSV Type Removal.

2. Unbolt and remove the diaphragm housing and main spring.

3. Remove the diaphragm ring with a screwdriver.

4. Remove the cotter pin from the connecting rod bolt with a needle-nosed pliers.

5. Remove the diaphragm assembly from the control rack.

6. Remove the five set screws and remove the governor body by applying force with a screwdriver blade in the slit between the governor and pump housings.

7. Remove the timer.

RSV TYPE INSTALLATION

1. Apply RTV silicone gasket material to the governor body and install the governor on the injection pump.

2. Tighten the upper spring eye screw holding the starting spring.

3. Install the timer.

4. Install the flyweight assembly.

5. Apply RTV silicone gasket material to the governor cover and install the starting spring on the housing side of the spring eye.

6. Install the link leaf spring in the hole in the end of the control rack.

7. Install the cover and set screws.

MZ TYPE INSTALLATION

1. Apply RTV silicone gasket material to the governor body, position it on the pump body and tap it into position with a plastic mallet. Install the set screws.

2. Install the diaphragm and balance spring on the control rack connecting bolt and lock with a new cotter pin. Apply chassis lube to the diaphragm ring.

3. Insert the main spring and install diaphragm housing with the four bolts.

Injection Pump Service

REPLACING THE DELIVERY VALVE

1. Thoroughly clean the area around the nozzle tube and delivery valve.

2. Remove the nozzle tube.

3. Remove the delivery valve holder lock plate.

4. Remove the delivery valve holder and spring.

5. Using ST57930-032, remove the delivery valve.

6. Position the delivery valve in the pump housing making sure no dirt gets between the top of the plunger barrel and the delivery valve.

7. Install a new delivery valve gasket. The gasket is installed with the larger face downward and may be tapped into place through the extractor.

8. Install the delivery valve spring.

9. Install the delivery valve holder and torque it to 22–25 ft. lbs.

10. Loosen the holder and retorque it.

11. Install the lock plate, nozzle tube and nozzle clamp.

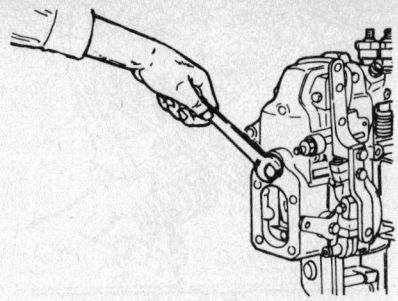

Removing the idling sub spring

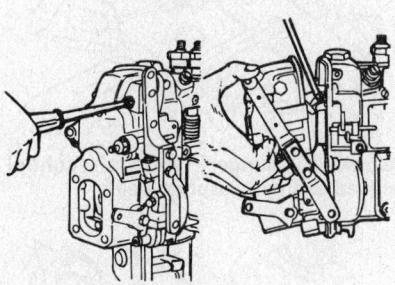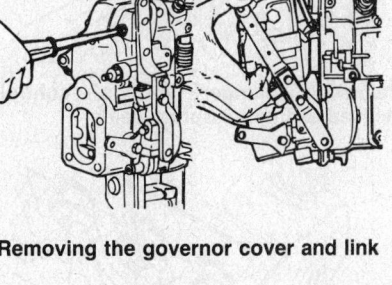

Removing the governor cover and link

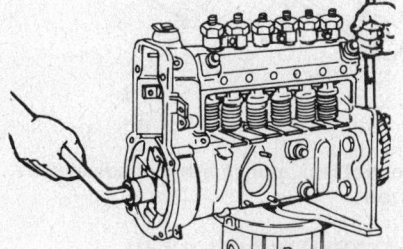

Removing the counterweights

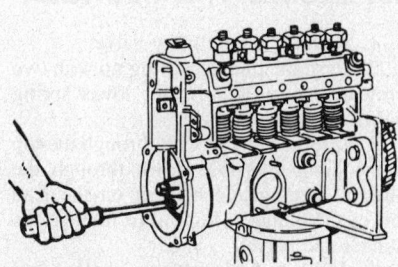

Removing the governor body

Removing the timer

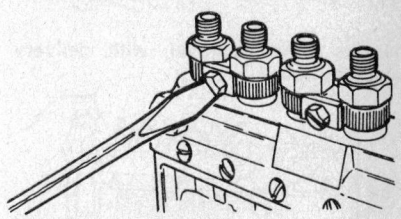

Removing delivery valve holder lock plate

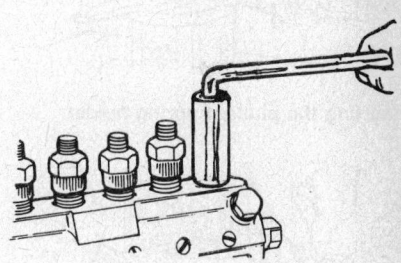

Loosening the delivery valve holder

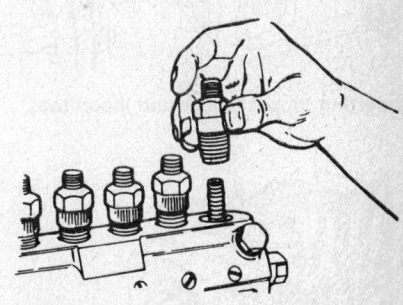

Removing the delivery valve holder and spring

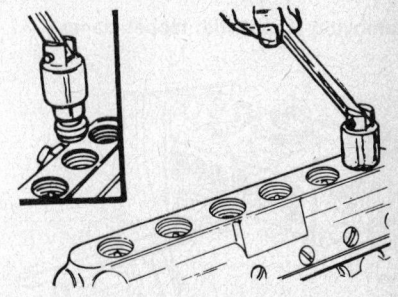

Removing the delivery valve with tool 57930-032

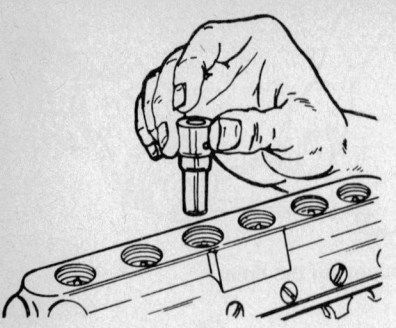

Plunger barrel removal, with delivery valves removed

Inserting the plunger spring holder

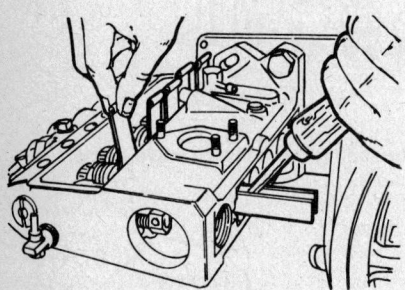

Inserting tappet holder and insert tool

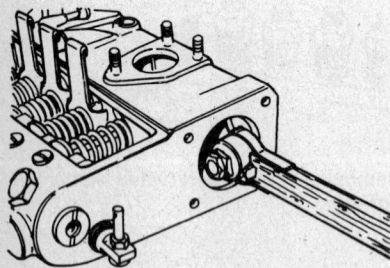

Removing tappet with tappet clamp

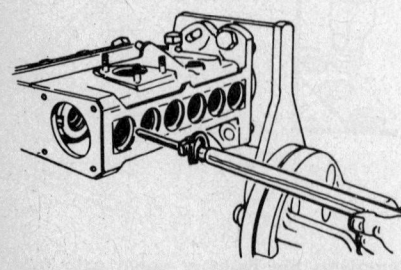

Removing plungers with tool 57921-412

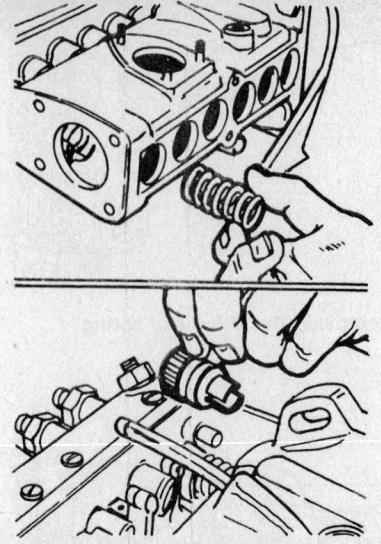

Removing plunger springs, control sleeves and upper spring seats

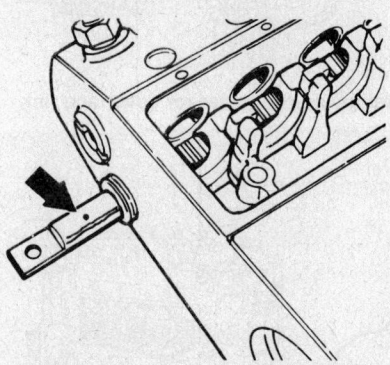

Control rack; punch mark is indicated by arrow

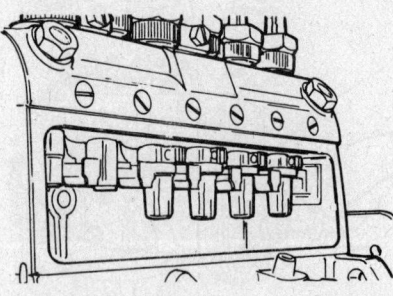

Control sleeves installed

REPLACING THE PLUNGER

1. Remove the delivery valve.
2. Push the plunger spring up with two screwdrivers and remove the lower spring seat from the plunger.
3. Insert a hooked wire through the top of the pump housing, down through the plunger opening and hook it on the lead unit of the plunger. Pull up to remove the plunger and barrel.
4. Immerse a new plunger in clean fuel oil and thoroughly wash off the rust preventive.

NOTE: The plunger was lapped at the factory. Do not hold it by the lapped section.

5. Operate the plunger in clean fuel oil to check its operation.
6. Slowly insert the plunger and barrel into the pump with the barrel groove and plunger notch facing forward. Make certain the plunger piston pin is properly seated in the groove in the control sleeve.
7. Push the plunger spring up with two screwdrivers and insert the lower spring seat.
8. Install the remaining parts in reverse of disassembly.

REPLACING THE TAPPETS

1. Remove the delivery valve, plunger and plunger barrel.
2. Remove the plunger spring.
3. Remove the tappet.
4. Installation is the reverse of removal.

TESTING AND ADJUSTING THE FUEL INJECTION PUMP

NOTE: It is necessary to inspect and adjust the pump, using a pump tester, whenever it has been disassembled and assembled, when the plunger or plunger barrel have been replaced or when any of the component parts have been replaced. Use nozzle tube 57805-002 and test nozzle 5000-101, starting pressure 1422.3 psi. Clean No. 2 fuel should be used. Rotating direction, from drive side, is clockwise. Sequence is 1-4-2-6-3-5.

1. Remove the fuel feed pump and cover plate from the injection pump.
2. Install the injection pump on the tester and holding fixture.
3. Connect the test coupling to the tester drive shaft with the coupling disc.
4. Remove the cap and position the tester dial to measure the camshaft rotating angle.
5. Install a tappet lift gauge on the #1 tappet.
6. Bottom the tappet and set the dial gauge to 0.
7. Bleed the pump at the bleeder screw.
8. Loosen the nozzle holder ball valve.
9. Feed fuel to the pump inlet while slowly turning the pump tester by hand in the normal engine rotation direction. Fuel will flow from the test nozzle. When the fuel stops flowing the injection point has been reached. The tappet, at this precise point, must be .08858–.09251" above BDC.
10. If the fuel does not stop flowing after .0926", turn the adjusting bolt counterclockwise to raise the position of the plunger.

11. If the fuel stops flowing before .0886″, turn the adjusting bolt clockwise to lower the plunger position.

12. When adjustment is made, torque the locknut to 43–50 ft. lbs.

13. With the pump set at initial injection, set the angle scale mark on the tester flywheel at 0 or 180°.

14. If adjustment is correct, fuel should stop flowing at #4 cylinder when the tester has been turned 60° in normal rotation. If fuel does not stop flowing at the correct time, adjust as above.

15. Check and adjust each cylinder in turn.

16. When timing for each cylinder is correct, position the cam at TDC, check the plunger piston pin-to-plunger barrel clearance and make sure that the tappet vertical clearance is at least .0118″ for each tappet.

STANDARD FUEL INJECTION VOLUME ADJUSTMENT

1. Determine the zero position of the control by attaching the measuring device to the pump and pushing the index all the way to governor side. Match the scale on the left end of the index and set the 0 (zero) position of the scale at the position at which the measuring device index stops. On RSV mechanical governors, loosen the stop bolt to align this index.

2. Remove the rack guide screw from the rear of the pump housing and apply the lock screw attached to the tester. Secure the control rack in the standard position for adjustment.

NOTE: The lock screw should be tightened by hand; overtightening will bend the rack.

3. Start the tester and run the pump at rated speed.

4. Set the pump feed pressure at 21.3–22.75 psi and measure the injection volume at the rated stroke of the female cylinder.

5. In the same manner, measure the injection volume at rated speed and standard rack position. Compute the rate of unevenness of the injection.

6. If the results show that the mean injection volume and rate of unevenness are not within the limits, adjust by changing the relative position of the control pinion and control sleeve. This may be done by:

   a. Loosen the pinion set screw.

   b. Place a pin in the hole in the control sleeve and adjust by moving the control sleeve along the control rack a little at a time.

   c. When adjustment is completed, secure the pinion set screw.

   d. Remove the lock screw from the control rack and reinstall the guide screw.

Testing and Adjusting the Governor

RSV MECHANICAL GOVERNOR

1. Match the adjusting device index to the zero point on the scale and set the control rack to the zero position.

2. Operate the control lever and make certain the full stroke of the rack is .827″.

3. Make certain that the rack moves freely in the direction for maximum fuel injection by the spring force of the starting spring.

4. Set the stop bolt to remove any significant load on the governor linkage.

5. Set the stop bolt to give a control rack setting of .0197–.03937″.

HIGH SPEED ADJUSTMENT

6. Remove the governor rear cover.

7. Loosen the full load stop lock nut and adjust the full load stop so that its setting corresponds to an A rack position be-

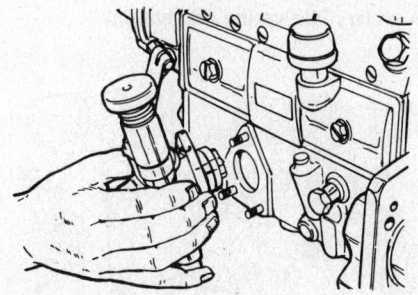

Fuel feed pump removal

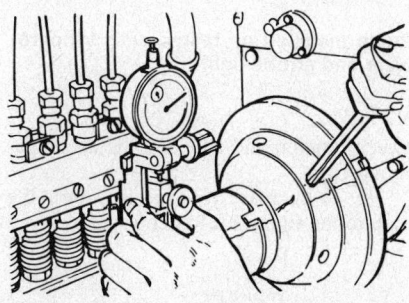

Checking injection start timing with a lift guage

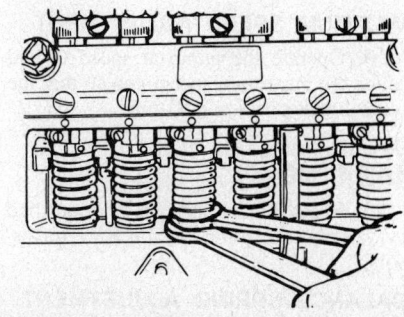

Turning the adjusting bolt

Checking tappet clearance

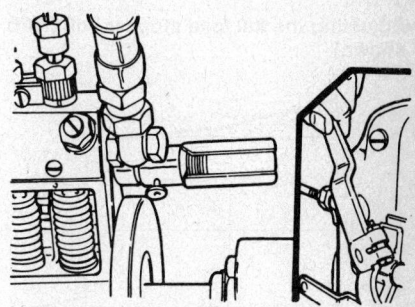

Attaching a measuring device to the pump

Installing the tester lock screw

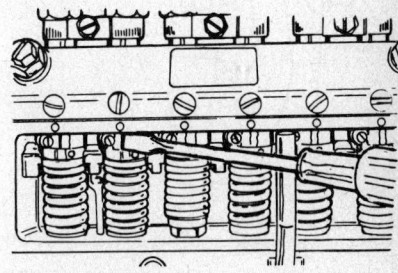

Loosening the pinion set screw

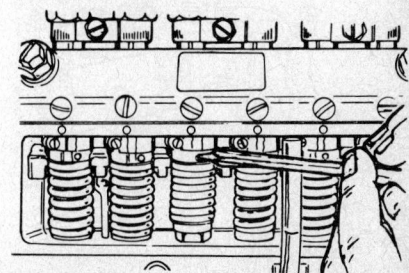

Installing the appropriate sized pin

Adjusting the full load stopper bolt (RAD shown)

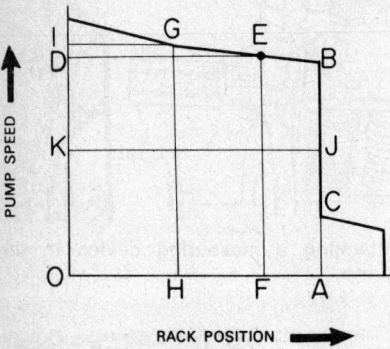

Schematic diagram of the governor

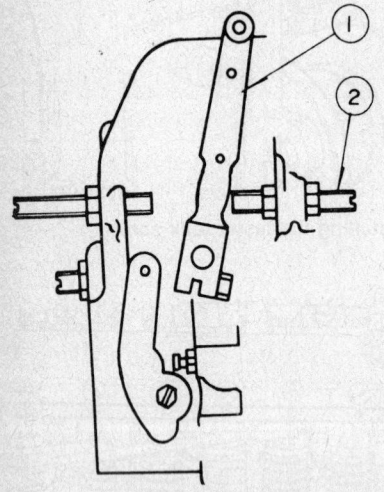

1. Speed control lever
2. Speed adjusting bolt (stopper bolt)

Adjusting the speed adjustment bolt (RSV shown)

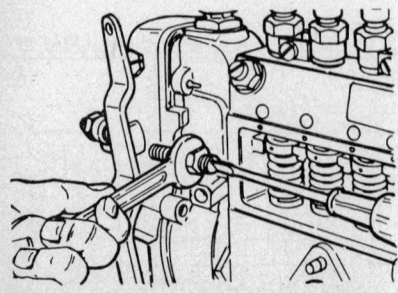

Maximum speed stopper adjustment

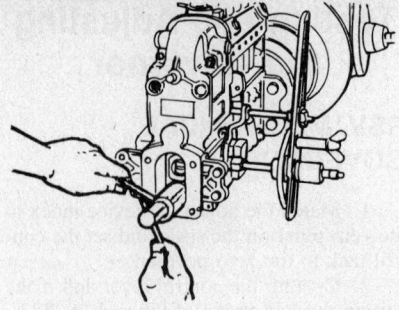

Adjusting the idling spring

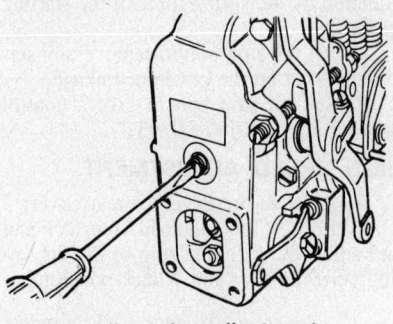

Auxiliary idle spring adjustment

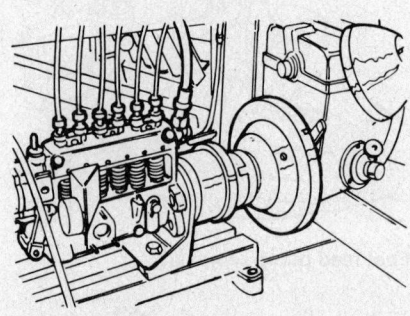

Pump installed on tester, with synchronizer and strobe light

tween rotation and BC. See the accompanying chart.

8. To increase the volume, turn the stop to the right; left to decrease.

$$\text{Unevenness} = \frac{\begin{array}{c}\text{Max or min}\\\text{injection}\\\text{volume for}\\\text{each plunger}\end{array} - \begin{array}{c}\text{Main}\\\text{injection}\\\text{volume}\end{array}}{\begin{array}{c}\text{Mean injection}\\\text{volume}\end{array}} \times 100$$

MAXIMUM SPEED ADJUSTMENT

9. Operate the pump at speed G and adjust the maximum speed stop so that the control rack position is G mm.

SPEED FLUCTUATION ADJUSTMENT

10. Speed fluctuation can be controlled by varying the spring rate on RSV governors.

BALANCE SPRING ADJUSTMENT

11. Set the control lever to the point where it contacts the maximum speed stop and operate the pump at a rate of F, between A and B.

12. Install the balance spring assembly under the tension lever.

13. Tighten the balance spring assembly with tool 57916-212 until the control rack position G is H mm. and secure with the lock nut.

14. Gradually accelerate the engine from speed D and make certain that the control rack is at G mm when the action of the spring ends at speed E.

IDLE SPEED ADJUSTMENT

15. Set the control lever at the stop position so that the control rack is at point B.

16. Set the speed to D and tighten the idle auxiliary spring so that the position of the rack is C mm. Secure with the lock nut.

NOTE: Do not tighten the auxiliary idle spring too much or overspeeding will result.

MZ PNEUMATIC GOVERNOR

1. Set the measuring device index at the zero point on the scale and set the control rack at the zero position.

2. Operate the control lever and make certain the full stroke of the control rack is .827″.

3. Connect a hose between the vacuum pump of the tester and the negative pressure chamber of the governor. Apply negative pressure equal to engine operation.

4. Operate the pump at 500 rpm and adjust the governor.

5. Tighten the stroke set screw so that the control rack is set at a position equal to zero.

6. Adjust the stroke of the balance spring to .236″.

7. If movement of the control rack deviates considerably from the performance curve, adjust by increasing or decreasing the thickness of the adjusting shims.

8. Operate the tester vacuum pump and check the control rack position and movement in relation to the pressure shown on the gauge. If the movement of the control rack for pressure variations does not conform to the performance curve, the idle speed is either too high or too low. Turn the auxiliary idle spring right to increase and left to decrease speed.

TESTING AND ADJUSTING THE TIMER

1. Install a timing light, such as tool 5783-001 on the tester using the cover plate attaching bolts, so that the synchronizer lever attachment is applied to the tappet.

2. Start the pump and turn on the timing light.

3. Direct the light at the angle scale on

the flywheel and measure the angular change based on variations in pump speed.

4. If the tester does not have an angle scale:

a. Attach an angle scale to the timer coupling and mount a pointer on the tester drive shaft.

b. Operate the pump and direct the light on the scale.

5. If the angular change is not within limits, disassemble the timer and adjust the spring force by increasing or decreasing the shims, or if necessary, replace the spring.

ENGINE ELECTRICAL

Distributor

REMOVAL

1. Remove the distributor wire harness connected to the coil.

2. Remove the distributor cap by either unsnapping the retaining clips or twisting the retaining clamps with a screwdriver. Bump the engine until the top dead center marks on the timing case and pointer are aligned on the compression stroke.

3. Using chalk or paint, carefully mark the position of the distributor rotor in relation to the distributor housing, and the position of the distributor housing in relation to the engine block. When this is done, you should have a line on the distributor housing directly in line with the tip of the rotor and another line on the engine block directly in line with the mark on the distributor housing. These markings are important because the distributor must be installed in the *exact* same position to avoid having to retime the engine.

4. Remove the vacuum line(s) from the advance diaphragm.

5. Remove the bolt that attaches the distributor to the engine block and pull the unit straight up and out of the engine.

INSTALLATION—ENGINE NOT DISTURBED

1. Before installing the distributor, replace the distributor mounting gasket in the engine counterbore.

2. Turn the rotor so the tip is aligned with the mark made on the housing during removal. Then turn the rotor about 1/8 turn in the opposite direction of distributor rotation past the mark.

3. Lower the distributor into the mounting hole and align the mark on the distributor housing with the one on the engine block.

NOTE: It may be necessary to move the rotor slightly to start the gear into mesh with the camshaft gear, but the rotor should align with the mark on the distributor housing when the distributor is down in place.

4. Install the distributor hold-down bolt and lockwasher but do not fully tighten.

5. Connect the distributor wire to the negative pole of the coil.

6. Install the distributor cap making certain that all the leads are all the way into the cap. Secure the cap.

NOTE: If the distributor cap is misaligned on its locating slots, the rotor and the cap will be damaged.

7. Start the engine and set the timing.

INSTALLATION WHEN THE ENGINE HAS BEEN DISTURBED

If the engine was turned over with the distributor removed or if you have installed the distributor incorrectly and the engine will not start, it will be necessary to time the engine from scratch.

1. Remove No. 1 spark plug. Have an assistant rotate the engine while you hold your finger over the plug port. Continue rotating slowly until you feel pressure and the timing mark on the crankshaft pulley lines up with the mark on the timing tab.

2. Install a new distributor mounting gasket in the counterbore of the engine.

3. Locate the No. 1 spark plug wire tower on the distributor cap.

4. Scribe a locating mark on the body of the distributor directly below the No. 1 spark plug wire tower with the cap installed.

5. Remove the cap, install the distributor, and align the rotor with the mark on the housing.

6. It may be necessary to turn the rotor slightly to get the distributor and the camshaft gears to mesh but the rotor should still align when the distributor is bottomed.

7. Install the distributor hold-down bolt and hand tighten.

8. Install the No. 1 spark plug, the distributor lead to the coil, and any plug wires which were removed.

9. Install the distributor cap making certain that the tang on the distributor body aligns with the slot in the distributor cap.

10. Start the engine and check the timing.

Alternator

PRECAUTIONS

Rectifiers and regulators in alternator systems are easily damaged by incorrect polarity. Observe the following precautions

when wiring and testing circuits:

1. Always be certain of battery polarity.

2. Always connect booster battery negative to negative and positive to positive.

3. Never ground alternator output terminal.

4. When adjusting voltage regulator, be careful not to short adjusting tool.

5. Before making any tests, turn off ignition switch and disconnect battery ground.

6. Never use a fast charge with the battery connected unless charging unit is equipped with a special alternator protector.

7. Never try to polarize the alternator regulator, this will cause severe damage to the regulator and alternator.

REMOVAL AND INSTALLATION

1. Disconnect the negative battery cable.

2. Remove the wire terminals from the rear of the alternator.

3. Loosen the adjusting strap and pivot bolts. Push inward on the alternator to loosen the belt and slip it off the pulley.

4. Remove the adjusting strap and pivot bolts, and remove the alternator from the engine.

5. Installation is in the reverse of the removal. Adjust the belt to have no more than 1/2 inch deflection on the longest span of the belt.

Voltage Regulators

Two types of voltage regulators are used to control the output of the alternators. One type is the internal unit, mounted with-in the alternator, and the second is an external type, normally mounted on the inner fender panel or the firewall.

VOLTAGE REGULATOR REMOVAL

External Type

1. Disconnect clamp lead at the negative terminal of battery.

2. Disconnect the wiring harness connector at regulator terminals.

3. Remove mounting screws and regulator unit from vehicle.

4. To install, reverse the above procedure.

5. Reconnect cable clamp to battery terminal, checking polarity first.

Internal Type

1. Remove the alternator as outlined.

2. Mark and separate the front housing from the rear housing.

3. Remove the diode trio screws and nuts, and remove the trio assembly.

4. Remove the two remaining screws in the regulator, and remove the brush holder and the regulator from the rear housing.

5. Installation is the reverse order of the removal, assuring that the insulated sleeves are installed on the proper screws, during installation.

NOTE: Refer to the General Repair Section for more repair information.

Starter

For servicing and overhauling starter motors, see General Repair Section.

REMOVAL AND INSTALLATION

1. Disconnect cable clamp from negative terminal of battery.
2. Disconnect cable and wire leads from terminals of solenoid assembly, identifying leads with tags. If the solenoid is not mounted directly on the starter motor, disconnect the cable from the solenoid to the motor at the motor terminal.
3. Remove starter motor mounting bolts or stud nuts.
4. Pull starter assembly forward to clear housing and remove starter.
5. To install, reverse the above procedure, installing new tang lockwashers where removed.

ENGINE MECHANICAL

Design

4 CYLINDER

The 196 cubic inch engine is a slant model with overhead valves and hydraulic lifters. The cylinder block and head are cast iron. The crankshaft is supported by five main bearings.

6 CYLINDER DIESEL

The six cylinder diesel engine is built for IHC by Nissan. Between 1976 and 1979, the engine was normally aspirated. In 1980, it was offered in a turbocharged mode.

V8 ENGINES

The V8 engines are overhead valve, 90° engines, all using a cast iron block and heads. The crankshaft is forged steel and is supported by five main bearings. Pistons are aluminum alloy and use cast iron connecting rods. Piston pins are press fit with

the lower end of the connecting rod and cap containing a locking type bearing insert.

Hydraulic lifters are used in all V8s and maintain a zero valve lash.

The cylinder heads use positive valve rotators on the exhaust valves. This device is called a "rotocap" and is located at the base of each valve spring.

The distributor, which is located at the front of the engine, is driven directly by the camshaft.

ENGINE REMOVAL AND INSTALLATION

The following is an outline of general engine removal. Removal procedure will vary from truck to truck due to the variety of body models and accessory equipment. Before lifting out engine be certain that everything has been disconnected. Remove anything that might be in the way of the actual lifting.

1. Drain water from radiator and engine block.
2. Drain crankcase oil.
3. Disconnect negative battery ground cable and remove cable clamp from hot terminal of battery.
4. Remove all water hoses to radiator and heater.
5. Remove fan blades and fan shroud.
6. Remove any radiator cross-brace rods or brackets.
7. Remove radiator mounting bolts and lift out radiator.
8. Remove hood hinge bracket mounting bolts and remove hood assembly.
9. Disconnect and remove air filter from engine. Remove breather hose from air cleaner, if applicable.
10. Disconnect fuel pump inlet line.
11. Remove vacuum lines from manifold and all other components, and lines from air compressor, and air pump, if applicable.
12. Disconnect throttle linkage, choke control wire and hand throttle control wire, if applicable. On V-304, 345, 392 engines remove the carburetor, if necessary, for the fitting of the lifting fixture.
13. If so equipped, disconnect wire from heater control valve.
14. Disconnect all wiring from engine:
    a. Water temperature gauge sender.
    b. Oil pressure gauge sender.
    c. Generator wires.
    d. Primary ignition wire to resistor.
    e. Starter solenoid wires and battery cable.
15. If so equipped, remove tachometer drive at the distributor on the small V8—or at the rear of the block on the big V8.
16. Disconnect exhaust pipes at manifolds.

— CAUTION —
Have the air conditioning system "bled" by a professional using the proper tools and safe procedures.

17. If so equipped, remove automatic transmission filler tube, freon compressor lines and disconnect power steering pump line and hose.
18. Install lifting fixtures and suitable sling. On V-304, 345, 392 models the lifting fixture is mounted on the intake manifold where the carburetor was removed.
19. Connect hoisting equipment to lifting fixture and hoist enough to support engine.
20. Remove bell housing mounting bolts. On V8 engines the flywheel housing front cover is removed before the flywheel housing is removed from crankcase.
21. Disconnect clutch linkage.
22. Remove front engine mounting bolts. On some models it is easier to unbolt the mount from the frame crossmember.
23. Remove side engine mount bolts.
24. In hoisting out engine, first pull engine forward to clear clutch assembly from transmission, then tilt front up and carefully out of the chassis.

— CAUTION —
Avoid damaging clutch driven disc.

25. Installation of the engine is in general the reverse of the above described procedure. Be careful when installing that wires are not pinched between engine and frame. Lower the engine until transmission main drive gear spline can be aligned with the clutch driven disc. The weight of the engine must remain supported until the bell housing is secured to flywheel housing. After engine has been secured to chassis, remove hoisting equipment and lifting fixtures.

Cylinder Head

CYLINDER HEAD REMOVAL AND INSTALLATION

V8 and 4 Cylinder Engines

1. Disconnect negative battery cable. Remove spark plug wires and spark plugs. Remove intake and exhaust manifolds as described in the following section. On V8's, this may entail removal of the air compressor and air compressor mounting bracket.
2. Remove valve covers and gaskets.
3. Loosen rocker arm shaft bracket bolts and remove the rocker arm assembly.

NOTE: Be sure to remove and keep track of the two dowel sleeves on the end brackets of the rocker arm assembly.

4. Remove pushrods, marking them so that they may be installed in their same locations.
5. Remove cylinder head bolts.
6. When lifting off cylinder, do not lose the two locating dowel sleeves.
7. Installation is basically the reverse

of the above procedure, with the exception of the following additional steps.

8. Be sure to use a new head gasket and to reinstall dowel sleeves when positioning the head and mounting the rocker assembly. Reinstall pushrods in their original locations.

9. On 4-196 and V-304, 345, 392, turn engine crankshaft until leading edge of balance weight on crankshaft pulley is aligned with the zero degree mark on the timing indicator before installing rocker arm assembly.

10. On 4-196 engines, be sure to install rocker assembly so that the oil feed shaft bracket is third from the rear.

11. On V-304, 345, 392 engines, install rocker arm assembly so that the notches at the end of the shaft are facing upward. Oil feed brackets are third from the rear on the right (even numbers) bank and third from the front on the left (odd numbers) bank.

--- CAUTION ---

Do not use a power wrench on heads of engines with hydraulic lifters. Torque head bolts slowly so that the leakdown of the lifters may relieve strain from the valve train.

12. On 4-196 and V-304, 345, 392 engines, tighten the head bolts in the sequence illustrated to 90–100 ft. lbs.

13. Retorque head bolts to the specified torque after 1000 miles of operation.

14. Install rocker covers and any other equipment removed for head work. Replace rocker cover gasket if necessary.

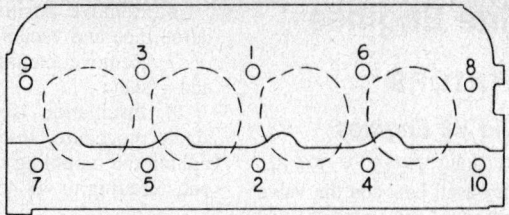

Gas engine—6 cyl head tightening sequence

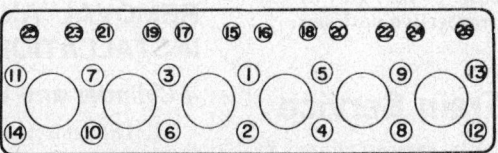

Diesel engine—cylinder head tightening sequence

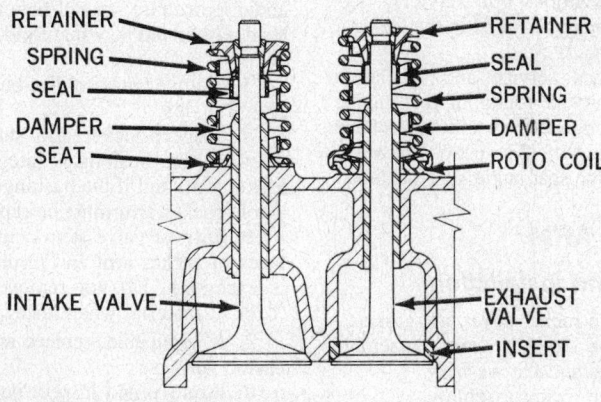

Rotator used under the exhaust valve spring

Diesel Engine

1. Remove the air cleaner.
2. Remove the crankcase vent hose and remove the intake and exhaust manifolds. These are bolted together.
3. Remove the alternator, bracket and belts.
4. Disconnect the coolant hose between the head and the oil cooler.
5. Remove the fuel filter assembly.
6. Disconnect the injection lines from the pump and the injectors. Cap all openings at once.
7. Remove the bypass hoses between the coolant pump and the thermostat housing.
8. Remove the fan.
9. Remove the rocker arm cover.
10. Remove the rocker arm shaft assembly.
11. Remove the pushrods and keep them in order.
12. Remove the fuel return lines.
13. Remove the nozzles from the head.
14. Remove the cylinder head bolts in the sequence shown.
15. Attach a hoist to the head and lift it clear of the block. On occasion, the pre-

combustion chambers may fall out, especially if the head is bumped or handled roughly. Take care that they are returned to their original positions if this occurs.

16. Remove the head gasket and O-rings.

NOTE: Before disassembling the head, make all necessary valve train measurements.

17. Place the head in a holding fixture.
18. Disassemble the valves. Mark all parts for assembly in their original positions.
19. Remove the retaining wire and lift off the valve stem seals.
20. Unscrew the glow plugs.
21. Disassemble the rocker arm shaft by removing the cotter pins at either end. Keep all parts in order. If rocker arm brackets prove to be difficult to remove, immerse the assembly in water heated to about 160°F. Immersion for a few minutes will loosen the parts.
22. Clean and inspect all parts.
23. Check the head with a straightedge. Maximum warpage is .0079″. Do not remove more than .011″ from the head.
24. Check the valve springs for free length and tilt. Free length must not be less

than 1.850″ and tilt must not exceed .03937″ (1mm).

25. Valve seats may be removed by cracking with a cold chisel or with a valve seat remover. New valve seats should be put in dry ice for five minutes prior to installation, at the same time the head should be immersed in 175°F water.

26. Assemble the head in reverse order of disassembly.

27. Place a new cylinder head gasket on the block with the stainless steel inset side facing up.

28. Install the O-rings around the water and oil passages.

29. Position the head on the block.

30. Coat the head bolts with clean engine oil and torque them in sequence, in stages as follows:
a. Large: 43, 94
b. Small: 21, 36

31. Install the pushrods, pressing down and turning them to be sure of proper seating.

32. Install the rocker arm shaft assembly, torquing the bolts to 18 ft. lbs. in sequence from the center to each end.

33. Install the injection nozzles.

34. Install all other parts in reverse order of removal.

Gasoline Engines

VALVE ROTATORS

4 Cylinder and V8 Engines

On the 4-196, V-304, V-345, V-392 engines, rotators are used between the valve spring and the cylinder head on the exhaust valve only.

NOTE: Keep the valves and their related parts together so they may be reinstalled in their respective positions.

Valve Train Service

The 4-196 and V-8 engines utilized hydraulic lifters for which there is no lash adjustment. Excess noise in the valve train of these engines indicates that service is required. Instructions for servicing hydraulic lifters may be found in the General Repair Section.

Valve removal, service, and installation procedures may be found in the Engine Rebuilding section. See specifications table at the beginning of this section for valve spring and valve seat angle specifications.

ROCKER ARM

Removal and Installation

1. Remove rocker cover and gasket.
2. Remove rocker arm assembly mounting bolts and flat washers.
3. Remove rocker assembly.
4. If applicable, remove clip-ring and retainer to disassemble rocker components. Be sure to keep all parts in order so that they may be replaced in their original positions.
5. Clean all parts thoroughly, making sure that oil passages are clear. If necessary to remove plugs from ends of shaft, drill a hole in one plug, knock out the other with a steel rod, then knock out the drilled plug.
6. Inspect shaft for wear and warpage. Replace bent or worn shaft.

Intake Manifold

REMOVAL AND INSTALLATION

4 Cylinder and V8 Engines

1. If engine is in vehicle, remove air cleaner and, if applicable, governor vacuum line.
2. Disconnect throttle linkage, choke cable and fuel line.
3. Remove carburetor.
4. On V-304, 345, 392, 400 engines, disconnect hose from thermostat housing and bracket for spark plug wires.
5. On 4 cylinder models, remove coil, coil mounting bracket and ignition resistor from intake manifold.
6. Remove positive crankcase ventilation pipe and vacuum line.
7. Remove mounting bolts, manifold and gasket.
8. Installation is the reverse of the above procedure. Install new gaskets and tighten the mounting bolts from the center out, torquing to 40–45 ft. lbs.

Exhaust Manifold

REMOVAL AND INSTALLATION

4 Cylinder and V8 Engines

1. Disconnect exhaust pipe from manifold.
2. Unbolt exhaust manifold from head.
3. Remove manifold.
4. Installation is the reverse of the above procedure. Install new manifold-to-head gasket and new manifold-to-pipe gasket.
5. Torque manifold-to-head bolts to 25–30 ft. lbs.
7. Inspect rocker arm shaft bushings for wear, the bushing is integral with the rocker arm, and if the bushing is worn, the whole rocker arm must be replaced.
8. Inspect valve stem contact pad surfaces of rocker arm and resurface if wear is excessive. Do not remove more than .010″ of material when resurfacing.
9. If applicable, replace any defective tension springs.
10. Remove and inspect push rods one by one (to insure original position). Roll them on a flat surface to check for straightness. Replace any pushrods that are bent, have loose ends or are worn.
11. Reassemble all rocker arm assembly components in their original order.
12. Install rocker arm assembly, making sure that the oil feed bracket is in the proper position and that dowel sleeves are in place. On 4-196 and V-304, 345, 392 engines turn the crankshaft until leading edge of balance weight on crankshaft pulley is aligned with the zero degree mark on the timing indicator before installing rocker arm assembly.
13. Tighten mounting bolts.
14. Adjust rocker arm to valve stem clearance as described above.
15. Install rocker cover, replacing gasket if necessary.

Timing Case & Gears

4-196 AND V8 ENGINES CRANKSHAFT PULLEY REMOVAL

Accessibility of the crankcase pulley and front (timing) cover will vary according to the model. On some vehicles the timing case will be accessible only if the engine is completely removed. The following instructions are general and apply to most front cover repairs and service.

1. Drain cooling system.
2. Disconnect radiator hoses and remove radiator. In some cases the radiator shroud and truck hood must be removed.
3. Loosen front engine mounts and jack up engine enough to provide access to the crankshaft pulley with a puller.
4. Loosen and remove fan belts and remove fan blades.
5. Remove crankshaft pulley retaining bolt. The vibration damper behind the pulley must be removed with a puller.
6. Using a suitable puller, remove the pulley from the crankshaft. On some models the pulley is in two pieces and the pulley must be unbolted from its hub before the hub is removed with a puller.

FRONT OIL SEAL REMOVAL AND INSTALLATION

1. Remove crankshaft pulley as described in the preceding procedure, steps 1 through 6.
2. Remove seal. It is preferable to use an appropriate seal puller. Use a new gasket when installing front cover and be sure to align cover before tightening.
3. Install a new seal using a suitable seal installing tool if possible. Lubricate first and be careful not to damage seal or seating surface of cover.
4. Install crankshaft pulley, fan belt and fan blades.
5. Lower engine and tighten mounting bolts.
6. Install radiator, shroud, hoses and whatever else was removed.
7. Fill cooling system.

TIMING GEAR REMOVAL

Timing gears can be removed without disassembling the engine. In some cases,

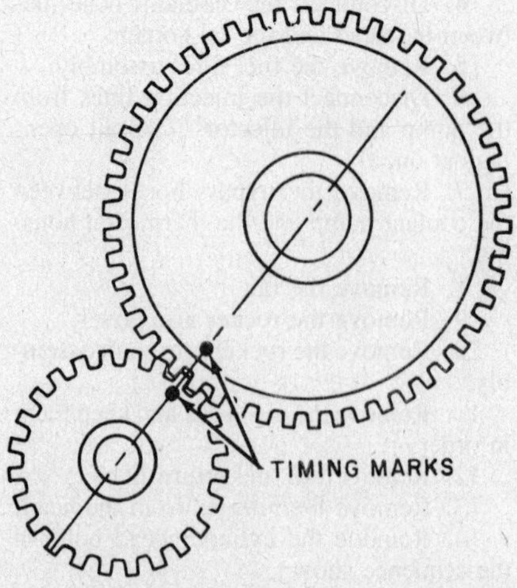

Timing gear alignment

however, the engine must be removed.

1. Remove crankcase pulley as described in steps 1 through 6 of Crankshaft Pulley Removal.

2. Remove engine front cover.

3. Rotate engine to align timing marks on crankshaft gear and camshaft gear.

4. To remove either gear, remove bolt and washer. Use a suitable puller.

NOTE: Replace both the cam gear and crankshaft gear, due to being serviced in matched sets.

5. Use a suitable installing tool to install gears. Lubricate with engine oil and insert key in shaft to align gear. Align timing marks as illustrated. Be careful not to damage threads on shaft. Install and tighten retaining bolt.

6. Rotate engine to check that gears are not binding.

7. Check gear backlash with a dial indicator. It should be within .0005–.0045″ on OHV4 and V8 engines.

8. Use a new gasket when installing front cover and be sure to align cover before tightening. On some models there is an oil slinger on the crankshaft.

9. Install crankshaft pulley, belt and fan blades. Tighten retaining bolt.

10. Lower engine and tighten engine mounting bolts.

11. Install radiator and hoses.

12. Fill cooling system.

CAMSHAFT REMOVAL AND INSTALLATION

On most models, it is possible to remove the camshaft with the engine remaining in the vehicle. However, the body grille work, radiator, A/C condensor (if equipped), hood, bumper, and braces must be removed to allow clearance for the camshaft to be withdrawn from the engine block. In some cases, it would be more advantageous to remove the engine from the vehicle to replace the camshaft. The decision would depend upon the individual and his shop facilities.

1. Remove the intake manifolds on the V8 engines, and the rocker covers on all engines.

2. Remove the rocker arms or assemblies, pushrods and tappets.

3. Remove the distributor and mechanical fuel pump.

4. Remove the oil pan and oil pump, if necessary.

5. Remove the crankshaft pulley as previously described.

6. Remove the front timing cover, gasket and seal.

7. Remove the two screws securing the camshaft thrust flange to the block.

8. Remove the camshaft and gear. To prevent nicking and damaging the camshaft or bearings, use a camshaft removal and installation tool, which is an extension on the front of the camshaft to act as a handle.

9. When installing the camshaft and gear, coat the bearing surfaces and lobes with lubricant and use the installing tool if possible, to aid in the installation of the camshaft. Make sure the gear timing marks align properly.

10. Working through the two large holes in the camshaft gear, install the two thrust flange screws and tighten to proper torque specifications.

11. Check timing gear backlash. If the end play exceeds the allowable limits, replace the thrust flange.

12. Place the oil slinger over the end of the crankshaft.

13. Install the front cover, using a new seal and gasket. Align the cover before tightening the bolts to the specified torque.

14. Install the crankshaft pulley, tightening to the proper torque.

15. Install the cylinder head, if removed, the intake manifold, tappets, pushrods, and rocker arms. Torque all bolts to the specified torque.

16. Install the fan pulley, blades and belts.

17. Install the distributor and fuel pump.

18. Install the oil pump and oil pan.

19. If the engine was raised, lower and tighten the engine mounts.

20. Complete the assembly as necessary for the removed body parts.

21. Start the engine, time it to specifications, and check for proper operation.

Pistons and Connecting Rods

For piston and connecting rod overhaul procedures see Engine Rebuilding General Sections.

PISTON REMOVAL AND INSTALLATION

1. Remove the cylinder head, the oil pan and the oil pump.

2. It may be necessary, on some models, to raise and block the front of the engine in order to gain enough room to drop the oil pan.

3. Use a ridge reamer and remove the ridge from the top of each cylinder.

4. Rotate the crankshaft until a connecting rod is to the bottom of its travel. Remove the connecting rod bearing cap. Place a piece of rubber tubing on each rod bolt to protect the crankshaft and cylinder wall. Push the connecting rod and piston assembly up and out of the cylinder. Remove all pistons in a like manner.

5. Place the crank journal at the bottom of its travel. Correctly seat rod bearing insert in rod then dip piston assembly in clean oil to lubricate rings. Using a ring compressor, install piston and rod in cylinder. Push piston in, do not strike. On 4-196 and all V8 engines, the piston assembly is in-

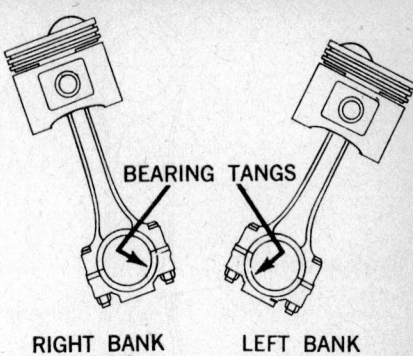

BEARING TANGS

RIGHT BANK
2-4-6-8

LEFT BANK
1-3-5-7

V8 engine—piston and rod assembly

stalled with the word "UP" toward the top (camshaft) side of the engine block.

6. Place lower half of bearing insert in rod cap and lubricate with oil. Assemble bearing cap to connecting rod with the number side of cap on the same side as the number on the connecting rod. Lubricate threads of bolts with engine oil and install bolts, tightening to the correct torque (see Specifications at the beginning of this section).

7. Rotate crankshaft and repeat installation procedure with the rest of the pistons and connecting rods.

8. Install oil pump and oil pan, using a new pan gasket.

9. Install cylinder head as described in Cylinder Head Removal and Installation.

10. If engine was raised, remove spacers and lower engine. Tighten engine mount bolts.

Piston Ring Replacement

1. Remove pistons as described above.

2. Remove both compression rings and three-piece oil ring.

3. Using rings which correspond to the piston size (standard or oversize), check rings for gap clearance and ring-to-groove side clearance.

4. Install rings on piston with a suitable ring expander tool.

5. Install piston assembly as described above.

Oil Pan

REMOVAL AND INSTALLATION

The engine and mounts may have to be loosened from the crossmember and lifted, and spacer blocks installed between the mounts and crossmember, to gain clearance to remove the oil pan from the engine. Other engine applications may only require the removal of steering linkage to gain suf-

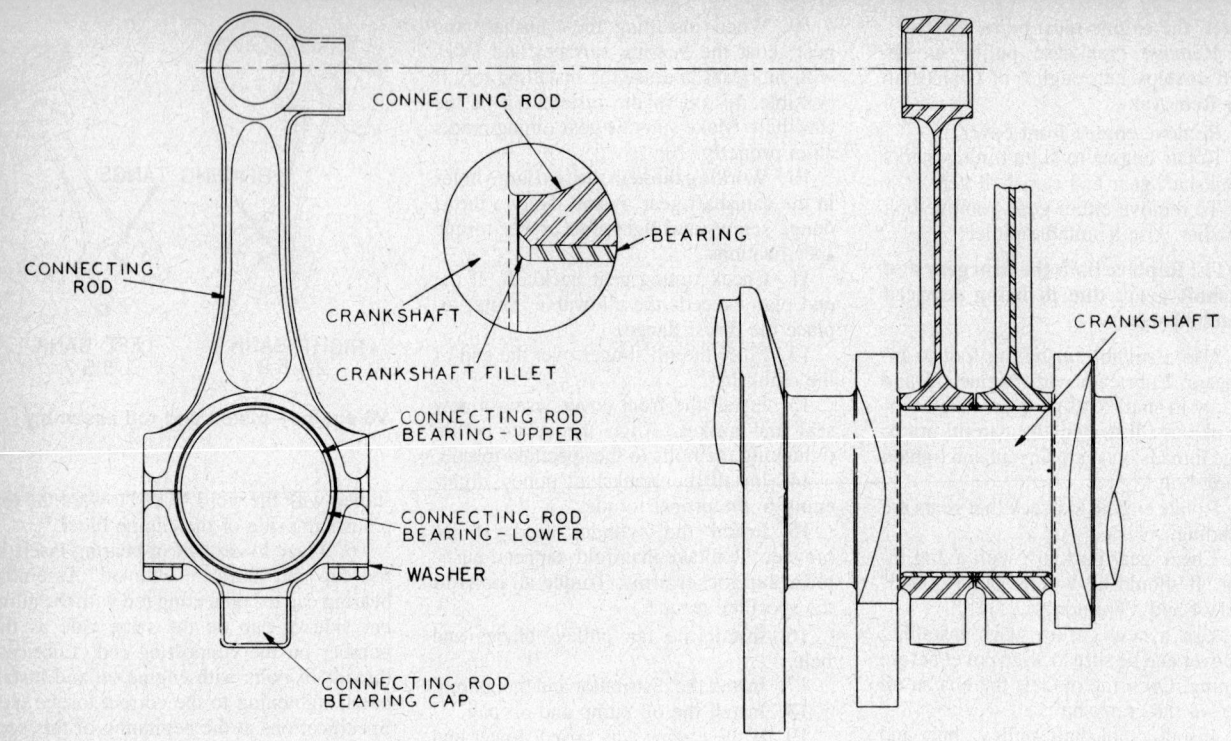

Installation of connecting rod to crankshaft

ficient clearance. Be sure to clean all old gasket material from the oil pan and the block before installing the oil pan and new gasket.

Main Bearing Replacement

On most models it is possible to replace main bearings without removing the engine from the vehicle. However, it is easier to do a better job with the engine removed and, if facilities are available for pulling the engine, this is the preferable method. See Engine Removal and Installation. For detailed procedures on main bearing, rod bearing and crankshaft servicing see General Repair Section.

1. Remove crankshaft pulley and front (timing) cover.

2. Remove cylinder head(s) and piston assemblies.

3. If the bell housing and transmission were not removed during engine removal, remove them now.

4. On many engines the clutch plate may be compressed by installing three cap screws ⅜"–16 × 2" for V-304, 345, 392 engines. If the clutch plate cannot be compressed in this way, cut three ½" × 1" × 3" wood blocks and insert them between the clutch fingers and back plate. Loosen backing plate mounting bolts slightly if it is difficult to insert wood blocks. A third alternative procedure for compressing the clutch plate is to insert three retaining clips. The clutch plate is compressed during re-

moval and installation of the clutch to prevent warpage.

5. Remove the backing plate mounting bolts and clutch assembly.

6. Remove flywheel bolts and pull off flywheel.

7. Remove main bearing caps. On OHV4, V-304, 345, 392, engines use a rear main bearing cap puller to remove rear main bearing cap. Note that the caps are numbered and should be reinstalled in their original positions.

8. When installing new main bearings make sure that the oil holes are properly aligned and that bearing tangs are fitted into tang recesses. Thoroughly clean all surfaces and coat lightly with oil. Be sure to align timing marks when positioning crankshaft. On the OHV4 and V-304, 345, 392 engines the numbered sides of the main bearing caps face the left side of the engine. When tightening main bearing caps, first tap them lightly into place, then tighten bolts in an alternating manner until the specified torque is reached. See Specifications for correct torque.

9. Install a new rear main bearing oil seal. On OHV4 and V-304, 345, 392 engines the round seal is pressed in after the rear main bearing cap is installed. Rear main bearing cap side oil seals are installed on these engines with an installer tool made from a piece of ⅛" welding rod. Puddle a ball on the end of the rod and file the ball to approximately 5.32" diameter.

10. Check main bearing clearance and crankshaft endplay and compare to clearance limits listed in Specifications at the beginning of this section. See Engine Re-

building General Section for clearance measurement and service procedures.

11. Reassemble engine following Steps 1 through 7 in reverse order. Be sure to align clutch driven disc with transmission shaft or clutch aligning tool before tightening clutch plate mounting bolts.

Rear Main Bearing Seal Replacement

4-196 AND V8 ENGINES

The rear main bearing cap seal can be replaced with the engine in the chassis, but the transmission, clutch assembly, and flywheel must be removed to gain access to the seal.

1. Remove the transmission, clutch assembly, and the flywheel.

2. Remove the engine oil pan.

3. With a slide hammer with a screw end adapter pierce the seal and remove it from the recess in the cap and block.

4. Lubricate the new seal, seat it squarely with a seal installer tool .085 inch from the rear face of the block.

NOTE: Production installed seals are seated flush with the rear of the block.

5. Install the bearing cap side seals with the use of a ⅛ inch welding rod, 8 inches long, with a 5/32 inch puddled ball on the end. Cut off any excess side seal, flush with the oil pan block surface.

6. Install the oil pan, flywheel, clutch assembly, and transmission.

Oil Filter Replacement

The oil filter unit is on the left side of the engine block. All engines use a spin-on type oil filter, which is replaced as a complete unit, using a strap wrench to remove it from the engine. Follow the instructions printed on the filter assembly to install.

Oil Pump

REMOVAL AND INSTALLATION

1. Drain crankcase and remove oil pan.
2. Remove oil pump mounting bolts and pull straight down on pump to remove.
3. When installing oil pump, guide pump shaft into position and rotate shaft until tang of drive gear is engaged.
4. Tighten oil pump mounting bolts to: 25–30 ft. lbs.
5. Install oil pan and fill crankcase.

OIL PUMP SERVICE

1. Thoroughly clean oil pump. Do not disturb or remove pickup tube unless absolutely necessary.
2. Remove pump cover bolts and pump cover.
3. Check gear to body clearance. If it is not within .0007–.0027″ on the OHV4 and V8 engines, obtain new parts.
4. Check gear backlash. If it exceeds .011″ on OHV4 and V8 engines replace gears.
5. Check pump shaft clearance in bore. If it exceeds .003″ on V8 and OHV4 engines, replace the whole pump assembly.
6. Remove relief valve and spring. Remove any burrs and clean. Be sure to install with bevelled or pointed end in seat. Check that valve moves freely in bore.
7. Check body and gear clearance. This is the distance between the pump gears and the pump cover. Adjustment of this clearance is made by the addition or removal of cover gaskets. On the OHV4 and V-304, 345, 392 engines the clearance is .0015–.006″.
8. When installing drive gears on pump shaft be sure that the correct drive gear to pump body clearance is obtained. On OHV4 and V-304, 345, 392 engines the oil pump shaft sleeve is crimped onto the shaft. On the OHV4 the assembly dimension is .200″ and on the V-304, 345, 392 engines the assembly dimension is .375″.

Lubrication System Priming

The recommended procedure to prime the internal parts and the oil pump is to attach a bearing leak detector or similar tool to a suitable fitting on the oil gallery, located

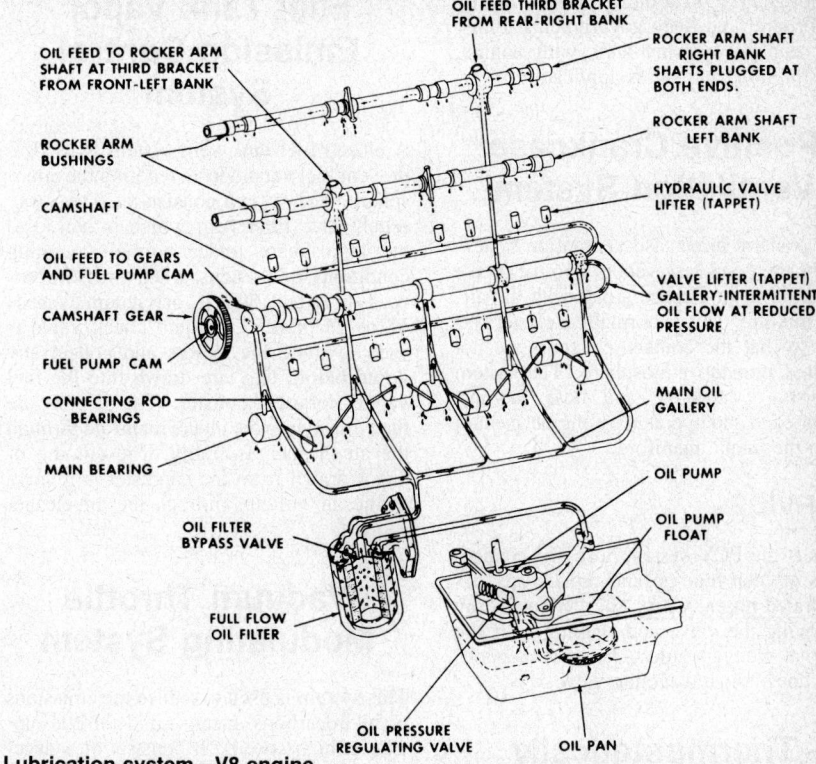

Lubrication system—V8 engine

on the left side of the engine block. Inject enough oil into the engine to fill the oil filter and the various passage ways for the lubrication system. Disconnect the primary coil wire and turn the engine over, while the priming operation is in process. Do not overfill the crankcase when this method is used. This type of priming will minimize the possibility of scuffing or heat build-up in the areas of friction, which could cause premature engine failure.

ENGINE COOLING

The cooling system is a closed type, utilizing a two valve pressure cap. One valve is used to relieve excessive pressure from the system, and the second valve is used to allow atmospheric air to enter the system during the cooling down period. The engine temperature is controlled by a thermostat, located on the front of the engine block or cylinder head. The coolant is forced through the engine and radiator by the water pump, located on the front of the engine, which is belt driven by the crankshaft pulley.

——— CAUTION ———

To avoid personal injury, remove the pressure cap from the radiator in two steps. Loosen the cap to its first notch and allow the pressure to escape through the over-flow pipe. After the pressure has been released, press on the cap and continue to turn until the prongs on the cap disengage from the radiator neck.

Water Pump

REMOVAL AND INSTALLATION

1. Drain cooling system.
2. If radiator shrouds hinder access they must be removed before proceeding.
3. Loosen alternator pivot bolts and adjusting bolt on bracket to relieve tension on the fan belt and remove belt from water pump pulley.
4. Remove all pipes and hoses connected to the water pump.
5. Remove mounting bolts or stud nuts and water pump.
6. Installation is the reverse of the above procedure. Be sure to install new gaskets and, if applicable, new O-rings on pipe end fittings.

EMISSION CONTROLS

Emission control systems are designed to control the emissions of hydrocarbons (HC), carbon monoxide (CO), and oxides of nitrogen (NOx) at the levels specified by the Federal and State governments. Emission control systems vary with engine, transmission, and series applications.

Positive Crankcase Ventilation System

The positive crankcase ventilation system draws the crankcase vapors into the intake manifold to be burned along with the air-fuel mixture. This is normally a closed system so that the crankcase vapors are not emitted into the atmosphere. The system consists of a valve and hose routings mounted to and operated by engine vacuum from the intake manifold.

SERVICE

Inspect the PCV system hose and connections at each tune-up and replace any deteriorated hoses. Check the PCV valve by removing the valve and shaking it. If the internal plunger rattles, the valve is good. If it does not, replace the valve.

Thermostatically Controlled Air Cleaner System

The air cleaner snorkel incorporates a thermostatically controlled valve, which directs air from the exhaust manifold area and from the engine compartment, depending upon the underhood temperature, to insure the carburetor induction air is warm before entry into the engine.

Air Guard System

This system is used to inject air into the exhaust ports to mix with the hot unburned gases, and to further burn the combustion mixture and reduce the emissions of hydrocarbons and carbon monoxide into the atmosphere. The system includes an air pump, a diverter valve, hose routings, and air injector manifolds and tubes.

Exhaust Gas Recirculation System

This system is used to meter exhaust gases into the combustion chambers to dilute the intake charge, thereby reducing the peak temperature of the gases and limit the formation of the oxides of nitrogen that form as the result of the high temperature during the combustion process. The system consists of a exhaust gas recirculating valve which connects the intake manifold to the exhaust manifold, and is operated by vacuum and temperature.

Fuel Tank Vapor Emission Control System

A closed fuel tank vent system is used to prevent fuel vapors from entering the atmosphere. The system consists of a two-way relief valve filler cap, which is closed to the atmosphere under normal operating conditions and opens when pressure exceeds 0.75 to 1.50 PSI, or vacuum exceeds 15 to 25 inches. A liquid check valve is used to route the vapors and collect any liquid before they are drawn into the fuel vapor storage cannister. The vapors are then drawn into the intake manifold through the air cleaner assembly. The amount of vapor drawn from the cannister is relative to the air volicity through the air cleaner snorkel.

Vacuum Throttle Modulating System

This system is used to reduce the emissions of hydrocarbons during rapid throttle closure at high speeds. It consists of a deceleration valve and a throttle modulating diaphragm located on the carburetor base to allow the throttle to remain slightly open and admit more air into the combustion chambers to lean out the overrich mixture. The decel valve and the modulator diaphragm are operated by engine vacuum signals.

Electric Choke

This system is used to assist in maintaining an open choke butterfly during cruising conditions, when vacuum may not be sufficient to draw enough heated air from the manifold to the choke assembly. When the engine cylinder head temperature is below 130 degrees, the electric choke is inoperative and the choke operates in the normal manner. Above the stated temperature, the electric choke is in operation.

FUEL SYSTEM

Fuel Pump

REMOVAL

1. Remove the fuel inlet pipe or hose and the outlet fuel pipe to the carburetor from the fuel pump fittings.
2. Remove the attaching bolts from the fuel pump housing to engine block and remove the fuel pump.
3. Clean the gasket surfaces of all gasket particles.

INSTALLATION

1. Install new gasket on the fuel pump mounting flange and install the fuel pump operating arm into the hole in the block, and into contact with the eccentric lobe on the camshaft.
2. Install the attaching bolts and tighten the pump to the block securely.
3. Install the inlet hose or pipe, and the outlet pipe to the fuel pump and tighten securely to avoid air leaks.

FUEL PUMP PRESSURE TEST

1. Disconnect fuel line at carburetor inlet and attach pressure gauge between the inlet and disconnected line.
2. Start engine and take reading. Consult Tune-up Specifications at the beginning of this section for correct pump pressure.
3. When engine is stopped, the pressure should remain constant or very slowly return to zero.

FUEL PUMP CAPACITY TEST

1. Disconnect fuel line from the fuel pump.
2. Connect a piece of hose to the line so that fuel can be directed into a measuring container.
3. Start engine and note time it takes to fill a pint container. Pump should fill one pint within 20–30 seconds.

Carburetor

REMOVAL

Single-Barrel Holley Model 1940

1. Remove the air cleaner, fuel lines, vacuum lines and any other lines or linkage attached to the carburetor.
2. Remove the attaching bolts from the base of the carburetor and remove the carburetor from the manifold. Remove and discard the old gasket from under the carburetor.
3. To install reverse the removal procedure making sure to install a new gasket under the carburetor base.

Two-Barrel Models

1. Remove air cleaner, throttle linkage and choke cable.
2. Disconnect fuel line and distributor vacuum lines.
3. Remove bolts from mounting studs and lift off carburetor.
4. To install, clean manifold mating surface and install a new flange gasket.
5. Install carburetor but do not tighten down stud nuts.
6. Connect fuel line and vacuum lines.

7. Tighten nuts on mounting studs in an alternating fashion so that flange gasket compresses evenly for a good seal.

8. Connect throttle linkage and choke cable, making sure that choke plates are fully open when the choke knob is pushed in.

9. Check throttle for complete travel.

10. Install air cleaner.

11. Adjust carburetor.

4-Barrel Models

1. Remove the air cleaner, throttle linkage, vacuum hoses, fuel lines, and any other hoses and linkages attached to the carburetor.

2. Remove the bolts or nuts holding the carburetor to the manifold, and remove the carburetor from the intake manifold.

3. Discard the base gasket and clean the base and manifold surface of gasket particles.

4. To install the carburetor, reverse the removal procedure, using a new base gasket.

5. Adjust the idle speed and air mixture.

NOTE: Refer to the Unit Repair Section for more repair information.

1. Lever, cam
2. Spring, cam lever return
3. Plug
4. Pin
5. Diaphragm assembly
6. Screw and lockwasher
7. Housing, valve assembly
8. Screw and lockwasher
9. Diaphragm, air dome
10. Air dome and filter assembly
11. Gasket, filter bowl
12. Filter
13. Elbow
14. Spring
15. Filter bowl
16. Retainer
17. Washer
18. Bolt
19. Lockwasher
20. Pump body
21. Pin, cam lever
22. Gasket, mounting

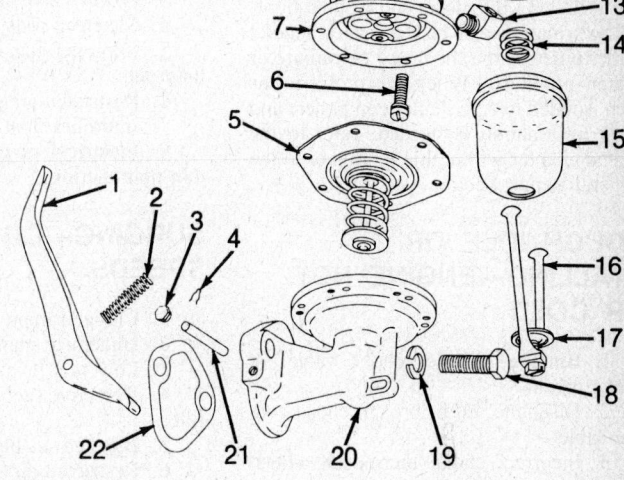

Exploded view of a typical fuel pump

OVERHAUL NOTES

All Types

Efficient carburetion depends greatly on careful cleaning and inspection during overhaul since dirt, gum, water, or varnish in or on the carburetor parts are often responsible for poor performance.

Overhaul in a clean, dust-free area. Carefully disassemble the carburetor, referring often to the exploded views. Keep all similar and look-alike parts segregated during disassembly and cleaning to avoid accidental interchange during assembly. Make a note of all jet sizes.

When the carburetor is disassembled, wash all parts (except diaphragms, electric choke units, pump plunger, and any other plastic, leather, fiber, or rubber parts) in clean carburetor solvent. Do not leave parts in the solvent any long than is necessary to sufficiently loosen the deposits. Excessive cleaning may remove the special finish from the float bowl and choke valve bodies, leaving these parts unfit for service. Rinse all parts in clean solvent and blow them dry with compressed air or allow to air dry. Wipe clean all cork, plastic, leather, and fiber parts with a clean, lint-free cloth.

Blow out all passages and jets with compressed air and be sure that there are no restrictions or blockages. Never use wire or similar tools to clean jets, fuel passages, or air bleeds. Clean all jets and valves separately to avoid accidental interchange.

Check all parts for wear or damage. If wear or damage is found, replace the defective parts. Especially check the following:

1. Check the float needle and seat for wear. If wear is found, replace the complete assembly.

2. Check the float hinge pin for wear and the float(s) for dents or distortion. Replace the float if fuel has leaked into it.

3. Check the throttle and choke shaft bores for wear or an out-of-round condition. Damage or wear to the throttle arm, shaft, or shaft bore will often require replacement of the throttle body. These parts require a close tolerance fit, wear may allow air leakage, which could effect starting and idling.

NOTE: Throttle shafts and bushings are not included in overhaul kits. They can be purchased separately.

4. Inspect the idle mixture adjusting needles for burrs or grooves. Any such condition requires replacement of the needle, since you will not be able to obtain a satisfactory idle.

5. Test the accelerator pump check valves. They should pass air one way but not the other. Test for proper seating by blowing and sucking on the valve. Replace the valve if necessary. If the valve is satisfactory, wash the valve again to remove breath moisture.

6. Check the bowl cover for warped surfaces with a straight edge.

7. Closely inspect the valves and seats for wear and damage, replacing as necessary.

8. After the carburetor is assembled, check the choke valve for freedom of operation.

Carburetor overhaul kits are recommended for each overhaul. These kits contain all gaskets and new parts to replace those that deteriorate most rapidly. Failure to replace all parts supplied with the kit (especially gaskets) can result in poor performance later.

Some carburetor manufacturers supply overhaul kits of three basic types: minor repair; major repair; and gasket kits. Basically, they contain the following:

1. Minor Repair Kits:
   a. All gaskets
   b. Float needle valve
   c. Volume control screw
   d. All diaphragms
   e. Spring for the pump diaphragm
2. Major Repair Kits:
   a. All jets and gaskets
   b. All diaphragms
   c. Float needle valve
   d. Volume control screw
   e. Pump ball valve
   f. Main jet carrier
   g. Float
   h. Complete intermediate rod
   i. Intermediate pump lever
   j. Complete injector tube
   k. Some cover hold-down screws and washers
3. Gasket Kits: All gaskets

After cleaning and checking all components, reassemble the carburetor, using new parts and referring to the exploded view. When reassembling, make sure all screws and jets are tight in their seats, but do not overtighten as the tips will be distorted. Tighten all screws gradually, in rotation.

Do not tighten needle valves into their seats; uneven jetting will result. Always use new gaskets. Be sure to adjust the float level when reassembling.

Carburetor Diagnosis Service

The following diagnosis and troubleshooting information can be used as a general guide to determine the cause of carburetor related problems. When the problem has been isolated to a particular component and more information is needed, refer to the related chapter within this section or to the General Repair Section.

ROUGH IDLE OR STALLING—ENGINE HOT OR COLD

1. Binding linkage, choke valve, or choke piston
2. Disconnected or broken choke control cable
3. Incorrect choke thermostat adjustment
4. Fast idle linkage and cam not properly adjusted
5. Idle mixture screw(s) out of adjustment
6. Idle speed screw out of adjustment
7. Air cleaner air flow restricted
8. Hot idle compensator valve stuck
9. Secondary throttle plates open (4V carburetors)
10. Clogged air bleed or idle passages
11. Vacuum leakage
12. Improper float level
13. Electrical or emission control systems malfunction

POOR LOW SPEED OPERATION

1. Clogged idle transfer slots
2. Clogged air bleed or idle passages
3. Air cleaner air flow restricted
4. Improper float level
5. Faulty automatic choke operation
6. Improper use of hand controlled choke
7. Vacuum leakage
8. Electrical or emission control system malfunction

POOR ENGINE ACCELERATION

1. Improper acceleration pump stroke
2. Inoperative or missing pump discharge check valve, ball, or needle
3. Damaged or worn pump diaphragm or piston
4. Leaking gaskets
5. Defective fuel pump
6. Clogged discharge jets

7. Electrical or emission control systems malfunction

POOR HIGH SPEED OPERATION

1. Defective fuel pump or clogged fuel filter
2. Clogged vacuum passages
3. Power valve stuck
4. Metering rods stuck
5. Improper size or obstructions in the main jets
6. Restricted air supply to air cleaner
7. Improper float level
8. Electrical or emission control system malfunction

SURGING—CRUISING SPEEDS

1. Clogged main jets
2. Undersize main jets
3. Low fuel level
4. Defective fuel pump or clogged fuel filter
5. Blocked air bleeds
6. Restricted air supply to air cleaner
7. Vacuum leakage
8. Metering rods out of adjustment
9. Power valve sticking
10. Electrical or emission control system malfunction

STALLING WHEN THE ACCELERATOR IS CLOSED QUICKLY

1. Improperly adjusted or defective throttle modulator or dash pot
2. Clogged air bleed or idle passages
3. Vacuum leakage
4. Throttle plates not closing

CLUTCH

REMOVAL AND INSTALLATION

1. Remove transmission. Extreme care should be taken to support the transmission until it is completely removed so that the main shaft splines will clear the driven member. For transmission removal procedures see Transmission Removal and Installation.
2. Remove flywheel housing cover.
3. Disconnect clevis yoke from clutch release lever.
4. Compress clutch assembly. On 9 spring clutches, the pressure plate is drilled and tapped so that three retaining cap screws and flat washers may be installed. Tighten the cap screws until flat washers and cap screw heads are seated on the back plate. On the 11″, 12″ and 10″ (6 spring, open back plate type) clutches, three re-

taining spacers are used to hold the clutch assembly compressed during removal. Slightly loosen the back plate to flywheel mounting screws to wedge the retaining spacers into place. On the 10″ six spring (full back plate type) clutch, three ⅝″ × 3″ × ¼″ hardwood blocks are used to compress the clutch during removal. Loosen back plate to flywheel retaining screws enough to wedge the blocks between the back plate inner flange and release fingers.
5. Remove back plate to flywheel screws and remove back plate assembly and driven disc.
6. When removing the clutch assembly, observe that the balance mark (spot of white paint) on the back plate flange is located as near as possible to the balance mark (''L'') stamped on the flywheel face. These balance marks should be located in the same relative position at clutch installation. If there are no marks, scribe a line to indicate correct position.
7. To install clutch, position the clutch driven member so that the long portion of the hub is toward the rear (all except the 10″ 6 spring open back plate type, which may be fitted either way). Clutch must be compressed for correct installation.
8. Place clutch assembly over the driven member on the flywheel so that the balance mark (spot of white paint) is as near as possible to the flywheel balance mark (''L''). Loosely install two or three back plate to flywheel mounting screws.
9. Using a clutch aligning arbor or transmission main drive gear shaft to hold the driven member in place, complete installation of the remaining back plate to flywheel mounting screws and lockwashers. Tighten capscrews alternately and evenly.
10. Remove retaining capscrews, wood blocks or retaining spacers which were used to hold the clutch compressed.
11. Install transmission as described in Transmission Removal and Installation.
12. Connect linkage to clutch release lever.
13. Install flywheel housing cover. Adjust linkage or cable as described.

Clutch Adjustment

1. Measure and correct the clutch pedal height to approximately 9 inches.

NOTE: On some models it may be necessary to increase the clutch pedal height setting slightly over the amount specified, in order to obtain complete clutch release.

2. Disconnect the return spring on release fork.
3. Loosen the nut on the cable or linkage rod.
4. Hold the pedal assembly against the pedal stop and lengthen or shorten the rod or cable to obtain zero clearance at the release bearing face and the pressure plate fingers.

5. After obtaining zero clearance, lengthen or shorten cable or linkage to obtain 3/32 inch between the bearing face and the fingers of the pressure plate.

6. Tighten nut on the cable or linkage rod.

7. Reconnect the return spring.

MANUAL TRANSMISSION

NOTE: For manual transmission overhaul procedures see Manual Transmission in the General Repair Section.

REMOVAL AND INSTALLATION

Removal and installation of manual transmissions will vary in detail, depending on which vehicle is being serviced. The following general procedure includes the basic steps common to all models.

1. Access to the transmission may be improved by removing cab floor panels if vehicle is equipped.

2. Raise vehicle on a hoist or jack up and support with jack stands.

3. Drain the transmission lubricant.

4. Disconnect drive shaft at the transmission. If the vehicle is equipped with a transfer case which is not mounted directly to the transmission, disconnect the shaft between the transfer case and transmission at the yoke. If the vehicle is equipped with a transfer case which is mounted directly to the transmission, it must be removed with the transmission as a unit and the forward and rear drive shafts must be disconnected. Secure shaft out of the way with wire.

5. Disconnect shift linkage from transmission shift levers. If the vehicle is equipped with a transfer case which is mounted directly to the transmission, disconnect the shift linkage from the transfer case shift levers.

6. If the vehicle is equipped with a transmission mounted handbrake, disconnect the handbrake cable at the relay lever.

7. Disconnect speedometer cable from the transmission.

8. On some models it may be necessary to remove the starter motor.

9. Support the rear of engine by means of a hydraulic jack.

10. Remove the transmission mounting bolts and insulators at the engine rear crossmember. If possible, remove the rear engine crossmember. Remove gear shift lever and housing from top of transmission if applicable.

11. Attach suitable hoisting equipment or jack to transmission and raise enough to support the transmission assembly.

12. Remove top transmission to clutch housing bolts and install transmission guide pins.

13. Remove remaining transmission to clutch housing bolts.

14. Carefully pull transmission rearward, keeping it in line until the main drive gear shaft is clear of the clutch.

CAUTION

Extreme care must be exercised to insure that the weight of the transmission does not rest on the hub of the clutch driven disc.

15. Depending on vehicle model, either lift the transmission up through the floorboard and out the right door or lower it with a jack.

16. Installation is the reverse of the above procedure.

17. Fill transmission with fluid.

Shift Linkage

Different types of transmissions are used which may require the shift linkage to be either mounted in the transmission and controlled by a shift lever, or to have a slight lever mounted remotely with linkage rods connecting the lever to the transmission. No adjustment is provided when the linkage is mounted in the transmission. When the shift lever is remotely mounted, the connecting rods have adjustment provisions. The adjustments are made with the shift control and the transmission arms in the neutral position, and the control rods adjusted to enter either the transmission arms or the shift lever arms with a free fit. Normally the control rods are threaded and trunnions and jam nuts are used to position the rods.

LINKAGE AND CABLE ADJUSTMENT

Shifter rods connect the shift arms of the transfer case to the shift lever arms. Nonadjustable and adjustable links are used on the various models of vehicles. To insure the proper alignment of the rods to the arms, use the following procedure.

Linkage Adjustment

1. Place the shift lever in the neutral position.

2. Remove the shift control rod at the transfer case.

3. Assure that the shift arm of the transfer case is in the center or neutral position.

4. If the control rod is adjustable, position the trunnion or clevis to align with the hole in the shift arm of the transfer case.

5. If the control rod is non-adjustable and the rod does not line up with the hole in the shift arm of the transfer case, replacement or bending will be necessary for the control rod.

6. Reconnect the control rod to the transfer case shift arm and check for proper operation.

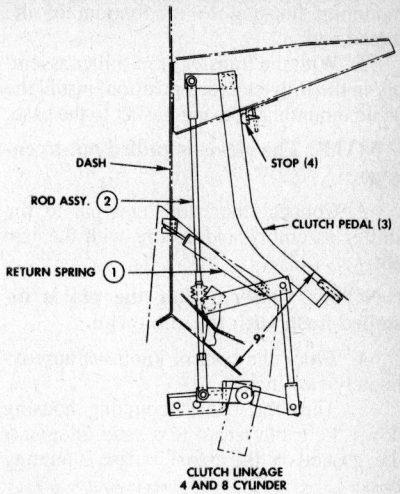

Clutch linkage

Cable Adjustment

A pull on the cable will engage the gears. To disengage, merely push the control cable in. To adjust, follow this procedure.

1. Pull the control cable knob out approximately two inches and block in this position.

2. Loosen the cable mounting housing jam nut.

3. Remove the two cable mounting housing bolts.

4. Unscrew the cable mounting housing away from the transfer case housing.

5. Confirm the inner clevis is positioned in the engaged position.

6. Turn the cable housing down the cable jacket to a snug fit against the gasket on the transfer case mounting boss. Install the two retaining screws.

7. Turn the jam nut down the cable jacket and secure against the cable mounting housing.

8. Remove the control cable knob block and operate the cable assembly to check the shifter operation.

CABLE

Removal

1. Leave the control knob pushed in.

2. Loosen the cable jam nut at the cable mounting housing on the transfer case and turn it back to the end of the threads.

3. Remove the two bolts holding the cable mounting housing to the transfer case.

4. Unscrew the housing all the way to the jam nut.

5. Pull the cable mounting housing forward until the inner cable jam nut is clear.

6. Loosen the inner cable jam nut at the shift clevis and unhook the cable end pin from the clevis.

7. Position the shift cable to obtain working clearance.

Installation

1. Turn the jam nut and the cable

mounting housing to the bottom of the thread end.

2. With the transfer case shifter assembly in the fully engaged position, install the cable mounting housing gasket to the case.

NOTE: The clevis is pulled out to engage.

3. Connect the cable end pin to the shifter assembly and secure with the jam nut.

NOTE: Confirm that the pin is installed flush with the cable end.

4. Block the control knob out approximately two inches.

5. Turn the cable mounting housing down the cable jacket to a snug fit against the gasket on the transfer case mounting boss.

6. Secure the cable mounting housing with the two mounting bolts to the transfer case.

7. Turn the jam nut down the cable jacket and lock against the cable mounting housing.

8. Remove the block from the shift control cable knob and operate the cable to check the shifter operation.

TRANSFER CASE

REMOVAL AND INSTALLATION

Frame Mounted

1. Drain the transfer case and disconnect the rear axle drive shaft at the transfer case.

2. Disconnect the front drive shaft at the transfer case.

3. Disconnect the speedometer cable, and indicator light switch wire, if equipped.

4. Disconnect the shift linkage. If equipped with a shift cable, refer to the cable removal and installation outlined previously.

5. Place a transmission jack under the transfer case and remove the mounting bolts from the frame to case.

6. Remove the transfer case from the vehicle.

7. The installation of the transfer case is the reverse of removal.

Transmission Mounted

1. Disconnect the rear driveshaft at the transfer case and drain the case assembly.

2. Disconnect the front driveshaft at the transfer case.

3. Disconnect the speedometer cable and the indicator light switch wire, if equipped.

4. Disconnect the shift linkage or cable.

5. Place a transmission jack under the transfer case and remove the flange bolts holding the transfer case to the transmission.

6. Pull the transfer case rearward to disengage the transmission output shaft from the coupler.

7. Lower the transfer case and remove from the vehicle.

8. The installation of the transfer case is the reverse of removal.

AUTOMATIC TRANSMISSION

Model T-407

REMOVAL

NOTE: The transmission and converter must be removed as a unit assembly. Damage can result to the converter drive plate, pump bushing, or to the pump seal, if the converter is allowed to remain on the converter drive plate.

1. Connect a remote switch to the starter solenoid so that the engine can be rotated from under the vehicle.

2. Disconnect the coil high tension cable.

3. Raise the vehicle and support safely.

4. Remove the engine rear crossmember on 4 × 4 vehicles, if necessary.

5. Remove the cover plate from the front of the converter housing to provide access to the converter drain plug and mounting bolts.

6. Rotate the engine to bring the drain plug to the six o'clock position. Drain the converter and loosen the pan bolts to drain the transmission.

7. Mark the converter and drive plate to aid in the assembly. Rotate the engine to locate the converter-to-drive plate bolts and remove the bolts.

8. Disconnect the negative battery cable and remove the starter motor assembly.

9. Disconnect the wires from the back-up light and neutral start switch.

10. Disconnect the gearshift cable or rod and bellcrank from the transmission.

11. Disconnect the throttle rod from the left side of the transmission.

12. Disconnect the cooler lines at the transmission and remove the filler tube.

13. Disconnect the speedometer cable, and move cable away from the transmission.

14. Disconnect the front universal joint and secure the shaft out of the way.

15. On vehicles equipped with parking brake mounted on the rear extension, re-move the parking brake cable.

16. On vehicles equipped with dual exhaust, the left exhaust system may have to be removed.

17. Install an engine support fixture to hold the rear of the engine.

18. Raise the transmission slightly, and remove the support crossmember holding the rear mount assembly.

19. Remove all bell housing bolts.

20. Carefully move the transmission assembly rearward off the block dowels and disengage the converter hub from the end of the crankshaft. Place a converter holding tool on the bell housing to hold the converter in place.

21. Lower the transmission assembly and remove the transmission from the vehicle.

22. To remove the converter assembly from the transmission, remove the holding tool and carefully slide the converter out of the transmission.

INSTALLATION

1. Rotate the pump rotors with tool SE-2402 or its equivalent, so that the lugs on the pump inner rotor are vertical.

2. Position the converter so that the impeller shaft slots are vertical and carefully slide the converter assembly over the input shaft and reaction shaft. Make sure that the converter slots fully engage the pump inner rotor lugs.

NOTE: The surface of the converter front cover lug should be at least ½ inch to the rear of a straightedge, placed on the face of the bell housing, when the converter is pushed all the way into the transmission.

3. Install the converter holding tool to hold the converter in place.

4. Position the transmission on a jack assembly and move the unit under the vehicle.

5. Rotate the converter to align the previously made marks on the drive plate and converter.

6. Raise the transmission and align with the engine. Install a pilot stud to aid in the alignment of the converter to the drive plate. Carefully work the transmission assembly forward over the engine block dowels with the converter hub entering the crankshaft opening.

7. Install the converter housing bolts and tighten to specified torque.

8. Install the crossmember and mount at the rear of the transmission. Remove the engine support fixture.

9. Install the oil filler tube and speedometer cable.

10. Connect the throttle rod and the gear shift rod to the transmission levers.

11. Connect the wires to the neutral start and back-up light switch.

12. Install the drive shaft and front universal joint.

13. Install the starter motor assembly.

14. Remove the pilot stud from the converter and install the bolts to the converter-drive plate assembly.

15. Install the cooler lines to the transmission.

16. Install the converter access plate on the front of the converter housing.

17. If the left exhaust system was removed, replace the pipes and brackets.

18. Install the parking brake cable and adjust, if equipped with the extension housing parking brake assembly.

19. Adjust the shift and throttle linkage.

20. Fill the transmission and connect the negative battery cable, if not done, and start the engine. Recheck the fluid level and refill as necessary.

TRANSMISSION FLUID DRAIN AND REFILL

1. Raise the vehicle on a jack or hoist. Support safely.

2. Place a large drain container under the transmission oil pan.

3. Loosen the pan bolts and tap one corner of the pan to break it loose, allowing the fluid to drain.

4. Remove the access plate from the front of the converter housing. Remove the converter drain plug and allow the fluid to drain.

5. Remove and clean the pan, remove the fluid filter and discard.

6. Install a new filter assembly on the valve body and tighten the screws securely.

7. Using a new pan gasket, install the pan and tighten the bolts securely.

8. Install and tighten the converter drain plug.

9. Install the converter housing access plate.

10. Install six quarts of transmission fluid into the transmission. Start the engine and allow to run for two minutes. Check the fluid level and add enough oil to bring the level to the ''ADD ONE PINT'' mark.

11. Recheck the level after moving the selector lever through all the gear positions and after the transmission has reached normal operating temperature. The level should be between the ''FULL'' mark and the ''ADD ONE PINT'' mark.

KICKDOWN BAND ADJUSTMENT

NOTE: The kickdown band is located on the left side of the transmission case near the throttle lever shaft.

1. Loosen the locknut and back off approximately five turns.

2. Tighten the adjusting screw to 10 ft. lbs.

3. Back off the adjusting screw 2¼ turns with the 6 and 8 cylinder engines. Hold the adjusting screw in position and tighten the lock nut to 29 ft. lbs.

LOW AND REVERSE BAND ADJUSTMENT

1. Raise the vehicle, support safely, drain the transmission fluid, and remove the pan.

2. Loosen the lock nut on the adjusting screw.

3. Tighten the adjusting screw to 10 ft. lbs.

4. Tighten the lock nut to 30 ft. lbs.

5. Install the pan using a new pan gasket.

6. Fill the transmission with fluid, start the engine and recheck the level. Add as necessary.

BACK-UP LIGHT AND NEUTRAL START SWITCH

No provisions are made for any adjustments of the back-up light and neutral start switch. The neutral start circuit is controlled by the inner terminal and the back-up light circuits are controlled by the two outside terminals.

The replacement of the switch is accomplished by unscrewing the switch from the transmission case, and screwing a new switch into the case. Since fluid leakage will occur when removing the switch, fluid must be added after the new switch is installed.

SHIFT LINKAGE

Adjustable Cable Control

1. Install cable conduit anchor clamps at both ends.

2. Install swivel on the control lever so that a distance of .55 inch exists from the end of the cable to the opposite side of the trunnion. Tighten the jam nut securely.

3. With the control in PARK position and transmission lever in the full rearward position (PARK detent), adjust the yoke so that the rod end pin installs freely and secure the yoke nut and install the cotter pin.

Column Shift

1. Assemble all linkage parts, but leave the upper control rod bolt loose.

2. Place the selector lever in DRIVE position.

3. Move the shift control lever on the transmission to the DRIVE position.

4. Tighten the upper bolt on the control rod to 14–16 ft. lbs.

5. Check the adjustment as follows:

a. Shift effort must be free and detents feel crisp. All gate stops must be positive.

b. Key start must only occur in the PARK or NEUTRAL positions.

c. Detent positions must be in proper relationship to the transmission lever positions.

THROTTLE VALVE LINKAGE ADJUSTMENT

1. With the engine off and an assistant holding the accelerator pedal to the floor, check for full carburetor throttle plate opening.

2. If necessary, adjust the throttle cable and pedal floor stop to obtain wide open throttle.

3. If necessary, adjust the idle speed of the engine with the use of a tachometer and with the engine at normal operating temperature and the carburetor off the fast idle cam. Adjust the curb idle speed, (throttle stop solenoid activated) with the transmission in neutral and the air conditioning in the OFF position.

NOTE: Be sure that carburetor is not being held open by a deceleration valve dashpot, solenoid valve, or a vacuum throttle modulator valve.

--- CAUTION ---

All components in the throttle control and transmission linkage system must operate freely with absolutely no sticking, excessive friction, or interference from other chassis components.

DRIVETRAIN

Front Driveshaft

The front driveshaft connects from the transfer case to the front axle companion flange. The U-joints are attached to the differential by bearing flanges on older models and U-bolts on newer ones.

REMOVAL AND INSTALLATION

1. Raise the front of the vehicle and place it on jackstands.

2. Place the transfer case in gear.

3. Remove the attaching bolts from the flange on the transfer case. Lower the driveshaft slowly to the ground.

4. Remove the attaching bolts from the flange on the front axle and pull the shaft from the vehicle.

To install:

5. Attach the front and rear universal joints.

6. Lower the vehicle.

Rear Driveshaft

REMOVAL AND INSTALLATION

2WD

1. Raise the vehicle and support it securely.

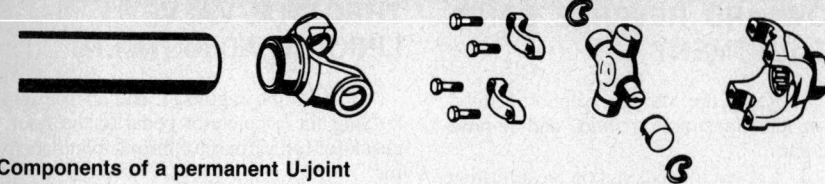

Components of a permanent U-joint

Components of a center bearing assembly

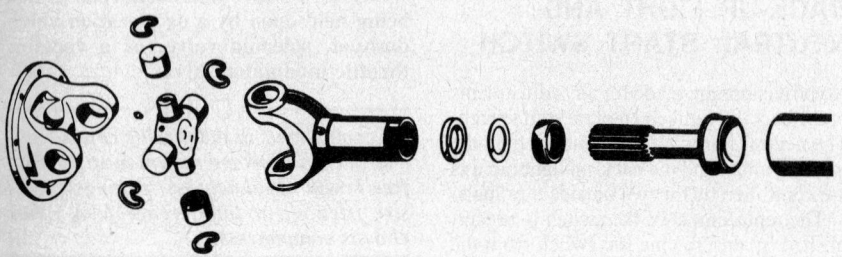

Components of a slip joint

2. Remove the attaching bolts from the companion flange and lower the end of the driveshaft to the floor.

3. Partially drain the transmission lubricant.

4. Pull the yoke from the rear of the transmission.

To install:

5. Insert the yoke onto the transmission output shaft.

--- **CAUTION** ---

Be careful not to damage the rear transmission seal.

6. Attach the rear U-joint to the companion flange.

7. Fill the transmission to the proper level.

8. Lower the vehicle.

4WD

1. Raise and securely support the vehicle.

2. Disconnect the rear driveshaft bolts from the companion flange.

3. Remove the driveshaft-to-transfer case flange attaching bolts.

4. Remove the driveshaft.

To install:

5. Attach the front U-joint to the transfer case flange.

6. Connect the rear end of the driveshaft to the companion flange of the rear axle.

7. Lower the vehicle.

U-Joints (Driveshaft)

Scout uses conventional roller bearing U-joints. Snap-rings hold the bearing cups to the yoke. 2WD models use two U-joints while 4WD models have four.

OVERHAUL

1. Remove the yoke and U-joint assembly from the transmission.

NOTE: Align the arrows on the yoke and transmission shaft when assembling.

2. Place the yoke assembly in a vise.

--- **CAUTION** ---

A soft-jawed vise should be used so that the yoke will not be damaged.

3. Remove the needle bearing assembly from the end of the cross.

4. Rotate the yoke in the vise so that a snap-ring journal is facing upward.

5. Tap the snap-ring to loosen it in its groove.

6. Using a pair of needle nose pliers, remove the snap-ring. Repeat the same procedure for the other snap-ring.

7. Tap the bearing on one side with a small brass drift to loosen the opposite side bearing cup.

8. Remove the bearing cup, turn the assembly over, and tap out the cup on the other side.

9. Remove the journal cross from the

yoke by tipping it to one side and pulling it out.

10. Installation is in the reverse of removal.

FRONT DRIVE AXLE

Leaf Spring

REMOVAL AND INSTALLATION

1. Raise the vehicle and support on the frame rails behind the front springs with floor stands.

2. Remove the shock absorber from the spring.

3. Remove the U-bolts, spring bumpers and retainer, or the U-bolt seat.

4. Remove the lubricators, if used.

5. Remove the nuts from the shackles and bracket pins.

6. Slide the spring off the bracket and shackle pins.

7. Remove the spring from the vehicle.

8. Installation is the reverse of removal. Tighten all nuts and bolts securely.

Front Drive Axle Removal

1. Jack up truck until load is removed from springs and block up frame to safely hold weight.

2. Drain lubricant from main housing and, if applicable, from wheel end housings.

3. Disconnect brakes.

4. Disconnect drag link from ball stud bracket.

5. Disconnect drive shaft from pinion shaft yoke.

6. Supporting axle with a portable floor jack, remove spring U-bolts.

7. Roll axle assembly out from under truck.

8. To install, reverse the above procedure.

Front Drive Axle Adjustments

Preload on the knuckle bearings of these front axles must be maintained at all times. Check for looseness each time knuckle is lubricated.

1. Jack up front end of truck until off-

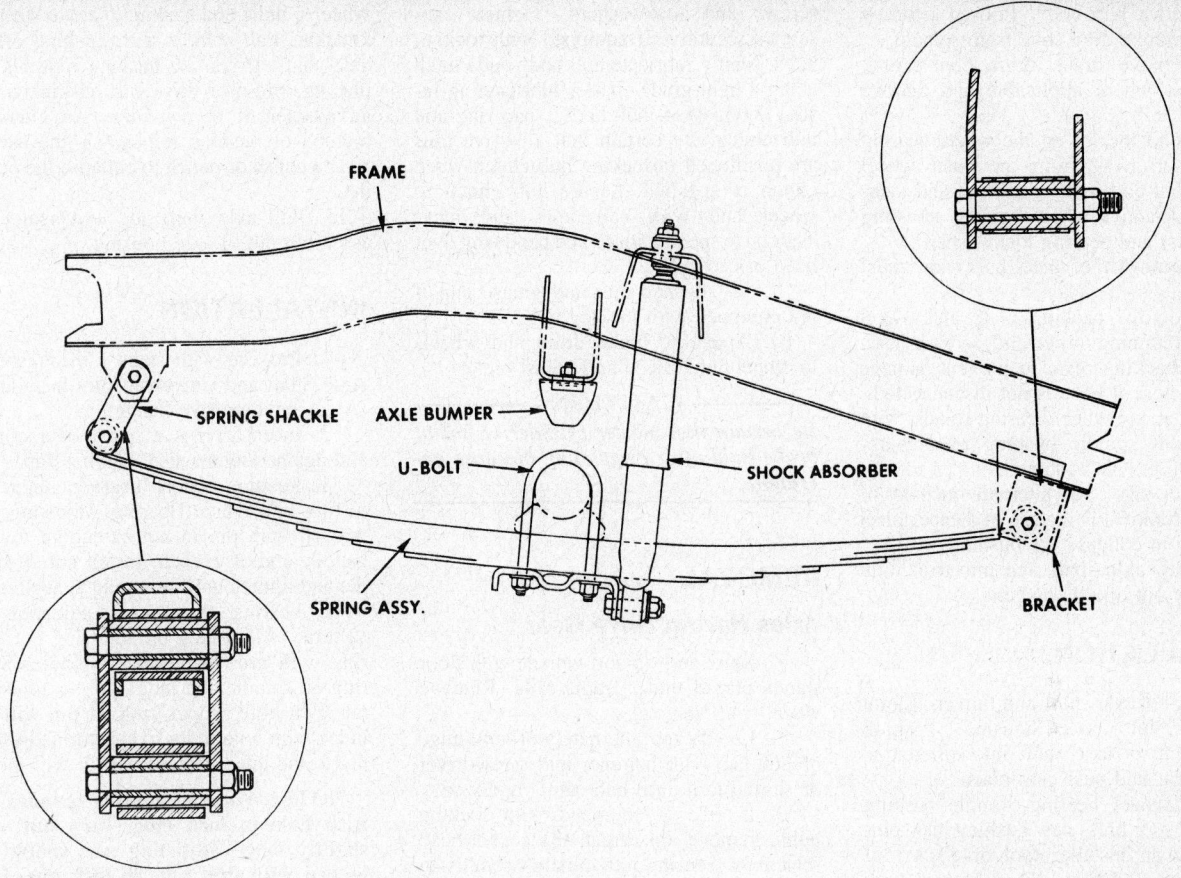

Front spring mounting

center weight of the wheel is relieved (wheel just barely touching ground).

2. Remove wheel and wheel adapter from hub.

3. Disconnect tie rod and drag link.

4. Remove axle shaft.

5. To remove play (check for play by pushing and pulling on top and bottom of knuckle) and increase preload drag, turn adjusting bolt into back of knuckle. Preload should read (spring scale hooked into end of steering arm) 12 lbs.

Front Wheel Bearing Adjustment

1. Remove wheel and adapter from hub.

2. Remove axle shaft or internal gear, and adjusting nut lock plate.

3. Tighten nut until just against bearing.

4. Rotate the wheel forward and backward until a slight drag can be felt. Turn nut back to the first lock hole to obtain about a ½ hole relief.

5. Bearing adjustment is correct when no play can be felt when pushing and pull at top and bottom of wheel.

NOTE: For overhaul procedures see Rear Axle in the General Repair Section.

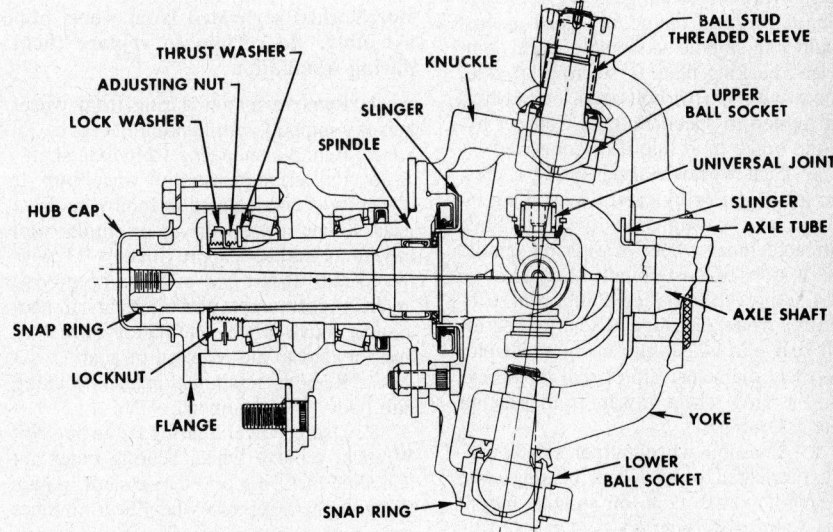

Typical front drive mounting

Front Axle Shaft

Removal

Axles Having Drive Flange

1. Raise vehicle, support with floor stands and remove wheel from vehicle.

2. Remove grease cap and snap-ring from end of axle shaft.

3. Remove drive flange cap screws, lock-washer, flange and gasket. If equipped with locking hubs, bend up locking tab, take out capscrews and remove clutch body.

NOTE: Lift off clutch body holding it erect so as not to let drive pins fall out of body. If they do fall out, be certain to install them during reassembly.

Remove hub body. Loosen setscrew and unscrew drag shoe from spindle.

4. Remove brake drum countersunk setscrews, where applicable and remove drum.

5. Bend the lip on the wheel bearing lockwasher away from the outer wheel bearing nut and remove the nut and lockwasher. Remove wheel bearing adjusting nut (inner) and bearing lockwasher.

6. Remove the wheel hub with wheel bearing.

7. Remove backing plate and wheel spindle retaining bolts and lockwashers. Support backing plate to prevent damage to brake hose if hose is not disconnected.

8. Remove wheel bearing spindle with bushing. If spindle bushing requires replacing, press out bushing using an adapter of correct size. An alternate method of bushing removal is the use of a cape chisel or punch to collapse the bushing.

9. Pull axle shaft and universal joint assembly out of axle housing.

INSTALLATION

1. Insert axle shaft and universal joint assembly into axle housing. Position splined end of axle shaft into differential pinion gear and push into place.

2. If wheel bearing spindle bushing was removed, press new bushing into spindle using an installer tool or adapter of proper size. Lubricate ID of bushing with chassis lube when installed to provide initial lubrication. Bushing should be pressed in until bushing flange is seated against shoulder in spindle. Assemble wheel spindle and backing plate to steering knuckle. Secure with six (6) bolts and lockwashers and tighten to specifications. Connect hydraulic brake fluid line if disconnected.

3. Pack wheel bearings using a pressure lubricator or by carefully working lubricant into bearing cones by hand. Slide lubricated inner wheel bearing on spindle until it stops against spindle shoulder.

4. Apply thin coating of lubricant specified for wheel bearings to seal lip and install seal into wheel hub using an adapter of correct diameter. Lip of seal should extend towards wheel (away from backing plate assembly).

5. Assemble wheel hub on spindle. Install lubricated outer wheel bearing cone on spindle. Push cone on spindle until it rests against bearing cup.

6. Install wheel bearing lockwasher and adjusting (inner) nut. Tighten adjusting nut until there is a slight drag on the bearings when the hub is turned; then back-off approximately one-sixth turn.

7. Install tang-type lockwasher and lock nut (outer). Tighten nut and bend lockwasher tang over lock nut. If axle is equipped with locking hubs, install drag shoe on spindle and tighten setscrew.

8. Align splines of drive flange with those of axle shaft and secure drive flange and new gasket to wheel hub with cap-

screws and lockwashers. Tighten capscrews securely. If equipped with locking hubs, lightly lubricate hub body and clutch using a light grade chassis lubricant an install new gasket, hub body, snap ring and hub clutch. Be certain that all drive pins are positioned in locking hub clutch when clutch is installed. Secure hub clutch to wheel hub with capscrews and lock. Tighten to specifications and bend tang over head of capscrew.

9. Install snap-ring and grease cup if not equipped with locking hubs.

10. Assemble brake drum and wheels to wheel hub. Bleed and adjust brakes.

--- CAUTION ---
Be certain that master cylinder is full of brake fluid after completing bleeding operation.

REMOVAL

Axles Having Drive Gear

1. Raise and support vehicle with floor stands placed under frame rails. Remove wheel from vehicle.

2. Lightly tap alternately around edge of hub cap with hammer and screwdriver or similar tool until hub cap is removed.

3. If axle is equipped with locking hubs, remove the eight (8) socket-head setscrews securing hub clutch assembly to wheel hub assembly.

NOTE: Drive pins may fall out of hub clutch when separated from wheel hub assembly. Be certain to replace them during installation.

4. Remove retaining ring from wheel hub if equipped with locking hubs.

5. Remove snap-ring from axle shaft.

6. Pull drive gear out of wheel hub. If difficulty is encountered in removing drive gear, obtain a screwdriver or similar tool having the end bent approximately 90° with the handle. Insert end of tool into groove in drive gear and withdraw gear. If necessary, move wheel alternately backward and forward to aid removal of gear.

7. Remove retaining ring and locking hub body, if so equipped.

8. Using Wheel Bearing Adjusting Nut Wrench, remove wheel bearing outer nut and slide lock ring off of axle shaft. Again using wrench, remove wheel bearing inner nut.

9. Pull drive gear spacer out of wheel hub.

10. Remove brake drum or disc brake assembly from wheel hub and slide wheel hub assembly off of spindle.

NOTE: Do not allow tapered roller bearings to drop on floor as bearings may be damaged.

11. Remove screws retaining grease guard to backing plate. Take off grease guard and gasket.

12. Remove the six (6) bolts securing

wheel spindle and backing plate to steering knuckle. Pull spindle with bushing off of axle shaft. If spindle bushing requires replacing, press or drive out bushing using an adapter of correct size. An alternate method of bushing removal is the use of a cape chisel or punch to collapse the bushing.

13. Pull axle shaft and universal joint assembly out of axle housing.

INSTALLATION

1. Proceed with steps 1 through 5 of Axle Shaft and Universal Joint Installation (Axles having drive flange).

2. Insert drive gear spacer over spindle and against outer wheel bearing cup.

3. Position wheel bearing inner adjusting nut Wheel Bearing Adjusting Nut wrench with pin in nut extending toward handlle end of wrench. Install nut on spindle and tighten until it is snug against outer wheel bearing; then loosen adjusting nut ¼ turn.. Align tang on adjusting nut lock ring with groove in wheel spindle. Slide ring on spindle and index pin on adjusting nut with hole in lock ring. If pin will not index with hole in lock ring, turn adjusting nut to the left (Loosen) until it will index.

NOTE: When attempting to index pin with hole in lock ring, turn nut very slightly since adjusting nut should be locked with first hole in lock ring past ¼ turn lose. Position wheel bearing out nut in adjusting nut wrench and install on spindle. Tighten nut securely.

4. Align splines on axle shaft and splines in wheel hub with those of drive gear. Insert drive gear on axle shaft. Push gear into hub until it rests again drive gear spacer.

NOTE: Groove on side of gear must be toward hub cap.

5. If axle is equipped with locking hubs, lightly lubricate locking hub body using a light grade chassis lubricant. Align splines and insert hub body into wheel hub.

6. Install snap-ring on end of axle shaft.

7. Place retaining groove in wheel hub, if equipped with locking hub.

8. If applicable, lightly grease hub clutch assembly using a light grade chasis lubricant. Be sure that all eight (8) drive pins are positioned in the locking hub clutch. Assemble hub clutch to hub body and secure with eight (8) socket head setscrews.

9. Position hub cap on wheel hub and lightly tap alternately around cap until flange is against edge of hub.

10. Assemble brake or disc brake assembly and wheel to wheel hub. Bleed and adjust brakes.

--- CAUTION ---
Be certain that the master cylinder is full of brake fluid after bleeding operation.

Steering Knuckle (Ball Joint)

REMOVAL

1. With the vehicle safely supported, remove the wheel, caliper and rotor.

2. Remove the backing plate and the spindle from the knuckle.

NOTE: If necessary, tap the spindle lightly with a soft hammer to loosen it from the knuckle bolts. The spindle oil seal, needle bearings, and bronze spacer can be removed and replaced at this time.

3. Remove the axle from the housing.

NOTE: The slingers can be removed from the axle by using pullers or tapping the axle through the slingers.

4. Disconnect and remove the tie rod from the steering arm.

5. Remove the cotter pin from the upper ball socket stud and remove the nut.

6. Remove the nut from the lowerball socket stud and discard.

NOTE: This nut is of a special torque design and should only be used one time.

7. Remove the lower ball socket snapring (used on 4 × 4 applications only), and unseat the upper and lower ball socket studs with a lead hammer or with a puller tool arrangement, to separate the knuckle from the yoke.

NOTE: If the upper ball socket stud remains in the yoke flange, remove it by striking it on the stud with a soft hammer.

8. With the aid of puller tools or a press and ram, remove the bottom ball socket.

9. Reverse the knuckle and remove the upper ball socket.

10. With the aid of a special socket, remove the threaded sleeve in the top flange of the yoke.

INSTALLATION

1. Assemble the lower ball socket into the knuckle with a press and ram or a puller tool arrangements, making sure that the ball socket is firmly seated against the knuckle. Install the snap-ring on the 4 × 4 application.

2. Assemble the upper ball socket into the knuckle with a press and ram or a puller type tool arrangement, making sure that the ball socket is firmly seated against the knuckle.

NOTE: Use a .0015 inch feeler gauge blade between the socket and knuckle. The blade should not enter at the minimum area of contact.

3. Install new threaded sleeve into the top flange of the yoke, leaving approximately two threads exposed.

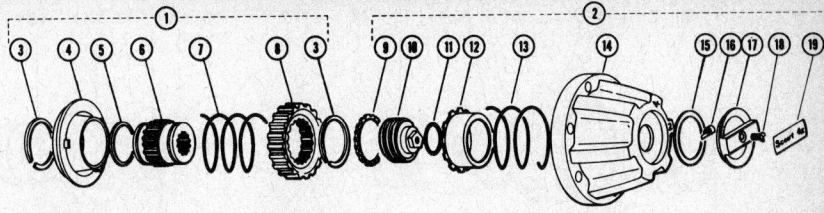

1. Clutch and bearing assembly	5. Washer	10. Dial screw	15. Washer
2. Cap assembly	6. Hub	11. O-ring seal	16. Detent dial
3. Retaining ring	7. Compression spring	12. Clutch cup	17. Control dial
4. Bearing hub	8. Clutch ring	13. Compression spring	18. Screw
	9. Clutch nut	14. Hub cap	19. Label

Components of a manual locking hub

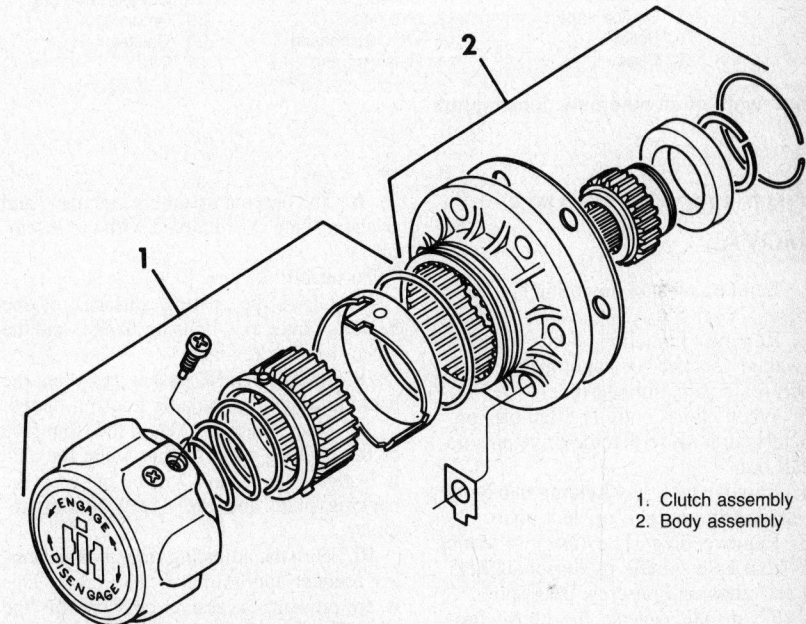

1. Clutch assembly
2. Body assembly

Components of a Dualmatic locking hub

4. Install the knuckle assembly to the yoke, using a new nut on the lower ball socket stud. Torque the lower nut to 80 ft. lbs.

5. With the use of a special socket, torque the threaded sleeve to 50 ft. lbs. in the upper yoke flange.

6. Install the top ball socket stud nut and torque to 100 ft. lbs. Align the cotterpin holes between the stud and the castellated nut. Do not loosen nut to align the holes. Install the cotter pin.

7. Assemble the tie rod to the steering arm.

8. Assure that slingers are properly installed on the axle shaft and install the shaft into the housing.

9. Position the spindle over the axle end with the bronze bushing in place.

10. Install the backing plate.

11. Install the hub rotor, caliper and wheel assembly, and lower the vehicle.

Checking Ball Sockets For Looseness

To check the ball sockets for excessive looseness, raise the vehicle and attach a dial indicator to the lower yoke or axle tube and set the indicator against the knuckle or lower ball socket, with a loaded pressure so as to read in both directions. Grasp the wheel at the top and bottom and move the wheel inward and outward. If the total indicator reading exceeds .020 inch, both the upper and lower ball sockets should be replaced.

Front Drive Locking Hubs

Three types of locking hubs are used: Manual, Lock-O-Matic and Warn. Manual locking hubs are either engaged or disengaged, depending on how they are set. Lock-O-Matic hubs, when in "free" position, automatically engage axle and wheel when forward torque is applied by the axle shaft. Thus, whenever front wheel drive is disengaged at the transmission, the wheels free wheel. "Lock" position is required only when engine braking control on the front wheel is desired.

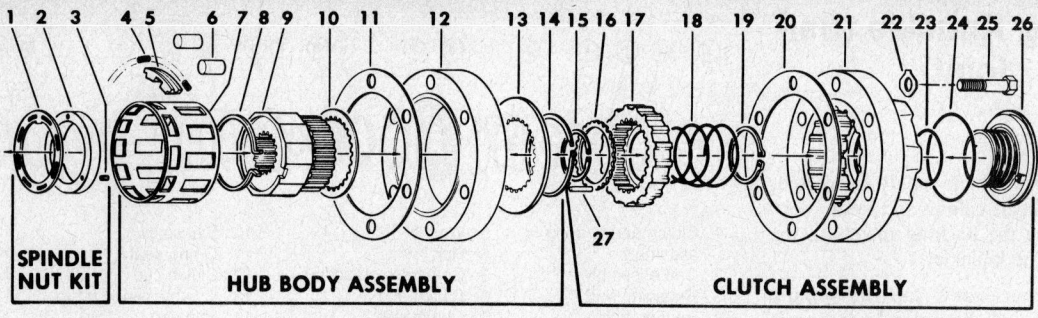

| SPINDLE NUT KIT | HUB BODY ASSEMBLY | | CLUTCH ASSEMBLY |

1. Lockwasher
2. Spindle nut
3. Set screw
4. Garter spring
5. Friction shoe
6. Roller
7. Cage
8. Centering spring
9. Shaft axle hub
10. Centering spring
11. Gasket
12. Hub body
13. Washer, bearing
14. Retaining ring
15. Retaining ring
16. Clutch nut
17. Clutch, ring and cup
18. Compression ring
19. Retaining ring
20. Gasket
21. Cap
22. Lockwasher tab
23. O-ring
24. U-ring
25. Cap screw
26. Control dial
27. Groove pin

Components of an automatic locking hub

FRONT LOCKING HUBS REMOVAL

1. Bend up tabs on mounting bolt lock washers.

2. Remove mounting bolts using a thin-walled socket or appropriate hex wrench (externally splined type).

3. When clutch body is lifted off, immediately tilt it up so that the drive pins do not fall out.

4. Remove lock ring holding hub body onto axle shaft and pull off hub body.

5. Remove drag shoe (Lock-O-Matic only) from axle spindle by loosening hex-head set screw and unscrew drag shoe.

6. To install, reverse the above procedure.

REAR AXLE

BEARING AND SEAL REPLACEMENT

Adjustable Bearing Ring Type

1. Raise and support the vehicle securely using jackstands.

2. Remove the rear wheels.

3. Remove the metal retaining clips from the wheel lugs and pull off the brake drum.

--- CAUTION ---

It may be necessary to back off the brake shoe adjuster to prevent binding between the shoes and the drum.

4. Remove the backing plate retaining bolts. These bolts also run through the axle retaining plate.

5. Pull the axle from the housing with a puller or similar tool.

--- CAUTION ---

Never strike the axle shaft during removal as permanent damage will result.

6. The bearing assembly, retainer, and adjusting ring are removed with the assembly.

To install:

7. Clean the mating surfaces of the backing plate, axle housing flange, and the wheel bearing retainer.

8. Install a new gasket between the backing plate and the axle housing flange.

9. Place a new gasket on the front face of the backing plate so that when the axle is installed the gasket will be between the backing plate and the wheel bearing retainer.

10. Turn the adjusting ring into the bearing retainer approximately two turns. This is to prevent excessive pressure on the wheel bearings or movement of the bearing cone or the clinch ring on the axle shaft.

NOTE: Do not thread the adjusting ring completely into the bearing retainer until the retainer and the backing plate have been bolted to the axle housing flange and tightened to the correct torque.

11. Install the axle shaft assembly.

--- CAUTION ---

Do not damage the axle seal when inserting the shaft.

12. Install the adjuster ring lock and secure the lock.

13. Secure the bearing retainer and the backing plate to the axle housing flange and torque to 40–45 ft. lbs.

NOTE: There is a fifth hole in the axle housing flange. This is for lubricant drain in case of axle seal leakage.

14. Coat the threads on the adjuster with a good waterproof sealer and install the adjusting ring into the wheel bearing retainer.

15. Adjust the axle shaft end-play.

16. Install the brake drums and retaining clips.

Unit Bearing Type

1. Raise the rear of the vehicle and support securely.

2. Remove the tires and wheels.

3. Remove the brake drums.

NOTE: It might be necessary to back off the brake adjusting mechanism to avoid contact between the brake shoes and the drum. Make certain to hold the automatic self-adjuster away before turning the adjuster screw.

4. Turn the axle shaft until the access hole in the axle flange is aligned with the backing plate retaining bolts. Remove the bolts and nuts.

5. Using a puller or other tool, pull the axle assembly from the axle housing. If a puller is not available, install the brake drum backwards and tighten two lug nuts. Exert outward pressure to remove the outside seal from the housing bore.

6. Remove the wheel bearing cup and the inside oil seal from the axle housing.

NOTE: The bearing cup is a loose fit in the housing but the clearance may not be sufficient to permit removal with your fingers.

7. Install the new oil seal with the closed side of the seal toward the housing flange. The seal should fit squarely against the seat in the housing bore. Lubricate the lip of the seal with rear axle lube.

8. Install the wheel bearing cup in the axle housing bore. The cup is installed with the thin side toward the housing flange. It may be necessary to lightly tap around the cup to ensure that the cup is tight around its seat.

NOTE: If a new wheel bearing is used, the bearing cup will be bonded to the rib ring and the cup will be installed with the axle shaft. Do not break the bond or install the cup separately.

9. Install the splined end of the axle shaft into the housing and start the splines into the differential pinion gears.

----- **CAUTION** -----
Be careful when inserting the axle shaft that the splines do not cut the inside oil seal.

10. Align the retaining plate and the backing plate mounting holes with those in the axle housing flange and push the axle shaft into the housing as far as possible.

11. Install the backing plate mounting bolts and tighten the nuts finger tight. Tighten the nuts alternately to approximately 15 ft. lbs. working through the hole in the axle shaft flange.

NOTE: The nuts should be tightened so that the seal and the wheel bearing are drawn tight against their seats.

12. Torque the backing plate mounting bolts to 50–60 ft. lbs.

13. Adjust the brakes until the brake drum will just slip over the shoes. Install the drum.

14. Install the rear wheels and tighten the lug nuts. Back the vehicle up and apply the brakes. This will activate the automatic brake adjusters.

Locking Differentials

For overhaul procedures of differentials with "NoSPIN" and "PowrLok" locking units, see Rear Axle in the General Repair Section.

STEERING AND SUSPENSION

STEERING WHEEL

Removal and Installation

1. Raise the hood and disconnect the battery cables.

2. Remove the horn cap, spring, and horn button baseplate.

3. Remove the retaining bolt and washer from the center shaft.

NOTE: Note the position of the long screw.

4. Using a puller, remove the wheel from the steering column.

5. To install, reverse the removal procedure.

TURN SIGNAL SWITCH REPLACEMENT

1. Disconnect the battery cables.

2. Remove the horn button and spring.

3. Remove the three screws which hold the horn button retaining plate.

4. Remove the steering wheel.

5. Remove the horn button contact ring located at the upper end of the column assembly.

6. Remove the turn signal switch retaining screws and pull out the switch assembly.

7. Installation is in the reverse of removal.

Steering Gear

For manual steering gear overhaul, see the General Repair Section.

STEERING GEAR REMOVAL

1. Loosen collar clamp at bottom of steering wheel column. Disconnect any wiring.

2. Remove nut or loosen clamp bolt which secures steering arm to lever shaft, removing steering arm from lever shaft using a suitable puller if necessary.

3. Remove mounting bolts and steering gear assembly.

4. To install, reverse the above procedure, taking special care not to bind steering column if there is no universal joint.

DRAG LINK ADJUSTMENT

To adjust the drag link, remove the cotter pin and turn the adjusting plug in the desired direction. If excess play is present in the link, turn the adjusting plug inward until it is tight and then back off to the first cotter pin hole. Install a new cotter pin of the correct size.

Power Steering Pump

REMOVAL AND INSTALLATION

1. Disconnect the reservoir hoses at the pump. Fasten the hoses with the ends raised upward to prevent fluid leakage.

2. Plug the pump fittings to prevent leakage of oil from the pump.

3. Loosen the pump-to-bracket mounting bolts, lean the pump to one side, and remove the drive belt.

4. Remove the bolts which hold the pump to the mounting bracket and remove the pump assembly.

5. Installation is the reverse of removal.

Tie Rod End

REMOVAL AND INSTALLATION

1. Remove the cotter pins and retaining nuts at both ends of the tie rod and from the end of the connecting rod where it attaches to the tie rod.

2. Remove the nut attaching the steering damper push rod to the tie rod bracket and move the damper aside.

3. Remove the tie rod ends from the steering arms and connecting rod with a puller.

4. Count the number of threads showing on the tie rod before removing the ends, as a guide to installation.

5. Loosen the adjusting tube clamp bolts and unthread the ends.

6. Installation is the reverse of removal. Adjust toe-in, if necessary.

Shock Absorbers

REMOVAL AND INSTALLATION

NOTE: Before installing new shocks, they should be purged of air. To do this, hold the shock upright and fully extend it, then invert and compress it. Do this several times.

1. Remove the locknuts and washers.

2. Pull the shock absorber eyes and rubber bushings from the mounting pins.

3. Install the shocks in the reverse order of the removal procedure.

NOTE: Squeaking usually occurs when movement takes place between the rubber bushings and the metal parts. The squeaking may be eliminated by placing the bushings under greater pressure. This is accomplished either by adding additional washers or by tightening the locknuts. Do not use mineral lubricant to stop the squeaking as it will deteriorate the rubber.

Front End Alignment

Proper alignment of the front wheels must be maintained in order to ensure ease of steering and satisfactory tire life.

The most important factors of front wheel alignment are wheel camber, axle caster, and wheel toe-in.

Wheel toe-in is the distance by which the wheels are closer together at the front than at the rear.

Wheel camber is the amount the top of the wheels incline outward from the vertical.

Front axle caster is the amount in degrees that the steering pivot pins are tilted toward the rear of the vehicle. Positive caster is inclination of the top of the pivot pin toward the rear of the vehicle.

These points should be checked at regular intervals, particularly when the front axle has been subjected to a heavy impact. When checking wheel alignment, it is important that wheel bearings and knuckle bearings be in proper adjustment. Loose bearings will affect instrument readings when checking the camber, pivot pin inclination, and toe-in.

Front wheel camber is preset. Caster can be altered by use of shims between the axle pad and the springs. Wheel toe-in may be adjusted. To measure wheel toe-in, follow the procedure given later on in this section.

CASTER ADJUSTMENT

Caster angle is established in the axle design by tilting the top of the mount toward the rear, and the bottom of the mount forward so that an imaginary line through the center of the mounts would strike the ground at a point ahead of the point of tire contact.

The purpose of caster is to provide steering stability which will keep the front wheels in the straight ahead position and also assist in straightening the wheels when coming out of a turn.

Caster is corrected by installing shims between the axle pad and the springs.

If the chamber and toe-in are correct and it is known that the axle is not twisted, a satisfactory check may be made by testing the vehicle on the road. Before road testing, make sure all tires are properly inflated, being particularly careful that both front tires are inflated to exactly the same pressure.

If the vehicle turns easily to either side but is hard to straighten out, insufficient caster for easy handling of the vehicle is indicated. If correction is necessary, it can usually be accomplished by installing shims between the springs and axle pads to secure the desired result.

CAMBER ADJUSTMENT

The purpose of camber is to more nearly place the weight of the vehicle over the tire contact patch on the road to facilitate ease of steering. The result of excessive camber is irregular wear of the tires on the outside shoulders and is usually caused by bent axle parts.

The result of excessive negative or reverse camber will be hard steering and possibly a wandering condition. Tires will also wear on the inside shoulders.

Unequal camber may cause any or a combination of the following conditions: unstable steering, wandering, kick-back or road shock, shimmy or excessive tire wear. The cause of unequal camber is usually a bent steering knuckle or axle end.

Correct wheel camber is set in the axle at the time of manufacture and cannot be altered by any adjustment. It is important that the camber be the same on both front wheels. Heating of any parts to facilitate straightening usually destroys the heat treatment given them at the factory. Cold bending may cause a fracture of the steel and is also unsafe. Replacement with new parts is recommended rather than any straightening of damaged parts.

TOE-IN ADJUSTMENT

First raise the front of the vehicle to free the front wheels. Turn the wheels to the straight ahead position. Use a steady rest to scribe a pencil line in the center of each tire tread as the wheel is turned by hand. A good way to do this is to first coat the wheel with a strip with chalk around the circumference of the tread at the center to form a base for a fine pencil line.

Measure the distance between the scribed lines at the front and rear of the wheels using care that both measurements are made at an equal distance from the floor. The distance between the lines should be greater at the rear than at the front by 3/64 in. to 3/32 in. To adjust, loosen the clamp bolts and turn the tie rod with a small pipe wrench. The tie rod is threaded with right and left hand threads to provide equal adjustment at both wheels. Do not overlook retightening the clamp bolts to 15–20 ft. lbs.

It is common practice to measure between the wheel rims. This is satisfactory providing the wheels run true. By scribing a line on the tire tread, measurement is taken between the road contact points reducing error by wheel run-out.

BRAKES

Late model trucks are equipped with a dual hydraulic brake system in which there are separate hydraulic systems for the front and rear brakes. In this dual system a warning light switch operates a warning light on the dashboard when there is a pressure failure in either the front or rear system. A power system may be employed to reduce the effort applied to the brake pedal.

NOTE: See General Repair Section for hydraulic brake service and overhaul.

Master Cylinder R & R

1. Disconnect hydraulic lines from master cylinder.
2. Disconnect master cylinder pushrod at brake pedal and remove nuts securing cylinder to dash panel.
3. If master cylinder is mounted on power unit, remove nuts securing master cylinder to power unit and remove cylinder from vehicle.
4. Installation is the reverse of the above procedure.
5. Bleed system.

RESETTING THE WARNING LIGHT SWITCH

Once a difference of 85–150 psi pressure between the front and rear systems has activated the warning light switch, it will not go off by itself and must be manually reset.

1. Clean switch and disconnect wire from terminal.

2. Unscrew and completely remove switch from body. This will allow the pistons to center and hold the switch in "off" position.
3. Screw switch back into body and reconnect wire to terminal.

4. **NOTE: If fluid is in the switch cavity, press brake pedal to see if pistol O-ring seals are leaking. If there is leakage, the O-rings must be replaced.**
5. Warning light switch should be checked periodically for proper function and the presence of foreign matter and dirt.

Adjusting Brake Shoes

1. Remove rubber dust cover from access hole.
2. Using an adjusting tool or screwdriver, turn star screw until shoes drag on the drum.
3. Rotate star screw back from drag position until drag is completely eliminated.
4. On brakes equipped with automatic adjusters it will be necessary to hold the adjusting lever away from the star wheel with a screwdriver while the adjustment is made.

Bleeding Hydraulic Brakes

1. Before bleeding the brake system, disconnect electrical wire from warning light switch and remove any foreign material or dirt accumulation around warning light switch. Then remove the switch from body. The switch must be removed to prevent shearing of the end of the pin due to unequal pressures created between front and rear systems while bleeding.
2. Fill master cylinder reservoir(s) with clean brake fluid.
3. Attach bleeder hose to bleeder valve on wheel cylinder and place free end of bleeder hose in a jar partially filled with fluid. On some models it may be necessary to take the wheel off to get at the bleeder valve.
4. While the brake pedal is being pressed steadily, open the bleeder valve until the fluid coming from the hose is clean and free of air bubbles, then close bleeder valve and release brake pedal.
5. If the brake pedal goes to the floorboard before the bleeding becomes clean, more fluid will have to be added to the reservoir and the above process repeated.
6. Repeat the above procedure for each wheel cylinder, making sure to check the level of fluid in the reservoir frequently.

NOTE: On models equipped with power boosters, the booster must be bled first.

Wheel Cylinder (Rear Wheel)

REMOVAL

1. Raise the rear of the vehicle and support it safely.
2. Remove the drum.
3. Remove the brake lining from the brake support plate.
4. Remove the hydraulic line from the wheel cylinder.
5. Remove the wheel cylinder attaching bolts and remove the cylinder.

INSTALLATION

1. Install the wheel cylinder on the brake support plate.
2. Install the hydraulic line to the wheel cylinder.
3. Install the brake shoes on the brake support plate.
4. Install the drum.
5. Install the wheel assembly.
6. Bleed the system and refill the master cylinder.

Disc Brakes

The disc brakes are the sliding caliper, single piston type, and are used on the front wheels in combination with drum type brakes on the rear.

REMOVAL

1. Raise the front of the vehicle and support it safely.
2. Remove the front wheels from the hub.
3. Remove approximately a third of the fluid from the large reservoir of the master cylinder, to avoid leakage of fluid when the pistons are forced back into the calipers.
4. Position a large C-clamp over the caliper and engage the rear of the caliper with the shoe of the clamp, and place the screw on the outboard disc pad. Tightening the screw will cause the piston to be forced deeper in the bore, by the movement of the caliper.
5. Remove the key retaining screw and drive the support key and support spring from the caliper and support, using a brass drift and a light hammer.
6. Remove the caliper from the support bracket and support the assembly on a wire.

—————— CAUTION ——————
Do not support the assembly by the brake hose.

NOTE: It is not necessary to remove the brake hose from the caliper when only replacing the disc pads, and therefore it would not be necessary to bleed the caliper when reinstalled.

7. Remove the disc pads from the calipers.

INSTALLATION

1. Position the new disc pads into the calipers, using a new anti-rattle spring clip, and position it on the inboard pad.
2. Place the caliper assembly over the rotor and engage the anchor bracket.
3. Position the caliper support spring and support key between the bottom edge of the caliper and the anchor bracket.
4. With the use of a brass drift and hammer, drive the key and spring assembly into position and install the key retaining screw.
5. Refill the master cylinder as needed, apply the brakes several times to seat the pads, and recheck the master cylinder fluid level.
6. Install the wheels and lower the vehicle.

Brake Pedal Adjustment

There are no provisions available for the adjustment of the brake pedal height. However, it should be checked to determine if sufficient height exists. Corrections can only be made by replacement of parts, alignment, or straightening of the affected parts. To determine if sufficient pedal height exists, open a wheel cylinder bleed valve to simulate a failed system, and depress the brake pedal. The pedal should not contact the floor board during this test.

NOTE: Close the bleeder valve before releasing the brake pedal. The brake warning light switch will have to be reset after the test is completed.

Stoplight Switch Adjustment

No stoplight switch adjustments are provided. If the stop lamps are inoperative, a defective switch, defective bulbs, loose or broken connections, or an improper positioned switch would be indicated. A mechanical type switch is located on the brake pedal, at the pushrod location, while the hydraulic type switch is located on or near the master cylinder, and operated by hydraulic pressure.

Parking Brake Adjustment

1. Loosen locknut on the equalizer rod and turn front nut forward several turns.
2. Turn the locknut (rear) forward just enough to remove any slack but not so much that the brake shoes lift of their anchors.

Master cylinder disconnect points

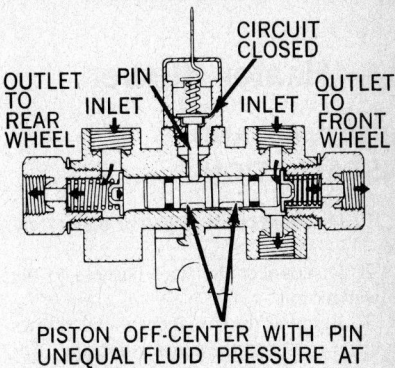

Warning light switch circuit closed

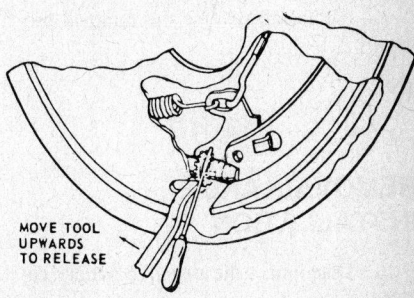

Backing off adjustment—self-adjusting brakes

3. Tighten both nuts against the equalizer.

CHASSIS ELECTRICAL

Heater

The Scout heater core and blower motor assembly are located in the right rear corner of the engine compartment.

Heater Core
REMOVAL AND INSTALLATION

1. Drain the cooling system and remove the negative battery cable.
2. Remove the heater hoses from the heater core outlets.
3. Remove the windshield washer bottle from the firewall.

4. Remove the cover plate from the heater box and remove the heater core from the housing.

5. Remove the core end cover.

NOTE: Do not damage the core fins during the removal and installation procedure.

6. Installation is the reverse of removal. Fill the cooling system and check the operation of the heater system.

Heater Blower

REMOVAL AND INSTALLATION

1. Disconnect the negative battery cable.

2. Disconnect the wire harness to the blower motor.

3. Remove the six sheet metal screws securing motor to the blower housing. Remove the motor with the blower.

4. Loosen and remove the bolt from the end of the motor shaft and detach the squirrel cage.

5. To install reverse the removal procedure.

Radio

REMOVAL AND INSTALLATION

1. Disconnect the negative battery cable.

2. Remove the bolts which hold the radio to the radio support.

3. Remove the attaching screws which hold the radio cover bezel to the instrument panel.

4. Pull the radio from the instrument panel and disconnect the radio lead wires.

5. Remove the radio from the car.

6. Installation is in reverse order of removal.

Wiper Motor and Linkage

REMOVAL AND INSTALLATION

1. Raise the hood and disconnect the windshield washer hose from the cowl.

2. Remove the attaching screws and pull off the cowl.

3. Remove the bolts from the wiper mounting bracket.

4. Release the attaching link from the motor to the wiper arm linkage.

5. Disconnect the motor wiring.

6. Remove the motor with the link assembly from the vehicle.

To install:

7. Position the wiper motor on the mounting bracket and connect the wiring.

8. Connect the wiper linkage to the motor.

9. Install the cowl and the windshield washer hose.

Instrument Cluster

REMOVAL AND INSTALLATION

Scouts use eight securing screws to mount the dash. Remove the screws and pull the panel out. It will be necessary to remove the speedometer cable and the electrical connections from the gauges if the cluster is to be totally removed. If an oil pressure gauge is used, plug the capillary tube to prevent leakage. To install, reverse the removal procedure.

Turn Signal and Hazard Flasher Locations

The turn signal indicator is located on the left side of the steering column below the steering wheel.

On some Scout models the turn signal indicator has two positions, one for lane change and the other for full turn. Moving the indicator one stop, either upward or downward, will activate the signal. The indicator must be held in position for the signal to work. Moving the indicator two stops to the lock position will activate the signal for a turn. The indicator will stay in a lock position until the turn is completed.

Headlights

REMOVAL AND INSTALLATION

1. Remove the screws retaining the headlight door and remove the door.

2. Remove the screws retaining the retaining ring and remove the ring.

3. Pull the headlight out, disconnect the wire harness and remove the headlight from the vehicle.

4. Install the headlight in the reverse order of removal.

Jeep

INDEX

BEFORE SERVICING, SEE THE SAFETY NOTICE AT THE FRONT OF THE BOOK

ENGINE IDENTIFICATION SPECIFICATIONS

The Engine Identification Code letter is the 6th character (4th from 1980) in the vehicle identification number for Jeep vehicles.

Engines	'75	'76	'77	'78	'79	'80	'81	'82
151-4 cyl	—	—	—	—	—	—	B	B
258-6 cyl.-Reg.	A	A	A	A	—	—	—	—
258-6 cyl.-L/C①	—	—	—	—	—	—	—	—
258-6 cyl. 2 bbl.	—	—	C	C	C	C	C	C
232-6 cyl.-Reg.	E	E	E	E	—	—	—	—
232-6 cyl.-L/C①	—	—	—	—	—	—	—	—
304-V8-2bbl.	H	H	H	H	H	H	H	—
360-V8-2bbl.	N	N	N	N	N	N	N	N
360-V8-4bbl.	P	P	P	P	—	—	—	—
401-V8-4bbl.	Z	Z	Z	Z	—	—	—	—

① Low compression engine.

GENERAL ENGINE SPECIFICATIONS

Engine Year	Carburetor Type	Horsepower at rpm	Torque (ft. lb.) at rpm	Bore × Stroke	Ratio Compression	Cranking Compression Pressure	Oil Pressure (psi) at 2000 rpm
4-151, '80–'82	2 bbl	90 @ 4400	128 @ 2400	4.000 × 3.000	8.24:1	140	38
6-232, '75	1 bbl	100 @ 3600	185 @ 1800	3.750 × 3.500	8.0:1	140 Minimum	50
6-232, '76–'78	1 bbl	90 @ 3050	170 @ 2000	3.750 × 3.500	8.0:1	140 Minimum	50
6-258, '75	1 bbl	110 @ 3500	195 @ 2000	3.750 × 3.895	8.0:1	150 Minimum	50
6-258, '76–'78	1 bbl	95 @ 3050	180 @ 2100	3.750 × 3.895	8.0:1	120–150	50
6-258, '79–'82	2 bbl	114 @ 3600	196 @ 2000	3.750 × 3.895	8.0:1	120–150	50
V8-304, '75	2 bbl	150 @ 4200	245 @ 2500	3.750 × 3.440	8.4:1	150 Minimum	50
V8-304, '76–'81	2 bbl	120 @ 3200	220 @ 2200	3.750 × 3.440	8.4:1	120–150	50
V8-360, '75–'82	2 bbl	175 @ 4000	285 @ 2900	4.080 × 3.440	8.25:1	120–150	50
V8-401, '75–'78	4 bbl	215 @ 4400	320 @ 2800	4.165 × 3.680	8.25:1	120–150	50

TUNE-UP SPECIFICATIONS

When analyzing compression test results, look for uniformity among cylinders rather than specific pressures.

Year	Engine No. Cyl Displacement (cu. in.)	hp	Spark Plugs Type	Gap (in.)	Distributor Point Dwell (deg)	Point Gap (in.)	Ignition Timing (deg) ▲	Valves Intake Opens (deg)■	Fuel Pump Pressure (psi)	Idle Speed (rpm)● Man Trans	Auto Trans
'75	6-232	100	N-12Y	.035	Electronic		5B	12	4–5	700(600)	—
	6-258	110	N-12Y	.035	Electronic		3B	12	4–5	700①(600)	550
	8-304	150	N-12Y	.035	Electronic		5B	14¾	5–6½	750	—
	8-360	175	N-12Y	.035	Electronic		2–5B	14¾	5–6½	750	700
	8-360	195	N-12Y	.035	Electronic		2–5B	14¾	5–6½	750	700
	8-401	215	N-12Y	.035	Electronic		2–5B	25½	5–6½	750	700
'76–'77	6-232	90	N-12Y	.035	Electronic		8B	12	4–5	600	—
	6-258	95	N-12Y	.035	Electronic		6B②	12	4–5	600	550(700)
	8-304	120	N-12Y	.035	Electronic		5B③	14¾	5–6½	750	700
	8-360	175	N-12Y	.035	Electronic		5B④	14¾	5–6½	750	700
	8-401	215	N-12Y	.035	Electronic		5B④	25½	5–6½	750	700
'78	6-232	90	N-13L	.035	Electronic		5B⑤	12	4–5	850⑥	—
	6-258	100	N-13L	.035	Electronic		6B⑦⑧	14½	4–5	850⑨⑩	550
	8-304	130	N-12Y	.035	Electronic		5B⑪	14¾	5–6½	750	700
	8-360	140	N-12Y	.035	Electronic		5B	14¾	5–6½	750	700
	8-401	215	N-12Y	.035	Electronic		8B	25½	5–6½	—	700
'79	6-258	110	N-13L	.035	Electronic		8B⑫	14½	4–5	700	600
	8-304	125	N-12Y	.035	Electronic		8B⑬	14¾	5–6½	700(750)	600
	8-360	175	N-12Y	.035	Electronic		8B	14¾	5–6½	800	600
'80–'82	4-151	80	R44TSX	.060	Electronic		10B⑰	33B	6½–8	900	700
	6-258	110	N-14L	.035	Electronic		8B⑭	14½	4–5	700	600⑮
	8-304	125	N-12Y	.035	Electronic		⑯	14¾	5–6	700	600
	8-360	175	N-12Y	.035	Electronic		8B	14¾	5–6	800	600

NOTE: If the information given in this chart disagrees with the information on the engine tune-up decal, use the specifications on the decal—they are current for the engine in your car.

NOTE: Figures in parentheses are for California engines

▲ With vacuum advance disconnected

■ All figures before TDC (BTDC)

● With manual transmission in Neutral and automatic transmission in Drive

B Before top dead center (BTDC)

① 650 rpm w/EGR
② 8B w/Automatic transmission
③ 10B w/Automatic transmission; 5B in California
④ 8B w/Automatic transmission; 5B in California
⑤ 10B for altitude
⑥ 600 rpm for altitude
⑦ w/Manual transmission; 10B altitude, 8B Calif.
⑧ w/Auto transmission; 8B 49 states and Calif., 10B altitude

⑨ w/Manual transmission and 1 bbl. carb 600 rpm for altitude
⑩ w/Manual transmission and 2 bbl. carb 650 rpm
⑪ w/Auto transmission; 10B 49 states and Calif.
⑫ w/Manual transmission; 4B w/Auto transmission; 6B, CJ model only
⑬ w/Manual transmission; 5B, CJ model only
⑭ California CJ with manual transmission, 6B
⑮ Cherokee, Wagoneer and J series; 700
⑯ Manual transmission, except Calif. and hilly terrain; 8B at 700 rpm
⑰ w/Automatic transmission; 12B

307

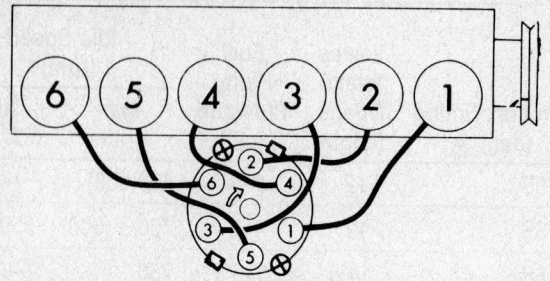

6 cylinder firing order: 1-5-3-6-2-4

4 cylinder firing order: 1-3-4-2

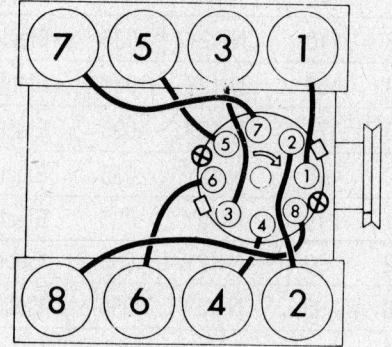

V8 firing order: 1-8-4-3-6-5-7-2

VALVE SPECIFICATIONS

Year	Engine No. Cyl. Displacement (cu in.)	Seat Angle (deg)①	Face Angle (deg)②	Spring Test Pressure (lbs. @ in.)	Spring Installed Height (in.)	Stem to Guide Clearance (in.)		Stem Diameter (in.)	
						Intake	Exhaust	Intake	Exhaust
'81–'82	4-151	46	45	176 @ 1.250	1.660	.0010–.0030	.0010–.0027	.3422	.3422
'75–'82	6-232	44½	44	100 @ 1¹³⁄₁₆	2¹⁵⁄₆₄③	.0010–.0030	.0010–.0030	.3720	.3720
	6-258	44½	44	100 @ 1¹³⁄₁₆	2¹⁵⁄₆₄③	.0010–.0030	.0010–.0030	.3720	.3720
	8-304	44½	44	84 @ 1¹³⁄₁₆	2⁷⁄₃₂③	.0010–.0030	.0010–.0030	.3720	.3720
	8-360	44½	44	84 @ 1¹³⁄₁₆	2⁷⁄₃₂③	.0010–.0030	.0010–.0030	.3720	.3720
'75–'78	8-401	44½	44	84 @ 1¹³⁄₁₆	2⁷⁄₃₂③	.0010–.0030	.0010–.0030	.3720	.3720

① Exhaust valve seat angle given; all intake valve seat angles are 30° unless otherwise noted
② Exhaust valve face angle given; all intake valve face angles are 29° unless otherwise noted
③ '78–'82—2″; except 1978—304, 360, 401—2⅕

CRANKSHAFT AND CONNECTING ROD SPECIFICATIONS
(All measurements given in inches)

| Engine | Crankshaft | | | | Connecting Rod | | |
	Main Bearing Journal Dia	Main Bearing Oil Clearance	Shaft End Play	Thrust on No.	Journal Dia	Oil Clearance	Side Clearance
4-151	2.2988	.0005–.0022	.0035–.0085	5	1.8690	.0007–.0027	.006–.022
6-232	2.4986–2.5001	.0010–.0020	.0015–.0065	3	2.0934–2.0955	.0010–.0020	.005–.014
6-258	2.4986–2.5001	.0010–.0020 ①	.0015–.0065 ⑤	3	2.0934–2.0955	.0010–.0020 ②	.005–.014
V8-304	2.7474–2.7489 ③	.0010–.0020 ④	.003–.008 ⑥	3	2.0934–2.0955	.0010–.0020	.006–.018

① '74–'79: .0010–.0030 (.0025 preferred)
② '74–'76: .0010–.0030 (.0025 preferred)
  '77–'82: .0010–.0025 (.0015–.0020 preferred)
③ #5: 2.7464–2.7479
④ #5: .0020–.0030
⑤ '81–'82: #1: .005–.0026
  2, 3, 4, 5, 6: .0005–.0030
  7: .0011–.0035
⑥ '81–'82: .0010–.0030 #5: .0020–.0040

PISTON RING SPECIFICATIONS

| | | Ring Gap | | | Ring Side Clearance | | | Piston to Bore Clearance |
	Engine	Top Compression	Bottom Compression	Oil Control	Top Compression	Bottom Compression	Oil Control	
'81–'82	4-151	.0027–.0033	.009–.019	.015–.055	.0025–.0033	.0025–.0033	.0025–.0033	.0025–.0033
'75–'82	6-232	.010–.020	.010–.020	.010–.025	.0015–.003	.0015–.003	.001–.008	.0009–.0017
	6-258	.010–.020	.010–.020	.010–.025	.0015–.003	.0015–.003	.001–.008	.0009–.0017
	8-304	.010–.020	.010–.020	.010–.025	.0015–.0035	.0015–.003	.0011–.008	.0010–.0018
	8-360	.010–.020	.010–.020	.015–.045	.0015–.0035	.0015–.0035	.000–.007	.0012–.0020
	8-401	.010–.020	.010–.020	.0015–.055	.0015–.003	.0015–.0035	.000–.007	.0010–.0018

WHEEL ALIGNMENT

| Model | Caster Pref. Setting (deg) | Camber Pref. Setting (deg) | Toe-IN (in.) | King-Pin Inclination (deg) | Wheel Pivot Ratio | |
					Inner Wheel	Outer Wheel
CJ-5, CJ-6, CJ-7, DJ-5, DJ-6, CJ-5A, CJ-6A	3 ①	1°30′ ②	³⁄₆₄–³⁄₃₂	8½	20	20
Commando	3	1°30′	³⁄₆₄–³⁄₃₂	7½	31	32
Wagoneer, Cherokee, J-10, J-20	4 ①	1°30′	³⁄₆₄–³⁄₃₂	8½	37	38

① '81–'82: 6°
② '81–'82: 0°

TORQUE SPECIFICATIONS
(All readings in ft. lbs.)

Engine No. Cyl. Displacement (cu. in.)	Cylinder Head Bolts	Rod Bearing Bolts	Main Bearing Bolts	Crankshaft Balancer Bolt	Flywheel to Crankshaft Bolts	Manifold	
						Intake	Exhaust
4-151	95	30	65	160	35	Bolt:40 Nut: 30	Bolt: 40 Nut: 30
6-232, 258	95–115	26–30①	75–85	50–64	95–120	37–47②	20–30②
8-304, 360	100–120	26–30①	90–105	48–64	95–120	37–47	20–30③
8-401	100–120	35–40	90–105	48–64	95–120	37–47	20–30

① 30–35 for '78–'80
② 18–20 for '74–'80
③ 20–30, center two bolts; 12–18, outer four bolts for '79–'80

TUNE-UP

Spark Plugs

Spark plugs ignite the air and fuel mixture in the cylinder as the piston reaches the top of the compression stroke. The controlled explosion that results forces the piston down, turning the crankshaft and the rest of the drive train.

The average lift of a spark plug is dependent on a number of factors: the mechanical condition of the engine; the type of fuel; driving conditions; and the driver.

When you remove the spark plugs, check their condition. They are a good indicator of the condition of the engine.

A small deposit of light tan or gray material on a spark plug that has been used for any period of time is to be considered normal. Additives in unleaded fuels may give a number of unusual color indications; for instance, MMT (a manganese anti-knock compound) will cause rust red deposits.

The gap between the center electrode and the side or ground electrode can be expected to increase not more than 0.001 in. every 1,000 miles under normal conditions.

When a spark plug is functioning normally or, more accurately, when the plug is installed in an engine that is functioning properly, the plugs can be taken out, cleaned, regapped, and reinstalled in the engine without doing the engine any harm.

When, and if, a plug fouls and begins to misfire, you will have to investigate, correct the cause of the fouling, and either clean or replace the plug.

There are several reasons why a spark plug will foul and you can learn which reason by just looking at the plug. A few of the most common reasons for plug fouling, and a description of the fouled plug's appearance, is listed in the electrical unit repair section which also offers solutions to the problems.

REMOVAL

1. Number the wires so you won't cross them when you replace them.
2. Remove the wire from the end of

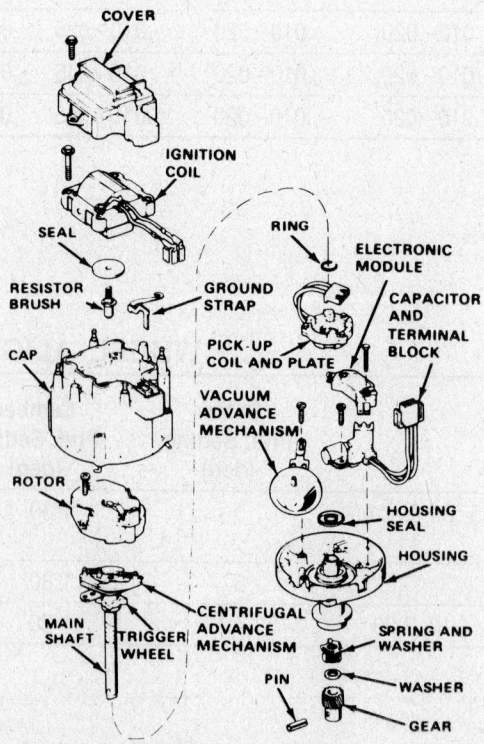

Exploded view of 4 cylinder distributor

the spark plug by grasping the wire by the rubber boot. If the boot sticks to the plug, remove it by twisting and pulling at the same time. Do not pull the wire itself or you will most certainly damage the delicate carbon core.

3. Use a spark plug plug socket to loosen all of the plugs about two turns.

4. If compressed air is available, blow off the area around the spark plug holes. Otherwise, use a rag or a brush to clean the area. Be careful not to allow any foreign material to drop into the spark plug holes.

5. Remove the plugs by unscrewing them the rest of the way from the engine.

INSPECTION

Check the plugs for deposits and wear. If they are not going to be replaced, clean the plugs thoroughly. Remember that any kind of deposit will decrease the efficiency of the plug. Plugs can be cleaned on a spark plug cleaning machine, which can sometimes be found in service stations, or you can do an acceptable job of cleaning with a stiff brush.

Check spark plug gap before installation. The ground electrode must be parallel to the center electrode and the specified size wire gauge should pass theough the gap with a slight drag. If the electrodes are worn, it is possible to file them level.

INSTALLATION

1. Insert the plugs in the spark plug hole and tighten them hand-tight. Take care not to cross-thread them.

2. Tighten the plugs firmly. The correct torque for all engines is 28 ft. lbs.

3. Install the spark plugs wires on their plugs. Make sure that each wire is firmly connected to each plug.

Electronic Ignition

1975 and all later models are equipped with an electronic ignition system.

NOTE: Refer to the Electrical General Repair section for detailed procedures on troubleshooting and repairing the electronic ignition.

Ignition Timing

All Engines

1. Locate the timing marks on the crankshaft pulley and the front of the timing case cover.

2. Clean off the timing marks, so that you can see them.

3. Use chalk or white paint to color the mark on the scale that will indicate the correct timing, when aligned with the mark on the pulley or the pointer. It is also helpful to mark the notch in the pulley or the tip of the pointer with a small dab of color.

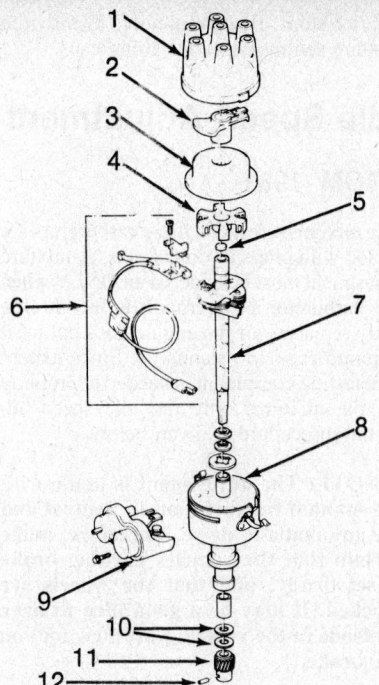

Exploded view of typical 6 cylinder distributor

1. Distributor cap
2. Rotor
3. Dust shield
4. Trigger wheel
5. Felt wick
6. Sensor assembly
7. Shaft assembly
8. Housing
9. Vacuum control
10. Shim
11. Drive gear
12. Pin

4. Attach a tachometer to the engine.

5. Attach a timing light to the engine.

6. Disconnect the vacuum lines to the distributor at the distributor and plug the vacuum lines. Disconnect the TCS switch if so equipped. Loosen the distributor lockbolt just enough so that the distributor can be turned with a little resistance.

7. Check to make sure that all of the wires clear the fan and then start the engine.

8. Adjust the idle to the correct specification.

9. With the timing light aimed at the pulley and the marks on the engine, turn the distributor in the direction of rotor rotation to retard the spark, and in the opposite direction of rotor rotation to advance the spark. Align the marks on the pulley and the engine with the flushes of the timing light.

10. When the marks are aligned, tighten the distributor locknut and recheck the timing with the timing light to make sure that the distributor did not move when you tightened the locknut.

11. Turn off the engine and disconnect the test equipment.

MAGNETIC TIMING PROBE

A bracket and hole are cast into the timing case cover for the use of a magnetic timing probe, connected to a special electronic timing meter for precise ignition timing.

The probe is inserted into the hole of the bracket until the vibration damper is touched. When the engine is started, the probe is automatically spaced away from the damper by the damper's eccentricity, or being slightly out of center. The probe senses a milled slot on the damper and compensating for the bracket's 9.5° ATDC position, registers the reading on the timing meter. Any

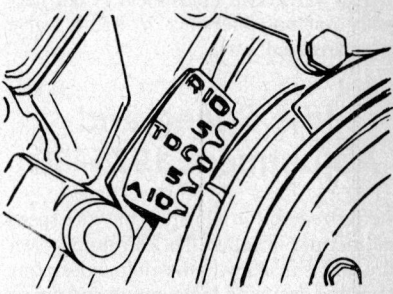

V8 engine timing marks

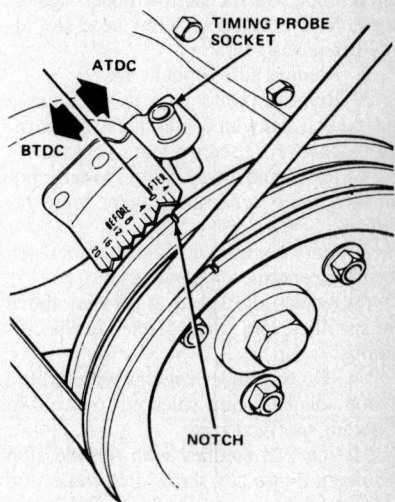

4 cylinder timing marks

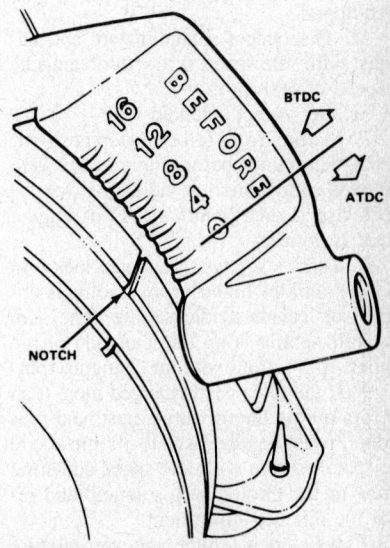

6 cylinder timing marks

necessary corrections can then be made to the ignition timing.

NOTE: Do not use the probe bracket and hole the check the ignition timing, using a conventional timing light.

Valve Lash Adjustment

Manual valve lash adjustment is not necessary nor possible since hydraulic valve lifters are used.

Idle Speed and Adjustment 1975–80

The procedure for adjusting the idle speed and mixture is called the lean drop procedure and is made with the engine operating at normal operating temperature and the air cleaner in place as follows:

1. Turn the mixture screws to the full rich position with the tabs on limiters against stops. Note position of screw head slot inside limiter cap slots.
2. Remove idle limiter caps.
3. Remove limiter caps by threading a sheet metal screw in center of cap and turning clockwise. Discard limiter caps.
4. Reset adjustment screws to same position noted before limiter caps were removed.
5. Start engine and allow it to reach normal operating temperature.
6. Adjust idle speed to 30 rpm above the specified rpm. See "Tune-Up Specifications" chart.
   a. On 6 cylinder engines with throttle stop solenoid, turn solenoid in or out to obtain specified rpm;
   b. On V8 engines with throttle stop solenoid, turn hex screw on throttle stop solenoid carriage to obtain specified rpm. This is done with solenoid wire connected;
   c. Tighten solenoid locknut, if so equipped.
   d. Disconnect solenoid wire and adjust curb idle speed screw to obtain idle speed of 500 rpm;
   e. Reconnect solenoid wire.
7. Starting from full rich stop position, as was determined before limiter caps were removed, turn mixture adjusting screws clockwise (leaner) until a loss of engine speed is noticed.
8. Turn screws counterclockwise (richer) until the highest rpm reading is obtained at lean best idle setting. The lean best idle setting is on the lean side of the highest rpm setting without changing rpm.
9. If the idle speed changed more than 30 rpm during the mixture adjustment procedure, reset the idle speed to 30 rpm above the specified rpm with idle speed adjusting screw or the throttle stop solenoid and repeat the mixture adjustment.
10. Install new limiter caps over mixture adjusting screws with tabs positioned against

full rich stops. Be careful not to disturb idle mixture setting while installing caps.

Idle Speed Adjustment

FROM 1981

Idle mixture screws on these carburetors are sealed with plugs or dowel pins. A mixture adjustment must be undertaken ONLY when the carburetor is overhauled, the throttle body replaced, or the engine does not meet required emission standards. Since expensive testing equipment is needed to properly set the mixture, only the idle speed adjusting procedure is given below.

NOTE: The adjustment is made with the manual transmission in neutral and the automatic in drive. Therefore, make certain that the vehicles parking brake is set firmly, and that the wheels are blocked. It may be a good idea to have someone in the vehicle with their foot on the brake.

1. Connect tachometer, start engine and warm to normal operating temperature. Choke and intake manifold heater (six-cylinder engine only) must be off.
2. If not within OK range, turn curb idle adjustment screw to obtain specified curb idle rpm.
3. For six cylinder engine (BBD carburetor):
   a. Disconnect vacuum hose from vacuum actuator and holding solenoid wire connector. Adjust curb (slow) idle speed adjustment screw to obtain specified curb (slow) idle rpm if not within OK range. Refer to Emission Control Information label, and Tune-Up Specifications.
   b. Apply direct source of vacuum to vacuum actuator.
   c. Turn vacuum actuator adjustment screw on throttle lever until specified rpm is obtained (900 rpm for manual transmissions, and 800 rpm for automatic transmissions).
   d. Disconnect manifold vacuum source from vacuum actuator.
   e. With jumper wire apply battery voltage (12V) to energize holding solenoid. Turn A/C on, if equipped.

NOTE: Throttle must be opened manually to allow Sol-Vac throttle positioner to be extended.

   f. With Sol-Vac throttle positioner extended, idle speed should be 650 rpm for automatic transmission equipped vehicles and 750 rpm for manual transmission equipped vehicles.
   g. If idle speed is not within tolerance, adjust Sol-Vac (hex-head adjustment screw) to obtain specified rpm.
   h. Remove jumper wire from Sol-Vac holding solenoid wire connector.
   i. Connect Sol-Vac holding solenoid wire connector.

   j. Connect original hose to vacuum actuator.
4. For four and eight cylinder engines (2SE, E2SE or 2150 carburetor, turn nut on solenoid plunger or hex screw on solenoid carriage to obtain specified idle rpm:
   a. Tighten locknut, if equipped.
   b. Disconnect solenoid wire connector and adjust curb idle screw to obtain 500 rpm idle speed.
   c. Connect solenoid wire connector.
   d. If model 2150 carburetor (eight-cylinder engine, is equipped with dashpot. With throttle at curb idle position, fully depress dashpot stem and measure clearance between stem and throttle lever. Clearance should be 0.032 inch (0.813 mm). Adjust by loosening locknut and turning dashpot.

ENGINE ELECTRICAL

Distributor

REMOVAL

1. Remove the air cleaner assembly and any other component that will interfere with distributor removal.
2. Disconnect the distributor wiring connector at the harness plug.

NOTE: The wire connector (from 1978) will contain special conductive grease. Do not remove the grease. The same grease will also be found on the metal parts of the rotor. Do not remove it even if it looks charred.

3. If the distributor is equipped with a vacuum diaphragm, disconnect the vacuum hose(s).
4. Release the distributor cap retainers, remove the cap and position it out of the way. If it is necessary to disconnect any plug wires, be sure to mark them for proper location.
5. Use chalk or paint and carefully mark the distributor body that the center of the rotor tip points to. Mark the engine block in relation to the mark on the distributor body. When this is done, the tip of the rotor, the line on the distributor and the engine block mark should match. When the distributor is reinstalled in the engine the distributor must be in the same position if correct ignition timing is to be maintained.
6. Remove the distributor hold-down bolt(s), lockwasher and clamp. Lift the distributor from the engine.

NOTE: The shaft and rotor will move slightly (about an ⅛ of a turn) away from the mark on the distributor body when the distributor (lifted for removal. When reinstalling the distributor, the rotor must

be keyed to the same position, to insure gear mesh.

INSTALLATION

1. Align the rotor with the mark on the distributor body. Turn the rotor about an ⅛ turn counterclockwise and install the distributor into the engine. The rotor should turn back to align with the mark if the distributor body has not rotated and is fully seated. Install the hold-down clamp, lockwasher and bolt(s) but do not tighten fully.

2. Connect the wiring harness and install the distributor cap. If any plug wires were removed from the cap reinstall them.

3. Start the engine, allow it to reach normal operating temperature and check/reset the ignition timing.

NOTE: If the engine has been turned with the distributor removed, or if marks were not drawn, it will be necessary to initially time the engine. Follow the next procedure.

INSTALLATION, ENGINE DISTURBED

1. It is necessary to place the no. 1 cylinder in the firing position to correctly install the distributor.

2. Remove the no. 1 cylinder spark plug.

Turn the engine until the piston in no. 1 cylinder is moving up on the compression stroke. This can be determined by placing your thumb over the spark plug hole and feeling the air being forced out of the cylinder. Stop turning the engine when the marks on the crankshaft pulley and the timing gear cover are in alignment at TDC ("O" mark).

3. Install the rotor and align the rotor tip with no. 1 spark plug terminal tower position when the cap is installed. To locate no. 1 position, temporarily install the distributor cap and mark the side of the distributor body just below the cap terminal tower.

4. Remove the cap. Align the rotor with the no. 1 mark on the distributor body.

5. Refer to Steps 1–3 of proceeding distributor installation.

Alternator

Refer to the Electrical section of the Unit Repair for detailed alternator test and overhaul procedures.

——— CAUTION ———
Since the AC generator and regulator are designed for use on only one polarity system, the following precautions must be

1. The polarity of the battery, generator and regulator must be matched and considered before making any electrical connections in the system.

2. When connecting a booster battery, be sure to connect the negative battery terminal to ground and the positive battery terminals together.

3. When connecting a charger to the battery, connect the charger positive lead to the battery positive terminal. Connect the charger negative lead to the battery negative terminal.

4. Never operate the AC generator on open circuit. Be sure that all connections in the circuit are clean and tight.

5. Do not short across or ground any of the terminals on the AC generator.

6. Do not attempt to polarize the AC generator.

7. Do not use test lamps of more than 12V for checking diode continuity.

8. Avoid long soldering times when replacing diodes or transistors. Prolonged heat is damaging to these units.

9. Disconnect the battery ground terminal when servicing any AC system. This will prevent the possibility of accidentally reversing polarity.

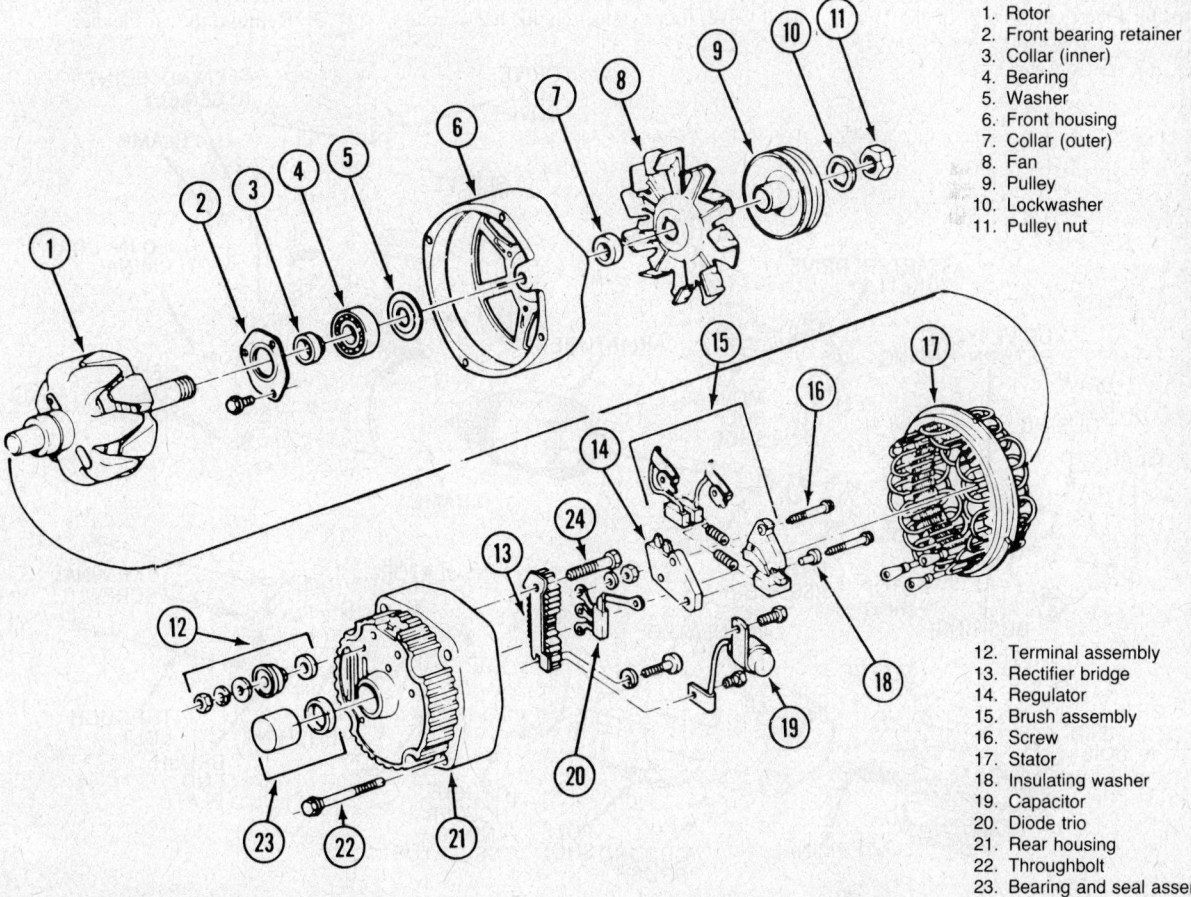

1. Rotor
2. Front bearing retainer
3. Collar (inner)
4. Bearing
5. Washer
6. Front housing
7. Collar (outer)
8. Fan
9. Pulley
10. Lockwasher
11. Pulley nut

12. Terminal assembly
13. Rectifier bridge
14. Regulator
15. Brush assembly
16. Screw
17. Stator
18. Insulating washer
19. Capacitor
20. Diode trio
21. Rear housing
22. Throughbolt
23. Bearing and seal assembly

Exploded view of an alternator

REMOVAL AND INSTALLATION

1. Remove the negative battery cable from the battery.
2. Remove the wire terminals attached to the rear of the alternator.
3. Loosen the bolt holding the adjusting bar and the pivot bolt at the opposite side of the alternator.
4. Move the alternator inward to relieve the belt tension and remove the belt.
5. Remove the adjusting bar and pivot bolts and remove the alternator from the engine.
6. Install the alternator in the reverse procedure of the disassembly.
7. When installing the belt, adjust to allow ½ inch play on the longest run between the pulleys.

Voltage Regulator

The voltage regulator is an integral part of the Delco alternator. Refer to the Unit Repair Section for the integral voltage regulator removal and installation procedures.

Starter

REFERENCE

Refer to the Electrical section of the Unit Repair for detailed starter test and overhaul procedures.

REMOVAL AND INSTALLATION

1. Disconnect the battery ground cable.
2. If necessary, raise the vehicle to gain working clearance.
3. Remove the positive battery lead from the starter or solenoid. Remove remaining wires as necessary.
4. Remove the starter retaining bolts and remove the starter from the vehicle.
5. The installation is in the reverse order of the removal procedure.

On some models, the transmission oil filler tube may have to be removed.

ENGINE MECHANICAL

Design

4–151

The 151 cid General Motors-built, overhead valve, four cylinder engine has a cross-flow cylinder head, five main crankshaft bearings, hydraulic lifters, conventional ball socket rocker arms, exceptionally long pushrods, a gear driven camshaft and a coolant heated aluminum intake manifold.

232 AND 258 SIXES

The American Motors six-cylinder engines are inline sixes with overhead intake and exhaust valves. The valves are operated by paired bridged pivot non-adjustable rocker arms. The 232 was last used in the 1978 model year.

304, 360 AND 401 V8 ENGINES

The V8 has two banks of four cylinders each which are opposed to each other at a 90° angle. The camshaft is located above the crankshaft, between the two banks. It operates the valves through the use of hydraulic lifters, pushrods rocker arms.

Engine

REMOVAL AND INSTALLATION

4–151

1. Disconnect the battery.
2. Remove the air cleaner.

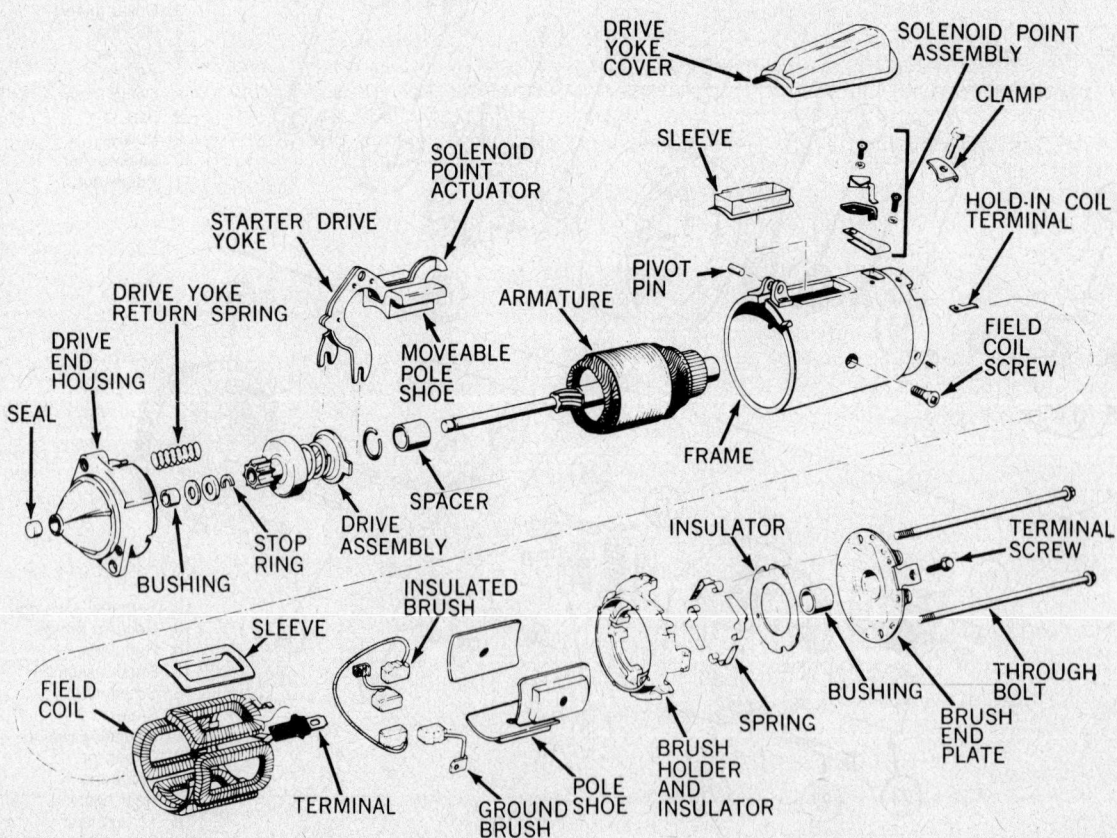

Exploded view of a starter motor

3. Jack up the vehicle and support it on jackstands.

4. Disconnect the exhaust pipe from the manifold.

5. Disconnect the oxygen sensor.

6. Disconnect the wires from the starter.

7. Unbolt the starter and remove it from the vehicle.

8. Disconnect the wires from the distributor and oil pressure sending unit.

9. Remove the engine mount nuts.

10. On vehicles with manual transmission, remove the clutch slave cylinder and flywheel inspection plate.

11. Remove the clutch or converter housing-to-engine bolts.

12. On vehicle with automatic transmission, disconnect the converter from the drive plate.

13. Lower the vehicle.

14. Support the transmission with a jack.

15. Tag all hoses at the carburetor and remove them.

16. Disconnect the mixture control solenoid wire from the carburetor. (not all vehicles have these)

17. Disconnect the wires from the alternator.

18. Disconnect the throttle cable from the bracket and the carburetor.

19. Disconnect the choke and solenoid wires at the carburetor.

20. Disconnect the temperature sender wire.

21. Drain the radiator at the drain cock, then remove the lower hose.

22. Remove the upper radiator hose and the heater hoses.

23. Remove the fan shroud, and radiator.

24. Remove the power steering hoses at the pump.

25. Attach a shop crane to the engine and lift it out of the vehicle.

NOTE: The manual transmission may have to be raised slightly to allow a smooth separation.

26. Installation is the reverse of removal.

Observe the following torque values:

Item	Ft. Lbs.
Clutch/converter housing-to-engine	35
Clutch slave cylinder	18
Engine mount nuts	34
Starter mounting bolts	27
Starter bracket nut	40 in. lbs.
Exhaust pipe-to-manifold nuts	35

232 and 258 Sixes

NOTE: This operation requires discharging the air conditioning system. This requires special tools and skills for safety reasons. It should not be attempted by untrained persons.

1. Remove the hood after marking the hinge locations. The hood need not be removed on most CJ series.

2. Remove the air cleaner.

3. Drain the coolant. Disconnect the radiator hoses. Disconnect automatic transmission cooler lines from the radiator. If there is a radiator shroud, remove it, then remove the radiator.

4. Remove the fan.

5. Remove and set aside the power steering pump and belt. Do not disconnect the hydralic lines.

6. Bleed the compressor refrigerant charge. See the note at the start of this procedure. Remove the condenser and receiver assembly.

7. Disconnect all wires, lines, linkage, and hoses from the engine.

8. Drain the oil and remove the filter.

9. Remove both engine front support cushion-to-frame retaining nuts.

10. Disconnect the exhaust pipe at the support bracket and the manifold.

11. Support the engine with the lifting equipment.

12. Remove the front support cushion and bracket assemblies from the engine.

13. Remove the transfer case lever boot, the floor mat, and the transmission access cover.

14. On automatic transmissions, remove the upper bolts holding the bellhousing to the engine adapter plate. On manual transmissions, remove the upper bolts holding the clutch housing to the engine.

15. Remove the starter.

16. On automatics, remove the two adapter plate inspection covers. Mark the relationship of the converter to the flex plate and remove the converter-to-flex plate bolts. Remove the rest of the bolts holding the bellhousing to the adapter plate. On manual transmissions, remove the clutch housing lower cover and the rest of the bolts holding the clutch housing to the engine.

17. Support the transmission with a floor jack and remove the engine by pulling it forward and upward.

To install the engines:

1. Lower the engine into place and align it with the bellhousing or clutch housing. Make sure the manual transmission clutch shaft aligns with the splines of the clutch driven plate.

2. On automatics, install the bellhousing-to-engine adapter plate bolts. On manuals, install the clutch housing-to-engine bolts. Torque the bolts to 25–28 ft. lbs. at the top and 40–45 ft. lbs. at the bottom.

3. Remove the floor jack.

4. Align the marks made in step 16 and install the converter-to-flex plate bolts, torquing them to 21–23 ft. lbs.

5. Install the two engine adapter plate inspection covers or the clutch housing lower cover.

6. Replace the starter.

7. Install the front support cushion and bracket assemblies to the engine, torquing the bolts to 25–30 ft. lbs. Lower the engine

onto the frame supports. Install the front support cushion retaining nuts, torquing them to 25–30 ft. lbs.

8. Connect the exhaust pipe at the support bracket and manifold. A new manifold seal is advisable.

9. Install the oil filter.

10. Replace all the items removed in step seven.

11. Replace the air conditioning condenser and receiver assembly and recharge the system.

12. Replace the power steering pump and belt. Install the fan and tighten the bolts to 15–25 ft. lbs.

13. Replace and reconnect the radiator. Replace the oil cooler lines. Fill the cooling system.

14. Fill the crankcase and replace the air cleaner. Install the transmission access cover, floor mat, and transfer case lever boot. Replace the hood.

304, 360 and 401 V8

NOTE: This operation requires discharging the air conditioning system. This requires special tools and skills. For safety reasons, it should not be attempted by untrained persons.

The engine is removed without the transmission and bellhousing.

1. On the Commando, Cherokee, Truck, and Wagoneer, the hood must be removed. Mark the hinge locations at the hood panel for alignment during installation. Remove the hood from the hinges.

2. Remove the air cleaner assembly.

3. Drain the cooling system and disconnect the upper and lower radiator hoses. If equipped with automatic transmission, disconnect the cooler lines from the radiator.

NOTE: If the vehicle is equipped with a radiator shroud, it is necessary to separate the shroud from the radiator to facilitate removal and installation of the radiator and engine fan.

4. Remove the radiator.

5. Remove the engine fan.

6. If equipped with power steering, remove the pump from the engine and lay it aside. Do not disconnect the hoses.

7. If equipped with air conditioning, turn both service valves clockwise to the front seated position. Bleed the compressor refrigerant charge by slowly loosening the service valve fittings. Disconnect the condenser and evaporator lines from the compressor. Disconnect the receiver outlet at the disconnect coupling. Remove the condenser and receiver assembly.

8. Remove the battery and tray.

9. On Wagoneers and Cherokees, (1975) remove the heater core housing and charcoal canister from the firewall.

10. If equipped, remove cruise command vacuum servo bellows and mounting bracket as a complete assembly.

11. On CJ models, (1976–82) remove

left cushion front support cushion and bracket from cylinder block.

12. Disconnect all wires, lines linkage, and hoses which are connected to the engine.

13. If equipped with automatic transmission, disconnect the transmission filler tube bracket from the right cylinder head. Do not remove the filler tube from the transmission.

14. Remove both engine front support cushion-to-frame retaining nuts.

15. Support the weight of the engine with a lifting device.

16. On CJ and Commando models, remove the transfer case shift lever boot, floor (if so equipped), and transmission access cover.

17. Remove the upper bolts which secure the transmission bellhousing to the engine adapter plate on vehicles equipped with automatic transmission. If equipped with manual transmission, remove the upper bolts which secure the clutch housing to the engine.

18. Disconnect the exhaust pipes at the exhaust manifolds and support bracket.

19. Remove the starter motor.

20. Support the transmission with a floor jack.

21. If equipped with automatic transmission, remove the two engine adapter plate inspection covers. Mark the assembled position of the converter and flex plate and remove the converter-to-flex plate cap screws. Remove the remaining bolts which secure the transmission bellhousing to the engine adapter plate.

22. If equipped with manual transmission, remove the clutch housing lower cover and the remaining bolts which secure the clutch housing to the engine.

23. Remove the engine by pulling upward and forward.

NOTE: If equipped with power brakes, care must be taken to avoid damaging the power unit while removing the engine.

To install the engine:

1. Lower the engine slowly into the engine compartment and align with the transmission bellhousing (automatic transmission) or clutch housing (manual transmission). On manual transmissions, make certain the clutch shaft is aligned properly with the splines of the clutch driven plate.

2. Install the transmission bellhousing-to-engine adapter plate bolts (automatic transmission) or the clutch housing to engine bolts (manual transmission). Tighten the bolts to the specified torque. Remove the floor jack which was used to support the transmission.

3. If equipped with automatic transmission, align the marks previously made on the converter and flex plate, install the converter-to-flex plate cap screws and tighten to the specified torque.

4. Install the two engine adapter plate inspection covers (automatic transmission)

or the clutch housing lower cover (manual transmission).

5. Install the starter motor.

6. Lower the engine onto the frame supports, remove the lifting device and install the front support cushion retaining nuts. Tighten the nuts to the specified torque.

7. Connect the exhaust pipes at the exhaust manifolds and support bracket.

8. If equipped with automatic transmission, connect the transmission filler tube bracket to the right cylinder head.

9. On Wagoneers and Cherokees, install the heater core housing and charcoal canister to the firewall.

10. If removed, install the battery and tray.

11. Connect all wires, lines linkage and hoses which were previously disconnected from the engine.

12. If removed, install the air conditioning condenser and receiver assembly. Connect the receiver outlet to the disconnect coupling. Connect the condenser and evaporator lines to the compressor. Purge the compressor of air.

NOTE: Both service valves must be open before the air conditioning system is operated.

13. If equipped with power steering, connect the power steering, pump to the engine.

14. Install the engine fan and tighten the retaining bolts to the specified torque.

15. Install the radiator and connect the upper and lower hoses. If equipped with automatic transmission, connect the cooler lines.

16. Fill the cooling system to the specified level.

17. Install the air cleaner assembly. Install cruise command vacuum servo bellows and mounting bracket.

18. Start the engine. Check all connections for leaks. Stop the engine.

19. If removed, install the transmission access cover, floor mat and transfer case shift lever boot.

20. If removed, install the transmission access cover, floor mat and transfer case shift level boot.

Rocker Shafts and Rocker Studs

REMOVAL AND INSTALLATION

4-151

1. Remove the rocker arm cover.
2. Remove the rocker arm capscrew and ball.
3. Remove the rocker arm.
4. Installation is the reverse of removal. Torque the capscrew to 20 ft. lbs. DO NOT OVERTORQUE!

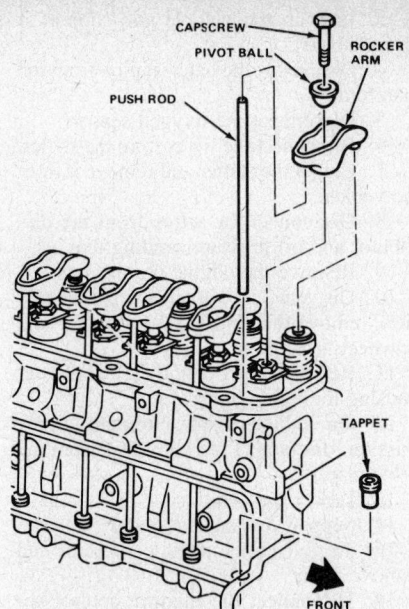

4 cylinder engine rocker arm and pushrod removal and installation

6-232 and 258

On these engines the rocker arms pivot on a bridged pivot that is secured with two capscrews. The bridged pivots maintain proper rocker arm-to-valve tip alignment.

1. Remove the rocker cover and gasket.

2. Remove the two capscrews at each bridged pivot, backing off each capscrew one turn at a time to avoid breaking the bridge.

3. Remove each bridged pivot and corresponding pair of rocker arms and place them on a clean surface in the same order as they are removed.

NOTE: Bridged pivots, capscrews, rockers, and pushrods must all be reinstalled in their original positions.

4. Clean all the parts in a suitable sol-

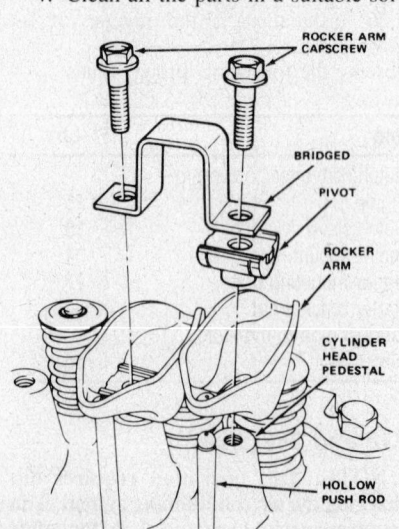

Bridged pivot type rocker arms found on 6 and V8 engines

vent and use compressed air to blow out the oil passages in the pushrods and the rocker arms. Replace any excessively worn parts.

5. Install rocker arms, pushrods and bridged pivots in the same positions from which they were removed.

NOTE: Be sure that the bottom end of each pushrod is centered in the plunger cap of each hydraulic valve tappet.

6. Install the capscrews and tighten them one turn at a time, alternating between the two screws on each bridge. Tighten the capscrews to 21 ft. lbs.

7. Install the rocker cover with new gasket.

V8 Engines

1. Remove the cylinder head cover and gasket.

2. Loosen the bridged pivot capscrews a turn at a time, so as not to break the bridge.

3. Remove the rocker arm and bridge assembly from the cylinder head.

To install:

1. Install the rocker arms and bridge assembly on the cylinder head, and align the push rods.

2. Install the capscrews and tighten each one a turn at a time to avoid breaking the bridge. Tighten the capscrews to 19 ft. lbs. torque.

3. Install the cylinder head cover with a new gasket and torque the cover bolts to 50 in. lbs.

Valve Arrangement

4 Cylinder Engines:
I E I E E I E I → Front
6 Cylinder Engines:
E I I E E I I E E I I E → Front
V8 Engines:
E I I E E I I E
E I I E E I I E → Front

Crankshaft Pulley Assembly (Vibration Damper)

REMOVAL AND INSTALLATION

1. Remove drive belts from pulley.

2. Remove the retaining bolts and separate the pulley from the vibration damper.

3. Remove the vibration damper retaining bolt from the crankshaft end.

4. Using a vibration damper puller, remove the damper from the crankshaft.

5. Upon installation, align the key slot of the pulley hub to the crankshaft key. Complete the assembly in the reverse order of removal. Torque the retaining bolts to specifications.

Cylinder Head

REMOVAL AND INSTALLATION

4-151 and 232 and 258 Sixes

NOTE: The 151 rocker cover is sealed with RTV silicone gasket material. Do not use a conventional Gasket.

1. Drain the cooling system and disconnect the hoses at the thermostat housing.

2. Remove the cylinder head cover (valve cover), the gasket, the rocker arm assembly, and the pushrods.

NOTE: The push rods must be replaced in their original positions.

3. Remove the intake and exhaust manifold from the cylinder head.

4. Disconnect the spark plug wires and remove the spark plugs to avoid damaging them.

5. Disconnect the temperature sending unit wire, ignition coil and bracket assembly and battery ground cable from the engine.

6. Remove the cylinder head bolts, the cylinder head and gasket from the block.

7. To install reverse the procedure. Tighten the headbolts to the specified torque, in the proper sequence.

V8 Engines

1. Drain the cooling system and cylinder block.

2. When removing the right cylinder head, it may be necessary to remove the heater core housing from the firewall.

3. Remove the valve cover(s) and gasket(s).

4. Remove the rocker arm assemblies and the push rods.

NOTE: The valve train components must be replaced in their original positions.

5. Remove the spark plugs to avoid damaging them.

6. Remove the intake manifold with the carburetor still attached.

7. Remove the exhaust pipes at the flange of the exhaust manifold. When replacing the exhaust pipes it is advisable to install new gaskets at the flange.

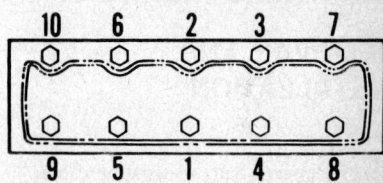

4 cylinder engine cylinder head bolt tightening sequence

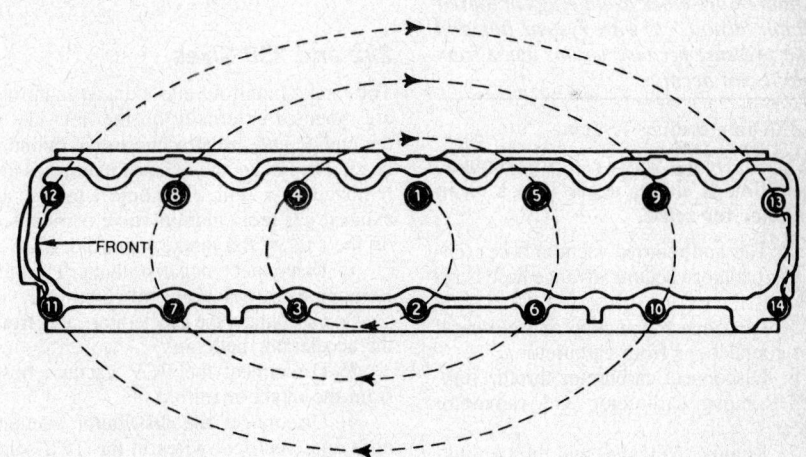

6 cylinder engine cylinder head bolt tightening sequence

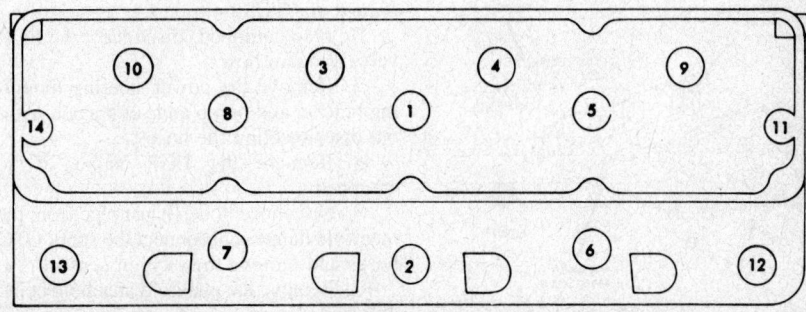

V8 engine cylinder head bolt tightening sequence

317

8. Loosen all of the drive belts.

9. Disconnect the battery ground cable and alternator bracket from the right cylinder head.

10. Disconnect the air pump and power steering pump brackets from the left cylinder head.

11. Remove the cylinder head bolts and lift the head(s) from the cylinder block.

12. Remove the cylinder head gasket from the head or the block.

13. To install, reverse the above procedure.

NOTE: Apply an even coat of sealing compound to both sides of the new head gasket only. Wire brush the cylinder head bolts, then lightly oil them prior to installation. First, tighten all bolts to 80 ft. lbs. then tighten to the specified torque. Follow the correct sequence.

Intake Manifold

REMOVAL AND INSTALLATION

4-151

1. Remove battery negative cable.

2. Remove air cleaner and PCV valve hose.

——— **CAUTION** ———

Do not remove block drain plugs or loosen radiator draincock with system hot and under pressure because serious burns from coolant can occur.

3. Drain cooling system.

NOTE: Do not waste reusable coolant. If solution is clean, drain into a clean container for reuse.

4. Tag and remove vacuum hoses (ensure distributor vacuum advance hose is removed).

5. Disconnect fuel pipe and electrical wire connections from carburetor.

6. Disconnect carburetor throttle linkage. Remove carburetor and carburetor spacer.

7. Remove bellcrank and throttle linkage brackets and move to one side for clearance.

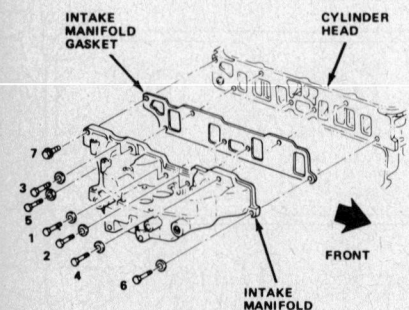

4 cylinder engine intake manifold bolt tightening sequence

8. Remove heater hose at intake manifold.

9. Remove alternator. Note position of spacers for installation.

10. Remove manifold-to-cylinder head bolts and remove manifold.

11. Position replacement gasket and install replacement manifold on cylinder head. Start all bolts.

12. Tighten all bolts with 37 ft. lbs. torque.

13. Connect heater hose to intake manifold.

14. Install bellcrank and throttle linkage brackets.

15. Connect carburetor throttle linkage to brackets and bellcrank.

16. Install carburetor spacer and tighten bolts with 15 ft. lbs. torque.

17. Install carburetor and gasket. Tighten nuts with 15 ft. lbs. torque.

18. Install fuel pipe and electrical wire connections. Install vacuum hoses.

19. Install battery negative cable.

——— **CAUTION** ———

Use extreme caution when engine is operating. Do not stand in direct line with fan. Do not put hands near pulleys, belts or fan. Do not wear loose clothing.

20. Refill cooling system. Start engine and inspect for leaks.

21. Install air cleaner and PCV valve hose.

232 and 258 Sixes

The intake manifold and exhaust manifold are mounted externally on the left side of the engine and are attached to the cylinder head. The intake and exhaust manifolds are removed as a unit. On some engines, an exhaust gas recirculation valve is mounted on the side of the intake manifold.

1. Disconnect negative battery cable. Remove the air cleaner and carburetor.

2. Disconnect the accelerator cable from the accelerator bellcrank.

3. Disconnect the PCV vacuum hose from the intake manifold.

4. Disconnect the distributor vacuum hose and electrical wires at the TCS solenoid vacuum valve.

5. Remove the TCS solenoid vacuum valve and bracket from the intake manifold. In some cases it might not be necessary to remove the TCS unit.

6. If so equipped, disconnect the EGR valve vacuum hoses.

7. Remove the power steering mounting bracket and pump and set it aside without disconnecting the hoses.

8. Remove the EGR valve, if so equipped.

9. Disconnect the exhaust pipe from the manifold flange. Disconnect the spark CTO hoses and remove the oxygen sensor.

10. Remove the manifold attaching bolts, nuts and clamps.

11. Separate the intake manifold and exhaust manifold from the engine as an assembly. Discard the gasket.

12. If either manifold is to be replaced, they should be separated at the heat riser area.

13. Clean the mating surfaces of the manifolds and the cylinder head before replacing the manifolds. Replace them in reverse order of the above procedure with a new gasket. Tighten the bolts and nuts to the specified torque in the proper sequence.

V8 Engines

1. Disconnect negative battery cable. Drain the coolant from the radiator.

2. Remove the air cleaner assembly.

3. Disconnect the spark plug wires. Remove the spark plug wire brackets from the valve covers, and the bypass valve bracket.

4. Disconnect the upper radiator hose and the by-pass hose from the intake manifold. Disconnect the heater hose from the rear of the manifold.

5. Disconnect the ignition coil bracket and lay the coil aside.

6. Disconnect the TCS solenoid vacuum valve from the right side valve cover.

7. Disconnect all lines, hoses, linkages and wires from the carburetor and intake manifold and TCS components as required.

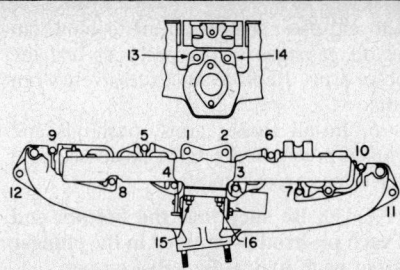

6 cylinder engine intake manifold bolt tightening sequence

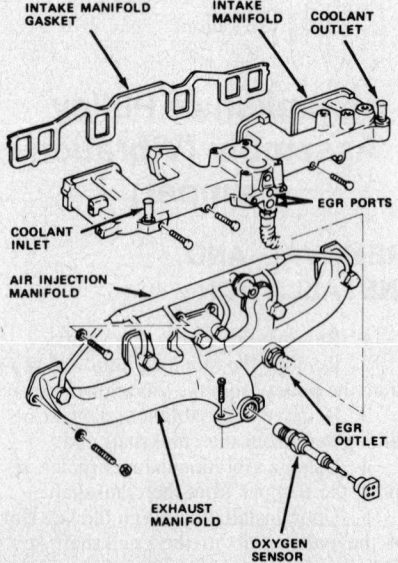

Intake and exhaust manifolds on 6 cylinder engine with oxygen sensor

8. Disconnect the air delivery hoses at the air distribution manifolds.

9. Disconnect the air pump diverter valve and lay the valve and the bracket assembly, including the hoses, forward of the engine.

10. Remove the intake manifold after removing the cap bolts that hold it in place. Remove and discard the side gaskets and the end seals.

11. Clean the mating surfaces of the intake manifold and the cylinder head before replacing the intake manifold. Use new gaskets and tighten the cap bolts to the correct torque. Install in reverse order of the above procedure.

NOTE: There is no specified tightening sequence for this intake manifold. Start at the center bolts and work outward.

Exhaust Manifolds

REMOVAL AND INSTALLATION

4-151

1. Remove air cleaner and heated air tube.

2. Remove engine oil dipstick tube attaching bolt.

3. Remove oxygen sensor, if equipped.

4. Raise vehicle and disconnect exhaust pipe from manifold. Lower vehicle.

5. Remove exhaust manifold bolts and remove manifold and gasket.

6. Install replacement gasket and exhaust manifold on cylinder head. Tighten all bolts to 39 foot-pounds torque.

7. Install dipstick tube attaching bolt.

232 and 258 Sixes

The intake and exhaust manifolds of the 232 and 258 cu. in. Sixes must be removed together. See the procedure for removing and installing the intake manifold.

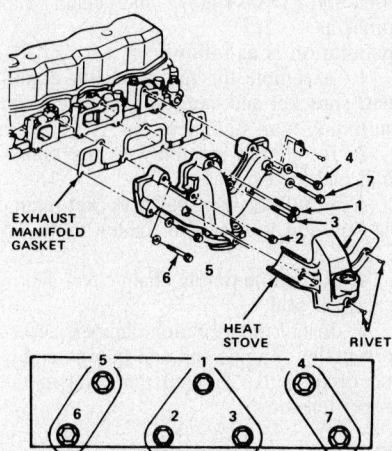

4 cylinder engine exhaust manifold bolt tightening sequence

V8 Engines

1. Disconnect the spark plug wires.

2. Disconnect the air delivery hose at the distribution manifold.

3. Remove the air distribution manifold and the injection trubes.

4. Disconnect the exhaust pipe at the manifold.

5. Remove the exhaust manifold attaching bolts and washers along with the spark plug shields.

6. Separate the exhaust manifold from the cylinder head.

7. Install in reverse order of the above procedure. Clean the mating surfaces and tighten the attaching bolts to the correct torque.

Timing Gear Cover

TIMING GEAR COVER AND OIL SEAL REPLACEMENT

4-151

1. Disconnect the battery ground.

2. Remove the crankshaft pulley hub.

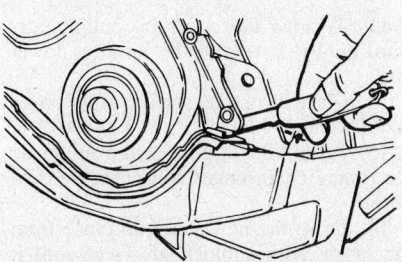

Cutting the pan gasket on the 4 cylinder engine

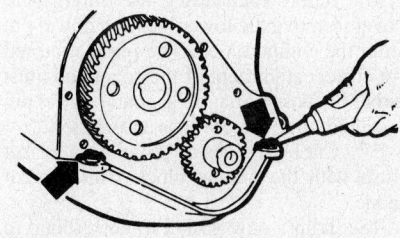

Applying RTV sealant on 4 cylinder engine

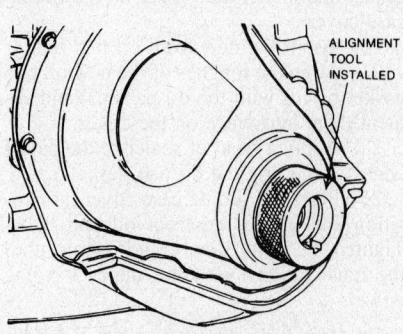

Timing case cover alignment tool installed on 4 cylinder engine

3. Remove the alternator bracket.

4. Remove the fan and radiator shroud.

5. Remove the oil pan-to-timing case cover bolts.

6. Pull the cover forward just enough to allow cutting the oil pan front seal flush with the block on both sides of the cover. Use a sharp knife or razor.

7. Remove the front cover.

8. Clean the gasket surface on the block and cover.

9. Cut the tabs from the new oil pan front seal.

10. Install the seal on the cover, pressing the tips into the holes provided in the cover.

11. Coat a new gasket with sealer and place on the cover.

12. Apply a ⅛ inch bead of RTV sealant to the joint formed at the oil pan and block.

13. Install an aligning tool such as tool J-23042 in the timing case cover seal.

NOTE: It is important that an aligning tool is used to avoid seal damage and to ensure a tight, even seal fit.

14. Position the cover on the block and partially tighten the two oil pan-to-cover bolts.

15. Install the remaining bolts, and tighten all bolts to 45 in. lbs.

16. Install all other parts in reverse order of removal. Torque the fan assembly bolts to 18 ft. lbs.

232 and 258 Sixes

1. Remove the drive belts, engine fan and hub assembly, the accessory pulley, and vibration damper.

2. Remove the oil pan to timing chain cover screws and the screws that attach the cover to the block.

3. Raise the timing chain cover just high enough to detach the retaining nibs of the oil pan neoprene seal from the bottom side of the cover. This must be done to prevent pulling the seal end tabs away from the tongues of the oil pan gaskets which would cause a leak.

4. Remove the timing chain cover and gasket from the engine.

5. Use a razor blade to cut off the oil pan seal end tabs flush with the front face of the cylinder block and remove the seal.

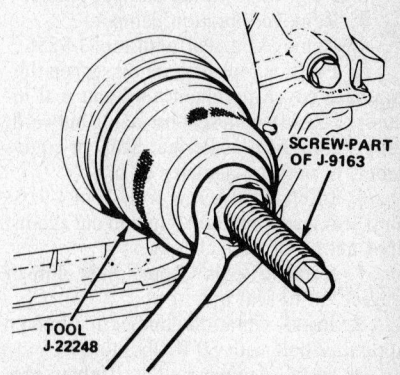

Timing case cover seal installation 6 cylinder engine

Clean the timing chain cover, oil pan, and cylinder block surfaces.

6. Apply seal compound (Perfect Seal, or equivalent) to both sides of replacement timing case cover gasket and position gasket on cylinder block.

7. Cut end tabs off replacement oil pan gasket corresponding to pieces cut off original gasket. Cement these pieces on oil pan.

8. Coat oil pan seal end tabs generously with Permatex No. 2, or equivalent, and position seal on timing case cover.

9. Position timing case cover on engine. Place timing case cover alignment tool and seal installer J-22248 in crankshaft opening of cover.

10. Install cover-to-block screws and oil pan-to-cover screws. Tighten cover-to-block screws with 5 ft. lbs. torque and oil pan-to-cover screws with 11 ft. lbs. torque.

11. Remove cover aligning tool and position replacement oil seal on tool with seal lip facing outward. Apply light film of Perfect Seal, or equivalent, on outside diameter of seal.

12. Insert draw screw from tool J-9163 into seal installing tool. Tighten nut against tool until tool contacts cover.

13. Remove tools and apply light film of engine oil to seal lip.

14. Install vibration damper and tighten retaining screw with 80 ft. lbs. torque.

15. Install damper pulley. Tighten capscrews with 20 ft. lbs. torque.

16. Install engine fan and hub assembly.

17. Install drive belt(s).

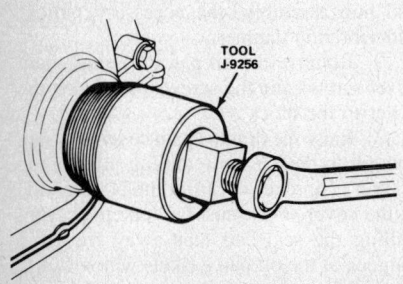

6 cylinder engine timing case cover seal removal

Cover on Engine

1. Remove drive belts.
2. Remove vibration damper pulley.
3. Remove vibration damper.
4. Remove oil seal with tool J-9256.
5. Position replacement oil seal on timing case cover alignment tool and seal installer J-22248 with seal lip facing outward. Apply light film of Perfect Seal, or equivalent, to outside diameter of seal.
6. Insert draw screw from tool J-9163 into seal installing tool. Tighten nut against tool until tool contacts cover.
7. Remove tools. Apply light film of engine oil to seal lip.
8. Install vibration damper and tighten retaining bolt with 80 ft. lbs. torque.
9. Install damper pulley. Tighten capscrews with 20 ft. lbs. torque.
10. Install drive belt(s).

V8 Engines

1. Remove the negative battery cable.
2. Drain the cooling system and disconnect the radiator hoses and by-pass hose.
3. Remove all of the drive belts and the fan and spacer assembly.
4. Remove the alternator and the front portion of the alternator bracket as an assembly.
5. Disconnect the heater hose.
6. Remove the power steering pump, and/or the air pump, and the mounting bracket as an assembly. Do not disconnect the power steering hoses.
7. Remove the distributor cap and note the position of the rotor. Remove the distributor. (See the Engine Electrical Section.)
8. Remove the fuel pump.
9. Remove the vibration damper and pulley.
10. Remove the two front oil pan bolts and the bolts which secure the timing chain cover to the engine block.

NOTE: The timing gear cover retaining bolts vary in length and must be installed in the same locations from which they were removed.

11. Remove the cover by pulling forward until it is free of the locating dowel pins.

12. Clean the gasket surface of the cover and the engine block.

13. Pry out the original seal from inside the timing chain cover and clean the seal bore.

14. Drive the new seal into place from the inside with a block of wood until it contacts the outer flange of the cover.

15. Apply a light film of motor oil to the lips of the new seal.

16. Before reinstalling the timing gear cover, remove the lower locating dowel pin from the engine block. The pin is required for correct alignment of the cover and must either be reused or a replacement dowel pin installed after the cover is in position.

17. Cut both sides of the oil pan gasket flush with the engine block with a razor blade.

18. Trim a new gasket to correspond to the amount cut off at the oil pan.

19. Apply sealer to both sides of the new gasket and install the gasket on the timing case cover.

20. Install the new front oil pan seal.

21. Align the tongues of the new oil pan gasket pieces with the oil pan seal and cement them into place on the cover.

22. Apply a bead of sealer to the cutoff edges of the original oil pan gaskets.

23. Place the timing case cover into position and install the front oil pan bolts. Tighten the bolts slowly and evenly until the cover aligns with the upper locating dowel.

24. Install the lower dowel through the cover and drive it into the corresponding hole in the engine block.

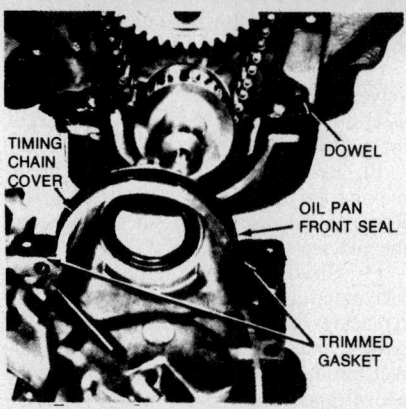

Trim the timing gear cover gasket as indicated before installing on V8 engine

25. Install the cover retaining bolts in the same locations from which they were removed. Tighten to 25 ft. lbs.

26. Assemble the remaining components in the reverse order of removal.

Timing Chain or Gears

REMOVAL AND INSTALLATION

4-151

Refer to Camshaft removal and installation.

232 and 258 Sixes

1. Remove the drive belts, engine fan and hub assembly, accessory pulley, vibration damper and timing chain cover.

2. Remove the oil seal from the timing chain cover.

3. Remove the camshaft sprocket retaining bolt and washer.

4. Rotate the crankshaft until the timing mark on the crankshaft sprocket is closest to and in a center line with the timing pointer of the camshaft sprocket.

5. Remove the crankshaft sprocket, camshaft sprocket and timing chain as an assembly. Disassemble the chain and sprockets.

Installation is as follows:

1. Assemble the timing chain, crankshaft sprocket and camshaft sprocket with the timing marks aligned.

2. Install the assembly to the crankshaft and the camshaft.

3. Install the camshaft sprocket retaining bolt and washer and tighten to 45–55 ft. lbs.

4. Install the timing chain cover and in a new oil seal.

5. Install the vibration damper, accessory pulley, engine fan and hub assembly and drive belts. Tighten the belts to the proper tension.

304, 360 and 401 V8s

1. Remove the timing chain cover and gasket.

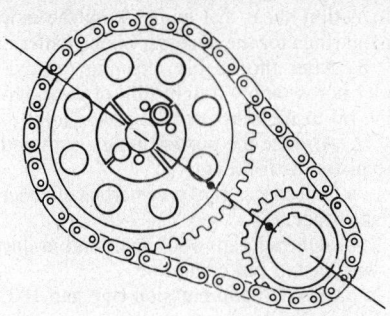

6 cylinder 232 and 258 timing gear alignment

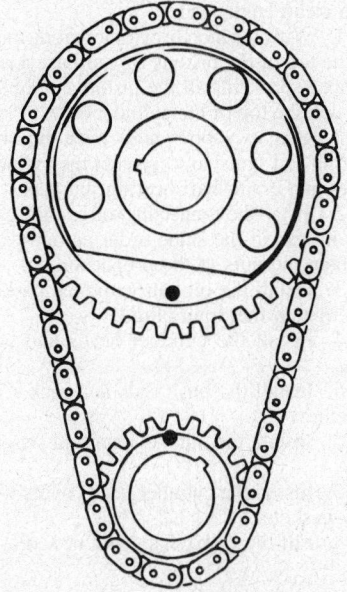

Timing gear alignment—V8 engines

2. Remove the crankshaft oil slinger.
3. Remove the camshaft sprocket retaining bolt and washer, distributor drive gear and fuel pump eccentric.
4. Rotate the crankshaft until the timing mark on the crankshaft sprocket is adjacent to, and on a center line with, the timing mark on the camshaft sprocket.
5. Remove the crankshaft sprocket, camshaft sprocket and timing chain as an assembly. Disassemble the chain and sprockets.

Installation is as follows:
1. Assemble the timing chain, crankshaft sprocket and camshaft sprocket with the timing marks on both sprockets aligned.
2. Install the assembly to the crankshaft and the camshaft.
3. Install the fuel pump eccentric, distributor drive gear, washer and retaining bolt. Tighten the bolt to 25–35 ft. lbs.

NOTE: The fuel pump eccentric must be installed with the stamped word "REAR" facing the camshaft sprocket.

4. Install the crankshaft oil slinger.
5. Install the timing chain cover using a new gasket and oil seal.

Camshaft

REMOVAL AND INSTALLATION

4-151

NOTE: Replacement of the cam gear requires the removal of the camshaft.

Removing Camshaft

1. Disconnect the negative battery cable.
2. Drain the coolant. Disconnect the radiator hoses at the radiator. Remove fan, shroud and radiator.
3. Remove the timing case cover. Refer to previous section.

NOTE: Keep all valve train components in order to position and cylinder. They must be returned to their original positions.

4. Remove valve cover, rocker arms and push rods. Remove side cover and lifters.
5. Remove distributor, oil pump drive and fuel pump.
6. Remove the camshaft thrust plate screws. Remove the camshaft and gear assembly by pulling them from the engine block.

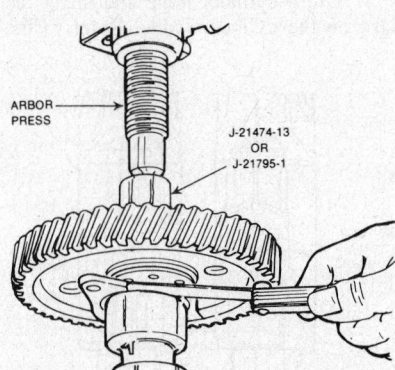

Installing 4-151 camshaft timing gear and measuring thrust plate end clearance

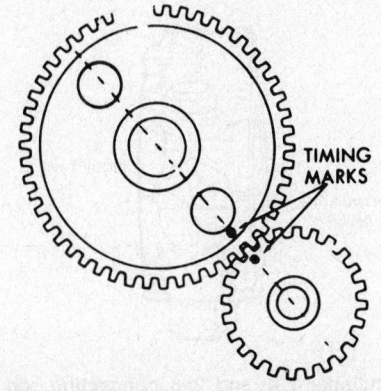

Timing gear alignment—4-151 engine

Removing Cam Gear

4-151

NOTE: Removal of the camshaft gear requires a special adapter and the use of a press. Camshaft removal is necessary.

1. Place the adapter on the press and place the camshaft through the opening.
2. Press the shaft out of the gear using a socket or other suitable tool.

— CAUTION —
The thrust plate must be in position so that the Woodruff key does not damage the gear when the shaft is pressed out.

3. To install the gear firmly support the shaft at the back of the front journal in an arbor press using press plate adapters.
4. Place the gear spacer ring and thrust plate over the end of the shaft, and install the Woodruff key in the shaft keyway.
5. Install the camshaft gear and press it onto the shaft until it bottoms against the gear spacer ring. The end clearance of the thrust plate should be .0015″ to .0050″. If less than .0015″, the spacer ring should be replaced. If more than .0050″, the thrust plate should be replaced.

INSTALLING THE CAMSHAFT

1. Thoroughly coat camshaft journals with high quality engine oil supplement such as STP or its equivalent.
2. Install camshaft assembly in engine block. Use care to prevent damaging bearings or camshaft.
3. Turn crankshaft and camshaft so that valve timing marks on gear teeth are aligned. Engine is now in number four cylinder firing position. Install camshaft thrust plate-to-block screws and tighten with 75 inch-pounds torque.
4. Install timing gear cover and gasket.
5. Line up keyway in hub with key on crankshaft and slide hub onto shaft. Install center bolt and tighten with 160 ft. lbs. torque.
6. Install valve tappets, push rods, push rod cover, oil pump shaft and gear assembly and fuel pump. Install distributor according to following procedure.
   a. Turn crankshaft 360 degrees to firing position of number one cylinder (number one exhaust and intake valve tappets both on base circle (heel) of camshaft and timing notch on vibration damper indexed with top dead center mark [TDC] on timing degree scale).
   b. Install distributor and align shaft so that rotor arm points toward number one cylinder spark plug contact.
7. Install rocker arms and pivot balls over push rods. With tappets on base circle (heel) of camshaft, tighten rocker arm capscrews with 20 ft. lbs. torque. Do not overtighten.

8. Install cylinder head cover.

9. Install intake manifold.

10. Install radiator and lower radiator hose.

11. Install belt, fan and shroud. Tighten fan bolts with 18 ft. lbs. torque. Install upper radiator hose. Tighten belts.

232 and 258 Sixes

1. Drain and remove radiator.

2. If equipped, remove air conditioning condenser and receiver assembly as a charged unit.

3. Remove fuel pump, distributor and ignition wires.

4. Remove cylinder head cover and gasket.

5. Remove rocker arms, bridged pivot assemblies and pushrods. Be sure to replace these parts in the same order as removed.

6. Remove cylinder head and gasket and lifters.

7. Remove timing case cover.

8. Remove timing chain and sprockets as one assembly, being careful to rotate the crankshaft until the timing mark on the crankshaft sprocket is lined up with the timing pointer on the camshaft sprocket.

9. Remove the front bumper or grill as required.

10. Carefully remove the camshaft from the engine.

11. Installation is the reverse of removal.

V8

1. Drain and remove radiator.

2. If equipped, remove air conditioning condenser and receiver assembly as a charged unit.

3. Remove fuel pump, distributor and ignition wires.

4. Remove cylinder head cover and gasket.

5. Remove drive belts, fan, and hub assembly.

6. Remove intake manifold.

7. Remove rocker arms, bridged pivot assemblies and pushrods. Be sure to replace these parts in the same order as removed.

8. Remove cylinder head and gasket and lifters.

9. Remove timing case cover.

10. Remove distributor drive gear and fuel pump eccentric from the camshaft.

NOTE: The fuel pump eccentric must be installed with the word "REAR" facing the camshaft sprocket.

11. Remove timing chain and sprocket as assembly, being careful to rotate the crankshaft until the timing mark on the crankshaft sprocket is lined up with the timing pointer on the camshaft sprocket.

12. Remove the front bumper or grill, and hood latch support bracket as required.

13. Carefully remove the camshaft from the engine.

14. Installation is the reverse of removal.

Pistons and Connecting Rods

REMOVAL AND INSTALLATION

1. Remove the cylinder head. (See previous section).

2. Raise the vehicle and safely support on jackstands. Drain the engine oil. Remove the oil pan. (See following section).

3. Position the pistons, one at a time, near the bottom of their stroke and use a ridge reamer to remove any ridge from the top of the cylinder walls.

4. Inspect the connecting rod and cap for cylinder number identification, if not identified mark them.

5. Remove the connecting rod bearing caps and bearing inserts, retain them in the same order they were removed.

6. Remove the connecting rod and piston assembly through the top of the cylinder.

NOTE: When removing the pistons and connecting rods, have the crank at the bottom of its stroke on the cylinder you are removing the piston from. After the rod cap has been removed, place two pieces of rubber tubing on the rod bolts to prevent damage to the crankshaft when removing the piston.

7. Use a cylinder hone and break the glaze on the cylinder walls. Refer to the instruction sheet that comes with the new piston rings for the necessary hone pattern.

8. After thoroughly cleaning the cylinder bores, apply a light film of clean engine oil to the bores with a clean cloth.

9. Arrange the piston ring gaps around the piston as follows:

    a. Oil spacer gap on centerline of either skirt face.

    b. Oil rail gaps 180° apart and in line with piston pin centerline.

    c. Second compression ring gap 180° from top oil rail gap.

    d. First compression ring gap 180° from second compression ring gap.

10. Lubricate piston and ring surfaces with clean engine oil.

11. With the notch or other front mark on the top of the pistons forward use a ring compressor to install the piston assemblies through the top of the cylinder bores. Place the lengths of rubber hose over the connecting rod bolts so to protect the cylinder bores and crankshaft bearing journals.

12. Install the connecting rod bearing caps and inserts in the same order as removed. Tighten the nuts to the proper torque.

13. Install the oil pan with new gaskets and tighten the drain plug.

14. Install the cylinder heads and gaskets.

15. Install the push rods and rocker assemblies.

16. Install the intake manifold assembly.

17. Install the cylinder head covers with new gaskets.

18. Fill the crankshaft with new oil.

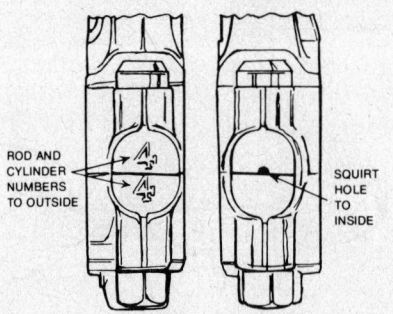

4-151 connecting rod numbers and squirt hole

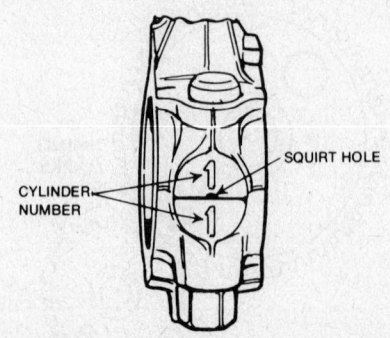

6 cylinder 232 and 258 connecting rod numbering

Piston Identification

NOTE: If there is a notch on top of the piston or an F mark anywhere on the piston, it must face to the front of the engine.

4-151

The letter F, or the notches in the edge of the piston, goes toward the front of the engine.

On the 151 4 cylinder engine the notch on the connecting rod should be opposite the notch on the piston.

232, 258 SIXES AND V8 ENGINES

The connecting rods and caps are stamped with the number of the cylinder to which they belong. Replace them in their original positions.

The numbered sides and squirt hole must face the camshaft when assembled in the Sixes. The numbered sides must face out on the V8s.

Crankshaft

REMOVAL AND INSTALLATION

4-151

1. Remove the engine and mount it on a work stand.
2. Remove the spark plugs.
3. Remove the fan and pulley.
4. Remove the vibration damper and hub.
5. Remove the oil pan and oil pump.
6. Remove the timing case cover.
7. Remove the crankshaft timing gear.
8. Remove the connecting rod bearing caps. Mark each for reassembly.
9. Remove the main bearing caps, marking each for reassembly.
10. Remove the crankshaft.
11. Installation is the reverse of removal.

Note the following points:
   a. Oil all parts with clean engine oil.
   b. After installing the crankshaft, install the main and rod bearing caps loosely and strike both ends of the crankshaft with a rubber mallet, first the front, then the rear, to center the thrust bearing.
   c. Tighten all bearing caps to the values shown in the torque chart. If new bearings are used, check the clearances with Plastigage.
   d. Make sure timing marks are aligned in timing gears.

232, 258 Sixes and V8 Engines

1. Remove the engine from the vehicle and mount it on a work stand.
2. Drain the oil.
3. Remove the flywheel or torque converter, match marking the pieces for installation.
4. Remove all drive belts.
5. Remove the fan and hub assembly.
6. Remove the crankshaft pulley and vibration damper.
7. Remove the timing case cover.
8. Remove the oil pan.
9. Remove the oil pump and pickup.
10. Remove the rod bearing caps, marking them for installation.
11. Remove the main bearing caps, marking them for installation.
12. Lift out the crankshaft.
13. Installation is the reverse of removal. Coat all moving parts with clean engine oil. Observe all torque values listed in the torque chart.

NOTE: A replacement oil pickup tube must be used. Do not attempt to install the original. Make sure the plastic button is inserted in the bottom of the pickup screen. Always use a new rear main seal. If new bearings are installed, check clearances with Plastigage.

ENGINE LUBRICATION

Oil Pan

REMOVAL AND INSTALLATION

4-151

1. Disconnect the battery ground.
2. Raise the vehicle and support it on jackstands.
3. Drain the oil.
4. Remove the starter.
5. Unbolt and remove the oil pan.
6. Clean all gasket surfaces, and remove all sludge and deposits from the pan.
7. Install the rear pan gasket in the main bearing cap and apply a small amount of RTV sealant in the depressions where the pan gasket contacts the block.
8. Position the gasket on the pan. Apply a 1/8 × 1/4 inch bead of RTV sealant at the split lines of the front and side gaskets.
9. Position the pan on the block carefully to avoid gasket misalignment. Install the bolts and tighten them to 45 in. lbs.
10. Install the starter. Tighten the bolts to 17 ft. lbs.; the nut to 40 in. lbs.
11. Connect the starter cables, lower the vehicle, fill the crankcase and run the engine to operating temperature, checking for leaks.

232, 258 Sixes and V8 Engines

1. Raise the vehicle and safely support it on jackstands. Disconnect the negative battery cable. Drain the engine oil.
2. Remove the starter motor.
3. If clearance is insufficient, place a jack under the transmission bell housing. Disconnect the engine right support cushion bracket from the block and raise the engine to allow sufficient clearance for oil pan removal.
4. Remove the oil pan attaching bolts and remove the oil pan.

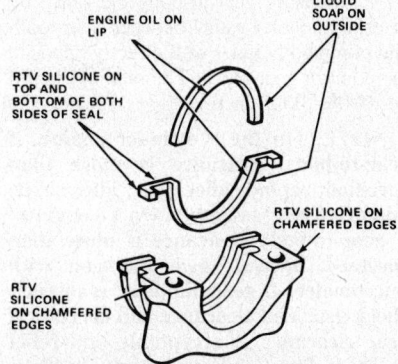

Rear main bearing oil seal installation—6 and V8 engines

5. Remove the oil pan front and rear neoprene oil seals and the side gaskets. Thoroughly clean the gasket surfaces of the oil pan and the engine block. Remove all of the sludge and dirt from the oil pan sump.
6. Apply a generous amount of RTV silicone to the end tabs of a new oil pan front seal and install the seal to the timing case cover.
7. Cement new oil pan side gaskets into position on the engine block and apply a generous amount of RTV silicone to the side gasket contacting surface of the seal end tabs.
8. Install the seal in the recess of the rear main bearing cap, making sure that it is fully seated.
9. Coat the oil pan contacting surface of the front and rear oil pan seals with engine oil.
10. Install the oil pan and assemble the engine mount in the reverse order of removal.

Rear Main Oil Seal

REPLACEMENT

4-151

NOTE: The seal is a one piece unit that can be removed and installed without removing the oil pan or crankshaft.

1. Raise and support the vehicle on jackstands.
2. Remove the transmission and transfer case as an assembly.
3. Disconnect and remove the starter.
4. On manual transmission vehicles, remove the flywheel inspection plate, and clutch slave cylinder.

232, 258 Sixes and V8 Engines

This seal is a two-piece neoprene type with a single lip.

1. Raise and support the vehicle on jackstands.
2. Remove the oil pan.
3. Remove the rear main bearing cap and discard the lower seal.
4. Loosen all remaining main bearing caps.
5. Using a center punch, carefully drive the upper half of the seal out of the block just far enough to grasp with a pliers and pull out.
6. Remove the oil pan front and rear seals and the side gaskets.
7. Clean all gasket surfaces.
8. Wipe clean the sealing surface of the crankshaft and coat it lightly with engine oil.
9. Coat the lip of the upper seal with engine oil and install it in the block. The lip faces forward.
10. Coat both end tabs of the lower seal with RTV silicone sealer. Do not get any RTV sealer on the seal lip.
11. Coat the outer curved surface of the

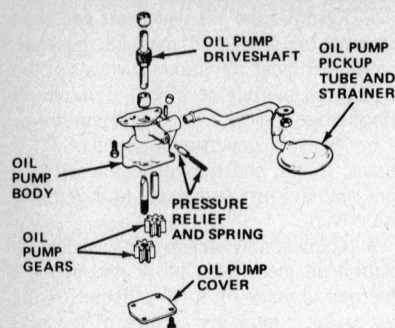

4-151 oil pump

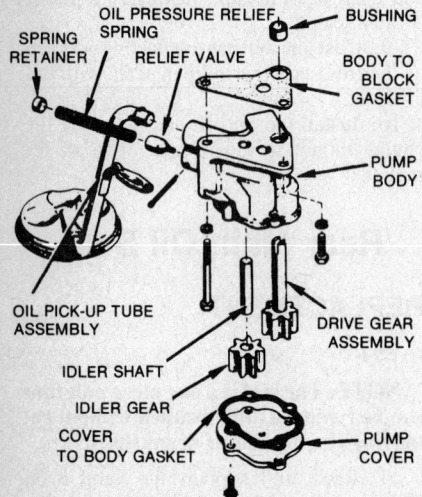

Inline six oil pump

seal with liquid soap. Coat the seal lip with engine oil.

12. Install the seal into the cap, pressing firmly.

13. Coat both chamfered edges of the cap with RTV sealer.

--- CAUTION ---
Do not allow any RTV sealer to get on the mating surfaces of the cap or block as this will affect bearing clearance.

14. Install the rear main cap.

15. Tighten all main bearing cap bolts gradually to 80 ft. lbs.

16. Replace the oil pan.

Oil Pump

REMOVAL AND INSTALLATION

4-151, 232, 258 Sixes

1. Drain the oil and remove the oil pan.

2. Remove the oil pump retaining screws and separate the oil pump and gasket from the engine block.

NOTE: On 6-cyl. engines, do not disturb the position of the oil pick-up tube and screen assembly in the pump body. If the tube is moved within the pump

body, a new assembly must be installed to assure an airtight seal.

3. Install in reverse order of the above procedure.

V8 Engines
Removal

1. Remove the oil pump cover from the timing chain cover and remove the oil pump gears and shaft.

2. Remove the oil pressure relief valve from the body.

3. Inspect the gears for abnormal wear, chips, looseness on the shafts, galling, and scoring.

4. Inspect the cover and cavity for breaks, cracks, distortion, and abnormal wear.

5. Install the gears into the pump cavity, and with the use of a straight edge and feeler gauge, check the gear to housing clearance.

6. If the clearances measure out of the allowable span, the timing chain cover and gears should be replaced.

Installation

1. Install the pressure relief valve if previously removed.

2. Install the gears into the gear cavity, and pack the cavity with petroleum jelly to insure the self priming of the pump.

NOTE: Never use chassis or wheel bearing grease to pack the gear cavity.

3. Install the gear cover, using a new gasket.

OIL PUMP CLEARANCES— CHECKING 6 CYL. AND V8 ENGINES

1. Remove cover and gasket from pump body.

2. Place a strip of plastigage across the full width of each gear.

3. Install pump cover with gasket and tighten.

4. Remove pump cover and determine the amount of clearance by measuring the width of the compressed plastigage. Clearance should be .002–.006 inch for 1975–76 and .002–.008 inch for 1977–82.

5. Measure gear-to-body clearance by inserting a feeler gauge between gear tooth and pump body inner wall directly opposite the point of gear mesh. The reading should be .0005–.0025 inch.

NOTE: On the 6 cylinder engine, if gear-to-body clearance is more than specified, replace idler gear, idler shaft, and drive gear assembly. On V8 engines, if gear-to-body clearance is more than specified, measure gear diameter with micrometer. If gear diameter is correct, check gear end clearance and correct. If gear clearance is acceptable and relief valve is functioning properly, replace timing case cover. If gear diameter is incorrect, replace gears and idler shaft.

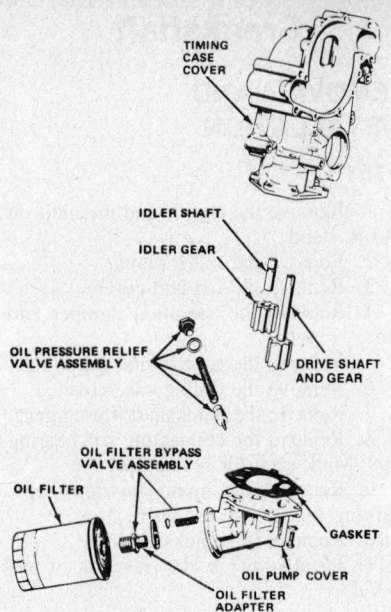

Typical V8 oil pump

ENGINE COOLING

The satisfactory performance of any water cooled engine is controlled to a great extent by the proper operation of the cooling system. The engine block is fully water jacketed to prevent distortion of the cylinder walls. Directed cooling and water holes in the cylinder head cause water to flow past the valve seats, which are one of the hottest parts of any engine, and carry the heat away from the valves and seats.

The minimum temperature of the coolant is controlled by a thermostat mounted in the outlet passage of the engine. When the coolant temperature is below the temperature rating of the thermostat, the thermostat remains closed and the coolant is directed through the radiator-by-pass hose to the water pump. If the coolant temperature is too high, the thermostat opens and coolant flow is directed to the top of the radiator. The radiator dissipates the excess engine heat before the coolant is recirculated through the engine.

The cooling system is pressurized and the operating pressure is regulated by the rating of the radiator cap which contains a relief valve.

Radiator

REMOVAL AND INSTALLATION

1. Drain the radiator by opening the drain cock and removing the radiator pressure cap.

2. Remove the upper and lower hose clamps and hoses at the radiator.

3. Disconnect the automatic transmission oil cooler lines at the radiator, if so equipped. Remove the radiator shroud from the radiator, if so equipped.

4. Remove all attaching screws that secure the radiator to the radiator body support.

5. Remove the radiator.

6. Replace in reverse order of the above procedure.

Thermostat

REMOVAL AND INSTALLATION

The thermostat is located in the water outlet housing at the front or on top of the engine. On the V8 the water outlet housing is located in the front of the intake manifold.

To remove the thermostats from all of these engines, first drain the cooling system. It is not necessary to disconnect or remove any of the hoses. Remove the two attaching screws and lift the housing from the engine. Remove the thermostat and the gasket. To install, place the thermostat in the housing with the spring inside the engine. Install a new gasket with a small amount of sealing compound applied to both sides. Install the water outlet and tighten the attaching bolts to 30 ft. lbs. Refill the cooling system.

Water Pump

REMOVAL AND INSTALLATION

4–151

1. Remove the fan belt.
2. Remove the fan and hub assembly.
3. Disconnect the hoses at the pump.
4. Unbolt and remove the pump.
5. Installation is the reverse of removal. Always use a new gasket coated with sealer. Torque the water pump bolts to 25 ft. lbs. Tighten the fan and hub bolts to 18 ft. lbs.

232 and 258 Sixes

1. Disconnect all hoses at the pump.
2. Remove the drive belts.
3. Remove the fan shroud attaching screws.
4. Unbolt the fan and fan drive assembly and remove along with the shroud. On some models it may be easier to turn the shroud ½ turn.
5. Unbolt and remove the pump.

—————— **CAUTION** ——————
Engines built for sale in California having a single, serpentine drive belt and viscous fan drive, have a reverse rotating pump

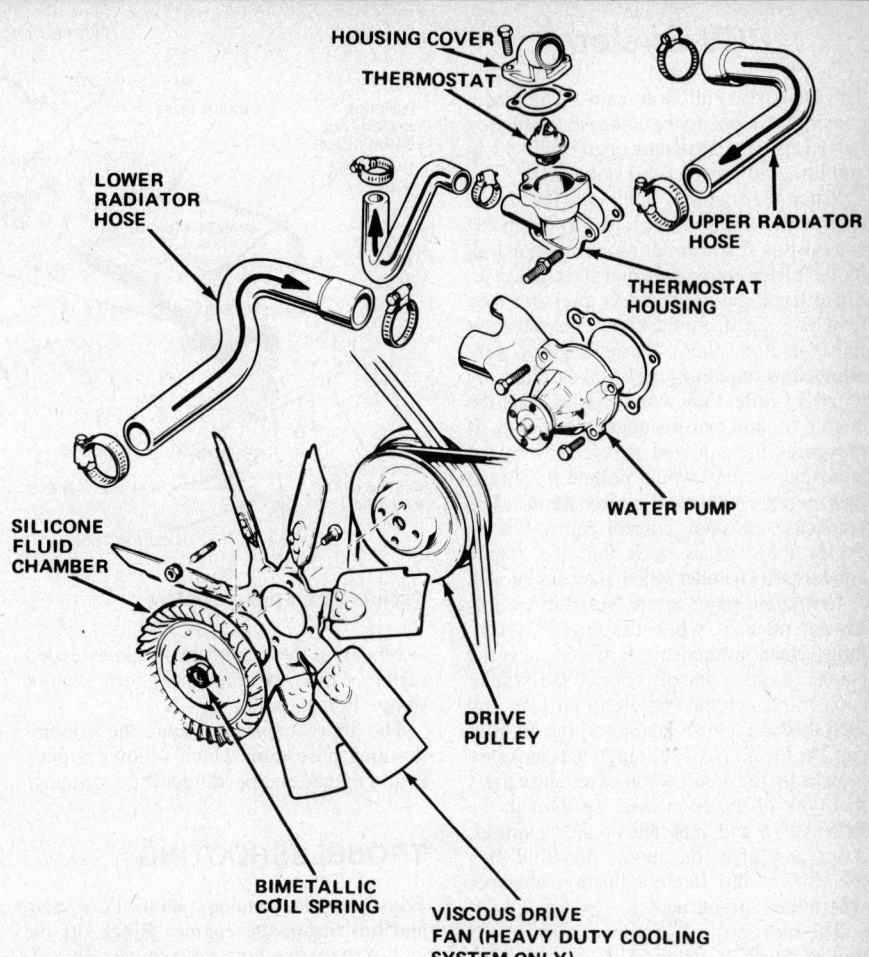

4-151 water pump and related parts

and drive. These components are identified by the word REVERSE stamped on the drive cover and inner side of the fan, and REV cast into the water pump body. Never interchange standard rotating parts with these.

6. Installation is the reverse of removal. Always use a new gasket coated with sealer. Torque the water pump bolts to 13 ft. lbs.; the fan bolts to 18 ft. lbs.

V8 Engines

1. Disconnect all hoses at the pump.
2. Loosen all drive belts.
3. Remove the shroud, but reinsert one bolt to hold the radiator.
4. Remove the fan and hub.
5. If the vehicle is equipped with A/C install a double nut on the compressor bracket-to-water pump stud and remove the stud.
6. Remove, but do not disconnect the alternator and bracket.
7. If so equipped, remove the nuts that attach the power steering pump to the rear half of the pump bracket.
8. Remove the two bolts that attach the front half to the rear half of the bracket.

9. Remove the remaining upper screw from the inner air pump support bracket, loosen the lower bolt and drop the bracket away from the power steering front bracket.

10. Remove the front half of the power steering bracket from the water pump mounting stud.

11. Unbolt and remove the water pump.

12. Installation is the reverse of removal. Always use a new gasket coated with sealer. Torque the pump-to timing case bolts to 48 in. lbs. and the pump-to-block bolts to 25 ft. lbs. Torque the power steering pulley nut to 60 ft. lbs.

EMISSION CONTROLS

There are three types of automotive pollutants; crankcase fumes, exhaust gases and gasoline evaporation. The equipment that is used to limit these pollutants is commonly called emission control equipment.

PCV System

The crankcase emission control equipment consists of a positive crankcase ventilation valve (PCV), a closed or open oil filler cap and hoses to connect this equipment.

When the engine is running, a small portion of the gases which are formed in the combustion chamber during combustion leak by the piston rings and enter the crankcase. Since these gases are under pressure they tend to escape from the crankcase and enter into the atmosphere. If these gases were allowed to remain in the crankcase for any length of time, they would contaminate the engine oil and cause sludge to build up. If the gases are allowed to escape into the atmosphere, they would pollute the air, as they contain unburned hydrocarbons. The crankcase emission control equipment recycles these gases back into the engine combustion chamber where they are burned.

Crankcase gases are recycled in the following manner: while the engine is running, clean filtered air is drawn into the crankcase either directly through the oil filler cap, or through the carburetor air filter and then through a hose leading to the oil filler cap. As the air passes through the crankcase it picks up the combustion gases and carries them out of the crankcase, up through the PCV valve and into the intake manifold. After they enter the intake manifold they are drawn into the combustion chamber where they are burned.

The most critical component in the system is the PCV valve. This vacuum controlled valve regulates the amount of gases which are recycled into the combustion chamber. At low engine speeds the valve is partially closed, limiting the flow of gases into the intake manifold. As engine speed increases, the valve opens to admit greater quantities of the gases into the intake manifold. If the valve should become blocked or plugged, the gases will be prevented from escaping from the crankcases by the normal route. Since these gases are under pressure, they will find their own way out of the crankcase. This alternate route is usually a weak oil seal or gasket in the engine. As the gas escapes by the gasket, it also creates an oil leak. Besides causing oil leaks, a clogged PCV valve also allows these gases

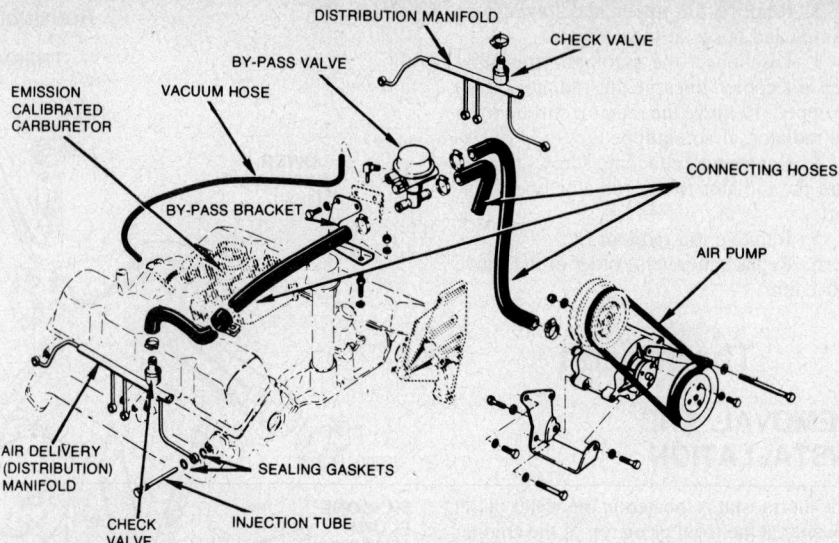

Typical V8 air pump system

to remain in the crankcase for an extended period of time, promoting the formation of sludge in the engine.

The above explanation and the troubleshooting procedure which follows applies to all engines equipped with PCV systems.

TROUBLESHOOTING

With the engine running, pull the PCV valve and hose from the engine. Block off the end of the valve with your finger. The engine speed should drop at least 50 rpm when the end of the valve is blocked. If the engine speed does not drop at least 50 rpm, then the valve is defective and should be replaced. Shake the valve; if it rattles it probably isn't clogged.

REMOVAL AND INSTALLATION

1. Pull the PCV valve and hose from the engine.
2. Remove the PCV valve from the hose. Inspect the inside of the PCV valve hose. If it is dirty, disconnect it from the intake manifold and clean it.

To install, proceed as follows:
1. If the PCV valve hose was removed, connect it to the intake manifold.
2. Connect the PCV valve to its hose.
3. Install the PCV valve on the engine.

Air Injection System

All of the engines used except the 4–151 at some point incorporated the air injection system for controlling the emission of exhaust gases into the atmosphere.

The exhaust emission control air injection system consists of a belt driven air pump which directs compressed air through connecting hoses to a steel distribution manifold into stainless steel injection tubes in the exhaust port adjacent to each exhaust valve. The air, with its normal oxygen content, reacts with the hot, but incompletely burned exhaust gases and permits further combustion in the exhaust port or manifold.

Air Pump

The air injection pump is a positive displacement vane type which is permanently lubricated and requires little periodic maintenance. The only serviceable parts on the air pump are the filter, exhaust tube, and relief valve. The relief valve relieves the air flow when the pump pressure reaches a preset level. This occurs at high engine rpm. This serves to prevent damage to the pump and to limit maximum exhaust manifold temperatures.

NOTE: On some models the relief valve assembly is incorporated in the diverter valve. If the relief valve is believed to be defective, the diverter valve assembly must be replaced.

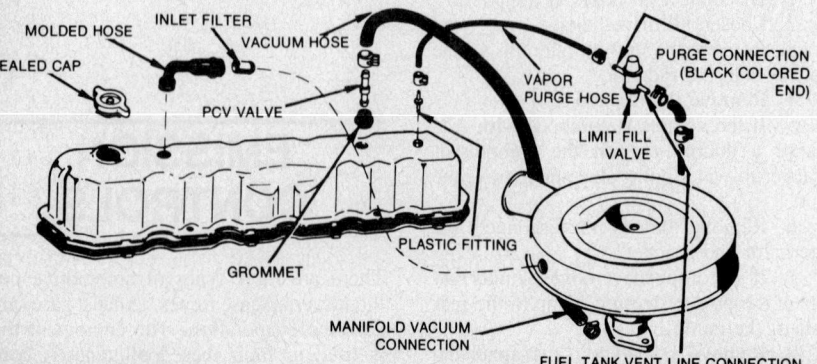
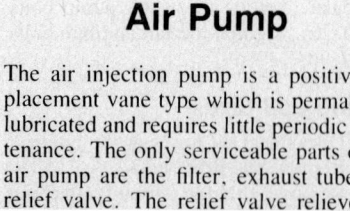

Typical PCV system

Air Delivery Manifold

The air delivery manifold distributes the air from the pump to each of the air delivery tubes in a uniform manner. A check valve is integral with the air delivery manifold. Its function is to prevent the reverse flow of exhaust gases to the pump should the pump fail. The reverse flow would damage the air pump and connecting hose.

Air Injection Tubes

The air injection tubes are inserted into the exhaust ports. The tubes project into the exhaust ports, directing air into the vicinity of the exhaust valve.

Anti-Backfire Valve

The anti-backfire diverter valve prevents engine backfire by briefly interrupting the air being injected into the exhaust manifold during periods of deceleration or rapid throttle closure. The valve opens when a sudden increase in manifold vacuum overcomes the diaphragm spring tension. With the valve in the open position the air flow is directed to the atmosphere.

The valve prevents backfiring in the exhaust manifold and also prevents an over rich fuel mixture from being burned in the exhaust manifold, which would cause backfiring and possible damage to the engine.

Thermostatically Controlled Air Cleaner System (TAC)

232 AND 258 SIXES THROUGH 1977

The TAC system consists of a two-piece heat shroud positioned on the exhaust manifold, a hot air hose, and an air duct and valve assembly located in the air cleaner snorkel.

The air duct and valve assembly incorporates an air valve, a thermostat mechanism, and a spring.

The temperature of the air entering the air cleaner is thermostatically regulated by the air duct and valve assembly. Cold air is supplied from the engine compartment and hot air from the shrouded exhaust manifold.

The thermostat unit in the air duct is exposed to incoming air on the air filter side of the air valve. The spring-loaded air valve is connected to the thermostat unit through linkage. The spring holds the valve in the closed (heat on) position until the thermostat overcomes the spring tension.

While the engine is warming up and the air temperature entering the air duct is less than 105°F, the thermostat is in the re-

tracted position and the air valve is held in the closed (heat on) position.

As the temperature of the air passing over the thermostat unit rises, the thermostat starts to open and pulls the air valve down, closing off the heated air intake and opening the cool air intake, allowing cooler engine compartment air to enter the air cleaner.

When the temperature of the air reaches 130°F, the air valve is completely open to engine compartment air.

4–151, 1978–82 SIXES AND V8 ENGINES

This system consists of a heat shroud which is integral with the right side exhaust manifold, a hot air hose and a special air cleaner assembly equipped with a thermal sensor and a vacuum motor and air valve assembly.

The thermal sensor incorporates an air bleed valve which regulates the amount of vacuum applied to the vacuum motor, controlling the air valve position to supply either heated air from the exhaust manifold or air from the engine compartment.

During the warm-up period when underhood temperatures are low, the air bleed valve is closed and sufficient vacuum is applied to the vacuum motor to hold the air valve in the closed (heat on) position.

As the temperature of the air entering the air cleaner approaches approximately 115°F, the air bled valve opens to decrease the amount of vacuum applied to the vacuum motor. The diaphragm spring in the vacuum motor then moves the air valve into the open (heat off) position, allowing only underhood air to enter the air cleaner.

The air valve in the air cleaner will also open, regardless of air temperature, during heavy acceleration to obtain maximum air flow through the air cleaner.

Solenoid Vacuum Valve

This valve is attached to the right rear intake manifold (V8), or to a bracket at the rear of the intake manifold (Sixes). When the valve is energized, carburetor vacuum is blocked off and the distributor vacuum line is vented to the atmosphere through a port in the valve, resulting in no vacuum advance. When the valve is de-energized, vacuum is applied to the distributor resulting in normal vacuum advance.

Solenoid Control Switch

This switch is located on the transmission on vehicles with manual transmissions. It opens or closes in relation to speed and gear range. When the transmission is in high gear, the switch opens and breaks the ground

circuit to the solenoid vacuum valve. In lower gear ranges the switch closes and completes the ground circuit to the solenoid vacuum valve. The switch is operated by the transmission shifter shaft.

On vehicles equipped with an automatic transmission, the switch is located along the speedometer cable on the firewall. The switch is operated by speedometer cable rpm. At about 32 to 36 mph the switch will open the electrical ground circuit to the solenoid vacuum valve.

NOTE: From 1976, the switch closes at a lower speed (22–28 mph) on deceleration.

Coolant Temperature Override Switch

The switch reacts to coolant temperatures to route either intake manifold or carburetor vacuum to the distributor vacuum advance diaphragm.

When the coolant temperature is below 160°F, intake manifold vacuum is applied through a hose connection to the distributor advance diaphragm, resulting in full vacuum advance.

When the coolant temperature is above 160°F, intake manifold vacuum is blocked off and carburetor vacuum is then applied through the solenoid vacuum valve to the distributor advance diaphragm, resulting in decreased vacuum advance.

NOTE: Some vehicles made for California, intake manifold vacuum routed through the TCS solenoid is applied to the distributor when the coolant temperature is above 160°F.

The relationship between distributor vacuum advance and the operation of the TCS system and coolant temperature override switch can be determined by referring to the Emission Control Distributor Vacuum Application Chart.

Exhaust Gas Recirculation (EGR) System

The EGR system consists of a diaphragm actuated flow control valve (EGR valve), coolant temperature override switch (EGR CTO) and connecting hoses. In 1980, a Thermal Vacuum Switch, located in the air cleaner, was added to control the vacuum signal between the EGR and CTO.

The purpose of the EGR system is to limit the formation of oxides of nitrogen by diluting the fresh air intake charge with a metered amount of exhaust gas, thereby reducing the peak temperatures of the burning gases in the combustion chambers.

EMISSION CONTROL DISTRIBUTOR VACUUM APPLICATION CHART

Transmission Gear			Coolant Temperature	Vacuum Source
3 Speed	4 Speed	Automatic		
1–2	1–2–3	Below 32–36 mph	Below 160°F	Manifold
1–2	1–2–3	Below 32–36 mph	Above 160°F	Through the Solenoid Vacuum Valve
3	4	Above 32–36 mph	Below 160°F	Manifold
3	4	Above 32–36 mph	Above 160°F	No Vacuum

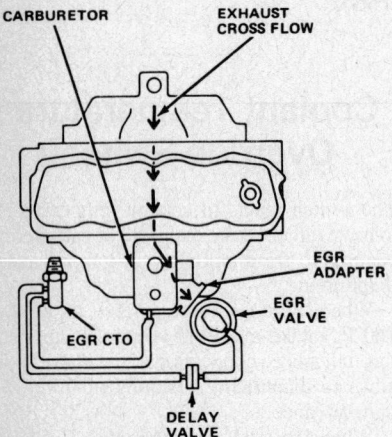

EGR system 4-151 (typical)

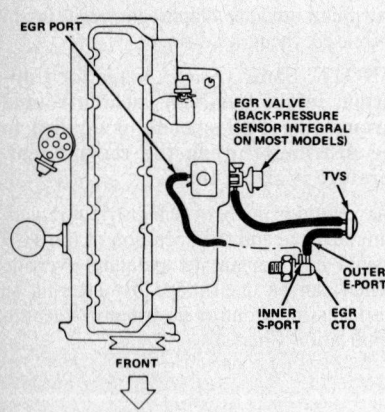

Typical 6-258 EGR system

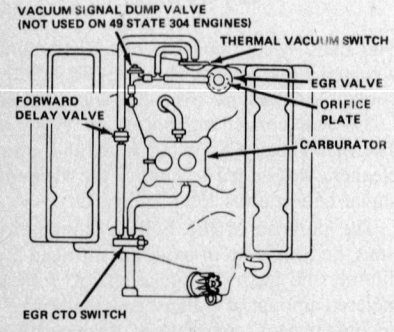

Typical V8 EGR system

EGR Valve

The EGR valve is mounted on a machined surface at the rear of the intake manifold on V8 engines and on the side of the intake manifold on the Sixes. When a backpressure sensor is used, the EGR valve is mounted on a spacer which is an integral part of the backpressure sensor.

The valve is held in a normally closed position by a coil spring located above the diaphragm. A special fitting is provided at the carburetor to route ported (above the throttle plates) vacuum through the CTO and a TVS or BPS (when used) and hose connections to a fitting located above the diaphragm on the valve. A passage in the intake manifold directs exhaust gas from the exhaust crossover passage on V8s and from near the heat riser on the Sixes, to the EGR valve. When the diaphragm is actuated by vacuum, the valve opens and meters exhaust gas through special passages into the intake manifold below the carburetor.

Coolant Temperature Override Switch

This switch is located in the intake manifold at the coolant passage adjacent to the oil filler tube on V8s and on the left-side of the cylinder block on the Sixes. The outer port of the switch is connected to either the EGR valve or BPS (when used). The inner port is connected by a hose to the EGR fitting at the carburetor. When the coolant temperature reaches 115°F the inner port of the switch opens and a vacuum signal is applied to the EGR valve. This vacuum signal is subject to regulation by the BPS when used.

Thermal Vacuum Switch (TVS)

The TVS is located in the air cleaner on all 1980 and later engines, and functions as an on/off switch controlled by air cleaner air temperature. The TVS controls the vacuum passage between the EGR CTO valve and the EGR valve. Air temperature in the 40–50°F range cause the TVS to limit the vacuum applied to the EGR valve, thus improving cold engine driveability.

Exhaust Backpressure Sensor (BPS)

This device is used on 1975 California vehicles, on all 1976 models, and on some 1977–81 models in conjunction with the EGR system.

The BPS monitors exhaust backpressure and permits EGR operation only when engine operating conditions are favorable. The BPR units are variously calibrated, are not serviceable, and must be replaced with the identical part as a unit when necessary.

The BPS consists of a diaphragm valve and a spacer connected by a metal tube projecting into an exhaust port in the spacer body. The EGR valve mounts directly on the spacer. On some 1977–81 sixes, the sensor is integral with the EGR valve.

In operation, the metal tube connecting the diaphragm valve to the spacer routes exhaust backpressure from the particular exhaust port to the sensor. When the backpressure reaches a certain level the diaphragm valve spring pressure is overcome, permitting a vacuum signal to the EGR valve, providing that the CTO switch is open.

Thus, EGR operations is only permitted when the engine is warmed up sufficiently and exhaust backpressure relatively high, such as during acceleration and at some cruising speeds. When temperature or backpressure conditions are not met, the vacuum signal is vented to the atmosphere from a vent at the diaphragm valve.

Feedback Systems

Two different feedback systems are used with 1981 and later Jeep vehicles. One, the C4 system is used with 4-151 engines built for sale in California; the other, the Computerized Emission Control (CEC) System is used on 6-258 engines built for sale in California. Each system is designed for the same purpose, to reduce exhaust emission using a Three-Way Catalytic Converter (TWC).

Each system is computerized, utilizing

microprocessors, and each is highly complex, requiring professional service. Therefore, no service procedures are given in this book for the diagnosis or repair of these systems.

Catalytic Converter

The catalytic converter is a muffler-like device inserted in the exhaust system. Exhaust gases flow through the converter where a chemical change takes place, reducing carbon monoxide and hydrocarbons to carbon dioxide and water; the latter two elements being harmless. The catalysts promoting this reaction are platinum and palladium-coated beads of alumina.

Because of the chemical reaction which does take place in the converter, the temperature of the converter during operation is higher than the exhaust gases when they leave the engine. However, insulation keeps the outside skin of the converter about the same temperature as the muffler.

An improperly adjusted carburetor or ignition problem which would permit unburned fuel to enter the converter could produce excessive heat. Excessive heat in the converter could result in bulging or other distortion of the converter's shape. If the converter is heat-damaged and must be replaced, the ignition or carburetor problem must be corrected also.

Fuel Tank Vapor Emission Control System

On 1975–76 models, the fuel vapor is routed from the fuel tank through vapor vent hoses to the liquid check valve. From the liquid check valve, the fuel vapor is routed to the vapor storage canister which is filled with charcoal. When the engine is not operating the charcoal retains the vapors. When the engine is started vacuum from the air cleaner snorkle routed through a hose leading to the top of the vapor storage canister sucks the vapors from the storage canister. There are three nipples on the top of the canister; one for vapors coming from the fuel tank, one for vapors going to the air cleaner snorkle, and the other nipple is plugged (for use with 4 bbl carburetors on other AMC engines). Fresh air is drawn up through the canister from the bottom through a replaceable filter during operation.

Limit Fill Valve

This valve is essentially a combination vapor flow regulator and pressure relief valve. It regulates vapor flow from the fuel tank vent line into the valve cover. The valve consists of a housing, a spring loaded diaphragm and a diaphragm cover. As tank vent pressure increases, the diaphragm lifts permitting vapor to flow through. The pressure at which this occurs is 4–6 in. of water column. This action regulates the flow of vapors under severe conditions but generally prohibits the flow of vapor during normal temperature operation, thus minimizing driveability problems.

LIQUID CHECK VALVE

The liquid check valve prevents liquid fuel from entering the vapor lines leading to the storage canister. The check valve incorporates a float and needle valve assembly. If liquid fuel should enter the check valve, the float will rise and force the needle upward to close the vent passage. With no liquid fuel present in the check valve, fuel vapors pass freely from the tank, through the check valve, and on to the storage canister.

Choke Heat By-Pass Valve (CHBPV) 1976 and later V8

When the engine is first started and begins to warm up, heated air from the exhaust crossover passage in the intake manifold is routed through a heat tube to the choke housing containing the thermostatic spring for regulating the choke flap. A thermostatic by-pass valve, which is integral with the choke heat tube, helps prevent premature choke valve opening during the early part of the warmup period. This is important when ambient temperatures are relatively low and adverse drivability could occur if the choke was opened too soon.

The thermostatic by-pass valve regulates the temperature of the hot airflow to the choke housing by allowing outside unheated air to enter the heat tube. A thermostatic disc in the valve is calibrated to close the valve at 75°F and open it at 55°F.

Fuel Return System

The purpose of the fuel return system is to reduce high temperature fuel vapor problems. The system consists of a fuel return line to the fuel tank and a special fuel filter with an extra outlet nipple to which the return line is connected. During normal operation, a small amount of fuel is returned to the fuel tank. During periods of high underhood temperatures, vaporized fuel in the fuel line is returned to the fuel tank and not passed through the carburetor.

NOTE: The extra nipple on the special fuel filter should be positioned upward to ensure proper operation of the system.

Emission Control Checks

ANTI-BACKFIRE DIVERTER VALVE

To check the diverter valve start the engine and let it idle. With the engine idling, there should be little or no air coming out the vents. When the engine is accelerated to 2,000–3,000 rpm, a strong flow of air should be felt at the vents. If the flow of air from the air pump is not diverted through the diverter valve vents when the engine is accelerated to the above mentioned rpm, check and make sure that the vacuum sensing line leading to the valve has vacuum and is not leaking or disconnected. The diverter valve should bleed air when 20 in. Hg or more vacuum is applied to the vacuum sensing line or when the output of the air pump exceeds 5 psi. When the engine is slowly accelerated, the diverter valve should begin to bleed off air between 2,500 and 3,500 rpm.

CHECK VALVE

The check valve in the air distribution manifold prevents the reverse flow of exhaust gases to the pump in the event the pump should become inoperative or should exhaust pressure ever exceed the pump pressure.

To check this valve for proper operation, remove the air supply hose from the pump at the distribution manifold. With the engine running, listen for exhaust leakage where the check valve is connected to the distribution manifold. If leakage is audible, the valve is not operating correctly. A small amount of leakage is normal.

AIR PUMP

Check for the proper drive belt tension and adjust as necessary. Do not pry on the die cast pump housing. Check to see if the pump is discharging air. Remove the air outlet hose at the pump. With the engine running, air should be felt at the pump outlet opening.

EGR VALVE

With the engine idling and at normal operating temperature, manually depress the EGR valve diaphragm. This should cause engine speed to drop about 200 rpm. This indicates that the EGR valve had been properly cutting off the flow of exhaust gas at idle and is operating properly.

If the engine speed did not change and the idle is smooth, exhaust gases are not reaching the combustion chambers. The probable cause of this is a plugged passage between the EGR valve and the intake manifold.

If the engine idle is rough and rpm is not

affected by depressing the EGR valve diaphragm, the EGR valve is not closing off the flow of exhaust at idle like it's supposed to and there is most likely a fault in the hoses, hose routing, or the EGR valve itself.

NOTE: The EGR valve can be removed and cleaned with a wire brush and a ⁹⁄₁₆ in. drill bit coated with grease (to hold dirt particles) inserted in discharge passage. The drill should be held with a pair of pliers only.

EGR CTO SWITCH

Before checking the operating of the EGR CTO switch, make sure that the engine coolant is below 100°F.

1. Check the vacuum lines for leaks and proper routing.
2. Disconnect the vacuum line at the backpressure sensor, if so equipped, or at the EGR valve, and connect the line to a vacuum gauge.
3. Operate the engine at 1,500 rpm. No vacuum should be indicated at the gauge. If vacuum is indicated, replace the EGR CTO switch.
4. Allow the engine to idle until the coolant temperature exceeds 115°F.
5. Accelerate the engine to 1,500 rpm. Vacuum should be present at the gauge. If not, replace the EGR CTO switch.

EXHAUST BPS UNIT

1. Make sure that all the EGR vacuum lines are routed correctly and are not leaking.
2. Install a "T" in the vacuum line between the EGR valve and BPS, and attach a vacuum gauge to the "T".
3. Start the engine and allow it to idle. No vacuum should be present.
   If vacuum is indicated at idle speed, make sure of correct line connections. Also, be sure that manifold vacuum is not the source. If the carburetor is providing the vacuum, look for a partially open throttle plate which could cause premature ported vacuum to the BPS unit.
4. Accelerate the engine to 2,000 rpm and observe the vacuum gauge for the following:
   a. If the coolant is below 115°F, no vacuum should be present;
   b. With coolant temperature above 115°F, ported vacuum should be indicated;
   c. If no vacuum is indicated at any time, make sure that vacuum is being applied to the inlet side of the BPS. If correct, remove the BPS and either clean it with a wire brush (if blocked) or replace it.

SPARK CTO SWITCH

Before testing the spark CTO switch, make

sure that the engine coolant temperature is below 160°F.

1. Remove all the hoses from the CTO switch and plug those which will create a vacuum leak.
2. Connect a vacuum line from a manifold vacuum source to the top port of the CTO switch.
3. Connect a vacuum gauge to the center port.
4. Start the engine. Manifold vacuum should be indicated on the gauge. If not, replace the switch.
5. With the engine still running and the coolant temperature still below 160°F, disconnect the vacuum line from the top port and connect it to the bottom port.
6. No vacuum should be indicated. Replace the switch if there is vacuum.
7. Allow the engine to run until the coolant temperature exceeds 160°F. Manifold vacuum should be indicated. If not, replace the CTO switch.
8. Disconnect the hose from the bottom port and connect it to the top port again. With the coolant temperature above 160°F, no vacuum should be indicated. If there is, replace the CTO switch.

TVS FUNCTIONAL TEST

1. Allow the air cleaner to cool to between 40 and 50°F.
2. Disconnect the vacuum hoses from the TVS and connect an external vacuum source to one nipple and a vacuum gauge to the other.
3. Apply vacuum to the TVS. Vacuum should not be present when the air temperature is 40–50°F. If vacuum is present, replace the switch.
4. Start the engine and allow the air cleaner to warm above 50°F. Vacuum should be present.

FUEL SYSTEM

Fuel Pump

REMOVAL AND INSTALLATION

All Engines

1. Disconnect the inlet and outlet fuel lines, and any vacuum lines.
2. Remove the two fuel pump body attaching nuts and lockwashers.
3. Pull the pump and gasket free of the engine. Make sure that the mating surfaces of the fuel pump and the engine are clean.
4. Cement a new gasket to the mounting flange of the fuel pump.
5. Position the fuel pump on the engine block so that the lever of the fuel pump rests on the fuel pump cam of the camshaft.

6. Secure the fuel pump to the block with the two cap screws and lock washers.
7. Connect the intake and outlet fuel lines to the fuel pump, and any vacuum lines.

FUEL PUMP TESTING

Volume Check

Disconnect the fuel line from the carburetor. Place the open end in a suitable container. Start the engine and operate it at normal idle speed. The pump should deliver at least one pin in 30 seconds.

Pressure Check

Disconnect the fuel line at the carburetor. Disconnect the fuel return line from the fuel filter if so equipped, and plug the nipple on the filter. Install a T-fitting on the open end of the fuel line and refit the line to the carburetor. Plug a pressure gauge into the remaining opening of the T-fitting. The hose leading to the pressure gauge should not be any longer than 6 inches. Start the engine and let it run at idle speed. Bleed any air out of the hose between the gauge and the T-fitting. Pressure readings are given in the Tune-up Specifications Chart.

Carburetors

NOTE: For detailed rebuilding and settings refer to the Unit Repair Section on carburetors.

REMOVAL AND INSTALLATION

All Engines

To remove the carburetor from any engine, first remove the air cleaner from the top of the carburetor. Remove all lines and hoses, noting their positions to facilitate installation. Remove all throttle and choke linkage at the carburetor. Remove the carburetor attaching nuts which hold it to the intake manifold. Lift the carburetor from the engine along with the carburetor base gasket. Discard the gasket. Install the carburetor in the reverse order of removal, using a new base gasket.

OVERHAUL

Efficient carburetion depends greatly on careful cleaning and inspection during overhaul since dirt, gum, water, or varnish in or on the carburetor parts are often responsible for poor performance.

Overhaul your carburetor in a clean, dust-free area. Carefully disassemble the carburetor, referring often to the exploded views. Keep all similar and look-alike parts segregated during disassembly and cleaning to avoid accidental interchange during assembly. Make a note of all jet sizes.

When the carburetor is disassembled, wash all parts (except diaphragms, electric choke units, pump plunger, and any other plastic, leather, fiber, or rubber parts) in clean carburetor solvent. Do not leave parts in the solvent any longer than is necessary to sufficiently loosen the deposits. Excessive cleaning may remove the special finish from the float bowl and choke valve bodies, leaving these parts unfit for service. Rinse all parts in clean solvent and blow them dry with compressed air or allow them to air dry. Wipe clean all cork, plastic, leather, and fiber parts with a clean, lint-free cloth.

Bow out all passages and jets with compressed air and be sure that there are no restrictions or blockages. Never use wire or similar tools to clean jets, fuel passages, or air bleeds. Clean all jets and valves separately to avoid accidental interchange.

Check all parts for wear or damage. If wear or damage is found, replace the defective parts. Especially check the following:

1. Check the float needle and seat for wear. If wear is found, replace the complete assembly.

2. Check the float hinge pin for wear and the float(s) for dents or distortion. Replace the float if fuel has leaked into it.

3. Check the throttle and choke shaft bores for wear or an out-of-round condition. Damage or wear to the throttle arm, shaft, or shaft bore will often require replacement of the throttle body. These parts require a close tolerance of fit; wear may allow air leakage, which could affect starting and idling.

NOTE: Throttle shafts and bushings are not included in overhaul kits. They can be purchased separately.

4. Inspect the idle mixture adjusting needles for burrs or grooves. Any such condition requires replacement of the needle, since you will not be able to obtain a satisfactory idle.

5. Test the accelerator pump check valves. They should pass air one way but not the other. Test for proper seating by blowing and sucking on the valve. Replace the valve if necessary. If the valve is satisfactory, wash the valve again to remove breath moisture.

6. Check the bowl cover for warped surfaces with a straightedge.

7. Closely inspect the valves and seats for wear and damage, replacing as necessary.

8. After the carburetor is assembled, check the choke valve for freedom of operation.

Carburetor overhaul kits are recommended for each overhaul. These kits contain all gaskets and new parts to replace those that deteriorate most rapidly. Failure to replace all parts supplied with the kit (especially gaskets) can result in poor performance later.

After cleaning and checking all components, reassemble the carburetor, using new parts and referring to the exploded view. When reassembling, make sure that all screws and jets are tight in their seats, but do not overtighten, as the tips will be distorted. Tighten all screws gradually, in rotation. Do not tighten needle valves into their seats, uneven jetting will result. Always use new gaskets. Be sure to adjust the float level when reassembling.

Fuel Tank

REMOVAL AND INSTALLATION

The fuel tank is attached to the frame by brackets and bolts. The brackets are attached to the tank at the seam flange or the skid plate.

Before removing the fuel tank, make sure that the level of the fuel inside the tank is at least below any of the various hoses connected. It is best to either drain or siphon the majority of fuel out of the tank to make it easier to handle while removing it.

CLUTCH

REMOVAL AND INSTALLATION

4-151

1. Remove the shift lever boot.
2. Remove the shift lever assembly.
3. Raise the vehicle and support it on jack stands.
4. Remove the transmission and transfer case.
5. Remove the slave cylinder-to-clutch housing bolts.
6. Disengage the slave cylinder pushrod from the throwout lever and move the cylinder out of the way.
7. Remove the starter.
8. Remove the throwout bearing.

9. Unbolt and remove the clutch housing.

10. Mark the position of the clutch pressure plate and remove the pressure plate bolts evenly, a little at a time in rotation.

11. Remove the pilot bushing lubricating wick from its bore in the crankshaft and soak the wick in clean engine oil.

12. Installation is the reverse of removal. Torque the pressure plate bolts to 23 ft. lbs., tightening them evenly, a little at a time in rotation. Torque the clutch housing to 54 ft. lbs.; the transmission-to-clutch housing bolts to 54 ft. lbs.; the transfer case-to-transmission bolts to 30 ft. lbs. See Note below.

Except 4-151

1. Remove the transmission.
2. Remove the starter.
3. Remove the throwout bearing and sleeve assembly.
4. Remove the bell housing.
5. Mark the clutch cover, pressure plate and the flywheel with a center punch so that these parts can be later installed in the same position.
6. Remove the clutch cover-to-flywheel attaching bolts. When removing these bolts, loosen them in rotation, one or two turns at a time, until the spring tension is released. The clutch cover is a steel stamping which could be warped by improper removal procedures, resulting in clutch chatter when reused.
7. Remove the clutch assembly from the flywheel. Install in reverse order of removal. Torque pressure plate bolts to 40 ft. lb. See Note below.

NOTE: Use extreme care at all times not to get the clutch driven plate dirty in any way. Lightly lubricate the inside of the clutch driven plate's spline with a coat of wheel bearing grease. Do the same to the input shaft of the transmission. Wipe off all excess grease so that none will fly off and get onto the driven plate. Lubricate the throwout bearing collar, the ball stud and the clutch fork with wheel bearing grease. Use a pilot shaft

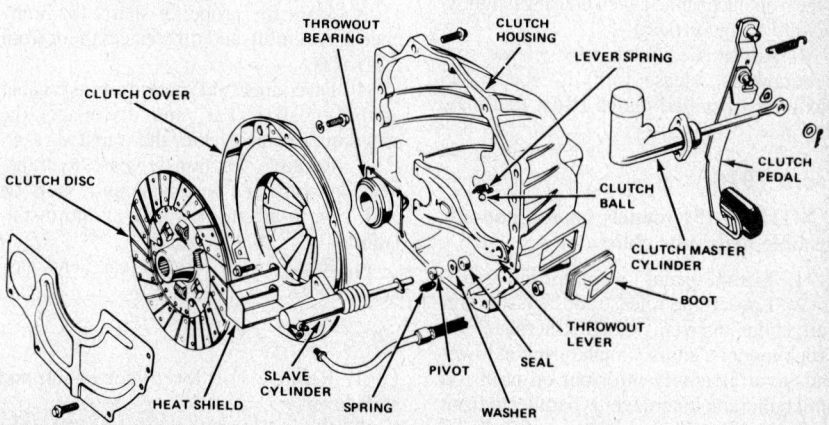

4-151, exploded view clutch assembly

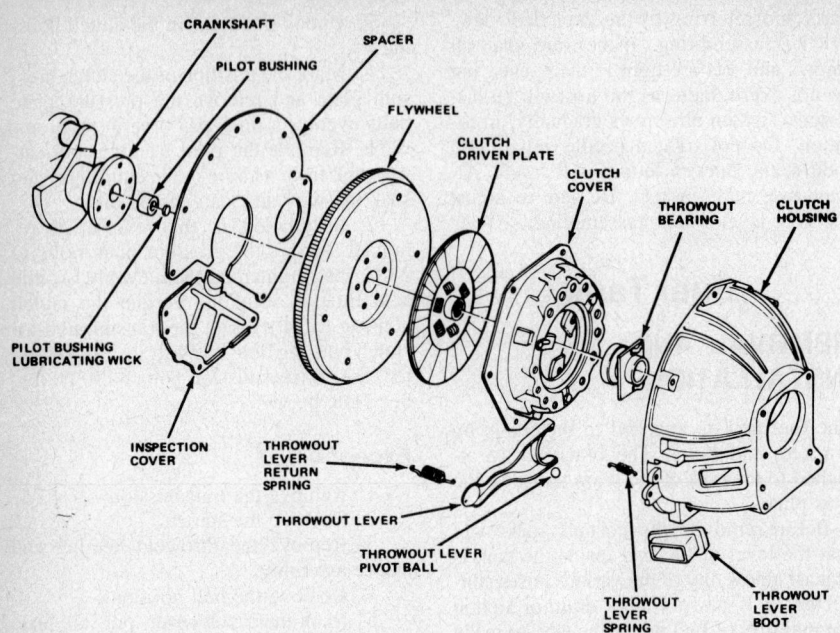

Typical 6 and V8 clutch assembly

or a spare transmission main shaft to align the driven shaft and the clutch pressure plate when attaching the assembly to the flywheel. Tighten down on the clutch-to-flywheel attaching bolts alternately so that the clutch is drawn squarely into position on the flywheel. Each bolt must be tightened one turn at a time to avoid bending the clutch cover flange.

CLUTCH PEDAL FREE-PLAY ADJUSTMENT

1975

1. Adjust the bellcrank outer support bracket to provide approximately ⅛ in. of bellcrank end play.
2. Lift up the clutch pedal against the pedal stop.
3. On the clutch push rod (pedal to bellcrank) adjust the lower ball pivot assembly onto or off the rod (as required) to position the bellcrank inner lever parallel to the front face of the clutch housing (slightly forward from vertical).
4. Adjust the clutch fork release rod (bellcrank to release fork) to obtain the maximum specified clutch pedal free play of 1 in.

From 1976

NOTE: 4-151 models have a non-adjustable hydraulic clutch.

1. Lift the pedal up against the stop.
2. Loosen the release rod adjuster jam nut, under the vehicle. On Cherokee and Truck models, adjust clutch push rod lower ball pivot assembly in-or-out on push rod until bellcrank inner lever is parallel to front face of clutch housing. Lever should be slightly forward from vertical.

3. Adjust the pedal free-play to about one inch.
4. Tighten the jam nut.

TRANSFER CASE

Refer to the Transfer Case General Repair Section for troubleshooting and overhaul procedures.

Transfer Case—Spicer Model 20

REMOVAL

1975

1. Remove the shift lever knob, boot, and shift lever.
2. Raise and support the vehicle safely.
3. Mark the propeller shafts for reference at assembly and disconnect them from the yokes.
4. Disconnect the parking brake cable at the equalizer bar, and disconnect the speedometer cable from the transfer case.
5. Remove the transfer case to transmission bolts and install a guide bolt on each side to aid in the removal and installation.
6. Remove the transfer case and gasket.

1976–79

1. Remove shift lever knob, boot, and shift lever.
2. Remove floor covering and remove transmission access cover from floorpan.

3. Drain lubricant from transfer case. On CJ models drain the transmission also.
4. If equipped, disconnect torque reaction bracket from crossmember. Disconnect speedometer at transfer case.
5. On CJ models, place support stand under clutch housing to support engine and transmission, and remove rear crossmember.
6. Disconnect front and rear driveshafts at transfer case, making sure to mark shaft yokes for assembly.
7. On Cherokee and Truck models, disconnect parking brake cable at equalizer and exhaust pipe support bracket at transfer case.
8. Remove bolts attaching transfer case to transmission and remove transfer case.

NOTE: One transfer case attaching bolt must be removed from front end of the case. This bolt is located at the bottom right corner of the transmission.

INSTALLATION

1975–79

1. Install a new gasket on the transmission.
2. Shift the transfer case into 4WD low and install the case assembly on the guide bolts.
3. Rotate the transfer case output shaft until the transmission main shaft gear engages the rear output shaft gear of the transfer case.
4. Slide the transfer case forward until the two units mate flush.
5. Install one upper bolt, remove the dowel guide bolts and install the remaining bolts. Torque to 30 ft. lbs.
6. Connect the speedometer cable and parking brake cable.
7. Install the propeller shafts after aligning the indexing marks.
8. Fill the unit with gear lube, and lower the vehicle.
9. Install the transfer case shift lever, boot, and knob.

MODELS 208 AND 300

From 1980
Removal and Installation

CHEROKEE, WAGONEER AND TRUCK MODELS

1. Raise and safely support the vehicle on jackstands.
2. Drain the lubricant from the transfer case.
3. Disconnect the speedometer cable and indicator switch wires. Disconnect the transfer case shift lever link at the operating lever.
4. Support the rear of the transmission and remove the rear crossmember.
5. Mark the transfer case front and rear output shaft yokes and driveshafts for assembly alignment reference.

6. Disconnect the front and rear drive-shafts at the transfer case yokes. Secure the shafts to the frame rails with wires to keep them out of the way.

7. Disconnect the parking brake cable guide from the pivot located on the right frame rail, if necessary.

8. Remove the bolts that attach the exhaust pipe support bracket to transfer case, if necessary.

9. Remove the bolts that attach the transfer case to the transmission.

10. Move the transfer case assembly rearward until it is free of the transmission output shaft. Remove and lower the transfer case.

11. Installation is in the reverse order of removal. Torque the transfer case mounting bolts to 40 ft. lbs.

CJ AND SCRAMBLER MODELS

1. On models with an automatic transmission; remove the shift lever knob, trim ring and boot from the transfer case shift lever.

2. On models with a manual transmission; remove the shift lever knob, trim ring and boot from the transmission and transfer case shift levers.

3. Remove the floor covering and remove the transmission access cover from the floorpan.

4. Raise and safely support the vehicle on jackstands. Drain the lubricant from the transfer case.

5. Support the engine and transmission under the clutch bell housing and remove the rear crossmember.

6. Mark the transfer case front and rear yokes and driveshafts for assembly alignment reference.

7. Disconnect the front and rear drive-shafts at the transfer case. Secure the shafts out of the way.

8. Disconnect the speedometer cable at the transfer case. Disconnect the parking brake cable at the equalizer and the exhaust pipe support bracket at the transfer case to gain any needed clearance.

9. Remove the bolts mounting the transfer case to the transmission. Remove the transfer case.

10. Installation is in the reverse order of removal. The transfer case should be shifted into the 4L position before installation. Rotate the output shaft yoke until the transmission output shaft gear engages the transfer case input shaft. Torque the mounting bolts to 30 ft. lbs.

QUADRA-TRAC®

Removal

1. Lift and support the vehicle safely.

2. Remove reduction unit on Cherokee, Wagoneer, and Truck models, if equipped.

3. Index the marks on the front and rear yokes and propeller shafts for proper alignment during assembly.

4. Disconnect both the front and rear propeller shafts. On CJ-7 models, place support stand under transmission and remove crossmember.

5. Mark the vacuum diaphragm control for identification during the assembly, and then disconnect the vacuum hoses, wiring, and speedometer cable.

6. Disconnect the parking brake cable guide from the pivot on the right frame side.

7. Remove the two front side transfer case to transmission bolts, and install a guide bolt into the upper hole.

8. Remove the two rear side bolts, holding the transfer case to the transmission, and install a guide bolt into the upper hole.

9. Move the transfer case rearward until the unit is free of the transmission output shaft and guide pins. Lower the assembly to the floor.

10. Remove all gasket material from the rear of the transmission.

Installation

1. Install a new gasket on the rear of the transmission.

2. Install the guide bolts in the upper transmission adapter and transfer case, if they were removed.

3. Raise the transfer case, engage the guide bolts, and move the case assembly forward to the transmission. Make sure a flush fit is achieved.

4. If necessary, rotate the transfer case rear output shaft yoke until the drive hub splines align with the transmission output shaft.

5. Install front and rear attaching bolts, and remove the guide bolts during this operation.

6. Attach the exhaust pipe bracket support, if removed.

7. Align the propeller shaft and indexing marks on the yokes and attach the propeller shafts.

8. Connect the speedometer cable, wiring, and vacuum hoses.

9. Connect the parking brake cable guide to the pivot bracket on the right frame side.

10. Install the specified lubricant, and lower the vehicle.

LINKAGE ADJUSTMENTS

The Shifter rails of the transfer case lever assembly connect to the shifter rails of the transfer case either directly or through non-adjustable links on vehicles with manual transmissions. An adjustable trunnion is provided on the lower shift rod to provide desired adjustment on automatic transmission equipped models. The linkage should be lubricated periodically.

QUADRA-TRAC®

Since the Quadra-Trac® system is a ''full time 4WD'' system, and is constantly engaged in 4WD, there is no ''shift linkage''

as such. There are two features which can be operated manually concerning the transfer case: the ''Lock-Out'' feature and the engagement of the optional ''Low Range Reduction Unit.''

Since the ''Lock-Out'' feature is a vacuum actuated unit, there are no external adjustments that can be made other than making sure that all vacuum lines are in place, connected and not damaged in any way.

The reduction unit is actuated by a shift cable and can be adjusted in the following manner:

1. Loosen the nut which clamps the cable to the shift lever pivot. Be sure that the cable can move freely in the pivot.

2. Move the reduction shift lever to the most rearward detent position (Hi-Range position).

3. Push the Low Range lever inward until it stops. Pull the Low Range lever out slightly, no more than $1/16$ in.

4. Tighten the cable clamp nut at the reduction unit shift lever.

NOTE: This procedure only applies to the Quadra-Trac transfer case equipped with a reduction unit.

MANUAL TRANSMISSION

Refer to the Manual Transmission General Repair Section for application, trouble-shooting and overhaul.

Transmission

REMOVAL AND INSTALLATION

The transmission and transfer case can be removed as a unit. These instructions apply to both three and four-speed transmission.

1. Remove the shift level knobs, trim rings, and bolts.

2. On three-speed floorshift models, remove the floor covering. Remove the floor pan section from above the transmission. Remove the shift control and level assembly. On some four-speed models, remove the shift control housing cap, washer, spring, shift lever, and pin. Other four-speed models (SR4, T4 and T5) require the removal of the shift lever housing assembly.

3. Remove the transfer case shift lever and bracket.

4. Raise the vehicle on a lift.

5. Disconnect the column shift rods.

6. Remove the front driveshaft and disconnect the front of the rear driveshaft. Disconnect the vacuum line and electrical lead on a Quadra-Trac unit.

7. Disconnect the clutch cable, if so

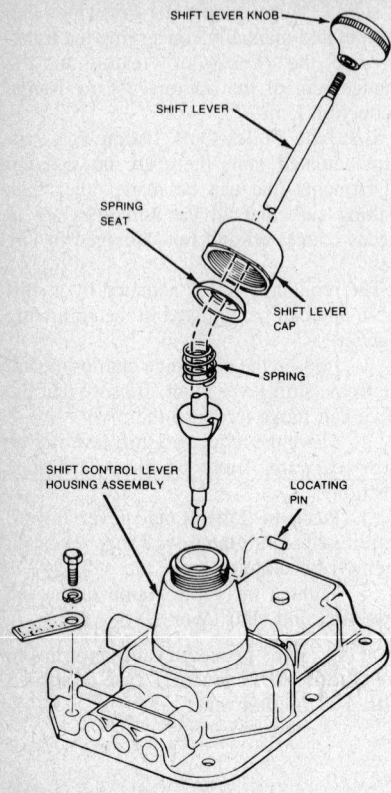

Shift lever removal for T-18A and all 3-speed units

equipped and remove the cable mounting bracket from the transfer case.

8. Disconnect the speedometer cable, TCS switch, and back-up light switch. Disconnect the parking brake cable if it is connected to the crossmember.

9. On models equipped with V8 engines, disconnect and lower the exhaust pipes from the exhaust manifolds, and catalytic converter, if equipped.

10. Support the transmission with a floor jack.

11. Unbolt the crossmember from the frame. Unbolt the transmission from the clutch housing.

12. Lower the transmission slightly and move it to the rear to disengage the clutch shaft. Remove the unit.

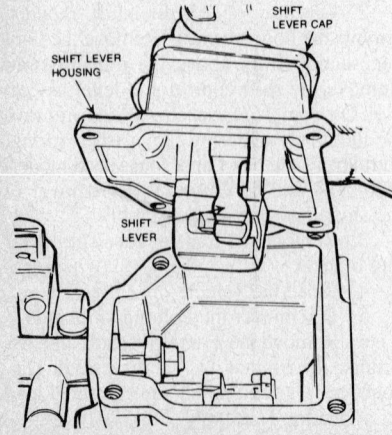

SR-4 shift lever removal

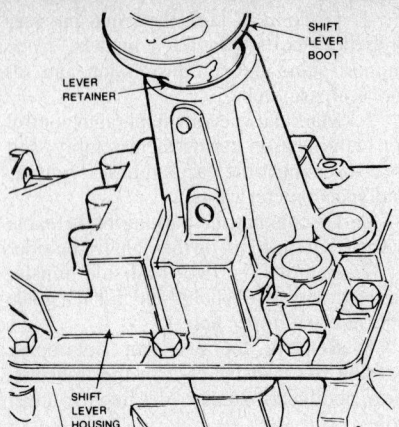

T-176 shift lever removal

To replace the transmission:

13. Place the wave washer and throwout bearing and sleeve assembly in the fork. Center the bearing over the release levers.

14. Slide the transmission into place, being careful to align the transmission splines with those on the clutch plate. Bolt the transmission to the clutch housing and torque the bolts.

15. Bolt the crossmember to the frame. Remove the jack.

16. On models equipped with V8 engines, connect the exhaust pipes to the exhaust manifolds, and catalytic converter, if equipped.

17. Connect the speedometer cable, backup light switch, TCS switch, parking brake cable, clutch cable and cable mounting bracket.

18. Install the driveshafts. Flange bolts should be torqued to 25–45 ft. lbs.

19. Replace the column shift linkage.

20. Lower the vehicle.

21. Replace the transfer case shift lever and bracket.

22. On four-speeds, install the lever pivot pin, shift lever, spring, washer, and control housing cap or shift lever and housing. On three-speeds, install the shift control and lever assembly. Set the gears and the cover in the neutral position. Install the cover, placing the shift forks into the sleeves.

23. Replace the floor covering, boots, trim rings, and shift lever knobs.

LINKAGE ADJUSTMENTS

The shift lever is connected to the transfer case shift rails through rods and nonadjustable links, therefore external adjustments are not possible.

AUTOMATIC TRANSMISSION

The General Motors Turbo-Hydramatic 400 transmission was used through 1979. From 1980, depending on the engine and model, either a Chrysler Loadflite 727, 904 or 999 transmission was installed. The 904 was discontinued in 1982. A lockup torque converter is used on some models.

REMOVAL AND INSTALLATION

1975

1. Remove the dipstick tube attaching bolt at the engine block.

2. Remove the carpet trim ring (if equipped).

3. If equipped with the Spicer Model 20 transfer case, remove the top cover and lever.

4. Mark and remove the rear propeller shaft.

5. Remove the exhaust pipe clamp bolt, shift lever, detent solenoid wire and speedometer cable.

6. Support the transmission and remove the rear cross member.

7. Remove the exhaust pipes.

8. Mark and remove the front propeller shaft from the transfer case end.

9. Remove the vacuum lines and the oil cooler lines from the transmission.

10. When equipped with the Quadra-Trac transfer case, remove the lockout signal wire and the diaphragm control hoses.

11. Disconnect the low range cable (if equipped), and the converter housing splash pan.

12. Mark the converter and flywheel for alignment at assembly and remove the converter to flywheel bolts.

13. Remove the converter housing to engine bolts and remove the transmission.

14. Installation is the reverse of removal. Torque the converter-to-flywheel bolts to 33 ft. lbs.

1976–79

1. Remove transmission dipstick.

2. If vehicle is equipped with radiator shroud, remove bolts attaching shroud to core support. Raise vehicle and support safety.

3. Mark front and rear universal joints and axle yokes.

4. On Cherokee, Wagoneer, and Truck models, remove parking brake cable jamnut and adjuster nut, remove clip attaching parking brake cable to crossmember and pull out of crossmember.

5. On CJ, and Truck models, with low range reduction unit, disconnect shift rod at reduction unit shift lever and remove reduction unit. On all other models, remove reduction unit shift lever from shift shaft and remove reduction unit.

6. Disconnect speedometer cable. Disconnect and mark emergency drive control vacuum lines and indicator lamp wire. Remove bolt attaching vacuum line routing bracket to rear of transfer case.

7. Disconnect detent solenoid wire at

transmission case connector. Remove starter. Remove converter housing inspection cover and mark the torque converter. Remove converter-to-drive plate attaching bolts.

8. Support the transmission and remove the rear crossmember. Disconnect exhaust system components where necessary.

9. Remove spring clip and flat washer attaching transmission gearshift rod trunion to outer range selector lever. Do not loosen trunnion locknut. Disengage gearshift rod and trunnion from outer range selector lever. Remove spring clip and spring attaching outer range selector lever to transmission selector lever. Remove bolts attaching outer range selector lever bracket and bushing to frame and remove bracket, lever, and bushing as an assembly.

10. Disconnect front propeller shaft at transfer case yoke and secure shaft. Disconnect transmission oil cooler lines. Disconnect engine-to-modulator vacuum hose, and remove transmission filler tube.

11. Position a support stand under the engine. Remove the transmission filler tube.

12. Remove the converter housing to engine attaching bolts and move the transmission assembly rearward with a supporting jack until it clears the crankshaft.

13. Hold the converter in place and lower the transmission from the vehicle.

14. The installation of the transmission is in the reverse of the removal procedure. Be sure the converter is properly aligned to the drive plate during installation.

From 1980

1. Disconnect the negative battery cable.

2. Disconnect the fan shroud, if equipped.

3. Disconnect the transmission oil fill tube top bracket.

4. Raise the vehicle and safely support it on jackstands.

5. Remove the inspection cover from the lower part of the converter housing.

6. Remove the oil filler tube and dipstick.

7. Remove the starter motor.

8. Mark the driveshafts and yokes for position. Disconnect the driveshafts from the transfer case yokes. Secure the shafts to the frame with wire so they are out of the way.

9. On eight cylinder models, disconnect the exhaust pipes at the exhaust manifolds and remove, if necessary, to gain clearance.

10. Drain the transfer case lubricant and transmission fluid.

11. Disconnect the speedometer cable, gearshift linkage, throttle linkage and the wires to the neutral safety switch.

12. Mark the converter drive plate and converter for location reference.

13. Remove the bolts that attach the converter to the drive plate. Use a ratchet and socket on the crankshaft pulley bolt to turn the engine when removing the converter mounting bolts.

14. Support the transmission-transfer case assembly on a suitable jack (transmission type jack if possible). Be sure the transmission assembly is firmly chained or secured on the jack for removal.

15. Remove the rear crossmember. Lower the transmission slightly and disconnect the oil coller lines.

16. Remove the bolts that mount the transmission to the engine.

17. Move the transmission and converter back and away from the engine. Make sure the converter breaks loose from the drive plate and is firmly mounted on the transmission.

18. Hold the converter in position and lower the transmission assembly until the converter housing clears the engine.

19. Remove the transmission and transfer case assembly from under the vehicle.

20. Remove the transfer case.

21. Installation is in the reverse order of removal. Be sure to line up the marks on the converter and drive plate when reinstalling. Transmission mounting bolts are torqued to 28 ft. lbs.

LINKAGE ADJUSTMENT

Through 1979

1. Place the steering column gearshift lever in the Neutral position.

2. Raise the vehicle on a hoist.

3. Loosen the locknut on the gearshift rod trunnion just enough to permit movement of the gearshift rod in the trunnion.

4. Place the outer range selector lever at the transmission, fully into the Neutral detent position and tighten the locknut at the trunnion to 9 ft. lbs.

5. Lower the car and operate the steering column gearshift in all ranges. The car should start in Park and Neutral only and the column gearshift lever engage properly in all detent positions.

From 1980

1. Raise and safely support the vehicle on jackstands.

2. Loosen the shift rod trunnion jamnuts.

3. Remove the lockpin that retains the shift rod trunnion to the bell crank. Disengage the trunnion and shift rod at the bell crank.

4. Place the gear shift lever in the Park position and lock the steering column.

5. Move the transmission lever rearward into the Park detent. Be sure the lever is as far rearward as it will go.

6. Check the engagement of the Park detent by trying to rotate the driveshaft (rear wheels must be off of the ground). The shaft will not rotate if the Park detent is engaged.

7. Adjust the trunnion until it will fit in the bell crank arm freely. Tighten the jamnuts. Install the lock pin.

8. Check engine starting in Park and Neutral, be sure it will not start in any other gear.

9. Lower vehicle from stands.

BAND ADJUSTMENT

Through 1979

No provisions are made for the external band adjustments of this transmission. Only during the assembly, can a different sized pin be installed in the rear band apply system, to compensate for lining wear.

FRONT BAND

From 1980

The front band adjusting screw is located on the left side of the transmission case just above the manual valve and throttle control levers.

1. Raise and safely support the vehicle on jackstands.

2. Loosen the adjusting screw locknut and back if off five turns.

3. Check the adjusting screw to make sure it turns freely, lubricate it if necessary.

4. Tighten the adjusting screw to 36 in. lbs.

5. Back of the adjusting screw two turns. Tighten the locknut. Do not allow the ad-

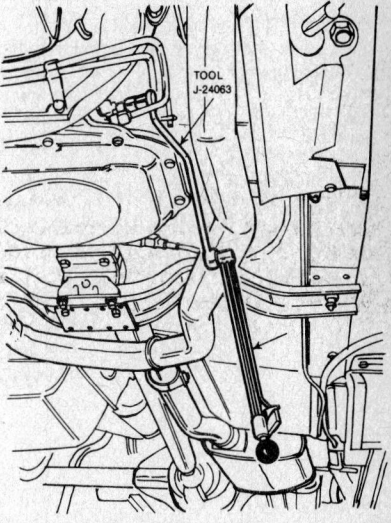

Front band adjustment-TorqueFlite

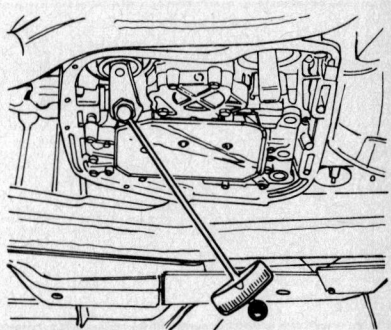

Rear band adjustment-TorqueFlite

justing screw to turn when tightening the locknut.

REAR BAND ADJUSTMENT

From 1980

NOTE: The transmission oil pan must be removed to gain access to the adjusting screw. See Pan and Filter Removal Section.

1. Raise and safely support the vehicle on jackstands.
2. Remove the oil pan and drain the fluid.
3. The adjusting screw is located on the right rear side above the rear side edge of the filter.
4. Loosen the locknut. Tighten the adjusting screw to 41 in. lbs. Back off the adjusting screw four turns on models 904 and 999, two turns on model 727.
5. Hold the adjusting screw so that it will not turn and tighten the locknut.
6. Install the oil pan and new gasket.
7. Lower the vehicle and fill the transmission to the correct level.

NEUTRAL SWITCH ADJUSTMENT

Through 1979

1. Apply the parking brake.
2. Check and adjust the manual linkage, if necessary.

3. Remove the Neutral switch from the steering column.
4. Place the selector lever in Park and lock the steering column.
5. Move the switch actuating lever until it is aligned with the letter ''P'' stamped on the back of the switch.
6. Insert a $3/32$ in. drill in the hole located below the letter ''N'' stamped on the back of the switch.
7. Move the switch actuating lever until it stops against the drill.
8. Position the switch on the steering column, install the attaching screws and remove the drill.
9. Check the operation of the switch. The engine should start in Park and Neutral only. The backup light should glow only in the Reverse position.

From 1980

The neutral safety switch is located on the side of the transmission by the manual linkage. It is an electrical switch that is thread mounted. The neutral starting section of the switch is contained in the center terminal of the three terminal switch. The other terminals control the backup lights.

TEST AND REPLACEMENT

1. Remove the wiring connector from the switch. Test for continuity between the center terminal pin and the transmission case. Continuity should exist only when the transmission control is in Park or Neutral.

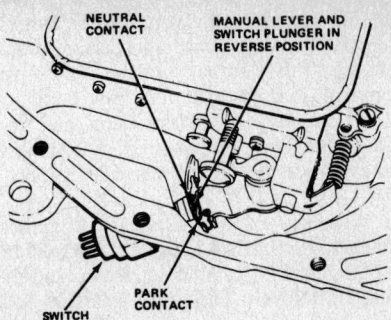

Torqueflite neutral start and backup light switch

2. If test shows that the switch is defective, check the gearshift linkage adjustment before replacing the switch.
3. Remove the switch from the transmission. A certain amount of fluid will leak out when the switch is removed, have a container ready to catch the fluid.
4. Move the gearshift lever to Park and neutral positions. Inspect the switch operating lever fingers and manual lever and shaft for proper alignment with the switch opening in the transmission case.
5. Install a new switch and seal into the transmission case. Tighten to 24 ft. lbs. Test for continuity.
6. Correct the transmission fluid level. Lower vehicle from stands.

Transmission Oil Pan and Filter

REMOVAL

1. Raise the vehicle and support safely.
2. Position a drain pan under the transmission and remove the oil pan bolts, except the four corner ones.
3. Loosen the corner bolts and pry the oil pan loose from the transmission case.
4. Allow the oil to drain from the corners of the oil pan, while tilting the pan to remove as much oil as possible.
5. Carefully remove the corner bolts and the oil pan from the transmission case.
6. Remove the oil filter, oil pan gasket, and through 1979, the intake tube O-ring seal.

INSTALLATION

1. Place a new O-ring on the intake tube and install the tube in place through 1979.
2. Install a new filter and retain it to the control valve assembly with the attaching bolt.
3. Install the oil pan and gasket. Torque the pan bolts to 10 ft. lbs.
4. Lower the vehicle and fill the transmission with the specified fluid. (Dexron® II equivalent).

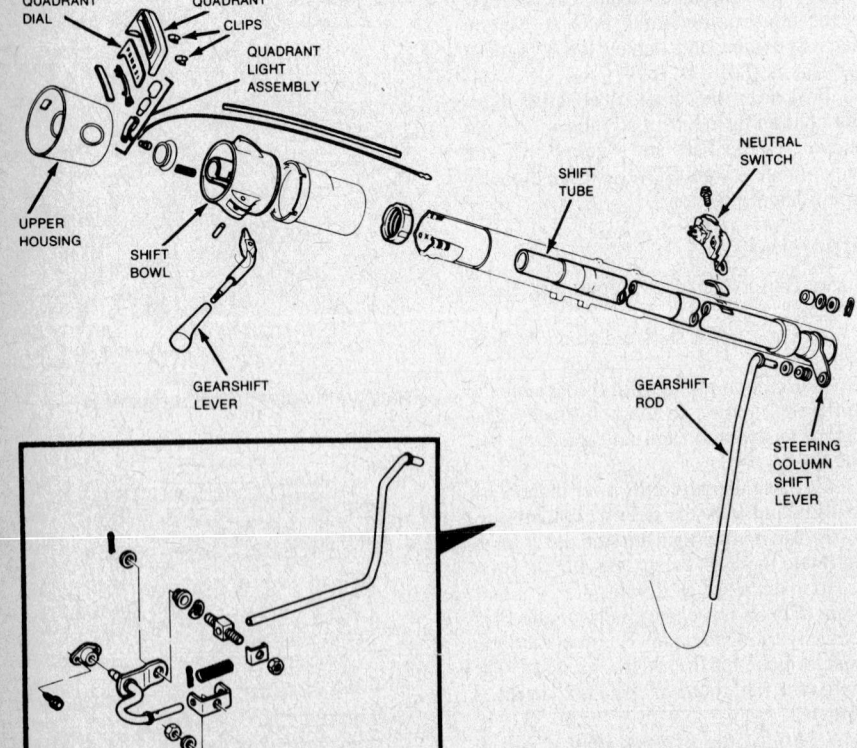

Turbo Hydra-Matic 400 shift linkage and neutral start switch

THROTTLE LINKAGE ADJUSTMENT 1980–81

4-151

1. Remove the air cleaner.
2. Remove the spark plug wire holder from the throttle cable bracket and move the holder and wires aside.
3. Raise and support the vehicle on jackstands.
4. Hold the throttle control lever rearward against its stop. Hook one end of a spare spring to the lever and hook the opposite end to any convenient point. This will hold the lever in position.
5. Lower the vehicle.
6. Block the choke open and move the carburetor linkage completely off the fast idle cam.
7. On vehicles without air conditioning, turn the ignition to ON to energize the solenoid.
8. Unlock the throttle control cable by releasing the T shaped adjuster clamp on the cable by lifting it upward with a small screwdriver.
9. Grasp the outer sheath of the cable and move the cable and sheath forward to remove any load on the cable bell crank.
10. Adjust the cable by removing the cable and sheath rearward until there is no play at all between the plastic cable and the bell crank ball.
11. When play has been eliminated, lock the cable by pressing the T shaped clamp downward until it snaps into place.
12. Turn the ignition off. Install all parts and remove the spare spring.

6-258

1. Disconnect the throttle control rod spring at the carburetor.
2. Raise and support the vehicle on jackstands.
3. Use the throttle control rod spring to hold the throttle control lever forward against its stop, by hooking one end of the spring on the throttle control lever and the other end on the throttle linkage bell crank bracket which is attached to the transmission housing.
4. Block the choke plate open and move the throttle linkage off the fast idle cam.
5. On carburetors equipped with a throttle operated solenoid valve, turn the ignition ON to energize the solenoid, then open the throttle halfway to allow the solenoid to lock and return the carburetor to the idle position.
6. Loosen the retaining bolt on the throttle control adjusting link. DO NOT REMOVE THE SPRING CLIP AND NYLON WASHER!
7. Pull on the end of the link to eliminate play and tighten the retaining bolt.
8. Remove the throttle control rod spring and install it on the control rod from where it came.
9. Lower the vehicle.

V8 Engines

1. Disconnect the throttle control rod spring at the carburetor.
2. Raise and support the vehicle on jackstands.
3. Use the throttle control rod spring to hold the transmission throttle valve control lever against its stop.
4. Block the choke plate open and make sure the throttle linkage is off the fast idle cam.

NOTE: On carburetors equipped with a throttle operated solenoid valve, turn the ignition to ON to energize the solenoid. Then turn the throttle halfway to allow the solenoid to lock and return the carburetor to idle.

5. Loosen the retaining bolt on the throttle control rod adjuster link. Remove the spring clip and move the nylon washer to the rear of the link.
6. Push on the end of the link to eliminate play and tighten the link retaining bolt.
7. Install the nylon washer and spring clip.
8. Remove the throttle control rod spring and install it in its intended position.
9. Lower the vehicle.

FRONT DRIVE AXLE

Selective Drive Hubs

Selective drive hubs are used to disengage the front axles from the drive train when the vehicle is used in two-wheel drive. When Quadra-Trac® is used, the selector hubs are not used. Two different types are used, automatic and manual.

CJ MODELS, AUTOMATIC HUBS

Removal

1. Remove the allen screws from the clutch assembly and remove the assembly from the hub body assembly.
2. Remove the retaining ring from the axle shaft end.
3. Straighten lock tabs and remove the screws attaching the hub body assembly to the front hub. Remove the hub body assembly.

CLUTCH ASSEMBLY OVERHAUL—AUTOMATIC HUBS

1. Push out the control dial, turn the unit over and remove the cluster ring and disc.
2. Clean and inspect all parts for damage. Replace U-ring and O-ring seals on the control dial.
3. Install the control dial assembly and install the disc.

NOTE: Lubricate O-ring and inside of cap.

4. Rotate the control dial to "FREE" position. Install the clutch ring and thread to the bottom.
5. Turn back the clutch ring until the holes align and install in the body assembly.
6. Turn the control from "FREE" to "LOCK" and check the operation.

BODY ASSEMBLY

Overhaul

1. Remove the friction shoe spring, retaining ring, and separate the hub body from the roller clutch.
2. Remove the centering spring, and spirolock ring. Separate the cage and axle shaft hub.
3. Clean and inspect all parts, coat lightly with grease.
4. Install the friction shoe on the cage, (avoid stretching the shoe) and lubricate the friction shoes liberally, and install.

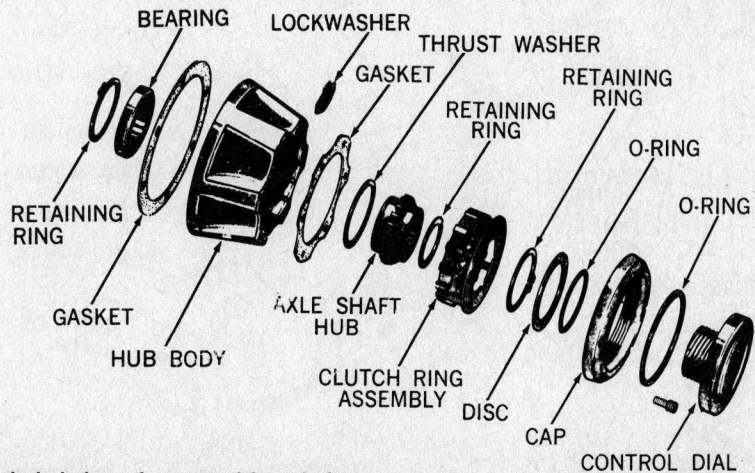

Exploded view of a manual front hub

Installation

1. Position the gasket and body assembly on the wheel hub.
2. Install the tab lock washer and screws. Torque the screws to 40–45 ft. lbs. and secure with the lock washer tabs.
3. Install the retaining ring on the axle shaft end.
4. Place the gasket and cap assembly on the body assembly and torque the allen headed screws to 6–8 ft. lbs.

CHEROKEE AND TRUCK

Removal

1. Remove the six allen screws and remove the clutch assembly.
2. Remove the capscrews, lock washers, and stop-ring on the axle shaft end.
3. Remove the retaining ring(s) and slide the hub body off the axle end.

Clutch Assembly—Automatic Hubs

OVERHAUL

1. Remove the taper headed screw from the clutch screw unit.
2. Push out the control dial, turn the assembly over and push out the clutch and clutch screw.
3. Clean and inspect all parts. Replace the U-ring and O-ring seals on the control dial.
4. Lubricate the clutch ring and thread the clutch screw into the clutch ring until the ring raises slightly.
5. Install the taper headed screw and stake it in place.

NOTE: If new parts are used, drill a ³⁄₁₆ inch hole through the clutch screw into the thick webbing on the control dial ⅝ inch deep. Install a pin and stake into place.

6. Turn the dial from "FREE" to "LOCK" and check the operation.

Hub Body—Automatic Hubs

OVERHAUL

1. Remove the friction shoe spring and the retaining ring.
2. Clean and inspect all parts.
3. Lubricate the bearing race lightly.
4. Place the cage into the body and pack rollers with chassis lub.
5. Place the body over the axle shaft hub, carefully, and install the retaining ring.

Installation

1. Carefully install the friction shoe spring and lubricate the shoes with chassis lube, and slide the body assembly into the hub.

NOTE: The body assembly will stop about ¼ inch from full position. Allow the body to slide to full position by pushing the assembly to expand the friction shoes over the drag shoe nut.

2. Install the retaining ring to hold the body assembly to the hub.
3. Install the screw, lock washer, and stop ring in the axle end and torque to 35–40 ft. lbs.
4. Install the clutch assembly to the body assembly with the allen headed screws, and torque to 4–6 ft. lbs.
5. Rotate the wheel and check for freedom of movement.

Manual Hubs

REMOVAL

1. Remove the allen screws from the clutch hub.
2. Remove the hub body bolts from the front hub.
3. Remove the retaining ring and pull the clutch ring assembly and axle shaft hub body from the axle.

NOTE: The clutch ring assembly cannot be disassembled. The control assembly and the clutch screw cannot be separated.

DISASSEMBLY

1. Remove the snap-ring from the hub bore.
2. Remove the needle bearing and thrust washer from the clutch hub body and the axle shaft hub, noting the side of the hub body from which the axle shaft hub is removed.

ASSEMBLY

1. Install the axle shaft hub into the hub body from the same side as it was removed.
2. Install the needle bearings in the hub and install the snap ring.

INSTALLATION

1. With a new gasket, install the hub body assembly onto the wheel hub and over the axle shaft, and install the attaching bolts.
2. Install the retaining ring in the groove at the end of the axle shaft hub.
3. Lubricate the bearing side and the grooves of the control assembly and install the new O-rings.
4. Insert the clutch ring assembly into the hub body and retain it with the snap-ring.

NOTE: Try the clutch ring for a free sliding fit on the drive pins. If a binding occurs, lift the unit out and reposition it. If the binding still exists, remove and examine for damage.

5. Position the control assembly with the dowel pin into the face of the clutch body, so that the arrow stops on the dot marked "FREE".
6. Install the control assembly over the axle end and retain it to the hub body with the allen headed screws. Use a new gasket.
7. Move the control from the "FREE" position to the "LOCK" position and assure that the unit is operating satisfactorily.

Axle Shaft

REMOVAL AND INSTALLATION

1. Raise and support the vehicle.

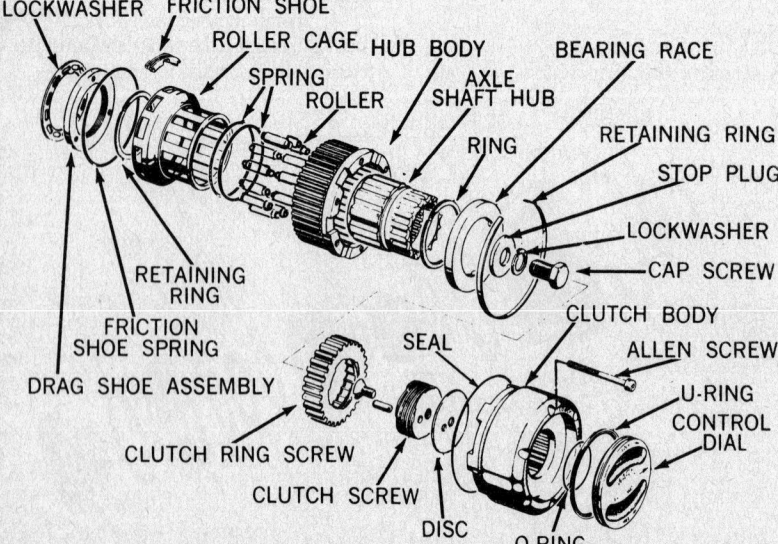

Exploded view of an automatic front hub

LOCKWASHER   FRICTION SHOE
ROLLER CAGE   HUB BODY   BEARING RACE
SPRING   AXLE SHAFT HUB
ROLLER   RING   RETAINING RING
STOP PLUG
LOCKWASHER
CAP SCREW
RETAINING RING
FRICTION SHOE SPRING
DRAG SHOE ASSEMBLY
CLUTCH RING SCREW
CLUTCH SCREW
SEAL
DISC   O-RING
CLUTCH BODY
ALLEN SCREW
U-RING
CONTROL DIAL

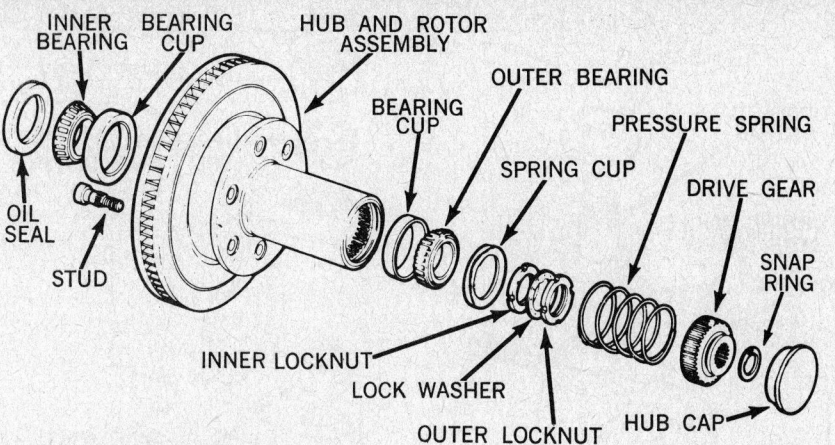

Typical front hub and rotor assembly

2. Remove the wheel and dust cover.

3. Remove the axle shaft snap-ring, drive flange, pressure spring and spring retainer. If the drive flange is stuck to the shaft, use a pry bar to pry it out.

4. Use the special nut wrench to remove the wheel bearing locknut, lockring, and wheel bearing adjusting nut.

5. Remove the two bolts securing the brake caliper assembly to the disc brake shield and move the caliper assembly aside.

6. Remove the rotor and hub assembly. The spring retainer and outer wheel bearing will slide out as the hub assembly is removed.

7. Remove the nuts and bolts attaching the spindle and disc brake shield.

8. Remove the spindle and disc brake shield. It may be necessary to tap the spindle lightly to free it.

9. Remove the axle shaft.

10. Install the new axle shaft, spindle, and bearing assembly.

11. Install the hub, brake shield, rotor, and the brake caliper assembly.

12. Install the inner wheel bearing adjusting nut. This is the nut with the peg on the side. Tighten the nut to 50 ft. lbs. with the special wheel bearing nut wrench. Rotate the hub and back off the adjusting nut ¼ turn maximum.

13. Install the lockwasher with the inner tab lined up with the keyway spindle. Turn the inner adjusting nut until the peg engages the nearest hole in the lockwasher. Install the outer locknut and tighten it to 50 ft. lbs. Install the spring retainer, pressure spring and drive flange.

14. Push the drive flange inward to provide clearance and install the axle shaft snap-ring.

15. Install the wheel and dust cover and lower the vehicle.

Axle Shaft Seal

REMOVAL AND INSTALLATION

1. Remove axle shaft.

2. Remove seal and bronze thrust washer. If washer is worn it must be replaced.

3. Install seal and washer with washer chamfered side toward the axle shaft seal.

4. Installation is the reverse of removal

NOTE: Pack wheel bearing grease around thrust face of shaft and seal and fill seal area of spindle with wheel bearing grease.

Wheel Bearing Adjustment

CJ MODELS

1. With the front of the vehicle raised, remove the hubcaps, snapsprings, capscrews, and washers attaching the drive flange to the hub.

2. Remove the drive flange from the front hub.

NOTE: A puller may be needed for this operation.

3. Straighten the edge of the lock washer, so that the lock nut and lock washer can be removed.

4. With a special wrench or equivalent, tighten the adjusting nut until the wheel binds, and back off approximately ⅙ turn, so that the wheel turns freely without any lateral shake.

5. Install the lock washer and lock nut on the housing end, tighten the lock nut and crimp the lock washer edge over the lock nut.

6. Assemble the drive flange, bolts, and the hub cap. Assure that the gasket is properly installed between the hub and the flange.

CHEROKEE, WAGONEER, AND TRUCKS

1. Remove the hub caps, snap-ring, drive gear pressure spring, outer lock nut, and lock washer.

2. Loosen the inner wheel bearing nut, and then retighten to 50 ft. lbs. torque (inner nut has peg on outer side).

3. Rotate the hub, back off the adjusting nut ¼ turn maximum.

4. Install the lock washer to have the tab engage the key way in the spindle and move the adjusting nut until the peg engages the nearest hole in the lock washer.

5. Install the outer lock washer and tighten to 50 ft. lbs.

Steering Knuckle Service

REMOVAL

1. Follow the Axle Removal procedure as outlined previously.

2. Remove the steering rods from the steering arm.

3. Remove the lower ball stud nut.

NOTE: This nut is a self-locking nut and should be discarded and replaced with a new nut upon assembly.

4. Remove the cotter pin from the upper ball stud nut and loosen it to the top of the stud in a flush manner. With the aid of a lead hammer, unseat the upper and lower ball studs from the yoke.

5. Remove the knuckle assembly from the axle.

6. With the use of a suitable tool remove the upper ball stud seat from the axle yoke.

Ball Joints

REMOVAL AND REPLACEMENT

1. With the aid of a puller or a press, position the tool to force the lower ball joint from the knuckle.

2. Position the puller or the press to force the upper ball joint from the knuckle.

3. To install the ball joints, press the lower joint into place and follow with the upper ball joint.

INSTALLATION

1. Install the upper ball stud seat into the axle yoke, until the top of the seat is flush with the top of the yoke.

2. Install the knuckle assembly onto the axle yoke by inserting the ball studs into their respective holes in the yoke. Install the new lower stud nut and tighten to 79-90 ft. lbs. torque.

3. Tighten the upper ball stud seat to 60 ft. lbs. torque, and install the upper ball stud nut and torque to 100 ft. lbs. torque.

4. If the cotter pin holes do not align, tighten the nut until the pin can be installed. Never loosen the nut to install the cotter pin.

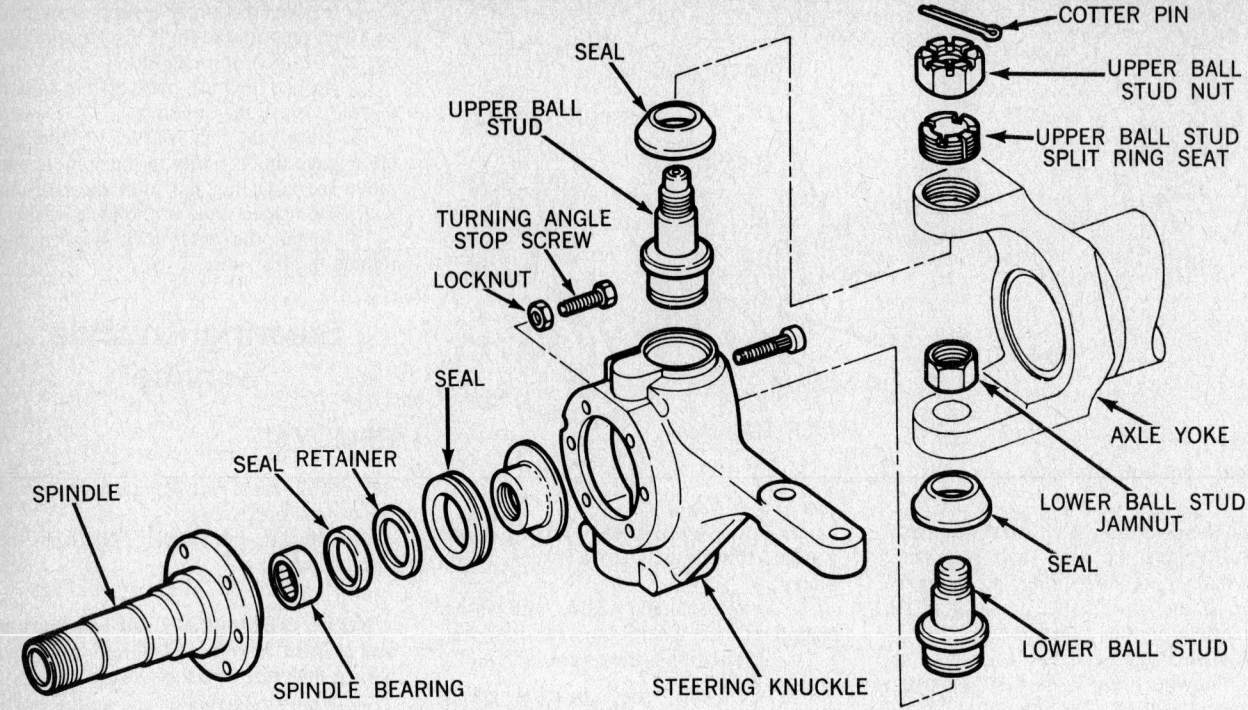

Steering knuckle components-typical

5. Continue with the assembly as previously outlined.

Upper Ball Joint Adjustment

Adjustment of the upper ball joint is necessary only when there is excessive play in the steering, persistent loosening of the steering linkage, or abnormal wear of the tires.

ADJUSTMENT PROCEDURE

1. Raise the vehicle on a hoist or jack and support with stands if necessary.
2. Disconnect the steering linkage from the left and right knuckle assemblies.
3. Attach a torque wrench and socket to a steering arm stud and check the torque needed to move the knuckle through its arc.
4. Maximum torque is 12–16 lbs. on model 30 axle, and 15–20 lbs. on model 44 axle.

NOTE: The knuckle should turn smoothly through the turning arc and have no vertical end play.

5. If the torque is too low, perform the following procedures.
   a. Remove the upper ball stud cotter pin.
   b. Torque the stud adjusting sleeve to 50 ft. lbs.
   c. Install the lock nut and a new cotter pin.
   d. Recheck the torque necessary to turn the knuckle through its arc, and if the

torque is still too low, retorque the sleeve to 60 ft. lbs. and recheck.
   e. If the torque specifications can not be obtained, it will be necessary to replace parts in the knuckle assembly.

NOTE: Temperature will affect the turning torque, therefore, allowances in the torque reading should be made.

Front Axle Assembly

REMOVAL

1. Raise and support the front of the vehicle, supporting the weight at the rear of the front spring.
2. Remove the wheel covers and wheels.
3. Index the propeller shaft to the differential yoke for the proper alignment upon installation.
4. Disconnect the steering linkage from the steering knuckles.
5. On vehicles equipped with sway bar, remove nuts attaching sway bar connecting links to spring tie plates.
6. Disconnect the shock absorbers and breather tube from the axle housing.
7. Remove the brake calipers, hub and rotor, and the brake shield.
8. Remove the spring clips and the spring clip plates.
9. Support the assembly on a jack and loosen the nuts securing the rear shackles, but do not remove the bolts.
10. Remove the front spring shackle bolts and rest the front of the spring on the floor.
11. Pull the jack and axle housing from underneath the vehicle.

INSTALLATION

1. Support the axle on a jack and slide the assembly under the vehicle, and position it over the springs.
2. Raise the front of the springs and install the front shackle bolts, but do not tighten.
3. Position the axle on the springs and install the spring clips and spring clip plates.
4. Tighten the front and rear shackle bolts.
5. Install the brake shield, hub and rotor, and brake calipers.
6. Connect the breather tube and shock absorbers.
7. Connect the steering linkage at the steering knuckles.
8. Align the indexing marks and install the propeller shaft.
9. Install the wheels and tighten. Install the wheel covers.
10. Lower the vehicle and check the wheel alignment and turning angle.

Driveshaft

REMOVAL AND INSTALLATION

In order to remove the front and rear driveshafts, unscrew the attaching nuts from the universal joint's U-bolts, remove the U-bolts and slide the shaft forward or backward toward the slip-joint. The shaft can then be removed from the end yokes and removed from under the vehicle. Install the driveshaft in the reverse order.

NOTE: Some driveshafts are marked at the slip-joints with arrows on the spline and sleeve yoke. When installing the driveshaft, align the arrows to have the yokes at the front and rear of the shaft in the same parallel plane.

U-Joint Overhaul

SNAP-RING TYPE DISASSEMBLY AND REPAIR

1. Remove the snap-rings.
2. Press on the end of one bearing until the opposite bearing is pushed from the yoke arm.
3. Turn the joint over. Press the first bearing back out of the arm by pressing on the exposed end of the journal shaft. Repeat this operation for the other two bearings, then lift out the journal assembly by sliding it to one side.
4. Wash all parts in solvent and inspect for wear. Replace all worn parts.
5. Install new gaskets on the journal assembly. Make certain that the grease channel in each journal trunnion is open.
6. Pack the bearing cones one-third full of grease and install the rollers.
7. Assemble in the reverse order of disassembly. If the joint binds when assembled, tap the arms lightly to relieve any pressure on the bearings at the end of the journal.

U-BOLT TYPE DISASSEMBLY AND REPAIR

Remove the attaching U-bolts to release one set of bearing races. Slide the driveshaft into the yoke flange to remove the races. The rest of the disassembly and repair procedure is the same as that given above for the snap-ring type of cross and roller joint. The correct U-bolt torque is 15–20 ft. lbs.

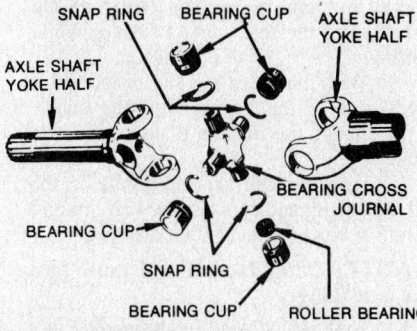

Exploded view of typical U-joint

REAR AXLE

Refer to the Drive Axle General Repair Section for application, troubleshooting, and overhaul procedures.

Rear Axle Assembly

REMOVAL

1. Raise the vehicle and place jack stands forward of the rear springs.
2. Remove the rear wheels.
3. Place an indexing mark on the rear yoke and propeller shaft, and disconnect the shaft.
4. Disconnect the shock absorbers from the axle tubes.
5. Disconnect the brake hose from the tee fitting on the axle housing.
6. Disconnect the parking brake cable at the frame mounting.
7. Remove U-Bolts. On vehicles with spring mounted above axle, disconnect spring at rear shackle.
8. Support the axle on a Jack, remove the spring clips, and remove the axle assembly from under the vehicle.
9. Installation is the reverse of removal.

NOTE: Bleed and adjust brakes accordingly.

Axle Shaft

REMOVAL AND INSTALLATION

Tapered Shaft

1. Jack up the vehicle and remove the hub cap.

2. Remove the wheel.
3. Remove the axle nut dust cap.
4. Remove the axle shaft cotter pin, castle nut and flat washer.
5. Back-off the brake adjustment.
6. Use a puller to remove the wheel hub.
7. Remove the screws attaching the brake dust protector, grease and bearing retainers, brake assembly and shim to the housing.
8. Remove the hydraulic line from the brake assembly.
9. Remove the dust shield and oil seal.
10. Use a puller to remove the axle shaft.
11. Install the axle shaft in the reverse order of removal, using a new grease seal and installing the hub assembly before the woodruff key.

NOTE: Should the axle shaft be broken, the inner end can usually be drawn out of the housing with a wire loop after the outer oil seal is removed. However, if the broken end is less than 8 in. long, it usually is necessary to remove the differential assembly.

Axle Shaft Bearing

REMOVAL AND INSTALLATION (AXLE OUT)

1. With the aid of a combination puller, remove the bearing from the axle shaft.

NOTE: If a puller is not available, place the threaded end of the axle on a heavy block of wood and with the aid of an assistant, drive the bearing from the axle shaft with a punch and hammer. Contact the inner race only with the punch.

2. The new bearing can be installed with the use of a combination puller, or with the

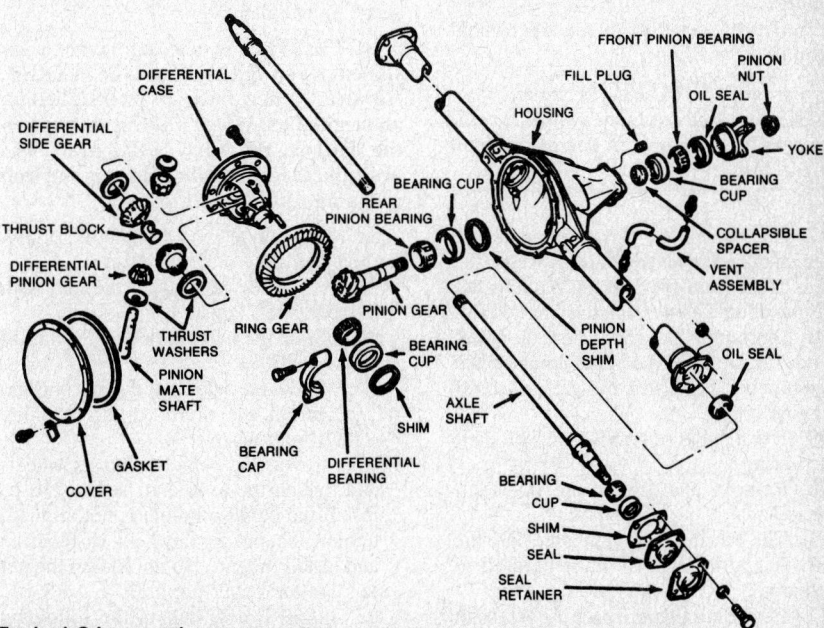

Typical CJ rear axle components

use of a length of pipe, fitted to the diameter of the inner bearing race, and slipped over the axle end to contact and drive the bearing to its seat on the axle shaft.

3. Lubricate the bearing with wheel bearing grease, making sure the grease fills the cavities between the bearing rollers.

Inner Oil Seal

REMOVAL AND INSTALLATION (AXLE OUT)

1. Insert the splined end of the axle shaft into the inner seal, hooking the axle end to the seal, and prying downward. The seal will move outward from the housing tube.

2. Install a new seal into the housing tube with the aid of a seal installer or its equivalent.

4. Seat the seal and lubricate the lip.

NOTE: The lip of the seal should point towards the center of the axle housing.

5. The outer seal is installed during the assembly of the brake support plate.

CJ MODELS ONLY, 1976 AND LATER

1. With the wheel on the ground, remove the axle shaft cotter pin and nut. Loosen the wheel nuts.

2. Raise and support the rear of the car, preferably with jackstands under the axle housing.

3. Remove the wheel.

4. Remove the drum retaining screws, 3 per drum

5. Remove the drum from the hub. If the brake shoes hold the drum, the brake adjustment will have to be backed off slightly.

6. Attach a puller to the wheel bolts and pull off the hub.

─────── CAUTION ───────

Don't use a knockout type puller. It could damage the rear wheel bearings or the differential.

7. Disconnect the parking brake cable at the equalizer. The equalizer is where the single cable from the parking brake pedal joins the double cable from the rear wheels.

8. Disconnect the brake tube at the wheel cylinder and remove the brake support plate assembly (backing plate), oil seal, and shims (left-side only).

9. Use a puller to remove the axle shaft and bearing.

10. Remove and discard the axle shaft inner oil seal.

11. The bearing cone is pressed onto the shaft. A hydraulic press must be used to remove it.

12. Before installation, pack the axle shaft bearings with high quality grease. Place a healthy glob of grease in the palm of one hand and force the edge of the bearing into it so that grease fills the bearing. Do this until the whole bearing is packed. Grease packing tools are available which make this task much easier.

13. Press the axle shaft bearings onto the axle shafts with the small diameter of the cone toward the outer end of the shaft.

─────── CAUTION ───────

Always press on the inner bearing race.

14. Coat the inner axle shaft seal with light oil.

15. Coat the outer surface of the metal seal retainer with sealant.

16. Use a seal driver to install the inner oil seal in the axle housing.

17. Install the axle shaft(s), turning them as necessary to fit the splines into the differential.

18. Install the outer bearing cup.

19. Apply sealant to the axle housing flange and brake support plate mounting areas. Install the original shims in their original locations, oil seal assembly, and brake support plate. Tighten the retaining bolts to 35 ft. lbs.

NOTE: The oil seal and retainer go on the outside of the brake support plate.

20. Axle shaft end-play can be measured by installing the hub retaining nut on the shaft so it can be pushed and pulled with relative ease. Strike the end of each axle shaft with a lead hammer to seat the bearing cups against the support plate. Mount a dial indicator on the left side support plate with the stylus resting on the end of the axle shaft. Check the end-play while pushing and pulling on the axle shaft. End play should be within 0.004–0.008 in., with 0.006 in. ideal. Add shims to increase end play and subtract whims to decrease endplay. Remove the hub retaining nut when finished checking endplay.

NOTE: When a new axle shaft is installed, a new hub must also be installed. However, a new hub can be installed on an original axle shaft if the serrations on the shaft are not worn or damaged. The procedures for installing an original hub and a new hub are different.

21. Install an original hub in the following manner:

a. Align the keyway in the hub with the axle shaft key.

b. Slide the hub onto the axle shaft as far as possible.

c. Install the axle shaft nut and washer.

d. Install the drum, drum retaining screws, and wheel.

e. Lower the vehicle onto its wheels and tighten the axle shaft nut to 250 ft. lbs. If the cotter pin hole is not aligned, tighten the nut to the next castellation and install the pin. Do not loosen the nut to align the cotter pin hole.

22. Install a new hub in the following manner:

a. Align the keyway in the hub with the axle shaft key.

b. Slide the hub onto the axle shaft as far as possible.

c. Install two well-lubricated thrust washers and the axle shaft nut.

d. Install the brake drum, drum retaining screws, and wheel.

e. Lower the vehicle onto its wheels.

f. Tighten the axle shaft nut until the distance from the outer face of the hub eto the outer end of the axle shaft is 1 5/16 in. Pressing the hub onto the axle to the specified distance is necessary to form the hub serrations properly.

g. Remove the axle shaft nut and one thrust washer.

h. Install the axle shaft nut and tighten it to 250 ft. lbs. If the cotter pin hole is not aligned, tighten the nut to the next castellation and install the pin. Do not loosen the nut to install the cotter pin.

23. Connect the brake line to the wheel cylinder and bleed the brake hydraulic system and adjust the brake shoes.

Flanged Shaft

REMOVAL AND INSTALLATION

1. Raise the vehicle and support safely. Remove the wheel.

2. Remove the brake drum spring lock nuts and remove the drum.

3. Remove the axle shaft flange cup plug by piercing the center with a sharp tool and prying it out.

4. Using the access hole in the axle shaft flange, remove the nuts which attach the brake support plate and retainer to the axle tube flange.

5. Remove the axle shaft from the housing with an axle puller.

6. Remove the inner oil seal from the axle housing tube. Install a new seal in the tube.

NOTE: Lip of seal must be facing towards the center of the differential.

7. Mount the axle in a vise, and with a chisel, cut the bearing retaining ring and drive the ring off the axle shaft.

8. Using a hacksaw, cut through the oil seal and remove from the axle shaft. Do not damage the seal contact surface while cutting.

9. With the aid of a puller or its equivalent, remove the bearing from the shaft.

10. Install the retainer plate on the axle shaft.

11. Apply wheel bearing grease to the oil seal cavity and between the seal lips and install seal on the axle shaft seal seat.

NOTE: Outer face of seal must face the axle flange.

12. Pack wheel bearing with grease and install on the axle shaft.

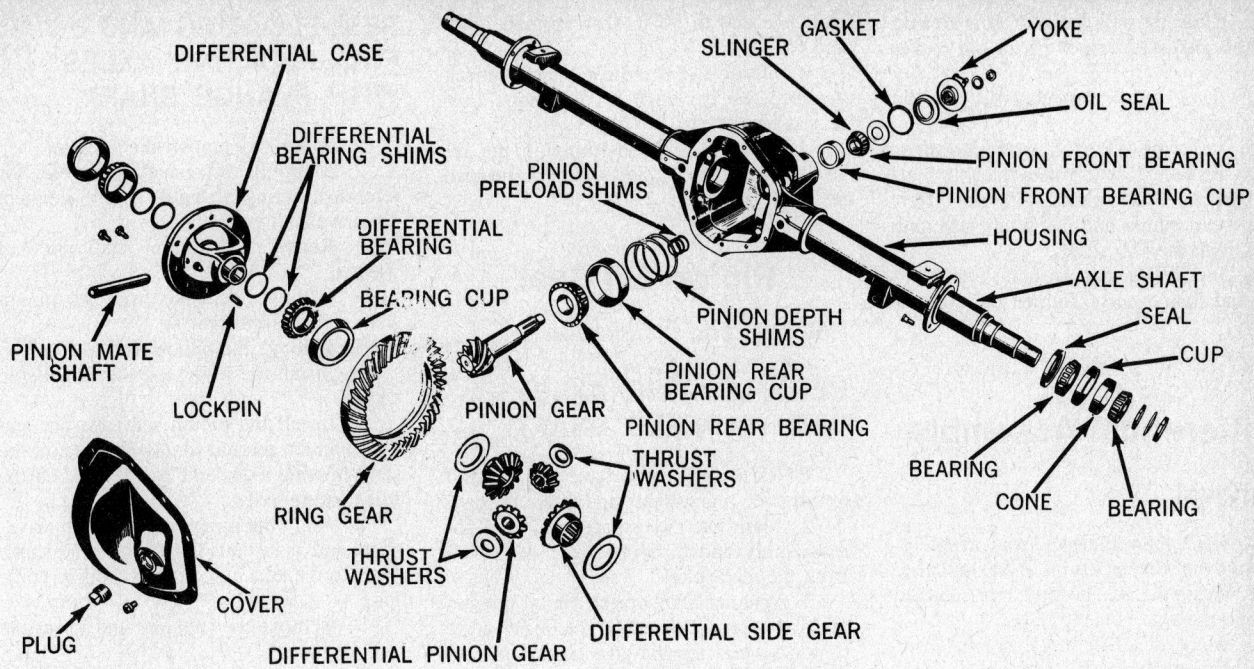

Full-floating rear axle assembly

NOTE: Cup rib ring should be facing the axle flange.

13. Install the retainer ring on the axle shaft, and press both the retainer and the bearing on the shaft at the same time, until both are seated against the shaft shoulder.

14. Install the axle shaft into the housing bore, being careful not to damage the inner seal.

15. Lubricate the outer surface of the bearing cup before installing into the bearing bore.

16. Tap the flanged end of the axle to position it into the bearing bore.

17. Attach the axle shaft retainer and brake support plate to the axle tube flange, and secure with the nuts and lockwashers.

18. Install the brake drum, spring type locknuts, and rear wheels.

19. Remove the safety stands and lower the vehicle.

Full-Floating Axle Shaft

It is not necessary to raise the rear wheels in order to remove the rear axle shaft on full-floating rear axles.

1. Remove the axle flange nuts, lock washers, and split washers retaining the axle shaft flange.

2. Remove the axle shaft from the axle housing.

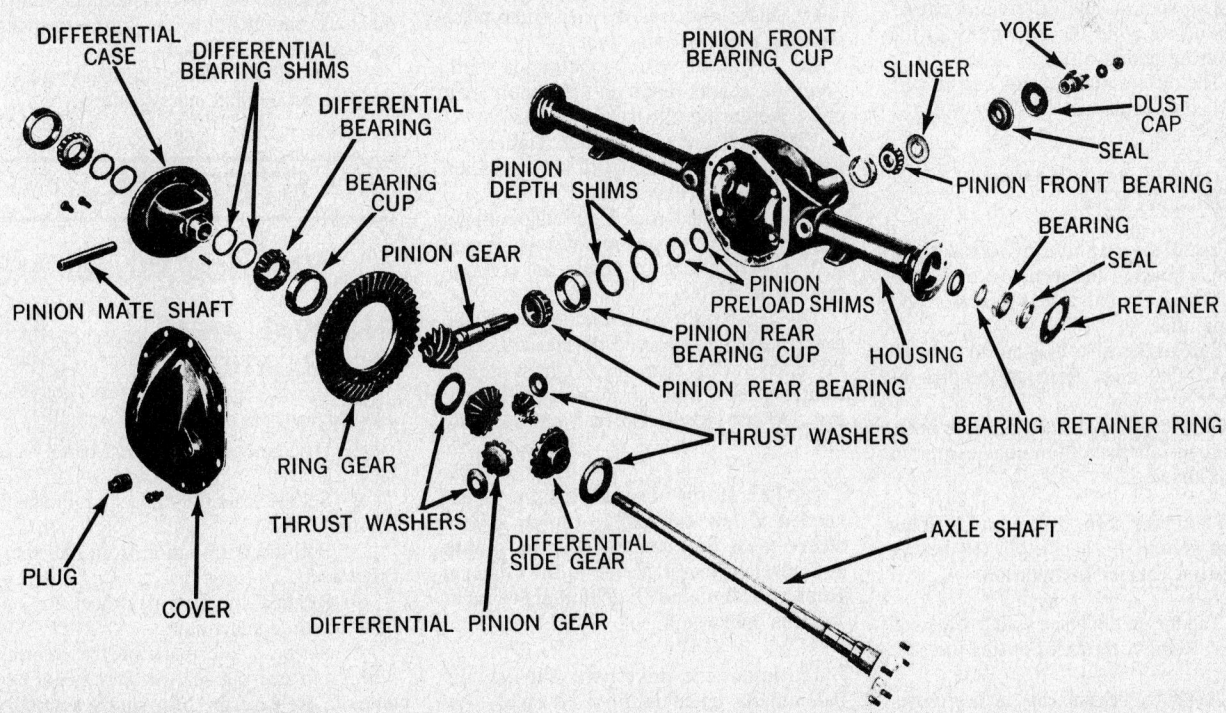

Semi-floating rear axle assembly

3. Clean the axle flange mating area on the hub and axle, removing all old gasket material.

4. Install a new flange gasket onto the hub studs.

5. Insert the axle shaft into the housing. It may be necessary to rotate the axle shaft to align the shaft splines with the differential gear splines and the flange attaching holes with the hub studs.

6. Install the split washers, lockwashers, and flange nuts. Tighten the nuts securely.

Differential Assembly

Removal

1. Raise the vehicle and support safely. Remove the wheels, drums and axle shafts.

2. Drain the axle housing lubricant and remove the axle housing cover.

3. Mark the differential bearing caps for alignment during the assembly.

4. Loosen the bearing cap bolts, but do not remove.

5. Install an axle housing spreader tool on the axle housing and secure with the hold-down clamps.

6. Mount a dial indicator on the axle housing to measure the amount of spread. Zero the indicator dial.

7. Spread the axle housing no more than 0.020 inch.

8. Remove the differential bearing caps and the dial indicator from the housing.

9. Using two pry bars, remove the differential carrier from the axle housing.

10. Remove the spreader tool from the housing as soon as the differential carrier is removed to avoid the possibility of the axle housing taking a set.

11. The differential housing can now be overhauled or replaced.

INSTALLATION

1. Install the axle housing spreader tool on the axle housing and secure with the hold down clamps. Install a dial indicator and center the dial.

2. Spread the axle housing to a maximum of 0.020 inch. Remove the dial indicator.

3. Lubricate the differential side bearings and install the differential carrier in the axle housing.

NOTE: Prior shim fitting and bearing preload should be accomplished before differential carrier installation.

4. Tap the unit in place with a soft faced hammer. Remove the axle housing spreader tool.

5. Install the bearing caps in their proper place and torque to 40 ft. lbs. on model 30

rear axle and to 80 ft. lbs. on models 44 and 60.

6. Install a dial indicator and recheck the ring gear backlash at two points. Correct as necessary.

7. Complete the assembly in the reverse of the removal, add lubricant and road test.

Pinion Oil Seal

Removal and Installation

SEMI-FLOATING AXLE WITH TAPERED SHAFT

1. Raise and support the vehicle and remove the rear wheels and brake drums.

2. Mark the driveshaft and yoke for reassembly and disconnect the driveshaft from the rear yoke.

3. With a socket on the pinion nut and an in. lb. torque wrench, rotate the drive pinion several revolutions. Check and record the torque required to turn the drive pinion.

4. Remove the pinion nut. Use a flange holding tool to hold the flange while removing the pinion nut. Discard the pinion nut.

5. Mark the yoke and the drive pinion shaft for reassembly reference.

6. Remove the rear yoke with a puller.

7. Inspect the seal surface of the yoke and replace it with a new one if the seal surface is pitted, grooved, or otherwise damaged.

8. Remove the pinion oil seal.

9. Before installing the new seal, coat the lip of the seal with rear axle lubricant.

10. Install the seal, driving it into place with the proper driving tool.

11. Install the yoke on the pinion shaft. Align the marks made on the pinion shaft and yoke during disassembly.

12. Install a new pinion nut. Tighten nut until end play is removed from the pinion bearing. Do not overtighten.

13. Check the torque required to turn the drive pinion. The pinion must be turned several revolutions to obtain an accurate reading.

14. Tighten the pinion nut to obtain the torque reading observed during disassembly (step 3) plus 5 in. lbs. Tighten the nut minutely each time, to avoid overtightening. Do not loosen and then retighten the nut.

NOTE: If the desired torque is exceeded a new collapsible pinion spacer sleeve must be installed and the pinion gear preload reset. Refer to the General Repair Section and Overhaul procedures for this operation.

15. Install the driveshaft, aligning the index marks made during disassembly. Install the rear brake drums and wheels.

SEMI-FLOATING AND FULL-FLOATING AXLES WITH FLANGE SHAFT

1. Raise and support the vehicle.

2. Mark the driveshaft and yoke for reference during assembly and disconnect the driveshaft at the yoke.

3. Remove the pinion shaft nut and washer.

4. Remove the yoke from the pinion shaft, using a puller.

5. Remove the pinion shaft oil seal.

6. Install the new seal with a suitable driver.

7. Install the pinion shaft washer and nut. Tighten the nut to 210 ft. lbs. on the semi-floating axles and 260 ft. lbs. on the full-floating axles.

8. Align the index marks on the driveshaft and yoke and install the driveshaft. Tighten the attaching bolts or nuts to 16 ft. lbs.

9. Remove the supports and lower the vehicle.

WHEEL BEARING ADJUSTMENT FULL FLOATING AXLE

1. Raise the vehicle so that the wheel can be rotated. Support the vehicle safely.

2. Remove the axle shaft.

3. Straighten the lip of the lock washer and remove the lock washer and lock nut.

4. Tighten the adjusting nut and rotate the wheel until binding exists. Back off the adjusting nut 1/16 turn until the wheel rotates freely without any lateral shake.

5. Replace the lock washer and tighten the lock nut, bending the lip of the lock washer over the lock nut.

6. Install the axle with a new gasket and tighten the axle nuts securely.

STEERING

Steering Wheel

REMOVAL AND INSTALLATION

1975

1. Disconnect the negative battery cable.

2. Set the front tires in a straight ahead position.

3. Pull the horn button from the steering wheel.

4. Remove the steering wheel nut and horn button contact cup.

5. Scribe a line mark on the steering wheel and steering shaft if there is not one already. Release the turn signal assembly from the steering post and install a puller.

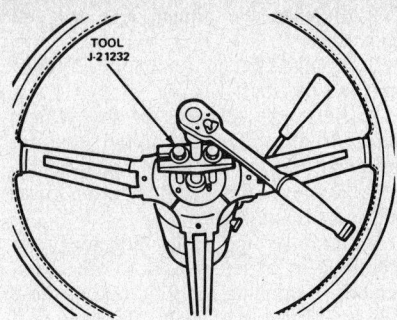

Steering wheel removal

6. Remove the steering wheel and spring.

7. To install, align the scribe marks on the steering shaft with the steering wheel and secure the steering wheel spring, steering wheel, and horn button contact cup with the steering wheel nut.

8. Install the horn button.

9. Connect the battery cable and test the horn.

From 1976

1. Disconnect the negative battery cable.

2. Place the front wheels in the straight-ahead position.

3. Remove the horn button from the steering wheel. Turn the botton until the locktabe on the button align with the notches in the contact cup and pull upward to remove it. With the sport wheel, just pull the button up.

4. Remove the steering wheel nut and washer.

5. If the Jeep is equipped with a sport style steering wheel, remove the horn button, nut and washer, bottom retaining ring, and horn contact ring.

6. Remove the plastic horn contact cup retainer and remove the cup and contact plate from the steering wheel.

7. Remove the horn contact pin and bushing from the steering wheel.

8. Paint or scribe alignment marks on the steering wheel and shaft for reference during assembly.

9. Remove the steering wheel using a puller.

10. Install the steering wheel in the reverse order, tightening the nut to 20 ft. lbs. for 1976-77, and 30 ft. lbs. for 1978-81.

Turn Signal Switch Replacement

1975

The turn signal switch is attached to the steering column; the whole unit is mounted externally. To remove the switch assembly, remove the attaching screws, unfasten the wires and remove the unit from the steering column.

The most frequent causes of failure in the directional signal system are loose connections and burned out bulbs. A flashing rate of approximately twice normal usually indicates a burned-out bulb in the circuit.

When trouble in the signal switch is suspected, it is advisable to make a few checks to definitely locate the trouble before going to the effort of removing the signal switch.

First check the fuse. There is an inline fuse located between the ignition switch and the turn signal flasher.

If the fuse checks out OK, next eliminate the flasher unit by substituting a known good flasher. If a new flasher does not cure the trouble, check the signal system wiring connections at the fuse and at the steering column connector.

1976-79

1. Disconnect the negative battery cable.

2. Remove the steering wheel.

3. Loosen the anti-theft cover retaining screws on 1976 models and lift the cover from the steering column. It is not necessary to completely remove these screws.

4. Depress the lockplate and pry the round wire snap-ring from the steering shaft groove. A lockplate compressor tool is available for compressing the lockplate.

5. Remove the lockplate, directional signal canceling cam, upper bearing preload spring, and thrust washer from the steering shaft.

6. Move the directional signal actuating lever to the right turn position and remove the lever.

7. Depress the hazard warning light switch and remove the button by turning it counterclockwise.

8. Remove the directional signal wiring harness connector block from its mounting bracket on the right-side of the lower column.

9. On vehicles equipped with an automatic transmission, use a stiff wire, such as a paper clip, to depress the lock tab which retains the shift quadrant light wire in the connector block.

10. Remove the directional signal switch retaining screws and pull the switch and wiring harness from the steering column.

11. Guide the wiring harness of the new switch into position and carefully align the switch assembly. Make sure that the actuating lever pivot is correctly aligned and seated in the upper housing pivot boss prior to installing the retaining screws.

12. Install the directional signal lever and actuate the directional signal switch to assure correct operation.

13. Place the thrust washer, spring, and directional signal canceling cam on the upper end of the steering shaft.

14. Align the lockplate splines with the steering shaft splines and place the lockplate in position with the directional signal canceling cam shaft protruding through the dogleg opening in the lockplate.

15. Install the snap-ring.

16. Install the anti-theft cover.

17. Install the steering wheel and connect the negative battery cable.

18. Check the operation of the turn signal switch.

FROM 1980

1. Disconnect the battery ground.

2. Cover the painted areas of the column.

3. Remove the column-to-dash bezel.

4. Loosen the toe plate screws.

5. With tilt columns, place the column in the non-tilt position.

6. Remove the steering wheel.

7. Remove the lockplate cover.

8. Compress the lockplate and unseat the steering shaft snap-ring as follows:

   a. Check the steering shaft nut threads. Metric threads have an identifying groove in the steering wheel splines. SAE threads do not.

   b. With SAE threads use a compressor tool such as tool J-23653 to compress the lockplate and remove the snap-ring.

   c. If the shaft has metric threads, replace the forcing screw in the compressor with metric forcing screw J-23653-4 before using.

9. Remove the compressor and snap-ring.

10. Remove the lockplate, canceling cam and upper bearing preload spring.

11. Place the turn signal lever in the right turn position and remove the lever.

12. Remove the hazard warning knob. Press the knob inward and turn counterclockwise to remove it.

13. Remove the wiring harness protectors.

14. Disconnect the wiring harness connectors.

15. Remove the turn signal switch attaching screws and lift out the switch.

Ignition Switch

REPLACEMENT

1975

1. Disconnect the battery ground cable.

2. Reach behind the panel and press the switch in against the spring. Turn the bezel counterclockwise to release.

3. Lower the switch and detach the wiring.

4. Reverse the procedure for installation.

From 1976

The ignition switch is on top of the lower part of the steering column, inside the vehicle.

1. Put the key in the lock and turn to the Off-unlocked position.

2. Disconnect the battery ground cable.

3. Detach the wire connectors at the switch.

4. Remove the switch screws.

5. Disconnect the actuating rod from the switch and remove the switch.

6. Move the switch slider all the way down the column. Move it back toward the steering wheel two clicks to the center Off-unlocked position.

7. Engage the column actuating rod in the switch slider and fasten the switch down.

8. Connect the wire connectors, then the battery ground cable.

Ignition Lock Cylinder

REPLACEMENT

1975

1. Remove the ignition switch.

2. Put the key in the lock and turn it to the On position.

3. Insert a heavy paper clip wire or something similar through the release hole in the side of the switch. Push in the retaining ring until the lock cylinder can be pulled out.

4. To install the new lock cylinder, line up the tang on the cylinder with the slot in the case and push the cylinder in.

5. Replace the switch.

From 1976

1. Disconnect the battery ground cable.

2. Remove the turn signal switch as described earlier in this chapter. You don't have to remove the switch completely, just set it aside.

3. Insert the key. With manual transmission, put it in the On position: with automatic, put it in Off-Lock.

4. Working through the slot next to the turn signal switch mounting boss, use a thin screwdriver to release the lock cylinder.

5. To install, insert the key in the new lock cylinder. Hold the sleeve and turn the key clockwise until it stops. Align the cylinder retaining tab with the housing slot and insert the cylinder. Push the cylinder in, rotate to engage, then push in until the retaining tab engages the housing groove.

6. The rest of the procedure is the reverse of removal.

Power Steering Pump

REMOVAL AND INSTALLATION

If the power steering pump has to be removed to service another component, it is not necessary to remove the hoses from the pump. Just disconnect the mounting fixtures and lift the pump away from the engine and lay it out of the way. The only time the power steering hoses have to be removed from the pump is when the pump has to be removed from the vehicle for service or replacement.

1. Remove the pump drive belt tension adjusting bolt. Disconnect the belt from the pump.

2. Disconnect the return and pressure hoses from the pump. Cover the hose connector and union on the pump and open ends of the hoses to avoid the entrance of dirt.

3. On the 304 v8, remove the front bracket from the engine.

4. Remove the two nuts which secure the rear of the pump to the bracket, and the two bolts which secure the front of the pump to the bracket and remove the pump.

5. To install, position the pump in the bracket and install the rear attaching screws. On the 304 V8, install the front bracket.

6. Connect the hydraulic hoses. Adjust the drive belt tension.

7. Fill the pump reservoir to the correct level.

8. Start the engine and wait for at least three minutes before turning the steering wheel. Check the level frequently during this time.

9. Slowly turn the steering wheel through its entire range a few times with the engine running. Recheck the level and inspect for possible leaks.

NOTE: If air becomes trapped in the fluid, the pump may become noisy until all of the air is out. This may take some time since trapped air does not bleed out rapidly.

Manual Steering Gear

REMOVAL AND INSTALLATION

1975

1. Disconnect the steering gear from the lower steering shaft by removing the bolt and nut attaching the coupling to the worm shaft.

2. Disconnect the steering arm from the connecting rod.

3. Remove the upper steering gear-to-frame bracket bolt.

4. Remove the two lower steering gear-to-frame bracket bolts and remove the gear.

5. Installation is the reverse of removal. Torque the pitman arm-to-shaft nut to 160–210 ft. lbs.; the steering bracket-to-frame 3/8 in. bolt to 35–45 ft. lbs.; the steering bracket-to-frame 7/16 in. bolt to 60–70 ft. lbs.; the steering gear-to-bracket bolts to 60–80 ft. lbs.

From 1976

1. Remove the intermediate shaft-to-wormshaft coupling clamp bolt and disconnect the intermediate shaft.

2. Remove the pitman arm nut and lockwasher.

3. Using a puller, remove the Pitman arm from the shaft.

4. Raise the left side of the vehicle slightly to relieve tension on the left front spring and rest the frame on a jackstand.

5. Remove the steering gear lower bracket-to-frame bolts.

6. Remove the bolts attaching the steering gear upper bracket to the cross-member. Beginning in 1979, one of these bolts is a Torx® head bolt. This bolt, and some others may be removed with the aid of a 9 inch extension. Remove the gear.

NOTE: Loctite 271® or similar material must be applied to all attaching bolt threads prior to installation.

7. Position the tie plate upper and lower mounting brackets on the gear and install the bolts. Torque the bracket-to-gear bolts to 70 ft. lbs. and the bracket-to-tie plate bolt to 55 ft. lbs.

8. Align and engage the intermediate shaft coupling with the steering gear worm-shaft splines.

9. Position the steering gear on the frame and install the mounting bolts. Torque the bolts to 55 ft. lbs. Install the Pitman arm and torque the nut to 185 ft. lbs.

NOTE: The steering gear may produce a slight roughness, this can be eliminated by turning the steering wheel full left and right 10–15 times.

Manual Steering Gear Adjustments

WORM BEARING PRELOAD ADJUSTMENT

1975

1. Loosen the steering gear end cover.

2. Add to or subtract from the number of shims under the cover to obtain a rolling torque of 2–5 in. lbs.

3. Tighten the cover bolts alternately and evenly to 18–22 ft. lbs.

STEERING GEAR CLEARANCE ADJUSTMENT

1. Loosen the locknut and turn the adjusting screw on the side cover, counterclockwise until the worm gear shaft turns freely through its entire range of travel.

2. Count the number of turns necessary to rotate the worm gear shaft through its travel.

3. Turn the shaft to center point.

4. Rotate the shaft back and forth over center, and tighten the adjusting screw until the shaft binds slightly at the center point.

5. Adjust the screw to obtain a rolling torque of 7–12 in. lbs. through the center.

6. Hold the adjusting screw and tighten the locknut to 16–20 ft. lbs.

WORM BEARING PRELOAD ADJUSTMENT

1. Tighten the worm bearing adjuster until it bottoms, then back it off ¼ turn.
2. Install a torque wrench and socket J-7754 or its equivalent on the splined end of the wormshaft.
3. Rotate the wormshaft clockwise until it hits the stop, then back it off ½ turn.
4. Tighten the wormshaft bearing adjuster until the torque required to rotate the shaft is 5–8 in. lbs.

NOTE: The adjustment must be made with the wormshaft no more than ½ turn from the stop.

5. Tighten the worm bearing adjuster locknut to 23 ft. lbs. Check rotating torque. Check and record the worm bearing preload reading.

PITMAN SHAFT OVERCENTER ADJUSTMENT

1. Rotate the wormshaft from stop-to-stop and count the number of turns.
2. Rotate the wormshaft back from the stop, ½ the total number of turns.
3. Install a torque wrench and socket J-7754 on the splined end of the wormshaft.
4. Tighten the pitman shaft adjuster screw, while rotating the shaft back and forth over center, until the torque equals the worm bearing preload setting of 5–8 in. lbs. previously recorded.
5. Rotate the shaft over center and continue tightening the adjuster until the drag torque is increased by an additional 4–10 in. lbs., but do not exceed 16 in. lbs. combined total.
6. Hold the adjuster screw and tighten the locknut to 23 ft. lbs. Do not allow the adjuster to turn, or the adjustment will have to be made over again!

Power Steering Gear

REMOVAL AND INSTALLATION

1975

1. Disconnect the hoses at the gear and raise them above the pump to prevent fluid loss.
2. Remove the pinch bolt from the lower flange.
3. Remove the Pitman arm nut and lockwasher, and remove the Pitman arm with a puller.
4. Unbolt and remove the pump.
5. Installation is the reverse of removal. Torque the Pitman arm nut to 160–210 ft. lbs. and the gear-to-frame bolts to 55 ft. lbs.

From 1976

1. Disconnect the hoses at the gear and raise them above the pump to prevent fluid loss.
2. Remove the clamp bolt and nut attaching the intermediate shaft coupling to the steering gear stub shaft and disconnect the intermediate shaft.
3. Mark the Pitman shaft and arm for alignment. Remove the Pitman nut and lockwasher and remove the Pitman arm with a puller.
4. Raise the left side of the vehicle slightly to relieve tension from the spring. Support with a jack stand under the frame.
5. Remove the three lower steering gear mounting bracket-to-frame bolts.
6. Remove the two steering gear-to-crossmember upper bolts. Remove the gear and brackets as an assembly.
7. Remove the brackets from the gear.

NOTE: Prior to installation, all bolts must be coated with Loctite 271® or its equivalent.

8. Position the mounting brackets on the gear and torque the bolts to 70 ft. lbs.
9. Align and connect the intermediate shaft coupling to the steering gear stub shaft.
10. Position the steering gear on the frame and crossmember. Install and tighten the bolts to 55 ft. lbs.
11. Lower the vehicle.
12. Install the intermediate shaft coupling-to-steering gear stub shaft clamp bolt and nut. Tighten the nut to 45 ft. lbs.
13. Align and install the Pitman arm, nut and lockwasher. Torque the nut to 185 ft. lbs. Stake the nut in two places.
14. Connect the hoses. Torque the hose connections to 25 ft. lbs.

Power Steering Gear Adjustments

NOTE: The gear must be adjusted off the vehicle. All adjustments must be made in the sequence described below. Worm bearing preload is always adjusted first!

WORM BEARING PRELOAD ADJUSTMENT

1. Mount the gear assembly in a vise.
2. Torque the adjuster plug to 20 ft. lbs.
3. Mark the gear housing in line with one of the adjuster plug holes.
4. Measure counterclockwise ³⁄₁₆–¼ in from the first mark on models through 1979 and ½ inch from the first mark on 1980–81 models, and make another mark.
5. Turn the adjuster plug counterclockwise to align the hole with the second mark.
6. Hold the adjuster plug and torque the locknut to 85 ft. lbs. Do not allow the adjuster to turn.
7. Turn the stubshaft clockwise to its stop, then back ¼ turn.
8. Using a torque wrench of no more than 50 in. lb. capacity and a 12 point deep socket, check the rotating torque at the splined end of the stub shaft at or near a vertical position. Torque should be 4–10 in. lbs.
9. If the torque cannot be adjusted within these limits, the gear will have to be rebuilt.

PITMAN SHAFT OVERCENTER ADJUSTMENT

1. Loosen the adjuster screw locknut.
2. Turn the adjuster screw counterclockwise until the screw is fully extended. Turn the screw back in one full turn.
3. Count the number of turns to rotate the stubshaft from stop-to-stop.
4. Turn the shaft back ½ the number of turns. At this point the flat surface of the stubshaft should be upward and the master spline on the Pitman shaft should be aligned with the adjuster screw.
5. Install a 50 in. lbs. torque wrench

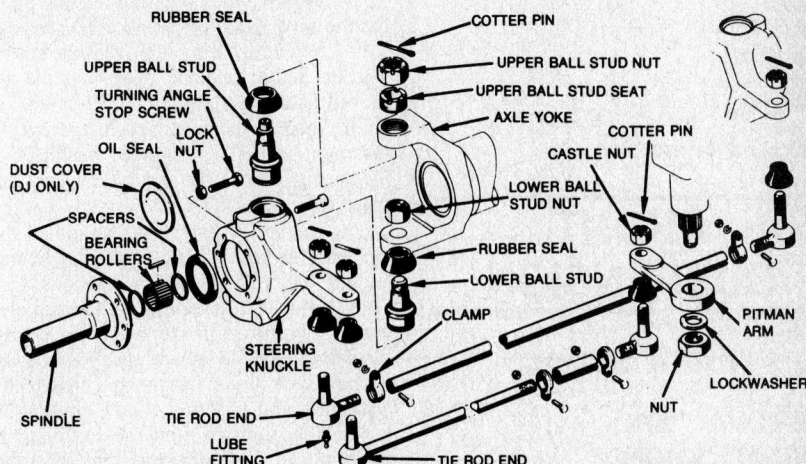

RUBBER SEAL — COTTER PIN — UPPER BALL STUD — UPPER BALL STUD NUT — TURNING ANGLE STOP SCREW — UPPER BALL STUD SEAT — OIL SEAL — LOCK NUT — AXLE YOKE — DUST COVER (DJ ONLY) — COTTER PIN — CASTLE NUT — SPACERS — LOWER BALL STUD NUT — BEARING ROLLERS — RUBBER SEAL — LOWER BALL STUD — STEERING KNUCKLE — CLAMP — PITMAN ARM — SPINDLE — TIE ROD END — LOCKWASHER — LUBE FITTING — TIE ROD END — NUT

Typical steering linkage

and deep 12 point socket on the splined end of the stub shaft. Place the torque wrench in a vertical position.

6. Rotate the torque wrench 45° to each side and record the highest torque at or near center. Record this reading.

7. Adjust the torque by turning the adjuster screw clockwise. Adjustment is: the recorded reading plus 4–8 in. lbs. for new gears, but not exceeding 14 in. lbs. total; the previously recorded reading plus 4–5 in. lbs. for used gears, but not exceeding 14 in. lbs. combined total.

8. Tighten the adjuster screw locknut to 20 ft. lbs. while holding the adjuster screw.

9. Install the gear.

Tie Rod End

REMOVAL AND INSTALLATION

1. Remove the cotter pins and retaining nuts at both ends of the tie rod and from the end of the connecting rod where it attaches to the tie rod.

2. Remove the nut attaching the steering damper push rod to the tie rod bracket and move the damper aside.

3. Remove the tie rod ends from the steering arms and connecting rod with a puller.

4. Count the number of threads showing on the tie rod before removing the ends, as a guide to installation.

5. Loosen the adjusting tube clamp bolts and unthread the ends.

6. Installation is the reverse of removal. Torque the connecting rod-to-tie rod nut to 70 ft. lbs.

7. Adjust toe-in, if necessary.

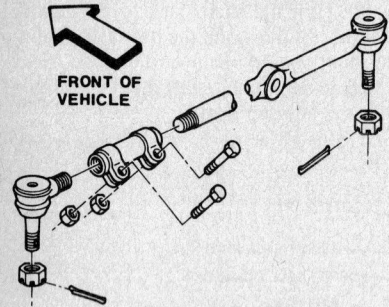

FRONT OF VEHICLE

Typical tie-rod assembly

FRONT SUSPENSION

Front Spring

REMOVAL AND INSTALLATION

1. Raise the vehicle with a jack under

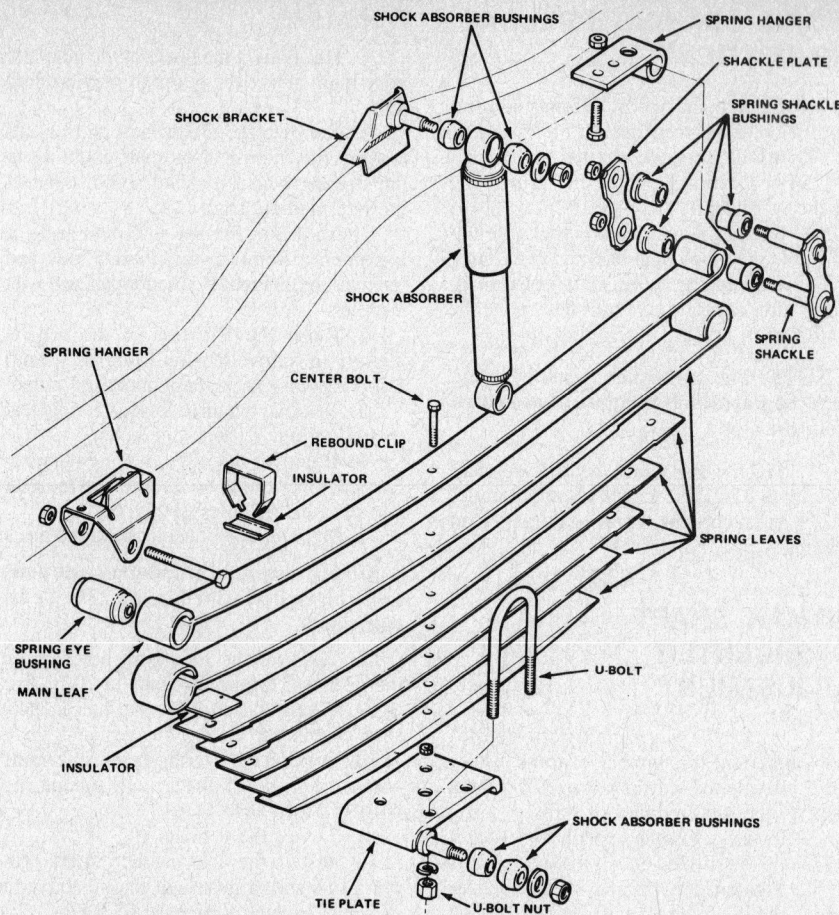

Typical front spring and shock absorber

the axle. Place a jackstand under the frame side rail. Then lower the axle jack so the load is relieved from the spring and the wheels just touch the floor.

2. Disconnect the shock absorber from the spring clip plate. Disconnect the front stabilizer bar, if any.

3. Remove the nuts which secure the spring clips (U-bolts). Remove the spring plate and spring clips. Free the spring from the axle by raising the axle.

4. Remove the pivot bolt nut and drive out the pivot bolt. Disconnect the shackle.

5. With the spring removed, the spring shackle and/or shackle plate may be removed from the spring.

6. Inspect the bushings in the eye of the main spring leaf and the bushings of the spring shackle for excessive wear. Replace if necessary.

7. The spring can be disassembled for replacing an individual spring leaf by removing the clips and the center bolts.

8. To install the spring on the vehicle, with the bushings in place and the spring shackle attached to the springs, position the spring in the pivot hanger and install the pivot bolt and lock nut. Only tighten the lock nut enough to hold the bushings in position until the vehicle is lowered from the jack.

9. Position the spring and install the shackle, shackle bolts, shackle plate if applicable, lockwasher, and nut. Only finger tighten the nuts at this time.

10. Move the axle into position on the spring by lowering the axle jack. Place the spring center bolt in the axle saddle hole. Install the spring clips, spring plate, lockwashers and nuts. Torque the 7/16 in. nuts to 36–42 ft. lbs and the 1/2 in. nuts to 45–65 ft. lbs. and the 9/16 nuts to 100 ft. lbs.

NOTE: Be sure that the center bolt is properly centered in the axle saddle.

11. Connect the shock absorber.

12. Remove the axle and allow the weight of the vehicle to seat the bushings in their operating positions. Then torque the 7/16 in. spring pivot bolt nuts and spring shackle nuts.

TOE-IN ADJUSTMENT

First raise the front of the vehicle to free the front wheels. Turn the wheels to the straight ahead position. Use a steadyrest to scribe a pencil line in the center of each tire tread as the wheel is turned by hand. A good way to do this is to first coat a strip with chalk around the circumference of the tread at the center to form a base for a fine pencil line.

Measure the distance between the scribed

lines at the front and rear of the wheels using care that both measurements are made at an equal distance from the floor. The distance between the lines should be greater at the rear than at the front by $3/64$ in. to $3/32$ in. To adjust, loosen the clamp bolts and turn the tie rod with a small pipe wrench. The tie rod is threaded with right and left hand threads to provide equal adjustment at both wheels. Do not overlook retightening the clamp bolts.

It is common practice to measure between the wheel rims. This is satisfactory providing the wheels run true. By scribing a line on the tire tread, measurement is taken between the road contact points reducing error caused by wheel run-out.

Shock Absorbers

REMOVAL AND INSTALLATION

1. Remove the locknuts and washers.
2. Pull the shock absorber eyes and rubber bushings from the mounting pins.
3. Install the shocks in reverse order of the removal procedure. Torque the upper bolt to 35 ft. lbs. and the lower bolt to 45 ft. lbs.

NOTE: Squeaking usually occurs when movement takes place between the rubber bushings and the metal parts. The squeaking may be eliminated by placing the bushings under great pressure. This is accomplished either by adding additional washers where the cotter pins are used or by tightening the locknuts. Do not use mineral lubricant to stop the squeaking as it will deteriorate the rubber.

REAR SUSPENSION

Spring

REMOVAL AND INSTALLATION

Mounted Below the Axle

1. Raise the vehicle and support the axle.
2. Disconnect the shock absorber and stabilizer bar, if so equipped.
3. Remove the U-bolts and tie plates.
4. Disconnect the front and rear ends of the spring and remove the spring.
5. The spring can be disassembled by removing the spring rebound clips and the center bolt.
6. Mount the spring in the vehicle, but do not tighten the pivot bolts.

7. Align the spring center bolt and install the tie plate and U-bolts.
8. Connect the shock absorber and stabilizer bar, if so equipped.
9. Remove the axle support and lower the vehicle.
10. Tighten the pivot bolts with the weight of the vehicle on the springs to 45 ft. lbs. on CJ models and 75 ft. lbs. on all other models. Tighten $9/16$ in. U-bolt nuts to 100 ft. lbs., $1/2$ in. nuts to 55 ft. lbs. and $7/16$ in. U-bolt nuts to 40 ft. lbs.

NOTE: If left-side spring is to be serviced, remove fuel tank skid plate.

Mounted Above the Axle

1. Raise the vehicle and support the frame ahead of the axle.
2. Remove the U-bolts.
3. Unclip the axle vent hose from the frame.
4. Disconnect the shock absorber.
5. Remove the spring pivot bolts.
6. Lower the axle enough so the spring can be turned over and remove the spring. The spring can be disassembled by removing the rebound clips and center bolt.
7. Mount the spring in the vehicle and install the pivot bolts and nuts.
8. Raise the axle, align the spring center bolt, and install the U-bolts.

9. Connect the shock absorber, vent hose, and remove the supports and lower the vehicle.
10. Tighten the spring pivot bolts with the weight of the vehicle on the springs. Tighten the pivot bolts to 75 ft. lbs. Tighten $9/16$ in. U-bolt nuts to 100 ft. lbs., $1/2$ in. nuts to 55 ft. lbs., and $7/16$ in. U-bolt nuts to 40 ft. lbs.

Spring Bushing

REMOVAL AND INSTALLATION

Small Bushing

1. Install an 8 in. length of threaded rod halfway through the bushing and place a 1 $1/8$ in. socket with the open end toward the bushing, one $1/2$ in. flat washer, and one $3/8$ in. hex nut on one end of the rod.
2. Place a 2 in. section of 1 $5/8$ in. or 1 $3/8$ in. ID pipe, one $3/4$ in. flat washer, or $1/2$ in. flat washer and on $3/8$ in. hex nut on the opposite end of the threaded rod.
3. Tighten both of the $3/8$ in. nuts finger-tight and align all of the components. Make sure the socket is positioned in the eye of the spring and aligns with the bushing. The pipe section must butt against the

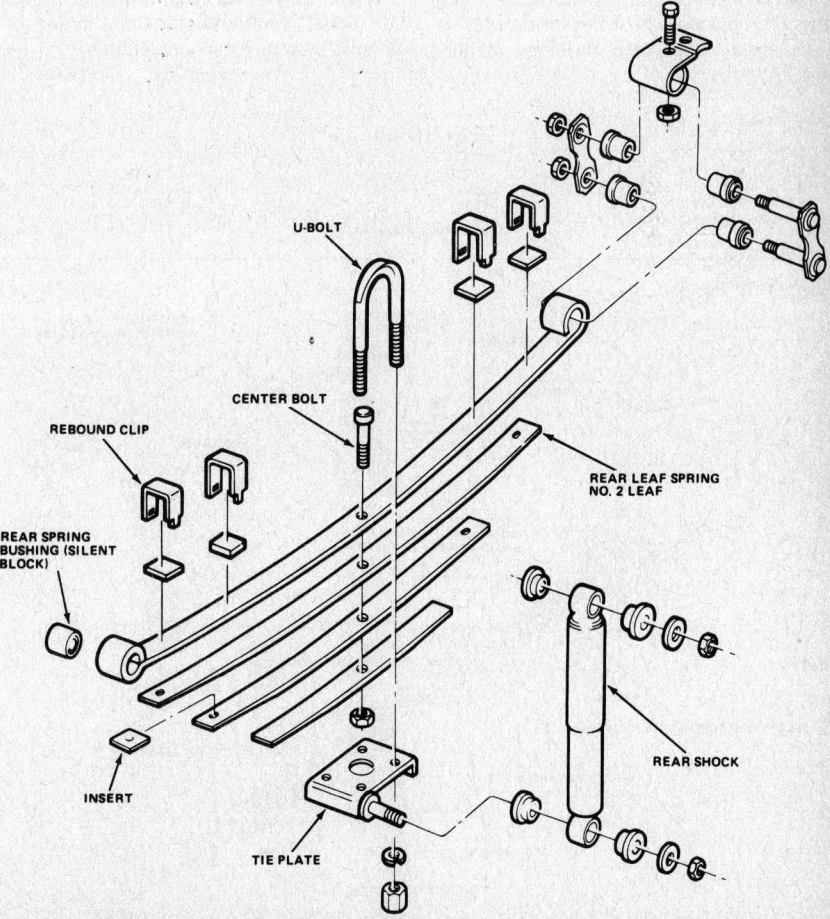

U-BOLT

CENTER BOLT

REBOUND CLIP

REAR SPRING BUSHING (SILENT BLOCK)

REAR LEAF SPRING NO. 2 LEAF

REAR SHOCK

INSERT

TIE PLATE

Typical rear spring and shock absorber assembly

spring eye so the bushing can pass through it. The socket will act as a press and will press the bushing out of the spring eye.

4. Tighten the nut at the socket end of the rod until the bushing is pressed out of the spring eye. Remove the tools and the bushing.

5. Install the replacement bushing on the threaded rod and assemble the bushing tools as outlined in steps 1 and 2, and press the bushing into the spring eye. Make sure the bushing is centered in the spring eye.

Large Bushing

1. Place ½ × 11 in. length of threaded rod half-way through the bushing and install 1 ¹⁄₁₆ in. deep socket with the open end toward the bushing, one ½ in. flat washer, and one ½ in. nut on the end of the rod.

2. Install a 3 in. length of 1 ½ in. ID pipe, one ½ in. flat washer and one ½ in. nut on the opposite end of the threaded rod.

3. Tighten both nuts finger tight and align all of the components. Make sure the socket is positioned in the eye of the spring and aligns with the bushing. The pipe section must butt against the spring eye so the bushing can pass through it. The socket will act as a press ram and press the bushing out of the spring eye.

4. Tighten the nut at the socket and press the bushing out of the spring eye.

5. Install the new bushing on the threaded rod and assemble the tushing tools as outlined in steps 1 and 2. Press the bushing into the spring eye until it is centered in the eye.

Shock Absorber

REMOVAL AND INSTALLATION

1. Raise the vehicle for working clearance and support safely.

2. Place a jack under the axle assembly and raise to relieve the springs of axle weight and to place the shock absorber in its mid stroke.

3. Remove the retaining nuts or bolts and remove the shock absorber from the vehicle.

4. Install the new shock absorber and tighten the attaching nuts or bolts.

5. Lower the vehicle to the ground.

BRAKES

Refer to the Brakes General Repair Section for detail troubleshooting and brake hydraulic system repair procedures.

Master Cylinder

REMOVAL AND INSTALLATION

1. Disconnect and plug the brake lines at the master cylinder.

2. Disconnect the wires from the stoplight switch.

3. Disconnect the master cylinder push rod at the brake pedal on vehicles with manual brakes.

4. Remove all attaching bolts and nuts and lift the master cylinder from the vehicle.

5. Install the master cylinder in the reverse order of removal and bleed the hydraulic system.

Power Unit

REMOVAL AND INSTALLATION

1975–1977

1. Clean the master cylinder and booster unit.

2. Remove the cotter and clevis pins securing the booster pushrod to the pedal linkage.

3. Disconnect the vacuum hose from the booster check valve.

4. Disconnect the fluid lines from the master cylinder. Plug the ends and catch any escaping fluid. Do not reuse brake fluid.

5. Disconnect the stoplight wires from the switch.

6. Remove the attaching nuts, booster unit assembly, and block spacers.

7. Remove the attaching nuts and separate the master cylinder from the booster.

To install the booster unit, reverse the removal procedure and bleed the brakes.

--- CAUTION ---
Do not pressure-bleed power-assisted brake systems.

From 1978

1. Disconnect brake pedal pushrod rod at brake pedal.

2. Disconnect vacuum hose from booster check valve.

3. Remove attaching nuts and separate master cylinder from brake booster. Do not disconnect brake lines at master cylinder.

4. On CJ models, remove bolts holding power unit bellcrank to dash panel and remove power unit and bellcrank as one assembly. Remove the bellcrank from the original power unit and lubricate the pivot pins with chassis lubricant before installing it on the replacement unit.

5. On all other models, remove bolts attaching power unit to dash panel and remove the unit.

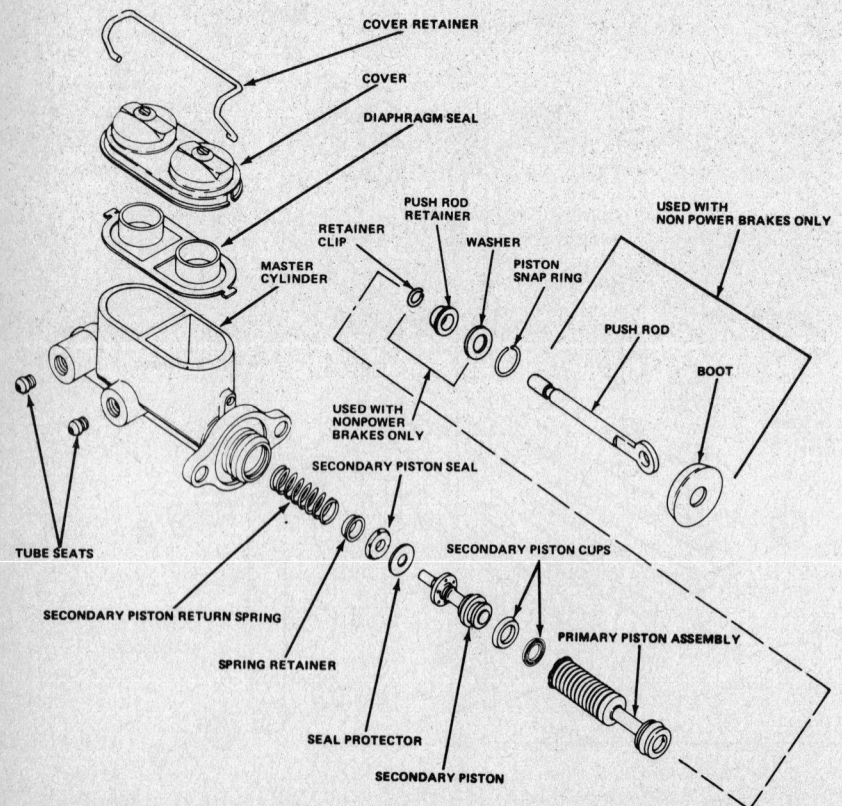

Exploded view of a typical master cylinder

COVER RETAINER
COVER
DIAPHRAGM SEAL
PUSH ROD RETAINER
RETAINER CLIP
WASHER
USED WITH NON POWER BRAKES ONLY
MASTER CYLINDER
PISTON SNAP RING
PUSH ROD
BOOT
USED WITH NONPOWER BRAKES ONLY
SECONDARY PISTON SEAL
TUBE SEATS
SECONDARY PISTON CUPS
SECONDARY PISTON RETURN SPRING
SPRING RETAINER
PRIMARY PISTON ASSEMBLY
SEAL PROTECTOR
SECONDARY PISTON

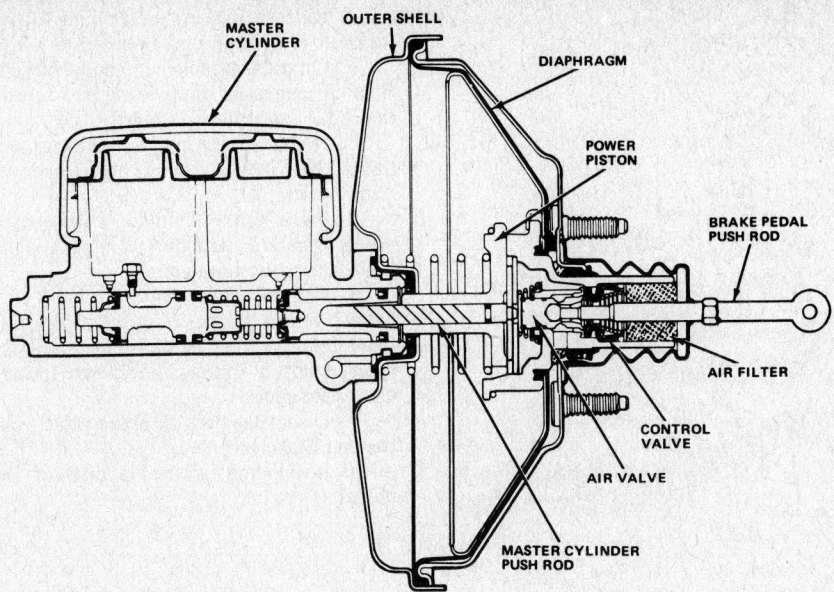

Power brake booster—typical

6. Installation is the reverse of removal.

NOTE: When replacing the power brake unit, use the push rod that is supplied with the new unit, as it has been correctly gauged and preset to the new unit.

Wheel Cylinder

Removal and Installation

1. Raise and support the vehicle and remove the brake drums and brake shoes.

2. Disconnect the brake line. Do not bend the line away from the wheel cylinder. When the cylinder is removed from the support plate, the line will separate from the wheel cylinder easily.

3. Remove the wheel cylinder mounting bolts and remove the wheel cylinder from the brake backing plate.

4. Clean the wheel cylinder mounting surface on the brake support plate. Clean the brake line fitting and threads.

5. Start the brake line fitting into the wheel cylinder and attach the wheel cylinder to the support plate and tighten the brake line fitting. Tighten the wheel cylinder mounting bolts to 18 ft. lbs.

Disc Brakes

Floating caliper, single piston type disc brakes are used on the front wheels of the Jeep vehicles, and consists of three assemblies, the caliper assembly, the hub and rotor assembly, and the support and shield assembly.

The caliper is attached to the support and shield assembly and upon hydraulic pressure application, the piston within the cal-

iper is forced outward and pushes the inboard shoe against the rotor face. The reaction force moves the caliper body and the outboard shoe against the opposite rotor face, causing a pinching action of the two brake shoes against the rotor and bringing the vehicle to a stop. Brake adjustment is not needed because wear is automatically compensated for by the sliding movement of the caliper and the increased piston extension.

Brake Pads

Replace the brake shoes when the linings are worn within $\frac{1}{32}$ inch of the shoe or rivets.

REMOVAL

1. Remove the wheel and tire assembly.

2. Remove approximately $\frac{2}{3}$ of the brake fluid from the front section of the master cylinder.

3. Using a C-clamp, bottom the piston in its bore by placing the solid end of the clamp on the back of the caliper and the screw end contacting the metal part of the out board shoe, and tighten the clamp screw.

NOTE: This procedure backs the brake shoes off the rotor surface, easing the lining replacement.

4. Remove both allen head mounting screws from the caliper to support, and lift the caliper off the rotor.

NOTE: Hang the caliper by a wire hook or tie it to the frame, to avoid allowing the brake hose to support the weight of the caliper assembly.

5. Remove both disc brake shoes from the caliper, and note the position of the support spring on the inboard shoe for later installation, and remove the spring from the shoe.

6. Remove the sleeves and rubber bushings from the ears of the calipers.

CLEANING AND INSPECTION

Clean the sliding surfaces of the caliper and clean any dirt from the mounting bolts, clips or keys. Inspect the boot on the piston for signs of cracks, cuts of any other damage. Check to see if there is any signs of fluid leakage around the seal on the piston. This will show up in the boot.

If there is any indication of a fluid leak,

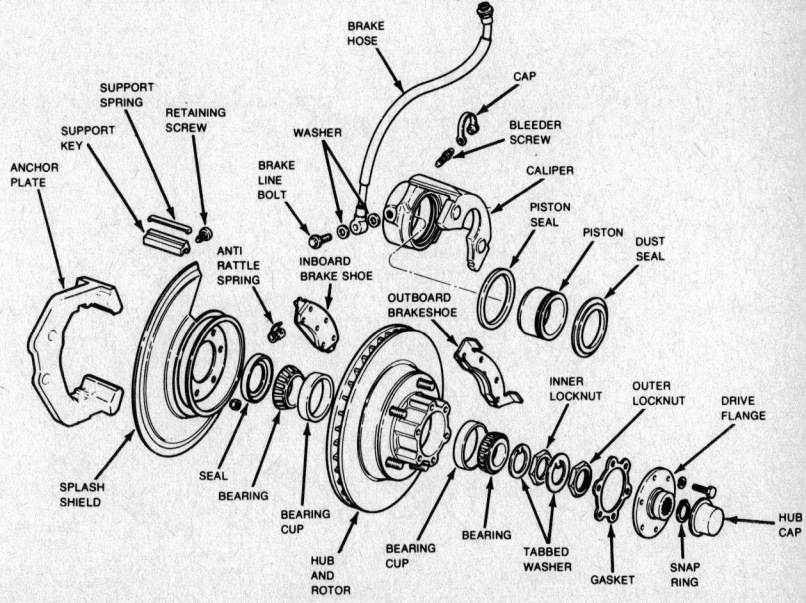

Typical disc brake details—models without locking hubs

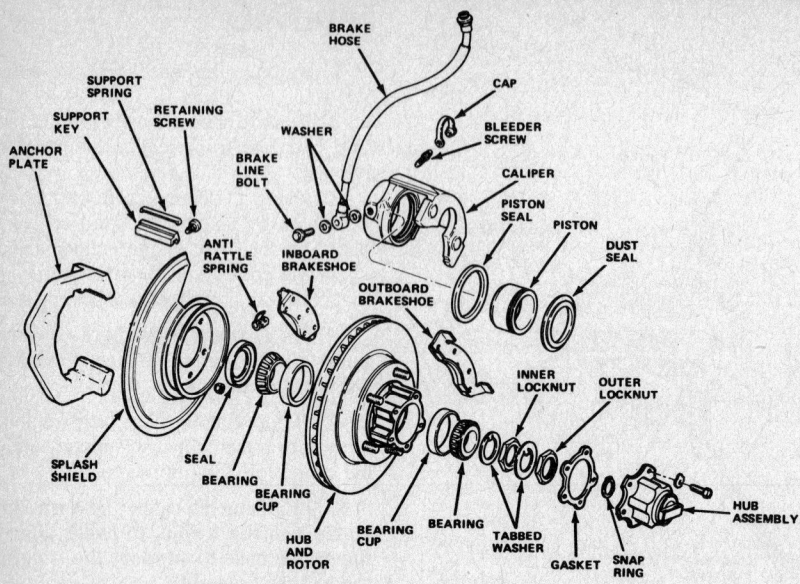

Typical disc brake details—models with locking hubs

the entire caliper will have to be over-hauled.

NOTE: Refer to the Brake General Repair Section for caliper overhaul procedures.

INSTALLATION

1. Clean all mounting holes, bolts, and bushing grooves. Lubricate and install new bushings and sleeves.

NOTE: Sleeves should be installed in the inboard mounting ears of the caliper, and positioned so the sleeve end facing the shoe and lining, is flush with the mounting ear.

2. Install the support spring on the inboard shoe. Place the single tang end of the spring over the notch in the shoe.

3. Install the two brake shoes into the caliper and assure that both shoes are fully seated by having the ears of the shoes resting on the ears of the caliper.

4. Position the caliper over the rotor and install the mounting bolts. Assure that the bolts pass through the holes of the outboard shoes and caliper ears, and that the retaining ears of the inboard shoes are over the bolts. Torque the bolts to 35 ft. lbs.

5. Fill the master cylinder and pump the brake pedal to seat the shoes to the rotor.

6. Bend the upper ears of the outboard shoe until the radial clearance between the shoe and the caliper is eliminated.

Drum Brakes
REMOVAL AND INSTALLATION

1. Remove wheel and brake drum.

2. Release parking brake and loosen locknuts at parking brake equalizer.

3. On truck models with model 60 full-floating rear axle, remove the two screws that hold rear drums on hubs.

4. Remove lever tang from hole in secondary shoe by grasping the adjusting lever with a pliers.

5. Place brake cylinder clamp over wheel cylinder to hold pistons in place while brake shoes are removed.

6. Remove brake return springs, secondary return spring, adjuster cable, primary return spring, cable guide, adjuster lever, adjuster springs, holddown springs and brake shoes.

7. Disengage parking brake cable from parking brake lever.

8. Installation is the reverse of removal.

Stop Light Switch

Two types of switches are used on the Jeep vehicles. One type is attached to the brake pedal rod end of the push rod, and cannot be adjusted. The second type is mounted on a flange attached to the brake pedal support bracket and is held in the otf position by the brake pedal being in its released position. Upon depressing the brake pedal, the switch plunger is allowed to move outward and contact is made within the switch to allow current to pass the operate the stop lights.

SWITCH ADJUSTMENT
1975–76

1. Release the brake pedal, unhook the retaining fingers of the wire connector from the switch and remove the wire harness.

2. Adjust the switch by turning it in or out of the mounting bracket. The switch should operate after $3/8$ to $5/8$ inch of brake pedal travel.

3. Connect the wire harness and re-check the switch operation.

From 1977

NOTE: CJ models with air conditioning, remove screws attaching the evaporator housing to the instrument panel and move housing away from the panel.

1. Hold the brake pedal in the applied position.

2. Push the stop light switch through the mounting bracket until it stops against the brake pedal bracket. Release the pedal to set the switch in the proper position.

3. Check the position of the switch. The switch plunger should be in the ON position and activate the brake lights after a brake pedal travel of $3/8$ to $5/8$ inch.

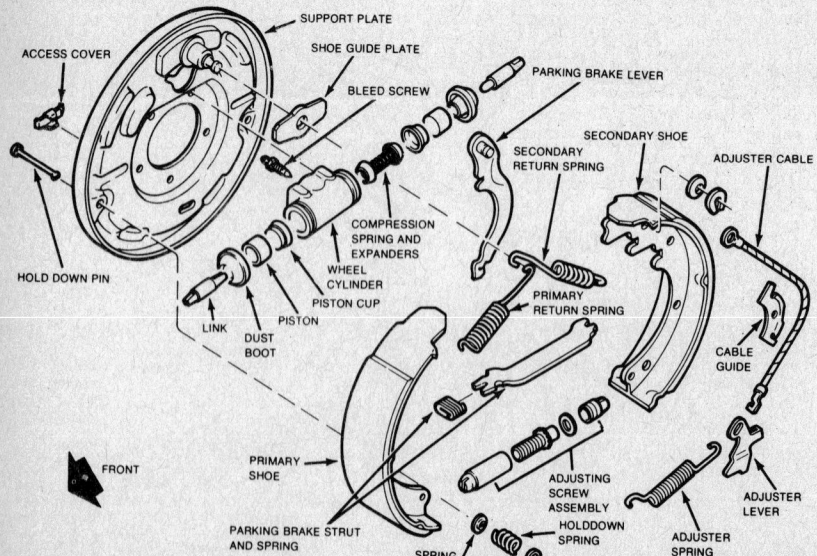

Typical rear brake components

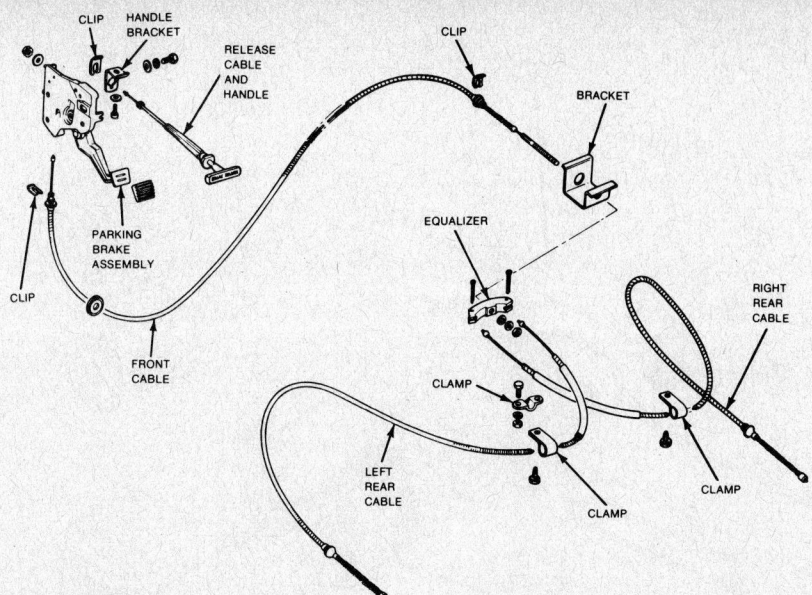

Parking brake components—typical

Parking Brakes

ADJUSTMENTS—TYPICAL

1. Make sure that the hydraulic brakes are in satisfactory adjustment.

2. Raise the rear wheels off the ground and disengage the parking brake pedal.

3. Loosen the locknut on the brake cable adjusting rod, located directly behind the frame center crossmember.

4. Spin the wheels and tighten the adjustment until the rear wheels drag slightly. Loosen the adjustment until there is no drag and the wheels spin freely.

5. Tighten the locknut to lock the adjusting nut.

CHASSIS ELECTRICAL

Heater Core

NOTE: (All models) If equipped with air conditioning, the unit must be removed from the dash and lowered to gain access to the heater control box for the removal of the heater core.

CJ MODELS

Removal

1. Remove the battery, drain the cooling system, and disconnect the heater hoses.

2. Disconnect the damper door control cable.

3. Disconnect the blower motor wire harness and ground wire at the switch and instrument panel.

4. Remove the glove box; water drain hose and defroster duct hose.

5. Disconnect the heater to air deflector duct at the heater housing.

6. Remove the nuts from the heater housing studs, protruding into the engine compartment.

7. Remove the heater housing assembly from the vehicle and remove the core from the housing.

Installation

1. The assembly is in the reverse of the disassembly.

2. When the assembly is completed, test the heater for proper operation.

CHEROKEE-WAGONEER— TRUCK

Removal

1. Remove the negative battery cable and drain the cooling system.

2. Disconnect the temperature control cable from the blend air door.

3. Remove the heater hoses and blower motor resistor wires.

4. Remove the heater core housing to dash panel attaching screws or nuts, projecting into the engine compartment.

5. Remove the heater housing assembly from the vehicle.

6. Separate the halves of the housing, after scribing a mark on the two halves, remove the core retaining screws and remove the heater core.

Assembly

1. The assembly is in the reverse of the disassembly.

2. When the assembly is completed, test the heater for proper operation.

Blower Motor
REMOVAL AND INSTALLATION

CJ Models

The heater housing assembly has to be removed to get out the blower motor.

1. Drain about two quarts of coolant.

2. Disconnect the heater hoses at the engine side of the firewall.

3. Detach the heater control cables.

4. Disconnect the motor wiring.

5. Detach the water drain hose and the defroster hose.

6. Remove the nuts from the studs in the engine compartment.

Cherokee-Wagoneer-Truck

1. Disconnect the blower motor wiring connector.

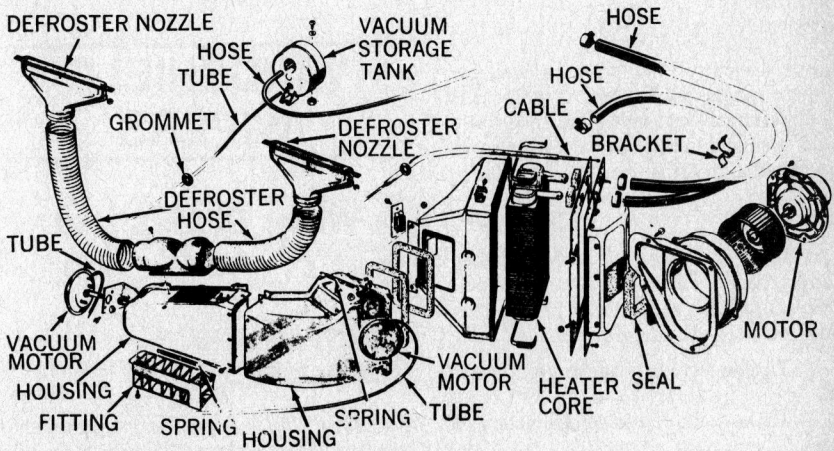

Typical Cherokee, Wagoneer and Truck heater/defroster assembly

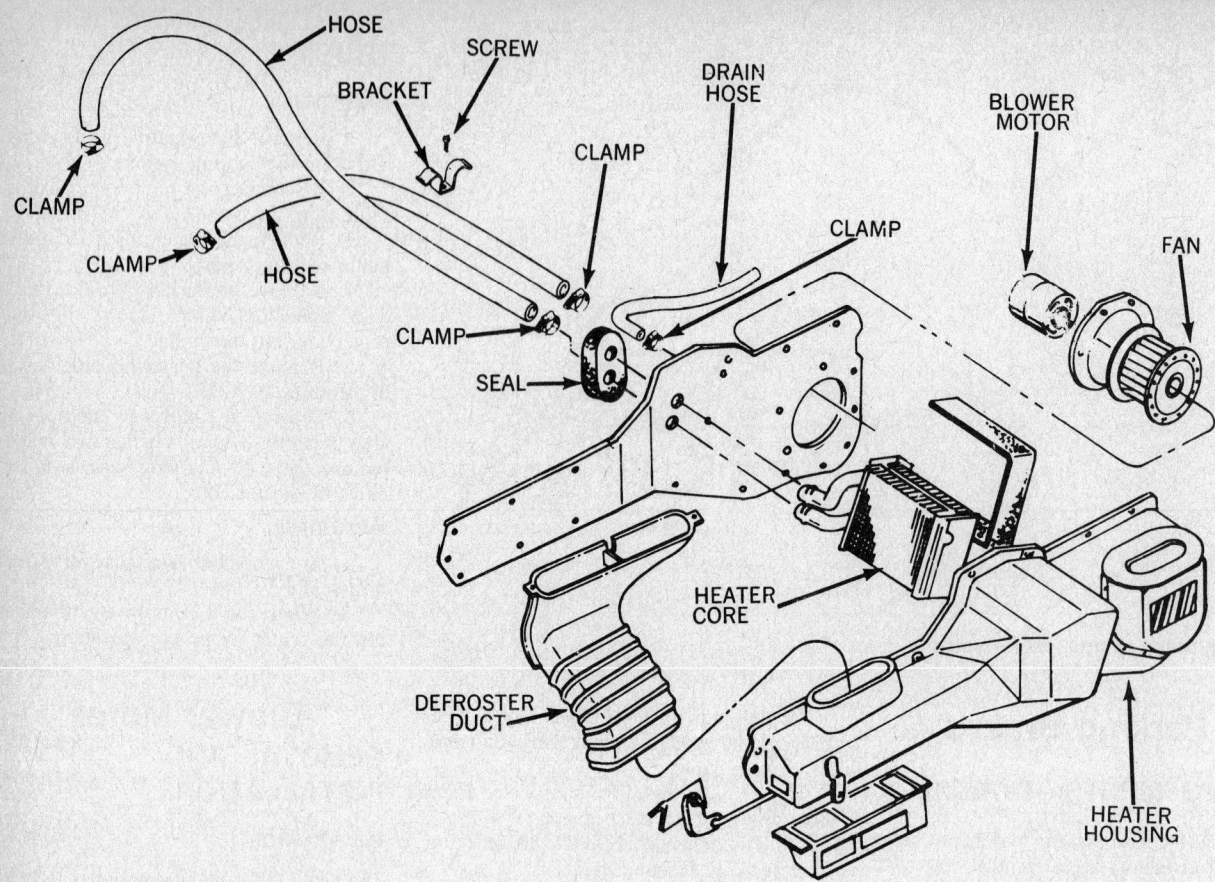

Typical CJ heater/defroster assembly

2. Remove the blower motor to blower housing mounting screws. Remove the blower motor and fan assembly.

3. Installation is in the reverse order of removal.

Radio

REMOVAL AND INSTALLATION

1975

The only factory installed radio available on these models was offered in 1975. It is a simple under-dash unit, similar to those dealer installed in earlier models. Removal and installation are obvious.

From 1976

NOTE: On Wagoneer and Cherokee models the glove box door, liner and lock striker must be removed. The radio is removed through the glove box.

1. Disconnect the battery ground cable.

2. Remove the control knobs, nuts, and bezel.

3. On 1976 and early 1977 models, you may have to detach the defroster hose. With air conditioning, remove the screws and lower the assembly.

4. Disconnect the radio bracket from the instrument panel.

5. Tilt the radio down and remove it toward the steering wheel.

6. Detach the antenna, speaker and power wires.

7. Reverse the procedure for installation.

WINDSHIELD WIPERS

Wiper Blades and Arms

REMOVAL AND INSTALLATION

To remove the blade, pull it away from the windshield. Push against the tip of the wiper arm to compress the locking spring and disengage the retaining pin. Pivot the blade clockwise to unhook it from the arm. To install the blade, just snap it into position.

To remove the arm, simply pry it straight off carefully. When you reinstall it, make sure that it doesn't hit the rubber moulding at either edge of the windshield while running. Install in the reverse order.

Motor

REMOVAL AND INSTALLATION

1975 CJ Models

1. Remove the crash pad, if any. Remove the extreme left plastic hole plug from the bottom of the windshield frame air duct and disconnect the drive link from the motor crank.

2. Loosen the wiper control knob setscrew.

3. Remove the control switch and mark the location of the wires on the switch prior to removing them from the switch.

4. Remove the motor cover and the motor.

5. Install in the reverse order of the above procedure.

NOTE: The motor cover must be sealed when installing.

From 1976 CJ Models

1. If your Jeep has crash padding, you have to fold the windshield down for access. Even if you don't have the padding, you can't get the wires out to remove the motor from the vehicle, unless the windshield is down.

2. Remove the wiper motor cover.

3. Remove the left access plug from the bottom of the windshield.

4. Disconnect the drive link from the left wiper pivot by sliding the clip off.

5. Detach the wiring from the switch.

6. Remove the mounting screws and the wiper motor.

7. Reverse the procedure for installation.

Wagoneer and Cherokee

1. Disconnect the wiper drive link from the crank under the instrument panel.

2. Mark the locations of the wires at the motor to facilitate proper assembly under the hood.

3. Disconnect the motor and washer pump wires at the motor under the hood.

4. Remove the motor-to-dash mounting screws and remove the motor from the vehicle.

5. Install the windshield wiper motor in the reverse order of removal.

Commando

1. Disconnect the wire harness plug and speedometer cable from the instrument cluster.

2. Remove the instrument cluster from the instrument panel by depressing the retainer springs at each corner.

3. Remove the 3 motor-to-brake and clutch pedal mounting bracket screws.

4. Disconnect the wiper drive link from the motor crank.

5. Disconnect the washer hoses from the washer pump. Pivot the motor assembly to the right and drop it below the instrument panel.

6. Mark the wire locations for proper assembly.

7. Disconnect the wire harness from the motor and washer pump and remove the motor.

8. Install the windshield wiper motor in the reverse order of removal.

Linkage

REMOVAL AND INSTALLATION

1975 CJ Models

1. Remove the wiper arms and pivot shaft nuts, washers, escutcheons and gaskets.

2. Disconnect the drive arm from the motor crank.

3. Remove the individual links where necessary, to remove the pivot shaft bodies without excessive interference.

4. Reverse the procedure for installation.

From 1976 CJ Models

1. Remove the wiper arms.

2. Remove the nuts attaching the pivots to the windshield frame.

3. Remove the necessary components from the top of the windshield frame.

4. Remove the windshield hold-down knobs and fold the windshield forward.

5. Remove the access hole covers on both sides of the windshield.

6. Disconnect the wiper motor drive link from the left wiper pivot.

7. Remove the wiper pivot shafts and linkage from the access hole.

8. Install the linkage in the reverse order.

Wagoneer, Cherokee and Commando

1. Remove the wiper arms and pivot shaft nuts, washers, escutcheons and gaskets.

2. Disconnect the drive arm from the motor crank.

3. Remove individual links where nec-

essary, to remove the pivot shaft bodies without excessive interference.

4. Install in the reverse order of removal.

Instrument Cluster

REMOVAL AND INSTALLATION

1975 CJ Models

1. Disconnect one battery cable.

2. Separate the speedometer cable from the speedometer head.

3. Remove the screws that hold up the heater control bracket. (1972 and later only)

4. Remove the attaching nuts that hold the cluster to the dash.

5. Remove the gauge wires and cluster lamps and remove the cluster assembly.

6. Install in the reverse order. After installing the cluster, connect the battery and check all of the lights and gauges for proper operation.

From 1976 CJ Models

1. Disconnect the negative battery cable.

2. Disconnect the speedometer cable from the back of the speedometer.

3. Remove the instrument cluster attaching screws/nuts and remove the cluster.

4. Disconnect the instrument cluster electrical connectors and remove the cluster from the vehicle.

5. Install in the reverse order.

Wagoneer, Cherokee and Commando

1. Disconnect the battery ground.

2. Disconnect the speedometer cable.

3. Cover the steering column.

4. Remove the cluster attaching screws and tilt the top toward the interior of the vehicle.

5. Mark the electrical connectors and hoses, disconnect them and the blend door air cable.

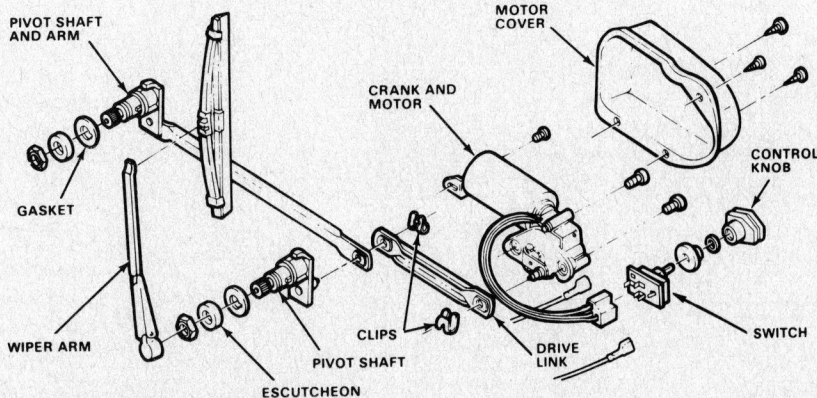

Typical windshield wiper components

6. Remove the cluster.

7. Installation is the reverse of removal.

Speedometer Cable Replacement

1. Reach up behind the center of the speedometer head. The cable is connected by a threaded ring. Unscrew the ring and pull the cable sheath from the head.

2. The cable core can be pulled from the sheath.

3. If the core is broken, detach the other end of the sheath from the transmission. Pull out the broken end.

4. When installing the cable, apply a very small amount of speedometer cable graphite lubricant.

LIGHTING

Headlight

REMOVAL AND INSTALLATION

1. Remove the attaching screws from the headlight trim ring. Pull out slightly at the bottom and push up to disengage the upper retaining tab.

2. Remove the trim ring.

3. Remove the three retaining screws from the retaining ring.

4. Pull the headlamp out and disconnect the wire harness.

5. Install in reverse order of the above procedure. Check for proper seating of the lamp in its mounting ring and check for proper alignment.

Fusible Links

Fusible links are sections of wire, with special insulation, designed to melt under electrical overload. There is usually one in the main wire from the battery, and near the alternator output side. If one melts, it must be replaced with a new link of the correct amperage rating. Never replace a melted link with ordinary wire; you run the risk of melting your entire wiring harness.

IMPORT
TRUCK
SECTION

Courier

INDEX

BEFORE SERVICING, SEE THE SAFETY NOTICE AT THE FRONT OF THE BOOK

COURIER

GENERAL ENGINE SPECIFICATIONS

Year	Engine Displacement cu. in. (ltrs.)	Carb. Type	Horsepower @ rpm	Torque @ rpm	Bore × Stroke (in.)	Compression Ratio	Oil Pressure psi @ rpm
'75	109.6 (1.8)	2 bbl.	74 @ 5000	92 @ 3500	3.07 × 3.70	8.6:1	50–64 @ 3000
'76–'78	109.6 (1.8)	2 bbl.	67 @ 5000	88 @ 3000	3.07 × 3.70	8.6:1	50–64 @ 3000
'77–'82	140.3 (2.3)	2 bbl.	92 @ 5000	121 @ 3000	3.78 × 3.126	9.0:1	40–60 @ 2000
'79–'82	120.2 (2.0)	2 bbl.	NA	NA	3.15 × 3.86	8.6:1	50–64 @ 3000

NA: Not available

TUNE-UP SPECIFICATIONS

Year	Engine Displacement cu. in. (liters)	Spark Plugs Type	Gap (in.)	Point Dwell (deg.)	Point Gap (in.)	Ignition Timing (BTDC)	Intake Valve Opens (BTDC)	Fuel Pump Pressure (psi)	Compression Pressure (psi)	Idle Speed ② MT (rpm)	AT (rpm)	Valve Clearance ③ Intake (in.)	Exhaust (in.)
'75–'76	109.6 (1.8)	AG32A ④	0.032	49–55	0.020	5°	13°	2.8–3.6	①	750	750	0.012	0.012
77	109.6 (1.8)	AG32	0.032	49–55	0.020	5°	13°	2.8–3.6	①	700	700	0.012	0.012
	140.3 (2.3)	AGRF52	0.034	Electronic		6°	NA	2.8–3.6	①	825	700	⑤	⑤
'78	109.6 (1.8)	AG32	0.032	49–55	0.020	8°	18°	2.8–3.6	①	700	700	0.012	0.012
	140.3 (2.3)	AGRF52	0.034	Electronic		6°	NA	2.8–3.6	①	825	700	⑤	⑤
'79–'80	120.2 (2.0)	AGR32	0.031	Electronic		8°	14°	2.8–3.6	①	650	650	0.012	0.012
	140.3 (2.3)	AGRF52	0.043	Electronic		6°	NA	2.8–3.6	①	800	700	⑤	⑤
'81–'82	120.2 (2.0)	AGR32	0.031	Electronic		8°	14°	2.8–3.6	①	650 ⑥	650 ⑥	0.012	0.012
	140.3 (2.3)	AGRF52	0.034	Electronic		6°	NA	2.8–3.6	①	850	700	⑤	⑤

NOTE: If the specifications on the engine decal differs from the above information, use the specifications as listed on the engine decal.
BTDC: Before top dead center

① The lowest reading cylinder should be within 75% of the highest.
② MT: Manual transmission (adjusted in NEUTRAL)
  AT: Automatic transmission (adjusted in DRIVE)
③ Adjusted with the engine at normal operating temperature.
④ For 1975 models. Use type AG32 for 1976 models.
⑤ Adjustment is not required.
⑥ 600 for California vehicles.

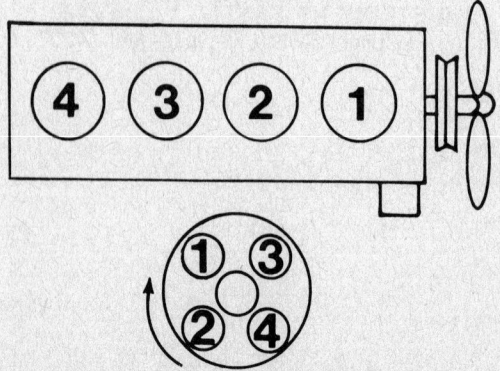

Firing order—1.8 and 2.0 liter engines

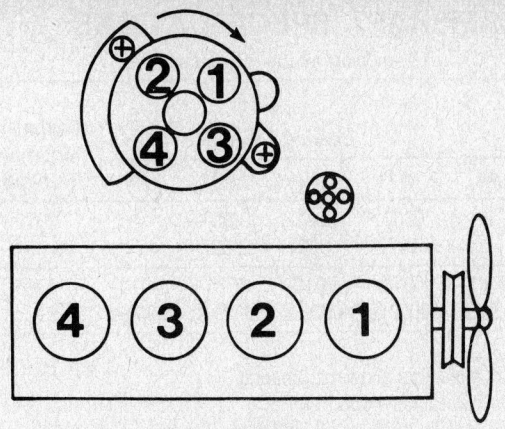

Firing order—2.3 liter engines

CAPACITIES

Year	Engine Crankcase With Filter qts. (L)	Without Filter qts. (L)	Transmission 4-Speed pts. (L)	5-Speed pts. (L)	Automatic qts. (L)	Rear Axle pts. (L)	Gas Tank gals. (L)	Cooling System qts. (L)
'75–'76	5 (4.7)	4 (3.8)	3 (1.4)	3.6 (1.7)	6.6 (6.3)	3.2 (1.5)	11.7 (44)	7.5 (7.2)
'77–'82	5 (4.7)	4 (3.8)	3 (1.4)	3.6 (1.7)	6.6 (6.3)	2.8 (1.3)	①	②

① Short bed truck—15 (57)
   Long bed truck—17.5 (66)
② With 1.8 or 2.0 liter engines—7.5 (7.2)
   With 2.3 liter engine—8.8 (8.3)

VALVE SPECIFICATIONS

Year	Engine Displacement cu in. (liters)	Seat Angle (deg)	Face Angle (deg)	Spring Test Pressure (lbs. @ in.)	Spring Free Length (in.)	Stem to Guide Clearance (in.) Intake	Exhaust	Stem Diameter (in.) Intake	Exhaust
'75–'78	109.6 (1.8)	45	45	16.3 @ 1.30① 26.8 @ 1.36②	1.438① 1.469②	.0007–.0021③	.0007–.0023③	.3161–.3167	.3159–.3167
'79–'81	120.2 (2.0)	45	45	20.9 @ 1.26① 31.4 @ 1.34②	1.438① 1.469②	.0007–.0021③	.0007–.0023③	.3162–.3168	.3160–.3168
'77–'81	140.3 (2.3)	45	44	71–79 @ 1.56	1.820	.0010–.0027④	.0015–.0032④	.3416–.3423	.3411–.3418
'82	120.2 (2.0)	45	45	56.8 @ 1.35	1.598	.0007–.0021③	.0007–.0023③	.3162–.3168	.3160–.3168
	140.3 (2.3)	45	44	71–79 @ 1.56	1.890	.0010–.0027④	.0015–.0032④	.3416–.3423	.3411–.3418

① Inner spring only
② Outer spring only
③ Wear limit: 0.008 in.
④ Service clearance 0.0055 in.

COURIER

CAMSHAFT SPECIFICATIONS
(All measurements in inches)

Engine Displacement cu. in. (liters)	Journal Diameter				Bearing Clearance				Maximum Journal Run-out	Lobe Lift①		End-Play	
	#1	#2	#3	#4	#1	#2	#3	#4		Int.	Exh.	Pref.	Max.
109.6 & 120.2 (1.8) (2.0)	1.7695–1.7701	1.7691–1.7697	1.7695–1.7701	—	.0007–.0027	.0011–.0031	.0007–.0027	—	.0012	NA	NA	.0010–.0070	.0080
140.3 (2.3)	1.7713–1.7720	1.7713–1.7720	1.7713–1.7720	1.7713–1.7720	.0010–.0030②	.0010–.0030②	.0010–.0030②	.0010–.0030②	.0005	.2437③	.2437③	.0010–.0070	.0090

① Subtract the small diameter (base circle) of the cam lobe from the large diameter (total lobe height) of the cam lobe to determine the lobe lift.
② Maximum allowable bearing clearance—.006 in.
③ Maximum allowable lift loss—.005 in.

CRANKSHAFT AND CONNECTING ROD SPECIFICATIONS
(All measurements in inches)

Year	Engine Displacement cu in. (liters)	Crankshaft				Connecting Rod		
		Main Brg Journal Dia	Main Brg Oil Clearance	Shaft End-Play	Thrust on No	Journal Dia	Oil Clearance	Side Clearance
'75–'78	109.6 (1.8)	2.4779–2.4785	0.0005–0.0015①	0.003–0.010	4	2.0842–2.0848	0.001–0.0011③	0.004–0.008②
'79–'82	120.2 (2.0)	2.4780–2.4786	0.0005–0.0015①	0.003–0.009	4	2.0842–2.0848	0.001–0.0026③	0.004–0.008②
'77–'82	140.3 (2.3)	2.3990–2.3982	0.0008–0.0015④	0.004–0.008	4	2.0464–2.0472	0.0008–0.0015④	0.0035–0.0105⑤

① Wear limit: 0.0012–0.0024 in.
② Wear limit: 0.014
③ Wear limit: 0.001–0.003 in.
④ Wear limit: 0.0008–0.0026 in.
⑤ Wear limit: 0.0150

TORQUE SPECIFICATIONS
(All readings in ft. lbs. unless noted)

Engine Displacement cu. in. (liters)	Cylinder Head Bolts	Rod Bearing Bolts	Main Bearing Bolts	Camshaft Sprocket-to-Cam	Flywheel-to Crankshaft Bolts	Manifolds	
						Intake	Exhaust
109.6 (1.8)	①	29–33	60–65	50–64	112–118	14–19	16–21
120.2 (2.0)	②	36–40	61–65	51–58	112–118	14–20	16–21
140.3 (2.3)	④	30–36	80–90	⑤	54–64	14–21③	27–38

① Torque to 63–68 ft. lbs. cold; re-torque to 69–73 ft. lbs. hot.
② Torque to 59–64 ft. lbs. cold; re-torque to 69–72 ft. lbs. hot.
③ Torque in two steps: 1st—5–7 ft. lbs.; 2nd—14–21 ft. lbs.
④ Torque in two steps: 1st—50–60 ft. lbs.; 2nd—80–90 ft. lbs.
⑤ '75–'81 models: 80–90 ft. lbs. '82 models: 50–71 ft. lbs.

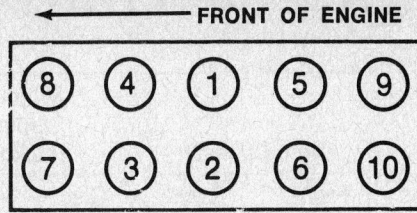

Cylinder head bolt torque sequence—1.8 and 2.0 liter engines

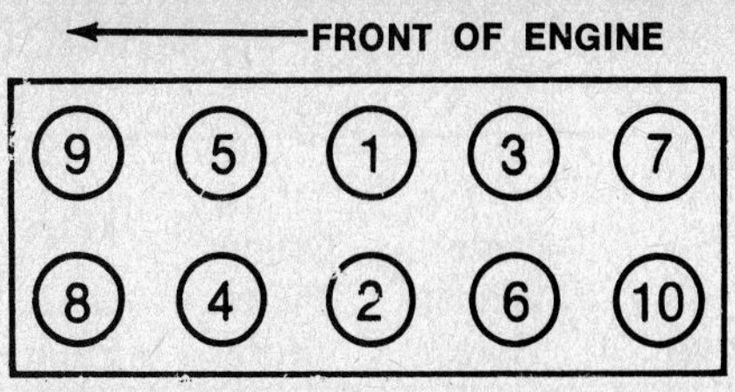

Cylinder head bolt torque sequence—2.3 liter engines

PISTON AND RING SPECIFICATIONS

(All measurements in inches)

Engine Displacement cu. in. (liters)	Piston to-bore Clearance	Ring Gap			Ring Side Clearance		
		First	Second	Oil Control	First	Second	Oil Control
109.6 (1.8)	0.0022–0.0028	0.008–0.016	0.008–0.016	0.008–0.016	0.0014–0.0028	0.0012–0.0025	0.0012–0.0024
120.2 (2.0)	0.0014–0.0030	0.008–0.016	0.008–0.016	0.012–0.035	0.0011–0.0027	0.0011–0.0025	Snug
140.3 (2.3)	0.0014–0.0022	0.010–0.020	0.010–0.020	0.015–0.055	0.002–0.004①	0.002–0.004①	Snug

① Service Limit—0.006 in.

WHEEL ALIGNMENT SPECIFICATIONS

Year	Model	Caster		Camber		Toe-in (in.)	Front Wheel Turning Angle (deg)	
		Range (deg)	Pref Setting (deg)	Range (deg)	Pref Setting (deg)		Inward	Outward
'75–'76	All	¾P–1¼P	1P	1P–1¾P	⅜P	0–¼	34–38	32–33
'77–'81	All	¾P–1¼P	1P	½P–1¼P	⅞P	0–¼	32°30′①	30°40′①
'82	All	¾P–1¼P	1P	½P–1¼P	⅞P	0–¼	33°53′②	30°38′②

P—Positive
① Maximum
② Except 600-14 tires. With 600-14 tires:
  Inward 32°34′
  Outward 30°48′

BATTERY AND STARTER SPECIFICATIONS

Year	Engine	Battery			Starter						Brush Spring Tension (oz)
		Amp Hour Capacity	Volts	Ground	Lock Test			No Load Test			
					Amps	Volts	Torque (ft. lbs.)	Amps	Volts	RPM	
'75–'82	All	①	12	Neg	Not Recommended			50 (or less)	11	5000 (or more)	38

① '75–'78 models: 60 amp standard; 70 amp optional
  '79–'82 models: 45 amp standard; 70 amp optional

BRAKE SPECIFICATIONS

(All measurements in inches)

Year	Model	Master Cylinder Bore	Caliper Piston Bore	Wheel Cylinder Bore		Front Disc Thickness	Drum Diameter		Minimum Lining Thickness	
				Front	Rear		Front	Rear	Disc	Drum ①
'75–'76	All	0.750	—	1.0	0.813	—	10.24	10.24 ③	—	1/32
'77–'78	All	0.875	2.1248	—	0.750	0.4724 ②	—	10.24 ③	0.315	1/32
'79–'82	All	0.875	2.1248	—	0.875	0.4724 ②	—	10.24 ③	0.276	1/32

① Measured from the brake shoe to the outermost portion of the lining.
② Minimum thickness—0.4331 in.; maximum run-out—0.004
③ Exact dimension—10.2362—10.2445; wear limit—10.2756

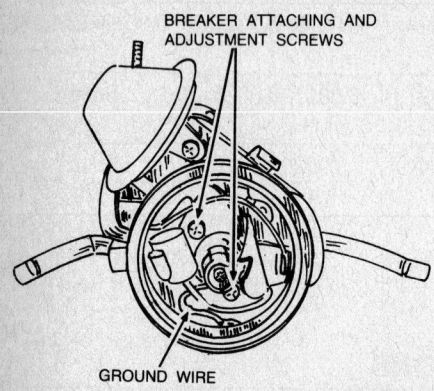

Breaker point replacement—1.8 engines

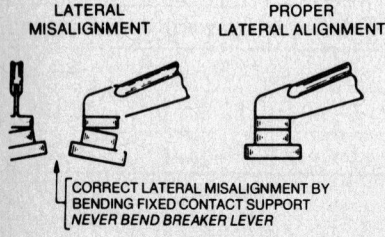

Breaker point alignment—1.8 engines

TUNE-UP

Spark Plugs

REPLACEMENT

1. Raise the hood and locate all the spark plugs.
2. If the spark plug wires are not numbered, mark each one with a small piece of masking tape. Print the number of the cylinder on the piece of tape.
3. Disconnect the wire from the plug by grasping, twisting and pulling the molded cap from the plug. Do not simply yank the wire from the plug, as the connection inside the cap can become damaged.
4. Using a spark plug socket, loosen the plug a few turns.
5. If compressed air is available, blow out the area around the base of the spark plug to remove foreign matter.
6. Remove the plug the rest of the way and inspect it. It is a good idea to inspect the plugs whether or not they are going to be reused.
7. If the plugs are to be reused, they may be cleaned with a wire brush. Hard deposits can be scraped off with a penknife. The electrodes can be filed flat with a fine points file, but if you do this, be sure the surfaces are flat, with sharp edges.
8. Check the plug gaps on the plugs before installing them in the engine. The ground electrode must be parallel to the center electrode and the specified size wire gauge should pass through the opening with a slight drag. If the gap is not as specified, use the adjusting device on the gap gauge to bend the outside electrode. Be careful not to bend the electrode too far or too often, because excessive bending may cause it to break off and fall into the combustion chamber, requiring removal of the cylinder head to retrieve it.
9. Insert the plugs into the engine and tighten them finger-tight.
10. Be sure that the plugs are not cross-threaded. If the plugs use metal gaskets, new gaskets should also be installed each time the plugs are removed and installed.
11. Tighten the spark plugs to 5–10 ft. lbs. if a torque wrench is available. Otherwise, just snug them in.
12. Install the spark plug wires on their respective plugs. Be sure that each wire is firmly connected.
13. While you are about the task of checking the spark plugs, the spark plug wires should also be checked. Any wires that are cracked or brittle should be replaced. Generally, spark plug wires may require replacement every fourth tune-up.

Breaker Points and Condenser

REPLACEMENT

1. Raise the hood and locate the distributor.
2. Scribe an alignment mark on the distributor cap and the distributor body. This way you will get the cap on the right way.
3. Remove the distributor cap with the wires attached and rotor. The cap is held on by two spring clips which can be levered off with a screwdriver. The rotor is simply pressed on the shaft, and is removed by pulling straight up. Clean off the cap inside and out with a clean rag, and check for cracks or carbon paths. A carbon path is a thin black line, usually running from one of the terminals to the bottom of the cap. Replace the cap if it has one of these, as it cannot be successfully scraped off. Check the condition of the carbon button in the center of the cap. Clean off the metal tip of the rotor with a rag, but don't file it. If it is badly corroded, replace the rotor.
4. Disconnect the primary and condenser wires from the breaker point terminal. Note the position of the wires before removing them from the terminal.
5. Remove the screws attaching the breaker points to the base plate. If possible, it is best to use a magnetic screwdriver to do this. The screws are very small and can be dropped easily.
6. Lift the breaker point assembly from the distributor. Remove the condenser from the side of the distributor case.
7. If the points are to be reused, clean them with a few strokes of a special points file. This is done with the points removed to prevent tiny metal filings from falling into the distributor. Don't use sandpaper or an emery board; they will cause rapid point burning.
8. Clean the distributor cam (which actuates the points). Apply a light film of

grease to the cam. If you have bought a tune-up kit containing points and rotor, it probably also contains a small vial of distributor cam grease. If not, a matchhead-sized dab of grease applied evenly will work just as well. Do not use oil to lubricate the cam or wick. It will get onto the points, causing rapid burning and pitting.

9. Place the breaker point(s) assemblies on the base plate. Install the attaching screws, again using a magnetic screwdriver.

10. Install the condenser. It is always best to install a new condenser each time you replace the points.

11. Connect the primary and condenser wires to the points(s) terminal and tighten the connection.

12. Check that the points meet squarely. If not, gently bend the fixed point with a pair of needle nose pliers until they do.

13. Set the point gap or dwell angle and install the rotor and distributor cap. Use the alignment marks made previously to get the cap on correctly.

ADJUSTMENT

There are two methods used to adjust breaker point gap. The first uses flat feeler gauges of a specified size which are inserted between the points. The movable point is adjusted until the proper clearance is obtained. The second method of adjustment is made after the first, and while not mandatory, is much more accurate, especially with worn points. In this method, a dwell meter is used to fine tune the point gap, so that the points remain open for only an exact number of degrees of distributor cam rotation.

If you do not have a dwell meter, the feeler blade method is adequate. If a dwell meter is available, perform the dwell meter adjustment after the initial feeler gauge setting is made.

Feeler Blade Method

1. Check the breaker point alignment and adjust if necessary, as outlined earlier.

2. Turn the engine until the rubbing block of the points rests on a high spot of the distributor cam. You can rotate the engine by putting the truck into high gear and pushing it forward, if you have a manual transmission. Otherwise, use the starter to bump the engine around in short bursts. The important thing here is to get the point block on one of the four corners of the cam, so that the points are at the widest possible opening. The object is to set the points correctly to the specified gap when wide open.

3. Insert a flat feeler blade of the correct size (found in the "Tune-Up Specifications" chart) between the points. The blades can be stacked to obtain the correct width, if necessary. The point gap setting is correct if the blade slips through with a slight drag. To adjust, slightly loosen the screw holding the movable point. There is a slot at the end of this point. By levering

the slot with a screwdriver, the points can be adjusted. It isn't easy to get the correct setting right away. Try gauges 0.001–0.002 in. larger and smaller than the setting size. The larger should spread the points slightly, while the smaller should not drag at all. When correct, tighten the hold down screw.

4. The gap often changes during the tightening process, so check it afterward and readjust if necessary.

5. If you have a dwell meter, go on to the following operation. If not, replace the rotor and distributor cap, and go on to the "Ignition Timing" section. The ignition timing must be checked, as a 1° increase in dwell results in an ignition timing retard of 2°, and vice versa.

Dwell Meter Method

The dwell angle is the number of degrees of distributor cam rotation through which the points remain closed (conducting electricity). Increasing the point gap decreases dwell, while decreasing the gap increases dwell.

The dwell angle may be checked with the distributor cap and rotor installed and the engine running or with the cap and rotor removed and the engine cranking at starter speed. The meter gives a constant reading with the engine running. With the engine cranking, the meter will fluctuate between zero degrees dwell and the maximum figure for that setting. Never attempt to adjust the points when the ignition is on, or you may receive a shock.

1. Connect the meter as per the manufacturer's instructions (usually red lead to the positive (+) primary terminal of the coil and black wire to a ground). Zero the meter if necessary.

2. Check the dwell by either the cranking method, or with the engine running. If the setting is incorrect, the points must be adjusted.

3. To change the dwell angle, loosen the point hold down screw and insert a screwdriver into the adjustment slot. Increase point gap to decrease dwell, and vice versa. Tighten the hold down screw and check the dwell angle with the engine cranking. If it seems to be correct, replace the cap and rotor and check dwell with the engine running. Readjust as necessary.

4. Run the engine speed up to about 2,500 rpm and then let the speed drop abruptly; the dwell reading should not fluctuate. If it does, a worn distributor shaft, bushing or cam, or a worn breaker plate is indicated. The parts should be inspected and replaced if necessary.

5. After adjusting dwell angle, go on to the Ignition Timing section.

Electronic Ignition

The 2.0 and 2.3 liter engines use an electronic ignition system which eliminates the points and condenser. Located in the distributor, in addition to the normal ignition

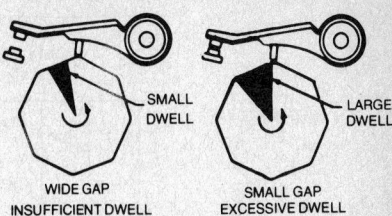

Dwell as a function of point gap

rotor, is a four spoke signal rotor which turns on the shaft in the same manner as the points cam found in conventional systems. A magnetic pickup coil is the only other component in the distributor. The system also includes an ignition module, mounted on the left fender apron on 2.3 liter engines or right fender apron on 1979 2.0 liter engines; the module is mounted on the distributor on the 1980 and later 2.0 liter engines. A conventional ignition coil is also used.

When a rotor spoke is not lined up with the pickup coil, it generates large lines of flux between itself, the magnet, and the pickup coil. This large flux variation results in a high generated voltage in the pickup coil, preventing battery current from flowing to the pickup coil. When a rotor spoke lines up with the coil, the flux variation is low—thus, zero voltage is generated in the pickup coil, allowing current to flow to it. Ignition primary current is then cut off by the ignition module, causing high voltage to be induced in the ignition coil secondary windings. The high voltage flows through the distributor to the spark plug.

Because no points or condenser are used, and because dwell is determined by the module, no adjustments are necessary. Ignition timing is checked in the usual way, but unless the distributor is disturbed it is not likely to change.

Service for the electronic ignition consists of inspection of the distributor cap, rotor, and ignition wires, replacing when necessary. These parts can be expected to last for at least 40,000 miles.

1. The cap is held on by two screws. After unscrewing them, lift the cap straight up and off, with the wires attached. Inspect the cap for cracks, carbon paths, or a worn center contact. Replace it if necessary, transferring the wires one at a time from the old cap to the new.

2. On all models except 1980 and later 2.0 liter engines, pull the ignition rotor (not the spoked timing rotor) straight up to remove. The ignition rotor on 1980 and later 2.0 liter engines is retained by two screws. Use a magnetic screwdriver to remove the screws, and remove the rotor from the distributor shaft. Inspect the rotor, and replace it if the contacts are worn, burned or pitted. Do not file the contacts. Replace the rotor: on 2.3 liter and 1979 2.0 liter engines, press the rotor onto the shaft, and check to see that it is fully seated; on 1980 and later 2.0 liter models, replace the retaining screws

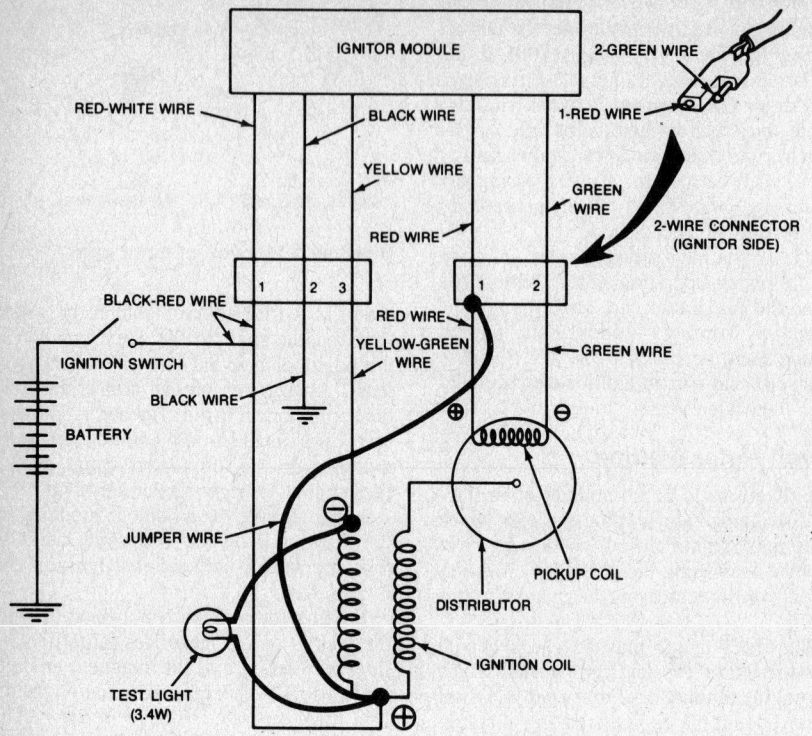

Electronic ignition troubleshooting

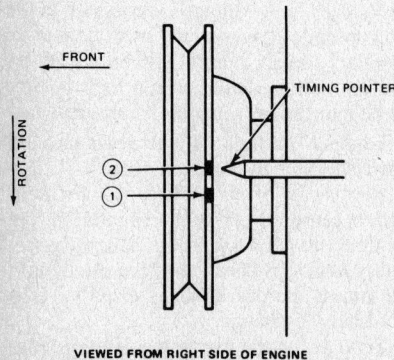

VIEWED FROM RIGHT SIDE OF ENGINE

1. Denotes 5° BTDC on 1975–77 and 1980 models; denotes 8° BTDC on 1978–79 and 1981–82 models.
2. Denotes TDC—all models

Timing mark identification. The ATDC mark is to the right of top dead center (above it in the illustration).

and washers.

3. Inspect the wires for cracks or brittleness. Replace them one at a time to prevent crosswiring, carefully pressing the replacement wires into place. The cores of electronic ignition wires are more susceptible to breakage than those of standard wires, so handle them carefully.

TROUBLESHOOTING

Troubleshooting the electronic ignition is easy, but you will need an accurate ohmmeter, a jumper wire, and a 3.4 watt test light.

Before suspecting the module or pickup coil, inspect all connections for breaks, improper hookups, shorts, or corrosion. Repair any faults before proceeding.

1. Check for a spark at the coil high tension lead: remove the coil high tension lead from the distributor and position it approximately ¼ inch from the engine block or other suitable ground. Hold the lead with a pair of insulated pliers and a heavy glove. Crank the engine and check for a spark. If the spark is good and consistent, inspect the cap and rotor. If the spark is weak or nonexistent, replace the high tension lead, clean and tighten all connections, and retest. If the spark is still weak, go to the next step.

2. Check the coil primary resistance: connect an ohmmeter across the coil primary terminals and read the resistance on the low scale. Resistance should measure approximately .9 ± .09 ohms @ 68°F. If the reading is far different, replace the coil.

3. Check the coil secondary resistance: connect an ohmmeter across the distributor side of the coil and the coil center tower. Read the resistance on the high scale of the meter. Resistance should measure 6,800–9,200 ohms @ 70°F. If the resistance is much higher (30,000–40,000 ohms), replace the coil.

4. Next, remove the distributor cap and ignition rotor. Crank the engine around until a rotor spoke of the armature is aligned with the pickup coil. Use a flat feeler gauge to check the armature gap. It should measure 0.008–0.024 in. (0.20–0.60 mm). If it does not, gently bend the pickup coil to adjust.

NOTE: This does not apply to 1980 and later 2.0 liter engines. The armature gap is not adjustable on these models.

5. Using the ohmmeter, measure the pickup coil resistance. Disconnect the 2 wire (red and green) connector at the distributor. The ignition switch should be OFF. Insert the probes of the ohmmeter into the pickup coil side of the connector. Resistance should be 760–840 ohms for the 2.3 liter and 1979 2.0 liter models. Resistance should be 1,050 ± 10% ohms @ 68°F for 1980 and later 2.0 liter models. If resistance is not within specifications, replace the pickup coil.

6. Finally, test the ignition module. On 2.3 liter and 1979 2.0 liter models, connect the test light between the positive and negative terminals of the ignition coil. Connect a jumper wire between the positive coil terminal and the red wire of the pickup coil (at the connector unplugged in the preceding pickup coil test). Be sure you are attaching the wire to the pickup coil side of the connector. Turn the ignition switch ON. The test light should come on. Disconnect the jumper wire from the red wire at the electrical connector. The test light should go out. If the module does not test out correctly, replace it.

On 1980 and later 2.0 liter models, the only way to test the ignition module is through a substitution test. If all other systems have been checked and are working correctly, remove the ignition module and install a new module known to be good. If the ignition system operates properly with the new module installed, the original one can be considered to be defective.

Ignition Timing

Timing should be checked at each tune-up and any time the points are adjusted or replaced. It is not likely to change very much on engines with electronic ignition.

If the ignition is set too far advanced (BTDC), the ignition and expansion of the fuel in the cylinder will occur too soon and tend to force the piston down while it is still traveling up. This causes engine ping. If the ignition spark is set too far retarded, after TDC (ATDC), the piston will have already passed TDC and started on its way down when the fuel is ignited. This will cause the piston to be forced down for only a portion of its travel, resulting in poor engine performance and lack of power.

To check and adjust the timing:

1. Warm the engine to normal operating temperature. Stop the engine and clean off the notches in the crankshaft pulley. Use some paint or chalk to make the marks more visible, if necessary. You will probably have to "bump" the engine around with the starter to get the notches into an accessible position.

2. There are two notches cut into the crankshaft pulley. Looking down at the marks, the Top Dead Center (TDC) mark

is on the exhaust system side of the engine. The one on the carburetor side indicates the proper number of degrees before TDC (BTDC) at which the spark plug is to fire. On 1975–78 models, TDC is marked with white paint and the BTDC timing mark is colored with yellow paint. On 1979 and later models, TDC is not colored at all, and the BTDC timing mark is colored white.

3. Disconnect and plug the vacuum hose at the distributor. The line must be plugged to prevent a vacuum leak.

4. Connect the timing light according to the manufacturer's instructions to the Number 1 spark plug (at the front of the engine). Connect a tachometer according to the manufacturer's instructions.

5. Set the parking brake, block the front wheels, put the transmission in Neutral, and start the engine.

——— CAUTION ———
Keep your hands, hair, clothes, and the various wires clear of the fan, belts and pulleys.

Reduce the idle speed by means of the idle speed screw. Adjust the idle to 700–750 rpm (800–850 rpm with the 2.3 and manual transmission). This prevents the centrifugal advance mechanism from affecting the timing.

6. Aim the timing light at the timing marks. If the BTDC mark on the pulley and the pointer are lined up, the timing is okay.

7. If the timing marks are not aligned, adjust by loosening the distributor hold-down clamp bolt at the base of the distributor shaft and turning the distributor slightly in one direction or the other until the marks coincide. Hold the distributor body, not the cap. When the marks are aligned, tighten the bolt.

8. Check the timing again to be sure it didn't change during the tightening process.

9. Check the centrifugal advance mechanism by accelerating the engine to 2000 rpm. The timing should advance (the marks should move away from the pointer, towards the carburetor side of the engine). Note the speed at which the advance begins.

10. Unplug and reattach the vacuum hose. Accelerate the engine to 2000 rpm. The engine speed at which advance begins should be sooner (and the advance should be greater) than with only the centrifugal advance operating. If this does not occur, the vacuum advance unit should be inspected for free operation, and the hose checked for vacuum. Reset the idle to specification.

11. Shut off the engine, and disconnect the timing light and tachometer.

Valve Adjustment

NOTE: While all valve adjustments must be made as accurately as possible, it is better to have the valve adjustment slightly loose than slightly tight, as burned valves may result from overly tight adjustments.

1.8 and 2.0 Liter Engines

1. Start the engine and allow it to reach normal operating temperature.

2. Turn the engine off.

3. Note the location of any wires and hoses which may interfere with cam cover removal, disconnect them and move them aside. Then remove the bolts which hold the cam cover in place and remove the cam cover.

4. Torque the cylinder head bolts to 70 ft. lbs. in sequence. The pattern is shown in the beginning of this section. When tightening the bolts, the proper procedure is to slightly loosen each bolt in turn, then tighten the bolt to the proper torque specification.

5. Place a wrench on the crankshaft pulley bolt and turn the engine over until the valves for no. 1 cylinder are closed. This is easier to do if the spark plugs are removed. When both camshaft lobes are pointing up, the valves are closed. If you have not done this before, it is a good idea to turn the engine over slowly several times and watch the valve action until you have a clear idea of just when the valves are closed.

6. Check the clearance of the valves. The correct size flat feeler gauge should pass between the base circle of the cam and the valve rocker arm with just a slight drag. Be sure the feeler gauge is inserted straight and not on an angle. You can also measure the clearance at the valve, if it is easier.

7. If the valves need adjustment, loosen the locking nut and then adjust the clearance with the adjusting screw. You will probably find it necessary to hold the locking nut while you turn the adjuster. After you have the correct clearance, tighten the locking nut and recheck the clearance. Remember, it's better to have them too loose than too tight, especially exhaust valves.

8. Repeat this procedure until you have checked and/or adjusted all the valves. Keep in mind that all that is necessary is to have the valves closed and the camshaft lobes pointing up. It is not particularly important what stroke the engine is on.

9. Install the cam cover gasket, the cam cover, and any wires and hoses which were removed.

2.3 Liter Engine

Valve clearances in the 2.3 liter engine are automatically adjusted by hydraulic valve lash adjusters, which resemble hydraulic valve lifters both in appearance and in function. Adjustments are not necessary.

Carburetor

IDLE SPEED AND MIXTURE ADJUSTMENTS

1. Put the transmission in Neutral.

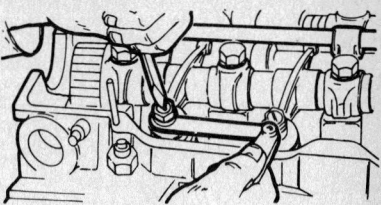

Checking the valve clearances at the valve

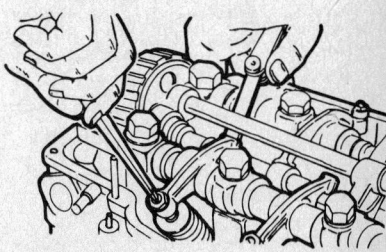

Checking the valve clearances at the camshaft

2. Connect a tachometer to the engine.

3. Start the engine and allow it to reach normal operating temperature. The choke should be fully open and the air cleaner on.

4. On 1978 and later models, run the engine for 3 minutes at 2000 rpm. Disconnect the canister purge hose between the canister and the air cleaner case.

5. Set the curb idle speed to specifications, using the curb idle speed adjusting screw. The correct idle speed can be found in the "Tune-Up Specifications" chart located at the beginning of this section, or on the emission control information label in the engine compartment.

6. The carburetor is probably equipped with idle limiter caps, which are small caps designed to provide a limited range of mixture adjustment.

7. The mixture can be checked only with the truck hooked up to an exhaust emission HC/CO analyzer. Your dealer, state inspection center, or service station may have one of these. The mixture is adjusted after the idle speed. The engine should be warm, choke open, and air cleaner on.

8. Disconnect the air hose between the air pump and the check valve, and plug the port of the check valve. See the Emission Control chapter for the location of these parts.

9. Turn the idle mixture adjusting screw in or out to obtain the specified idle/CO setting. The proper figure is given on the emission control information label in the engine compartment.

10. Unplug the check valve port and reconnect the hose. On 1978 and later models, connect the canister purge hose.

Supplemental Checks

If a satisfactory idle speed cannot be obtained after the normal idle adjustments, check the following:

1. Vacuum leaks;

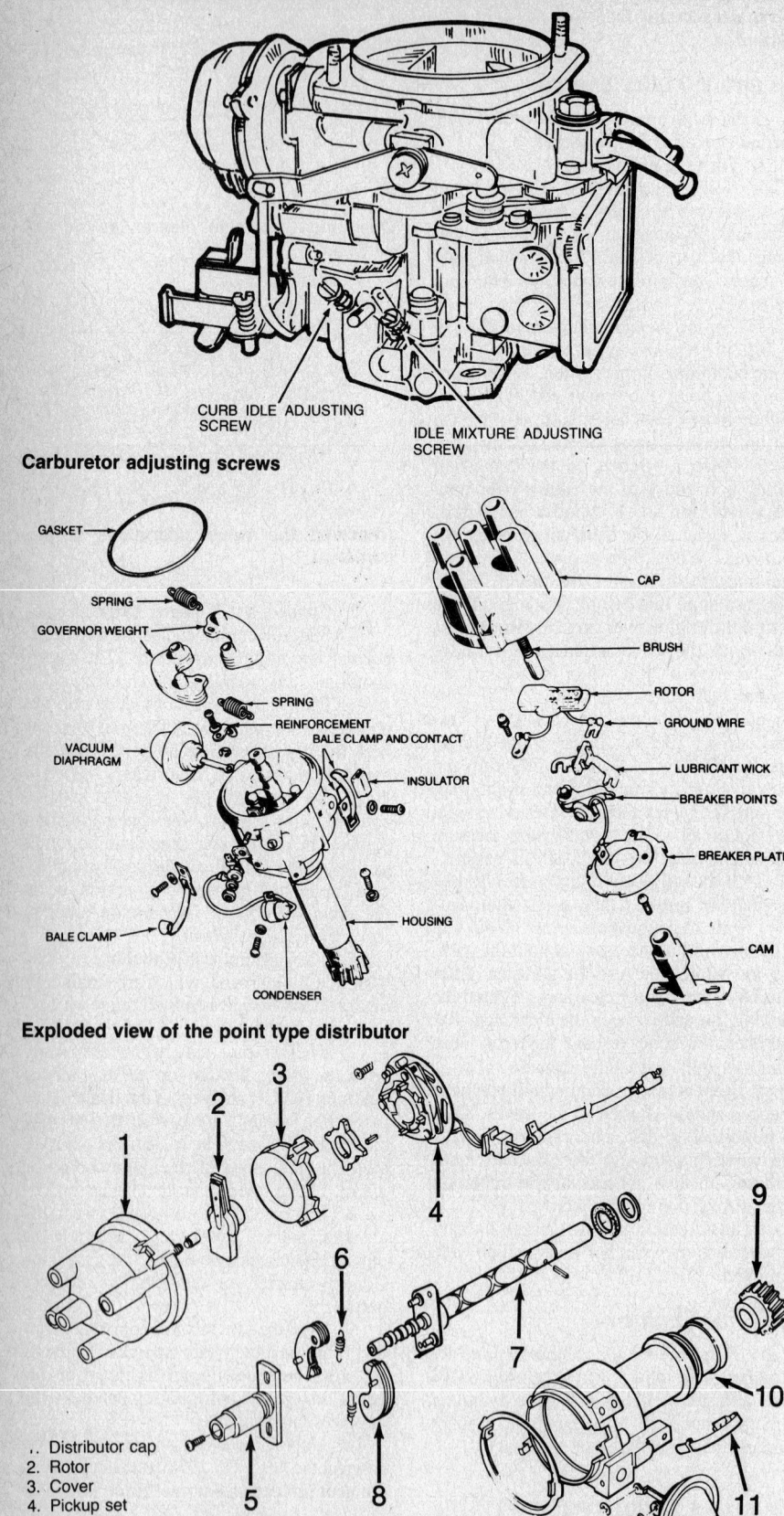

CURB IDLE ADJUSTING
SCREW

IDLE MIXTURE ADJUSTING
SCREW

Carburetor adjusting screws

GASKET

SPRING

GOVERNOR WEIGHT

SPRING

REINFORCEMENT
BALE CLAMP AND CONTACT

VACUUM
DIAPHRAGM

INSULATOR

BALE CLAMP

HOUSING

CONDENSER

CAP

BRUSH

ROTOR

GROUND WIRE

LUBRICANT WICK

BREAKER POINTS

BREAKER PLATE

CAM

Exploded view of the point type distributor

.. Distributor cap
2. Rotor
3. Cover
4. Pickup set
5. Cam
6. Spring
7. Shaft
8. Governor weight
9. Gear
10. Housing
11. Bale clamp

Exploded view of the electronic distributor used on 2.3 engines (1979 and earlier 2.0 engines similar)

2. Ignition system wiring;
3. Spark plugs;
4. Dwell angle;
5. Distributor point condition, and;
6. Ignition timing.

If the idle condition does not improve, check these items, and correct, if necessary:
1. Fuel level;
2. Crankcase ventilation system;
3. Valve clearance; and,
4. Engine compression.

If a satisfactory idle still cannot be obtained, have someone with an exhaust gas analyzer look into the problem for a possible too lean mixture or over-rich mixture.

ENGINE ELECTRICAL

Distributor

REMOVAL AND INSTALLATION

1. Matchmark the distributor cap and the body of the distributor. Remove the distributor cap.
2. Disconnect the vacuum hose from the diaphragm.
3. On 2.3 liter engines, remove the rubber plug from the timing belt cover. On all engines, scribe matchmarks on the distributor body and the cylinder block to indicate their relative positions.
4. Scribe another mark on the distributor body indicating the position of the rotor. On 2.3 liter engines, also scribe a mark on the cam pulley and on the indicator inside the timing belt cover to mark the position of the pulley relative to the indicator.
5. Disconnect the primary wires from the distributor.
6. Remove the distributor hold-down nut, lockwasher and flat washer.
7. Remove the distributor from the engine.

NOTE: Do not crank the engine while the distributor is removed. All distributors have a helical drive gear, which will cause the rotor to turn slightly when the distributor is removed. If the amount of movement is noted during removal, the rotor can be adjusted slightly before installation to compensate. Lubricate the drive gear and distributor shaft with engine oil before installation.

To install the distributor:
8. If the engine was cranked while the distributor was removed, turn the crankshaft until no. 1 cylinder is at the top of the compression stroke. This can be determined by feeling compression with your thumb through the spark plug port. The

TDC mark on the crankshaft pulley should also be aligned with the timing pointer. On 2.3 liter engines, watch the mark on the cam pulley and the TDC mark on the crankshaft pulley. Slide the distributor into the engine with the rotor pointing to no. 1 firing position.

9. If the engine has not been cranked while the distributor was removed, slide the distributor (with the O-ring) into the engine, aligning the matchmarks made during removal.

10. Install the flat washer, lockwasher and hold-down nut, but do not tighten the nut.

11. Install the distributor cap and connect the primary wires.

12. Set the ignition timing as previously outlined and tighten the hold-down nut.

13. Connect the vacuum line.

Alternator

PRECAUTIONS

Some precautions should be taken when working on this, or any other, AC charging system.

1. Never switch battery polarity.

2. When installing a battery, always connect the grounded terminal first.

3. Never disconnect the battery while the engine is running.

4. If the molded connector is disconnected from the alternator, never ground the hot wire.

5. Never run the alternator with the main output cable disconnected.

6. Never electric weld around the truck without disconnecting the alternator.

7. Never apply any voltage in excess of battery voltage while testing.

8. Never "jump" a battery for starting purposes with more than 12 volts.

REMOVAL AND INSTALLATION

1. Open the hood and remove the battery. Disconnect the negative (ground) cable first.

2. Remove the nut holding the alternator wire to the terminal at the rear of the alternator.

3. Pull the multiple connector from the rear of the alternator.

4. Remove the alternator adjusting arm bolt. Swing the alternator in and disengage the fan belt.

5. Remove the distributor cap and rotor from the distributor on 1.8s only to provide clearance.

6. Remove the alternator pivot bolt and remove the alternator from the truck.

7. Installation is the reverse of removal. Be sure to adjust the drive belt tension and to connect the battery properly.

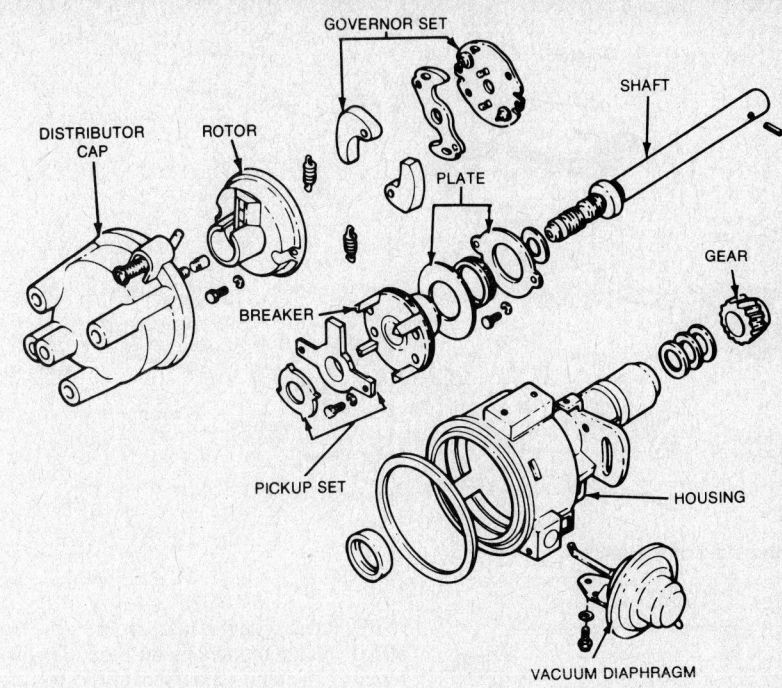

Exploded view of the electronic distributor used on 1980 and later 2.0 engines

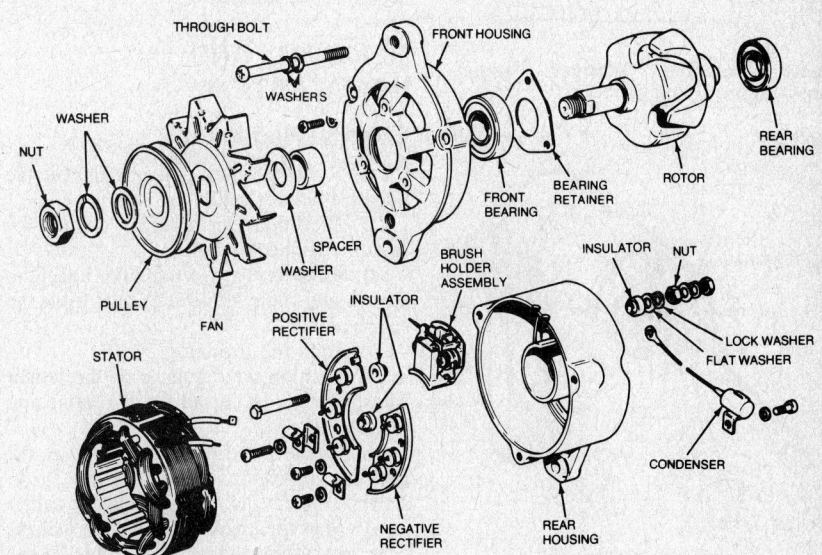

Exploded view of the alternator

BELT TENSION ADJUSTMENT

1. Check the alternator drive belt tension by applying thumb pressure to the belt midway between the fan pulley and the alternator. It should deflect 3/8–1/2 in. with a new belt or 1/2–5/8 in. with a used belt.

2. If it does not have the correct tension, loosen the alternator mounting bolts slightly and loosen the adjusting arm bolt.

3. Apply pressure on the alternator front housing until the correct tension is obtained. Tighten the adjusting arm bolt securely.

4. Tighten the alternator mounting bolts securely.

5. Recheck the tension.

Voltage Regulator

External regulators have been used on the courier from 1975–81. The external regulator is mounted on the fender splash shield.

367

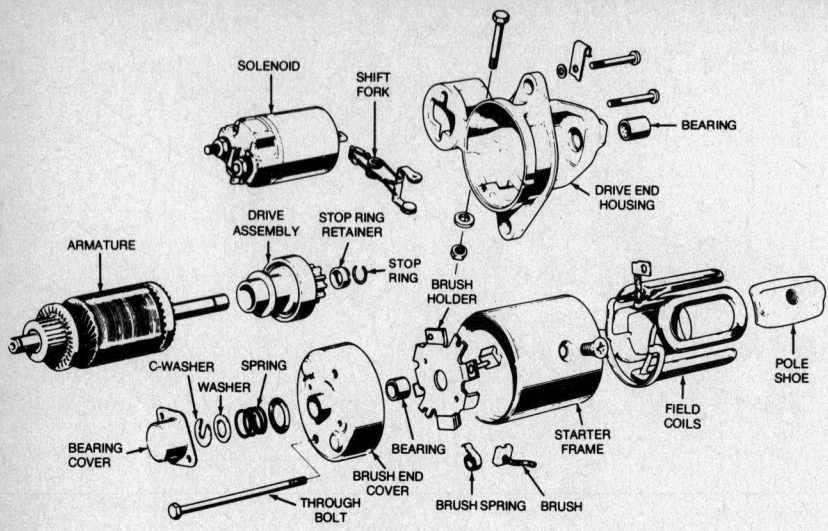

Exploded view of the starter

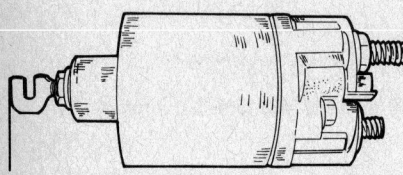

Starter solenoid plunger adjustment—adjust to 0.8 in.

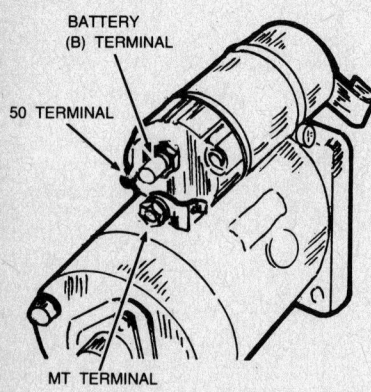

Starter solenoid terminals

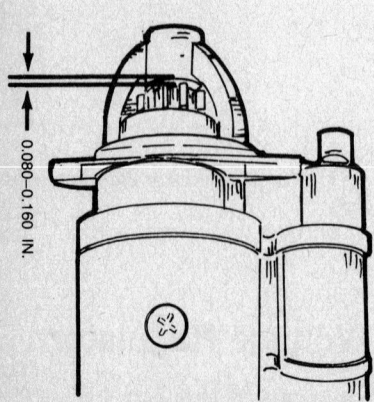

Starter drive end clearance

Beginning with the 1982 model year, internal voltage regulators are used. The internal regulator is mounted inside the alternator assembly. The alternator must be removed and disassembled in order to gain access to the internal regulator.

REMOVAL AND INSTALLATION

External Regulator

1. Raise the hood and disconnect the negative battery cable.
2. Disconnect the regulator wires at the multiple connector.
3. Remove the two regulator attaching screws and remove the regulator from the splash shield.
To install the regulator:
4. Position the regulator on the fender splash shield and install the two attaching screws.
5. Connect the regulator wires at the multiple connector.
6. Connect the negative battery cable.
7. Start the engine and be sure that the charging system indicator light goes out.

TESTING

The alternator regulator is not adjustable, but if it is suspected to be malfunctioning, the following test can be performed.

1. Connect a tachometer to the engine. Follow the manufacturer's hook-up instructions.
2. Connect the positive lead of a voltmeter to the alternator B terminal.
3. Connect the negative lead of a voltmeter to the regulator body (ground).
4. Set the voltmeter on the 20 volt scale.
5. Put the transmission in Neutral and set the parking brake.
6. Start the engine and run it at 1,800 rpm. The voltmeter should read 14–15 volts. If not the regulator should be replaced.

Starter

REMOVAL AND INSTALLATION

1. Raise the hood and disconnect the battery ground cable.
2. Remove the carburetor air cleaner and air intake tube to provide clearance, if necessary.
3. Disconnect the battery cable from the starter solenoid battery terminal.
4. Pull the ignition switch wire from the solenoid 50 terminal.
5. Raise and support the truck on jackstands.
6. Working under the truck, remove the starter attaching bolts, washers and nuts.
7. Tilt the drive end of the starter and remove the starter by working it out below the emission system hoses.
To install the starter:
8. Install the starter and bolts, washers and nuts.
9. Connect the ignition switch wire to the solenoid 50 terminal.
10. Connect the battery cable to the solenoid battery terminal.
11. Install the carburetor air cleaner and air intake tube, if removed.
12. Connect the ground cable to the battery.
13. Lower the truck to the ground and check the operation of the starter.

BRUSH REPLACEMENT

1. Remove the starter. Remove the two screws attaching the brush end bearing cover and remove the bearing cover.
2. Remove the through-bolts.
3. Remove the C-washer, washer and spring from the brush end of the armature shaft.
4. Pull the brush end cover from the starter frame.
5. Unsolder the two brushes from the field terminals and slide the brush holder from the armature shaft.
6. Cut the two brush wires at the brush holder and solder two new brushes to the brush holder. Solder two new brushes to the field coil terminals.
7. Install the brush holder on the armature shaft and install the brushes in the brush holder.
8. Install the brush end cover on the starter frame and be sure that the ear tabs of the brush holder are aligned with the through-bolt holes.
9. Install the through-bolts.
10. Install the rubber gasket, spring, washer and C-washer on the armature shaft.
11. Install the brush end bearing cover on the brush end cover and install the two screws. If the brush holder tabs are not aligned with the through-bolts, the bearing cover screws cannot be installed.

DRIVE REPLACEMENT

1. Remove the starter from the truck.
2. Disconnect the field strap from the solenoid MT terminal.
3. Remove the screws attaching the solenoid to the drive end housing. Disengage the solenoid plunger hook from the shift fork and remove the solenoid.
4. Remove the shift fork pivot bolt, nut and lockwasher. Later models don't have the nut and washer.
5. Remove the through-bolts and separate the drive end housing from the starter frame. At the same time, disengage the shift fork from the drive assembly.
6. Slide the drive stop-ring retainer toward the armature and remove the stop-ring. Slide the retainer and drive assembly off the armature shaft.

To assemble:

7. Position the drive assembly on the armature shaft.
8. Position the drive stop-ring retainer on the armature shaft and install the drive stop-ring. Slide the stop-ring retainer over the stop-ring to secure the stop-ring on the shaft.
9. Install the drive end housing on the armature shaft and starter housing. Engage the shift fork with the starter drive assembly as you move the drive end housing toward the starter frame.
10. Install the through-bolts.
11. Align the shift fork with the pivot bolt hole and install the pivot bolt, lockwasher and nut. Tighten the nut securely. On 1977 and later models, install the pivot bolt through the shift fork to locate it in place.
12. Check the solenoid plunger length. The tip of the solenoid plunger should be 0.8 in. from the front edge of the solenoid body. If the dimension is not correct, loosen the locknut and adjust the plunger length as necessary. Tighten the locknut.
13. Position the solenoid on the drive end housing. Be sure that the solenoid plunger hook is engaged with the shift fork.
14. Install the two solenoid retaining screws and washers.
15. Apply a minimum of 8 volts to the solenoid 50 terminal and check the clearance between the starter drive and the stop-ring retainer. The clearance should be 0.080–0.160 in. If not, the solenoid plunger is not properly adjusted. To increase the clearance, lengthen the solenoid plunger and shorten the plunger to decrease the clearance.
16. Install the field strap on the solenoid MT terminal and tighten the nut.
17. Install the starter. Check the operation of the starter.

SOLENOID REPLACEMENT

Follow steps 1, 2, 3, 12, 13, 14, 15, 16, and 17 of the Starter Drive Replacement procedure.

ENGINE MECHANICAL

Design

Couriers used a 1.8 liter (1796 cc), single overhead camshaft four cylinder as the standard engine from 1975 to 1978. In 1979, the engine was enlarged to 2.0 liter (2000 cc). Water cools the thin cast iron block and cast aluminum alloy cylinder head with multispherical type combustion chambers.

The camshaft bearing caps are machined with the cylinder head and are not interchangeable. The cylinder head bolts also retain the camshaft bearing caps and the rocker arm shaft supports.

Exhaust valves are free rotating to prevent uneven valve wear. Intake rocker arm shafts are 2-piece units, while the exhaust rocker arm shafts are single-piece units.

The timing chain is a dual cog type encircling the crankshaft and camshaft sprockets. The crankshaft sprocket also holds the rotor type oil pump drive chain.

An all iron four cylinder overhead camshaft 2.3 liter (2300 cc) engine was made available in 1977. First designed for use in the Pinto, the Courier's all-metric 2.3 liter is built in Brazil. The crankshaft runs in five main bearings, the camshaft in four. The camshaft is driven from the crankshaft pulley by a cogged belt, which also turns an auxiliary shaft, located on the left side of the engine. Oil pump and distributor drives are taken from the auxiliary shaft. A conventional fan belt, taking power from the crankshaft pulley, drives the water pump, alternator, and fan.

The cylinder head is a crossflow design; gases enter through the intake manifold on the left side of the head, and exit through the exhaust manifold on the right. This design produces a more efficient flow, and the swirl pattern it develops results in more efficient combustion. Valve adjustments are eliminated through the use of hydraulic lash adjusters.

Engine Removal and Installation

The engine is removed through the engine compartment leaving the transmission in place. When installing nuts or bolts, lubricate the threads with light engine oil, but do not oil threads which require oil-resistant or water-resistant sealer.

NOTE: Always label all disconnected hoses as they are removed, as an aid to correct installation.

1. Scribe the locations of the hood hinges and remove the hood.
2. Drain the coolant.
3. Remove the air cleaner and, on the 2.3, the heat stove.

4. Disconnect the upper radiator hose at the engine and the lower radiator hose at the radiator on the 1.8 and 2.0. With the 2.3, disconnect both at the radiator. If you have an automatic transmission, also disconnect and plug the two fluid cooler lines at the radiator.
5. Unbolt and remove the radiator. With the 2.3, you will first have to loosen the shroud mounting bolts and slide the shroud rearward.
6. Disconnect the accelerator linkage at the carburetor.
7. Disconnect and plug the fuel line at the carburetor.
8. Remove the linkage attaching nuts at the intake manifold and remove the linkage.
9. Disconnect the cable at the air by-pass valve (if equipped).
10. Disconnect the choke cable.
11. Disconnect the battery cables, negative cable first.
12. Disconnect the coil high tension wire at the distributor. Disconnect the coil lead wire.
13. Remove the fan.
14. Loosen the alternator retaining bolts and remove the alternator drive belt.
15. If equipped, remove the Thermactor air pump drive belt.
16. Remove the alternator bracket and adjusting arm bolts. Position the alternator out of the way. If your Courier has air conditioning, unbolt the compressor and set it aside without detaching any lines.

CAUTION

Never open any air conditioning lines. Escaping compressed refrigerant can freeze any body surface, including the eyes, that it contacts. It also decomposes into a poisonous gas in the presence of flame.

17. If equipped, disconnect the Thermactor hoses at the pump. Remove the Thermactor bracket and adjusting arm bolt and lay the Thermactor pump aside. On the 2.3, disconnect the brake vacuum booster hose at the engine, and the vacuum lines at the vacuum amplifier.
18. Remove the heater hoses from the front and rear of the intake manifold on the 1.8 and 2.0. On the 2.3, remove the heater hoses altogether.
19. If equipped, disconnect the Thermactor air filter hose at the air by-pass valve.
20. Disconnect the oil pressure gauge lead wire and boot from the sending unit.
21. Disconnect the battery ground cable from the block.
22. Disconnect the wires from the starter solenoid.
23. Raise and support the vehicle and drain the oil from the engine.
24. Remove the engine front lower skid plate, 1.8 and 2.0 only.
25. Disconnect the exhaust pipe at the exhaust manifold. With the 2.3 also unbolt the exhaust pipe hanger from the transmission.
26. With manual transmission, on the

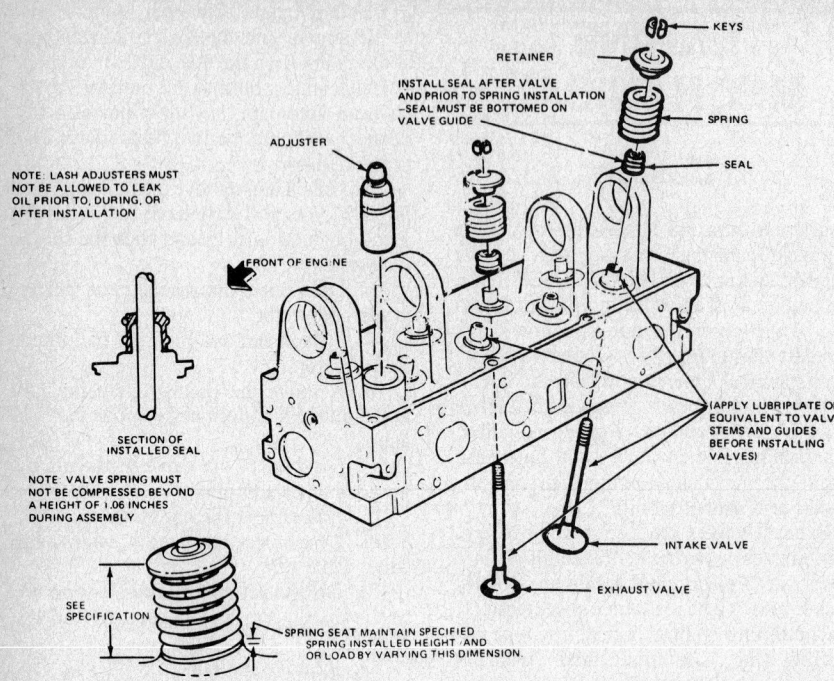

NOTE: LASH ADJUSTERS MUST NOT BE ALLOWED TO LEAK OIL PRIOR TO, DURING, OR AFTER INSTALLATION

KEYS

RETAINER

INSTALL SEAL AFTER VALVE AND PRIOR TO SPRING INSTALLATION —SEAL MUST BE BOTTOMED ON VALVE GUIDE

SPRING

SEAL

ADJUSTER

FRONT OF ENGINE

SECTION OF INSTALLED SEAL

(APPLY LUBRIPLATE OR EQUIVALENT TO VALVE STEMS AND GUIDES BEFORE INSTALLING VALVES)

NOTE: VALVE SPRING MUST NOT BE COMPRESSED BEYOND A HEIGHT OF 1.06 INCHES DURING ASSEMBLY

INTAKE VALVE

EXHAUST VALVE

SEE SPECIFICATION

SPRING SEAT MAINTAIN SPECIFIED SPRING INSTALLED HEIGHT AND OR LOAD BY VARYING THIS DIMENSION.

Valve components of the 2.3 engine

1.8 and 2.0 remove the flywheel housing bolt and the lower starter nuts and one lower bolt. On the 2.3, just remove the lower transmission-to-engine bolts at this time. With automatic transmission, first disconnect the vacuum hose from the diaphragm. Unbolt the access cover from the lower end of the torque converter housing. Match-mark the driveplate (flywheel) and the torque converter for later alignment, then remove the four bolts connecting the driveplate to the torque converter. Disconnect the throttle linkage from the transmission.

27. Remove the lower exhaust pipe bolt and let the pipe hang on the 1.8 and 2.0. Remove the engine support bolts and remove the right engine mount bracket, with the 2.3.

28. Lower the truck.

29. Remove the starter upper bolts and remove the starter on the 1.8 and 2.0.

30. Support the transmission with a jack. Remove the remaining transmission-to-engine bolts on the 2.3.

31. Install a lifting sling on the engine at the engine hanger brackets. Remove the clutch slave cylinder from the transmission on the 2.3.

32. Attach a sling to the hoist and pull the engine forward until it clears the transmission shaft. Be sure that the transmission is not dislodged from the jack. Unbolt the engine from the mounts.

33. Lift the engine from the truck. If your truck has an automatic transmission, be careful not to let the torque converter fall out of its housing.

To install the engine:

34. Lower the engine into the chassis. Loosely install several clutch housing bolts.

35. Install the engine mount bolts. In-stall the 2.3s right engine mount and the clutch slave cylinder.

36. Remove the lifting sling and transmission jack. Be sure that the mainshaft is engaged with the engine.

37. Install the starter and upper attaching bolt on the 1.8 and 2.0.

38. Raise and support the truck.

39. Install the flywheel housing bolts with manual transmission. With automatic, line up the marks made earlier on the driveplate and the torque converter, and install the four bolts. Torque them to 25–36 ft. lbs. Install the torque converter housing-to-engine bolts, and torque to 23–34 ft. lbs. Replace the access cover on the torque converter housing.

40. Connect the exhaust pipe to the exhaust manifold. Install the bracket bolt. Install the exhaust pipe hanger to the transmission on 2.3s.

41. Install the lower starter bolts on the 1.8 and 2.0.

42. Install the 1.8 and 2.0 engine front skid plate.

43. Connect the starter wires and lower the vehicle.

44. Install the accelerator linkage. Connect the fuel line and choke cable. With automatics, also connect the throttle linkage and the vacuum hose.

45. Connect the heater hoses. If equipped, connect the Thermactor air filter hose. Connect the 2.3s brake vacuum booster hose and the vacuum line at the amplifier.

46. Install the battery ground cable to the block. Install the coil wires.

47. Install the alternator on the bracket and install the bolts. Install the air conditioning compressor, if removed.

48. If equipped, install the Thermactor air pump.

49. Install the fan.

50. Install the drive belts and adjust the tension.

51. Install the radiator. Connect the upper and lower hoses. Connect the automatic transmission cooler lines, if equipped.

52. Connect the oil pressure sending unit.

53. Fill the cooling system and crank-case with the specified type and amount of fluid. Install the air cleaner (and heat stove on 2.3s).

54. Install the hood. Connect the battery cables. Start the engine and check for leaks and proper operation.

Cylinder Head

REMOVAL AND INSTALLATION

1.8 and 2.0 Liter Engines

Be sure that the cylinder head is cold before removal. This will prevent warpage.

1. Drain the cooling system.

2. On 1977 and earlier models, scribe alignment marks around the hood hinges and remove the hood.

3. Remove the air cleaner.

4. Disconnect the coil wire and vacuum line from the distributor.

5. Rotate the crankshaft to place no. 1 cylinder at TDC, on the compression stroke.

6. Remove the plug wires and distributor cap as a unit. Number wires.

7. Remove the distributor.

8. Remove the rocker arm cover.

9. Raise and support the truck. Disconnect the exhaust pipe from the manifold.

10. Remove the accelerator linkage. Disconnect the wire from the water thermo switch, under the intake manifold and behind the carburetor, which should be disconnected. Disconnect the throttle cable at the air by-pass valve, and the choke cable and fuel line at the carburetor.

11. If your Courier has an air pump, remove the hoses from the pump. Disconnect the heater return hose at the intake manifold, the coolant by-pass hose, the water pump hose, and the upper radiator hose (at the engine).

12. Disconnect the wire from the slow fuel valve (throttle solenoid on the carburetor). Remove the intake manifold bracket.

13. Remove the water pump.

14. Remove the nut, washer, and the distributor gear from the camshaft.

15. Remove the nut and washer from the camshaft gear. You will have to lock up the engine to do this. The best way is with a tool which locks onto the flywheel teeth. These tools are available in auto parts stores or from your dealer. Support the timing chain in such a way that it cannot fall into the timing chain case. Do not remove the cam gear from the timing chain. The relationship between the chain and the gear teeth should not be disturbed, since cam

timing is dependent on this relationship. You can wire the chain and gear together to keep them in position.

16. Loosen the cylinder head bolts a little at a time in the reverse order of the tightening sequence, and remove them. Also remove the cylinder head-to-front cover bolt.

17. Remove the rocker arm assembly.

18. Remove the camshaft from the camshaft gear. See the "Camshaft Removal" section.

19. Lift off the cylinder head being careful not to let the timing chain and gear fall into the timing case.

20. Remove all tension from the timing chain. See the Timing Chain Tensioner Adjustment procedure.

To install the cylinder head:

1. Clean the rocker cover gasket surface at the head and the cover. Clean the head gasket surface at the head and the block. Clean the water pump gasket surface at the head gasket surface and the front cover. Be careful not to scratch the flat surfaces. Vacuum out any bits that fall into the cylinders or passages, being careful not to nick the cylinder walls.

2. Check the cylinder head flatness with a straightedge and feeler blades. It should not exceed 0.003 in. in any 6 in. span or 0.006 in. overall.

3. Clean the cylinder head bolt holes of oil and dirt.

4. Position a new head gasket on the cylinder block.

5. Install the cylinder head on the block using the guides at either end of the block.

6. Coat the camshaft bearings and camshaft with engine oil, and install the camshaft to the camshaft gear. See the Camshaft Installation procedure.

7. Install the rocker arm assembly.

8. Install the head bolts. Torque the bolts to specifications in three passes.

9. Install the camshaft gear washer and nut. Torque to specifications.

10. Install the distributor gear, washer and nut.

11. Time the engine. Follow the instructions under "Timing Chain and Sprocket Installation."

12. Adjust the timing chain tension. See "Timing Chain Tensioner Adjustment."

13. Connect the exhaust pipe to the exhaust manifold. Lower the truck.

14. Install the distributor, distributor cap and plug wires.

15. Install the water pump.

16. Install the lower intake bracket bolt.

17. Install the accelerator linkage.

18. Connect the vacuum line and coil wire. Connect all the hoses and wires disconnected earlier.

19. Adjust the valve clearance cold.

20. Install the rocker arm cover. Fill the cooling system.

21. Run the engine until normal operating temperature is reached, and check for leaks. Adjust the valve clearance hot.

22. Adjust the carburetor and ignition timing. Install the air cleaner and install the hood.

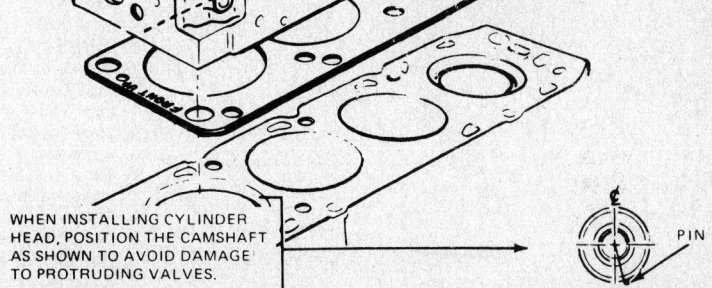

Cylinder head removal and installation—2.3 engines

2.3 Liter Engines

It is easier to remove the cylinder head if the intake and exhaust manifolds are removed first. It is not necessary to remove the camshaft. The engine should be cold to reduce the chance of warpage when the cylinder head bolts are removed.

1. Drain the cooling system.

2. Remove the air cleaner. Remove the spark plug wires from the plugs. Remove the spark plugs.

3. Remove the valve cover. It is held on by eight bolts.

4. Remove the intake and exhaust manifolds from the head. See the appropriate procedures for each.

5. Remove the camshaft drive belt cover. There are tubular spacers underneath the two bolts directly above the crankshaft pulley.

6. Loosen the drive belt tensioner and slip the belt off of the cam sprocket and tensioner. See the "Belt Tensioner Adjustment" section. It is not necessary to remove the tensioner from the head.

7. Remove the coolant outlet elbow, with the hose attached, from the cylinder head.

8. Loosen the cylinder head bolts a little at a time in the reverse order of the torque sequence shown for tightening.

9. Remove the cylinder head.

To install:

1. Clean all the gasket material and sealer from the cylinder head, engine block, valve cover, and water outlet. Be careful not to scratch the surfaces. Vacuum out any particles which fall into the cylinders or passages, being careful not to nick the cylinder walls.

2. Check the cylinder head for flatness. It should not exceed 0.003 in. in any 6 in. span, or 0.006 in. overall. If the head must be machined, do not remove more than 0.010 in. from the original surface. Remove any burrs or scratches with an oil stone.

3. Clean the cylinder head and block bolt holes of any oil or dirt.

4. Place a new gasket on the cylinder block.

5. Position the cam with the pin in the position shown in the illustration.

6. Lower the head carefully onto the block and gasket.

7. Lightly oil the threads of the cylinder head bolts before installation. Torque the bolts to specification in at least three passes, increasing the amount of torque used each time. Torque the bolts in the sequence shown.

8. Slip the camshaft drive belt back over the cam sprocket and tensioner, then time the camshaft. See the "Camshaft Timing Belt" removal and installation procedure for instructions.

9. Install the camshaft drive belt cover and its attaching bolts. Make sure the two spacers are installed correctly. Tighten the bolts to 6–13 ft. lbs.

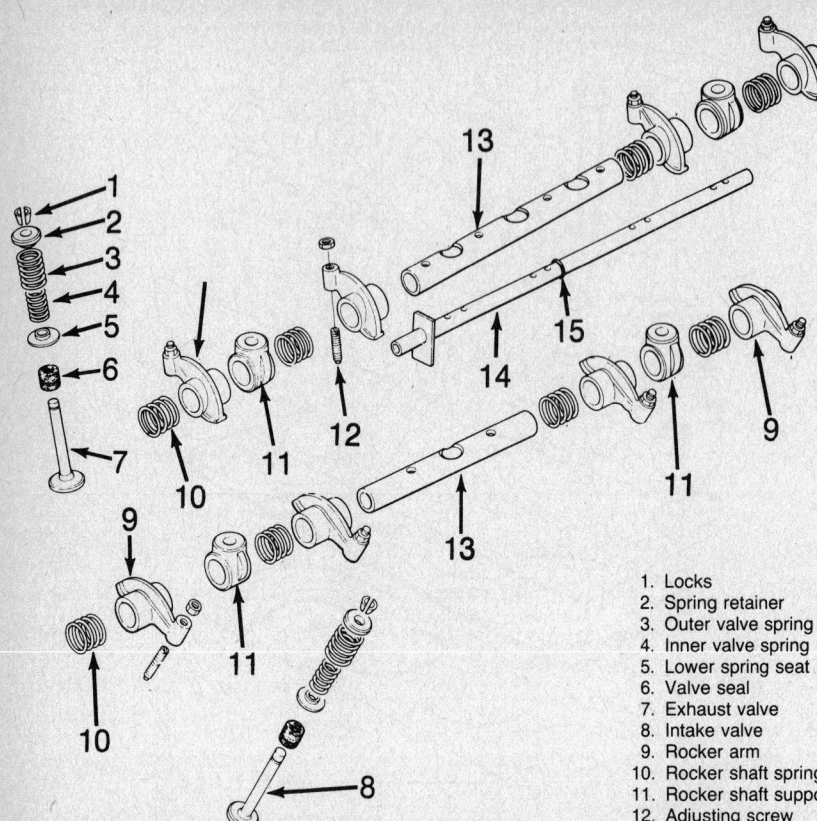

Rocker arms, shafts and valves—1.8 and 2.0 engines

1. Locks
2. Spring retainer
3. Outer valve spring
4. Inner valve spring
5. Lower spring seat
6. Valve seal
7. Exhaust valve
8. Intake valve
9. Rocker arm
10. Rocker shaft spring
11. Rocker shaft support
12. Adjusting screw
13. Rocker shaft
14. Lubrication tube
15. Seal

10. Install the water outlet elbow and a new gasket onto the head. Tighten the bolts to 12–15 ft. lbs.

11. Install the intake and exhaust manifolds. See the appropriate section for each.

12. Install the valve cover, using a new gasket. Use an oil resistant sealer, such as silicone, on both sides of the gasket. Install the air cleaner. Install the spark plugs and wires.

13. Fill the cooling system.

Rocker Shafts

REMOVAL AND INSTALLATION

1.8 and 2.0 Liter Engines Only

This operation should only be performed on a cold engine; the bolts which hold the rocker shafts in place also hold the cylinder head to the block.

1. Raise the hood and cover the fenders.

2. Disconnect the choke cable.

3. If equipped, disconnect the air by-pass valve cable.

4. Label the spark plug wires to prevent crosswiring upon installation and disconnect them from the spark plugs. Remove the wires from the clips on the rocker cover and position them out of the way.

5. Remove the rocker cover and discard the gasket.

6. Remove the rocker arm shaft attaching bolts evenly and remove the rocker arm shafts.

To install the rocker shafts:

7. Install the rocker arm assemblies on the cylinder head. Torque the bolts to specifications in sequence.

8. Adjust the valves cold.

9. Clean the mating surfaces of the cylinder head and rocker cover.

10. Install the rocker cover with a new gasket.

11. Install the spark plug wires on the plugs. Place the wires in the clips on the rocker cover. Connect the choke and air by-pass valve cable.

12. Start the engine and check for leaks.

13. Allow the engine to reach operating temperature, torque the head bolts to specifications and adjust the valves hot.

Intake Manifold

REMOVAL AND INSTALLATION

1.8 and 2.0 Liter Engines

1975–77

1. Drain the cooling system.

2. Remove the air cleaner.

3. Remove the accelerator linkage, vacuum hoses, solenoid wire (at the quick-disconnect plug), and deceleration control lines from the carburetor and intake manifold. Label all of these wires and hoses as they are removed, to make reconnection easier.

4. Disconnect the choke cable and fuel line. Plug the fuel line.

5. Disconnect the Thermactor hoses, if equipped.

6. Disconnect the PCV valve hose.

7. Disconnect the heater return hose and by-pass hose.

8. Remove the intake manifold-to-cylinder head attaching nuts.

9. Remove the manifold and carburetor as an assembly.

To install the manifold:

10. Clean the gasket mating surfaces.

11. Install a new gasket and the manifold on the studs. Torque the attaching nuts to specification, working from the center outward.

12. Connect the PCV valve hose to the manifold.

13. Connect the by-pass and heater return hose.

14. If equipped, connect the Thermactor hose.

15. Install the accelerator linkage.

16. Connect the fuel line, choke cable, vacuum hoses, and solenoid wire.

17. Replace the air cleaner.

18. Fill the cooling system. Run the engine and check for leaks.

1978–82

1. Drain the cooling system and remove the air cleaner assembly.

2. Disconnect the following items at the carburetor:
   a. Accelerator linkage
   b. Choke cable
   c. Fuel line

3. Disconnect the heater return hose and by-pass hose.

4. Disconnect the electrical connectors from both the carburetor solenoid and the water temperature sender.

5. Disconnect all of the vacuum hoses from the carburetor and the intake manifold. Tag the hoses so that they may be reinstalled correctly.

6. Disconnect the air injection system hoses at the air by-pass valve (or the anti-afterburn valve for Calif.) and remove the valve.

7. Disconnect and remove the EGR control valve and pipe assembly.

8. Remove the PCV valve.

9. Disconnect the servo diaphragm (for the throttle positioner system) and remove the diaphragm.

10. Remove the intake manifold-to-cylinder head fasteners and remove the manifold and carburetor as an assembly.

11. Clean the gasket mating surfaces.

12. Installation is the reverse of the previous steps. Replenish the cooling system

with coolant and check the system for leaks after the engine is started.

NOTE: Torque the manifold fasteners starting from the center and work outward in a circular pattern.

2.3 Liter Engines

1. Drain the cooling system and remove the air cleaner assembly.

2. Disconnect the accelerator cable at the carburetor.

3. Disconnect all of the vacuum hoses from the carburetor and the intake manifold. Tag the hoses so that they may be reinstalled correctly.

4. Disconnect the heat tube at the EGR valve.

5. Remove the engine oil dipstick and tube assembly.

6. Disconnect the fuel lines at the carburetor.

7. Remove the PCV valve.

8. Remove the two distributor cap screws and move the distributor cap aside.

9. Remove the intake manifold retaining bolts and remove the manifold and carburetor as an assembly.

10. Clean the gasket mating surfaces.

11. Installation is the reverse of the previous steps. Replenish the cooling system with coolant and check the system for leaks after the engine is started.

NOTE: Torque the manifold fasteners according to the accompanying illustration.

Exhaust Manifold

REMOVAL AND INSTALLATION

1. Remove the hot air duct which runs to the air cleaner case, if equipped. Remove the air injection nozzles or air pipe assembly, if equipped, on the 1.8 and 2.0. If the engine has a hot air duct, remove the upper and lower heat insulators. If the engine has an EGR valve, remove it.

2. Raise and support the truck.

3. Remove the two attaching nuts from the exhaust pipe at the manifold. Discard the old gasket.

4. Remove the manifold attaching nuts. On 2.3s, disconnect the air pump check valve hose.

5. Remove the manifold.

To install the manifold:

6. Apply a light film of graphite grease to the exhaust manifold mating surfaces before installation.

7. Install the manifold on the studs and install the attaching nuts. Tighten the nuts to 16–21 ft. lbs. on the 1.8 and 2.0. Final torque for the 2.3 is 16–23 ft. lbs., 1977–78, or 27–38 ft. lbs., 1979 and later. Tighten the nuts in a circular pattern, working from the center out towards the ends, on the 1.8 and 2.0. On the 2.3, follow the pattern illustrated.

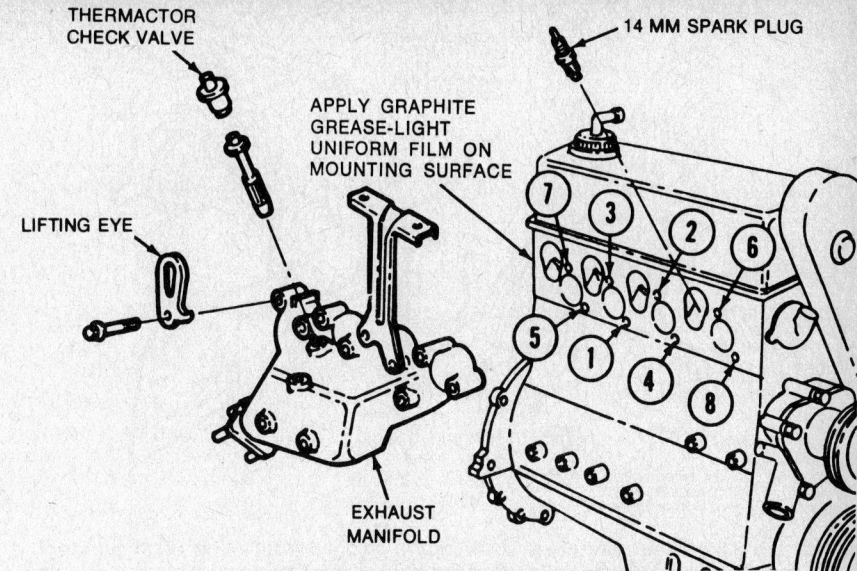

TORQUE THE MANIFOLD BOLTS TO SPECIFICATIONS IN TWO PROGRESSIVE STEPS IN THE SEQUENCE SHOWN

Exhaust manifold torque sequence for the 2.3 engine

8. Install a new exhaust pipe gasket. Connect the exhaust pipe and torque the nuts to 15 ft. lbs.

9. On 2.3s, connect the hose to the air pump check valve. Install the EGR valve, heat insulators, air injection nozzles or air pipe, and hot air duct, as applicable.

Engine Front Cover

REMOVAL AND INSTALLATION

1.8 and 2.0 Liter Engines

1. On 1977 and earlier models, scribe alignment marks on the hood hinges and remove the hood.

2. Drain the cooling system.

3. Disconnect the upper and lower radiator hoses. Remove the radiator.

4. Remove the accessory drive belts.

5. Remove the crankshaft pulley, water pump, and engine cooling fan.

6. Remove the cylinder head-to-front cover bolt.

7. Raise and support the truck.

8. Remove the engine skid plate.

9. Disconnect the emission line from the oil pan, if equipped. Drain the oil from the engine.

10. Remove the oil pan.

11. Remove the alternator and bracket and lay the alternator aside.

12. Remove the Thermactor pump (if equipped) and lay the pump aside.

13. Remove the steel tube from the front of the engine.

14. Unbolt and remove the front cover.

To install the front cover:

15. Clean all the gasket mating surfaces.

16. Clean the crankshaft pulley.

17. Use contact cement and cement a new front cover gasket on the block.

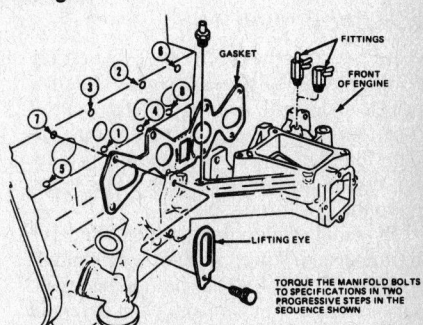

Intake manifold torque sequence for the 2.3 engine

18. Install the front cover and torque the attaching bolts to specifications.

19. Install the Thermactor pump (if equipped).

20. Install the alternator and bracket.

21. Install the water pump and a new gasket. Torque the bolts to specifications.

22. Connect the by-pass hose and heater hose to the water pump.

23. Install the crankshaft pulley and attaching bolt. Torque the bolt to specifications.

24. Install the Thermactor (if equipped), and alternator belts. Install the water pump pulley and the engine cooling fan.

25. Install the fan. Adjust the tension of the belt(s).

26. Install the radiator and the upper and lower hoses.

27. Install the air cleaner.

28. Install the oil pan and the emission line.

29. Install the engine skid plate.

30. Lower the truck to the ground.

31. Fill the engine with oil and fill the cooling system. Run the engine and check for leaks.

32. Install the hood on 1977 and earlier models.

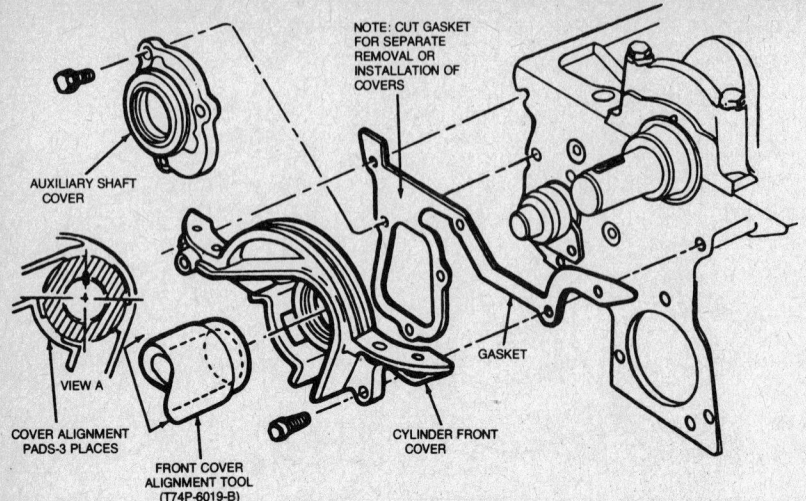

View of the 2.3 engine front cover showing the stepped front cover alignment tool which must be used during installation of the front cover. The cylinder block is shown inverted for clarity.

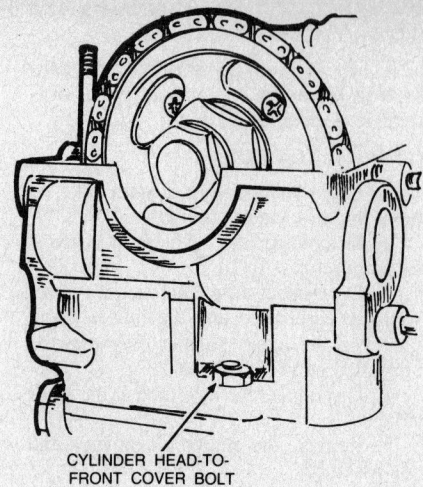

Cylinder head-to-front cover bolt on the 1.8 and the 2.0 engines

2.3 Liter Engine

There are actually two front covers on the 2.3 liter engine, which share a common gasket. You will need either the special Ford tool or a stepped socket (or pipe) to align the crankshaft cover upon reinstallation, and a thin-fingered gear puller to remove the crankshaft sprocket.

1. Drain the cooling system. Remove the upper and lower radiator hoses at the radiator. If your Courier has an automatic transmission, remove and plug the fluid cooler lines from the bottom of the radiator. Remove the radiator.

2. Remove the drive belts to the alternator, air pump and air conditioning compressor, if so equipped, and move the components out of the way. Do NOT disconnect any air conditioning lines. Unbolt and remove the fan and its pulley from the water pump shaft.

3. Remove the camshaft belt outer cover. There are tubular spacers underneath the two bolts directly above the crankshaft pulley.

4. Remove the crankshaft pulley. It is held on with a single center bolt. Remove the belt guide underneath the pulley. It is pressed onto the crankshaft over the locating key.

5. Loosen the cam belt tensioner and remove the belt. See the Timing Belt and Tensioner procedure section.

6. Remove the belt inner cover.

7. Use a puller to remove the crankshaft cam belt sprocket. Be sure that the puller does not cock the sprocket on the shaft.

8. Drain the engine oil and remove the oil pan. See the appropriate section in this chapter.

9. Unbolt and remove the cylinder front cover and the auxiliary shaft cover, and the common gasket.

If only one cover is to be removed, cut the gasket around the remaining cover, then use the necessary half of a new gasket when the cover is replaced.

Before reinstalling the cover(s), clean all the gasket surfaces thoroughly. Pry out the old seals from the covers, but do not install new shaft seals until the covers are in place. Position a new gasket on the front of the engine, install the covers and bolts, but do not tighten them. Using either the Ford tool (illustrated) or a stepped pipe, align the cylinder cover and the crankshaft, so that the timing belt will not interfere with the front cover. Torque the bolts to 6–9 ft. lbs. with the tool in place.

Install new shaft seals after the covers have been installed. Oil the lips of the seals before installation. The rest of the installation process is the reverse of removal. Be sure to use sealer on the oil pan gasket, front cover and rear main bearing cap seals. No special tool is necessary to replace the crankshaft sprocket; just align it with the key and press it into place. After assembly, fill the crankcase with oil, the cooling system with coolant, and adjust the belt tension. Start the engine, check for leaks, and adjust the initial ignition and engine (belt) timing.

Front Cover Oil Seal

REMOVAL AND INSTALLATION

1.8 and 2.0 Liter Engines

The front cover oil seal can be removed and a new one installed without removing the front cover.

1. On 1977 and earlier models, scribe alignment marks on the hood hinges and remove the hood.

2. Drain the cooling system.

3. Disconnect the upper and lower radiator hoses and remove the radiator.

4. Remove the drive belt(s).

5. Remove the crankshaft pulley.

6. Pry the front oil seal from the front cover.

To install a new oil seal:

7. Clean the pulley and seal area.

8. Press a new front seal into position (flush).

9. Install the crankshaft pulley and torque the bolt to specifications.

10. Install the drive belt(s) and adjust the tension.

11. Install the radiator and connect the upper and lower hoses. Fill the cooling system.

12. Start the engine and check for leaks.

13. Install the hood on 1977 and earlier models.

2.3 Liter Engine

The cylinder and auxiliary shaft front cover seals can be replaced without removing the covers. Follow steps 1, 2, 3, 4, 5, and 7 of the 2.3 Engine Front Cover procedure. Ford recommends the use of a puller to remove the old seal; you can also use a sharp pointed piece of plastic or wood to pry it out. Do not use a screwdriver, though, because you may damage the seal seat. Coat the lips of the new seal with engine oil and press it into place. Ford has a threaded arbor press available for this job. You should also be able to press it home using a socket with a diameter slightly smaller than that of the seal (the socket should just clear the seal seat in the front cover). Place a block of wood on the socket, and tap the seal into place with light hammer blows on the wood.

After installing the new seals, replace the crankshaft sprocket, cam belt, belt guide, crankshaft pulley, belt outer cover, fan drive belts, and radiator. Replace the coolant, adjust the tension of the various belts, and check the initial ignition timing and the engine (belt) timing.

Timing Chain or Belt

CHAIN REMOVAL AND INSTALLATION

1.8 and 2.0 Liter Engines

1. Remove the cylinder head and front cover as previously outlined. It is not necessary to remove the intake and exhaust manifolds from the head.

2. Remove the timing chain tensioner.

3. Loosen the timing chain guide strip screws.

4. Remove the oil slinger.

5. Straighten the locktab on the oil pump gear nut washer. Remove the nut. Remove the oil pump gear and chain as an assembly.

6. Remove the timing chain, crankshaft gear and camshaft gears from the engine.

To install the timing chain, timing gears and tensioner:

7. Position the crankshaft gear in the timing chain as shown. The two bright links must align with the timing mark (notch).

8. Position the oil pump chain and gear on the crankshaft and oil pump.

9. Install the oil slinger.

10. Install the oil pump washer and nut. Bend the washer over the nut.

11. Install the timing chain tensioner. Fully compress the snubber spring and wedge a screwdriver into the tensioner release mechanism. Without removing the screwdriver, install the tensioner.

12. Install the cylinder head and camshaft. Be sure that the valve timing is as illustrated. It must be exact. You may have to move the cam gear one or two teeth to obtain the correct alignment.

13. Install the rocker arm shafts and cam bearing caps.

14. Install and torque the cylinder head bolts.

15. Adjust the timing chain tension. Press in on the chain guide strip. Tighten the guide strip attaching screws. Remove the screwdriver from the tensioner, allowing the snubber to take up the chain slack.

16. Replace the front cover.

17. Adjust the valve clearance cold. Run the engine until it reaches normal operating temperature. Retorque the cylinder head bolts and readjust the valve clearances.

BELT REMOVAL AND INSTALLATION

2.3 Liter Engines

1. Remove the access plug from the front of the belt cover.

2. Turn the crankshaft until the engine is at TDC, indicated when the timing pointer is aligned with the TDC notch on the crankshaft pulley. You can turn the crankshaft with a wrench on the pulley bolt; it is also easier with the spark plugs removed.

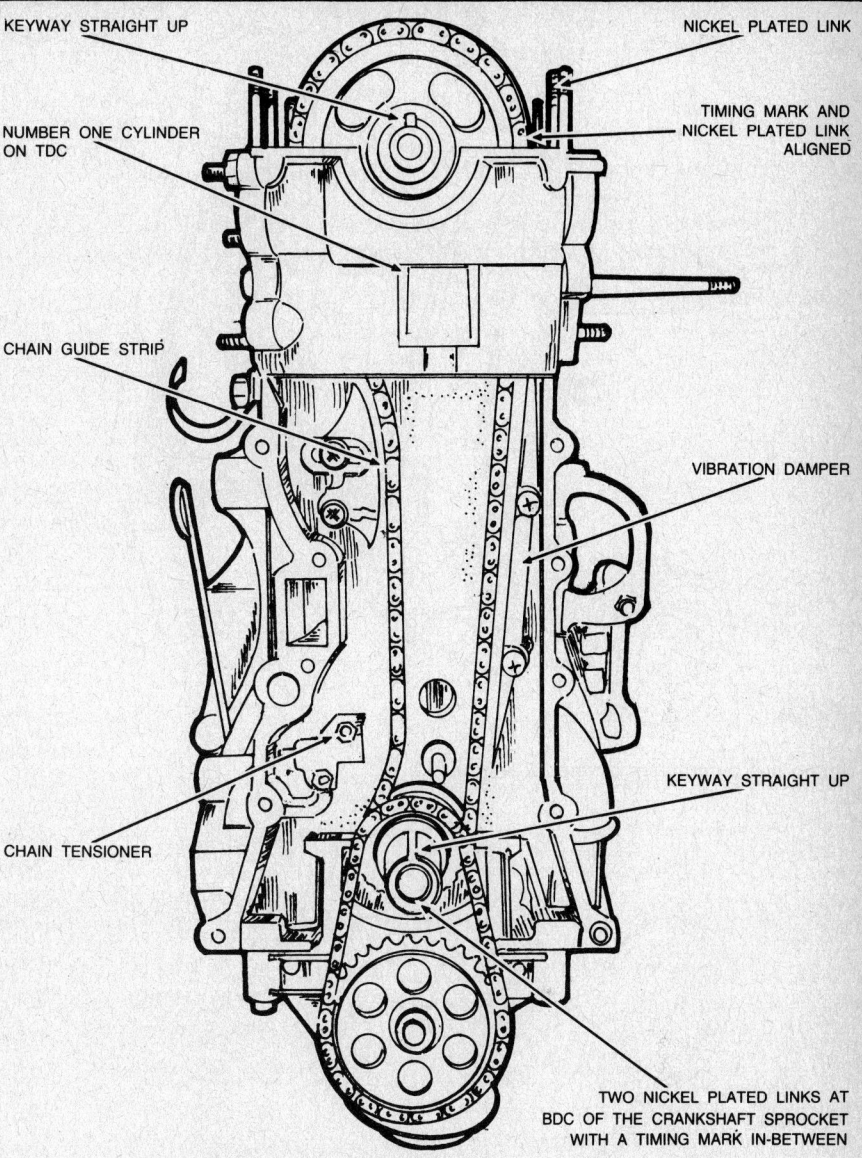

Positions of the timing chain and related components for the 1.8 and 2.0 engines. Align all marks as illustrated during installation of the chain.

CAUTION

Always turn the engine in the direction of normal rotation (clockwise as you face it). Backward rotation will cause the belt to jump time or lose teeth.

3. Remove the distributor cap. The rotor should point to the no. 1 cylinder plug wire tower.

4. Look through the access hole in the belt cover. The cam sprocket timing mark should be aligned with the timing pointer attached to the inner belt cover.

5. Loosen the adjustment bolts on the alternator, air pump, and a/c compressor (if equipped), and remove their drive belts. To provide clearance for removing the camshaft belt, remove the fan and its pulley from the water pump shaft.

6. Remove the belt outer cover. Note that there are tubular spacers underneath the two lower bolts.

7. Loosen the belt tensioner adjustment and pivot bolts. Lever the belt tensioner away from the belt and retighten the adjustment bolt to hold it away.

8. Remove the crankshaft pulley. It is held on by a single center bolt. Remove the belt guide behind it also.

9. Remove the camshaft drive belt. If it is not to be replaced, inspect it carefully for wear, cracks, or broken or missing teeth. If it shows any signs of wear, replace it.

10. With the belt still removed, turn the crankshaft until the key is vertical. Remove the distributor cap and set the distributor rotor to the no. 1 firing position by turning the auxiliary shaft sprocket. Turn the camshaft sprocket until its timing mark is aligned with the pointer attached to the inner belt cover. (This step is not necessary if the engine is in time and set to TDC).

11. Install the timing belt, first over the crankshaft sprocket. Then push it on coun-

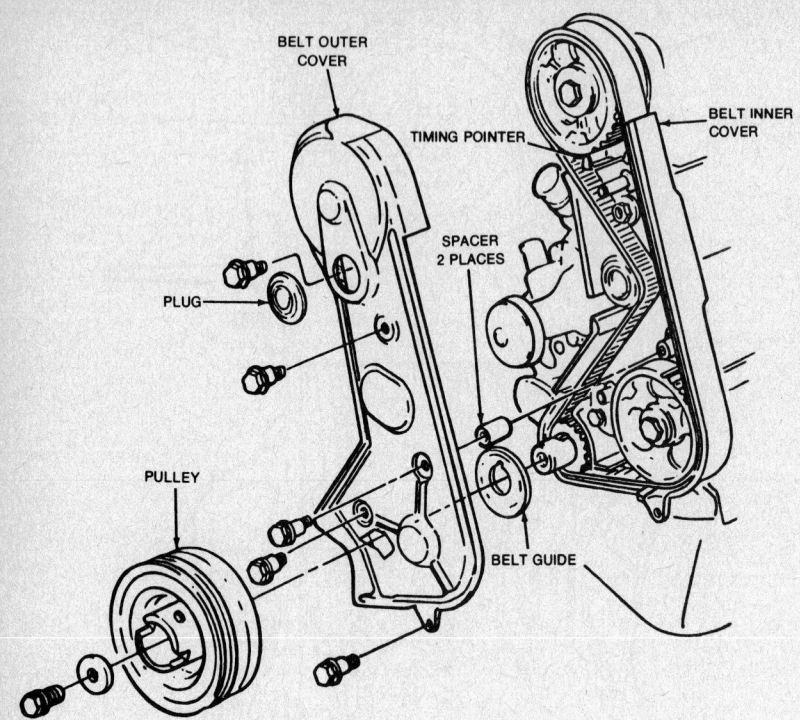

Timing belt outer cover on the 2.3 engine

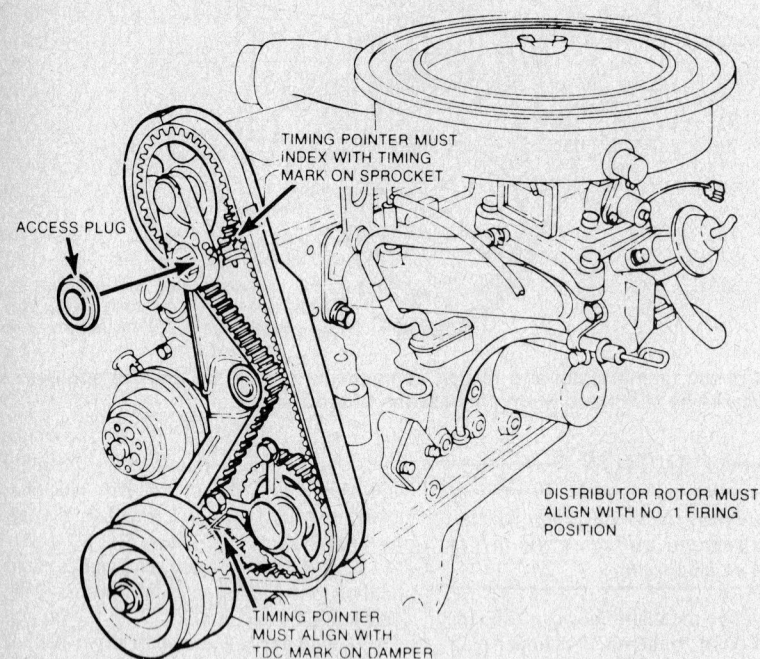

Proper timing belt alignment during belt installation on the 2.3 engine

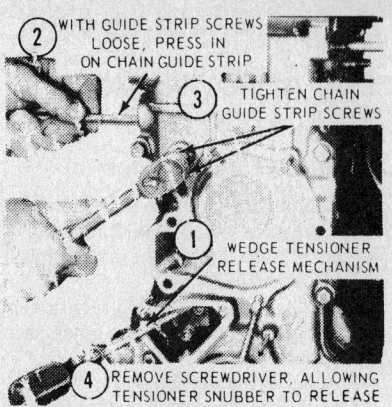

Timing chain tensioner adjustment with the front cover installed—1.8 and 2.0 engines

just the drive belt tension. Start the engine and check the ignition timing; adjusting as necessary.

Timing Chain or Belt Tensioner

REMOVAL, INSTALLATION AND ADJUSTMENT

1.8 and 2.0 Liter Engines

1. Remove the water pump.
2. Remove the tensioner cover.
3. Remove the attaching bolts from the tensioner. Remove the tensioner.

To install the tensioner:

4. Fully compress the snubber spring. Insert a screwdriver into the tensioner release mechanism.

5. Without removing the screwdriver, insert the tensioner and align the bolt holes. Install and torque the bolts.

6. Adjust the chain tension as follows:

a. Remove the two blind plugs and aluminum washers from the front cover.

b. Loosen the guide strip attaching screws.

c. Press the top of the chain guide strip through the adjusting hole in the cylinder head.

d. Tighten the guide strip attaching screws.

e. Remove the screwdriver drom the tensioner and let the snubber take up the slack in the chain.

f. Install the blind plugs and aluminum washers.

g. Install the tensioner cover and gasket.

h. Install a new gasket and water pump. Install the crankshaft pulley and drive belt and adjust the tension. Check the coolant system level.

2.3 Liter Engines

Refer to the text and illustrations, concerning timing belt replacement.

terclockwise over the auxiliary sprocket and cam sprocket (from the bottom up on the auxiliary sprocket and from the intake to exhaust side on the cam sprocket). Adjust the belt fore and aft so it is centered on the sprockets.

12. Loosen the tensioner adjustment bolt, allowing it to spring back against the belt.

13. With the spark plugs removed, rotate the crankshaft two complete turns in the direction of normal rotation (clockwise as you face it). This will remove any slack from the belt. Torque the tensioner adjustment bolt to 14–21 ft. lbs., and pivot bolt to 28–40 ft. lbs.

14. Replace the belt guide and crankshaft pulley.

15. Replace the spark plugs, distributor cap, outer cover, fan and pulley, and drive belts for the alternator and accessories. Ad-

Camshaft

REMOVAL AND INSTALLATION

1.8 and 2.0 Liter Engines

Perform this operation on a cold engine only.

1. On 1977 and earlier models, scribe alignment marks on the hood hinges and remove the hood.

2. Drain the cooling system and remove the water pump.

3. Disconnect the coil wire and vacuum line from the distributor.

4. Rotate the crankshaft to place no. 1 cylinder on TDC of the compression stroke. This can be determined by removing the spark plug and feeling compression with your thumb. When compression is felt, rotate the crankshaft until the pointer aligns with the TDC mark on the pulley.

5. Remove the plug wires and distributor cap. Remove the distributor.

6. Remove the valve cover.

7. Release the tension on the timing chain.

8. Remove the cylinder head bolts. Only do this on a cold engine.

9. Remove the rocker arm assembly.

10. Remove the nut, washer and distributor gear from the camshaft.

11. Remove the nut and washer holding the camshaft gear.

12. Remove the camshaft. Do not remove the camshaft gear from the timing chain. Be sure that the gear teeth and chain relationship is not distrubed. Wire the chain and cam gear in place so that they will not fall into the front cover.

To install the camshaft:

13. Clean all the gasket surfaces.

14. Clean the cylinder head bolt holes.

15. Coat the camshaft and bearings thoroughly with engine oil. Install the camshaft on the head and install the camshaft gear.

16. Check the valve timing.

17. Install the rocker arm assembly.

18. Install and torque the head bolts.

19. Install the cam gear washer and nut.

20. Install the distributor gear, washer, and nut.

21. Adjust the timing chain tension.

22. Check the camshaft end-play. It should be 0.001–0.007 in. If it exceeds 0.008 in., replace the thrust plate with a new one.

23. Install the distributor, distributor cap and plug wires.

24. Connect the vacuum line and coil wire.

25. Adjust the valve clearance cold. Install the valve cover and water pump. Fill the cooling system.

26. Run the engine and check for leaks. When normal operating temperature is reached, adjust the hot valve clearance.

27. Adjust the carburetor and ignition timing.

28. Install the air cleaner.

29. On 1977 and earlier models, install the hood.

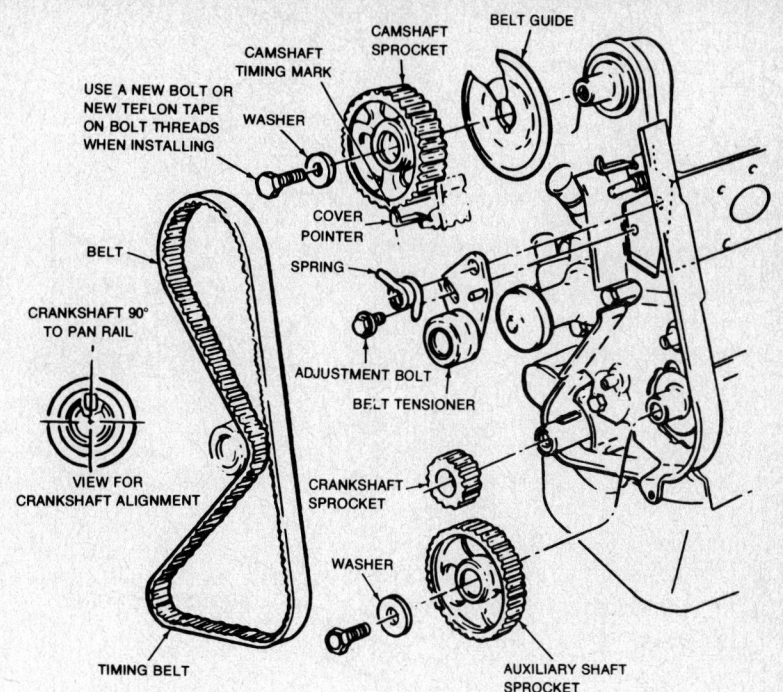

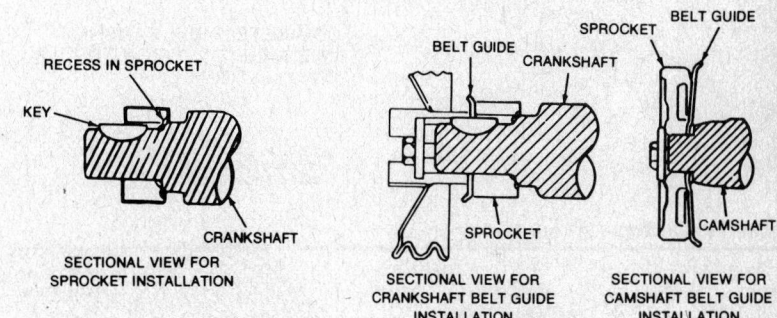

Camshaft drive system components on the 2.3 engine

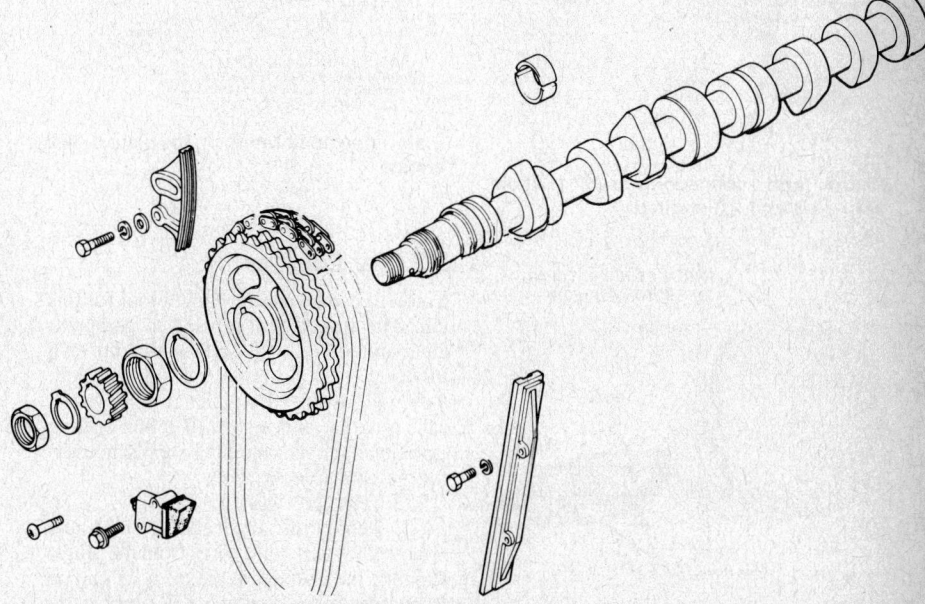

Camshaft and related components—1.8 and 2.0 engines

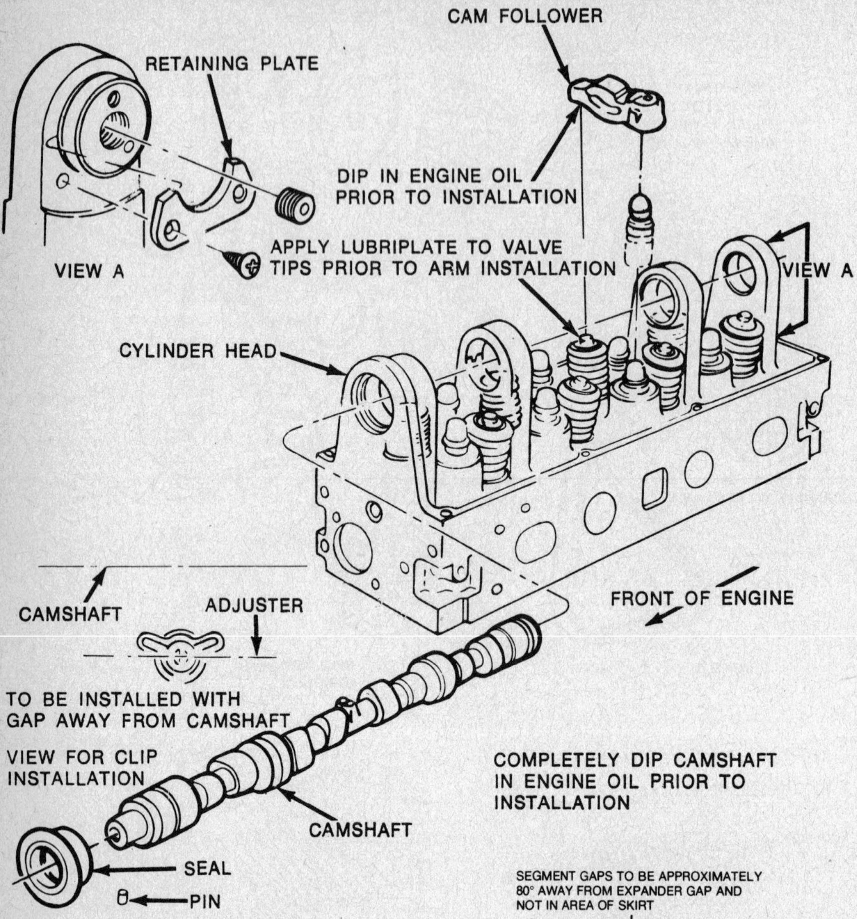

RETAINING PLATE

CAM FOLLOWER

DIP IN ENGINE OIL
PRIOR TO INSTALLATION

APPLY LUBRIPLATE TO VALVE
TIPS PRIOR TO ARM INSTALLATION

VIEW A

VIEW A

CYLINDER HEAD

CAMSHAFT   ADJUSTER

FRONT OF ENGINE

TO BE INSTALLED WITH
GAP AWAY FROM CAMSHAFT

VIEW FOR CLIP
INSTALLATION

COMPLETELY DIP CAMSHAFT
IN ENGINE OIL PRIOR TO
INSTALLATION

SEAL

PIN

CAMSHAFT

Camshaft installation—2.3 engine

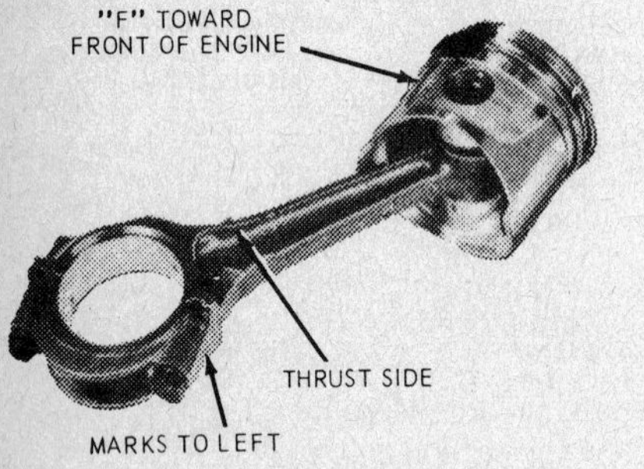

"F" TOWARD
FRONT OF ENGINE

SEGMENT GAPS TO BE APPROXIMATELY
80° AWAY FROM EXPANDER GAP AND
NOT IN AREA OF SKIRT

PISTON NOTCH
TO FRONT OF ENGINE
AT INSTALLATION

₵ EXPANDER

₵ SEGMENT

INSTALL PISTON INTO BLOCK
WITH RING GAPS AS FOLLOWS
EXPANDER—TO FRONT OF PISTON
SEGMENT—TO REAR OF PISTON

THRUST SIDE

MARKS TO LEFT

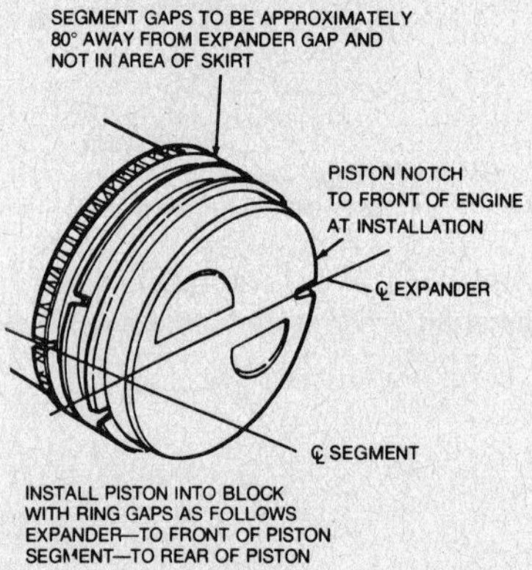

Piston ring positioning on the piston—2.3 engine

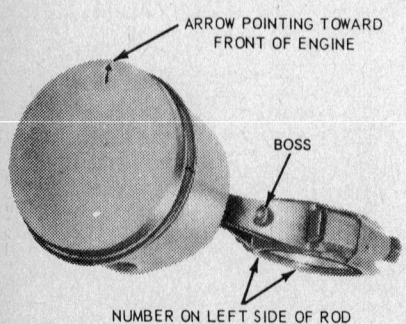

Piston and connecting rod relationship—1.8 and 2.0 engines

2.3 Liter Engines

You will need a special forked tool for this job. The forked tool is used to compress the hydraulic lash adjusters so that the cam followers may be removed and installed. You will also need a puller to remove the cam sprocket and a strip of teflon sealing tape (available at plumbing supply houses) for the cam sprocket bolt.

1. Turn the engine to TDC.
2. Remove the air cleaner. Number and remove the spark plug wires from the plugs. Remove the hose from the oil filler cap on the valve cover. Remove any other wires or hoses crossing the valve cover, and remove the valve cover.

ARROW POINTING TOWARD
FRONT OF ENGINE

BOSS

NUMBER ON LEFT SIDE OF ROD

Piston and connecting rod relationship—2.3 engine

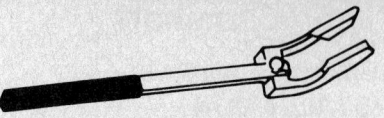

You will need a forked compressing tool like this to remove the 2.3 cam followers

Camshaft follower depressing tool used on the 2.3 engine—see text

3. Remove the camshaft belt outer cover.
4. Loosen the belt tensioner adjuster and pivot bolts, and lever the tensioner away from the belt. Retighten the adjuster bolt to hold it away.
5. Slip the cam belt off the cam sprocket.
6. Remove the cam sprocket bolt and washer. Use a puller to remove the cam sprocket. Remove the belt guide.
7. Position the camshaft so that the base circle (low point) of the cam lobe is on the cam follower of the rearmost valve (#4 intake). Compress the lash adjuster with the forked tool, and withdraw the cam follower over the lash adjuster and out. It may also be necessary to compress the valve spring.
8. Repeat this procedure with all eight cam followers, working from the rear of the head to the front. Keep the folllowers in order; they must be returned to their original positions.
9. When all the followers have been removed, remove the two phillips head screws and washers and the retaining plate from the rear of the rear cam bearing tower.
10. Using a puller or a pointed piece of wood or plastic, pry the seal from the front of the camshaft. Slide the camshaft out through the front of the head.

To install:
1. Coat the camshaft and bearings thoroughly with engine oil. Slide the cam into the head.
2. Replace the retaining plate, screws and washers. Press a new front cam seal into place. Oil the lips of the seal before installation.
3. Coat the valve tips with Lubriplate® or its equivalent. Coat each cam follower with engine oil.
4. Working from the front to the rear, replace the cam followers. Rotate the cam so that the base circle of the cam lobe for the appropriate valve is facing the head. Use the forked tool to compress the lash adjuster, and install the follower over the lash adjuster and valve stem. It may also be necessary to compress the valve spring, using the same tool. Be sure the cam followers are returned to their original valves.

Before rotating the camshaft to the proper position for the next valve, fully compress and release the lash adjuster of the cam follower just installed. It is imperative that this is done to prevent the adjusters from pumping up and providing incorrect clearance.
5. Slide the cam belt guide into place over the key. Install the cam sprocket over

the key. Wrap the sprocket bolt threads with teflon tape, and install the bolt and washer.

6. Measure the camshaft end play. Push the cam to the rear of the head. Install a dial indicator so that the point is on the cam sprocket. By inserting a large screwdriver between the cam sprocket and head, lever the cam forward and release it. If the end play measures more than 0.009 in., the retaining plate must be replaced.

7. Turn the cam until its sprocket timing mark lines up with the indicator on the belt sprocket, pushing it on from the intake side to the exhaust side. Adjust the belt fore and aft on the sprocket so that it is centered.

8. Release the cam belt tensioner so that it springs back against the belt. Remove the spark plugs. Using a wrench on the crankshaft pulley, rotate the engine two complete turns to remove slack from the belt. Rotate the engine in the normal direction of rotation (clockwise as you face it).

9. Tighten the belt tensioner adjuster bolt to 14–21 ft. lbs., the pivot bolt to 28–40 ft. lbs. Check the belt timing.

10. Replace the belt outer cover.

11. Install a new gasket on the valve cover with sealer, and install the valve cover. Replace the spark plugs, spark plug wires, oil filler cap hose, air cleaner, and any other hoses or wires disconnected.

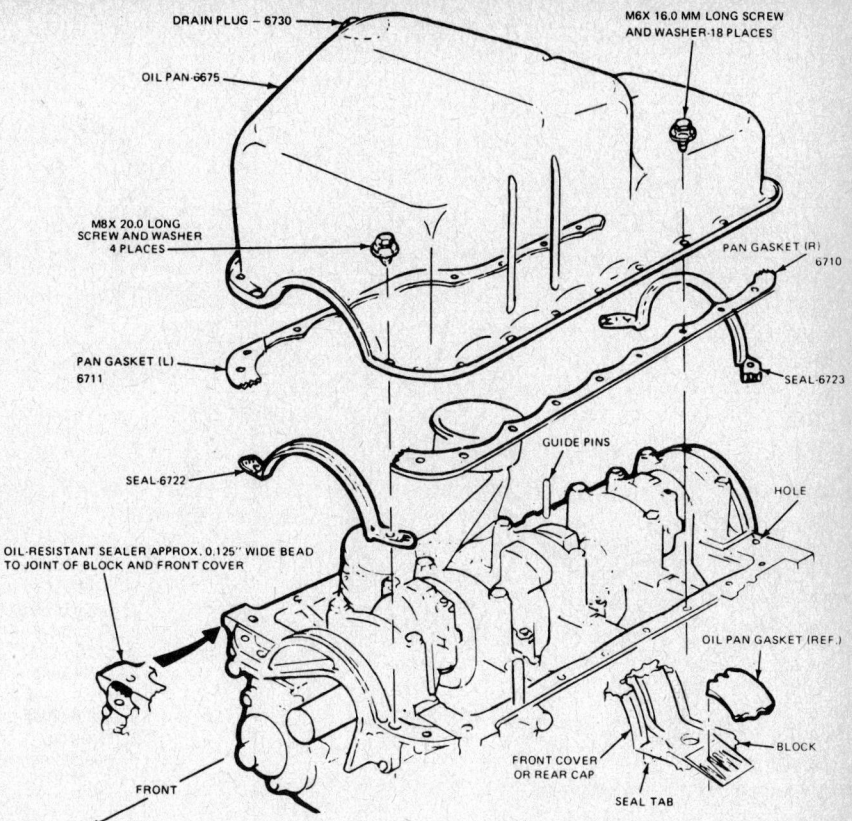

Oil pan gasket installation—2.3 engine

Auxiliary Shaft

REMOVAL AND INSTALLATION

2.3 Liter Engine Only

1. Set the engine to TDC.

2. Remove the camshaft drive (timing) belt as previously outlined.

3. Remove the auxiliary shaft sprocket. It is held on by a single center bolt and washer. You will probably need a puller to get the sprocket off the shaft.

4. Remove the distributor as previously outlined.

5. Remove the auxiliary shaft cover and retaining plate.

6. Remove the shaft through the front of the block.

NOTE: Do not allow the distributor drive gear to touch the bearing surfaces in the block.

To install:

1. Because the auxiliary shaft cover gasket is shared with the cylinder front (timing) cover, you will have to carefully cut off the old gasket around the marks left by the cover, if it did not tear and pull off when you removed the cover. Scrape off any traces of the old gasket, and cut a new gasket to fit. Do not install the new gasket yet.

2. Coat the auxiliary shaft, bearings, and gear with engine oil.

3. Slide the shaft into place, being careful not to bang the gear into the bearings.

4. Replace the retaining plate. Coat the new gasket with a thin layer of sealer and install onto the front of the block. Install the cover.

5. Install the distributor.

6. Install the auxiliary shaft sprocket, washer, and bolt.

7. Remove the distributor cap. Turn the auxiliary shaft sprocket until the distributor rotor points to the no. 1 spark plug tower position. The camshaft and crankshaft should still be at the TDC position.

8. Install the camshaft drive belt, outer cover, belts, fan and pulley as previously outlined.

Pistons and Connecting Rods

Piston, connecting rod, and piston ring removal and installation are detailed in the Engine Rebuilding section at the end of this chapter. Removal and installation are outlined with the engine out of the truck, but the same procedures may be used with the block in the chassis.

Apply a light coat of oil to all parts before reassembly. You may need to start the piston pin back into place with a few taps of a soft mallet. Always check the fit of new rings in the cylinder in which they are to be used before installing. Press them square in the bore with a piston before measuring.

Piston installation position is shown in the illustrations. On the 1.8 and 2.0 space the piston rings 120° apart, so that the gaps are not located on the thrust side or piston pin side.

On the 2.3, install the rings as shown. Be very careful when reinstalling when reinstalling pistons not to nick the crankshaft journals with the connecting rod bolts. Cover the bolts with a length of hose for protection.

Crankshaft

Main bearings may be replaced without removing the crankshaft. If the crankshaft must be removed, it is recommended that the engine be removed from the vehicle and mounted in a work stand. Refer to the Engine Rebuilding section.

Engine Lubrication

OIL PAN

Removal and Installation

1. Raise and support the truck.

2. Remove the engine skid plate (1.8 and 2.0).

3. Drain the engine oil.

4. Remove the clutch release cylinder attaching nuts. Let the cylinder hang.

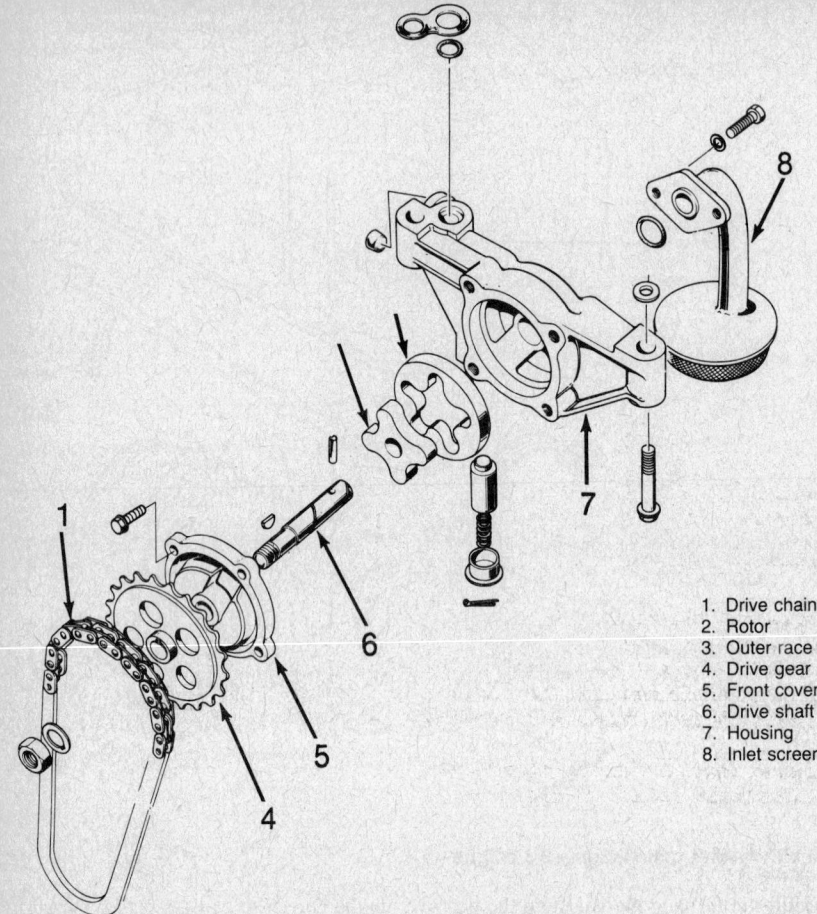

1. Drive chain
2. Rotor
3. Outer race
4. Drive gear
5. Front cover
6. Drive shaft
7. Housing
8. Inlet screen

Oil pump and related components—1.8 and 2.0 engines

5. Remove the engine rear brace attaching bolts and loosen the bolts on the left side.

6. Disconnect the emission line from the oil pan (some 1.8s).

7. Remove the oil pan nuts and bolts and let the oil pan rest on the crossmember. The 2.3 oil pan is held on by 18 16 mm long bolts and washers around the perimeter, and 4 20mm long bolts and washers. These must be returned to their original positions.

8. Remove the oil pump pickup tube from the pump (1.8 and 2.0).

9. Remove the oil pan.

To install the oil pan:

10. Clean all the gasket surfaces.

11. Clean the oil pan, oil pump pickup tube and oil pump screen.

12. Install a new oil pan gasket with oil-resistant sealer. There are two side gaskets and a front and rear seal on the 2.3. The seals go on to the engine block, and the side pan gaskets go onto the pan. Refer to the illustration.

13. Install the oil pump pickup tube and screen (1.8 and 2.0).

14. Install the oil pan on the block. Torque the bolts to 5–8 ft. lbs.

15. Connect the emission line to the oil pan, if applicable.

16. Attach the rear engine bracket. Torque the bolts to specification.

17. Install the clutch release cylinder.

18. Replace the engine skid plate.

19. Lower the truck. Fill the crankcase, and run the engine. Check for leaks and oil pressure.

Oil Pump

REMOVAL AND INSTALLATION

1.8 and 2.0 Liter Engines

1. Remove the oil pan.

2. Remove the oil pump gear attaching nut.

3. Remove the bolts attaching the oil pump to the block. Loosen the gear on the pump.

4. Remove the oil pump and gear.

To install the oil pump:

5. Install the oil pump gear in the chain.

6. Prime the oil pump and install it on the gear and cylinder block. Install the bolts

and torque them to 13–20 ft. lbs.

7. Install the washer, gear and nut. Bend the locktab on the washer.

8. Install the oil pan. Fill the engine with oil. Start the engine and check for oil pressure. Check for leaks.

2.3 Liter Engine

The oil pump is mounted on the bottom of the engine block and is enclosed by the oil pan. To remove the pump, remove the oil pan, attaching bolts, and the pump. When installing, use a new gasket, and fill the pump with oil to prime it.

INSPECTION

1. Thoroughly wash the pump with cleaning solvent.

2. Visually inspect the pump rotor and race for damage.

3. Visually check the mating surface of the pump cover for excessive wear and/or damage. Replace the pump cover if necessary.

4. Using a feeler gauge, measure the clearance between the pump (outer) race and the pump body. The measurement should be within the following range: .001–.013 in. for 2.3 liter engines; .006–.010 in. for 1.8 and 2.0 liter engines.

5. Place a straightedge across the pump housing and measure the distance between the pump housing and the pump rotor/race, using a feeler gauge. The total clearance (rotor end-play) should be within the following range: .002–.004.

6. Measure the outer diameter of the pump shaft and the inner diameter of the corresponding housing bearing bore. The difference between these two measurements should be within the following range: .0015–.0030.

The pump cover is the only part of the pump which is serviced separately from the pump assembly. If any of the previous measurements exceed the specification limits, or if damage to the pump is apparent, the entire pump assembly must be replaced.

Oil Pump Chain

TENSION CHECK AND ADJUSTMENT

1.8 and 2.0 Liter Engines Only

Oil pump chain tension can be checked with a straightedge and a ruler. Lay the straightedge against the oil pump and crankshaft gears, alongside the chain. Depress the chain and measure the slack with a ruler. If slack exceeds 0.157 inches, the chain tension will have to be adjusted. Chain slack is reduced by the addition of shims between the oil pump and the cylinder block. The shims should be of equal thickness on each side of the pump.

Rear Main Oil Seal

REPLACEMENT

1.8 and 2.0 Liter Engines

If the rear main oil seal is being replaced independently of any other parts, it can be done with the engine in place. If the rear main oil seal and the rear main bearing are being replaced together, the engine must be removed from the truck.

1. Remove the transmission.
2. Remove the clutch disc, pressure plate and flywheel.
3. Using an awl, punch two holes in the crankshaft rear oil seal. They should be punched on opposite sides of the crankshaft, just above the bearing cap-to-cylinder block split line.
4. Install a sheet metal screw in each hole. Pry against both screws at the same time to remove the oil seal. Do not scratch the oil seal surface on the crankshaft.
5. Clean the oil recess in the cylinder block and bearing cap. Clean the oil seal surface on the crankshaft.
6. Coat the oil seal surfaces with oil. Coat the oil seal surface and the seal surface on the crankshaft with Lubriplate®. Install the oil seal and be sure that it is not cocked. Be sure that the seal surface was not damaged.
7. Install the flywheel. Coat the threads of the flywheel attaching bolts with oil-resistant sealer. Torque the bolts to specification, in sequence, across from each other.
8. Install the clutch, pressure plate, and transmission.

2.3 Liter Engines

1. Remove the oil pan. It may also be necessary to remove the oil pump to provide access to the main bearing cap bolts.
2. Loosen all the main bearing cap bolts, thereby lowering the crankshaft slightly, but not more than 1/32 in.
3. Remove the rear main bearing cap, and remove the oil seal from the bearing cap and cylinder block. Install a small sheet metal screw in one end of the cylinder block half of the seal, and pull on the screw to remove the seal. Be careful not to scratch the seal surfaces.
4. Clean the seal grooves in the cap and block with solvent (such as lacquer thinner). Use a brush to get behind the groove lip. Dry the area thoroughly. No solvent should remain to come in contact with the seal.
5. Dip the new seal halves in clean engine oil.
6. Carefully install the upper seal (block half) into its groove with the undercut side of the seal toward the front of the engine, by rotating it on the seal journal of the crankshaft until the ends are flush with the parting surface. Be sure that no rubber has been shaved off. Wipe the oil from the mating surface of the bearing cap and cylinder block.

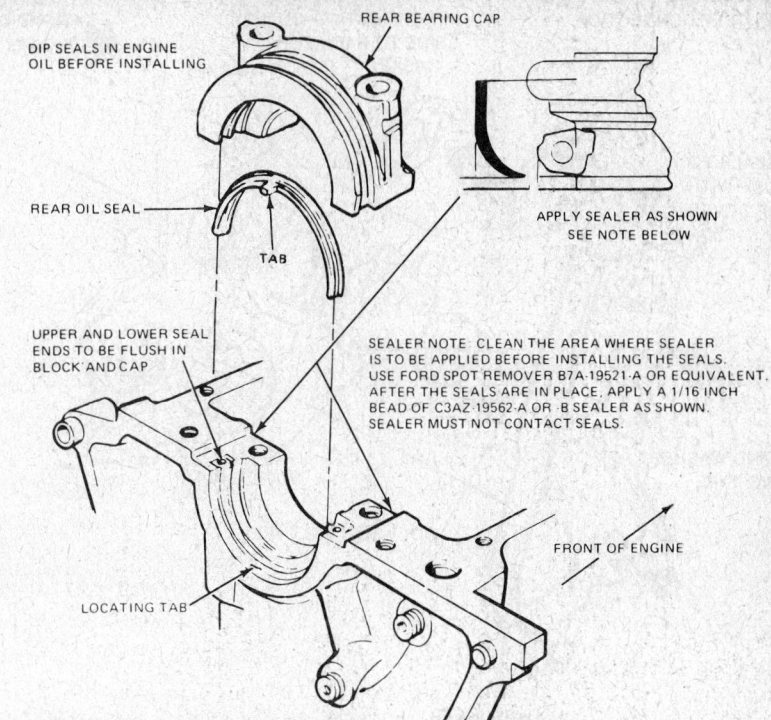

Rear main seal installation—2.3 engine

7. Tighten the bearing cap bolts to 80–90 ft. lbs.
8. Install the lower seal in the rear main bearing cap with the undercut side of the seal toward the front of the engine. Be sure that the seal ends are flush with the parting surface to mate with the upper seal when the cap is installed.

NOTE: Install the seals so that the locating tab faces the rear of the engine.

9. Apply a *small* amount of silicone sealer to the mating surface of the bearing cap. No sealer should come in contact with the rubber seals when the bearing cap is installed and tightened.
10. Install the rear main bearing cap and torque to 80–90 ft. lbs.
11. Install the oil pump (if removed) and oil pan. Fill the crankcase with oil, and operate the engine, checking for leaks.

ENGINE COOLING

Radiator

REMOVAL AND INSTALLATION

1. Drain the cooling system.
2. If equipped, remove the fan shroud.
3. Remove the fan. On California models, remove the fan clutch.
4. Disconnect the upper and lower radiator hoses. If your truck has automatic transmission, disconnect and plug the fluid cooler lines at the bottom of the radiator.
5. Unbolt and remove the radiator.

To install the radiator:

6. Install the radiator against the supports and tighten the mounting bolts.
7. Install the hoses on the radiator. Tighten the clamps. Install the automatic transmission cooler lines, if removed.
8. Install the fan and fan clutch (California models).
9. If equipped, install the fan shroud.
10. Refill the cooling system with the specified amount and type of coolant. Run the engine and check for leaks.

Water Pump

REMOVAL AND INSTALLATION

1.8 and 2.0 Liter Engines

1. Drain the cooling system.
2. Remove the lower hose from the water pump.
3. Disconnect the upper radiator hose from the engine and the lower radiator hose at the radiator.
4. Remove the radiator.
5. Remove the drive belts.
6. Remove the fan and pulley. Remove the crankshaft pulley.
7. Disconnect the coolant bypass hoses from the water pump.
8. Unbolt and remove the water pump.

To install the water pump:

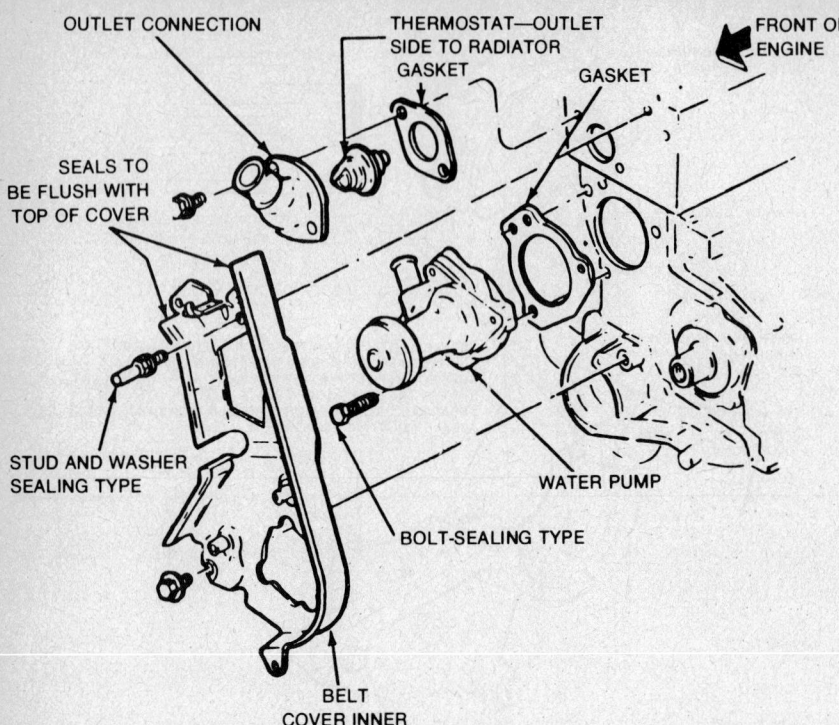

OUTLET CONNECTION

THERMOSTAT—OUTLET
SIDE TO RADIATOR
GASKET

GASKET

FRONT OF
ENGINE

SEALS TO
BE FLUSH WITH
TOP OF COVER

STUD AND WASHER
SEALING TYPE

WATER PUMP

BOLT-SEALING TYPE

BELT
COVER INNER

Water pump and thermostat—2.3 engine. It is not necessary to remove the inner timing belt cover to replace the pump.

9. Clean the gasket surfaces of the water pump and cylinder block.

10. Install the water pump and new gasket on the block. Torque the bolts to specification.

11. Install the lower hose on the water pump. Install the bypass hoses.

12. Install the fan and pulley. Install the crankshaft pulley.

13. Install the drive belts and adjust the crankshaft pulley.

14. Install the radiator.

15. Refill the cooling system with the specified amount and type of coolant. Install the radiator cap and start the engine. Check for leaks.

2.3 Liter Engine

1. Drain the cooling system.

2. Disconnect the lower radiator hose and heater hose from the water pump.

3. Remove the alternator, air pump, and air conditioner drive belts. Remove the fan shroud, if your truck has one.

4. Remove the fan and pulley.

5. Remove the camshaft drive belt outer cover.

6. Remove the water pump attaching bolts and the water pump. It is not necessary to remove the belt inner cover.

To install:

1. Clean all gasket material from the mating surfaces.

2. Transfer the heater hose fitting to the new water pump.

3. Coat the new gasket with sealer and position the pump and gasket on the engine.

4. Install the pump mounting bolts.

5. Install the belt outer cover, fan and pulley, and accessory drive belts. Install the fan shroud, if equipped.

6. Connect the radiator hose.

7. Fill the cooling system. Turn the heater on, install the radiator and coolant recovery tank caps, and run the engine. Check for leaks. When the engine has cooled, check the coolant level, and add as necessary.

Thermostat

REMOVAL AND INSTALLATION

1.8 and 2.0 Liter Engines

1. Drain enough coolant to bring the coolant level down below the thermostat housing. The thermostat housing is located on the left front side of the cylinder block. Disconnect the temperature sending unit wire.

2. Remove the coolant outlet elbow. If so equipped, position the vacuum control valve out of the way. The vacuum control valve is not used on California models.

3. Disconnect the coolant by-pass hose from the thermostat housing.

4. Remove the thermostat and housing from the engine.

5. Remove the thermostat from the housing and note the position of the jiggle pin.

To install the thermostat:

6. Remove all gasket material from the parts.

7. Install the thermostat housing using a new gasket with water-resistant sealer.

8. Position the thermostat in the housing with the jiggle pin up. Coat a new gasket with sealer and install it on the thermostat housing.

9. Install the coolant outlet elbow and vacuum control valve (if equipped).

10. Connect the by-pass and radiator hoses.

11. Connect the temperature sending unit wire.

12. Fill the cooling system with the proper coolant. Operate the engine and check the coolant level. Check for leaks.

2.3 Liter Engine

1. Drain the coolant so that the level is below the thermostat.

2. It is not necessary to remove the hose from the outlet connection, if you're careful. Remove the two bolts holding the outlet to the block and pull it away enough to provide access to the thermostat.

3. Remove the thermostat and gasket.

To install:

1. Clean the mouting surface and outlet housing of all old gasket material.

2. Coat a new gasket with silicone sealer. The gasket must go on before the thermostat.

3. Position the gasket against the engine, then place the thermostat on top of it with the outlet side towards the radiator.

4. Install the coolant outlet and the two retaining bolts. Torque the bolts to 14–21 ft. lbs. Refill the cooling system, start the engine, and check for leaks and proper thermostat operation.

EMISSION CONTROLS

Since their introduction into the United States, Couriers have been equipped with air pollution control systems.

Hydrocarbons (HC), carbon monoxide (CO), oxides of nitrogen (NO$_x$) and fuel vapors are controlled by four basic systems. A Thermactor air injection system is used to control harmful composites in the exhaust gases by introducing fresh air to aid in more complete combustion. A positive crankcase ventilation (PCV) system is used on all trucks to route blow-by gases from the crankcase into the combustion chamber. All Couriers use an evaporative emission control system to absorb fuel vapors emitted from the fuel tank by evaporation. All Couriers also use a deceleration control system to augment the Thermactor air pump.

In addition, three systems were introduced in 1976 and 1977. Exhaust gas recirculation (EGR) is used on 1976 California Couriers with manual transmission, and all 1977–80 models. Its purpose is to recycle a small portion of the exhaust gas by

THERMACTOR SYSTEM COMPONENT USAGE

Year	Engine Displacement (Liters)	Air Pump	Check Valve	Air Injection Nozzle(s)	Manifold	Air Control Valve	Reed Valve and Air Pipe Assembly	Vacuum Delay Valve(s)
'75–'76	1.8	yes	yes	yes	yes	yes	no	no
'77–'78	1.8	yes	yes	yes	yes	yes①	no	no
	2.3	yes	yes	yes	no②	yes③	no	yes④
'79–'81	Fed. 2.0	no	no	no	yes	no	yes	no
	Cal. 2.0	yes	yes	yes	yes	yes	no	yes④
	Can. 2.0	yes	yes	yes	yes	no	no	no
	Fed. 2.3	no	no	no	no②	no	yes	no
	Cal. 2.3	yes	yes	yes	no②	yes	no	yes④
	Can. 2.3	yes	yes	yes	no②	no	no	no
'82	Fed. and Can. 2.0	no	no	no	yes	no	yes	no
	Cal. 2.0	yes	yes	yes	yes	yes	no	yes④
	Fed. and Can. 2.3	no	no	no	no②	no	yes	no
	Cal. 2.3	yes	yes	yes	no②	yes	no	yes④

Fed.: Federal (49 state) usage
Cal.: California usage
Can.: Canada usage
① '77 California models only
② Passages integral with exhaust manifold and/or cylinder head
③ 1978 California models only
④ Some California models

returning it to the combustion chamber, thus reducing combustion temperatures and the formation of No_x. The catalytic converter, used on some 1976–78 California trucks and most 1979 and later models, chemically alters the composition of exhaust gases which pass through it. In addition, a spark delay system is used on 1977 and later 1.8 and 2.0 engines and all 1981–82 engines, which retards the ignition spark curve during acceleration to promote more thorough combustion.

Thermactor Air Injection System

Because of the many variables under which the engine operates, some hydrocarbon and carbon monoxide gases escape unburnt from the combustion chamber. To burn these gases more thoroughly, a belt-driven air pump is used to supply fresh air to an air injection manifold located on the exhaust manifold. The injection of fresh air supports combustion of the hot unburned HC and CO gases within the exhaust manifold.

AIR PUMP

The air pump is a belt-driven vane-type pump which is located at the front of the engine. The pump pressurizes fresh air which is then delivered to the remaining Thermactor system components.

The pump incorporates a relief valve which relieves excess pressure in the pump. This action prevents excessive engine power loss and protects the pump from internal damage due to excessive pressure.

In the event of pump failure, the entire air pump and relief valve assembly must be replaced.

Belt Adjustment

1. Loosen the pump adjusting bolt and lower mounting bolt.
2. Pry the pump outward until the center of the belt can be deflected the following amounts by applying about 22 lbs. of pressure on the belt:
   a. 1.8 and 2.0 engines—.4–.6″(new); .6–.7″(used)
   b. 2.3 engines—.5–.7″(new); .8–.9″(used)
3. When the proper belt deflection is obtained, tighten both pump bolts.

Air Pump Testing

1. Adjust the pump drive belt tension as previously outlined.
2. Disconnect the pump outlet hose from the air by-pass (exc. Calif.) or anti-afterburn (Calif.) valve.

NOTE: The air by-pass and anti-afterburn valves are considered to be part of the Deceleration Control System. Refer to the appropriate section for identification of the valve.

3. Attach a pressure gauge to the end of the hose, using a tee fitting if necessary.
4. Start the engine and raise the engine rpm to 1500.
5. Note the reading on the pressure gauge. If the reading is below 1 psi, the pump must be replaced.
6. Remove the pressure gauge and reattach the pump outlet hose.

Air Pump Relief Valve Testing

1. Remove the air hose from the relief valve port.
2. Start the engine and allow it to idle.
3. Check for air flow at the relief valve. No air flow should be apparent. If there is air flow from the relief valve at idle, the air pump and relief valve assembly must be replaced.
4. Increase the engine rpm to 4500. Air should flow from the relief valve. If air does not flow from the valve or if the valve is excessively noisy, replace the air pump and relief valve assembly.

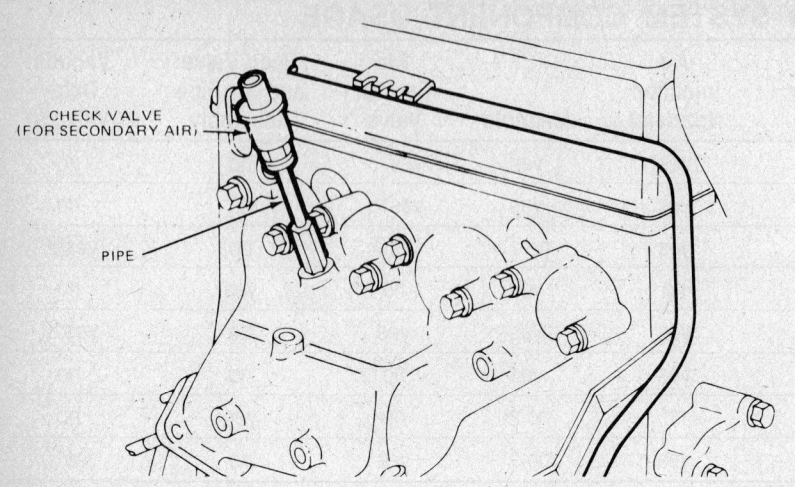

Air injection nozzle—2.3 engines

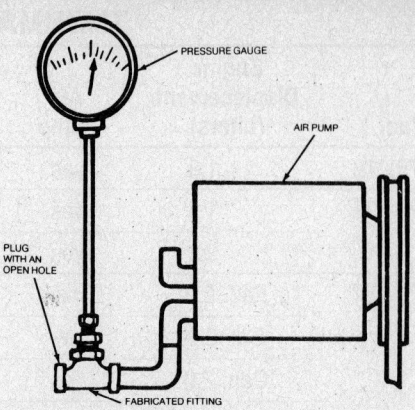

Checking the air pump output pressure

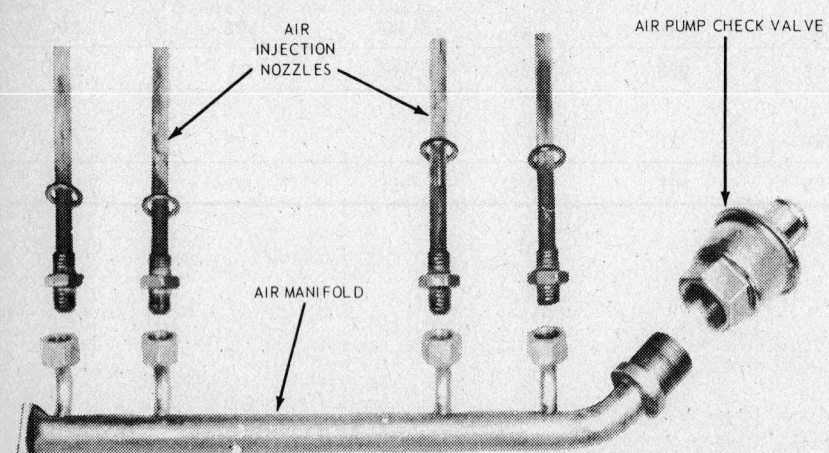

Air injection manifold and related parts—1.8 and 2.0 engines (typical). Some models use a secondary air injection system which is similar to that used on some 2.3 engines. See text for details.

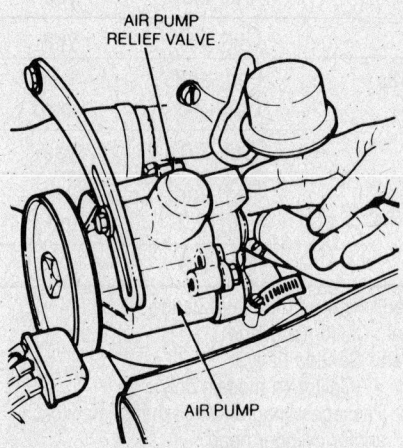

Checking the air pump relief valve

Pump Removal and Installation

1. On 1978 and later 1.8 and 2.0 engines, remove the air cleaner assembly.

NOTE: Step 2 is not necessary on 1978 and later models.

2. Remove the battery, alternator drive belt and alternator.

3. Disconnect the hoses from the air pump. Tag the hoses so that they may be correctly reinstalled.

4. Remove the pump adjusting bolt and drive belt.

5. Remove the pump mounting bolt and remove the pump.

6. Installation is the reverse of the previous steps. Adjust the tension of the alternator and air pump drive belts.

CHECK VALVE

The check valve is used to prevent the entrance of hot exhaust gas into the Thermactor system at times when the exhaust pressure is higher than the air pump output

pressure (e.g.,—engine backfire).

During normal operation, the air pump output pressure opens the check valve to allow air from the pump into the exhaust tract of the engine.

Removal and Installation

1. Disconnect the rubber hose from the check valve.

2. Unscrew the valve from either the Thermactor manifold (1.8 and 2.0 engines) or the air inlet pipe (2.3 engines).

3. Installation is the reverse of the previous steps.

Testing

1. Remove the check valve as previously outlined.

2. Blow into the side of the valve which attaches to the rubber hose. Air should flow freely in this direction.

3. Blow into the opposite (threaded) side of the valve. Air should not pass in this direction.

4. Replace the valve if it failed either of the previous tests.

AIR INJECTION NOZZLE(S)

The function of the injection nozzle is to direct air from the manifold (except 2.3 engines) to the proper location. 2.3 engines use only one injection nozzle; the direction of the air from that point is through the passages within the exhaust manifold.

Service of the nozzle(s) is not necessary as long as the nozzles are clear.

Removal and Installation

1. Disconnect the rubber hose from the check valve.

2. Remove the check valve.

3. On 1.8 and 2.0 engines, remove the air injection manifold.

4. Remove the injection nozzle(s) from the exhaust manifold.

5. Installation is the reverse of the previous steps.

INJECTION MANIFOLD

A manifold is used only on 1.8 and 2.0 engines. The manifold merely distributes the air from the pump to the individual air injection nozzles.

Service of the manifold is not necessary as long as the manifold passages are clear.

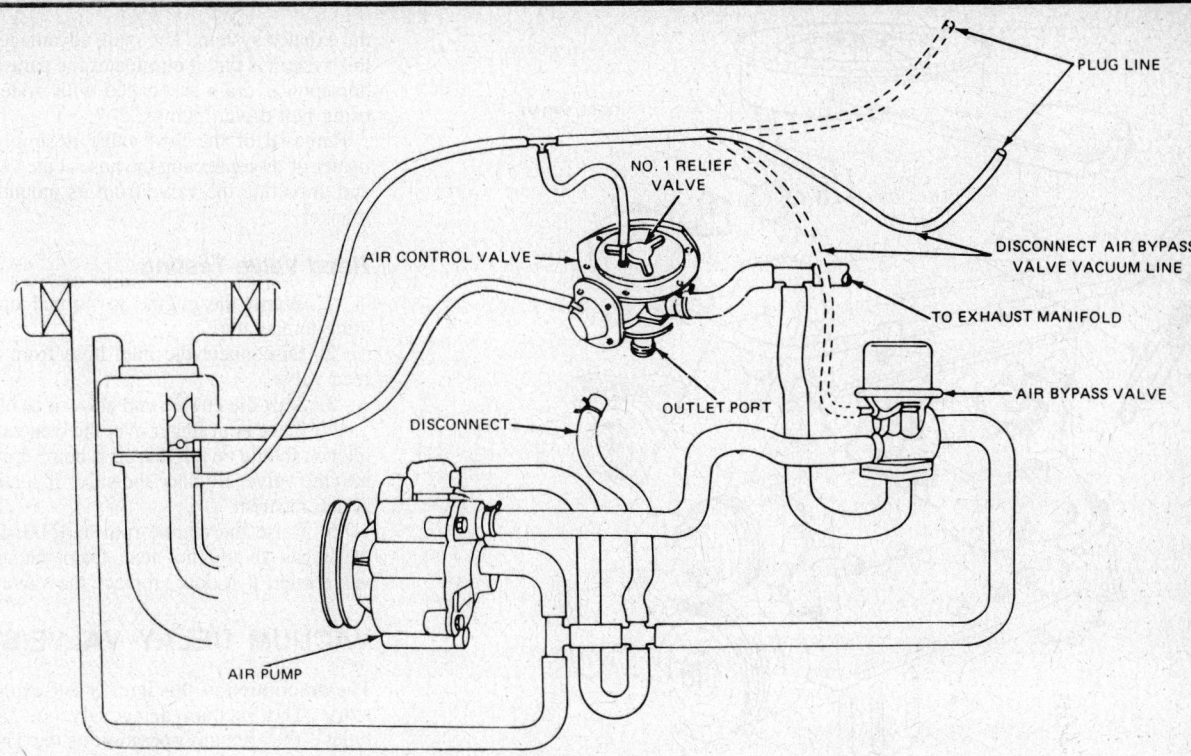

Testing the no. 1 relief valve of the air control valve—typical

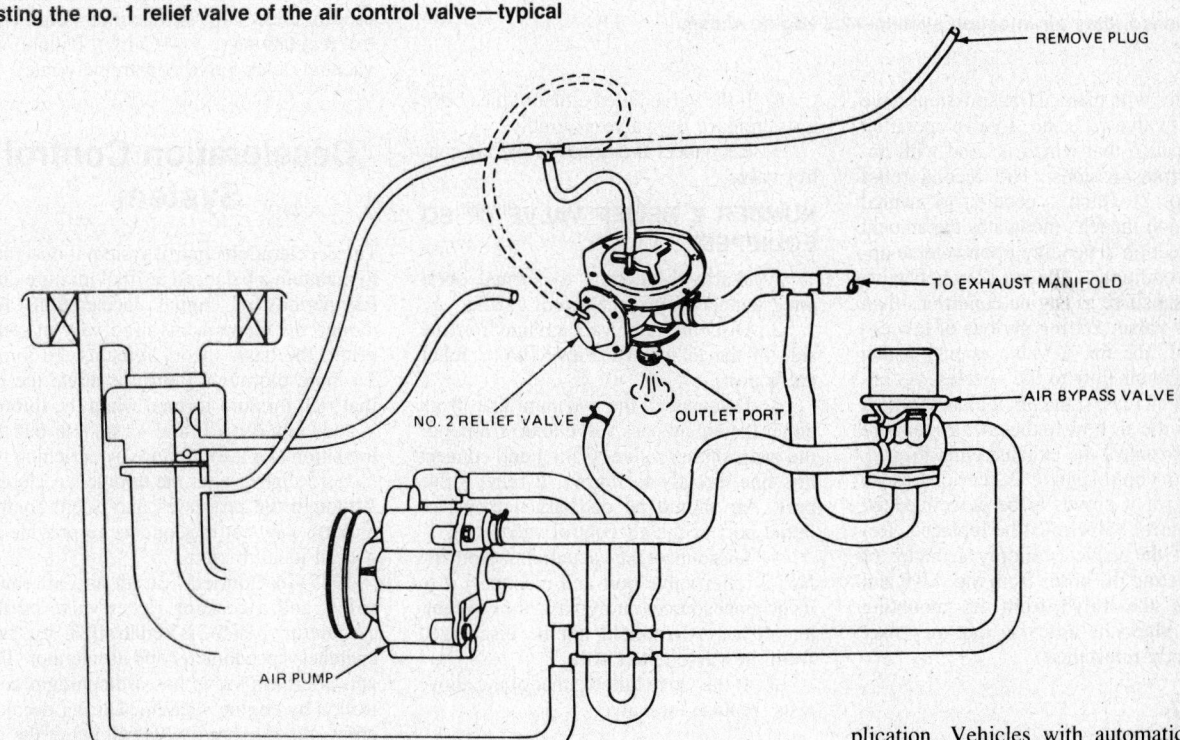

Testing the no. 2 relief valve of the air control valve—typical

Removal and Installation

1. Disconnect the rubber hose from the check valve.

2. Unscrew the check valve from the manifold.

3. Disconnect the manifold from the nozzles and remove the manifold.

4. Installation is the reverse of the previous steps.

AIR CONTROL VALVE

The air control valve contains either one or two relief valves depending upon the application. Vehicles with automatic transmissions have one relief valve (no. 1) which is actuated by intake manifold vacuum. At low engine loads, the no. 1 valve is closed, which directs air from the pump through the Thermactor system and to the nozzles. During periods of high engine loads, the no. 1 valve closes which stops air flow to the nozzles. The pump output air is diverted back to the pump air inlet. Also, the closing of the no. 1 valve during periods of high engine load prevents exhaust system overheating.

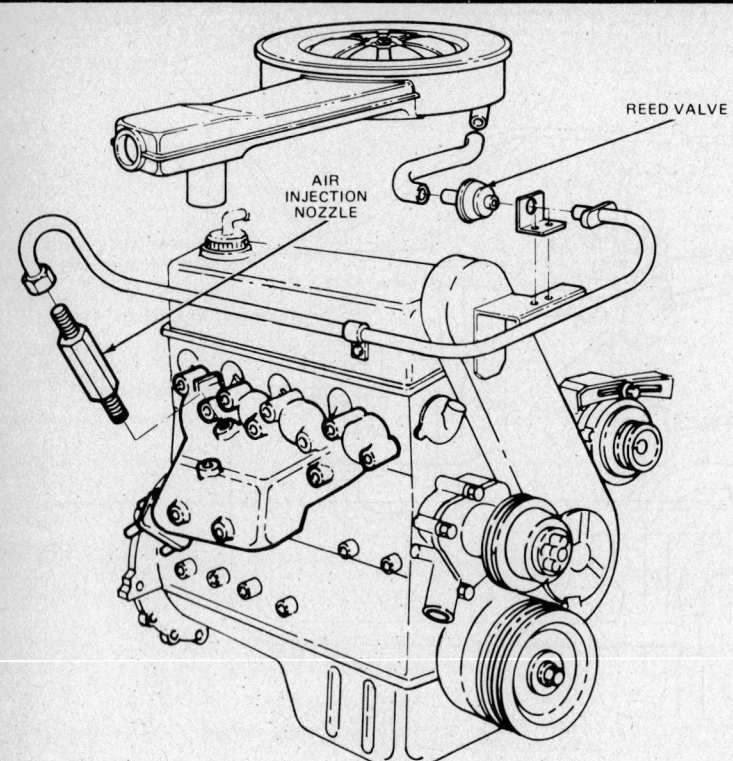

REED VALVE

AIR INJECTION NOZZLE

Typical secondary air injection system—2.3 engine shown

Vehicles with manual transmissions have two relief valves. The no. 1 valve operation is identical to that which is used with automatic transmissions. The second relief valve (no. 2) which is peculiar to manual transmission models, modulates the amount of air injection depending upon vehicle operating conditions. The no. 2 relief valve is more sensitive to engine conditions than the no. 1 valve. During periods of low engine load, the no. 2 valve opens, which reduces the air flow to the nozzles. As engine load increases, the no. 2 closes, which increases the air flow to the nozzles to more precisely control the exhaust emissions.

The air control valve is serviced as an assembly; if it proves to be defective, the entire control valve must be replaced. Removal of the valve is simply a matter of disconnecting the hoses from the valve and unbolting the valve from its mounting bracket. Mark the hoses so that they may be correctly reinstalled.

Testing

NUMBER 1 RELIEF VALVE

1. Disconnect the air hose from the bottom of the air control valve.
2. Start the engine and allow it to idle.
3. Air should not be discharged from the valve port (where the hose was disconnected).
4. Disconnect the vacuum line from the top of the air control valve (no. 1 relief valve port).
5. Air should not be discharged from the valve outlet port.

6. If the valve failed either of the above tests, replace the valve assembly.
7. Reconnect the hoses to the air control valve.

NUMBER 2 RELIEF VALVE (IF SO EQUIPPED)

1. Warm the engine to normal operating temperature and allow it to idle.
2. Disconnect the vacuum line from the side of the air control valve (no. 2 relief valve port).
3. Disconnect the vacuum line from either the air by-pass valve (exc. Calif.) or the evap shutter valve (Calif.) and connect this line directly to the no. 2 relief valve port. Air should be discharged from the outlet port of the air control valve.
4. Disconnect the vacuum line from the No. 2 relief valve port and reconnect it to its original source (air by-pass or evap shutter valve). Air should not be discharged from the valve outlet port.
5. If the valve failed either of the above tests, replace the valve.

REED VALVE AND AIR PIPE ASSEMBLY

This assembly is the main component of what is termed the secondary air injection system. Vehicles having this system are not equipped with air pumps.

The secondary system operates by sensing exhaust gas pulsations which in turn causes the reed valve to draw fresh air from the air cleaner and inject the fresh air into

the exhaust system. The main advantage of this system is that it eliminates the parasitic horsepower drain associated with systems using belt driven pumps.

Removal of the reed valve is simply a matter of disconnecting the hose at the valve and unbolting the valve from its mounting bracket.

Reed Valve Testing

1. Warm the engine to normal operating temperature.
2. Disconnect the inlet hose from the reed valve.
3. Start the engine and allow it to idle.
4. Place your finger over the reed valve inlet. It should be felt that air is being drawn into the valve. Replace the valve if suction is not apparent.
5. Raise the engine rpm to 1500. Exhaust gas should not leak from the reed valve inlet; if it does, replace the valve.

VACUUM DELAY VALVE(S)

The description of this item is self-explanatory. The vacuum delay valve(s) "fine tunes" the vacuum operation of the Thermactor system for vehicles which are to be used in areas with stringent emission control regulations (e.g.—Calif.). Failure of a vacuum delay valve is extremely rare.

Deceleration Control System

The deceleration control system is designed to maintain a balanced air/fuel mixture during periods of engine deceleration. Although the components used vary in some years, the basic theory remains the same: To more thoroughly burn or dilute the initial rich mixture formed when the throttle is suddenly closed, and to smooth out the transition to a lean mixture by enriching the mixture slightly after the throttle has closed. Although the processes may seem contradictory, they act in sequence to provide an overall ideal mixture.

1975–76 Couriers use an anti-afterburn valve, and a coasting richer valve on the carburetor which is controlled by two switches: speedometer and accelerator. The anti-afterburn valve has a diaphragm controlled by engine vacuum. During deceleration, the diaphragm lifts allowing the air pump to inject air into the intake manifold. This dilutes the incoming rich mixture, preventing detonation in the exhaust system, which would occur if the injected air from the air pump were to burn this rich mixture in the exhaust manifold. The coasting richer valve acts to add additional fuel to the lean intake mixture as soon as the anti-afterburn valve has shut off. The speed, accelerator and clutch switches must be closed to allow the coasting richer valve to operate. The accelerator switch closes when the accel-

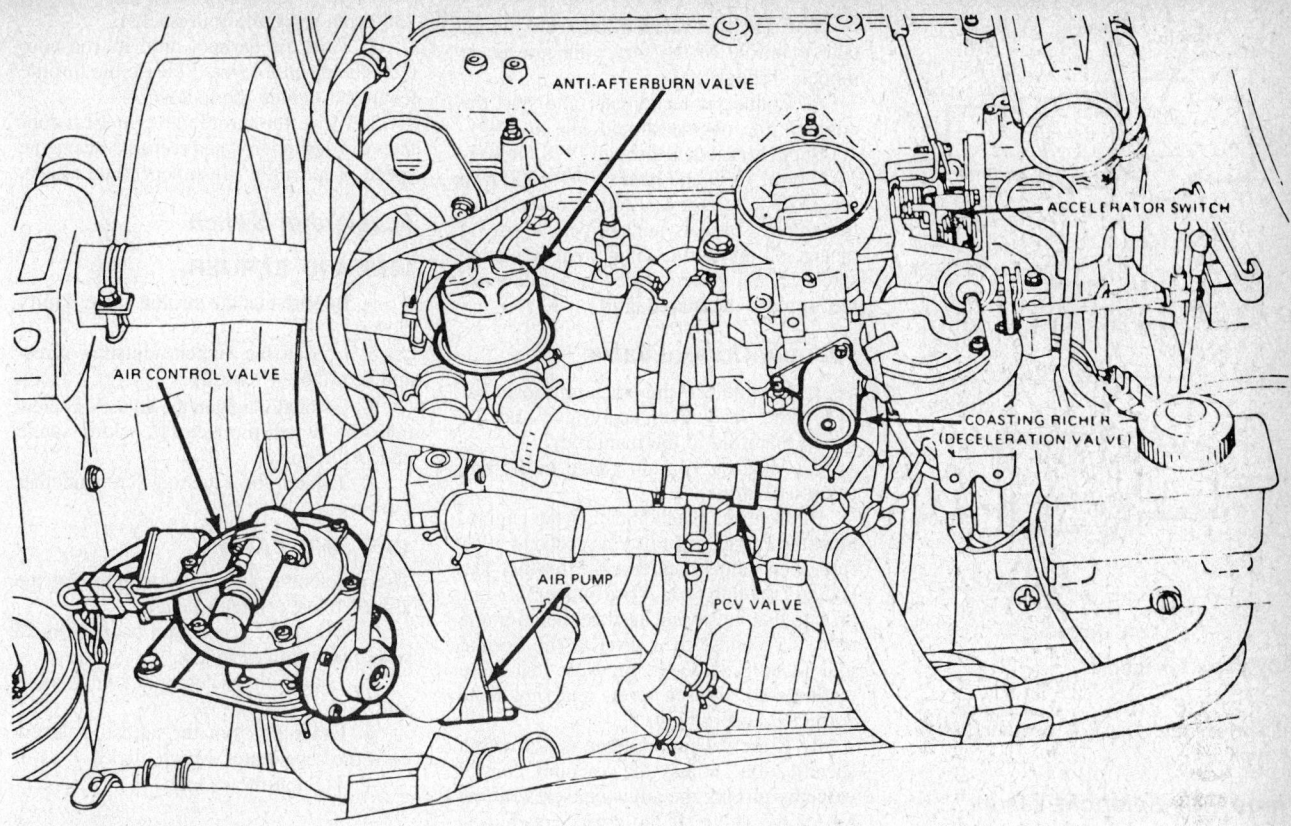

Typical Deceleration Control System

erator pedal is released. The speedometer switch closes when the truck speed is above 17–23 mph.

1977–78 Couriers with 1.8 engines use an air by-pass valve, a carburetor dashpot, and a throttle opener system comprised of a servo diaphragm connected to the throttle and a vacuum control valve. The air by-pass valve prevents afterburn in the exhaust by shutting off air to the exhaust manifold from the air pump during deceleration. The dashpot holds the throttle open slightly for an instant during sudden deceleration.

1977–78 2.3 engine 49 states and Canada trucks use an air by-pass valve, a dashpot (on trucks with manual transmissions only), and a coasting richer valve controlled by speed and accelerator switches. The air by-pass valve and dashpot are the same as those used on the 1977–78 1.8 and the coasting richer valve is the same as that on 1975–76 Couriers. 1977–78 California Couriers use the air by-pass valve, and the dashpot if the truck has a manual transmission.

1979–82 2.0 liter 49 states models use an anti-afterburn valve and a throttle positioner. California models have an air by-pass valve and a throttle positioner. Canadian models have an air by-pass valve, a dashpot, and a throttle positioner.

1979–82 2.3 liter 49 states models have a coasting richer solenoid valve activated by a speed switch and an accelerator switch; this system is the same as that used on earlier models. California and Canada models have an air by-pass valve, and a coasting richer solenoid valve activated by a speed switch and an accelerator switch; manual transmission models add a dashpot to these systems.

COMPONENT TESTS

Anti-Afterburn Valve

1. Remove the outlet hose from the anti-afterburn valve.

2. Hold a hand over the outlet fitting and raise the engine rpm. Quickly release the accelerator. Air should flow for approximately three seconds. If the valve passes air for more than three seconds, or does not pass air at all, it should be replaced.

Coasting Richer Valve (Deceleration Valve)

1. Remove the coasting richer valve from the carburetor.

2. Connect the coasting richer valve to the battery.

3. As power is applied to the valve, the solenoid plunger should be pulled into the valve body.

4. Reinstall the coasting richer valve. Connect a test light.

5. Raise the rear wheels and support the truck on stands. Block the front wheels.

6. Start the engine and raise the engine speed above 30 mph. Release the accelerator pedal. The test light should come ON and remain ON until the speed falls below 17–23 mph.

7. If the system is operating properly, no further tests are required. If not, proceed with the other tests.

8. Remove the stands and lower the truck. Disconnect the test light.

Accelerator Switch

The accelerator switch is actuated by a throttle lever link on the carburetor through 1978; the switch is located on the accelerator pedal on 1979–80 models. When checking the switch with a circuit tester, the test light should be ON when the accelerator pedal is fully released and should be OFF when the pedal is depressed.

Speed Switch

1. Remove the instrument cluster and attach a test light to the speedometer switch.

2. Reconnect the speedometer cable and ground wire.

3. Raise both wheels off the ground and support the truck on stands. Block the front wheels.

4. Start the engine.

5. Depress the accelerator pedal to accelerate the engine and confirm that the speed switch is ON at speeds of 17–23 mph and OFF at speeds below 17–23 mph.

6. If not, replace the switch.

7. Lower the truck and remove the test light. Reinstall the instrument cluster.

Speed Switch Relay

Check the speed switch relay with a test

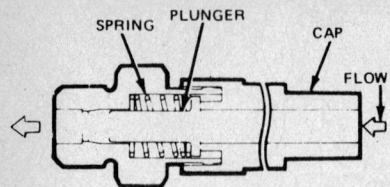

2.0L ENGINE

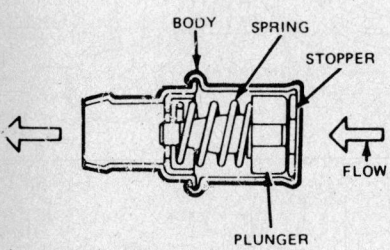

2.3L ENGINE

PCV valve operation

light to be sure that it is operating at 17–23 mph.

Three Way Solenoid Valve

1979–82 2.0 ENGINES ONLY

1. Start the engine and allow it to reach normal operating temperature. Check the idle speed and adjust as necessary.
2. Disconnect the wire at the three way solenoid valve. This wire is coded either black with a white stripe or brown with a red stripe on some models.
3. When the wire is disconnected, the engine speed should increase to 1000 rpm for 49 States trucks, or 1100 rpm for California models.
4. If the engine speed does not increase, the three way solenoid valve or the servo diaphragm is not operating correctly. Check the servo diaphragm using the following procedure; if the servo diaphragm is operating correctly, the three way valve is faulty and should be replaced.

Servo Diaphragm

1. Start the engine and set the idle speed to specification.
2. Stop the engine and disconnect the vacuum line between the vacuum control valve and the diaphragm at the diaphragm.
3. Disconnect the vacuum line between the intake manifold and the vacuum control valve at the manifold on models through 1978. On 1979–82 models, disconnect the vacuum hose at the vacuum amplifier and the vacuum hose at the three way solenoid valve. Connect the vacuum hose from the servo diaphragm to the vacuum amplifier so that the intake manifold vacuum is applied directly to the servo diaphragm.
4. Disconnect and plug the vacuum line between the carburetor and the distributor.

5. Connect a vacuum line from the intake manifold to the servo diaphragm on models through 1978.
6. Connect a tachometer and start the engine. The engine should idle at 1300–1500 rpm for models through 1978, or 900–1100 rpm, 1979 and later (1000–1200 rpm for 1979 and later California models). If the engine speed is not correct, adjust by means of the servo diaphragm adjusting screw. If the correct speed is not obtainable, replace the diaphragm.

Vacuum Control Valve

1. Disconnect the vacuum hose between the vacuum control valve and the intake manifold at the manifold.
2. Attach a vacuum gauge in the line using a T-fitting.
3. Connect a tachometer to the engine. Start the engine and raise the speed to 3000 rpm, then suddenly release the throttle. The vacuum reading should rise above 21.3 in., drop to that figure and hesitate there for one or two seconds, then drop to the normal idle vacuum of 16–18 in. Note that these readings are for sea level, and should be corrected accordingly.
4. If the vacuum reading is not within specification, adjust the vacuum control valve by turning the adjusting screw in the top of the valve. If the correct reading is unobtainable, replace the valve.

Vacuum Switch

1. Disconnect the vacuum hose between the vacuum switch and the vacuum control valve.
2. Using a T-fitting, connect a vacuum gauge between the vacuum switch and an external vacuum source.
3. Raise the vacuum reading above 8 in., then allow the vacuum to drop. The switch should click at approximately 6 in. If it does not, or if it clicks at a higher reading, replace the switch.

Air By-Pass Valve

1. Disconnect the air hose from the side of the air by-pass valve.
2. Connect a tachometer to the engine. Start the engine and raise the speed above 2000 rpm.
3. Release the throttle and check for air flow from the port on the side of the air by-pass valve. If there is no airflow, replace the valve.

COMPONENT ADJUSTMENTS

Dashpot

1. Check the engine idle speed and mixture, and adjust as necessary.
2. Remove the air cleaner.
3. With the tachometer still connected to the engine, loosen the dashpot locknut. Move the throttle lever and hold to maintain the engine speed at 2400–2600 rpm (2100–

2300 rpm for California trucks).
4. Turn the dashpot until its rod contacts the throttle lever. Release the throttle lever and tighten the locknut.
5. Move the throttle lever until it contacts the dashpot rod and recheck the engine speed. Repeat the adjustment if necessary.

Accelerator Switch

1978 AND EARLIER

1. Be sure that the throttle valve is fully closed.
2. Loosen the switch adjusting screw and turn the switch off.
3. Gradually tighten the adjusting screw until the switch produces a clicking sound and is turned on.
4. Tighten the adjusting screw another 1½ turns.

1979 AND LATER

The accelerator switch is mounted on the arm of the accelerator pedal.
1. Check the accelerator pedal to make sure that it moves freely.
2. Loosen the accelerator switch locknut.
3. Gradually turn the adjusting screw until the accelerator switch clicks.
4. Tighten the locknut.

COMPONENT REPLACEMENT

With the exception of the speed switch, replacement of the various components is simply a matter of disconnecting hoses, wires, etc., and dismounting the component. Mark all disconnected items so that they may be properly reconnected.

The speed switch is integrated with the speedometer assembly. To replace the speed switch, remove the speedometer as outlined later in the Courier section.

Positive Crankcase Ventilation (PCV) System

The function of the PCV valve is to divert blow-by gases from the crankcase to the intake manifold to be burned in the cylinders. The system consists of a PCV valve and the hoses necessary to connect the components.

Ventilating air is routed into the rocker cover from the air cleaner. The air is then moved to the PCV valve. The PCV valve is operated by differences in air pressure between the intake manifold and the rocker cover.

TESTING

1.8 and 2.0 Engines

1. Remove the hose from the PCV valve.

2. Start the engine and run it at approximately 700–1,000 rpm.

3. Cover the end of the PCV valve with a finger. A distinct vacuum should be felt. If no vacuum is felt, replace the valve.

2.3

Remove the PCV valve from the engine. Install a PCV valve known to be good. If the idle quality improves, the original valve was bad.

Evaporative Emission Control System

The evaporative emission system is designed to control the emission of gasoline vapors into the atmosphere. The system consists of a fuel tank, a condenser tank, a check valve, and a charcoal canister for 1975–76 models. In 1977, the system was changed slightly to consist of a sealed fuel tank, a vapor controlling orifice in the line between the tank and the charcoal canister, and the canister. The check valve of the previous system was eliminated through substitution of a filler cap with vacuum and pressure relief valves, and a fuel vapor valve on the tank.

When the engine is not running, fuel vapors are channeled to the condenser tank. The fuel returns to the fuel tank as the vapors condense. During periods of engine operation, fuel vapor that has not condensed in the condenser tank moves to the carbon canister. The stored vapors are removed from the charcoal by fresh air moving through the inlet hole in the bottom of the canister.

The check valve (1975–76), located between the condenser tank and the canister, allows fuel vapor and ventilation to flow during normal operation. If the system becomes clogged or frozen, the valve opens (by negative pressure in the fuel tank) to allow fuel to be drawn from the tank. The valve also opens to vent internal tank pressure under hot conditions. The fuel tank cap and fuel vapor valve replace the check valve on 1977 and later models, and perform essentially the same functions.

The only service necessary for this system is replacement of the charcoal canister at regular intervals and inspection of the rubber hoses at the same time for cracks or breaks. Any deteriorated hoses should be replaced.

Replacement of the canister is a basic procedure requiring only to disconnect the hoses at the canister and dismount the canister. Mark the hoses for proper installation.

Exhaust Gas Recirculation System

Oxides of nitrogen are formed under conditions of high temperatures and high pres-

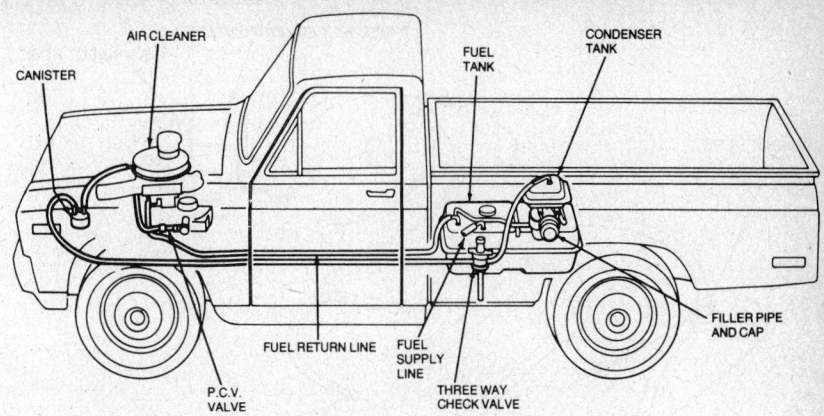

Evaporative emission control system—typical of 1975–77 models

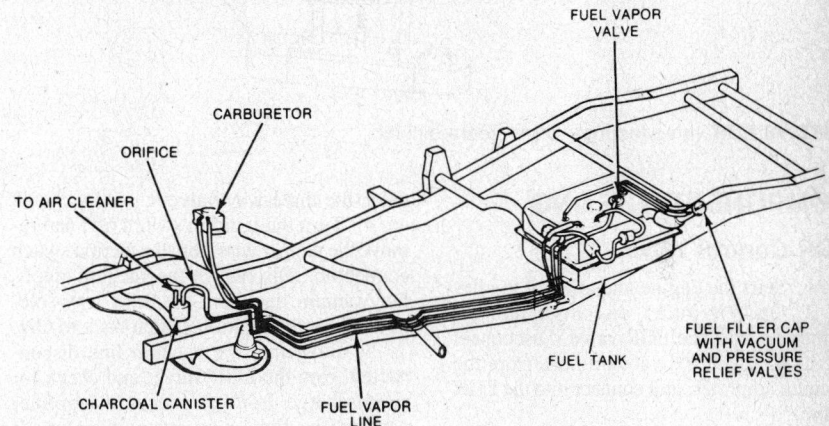

Evaporative emission control system—typical for 1978 and later models

sure. By eliminating one of these conditions, the production of NOx is restricted. The exhaust gas recirculation system (EGR) reintroduces a small portion of the exhaust gases into the combustion chamber with the intake charge, thus reducing peak combustion temperature. The EGR system is used on 1976 Couriers with manual transmission sold in California, and all 1977 and later trucks.

Components used through 1978 include an EGR control valve, a three-way solenoid valve, a vacuum amplifier, and a water thermo switch. The control valve, operated by engine vacuum, opens to allow exhaust gases into the intake manifold, and closes to shut them off. The solenoid valve regulates vacuum to the EGR valve. It is governed by the thermo switch. At coolant temperatures below 122°F (131°F for 1976 only), the thermo switch is closed. This closes the vacuum passage in the solenoid valve, cutting vacuum to the control valve which prevents exhaust recirculation when the engine is cold. At temperatures above 131°F, the thermo switch opens, allowing intake manifold vacuum to raise the control valve diaphragm, allowing recirculation of exhaust gases. The vacuum amplifier supplies varying amounts of vacuum to the control valve through the solenoid valve, opening or closing it during acceleration or at varying

engine speeds.

A slightly different EGR system is used on 1979 and later models. Components include the EGR valve, a water thermo valve, and a vacuum amplifier. The three-way solenoid valve is used on 2.0 liter engines only. The EGR valve is the same vacuum operated unit used in earlier years, and operates in the same manner. The water thermo valve controls the EGR valve, except on California models; on California models, the thermo valve actuates the no. 2 relief valve in the air control valve, and the air control valve regulates the EGR vacuum signal. The thermo valve is closed when coolant temperatures are below 115°F. Above that temperature, the valve opens, allowing vacuum to be transmitted to the EGR valve. The vacuum amplifier performs the same function as in earlier years.

NOTE: 1979 and 1980 2.0 liter Couriers sold in California have two water thermo valves. One is for the EGR system and the other is for the Spark Timing Control system. The thermo valve used in the EGR system has two vacuum hoses: one runs to the vacuum amplifier, and the other runs to the EGR valve. 1981 and 1982 California 2.0 engines use three water thermo valves; the valves are used in the EGR, purge control and spark timing control systems.

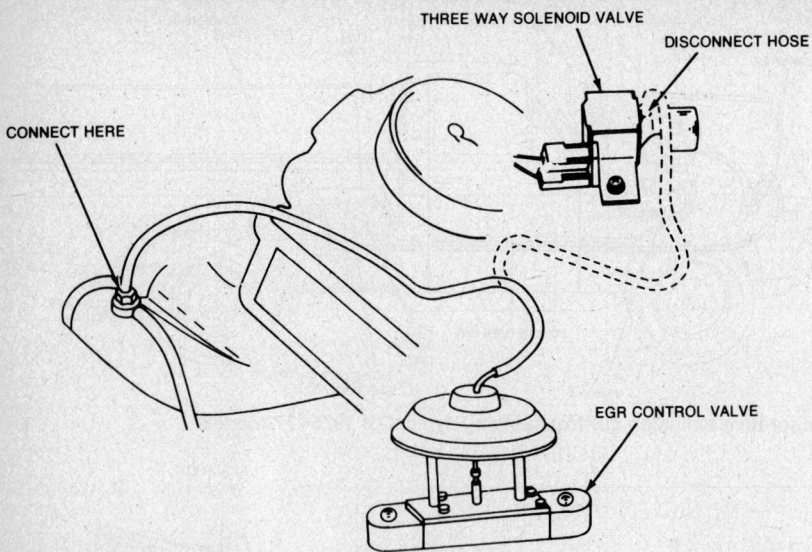

THREE WAY SOLENOID VALVE

DISCONNECT HOSE

CONNECT HERE

EGR CONTROL VALVE

1977–78 EGR valve testing—other years similar

COMPONENT TESTING

EGR Control Valve

1. Start the engine and allow it to idle.
2. On 1976 trucks, disconnect the vacuum hose from the EGR valve. Disconnect the intake manifold vacuum hose from the vacuum amplifier, and connect it to the EGR valve.
3. On 1977–78 trucks, disconnect the vacuum hose which runs from the EGR valve to the three-way solenoid valve at the solenoid valve. Disconnect the intake manifold vacuum hose at the manifold, and connect the EGR valve vacuum hose to the intake manifold fitting.
4. On 1979 and later models, disconnect the vacuum hose from the EGR water thermo valve. The valve is installed in the intake manifold. Disconnect the intake manifold vacuum hose and connect the EGR valve vacuum hose to the intake manifold vacuum fitting.
5. The engine should stall or idle roughly. If it does not, shut off the engine and remove the EGR valve and pipe from the engine. Clean the passages of the valve and pipe with a brush and a wire. Reinstall the parts and repeat the test.
6. If the test is not successful, replace the EGR valve. When engine stall or idle roughness occurs with the manifold vacuum hose connected to the EGR valve, return the hoses to their original positions.

Three-Way Solenoid Valve

1. Disconnect the electrical connectors from the thermo switch. Connect a jumper wire between the connectors to simulate a complete circuit.
2. Turn the ignition switch to ON.
3. Disconnect the vacuum hose from the EGR valve and blow into the hose. Air should be discharged from the three-way solenoid valve relief port. If it is not, re-

place the three-way valve.
4. Turn the ignition switch off, and remove the jumper wire from the thermo switch connectors. Disconnect the vacuum amplifier vacuum line from the three-way solenoid. Turn the ignition switch back to ON.
5. Blow into the vacuum line disconnected from the EGR valve, and check for air discharge from the vacuum amplifier port on the three-way solenoid valve. If there is no discharge, replace the solenoid valve.
6. After completion of all tests, reconnect the hoses to their original locations.

Vacuum Amplifier

1. Start the engine and warm it to normal operating temperature.
2. Disconnect the vacuum amplifier vacuum hose from the solenoid valve or thermo valve. Connect a vacuum gauge to this hose.
3. Disconnect the vacuum amplifier vacuum hose from the carburetor. The vacuum hose to the intake manifold should remain connected.
4. Depress and release the accelerator several times, then allow the engine to idle. The vacuum gauge reading should be 2.0 ± .04 in. Hg.
5. Reconnect the vacuum amplifier vacuum hose to the carburetor.
6. Increase engine speed to 3500 rpm. The vacuum gauge reading should be 3.54 in. Hg. If the vacuum amplifier does not test properly, replace it.
7. After all tests are completed, return the hoses to their original positions.

Water Thermo Valve

1. Drain the cooling system until the coolant level is below the intake manifold. Remove the water thermo valve from the manifold.
2. Place the valve in a container of

water. Attach a length of vacuum hose to each of the two fittings.
3. Gradually heat the water while observing the temperature.
4. By blowing through one of the vacuum hoses, you will be able to tell when the valve opens. The valve should block the passage of air until the water temperature reaches approximately 115°F. If this is not the case, the valve is faulty and must be replaced.

EGR WARNING LIGHT— 1976 ONLY

1976 Couriers with EGR are equipped with a maintenance warning light on the instrument panel, which lights every 12,500 miles. The light indicates that the EGR system should be checked for proper operation, using the procedures outlined. The EGR valve should be removed and cleaned every 25,000 miles.

The switch controlling the light is installed behind the speedometer. To reset the switch after the maintenance has been performed, remove the cover from the switch, and move the switch knob to the opposite position.

Catalytic Converter

All 1976 and later trucks sold in California, and almost all 1979 and later trucks have a catalytic converter installed in the exhaust system to aid in the reduction of hydrocarbon and carbonmonoxide emissions. The only exceptions are some 1979 and later models sold in Canada.

The catalytic converter is a muffler-shaped device located between the exhaust manifold and the muffler. It is filled with beads containing platinum and palladium which, through catalytic action, enable the hydrocarbon (HC) and carbon monoxide (CO) gases to be converted into water vapor (H_2O) and carbon dioxide (CO_2). The converter has a warning system (1976 only), consisting of a thermo sensor inserted into the side of the converter, which monitors temperatures, and a warning light on the instrument panel which lights when the sensor detects converter temperatures exceeding 1,742°F. The converter should be inspected periodically for cracks, corrosion, and any signs of external burning, and replaced as required.

WARNING SYSTEM TEST (1976 ONLY)

1. Turn the ignition switch ON. The warning light on the instrument panel should light. Start the engine. The warning light should go off.
2. If the light does not light, check the bulb. If burned out, replace and re-test the system.
3. If the light does not go out after the

engine has started, shut off the engine and tilt the seatback forward.

4. Disconnect the thermo sensor wire electrical connectors.

5. Using an ohmmeter, check the thermo sensor circuit for continuity, on the sensor side of the wiring. If there is no continuity, replace the sensor. Reconnect the wires and repeat the test.

CONVERTER REMOVAL AND INSTALLATION

1. Raise the truck and support it on safety stands.

--- **CAUTION** ---

Be very careful when working on or near the converter. External temperatures can reach 1,500°F. and more, causing severe burns. Removal or installation should only be performed on a cold exhaust system.

2. Loosen the nut and remove the thermo sensor from the side of the converter (1976 models).

3. Remove the front and rear flange attaching nuts.

4. Remove the nut and rubber support which secures the converter bracket, and remove the converter.

5. Installation is the reverse of removal.

Spark Timing Control System

A spark delay system is used on 1977–78 1.8 liter engines; 1979 and later 2.0 liter engines; and 1981 and later 2.3 engines made for California. Its purpose is to reduce the formation of CO and NO_x emissions by delaying the vacuum advance to the distributor during normal acceleration. The system consists of a spark delay valve installed in the vacuum hose between the carburetor and the distributor vacuum advance diaphragm, on all 1977–78 models, and all 1979 and later 49 States models. The spark delay valve is installed in the vacuum line between the water thermo valve and the distributor diaphragm on 1979 and later models sold in California. The water thermo valve is installed in the intake manifold. The spark delay valve has an internal restrictor to slow the air flow in one direction, and a check valve which allows air to flow freely in the opposite direction. In addition, 2.3 engines use a distributor solenoid valve and an electrical timer.

TESTING

Spark Delay Valve

1975–81

1. Remove the air cleaner. Disconnect the vacuum hose from the distributor.

2. On 1977–78 models, disconnect the

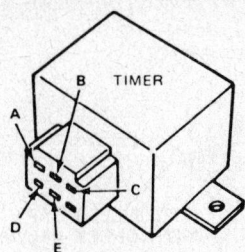

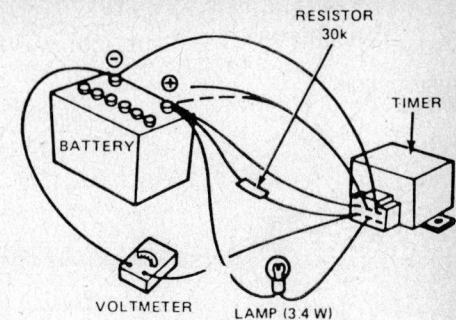

Testing arrangement for the electrical timer of the Spark Control System

vacuum control valve hose at the intake manifold fitting, and install the distributor hose on that fitting. On 1979–81 49 states models, disconnect the anti-afterburn valve line at the intake manifold fitting and install the distributor vacuum line to the intake manifold fitting. On 1979–81 California models, disconnect the air bypass valve hose from the intake manifold fitting and install the distributor vacuum line to the intake manifold fitting.

3. Remove the vacuum hose from the carburetor side of the spark delay valve. Plug this hose, and attach a vacuum gauge to the delay valve.

4. Start the engine and allow it to idle.

5. Disconnect the vacuum hose from the intake manifold fitting (the hose from the spark delay valve to the distributor which has been connected to the intake manifold in step 2) and note the time for the vacuum gauge reading to drop to 11.8 in. Hg. It should drop to this figure within 2–7 seconds (2–10 seconds on California models), 1977–78, or 4–6 seconds, 1979–81. If the reading is not correct, replace the spark delay valve.

6. After all tests have been completed, return the hoses to their original positions.

1982

The procedure for testing the delay valve on 1982 models is identical to the 1975–81 procedure with the following exception: During step 3 of the 1975–81 procedure, a 30 cc vacuum reservoir must be installed BETWEEN the spark delay valve and the vacuum gauge.

Distributor Solenoid Valve

1982 2.3 LITER CALIFORNIA ENGINES ONLY

1. Start the engine and allow it to idle.

2. Disconnect the electrical connector at the solenoid valve.

3. Apply battery power to the terminals of the solenoid valve to energize the solenoid.

4. Disconnect the vacuum hose from the distributor vacuum unit. There should be no vacuum at this hose.

5. Remove the battery power from the solenoid valve. Vacuum should be available at the hose as soon as the solenoid is de-energized.

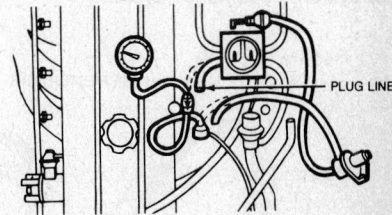

Spark delay valve testing arrangement

6. If the vacuum did not react as stated in steps 4 and 5, replace the solenoid valve.

7. Reconnect the electrical connector at the solenoid valve.

Electrical Timer

1982 2.3 LITER CALIFORNIA ENGINES ONLY

1. Disconnect the wiring from the timer and remove the timer.

2. Connect three separate wires to the timer as follows: one wire to the A terminal; one wire to the B terminal; one wire to the C terminal.

3. Connect a wire with an in-line 30K ohm resistor to the D terminal of the timer.

4. Connect a wire with a test lamp (12V-3.4W) to the E terminal of the timer.

5. Connect a voltmeter to the timer and battery as follows: positive voltmeter lead to the D terminal of the timer; negative voltmeter lead to the battery negative terminal.

6. Connect the wires which were previously connected to the A, D, and E timer terminals to the positive battery terminals. Do not connect the wire from the B terminal of the timer.

7. Connect the wire previously connected to the C timer terminal to the battery negative terminal.

8. Check the voltmeter reading. The voltmeter should read no less than six volts at this time.

9. Connect the opposite end of the B timer terminal wire to the battery positive terminal. As soon as the connection is made, the voltmeter reading should drop to one volt or less. Leave this connection intact for approximately two minutes. At the end of the two minutes, the voltmeter should read approximately eight volts.

10. If the voltmeter did not react as spec-

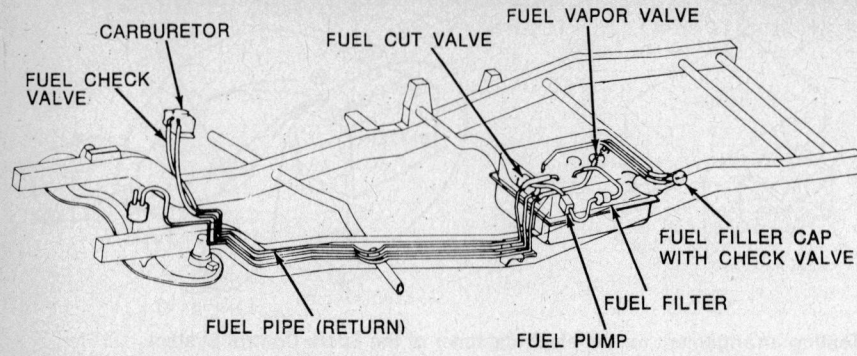

Fuel system schematic—typical

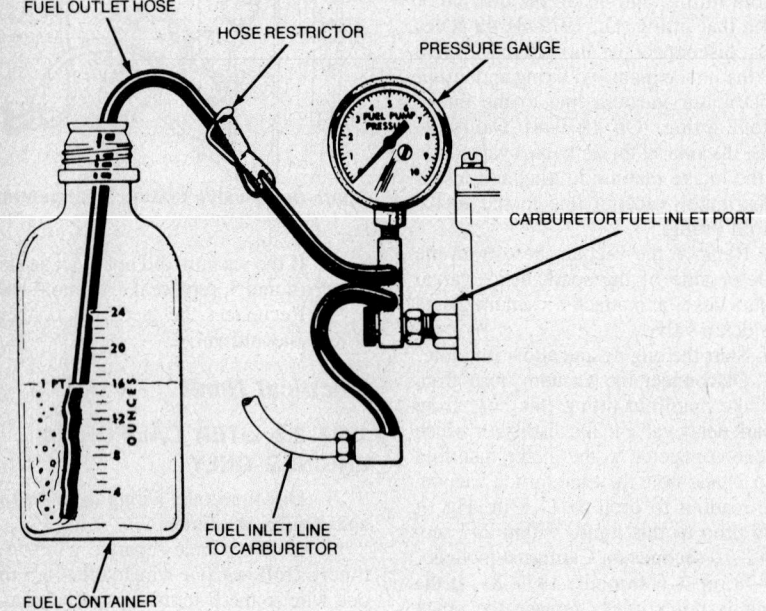

Fuel pump testing

operate the engine at idle speed and vent the system into the container by momentarily opening the hose restrictor.

5. Close the hose restrictor and allow the pressure to stabilize and note the reading. It should be 2.8–3.6 psi.

6. If the pump pressure is not within specifications, and the fuel filter and fuel lines are not blocked, the pump is malfunctioning and should be replaced. If the pressure is within specifications, perform the volume test.

7. Open the hose restrictor and expel the fuel into the container, while observing the time required to discharge 1 pint. Close the restrictor. Fuel pump volume should be approximately 2 pints/minute.

8. If the pump volume is below specifications, repeat the test using an auxiliary fuel supply and a new filter. If the pump volume meets specifications while using the auxiliary fuel supply, check for a restriction in the fuel lines or vent.

Carburetor

REMOVAL AND INSTALLATION

1. Remove the air cleaner and duct.
2. Disconnect the accelerator shaft from the throttle lever.
3. Disconnect and plug the fuel supply and fuel return lines.
4. Disconnect the leads from the throttle solenoid and deceleration valve at the quick-disconnects.
5. Disconnect all vacuum hoses from the carburetor. Tag the hoses so that they may be properly reinstalled.
6. Disconnect the throttle return spring.
7. Disconnect the choke cable or electrical lead. On 1978 and later models, remove the servo diaphragm link for the throttle opener.
8. Remove the carburetor attaching nuts from the intake manifold studs and remove the carburetor.
9. Installation is the reverse of the previous steps. Adjust the choke cable if so equipped.

OVERHAUL

Efficient carburetion depends greatly on careful cleaning and inspection during overhaul, since dirt, gum, water, or varnish in or on the carburetor parts are often responsible for poor performance.

Overhaul your carburetor in a clean, dust-free area. Carefully disassemble the carburetor, referring often to the exploded views. Keep all similar and look-alike parts segregated during disassembly and cleaning to avoid accidental interchange during assembly. Make a note of all jet sizes.

When the carburetor is disassembled, wash all parts (except diaphragms, electric choke units, pump plunger, and any other

---

ified, replace the timer unit.

11. Disconnect all of the test wires from both the timer and the battery and reinstall the timer unit.

FUEL SYSTEM

Fuel Pump

REMOVAL AND INSTALLATION

1. Remove the fuel pump shield from the frame (if equipped). Disconnect the electrical leads from the pump.
2. Disconnect the inlet and outlet lines from the pump. Plug the lines.
3. Unbolt and remove the pump from its mounting bracket.

To install the fuel pump:

4. Position the fuel pump on the mounting bracket and install the bolts. Be sure that both mounting surfaces are clean.

5. Connect the inlet and outlet hoses.
6. Connect the electrical leads to the pump.
7. Install the fuel pump shield.

TESTING

To determine that the fuel pump is in good operating condition, tests for both volume and pressure should be performed. The tests are performed with the fuel pump installed, and the engine at normal operating temperature and idle speed.

NOTE: Steps 1 through 6 test the fuel pump for proper pressure; steps 7 and 8 test the pump for proper output volume.

1. Remove the air cleaner.
2. Disconnect the fuel inlet line at the carburetor.
3. Connect a pressure gauge, a restrictor and a flexible hose between the fuel filter and the carburetor. Position the flexible hose and restrictor so that the fuel can be discharged into a suitable graduated container.
4. Before taking a pressure reading,

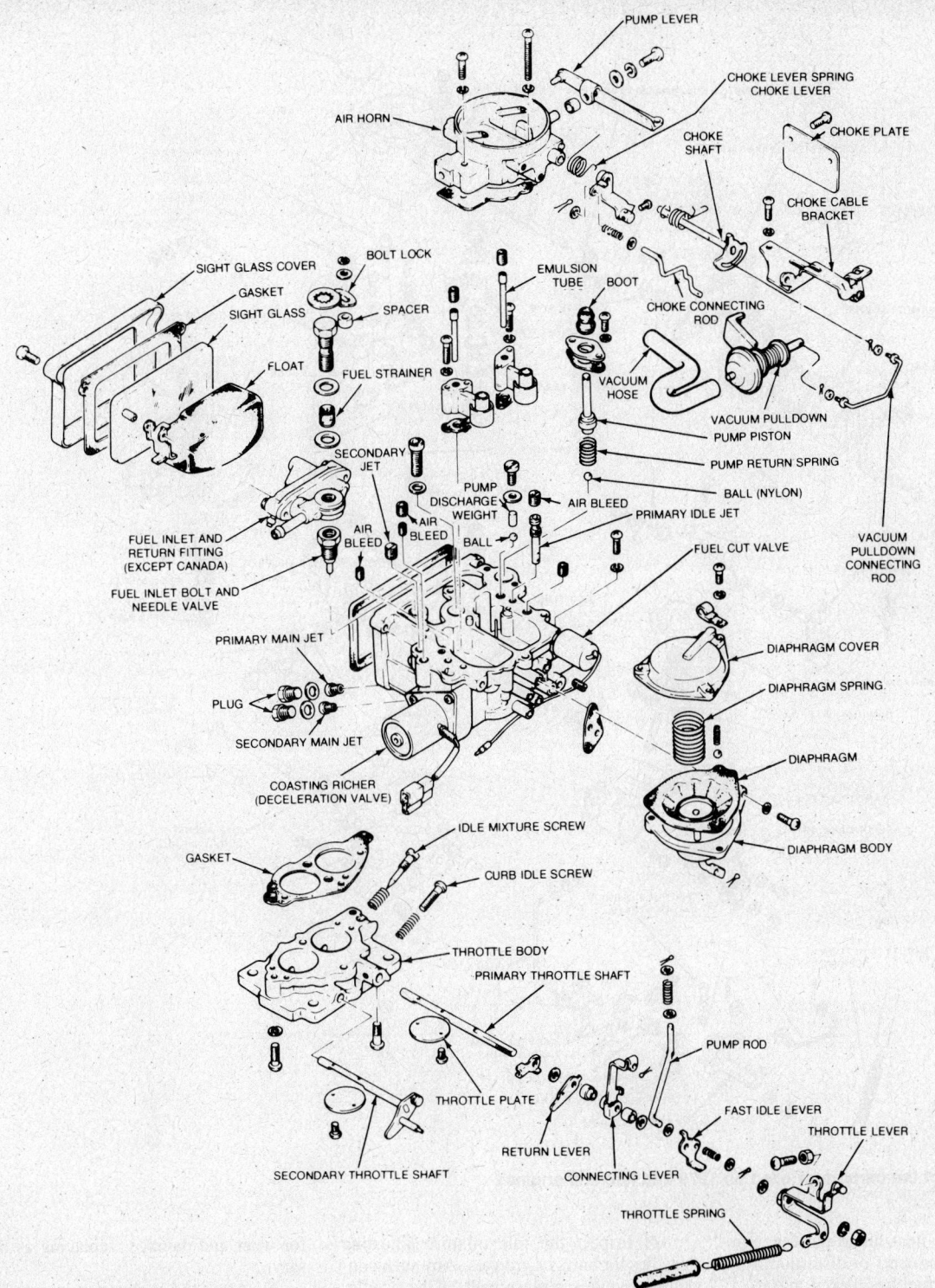

Exploded view of the carburetor used on 1978 and earlier models. Only 1.8 engines use the diaphragm assembly.

plastic, leather, fiber, or rubber parts) in clean carburetor solvent. Do not leave parts in the solvent any longer than is necessary to sufficiently loosen the deposits. Excessive cleaning may remove the special finish from the float bowl and choke valve bodies, leaving these parts unfit for service. Rinse all parts in clean solvent and blow them dry

with compressed air or allow them to air dry. Wipe clean all cork, plastic, leather, and fiber parts with a clean, lint-free cloth.

Blow out all passages and jets with compressed air and be sure that there are no restrictions or blockages. Never use wire or similar tools to clean jets, fuel passages, or air bleeds. Clean all jets and valves sep-

arately to avoid accidental interchange.

Check all parts for wear or damage. If wear or damage is found, replace the defective parts. Especially check the following:

1. Check the float needle and seat for wear. If wear is found, replace the complete assembly.

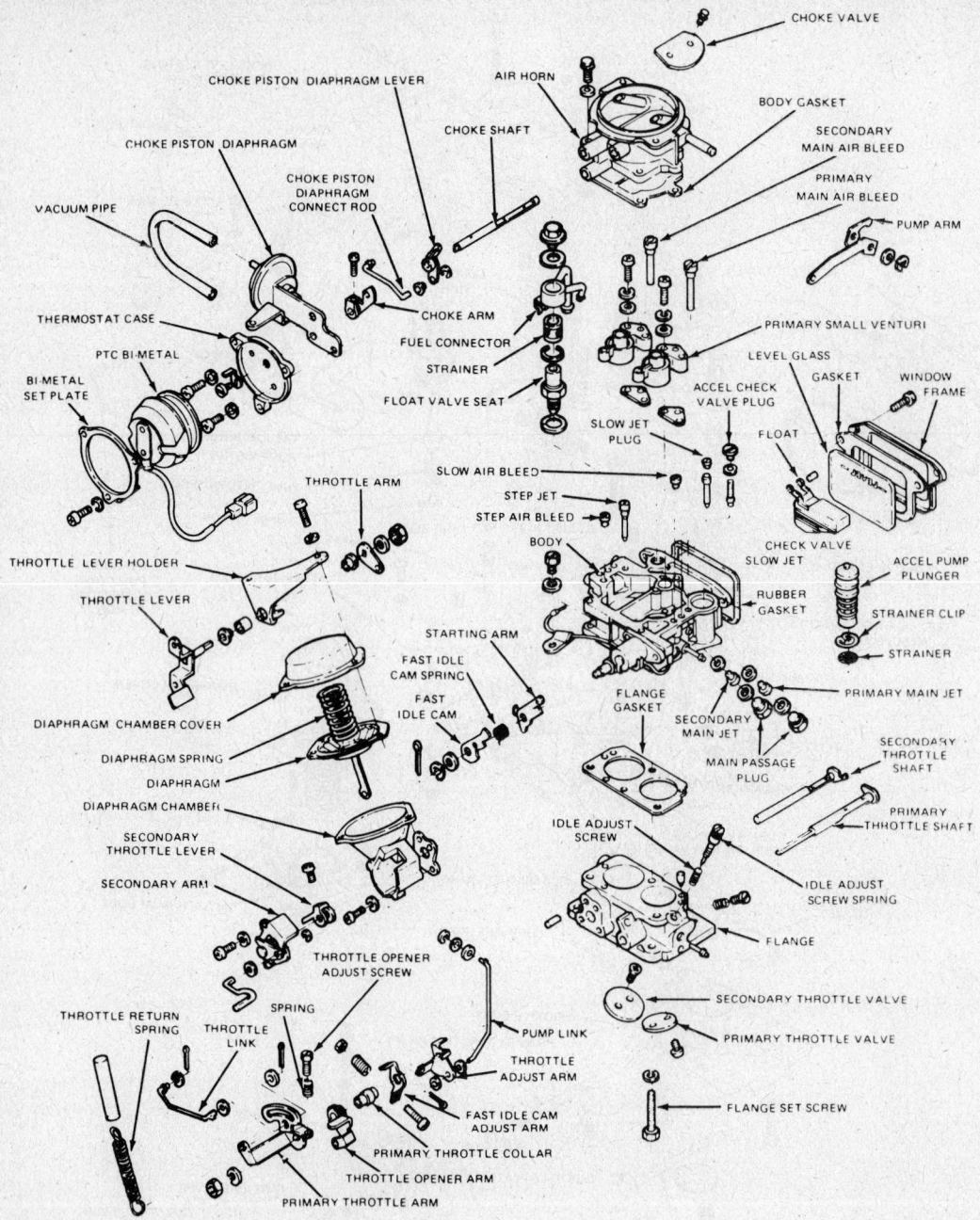

Exploded view of the carburetor used on 1979 and later 2.0 engines

2. Check the float hinge pin for wear and the float(s) for dents or distortion. Replace the float if fuel has leaked into it.

3. Check the throttle and choke shaft bores for wear or an out-of-round condition. Damage or wear to the throttle arm, shaft, or shaft bore will often require replacement of the throttle body. These parts require a close tolerance of fit; wear may allow air leakage, which could affect starting and idling.

NOTE: Throttle shafts and bushings are not included in overhaul kits. They can be purchased separately.

4. Inspect the idle mixture adjusting needles for burrs or grooves. Any such condition requires replacement of the needle, since you will not be able to obtain a satisfactory idle.

5. Test the accelerator pump check valves. They should pass air one way but not the other. Test for proper seating by blowing and sucking on the valve. Replace the valve if necessary. If the valve is satisfactory, wash the valve again to remove breath moisture.

6. Check the bowl cover for warped surfaces with a straightedge.

7. Closely inspect the valves and seats

for wear and damage, replacing as necessary.

8. After the carburetor is assembled, check the choke valve for freedom of operation.

Carburetor overhaul kits are recommended for each overhaul. These kits contain all gaskets and new parts to replace those which deteriorate most rapidly. Failure to replace all parts supplied with the kit (especially gaskets) can result in poor performance later.

Some carburetor manufacturers supply overhaul kits of three basic types: minor repair; major repair; and gasket kits.

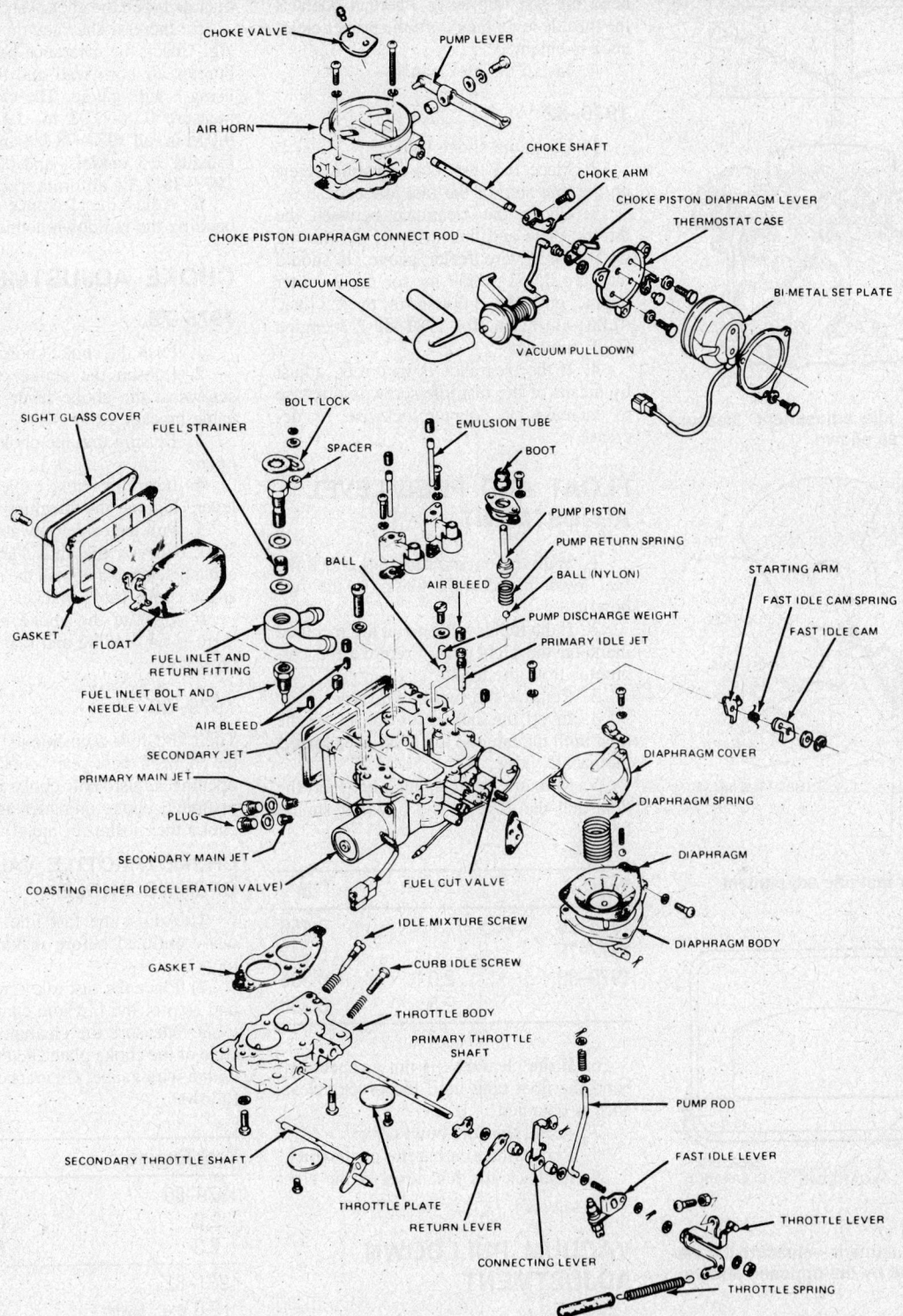

CHOKE VALVE — PUMP LEVER

AIR HORN

CHOKE SHAFT
CHOKE ARM
CHOKE PISTON DIAPHRAGM LEVER
THERMOSTAT CASE
CHOKE PISTON DIAPHRAGM CONNECT ROD
BI-METAL SET PLATE
VACUUM HOSE
VACUUM PULLDOWN

SIGHT GLASS COVER
FUEL STRAINER
BOLT LOCK
SPACER
EMULSION TUBE
BOOT
PUMP PISTON
PUMP RETURN SPRING
STARTING ARM
FAST IDLE CAM SPRING
FAST IDLE CAM
BALL
AIR BLEED
BALL (NYLON)
PUMP DISCHARGE WEIGHT
GASKET
FLOAT
FUEL INLET AND RETURN FITTING
PRIMARY IDLE JET
FUEL INLET BOLT AND NEEDLE VALVE
AIR BLEED
SECONDARY JET
DIAPHRAGM COVER
PRIMARY MAIN JET
DIAPHRAGM SPRING
PLUG
SECONDARY MAIN JET
DIAPHRAGM
COASTING RICHER (DECELERATION VALVE)
FUEL CUT VALVE
DIAPHRAGM BODY
IDLE MIXTURE SCREW
GASKET
CURB IDLE SCREW
THROTTLE BODY
PRIMARY THROTTLE SHAFT
PUMP ROD
SECONDARY THROTTLE SHAFT
FAST IDLE LEVER
THROTTLE PLATE
THROTTLE LEVER
RETURN LEVER
CONNECTING LEVER
THROTTLE SPRING

Exploded view of the carburetor used on 1979 and later 2.3 engines

After cleaning and checking all components, reassemble the carburetor, using new parts and referring to the exploded view. When reassembling, make sure that all screws and jets are tight in their seats, but do not overtighten as the tips will be distorted. Tighten all screws gradually, in rotation. Do not tighten needle valves into their seats; uneven jetting will result. Always use new gaskets. Be sure to adjust the float level when reassembling.

FAST IDLE ADJUSTMENT

1975–78

1. Remove the air cleaner.

2. With the choke plate fully closed, measure the clearance between the primary throttle plate and the wall of the throttle bore. The clearance should measure 0.063–0.067 in. for 1975–76, and 0.071 in 1977–78, or 0.067 in. for 1977–78 California models.

3. If the clearance is not as specified,

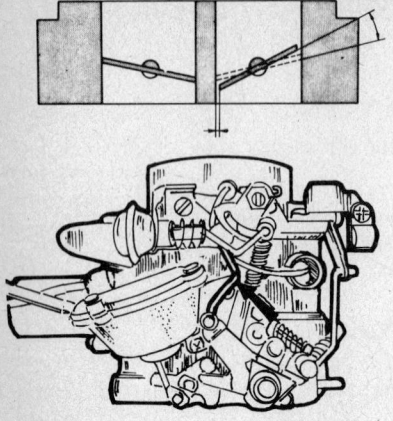

1975–78 fast idle adjustment. Measure the clearance as shown.

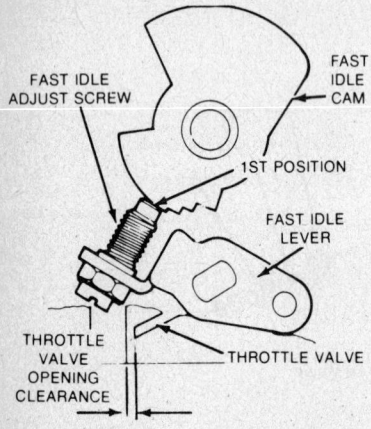

1979 and later fast idle adjustment

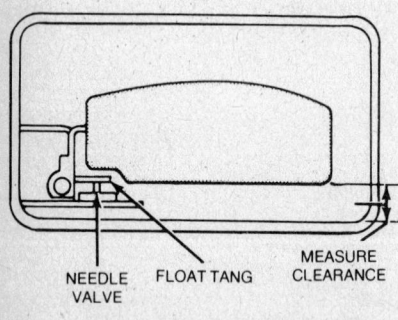

Float level adjustment—measure the distance indicated by the opposed arrows

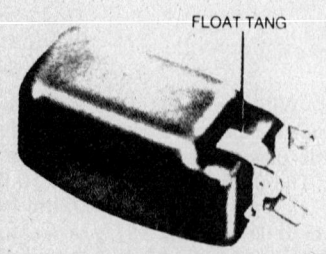

Bend this tang to adjust the float level

bend the fast idle lever where it contacts the throttle lever tang until the proper clearance is obtained.

4. Install the air cleaner.

1979–82

1. Close the choke fully.

2. Place the fast idle adjusting screw on the first step of the fast idle cam.

3. Check the clearance between the throttle plate and the inside of the throttle wall with a wire feeler gauge. It should measure 0.051–0.059 in. for the 2.0 liter engine, or 0.058–0.066 in. for the 2.3 liter. (0.061–0.071 in. for 1981–82 2.3 engine Calif. models)

4. If the clearance is incorrect, adjust by means of the fast idle screw, clockwise to increase or counterclockwise to decrease.

FLOAT AND FUEL LEVEL ADJUSTMENT

1. With the engine running, check the fuel level in the sight glass (in the fuel bowl).

2. If the fuel level is not at the specified mark on the sight glass, remove the carburetor from the truck.

3. Remove the fuel bowl cover.

4. Invert the carburetor and lower the float until the tang on the float just contacts the needle valve.

5. Measure the clearance between the float and the edge of the bowl. It should be:

Year		In
1975–76		0.256
1977–78		0.047
1979–82	2.0	0.335
	2.3	0.236

6. If the clearance is not as specified, bend the float tang until the proper clearance is obtained.

7. Install the fuel bowl cover.

8. Reinstall the carburetor on the truck.

9. Recheck the fuel level at the sight glass.

VACUUM PULLDOWN ADJUSTMENT

1975–78 Only

1. On California Couriers, unplug the electrical connectors from the water thermo switch and connect a jumper wire between the connectors. Turn the ignition switch on.

2. Pull the choke knob out to fully close the choke.

3. Disconnect the vacuum hose from the pulldown diaphragm.

4. Connect an external vacuum source to the pulldown diaphragm. Gradually apply vacuum. The pulldown should start to operate (open the choke) at 5.9–7.5 in. Hg.

5. Increase the vacuum to 9.8–12.0 in. Hg. Check the clearance between the carburetor air horn wall and the choke plate using a wire gauge. The clearance should measure 0.06–0.08 in. 1975–76, 0.066–0.075 in. all 1977–78 1.8 and 49 states and Canada 2.3 models, and 0.075–0.084 in. 1977–78 2.3 California trucks.

6. Adjust the clearance if necessary by bending the pulldown connecting rod.

CHOKE ADJUSTMENT

1975–78

1. Push the choke knob all the way in.

2. Loosen the choke cable attaching screws at the choke lever and the choke cable bracket.

3. Be sure that the choke plate is fully open.

4. Insert the choke cable into the choke lever. Tighten the attaching screw.

5. Pull the cable outward to remove all slack between the choke lever and choke cable bracket and tighten the attaching screw at the choke cable bracket.

6. Operate the choke to be sure that there is no binding and that it is operating properly.

1979–80

There are four adjustments to be made to the choke in these years: choke/throttle valve opening adjustment; choke diaphragm adjustment; choke unloader adjustment; and choke thermostat (bi-metal) adjustment.

CHOKE/THROTTLE VALVE OPENING ANGLE

1. Adjust the fast idle cam as previously outlined before making this adjustment.

2. Place the fast idle screw on the second step of the fast idle cam.

3. Measure the clearance between the edge of the choke plate and the throttle bore with a wire gauge. Clearances should be as follows:

Year/Engine	In.
1979–80	
2.0	0.047–0.067
2.3	0.051–0.071
1981–82	
2.0 exc. Calif.	0.016–0.028
2.0 Calif.	0.024–0.036
2.3 exc. Calif.	0.039–0.051
2.3 Calif.	0.041–0.067

4. If the clearance is incorrect, adjust by bending the starting arm. If a large adjustment is required, the choke rod can be bent slightly.

CHOKE DIAPHRAGM

1. Remove the vacuum hose from the

choke diaphragm. Attach a vacuum pump to the diaphragm fitting and apply approximately 15.6 inches of mercury vacuum to the diaphragm.

2. Check to see that the fast idle screw is on the first step of the fast idle cam.

3. Press on the choke plate slightly to settle it. Measure the clearance between the edge of the choke plate and the throttle bore. Clearances should be as follows:

Year/Engine	In.
Except 1981–82 California models	
2.0	0.047–0.067
2.3	0.051–0.071
1981–82 California models	
2.0	0.065–0.085
2.3	0.063–0.079

4. If the clearance is incorrect, adjust by bending the choke lever.

CHOKE UNLOADER

1. Close the choke plate fully. Open the throttle plate fully.

2. Measure the clearance between the edge of the choke plate and the throttle bore with a wire gauge. Clearances should be as follows:

Year/Engine	In.
Models through 1981 exc. 1981 Calif.	
2.0	0.079–0.099
2.3	0.090–0.110
1981 California models	
2.0	0.079–0.099
2.3	0.094–0.126
1982 models exc. California	
2.0	0.075–0.107
2.3	0.090–0.110
1982 California models	
2.0	0.075–0.107
2.3	0.094–0.126

3. If the clearance is incorrect, bend the choke unloader adjusting nail (tang).

THERMOSTAT

1. The index mark on the thermostat cover should be aligned with the center mark on the choke housing.

2. Adjust by loosening the thermostat cover retaining screws slightly and shifting the position of the cover. Tighten the screws after adjustment.

THROTTLE LINKAGE ADJUSTMENT

1. Loosen the locknuts on the longer linkage rod and rotate both ends in the sockets until the proper accelerator travel from

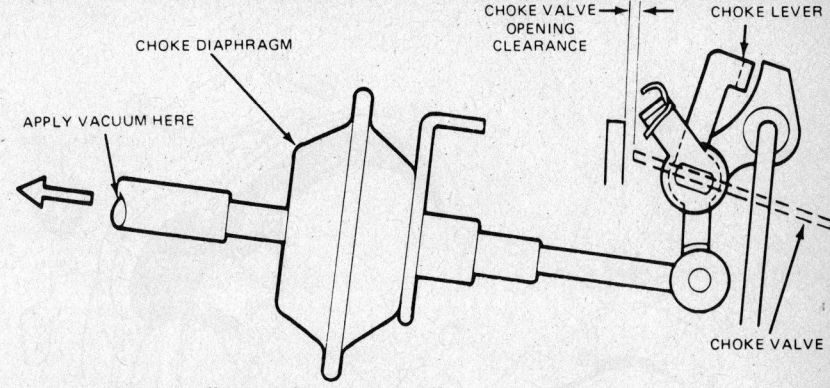

Vacuum pulldown adjustment

idle to wide-open throttle is obtained.

2. Tighten the locknuts to set the adjustment.

Fuel Tank

REMOVAL AND INSTALLATION

NOTE: It is best to run the fuel tank as low as possible before removing the tank.

1. Raise and support the rear of the truck.

2. Remove the fuel tank drain plug and drain the gasoline into a metal container.

3. Install the drain plug.

NOTE: On models not equipped with a drain plug, disconnect the line which runs to the fuel pump at the tank and allow the tank to drain. Plug the line connection at the tank before proceeding.

4. Disconnect and plug the fuel pump line at the tank.

5. Disconnect the line from the condenser tank or vapor valve at the fuel tank.

6. If so equipped, disconnect the fuel return line.

7. Disconnect the fuel sending unit lead and the electrical connector.

8. Remove the fuel tank attaching bolts at the mounting bracket and lower the tank.
To install:

1. Raise the tank into position and install the attaching bolts securely.

2. Connect the fuel sending unit lead.

3. Connect the fuel return line if equipped.

4. Connect the condenser tank or vapor valve line.

5. Connect the fuel pump line.

CLUTCH

The clutch is a dry single disc type, consisting of a clutch disc, clutch cover and

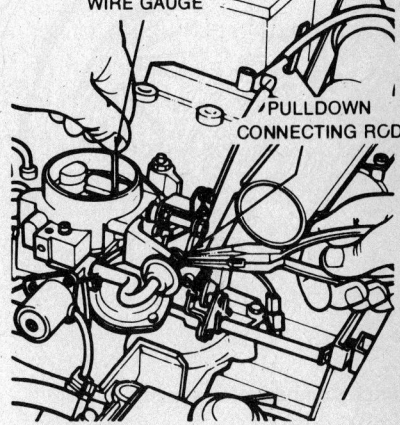

1979 and later choke/throttle valve opening adjustment

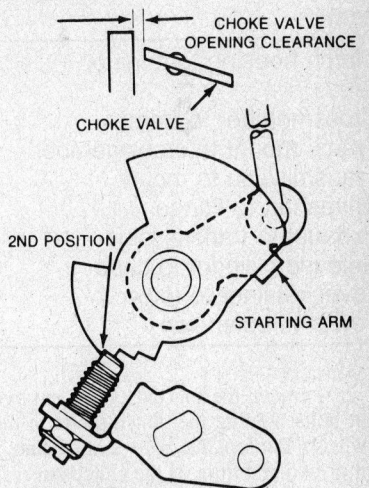

1979 and later choke diaphragm adjustment

pressure plate and a clutch release mechanism. It is hydraulically operated by a firewall mounted master cylinder and clutch release slave cylinder mounted on the flywheel housing.

REMOVAL AND INSTALLATION

1. Remove the transmission as outlined later in this section.

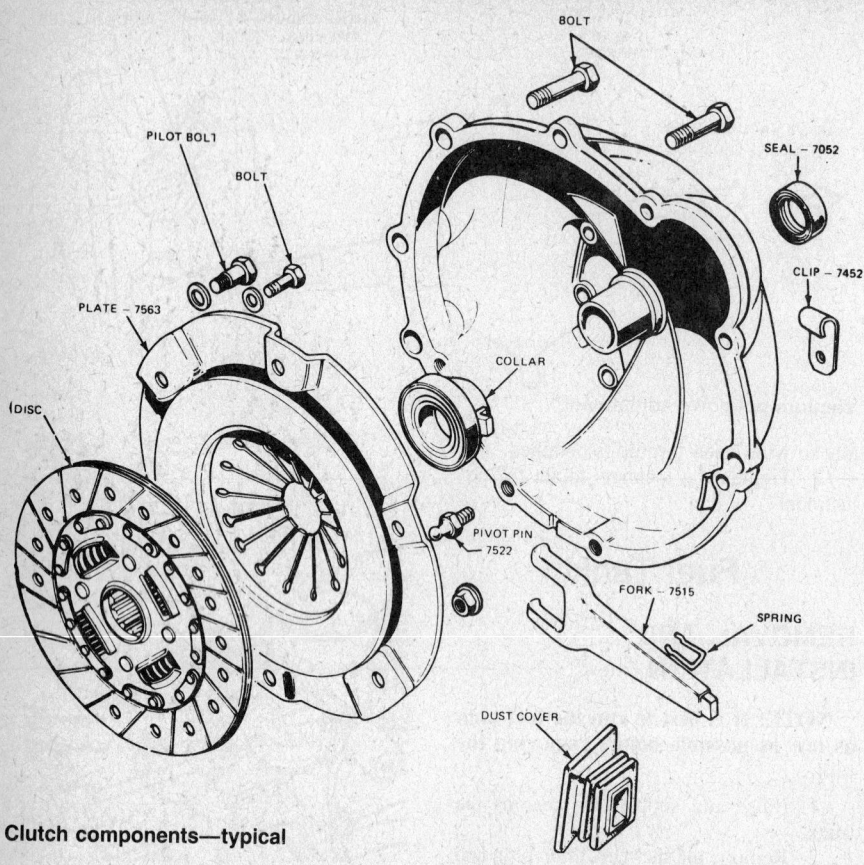

Clutch components—typical

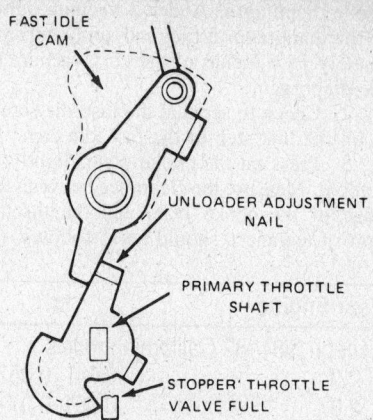

1979 and later choke unloader adjustment

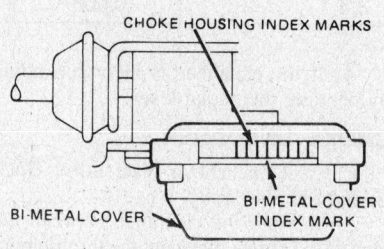

1979 and later choke thermostat adjustment

CLUTCH INSTALLATION TORQUES

Item	Ft. Lbs.
Clutch housing to engine	34–45 (1.8 and 2.0)
	28–40 (2.3)
Crossmember to frame	23–34
Trans. mount to crossmember	23–34
Transmission to mount	12–17
Driveshaft to flange	40–47
Exhaust to transmission	12–17
Release cylinder to case	12–17
Lever retainer to tower	5–8
Tower to extension	12–17

2. Remove the four attaching and two pilot bolts holding the clutch cover to the flywheel. Loosen the bolts evenly and a turn or two at a time. If the clutch cover is to be reinstalled, mark the flywheel and clutch cover to show the location of the two pilot holes.

3. Remove the clutch disc.

Inspect the old clutch for signs of oil or grease contamination. If present, correct the cause before installing a new clutch. Probable sources of leakage would include the transmission input shaft seal and the engine rear main bearing seal. Inspect the flywheel and pressure plate for signs of scoring, wear, or overheating. Light scoring can be cleaned up with crocus cloth, or by refacing the flywheel; however, heavy wear warrants replacement of the part. Overheated parts will usually be discolored (dark blue or black) and should be replaced. Check the fit of the clutch pilot bearing in the bore of the crankshaft. If it is loose or rough, it should be replaced.

To install the clutch:

4. Install the clutch disc on the flywheel. Do not touch the facing or allow the facing to come in contact with grease or oil. The clutch disc can be aligned using a tool made for that purpose, or with an old input shaft.

5. Install the clutch cover on the flywheel aligning the marks made during removal, and install the four standard bolts and the two pilot bolts.

6. To avoid distorting the pressure plate, tighten the bolts evenly a few turns at a time until they are all tight.

7. Torque the bolts to 13–20 ft. lbs. using a crossing pattern.

8. Remove the aligning tool.

9. Apply a light film of lubricant to the release bearing, release lever contact area on the release bearing hub and to the input shaft bearing retainer. Check the release lever for free operation.

10. Install the transmission.

11. Check the operation of the clutch and if necessary, adjust the pedal free-play and the release lever.

PEDAL HEIGHT ADJUSTMENT (FREE-PLAY)

1. The clutch pedal free-play is adjusted by loosening the locknut on the pushrod and adjusting the pushrod length by rotating the rod. The clutch should have a free travel of 13/16–1 3/16 in. for 1975 models measured at the pedal pad. The free travel should measure 0.025–0.121 in., 1976–80; 0.80–1.18 in. for 1981–82 models. Tighten the locknut when the adjustment is complete.

CLUTCH RELEASE LEVER ADJUSTMENT

This adjustment must be maintained to prevent release bearing and clutch damage.

1975

1. Raise and support the truck.
2. Disconnect the release lever return

spring at the lever.

3. Loosen the locknut and rotate the adjusting nut until a clearance of ⅛–⁹⁄₆₄ in. (0.12–0.14 in.) is obtained between the bullet nosed end of the adjusting nut and the release lever.

4. Tighten the locknut and hook the return spring.

5. Lower the truck.

1976–82

No adjustment is possible on 1976 and later trucks. Instead, the stroke can be checked by raising the truck and moving the release rod. If the stroke measures less than 5mm (0.196 in.) the clutch plate should be replaced.

Clutch Master Cylinder

REMOVAL AND INSTALLATION

1. Disconnect and plug the fluid outlet line at the outlet fitting on the master cylinder one-way valve.

2. Remove the nuts and bolts attaching the master cylinder to the firewall.

3. Remove the cylinder straight out away from the firewall.

To install the master cylinder:

4. Start the pedal pushrod into the master cylinder and position the master cylinder on the firewall.

5. Install the attaching nuts and bolts. Torque the nuts to 12–17 ft. lbs.

6. Connect the fluid outlet line to the master cylinder fitting.

7. Bleed the hydraulic system.

8. Check the clutch pedal free-travel and adjust as necessary.

OVERHAUL

1. Remove the master cylinder.

2. Clean the outside of the cylinder thoroughly and drain the fluid.

3. Remove the boot (1975).

4. Use a screwdriver to remove the piston stop-ring. Remove the stop washer.

5. Remove the piston, piston cup and piston return spring from the cylinder.

6. Carefully remove and disassemble the one-way valve. 1976 and later 1.8s don't have one.

7. Wash all parts (except rubber parts) in clean alcohol or brake fluid. Never use mineral spirits of any kind to clean a master cylinder.

8. Check the rubber cups. If they have become worn, softened or swollen, replace them.

9. Check the clearance between the cylinder bore and piston. If it exceeds 0.004 in., replace the cylinder or piston.

10. Be sure that the one-way valve is free to operate. 1976 and later 1.8s have a compensating port which must be open.

To assemble the master cylinder:

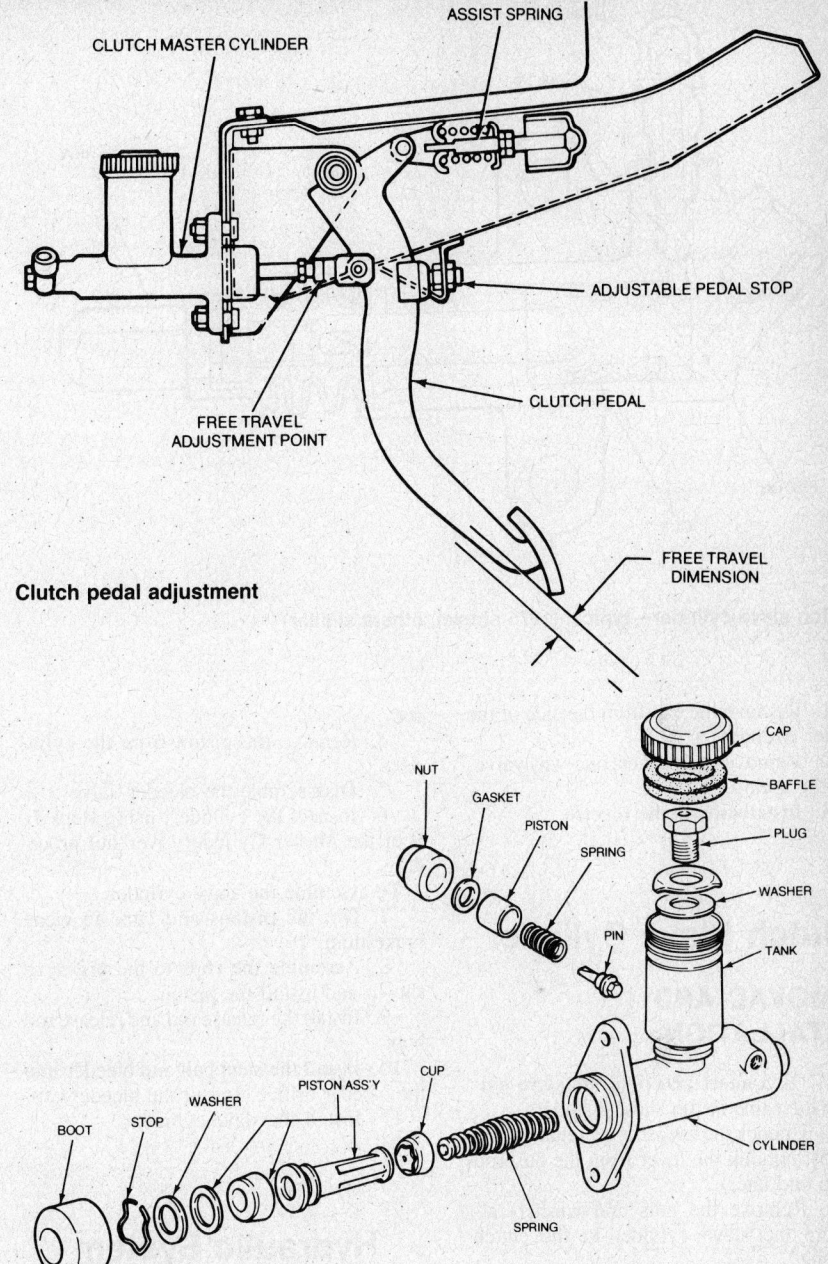

Clutch pedal adjustment

Clutch master cylinder—typical

11. Dip the piston and cups in clean brake fluid.

12. Install the return spring in the cylinder bore.

13. Install the primary cup so that the flat side of the cup is toward the piston.

14. Install the secondary cup on the piston and insert the cup and piston into the cylinder.

15. Install the stop washer and stop-ring.

16. Assemble and install the one-way valve, if equipped.

17. Fill the reservoir with clean brake fluid and operate the piston with a screwdriver until fluid is ejected through the outlet fitting.

18. Install the master cylinder.

19. Bleed the hydraulic system.

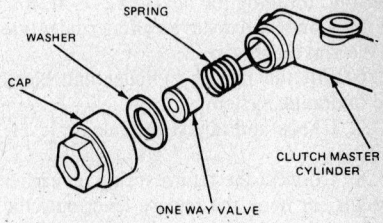

Clutch master cylinder one-way valve

One-Way Valve Removal and Installation

A one-way valve is used on all master cylinders except 1976–78 1.8 liter models, which have a compensating port instead.

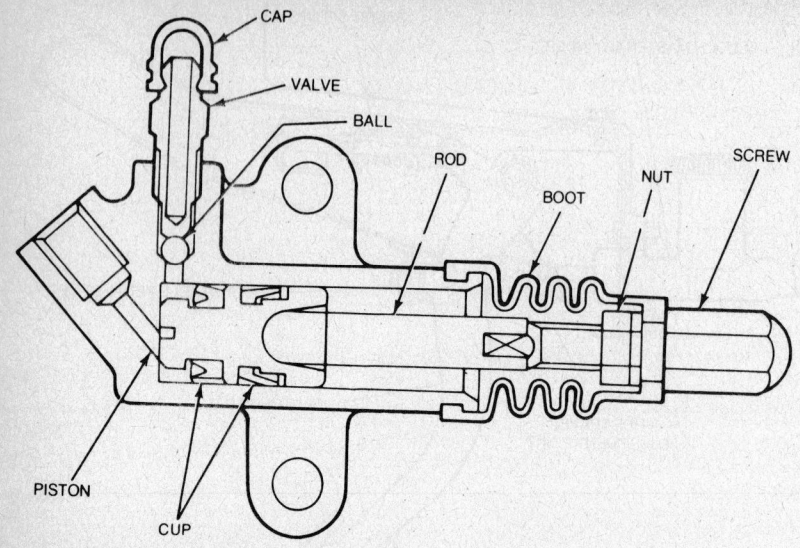

Clutch slave cylinder—typical (1975 shown, others similar)

1. Remove the cap from the side of the master cylinder.
2. Remove the washer, one-way valve, and the spring.
3. Installation is the reverse.

Clutch Slave Cylinder

REMOVAL AND INSTALLATION

1. Disconnect and plug the slave cylinder inlet line at the slave cylinder.
2. Unhook the release lever return spring (1975); unhook the lever from the pushrod (1976 and later).
3. Remove the nuts and washers attaching the slave cylinder to the clutch housing.
To install the slave cylinder:
4. Install the slave cylinder on the clutch housing, torquing the nuts to 12–17 ft. lbs.
5. Connect the slave cylinder inlet line to the slave cylinder.
6. Fill the master cylinder and bleed the hydraulic system.
7. Check and adjust the release lever, (1975).
8. Connect the return spring on earlier models, or hook the release lever onto the pushrod after 1975.
9. Check the system for proper operation.

OVERHAUL

1. Remove the slave cylinder.
2. Clean the outside thoroughly.
3. Remove the dust cover and release rod.
4. Remove the piston from the cylinder.
5. Disassemble the bleeder valve.
6. Inspect the cylinder, using steps 7–9 of the Master Cylinder Overhaul procedure.
To assemble the slave cylinder:
7. Dip the pistons and cups in clean brake fluid.
8. Assemble the cups to the piston as shown and install the piston.
9. Install the release rod and release rod boot.
10. Install the steel ball and bleeder into the bleeder orifice. Install the bleeder cap.
11. Install the slave cylinder.

Hydraulic System Bleeding

The clutch hydraulic system must be bled whenever the line has been disconnected or air has entered the system.

To bleed the system, remove the rubber cap from the bleeder valve and attach a rubber hose to the valve. Submerge the other end of the hose in a large jar of clean brake fluid. Open the bleeder valve. Have an assistant depress the clutch pedal and allow it to return slowly. Continue this pumping action and watch the jar of brake fluid. When air bubbles stop appearing, close the bleeder valve and remove the tube.

During the bleeding process, the master cylinder must be kept at least ¾ full. After the bleeding operation is finished, install the cap on the bleeder valve and fill the master cylinder to the proper level. Always use fresh brake fluid, and above all, do not use the fluid that was in the jar for bleeding, since it contains air. Install the master cylinder reservoir cap.

Clutch Release Lever and Bearing

REMOVAL AND INSTALLATION

1. Most earlier models have a spring attached to the release bearing (throwout bearing) collar. If present, remove this spring. The release lever (fork) is retained by either a spring (1975) or a spring clip (1976 and later). Remove the spring and pull the fork from the pivot pin.
2. Remove the lever, dust cover boot and the release (throwout) bearing.
3. Inspect the parts carefully. Wipe off all the oil and dirt from the bearing, but do not soak it in solvent; it is prelubricated. Any burrs should be smoothed with crocus cloth. If burrs are present, inspect the transmission input shaft bearing retainer, and smooth any scoring with crocus cloth.
4. Coat the bearing retainer with a thin film of lithium base grease (Ford specification C3VY-19586-A or equivalent). Apply a thin film of this grease to both sides of the fork at contact points. Also lightly coat the release bearing surface where it contacts the pressure plate fingers.
5. Fill the grease groove inside the bearing hub with the lithium grease. Do not use polyethylene grease. Clean any excess grease from the bore of the hub, because excess grease will eventually work its way onto the clutch disc.
6. Before installing the bearing, hold the inner race and rotate the outer race, applying pressure. If the rotation is noisy or rough, replace the bearing. Bearing failure is generally caused by improper free-play settings at the release cylinder or pedal. Riding the pedal can reduce clearance, causing the bearing to constantly spin, increasing wear. The bearing can also fail due to release lever misalignment (bent out of plane or not centered on the housing bracket) or misalignment between the engine and transmission.
To install:
7. Apply a thin of lithium grease to the input shaft bearing retainer portion of the clutch housing.
8. Dab the end of the pivot pin with grease, and drive the release lever onto it. Apply a thin film of grease to the contact points of the release lever, and install the release bearing. Hook the release collar spring back into place (if applicable).
9. Check the operation of the release bearing hub. It should slide freely on the input shaft bearing retainer.
10. Install the dust boot.

MANUAL TRANSMISSION

The 4-speed manual transmission is synchronized in all forward gears. The transmission case is of light metal construction, manufactured as two mated halves. There is no external shift linkage; all the shifting mechanisms are contained within the case. There are no linkage or shifter adjustments.

The optional 5-speed manual, first available in 1976, is synchronized in all forward gears. The transmission case is cast aluminum, with a bottom cover and removable clutch and extension housings. The gearshift lever is connected directly to the shift forks; thus, there is no external linkage, and no adjustments are necessary.

REMOVAL AND INSTALLATION

1. Put the gearshift in Neutral.
2. Lift up the boot covering the shift lever and detach the gearshift tower from the extension housing. Remove the shift lever, tower and gasket as an assembly.
3. Cover the opening in the case with a heavy rag to keep dirt out.
4. Remove the negative battery cable. Raise and support the truck.
5. Disconnect the driveshaft at the rear axle.
6. Remove the driveshaft center bearing support and pull the driveshaft rearward to disconnect the driveshaft from the transmission. Install a plug in the extension housing to prevent lubricant from leaking out.
7. Remove the exhaust pipe brackets from the transmission case.
8. Disconnect the exhaust pipe hanger from the clutch housing.
9. Disconnect the exhaust pipe at the manifold and muffler and remove the exhaust pipe-resonator assembly or catalytic converter.
10. Unhook the clutch release lever return spring. Remove the clutch release cylinder and secure it out of the way.
11. Remove the speedometer cable from the extension housing.
12. Disconnect the starter motor and back-up light wires.
13. Protect the oil pan with a block of wood and support the engine with a jack. Support the transmission with a separate jack.
14. Remove the starter.
15. Unbolt the transmission from the engine rear plate.
16. Unbolt the transmission mount from the crossmember.
17. Remove the crossmember.
18. Work the clutch housing off the locating dowels. Slide the transmission rearward until the input shaft spline clears the clutch disc.

19. Remove the transmission from the truck. Refer to the Unit Repair Section for overhaul procedures.
   To install the transmission:
20. Be sure that all mating surfaces are free of dirt, burrs and paint.
21. Lift the transmission into place and start the input shaft into the clutch disc. Be sure that the splines align and move the transmission forward until the clutch housing seats on the locating dowels of the engine rear plate.
22. Bolt the clutch housing to the rear plate.
23. Install the starter motor.
24. Raise the engine and install the rear crossmember.
25. Install the rear transmission mount on the crossmember. Bolt the transmission to the rear mount.
26. Remove the jacks.
27. Install the driveshaft in the transmission extension housing. Install the center bearing.
28. Connect the driveshaft to the rear axle flange.
29. Install the exhaust pipe and resonator.
30. Connect the exhaust pipe to the flywheel housing and transmission brackets.
31. Connect the starter and back-up light wires.
32. Install the clutch release cylinder.
33. Adjust the clutch release lever free travel. Connect the return spring.
34. Connect the speedometer cable.
35. Fill the transmission with lubricant.
36. Lower the truck.
37. Install the shift tower and gasket. Install the boot.
38. Road test the truck and check for leaks.

LINKAGE ADJUSTMENT

The shifting mechanism of either Courier transmission is built into the transmission extension housing, therefore adjustments are not required.

AUTOMATIC TRANSMISSION

Couriers use a JATCO automatic transmission. It is model 3N71B, a 3-speed unit with manual selection of 1st and 2nd gears possible.

There are no internal points to adjust except for an intermediate band.

REMOVAL AND INSTALLATION

1. Disconnect the negative cable from the battery.

2. Raise and support the truck.
3. Drain the transmission fluid, but do not remove the pan. After the fluid has drained, install a few bolts to hold the pan in place, temporarily.
4. Remove the exhaust pipe bracket bolt from the right side of the converter housing.
5. Remove the exhaust pipe flange bolts from the rear of the resonator or catalytic converter, and disconnect the pipe.
6. Disconnect the driveshaft from the rear axle flange.
7. Remove the driveshaft center bearing support nuts, washers, and lockwashers. Lower the driveshaft and remove it from the transmission.
8. Disconnect the speedometer cable.
9. Disconnect the shift rod from the manual lever.
10. Remove the vacuum hose from the diaphragm. Disconnect the electrical connectors from the downshift solenoid and inhibitor switch, and remove their wires from the clip.
11. Disconnect and plug the cooler lines from the radiator at the transmission. Use a flare nut wrench if one is available.
12. Remove the access cover from the lower front of the converter housing.
13. Matchmark the drive plate (flywheel) and torque converter for reassembly. Remove the four bolts holding the torque converter to the drive plate.
14. Remove the bolts connecting the crossmember to the transmission.
15. Support the transmission with a jack. Remove the crossmember-to-frame bolts, and remove the crossmember.
16. Make sure that the transmission is securely supported. Secure it to the jack with a safety chain, if necessary.
17. Lower the transmission to provide working clearance, and remove the starter.
18. Remove the converter housing-to-engine bolts.
19. Remove the fluid filler tube.
20. With a pry bar, exert light pressure between the converter and the drive plate to prevent the converter from disengaging from the transmission as it is removed.
21. Lower the transmission and converter as an assembly. Be careful not to let the converter fall out.
   To install:
22. Place the transmission on the jack. Be sure that the converter is properly installed.
23. Raise the transmission into place. Install the converter housing-to-engine bolts, and torque in two stages to 23–34 ft. lbs.
24. Lower the transmission on the jack and install the starter.
25. Install the fluid filler tube with a new O-ring.
26. Raise the transmission slightly, and install the crossmember to the frame. Tighten the bolts to 23–34 ft. lbs.
27. Lower the transmission and install the transmission-to-crossmember bolts. Tighten to 23–34 ft. lbs.
28. Align the matchmarks made earlier

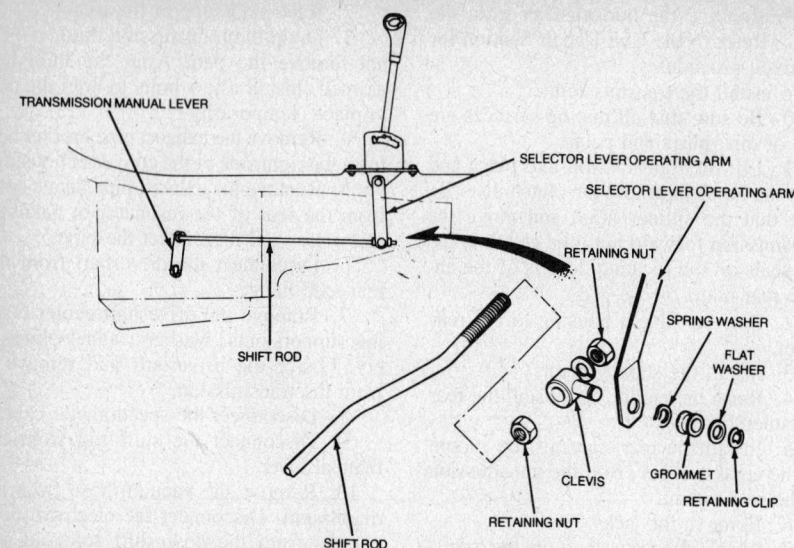

Automatic transmission shift linkage

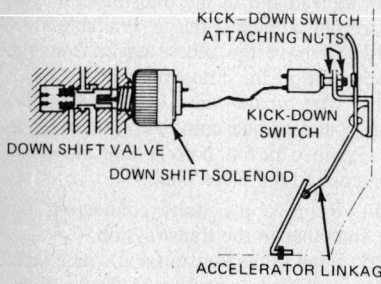

Automatic transmission kick-down switch adjustment

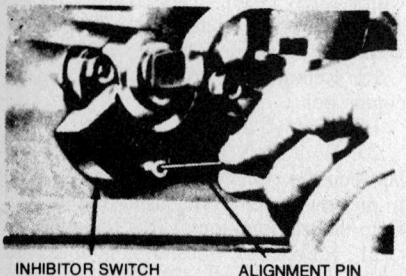

Automatic transmission neutral start switch adjustment

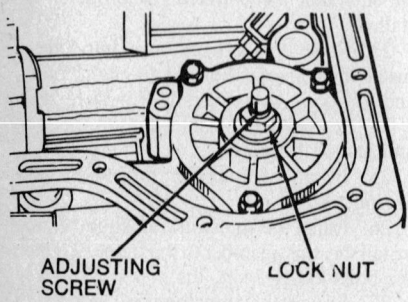

Automatic transmission intermediate band adjustment—models through 1976

on the torque converter and drive plate. Install the four attaching bolts and torque to 25–36 ft. lbs. in three stages.

29. Install the access cover. Remove the jack.

30. Connect the cooler lines.

31. Install the electrical connectors to the switch and solenoid, and replace the wires in the clip. Install the diaphragm vacuum hose.

32. Connect the shift rod to the lever.

33. Reconnect the speedometer cable.

34. Insert the driveshaft into the transmission. Install the center bearing support. Bolt the driveshaft to the rear axle flange.

35. Connect the exhaust pipe to the resonator or catalytic converter, using a new gasket. Reinstall the exhaust pipe clamp onto the converter housing, and torque the bolt to 10–15 ft. lbs.

36. Install a new pan gasket and the fluid pan, if this has not already been done.

37. Lower the truck. Connect the battery cable. Fill the transmission through the dipstick tube with the specified fluid, being careful not to overfill, and check for leaks.

Shift Linkage Adjustment

1. Put the gearshift lever in Neutral.
2. Raise and support the truck.
3. Disconnect the clevis from the lower end of the selector lever operating arm.
4. Move the transmission manual lever to Neutral, the 3rd detent position from the rear of the transmission.
5. Loosen the two clevis retaining nuts and adjust the clevis so that it freely enters the hole of the lever. Tighten the retaining nuts to secure the adjustment.
6. Connect the clevis to the lever and attach it with the spring washer, flat washer and retaining clip.
7. Lower the truck and check the operation of the linkage. Be sure that all gears engage properly.

THROTTLE LINKAGE ADJUSTMENT

See Fuel System section.

KICK-DOWN SWITCH ADJUSTMENT

1. Turn the ignition switch to the ON position.
2. Loosen the kick-down switch attaching nut and adjust the switch to engage when the accelerator pedal is depressed about ⅞ of the way. The down-shift solenoid will click when the switch engages.
3. Tighten the attaching nut and check the switch for proper operation.

NEUTRAL START SWITCH ADJUSTMENT

1. Adjust the manual linkage.
2. Place the transmission manual lever in Neutral (3rd detent from the rear of the transmission).
3. Remove the transmission manual lever retaining nut and lever.
4. Loosen the inhibitor switch attaching bolts. Remove the screw from the alignment pin hole at the bottom of the switch.
5. Rotate the switch and insert an alignment pin (0.079 in. diameter) into the alignment pin hole and internal rotor.
6. Tighten the two switch attaching bolts and remove the alignment pin.
7. Reinstall the alignment pin hole screw in the switch body.
8. Install the manual lever.
9. Check the operation of the switch. The engine should only start with the transmission selector lever in Neutral or Park.

INTERMEDIATE BAND ADJUSTMENT

1975–76

1. Raise and support the truck.
2. Place a drain pan under the transmission and loosen the pan attaching bolts to drain the fluid. Finally remove all the bolts except the two at the front.
3. When the fluid has drained, remove and thoroughly clean the pan.
4. Discard the pan gasket.
5. Loosen the brake band adjusting screw locknut and tighten the adjusting screw to 9–11 ft. lbs.
6. Back the adjusting screw off two turns.
7. Hold the adjusting screw stationary and tighten the adjusting screw locknut to 22–29 ft. lbs.
8. Install a new pan gasket and install the pan on the transmission.
9. Lower the truck and fill the transmission with fluid.

1977 and Later

The adjuster screw is located on the right front side of the case, under the servo cover. Removal of the pan is unnecessary. Remove the servo cover and follow steps 5, 6, and 7 of the 1975–76 procedure.

DRIVE TRAIN

Driveshaft(s)

The two piece driveshaft assembly consists of the front shaft, the rear shaft, a center support bearing and U-joints and yokes. The rear end of the driveshaft is attached to the companion flange at the rear axle through a U-joint, and at the front to the mainshaft by means of a sliding yoke. This arrangement provides for fore-and-aft movement of the driveshaft as the truck moves up and down. The center of the driveshaft is supported by the bearing attached to the underbody of the truck. The two piece driveshaft is used on all 1975–76 Couriers, and some 1977–82 models.

Some 1977 and later Couriers may have a one piece driveshaft, consisting of the shaft, universal joints at each end, a coupling yoke at the rear which bolts to the axle flange, and a splined sliding yoke at the front which mates to the transmission mainshaft. No center bearing is used. The one piece shaft looks like the rear half of the two piece driveshaft shown in the illustration, with the addition of the sliding yoke assembly from the front half.

REMOVAL AND INSTALLATION

The two piece driveshaft is removed as an assembly. It is not necessary to disassemble the center bearing.

1. Raise and support the rear of the truck.
2. Paint or scribe a matchmark across the universal joint yoke and the axle flange. The driveshaft was balanced at the factory as an assembly, and should be replaced in its original position to avoid driveline vibrations or imbalances.
3. On two piece driveshafts only, remove the two nuts and their washers securing the center bearing support bracket to the frame, and remove the bracket.
4. Remove the four bolts from the universal joint yoke and axle flange. On some earlier models, the axle flange has studs, and the universal joint yoke is retained by nuts, instead of bolts.
5. Drop the rear end of the driveshaft down, and slide the splined sliding yoke out of the transmission.

NOTE: Plug the end of the transmission to avoid the loss of gear oil.

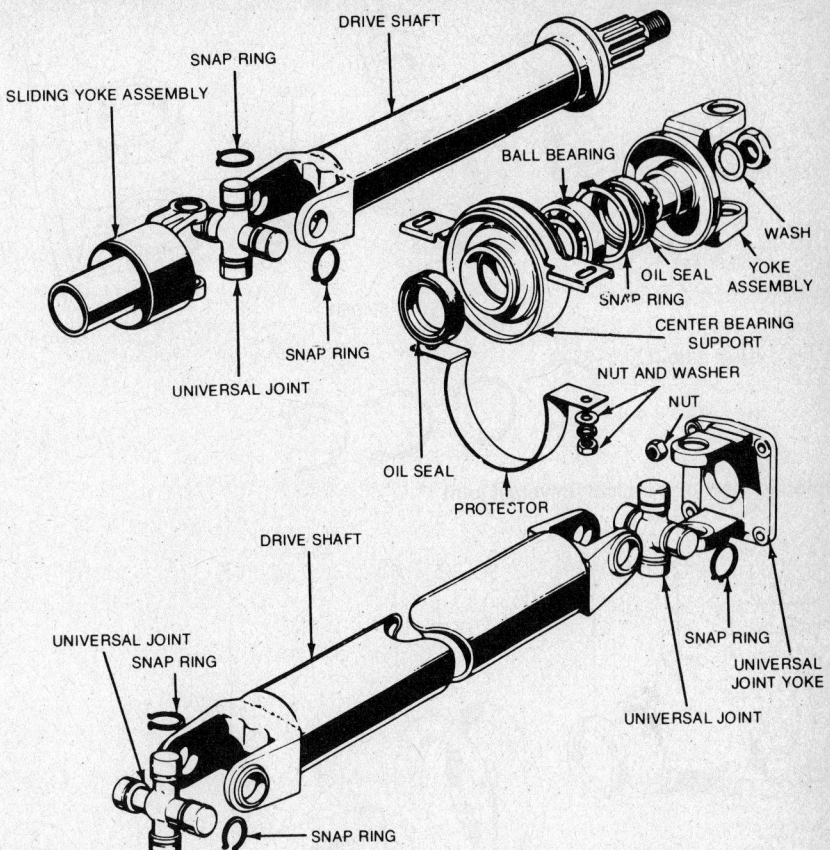

Disassembled view of the two-piece driveshaft

To install:

6. Apply a lithium grease to the interior splines of the sliding yoke.
7. Unplug the transmission end. Slide the yoke into the extension housing. Be careful not to damage the extension housing seal.
8. Align the mating marks on the rear flange. Install the bolts and tighten to 40–47 ft. lbs.
9. On two piece driveshafts only, install the center support bracket, and tighten the nuts to 27–38 ft. lbs.
10. Lower the truck.

Center Bearing

REPLACEMENT

The center support bearing is a sealed unit which requires no periodic maintenance. The following procedure should be used if it becomes necessary to replace the bearing. You will need a pair of snap-ring pliers for this job.

1. Remove the driveshaft assembly.
2. To maintain driveline balance, matchmark the rear driveshaft, the center yoke and the front driveshaft so that they may be installed in their original positions.
3. Remove the center universal joint from the center yoke, leaving it attached to the rear driveshaft. See the following sec-

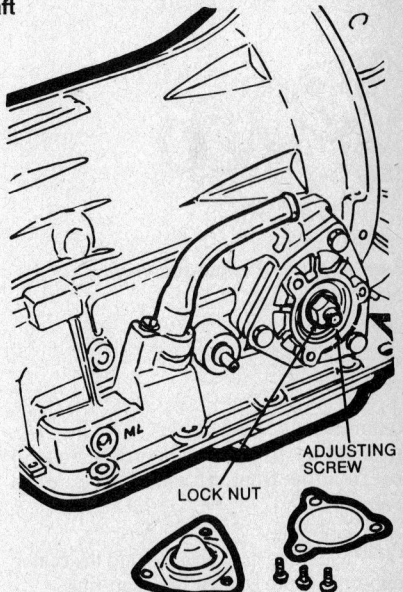

Automatic transmission intermediate band adjustment—1977 and later models

tion for the correct procedure.

4. Remove the nut and washer securing the center yoke to the front driveshaft.
5. Slide the center yoke off the splines. The rear oil seal should slide off with it.
6. If the oil seal has remained on top of the snap-ring, remove and discard the seal. Remove the snap-ring from its groove.

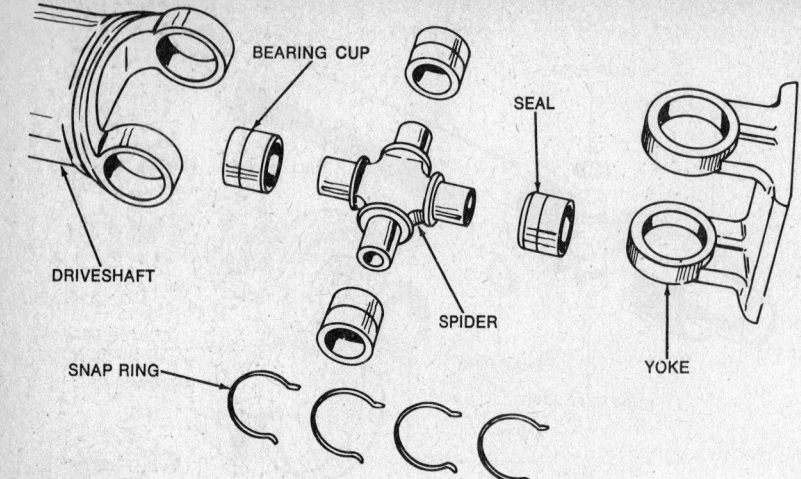

Exploded view of a typical universal joint

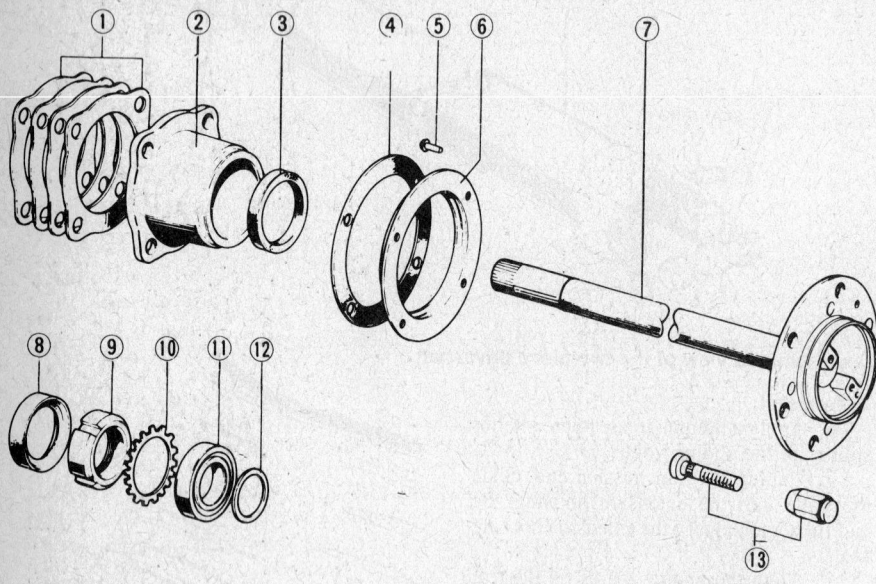

Rear axle shaft exploded view

1. Shims
2. Bearing housing
3. Outer oil seal
4. Gasket
5. Rivet
6. Baffle seal
7. Axle shaft
8. Inner oil seal
9. Lock nut
10. Lock washer
11. Bearing
12. Spacer
13. Hub bolt and lug nut

Remove the bearing.

7. Slide the center support and front oil seal from the front driveshaft. Discard the seal.

To assemble:

8. Install the new bearing into the center support. Secure it with the snap-ring.

9. Apply a coat of grease to the lips of the new oil seals, and install them into the center support on either side of the bearing.

10. Coat the splines of the front driveshaft with grease. Install the center support assembly and the center yoke onto the front driveshaft, being sure to match up the marks made during disassembly.

11. Install the washer and nut. Torque the nut to 116–130 ft. lbs.

12. Check that the center support assembly rotates smoothly around the driveshaft.

13. Align the mating marks on the center yoke and the rear driveshaft, and assemble the center universal joint.

14. Install the driveshaft. Be sure that the rear yoke and the axle flange are aligned properly.

Universal Joint

REPLACEMENT

1. Remove the driveshaft from the vehicle.

2. Remove the snap-rings which retain the U-joint bearings in the flange and in the driveshaft.

3. Position the U-joint in a vise with a socket smaller than the bearing cap on one side and a socket larger than the bearing cap on the other side.

4. Slowly tighten the jaws of the vise so that the smaller socket forces the U-joint spider and the opposite bearing into the larger socket. If the bearing cannot be pressed entirely out, remove it with a pair of channel lock pliers.

5. Remove the other side of the spider in the same manner (if applicable) and remove the spider assembly from the driveshaft. Discard the spider assemblies.

6. Clean all foreign matter from the yoke areas at the end of the driveshaft(s).

7. Start the new spider and one of the bearing cap assemblies into a yoke by positioning the yoke in a vise with the spider positioned in place with one of the bearing cap assemblies positioned over one of the holes in the yoke. Slowly close the vise, pressing the bearing cap assembly in the yoke. Press the cap in far enough so that the retaining snap-ring can be installed. Use the smaller socket to recess the bearing cap.

8. Open the vise and position the opposite bearing cap assembly over the proper hole in the yoke with the socket that is smaller than the diameter of the bearing cap located on the cap. Slowly close the vise, pressing the bearing cap into the hole in the yoke with the socket. Make sure that the spider assembly is in line with the bearing cap as it is pressed in. Press the bearing cap in far enough so that the retaining snap-ring can be installed. Snap-rings are available in 0.057–0.064 in. thickness to assure good centering of the yokes and spiders, preventing out-of-balance. When selecting snap-rings, to give a suitable slight drag fit (not binding), use similar snap-rings in any given yoke. For example, do not use a 0.059 in. snap-ring opposite a 0.063 in. snap-ring, as this would create an out-of-balance condition.

9. Install all remaining U-joints in the same manner.

10. Install the driveshaft.

REAR DRIVE AXLE

The Courier uses a removable carrier axle with a hypoid ring and pinion and a semifloating axle.

Axle Shaft, Bearing, and Seal

REMOVAL AND INSTALLATION

1. Loosen the wheel lug nuts. Raise and support the rear of the truck with jackstands under the axle housing. Remove the wheel.

2. Remove the brake drum and brake shoes, and the parking cable retainer. Disconnect and plug the hydraulic lines at the wheel cylinders.

3. Remove the nuts holding the brake backing plate and the bearing housing to the axle housing.

4. Pull the axle shaft, backing plate, bearing housing assembly, and shims out from the axle housing.

To replace the bearing and seals:

5. Remove the inner oil seal from the bearing housing.

6. Loosen the locknut and remove the locknut and lockwasher. There are special wrenches available to fit the locknut, but you can remove it with a hammer and a flat-nosed punch, if you work carefully.

7. Remove the bearing and housing assembly from the axle shaft, using either a puller on the housing, or a press on the axle shaft while supporting the housing.

8. Remove the bearing, spacer, and outer oil seal.

9. Oil the lips of a new oil seal, and press it into place in the housing.

10. Install the spacer and a new bearing into the housing.

11. Press the bearing housing assembly onto the axle shaft. Install a new lockwasher and the locknut.

12. Oil the lips of a new inner seal, and press it into place. Check that the bearing and housing assembly rotate smoothly on the axle shaft.

To install the axle shaft:

13. Install the axle shaft, backing plate, and bearing housing assembly, but no shims, into the axle housing. Insert it carefully to avoid damage to the splines.

14. Using two bolts and nuts, temporarily install the bearing housing and backing plate to the housing flange.

15. Check the axle shaft end-play with a dial indicator mounted on the backing plate.

16. If only one axle shaft has been removed, the end-play should be 0.002–0.006 in. If both axle shafts have been removed, check the end-play after the first shaft is installed. Don't wait until after both shafts are installed. It should be 0.026–0.033 in. The end-play of the second shaft should then be 0.002–0.006 in. Shims are available to adjust the end-play.

17. After adjusting the end-play, install all bolts and torque them to 40–50 ft. lbs.

18. Install the brake shoe, parking brake cable retainer, and brake drum. Connect the hydraulic lines to the wheel cylinders, and bleed the brakes.

19. Install the wheel and lower the truck. Check the axle lubricant level and add if necessary.

Differential

Overhaul of the differential carrier is a complex operation requiring special tools and technical knowledge. If either of these is

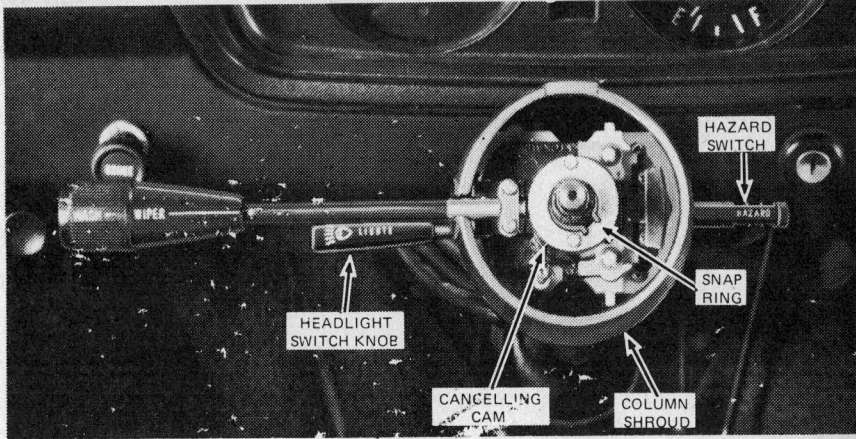

Combination switch installed. Some models also have a LIGHTS-HAZARD indicator at the top of the shroud.

not available, it may be wise (economically) to remove the carrier yourself and have a professional perform the overhaul, rather than purchase special (and expensive) tools or take the vehicle to a shop.

REMOVAL AND INSTALLATION

1. Raise the vehicle and support it safely with jackstands.

2. Remove the differential drain plug and drain the lubricant from the differential. Install the plug after all of the fluid has drained.

3. Remove the axle shafts as previously outlined.

4. Remove the driveshaft(s) as previously outlined.

5. Remove the carrier-to-differential housing retaining fasteners and remove the carrier assembly from the housing.

Installation is performed in the following manner:

6. Clean the carrier and axle housing mating surfaces.

7. If the differential originally used a gasket between the carrier and the differential housing, replace the gasket. If the unit had no gasket, apply a thin film of oil-resistant silicone sealer to the mating surfaces of both the carrier and the housing and allow the sealer to set according to the manufacturer's instructions.

8. Place the carrier assembly onto the housing and install the carrier-to-housing fasteners. Torque the fasteners to 12–17 ft. lbs.

9. Install the driveshaft(s) and axle shafts as previously outlined.

10. Install the brake drums and wheels.

11. Fill the differential with the proper amount of fluid. See the Capacities Chart at the beginning of the Courier section.

NOTE: The lubricant must meet or exceed the following Ford specifications: 1975 vehicles—ESW-M2628-BA (for use above 0°F.) or ESW-M2C28-AA (for use

below 0°F.); 1976 and later vehicles—ESW-M2C105-A.

12. Lower the vehicle and road test for proper operation.

STEERING

Steering Wheel

REMOVAL AND INSTALLATION

1. Disconnect the negative battery cable.

2. Remove the horn button by turning it counterclockwise. Remove the horn contact spring.

3. Matchmark the steering wheel and shaft.

4. Remove the wheel attaching nut and remove the steering wheel with a puller.

NOTE: Do not use a hammer for removal, and under no circumstances hammer on the steering shaft.

5. Installation is the reverse of removal.

Use the matchmarks to assemble properly. Torque the steering wheel nut to 22–29 ft. lbs.

Turn Signal Switch

The combination turn signal, windshield wiper, and headlight switch is mounted on the steering column, and must be replaced as an assembly.

REMOVAL AND INSTALLATION

1. Disconnect the negative battery cable.

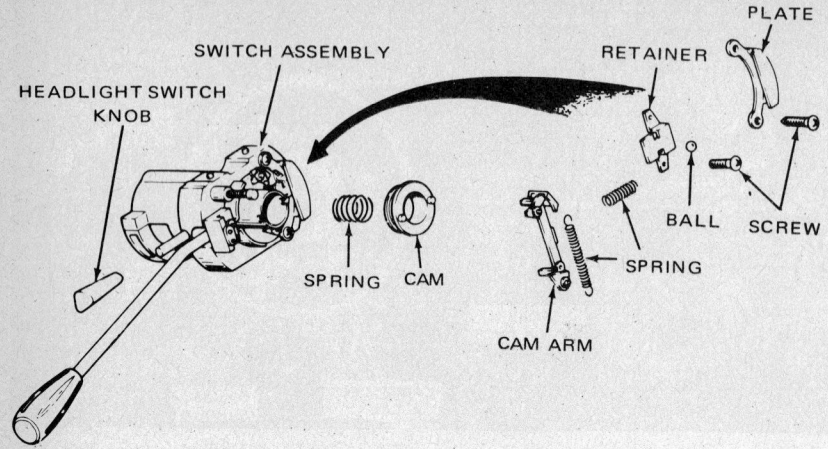

Turn signal arm and related components

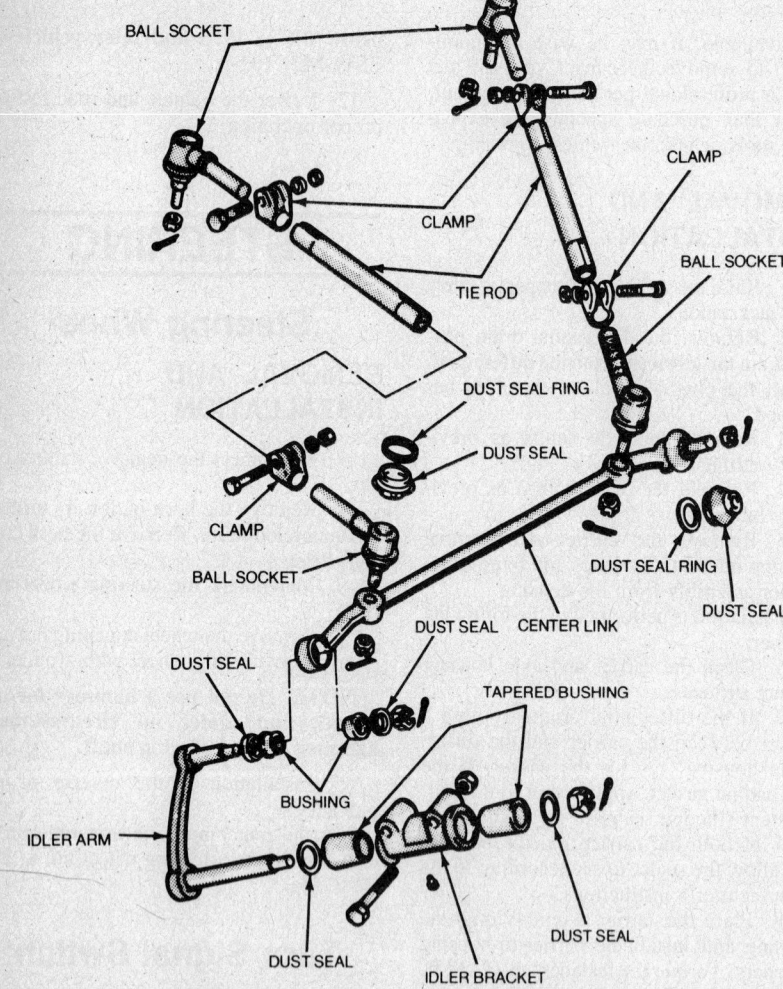

Exploded view of the steering linkage. 1977 and later models use jam nuts instead of clamps to lock the tie rods in place.

2. Remove the steering wheel.

3. Remove the "Lights-Hazard" Indicator and the steering column shroud.

4. Unplug the electrical multiple connectors at the base of the steering column.

5. Pull the headlight knob from its shaft.

6. Remove the snap-ring, which retains the switch, from the steering shaft. Pull the turn indicator canceling cam from the shaft.

7. Remove the single retaining bolt near the bottom of the switch. Remove the complete switch from the column.

Installation is the reverse of removal.

Check the operation of the switch before installing the steering wheel.

Steering Linkage

REMOVAL AND INSTALLATION

The center link can be removed from both tie-rods, Pitman arm and idler arm by removing the ball socket nuts and using a ball socket puller to remove the ball socket. After removing the center link, the Pitman arm can be removed from the sector shaft by removing the nut and using the puller. Tie rods can also be removed by use of a puller. Toe-in must be reset when tie rods or ball sockets are replaced.

Tie Rod Ends

REMOVAL AND INSTALLATION

1. Loosen the tie rod clamp nuts (jam nuts, 1977 and later).

2. Remove and discard the cotter pin from the ball socket end, and remove the nut.

3. Use a ball joint puller to loosen the ball socket stud from the center link. Remove the stud from the kingpin steering arm in the same way.

4. Unscrew the tie rod end from the threaded sleeve. The threads may be left or right hand threads. Count the number of threads required to remove it.

5. To install, lightly coat the threads with grease, and turn the new end in as many turns as were required to remove it. This will give approximately correct toe-in.

6. Install the ball socket studs into center link and kingpin steering arm. Tighten the nuts to 22–29 ft. lbs. Install a new cotter pin. You may tighten the nut to fit the cotter pin, but don't loosen it.

7. Check and adjust the toe-in, and tighten the tie rod clamps or jam nuts.

Steering Column and Gear

REMOVAL AND INSTALLATION

1975–78

1. Disconnect the negative battery cable at the battery.

2. Rotate the horn button counterclockwise and remove the horn button and the horn button contact spring.

3. Remove the steering wheel as previously outlined.

4. Remove the turn signal cancelling

cam snap-ring and the cancelling cam from the top of the steering shaft.

5. Disconnect the steering column wiring by disconnecting the snap connectors.

6. Remove the steering column support bracket.

7. Move the floor covering and insulation away from the bottom of the steering column. Remove the four screws and two bolts which secure the toe plate and boot to the dash panel.

8. Loosen the bolt which secures the bottom of the steering column jacket and remove the jacket from the shaft.

9. Remove the air cleaner assembly.

10. Dismount the heater (coolant) hoses from their brackets and move the hoses out of the way.

11. Remove and plug the hydraulic lines from both the brake and clutch master cylinders.

12. Remove the brake and clutch master cylinders from the vehicle.

13. Raise the vehicle and support it safely with jackstands.

14. Disconnect the Pitman arm from the steering gear shaft using a puller.

15. Remove the steering gear-to-frame fasteners and remove the steering gear from the vehicle. Note the position of the shim(s) located between the gear and the frame, if so equipped. During installation, place the shim(s) in its original position.

16. Installation of the gear and column is the reverse of the previous steps. Note the following points during installation:

   a. Align the steering wheel and steering column shaft markings made during step 3.

   b. Bleed the hydraulic clutch system as previously outlined.

   c. Bleed the brake system. Refer to the Brake Section for the appropriate procedure.

1979–81

1. Follow steps 1–11 of the previous 1975–78 procedure.

NOTE: After performing step 3, remove the light switch knob, then proceed.

2. Remove the intake manifold and carburetor assembly. Refer to the appropriate sections (Fuel and Engine).

3. Remove the dust cover from the tire apron panel.

4. Raise the front of the vehicle and support it safely with jackstands.

5. Remove the left side wheel and tire assembly.

6. Disconnect the steering center link from the Pitman arm using a puller.

7. Remove the Pitman arm nut and the Pitman arm.

8. Jack up the left side lower control arm.

9. Remove the left upper control arm. Note the position and number of alignment shims so that proper front end alignment is retained after installation.

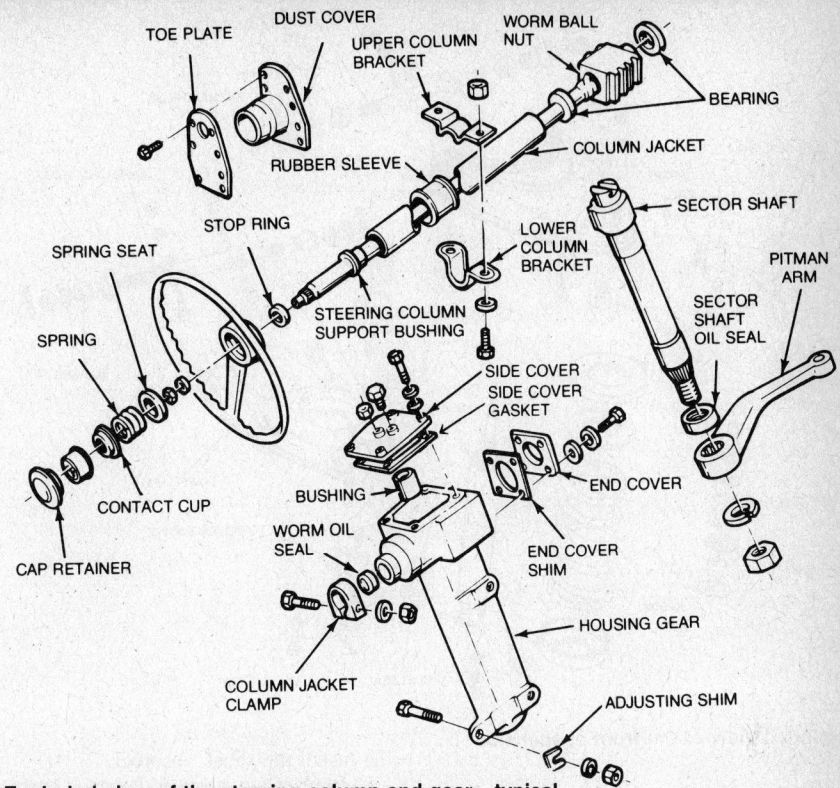

Exploded view of the steering column and gear—typical

10. Remove the steering gear-to-frame fasteners and remove the steering gear from the vehicle.

11. Installation of the components is the reverse of the previous steps. Refer to step 16 of the 1975–78 procedure for points which should be noted during installation.

1982

1. Disconnect the negative battery cable at the battery.

2. Remove the horn cap from the steering wheel and remove the steering wheel as previously outlined.

3. Remove the screws which retain the steering column cover and remove the cover.

4. Remove the stop ring, cancelling cam and spring from the top of the steering column shaft.

5. Disconnect the wiring couplings for the combination switch.

6. Remove the combination switch retaining screws and remove the combination switch.

7. Remove the steering column mounting bracket-to-dash panel bolts.

8. Move the floor covering and insulation out of the way and remove the bolts which attach the steering column set plate to the dash panel.

9. Pull the steering column jacket off of the steering shaft.

10. Remove the yoke joint-to-worm shaft bolts and remove the steering shaft.

11. Remove the air cleaner assembly.

12. Disconnect and plug the hydraulic lines from both the brake and clutch master cylinders.

13. Remove both the brake and clutch

master cylinders from the vehicle.

14. Raise the front of the vehicle and support it safely with jackstands.

15. Remove the left side wheel and tire assembly.

16. Disconnect the center steering link from the Pitman arm using a puller.

17. Remove the steering gear-to-frame fasteners and remove the steering gear from the vehicle.

18. Installation of the components is the reverse of the previous steps. Refer to step 16 of the 1975–78 procedure for points which should be noted during installation.

NOTE: To secure the steering column jacket, insert U-pins into the holes of the steering column jacket to centralize the jacket as shown in the accompanying illustration. Tighten the steering column jacket bolts and remove the U-pins from the jacket.

WORM BEARING PRELOAD ADJUSTMENT

1. It is necessary to drain the steering gear to make this adjustment. Refill the steering gear after adjustment.

2. Disconnect the Pitman arm from the gear.

3. Loosen the sector adjusting screw locknut and turn the adjusting screw counterclockwise.

4. Rotate the worm shaft with a torque wrench. The preload should be 1–3.5 in. lbs. for 1975–76 models; 5.2–7.8 in. lbs. for 1977 and later models. If it is not, unscrew the end cover bolts and remove the

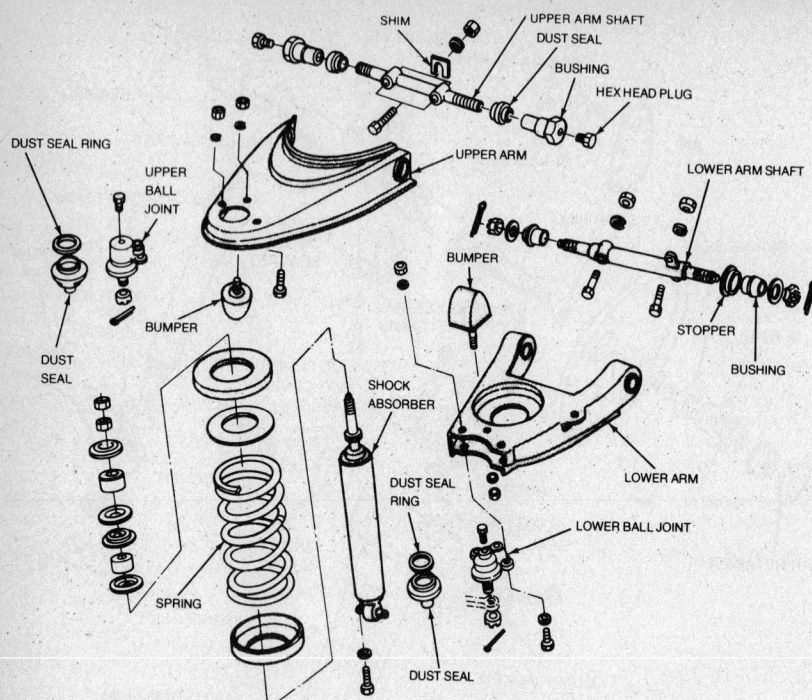

Exploded view of the front suspension

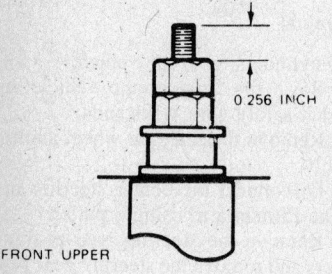

Shock absorber upper mount installation

end cover with the shim pack. If the preload is less than specified, reduce the shim size. If it is more than specified, increase the shim size. Shims are available in 0.002, 0.003, 0.004 and 0.008 in.

5. Reconnect the Pitman arm.

FRONT SUSPENSION

Shock Absorbers

REMOVAL AND INSTALLATION

1. Remove the nuts attaching the upper end of the shock absorber to the crossmember.

2. Remove the rubber bushings and washers.

3. Remove the bolts attaching the lower end of the shock absorber to the lower control arm.

4. Remove the shock from under the lower control arm.

To install the shock absorber:

5. Replace any worn or damaged bushings.

6. From under the lower control arm, install the shock with bushings and attach the shock to the lower control arm. Torque the lower mount to 12–17 ft. lbs.

7. Attach the upper end of the shock to the crossmember and tighten the nuts so that there is 0.256 in. between the top of the shock absorber rod and the top of the upper nut.

Springs

REMOVAL AND INSTALLATION

Refer to the Lower Control Arm Removal and Installation procedure to replace the spring(s).

Upper Control Arm

REMOVAL AND INSTALLATION

1. Raise the front of the vehicle.

2. Place jackstands under the lower control arms and lower the vehicle onto the jackstands until the upper arm is off of the frame bumper.

3. Remove the wheel. Install a chain around the coil spring as a safety measure.

4. Remove the cotter pin and nut retaining the upper ball joint.

5. Break the tapered fit loose by striking it with a hammer and separate the ball joint from the spindle.

6. From under the hood, remove the two upper arm retaining bolts and remove the arm from the vehicle. Keep track of the shims under the bolts.

7. Remove the three ball joint retaining bolts and remove the ball joint from the upper arm.

To install the upper control arm:

8. Install the ball joint in the upper control arm and torque the retaining bolts to 15–20 ft. lbs.

9. Position the upper control arm in the truck and install the alignment shims from where they were removed. Install the retaining nuts and bolts on the shaft and torque them to 62–76 ft. lbs.

10. Position the spindle on the ball joint and install the retaining nut and cotter pin. The nut should be torqued to 40–55 ft. lbs.

11. Remove the safety chain.

12. Install the wheel.

13. Remove the jackstands and lower the truck. Have the front end alignment checked.

Lower Control Arm

REMOVAL AND INSTALLATION

———— **CAUTION** ————
Be extremely careful while working with coil springs. Failure to follow safety measures could result in personal injury.

1. Raise the front of the truck and position jackstands under both sides of the frame just behind the lower control arms.

2. Remove the wheel.

3. Remove the lower shock absorber retaining bolts and push the shock up into the spring.

4. Remove the front stabilizer bar retaining bolt, nut and bushings and disconnect the stabilizer bar from the lower control arm.

5. Position a floor jack under the lower control arm and raise the arm to take the spring pressure off. Install a safety chain on the spring.

6. Unbolt the ball joint from the lower control arm.

7. Pull the spindle and ball joint away from the lower arm.

8. If necessary, the lower ball joint can be removed by removing the cotter pin and nut and loosening the ball joint with a hammer.

9. Carefully lower the control arm on the jack, being careful that the spring does not fly out.

10. Remove the three lower control arm retaining bolts and remove the lower control arm.

To install the lower control arm:

11. Position the lower control arm in place and install the three retaining bolts and nuts. Do not tighten. If removed, install the ball joint in the spindle. Tighten to 60–70 ft. lbs.

12. Position the spring on the lower con-

trol arm and in the upper frame retaining pocket.

13. Use a C-clamp to clamp the spring to the lower control arm.

14. Raise the lower control arm with a floor jack and position the ball joint and spindle in the lower arm.

15. Loosely install the three lower arm-to-ball joint bolts. Remove the safety chain from the spring, and remove the floor jack and C-clamp.

16. Torque the three ball joint retaining nuts to 60–70 ft. lbs.

17. Pull the shock absorber down and install the bolts and nuts. Torque to 12–17 ft. lbs.

18. Install the stabilizer bar on the lower control arm.

19. Install the front wheel. Lower the truck and have the front wheel alignment checked.

Ball Joints

INSPECTION

1. Check the ball joint dust seals and replace them if they are defective.

2. Check the end-play of the upper and lower ball joints. If the end-play exceeds 0.031 in., replace the ball joint.

REPLACEMENT

Use the applicable procedures under ''Upper Control Arm Removal and Installation,'' or ''Lower Control Arm Removal and Installation.''

Front End Alignment

Caster and camber cannot be set or measured accurately without professional equipment. Toe-in can be adjusted with some degree of success without any special equipment.

CASTER

Caster is the forward or rearward tilt of the upper ball joint. Rearward tilt is referred to as positive caster, while forward tilt is referred to as negative caster.

Caster is adjusted by changing the shim(s) between the upper arm shaft and the frame, or by turning the shaft until the correct angle is obtained.

CAMBER

Camber is the inward or outward tilt from the vertical, measured in degrees, of the front wheels at the top. An outward tilt gives the wheel positive camber. Proper camber is critical to assure even tire wear.

Camber is adjusted by adding or subtracting the shim(s) between the upper arm shaft and the frame. The shim is available in thicknesses of 0.040 in., 0.064 in., 0.080 in., and 0.128 in.

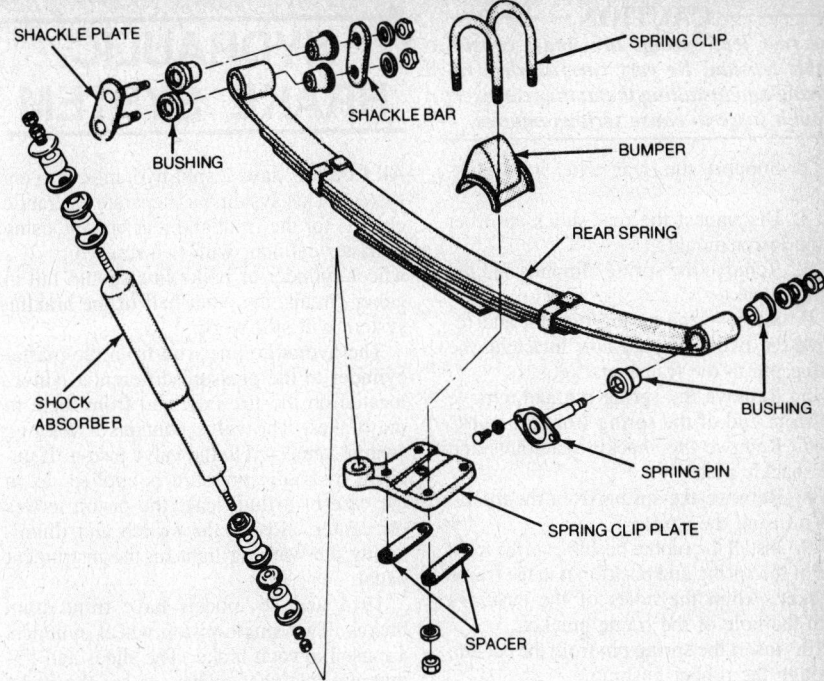

Exploded view of the rear suspension

TOE-IN

Toe-in is the amount, measured in a fraction of an inch, that the wheels are closer together in front than at the rear.

Toe-in can be increased or decreased by changing the length of the tie rods. Threaded sleeves are provided for this purpose.

Toe-in must be checked after caster and camber have been adjusted, but it can be adjusted without disturbing the other two settings. You can make this adjustment without special equipment if you make careful measurements. The adjustment is made at the tie-rod sleeves. The wheels must be straight ahead.

1. Toe-in can be determined by measuring the distance between the centers of the tire treads, front and rear. If the tread pattern of your tires makes this impossible, you can measure between the edges of the wheel rims, but make sure to move the truck forward and measure in a couple of places to avoid errors caused by bent rims or wheel runout.

2. If the measurement is not within specifications, loosen the clamp bolts on the tie rod sleeves (1975–76). For 1977 and later models, loosen the jam nuts next to the tie rod ends.

3. Rotate the sleeves equally (in opposite directions) to obtain the correct measurement. If the sleeves are not adjusted equally, the steering wheel will be crooked when you're done.

NOTE: If your steering wheel is already crooked, it can be straightened by turning the sleeves equally in the same direction.

4. When measurement is within spe-

cifications, check the position of the clamps on 1975–76 models. The clamps must be positioned with the open areas 20°–50° forward of the vertical centerline of the tie rod, to prevent interference with the center link. If the open areas are not within this range, rotate the clamps until they are. Tighten the clamps, and recheck the measurement. For 1977 and later models, tighten the jam nuts against the tie rods and re-check the measurement.

FRONT WHEEL TURNING ANGLE

The turning stop screws are located at the steering knuckle. If necessary, the screws can be adjusted to adjust the turning angle.

NOTE: This should not be attempted unless you are equipped with the necessary measuring equipment and a knowledge of front end alignment.

REAR SUSPENSION

The rear suspension consists of semi-elliptic leaf springs and hydraulic double-action shock absorbers.

Springs

REMOVAL AND INSTALLATION

1. Raise and support the truck, allowing the spring to hang freely.

2. Support the rear axle with jackstands.

3. Disconnect the rear shock absorber at the lower mount.

4. Remove the spring clip nuts and the spring plate.

5. Remove the spring pin nut and remove the two bolts and nuts attaching the spring pin to the frame bracket.

6. Remove the spring pin and remove the front end of the spring from the truck.

7. Remove the shackle plate nuts and the shackle plate.

8. Remove the spring from the truck.

To install the spring:

9. Install the rubber bushings in the front eye of the spring and position it in the frame bracket. Align the holes of the bushings with the hole of the frame bracket.

10. Insert the spring pin from the outside through the rubber bushing.

11. Install the spring pin plate to the frame bracket and torque the nuts to 15–18 ft. lbs.

12. Install the rubber bushings in the rear spring eye and shackle plate. Install the spring and shackle plate to the frame bracket. Do not tighten the nuts.

13. Lower the rear axle and place the center hole of the axle spring clip plate over the head of the spring center bolt.

14. Install the spring plate under the spring and install the spring clips. Torque the nuts to 46–58 ft. lbs.

15. Connect the shock absorber at the lower mount and torque the mount to 18–26 ft. lbs.

16. Lower the vehicle and bounce it several times to seat the springs.

17. Tighten the spring pin nuts to 62–76 ft. lbs. and the shackle plate nuts to 44–58 ft. lbs.

Shock Absorbers

REMOVAL AND INSTALLATION

1. Remove the nuts, washers and bushings from the upper and lower shock mounts.

2. Compress the shock absorber and remove it.

To install the shock absorber:

3. If the rubber bushings are worn or damaged, use new ones.

4. Compress the shock absorber and install it in the truck.

5. Install the rubber bushings, washers and nuts on both the upper and lower mounts. Both the lower and upper mounts must be tightened to provide 0.138 in. between the outside nut and the end of the shock rod in 1975, and 0.217 in. for 1976 and later models. See the front shock absorber installation section for an illustration of this measurement.

HYDRAULIC BRAKE SYSTEM

All Couriers have a split hydraulic braking system. This system has separate hydraulic circuits for the front and rear brakes, using a master cylinder with two reservoirs. If a wheel cylinder or brake line should fail in either circuit, the other half of the braking system will still work.

The hydraulic lines run from the master cylinder to the pressure differential valve, located on the firewall, and from there to the brakes. The valve contains a warning switch connected to the valve piston. If unequal hydraulic pressure is applied, as in the case of a fluid leak, the piston moves off center, closing the switch and illuminating the warning light on the instrument panel.

1975 and 76 models have front drum brakes. Two single-piston wheel cylinders are used in each brake. The shoes and linings are interchangeable, as are the brake return springs. 1977–82 Couriers have single piston caliper front disc brakes. All Couriers through 1978 have two dual piston wheel cylinders in each rear drum brake. The rear brakes are not self-adjusting on those models, and adjustments must be made to each of the two wheel cylinders in each brake. 1979 and later models have one dual piston wheel cylinder in each rear drum brake; the brakes are self-adjusting, requiring manual adjustment only when the linings are replaced. As in the front drum brakes, the shoes, linings, and return springs are interchangeable in the rear brakes (but 1975–78 brake components are not interchangeable with 1979–82 brake parts). The brake system is vacuum boosted in all 1977 and later models.

An independent hand-operated parking brake actuates the rear wheel brakes through a cable linkage.

Adjustments

FRONT DISC BRAKES

The front disc brakes are self adjusting. No adjustment is either necessary or possible.

FRONT DRUM BRAKES

The brake shoes should be at normal room temperature. Adjust each front brake shoe as follows:

1. Raise and support the truck. The wheels must be able to turn freely.

2. Remove the adjusting slot covers from the brake backing plate.

3. Insert a brake adjusting spoon (a screwdriver will do in a pinch) to grab the starwheel of the wheel cylinder.

4. Rotate the starwheel of one wheel cylinder toward the inside of the brake drum until the wheel is locked. Then back off the starwheel five notches.

5. Repeat step 4 for all the wheel cylinders.

6. Install the adjusting slot covers.

7. Check the brake adjustment by spinning the wheel by hand. There should be no drag.

8. Lower the truck.

REAR BRAKES

1978 and Earlier Models

The brake shoes should be at normal room temperature. Make the adjustment as follows:

1. Be sure that the parking brake is fully released. Disconnect the equalizer clevis pin.

2. Raise and support the truck so that the wheels are free to turn.

3. Remove the adjusting slot covers from the brake backing plate.

4. Insert a brake spoon (or screwdriver) into the lower adjusting slot to contact the starwheel of the lower wheel cylinder.

5. Turn the lower wheel cylinder star wheel to expand the brake shoe until it locks against the drum. Back the starwheel off five notches. Check the wheel, by rotating it, to be sure that there is no drag.

6. Repeat step 5 for all the wheel cylinders.

7. Connect the parking brake equalizer clevis pin and check the parking brake adjustment.

8. Install the adjusting hole covers.

9. Lower the truck and road-test the brakes. Readjust if necessary.

1979 and Later Models

The rear drum brakes are self-adjusting on these models. Manual adjustment is required only when the brake shoes have been replaced, or when the length of the self-adjusting rod has been changed for some reason. The brakes should be cold (room temperature).

1. If the shoe retaining spring has been removed, first retract the pushrod fully (drum removed).

2. Raise and support the rear of the truck. The wheels must be free to turn.

3. Make sure the parking brake is fully released.

4. Remove the two adjusting hole plugs from the brake backing plate.

5. An arrow stamped on the backing plate indicates the direction to turn the adjuster starwheel to expand the shoes. Insert a screwdriver through the adjuster hole and turn the starwheel until the brakes are locked.

6. Insert a drift through the other adjuster hole. Use the drift to hold the pole lever of the self-adjuster firmly. Back off the starwheel three or four notches; the wheel should rotate freely (no drag).

7. Repeat the adjustment on the other wheel. Make sure the adjustment is exactly the same. Road test for equal brake action and readjust as necessary.

BRAKE PEDAL FREE-TRAVEL

There should be 0.12–0.34 in. of brake pedal free-travel before the brakes are applied on 1975–76 trucks. 1977 and later vacuum boosted models should have 0.33–0.39 in. of play.

1. Loosen the locknut on the master cylinder pushrod at the clevis, which attaches the pushrod to the pedal.

2. Turn the master cylinder pushrod either in or out to obtain the specified clearance.

3. When the adjustment is complete, tighten the locknut to 8–13 ft. lbs.

Master Cylinder

REMOVAL AND INSTALLATION

1. Wipe off the master cylinder and lines, then place cloths under it to absorb spilled fluid. Disconnect and plug the brake lines from the master cylinder outlets. The 1977 and later models have a remote reservoir, so the two inlet hoses should be disconnected at the master cylinder and plugged. If you pinch the reservoir hoses while removing them, and then raise their ends above the level of the reservoir, spillage will be reduced.

NOTE: Brake fluid destroys paint. Be careful not to spill fluid on painted surfaces.

2. Remove the two nuts and lockwashers which secure the master cylinder to the firewall or vacuum booster.

3. Lift the master cylinder (and boot on units through 1976) outward and upward away from the firewall and brake pushrod.

To install the master cylinder:

4. Install the master cylinder (and boot if equipped) on the firewall or booster, while carefully guiding the brake pushrod into contact with the master cylinder piston.

5. Install the two nuts and lockwashers and tighten the nuts to 11–17 ft. lbs.

6. Connect the brake lines to the master cylinder ports.

7. Bleed the brake system.

8. Check the brake pedal free-travel adjustment.

OVERHAUL

1. Remove the master cylinder.

2. Remove the master cylinder reservoir, through 1976, and drain the master cylinder.

3. Remove the two grommets from the master cylinder body through 1976. Remove the elbow connectors 1977 and later.

4. Remove the dust boot (through 1976).

5. Use a small screwdriver to remove the piston stop ring.

6. Remove the piston stop washer, primary piston and primary piston return spring.

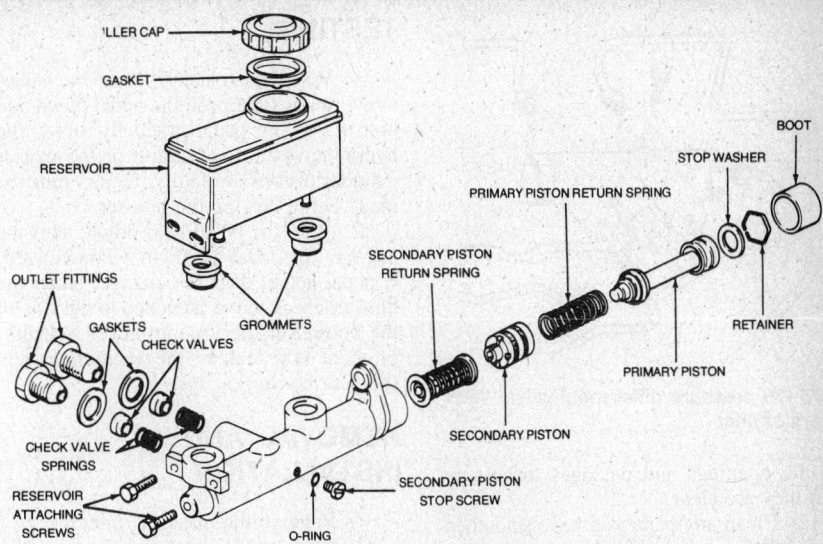

Exploded view of the 1975–76 brake master cylinder

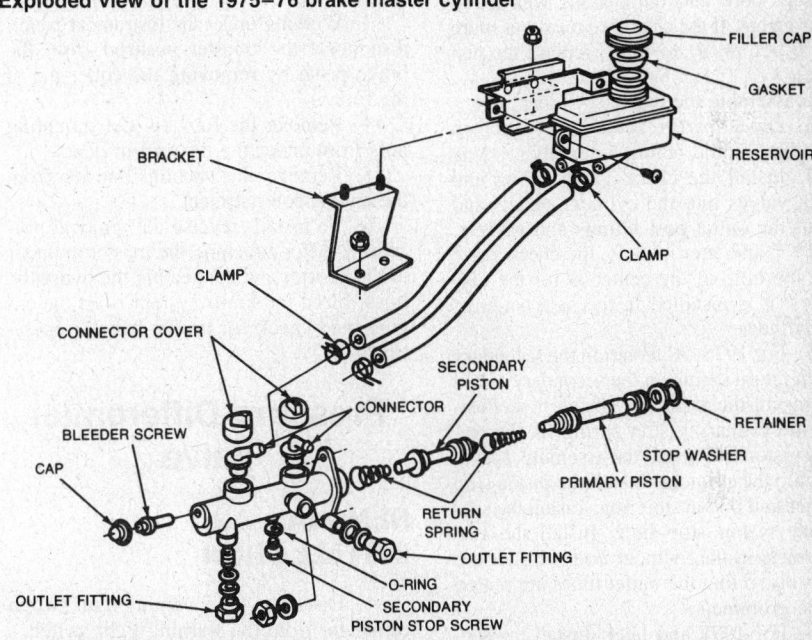

Exploded view of the 1977–78 brake master cylinder—later models similar

7. Remove the secondary piston stop screw and O-ring through 1976. On 1977 and later models, you must first fabricate a guide pin according to the dimensions in the illustration. The guide pin is necessary to prevent damage to the secondary piston cup as it passes over the secondary piston stop screw hole. Push the secondary piston toward the front of the cylinder with a screwdriver, then remove the stop screw and its O-ring. Then insert the guide pin, slowly release pressure on the secondary piston, and allow it to pass over the guide pin and out.

8. Remove the secondary piston and secondary return spring. If necessary, you can use low air pressure applied to the outlet hole.

9. Remove the outlet port fittings, gaskets, check valves and check valve springs.

10. Clean all the parts (except rubber) in isopropyl alcohol. Do not use mineral

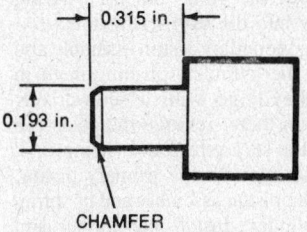

Guide pin dimensions for removing the secondary piston from 1977 and later master cylinders.

base fluids. Allow all parts to air dry.

11. Inspect the piston cups for damage, wear, softening, or swelling, and replace as necessary. Examine the pistons and cylinder bore for wear, scoring, corrosion, or roughness. If the damage is minor, it can be smoothed with crocus cloth, but be careful not to remove too much material. The pistons are a close fit in the bore. Check

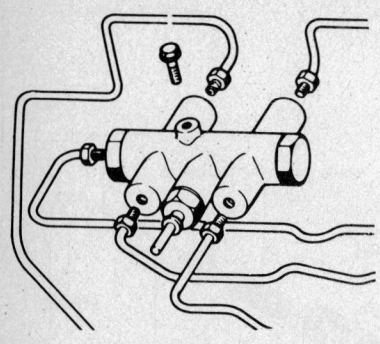

1975–76 pressure differential valve—later years similar

all the openings and passages to be sure that they are clear.

12. Clean any parts you have smoothed again, then check the clearance between the cylinder bore and the pistons with a flat feeler gauge. If the clearance measures more than 0.006 in. (0.15 mm), replace the piston(s).

To assemble the master cylinder:

13. Dip all parts (except the cylinder) in clean brake fluid before assembly.

14. Install the check valve spring and check valves into the cylinder outlets and install the outlet port fittings and gaskets. On 1977 and later models, the check valve with the hole in the center is for the disc brakes; it is installed in the side outlet of the cylinder.

15. For 1975–76: Position the secondary piston return spring on the secondary piston and install the assembly spring first. Position the primary piston spring on the primary piston and install the assembly, spring first into the cylinder. Install the piston stop washer and piston stop ring. Install the secondary piston stop bolt. Install the two grommets in the cylinder body. Install the reservoir so that the outlet tubes are seated in the grommets.

16. For 1977 and later: Install the secondary and primary cups on the secondary piston. Install the guide pin used during disassembly into the stop screw hole.

Install the secondary piston assembly and spring into the cylinder, pushing them in as far as they'll go with a screwdriver. Holding them there, remove the guide pin and install the stop screw and O-ring.

Install the cups on the primary piston, and install the piston assembly and its spring into the cylinder. Install the washer and snap-ring into the end of the cylinder.

17. Fill the master cylinder and pump the piston with a screwdriver until fluid flows from the outlet ports.

18. Install the master cylinder and bleed the brakes.

Vacuum Booster

Brakes are vacuum boosted starting in 1977, with the introduction of front disc brakes. The booster obtains vacuum from the engine intake manifold.

TESTING

1. With the engine off, pump the brakes a few times, then push the pedal down and hold it. (If the pedal gradually sinks, the hydraulic system is leaking or the master cylinder pistons are faulty; repairs must be made before testing the booster.)

2. With the pedal held down, start the engine. The pedal should move downward. If pedal height does not change, either the booster check valve (attached to the side of the booster at the vacuum hose) is faulty, or there is a leak in the vacuum system (hose or booster).

REMOVAL AND INSTALLATION

1. Remove the master cylinder.

2. Remove the vacuum hose from the check valve.

3. Working under the instrument panel, disconnect the booster pushrod from the brake pedal by removing the cotter pin at the fork.

4. Remove the four booster mounting nuts from under the instrument panel.

5. Remove the vacuum booster from the engine compartment.

6. To install, reverse the removal procedure. After attaching the master cylinder to the booster and connecting the hydraulic lines, bleed the brake system, start the engine, and check for proper booster operation.

Pressure Differential Valve

REMOVAL AND INSTALLATION

1. Disconnect the warning light switch connector from the warning light switch.

2. Disconnect the brake inlet and outlet lines. Plug the lines.

3. Remove the valve assembly-to-cowl attaching bolt and remove the valve and switch assembly.

To install the valve and switch:

4. Position the valve and switch on the cowl. Install the retaining bolt.

5. Connect the brake lines to the valve.

6. Connect the warning light to the switch wiring connector.

7. Depress the brake pedal several times, then bleed the brake system.

8. Fill the master cylinder and check for proper operation.

CENTRALIZING THE PRESSURE DIFFERENTIAL VALVE

Normally, the brake warning light will remain ON after any repairs to the brake system, or after bleeding the brakes. This is caused by the pressure differential valve remaining in the off center position.

To centralize the pressure differential valve and turn the warning light OFF:

1. Turn the ignition switch to ON.

2. Check the fluid levels in the master cylinder reservoirs and fill them to within ¼ in. of the top, if necessary.

3. Depress the brake pedal and the piston will center itself, causing the warning light to go out.

4. Turn the ignition switch OFF.

5. Before driving the truck, check the operation of the brakes to be sure that a firm pedal has been obtained.

Bleeding the System

The purpose of bleeding the brakes is to expel air trapped in the hydraulic system. The system must be bled whenever the pedal feels spongy, indicating that compressible air has entered the system, or whenever the system has been opened or leaking. You will need a helper for this job.

The primary and secondary (front and rear) systems are independent systems and are bled separately. Bleed the longest line first on an individual system. In the case of the rear brakes through 1978, bleed at the lower right rear wheel cylinder then at the upper right rear wheel cylinder.

During the bleeding operation, do not allow the master cylinder to run dry. Keep the master cylinder reservoirs full of extra heavy duty brake fluid (ESA-M6C25-A or the equivalent). Immediately after bleeding, throw out the fluid that was bled from the system. It is useless since it contains air bubbles.

Do not use the secondary piston stop screw located on the side of the master cylinder to bleed, as damage to the secondary piston could result.

1. Bleed the rear (secondary) brake system first. Remove the bleed fitting cap and attach a rubber hose snugly over the fitting at the right rear lower wheel cylinder.

2. Submerge the other end of the hose in a jar half filled with brake fluid.

3. Open the bleeder valve ¾ of a turn with an 8 mm box wrench.

4. Have your helper push the brake pedal down slowly through its full travel. Close the bleeder fitting and let the pedal return. Repeat this operation until air bubbles cease to appear at the submerged end of the bleeder tube.

5. When the fluid is completely free of bubbles, remove the tube and install the bleeder fitting cap.

6. Repeat this procedure at the upper right wheel cylinder (through 1978 only).

7. Repeat the procedure at the left rear wheel cylinders. Refill the master cylinder reservoir after each wheel cylinder is bled.

NOTE: Brake fluid picks up moisture from the air. Don't leave the master cylinder or the fluid container uncovered

for any longer than necessary. Be careful—brake fluid destroys paint.

8. Bleed the primary (front) brake system in the same manner, ending by bleeding each left front wheel cylinder or the caliper.

9. When the bleeding operation is complete, the master cylinder should be filled to within ¼ in. of the top. Install the master cylinder cover.

10. Centralize the pressure differential valve.

Front Disc Brakes

PADS

Inspection

The caliper must be removed to check the pad wear. Follow the procedure under "Pad Replacement". Measure the lining thickness. Pads should be replaced if the lining is 0.315 inches thick or less, 1977–78, or 0.276 inches thick or less, 1979 and later.

NOTE: This measurement may disagree with your state inspection laws.

Replacement

1. Loosen the wheel lug nuts. Raise and support the truck. Remove the wheel.
2. Remove the four locking clips (retainer pins).
3. Remove the two stopper plates (wedges). These can be gently pushed out toward the outside of the hub with a hammer and drift.
4. Remove the caliper body and anti-rattle spring. Support the caliper with a block of wood, a length of wire or the like. Do not allow it to hang by the brake hose.
5. Pull out the brake pads.
To install:
6. You will first have to press the piston back into the caliper body. If you have a large pair of channel lock pliers, you can usually push it right back in. Otherwise, use a C-clamp. The piston may want to spring back out again. If this is the case, slightly open the bleeder valve as you squeeze the piston back into place, then close the valve as you hold the piston back. If you do this quickly, no air should enter the system. It would be best, however, to bleed the brakes afterward to be sure.
7. Install new pads (and shims, if necessary). When you replace pads, all pads on both front wheels must be replaced at the same time. Do not mix different types of linings.
8. Replace the anti-rattle spring and the caliper body.
9. Apply a thin coat of grease to the stopper plates, and push them into place. Install the four locking clips.
10. Install the wheel and lower the truck. Check the fluid level in the master cylinder, and add if necessary. Check for a hard brake pedal. Do not move the truck until a hard pedal is obtained.

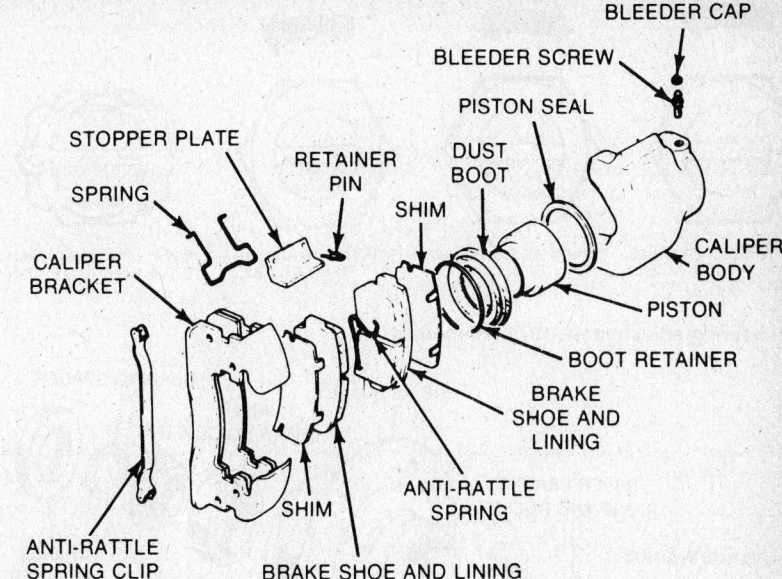

Front disc brake components—typical

CALIPER

Removal and Installation

1. Follow steps 1–5 of the Pad Replacement procedure.
2. Disconnect and plug the brake hose. It may be easier to disconnect the hose at the fender apron and plug it there, and then remove the hose from the caliper when it is off the truck.
3. Remove the caliper body.
4. If necessary, remove the caliper bracket by removing the two retaining bolts.
5. Installation is the reverse of removal. Be sure to bleed the system after installation.

Overhaul

Any brake overhaul work must be performed on a perfectly clean surface. If there is any question of a part's cleanliness after work has been performed, clean it again and allow it to dry.

1. Clean off the outside of the caliper.
2. Remove the boot retainer and dust boot.
3. Place a slat of wood or some cloths in front of the piston to prevent damage. Apply compressed air to the brake line hole, and remove the piston. If the piston is seized in its bore, lightly tap around the piston with a plastic mallet while applying air pressure.
4. Remove the piston seal from the caliper bore with a blunt piece of plastic or wood to avoid damage to the bore. Discard the seal and boot.
5. If necessary, remove the bleeder valve.
6. Clean all the parts in clean brake fluid or denatured alcohol.

NOTE: Do not use gasoline, kerosene, or anything else.

Allow the parts to air dry, or use com-

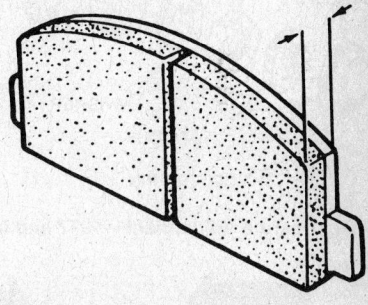

Gauging the front disc pad thickness

pressed air.

7. Inspect the caliper bore and the piston for scratches, scoring, or corrosion. If damaged, replace the parts. Minor scratches can be removed with crocus cloth, but be careful not to remove too much material. Clean the parts again afterwards.
8. Coat the new seal with brake fluid, and install it into the groove in the caliper bore. Be sure it is firmly seated and not twisted.
9. Coat the piston and bore with clean brake fluid, and install the piston.
10. Install the dust boot by pressing its flange squarely into the inner groove of the caliper bore. Install the boot retainer.
11. Install the caliper, being certain to bleed the system after installation.

DISC (ROTOR)

Removal and Installation

Refer to the Hub and Wheel Bearing procedure which follows.

Inspection

Inspect the surface of the disc for scratches, scoring, and deep rust pitting. If these conditions exist, the disc should be taken to a machine shop or garage for refinishing. When refacing the disc, as little material as possible should be removed. If the disc

 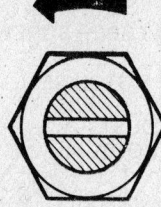 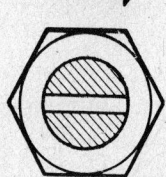 

| WITH WHEEL ROTATING, TORQUE ADJUSTING NUT TO 17-25 FT. LBS. | BACK ADJUSTING NUT OFF 1/2 TURN | TIGHTEN ADJUSTING NUT TO 6-8 FT. LBS. | INSTALL THE RETAINER AND A NEW COTTER PIN |

Wheel bearing adjustment—1975–76 models

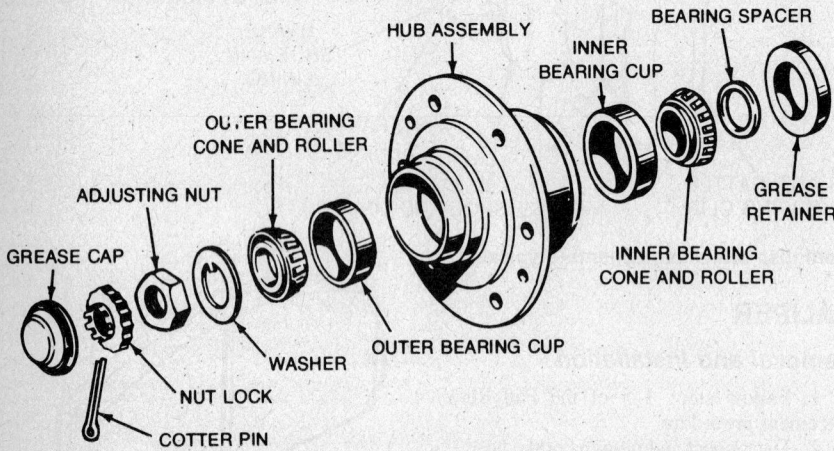

Wheel bearing adjustment—1977 and later models

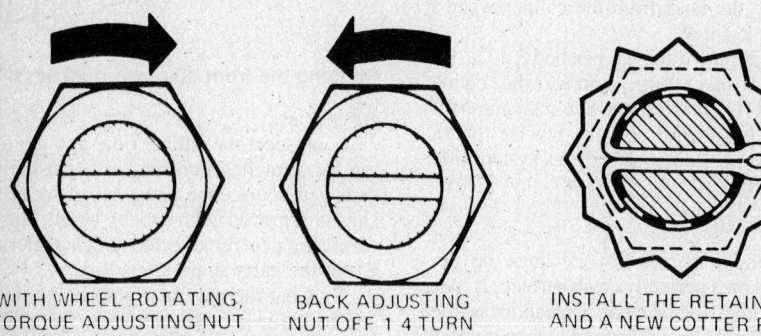

| WITH WHEEL ROTATING, TORQUE ADJUSTING NUT TO 17-25 FT. LBS. | BACK ADJUSTING NUT OFF 1 4 TURN | INSTALL THE RETAINER AND A NEW COTTER PIN |

Front hub and related components—typical

is less than 0.433 in. thick after refinishing, replace it.

The lateral runout of the disc should be checked at every brake pad replacement. Measure the run out with a dial replacement. Measure the run out with a dial indicator. If it measures more than 0.004 in., the disc should be either refinished or replaced. Make sure that the bearings are properly adjusted before making this measurement.

FRONT HUB AND WHEEL BEARINGS

BEARING ADJUSTMENT

The front wheel bearings should be adjusted if the wheel is loose on the spindle or if the wheel does not rotate freely.

1. Raise and support the truck.
2. Remove the wheel cover and pry the grease cap from the hub.
3. Remove the cotter pin and locknut.
4. While rotating the wheel, drum and hub, tighten the adjusting nut to 17–25 ft. lbs.
5. Back off the adjusting nut ½ turn, then tighten the nut or 6–8 ft. lbs. (1975–76) For 1977 and later trucks, simply back off the adjusting nut ¼ turn.
6. Install the nut lock on the adjusting nut so that the castellations are aligned with the cotter pin hole in the spindle.
7. Install a new cotter pin.

Hub Removal and Installation (Includes Bearing Replacement)

1. Raise and support the truck.

2. Remove the wheel cover.
3. Remove the wheel and tire.
4. Remove the grease cap from the hub. Remove the cotter pin, nut lock, adjusting nut and flat washer from the spindle.
5. Remove the hub and drum (or disc rotor).
6. Remove and discard the old grease retainer. Remove the inner bearing cone and roller from the hub.
7. Clean the grease from the inner and outer bearing cups with solvent and inspect the cups for scratches, pits, or wear.
8. If the cups are worn or damaged, remove them with a drift.
9. Thoroughly clean the inner and outer bearing cones and rollers. DO NOT SPIN THE BEARINGS TO DRY THEM.
10. Inspect the cones and roller for wear and replace as necessary. The cone and roller assemblies should be replaced as a set. Do not use new bearings or cups with old bearings or cups.
11. Clean the spindle and the inside of the hub with solvent to remove all of the old grease.
12. Cover the spindle with a cloth and clean the dirt from the dustshield. Remove the cloth carefully. Do not get dirt on the spindle.
13. If the inner or outer bearing cups were removed, install the new replacement cups in the hub. Be sure that they are seated squarely and properly.
14. Pack the inside of the hub with wheel bearing grease.

NOTE: It is important that all the old grease is removed, because lithium base grease is not compatible with the sodium base grease that was originally installed.

15. Pack the bearing cone and roller with wheel bearing grease. Work as much grease as possible between the cone and rollers. Lubricate the outside cone surfaces with grease.
16. Installing the inner bearing cone and roller in the inner cup. Apply a light film of grease to the grease seal and install the seal. Be sure that the seal is properly seated.
17. Install the hub and drum on the spindle. Keep the hub centered on the spindle to prevent damaging the grease seal.
18. Install the outer bearing cone and roller and the flat washer on the spindle. Install the adjusting nut.
19. Install the wheel and tire.
20. Adjust the wheel bearings.
21. Install the hub cap.
22. Pump the brake pedal several times to restore normal brake lining-to-drum clearance and normal brake pedal pressure.

Drum Brakes

BRAKE DRUM

Removal and Installation

1. Raise and support the truck.
2. Remove the wheel.

3. Remove the brake drum attaching screws and install them in the tapped holes in the brake drum.

4. Turn these screws in evenly to force the brake drum away from the wheel hub. If the brake drum seems to be locked in place, the shoes may be dragging against it. Back off the adjusting nut 5 or 6 turns to move the shoes away from the drum. See the adjustment section at the beginning of the Brake section.

5. Remove and inspect the brake drum. See Inspection.

To install the brake drum:

6. Install the brake drum with the attaching screw holes aligned with the holes in the hub.

7. Transfer the attaching screws from the tapped holes in the brake drum to the attaching holes in the hub.

8. Tighten the screws evenly to secure the hub.

9. Install the wheel.

10. Lower the truck and check the brake adjustment.

Inspection

1. Wipe all dust from the inside of the brake drum.

CAUTION

Do not blow the brake dust out of the drums with compressed air or lung power. Brake linings contain asbestos, a known cancer causing substance. Wipe the drums with a cloth dampened with water, and dispose of the cloth after use.

---

2. Check the brake drum diameter with a brake drum gauge. Refer to the Brake Specification chart at the beginning of this section for allowable wear limits.

3. Inspect the brake drums for cracks. Replace any cracked drums.

4. Look carefully for any scoring of the drums. If the drums are scored, have them reground professionally.

BRAKE SHOES

Inspection

1. Wipe out the accumulated dust and grit.

2. Inspect for excessive lining wear or shoe damage. Replace any cracked shoes.

3. If the lining is worn to within $\frac{1}{32}$ in. of the shoe or if the shoes are damaged, they must be replaced.

NOTE: This wear measurement may disagree with your state inspection laws.

4. Replace any linings that are contaminated with grease or brake fluid from leaking wheel cylinders. Replace linings in axle sets only.

5. Check the condition of the shoes, retracting springs and hold-down springs for signs of overheating. If the shoes have a slight blue color, this indicates overheating and replacement of the springs as well as the linings is recommended.

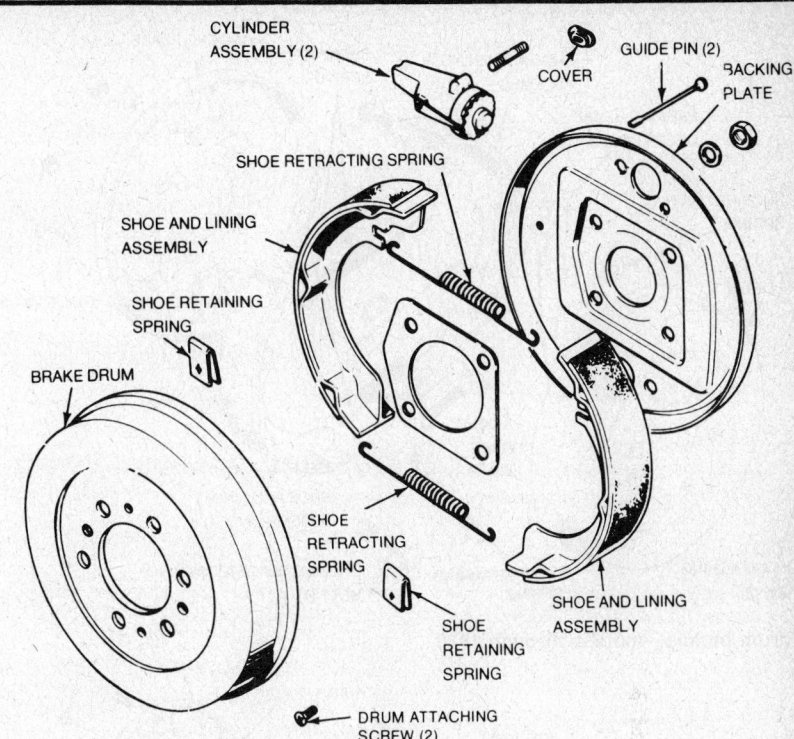

Front drum brakes and related components

6. If signs of overheating are present, the wheel cylinders should be rebuilt as a precaution against future problems.

Removal and Installation

1. Raise and support the truck.

2. Remove the wheel.

3. Remove the brake drum.

4. Remove the brake shoe retracting springs.

5. Remove the shoe retaining spring guide pin and the retaining spring, by holding the guide pin to the backing plate and compressing and turning the spring 90°. A brake spring tool to do this easily is available, inexpensively, from most auto parts stores.

6. On rear brakes only, remove the parking brake cable from the parking brake lever.

7. Remove the brake shoes, noting their positions.

To install new brake shoes:

8. Lubricate the threads of the adjusting screw with brake paste and one or two spots on the adjuster wheel inside threads. Lubricate the backing plate shoe pads.

9. On front wheel brakes, position each brake shoe on the brake backing plate so that the slot in the shoe web is toward the starwheel in the wheel cylinder.

10. On rear brakes, install the parking brake lever on the rear shoe and install the retaining clip. Hold the rear brake shoe near the brake backing plate and connect the eye of the parking brake cable to the parking brake operating lever. Position both shoes on the backing plate and connect the parking brake link between both shoes. Engage

the brake shoes with the slots in the wheel cylinder pistons and adjusting screws.

11. Install the shoe retaining spring guide pins. Install the retaining spring over the guide pin, hold the guide pin in place and depress the retaining spring. Turn it 90° to lock the spring in place.

12. Install the brake shoe retracting springs. Be careful not to bend the springs or stretch the hooks.

13. Install the brake drum.

14. Install the wheel.

15. Adjust the brakes.

16. Bleed the brakes.

17. Lower the truck and check for proper operation.

WHEEL CYLINDER

Removal and Installation

1. Raise and support the truck.

2. Remove the wheel.

3. Remove the brake drum and brake shoes.

4. Disconnect and plug the brake line at the wheel cylinder.

5. Remove the stud nuts and bolt attaching the wheel cylinder to the backing plate and remove the wheel cylinder.

To install the wheel cylinder:

6. Install the wheel cylinder on the backing plate.

7. Clean the end of the brake line and attach it to the wheel cylinder. Tighten the tube fitting nut.

8. Install the links in the end of the wheel cylinder.

9. Install the shoes and adjuster assemblies.

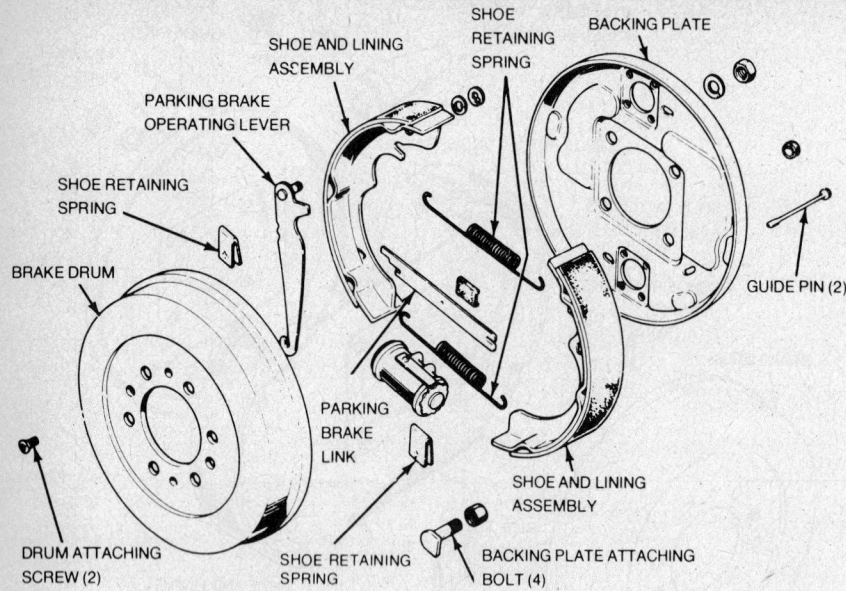

Rear drum brakes—models through 1978

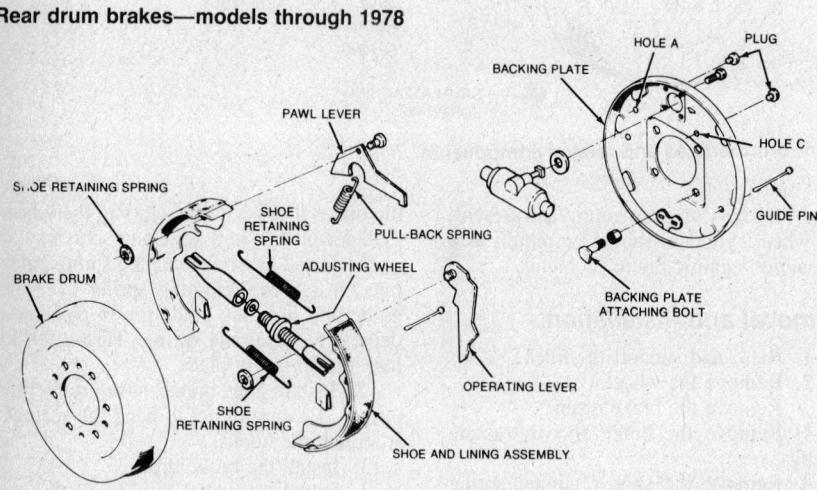

Rear drum brakes—1979 and later models

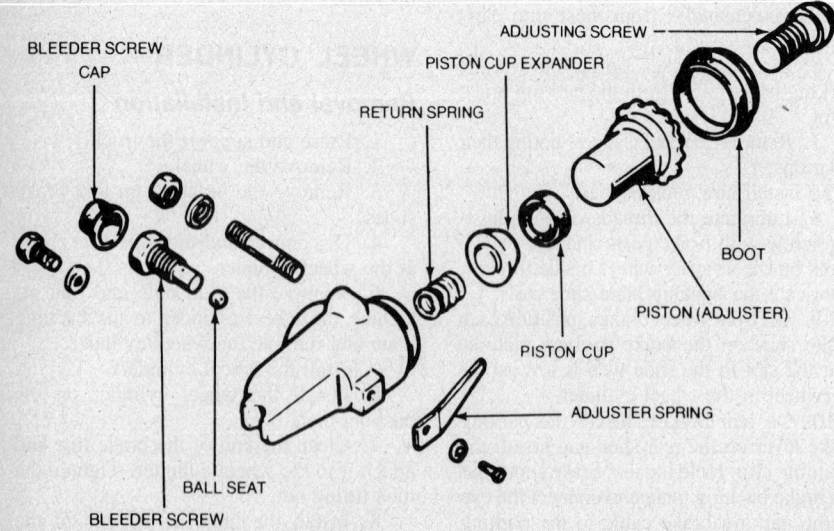

Exploded view of the front wheel cylinder

10. Install the brake drum and wheel.

11. Adjust the brakes.

12. Bleed the brakes and centralize the pressure differential valve.

13. Lower the truck.

Overhaul

1. Remove the wheel cylinder.

2. 1978 and earlier: Remove the piston and adjusting screw with the boot attached to the adjuster. Separate the adjuster screw and boot from the adjuster. On rear wheel cylinders, also remove the other piston and boot and separate the parts.

1979 and later: Remove the piston and boot and separate the boot from the piston.

3. On front cylinders, using compressed air (if possible), remove the piston cup, expander and spring. Lay the cylinder face down and apply air pressure to the brake line port. On rear cylinders, press in on either piston cup and force the piston cups, expanders, and return spring from the cylinder.

4. Wash all parts in isopropyl alcohol, except the rubber boot(s). Discard the piston cups.

5. Examine the cylinder bore, piston and adjuster for wear roughness or damage. Check the clearance between the piston and cylinder bore. If the clearance is greater than 0.006 in., replace with new parts.

To assemble the wheel cylinder:

6. Lubricate the cylinder bore, adjuster and new piston cup(s) with clean brake fluid. Always use new piston cups.

7. Position the piston return spring in the piston cup expander. On rear cylinders, use either expander, then place the other piston cup expander and a new piston cup on the return spring. On all cylinders, install the return spring, piston cup expander(s) and cup(s) into the cylinders. The flat side of the cup faces out.

8. Install the piston boot to the piston adjuster (smaller lip of the boot in the groove of the piston adjuster).

9. Insert the piston adjuster into the cylinder and install the larger lip of the boot in the groove on the cylinder body.

10. Install the adjusting screw in the piston adjuster.

11. Install the wheel cylinder.

Parking Brake Adjustment

1. Adjust the service brakes before attempting to adjust the parking brake.

2. Use the adjusting nut to adjust the length of the front cable so that the rear brakes are locked when the parking brake lever is pulled out 5–10 notches.

3. After adjustment, apply the parking brake several times. Release the parking brake and make sure that the rear wheels rotate without dragging. If they drag, repeat the adjustment.

NOTE: If the parking brake cable is

replaced, prestretch it by applying the parking brake hard three or four times before attempting adjustment.

PARKING BRAKE WARNING LIGHT SWITCH

Removal and Installation

1. Apply the parking brake to provide clearance between the switch assembly and the switch stop tab on the parking brake lever shaft.

2. Disconnect the switch wiring connector.

3. Remove the switch from its mounting bracket.

To install the switch:

4. Install the switch on the mounting bracket.

5. Install the attaching screws.

6. Connect the switch wire connector.

7. Turn the ignition switch ON and check the operation of the switch. No adjustment to the switch is possible. If it is defective, replace the switch.

CHASSIS ELECTRICAL

Heater Assembly

REMOVAL AND INSTALLATION

1. Disconnect the battery ground cable.

2. Drain the cooling system.

3. Remove the water valve shield at the left side of the heater.

4. Disconnect the two hoses from the left side of the heater.

5. At the heat-defoster door, at the water valve and at the outside recirculation door, disengage the control cable housing from the mounting clip on the heater. Disconnect each of the three cable wires from the crank arms.

6. Disconnect the fan motor electrical lead.

7. On 1975–77 models, remove the glove compartment for clearance.

8. Working inside the engine compartment, remove the two retaining nuts and the single bolt and washer which hold the heater to the firewall. 1978 and later models also have a retaining bolt inside the passenger compartment which must be removed.

9. Disconnect the two defroster ducts from the heater and remove the heater.

To install the heater:

10. Install the heater on the dash so that the heater duct indexes with the air intake duct and the two mounting studs enter their respective holes.

11. From the engine side of the firewall,

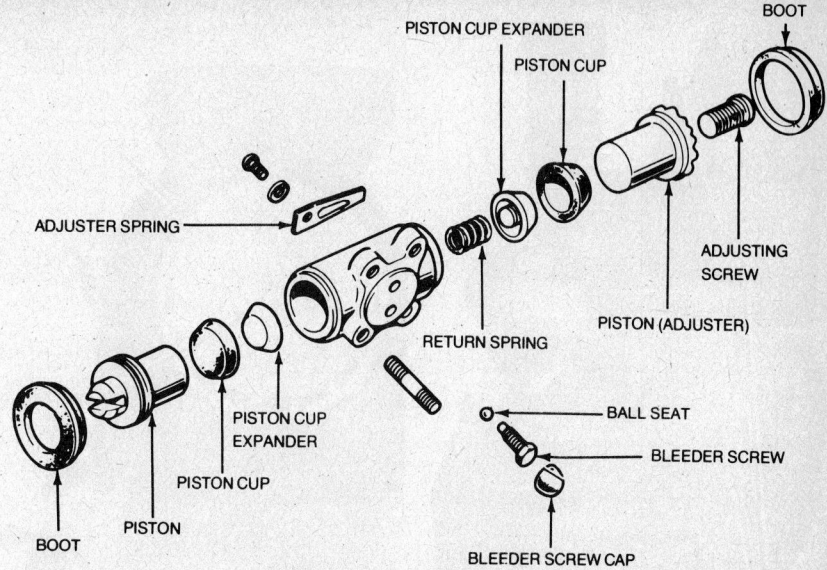

Exploded view of the rear wheel cylinder through 1978

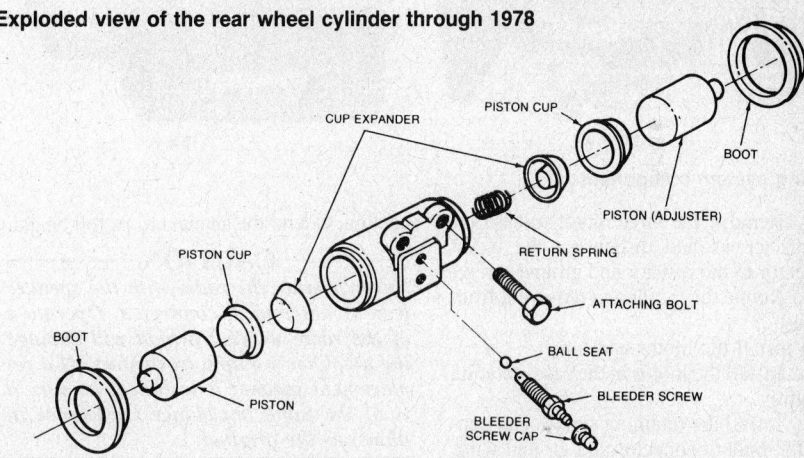

Exploded view of the rear wheel cylinder—1979 and later models

install the nuts on the mounting studs. While an assistant holds the heater in position, install the mounting bolt.

12. Connect the defroster ducts.

13. Connect the heat-defrost door control cable to the door crank arm. Set the control lever (upper) in the HEAT position and turn the crank arm toward the mounting clip as far as it will go. Engage the cable housing in the clip and install the screw in the clip.

14. Connect the water valve control cable wire to the crank arm on the water valve lever. Locate the cable housing in the mounting clip. Set the control lever in the HOT position and pull the valve plunger and lever to the full outward position. This will move the lever crank arm toward the cable mounting clip as far as it will go. Tighten the clip and screw.

15. Insert the outside-recirculation door control cable into the hole in the door crank arm. Bend the wire over and tighten the screw. Set the center control lever in the REC position and turn the door crank arm toward the mounting clip as far as it will go. Engage the cable housing in the clip and install the screw in the clip.

16. Connect the fan motor electrical lead.

17. Connect the two hoses to the heater core tubes, at the left side of the heater, and tighten the clamp.

18. Install the water valve shield and tighten the three screws (left side of the heater).

19. Refill the cooling system and connect the battery ground cable.

20. Run the engine and check for leaks. Check the operation of the heater.

21. On 1975–77 models replace the glove compartment.

Heater Motor and Blower Fan

REMOVAL AND INSTALLATION

1. Remove the heater assembly.

2. Remove the five screws and separate the halves of the heater assembly.

3. Loosen the fan retaining nut. Lightly tap on the nut to loosen the fan. Remove the fan and nut from the motor shaft.

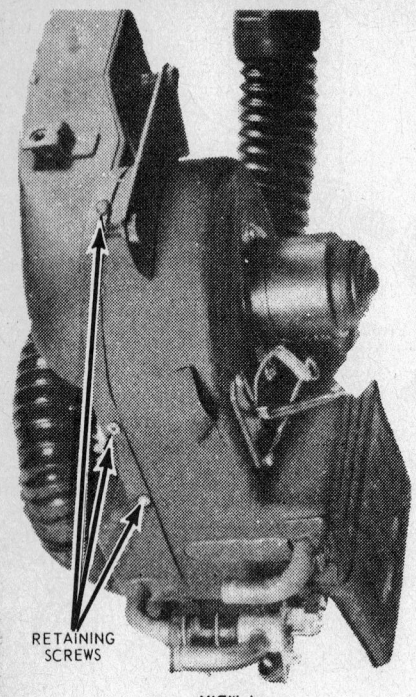

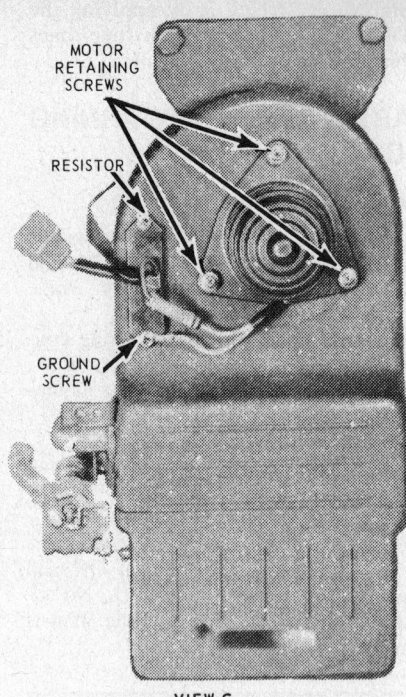

VIEW A

VIEW B

VIEW C

Heating system components

4. Remove the three motor-to-case retaining screws and disconnect the bullet connector to the resistor and ground screw.

5. Rotate the motor and remove it from the case.

To install the motor and fan:

6. Install the motor in the case, rotating it slightly.

7. Install the retaining screws and connect the bullet connector and ground wire.

8. Install the fan on the shaft and install the nut.

9. Assemble the halves together and install the five retaining screws.

10. Install the heater in the truck. Check the operation of the heater.

Heater Core

REMOVAL AND INSTALLATION

1. Remove the heater from the truck.

2. Remove the five screws and separate the halves of the case.

3. Loosen the hose clamps and slide the heater core from the case.

4. Slide the replacement core into the case. At the same time, connect the core tube to the water valve tube with the short hose and clamps.

5. Assemble the halves of the heater and install the five screws.

6. Install the heater in the truck. Check the operation of the heater.

Radio

For best FM reception, adjust the antenna to a height of 31 inches. For best AM re-ception, extend the antenna to its full height.

CAUTION

Never operate the radio with the speaker lead or antenna disconnected. Operation of the radio without a load will damage the amplifier's output transistors. If a replacement speaker is installed, be sure it is of the same impedance (resistance in ohms) as the original.

REMOVAL AND INSTALLATION

1978 and Earlier

1. Remove the ash tray, ash tray retainer and rear retainer support. Remove the heater control knobs, heater control bezel and right-hand defroster hose.

2. Remove the heater control and position it to the left.

3. Remove the radio chassis rear support bracket.

4. Bend the bracket down 90°.

5. Remove the radio knobs, attaching nuts and bezel.

6. Pull the chassis forward until the control shafts clear the holes in the instrument panel. Disconnect the speaker wires, power lead and antenna lead. Rotate the chassis so that the control shafts point upward and lower the radio.

To install the radio:

7. Install the radio vertically, with the control shafts pointed upward.

8. Connect the speaker wires, power lead and antenna cable.

9. Slide the chassis upward and position it with the control shafts in the holes in the instrument panel.

10. Install the radio attaching nuts, and control knobs.

11. Bend the bracket on the dash panel back into position.

12. Install the radio rear support nut to the ash tray retainer rear support.

13. Install the ash tray retainer, heater control bezel and knobs, ash tray, and right-hand defroster hose.

1979 and Later

1. Disconnect the negative battery cable.

2. Pull off the heater control knobs, the instrument light brightness control knob, and the radio knobs.

3. Remove the ring nut and fiber washer for the brightness control. Remove the radio attaching nuts (shaft nuts). Remove the four screws for the meter hood (instrument trim panel) and remove the hood.

4. Slide the radio to the left until the rear support pin clears the support bracket. Pull the radio out from the instrument panel far enough to gain access to the wires at the rear of the radio chassis.

5. Disconnect the power lead, speaker leads and the antenna cable. Remove the radio.

6. To install, connect the wires to the radio.

7. Slide the radio into place. Move the radio to the left, engage the support pin with its bracket, then slide the radio to the right.

8. Install the meter hood, inserting the radio shafts and heater knobs through it as it is fitted into place. Install the four retaining screws but do not tighten them yet.

9. Install the washer and ring nut for the brightness control. Install the radio shaft nuts loosely. Tighten the meter hood screws,

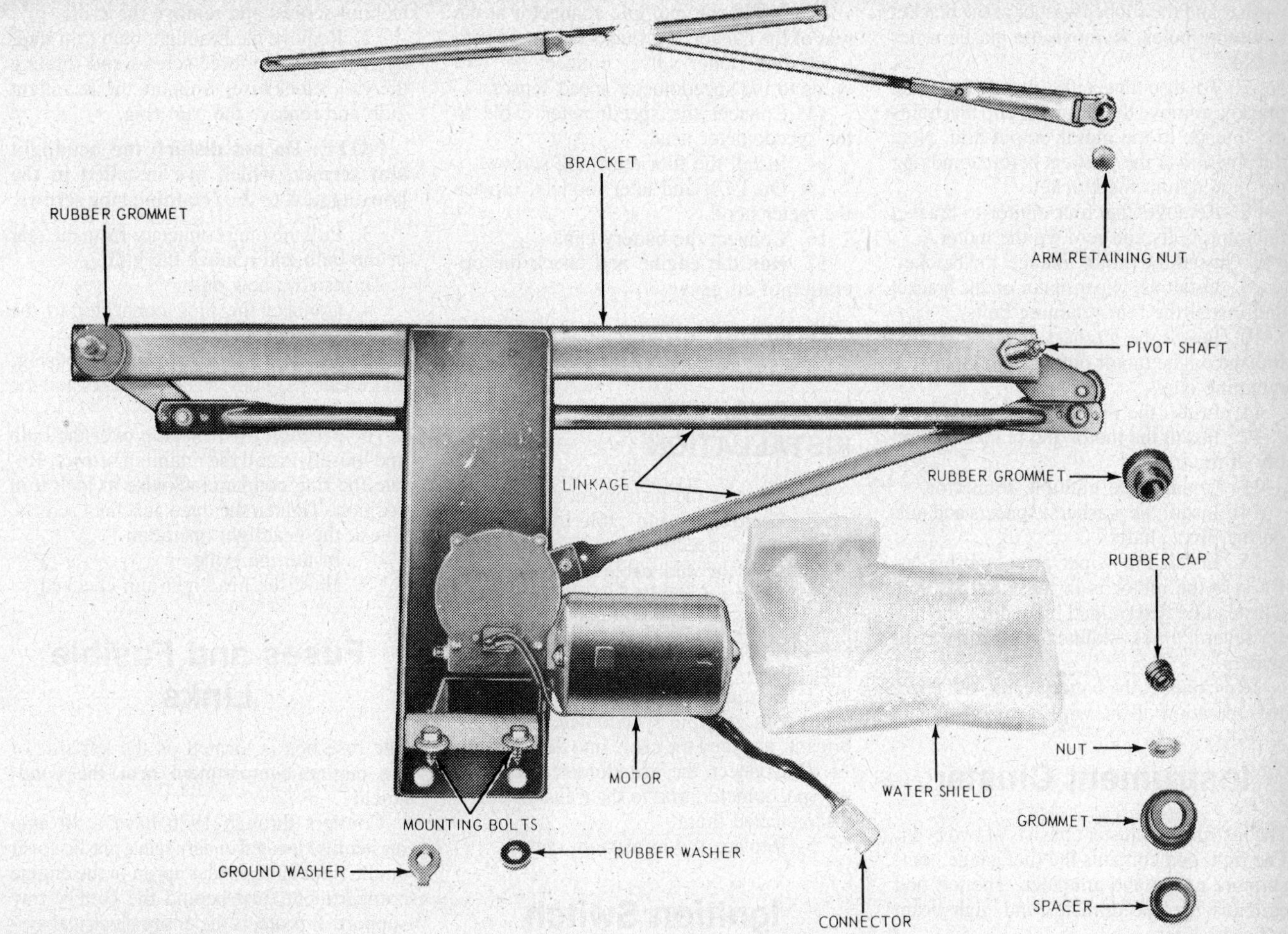

RUBBER GROMMET

BRACKET

ARM RETAINING NUT

PIVOT SHAFT

LINKAGE

RUBBER GROMMET

RUBBER CAP

MOTOR

WATER SHIELD

NUT

GROMMET

MOUNTING BOLTS

RUBBER WASHER

SPACER

GROUND WASHER

CONNECTOR

Windshield wiper components

then tighten the radio shaft nuts.

10. Install the knobs. Connect the negative battery cable.

Windshield Wipers

BLADE AND ARM

Removal and Installation

1. To remove the blade and arm, unscrew the retaing nut and pry the blade and arm from the pivot shaft. The shaft and arm are serrated to provide for adjustment of the wiper pattern on the glass.

2. To set the arms back in the proper park position, turn the wiper switch on and allow the motor to cycle three or four times. Then turn off the wiper switch (do not turn off the wiper motor with the ignition key). This will place the wiper shafts in the proper park position.

3. Install the blade and arm on the shaft and install the retaining nut. The blades and arms should be positioned according to the illustration.

WIPER MOTOR, LINKAGE AND BRACKET

Removal and Installation

1. Disconnect the battery ground ca-

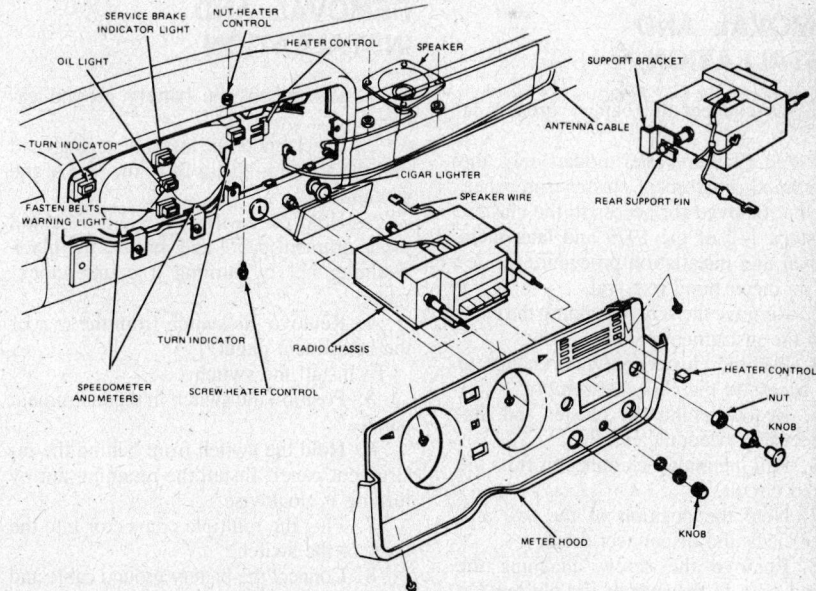

SERVICE BRAKE INDICATOR LIGHT

NUT-HEATER CONTROL

HEATER CONTROL

SPEAKER

OIL LIGHT

SUPPORT BRACKET

ANTENNA CABLE

TURN INDICATOR

CIGAR LIGHTER

SPEAKER WIRE

REAR SUPPORT PIN

FASTEN BELTS WARNING LIGHT

TURN INDICATOR

RADIO CHASSIS

SPEEDOMETER AND METERS

SCREW-HEATER CONTROL

HEATER CONTROL

NUT

KNOB

KNOB

METER HOOD

KNOB

Radio removal and installation—1979 and later models

ble.

2. Remove the wiper arms and blades by removing the retaining nuts.

3. Remove the rubber cap, nut, tapered spacer and rubber grommet from each pivot shaft.

4. Remove the two motor and bracket retaining bolts and washers.

5. Disconnect the wiper motor leads at the multiple connector.

6. Remove the motor and bracket assembly. Note the position of the ground

washer and the rubber washer at the bracket mounting holes. Remove the plastic water shield.

7. To disconnect the motor from the bracket, remove the retaining clip that holds the linkage to the motor output arm. Note the position of the washers before removing the motor from the bracket.

8. Remove the four motor-to-bracket retaining bolts and remove the motor.

To install the motor linkage and bracket:

9. Install the wiper motor on the bracket and install the four retaining bolts.

10. Install the washers and position the linkage on the motor output arm. Install the retaining clip.

11. Install the plastic water shield.

12. Install the motor and bracket assembly in the truck.

13. Connect the multiple connector.

14. Install the washers, spacers and nuts on the pivot shafts.

15. Install the wiper arms and blades. Be sure the motor is in the Park position. This can be determined by cycling the motor several times. Adjust the position of the wipers.

16. Connect the battery cable and check the operation of the wipers.

Instrument Cluster

The instrument cluster consists of two pods. The right pod contains the fuel gauge, temperature gauge and ammeter. The left pod contains the speedometer and high beam indicator light.

REMOVAL AND INSTALLATION

1. Disconnect the battery ground cable.

2. On 1979 and later models only, the meter hood (instrument cluster trim panel) must be removed for access to the cluster. See steps 1–3 of the 1979 and later radio removal and installation procedure for details on meter hood removal.

3. Remove the screws holding the cluster to the instrument panel.

4. Pull the cluster rearward enough to gain access to the cluster assembly.

5. Reach behind the cluster and disconnect the speedometer cable.

6. Pull the multiple connector from the printed circuit.

7. Note the position of the two ammeter leads and disconnect them.

8. Remove the screw attaching the ground wire to the rear of the cluster. On trucks equipped with a coasting richer valve, remove the two connectors at the speedometer sensor switch.

9. Remove the instrument cluster.

To install the instrument cluster:

10. Position the cluster assembly near the opening and connect the ground lead.

11. Connect the two ammeter leads to the ammeter.

12. Install the multiple connector at the rear of the cluster. On trucks equipped with a coasting richer valve, connect the two wires to the speedometer speed sensor.

13. Connect the speedometer cable to the speedometer head.

14. Install the four attaching screws.

15. On 1979 and later models, replace the meter hood.

16. Connect the battery cable.

17. Run the engine and check the operation of all gauges.

Speedometer Cable

REMOVAL AND INSTALLATION

1. Remove the instrument cluster.

2. Remove the old cable by pulling it out from the speedometer end of the cable housing. If the old cable is broken, the speedometer cable will have to be disconnected from the transmission and the broken piece removed from the transmission end.

3. Lubricate the lower ¾ of the new cable with graphite speedometer cable lubricant, and feed the cable into the housing.

4. Connect the speedometer cable to the speedometer, and to the transmission if disconnected there.

5. Replace the instrument cluster.

Ignition Switch

REMOVAL AND INSTALLATION

1. Disconnect the battery ground cable.

2. Reach under the instrument panel and pull the wire connector from the rear of the switch.

3. Hold the switch body from behind the instrument panel and remove the black retaining nut by turning it counterclockwise.

4. Remove the switch from the rear of the instrument panel.

To install the switch:

5. Position the switch in the instrument panel.

6. Hold the switch from behind the instrument panel. Install the retaining nut by turning it clockwise.

7. Plug the multiple connector into the back of the switch.

8. Connect the battery ground cable and check the operation of the switch.

Headlights

REMOVAL AND INSTALLATION

1. Remove the six radiator grille at-

taching screws and remove the grille.

2. Remove the headlight bulb trim ring, by removing the three screws and rotating the ring clockwise. Support the headlight bulb and remove the trim ring.

NOTE: Do not disturb the headlight aim screws, which are installed in the housing next to the retaining ring screws.

3. Pull the plug connector from the rear of the bulb and remove the bulb.

To install a new bulb:

4. Connect the plug connector to the rear of a new headlight.

5. Install the headlight in the housing, and locate the bulb tabs in the slots and the housing.

6. Position the trim ring over the bulb and loosely install the retaining screws. Rotate the ring counterclockwise to lock it in position. Tighten the three attaching screws. Check the headlight operation.

7. Install the grille.

8. Have the headlight aim checked.

Fuses and Fusible Links

The fuse box is located on the left side of the engine compartment near the windshield

Couriers through 1976 have a 40 amp master fuse located underneath a plastic cover on the right hand fender apron in the engine compartment, just behind the battery tray support. It protects the entire electrical system; all systems will be dead if it has blown. To replace it, first disconnect the battery ground cable. Then remove the plastic cover and the fuse.

Couriers built after 1977 have a fusible link instead of the master fuse. The fusible link is a length of wire specially designed to melt under excessive electrical loads. It protects the entire electrical system. Replacements are made by splicing a new section into place. To replace the fusible link, first disconnect the battery negative cable. Then remove the old link and replace it with a link of similar capacity, available at your dealer.

Flashers and Relays

The hazard warning flasher is located to the left of the steering column, beneath the instrument panel, and is secured by a clamp and one screw. To remove it, simply unplug the electrical connector, loosen the screw, and slide the flasher out of the clamp. The turn signal flasher is located to the right of the steering column, beneath the instrument panel, and is secured in the same way as the hazard flasher.

The turn signal relay is located to the immediate right of the hazard flasher, and is secured by two screws. To remove it, unplug the electrical connector and remove the screws.

Dodge D-50
Arrow

INDEX

BEFORE SERVICING, SEE THE SAFETY NOTICE AT THE FRONT OF THE BOOK

D-50/ARROW

VEHICLE IDENTIFICATION THROUGH 1980

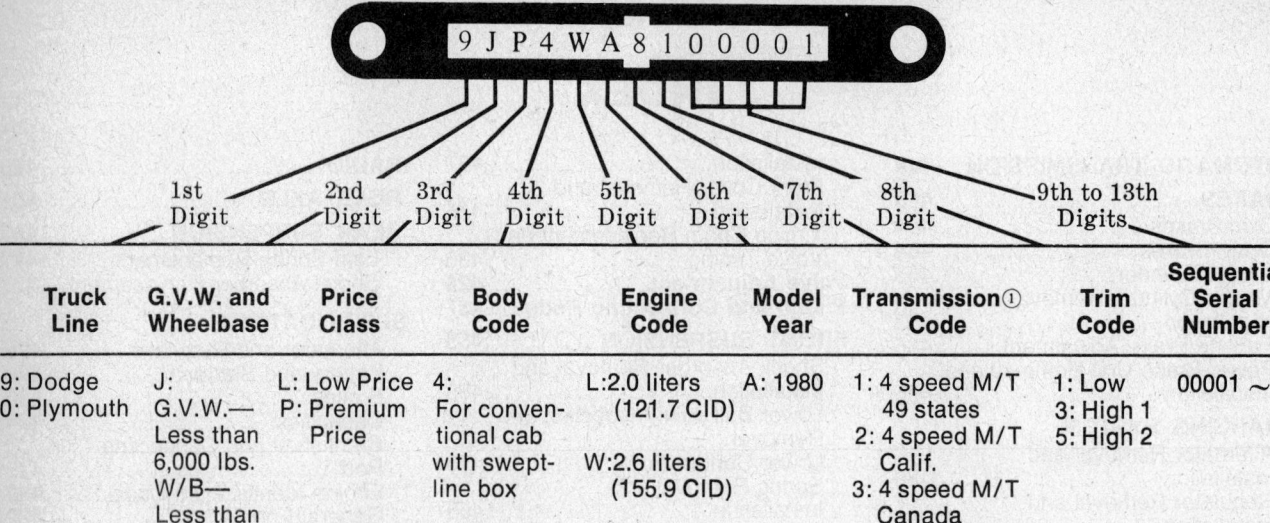

9 J P 4 W A 8 1 0 0 0 0 1

	1st Digit	2nd Digit	3rd Digit	4th Digit	5th Digit	6th Digit	7th Digit	8th Digit	9th to 13th Digits
	Truck Line	G.V.W. and Wheelbase	Price Class	Body Code	Engine Code	Model Year	Transmission① Code	Trim Code	Sequential Serial Number
	9: Dodge 0: Plymouth	J: G.V.W.— Less than 6,000 lbs. W/B— Less than 110.2 in.	L: Low Price P: Premium Price	4: For conven- tional cab with swept- line box	L:2.0 liters (121.7 CID) W:2.6 liters (155.9 CID)	A: 1980	1: 4 speed M/T 49 states 2: 4 speed M/T Calif. 3: 4 speed M/T Canada 4: 5 speed M/T 49 states 5: 5 speed M/T Calif. 6: 5 speed M/T Canada 7: A/T 49 states 8: A/T Calif. 9: A/T Canada	1: Low 3: High 1 5: High 2	00001 ~

① M/T: Manual transmission,　　　　G.V.W. Gross Vehicle Weight　　　　W/B: Wheel Base
　A/T: Automatic transmission

ENGINE IDENTIFICATION

Model	Year	Cu. in. (cm³)	Number of Cylinders	Type	Engine Series Identification
Dodge D-50/RAM-50	'79-'82	121.7 (2000)	4	OHC	U
Plymouth Arrow	'79-'82	121.7 (2000)	4	OHC	U
Dodge D-50 Sport, RAM-50, Bighorn	'79-'82	155.92 (2555)	4	OHC	W
Plymouth Arrow Sport	'79-'82	155.92 (2555)	4	OHC	W

OHC: overhead cam

GENERAL ENGINE SPECIFICATIONS

Year	Engine Displacement cu in. (cc)	Carburetor Type	Horsepower @ rpm	Torque @ rpm (ft-lbs)	Bore X Stroke (in.)	Compres-sion Ratio	Oil Pressure (psi)
'79-'82	121.7 (1995)	1 × 2 bbl	93 @ 5200①⑤	108 @ 3000②	3.31 × 3.54	8.5:1	50-64
	155.92(2555)	1 × 2 bbl	105 @ 5000③⑥	139 @ 2500④	3.59 × 3.86	8.2:1	50-64

① Canada: 96 @ 5500 HP　　　　　　　　　　④ Canada: 140 @ 2500 torque (thru '80)
② Canada: 109 @ 3500 torque　　　　　　　　⑤ '82 California 88 @ 5000
③ Canada: 108 @ 5000 HP (thru '80)　　　　　⑥ '82 California 103 @ 5000

VEHICLE IDENTIFICATION FROM 1981

All vehicle identification number contains 17 digits. The vehicle number is a code which tells destination, brand, sales code, price class, engine displacement, type of body, etc.

J B 7 F P 2 4 5 1 C Y 1 0 0 1 0 1

1st Digit	2nd Digit	3rd Digit	4th Digit	5th Digit	6th Digit	7th Digit	8th Digit	9th Digit	10th Digit	11th Digit	12th Digit	13th to 17th Digit
Manufacturing Country	Sales Channel	Vehicle Type	Other	Vehicle Line	Trim Code	Body Type	Engine Displacement	*Check Digits	Model Year	Assembly Plant	Transmission Code	Sequence Number
J-Japan	B-Dodge P-Plymouth	7-Truck	F-4000 lbs. more and with hydraulic brake	P-RAM50/ ARROW PICK-UP	2-Low 4-High 5-Premium	4-Convenience Cab	5-2.0 liters (121.7 CID) 7-2.6 liters (155.9 CID)	1 2 . . 9 X	C-1982 'year	Y-OYE plant	1-4 speed Federal 2-4 speed ** California 3-4 speed Canada 4-5 speed Federal 5-5 speed ** California 7-A/T Federal 8-A/T ** California 9-A/T Canada	00101~

* "Check Digit" means a single number or letter ✕ used to verify the accuracy of transcription of vehicle identification number.

** can also be sold in Federal States.

ENGINE TUNE-UP SPECIFICATIONS
U.S.A. Engines

Engine	Transmission	Curb Idle Speed	Curb Idle CO	Enriched Idle Speed	Enriched Idle CO	Ignition Timing
49-state						
U-engine	Manual	650 ± 50 rpm	Below 0.1%	730 ± 10	1.0 ± 0.1%	5° BTDC ± 1°
	Automatic	700 ± 50 rpm	Below 0.1%	780 ± 10	1.0 ± 0.1%	5° BTDC ± 1°
W-engine	Manual	750 ± 50 rpm	1.0 ± 0.5%①	—	—	7° BTDC ± 1°
	Automatic	750 ± 50 rpm	1.0 ± 0.5%①	—	—	7° BTDC ± 1°
California						
U-engine	Manual	650 ± 50 rpm	1.0 ± 0.5%①	—	—	5° BTDC ± 1°
	Automatic	700 ± 50 rpm	1.0 ± 0.5%①	—	—	5° BTDC ± 1°
W-engine	Manual	750 ± 50 rpm	1.0 ± 0.5%①	—	—	7° BTDC ± 1°
	Automatic	750 ± 50 rpm	1.0 ± 0.5%①	—	—	7° BTDC ± 1°

①With air injection system disconnected

TUNE-UP SPECIFICATIONS

(When analyzing compression test results, look for uniformity among cylinders, rather than specific pressures)

Year	Engine Displacement cu in. (cc)	Spark Plug Gap (in.)	Ignition Timing (deg) MT	Ignition Timing (deg) AT	Intake Valve Opens (deg) BTDC	Fuel Pump Pressure (psi)	Idle Speed (rpm)	Valve Clearance (in.) In	Valve Clearance (in.) Ex
'79–'82	121.7 (2000)	0.039–0.043①	5B	5B	25	4.6–6.0	650±50③	0.006② Hot	0.010 Hot
	155.92 (2555)	0.039–0.043①	7B	7B	25	4.6–6.0	750±50	0.006② Hot	0.010 Hot

NOTE: The underhood specification sticker sometimes reflects tune-up specification changes made in production. Sticker figures must be used if they disagree with this chart.

① Canada: 0.028–0.031 in.
② Jet valve clearance: 0.006 (Hot)
③ Automatic transmission: 700±50 rpm.
MT: manual transmission
AT: automatic transmission

FIRING ORDER

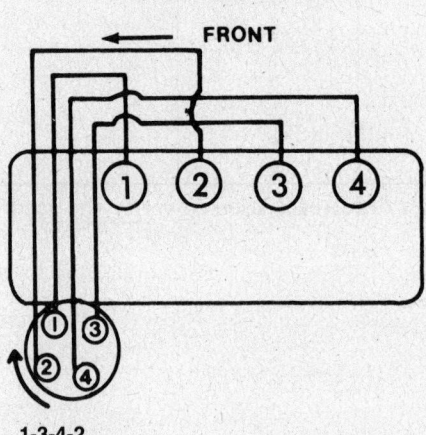

FRONT

1-3-4-2

CAPACITIES

Year	Model	Engine Displacement (cc)	Crankcase (qts) With Filter	Crankcase (qts) Without Filter	Transmission (qts) Manual 4-spd	Transmission (qts) Manual 5-spd	Transmission (qts) Automatic	Drive Axle (pts)	Gasoline Tank (gals)	Cooling System (qts) With AC	Cooling System (qts) Without AC
'79–'82	All	2000	4.5	4.0	2.2	—	6.8①	2.8	15.8②	9.5	9.5
		2555	4.5	4.0	—	2.4	6.8①	2.8	15.8②	9.7	9.7

① '80–'82: 7.2 U.S. quarts
② '81 (2000) 15.1 gal
    (2555) 18.0 gal. also optional with 2000
 '82 All; 18.0 gal

CRANKSHAFT AND CONNECTING ROD SPECIFICATIONS

(All measurements given in inches)

Year	Engine cu. in.	Crankshaft				Connecting Rod		
		Main Brg. Journal Dia.	Main Brg. Oil Clearance	Shaft End Play	Thrust on No.	Journal Diameter	Oil Clearance	Side Clearance
'79–'82	121.7 155.9	2.3622	0.0008–0.0028	0.002–0.007	3	2.0866	0.0008–0.0028	0.004–0.010

VALVE SPECIFICATIONS

Year	Engine Displacement cu in. (cc)	Seat Angle (deg)	Face Angle (deg)	Spring Test Pressure (lbs @ in.)	Spring Installed Height (in.)	Stem to Guide Clearance (in.)		Stem Diameter (in.)	
						Intake	Exhaust	Intake	Exhaust
'79–'82	121.7 (2000)	45	45	61 @ 1.59	1.590	0.0012–0.0024	0.002–0.0035	0.315	0.315
	155.92 (2555)	45	45	61 @ 1.59	1.590	0.0012–0.0024	0.002–0.0035	0.315	0.315
	Jet valve	45	45	5.5 @ .846	—	—	—	0.1693	0.1693

PISTON AND RING SPECIFICATIONS

(All measurements given in inches)

Year	Engine cu in.	Piston to Bore Clearance	Ring Side Clearance			Ring Gap		
			Top Compression	Bottom Compression	Oil Control	Top Compression	Bottom Compression	Oil Control
'79–'82	121.7 155.92	0.0008–0.0016	0.0024–0.0039	0.0008–0.0024	—	0.010–0.018	0.010–0.018	0.0078–0.035

TORQUE SPECIFICATIONS

(All readings in ft. lbs.)

Year	Engine Displacement cu in. (cc)	Cylinder Head Bolts	Rod Bearing Bolts	Main Bearing Bolts	Crankshaft Pulley Bolt	Flywheel to Crankshaft Bolts	Manifolds	
							Intake	Exhaust
'79–'82	All	65–72	33–34	55–61	80–94	94–101	11–14	11–14

TORQUE SEQUENCE

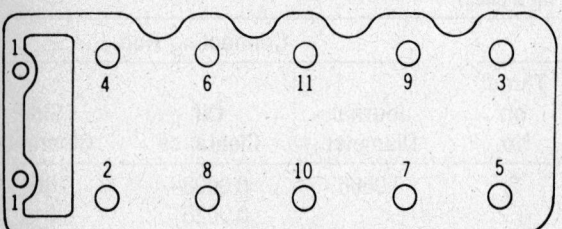

Removal

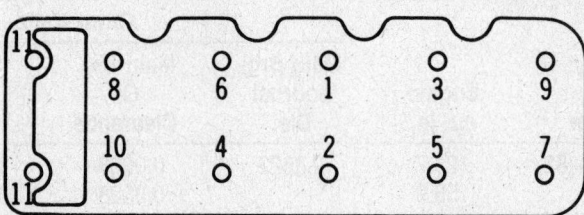

Installation

ALTERNATOR AND REGULATOR SPECIFICATIONS

Model	Year	Alternator Identification Number	Rated Output @ 5000	Rated Output @ 2500	Brush Length (in.)	Brush Spring Tension (lbs.)	Regulated Voltage
All	'79	AQ2245G	41 amps	34 amps	0.669①	2.9–3.7②	14.1–14.7
	'80–'82	A2T16471	44 amps	37 amps	0.709	0.7–1	14.1–14.7

① Built-in type brush: 0.709 in.
② Built-in type spring: 0.71–1 lbs.

BATTERY AND STARTER SPECIFICATIONS

Year	Engine Model	Battery Amp Hour Capacity	Amps	Starter					Type of Starter
				No Load Test Volts	RPM	Brush Spring Tension (lbs)	Min. Brush Length (in.)		
'79–'82	U, W w/MT	45, 60①	60	11.5	6,600	2.9–3.7	0.453		Direct Drive
	U, W w/AT	45, 60①	90④	11.5③	②3,300	2.9–3.7	0.453		Gear Reduction

MT: Manual Transmission
AT: Automatic Transmission
① 60 amp for Canada
② 1979: 4,500 rpm
③ 1979: 11 volts
④ 1979: 62 amps

BRAKE SPECIFICATIONS
(All measurements are given in inches unless noted)

Model	Year	Lug Nut Torque Ft-lb	Master Cylinder Bore	Brake Disc Thickness			Brake Drum		Lining Thickness	
				Std.	Min.	Runout	Diameter	Maximum Wear	Front Min.	Rear Min.
All	'79	51–58	⅞	0.79	0.72	0.006	9.5	9.579	0.04①	0.04①
	'80–'82	51–58	⅞	0.79	0.72	0.006	9.5	9.579	0.04①	0.04①

① Due to the variations in state inspection regulations, the minimum allowable lining thickness may be different from that recommended by the manufacturer.

WHEEL ALIGNMENT

| Year | Model | Caster (degrees) | Camber (degrees) | Toe-in (in.) | Steering Angle | | King Pin Angle |
					Inner Wheel (degrees)	Outer Wheel (degrees)	
'79	All	3° ± 1°	1° ± 30'	0.08–0.35	37°	30.5°	8°
'80–'82	All	2°30' ± 1°	1° ± 30'	0.08–0.35	37°	30.5°	8°

TUNE-UP

NOTE: The procedures outlined below are the specific procedures for the Dodge and Plymouth pick-up truck. General tune-up procedures may be found in the section at the end of this book.

Spark Plugs

Check, clean and adjust the spark plugs every 12,000 miles. Replace them every 30,000 miles.

Clean any foreign material from around the spark plugs before removing them. When removing plug cables, grasp them at the cable caps.

Inspect the plugs for cracked or damaged threads or insulators, worn electrodes and damaged or worn plug gaskets. Always replace all four plugs as a set, it will be cheaper and more effective in the long run.

Set the plug gap to 0.039–0.043 in. (USA), 0.028–0.031 in. (Canada) using a wire feeler gauge.

NOTE: Do not use a flat gauge; an inaccurate reading will result. Hand start, then torque each plug into its hole at 18–21 ft. lbs.

--------- CAUTION ---------
Don't over-torque plugs or thread stripping could result.

Electronic Ignition System (EIS)

All pick-ups are equipped with electronic ignition systems which replace the contact points and condenser with a transistorized integrated circuit. No adjustments can be done on this type of ignition system.

IGNITION SYSTEM TEST

NOTE: If engine will not start, go to test 1 or test 2, depending on the year of your truck.

If the engine will run:

1. Start the engine, allow to idle until the normal operating temperature is reached.

2. Check the ignition timing, adjust if necessary.

3. Visually check electrical connections for frayed insulation or bare wires. Make sure all plug-in connectors are clean and tight. Check the spark plug and coil wires for cracking, crossfiring, corroded terminals, continuity and resistance.

Check the distributor cap for cracks or carbon tracking. Check any suspect parts. Check the spark plugs for foiling, nonfiring and correct gap.

4. If none of the checks have solved the problem, or the car fails to start, proceed to the following tests.

1979–80 TEST 1

1. Remove the distributor cap by inserting a screwdriver in the ends of the two

retaining screws, pushing in and turning the screws clockwise.

2. Remove the screws holding the rotor assembly and lift out the rotor.

3. Turn the ignition switch to the ON position.

4. Disconnect the high tension cable (coil wire) from the center terminal of the distributor cap and hold its end about a quarter of an inch away from a ground (cylinder block etc.).

NOTE: Use insulated pliers to hold the cable.

Insert a flatblade screwdriver between the reluctor and the stator. A spark should jump from the high tension wire to the ground. If a spark is not produced, a defective control unit, pick-up coil, ignition coil or faulty wiring may be the problem. Further service should be left to a qualified service technician. However, in the paragraphs that follow further tests are described.

FROM 1981 TEST 2

Remove the coil wire from the distributor cap tower. Hold the end of the wire with insulated pliers (prevents you from getting a shock). Locate the end of the wire about a quarter of an inch away from the cylinder head and have a friend crank the engine with the starter. Observe the spark or no spark condition. If a spark is produced, the IC igniter and ignition coil may be considered in good condition. Remove the distributor cap and check it for cracks, carbon tracking or dirt. Check the rotor for wear. Replace as necessary. If no sparks are

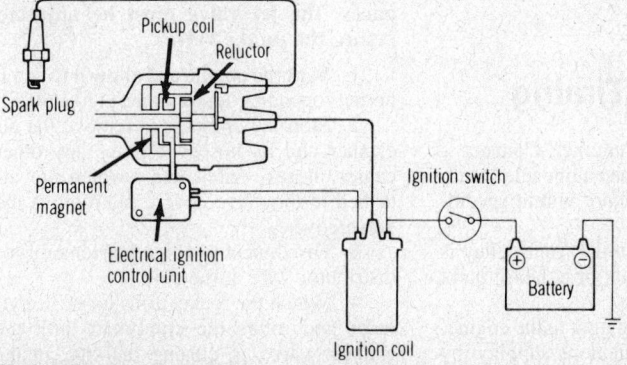

Electronic ignition to 1980

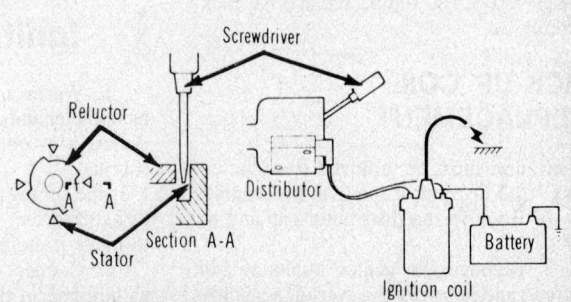

Testing ignition through 1980

produced a defective control unit (internal), pick-up coil, ignition coil or faulty wiring may be the problem.

IGNITION COIL

If either test 1 or test 2 produces no spark, the ignition coil could be at fault. The fastest way to check is by substituting a known good coil. If a coil is not on hand, proceed with one or more of the following tests.

1. With the ignition switch in the ON position measure the voltage at the negative terminal of the ignition coil. If zero volts are shown, there is an open circuit in the coil.

2. Check the ignition coil resistance. If the engine will run allow it to reach normal operating temperature (the ignition coil should be hot). Shut off the engine and disconnect the high tension lead (coil wire) from the coil tower.

2a. Measure primary resistance with an ohmmeter, connecting the coil minus and plus primary terminals. Resistance should be; 0.7–0.85 ohms.

2b. Measure the secondary resistance by connecting the ohmmeter between the contacts in the coil tower and the plus primary terminal. Resistance should be; 9–11 k ohms.

3. Replace the coil if the voltage tests show zero volts or the resistances are not within specifications.

TESTING THE EXTERNAL RESISTOR

1. With the ignition switch off: connect an ohmmeter between the terminals of the external resistor.

2. Obtain a reading from the ohmmeter. Resistance should be 1.22–1.49 ohms.

3. If the reading on the ohmmeter is zero or not within specs, replace the resistor.

TESTING THE PICK-UP COIL

The pick-up coil may be tested while mounted in the distributor. Remove the cap and rotor and connect an ohmmeter between the two terminals of the pick-up coil. If the resistance is not within the limits; (1980) 1,050 plus or minus 50 ohms: (from 1981) 920–1.120 ohms; replace the pick-up coil.

PICK-UP COIL REPLACEMENT

Distributor must be removed from the engine. (see distributor removal procedure).

1. Remove the distributor cap and rotor.

2. Remove the center mounting bolt (screw) and remove the governor assembly. Take care not to mix up the governor

springs they must be installed in the same position. Remove the reluctor.

3. Remove the two mounting screws and take out the pick-up coil (79–80) or the pick-up coil and IC Igniter (81–82). Carefully pull the Igniter from the pick-up coil (81–82).

4. Installation of the new pick-up coil is the reverse of the removal.

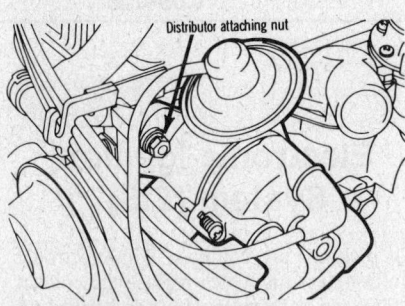

Distributor locknut location

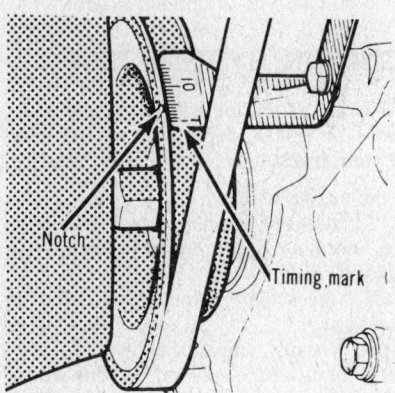

Timing marks

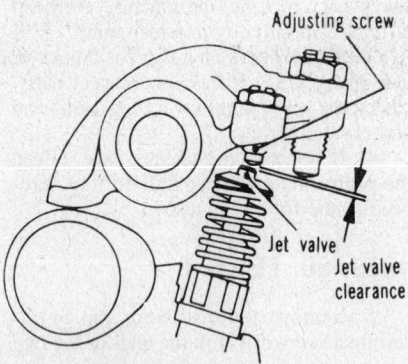

Jet valve adjustment

Ignition Timing

1. Warm up the engine. Connect a tachometer and check the engine idle speed. Adjust it as outlined if not within specifications.

If the timing mark on the front pulley is difficult to see, use chalk or a dab of paint to make it more visible.

2. Connect a timing light to the engine, as outlined in the instructions supplied by the manufacturer of the light.

Valve adjustment

3. Allow the engine to run at the specified idle speed with the gear shift in Neutral (Park, if automatic) and the air conditioning compressor and lights off.

CAUTION
Be sure the parking brake is firmly set and that the wheels are chocked.

4. Point the timing light at the timing marks indicated on the front timing chain cover. With engine at idle, timing should be at the specifications given in the tune-up chart at the beginning of this section. If it is not, loosen the attaching nut at the base of the distributor and rotate the distributor until the correct timing is achieved.

5. Stop the engine and retighten the attaching nut. Start the engine and recheck the timing.

6. Stop the engine and disconnect the timing light and tachometer.

Valve Lash

Both the U engine (1995 c.c.) and the W engine (2555 c.c.) which are sold in the United States have a jet valve located beside the intake valve of each cylinder. The jet valve works off the intake valve rocker arm and injects a swirl of air into the combustion chamber to promote more complete burning of fuel.

NOTE: When adjusting valve clearances, the jet valve must be adjusted before the intake valve.

1. Start the engine and allow it to reach normal operating temperature (170–190°F).

2. Stop the engine and remove the air cleaner and its hoses. Remove any other cables, hoses, wires, etc., which are attached to the valve cover, and remove the valve cover.

3. Disconnect the high tension coil-to-distributor wire at the coil.

4. Watch the rocker arms for no. 1 cylinder and rotate the crankshaft until the exhaust valve is closing and the intake valve has just started to open. At this point,

no. 4 cylinder will be at top dead center (TDC) commencing its firing stroke.

5. Loosen the lock nut on cylinder no. 4 intake valve and back off the intake valve adjusting screw 2 or more turns.

6. Loosen the lock nut on the jet valve adjusting screw.

7. Turn the jet valve adjusting screw counter-clockwise and insert a 0.006 in. feeler gauge between the jet valve stem and the adjusting screw.

8. Tighten the adjusting screw until it touches the feeler gauge.

Take care not to press in the valve while adjusting because the jet valve spring is very weak.

NOTE: If the adjusting screw is tight, special care must be taken to avoid pressing down on the jet valve when adjusting the clearance or a false reading will result.

9. Tighten the lock nut securely while holding the rocker arm adjusting screw with a screwdriver to prevent it from turning.

10. Make sure that a 0.006 in. feeler gauge can be easily inserted between the jet valve and the rocker arm.

11. Adjust no. 4 cylinder's intake valve to 0.006 in. and its exhaust valve to 0.010 in. Tighten the adjusting screw locknuts and re-check each clearance.

12. Perform step 4 in conjunction with the chart below to set up the remaining three cylinders for valve adjustments.

13. Replace the valve cover and all other components. Run the engine and check for oil leaks at the valve cover.

Exhaust Valve Closing	Adjust
No. 1 cylinder	No. 4 cylinder valves
No. 2 cylinder	No. 3 cylinder valves
No. 3 cylinder	No. 2 cylinder valves
No. 4 cylinder	No. 1 cylinder valves

Carburetor

NOTE: See Fuel System for other carburetor adjustments.

IDLE SPEED AND MIXTURE ADJUSTMENTS

1. Start and run the engine at idle until normal operating temperature is reached.

2. Check the tune-up specifications chart or the underhood decal for the correct curb idle speed.

3. Connect a tachometer (follow the instructions that came with the meter) and adjust the idle speed screw until the correct rpm is reached.

4. *Idle mixture adjustments should be made by an authorized garage using a CO meter.* However, a small amount of adjustment is possible (within the limits of the idle mixture screw limiter cap—which must not be removed).

NOTE: Some late model carburetors have a tamperproof, sealed idle mixture screw—these cannot be adjusted, except by an authorized garage.

5. To adjust the idle mixture; first, adjust carb to correct curb idle speed. Next, watch the tachometer scale, listen to the engine and slowly turn the idle mixture screw clockwise. A drop in engine rpm or engine roughness will tell you when to stop. Then, slowly turn the mixture screw counterclockwise until once again you encounter rpm drop or engine roughness. A point, in between the clockwise or counterclockwise positions that gives you the highest rpm or smoothest running engine, is the best setting.

6. Check and readjust the curb idle speed, if necessary.

7. Have your adjustment checked with a CO meter as soon as possible.

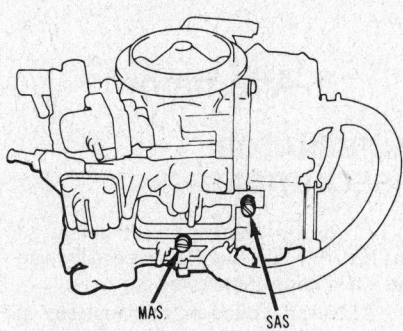

Carburetor idle adjustments

ENGINE ELECTRICAL

Distributor

REMOVAL

1. Disconnect the battery ground cable.

2. Disconnect the wiring harness from the distributor control unit.

3. Mark the spark plug cables and pull them off the spark plugs.

NOTE: Always pull spark plug and coil cables at their boots to avoid breaking the wires inside the cables.

4. Remove the distributor cap by inserting a screwdriver into the two retaining screws, pushing in and turning clockwise.

5. Match-mark the distributor housing and the engine block; mark the rotor position in the distributor as well. This will aid in correct positioning of the distributor during installation.

6. Disconnect the vacuum hose from the vacuum control unit.

7. Remove the distributor mounting nut and lift off the distributor assembly.

INSTALLATION—ENGINE DISTURBED

1. Turn the engine crankshaft until the No. 1 cylinder is at top dead center on compression stroke. To find No. 1 cylinder, compression stroke, take off the distributor cap and turn the rotor and shaft until the rotor assembly is pointing toward the No. 1 cylinder lead in the distributor cap. Verify top dead center on the crankshaft pulley.

2. Align the mating mark (line) on the distributor housing with the mating mark (punch mark) on the distributor driven gear.

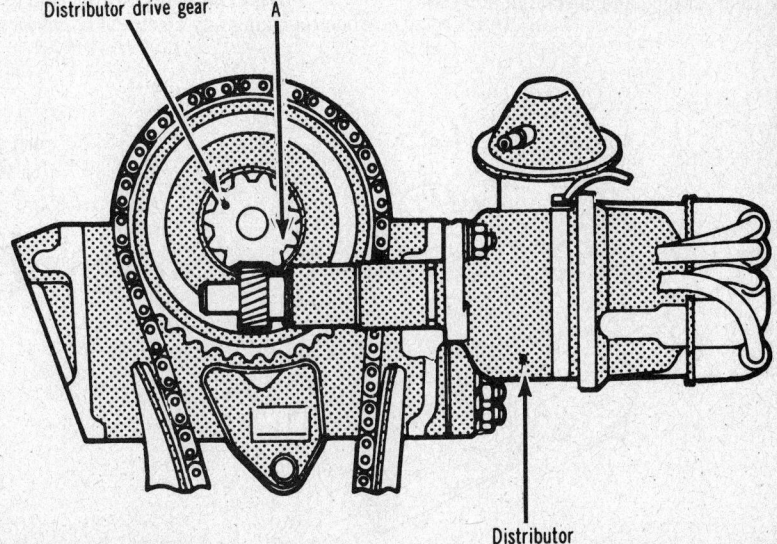

Distributor mounting

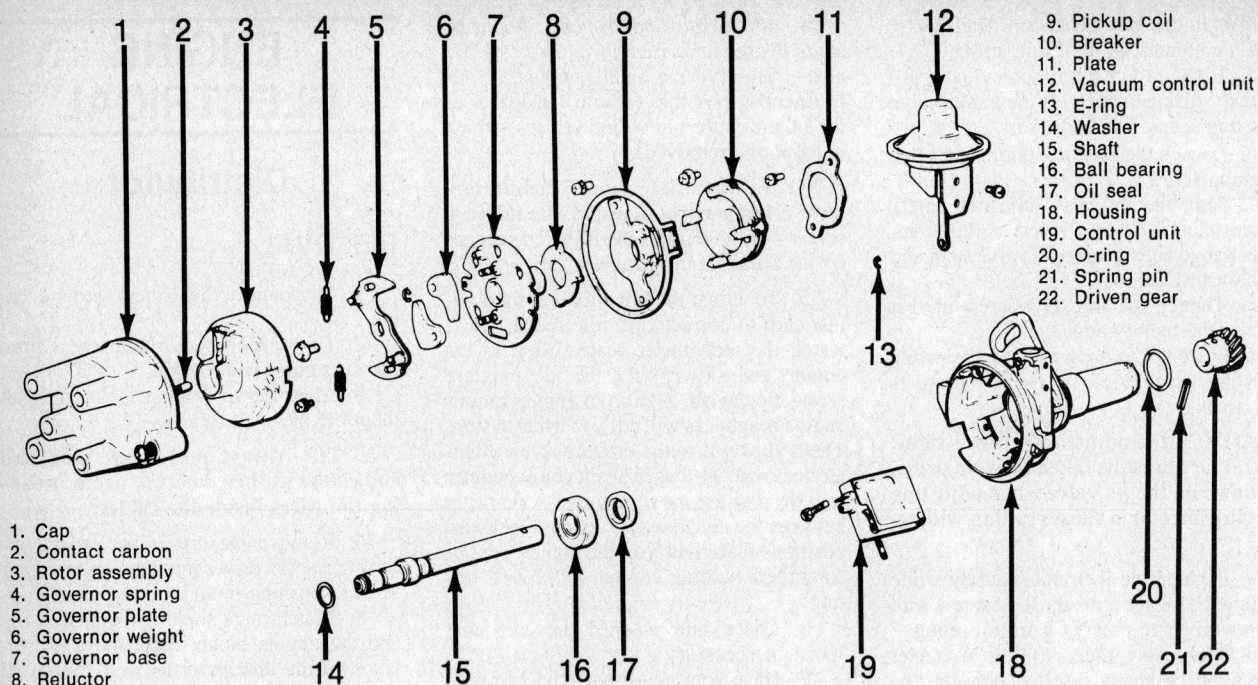

1. Cap
2. Contact carbon
3. Rotor assembly
4. Governor spring
5. Governor plate
6. Governor weight
7. Governor base
8. Reluctor

9. Pickup coil
10. Breaker
11. Plate
12. Vacuum control unit
13. E-ring
14. Washer
15. Shaft
16. Ball bearing
17. Oil seal
18. Housing
19. Control unit
20. O-ring
21. Spring pin
22. Driven gear

Exploded view of distributor—typical

3. Install the distributor with the mating mark on the distributor attaching flange even with the center of the distributor retaining stud. Tighten the nut and replace the distributor cap, wires, and plug wires.

4. Set ignition timing as described above.

INSTALLATION—ENGINE NOT DISTURBED

1. Insert the distributor in the engine and align the marks made during removal.

2. Install the mounting nut, distributor cap, wires and plug wires, and vacuum line.

3. Start engine and check ignition timing.

Alternator

ALTERNATOR PRECAUTIONS

1. Always observe proper polarity of the battery connections; be especially careful when jump-starting the car.

2. Never ground or short out any alternator or alternator regulator terminals.

3. Never operate the alternator with any of its or the battery's leads disconnected.

4. Always remove the battery or disconnect the cables while charging it.

5. Always disconnect the ground cable when replacing any electrical components.

6. Never subject the alternator to excessive heat or dampness if the engine is being steam-cleaned.

7. Never use arc-welding equipment with the alternator connected.

REMOVAL AND INSTALLATION

1. Disconnect the battery ground cable.

2. Disconnect the cable from terminal "B" on the back of the alternator. Disconnect the other cables.

3. Remove the alternator brace bolt and the support bolt nut. Remove the drive belt.

4. Pull out the support bolt and remove the alternator assembly.

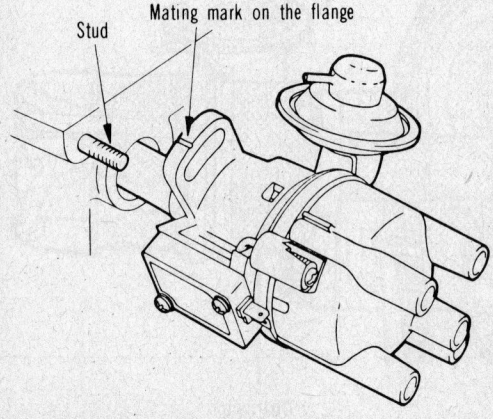

Align mark on flange with stud

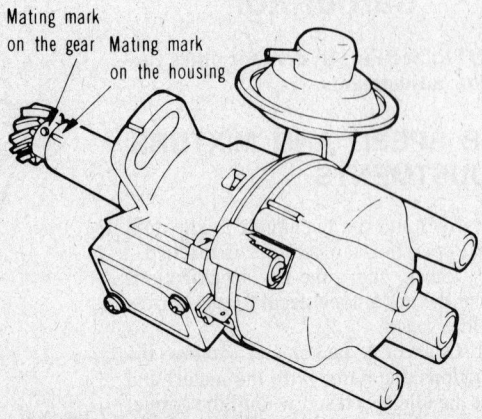

Mating mark alignment

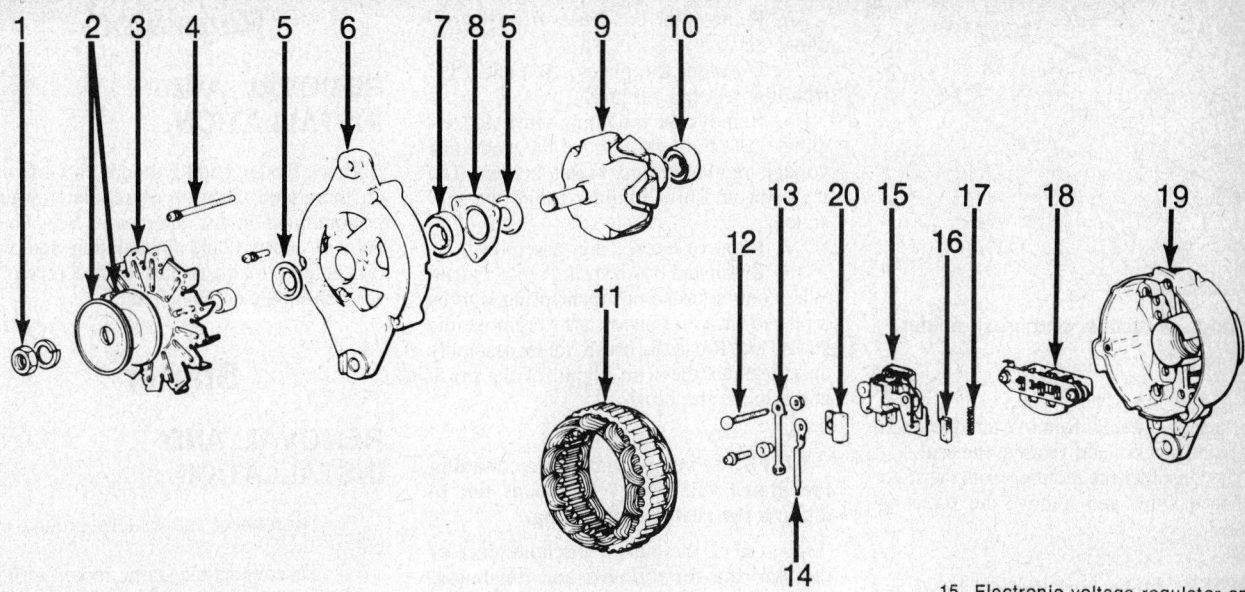

Exploded view of alternator

1. Pulley nut
2. Pulley
3. Fan
4. Through bolt
5. Seal
6. Front bracket
7. Ball bearing
8. Bearing retainer
9. Rotor assembly
10. Ball bearing
11. Stator assembly
12. Terminal "B" bolt
13. Plate "B"
14. Plate "L"
15. Electronic voltage regulator and brush holder
16. Brush
17. Brush spring
18. Rectifier assembly
19. Rear bracket
20. Condenser

To install alternator:

1. Align the hole in the alternator leg with the hole in the front case and insert the alternator support bolt from the front bracket side.

2. Install the brace bolt.

3. Install drive belt.

4. Push the alternator toward the front of the engine and check the clearance between the alternator leg and the front case. If the clearance is more than 0.008 in., insert spacers as required. 0.0078 in. thick spacers are available.

5. Adjust the belt tension as described below.

6. Tighten the alternator support bolt nut to 15–18 ft. lbs. and the brace bolt to 9–11 ft. lbs.

Belt Adjustment

Inspection and adjustment to the alternator drive belt should be performed every 15,-000 miles. The belt should be replaced every 30,000 miles.

1. Inspect the drive belt to see that it is not cracked or worn. Be sure that its surfaces are free of grease or oil.

2. Pull the belt with a force of about 22 lbs. at a point halfway between the alternator pulley and the water pump pulley. The belt deflection should be ¼ to ⅜ in.

3. If the belt requires adjustment, loosen the alternator support bolt and alternator brace bolt and move the alternator to obtain specified deflection at 22 lbs. pressure.

4. After adjustment, tighten the alter-

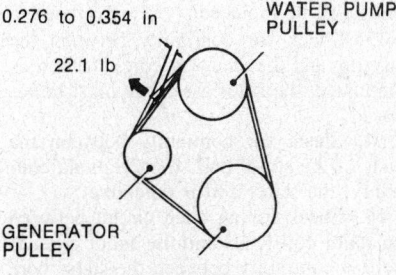

Drive belt tension adjustment

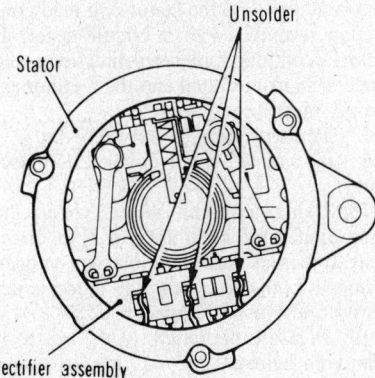

Unsolder the three wires to remove the stator assembly

nator support bolt to 14–18 ft. lbs., and the alternator brace bolt to 9 to 11 ft. lbs.

— CAUTION —
Do not overtighten the belt, or damage to the alternator bearings might result.

Charging System Test (On-Vehicle)

1. Place the ignition switch at off.

2. Disconnect the battery ground cable.

3. Disconnect the cable from terminal "B" of the alternator and connect an ammeter between the terminal "B" and the cable.

4. Connect a voltmeter between terminal "B" (+) and ground (−).

5. Set the engine tachometer.

6. Connect the battery ground cable to the battery. The voltmeter should indicate the battery voltage.

7. Start the engine.

8. Turn on the lamps, accelerate the engine to the speed specified in the chart at the beginning of this section and measure the output current. Check it against the chart.

OVERHAUL

1. Remove alternator from vehicle.

2. Remove the three through bolts from the alternator body.

3. Insert a screwdriver between the front bracket and stator (see illustration). Pry the front bracket away from the stator. Remove the front bracket along with the rotor.

NOTE: If the screwdriver is inserted too deeply, the stator coil might be damaged.

4. Hold the rotor in a vise and remove

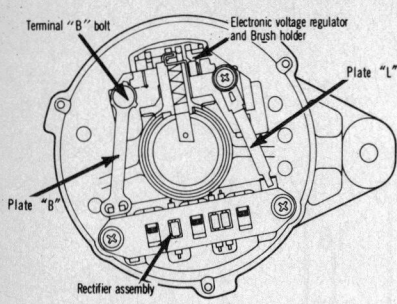

Location of rectifier and brush holder

the pulley nut. Then remove the pulley, fan, spacer and seal. Remove the rotor from the front bracket and remove the seal.

5. Unsolder the rectifier from the stator coil lead wires and remove the stator assembly.

NOTE: Make sure the solder is removed quickly (in less than five seconds). If a diode is heated to more than 150°C, it might be damaged.

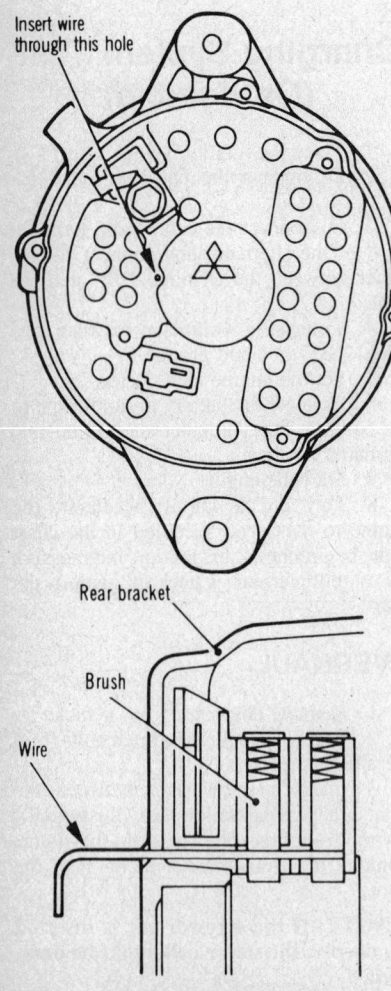

Insert a wire to hold the brushes

6. Remove the condenser from the terminal "B".

7. Unsolder the plates "B" and "L" from the rectifier assembly.

8. Remove the mounting screw and terminal "B" bolt and remove the electronic voltage regulator and brush holder. The regulator and brush holder cannot be separated.

9. Remove the rectifier assembly.

10. Brush and brush spring replacement; When only a brush or brush spring is to be replaced, it is not necessary to remove the stator, etc. Raise the brush holder assembly and unsolder the wire pigtail of the brush and remove the brush.

NOTE: Be very careful when bending the plates "B" and "L" so as not to disturb the rectifier moulding.

11. Check the outside circumference of the slip ring for dirtiness and roughness. Clean or polish with armature paper, if required. A badly damaged slip ring or a slip ring worn down beyond the service limit should also be replaced. The service limit for the slip ring outside diameter is 1.268 in.

12. Check for continuity between the field coil and slip ring. If there is not continuity, the field coil is defective and the rotor must be replaced.

13. Check for continuity between the slip ring and the shaft (or core). If there is continuity, the rotor assembly must be replaced.

14. Check for continuity between the leads of the stator coil. If there is no continuity, the stator coil is defective.

15. Check for an open circuit between the stator coil leads and the stator core. If there is continuity between the stator core and the coil leads, the stator assembly must be replaced.

16. Check for continuity between the (+) heat sink and the stator coil lead connection terminal with a circuit tester. If there is continuity in both directions, the diode is short-circuited and the rectifier assembly must be replaced.

17. Perform step 16 between the (−) heat sink and the stator coil lead connection.

18. Using a circuit tester, check the three diodes for continuity in both directions. If there is either continuity or an open circuit in both directions, the diode is defective and must be replaced.

19. Measure the length of the brush. If it is worn below 0.315 in., it must be replaced.

Assembly is the reverse of disassembly with the following notes:

1. Be sure to install both the front and rear seals on the front bearing.

2. To install the rotor assembly in the rear bracket, push the brushes into the brush holder, insert a wire to hold them in the raised position and install the rotor. Remove the wire.

Regulator

REMOVAL AND INSTALLATION

Both the Dodge and Plymouth Pick-ups use an integrated circuit-type regulator which is contained in the alternator. See Alternator Removal and Installation removal procedures. Adjustments of the regulator are confined to replacement.

Starter

REMOVAL AND INSTALLATION

1. Disconnect the battery ground cable.

2. Disconnect the starter motor wiring.

3. Loosen and remove the two starter motor mounting bolts and remove the starter motor.

4. Installation is the reverse of removal.

STARTER DRIVE, SOLENOID AND BRUSH REPLACEMENT

NOTE: Starter must be removed from vehicle for this operation.

Direct Drive Type

1. Remove the wire connecting the starter solenoid to the starter.

2. Remove the two screws holding the starter solenoid on the starter-drive housing and remove the solenoid.

3. Remove the two long through bolts at the rear of the starter and separate the armature yoke from the armature.

4. Carefully remove the armature and the starter drive engagement lever from the front bracket, after making a mental note of the way they are positioned along with the attendant spring and spring retainer.

5. Loosen the two screws and remove the rear bracket.

6. Tap the stopper ring at the end of the drive gear engagement shaft in towards the drive gear to expose the snap-ring. Remove the snap-ring.

7. Pull the stopper, drive gear and overrunning clutch from the end of the shaft. For 1979 models with automatic transmissions, remove the center bracket, spring and spring retainer.

Inspect the pinion and spline teeth for wear or damage. If the engagement teeth are damaged, visually check the flywheel ring gear through the starter hole to insure that it is not damaged. It will be necessary to turn the engine over by hand to completely inspect the ring gear.

Check the brushes for wear. Their ser-

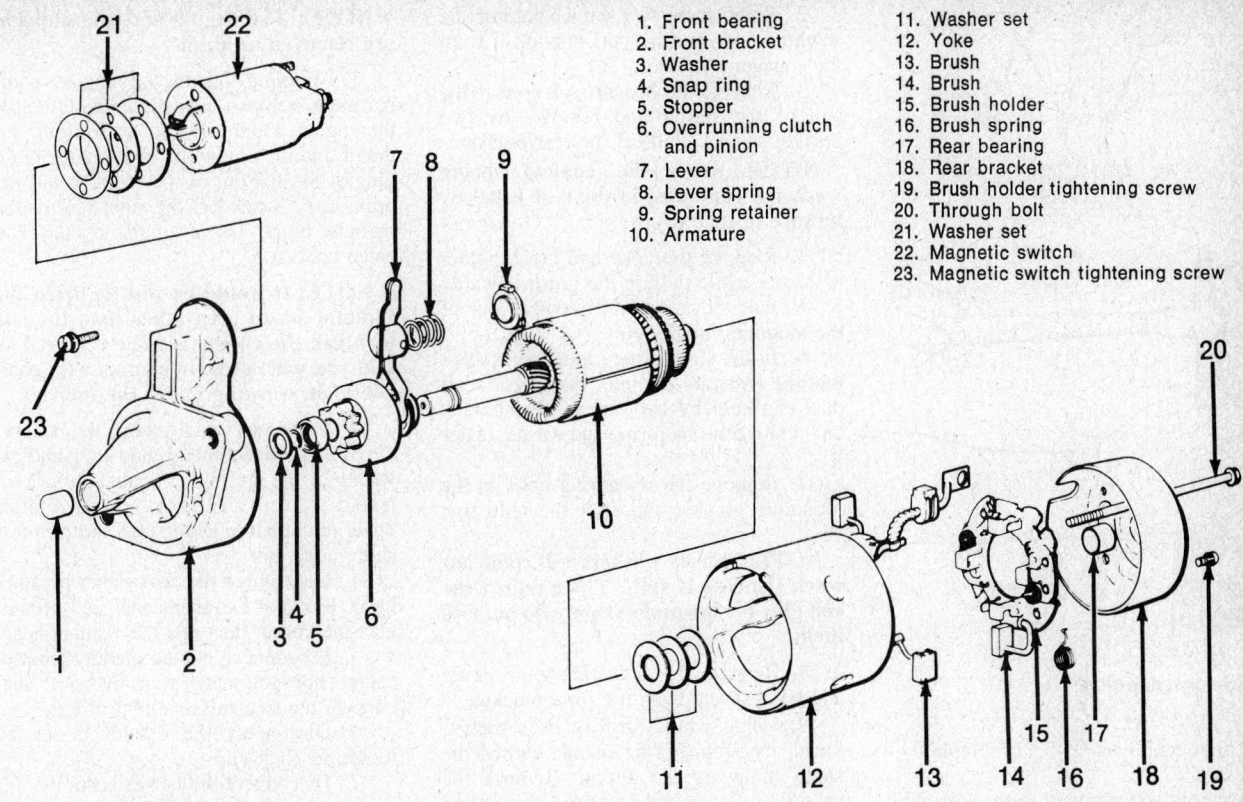

1. Front bearing
2. Front bracket
3. Washer
4. Snap ring
5. Stopper
6. Overrunning clutch and pinion
7. Lever
8. Lever spring
9. Spring retainer
10. Armature
11. Washer set
12. Yoke
13. Brush
14. Brush
15. Brush holder
16. Brush spring
17. Rear bearing
18. Rear bracket
19. Brush holder tightening screw
20. Through bolt
21. Washer set
22. Magnetic switch
23. Magnetic switch tightening screw

Exploded view of direct drive starter

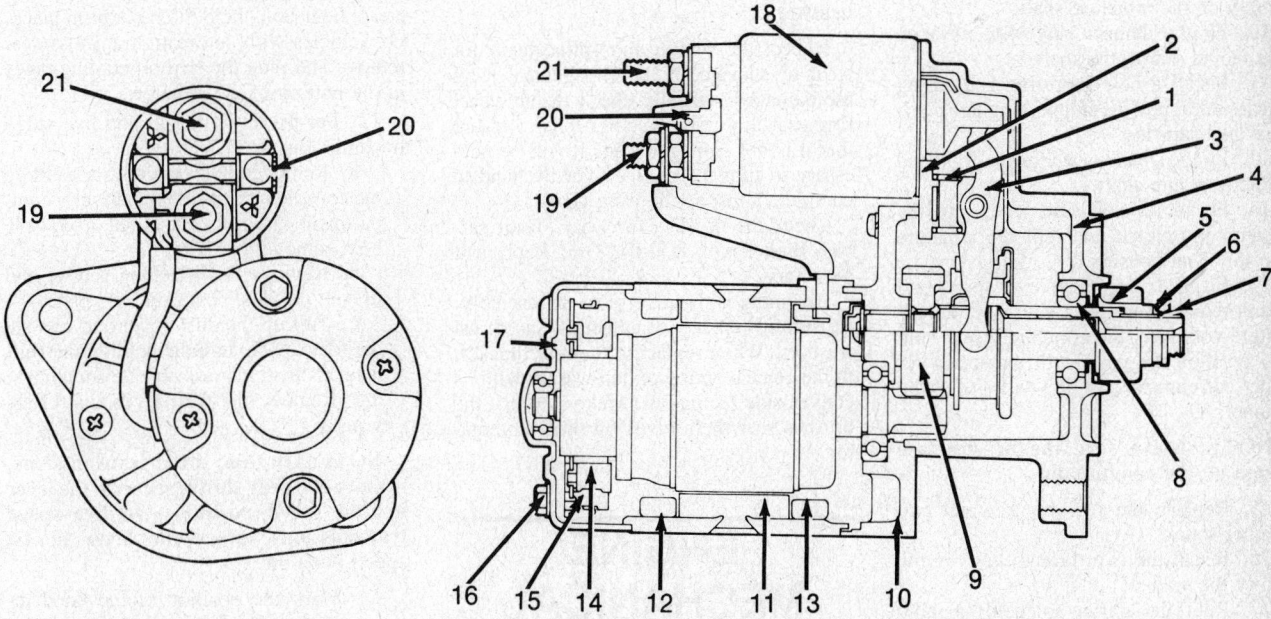

Gear reduction starter

1. Lever spring
2. Packing
3. Lever
4. Front bracket
5. Pinion
6. Stopper
7. Ring
8. Pinion shaft assy
9. Gear
10. Center bracket
11. Pole
12. Yoke
13. Field coil
14. Brush
15. Brush holder
16. Through bolt
17. Rear bracket
18. Magnetic switch
19. Terminal "M"
20. Terminal "S"
21. Terminal "B"

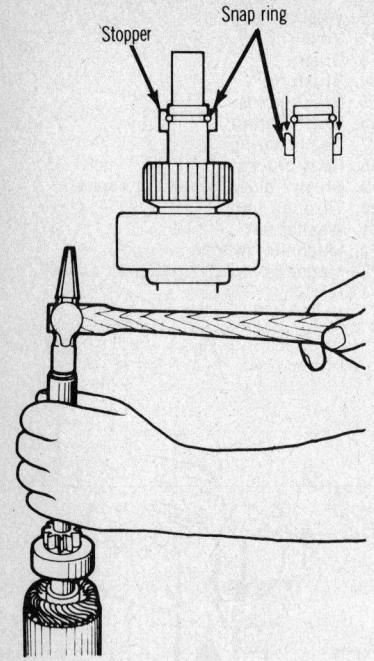

Stopper Snap ring

Removing snap-ring

vice limit length is 0.453 in. Replace if necessary.

Assembly is performed in the following manner. For 1979 models with automatic transmissions, fit the spring retainer, spring and center bracket on the shaft.

8. Install the spring retainer and spring on the armature shaft.

9. Install the overrunning clutch assembly on the armature shaft.

10. Fit the stopper ring with its open side facing out on the shaft.

11. Install a new snap-ring and, using a gear puller, pull the stopper ring into place over the snap-ring.

12. Fit the small washer on the front end of the armature shaft.

13. Fit the engagement lever into the overrunning clutch and refit the armature into the front housing.

14. Fit the engagement lever spring and spring retainer into place and slide the armature yoke over the armature. Make sure you position the yoke with the spring retainer cut-out space in line with the spring retainer.

NOTE: Make sure the brushes are seated on the commutator.

15. Replace the rear bracket and two retainer screws.

16. Install the two through bolts in the end of the yoke.

17. Refit the starter solenoid, making sure you fit the plunger over the engagement lever. Install the screws and connect the wire running from the starter yoke to the starter solenoid.

Gear Reduction Type

1. Remove the wire connecting the starter solenoid to the starter.

2. Remove the two screws holding the solenoid and, pulling out, unhook it from the engagement lever.

3. Remove the two through bolts in the end of the starter and remove the two bracket screws. Pull off the rear bracket.

NOTE: Since the conical spring washer is contained in the rear bracket, be sure to take it out.

4. Remove the yoke and brush holder assembly while pulling the brush upward.

5. Pull the armature assembly out of the mounting bracket.

6. In the side of the mounting bracket that the armature fits into, there is a small dust cap held by two screws. Remove it and remove the snap-ring and washer under it.

7. Remove the remaining bolts in the mounting bracket and split the reduction case.

NOTE: Several washers will come out when the case is split. These adjust the end play for the pinion shaft. Do not lose them.

8. Remove the reduction gear, lever and lever spring from the front bracket.

9. Using a brass drift or deep socket, knock the stopper ring on the end of the shaft in toward the pinion. Remove the snap-ring. Remove the stopper, pinion and pinion shaft assembly.

10. Remove the ball bearings at both ends of the armature.

NOTE: The ball bearings are pressed in the front bracket and are not replaceable. Replace them together with the bracket.

Inspect the pinion and spline teeth for wear or damage. If the engagement teeth are damaged, visually check the flywheel ring gear through the starter hole to insure that it is not damaged also. It will be necessary to turn the engine over by hand to completely inspect the ring gear.

Check the brushes for wear. Their service limit length is 0.0453 in. Replace if necessary.

Assembly is the reverse of disassembly. Be sure to replace all adjusting and thrust washers. When replacing the rear bracket, fit the conical spring pinion washer with its convex side facing out. Make sure that the brushes seat themselves on the commutator.

ENGINE MECHANICAL

REMOVAL AND INSTALLATION

——— CAUTION ———
Be sure the car is supported securely during engine removal.

NOTE: The engine and transmission are removed as a unit.

1. Working inside the engine compartment, remove the splash shield below the engine. Drain the coolant from the radiator and the engine by opening the drain plug at the bottom of the radiator and the drain cock located at the right rear of the cylinder block. Use a suitable container to catch coolant.

NOTE: It would be wise to drain the radiator in an area other than the one in which the engine is to be removed so that you will not be in contact with coolant when working under the vehicle.

2. Disconnect and remove the battery.

3. Disconnect the ground strap and the wiring of the ignition coil, fuel cut-off solenoid valve, alternator, starter motor, water temperature gauge unit and oil pressure gauge unit.

4. Disconnect the air cleaner breather hose. Remove the air cleaner and disconnect the hot air duct and the vacuum hose.

5. Disconnect the accelerator control cable. For automatic transmissions, disconnect the transmission control rod.

6. Disconnect the radiator hoses by loosening their clips.

7. Disconnect the heater hose.

8. Disconnect the exhaust pipe from the exhaust manifold. The muffler pipe bracket should be detached at the transmission.

9. Disconnect the fuel hoses and vapor hose.

10. Remove the radiator and radiator cowl. Four bolts hold the radiator in place. On vehicles with automatic transmissions, remove and plug the two oil cooling pipes in the bottom of the radiator.

11. For trucks with four and five speed transmissions:

   a. Remove the lock screws and lift up the console box, inside the driver's compartment. In trucks without a console box, remove the carpet.

   b. Remove the attaching screws and lift out the dust cover retainer plate.

   c. Pull up the dust cover and remove the four attaching bolts holding the shift lever to the transmission extension housing. Remove the shift lever control assembly.

NOTE: On four speed transmissions, remove the gear shift lever with the lever in 2nd speed position. On five speed transmissions, place the lever in 1st speed position.

12. Mark the position of the hood retaining bolts in relation to the hood and remove the hood.

13. Jack up the vehicle and support it on stands.

14. Disconnect the speedometer cable and backup light switch wiring from the transmission.

15. For trucks with manual transmissions, disconnect the clutch cable from the

transmission by removing the cotter key and sliding it off the arm. Disconnect the cable from the cable bracket. For automatic transmissions, remove shift linkage between transmission and shift lever.

16. Drain the transmission.

17. Remove the bolts holding the rear of the driveshaft to the rear axle. Remove the two nuts holding the center bearing assembly of the driveshaft to the frame and pull the driveshaft out of the rear of the transmission.

18. Support the transmission on a jack and remove the bolts holding the front motor mounts.

19. Unbolt the rear transmission mount crossmember and remove the two bolts holding it to the transmission. Remove the crossmember.

20. Attach steel lifting cables to the engine front and rear hangers and attach the cables to a suitable hoist.

21. Have an assistant slowly lower the jack under the transmission and pull the engine/transmission out of the vehicle by tilting it upwards and pulling forward.

NOTE: If the transmission will not clear the steering relay rod, raise it until the bell housing is above the rod, then remove the engine/transmission from the truck.

Installation is the reverse of removal. Adjust all transmission and carburetor linkages as detailed in the appropriate sections. Install and adjust the hood. Refill the engine, transmission and radiator to capacity.

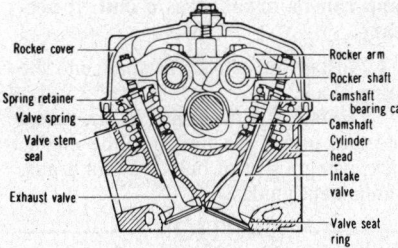

Cross section of cylinder head

Cylinder Head

REMOVAL AND INSTALLATION

— CAUTION —

Do not perform this operation on a warm engine. Remove the head bolts in the sequence shown at the front of this section and in several steps. Loosen the head bolts evenly, not one at a time. Do not attempt to slide the cylinder head off the block, as it is located with dowel pins. Lift the head straight up and off the block.

1. Disconnect the battery and drain the cooling system. Disconnect the upper radiator hose.

2. Remove the breather hoses and purge hose.

3. Remove the air cleaner and fuel line.

4. Remove the vacuum hose at the distributor and purge control valve.

5. Disconnect the spark plug wires after marking them for reinstallation.

6. Remove the distributor cap, and distributor by removing the retainer nut and pulling the unit out.

7. Disconnect the heater hose at the intake manifold.

8. Disconnect the water temperature gauge unit wire.

9. Place no. 1 piston in the Top Dead Center position to take pressure off the fuel pump rocker arm. Disconnect the fuel hoses and plug the line leading to the gas tank to prevent fuel leakage.

10. Remove the fuel pump mounting nuts or bolts and remove the fuel assembly. Remove the insulator and gaskets.

11. Disconnect the exhaust pipe at the exhaust manifold flange.

12. Remove the rocker cover.

13. Remove its breather and semi-circular seal.

14. After slightly loosening the camshaft sprocket bolt, turn the crankshaft until no. 1 piston is at top dead center on compression stroke (both valves closed).

NOTE: Never turn the engine over using the camshaft bolt: it puts undue strain on the chain and other components.

15. Remove the camshaft sprocket bolt and distributor drive gear. Remove the camshaft sprocket and allow it to rest in the chain on the holder below.

16. Remove the cylinder head bolts in the sequence shown in the illustration. Head bolts should be loosened in two or three stages to prevent head warpage.

NOTE: The cylinder head assembly is located with two dowel pins, front and rear, on the cylinder block. When removing, be careful not to slide it, or twist the camshaft sprocket and chain.

17. Remove the cylinder head assembly and cylinder head gasket.

Installation is performed in the following manner.

18. Clean all gasket surfaces of cylinder block and cylinder head.

19. Install a new cylinder head gasket. Install the cylinder head assembly.

NOTE: Do not apply sealant to the head gasket and do not reuse an old head gasket.

20. Install the ten cylinder head bolts. Starting at top center, tighten all cylinder head bolts to 35 ft. lbs. in the sequence shown in the illustration. Repeat the tightening procedure, this time torque the bolts to 65–72 ft. lbs. (cold engine), (72–80 ft. lbs. hot engine).

21. Tighten the two front bolts (number 11 in illustration) to 11–15 ft. lbs.

22. Verify that no. 1 cylinder is at top dead center. Align the dowel pin in the end of the camshaft sprocket with the groove in the top of the front camshaft bearing cap and install the camshaft sprocket and chain while pulling up on the sprocket.

23. Install the distributor drive gear and the sprocket bolt.

24. Turn the crankshaft about 90° back, and tighten the camshaft sprocket bolt to 37–43 ft. lbs.

Very slowly turn the engine over two times to make sure the valve timing is correct. If the engine locks at a certain point in these two revolutions, the valve timing is not correct. Repeat steps 22–24.

— CAUTION —

At this point, do not turn the engine over using the starter. If the valve timing is off, several of the valves could be bent.

25. Install the breather and semicircular seal to the cylinder head after applying sealant to surface contact points. Install the rocker cover with a new gasket.

26. Connect the exhaust pipe to the exhaust manifold flange. Tighten the bolts to 11–18 ft. lbs.

27. Put no. 1 cylinder at top dead cente and install the fuel pump with a new gaske and insulator. Connect all hoses.

28. Connect the water temperature gauge unit wire. Connect the heater hose to the intake manifold.

Install the distributor and spark plug cables. See distributor section, above, for procedure.

29. Connect the vacuum hose to the distributor and purge control valve. Connect the upper radiator hose and fill the cooling system with coolant.

Many mechanics recommend that the engine oil be replaced after the head is removed to avoid water contamination from the coolant.

Intake Manifold

REMOVAL AND INSTALLATION

1. Drain the cooling system.

2. Remove the air cleaner assembly with its hoses from the engine.

3. Disconnect the fuel line and EGR lines.

4. Disconnect the accelerator linkage and, if so equipped, the automatic transmission shift cables at the carburetor.

5. Remove the water hose at the intake manifold. Remove the water hose at the carburetor.

6. Disconnect the water temperature sending unit.

7. Remove the manifold with the carburetor as a unit.

Installation is the reverse of removal. Tighten manifold nuts to 11–14 ft. lbs.

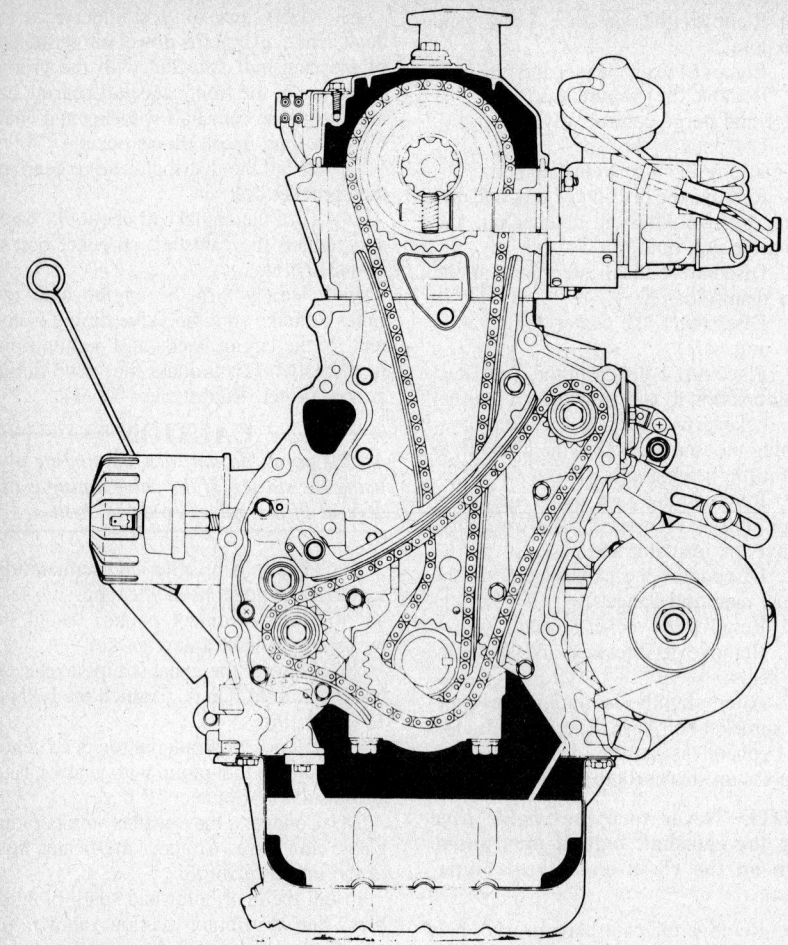

Front view of engine showing timing chain

Exhaust Manifold

REMOVAL AND INSTALLATION

1. Remove air cleaner.
2. Remove the heat shield from the exhaust manifold. Remove the EGR lines and reed valve, if equipped.
3. Unbolt the exhaust flange connection.
4. Remove nuts holding manifold to cylinder head.
5. Remove manifold.

Installation is the reverse of removal. Tighten flange connection bolts to 11–18 ft. lbs. Tighten manifold bolts to 11–14 ft. lbs.

Timing Chain, Cover, "Silent Shafts" and Tensioner

REMOVAL AND INSTALLATION

NOTE: All pick-ups are equipped with two "Silent Shafts" which cancel the vertical vibrating force of the engine and the secondary vibrating forces, which include the sideways rocking of the engine due to the turning direction of the crankshaft and other rolling parts. The secondary vibrating forces can be cancelled if forces equivalent in magnitude but opposite in direction are produced. In these engines, the opposite force is produced by silent shafts located in the upper left and lower right sides in the front of the cylinder block. The shafts are driven by a duplex chain and are turned by the crankshaft. The silent shaft chain assembly is mounted in front of the timing chain assembly and must be removed to service the timing chain.

1. Remove the battery cables.
2. Drain the radiator and remove it from the vehicle.
3. Remove the cylinder head (refer to cylinder head section for procedures).
4. Remove the cooling fan, spacer, water pump pulley and belt.
5. Remove the alternator. Remove the water pump.
6. Raise the front of the vehicle and support it on jack stands.
7. Remove the oil pan and screen. Remove the crankshaft pulley.
8. Remove the timing case cover.

9. Remove the chain guides, side (A), top (B), bottom (C), from the "B" chain (outer).
10. Remove the locking bolts from the "B" chain sprockets.
11. Remove the crankshaft sprocket, silent shaft sprocket and the outer chain.
12. Remove the crankshaft and camshaft sprockets and the timing chain.
13. Remove the camshaft sprocket holder and the chain guides, both left and right.
14. Remove the tensioner.
15. Remove the sleeve from the oil pump. Remove the oil pump by first removing the bolt locking the oil pump driven gear and the right silent shaft, then remove the oil pump mounting bolts. Remove the silent shaft from the engine block.

NOTE: If the bolt locking the oil pump and the silent shaft is hard to loosen, remove the oil pump and the shaft as a unit.

16. Remove the left silent shaft thrust washer and take the shaft from the engine block.

Installation is performed in the following manner:

1. Install the right silent shaft into the engine block.
2. Install the oil pump assembly. Do not lose the woodruff key from the end of the silent shaft. Torque the oil pump mounting bolts to 6 to 7 ft. lbs.
3. Tighten the silent shaft and the oil pump driven gear mounting bolt.

NOTE: The silent shaft and the oil pump can be installed as a unit, if necessary.

4. Install the left silent shaft into the engine block.
5. Install a new O-ring on the thrust plate and install the unit into the engine block, using a pair of bolts without heads, as alignment guides.

CAUTION
If the thrust plate is turned to align the bolt holes, the O-ring may be damaged.

6. Remove the guide bolts and install the regular bolts into the thrust plate and tighten securely.
7. Rotate the crankshaft to bring no. 1 piston to TDC.
8. Install the cylinder head.
9. Install the sprocket holder and the right and left chain guides.
10. Install the tensioner spring and sleeve on the oil pump body.
11. Install the camshaft and crankshaft sprockets on the timing chain, aligning the sprocket punch marks to the plated chain links.
12. While holding the sprocket and chain as a unit, install the crankshaft sprocket over the crankshaft and align it with the keyway.
13. Keeping the dowel pin hole on the camshaft in a vertical position, install the

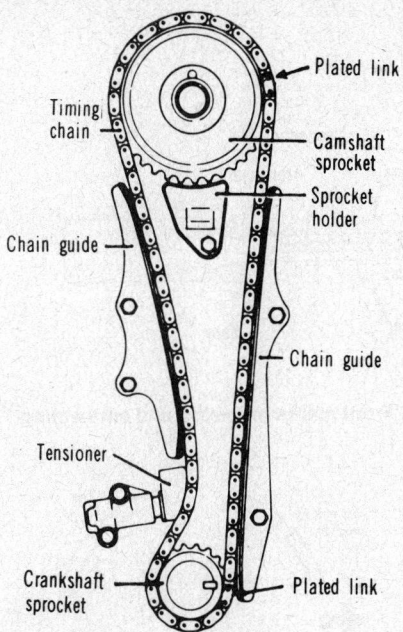

Timing chain installation: align the plated links with the punch-marks on the cam sprocket and the crankshaft sprocket

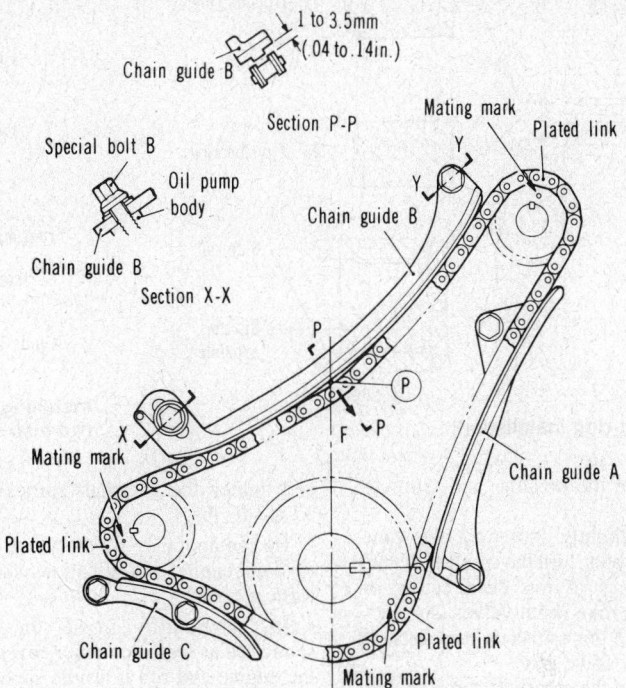

"Silent Shaft" balancing system

camshaft sprocket and chain on the camshaft.

NOTE: The sprocket timing mark and the plated chain link should be at the 2 to 3 O'clock position when correctly installed.

--- CAUTION ---
The chain must be aligned in the right and left chain guides with the tensioner pushing against the chain. The tension for the inner chain is predetermined by spring tension.

14. Install the crankshaft sprocket for the outer or "B" chain.

15. Install the two silent shaft sprockets and align the punched mating marks with the plated links of the chain.

16. Holding the two shaft sprockets and chain, install the outer chain in alignment with the mark on the crankshaft sprocket. Install the shaft sprockets on the silent shaft and the oil pump driver gear. Install the lock bolts and recheck the alignment of the punch marks and the plated links.

17. Temporarily install the chain guides, side (A), top (B), and bottom (C).

18. Tighten side (A) chain guide securely.

19. Tighten bottom (B) chain guide securely.

20. Adjust the position of the top (B) chain guide, after shaking the right and left sprockets to collect any chain slack, so that when the chain is moved toward the center, the clearance between the chain guide and the chain links will be approximately ⁹⁄₆₄ inch. Tighten the top (B) chain guide bolts.

21. Install the timing chain cover using a new gasket, being careful not to damage the front seal.

22. Install the oil screen and the oil pan, using a new gasket. Torque the bolts to 4.5–5.5 ft. lbs.

23. Install the crankshaft pulley, alternator and accessory belts, and the distributor.

24. Install the oil pressure switch, if removed, and install the battery ground cable.

25. Install the fan blades, radiator, fill the system with coolant and start the engine.

Camshaft

REMOVAL AND INSTALLATION

1. Remove the breather hoses and purge hose.
2. Remove the air cleaner and fuel line.
3. Remove the fuel pump. Remove the distributor.
4. Diconnect the spark plug cables.
5. Remove the rocker cover.

PISTON AND PISTON RING APPLICATION

Description	Engine	Identification Mark
Piston	U (for U.S.A.)	52J①
	U (for Canada)	52①
	W (for U.S.A.)	54J①
	W (for Canada)	54①
Piston ring No. 1	U	N1②
	W	T②
No. 2	U	N②
	W	2T②
Oil ring		None

①Stamped on top of piston
②Stamped on ring end

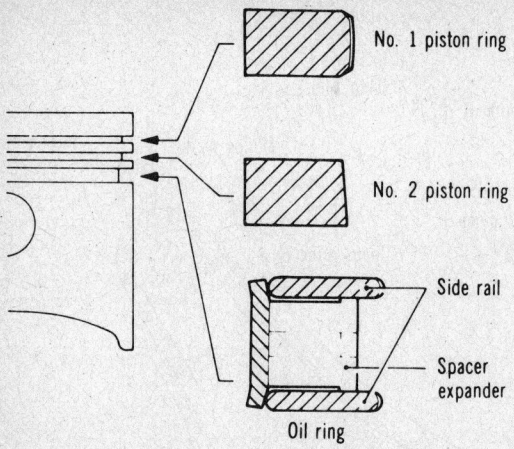

Piston ring installation

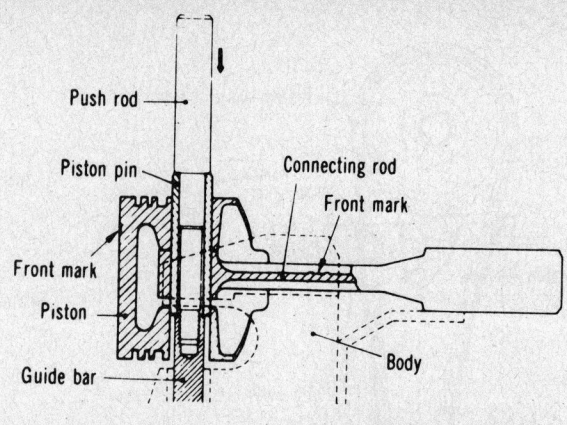

Installing the piston pin. Front marks on piston and connecting rod also shown

6. Remove the breather and semi-circular seal.

7. After slightly loosening the camshaft sprocket bolt, turn the crankshaft until no. 1 piston is at top dead center on compression stroke (both valves closed).

8. Remove the camshaft sprocket bolt and distributor drive gear.

9. Remove the camshaft sprocket with chain and allow it to rest on the camshaft sprocket holder.

10. Remove the camshaft bearing cap tightening bolts. Do not remove the front and rear bearing cap bolts altogether, but keep them inserted in the bearing caps so that the rocker assembly can be removed as a unit.

11. Remove the rocker arms, rocker shafts and bearing caps as an assembly.

12. Remove the camshaft.

Installation is performed in the following manner.

13. Lubricate the camshaft lobes and bearings and fit camshaft into head.

14. Install the assembled rocker arm shaft assembly. The camshaft should be positioned so that the dowel pin on the front end of the cam is in the 12 o'clock position and in line with the notch in the top of the front bearing cap.

15. Install the bearing cap bolts. Starting at the center and working out, tighten the bolts to 7 ft. lbs. Repeat the procedure, this time tightening them to 14–15 ft. lbs.

16. Install the camshaft sprocket and distributor drive gear onto the camshaft while pulling it upward. Temporarily tighten the locking bolt.

17. Turn the crankshaft about 90° back

and tighten the camshaft sprocket bolt to 37–43 ft. lbs.

18. Temporarily set the valve clearance to cold engine specifications (see Valve Lash section).

19. Temporarily install the breather, semicircular seal and rocker cover and start the engine and run it at idle speed.

20. After the engine is at normal operational temperature, adjust the valves to hot engine specifications (see Valve Lash section).

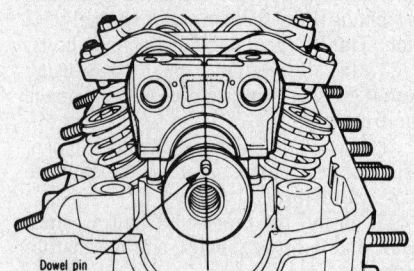

Installing the camshaft: align the dowel pin with the notch in the top of the front bearing cap

21. Install breather and seal and apply sealant to the contact surfaces.

22. Install the rocker cover and tighten to 4–5 ft. lbs.

23. Install distributor, fuel pump, air cleaner, fuel line, plug leads and other assemblies.

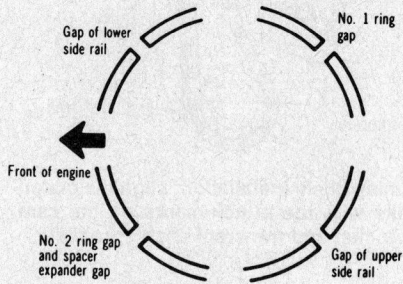

Ring end gap positioning

ENGINE LUBRICATION

Oil Pan

REMOVAL AND INSTALLATION

The engine must be raised off its mounts and safely blocked, for the pan to clear the suspension crossmember.

1. Remove the underbody splash shield.

2. Unbolt the left and right engine mounts.

3. Jack up the engine under the bell housing.

4. Remove the oil pan.

5. Installation is the reverse of removal.

OIL PUMP SPECIFICATIONS

Engine	Type	Drive Gear Rear End Clearance With Bearing	Tip Clearance: Gear to Cover (in.)	Maximum Oil Pressure (psi)	Relief Valve Spring Free Length (in.)	Relief Valve Opening Pressure (psi)
U. W	Gear	0.0016-0.0028	0.0043-0.0059	64.0	1.850	49.8-64

PISTON RING SERVICE SIZE

Size mm (in.)	Size Mark
STD	None
0.25 (.010) O.S.	25
0.50 (.020) O.S.	50
0.75 (.030) O.S.	75
1.00 (.039) O.S.	100

Rear Main Oil Seal

REPLACEMENT

The rear main oil seal is located in a housing on the rear of the block. To replace the seal, remove the transmission and do the work from underneath the vehicle or remove the engine and do the work on the bench.

1. Remove the housing from the block.
2. Remove the separator from the housing.
3. Pry out the old seal.
4. Lightly oil the replacement seal. The oil seal should be installed so that the seal plate fits into the inner contact surface of the seal case. Install the separator with the oil holes facing down.

Oil Pump

REMOVAL AND INSTALLATION

See Timing Chain, Cover, "Silent Shaft" and Tensioner Removal and Installation procedure.

OVERHAUL

1. Remove the two screws at the rear of the oil pump and remove the cover and gear.
2. Remove the relief valve plug and withdraw the relief spring and plunger.
3. Check the pump for cracks and wear. Check all oil holes for clogging.
4. Clearance between the gears and the pump assembly (tip clearance) should be 0.0043–0.0059 in.
5. Both gears front bearing clearance should be within 0.0008 and 0.0020 in.

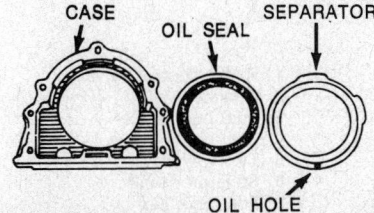

Rear main oil seal

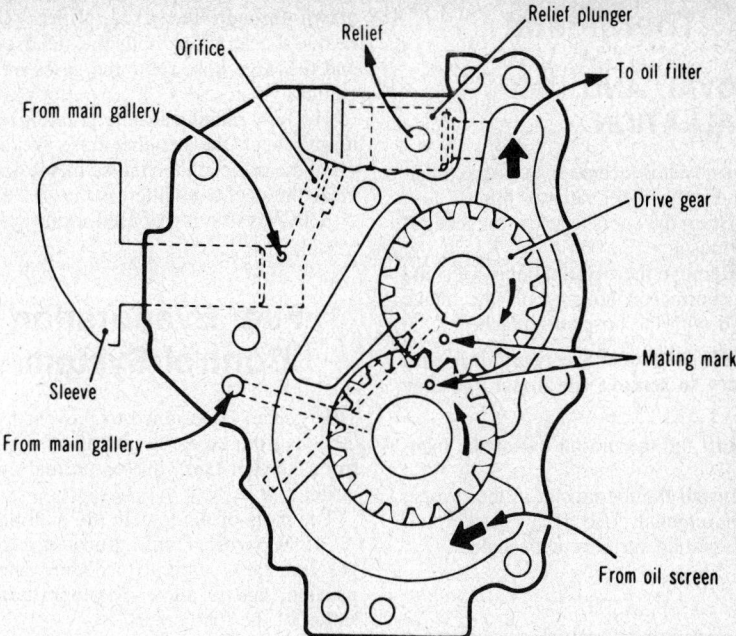

Oil pump layout—Notice mating marks on gears

6. The rear bearing clearance of the drive gear should be 0.0016–0.0028 in.

NOTE: When bearing replacement is necessary, replace the oil pump body assembly.

7. Insert the relief plunger into the pump body and make sure it operates smoothly. Check the relief spring for breakage or sagging.

When reassembling, observe the following:

8. Coat all parts in oil before reassembling.
9. Match the two punch marks on the gears so that they mate where the gears meet.
10. Check for smooth rotation after assembly.

— **CAUTION** —
Make sure the mating marks meet, or the silent shaft will be out of time and cause vibration.

Before installing the pump, fill the delivery port with clean oil to prime it.

ENGINE COOLING

Radiator

REMOVAL AND INSTALLATION

1. Remove the splash panel from the bottom of the vehicle. Drain the radiator by opening the petcock. Remove the shroud on models so equipped.
2. Disconnect the radiator hoses at the engine. On automatic transmission vehicles, disconnect and plug the transmission lines to the bottom of the radiator.
3. Remove the two retaining bolts from either side of the radiator. Lift out the radiator.
4. Install the radiator in the reverse order of removal. Tighten the retaining bolts gradually in a criss-cross pattern.

Water Pump

REMOVAL

1. Drain the cooling system.
2. Remove the fan shroud and radiator if necessary for working room.
3. Remove the alternator and accessory belts.
4. Remove the fan blades and/or automatic hub, if equipped.
5. Remove the water pump assembly from the timing chain case or the cylinder block.

INSTALLATION

1. Install the water pump to the timing chain case or the engine block and tighten the bolts securely.
2. Install the fan blades and/or the automatic clutch fan hub.
3. Install the alternator and accessory belts and adjust as necessary.
4. Install the fan shroud and the radiator, if removed.
5. Fill the cooling system, start the engine, and check for coolant leakage.

Thermostat

REMOVAL AND INSTALLATION

The thermostat is located in the intake manifold under the upper radiator hose.

1. Drain the coolant below the level of the thermostat.

2. Remove the two retaining bolts and lift the thermostat housing off the intake manifold with the hose still attached.

NOTE: If you are careful, it is not necessary to remove the upper radiator hose.

3. Lift the thermostat out of the manifold.

4. Install the thermostat in the reverse order of removal. Use a new gasket and coat the mating surfaces with sealer.

EMISSION CONTROLS

Crankcase Emission Control System

A closed-type crankcase ventilation system is used to prevent engine blow-by gases from escaping into the atmosphere.

A small fixed orifice, located in the intake manifold, is connected to the rear section of the rocker arm cover by a hose.

A larger hose is connected from the front of the rocker arm cover to the air cleaner assembly. Under light to medium carburetor throttle opening, the blow-by gases are drawn through the fixed orifice. Under heavy acceleration, both the fixed orifice and the large hose route the gases into the engine.

The only maintenance required is to regularly check the breather hose condition, clean the orifice in the intake manifold, and clean the steel wool filter, in the air cleaner.

A PCV valve is not used in the system.

Fuel Evaporation Control System

This system is designed to prevent hydrocarbons from escaping into the atmosphere from the fuel tank, due to normal evaporation.

The parts of the system are as follow:

1. **Separator tank:** Located near the gasoline tank, used to accommodate expansion, and to allow maximum condensation of the fuel vapors.

2. **Canister:** Located in the engine compartment to trap and retain gasoline vapors while the engine is not operating. When the engine is started, fresh air is drawn into the canister, removing the stored vapors, and is directed to the air cleaner.

3. **Two-way Valve:** Because of different methods of tank venting and the use of sealed gasoline tank cap, the two-way valve is used in the vapor lines. The valve relieves either pressure or vacuum in the tank.

4. **Purge Control Valve:** The purge control valve replaces the check valve used in previous years. During idle, the valve closes off the vapor passage to the air cleaner.

5. **Fuel Check Valve:** This valve is used to prevent fuel leakage in case of roll over. It is installed in the vapor line between the separator and the two-way valve.

MAINTENANCE

Be sure that all hoses are clamped and not dry-rotted or broken. Check the valves for cracks, signs of gasoline leakage, and proper operating condition. The canister air filter should be inspected and changed at least every 24,000 miles.

Heated Air Intake System

All models are equipped with a temperature regulated air control valve in the air cleaner snorkel.

When the underhood air temperature is 41 degrees or lower, the air control valve allows preheated air to flow through the heat cowl of the exhaust manifold, via a flexible hose, to the air cleaner and into the carburetor.

When the underhood temperature is 108 degrees or above, the air flow is directed through the air cleaner snorkel.

At intermediate temperature, the carburetor intake air is a blend of the direct underhood and preheated air.

MAINTENANCE

Visually check the control valve assembly when the engine is cold, to be sure that the valve is closed.

Warm up the engine and check that the control valve opens to the outside air.

Secondary Air Supply System

This system supplies air for the further combustion of unburned gases in the ther-

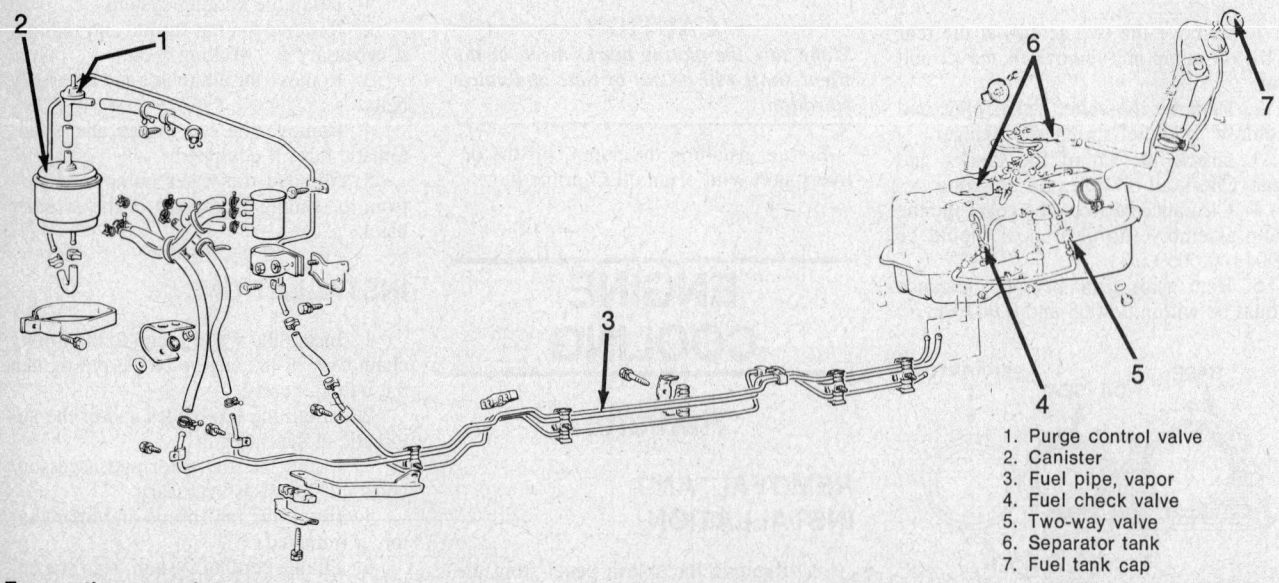

1. Purge control valve
2. Canister
3. Fuel pipe, vapor
4. Fuel check valve
5. Two-way valve
6. Separator tank
7. Fuel tank cap

Evaporation control system

mal reactor (California only) or exhaust manifold and consists of a reed valve, air hoses, and air passages built into the cylinder head.

The reed valve is operated by exhaust pulsations in the exhaust manifold. It draws fresh air through the air cleaner and supplies it to the exhaust ports.

MAINTENANCE

Check for damage to the air hoses and air pipes. Make sure the air passages are open in the head.

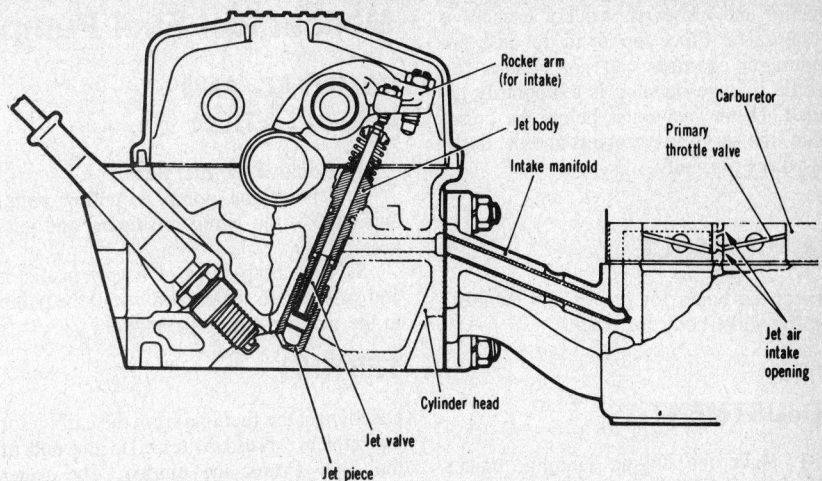

Cross section of Jet Valve (U.S.A. only)

Exhaust Gas Recirculation System

The EGR system recirculates part of the exhaust gases into the combustion chambers. This dilutes the air/fuel mixture, reducing formation of oxides of nitrogen in the exhaust gases by lowering the peak combustion temperatures.

The parts of the EGR system are:

1. **EGR Valve:** Operated by vacuum drawn from a point above the carburetor throttle plate. The vacuum controls the raising and lowering of the valve pintle to allow exhaust gases to pass from the exhaust system to the intake manifold.

2. **Thermo Valve:** Used to stop EGR valve operation below approximately 131 degrees, in order to improve cold driveability and starting.

Dual EGR Control Valve

The EGR vacuum flow is suspended during idle and wide open throttle operation.

The primary valve controls EGR flow when the throttle valve opening is relatively narrow, while the secondary control valve operates at wider openings.

Sub-EGR control valve is linked to the throttle valve to closely modulate the EGR gas flow.

EGR Maintenance Warning Light

A light in the speedometer assembly to alert the driver to the need for EGR system maintenance.

This device has a mileage sensor to light the visual signal at 15,000 mile intervals.

Upon completion of the required EGR system maintenance, the warning light can be turned off by resetting the switch. It is in the speedometer cable, under the instrument panel.

MAINTENANCE

1. Check all vacuum hoses for cracks, breakage and correct installation.

2. Check EGR valve operation by applying vacuum to the EGR valve vacuum nipple with the engine idling. The idle should become rough.

3. Check the passages in the cylinder head and intake manifold for clogging. Clean as necessary.

4. Cold start the engine. The EGR port nipple should be open. When the coolant is warmed to over 131 degrees, the port should be closed.

Catalytic Converter

This unit replaces the thermal reactor. It is filled with catalyst to oxidize hydrocarbons and carbon monoxide in the exhaust gases.

MAINTENANCE

1. Check the core for cracks and damages.

2. If the idle carbon monoxide and hydrocarbon content exceeds specifications and the ignition timing and idle mixture are correct, the converter must be replaced.

Jet Air System

A jet air passage is provided in the carburetor, intake manifold, and cylinder head to direct air to a jet valve, operated simultaneously with the intake valve.

On the intake stroke, jet air is forced into the combustion chamber because of the pressure difference between the ends of the air jet passage.

This jet of air produces a strong swirl in the combustion chamber scavenging the residual gases around the spark plug.

The jet air volume lessens with increased throttle opening. It is at a maximum at idle.

MAINTENANCE

NOTE: Refer to Valve Lash Adjustment for adjusting jet valve clearance.

No maintenance is required other than clearance adjustment during valve adjustment. The valve can be removed from the cylinder head for service or replacement.

Ignition Timing Control System

When the engine is idling or operating at low speeds under light load or deceleration, the exhaust gas temperature is low, resulting in incomplete combustion of the air/fuel mixture. To prevent this, ignition timing is retarded under these conditions to maintain high exhaust gas temperature.

The units in the Ignition Timing Control system are as follow:

1. **Thermo Valve:** This valve is used to protect the engine from overheating. When coolant temperature reaches 203 degrees, the advance unit is allowed to operate, causing an increase in engine speed and a decrease in coolant temperature.

2. **Single Diaphragm Distributor:** This distributor has a single diaphragm vacuum advance unit, which advances the ignition timing as engine vacuum dictates. The single diaphragm distributor must not be interchanged with the dual diaphragm distributor. The distributor operating curves are different and would cause increased emissions. A thermo valve is not used with this type of distributor.

Deceleration Device

Closing of the throttle valve on deceleration is delayed in order to burn the air/fuel mixture more thoroughly. A vacuum controlled dashpot, attached to the carburetor linkage is used.

A servo valve detects intake manifold

vacuum and closes if vacuum exceeds a preset valve. Since the air in the dash pot diaphragm chamber can not escape, the throttle linkage opening is temporarily retained. If the vacuum is below the preset value, the servo valve opens and the dashpot works normally.

MAINTENANCE

Inspect the hoses for breaks and damage, and the valve body for cracks.

ADJUSTMENT

1. Have the engine running, brakes locked, and a tachometer attached.
2. Push the dashpot rod, connected to the carburetor arm, upward and into the dashpot until it stops.
3. Note the rpm at the dashpot stop and adjust to specifications. Note the time required between suddenly releasing the dashpot rod and the return to normal curb idle.

Mixture Control Valve

This control valve is used to supply additional air into the intake manifold to decrease manifold vacuum during deceleration, and is activated by the intake manifold vacuum level.

Manual Altitude Compensation System

An off-on valve is used to increase the air supply to the carburetor to lean the mixture and decrease the EGR flow for high altitude operation.

MAINTENANCE

The required maintenance is to inspect any vacuum hoses and routing for kinks, breakage and cracks. The off-on valve should be on for high altitude and off for driving under 4000 ft.

FUEL SYSTEM

Fuel Filter

REPLACEMENT

All models use an in-line filter which should be replaced every 12,000 miles.

Mechanical Fuel Pump

REMOVAL AND INSTALLATION

1. Remove the fuel lines.
2. Unbolt the pump mounting bolts, and remove the pump, insulator, and gasket.
3. Coat both sides of a new insulator and gasket with sealer, and install the pump in the reverse order of removal.

TESTING

Disconnect the fuel line from the carburetor and attach a pressure tester to the end of the line. Crank the engine. The tester should show 4.6–6 psi.

Carburetors

REMOVAL AND INSTALLATION

1. Remove the solenoid valve wiring.
2. Disconnect the air cleaner breather hose, air duct and vacuum tube.
3. Remove the air cleaner.
4. Remove the air cleaner case.
5. Disconnect the accelerator and shift cables (automatic transmission) at the carburetor.
6. Disconnect the purge valve hose; remove the vacuum compensator, and fuel lines.

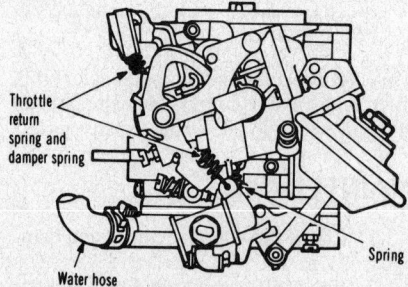

Throttle return spring and damper spring
Water hose
Spring

Removing springs

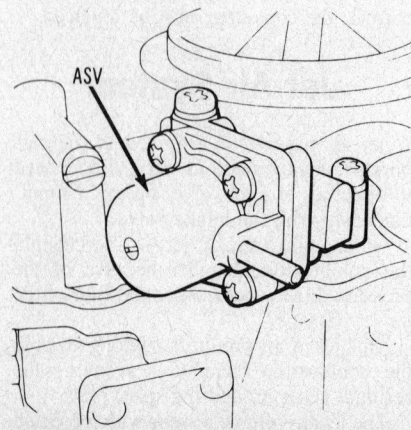

ASV

Removing the air switching valve (ASV)

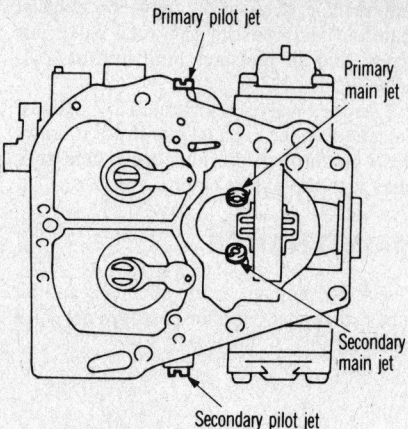

Primary pilot jet
Primary main jet
Secondary main jet
Secondary pilot jet

Location of jets

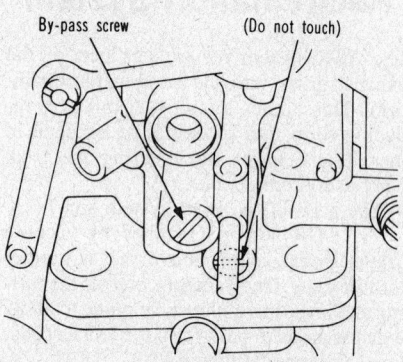

By-pass screw
(Do not touch)

Do not touch these screws (painted white) when disassembling the carburetor

7. Drain the coolant.
8. Remove the water hose between the carburetor and the cylinder head.
9. Remove the carburetor.
10. Installation is the reverse of removal.

OVERHAUL—THROUGH 1980

1. Disconnect the water hose.
2. Remove the throttle return spring and damper spring.
3. Remove the throttle adjuster lever spring and the secondary return spring.
4. Remove the choke unloader link retaining clip and disconnect the choke unloader link.
5. Disconnect the vacuum hose.
6. Disconnect the lower end of the diaphragm chamber link and remove the diaphragm chamber. *Do not immerse the diaphragm chamber assembly in cleaner.*
7. Remove the two screws and remove the air switching valve (ASV).
8. Remove the six float chamber cover screws. Separate the float chamber cover from the carburetor main body by tapping with a plastic hammer. Do not pry it off.
9. Remove the float chamber cover gasket.
10. Remove the float lever pin and the float.

11. Remove the needle valve assembly, gasket and filter.

12. Do not remove the automatic choke system because the factory setting will be disturbed.

13. Turn the main body upside down and remove the pump discharge check ball and weight.

14. Remove the fuel cut-off solenoid.

15. Remove the main jets and pilot jets. Do not tamper with the screws with white paint on heads.

16. Remove the enrichment assembly.

17. Disconnect the pump rod from the throttle shaft lever and remove the accelerator pump assembly.

18. Remove the sub-EGR valve link retaining clip and remove the washer and spring, then disconnect the link. Do not touch the EGR adjusting screw because it was preset at the factory. Do not distort the sub-EGR valve link.

19. Remove the two main body-to-throttle body screws. Separate the throttle body from the main body and remove the gasket.

20. Remove the idle speed adjusting screw, spring washer and packing from the throttle body.

Assembly is the reverse of disassembly.

OVERHAUL—FROM 1981

NOTE: A thorough test and check of minor carburetor adjustments should precede any major carburetor overhauls. Sometimes poor performance can be the result of loose, misadjusted or malfunctioning engine or electrical components.

Disassembly

1. Pull the water hose off the nipple of throttle body and off the nipple of wax element portion.

2. Grind down the head of choke cover lock screws (in 2 positions) by using a hand grinder or other instruments.

3. Disconnect the ground line of the fuel cut-off solenoid at the float chamber cover.

4. Remove the throttle return spring and the damper spring.

5. Pull of the vacuum hose connecting the depression chamber and the throttle body.

6. Remove the accelerator pump rod from the throttle lever.

7. Remove the dashpot rod (manual transmission) or throttle opener rod (automatic transmission) from the free lever.

8. Remove the depression chamber rod from the secondary throttle lever.

9. Remove the float chamber cover screws (6). Four screws connect the float chamber cover to the main body. Two screws connect the cover to the throttle body.

10. Remove only the main body by lifting the float chamber cover (the cover can not be removed because the choke unloader rod is connected to the throttle shaft.) Don't turn the carburetor up side down, during the procedure. Turning the carburetor causes accelerator pump check weight, ball, and steel ball of anti-overfill device to drop.

NOTE: When lifting the chamber cover, the venturi retaining spring may drop down.

11. Remove the E-ring at the lower end of the choke unloader rod, and disconnect the rod from the lever.

12. Do not remove any device from the float chamber unless necessary, especially the autochoke system.

13. The float can be removed by pulling the pin off.

14. The needle valve can be removed by removing the screw and retainer.

15. Remove the accelerator pump and fuel cut off solenoid.

16. Don't remove parts without necessity.

Don't remove the throttle valves and don't touch SAS and dashpot adjusting screws.

17. Assembly is the reverse of disassembly.

OVERHAUL TIPS

When the carburetor is disassembled, wash all parts (except diaphragms, electric choke units, pump plunger, and any other plastic, leather, fiber, or rubber parts) in clean carburetor solvent. Do not leave parts in the solvent any longer than is necessary to sufficiently loosen the deposits. Excessive cleaning may remove the special finish from the float bowl and choke valve bodies, leaving these parts unfit for service. Rinse all parts in clean solvent and blow them dry with compressed air or allow them to air dry. Wipe clean all cork, plastic, leather, and fiber parts with a clean, lint-free cloth.

Blow out all passages and jets with compressed air and be sure that there are no restrictions or blockages. Never use wire or similar tools to clean jets, fuel passages, or air bleeds. Clean all jets and valves separately to avoid accidental interchange.

Check all parts for wear or damage. If wear or damage is found, replace the defective parts. Especially check the following:

1. Check the float needle and seat for wear. If wear is found; replace the complete assembly.

2. Check the float hinge pin for wear and the float(s) for dents or distortion. Replace the float if fuel has leaked into it.

3. Check the throttle and choke shaft bores for wear or an out-of-round condition. Damage or wear to the throttle arm, shaft, or shaft bore will often require replacement of the throttle body. These parts require a close tolerance of fit; wear may allow air leakage, which could affect starting and idling.

NOTE: Throttle shafts and bushings are not included in overhaul kits. They can be purchased separately.

4. Inspect the idle mixture adjusting needles for burrs or grooves. Any such condition requires replacement of the needle, since you will not be able to obtain a satisfactory idle.

5. Test the accelerator pump check valves. They should pass air one way but not the other. Test for proper seating by blowing and sucking on the valve. Replace the valve if necessary. If the valve is satisfactory, wash the valve again to remove breath moisture.

6. Check the bowl cover for warped surfaces with a straight edge.

7. Closely inspect the valves and seats for wear and damage, replacing as necessary.

8. After the carburetor is assembled, check the choke valve for freedom of operation.

Carburetor overhaul kits are recommended for each overhaul. These kits contain all gaskets and new parts to replace those that deteriorate most rapidly. Failure to replace all parts supplied with the kit (especially gaskets) can result in poor performance later.

After cleaning and checking all components, reassemble the carburetor, using new parts and referring to the exploded view. When reassembling, make sure that all screws and jets are tight in their seats, but do not overtighten as the tips will be distorted. Tighten all screws gradually, in rotation. Do not tighten needle valves into their seats; uneven jetting will result. Always use new gaskets. Be sure to adjust the float level, following the instructions contained in the rebuilding kit, when reassembling.

Fast Idle Adjustment

1. Start the engine and open the throttle valve about 45 degrees. Manually close the choke valve and slowly return the throttle valve to the stop position.

2. With a tachometer, check that the fast idle speed is 2,000 rpm or lower (not less than 1700 rpm). Adjust the speed as necessary with the fast idle speed screw.

3. Cold start the engine and check the automatic choke and fast idle operation.

Automatic Choke Adjustment

The choke case has five small projections. Align the center projection with the yellow punch mark of the bimetal case.

MANUAL TRANSMISSION

Four and Five Speed

REMOVAL AND INSTALLATION

1. Disconnect the battery ground cable, remove the air cleaner and the starter.

2. Remove the top transmission mounting bolts from the bell housing.

3. From inside the vehicle, raise the console assembly, if equipped, or the carpet and remove the dust cover retaining plate at the shift lever.

4. Place the four speed transmission in second gear and the five speed transmission in first gear. Remove the control lever assembly.

5. Raise the vehicle and support it safely. Drain the transmission. Disconnect the speedometer and the back up light switch.

6. Remove the drive shaft, exhaust pipe, and the clutch cable.

7. Support the transmission and remove the engine rear support bracket.

8. Remove the bell housing cover and bolts, move the transmission rearward, and lower it carefully to the floor. Remove the transmission from under the vehicle.

9. To install the transmission, reverse the removal procedure. Make sure the transmission is in the proper gear before installing the gear shift lever.

OVERHAUL

NOTE: Proper transmission overhaul requires the use of certain special tools. If these are not available, the job should not be undertaken.

4-Speed

1. Remove the undercover.

2. Remove the backup light switch. Be careful not to lose the steel ball.

3. Remove the speedometer gear sleeve clamp and remove the speedometer driven gear and sleeve assembly from the extension housing assembly.

4. Remove the extension housing bolts. Turn the shift lever to the left and pull off the extension housing.

5. Loosen the three poppet plugs, then remove the three poppet springs and the three steel balls.

6. Place the 1st–2nd speed shift rod in Neutral position.

7. Remove the reverse shift rail and fork assembly together with the reverse idler gear.

8. Using a 3/16 in. punch, drive off the 3rd–4th and 1st–2nd speed shift fork spring pins. Push each shift rod toward the rear of the transmission case and remove the shift forks. Remember to remove the interlock plunger.

9. Remove the snap-ring from the rear end of the counter gear and then remove the reverse counter gear.

10. Unlock the main shaft lock nut and remove the lock nut. The lock nut can be loosened by double-engaging the 3rd speed gear and the 1st speed gear.

11. Remove the reverse gear from the main shaft.

12. Remove the five attaching screws and then remove the rear bearing retainer.

13. Remove the front bearing retainer.

14. With the counter gear pressed to the rear, remove the rear bearing snap-ring. Then using a bearing puller remove the rear counter bearing.

15. Remove the snap-ring from the front counter bearing. Pull off the bearing with a bearing puller.

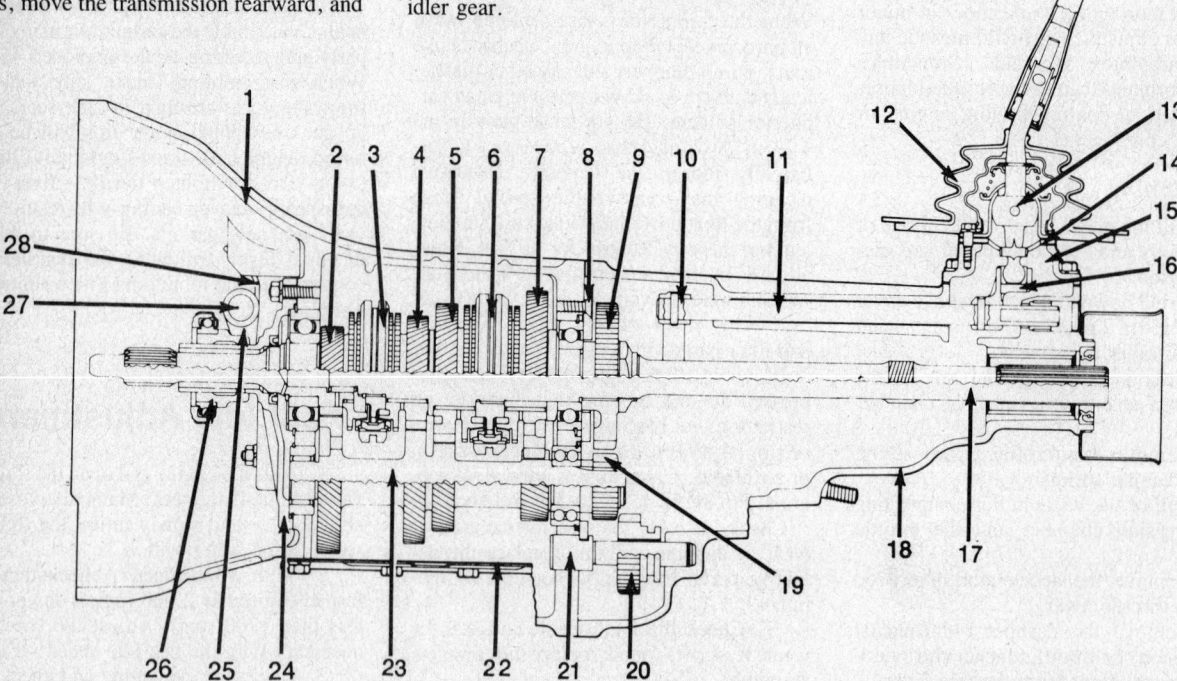

Cross section of four speed transmission

1. Transmission case
2. Main drive pinion
3. Synchronizer assy (3-4 speed)
4. 3rd speed gear
5. 2nd speed gear
6. Synchronizer assy (1-2 speed)
7. 1st speed gear
8. Rear bearing retainer
9. Reverse gear
10. Control finger
11. Control shaft
12. Control lever cover
13. Control level assy
14. Stopper plate
15. Control housing
16. Change shifter
17. Mainshaft
18. Extension housing
19. Counter reverse gear
20. Reverse idler gear
21. Reverse idler gear shaft
22. Under cover
23. Counter gear
24. Front bearing retainer
25. Clutch shift arm
26. Release bearing carrier
27. Clutch control shaft
28. Return spring

16. Pull the counter gear out of the case.

17. Remove the main drive pinion from the front of the case. To remove the bearing from the main drive pinion, remove the two snap-rings and then remove the bearing with a bearing puller.

18. Remove the mainshaft bearing snap-ring and remove the bearing using a dual post bearing puller (D-50/Plymouth Arrow special tool MD998056-10 and MD998056).

19. Remove the main shaft assembly by lifting it up through the case.

20. Disassemble the mainshaft assembly in the following order.

   a. Pull off the 1st speed gear, the 1st–2nd speed synchronizer and the 2nd speed gear toward the rear of the mainshaft.

   b. Remove the snap-ring from the forward end of the mainshaft, then remove the 3rd–4th speed synchronizer and the 3rd speed gear.

21. If removing the shift control shaft assembly, remove the pin locking the gear shifter using a ³⁄₁₆ in. punch. To remove the lock pin, press the gear shifter forward and drive the lock pin off, being careful not to bend the control shaft.

Inspect the parts after cleaning. Replace any worn, damaged or defective.

Assembly is as follows.

22. If the main drive pinion bearing has been removed, replace it using a pipe fit over the end of the pinion shaft.

CAUTION

Make sure the pipe does not apply pressure on the ball bearings but only on the bearing race, or bearing damage could result.

23. Fit a snap-ring which gives a clearance of no more than 0–0.002 in. and install it on the drive pinion.

24. Assemble the main shaft in the following order.

   a. Assemble the 3rd–4th speed and the 1st–2nd speed synchronizers. The front and rear ends of the synchronizer sleeve and hub can be identified as shown in the illustration. The synchronizer spring is installed as shown.

   b. Install the needle bearing, 3rd speed gear, synchronizer ring and the 3rd–4th speed synchronizer assembly onto the mainshaft from the front end. Be careful not to confuse the front and the rear of the synchronizer assembly.

25. Select and install a snap-ring that will give the 3rd–4th speed synchronizer hub an end-play from 0.0 to 0.003 in.

26. Third speed gear end-play should be from 0.002 to 0.008 in.

27. Install the needle bearing, the 2nd speed gear, the synchronizer assembly, the bearing sleeve, the needle bearing, the 1st speed gear, and the bearing spacer onto the mainshaft from the rear end.

28. Push the bearing spacer forward and check the 1st and 2nd speed gear end play. Clearance should be within 0.002–0.008 in.

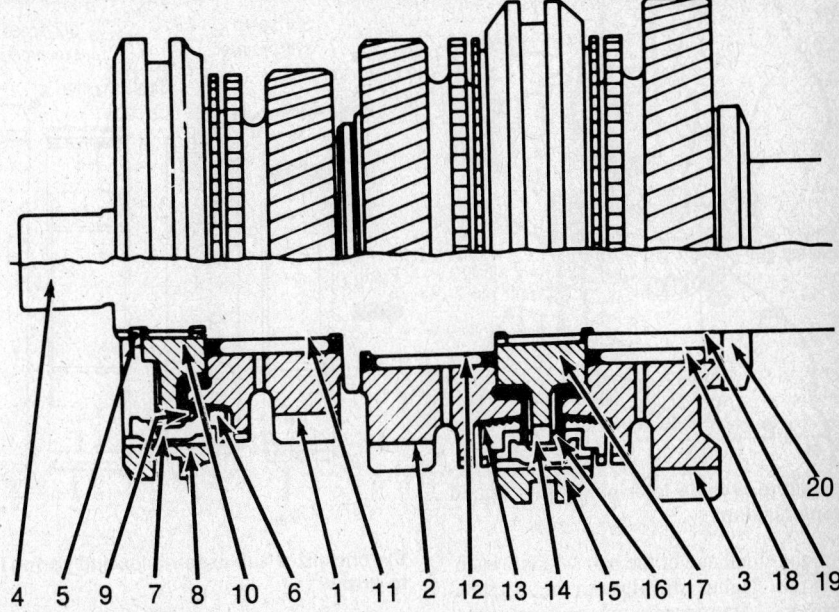

Mainshaft assembly—four and five speed transmissions

1. 3rd speed gear
2. 2nd speed gear
3. 1st speed gear
4. Mainshaft
5. Snap ring
6. Synchronizer ring (3-4 speed)
7. Synchronizer piece
8. Synchronizer sleeve (3-4 speed)
9. Synchronizer spring (3-4 speed)
10. Synchronizer hub (3-4 speed)
11. Needle bearing (3rd speed gear)
12. Needle bearing (2nd speed gear)
13. Synchronizer ring (1-2 speed)
14. Synchronizer piece
15. Synchronizer sleeve (1-2 speed)
16. Synchronizer spring (1-2 speed)
17. Synchronizer hub (1-2 speed)
18. Needle bearing (1st speed gear)
19. 1st gear bearing sleeve
20. Bearing spacer

29. Insert the mainshaft assembly into the transmission case and fit the mainshaft center bearing using a bearing driver. Hold the forward end of the mainshaft by hand at the front of the case.

30. Install the needle bearing and the synchronizer ring, then insert the main drive pinion assembly into the case from the front.

31. Insert the countershaft gear into the case. With a snap-ring fitted to the countershaft front needle bearing, drive the bearing into the case by hammering on the outer race of the bearing.

32. Fit a snap-ring to the countershaft rear ball bearing and then install the bearing with a bearing installer.

33. Install the front bearing retainer. When installing the retainer, install a spacer that will give a clearance (C) of 0.0–0.004 in. (see illustration). Apply sealant to both sides of the front bearing retainer packing and apply gear oil to the oil seal lip. Install packing and oil seal.

34. Install the rear bearing retainer and its five screws. It is suggested that each screw head be staked with a pointed punch to prevent them from coming loose.

35. Install the reverse gear on the mainshaft and tighten the lock nut to 73–94 ft. lbs. Lock the nut at the notch of the mainshaft.

36. Install the spacer and counter reverse gear to the counter gear rear end.

37. Install a snap-ring of the proper size so that the reverse counter gear and play will be from 0.0 to 0.003 in.

38. Install the 3rd–4th and 1st–2nd speed shift forks into their respective synchronizer sleeves. Insert each shift rod from the rear of the case. Lock the shift forks and rod with spring pins, install the interlock plunger between the shift rods.

NOTE: The spring pins should be installed with the slits parallel to the shift rod.

39. Install the reverse shift rod and fork assembly together with the reverse idler gear.

40. Insert the ball and poppet spring

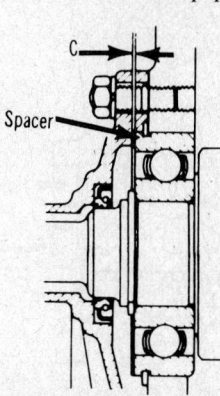

Retainer-to-bearing clearance adjustment

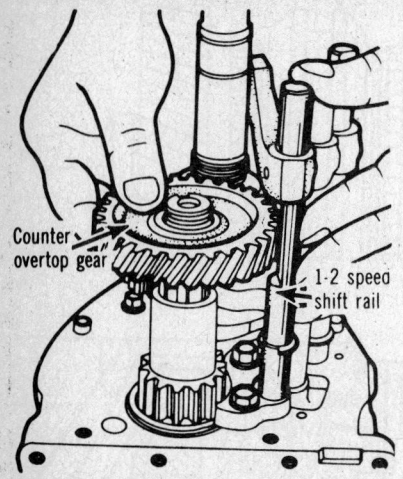

Installing reverse idler gear—four speed transmission

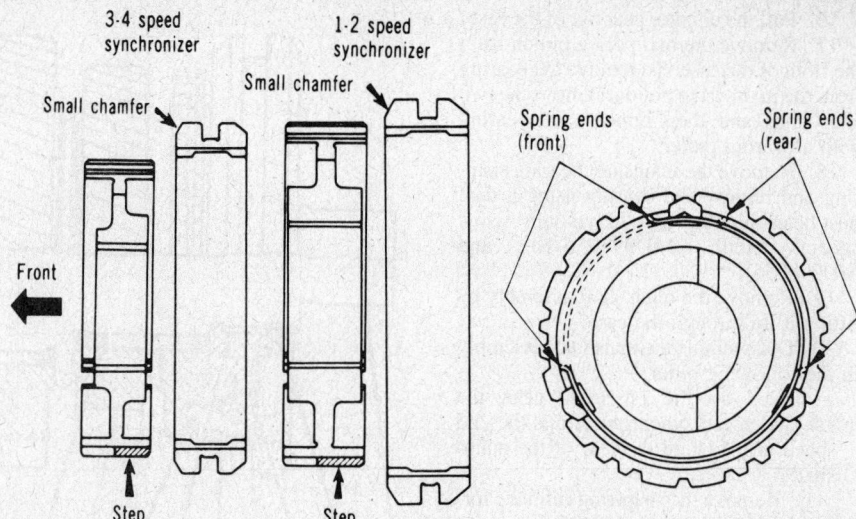

Synchronizer hub assemblies and spring installation. Note direction of hubs in relation to arrow

with the small end of the ball side into each shift rod. Tighten the plugs to the specified positions. After installation, seal each plug head with sealant.

41. Apply sealant to both sides of the extension housing packing and fit the packing into the housing.

42. Turn the gear shift control down to the left and install the extension to the transmission case.

43. Make sure the forward end of the control finger is snug in the slot of the shift lug and fit the extension housing bolts after coating their threads with sealant.

44. Apply gear oil to the speedometer driven gear and install the gear and sleeve assembly in the extension housing. Make sure the sleeve flange and its mating areas on the extension housing are free of dirt, or it will cause the gears to be misaligned and could damage them.

45. Rotate the speedometer driven gear and sleeve assembly so that the number on the sleeve, which is the same as the number of teeth on the gear, is in the "U" mark position as the assembly is installed.

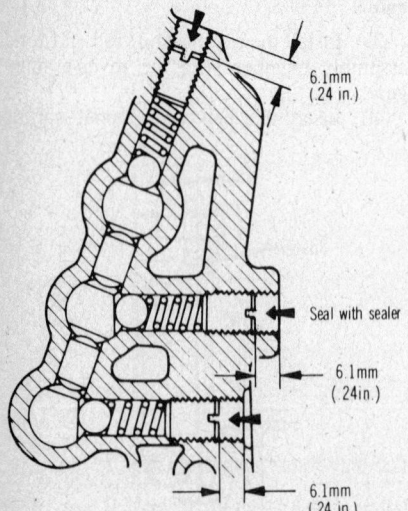

Installing poppet spring and plug assembly—four and five speed transmissions

46. Install the speedometer gear clamp with its tongs in the sleeve positioning slots.

47. Install the backup light switch with its steel ball.

48. Refit the under cover and torque the bolts to 6–7 ft. lbs.

49. Install the transmission control lever assembly and fill the gear shifter area with grease. Fill the transmission with lubricant.

5 Speed

1. Drain the oil and remove the case cover.

2. Remove the backup light switch and ball.

3. Remove the extension housing attaching bolts, back off the plug of the neutral return plunger, turn the shift lever down to the left and pull off the extension housing.

4. Remove the snap-ring and speedometer drive gear.

5. Remove the snap-ring and mainshaft rear bearing.

6. Remove the three plugs and remove the poppet springs and balls.

7. Remove the 1–2 and 3–4 shift fork pins with a 3/16" punch. Pull each rail toward the rear of the case and remove the forks and interlock plunger.

8. In the same manner, remove the 5th-reverse forks.

9. Engage the reverse and 2nd gears and remove the mainshaft and countershaft rear locknuts.

10. Remove the 5th counter gear and bearing with a puller. Remove the spacer and reverse counter gear.

11. Remove the 5th gear and sleeve from the mainshaft. Remove the 5th synchronizer and spacer.

12. Remove the cotter pin, nut and reverse idler gear.

13. Remove the rear bearing retainer.

14. Drive the reverse idler gear shaft from the case.

15. Remove the front bearing retainer.

16. Press the countergear to the rear and remove the rear bearing snap-ring.

17. Using a puller, remove the counter rear bearing.

18. Remove the snap-ring and pull the counter front bearing. Remove the countergear from the case.

19. Remove the main drive pinion from the case.

20. Remove the two snap-rings and pull the bearing.

21. Remove the snap-ring and pull the mainshaft bearing.

22. Remove the mainshaft from the case.

23. Disassemble the mainshaft.

24. Disassemble the extension housing. To assemble:

25. Install the bearing on the main drive pinion and select a snap-ring which will give a clearance of 0–0.0024 in. between the snap-ring and the bearing.

26. Assemble the mainshaft. Use a spacer which will give a 3–4 synchronizer end play of 0–0.003". Use a snap-ring which will give a 1–2 gear end play of 0.002–0.008".

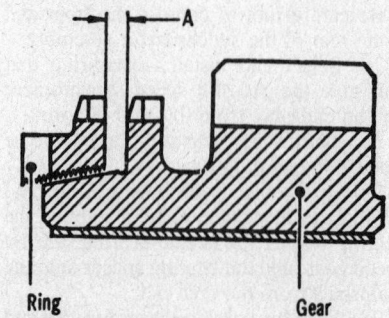

Synchronizer ring to gear clearance: "A" equals 0.032 in. on both four and five speed transmissions

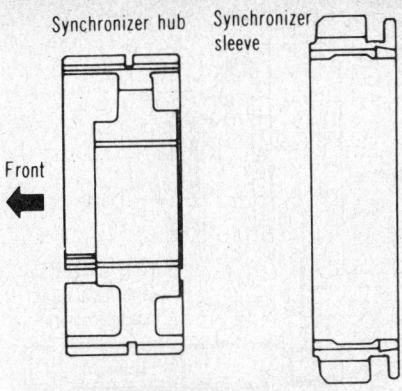

Fifth speed (overdrive) synchronizer hub installation direction

27. Insert the mainshaft into the case and drive in the center bearing.

28. Install the needle bearing and synchronizer ring, then insert the main drive pinion into the case from the front.

29. Insert the countershaft gear into the case.

30. Install the snap-ring on the countershaft front needle bearing and drive the bearing into the case by hammering the outer race.

31. Install the snap-ring on the countershaft rear bearing and install it in place.

32. Install the front bearing retainer using a spacer which will give clearance of 0–0.004″ between the bearing and retainer.

33. Install the front retainer oil seal.

34. Install the rear retainer.

35. Install the reverse idler gear shaft.

36. Install the needle bearing, reverse idler gear and thrust washer. Tighten the locknut and install the cotter pin. Idler gear end play should be 0.0047–0.0110″. If not, replace the thrust washer.

37. Assemble the 5th synchronizer.

38. Install the spacer, stop plate and 5th synchronizer assembly, the 5th gear bearing sleeve and needle bearing, the synchronizer ring and 5th gear, in that order, to the mainshaft from the rear. 5th gear end play should be 0.004–0.010″.

39. Install the spacer, counter reverse gear spacer, counter 5th gear and the ball bearing onto the countershaft gear from the rear. Tighten and lock the nut.

40. Insert the 3–4 and 1–2 forks into their synchronizer sleeves. Insert each shift rail from the rear of the case. Install the spring pins and interlock plunger.

NOTE: The slit in the pins should be parallel with the rail.

41. Insert the ball and poppet spring into each shift rail. Tighten the plugs flush with the case.

42. Install the ball bearing on the rear of the mainshaft.

43. Install the speedometer drive gear.

44. Turn the shifter down and to the left and install the extension housing.

45. Install the neutral return plungers, spring, and resistance spring and ball. Tighten the plugs flush with the case.

46. Install the speedometer driven gear sleeve and lock plate.

47. Install the backup light switch and ball.

48. Install the bottom cover and torque the bolts to 6–7 ft. lbs.

49. Install the control lever assembly.

CLUTCH

Clutch Cable

REMOVAL AND INSTALLATION

1. Loosen the cable adjusting wheel inside the engine compartment.

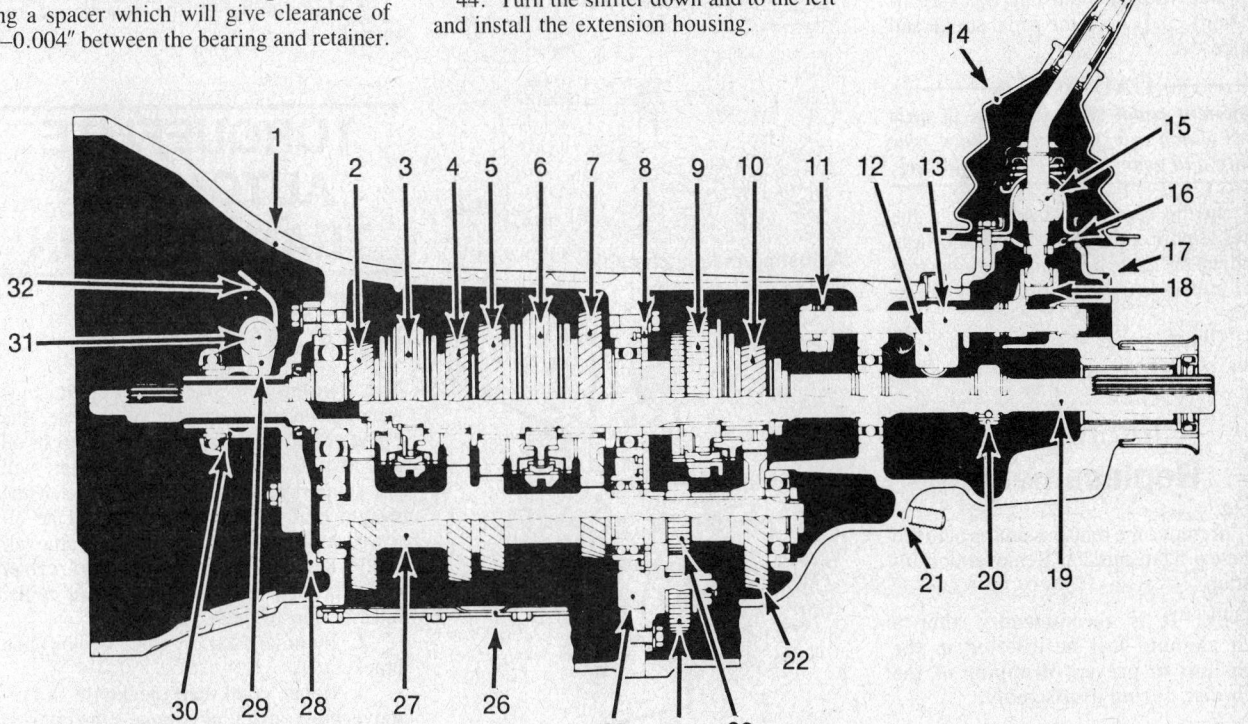

Cross section of five speed transmission

1. Transmission case
2. Main drive pinion
3. Synchronizer assy (3-4 speed)
4. 3rd speed gear
5. 2nd speed gear
6. Synchronizer assy (1-2 speed)
7. 1st speed gear
8. Rear bearing retainer
9. Synchronizer assy (overdrive)
10. Overdrive gear
11. Control finger
12. Neutral return finger
13. Control shaft
14. Control lever cover
15. Control lever assy
16. Stopper plate
17. Control housing
18. Change shifter
19. Mainshaft
20. Speedometer drive gear
21. Extension housing
22. Counter overdrive gear
23. Counter reverse gear
24. Reverse idler gear
25. Reverse idler gear shaft
26. Under cover
27. Counter gear
28. Front bearing retainer
29. Clutch shift arm
30. Release bearing carrier
31. Clutch control shaft
32. Return spring

PEDAL HEIGHT ADJUSTMENT

Description	Standard valve mm (in.)	
	U-engine	W-engine
Distance A	22 (.9)	20 (.8)
Pedal height	166 (6.5)	176 (6.9)
Pedal stroke	140 (5.5)	150 (5.9)

2. Loosen the clutch pedal adjusting bolt locknut and loosen the adjusting bolt.

3. Remove the cable end from the clutch throwout lever.

4. Remove the cable end from the clutch pedal.

5. Installation is the reverse of removal.

NOTE: Apply engine oil to the cable before replacing. Make sure the isolating pad is fitted on the cable after installation to keep the cable from rubbing the motor mount during operation.

Adjustment

PEDAL HEIGHT

1. Adjust the pedal height to the standard value with the adjusting bolt (see illustration), and check the pedal stroke and distance "A".

————— CAUTION —————
Insufficient pedal stroke results in only partial clutch release, causing hard gear shifting and gear grinding when shifting.

2. In the engine compartment, at the fire wall, pull out the clutch cable a little and adjust the cable by turning the adjusting wheel until it is 0.12–0.16 in from the insulator.

3. Clutch pedal free play should be within 0.8–1.4 in.

Clutch Disc Replacement

1. Remove the transmission as outlined in Manual Transmission Removal and Installation.

NOTE: It is recommended that a clutch aligning tool be inserted in the clutch hub to prevent dropping of the clutch disc during disassembly.

2. Remove pressure plate bolts, pressure plate and clutch disc.

3. From inside the transmission bell housing, remove the return spring clip and remove the release bearing assembly.

4. If necessary, remove the release control lever and spring pin with a 3/16 inch punch. Remove the control lever shaft assembly and clutch shift arm, two felt packings and two return springs.

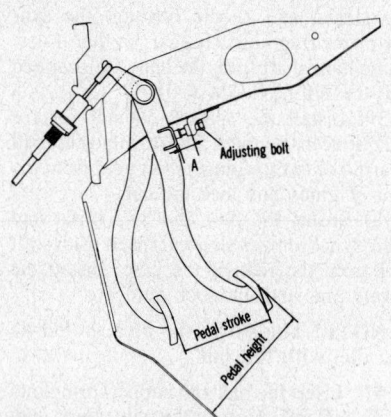

Adjusting clutch pedal height

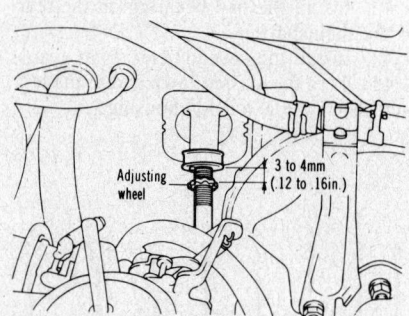

Adjusting the clutch cable

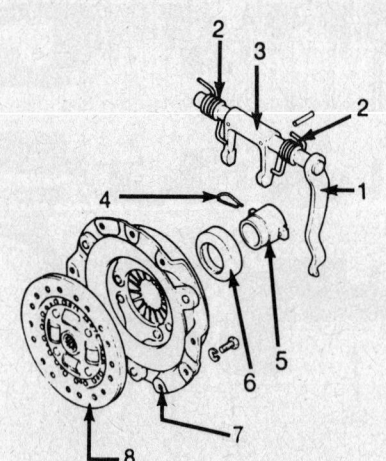

Exploded view of clutch assembly

1. Clutch control shaft
2. Return spring
3. Clutch shift arm
4. Return clip
5. Release bearing carrier
6. Release bearing
7. Pressure plate assembly
8. Clutch disc

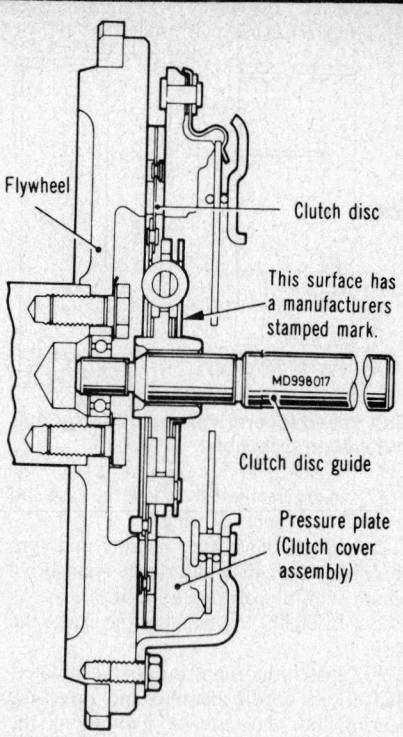

Installing the clutch disc—use clutch disc guide as shown

5. Installation is the reverse of removal.

TORQUEFLITE AUTOMATIC TRANSMISSION

REMOVAL AND INSTALLATION

The transmission and converter must be removed as an assembly; otherwise, the converter drive plate, pump bushing, or oil seal may be damaged. The drive plate will not support a load; therefore, none of the weight of the transmission should be allowed to rest on the plate during removal.

1. Disconnect battery ground cable, drain the transmission, and remove cooler lines at transmission.

2. Remove starter and cooler line bracket.

3. Rotate crankshaft clockwise and remove bolts attaching torque converter to drive plate.

4. Remove the driveshaft.

5. Disconnect gearshift rod and torque shaft.

6. Disconnect throttle rod from lever at the left side of transmission. Remove linkage bellcrank from transmission if so equipped.

7. Remove the oil filler tube and speedometer cable.

8. Support the rear of the engine with jack.

9. Raise transmission slightly.

10. Remove crossmember.

11. Remove all bell housing bolts.

12. Carefully work transmission converter assembly rearward off engine block dowels and disengage converter hub from end of crankshaft. Attach a small C-clamp to edge of bell housing to hold converter in place during transmission removal.

13. Remove transmission.

14. Installation is the reverse of removal.

Pan and Filter

REMOVAL AND INSTALLATION

1. Raise and support vehicle.

2. Loosen the pan bolts from one end to the other allowing the fluid to drain out.

3. Unbolt the old filter from the pan.

4. Clean the pan and install a new filter. Tighten filter bolts to 35 in. lbs.

5. Install the pan and new gasket. Torque pan bolts to 6–9 ft. lbs.

6. Add four quarts of Dexron fluid, start the engine and move the lever through all positions, pausing momentarily in each. Add enough fluid to bring the level to the full mark on the dipstick.

Adjustments

THROTTLE LINKAGE

The throttle rod adjustment is very important to proper transmission operation. This adjustment positions a valve which controls shift speed, shift quality and part throttle-down shift sensitivity. If the setting is too short, early shifts and slippage between shifts may occur. If the setting is too long, shifts may be delayed and part throttle-down shifts may be very sensitive.

To adjust the throttle rod:

1. Warm up the engine until it reaches the normal operating temperature. With the

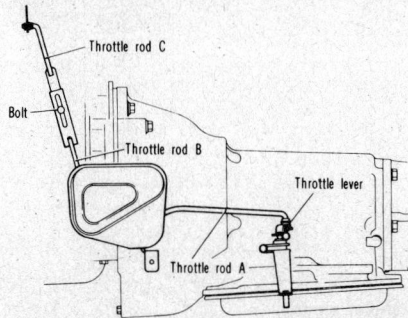

Throttle rod adjustment—automatic transmission

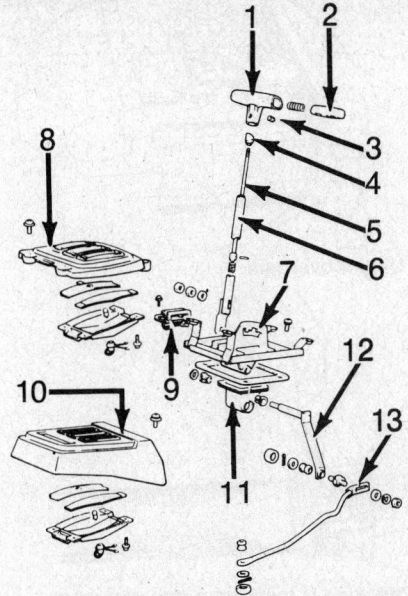

Exploded view of automatic transmission shift control

1. Selector handle
2. Push button
3. Set screw
4. Rod adjusting cam
5. Selector lever rod
6. Selector lever
7. Detent plate
8. Position indicator cover (for sports)
9. Inhibitor switch
10. Position indicator cover
11. Lever bracket cover
12. Control cover
13. Control rod

carburetor automatic choke disengaged from the fast idle cam, adjust the engine idle speed by rotating speed adjusting screw (SAS). See "Tune-up Procedures" at the beginning of this section.

2. Loosen the bolts on the linkage so that both rod "B" and "C" can slide properly.

3. Lightly push rod "A" or the transmission throttle lever and rod "C" toward the idle stopper, and set the rods to the idle position. Tighten the bolt securely that connects rods "B" and "C".

4. Make sure that when the carburetor throttle valve is wide-open, the transmission throttle lever smoothly moves from the IDLE to the WIDE OPEN position (from 47.5° to 54°), and that there is some range in the lever stroke.

5. Also make sure that when the throttle linkage alone is slowly returned from the fully closed position, the transmission throttle lever completely returns to *idle* by return spring force.

KICKDOWN BAND

The kickdown band adjusting screw is located on the left side of the transmission case.

1. Loosen locknut and back off approximately 5 turns. Test adjusting screw for free turning in the transmission case.

2. Tighten the adjusting screw to 72 in. lbs.

3. Back off adjusting screw 3 turns from step 2. Tighten the locknut to 35 ft. lbs.

LOW & REVERSE BAND

1. Raise vehicle, drain transmission fluid and remove the pan.

2. This transmission has an allen socket adjustment screw at the servo end of lever. After removing the locknut this screw is tightened to 41 in. lbs. torque then backed off 7½ turns. Tighten locknut to 30 ft. lbs.

3. Reinstall the pan.

NEUTRAL SAFETY SWITCH

1. When testing the safety switch, check to see if the switch has been properly installed. Move the selector lever into N position and adjust the switch by moving it so that the pin on the forward end of the rod assembly will be in the position near the lobe of detent plate and that this position will be at the front end of the range of N connection of the switch. Temporarily tighten the attaching screws. After adjusting the selection lever clearance to 0.059 in. securely tighten the screws.

2. Test the continuity of the switch circuit by using a test light with switch connector disconnected.

SHIFT LINKAGE ADJUSTMENT

To adjust the shift linkage, the control cover must be removed.

Removal and Installation

1. Remove the shift handle assembly from the lever.

2. Take the position indicator assembly out upward.

Remove the position indicator lamp.

3. Disconnect the control rod from the arm.

Remove the lever bracket assembly.

4. Installation is the reverse of removal.

If the proper turning effort (13–29 in. lbs.) is not obtained, adjust it by using a selective wave-washer of proper size.

CAUTION

When the turning effort at the pivot A is checked, the pin at the forward end of the rod assembly must not slide with the detent plate. If the arm is loose, the bushing should be replaced.

DRIVELINE

Driveshaft

REMOVAL AND INSTALLATION

1. Make mating marks on the flange yoke and the differential companion flange.
2. Remove the bolts connecting the flange yoke to the differential companion flange, and remove the nuts attaching the center bearing assembly.
3. Remove the propeller shaft by drawing it out. Installation is reverse of removal.

NOTE: When the sleeve yoke end of the propeller shaft is pulled out from the transmission extension housing, transmission oil will flow out it if the front of the truck is raised higher, than the rear.

——— CAUTION ———
When removing the propeller shaft, be careful not to damage the oil seal lip and see that no foreign substance is present in the lip area.

U-Joint Overhaul

1. Remove the bearing retainer snaprings from the flange yoke.
2. With a vise and suitable sockets, force one needle bearing cup outward from the yoke, using the cross as a ram.
3. Grasp the protruding bearing with pliers or vise grips and remove it from the yoke.
4. Reverse the sockets and again using the cross as a ram, force the opposite bearing outward from the yoke and remove it with pliers or vise grips.
5. Follow the same procedure to remove the remaining bearing in the yoke.
6. To install, place the cross in the yoke and start a bearing cup into the yoke collar, engaging the cross arm.
7. With the aid of a vise, force the bearing cup into the yoke collar until it bottoms. Install the opposite bearing cup in the same manner.

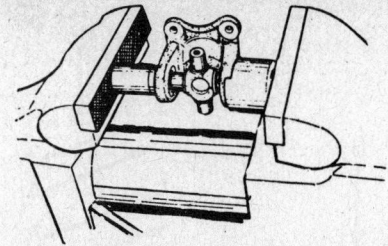

U-joint overhaul

Checking U-joint snap-ring clearance

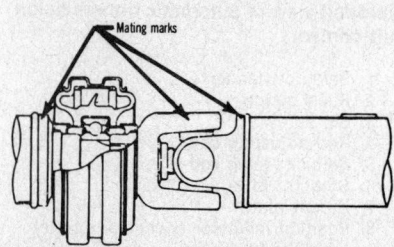

When installing center bearing align three mating marks

NOTE: Sockets may be used to force the bearing cup inward so that the retaining snap-rings can be installed.

8. Different thickness snap-rings are used to control the clearance between the bearing and the snap-ring.
9. Install a snap-ring and measure the clearance with a feeler gauge. Replace the snap-ring with one of the proper thickness

to have a total clearance tolerance of .000 to .001 inch.
Snap-ring selection range:
No color—0.0504 inch
Yellow—0.0561 inch
Blue—0.0528 inch
Purple—0.0539 inch

NOTE: When snap-rings are installed, press each bearing towards the opposite side to measure the maximum clearance.

Center Bearing

REMOVAL AND INSTALLATION

1. Remove driveshaft.
2. Disconnect the center universal joint.
3. Remove the nut holding the center yoke and remove the yoke. Remove the center bearing bracket from the bearing by prying on it.
4. Remove the center bearing using a gear puller.

NOTE: The center bracket and the mounting rubber are welded together and must be replaced as a unit.

To assemble:
5. Fill the bearing grease cavity with multipurpose grease.
6. Partially insert the center bearing into the shaft and install the bracket to the bearing.
7. Verify that the bracket mounting rubber is properly fitted in the bearing groove.
8. Refit the center yoke, making sure you align the notch on the yoke with the notch on the front propeller shaft. Replace

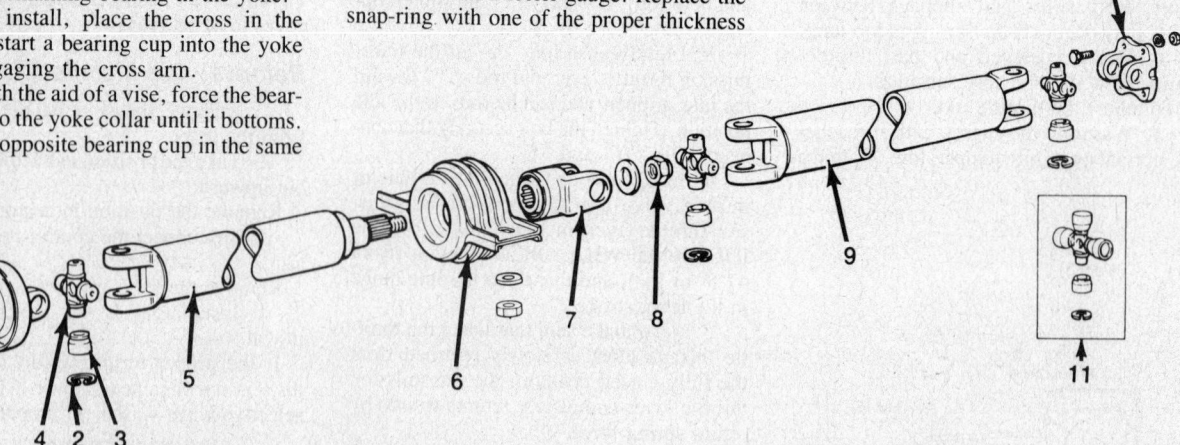

Exploded view of driveshaft

1. Sleeve yoke
2. Snap ring
3. Needle bearing
4. Universal joint journal
5. Front propeller shaft
6. Center bearing assembly
7. Center yoke
8. Center yoke attaching nut
9. Rear propeller shaft
10. Propeller shaft flange yoke
11. Universal joint journal kit

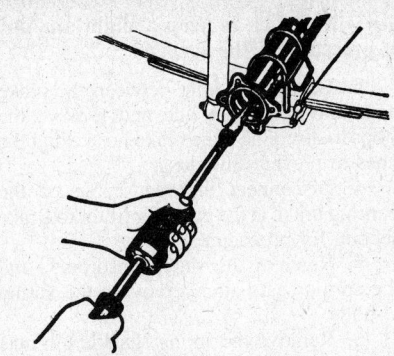

Removing the oil seal

the attaching nut and tighten to 116–159 ft. lbs.

9. Replace the center universal joint, making sure you align the notch on the rear propeller shaft with the notch on the yoke.

10. Install the driveshaft.

NOTE: The manufacturer suggests that a new center yoke locking nut be used when the center bearing is removed.

DRIVE AXLE

Axle Shaft, Bearing and Seal

REMOVAL AND INSTALLATION

1. Jack up the vehicle and support it on stands.

2. Remove the rear wheels and brake drums.

3. Disconnect the brake line from the wheel cylinder and plug it to prevent fluid loss.

4. Remove the four nuts behind the brake backing plate holding the bearing case to the axle housing assembly.

5. Remove the braking plate, bearing case and the axle shaft as an assembly.

NOTE: It may be necessary to use a slide hammer to remove the assembly.

6. Remove the O-ring and the bearing preload shims. Save the preload shims, as you will need them for reassembly.

7. Remove the oil seal with a hooked slide hammer.

8. To remove the axle shaft bearing, remove the notched locknut. This calls for a special tool, but you should be able to use a brass drift to knock it loose.

9. Remove the lock washer and plain washer.

10. Screw the lock nut back on to the axle shaft about three turns.

11. It will be necessary to fabricate a metal plate that fits over the axle shaft and butts the lock nut. Drill four holes in the plate that align with the four bearing case studs and fit the plate. Refit two nuts and washers to the bearing case studs diagonally across from each other and tighten them evenly to free the bearing case and the bearing.

12. Use a hammer and drift to remove the bearing outer race from the bearing case.

13. Remove the outer oil seal from the bearing case.

To assemble:

NOTE: Always use new O-rings and check the condition of all oil seals and dust covers.

14. Apply grease to the outer surface on

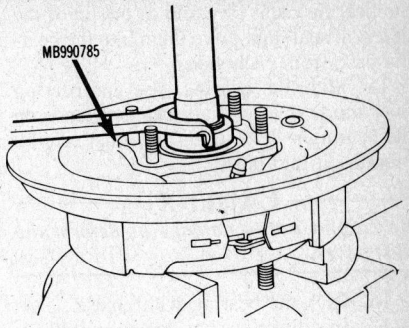

Removing axle shaft locknut

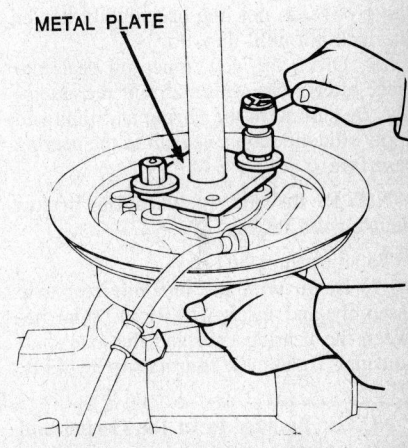

Removing axle bearing-fabricate metal plate indicated in picture

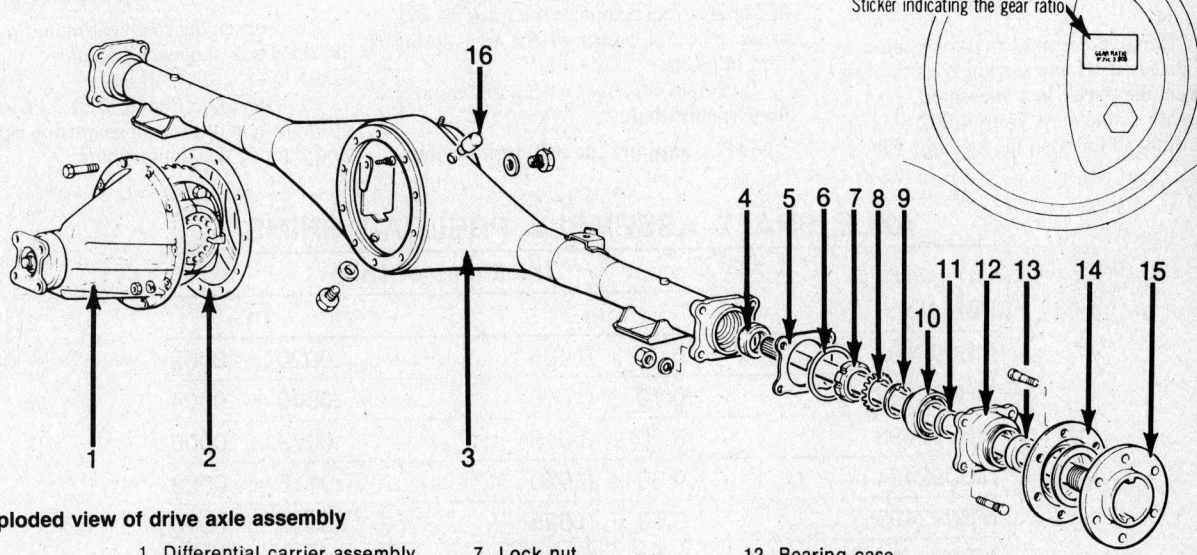

Exploded view of drive axle assembly

1. Differential carrier assembly	7. Lock nut
2. Packing	8. Lock washer
3. Rear axle housing	9. Washer
4. Rear axle shaft oil seal (Inner)	10. Rear axle shaft bearing
5. Shim	11. Collar
6. O-ring	

12. Bearing case	
13. Rear axle shaft oil seal (Outer)	
14. Dust cover	
15. Rear axle shaft	
16. Air breather	

the bearing outer race and to the lip of the outer oil seal, and drive them into the bearing case from each side.

15. Slide the bearing case and bearing over the rear axle shaft. Apply grease on the bearing rollers and fit the inner race by pressing it into place.

— **CAUTION** —

Be careful not to damage or deform the dust cover.

16. Pack the bearing with grease.

17. Install the washer, the crowned lock washer and the lock nut in the order just given and tighten the lock nut to 130–159 ft. lbs. if possible.

18. Bend the tab on the lock washer into the groove on the lock nut. If the tab and the groove do not line up, slightly tighten the lock nut until they do.

19. Drive the new inner oil seal into place after greasing it and refit the assembly. Be sure to fit the O-ring and shim and apply silicone rubber sealant to the bearing case face.

NOTE: Be sure to bleed the brakes before road testing!

To adjust preload:

1. Begin with the left side rear axle assembly and insert a 0.04 in. shim between the bearing case and the axle shaft housing. Tighten the four nuts to 36–43 ft. lbs.

NOTE: Be sure to fit the O-ring and apply sealant.

2. Install the right side axle assembly into the right side housing without its shim and O-ring. Tighten the four nuts to 0.4 ft. lbs.

3. Using a flat blade feeler gauge, measure the gap between the bearing case and the axle housing face. It should range between 0.002–0.008 in. Record the measurement.

4. Remove the axle shaft and select a shim that is the same thickness as the gap between the faces just measured, plus a shim with a thickness from 0.002–0.0079 in. and install them on the housing. Fit the

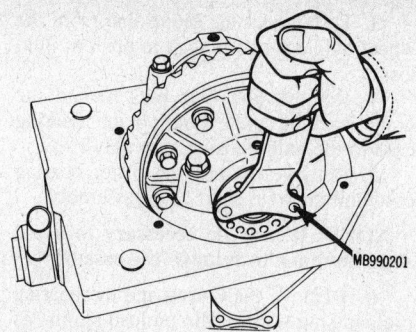

Removing side bearing nuts with special spanner

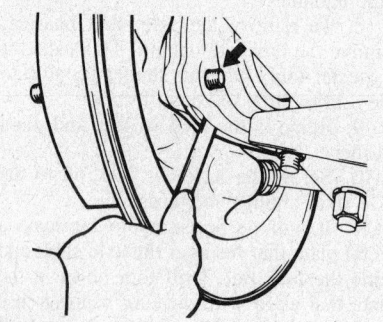

Measuring clearance between bearing case and axle housing face

O-ring and apply sealant. Fit the axle assembly and tighten the four nuts to 36–43 ft. lbs.

5. Assemble remaining components. Be sure to bleed the brakes.

Rear Axle Assembly

REMOVAL AND INSTALLATION

1. Loosen the rear wheel hub nuts and jack up the truck. Support the truck on jack stands placed forward of the rear spring front brackets.

2. Remove the rear wheels and remove the propeller shaft.

NOTE: Support the differential hous-

ing with a jack to keep a slight amount of pressure on the springs.

3. Loosen the joint between the brake hose and the brake line and remove the stops to disconnect the brake hose. Plug the lines to prevent fluid loss.

4. Disconnect the rear cable of the parking brake at the balancer (refer to Brake section for procedure.)

5. Remove the shock absorbers, and the spring seats after removing the spring U-bolts.

6. Remove the spring shackle pin nuts and the shackle plate.

— **CAUTION** —

The axle assembly will be supported solely by the jack under the differential case. Be careful not to allow it to drop.

7. With an assistant holding the axle assembly, slowly lower it to the ground.

Installation is the reverse of removal. Bleed the brakes after assembly.

OVERHAUL

Differential overhaul requires many special tools and access to a range of preload shims and other dealer equipment. If you have never overhauled a rear axle assembly before, it would be wise to let your dealer perform this operation for you.

1. Remove the lock bolts and plates holding the side bearing nut in place.

2. Remove the side bearing nuts with the special adjusting spanner no. MB990201.

3. Remove the carrier caps and pry out the differential.

4. Pull off the differential side bearings.

NOTE: Be sure to keep the right and left bearings and shims separated.

5. Loosen the ring gear mounting bolts in diagonal sequence. Remove the ring gear.

6. Drive the pinion shaft lock pin out from the rear of the ring gear using a punch, and remove the pinion shaft.

AXLE SHAFT ASSEMBLY PRELOAD SHIMS

Part No.	Thickness of shim	
	mm	in.
MB092491	0.05 ± 0.005	.0020 ± .0002
MB092492	0.10 ± 0.010	.0040 ± .0004
MB092493	0.20 ± 0.015	.0079 ± .0006
MB092494	0.30 ± 0.020	.0118 ± .0008
MB092495	0.50 ± 0.025	.0197 ± .0010
MB092496	1.00 ± 0.040	.0394 ± .0016
MB092497	1.50 ± 0.050	.0591 ± .0020
MB092498	2.00 ± 0.055	.0787 ± .0022

1. Self-locking nut
2. Washer
3. End yoke (companion flange)
4. Dust cover
5. Oil seal
6. Drive pinion bearing, front
7. Preload adjusting shim
8. Gear carrier
9. Carrier cap
10. Drive pinion spacer

Exploded view of rear end drive gears

11. Drive pinion bearing, rear	15. Side gear thrust spacer	19. Pinion gear	23. Final gear set
12. Drive pinion height adjusting shim	16. Side gear	20. Pinion washer	24. Differential case
13. Side bearing nut	17. Center block	21. Lock pin	25. Lock bolt
14. Side bearing	18. Pinion shaft	22. Packing	26. Lock plate

7. Remove the side gears with their spacers. Keep left and right side gears and spacers separate.

8. Hold the end yoke and remove the pinion lock nut.

9. Remove the end yoke.

10. Tap the end of the drive pinion shaft with a plastic hammer and force out the drive pinion along with its adjusting shim, the rear inner race, the drive pinion spacer and the preload adjusting shim. The rear bearing inner race can be pressed off the pinion shaft.

11. Remove the front and rear pinion bearing outer races. The front race should be removed with its oil seal.

NOTE: Do not reuse the old oil seal. If the unit is to be assembled using no replacement parts except oil seals, the same spacers and shims can generally be used. If either pinion bearing or ring gear and drive pinion are being replaced, new shims should be used. Only replace the drive pinion and ring gear in matched sets.

Assemble the side gears in the differential case. Install the spacers in the same positions they were in when removed.

12. With the washers, insert both differential gears at the same time to mesh with the side gears. Insert the pinion shaft.

13. Measure the backlash of the differential pinion gears and the side gears. Backlash should be within 0.002–0.005 in. If not, replace the side gear spacers with the appropriate ones listed below.

14. Align the differential drive pinion shaft with the lock pin hole in the differential case and drive the pin in from the

rear of the case. Stake the pin with a small pointed punch to secure it.

15. Remove the old adhesive from the ring gear mounting bolts and apply new adhesive. Snug up all bolts then tighten them on a criss-cross pattern of 58–65 ft. lbs.

NOTE: To allow the adhesive to set on the bolt threads, keep the unit stationary for about an hour.

16. Press the front and rear bearing outer races into the gear carrier.

--- **CAUTION** ---
Make sure that the races do not tilt and that they sit fully in the case.

Look at the top face of the drive pinion (gear side). If there is an etched number, such as −0, −1, −2, +1, +2, etc., complete step 17. If not, skip step 17 and go on to step 18.

17. Insert a shim between the drive pinion and rear bearing. If the original gear set is being replaced, the original shims may be used. If a new gear set is being installed, calculate the shim dimension in the following manner. Assuming the pinion height before disassembly is correct, subtract the new pinion variation marking (on the pinion head) from the old pinion variation marking. If the answer is positive, add shims in the corresponding amount. If the answer is negative, subract shims in the corresponding amount. This will produce a reasonable starting point for assembly. If the shim choice is proved incorrect, the entire pinion must be disassembled, and the shim changed accordingly. The etched marking on the face of the pinion represents

a positive or negative variation from the standard in millimeters.

NOTE: If the original gear set is being reused in the differential case, the original shims may be used.

18. If the drive pinion has no marking on its gear-side face, it will be necessary to obtain two D-50/Plymouth Arrow dealer special tools; MB990819 and MB990552. Install parts marked 1,6,2,7,3,4, and 5 in the illustration labeled "Measuring pinion

Pinion and ring gear markings

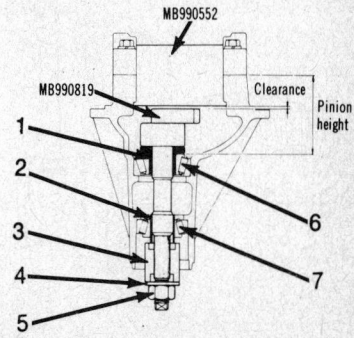

Measuring pinion height (clearance)

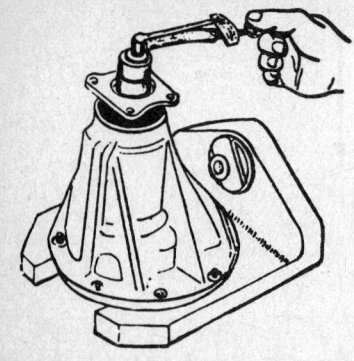

Measuring pinion preload

SIDE GEAR SPACERS

Part No.	Thickness of spacer	
	mm	in.
MB092034	0.8 $^{-0.08}_{-0.17}$	.0315 $^{-.0031}_{-.0067}$
MB092035	0.8 $^{-0.18}_{-0.27}$	.0315 $^{-.0071}_{-.0106}$
MB092036	0.8 $^{0}_{-0.07}$	.0315 $^{0}_{-.0028}$

DRIVE PINION HEIGHT SHIMS

Part No.	Thickness of shim	
	Mm	In.
MB092160	1.38 ± 0.01	.0543 ± .0004
MB092161	1.41 ± 0.01	.0555 ± .0004
MB092162	1.44 ± 0.01	.0567 ± .0004
MB092163	1.47 ± 0.01	.0579 ± .0004
MB092164	1.50 ± 0.01	.0591 ± .0004
MB092165	1.53 ± 0.01	.0603 ± .0004
MB092166	1.56 ± 0.01	.0614 ± .0004
MB092167	1.59 ± 0.01	.0626 ± .0004
MB092168	1.62 ± 0.01	.0638 ± .0004
MB092169	1.65 ± 0.01	.0650 ± .0004
MB092170	0.30 ± 0.013	.0118 ± .0005

height (clearance)'' with special tool MB990819 into the carrier case. Gradually tighten the nut to produce 6–9 in. lbs. without the oil seal. Fit special tool MB990552 in the differential caps and replace the caps on the case. Measure the clearance between the two special tools (see illustration) and select a shim of an equivalent thickness to the clearance to make the pinion height within tolerance of ±0.0012 in.

NOTE: If the pinion height has to be adjusted by more than 0.0650 in. use two shims including one 0.0118 in. thick.

19. Install the selected shim between the drive pinion and the rear bearing. Press the bearing onto the drive pinion shaft.

20. Assemble the drive pinion in the case and torque the pinion nut gradually to 137–180 ft. lbs. Check the pinion preload. With oil seal, it should be between 9–11 in. lbs. Without the oil seal, it should be 6–9 in. lbs. The preload shim selection ranges from 0.0118 to 0.0917 in.

21. If you have not already done so, apply a thin coat of grease to the drive pinion oil seal and insert it in the case. Refit the yoke and tighten to 137–180 ft. lbs.

22. Press the side bearings into the differential case and fit the case into the carrier.

23. Install the carrier caps with their mating marks in line with the marks on the carriers and finger tighten the four set bolts.

24. Install the side bearing nuts, and tighten the carrier cap bolts to 40–47 ft. lbs.

25. Screw in the side bearing nuts to

PINION BEARING PRELOAD SHIMS

Part No.	Thickness of shim	
	Mm	In.
MB092130	0.30 ± 0.01	.0118 ± .0004
MB092131	2.00 ± 0.01	.0787 ± .0004
MB092132	2.03 ± 0.01	.0799 ± .0004
MB092133	2.06 ± 0.01	.0811 ± .0004
MB092134	2.09 ± 0.01	.0823 ± .0004
MB092135	2.12 ± 0.01	.0835 ± .0004
MB092136	2.15 ± 0.01	.0846 ± .0004
MB092137	2.18 ± 0.01	.0858 ± .0004
MB092138	2.21 ± 0.01	.0870 ± .0004
MB092139	2.24 ± 0.01	.0882 ± .0004
MB092140	2.27 ± 0.01	.0894 ± .0004
MB092141	2.30 ± 0.01	.0906 ± .0004
MB092142	2.33 ± 0.01	.0917 ± .0004

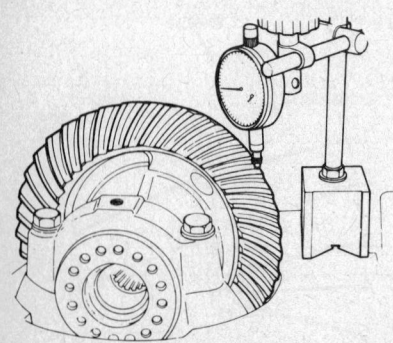

Backlash adjustment

adjust the standard backlash value. Each nut should be tightened to 11 lbs. Repeatedly loosen and tighten the bearing nuts to insure smooth operation, then tighten them until they become hard to turn.

26. Attach a dial indicator to the ring gear teeth and make certain the backlash is between 0.005–0.007 in.

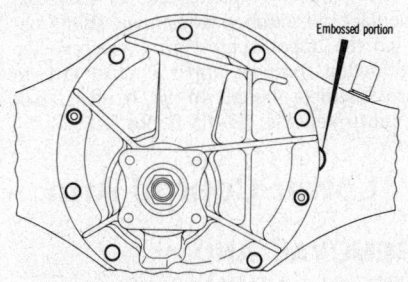

Installing the packing

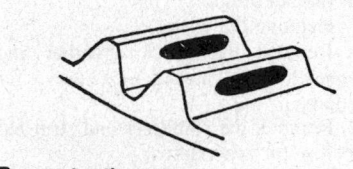

Proper tooth contact

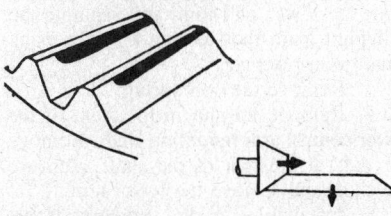

Face contact

Heel contact

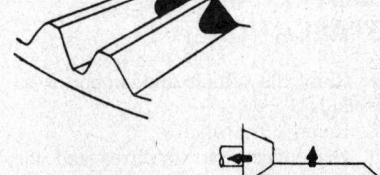

Toe contact

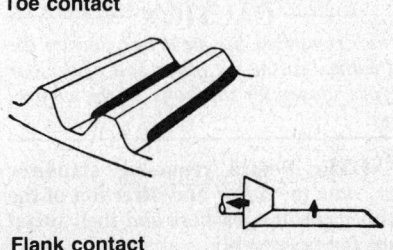

Flank contact

NOTE: If the backlash is less than the limit, loosen the bearing nut on the back side of the ring gear and tighten the bearing nut on the teeth side by the same amount.

27. After adjusting backlash, tighten the bearing nuts ½ pitch.

NOTE: One pitch is the space between two adjacent holes on the side of the bearing nut.

28. Again measure the backlash and install a one or two pronged lock plate whichever lines up with the bearing nut holes. Tighten the lock plate bolts to 11–16 ft. lbs.

29. Measure the ring gear runout in four or more spots. Runout should be 0.002 in. or less.

30. Make a ring gear tooth pattern check.

31. Apply gear oil to all moving parts and use sealant when assembling. Install the packing with the embossed portion at about 3 o'clock position on the axle housing.

32. Fit the differential and tighten the mounting nuts to 18–22 ft. lbs.

33. Be sure to fill the rear axle with about 3 pints of gear oil before testing.

FRONT SUSPENSION

Coil Spring

REMOVAL AND INSTALLATION

1. Raise the front of the vehicle and support it on jack stands.
2. Remove the wheel.
3. Remove the shock absorber (see below for procedures).
4. Remove stabilizer and strut bar (see below for procedures).
5. Compress the coil spring with a spring compressor.
6. Remove the relay rod from the steering arm.
7. Remove the upper knd lower ball joints using a ball joint remover.
8. Remove the coil spring.
Installation is the reverse of removal.

NOTE: The coil springs are color coded. The left side spring has a green band on it and the right side spring has a pink band on it. Do not mix the left and right springs.

9. Tighten the ball joint castle nuts to: upper, 43–65 ft. lbs.; lower, 87–130 ft. lbs.

Shock Absorbers

REMOVAL AND INSTALLATION

1. Raise the vehicle and support it on jack stands.
2. Remove the wheel.
3. Remove the double lock nuts at the top of the shock absorber along with the rubber washer and its metal caps.
4. Remove the two bolts at the bottom of the shock absorber and withdraw the shock absorber through the bottom arm.
Installation is the reverse of removal.
5. Be sure to refit all of the rubber cushion washers and their metal caps in the correct order. Tighten the upper shock absorber nut to 9–13 ft. lbs. and install the lock nut. Tighten the two lower shock absorber bolts to 6–9 ft. lbs.

Steering Knuckle

REMOVAL AND INSTALLATION

1. Raise the vehicle and support it on jack stands.
2. Remove the wheel.
3. Remove the brake caliper assembly and the front hub assembly (see brake caliper and hub removal section, below).
4. Disconnect the stabilizer and strut bar from the lower arm (see stabilizer and strut bar removal section, below).
5. Remove the shock absorber and compress the coil spring (see above for shock absorber removal).
6. Remove the relay rod from the steering arm using a ball joint remover.
7. Remove the cotter pins and castle nuts from the steering knuckle ball joints, and using either a gear puller or a ball joint remover, free the ball joints from the knuckle. Remove the knuckle.

When installing, tighten the upper ball joint castle nut to 43–65 ft. lbs. and the lower ball joint nut to 87–130 ft. lbs. Tighten the tie rod end ball joint nut to 25–33 ft. lbs. Fit new cotter keys. Installation is the reverse of removal.

Upper Control Arm

REMOVAL AND INSTALLATION

1. Jack up the front of the truck and support it on stands.
2. Remove the wheel.
3. Remove the shock absorber and compress the coil spring.
4. Remove the cotter pin and castle nut from the upper ball joint.
5. Using a gear puller or ball joint re-

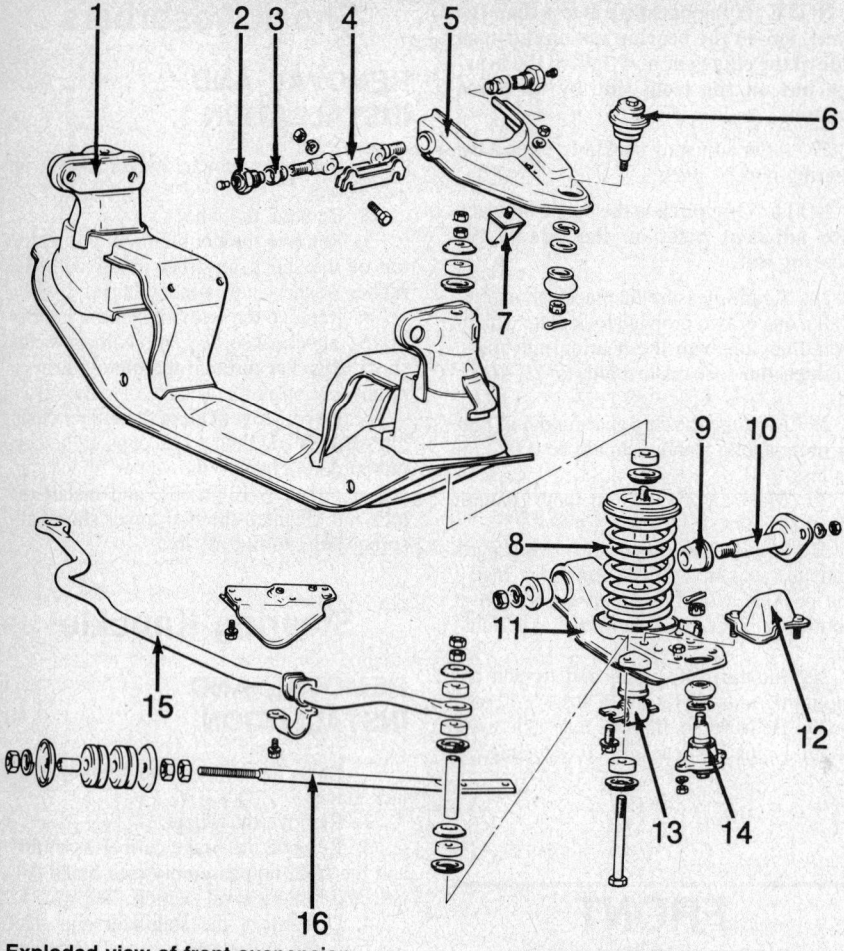

Exploded view of front suspension

1. Crossmember
2. Pivot bushing
3. Dust seal
4. Upper arm shaft
5. Upper arm
6. Upper ball joint
7. Rebound stop
8. Front coil spring
9. Lower arm bushing
10. Lower arm shaft
11. Lower arm
12. Bump stop
13. Shock absorber
14. Lower ball joint
15. Stabilizer
16. Strut bar

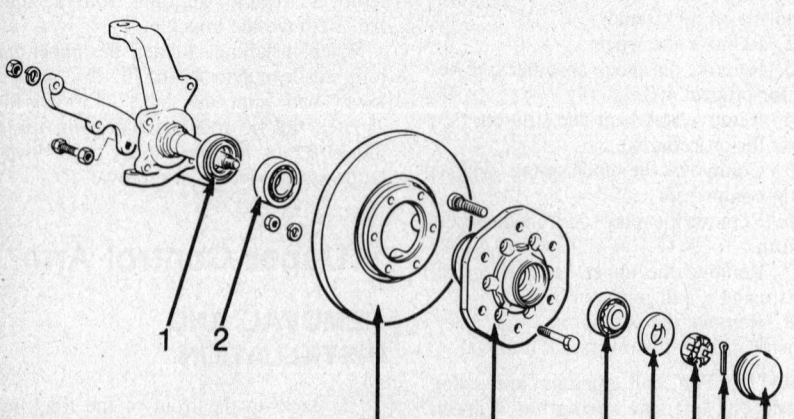

Steering knuckle and hub assembly

1. Oil seal
2. Wheel bearing (inner)
3. Brake disc
4. Wheel hub
5. Wheel bearing (outer)
6. Washer
7. Hub nut
8. Cotter pin
9. Hub cap

mover, free the ball joint from the steering knuckle.

6. Remove the bolts holding the upper control arm to the crossmember and remove the control arm as an assembly.

NOTE: Save all of the adjustment shims from the upper control arm for reassembly.

Installation is the reverse of removal. Replace all camber adjustment shims behind the upper control arm. Observe the following torques: upper control arm to crossmember bolts, 40–54 ft. lbs., ball joint to knuckle, 43–65 ft. lbs.

Lower Control Arm

REMOVAL AND INSTALLATION

1. Raise the front of the truck and support it on jackstands.
2. Remove the wheel.
3. Remove the shock absorber and compress the coil spring (see above for procedure).
4. Remove the stabilizer and strut bar (see below for procedures).
5. Remove the cotter pin and castle nut from the lower ball joint and separate the ball joint from the steering knuckle using a ball joint remover.
6. Remove the coil spring.
7. Remove the nut in the front of the lower control arm mounting shaft. Remove the nuts at the rear of the shaft. Remove the shaft and remove the lower arm.
8. Installation is the reverse of removal. Tighten the front mounting shaft nut to 40–54 ft. lbs. Tighten the rear nut to 6–9 ft. lbs. Tighten the ball joint castle nut to 87–130 ft. lbs. Tighten control arm shaft only after truck is on the ground.

Stabilizer and Strut Bar

REMOVAL AND INSTALLATION

1. Raise the vehicle and support it on jack stands.
2. Remove the wheels.
3. Disconnect the stabilizer and the strut bars from the lower control arms.

——— CAUTION ———
When removing the strut bar, loosen the adjusting nut at the other end of the bar before loosening the bolts at the control arm.

NOTE: Before removing stabilizer bar, note the order and direction of the rubber cushion washers and their metal caps for reassembly.

4. Remove the nut and spacers at the threaded end of the strut bar and remove the bar.

5. Remove the two stabilizer brackets and remove the stabilizer.

Installation is the reverse of removal. Observe the following.

There is a letter ''L'' on the left side strut bar, do not confuse it with the right side bar. The rubber cushions on the front of the strut bar are different; the cushion with a protruded lip is mounted at the front and the regular cushion is mounted at the back.

When installing the strut bar, set the standard distance of 3.8 in. from the tip of the threaded end of the bar to the rear face of the rear double nut. Lower the vehicle to the ground and tighten all nuts and bolts.

— CAUTION —

Make sure you check the front wheel alignment after installing the strut bar in order to obtain the correct caster, and then re-adjust the distance as required.

When installing both ends of the stabilizer, tighten the first nut (adjustment nut) to obtain length 0.87–0.94 in., then tighten the lock nut to 18–25 ft. lbs.

Upper Ball Joint

REMOVAL AND INSTALLATION

1. Remove the upper control arm from the vehicle (see above for procedure).

2. Remove the ball joint dust seal by prying up the dust seal ring evenly.

3. Remove the snap ring using snap ring pliers.

4. Using a ball joint remover and installer tool, press off the ball joint.

NOTE: A minimum of 2200 lb. pressure will be required to remove the upper ball joint from the control arm.

5. To install the ball joint, press it into the burred hole, with the ball joint and upper arm mating marks aligned.

6. Make sure the ball joint snap-ring is a tight fit and install the dust cover.

Lower Ball Joint

REMOVAL AND INSTALLATION

1. Jack up and safely support the vehicle. Remove the wheel.

2. Remove the coil spring (see above for procedures).

3. If you have not already done so, free the lower ball joint from the steering knuckle using a ball joint remover. Remove the dust cover from the ball joint.

4. Unbolt and remove the ball joint.

5. Installation is the reverse of removal. Install the ball joint with its tab side pointing to the rear of the vehicle. Tighten the ball joint to lower control arm bolts to 22–30 ft. lbs.

REAR SUSPENSION

Leaf Springs

REMOVAL AND INSTALLATION

1. Loosen the wheel nuts and jack up the vehicle. Support the frame on jack stands and lower the jack under the rear axle housing.

— CAUTION —

Do not put jack stands under axle housing shafts.

2. Remove the parking brake cable clamp from the leaf spring.

3. Disconnect the upper end of the shock absorber and the lower end at the spring U-bolt seat.

NOTE: If the shock absorber is not going to be replaced or serviced, leave the lower end on the spring U-bolt seat.

4. Loosen the U-bolt nuts and jack up the rear axle housing until it clears the spring seat. Remove the spring seat.

5. Remove the front spring pin and the rear shackle pin and remove the spring.

Installation is the reverse of removal. Observe the following:

6. Install the spring front eye bushings from both sides of the eye with the bushing flanges facing out. Insert the spring pin assembly from the wheel side and secure it to the hanger bracket with its bolt. Temporarily tighten the spring pin nut.

7. Repeat step 6 on the rear spring mount.

8. Align the center of the U-bolt seat with the center bolt hole in the spring. Tighten the U-bolts to 47–54 ft. lbs.

NOTE: Tighten the nuts on the U-bolts until all of the U-bolt threads protrude evenly.

Tighten the spring pins and shackle pins to 22–33 ft. lbs.

Shock Absorbers

REMOVAL AND INSTALLATION

1. Jack up the vehicle and remove the wheel.

2. Unbolt the top and bottom of the shock absorber and remove.

Installation is the reverse of removal. Tighten the shock absorber upper and lower mounting nuts to 13–18 ft. lbs.

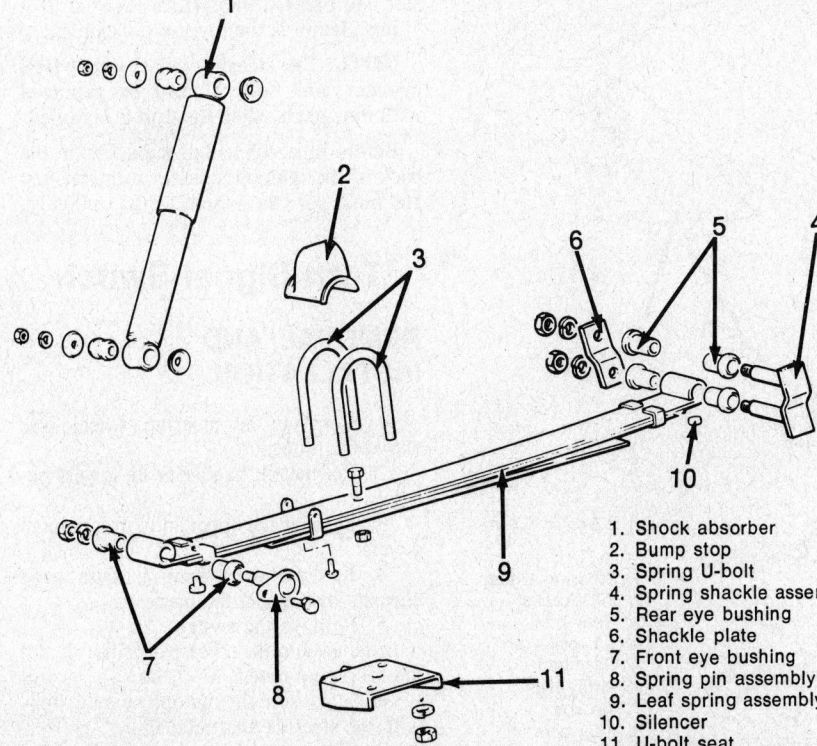

1. Shock absorber
2. Bump stop
3. Spring U-bolt
4. Spring shackle assembly
5. Rear eye bushing
6. Shackle plate
7. Front eye bushing
8. Spring pin assembly
9. Leaf spring assembly
10. Silencer
11. U-bolt seat

Rear suspension

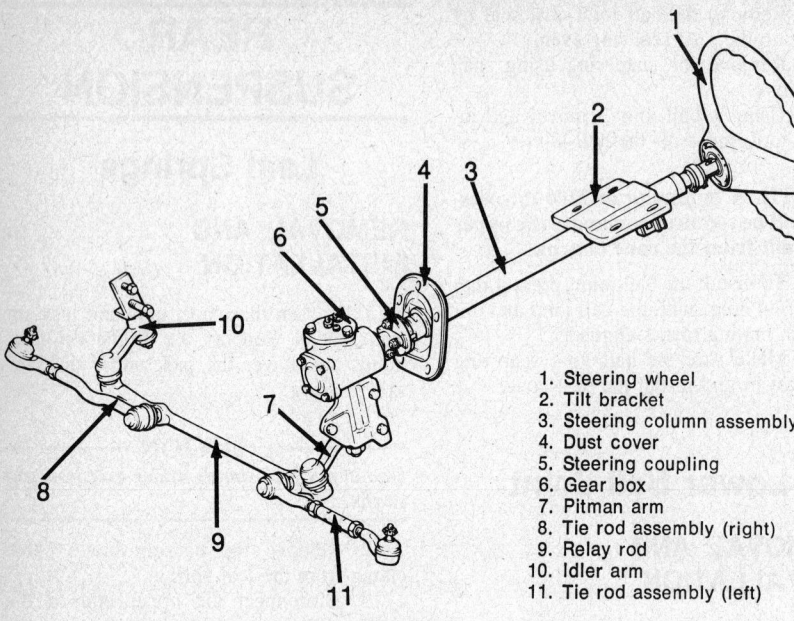

1. Steering wheel
2. Tilt bracket
3. Steering column assembly
4. Dust cover
5. Steering coupling
6. Gear box
7. Pitman arm
8. Tie rod assembly (right)
9. Relay rod
10. Idler arm
11. Tie rod assembly (left)

Manual steering column and gear assembly

STEERING

Steering Wheel

REMOVAL AND INSTALLATION

1. Pry off the steering wheel center foam pad.
2. Remove the steering wheel retaining nut.
3. Using a steering wheel puller, remove the wheel.
4. Be sure the front wheels are in a straight ahead position. Reverse the removal procedure for installation.

Steering Column

REMOVAL AND INSTALLATION

1. Remove the air cleaner. Match mark the column shaft on the steering gear shaft.
2. Remove the clamp bolt which holds

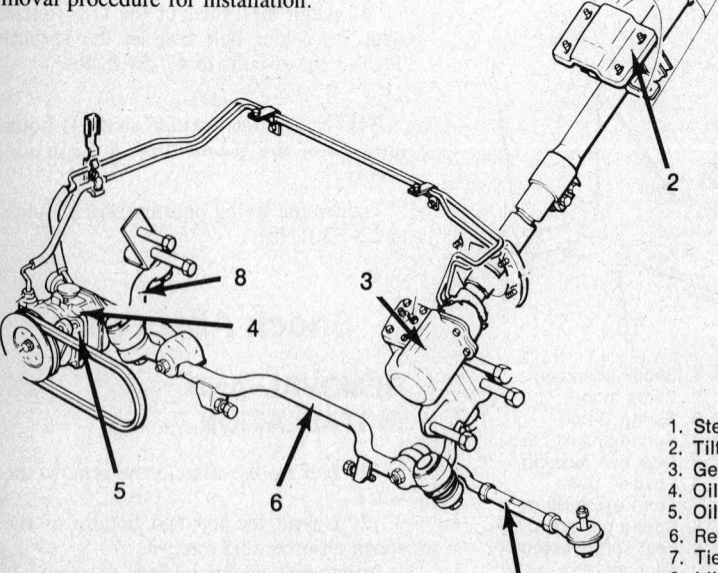

1. Steering wheel
2. Tilt bracket
3. Gear box
4. Oil reservoir
5. Oil pump
6. Relay rod
7. Tie rod
8. Idler arm

Power steering column and assembly

the steering column shaft on the steering gear shaft.

NOTE: On vehicles with air conditioning, step 2 must be done from under the truck.

3. Remove the horn pad and steering wheel retaining nut, then remove the steering wheel using a puller.
4. Loosen the tilt lock knob and lower the steering column fully.
5. Remove the steering column cover and disconnect the column wiring under the dashboard.
6. Remove the five bolts holding the base of the column at the fire wall.
7. Remove the four bolts holding the tilt column and remove the steering column from the vehicle.

Installation is the reverse of removal. Align the match marks on the steering column shaft and the steering gear shaft and couple the shafts before installing any bolts. Tighten the clamp bolt to 15–18 ft. lbs.

Ignition Switch/Lock

REMOVAL AND INSTALLATION

1. Remove the column cover.
2. Cut a notch in the lock bracket bolt head with a hack saw.
3. Remove the lock bolts.
4. Disconnect the ignition harness and remove the switch/lock as a unit.
5. To remove the ignition switch, remove the screw holding it on the harness side and pull out the switch.

Installation is the reverse of removal.

NOTE: The steering wheel upper lock bracket and bolts should be replaced with new parts when the unit is installed.

Before fully tightening the screw in the back of the ignition switch, insert the key and make sure the switch works smoothly.

Turn Signal Switch

REMOVAL AND INSTALLATION

1. Remove the steering wheel (see above for procedure).
2. Put the tilt handle in its lowest position.
3. Remove the upper and lower column covers.
4. Remove the wiring harness band clip and disconnect the harness.
5. Remove the switch.

Installation is the reverse of removal with the following notes.

6. Make sure the column switch aligns with the steering shaft center.
7. Place the wiring harness along the column tube as close as possible to the cen-

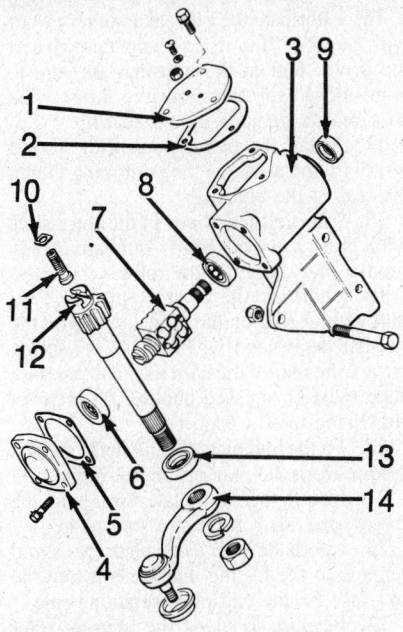

Exploded view of manual steering gear

1. Gear housing upper cover
2. Packing
3. Gear housing
4. Gear housing end cover
5. Mainshaft adjusting shim
6. Mainshaft bearing
7. Mainshaft assembly
8. Mainshaft bearing
9. Mainshaft oil seal
10. Gear adjusting spacer
11. Gear adjusting bolt
12. Cross shaft
13. Cross shaft oil seal
14. Pitman arm

MANUAL STEERING MAINSHAFT SHIMS

Part No.	Thickness	
	Mm	In.
MB005890	0.05	.0020
MB005891	0.06	.0024
MB005892	0.07	.0030
MB005893	0.10	.0040
MB005894	0.20	.0080
MB005895	0.30	.0120
MB005896	0.50	.0200

Manual Steering

GEAR BOX

Removal and Installation

1. Remove the clamp bolt connecting the steering shaft with the steering gear housing mainshaft.
2. Disconnect the tie rod and Pitman arm from the relay rod using a ball joint remover or gear puller.
3. Remove the three bolts holding the gear box to the frame and remove the gear box from under the vehicle.

Installation is the reverse of removal. Tighten the Pitman arm to relay rod nut to 94–109 ft. lbs. and the tie rod socket to relay rod to 29–33 ft. lbs.

Overhaul and Adjustments

1. Remove the gear box from the vehicle.
2. Remove the nut holding the Pitman arm on the cross shaft and using a gear puller, pull the arm from the shaft.
3. Before disassembling any further, record the starting preload of the mainshaft as a guide for reassembly.
4. Loosen the lock nut on the cross shaft adjusting bolt and turn the bolt slightly counterclockwise. Remove the cover bolts.
5. Lift the cover up slightly and turn the adjusting bolt in until it unfastens from the cover and remove the cover.
6. Turn the cross shaft until its teeth will fit through the cover hole and pull it out of the gear housing.

NOTE: Use care not to damage the cross shaft splines and the oil seal when removing the cross shaft.

7. Measure the main shaft starting preload with the cross shaft removed.
8. Loosen the end cover attaching bolts and remove the end cover and shim.

NOTE: Keep the shim for reassembly.

9. Gently pull out the main shaft, ball nut assembly and the bearings.

— CAUTION —
Never attempt to disassemble the main shaft and ball nut assembly.

Check the component parts for wear or damage. Make sure the ball nut slides easily on the mainshaft. There should not be excessive free play.

---

ter line. Be sure to replace the adjustable wiring harness bands.

Steering Linkage

REMOVAL AND INSTALLATION

1. Jack up the vehicle and support it on stands.
2. Remove the cotter pins and castle nuts holding the tie rod ends to the steering arms and the relay rod, and free the tie rods using either a suitable gear puller or a ball joint remover.
3. Unbolt and remove the relay rod in the same manner.
4. To remove the idler arm, remove the two bolts holding it to the frame and pull it out.

NOTE: The outer tie rod end has a left hand thread and the inner tie rod has a right handed thread on the driver's side.

Installation is the reverse of removal. Tighten all tie rod end nuts and relay rod nuts to 25–33 ft. lbs.

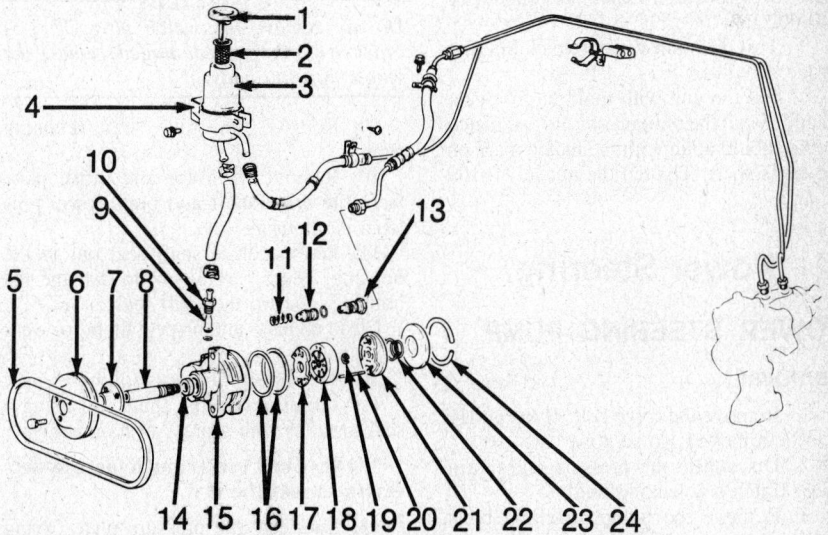

Separate reservoir power steering pump assembly—others similar

1. Oil reservoir cap	9. Fitting pipe
2. Oil filter	10. Fitting connector
3. Oil reservoir	11. Flow control spring
4. Oil reservoir bracket	12. Flow control plunger
5. Drive belt	13. Connector & fitting assembly
6. Oil pump pulley	14. Drive shaft seal
7. Pulley bracket	15. Oil pump body
8. Drive shaft	16. O-ring
17. Thrust plate	
18. Pump ring & rotor	
19. Drive shaft retaining ring	
20. Dowel	
21. Pressure plate	
22. End plate spring	
23. End plate	
24. Retaining ring	

To assemble:

10. Insert the main shaft assembly into the gear housing. Hold the main shaft horizontally.

11. Install the oil seal after applying a small amount of grease to its lip.

12. Install the gasket, shim and gasket end cover to the housing. Tighten the four end cover bolts to 11–45 ft. lbs. Use sealant on both the cover gasket and the bolt threads.

13. Measure the main shaft preload. It should be between 3–4.8 ft. lbs. If not, adjust it replacing the shim with a thicker or thinner shim. Shims come in thicknesses from 0.0020 to 0.0200 in.

14. Fit the adjusting bolt and shim in the top of the cross shaft and, using a feeler gauge, check the clearance between the adjusting bolt head and the cross shaft. Clearance should be 0–0.002. If not, replace the shim.

15. Insert the cross shaft into the gear housing. Be sure to align the teeth on both shafts in the center of their travel.

16. Install the cover and torque the bolts to 11–14 ft. lbs. Apply sealant to the cover gasket and the threads of the bolts.

17. Verify that the unit works smoothly, then screw the adjusting bolt in and out of the cover two or three times to adjust the cross shaft into proper mesh with the main shaft.

18. Then loosen the adjusting bolt, making sure there is no free play at the mainshaft center position. Back lash should be 0–0.002 in.

19. Test the main shaft preload. Starting torque should be 5.7–7.4 ft. lbs.

20. Fill the unit with multipurpose gear oil and install the pitman arm. Its two match marks should align with the match mark on the cross shaft. Tighten the nut to 94–109 ft. lbs.

Power Steering

POWER STEERING PUMP

Removal

1. Remove the drive belt. If the pulley is to be removed, do so now.

2. Disconnect the pressure and return lines. Catch any leaking fluid.

3. Remove the pump attaching bolts and lift the pump from the brackets.

Installation

1. Make sure the bracket bolts are tight and install the pump to the brackets.

2. If pulley had been removed, install it and tighten the nut securely. Bend the lock tab over the nut.

3. Install the drive belt and adjust to a tension of 22 lbs. at a deflection of .28 to .39 inches at the top center of the belt. Tighten the pump bolts securely to hold the tension.

4. Connect the pressure and return lines and fill the reservoir with approved fluid. (Dexron® I).

5. Bleed the system (refer to the bleeding procedure).

OVERHAUL

Separate Reservoir Type

1. Remove the pulley bracket with a gear puller.

2. Loosen and remove the suction port assembly.

3. Remove the pressure hose fitting assembly.

4. Remove the end plate retaining ring by inserting a small punch in the 0.13 in. diameter hole in the housing opposite the flow control valve hole. Compress the retaining ring with the punch and remove it by inserting a screwdriver under the ring and twisting.

5. Remove the end plate and the end plate O-ring. The end plate is spring loaded and should pop out. If it sticks, rocking it from side to side should free it.

6. Turn the pump over and allow the flow control valve and the valve spring to fall out.

7. With the end cover O-ring removed, tap lightly on the end of the drive shaft to free the pressure plate.

8. Remove the pressure plate, drive shaft, pump ring, vanes and rotor.

9. Remove the drive shaft retaining ring.

10. Remove the rotor and thrust plate from the drive shaft and both dowel pins from the housing.

11. Pry the drive shaft seal out of the housing, being careful not to damage the housing, discard the shaft seal.

Clean all parts and inspect them for wear or damage.

To assemble, proceed as follows.

12. Install new drive shaft seal using a seal installer with a press or hammer.

NOTE: Only use as much force as necessary to seat the seal.

13. Lubricate the pressure plate O-ring with Dexron® II or its equivalent, and install it in the third groove from the rear of the housing.

14. Insert both dowel pins in the housing.

15. Assemble the drive shaft, thrust plate and rotor, then fit a new snap-ring on the drive shaft. The rotor must have its countersunk side toward the thrust plate.

16. Lubricate the oil seal and drive shaft with Dexron® II or its equivalent, and insert the drive shaft in the housing. Be sure to align the dowel pins with the thrust plate so as not to damage the oil seal lip.

17. Install the pump ring on the dowel pins with the arrow in the pump ring facing the rear of the housing.

18. Insert all ten vanes in the rotor slots with their rounded edges outward. They should slide freely in the rotor.

19. Lubricate the pressure plate and install with O-ring on the dowel pins with the circular depression which holds the spring toward the rear of the housing. The pressure plate must be pressed about 0.06 in. over the O-ring to seat properly.

20. Fit the end plate O-ring in the second groove from the rear of the housing.

21. Install the end plate spring in the groove provided in the pressure plate.

22. Lubricate the end plate to avoid damage to the O-ring and press it into the housing. Fit the end plate retaining ring.

23. Be sure to bleed the system (refer to bleeding procedure).

Reservoir in Unit Type

1. Remove the oil reservoir.

2. Hold the pump in a vise, loosen the pump cover bolts and remove the cover.

3. Remove the following parts from the pump body: cam ring, vanes, O-ring, side plate assembly, and the shaft assembly which includes the shaft, rotor, side plate, collar and snap-ring.

4. Remove the shaft assembly snap-ring and remove the collar, rotor side plate.

5. Remove the oil seal with a screw driver. Remove the suction connector.

6. Remove the connector at the top of the pump body and remove the flow control valve assembly and flow control spring.

7. Clean and check all parts for wear. Always use new gaskets and lubricate all parts with Dexron® II before assembling.

Assembly is the reverse of disassembly with the following notes.

8. Pay close attention to the illustrations for the installing direction of the side plate, rotor and collar.

9. When installing the cam ring, the counter-sunk holes at the end of the vanes face toward the cover.

10. Fit the vanes with their rounded sides pointed out.

11. Bleed the system (see bleeding procedures).

Power Steering Gear

REMOVAL AND INSTALLATION

1. Disconnect the steering shaft from the gear box mainshaft.

2. Disconnect the tie rod from the relay rod, and the Pitman arm from the relay rod using a gear puller.

3. Remove the air cleaner and disconnect the pressure hose and the return hose from the gear box using a pipe wrench, then remove the undercover.

4. Loosen the gear box mounting bolts. On vehicles with automatic transmissions, remove the throttle linkage with the throttle linkage splash shield. On vehicles with manual transmissions, remove the starter on the transmission.

5. Remove the gear box from under the vehicle.

6. Remove the Pitman arm with a gear puller.

Installation is the reverse of removal. Observe the following torques: gear box to frame, 40–47 ft. lbs.; tie rod socket and relay rod connection, 25–33 ft. lbs.; pressure hose connection, 22–29 ft. lbs.; return hose connection 29–36 ft. lbs.

OVERHAUL

1. Loosen the adjusting lock nut and remove it.

2. With the gear in neutral position, tap the bottom of the cross shaft with a plastic hammer to remove the cross shaft.

3. Remove the side cover bolts, and screw in the adjusting bolt two or three turns.

4. Remove the valve housing nut.

5. Remove the valve housing bolts and take out the valve housing and rack piston, holding the rack piston to avoid turning it.

NOTE: Be careful not to let the rack piston fall off of the shaft.

6. Hold the valve housing in a vise and move the rack piston up and down to check the backlash between the groove of the rack piston and the balls. Measure the backlash after fully tightening the rack piston on the shaft and then loosening it two turns. Service limit is 0.008 in. If backlash exceeds the service limit, replace the ball screw unit and the rack piston as an assembly.

7. To remove the rack piston, turn it counter-clockwise.

━━━ CAUTION ━━━
There are twenty-six steel balls in the rack piston which will probably fall out when you remove it from the shaft. Do not lose them.

8. To disassemble the rack piston, remove the circular holder, the circulator, the steel balls, the seal ring and the O-ring. Do not disassemble the rack piston end cap.

9. Loosen the top cover and remove ti and the input worm shaft from the valve housing.

10. Remove worm shaft thrust plate, thrust needle roller bearing, two seal rings and two O-rings.

11. Screw in the adjusting bolt at the tip of the cross shaft and remove the side cover.

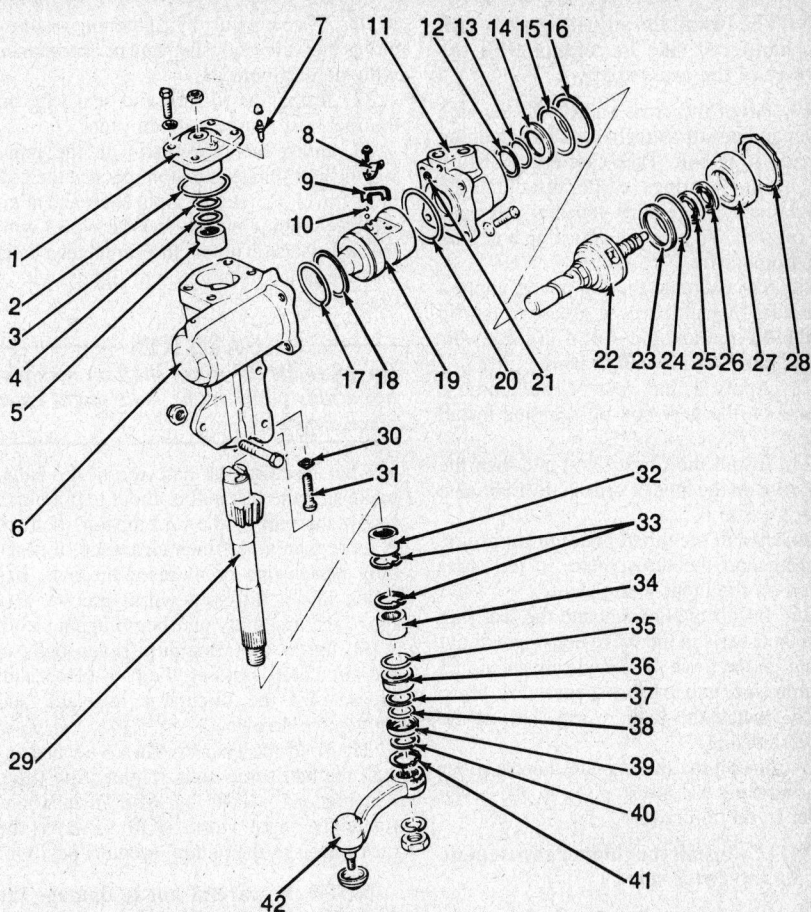

Exploded view of power steering gear assembly

1. Side cover	15. O-ring	29. Cross shaft
2. O-ring	16. Seal ring	30. Adjusting plate
3. O-ring	17. O-ring	31. Adjusting bolt
4. Seal ring	18. Seal ring	32. Needle bearing, upper
5. Needle bearing	19. Rack piston	33. Snap ring
6. Gear box	20. O-ring	34. Needle bearing, lower
7. Bleeder plug	21. O-ring	35. O-ring
8. Circulator holder	22. Input worm shaft	36. Seal housing
8. Circulator	23. Thrust needle bearing	37. Seal ring
10. Ball	24. O-ring	38. O-ring
11. Valve housing	25. Ball bearing	39. Oil seal
12. Seal ring	26. Oil seal	40. Backup ring
13. O-ring	27. Top cover	41. Snap ring
14. Thrust needle bearing	28. Nut	42. Pitman arm

━━━ CAUTION ━━━
There are thirty-three needle bearing rollers which may fall out when you remove the cross shaft. Do not lose them.

12. Remove the following parts from the side cover: O-ring, needle bearings, adjusting bolt and adjusting plate.

NOTE: If no oil leaks through the threads of the adjusting bolt, do not remove the sealing at the rear of the needle bearing seat.

13. Remove the seal ring and O-ring from the valve housing.

14. To remove the ball bearing and oil seal in the top cover, use a brass drift.

15. Remove the oil seal and seal ring from the gear box using a screwdriver.

Clean and inspect all parts for wear or damage. Always use new gaskets and oil seals and coat indicated parts with Dexron® II before installing.

To assemble, proceed as follows.

16. Apply a thin coat of multipurpose grease to the bearing race in the side cover and insert the thirty-three roller bearings. Apply a dab of grease to bottom of the side cover. Be careful not to disturb the needle bearings.

17. Install the side cover O-ring.

18. With the adjusting bolt and adjusting plate inserted in the top of the cross shaft, measure the clearance between the bolt head and the cross shaft. It should be from 0 to 0.002 in. Adjust clearance by replacing shim plate.

NOTE: Install the adjusting plate with its chamfered side in contact with the surface of the cross shaft.

19. Align the cross shaft with the side cover and install. Attach them by tightening the adjusting bolt. Take care not to disturb the needle bearings while installing the cross shaft. Make sure you don't damage the oil seal. Tighten the adjusting bolt lock nut temporarily.

20. To assemble the top cover, apply a thin coat of multipurpose grease to the lip of the oil seal and press fit it in the cover.

21. Press fit the ball bearing.

22. Apply a thin coat of multipurpose grease on the gear box oil seal and install it.

23. Install the O-ring first and then the seal ring on the input worm shaft. Lubricate with Dexron.

24. Install the thrust plate, thrust needle bearing and the thrust plate in the order given on the input worm shaft.

25. Install the O-rings and the seal ring into their seats in the valve housing without using undue force. The seal ring should be compressed into a heart shape when fit.

26. Install the input worm shaft in the valve housing.

27. Install the thrust plate, needle roller bearing and the thrust plate in the given order in the top cover.

NOTE: Install the thinner thrust plate on the top cover side.

28. Temporarily tighten the top cover to the valve housing.

NOTE: Take care not to distrub the thrust plate and needle roller bearing in the top cover.

29. Tighten the top cover bolts to 12–16 in. lbs.

NOTE: Turn the input worm shaft and check for smooth rotation and noise.

30. Tighten the valve housing nut to 130–166 ft. lbs.

NOTE: Do not allow the top cover to rotate while tightening the nut.

31. Measure the starting preload of the input worm shaft. It should be from 3–5

POWER STEERING CROSS SHAFT SHIM PLATES

Part No.	Thickness	
	Mm	In.
MB076596	1.95	.077
MB076196	2.00	.079
MB076597	2.05	.081
MB076598	2.10	.083
MB076599	2.15	.085

in. lbs. If not, adjust by tightening or loosening the valve housing nut in accordance with steps 30 and 31.

32. Install the O-ring and seal ring on the rack piston in the given order.

33. Insert the rack piston in the input worm shaft until the piston reaches the end of its travel. Rotate the input shaft and align the ball running surface on the worm with the ball insertion holes. Insert nineteen balls into the hole, pushing them lightly with a brass rod.

————— CAUTION —————

Do not rotate the worm shaft on rack piston at this point or the balls might enter other grooves.

After installing all nineteen of the balls, make sure the last ball is about half an inch below the end of the rack piston. If there is more than a half inch clearance, it probably means one or more of the balls has fallen into a different worm groove. Remove the assembly and begin again.

34. Insert the remaining seven balls in the circulator, holding them in place with grease. Fit the circulator in place and tighten the screws.

35. Hold the gear box in a vise and install the ball screw unit. Tighten the valve housing to 33–40 ft. lbs. After installation, rotate the input worm shaft to move the rack piston to the neutral (center) position.

NOTE: Be careful not to damage the seal ring when installing the rack piston.

36. Install the cross shaft assembly (with side cover) in to the gear box and tighten the side cover to 33–40 ft. lbs. When installing the cross shaft, apply a thin coat of ATF to the teeth and shaft of the rack piston and multipurpose grease to the oil seal lip. Do not rotate the side cover during installation or risk damage to the O-ring. It might be a good idea to wrap tape around the splined end of the cross shaft to prevent damage to the seals.

37. Measure the total starting torque of the input worm shaft to neutral position (center). Make sure the ball screw operates smoothly through its entire travel. Starting torque should be between 4–6 in. lbs. Tighten the valve housing nut to 130–166 ft. lbs. Measure the preload after tightening.

38. Install the Pitman arm on the cross shaft aligning the slit in the end of the shaft with the two slits on the Pitman arm. Tighten the Pitman nut to 94–109 ft. lbs.

39. After tightening the Pitman arm, measure the distance between the center of the frame mounting bolt hole closest to the Pitman arm and the inner surface of the Pitman arm. This length should be about 0.77 in.

BLEEDING THE SYSTEM

1. The reservoir should be full of Dexron® II.

2. Jack up the front wheels and support the vehicle safely.

3. Turn the steering wheel fully to the right and left until no air bubbles appear in the fluid. Maintain the reservoir level.

4. Lower the vehicle and with the engine idling, turn the wheels fully to the right and left. Stop the engine.

5. Install a tube from the bleeder screw on the steering gear box to the reservoir.

6. Start the engine, turn the steering wheel fully to the left and loosen the bleeder screw.

7. Repeat the procedure until no air bubbles pass through the tube.

8. Tighten the bleeder screw and remove the tube. Refill the reservoir as needed, and check that no further bubbles are present in the fluid.

————— CAUTION —————

An abrupt rise in the fluid level after stopping the engine is a sign of incomplete bleeding. This will cause noise from the pump or control valve.

Front End Alignment

CASTER AND CAMBER

To adjust caster, adjust the tightening of the upper arm shaft. A half turn of the upper arm shaft will cause 0.049 in. play in the upper arm shaft resulting in a ¼ degree caster adjustment. The standard caster value and other wheel alignment specifications can be found at the beginning of this chapter.

To adjust the camber, it is necessary to adjust the number and thickness of the shims under the upper arm shaft. A total of 0.16 in. shim thickness between the upper arm shaft and the crossmember is normally required for standard camber. A 0.024 in. adjustment in thickness of shims will provide about 8 minutes adjustment of camber.

TOE-IN

Toe-in can be adjusted by screwing the left tie rod turnbuckle in or out. One revolution of the turnbuckle will vary in about 0.3 in. of toe-in adjustment. The toe-in may be increased or decreased by turning the tie rod turnbuckle toward the front or the rear of the vehicle respectively. After completion of the toe-in adjustment, check the difference in the length of the left and the right tie rods. If the difference exceeds 0.2 in., remove the right tie rod and adjust the length until the difference is reduced to 0.2 in. or less. An "L" stamped on the outer surface of the tie rod stands for left-hand thread end.

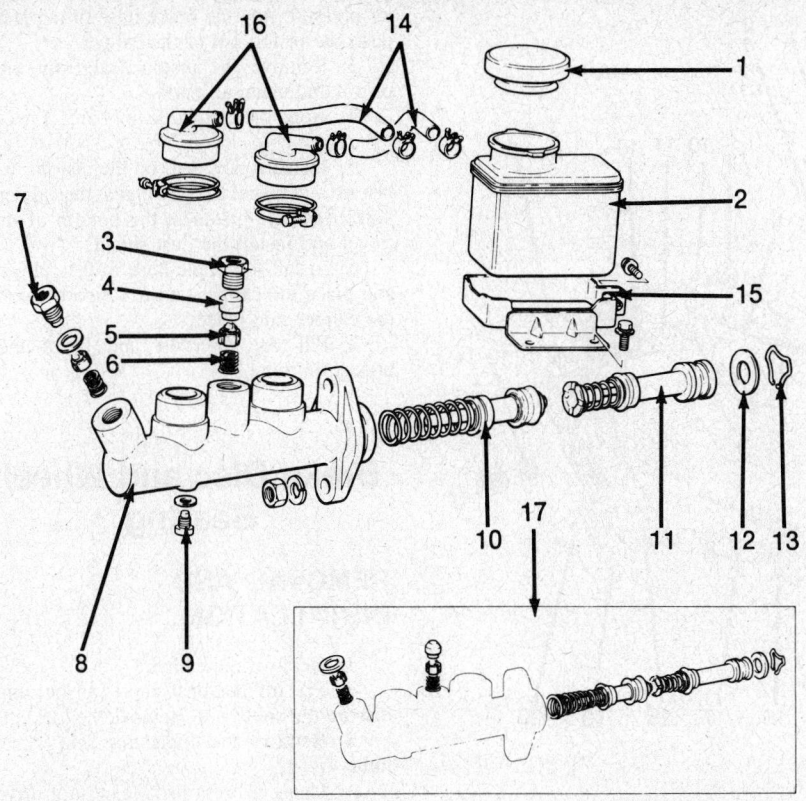

Master cylinder

1. Reservoir cap	7. Valve case	13. Stop ring
2. Fluid reservoir	8. Master cylinder	14. Reservoir hose
3. Check valve cap	9. Secondary piston stop	15. Bracket
4. Outer pipe seat	10. Secondary piston assembly	16. Nipple
5. Check valve	11. Primary piston assembly	17. Master cylinder kit
6. Check valve spring	12. Piston stop	

CAUTION

Do not attempt to disassemble the primary piston assembly; its length is factory adjusted.

NOTE: When any related parts such as the return spring, piston cup and piston require replacement, you must replace the entire piston assembly.

To assemble:

4. Hone the master cylinder slightly. The cylinder bore inside diameter should be between 0.8748–0.8768 in. If not, replace cylinder. Coat the cylinder with brake fluid.

5. Measure the piston outside diameter. It should be between 0.8719–0.8732. If not replace.

6. Assemble the master cylinder components in the master cylinder after coating the rubber seals with brake fluid. Bleed the brakes after installation.

NOTE: Prime the cylinder by pouring a little fluid in the reservoirs and working the piston until fluid squirts out of the two brake line ports.

SYSTEM BLEEDING

1. Check the master cylinder fluid level.
2. Remove the cap from the bleeder screw of the wheel farthest from the master cylinder.

BRAKES

Master Cylinder

REMOVAL AND INSTALLATION

1. Remove all lines connected to the master cylinder. Slowly depress the brake pedal to remove the fluid.

2. Remove the master cylinder from the booster assembly.

3. Installation is the reverse of removal. Bleed the brakes.

OVERHAUL

1. Remove the stop ring, piston stop, primary piston assembly, secondary piston assembly and the secondary return spring in the given order.

2. Loosen the valve case and remove the check valve and the check valve spring.

3. Wash the master cylinder, pistons and cups in brake fluid. Use care not to damage the cylinder, piston or cups.

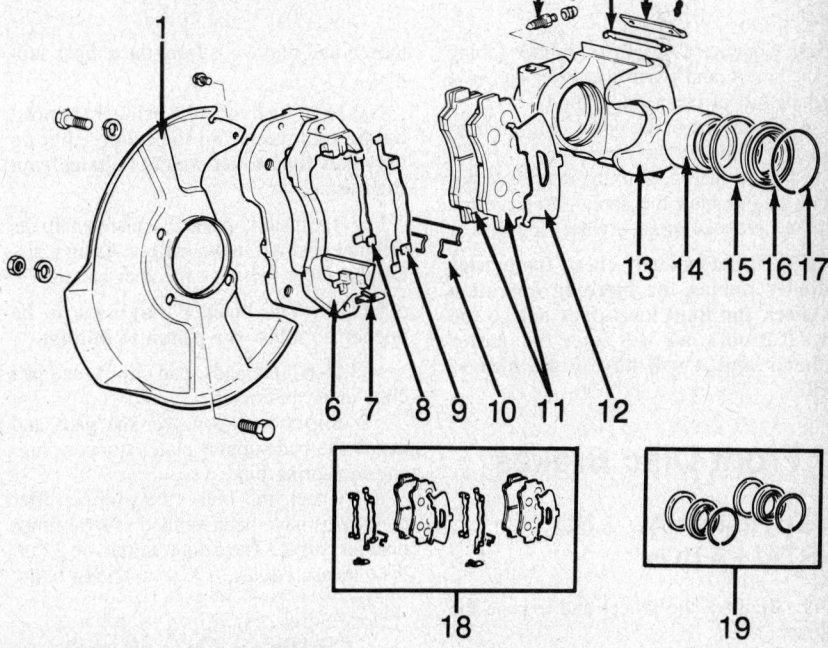

Front disc brake caliper assembly

1. Dust cover	6. Caliper support	11. Brake pad	16. Dust boot
2. Bleeder screw	7. Pad clip (inner)	12. Anti-squeak shim	17. Boot ring
3. Pad support plate	8. Pad clip B	13. Caliper body	18. Pad repair kit
4. Stopper plug	9. Pad clip (outer)	14. Piston	19. Seal and boot
5. Spigot pin	10. Anti-rattle spring	15. Piston seal	repair kit

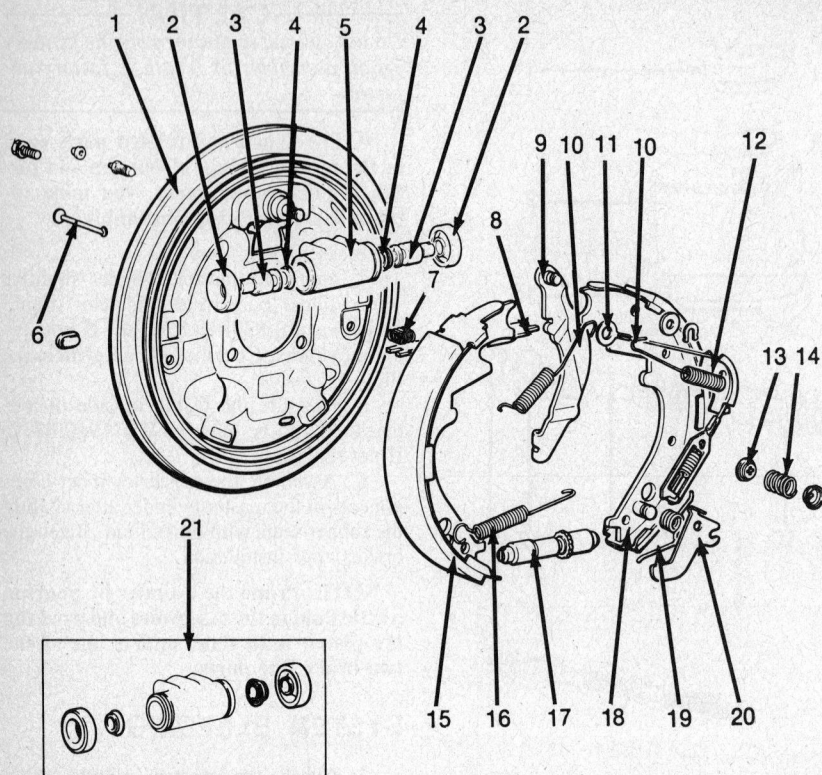

Rear brake drum components

1. Backing plate
2. Wheel cylinder boot
3. Wheel cylinder piston
4. Wheel cylinder piston cup
5. Wheel cylinder body
6. Shoe hold-down pin
7. Anti-rattle spring
8. Parking brake strut
9. Parking brake lever
10. Shoe return spring
11. Adjusting cable
12. Cable guide
13. Shoe hold-down cup
14. Shoe hold-down spring
15. Primary shoe assembly
16. Adjusting spring
17. Adjuster assembly
18. Secondary shoe assembly
19. Adjuster spring
20. Autoadjuster lever
21. Wheel cylinder repair kit

3. Connect a length of rubber tubing to the screw and place the other end in a jar half full of clean brake fluid.

4. Pump the brake pedal until no bubbles are visible in the container.

5. Hold the pedal in the depressed position and tighten the screw. Replace the cap and proceed to each wheel in turn.

NOTE: Periodically check the master cylinder during the bleeding operation to check the fluid level does not go too low. If it does, air will enter the master cylinder and it will have to be bled as well.

Front Disc Brakes

PAD REMOVAL AND INSTALLATION

1. Remove the wheel and expose the caliper.

2. Remove approximately ½ the fluid from the master cylinder reservoir.

3. Remove the spring (spigot) pin and pull the stopper plug from the upper end of the caliper.

4. Move the caliper back and forth to loosen and remove it from the caliper support.

NOTE: The hydraulic brake hose need not be removed from the caliper, but do not allow the caliper weight to hang from the hose.

5. To install, push the piston into its original position in the caliper, using a piston expander tool or a hammer handle.

NOTE: The bleeder may have to be opened to allow the piston to bottom.

6. Install the pads, pad clip B, and pad clips inner and outer.

7. Slip the caliper over the pads and install the pad support plate, stopper plug, and the spring pin.

8. Check the brake drag torque after the brakes have been applied several times on a test drive. The torque should be 29 in. lbs., measured at a wheel mounting bolt.

Caliper Overhaul

1. Remove the wheel and caliper. Disconnect the hydraulic brake line.

2. Remove the dust boot. Cover the outer side of the caliper with a cloth, inject

air pressure into the brake hose fitting and push the piston out of the caliper.

3. Remove the piston seal from the piston and clean all parts.

4. Hone the caliper piston bore, if necessary.

5. Install a new seal on the piston, lubricate and install the piston into the caliper bore. Seat the piston at the bottom of its travel and install the dust shield.

6. Install the brake hose to the caliper and place the caliper on the support. Lock the caliper into place.

7. Fill the reservoir and bleed the brakes thoroughly.

Brake Disc and Wheel Bearing

REMOVAL AND INSTALLATION

1. Remove the caliper.

2. Pry off the dust cap. Tap out and discard the cotter pin. Remove the locknut.

3. Remove the brake disc and wheel hub.

4. Using a brass drift, carefully drive the outer bearing race out of the hub.

5. Remove the inner bearing seal and bearing.

6. Check the bearings for wear or damage and replace them if necessary. Drift the bearing race into place in the hub.

7. Pack the inner and outer wheel bearings with grease.

8. Install the inner bearing in the hub. Drive the seal on until its outer edge is even with the edge of the hub.

9. Install the hub/disc assembly on the spindle, being careful not to damage the oil seal.

10. Install the outer bearing, washer, and spindle nut. Adjust the bearing.

ADJUSTMENT

1. Tighten the spindle nut to 22 ft. lbs. and then loosen it.

2. Tighten the nut to 6 ft. lbs.

3. Install the cap on the nut. Do not back off the nut more than 30° for cotter pin hole-to-slot alignment.

Drum Brakes

Installation

1. Release the parking brake. Block the front wheels.

2. Jack up the rear of the truck and support it on stands.

3. Remove the wheel.

4. Remove the brake drum.

Installation is the reverse of removal.

Brake Shoes

REMOVAL AND INSTALLATION

1. Remove the wheel and the brake drum.

2. Using a standard brake return spring tool, remove the return spring.

3. Remove the adjusting spring and the adjusting lever.

4. Remove the brake shoes and the adjusting assembly then remove the cable from the parking brake lever.

Installation is the reverse of removal with the following notes.

5. After the primary shoes have been installed, install the parking brake cable. Set the adjuster assembly, then secure the secondary shoes.

NOTE: Grease the threaded area on the adjuster assembly and make sure it turns smoothly.

6. Install the primary shoe return springs, adjusting cable and the secondary shoe return springs in the given order.

NOTE: The spring for the primary shoe is colored green, while the spring for the secondary shoe is gray. Do not mix them, as they are different lengths.

7. To check the adjuster assembly operation: pull the adjuster cable toward you to see if the adjuster lever goes into mesh with the next tooth on the adjuster wheel. Make sure that when the cable is released, the adjuster lever returns to its original position after the adjuster wheel has moved a tooth ahead.

Wheel Cylinder

REMOVAL AND INSTALLATION

1. Remove brake shoes.

2. Disconnect the brake pipe from the rear of the wheel cylinder and plug it to prevent it from leaking fluid.

3. Remove the wheel cylinder from the brake backing plate.

Installation is the reverse of removal.

OVERHAUL

1. Remove dust caps from both ends of the wheel cylinder.

2. Pull out the plungers, rubber seals and piston cups.

Clean and lightly hone the wheel cylinder.

Assembly is the reverse of disassembly. Lubricate all parts with brake fluid before assembly.

Power Brake Unit

REMOVAL AND INSTALLATION

1. Remove the master cylinder.

2. Disconnect the vacuum hose from the power brake.

3. Remove the pin connecting the power brake operating rod to the pedal.

4. Loosen the nuts attaching the power brake to the fire wall and remove the power brake.

Installation is the reverse of removal. Apply sealer to all mounting surfaces before assembling.

Parking Brake

ADJUSTMENT

1. Release the parking brake.

2. Jack up the vehicle and support it on jack stands.

3. Make sure the balancer that the front of the cable rides in is parallel with the center line of the truck. The clearance between the balancer and the crossmember should be about 8 in.

4. Adjust the parking brake by turning the turnbuckle on the cable. The brake is properly adjusted when the parking brake handle can be pulled 16 to 17 notches (approx. 4.3 in.).

5. After adjusting the parking brake, make sure there is slack in the cable when the brake is in the off position.

If the brake will not adjust correctly or fails on a hill, the rear brake shoes should be inspected for wear, oil or grease covered surfaces or malfunction.

CHASSIS ELECTRICAL

Blower Motor Without Air Conditioning

REMOVAL AND INSTALLATION

1. Remove the cluster panel.

2. Disconnect the cable between the motor and the heater unit.

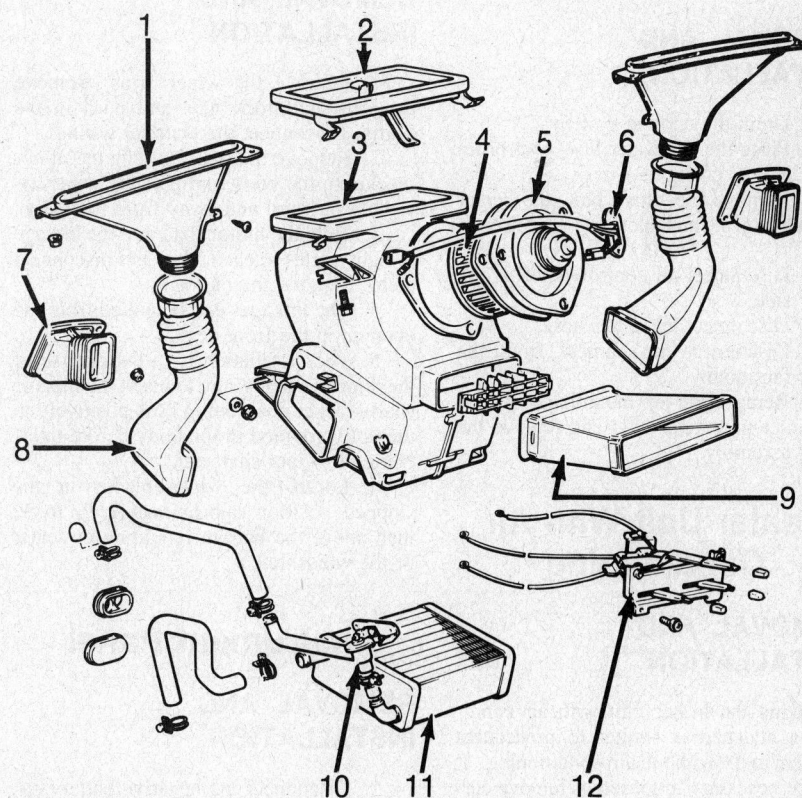

Heater assembly

1. Defroster nozzle
2. Ventilator assembly
3. Heater assembly
4. Turbo fan
5. Motor
6. Heater resistor
7. Side ventilation duct
8. Defroster duct
9. Center ventilation duct
10. Water valve
11. Heater core
12. Heater control panel assembly

3. Remove the three bolts holding the motor in the heater unit and pull out the fan.

NOTE: It may be necessary to unfasten the fan from the motor to remove them from under the dashboard.

Installation is the reverse of removal.

Blower Motor With Air Conditioning

REMOVAL AND INSTALLATION

The air conditioning system used on Dodge and Plymouth pick-up trucks utilizes the blower motor assembly of the heater unit. However, it may be necessary to remove some of the air conditioning components to gain access to the motor. If this is the case, never attempt to loosen any of the air conditioning hoses during your work. They contain refrigerant under pressure, which could severely damage your eyes or skin on contact.

Heater Unit Without Air Conditioning

REMOVAL AND INSTALLATION

1. Drain the cooling system.
2. Place the hot water flow control lever in the off position.
3. Remove the glove box, the center ventilation grille and duct, and the defroster duct.
4. Disconnect all control cables at the heater side.
5. Disconnect the water hoses.
6. Disconnect the harness from the heater fan motor.
7. Remove the top mounting bolts and the center mounting nuts, and remove the heater assembly.

Heater Unit With Air Conditioning

REMOVAL AND INSTALLATION

Removing the heater unit with air conditioning attached is similar to procedures used on units without air conditioning. It may be necessary to loosen or remove certain components of the air conditioning sys-

tem to facilitate heater unit removal, however, *never* loosen the refrigerant pipes that lead into the air conditioning evaporator assembly. They are filled with a noxious fluid which, under certain conditions, could cause severe damage to your face or skin. Always leave all air conditioning work to skilled professionals.

Radio

REMOVAL AND INSTALLATION

1. Remove the instrument cluster bezel.
2. Remove the radio bracket attaching screws from the instrument panel, and remove the radio bracket.
3. Pull the radio out slightly, disconnect the antenna lead-in, speaker connector and the power supply connector.
4. Take out the radio.
Installation is the reverse of removal.

Windshield Wipers Motor and Linkage

REMOVAL AND INSTALLATION

1. Remove the wiper arms. Remove the arm shaft lock nuts and push in the shafts. Disconnect the elctrical wiring.
2. Remove the bolts holding the motor bracket to the body and pull the wiper assembly outward and away from the body.
3. Hold the motor shaft and the linkage at right angles to each other and disconnect them. Remove the motor.
4. The linkages can be pulled from the opening in the front deck.
5. The installation is in the reverse of the removal, being sure to insert the linkage shaft bracket positioning boss positively in the hole provided in the body before tightening the wiper shaft nut.
6. Locate the wiper blades in the stopped position approximately ½ to ¾ inch above the bottom moulding or sealer of the windshield.

Instrument Panel

REMOVAL AND INSTALLATION

1. Disconnect the negative battery cable.

2. Remove the heater fan control knob, heater control knobs and the radio knobs.
3. Remove the ash tray and remove the two screws behind it holding the instrument panel bezel. Remove the two screws at tbe top of the bezel and remove the bezel.
4. Remove the four screws in the corners of the meter case.
5. Disconnect the speedometer cable and connectors from the back of the meter, and remove the meter assembly.
Installation is the reverse of removal.

Speedometer Cable

REMOVAL AND INSTALLATION

1. Unfasten the speedometer cable from the rear of the speedometer. The instrument panel may have to be removed.

NOTE: The cable is fastened to tbe speedometer via a snap clip, which must be pressed down while the cable is being unfastened.

2. Unfasten the speedometer cable from the transmission.
3. Remove the bands holding the cable with the wiring harness and withdraw the cable through the engine compartment.
Installation is the reverse of removal.

— **CAUTION** —
Always install the speedometer cable with the largest radius possible to prevent cable binding and noise.

Circuit Protection

FUSE BOX LOCATION

The fuse box is located below the hood release handle on the driver's side of the vehicle.

FUSIBLE LINK

The fusible link is located on the battery running from the positive (+) battery terminal. It is necessary to test the link for continuity with a circuit tester, since visual inspection is not enough to detect a melted fusible link. When the fusible link is melted, a dead short may be the cause.

Datsun

INDEX

BEFORE SERVICING, SEE THE SAFETY NOTICE AT THE FRONT OF THE BOOK

DATSUN

GENERAL ENGINE SPECIFICATIONS

Year	Engine Displacement cc (cu. in.)	Carb Type	Advertised Horsepower @ rpm	Advertised Torque @ rpm (ft. lbs.)	Bore and Stroke (in.)	Advertised Compression Ratio	Oil Pressure (psi/idle)
'75	1952 (119)	2 bbl	112 @ 5600	108 @ 3600	3.35 × 3.39	8.5:1	50–57
'76–'80	1952 (119)	2 bbl	97 @ 5600	102 @ 3200	3.35 × 3.39	8.5:1	50–57
'81	2164 (132)	Diesel	61 @ 4000	102 @ 1800	3.27 × 3.94	21.6:1	60
	2187 (133.5)	2 bbl	98 @ 4000	117 @ 1800	3.43 × 3.62	8.5:1	60
'82	2187 (133.5)	2 bbl	98 @ 4000	117 @ 1800	3.43 × 3.62	8.5:1	60
	2164 (132)	Diesel	61 @ 4000	102 @ 1800	3.27 × 3.94	21.6:1	60

CAPACITIES

Year	Engine Displacement cc (cu in.)	Crankcase L (qts) w/filter	Crankcase L (qts) wo/filter	Transmission L (pts) 4sp	Transmission L (pts) 5sp	Transmission L (pts) Auto	Transfer Case L (pts)	Rear Drive Axle L (pts)	Front Drive Axle L (pts)	Gas Tank L (gal)	Cooling System L (qts) Manual	Cooling System L (qts) Auto
'75	1952 (119.1)	4.8(5.1)	4.1(4.3)	1.7(3.6)	—	5.5 (11.7)	—	1.0 (2.1)	—	45(11.8)	6.0 (6.3)	6.0 (6.3)
'76–'77	1952 (119.1)	4.3(4.5)	3.8(4.0)	1.7(3.6)	2.0(4.2)	5.5 (11.7)	—	1.0 (2.1)	—	45(11.8)	8.0 (8.5)	7.8 (8.2)
'78	1952 (119.1)	4.3(4.5)	3.8(4.0)	1.7(3.6)	2.0(4.2)	5.5 (11.7)	—	1.0 (2.1)	—	45(11.8)	8.9 (9.3)	8.7 (9.2)
'79	1952 (119.1)	4.3(4.5)	3.8(4.0)	1.7(3.6)	2.0(4.2)	5.5 (11.7)	—	1.0 (2.1)	—	50(13.2)①	8.9 (9.3)	8.7 (9.2)
'80	1952 (119.1)	4.3(4.5)	3.8(4.0)	1.7(3.6)	2.0(4.2)	5.5 (11.7)	1.4(3.0)	1.25(2.6)	1.0(2.1)	50(13.2)①	8.9 (9.3)	8.7 (9.2)
'81 2-WD	2187 (133.5)	4.4(4.6)	3.9(4.12)	1.7(3.6)	2.0(4.2)	5.5 (11.7)	—	1.25(2.6)	—	50(13.2)①	10.2(10.75)	10.1(10.6)
4-WD	2187 (133.5)	4.2(4.5)	3.7(3.8)	1.7(3.6)	2.0(4.2)	5.5 (11.7)	1.4(3.0)	1.25(2.6)	1.0(2.1)	60(15.8)②	10.2(10.75)	10.1(10.6)
Diesel	2164 (132)	5.5(5.8)	—	—	2.0(4.2)	—	—	1.25(2.6)	—	60(15.8)②	—	—
'82 2-WD	2187 (133.5)	4.4(4.6)	3.9(4.12)	1.7(3.6)	2.0(4.2)	5.5 (11.7)	—	1.25(2.6)	—	50(13.25)①	10.2(10.75)	10.1(10.6)
4-WD	2187 (133.5)	4.2(4.5)	3.7(3.8)	1.7(3.6)	2.0(4.2)	5.5 (11.7)	1.4(3.0)	1.25(2.6)	1.0(2.12)	60(15.8)②	10.2(10.75)	10.1(10.6)
Diesel	2164 (132)	6.0(6.4)	—	—	2.0(4.2)	—	—	1.25(2.6)	—	50(13.25)①	9.9(10.5)	—

① Long bed: 64(16.8)
② Longbed w/4-WD: 75(19.8)
—Not applicable

DIESEL ENGINE TUNE-UP SPECIFICATIONS

Injector Opening Pressure (psi)	Low Idle (rpm)	Dashpot Speed (rpm)	Valve Clearance (in.)		Intake Valve Opens (deg.)	Injection Timing rpm	Firing Order
			Intake	Exhaust			
1422.5	550–700	1280–1350	.014	.014	28	20 BTDC	1-4-3-2

GASOLINE ENGINE TUNE-UP SPECIFICATIONS

Year	Engine Displacement cu in. (cc)	Spark Plug		Distributor		Ignition Timing (deg)		Intake Valve Opens (deg)	Fuel Pump Pressure (psi)	Compression Pressure (psi)▲	Idle Speed (rpm)		Valve Clearance (in.)●	
		Type	Gap (in.)	Point Dwell (deg)	Point Gap (in.)	MT	AT				MT	AT	In	Ex
'75	4-119 (1952)	BP6ES	0.034	52	0.020	12B⑤	12B	16B	3.0–3.8	171②	750	650①	0.010	0.012
'76–'77	4-119 (1952)	BP6ES④	0.033⑤	52	0.020⑥	12B③	12B	16B	3.0–3.8	171②	750	650①	0.010	0.012
'78	4-119 (1952)	BP6ES-11	0.041	—	⑥	12B	12B	16B	3.0–3.9⑦	171②	600	600①	0.010	0.012
'79	4-119 (1952)	BP6ES-11	0.041	—	⑧	12B	12B	16B	3.0–3.9⑦	171②	650	630①	0.010	0.012
'80	4-119 (1952)	BP6ES-11	0.041	—	⑧	12B⑨	12B⑨	16B	3.0–3.9⑦	171②	600	600	0.010	0.012
'81	4-133.5 (2187)	BP6ES⑩	0.033	—	⑧	5B	5B	16B	3.0–3.9	171②	650⑪	650	0.012	0.012
'82	4-133.5 (2187)	⑫	0.033	—	⑧	3B	3B	16B	3.0–3.9	171②	650⑪	650	0.012	0.012

NOTE: Part numbers in this chart are not recommendations by Chilton for any product by brand name.
● Measured with engine hot
▲ Lowest reading must be at least 80% of the highest
B Before top dead center
① Transmission in Drive
② 128 psi minimum
③ 10° B in California
④ BP6ES-11, Transistor ignition; BPR6ES, Canada, 1977 and later with conventional ignition
⑤ 0.041, Transistor ignition
⑥ 0.008–0.016, Transistor ignition air gap
⑦ 4.6 or less with electric fuel pump (air conditioned models)
⑧ 0.012—0.020, Transistor ignition air gap
⑨ Calif. Heavy Duty models: 10B
⑩ Canada: BPR6ES
⑪ 4-WD: 800
⑫ Intake side: BPR6ES
Exhaust side: BPR5ES

L20B firing order

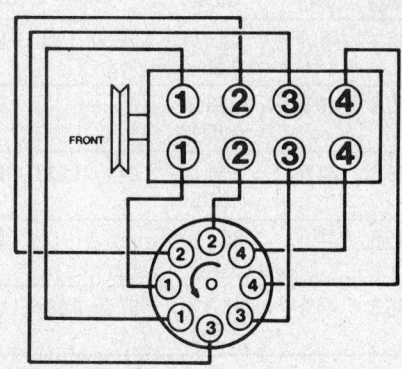

Z22 firing order

CRANKSHAFT AND CONNECTING ROD SPECIFICATIONS

(All measurements given in in.)

Year	Engine Displacement cc (cu in.)	Crankshaft					Connecting Rod		
		Main Brg Journal Dia	Main Brg Oil Clearance	Shaft End-Play	Thrust on No.	Journal Dia	Oil Clearance	Side Clearance
'75	1952 (119)	2.3599–2.3600	0.0008–0.0024	0.0020–0.0071	3	1.9660–1.9670	0.0010–0.0022	0.0079–0.0118
'76–'78	1952 (119)	2.3599–2.3604	0.0008–0.0024	0.0020–0.0071	3	1.9670–1.9675	0.0010–0.0020	0.008–0.012
'79–'80	1952 (119)	2.3599–2.3604	0.0008–0.0026	0.0020–0.0071	3	1.9670–1.9675	0.0009–0.0026	0.008–0.012
'81	2164 (132)	2.7918–2.7988	0.0013–0.0038	0.0024–0.0094	3	2.0840–2.0906	0.0013–0.0038	0.0039–0.0079
	2187 (133.5)	2.1631–2.1636	0.0008–0.0024	0.0021–0.0070	3	1.9670–1.9675	0.0010–0.0022	0.008–0.012
'82	2164 (132)	2.7916–2.7921	0.0014–0.0037	0.0024–0.0055	3	2.0832–2.0837	0.0014–0.0034	0.004–0.008
	2187 (133.5)	2.1631–2.1636	0.0008–0.0024	0.0020–0.0071	3	1.9670–1.9675	0.0010–0.0022	0.008–0.012

VALVE SPECIFICATIONS

Year	Engine Displacement cc (cu in.)	Seat Angle (deg)	Face Angle (deg)	Spring Test Pressure (lbs. @ in.)		Free Length (in.)		Stem-to-Guide Clearance (in.)		Stem Diameter (in.)	
				Outer	Inner	Outer	Inner	Intake	Exhaust	Intake	Exhaust
'75–'80	1952 (119)	45	45①	47 @ 1.58	27 @ 1.38	1.97	1.77	0.0008–0.0021	0.0016–0.0029	0.3139	0.3131
'81	2164 (132)	45.5	44.5	33 @ 1.634	—	1.929	—	0.0006–0.0018	0.0016–0.0028	0.3137–0.3143	0.3137–0.3143
	2187 (133.5)	45.5	44.5	51 @ 1.575	24 @ 1.378	1.959	1.736	0.0008–0.0021	0.0016–0.0029	0.3136–0.3142	0.3128–0.3134
'82	2164 (132)	45.5	44.5	134.7 @ 1.197	—	1.9764	—	0.0006–0.0018	0.0016–0.0028	0.3138–0.3144	0.3128–0.3134
	2187 (133.5)	45.5	44.5	115.3 @ 1.180	57 @ 0.98	1.9594	1.7362	0.0008–0.0021	0.0016–0.0029	0.3136–0.3142	0.3128–0.3134

① 45°30 '78–'79

PISTON CLEARANCE
(All measurements given in in.)

Year	Engine Displacement cc (cu. in.)	Minimum	Maximum
'75–'80	1770 (108) 1952 (119)	0.0010	0.0018
'81	2187 (133.5)	0.0010	0.0018
	2164 (132)	0.0047	0.0075
'82	2187 (133.5)	0.0010	0.0018
	2164 (132)	0.0016	0.0043

PISTON RING GAPS
(All measurements given in in.)

Year	Engine Displacement cc (cu in.)	Top Compression		Middle Compression		Oil Control	
		Min	Max	Min	Max	Min	Max
'75–'80	1952 (119)	0.0098	0.0157	0.0118	0.0197	0.0118	0.0354
'81	2187 (133.5)	0.0098	0.0157	0.0059	0.0118	0.0118	0.0354
	2164 (132)	0.0118	0.0197	0.0118	0.0197	0.0118	0.0197
'82	2187 (133.5)	0.0098	0.0157	0.0059	0.0118	0.0118	0.0354
	2164 (132)	0.0118	0.0177	0.0079	0.0138	0.0059	0.0118

PISTON RING SIDE CLEARANCE
(All measurements given in in.)

Year	Engine Displacement cc (in.)	Top Compression		Middle Compression		Oil Control	
		Min	Max	Min	Max	Min	Max
'75–'80	1770 (108) 1952 (119)	0.0016	0.0029	0.0012	0.0028	Snug	Snug
'81–'82	2187 (133.5)	0.0016	0.0029	0.0012	0.0025	Snug	Snug
	2164 (132)	0.0024	0.0039	0.0016①	0.0032①	0.0008	0.0024

① Diesel: 2nd and 3rd rings

DATSUN

TORQUE SPECIFICATIONS
(All readings in ft. lbs. unless noted)

Year	Engine Displacement cc (cu in.)	Cylinder Head Bolts	Rod Bearing Bolts	Main Bearing Bolts	Crankshaft Pulley Bolts	Flywheel to Crankshaft Bolts	Manifolds Intake	Manifolds Exhaust
'75–'80	1952 (119)	61	37	37	102	109	11	11
'81–'82	2187 (133.5)	51–58	33–40	33–40	87–116	101–116	12–15	12–16
	2164 (132)	94 large 40 small	36–40	109–116①	217–239	33–36	11–13	11–13

① 1982: 123–127

BATTERY AND STARTER SPECIFICATIONS

Year	Engine Displacement cc (cu in.)	Battery Amp Hour Capacity	Battery Volts	Battery Ground	Starter Lock Test Amps	Starter Lock Test Volts	Starter Lock Test Torque (ft. lbs.)	Starter No Load Test Amps	Starter No Load Test Volts	Starter No Load Test RPM	Brush Spring Tension (oz)
'75–'80	1952 (119)	①	12	Neg	Not Recommended			60—	12	7000 + ②	56
'81–'82	2187 (133.5)	①	12	Neg	Not Recommended			60③	11.5④	6000–7000⑤	56
	2164 (132)	①	12	Neg	800	5.0	21.0	150	12	3500	123.2

① 60 and 80 amp hour batteries were available
② 6000 + if equipped with automatic transmission
③ Canada: 100
④ Canada: 11.0
⑤ 3900

ALTERNATOR AND REGULATOR SPECIFICATIONS

Year	Alternator Manufacturer and/or Part Number	Alternator Output @ Alternator rpm	Charge Indicator Relay Back Gap (in.)	Charge Indicator Relay Air Gap (in.)	Charge Indicator Relay Point Gap (in.)	Voltage Regulator Back Gap (in.)	Voltage Regulator Air Gap (in.)	Voltage Regulator Point Gap (in.)	Regulated Voltage
'75	Hitachi LT135-13B LT135-19B①	28 Amp @ 2500 (14 volts)	—	0.035	0.020	—	0.032	0.014	14–15
'76	Hitachi LT135-13B LT135-19B①	28 @ 2500	—	0.035	0.020	—	0.032	0.016	14.3–15.3
'77	Hitachi LT135-36B LT138-01B①	28 @ 2500 30 @ 2500	—	0.035	0.020	—	0.032	0.016	14.3–15.3

ALTERNATOR AND REGULATOR SPECIFICATIONS

Year	Manufacturer and/or Part Number	Output @ Alternator rpm	Charge Indicator Relay Back Gap (in.)	Air Gap (in.)	Point Gap (in.)	Voltage Regulator Back Gap (in.)	Air Gap (in.)	Point Gap (in.)	Regulated Voltage
'78–'80	Hitachi LT135-44	27.5 @ 2500	—Transistorized Non-Adjustable Relay—						14.4–15.0
	LR138-01 ①	30.0 @ 2500							
'81	Hitachi LR150-98	50 @ 5000	—Transistorized Non-Adjustable Relay—						14.4–15.0
	LR160-78	60 @ 5000							
	LR150-52	50 @ 5000							
	LR160-78	60 @ 5000							
'82	Hitachi LR150-98B	40 @ 2500	—Transistorized Non-Adjustable Relay—						14.4–15.0
	LR160-78 & 78B	50 @ 2500	—Transistorized Non-Adjustable Relay—						14.4–15.0
	LR160-97B	52 @ 2500	—Transistorized Non-Adjustable Relay—						14.4–15.0

① With air conditioning
—Not applicable

BRAKE SPECIFICATIONS
(All measurements are given in in.)

Year	Master Cylinder Bore	Wheel Cylinder or Caliper Bore Front	Rear	Piston-to-Bore Clearance	Brake Drum or Rotor Diameter Front	Rear	Minimum Lining Thickness	Brake Disc Minimum Thickness	Maximum Run-out
'75	0.750	0.750	0.688	0.006	10.00	10.00	0.0394	—	—
'76–'77	0.750	0.750	0.750	0.006	10.00	10.00	0.0394	—	—
'78–'79	0.813	2.125	0.625	0.006	10.67	10.00	0.08 (disc) 0.06 (drum)	0.413	0.0059
'80–'82	0.875	2.125	0.625	0.006	10.67	10.00	0.08 (disc) 0.06 (drum)	0.413	0.0059

WHEEL ALIGNMENT SPECIFICATIONS

Year	Toe-In Range (in.)	Preferred (in.)	Camber Range (deg)	Preferred (deg)	Caster Range (deg)	Preferred (deg)	Kingpin Inclination (deg)	Steering Angle Inner Wheel (deg)	Outer Wheel (deg)
'75–'76	0.0394–0.1969	0.1182	15'–2°15'	1°15'	1°5'–2°35'	1°50'	6°15'	36° ± 1°	31° ± 1°
'77	0.079–0.118	0.100	15'–2°15'	1°15'	1°5'–2°35'	1°50'	6°15'	36° ± 1°	31° ± 1°
'78–'79	0.20–0.28	0.240	15'–1°15'	1°	35'–2°05'	1°30'	9°	35° ± 1°	30°30' ± 1°
'80	0.20–0.28	0.240	0–1°	½°	50'–1°50'	1°25'	9°	35° ± 1°	31° ± 1°
'81 2-wd	0.20–0.28	0.240	0–1°	½°	50'–1°50'	1°25'	9°	35° ± 1°	31° ± 1°
'81 4-wd	0.20–0.28	0.240	0–1°	½°	1°10'–2°10'	1°40'	9°	31° ± 2°	28° ± 1°
'82 2-wd	0.20–0.28	0.240	0–1°	½°	50'–1°50'	1°	8°45'	35° ± 1°	31° ± 1°
'82 4-wd	0.20–0.28	0.240	0–1°	½°	1°10'–2°10'	.6°	11°	31° ± 2°	28° ± 1°

DATSUN

TUNE-UP

NOTE: All 1975 Datsun pick-ups use a conventional breaker points ignition system. 1976 and later trucks sold in California, and all 1978 and later models sold in the U.S. use a fully transistorized ignition system. 1976–77 49 States and Canada models use the single breaker points system used in all models in 1975.

Breaker Points and Condenser

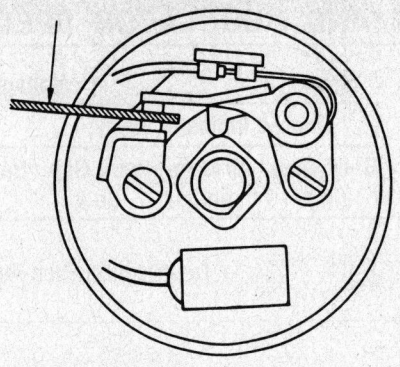

Arrow indicates the feeler gauge used to measure point gap

INSPECTION OF THE POINTS

1. Disconnect the high-tension wire from the top of the distributor and the coil.

2. The distributor cap is retained by two spring clips. Insert a screwdriver under their ends and release them. Lift off the cap with the spark plug wires attached. Inspect the inside of the cap. Wipe it clean with a rag and check for burned contacts, cracks and carbon tracks. A carbon track shows as a dark line running from one terminal to another. It cannot be successfully removed, so replace the cap if it has one of these. Generally, a cap and rotor will last 36,000 miles.

3. Remove the rotor from the distributor shaft by pulling it straight up. Examine the condition of the rotor. If it is cracked or the metal tip is excessively worn or burned, it should be replaced. Clean the metal tip with a clean cloth, but don't file it.

4. Pry open the contacts of the points with a screwdriver and check the condition of the contacts. If they are excessively worn, burned or pitted, they should be replaced.

5. If the points are in good condition, adjust them and replace the rotor and the distributor cap. If the points need to be replaced, follow the replacement procedure given next.

REPLACEMENT OF THE BREAKER POINTS AND CONDENSER

1. Remove the cap and rotor as outlined in steps 1–3 of the preceding section.

2. Loosen the two screws securing the points. Use a magnetic screwdriver to avoid losing a screw down the distributor. Loosen the screw in the side of the distributor and slip the points wire out. Remove the point set.

To remove the distributor, first note and mark the position of the distributor on the small timing scale on the front of the distributor. Then mark the position of the rotor in relation to the distributor body. Do this by simply replacing the rotor on the distributor shaft and marking the spot on the distributor body where the rotor is pointing. Remove the small bolt at the rear of the distributor, and lift the distributor out of the block. DO NOT CRANK THE ENGINE WITH THE DISTRIBUTOR REMOVED.

3. The condenser is held in place by the same screw as the points mounting screw, and its lead is attached at the same place as the points wire. Simply remove the condenser.

4. Before installing the new points and condenser, place a matchhead-sized dab of grease on the distributor shaft cam and smear it evenly around the cam. Do not use oil, because it will lead to rapid point burning.

5. Install the new points set and condenser. Tighten the condenser mounting screws, but leave the points screws slightly loose.

6. Check that the faces of the points meet squarely. If not, the *fixed* mount can be bent slightly with gentle force and a set of needlenose pliers. Do not bend the movable contact.

7. The point gap must be adjusted next. The gap is adjusted with the rubbing block of the points resting on one of the four high spots of the distributor cam. To get it there, the engine can be rotated by bumping the starter with the ignition key, or the crankshaft can be turned with a wrench on the crankshaft pulley bolt; this is easier to do with the spark plugs removed.

If the distributor shaft can be rotated until the points blocks are resting on the high spots of the cam. It won't matter if you move the distributor shaft; it can only go back into the engine one way. Just note the position from which it is moved, and move it back there prior to replacing the distributor in the engine.

8. Insert a 0.020 in. thick flat feeler gauge between the points. A slight drag should be felt. If no drag can be felt, or if the gauge cannot be inserted at all, insert a screwdriver into the eccentric adjusting screw, or into the notch provided for adjustment, and use it to open or close the gap between the points until it is correct.

9. When the gap is set, tighten the points screws, and then recheck the gap. Sometimes it takes three or four tries to get it correct, so don't feel frustrated if they seem to move around on you a little. It is not easy to feel the correct gap, either. Use gauges 0.002 in. larger and smaller than 0.020 as a test. If the points are spread slightly by a 0.022 in. gauge, and not touched at all by a 0.018 in. gauge, the setting should be right.

10. After all the adjustments are complete, pull a clean piece of tissue or a white business card between the points to clear any bits of grit.

11. Replace the rotor and distributor cap, and snap on the clips. If you have a dwell meter (recommended) you should next set the dwell. Otherwise, go on to the ignition timing.

ADJUSTMENT OF THE BREAKER POINTS WITH A DWELL METER

The dwell angle is the number of degrees of distributor cam rotation through which the points remain closed (conducting electricity). Increasing the point gap decreases dwell, while decreasing the gap increases dwell.

The dwell angle may be checked with the distributor cap and rotor installed and the engine running, or with the cap and rotor removed and the engine cranking at starter speed. The meter gives a constant reading with the engine running. With the engine cranking, the meter will fluctuate between zero degrees dwell and the maximum figure for that setting. Never attempt to adjust the points when the ignition is on, or you may receive a shock.

1. Connect a meter as per the manufacturer's instructions (usually one lead to the distributor terminal of the coil and the other lead to a ground). Zero the meter, if necessary.

NOTE: If the dwell meter does not have a four cylinder scale, multiply the eight cylinder reading by two.

2. Check the dwell by either the cranking method, or with the engine running. If the setting is incorrect, the points must be adjusted.

—— **CAUTION** ——

Keep your hands, hair and clothing clear of the engine fan and pulleys. Be sure the wires from the dwell meter are routed out of the way. If the engine is running, block the front wheels, put the transmission in Neutral, and set the parking brake.

3. To change the dwell angle, turn the ignition off, loosen the points hold down screw and adjust the point gap; increase the gap to decrease dwell, and vice versa. Tighten the hold down screw and check the dwell angle with the engine cranking. If it seems to be correct, replace the cap and rotor and check dwell with the engine run-

ning. Readjust as necessary.

4. Run the engine speed up to about 2,500 rpm, and then let the speed drop abruptly; the dwell reading should not change. If it does, a worn distributor shaft, bushing or cam, or a worn breaker plate is indicated. The parts must be inspected and replaced, if necessary.

5. After adjusting dwell angle, go on to the Ignition Timing section following. Ignition timing must be checked after adjusting the point gap, as a 1° increase in dwell results in an ignition timing retard of 2°, and vice versa.

Electronic Ignition

Datsun pick-ups sold in California beginning in 1976 were equipped with electronic ignition, and all 1978 and later trucks are equipped with the system. The 1978 system differs somewhat from the earlier system; the 1979 and later system is markedly different.

The electronic ignition differs from its conventional counterpart only in the distributor component area. The secondary side of the ignition system is the same as a conventional breaker points system.

Located in the distributor, in addition to the normal ignition rotor, is a four spoke rotor (reluctor) which rests on the distributor shaft where the breaker points cam is found on earlier systems. A pick-up coil, consisting of a magnet, coil, and wiring, rests on the "breaker plate" next to the reluctor. The system also uses a transistor ignition unit, located on the right side of the firewall in the passenger compartment, through 1978, 1979 and later models have an integrated circuit (IC) ignition unit, which is mounted on the side of the distributor. In addition, 1979 and later models use a ring-type pick-up coil, which surrounds the reluctor, rather than the arm-type coil used through 1978.

When a reluctor spoke is not aligned with the pick-up coil, it generates large lines of flux between itself, the magnet, and the pick-up coil. This large flux variation results in a high generated voltage in the pick-up coil, preventing current from flowing to the pick-up coil. When a reluctor spoke lines up with the pick-up coil, the flux variation is low—thus, zero voltage is generated, allowing current to flow to the pick-up coil. Ignition primary current is then cut off by the electronic unit, allowing the field in the ignition coil to collapse, inducing high secondary voltage in the conventional manner. The high voltage then flows through the distributor to the spark plug, as usual.

Because no points or condenser are used, and because dwell is determined by the electronic unit, no adjustments are necessary. Ignition timing is checked in the usual way, but unless the distributor is disturbed it is not likely to ever change very much.

Service consists of inspection of the distributor cap, rotor, and ignition wires, re-placing when necessary. These parts can be expected to last for at least 40,000 miles. In addition, the reluctor air gap should be checked periodically.

1. The distributor cap is held on by two clips. Release them with a screwdriver and lift the cap straight up and off, with the wires attached. Inspect the cap for cracks, carbon tracks, or a worn center contact. Replace it if necessary, transferring the wires one at a time from the old cap to the new.

2. Pull the ignition rotor (not the spoked reluctor) straight up to remove. Replace it if its contacts are worn, burned, or pitted. Do not file the contacts. To replace, press it firmly onto the shaft. It only goes on one way, so be sure it is fully seated.

3. Before replacing the ignition rotor, check the reluctor air gap. Use a non-magnetic feeler gauge. Rotate the engine until a reluctor spoke is aligned with the pick-up coil (either bump the engine around with the starter, or turn it with a wrench on the crankshaft pulley bolt). The gap should measure 0.008–0.016 in. through 1978, or 0.012–0.020 in. for 1979 and later. Adjustment, if necessary, is made by loosening the pick-up coil mounting screws and shifting its position on the "breaker plate" either closer to or farther from the reluctor. On 1979 and later models, center the pick-up coil (ring) around the reluctor. Tighten the screws and recheck the gap.

4. Inspect the wires for cracks or brittleness. Replace them one at a time to prevent crosswiring, carefully pressing the replacement wires into place. The cores of electronic wires are more susceptible to breakage than those of standard wires, so treat them gently.

TROUBLESHOOTING

1976–78

The main differences between the 1976–77 and 1978 systems are: (1) the 1976–77 system uses an external ballast resistor located next to the ignition coil, and (2) the earlier system uses a wiring harness with individual eyelet connectors to the electronic unit, while the later system uses a multiple plug connector. You will need an accurate voltmeter and ohmmeter for these tests, which must be performed in the order given.

1. Check all connections for corrosion, looseness, breaks, etc., and correct if necessary. Clean and gap the spark plugs.

2a. Disconnect the harness (connector or plug) from the electronic unit. Turn the ignition switch On. Set the voltmeter to the DC 50V range. Connect the positive (+) voltmeter lead to the black/white wire terminal, and the negative (−) lead to the black wire terminal. Battery voltage should be obtained. If not, check the black/white and black wires for continuity; check the battery terminals for corrosion; check the battery state of charge.

2b. Next, connect the voltmeter + lead to the blue wire and the − lead to the black

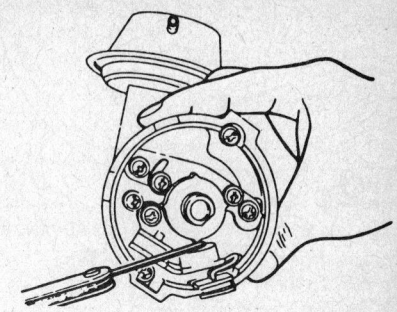

1976–78 air gap adjustment

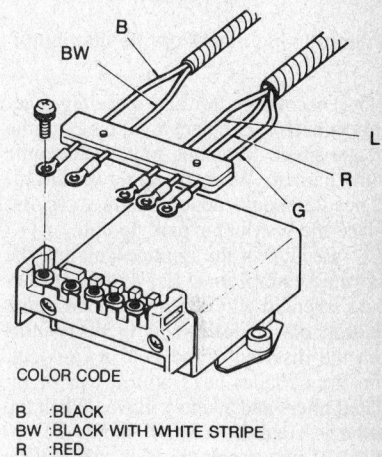

COLOR CODE

B : BLACK
BW : BLACK WITH WHITE STRIPE
R : RED
G : GREEN
L : BLUE

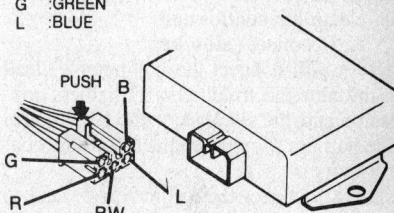

Electronic control unit connection: upper 1976–77, lower 1978 and later

wire. Battery voltage should be obtained. If not, check the blue wire for continuity; check the ignition coil terminals for corrosion or looseness; check the coil for continuity. On 1976–77 models, also check the external ballast resistor.

3. Disconnect the distributor harness wires from the ignition coil ballast resistor on 1976–77 models, leaving the ballast resistor-to-coil wires attached. On 1978 models, disconnect the ignition coil wires. Connect the leads of an ohmmeter to the ballast resistor outside terminals (at each end) through 1977; resistance should be 1.6–2.0 ohms. In 1978, connect the ohmmeter to the coil terminals: resistance should be 0 ohs. If more than 2.0 ohms, 1976–77, or 1.8 ohms, 1978, replace the coil.

4. Disconnect the harness from the electronic control unit. Connect an ohmmeter to the red and the green wire terminals. Resistance should be 720 ohms. If far more or far less, replace the distributor pick-up coil.

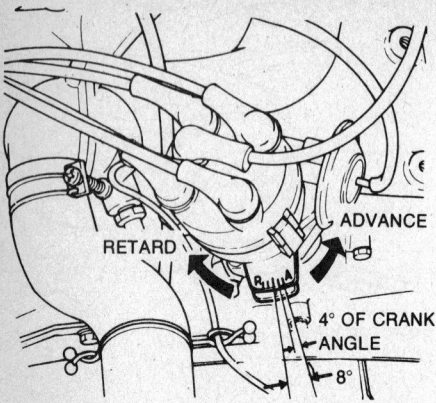

Ignition timing marks on the distributor

5. Disconnect the anti-dieseling solenoid connector. Connect a voltmeter to the red and green terminals of the electronic control harness. When the starter is cranked, the needle should deflect slightly. If not, replace the distributor pick-up coil.

6. Reconnect the ignition coil and the electronic control unit. Leave the anti-dieseling solenoid wire disconnected. Unplug the high ension lead (coil to distributor) from the distributor and hold it ⅛–¼ in. from the cylinder head with a pair of insulated pliers and a heavy glove. When the engine is cranked, a spark should be observed. If not, check the lead, and replace the electronic control unit.

7. Reconnect all wires:

1976–77: connect the voltmeter + lead to the blue electronic control harness connector and the − lead to the black wire. The harness should be attached to the control unit.

1978: connect the voltmeter + lead to the − terminal of the ignition coil and the − lead to ground.

As soon as the ignition switch is turned ON, the meter should indicate battery voltage. If not, replace the electronic control unit.

1979 and Later

1. Make a check of the power supply circuit. Turn the ignition OFF. Disconnect the connector from the top of the IC unit. Turn the ignition ON. Measure the voltage at each terminal of the connector in turn by touching the probe of the positive lead of the voltmeter to one of the terminals, and touching the probe of the negative lead of the voltmeter to a ground, such as the engine. In each case, battery voltage should be indicated. If not, check all wiring, the ignition switch, and all connectors for breaks, corrosion, discontinuity, etc., and repair as necessary.

2. Check the primary windings off the ignition coil. Turn the ignition OFF. Disconnect the harness connector from the negative coil terminals. Use an ohmmeter to measure the resistance between the positive and negative coil terminals. If resistance is 0.84–1.02 ohms, the coil is OK.

Replace if far from this range.

If the power supply, circuits, wiring, and coil are in good shape, check the IC unit and pick-up coil, as follows:

3. Turn the ignition OFF. Remove the distributor cap and ignition rotor. Use an ohmmeter to measure the resistance between the two terminals of the pick-up coil, where they attach to the IC unit. Measure the resistance by reversing the polarity of the probes. If approximately 400 ohms are indicated, the pick-up coil is OK, but the IC unit is bad and must be replaced. If other than 400 ohms are measured, go to the next step.

4. Be certain the two pin connector to the IC unit is secure. Turn the ignition ON. Measure the voltage at the ignition coil negative terminal. Turn the ignition OFF.

--- **CAUTION** ---

Remove the tester probe from the coil negative terminal before switching the ignition OFF, to prevent burning out the tester.

If zero voltage is indicated, the IC unit is bad and must be replaced. If battery voltage is indicated, proceed.

5. Remove the IC unit from the distributor:

a. Disconnect the battery ground (negative) cable.

b. Remove the distributor cap and ignition rotor.

c. Disconnect the harness connector at the top of the IC unit.

d. Remove the two screws securing the IC unit to the distributor.

e. Disconnect the two pick-up coil wires from the IC unit.

--- **CAUTION** ---

Pull the connectors free with a pair of needlenosed pliers. Do not pull on the wires to detach the connectors.

f. Remove the IC unit.

6. Measure the resistance between the terminals of the pick-up coil. It should be approximately 400 ohms. If so, the pick-up coil is OK, and the IC unit is bad. If not approximately 400 ohms, the pick-up coil is bad and must be replaced.

7. With a new pick-up coil installed, install the IC unit. Check for a spark at one of the spark plugs. If a good spark is obtained, the IC unit is OK. If not, replace the IC unit.

Ignition Timing

NOTE: For diesel engine injection pump timing, see the fuel system section.

Ignition timing is the measurement, in degrees of crankshaft rotation, of the point at which the spark plugs fire in each of the cylinders. It is measured in degrees before or after Top Dead Center (TDC) of the compression stroke.

Because it takes a fraction of a second for the spark plug to ignite the mixture in

the cylinder, the spark plug must fire a little before the piston reaches TDC. Otherwise, the mixture will not be completely ignited as the piston passes TDC and the full power of the explosion will not be used by the engine.

The timing measurement is given in degrees of crankshaft rotation before the piston reaches TDC (BTDC). If the setting for the ignition timing is 5° BTDC, the spark plug must fire 5° before each piston reaches TDC. This only holds true, however, when the engine is at idle speed.

As the engine speed increases, the pistons go faster. The spark plugs have to ignite the fuel even sooner if it is to be completely ignited when the piston reaches TDC. To do this, the distributor has a means to advance the timing of the spark as the engine speed increases. This is accomplished by centrifugal weights within the distributor and a vacuum diaphragm, mounted on the side of the distributor. On Datsun pick-ups, it is not necessary to disconnect the vacuum line from the diaphragm when the ignition timing is being set.

If the ignition is set too far advanced (BTDC), the ignition and expansion of the fuel in the cylinder will occur too soon and tend to force the piston down while it is still traveling up. This causes engine ping. If the ignition spark is set too far retarded, after TDC (ATDC), the piston will have already passed TDC and started on its way down when the fuel is ignited. This will cause the piston to be forced down for only a portion of its travel. This will result in poor engine performance and lack of power.

Timing marks consist of a notch on the rim of the crankshaft pulley and a scale of degrees attached to the front of the engine. The notch correponds to the position of the piston in the no. 1 cylinder. A stroboscopic (dynamic) timing light is used, which is hooked into the circuit of the no. 1 cylinder spark plug. Every time the spark plug fires, the timing light flashes. By aiming the timing light at the timing marks, the exact position of the piston within the cylinder can be read, since the stroboscopic flash makes the mark on the pulley appear to be standing still. Proper timing is indicated when the notch is aligned with the correct number on the scale. There are three basic types of timing light available. The first is a simple neon bulb with two wire connections (one for the spark plug and one for the plug wire, connecting the light in a series). This type of light is quite dim, and must be held closely to the marks to be seen, but it is quite inexpensive. The second type of light operates from the truck battery. Two alligator clips connect to the battery terminals, while a third wire connects to the spark plug with an adapter. This type of light is more expensive, but the xenon bulb provides a nice bright flash which can even be seen in sunlight. The third type replaces the battery source with 110 volt house current. Some timing lights have other functions built into them, such as dwell meters, tachometers, or remote starting switches. These are convenient, in that they reduce the tangle of wires under the hood, but may duplicate the functions of tools you already have.

If your Datsun has electronic ignition, you should use a timing light with an inductive pickup. This pickup simply clamps onto the no. 1 plug wire, eliminating the adapter. It is not susceptible to crossfiring or false triggering, which may occur with a conventional light, due to the greater voltages produced by electronic ignition.

IGNITION TIMING ADJUSTMENT

NOTE: Refer to Fuel System for the procedure to time diesel engines

1. Set the dwell of the breaker points to the proper specification.
2. Locate the timing marks on the crankshaft pulley and the front of the engine.
3. Clean off the timing marks, so that you can see them.
4. Use chalk or white paint to color the mark on the crankshaft pulley and the mark on the scale which will indicate the correct timing when aligned with the notch on the crankshaft pulley.
5. Attach a tachometer to the engine.
6. Attach a timing light to the engine, according to the manufacturer's instructions. If the timing light has three wires, one, usually green or blue, is attached to the no. 1 spark plug with an adapter. The other wires are connected to the battery. The red wire goes to the positive side of the battery and the black wire is connected to the negative terminal of the battery.
7. Leave the vacuum line connected to the distributor vacuum diaphragm.
8. Check to make sure that all of the wires clear the fan and then start the engine. Allow the engine to reach normal operating temperature.

———— CAUTION ————
Block the front wheels and set the parking brake. Shift the manual transmission to Neutral or the automatic to Drive. Do not stand in front of the truck when making adjustments!

9. Adjust the idle to the correct setting.
10. Aim the timing light at the timing marks. If the marks which you put on the pulley and the engine are aligned when the light flashes, the timing is correct. Turn off the engine and remove the tachometer and the timing light. If the marks are not in alignment, proceed with the following steps.
11. Turn off the engine.
12. Loosen the distributor lockbolt just enough so that the distributor can be turned with a little effort.
13. Start the engine. Keep the wires of the timing light clear of the fan.
14. With the timing light aimed at the

pulley and the marks on the engine, turn the distributor in the direction of rotor rotation to retard the spark, and in the opposite direction of rotor rotation to advance the spark. Align the marks on the pulley and the engine with the flashes of the timing light.
15. Tighten the distributor lockbolt and recheck the timing.

Valve Lash

Valve adjustment determines how far the valves enter the cylinder and how long they stay open and closed.

If the valve clearance is too large, part of the lift of the camshaft will be used in removing the excessive clearance. Consequently, the valve will not be opening for as long as it should. This condition has two effects; the valve train components will emit a tapping sound as they take up the excessive clearance and the engine will perform poorly because the valves don't open fully and allow the proper amount of gases to flow into and out of the engine.

If the valve clearance is too small, the intake valves and the exhaust valves will open too far and they will not fully seat on the cylinder head when they close. When a valve seats itself on the cylinder head, it does two things: it seals the combustion chamber so that none of the gases in the cylinder escape and it cools itself by transferring some of the heat it absorbs from the combustion in the cylinder to the cylinder head and to the engine's cooling system. If the valve clearance is too small, the engine will run poorly because of the gases escaping from the combustion chamber. The valves will also become overheated and will warp, since they cannot transfer heat unless they are touching the valve seat in the cylinder head.

NOTE: While all valve adjustments must be made as accurately as possible, it is better to have the valve adjustment slightly loose than slightly tight, as a burned valve may result from overly tight adjustments.

ADJUSTMENT

All Except 1981–82 Gasoline Engine

1. The valves are adjusted with the engine at normal operating temperature. Oil temperature, and the resultant parts expansion, is much more important than water temperature. Run the engine for at least fifteen minutes to ensure that all the parts have reached their full expansion. After the engine is warmed up, shut it off.
2. Purchase either a new gasket or some silicone gasket seal before removing the camshaft cover. Note the location of any wires and hoses which may interfere with cam cover removal, disconnect them and move them aside. Then remove the bolts

which hold the cam cover in place and remove the cam cover.

3. Place a wrench on the crankshaft pulley bolt and turn the engine over until the valves for no. 1 cylinder are closed. When both cam lobes are pointing up, the valves are closed. If you have not done this before, it is a good idea to turn the engine over slowly several times and watch the valve action until you have a clear idea of just when the valve is closed.
4. Check the clearance of the intake and exhaust valves. You can differentiate between them by lining them up with the tubes of the intake and exhaust manifolds. The correct size feeler gauge should pass between the base circle of the cam and the rocker arm with just a slight drag. Be sure the feeler gauge is inserted *straight* and not on an angle.
5. If the valves need adjustment, loosen the locking nut and then adjust the clearance with the adjusting screw. You will probably find it necessary to hold the locking nut while you turn the adjuster. After you have the correct clearance, tighten the locking nut and recheck the clearance. Remember, it's better to have them too loose than too tight, especially exhaust valves.
6. Repeat this procedure until you have checked and/or adjusted all the valves. Keep in mind that all that is necessary is to have the valves closed and the camshaft lobes pointing up. It is not particularly important what stroke the engine is on.

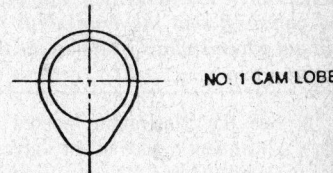

NO. 1 CAM LOBE

Cam lobe pointing straight down—Z series engines

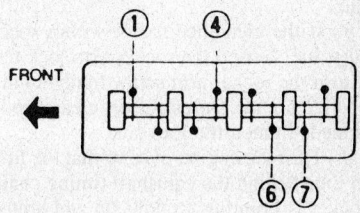

Primary adjustment—Z series engines

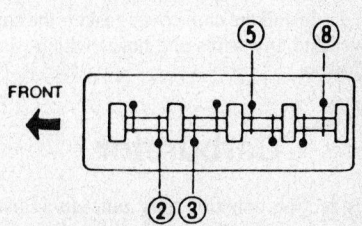

Secondary adjustment—Z series engines

7. Install the cam cover gasket, the cam cover, and any wires and hoses which were removed.

1981–82 Z22 Engine

1. The valves must be adjusted with the engine warm, so start the truck and run the engine until the needle on the temperature gauge reaches the middle of the gauge. After the engine is warm, shut it off.

2. Purchase either a new gasket or some silicone gasket sealer before removing the camshaft cover. Counting on the old gasket to be in good shape is a losing proposition; always use new gaskets. Note the location of any wires and hoses which may interfere with cam cover removal, disconnect them and move them to one side. Remove the bolts holding the cover in place and remove the cover. Remember, the engine will be hot, so be careful.

3. Place a wrench on the crankshaft pulley bolt and turn the engine over until the first cam lobe behind the camshaft timing chain sprocket is pointing straight down.

NOTE: If you decide to turn the engine by "bumping" it with the starter, be sure to disconnect the high tension wire from the coil(s) to prevent the engine from accidentally starting and spewing oil all over the engine compartment.

—— **CAUTION** ——
Never attempt to turn the engine by using a wrench on the camshaft sprocket bolt; there is a one to two turning ratio between the camshaft and the crankshaft which will put a tremendous strain on the timing chain.

4. See the illustration marked "Primary adjustment" and adjust valves (1), (4), (6), and (7) to 0.012 in. using a flat-bladed feeler gauge. The feeler gauge should pass between the valve stem end and the rocker arm screw with a very slight drag. Insert the feeler gauge *straight*, not at an angle.

5. If the clearance is not within specified value, loosen the rocker arm lock nut and turn the rocker arm screw to obtain the proper clearance. After correct clearance is obtained, tighten the lock nut.

6. Turn the engine over so that the first cam lobe behind the camshaft timing chain sprocket is pointing straight up and adjust the valves marked (2), (3), (5), and (8) in the "Secondary adjustment" illustration. They, too, should have a clearance of 0.012 in.

7. Install the cam cover gasket, the cam cover and any wires and hoses which were removed.

Carburetor

This section contains only tune-up adjustment procedures for carburetors. Descriptions, adjustments, and overhaul procedures for carburetors can be found in the Fuel System section.

When the engine in your Datsun is running, the air-fuel mixture from the carburetor is being drawn into the engine by a partial vacuum which is created by the movement of the pistons downward on the intake stroke. The amount of air-fuel mixture that enters into the engine is controlled by the throttle plates in the bottom of the carburetor. When the engine is not running the throttle plates are closed, completely blocking off the bottom of the carburetor from the inside of the engine. The throttle plates are connected by the throttle linkage to the accelerator pedal in the passenger compartment of the Datsun. When you depress the pedal, you open the throttle plates in the carburetor to admit more air-fuel mixture to the engine.

When the engine is not running, the throttle plates are closed. When the engine is idling, it is necessary to have the throttle plates open slightly. To prevent having to hold your foot on the pedal when the engine is idling, an idle speed adjusting screw is added to the carburetor linkage.

The idle adjusting screw contacts a lever (throttle lever) on the outside of the carburetor. When the screw is turned, it either opens or closes the throttle plates of the carburetor, raising or lowering the idle speed of the engine. This screw is called the curb idle adjusting screw.

A special mixture circuit is incorporated into the carburetor to enable the engine to run smoothly at idle. This circuit is controlled by the mixture screw, which determines the amount of fuel admitted at idle.

IDLE SPEED AND MIXTURE ADJUSTMENT

1. Start the engine and run it until it reaches operating temperature.

2. Allow the engine idle speed to stabilize by running the engine at idle for at least one minute.

3. If it hasn't already been done, check and adjust the ignition timing to the proper setting.

4. Turn off the engine and connect a tachometer to the engine.

5. Disconnect and plug the air hose between the three way connector and the check valve, if equipped. Start the engine. With the transmission in Neutral, check the idle speed on the tachometer. If the reading on the tachometer is correct, turn the idle adjusting screw clockwise with a screwdriver to increase the idle speed and counterclockwise to decrease it.

6. With an automatic transmission in Drive (wheels chocked and parking brake applied) or a manual transmission in Neutral, turn the mixture screw out until the engine rpm starts to drop due to an overly rich mixture.

7. Turn the screw in past the starting point until the engine rpm start to drop be-

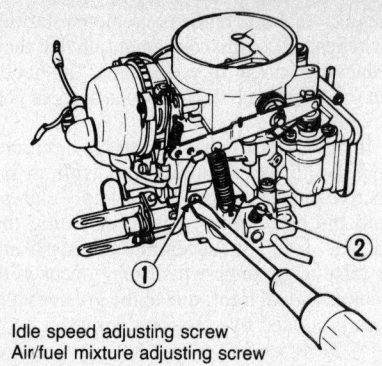

1. Idle speed adjusting screw
2. Air/fuel mixture adjusting screw

Idle speed and mixture adjustments

cause of a too lean mixture. On 1975–77 models, turn the mixture screw in until the idle speed drops 60–70 rpm with manual transmission, or 15–25 rpm with automatic transmission (in Drive). On 1978 models, the rpm drop should be 45–55 rpm for all trucks. For 1979 and later the rpm drop should be 45–55 rpm with manual transmission, or 25–35 rpm with automatic transmission (in Drive). If the mixture limiter cap will not allow this adjustment, remove it, make the adjustment, and reinstall it.

8. Install the air hose. If the engine speed increases, reduce it with the idle speed screw.

NOTE: To be sure that the vehicle is complying with emission laws, have the exhaust checked with a "CO" meter. The percentages of CO should be 2% 1975–77, and 1% 1978–82 at idle speed.

NOTE: Idle limiter caps are installed on the mixture adjusting screws so that an incorrect adjustment cannot be made. If a satisfactory idle cannot be obtained within the range of the limiter caps, remove them and make the adjustment as outlined above. Reinstall the limiter caps so that the cap can be turned only 1/8 of a turn counterclockwise before it reaches the stop. Have the engine checked with a CO meter after making the adjustment.

ENGINE ELECTRICAL

Distributor

REMOVAL

1. Remove the high-tension wires from the distributor cap terminal towers, noting their positions to assure correct reassembly. Number the wires with pieces of adhesive tape if they are not already numbered.

2. Disconnect the distributor wiring harness.

3. Disconnect the vacuum line(s).

4. Unlatch the two distributor cap retaining clips and remove the distributor cap.

5. Note the position of the rotor in relation to the base. Scribe a mark on the base of the distributor and on the engine block to facilitate reinstallation. Align the marks with the direction the metal tip of the rotor is pointing.

6. Remove the bolt which holds the distributor to the engine.

7. Lift the distributor assembly from the engine.

INSTALLATION

1. Insert the distributor shaft and assembly into the engine. Line up the mark on the distributor and the one on the engine with the metal tip of the rotor. Make sure that the vacuum advance diaphragm is pointed in the same direction as it was pointed originally. This will be done automatically if the marks on the engine and the distributor are lined up with the rotor.

2. Install the distributor hold-down bolt and clamp. Leave the screw loose enough so that you can move the distributor with heavy hand pressure.

3. Connect the distributor wiring harness. Install the distributor cap on the distributor housing. Secure the distributor cap with the spring clips.

4. Install the spark plug wires. Make sure that the wires are pressed all the way into the top of the distributor cap and firmly onto the spark plug.

5. Adjust the point dwell and set the ignition timing.

NOTE: If the crankshaft has been turned or the engine disturbed in any manner (i.e., disassembled and rebuilt) while the distributor was removed, or if the marks were not drawn, it will be necessary to initially time the engine. Follow the procedure given below.

1. It is necessary to place the no. 1 cylinder in the firing position to correctly install the distributor. To locate this position, the ignition timing marks on the crankshaft front pulley are used.

2. Remove the no. 1 cylinder spark plug. Turn the crankshaft until the piston in the no. 1 cylinder is moving up on the compression stroke. This can be determined by placing your thumb over the spark plug hole and feeling the air being forced out of the cylinder. Stop turning the crankshaft when the timing marks that are used to time the engine are aligned.

3. Oil the distributor housing lightly where the distributor bears on the cylinder block.

4. Install the distributor so that the rotor, which is mounted on the shaft, points toward the no. 1 spark plug terminal tower position when the cap is installed. Of course you won't be able to see the direction in which the rotor is pointing if the cap is on the distributor. Lay the cap on the top of

1. Cap assembly
2. Rotor head assembly
3. Roll pin
4. Reluctor
5. Pick-up coil
6. Contactor
7. Breaker plate assembly
8. Packing
9. Rotor shaft
10. Governor spring
11. Governor weight
12. Shaft assembly
13. Cap setter
14. Vacuum controller
15. Housing
16. Fixing plate
17. O-ring
18. Collar

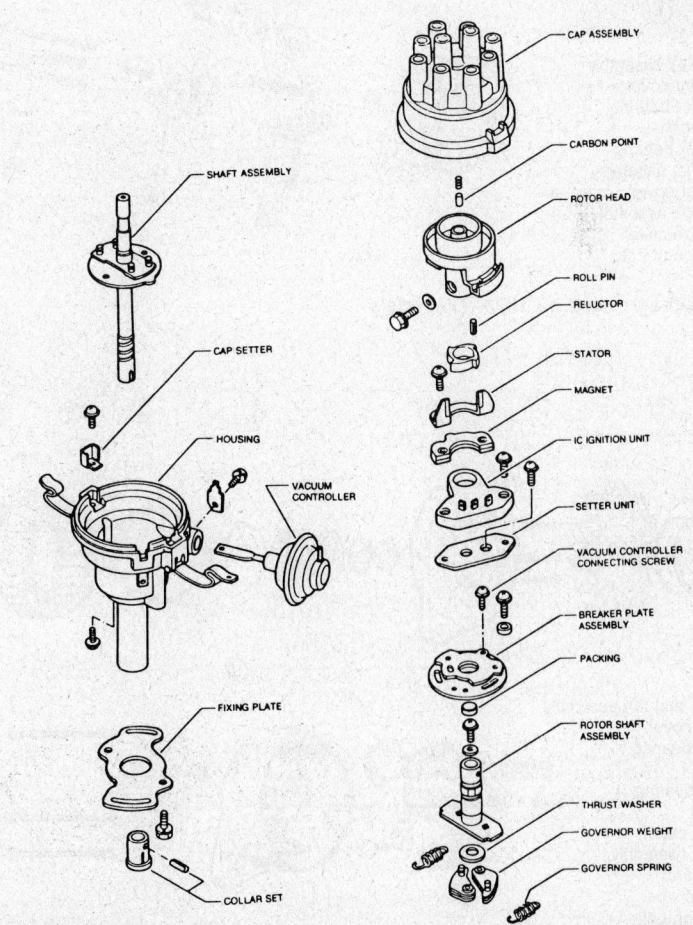

Exploded view of the electronic ignition distributor

CAP ASSEMBLY
CARBON POINT
ROTOR HEAD
ROLL PIN
RELUCTOR
STATOR
MAGNET
IC IGNITION UNIT
SETTER UNIT
VACUUM CONTROLLER CONNECTING SCREW
BREAKER PLATE ASSEMBLY
PACKING
ROTOR SHAFT ASSEMBLY
THRUST WASHER
GOVERNOR WEIGHT
GOVERNOR SPRING

SHAFT ASSEMBLY
CAP SETTER
HOUSING
VACUUM CONTROLLER
FIXING PLATE
COLLAR SET

Z22 engine distributor

the distributor and make a mark on the side of the distributor housing just below the no. 1 spark plug terminal. Make sure that the rotor points toward that mark when you install the distributor.

5. When the distributor shaft has reached the bottom of the hole, move the rotor back and forth slightly until the driving lug on the end of the shaft enters the slots cut in the end of the oil pump shaft and the distributor assembly slides down into place.

6. When the distributor is correctly installed, the breaker points should be in such a position that they are just ready to break contact with each other. This is accomplished by rotating the distributor body after it has been installed in the engine. Once again, line up the marks that you made before the distributor was removed from the engine.

7. Install the distributor hold-down bolt.

8. Install the spark plug into the no. 1 spark plug hole and continue from step 3 of the distributor installation procedure.

Alternator

Datsun pick-ups are equipped with a 35 amp alternator with electromechanical, adjustable voltage regulators through 1976. 1977 models are the same, except that trucks with factory air conditioning have 38 amp alternators. 1978–80 models use 35 amp alternators (38 amp with A/C), but have a transistorized, non-adjustable regulator integral with the alternator. 1981–82 models have a 40, 50, or 60 amp unit, with the diesel featuring a 70 or 80 amp unit.

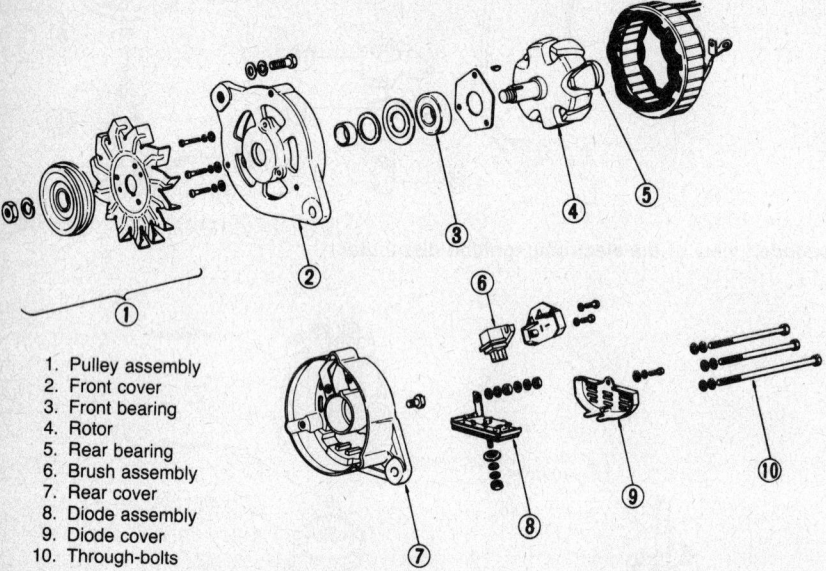

1. Pulley assembly
2. Front cover
3. Front bearing
4. Rotor
5. Rear bearing
6. Brush assembly
7. Rear cover
8. Diode assembly
9. Diode cover
10. Through-bolts

Typical alternator used on 1975–77 models

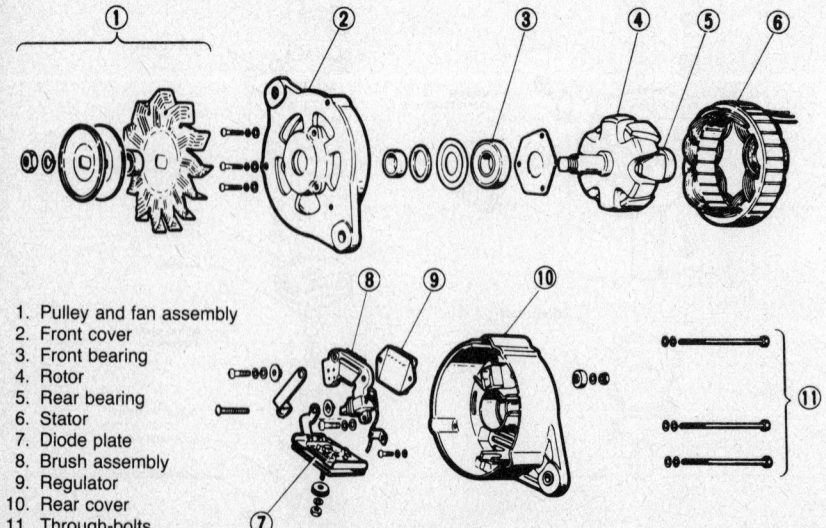

1. Pulley and fan assembly
2. Front cover
3. Front bearing
4. Rotor
5. Rear bearing
6. Stator
7. Diode plate
8. Brush assembly
9. Regulator
10. Rear cover
11. Through-bolts

Typical alternator used on 1978 and later models

ALTERNATOR PRECAUTIONS

To prevent damage to the alternator and regulator, the following precautionary measures must be taken when working with the electrical system.

1. Never reverse battery connections. Always check the battery polarity visually. This is to be done before any connections are made to be sure that all of the connections correspond to the battery ground polarity of the truck.

2. Booster batteries for starting must be connected properly. Make sure that the positive cable of the booster battery is connected to the positive terminal of the battery which is getting the boost.

3. Disconnect the battery cables before using a fast charger; the charger has a tendency to force current through the diodes in the opposite direction for which they were designed. This burns out the diodes.

4. Never use a fast charger as a booster for starting the vehicle.

5. Never disconnect the voltage regulator while the engine is running.

6. Do not ground the alternator output terminal.

7. Do not operate the alternator on an open circuit with the field energized.

8. Do not attempt to polarize an alternator.

9. Disconnect the battery cables before using an electric arc welder on the truck.

REMOVAL AND INSTALLATION

1. Disconnect the negative battery terminal.

2. Disconnect the two lead wires and connector from the alternator.

3. Loosen the drive belt adjusting bolt and remove the belt.

4. Unscrew the alternator attaching bolts and remove the alternator from the vehicle.

5. Install the alternator in the reverse order of removal.

Regulator

REMOVAL AND INSTALLATION

1975–77

1. Disconnect the negative battery terminal.

2. Disconnect the electrical lead connector of the regulator.

3. Remove the two mounting screws and remove the regulator from the vehicle.

4. Install the regulator in the reverse order of removal.

1978–82

The transistorized regulator is soldered to the brush assembly inside the alternator. It is non-adjustable, and must be replaced together with the brush assembly if faulty.

1. Remove the alternator.

2. Remove the through bolts and separate the front cover from the stator housing.

3. Unsolder the wire connecting the diode plate to the brush at the brush terminal.

4. Remove the bolt retaining the diode plate to the rear cover.

5. Remove the nut securing the battery terminal bolt.

6. Lift the stator slightly, together with the diode plate, to gain access to the diode plate screw. Remove the screw.

7. Separate the stator and diode, and remove the brush and regulator assembly.

8. Assembly is the reverse. Apply soldering heat sparingly, carrying out the operation as quickly as possible, to avoid heat damage to the transistors and diodes. Before assembling the alternator halves, bend a piece of wire in an "L" and slip it through the rear cover next to the brushes. Use the wire to hold the brushes in a retracted position until the case halves are assembled. Remove the wire carefully, to prevent damage to the slip rings.

ADJUSTMENT

1975–77

1. Adjust the voltage regulator core gap by loosening the screw which is used to secure the contact set on the yoke, and move the contact up or down as necessary. Retighten the screw. The gap should be 0.024–0.039 in.

2. Adjust the point gap of the voltage regulator coil by loosening the screw used to secure the upper contact and move the upper contact up or down. The gap should be 0.012–0.016 in. for 1975, 0.014–0.018 1976–77.

3. The core gap and point gap on the charge relay coil is or are adjusted in the same manner as previously outlined for the voltage regulator coil. The core gap is to be set at 0.032–0.039 in. and the point gap adjusted to 0.016–0.024in.

4. The regulated voltage is adjusted by loosening the locknut and turning the adjusting screw clockwise to increase, or counterclockwise to decrease the regulated voltage. The voltage should be between 14.3–15.3 volts at 68°F.

Starter

A standard non-reduction gear starting motor is used on all models through 1977, and most 1978–79 models. This motor has its brushes located within the rear cover. A reduction gear starting motor is installed in all 1978–79 Canadian models, and is optional for 1979–82 U.S. trucks. The reduction gear motor brushes are on a plate located just behind the starter drive housing.

REMOVAL AND INSTALLATION

1. Disconnect the negative battery cable from the battery.

2. Disconnect the starter wiring at the starter, taking note of the positions for correct reinstallation.

3. Remove the bolts attaching the starter to the engine and remove the starter from the vehicle.

4. Install the starter in the reverse order of removal.

BRUSH REPLACEMENT

Non-Reduction Gear Type

1. With the starter out of the vehicle, remove the bolts holding the solenoid to the top of the starter and remove the solenoid.

2. To remove the brushes, remove the two thru-bolts, and the two rear cover attaching screws and remove the rear cover.

3. Disconnect the electrical leads and remove the brushes.

4. Install the brushes in the reverse order of removal.

Reduction Gear Type

1. Remove the starter. Remove the solenoid.

2. Remove the through bolts and the rear cover. The rear cover can be pried off with a screwdriver, but be careful not to damage the O-ring.

3. Remove the starter housing, armature, and brush holder from the center housing. They can be removed as an assembly.

4. Remove the positive side brush from its holder. The positive brush is insulated from the brush holder, and its lead wire is connected to the field coil.

5. Carefully lift the negative brush from the commutator and remove it from the holder.

6. Installation is the reverse.

STARTER DRIVE REPLACEMENT

Non-Reduction Gear Type

1. With the starter motor removed from the vehicle, remove the solenoid from the starter.

2. Remove the two thru-bolts and separate the gear from the yoke housing.

3. Remove the pinion stopper clip and the pinion stopper.

4. Slide the starter drive off the armature shaft.

5. Install the starter drive and reassemble the starter in the reverse order of removal.

Reduction Gear Type

1. Remove the starter.

2. Remove the solenoid and the shift

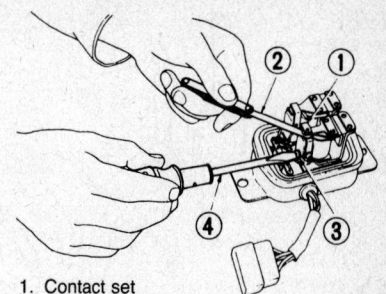

1. Contact set
2. Thickness gauge
3. 4 mm (0.1575 in.) dia. screw
4. Crosshead screwdriver

1975–77 voltage regulator core gap adjustment

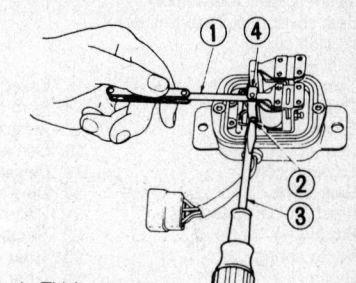

1. Thickness gauge
2. 3 mm (0.1181 in.) dia. screw
3. Crosshead screwdriver
4. Upper contact

1975–77 voltage regulator coil point adjustment

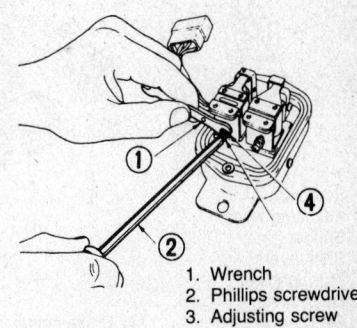

1. Wrench
2. Phillips screwdriver
3. Adjusting screw
4. Locknut

1975–77 regulated voltage adjustment

lever.

3. Remove the bolts securing the center housing to the front cover and separate the parts.

4. Remove the gears and starter drive.

5. Installation is the reverse.

Battery

REMOVAL AND INSTALLATION

1. Disconnect the negative (ground) cable from the terminal, and then the positive cable. Special pullers are available to remove the cable clamps.

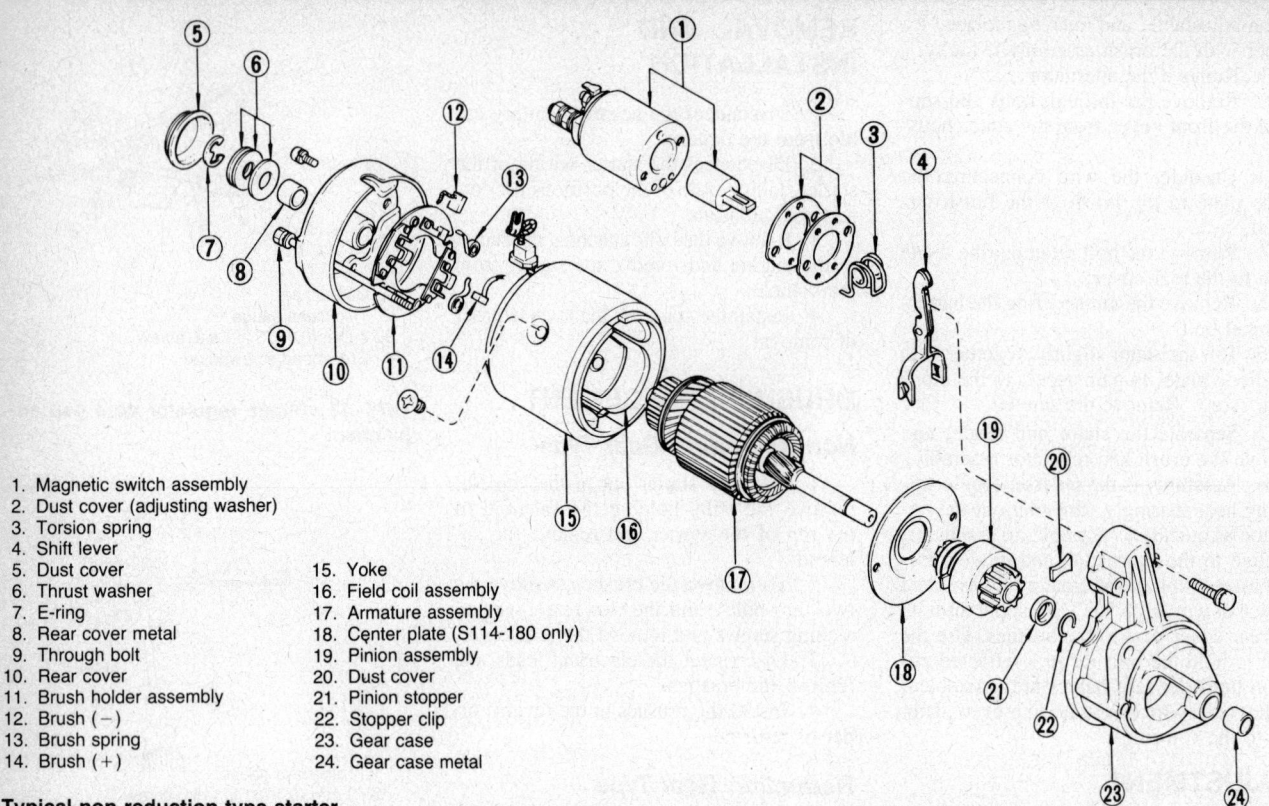

1. Magnetic switch assembly
2. Dust cover (adjusting washer)
3. Torsion spring
4. Shift lever
5. Dust cover
6. Thrust washer
7. E-ring
8. Rear cover metal
9. Through bolt
10. Rear cover
11. Brush holder assembly
12. Brush (−)
13. Brush spring
14. Brush (+)
15. Yoke
16. Field coil assembly
17. Armature assembly
18. Center plate (S114-180 only)
19. Pinion assembly
20. Dust cover
21. Pinion stopper
22. Stopper clip
23. Gear case
24. Gear case metal

Typical non reduction type starter

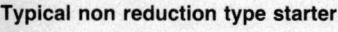

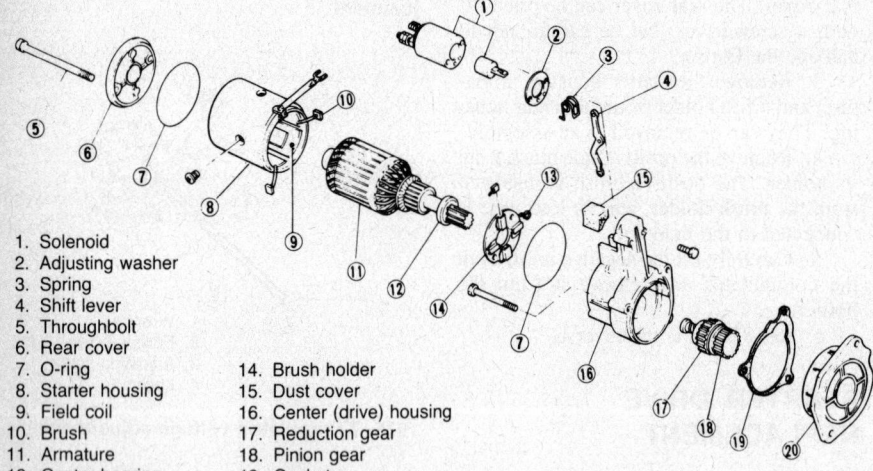

1. Solenoid
2. Adjusting washer
3. Spring
4. Shift lever
5. Throughbolt
6. Rear cover
7. O-ring
8. Starter housing
9. Field coil
10. Brush
11. Armature
12. Center bearing
13. Brush spring
14. Brush holder
15. Dust cover
16. Center (drive) housing
17. Reduction gear
18. Pinion gear
19. Gasket
20. Front cover

Typical reduction gear starter

NOTE: To avoid sparks, always disconnect the ground cable first, and connect it last.

2. Remove the battery hold-down clamp.

3. Remove the battery, being careful not to spill the acid.

NOTE: Spilled acid can be neutralized with a baking soda/water solution. If you somehow get acid into your eyes, flush it out with lots of water and get to a doctor.

4. Clean the battery posts thoroughly before reinstalling, or when installing a new battery.

5. Clean the cable clamps, using a wire brush, both inside and out.

6. Install the battery and the hold-down clamp or strap. Connect the positive, and then the negative cable. Do not hammer them in place. The terminals should be coated lightly (externally) with grease to prevent corrosion. There are also felt washers impregnated with an anti-corrosion substance

which are slipped over the battery posts before installing the cables; these are available in auto parts stores.

CAUTION

Make absolutely sure that the battery is connected properly before you turn on the ignition switch. Reversed polarity can burn out your alternator and regulator within a matter of seconds.

ENGINE MECHANICAL

Design

The L20B gasoline engine used in the Datsun pick-up through 1980, is a water-cooled, 4 cycle, 4 cylinder, overhead camshaft gasoline engine.

The cylinder head is cast aluminum alloy with wedge-type combustion chambers.

The valve system consists of a chain-driven overhead camshaft working directly on the rocker arms which operate valves with dual valve springs.

The crankshaft is fully balanced and is supported by five main bearings.

The intake and exhaust manifolds are mounted on the same side of the engine. The intake manifold is of cast aluminum upon which is mounted a single, two barrel, downdraft carburetor.

The Z22 gasoline engine, new in 1981, is a four cylinder, overhead camshaft engine with a cast iron block and a cross-flow aluminum cylinder head. Hemispherical combustion chambers are employed. This engine has two spark plugs per cylinder which fire simultaneously, effectively burning all of the recirculated exhaust gases and improving idle and performance. The crankshaft employs five main bearings with the thrust on the center bearing.

The SD22 diesel engine is also new for 1981. It has a cast iron block with dry-type, pressed-in cylinder liners. The one-piece cylinder head has swirl-type combustion chambers. Both intake and exhaust valves have cold-fitted, cast iron seats. The camshaft is gear-driven. Also gear-driven is the Bosch-Diesel Kikki injection pump.

Engine Removal and Installation

It is much easier to remove the engine and the transmission together as an assembly than to remove only the engine from the engine compartment. After the engine and transmission are removed from the vehicle, the two can be separated.

1. Disconnect the battery ground cable. Remove the battery.

2. Mark the location of the hood hinges on the body in order to facilitate installation and remove the hood.

3. Remove the air cleaner after disconnecting the PCV hose from the rocker cover.

4. Drain the radiator of coolant and the engine crankcase of oil.

5. Disconnect the upper and lower radiator hoses from the engine. Disconnect and plug the automatic transmission cooler lines at the radiator, if so equipped. Use a flare nut wrench if one is available.

6. Remove the four bolts securing the radiator and remove the radiator from the vehicle.

7. Disconnect the engine ground cable at the cylinder head.

8. Disconnect the electrical leads at the starter, alternator, distributor, the high-tension ignition coil cable, and the oil pressure and temperature sending units' wires.

9. Disconnect the fuel pump (or filter on electric pump models), the heater hose at the engine side, and the choke wire and accelerator cable at the carburetor. Disconnect the emission hoses or wires to the carbon canister, air pump, B.C.D.D. solenoid, and fuel cut solenoid; the vacuum hose to the brake booster (on models so equipped), and any other wires or hoses running to the engine. Tag all wires as they are disconnected for assembly.

10. Remove the transmission control linkage from the transmission; in the case of an automatic transmission, remove the cross-shaft assembly from the transmis-

sion. Remove the selector rod from the selector lever on the automatic transmission. On manual transmissions, lift the rubber boot and remove the nut or C-clip from the shift lever and detach the shift lever from the transmission.

11. Remove the two bolts securing the clutch slave cylinder. Disconnect the clutch slave cylinder and flexible tubing as an assembly.

12. Disconnect the speedometer cable and the back-up light wiring (and neutral switch, if equipped) from the rear section of the transmission.

13. Disconnect the exhaust pipe from the exhaust manifold.

14. Disconnect the driveshaft center bearing bracket from the third crossmember of the frame. Disconnect the driveshaft at the differential housing. Remove the driveshaft assembly from the vehicle and plug the rear end of the transmission extension housing to prevent loss of transmission lubricant.

15. Attach a suitable lifting device to the engine and lift the engine slightly.

16. Remove the front engine mount bolts on both sides of the engine.

17. Place a jack under the transmission and lift it slightly.

18. Loosen the two combination engine rear mounting/transmission mounting bolts. On models with a catalytic converter, loosen the two exhaust pipe hanger bolts.

19. On 1975 models, remove the four bolts (two on each side) securing the engine rear mounting/transmission support side member and detach the support from the frame.

20. On 1976 and later models, remove the bolts securing the idler arm to the frame, and push down the tie-rod.

21. Pull the engine toward the front as far as possible and carefully raise the engine with the transmission up and out of the vehicle.

22. Install the engine in the reverse order of removal, taking note of the following:

Do not connect any parts to the engine or transmission until the engine and transmission are in place on the engine/transmission mounts and secured by the mounting bolts. Secure the rear support first and then the front engine mounts, using the upper bolt hole as a guide.

Cylinder Head

REMOVAL AND INSTALLATION

L20B Engines

1. Crank the engine until the no. 1 piston is at TDC of the compression stroke and disconnect the negative battery cable, drain the cooling system, and remove the air cleaner and attending hoses.

2. Remove the alternator.

3. If equipped with air conditioning,

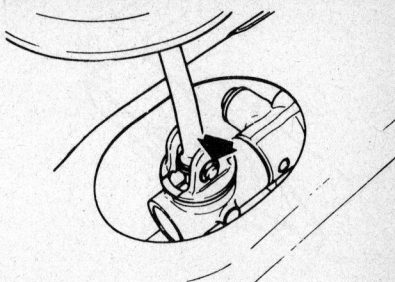

Remove the C-clip and pin on later models for shift lever removal

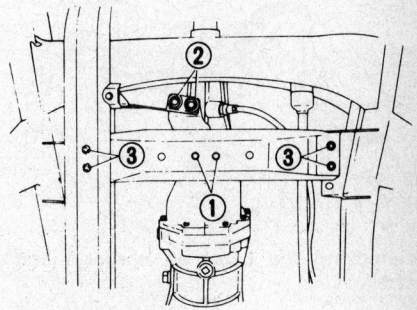

1. Engine mount bolts
2. Exhaust pipe bolts
3. Crossmember bolts

Engine and transmission cross member removal

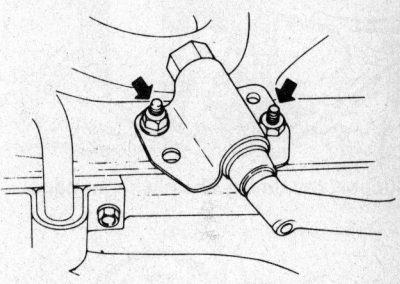

Idler arm removal

unbolt the compressor and move it aside onto the fender. Do not detach any of the compressor lines; the escaping refrigerant will freeze any surface it contacts, including your skin.

4. Disconnect the carburetor throttle linkage, the fuel line and any other vacuum lines or electrical leads, and remove the carburetor.

5. Disconnect the exhaust pipe from the exhaust manifold.

6. Remove the fan and fan pulley.

7. Remove the spark plugs to protect them from damage. Lay the spark plugs aside and out of the way.

8. Remove the rocker cover.

9. Remove the water pump.

10. Remove the fuel pump from the head, on models without the electric pump.

11. Remove the fuel pump drive cam.

12. Mark the relationship of the camshaft sprocket to the timing chain with paint or chalk. If this is done, it will not be nec-

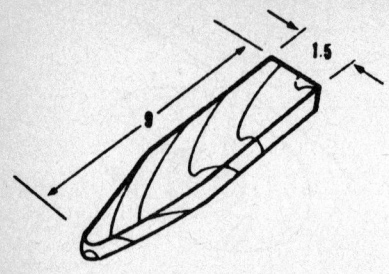

Dimensions for fabricating the wooden wedge used to support the timing chain

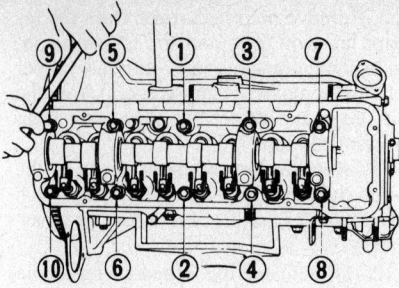

L20B head bolt tightening sequence

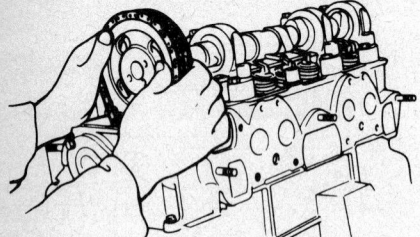

Removing the camshaft sprocket and chain

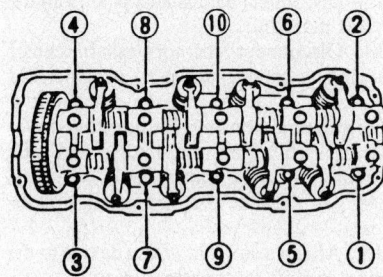

Z22 head bolt loosening sequence

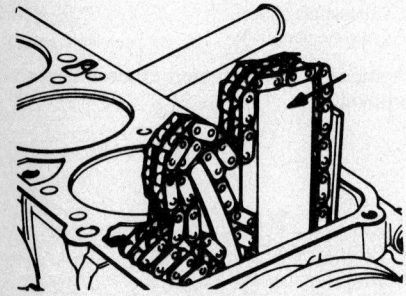

Support the timing chain with a wedge

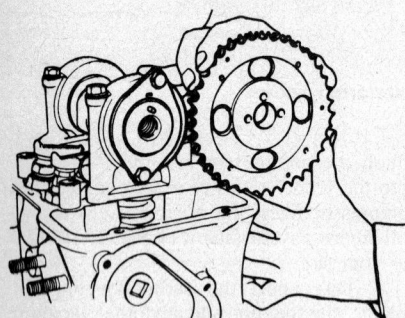

Installing the camshaft sprocket

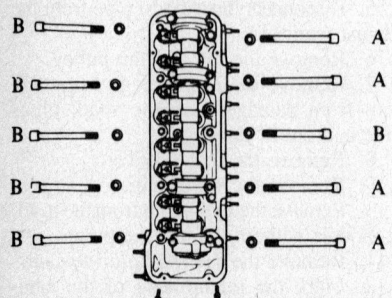

Different size cylinder head bolts

of possible damage which might occur to the valves.

17. Temporarily tighten the two center right and left cylinder head bolts to 14.5 ft. lbs.

18. Install the camshaft sprocket together with the timing chain to the camshaft. Make sure that the marks you made earlier line up. If the chain will not stretch over the sprocket, the problem lies in the tensioner. See "Timing Chain Removal and Installation" for timing procedure, if necessary.

19. Install the cylinder head bolts. Note that there are two sizes of bolts used; the longer bolts are installed on the driver side of the engine with a smaller bolt in the center position. The remaining small bolts are installed on the opposite side of the cylinder head.

20. Tighten the cylinder head bolts in three stages: first to 29 ft. lbs, second to 43 ft. lbs, and lastly to 47–62 ft. lbs.

Tighten the cylinder head bolts on all models in the proper sequence.

21. Install and assemble the remaining components of the engine in the reverse order of removal.

Z22 Engine

1. Complete steps 1 through 5 under L20 Overhead Camshaft Engine. Observe the following note for step 5.

NOTE: The spark plug leads should be marked, however it would be wise to mark them yourself.

2. Disconnect the throttle linkage, the air cleaner or its intake hose assembly (fuel injection). Disconnect the fuel line, the return fuel line and any other vacuum lines or electrical leads. Remove the carburetor to avoid damaging it while removing the head.

NOTE: A good rule of thumb when disconnecting the rather complex engine wiring of today's automobiles is to put a piece of masking tape on the wire or hose and on the connection you removed the wire or hose from, then mark both pieces of tape 1, 2, 3, etc. When replacing wiring, simply match the pieces of tape.

3. Remove the EGR tube from around the rear of the engine.

4. Remove the exhaust air induction tubes from around the front of the engine.

5. Unbolt the exhaust manifold from the exhaust pipe. Remove the fuel pump.

6. Remove the PCV valve from around the rear of the engine if necessary.

7. Remove the spark plugs to protect them from damage. Remove the valve cover.

8. Mark the relationship of the camshaft sprocket to the timing chain with paint or chalk. If this is done, it will not be necessary to locate the factory timing marks. Before removing the camshaft sprocket, it will be necessary to wedge the chain in place so that it will not fall down into the front cover. The factory procedure is to

essary to locate the factory timing marks. Before removing the camshaft sprocket, it will be necessary to wedge the chain in place so that it will not fall down into the front cover. The factory procedure is to wedge the timing chain in place with the wooden wedge shown here. The problem with this is that it may allow the chain tensioner to move out far enough to cock itself against the chain. If this happens, you'll find that the chain won't go back over the sprocket after you've put the sprocket back on. In this case, you'll have to remove the front cover and push the tensioner back.

After installing the wedge, unbolt and remove the camshaft sprocket.

13. Loosen and remove the cylinder head bolts. You will need a 10 mm Allen wrench to remove the head bolts. Keep the bolts in order, because they are different sizes. Lift the cylinder head assembly from the engine. Remove the intake and exhaust manifolds as necessary.

14. Thoroughly clean the cylinder block and head mating surfaces. Check the block and head for flatness before installing the head. Install a new cylinder head gasket. Do not use sealer on the cylinder head gasket.

15. With the crankshaft turned so that the no. 1 piston is at TDC of the compression stroke (if not already done so as mentioned in step 1), make sure that the camshaft sprocket timing mark and the oblong groove in the camshaft retaining plate are aligned.

16. Place the cylinder head in position on the cylinder block, being careful not to allow any of the valves to come in contact with any of the pistons. Do not rotate the crankshaft or camshaft separately because

wedge the timing chain in place with the wooden wedge shown here. The problem with this procedure is that it may allow the chain tensioner to move out far enough to cock itself against the chain. If this happens, you'll find that the chain won't go back on. In this case, you'll have to remove the front cover and push the tensioner back. After you've wedged the chain, unbolt the camshaft sprocket and remove it.

9. Working from both ends in, loosen the cylinder head bolts and remove them. Remove the bolts securing the cylinder head to the front cover assembly.

10. Lift the cylinder head off the engine block. It may be necessary to tap the head lightly with a copper or brass mallet to loosen it.

To install the cylinder head:

11. Thoroughly clean the cylinder block and head surfaces and check both for warpage.

12. Fit the new head gasket. Don't use sealant. Make sure that no open valves are in the way of raised pistons, and do not rotate the crankshaft or camshaft separately because of possible damage which might occur to the valves.

13. Temporarily tighten the two center right and left cylinder head bolts to 14 ft. lbs.

14. Install the camshaft sprocket together with the timing chain to the camshaft. Make sure the marks you made earlier line up with each other. If you get into trouble, see "Timing Chain Removal and Installation" for timing procedures.

15. Install the cylinder head bolts and torque them to 20 ft. lbs., then 40 ft. lbs., then 58 ft. lbs. in the order shown in the illustration.

16. Assemble the rest of the components in the reverse order of disassembly.

NOTE: It is always wise to drain the crankcase oil after the cylinder head has been installed to avoid coolant contamination.

Overhaul

Cylinder head overhaul should be referred to a competent automotive machine shop. Valve guides and seats are removable and oversizes are available from Datsun. See overhaul section of Unit Repair.

SD22 Diesel

1. Remove the air cleaner.

2. Remove the crankcase vent hose and remove the intake and exhaust manifolds. These are bolted together.

3. Remove the alternator, bracket and belts.

4. Disconnect the coolant hose between the head and the oil cooler.

5. Remove the fuel filter assembly.

6. Disconnect the injection lines from the pump and the injectors. Cap all openings at once.

7. Remove the bypass hoses between the coolant pump and the thermostat housing.

8. Remove the fan.

9. Remove the rocker arm cover.

10. Remove the rocker arm shaft assembly.

11. Remove the pushrods and keep them in order.

12. Remove the fuel return lines.

13. Remove the nozzles from the head.

14. Remove the cylinder head bolts in the sequence shown.

15. Attach a hoist to the head and lift it clear of the block. On occasion, the precombustion chambers may fall out, especially if the head is bumped or handled roughly. Take care that they are returned to their original positions if this occurs.

16. Remove the head gasket and O-rings.

17. Clean and inspect all parts.

18. Check the head with a straight-edge. Maximum warpage is .0079″. Do not remove more than .011″ from the head.

19. Place a new cylinder head gasket on the block with the stainless steel inset side facing up.

20. Install the O-rings around the water and oil passages.

21. Position the head on the block.

22. Coat the head bolts with clean engine oil and torque them in sequence, in stages as follows:

Large: 43, 94
Small: 21, 36

23. Install the pushrods, pressing down and turning them to be sure of proper seating.

24. Install the rocker arm shaft assembly, torquing the bolts to 18 ft. lbs. in sequence from the center to each end.

25. Install the injection nozzles.

26. Install all other parts in reverse order of removal.

VALVE GUIDE REMOVAL AND INSTALLATION

Gasoline Engines

1. With the cylinder head removed from the engine, and the valves removed from the head, use a drift and a hammer or press. Drive the valve guides out from the combustion chamber side toward the rocker cover side. A heated cylinder head will facilitate the operation.

2. Ream the cylinder head side guide hole at room temperature. The guide hole should be 0.4719–0.4723 in. for standard

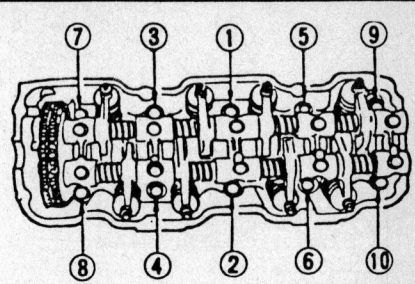

Z22 head bolt tightening sequence

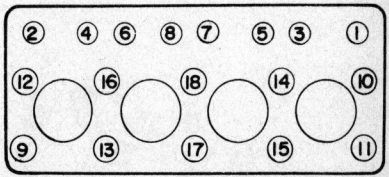

SD22 head bolt loosening sequence

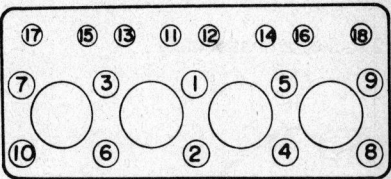

SD22 head bolt tightening sequence

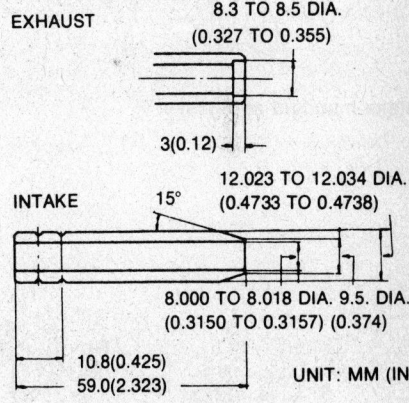

Valve guide dimensions

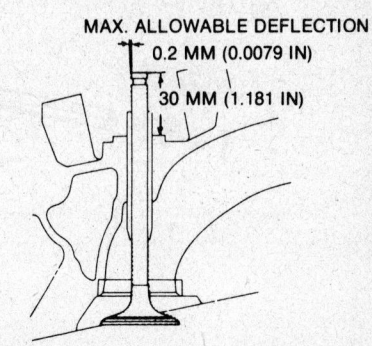

Measuring the valve stem-to-guide clearance

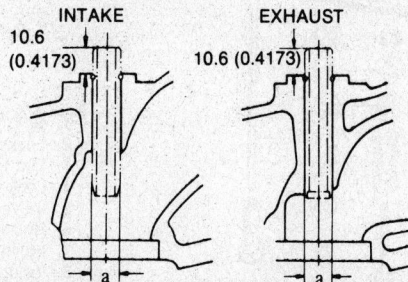

Gasoline engine valve guide installation

DATSUN

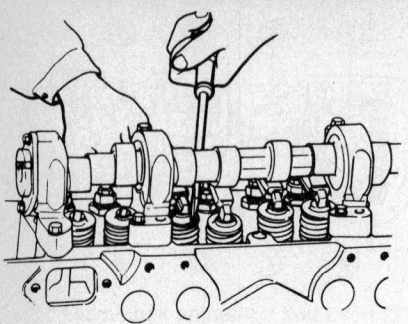

L20B rocker arm removal

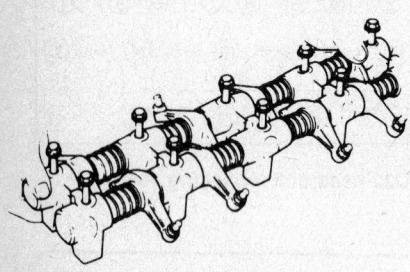

Z22 rocker arm assembly

Intake manifold and gasket

valves and 0.4797–0.4802 in. for 0.0079 in. oversize valves which are available for service.

3. After heating the cylinder head to 302–392°F, press the new valve guide carefully into the cylinder head. The top of the valve guide should protrude out the top of the guide hole 0.4173 in.

4. Ream the bore of the valve guide with the valve guide pressed into the cylinder head. The standard valve guide bore size is 0.3150–0.3157 in.

5. Assemble the cylinder head and install it on the engine in the reverse order of removal.

Diesel Engine

The guides are not replaceable.

VALVE SEAT REMOVAL AND INSTALLATION

Gasoline Engines

1. With the cylinder head removed from the engine and the valves removed from the cylinder head, old valve seat inserts can be removed by boring them out until they collapse. Be careful that the boring doesn't continue beyond the bottom face of the insert recess in the cylinder head.

2. Select the suitable valve seat insert and check its outside diameter.

3. Machine the cylinder head recess using the center of the valve guide as the center of the valve seat insert so that the insert will have the correct fit.

4. Ream the cylinder head recess at room temperature.

5. Heat the cylinder head to 302–392°F.

6. Fit the insert, making sure that it seats fully in the recess in the cylinder head.

Peen the insert with a punch in at least four places equally spaced around its circumference.

7. Grind the valve seats to the proper angle.

8. Lap the valves with lapping compound to each seat to which they are to be mated. Thoroughly clean both the valve and the seat of all lapping compound before installing the valves.

Diesel Engines

1. The seats may be removed by cracking with a cold chisel.

2. Immerse the head in water at 175°F while at the same time cool the valve seats in dry ice. The processes should take about 5–10 minutes.

3. Install the seats and reface and lap according to specifications.

Valve Rockers and Rocker Pivots

REMOVAL AND INSTALLATION

L20B

1. Loosen the rocker pivot locknut, lower the pivot by screwing it down into the cylinder head, and remove the rocker arm by pressing down on the valve spring.

2. To remove the rocker pivots, loosen the locknut, then unscrew the pivot from the cylinder head.

3. Install the pivots and rockers and assemble the engine in the reverse order of removal.

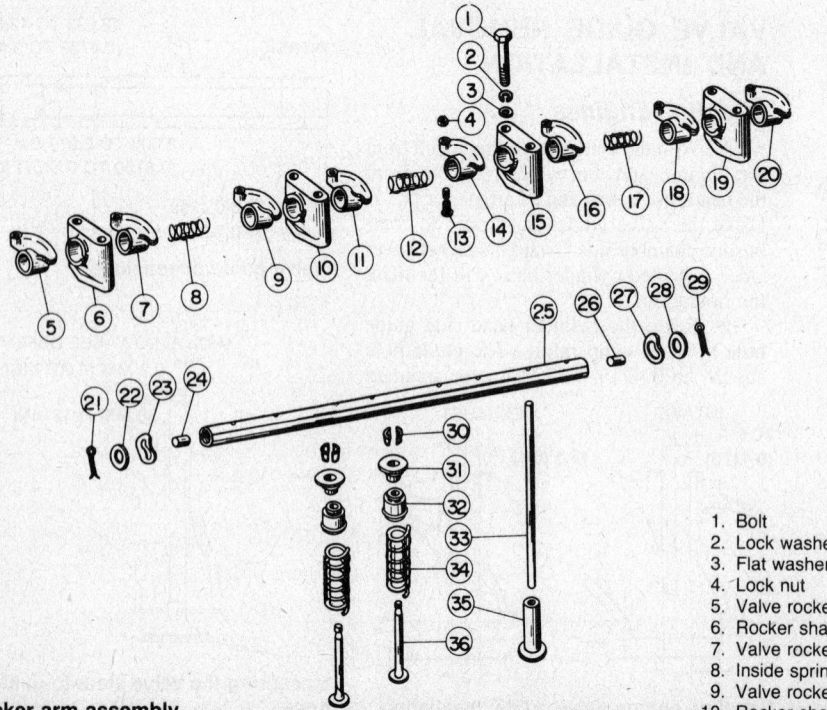

1. Bolt
2. Lock washer
3. Flat washer
4. Lock nut
5. Valve rocker A
6. Rocker shaft bracket
7. Valve rocker B
8. Inside spring
9. Valve rocker C
10. Rocker shaft bracket
11. Valve rocker D
12. Inside spring
13. Adjusting screw
14. Valve rocker A
15. Rocker shaft bracket
16. Valve rocker B
17. Inside spring
18. Valve rocker C
19. Rocker shaft bracket
20. Valve rocker D
21. Cotter pin
22. Washer
23. Outside spring
24. Plug
25. Rocker shaft
26. Plug
27. Outside spring
28. Washer
29. Cotter pin
30. Split collar
31. Spring seat
32. Valve stem seal
33. Push rod
34. Valve spring
35. Valve lifter
36. Valve

SD22 rocker arm assembly

Rocker Shaft Assembly

REMOVAL AND INSTALLATION

Z22

1. The rocker shaft assembly is removed by simply removing the retaining bolts.

NOTE: When removing the bolts, DO NOT REMOVE THE NO. 1 AND NO. 5 BRACKET BOLTS SINCE THE ROCKER SHAFT BRACKET AND ROCKER ARM WILL SPRING OUT!

2. Installation is the reverse of removal. Torque the bolts evenly from the ends toward the center to 11–18 ft. lbs.

SD22 Diesel

1. Remove the shaft retaining bolts evenly, from the center towards the ends.
2. Lift the shaft assembly off the head.
3. If you are disassembling the shaft and rocker arms, it may be necessary to immerse the assembly in water heated to 160°F for a few minutes to free the rocker arms. NEVER HAMMER THEM OFF!
4. Installation is the reverse of removal. Torque the retaining bolts evenly from the ends toward the center to 14–18 ft. lbs.

Intake Manifold

REMOVAL AND INSTALLATION

All Engines

1. Remove the air cleaner assembly together with all of the attending hoses. Remove the EGR tube.

NOTE: It is important to replace the gasket whenever the intake manifold is removed. Because the intake and exhaust manifolds share a common gasket, whenever the intake manifold is removed, the exhaust manifold must also be removed, so that the gasket can be replaced.

2. Disconnect the throttle linkage, fuel, and vacuum lines from the carburetor. Label all wires and hoses as they are removed to simplify installation.
3. The carburetor can be removed from the manifold at this point or can be removed as an assembly with the intake manifold.
4. Loosen the intake manifold attaching nuts, working from the two ends toward the center, and then remove them.
5. Remove the intake manifold from the engine.
6. Install the intake manifold in the reverse order of removal. Always use a new gasket when installing the manifold; air leaks will cause burnt valves. Tighten the man-

ifold bolts from the center outwards, in two progressive steps, to 9–12 ft. lbs.

Exhaust Manifold

REMOVAL AND INSTALLATION

All Engines

1. Remove the air cleaner assembly.
2. Disconnect the exhaust pipe from the exhaust manifold.

NOTE: It is not absolutely necessary to replace the gasket when only the exhaust manifold is removed, unless the gasket is damaged, or leaks develop.

3. Loosen and remove the exhaust manifold attaching nuts and remove the manifold from the engine.
4. Install the exhaust manifold in the reverse order of removal. Use new gaskets at the cylinder head (if necessary) and exhaust pipe. Tighten the mounting bolts in a circular pattern, working from the center to the ends, in two progressive steps to the figures in the torque chart.

NOTE: On 1978–82 gasoline models, install the stud bolt into the center of the outermost guide hole (no. 4 cylinder) of the manifold.

Timing Gear Cover

REMOVAL AND INSTALLATION

Gasoline Engines

1. Disconnect the negative battery cable from the battery, drain the cooling system, and remove the radiator together with the upper and lower radiator hoses.
2. Loosen the alternator drive belt adjusting screw and remove the drive belt. Remove the bolts which attach the alternator bracket to the engine and set the alternator aside out of the way.
3. Remove the distributor.
4. Remove the oil pump attaching screws, and take out the pump and its drive spindle.
5. Remove the cooling fan and the fan pulley together with the drive belt.
6. Remove the water pump.
7. Remove the crankshaft pulley bolt and remove the crankshaft pulley.
8. Remove the bolts holding the front cover to the front of the cylinder block, the four bolts which retain the front of the oil pan to the bottom of the front cover and the two bolts which are screwed down through the front of the cylinder head and into the top of the front cover.
9. Carefully pry the front cover off the front of the engine.
10. Cut the exposed front section of the oil pan gasket away from the oil pan. Do

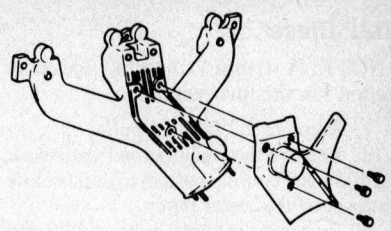

Exhaust manifold and heat stove

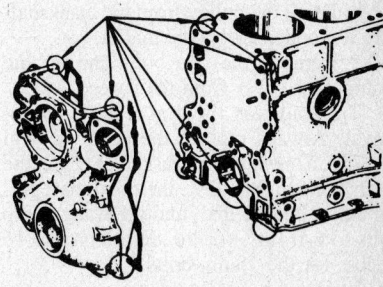

APPLY SEALANT AT THESE POINTS

Gasoline engine front cover installation

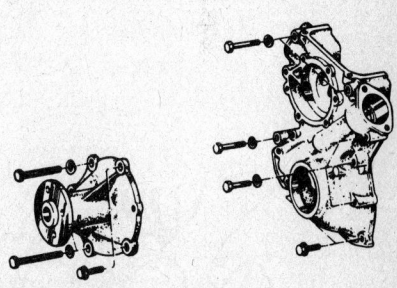

Gasoline engine front cover bolts

the same to the gasket at the top of the front cover. Remove the two side gaskets and clean all of the mating surfaces.

11. Cut the portions needed from a new oil pan gasket and top front cover gasket.
12. Apply sealer to all of the gaskets and position them on the engine in their proper places.
13. Apply a light coating of oil to the crankshaft oil seal and carefully mount the front cover to the front of the engine and install all of the mounting bolts.

Tighten the 8 mm bolts to 7–12 ft. lbs. and the 6 mm bolts to 3–6 ft. lbs. Tighten the oil pan attaching bolts to 4–7 ft. lbs.

14. Before installing the oil pump, place the gasket over the shaft and make sure that the mark on the drive spindle faces (aligned with) the oil pump hole. Install the oil pump so that the projection on the top of the shaft is located in the exact position as when it was removed or is in the 11:25 o'clock position with the piston in the no. 1 cylinder is placed at TDC on the compression stroke, if the engine was disturbed since disassembly. Tighten the oil pump attaching screws to 8–10 ft. lbs. See Oil Pump Removal and Installation.

SD22 Diesel

NOTE: A 41mm (1.614 in.) socket is needed for this procedure.

1. Remove the fan and pulley.
2. Remove the water pump bypass hose and allow the cooling system to drain below the level of the water pump.
3. Remove the three bolts and lift the water pump and gasket off the block. Discard the gasket.
4. Remove the crankshaft pulley nut with a 41mm socket.
5. Drive the pulley from the crankshaft with a wooden or plastic mallet.
6. Remove the five bolts and lift the timing gear cover from the case.
7. Installation is the reverse of removal. Always replace the cover oil seal and use a new cover gasket. Torque the cover bolts to 8 ft. lbs., the crankshaft pulley nut to 238 ft. lbs., and the water pump bolts to 8 ft. lbs. for the 8mm bolt and 16 ft. lbs. for the 10mm bolts.

NOTE: Do not tighten the water pump bolts until the belt adjuster is installed when installing the alternator.

Timing Gear Cover Oil Seal

REMOVAL AND INSTALLATION

1. Remove the front cover.
2. Pry the old seal from the cover with a pointed piece of plastic or wood. Do not use a screwdriver to avoid scratching the seal surface.
3. Oil the lip of the new seal. Do not use grease. Press it into place, making sure the flat side faces forward and the lip faces the engine.
4. Install the front cover.

Timing Gears and Case

The following requires use of special tools.

REMOVAL AND INSTALLATION

SD22 Diesel

1. Remove the timing gear cover.
2. Remove the timing gear round nut.
3. Using timer extractor 57926-581, thread the tool into the timer weight holder. Remove the timing gear assembly by threading in the extractor tool bolt.
4. Unbolt and remove the camshaft gear set.
5. Remove the oil slinger. Unbolt the crankshaft gear and remove it with a gear puller.
6. Install the camshaft gear.
7. Install the crankshaft gear and oil slinger while carefully aligning the timing marks as shown. Measure the gear backlash. Backlash should be 0.0028–0.0079 in.
8. With the no. 1 piston at TDC, mesh the timing gear and idler gear at the "Y" marks. After aligning the gear with the keyway, secure the timer assembly with a lock

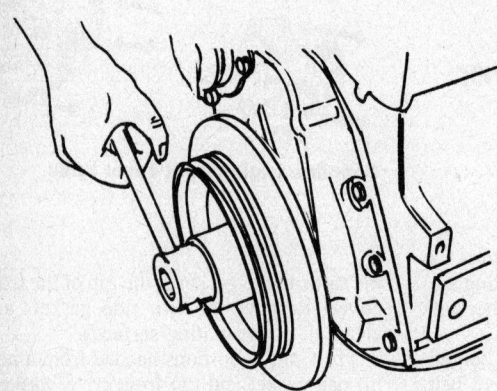

Crankshaft pulley nut removal

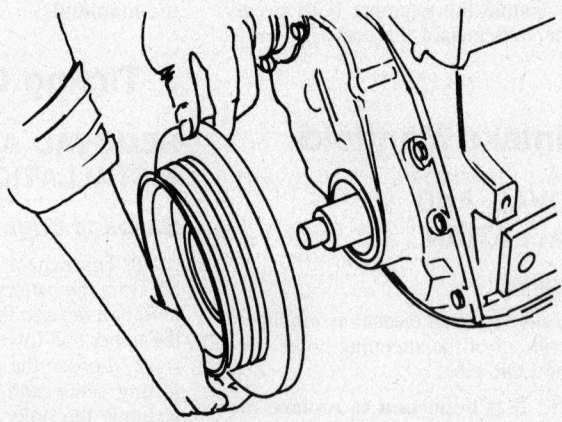

Lifting the pulley assembly

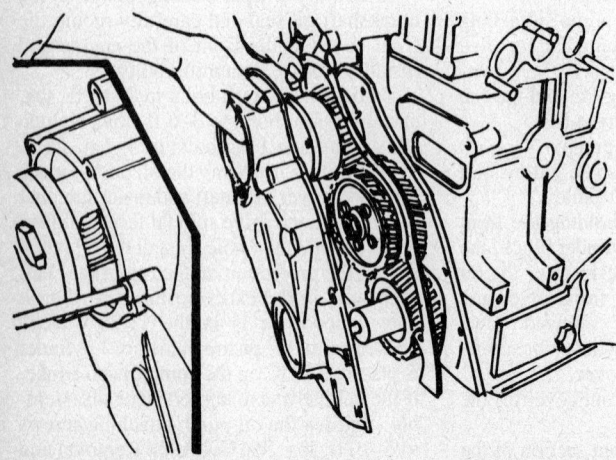

Timing gear case removal

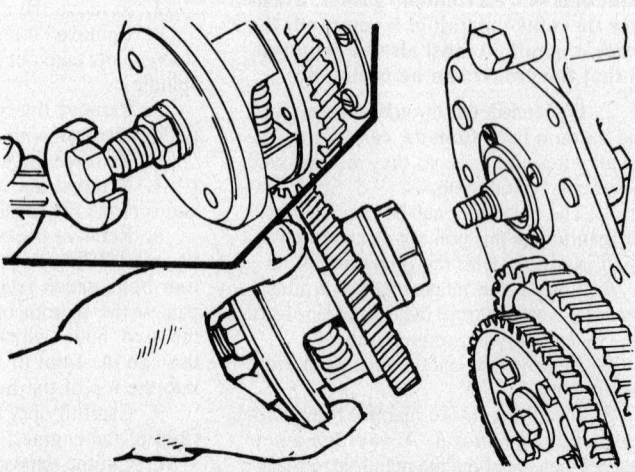

Timer removal

washer and the round nut. Torque the nut to 50–58 ft. lbs.

9. Install the cover.

NOTE: If the gear case oil jet was removed, install in the relationship as shown.

Timing Chain and Tensioner

REMOVAL AND INSTALLATION

Gasoline Engines

1. Before beginning any disassembly procedures, position the no. 1 piston at TDC on the compression stroke.

2. Remove the front cover. Remove the camshaft cover.

3. With the no. 1 piston at TDC, the timing marks on the camshaft sprocket and the timing chain should be visible. Mark both of them with paint. Also mark the relationship of the camshaft sprocket to the camshaft. At this point you will see that

there are three sets of timing marks and locating holes in the sprocket. They are for making adjustments to compensate for timing chain stretch. See the "Timing Chain Adjustment" section following for details.

4. With the timing marks on the cam sprocket clearly marked, locate and mark the timing marks on the crankshaft sprocket. Also mark the chain timing mark. Of course, if the chain is not to be reused, marking it is useless.

5. Unbolt the camshaft sprocket and remove the sprocket along with the chain. As you remove the chain, hold it where the chain tensioner contacts it. When the chain is removed, the tensioner is going to come apart. Hold on to it and you won't lose any of the parts.

The crankshaft sprocket can be removed with a puller, if necessary. There is no need to remove the chain guide unless it is being replaced.

6. Install the timing chain and the camshaft sprocket together after first positioning the chain over the crankshaft sprocket. Position the sprocket so that the marks made earlier line up. This is assuming that the engine has not been disturbed. The cam-

shaft and the crankshaft keys should both be pointing upward. If a new chain and/or gear is being installed, position the sprocket so that the timing marks on the chain align with the marks on the sprocket (with both keys pointing up). The marks are on the right-hand side of the sprockets as you face the engine. Engines have 44 pins between the mating marks of the chain and sprockets when the chain is installed correctly. The factory refers to the pins as links, but in American terminology this is incorrect. Count the pins. There are two pins per chain link. This is an important step. If you do

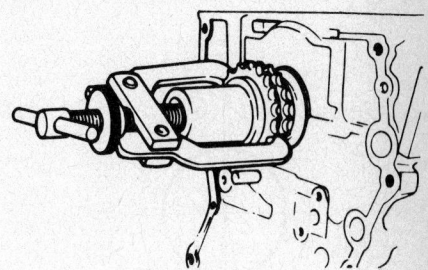

Gasoline engine crankshaft sprocket removal

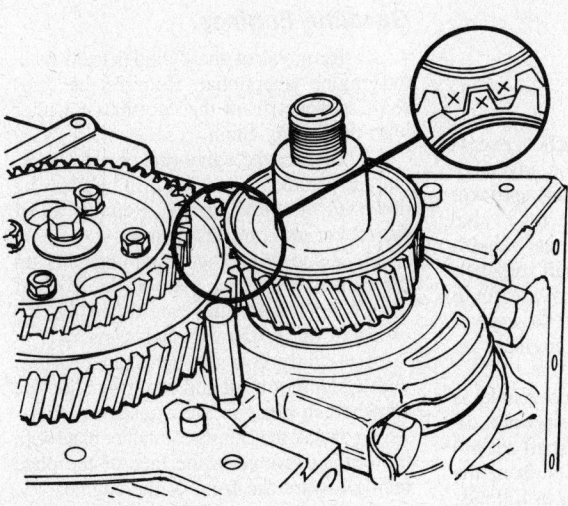

Timing mark alignment

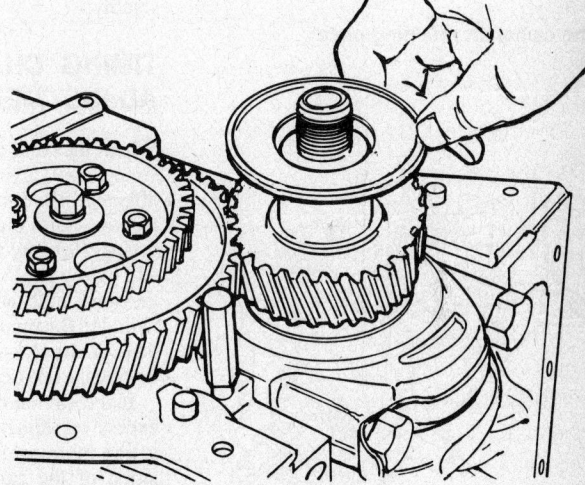

Oil slinger installation

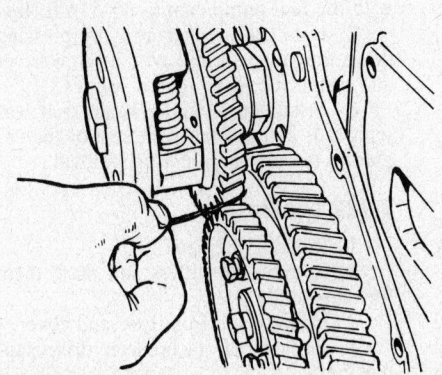

Measuring backlash

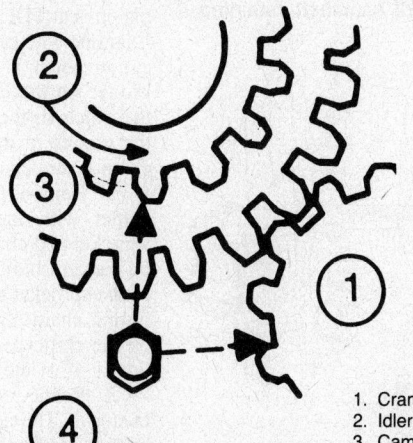

Oil jet orientation

1. Crankshaft gear
2. Idler
3. Camshaft gear
4. Oil jet

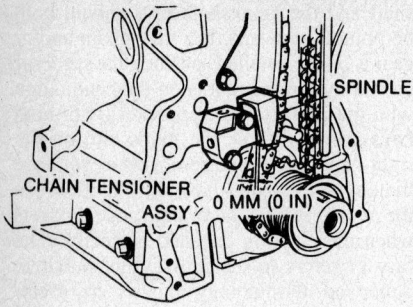

Installing the timing chain tensioner

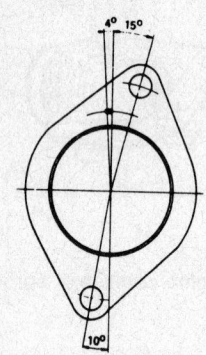

The camshaft retaining plate

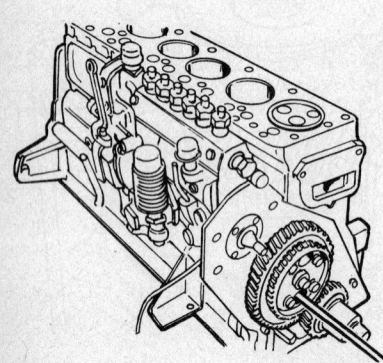

Removing the SD22 camshaft retaining bolts

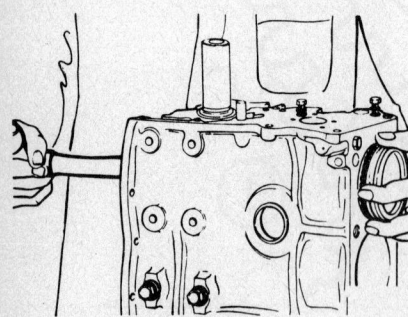

Removing the piston and connecting rod assemblies from the block

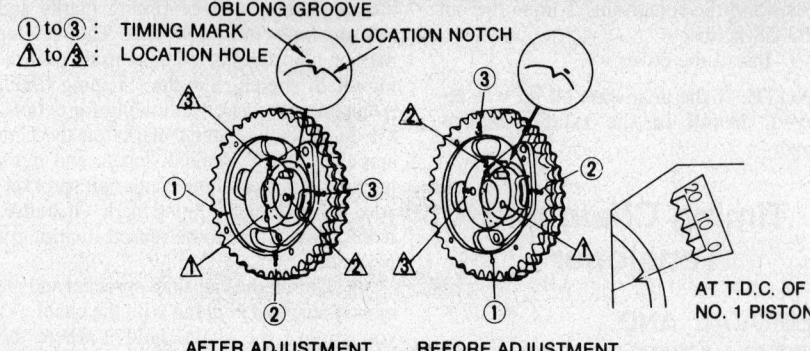

Adjusting the camshaft sprocket to obtain proper valve timing due to a worn timing chain

not get the exact number of pins between the timing marks, valve timing will be incorrect, and the engine will either not run at all or run very badly.

7. Install the chain tensioner. Adjust the protrusion of the chain tensioner spindle to zero clearance.

8. With a new seal installed in the front cover and a light coat of oil applied to the seal, assemble the remaining components of the engine in the reverse order of disassembly.

TIMING CHAIN ADJUSTMENT

When the timing chain stretches excessively, the valve timing will be adversely affected. There are two camshaft sprocket locating holes provided to correct the valve timing. Actually there are three sets of holes and timing marks on the camshaft sprocket; the third hole and timing mark are for 6 cylinder Datsun engines and in the case of the Datsun pick-up 4 cylinder engines, are obviously ignored.

If the stretch of the chain roller links is excessive, adjust the camshaft sprocket location by transferring the camshaft set position of the camshaft sprocket from the factory position of no. 1 to no. 2 as follows:

1. Turn the crankshaft until the no. 1 piston is at TDC on its compression stroke. Examine whether the camshaft sprocket location notch is to the left of the oblong groove on the camshaft retaining plate. If the notch in the sprocket is to the left of the groove in the retaining plate, then the chain is stretched and needs adjusting.

2. Remove the camshaft sprocket together with the chain and reinstall the sprocket and chain with the locating dowel on the camshaft inserted into the no. 2 hole of the sprocket and the timing mark on the timing chain aligned with the no. 2 mark on the sprocket. The amount of modification is 4° of the crankshaft rotation.

3. Recheck the valve timing as outlined in step 1. The notch in the sprocket should be to the right of the groove in the camshaft retaining plate.

4. If and when the notch cannot be

brought to the right of the groove with the sprocket installed in the no. 2 hole, the timing chain must be replaced to gain the proper valve timing.

Camshaft

REMOVAL AND INSTALLATION

Gasoline Engines

1. Removal of the cylinder head from the engine is optional. Remove the camshaft sprocket from the camshaft together with the timing chain.

2. Loosen the valve rocker pivot locknut and remove the rocker arm by pressing down on the valve spring. Remove all of the rocker arms in this manner.

3. Remove the two retaining nuts on the camshaft retainer plate at the front of the cylinder head and carefully slide the camshaft out of the camshaft carrier.

4. Lightly coat the camshaft bearings with clean motor oil and carefully slide the camshaft in place in the camshaft carrier.

5. Install the camshaft retainer plate with the oblong groove in the face of the plate facing toward the front of the engine.

6. Check the valve timing as outlined under "Timing Chain Removal and Installation" and install the timing sprocket on the camshaft, tightening the bolt together with the fuel pump cam to 86–116 ft. lbs.

7. Install the rocker arms by pressing down the valve springs with a screwdriver and install the valve rocker springs.

8. Install the cylinder head, if it was removed, and assemble the rest of the engine in the reverse order of removal.

SD22 Diesel

1. Remove the head.

2. Remove the lifters and mark them for reassembly.

3. Remove the front case and cover.

4. Remove the tachometer drive support nuts.

5. Remove the timer round nut.

6. Thread the timer extractor, ST 57926-

581, into the timer weight holder. Remove the timer assembly by tightening the extractor bolt.

7. Remove the oil pump drive spindle.

8. Remove the camshaft locating plate bolts and carefully slide the camshaft from the engine.

9. Coat the camshaft with clean engine oil and carefully slide it into the block. Install the locating plate.

10. Install the oil pump drive spindle by aligning the oil pump drive shaft groove and the camshaft oil pump drive gear with the spindle.

11. Install all other parts in reverse order.

Pistons and Connecting Rods

REMOVAL AND INSTALLATION

See the "Engine Rebuilding" section for general procedures.

1. Remove the cylinder head.

2. Remove the oil pan.

3. Remove any carbon buildup from the cylinder wall at the top end of the piston travel with a ridge reamer tool.

4. Position the piston to be removed at the bottom of its stroke so that the connecting rod bearing cap can be reached easily from under the engine.

5. Unscrew the connecting rod bearing cap and remove the cap and lower half of the bearing.

6. Push the piston and connecting rod up and out of the cylinder block with a length of wood. Use care not to scratch the cylinder wall with the connecting rod or the wooden tool.

7. Keep all of the components from each cylinder together and install them in the cylinder from which they were removed.

8. Coat the bearing face of the connecting rod and the outer face of the pistons with engine oil.

9. Turn the top compression ring to bring its gap to about the 1:30 o'clock position. Set the remaining rings so that their gaps are positioned 180° apart around the piston. The oil ring gap will be directly under the top compression ring gap.

10. Turn the crankshaft until the rod journal of the particular cylinder you are working on is brought to the TDC position.

11. With the piston and rings clamped in a ring compressor, the notched mark on the head of the piston toward the front of the engine, and the oil hole side of the connecting rod toward the right side of the engine, push the piston and connecting rod assembly into the cylinder bore until the big bearing end of the connecting rod contacts and is seated on the rod journal of the crankshaft. Use care not to scratch the cylinder wall with the connecting rod.

12. Push down farther on the piston and turn the crankshaft while the connecting rod rides around on the crankshaft rod journal. Turn the crankshaft until the crankshaft rod journal is at BDC (bottom dead center).

13. Align the mark on the connecting rod bearing cap with that on the connecting rod and tighten the bearing cap bolts to the specified torque.

14. Install all of the piston/connecting rod assemblies in the manner outlined above and assemble the oil pan and cylinder head to the engine in the reverse order of removal.

PISTON AND CONNECTING ROD IDENTIFICATION AND POSITIONING

The pistons are marked with a notch in the piston head. When installed in the engine, the notch markings are to be facing toward the front of the engine.

The connecting rods are installed in the engine with the oil hole facing toward the fuel pump side (right) of the engine.

NOTE: It is advisable to number the pistons, connecting rods, and bearing caps in some manner so that they can be reinstalled in the same cylinder, facing the same direction from which they are removed.

ENGINE LUBRICATION

Oil Pan

REMOVAL AND INSTALLATION

To remove the oil pan it will be necessary to unbolt the motor mounts and jack the engine to gain clearance. Drain the oil and remove the attaching screws and remove the oil pan and gasket. Install the oil pan in the reverse order with a new gasket. Apply a thin bead of silicone seal to the engine block at the junction of the block and front cover, and the junction of the block and main bearing cap. Then apply a thin coat of silicone seal to the new oil pan gasket, install the gasket to the block, and install the pan. Tighten the pan bolts in a circular pattern from the center to the ends, to 4–7 ft. lbs. Overtightening will distort the pan lip, causing leakage.

Rear Main Oil Seal

REPLACEMENT

In order to replace the rear main oil seal, the rear main bearing cap must be removed.

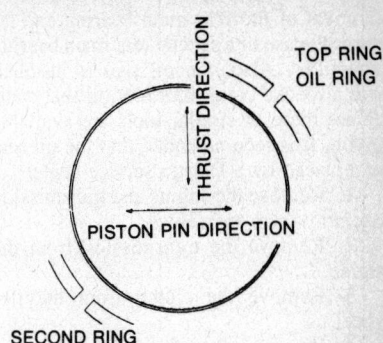

Arrangement of the piston ring gaps around the piston

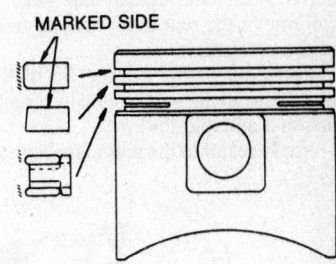

Piston ring installation

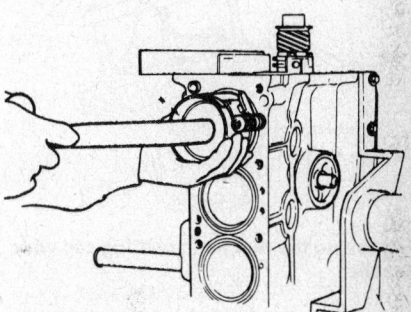

Installing the piston and connecting rod

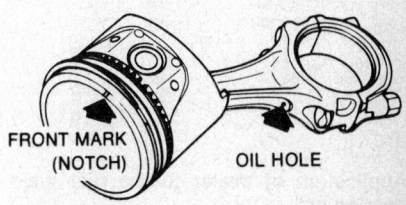

Piston and rod identification and positioning

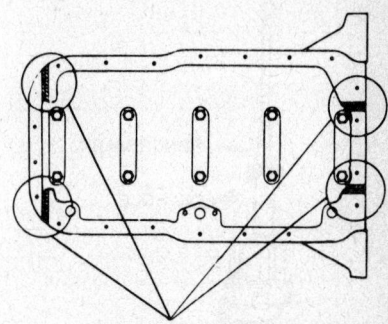

Apply a thin bead of silicone sealer to these areas before installation

Removal of the rear main bearing cap requires the use of a special rear main bearing cap puller. Also, the oil seal is installed with a special crankshaft rear oil seal drift. Unless these or similar tools are available to you, it is recommended that the oil seal be replaced by a Datsun service center.

1. Remove the engine and transmission assembly from the vehicle.

2. Remove the transmission from the engine.

3. Remove the clutch from the flywheel.

4. Remove the flywheel from the crankshaft.

5. Remove the rear main bearing cap together with the bearing cap side seals.

6. Remove the rear main oil seal from around the crankshaft.

7. Apply oil to the sealing lip of the oil seal and install the seal around the crankshaft using a suitable tool.

8. Apply sealer to the rear main bearing cap as indicated and install the rear main bearing cap and tighten the cap bolts to 33–40 ft. lbs.

9. Apply sealant to the rear main bearing cap side seals and install the side seals, driving the seals into place with a suitable drift.

10. Assemble the engine and install it in the vehicle in the reverse order of removal.

Oil Pump

REMOVAL AND INSTALLATION

Gasoline Engines

The oil pump is mounted externally on the engine, eliminating the need to remove the oil pan in order to remove the oil pump.

1. Remove the distributor.

2. Drain the engine oil.

3. Remove the front stabilizer.

4. Remove the splash shield board.

5. Remove the oil pump body with the drive spindle assembly.

6. Before installing the oil pump in the engine, turn the crankshaft so that the no. 1 piston is at TDC of the compression stroke.

7. Fill the pump housing with engine oil, then align the punch mark on the spindle with the hole in the oil pump.

8. With a new gasket placed over the drive spindle, install the oil pump and drive spindle assembly so that the projection on

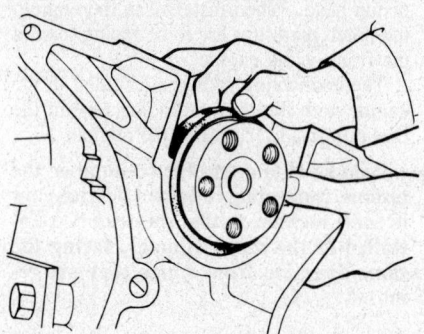

Removing the rear main bearing cap with a puller

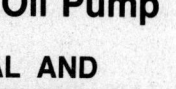

Application of sealer to the rear main bearing cap

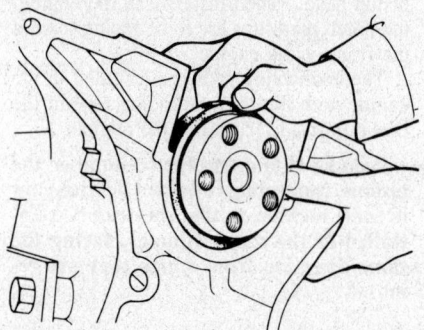

Removing the rear main seal

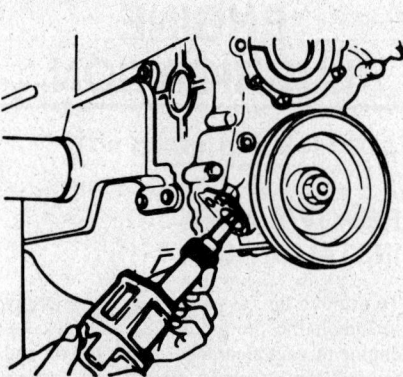

Removing the gasoline engine oil pump

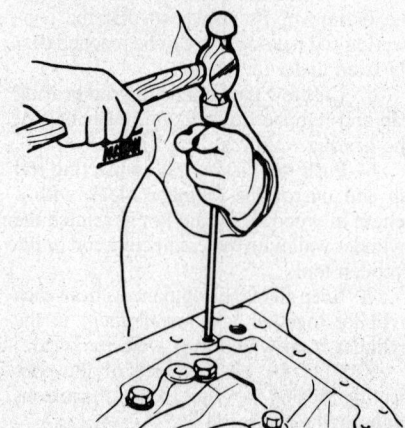

Installing the rear main seal

Installing the rear main bearing cap side seals

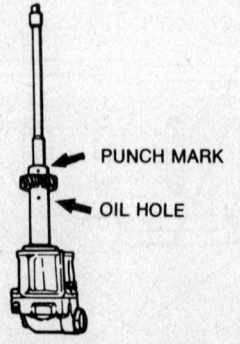

PUNCH MARK

OIL HOLE

Aligning the punch mark on the spindle with the hole in the oil pump on gasoline engines

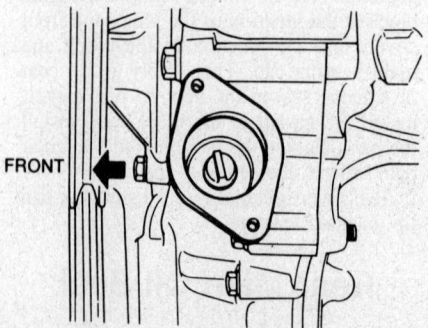

FRONT

The projection on the top of the oil pump drive spindle located at the 11:25 o'clock position. The smaller crescent formed by the notch faces forward.

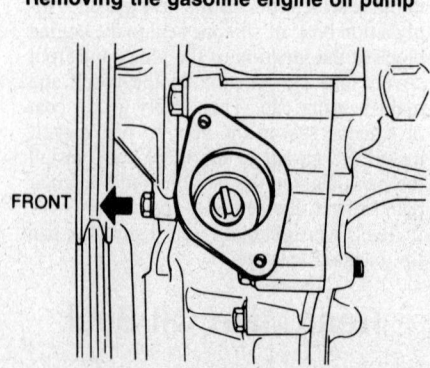

Diesel engine oil pump drive spindle removal

the top of the drive spindle is located in the 11:25 o'clock position.

9. Install the distributor with the metal tip of the rotor pointing toward the no. 1 spark plug tower of the distributor.

SD22 Diesel

1. Remove the oil pump drive spindle.
2. Remove the oil pan.
3. Unbolt and remove the oil pump. Discard the gasket.
4. Using a new gasket, install the oil pump. Torque the bolts to 7–9 ft. lbs.
5. Install the drive spindle by aligning it with the oil pump drive shaft groove in the cylinder block and the camshaft oil pump drive gear.
6. Place a new O-ring on the spindle support and bolt it to the block.

Oil Filter Canister Assembly

REMOVAL AND INSTALLATION

SD22 Diesel

1. Remove the bolts at the oil filter end

of the oil inlet and outlet lines.

2. Remove the four filter assembly mounting bolts and separate the filter from the block.

NOTE: Have a drip pan ready, since some oil will drain out.

3. Installation is the reverse of removal. Torque the bolts to 14–18 ft. lbs.

Oil Cooler

REMOVAL AND INSTALLATION

SD22 Diesel

1. Remove the water hose from the cooler.
2. Remove the eight mounting bolts and lift the cooler from the block.

NOTE: Have a drip pan ready, since some oil will drain out.

3. Installation is the reverse of removal. Torque bolts to 14–18 ft. lbs

ENGINE COOLING

Radiator

REMOVAL AND INSTALLATION

1. Drain the engine coolant into a clean container.
2. Remove the front grille.
3. Disconnect the upper and lower radiator hoses. On a truck with an automatic transmission, disconnect the fluid cooler inlet and outlet lines from the radiator. Plug the lines to prevent the loss of transmission fluid and the entrance of dirt. Remove the fan shroud, if equipped.
4. Remove the bolts retaining the radiator from the radiator side supports and remove the radiator upward.
5. Install the radiator in the reverse order of removal.

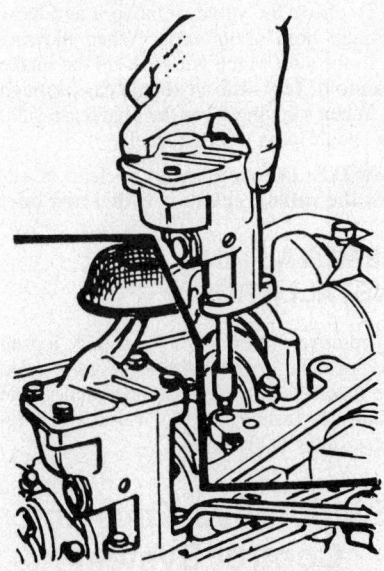

Removing the diesel engine oil pump

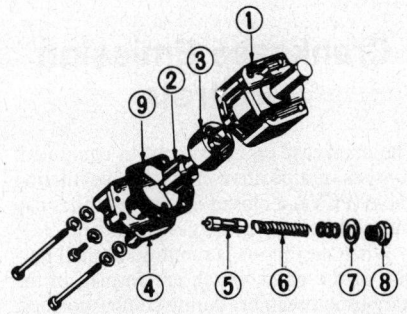

1. Oil pump body
2. Inner rotor and shaft
3. Outer rotor
4. Oil pump cover
5. Regulator valve
6. Regulator spring
7. Washer
8. Regulator cap
9. Cover gasket

Gasoline engine oil pump

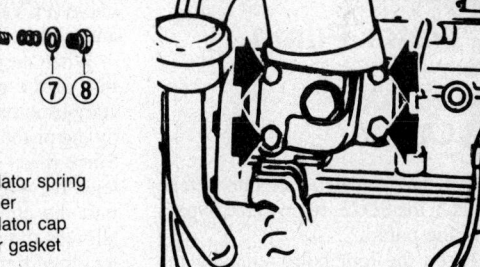

Oil filter showing the four mounting bolts

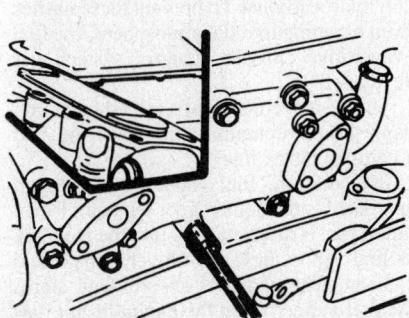

Oil cooler removal

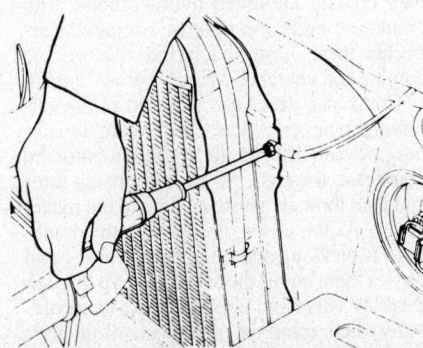

Removing the radiator securing bolts

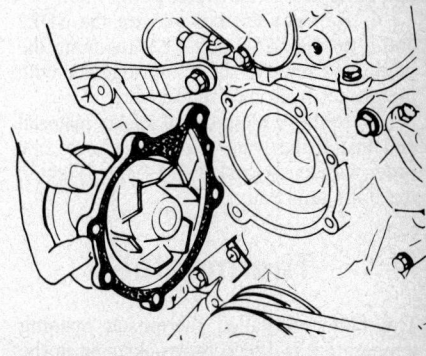

Removing the water pump

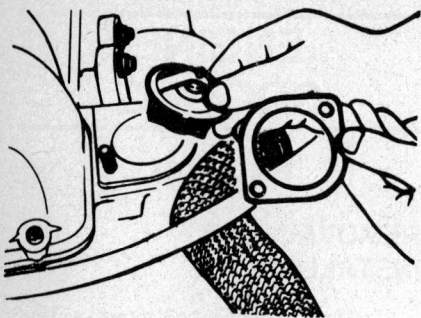

Removing the thermostat

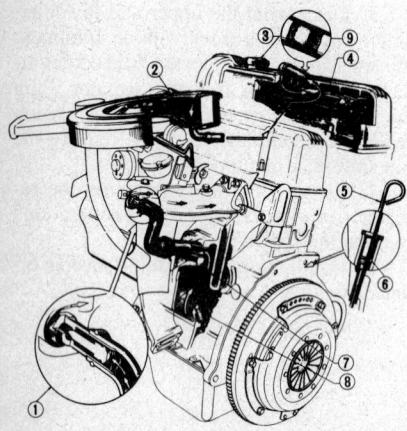

1. Crankcase ventilation control valve
2. Flame arrester
3. Sealed filler cap
4. Baffle plate
5. Oil level gauge
6. O-ring
7. Oil separator
8. Baffle plate
9. Flame arrester

Positive crankcase ventilation system

Water Pump

REMOVAL AND INSTALLATION

1. Drain the engine coolant into a clean container. On the SD22, remove the bypass hose from the pump.

2. Loosen the four bolts retaining the fan shroud to the radiator and remove the shroud.

3. Loosen the belt, then remove the fan and pulley from the water pump hub.

4. Remove the bolts (3 on the SD22 and 5 on the L20B and Z22) retaining the pump and remove the pump together with the gasket from the front cover.

5. Remove all traces of gasket material and install the water pump in the reverse order with a new gasket and sealer. Tighten the bolts uniformly.

Thermostat

The factory-installed thermostat opening temperature is 180°F for trucks sold in the U.S., 190°F for trucks sold in Canada.

REMOVAL AND INSTALLATION

1. Drain the engine coolant into a clean container so that the level is below the thermostat housing.

2. Disconnect the upper radiator hose at the water outlet.

3. Loosen the two securing nuts and remove the water outlet, gasket, and the thermostat from the thermostat housing.

4. Install the thermostat in the reverse order of removal, using a new gasket with sealer and with the thermostat spring toward the inside of the engine.

EMISSION CONTROLS

There are three sources of automotive pollutants: crankcase fumes, exhaust gases and gasoline evaporation. The pollutants formed from these substances fall into three categories: unburnt hydrocarbons (HC), carbon monoxide (CO), and oxides of nitrogen (NO_x). The equipment that is used to limit these pollutants is commonly called emission control equipment.

Crankcase Emission Controls

The crankcase emission control equipment consists of a positive crankcase ventilation valve (PCV), a closed or open oil filler cap and hoses to connect this equipment.

When the engine is running, a small portion of the gases which are formed in the combustion chamber during combustion leak by the piston rings and enter the crankcase. Since these gases are under pressure they tend to escape from the crankcase and enter into the atmosphere. If these gases were allowed to remain in the crankcase for any length of time, they would contaminate the engine oil and cause sludge to build up. If the gases were allowed to escape into the atmosphere, they would pollute the air, as they contain unburned hydrocarbons. The crankcase emission control equipment recycles these gases back into the engine combustion chamber where they are burned.

Crankcase gases are recycled in the following manner: while the engine is running, clean filtered air is drawn into the crankcase through the carburetor air filter and then through a hose leading to the rocker cover. As the air passes through the crankcase it picks up the combustion gases and carries them out of the crankcase, up through the PCV valve and into the intake manifold. After they enter the intake manifold they are drawn into the combustion chamber and burned.

The most critical component in the system is the PCV valve. This vacuum controlled valve regulates the amount of gases which are recycled into the combustion chamber. At low engine speeds the valve is partially closed, limiting the flow of gases into the intake manifold. As engine speed increases, the valve opens to admit greater quantities of the gases into the intake manifold. If the valve should become blocked or plugged, the gases will be prevented from escaping from the crankcase by the normal route. Since these gases are under pressure, they will find their own way out of the crankcase. This alternate route is usually a weak oil seal or gasket in the engine. As the gas escapes by the gasket, it also creates an oil leak. Besides causing oil leaks, a clogged PCV valve also allows these gases to remain in the crankcase for an extended period of time, promoting the formation of sludge in the engine.

The above explanation and the troubleshooting procedure which follows applies to all engines with PCV systems.

TESTING

Check the PCV system hoses and connections, to see that there are no leaks; then replace or tighten, as necessary.

To check the valve, remove it and blow through both of its ends. When blowing from the side which goes toward the intake manifold, very little air should pass through it. When blowing from the crankcase side, air should pass through freely.

NOTE: Do not attempt to clean or adjust the valve; replace it with a new one.

REMOVAL AND INSTALLATION

To remove the PCV valve, simply loosen the hose clamp and remove the valve from the manifold-to-crankcase hose and intake manifold. Install the PCV valve in the reverse order of removal.

Evaporative Emission Control System

When raw fuel evaporates, the vapors contain hydrocarbons. To prevent these nasties from escaping into the atmosphere, the fuel evaporative emission control system was developed.

The system consists of a sealed fuel tank, vapor-liquid separator, vapor vent line, and a canister purge line.

In operation, fuel vapors and/or liquid are routed to the liquid/vapor separator where liquid fuel is directed back into the fuel tank as fuel vapors flow into the charcoal-filled canister. The charcoal absorbs and stores the fuel vapors when the engine is not running or is at idle. When the throttle valves in the carburetor are opened, vacuum from above the throttle valves is routed through a vacuum signal line to the purge control valve on the canister. The control valve opens and allows the fuel vapors to be drawn from the canister through a purge line and into the intake manifold and combustion chambers.

INSPECTION AND SERVICE

Check the hoses for proper connections and damage. Replace as necessary. Check the vapor separator tank for fuel leaks, distortion and dents, and replace as necessary.

Carbon Canister and Purge Control Valve

To check the operation of the carbon canister purge control valve, disconnect the rubber hose between the canister control valve and the T-fitting, at the T-fitting. Apply vacuum to the hose leading to the control valve. The vacuum condition should be maintained indefinitely. If the control valve leaks, remove the top cover of the valve and check for a dislocated or cracked diaphragm. If the diaphragm is damaged, a repair kit containing a new diaphragm, retainer, and spring is available and should be installed.

The carbon canister has an air filter in the bottom of the canister. The filter element should be checked once a year or every 12,000 miles; more frequently if the truck is operated in dusty areas. Replace the filter by pulling it out of the bottom of the canister and installing a new one.

Removal and Installation

Removal and installation of the various evaporative emission control system components consists of disconnecting the hoses, loosening retaining screws, and removing the part which is to be replaced or checked. Install in the reverse order. When replacing hose, make sure that it is fuel and vapor resistant.

Exhaust Emission Control

Air Injection System (AIS)

In gasoline engines, it is difficult to burn the air/fuel mixture completely through normal combustion in the combustion chambers. Under certain operating conditions, unburned fuel is exhausted into the atmosphere.

The air injection reactor system is designed so that ambient air, pressurized by an air pump, is injected through the injection nozzles into exhaust ports near each exhaust valve. The exhaust gases are at high temperatures and ignite when brought into

contact with the oxygen of the ambient air. Thus, the unburned fuel is burned in the exhaust ports and manifold.

A check valve is installed in the air pump discharge line to prevent the airflow from reversing due to a broken drive belt, relief valve spring failure, or backfire in the exhaust manifold. Reversed airflow could damage the air pump.

The air pump relief valve bleeds off excess air from the pump at high speeds. The valve is mounted on the carburetor air cleaner.

Trucks with a catalytic converter (1976 and later pick-ups sold in California) have protection devices to prevent converter overheating due to large quantities of injected air. 1976–77 models use an emergency air relief valve and an air control

valve. The emergency valve has a diaphragm operated by engine vacuum. When intake manifold vacuum reaches a predetermined level, the valve opens, diverting air from the pump into the atmosphere. When vacuum drops, the valve closes allowing normal AIS operation.

The air control valve is also controlled by engine vacuum. High vacuum and high pressure from the air pump open the control valve, venting air from the pump into the air cleaner.

1978–79 models have a combined air control valve instead of the relief valve, emergency valve, and air control valve. The combined air control valve regulates the amount of injected air according to intake manifold and air pump discharge pressure, to prevent the converter from overheating.

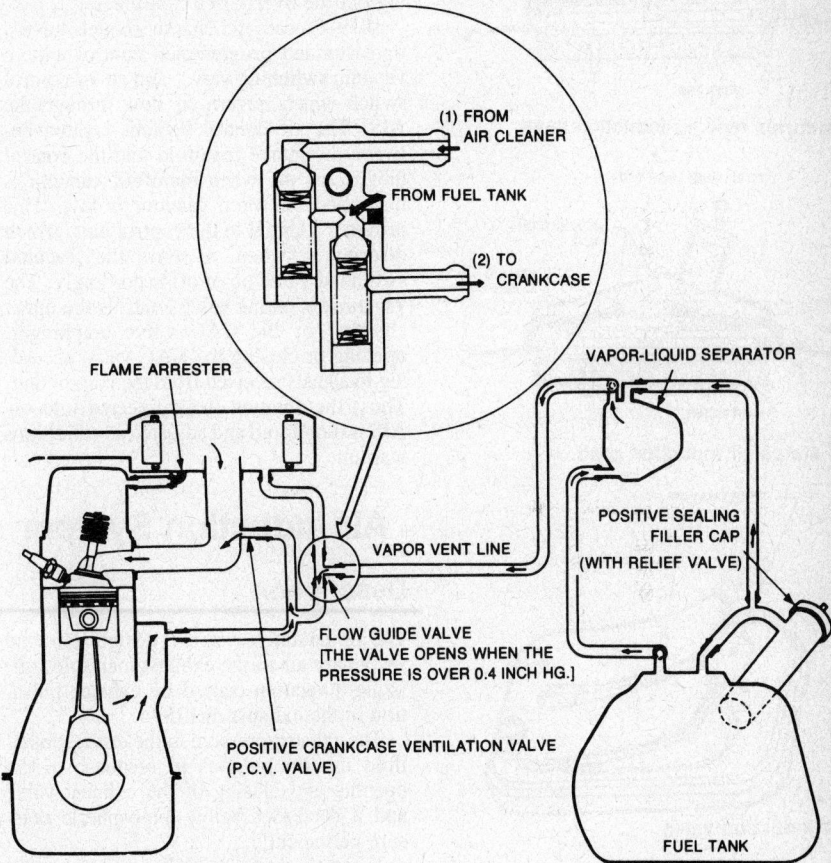

Evaporative emission control system

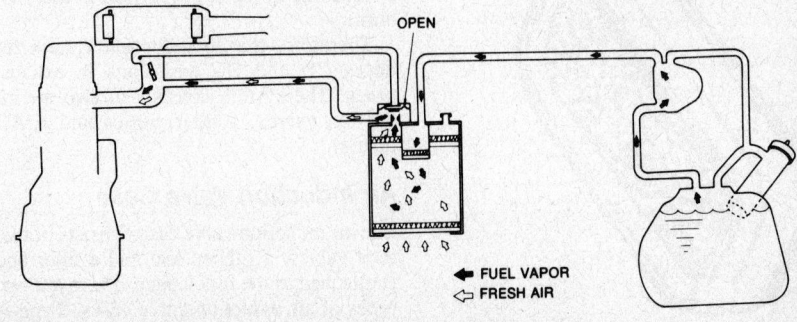

The evaporative emission control system running above idle

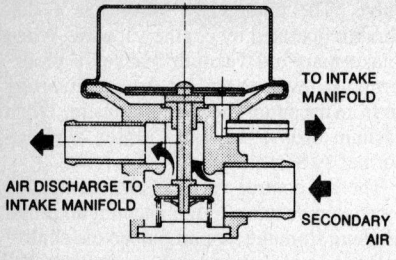

Anti-backfire valve operation

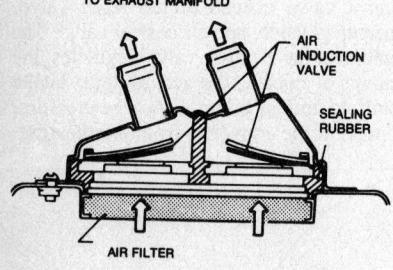

California type air induction case

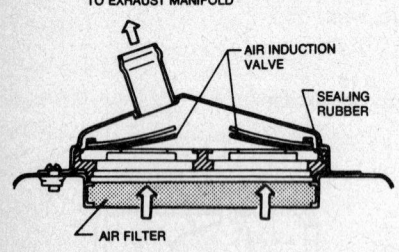

49 states air induction case

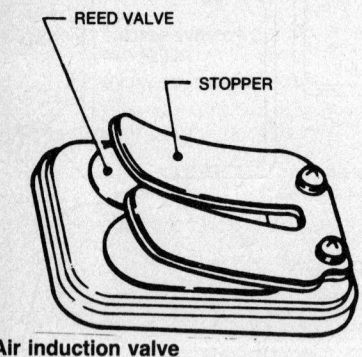

Air induction valve

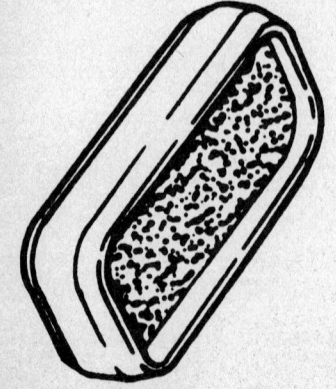

Air induction filter

An anti-backfire valve is installed in an air delivery hose. The purpose of the valve is to prevent backfiring in the exhaust manifold during deceleration. When the throttle closes suddenly, an overly rich air/fuel mixture exists in the intake manifold due to the lack of air getting past the throttle valves. This rich mixture will not completely burn in the combustion chamber. If the unburned gases were to come in contact with the oxygen pumped into the exhaust ports by the air pump, they would ignite and cause backfiring and possible damage.

The anti-backfire valve is connected to the intake manifold by a vacuum line and when the vacuum rises, the valve opens a port in the intake manifold, allowing extra filtered air from the air cleaner to be admitted into the combustion chambers, leaning out the overly rich mixture.

1979–82 cab and chassis models have a transistorized programmed control unit, a vacuum switching valve, and an air control switch which govern air flow through the AIS. The air control switch, located between the intake manifold and the control unit, turns off when manifold vacuum is high, and on when vacuum is low. This provides a signal to the control unit, which determines when to turn the vacuum switching valve on or off accordingly. The vacuum switching valve controls the upper chamber of the CAC valve diaphragm, opening or closing the CAC valve according to signals received from the control unit. Thus, the amount of air injected into the AIS is monitored and adjusted as conditions warrant.

Air Induction System

Description

The air induction system is designed to send secondary air to the exhaust manifold, utilizing a vacuum caused by exhaust pulsation in the exhaust manifold.

The exhaust pressure in the exhaust manifold usually pulsates in response to the opening and closing of the exhaust valve and it decreases below atmospheric pressure periodically.

If a secondary air intake pipe is opened to the atmosphere under vacuum conditions, secondary air can be drawn into the exhaust manifold in proportion to the vacuum.

Therefore, the air induction system reduces CO and HC emissions in exhaust gases. The system consists of two air induction valves, a filter, hoses and E.A.I tube(s).

Air Induction Valve Case

The air induction valve case consists of two reed valves, a rubber seal and a filter and is attached to the air cleaner. There are two types of air induction valve cases. Type-A is equipped with two hose connectors and is installed on California models, while Type-B is equipped with one connector and is installed on non-California models.

Air Induction Valve

Two reed valve type check valves are installed in the air cleaner. When the exhaust pressure is below atmospheric pressure (negative pressure), secondary air is sent to the exhaust manifold.

When the exhaust pressure is above atmospheric pressure, the reed valves prevent secondary air from being sent back to the air cleaner.

Air Induction Valve Filter

The air induction valve filter is installed at the dust side of the air cleaner. It purifies secondary air to be sent to the exhaust manifold.

Air Induction Pipe

The secondary air fed from the air induction valve goes through the E.A.I. pipe to the exhaust manifold.

Anti-Backfire (A.B.) Valve

This valve is actuated by intake manifold vacuum to prevent backfire in the exhaust system at the initial period of deceleration.

At this period, the mixture in the intake manifold becomes too rich to ignite and burn in the combustion chamber and burns easily in the exhaust system with injected air in the exhaust manifold.

The A.B. valve provides air to the intake manifold to make the air-fuel mixture leaner and prevents backfire.

The correct function of this valve reduces hydrocarbon emission during deceleration.

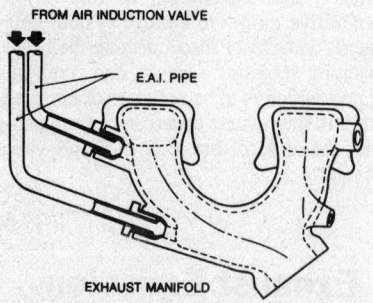

Air induction pipes on California trucks

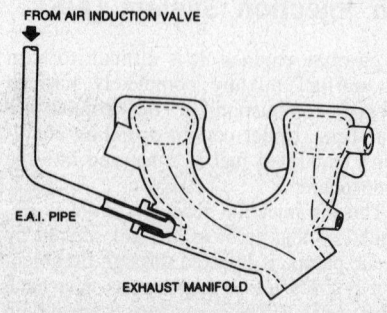

Air induction pipe on non-California trucks

Boost Control Deceleration Device (BCDD)

The BCDD reduces hydrocarbon emissions during coasting conditions.

High manifold vacuum during coasting prevents the complete combustion of the air/fuel mixture because of the reduced amount of air. This condition will result in large HC emissions. Enriching the air/fuel mixture for a short time (during the high vacuum condition) will reduce the emission of HC in conjunction with the AIR system.

However, enriching the air/fuel mixture with only the mixture adjusting screw will cause poor engine idle, or invite an increase in the carbon monoxide (CO) content of the exhaust gases.

The BCDD consists of an independently operated auxiliary fuel system. This system functions when the engine is coasting to enrich the air-fuel mixture which minimizes the hydrocarbon content of the exhaust gases through more efficient combustion. This is accomplished without adversely affecting engine idle and the carbon monoxide content of the exhaust gases.

When intake manifold vacuum exceeds a predetermined value, a vacuum-actuated diaphragm opens an air passage allowing additional air to enter the intake manifold. When the additional air passage is opened, vacuum is brought to bear on another diaphragm which opens a fuel passage allowing additional fuel to enter the intake manifold.

When the engine changes from a coasting condition to that of idling, the transmission speed sensor closes an electrical circuit, energizing the vacuum control solenoid valve. When energized, the vacuum control solenoid valve vents the intake manifold vacuum to the atmosphere, thus causing the two diaphragms to return to their normal positions, closing off the additional air and fuel mixture. The transmission switch is not used on 1978–79 models.

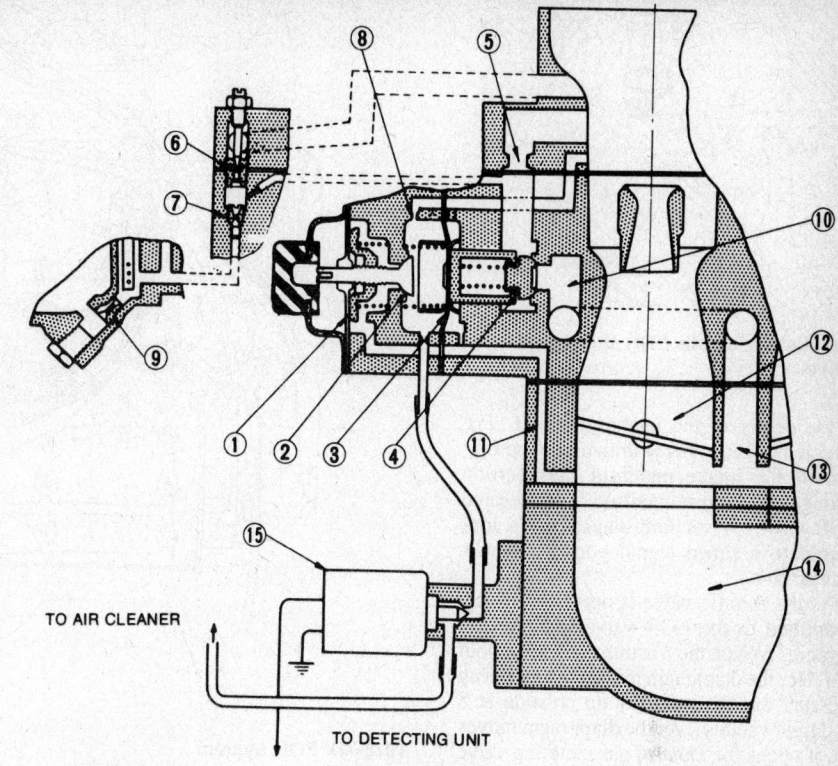

1. Diaphragm I
2. Vacuum control valve
3. Diaphragm II
4. Mixture control valve
5. Coasting air bleed II
6. Coasting air bleed I
7. Coasting jet
8. Air jet
9. Secondary main jet
10. Mixture air passage
11. Boost passage
12. Secondary barrel
13. Mixture outlet
14. Intake manifold
15. Vacuum control solenoid valve

Boost Control Deceleration Device

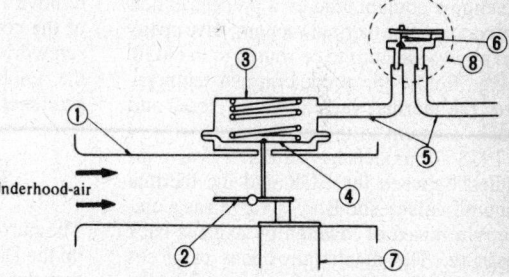

1. Air inlet pipe
2. Air control valve
3. Diaphragm spring
4. Diaphragm
5. Vacuum hoses
6. Air bleed valve (fully open)
7. Hot air pipe
8. Temperature sensor assembly

Automatic temperature control air cleaner open to underhood, warm air

Automatic Temperature Controlled (ATC) Air Cleaner

The rate of fuel atomization varies with the temperature of the air with which the fuel is being mixed. The air/fuel ratio cannot be held constant for efficient fuel combustion with a wide range of air temperatures. Cold air being drawn into the engine causes a denser and richer air/fuel mixture, inefficient fuel atomization, and thus, more hydrocarbons in the exhaust gas. Hot air being drawn into the engine causes a leaner air/fuel mixture and more efficient atomization

and combustion for less hydrocarbons in the exhause gases.

The automatic temperature controlled air cleaner is designed so that the temperature of the ambient air being drawn into the engine is automatically controlled, to hold the temperature of the air and, consequently, the fuel/air ratio at a constant rate for efficient fuel combusion.

A temperature sensing vacuum switch controls vacuum applied to a vacuum motor operating a valve in the intake snorkle of the air cleaner. When the engine is cold or the air being drawn into the engine is cold, the vacuum motor opens the valve, allowing air heated by the exhaust manifold to be drawn into the engine. As the engine warms up, the temperature sensing unit shuts

off the vacuum applied to the vacuum motor which allows the valve to close, shutting off the heated air and allowing cooler, outside (underhood) air to be drawn into the engine.

Exhaust Gas Recirculation System (EGR)

Exhaust gas recirculation is used to reduce combustion temperatures in the engine, thereby reducing the oxides of nitrogen emissions.

An EGR valve is mounted on the center

DATSUN

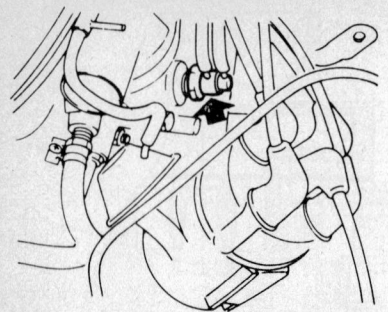

Installation of the EGR thermal vacuum valve

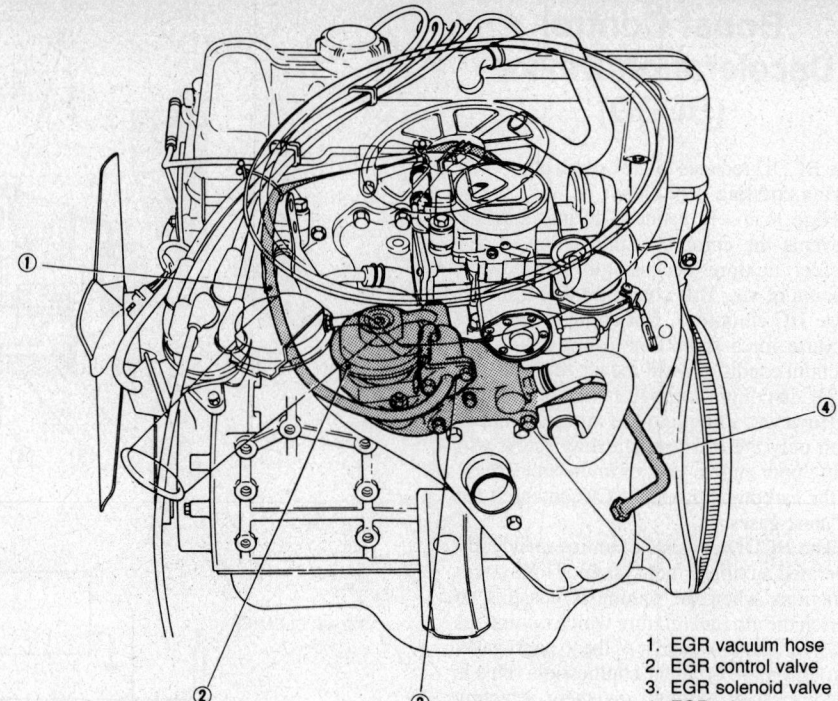

1. EGR vacuum hose
2. EGR control valve
3. EGR solenoid valve
4. EGR tube

1975–77 EGR system

of the center of the intake manifold. The recycled exhaust gas is drawn into the bottom of the intake manifold riser portion through the exhaust manifold heat stove and EGR valve. A vacuum diaphragm is connected to a timed signal port at the carburetor flange.

As the throttle valve is opened, vacuum is applied to the EGR valve vacuum diaphragm. When the vacuum reaches about 2 in. Hg, the diaphragm moves against spring pressure and is in a fully up position at 8 in. Hg of vacuum. As the diaphragm moves up, it opens the exhaust gas metering valve which allows exhaust gas to be pulled into the engine intake manifold. The system does not operate when the engine is idling because the exhaust gas recirculation would cause a rough idle.

A thermal vacuum valve inserted in the engine thermostat housing controls the application of vacuum to the EGR valve. When the engine coolant reaches a predetermined temperature, the thermal vacuum valve opens and allows vacuum to be routed to the EGR valve. Below the predetermined temperature, the thermal vacuum valve closes and blocks vacuum to the EGR valve.

1978–79 models have a B.P.T. valve installed between the EGR and the thermal vacuum valve. The B.P.T. valve has a diaphragm raised or lowered by exhaust back pressure. The diaphragm opens or closes an air bleed, which is connected into the EGR vacuum line. High pressure results in higher levels of EGR, because the diaphragm is raised, closing off the air bleed, which allows more vacuum to reach and open the EGR valve. Thus, the amount of recirculated exhaust gas varies with exhaust pressure.

1978–79 California models have a vacuum delay valve installed in the line between the thermal vacuum valve and the EGR valve. This valve delays rapid drops in vacuum in the EGR line, thus effecting a longer EGR time.

On all 1975 model trucks (except Canadian models) and all 1976–77 49 States model trucks, the EGR system is equipped with a warning system which monitors the distance the pick-up has traveled and activates a warning light when the EGR system must be checked and possibly serviced. The EGR warning light, mounted on top

of the dash, comes on when a predetermined number of miles has been traveled and every time the starter is engaged as a check for a burned-out bulb.

To reset the counter, which is mounted on the right fender apron under the hood, remove the grommet installed in the side of the counter and insert the tip of a small screwdriver into the hole. Press down on the knob inside the hole. Reinstall the grommet.

Electric Choke

The purpose of the electric choke installed on the Datsun pick-up is to shorten the time that the choke is in operation after the engine is started, thus shortening the time of high HC output.

An electric heater warms the bimetal spring which controls the opening and closing of the choke valve. The heater starts to heat as soon as the engine starts.

Catalytic Converter

1976 and later trucks sold in California have a catalytic converter, which is a muffler-shaped device installed into the exhaust system. The converter is filled with a monolithic substrate coated with small amounts of platinum and palladium. Through catalytic action, a chemical change converts carbon monoxide and hydrocarbons into carbon dioxide and water. The catalytic process is aided by the injection of air from the air pump system, which oxidizes the

HC and CO before they reach the converter.

1976–78 catalyst-equipped trucks have a floor temperature warning system, consisting of a temperature sensor, installed onto the floor of the cab above the converter; a relay, located with the other relays on the right fender of the engine compartment, and a light installed on the instrument panel. The lamp turns on when floor temperatures become abnormally high, due to converter or engine malfunction. The light also comes on when the ignition switch is turned to Start, to check its operation. 1979 and later models do not have the warning system.

Trucks with the catalytic converter also have a combined air control valve in 1978 and later, which controls the amount of secondary air injected into the exhaust manifold. It is regulated by engine vacuum and air pump pressure, and works to keep the converter temperatures within proper limits. The combined air control valve replaces the air pump relief valve, found in the air pump system of trucks not equipped with a catalytic converter. 1976–77 models have an emergency air relief valve for catalyst protection. See the AIS section for a description.

Spark Timing Control System

A spark timing control system is added to manual transmission models sold in the U.S. in 1979. The system controls distributor vacuum advance, giving full vacuum advance when the transmission is in 4th or

5th, and partial advance in the first three gears. This provides better control of the combustion process, lowering emissions of HC and NO.

The system components include a top detecting switch, installed into the transmission, and a vacuum switching valve spliced into the distributor vacuum advance hose by means of a three way connector. When the transmission is shifted into either of the two top gears, the transmission switch goes on, thus activating the vacuum switching valve which closes its air bleed, giving full advance. Shifting into any gear but 4th or 5th turns the transmission switch off, deactivating the vacuum switching valve. The valve opens a vacuum leak, providing only partial vacuum advance to the distributor.

Inspection and Adjustments

AIR INJECTION SYSTEM

Air Pump

If the air pump makes an abnormal noise and cannot be corrected without removing the pump from the vehicle, check the following in sequence:

1. Turn the pulley ¾ of a turn in the clockwise direction and ¼ of a turn in the counterclockwise direction. If the pulley is binding and if rotation is not smooth, a defective bearing is indicated.

2. Check the inner wall of the pump body, vanes, and rotor for wear. If the rotor has abnormal wear, replace the air pump.

3. Check the needle roller bearing for wear and damage. If the bearings are defective, the air pump should be replaced.

4. Check and replace the rear side seal if abnormal wear or damage is noticed.

5. Check and replace the carbon shoes holding the vanes if they are found to be worn or damaged.

6. A deposit of carbon particles on the inner wall of the pump body and vanes is normal, but should be removed with compressed air before reassembling the air pump.

Check Valve

Remove the check valve from the air pump discharge line. Test it for leakage by blowing air into the valve from the air pump side and from the air manifold side. Air should only pass through the valve from the air pump side if the valve is functioning normally. A small amount of air leakage from the manifold side can be overlooked. Replace the check valve if it is found to be defective.

Anti-Backfire Valve

To check the valve, disconnect the hose from the air cleaner and place a finger on the end. Run the engine up to about 3,000 rpm, then quickly release the throttle. If the

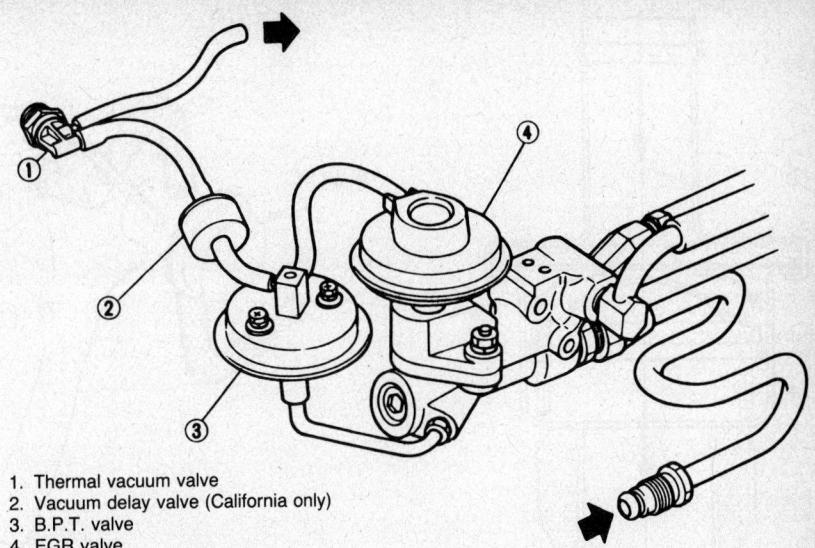

1. Thermal vacuum valve
2. Vacuum delay valve (California only)
3. B.P.T. valve
4. EGR valve

1978 and later EGR system components. The hose at top runs to the carburetor; the hose at the bottom runs to the exhaust manifold

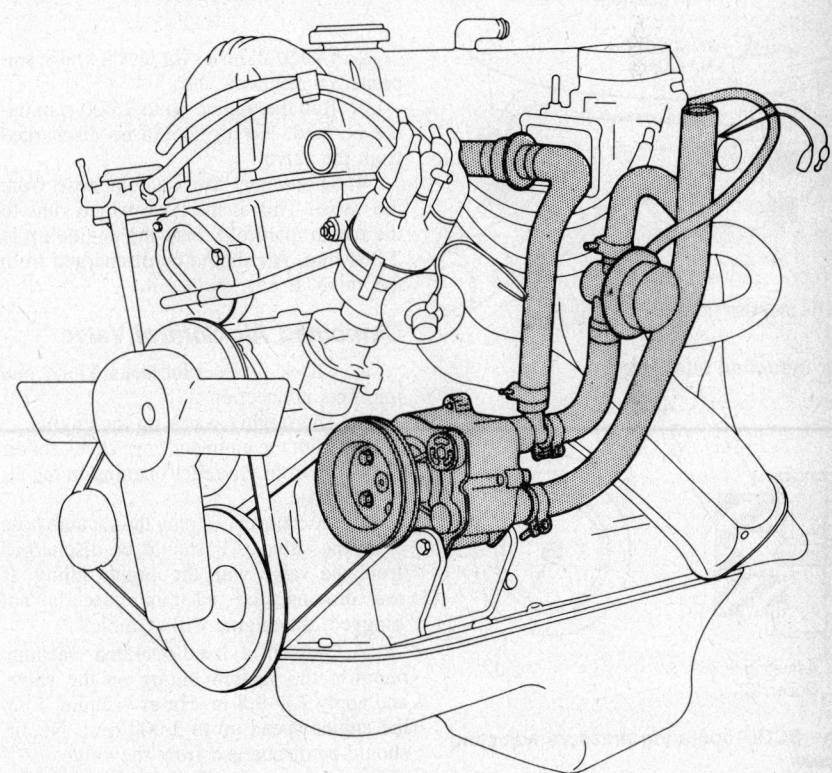

The air injection system

valve is performing correctly, suction should be felt at the end of the hose. If no suction is felt, replace the anti-backfire valve.

Air Pump Relief Valve

1. Disconnect the hoses leading to the check valve (on the air injection manifold) and the air control valve from the air hose connector. Plug the connector.

2. Start the engine and increase the engine speed to about 3,000 rpm. Place your finger on the outlet of the relief valve (inside the air cleaner housing) and check for air discharge. If you do not feel any air coming out, the relief valve is faulty, and must be replaced.

Air Injection Nozzles

Check around the air manifold for air leakage with the engine running at 2,000 rpm. If air is leaking from the eye joint bolt, retighten or replace the gasket. Check the

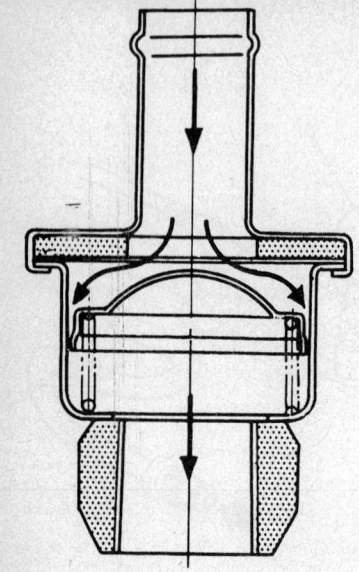

The AIR check valve

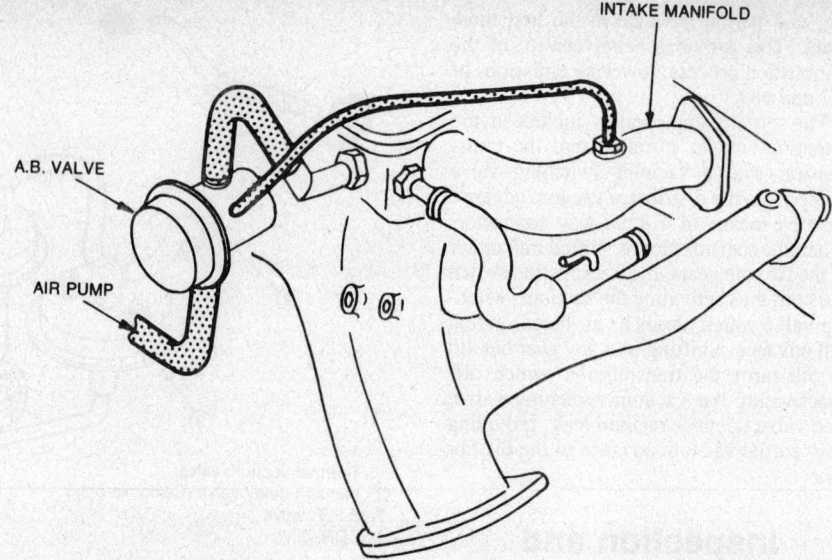

The AIR anti-backfire valve

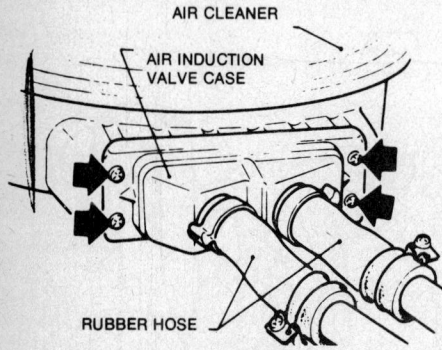

Air induction filter location

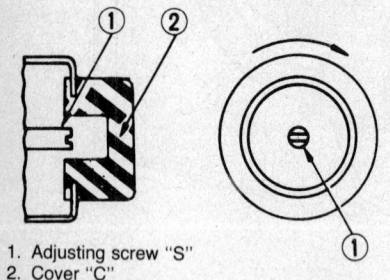

1. Adjusting screw "S"
2. Cover "C"

The BCDD operating pressure adjusting screw

air nozzles for restrictions by blowing air into the nozzles.

Hoses

Check and replace hoses if they are found to be weakened or cracked. Check all hose connections and clips. Be sure that the hoses are not in contact with other parts of the engine.

Emergency Air Relief Valve

1. Warm up the engine.

2. Check all hoses for leaks, kinks, improper connections, etc.

3. Run the engine up to 2,000 rpm under no load. No air should be discharged from the valve.

4. Disconnect the vacuum hose from the valve. This is the hose which runs to the intake manifold. Run the engine up to 2,000 rpm. Air should be discharged from the valve. If not, replace it.

Combined Air Control Valve

1. Check all hoses for leaks, kinks, and improper connections.

2. Thoroughly warm up the engine.

3. With the engine idling, check for air discharge from the relief opening in the air cleaner case.

4. Disconnect and plug the vacuum hose from the valve. Air should be discharged from the valve with the engine idling. If the disconnected vacuum hose is not plugged, the engine will stumble.

5. Connect a hand-operated vacuum pump to the vacuum fitting on the valve and apply 7.8–9.8 in. Hg of vacuum. Run the engine speed up to 3,000 rpm. No air should be discharged from the valve.

6. Disconnect and plug the air hose at the check valve, with the conditions as in the preceding step. This should cause the valve to discharge air. If not, or if any of the conditions in this procedure are not met, replace the valve.

AIR INDUCTION SYSTEM

Air Induction Valve and Filter

Remove the valve and filter on the air cleaner. The air induction valve and valve filter can then be taken out easily. Installation is in the reverse sequence of removal.

Air Induction Pipe

Remove nut securing the pipe to the exhaust manifold. At the same time, remove the screws securing the bracket and rubber hose clamp.

The air induction pipe can then be taken out. Installation is in the reverse sequence of removal.

A.B. Valve

1. Remove air cleaner.
2. Remove air hoses and vacuum tube. Then the A.B. valve can be taken out.

BOOST CONTROLLED DECELERATION DEVICE (BCDD)

Normally, the BCDD never needs adjustment. However, if the need should arise because of suspected malfunction of the system, proceed as follows:

1. Connect a tachometer to the engine.

2. Connect a quick-response vacuum gauge to the intake manifold.

3. Disconnect the BCDD solenoid valve electrical leads.

4. Start and warm up the engine until it reaches normal operating temperature.

5. Adjust the idle speed to the proper specification.

6. Raise the engine speed to 3,000–3,500 rpm under no-load (transmission in Neutral or Park), then allow the throttle to close quickly. Take notice as to whether or not the engine rpm returns to idle speed and if it does, how long the fall in rpm is interrupted before it reaches idle speed.

At the moment the throttle is snapped closed at high engine rpm, the vacuum in the intake manifold reaches −23.6 in. Hg on 1975 models, and then gradually falls to about −16.5 in. Hg at idle speed. The process of the fall of intake manifold vacuum and engine rpm will take one of the following three forms:

a. When the operating pressure of the BCDD is too high, the system remains inoperative, and the vacuum in the intake manifold decreases without interruption just like that of an engine without a BCDD;

b. When the operating pressure is lower than that of the case given, but still higher than the properly set pressure, the fall of vacuum in the intake manifold is interrupted and kept constant at a certain level (operating pressure) for about one second and then gradually falls down to the normal vacuum at idle speed;

c. When the set operating pressure of the BCDD is lower than the intake manifold vacuum when the throttle is suddenly released, the engine speed will not lower to idle speed.

To adjust the set operating pressure of the BCDD, remove the adjusting screw cover from the BCDD mechanism mounted on the side of the carburetor.

The adjusting screw is a left-hand threaded screw. Turning the screw ⅛ of a turn in either direction will change the operation pressure about 0.79 in. Hg. Turning the screw counterclockwise will increase the amount of vacuum needed to operate the mechanism and turning the screw clockwise will decrease the amount of vacuum needed to operate the mechanism.

The operating pressure for the BCDD is listed below. The decrease in intake manifold vacuum should be interrupted at these levels for about one second when the BCDD is operating correctly.

1975–76:
−20.7 to −21.1, manual transmission;
−19.9 to −20.3, automatic transmission;

1977:
−20.1 to −21.7, manual transmission;
−19.3 to −20.9, automatic transmission;

1978:
−22.05 ± 0.79, all models;

1979
−21.65 ± 0.75, all models.

Don't forget to install the adjusting screw cover when the system is adjusted.

AUTOMATIC TEMPERATURE CONTROLLED AIR CLEANER

When the air around the temperature sensor of the unit mounted inside the air cleaner housing reaches 100°F, the sensor should block the flow of vacuum to the air control valve vacuum motor. When the temperature around the temperature sensor is below 100°F, the sensor should allow vacuum to pass onto the air valve vacuum motor, thus blocking off the air cleaner snorkle to underhood (unheated) air.

When the temperature around the sensor is about 118°F, the air control valve should be completely open to underhood air.

When the engine is operating under a heavy load (wide open throttle acceleration), the air control valve fully opens to underhood air to obtain full power no matter what the temperature is around the temperature sensor.

EXHAUST GAS RECIRCULATION

1. Remove the EGR valve and apply enough vacuum to the diaphragm to open the valve.

2. The valve should remain open for over 30 seconds after the vacuum is removed.

3. Check the valve for damage, such as warpage, cracks, and excessive wear around the valve and seat.

4. Clean the seat with a brush and compressed air and remove any deposits from around the valve and port (seat).

5. To check the operation of the thermal vacuum valve, remove the valve from the engine and apply vacuum to the ports of the valve. The valve should not allow vacuum to pass.

6. Place the valve in a container of water with a thermometer and heat the water. When the temperature of the water reaches 134°–145°F, remove the valve and apply vacuum to the ports; the valve should allow vacuum to pass through it.

7. To test the B.P.T. valve installed on 1978 and later models, disconnect the two vacuum hoses from the valve. Plug one of the ports. While applying pressure to the bottom of the valve, apply vacuum to the unplugged port and check for leakage. If any exists, replace the valve.

8. To test the check valve installed in some 1978 and later models, remove the valve and blow into the side which connects to the EGR valve. Air should flow. When air is applied to the other side, air flow resistance should be greater. If not, replace the valve.

SPARK TIMING CONTROL SYSTEM

1. Check all hoses and electrical wires for proper connections, leaks or corrosion, and so on.

2. Check the distributor vacuum advance unit for proper operation. This can be checked by hooking up a timing light, starting the engine, then increasing engine speed and observing whether or not the timing marks advance. If not, the advance unit must be checked for binding or leaks.

3. With the timing light installed, increase the engine speed to 2,000 rpm. Have an assistant disengage the clutch, then shift between 3, 4, and 5, then back down and into neutral. Spark timing should vary when the transmission is in 4 or 5 (advance should

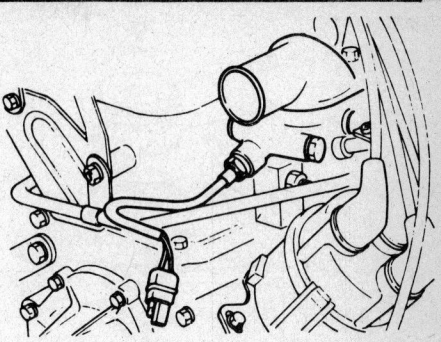

The EGR water temperature sensing switch

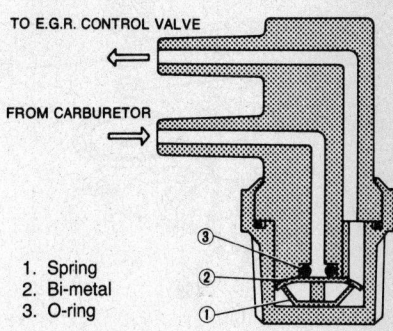

TO E.G.R. CONTROL VALVE

FROM CARBURETOR

1. Spring
2. Bi-metal
3. O-ring

Cutaway view of the EGR thermal vacuum valve

be greater). If this is not the case, check the vacuum switching valve.

Vacuum Switching Valve

1. Disconnect the valve's electrical connectors. With the timing light installed, run the engine up to about 2,000 rpm and keep it there. Check the timing.

2. Connect the valve's electrical connectors directly to the battery with a pair of jumper wires. Be sure to observe correct polarity. If spark timing varies, the valve is ok. If not, replace it.

Transmission Switch

The switch can be checked easily with an ohmmeter. Connect the ohmmeter leads to the switch leads on the transmission. Shift back and forth between either 4 or 5 and one of the other gears. If the resistance does not change, replace the switch.

GASOLINE ENGINE FUEL SYSTEM

If the fuel pump is suspected as being faulty, tests for both pressure and volume should be performed. Never replace the pump without performing these simple tests first.

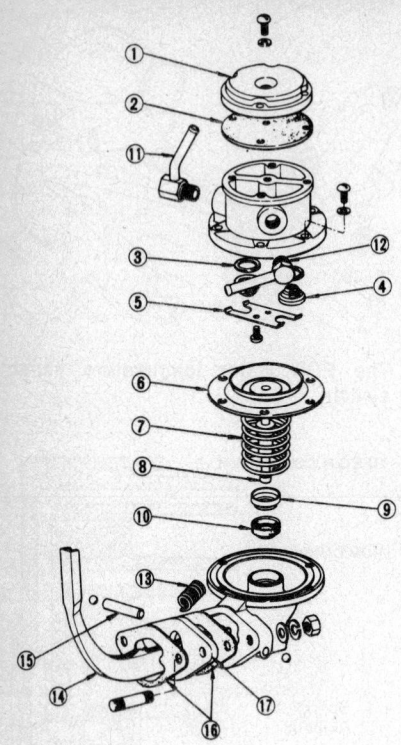

The mechanical fuel pump

1. Fuel pump cap
2. Cap gasket
3. Valve packing
4. Fuel pump valve
5. Valve retainer
6. Diaphragm
7. Diaphragm spring
8. Pull rod
9. Lower body seal washer
10. Lower body seal
11. Inlet connector
12. Outlet connector
13. Rocker arm spring
14. Rocker arm
15. Rocker arm side pin
16. Fuel pump packing
17. Spacer—fuel pump to cylinder block

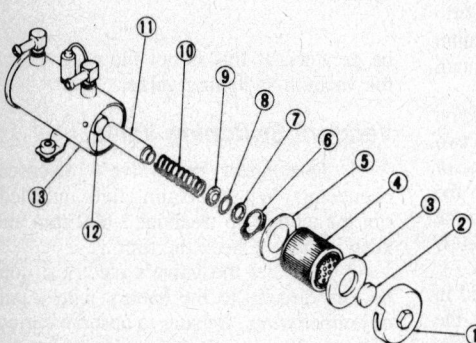

The electric fuel pump

1. End cover
2. Magnet
3. Gasket
4. Filter
5. Gasket
6. Retainer
7. Washer
8. O-ring
9. Inlet valve
10. Return spring
11. Plunger
12. Plunger cylinder
13. Body

TESTING

1. Disconnect the line between the carburetor and the pump at the carburetor.

2. Connect a fuel pump pressure gauge into the line.

3. Start the engine. The pressure should be between 3.0 and 3.9 psi. There is usually enough gas in the float bowl to perform this test.

4. If the pressure is ok, perform a capacity test. Remove the gauge from the line. Use a graduated container to catch the gas from the fuel line. Fill the carburetor float bowl with gas. Run the engine for one minute at about 1,000 rpm. The pump should deliver 1,000cc in one minute or less.

REMOVAL AND INSTALLATION

1. Disconnect the two fuel lines from the fuel pump. Be sure to keep the line leading from the fuel tank up high to prevent the excessive loss of fuel.

2. Remove the two fuel pump mounting nuts and remove the fuel pump assembly from the side of the engine.

3. Install the fuel pump in the reverse order of removal, using a new gasket and sealer on the mating surface.

Electric Fuel Pump

An electric fuel pump is used on 1977 and later models with factory-installed air conditioning, and also on 1979 and later cab and chassis models. The pump is mounted on a bracket located on the right frame rail next to the fuel tank. There is a filter mounted in the body of the pump, which does not normally require service. The pump can be disassembled, if necessary, but all electronic parts within the body (one transistor, two diodes, and three resistors) must be replaced as an assembly.

TESTING

1. Disconnect the hose from the pump outlet at the pump.

2. Connect a length of hose to the outlet. The hose should have an inside diameter of 1/4 in. (6mm.). The diameter of the hose is important for accurate measurements.

3. Raise the end of the hose above the level of the pump. Turn the ignition switch on and catch the gasoline in a graduated container. Pump output should be 1,400cc in one minute or less.

4. Fuel pump pressure should be 4.6 psi through 1978, and between 3.1 and 3.8 psi in 1979 and later.

REMOVAL AND INSTALLATION

1. Remove the inlet and outlet hoses,

Always check all hoses for leaks or clogs before testing the pump.

Fuel Filter

The gasoline fuel filter is located on the right inner fender in the engine compartment. It is a disposable cartridge type, and should be replaced every 24,000 miles.

To replace the filter, loosen the clamps on the fuel lines and slide the clamps down the hoses past the point to which the filter pipes extend. Gently twist and pull on the hoses to remove them from the filter. Be careful, because some gas will spill from the bottom fuel line. Remove the old filter from the clip, install a new filter, and replace the hoses and clamps. Be certain that the line from the fuel tank connects to the fuel inlet, and that the carburetor line con-

nects to the outlet. Start the engine and check for leaks.

The diesel fuel filter is located on the upper right front of the engine. It is the canister type with a paper cartridge inside. To replace the filter, unbolt the top of the canister and lift out the old filter. Insert the new filter using new gaskets and O-rings. Replace the top. The filter should be replaced every 6,000 miles.

Mechanical Fuel Pump

The fuel pump is a mechanically-operated, diaphragm-type driven by the fuel pump eccentric cam on the front of the camshaft.

Design of the fuel pump permits disassembly, cleaning, and repair or replacement of defective parts.

catching the fuel that drains in a metal container.

2. Disconnect the wiring at the connector.

3. Remove the two bolts securing the pump to the bracket and remove the pump.

4. Installation is the reverse. Replace the hose clamps if their condition warrants.

Carburetor

The carburetor used on the Datsun pick-up is a two-barrel, downdraft-type with a low-speed (primary) side and a high-speed (secondary) side.

The carburetor has an electrically-operated anti-dieseling solenoid. As the ignition switch is turned off, the valve is energized and shuts off the supply of fuel to the idle circuit of the carburetor.

REMOVAL AND INSTALLATION

1. Remove the air cleaner.

2. Disconnect and label the fuel and vacuum lines from the carburetor.

3. Remove the throttle linkage.

4. Remove the four nuts and washers retaining the carburetor to the manifold.

5. Lift the carburetor from the manifold.

6. Remove and discard the gasket used between the carburetor and the manifold.

7. Install the carburetor in the reverse order of removal using a new carburetor base gasket.

AUTOMATIC CHOKE ADJUSTMENT

1. With the engine cold, make sure the choke is fully closed (press the gas pedal all the way to the floor and release, or pull the choke knob out on early models with that system).

2. Check the choke linkage for binding. The choke plate should be easily opened and closed with your finger. If the choke sticks or binds, it can usually be freed with a liberal application of a carburetor cleaner made for the purpose. A couple of quick shots from a spray can of this stuff normally does the trick. If not, the carburetor will have to be disassembled for repairs.

3. The choke is correctly adjusted when the index mark on the choke housing (notch) aligns with the center mark on the carburetor body. If the setting is incorrect, loosen the three screws clamping the choke body in place and rotate the choke cover left or right until the marks align. Tighten the screws carefully to avoid cracking the housing.

THROTTLE LINKAGE ADJUSTMENT

When the primary throttle valve is opened

to an angle of 50° from its closed position, the adjust plate which is integral with the primary throttle valve, is brought into contact with portion A (see illustration) of the return plate. When the primary throttle valve is opened farther, the return plate is pulled apart from the stopper (B in the illustration), allowing the secondary throttle valve to open.

To adjust the linkage:

1. Measure the clearance between the primary throttle valve and the wall of the throttle chamber at the center of the throttle valve when the adjust plate is brought into contact with portion A of the return plate. Standard clearance is 0.26–0.32 in.

2. If necessary, make the adjustment by bending the portion A of the return plate.

FLOAT LEVEL ADJUSTMENT

The fuel level is normal if it is within the lines on the window glass of the float chamber when the vehicle is resting on level ground and the engine is off.

If the fuel level is outside the lines, remove the float housing cover. Have an absorbent cloth under the cover to catch the fuel from the fuel bowl. Adjust the float level by bending the needle seat on the float.

The needle valve should have an effective stroke of about 0.0591 in. When necessary, the needle valve stroke can be adjusted by bending the float stopper.

NOTE: Be careful not to bend the needle valve rod when installing the float and baffle plate, if removed.

FAST IDLE ADJUSTMENT

1. With the carburetor removed from the vehicle, place the upper side of the fast idle screw on the second step of the fast idle cam and measure the clearance between the throttle valve and the wall of the

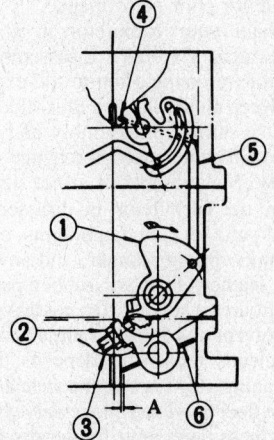

1. Fast idle cam   4. Choke valve
2. Nut   5. Choke connecting rod
3. Fast idle screw 6. Throttle valve

Fast idle screw

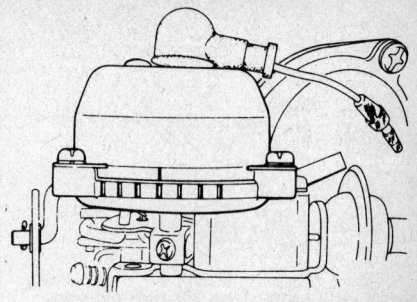

Align the choke cover mark with the center notch on the carburetor

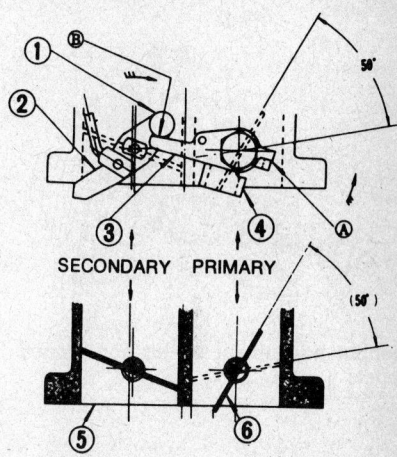

SECONDARY   PRIMARY

1. Roller   4. Adjust plate
2. Connecting lever 5. Throttle chamber
3. Return plate   6. Throttle valve

Throttle linkage adjustment

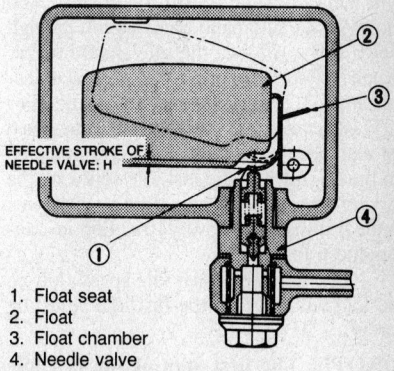

EFFECTIVE STROKE OF NEEDLE VALVE: H

1. Float seat
2. Float
3. Float chamber
4. Needle valve

Float level adjustment

throttle valve chamber at the center of the throttle valve (A in the illustration). The clearance should be 0.040–0.048 in., manual, 0.048–0.052 in. automatic.

For 1977–82 models, the fast idle screw should be placed on the first step of the fast idle cam. This is the highest of the four. Clearance A should be 0.052–0.058 in., manual transmission, or 0.062–0.068 in. automatic.

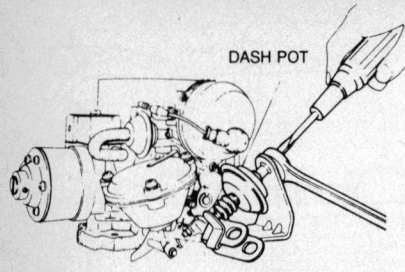

DASH POT

Dashpot adjustment on all non-air conditioned models

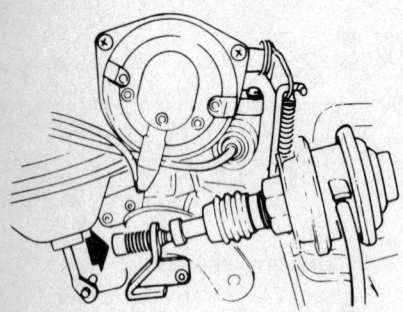

Dashpot adjustment on air conditioned models

2. Install the carburetor on the engine. Place the fast idle screw on the second step of the cam for all years, including 1977–82 models.

3. Start the engine and measure the fast idle rpm with the engine at operating temperature. The rpm should be about 2,000 rpm with a manual transmission and 2,400 rpm with an automatic transmission through 1976. For 1977–82, the idle should be between 1,900 and 2,800 for manual transmission, 2,200–3,200 for automatic. For 1977–82, there is a "reference" value given for distance A, with the carburetor mounted on the engine and the fast idle screw on the *second* step of the cam: 0.037–0.046 in., manual transmission, 0.046–0.055 in., automatic transmission.

4. To adjust the fast idle speed, loosen the locknut and turn the fast idle adjusting screw.

NOTE: The first step of the fast idle adjustment procedure is not absolutely necessary; it should be used as a guide to correct adjustment at overhaul.

CHOKE UNLOADER ADJUSTMENT

1. Close the choke valve completely.
2. Hold the choke valve closed by stretching a rubber band between the choke piston lever and a stationary part of the carburetor.
3. Open the throttle lever fully.

4. With the throttle lever fully open, adjust the clearance between the choke valve and the carburetor body to 0.096 in., by bending the unloader tongue.

NOTE: Make sure that the throttle valve opens completely when the carburetor is mounted on the engine.

DASHPOT ADJUSTMENT

The purpose of this device is to prevent the throttle from suddenly snapping shut. The dashpot has a plunger which extends when the throttle is closed suddenly. The plunger contacts a tab on the throttle lever and holds the throttle open slightly for a second, then closes the throttle slowly over the period of another second or so.

1. Adjust the idle speed and mixture before making adjustments to the dashpot. Warm the engine to operating temperature, and connect a tachometer to the engine.

2. Move the throttle lever by hand, and note the engine speed when the dashpot plunger just touches the throttle lever.

3. The engine speed should be 1,650–1,850 rpm with automatic transmission, or 1,900–2,100 rpm with manual transmission through 1980. On 1981–82 models the speed is 1,600 rpm.

4. If not, loosen the locknut and turn the adjusting screw until the engine speed is in the proper range. Tighten the locknut. On 1978–79 models with air conditioning, a different dashpot is used. Adjustment is made by turning the screw on the throttle lever which contacts the plunger.

5. Open the throttle and allow it to close by itself. The dashpot should smoothly reduce the idling speed from 2,000 to 1,000 rpm in about three seconds.

OVERHAUL

Efficient carburetion depends greatly on careful cleaning and inspection during overhaul, since dirt, gum, water, or varnish in or on the carburetor parts are often responsible for poor performance.

Overhaul your carburetor in a clean, dustfree area. Carefully disassemble the carburetor, referring often to the exploded views. Keep all similar and look-alike parts segregated during disassembly and cleaning to avoid accidental interchange during assembly. Make a note of all jet sizes.

When the carburetor is disassembled, wash all parts (except diaphragms, electric choke units, pump plunger, and any other plastic, leather, fiber, or rubber parts) in clean carburetor solvent. Do not leave parts in the solvent any longer than is necessary to sufficiently loosen the deposits. Excessive cleaning may remove the special finish from the float bowl and choke valve bodies, leaving these parts unfit for service. Rinse all parts in clean solvent and blow them dry with compressed air or allow them to air dry. Wipe clean all cork, plastic, leather,

and fiber parts with a clean, lint-free cloth.

Blow out all passages and jets with compressed air and be sure that there are no restrictions or blockages. Never use wire or similar tools to clean jets, fuel passages, or air bleeds. Clean all jets and valves separately to avoid accidental interchange.

Check all parts for wear or damage. If wear or damage is found, replace the defective parts. Especially check the following:

1. Check the float needle and seat for wear. If wear is found, replace the complete assembly.

2. Check the float hinge pin for wear and the float(s) for dents or distortion. Replace the float if fuel has leaked into it.

3. Check the throttle and choke shaft bores for wear or an out-of-round condition. Damage or wear to the throttle arm, shaft, or shaft bore will often require replacements of the throttle body. These parts require a close tolerance of fit; wear may allow air leakage, which could affect starting and idling.

NOTE: Throttle shafts and bushings are not included in overhaul kits. They can be purchased separately.

4. Inspect the idle mixture adjusting needles for burrs or grooves. Any such condition requires replacement of the needle, since you will not be able to obtain a satisfactory idle.

5. Test the accelerator pump check valves. They should pass air one way but not the other. Test for proper seating by blowing and sucking on the valve. Replace the valve if necessary. If the valve is satisfactory, wash the valve again to remove breath moisture.

6. Check the bowl cover for warped surfaces with a straightedge.

7. Closely inspect the valves and seats for wear and damage, replacing as necessary.

8. After the carburetor is assembled, check the choke valve for freedom of operation

Carburetor overhaul kits are recommended for each overhaul. These kits contain all gaskets and new parts to replace those that deteriorate most rapidly. Failure to replace all parts supplied with the kit (especially gaskets) can result in poor performance later.

Some carburetor manufacturers supply overhaul kits of three basic types: minor repair; major repair; and gasket kits.

After cleaning and checking all components, reassemble the carburetor, using new parts and referring to the exploded view. When reassembling, make sure that all screws and jets are tight in their seats, but do not overtighten as the tips will be distorted. Tighten all screws gradually, in rotation. Do not tighten needle valves into their seats; uneven jetting will result. Always use new gaskets. Be sure to adjust the float level when reassembling.

CARBURETOR SPECIFICATIONS

Year	Engine Displacement cc (cu in.)	Model Number	Main Jet Primary	Main Jet Secondary	Main Air Bleed Primary	Main Air Bleed Secondary	Slow Jet Primary	Slow Jet Secondary	Slow Jet Air Bleed Primary	Slow Jet Air Bleed Secondary	Float Level (in.)	Power Jet
'75	1952(119)	①	#99	#160	#70	#60	#48	#80	NA	NA	0.906	#43
'76	1952(119)	②	#99	#160	#70	#60	#48	#100	NA	NA	0.906	#43
		③	#101	#160	#70	#60	#48	#80	NA	NA	0.906	#40
'77	1952(119)	④	#99	#160	#70	#60	#48	#100	NA	NA	0.906	#43
		⑤	#101	#160	#70	#60	#48	#100	NA	NA	0.906	#40
		⑥	#101	#160	#70	#60	#48	#80	NA	NA	0.906	#40
'78	1952(119)	⑦	#101	#158	#70	#60	#48	#70	NA	NA	0.910	#40
		⑧	#103	#160	#60	#60	#48	#70	NA	NA	0.910	#43
'79	1952(119)	⑨	#103⑩	#158	#70	#60	#48	#70⑪	NA	NA	0.901	#43
		⑫	#103⑬	#160	#60	#60	#48	#70	NA	NA	0.910	#35
		⑭	#103	#150	#60	#60	#48	#50	NA	NA	0.910	#35
'80	1952(119)	DCH340–111,112	#104	#158	#70	#60	#48	#70	—	—	0.910	#35
		DCH340–115	#103	#140	#70	#60	#48	#60	—	—	0.910	#35
		DCH340–113	#105	#158	#60	#60	#48	#70	—	—	0.910	#35
		DCH340–116	#103	#140	#60	#60	#48	#50	—	—	0.910	#35
		DCH340–114	#105	#158	#60	#60	#48	#70	—	—	0.910	#35
		DCH340–117,118	#106	#160	#60	#60	#48	#70	—	—	0.910	#35
'81	2187 (133.5)	DCR342–11, DCR342–12, DCR342–13	#112	#155	#90	#60	#47	#100	—	—	0.910	#35
		DCR342–21 DCR342–22	#110	#145	#90	#60	#47	#80	—	—	0.910	#35
		DCR342–17, DCR342–18	#110	#155	#90	#60	#47	#100	—	—	0.910	#35
		DCR342–14, DCR342–15	#105	#155	#80	#60	#47	#100	—	—	0.910	#40
		DCR342–23, DCR342–24	#105	#155	#80	#60	#47	#100	—	—	0.910	#40
'82	2187 (133.5)	DCR342-11A DCR342-13A	#113	#155	#80	#60	#47	#100	—	—	0.910	#35
		DCR342-21A	#112	#145	#80	#60	#47	#80	—	—	0.910	#35
		DCR342-17A	#112	#155	#80	#60	#47	#100	—	—	0.910	#35
		DCR342-14A DCR342-16A	#105	#155	#80	#60	#47	#100	—	—	0.910	#40
		DCR342-23A	#105	#155	#80	#60	#47	#100	—	—	0.910	#40

① Manual Transmission
② Automatic Transmission
③ DCH340-47 with manual transmission
DCH340-48 with automatic transmission
④ DCH340-47—49 States and Canada, manual transmission
DCH340-48—49 States and Canada, automatic transmission
DCH340-45A—California, manual transmission
⑤ DCH340-46—California, automatic transmission

⑥ DCH340-47A—49 States and Canada, manual transmission
DCH340-48A—49 States and Canada, automatic transmission
⑦ DCH340-45B—California, manual transmission
⑧ DCH340-46A—California, automatic transmission
⑨ DCH340-95—California, manual transmission
DCH340-96—California, automatic transmission

⑩ DCH340-97—49 States and Canada, manual transmission
DCH340-98—49 States and Canada, automatic transmission
⑪ DCH340-95C—California, manual transmission except cab and chassis
DCH340-65A—California, manual transmission, cab and chassis
DCH340-96C—California, automatic transmission
⑫ #101, DCH340-65A
⑬ #60, DCH340-65A

⑭ DCH340-97C—49 States, manual transmission
DCH340-57A—Canada, manual transmission
DCH340-98B—49 States, automatic transmission
DCH340-58A—Canada, automatic transmission
⑮ #106, DCH340-57A and B
⑯ #106, DCH340-67A—49 States, manual transmission, cab and chassis
NA Not available
—Not used

Fuel line removal

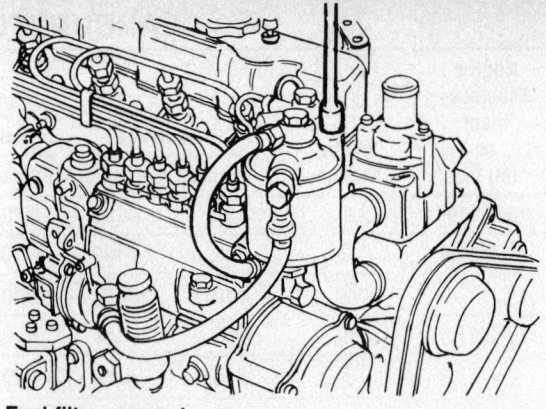

Fuel filter removal

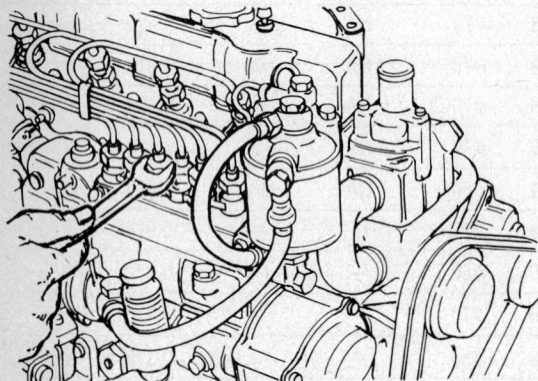

Injection line removal

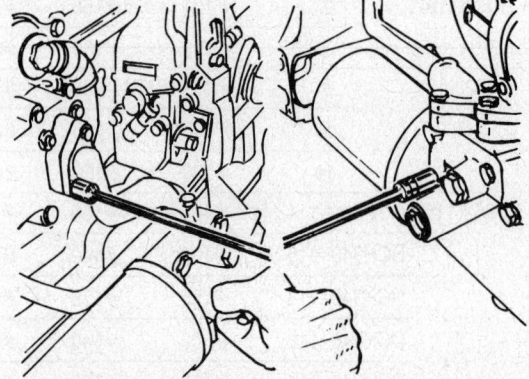

Water passage removal

DIESEL ENGINE FUEL SYSTEM

Injection Pump

REMOVAL AND INSTALLATION

The following procedure requires the use of special tools.

NOTE: In some applications, this procedure is best done with the engine removed from the vehicle.

1. Remove the inlet and outlet lines from the oil cooler.
2. Remove the bolts (4) and separate the oil filter and lines from the cooler.
3. Remove the coolant hose between the oil cooler and the head.
4. Remove the bolts (10) and separate the cooler from the block.
5. Disconnect the fuel lines and remove the fuel filter from the bracket.
6. Remove the injection lines from the nozzles and pump. Cover all openings immediately.
7. Remove the fan, spacer and pulley from the water pump.
8. Remove the bypass hose from the pump and thermostat housing.
9. Remove the three bolts and lift off the water pump and gasket.
10. Remove the inspection cover and pointer from the flywheel housing and lock the flywheel in place with a locking tool.
11. Flatten the lockwasher and remove the crankshaft pulley nut.
12. Tap evenly around the edge of the pulley using a brass drift, until the cone protrudes from the pulley. Remove the cone.
13. Drive the pulley and damper from the crankshaft with a soft mallet.
14. Remove the inner cover from the timing gear case.
15. Pry out the oil seal.
16. Remove the mounting bolts and tap the case loose with a soft mallet.
17. Remove the tachometer drive support nuts.
18. Remove the timer round nut.
19. Thread the timer extractor, special tool #57926-581 into the timer weight holder. Remove the timer assembly by tightening the extractor bolt.
20. Unbolt and separate the injection pump from the front end plate.
21. Temporarily install the injection pump and gasket on the front plate.
22. Check the timing marks and bring the #1 piston to TDC.
23. Mesh the injection pump drive gear and idler gear at the timing marks.
24. After aligning the injection pump keyway, install the lockwasher and round nut and torque to 50–58 ft. lbs.
25. Install the tachometer drive coupling.
26. Check the backlash between the pump drive gear and the idler gear. Backlash should be .0028–0079″. Adjust if necessary.
27. Remove the no.1 cylinder holder clamp, loosen the delivery valve and pull out the delivery spring. Tighten the valve holder to 22–25 ft. lbs.
28. Connect the fuel supply lines.
29. Bring the no. 1 piston to 20° BTDC. This can be done by aligning the first mark, in normal rotation, on the crankshaft pulley with the raised line on the gear case.
30. Hand prime the pump. Push the pump in all the way toward the block. Move the pump slowly away from the block until the fuel just stops flowing from the valve holder. Lock the pump in place.
31. Remove the delivery holder and assemble the spring. Torque the holder to 22–25 ft. lbs.
32. Install remaining parts in reverse order of removal.

NOTE: Oil filter bolt torque is 15–18 ft. lbs.

Injection Nozzle

REMOVAL, OVERHAUL AND INSTALLATION

1. Loosen the injection lines at the pump and nozzles and remove the lines. Cap the openings immediately.

Timing cover removal

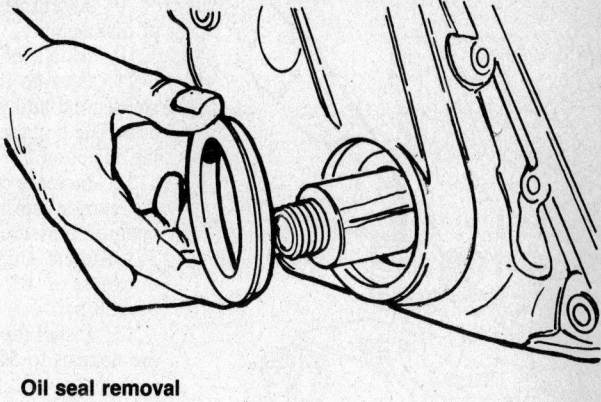

Oil seal removal

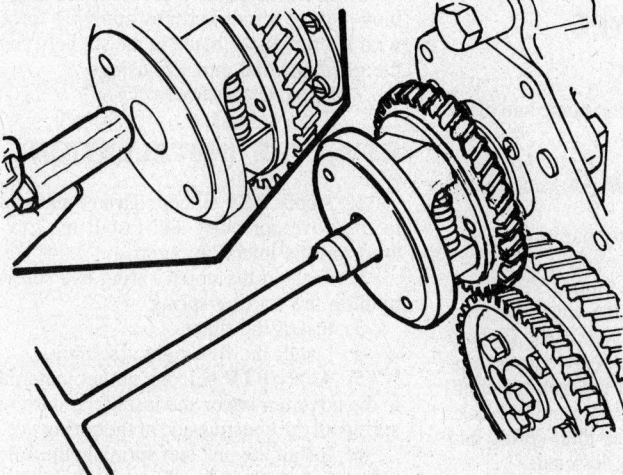

Removing the timer round nut

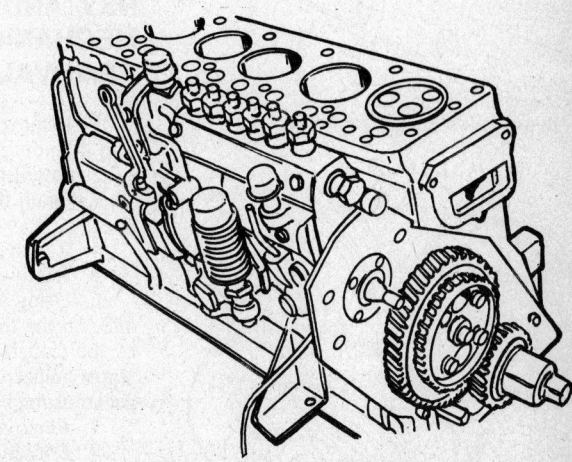

Injection pump and end plate assembly

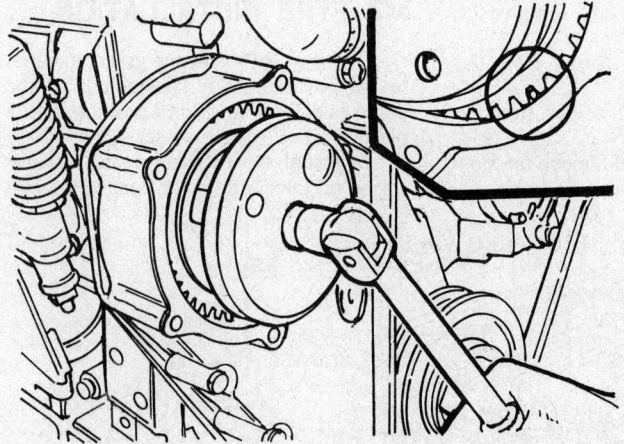

Timer installation

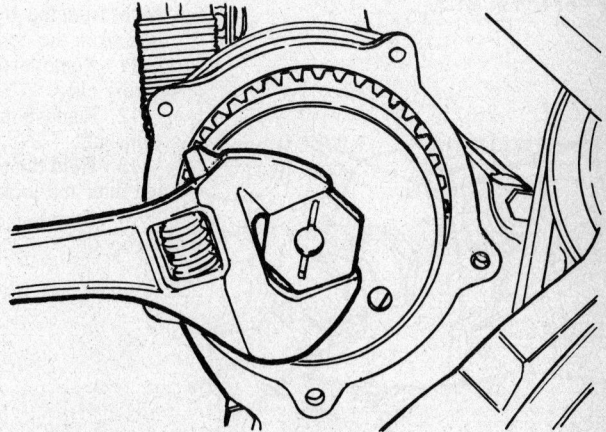

Tachometer drive coupling installation

2. Unscrew the injector and holder from the head.

3. Secure the nozzle holder in a vise and remove the lock nut.

4. Remove the nipple.

5. Remove the nozzle holder body from the nozzle nut.

6. Remove the spacer collar and push-rod.

7. Remove the nozzle holder body from the vise and remove the nozzle spring and adjusting shims.

NOTE: The adjusting shims may be

removed with a piece of wire, but great care must be taken to avoid damage to the nozzle tip.

8. Clean fuel oil may be used to clean all parts. Inspect all parts for damage and good fit.

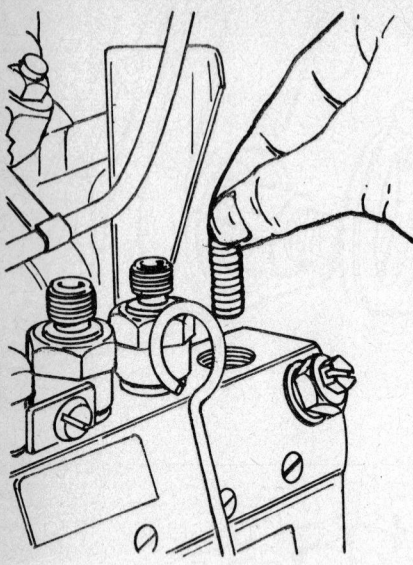

Delivery valve spring removal

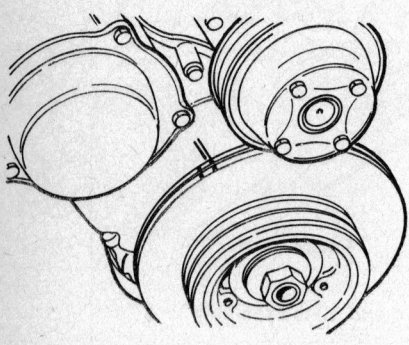

#1 piston at BTDC

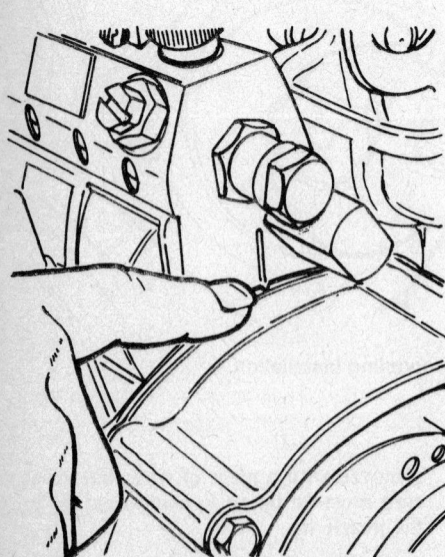

Lock the pump at this point which is the beginning of injection

9. Assemble the nozzle in reverse order of disassembly.

10. Install the nozzle in a tester.

11. Operate the tester lever at 1 stroke per second and read the pressure at injection. The pointer will oscillate slightly during injection.

12. Increase or decrease the thickness of the nozzle spring adjusting shims until opening pressure is 1,422.3 psi. A total of 31 different shims are available. A shim thickness of .05 mm equals a difference of 85.338 psi.

13. Install the nozzles and lines. Torque the nozzles to 50–65 ft. lbs.

Governor

RSV AND RAD MECHANICAL TYPE REMOVAL

1. Remove the injection pump and place it in a holding fixture.

2. Install the timer.

3. Drain the cam and governor chambers.

4. Remove the supply pump.

5. Remove the cam cover.

6. Using a special wrench, ST-57916-432, on the timer, turn the camshaft until all the tappets are raised to TDC. Place a tappet holder, 57931-210, between the tappet adjusting bolt and nut for each cylinder.

7. Remove the rear cover and dipstick.

8. Loosen the balance idler spring and the auxiliary idler spring lock nut.

9. Loosen the governor cover lock screw.

10. Unbolt and remove the governor cover from the governor body. Remove the link from the control rack.

11. Remove the start spring from the spring eye.

12. Remove the counterweights from the camshaft.

13. Hold the timer and remove the slotted nuts and lockwashers.

14. Using a puller, ST57926-512, remove the flyweight assembly.

15. Remove the timer.

16. Unbolt and remove the governor body.

MZ PNEUMATIC TYPE REMOVAL

1. Follow steps 1 through 6 of RSV Type Removal.

2. Unbolt and remove the diaphragm housing and main spring.

3. Remove the diaphragm ring with a screwdriver.

4. Remove the cotter pin from the connecting rod bolt with a needle-nosed pliers.

5. Remove the diaphragm assembly from the control rack.

6. Remove the five set screws and remove the governor body by applying force with a screwdriver blade in the slit between the governor and pump housings.

7. Remove the timer.

RSV TYPE INSTALLATION

1. Apply RTV silicone gasket material to the governor body and install the governor on the injection pump.

2. Tighten the upper spring eye screw holding the starting spring.

3. Install the timer.

4. Install the flyweight assembly.

5. Apply RTV silicone gasket material to the governor cover and install the starting spring on the housing side of the spring eye.

6. Install the link leaf spring in the hole in the end of the control rack.

7. Install the cover and set screws.

MZ TYPE INSTALLATION

1. Apply RTV silicone gasket material to the governor body, position it on the pump body and tap it into position with a plastic mallet. Install the set screw.

2. Install the diaphragm and balance spring on the control rack connecting bolt

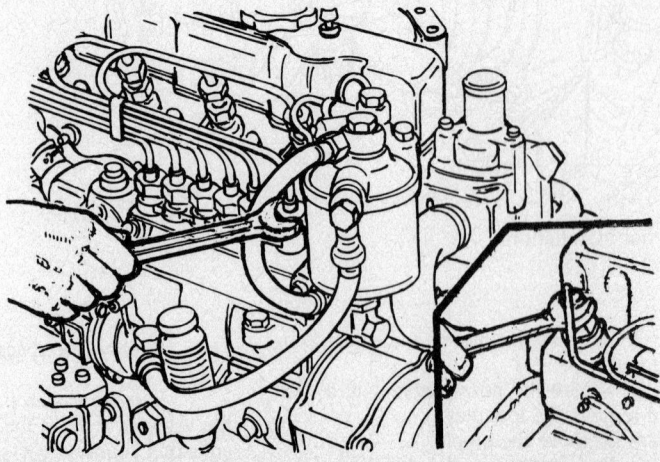

Connecting the injection lines

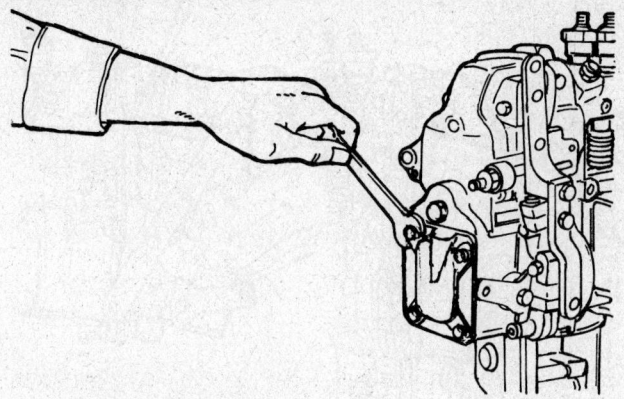

Removing the cam cover

Feed pump removal

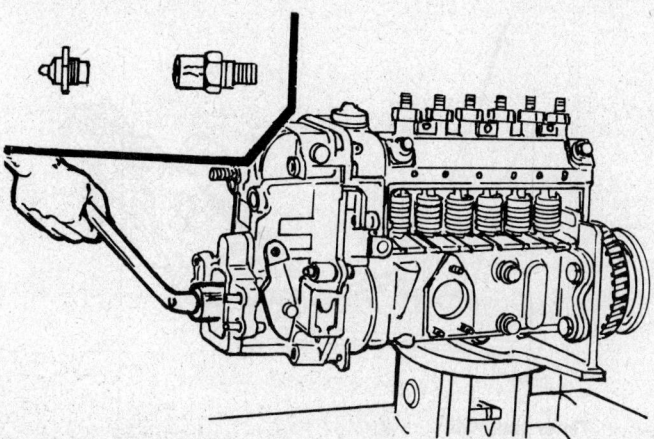

Removing the idle spring from RAD type governors

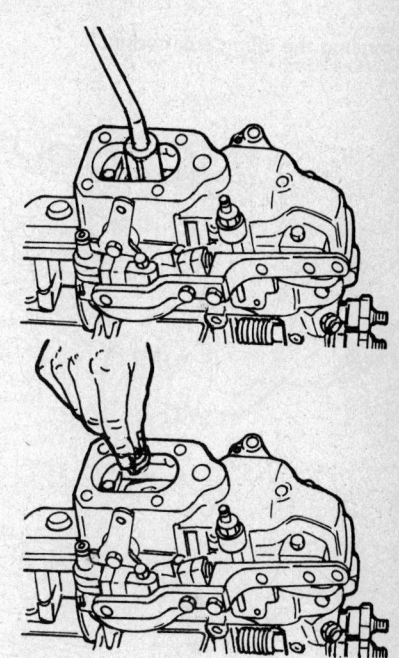

and lock with a new cotter pin. Apply chassis lube to the diaphragm ring.

3. Insert the main spring and install diaphragm housing with the four bolts.

Injection Pump Service

REPLACING THE DELIVERY VALVE

1. Thoroughly clean the area around the nozzle tube and delivery valve.

2. Remove the nozzle tube.

3. Remove the delivery valve holder lock plate.

4. Remove the delivery valve holder and spring.

5. Using ST57930-032, remove the delivery valve.

6. Position the delivery valve in the pump housing making sure no dirt gets between the top of the plunger barrel and the delivery valve.

7. Install a new delivery valve gasket. The gasket is installed with the larger face downward and may be tapped into place through the extractor.

8. Install the delivery valve spring.

9. Install the delivery valve holder and

torque it to 22–25 ft. lbs.

10. Loosen the holder and retorque it.

11. Install the lock plate, nozzle tube and nozzle clamp.

REPLACING THE PLUNGER

1. Remove the delivery valve.

2. Push the plunger spring up with two screwdrivers and remove the lower spring seat from the plunger.

3. Insert a hooked wire through the top of the pump housing, down through the plunger opening and hook it on the lead unit of the plunger. Pull up to remove the plunger and barrel.

4. Immerse a new plunger in clean fuel oil and thoroughly wash off the rust preventive.

NOTE: The plunger was lapped at the factory. Do not hold it by the lapped section.

5. Operate the plunger in clean fuel oil to check its operation.

6. Slowly insert the plunger and barrel into the pump with the barrel groove and plunger notch facing forward. Make certain the plunger piston pin is properly seated in the groove in the control sleeve.

Removing the idling spring from RSV type governors

7. Push the plunger spring up with two screwdrivers and insert the lower spring seat.

8. Install the remaining parts in reverse of disassembly.

CAMSHAFT REMOVAL AND INSTALLATION

1. Remove the key from the camshaft and remove the four setscrews on the drive side of the pump housing. Remove the bearing cover.

2. Lay the pump on its side and remove the screw plugs from the bottom of the housing with tool 57910-112 or a ratchet handle.

3. Remove the set screws from the center bearing.

4. Remove the camshaft from the housing.

5. Install the bearing cover on the timer side of the housing.

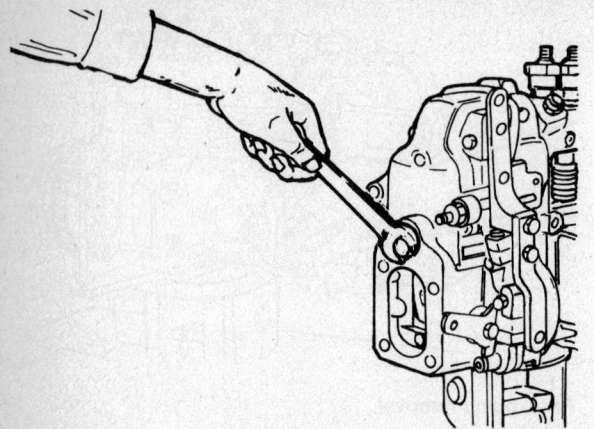

Removing the idling sub spring

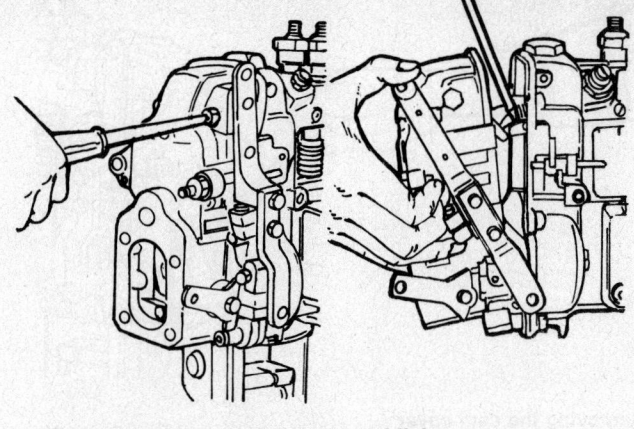

Removing the governor cover and link

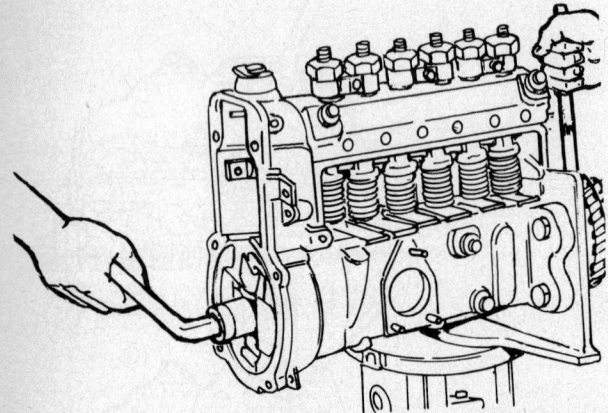

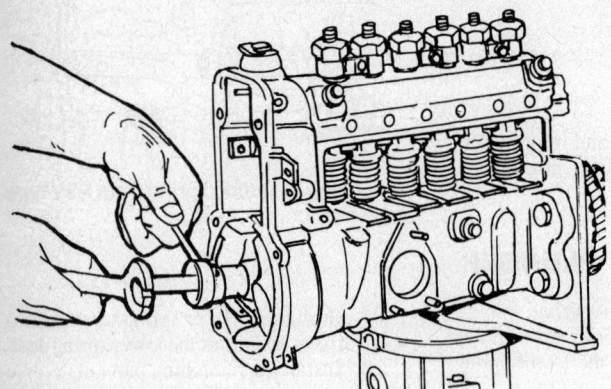

Timer removal

Counterweight removal

Removing the delivery valve holder lock plate

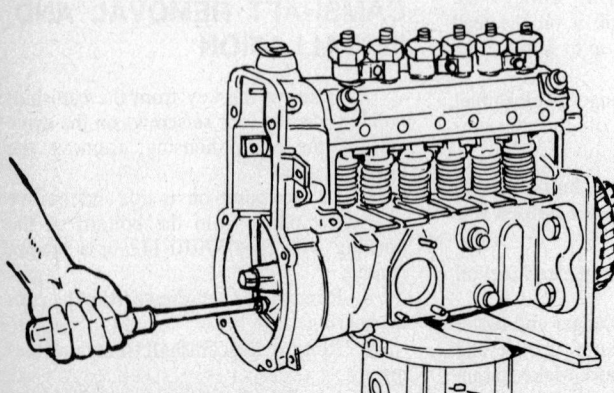

Removing the governor body

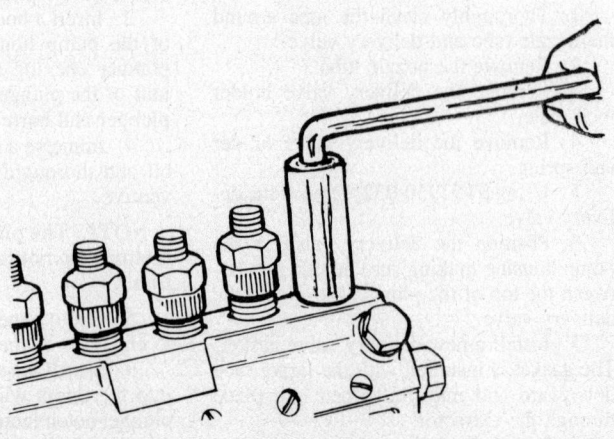

Loosening the delivery valve holder

6. Install the camshaft so that alignment mark "A" is toward the timer.

7. Check end play as illustrated. End play is 0-.0012 in.

TAPPET REMOVAL AND INSTALLATION

1. Remove the camshaft.

2. Install a tappet insert tool 57912-012 and remove the tappet holder, at the same time, removing the tappet from the holder. Be careful to avoid damaging the housing plug hole threads.

3. Lossen the tappet insert tool, withdraw the tappet assembly into the camshaft chamber and remove the tappet from the housing with a tappet clamp.

4. Installation is the reverse of removal. Make sure that the mechanism works smoothly.

PLUNGER REMOVAL AND INSTALLATION

1. Remove the tappets.

2. Remove the plungers using plunger pinchers 57921-412 or equivalent, together with the lower spring seat.

3. Place any reusable plungers in the corresponding plunger barrels and immerse them in kerosene or safe solvent.

4. Remove the plunger springs, upper spring seats and control sleeves.

5. Lay the housing on its side and position the control rack so that the punch marks on both sides are the same distance from each end of the housing.

6. Install the control sleeve with the gap in the sleeve facing straight upward. At the same time install the spring seats.

7. Install the plunger spring in the housing.

8. Install the plunger in the barrel using tool 57921-412, along with the lower spring seat.

9. Make sure the mechanism functions smoothly.

TESTING AND ADJUSTING THE FUEL INJECTION PUMP

NOTE: It is necessary to inspect and adjust the pump, using a pump tester, whenever it has been disassembled and assembled, when the plunger or plunger barrel have been replaced or when any of the component parts have been replaced. Use nozzle tube 57805-002 and test nozzle 5000-101, starting pressure 1422.3 psi. Clean no. 2 fuel should be used. Rotating direction, from drive side, is clockwise. Sequence is 1-4-3-2.

Starting Timing

1. Remove the fuel feed pump and cover plate from the injection pump.

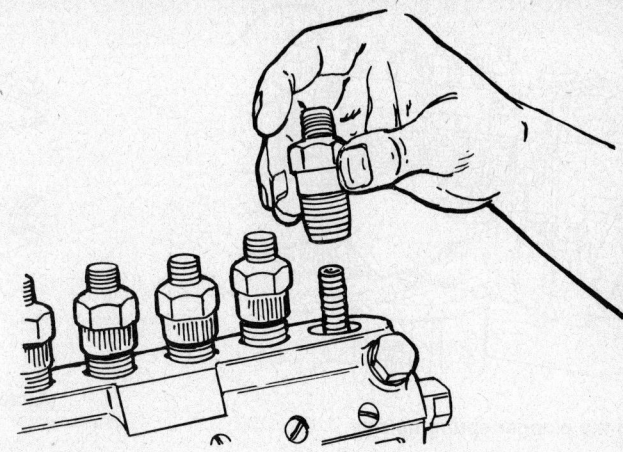

Removing the delivery valve holder and spring

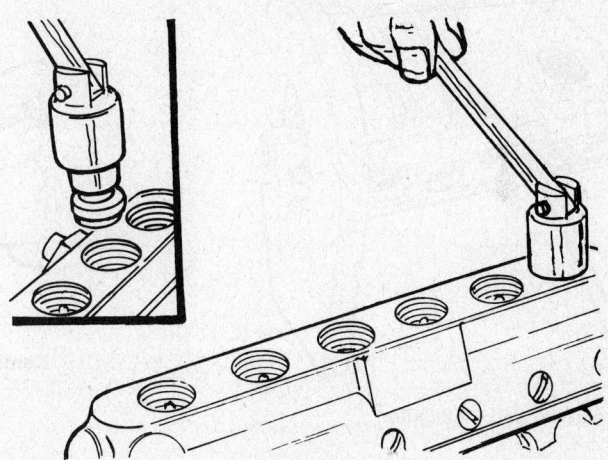

Removing the delivery valve with tool 57930-032

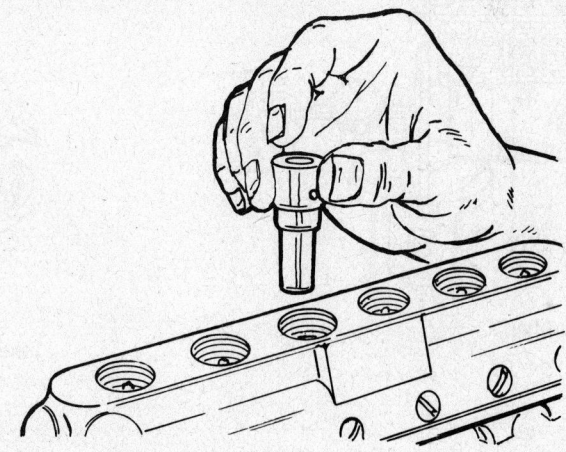

Plunger barrel removal with delivery valves removed

2. Install the injection pump on the tester and holding fixture.

3. Connect the test coupling to the tester drive shaft with the coupling disc.

4. Remove the cap and position the tester dial to measure the camshaft rotating angle.

5. Install a tappet lift gauge on the #1 tappet.

6. Bottom the tappet and set the dial gauge to 0.

7. Bleed the pump at the bleeder screw.

8. Loosen the nozzle holder ball valve.

9. Feed fuel to the pump inlet while slowly turning the pump tester by hand in the normal engine rotation direction. Fuel will flow from the test nozzle. When the

Inserting the plunger spring holder

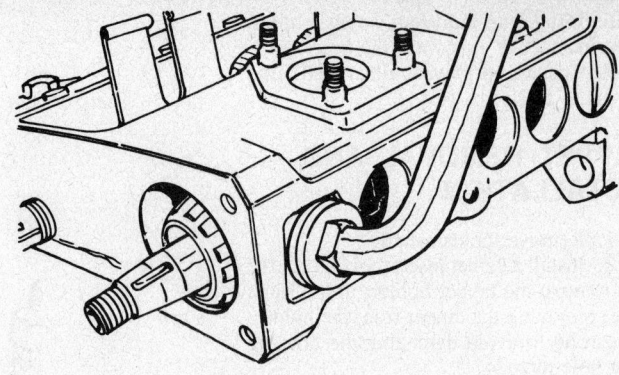

Screw plug removal and installation

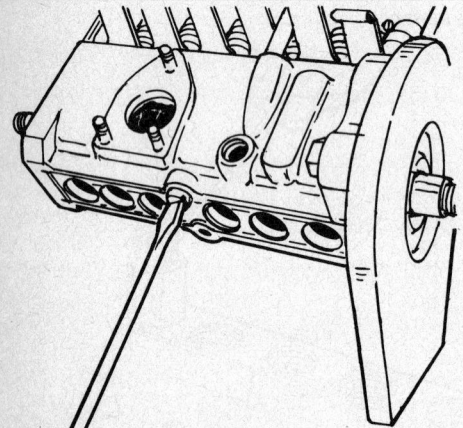

Setscrew removal and installation

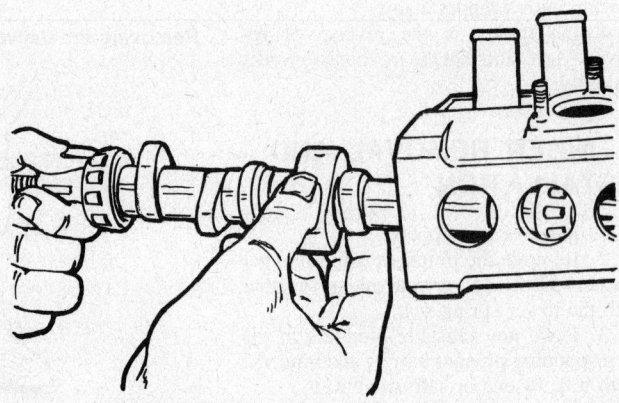

Camshaft removal

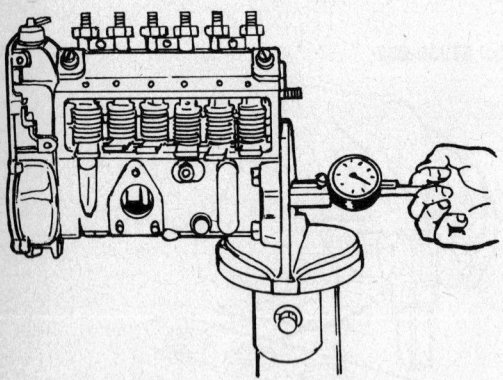

Measuring end-play

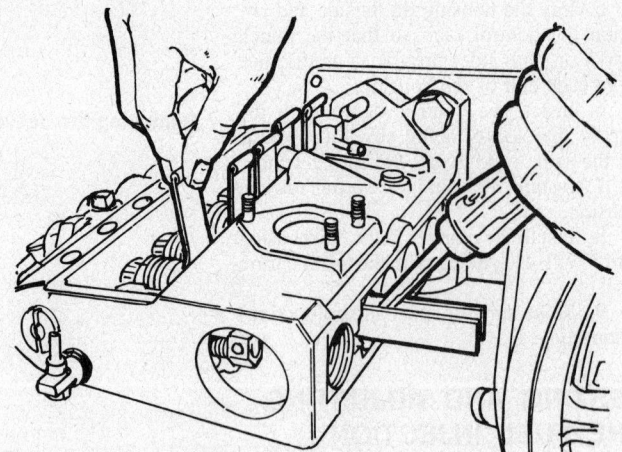

Inserting tappet holder and insert tool

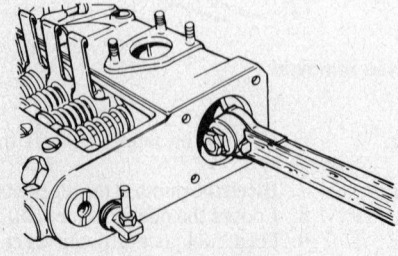

Removing tappet with tappet clamp

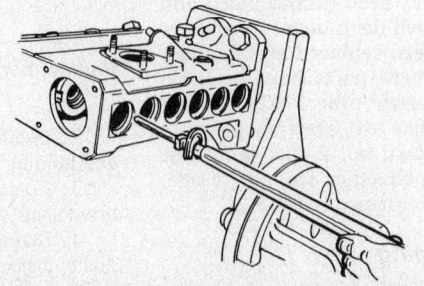

Removing plungers with tool 57921-412

fuel stops flowing the injection point has been reached. The tappet, at this precise point, must be .08858–.09251″ above BDC.

10. If the fuel does not stop flowing after .0926″, turn the adjusting bolt counter-clockwise to raise the position of the plunger.

11. If the fuel stops flowing before .0886″, turn the adjusting bolt clockwise to lower the plunger position.

12. When adjustment is made, torque the locknut to 43–50 ft. lbs.

13. With the pump set at initial injection, set the angle scale mark on the tester flywheel at 0 or 180°.

14. If adjustment is correct, fuel should stop flowing at no. 4 cylinder when the tester has been turned 60° in normal rotation. If fuel does not stop flowing at the correct time, adjust as above.

15. Check and adjust each cylinder in turn.

16. When timing for each cylinder is correct, position the cam at TDC, check the plunger piston pin-to-plunger barrel clearance and make sure that the tappet vertical clearance is at least .0118″ for each tappet.

Standard Fuel Injection Volume Adjustment

1. Determine the zero position of the control by attaching the measuring device to the pump and pushing the index all the way to governor side. Match the scale on the left end of the index and set the 0(zero) position of the scale at the position at which the measuring device index stops. On RSV mechanical governors, loosen the stop bolt to align this index.

2. Remove the rack guide screw from the rear of the pump housing and apply the lock screw attached to the tester. Secure the control rack in the standard position for adjustment.

NOTE: The lock screw should be tightened by hand; overtightening will bend the rack.

3. Start the tester and run the pump at rated speed.

4. Set the pump feed pressure at 21.3–22.75 psi and measure the injection volume at the rated stroke of the female cylinder.

5. In the same manner, measure the injection volume at rated speed and standard rack position. Compute the rate of unevenness of the injection.

6. If the results show that the mean injection volume and rate of unevenness are not within the limits, adjust by changing the relative position of the control pinion and control sleeve. This may be done as follows:

    a. Loosen the pinion set screw.

    b. Place a pin in the hole in the control sleeve and adjust by moving the control sleeve along the control rack a little at a time.

    c. When adjustment is completed, secure the pinion set screw.

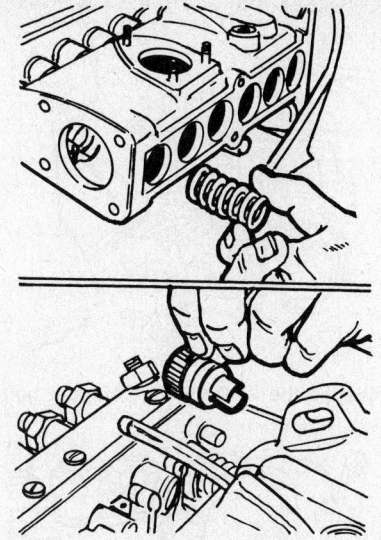

Removing plunger springs, control sleeves and upper spring seats

    d. Remove the lock screw from the control rack and reinstall the guide screw.

Testing and Adjusting the Governor

RSV AND RAD MECHANICAL GOVERNOR

1. Match the adjusting device index to the zero point on the scale and set the control rack to the zero position.

2. Operate the control lever and make certain the full stroke of the rack is .827″.

3. Make certain that the rack moves freely in the direction for maximum fuel injection by the spring force of the starting spring.

4. Set the stop bolt to remove any significant load on the governor linkage.

5. Set the stop bolt to give a control rack setting of .0197–.03937dp.

High Speed Adjustment

6. Remove the governor rear cover.

7. Loosen the full load stop lock nut and adjust the full load stop so that its setting corresponds to an A rack position between "K" rotation and BC. See the accompanying chart for the uneveness formula:

$$\frac{\text{Max. or min. injection volume for each plunger} - \text{Main injection volume}}{\text{Mean injection volume}} \times 100$$

8. To increase the volume, turn the stop to the right; left to decrease.

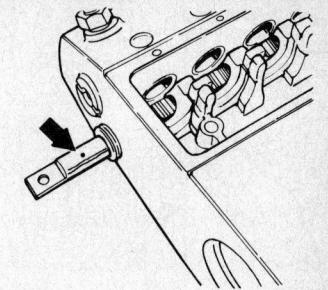

Control rack: punch mark is indicated by arrow

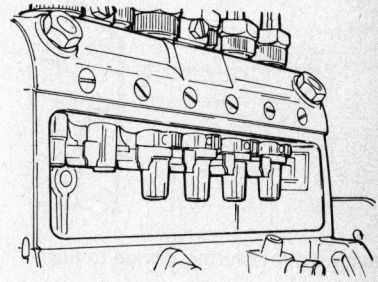

Control sleeves installed

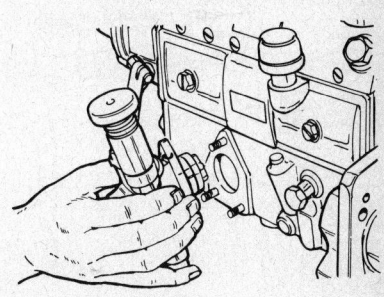

Feed pump removal

Checking injection start timing with a lift gauge

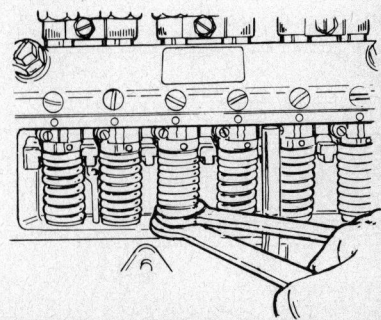

Turning the adjusting bolt

Checking tappet clearance

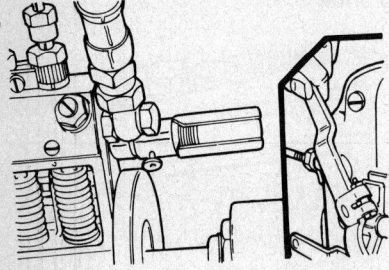

Attaching a measuring device to the pump

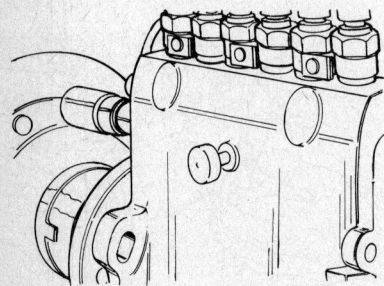

Installing the tester lock screw

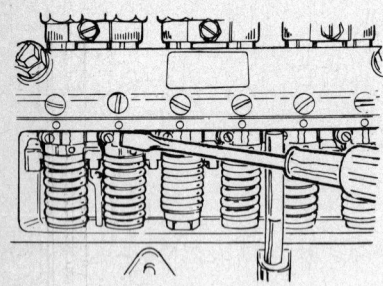

Loosening the pinion setscrew

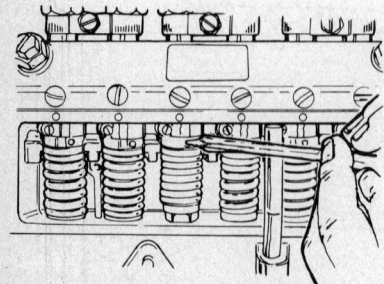

Installing the appropriate sized pin

Adjusting the RAD full load stopper bolt

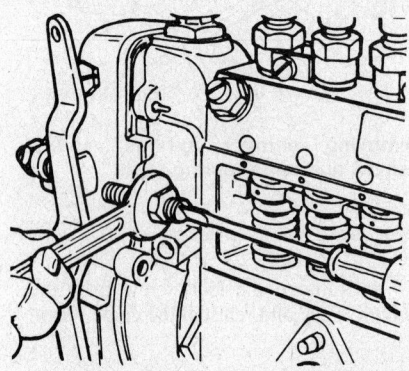

Maximum speed stopper adjustment

Maximum Speed Adjustment

9. Operate the pump at speed G and adjust the maximum speed stop so that the control rack position is G mm.

Speed Fluctuation Adjustment

10. Speed fluctuation can be controlled by varying the spring rate on RSV governors.

Balance Spring Adjustment

11. Set the control lever to the point where it contacts the maximum speed stop and operate the pump at a rate of F, between A and B.

12. Install the balance spring assembly under the tension lever.

13. Tighten the balance spring assembly with tool 57916-212 until the control rack position G is H mm. and secure with the lock nut.

14. Gradually accelerate the engine from speed D and make certain that the control rack is at G mm when the action of the spring ends at speed E.

Idle Speed Adjustment

15. Set the control lever at the stop position so that the control rack is at point B.

16. Set the speed to D and tighten the idle auxiliary spring so that the position of the rack is C mm. Secure with the lock nut.

NOTE: Do not tighten the auxiliary idle spring too much or overspeeding will result.

Testing and Adjusting the Timer

1. Install a timing light, such as tool 5783-001 on the tester using the cover plate attaching bolts, so that the synchronizer lever attachment is applied to the tappet.

2. Start the pump and turn on the timing light.

3. Direct the light at the angle scale on the flywheel and measure the angular change based on variations in pump speed.

4. If the tester does not have an angle scale:

   a. Attach an angle scale to the timer coupling and mount a pointer on the tester drive shaft.

   b. Operate the pump and direct the light on the scale.

5. If the angular change is not within limits, disassemble the timer and adjust the spring force by increasing or decreasing the shims, or if necessary, replace the spring.

FUEL TANK

The fuel tank is located under the floor of the bed on the right side, directly behind the cab.

REMOVAL AND INSTALLATION

1. Disconnect the negative cable from the battery.

2. Remove the drain plug at the bottom of the tank and drain the fuel into a suitable container.

3. Disconnect the filler tube from the filler hose.

4. Disconnect the ventilation hoses, the fuel return hose and fuel outlet hose from the tank. Disconnect the gauge unit wires at the electrical connector.

5. Remove the mounting bolts and remove the fuel tank.

6. Installation is the reverse. Install the clamps securely, but do not crimp any of the lines. Install the clips holding the fuel tube to the underbody securely. Do not attach the filler hose to the tube until the tank is in place. Failure to do this will cause leaks around the connection.

GAUGE UNIT

The fuel tank must be removed for access to the gauge unit. The unit is installed into the tank with a bayonet-type of mount. Turn it counterclockwise with a screwdriver to remove. Use a new O-ring when installing, aligning the tab in the unit with the notch in the tank.

MANUAL TRANSMISSION

The Datsun pick-up uses an F4W71B four speed or an optional FS5W71B five speed transmission. The two models have a one piece case, an adapter plate which supports the mainshaft and countershaft, and an extension housing. All units have internal shift rails; no linkage adjustments are necessary.

REMOVAL AND INSTALLATION

1. Disconnect the battery ground cable from the battery.

2. Remove the shift lever from inside the cab. It is retained to the shift rail by a C-clip, accessible under the boot. Remove the C-clip and retaining pin, and remove the lever.

3. Jack up the vehicle and support it with jackstands.

4. Disconnect the exhaust pipe from the exhaust manifold. On trucks with a catalytic converter, also remove the exhaust pipe bracket next to the speedometer cable by unscrewing the two mounting bolts.

5. Remove the clutch slave cylinder from the transmission case.

6. Disconnect the speedometer cable from the transmission extension housing, and the back-up light and transmission switch wires at the switch(es).

7. Remove the bracket holding the center bearing of the driveshaft on the third crossmember of the frame.

8. Remove the driveshaft(s).

NOTE: On 4-wheel drive models, this requires removal of the transfer case, which should be performed at this time.

9. Support the engine with a jack located under the oil pan. Place a block of wood between the jack and the oil pan to prevent damage to the oil pan. Support the transmission with a jack.

10. Remove the rear engine mount securing bolts and the crossmember mounting bolts. Only the rear engine/transmission extension housing mount is removable from the crossmember.

11. Remove the starter motor.

12. Remove the bolts securing the transmission to the engine, pull the transmission toward the rear until the transmission mainshaft is free of the back of the engine. Separate the transmission from the engine, then lower the transmission out from under the truck.

14. Install the transmission in the reverse order of removal. Before installing, clean the mating surfaces of the engine and transmission thoroughly. Lightly coat the input shaft splines with grease. Tighten the engine-to-transmission bolts to 29–36 ft. lbs. 1975–76; or 32–43 ft. lbs., 1977 and

later. Tighten the crossmember to chassis bolts to 20–27 ft. lbs. and the clutch slave cylinder mounting bolts to 18–22 ft. lbs. Be sure to align the marks made earlier on the U-joint and differential flange when installing the driveshaft, to maintain driveline balance.

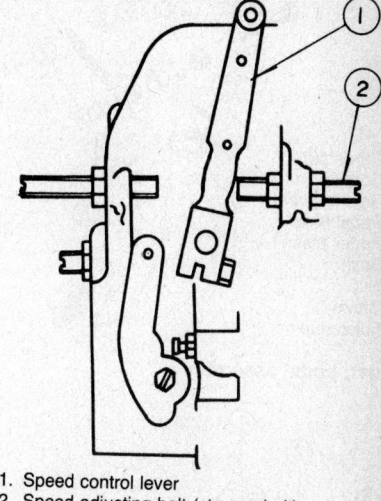

1. Speed control lever
2. Speed adjusting bolt (stopper bolt)

Adjusting the RSV speed adjustment bolt

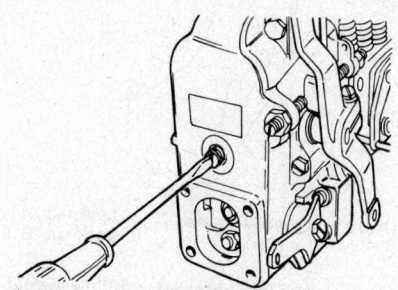

Auxiliary idle spring adjustment

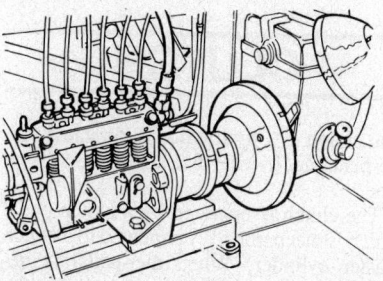

Pump installed on a tester with synchronizer and strobe light

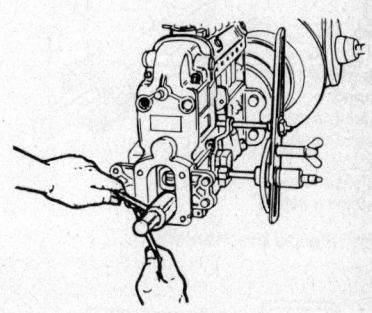

Adjusting the idling spring

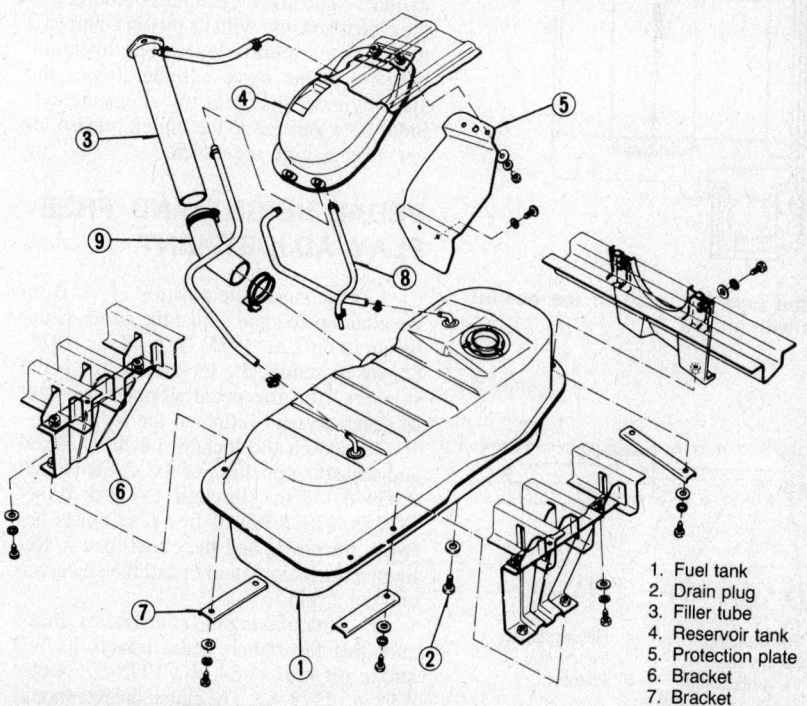

1. Fuel tank
2. Drain plug
3. Filler tube
4. Reservoir tank
5. Protection plate
6. Bracket
7. Bracket
8. Ventilation hose
9. Filler hose

Fuel tank and lines

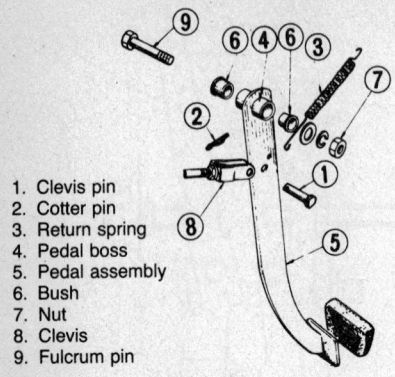

1. Clevis pin
2. Cotter pin
3. Return spring
4. Pedal boss
5. Pedal assembly
6. Bush
7. Nut
8. Clevis
9. Fulcrum pin

Clutch pedal assembly

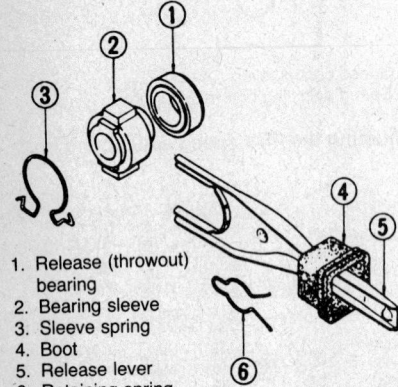

1. Release (throwout) bearing
2. Bearing sleeve
3. Sleeve spring
4. Boot
5. Release lever
6. Retaining spring

Clutch release mechanism

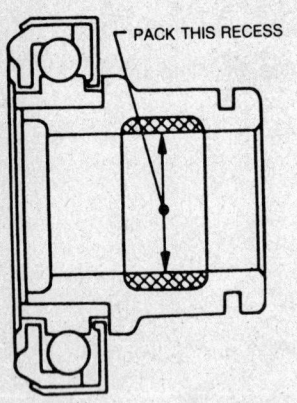

PACK THIS RECESS

Coat the area indicated in the bearing sleeve with grease

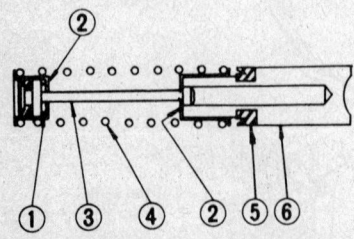

1. Valve spring
2. Spring seat
3. Valve assembly
4. Return spring
5. Piston cup
6. Piston

Cutaway view of the clutch master cylinder piston

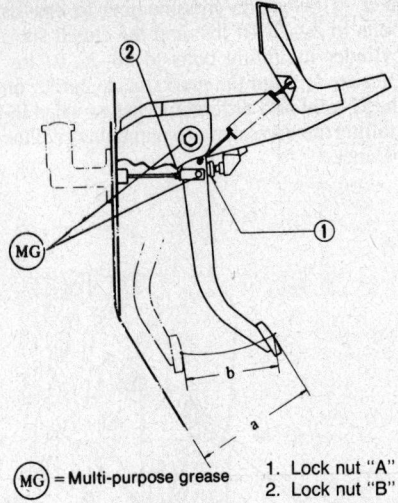

(MG) = Multi-purpose grease

1. Lock nut "A"
2. Lock nut "B"

Clutch pedal adjustment: "a" is pedal height, "b" is pedal stroke

CLUTCH

The clutch is a hydraulically-operated single-plate, dry friction disc, diaphragm spring type.

The clutch is operated by a clutch pedal which is mechanically connected to a clutch master cylinder. When the pedal is depressed, the piston in the master cylinder is moved in the master cylinder bore. This movement compresses the fluid in the master cylinder causing hydraulic pressure which is transferred through a tube to the slave cylinder. The slave cylinder is mounted to the clutch housing with its piston connected to the clutch release lever. The hydraulic pressure in the slave cylinder forces the slave cylinder piston to travel out the cylinder bore and move the clutch release lever, disengaging the clutch.

PEDAL HEIGHT AND FREE-PLAY ADJUSTMENT

1. Disconnect the pushrod clevis from the clutch pedal and adjust the clutch pedal height to 6.02 in. 1975-77; 6.42 in., 1978-82, by loosening the locknut on the pedal stopper. Turn the pedal stopper in or out as necessary and retighten the locknut.

2. Loosen the locknut on the pushrod and adjust the position of the clevis so that 0.039–0.118 in. (through 1977) or 0.04–0.20 in. (1978-82) of free-play exists between the clevis and the clutch pedal. Retighten the locknut and install the clevis pin and cotter pin.

3. After making the adjustments, make sure that the clutch pedal travels its full stroke of: 4.61–4.84 in., 1975–77; 4.69–4.92 in., 1978–82. The clutch linkage should operate smoothly and completely disengage and engage the clutch.

REMOVAL AND INSTALLATION

1. Raise the vehicle on a hoist.
2. Remove the transmission.
3. Mark the clutch assembly-to-flywheel relationship with paint or a center punch so that the clutch assembly can be reassembled in the same position from which it is removed. Insert a clutch aligning tool (dummy shaft) into the hub. This tool is available from your dealer or an auto parts store. It is important to support the weight of the clutch while the retaining bolts are being removed.
4. Loosen the six clutch cover-to-flywheel attaching bolts, one turn at a time in an alternating sequence, until the spring tension is relieved to avoid distorting or bending the clutch cover. Remove the clutch assembly.
5. Inspect the flywheel for scoring, roughness, or signs of overheating. Light scoring may be cleaned up with emery cloth, but any deep grooves or scoring warrant replacement or refacing (if possible) of the flywheel. If the clutch facings or flywheel are oily, inspect the transmission front cover oil seal, the pilot bushing, and engine rear seals, etc. for leakage, and correct before replacing the clutch. If the pilot bushing in the crankshaft is worn, replace it. Install it using a soft hammer. The factory-supplied part does not have to be oiled, but check the procedure if you are using an after-market part. Inspect the clutch cover for wear or scoring, and replace as necessary. The pressure plate and spring cannot be disassembled; you must replace the clutch cover as an assembly.
6. Inspect the clutch release bearing. If it is rough or noisy, it should be replaced. The bearing can be removed from the sleeve with a puller; this requires a press to install the new bearing. After installation, coat the groove in the sleeve, the contact surfaces of the release lever, pivot pin and sleeve, and the release bearing contact surfaces on the transmission front cover with a light coat of grease. Be careful not to use too much grease, which will run at high temperatures and get onto the clutch facings. Reinstall the release bearing on the lever.
7. Apply a thin coat of grease to the pressure plate wire ring, diaphragm spring, clutch cover grooves and the drive bosses on the pressure plate.
8. Apply a thin coat of Lubriplate to the splines in the driven plate. Slide the clutch disc onto the splines, and move it back and forth several times. Remove the disc and wipe off the excess lubricant. Be very careful not to get any grease on the clutch facings.
9. Assemble the clutch cover and the clutch plate on the clutch alignment arbor.
10. Align the marks made on the clutch cover and the flywheel (if the old cover is being used) and install the six clutch cover-to-flywheel attaching bolts. Three dowels are used to locate the clutch cover on the

flywheel properly. Tighten the bolts in an alternating sequence one turn at a time to 12-15 ft. lbs. Remove the aligning arbor.

11. Install the transmission.

Clutch Master Cylinder

REMOVAL AND INSTALLATION

1. Disconnect the clutch pedal arm from the pushrod clevis. Remove the dust cover (boot) from the master cylinder body and pushrod. It will not go through the firewall without tearing.

2. Disconnect the clutch hydraulic line from the master cylinder.

NOTE: Take precautions to keep brake fluid from coming in contact with any painted surfaces.

3. Remove the nuts attaching the master cylinder and remove the master cylinder and pushrod toward the engine compartment side.

4. Install the master cylinder in the reverse order of removal and bleed the clutch hydraulic system.

OVERHAUL

NOTE: Datsun obtains its clutch master cylinder parts from two suppliers: Nabco and Tokico. There is no interchangeability between the parts. Be absolutely certain that you get the correct parts for the master cylinder installed on your truck. The manufacturer's name is clearly written on the cylinder.

1. Remove the master cylinder.

2. Drain the clutch fluid from the master cylinder reservoir.

3. Remove the circlip and remove the pushrod.

4. Remove the stopper, piston, cup, and return spring.

5. Clean all of the parts in clean brake fluid.

6. Check the master cylinder and piston for wear, corrosion and scores, and replace the parts as necessary. Light scoring and glaze can be removed with crocus cloth soaked in brake fluid. Move the crocus cloth in a circular motion; not in and out.

7. Generally, the cup seal should be replaced each time the master cylinder is disassembled. Check the cup and replace it if it is worn, fatigued, or damaged.

8. Check the clutch fluid reservoir, filler cap, dust cover, and the pipe for distortion and damage and replace the parts as necessary.

9. Lubricate all new parts with clean brake fluid.

10. Reassemble the master cylinder parts in the reverse order of disassembly, taking note of the following:

    a. Reinstall the cup seal carefully to prevent damaging the lipped portions;

    b. Adjust the height of the clutch pedal after installing the master cylinder in position on the vehicle;

    c. Fill the master cylinder and clutch fluid reservoir and then bleed the clutch hydraulic system.

Clutch Slave Cylinder

REMOVAL AND INSTALLATION

1. Remove the slave cylinder attaching bolts and the pushrod from the shift fork.

2. Disconnect the flexible fluid hose from the slave cylinder and remove the unit from the vehicle.

3. Install the slave cylinder in the reverse order of removal and bleed the clutch hydraulic system. Tighten the attaching bolts to 18–25 ft. lbs.

OVERHAUL

NOTE: Datsun obtains its slave cylinders from two manufacturers: Nabco and Tokico. Parts are not interchangeable. Be sure you get the correct rebuilding parts for the model on your truck.

1. Remove the slave cylinder from the vehicle.

2. Remove the pushrod and boot.

3. Force out the piston by blowing compressed air into the slave cylinder at the hose connection.

NOTE: Be careful not to apply excess air pressure to avoid possible injury.

4. Clean all of the parts in clean brake fluid.

5. Check and replace the slave cylinder bore and piston if wear or severe scoring exists. Light scoring and glaze can be removed with crocus cloth soaked in brake fluid. Move the crocus cloth in a circular motion; not in and out.

6. Normally the piston cup should be replaced when the slave cylinder is disassembled. Check the piston cup and replace it if it is found to be worn, fatigued or scored.

7. Replace the rubber boot if it is cracked or broken.

8. Lubricate all of the new parts in clean brake fluid and reassemble in the reverse order of disassembly, taking note of the following:

    a. Use care when reassembling the piston cup to prevent damaging the lipped portion of the piston cup;

    b. Fill the master cylinder with brake fluid and bleed the clutch hydraulic system:

Bleeding the Clutch Hydraulic System

1. Check and fill the clutch fluid res-

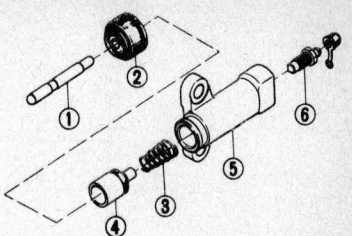

1. Push rod
2. Dust cover
3. Piston spring
4. Piston
5. Operating cylinder
6. Bleeder screw

Clutch slave cylinder

ervoir to the full mark if necessary. During the bleeding process, continue to check and replenish the reservoir to prevent the fluid level from getting lower than ½ full.

2. Connect a clear vinyl hose to the bleeder screw on the slave cylinder. Immerse the other end of the hose in a clear jar half filled with brake fluid.

NOTE: Don't drip brake fluid on any painted surfaces.

3. Have an assistant pump the clutch pedal several times and hold it down. Loosen the bleeder screw slowly.

4. Tighten the bleeder screw and release the clutch pedal gradually. Repeat this operation until air bubbles disappear from the brake fluid being expelled out through the bleeder screw.

5. When the air is completely removed, securely tighten the bleeder screw and replace the dust cap.

6. Check and refill the master cylinder reservoir as necessary.

7. Depress the clutch pedal several times to check the operation of the clutch and check for leaks.

AUTOMATIC TRANSMISSION

The optional automatic transmission is a JATCO (Japan Automatic Transmission Co., Ltd.) model 3N71B. It is a fully automatic unit, with a three element torque converter and two planetary gear sets. The transmission shifts gears in response to signals of both engine speed and manifold vacuum.

PAN REMOVAL

Loosen the automatic transmission pan attaching bolts more at one corner than the other three corners. Allow the fluid to drain out the one corner. Remove all of the pan attaching bolts and remove the pan. Install the pan in the reverse order of removal. Always use a new gasket.

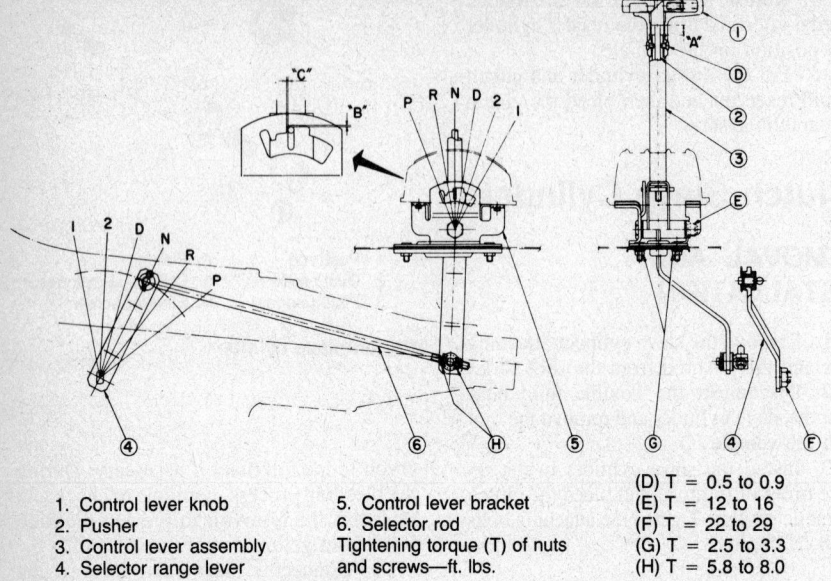

1. Control lever knob
2. Pusher
3. Control lever assembly
4. Selector range lever
5. Control lever bracket
6. Selector rod
Tightening torque (T) of nuts and screws—ft. lbs.

(D) T = 0.5 to 0.9
(E) T = 12 to 16
(F) T = 22 to 29
(G) T = 2.5 to 3.3
(H) T = 5.8 to 8.0

Automatic transmission shift linkage

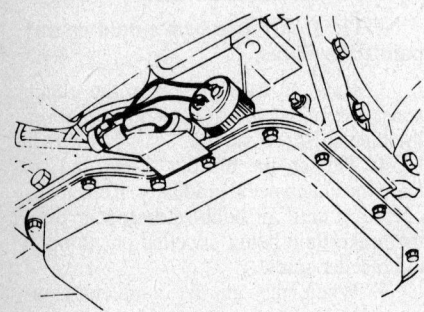

Downshift solenoid

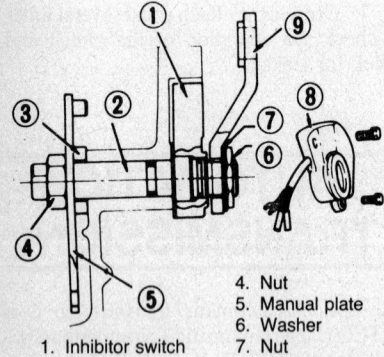

1. Inhibitor switch
2. Manual shaft
3. Washer
4. Nut
5. Manual plate
6. Washer
7. Nut
8. Inhibitor switch
9. Selector lever

Neutral safety switch

Adjustments

SHIFT LINKAGE ADJUSTMENT

Adjustment of the shift linkage is a critical operation. If the adjustment is made sloppily, the result will be partial application of the band or clutches, and will eventually burn up the transmission.

1. If the control knob is removed, prior to installation set dimension "A" in the illustration to 0.43–0.47 in.

2. Install the control knob, adjusting dimension "B" to 0.004–0.043 in. by turning the pushing rod (2).

3. Loosen the adjusting nuts ("H"). Set both the shift lever (3) and the transmission selector lever (4) into the neutral positions. Set clearance "C" to 0.04 in. (1 mm) by turning the adjusting nuts which connect to the selector rod (6).

After making the adjustments, check for proper engagement in each gear, and that the mechanism operates without binding. Readjust as necessary.

KICK-DOWN SWITCH AND DOWNSHIFT SOLENOID

With the ignition switch in the ON position and the engine off, when the accelerator pedal is depressed fully, the kick-down switch contacts should be closed and the downshift solenoid activated, emitting a clicking sound. If the components fail to operate in this manner, check for continuity first at the switch and then at the solenoid if the switch checks out as being satisfactory. Replace either of the components as necessary.

NEUTRAL SAFETY SWITCH

The neutral safety switch is located on the transmission range selector lever. The switch operates the back-up lights and controls the operation of the starter. The starter should only operate when the transmission is in Park or Neutral.

To adjust the neutral safety switch, unscrew the securing nut of the range selector lever and the two bolts securing the switch body. Remove the machine screw under the switch body. Adjust the shift selector to the Neutral position (in vertical position and detent clicks).

Move the switch slightly aside so that the screw hole will be aligned with the pin hole of the internal rotor combined with the manual shaft and check their alignment by inserting a 0.0591 in. (1.5 mm) diameter pin into the holes. A #53 drill bit will work for this. Fasten the switch body with the bolts, pull out the pin, and tighten the screw into the hole. Connect the selector lever.

If the neutral safety switch does not perform satisfactorily after adjustment, replace it with a new one.

Transmission Removal and Installation

1. Disconnect the negative battery cable.

2. Disconnect the shaft from the accelerator linkage.

3. Raise and support the truck.

4. Matchmark the U-joint and differential flange and disconnect them. Remove the center bearing mounting bolts and remove the driveshaft. Plug the transmission extension housing.

5. Disconnect the exhaust pipe from the manifold and discard the gasket. Use a new gasket upon assembly. On trucks with a catalytic converter, disconnect the exhaust pipe bracket.

6. Disconnect the shift linkage at the transmission.

7. Disconnect the neutral switch wires. Disconnect the vacuum hose from the diaphragm, and the wire from the downshift solenoid. Disconnect the speedometer cable from the extension housing.

8. Remove the fluid filler tube.

9. Disconnect the fluid cooler lines at the transmission. Use a flare nut wrench if one is available.

10. Support the engine with a jack under the oil pan, placing a wooden block between the pan and the jack as a buffer. Also support the transmission with a jack.

11. Remove the torque converter cover. Matchmark the converter and the drive plate for reassembly; they were balanced as a unit at the factory. Remove the bolts attaching the converter to the drive plate (flywheel). You will have to rotate the engine to do this, using a wrench on the crankshaft pulley bolt.

12. Remove the bolts for the rear engine mount and the crossmember. Remove the crossmember.

13. Remove the starter.

14. Remove the transmission-to-engine bolts. Lower the transmission back and down, out from under the truck.

15. Before installing the transmission, check the drive plate runout with a dial indicator. Turn the crankshaft one full turn.

Maximum allowable runout is 0.012 in. (0.3 mm). Replace the drive plate if runout exceeds 0.020 in. (0.5 mm); otherwise, reface it.

16. When installing the torque converter, be sure to line up the notch in the converter with the projection on the oil pump. Align the marks made during removal and bolt the converter to the drive plate, tightening the bolts to 29–36 ft. lbs. Then rotate the engine a few turns to make sure the transmission rotates freely without binding. The engine-to-transmission bolt torque is 29–36 ft. lbs. Adjust the shift linkage and neutral switch after installation.

TRANSFER CASE

Removal and Installation

1. Disconnect the battery ground.
2. Raise the vehicle and support it on stands.
3. Remove the transfer case shield.
4. Remove the primary driveshaft securing nuts.
5. Remove the front and rear driveshafts.
6. Disconnect the 4-wd switch wire.
7. Disconnect the speedometer cable.
8. Remove the exhaust pipe.
9. Support the transfer case with a jack.
10. Temporarily loosen the transfer case insulator bolts.
11. Remove the shift lever rubber boot from the floor.
12. Unbolt and remove the transfer case and primary driveshaft from the vehicle.
13. Installation is the reverse of removal. Torque all mounting bolts to 20–26 ft. lbs.

DRIVELINE

2-Wheel Drive

REMOVAL AND INSTALLATION

Driveshaft and U-Joints

1. Raise the truck on a hoist. Mark the relationship of the driveshaft to the companion flange at the differential housing so that the driveshaft can be reinstalled in the same position.
2. Remove the bolts retaining the center bearing bracket.
3. Remove the bolts connecting the driveshaft to the companion flange at the differential housing (and at the front flange on early models).
4. Move the driveshaft assembly toward the rear of the truck, passing it under the rear axle, removing the sleeve yoke from the transmission. Watch for oil leaking out the end of the transmission. Plug if necessary.
5. Install the driveshaft in the reverse order of removal. Be careful not to bang the sleeve yoke into the seal inside the transmission extension housing, which will damage the seal, causing leakage. Align the driveshaft with the differential housing companion flange in their original position. Tighten the U-joint nuts to 17–24 ft. lbs., and the nuts retaining the center bearing bracket to 12–16 ft. lbs.

4-Wheel Drive 1981–82

REMOVAL AND INSTALLATION

Primary Driveshaft

1. Match-mark the flanges and separate the primary driveshaft from the transfer case.
2. Remove the transfer case.
3. Pull the primary shaft from the transmission and plug the opening.
4. Installation is the reverse of removal. Align your match-marks.

Front Driveshaft

1. Match-mark the flanges and unbolt the front shaft from the front differential.
2. Pull the shaft from the transfer case and plug the opening.
3. Installation is the reverse of removal. Align your match-marks.

Rear Driveshaft

1. Match-mark the flanges and unbolt the shaft from the rear differential.
2. Remove the center bearing bracket.
3. Pull the shaft from the transmission and plug the opening.
4. Installation is the reverse of removal. Align your match-marks.

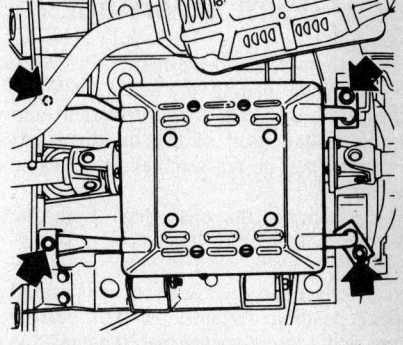

Transfer case shield bolts

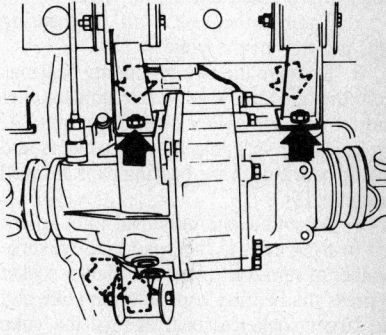

Transfer case mounting bolts

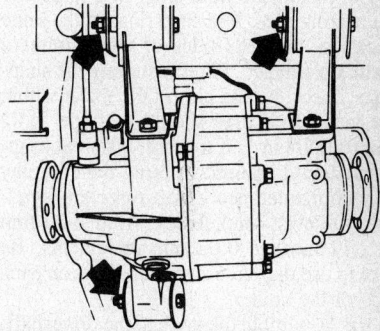

Transfer case insulator bolts

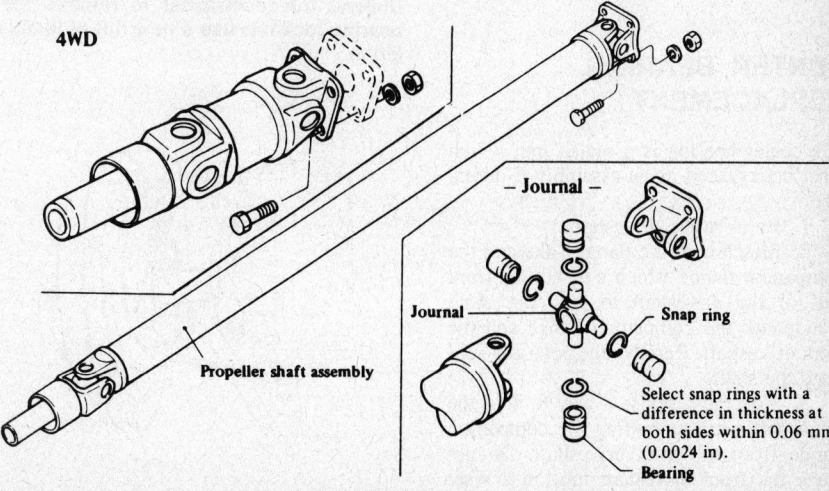

Front axle propellor shaft: the left insert shows the primary driveshaft which connects the transfer case with the transmission

U-Joint Overhaul

1. Remove the driveshaft.

2. Punch mating marks on both the yokes at either end of the driveshaft and the driveshaft itself so that the driveshaft assembly can be reassembled in the same position.

3. Remove the snap-rings from the bearing hole of the yokes with a screwdriver.

4. Place the yoke in a vise with a small socket positioned against one of the bearing cups and a larger socket placed against the yoke on the opposite side. The larger socket must be able to receive the bearing cap when it is pressed out of the yoke.

5. Tighten the vise until the bearing caps are free of the yoke.

6. Remove the two remaining bearings from the opposite yoke in the same manner and remove the spider bearing journal.

7. Make sure that the new spiders and needle bearings in the bearing caps are well lubricated.

8. Assemble the universal joint spider and bearing caps to the yoke in the reverse manner of removal, using the smaller socket to press the bearing caps into the yoke and the larger socket to bear against the yoke bearing cap hole at the opposite end. Use a vise to press the bearing caps in place.

9. Install the hole snap-ring to secure the bearing caps. Use snap-rings of the same thickness on both sides of the U-joint to maintain balance. After installing the snap-rings, check the end play of the spider within the yoke. End play should be under 0.02 mm (0.0008 in.). If it is not, different snap-rings should be used to bring the end play to within tolerance. Snap-rings are available in seven thicknesses, from 2.00 mm to 2.12 mm, in 0.02 mm increments. Be sure to use the same size snap-rings on each side of the spider.

10. Assemble the yoke to the driveshaft, aligning the marks made prior to disassembly.

11. Install the driveshaft.

CENTER BEARING REPLACEMENT

The center bearing is a sealed unit which must be replaced as an assembly if defective.

1. Remove the driveshaft.

2. Matchmark the flange yoke and the companion flange which connect the front half of the driveshaft to the rear. Also matchmark the companion flange and the front driveshaft. Remove the bolts and separate the shafts.

3. You must devise a way to hold the driveshaft while unbolting the companion flange from the front driveshaft. Do not place the front driveshaft tube in a vise, because the chances are it will get crushed. The best way is to grip the flange somehow while loosening the nut. It is going to re-

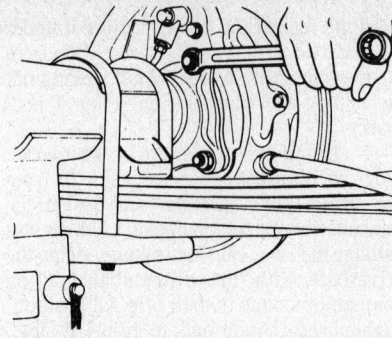

Disconnecting the brake backing plate from the axle housing

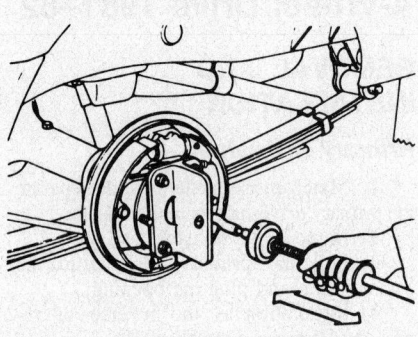

Removing the axle shaft with a slide hammer

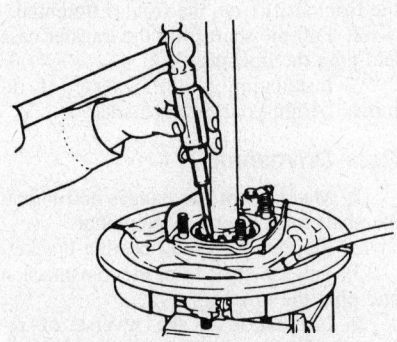

Unbend the lockwasher to remove the bearing locknut; use a new nut at installation

Axle shaft end play is adjusted by the addition or subtraction of shims behind the brake backing plate

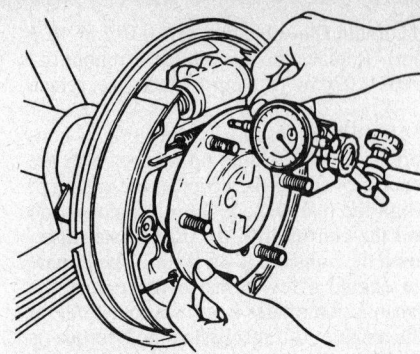

Measure the axial end-play with a dial indicator

quire some strength to remove.

4. Slide the companion flange off the front driveshaft and remove the center bearing from its mount.

5. The new bearing is already lubricated. Install it into the mount, making sure that the seals and so on are facing the same way as when removed.

6. Slide the companion flange onto the front driveshaft, aligning the marks made during removal. Install the washer and locknut. Tighten the nut to 145–175 ft. lbs. Check that the bearing rotates freely around the driveshaft.

7. Connect the companion flange to the flange yoke, aligning the marks made during disassembly. Torque to 18–23 ft. lbs.

8. Install the driveshaft, aligning the marks made at the axle flange during removal.

REAR AXLE

Axle Shaft, Bearing and Seal

REMOVAL AND INSTALLATION

1. Raise the rear of the vehicle and support it. Remove the rear wheel and tire.

2. Disconnect the rear parking brake cable by removing the adjusting nut and clamps.

3. Disconnect the brake tube at the rear brake backing plate. Plug the end of the brake tube to prevent loss of brake fluid.

4. Remove the brake drum.

5. Remove the nuts securing the wheel bearing retainer to the brake backing plate.

6. Pull out the axle shaft assembly together with the brake backing plate using a slide hammer.

7. Remove the oil seal in the axle housing if necessary. It can be pried out with a screwdriver. Oil the lips of the new seal and install it carefully to avoid damage to the lip.

8. To replace the bearing, unbend and discard the lockwasher. Remove the locknut with a soft drift and a hammer.

9. Press the old bearing and cage off the shaft.

10. Remove the oil seal in the cage. Use a brass drift to remove the bearing cup after the seal has been removed.

11. Install the new cup with a brass drift. Install a new oil seal over the bearing cup. Lubricate the area between the seal lips with grease after installation.

12. Place the bearing cage and spacer on the axle shaft, then fit the bearing, tapping it into place with a soft drift and light hammer blows.

13. Place the flat bearing lockwasher over the bearing, then the new nut lockwasher. Install the locknut, tightening to 108 ft. lbs. Continue to tighten after that until the grooves line up with the lockwasher tabs. The nut can be tightened up to 145 ft. lbs. Bend the lockwasher tabs into place.

14. Lubricate the bearing and the recess in the axle housing with wheel bearing grease. Coat the axle splines with gear oil. Coat the seal surface of the shaft with grease.

15. Install the axle shaft in the reverse order of removal. The axle end-play should be 0.012–0.035 in. The end-play is adjusted by adding or removing shims behind the brake backing plate. Tighten the backing plate attaching nuts to 39–46 ft. lbs.

FRONT AXLE

Free Running Hub

REMOVAL AND INSTALLATION

1. Raise and support the front axle on stands.

2. Set the hub in the lock position.

3. Remove the driven clutch by turning it clockwise.

NOTE: A pin is located inside the hub case to lock the driven clutch. Pull and turn the clutch while attracting the pin with a magnet.

4. Remove the lock pin.

5. Set the hub at the free position.

6. Screw the driven clutch into place by turning it counterclockwise until it bottoms.

7. Turn it clockwise until it aligns with the bolt hole.

8. Install the lock pin.

Axle Shaft

REMOVAL AND INSTALLATION

1. Remove the free running hub.

2. Remove the snap-ring and remove the driven clutch.

3. Remove the rebound bumper.

4. Disconnect the stabilizer bar at the lower link.

5. Remove the bolts attaching the axle shaft to the carrier. DO NOT REMOVE THE RUBBER BOOTS!

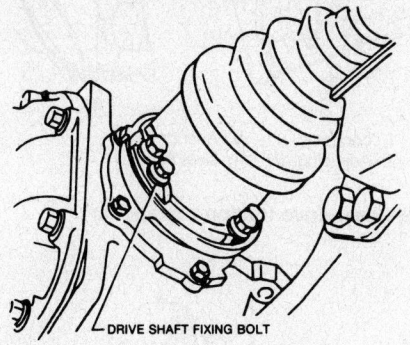

DRIVE SHAFT FIXING BOLT

Axle shaft-to-carrier bolts

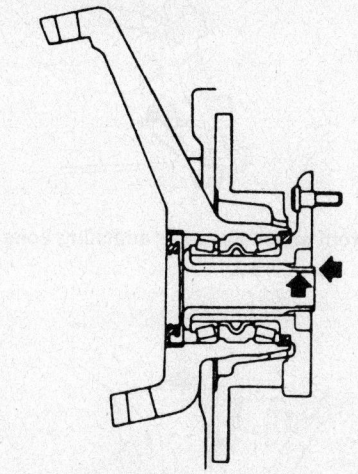

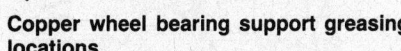

◀ : GREASING POINT

Copper wheel bearing support greasing locations

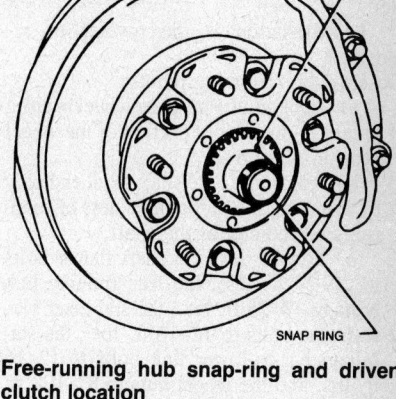

Free-running hub snap-ring and driven clutch location

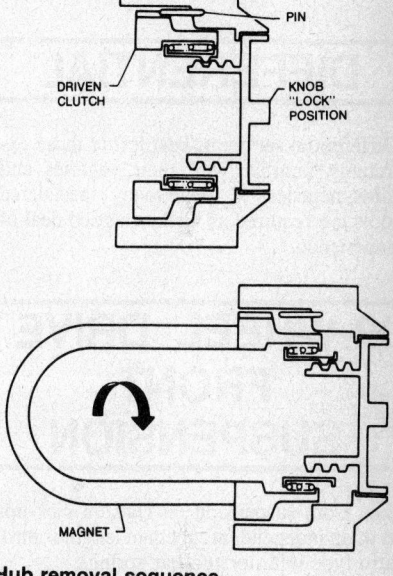

Hub removal sequence

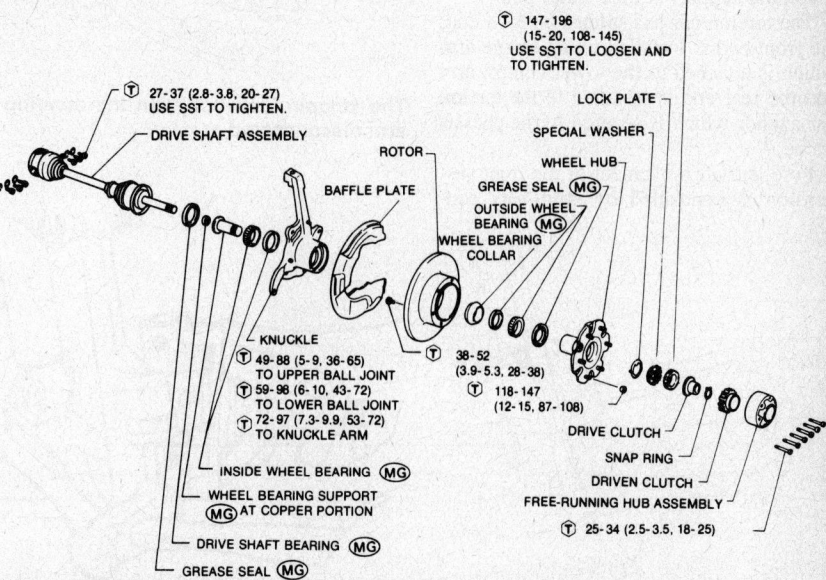

MG: MULTI-PURPOSE GREASE POINTS
Ⓣ : N·m (KG-M, FT-LB)

Front drive axle

6. Pull the axle shaft from the suspension.

7. Installation is the reverse of removal. Observe the following points:

   a. Apply multi-purpose wheel bearing grease to the copper portion of the wheel bearing support.

   b. Adjust the axle shaft axial end play by installing the proper thickness of snaprings on the end of the shaft.

   c. Torque the axle shaft flange bolts to 20–27 ft. lbs.; the free running hub bolts to 18–25 ft. lbs.; the stabilizer bar-to-frame bolts to 12–16 ft. lbs.; the stabilizer bar-to-lower link bolts to 12–16 ft. lbs. and the wheel nuts to 87–108 ft. lbs.

DIFFERENTIAL

Differential service is best left to those extremely familiar with their vagaries and idiosyncrasies. A great many specialized tools are required as well as a good deal of experience.

2-WHEEL DRIVE FRONT SUSPENSION

The front suspension on Datsum pick-ups is of an independent, unequal length control arm type with torsion bar springs.

The control arms are attached to a bracket which is welded to the frame at their inner pivot points and to the steering knuckle/spindle support at their outer points.

The torsion bar has splines on each end; the front end is installed to the torque arm which is attached to the lower control arm and the rear end is installed to the torsion bar anchor which is secured to the chassis frame.

Fore-and-aft movement of the front suspension is controlled by strut bars con-

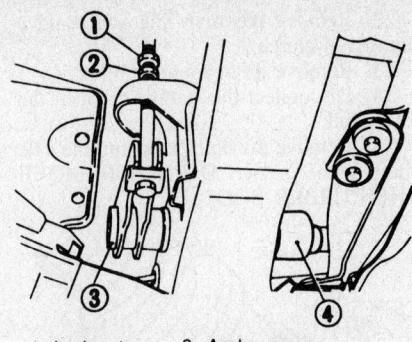

1. Lock nut   3. Anchor arm
2. Adjusting nut   4. Dust cover

2-wheel drive torsion bar anchor

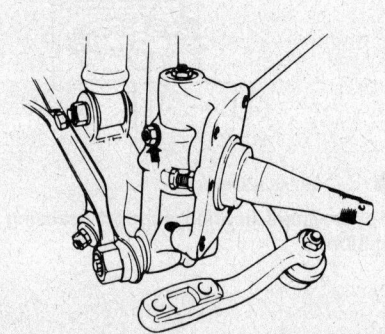

Front shock absorber attaching bolts

The kingpin lock bolt with the steering arm disconnected

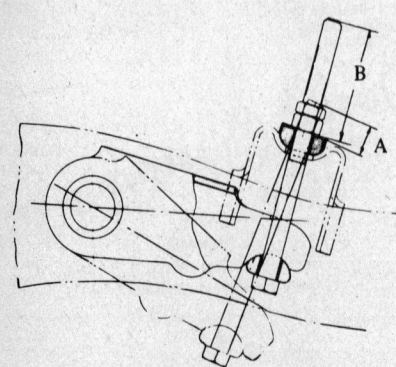

Installing the torsion bar anchor end on 2-wheel drive models

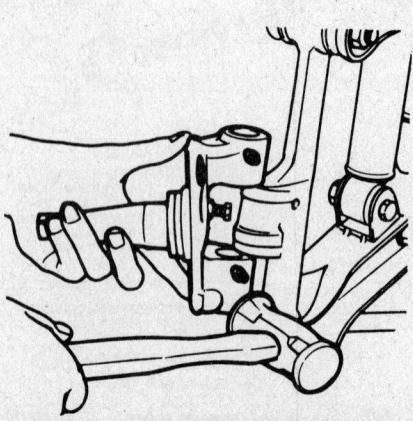

Removing the steering knuckle/spindle

nected to the lower control arms at one end and mounted to the chassis frame at the forward end.

An optional torsion bar type stabilizer is connected to the lower control arms through vertical stabilizer links.

The steering knuckle/spindle is attached to the steering knuckle/spindle support by a kingpin through 1977. Ball joints are used from 1978.

Torsion Bars

REMOVAL AND INSTALLATION

1. Jack up the front of the vehicle and support it with jackstands. Remove the wheel. On trucks with a catalytic converter, the converter must be removed if the left torsion bar is being removed.

2. Loosen the ride height adjusting nuts at the anchor (rear) end of the torsion bar, allowing the anchor arm to hang down.

3. Remove the dust cover at the rear end of the torsion bar and remove the snapring.

4. Pull the anchor arm rearward and off the torsion bar. Withdraw the torsion bar from the lower control arm and remove it from under the vehicle.

5. Before installing the torsion bar, apply a light coat of grease to the splines. Install the torsion bar to the lower control arm.

NOTE: The torsion bars are marked on the end with an "L" (left) or an "R" (right). The torsion bars must be installed on the same side from which they are removed.

6. Install the anchor arm on the rear end of the torsion bar. Dimension "A" must be:

1975–76: 0.20–0.60 in. standard bed, 0.59–0.98 in., long bed;
1977: 0.59–0.98 in. all models;
1978–82: 0.28–0.67 in., all models.

Note that there are two different methods used for measuring this distance. Be sure you are using the correct illustration for your truck.

7. Install a new retaining snap-ring and dust boot to the anchor arm end of the torsion bar.

NOTE: Always use a new snap-ring. Never reinstall the old one.

8. Tighten the adjusting nut until the link protrudes above the support bracket 2.36–2.76 in. on all models (dimension "B").

9. Install the wheel and lower the vehicle.

10. Adjust the vehicle ride height with the truck at curb weight (full tank of gas and no passengers). Refer to "Ride Height Adjustment." Tighten the locknut to 23–30 ft. lbs.

Shock Absorbers

TESTING

Visually inspect the shock absorber. If there is evidence of leakage and the shock absorber is covered with oil, the shock is defective and must be replaced.

If there is no sign of excessive leakage (a small amount of weeping is natural) bounce the truck at one corner by pressing up and down on the fender or bumper. When you have the truck bouncing as much as you can, stop bouncing it, and release the fender or bumper. The truck should stop bouncing after the first rebound. If the bouncing continues past the center point of the bounce more than once, the shock absorbers are worn and should be replaced.

REMOVAL AND INSTALLATION

1. Jack up the vehicle and support it. Remove the wheel.
2. Hold the upper stem of the shock absorber and remove the nuts, washer, and rubber bushing.
3. Remove the bolt from the lower end of the shock absorber and remove the shock absorber from the vehicle.
4. Install the shock absorber in the reverse order of removal. Replace all of the rubber bushings with new ones if a new shock absorber is being installed. Install the lower retaining bolt from the front of the truck. Tighten the upper attaching nut to 12–16 ft. lbs. and the lower nut to 23–30 ft. lbs.

Kingpins

INSPECTION

1. Jack the vehicle so that the tire on the side to be checked is off the ground. Adjust wheel bearing preload to the proper specification.
2. Grasp the top and bottom of the tire and try to move the top and bottom of the tire alternately in and out. If there is noticeable play between the steering knuckle/spindle and the spindle support then it can be assumed that the kingpins or bushings are worn and should be replaced.

NOTE: Before performing this test make sure that the wheel bearings are properly adjusted.

REMOVAL AND INSTALLATION

1. Jack up the front of the vehicle and support it by placing jackstands under the frame.
2. Remove the front wheel.
3. Remove the brake hose and connector from the wheel cylinder.

NOTE: It is not absolutely necessary to remove the drum, hub, brake, and backing plate from the spindle, although it will make working with the spindle a great deal easier. If you choose to leave the parts in place, skip down to step 8.

4. Remove the brake drum.
5. Remove the hub dust cap, cotter pin, adjusting cap, and spindle nut from the spindle.
6. Remove the wheel hub, inner and outer wheel bearings, bearing washer, and grease seal from the spindle.
7. Remove the brake backing plate from the knuckle/spindle flange.
8. Remove the knuckle/spindle steering arm from the knuckle/spindle.
9. Remove the kingpin lockbolt.
10. Remove the plug from the top of the kingpin by drilling a small hole in the plug, screwing a sheet metal screw into the hole, and pulling out the plug.
11. Drive out the kingpin together with the lower plug with a suitable drift and a hammer.
12. Tap the steering knuckle/spindle lightly with a hammer and detach it from knuckle/spindle support. Be careful not to drop the thrust bearing.
13. Drive the steering knuckle/spindle bushing and grease seal out of the kingpin bore with a kingpin bushing driver. Do not try to use a drift, because it will probably score the inner wall of the knuckle spindle.
14. After cleaning the pin bores thoroughly, install the new bushing carefully by using a bushing driver. Position the bushings in the spindle so that they are flush with the counterbores for the plugs. The bushings in the factory rebuilding kit have a grease gallery which should align with the grease nipple hole in the spindle (see the illustration).
15. Remove the grease nipples and drill grease holes through the bushings, placing the drill through the threaded grease nipple hole. The grease hole should be 1/8 in. or less. Remove *all* metal filings and burrs after drilling the grease holes. This step is not necessary if you have used the factory bushings and installed them as outlined in step 14.
16. Ream the inside of the kingpin bushings, if necessary, to 0.7878–0.7888 in. The fit should be such that the kingpin, when greased, can be turned or pushed in or out with thumb pressure. Use the lower bore as a guide for reaming the upper bore, and vice versa, to keep the bores aligned.
17. Press fit the grease seal on the upper bushing. Take care not to damage the grease seal lip.
18. Install the steering knuckle/spindle to the steering knuckle/spindle support in the reverse order of removal as follows:
19. Insert the O-ring in the lower end of the knuckle/spindle support. Install the thrust bearing and shim together with the steering knuckle/spindle to the knuckle/spindle support.

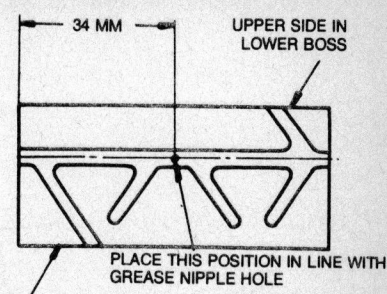

The kingpin bushings should be aligned with the grease nipple hole in the spindle

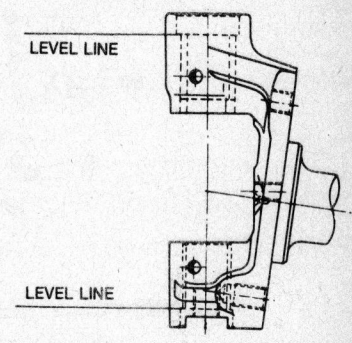

Installing the kingpin bushings flush with the plug counterbores

Select the spindle shims which will obtain 0.004 in. or less clearance between the steering knuckle/spindle and the support. To measure this clearance with a feeler gauge, jack up the bottom of the spindle slightly.

NOTE: The thrust bearing is installed so that the covered side faces upward. You will probably be able to use the same shims that were originally installed.

20. Drive the new kingpin into the kingpin bores, securing the steering knuckle/spindle to the support.
21. Align the locking bolt hole of the knuckle/spindle support with the notch in the kingpin and install the lockbolt.
22. Install the upper and lower kingpin plugs.
23. Install the steering knuckle/spindle arm to the steering knuckle/spindle arm together with a new lockplate. Tighten the steering knuckle arm attaching bolts to 75–88 ft. lbs. Bend the tabs of the lockplate to engage the flats on the bolt head.
24. Install the brake backing plate, hub and wheel bearings, brake drum, and wheel. Bleed the brake hydraulic system and grease the newly installed bushings until grease is visible around the upper and lower grease seals.

Ball Joints

Ball joints are used on 1978 and later trucks, replacing the kingpins used previously.

DATSUN

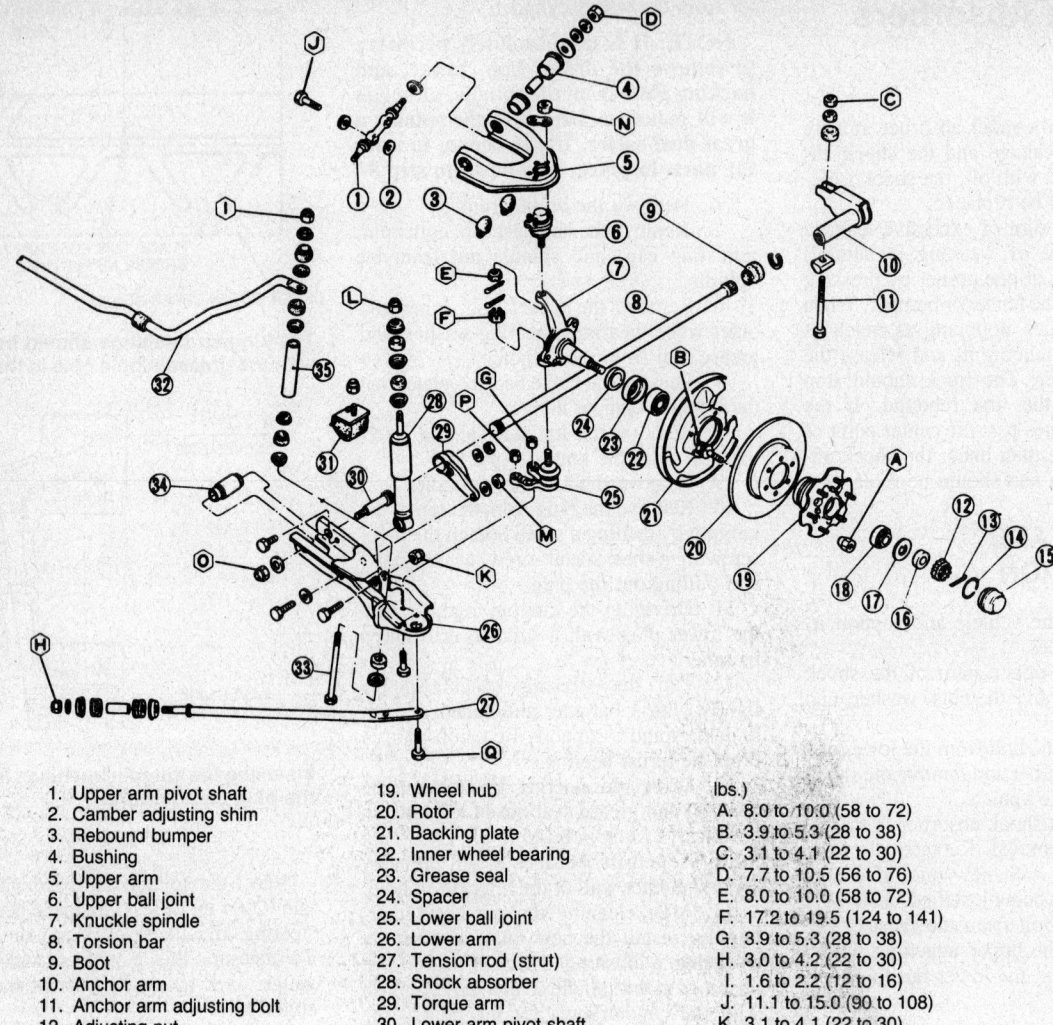

1. Upper arm pivot shaft	19. Wheel hub
2. Camber adjusting shim	20. Rotor
3. Rebound bumper	21. Backing plate
4. Bushing	22. Inner wheel bearing
5. Upper arm	23. Grease seal
6. Upper ball joint	24. Spacer
7. Knuckle spindle	25. Lower ball joint
8. Torsion bar	26. Lower arm
9. Boot	27. Tension rod (strut)
10. Anchor arm	28. Shock absorber
11. Anchor arm adjusting bolt	29. Torque arm
12. Adjusting nut	30. Lower arm pivot shaft
13. Cotter pin	31. Bumper stop
14. O-ring	32. Stabilizer (optional)
15. Hub cap	33. Stabilizer connecting bolt
16. Spindle nut	34. Lower arm bushing
17. Washer	35. Stabilizer collar
18. Outer wheel bearing	Tightening torque kg-m (ft.

lbs.)	
A.	8.0 to 10.0 (58 to 72)
B.	3.9 to 5.3 (28 to 38)
C.	3.1 to 4.1 (22 to 30)
D.	7.7 to 10.5 (56 to 76)
E.	8.0 to 10.0 (58 to 72)
F.	17.2 to 19.5 (124 to 141)
G.	3.9 to 5.3 (28 to 38)
H.	3.0 to 4.2 (22 to 30)
I.	1.6 to 2.2 (12 to 16)
J.	11.1 to 15.0 (90 to 108)
K.	3.1 to 4.1 (22 to 30)
L.	1.6 to 2.2 (12 to 16)
M.	2.7 to 3.7 (20 to 27)
N.	1.7 to 2.2 (12 to 16)
O.	11.1 to 15.0 (80 to 108)
P.	3.6 to 4.6 (26 to 33)
Q.	3.9 to 5.3 (28 to 38)

1978–82 front suspension

INSPECTION

The ball joint should be replaced when play becomes excessive. Datsun does not publish specifications on just what constitutes excessive play, relying instead on a method of determining the force (in inch pounds) required to keep the ball joint turning. This method is not very helpful to the backyard mechanic since it involves removing the ball joint, which is what we are trying to avoid in the first place. An effective way to determine ball joint play is to jack up the truck until the wheel is just a couple of inches off the ground and the ball joint is unloaded, which means that you can't jack directly under the ball joint. Place a long bar under the tire and move the wheel and tire assembly up and down. Keep one hand on top of the tire while you are doing this. If there is over ¼ inch of play at the top

of the tire, the ball joint is probably bad. This assuming that the wheel bearings are in good shape and properly adjusted. As a double check, have someone watch the ball joint while you move the tire up and down with the bar. If considerable play is seen, besides feeling play at the top of the wheel, the ball joints need to be replaced.

REMOVAL AND INSTALLATION

Upper

1. Raise and support the truck on stands placed on the frame rails.
2. Remove the wheels.
3. Loosen the torsion bar anchor lock and adjusting nuts to relieve spring tension.
4. Remove and discard the cotter pin from the ball joint stud and remove the nut.

Separate the stud from the knuckle spindle with a ball joint removal tool.

5. Loosen the bolts retaining the ball joint to the control arm, and remove the joint.

6. Install the new ball joint into the control arm, tightening the bolts to 12–16 ft. lbs. Install the ball joint stud into the knuckle spindle and install the nut. Tighten the nut to 60 ft. lbs., then continue to tighten until the holes align (limit: 72 ft. lbs.). Install a new cotter pin. Install the wheel, lower the truck, and adjust the ride height. Have the alignment checked.

Lower

1. Perform steps 1 and 2 of the upper ball joint removal procedure. Remove the lower shock absorber mounting bolt.

2. Loosen the torsion bar spring anchor

lock and adjusting nuts, and remove the anchor arm bolt from the anchor arm.

3. Remove the snap-ring, then move the anchor arm and torsion bar fully rearward.

4. Disconnect the stabilizer bar from the lower arm, if equipped.

5. Disconnect the strut (tension rod) from the lower arm.

6. Remove and discard the cotter pin from the ball joint stud, and remove the nut. Separate the ball joint from the knuckle spindle with a ball joint removal tool.

7. Remove the attaching bolts, and remove the ball joint from the lower arm.

8. Install the new ball joint in the arm, tightening the bolts to 28–38 ft. lbs. Install the ball joint stud into the knuckle spindle and tighten the nut to 127 ft. lbs. Continue to tighten until the holes align, then install the new cotter pin (limit: 141 ft. lbs.). The torsion bar ride height must be adjusted after assembly.

Upper and Lower Control Arms

REMOVAL AND INSTALLATION

1975–77

1. Raise the truck on a hoist or jack up the front end and support it with jackstands placed under the frame.

2. Remove the wheel and brake drum.

3. Remove the hub.

4. Remove the brake backing plate from the steering knuckle/spindle support.

5. Remove the steering knuckle/spindle arm, torsion bar, stabilizer bar, shock absorber, and strut rod, in this order.

6. Remove the upper fulcrum bolt securing the knuckle/spindle support to the upper control arm assembly and detach the two.

7. Remove the upper control arm bushings from the knuckle/spindle support.

8. Remove the screw bushings from both ends of the lower control arm fulcrum pin.

9. Loosen the nut at the lower end of the knuckle/spindle support from the inside and pull out the cotter pin retaining the fulcrum.

10. Drive the fulcrum pin out of the lower control arm and remove the knuckle/spindle support and steering knuckle/spindle from the lower control arm.

11. Remove the bolts retaining the upper control arm pivot shaft and remove the upper control arm pivot shaft with the camber adjusting shims from the body bracket.

12. Remove the nut retaining the lower control arm pivot shaft and remove the lower control arm pivot shaft. Remove the lower control arm with the torque arm from the mounting bracket.

13. The lower control arm bushing is removed with a drift and hammer.

14. Install the upper and lower control

arms in the reverse order of removal. Tighten the lower control arm attaching nut to 54–58 ft. lbs. Tighten the upper control arm and camber adjusting shim bolts to 51–65 ft. lbs.

15. Coat the threads of the fulcrum pin with grease and line up the notch of the fulcrum pin with the knuckle/spindle support for the insertion of the cotter pin. Install the fulcrum pin to the knuckle/spindle support with a soft hammer, attaching the support to the upper control arm. Install the cotter pin and tighten the locknut to 5.8–8.0 ft. lbs.

16. Coat the threaded portion inside of the screw bushing liberally with grease. Position the support at the center of the lower control arm and install the screw bushings. Check the dimensions of the installed screw bushing against those in the illustration, then tighten the bushing to 145–216 ft. lbs.

17. Replace the grease filler plug with a grease fitting and pump grease in until grease comes out around the dust cover. Reinstall the filler plug.

18. Install the upper control arm bushing to the knuckle/spindle support and then connect the knuckle/spindle support to the upper control arm. Insert the connecting bolt from the rear and tighten the nut to 28–38 ft. lbs.

19. Install the strut rod, shock absorber, stabilizer rod, torsion bar, and steering knuckle arm.

20. Install the brake backing plate to the steering knuckle/spindle and tighten the attaching bolts to 30–36 ft. lbs.

21. Install the brake drum and wheel and adjust the wheel bearing preload.

1978–82

UPPER

1. Perform steps 1–4 of the upper ball joint removal procedure.

2. Remove the bolts retaining the upper arm pivot shaft and remove the shaft, arm, and camber adjusting shims from the body. Note the location of the shims so that they may be installed in their original positions during assembly.

3. To remove the upper arm shaft and bushings from the arm, remove the nuts and washers from the shaft. Use a press, first on one end of the shaft and then the other, to press out the bushings. Remove the shaft.

4. To install, coat the bushing with soapy water and press it into the upper arm. Install the washers onto the shaft and install the shaft into the arm. Be sure the chamfered side of the washer is against the shaft flange. Measure the distance between the outer collar on the bushing and the washer on the shaft (dimension "C" in the illustration); it should exceed 4.5 mm (0.177 in.).

5. Press the other bushing into the arm, and check dimension "C." Also check the distance between the outer collars of both bushings (dimension "D") and the distance between the end of the bushing and the centerline of the shaft mounting bolt bore

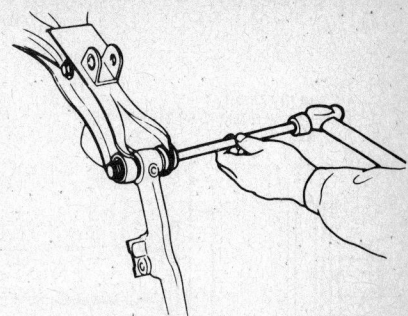
Driving the fulcrum pin out of the lower control arm in order to remove the steering knuckle support

The upper control arm pivot shaft

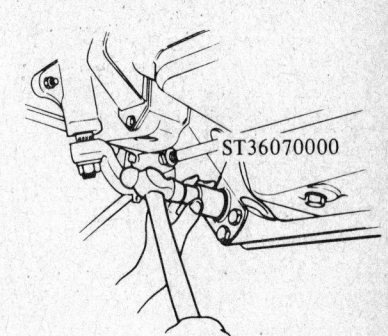
ST36070000

Removing the lower control arm pivot shaft bushing

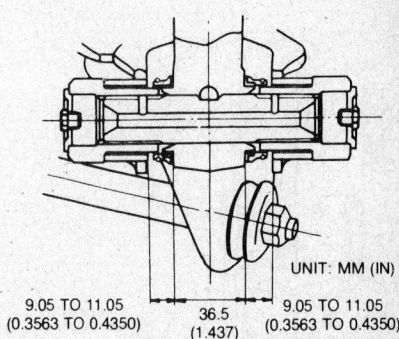
9.05 TO 11.05 (0.3563 TO 0.4350) 36.5 (1.437) 9.05 TO 11.05 (0.3563 TO 0.4350) UNIT: MM (IN)

Installation of the lower control arm-to-knuckle screw bushing

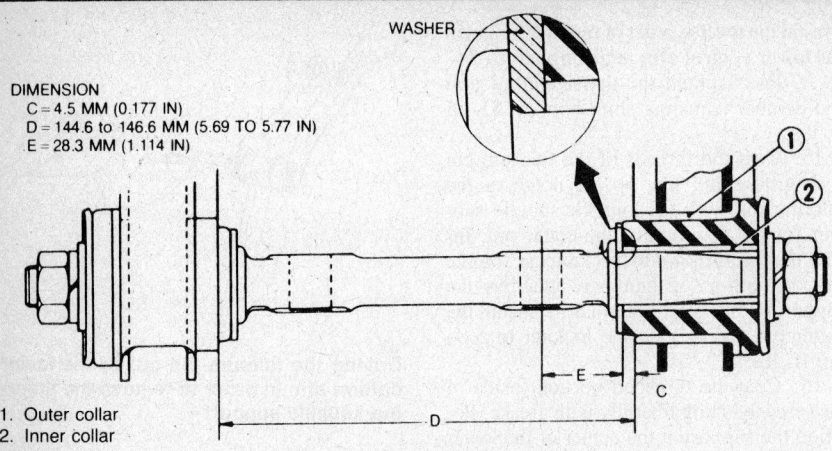

DIMENSION
C = 4.5 MM (0.177 IN)
D = 144.6 to 146.6 MM (5.69 TO 5.77 IN)
E = 28.3 MM (1.114 IN)

WASHER

1. Outer collar
2. Inner collar

Upper arm pivot shaft and bushing installation dimensions, 1978–82

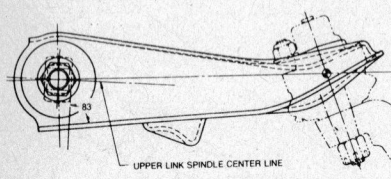

UPPER LINK SPINDLE CENTER LINE

Upper arm pivot shaft installation before tightening the shaft nuts, 1978–82

Knuckle arm attaching bolt

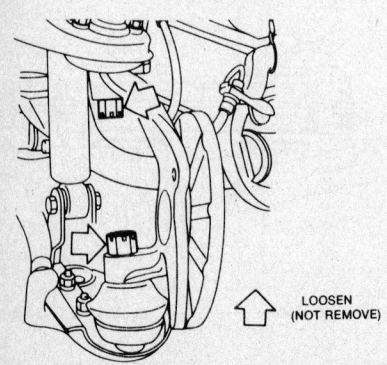

LOOSEN
(NOT REMOVE)

Upper and lower ball joint nuts

(dimension ''E''). D should be 144.6–146.6 mm (5.69–5.77 in.); E should be 28.3 mm (1.114 in.).

6. Rotate the pivot shaft in the arm until the angle is as specified in the illustration. Install the nuts and washers on the shaft. Tighten the bushings to 56–76 ft. lbs.

7. Install the upper arm and shaft assembly to the body, replacing the camber shims in their original locations. Tighten the bolts to 80–108 ft. lbs.

8. Follow step 6 of the upper ball joint removal procedure.

LOWER

1. Perform steps 1–6 of the lower ball joint removal procedure.

2. Remove the lower arm pivot shaft bolt and washer. Tap the pivot shaft out of the bushing. Push down on the torsion bar and remove the lower arm.

3. Use a bushing driver to tap the lower arm bushing from the frame.

4. Drive the new bushing into the frame.

5. Install the arm and pivot shaft, tightening the nut to 80–108 ft. lbs.

6. Follow step 8 of the lower ball joint removal procedure.

4-WHEEL DRIVE FRONT SUSPENSION

Hub and Knuckle

REMOVAL AND INSTALLATION

1. Block the rear wheels, raise and support the front of the vehicle on jackstands.

2. Remove the wheels.

3. Remove the brake caliper and suspend it out the way. DO NOT DISCONNECT THE BRAKE HOSE!

4. Remove the axle shaft.

5. Remove the bolt securing the knuckle arm to the knuckle.

6. Loosen, but do not remove the upper and lower ball joint tightening nuts.

7. Separate the ball joints from the knuckle with a ball joint removing tool.

——— CAUTION ———
NEVER REMOVE THE BALLJOINT NUT IN THE PREVIOUS STEP!

8. Jack up the lower link and remove the ball joint tightening nut.

9. Remove the knuckle.

10. Unbend the lockwasher with a screwdriver and remove the front hub locknut.

11. Remove the lockwasher and special washer.

12. Push the wheel bearing support out of the hub.

13. Separate the knuckle from the hub with a puller.

14. Remove the bearing collar.

15. Remove the inside bearing and seal. Drive the race out with a brass driver.

16. Separate the hub from the rotor.

17. Knock the hub on a wood block to move the outer bearing away from the hub surface, then pull it the rest of the way with a bearing puller. Remove the grease seal.

18. Remove the axle shaft bearing from the bearing support with a brass driver.

19. Clean and thoroughly repack the bearings.

20. Assembly is the reverse of removal. Note the following points:

   a. Install the bearing outer race into each side of the knuckle with a brass driver.

   b. Install the outer grease seal and bearing with a brass driver.

   c. Pack the seal lip with wheel bearing grease. Be sure that the seal faces the right direction.

   d. The wheel bearing collar thickness determines end-play. Determine what thickness to use as follows:

Determining Bearing Collar Thickness

1. Install the collar which was removed.

2. Install the inside bearing with a brass driver.

3. Install the special washer and lockwasher.

4. Tighten the locknut to 108–145 ft. lbs.

5. Turn the hub several times in both directions to seat the bearings.

6. Using a spring scale as shown, check the preload to see that it falls between 2.2 and 9.5 ft. lbs.

7. If not, adjust by replacing the collar with one of a different thickness, as shown by the number stamped on the collar. The larger the number, the thicker the collar.

8. When preload has been correctly set, secure the nut by bending the lockwasher tip.

Observe the following torques:

Item	ft. lbs.
Upper ball joint-to-knuckle	36–65
Lower ball joint-to-knuckle	43–72
Knuckle arm-to-knuckle	53–72
Caliper-to-knuckle	53–72
Axle shaft-to-carrier	20–27
Free running hub	18–25
Stabilizer bar	12–16
Wheel nut	87–108

Shock Absorbers

See the 2-wheel drive section.

Torsion Bars

REMOVAL AND INSTALLATION

1. Raise and support the front end on jack stands.
2. Remove the torsion bar spring anchor bolt.
3. Pull the anchor arm out rearward.
4. Pull the torsion bar spring rearward.
5. Remove the torsion bar.
6. Install the torsion arm to the lower link. Torque the outer bolt to 20–27 ft. lbs. and the inner to 26–33 ft. lbs.
7. Place a coating of grease on the torsion bar spring serrated end and install it in the torsion arm.
8. Install the anchor arm to the serrated end of the torsion bar spring and install the anchor arm adjusting bolt. Turn the bolt until the bottom of the nut is about ½ (Dimension A) inch from the end of the bolt.
9. Install the dust cover.
10. Adjust the anchor arm position until the distance between the end of the dust cover and the bottom of the nut (Dimension B) is about 2½ inches.
11. Lower the vehicle.
12. Turn the anchor bolt adjusting nut until the center line of the lower link spindle is 5.28–5.47 inches above the tension rod attaching bolts. This is dimension H in the accompanying figure.

Tension Bar and Stabilizer Link

See the 2-wheel drive section.

Ball Joints and Control Arms

See the 2-wheel drive section with the following exceptions:

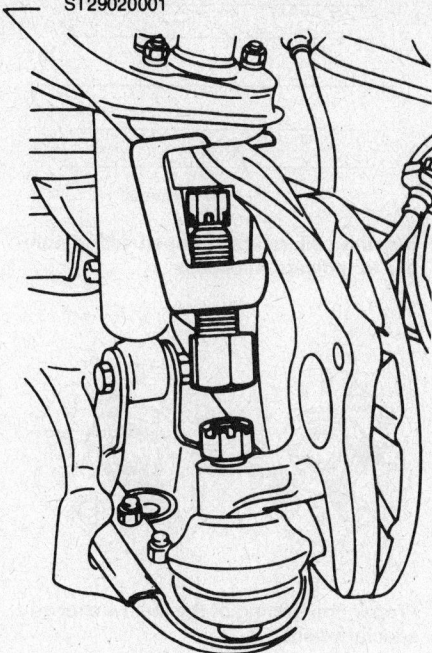

Removing the ball joint using a ball joint tool

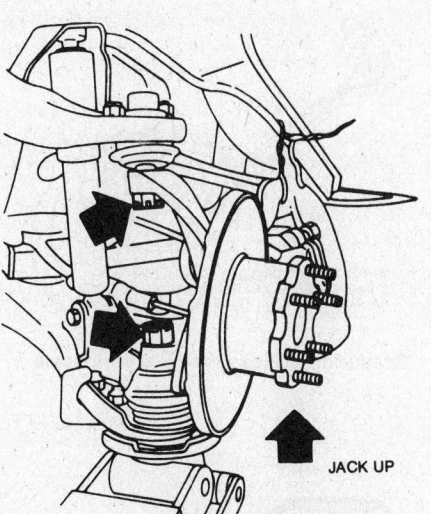

Removing the ball joint tightening nuts

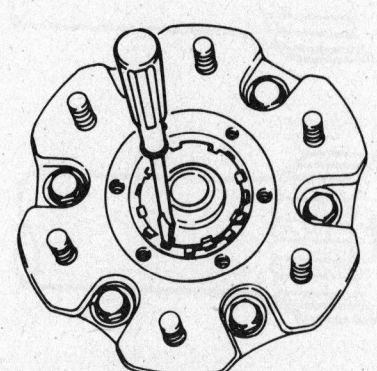

Unbending the lockwasher

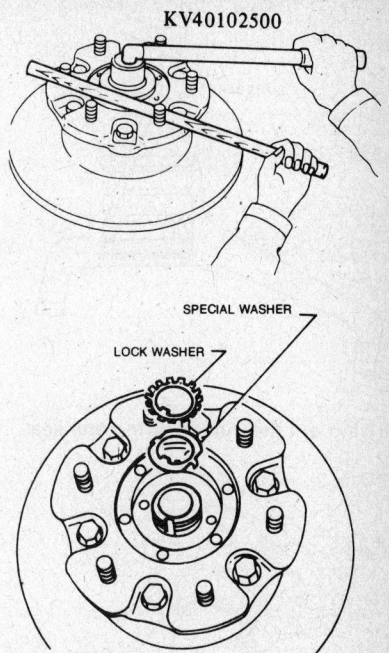

Removing the special washer and lockwasher

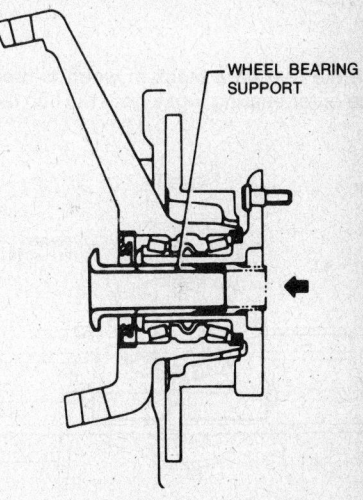

Wheel bearing support greasing location

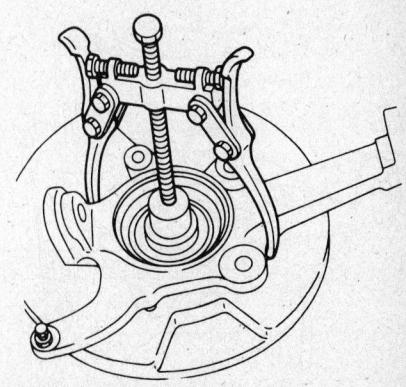

Using a puller to separate the hub from the knuckle

DATSUN

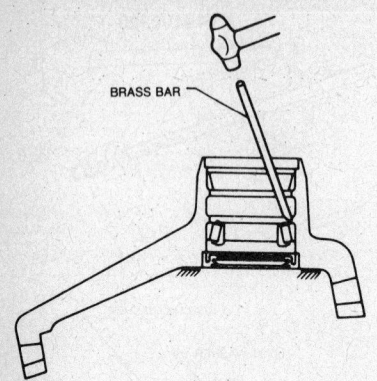

Driving out the inner bearing and seal

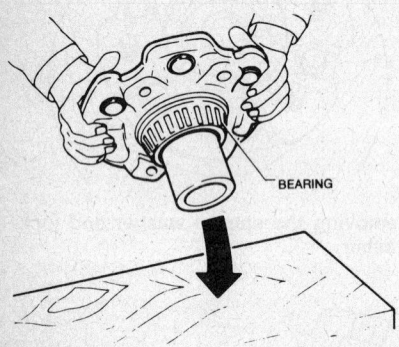

Hit the hub on a block of wood to break the outer bearing loose from the hub face

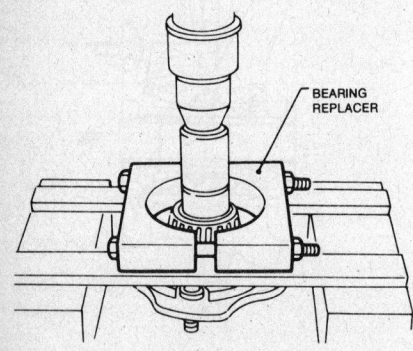

Removing the outer bearing with a puller

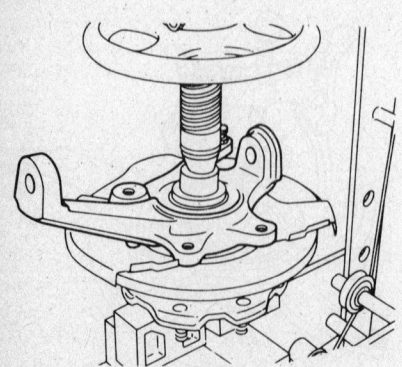

Installing the outer bearing into the knuckle

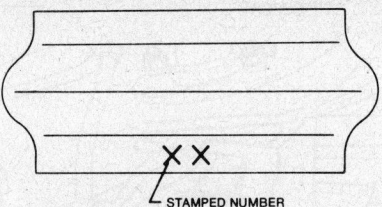

Bearing collars are stamped with a number to indicate thickness

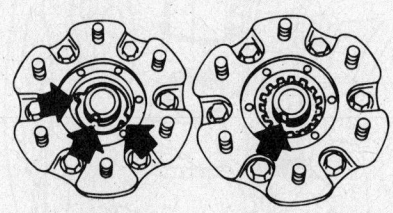

Proper positioning of the lockwasher and special washer

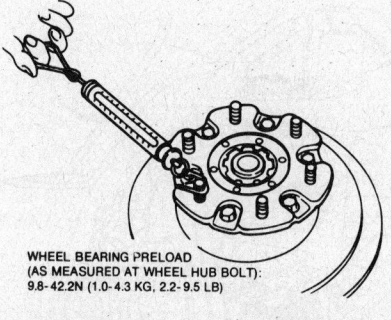

WHEEL BEARING PRELOAD
(AS MEASURED AT WHEEL HUB BOLT):
9.8-42.2N (1.0-4.3 KG, 2.2-9.5 LB)

Measuring preload with a spring scale

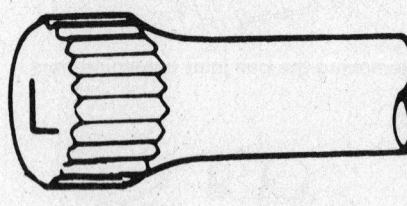

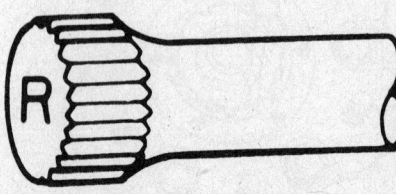

Torsion bar spring serrated ends. Note that they are marked and not interchangeable

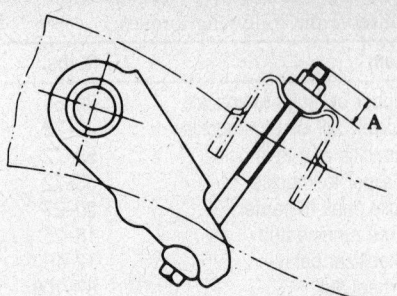

A: 7 - 17 mm (0.28 - 0.67 in)

Anchor arm adjusting bolt measurement

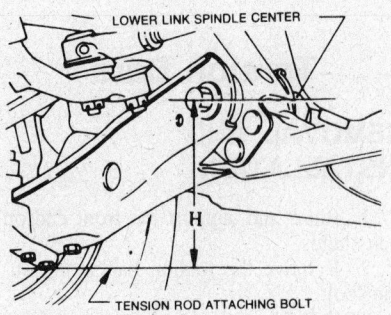

Ride height adjustment

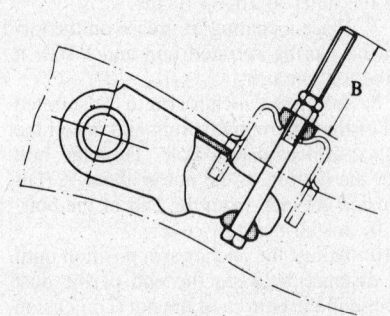

B: 60 - 70 mm (2.36 - 2.76 in)

Anchor arm position adjustment

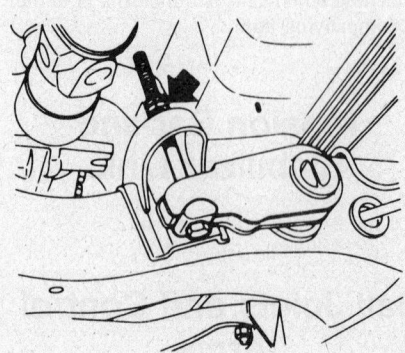

Torsion bar spring anchor bolt

INSTALLATION

1. Install the lower ball joint to the control arm. Torque the attaching bolts to 28–38 ft. lbs.

2. Install the lower control arm spindle bushing to the frame.

3. Attach the torque arm to the torsion bar.

4. Install the lower control arm.

5. Install the torque arm on the lower control arm. Torque the inner side to 26–33 ft. lbs. and the outer side to 20–27 ft. lbs.

6. Jack up the lower link.

7. Install the lower ball joint in the spindle and torque the nut to 43–72 ft. lbs.

8. Install the shock absorber lower end to the control arm and torque to 22–30 ft. lbs.

9. Install the tension rod and stabilizer connecting rod to the control arm.

10. Lower the vehicle.

11. Turn the anchor bolt adjusting nut to obtain the dimension specified in step 12 of Torsion Bar Removal and Installation.

12. After installation, check wheel alignment.

FRONT END ALIGNMENT

Caster

Caster is the forward or rearward tilt of the upper end of the kingpin, or the upper ball joint, which results in a slight tilt of the steering axis forward or backward. Rearward tilt is referred to as positive caster, while forward tilt is referred to as negative caster.

Caster is adjusted by creating a difference in the total number (thickness) of shims front and rear between the upper control arm pivot shaft and its mounting bracket. Adjustment requires the use of special equipment, thus, it is not covered here.

Camber

Camber is the inward or outward tilt from the vertical, measured in degrees, of the front wheels at the top. An outward tilt gives the wheel positive camber. Proper camber is critical to assure even tire wear.

Camber is adjusted by adding or subtracting the same number and thickness of shims at the front and rear upper arm pivot shaft attaching bolts. Adjustment requires the use of special equipment; thus, it is not covered here.

Toe

Toe is the amount, measured in a fraction

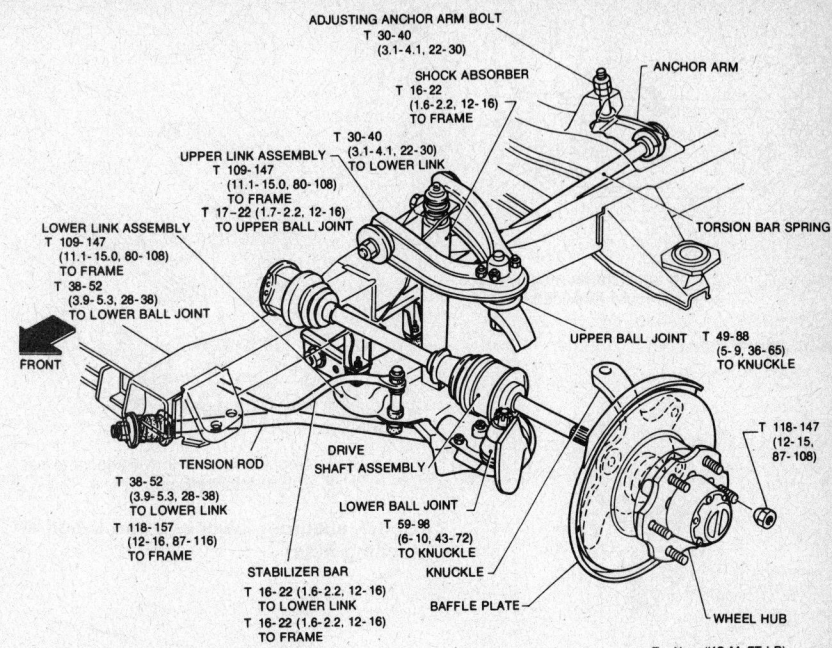

Four wheel drive front suspension

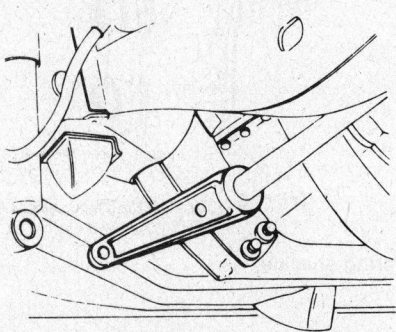

Torque arm-to-torsion bar attachment

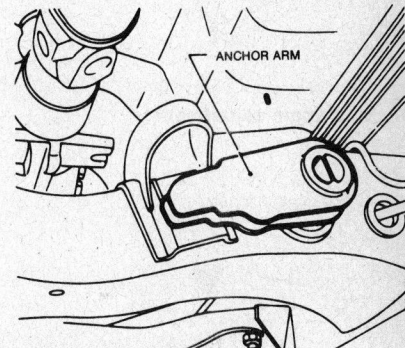

Torsion bar anchor arm

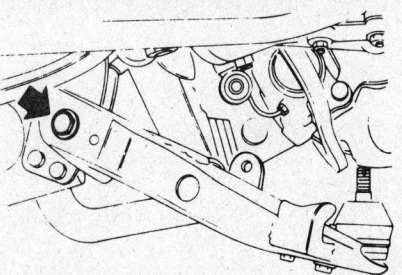

Torque arm-to-lower control arm attachment

$\top$: N·m (kg-m, ft-lb)

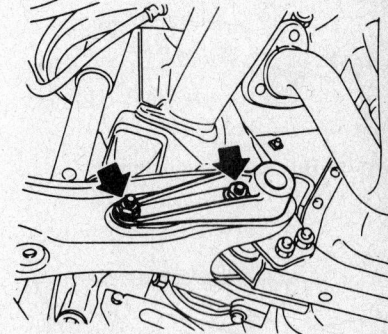

Torsion arm-to-link bolts

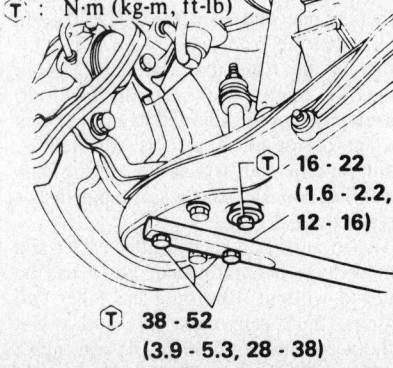

Attaching the tension rod and stabilizer bar to the lower control arm

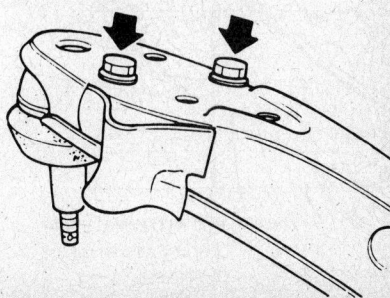

Ball joint-to-control arm bolts

529

DATSUN

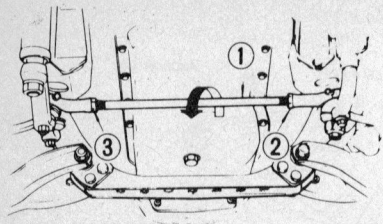

1. Tie-rod
2. Left-hand threaded locknut
3. Right-hand threaded locknut

Toe-in adjustment

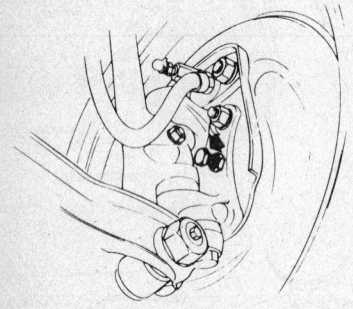

Steering angle adjustment

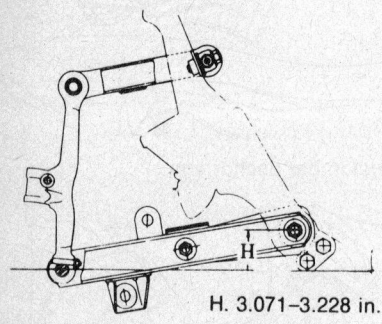

H. 3.071–3.228 in.

1975–77 ride height adjustment

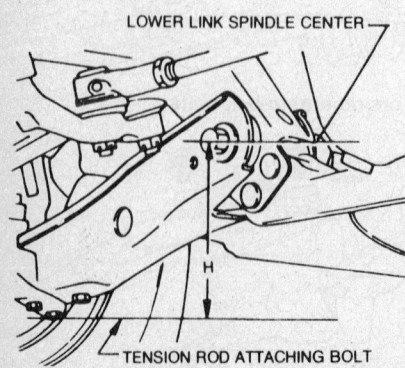

LOWER LINK SPINDLE CENTER

TENSION ROD ATTACHING BOLT

1978–82 ride height adjustment

530

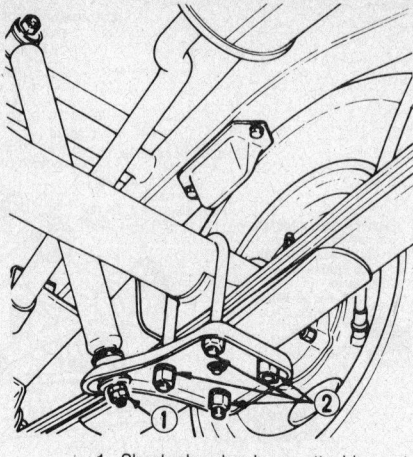

1. Shock absorber lower attaching nut
2. U-bolt attaching nut

Shock absorber lower end and U-bolt attaching nuts

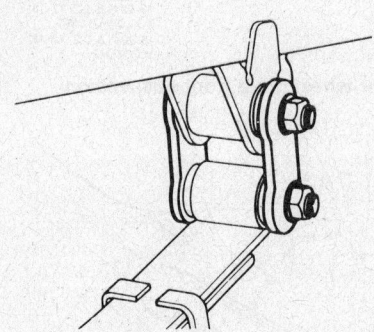

Spring shackle

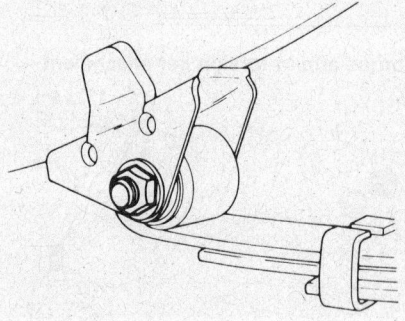

Spring pin

of an inch, that the wheels are closer together at one end than the other. Toe-in means that the front wheels are closer together at the front than the rear; toe-out means the rears are closer than the front. Datsun pick-ups are adjusted to have a slight amount of toe-in. Toe-in is adjusted by turning the tie-rod, which has a right-hand thread on one end and a left-hand thread on the other.

Toe-in must be checked after caster and camber have been adjusted, but it can be adjusted without disturbing the other two settings. You can make this adjustment without special equipment if you make careful measurements. The wheels must be straight ahead.

1. Toe-in can be determined by measuring the distance between the centers of the tire treads, at the front of the tire and at the rear. If the tread pattern of your truck's tires makes this impossible, you can measure between the edges of the wheel rims, but make sure to move the truck forward and measure in a couple of places to avoid errors caused by bent rims or wheel runout.

2. If the measurement is not within specifications, loosen the locknuts at both ends of the tie-rod (the driver's side locknut is left-hand threaded).

3. Turn the top of the tie-rod toward the front of the truck to reduce toe-in, or toward the rear to increase it. When the correct dimension is reached, tighten the locknuts to 58–72 ft. lbs. and check the adjustment.

Steering Angle Adjustment

The maximum steering angle is adjusted by stopper bolts located on the inside of the steering knuckle/spindle. Loosen the locknut on the stopper bolt, turn the stopper bolt in or out as required to obtain the proper maximum steering angle and retighten the locknut.

Ride Height Adjustment

The vehicle ride height is adjusted by turning the torsion bar anchor adjusting nut after loosening the locknut. The ride height adjustment should be performed with the gas tank full, the radiator and engine oil at the proper level, the spare tire/wheel, jack, and jack handle in the vehicle and no passengers. Also make sure that the tires are inflated to the proper pressure.

1. Raise and support the truck under the front suspension crossmember to unload the torsion bars.

2. Turn the rear torsion bar anchor bolt to the right to lower the truck or to the left to raise it.

3. For trucks through 1976, dimension ''H'' in the illustration should be 3.07–3.23 in. with the truck empty and resting on its wheels. For 1977 models, the distance should be 3.11–3.31 in.

4. For 1978–82 models, measure the distance ''H'' between the center of the lower control arm pivot bolt and the tension rod (strut) attaching bolt, as shown in the other illustration; ''H'' should be 4.92 in.

REAR SUSPENSION

The rear suspension consists of semielliptic

leaf springs and telescopic hydraulic shock absorbers. There are rubber bushings at either end of the leaf springs and shock absorbers to absorb vibration and noise.

Springs

REMOVAL AND INSTALLATION

———— CAUTION ————
The leaf springs are under a considerable amount of tension. Be very careful when removing or installing them; they can exert enough force to cause serious injuries.

1. Jack up the rear of the truck and support it with jackstands placed under the frame.
2. Disconnect the shock absorbers at their lower end.
3. Remove the nuts securing the U-bolts around the axle housing.
4. Place a jack under the rear axle housing and raise the housing to remove the weight off the spring.
5. Remove the nuts from the spring shackles, drive out the shackle pins and remove the spring from the vehicle.
6. Install the spring in the reverse order of removal. The weight of the truck must be on the rear wheels before tightening the front pin, shackle, and shock absorber attaching nuts. Tighten the front pin and shackle nuts to 83–94 ft. lbs. (37–50 ft. lbs. for the spring shackle nuts, 1978–82), the U-bolt nuts to 53–72 ft. lbs., and the shock absorber lower end nut to 12–16 ft. lbs.

Shock Absorbers

INSPECTION AND TESTING

Inspect and test the rear shock absorbers in the same manner as outlined for the front shock absorbers.

REMOVAL AND INSTALLATION

The rear shock absorbers are removed simply by removing the upper and lower at-

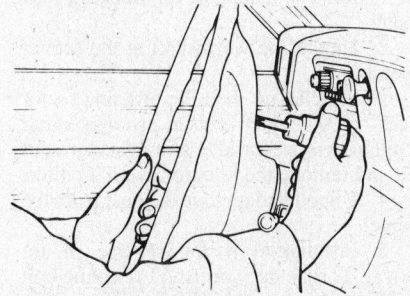

Removing the horn pad from the steering wheel

taching nuts, and removing the component from the vehicle. They are installed in the reverse order. The weight of the vehicle must be on the rear wheels before tightening the shock absorber attaching nuts to 12–16 ft. lbs.

STEERING

Steering Wheel

REMOVAL AND INSTALLATION

1. Position the wheels in the straight-ahead position.
2. Disconnect the battery ground cable from the battery.
3. Remove the horn pad by unscrewing the two screws from the rear side of the steering wheel crossbar.
4. Punch mark the top of the steering column shaft and the steering wheel flange.
5. Remove the attaching nut and remove the steering wheel with a puller.

———— CAUTION ————
Do not strike the shaft with a hammer, which may cause the column to collapse.

6. Install the steering wheel in the reverse order of removal aligning the punch marks. Tighten the steering wheel attaching nut to 51–54 ft. lbs.

Turn Signal and Dimmer Switch

REMOVAL AND INSTALLATION

1. Disconnect the negative cable from

the battery.
2. Remove the steering wheel.
3. Disconnect the wiring harness from the clip which retains it to the lower instrument panel.
4. Disconnect the multiple connector and lead wire from the instrument panel wiring harness.
5. Remove the steering column shell covers (upper and lower).
6. Loosen the two screws attaching the

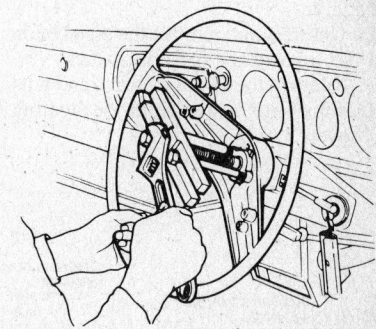

Removing the steering wheel with a puller

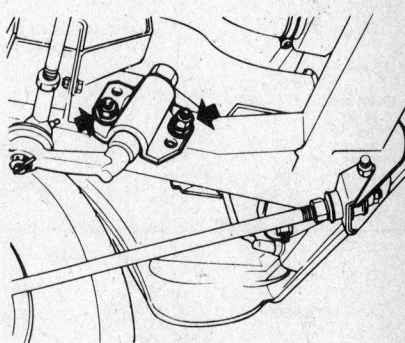

The idler arm attaching nuts

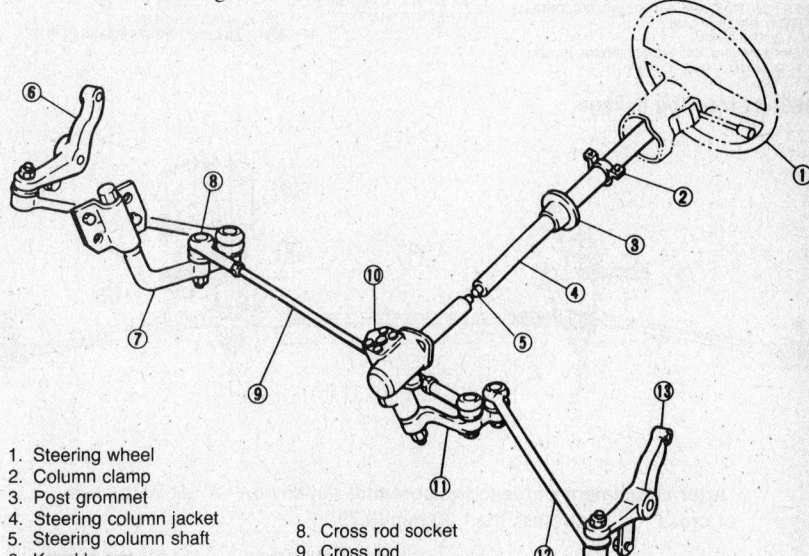

1. Steering wheel
2. Column clamp
3. Post grommet
4. Steering column jacket
5. Steering column shaft
6. Knuckle arm
7. Idler arm assembly
8. Cross rod socket
9. Cross rod
10. Steering gear assembly
11. Steering gear arm
12. Side rod
13. Knuckle arm

1975–79 steering linkage

DATSUN

switch assembly to the steering column jacket and remove the switch assembly.

7. Install the turn signal and dimmer switch and the steering wheel in the reverse order of removal.

Ignition Switch

REMOVAL AND INSTALLATION

1. Disconnect the negative cable from the battery.
2. Unscrew and remove the escutcheon from the front of the ignition switch.
3. Remove the ignition switch and wiring harness with spacer from the steering shell cover.

4. Disconnect the wiring connector from the back of the ignition switch.

5. Install the ignition switch in the reverse order of removal.

NOTE: On models with the optional steering lock cylinder, remove the switch by removing the two retaining screws from the back of the steering lock cylinder.

Steering Lock

REMOVAL AND INSTALLATION

1. Remove the ignition switch.
2. Drill out the two shear screws.
3. Remove the two other normal type

screws and dismount the steering lock from the steering jacket tube.

4. Install a new steering lock in the reverse order, being sure to tighten the two shear screws until they shear.

Steering Linkage

REMOVAL AND INSTALLATION

1. Jack up the front of the truck and support it with jackstands placed under the frame.
2. Remove the cotter pins and nuts securing the side rod ball studs to the steering knuckle/spindle arms.
3. Use a puller to disconnect the side rod ball studs from the steering knuckle arms. If a puller is not available, strike the side of the steering knuckle arm boss with a hammer, backing it up with a heavy hammer on the opposite side, and at the same time having an assistant pull the ball stud out of the steering knuckle arm.

NOTE: Do not strike the ball stud head, the ball socket on the side rod, or the side rod with the hammer.

4. Remove the nut securing the steering gear arm on the sector shaft and remove the gear arm with a puller. If a puller is not available, and the steering gear arm need not be removed, disconnect the side arm and tie-rod ball studs from the steering gear arm in the same manner as outlined in Step 3.
5. Remove the idler arm assembly from the frame by unscrewing the two attaching nuts.
6. Install the steering linkage in the reverse order of removal. Tighten the ball stud nuts to 40–55 ft. lbs. idler arm assembly attaching nuts to 23–27 ft. lbs., and the tie-rod adjustment locknuts to 58–72 ft. lbs. Adjust the toe-in and steering angle.

MG SLIDING PORTION

STEERING WHEEL
• DO NOT STRIKE END OF STEERING COLUMN SHAFT WITH A HAMMER. STRIKING SHAFT WILL DAMAGE NEEDLE BEARING OR COLUMN SHAFT.
• BE CAREFUL NOT TO DAMAGE CANCEL POLE.

STEERING COLUMN MOUNTING BRACKET
T 9-11 (0.9-1.1, 6.5-8.0)

RUBBER COUPLING
T 39-49 (4.0-5.0, 29-36) MAKE SURE THAT UNDUE STRESS IS NOT APPLIED TO IT.

JACKET TUBE BRACKET
T 2.9-4.3 (0.30-0.44, 2.2-3.2)

STEERING LOCK

IDLER ARM
T 49-69 (5.0-7.0, 36-51) TO FRAME

STEERING COLUMN TUBE
• NEVER IN ANY CASE SHOULD UNDUE STRESS BE APPLIED TO STEERING COLUMN IN AXIAL DIRECTION.
• WHEN INSTALLING, DO NOT APPLY BENDING FORCE TO STEERING COLUMN.

CROSS ROD

SIDE ROD

SIDE ROD CLAMP   T 11-17 (1.1-1.7, 8-12)

BALL JOINT
T 54-98 (5.5-10.0, 40-72) TO KNUCKLE ARM

STEERING GEAR
T 84-96 (8.6-9.8, 62-71) TO FRAME
STEERING WHEEL COLUMN AND STEERING LOCK WHEN REMOVING AND INSTALLING, DISCONNECT BATTERY GROUND CABLE.
EACH DUST COVER
WHEN REMOVING AND INSTALLING, BE CAREFUL NOT TO DAMAGE DUST COVER.

GEAR ARM
T 127-147 (13-15, 94-108) TO SECTOR SHAFT

Ⓣ : N·m (KG-M, FT-LB)
ⓂⒼ : MULTI-PURPOSE GREASE POINTS

1980–82 steering linkage

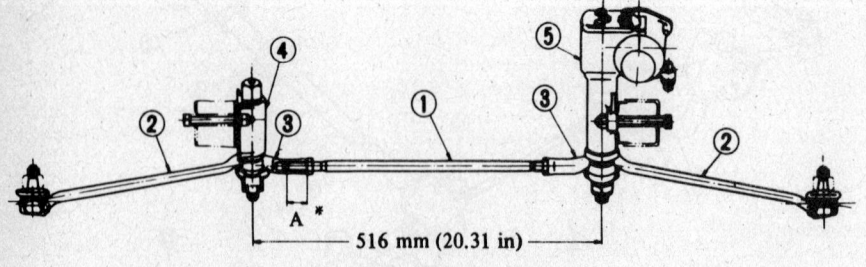

516 mm (20.31 in)

*After adjustment of toe-in, be sure that dimension "A" at both ends of cross rod is not less than 20 mm (0.79 in).

1. Cross rod (tie rod)   4. Idler arm assembly
2. Side rod   5. Steering gear assembly
3. Ball socket

Steering linkage installation dimensions, all models

Steering Gear

REMOVAL AND INSTALLATION

1. Raise and support the truck on jack stands.
2. Unbolt the wormshaft at the rubber coupling.
3. Matchmark the idler arm and sector shaft, and with the wheels in a straight ahead position, remove the idler arm-to-sector shaft nut and remove the idler arm with a puller.
4. Unbolt and remove the gear from the frame.
5. Installation is the reverse of removal. Torque the wormshaft coupling bolt to 29–36 ft. lbs.; the idle arm nut to 94–108 ft. lbs. and the gear-to-frame bolts to 62–71 ft. lbs.

BRAKE SYSTEM

Adjustment

DISC BRAKES

The front disc brakes are inherently self-adjusting. No adjustments are either necessary or possible.

DRUM BRAKES

1. Jack up the wheel to be adjusted until it completely clears the ground.

2. Make sure that the parking brake is completely released if the rear brakes are being adjusted.

3. Remove the rubber boot from the rear of the brake backing plate.

4. Lightly tap the adjuster housing forward with a hammer and screwdriver.

5. Turn the adjuster wheel downward with a screwdriver to spread the brake shoes. Stop turning the adjuster wheel when the brake drum is locked and the wheel cannot be turned by hand.

6. Turn the adjuster wheel upward, backing off the shoes from the brake drum 12 notches, to obtain the correct clearance between the brake shoes and drum. Turn the wheel to make sure that the brake drum turns without dragging.

7. Install the rubber boot.

BRAKE PEDAL ADJUSTMENT

The trucks are equipped with an adjustable master cylinder pushrod for setting free-play.

1. Adjust the height of the stop light switch so that the top surface of the brake pedal is 5.5 in. off the surface of the floor board (without rugs) in 1975. The distance should be 5.8 in., 1976–77, 6.06 in., 1978–79, and 6.7 in. for 1980–82. Tighten the stop light switch locknut.

2. Adjust the length of the master cylinder pushrod (booster pushrod on vehicles so equipped) clevis so that 0.04–0.12 in. of free-play exists between the brake pedal and the pushrod in 1975. Free-play should be 0.024–0.047 in., 1976–77, or 0.04–0.20 in., 1978–82.

3. Operate the brake pedal to make sure that it operates freely with no noise or interference.

Master Cylinder

REMOVAL AND INSTALLATION

1. On a truck not equipped with power brakes, remove the cotter pin, pull out the

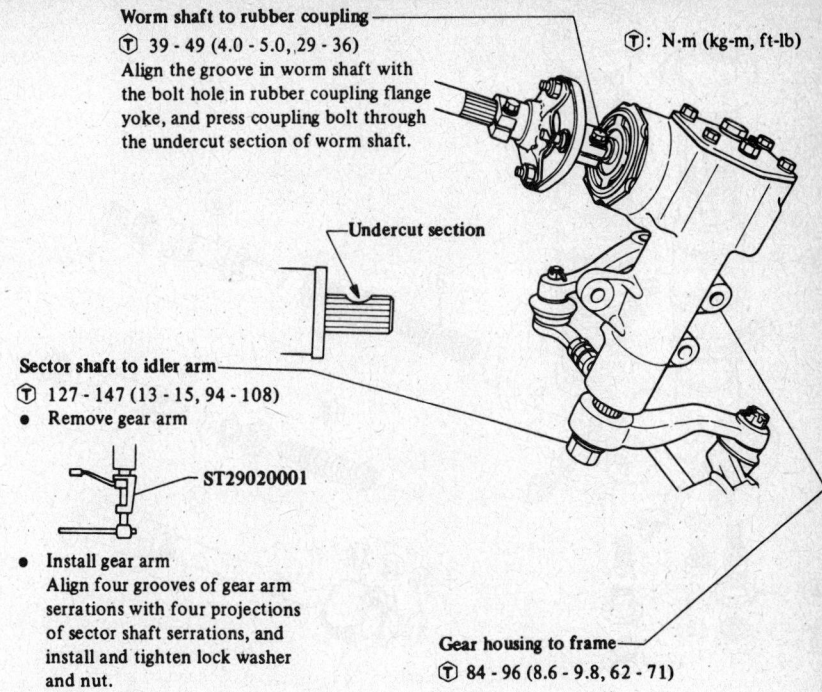

Worm shaft to rubber coupling
Ⓣ 39 - 49 (4.0 - 5.0, 29 - 36)
Align the groove in worm shaft with the bolt hole in rubber coupling flange yoke, and press coupling bolt through the undercut section of worm shaft.

Undercut section

Sector shaft to idler arm
Ⓣ 127 - 147 (13 - 15, 94 - 108)
● Remove gear arm

ST29020001

● Install gear arm
Align four grooves of gear arm serrations with four projections of sector shaft serrations, and install and tighten lock washer and nut.

Ⓣ: N·m (kg-m, ft-lb)

Gear housing to frame
Ⓣ 84 - 96 (8.6 - 9.8, 62 - 71)

Steering gear removal and installation

clevis pin, and separate the brake pedal from the master cylinder pushrod.

2. Place a number of cloths or a container under the master cylinder to catch the brake fluid. Disconnect the brake tubes from the master cylinder; use a flare nut wrench if one is available.

NOTE: Brake fluid eats paint; wipe up any spilled fluid immediately, then flush the area with clear water.

3. Remove the master cylinder securing nuts and withdraw the master cylinder from the firewall or power brake booster.

4. Install the master cylinder in the reverse order of removal and bleed the brake hydraulic system.

OVERHAUL

This is a tedious, time-consuming job. You can save yourself a lot of trouble by buying a rebuilt master cylinder from your dealer or parts supply house. The small difference in price between a rebuilding kit and a rebuilt part usually makes it more economical, in terms of time and work, to buy the rebuilt part.

NOTE: Datsun has two suppliers for brake parts: Nabco and Tokico. These parts are not interchangeable. Be certain to get the correct parts for the model installed on your truck. The manufacturer's name is clearly stamped on the part.

1. Remove the master cylinder from the vehicle.

2. Remove the reservoir caps and filters and drain the brake fluid.

3. Withdraw the pushrod and remove the rubber dust boot from the open end of the master cylinder.

4. Pry the piston stopper snap-ring from the open end of the master cylinder with a screwdriver.

5. Remove the stopper screw and washer from the bottom of the master cylinder and then remove the primary and secondary piston assemblies from the master cylinder bore.

6. Remove the caps on the underside of the master cylinder to gain access to the check valves for cleaning.

7. Discard all used rubber parts and gaskets. These parts should be replaced with new components which are usually contained in rebuilding kits.

NOTE: Never remove the master cylinder reservoir tanks. If they are removed for any reason, they must be replaced with new ones.

8. Clean all of the parts in clean brake fluid.

9. Check the cylinder bore and piston for wear, scoring, corrosion, or any other damage. The piston and cylinder bore can be dressed with crocus cloth soaked in brake fluid. Move the crocus cloth around the cylinder bore, not in and out. Do the same to the piston, if necessary. Wash both the cylinder bore and the piston in clean brake fluid after cleaning them with crocus cloth.

10. Check the piston-to-cylinder bore clearance; it should measure less than 0.15 mm (0.0059 in.) for all models. If greater clearance exists, replace the piston, or cylinder, or both. The cylinder bore diameter should be 19.05 mm (¾ in.) through 1977, 20.64 mm (¹³/₁₆ in.), 1978–79, or 22.23

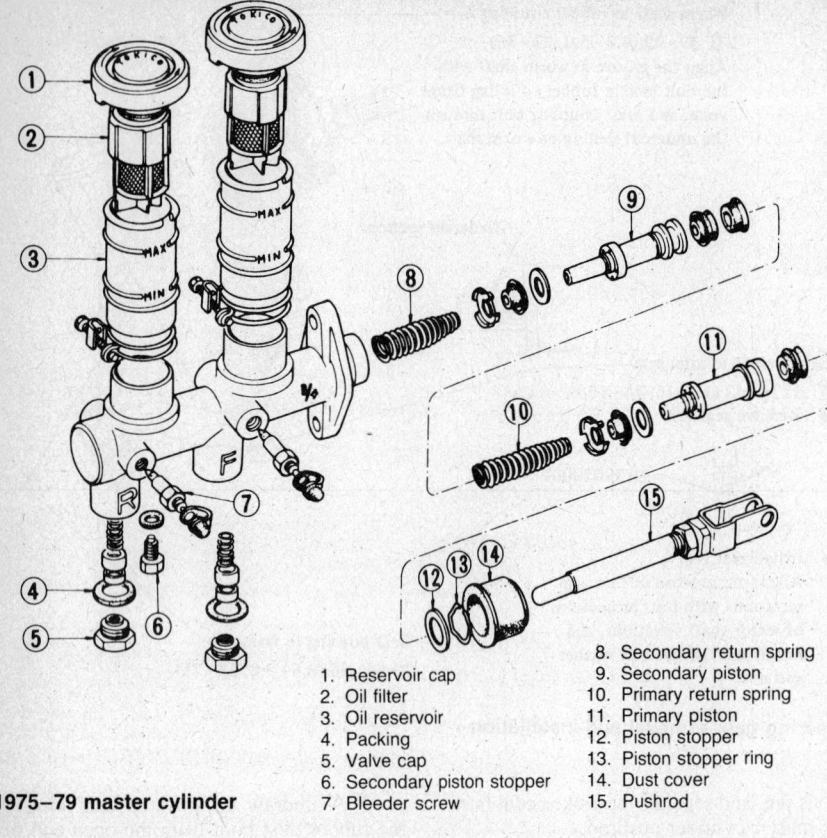

1. Reservoir cap
2. Oil filter
3. Oil reservoir
4. Packing
5. Valve cap
6. Secondary piston stopper
7. Bleeder screw
8. Secondary return spring
9. Secondary piston
10. Primary return spring
11. Primary piston
12. Piston stopper
13. Piston stopper ring
14. Dust cover
15. Pushrod

1975–79 master cylinder

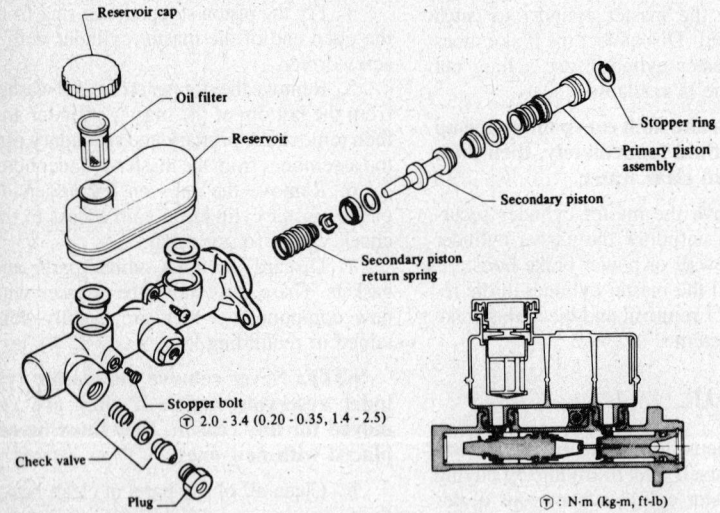

Reservoir cap

Oil filter

Reservoir

Stopper ring

Primary piston assembly

Secondary piston

Secondary piston return spring

Stopper bolt
Ⓣ 2.0 - 3.4 (0.20 - 0.35, 1.4 - 2.5)

Check valve

Plug
Ⓣ 44 - 54 (4.5 - 5.5, 33 - 40)

Ⓣ : N·m (kg-m, ft-lb)

1980–82 master cylinder

mm (⅞ in.) for 1980–82.

11. Assemble the master cylinder in the reverse order of removal. Soak all of the components in clean brake fluid before assembling them. Clamp the master cylinder in a vise. Fill the reservoir(s) with fresh fluid, and pump the piston with a screwdriver until fluid squirts from the outlet ports. Install the master cylinder and bleed the brakes.

NLSV

The Nissan Load Sensing Valve is a proportioning valve installed between the master cylinder and the brakes. It limits fluid pressure to the rear brakes to prevent rear wheel lock-up. The valve is not rebuildable, and must be replaced as an assembly if defective. It should be replaced if, in a

stop on dry pavement from 30 mph, the rear wheels lock prior to the front wheels (although ideally, no wheel will lock).

Bleeding

The purpose of bleeding the brakes is to expel air trapped in the hydraulic system. The system must be bled whenever the pedal feels spongy, indicating that compressible air has entered the system. It must also be bled whenever the system has been opened or repaired. You will need a helper for this job.

—————— CAUTION ——————
Never reuse brake fluid which has been bled from the brake system.

1. The sequence for bleeding is as follows:
1975: Master cylinder front, master cylinder rear, then the right rear, left rear, right front, left front. 1976–82: Master cylinder front, master cylinder rear, NLSV front, right front, left front, left rear, right rear, NLSV rear, NLSV center.

It is not necessary to run the engine with a vacuum booster.

2. Clean all the bleeder screws. You may want to give each one a shot of a penetrating lubricant to loosen it up; seizure is a common problem with bleeder screws, which then break off, sometimes requiring replacement of the part to which they are attached.

3. Fill the master cylinder with DOT 3 brake fluid.

NOTE: Brake fluid picks up moisture from the air. Don't leave the master cylinder or the fluid container uncovered any longer than necessary. Be careful— brake fluid eats paint.

Check the level of the fluid often when bleeding and refill the reservoirs as necessary. Don't let them run dry, or you will have to repeat the process.

4. Attach a length of clear vinyl tubing to the bleeder screw on the wheel cylinder (or master cylinder). Insert the other end of the tube into a clear, clean jar half filled with brake fluid.

5. Have your helper slowly depress the brake pedal. As this is done, open the bleeder screw ⅓–½ of a turn, and allow the fluid to run through the tube. Then close the bleeder screw before the pedal reaches the end of its travel. Have your assistant slowly release the pedal. Repeat this process until no air bubbles appear in the expelled fluid.

NOTE: If the brake pedal is depressed too fast, small air bubbles will form in the brake fluid.

6. Repeat the procedure on the other three brakes, checking the level of fluid in the cylinder reservoirs often.

Disc Pads

INSPECTION

The pads should be removed so that the thickness of the remaining friction material can be measured. If the pads are less than 2 mm (0.08 in.) thick, they must be replaced. This measurement may disagree with your state inspection laws.

NOTE: Always replace all pads on both wheels at the same time. The factory kit includes four pads, clips, pins, and springs; all parts should be used.

REMOVAL AND INSTALLATION

1. Raise and support the front of the truck. Remove the wheels.
2. Remove the retaining clip from the outboard pad.
3. Remove the pad pins retaining the antisqueal springs.
4. Remove the pads.

NOTE: When replacing the pads, always check the surface of the rotors for scoring or wear. The rotors should be removed for resurfacing if badly worn.

5. To install, open the bleeder screw slightly and push the outer piston into the cylinder until the dust seal groove aligns with the end of the seal retaining ring, then close the bleeder screw. Be careful, because the piston can be pushed too far, requiring disassembly of the caliper to repair. Install the inner pad.
6. Pull the yoke to push the inner piston into place. Install the outer pad.
7. Lightly coat the areas where the pins touch the pads, and where the pads touch the caliper (at the top) with grease. Do not allow the grease to get on the pad friction surfaces.
8. Install the anti-squeal springs and pad pins. Install the clip.
9. Apply the brakes a few times to seat the pads. Check the master cylinder level; add fluid if necessary. Bleed the brakes if necessary.

Caliper

REMOVAL AND INSTALLATION

1. Remove and plug the brake tube.
2. Unbolt and remove the caliper from the spindle.
3. Installation is the reverse. Tighten the mounting bolts to 53–72 ft. lbs.

OVERHAUL

1. Remove the caliper.
2. Remove the pads.
3. Remove the gripper pin attaching nuts and separate the yoke from the caliper body.
4. Remove the yoke holder from the piston and remove the retaining rings and dust seals from the ends of both pistons.
5. Apply air pressure gradually into the fluid chamber of the caliper, to force the pistons from the cylinders.
6. Remove the piston seals.
7. Inspect the parts for wear or damage. Check the inside surface of the cylinder for scoring or wear, and replace the caliper as necessary. Minor damage can be cleaned up with crocus cloth, but deep pitting or scoring warrants replacement of the caliper. The piston should be examined for wear, but do not polish it with crocus cloth; it has a plated surface which will be damaged by sanding. Replace the piston as necessary.
8. To assemble, coat the seals and pistons with clean brake fluid. Install the seals into the cylinder bore.
9. Slide the "A" piston into the cylinder, followed by the "B" piston, so that its yoke groove coincides with the yoke groove of the cylinder.
10. Install the dust seal and secure tightly with the retaining ring.
11. Install the yoke holder onto the "A" piston and install the gripper to the yoke. If you lightly coat the gripper pins with soapy water, they will be easier to install.
12. Support the end of the "B" piston, and press the yoke into the yoke holder. This will require a good deal of force. Be careful to insert the yoke straight into the holder, to avoid cracking the yoke holder.

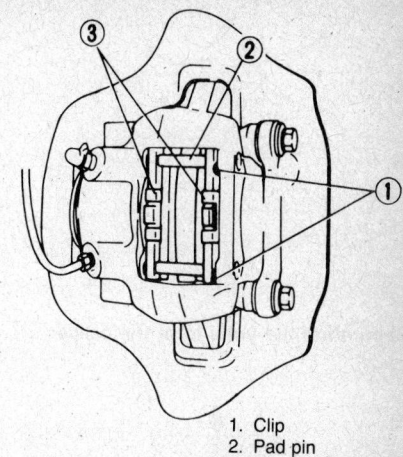

1. Clip
2. Pad pin
3. Anti-squeal spring

Removing the disc brake pads

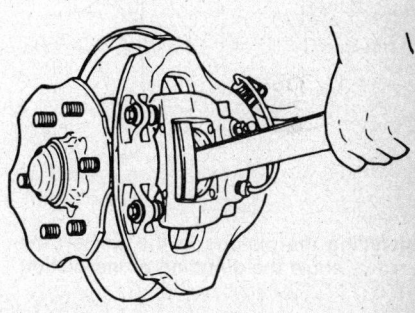

Pressing the piston into place

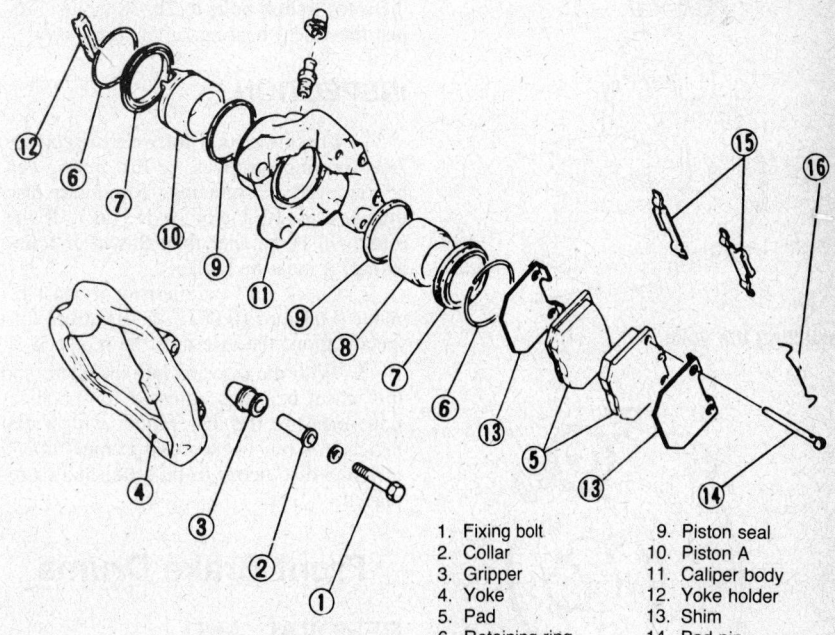

1. Fixing bolt	9. Piston seal
2. Collar	10. Piston A
3. Gripper	11. Caliper body
4. Yoke	12. Yoke holder
5. Pad	13. Shim
6. Retaining ring	14. Pad pin
7. Dust seal	15. Anti-squeal spring
8. Piston B	16. Clip

Disc brake caliper

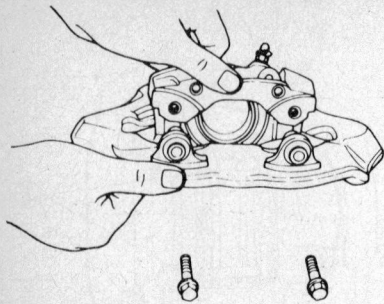

Separating the yoke from the caliper

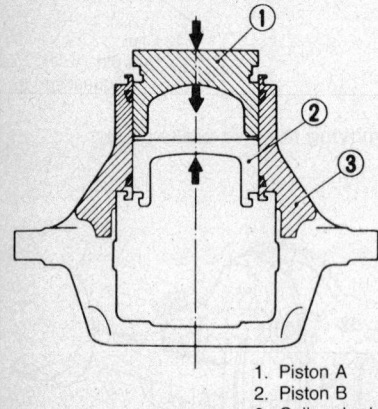

1. Piston A
2. Piston B
3. Caliper body

Installing the pistons in the caliper: the arrows show the direction of installation

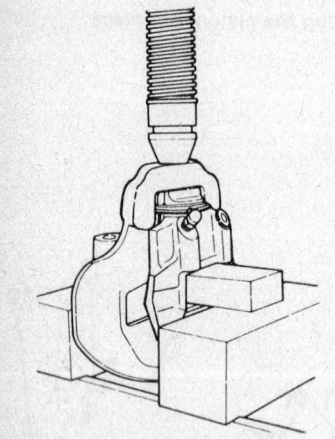

Installing the yoke

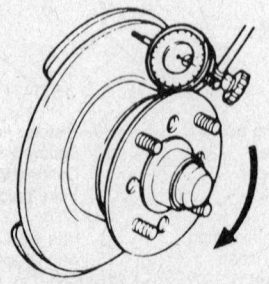

Measuring the disc runout with a dial indicator

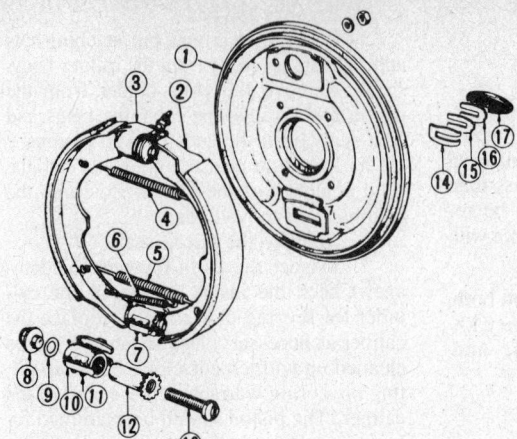

Front drum brake

1. Brake backing plate
2. Brake shoe assembly
3. Wheel cylinder assembly
4. Brake shoe upper return spring
5. Brake shoe lower return spring
6. After shoe return spring
7. Adjuster assembly
8. Adjuster head
9. Adjuster head shim
10. Lock spring
11. Adjuster housing
12. Adjuster wheel
13. Adjuster screw
14. Retaining spring
15. Lockplate
16. Adjuster shim
17. Rubber boot

13. Install the pads, anti-squeal springs, and pad pins and retain with the clip.

14. Tighten the gripper pin attaching nuts to 12–15 ft. lbs., and install the caliper on the spindle.

Disc (Rotor)

REMOVAL AND INSTALLATION

1. Remove the caliper.
2. Remove the hub cap, cotter pin, and adjusting nut.
3. Remove the wheel bearing nut and remove the hub and rotor.
4. Hold the hub in a vise and loosen the bolts to remove the rotor from the hub.
5. Installation is the reverse. Tighten the rotor-to-hub bolts to 28–38 ft. lbs. Adjust the wheel bearings after installation.

INSPECTION

1. Check the rotor for wear or scoring. Deep scoring, grooves, or rust pitting can be removed by refacing. Minimum disc thickness is 10.5 mm (0.413 in.). If the rotor will be thinner than this after refinishing, it must be replaced.
2. Check disc parallelism; it must be under 0.03 mm (0.0012 in.). If over this specification, the disc must be replaced.
3. With the disc and hub installed, and the wheel bearings adjusted to specification, measure the disc runout with a dial indicator. If runout exceeds 0.15 mm (0.0059 in.), the disc needs to be refinished or replaced.

Front Brake Drums

REMOVAL AND INSTALLATION

1. Jack up the front of the vehicle so that the wheel which is to be serviced is off the ground. Be sure to loosen the lug nuts before the wheel comes off the ground.

2. Remove the wheel and tire assembly.

3. Pull the brake drum off of the hub. If the drum cannot be easily removed, back off on the brake adjustment.

NOTE: Never depress the brake pedal while the brake drum is removed.

4. Install the brake drum in the reverse order of removal and adjust the brakes.

INSPECTION

After removing the brake drum, wipe out the accumulated dust with a damp cloth.

--- CAUTION ---
Do not blow the brake dust out of the drums with compressed air or lung power. Brake linings contain asbestos, a known cancer causing substance. Dispose of the cloth after use.

Inspect the drum for cracks, deep grooves, roughness, scoring, or out-of-roundness. Replace any brake drum which is cracked.

Smooth any slight scores by polishing the friction surface with fine emery cloth. Heavy or extensive scoring will cause excessive brake lining wear and should be removed from the brake drum through resurfacing. The maximum finished diameter of the brake drums must not exceed 10.059 in. The brake drum must be replaced if the diameter is 10.079 in. or greater.

Front Brake Shoes

INSPECTION

After removing the brake drum, inspect the brake shoes. If the lining is worn down so that the thickness is less than 0.0394 in., the brake shoes must be replaced.

NOTE: This figure may disagree with your state inspection laws.

If the brake lining is soaked with brake

fluid, it must be replaced. Also the brake drum should be sanded with crocus cloth to remove all traces of brake fluid and the wheel cylinders rebuilt. Clean all grit off the brake drum before installing it.

If the brake lining is chipped, cracked, or otherwise damaged, it must be replaced with new lining.

NOTE: Always replace the brake linings (shoes) in sets of two on both ends of the axle. Never replace just one shoe or both shoes on just one side.

Check the condition of the shoes, retracting springs and hold-down springs for signs of overheating. If the shoes or springs have a slight blue color, this indicates overheating and replacement of the springs and shoes is recommended. The wheel cylinders should be rebuilt as a precaution against future problems.

REMOVAL AND INSTALLATION

1. Jack up the vehicle until the wheel which is to be serviced is off the ground. Remove the wheel and brake drum.

NOTE: It is not absolutely essential to remove the hub assembly from the spindle, but it makes the job a great deal easier. If you can work with the hub in place, skip down to step 7.

2. Remove the hub dust cap.
3. Straighten the cotter pin and remove it from the spindle.
4. Unscrew the spindle nut and remove the adjusting cap, spindle nut, and spindle washer.
5. Wiggle the hub assembly until the outer bearing comes unseated and can be removed from the hub. Remove the outer bearing.
6. Pull the hub assembly off the spindle.
7. Unhook the upper, lower, and after shoe return springs, and remove them from the brake assembly.
8. Remove the brake shoes from the wheel cylinder at the top and the adjuster assembly at the bottom.
9. Clean the backing plate and adjuster assembly free of all dust and dirt. To remove the adjuster assembly for cleaning, remove the rubber boot at the back of the adjuster assembly and slide the adjuster shim, lockplate and retaining spring off the rear of the adjuster assembly.
10. Check the wheel cylinders by carefully pulling the lower edges of the wheel cylinder boots away from the cylinders. If there is leakage, the inside of the cylinder will be wet with fluid. If leakage exists, a wheel cylinder overhaul is in order. Do not delay, because brake failure could result.

NOTE: A trace of fluid will be present, which acts as a lubricant for the wheel cylinder pistons.

11. Apply brake grease to the adjuster

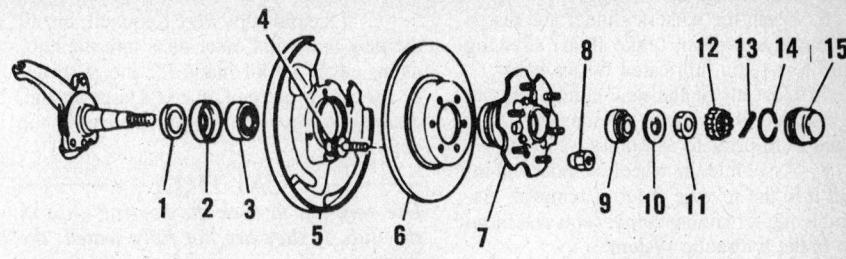

1. Spacer
2. Grease seal
3. Inner bearing
4. Hub bolt
5. Backing plate
6. Disc (rotor)
7. Hub
8. Lug nut
9. Outer bearing
10. Washer
11. Adjusting nut
12. Lock (castle) nut
13. Cotter pin
14. O-ring
15. Grease cap

2-wheel drive hub and bearings with disc brakes. Drum brakes are similar

assembly housing bore, adjuster wheel, and adjuster screw. Assemble the adjuster assembly with the adjuster screw turned all the way *in*. Apply brake grease to the sliding surfaces of the adjuster assembly, brake backing plate, and the retaining spring. Install the adjuster assembly to the backing plate in the reverse order of removal.

12. Before installing the brake shoes, apply brake grease to the notches into which the brake shoes fit on the wheel cylinder and adjuster mechanism, and brake shoe-to-backing plate contact surfaces.
13. Install the brake shoes in the reverse order of removal.
14. Install the hub, brake drum, and wheel in the reverse order of removal and adjust the wheel bearings and the brake shoes. Bleed the brakes. Lower the vehicle and roadtest it.

Front Wheel Cylinders

REMOVAL AND INSTALLATION

1. Jack up the wheel to be serviced.
2. Remove the wheel, brake drum, hub assembly, and brake shoes.
3. Disconnect the brake hose from the wheel cylinder.
4. Unscrew the wheel cylinder securing nut and remove the wheel cylinder from the brake backing plate.
5. Install the wheel cylinder in the reverse order of removal, assemble the remaining components, and bleed the brake hydraulic system.

OVERHAUL

NOTE: This is one of those jobs where it is usually easier just to replace the part rather than rebuild it. If you decide to rebuild the wheel cylinders, be sure you get the correct parts for your truck. Datsun obtains parts from two manufacturers: Nabco and Tokico. Parts are not interchangeable. The name of the manufacturer is on the part.

1. Remove the wheel cylinder from the

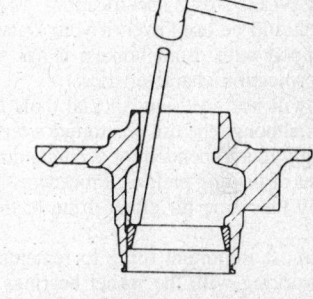

Drive worn bearing cups from the hub with a soft drift and hammer

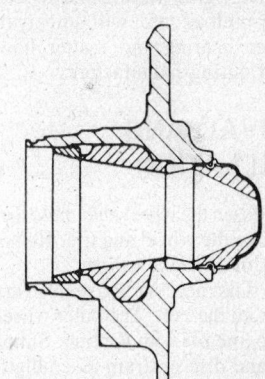

Fill the shaded portion of the hub and grease cap with wheel bearing grease. Also coat the cups with grease

backing plate.
2. Remove the snap-ring from the piston bore.
3. Remove the dust boot and take out the piston. Discard the piston cup. The dust boot can be reused, if necessary, but it is better to replace it.
4. Wash all of the components in clean brake fluid.
5. Inspect the piston and piston bore. Replace any components which are severely corroded, scored, or worn. The piston and piston bore can be polished lightly with crocus cloth. Move the crocus cloth around the piston bore; *not* in and out of the piston bore.

6. Wash the wheel cylinder and piston thoroughly in clean brake fluid, allowing them to remain lubricated for assembly.

7. Coat all of the new components to be installed in the wheel cylinder with clean brake fluid prior to assembly.

8. Assemble the wheel cylinder and install it in the reverse order of removal. Assemble the remaining components and bleed the brake hydraulic system.

Wheel Bearings

The following is for 2-wheel drive only. For 4-wheel drive vehicles, see the Front Drive Axle section.

Only the front wheel bearings require periodic service. The lubricant to use is high temperature disc brake wheel bearing grease meeting NLGI No. 2 specifications. (This grease should be used even if your Datsun is equipped with drum brakes; it has superior protection characteristics.)

You will not need any special tools for this job, although the use of a torque wrench is strongly recommended for accurate measurement of bearing preload. Procedures are basically the same for either drum or disc brakes.

The most important thing to remember when working with the wheel bearings is that although they are basically durable, in some ways they are remarkably fragile. Mishandling, grit, misalignment, scratches, improper preload, etc. will quickly destroy any roller bearing, no matter how well hardened during manufacture.

REMOVAL AND INSTALLATION

1. Loosen the wheel nuts, raise the truck, and remove the wheel and tire. Remove the brake drum or brake caliper.

2. It is not necessary to remove the drum or disc from the hub. The outer wheel bearing will come off with the hub. Simply pull the hub and disc or drum assembly toward you off the spindle. Be sure to catch the bearing before it falls to the ground.

3. From the inner side of the hub, remove the inner grease seal, and lift the inner bearing from the hub. Discard the grease seal.

4. Clean the bearings in solvent and allow them to air dry. You risk leaving bits of lint in the races if you dry them with a rag. Clean the grease cap, nuts, spindle, and the races in the hub thoroughly, and allow the parts to dry.

5. Inspect the bearing carefully. If they are worn, cracked, brinelled, pitted, burned, scored, etc., they should be replaced, along with the bearing cups in which they run in the hub. Do not mix old and new parts.

6. If the cups are worn, remove them from the hub, by using a brass rod as a drift.

To install:

7. If the old cups were removed, install the new inner and outer cups into the hub, using either a tool made for the purpose, or a socket or piece of pipe of a large enough diameter to press on the outside rim of the cup only.

— CAUTION —
Use care not to cock the bearing cups in the hub. If they are not fully seated, the bearings will be impossible to adjust properly.

8. Pack the inside area of the hub and cups with grease, according to the illustration given. Pack the inside of the grease cap while you're at it, but do not install the cap into the hub.

9. Pack the inner bearing with grease. Place a large glob of grease into the palm of one hand and push the inner bearing through it with a sliding motion. The grease must be forced through the side of the bearing and in between each roller. Continue until the grease begins to ooze out the other side through the gaps between the rollers; the bearing must be completely packed with grease. Install the inner bearing into its cup in the hub, then press a new grease seal into place over it.

10. Install the hub and rotor or drum assembly onto the spindle. Pack the outer bearing with grease in the same manner as the inner bearing, then install the outer bearing into place in the hub.

11. Apply a thin coat of grease to the washer and the threaded portion of the spindle, then loosely install the washer and adjusting nut. Go on to the bearing preload adjustment following.

BEARING PRELOAD ADJUSTMENT

1. While turning the hub forward, tighten the adjusting nut to 22–29 ft. lbs.

2. Rotate the hub a few more times to snug down the bearings.

3. Retighten the nut to 22–29 ft. lbs. Unscrew the adjusting nut 1/8 of a turn (45 degrees). Install the lock nut (castellated nut) and snug it down against the adjusting nut until one of its grooves lines up with the hole in the spindle. It is okay to tighten the adjusting nut up to 15 degrees to allow the lock nut holes to align. Install a new cotter pin, bending its ends around the lock nut.

4. Install the wheel and a couple of lug nuts. Check the axial play of the wheel by shaking it back and forth. The bearing free play should feel close to zero, but the wheel should spin freely. Be sure the brake shoes are not dragging against the drum, if your truck has drum brakes.

5. If the bearing play is correct, with drum brakes you can install the grease cap and the rest of the lug nuts. With disc brakes, remove the wheel, replace the caliper, then install the wheel and grease cap.

Rear Brake Drums

INSPECTION

The inspection procedures for the rear brake drums are the same as those previously outlined for the front brake drums.

REMOVAL AND INSTALLATION

Remove the rear brake drum in the same manner as outlined for the front brake drums.

Rear Brake Shoes

REMOVAL AND INSTALLATION

1. Jack up the vehicle until the wheel to be serviced is off the ground and remove the wheel and brake drum.

2. With a pair of pliers, remove the brake shoe hold-down anti-rattle spring retainers. Depress the retainer while rotating it 90° to align the slot in the retainer with the flanged end of the pin. Remove the retainers, springs, spring seats, and pins.

3. Open the brake shoes outward against the return springs and remove the parking brake extension link.

4. Disconnect the brake shoe return springs.

5. Remove the brake shoes from the backing plate. The secondary (after) brake shoe must be disconnected from the parking brake toggle lever after withdrawing the toggle lever clevis pin.

6. Remove the rubber boot from behind the brake backing plate and slide the adjuster shim, lockplate, and adjuster springs off the back of the adjuster assembly. Remove the adjuster assembly from the backing plate.

7. Clean the backing plate and adjuster assembly free of all dust and dirt.

8. Check the wheel cylinders as outlined in Step 10 of the front brake procedure.

9. Apply brake grease to the adjuster assembly housing bore, adjuster wheel, and adjuster screw. Assemble the adjuster assembly with the adjuster screw turned all the way *in*. Apply brake grease to the sliding surfaces of the adjuster assembly, brake backing plate, and the retaining spring. Install the adjuster assembly to the backing plate in the reverse order of removal.

10. Assemble the secondary (after) brake shoe to the parking brake toggle lever and adjust the clearance between the toggle lever and the brake shoe. Use the proper thickness toggle pin washer to adjust the clearance which should be 0.012 in. Toggle pin washers are available in the following thicknesses: 0.079, 0.091, 0.102, 0.114, and 0.126 in.

11. Before assembling the brake shoes

to the backing plate apply brake grease to the following areas: the brake shoe grooves in the parking brake extension link, the inside surfaces of the anti-rattle (retaining) spring seats, and the contact surfaces between the brake backing plate and the brake shoes.

12. Assemble the brake shoes to the backing plate in the reverse order of removal.

13. Install the brake drum and the wheel.

14. Adjust the brakes. Bleed the brakes.

Rear Wheel Cylinders

REMOVAL AND INSTALLATION

1. Jack up the vehicle, remove the wheel, brake drum, and brake shoes.

2. Disconnect the brake tube from the rear of the wheel cylinder.

3. Remove the wheel cylinder retaining nuts and remove the wheel cylinder from the backing plate.

4. Install the wheel cylinder and assemble the brake in the reverse order of removal and disassembly.

5. Bleed the brake hydraulic system.

OVERHAUL

The rear wheel cylinders are overhauled in the same manner as is outlined for the front wheel cylinders. The only difference is that the rear wheel cylinder bores are open at both ends and contain two pistons, piston heads, and dust boots.

Parking Brake Cable

ADJUSTMENT

1. Jack up the rear of the vehicle until the rear wheels clear the ground.

2. Adjust the rear brakes as outlined under "Brake System Adjustment."

3. Loosen the locknut at the parking cable lever assembly mounted on the driveshaft center bearing crossmember.

4. Turn the adjusting nut until the parking brake control lever operating stroke is between 3 in. and 4 in.

5. Release the parking brake and make sure that the rear wheels turn freely with no drag.

6. Lower the vehicle.

REMOVAL AND INSTALLATION

1. Fully release the parking brake control lever.

2. Loosen the adjusting nut at the cable lever mounted to the frame crossmember.

3. Disconnect the cable from the control lever.

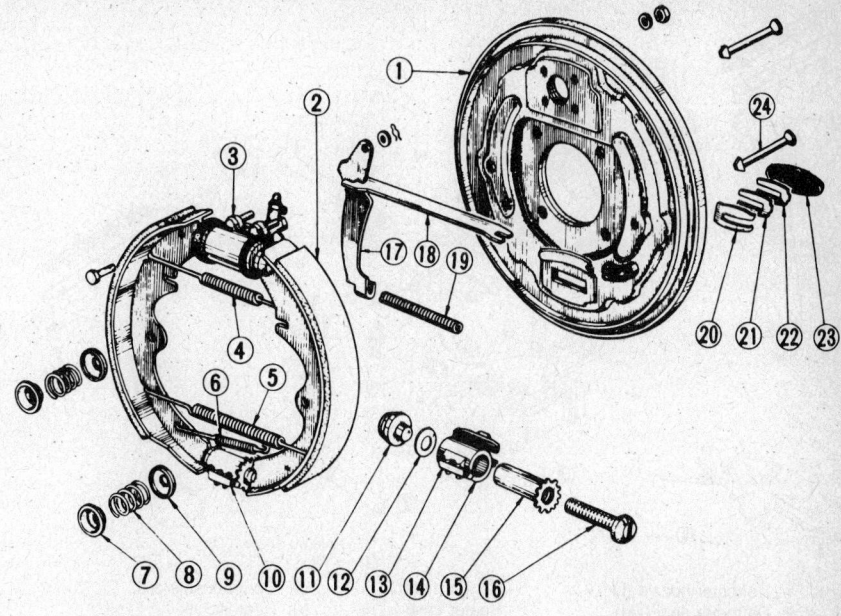

1. Brake backing plate	9. Spring seat	17. Toggle lever
2. Brake shoe	10. Adjuster assembly	18. Extension link
3. Wheel cylinder	11. Adjuster head	19. Return spring
4. Return upper spring	12. Adjuster head shim	20. Adjuster spring
5. Return lower spring	13. Lock-spring	21. Lockplate
6. After shoe return spring	14. Adjuster housing	22. Adjuster shim
7. Retainer	15. Adjuster wheel	23. Rubber boot
8. Anti-rattle spring	16. Adjuster screw	24. Anti-rattle pin

Rear brake

4. Remove the rear brake drums, and disconnect the parking brake cables from the parking brake toggle levers of the rear service brake assemblies.

5. Remove lockplate, spring and clip, and pull the parking brake cable out toward the cable lever.

6. Remove the cotter pin at the cable lever and disconnect the cable.

7. Install the cables in the reverse order of removal. Apply a light coat of grease to the cables to make sure that they slide properly. Adjust the parking brake cables.

CHASSIS ELECTRICAL

Heater Assembly

REMOVAL AND INSTALLATION

1975–79

1. Disconnect the battery ground cable.

2. Drain the engine coolant.

3. Remove the defroster hoses.

4. Remove the three cable retaining clips and disconnect the control cables from the valves and water cock.

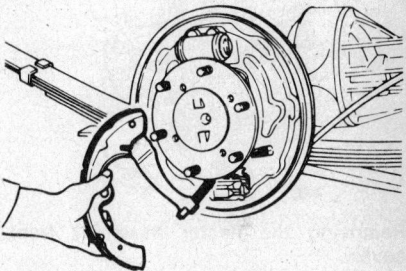

Removing the parking brake toggle lever from the secondary shoe

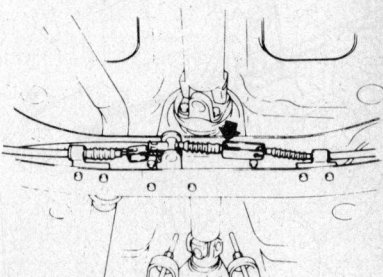

Parking brake adjusting nut

5. Disconnect the two fan motor leads from each connector.

6. Disconnect the two resistor lead wires from each connector.

7. Disconnect the water hoses from the heater core and water cock.

8. Remove the three heater housing mounting bolts and remove the heater assembly from the vehicle.

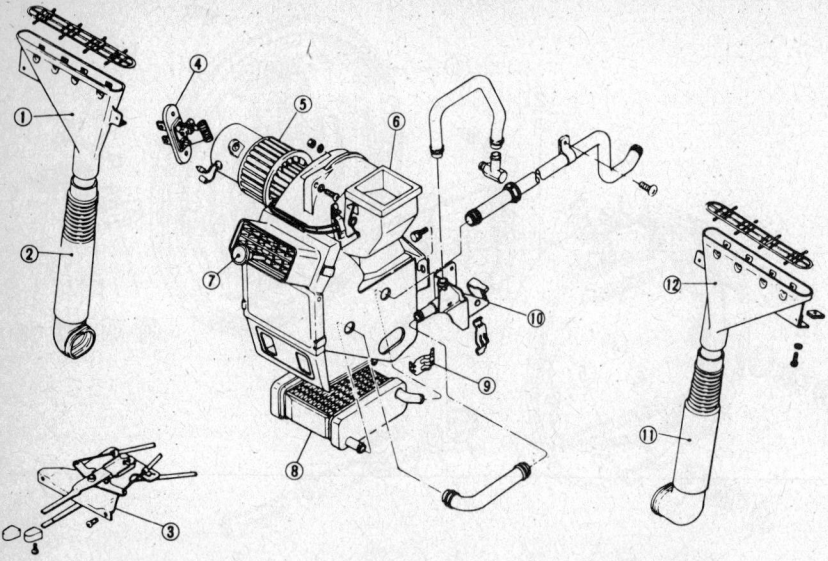

1. Defroster nozzle (LH)
2. Defroster duct (LH)
3. Heater control
4. Resistor
5. Heater motor
6. Heater case
7. Ventilator knob
8. Heater core
9. Control cable clip
10. Heater cock
11. Defroster duct (RH)
12. Defroster nozzle (RH)

1975–79 heater assembly

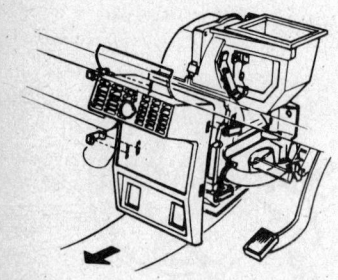

Removing the heater assembly front cover

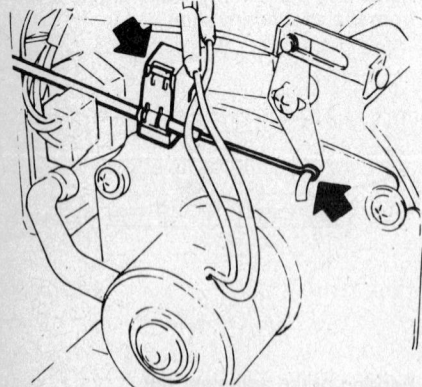

Control cable positioning

9. Install the heater assembly in the reverse order of removal.

1980–82

1. Disconnect the battery ground cable.
2. Drain the cooling system.
3. On models with air conditioning,

disconnect the heater hose from the engine.

4. On models without air conditioning, remove the heater duct and disconnect the heater hose at the heater.

5. Remove the console box and instrument panel assembly.

6. Disconnect the air intake control cable from the blower.

7. On models equipped with A/C, remove the blower. Remove the evaporator unit nuts and bolts, but do not remove the evaporator unit.

8. Remove the heater assembly.

9. Installation is the reverse of removal. Adjust the control cable for proper operation.

Blower

REMOVAL AND INSTALLATION

1975–79

1. Remove the heater assembly from the vehicle as previously outlined.

2. Remove the nine spring clips and disassemble the heater housing.

3. Remove the fan from the electric motor.

4. Remove the fan motor retaining screws and remove the motor.

5. Install the blower motor and heater assembly in the reverse order.

1980–82

1. Disconnect the battery ground.
2. Remove the package tray.
3. Remove the heater duct on models without air conditioning.

4. Remove the resistor connector and disconnect the control cable.

5. Remove the blower.

6. Installation is the reverse of removal. Adjust the control cable for proper operation.

Heater Core

REMOVAL AND INSTALLATION

1. Drain the engine coolant.
2. Remove the defroster hoses.
3. Disconnect the water hoses from the inlet and outlet pipes of the heater core.
4. Remove the four clips and front cover.
5. Remove the heater core from the heater housing.
6. Install the heater core in the reverse order of removal.

Radio

Observe the following cautions when working on the radio:

1. Always observe the proper polarity of the connections (positive to positive and negative to negative).

2. Never operate the radio without a speaker, to prevent damage to the output transistors. If a new speaker is installed, make sure it has the correct impedance (ohms) for the radio.

If a new antenna or antenna cable is used, or if poor AM reception is noted, the antenna trimmer can be adjusted. Tune the radio to a weak station around 1400kc. Adjust the trimmer screw until best reception and maximum volume are obtained. The trimmer screw for the factory-installed radio is located in the lower left corner of the rear of the radio case 1975–78 and above the left knob on the front of the radio in 1979. For best FM reception, raise the antenna to 31 inches. For best AM reception, raise the antenna to its full height.

REMOVAL AND INSTALLATION

1975–79

1. Pull the knobs off the radio control shafts.

2. Remove the radio retaining nuts and washer from the radio control shafts.

3. Remove the bezel plate from the front of the radio.

4. Disconnect the antenna cable and the power and speaker wires from under the instrument panel.

5. Remove the radio from the instrument panel.

6. Install the radio in the reverse order of removal.

1980–82

1. Disconnect the battery ground.
2. Remove the ash tray and heater/air conditioner control panel.
3. Disconnect the wiring plug at the back of the radio.
4. Remove the plug covering the mounting screws, remove the screws and pull the radio from the dash.
5. Disconnect the wiring harness and the antenna.
6. Installation is the reverse of removal.

Windshield Wiper Motor

REMOVAL AND INSTALLATION

1. Remove the wiper blades and arms as an assembly from the pivots. The arms are retained to the pivots by nuts. Remove the nuts and pull the arms straight off.
2. Remove the cowl top grille. It is retained by four screws at its front edge. Remove the screws and pull the grille forward to disengage the tabs at the rear.
3. Remove the stop ring which connects the wiper motor arm to the connecting rod.
4. Disconnect the wiper motor harness at the connector on the wiper motor body from under the instrument panel.
5. Remove the three retaining screws and pull the wiper motor outward and remove the motor from the vehicle.
6. Install the wiper motor in the reverse order of removal. The wiper arms should be installed so that the blades are .98 in. (25 mm) above, and parallel to, the windshield molding. If the motor has been run, be sure the motor and linkage is in its parked position before installing the wiper arms. To do this, turn the ignition switch on, and cycle the motor three or four times. Shut off the motor with the wiper switch (not the ignition switch), and allow the motor to return to the park position.

Wiper Linkage

REMOVAL AND INSTALLATION

1. Remove the wiper blade and arm from the pivot.
2. Remove the cowl top grille.
3. Remove the two flange nuts retaining the wiper linkage pivot to the cowl top.
4. Remove the stop ring which retains the connecting rod to the wiper motor arm.
5. Remove the wiper motor linkage assembly from the truck.
6. Install the linkage in the reverse order of removal.

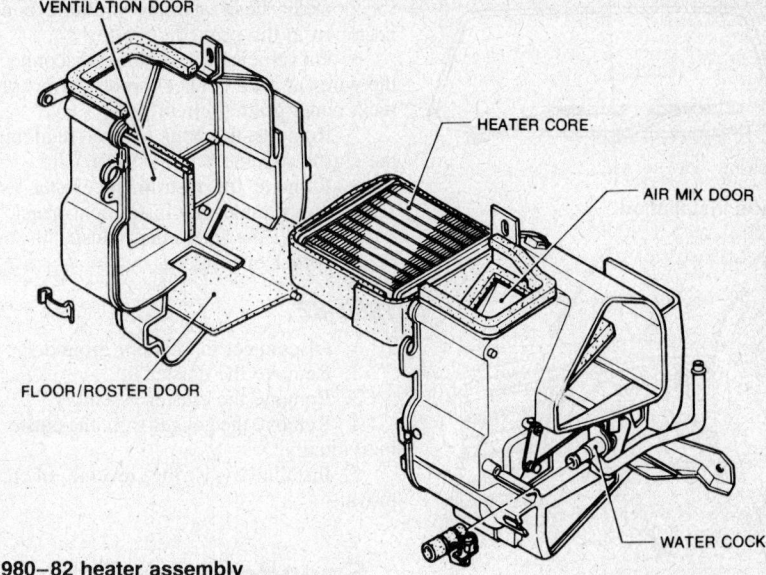

1980–82 heater assembly

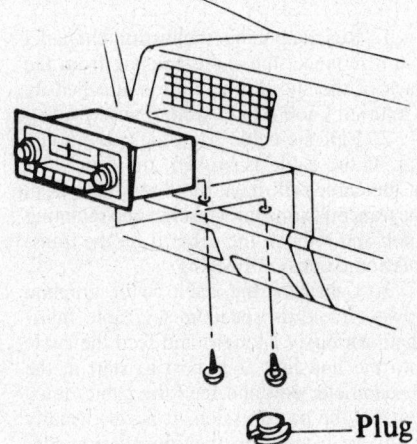

1980–82 radio removal

Instrument Cluster

REMOVAL AND INSTALLATION

1975–79

1. Disconnect the battery ground (negative) cable.
2. Working through the openings of the instrument cluster cover, remove the three screws retaining the cluster cover to the instrument panel and remove cover.
3. From underneath the instrument panel, remove the one screw retaining the cluster assembly to the lower instrument panel.
4. Withdraw the cluster lid slightly. Press the windshield wiper control knob in, turn it counterclockwise and pull it off the switch. Remove the headlight/parking light switch knob in the same manner.
5. From behind the instrument cluster, disconnect the speedometer cable at the

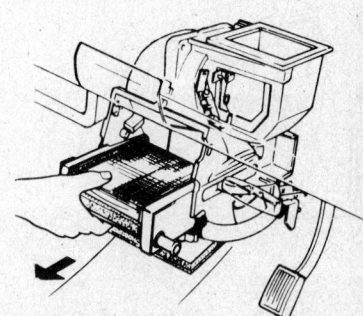

Removing the heater core

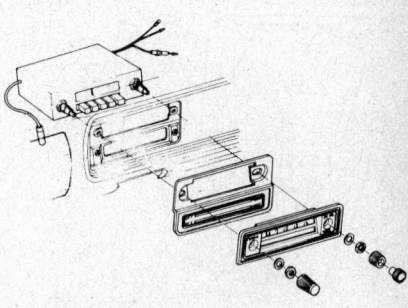

1975–79 radio removal

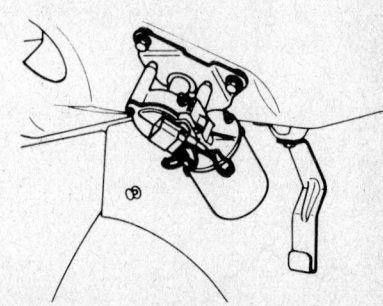

Windshield wiper motor

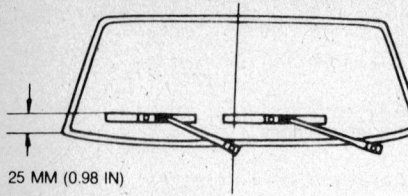

25 MM (0.98 IN)

Wiper arm installation

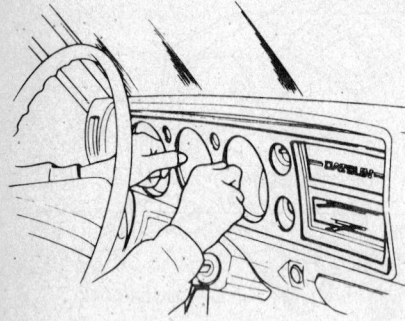

1975–79 cluster cover removal

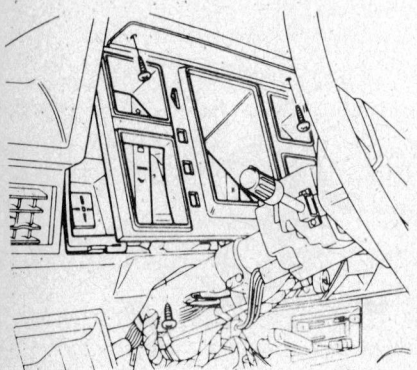

1980–82 cluster lid removal

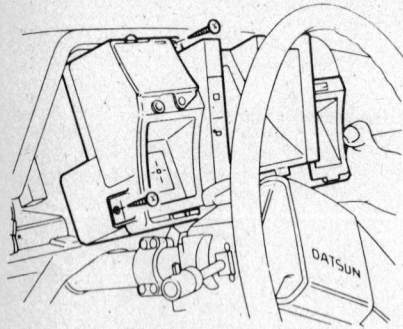

1980–82 cluster removal

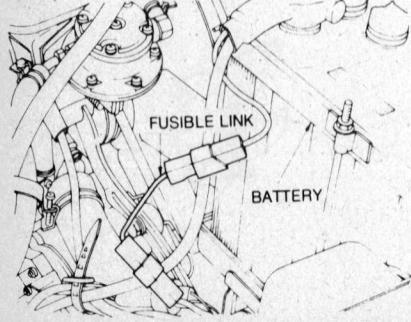

FUSIBLE LINK

BATTERY

Fusible link

speedometer head and the multiple connector from the printed circuit.

6. On vehicles with a clock, disconnect the wires at each connection on the instrument panel printed circuit.

7. Remove the four screws retaining the cluster assembly to the cluster lid.

8. Remove the instrument cluster assembly from under the instrument panel.

9. Install the instrument cluster in the reverse order of removal.

1980–82

1. Disconnect the battery ground.
2. Remove the cluster lid.
3. Remove the cluster assembly.
4. Remove the gauges from the cluster, individually.
5. Installation is the reverse of removal.

Speedometer Cable

REPLACEMENT

1. Reach up under the instrument panel and disconnect the cable housing from the back of the speedometer. It is attached by a knurled knob which simply unscrews.

2. Pull the cable from the cable housing. If the cable is broken, the other half of the cable will have to be removed from the transmission end. Unscrew the retaining knob and remove the cable from the transmission extension housing.

3. Lubricate the cable with graphite powder (sold as speedometer cable lubricant, curiously enough) and feed the cable into the housing. It is best to start at the speedometer end and feed the cable down towards the transmission. It is also usually necessary to unscrew the transmission connection and install the cable end to the gear, then reconnect the housing to the transmission. Slip the cable end into the speedometer, and reconnect the cable housing.

Headlights

REMOVAL AND INSTALLATION

1. Remove the radiator grille retaining screws and remove the radiator grille.

2. Loosen and remove, if necessary, the three retaining ring screws. Do not disturb the aiming adjusting screws.

3. Remove the retaining ring by rotating it clockwise.

4. Remove the headlight from the mounting ring and disconnect the electrical connector from behind the light.

5. Change the headlight and connect the wiring connector to the new light.

6. Place the headlight in position so that the three locating tabs behind the light fit in the three holes on the mounting ring.

7. Install the headlight retaining ring and tighten the retaining screws.

8. Install the radiator grille.

Fusible Links

A fusible link is a protective device used in an electrical circuit. When current increases beyond a certain amperage, the fusible metal wire of the link melts, thus breaking the electrical circuit and preventing further damage to other components and wiring. Whenever a fusible link is melted because of a short circuit, correct the cause before installing a new fusible link.

There is only one fusible link in Datsun pick-ups installed in the thinner of the two wires connected to the positive battery terminal. Replacements are simply plugged into the connectors in this wire.

—— **CAUTION** ——
Use only replacements of the same electrical capacity as the original, available from your dealer. Replacements of a different electrical value will not provide adequate system protection.

Fuses

Fuses protect all the major electrical systems in the truck. In case of an electrical overload, the fuse melts, breaking the circuit and stopping the flow of electricity.

If a fuse blows, the cause should be investigated and corrected before the installation of a new fuse. This, however, is easier to say than to do. Because each fuse protects a limited number of components, your job is narrowed down somewhat. Begin your investigation by looking for obvious fraying, loose connections, breaks in insulation, etc. Electrical problems are almost always a real headache to solve, but patience and persistence, coupled with logic, usually provide a solution.

The amperage of each fuse and the circuit it protects are marked on the cover of the fusebox, which is located under the instrument panel next to the steering column.

Flashers and Relays

The turn signal and four-way hazard flashers are located under the instrument panel on opposite sides of the steering column. The turn signal flasher is the larger of the two. Replacement is made by unplugging the old flasher and plugging in the new one.

Relays are used for the horn, headlights, wiper, heater, choke heater, catalyst floor sensor, air conditioner compressor, and transmission switches, although obviously not all relays are used on all models. All relays used are grouped together, and mounted on the right fender in the engine compartment.

Isuzu

INDEX

BEFORE SERVICING, SEE THE SAFETY NOTICE AT THE FRONT OF THE BOOK

ISUZU

GENERAL ENGINE SPECIFICATIONS

Engine Displacement cc (cu. in.)	Carb Type	Advertised Horsepower @ rpm	Advertised Torque @ rpm (ft. lbs.)	Bore and Stroke (in.)	Advertised Compression Ratio	Oil Pressure psi @ 1400 rpm
1800 (110.8)	2-bbl	80 @ 4800	95 @ 3000	3.31 × 3.23	8.5:1	57
2238 (136.6)	Diesel	58 @ 4300	93 @ 2200	3.46 × 3.62	21.0:1	55

CAPACITIES

Engine Displacement cc (cu in.)	Crankcase L (qts)	Transmission L (pts)			Transfer Case L (pts)	Rear Drive Axle L (pts)	Front Drive Axle L (pts)	Gas Tank L (gal)	Cooling System L (qts)	
		4 sp	5sp	Auto					Manual	Auto
1800 (110.8)	5.4 (5.72)	1.3 (2.7)	1.3 (2.7)	6.6 (14)	2.5 (5.2)	1.3 (2.7)	0.8 (1.7)	56 (13)	6.4 (6.7)	6.1 (6.4)
2238 (136.6)	4.8 (5.1)	1.3 (2.7)	1.3 (2.7)	6.6 (14)	2.5 (5.2)	1.3 (2.7)	0.8 (1.7)	56 (13)	6.4 (6.7)	6.1 (6.4)

GASOLINE ENGINE TUNE-UP SPECIFICATIONS

Engine Displacement cc (cu in.)	Spark Plug		Distributor		Ignition Timing (deg)		Intake Valve Opens (deg)	Fuel Pump Pressure (psi)	Idle Speed (rpm)		Valve Clearance (in.)	
	Type	Gap (in.)	Point Dwell (deg)	Point Gap (in.)	MT	AT			MT	AT	In	Ex
1800 (110.8)	BPR-6E511	0.040	Electronic		6B	6B	21B	3.0	800	900	0.006	0.010

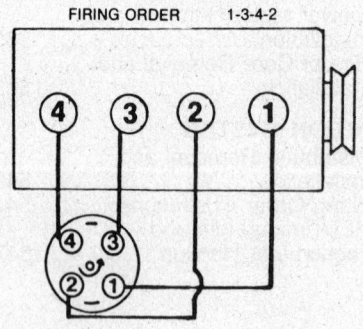

Gasoline engine firing order

DIESEL ENGINE TUNE-UP SPECIFICATIONS

Injector Opening Pressure (psi)	Low Idle (rpm)	Valve Clearance (in.)		Intake Valve Opens (deg)	Injection Timing (deg)	Firing Order
		Intake	Exhaust			
2133	750	0.016C	0.016C	16B	15B	1-3-4-2

CRANKSHAFT AND CONNECTING ROD SPECIFICATIONS

(All measurements given in in.)

Engine Displacement cc (cu in.)	Crankshaft					Connecting Rod		
	Main Brg Journal Dia	Main Brg Oil Clearance	Shaft End-Play	Thrust on No.		Journal Dia	Oil Clearance	Side Clearance
1800 (110.8)	2.2050	0.0008–0.0025	0.0117	3		1.9290	0.0007–0.0030	0.0137
2238 (136.6)	2.3593	0.0011–0.0033	0.0018	3		2.0837	0.0016–0.0047	0.0024

VALVE SPECIFICATIONS

Engine Displacement cc (cu in.)	Seat Angle (deg)	Face Angle (deg)	Spring Test Pressure (lbs. @ in.)		Stem-to-Guide Clearance (in.)		Stem Diameter (in.)	
			Outer	Inner	Intake	Exhaust	Intake	Exhaust
1800 (110.8)	45	45	35 @ 1.614	20 @ 1.516	0.0009–0.0022	0.0015–0.0031	0.3102	0.3091
2238 (136.6)	45	45	145 @ 1.535	44 @ 1.457	0.0015–0.0027	0.0025–0.0037	0.3150	0.3150

PISTON RING SIDE CLEARANCE

(All measurements given in in.)

Engine Displacement cc (in.)	Top Compression	Middle Compression	Oil Control
1800 (110.8)	0.0059	0.0059	0.0059
2238 (136.6)	0.0018–0.0028	0.0012–0.0021	0.0008–0.0021

PISTON RING GAPS

(All measurements given in in.)

Engine Displacement cc (cu in.)	Top Compression		Middle Compression		Oil Control	
	Min	Max	Min	Max	Min	Max
1800 (110.8)	0.008	0.016	0.008	0.016	0.008	0.035
2238 (136.6)	0.008	0.016	0.008	0.016	0.008	0.016

PISTON CLEARANCE

(All measurements given in in.)

Engine Displacement cc (cu in.)	Minimum	Maximum
1800 (110.8)	0.0018	0.0026
2238 (136.6)	0.0062	0.0070

TORQUE SPECIFICATIONS

(All readings in ft. lbs. unless noted)

Engine Displacement cc (cu in.)	Cylinder Head Bolts	Rod Bearing Bolts	Main Bearing Bolts	Crankshaft Pulley Bolts	Flywheel to Crankshaft Bolts	Manifolds	
						Intake	Exhaust
1800 (110.8)	72	43	72	87	69	13	15
2238 (136.6)	54–61	58–65	116–130	124–150	65–72	15	15

WHEEL ALIGNMENT SPECIFICATIONS

	Toe-In		Camber		Caster		Kingpin Inclination (deg)
	Range (mm)	Preferred (mm)	Range (deg)	Preferred (deg)	Range (deg)	Preferred (deg)	
2-wd	0 to 4	2	0 to 1P	30'P	0 to 1P	30'P	7°30'
4-wd	2 out to 2 in	0	5'P to 1°5'P	35'P	10'N to 50'P	20'P	7°25'

BRAKE SPECIFICATIONS

(All measurements are given in in.)

Master Cylinder Bore	Wheel Cylinder or Caliper Bore		Piston-to-Bore Clearance	Brake rotor or Drum Diameter		Minimum Lining Thickness	Brake Disc	
	Front	Rear		Front	Rear		Minimum Thickness	Maximum Run-out
0.875	—	1.00	0.006	10.00	10.00	0.039	0.453	0.005①

① Rate of change must not exceed 0.001 in. in 30°

ALTERNATOR AND REGULATOR SPECIFICATIONS

Manufacturer and/or Part Number	Alternator	Voltage Regulator						
	Output Amps @ Generator rpm	Charge Indicator Relay		Voltage Regulator			Regulated Voltage
		Back Gap (in.)	Point Gap (in.)	Back Gap (in.)	Air Gap (in.)	Point Gap (in.)	
LT140-126	40	0.036	0.020	0.015	0.014	0.012	13.8–14.8
LT150-144	50	0.036	0.020	0.015	0.014	0.012	13.8–14.8
LT150-131B	50	0.036	0.020	0.015	0.014	0.012	13.8–14.8

BATTERY AND STARTER SPECIFICATIONS

Engine Displacement cc (cu in.)	Battery			Starter						Brush Spring Tension (oz)
	Amp Hour Capacity	Volts	Ground	Lock Test			No Load Test			
				Amps	Volts	Torque (ft. lbs.)	Amps	Volts	RPM	
1800 (110.8)	50	12	N	Not Recommended						56
2238 (136.6)	80	12	N	Not Recommended						56

TUNE-UP

Electronic Ignition

AIR GAP SETTING

All models have electronic ignition. The only adjustment possible on this ignition is setting of the air gap.

1. Remove the distributor cap and O-ring.
2. Remove the rotor.
3. Use a feeler gauge to measure the air gap at the pick up coil projection. The gap should be 0.008–0.016 in. Adjust if necessary.
4. Loosen the screws and move the signal generator until the gap is correct. Tighten the screws and recheck the gap.

NOTE: The electrical parts in this system are not repairable. If found to be defective they must be replaced.

You can also check the signal generator by using an ohmmeter to determine its resistance. It should be 140–180 ohms. If the resistance is not correct, it must be replaced.

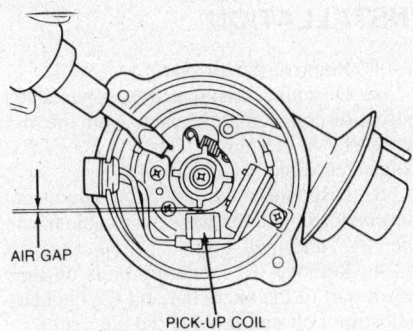

Adjusting the air gap

IGNITION TIMING ADJUSTMENT

NOTE: For diesel injection timing, see the Diesel Fuel System section.

1. Set the dwell of the breaker points to the proper specification.
2. Locate the timing marks on the crankshaft pulley and the front of the engine.
3. Clean off the timing marks, so that you can see them.
4. Use chalk or white paint to color the mark on the crankshaft pulley. This will help you see the timing mark when using the timing light.
5. Attach a tachometer to the engine.
6. Attach a timing light to the engine, according to the manufacturer's instructions. If the timing light has three wires, one is attached to the no. 1 spark plug with an adapter. The other wires go to the positive side of the battery and the black wire

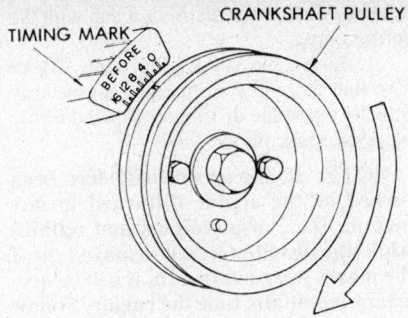

Ignition timing marks

is connected to the negative terminal of the battery.

7. Disconnect the vacuum line to the distributor at the distributor and plug the vacuum line. A golf tee does a fine job.
8. Check to make sure that all of the wires clear the fan and then start the engine.
9. Adjust the idle to the correct setting.
10. Aim the timing light at the timing marks. If the marks that you put on the pulley and the engine are aligned when the light flashes, the timing is correct. Turn off the engine and remove the tachometer and the timing light. If the marks are not in alignment, proceed with the following steps.
11. Turn off the engine.
12. Loosen the distributor lockbolt just enough so that the distributor can be turned with a little effort.
13. Start the engine. Keep the wires of the timing light clear of the fan.
14. With the timing light aimed at the pulley and the marks on the engine, turn the distributor in the direction of rotor rotation to retard the spark, and in the opposite direction of rotor rotation to advance the spark. Align the marks on the pulley and the engine with the flashes of the timing light.

Valve Lash

Valve adjustment determines how far the valves enter the cylinder and how long they stay open and closed.

NOTE: While all valve adjustments must be made as accurately as possible, it is better to have the valve adjustment slightly loose than slightly tight, as a burned valve may result from overly tight adjustments.

ADJUSTMENT

NOTE: The valves are adjusted with the engine cold.

1. Make sure that the cylinder head and camshaft retaining bolts are tightened to the proper torque.
2. Remove the camshaft carrier side cover.
3. Turn the crankshaft with a wrench on the front pulley attaching bolt or by bumping the engine with the starter or re-

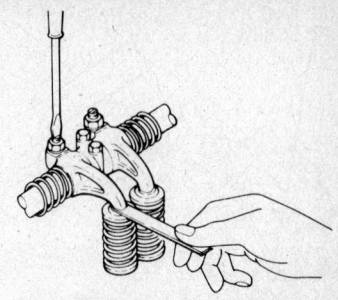

Valve clearance adjustment

Number of Cylinders	1		2		3		4	
Valve Arrangement	Exh.	In.	In.	Exh.	Exh.	In.	In.	Exh.
When piston in No. 1 cylinder is held at T.D.C.	0	0	0		0			
When piston in No. 4 cylinder is held at T.D.C.				0		0	0	0

Valve adjusting sequence

mote starter button until the no. 1 piston is at TDC of the compression stroke. You can tell when the piston is coming up on the compression stroke by removing the spark plug and placing your thumb over the hole and you will feel air being forced out of the spark plug hole past your thumb. Stop turning the crankshaft when the TDC timing mark on the crankshaft pulley is directly aligned with the timing mark pointer.

4. With the no. 1 piston at TDC of the compression stroke, check the clearance between the rocker arm and the camshaft with the proper thickness feeler gauge on nos. 1 and 2 intake valves and nos. 1 and 3 exhaust valves.
5. Adjust the clearance by loosening the locknut with an open-end wrench, turning the adjuster screw with a phillips head screwdriver and retightening the locknut. The proper thickness feeler gauge should pass between the camshaft and the rocker with a slight drag when the clearance is correct.
6. Turn the crankshaft one full turn to position the no. 4 piston at TDC of its compression stroke. Adjust the remaining valves: nos. 2 and 4 exhaust and nos. 3 and 4 intake in the same manner as outlined in step 5.
7. Install the camshaft carrier side-cover.

Idle Speed and Mixture Adjustment

In order to adjust the idle mixture you must first remove the plug that covers the mixture screw.

1. To remove the plug, first remove the carburetor and turn it upside down.
2. Remove the plug carefully with a hammer and screwdriver, (see illustration).
3. Reinstall the carburetor and adjust as necessary.

ISUZU

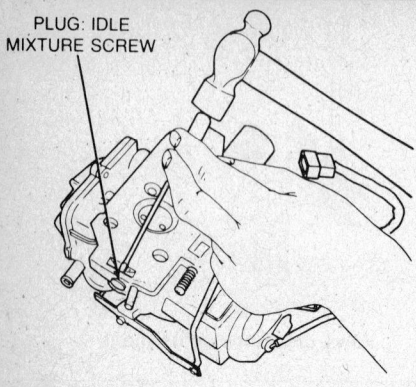

PLUG: IDLE MIXTURE SCREW

Removing the idle mixture plugs

4. Turn the mixture screw all the way in, and then back it out 2 turns (Federal) and 1 turn (California).

5. Readjust the idle if necessary.

ENGINE ELECTRICAL

Distributor

REMOVAL

1. Remove the high-tension wires from the distributor cap terminal towers, noting their positions to assure correct reassembly.

2. Remove the primary lead from the coil terminal.

3. Disconnect the vacuum line.

4. Unlatch the two distributor cap retaining clips and remove the distributor cap.

5. Note the position of the rotor in relation to the base. Scribe a mark on the base of the distributor and on the engine block to facilitate reinstallation. Align the marks with the direction the metal tip of the rotor is pointing.

6. Remove the bolt which holds the distributor to the engine.

7. Lift the distributor assembly from the engine.

INSTALLATION

1. Insert the distributor shaft and assembly into the engine. Line up the mark on the distributor and the one on the engine with the metal tip of the rotor. Make sure that the vacuum advance diaphragm is pointed in the same direction as it was pointed originally. This will be done automatically if the marks on the engine and the distributor are lined up with the rotor.

2. Install the distributor hold-down bolt and clamp. Leave the screw loose enough so that you can move the distributor with heavy hand pressure.

3. Connect the primary wire to the coil. Install the distributor cap on the distributor

housing. Secure the distributor cap with the spring clips.

4. Install the spark plug wires. Make sure that the wires are pressed all the way into the top of the distributor cap and firmly onto the spark plug.

NOTE: If the crankshaft has been turned or the engine disturbed in any manner (i.e., disassembled and rebuilt) while the distributor was removed, or if the marks were not drawn, it will be necessary to initially time the engine. Follow the procedure given below.

1. It is necessary to place the no. 1 cylinder in the firing position to correctly install the distributor. To locate this position, the ignition timing marks on the crankshaft front pulley are used.

2. Remove the no. 1 cylinder spark plug. Turn the crankshaft until the piston in the no. 1 cylinder is moving up on the compression stroke. This can be determined by placing your thumb over the spark plug hole and feeling the air being forced out of the cylinder. Stop turning the crankshaft when the timing marks that are used to time the engine are aligned.

3. Oil the distributor housing lightly where the distributor bears on the cylinder block.

4. Install the distributor so that the rotor, which is mounted on the shaft, points toward the no. 1 spark plug terminal tower position when the cap is installed. Of course you won't be able to see the direction in which the rotor is pointing if the cap is on the distributor, and make a mark on the side of the distributor housing just below the no. 1 spark plug terminal. Make sure that the rotor points toward that mark when you install the distributor.

5. When the distributor shaft has reached the bottom of the hole, move the rotor back and forth slightly until the driving lug on the end of the shaft enters the slots cut in the end of the oil pump shaft and the distributor assembly slides down into place.

6. When the distributor is correctly installed, the breaker points should be in such a position that they are just ready to break contact with each other. This is accomplished by rotating the distributor body after it has been installed in the engine. Once again, line up the marks that you made before the distributor was removed from the engine.

7. Install the distributor hold-down bolt.

8. Install the spark plug into the no. 1 spark plug hole and continue from step 3 of the distributor installation procedure.

Alternator

ALTERNATOR PRECAUTIONS

To prevent damage to the alternator and regulator, the following precautionary mea-

sures must be taken when working with the electrical system.

1. Never reverse battery connections. Always check the battery polarity visually. This is to be done before any connections are made to be sure that all of the connections correspond to the battery ground polarity.

2. Booster batteries for starting must be connected properly. Make sure that the positive cable of the booster battery is connected to the positive terminal of the battery that is getting the boost. This applies to both negative and ground cables.

3. Disconnect the battery cables before using a fast charger; the charger has a tendency to force current through the diodes in the opposite direction for which they were designed. This burns out the diodes.

4. Never use a fast charger as a booster for starting the vehicle.

5. Never disconnect the voltage regulator while the engine is running.

6. Do not ground the alternator output terminal.

7. Do not operate the alternator on an open circuit with the field energized.

8. Do not attempt to polarize an alternator.

REMOVAL AND INSTALLATION

1. Remove the air pump.

2. Disconnect the battery ground cable before disconnecting the cable from the alternator "A" terminal. This is a hot cable connected directly to the battery.

3. Disconnect the alternator circuit at the connector and disconnect the cable from the "A" terminal.

4. Remove the mounting bolts on the lower part of the alternator and the fan belt adjusting bolt and remove the alternator.

5. Install the alternator in the reverse order of removal and tighten the fan belt and air pump belt tension.

Regulator

REMOVAL AND INSTALLATION

1. Remove the negative battery cable from the battery.

2. Disconnect the electrical leads at the regulator, taking note of the positions in order to facilitate correct reconnection.

3. Remove the two mounting screws and remove the regulator.

4. Install the regulator in the reverse order of removal.

ADJUSTMENT

1. Remove the regulator from the vehicle and remove the regulator cover.

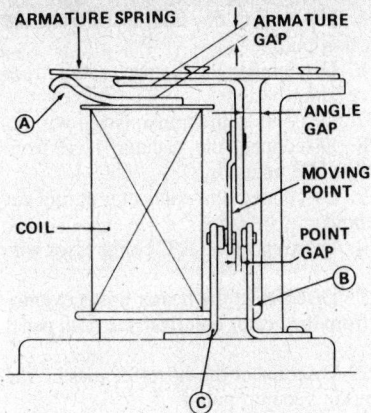

Voltage relay adjustment

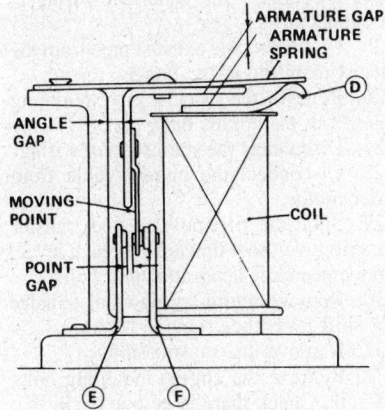

Voltage regulator adjustment

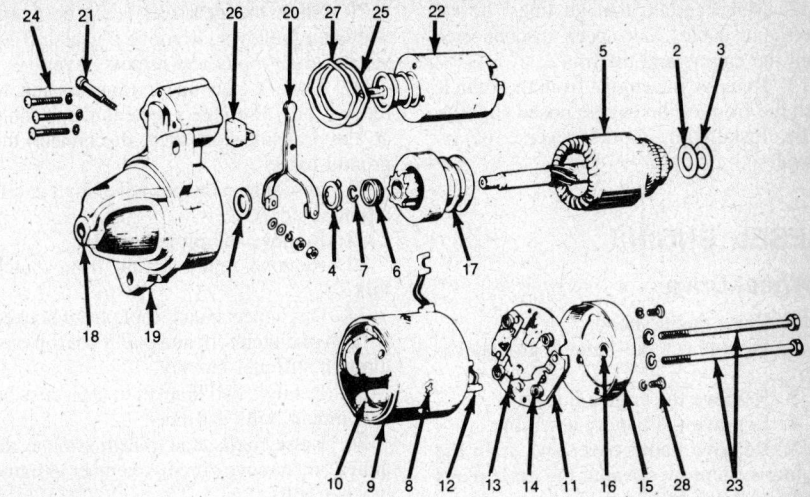

Starter motor

ISUZU

1. Thrust washer
2. Spacer
3. Washer
4. Stopper washer
5. Armature
6. Pinion stopper
7. Snap-ring
8. Field coil retaining screw
9. Yoke housing
10. Field coils
11. Brush holder
12. Brush (field coil)
13. Brush (ground)
14. Brush tension spring
15. Rear cover
16. Rear armature bearing
17. Clutch drive
18. Front armature bearing
19. Gear case
20. Shift lever
21. Shift lever pivot bolt
22. Solenoid switch
23. Through-bolts
24. Solenoid-to-gear case attaching bolts
25. Washer
26. Dust cover
27. Insulator
28. Brush holder-to-rear cover attaching screw

2. If the contact points are rough, dress them with fine sandpaper.

3. Check and adjust the gaps: core gap first, and then the point gap. Adjustment of the yoke gap is unnecessary.

4. Adjust the core gap by loosening the screws attaching the contact set to the yoke. Move the contact set up or down as required. Tighten the attaching screw.

5. Adjust the point gap by loosening the screw attaching the upper contact. Move the upper contact up or down as required.

6. Adjust the regulated voltage by means of the adjusting screw. Turn the adjusting screw in to increase voltage and out to reduce voltage. When the correct adjustment is obtained, secure the adjusting screw by tightening the locknut.

7. Install the regulator cover, reconnect the electrical leads and install the regulator.

Starter

REMOVAL AND INSTALLATION

1. Disconnect the negative battery cable from the battery.

2. Disconnect the starter wiring at the starter, taking note of the positions for correct reinstallation.

3. Remove the bolts attaching the starter to the engine and remove the starter from the vehicle.

4. Install the starter in the reverse order of removal.

BRUSH REPLACEMENT

1. With the starter out of the vehicle, remove the bolts holding the solenoid to the top of the starter and remove the solenoid.

2. To remove the brushes, remove the two thru-bolts and the two rear cover attaching screws and remove the rear cover.

3. Disconnect the brushes electrical leads and remove the brushes.

4. Install the brushes in the reverse order of removal.

STARTER DRIVE REPLACEMENT

1. With the starter motor removed from the vehicle, remove the solenoid from the starter.

2. Remove the two thru-bolts and separate the gear case from the yoke housing.

3. Remove the pinion stopper clip and the pinion stopper.

4. Slide the starter drive off the armature shaft.

5. Install the starter drive and reassemble the starter in the reverse order of removal.

ENGINE MECHANICAL

Engine Removal and Installation

GASOLINE ENGINE

1. Raise the hood and disconnect the battery cables.

2. Remove the skid plate and drain both the cooling system and the oil pan.

3. Remove the air cleaner assembly and vacuum hoses. Mark the vacuum hoses for reinstallation.

4. Disconnect all hoses, tubing and electrical leads from the engine and mark them for reinstallation.

5. Remove the radiator and fan blade assembly.

6. Disconnect the exhaust pipe from the exhaust manifold.

7. Raise the vehicle and, if equipped with a manual transmission, remove the clutch return spring and slave cylinder. Fasten the cylinder to the frame rail with a piece of wire.

8. Remove the starter motor and fasten it to the frame rail with a piece of wire.

9. Remove the flywheel cover pan.

10. Remove the bell housing bolts and support the transmission.

11. Lift the engine slightly and remove the engine mount nuts.

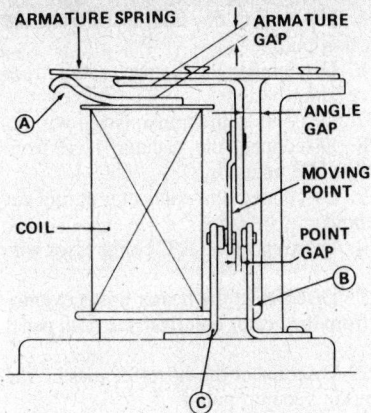

Voltage relay adjustment

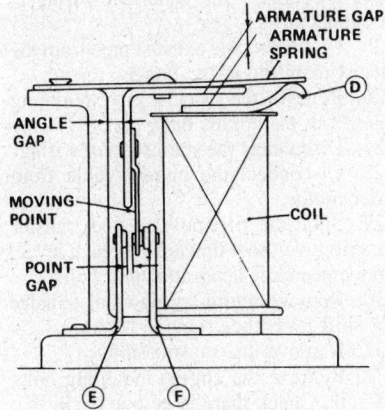

Voltage regulator adjustment

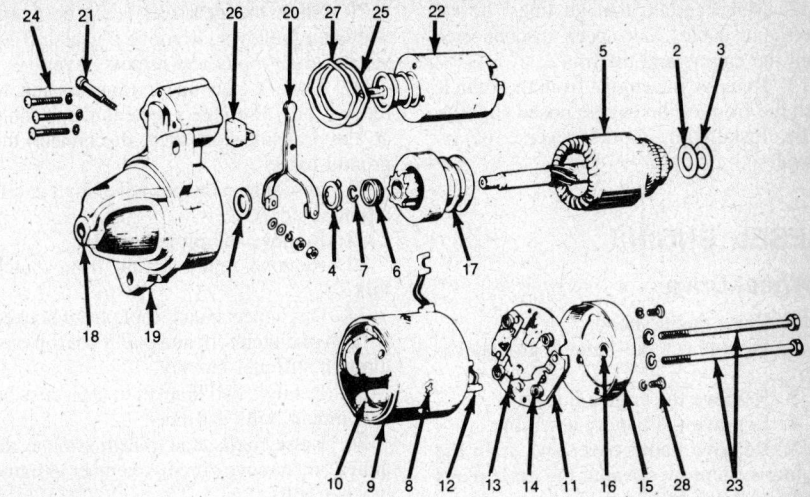

Starter motor

12. Make certain that all lines, hoses, wires and cables have been disconnected from the engine and the frame.

13. Remove the engine from the vehicle with the front of the engine raised slightly.

14. Installation is the reverse of removal.

DIESEL ENGINE

2-Wheel Drive

1. Raise engine hood.

2. Disconnect the battery ground cable.

3. Remove the engine hood.

4. Remove the battery assembly.

5. Remove under cover and drain the cooling system by opening the drain plugs on the radiator and on the cylinder block.

6. Remove the air cleaner assembly as follows:

   a. Remove the intake silencer.

   b. Remove the bolts fixing the air cleaner and loosen the clamp bolt.

   c. Lift the air cleaner slightly and disconnect the breather hose, then remove the air cleaner assembly.

7. Disconnect the upper water hose at the engine side.

8. Loosen the compressor drive belts by moving the power steering oil pump or idler (if so equipped).

9. Remove the cooling fan and fan shroud.

10. Disconnect the lower water hose at the engine side.

11. Remove the radiator grille.

12. Remove the radiator attaching bolts and remove the radiator.

13. Disconnect the accelerator control cable from the injection pump side.

14. Disconnect the air conditioner compressor control cable (if so equipped).

15. Disconnect the fuel hoses from the injection pump.

16. Disconnect the battery cable from the cylinder body.

17. Disconnect the transmission wiring.

18. Disconnect the vacuum hose from the fast idle actuator.

19. Disconnect the connector at fuel cut solenoid.

20. Disconnect the A/C compressor wiring.

21. Disconnect the heater hoses extending from the heater unit from the dash panel side.

22. Disconnect the hose for master-vac from the vacuum pump.

23. Disconnect vacuum hose from the vacuum pump.

24. Disconnect the generator wiring at the connector.

25. Disconnect the exhaust pipe from the exhaust manifold at the flange.

26. Remove the exhaust pipe mounting brake from the engine back plate.

27. Disconnect the starter motor wiring.

28. Disconnect the battery cable from starter motor.

29. Slide the gearshift lever boot upwards on the lever. Remove 2 gearshift lever attaching bolts and remove lever.

30. Place a pan under transmission to receive oil, disconnect speedometer cable at the transmission then disconnect the ground cable.

31. Disconnect the propeller shaft at differential side.

32. Remove the propeller shaft.

33. Remove return spring from clutch fork.

34. Disconnect clutch cable from hooked portion of clutch fork and pull it out forward through stiffener bracket.

35. Remove two bracket to transmission rear mount bolts and nuts.

36. Raise engine and transmission as required and remove (4) crossmember to frame bracket bolts.

37. Remove the rear mounting nuts from the transmission rear extension.

38. Disconnect electrical connectors at CRS switch and back-up lamp switch.

39. Remove the engine mounting bolt and nuts. Check that the engine is slightly lifted before removing the engine mounting bolt and nuts.

40. Engine removal:

   a. Check to make certain all the parts have been removed or disconnected from the engine that are fastened to the frame side.

   b. Remove the engine toward front of the vehicle by maneuvering the hoist, so that front part of the engine is lifted slightly.

4 Wheel Drive

1. Raise engine hood.

2. Disconnect the battery ground cable.

3. Remove the engine hood.

4. Remove the battery assembly.

5. Remove under cover and drain the cooling system by opening the drain plugs on the radiator and on the cylinder block.

6. Remove the air cleaner as follows:

   a. Remove the intake silencer.

   b. Remove the bolts fixing the air cleaner and loosen the clamp bolt.

   c. Lift the air cleaner slightly and disconnect the breather hose, then remove the air cleaner assembly.

7. Disconnect the upper water hose at the engine side.

8. Loosen the compressor drive belts by moving the power steering oil pump or idler (if so equipped).

9. Remove the cooling fan and fan shroud.

10. Disconnect the lower water hose at the engine side.

11. Remove the radiator grille.

12. Remove the radiator attaching bolts and remove the radiator.

13. Disconnect the accelerator control cable from the injection pump side.

14. Disconnect the air conditioner compressor control cable (if so equipped).

15. Disconnect the fuel hoses from the injection pump.

16. Disconnect the battery cable from the cylinder body.

17. Disconnect the transmission wiring.

18. Disconnect the vacuum hose from the fast idle actuator.

19. Disconnect the connector at fuel cut solenoid.

20. Disconnect the A/C compressor wiring.

21. Disconnect the heater hoses extending from the heater unit from the dash panel side.

22. Disconnect the hose for master-vac from the vacuum pump.

23. Disconnect the vacuum hose from the vacuum pump.

24. Disconnect the generator wiring at the connector.

25. Disconnect the exhaust pipe from the exhaust manifold at the flange.

26. Remove the exhaust pipe mounting brake from the engine back plate.

27. Disconnect the starter motor wiring.

28. Disconnect the battery cable from starter motor.

29. Slide the transmission and transfer gearshift lever boot upwards on each lever, remove gearshift lever attaching bolts.

30. Remove return spring from transfer gear shift lever then remove levers.

31. Remove the transmission.

32. Remove the engine mounting bolts and nuts. Check that the engine is slightly lifted before removing the engine mounting bolts and nuts.

33. Engine removal:

   a. Check to make certain all the parts have been removed or disconnected from the engine that are fastened to the frame side.

   b. Remove the engine toward front of the vehicle by maneuvering the hoist, so that front part of the engine is lifted slightly.

Cylinder Head

REMOVAL AND INSTALLATION

Gasoline Engine

1. Disconnect the negative battery cable, drain the cooling system and remove the air cleaner and hoses.

2. Remove the air pump.

3. Remove the alternator.

4. Disconnect the carburetor throttle linkage and fuel line together with the solenoid electrical lead.

5. Disconnect the exhaust pipe from the exhaust manifold.

6. Remove the six bolts retaining the camshaft carrier front cover and remove the front cover.

7. Remove the oil line from the secondary chain tensioner plug.

8. Remove the chain tensioner plug along with the tensioner spring.

9. Remove the bolt and plate washer retaining the timing (camshaft) sprocket.

10. Remove both upper secondary timing chain damper bolts, located in the front of the cylinder head.

11. Loosen both lower timing chain damper bolts.

12. Separate the timing (camshaft) sprocket from the camshaft, together with the chain.

13. Carefully separate the sprocket from the chain to prevent the timing sprocket pin from falling out.

NOTE: When removing the camshaft from the timing sprocket, the pin should be positioned in the top. Mark the position of the pin on the timing sprocket prior to disassembling the parts.

14. Hold the chain in position with a wire or cord.

15. Remove the 10 bolts retaining the camshaft cover and remove the cover.

16. Loosen the 12 camshaft carrier bolts evenly in progression and remove them. The camshaft carrier is under tension from the valve springs. Loosen all the bolts alternately in progression, so that a single bolt will not receive the tension of the valve springs. Care must be taken not to loosen the camshaft carrier locating dowel.

17. Loosen the sleeve nut on the air injection nozzle and remove the nozzle by turning it about 180°.

18. Remove the three bolts retaining the timing gear case to the cylinder head.

19. Loosen the cylinder head bolts in a progressional sequence.

20. Remove the cylinder head, gasket and O-rings.

Install the cylinder head in the reverse order of removal, as follows.

21. Position the cylinder head gasket on the block with the "Top" side up. Insert the O-rings into the oil ports.

22. Position a gear case-to-cylinder head gasket on the gear case, if necessary.

23. Install the cylinder head on the block and tighten the cylinder head bolts to specifications.

24. Tighten the three bolts attaching the timing gear case to the cylinder head.

25. Install the air injection nozzles. Do not tighten them securely at this time.

26. Align the setting mark on the camshaft thrust plate with the corresponding mark on the camshaft.

27. Position the O-rings to the camshaft carrier. Install these parts in position and lightly tighten the bolts retaining the dowels. Install the longest bolts in the position of the dowel.

28. Install the camshaft carrier bolts. Tighten the bolts alternately, in progression to 15 ft. lbs. to compress the valve springs evenly. Note that the camshaft carrier is also used to retain two portions of the air manifold bracket and PCV hose clips.

29. With the no. 4 cylinder at TDC of

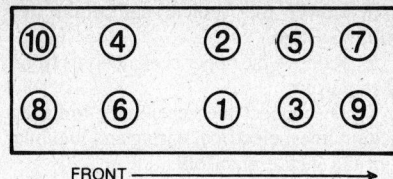

Gasoline engine head bolt torque sequence

the compression stroke, check that the setting mark on the camshaft and on the thrust plate are correctly aligned. If the setting marks are not in good alignment, make the necessary adjustment as follows:

a. If the setting mark on the camshaft and the thrust plate are not in alignment, attach the camshaft sprocket to the camshaft, insert the pin into a hole in the camshaft timing sprocket and turn the crankshaft until the marks line up. Then, bring the camshaft into a free state by removing the camshaft timing sprocket from the camshaft and, set the piston in the no. 4 cylinder to TDC of the compression stroke. If the engine has been turned in reverse in the course of this adjustment, make a final adjustment by turning the engine in the normal direction of rotation so that the marks are lined up, with the chain properly tensioned on the correct side.

b. When installing the camshaft timing sprocket on the camshaft, keep their mating faces free of foreign matter because the drive torque is relayed to the timing sprocket from the camshaft by means of frictional contact.

30. Bring the camshaft timing sprocket together with the timing chain, so that the punched mark on the sprocket is located at the 12 o'clock position. Assemble the sprocket to the camshaft.

31. Adjust the position of the camshaft timing sprocket, relative to the camshaft, so that the punched mark on the camshaft timing sprocket is turned up when the drive side of the timing chain is tensioned by pushing the chain tensioner shoe from the plug hole in the secondary chain tensioner. When the camshaft timing sprocket is correctly installed, the punched mark on the sprocket is brought to a position 6°20' from the top in the direction of rotation.

32. Hold the parts in their relative position. Look through each of the five holes in the camshaft timing sprocket to find a hole in alignment with the hole in the camshaft flange and insert the pin into that hole.

33. Tighten the camshaft timing sprocket attaching bolt, with the plate washer installed, to 33 ft. lbs.

34. Install the camshaft carrier front cover.

35. Install the secondary chain tensioner.

36. Assemble the remaining components to the engine in the reverse order of removal, working backwards from step 5.

37. Adjust the valves.

Diesel Engine

1. Follow the intake and exhaust manifold removal steps.

2. Remove the intake and exhaust manifold gasket.

3. Drain the cooling system by opening the drain plugs on the radiator and on the cylinder block.

4. Disconnect the upper water hose at the engine side.

5. Remove the cooling fan and fan shroud.

6. Remove the sleeve nuts and disconnect the injection pipes.

7. Remove the nozzle holder fixing nuts and remove the nozzle holder assembly.

8. Follow the rocker arm, bracket and shaft assembly removal steps.

9. Remove the pushrods.

10. Remove the joint bolt and disconnect the leak-off pipe.

11. Remove the 19 bolts fixing the cylinder head, then remove the cylinder head and gasket.

12. Install the cylinder head gasket with the TOP mark side up on the cylinder body by aligning the holes with the dowels.

13. Install the cylinder head.

14. Install the pushrod in position on the cylinder head.

15. Install the rocker arm assembly on the cylinder head. Tighten the bracket fixing bolts evenly in sequence commencing with the inner ones.

16. Follow the intake and exhaust manifold installation steps.

17. Install the cooling fan and fan shroud.

18. Connect the upper water hose to engine side.

19. Fill the engine cooling system.

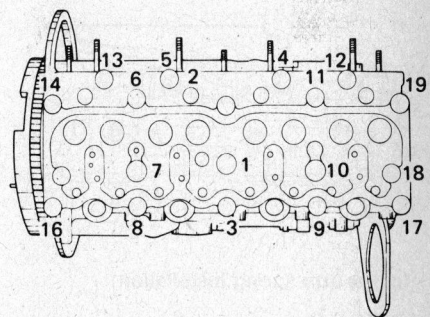

Diesel engine head bolt torque sequence

VALVE GUIDE REPLACEMENT

1. With the cylinder head removed from the vehicle and the valves removed from the head, drive the guides out toward the upper face of the cylinder head with a suitable driver. The valve guides cannot be driven out downward because they are secured in place with a snap-ring.

2. Lubricate the outside of the new valve guide with oil. Press it all the way into position, from the upper face of the cylinder head, until it is brought in contact with the

snap-ring. Allowable interference between the cylinder head and the valve guide is 0.0016 in.

NOTE: Standard interference on 1980 and later models is 0.0031–0.0047.

Valve Rockers

REMOVAL AND INSTALLATION

Gasoline Engine

1. Remove the camshaft carrier as outlined under Cylinder Head Removal.
2. Remove the rocker spring from the pivot and lift the rocker from the cylinder head. Be careful not to lose the rocker guide resting on the top of each of the valves.
3. Install in the reverse order of removal.

Diesel Engine

1. Remove the rocker cover.
2. Remove the 8 bolts fixing the rocker arm brackets in sequence commencing with the outer ones.
3. Remove the rocker arm, bracket and shaft assembly.
4. To install, follow the removal procedure in reverse order.
5. Tighten the bracket fixing bolts evenly in sequence commencing with the inner ones to 15 ft. lbs.

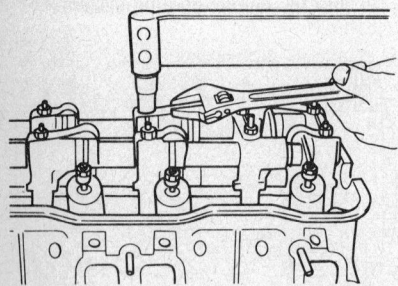

Rocker arm spring installation

Intake Manifold

REMOVAL AND INSTALLATION

Gasoline Engine

1. Disconnect the battery ground cable and remove the air cleaner assembly.
2. Remove the EGR pipe clamp bolt at the rear of the cylinder head.
3. Raise the vehicle and remove the EGR pipe from the intake and exhaust manifolds.
4. Remove the EGR valve and bracket assembly from the intake manifold.

5. Lower the vehicle and drain the cooling system.
6. Remove the upper coolant hoses from the manifold.
7. Disconnect the accelerator linkage, vacuum lines, electrical wiring and fuel line from the intake manifold.
8. Remove the retaining nuts and remove the manifold from the cylinder head.
9. Remove the lower heater hose while holding the manifold away from the engine. Remove the manifold from the vehicle.
10. Installation is the reverse of removal.

Diesel Engine

1. Raise engine hood.
2. Remove the bolts fixing the air cleaner and loosen the clamp bolt.
3. Lift the air cleaner slightly and disconnect the breather hose, then remove the air cleaner assembly.
4. Remove the 2 bolts and 4 nuts fixing the intake manifold.
5. Remove the intake manifold.
6. Installation is the reverse of removal. Torque the bolts to 15 ft. lbs.

Exhaust Manifold

REMOVAL AND INSTALLATION

Gasoline Engine

1. Disconnect the battery ground cable and remove the air cleaner assembly.
2. Remove the EGR pipe clamp bolt at the rear of the cylinder head.
3. Raise the vehicle and remove the EGR pipe from the intake and exhaust manifolds.
4. Separate the exhaust pipe from the manifold.
5. Remove the manifold shield and remove the heat stove.
6. Remove the manifold retaining nuts and remove the manifold from the engine.
7. Installation is the reverse of removal.

Diesel Engine

1. Raise engine hood.
2. Remove the bolts fixing the air cleaner and loosen the clamp bolt.
3. Lift the air cleaner slightly and disconnect the breather hose, then remove the air cleaner assembly.
4. Disconnect the exhaust pipe from the exhaust manifold at the flange.
5. Remove the 3 nuts fixing the exhaust manifold, then remove the engine hanger and exhaust manifold.
6. Installation is the reverse of removal. Torque the bolts to 15 ft. lbs.

Timing Gear Cover

REMOVAL AND INSTALLATION

Gasoline Engine

1. Disconnect the negative battery cable from the battery, drain the cooling system, and remove the alternator and air pump together with their respective mounting brackets and drive belts.
2. Remove the crankshaft pulley bolt and remove the pulley.
3. Remove the six bolts retaining the front cover and remove the front camshaft carrier cover.
4. Remove the 17 bolts retaining the timing gear case.
5. Remove the access plug and take out the bolt on the inner face of the gear case.
6. Insert the edge of a screwdriver into the cutaway portions on the outer rim of the timing gear case and pry it off the engine.
7. Install the timing gear case and the camshaft carrier front cover in the reverse order of removal and assemble the engine in the reverse order of disassembly.

Diesel Engine

1. Remove the radiator.
2. Remove the compressor drive belt by moving the powersteering oil pump or idler (if so equipped.)
3. Loosen the generator adjust plate bolt and fixing bolt, then remove the fan belt.
4. Remove the 4 bolts fixing the crankshaft pulley and remove the crankshaft pulley.
5. Remove the bolts fixing the timing pulley housing covers, then remove the covers.
6. Installation is the reverse of removal.

Timing Chains, Sprockets, and Tensioners

REMOVAL AND INSTALLATION

Gasoline Engine

1. Disconnect the battery ground cable, drain the cooling system, and remove the alternator and air pump together with their respective mounting bracket and drive belts. Remove the cooling fan.
2. Remove the timing gear cover.
3. Remove the oil line from the secondary chain tensioner plug.
4. Remove the chain tensioner plug with the tensioner spring.
5. Remove the bolt and plate washer retaining the camshaft timing sprocket.

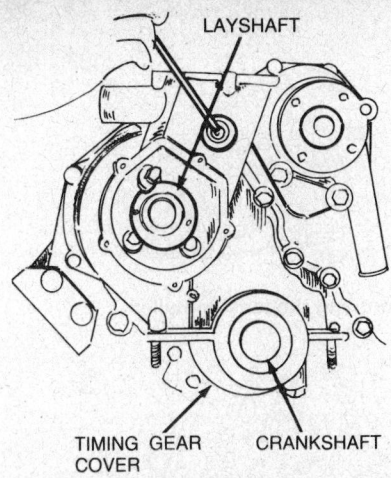

With the access plug removed, remove the bolt on the inner face of the gear cover

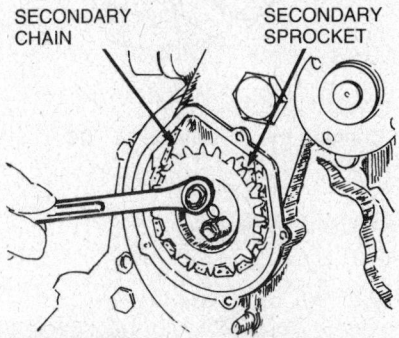

Removing the secondary timing sprocket from the jackshaft by installing the two screws in the holes provided and turning them alternately

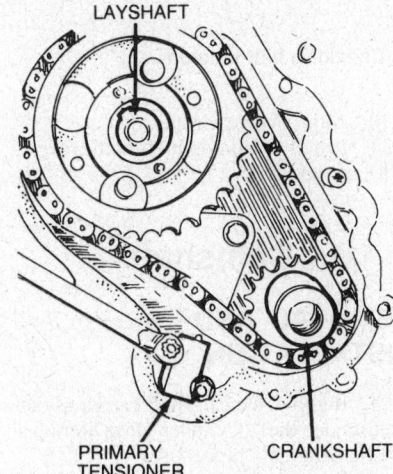

Removing the primary chain tensioner

6. Remove both of the upper secondary timing chain damper bolts, located in the front of the cylinder head.

7. Loosen both of the lower timing chain damper bolts.

8. Separate the timing sprocket from the camshaft, together with the chain. Then, carefully remove the timing sprocket from

the chain to prevent the timing sprocket pin from falling out. When removing the timing sprocket from the camshaft, the pin should be positioned at the top. Mark the position of the pin on the timing sprocket before disassembling the parts.

9. Remove the bolt retaining the secondary timing sprocket to the jackshaft. Remove the secondary sprocket by alternately screwing two bolts into the threaded holes in the timing sprocket one turn at a time.

10. Remove the secondary sprocket from the chain.

11. Remove the chain from the top, through the camshaft carrier front cover hole.

12. Remove the secondary chain tensioners from the cylinder head.

13. Remove the two nuts retaining the primary chain tensioner. Be careful to prevent the tensioner shoe from jumping out of position by the action of the spring. Remove the chain tensioner.

14. Remove the timing sprockets together with the chain, by inserting screws into the threaded holes in the jackshaft sprocket and turning them alternately and evenly until the sprockets are free.

To install the timing chains, tensioners and sprockets:

15. If the engine was not disturbed while the components were removed, then install everything in the reverse order of removal, using the procedure below as a guide. If, however, the crankshaft or camshaft was turned or the engine disassembled further, start the assembly procedure by bringing the no. 1 and no. 4 pistons to top dead center (TDC).

16. Check that the pistons are at TDC by positioning the timing gear cover on the locating dowels and place the crankshaft pulley in position. The TDC timing mark should be in direct line with the timing mark pointer.

17. Position the crankshaft and jackshaft timing sprocket into position with the primary chain attached to them. When installing the primary timing sprockets, the timing mark on the jackshaft sprocket must align with the timing mark on the crankshaft sprocket.

18. Align the keyway of the jackshaft with the key in the sprocket by turning the jackshaft, then set both sprockets in position by lightly tapping each sprocket alternately.

NOTE: The jackshaft can be prevented from turning while driving the sprockets into position by holding it through the fuel pump opening.

19. Install the primary chain tensioner.

20. Install a new oil seal in the timing gear case and fill the space between the lips of the oil seal with grease. Position a new gasket to the mating face of the gear case with adhesive. Align the locating dowels with the proper holes and mount the gear case onto the engine. Install and tighten the retaining screws.

21. With the no. 4 piston at TDC on the

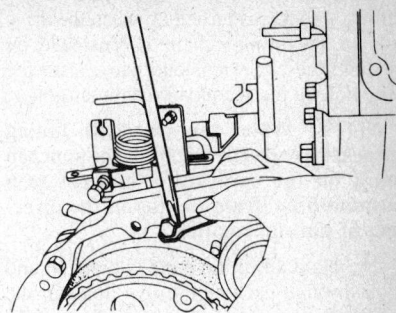

Removing the tension spring

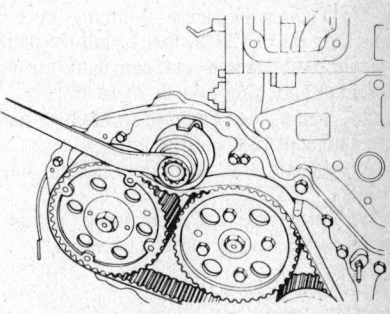

Removing the tension pulley

compression stroke, check to make sure that the setting mark on the camshaft and on the camshaft thrust plate are aligned. If they are not aligned, proceed as follows. If they are aligned, go on to the next numbered step.

    a. Attach the camshaft sprocket to the camshaft, insert the pin into a hole in the camshaft sprocket and turn the crankshaft until the marks on the camshaft and the thrust plate align.

    b. Remove the camshaft sprocket from the camshaft and bring the no. 4 piston to TDC of the compression stroke.

NOTE: If the engine has been turned in the opposite direction of normal rotation to align the marks on the thrust plate and the camshaft, make the final adjustment by turning the engine in the direction of normal rotation so that the marks are lined up and the chain is tensioned on the normal side.

22. Insert the timing chain into the gear case from the upper opening and hold it in position.

23. Bring the jackshaft timing sprocket together with the chain, and install it in position so that the punched mark on the sprocket is pointed to the key on the jackshaft. When the sprocket is correctly installed, the punched mark is located approximately at the 2 o'clock position.

24. Bring the camshaft timing sprocket together with the timing chain, so that the punched mark on the sprocket is located at the 12 o'clock position and assemble the sprocket to the camshaft.

25. Adjust the position of the camshaft timing sprocket, relative to the camshaft, so that the punched mark on the camshaft

timing sprocket is turned up when the drive side of the timing chain is tensioned by pushing the chain tensioner shoe from the plug hole in the secondary chain tensioner.

NOTE: When the camshaft timing sprocket is correctly installed, the punched mark on the sprocket is brought to a position 6°20′ from the top in the direction of normal rotation.

26. Hold all of the parts in position and look through each of the five holes in the camshaft timing sprocket to find a hole in alignment with the hole in the camshaft flange. Insert the pin into that hole.

27. Tighten the jackshaft timing sprocket attaching bolt to 33 ft. lbs. Install the plate washer and tighten the camshaft timing sprocket attaching bolt to 33 ft. lbs.

28. Install the gear case front cover and the camshaft carrier front cover.

29. Install the secondary chain tensioner.

30. Assemble the remaining components in the reverse order of removal.

Timing Belt

DIESEL ENGINE

Removal

1. Follow the timing pulley housing cover removal steps.

2. Remove the bolts fixing the injection pump timing pulley flange, then remove the flange.

3. When removing tension spring, avoid using excess force, or distortion of spring will result.

4. Remove the fixing nut of the tension pulley, then remove the tension pulley and tension center.

5. Remove the timing belt. Avoid twisting or kinking the belt and keep it free from water, oil, dust and other foreign matter.

Installation

No attempt should be made to readjust belt tension. If the belt has been loosened through service of the timing system, it should be replaced with a new one.

1. Check that the setting marks on the crank pulley, injection pump timing pulley, and camshaft timing pulley are in alignment, then install the timing belt in sequence of crankshaft timing pulley, camshaft timing pulley, and injection pump timing pulley.

Make an adjustment, so that slackness of the belt is taken up by the tension pulley.

When installing the belt, care should be taken so as not to damage the belt.

2. Install the tension center and tension pulley, making certain the end of the tension center is in proper contact with two pins on the timing pulley housing.

3. Hand-tighten the nut, so that tension pulley can slide freely.

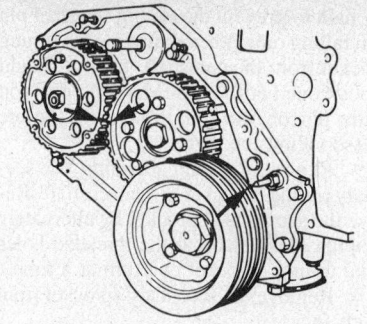

Timing marks aligned on the diesel

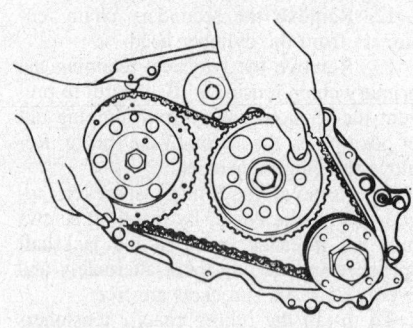

Installing belt

4. Install the tension spring correctly and semitighten the tension pulley fixing nut.

5. Turn the crankshaft 2 turns in normal direction of rotation to permit seating of the belt. Further rotate the crankshaft 90 degrees beyond top dead center to settle the injection pump. Never attempt to turn the crankshaft in reverse direction.

6. Loosen the tension pulley fixing nut completely, allowing the pulley to take up looseness of the belt. Then, tighten the nut to 78–95 ft. lbs.

7. Install the flange on the injection pump pulley. The hole in the outer circumference of the flange should be aligned with the timing mark "△" on the injection pump pulley.

8. Turn the crankshaft 2 turns in normal direction of rotation to bring the piston in no. 1 cylinder to top dead center on compression stroke and check that the mark "△" on the timing pulley is in alignment with the hole in the flange.

9. The belt tension should be checked at a point between the injection pump pulley and crankshaft pulley using tool J-29771, to a pull of 33–55 lbs.

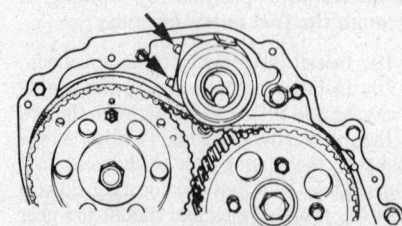

The tension pulley making proper contact with the two pins on the housing

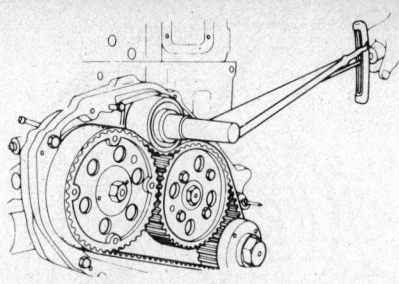

Torquing the tension pulley

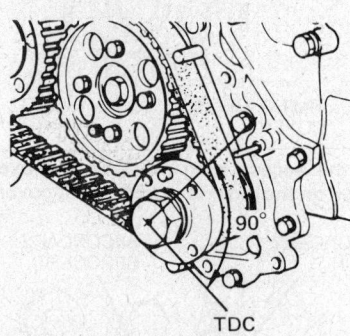

TDC

Bringing the #1 cylinder to TDC

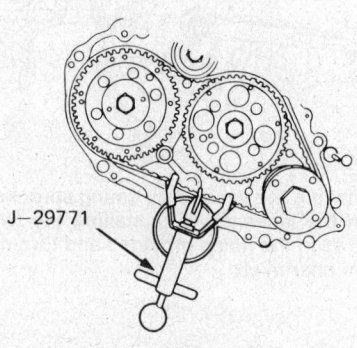

J–29771

Checking belt tension

10. Adjust valve clearances.

11. Install remaining parts in the reverse order of removal.

Camshaft

REMOVAL AND INSTALLATION

1. Remove the camshaft carrier as outlined under the "Cylinder Head Removal and Installation" procedure.

2. Remove the two bolts retaining the thrust plate in position on the front of the camshaft carrier.

3. Remove the thrust plate and carefully slide the camshaft out through the front of the carrier.

4. Install the camshaft in the carrier in the reverse order of removal, coating it liberally with engine oil before sliding it into position. Exercise care not to damage the camshaft bearing journals during the installation.

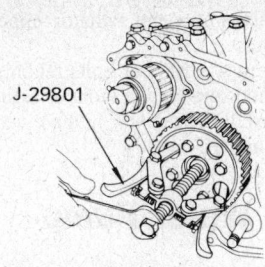

Removing camshaft pulley

Pistons and Connecting Rods

REMOVAL AND INSTALLATION

1. Remove the cylinder head.
2. Remove the oil pan.
3. Remove any carbon buildup from the cylinder wall at the top end of the piston travel with a ridge reamer tool.
4. Position the piston to be removed at the bottom of its stroke so that the connecting rod bearing cap can be reached easily from under the engine.
5. Unscrew the connecting rod bearing cap and remove the cap and lower half of the bearing.
6. Push the piston and connecting rod up and out of the cylinder block with a length of wood. Use care not to scratch the cylinder wall with the connecting rod or the wooden tool.
7. Keep all of the components from each cylinder together and install them in the cylinder from which they were removed.
8. Coat the bearing face of the connecting rod and the outer face of the pistons with engine oil.
9. Turn the top compression ring to bring its gap to the side of the piston marked "Front". Set the remaining rings so that their gaps are positioned 120° apart around the piston.
10. Turn the crankshaft until the rod journal of the particular cylinder you are working on is brought to the TDC position.
11. With the piston and rings clamped in a ring compressor, the notched mark on the head of the piston toward the front of the engine, and the marked side of the con-

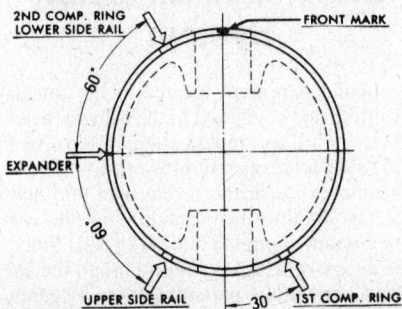

Piston ring positioning

necting rod toward the jackshaft, push the piston and connecting rod assembly into the cylinder bore until the big bearing end of the connecting rod contacts and is seated on the rod journal of the crankshaft. Use care not to scratch the cylinder wall with the connecting rod.

12. Push down farther on the piston and turn the crankshaft while the connecting rod rides around on the crankshaft rod journal. Turn the crankshaft until the crankshaft rod journal is at BDC (bottom dead center).
13. Align the mark on the connecting rod bearing cap with that on the connecting rod and tighten the bearing cap bolts to the specified torque.
14. Install all of the piston/connecting rod assemblies in the manner outlined above and assemble the oil pan and cylinder head to the engine in the reverse order of removal.

PISTON AND CONNECTING ROD IDENTIFICATION AND POSITIONING

The pistons are marked with the word "Front" and a notch in the piston head. When installed in the engine the "Front" and notch markings are to be facing the front of the engine. The connecting rods are numbered corresponding to the cylinders in which they are to be installed. Install the connecting rods in their correct cylinders with the marking to the right of the notch in the piston (looking from the rear of the engine), on the same side as the jackshaft.

ENGINE LUBRICATION

Oil Pan

REMOVAL AND INSTALLATION

Gasoline Engine

NOTE: On 4-wheel drive and diesel models, the engine must be removed before removing the oil pan.

1. Disconnect the negative battery terminal.
2. Jack up your vehicle and support it with jack stands.
3. Drain the oil.
4. Remove the front splash shield.
5. Remove the front crossmember, if necessary.
6. Disconnect the relay rod at the idler arm and lower the relay rod.
7. Remove the left side bellhousing bracket.

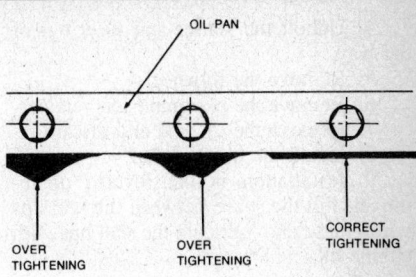

Correct tightening of the oil pan bolts

Use sealer at the points indicated when installing the pan gasket

8. Remove the vacuum line at the oil pan.
9. Remove the oil pan bolts and the pan.

NOTE: It may be necessary to remove the motor mounts and jack up the engine in order to remove the oil pan.

10. Installation is the reverse of removal.
Tighten the retaining bolts to 43 in. lbs.

Rear Main Oil Seal

REPLACEMENT

Gasoline Engine

1. Disconnect the negative battery terminal.
2. Remove the oil pan as previously described.
3. Remove the transmission.

NOTE: On manual transmissions, remove the clutch assembly.

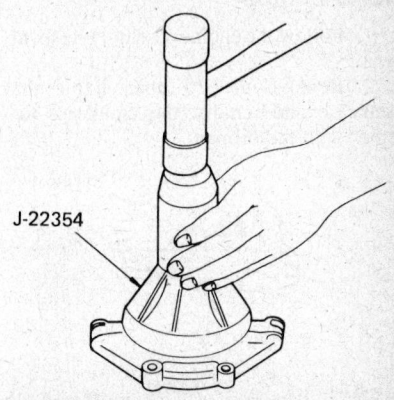

Installing the crankshaft rear seal on gasoline engines

4. Unbolt the starter and tie it out of the way.

5. Remove the flywheel.

6. Remove the rear main seal retainer.

7. Remove the oil seal and discard it.

8. Install the new oil seal.

9. Installation is the reverse of removal. Fill the space between the seal lips with grease and lubricate the seal lips with engine oil.

Diesel Engine

1. Follow the engine assembly removal steps.

2. Remove the 6 bolts mounting the flywheel and remove the flywheel assembly.

When loosening the flywheel bolts, hold the crankshaft front bolt with a wrench to prevent turning of the crankshaft.

3. Remove the crankshaft rear seal.

4. Install the new seal with seal installer J-22928 or equivalent. Reverse removal procedures for all other parts.

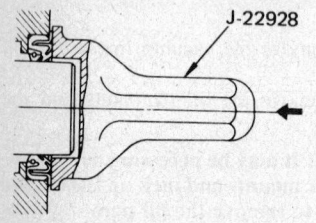

Installing the rear main seal on diesel engines

Oil Pump

REMOVAL AND INSTALLATION

Gasoline Engine

1. Drain and remove the oil pan.

2. Disconnect the oil feed pipe.

3. Remove the two bolts securing the oil pump to the cylinder block and remove the oil pump.

4. Install in the reverse order of removal.

Diesel Engine

1. Follow the engine assembly removal steps.

2. Remove the 20 bolts fixing the crankcase and remove the crankcase together with the oil pan.

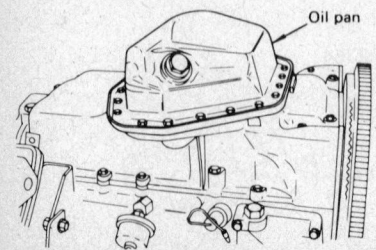

Diesel oil pan

NOTE: Pry off the crankcase by fitting a screwdriver into the slots in the crankcase.

3. Remove the oil pipe sleeve nut.

4. Remove the 2 bolts fixing the oil pump and remove the oil pump with oil pipe.

5. Install the oil pipe and leave the joints semi-tight.

6. Fully tighten the oil pump fixing screws, then tighten the oil pipe joints.

7. Reverse the removal procedure for the remaining parts.

Oil Cooler

REMOVAL AND INSTALLATION

Diesel

1. Place a suitable size tray under the oil filter to receive oil and water flowing out from the filter.

2. Drain the cooling system by opening the drain plugs on the radiator and on the cylinder block.

3. Remove the oil cooler water drain plug and drain the water.

4. Disconnect the oil cooler hoses at the cooler side.

5. Remove the oil filter cartridge using filter wrench.

6. Remove the nut fixing the oil cooler, then remove the oil cooler assembly.

7. Install the cooler using a new O-ring. Torque to 55–60 ft. lbs.

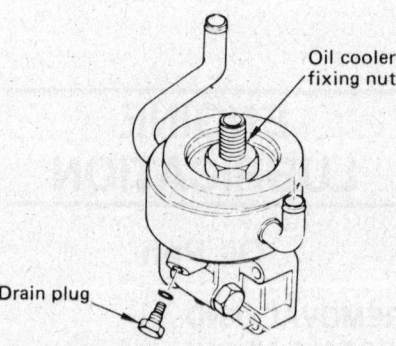

Diesel oil cooler

ENGINE COOLING

Radiator

REMOVAL AND INSTALLATION

1. Drain the radiator by opening the drain cock on the lower part of the radiator.

2. Disconnect the radiator upper and lower hoses.

3. Remove the four bolts retaining the radiator and remove the radiator assembly.

4. Install the radiator in the reverse order of removal.

Water Pump

REMOVAL AND INSTALLATION

1. Disconnect the battery ground cable.

2. Remove the lower cover and drain the cooling system. Remove the coolant hoses from the pump body.

3. On non–air conditioned models, remove the fan blades and pulleys from the hub.

4. On air conditioned models, remove the air pump and alternator belts, fan blades and pulleys.

5. Remove the water pump assembly.

6. Installation is the reverse of removal.

Thermostat

REMOVAL AND INSTALLATION

1. Drain the radiator by opening the petcock on the bottom of the radiator.

2. Disconnect the upper and lower radiator hoses.

3. Disconnect the water outlet from the engine.

4. Remove the thermostat.

5. Replace the thermostat in the reverse order of removal, using a new gasket under the new outlet housing and making sure that the thermostat is placed so that the spring end is inside the engine.

EMISSION CONTROLS

Crankcase Emission System

A regulated orifice, located in the intake manifold and connected to the cylinder head cover by a hose, replaces the PCV valve.

During wide open throttle operation, low vacuum exists in the intake manifold and the regulating orifice cannot admit the entire amount of engine blow-by gases. Since the air movement is greater through the air cleaner assembly, part of the blow-by gases are drawn in to the air cleaner from the rear end of the cylinder head cover.

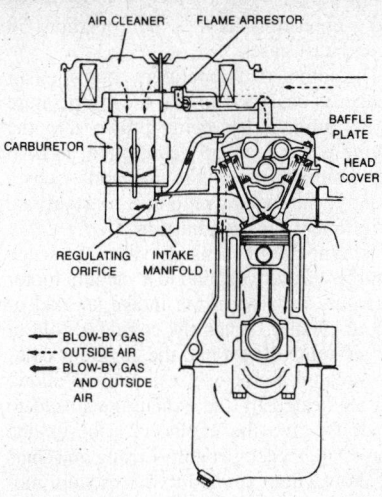

PCV system

SERVICE

1. Clean the internal parts of the hoses and regulating orifice.
2. Check the hoses for cracks, fatigue and swelling.

Evaporative Emission Control System

When raw fuel evaporates, the vapors contain hydrocarbons. To prevent these from escaping into the atmosphere, the fuel evaporative emission control system was developed.

The system consists of a sealed fuel tank, a vapor separator tank, check and relief valve and the hoses connecting these components, in the above order leading from the fuel tank, to the crankcase of the engine.

In operation, the vapor formed in the fuel tank passes through the vapor separator, which allows liquid fuel to flow back into fuel tank while allowing fuel vapor to pass onto the check and relief valve and the crankcase. When the engine is not running, if the fuel vapor pressure in the vapor separator becomes as high as 1 to 1.4 in. Hg, the check valve opens and allows the vapor to enter the engine crankcase. Otherwise the check valve is closed to the vapor separator while the engine is not running. When the engine is running, and a vacuum is developed in the fuel tank or in the engine crankcase and the difference of pressure between the relief side and the fuel tank or crankcase becomes 2 in. Hg, the relief valve opens and allows ambient air from the air cleaner into the fuel tank or the engine crankcase. This ambient air replaces the vapor within the fuel tank or crankcase, bringing the fuel tank or crankcase back into a neutral or positive pressure range.

INSPECTION AND SERVICE

Check the hoses for proper connections and damage. Replace as necessary. Check the vapor separator tank for fuel leaks, distortion and dents, and replace as necessary.

Remove the check valve and inspect it for leakage by blowing air into the ports in the check valve. When air is applied from the fuel tank side, the check valve is normal if air passes into the check side (crankcase side), but not leaking into the relief side (air cleaner side). When air is applied from the check side, the valve is normal if the passage of air is restricted. When air is applied from the relief side (air cleaner side), the valve is normal if air passes into the fuel tank side but not into the check side.

REMOVAL AND INSTALLATION

Removal and installation of the various evaporative emission control system components consists of disconnecting the hoses, loosening retaining screws, and removing the part which is to be replaced or checked. Install in the reverse order. When replacing hose, make sure that it is fuel and vapor resistant.

Exhaust Emission Control Systems

AIR INJECTION REACTOR SYSTEM

In gasoline engines, it is difficult to burn the air/fuel mixture completely through normal combustion in the combustion chambers. Under certain operating conditions, unburned fuel is exhausted into the atmosphere.

The air injection reactor system is designed so that ambient air, pressurized by the air pump, is injected through the injection nozzles into the exhaust ports near each exhaust valve. The exhaust gases are at high temperatures and ignite when brought into contact with the oxygen of the ambient air. Thus, the unburned fuel is burned in the exhaust ports and manifold.

To act against over-rich air/fuel mixture which occurs momentarily when the throttle plates in the carburetor are rapidly closed, additional ambient air is supplied intermittently into the intake manifold through the mixture control valve.

COASTING RICHER SYSTEM

While the engine is coasting the air/fuel mixture remains lean, preventing efficient reburning of unburned exhaust gases which can only be done with the addition of more air. Therefore, it is necessary to enrich the air/fuel mixture while the engine is coasting to attain efficient reburning of exhaust gases.

However, enriching the air/fuel mixture with only the mixture adjusting screw will

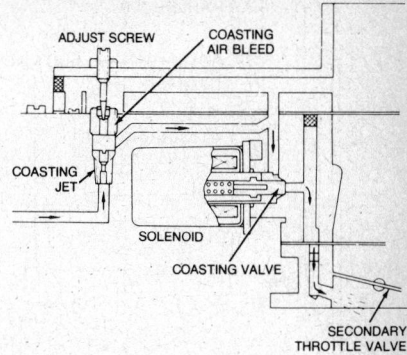

Coasting richer system solenoid

cause poor engine idle, or invite an increase in the carbon monoxide (CO) content of the exhaust gases.

The coasting richer system consists of an independent operative auxiliary fuel system. This system functions when the engine is coasting, to enrich the air/fuel mixture, which minimizes hydrocarbon content of the exhaust gases through efficient combustion. This is accomplished without adversely affecting engine idle and the carbon monoxide content of the exhaust gases.

A solenoid operated valve in the carburetor allows extra fuel to be drawn into the intake manifold. The solenoid valve is electrically connected in series to a transmission 4th/3rd gear switch, accelerator switch and a clutch switch, all of which are used to detect engine coasting conditions.

When all of these switches turn on or when the engine is coasting, the solenoid valve on the secondary side of the carburetor energizes and causes the valve to open. When the valve opens, fuel is drawn out of the float chamber by engine vacuum and metered via the coasting jet below the secondary throttle valve.

As a result of the operation of the coasting richer system, the air/fuel mixture becomes temporarily enriched to facilitate efficient reburning of exhaust gases in the exhaust manifold, thereby reducing hydrocarbon and carbon monoxide content in the exhaust gases exiting to the atmosphere.

When the engine coasting condition is halted or when the transmission is placed in Neutral, the coasting richer circuit is opened and causes the coasting richer valve to close, shutting off the supply of extra fuel.

The solenoid switch is linked to the secondary side of the carburetor. The solenoid valve is electrically controlled by means of the accelerator switch, clutch switch, and the transmission switch.

The accelerator switch is connected to the engine accelerator linkage and is turned Off when the throttle valve is open to an angle of 7°.

The clutch switch is installed in a position near the clutch pedal and turns Off when the clutch pedal is depressed.

The transmission switch is installed on the upper part of the transmission gearbox

ISUZU

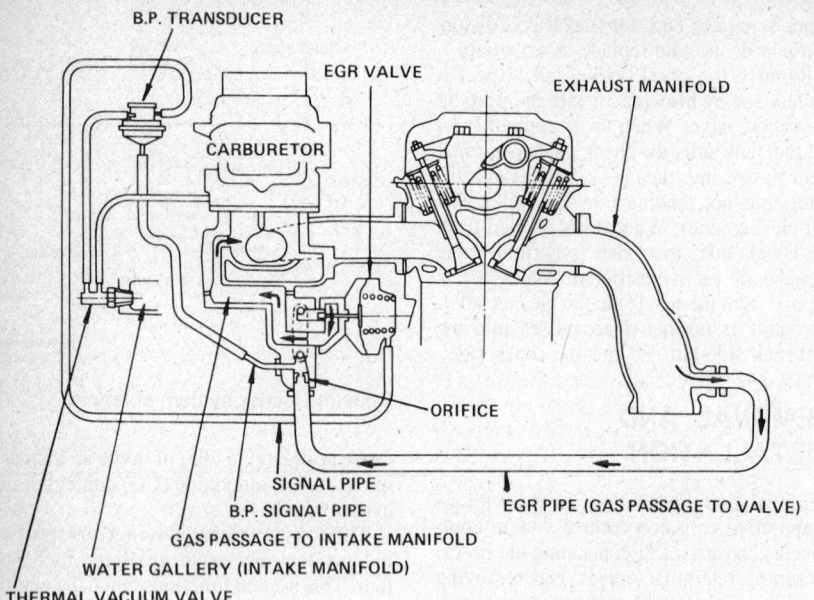

EGR system

and turns On when the transmission is shifted into 4th or 3rd gear. The switch is Off in all other gear ranges and the coasting richer circuit is broken and the system deenergized.

EXHAUST GAS RECIRCULATION SYSTEM (EGR)

The vacuum diaphragm is connected to the vacuum port in the carburetor flange through a thermal vacuum valve, and a back pressure transducer. As the throttle valve is opened, vacuum is applied to the vacuum diaphragm. When vacuum reaches the specified value, the diaphragm overcomes the spring force.

As the diaphragm moves up, it opens the exhaust gas metering valve thus allowing exhaust gas to be pulled into the engine intake.

THERMAL VACUUM VALVE

The thermal vacuum valve is mounted on the intake manifold and is connected in series between the vacuum port in the carburetor and the EGR valve. This valve is of the wax type, in that it opens as the engine coolant temperature increases. When the coolant temperature is below 115°F the valve is closed (the EGR system does not operate). When the temperature rises above 120°F the valve opens and the EGR system begins operation.

BACK PRESSURE TRANSDUCER

The back pressure transducer is responsive to exhaust pressure. Under normal oper-

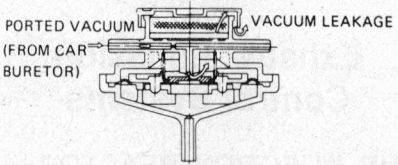

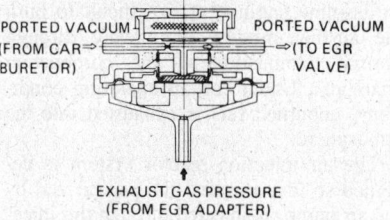

Back pressure transducer

ating conditions, ported vacuum leaks into the air, and is applied to the EGR valve under high pressure conditions thereby controlling the volume of recirculating exhaust gas.

TEMPERATURE CONTROLLED AIR CLEANER

The rate of fuel atomization varies with the temperature of the air that the fuel is being mixed with. The air/fuel ratio cannot be held constant for efficient fuel combustion with a wide range of air temperatures. Cold air being drawn into the engine causes a denser and richer air/fuel mixture, inefficient fuel atomization, and thus, more hydrocarbons in the exhaust gas. Hot air being drawn into the engine causes a leaner air/fuel mixture and more efficient atomization

and combustion for less hydrocarbons in the exhaust gases.

The automatic temperature controlled air cleaner is designed so that the temperature of the ambient air being drawn into the engine is automatically controlled, to hold the temperature of the air and, consequently, the fuel/air ratio at a constant rate for efficient fuel combustion.

A temperature sensing vacuum switch controls vacuum applied to a vacuum motor operating a valve in the intake snorkel of the air cleaner. When the engine is cold or the air being drawn into the engine is cold, the vacuum motor opens the valve, allowing air heated by the exhaust manifold to be drawn into the engine. As the engine warms up, the temperature sensing unit shuts off the vacuum applied to the vacuum motor which allows the valve to close, shutting off the heated air and allowing cooler, outside (under hood) air to be drawn into the engine.

OXIDIZING CATALYTIC CONVERTER SYSTEM

An oxidizing catalytic converter is used to control hydrocarbons and carbon monoxide. This is accomplished by placing the converter in the exhaust system so all exhaust must pass through it before it enters the air. The chemical reaction that happens in the converter is the changing of hydrocarbons and carbon monoxide into water and carbon dioxide.

OVER TEMPERATURE CONTROL SYSTEM

While the engine is coasting, the coasting richer system is operated to prevent the catalyst from overheating caused by poor combustion. The secondary air injection is operated simultaneously with the coasting richer system. When the catalyst temperature reaches 1350°F due to high speed and/or high load driving, the secondary air is diverted to the atmosphere to reduce chemical reaction in the catalyst. When the temperature reaches 180°F due to an engine malfunction or ignition system failure the warning light and buzzer are turned on. The buzzer will cease automatically when the catalyst temperature returns to normal; however the warning light will stay lit until you disconnect the positive battery terminal. When this terminal is reconnected the light will reset.

AIR SWITCHING VALVE

This valve is designed to switch air flow from the air pump. It is operated by vacuum and air pump pressure which are switched by a vacuum switching valve.

While air pump pressure acts in the diaphragm chamber "B" (see illustration)

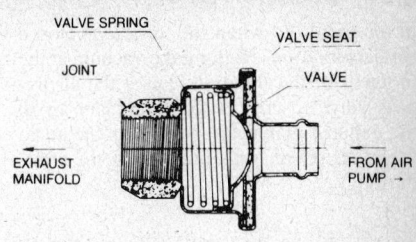

Check valve

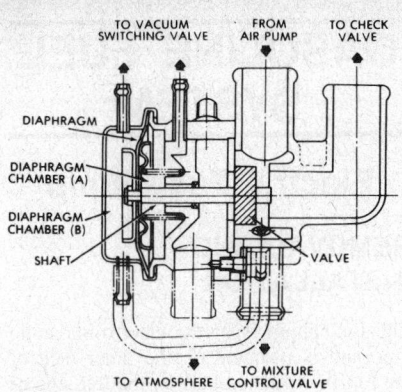

Air switching valve

through the vacuum switching valve, this valve flows the air from the air pump to the check valve. When manifold vacuum switched by the vacuum switching valve acts in the diaphragm chamber "B" the valve closes the air passage to the check valve, and at the same time opens the port to the atmosphere, so the air from the pump is diverted to the atmosphere.

VACUUM SWITCHING VALVE

The vacuum switching valve has 3-way ports, two of which are opened or closed by electrically controlling the solenoid plunger. The solenoid plunger is energized when the catalytic converter temperature exceeds 1350°F. When energized the vacuum switching valve connects the diaphragm chamber "B" (see illustration) of the air switching valve to the intake manifold permitting the manifold vacuum to be applied to the diaphragm chamber "B". When the solenoid plunger is de-energized it plugs the port, so the diaphragm chamber "B" of the air switching valve is connected to the diaphragm chamber "A".

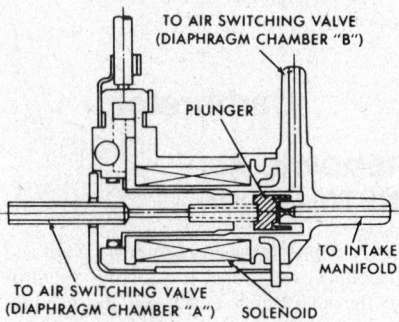

Vacuum switching valve

THERMO SENSOR AND THERMO CONTROLLER

The Thermo Sensor is installed to the front side of the catalytic converter. A thermistor

is used in this sensor and is covered with a stainless steel sheath.

Sensing electrical resistance of the thermo sensor, the thermo controller sends "ON and OFF" signals to the vacuum switching valve, and the warning light and buzzer. When converter temperatures reach 1350°F the controller sends "ON" signals to the vacuum switching valve and if temperatures exceed 1830°F it sends an "ON" signal to the warning light and buzzer.

VENT SWITCHING VALVE

This valve is an electrically operated solenoid type built into the carburetor.

Its functions are as follows:

1. When the engine is not running, the valve is open to allow fuel vapors into the canister.

2. When the engine is running, the valve is closed to prevent ambient air from flowing into the carburetor through the canister.

CHARCOAL CANISTER

The charcoal canister contains activated carbon to store up fuel vapor from the carburetor. The purge control valve, built into the canister, shuts off the purge line while the engine is not running. When the engine is started and the vacuum signal becomes higher than specification pressure, the purge control valve opens a passage, and fuel vapors are then drawn into the intake manifold.

Inspection and Adjustments

AIR PUMP

If the air pump makes an abnormal noise and cannot be corrected without removing the pump from the vehicle, check the following in sequence:

1. Turn the pulley ¾ of a turn in the clockwise direction and ¼ of a turn in the counterclockwise direction. If the pulley is binding and if rotation is not smooth, a defective bearing is indicated.

2. Check the inner wall of the pump body, vanes and rotor for wear. If the rotor has abnormal wear, replace the air pump.

3. Check the needle roller bearing for wear and damage. If the bearings are defective, the air pump should be replaced.

4. Check and replace the rear side seal if abnormal wear or damage is noticed.

5. Check and replace the carbon shoes holding the vanes if they are found to be worn or damaged.

6. A deposit of carbon particles on the inner wall of the pump body and vanes is normal, but should be removed with compressed air before reassembling the air pump.

CHECK VALVE

Remove the check valve from the air manifold. Test it for leakage by blowing air into the valve from the air pump side and from the air manifold side. Air should only pass through the valve from the air pump side if the valve is functioning normally. A small amount of air leakage from the manifold side can be overlooked. Replace the check valve if it is found to be defective.

MIXTURE CONTROL VALVE

Disconnect the rubber hose connecting the mixture control valve with the intake manifold and plug the intake manifold side of the valve. If the mixture control valve is operating correctly, air will continue to blow out the mixture control valve for a few seconds after the accelerator pedal is fully depressed (engine running) and released quickly. If air continues to blow out for more than five seconds, replace the mixture control valve.

AIR MANIFOLD AND AIR INJECTION NOZZLES

Check around the air manifold for air leakage with the engine running at 2,000 rpm. If air is leaking from the eye joint bolt, retighten or replace the gasket. Check the air nozzles for restrictions by blowing air into the nozzles.

AIR BY-PASS VALVE FEDERAL MODELS

The purpose of the air by-pass valve is to prevent the afterburning of the exhaust gases

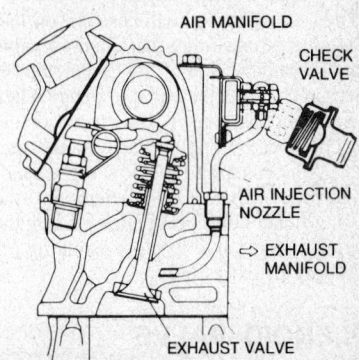

Air injection manifold and nozzles

in the manifold when the throttle is closed for deceleration. High intake vacuum at the moment of deceleration causes the air by-pass valve to cut off the secondary air to the exhaust manifold and diverts the air to the atmosphere, thus preventing the after-burning.

Testing

Remove the outlet hose and with the engine running, open the throttle completely and close it quickly. Air should flow out for a few seconds. If the air continues to flow out for more than five seconds, replace the air by-pass valve.

HOSES

Check and replace hoses if they are found to be weakened or cracked. Check all hose connections and clips. Be sure that the hoses are not in contact with other parts of the engine.

COASTING RICHER SYSTEM

This system functions when the engine is coasting to enrich the air/fuel mixture, which minimizes hydrocarbon content of the exhaust gases through efficient combustion.

A solenoid operated valve in the carburetor allows extra fuel to be drawn into the intake manifold during coasting.

The solenoid is energized by the following switches:

1. **Federal with manual transmission:**
   a. Accelerator switch.
   b. Clutch switch.
   c. 3rd–4th gear switch.
2. **California with manual transmission:**
   a. Accelerator switch.
   b. Clutch switch.
   c. Transmission neutral switch.
   d. Engine speed sensor.
3. **California with automatic transmission:**
   a. Accelerator switch.
   b. Inhibitor switch.
   c. Engine speed sensor.

When all of these switches turn on and the engine is coasting, the solenoid valve on the secondary side of the carburetor energizes and causes the valve to open. When the valve opens, fuel is drawn out of the float chamber by engine vacuum and metered by the coasting jet below the secondary throttle valve. On acceleration, the coasting richer circuit is opened causing the coasting richer valve to close, shutting off the supply of extra fuel.

SOLENOID VALVE

The valve should open when the circuit is energized. A clicking noise should be heard when the valve operates.

ACCELERATOR SWITCH

The accelerator switch should be closed when the pedal is not depressed and open when the pedal is depressed. Check with a test lamp.

CLUTCH SWITCH

When the clutch pedal is depressed, the switch contacts are opened and the coasting richer system is de-energized.

Test all years' clutch switches with a test lamp.

TRANSMISSION SWITCH

Federal Manual Transmission Models

The transmission switch turns on when the transmission is shifted into 3rd or 4th gear and energizes the coasting richer system. It de-energizes the system when the transmission is shifted into any other position.

California Manual Transmission Models

The transmission switch turns on when the transmission is shifted into any gear and turns off when it is shifted into neutral position. The solenoid is energized when the switch is in the On position. Test with a test lamp.

INHIBITOR SWITCH

California Automatic Transmission Models

The inhibitor switch is installed on the shift linkage lever and energizes the coasting richer system in drive, low or second gear positions. Test with a test lamp.

EGR VALVE

NOTE: The EGR valve cannot be disassembled. No actual service is required except to determine proper operation of the valve.

Check the valve shaft for proper movement by opening the throttle to give 2,000–2,500 rpm. The shaft should move upward at these speeds and return to the downward position when the engine speed is reduced to normal idle speed.

Check the vacuum diaphragm function by applying an outside vacuum source to the vacuum supply tube at the top of the vacuum diaphragm. The diaphragm should not leak down and should move to the fully up position at about 8–10 in. Hg. of vacuum.

GASOLINE FUEL SYSTEM

Electric Fuel Pump

REMOVAL AND INSTALLATION

The fuel pump is of the electro-magnetic type and is installed on the inner face of the fourth crossmember, on the left side of the truck.

This fuel pump is a totally enclosed type and can not be repaired. If you have determined that there is a problem with the fuel pump, it must be replaced as a unit.

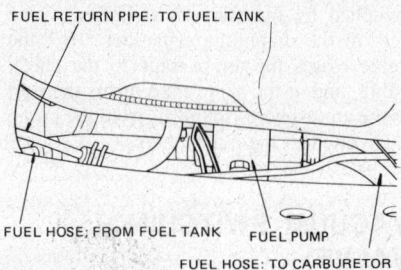

Fuel pump

1. Disconnect the negative battery terminal.
2. Disconnect the electrical lead and fuel lines.
3. Plug the fuel lines to prevent leaking.

NOTE: You can plug the fuel lines with a bolt that is approximately the same size as the fuel line or crimp the hose with Vise-grip® type pliers.

4. Remove the fuel pump mounting bolts and nuts.
5. Remove the fuel pump.
6. Installation is the reverse of removal.

Carburetor

REMOVAL AND INSTALLATION

1. Remove the air cleaner wing nut and disconnect the rubber hoses from the clips on the air cleaner cover and the vacuum hose from the vacuum motor.
2. Remove the bracket bolts at the air cleaner and remove the air cleaner cover and filter element.
3. Disconnect the hot air hose (to the hot air duct), the air hose to the air pump at the air cleaner, and the vacuum hose at the joint nipple side of the intake manifold.
4. Loosen the bolt clamping the air

cleaner to the carburetor. Separate the air cleaner body from the carburetor but do not remove it completely as the hoses remain connected.

5. Disconnect the PCV hose (to the camshaft cover), the rubber hoses to the check and relief valve and remove the air cleaner body.

6. Disconnect the choke control wire.

7. Disconnect the lead from the throttle solenoid.

8. Disconnect the throttle linkage return spring.

9. Disconnect the accelerator linkage wire.

10. Disconnect the fuel line at the carburetor.

11. Remove the check valve from the air manifold.

12. Remove the four retaining nuts and lockwashers securing the carburetor to the manifold and remove the carburetor.

13. Install the carburetor in the reverse order of removal.

THROTTLE LINKAGE ADJUSTMENT

When the primary throttle valve is opened to an angle of 50° from its closed position, the adjust plate which is interlocked with the primary throttle valve, is brought into contact with portion A (see illustration) of the return plate. When the primary throttle valve is opened farther, the return plate is pulled apart from the stopper (B in the illustration), allowing the secondary throttle valve to open.

To adjust the linkage:

1. Measure the clearance between the primary throttle valve and the wall of the throttle chamber at the center of the throttle valve when the adjust plate is brought into contact with portion A of the return plate. Standard clearance is 0.26–0.32 in.

2. If necessary, make the adjustment by bending the portion A of the return plate.

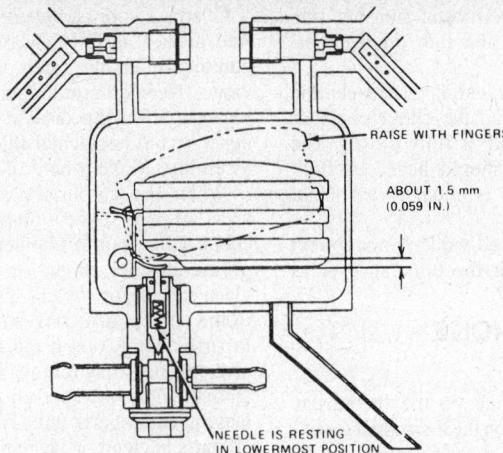

Float level adjustment

FLOAT LEVEL ADJUSTMENT

The fuel level is normal if it is within the lines on the window glass of the float chamber when the vehicle is resting on level ground and the engine is off.

If the fuel level is outside the lines, remove the float housing cover. Have an absorbent cloth under the cover to catch the fuel from the fuel bowl. Adjust the float level by bending the needle seat on the float.

The needle valve should have an effective stroke of about 0.059 in. When necessary, the needle valve stroke can be adjusted by bending the float stopper.

NOTE: Be careful not to bend the needle valve rod when installing the float and baffle plate, if removed.

KICK LEVER ADJUSTMENT

1. Bring the primary side throttle valve into the complete closed position, by turning the throttle adjustment screw.

2. On manual transmission models, with the throttle valve completely closed, loosen the lock nut on the kick lever screw and

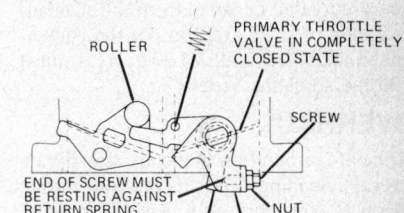

Kickdown lever

turn the screw until it is in contact with the return plate and tighten the lock nut (see illustration).

3. On automatic transmission models with the throttle valve completely closed, bend the end of the kick lever until it is in contact with the return plate (see illustration).

ELECTRIC AUTOMATIC CHOKE

1. Install the thermostat cover by fitting the end of the choke lever into the bimetal hook.

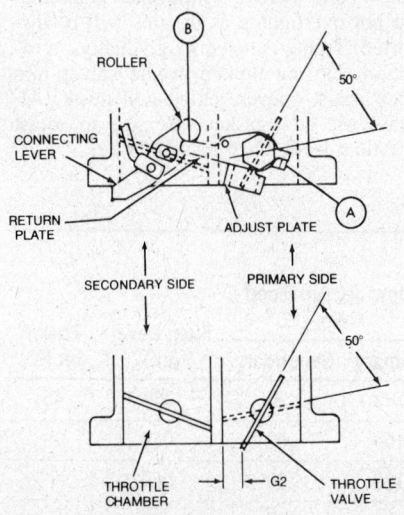

Throttle linkage adjustment

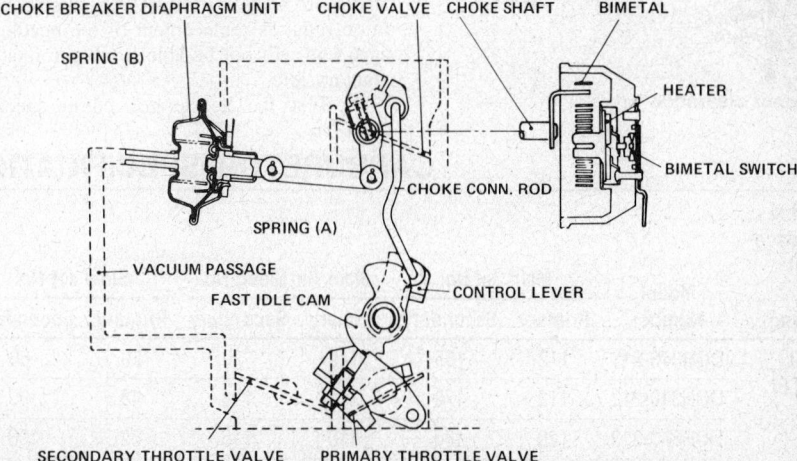

Electric choke

2. Align the thermostat housing line (thickest one) with the line on the thermostat cover.

3. Measure the clearance (between the choke valve edge and the choke chamber wall) when the choke is fully closed. The standard clearance should be (0.11–0.29 in.). This clearance is equal to a bimetal lever angle of 30°.

4. If the measured value is not correct adjust it by bending the bimetal lever as necessary.

ELECTRIC CHOKE ADJUSTMENT

Align the thickest line on the thermostat housing with the line on the thermostat cover. Measure clearance between the cover side stopper and the bimetal level side stopper when the diaphragm is fully stroked with negative pressure or finger pressure. If the measured value deviates from the standard clearance of 0.28–0.29 in. or the equivalent bimetal lever angle of 20 degrees adjust with the adjusting screw.

OVERHAUL

Efficient carburetion depends greatly on careful cleaning and inspection during overhaul, since dirt, gum, water, or varnish in or on the carburetor parts are often responsible for poor performance.

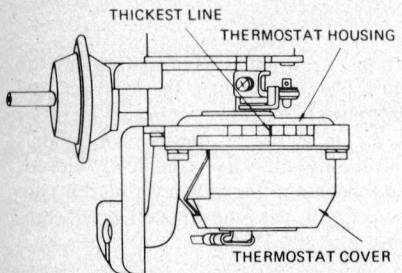

Choke thermostat housing alignment

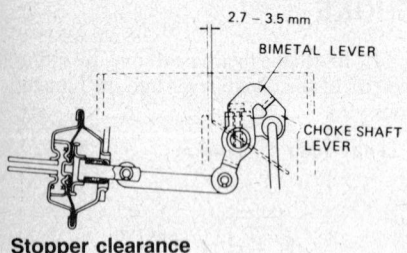

Stopper clearance

Overhaul your carburetor in a clean, dust-free area. Carefully disassemble the carburetor, referring often to the exploded views. Keep all similar and lookalike parts segregated during disassembly and cleaning to avoid accidental interchange during assembly. Make a note of all jet sizes.

When the carburetor is disassembled, wash all parts (except diaphragms, electric choke units, pump plunger, and any other plastic, leather, fiber, or rubber parts) in clean carburetor solvent. Do not leave parts in the solvent any longer than is necessary to sufficiently loosen the deposits. Excessive cleaning may remove the special finish from the float bowl and choke valve bodies, leaving these parts unfit for service. Rinse all parts in clean solvent and blow them dry with compressed air or allow them to air dry. Wipe clean all cork, plastic, leather and fiber parts with a clean, lint-free cloth.

Blow out all passages and jets with compressed air and be sure that there are no restrictions or blockages. Never use wire or similar tools to clean jets, fuel passages, or air bleeds. Clean all jets and valves separately to avoid accidental interchange.

Check all parts for wear or damage. If wear or damage is found, replace the defective parts. Especially check the following:

1. Check the float needle and seat for wear. If wear is found, replace the complete assembly.

2. Check the float hinge pin for wear and the float(s) for dents or distortion. Replace the float if fuel has leaked into it.

3. Check the throttle and choke shaft bores for wear or an out-of-round condition. Damage or wear to the throttle arm, shaft, or shaft bore will often require replacement of the throttle body. These parts require a close tolerance of fit; wear may allow air leakage, which could affect starting and idling.

NOTE: Throttle shafts and bushings are not included in overhaul kits. They can be purchased separately.

4. Inspect the idle mixture adjusting needles for burrs or grooves. Any such condition requires replacement of the needle, since you will not be able to obtain a satisfactory idle.

5. Test the accelerator pump check

valves. They should pass air one way but not the other. Test for proper seating by blowing and sucking on the valve. Replace the valve if necessary. If the valve is satisfactory, wash the valve again to remove breath moisture.

6. Check the bowl cover for warped surfaces with a straightedge.

7. Closely inspect the valves and seats for wear and damage, replacing as necessary.

8. After the carburetor is assembled, check the choke valve for freedom of operation.

Carburetor overhaul kits are recommended for each overhaul. These kits contain all gaskets and new parts to replace those that deteriorate most rapidly. Failure to replace all parts supplied with the kit (especially gaskets) can result in poor performance later.

Some carburetor manufacturers supply overhaul kits of three basic types: minor repair; major repair; and gasket kits. Basically, they contain the following:

1. **Minor repair kits:**
   a. All gaskets
   b. Float needle valve
   c. Volume control screw
   d. All diaphragms
   e. Spring for the pump diaphragm
2. **Major repair kits:**
   a. All jets and gaskets
   b. All diaphragms
   c. Float needle valve
   d. Volume control screw
   e. Pump ball valve
   f. Main jet carrier
   g. Float
   h. Complete intermediate rod
   i. Intermediate pump lever
   j. Complete injector tube
   k. Some cover hold-down screws and washers
3. **Gasket kits:** All gaskets

After cleaning and checking all components, reassemble the carburetor, using new parts and referring to the exploded view. When reassembling, make sure that all screws and jets are tight in their seats, but do not overtighten as the tips will be distorted. Tighten all screws gradually, in rotation. Do not tighten needle valves into their seats; uneven jetting will result. Always use new gaskets. Be sure to adjust the float level when reassembling.

CARBURETOR SPECIFICATIONS

Engine Displacement cc (cu in.)	Model Number	Main Jet No.		Main Air Bleed No.		Slow Jet No.		Slow Jet Air Bleed No.		Float Level (in.)	Power Jet No.
		Primary	Secondary	Primary	Secondary	Primary	Secondary	Primary	Secondary		
1800 (110.8)	DCH340-211	112	165	110	70	50	80	150	90	.059	45
	DCH340-212	112	170	110	115	48	90	150	100	.059	—
	DCH340-313	120	165	110	115	52	100	150	100	.059	—
	DCH340-214	120	165	110	115	52	100	150	100	.059	—

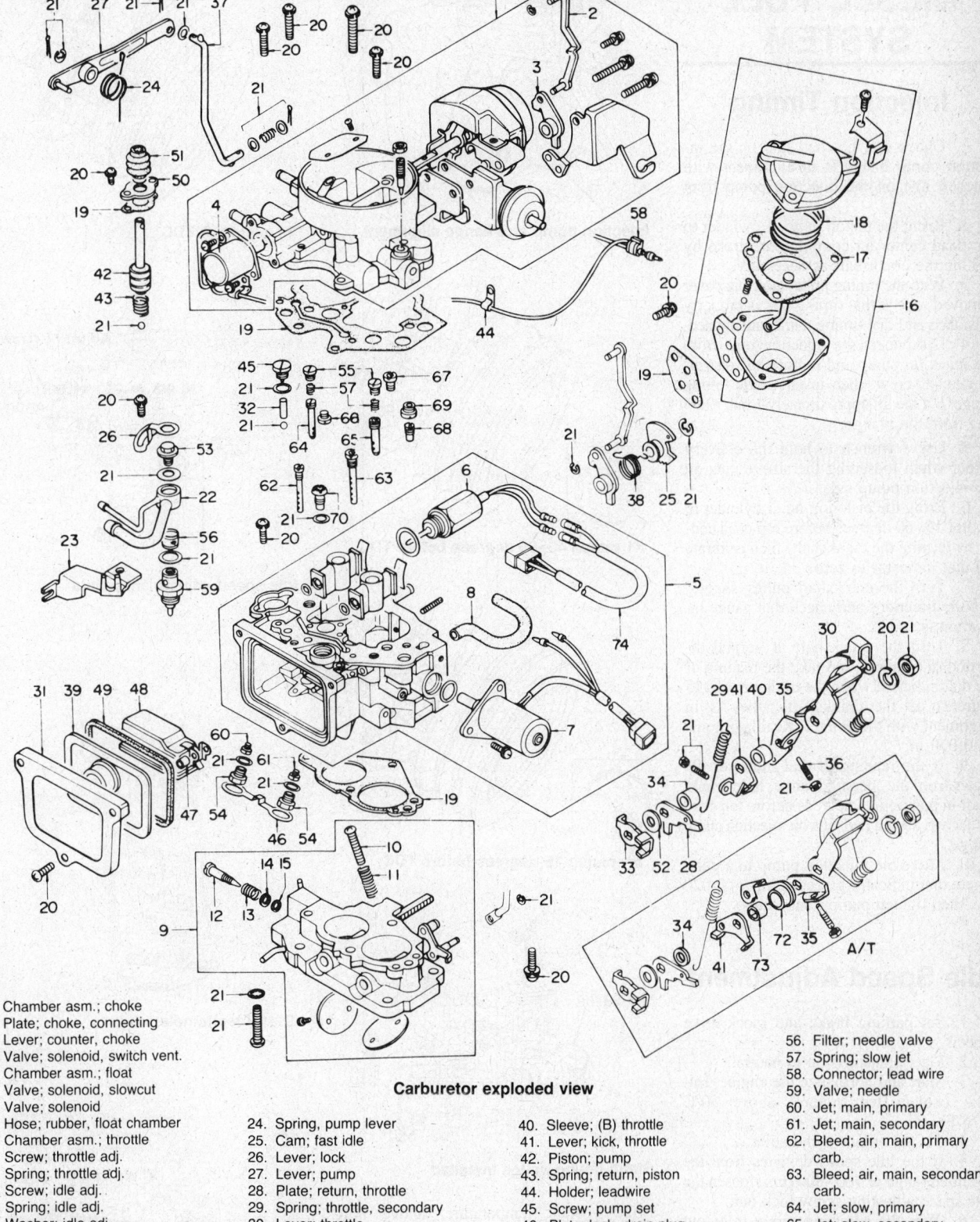

Carburetor exploded view

1. Chamber asm.; choke
2. Plate; choke, connecting
3. Lever; counter, choke
4. Valve; solenoid, switch vent.
5. Chamber asm.; float
6. Valve; solenoid, slowcut
7. Valve; solenoid
8. Hose; rubber, float chamber
9. Chamber asm.; throttle
10. Screw; throttle adj.
11. Spring; throttle adj.
12. Screw; idle adj.
13. Spring; idle adj.
14. Washer; idle adj.
15. Seal; rubber, idle adj.
16. Chamber asm.; diaphragm
17. Diaphragm
18. Spring; diaphragm
19. Gasket kit; carb. overhaul
20. Screw and washer kit (A)
21. Screw and washer kit (B)
22. Nipple; fuel
23. Plate; stopping

24. Spring, pump lever
25. Cam; fast idle
26. Lever; lock
27. Lever; pump
28. Plate; return, throttle
29. Spring; throttle, secondary
30. Lever; throttle
31. Cover; level gauge
32. Weight, injector
33. Lever; fast adj.
34. Sleeve; (A) throttle
35. Lever; fast adj.
36. Screw; fast idle
37. Rod; pump
38. Spring; fast idle cam
39. Gauge; level fuel

40. Sleeve; (B) throttle
41. Lever; kick, throttle
42. Piston; pump
43. Spring; return, piston
44. Holder; leadwire
45. Screw; pump set
46. Plate; lock, drain plug
47. Collar; (C) float set
48. Float; fuel level
49. Seal; ruber, level gauge
50. Plate; cylinder
51. Cover; dust
52. Washer; throttle shaft
53. Screw; nipple set
54. Plug; drain
55. Plug; taper, slow jet

56. Filter; needle valve
57. Spring; slow jet
58. Connector; lead wire
59. Valve; needle
60. Jet; main, primary
61. Jet; main, secondary
62. Bleed; air, main, primary carb.
63. Bleed; air, main, secondary carb.
64. Jet; slow, primary
65. Jet; slow, secondary
66. Bleed; slow air, primary
67. Bleed; slow air, secondary
68. Jet; coasting
69. Bleed; air coasting
70. Valve; power
71. Collar
72. Lever; down shift
73. Lever; connecting
74. Harness asm.; w/connector

DIESEL FUEL SYSTEM

Injection Timing

1. Check that notched line on the injection pump flange is in alignment with notched line on the injection pump front bracket.

2. Bring the piston in no. 1 cylinder to top dead center on compression stroke by turning the crankshaft as necessary.

3. With the timing pulley housing cover removed, check that timing belt is properly tensioned and that timing marks are aligned.

4. Disconnect the injection pipe from the injection pump and remove the distributor head screw, then install static timing gauge. Set the lift approximately 1 mm (0.04 in.) from the plunger.

5. Use a wrench to hold the delivery holder when loosening the sleeve nuts on the injection pump side.

6. Bring the piston in no. 1 cylinder to a point 45–60 degrees before top dead center by turning the crankshaft, then calibrate the dial indicator to zero.

7. Turn the crankshaft pulley slightly in both directions and check that gauge indication is stable.

8. Turn the crankshaft in normal direction of rotation, and take the reading of the dial indicator when the timing mark (15 degrees) on the crankshaft pulley is in alignment with the pointer. Reading should be 0.020 in.

9. If the reading of dial indicator deviates from the specified range, hold crankshaft in position 15 degrees before top dead center and loosen two nuts on injection pump flange.

10. Move the injection pump to a point where dial indicator gives reading of 0.020 in., then tighten pump flange nuts.

Idle Speed Adjustment

1. Set parking brake and block drive wheels.

2. Place transmission in neutral.

3. Start and normalize the engine. Engine coolant temperature: above 80°C (176°F).

4. Set the engine tachometer.

5. If the idle speed deviates from the specified range of 700–800 rpm, loosen the idle speed adjusting screw lock nut.

6. Turn the adjusting screw in or out until the idle speed is in the correct range. After tightening the lock nut, lock it in place.

Fast Idle Speed

1. Start and normalize the engine. En-

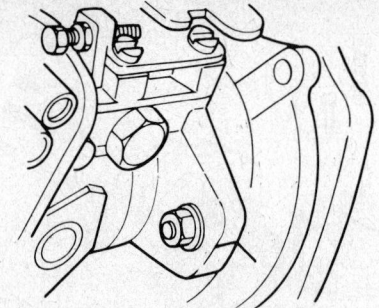

Injection pump and flange alignment

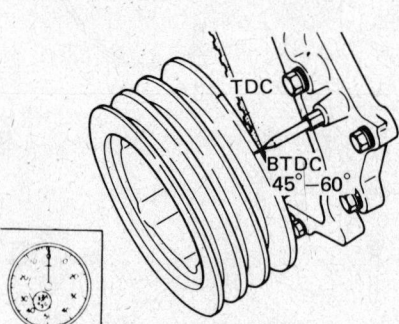

#1 piston 45–60 degrees before TDC

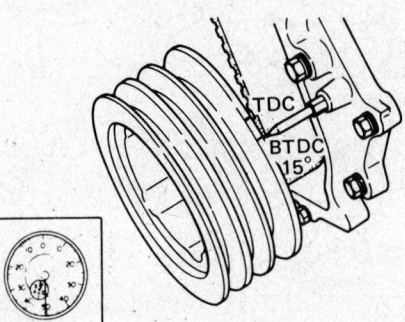

#1 piston 15 degrees before TDC

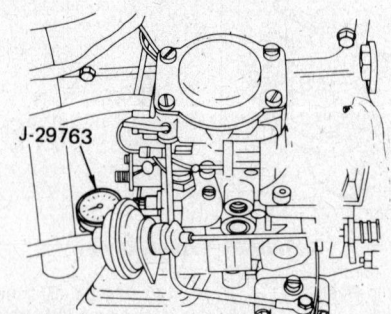

Static timing gauge installed

gine coolant temperature: above 80°C (176°F).

2. Set the engine tachometer.

3. Disconnect the hoses from the vacuum switch valve, then connect a pipe (4 mm dia.) in position between the hoses.

4. Loosen adjust nut and adjust engine idle speed by moving the nut. Fast idle should be 900–950 rpm.

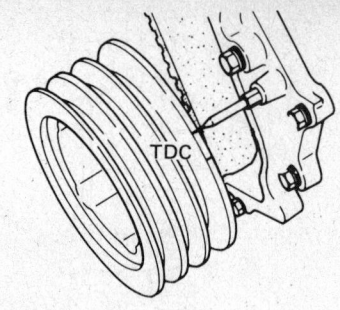

#1 piston at TDC

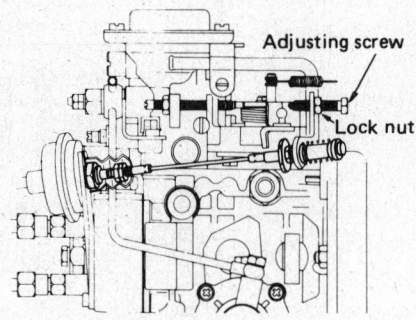

Idle speed adjustment points

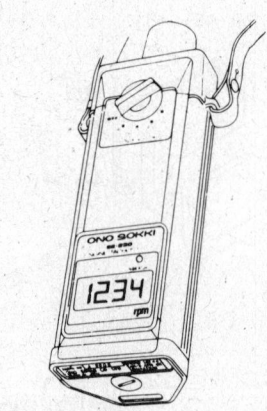

Diesel tachometer

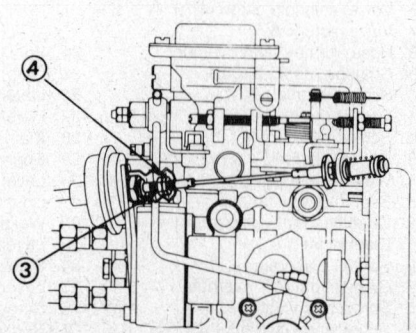

Fast idle adjusting points

5. Tighten the nut.

6. Remove engine tachometer.

Injection Pump

REMOVAL

1. Raise engine hood.

2. Disconnect the battery ground cable.

3. Remove the battery.

4. Remove the under cover.

5. Drain the cooling system by opening the drain plugs on the radiator and on the cylinder block.

6. Disconnect the upper water hose at the engine side.

7. Loosen the compressor drive belt by moving the power steering oil pump or idler. (If so equipped.)

8. Remove the cooling fan and fan shroud.

9. Disconnect the lower water hose at the engine side.

10. Remove the air conditioner compressor. (If so equipped.)

11. Remove the fan belt.

12. Remove the crankshaft pulley.

13. Remove the timing pulley housing covers.

14. Remove the tension spring and fixing bolt, then remove the tension center and pulley.

15. Remove the timing belt.

16. Remove the engine control cable and wiring harness of the fuel cut solenoid.

17. Remove the fuel hoses and injection pipes. Use a wrench to hold the delivery holder when loosening the sleeve nuts on the injection pump side.

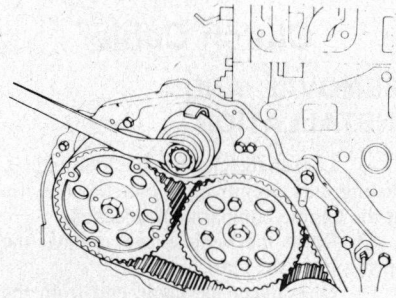

Loosening tension pulley

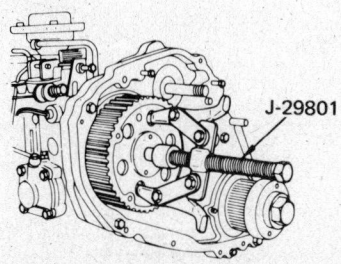

Removing timing pulley

18. Install a 6 mm bolt (with pitch of 1.25) into threaded hole in the timing pulley housing through the hole in pulley to prevent turning of the pulley.

Remove the bolts fixing the injection pump timing pulley, then remove the pulley using pulley puller.

19. Remove injection pump flange fixing nuts and rear bracket bolts, then remove the injection pump.

INSTALLATION

1. Install the injection pump by aligning notched line on the flange with the line on the front bracket.

2. Install the injection pump timing pulley by aligning it with the key groove. Torque to 42–52 ft. lbs.

3. Bring the piston in no. 1 cylinder to top dead center on compression stroke and align marks on the timing pulleys.

4. Follow the timing belt installation steps.

5. Check the injection timing.

6. To install remaining parts, follow the removal steps in reverse order.

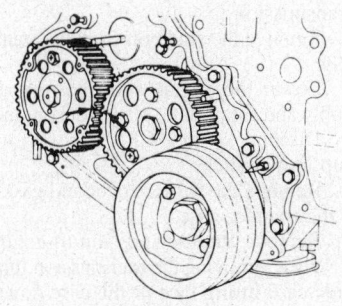

Timing marks aligned

Fuel Tank

REMOVAL AND INSTALLATION

———— CAUTION ————

Before attempting to remove the fuel tank, the following suggestions are recommended: Remove the negative battery terminal; Empty the fuel tank.

1. Remove the filler neck bolts, the hose clamps, the filler neck and the vent hose.

2. Disconnect the sending unit from the electrical terminal.

3. Disconnect the four rubber hoses on the left side of the tank.

4. Disconnect the feed and return lines.

NOTE: Plug the fuel lines to prevent fuel from leaking.

5. Remove the tank mounting bolts and remove the tank.

6. Installation is the reverse of removal.

MANUAL TRANSMISSION

2 Wheel Drive 4-Speed

REMOVAL AND INSTALLATION

1. Disconnect the negative battery cable.

2. Remove the air cleaner assembly, and disconnect the accelerator linkage at the carburetor throttle lever.

3. Slide the gearshift lever boot upward on the lever, remove the two gearshift lever attaching bolts and remove the lever.

4. Remove the starter attaching bolts and lay the starter assembly aside.

5. Raise the vehicle on a hoist and disconnect the exhaust pipe at the flange and disconnect the exhaust pipe hanger at the transmission.

6. Disconnect the speedometer cable at the transmission and disconnect the driveshaft at the differential. Remove the driveshaft. At this point you will have to either drain the transmission lubricant or plug the output shaft opening to prevent spillage.

7. Disconnect the clutch from the bell housing.

8. Remove the bolts attaching the stiffeners, then remove the stone shield (all models).

9. Remove the three frame bracket-to-rear transmission mount attaching bolts.

10. Raise the engine and transmission as required and remove the four cross-member-to-frame bracket bolts.

11. Remove the mounting from the transmission rear cover.

12. Lower the engine and transmission assembly and support the rear of the engine.

13. Disconnect the electrical connectors at the TCS switch and the back-up light switch.

14. Remove the transmission-to-engine attaching bolts and slide the transmission straight back until the input shaft is clear of the clutch. Tip the front of the transmission downward and remove the transmission from the vehicle.

15. Install the transmission in the reverse order of removal, using a clutch aligning arbor or discarded transmission input shaft to align the clutch disc and the pilot bearing, if necessary (if the clutch was removed).

5 Speed

REMOVAL

1. Disconnect battery ground cable.

2. Slide the gearshift lever boot upwards on the lever, remove two gearshift lever attaching bolts and remove lever.

3. Remove starter attaching bolts and lay starter assembly aside.

4. Raise vehicle on hoist and disconnect exhaust pipe hanger at transmission.

5. Place pan under transmission to catch the oil, then disconnect the speedometer cable at the transmission, disconnect ground cable and disconnect propeller shaft at differential. Remove propeller shaft.

6. Remove return spring from clutch fork.

7. Take out two bolts (lower bolts) mounting the flywheel stone guard.

8. Remove two frame bracket to transmission rear mount bolts and nuts.

9. Raise engine and transmission as required and remove four crossmember to frame bracket bolts.

10. Remove the rear mounting (2 nuts) from the transmission rear extension.

11. Lower engine and transmission assembly and support rear of engine.

12. Disconnect electrical connector at back-up lamp switch.

13. Remove transmission to engine attaching bolts.

14. Pull transmission straight back until disengaged from clutch. Tip front of transmission downward and remove.

INSTALLATION

1. Position transmission in vehicle and slide forward guiding clutch gear into pilot bearing.

2. Install transmission to engine attaching bolts.

3. Raise and lower engine and transmission as required and install crossmember frame bracket and rear mount.

4. Install the two bolts (lower bolts) mounting the flywheel stone guard.

5. Remove plug (if used) from rear extension and install propeller shaft.

6. Connect speedometer cable, ground cable and exhaust pipe hanger.

7. Connect clutch cable and adjust shift fork as outlined in Clutch Section.

8. Connect electrical connector at back-up lamp switch.

9. Lower vehicle and install starter assembly.

10. Connect battery negative cable.

11. Install gearshift lever and adjust clutch pedal height as outlined in Clutch Section.

12. Check transmission operation.

Manual Transmission and Transfer Case Assembly

REMOVAL AND INSTALLATION

1. Disconnect the negative battery terminal.

2. Drain the transmission oil.

3. Slide the shift lever boots upward and unbolt each lever.

4. Remove the return spring from the transfer case shift lever and remove both levers.

5. Remove the starter attaching bolts and remove the starter assembly.

6. Jack up your vehicle and support it with jackstands. Disconnect the exhaust pipe from the manifold and disconnect the pipe support from the transmission.

7. Disconnect the speedometer cable at the transmission. Disconnect the rear driveshaft at the differential. Disconnect the ground strap.

8. Remove the rear driveshaft from the transfer case. Remove the front driveshaft.

9. Disconnect the clutch return spring.

10. Disconnect the clutch cable at the fork.

11. Remove the flywheel stoneguard.

12. Remove the transmission rear crossmember bolts.

13. Raise the engine and transmission, and remove the rear crossmember-to-frame bolts.

14. Remove the rear mounting bolts from the transfer case.

15. Unbolt and remove the side case from the transmission.

16. Remove the stud bolt from the transfer case.

17. Lower the engine and transmission assembly and support the rear of the engine.

18. Disconnect the CRS switch and backup light switch.

19. Remove the shifter cover and gasket from the transfer case.

20. Remove the transmission-to-engine bolts. When removing the transmission, turn the side case fitting face of the case downward and pull the case straight back until free from the clutch. Tip the front of the transmission downward and remove it.

21. Installation is the reverse of removal. Torque shifter cover bolts to 14 ft. lbs.

CLUTCH

The clutch is a single-plate, dry friction disc, diaphragm spring type.

PEDAL HEIGHT ADJUSTMENT

Adjust the pedal stop so that the clutch and brake pedals are the same height. Make sure that the clutch switch is in contact with the clutch pedal bracket.

REMOVAL AND INSTALLATION

1. Raise the vehicle on a hoist.
2. Remove the transmission.

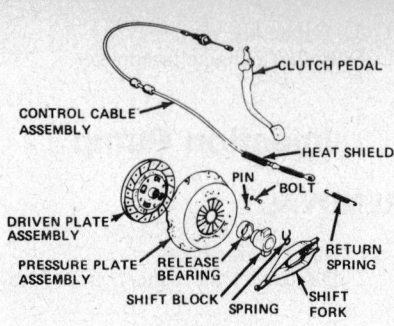

Clutch components

3. Mark the clutch assembly-to-flywheel relationship with paint or a center punch so that the clutch assembly can be reassembled in the same position from which it is removed.

4. Loosen the six clutch cover-to-flywheel attaching bolts, one turn at a time in an alternating sequence, until the spring tension is relieved to avoid distorting or bending the clutch cover.

5. Support the clutch pressure plate and cover assembly with a clutch aligning arbor, then remove the bolts and the clutch assembly.

6. Apply a thin coat of grease to the pressure plate wire ring, diaphragm spring, clutch cover grooves and the drive bosses on the pressure plate.

7. Apply a thin coat of Lubriplate® to the splines in the driven plate.

8. Assemble the clutch cover and pressure plate and the driven plate on a clutch alignment arbor.

9. Align the marks made on the clutch cover and the flywheel and install the six clutch cover-to-flywheel attaching bolts. Tighten the bolts to 50 in. lbs. Remove the aligning arbor.

10. Install the transmission.

Clutch Cable

REMOVAL AND INSTALLATION

1. Loosen the clutch cable lock and adjusting nuts. Remove the clutch cable clip at the engine compartment location.

2. Raise the vehicle and remove the spring from the shift fork end.

3. Disconnect the cable end from the shift fork and pull the cable assembly through the bracket.

4. Lower the vehicle enough to dis-

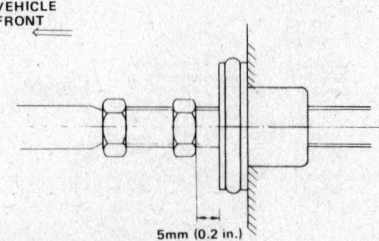

Clutch cable adjustment

engage the hooked part of the clutch pedal from the cable eye. Pull the cable assembly towards the engine compartment and remove the cable from the vehicle.

5. Installation is the reverse of removal.

ADJUSTMENT

1. Pull the outer cable forward and turn the adjusting nut inward until the rubber lip on the washer damper touches the firewall.

2. Depress and release the clutch pedal a few times.

3. Pull the outer cable forward again and fully tighten the adjusting nut. Back the adjusting nut off to provide a clearance of 0.20 in.

4. Release the outer cable and tighten the nut.

AUTOMATIC TRANSMISSION

The Turbo Hydra-Matic 200 transmission is a fully automatic unit consisting primarily of a 3 element hydraulic torque converter and a compound planetary gear set. Three multiple-disc clutches, a roller clutch, and a band provide the friction elements required to obtain the desired function of the compound planetary gear set.

NOTE: Because of the highly technical skill needed to repair this transmission, it is recommended that repairs be handled by a qualified mechanic.

REMOVAL AND INSTALLATION

1. Disconnect the negative battery cable and remove the throttle valve cable from the carburetor.

2. Remove the transmission dipstick assembly.

3. Raise the vehicle and remove the pan from the converter housing.

4. Remove the starter assembly.

5. Disconnect the driveshaft and remove it from the vehicle.

NOTE: Plug the rear of the transmission to avoid fluid leakage.

6. Disconnect the shift lever control rod from the transmission shift lever.

7. Remove the exhaust pipe bracket. Remove the speedometer cable from the transmission.

8. Remove the oil cooler lines and position them along the vehicle frame to prevent damage.

9. Remove the bolts and nuts coupling the drive plate to the converter.

10. Remove the bolts holding the frame bracket to the transmission rear mount.

11. Raise the engine and transmission assembly and remove the frame bracket from the crossmember. Remove the rear mount from the transmission.

12. Remove the bell housing bolts and move the transmission rearward together with the throttle cable and the oil filler tube.

CAUTION
Do not allow the torque converter to drop from the transmission.

SHIFT LINKAGE ADJUSTMENT

1. Loosen the control rod lock nuts so that trunnion will slide on the control rod.

2. Turn the lever shaft of the transmission counterclockwise, viewed from the left side of the transmission, as far as it will go.

3. Back off the lever shaft three stops to the neutral position.

4. Holding the shaft in this position, move the shift lever to the neutral position and push the shift control lower lever rearward to remove play. Tighten the lock nuts.

5. Check for proper operation of the transmission in all transmission ranges.

Throttle Valve Control Cable

REMOVAL AND INSTALLATION

1. Loosen the throttle valve control cable adjusting nuts and disconnect the cable from the carburetor throttle lever by removing the pin.

2. Remove the throttle valve cable clip from the right side of the cylinder body.

3. Remove the bolt holding the throttle cable to the transmission and pull the cable upward. Disconnect the end of the inner cable from the throttle lever link on the transmission side.

4. Remove the cable assembly from the vehicle.

5. Installation is the reverse of removal.

ADJUSTMENT

1. Loosen the throttle valve control cable adjusting nuts.

2. Open the carburetor throttle lever to the wide open position and adjust the inner cable by turning the adjustment nut (lower) on the outer cable by hand so that the inner cable has a free play of approximately 0.040 in.

3. Tighten the lock nut (upper) securely.

4. Make sure that the stroke of the inner cable from the wide open position to the closed position is within the range of 1.37 to 1.41 inches.

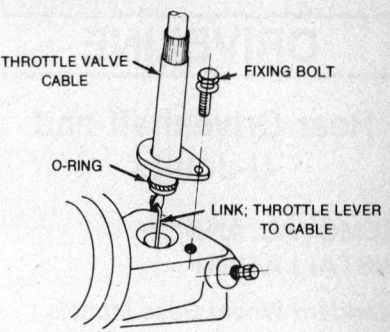

Throttle valve cable removal

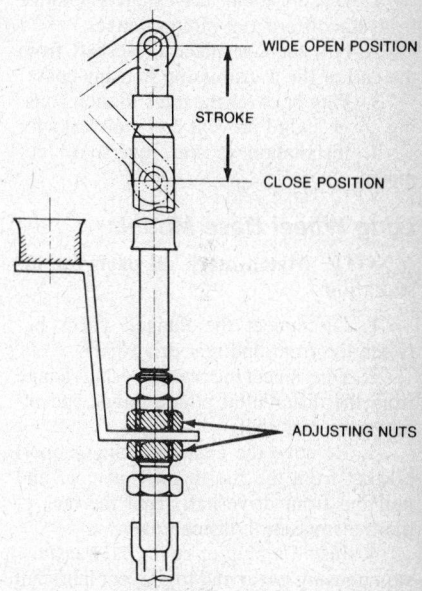

Throttle valve cable adjustment

Inhibitor Switch

ADJUSTMENT

1. Loosen the screws holding the switch. Move the switch body so that the center of the moveable part of the switch, aligns with the neutral position indicator line on the steel case when the shift lever is in the neutral position.

2. Tighten the holding screws and make sure that the engine does not start in gear.

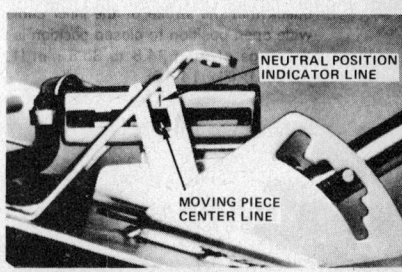

Inhibitor switch adjustment

DRIVELINE

Rear Driveshaft and U-Joints

REMOVAL AND INSTALLATION

Standard Wheel Base Models

NOTE: Match-mark all parts for installation.

1. Disconnect the driveshaft rear flange from the differential pinion flange.
2. Pull the one piece driveshaft from the end of the transmission housing cover.
3. Plug or cover the transmission housing cover end to prevent lubricant leakage.
4. Installation is the reverse of removal.

Long Wheel Base Models

NOTE: Match-mark all parts for installation.

1. Disconnect the flanged yokes between the front and rear driveshafts.
2. Disconnect the rear driveshaft flange from the differential pinion flange and remove the rear shaft.
3. Remove the center bearing support bracket from the fourth crossmember and pull the front driveshaft from the rear of the transmission housing cover.
4. Install a plug or cover the transmission housing cover end to prevent lubricant loss.
5. Installation is the reverse of removal.

Front Drive Shaft

REMOVAL AND INSTALLATION

1. Jack up your vehicle and support it with jack stands.

NOTE: You must raise the vehicle enough for the front wheels to turn freely.

2. Place the transmission and transfer case in the neutral position.
3. Match-mark each end of the driveshaft and the flanges on the rear and transfer case.
4. Remove the U-bolts from the rear and the transfer case flanges.
5. Remove the driveshaft.
6. Installation is the reverse of removal.

U-JOINT OVERHAUL

1. Remove the driveshaft from the vehicle.
2. Punch mating marks on both the

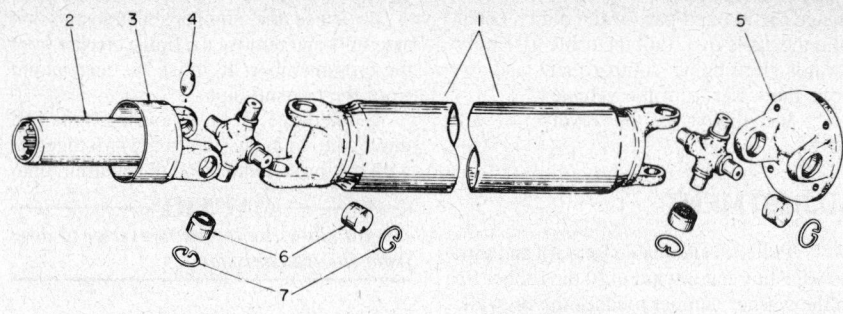

Driveshaft

1. Driveshaft
2. Spline yoke
3. Cover
4. Plate plug
5. Flange yoke
6. Bearing caps
7. Snap-rings

yokes at either end of the driveshaft and the driveshaft itself so that the driveshaft assembly can be reassembled in the same position.

3. Remove the snap-rings from the bearing hole of the yokes.
4. Place the yoke in a vise with a small socket positioned against one of the bearing cups and a larger socket placed against the yoke on the opposite side. The larger socket must be able to receive the bearing cap when it is pressed out of the yoke.
5. Tighten the vise until the bearing caps are free of the yoke.
6. Remove the two remaining bearings from the opposite yoke in the same manner and remove the spider bearing journal.
7. Make sure that the new spiders and needle bearings in the bearing caps are well lubricated.
8. Assemble the universal joint spider and bearing caps to the yoke in the reverse manner of removal, using the smaller socket to press the bearing caps into the yoke and the larger socket to bear against the yoke bearing cap hole at the opposite end. Use a vise to press the bearing caps in place.
9. Install the hole snap-ring to secure the bearing caps.
10. Assemble the slide yoke to the driveshaft, aligning the marks made prior to disassembly.
11. Install the driveshaft assembly on the vehicle.

Rear Axle Shaft

REMOVAL AND INSTALLATION

1. Raise the vehicle on a hoist.
2. Remove the rear wheel cover and the wheel and tire.
3. Remove the brake drum, brake shoes and disconnect the parking brake inner cable.
4. Disconnect the brake line at the wheel cylinder and plug the end of the line.
5. Remove the four nuts from the bearing holder through-bolts from the inside of the brake backing plate.

6. Using an axle puller, pull out the axle shaft assembly. Never strike the brake backing plate with a hammer in an attempt to remove the axle shaft.
7. Install the axle shaft in the reverse order of removal, tightening the bearing holding plate attaching nuts to 55 ft. lbs., bleeding the brake hydraulic system after installing the brakes and adjusting the parking brake cable as necessary.

Front Axle and Axle Shaft

REMOVAL AND INSTALLATION

1. Raise and support the vehicle.
2. Disconnect the front driveshaft at the differential.
3. Remove the wheels and skid plate.
4. Loosen the torsion bar completely with the height control adjusting bolts.
5. Remove the strut bars.
6. Disconnect the stabilizer bars at the lower control arms.
7. Remove the caliper assemblies and wire them to the frame. It is not necessary to disconnect the brake lines.
8. Remove the ball joints from the tie rods.
9. Disconnect the upper control arms at the frame. Make sure to note the number and positions of the shims.
10. Remove the steering link ends from the lower control arms.
11. Disconnect the shock absorbers from the lower control arms.
12. Disconnect the lower control arms from the frame.
13. Remove the free wheeling hub. See Front Bearing Removal.
14. Remove the rotors and upper links.
15. Remove the pitman arm and idler arm along with the steering linkage assembly.
16. Support the differential housing with a jack, lower it clear of the vehicle and roll it out. Take care to avoid damaging the birfield joints.

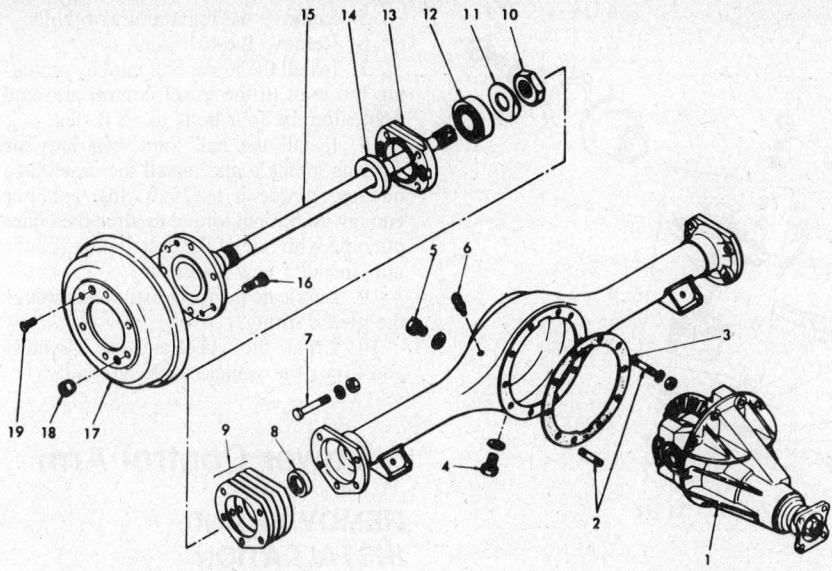

Axle shaft and housing

1. Differetial carrier and case assembly	5. Filler plug	10. Locknut	15. Axle shaft
2. Mounting bolt	6. Vent	11. Lockwasher	16. Wheel stud
3. Gasket	7. Through-bolt	12. Axle shaft bearing	17. Brake drum
4. Drain plug	8. Oil seal	13. Bearing holder	18. Wheel nut
	9. Shims	14. Grease seal	19. Drum-to-flange screw

17. Drain the differential case and remove the four bolts attaching the axle mounting bracket to the case.

18. Pull the shaft assemblies from the case on both sides.

19. Installation is the reverse of removal.

Observe the following torque values:

Item	Ft. Lbs.
Axle shaft-to-case	43
Differential case-to-frame	15
Pitman arm-to-sector shaft	160
Idler arm-to-pivot shaft	87
Lower control arm-to-frame	94
Ball joint castellated nut	100

2-WHEEL DRIVE FRONT SUSPENSION

Torsion Bars

REMOVAL AND INSTALLATION

1. Jack up the front of the vehicle and support it with jackstands.

2. Remove the adjusting bolt from the height control arm.

3. Mark the location and remove the height control arm from the torsion bar and the third crossmember.

4. Mark the location and withdraw the torsion bar from the lower control arm.

5. For installation, apply a generous amount of grease to the serrated ends of the torsion bars.

6. Hold the rubber bumpers in contact with the lower control arm. Jack the vehicle up under the lower control arm to accomplish this.

7. Insert the front end of the torsion bar into the control arm.

8. Install the height control arm in position so that its end is reaching the adjusting bolt. Be sure to lubricate the part of the height control arm that fits into the chassis with grease.

9. Install a new cotter pin in the control arm.

10. Turn the adjusting bolt to the location marked before removal.

11. Lower the vehicle and check the vehicle height.

Shock Absorbers

REMOVAL AND INSTALLATION

1. Raise the vehicle and support it with jackstands.

2. Hold the upper stem of the shock absorber from turning with an open-end wrench, and then, remove the upper stem retaining nut, retainer and rubber grommet.

3. Remove the bolt retaining the lower shock absorber pivot to the power control arm and remove the shock absorber from the vehicle.

4. Install the shock absorber by first installing the lower retainer and rubber grommet over the upper stem and then, installing the shock fully extended up through the upper control arm so that the upper stem passes through the mounting hole in the frame bracket.

5. Install the upper rubber grommet, retainer and attaching nut over the shock absorber upper stem.

6. Hold the upper stem of the shock absorber from turning with an open-end wrench and tighten the retaining nut.

7. Install the retainers attaching the shock absorber lower pivot to the lower control arm and tighten them.

8. Lower the vehicle.

Upper Control Arm and Ball Joint

REMOVAL AND INSTALLATION

NOTE: The upper control arm and ball joint are replaced as an assembly.

1. Raise the vehicle and support it on jackstands placed under the lower control arms.

2. Remove the wheel and tire assembly.

3. Remove the cotter pin nut fastening the upper control arm and upper ball joint assembly and disconnect the upper control arm from the steering knuckle.

NOTE: Do not allow the steering knuckle to hang by the flexible brake line. Wire the steering knuckle up to the frame temporarily.

4. Remove the two bolts from the upper pivot shaft and remove the upper control arm from the bracket. Be sure to note the position and number of shims used for adjusting the camber and caster angles when removing the upper control arm. This is to ensure that the shims are reinstalled in their original positions.

5. To remove the pivot shaft and bushings from the upper control arm assembly, remove the bushing nuts from the pivot shaft by loosening them alternately, then remove the pivot shaft.

6. To install the upper control arm and ball joint assembly, first install the pivot shaft boots to the pivot shaft.

7. Fill the internal part of the bushings with grease (molybdenum disulfide) and screw the bushings into the pivot shaft. Be sure to screw the right-side and the left-side bushings alternately into the pivot shafts carefully avoiding getting grease on the outer face of the bushings. Tighten the nuts to 250 ft. lbs. for 2-wheel drive and 220 ft. lbs. for 4-wheel drive.

NOTE: Be sure that the control arm and bushings are centered properly and that the control arm rotates with resistance but not binding on the pivot shaft when tightened to the proper torque.

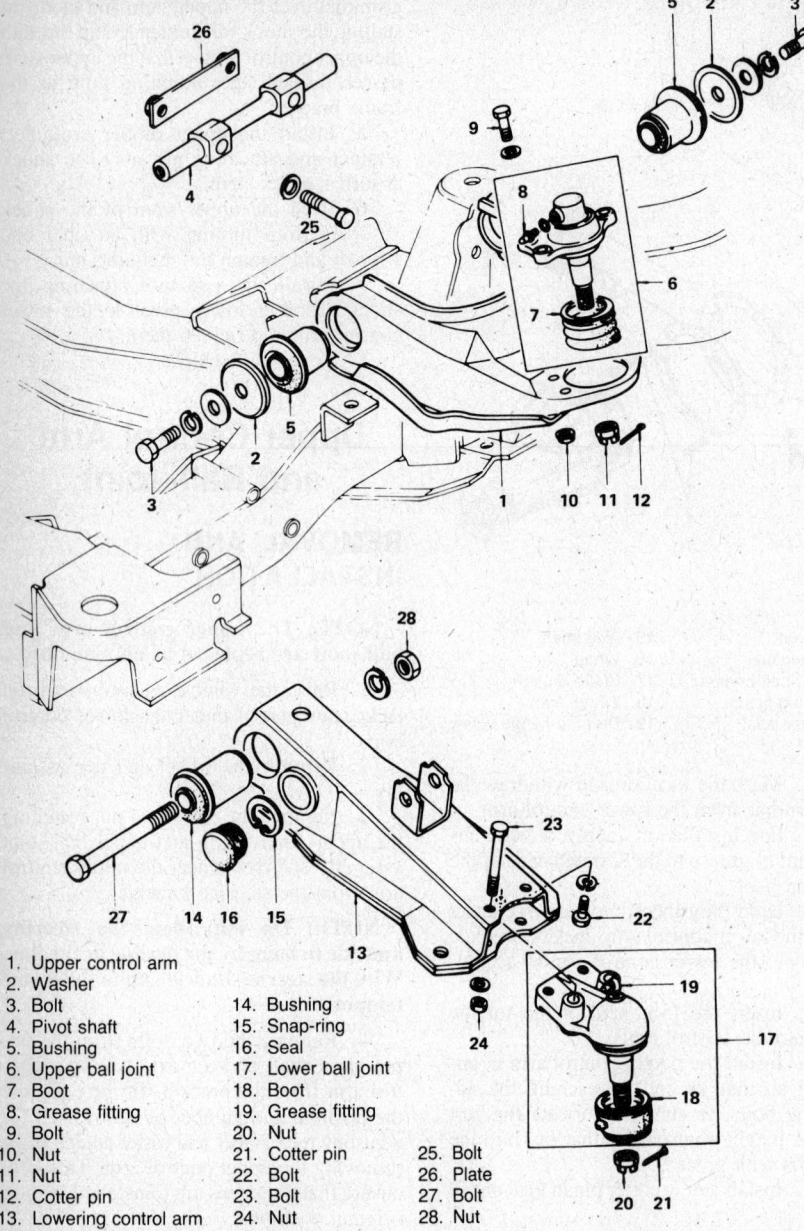

5. Remove the remaining two bolts.
6. Remove the ball joint.
7. Install the lower ball joint by mounting the joint to the lower control arm and tightening the four bolts to 45 ft. lbs.
8. Install the ball joint stud into the steering knuckle and install the castellated nut and torque it to 75 ft. lbs. and just enough additional torque to align the cotter pin hole with one of the castellations on the nut. Install a new cotter pin.
9. Lubricate the lower ball joint through the grease fitting.
10. Install the wheel and tire assembly and lower the vehicle to the ground.

Lower Control Arm

REMOVAL AND INSTALLATION

1. Jack up the vehicle and support it with jackstands.
2. Remove the wheel and tire.
3. Remove the strut bar by removing the frame side bracket and the double nuts, washer and the rubber bushing from the front side of the strut bar. Next, remove the two bolts fastening the strut bar to the lower control arm and remove the bar.
4. Disconnect the stabilizer bar from the lower control arm.
5. Remove the torsion bar.
6. Disconnect the shock absorber from the lower control arm.
7. If you so desire, remove the lower ball joint from the lower control arm joint at this time.
8. Remove the retaining nut and drive out the bolt holding the lower control arm to the chassis with a soft metal drift. Remove the lower control arm from the vehicle.
9. To install the lower control arm, first, install the lower ball joint to the lower control arm. Tighten the retaining nuts to 45 ft. lbs.
10. Mount the lower control arm to the frame. Drive the bolt into position carefully with a soft metal drift. Use care not to damage the serrated portions. Tighten the nut on the end of the pivot bolt to 135 ft. lbs.
11. Install the stabilizer bar to the lower control arm.
12. Place the washers and bushings on the strut rod and install it through the frame bracket. Install the second set of washers and bushings on the strut rod together with the lockwashers and nut. Leave the nut loose temporarily.
13. Install the strut rod to the lower control arm and tighten the bolts to 45 ft. lbs.
14. Assemble the lower ball joint to the steering knuckle.
15. Install the wheel and tire and lower the vehicle.
16. Tighten the first strut bar-to-chassis frame attaching nut to 175 ft. lbs., and the second locknut to 55 ft. lbs.

1. Upper control arm
2. Washer
3. Bolt
4. Pivot shaft
5. Bushing
6. Upper ball joint
7. Boot
8. Grease fitting
9. Bolt
10. Nut
11. Nut
12. Cotter pin
13. Lowering control arm
14. Bushing
15. Snap-ring
16. Seal
17. Lower ball joint
18. Boot
19. Grease fitting
20. Nut
21. Cotter pin
22. Bolt
23. Bolt
24. Nut
25. Bolt
26. Plate
27. Bolt
28. Nut

2-wheel drive front suspension

8. Install the grease fittings and lubricate the parts with grease through the grease fittings.
9. Install the ball joint stud through the steering knuckle. Install the castellated nut and tighten it to 75 ft. lbs. and just enough additional torque to install the cotter pin. Use a new cotter pin.
10. Mount the upper control arm to the chassis frame and install the shims in their original positions between the pivot shaft and bracket. Tighten the pivot shaft attaching nuts to 55 ft. lbs.

NOTE: Tighten the thinner shim pack's nut first for improved shaft-to-frame clamping force and torque retention.

11. Install the dust cover.

12. Install the wheel and tire assembly and lower the vehicle to the floor.

Lower Ball Joint

REMOVAL AND INSTALLATION

1. Raise the front of the vehicle and support it with jackstands.
2. Remove the wheel and tire assembly.
3. Remove the cotter pin and castellated nut which retains the ball joint to the steering knuckle.
4. Remove the two bolts retaining the lower ball joint and strut rod.

1. Torsion bar
2. Height control arm
3. Upper pivot nut
4. Lower pivot nut
5. Height control bolt
6. Stopper plate
7. Bolt
8. Strut rod
9. Strut rod bushing
10. Strut rod washer
11. Tube
12. Nut
13. Bolt
14. Bolt
15. Shock absorber
16. Shock absorber bushing
17. Bushing retainer
18. Nut
19. Bolt
20. Nut
21. Dust cover
22. Screw
23. Lower control arm bumper
24. Upper control arm bumper
25. Stabilizer bar
26. Bolt
27. Stabilizer bar bushing
28. Stabilizer bar upper clamp
29. Stabilizer bar lower clamp
30. Bolt
31. Nut
32. Bolt
33. Nut
34. Bracket, stabilizer bar to frame
35. Bolt
36. Bushing
37. Washer
38. Nut
39. Nut
40. Nut

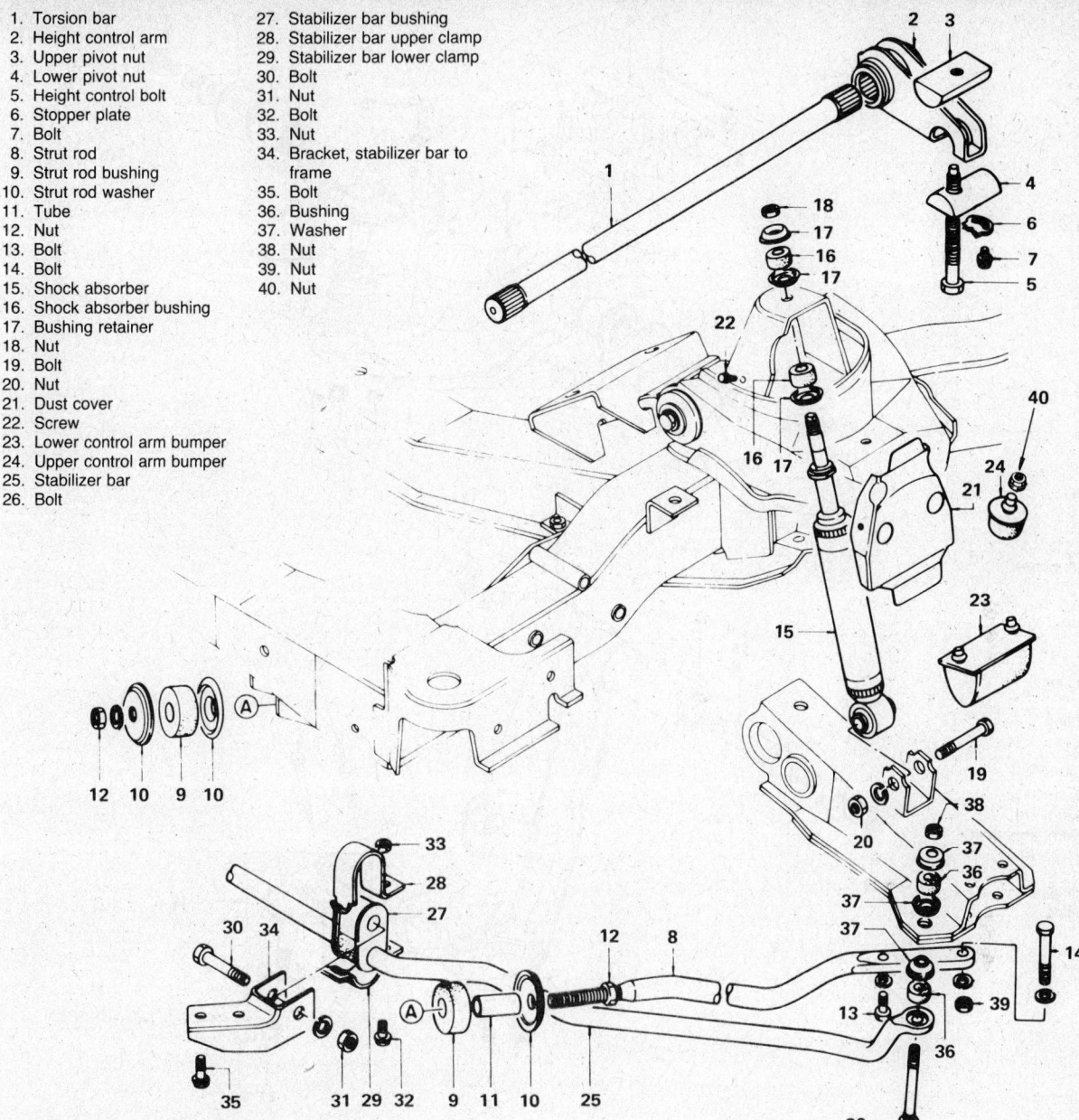

2-wheel drive torsion, strut and stabilizer bars

4-WHEEL DRIVE FRONT SUSPENSION

Locking Hub

REMOVAL AND INSTALLATION

1. Jack up your vehicle and support it with jackstands.

2. Place the transfer case in the 2H position.

3. Set the hubs in the free position.

4. Remove the hub cover bolts and remove the hub cover.

Cover Assembly

1. While pushing the follower toward the knob, turn the clutch assembly clockwise, and then remove the clutch assembly from the knob.

2. Remove the snap-ring and remove the knob from the cover.

NOTE: Do not lose the detent ball.

3. Remove the ball and spring from the knob.

4. Remove the X-ring from the knob by pressing it off with your fingers.

NOTE: Do not use a screwdriver to remove this ring because it may scratch the ring.

5. Remove the compression spring, retaining spring, and the follower from the clutch assembly.

6. Remove the retaining spring from the clutch assembly by turning it counterclockwise.

Body Assembly

1. Remove the snap-ring and then remove the inner assembly from the body.

2. Separate the ring, inner, and spacer by removing the snap-ring.

3. Installation is the reverse of removal with the following suggestions.

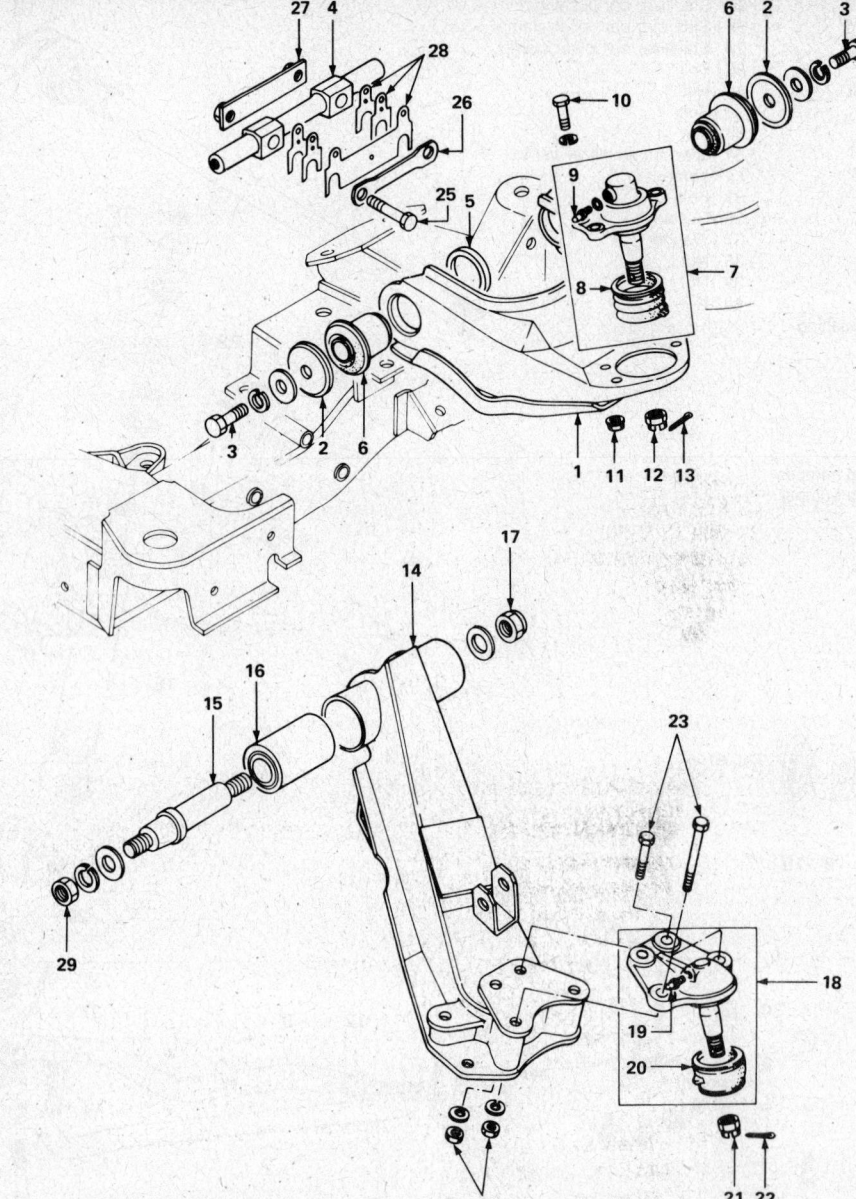

1. Upper control arm
2. Washer
3. Bolt
4. Pivot shaft
5. Collar
6. Bushing
7. Upper ball joint
8. Boot
9. Grease fitting
10. Bolt
11. Nut
12. Nut
13. Cotter pin
14. Lower control arm
15. Lower control arm shaft
16. Bushing
17. Nut
18. Lower ball joint
19. Grease fitting
20. Boot
21. Nut
22. Cotter pin
23. Bolt
24. Nut
25. Bolt
26. Plate
27. Plate
28. Shim
29. Nut

4-wheel drive front suspension

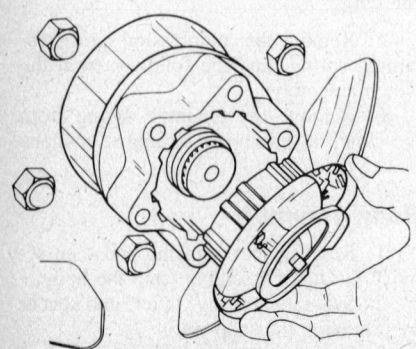

Front hub cover removal

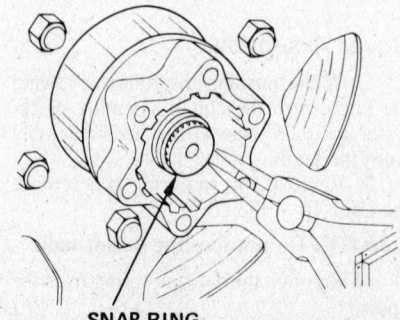

Hub snap-ring

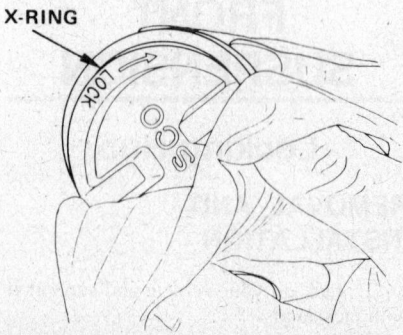

Removing X-ring

1. Torsion bar
2. Rubber seat
3. Height control arm
4. Pivot Nut
5. Height control seat and bolt
6. Strut bar
7. Strut bar bushing
8. Strut bar washer
9. Nut
10. Bolt
11. Bolt
12. Nut
13. Shock absorber
14. Bushing
15. Retainer
16. Nut
17. Bolt
18. Nut
19. Lower control arm bumper
20. Bolt
21. Upper control arm bumper
22. Stabilizer bar
23. Stabilizer bar bushing
24. Stabilizer bar support
25. Stabilizer bar bracket
26. Bolt
27. Bushing
28. Washer
29. Nut
30. Bolt
31. Bushing
32. Washer
33. Nut

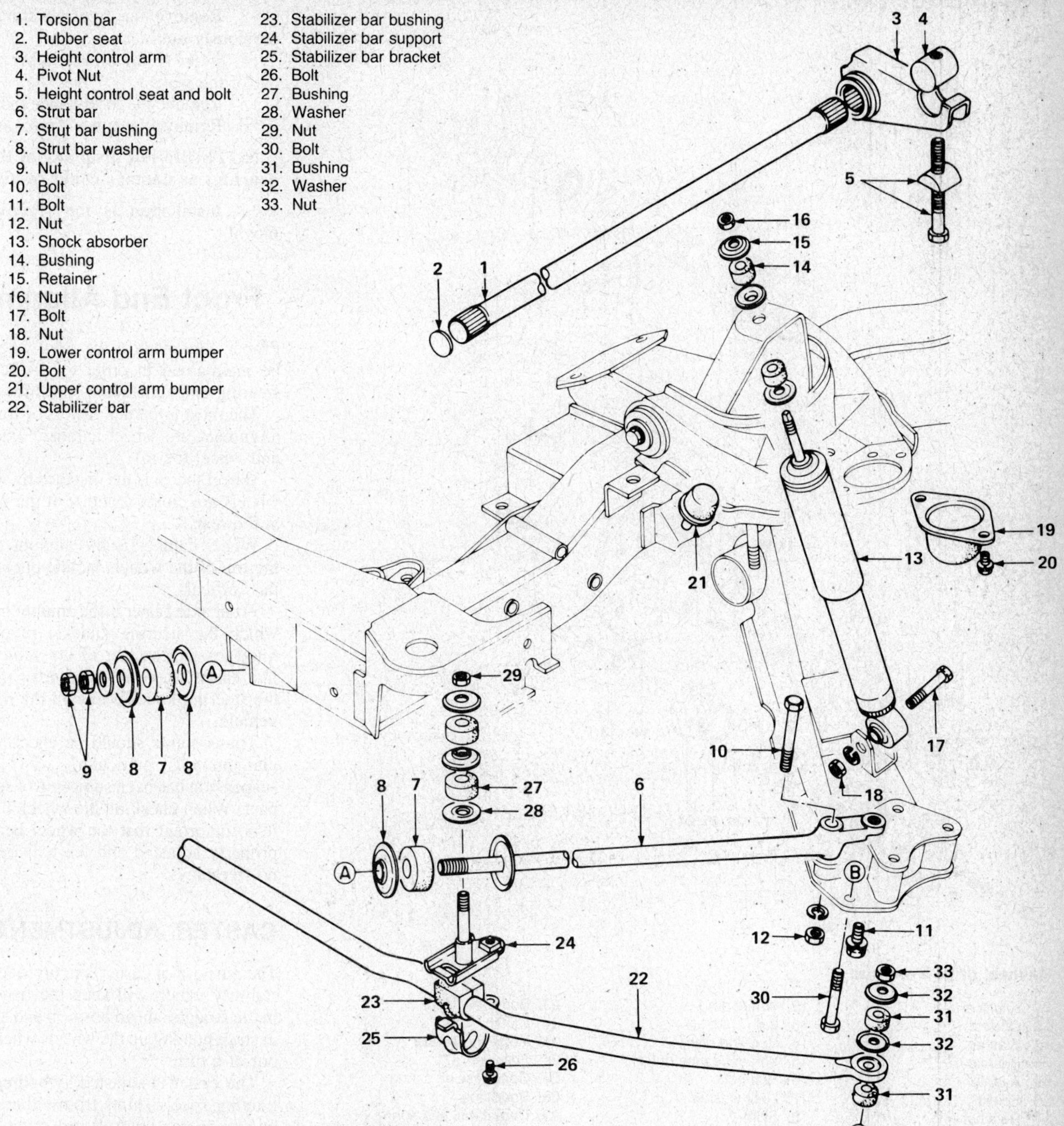

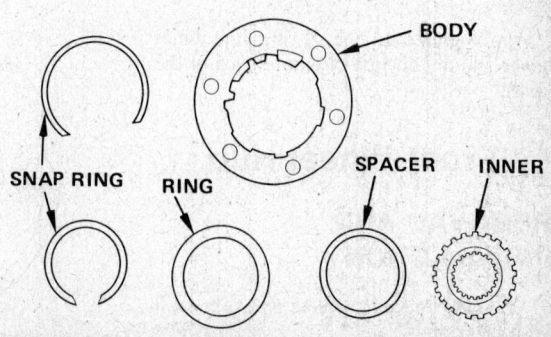

4-wheel drive torsion, strut and stabilizer bars

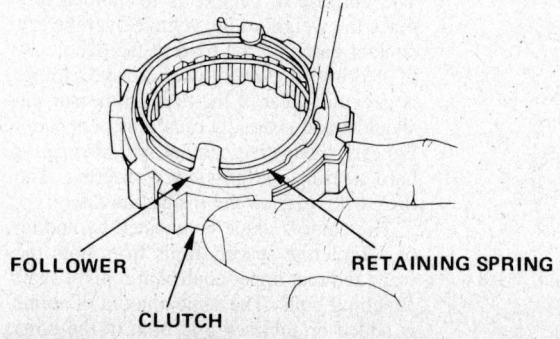

Removing clutch follower

FOLLOWER RETAINING SPRING CLUTCH

Hub body components

BODY SNAP RING RING SPACER INNER

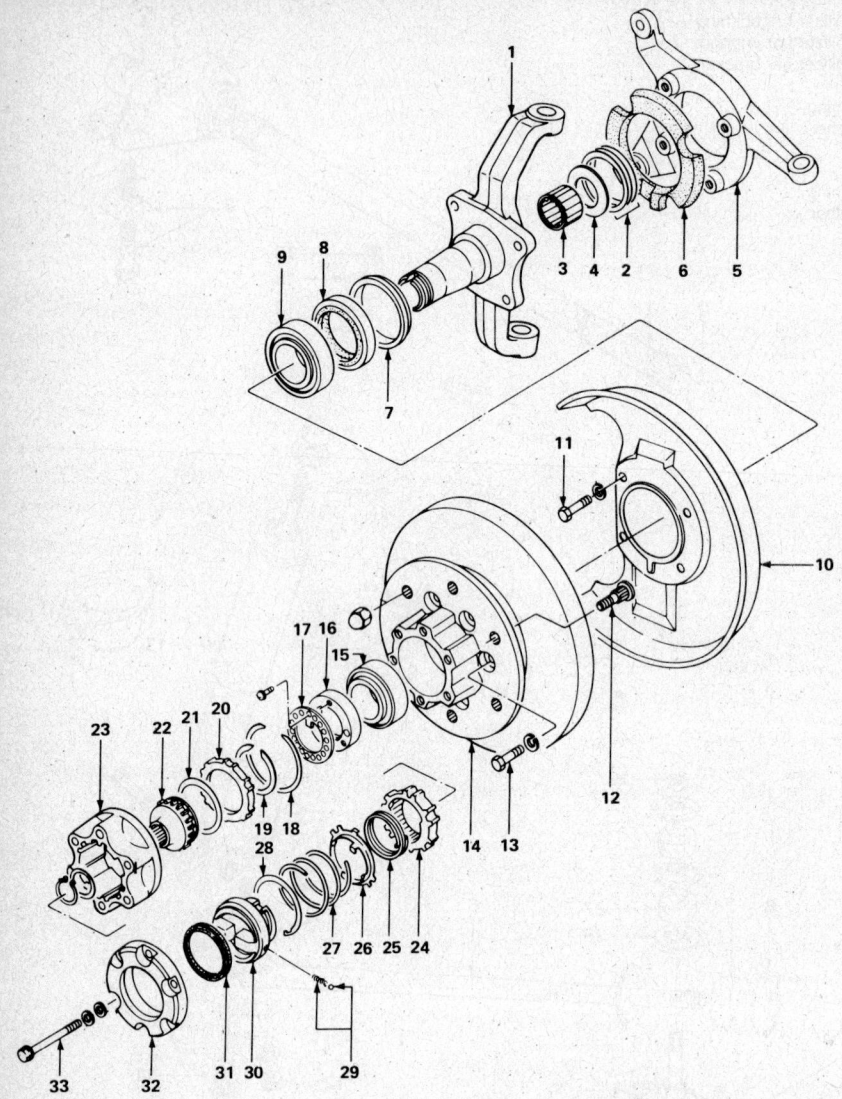

4-wheel drive front hub

1. Knuckle
2. Oil seal
3. Washer
4. Bearing
5. Adaptor
6. Shield
7. Retainer ring
8. Oil seal
9. Hub bearing inner
10. Dust shield
11. Bolt
12. Wheel pin
13. Bolt
14. Hub and disc
15. Wheel bearing outer
16. Hub nut
17. Lock washer
18. Shim
19. Snap-ring
20. Ring
21. Spacer
22. Inner
23. Body
24. Clutch
25. Retaining spring
26. Follower
27. Compression spring
28. Snap-ring
29. Detent ball and spring
30. Knob
31. X–Ring
32. Cover
33. Bolt

Apply grease to the X-ring, the inner cover and the outside circumference of the knob.

Front Wheel Hub

REMOVAL AND INSTALLATION

1. Jack up your vehicle and support it with jackstands.
2. Remove the front wheel.

FREE POSITION

Front hub knob

3. Remove the free wheeling hub as previously outlined.
4. Remove the brake caliper and tie it out of the way.
5. Remove the lockwasher and hub nut.
6. Remove the hub and rotor assembly.

NOTE: Do not drop any of the wheel bearings as damage could result.

7. Installation is the reverse of removal.

Front End Alignment

Proper alignment of the front wheels must be maintained in order to ensure ease of steering and satisfactory tire life.

The most important factors of front wheel alignment are wheel camber, axle caster, and wheel toe-in.

Wheel toe-in is the distance by which the wheels are closer together at the front than at the rear.

Wheel camber is the amount in which the top of the wheels incline outward from the vertical.

Front axle caster is the amount in degrees which the steering knuckle pivot axis is tilted toward the rear of the vehicle. Positive caster is the inclination of the top of the steering knuckle toward the rear of the vehicle.

These points should be checked at regular intervals, particularly when the front suspension has been subjected to severe impact. When checking the wheel alignment, it is important that the wheel bearings be properly adjusted and the ball joints have no free-play.

CASTER ADJUSTMENT

The purpose of caster is to provide steering stability which will keep the front wheels in the straight-ahead position and also assist in straightening up the wheels when coming out of a turn.

The caster is adjusted by adding or subtracting spacer shims from either the front or rear upper control arm pivot shaft attaching bolts.

CAMBER ADJUSTMENT

The purpose of camber is to more nearly place the weight of the vehicle over the tire contact patch on the road to facilitate ease of steering. The result of excessive camber is irregular wear of the tires on the outside shoulder and is usually caused by bent parts. Excessive negative camber will also cause hard steering and possibly wandering. The tires will wear on the inside shoulders.

The camber angle is adjusted by adding or subtracting spacer shims from both the front and rear upper control arm pivot shaft attaching bolts. The same amount of shims is added or subtracted to both of the bolts at the same time.

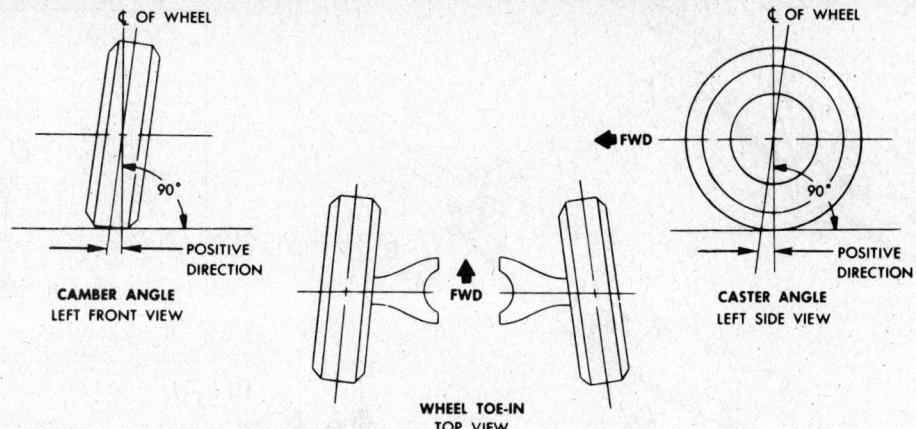

Caster, camber and toe-in

TOE-IN

The toe-in measurement is the difference between the distances between the front and rear center of the tread of the two front tires.

The toe-in can be adjusted by turning the intermediate rod after loosening the locknuts on the intermediate rod ends. The locknuts have left-hand and right-hand threads to allow for equal adjustment of both wheels at the same time. Turn the intermediate rod toward the front of the vehicle to reduce the toe-in angle and toward the rear of the vehicle to increase the toe-in angle.

RIDE HEIGHT ADJUSTMENT

NOTE: The ride height should be measured with a full tank of gas, spare tire, jack, no passengers, and with the tires inflated to the correct pressure.

1. Place the vehicle on a smooth level floor and bounce the front end several times. Raise the vehicle and then allow it to settle to a normal height.
2. Measure the distance between the bottom of the lower ball joint stud which fits through the steering knuckle and the

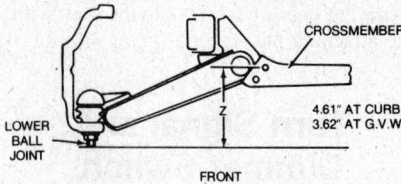

Ride height measurement, front

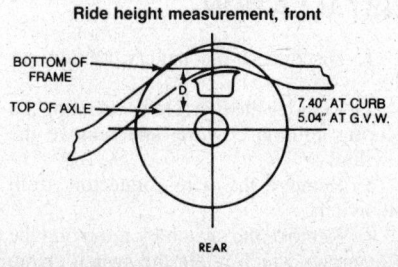

Ride height measurement, rear

ground and the distance between the frame crossmember that the lower control arm attaches to and the ground.

The difference between these two measurements should be 2.52 in. (1.54 in. with the vehicle loaded to GVW).

3. Adjust the vehicle height by first loosening the nuts on the front end of the strut bar and then turning the vehicle height adjusting bolt. Turn the bolt clockwise to raise the vehicle. As an additional check, measure the clearance between the rubber bumper and the lower control arm. The clearance should be 7/8 in.

4. Check the ride height at the front of the vehicle as outlined in step 2 above and the ride height at the rear axle by measuring the clearance between the top of the axle and the bottom of the frame where the frame rises to clear the axle. The clearance between the frame and axle at this point should be 7.90 in. (6.26 in. with the vehicle loaded to GVW).

5. After obtaining the correct clearances, securely tighten the strut bar attaching nuts to the proper torque.

REAR SUSPENSION

Springs

REMOVAL

1. Jack up the rear of the vehicle and place jackstands under the frame near the rear end of the rear spring brackets.
2. Remove the rear shock absorbers.
3. Remove the parking brake cable clips.
4. Remove the nuts from the U-bolts holding the springs to the axle housing.
5. Jack the rear axle up to remove the weight of the axle housing from the springs.
6. Remove the front and rear shackle pin nuts.
7. Drive out the rear shackle pin by

using a hammer and drift and lower the rear end of the leaf spring assembly to the floor.

8. Drive out the front shackle pin and remove the leaf spring assembly rearward.
9. Remove the shackle pin from the rear spring bracket and remove the shackle.

INSPECTION

1. Check the leaf springs for cracks, wear and broken leaves. Replace any leaves found to be cracked, broken, fatigued or seriously worn.
2. Check the shackles for bending and the pins for wear.
3. Check the U-bolts for distortion or other damage.

INSTALLATION

1. Mount the shackle to the bracket.
2. Align the front end of the leaf spring assembly with the front bracket and install the shackle pin.
3. Align the rear end of the leaf spring assembly with the shackle and install the shackle pin.
4. Loosely install the shackle pin nuts and install the U-bolts. Tighten the U-bolt nuts to 40 ft. lbs.
5. Install the shock absorbers.
6. Clip the parking brake cable to the bracket.
7. Remove the jackstands and lower the vehicle so that the vehicle weight is on the leaf springs.
8. Tighten the shackle pin nuts to 130 ft. lbs.

Shock Absorbers

REMOVAL AND INSTALLATION

Remove the rear shock absorbers by loosening and removing the upper and lower attaching nuts and pulling the shock absorber ends off the mounting studs, together

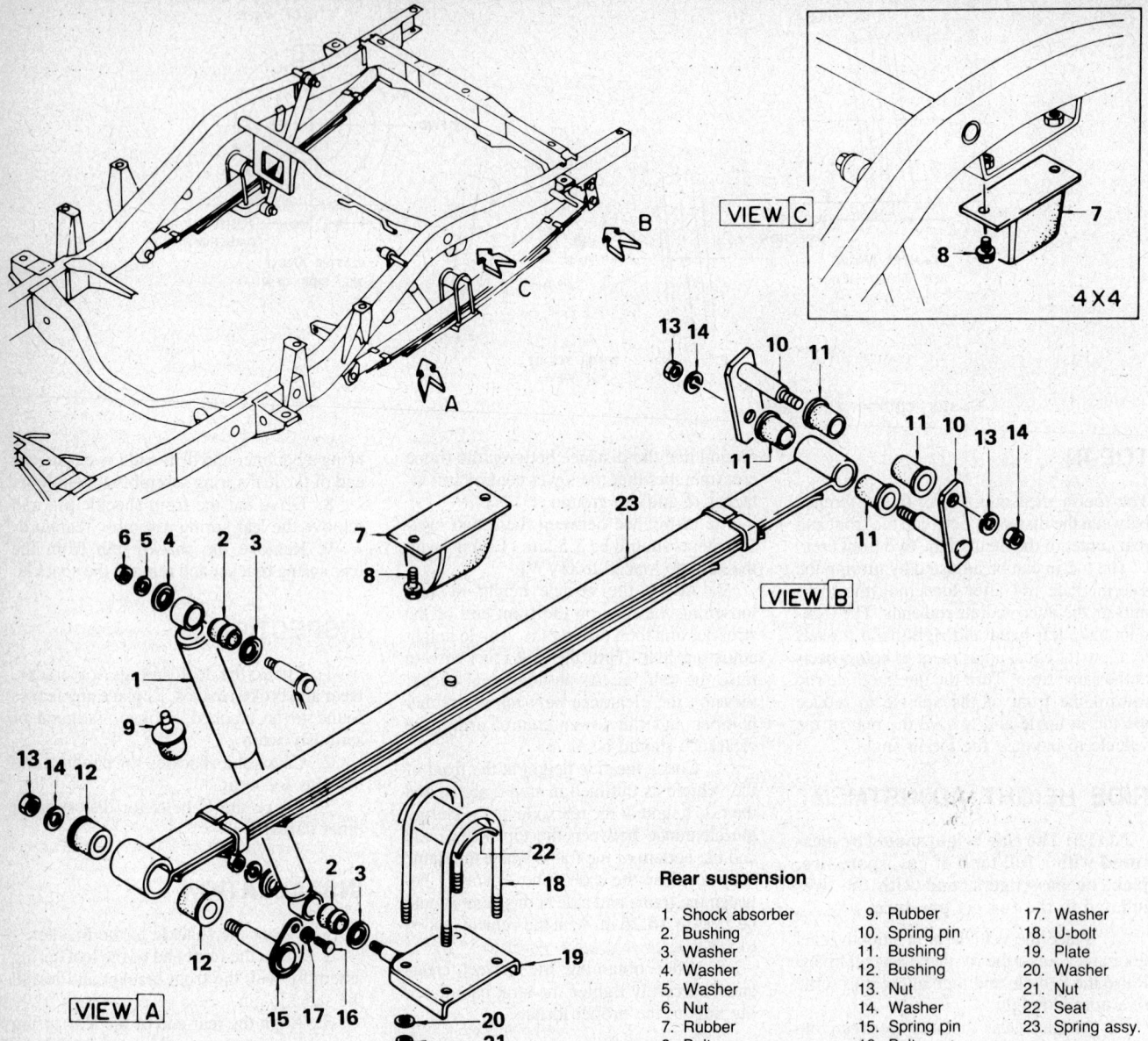

VIEW C

4 X 4

13 14   10   11

11 10 13 14

11

11

VIEW B

23

7

8

6 5 4   2 3

7

8

1

9

13 14 12

22

18

12

2 3

12

VIEW A

15 17 16

19

20

21

Rear suspension

1. Shock absorber	9. Rubber	17. Washer
2. Bushing	10. Spring pin	18. U-bolt
3. Washer	11. Bushing	19. Plate
4. Washer	12. Bushing	20. Washer
5. Washer	13. Nut	21. Nut
6. Nut	14. Washer	22. Seat
7. Rubber	15. Spring pin	23. Spring assy.
8. Bolt	16. Bolt	

with the washers and rubber bushings. Install the shock absorbers in the reverse order of removal, making sure that you use new rubber bushings and that they are installed correctly in the bevel shaped mounting holes in the end of the shock absorbers.

STEERING

Steering Wheel

REMOVAL AND INSTALLATION

1. Disconnect the battery ground cable.
2. Remove the horn shroud and spring

by pushing and turning it counterclockwise. Remove the horn contact ring and wire.

3. Remove the steering wheel-to-steering shaft retaining nut, washer and lockwasher.

4. Mark the relative position of the steering wheel and shaft to each other.

5. Remove the steering column cowling by removing the four attaching screws and washers.

6. Remove the steering wheel from the shaft with a puller.

NOTE: Under no circumstances is the steering shaft to be hammered upon, jarred, or leaned upon. The steering column is a collapsible, energy-absorbing type and can be easily damaged through mistreatment.

7. Install the steering wheel in the reverse order of removal, aligning the marks made on the steering wheel and the shaft.

Draw the steering wheel onto the shaft with the attaching nut.

Turn Signal and Dimmer Switch

REMOVAL AND INSTALLATION

1. Disconnect the battery ground cable.

2. Remove the five screws retaining the steering column cowling and remove the cowling.

3. Remove the wire connectors from the switch.

4. Remove the switch by removing the two screws which retain the switch clamp to the steering column mast jacket.

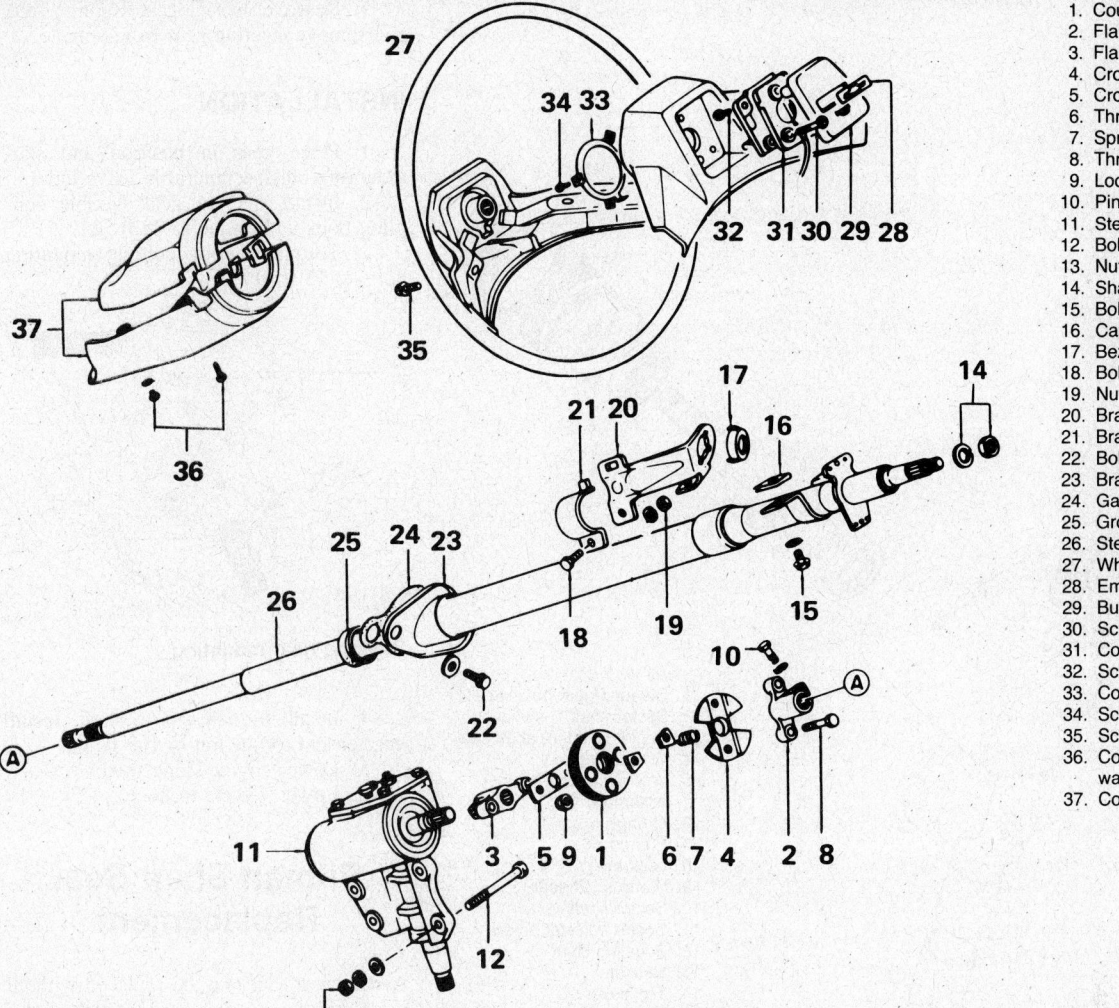

Steering column

1.	Coupling

1. Coupling
2. Flange, upper coupling
3. Flange, lower coupling
4. Cross-strap
5. Cross-strap
6. Thrust washer
7. Spring
8. Through-bolt
9. Lock nut
10. Pinch bolt, lock washer
11. Steering unit assembly
12. Bolt
13. Nut
14. Shaft nut and washer
15. Bolt
16. Capsule
17. Bezel, starter switch
18. Bolt
19. Nut
20. Bracket, RH
21. Bracket, LH
22. Bolt
23. Bracket
24. Gasket
25. Grommet
26. Steering shaft assembly
27. Wheel assembly
28. Emblem
29. Button
30. Screw
31. Contact plate
32. Screw
33. Contact ring
34. Screw
35. Screw
36. Cowling screws and washer
37. Column cowling

5. Replace the switch in the reverse order of removal.

Tie Rod Ends

REMOVAL AND INSTALLATION

1. Jack up your vehicle and support it with jackstands.
2. Match-mark the tie rod ends and the sleeves for installation.
3. Remove the cotter pin and nut from the tie rod end, and loosen the clamping bolts on the sleeve.
4. Use a puller to remove the tie rod from the steering knuckle.
5. Unscrew the tie rod and remove it.
6. Check it for damage and replace it if necessary.
7. Installation is the reverse of removal.

NOTE: Make sure to use a new cotter pin when installing the tie rod.

Steering Gear

ADJUSTMENTS

NOTE: These adjustments must be performed in the following sequence.

1. Disconnect the battery ground cable. Raise vehicle.
2. Remove the Pitman arm nut and lockwasher. Remove the Pitman arm.
3. Remove the horn shroud and spring.
4. Turn the steering wheel gently in one direction until stopped by the gear; then turn back half way.

NOTE: Do not turn the steering wheel hard against the stops when the steering linkage is disconnected from the gear as damage to the ball guides could result.

5. Measure and record "bearing drag" by applying a torque wrench with a socket on the steering wheel nut and rotating through a 90° arc.

Do not use a torque wrench having a maximum torque reading of more than 0.5 kg-m (50 in. lbs.).
6. Adjust "over-center preload" as follows:
a. Turn the steering wheel gently from one stop all the way to the other carefully counting the total number of turns. Turn the wheel back exactly half-way, to center position.
b. Loosen the lock nut and turn the lash adjuster screw clockwise to take out all lash between the ball nut and Pitman shaft sector teeth and then tighten the locknut.
c. Check the torque at the steering wheel, taking the highest reading as the wheel is turned through center position. Preload should be 4.3–10.5 in. lbs.
d. If necessary, loosen locknut and readjust lash adjuster screw to obtain proper torque. Tighten the locknut to 20 ft. lbs. and again check torque reading through center of travel. If maximum specification is exceeded, turn lash ad-

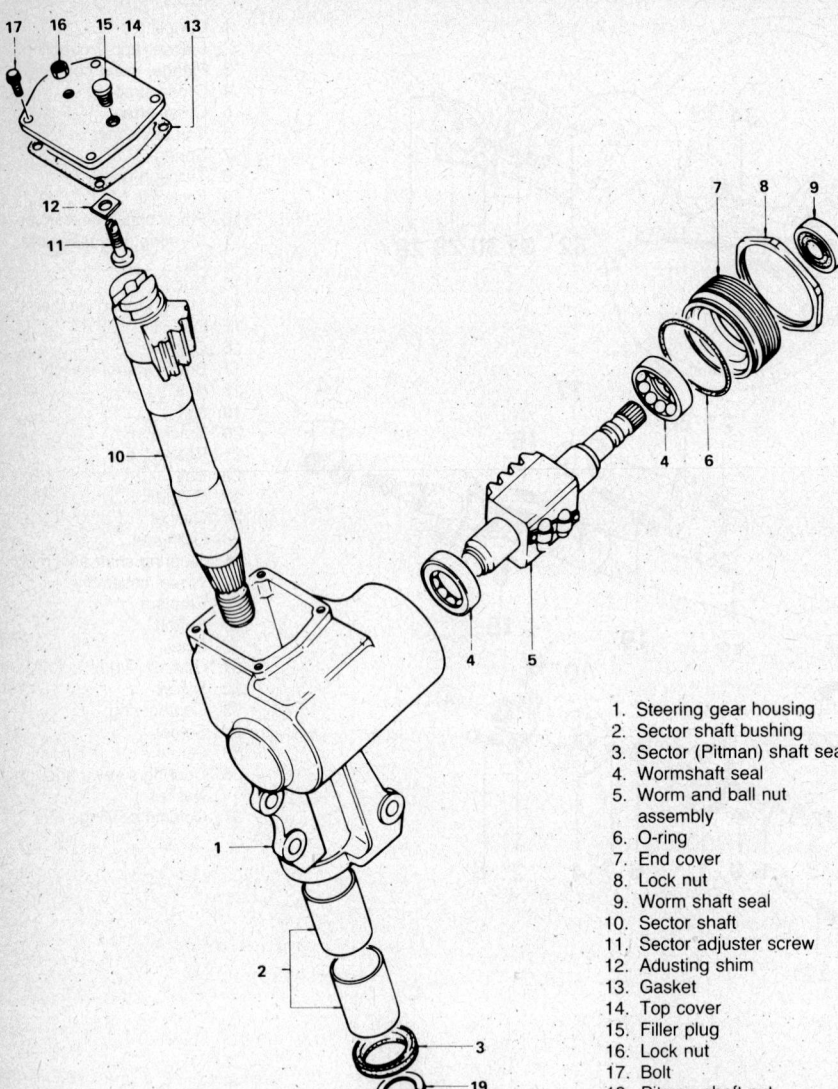

17 16 15 14 13

12

11

10

7 8 9

4 6

4 5

1

2

3

19

18

1. Steering gear housing
2. Sector shaft bushing
3. Sector (Pitman) shaft seal
4. Wormshaft seal
5. Worm and ball nut assembly
6. O-ring
7. End cover
8. Lock nut
9. Worm shaft seal
10. Sector shaft
11. Sector adjuster screw
12. Adusting shim
13. Gasket
14. Top cover
15. Filler plug
16. Lock nut
17. Bolt
18. Pitman shaft nut
19. Lock washer

Steering gear

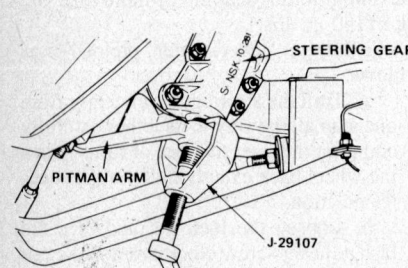

STEERING GEAR

PITMAN ARM

J-29107

Pitman arm removal

juster screw counterclockwise, then come up on adjustment by turning the adjuster locknut in a clockwise motion.

7. Reassemble the Pitman arm to the Pitman shaft. Tighten the Pitman shaft nut to 160 ft. lbs.

8. Install the horn spring and connect the battery ground cable.

9. Lower vehicle to floor.

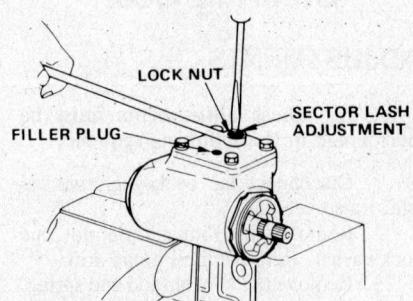

FILLER PLUG
LOCK NUT
SECTOR LASH ADJUSTMENT

Steering gear adjustment

REMOVAL

1. Raise vehicle on hoist.
2. Remove Pitman arm nut and washer and using puller J-29107 remove Pitman arm from Pitman shaft.
3. Remove engine stone shield.
4. Remove lower clamp to flexible coupling bolts.

5. Remove steering gear to frame bolts and remove steering gear from vehicle.

INSTALLATION

1. Place gear in position and start mounting bolts; temporarily leave loose.
2. Install steering gear flexible coupling bolts and torque to 22 ft. lbs.
3. Torque steering column mounting bolts to 13 ft. lbs.

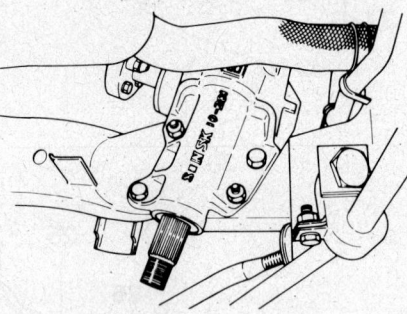

Steering gear mounting

4. Install Pitman arm to shaft. Install washer and torque nut to 160 ft. lbs.
5. Lower engine stone shield.
6. Lower vehicle to floor.

Pitman Shaft Seal Replacement

A defective seal may be replaced without removing the steering gear from the vehicle. If it has been diagnosed that the seal should be replaced proceed as follows:

REMOVAL

1. Raise vehicle on hoist.
2. Remove Pitman arm as previously described.
3. Wipe clean the area around the seal.
4. Using an awl, screwdriver or similar tool, pry out the old seal being careful not to damage the housing bore.

NOTE: Inspect the lubricant in the gear for contamination. If the lubricant is contaminated in any way, the gear must be removed from the vehicle and completely overhauled.

INSTALLATION

1. Coat the new Pitman shaft seal with steering gear lubricant (or equivalent). Position the seal in the Pitman shaft bore and tap into position using a suitable size socket.
2. Install Pitman arm as previously described.
3. Lower vehicle to floor.
4. Check lubricant level in gear box; total capacity 0.2L (7 oz.). Do not overfill.

Idler Arm, Idler Arm Pivot Shaft and/or Bracket

REMOVAL

1. Raise vehicle on hoist.
2. Remove lockwasher and nut that retain the intermediate rod to the idle arm.
3. The ball studs for the above may be removed using tool J-21687-02.
4. Remove the four bolts, nuts and washers retaining the bracket to the frame, and remove the idler arm pivot shaft and bracket with idler arm.
5. If the idler arm is being replaced proceed as follows:
   a. Remove idler arm to idler arm pivot shaft nut and lockwashers.
   b. Remove the idler arm from the pivot shaft.

INSTALLATION

1. Install bracket and shaft assembly to frame and torque to 29 ft. lbs.
2. Install the idler arm to the shaft and torque nut to 87 ft. lbs.
3. Install the ball studs and intermediate rod to the idler arm. Torque the castellated nuts to 50 ft. lbs. and just enough additional to line up cotter pin holes. Install new cotter pins.
4. Lubricate idler arm pivot shaft.
5. Lower vehicle to floor.

Intermediate Rod and Tie Rods

REMOVAL

1. Raise vehicle on hoist.
2. Remove cotter pin from the ball studs connecting tie rods to intermediate rod and steering damper. Remove the castellated nuts and disconnect the parts using special tool J-21687-02.
3. Remove the nut and lockwasher on ball stud connecting the intermediate rod to idler arm. Disconnect the parts using special tool J-21687-02.

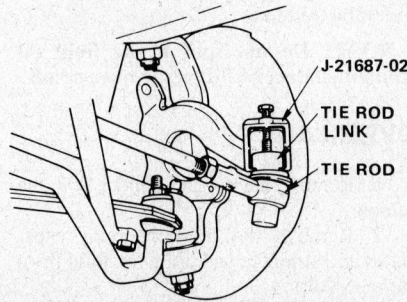

Tie-rod end removal

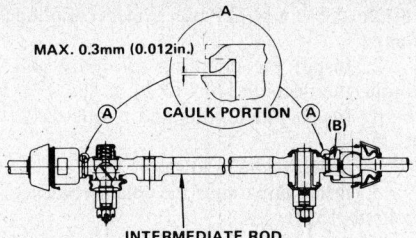

Installing tie rod to intermediate rod

4. Remove the intermediate rod together with tie rods.
5. If the tie rod is replaced, disconnect the intermediate rod from tie rod.

INSTALLATION

1. If the tie rod has been removed, proceed as follows:
   a. Apply liquid gasket (Felcobond 401) to portion B. Install and tighten tie rod end to specified torque of 9.0 kg-m (65 ft. lbs.).
   b. Caulk two portions (upper and lower portions) of A.
2. Make sure threads on ball studs and nuts are clean and smooth.
3. Install intermediate rod to idler arm, install lockwasher, nut, and torque nut to 50 ft. lbs.
4. Raise end of rod and install on Pitman arm. Torque nut to 44 ft. lbs., then advance nut just enough to insert cotter pin and install new cotter pin.
5. Install intermediate rod to steering damper end. Torque nut to 87 ft. lbs., then advance nut just enough to insert cotter pin and install new cotter pin.
6. Install the tie rods to adapter, torque nut to 44 ft. lbs., then advance nut just enough to insert cotter pin and install new cotter pin, and lubricate tie rod ball studs.

Steering Damper

REPLACEMENT

1. Raise vehicle on hoist.
2. Remove cotter pin and castellated nut on stud connecting the damper end with intermediate rod.
3. Remove the cotter pin and and castellated nut on the stud connecting the damper end to second crossmember (on 4 × 2 model) or to idler arm bracket (on 4 × 4 model).
4. Remove the steering damper.
5. To install, reverse steps 1–4.

Pitman Arm

REMOVAL

1. Raise vehicle on hoist.
2. Remove nut and lockwasher retaining Pitman arm to Pitman shaft.

3. Using tool J-29107 remove Pitman arm from pitman shaft.
4. Remove cotter pins and castellated nuts retaining the Pitman arm to the tie rod and intermediate rod.
5. The ball studs may be removed from the Pitman arm using tool J-21687-02.
6. Remove the Pitman arm.

INSTALLATION

1. Install Pitman arm to intermediate rod and tie rod ball studs. Install castellated nuts (do not torque yet).
2. Install Pitman arm to Pitman shaft.
3. Install Pitman shaft lockwashers and nut, and torque to 160 ft. lbs.
4. Torque ball stud nuts to 44 ft. lbs. and just enough additional to align cotter pin hole. Install new cotter pin.
5. Lower vehicle to floor.

Steering Column and Shaft Assembly

REMOVAL

1. Disconnect the battery ground cable.
2. Remove upper coupling clamp pinch bolt from the steering shaft flexible coupling in the engine compartment.

NOTE: Apply a setting mark across the steering shaft and coupling clamp.

3. Disconnect the combination switch and ignition switch wiring at the harness connector.
4. Remove the two column to instrument panel bolts.
5. Remove the steering column toward the cab being careful not to damage or jar the shaft as it is an energy absorbing unit.

DISASSEMBLY

1. Remove the five screws that retain the steering column cowling.
2. Remove the steering wheel as outlined previously.
3. Remove two screws that retain the combination switch to column on flange.
4. Remove the combination switch assembly.
5. Remove bolt that retains the ignition switch bracket.

Steering column flexible coupling

ISUZU

ASSEMBLY

1. Install the combination switch on the column flange using 2 screws.
2. Install the ignition switch to the column as previously described.
3. Install the steering wheel lockwasher and nut and torque the nut to 29 ft. lbs.
4. Install the horn shroud.
5. Install the steering column cowling.

INSTALLATION

1. Place column through cowl and move into position.
2. Install end of steering shaft into flexible coupling clamp. Install coupling to worm gear shaft. Torque pinch bolts to 22 ft. lbs.

NOTE: Align setting marks applied at disassembly when connecting steering shaft end to coupling clamp.

3. Install column to instrument panel unless vehicle is setting on its wheels or suspension.
4. Tighten the column to instrument panel bolts. Tightening torque 1.5 kg-m (11 ft. lbs.).
5. Make connections of combination switch and ignition switch wiring at the connector.
6. Check operation of horn and combination switch.
7. Check for interference between steering column cowling and steering wheel.
8. Check alignment between front wheels and steering wheel.
9. Check steering wheel free-play when the steering unit assembly is installed in position on the vehicle. The standard steering wheel play is about 10 mm (0.4 in.) when measured at the outside diameter of the steering wheel.

Steering Shaft Flexible Coupling

REMOVAL

1. Jack up front of vehicle until wheels are just off the ground.
2. Remove coupling through-bolts and lock nut. Only two bolts can be removed.
3. Remove the pinch bolts on the upper and lower flanges of the coupling.
4. Remove two bolts fixing the column bracket.
5. Pull the steering column and shaft approximately 50 mm (1.968 in.) in toward the cab.
6. Remove the upper coupling flange and coupling, then remove the lower coupling flange.

INSTALLATION

1. Install the lower coupling flange, then install the coupling and upper coupling flange.
2. Install the coupling assembly and torque the through bolts to 22 ft. lbs.
3. Install pinch bolts and torque to 22 ft. lbs.
4. Lower vehicle to floor.
5. Install and torque the column bracket bolts to 13. ft. lbs.

BRAKE SYSTEM

ADJUSTMENT

Disc brakes require no adjustments. Although the drum brakes are self-adjusting, an initial adjusting may be necessary after the brakes have been replaced, or whenever the adjuster position has been changed. The final adjustment is made by using the self-adjusting mechanism.

1. With the brake drum removed, remove actuator from the starwheel on the rear brakes.
2. Turn the starwheel until the brake drum slides over the brake shoes with a slight drag.
3. Turn the starwheel on the rear brakes 1¼ turns to retract the shoes.
4. Install the brake drums and wheels and lower the vehicle.
5. Perform the final adjustment by making a number of forward and reverse stops, applying the brakes with a firm pedal effort until a satisfactory brake pedal height and straight-line braking is achieved.

BRAKE PEDAL HEIGHT ADJUSTMENT

When the brake pedal is fully released, the pedal bumper bottoms on the stop light switch housing.

1. Disconnect the battery ground cable.
2. Measure the brake pedal height after making sure that the pedal is fully returned by the pedal return spring. The brake pedal height should be between 5.9 and 6.3 in.
3. If it is necessary to adjust the brake pedal height, disconnect the stop light switch wiring, remove the switch locknut, and remove the switch from the switch bracket by rotating it counterclockwise.
4. Loosen the locknut on the master cylinder pushrod.
5. Adjust the brake pedal to the specified height by rotating the pushrod in the appropriate direction. Tighten the locknut when the proper height is reached.
6. Install the stop light switch. Adjust the clearance between the switch housing and the brake pedal tab 0.02–0.04 in. Tighten the switch locknut.
7. Connect the stop light switch wires.
8. Connect the battery ground cable.

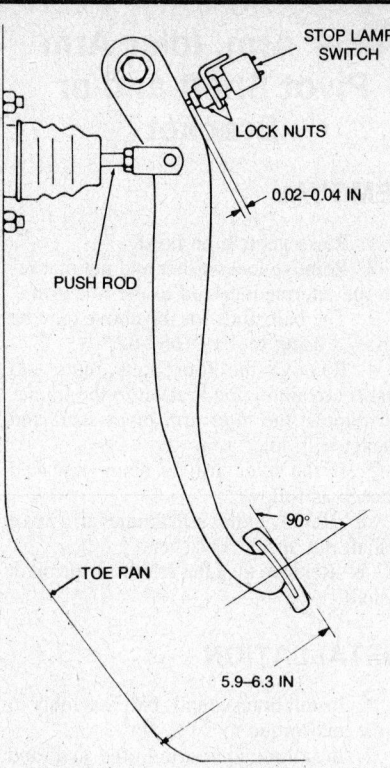

Brake pedal height adjustment

Master Cylinder

REMOVAL AND INSTALLATION

1. Disconnect the battery ground cable.
2. Wipe the master cylinder and brake lines clean. Place absorbent cloths below the master cylinder area to absorb any fluid leakage.
3. Disconnect the hydraulic lines at the connections on the master cylinder. Cover the ends of the brake lines to prevent the entrance of dirt.
4. Remove the master cylinder bracket bolt at the front end of the master cylinder.
5. Remove the master cylinder-to-booster attaching nuts and lockwashers and remove the master cylinder and gasket from the booster.
6. Install the master cylinder in the reverse order of removal, and bleed the brake hydraulic system.

NOTE: Do not spill brake fluid on painted surfaces as damage may result.

OVERHAUL

1. Remove the master cylinder from the vehicle.
2. Remove the fluid reservoir caps, plates and strainers and drain the fluid from the reservoirs.
3. Place the master cylinder in a vise.
4. Loosen the fluid reservoir clamp

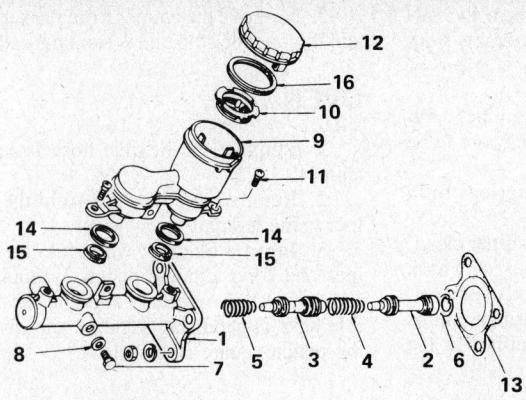

1. Master cylinder
2. Primary piston
3. Secondary piston
4. Spring; primary
5. Spring; secondary
6. Snap-ring
7. Stopper bolt
8. Gasket
9. Reservoir
10. Filter
11. Clamp screw
12. Clamp cap
13. Gasket
14. Upper rubber seal
15. Lower rubber seal
16. Cap seal

Master cylinder

screws and remove the plastic reservoirs from the master cylinder body.

5. Remove the connector bolt, connector and gaskets from the front system side (rear outlet). Then, remove the end plug, gasket, check valve, return spring and spring seat.

6. Remove the connector, gasket, check valve, return spring and spring seat from the rear system side (front outlet).

7. Push the primary piston all the way in and then remove the stopper bolt and gasket on the right-side of the master cylinder.

8. Using snap-ring pliers, remove the primary piston snap-ring.

9. Remove the primary and secondary piston assemblies from the cylinder bore.

10. Clean all of the parts in clean brake fluid. Blow out all passages, orifices, and valve holes with compressed air.

11. Inspect the master cylinder bore and pistons for scoring, corrosion, and rust. Slight scoring and rust can be removed by polishing with crocus cloth or fine emery paper soaked with brake fluid.

12. Soak all new and old parts in clean brake fluid before reassembling.

13. Insert the secondary piston assembly into the master cylinder bore, so that the primary stem guide is projected slightly beyond the cylinder bore end.

14. Insert the primary piston into the master cylinder bore so that the secondary piston stem guide enters the hole in the primary piston.

15. Install the snap-ring into the groove in the master cylinder housing.

16. Depress the primary piston and install the piston stopper bolt and new gasket.

17. Install the spring seat, return spring, check valve, new gasket and end plug in the front system side of the master cylinder (rear outlet).

18. Install a new gasket on either side of the connector and secure it into position with the connector bolt.

19. Install the spring seat, return spring, check valve, new gasket and connector in the rear system side of the master cylinder (front outlet).

20. Install the clamps over the lower ends of the fluid reservoirs, place the reservoirs

in position on the master cylinder body and then tighten the clamp bolts.

21. Install the reservoir filters, and fill the reservoirs with clean brake fluid.

Push in on the primary piston to determine that it returns smoothly. Test the piston assembly two or three times to make sure that fluid comes out of the front and rear outlets.

22. Install the plates and covers.

23. Install plugs in all of the connector outlet ports.

24. Fill the reservoirs to the proper level with clean brake fluid.

25. Insert a rod with a smooth round end to the piston end and press it in to compress the piston return spring.

26. Release the pressure on the rod. Watch for air bubbles in the reservoir fluid.

27. Repeat steps 25 and 26 as long as bubbles appear in the fluid.

28. Install the master cylinder on the vehicle and bleed the brake hydraulic system.

Power Booster

REMOVAL AND INSTALLATION

1. Disconnect the negative battery terminal.

2. Remove the brake lines from the master cylinder.

3. Remove the vacuum line from the power booster.

4. Disconnect the brake pedal return spring.

5. Remove the cotter pin, washer and pushrod clevis to brake pedal pin.

6. Remove the booster retaining nuts.

7. Remove the master cylinder and power brake booster as an assembly.

NOTE: Remember to bleed the brake system.

Bleeding

The brake hydraulic system must be bled after any line has been disconnected or air has somehow found its way into the system.

The bleeding operation should start with the wheel cylinder furthest from the master cylinder and end with the one nearest.

NOTE: Do not bleed the brakes with the brake drums or calipers removed.

1. Make sure that the master cylinder is full and kept at least ¾ full throughout the entire bleeding process. Check the fluid level in the master cylinder reservoirs frequently during the bleeding operation.

2. Remove the cap from the wheel cylinder or caliper bleeder valve. Position a wrench on the bleeder valve and place a rubber hose over the bleeder valve nipple.

3. Place the other end of the bleeder hose into a clear container containing enough brake fluid to ensure that the end of the bleeder hose will remain submerged.

4. Start the engine and allow it to run during the actual bleeding of each wheel cylinder. This is so to have vacuum applied to the brake booster during the bleeding process.

5. Open the wheel cylinder bleeder valve by turning the wrench counterclockwise about ¾ of a turn. Have an assistant depress the brake pedal. Just before the brake pedal reaches the end of its travel, close the bleeder valve and allow the brake pedal to return slowly to the released position. Repeat this operation until the brake fluid being expelled is free from air bubbles, then close the bleeder valve tightly.

6. Remove the bleeder hose and the wrench from the bleeder valve and install them onto the next wheel cylinder or caliper to be bled. Repeat step 5 on all of the remaining wheel cylinders. Don't forget to check and replenish the brake fluid in the master cylinder reservoirs.

7. After bleeding the brake hydraulic system, check the operation of the brakes. Depress the brake pedal several times then hold it depressed. Notice how far the pedal can be depressed. Release the pedal for about 10 seconds, then depress it again and hold it, taking notice of the distance which it can be depressed before it stops with the same amount of pedal pressure applied as before. If the pedal depresses further or can be "pumped up," then it can be assumed that there is still air in the hydraulic system and further bleeding is required.

Combination Valve

The combination valve consists of the differential valve (failure indicator) combined with the proportioning valve (pressure control valve). It is mounted on the left side inner fender and is connected to the master cylinder.

The fail indicator incorporates a hydraulic differential pressure switch. A wiring harness connects the electrical terminal of this switch to the brake warning light on the dashboard.

The pressure control valve is a proportioning valve that controls the fluid pressure

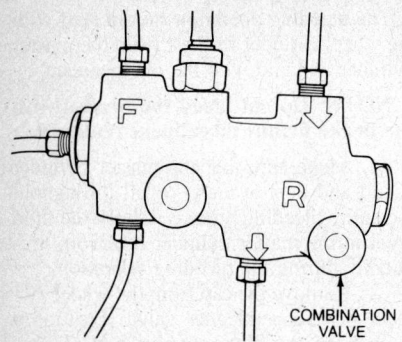

Combination valve

to the rear brakes to prevent wheel lockup.

This valve can not be repaired, if found to be defective it must be replaced.

Disc Brake Pads

INSPECTION

Replace the front disc brake linings whenever the lining wear indicator makes a squeaking noise or when the lining is worn to within .039" of the shoe surface. All four brake linings should always be replaced at the same time.

REMOVAL AND INSTALLATION

1. Raise the vehicle on a lift.
2. Remove the wheel and tire assembly.
3. Remove the pins from the caliper stops and then remove the stops.
4. Remove the caliper from the support, remove the stop plates from the caliper, then suspend the caliper assembly from the upper link or frame using a piece of heavy wire.
5. Remove the pad assemblies and shims. Mark their location if they are to be reinstalled.
6. Remove the anti-rattle springs from the support.
7. Wipe the inside of the caliper clean, including the exterior of the dust seal. Check to see that the dust seal is in good condition.
8. Install the anti-rattle springs, shims and the shoe and lining assemblies to the support.

NOTE: If original linings are being reinstalled, they must be installed in the original position. Also position the wear indicators to the lower side of the support.

9. Install new stop plates to the caliper, then install the caliper, stops and stop pins.
10. Install the wheel and tire assembly.

Disc Brake Calipers

REMOVAL AND INSTALLATION

1. Raise the vehicle on a lift.
2. Remove the wheel and tire assembly.
3. Remove the pins from the caliper stops and then remove the stops.
4. Disconnect the front flexible hose from the brake line.

NOTE: To keep dirt from entering, cap or tape the openings of the flexible hose and brake line.

5. Remove the caliper from the support and remove the stop plates from the caliper.

OVERHAUL

1. Remove the flexible hose from the caliper.
2. Remove the dust seal from the caliper using a small screwdriver.
3. Insert a block of wood into the caliper and force out the piston by applying compressed air into the caliper at the flexible hose attachment. Remove and discard the piston square ring seal.

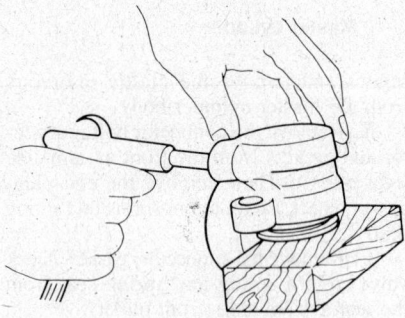

Removing caliper piston

--- **CAUTION** ---
Do not place fingers in front of the piston in an attempt to catch or protect it when applying compressed air.

4. Clean all parts in clean brake fluid. Check the cylinder bore and pistons for wear, scuffing or corrosion and replace as necessary.
5. Apply a silicone lube to the caliper bore and the piston square ring seal and insert the piston seal into the caliper bore using finger pressure only.
6. Apply a silicone lubricant to the piston and assemble the dust seal to the piston and caliper. Install the seal ring into the dust seal.
7. Install the flexible hose to the caliper using new gaskets.
8. Lubricate the stop plates and the sliding surfaces of the caliper then install the new stop plates to the caliper, install the caliper and the new stop pins.

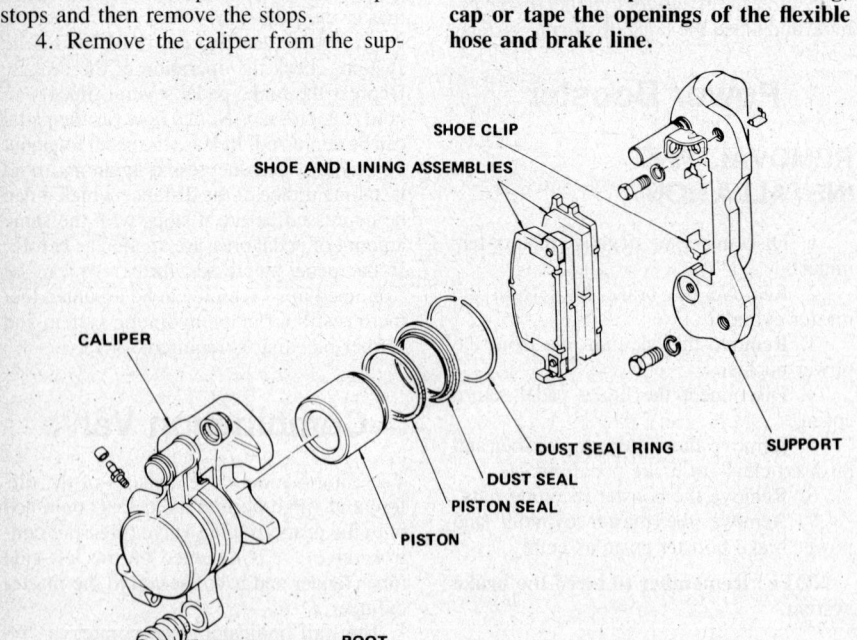

Disc brake components

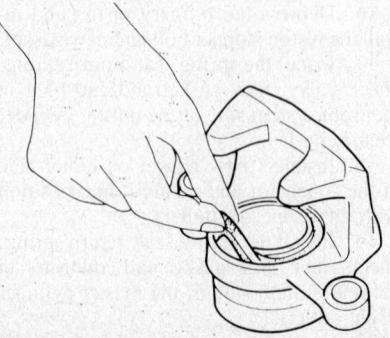

Removing dust seal

9. Connect the flexible brake hose to the brake line.

10. Install the wheel and tire assembly.

NOTE: Remember to bleed the brake system.

Brake Disc Assembly

REMOVAL AND INSTALLATION

1. Raise the vehicle on a lift.

2. Remove the front tire and wheel assembly.

3. Remove the bolts attaching the caliper support to the adapter and then suspend the caliper and support it from the upper link or frame using a piece of heavy wire.

4. Remove the hub grease cap, cotter pin, spindle nut retainer and nut and remove the hub and rotor assembly.

5. Replace the hub and disc as an assembly if either needs replacement.

NOTE: All brake discs have a minimum thickness dimension cast into them. This dimension is the minimum wear dimension and not a refinish dimension.

6. Install the dust shield and adapter to the steering knuckle and torque the long bolts to 55 ft. lbs. and the small bolts to 35 ft. lbs.

7. Install the front hub and disc assembly and adjust the wheel bearings.

8. Assemble the caliper and support assembly to the adapter and torque the bolts to 64 ft. lbs.

9. Install the front wheel and tire assembly.

NOTE: On 4 wheel drive vehicles see Free Wheel Hub Removal before attempting this procedure.

Wheel Cylinders

REMOVAL AND INSTALLATION

It is not necessary to remove the wheel cylinders from the backing plates to disassemble, inspect, and overhaul the cylinder. Removal is necessary only when the wheel cylinder is damaged beyond repair and must be replaced.

It is a good practice to inspect the wheel cylinders for leakage whenever the brake drums are removed. Simply pull the edge of the wheel cylinder boot carefully away from the cylinder and note whether or not the interior is wet with brake fluid. Excessive fluid at this point indicates leakage past the piston cup, requiring overhaul or replacement. A slight amount of fluid on the inside of the wheel cylinder is almost always present and acts as a lubricant for the piston.

1. Remove the wheel and tire assembly, the brake drum and the brake shoes.

2. Disconnect the brake system hydraulic line from the wheel cylinder at the rear of the backing plate.

3. Remove the screws securing the wheel cylinder to the backing plate and remove the wheel cylinder from the backing plate.

4. Install the wheel cylinder in the reverse order of removal and bleed the brake hydraulic system.

OVERHAUL

1. Either with the wheel cylinder removed or still on the brake backing plate, remove the boot(s) from the cylinder end(s).

2. Remove the piston(s) and cup(s).

NOTE: The front wheel cylinder pistons and cups are serviced as an assembly.

3. Inspect the cylinder bore. Check for staining and corrosion. Discard any wheel cylinder which is excessively corroded. Inspect the piston and discard it if it is excessively pitted, scored or damaged.

4. Polish any stained or slightly scored areas in the cylinder bore with crocus cloth. Move the crocus cloth in a circular motion around the circumference of the cylinder bore, not in a lengthwise manner.

5. Wash the wheel cylinder body thoroughly in clean brake fluid, allowing it to remain lubricated for assembly. Do not lubricate the pistons or cups prior to their installation in the cylinder.

6. On front wheel cylinders, install the piston assembly into the cylinder, being careful not to damage the boot.

7. On rear wheel cylinders, insert the spring-expander into the cylinder bore. Install the new cups with the flat surface toward the outer ends of the cylinder. Be sure that the cups are lint-free. Do not lubricate the cups prior to installation. Install the new pistons into the cylinder with the flat surfaces toward the center of the cylinder. Do not lubricate prior to installation.

8. Press the new boot(s) onto the wheel cylinder.

9. Install the wheel cylinder onto the brake backing plate. If it was removed, assemble the brake shoes to the backing plate, install the brake drum and bleed the brake hydraulic system.

Brake Drums

REMOVAL AND INSTALLATION

1. Raise the vehicle and support it on jackstands.

2. Remove the hub caps and remove the rear tire and wheel.

3. Loosen the check nuts at the parking brake equalizer sufficiently to remove all tension from the brake cable.

4. Remove the drum-to-hub retaining screws and remove the drum from the vehicle. Identify each brake drum so that it can be reinstalled in its original position. Never depress the brake pedal while any of the brake drums are removed.

5. Install the brake drums in the reverse order of removal.

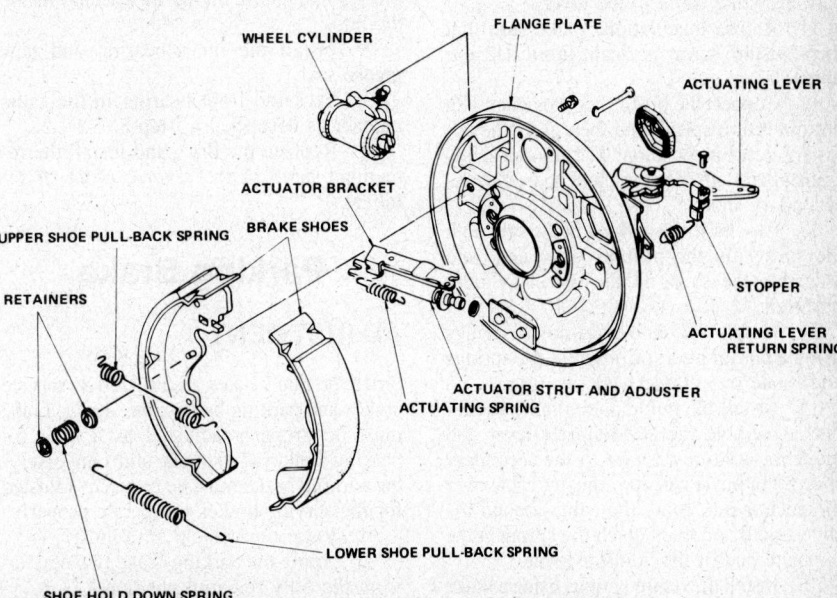

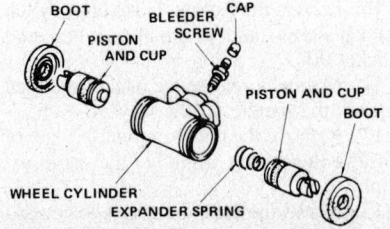

Wheel cylinder

Rear brake components

ISUZU

INSPECTION

Inspect the rear brake drums for growing, scoring or crack. Reface them if possible.

Brake Shoes

REMOVAL AND INSTALLATION

1. Remove the brake drums.
2. Unhook the brake return springs from the anchor pin using a brake tool and remove the springs.
3. Remove the brake shoe hold-down springs using pliers. Depress the spring retainer while rotating it 90° to align the slot in the retainer with the flanged end of the pin.
4. Remove the self-adjuster cable assembly by disconnecting the spring at the adjuster lever and removing the cable end from the anchor pin. Remove the guide plate from the anchor pin.
5. Remove the adjuster lever and the lever hold-down wire from the shoe pivot.
6. Separate the shoes from the wheel cylinder pushrods.
7. Separate the primary and secondary brake shoes, adjuster, return spring, and parking brake strut assemblies.

NOTE: If the brake shoes are to be reinstalled, be sure to identify them so that they can be reinstalled in their original positions.

8. Separate the parking brake lever and the rear cable. Remove the clip and washer and remove the parking brake lever from the secondary shoe.
9. Lubricate the parking brake cable with Lubriplate®.
10. Assemble the parking brake lever to the secondary shoe and then assemble the parking brake cable to the lever.
11. Before installation, make sure that the adjusting screw is clean, lubricated and operable.
12. Connect the brake shoes together with bottom return spring and then place the adjuster screw into position. The adjuster screw is installed with the starwheel nearest to the secondary shoe.
13. Assemble the parking brake strut with the spring on the primary shoe end, and assemble the shoes to the wheel cylinder pushrods.
14. Install the shoe hold-down springs using a pair of pliers. Compress the springs and rotate the retainers 90°.
15. Install the guide plate on the anchor pin. Assemble the self-adjuster lever and the lever hold-down wire to the secondary shoe pivot pin. Place the adjuster cable over the anchor pin, route the cable around the shoe shield and then attach the spring at the opposite end of the adjuster lever.
16. Install the return springs using a brake tool.
17. Pry the shoes away from the backing plate and lubricate the shoe contact areas with a thin coat of Lubriplate®.
18. Check the operation of the parking brake. *Do not step on the brake pedal.*
19. Install the brake drum and adjust the brake shoes.

Wheel Bearings

REMOVAL AND INSTALLATION

1. Jack up your vehicle and support it with jackstands.
2. Remove the front wheels.
3. Remove the brake caliper assembly and tie it out of the way.
4. Remove the bearing cap, cotter pin, locknut and washer. The outer bearing will come out at this time also.

NOTE: On 4-wheel drive vehicles you must remove the free wheeling hub before removing the disc and wheel bearings.

5. Remove the disc from the spindle.
6. Place the disc on two blocks of wood and drive out the grease seal.

NOTE: Be careful not to damage the inner bearing when removing the seal.

7. Clean the disc and bearings in solvent. Check the bearings and races for damage.

NOTE: If the races are damaged drive them out using a drift pin and hammer. Install them in the reverse manner being careful not to damage them.

8. Place a large amount of wheel bearing grease in the palm of your hand, and force the edge of the bearing into it so that grease fills the bearing. Do this until the whole bearing is completely filled. Also place some grease on the spindle and inside the hub.
9. Install the inner bearing and new grease seal.
10. Pack the front bearing in the same manner as described in step 8.
11. Replace the disc, and install the remaining parts in the reverse order of removal.

Parking Brake

ADJUSTMENT

Since the rear brakes are utilized as service brakes and parking brakes, the service brake must be properly adjusted as a base for parking brake adjustment and conversely, the parking brake must be properly adjusted for the service brakes to operate properly.

1. Raise the vehicle on a hoist.
2. Apply the parking brake two notches from the fully released position.
3. Loosen the equalizer check nut, and tighten or loosen the front jam nut until a

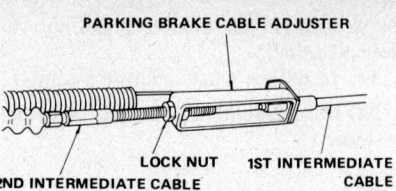

Parking brake adjuster

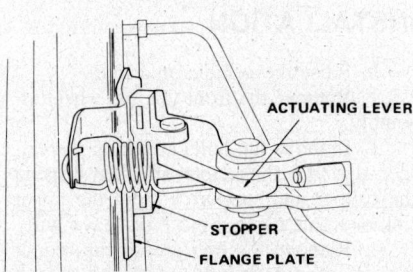

Actuating lever stopper

light to moderate drag is felt when the rear wheels are rotated frontward.
4. Tighten the nuts securely. Hold the front nut while tightening the jam nut.
5. Fully release the parking brake and rotate the rear wheels. No drag should be present.
6. Lower the vehicle.

CABLE REMOVAL AND INSTALLATION

Front Cable

1. Disconnect the battery ground cable.
2. Remove the carburetor air cleaner.
3. Drain the cooling system. Disconnect the heater hoses at the heater core outlet tubes at the dash panel and secure the hoses in an upright position to minimize coolant loss.
4. Disconnect the parking brake front cable at the control lever on the right-side of the engine compartment.
5. Remove the right-hand pulley center bolt and remove the pulley.
6. Remove the cable cover nuts at the dash panel and remove the cover.
7. Remove the windshield wiper switch on the instrument panel.
8. Remove the screws attaching the lever assembly to the instrument panel.
9. Pull the assembly rearward and lay it on the floor.
10. Loosen the parking brake light switch bracket screw and rotate the switch and bracket 90°.
11. Manually release the ratchet and then depress the handle all the way in.
12. Remove the cotter pin, washer, pivot pin and the pulley. Remove the cable assembly.
13. Install the cable to handle lower end and then pull the handle rearward seven notches.

14. Rotate the parking brake light switch and bracket into position and tighten the bracket screw.

15. Install the pulley, pivot pin, washer and cotter pin.

16. For the remainder of the installation procedure follow the removal procedure in reverse starting with step 8.

Intermediate Cable

1. Raise the vehicle on a hoist.
2. Disconnect the equalizer lever spring at the lever.
3. Loosen the cable guide nut and remove the cable assembly.
4. Install the intermediate cable in the reverse order of removal and adjust the parking brake.

Rear Cable

1. Raise the vehicle on a hoist.
2. Remove the rear cable retaining clamps on the left and right sides.
3. Disconnect the equalizer lever return spring at the lever.
4. Remove the cotter pin, washer and pin and remove the equalizer lever from the front cable and equalizer adjusting bolt clevis.
5. Remove the left and right rear wheel and tire assemblies.
6. Remove the brake drums and shoes, disconnecting the rear cable from the brake lever.
7. Remove the rear cable spring cup using a box wrench.
8. Withdraw the cable ends from the backing plates on either side and remove the cable assembly.
9. Install the cable in the reverse order of removal and adjust the parking brake.

CHASSIS ELECTRICAL

Blower

REMOVAL AND INSTALLATION

1. Disconnect the battery ground cable.
2. Disconnect the blower motor electrical leads.
3. Remove the blower-to-heater core screws and remove the blower motor assembly.
4. Install in the reverse order.

Heater Core

REMOVAL AND INSTALLATION

1. Disconnect the battery ground cable.

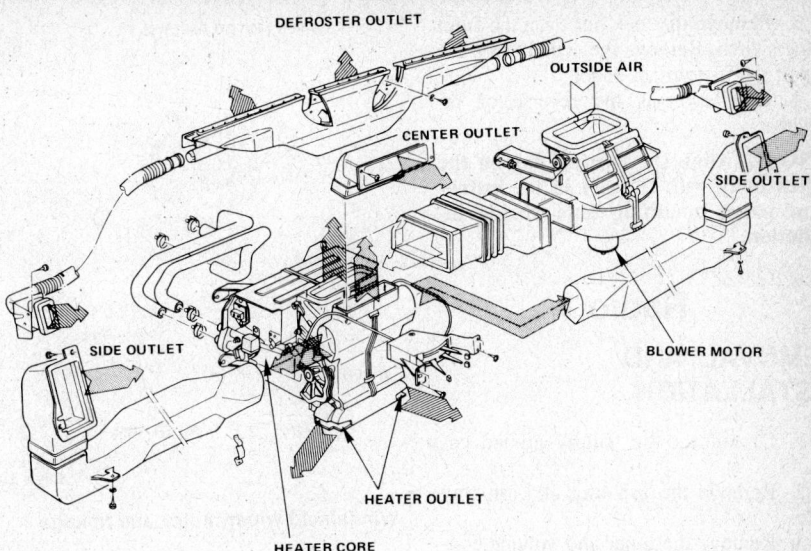

Heater

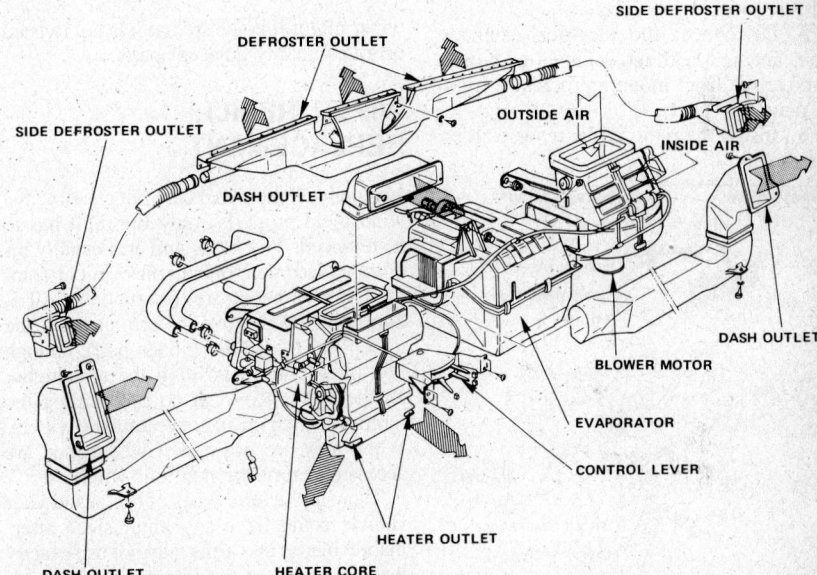

Heater-air conditioner

2. Place a drain pan under the heater hoses at the heater and remove the heater hoses from the core tubes, securing the heater hoses in a raised position to prevent further loss of coolant. Plug or tape the heater core tubes to prevent spillage of coolant in the passenger compartment when removing.

3. Remove the five parcel shelf attaching screws and remove the shelf.

4. Loosen the air diverter and defroster door bowden cable clamps at the heater case and disconnect the cables from the doors.

5. Disconnect the blower resistor leads.

6. Remove the control assembly-to-instrument panel screws and swing the control to the left and lay it on the floor. Be careful not to kink the water valve bowden cable.

7. Remove the four heater-to-firewall screws. Pull the heater rearward until the core tubes clear the dash opening, then re-

move the heater by moving it to the right and down.

8. Remove the core tube clamp screw and remove the clamp.

9. Remove the seven screws and separate the heater case halves.

10. Remove the core from the case.

11. Install and assemble the heater core and heater case in the reverse order of removal, using new seals around the heater core.

Ignition Switch

REMOVAL AND INSTALLATION

1. Disconnect the negative battery terminal.
2. Remove the multi-connector from the rear of the ignition switch.

3. Remove the lock nut from the front of the switch. Remove the switch from the rear of the instrument panel.

4. Installation is the reverse of removal.

NOTE: Align the locating lug on the switch body with the slot in the instrument panel mounting hole during installation.

Radio

REMOVAL AND INSTALLATION

1. Disconnect the battery ground cable.

2. Remove the ash tray and ash tray plate.

3. Remove the tuner and volume control knobs, jam nuts, washers and face panel.

4. Remove the screws from the front and rear mounting brackets.

5. Disconnect the electrical connections, antenna lead and remove the radio. Remove the front mounting brackets from the radio.

6. Install the radio in the reverse order of removal.

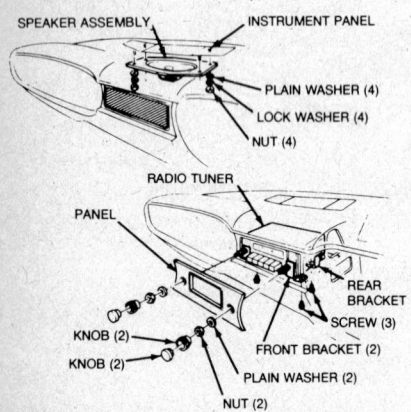

Radio installation

Windshield Wiper Motor and Linkage

REMOVAL AND INSTALLATION

1. Remove the wiper blades and arms.

2. Remove the two bolts attaching the pivot.

3. Remove the four wiper motor mounting bolts and remove the wiper motor and linkage.

4. To remove the motor independently, take out the motor shaft nut and three bolts and then pull off the connector and disconnect the ground cable.

5. Install and assemble in the reverse order of removal. Make sure to install the

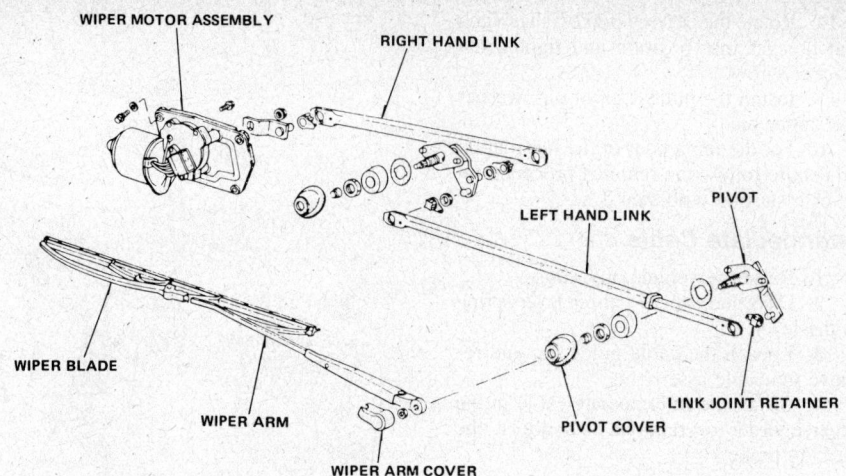

Windshield wiper motor and linkage

wiper motor linkage so that it is not twisted or touching any adjacent parts.

WIPER REFILL REPLACEMENT

Normally, if the wipers are not cleaning the windshield properly, only the refill has to be replaced. The blade and arm usually require replacement only in the event of damage. It is not necessary (except on new Tridon refills) to remove the arm or the blade to replace the refill (rubber part), though you may have to position the arm higher on the glass. You can do this turning the ignition switch on and operating the wipers. When they are positioned where they are accessible, turn the ignition switch off.

There are several types of refills and your vehicle could have any kind, since aftermarket blades and arms may not use exactly the same refill as the original equipment.

Most Trico styles use a release button that is pushed down to allow the refill to slide out of the yoke jaws. The new refill slides in and locks in place. Some Trico refills are removed by locating where the metal backing strip or the refill is wider. Insert a small screwdriver blade between the frame and metal backing strip. Press down to release the refill from the retaining tab.

The Anco style is unlocked at one end by squeezing 2 metal tabs, and the refill is slid out of the frame jaws. When the new refill is installed, the tabs will click into place, locking the refill.

The polycarbonate type is held in place by a locking lever that is pushed downward out of the groove in the arm to free the refill. When the new refill is installed, it will lock in place automatically.

The Tridon refill has a plastic backing strip with a notch about an inch from the end. Hold the blade (frame) on a hard surface so that the frame is tightly bowed. Grip the tip of the backing strip and pull up while twisting counterclockwise. The backing strip will snap out of the retaining tab. Do this for the remaining tabs until the refill is free of the arm. The length of these refills is molded into the end and they should be replaced with identical types.

No matter which type of refill you use, be sure that all of the frame claws engage the refill. Before operating the wipers, be sure that no part of the metal frame is contacting the windshield.

Instrument Cluster

REMOVAL AND INSTALLATION

1. Disconnect the speedometer cable.

2. Remove the wing nuts on the rear side of the instrument panel and pull the assembly part way out.

3. Disconnect the wiring harness at the connector and remove the instrument panel.

4. Install the instrument panel in the reverse order of removal.

Headlights

REMOVAL AND INSTALLATION

1. Remove the headlight trim rim.

2. Loosen the three screws attaching the sealed beam unit by turning the retaining ring counterclockwise.

3. Install the headlight by fitting the bosses on the headlight lens into the grooves so that the "TOP" mark is up.

4. Tighten the three attaching screws and install the headlight trim rim.

LUV

INDEX

MODEL IDENTIFICATION

The LUV is available in conventional pickup design with a ½-ton rating. Four-wheel drive, with an independent front axle, is available as an option beginning with the series 9 in the 1979 model year.

SERIAL NUMBER IDENTIFICATION

Vehicle

The chassis number plate is attached to the left-side rear door pillar within the cab. It has the date of manufacture and chassis number stamped on its face.

Location of chassis number plate on the left side door panel

Engine

The engine number is stamped on the right upper center part of the cylinder block, adjacent to the distributor.

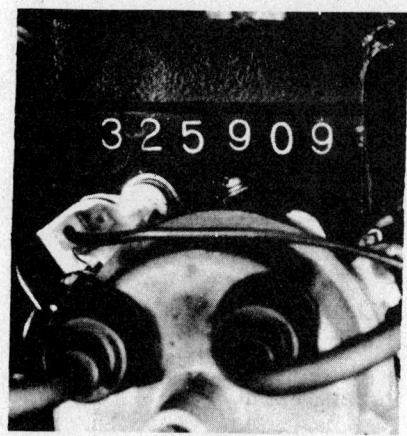

Location of the engine identification number on the center of the right side of the cylinder block

GENERAL ENGINE SPECIFICATIONS

Year	Engine Displacement cu in. (cc)	Carb Type	Advertised Horsepower (@ rpm)	Advertised Torque @ rpm (ft lbs)	Bore and Stroke (in.)	Advertised Compression Ratio	Oil Pressure (psi)
'75	110.8 (1817)	2-bbl	75 @ 5000	88 @ 3000	3.31 × 3.23	8.2:1	57
'76–'82	110.8 (1817)	2-bbl	80 @ 4800	95 @ 3000	3.31 × 3.23	8.5:1	64①
'82 Diesel	136.6 (2238)	Diesel	58 @ 4300	98 @ 2200	3.46 × 3.62	21.0:1	55

① '80–'82—58

TUNE-UP SPECIFICATIONS

(When analyzing compression results, look for uniformity among cylinders, rather than specific pressures)

Year	Engine No. Cyl. Displacement cu in. (cc)	Spark Plugs Type	Gap (in.)	Distributor Point Dwell (deg)	Distributor Point Gap (in.)	Ignition Timing (deg) MT	Ignition Timing (deg) AT	Intake Valve Opens (deg)	Fuel Pump Pressure (psi)	Idle Speed (rpm) MT	Idle Speed (rpm) AT	Valve Clearance (in.) In	Valve Clearance (in.) Ex
'75	4-110.8 (1817)	BP-6ES	0.030	49–55	0.018–0.022	12B	—	31	3–4.5	900	—	0.004	0.006
'76	4-110.8 (1817)	BPR-6ES	0.030	47–57	0.016–0.020	6B	6B	21	3–4.5	900	900	0.006	0.010
'77–'79	4-110.8 (1817)	BPR-6ES①	0.030	47–57	0.016–0.020	6B	6B	21B	2.6–3.3	900	900	0.006	0.010

TUNE-UP SPECIFICATIONS

(When analyzing compression results, look for uniformity among cylinders, rather than specific pressures)

Year	Engine No. Cyl. Displacement cu in. (cc)	Spark Plugs Type	Gap (in.)	Distributor Point Dwell (deg)	Point Gap (in.)	Ignition Timing (deg) MT	AT	Intake Valve Opens (deg)	Fuel Pump Pressure (psi)	Idle Speed (rpm) MT	AT	Valve Clearance (in.) In	Ex
'80	4-110.8 (1817)	BPR-6ES②	0.030	47–57	0.016–0.020	6B	6B	21B	—	900	900	0.006	0.010
'81–'82	4-110.8 (1817)	BPR-6ES11③	0.040	Electronic		6B	6B	21B	3.0	900	900	0.006	0.010

① AC-R44XLS
② AC-R44XLS in some models
③ AC-R22XLS in some models

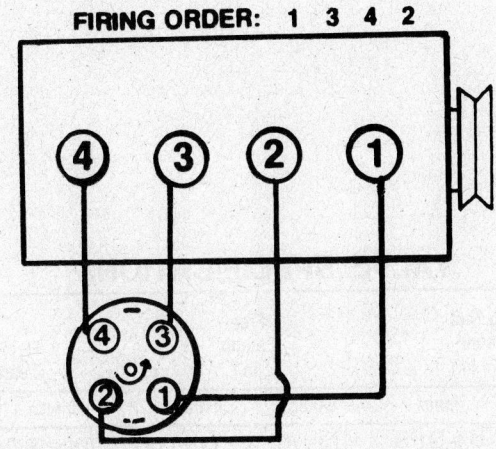

FIRING ORDER: 1 3 4 2

Firing order

DIESEL ENGINE TUNE-UP SPECIFICATIONS

Injector Opening Pressure	Low Idle (rpm)	Valve Clearance (in.) Intake	Exhaust	Intake Valve Opens (deg)	Injection Timing (deg)	Firing Order
2133	750	0.016C	0.016C	16B	15B	1-3-4-2

CRANKSHAFT AND CONNECTING ROD SPECIFICATIONS

(All measurements given in in.)

Year	Engine Displacement cu in. (cc)	Crankshaft Main Brg Journal Dia	Main Brg Oil Clearance	Shaft End-Play	Thrust on No.	Connecting Rod Journal Dia	Oil Clearance	Side Clearance
'75	110.8 (1817)	2.2016–2.2022	0.0015–0.0047	0.0059–0.0120	3	1.9262–1.9268	0.0020–0.0047	0.0079–0.0130
'76–'82	110.8 (1817)	2.2016–2.2022	0.0008–0.0025	0.0024–0.0094	3	1.9262–1.9268	0.0007–0.0030	0.0137–Max.
'82 Diesel	136.6 (2238)	2.3591–2.3594	0.0011–0.0033	0.0018–0.0039	3	2.0837	0.0016–0.0047	0.0024

CAPACITIES

Year	Engine Displacement cu. in. (cc)	Engine Crankcase (qts)	Transmission (pts)			Drive Axle (pts)	Fuel Tank (gals)	Cooling System (qts)	
			4sp	5sp	Auto			With Heater	Without Heater
'75–'79	110.8 (1817)	5.3	2.6①	—	6	2.7②	13.2	6.4	5.3
'80–'82	110.8 (1817)	4.2	2.7③	2.7③	7	2.7④	13.2⑤	6.4⑥	—
'82 Diesel	136.6 (2238)	6	2.7③	2.7	7	2.7④	13.2⑤	7	—

① w/transfer case—5.3 pts.
② Front and rear
③ w/transfer case—5.2 pts.
④ 1.7 front, rear
⑤ 18.5 gal. long bed '80–'81
   19.1 gal. long bed '82
⑥ 6.8 qts. manual trans., 6.4 qts. auto. trans.

VALVE SPECIFICATIONS

Year	Engine Displacement cu. in. (cc)	Seat Angle (deg)	Face Angle (deg)	Spring Test Pressure (lbs. @ in.)		Free Length (in.)		Stem-to-Guide Clearance (in.)		Stem Diameter (in.)	
				Outer	Inner	Outer	Inner	Intake	Exhaust	Intake	Exhaust
'75	110.8 (1817)	45	45	41.8–50.1 @ 1.58	15.4–19.0 @ 1.50	2.05–1.99	1.78–1.73	.0016–.0079	.0020–.0098	.3150–.3102	.3150–.3091
'76–'82	110.8 (1817)	45	45	32.2–37.0 @ 1.614	18.7–21.5 @ 1.516	1.7874–1.8465	1.7244–1.7835	0.0009–0.0022	0.0015–0.0031	0.3102	0.3091
'82 Diesel	136.6 (2238)	45	45	145 @ 1.535	44 @ 1.457	1.8636	1.8873	0.0015–0.0027	0.0025–0.0037	0.3150	0.3150

PISTON AND RING SPECIFICATIONS

(All measurements in inches)

Year	Engine Displacement cu. in. (cc)	Piston Clearance	Ring Gap			Ring Side Clearance		
			Top Compression	Bottom Compression	Oil Control	Top Compression	Bottom Compression	Oil Control
'75	110.8 (1817)	0.0018–0.0026	0.008–0.016	0.008–0.016	0.012–0.039①	0.0012–0.0028	0.0012–0.0028	0.0008–0.0024
'76–'82	110.8 (1817)	0.0018–0.0026	0.008–0.016	0.008–0.016	0.008–0.035	0.0059	0.0059	0.0059
'82 Diesel	136.6 (2238)	0.0062–0.0070	0.0079–0.0158	0.0079–0.0158	0.0079–0.0158	0.0018–0.0028	0.0012–0.0021	0.0008–0.0021

① '77—.008–.035

TORQUE SPECIFICATIONS

(All readings in ft. lbs. unless noted)

Year	Engine Displacement cu. in. (cc)	Cylinder Head Bolts	Rod Bearing Bolts	Main Bearing Bolts	Crankshaft Pulley Bolt	Flywheel-to-Crankshaft Bolts
'75–'79	110.8 (1817)	①	43	72	50②	69
'80–'82	110.8 (1817)	72③	43	72④	87⑤	—
'82 Diesel	136.6 (2238)	65⑥	61	123	136	68

① On '75 models, tighten to 43 ft. lbs. first, then loosen completely and re-tighten 1, 2, 3 and 6 to 70 ft. lbs., and the remaining bolts to 60 ft. lbs. On '76 and later models, tighten to 61 ft. lbs. first, retighten to 72 ft. lbs.

② '76–'79: 87 ft. lbs.

③ '81: 70 ft. lbs.

④ '81: Tighten in order 3, 4, 2, 5, 1 to 75 ft. lbs.

⑤ '81: 90 ft. lbs.

⑥ Tighten in 2 steps: 44 ft. lbs. first, then 65 ft. lbs. final torque.

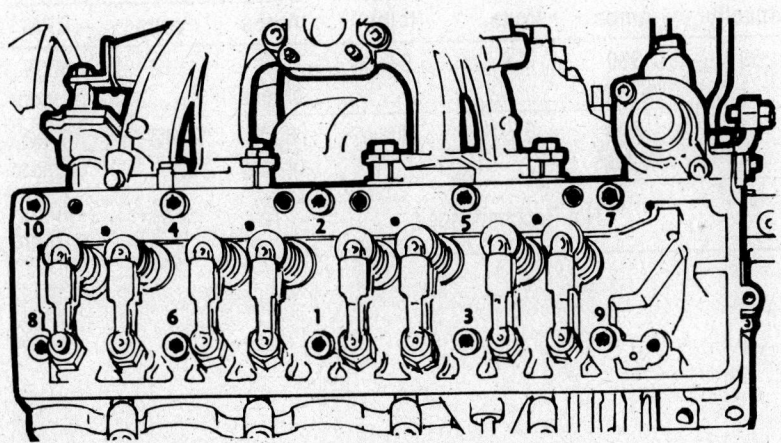

1975 torque sequence

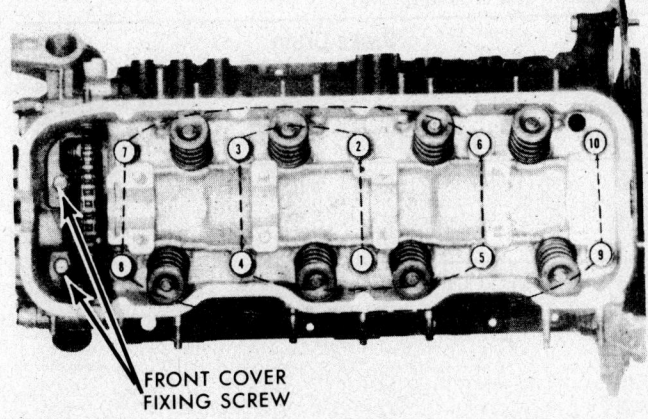

FRONT COVER FIXING SCREW

Diesel cylinder head bolt tightening sequence

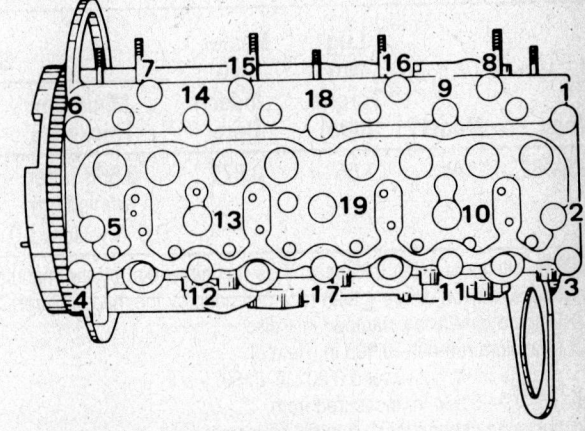

1976 and later torque sequence

ALTERNATOR AND REGULATOR SPECIFICATIONS

Year	Alternator			Charge Indicator Relay		Voltage Regulator				
	Part No.	Output (amps)		Back Gap (in.)	Point Gap (in.)	Back Gap (in.)	Core Gap (in.)	Air Gap (in.)	Point Gap (in.)	Volts @ 75°F
'75–'76	LT130-83	30		.032–.039	.016–.024	—	.024–.039	—	.012–.016	13.5–14.5
'77–'82	LT135-30①	35		.032–.039	.016–.024	—	.024–.039	—	.012–.016	13.8–14.8
	LT190-126	40		.036	.020	.015	—	.014	.012	13.8–14.8
	LT150-144	50		.036	.020	.015	—	.014	.012	13.8–14.8
	LT150-131B	50		.036	.020	.015	—	.014	.012	13.8–14.8

BATTERY AND STARTER SPECIFICATIONS

(All trucks use 12 volt, negative ground electrical systems)

Year	Model	Battery Amp Hour Capacity	Starter — Lock Test Amps	Volts	Torque (ft/lb)	No Load Test Amps	Volts	RPM	Brush Spring Tension (oz)	Min. Brush Length (in.)
'75–'79	All	50	330 or less	5.1	5.8	60 or less	12	6000 or more	56	0.49①
'80–'82	All	50	200 or less	5②	3.6	60③ or less	12	6000 or more	—	—
'82 Diesel	All	80	Not Recommended			120	12	4000 or more	56	0.787

① '77—0.47
② '81–'82—7.4 volts
③ '81–'82—70 amp or less

BRAKE SPECIFICATIONS

(All measurements given are (inches) unless noted)

Year	Model	Lug Nut Torque (ft/lb)	Master Cylinder Bore	Brake Disc — Minimum Thickness	Maximum Run-Out	Diameter	Brake Drum — Max. Machine O/S	Max. Wear Limit	Minimum Lining Thickness Front	Rear
'75–'82	All	65	0.875	0.668 (after refinishing) 0.653 (discard)①	②	10.00	10.059	10.079	0.059③	0.059

NOTE: Minimum lining thickness is as recommended by the manufacturer. Due to variations in state inspection regulations, the minimum allowable thickness may be different than recommended by the manufacturer.
① Discard dimension stamped into disc.
② Maximum run-out—0.005 in. Rate of change must not exceed 0.001 in. in 30°.
③ '76–'79—0.264 in. measured from backside of shoe table. Is point of contact of warning sensor.

WHEEL ALIGNMENT SPECIFICATIONS

Year	Model	Camber Range (deg)	Camber Preferred (deg)	Caster Range (deg)	Caster Preferred (deg)	Toe-in Range (in.)	Toe-in Preferred (in.)	Kingpin Inclination (deg)
'75	All	½P to 1½P	1P①	0 to 1P	½P②	+⅛ ± ¹⁄₁₆③	<0	7
'76	All	±¾	½P	±1	⅙N	0	<0	7
'77–'79	All	±¾	½P	±1	⅙P	0	<0	7½
'79–'81	4 × 4	±¾	⁷⁄₁₂P	±1	⅓P	0	<0	7¼
'80–'81	All	±¾	½P	±1	⅙P④	0	0.08	7½
'82	4 × 4	5'P to 1°5' P	35'P	10'N to 50'P	20'P	+¹⁄₁₆ to −¹⁄₁₆	0	7°25'
'82	All	0 to 1P	30'P	0 to 1P	30'P	±⅛	¹⁄₁₆	7°30'

① Camber should not vary more than ½°
from side-to-side
② Caster should not vary more than ½° from
side-to-side
③ Always adjust toe-in after adjusting caster
and camber
④ '81: ½P

TUNE-UP PROCEDURES

Spark Plugs

REMOVAL

1. Remove the wire from the end of the spark plug by grasping the wire by the rubber boot. If the boot sticks to the plug, remove it by twisting and pulling at the same time. Do not pull the wire itself or you will damage the delicate carbon core.
2. Use a ¹³⁄₁₆ in. spark plug socket to loosen all of the plugs about two turns.
3. If compressed air is available, blow off the area around the spark plug holes BEFORE removing plugs. Otherwise, use a rag or a brush to clean the area. Be careful not to allow any foreign material to drop into the spark plug holes.
4. Remove the plugs by unscrewing them the rest of the way from the engine.

INSPECTION

Check the plugs for deposits and wear. If they are not going to be replaced, clean the plugs thoroughly. Remember that any kind of deposit will decrease the efficiency of the plug. Plugs can be cleaned on a spark plug cleaning machine, or you can do an acceptable job of cleaning with a stiff wire brush.

Check the spark plug gap before installation. The ground electrode must be parallel to the center electrode and the specified size wire gauge should pass through the gap with a slight drag. If the electrodes are worn, it is possible to file them level. The best alternative, however is a brand-new set of spark plugs.

INSTALLATION

1. Insert the plugs in the spark plug holes and tighten them hand tight. Take care not to ''strip'' or cross-thread them.
2. Tighten the plugs to 18–25 ft. lbs.
3. Install the spark plug wires on their plugs. Make sure that each rubber boot is firmly connected to each plug.

Breaker Points And Condenser

When replacing the points, always install a new condenser.

Remember that a change in the point gap or dwell also changes the ignition timing. Therefore, if the points are adjusted, you must also correct the ignition timing.

INSPECTION OF POINTS

1. Disconnect the high-tension wire from the top of the distributor.
2. Remove the distributor cap by prying off the spring clips on the sides of the cap.
3. Remove the rotor from the distributor shaft by pulling it straight up. Examine the condition of the rotor. If it is cracked or the brass tip is excessively worn or burned, the rotor should be replaced. If not exces-

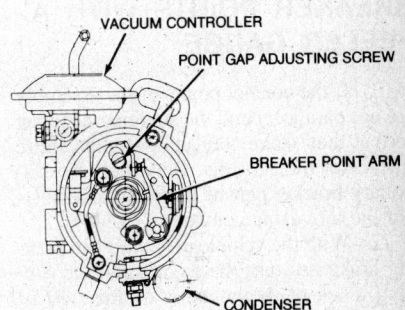

Distributor

sively worn, clean the brass tip with fine emery paper until shiny.
4. Pry open the contacts of the points with a screwdriver and check the condition of the contacts. If they are excessively worn, burned or pitted, they should be replaced.
5. If the points are in good condition, adjust them and replace the rotor and the distributor cap. If the points need to be replaced, follow the replacement procedure given below.

REMOVAL AND INSTALLATION

1. Remove the coil high-tension wire from top of the distributor cap. Remove the distributor cap from the distributor and place it out of the way. Remove the rotor from the distributor shaft.
2. Loosen the screw that holds the condenser lead to the body of the breaker points

and remove the condenser lead from the points.

3. Remove the screw that holds and grounds the condenser to the distributor body. Remove the condenser from the distributor and discard it.

4. Remove the points assembly attaching screws and adjustment lockscrews. A screwdriver with a holding mechanism will come in handy here, so that you don't drop a screw into the distributor and have to remove the entire distributor to retrieve it.

5. Remove the points by lifting them straight up and off the locating dowel on the plate. Wipe off the cam and apply new cam lubricant. Discard the old set of points.

6. Slip the new set of points onto the locating dowel and install the screws that hold the assembly onto the plate. Do not tighten them all the way.

7. Attach the new condenser to the plate with the ground screw.

8. Attach the condenser lead to the points at the proper place.

9. Apply a small amount of cam lubricant to the shaft where the rubbing block of the points touches.

ADJUSTMENT OF THE BREAKER POINTS WITH A FEELER GAUGE

1. If the contact points of the assembly are not parallel, bend the stationary contact so that they make contact across the entire surface of the contacts. Bend only the stationary bracket part of the point assembly; not the moveable contact.

2. With the vehicle in neutral and parking brake on, turn the engine untl the rubbing block of the points is on the crest of one of the high points of the distributor cam. You can do this by either having an assistant turn the ignition switch "on" and then releasing it quickly ("bumping" the engine) or by turning the crankshaft pulley bolt with a wrench or socket wrench.

3. Place the correct size feeler gauge between the contacts. Make sure it is parallel with the contact surfaces.

4. With your free hand, insert a screwdriver into the notch provided for adjustment or into the eccentric adjusting screw, then twist the screwdriver to either increase or decrease the gap to the proper setting.

5. Tighten the adjustment lockscrew, and turn the engine until the rubbing block of the points rests on the next crest of the distributor cam.

Recheck the contact gap to make sure that it didn't change when the lockscrew was tightened.

6. Replace the rotor and distributor cap, and the high-tension wire that connects the top of the distributor and the coil. Make sure that the rotor is firmly seated all the way onto the distributor shaft and that the tab of the rotor is aligned with the notch in the shaft. Align the tab in the base of the

distributor cap with the notch in the distributor body. Make sure that the cap is firmly seated on the distributor and that the retainer springs are in place. Make sure that the end of the high-tension wire is firmly placed in the top of the distributor and the coil.

ADJUSTMENT OF THE BREAKER POINTS WITH A DWELL METER

1. Adjust the points with a feeler gauge as previously described.

2. Connect the dwell meter to the ignition circuit according to the manufacturer's instructions. One lead of the meter is connected to a ground and the other lead is connected to the distributor post on the coil. An adapter is usually provided for this purpose.

3. If the dwell meter has a set line on it, adjust the meter to zero the indicator.

4. Start the engine.

NOTE: Be careful when working on any vehicle while the engine is running. Make sure that the transmission is in Neutral and that the parking brake is applied. Keep hands, clothing, tools and the wires of the test instruments clear of the rotating fan blades.

5. Observe the reading on the dwell meter. If the reading is within the specified range, turn off the engine and remove the dwell meter.

NOTE: If the meter does not have a scale for 4 cylinder engines, multiply the 8 cylinder reading by two.

6. If the reading is above the specified range, the breaker point gap is too small. If the reading is below the specified range, the gap is too large. In either case, the engine must be stopped and the gap adjusted in the manner previously covered. After making the adjustment, start the engine and check the reading on the dwell meter. When the correct reading is obtained, disconnect the dwell meter.

7. Check the adjustment of the ignition timing.

Electronic Ignition

AIR GAP SETTING

All 1981 and later models have electronic ignition. The only adjustment possible on this ignition is setting of the air gap.

1. Remove the distributor cap and O-ring.

2. Remove the rotor.

3. Use a feeler gauge to measure the air gap at the pick up coil projection. The gap should be 0.008–0.016 in. Adjust if necessary.

4. Loosen the screws and move the sig-

nal generator until the gap is correct. Tighten the screws and recheck the gap.

NOTE: The electrical parts in this system are not repairable. If found to be defective they must be replaced.

You can also check the signal generator by using an ohmmeter to determine its resistance. It should be 140–180 ohms. If the resistance is not correct, it must be replaced.

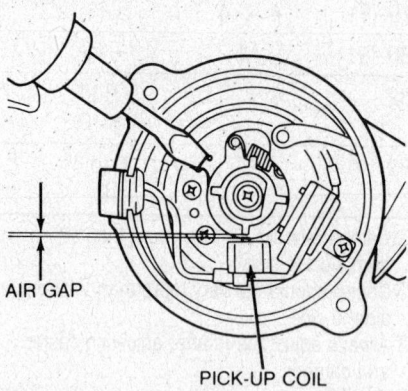

AIR GAP

PICK-UP COIL

Adjusting the air gap—1981–82 models

Ignition Timing

NOTE: For diesel injection timing, see Diesel Fuel System section.

The timing marks are located at the front crankshaft pulley and consist of a pointer attached to the engine block and graduations on the crankshaft pulley.

1. Set the dwell angle to the proper specification.

2. Locate the timing marks on the crankshaft pulley and the front of the engine.

3. Clean off the timing marks, so that you can see them.

4. Use chalk or white paint to color the mark on the crankshaft pulley that will indicate the correct timing, when aligned with the pointer. It is also helpful to mark the tip of the pointer with a small dab of color.

5. Attach a tachometer to the engine.

6. Attach a timing light to the engine according to the manufacturer's instructions. If the timing light has three wires, one, usually green or blue, is attached to the no. 1 spark plug with an adapter. The other wires are connected to the battery. The red wire goes to the positive side of the battery and the black wire is connected to the negative terminal of the battery.

7. Disconnect the vacuum line to the distributor at the distributor and plug the vacuum line. A golf tee does a good job.

8. Make sure that all wires from the timing light and tachometer are clear of the fan and belts. Start the engine.

9. Adjust the idle to the correct setting and rpm (900).

10. Aim the timing light at the timing marks. If the marks that you put on the

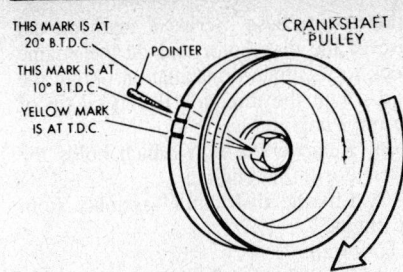

1975 timing marks

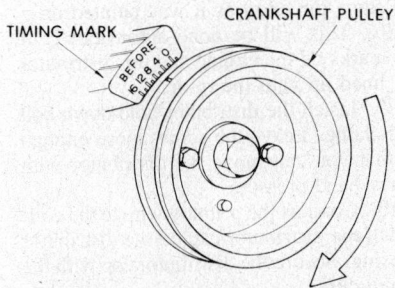

1976 and later timing marks

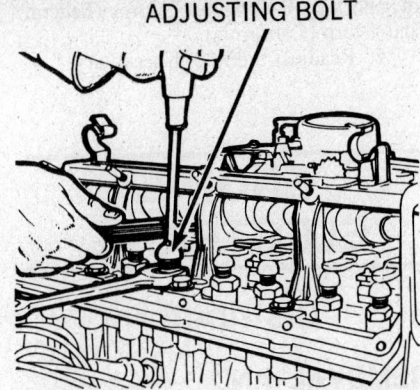

Valve adjustment—feeler gauge is placed between rocker arm and camshaft lobe; wrench holds locknut

Number of Cylinders	1		2		3		4	
Valve Arrangement	Exh.	In.	In.	Exh.	Exh.	In.	In.	Exh.
When piston in No. 1 cylinder is held at T.D.C.	0	0	0		0			
When piston in No. 4 cylinder is held at T.D.C.				0		0	0	0

Valve adjusting sequence

pulley and the engine are aligned when the light flashes, the timing is correct. Turn off the engine and remove the tachometer and the timing light. If the marks are not in alignment, proceed with the following steps.

11. Turn off the engine.

12. Loosen the distributor lockbolt just enough so that the distributor can be turned with a little effort.

13. Start the engine. Keep the wires of the timing light clear of the fan.

14. With the timing light aimed at the pulley and the marks on the engine, turn the distributor in the direction of rotor rotation to retard the spark, and in the opposite direction of the rotor rotation to advance the spark. Align the marks on the pulley and the engine with the flashes of the timing light.

15. Tighten distributor lockbolt, unplug vacuum line and test instruments, and reconnect.

Valve Lash

NOTE: The valves are adjusted with the engine COLD. It is best to allow an engine to sit overnight before beginning a valve adjustment.

NOTE: While all valve adjustments must be made as accurately as possible, it is better to have the valve adjustment slightly loose than slightly tight, as a burned valve may result from overly tight adjustments.

1. Make sure that both the cylinder head and camshaft retaining bolts are tightened to the proper torque.

2. Remove the camshaft carrier sidecover, and discard the gasket if it is torn, cracked, or worn in any way.

3. Turn the crankshaft with a wrench on the front pulley attaching bolt or by "bumping" the engine with the starter until the no. 1 piston is at TDC of the compression stroke. You can tell when the piston is coming up on the compression stroke by removing the spark plug and placing your thumb over the hole; you will feel air being forced out of the spark plug hole past your thumb. Both valves on no. 1 cylinder will be closed. Stop turning the crankshaft when the TDC timing mark on the crankshaft pulley is directly aligned with the timing mark pointer.

4. With the no. 1 piston at TDC of the compression stroke, check the clearance between the rocker arm and the camshaft on 1975–76 models, and between the rocker arm and valve stem on 1977–79 models with the proper thickness feeler gauge on nos. 1 and 2, intake valves and nos. 1 and 3 exhaust valves.

5. Adjust the clearance by loosening the locknut with an open-end wrench, turning the adjusting screw with a phillips head screwdriver and retightening the locknut. The proper thickness feeler gauge should pass between the camshaft or valve stem and the rocker with a slight drag when the clearance is corrected.

6. Turn the crankshaft one full turn to position the no. 4 piston at TDC of its compression stroke. Adjust the remaining valves: nos. 2 and 4 exhaust and nos. 3 and 4 intake in the same manner as outlined in step 5.

7. Install the camshaft carrier sidecover with a new gasket and sealer.

Carburetor

This section contains only tune-up adjustment procedures for carburetors. Descriptions, adjustments, and overhaul procedures for carburetors can be found in the Fuel System section.

IDLE SPEED AND MIXTURE ADJUSTMENT

1975–80

1. Start the engine and run it until it reaches operating temperature.

2. If it hasn't already been done, check and adjust the ignition timing. After you have set the timing, turn off the engine.

3. Attach tachometer to the engine.

4. Remove the air cleaner.

5. Start the engine and, with transmission in Neutral, check the idle speed on the tachometer. If the reading is correct (900 rpm), turn off the engine and remove the tachometer. If it is not correct, proceed to the following steps.

6. Turn the idle adjusting screw with a screwdriver—clockwise to increase idle speed and counterclockwise to decrease it.

7. If the vehicle is equipped with air conditioning:

   a. Turn on the AC to maximum cold and high blower. Disconnect the vacuum line to the air cleaner housing air compensator and plug the inlet manifold;

   b. Open the throttle approximately ⅓ and allow the throttle to close. This will allow the speed-up solenoid to reach full travel;

   c. Adjust the fast-idle screw to set the idle speed to 900 rpm;

   d. Open the throttle about ⅓ and allow it to close. Read the idle rpm. If it is not at 900 rpm, repeat step c until the correct reading is obtained. Shut off the engine.

8. Turn the mixture adjusting screw all the way. Seat the needle tip *lightly* to avoid damaging the tip. Back the screw out 3½ turns.

9. Start the engine. Turn the mixture screw until the maximum engine rpm is achieved.

10. Reset the engine idle speed to 900 rpm.

11. Turn the idle mixture screw clockwise (lean) until the engine speed drops to 850 rpm.

12. Reset the idle mixture screw ½ turn counter-clockwise (rich) from step 11 position.

13. Rest the throttle adjusting screw to 900 rpm.

14. Unplug and reconnect any vacuum lines that may have been disconnected.

1981 and Later Models

The idle mixture adjustment for 1981 models is the same as previously described with the following exceptions:

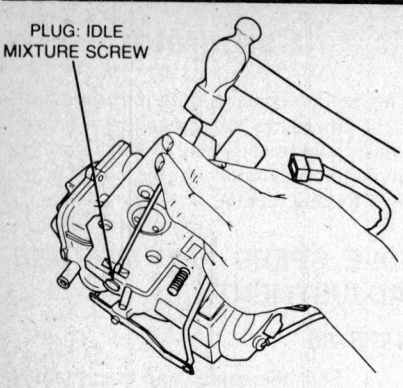

PLUG: IDLE MIXTURE SCREW

Removing the idle mixture plugs

In order to adjust the idle mixture on 1981 models you must first remove the plug that covers the mixture screw.

1. To remove the plug, first remove the carburetor and turn it upside down.

2. Remove the plug carefully with a hammer and screwdriver (see illustration).

3. Reinstall the carburetor and adjust as necessary.

4. Turn the mixture screw all the way in, and then back it out 2 turns (Federal) and 1 turn (California).

5. Readjust the idle if necessary.

ENGINE ELECTRICAL

Distributor

REMOVAL AND INSTALLATION

1. Remove the high-tension wires from the distributor cap terminal towers, noting their positions to assure correct reassembly.

2. Remove the primary lead from the coil terminal.

3. Disconnect the vacuum line.

4. Unlatch the two distributor cap retaining clips and remove the distributor cap.

5. Note the position of the rotor in relation to the base. Scribe a mark on the base of the distributor and on the engine block to facilitate reinstallation. Align the marks with the direction the metal tip of the rotor is pointing.

6. Remove the bolt which holds the distributor to the engine.

7. Lift the distributor assembly from the engine.

To install:

8. Insert the distributor into the engine. Line up the mark on the engine with the metal tip of the rotor. Make sure that the vacuum advance diaphragm is pointed in the same direction as it was pointed originally. This will be done automatically if the marks on the engine and the distributor are lined up with the rotor.

9. Install the distributor hold-down bolt and clamp. Leave the screw loose enough so that you can move the distributor with heavy hand pressure.

10. Connect the primary wire to the coil. Install the distributor cap on the distributor housing. Secure the distributor cap with the spring clips.

11. Install the spark plug wires, checking the wire placement with the firing order diagram in the front of this section. Make sure the wires are pressed all the way into the top of the distributor cap and firmly onto the spark plugs.

12. Adjust the point dwell and set the ignition timing.

NOTE: If the crankshaft has been turned or the engine disturbed in any manner while the distributor was removed, or if the marks were not drawn, it will be necessary to initially time the engine. Follow the procedure given below:

1. It is necessary to place the no. 1 cylinder in the firing position to correctly install the distributor. To locate this position, the ignition timing marks on the crankshaft front pulley are used.

2. Remove the no. 1 cylinder spark plug. Turn the crankshaft until the piston in the no. 1 cylinder is moving up on the compression stroke. This can be determined by placing your thumb over the spark plug hole and feeling the air being forced out of the cylinder. Stop turning the crankshaft when the timing marks that are used to time the engine are aligned.

3. Oil the distributor housing lightly where the distributor bears on the cylinder block.

4. Install the distributor so that the rotor, which is mounted on the shaft, points toward the no. 1 spark plug terminal tower position when the cap is installed. Of course you won't be able to see the direction in which the rotor is pointing if the cap is on the distributor. Lay the cap on the top of the distributor and make a mark on the side of the distributor housing just below the no. 1 spark plug terminal. Make sure that the rotor points toward the mark when you install the distributor.

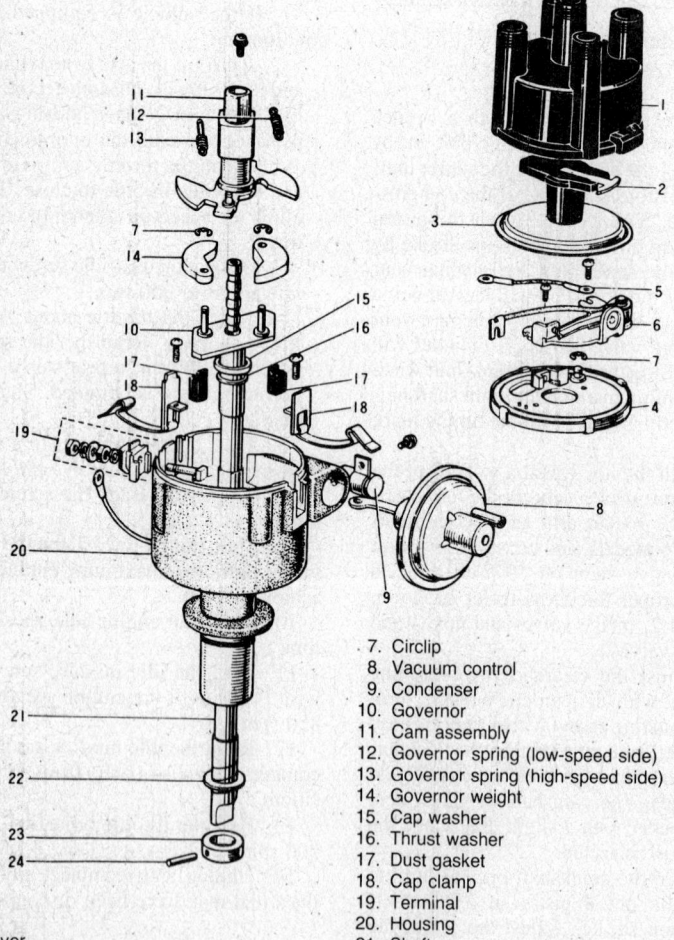

7. Circlip
8. Vacuum control
9. Condenser
10. Governor
11. Cam assembly
12. Governor spring (low-speed side)
13. Governor spring (high-speed side)
14. Governor weight
15. Cap washer
16. Thrust washer
17. Dust gasket
18. Cap clamp
19. Terminal
20. Housing
21. Shaft
22. O-ring
23. Collar
24. Pin

1. Cap
2. Rotor
3. Dust cover
4. Breaker plate
5. Lead wire
6. Breaker point

Exploded view of the distributor

5. When the distributor shaft has reached the bottom of the hole, move the rotor back and forth slightly until the driving lug on the end of the shaft enters the slots cut in the end of the oil pump shaft and the distributor assembly slides down into place.

6. When the distributor is correctly installed, the breaker points should be in such a position that they are just ready to break contact with each other. This is accomplished by rotating the distributor body after it has been installed in the engine. Once again, line up the marks that you made before the distributor was removed from the engine.

7. Install the distributor hold-down bolt.

8. Install the spark plug into the no. 1 spark plug hole and continue from step 9 of the distributor installation procedure.

Alternator

1975–76 Chevrolet LUV vehicles are equipped with a 30 amp alternator with an electro-mechanical, adjustable voltage regulator. 1977–80 models use a similar 35 amp unit. 1981 and later models use either 40 amp (LT 140-126) or 50 amp (LT 150-144 and LT 150-131B) units.

ALTERNATOR PRECAUTIONS

To prevent damage to the alternator and regulator, the following precautionary measures must be taken when working with the electrical system.

1. Never reverse battery connections. Always check the battery polarity visually. This is to be done before any connections are made to be sure that all of the connections correspond to the battery ground polarity of the LUV.

2. Booster batteries for starting must be connected properly. Make sure that the positive cable of the booster battery is connected to the positive terminal of the battery that is getting the boost. This applies to both negative and ground cables.

3. Disconnect the battery cables before using a fast charger; the charger has a tendency to force current through the diodes in the opposite direction for which they were designed. This burns out the diodes.

4. Never use a fast charger as a booster for starting the vehicle.

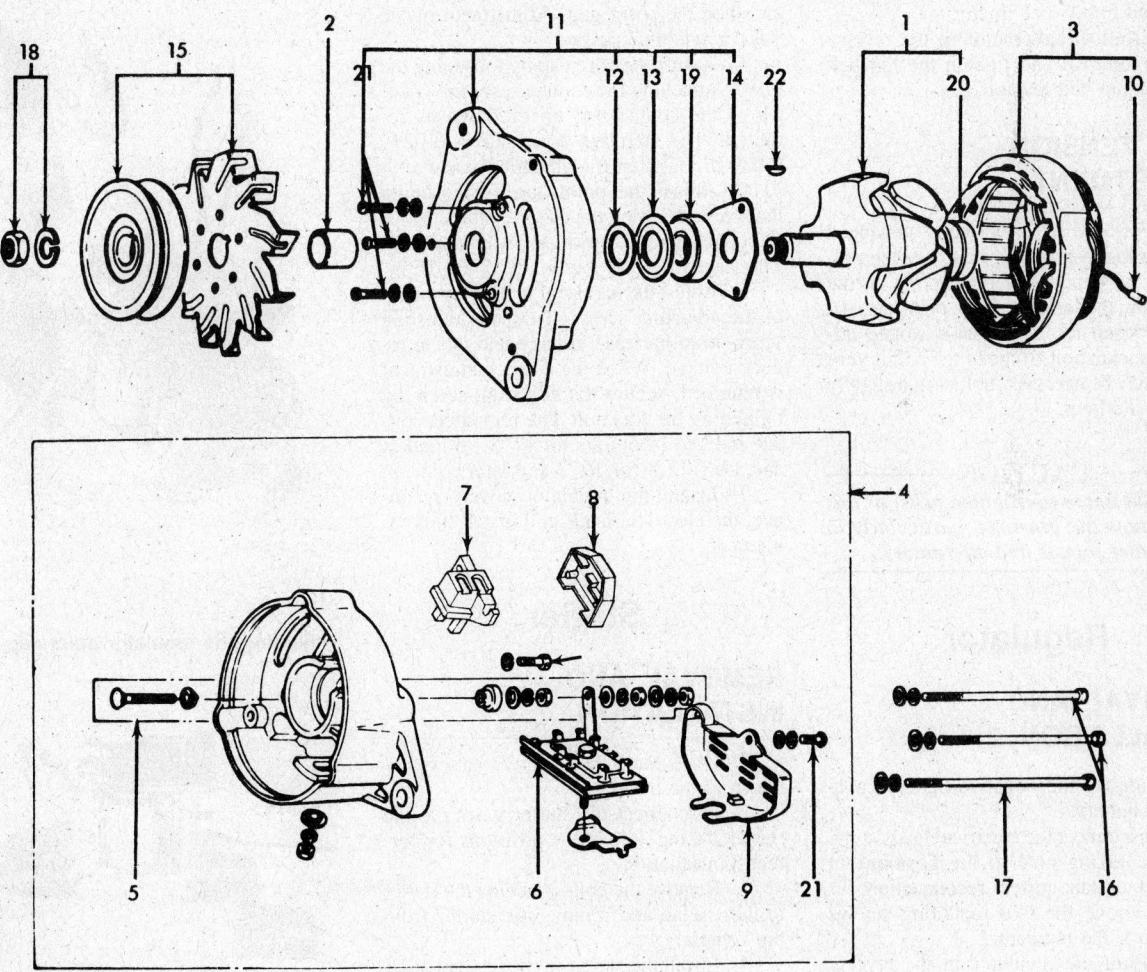

Exploded view of the alternator—typical

1. Rotor assembly
2. Spacer
3. Stator assembly
4. Rear cover assembly
5. Terminal bolt assembly
6. Diode assembly
7. Brush holder assembly
8. Cover
9. Diode cover
10. Terminal
11. Front cover assembly
12. Seal
13. Seal retainer
14. Bearing retainer
15. Pulley assembly w/fan
16. Throughbolt
17. Throughbolt
18. Nut and lockwasher assembly
19. Front ball bearing
20. Rear ball bearing
21. Screw
22. Key

5. Never disconnect the voltage regulator while the engine is running.

6. Do not ground the alternator output terminal.

7. Do not operate the alternator on an open circuit with the field energized.

8. Do not attempt to polarize an alternator.

REMOVAL AND INSTALLATION

1. Remove the air pump.

2. Disconnect the battery ground cable before disconnecting the cable from the alternator "A" terminal. This is a hot cable connected directly to the battery.

3. Disconnect the alternator circuit at the connector and disconnect the cable from the "A" terminal.

4. Remove the mounting bolts on the lower part of the alternator and the fan belt adjusting bolt. Pull belt clear of alternator pulley and remove alternator.

5. Install the alternator in the reverse order of removal and tighten the fan belt and air pump belt tension.

BELT TENSION ADJUSTMENT

Any engine V-belt is correctly tensioned when the longest span of belt between pulleys can be depressed about ¼ in. in the middle by moderate thumb pressure. To adjust, loosen the accessory's slotted adjusting bracket bolt. If the hinge bolt is very tight, it may be necessary to loosen it slightly to move the item.

———— CAUTION ————
Be careful not to overtighten belts, as this will damage the bearings, particularly in air or water pumps and alternators.

Regulator

REMOVAL AND INSTALLATION

1. Remove the negative battery cable from the battery.

2. Disconnect the electrical leads at the regulator, taking note to the positions in order to facilitate correct reconnection.

3. Remove the two mounting screws and remove the regulator.

4. Install the regulator in the reverse order of removal.

ADJUSTMENT

1. Remove the regulator from the vehicle and remove the regulator cover.

2. If the contact points are rough, carefully dress them with fine emery paper (a 400-grit autobody paper works fine).

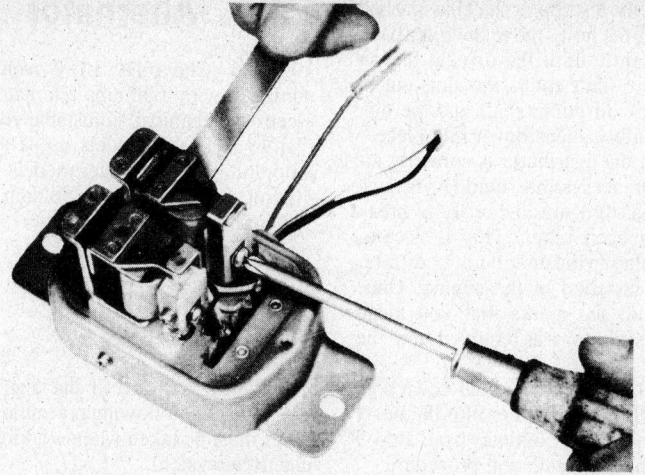

Adjusting the regulator core gap

3. Check and adjust the core gap first, and then the point gap. Adjustment of the yoke gap is unnecessary.

4. Adjust the core gap by loosening the screws attaching the contact set to the yoke. Move the contact set up or down as required. The standard core gap is 0.024–0.039 in. Tighten the attaching screw.

5. Adjust the point gap by loosening the screw attaching the upper contact. Move the upper contact up or down as required. The standard point gap is 0.012–0.016 in.

6. Adjust the regulated voltage by means of the adjusting screw. Turn the adjusting screw in to increase voltage and out to reduce voltage. When the correct adjustment is obtained, secure the adjusting screw by tightening the locknut. The regulated voltage is 13.5–14.5 volts for 1975–76 models and 13.8–14.8 for 1977 and later.

7. Install the regulator cover, reconnect the electrical leads and install the regulator.

Starter

REMOVAL AND INSTALLATION

1. Disconnect the negative battery cable from the battery.

2. Disconnect the starter wiring at the starter, taking note of the positions for correct reinstallation.

3. Remove the bolts attaching the starter to the engine and remove the starter from the vehicle.

4. Install the starter in the reverse order of removal.

BRUSH REPLACEMENT

1. With the starter out of the vehicle, remove the bolts holding the solenoid to the top of the starter and remove the solenoid.

2. To remove the brushes, remove the

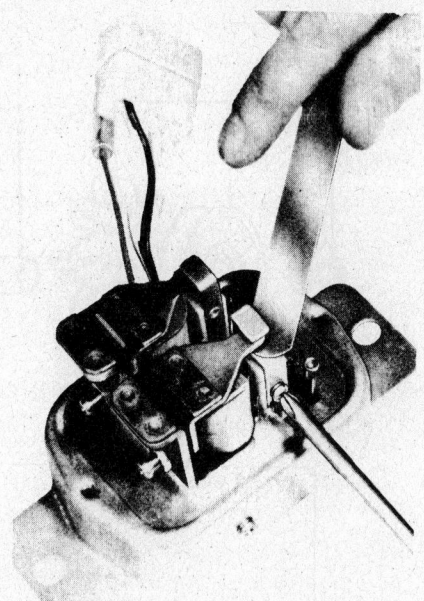

Adjusting the regulator point gap

Adjusting the regulator voltage

two through-bolts and the two rear cover attaching screws and remove the rear cover.

3. Disconnect the brushes, electrical leads and remove the brushes.

4. Install the brushes in the reverse order of removal.

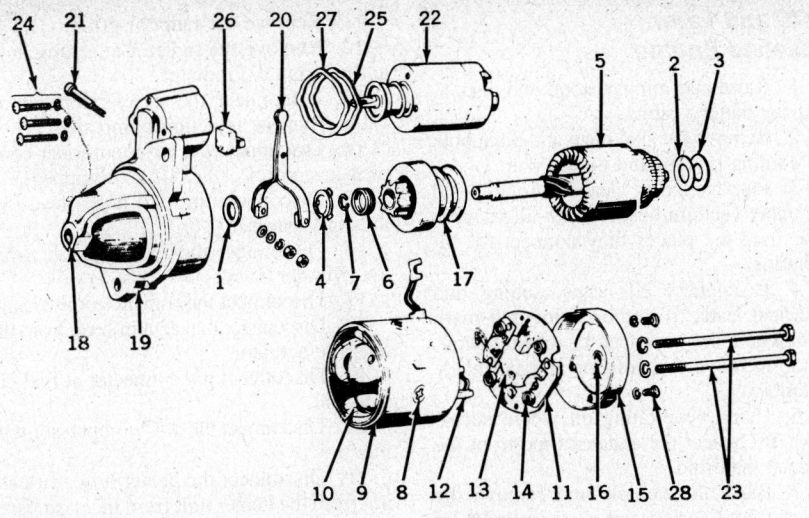

5.	Armature
6.	Pinion stopper
7.	Snap-ring
8.	Field coil retaining screw
9.	Yoke housing
10.	Field coils
11.	Brush holder
12.	Brush (field coil)
13.	Brush (ground)
14.	Brush tension spring
15.	Rear cover
16.	Rear armature bearing
17.	Clutch drive
18.	Front armature bearing
19.	Gear case
20.	Shift lever
21.	Shift lever pivot bolt
22.	Solenoid switch
23.	Through-bolts
24.	Solenoid-to-gear case attaching bolts
25.	Washer
26.	Dust cover
27.	Insulator
28.	Brush holder-to-rear cover attaching screw

1. Thrust washer
2. Spacer

3. Washer
4. Stopper washer

Exploded view of the starter—1975

STARTER DRIVE REPLACEMENT

1. With the starter motor removed from the vehicle, remove the solenoid from the starter.

2. Remove the two through-bolts and separate the gear case from the yoke housing.

3. Remove the pinion stopper clip and the pinion stopper.

4. Slide the starter drive off the armature shaft.

5. Install the starter drive and reassemble the starter in the reverse order of removal.

ENGINE MECHANICAL

Engine Removal and Installation

1975

1. Disconnect the battery ground cable.

2. Prior to removing the hood, scribe a line around the hood mounting brackets, outlining their position on the bottom of the hood. This ensures the hood is reinstalled in its original position. Remove the hood.

3. Drain the cooling system through the drain cock on the radiator and on the cylinder block.

4. Drain the engine oil.

5. Disconnect the upper and lower hoses from the radiator and remove the radiator assembly.

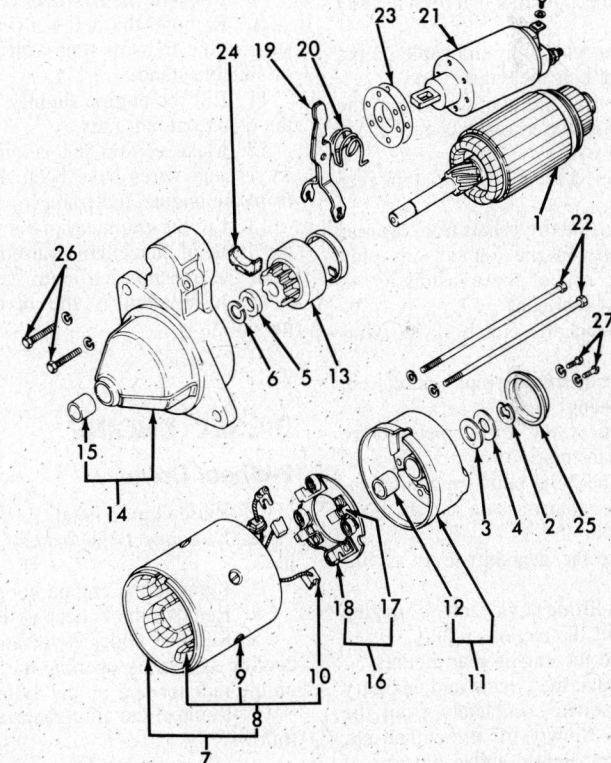

Exploded view of the starter—1976 and later

1. Armature
2. Snap-ring
3. Thrust washer
4. Thrust washer
5. Pinion stop
6. Pinion stop clip
7. Yoke
8. Field coil
9. Screw
10. Brush (+)
11. Rear cover assembly
12. Rear cover bushing
13. Pinion
14. Gear case assembly

15. Gear case bushing
16. Brush holder assembly
17. Brush (−)
18. Brush spring
19. Shift lever
20. Torsion spring
21. Magnetic switch
22. Bolt
23. Adjusting plates
24. Dust cover, gear case
25. Dust cover, rear cover
26. Bolt
27. Screw

6. Disconnect the hoses from the air cleaner and remove the air cleaner assembly.

7. Remove the carburetor control cable.

8. Remove the choke control cable.

9. Disconnect the carburetor wiring.

10. Using penetrating oil on the nuts first, disconnect the exhaust pipe from the exhaust manifold at the flange.

11. Disconnect the alternator and starter wiring.

12. Disconnect the heater hose at the fender side.

13. Disconnect the vacuum hose.

14. Disconnect the spark plug wires from the distributor.

15. Disconnect the grounding cable between the cylinder head cover and the dashboard at the cylinder head cover side.

16. Disconnect the engine wiring at the two connectors.

17. Disconnect the oil pressure unit cord and temperature sending unit lead and the distributor ground wire; remove the wire from the three clips on the engine.

18. Disconnect the fuel line from the fuel pump.

19. Disconnect the ground cable on the timing gear case at the engine side.

20. Disconnect the two hoses from the fuel tank evaporative emission control check and relief valve.

21. Disconnect the driveshaft at the rear axle.

22. Remove the driveshaft from the rear of the transmission and immediately plug a rag into the end of the transmission to prevent loss of lubricant.

23. Disconnect the clutch slave cylinder.

24. Remove the exhaust pipe bracket from the clutch housing.

25. Disconnect the speedometer drive cable at the transmission.

26. Disconnect the body grounding cable between the transmission and the body at the floor side.

27. Remove the gearshift lever assembly.

28. Insert a lifting device into the engine hangers and lift the engine slightly.

29. Remove the engine rear mounts.

30. Check that the engine and auxiliary parts are separated completely from the chassis frame. Slowly lift the engine up, tilting the front slightly above the rear of the engine, to clear the transmission input shaft. Lift the engine out of position.

31. When the front of the engine clears the deflector, continue raising and move the engine toward the front of the truck and out.

32. Install the engine in the reverse order of removal. After the installation is complete, fill the crankcase with oil, the cooling system with coolant, and adjust the clutch pedal free-play. If the engine has been rebuilt, or has had major repair (rings, bearings, etc.), follow the break-in procedure after starting. Check for leaks.

1976 and Later Gasoline Engine

1. Raise and remove hood and disconnect the battery cables.

2. Remove the skid plate and drain both the cooling system and the oil pan.

3. Remove the air cleaner assembly and the many vacuum hoses. Mark all vacuum hoses and the places they connect for installation.

4. Disconnect all hoses, tubing and electrical leads from the engine and mark them where they connect for reinstallation.

5. Remove the radiator and fan blade assembly.

6. Using penetrating oil where necessary, disconnect the exhaust pipe from the exhaust manifold.

7. Raise the vehicle and remove the clutch return spring and slave cylinder, if equipped with a manual transmission. Fasten the cylinder to the frame with a piece of wire or duct tape.

8. Remove the starter motor and fasten it to the frame rail with a piece of wire.

9. Remove the flywheel cover pan.

10. Remove the bell housing bolts and support the transmission with a floor jack or suitable stand.

11. Lift the engine slightly and remove the engine mount nuts.

12. Make certain that all lines, hoses, cables and wires have been disconnected from the engine and frame.

13. Lift the engine from the vehicle with the front of the engine raised slightly to clear the transmission input shaft.

14. Installation is the reverse of removal.

DIESEL ENGINE

2-Wheel Drive

1. Raise engine hood.

2. Disconnect the battery ground cable.

3. Remove the engine hood.

4. Remove the battery assembly.

5. Remove under cover and drain the cooling system by opening the drain plugs on the radiator and on the cylinder block.

6. Remove the air cleaner assembly as follows:

   a. Remove the intake silencer.

   b. Remove the bolts fixing the air cleaner and loosen the clamp bolt.

   c. Lift the air cleaner slightly and disconnect the breather hose, then remove the air cleaner assembly.

7. Disconnect the upper water hose at the engine side.

8. Loosen the compressor drive belts by moving the power steering oil pump or idler if so equipped.

9. Remove the cooling fan and fan shroud.

10. Disconnect the lower water hose at the engine side.

11. Remove the radiator grille.

12. Remove the radiator attaching bolts and remove the radiator.

13. Disconnect the accelerator control cable from the injection pump side.

14. Disconnect the air conditioner compressor control cable. (If so equipped).

15. Disconnect the fuel hoses from the injection pump.

16. Disconnect the battery cable from the cylinder body.

17. Disconnect the transmission wiring.

18. Disconnect the vacuum hose from the fast idle actuator.

19. Disconnect the connector at fuel cut solenoid.

20. Disconnect the A/C compressor wiring.

21. Disconnect the heater hoses extending from the heater unit from the dash panel side.

22. Disconnect the hose for master-vac from the vacuum pump.

23. Disconnect vacuum hose from the vacuum pump.

24. Disconnect the generator wiring at the connector.

25. Disconnect the exhaust pipe from the exhaust manifold at the flange.

26. Remove the exhaust pipe mounting brake from the engine back plate.

27. Disconnect the starter motor wiring.

28. Disconnect the battery cable from starter motor.

29. Slide the gearshift lever boot upwards on the lever. Remove 2 gearshift lever attaching bolts and remove lever.

30. Place a pan under transmission to receive oil, disconnect speedometer cable at the transmission then disconnect the ground cable.

31. Disconnect the propeller shaft at differential side.

32. Remove the propeller shaft.

33. Remove return spring from clutch fork.

34. Disconnect clutch cable from hooked portion of clutch fork and pull it out forward through stiffener bracket.

35. Remove two bracket to transmission rear mount bolts and nuts.

36. Raise engine and transmission as required and remove (4) crossmember to frame bracket bolts.

37. Remove the rear mounting nuts from the transmission rear extension.

38. Disconnect electrical connectors at CRS switch and back-up lamp switch.

39. Remove the engine mounting bolt and nuts. Check that the engine is slightly lifted before removing the engine mounting bolt and nuts.

40. Engine removal:

   a. Check to make certain all the parts have been removed or disconnected from the engine that are fastened to the frame side.

   b. Remove the engine toward front of the vehicle by maneuve the hoist, so that front part of the engine is lifted slightly above the level.

4 Wheel Drive

1. Raise engine hood.
2. Disconnect the battery ground cable.
3. Remove the engine hood.
4. Remove the battery assembly.
5. Remove under cover and drain the cooling system by opening the drain plugs on the radiator and on the cylinder block.
6. Remove the air cleaner as follows:
   a. Remove the intake silencer.
   b. Remove the bolts fixing the air cleaner and loosen the clamp bolt.
   c. Lift the air cleaner slightly and disconnect the breather hose, then remove the air cleaner assembly.
7. Disconnect the upper water hose at the engine side.
8. Loosen the compressor drive belts by moving the power steering oil pump or idler. (If so equipped).
9. Remove the cooling fan and fan shroud.
10. Disconnect the lower water hose at the engine side.
11. Remove the radiator grille.
12. Remove the radiator attaching bolts and remove the radiator.
13. Disconnect the accelerator control cable from the injection pump side.
14. Disconnect the air conditioner compressor control cable. (If so equipped).
15. Disconnect the fuel hoses from the injection pump.
16. Disconnect the battery cable from the cylinder body.
17. Disconnect the transmission wiring.
18. Disconnect the vacuum hose from the fast idle actuator.
19. Disconnect the connector at fuel cut solenoid.
20. Disconnect the A/C compressor wiring.
21. Disconnect the heater hoses extending from the heater unit from the dash panel side.
22. Disconnect the hose for master-vac from the vacuum pump.
23. Disconnect the vacuum hose from the vacuum pump.
24. Disconnect the generator wiring at the connector.
25. Disconnect the exhaust pipe from the exhaust manifold at the flange.
26. Remove the exhaust pipe mounting brake from the engine back plate.
27. Disconnect the starter motor wiring.
28. Disconnect the battery cable from starter motor.
29. Slide the transmission and transfer gearshift lever boot upwards on each lever, remove gearshift lever attaching bolts.
30. Remove return spring from transfer gear shift lever then remove levers.
31. Remove the transmission.
32. Remove the engine mounting bolts and nuts. Check that the engine is slightly lifted before removing the engine mounting bolts and nuts.
33. Engine removal:

   a. Check to make certain all the parts have been removed or disconnected frame the engine that are fastened to the frame side.
   b. Remove the engine toward front of the vehicle by maneuvering the hoist, so that front part of the engine is lifted slightly above the level.

Cylinder Head

REMOVAL AND INSTALLATION

1975

1. Disconnect the negative battery cable, drain the cooling system and remove the air cleaner and attendant hoses.
2. Remove the air pump.
3. Remove the alternator.
4. Disconnect the carburetor throttle linkage and fuel line together with the solenoid electrical lead.
5. Disconnect the exhaust pipe from exhaust manifold.
6. Remove the six bolts retaining the camshaft carrier front cover and remove the front cover.
7. Remove the oil line from the secondary chain tensioner plug.
8. Remove the chain tensioner plug along with the tensioner spring.
9. Remove the bolt and plate washer retaining the timing (camshaft) sprocket.
10. Remove both upper secondary timing chain damper bolts, located in the front of the cylinder head.
11. Loosen both lower timing chain damper bolts.
12. Separate the timing (camshaft) sprocket from the camshaft, together with the chain.
13. Carefully separate the sprocket from

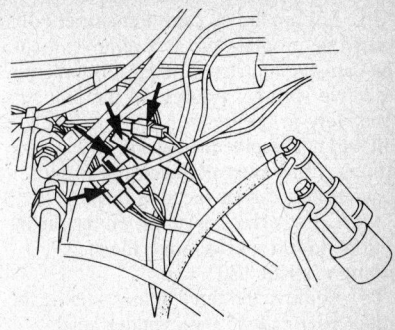

Diesel electrical connections, including sensing resistor, Thermoswitch and A/C compressor switch.

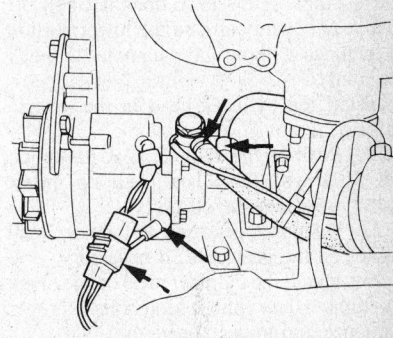

Vacuum pump hose and generator wiring connectors

the chain to prevent the timing sprocket pin from falling out.

NOTE: When removing the camshaft from the timing sprocket, the pin should be positioned in the top. Mark the position of the pin on the timing sprocket prior to disassembling the parts.

14. Hold the chain in position with a wire or cord.
15. Remove the 10 bolts retaining the camshaft cover and remove the cover.

Removing the camshaft carrier front cover—1975 models

16. Loosen the 12 camshaft carrier bolts evenly in progression and remove them. The camshaft carrier is under tension from the valve springs. Loosen all the bolts alternatively in progression, so that a single bolt will not receive the tension of the valve springs. Care must be taken not to loosen the camshaft carrier locating dowel.

17. Loosen the sleeve nut on the air injection nozzle and remove the nozzle by turning it about 180°.

18. Remove the three bolts retaining the timing gear case to the cylinder head.

19. Loosen the cylinder head bolts in a progressional sequence.

20. Remove the cylinder head, gasket and O-rings. If the head does not pull off easily, tap evenly around the lower portion of the head with a rubber hammer to break the joint.

Install the cylinder head in the reverse order of removal, as follows:

21. Position the cylinder head gasket on the block with the "Top" side up. Insert the O-rings into the oil ports.

22. Position a gear case-to-cylinder head gasket on the gear case, if necessary.

23. Install the cylinder head on the block and tighten the cylinder head bolts in proper sequence and to specifications.

24. Tighten the three bolts attaching the timing gear case to the cylinder head.

25. Install the air injection nozzles. Do not tighten them securely at this time.

26. Align the setting mark on the camshaft thrust plate with the corresponding mark on the camshaft.

27. Position the O-rings to the camshaft carrier. Install these parts in position and lightly tighten the bolts retaining the dowels. Install the longest bolts in the position of the dowel.

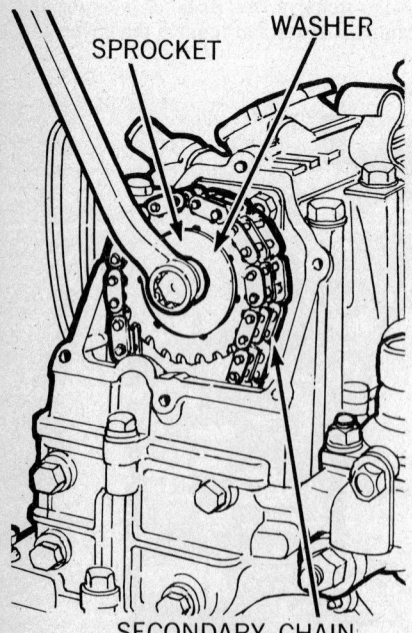

Removing the camshaft timing sprocket retaining bolt—1975

28. Install the camshaft carrier bolts. Tighten the bolts alternately, in progression to 15 ft. lbs. to compress the valve springs evenly. Note that the camshaft carrier is also used to retain two portions of the air manifold bracket and PCV hose clips.

29. With the no. 4 cylinder at TDC of the compression stroke, check that the setting mark on the camshaft and on the thrust plate are correctly aligned. If the setting marks are not in good alignment, make the necessary adjustment as follows:

a. If the setting mark on the camshaft and the thrust plate are not in alignment, attach the camshaft sprocket to the camshaft, insert the pin into a hole in the camshaft timing sprocket and turn the crankshaft until the marks line up. Then, bring the camshaft into a free state by removing the camshaft timing sprocket from the camshaft and, set the piston in the no. 4 cylinder to TDC of the compression stroke. If the engine has been turned in reverse in the course of this adjustment, make a final adjustment by turning the engine in the normal direction of rotation so that the marks are lined up, with the chain properly tensioned on the correct side.

b. When installing the camshaft timing sprocket on the camshaft, keep their mating faces free of foreign matter because the drive torque is relayed to the timing sprocket from the camshaft by means of frictional contact.

30. Bring the camshaft timing sprocket together with the timing chain, so that the punched mark on the sprocket is located at the 12 o'clock position. Assemble the sprocket to the camshaft.

31. Adjust the position of the camshaft timing sprocket, relative to the camshaft, so that the punched mark on the camshaft timing sprocket is turned up when the drive side of the timing chain is tensioned by pushing the chain tensioner shoe from the plug hole in the secondary chain tensioner. When the camshaft timing sprocket is correctly installed, the punched mark on the sprocket is brought to a position 6°20′ from the top in the direction of rotation.

32. Hold the parts in their relative position. Look through each of the five holes in the camshaft timing sprocket to find a hole in alignment with the hole in the camshaft flange and insert the pin into that hole.

33. Tighten the camshaft timing sprocket attaching bolt, with the plate washer installed, to 33 ft. lbs.

34. Install the camshaft carrier front cover.

35. Install the secondary chain tensioner.

36. Assemble the remaining components to the engine in the reverse order of removal, working backwards from Step 5.

37. Adjust the valves.

1976 and Later

1. Remove the cam cover.

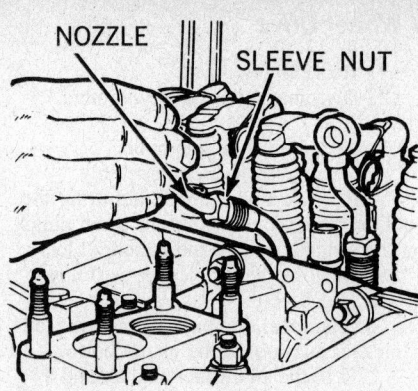

Removal of the air injection nozzle

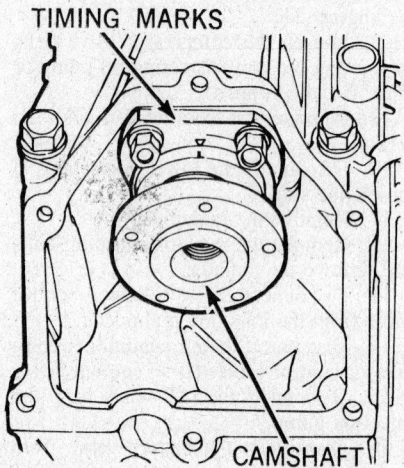

Camshaft timing marks—1975 models

2. Remove the EGR pipe clamp bolt at the rear of the cylinder head.

3. Jack up the vehicle and safely support it. Disconnect the exhaust pipe at the exhaust manifold, using plenty of penetrating oil.

4. Lower the vehicle from the hoist and drain the cooling system.

5. Disconnect the heater hoses at the inlet manifold and at the rear of the cylinder head.

6. Disconnect the accelerator linkage and fuel line at the carburetor, all necessary electrical connections, spark plug wires and vacuum lines.

7. Rotate the camshaft until the no. 4 cylinder is in the firing position. Remove the distributor cap and mark the rotor to housing relationship.

8. Lock the timing chain adjuster by depressing and turning the automatic adjuster side pin 90° clockwise.

9. Remove the timing sprocket to camshaft bolt and remove the sprocket from the camshaft.

NOTE: Keep the sprocket on the chain damper and chain.

10. Disconnect the AIR hose and the check valve at the exhaust manifold.

11. Remove the cylinder head to timing cover bolts.

12. Remove the cylinder head bolts in a progressional sequence, starting with the outer bolts.

13. Remove the cylinder head, intake and exhaust manifold as a unit.

14. To install, reverse the removal procedure and tighten the bolts in the sequence and torque shown in the specifications table in the front of the section.

Diesel Engine

1. Follow the intake and exhaust manifold removal steps.

2. Remove the intake and exhaust manifold gasket.

3. Drain the cooling system by opening the drain plugs on the radiator and on the cylinder block.

4. Disconnect the upper water hose at the engine side.

5. Remove the cooling fan and fan shroud.

6. Remove the sleeve nuts and disconnect the injection pipes.

7. Remove the nozzle holder fixing nuts and remove the nozzle holder assembly.

8. Follow the rocker arm, bracket and shaft assembly removal steps.

9. Remove the pushrods.

10. Remove the joint bolt and disconnect the leak-off pipe.

11. Remove the 19 bolts fixing the cylinder head, then remove the cylinder head and gasket.

12. Install the cylinder head gasket with the TOP mark side up on the cylinder body by aligning the holes with the dowels.

13. Install the cylinder head.

14. Install the pushrod in position on the cylinder head.

15. Install the rocker arm assembly on the cylinder head. Tighten the bracket fixing bolts evenly in sequence commencing with the inner ones.

16. Follow the intake and exhaust manifold installation steps.

17. Install the cooling fan and fan shroud.

18. Connect the upper water hose to engine side.

19. Fill the engine cooling system.

VALVE GUIDE REPLACEMENT

1. With the cylinder head removed from the vehicle and the valves removed from the head, drive the guides out toward the upper face of the cylinder head with a suitable driver. The valve guides cannot be driven out downward because they are secured in place with a snap-ring.

2. Lubricate the outside of the new valve guide with oil. Press it all the way into position, from the upper face of the cylinder head, until it is brought in contact with the snap-ring. Allowable interference between the cylinder head and the valve guide is 0.0016 in.

Valve Rockers

REMOVAL AND INSTALLATION

1975

1. Remove the camshaft cover as outlined under "Cylinder Head Removal."

2. Remove the rocker spring from the pivot and lift the rocker from the cylinder head. Be careful not to lose the rocker guide resting on the top of each of the valves.

3. Install in the reverse order of removal.

1976 and Later

1. Remove the cam cover.

2. Loosen the rocker arm shaft bracket nuts a little at a time, in sequence, starting with the outer brackets.

3. Remove the nuts from the rocker arm shaft brackets.

4. Remove the spring from the rocker arm shaft and remove the rocker brackets and arms.

5. Before installing apply a generous amount of clean engine oil to the rocker arm shaft, rocker arms and valve stems.

6. Install the longer shaft on the exhaust valve side and the shorter shaft on the intake side so that the aligning marks on the shafts are turned on the front (timing) side of the engine.

7. Assemble the rocker arm shaft brackets and rocker arms to the shafts so that the cylinder number that is on the upper face of the brackets is pointed toward the front of the engine.

8. Align the mark on the no. 1 rocker arm shaft bracket with the mark on the intake and exhaust valve side rocker arm shaft.

9. Make certain the amount of projection of the rocker arm shaft beyond the face of the no. 1 rocker arm shaft bracket is longer on the exhaust side shaft than on the intake shaft when the rocker arm shaft stud holes are aligned with the rocker arm shaft bracket stud holes.

10. Place the rocker arm shaft springs in position between the shaft bracket and rocker arm.

11. Check that the punch mark on the rocker arm shaft is turned upward, then install the rocker arm shaft bracket assembly onto the cylinder head studs. Align the mark on the camshaft with the mark on the no. 1 rocker arm shaft bracket.

12. Tighten the rocker arm shaft brackets stud nuts to 16 ft. lbs.

NOTE: Hold the rocker arm springs with an adjustable wrench while torquing nuts to prevent damage to the spring. Start with the center nut and work outward.

13. Adjust the valves and install the camshaft cover, with a new gasket and sealer.

Diesel Engine

1. Remove the rocker cover.

2. Remove the 8 bolts fixing the rocker arm brackets in sequence commencing with the outer ones.

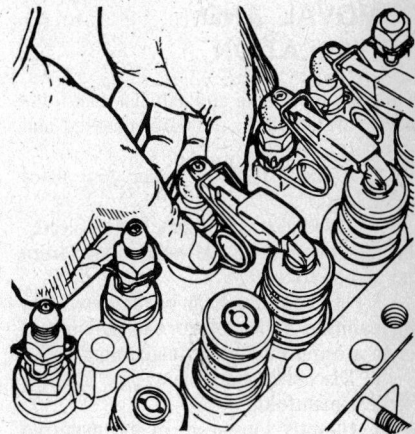

Removing or installing the rocker arm retaining spring

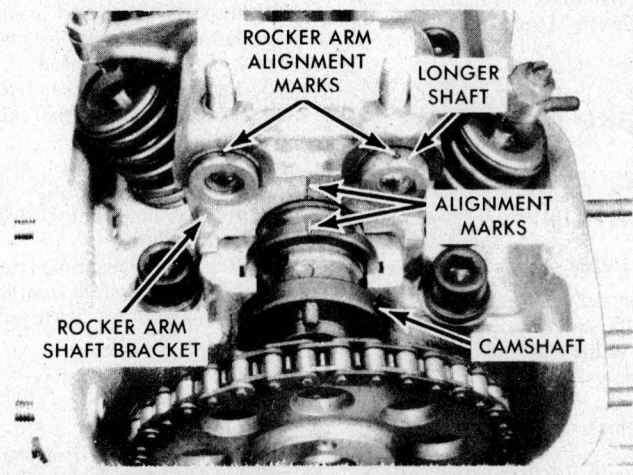

Rocker arm shaft installation—1976 and later

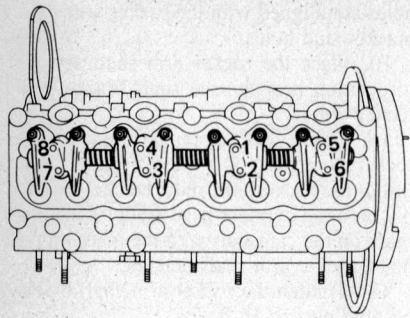

Diesel rocker shaft bolt tightening sequence

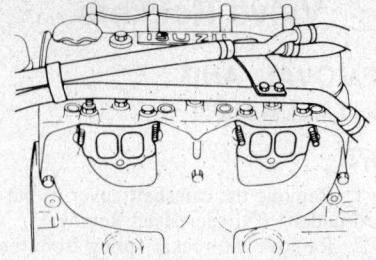

Intake manifold removed—diesel engine

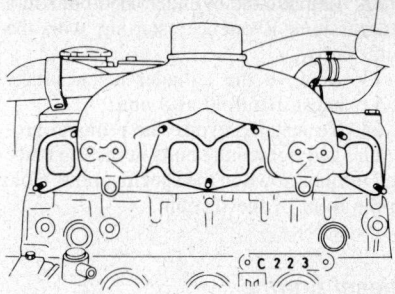

Diesel exhaust manifold mounting bosses

3. Remove the rocker arm, bracket and shaft assembly.

4. To install, follow the removal procedure in reverse order.

5. Tighten the bracket fixing bolts evenly in sequence commencing with the inner ones to 15 ft. lbs.

Combination Manifold

REMOVAL AND INSTALLATION

Although the intake and exhaust manifolds are separate pieces, they are removed and installed as a unit.

1. Remove the air cleaner with all of the hoses.

2. Disconnect all of the electrical leads, throttle linkage, fuel and vacuum lines from the carburetor.

3. The carburetor can be removed from the manifold at this point or can be removed as an assembly with the intake manifold.

4. Disconnect the exhaust pipe from the exhaust manifold.

5. Slightly loosen all of the manifold attaching nuts, and then remove them, working from the outside toward the center. Remove the two manifolds.

6. Install the manifolds in the reverse order of removal, making sure that the surfaces of the manifolds and head are clean before installation. Use a new gasket in assembly.

Intake Manifold

REMOVAL AND INSTALLATION

1976 and Later

1. Disconnect the battery ground cable and remove the air cleaner assembly.

2. Remove the EGR pipe clamp bolt at the rear of the cylinder head.

3. Raise the vehicle and remove the EGR pipe from the intake and exhaust manifolds.

4. Remove the EGR valve and bracket assembly from the intake manifold.

5. Lower the vehicle and drain the cooling system.

6. Remove the upper coolant hoses from the manifold.

7. Disconnect the accelerator linkage, vacuum lines, electrical wiring and fuel line from the intake manifold.

8. Remove the retaining nuts and remove the manifold from the cylinder head.

9. Remove the lower heater hose while holding the manifold away from the engine. Remove the manifold from the vehicle.

10. Installation is reverse of removal.

Diesel Engine

1. Raise engine hood.

2. Remove the bolts fixing the air cleaner and loosen the clamp bolt.

3. Lift the air cleaner slightly and disconnect the breather hose, then remove the air cleaner assembly.

4. Remove the 2 bolts and 4 nuts fixing the intake manifold.

5. Remove the intake manifold.

6. Installation is the reverse of removal. Torque the bolts to 15 ft. lbs.

Exhaust Manifold

REMOVAL AND INSTALLATION

1976 and Later

1. Disconnect the battery ground cable and remove the air cleaner assembly.

2. Remove the EGR pipe clamp bolt at the rear of the cylinder head.

3. Raise the vehicle and remove the EGR pipe from the intake and exhaust manifolds.

4. Separate the exhaust pipe from the manifold.

5. Remove the manifold shield and remove the heat stove.

6. Remove the manifold retaining nuts and remove the manifold from the engine.

7. Installation is the reverse of removal.

Diesel Engine

1 Raise engine hood.

2. Remove the bolts fixing the air cleaner and loosen the clamp bolt.

3. Lift the air cleaner slightly and dis-

connect the breather hose, then remove the air cleaner assembly.

4. Disconnect the exhaust pipe from the exhaust manifold at the flange.

5. Remove the 3 nuts fixing the exhaust manifold, then remove the engine hanger and exhaust manifold.

6. Installation is the reverse of removal. Torque the bolts to 15 ft. lbs.

Timing Gear Cover

REMOVAL AND INSTALLATION

1975

1. Disconnect the negative battery cable, drain the cooling system, and remove the alternator and air pump with their respective mounting brackets and drive belts.

2. Remove the crankshaft pulley bolt and remove the pulley.

3. Remove the six bolts retaining the front cover and remove the front camshaft carrier cover.

4. Remove the 17 bolts retaining the timing gear case.

5. Remove the access plug and take out the bolt on the inner face of the gear case.

6. Insert a small pry bar into the cutaway portions on the outer rim of the timing gear case and pry it off the engine.

7. Install the timing gear case and the camshaft carrier front cover in the reverse order of removal and assemble the engine in the reverse order of disassembly.

1976 and Later

1. Remove the cylinder head.

2. Remove the oil pan.

3. Remove the oil pickup tube from the oil pump.

4. Remove the harmonic balancer. (See Timing Cover Seal—Removal and Installation).

5. Remove the air pump drive belt.

6. If equipped with air conditioning, remove the compressor and lay it to one side. Then remove the mounting brackets.

7. Remove the distributor cap and the distributor.

8. Remove the front cover attaching bolts, then the cover.

9. Install a new gasket onto the cylinder block.

10. Align the oil pump drive gear punch mark with the oil filter side of the cover; then align the center of the dowel pin with the alignment mark on the oil pump case.

11. Rotate the crankshaft until the no. 1 and the no. 4 cylinders are at TDC.

12. Install the front cover by engaging the pinion gear with the oil pump drive gear on the crankshaft.

13. Check that the punch mark on the oil pump drive gear is turned to the rear side as viewed through the clearance between the front cover and the cylinder block.

14. Check that the slit at the end of the oil pump shaft is parallel with the front face of the cylinder block and is offset forward.

15. Reverse steps 1 through 7 for assembly, using new gaskets and sealer on the oil pan, and a new head gasket.

Diesel Engine

1. Remove the radiator.

2. Remove the compressor drive belt by moving the power steering oil pump or idler. (If so equipped.)

3. Loosen the generator adjust plate bolt and fixing bolt, then remove the fan belt.

4. Remove the 4 bolts fixing the crankshaft pulley and remove the crankshaft pulley.

5. Remove the bolts fixing the timing pulley housing covers, then remove the covers.

6. Installation is the reverse of removal.

Timing Cover Seal

REMOVAL AND INSTALLATION

1. Disconnect the negative battery cable.

2. Drain the cooling system.

3. Disconnect the radiator inlet and outlet hoses.

4. Remove the radiator assembly.

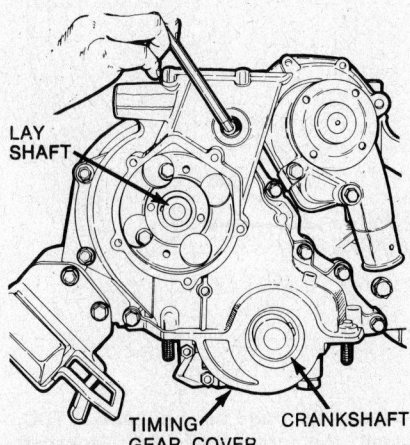

With the access cover removed, remove bolt on the inner face of the gear cover

5. Remove the generator and compressor drive belts.

6. Remove the engine fan.

7. Remove the crankshaft pulley center bolt and remove the pulley and balancer assembly.

8. Carefully pry out the timing cover seal using a small pry bar. (A brake adjusting spoon makes a good tool here).

9. Using the butt-end of a wooden-handled screwdriver or block of wood and hammer, carefully tap the new seal into place on the cover.

10. Reverse steps 1 through 7 for reassembly, using a new gasket and sealer between the timing cover and engine block.

Timing Chains, Sprockets, and Tensioner

REMOVAL AND INSTALLATION

1975

1. Disconnect the battery ground cable, drain the cooling system, and remove the alternator and air pump with their respective mounting brackets and drive belts. Remove the fan.

2. Remove the timing gear cover.

3. Remove the oil line from the secondary chain tensioner plug.

4. Remove the chain tensioner plug with the tensioner spring.

5. Remove the bolt and plate washer retaining the camshaft timing sprocket.

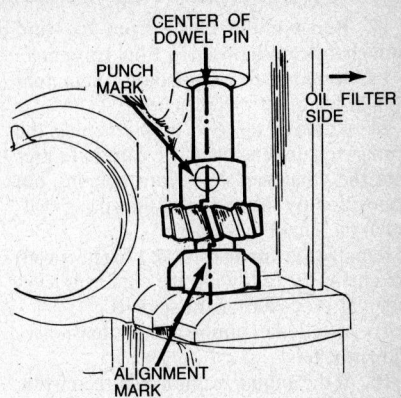

Oil pump alignment—1976 and later

6. Remove both of the upper secondary timing chain damper bolts, located in front of the cylinder head.

7. Loosen both of the lower timing chain damper bolts.

8. Mark the position of the timing sprocket pin with a scribe or yellow grease pencil. The pin should be positioned at the top when removing the sprocket.

9. Separate the timing sprocket from the camshaft, with the chain still attached. Carefully remove the timing sprocket from the chain to prevent the sprocket pin from falling out.

10. Remove the bolt retaining the secondary timing sprocket to the jackshaft. Remove the secondary sprocket by alternately screwing two bolts into the threaded holes in the timing sprocket, one turn at a time.

11. Remove the secondary sprocket from the chain.

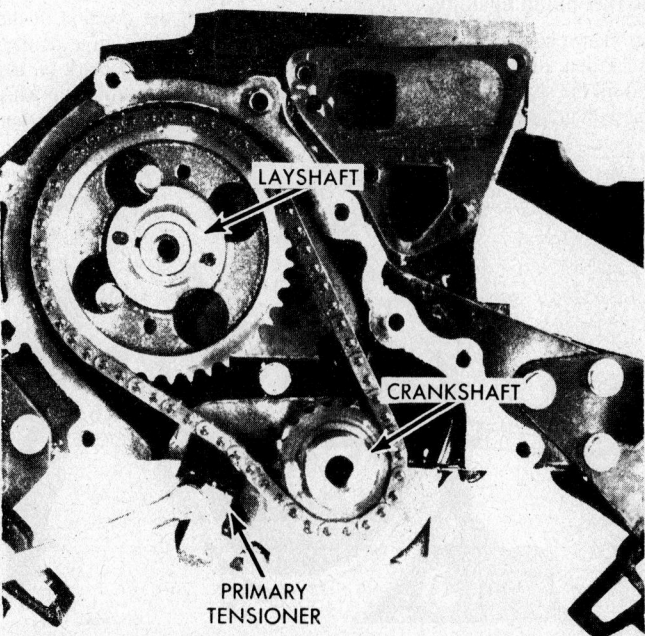

Removing the primary chain tensioner—the layshaft is the jackshaft referred to in the text

12. Remove the chain from the top, through the camshaft carrier front cover hole.

13. Remove the secondary chain tensioners from the cylinder head.

14. Remove the two nuts retaining the primary chain tensioner. Be careful to prevent the tensioner shoe from popping out of position by the action of the spring. Remove the chain tensioner.

Remove the timing sprockets together with the chain, by following the same sprocket removal procedure as in step 10.

To install the timing chain, tensioners and sprockets:

16. If the engine was not disturbed while the components were removed, then install everything in reverse order, using the procedure below as a guide. However, if the crankshaft or cam was turned at all or the engine disassembled further, start the assembly procedure by bringing the no. 1 and no. 4 pistons to TDC.

17. Check that both pistons are at TDC by positioning the timing cover on the locating dowels and place the crankshaft pulley in position. The TDC timing mark should be in direct line with the timing mark pointer.

18. Position the crankshaft and jackshaft timing sprocket into position with the primary chain attached to them. When installing the primary timing sprockets, the timing mark on the jackshaft sprocket must align with the timing mark on the crankshaft sprocket.

19. Align the keyway of the jackshaft with the key in the sprocket by turning the jackshaft, then set both sprockets in position by lightly tapping each sprocket alternately.

NOTE: The jackshaft can be prevented from turning while driving the sprockets into position by holding it through the fuel pump opening.

Install the primary chain tensioner.

20. Install a new oil seal in the timing gear case and fill the space between the lips of the oil seal with grease. Clean the mating

surfaces and position a new gasket to the face of the gear case with sealer. Align the locating dowels with the proper holes and mount the gear case onto the engine block. Install the retaining screws and tighten.

21. With the no. 4 piston at TDC on the compression stroke, check to make sure that the setting mark on the camshaft and on the camshaft thrust plate are aligned. If they are not aligned, go on to the next numbered step.

   a. Attach the camshaft sprocket to the camshaft, insert the pin into a hole in the camshaft sprocket and turn the crankshaft until the marks on the camshaft and the thrust plate align.

   b. Remove the camshaft sprocket from the camshaft and bring the no. 4 piston to TDC of the compression stroke.

NOTE: If the engine has been turned in the opposite direction of normal rotation to align the marks on the thrust plate and the camshaft, make the final adjustment by turning the engine in the direction of normal rotation so that the marks are lined up and the chain is tensioned on the normal side.

22. Insert the timing chain into the gear case from the upper opening and hold it in position.

23. Bring the jackshaft timing sprocket together with the chain, and install it in position so that the punched mark on the sprocket is pointed to the key on the jackshaft. When the sprocket is correctly installed, the punched mark is located approximately at the 2 o'clock position.

24. Bring the camshaft timing sprocket together with the timing chain, so that the punched mark on the sprocket is located at the 12 o'clock position and assemble the sprocket to the camshaft.

25. Adjust the position of the camshaft timing sprocket, relative to the camshaft, so that the punched mark on the camshaft timing sprocket is turned up when the drive side of the timing chain is tensioned by

pushing the chain tensioner shoe against the timing chain from the plug hole in the secondary chain tensioner.

NOTE: When the camshaft timing sprocket is correctly installed, the punched mark on the sprocket is brought to a position 6°20′ from the top in the direction of normal rotation.

26. Hold all of the parts in position and look through each of the five holes in the camshaft timing sprocket to find a hole in alignment with the hole in the camshaft flange. Insert the pin into that hole.

27. Tighten the jackshaft timing sprocket attaching bolt to 33 ft. lbs. Install the plate washer and tighten the camshaft timing sprocket attaching bolt to 33 ft. lbs.

28. Install the gear case front cover and the camshaft carrier front cover, along with new gaskets and sealer.

29. Install the secondary chain tensioner.

30. Assemble the remaining components in the reverse order of removal.

1976 and Later

1. Remove the front cover assembly as previously described.

2. Remove the timing chain from the crankshaft sprocket.

3. Remove the sprocket and the pinion gear from the crankshaft using a puller.

4. Remove the E-clip and remove the automatic chain adjuster.

5. Remove the E-clip and remove the chain tensioner.

6. Check the timing chain for wear. With a pull of approximately 22 lbs. as shown in the illustration the standard length is 15.00″; replace the chain if it is greater than 15.16″.

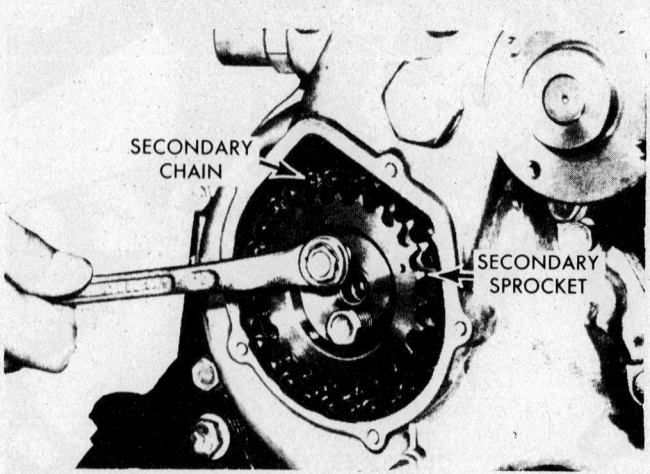

Removing the secondary timing sprocket from the jackshaft by installing two screws in the holes provided and turning them alternately

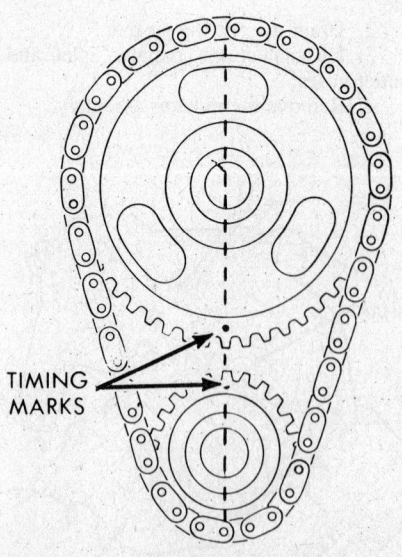

With the no. 1 and no. 4 pistons at TDC, install the crankshaft and jackshaft sprockets with the chain so the timing marks on the sprockets are aligned—1975 models

7. Check tensioner pins for wear or damage, and replace if necessary.

8. Replace the chain tensioner and adjuster using the E-clips.

9. Install the timing sprocket and pinion gear with the groove side toward the front cover. Align the key grooves with the key on the crankshaft, then drive into position using the appropriate tool.

10. Turn the crankshaft so that the key is turned toward the cylinder head side (no. 1 and no.4 pistons at top dead center).

11. Install the timing chain by aligning the mark plate on the chain with the mark on the crankshaft timing sprocket. The side of the chain with the mark plate is on the front side and the side of the chain with the most links between the mark plates is on the chain guide side.

12. Install the camshaft timing sprocket so that the mark side of the sprocket faces forward and so that the triangular mark aligns with the chain mark plate.

NOTE: Keep the timing chain engaged with the camshaft timing sprocket until the sprocket is installed on the camshaft.

13. Install the front cover assembly, using a new gasket and sealer.

Locking the timing chain adjuster—1976 and later

Camshaft

REMOVAL AND INSTALLATION

1975

1. Remove the camshaft carrier as outlined under Cylinder Head Removal and Installation.

2. Remove the two bolts retaining the thrust plate in position on the front of the camshaft carrier.

3. Remove the thrust plate and slide the camshaft out through the front of the carrier.

4. Liberally smear the camshaft with clean engine oil, and install it in the carrier in the reverse order of removal. Be careful not to damage the lobe faces or camshaft bearing journals during installation.

1976 and later

1. Remove the cam cover.

2. Rotate the camshaft until the no. 4 cylinder is in firing position. Remove the distributor cap and mark the rotor to housing position.

3. Lock the timing chain adjuster by depressing and turning the automatic adjuster slide pin 90° in a clockwise position.

NOTE: Make sure that the chain is in a free state, after locking the chain adjuster.

4. Remove the bolt retaining the sprocket to the camshaft and remove the sprocket.

Install the jackshaft secondary timing sprocket so that the punched mark aligns with the key on the jackshaft—1975 models

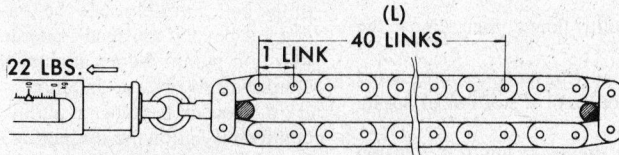

Checking timing chain wear—1976 and later

NOTE: Keep the timing sprocket on the chain damper and tensioner without removing the chain from the sprocket.

5. Remove the rocker arm, shaft and bracket assembly.

6. Remove the camshaft assembly.

7. To install reverse the removal procedure.

Timing Belt

DIESEL ENGINE

1. Follow the timing pulley housing cover removal steps.

2. Remove the bolts fixing the injection

LUV

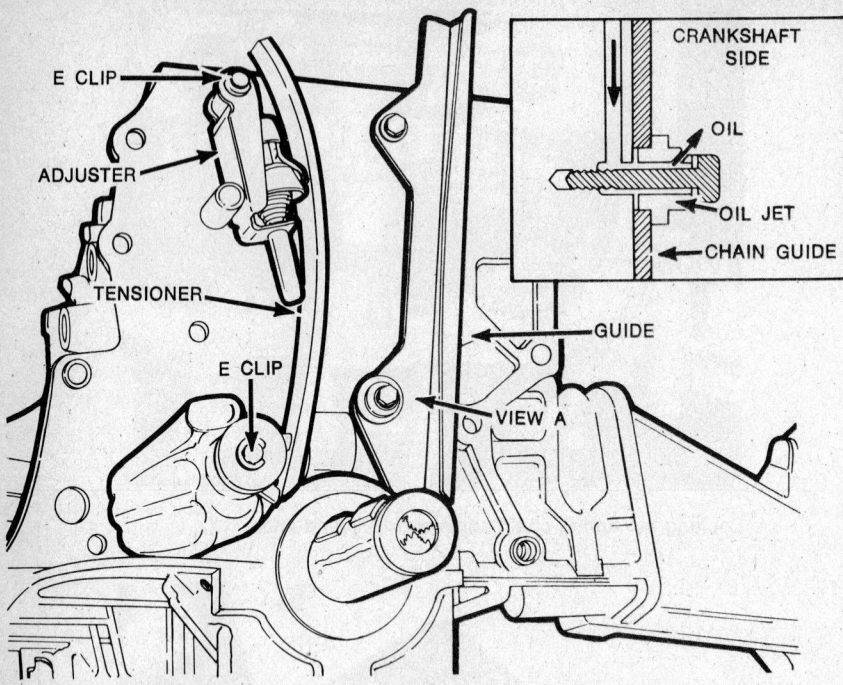

Timing chain adjuster—1976 and later

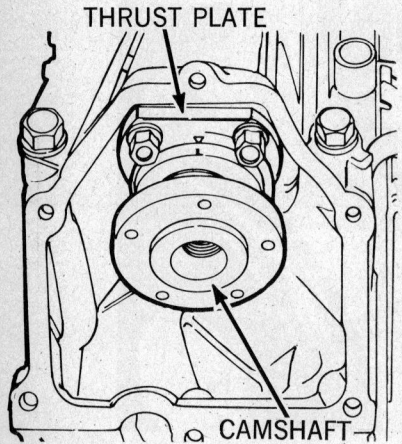

Removing the camshaft thrust plate—1975 models

pump timing pulley flange, then remove the flange.

3. When removing tension spring, avoid using excess force, or distortion of spring will result.

4. Remove the fixing nut of the tension pulley, then remove the tension pulley and tension center.

5. Remove the timing belt. Avoid twisting or kinking the belt and keep it free from water, oil, dust and other foreign matter.

Installation

No attempt should be made to readjust belt tension. If the belt has been loosened through service of the timing system, it should be replaced with a new one.

1. Check that the setting marks on the crank pulley, injection pump timing pulley, and camshaft timing pulley are in alignment, then install the timing belt in sequence of crankshaft timing pulley, camshaft timing pulley, and injection pump timing pulley.

Make an adjustment so that slackness of the belt is taken up by the tension pulley.

When installing the belt, care should be taken so as not to damage the belt.

2. Install the tension center and tension pulley, making certain the end of the tension center is in proper contact with two pins on the timing pulley housing.

3. Hand-tighten the nut so that tension pulley can slide freely.

4. Install the tension spring correctly and semitighten the tension pulley fixing nut.

5. Turn the crankshaft 2 turns in normal direction of rotation to permit seating of the belt. Further rotate the crankshaft 90 degrees beyond top dead center to settle the injection pump. Never attempt to turn the crankshaft in reverse direction.

6. Loosen the tension pulley fixing nut completely, allowing the pulley to take up looseness of the belt. Then, tighten the nut to 78–95 ft. lbs.

7. Install the flange on the injection pump pulley. The hole in the outer circumference of the flange should be aligned with the timing mark "△" on the injection pump pulley.

8. Turn the crankshaft 2 turns in normal direction of rotation to bring the piston in No. 1 cylinder to top dead center on compression stroke and check that the mark "△" on the timing pulley is in alignment with the hole in the flange.

9. The belt tension should be checked at a point between the injection pump pulley and crankshaft pulley using tool J-29771, to a pull of 33–55 lbs.

10. Adjust valve clearances.

11. Install remaining parts in the reverse order of removal.

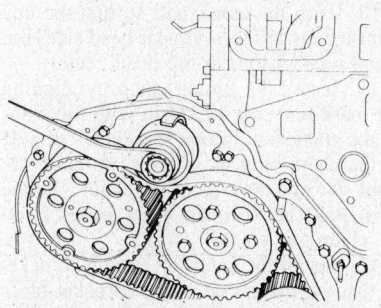

Removing tension pulley nut—diesel engine

Pistons and Connecting Rods

PISTON AND CONNECTING ROD IDENTIFICATION AND POSITIONING

The pistons are marked with the word "Front" and a notch in the piston head. When installed in the engine the "Front" and notch markings are to be facing the front of the engine. The connecting rods

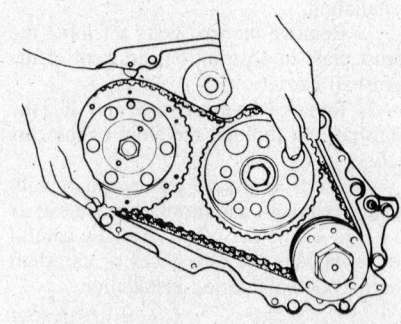

Installation sequence of belt: crankshaft timing pulley, camshaft timing pulley, and injection pump timing pulley

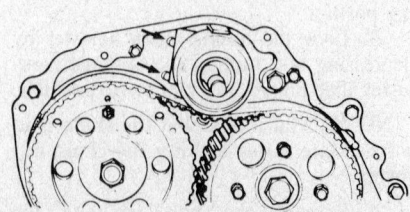

Make sure end of tension center fits against two pins on timing housing properly

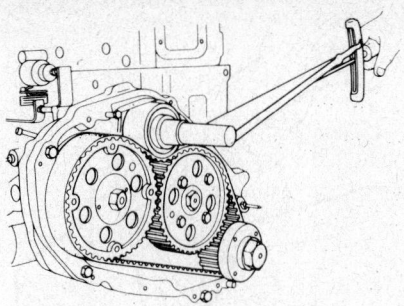

Semitighten tension pulley nuts to 29 ft. lbs.

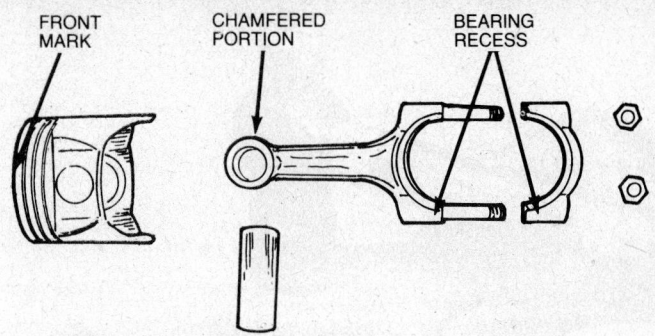

Piston and connecting rod assembly

are numbered corresponding to the cylinders in which they are to be installed. Install the connecting rods in their correct cylinders with the marking to the right of the notch in the piston (looking from the rear of the engine), on the same side as the jackshaft.

ENGINE LUBRICATION

Oil Pan

REMOVAL AND INSTALLATION

All models have a one-piece stamped steel oil pan attached to the crankcase.

NOTE: On 4-wheel drive models, the engine must be removed before removing the oil pan.

1975

To remove the oil pan it may be necessary to unbolt the motor mounts and lift the engine to gain clearance. Drain the oil, remove the attaching screws and remove the pan. Install in the reverse order of removal, using a new gasket and sealer. Tighten the retaining bolts to 50 in. lbs.

1976 and Later

1. Raise the hood and disconnect the battery ground cable.
2. Jack up the vehicle and safely support it.
3. Drain the oil.
4. Remove the front splash shield.
5. Remove the front crossmember, if necessary.
6. Disconnect the relay rod at the idler arm and lower the relay rod.
7. Remove the left side bellhousing bracket.

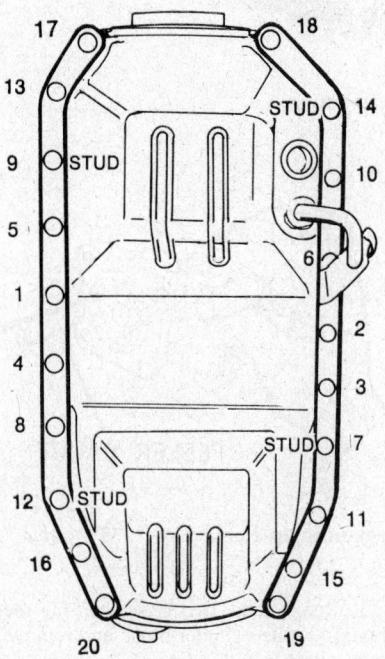

Oil pan tightening sequence—1975 models

8. Disconnect the vacuum line at the oil pan.
9. Remove the oil pan bolts and the pan.
10. Installation is the reverse of removal. Tighten the retaining bolts to 43 in. lbs. on 1976 and later models. On models with a separate crankcase tighten the bolts 15 ft. lbs. Use a new gasket and sealer.

Rear Main Oil Seal

REPLACEMENT

1. Disconnect the negative battery terminal.
2. Remove the oil pan as previously described.
3. Remove the transmission.

NOTE: On manual transmissions, remove the clutch assembly.

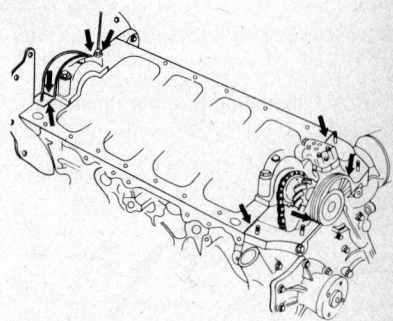

Use sealer at the points indicated when installing the pan gasket

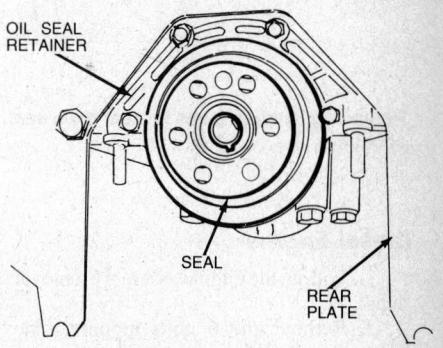

Rear main bearing oil seal

4. Unbolt the starter and tie it out of the way with a piece of wire or heavy twine.
5. Remove the flywheel.
6. Remove the rear main seal retainer.
7. Remove the oil seal, using a pin punch. Work the punch around the diameter of the seal with a hammer until the seal begins to lift out, using care not to damage the seat and area around the seal.
8. Install the new oil seal.
9. Installation is the reverse of removal. Fill the space between the seal lips with grease and lubricate the seal lips with clean engine oil.
10. Install the oil pan with a new gasket and sealer.

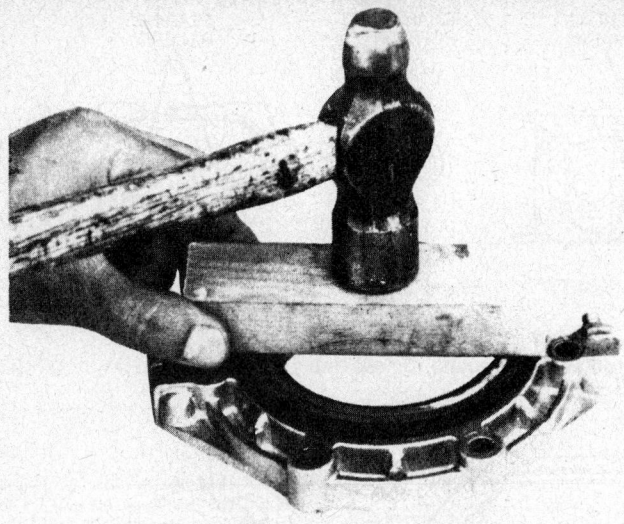

Installing the rear main seal using a seal driver

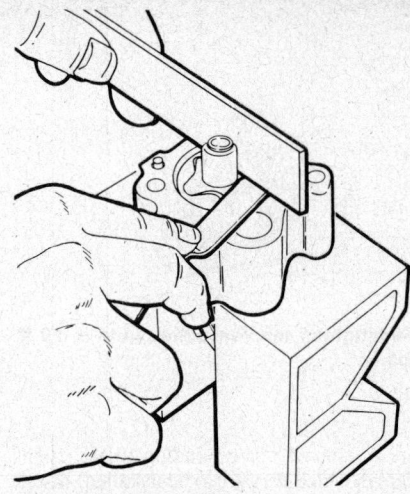

Measuring pump cover to rotor clearance—1976 and later

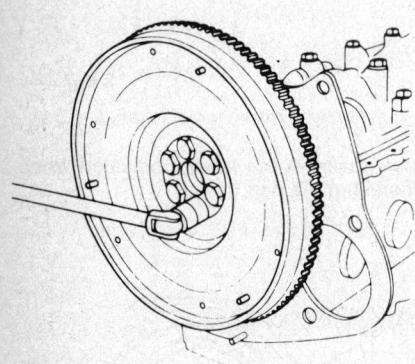

Removing flywheel bolts for rear main seal access

Diesel Engine

1. Follow the engine assembly removal steps.

2. Remove the 6 bolts mounting the flywheel and remove the flywheel assembly.

When loosening the flywheel bolts, hold the crankshaft front bolt with a wrench to prevent turning of the crankshaft.

3. Remove the crankshaft rear seal.

4. Install the new seal with seal installer J-22928 or equivalent. Reverse removal procedures for all other parts.

Oil Pump

REMOVAL AND INSTALLATION

1975

1. Drain and remove the oil pan or crankcase.

2. Disconnect the oil feed pipe.

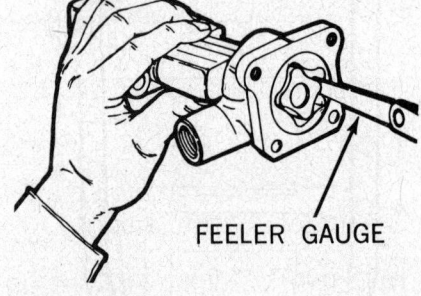

Measuring tip clearance—1975 models

3. Remove the two bolts securing the oil pump to the cylinder block and remove the oil pump.

4. Install in the reverse order of removal, using a new gasket.

1976 and Later

1. Remove the cam cover.

2. Remove the distributor cap, then the distributor.

3. Remove the engine oil pan.

4. Remove the bolt attaching the oil pickup tube to the block and remove the tube from the oil pump.

5. Remove the oil pump mounting bolts and remove the pump assembly.

6. To install align the mark on the camshaft with the mark on the no. 1 rocker arm shaft bracket. Align the notch on the crankshaft pulley with the "O" mark on the front cover. When the two sets of marks are aligned the no. 4 cylinder is at top dead center on the compression stroke.

7. Install the oil pump assembly by engaging the oil pump drive gear with the pinion gear on the crankshaft, so that the alignment mark on the drive gear is turned rearward and is away from the crankshaft by approximately 20° in a clockwise position.

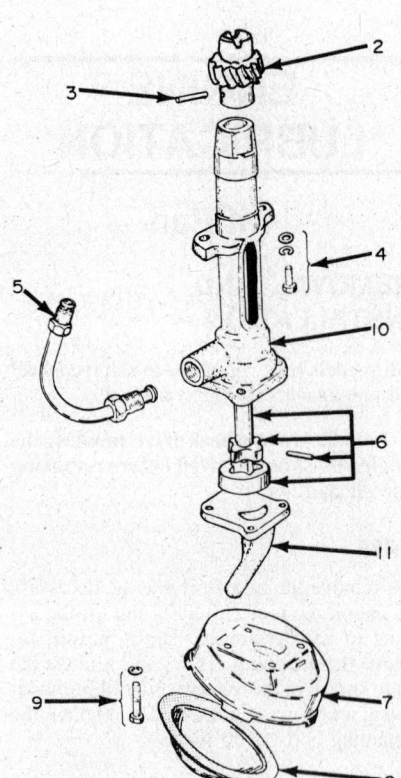

Exploded view of the oil pump—1975 models

1. Pump assembly
2. Pinion
3. Pin
4. Bolt, lockwasher, plain washer
5. Pipe assembly
6. Rotor set
7. Case
8. Screen
9. Bolt, lockwasher
10. Body
11. Cover

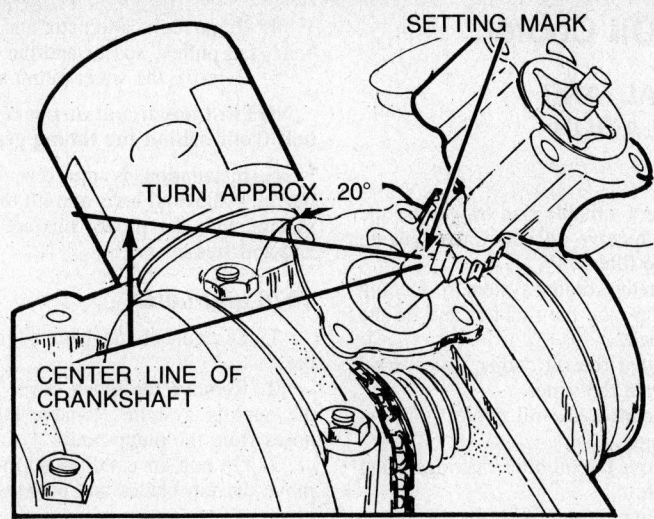

Installing oil pump—1976 and later

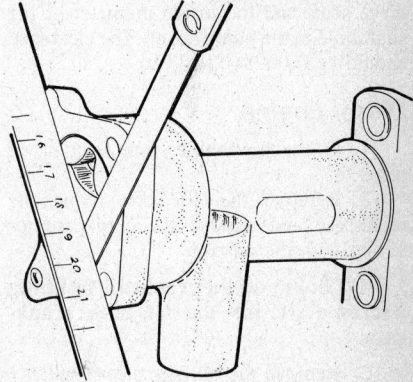

Measuring driven rotor to body clearance—1976 and later

8. Install the oil pump mounting bolts.

9. Connect the oil pipe to the rubber hose and attach the oil pipe to the cylinder block.

10. Install the oil pan and cam cover.

11. Install the distributor by turning the distributor shaft, so that the boss on the shaft is fitted into the slit at the end of the oil pump drive shaft.

12. Install the distributor cap.

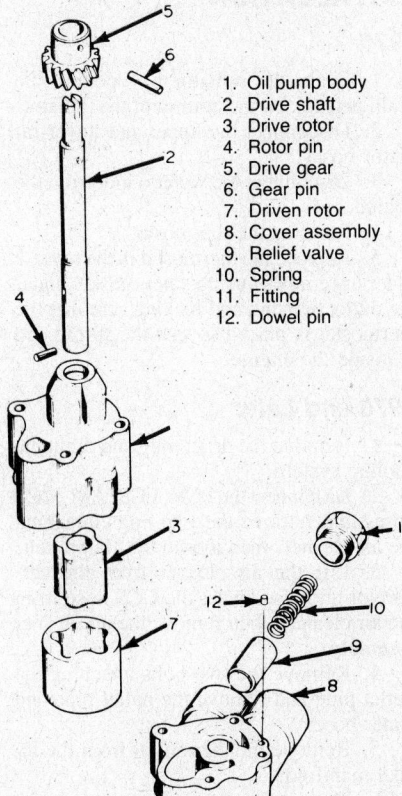

1. Oil pump body
2. Drive shaft
3. Drive rotor
4. Rotor pin
5. Drive gear
6. Gear pin
7. Driven rotor
8. Cover assembly
9. Relief valve
10. Spring
11. Fitting
12. Dowel pin

Exploded view of the oil pump—1976 and later

CHECKING CLEARANCES

NOTE: If measured values of the clearance exceed standard values (given here), or if considerable damage or wear to the sliding faces is evident, the entire oil pump assembly should be replaced with a new one.

1975

1. To disassemble the oil pump, first flatten out the tab bent to the case.

2. Remove the four bolts and remove the strainer case and pump body cover.

3. Measure the clearance between the tips of the rotor (center piece) and the high sections of the vane with a feeler gauge. The clearance should be between 0.0012–0.0059 in.

4. Measure the clearance between the vane and wall of the pump body with a feeler gauge. Replacement of either the vane or the pump body is necessary if the clearance is not within the limits of 0.008–0.011 in.

5. Place a straight edge over the rotor and vane, resting the straight edge on the pump cover mating surface of the pump body. Measure the clearance between the straight edge and the rotor and vane. The standard clearance should be between 0.0016–0.0035 in. Replace either the rotor, vane, or the pump body cover if the clearance is more than 0.0060 in.

6. Assemble the oil pump in the reverse order of disassembly.

1976 and Later

1. Measure tip clearance between the drive and the driven rotor with a feeler gauge. The clearance should be 0.005–0.0059 inch.

2. Measure the clearance between the driven rotor and the inner wall of the pump body. The clearance should be 0.0063–0.0087 inch.

Measuring body cover clearance—1975 models

Loosen, but do not remove, the bolt behind the timing cover when removing the 1975 oil pump

Oil pump showing oil pipe gland nuts

3. Measure the clearance between the rotors and oil pump cover with a square and feeler gauge. The clearance should be 0.0012–0.0035 inch.

4. Measure the outside diameter of the drive shaft and the inside diameter of the shaft hole in the pump cover. The clearance should be 0.0028–0.0043 in.

Diesel Engine

1. Follow the engine assembly removal steps.

2. Remove the 20 bolts fixing the crankcase and remove the crankcase together with the oil pan.

NOTE: Pry off the crankcase by fitting a screw driver into the slots in the crankcase.

3. Remove the oil pipe sleeve nut.

4. Remove the 2 bolts fixing the oil pump and remove the oil pump with oil pipe.

5. Install the oil pipe and leave the joints semi-tight.

6. Fully tighten the oil pump fixing screws, then tighten the oil pipe joints.

7. Reverse the removal procedure for the remaining parts.

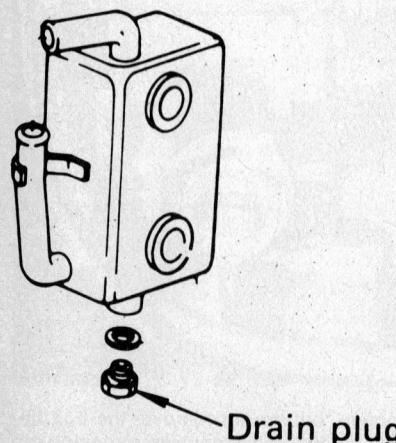

Drain plug

Oil cooler unit showing drain plug

Oil Cooler

REMOVAL AND INSTALLATION

Diesel

1. Place a suitable size tray under the oil filter to receive oil and water flowing out from the filter.

2. Drain the cooling system by opening the drain plugs on the radiator and on the cylinder block.

3. Remove the oil cooler water drain plug and drain the water.

4. Disconnect the oil cooler hoses at the cooler side.

5. Remove the oil filter cartridge using filter wrench.

6. Remove the nut fixing the oil cooler, then remove the oil cooler assembly.

7. Install the cooler using a new O-ring. Torque to 55–60 ft. lbs.

ENGINE COOLING

Radiator

REMOVAL AND INSTALLATION

1. Drain the radiator by opening the drain cock on the lower part of the radiator.

2. Disconnect the radiator upper and lower hoses.

3. Remove the four bolts retaining the radiator and remove the radiator assembly.

4. Install the radiator in the reverse order of removal.

Water Pump

REMOVAL AND INSTALLATION

NOTE: The water pump assembly cannot be disassembled and must be replaced entirely if service is necessary.

1975

1. Disconnect the battery ground cable.

2. Drain the cooling system and disconnect the upper and lower radiator hoses. Disconnect and move heater hose out of work area.

3. Remove the radiator and shroud assembly.

4. Remove the alternator and air pump belts, fan pulley, spacer and fan blades.

5. Remove the water pump assembly.

NOTE: Loosen, but do not remove the bolt from behind the timing gear cover.

6. Installation is the reverse of removal. Adjust all belts and fill the cooling system with the proper mixture of water and anti-freeze.

1976 and Later

1. Disconnect the battery ground cable.

2. Remove the lower cover and drain the cooling system. Remove the coolant hoses from the pump body.

3. On non air conditioned models, remove the fan blades and pulleys from the hub.

4. On air conditioned models, remove the air pump and alternator belts, fan blades and pulleys.

5. Remove the water pump assembly.

6. Installation is the reverse of removal. Adjust all belts and fill the cooling system with the proper mixture of water and anti-freeze.

Thermostat

REMOVAL AND INSTALLATION

1975

1. Drain the radiator by opening the drain petcock on the bottom of the radiator.

2. Disconnect the upper and lower radiator hoses.

3. Disconnect the water outlet from the engine.

4. Remove the thermostat.

5. Replace the thermostat in the reverse order of removal, using a new gasket under the outlet housing and making sure that the thermostat is placed so that the spring end is inside the engine.

1976 and Later

1. Remove the drain plug and drain the cooling system.

2. Disconnect the PCV, ECS, AIR, CCS hoses and remove the two bolts attaching the air cleaner, then loosen the clamp bolt.

3. Lift the air cleaner from the carburetor and disconnect the CCS hose from the air cleaner, then remove the air cleaner assembly.

4. Remove the two bolts attaching the outlet pipe and remove the outlet pipe and water hose.

5. Remove the thermostat from the intake manifold.

6. To install, reverse the removal procedure, using a new gasket under the outlet housing and making sure that the thermostat is placed so that the spring end is inside the engine.

EMISSION CONTROL SYSTEMS
APPLICATION CHART

Year	'75	'76	'77	'78–'82
Positive Crankcase Ventilation System (PCV)	X	X	X	X
Controlled Combustion System (CCS)	X	X	X	X
Evaporation Control System (ECS)	X	X	X	X
Exhaust Gas Recirculation System (EGR)	X	X	X	X
Air Injector Reactor System (AIR)	X	X①	X①	X①
Coasting Richer System	X	X②	X②	X②
Oxidizing Catalytic Converter System (OCS)		X③	X③	X③
Over Temperature Control System (OTC)		X③	X③	X③
Dashpot	X		X	X④
Transmission Control Spark System (TCS)	X			

① Federal uses Air By-pass Valve; California uses Mixture Control Valve
② Federal with manual transmission; California with automatic and manual trans.
③ California only
④ Federal cab and chassis only with manual transmission

EMISSION CONTROLS

There are three types of automotive pollutants; crankcase fumes, exhaust gases, and gasoline evaporation. The equipment that is used to limit these pollutants is commonly called emission control equipment.

Crankcase Emission Controls

1975

The crankcase emission control equipment consists of a positive crankcase ventilation valve (PCV), a closed or open oil filler cap and hoses to connect this equipment.

Crankcase gases are recycled in the following manner: while the engine is running, clean filtered air is drawn into the crankcase through the carburetor air filter and then through a hose leading to the rocker cover. As the air passes through the crankcase it picks up the combustion gases and carries them out of the crankcase, up through the PCV valve and into the intake manifold they are drawn into the combustion chamber and burned.

The most critical component in the system is the PCV valve. This vacuum controlled valve regulates the amount of gases which are recycled into the combustion chamber. At low engine speeds the valve is partially closed, limiting the flow of gases into the intake manifold. As engine speed increases, the valve opens to admit greater quantities of the gases into the intake manifold. If the valve should become blocked or plugged, the gases will be prevented from escaping from the crankcases by the normal route. Since these gases are under pressure, they will find their own way out of the crankcase. This alternate route is usually a weak oil seal or gasket in the engine. As the gas escapes by the gasket, it also creates an oil leak. Besides causing oil leaks, a clogged PCV valve also allows these gases to remain in the crankcase for an extended period of time, promoting the formation of sludge in the engine.

TESTING

Check the PCV system hoses and connec-tions, to see that there are no leaks; then replace or tighten, as necessary.

To check the valve, remove it and blow through both ends. When blowing from the side which goes toward the intake manifold, very little air should pass through it. When blowing from the crankcase (valve cover) side, air should pass through freely.

Replace the valve with a new one, if the valve fails to function as outlined.

NOTE: Do not attempt to clean or adjust the valve; replace it with a new one.

REMOVAL AND INSTALLATION

To remove the PCV valve, simply loosen the hose clamp and remove the valve from the manifold-to-crankcase hose and intake manifold. Install the PCV valve in the reverse order of removal.

1976 and Later

A regulated orifice, located in the intake manifold and connected to the cylinder head cover by a hose, replaces the PCV valve.

During wide open throttle operation, low vacuum exists in the intake manifold and

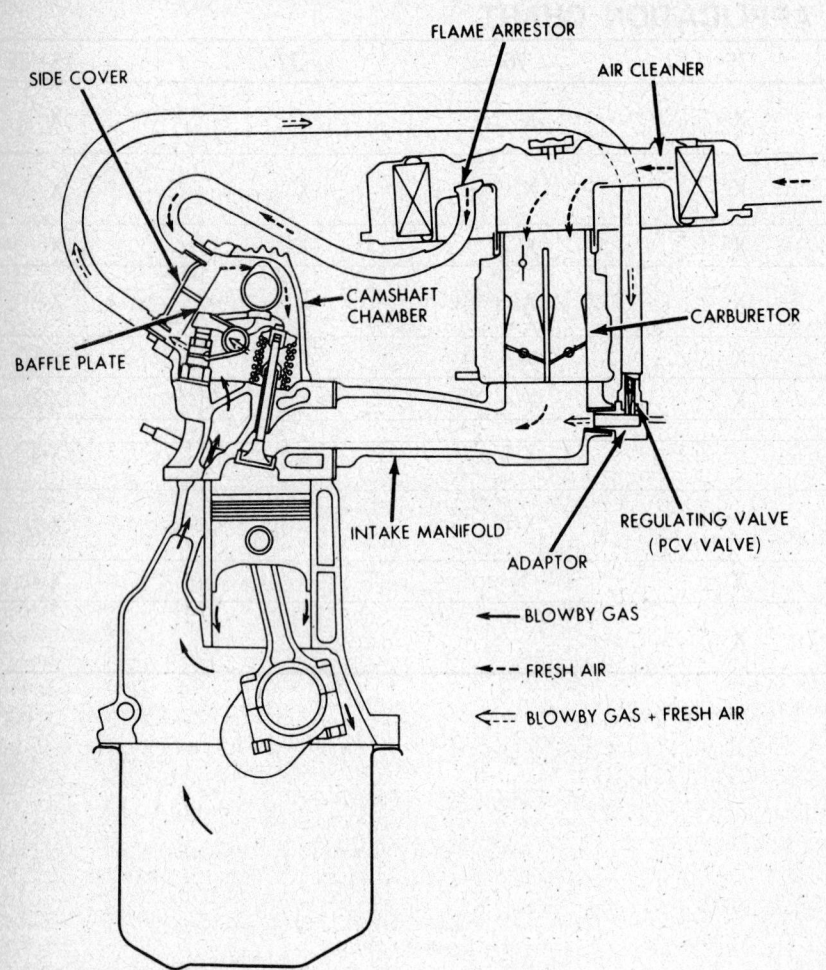

PCV system—1975 models

the regulating orifice cannot admit the entire amount of engine blow-by gases. Since the air movement is greater through the air cleaner assembly, part of the blow-by gases are drawn into the air cleaner from the rear end of the cylinder head cover.

SERVICE

1. Clean the internal parts of the hoses and regulating orifice.

2. Check the hoses thoroughly for cracks, fatigue or swelling. Replace any rubber hoses that seem brittle or hard.

Evaporative Emission Control System

When raw fuel evaporates, the vapors contain hydrocarbons. To prevent these nasties from escaping into the atmosphere, the fuel evaporative emission control system was developed.

The system consists of a sealed fuel tank, a vapor separator tank, check and relief valve and the hoses connecting these components, leading from the fuel tank, to the crankcase of the engine.

In operation, the vapor formed in the fuel tank passes through the vapor separator, which allows liquid fuel to flow back into the fuel tank while allowing fuel vapor to pass into the check and relief valve and the crankcase. When the engine is not running, if the fuel vapor pressure in the vapor separator becomes as high as 1 to 1.4 in. Hg, the check valve opens and allows the vapor to enter the engine crankcase.

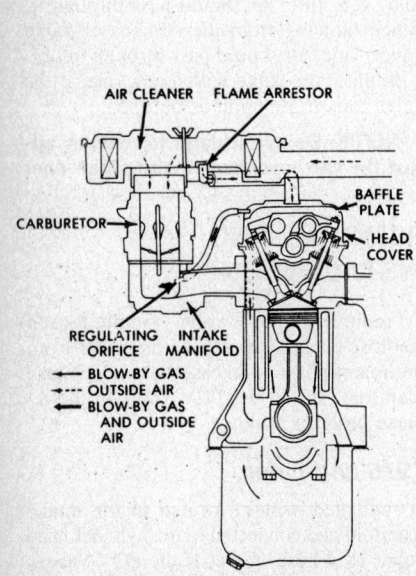

PCV system—1976 and later

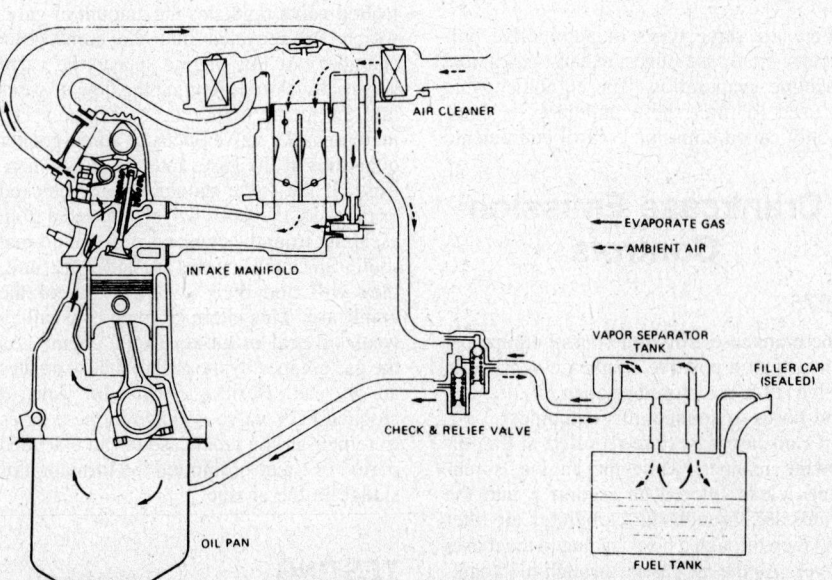

Evaporative Emission Control System—typical

INSPECTION AND SERVICE

Check the hoses for proper connections and damage. Replace as necessary. Check the vapor separator tank for fuel leaks, distortion and dents, and replace as necessary.

Remove the check valve and inspect it for leakage by blowing air into the ports in the check valve. When air is applied from the fuel tank side, the check valve is normal if air passes into the check side (crankcase side), but not leaking into the relief side (air cleaner side). When air is applied from the check side, the valve is normal if the passage of air is restricted. When air is applied from the relief side (air cleaner side), the valve is normal if air passes into the fuel tank side but not into the check side.

REMOVAL AND INSTALLATION

Removal and installation of the various evaporative emission control system components consists of disconnecting the hoses, loosening retaining screws, and removing the part which is to be replaced or checked. Install in the reverse order. When replacing hose, make sure that it is fuel and vapor resistant.

Exhaust Emission Control Systems

AIR INJECTION REACTOR SYSTEM

In gasoline engines, it is difficult to burn the air/fuel mixture completely through normal combustion in the combustion chambers. Under certain operating conditions, unburned fuel is exhausted into the atmosphere.

The air injection reactor system is designed so that ambient air, pressurized by the air pump, is injected through the injection nozzles into the exhaust ports near each exhaust valve. The exhaust gases are at high temperatures and ignite when brought into contact with the oxygen of the ambient air. Thus, the unburned fuel is burned in the exhaust ports and manifold.

To act against over-rich air/fuel mixture which occurs momentarily when the throttle plates in the carburetor are rapidly closed, additional ambient air is supplied intermittently into the intake manifold through the mixture control valve.

EXHAUST GAS RECIRCULATION SYSTEM (EGR)

Exhaust gas recirculation is used to reduce combustion temperatures in the engine, thereby reducing the oxides of nitrogen emissions.

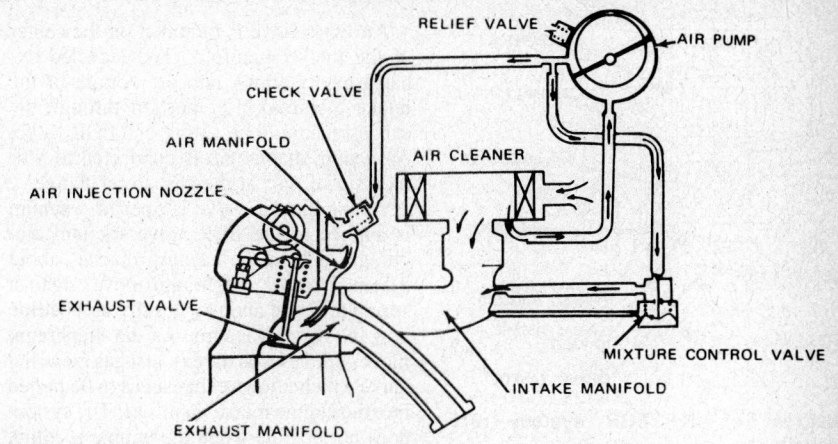

Diagram of the AIR system

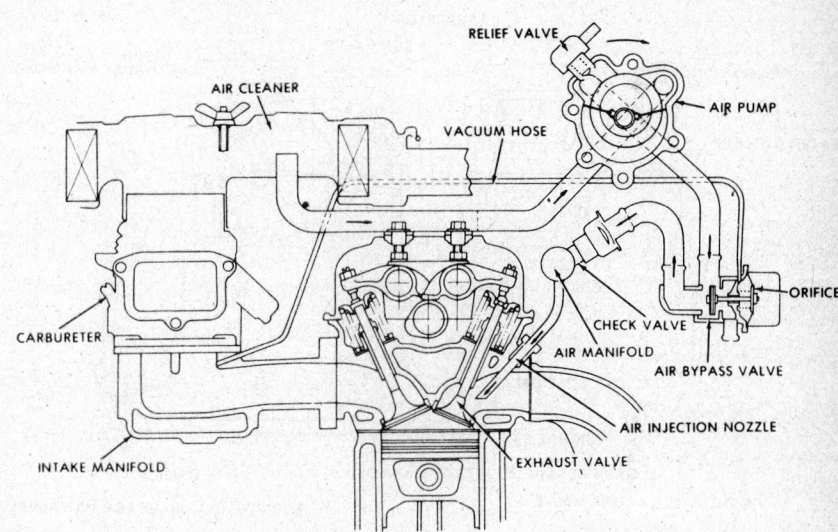

1976 and later AIR system—Federal models

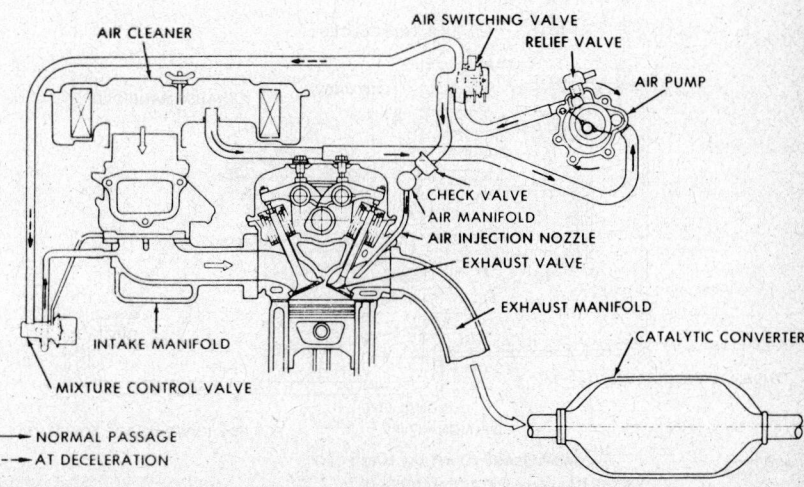

NORMAL PASSAGE
AT DECELERATION

1976 and later AIR system—California models

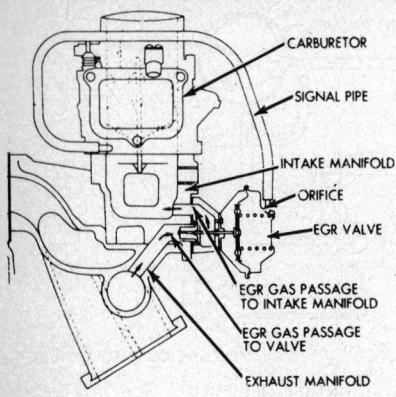

Diagram of the EGR system—1975 models

An EGR valve is mounted on the center of the intake manifold. The recycled exhaust gas is drawn into the bottom of the intake manifold riser portion through the exhaust manifold heat stove and EGR valve. A vacuum diaphragm is connected to a timed signal port at the carburetor flange.

As the throttle valve is opened, vacuum is applied to the EGR valve vacuum diaphragm. When the vacuum reaches about 3.5 in. Hg, the diaphragm moves against spring pressure and is in a fully up position at 8 in. Hg of vacuum. As the diaphragm moves up, it opens the exhaust gas metering valve which allows exhaust gas to be pulled into the engine intake manifold. The system does not operate when the engine is idling because the exhaust gas recirculation would cause a rough idle.

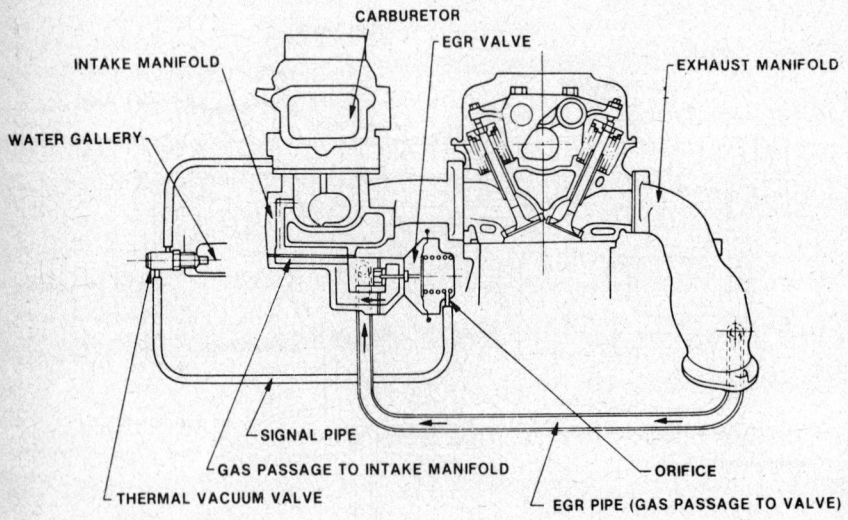

1976–78 EGR system

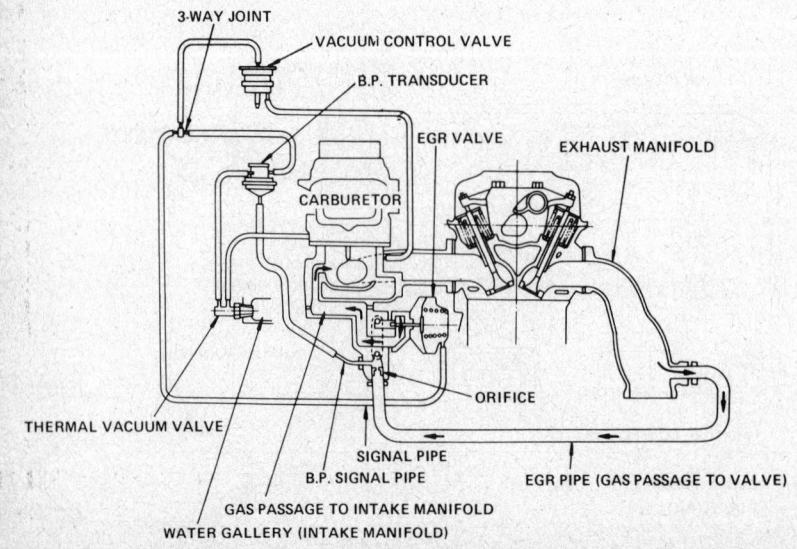

Early 1979 EGR system

THERMAL VACUUM VALVE

The thermal vacuum valve is mounted on the intake manifold and is connected in series between the vacuum port in the carburetor and the EGR valve. This valve is a wax-type device, that opens as the engine coolant temperature increases. When the coolant temperature is below 115°F the valve stays closed and the EGR system does not operate. When the temperature rises above 120°F the valve opens and the EGR system begins operation.

BACK PRESSURE TRANSDUCER

The back pressure transducer responds to exhaust pressure. Under normal operating conditions, ported vacuum leaks into the air, and is applied to the EGR valve under high pressure, thereby controlling the volume of recirculating exhaust gas.

TEMPERATURE CONTROLLED AIR CLEANER

The rate of fuel atomization varies with the temperature of the air that the fuel is being mixed with. The air/fuel ratio cannot be held constant for efficient fuel combustion with a wide range of air temperatures. Cold air being drawn into the engine causes a denser and richer air/fuel mixture, inefficient fuel atomization, and thus, more hydrocarbons in the exhaust gas. Hot air being drawn into the engine causes a leaner air/fuel mixture and more efficient atomization and combustion for less hydrocarbons in the exhaust gases.

The automatic temperature controlled air cleaner is designed so that the temperature of the ambient air being drawn into the engine is automatically controlled, to hold the temperature of the air and, consequently, the fuel/air ratio at a constant rate for efficient fuel combustion.

A temperature sensing vacuum switch controls vacuum applied to a vacuum motor operating a valve in the intake snorkel of the air cleaner. When the engine is cold or the air being drawn into the engine is cold, the vacuum motor opens the valve, allowing air heated by the exhaust manifold to be drawn into the engine. As the engine warms up, the temperature sensing unit shuts off the vacuum applied to the vacuum motor which allows the valve to close, shutting off the heated air and allowing cooler, outside (under hood) air to be drawn into the engine.

INSPECTION AND ADJUSTMENTS
AIR PUMP

If the air pump makes an abnormal noise and cannot be corrected without removing

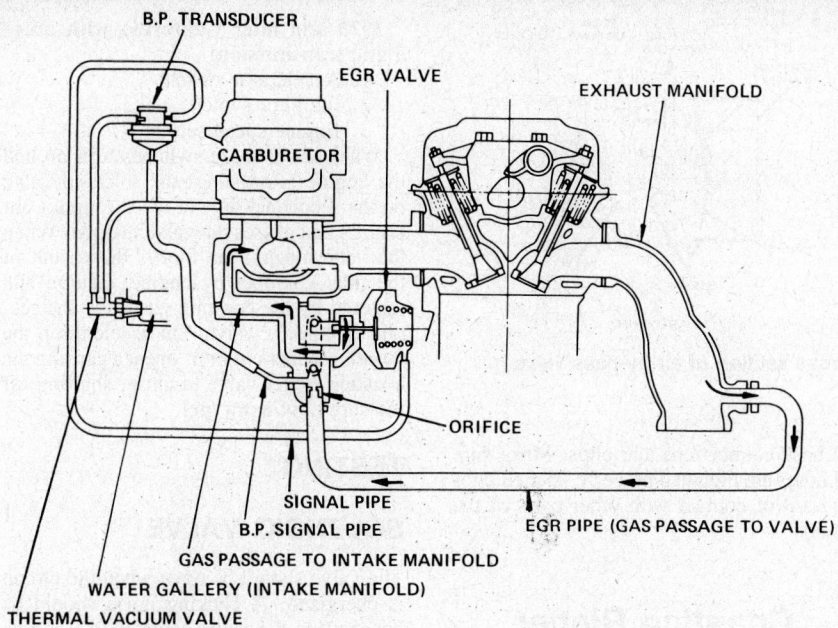

1979 and later EGR system

the pump from the vehicle, check the following in sequence:

1. Turn the pulley ¾ of a turn in the clockwise direction and ¼ turn in the counterclockwise direction. If the pulley is binding and if rotation is not smooth, a defective bearing is indicated.

2. Check the inner wall of the pump body, vanes and rotor for wear. If the rotor has abnormal wear, replace the air pump.

3. Check the needle roller bearing for wear and damage. If the bearings are defective, the air pump should be replaced.

4. Check and replace the rear side seal if abnormal wear or damage is noticed.

5. Check and replace the carbon shoes holding the vanes if they are found to be worn or damaged.

6. A deposit of carbon particles on the inner wall of the pump body and vanes is normal, but should be removed with compressed air before reassembling the air pump.

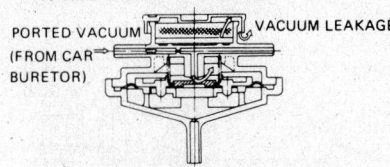

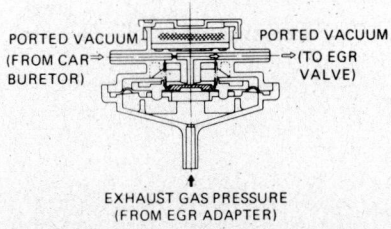

Back pressure transducer

CHECK VALVE

Remove the check valve from the air manifold. Test it for leakage by blowing air into the valve from the air pump side and from the air manifold side. Air should only pass through the valve from the air pump side if the valve is functioning properly. A small amount of air leakage from the manifold side can be overlooked. Replace the check valve if it is found to be defective.

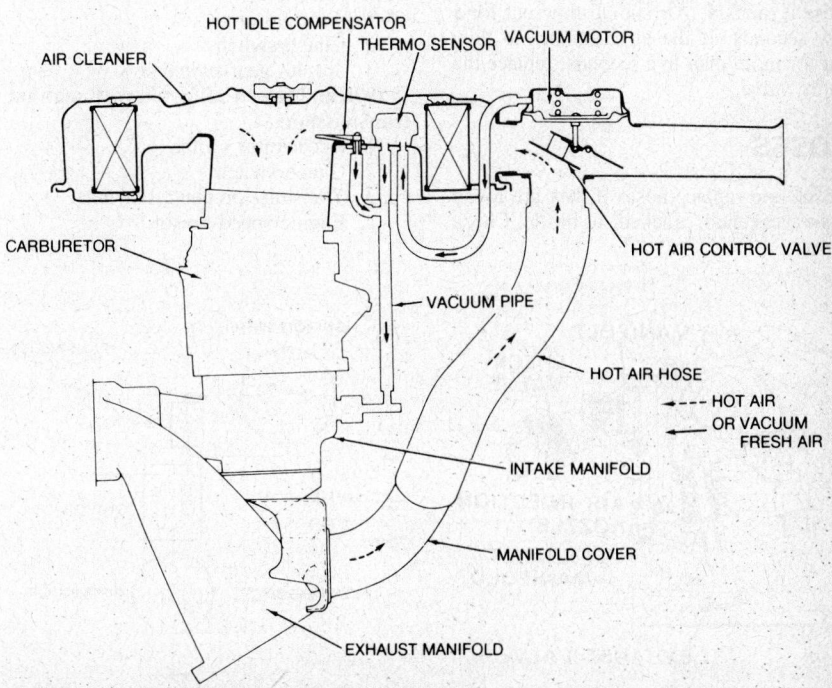

Diagram of the temperature controlled air cleaner

MIXTURE CONTROL VALVE

1976 and Later California And High Altitude Models

Disconnect the rubber hose connecting the mixture control valve with the intake manifold and plug the intake manifold side of the valve. If the mixture control valve is operating correctly, air will continue to blow out the mixture control valve for a few seconds after the accelerator pedal is fully depressed (engine running) and released quickly. If air continues to blow out for more than five seconds, replace the mixture control valve.

AIR MANIFOLD AND AIR INJECTION NOZZLES

Check around the air manifold for air leakage with the engine running 2000 rpm. If air is leaking from the eye joint bolt, retighten or replace the gasket. Check the air nozzles for blockage by blowing air into the nozzles.

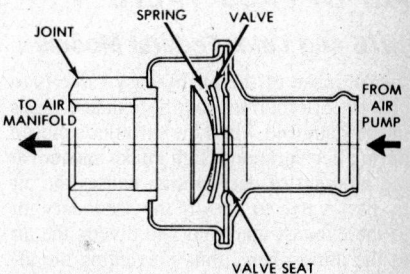

Check valve cross section

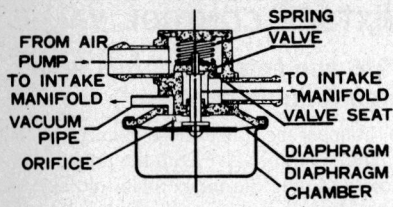

Cut-away of the mixture control valve

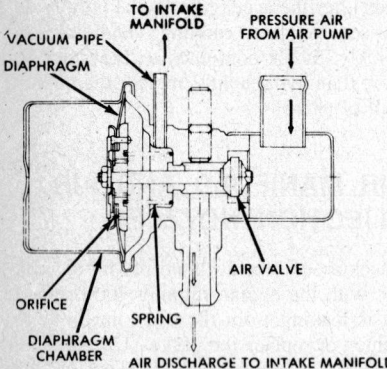

Cross-section of mixture control valve

AIR BY-PASS VALVE

1976 and Later Federal Models

The purpose of the air by-pass valve is to prevent afterburning of the exhaust gases in the manifold when the throttle is closed during deceleration. High intake vacuum at the moment of deceleration causes the air by-pass valve to cut off the secondary air to the exhaust manifold and diverts the air to the atmosphere, thus preventing the afterburning. To test the air by-pass valve, remove the outlet hose and with the engine running, open the throttle completely and close it quickly. Air should flow out for a few seconds. If the air continues to flow out for more than five seconds, replace the entire valve.

HOSES

Check and replace hoses if they are found to be weakened, cracked, or brittle. Check

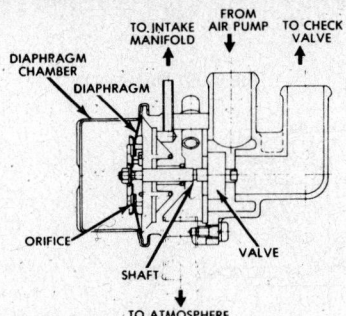

Cross section of air by-pass valve

all hose connections and clips. Make sure all hoses are mounted properly, in their clips and out of contact with other parts of the engine.

Coasting Richer System

This system functions when the engine is coasting, to enrich the air/fuel mixture, which minimizes hydrocarbon content of the exhaust gases through efficient combustion.

A solenoid operated valve in the carburetor allows extra fuel to be drawn into the intake manifold during coasting. The solenoid is energized by the following switches:

1975:
1. Accelerator switch
2. Clutch switch (two types)
3. 3rd-4th transmission switch

1976 and later Federal with manual transmission:
1. Accelerator switch
2. Clutch switch
3. 3rd-4th gear switch

1976 and later California with manual transmission:
1. Accelerator switch
2. Clutch switch
3. Transmission neutral switch
4. Engine speed sensor

1976 and later California with automatic transmission:
1. Accelerator switch
2. Inhibitor switch
3. Engine speed sensor

When all of these switches turn on and the engine is coasting, the solenoid valve on the secondary side of the carburetor energizes and causes the valve to open. When the valve opens, the fuel is drawn out of the float chamber by engine vacuum and metered by the coasting jet below the secondary throttle valve. On acceleration the coasting richer circuit is opened causing the coasting richer valve to close, shutting off the supply of extra fuel.

TESTING

SOLENOID VALVE

The valve should be open when the circuit is energized. A clicking noise should be heard when the valve operates.

ACCELERATOR SWITCH

The accelerator switch should be closed when the pedal is not depressed and open when the pedal is depressed. Check with a test lamp.

CLUTCH SWITCH

1975 and Later

When the clutch pedal is depressed, the switch contacts are opened and the coasting richer system is de-energized. Test all years' clutch switches with a test lamp.

TRANSMISSION SWITCH

Federal Manual Transmission Models

The transmission switch turns on when the transmission is shifted into 3rd or 4th gear and energizes the coasting richer system. It de-energizes the system when the transmission is shifted into any other position.

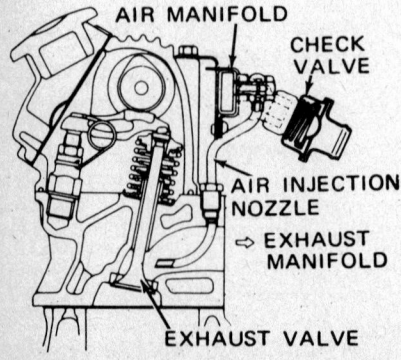

Air injection manifold and nozzles—1975 models

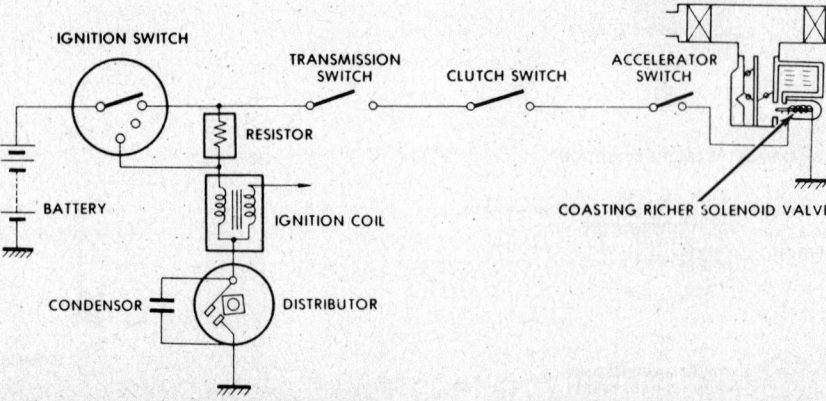

Coasting richer system—Federal models

SOLENOID VALVE CIRCUIT TEST

If the solenoid valve does not function properly when the ignition switch, transmission switch, clutch switch, and accelerator switch are turned ON, perform the following checks to determine the cause of trouble.

Test	Result	Cause
A. Check the solenoid valve terminal voltage.	One Terminal indicates 12V.	Solenoid valve defective or grounding cable poorly connected
	Both Terminals also indicate zero V.	Check parts mentioned under paragraph B.
B. Check voltage at ignition switch AM terminal and IG terminal.	Both terminals indicate zero V.	Cable between solenoid valve and ignition switch poorly connected.
	AM terminal indicates 12V and 1G terminal zero V.	Ignition switch defective.
	Both terminals indicate 12V.	Check parts metnioned under paragraph C.
C. Check voltage at transmission switch terminals.	Both terminals indicate indicate zero V.	Cable between ignition switch and transmission switch poorly connected.
	One of terminals indicates 12V and the other zero V.	Transmission switch defective or incorrectly installed.
	Both terminals indicate 12V.	Check parts mentioned under paragraph D.
D. Check voltage at clutch switch terminals	Both terminals indicate zero V.	Cables between transmission switch and clutch switch poorly connected.
	One of the terminals indicates 12V, other zero V.	Clutch switch defective or incorrectly installed.
	Both terminals indicate 12V.	Check parts mentioned under paragraph E.
E. Check voltage at accelerator switch terminals.	Both terminals indicate zero V.	Cable between clutch switch and accelerator switch poorly connected.
	One of the terminals indicates 12V and another zero V.	Accelerator switch defective or incorrectly installed.

TCS SYSTEM TROUBLESHOOTING

Test	Result	Cause
1. Check the vacuum switching valve terminal voltage.	One terminal indicates 12V.	Vacuum switching valve defective or grounding cable poorly connected.
	Both terminals also indicate zero V.	Check parts mentioned under Test 2.
2. Check voltage at ignition switch AM terminal and IG terminal.	Both terminals indicate zero V.	Cable between vacuum switching and ignition switch poorly connected.
	AM terminal indicates 12V and IG terminal zero V.	Ignition switch defective.
	Both terminals indicate 12V.	Check parts mentioned under Test 3.
3. Check voltage at transmission switch terminals.	Both terminals indicate zero V.	Cable between ignition switch and transmission switch poorly connected.

California Manual Transmission Models

The transmission switch turns on when the transmission is shifted into any gear and turns off when it is shifted into neutral position. The solenoid is energized when the switch is in the On position. Test with a test lamp.

INHIBITOR SWITCH

California Automatic Transmission Models

The inhibitor switch is installed on the shift linkage lever and energizes the coasting richer system in drive, low or second gear positions. Test the inhibitor switch with a test lamp.

EGR VALVE

NOTE: The EGR valve cannot be disassembled. No actual service is required except to determine proper operation of the valve.

LUV

Check the valve shaft for proper movement by opening the throttle to give 2,000–2,500 rpm. The shaft should move upward at these speeds and return to the downward position when the engine speed is reduced to normal idle speed.

Check the vacuum diaphragm function by applying an outside vacuum source to the vacuum supply tube at the top of the vacuum diaphragm. The diaphragm should not leak down and should move to the fully up position at about 8–10 in. Hg of vacuum.

Transmission Controlled Spark Advance System

1975 CALIFORNIA ONLY

This was used on the 1975 models and was designed to control the ignition timing while in third gear by eliminating the vacuum advance.

An electrically-operated switch, controlled by the transmission shift rail, controls distributor vacuum advance by the use of a vacuum switching valve, located on the firewall.

TESTING

Test the circuit with a test lamp. No current will flow through the transmission switch when in third gear. When energized, the switching valve should allow vacuum to the distributor.

Engine Speed Sensor—California Only

Disconnect the engine speed sensor wiring connector and connect "B", "BR", and "BY" color-coded wiring terminals to each other with suitable cables. Then start the engine and check for the continuity between "LgB" color-coded wiring terminals. When the engine runs over 1500–1700 rpm, the engine speed sensor is normal, if the continuity exists.

Catalytic Converter System—California Only

1976 AND LATER CALIFORNIA MODELS

A 2.6 liter converter is used to control hydrocarbon and carbon monoxide emissions.

The converter oxidizes hydrocarbons and carbon monoxide into water and carbon dioxide.

OVER-TEMPERATURE CONTROL SYSTEM

While the engine is coasting, the coasting richer system is operated to prevent catalyst overheating caused by poor combustion. The secondary air injection is operated simultaneously with the coasting richer system. When the catalyst temperature reaches 1350°F, due to high speed and/or high load driving, the secondary air is diverted to the atmosphere to reduce chemical reaction in the catalyst. When the catalyst temperature reaches 1830°F, due to engine malfunction or ignition system failure, the warning lamp and buzzer are turned on.

VACUUM SWITCHING VALVE

The Vacuum switching valve has three ports, two of which are activated electrically by the solenoid plunger. The plunger is energized when the catalyst temperature exceeds 1350°F. It connects the diaphragm chamber of the air switching valve with the intake manifold permitting manifold vacuum to be applied to the diaphragm chamber.

AIR SWITCHING VALVE

This valve diverts air flow from the pump and is operated by manifold vacuum and air pump pressure which are operated by the vacuum switching valve.

FUEL SYSTEM

Fuel Filter

GASOLINE ENGINES

A fuel filter is located in the fuel line leading from the fuel tank to the fuel pump. It is of the cartridge type with a replaceable paper filter element. If the fuel line is suspected of being clogged (rough running, hesitation, uneven throttle response), check the fuel filter. The fuel filter element should be checked once a year and replaced if excessively dirty.

NOTE: 1975–80 models require filter element replacement every 15,000 miles, 1981 and later models at 30,000 mile intervals.

FUEL FILTER (CARTRIDGE) REPLACEMENT DIESEL ENGINE

Removal and Installation

1. Disconnect water separator sensor wiring at the connector and water drain hose.
2. Remove the filter using a filter wrench. Use care so as not to spill fuel within the cartridge.
3. Drain the cartridge into a suitable pan, then remove the sensor from the filter cartridge.
4. Install the sensor on a new filter cartridge, applying clean diesel fuel to the O-ring before installation.

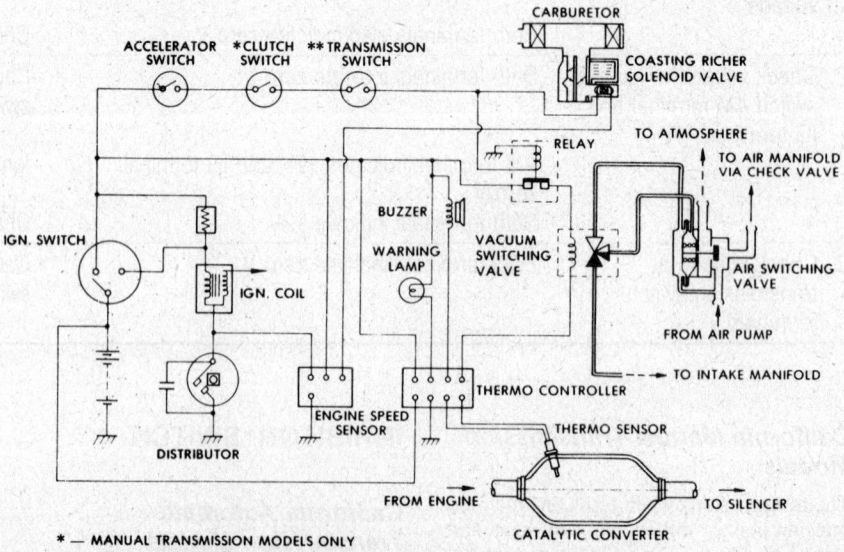

* — MANUAL TRANSMISSION MODELS ONLY

** — NEUTRAL SWITCH FOR MANUAL TRANSMISSION MODELS

— INHIBITOR SWITCH FOR AUTOMATIC TRANSMISSION MODELS

Overtemperature Control System—California models

5. Turn in the filter until sealing face is brought into contact with the O-ring. Further tighten 2/3 of a turn. Connect the connector to the sensor and install the water drain hose.

6. Fill the cartridge with fuel by operating the priming pump handle 30 to 40 times.

NOTE: The force needed to operate the priming pump increases when the filter becomes filled.

7. Start the engine and check for fuel leaks.

WATER SEPARATOR DRAINING PROCEDURE

1. Place a container (approx. ½ gal. capacity) at the end of the vinyl hose beneath the drain plug of the separator.
2. Loosen the drain plug approximately four turns.
3. Continue to operate the priming pump ten times by hand.
4. Tighten the drain plug, and continue to operate the priming pump again several strokes.
5. Start the engine and check for fuel leakage from around the sealing portions. Also check to see that the "FILTER" indicator light has turned off.

MECHANICAL FUEL PUMP GASOLINE ENGINES

The fuel pump is a mechanically-operated, diaphragm-type driven by the fuel pump eccentric cam on the jackshaft.

Design of the fuel pump permits disassembly, cleaning, and repair or replacement of defective parts.

REMOVAL AND INSTALLATION

1. Disconnect the rubber hose at the side of the fuel pump.
2. Remove the joint bolt and disconnect the fuel line at the side of the fuel pump. Be careful not to lose the joint bolt gaskets when removing the joint bolt.
3. Remove the two fuel pump mounting nuts and remove the fuel pump assembly from the side of the engine.
4. Install the fuel pump in the reverse order of removal, using a new gasket and sealer on the mating surface.

Electric Fuel Pump

The fuel pump is of the electro-magnetic type and is installed on the inner face of the third crossmember at the left hand side. This fuel pump is a totally enclosed type and cannot be disassembled.

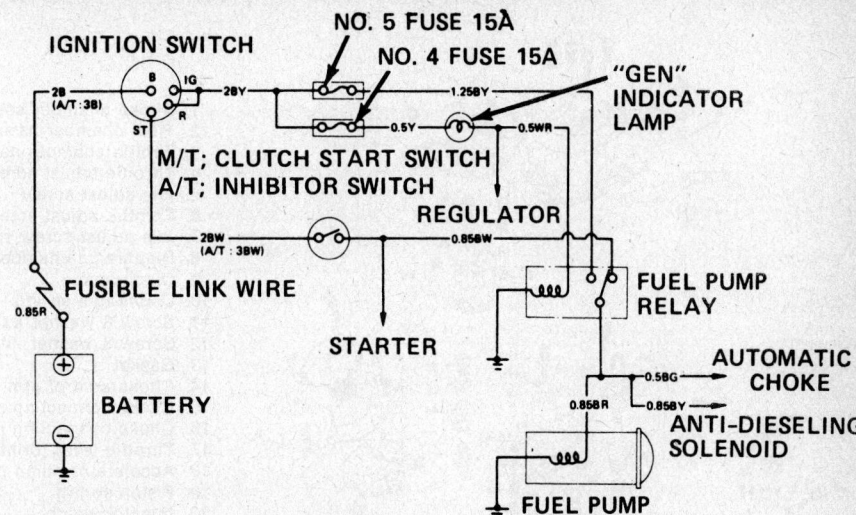

Electric fuel pump circuit schematic

REMOVAL AND INSTALLATION

1. Disconnect the hoses at the fuel pump.
2. Remove the two bolts and one nut mounting the fuel pump and remove the fuel pump assembly.

Carburetor

The carburetor used on all gas-engined Chevy LUV trucks is a two-barrel, downdraft type with a low-speed (primary) side and a high-speed (secondary) side.

REMOVAL AND INSTALLATION

1. Remove the air cleaner wing nut and disconnect the rubber hoses from the clips on the air cleaner cover and the vacuum hose from the vacuum motor.
2. Remove the bracket bolts at the air cleaner and remove the air cleaner cover and filter element.
3. Disconnect the hot air hose (to the hot air duct), the air hose to the air pump at the air cleaner, and the vacuum hose at the joint nipple side of the intake manifold.
4. Loosen the bolt clamping the air cleaner to the carburetor. Separate the air cleaner body from the carburetor but do not remove it completely as the hoses remain connected.
5. Disconnect the PCV hose (to the camshaft cover), the rubber hoses to the check and relief valve and remove the air cleaner body.
6. Disconnect the vacuum hoses from the EGR valve.
7. Disconect the choke control wire.
8. Disconnect the lead from the throttle solenoid.

9. Disconnect the throttle linkage return spring.
10. Disconnect the accelerator linkage wire.
11. Disconnect the fuel line at the carburetor.
12. On 1975 models, remove the check valve from the air manifold.
13. Remove the four retaining nuts and lockwashers securing the carburetor to the manifold and remove the carburetor.
14. Install the carburetor in the reverse order of removal.

OVERHAUL

Efficient carburetion depends greatly on careful cleaning and inspection during overhaul, since dirt, gum, water, or varnish in or on the carburetor parts are often responsible for poor performance.

Overhaul your carburetor in a clean, dust-free area. Carefully disassemble the carburetor, referring often to the exploded views. Keep all similar and look-alike parts segregated during disassembly and cleaning to avoid accidental interchange during assembly. Make a note of all jet sizes.

When the carburetor is disassembled, wash all parts (except diaphragms, electric choke units, pump plunger, and any other plastic, leather, fiber, or rubber parts) in clean carburetor solvent. Do not leave parts in the solvent any longer than is necessary to sufficiently loosen the deposits. Excessive cleaning may remove the special finish from the float bowl and choke valve bodies, leaving these parts unfit for service. Rinse all parts in clean solvent and blow them dry with compressed air or allow them to air dry. Wipe clean all cork, plastic, leather with lint-free cloth.

Blow out all passages and jets with compressed air and be sure that there are no restrictions or blockages. Never use wire or similar tools to clean jets, fuel passages,

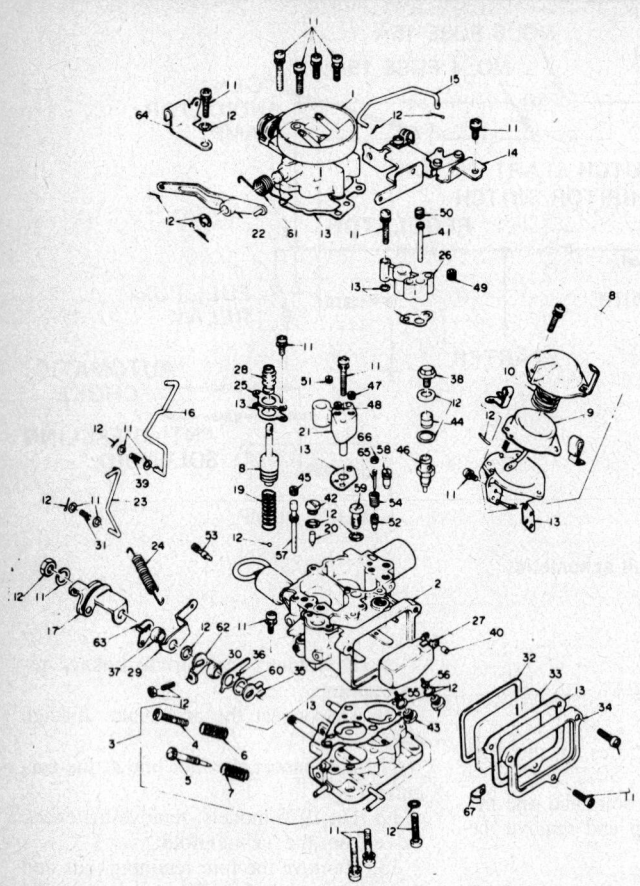

1. Choke chamber assembly
2. Float chamber assembly
3. Thottle chamber assembly
4. Throttle adjust screw
5. Idle adjust screw
6. Throttle adjust screw spring
7. Idle adjust screw spring
8. Diaphragm chamber assembly
9. Diaphragm
10. Diaphragm spring
11. Screw & washer kit, A
12. Screw & washer kit, B
13. Gasket
14. Choke control arm
15. Choke connecting rod
16. Choke connecting rod
17. Throttle lever (primary)
18. Accelerator pump piston
19. Piston spring
20. Injector weight
21. Small venturi (primary)
22. Accelerator pump lever
23. Connecting rod
24. Throttle return spring
25. Plate
26. Small venturi (secondary)
27. Float
28. Dust cover
29. Starting lever
30. Sleeve
31. Spring
32. Rubber seal
33. Fuel level gage
34. Cover
35. Adjust lever, B
36. Return plate
37. Sleeve
38. Filter set screw
39. Spring
40. Collar
41. Secondary emulsion tube
42. Plug
43. Drain plug
44. Filter
45. Slow jet plug (primary)
46. Needle valve
47. Accel air bleed
48. Main air bleed (primary)
49. Slow air bleed (secondary)
50. Main air bleed (secondary)
51. Slow air bleed (primary)
52. Coasting jet
53. Vacuum jet
54. Coasting air bleed
55. Main jet (primary)
56. Slow jet (secondary)
57. Slow jet (primary)
58. Slow jet (secondary)
59. Power valve
60. Thrust washer
61. Pump lever return spring
62. Kick lever
63. Crank
64. Choke control cable hanger
65. Coasting adjust screw
66. Coasting adjust screw

Exploded view of the 1975 carburetor

or air bleeds. Clean all jets and valves separately to avoid accidental interchange.

Check all parts for wear or damage. Replace any part that is worn or damaged. Especially check the following:

1. Check the float needle and seat for wear. Replace completely if wear is found.

2. Check the float hinge pin for wear and the float(s) for dents, distortion or cracks. Replace float if fuel has leaked into it (shake float and listen for any fuel inside).

3. Check the throttle and choke shaft bores for wear or an out-of-round condition. Damage or wear to the throttle arm, shaft, or shaft bore will often require replacement of the throttle body. These parts require a close tolerance of fit; wear may allow air leakage, which would affect starting and idling.

NOTE: Throttle shafts and bushings are not included in overhaul kits. They can be purchased separately.

4. Inspect the idle mixture adjusting needles for burrs or grooves. Any such condition requires replacement of the needle, since you will not be able to obtain a satisfactory idle.

5. Test the accelerator pump check valves. They should pass air one way but not the other. Test for proper setting by blowing and sucking on the valve. Replace the valve if necessary. If the valve is sat-

isfactory, wash the valve again to remove breath moisture.

6. Check the bowl cover for warped surfaces with a straightedge.

7. Closely inspect the valves and seats for wear and damage, replacing as necessary.

8. After the carburetor is assembled, check the choke valve for freedom of operation.

Carburetor overhaul kits are essential for each overhaul. These kits contain all gaskets and new parts to replace those that deteriorate most rapidly. New gaskets, O-rings and fiber washers are especially crucial in a carburetor overhaul. Failure to replace all parts supplied with the kit can result in problems and poor performance later.

After cleaning and checking all components, reassemble the carburetor, using new parts and referring to the exploded view. When reassembling, make sure that all screws are tight; make sure all jets are snug in their seats, but do not overtighten as damage to the jet tips and seats may occur. Tighten all screws gradually, in rotation. Do not tighten needle valves into their seats—uneven jetting will occur. Instead, screw them in to adjust slowly until the needle just seats itself, and then back the needle out. Always use new gaskets. Be sure to adjust the float level when reassembling.

THROTTLE LINKAGE ADJUSTMENT

When the primary throttle valve is opened to an angle of 50° for 1975 or 47° for 1976 and later from its closed position, the adjust plate which is interlocked with the primary throttle valve is brought into contact with portion A (see illustration) of the return

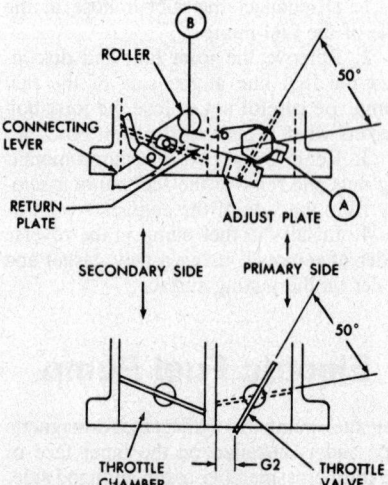

Throttle linkage adjustment

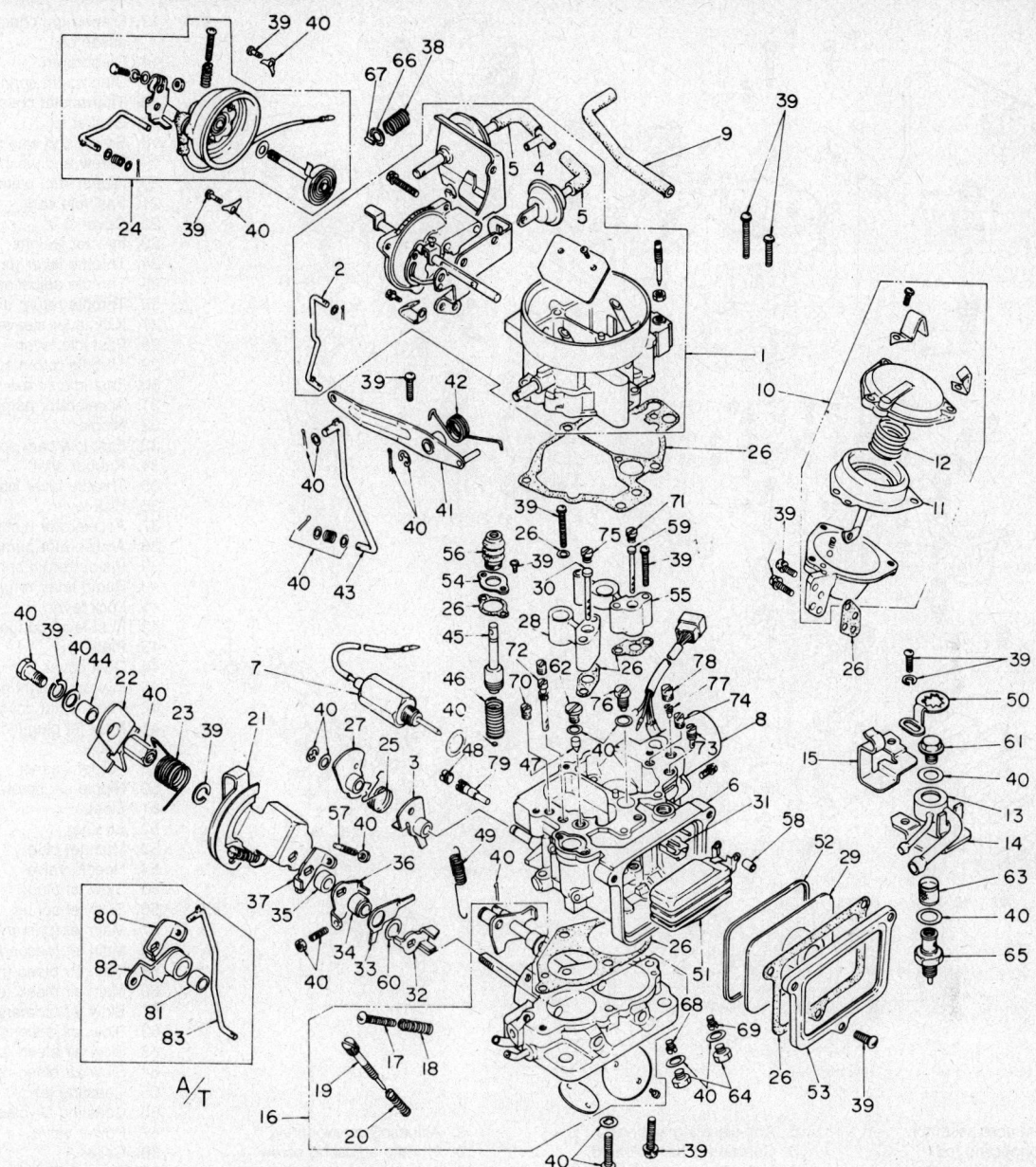

Exploded view of the carburetor—1976–78

1. Choke chamber assembly
2. Choke connecting rod
3. Counter lever
4. Nipple
5. Hose
6. Float chamber assembly
7. Anti-dieseling solenoid
8. Coasting richer solenoid
9. Hose
10. Diaphragm chamber assembly
11. Diaphragm
12. Diaphragm spring
13. Nipple
14. Nipple stop late
15. EGR vacuum hose clip
16. Throttle chamber assembly
17. Throttle adjusting screw
18. Adjusting screw spring
19. Idle adjusting screw
20. Adjusting screw spring
21. Throttle lever (Primary)

22. Fast idle lever
23. Fast idle lever spring
24. Thermostat cover assembly
25. Fast idle cam spring
26. Gasket kit
27. Fast idle cam
28. Small venture (Primary)
29. Fuel level gauge
30. Primary emulsion tube
31. Baffle plate
32. Throttle adjusting lever
33. Throttle return plate
34. Kick lever sleeve
35. Throttle lever sleeve
36. Kick lever
37. Fast idle lever
38. Auto choke piston spring
39. Screw & Washer kit, A
40. Screw & Washer kit, B
41. Accelerator pump lever
42. Pump lever return spring

43. Accelerator pump rod
44. Fast idle lever collar
45. Accelerator pump piston
46. Piston return spring
47. Injector weight
48. Vacuum jet plug
49. Throttle return spring
50. Lock lever
51. Float
52. Rubber seal
53. Cover
54. Plate
55. Small venturi (Secondary)
56. Dust cover
57. Fast idle adjusting screw
58. Collar
59. Secondary emulsion tube
60. Thrust washer
61. Filter set screw
62. Injector weight plug
63. Filter

64. Drain plug
65. Needle valve
66. Piston spring carrier
67. Piston spring stop pin
68. Main jet (Primary)
69. Main jet (Secondary)
70. Slow air bleed (Primary)
71. Main air bleed (Secondary)
72. Slow jet (Primary)
73. Slow jet (Secondary)
74. Slow air bleed (Secondary)
75. Main air bleed (Primary)
76. Power valve
77. Coasting jet
78. Coasting air bleed
79. Vacuum jet
80. Connecting lever
81. Collar A
82. Down shift lever
83. Pump rod

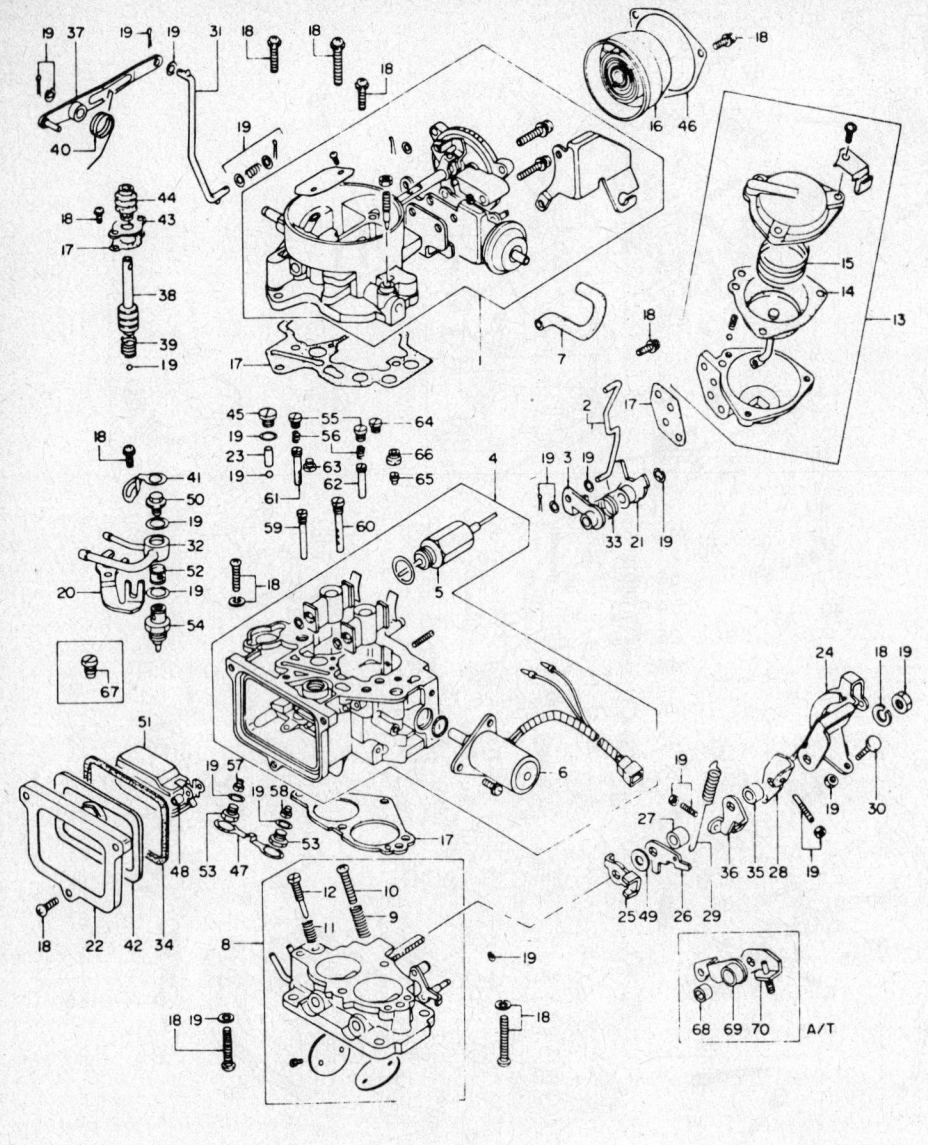

13. Diaphragm chamber assembly
14. Diaphragm
15. Diaphragm spring
16. Thermostat cover assembly
17. Gasket kit
18. Screw and washer kit, A
19. Screw and washer kit, B
20. Nipple stop plate
21. Fast idle cam
22. Cover
23. Injector weight
24. Throttle lever (primary)
25. Throttle adjusting lever
26. Throttle return plate
27. Kick lever sleeve
28. Fast idle lever
29. Throttle return spring
30. Fast idle screw
31. Accelerator pump rod
32. Nipple
33. Fast idle cam spring
34. Rubber seal
35. Throttle lever sleeve
36. Kick lever
37. Accelerator pump lever
38. Accelerator pump piston
39. Piston return spring
40. Pump lever return spring
41. Lock lever
42. Fuel level gauge
43. Plate
44. Dust cover
45. Injector weight plug
46. Thermostat cover fixing plate
47. Main jet plug lock plate
48. Collar
49. Thrust washer
50. Nipple set screw
51. Float
52. Strainer
53. Main jet plug
54. Needle valve
55. Slow jet plug
56. Slow jet spring
57. Main jet (primary)
58. Main jet (secondary)
59. Main air bleed (primary)
60. Main air bleed (secondary)
61. Slow jet (primary)
62. Slow jet (secondary)
63. Slow air bleed (primary)
64. Slow air bleed (secondary)
65. Coasting jet
66. Coasting air bleed
67. Power valve
68. Collar A
69. Down shift lever
70. Connecting lever

1. Choke chamber assembly
2. Choke connecting rod
3. Counter lever
4. Float chamber assembly
5. Anti-dieseling solenoid
6. Coasting richer solenoid
7. Hose
8. Throttle chamber assembly
9. Adjusting screw spring
10. Throttle adjusting screw
11. Adjusting screw spring
12. Idle adjusting screw

Carburetor exploded—1979

plate. When the primary throttle valve is opened farther, the return plate is pulled apart from the stopper (B in the illustration), allowing the secondary throttle valve to open.

To adjust linkage:

1. Measure the clearance between the primary throttle valve and the wall of the throttle chamber at the center of the throttle valve when the adjust plate is brought into contact with portion A of the return plate. Standard clearance is 0.26–0.32 in.—1975, 0.24–0.30 in.—1976 and later.

2. If necessary, make the adjustment by bending the portion A of the return plate.

FLOAT LEVEL ADJUSTMENT

The fuel level is normal if it is within the lines on the window glass of the float chamber when the vehicle is resting on level ground and the engine is off.

If the fuel level is outside the lines, remove the float housing cover. Have an absorbent cloth under the cover to catch the fuel from the fuel bowl. Adjust the float level by bending the needle seat on the float.

The needle valve should have an effective stroke of about 0.059 in. When nec-

essary, the needle valve stroke can be adjusted by bending the float stopper.

NOTE: Be careful not to bend the needle valve rod when installing the float and baffle plate, if removed.

CHOKE AND FAST IDLE ADJUSTMENT

When the choke is pulled completely closed, the primary throttle valve is opened, by means of the choke connecting rod to an angle of 17°.

To check the opening angle of the pri-

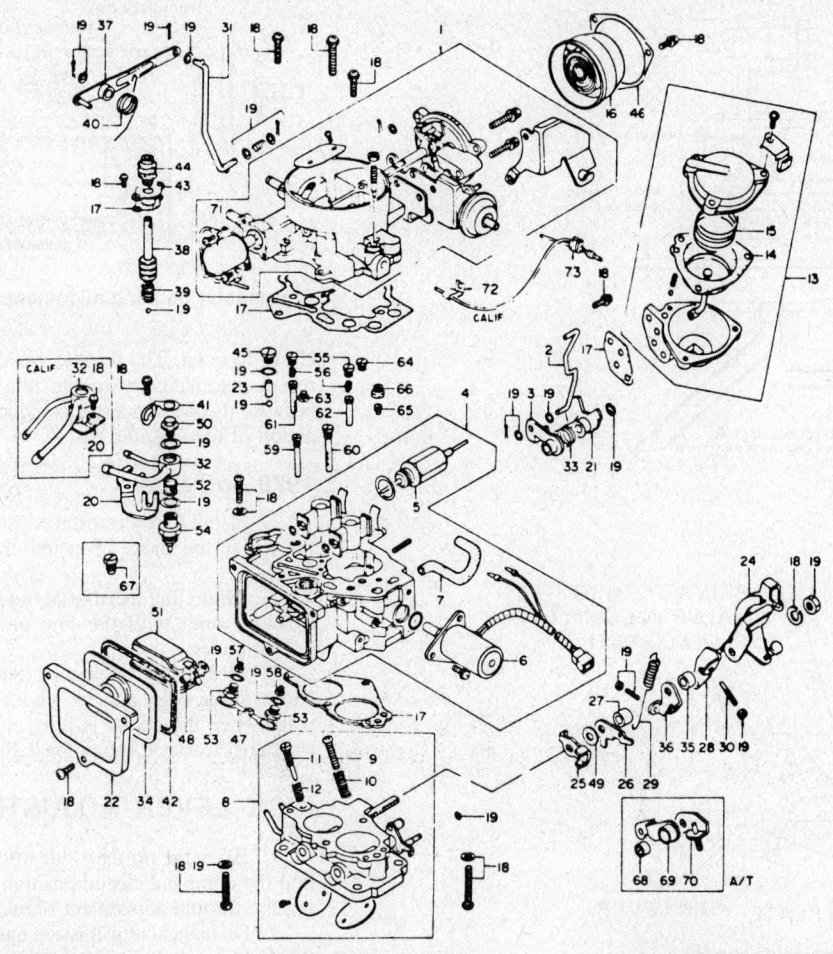

21. Fast idle cam
22. Cover
23. Injector weight
24. Throttle lever (primary)
25. Throttle adjusting lever
26. Throttle return plate
27. Kick lever sleeve
28. Fast idle lever
29. Throttle return spring
30. Fast idle screw
31. Accelerator pump rod
32. Nipple
33. Fast idle cam spring
34. Fuel level gauge
35. Throttle lever sleeve
36. Kick lever
37. Accelerator pump lever
38. Accelerator pump piston
39. Piston return spring
40. Pump lever return spring
41. Lock lever
42. Rubber seal
43. Plate
44. Dust cover
45. Injector weight plug
46. Thermostat cover fixing plate
47. Main jet plug lock plate
48. Collar
49. Thrust washer
50. Nipple set screw
51. Float
52. Strainer
53. Main jet plug
54. Needle valve
55. Slow jet plug
56. Slow jet spring
57. Main jet (primary)
58. Main jet (secondary)
59. Main air bleed (primary)
60. Main air bleed (secondary)
61. Slow jet (primary)
62. Slow jet (secondary)
63. Slow air bleed (primary)
64. Slow air bleed (secondary)
65. Coasting jet
66. Coasting air bleed
67. Power valve
68. Collar A
69. Down shift lever
70. Connecting lever
71. Vent switching valve solenoid
72. Harness clip
73. Harness clip

1. Choke chamber assembly
2. Choke connecting rod
3. Counter lever
4. Float chamber assembly
5. Anti-dieseling solenoid
6. Coasting richer solenoid
7. Hose
8. Throttle chamber assembly
9. Throttle adjusting screw
10. Adjusting screw spring
11. Idle adjusting screw
12. Adjusting screw spring
13. Diaphragm chamber assembly
14. Diaphragm
15. Diaphragm spring
16. Thermostat cover assembly
17. Gasket kit
18. Screw and washer kit, A
19. Screw and washer kit, B
20. Nipple stop plate

Exploded view of the carburetor—1980–82

mary throttle valve, close the choke valve completely and measure the clearance between the throttle valve and the wall of the throttle valve chamber at the center part of the throttle valve. The clearance should be

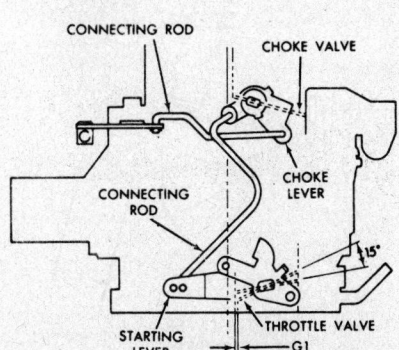

Choke and fast idle adjustment

0.047–0.051 in. If necessary, adjust the throttle valve opening angle by bending the connecting rod. Make sure to turn the throttle stop screw all the way in before measuring the clearance.

KICK LEVER ADJUSTMENT

1. Bring the primary side throttle valve into the complete closed position, by turning the throttle adjustment screw.

2. On manual transmission models, with the throttle valve completely closed, loosen the lock nut on the kick lever screw and turn the screw until it is in contact with the return plate and tighten the locknut (see illustration).

3. On automatic transmission models with the throttle valve completely closed, bend the end of the kick lever until it is in contact with the return plate (see illustration).

ELECTRIC AUTOMATIC CHOKE

Through 1978

The automatic choke assembly incorporates a thermostatic spring which automatically works in response to ambient air temperature changes, thereby allowing the engine to start.

The choke valve is set into position by the accelerator pedal. Depressing the pedal to the floor sets the choke mechanism.

When the engine starts, manifold vacuum is transmitted to the choke breaker diaphragm unit. This opens the choke valve to a point where the engine will run without stalling.

Two springs are in the choke breaker diaphragm unit. The purpose of spring "A" (see illustration), is to offset bimetal tension and balance the opening of the choke. This

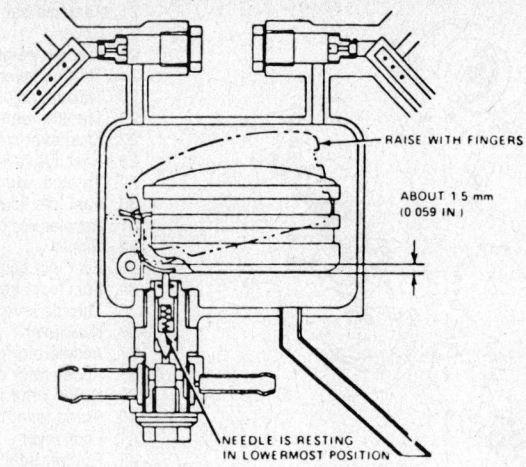

Float level adjustment

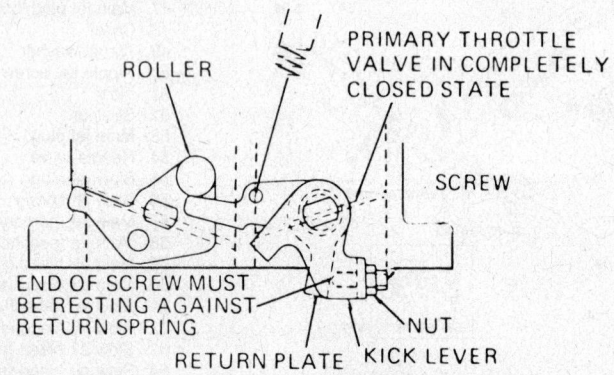

Kick lever—manual transmission model

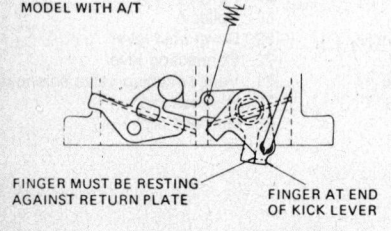

Kick lever—automatic transmission model

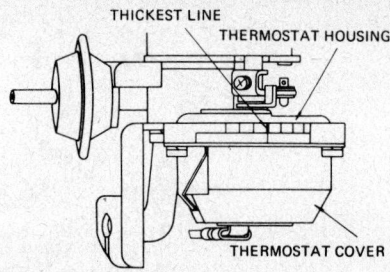

Thermostat housing alignment

choke to open. The throttle valve does not return automatically to the idle position, because its opening angle is reduced by the action of the fast idle cam.

1979 And Later

1. Install the thermostat cover by fitting the end of the choke lever into the bimetal hook.

2. Align the thermostat housing line (thickest one) with the line on the thermostat cover.

3. Measure the clearance (between the choke valve edge and the choke chamber wall) when the choke is fully closed. The standard clearance should be 0.11–0.29 in.

KICK LEVER ADJUSTMENT

1. Bring the primary side throttle valve into the complete closed position, by turning the throttle adjustment screw.

2. On manual transmission models, with the throttle valve completely closed, loosen the lock nut on the kick lever screw and turn the screw until it is in contact with the return plate and tighten the locknut (see illustration).

3. On the automatic transmission models with the throttle valve completely closed, bend the end of the kick lever until it is in contact with the return plate (see illustration).

enables further refinement of the choke mixture because the bimetal senses engine and ambient temperatures thereby varying choke valve opening.

The bimetal switch varies the amount of choke tension based on the air temperature.

When the engine is started the current flowing through the heater relay and element causes the bimetal to flex, causing the

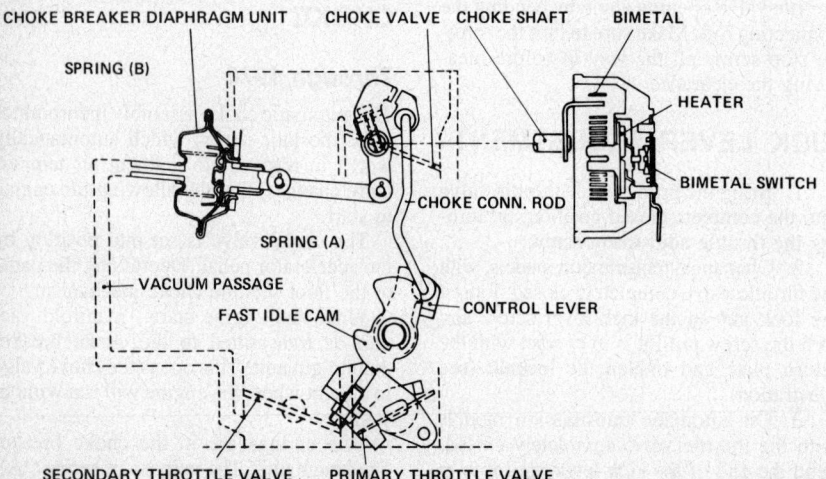

Automatic choke 1979 and later

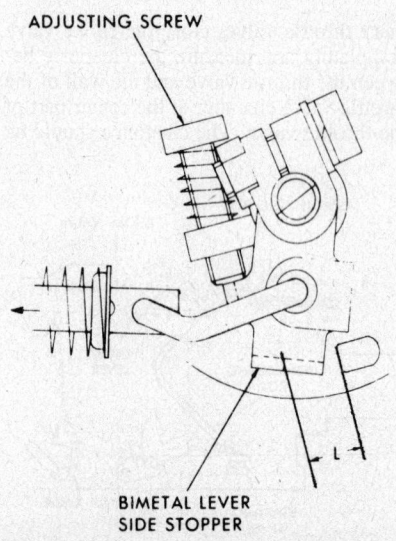

Electric choke stopper clearance

ELECTRIC CHOKE ADJUSTMENT

Align the thickest line on the thermostat housing with the line on the thermostat cover. Measure clearance between the cover side stopper and the bimetal level side stopper when the diaphragm (B) is fully stroked with negative pressure or finger pressure. If the measured valve deviates from the standard clearance of 0.28–0.29 in. or the equivalent bimetal lever angle of 20 degrees, adjust with the adjusting screw.

DIESEL FUEL SYSTEM

Injection Timing

1. Check that notched line on the injection pump flange is in alignment with notched line on the injection pump front bracket.

2. Bring the piston in No. 1 cylinder to top dead center on compression stroke by turning the crankshaft as necessary.

3. With the timing pulley housing cover removed, check that timing belt is properly tensioned and that timing marks are aligned.

4. Disconnect the injection pipe from the injection pump and remove the distributor head screw, then install static timing gauge. Set the lift approximately 1 mm (0.04 in.) from the plunger.

5. Use a wrench to hold the delivery holder when loosening the sleeve nuts on the injection pump side.

6. Bring the piston in no. 1 cylinder to a point 45–60 degrees before top dead cen-

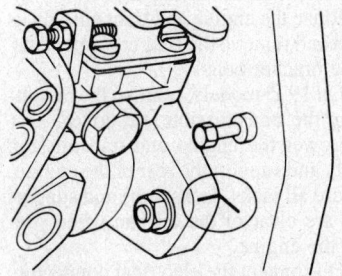

Check alignment of injector pump flange and front plate notched lines

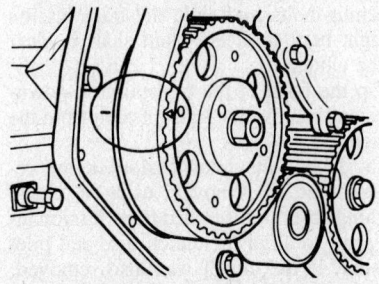

Timing mark alignment—diesel

ter by turning the crankshaft, then calibrate the dial indicator to zero.

7. Turn the crankshaft pulley slightly in both directions and check that gauge indication is stable.

8. Turn the crankshaft in normal direction of rotation, and take the reading of the dial indicator when the timing mark (15 degrees) on the crankshaft pulley is in alignment with the pointer. Reading should be 0.020 in.

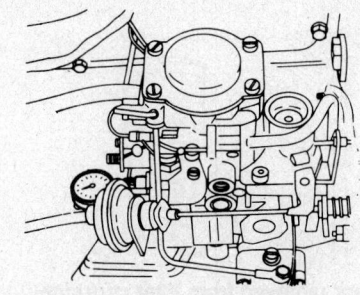

Installation of static timing gauge, injection pump

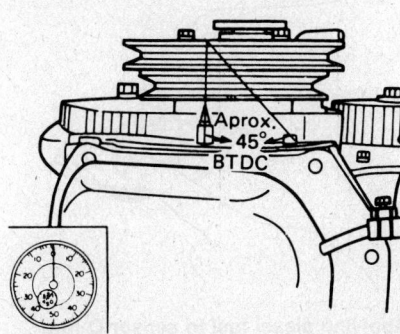

Setting NO. 1 piston 45–60 degrees B.T.D.C.

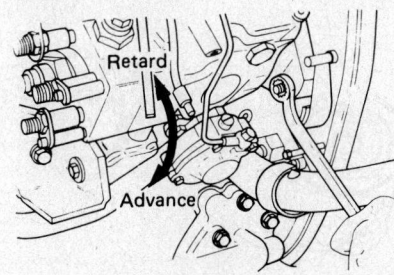

Injector pump adjustment

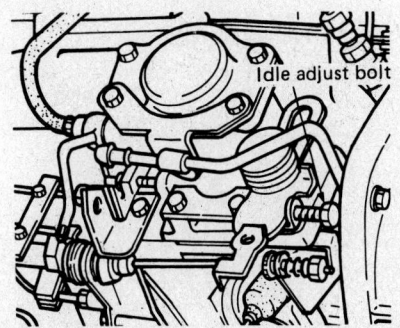

Diesel injection pump showing idle adjustment

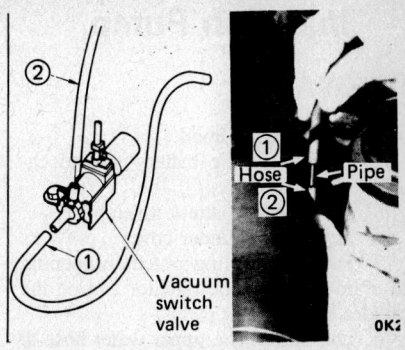

Hose connections, diesel fast idle

9. If the reading of dial indicator deviates from the specified range, hold crankshaft is position 15 degrees before top dead center and loosen two nuts on injection pump flange.

10. Move the injection pump to a point where dial indicator gives reading of 0.020 in., then tighten pump flange nuts.

Idle Speed Adjustment

1. Set parking brake and block drive wheels.

2. Place transmission in neutral.

3. Start and normalize the engine. Engine coolant temperature: above 80°C (176°F).

4. Set the engine tachometer.

5. If the idle speed deviates from the specified range of 700-800 rpm, loosen the idle speed adjusting screw lock nut.

6. Turn the adjusting screw in or out until the idle speed is in the correct range. After tightening the lock nut, lock it in place.

Fast Idle Speed

1. Start and normalize the engine. Engine coolant temperature: above 80°C (176°F).

2. Set the engine tachometer.

3. Disconnect the hoses from the vacuum switch valve, then connect a pipe (4mm dia.) in position between the hoses.

4. Loosen adjust nut and adjust engine idle speed by moving the nut. Fast idle should be 900–950 rpm.

5. Tighten the nut.

6. Remove engine tachometer.

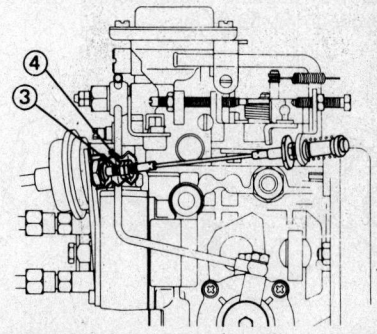

Diesel fast idle adjustments

Injection Pump

REMOVAL

1. Raise engine hood.
2. Disconnect the battery ground cable.
3. Remove the battery assembly.
4. Remove the under cover.
5. Drain the cooling system by opening the drain plugs on the radiator and on the cylinder block.
6. Disconnect the upper water hose at the engine side.
7. Loosen the compressor drive belt by moving the power-steering oil pump or idler. (If so equipped.)
8. Remove the cooling fan and fan shroud.
9. Disconnect the lower water hose at the engine side.
10. Remove the air conditioner compressor. (If so equipped.)
11. Remove the fan belt.
12. Remove the crankshaft pulley.
13. Remove the timing pulley housing covers.
14. Remove the tension spring and fixing bolt, then remove the tension center and pulley.
15. Remove the timing belt.
16. Remove the engine control cable and wiring harness of the fuel cut solenoid.
17. Remove the fuel hoses and injection pipes. Use a wrench to hold the delivery holder when loosening the sleeve nuts on the injection pump side.
18. Install a 6 mm bolt (with pitch of 1.25) into threaded hole in the timing pulley housing through the hole in pulley to prevent turning of the pulley.
   Remove the bolts fixing the injection pump timing pulley, then remove the pulley using pulley puller.
19. Remove injection pump flange fixing nuts and rear bracket bolts, then remove the injection pump.

INSTALLATION

1. Install the injection pump by aligning notched line on the flange with the line on the front bracket.
2. Install the injection pump timing pulley by aligning it with the key groove. Torque to 42–52 ft. lbs.

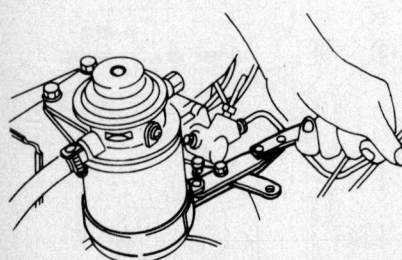

Removing filter cartridge using filter wrench

3. Bring the piston in No. 1 cylinder to top dead center on compression stroke and align marks on the timing pulleys.
4. Follow the timing belt installation steps.
5. Check the injection timing.
6. To install remaining parts, follow the removal steps in reverse order. flange.

Sensor removed from filter cartridge

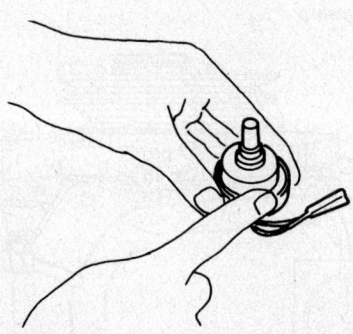

Applying diesel fuel to sensor O-ring

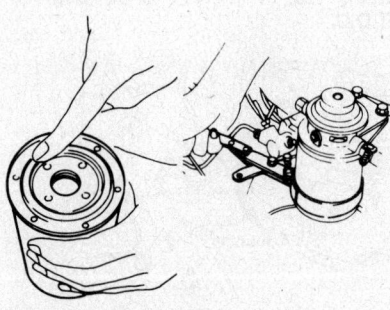

Applying diesel fuel to cartridge O-ring

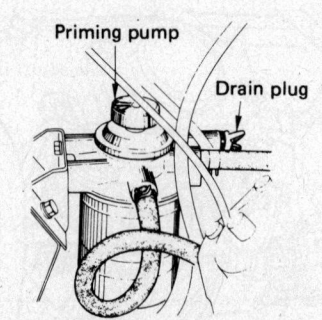

Priming pump and drain plug locations, fuel filter

MANUAL TRANSMISSION

2-Wheel Drive Models

REMOVAL AND INSTALLATION

4-Speed

1. Disconnect the negative battery cable.
2. Remove the air cleaner assembly, and disconnect the accelerator linkage at the carburetor throttle lever.
3. Slide the gearshift lever boot upward on the lever, remove the two gearshift lever attaching bolts and remove the lever.
4. Remove the starter attaching bolts and lay the starter assembly aside.
5. Jack up the vehicle and safely support it with jackstands. Disconnect the exhaust pipe at the flange and disconnect the exhaust pipe hanger at the transmission.
6. Disconnect the speedometer cable at the transmission and disconnect the driveshaft at the differential. Either drain the transmission oil or have a rag ready to plug the output shaft opening (at rear of trans) to prevent spillage. Remove the driveshaft.
7. On 1975–77 models, disconnect the clutch slave cylinder and pushrod from the transmission case and wire the slave cylinder to the frame. On 1978 and later models, disconnect the clutch cable from the bell housing and clutch fork.
8. Remove the bolts attaching the stiffeners, then remove the skid plate (all models).
9. Remove the three frame bracket-to-transmission rear mounting bolts.
10. Raise the engine and transmission as required and remove the four crossmember-to-frame bracket bolts.
11. On 1975 models, remove the mounting from the transmission rear cover.
12. Lower the engine and transmission assembly and support the rear of the engine. Make sure all jacks, jackstands and support devices are clear of the oil pan when supporting the engine.
13. Disconnect the electrical connectors at the TCS or CRS switch and the back-up light switch.
14. Remove the transmission-to-engine attaching bolts and slide the transmission straight back until the input shaft is clear of the clutch.
   Tip the front of the transmission downward and remove the transmission from the vehicle.
15. Install the transmission in the reverse order of removal, using a clutch aligning arbor or discarded transmission input shaft to align the clutch disc and pilot bearing, if the clutch was also removed. Coat the input shaft lightly with Lubriplate® or similar grease before installation.

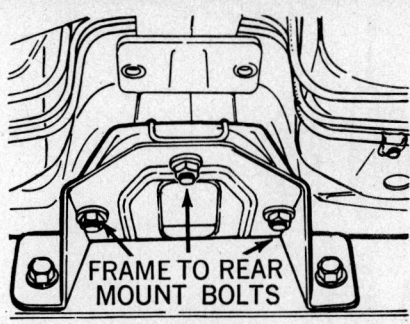

Remove the three frame bracket-to-transmission rear mounting bolts

5-Speed

Removal

1. Disconnect battery ground cable.
2. Slide the gearshift lever boot upwards on the lever, remove two gearshift lever attaching bolts and remove lever.
3. Remove starter attaching bolts and lay starter assembly aside.
4. Raise vehicle on hoist and disconnect exhaust pipe hanger at transmission.
5. Place pan under transmission to catch the oil, then disconnect the speedometer cable at the transmission, disconnect ground cable and disconnect propeller shaft at differential. Remove propeller shaft.
6. Remove return spring from clutch fork.
7. Take out two bolts (lower bolts) mounting the flywheel stone guard.
8. Remove two frame bracket to transmission rear mount bolts and nuts.
9. Raise engine and transmission as required and remove four crossmember to frame bracket bolts.
10. Remove the rear mounting (2 nuts) from the transmission rear extension.
11. Lower engine and transmission assembly and support rear of engine.
12. Disconnect electrical connector at back-up lamp switch.
13. Remove transmission to engine attaching bolts.
14. Pull transmission straight back until disengaged from clutch. Tip front of transmission downward and remove.

INSTALLATION

1. Position transmission in vehicle and slide forward guiding clutch gear into pilot bearing.
2. Install transmission to engine attaching bolts.
3. Raise and lower engine and transmission as required and install crossmember frame bracket and rear mount.
4. Install the two bolts (lower bolts) mounting the flywheel stone guard.
5. Remove plug (if used) from rear extension and install propeller shaft.

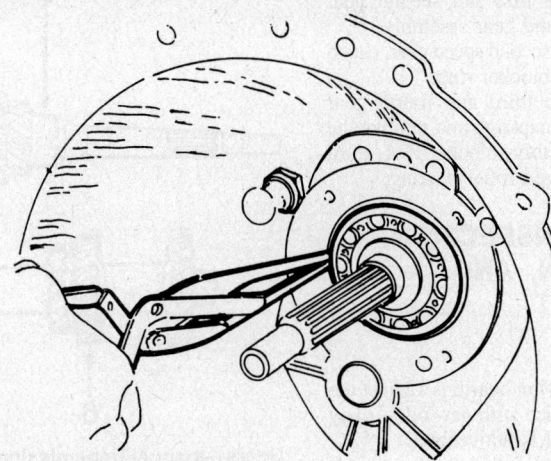

Removing bearing snap-ring

6. Connect speedometer cable, ground cable and exhaust pipe hanger.
7. Connect clutch cable and adjust shift fork as outlined in Clutch Section.
8. Connect electrical connector at back-up lamp switch.
9. Lower vehicle and install starter assembly.
10. Connect battery negative cable.
11. Install gearshift lever and adjust clutch pedal height as outlined in Clutch Section.
12. Check transmission operation.

OVERHAUL

1975 Models

1. Drain the transmission oil.
2. Remove the clutch fork, cover and release bearing.
3. Remove the five bolts from the front bearing retainer and the Belleville spring.
4. Remove the eight transmission top cover retaining bolts and remove the cover. Take care not to lose the three detent springs and balls.
5. Remove the four shift quadrant cover retaining bolts and remove the cover.
6. Remove the TCS or CRS switch and back-up lamp switch. Take care not to lose the back-up switch actuating pin and detent ball when removing the switch.
7. Remove the fulcrum bracket and the reverse idler gear control lever and the shift block.
8. Remove the three rollpins from the shift forks.
9. Remove the reverse shifter shaft through the front of the case and remove the shift fork. Be careful not to lose the three detent balls at the front of the case.
10. Remove the speedometer adapter from the transmission extension housing.
11. Remove the rear extension housing.
12. Remove the third and fourth gear shifter shaft through the rear of the case. Take care not to lose the two interlock balls at the front of the case.
13. Remove the first and second shifter shaft through the rear of the case. Avoid

losing the interlock pin through the front of the shaft.
14. Remove the first and second, and the third and fourth gear shift forks through the top of the case.
15. Remove the lock plate at the rear of the case and remove the reverse idler gear shaft through the rear of the case.
16. Drive the countergear shaft through the rear of the case with a drift.
17. Remove the mainshaft from the rear of the transmission case. Remove the clutch gear pilot roller from the clutch gear. Remove the clutch gear and the bearing assembly from the front of the case. Press the front bearing from the clutch gear.
18. Remove the countergear and reverse idler gear from the transmission case.
19. Remove the snap-ring and remove the front bearing from the clutch gear shaft.
20. Remove the rear speedometer drive gear snap-ring, speedometer gear and drive key, and remove the front snap-ring.
21. Remove the rear bearing retainer nut and lockwasher and remove the rear bearing retainer.
22. Press the rear bearing from the retainer.
23. Remove the first gear rear thrust washer, gear, caged roller bearing, sleeve and blocker ring.

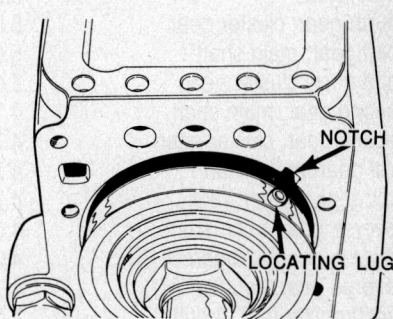

Insert the main drive assembly into the rear case insuring that the lug of the rear of the bearing retainer assembly is located in the notch in the rear of the case

24. Remove the first and second gear synchronizer hub and gear assembly.

25. Remove the second speed gear, caged roller bearing and blocker ring.

26. Remove the third and fourth gear synchronizer hub snap-ring and remove the synchronizer assembly, blocker ring, third speed gear and caged roller bearing.

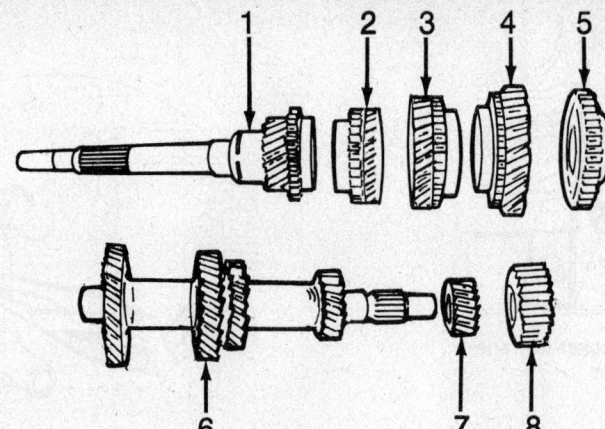

1. Clutch gear shaft
2. 3rd gear
3. 2nd gear
4. 1st gear
5. Reverse gear
6. Counter gear
7. Counter reverse gear
8. Reverse idle gear

Gears—manual transmission

BEARINGS INSPECTION, CORRECTION, AND ADJUSTMENT

All Models

Check all transmission bearings against the following and replace with new ones if any abnormal condition is noticeable:

1. Check for smoothness of rotation. Roughness of rotation usually indicates worn needles, balls, or their races.

2. Check for abnormal noises during rotation.

3. Check for wear, scratches, or corrosion.

4. Check for play in direction of thrust.

5. Check the needle rollers for cracking, wear, or corrosion.

Gears

Check the gears against the following:

1. If a slight amount of step wear or roughness is noticeable, correct with an oil stone or a pencil grinder. Replace the gear with a new one if the condition of wear or damage is beyond correction.

2. Check for chipped or damaged gear teeth.

3. Check conical tapered portion (blocker ring fitting face) for roughness or damage.

4. Check gear teeth for wear by measuring overall diameter.

5. Measure the inside diameter of the first, second and third gears. Replace the gears if the measured values are beyond the limit.

6. Measure the outside diameter of the reverse idle gear shaft and inside diameter of the idle gear bushing and compare the measured values to determine the clearance. If the amount of clearance is beyond 0.15 mm (0.006″), replace the bushing with a new one. The outside diameter of the idler shaft should be 22 mm (0.866″).

7. Measure the width of the 1st gear and collar and compare the measured values. If the amount of difference between the measured values is beyond 0.5 mm (0.0197″), replace the gear.

8. Check the speedometer drive and driven gears and bushing for wear or damage and replace the parts as necessary.

MAINSHAFT

1. Check the outer face, needle roller bearing fitting faces and splined portion of the mainshaft for wear or damage. If a slight amount of wear or damage is noticeable, correct with an oil stone. Replace the mainshaft with a new one if the amount of wear or damage is beyond correction.

2. Check the mainshaft for run-out using a dial indicator. The run-out limit is 0.05 mm (0.002″).

SYNCHRONIZER ASSEMBLY

Check the clutch hub, sliding sleeve, blocker ring, inserts, etc. against the following.

1. Correct minor damage or slight wear using an oil stone or a pencil grinder.

2. Replace the parts with new ones if the amount of wear is beyond the limit or if damage is beyond correction.

TRANSMISSION GEAR OVERALL DIAMETER
(4 × 2 Model)

Gears	Over Ball (Pin Diameter)		Standard Value For Assembly		Limit For Use	
	MM	Inches	MM	Inches	MM	Inches
Fourth gear	5.00	0.197	61.92	2.438	61.62	2.426
Fourth gear; cluster gear	5.00	0.197	93.73	3.690	93.43	3.678
Third gear; main shaft	5.00	0.197	75.07	2.956	74.77	2.944
Third gear; cluster gear	5.00	0.197	81.17	3.196	80.87	3.184
Second gear; main shaft	4.76	0.188	92.19	3.630	91.89	3.618
Second gear; cluster gear	4.76	0.188	63.00	2.480	62.70	2.468
First gear; main shaft	4.76	0.188	106.98	4.212	106.68	4.200
First gear; cluster gear	4.76	0.188	47.67	1.877	47.37	1.865
Reverse gear; main shaft	4.00	0.157	95.00	3.740	94.70	3.728
Reverse gear; idle gear	4.00	0.157	64.54	2.541	64.24	2.529
Reverse gear; counter	4.76	0.188	46.91	1.847	46.61	1.835
Synchronizer hub; 3rd/4th	4.00	0.157	75.45	2.970	75.15	2.958
Synchronizer hub; 1st/2nd	4.00	0.157	87.41	3.441	87.11	3.429
Sliding sleeve; 3rd/4th	4.00	0.157	64.18	2.527	63.88	2.515
Sliding sleeve; 1st/2nd	4.00	0.157	75.86	2.987	75.56	2.975

TRANSMISSION GEAR OVERALL DIAMETER

Model	Gear Name	Backlash			
		Standard Value For Assembly		Limit For Use	
		MM	Inches	MM	Inches
4 × 2 &	First gear	0.03–0.11	0.0012–0.0043	0.35	0.014
	Second gear	0.03–0.11	0.0012–0.0043	0.35	0.014
4 × 4	Third gear	0.03–0.10	0.0012–0.0039	0.35	0.014
	Fourth gear	0.03–0.11	0.0012–0.0043	0.35	0.014
4 × 2	Reverse gear, main-idle	0.07–0.14	0.0028–0.0055	0.35	0.014
	Reverse gear, idle-counter	0.03–0.11	0.0012–0.0043	0.35	0.014
4 × 4	Reverse gear; main-idle	0.05–0.13	0.0020–0.0051	0.35	0.014
	Reverse gear; idle-counter	0.05–0.13	0.0020–0.0051	0.35	0.014

INSIDE DIAMETER OF GEARS

Gear name	Standard value for assembly	Limit for use
First gear	45mm (1.773″)	45.1mm (1.776″)
Second gear	41mm (1.615″)	41.1mm (1.619″)
Third gear	41mm (1.615″)	41.1mm (1.619″)

3. Check the tapered portion, gear teeth and insert fitting grooves of the blocker ring for wear or damage.

4. Check the conical section and blocker ring fitting face of the gear for step wear, roughness or damage.

5. To check the tapered portions for wear, proceed as follows:

   a. Hold the blocker ring against the conical section of the gear and measure the amount of clearance at the portions indicated in the illustration. Replace the blocker ring if the amount of clearance is beyond 0.8 mm (0.032″).

6. Check the sliding faces, splines and insert fitting grooves of the clutch hub and sliding sleeve for wear or damage.

7. Measure the amount of play in the clutch hub splines and mainshaft splines in normal direction of rotation. Replace the clutch hub with a new one if the amount of play is beyond 0.2 mm (0.008″).

SHIFT MECHANISM INSPECTION

1. Check the shift mechanism for wear, bending or damage. The parts with a slight amount of wear or damage may be corrected. Replace the parts with new ones if the amount of wear is beyond the limit or condition of damage is beyond correction.

2. Check for grooves in the shift arms and shift blocks for wear or distortion. Check the shift arms for wear. Replace the shift arm with a new one if the thickness at the end is less than 6.5 mm (0.256″) for 3rd and 4th, 7.0 mm (0.276″) for 1st and 2nd and 7.0 mm (0.276″) for reverse.

3. Check the shift rods for bending or wear and replace as necessary.

4. Check the shift rod detent balls and springs for wear, weakening or damage. If the spring free length is less than 27.5 mm (1.083″) for forward gears or 26.7 mm (1.051″) for reverse replace the spring with a new one.

To assemble the transmission:

1. Lightly oil the third gear bearing journal on the mainshaft. Install the caged roller bearing, the third gear blocker ring, and the third and fourth gear synchronizer hub assembly with the chamfer on the synchronizer hub toward the front of the transmission. Install the snap-ring.

2. Hold the shaft in a vertical position so that the rearward end is up. Lightly oil the second speed journal on the main shaft. Install the clutch pilot roller bearing, second speed gear and blocker ring.

3. Install the first and second gear synchronizer hub and gear assembly. The toothed portion of the reverse sliding gear on the synchronizer assembly should be located toward the front of the transmission.

4. Install the first gear sleeve and lightly oil the sleeve. Install the caged roller bearing over the sleeve and install the blocker ring, first gear and the rear thrust washer. The thrust washer oil groove side faces first gear.

5. Press the rear bearing into the rear bearing retainer. The sealed portion of the bearing should be positioned toward the front of the retainer.

6. Install the rear bearing and retainer assembly on the rear of the main shaft and install the lockwasher and nut. Tighten the nut to 80 ft. lbs. and bend the tab on the lockwasher over one flat portion of the nut.

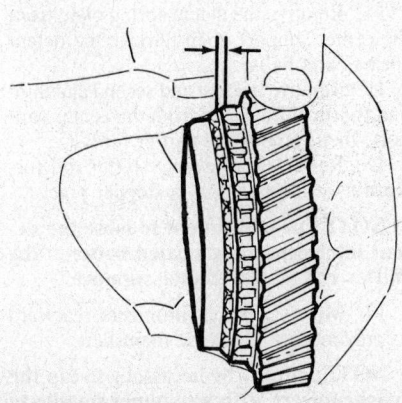

Checking blocker ring

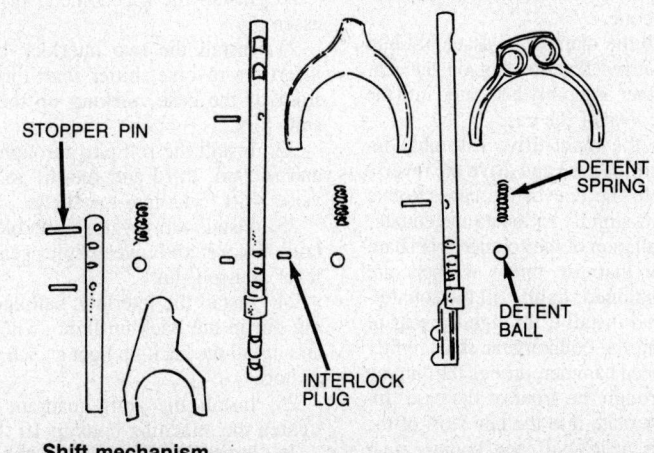

Shift mechanism

STOPPER PIN

DETENT SPRING

INTERLOCK PLUG

DETENT BALL

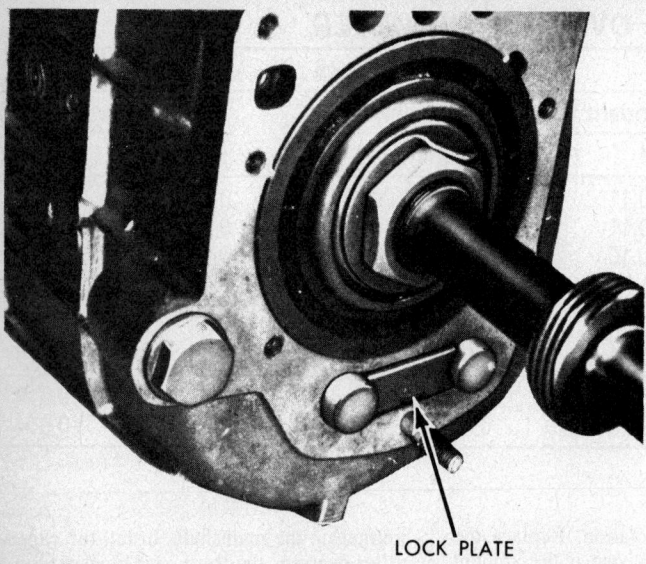

LOCK PLATE

Remove the lockplate at the rear of the transmission housing before removing the reverse idler gear shaft through the rear of the housing

Be sure the notches of the blocker rings align with the keys on the synchronizer assemblies.

7. Insert the reverse idler gear into the case. The shift fork groove should be toward the rear of the transmission.

8. Install the inner thrust washers, of which there are 46 (23 on each side). Using a bit of fresh chassis grease to retain the bearings during assembly, install the needle bearings and the outer thrust washers into the front and rear of the counter gear. Install the dummy shaft.

9. Install the front and rear countergear thrust washers and install the countergear into the case locating the large diameter gear toward the front of the case.

10. Install the front bearing onto the clutch gear and install the snap-ring.

11. Install the clutch gear into the transmission case. Make sure the clutch gear is properly positioned when driving it into the case so as not to gall the bearing race.

12. Install the clutch gear pilot roller into the clutch gear, pack the bearing with chassis lube and install the blocker ring on the clutch gear cone.

13. Install the main drive assembly into the case insuring that the lug on the rear bearing retainer assembly is located into the notch in the rear of the case.

14. With the main drive assembly installed, invert the case and drive the reverse idle shaft into the rear of the case. Rotate the mainshaft slightly to locate the counter gear for installation of the counter gear shaft.

To insure that the thrust washers are properly positioned, lightly oil the countergear shaft and install it through the rear of the case. Tap the countergear shaft lightly with a soft faced hammer, driving the dummy shaft out through the front of the case. Install the lock plate into the key slots of the reverse idler gear shaft and counter gear

shaft and drive the lock-plate against the rear of the case.

15. Install the shift forks into the case, positioning the shift forks into the grooves of the synchronizer sleeves on the first and second, and the third and fourth gear synchronizer assemblies. Install the reverse gear shift fork into the groove on the reverse idler gear.

16. Install the interlock pin into the first and second shifter shaft and install the shaft through the rear of the case, picking up the first and second gear shift fork.

17. Rotate the transmission case and install the two interlock balls into the front shifter shaft bosses. Install the third and fourth shifter shaft through the rear of the case, picking up the third and fourth shift fork and locate the shaft to the front of the case to retain the interlock balls.

18. Install the speedometer drive gear and snap-rings.

19. Install the rear extension housing and tighten the attaching bolts and nut to 10 ft. lbs. Install the extension housing seal.

20. Install the speedometer driven gear assembly.

21. Install the two interlock balls and insert the reverse shifter shaft through the front of the case, picking up the reverse shift fork.

22. Install the roll pins through the first and second, third and fourth, and the reverse shift forks into the shafts.

23. Install the reverse shift block, fulcrum bracket and reverse idler gear control lever and roll pin.

24. Install the interlock ball and actuating pin in the back-up light switch orifice and install the back-up light switch and TCS switch.

25. Install the shift quadrant top and tighten the attaching bolts to 10 ft. lbs.

26. Put the transmission in Neutral and

install the three detent balls, springs, gasket and top cover and tighten the cover attaching bolts to 10 ft. lbs.

27. Install the front cover attaching bolts to 10 ft. lbs.

28. Install the speedometer driven gear.

29. Install the shift fork ball stud and tighten to 65–70 ft. lbs.

30. Install the clutch shift fork and release the bearing assembly.

31. Fill the transmission with SAE 30 oil.

OVERHAUL

1976 and Later

1. Remove the drain plug and drain the transmission pan.

2. Remove the boot, clutch fork and throwout bearing.

3. Remove the four bearing retainer bolts and remove the retainer, gasket and spring washer.

4. Remove the bolt holding the speedometer gear bushing and remove the speedometer driven gear assembly.

5. Remove the four bolts holding the shifter cover and remove the shifter cover and gasket.

6. Remove the back-up switch on California vehicles and both back-up and CRS switches on all others.

7. Remove the eight bolts holding the rear extension, then remove the rear extension and gasket.

8. Remove the thrust washers and reverse idler gear from the reverse idler gear shaft.

9. Remove the snap-rings, speedometer drive gear and key from the mainshaft.

10. Remove the spring pin from the reverse shifter fork and reverse gear.

11. Remove the snap-ring from the outer circumference of the clutch gear shaft ball bearing.

12. Remove the center support assembly from the transmission case.

13. Drive out the spring pins from the third and fourth and first and second shift forks.

NOTE: When removing the spring pin, hold a round bar against the end of the shifter rods to prevent damage.

14. Remove the detent spring plate from the center support, then remove the detent springs and balls.

15. Remove the first and second and third and fourth shifter rods from the center support, then remove the shifter forks.

16. Remove the reverse shifter rod forward as it is fitted with a stopper pin.

NOTE: Be careful not to loose the detent interlock plugs located between the shifter rods in the center support.

17. Move both synchronizers rearward to prevent turning of the mainshaft.

NOTE: It may be necessary to tap the synchronizers with a hammer handle to get them engaged.

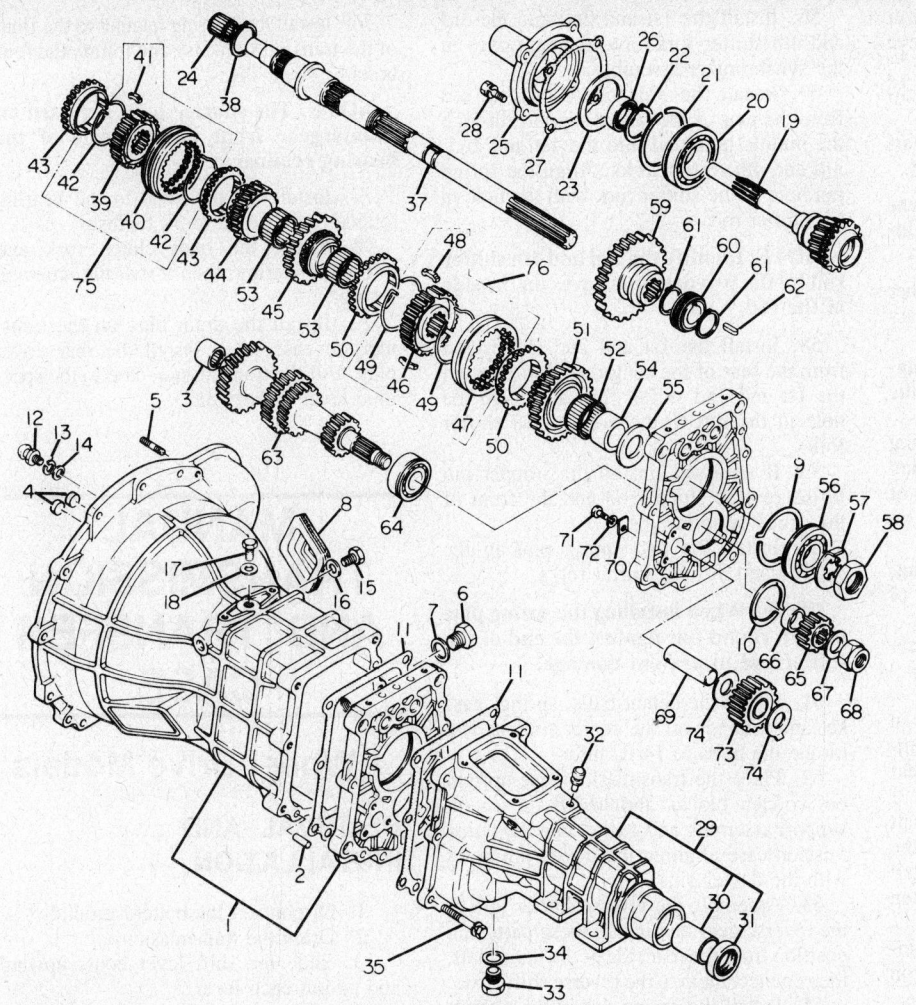

22. Ring, snap
23. Spring, Belleville
24. Bearing, needle
25. Bearing retainer
26. Seal, oil, bearing retainer
27. Gasket, bearing retainer
28. Bolt
29. Extension assembly, rear, w/bushing and seal
30. Bushing
31. Seal, oil, rear extension
32. Breather assembly
33. Plug, oil drain
34. O-ring, oil drain
35. Bolt
37. Shaft main
38. Ring, snap
39. Hub, synchronizer, 3rd-4th
40. Sleeve, synchronizer
41. Key, synchronizer
42. Spring, synchronizer
43. Ring, blocker
44. Gear assembly, 3rd
45. Gear assembly, 2nd
46. Hub, synchronizer, 1st-2nd
47. Sleeve, synchronizer
48. Key, synchronizer
49. Spring, synchronizer
50. Ring blocker
51. Gear assembly, 1st
52. Bearing needle, 1st
53. Bearing, needle, 2nd
54. Collar, needle bearing
55. Washer, thrust, 1st
56. Bearing, mainshaft
57. Washer, lock, mainshaft
58. Nut, mainshaft
59. Gear, reverse
60. Gear, speed drive
61. Ring, snap, drive gear
62. Key
63. Gear, counter
64. Bearing, angular ball
65. Gear, counter reverse
66. Spacer
67. Washer, plain
68. Nut, self lock
69. Shaft, reverse idle
70. Plate lock
71. Bolt, lock
72. Washer, spring
73. Gear, reverse idle
74. Washer, thrust
75. Synchronizer assembly, 3rd-4th
76. Synchronizer assembly, 1st-2nd

1. Case, w/center support
2. Pin, guide
3. Bearing, needle
4. Plug, shift rod
5. Stud
6. Plug, oil filler
7. O-ring, oil filler
8. Dust cover, shift fork
9. Ring, snap, mainshaft
10. Ring, snap counter gear
11. Gasket, case and rear cover
12. Ball stud
13. Washer, lock
14. Washer, plain
15. Plug, screw
16. Gasket, plug (Calif. spec.)
17. Plug, screw (Calif. spec.)
18. Gasket, plug (Calif. spec.)
19. Shaft, clutch gear
20. Bearing, ball
21. Ring, snap

1975 and later manual transmission—2-wheel drive

18. Flatten out the lock washer and remove the lock nut and washer from the mainshaft.

19. Remove the self locking nut, washer, countershaft reverse gear and collar from the rear of the countergear.

20. Insert the nose of snap-ring pliers into the countergear bearing snap-ring hole in the center support and disengage the snapring from the ring groove by tapping on the front face of the center support while expanding the countergear bearing snap-ring.

21. Remove the center support by expanding the mainshaft rear bearing snapring with the snap-ring pliers.

22. Separate the clutch gear, needle bearings and blocker ring from the mainshaft assembly.

23. Press the rear bearing from the mainshaft.

24. Remove the thrust washer, 1st speed gear, needle roller bearing, a collar and blocker ring.

25. Remove the 1st and 2nd gear synchronizer assembly.

26. Remove the 2nd gear, blocker ring and needle roller bearing from the mainshaft.

27. Remove the snap-ring, 3rd and 4th synchronizer assembly, and blocker ring from the mainshaft.

28. Remove 3rd gear and needle bearings.

29. Remove the snap-ring and press off the clutch bearing and countergear bearing from the shaft.

To assemble the transmission:

30. Stand the front of the mainshaft upward and install the 3rd speed gear and needle roller bearing with the tapered side of the gear facing the front of the mainshaft.

31. Install a blocker ring with the clutch-ing teeth upward over the synchronizing surface of the 3rd speed gear.

32. If it is necessary to reassemble the synchronizer assembly turn the face of the synchronizer hub with the heavy boss to the face of the sleeve with the light chamfering on the outer rim.

33. Fit the keys into the key groove and position the synchronizer springs into the hole in the side face of the hub.

34. Install the 3rd and 4th synchronizer assembly on the mainshaft with the face of the sleeve with the light chamfer rearward.

35. Install the snap-ring.

36. Now turn the rear of the mainshaft upward and install the 2nd speed gear and needle roller bearing on the mainshaft with the tapered surface of the gear facing the rear of the mainshaft.

37. Install a blocker ring with the clutch-ing teeth downward over the synchronizing surface of the 2nd speed gear.

38. Install the 1st and 2nd synchronizer assembly with the chamfer on the sleeve facing the front of the mainshaft.

39. Install a blocker ring with the clutching teeth rearward.

40. Install the collar, needle roller bearing and 1st speed gear on the mainshaft.

NOTE: The tapered side of the gear should be facing the front of the mainshaft.

40. Install the 1st speed gear thrust washer on the mainshaft with the grooved side facing 1st gear.

41. Press the rear bearing on the mainshaft with the snap-ring groove facing front of the mainshaft.

42. If removed, press the ball bearing on the clutch gear shaft with the snap-ring groove on the bearing facing the front of the transmission. Install the snap-ring on the clutch gear shaft.

43. Assemble the needle roller bearing, blocker ring and clutch gear to the front of the mainshaft.

44. If removed, press on the counter gear ball bearing with the snap-ring groove facing the rear of the transmission.

45. If removed, install the snap-rings in the snap-ring groove in the inner circumference of the mainshaft and countergear holes of the center support.

46. If removed, insert the idler gear shaft with the lock plate groove side into the center support from the rear, then install the lock plate into the groove and tighten the bolt to 14 ft. lbs.

47. Mesh the countergear with the mainshaft assembly and install a holding tool on the mainshaft and countergear.

48. Place the tool with mainshaft and countergear assembled into a vise, then install the center support.

49. Expand the mainshaft bearing snapring in the center support and press the center support onto the shaft until the countergear bearing is brought into contact with its snap-ring.

50. Expand the countergear bearing snapring and press the center support further until the mainshaft and countergear snaprings are fitted into their grooves.

51. Remove the holding tool from the mainshaft and countergear and remove the assembly from the vise.

52. Move both synchronizers rearward to prevent turning of the mainshaft.

53. Install the collar, countershaft reverse gear, washer and self locking nut on the rear of the countergear; torque the nut to 100 ft. lbs.

NOTE: New self-locking nuts should be used.

54. Install the lock nut and lock washer on the mainshaft and torque the nut to 94 ft. lbs., then bend down the lock washer.

NOTE: Install the lock nut so that the chamfered side is facing the lock washer.

55. Apply grease to the two detent holes from the middle hole of the center support.

56. Install the 1st and 2nd and the 3rd and 4th shifter forks into their grooves in the synchronizer assembly.

57. Install the 3rd and 4th shifter rod from the rear of the center support through the middle hole and into the 1st and 2nd, 3rd and 4th shifter forks. Align the spring pin hole in the shifter fork with the hole in the shifter rod.

NOTE: Identify the 3rd and 4th shifter rod by the two detent grooves on the side of the rod.

58. Install the 1st and 2nd shifter rod from the rear of the center support through the 1st and 2nd shifter fork and align the hole in the rod to the hole in the shifter fork.

59. If removed, install the stopper pin in the reverse shifter rod and the front of the center support.

60. Install the two spring pins in the 1st/2nd and 3rd/4th shifter forks.

NOTE: When installing the spring pins place a round bar against the end of the shifter rod to prevent damage.

61. Install the detent balls, spring, gasket and retainer on the center support and torque the bolts to 14 ft. lbs.

62. Place the transmission case upright on wooden blocks and install the center support assembly and gasket into the transmission case aligning the dowel pin holes with the dowel pins.

63. Assemble the reverse shifter fork to the reverse gear and install these parts into position from the rear side of the mainshaft, then connect them to the reverse shifter rod.

64. Install the spring pin in the reverse shifter fork.

65. Install the thrust washer and reverse idler gear on the idler shaft.

NOTE: The reverse idler gear should be installed with undercut teeth forward.

66. Install the speedometer drive gear snap-ring and key on the mainshaft.

67. If removed install a new oil seal to the rear extension.

68. Apply grease to the outer thrust washer of the reverse idler shaft and insert it in the rear extension.

69. Install the rear extension and gasket to the transmission case aligning the dowel pin hole with the dowel pin. Torque the eight bolts to 27 ft. lbs.

70. Install the back-up lamp switch and CRS switch if removed.

71. Install the shifter cover and gasket and torque the bolts to 10 ft. lbs.

72. Install the oil O-ring to the speedometer driven gear and install the gear to the rear extension.

73. Install the front bearing retainer seal.

74. Install a snap-ring to the outer circumference of the clutch gear bearing.

75. Apply grease to the bearing retainer spring washer and place it in the bearing retainer with the dished face turned to the bearing outer space.

76. Install the bearing retainer to the front of the transmission case and torque the four bolts to 14 ft. lbs.

NOTE: The shorter bolts are used on countergear front bearing side of the bearing retainer.

77. Install the ball stud to the bearing retainer and torque to 30 ft. lbs.

78. Install the boot clutch fork and throwout bearing, then install the retaining spring.

79. Install the drain plug on the transmission case, then install the rear cover plug. Fill the transmission case to the specified level of 1.35 qt.

MANUAL TRANSMISSION AND TRANSFER CASE

4 Wheel Drive Models

REMOVAL AND INSTALLATION

1. Disconnect the battery ground.

2. Drain the transmission oil.

3. Slide the shift lever boots upward and unbolt each lever.

4. Remove the return spring from the transfer case shift lever and remove both levers.

5. Remove the starter attaching bolts and remove the starter assembly.

6. Jack up the vehicle and safely support it with jackstands. Disconnect the exhaust pipe from the manifold and disconnect the pipe support from the transmission.

7. Disconnect the speedometer cable at the transmission. Disconnect the rear driveshaft at the differential. Disconnect the ground strap.

8. Remove the rear driveshaft from the transfer case. Remove the front driveshaft.

9. Disconnect the clutch return spring.

10. Disconnect the clutch cable at the fork.

11. Remove the flywheel stoneguard.

12. Remove the transmission rear crossmember bolts.

13. Raise the engine and transmission, and remove the rear crossmember-to-frame bolts.

14. Remove the rear mounting bolts from the transfer case.

15. Unbolt and remove the side case from the transmission.

16. Remove the stud bolt from the transfer case.

17. Lower the engine and transmission assembly and support the rear of the engine.

18. Disconnect the CRS switch and backup light switch.

19. Remove the shifter cover and gasket from the transfer case.

20. Remove the transmission-to-engine bolts. When removing the transmission, turn the side case fitting face of the case downward and pull the case straight back until free from the clutch. Tip the front of the transmission downward and remove it.

21. Installation is the reverse of removal. Torque shifter cover bolts to 14 ft. lbs.

CLUTCH

The clutch is a hydraulically-operated single-plate, dry friction disc, diaphragm spring type.

is moved in the master cylinder bore. This movement compresses the fluid in the master cylinder causing hydraulic pressure which is transferred through a tube to the slave cylinder. The slave cylinder is mounted to the clutch housing with its piston connected to the clutch release lever. The hydraulic pressure in the slave cylinder forces the slave cylinder piston to travel out the cylinder bore and move the clutch release lever, disengaging the clutch.

1975–77

The clutch is operated by a clutch pedal which is mechanically connected to a clutch master cylinder. When the pedal is depressed, the piston in the master cylinder

1978 and Later

The clutch is operated by a steel cable connecting the pedal with the throw-out arm.

REMOVAL AND INSTALLATION

1. Jack up the vehicle and safely support it using jackstands.

2. Remove the transmission.

3. Mark the clutch assembly-to-flywheel relationship with a center punch or scribe so that the clutch assembly can be reassembled in the same position from which it is removed.

4. Loosen the six clutch cover-to-flywheel attaching bolts, one turn at a time in an alternating sequence, until the spring tension is relieved to avoid distorting or bending the clutch cover.

5. Support the clutch pressure plate and cover assembly with a clutch aligning arbor, then remove the bolts and the clutch assembly.

6. Apply a thin coat of grease to the pressure plate wire ring, diaphragm spring,

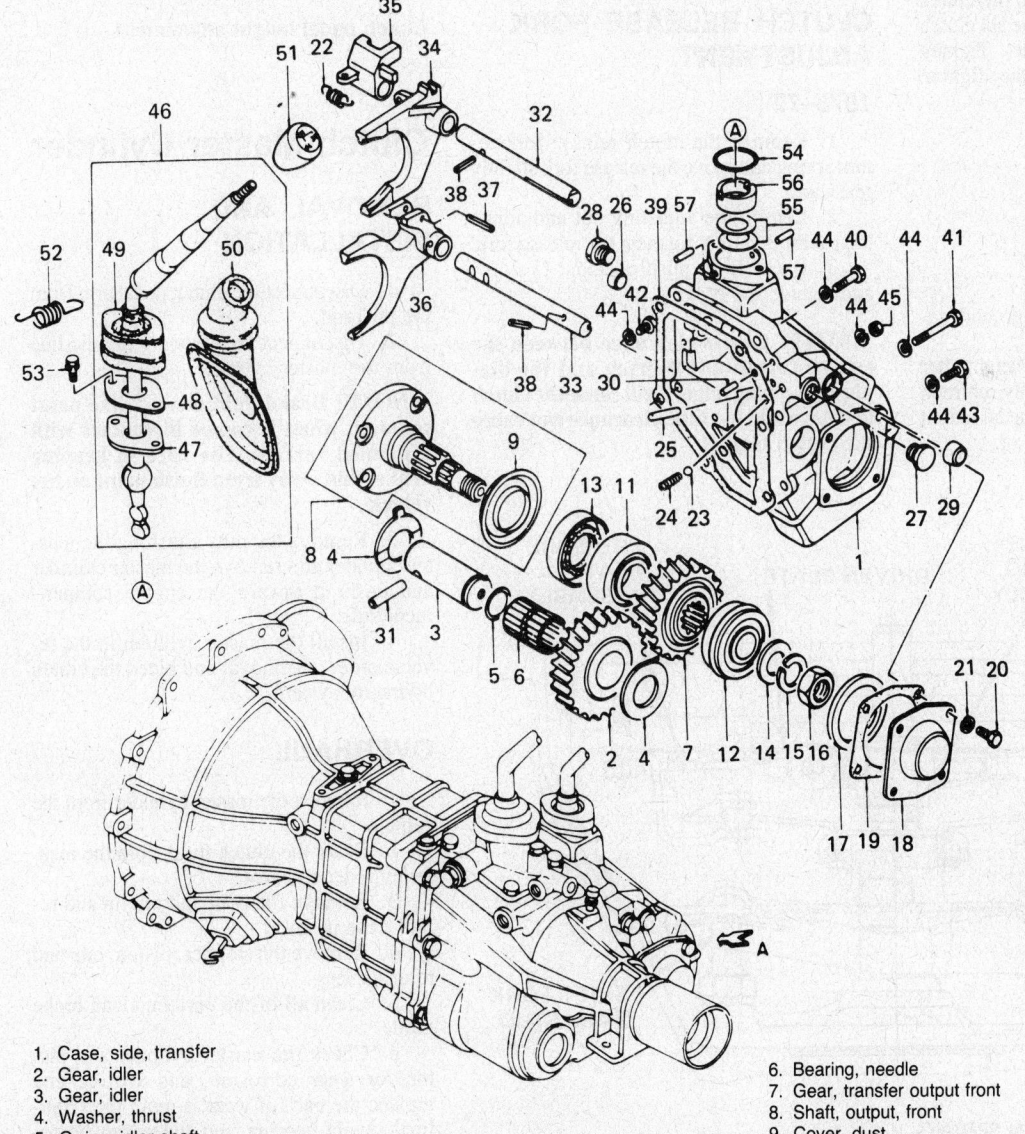

10. —
11. Bearing, ball, front, output shaft
12. Bearing, ball, rear, output shaft
13. Oil seal, front output shaft
14. Washer, plain
15. Washer, lock
16. Nut, front output shaft
17. Distance piece
18. Cover, front output shaft
19. Gasket, cover
20. Bolt
21. Washer, lock
22. Spring, gear lock release
23. Ball, detent
24. Spring, detent
25. Pin, interlock
26. Plug, shift rod
27. Plug, screw
28. Plug screw
29. Plug, shift rod
30. Pin, dowel
31. Pin, dowel
32. Rod, shift, 4-wheel
33. Rod, shift, range
34. Arm, shift, 4-wheel
35. Block, shift, 4-wheel
36. Arm, shift, range
37. Pin, spring, select stop
38. Pin, spring, shift arm
39. Gasket, side case and transfer case
40. Bolt
41. Bolt
42. Bolt
43. Bolt
44. Washer, lock
45. Nut
46. Lever, gear shift, transfer
47. Cover, ball seat
48. Retainer, gear shift lever
49. Cover, dust
50. Grommet, gear shift lever
51. Knob, gear shift lever
52. Spring, return, gear shift lever
53. Bolt
54. O-ring, gear shift lever
55. Spring, ball seat
56. Seat, ball
57. Pin, straight

1. Case, side, transfer
2. Gear, idler
3. Gear, idler
4. Washer, thrust
5. O-ring, idler shaft

6. Bearing, needle
7. Gear, transfer output front
8. Shaft, output, front
9. Cover, dust

Typical exploded view manual transmission w/transfer case

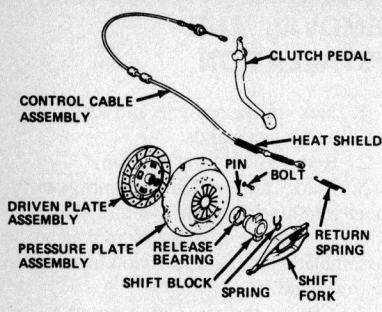

Clutch components

clutch cover grooves and the drive bosses on the pressure plate.

7. Apply a thin coat of Lubriplate® to the splines in the driven plate.

8. Assemble the clutch cover and pressure plate and the driven plate on a clutch alignment arbor.

9. Align the marks made on the clutch cover and flywheel and install the six clutch cover-to-flywheel attaching bolts. Tighten the bolts to 50 in. lbs. Remove the aligning arbor.

PEDAL HEIGHT ADJUSTMENT

1975–77

1. Disconnect the battery ground cable.

2. Measure the clutch pedal height after making sure that the pedal is fully returned by the pedal return spring. The pedal height should be between 5.9 and 6.3 in.

3. To adjust the height, disconnect the clutch switch and remove it from its mounting bracket.

4. Loosen the locknut on the master cylinder pushrod.

5. Adjust the clutch pedal to the specified height by rotating the pushrod in the appropriate direction. Tighten the locknut when finished with the adjustment.

6. Install the clutch switch. Adjust the clearance between the switch housing (not the switch actuating pin) and the clutch pedal tab to 0.02–0.04 in. Tighten the switch locknut.

7. Connect the electrical leads to the clutch switch and connect the negative battery cable.

1978 and Later

Adjust the pedal stop so that the clutch and brake pedals are the same height. Make sure that the clutch switch is in contact with the clutch pedal bracket.

CLUTCH RELEASE FORK ADJUSTMENT

1975–77

1. Remove the clutch release fork return spring and move the release fork slightly rearward.

2. Loosen the adjusting nut and adjust the pushrod until it contacts the release fork.

3. Back off the pushrod about 1¾ turns and tighten the locknut.

NOTE: Excess clearance between the release (throwout) bearing and the diaphragm spring fingers will cause the clutch to drag while too little clearance can cause the clutch to slip.

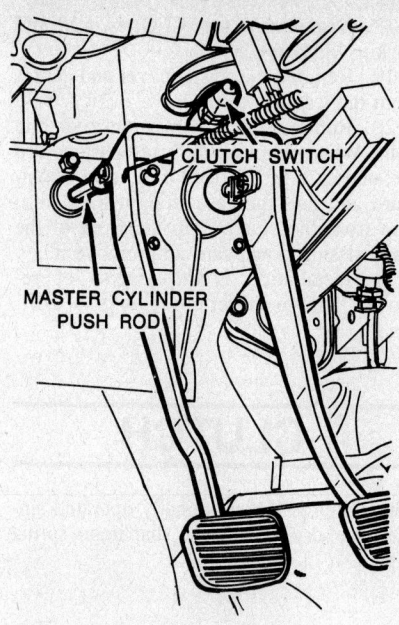

Clutch pedal height adjustment

Clutch Master Cylinder

REMOVAL AND INSTALLATION

1. Disconnect the clutch pedal arm from the pushrod.

2. Disconnect the clutch hydraulic line from the master cylinder.

NOTE: Brake fluid can act like paint remover when it comes in contact with a painted surface. Use care in keeping brake fluid away from finish paint on the vehicle.

3. Remove the nuts attaching the master cylinder and remove the master cylinder and pushrod toward the engine compartment side.

4. Install the master cylinder in the reverse order of removal and bleed the clutch hydraulic system.

OVERHAUL

1. Remove the master cylinder from the vehicle.

2. Drain the clutch fluid from the master cylinder reservoir.

3. Remove the boot and circlip and remove the pushrod.

4. Remove the stopper, piston, cup and return spring.

5. Clean all of the parts in clean brake fluid.

6. Check the master cylinder and piston for wear corrosion, and scoring and replace the parts if wear is more than minimal. Light scoring and glaze can be removed with crocus cloth soaked in brake fluid.

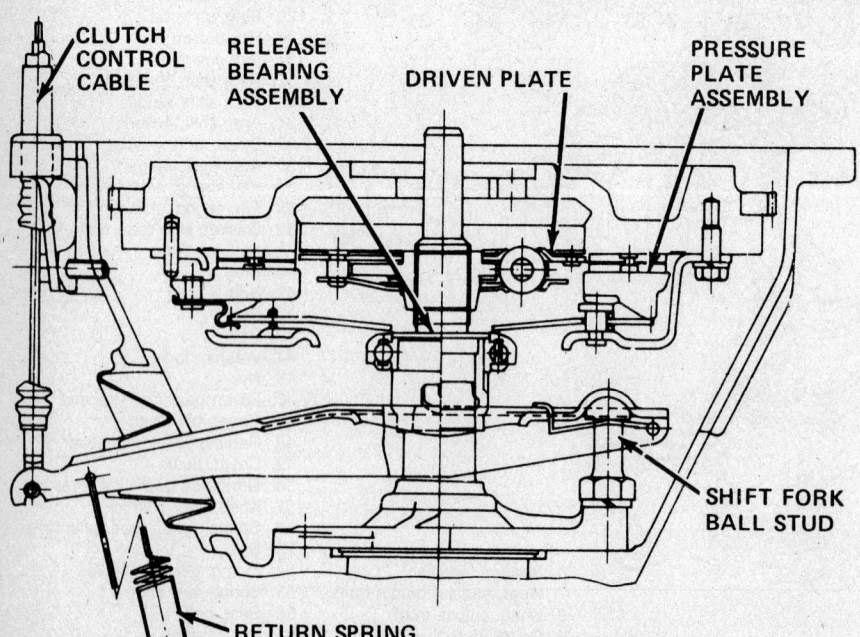

Exploded view of the 1978 and later cable-operated clutch assembly

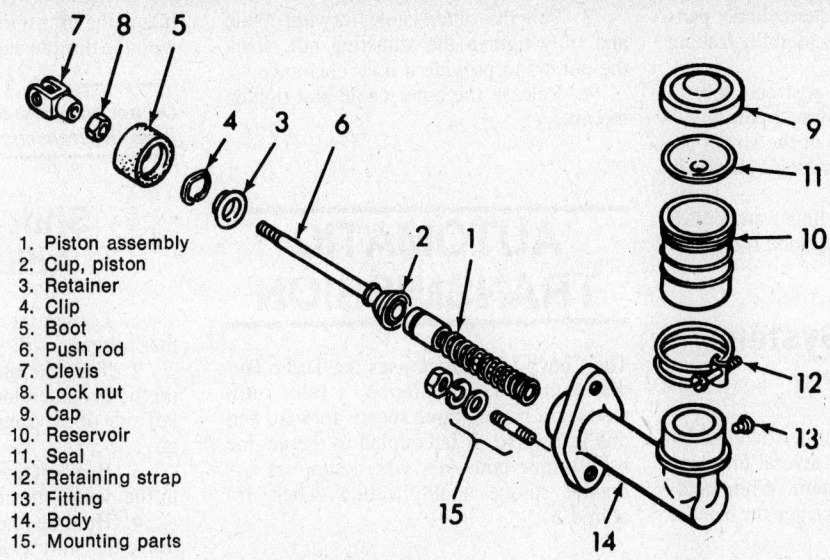

1. Piston assembly
2. Cup, piston
3. Retainer
4. Clip
5. Boot
6. Push rod
7. Clevis
8. Lock nut
9. Cap
10. Reservoir
11. Seal
12. Retaining strap
13. Fitting
14. Body
15. Mounting parts

Exploded view of the clutch master cylinder

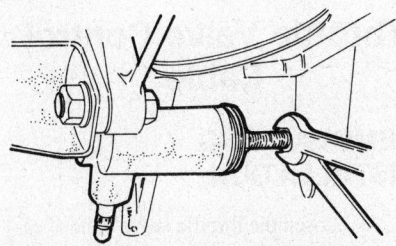

Clutch release fork adjustment

Clutch Slave Cylinder

REMOVAL AND INSTALLATION

1. Remove the slave cylinder attaching bolts and the pushrod from the shift fork.
2. Disconnect the flexible fluid hose from the slave cylinder and remove the unit from the vehicle.

3. Install the slave cylinder in the reverse order of removal and bleed the clutch hydraulic system.

OVERHAUL

1. Remove the slave cylinder from the vehicle.
2. Remove the pushrod and boot.
3. Force out the piston by blowing compressed air into the slave cylinder at the hose connection.

NOTE: Be careful not to apply excess air pressure to avoid possible injury.

4. Clean all of the parts in brake fluid.
5. Check and replace the slave cylinder bore and piston if wear or severe scoring exists. Light scoring and glaze can be removed with crocus clotch soaked in brake fluid.
6. Normally the piston cup should be replaced when the slave cylinder is disassembled. Check the piston cup and replace it if it is found to be worn, fatigued or scored.

7. Replace the rubber boot if it is cracked or broken.
8. Lubricate all of the new parts in clean brake fluid and reassemble in the reverse order of disassembly, taking note of the following:

  a. Use care when reassembling the piston cup to the piston and when inserting the piston assembly into the cylinder, to prevent damage to the lipped portion of the cup;

  b. Fill the master cylinder with brake fluid and bleed the clutch hydraulic system;

  c. Adjust the clearance between the pushrod and the shift fork to 5/64 in.

7. Generally, the cup seal should be replaced each time the master cylinder is disassembled. Check the cup and replace it if it is worn, fatigued, or damaged.
8. Check the clutch fluid reservoir, filler cap, dust cover and the pipe for distortion and damage and replace the parts as necessary.
9. Lubricate all new parts with clean brake fluid.

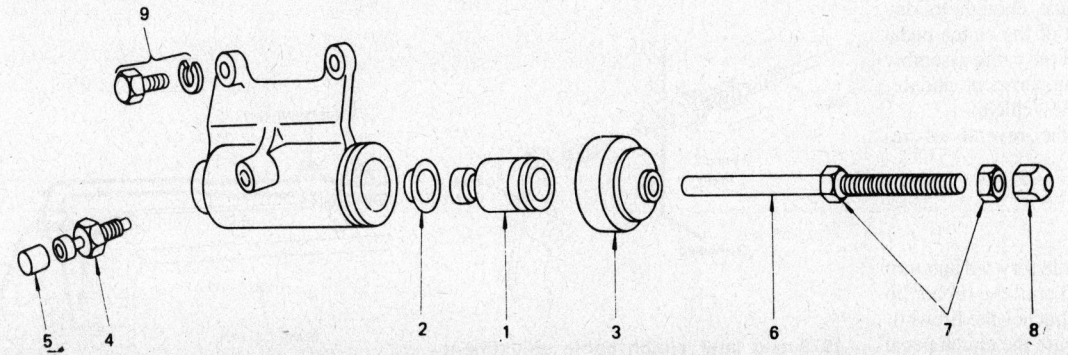

1. Piston
2. Piston cup
3. Boot
4. Bleeder screw
5. Cap
6. Push rod
7. Nut
8. Nut
9. Nut

Exploded view of the clutch slave cylinder

10. Reassemble the master cylinder parts in the reverse order of disassembly, taking note of the following:

a. Reinstall the cup seal carefully to prevent damaging the lipped portions;

b. Adjust the height of the clutch pedal after installing the master cylinder in position on the vehicle;

c. Fill the master cylinder and clutch fluid reservoir and then bleed the clutch hydraulic system.

Hydraulic System Bleeding

1. Bleed the clutch master cylinder by pumping the clutch pedal several times, to push the air out of the system. While holding the pedal down, slowly open the bleeder screw.

2. Repeat step one until all signs of air bubbles disappear in the released fluid.

—————— CAUTION ——————
Don't let the master cylinder fluid level get too low.

3. Connect a tube to the clutch slave cylinder bleeder screw and insert the other end into a clean glass container, ¼ to ½ filled with brake fluid.

4. Bleed the slave cylinder in the same manner as the master cylinder until the air bubbles disappear.

5. Refill the system reservoir and depress the clutch pedal several times.

6. Check for leaks and smooth operation.

Clutch Cable

REMOVAL AND INSTALLATION

1978 and Later

1. Loosen the clutch cable lock and adjusting nuts. Remove the clutch cable clip at the engine compartment location.

2. Raise the vehicle and remove the spring from the shift fork end.

3. Disconnect the cable end from the shift fork and pull the cable assembly through the bracket.

4. Lower the vehicle enough to disengage the hooked part of the clutch pedal from the cable eye. Pull the cable assembly towards the engine compartment and remove the cable from the vehicle.

5. Installation is the reverse of removal.

ADJUSTMENT

1. Pull the outer cable forward and turn the adjusting nut inward until the rubber lip on the washer damper touches the firewall.

2. Depress and release the clutch pedal a few times.

3. Pull the outer cable forward again and fully tighten the adjusting nut. Back the nut off to provide a 0.20 clearance.

4. Release the outer cable and tighten the nut.

AUTOMATIC TRANSMISSION

The Chevy LUV truck uses the Turbo Hydra-Matic 200 transmission, a fully automatic unit having three speeds forward and one in reverse. It is coupled to the engine by a torque converter which supplies hydraulic torque multiplication when required.

REMOVAL AND INSTALLATION

1. Disconnect the negative battery cable and remove the throttle valve cable from the carburetor.

2. Remove the transmission dipstick assembly.

3. Raise the vehicle and remove the pan from the converter housing.

4. Remove the starter assembly.

5. Have a clean rag ready to use as a plug for the end of the transmission. Disconnect the driveshaft and remove it from the vehicle. Plug the rear of the transmission to avoid oil leakage.

6. Disconnect the shift lever control rod from the transmission shift lever.

7. Remove the exhaust pipe bracket. Remove the speedometer cable from the transmission.

8. Remove the oil cooler lines and position them along the vehicle frame to prevent damage.

9. Remove the bolts and nuts coupling the drive plate to the converter.

10. Remove the bolts holding the frame bracket to the transmission rear mount.

11. Raise the engine and transmission assembly and remove the frame bracket from the cross member. Remove the rear mount from the transmission.

12. Remove the bell housing bolts and

move the transmission rearward together with the throttle cable and the oil filler tube.

—————— CAUTION ——————
Do not allow the torque converter to drop from the transmission during removal.

Shift Linkage Adjustment

1. Loosen the control rod lock nuts so that trunnion will slide on the control rod.

2. Turn the manual shaft of the transmission counterclockwise, viewed from the left side of the transmission, as far as it will go.

3. Back off the manual shaft three stops to the neutral position.

4. Holding the shaft in this position, move the shift lever to the neutral position and push the shift control lower lever rearward to remove play. Tighten the lock nuts.

5. Check for proper operation of the transmission in all transmission ranges.

Throttle Valve Control Cable

REMOVAL AND INSTALLATION

1. Loosen the throttle valve control cable adjusting nuts and disconnect the cable from the carburetor throttle lever by removing the pin.

2. Remove the throttle valve cable clip from the right side of the cylinder body.

3. Remove the bolt holding the throttle cable to the transmission and pull the cable upward. Disconnect the end of the inner cable from the throttle lever link on the transmission side.

4. Remove the cable assembly from the vehicle.

5. Installation is the reverse of removal.

ADJUSTMENT

1. Loosen the throttle valve control cable adjusting nuts.

1978 and later clutch cable adjustment locations

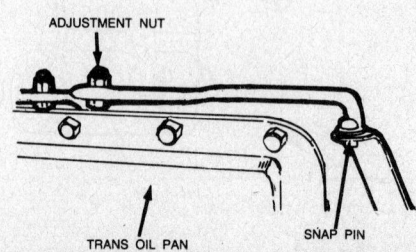
Shift linkage adjustment—Turbo 200

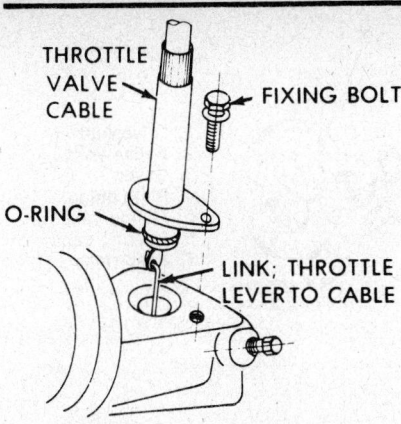

THROTTLE VALVE CABLE — FIXING BOLT

O-RING — LINK; THROTTLE LEVER TO CABLE

Throttle valve cable removal

2. Open the carburetor throttle lever to the wide open position and adjust the inner cable by turning the adjustment nut (lower) on the outer cable by hand so that the inner cable has a free play of approximately 0.040 in.

3. Tighten the lock nut (upper) securely.

4. Make sure that the stroke of the inner cable from the wide open position to the closed position is within the range of 1.37 to 1.41 inches.

Inhibitor Switch

ADJUSTMENT

1. Loosen the screws holding the switch. Move the switch body so that the center of the moveable part of the switch, aligns with the neutral position indicator line on the steel case when the shift lever is in the neutral position.

2. Tighten the holding screws, and make sure that the engine does not start in gear.

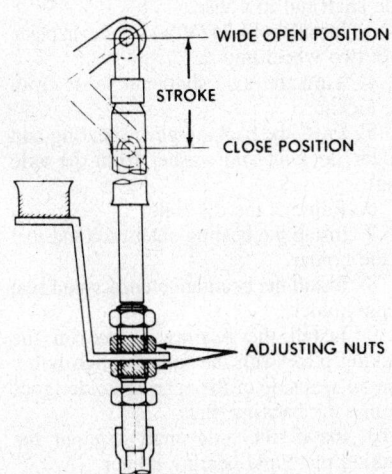

WIDE OPEN POSITION

STROKE

CLOSE POSITION

ADJUSTING NUTS

Checking throttle valve cable adjustment—Turbo 200 transmission

Intermediate Band

The bands are not adjustable. A selective band apply pin is installed at time of assembly or overhaul that compensates for normal band wear.

Transmission Fluid Drain and Refilling

1. Jack up the vehicle and support it with jackstands. Support the transmission at the vibration damper, and remove the oil pan retaining bolts from the front and sides of the fluid pan.

2. Loosen the rear fluid pan bolts approximately four (4) turns.

——————— CAUTION ———————
If the vehicle has been running, the transmission fluid will be HOT, exceeding 350°F.

3. Carefully pry the front of the fluid pan loose from the transmission case using a small pry bar or brake adjusting spoon. Allow the fluid to drain into a waste container.

4. Remove and clean the pan.

5. Remove the two retaining screen-to-valve body bolts, screen and gasket and clean the screen thoroughly.

6. Install screen and new gasket in place on valve body. Tighten retaining bolts to 6–10 ft. lbs.

7. Install the fluid pan with a new gasket and torque the pan retaining bolts to 10–13 ft. lbs.

8. Lower the vehicle and install six pints of Dexron® II in the transmission. Start the engine and move the selector lever through each gear position.

9. Recheck the fluid level and fill to the following levels.

   a. Fluid at room temperature: Level should be ⅛ to ⅜ in. below the add mark on the dip stick.

   b. Fluid at normal operating temperature:
Fluid level should be at the full mark on the dip stick.

NOTE: Normal operating temperature is reached after approximately 15 miles of highway type driving or equivalent.

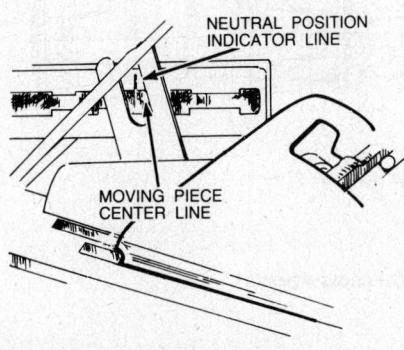

NEUTRAL POSITION INDICATOR LINE

MOVING PIECE CENTER LINE

Inhibitor switch adjustment

Driveshaft and U-Joints

STANDARD WHEELBASE MODELS

NOTE: Match-mark all parts with a scribe or center punch for later installation.

1. Disconnect the driveshaft rear flange from the differential pinion flange.

2. Pull the one piece driveshaft from the end of the transmission housing cover.

3. Plug or cover the transmission housing cover end to prevent lubricant leakage.

4. Installation is the reverse of removal.

LONG WHEEL BASE MODELS

NOTE: Match-mark all parts for installation.

1. Disconnect the flanged yokes between the front and the rear driveshafts.

2. Disconnect the rear driveshaft flange from the differential pinion flange and remove the rear shaft.

3. Have a clean rag ready to plug the end of the transmission housing when the driveshaft is removed. Remove the center bearing support bracket from the fourth crossmember and pull the front driveshaft from the housing. Plug the transmission end to prevent loss of lubricant.

4. Installation is the reverse of removal.

Front Drive Shaft

4-WHEEL DRIVE MODELS REMOVAL AND INSTALLATION

1. Jack up vehicle and safely support it with jackstands.

NOTE: You must raise the truck enough for the front wheels to turn freely.

2. Place the transmission and transfer case in the neutral position.

3. Match-mark each end of the driveshaft and the flanges on the rear of the transfer case with a scribe or center punch for later installation.

4. Remove the U-bolts from the rear and the transfer case flanges.

5. Remove the driveshaft.

6. Installation is the reverse of removal.

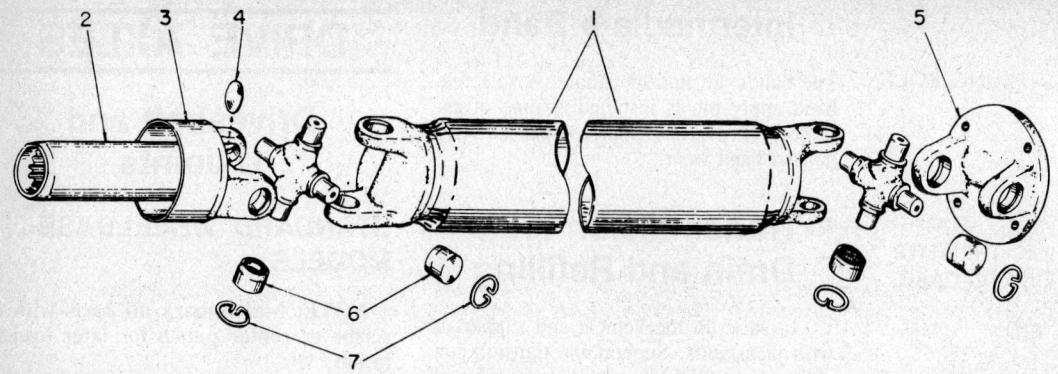

1. Driveshaft
2. Spline yoke
3. Cover
4. Plate plug
5. Flange yoke
6. Bearing caps
7. Snap-rings

Exploded view of the driveshaft and U-joints

U-Joint

OVERHAUL

1. Remove the driveshaft from the vehicle.

2. Punch mating marks on both the yokes at either end of the driveshaft and the driveshaft itself so that the driveshaft assembly can be reassembled in the same position.

3. Remove the snap-rings from the bearing hole of the yokes.

4. Place the yoke in a vise with a small socket positioned against one of the bearing caps and a larger socket placed against the yoke on the opposite side. The larger socket must be able to receive the bearing cap when it is pressed out of the yoke.

5. Tighten the vise until the bearing caps are free of the yoke.

6. Remove the two remaining bearings from the opposite yoke in the same manner and remove the spider bearing journal.

7. Carefully coat the spiders and ring of needle bearings around the inside of the bearing caps with grease before assembly. This will prevent the needle bearings from falling out or coming out of place in the caps. Also make sure the bearings are lined up squarely around the inside of the caps.

8. Assemble the universal joint spider and bearing caps to the yoke in the reverse manner of removal, using the smaller socket to press the bearing caps into the yoke and the larger socket to bear against the yoke bearing cap hole at the opposite end. Use a vise to press the bearing caps in place.

9. Install the hole snap-ring to secure the bearing caps.

10. Assemble the slide yoke to the driveshaft, aligning the marks made prior to disassembly.

11. Install the driveshaft assembly on the vehicle.

Axle Shaft, Bearing and Seal—2 Wheel Drive

AXLE SHAFT REMOVAL AND INSTALLATION

1. Jack up the vehicle and safely support it with jackstands.

2. Remove the rear wheel cover and the wheel and tire.

3. Remove the brake drum, brake shoes, and disconnect the parking brake inner cable.

4. Disconnect the brake line at the wheel cylinder and plug the end of the line.

5. Remove the four nuts from the bearing holder through-bolts from the inside of the brake backing plate.

6. Using an axle puller, pull out the axle shaft assembly. Never strike the brake backing plate with a hammer in an attempt to remove the axle shaft.

7. Install the axle shaft in the reverse order of removal, tighten the bearing holding plate attaching nuts to 55 ft. lbs.; bleeding the brake hydraulic system after installing the brakes and adjusting the parking brake cable as necessary.

BEARING AND/OR SEAL REMOVAL AND INSTALLATION AXLE SHAFT END-PLAY ADJUSTMENT

Tool J-24246 (or substitute) is necessary to break the locknut loose from the axle shaft. The locknuts is torqued to 190 ft. lbs. Adjust the axle shaft end-play.

1. Remove the axle shaft.

2. Flatten the locktab and clamp the axle shaft nut in a vise.

3. Install tool J-24246 and clamp in place with two wheel nuts.

4. Turn the axle shaft nut loose from the locknut.

5. Press the backing plate, bearing and holder, locknut and washer from the axle shaft.

6. Remove the oil seal.

7. Install the bearing outer race and seal in the holder.

8. Install the bearing outer race and seal in the holder.

9. Install the bearing holder on the backing plate with the four through bolts. The oil seal side of the bearing holder goes against the backing plate.

10. Install the axle shaft through the backing plate and bearing holder.

11. Install a new lockwasher with dished side away from the bearing.

12. Clamp the locknut in a vise and us-

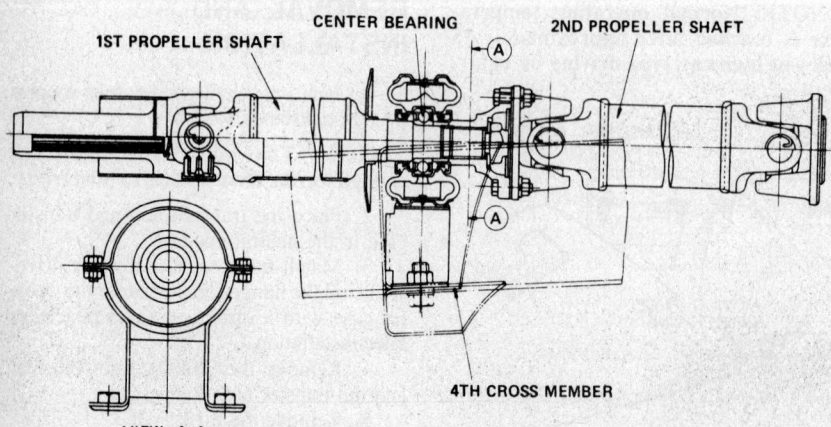

1ST PROPELLER SHAFT
CENTER BEARING
2ND PROPELLER SHAFT
(A)
(A)
4TH CROSS MEMBER
VIEW A-A

Exploded view of the driveshaft—long wheelbase models

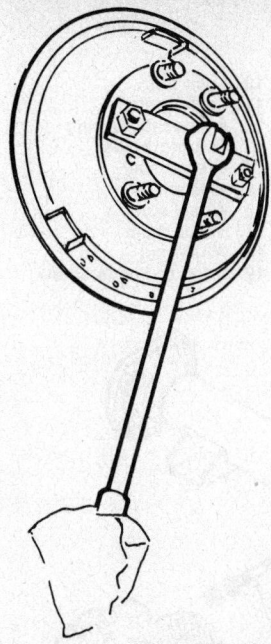

Removing the axle shaft from the brake backing plate using tool J-24246 or substitute

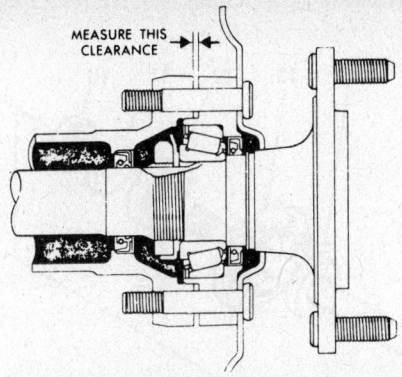

Axle shaft bearing holder-to-flange clearance—this dimension plus 0.0004 in. equals the thickness of the shim pack

ing tool J-24246 tighten the axle shaft into the locknut to 190 ft. lbs. Bend the locktab.

13. Install the axle shaft.

14. To adjust the end-play:

If one shaft has been serviced, start with step b.

a. Insert a .079 in. shim between bearing holder and axle tube flange. Install the axle shaft.

b. Install the opposite axle shaft without shims until it contacts the differential thrust block. Measure the clearance between the bearing holder and flange.

c. The proper shim size is this measurement (step b) plus 0.004 in.

d. Remove the axle shaft, install shim pack and reinstall the axle shaft.

FRONT AXLE AND AXLE SHAFT—4-WHEEL DRIVE REMOVAL AND INSTALLATION

1. Raise and support the vehicle.

2. Disconnect the front driveshaft at the differential.

3. Remove the wheels and skid plate.

4. Loosen the torsion bar completely with the height control adjusting bolts.

5. Remove the strut bars.

6. Disconnect the stabilizer bars at the lower control arms.

7. Remove the caliper assemblies and wire them to the frame. It is not necessary to disconnect the brake lines.

8. Remove the ball joints from the tie rods using a ball joint removal tool, and using care not to damage the rubber grease boots.

9. Disconnect the upper control arms at the frame. Make sure to note the number and positions of the shims.

10. Remove the steering link ends from the lower control arms.

11. Disconnect the shock absorbers from the lower control arms.

12. Disconnect the lower control arms from the frame.

13. Remove the free wheeling hub. See Front Bearing Removal.

14. Remove the rotors and upper links.

15. Remove the pitman arm and idler arm along with the steering linkage assembly.

16. Support the differential housing with a jack, lower it clear of the vehicle and roll it out. Take care to avoid damaging the U-joints.

17. Drain the differential case and remove the four bolts attaching the axle mounting bracket to the case.

18. Pull the shaft assemblies from the case on both sides.

19. Installation is the reverse of removal. Observe the following torque settings:

Item	Ft. Lbs.
Axle shaft-to-case	43
Differential case-to-frame	15
Pitman arm-to-sector shaft	160
Idler arm-to-pivot shaft	87
Lower control arm-to-frame	94
Ball joint castellated nut	100

Differential

REMOVAL AND INSTALLATION

1. Jack up the vehicle and safely support it with jackstands.

2. Remove the wheels and brake drums.

3. Remove the axle shafts.

4. Remove the driveshaft.

5. Remove the ten attaching nuts retaining the differential carrier and case assembly to the axle housing and remove the carrier from the vehicle.

6. Install the differential carrier in the reverse order of removal, tightening the nuts to 18 ft. lbs.

OVERHAUL DISASSEMBLY

1. Before disassembling the differential, make a pattern check of the ring gear.

2. Mark the side bearing caps so they can be reinstalled in the same positions.

3. Remove the nuts and the bearing caps, then remove the differential case and ring gear assembly. Keep left and right side bearings separate to avoid interchanging.

4. Remove the differential side bearings from the case. Carefully record the thickness of each side bearing and each shim pack removed and keep them separated.

5. Remove the ring gear bolts and separate the ring gear from the differential case.

6. Drive out the pinion shaft lock-pin with a long drift. It may be necessary to first remove the caulking in the lock-pin with a 5 mm drill.

7. Remove the pinion shaft with a drift and take out the thrust block, pinion gears, side gears and thrust washers from the differential case.

8. Remove the pinion nut.

9. Remove the companion flange.

10. Drive the pinion from the carrier by hitting a soft metal drift held against the splined end of the drive pinion. The outer (front) bearing will fall loose in the carrier, while the inner (rear) bearing will remain pressed on the drive pinion. Both bearing races will remain in the carrier bores.

11. Remove the rear bearing from the drive pinion by use of a press.

Wash all of the parts in a cleaning solvent, being careful not to interchange any. Look for damaged, excessively worn, or bent parts. Replace any defective parts.

NOTE: Ring gears and drive pinions come only in matched sets. If either part is defective, both must be replaced together.

It is crucial to clean and assemble the parts with care, and to follow adjustment procedures. Units that are contaminated with dirt or other foreign material, or which are incorrectly adjusted may be noisy and have a short service life. Be sure to use all new seals, gaskets and flange nuts when reassembling the axle.

PINION DEPTH ADJUSTMENT

If the old ring and pinion are going to be reinstalled and the contact pattern was found to be satisfactory before disassembly, install the pinion in the housing in the reverse order of removal, using the old shims installed in the original locations with a new collapsible spacer.

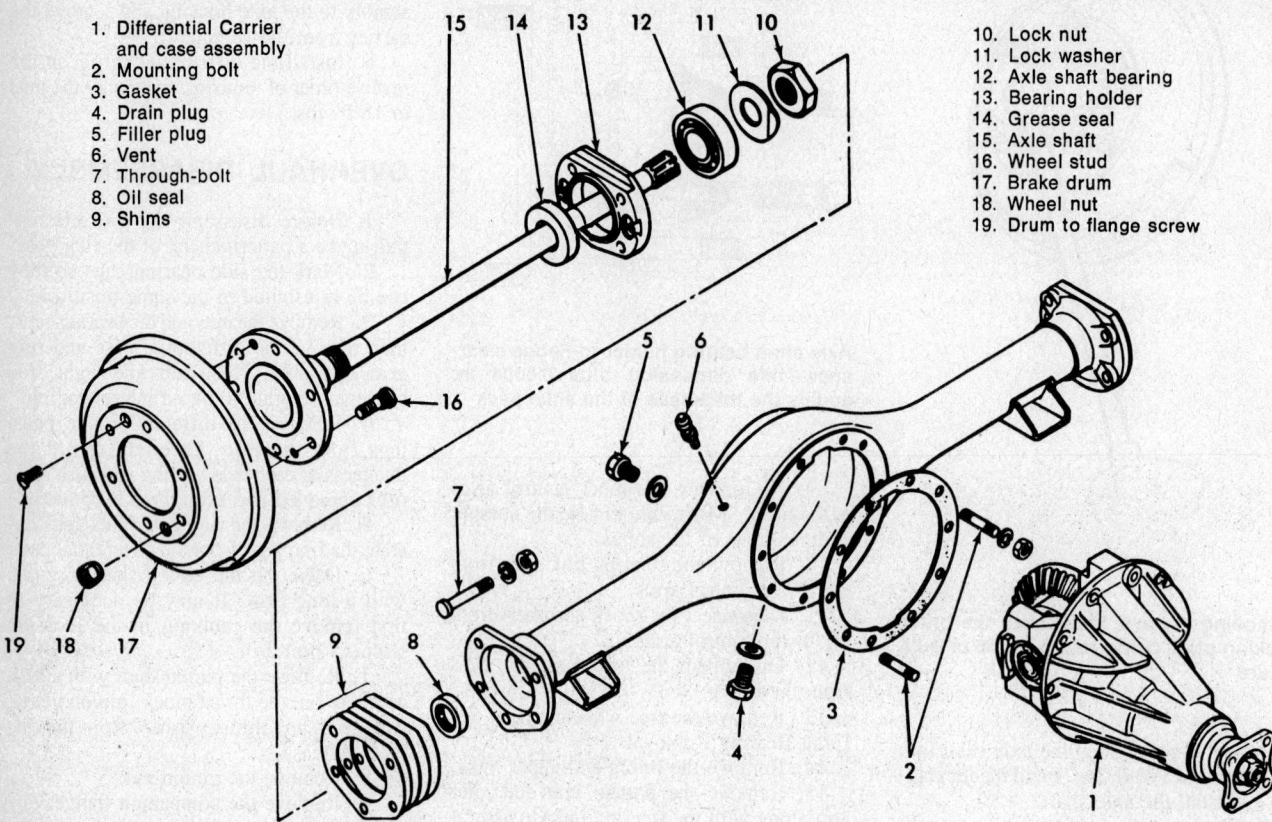

1. Differential Carrier and case assembly
2. Mounting bolt
3. Gasket
4. Drain plug
5. Filler plug
6. Vent
7. Through-bolt
8. Oil seal
9. Shims
10. Lock nut
11. Lock washer
12. Axle shaft bearing
13. Bearing holder
14. Grease seal
15. Axle shaft
16. Wheel stud
17. Brake drum
18. Wheel nut
19. Drum to flange screw

Exploded view of the axle shaft and housing assembly

However, if the contact pattern was found to be unsatisfactory due to assumed wear of a depth adjusting shim, measure the thickness of the shim(s) and install or subtract shims accordingly to gain a satisfactory contact pattern between the ring and pinion gear in regard to pinion depth.

NOTE: Shims are available in sizes ranging from 0.086 in. to 0.101 in.

If a new ring and pinion are being installed, compute the difference between the old and new pinions' depth code numbers then add or subtract shims accordingly as follows:

After installing a new ring and pinion together with the correct size shims, conduct another gear tooth contact pattern check. If the pattern is satisfactory, install the differential in the housing. If the pattern must be changed, disassemble the differential, install different shims accordingly, and reassemble the differential with a new crush collar (collapsible spacer). Make another gear tooth contact pattern check.

PINION BEARING PRELOAD ADJUSTMENT

Upon installation of the drive pinion, it is necessary to tighten the companion flange-to-pinion attaching nut to the proper specification in order to place the right amount of preload on the drive pinion bearings.

1. Place the drive pinion and the crush collar into the carrier.

2. Lubricate, then position the front bearing into the carrier. Install a new oil seal.

3. Mount the companion flange to the drive pinion. Apply hypoid lubricant to the pinion threads. Install a new pinion nut and tighten it to 85 ft. lbs.

4. Rotate the drive pinion to insure that the bearings are seated.

5. Wind a length of string around the pinion flange. Attach a pull scale to the loose end of the string. Note the scale reading required to rotate the pinion by pulling the scale.

6. Continue to tighten the pinion nut in small amounts until the pull required to rotate the drive pinion becomes 17 lbs. for new bearings and 7–9 lbs. for used bearings.

NOTE: Tighten the drive pinion nut in small increments only, so as to be sure of not exceeding the preload specifications. If the preload specifications are exceeded, the crush collar will be compressed too far and will require replacement.

PINION SHIM ADJUSTMENT CHART

Pinion Depth Code Number	Thickness Shim Required
+10	Subtract 0.005 in.
+8	Subtract 0.004 in.
+6	Subtract 0.003 in.
+4	Subtract 0.002 in.
+2	Subtract 0.001 in.
0	No shim required
−2	Add 0.001 in.
−4	Add 0.002 in.
−6	Add 0.003 in.
−8	Add 0.004 in.
−10	Add 0.005 in.

DIFFERENTIAL CASE REASSEMBLY

1. Install the side gears and thrust washers in the differential case.

2. Position the pinion gears 180° apart. Roll the gears into position, making sure they are in alignment, to allow installation of the pinion shaft.

3. Place the thrust block between the pinion gears, and drive the pinion shaft into

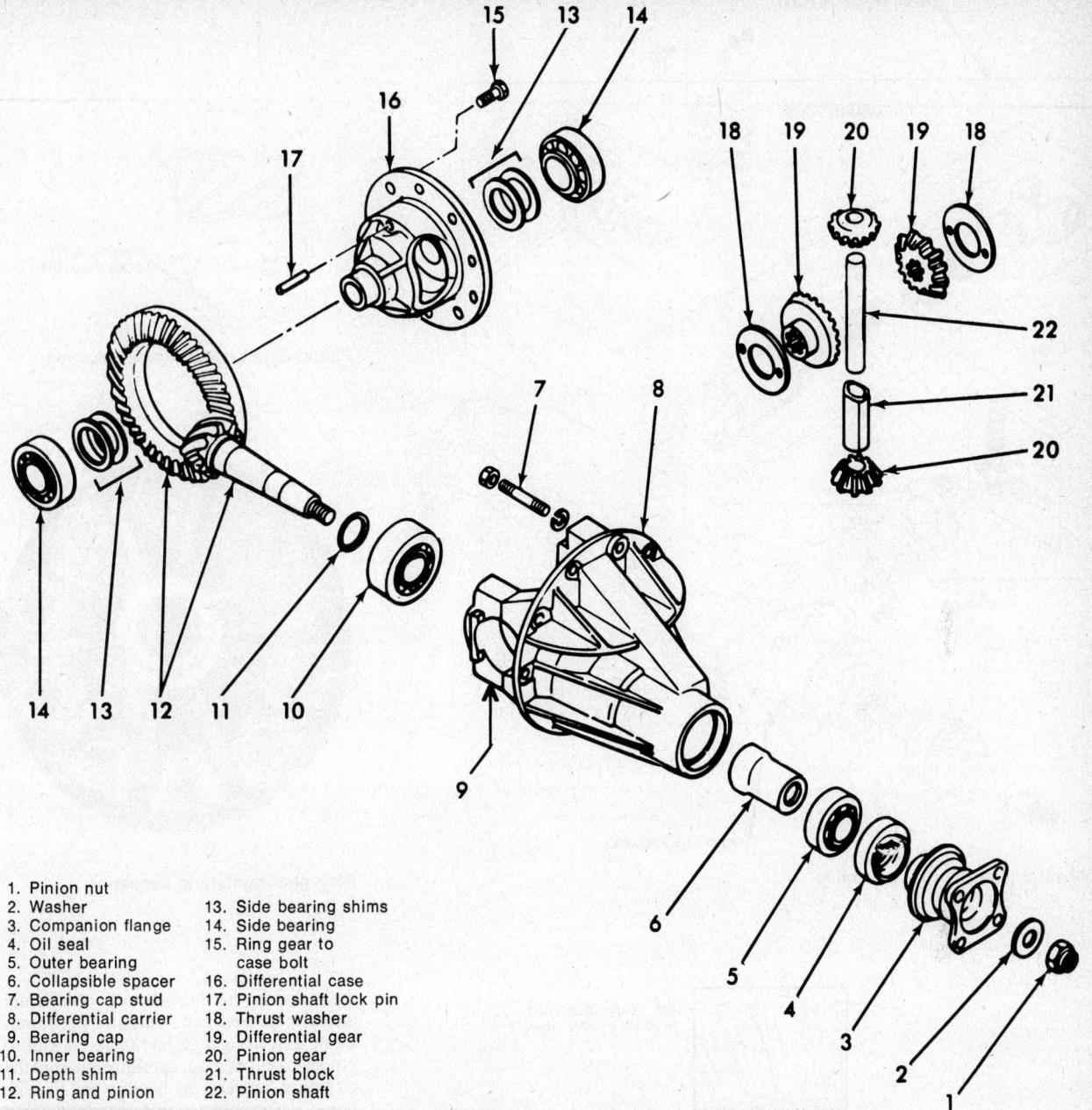

1. Pinion nut
2. Washer
3. Companion flange
4. Oil seal
5. Outer bearing
6. Collapsible spacer
7. Bearing cap stud
8. Differential carrier
9. Bearing cap
10. Inner bearing
11. Depth shim
12. Ring and pinion
13. Side bearing shims
14. Side bearing
15. Ring gear to
    case bolt
16. Differential case
17. Pinion shaft lock pin
18. Thrust washer
19. Differential gear
20. Pinion gear
21. Thrust block
22. Pinion shaft

Exploded view of the differential

position. Make sure that the lockpin hole in the cross shaft aligns with the hole in the case.

4. Measure the amount of backlash between the differential gears and the pinion gears. If the backlash is greater than 0.003 in., make the necessary adjustment with the thrust washers, available in thicknesses of 0.037 in., 0.041 in., and 0.045 in. Remember that increasing the thickness of the washers will decrease backlash and vice versa.

5. Install the lockpin into the cross-shaft and caulk its end to prevent loosening.

6. Clean the bolts and their threads. Apply Loctite® or a similar thread locking compound to the threaded portion of the bolts. Install the ring gear in position on the differential case. Torque the bolts in a diagonal sequence to 80–87 ft. lbs.

SIDE BEARING PRELOAD AND INITIAL BACKLASH ADJUSTMENT

If the original side bearings, differential case, ring and pinion, and differential carrier are being reused, and if the pattern check taken before disassembly showed a satisfactory contact pattern, the original shims (or new shims of the same dimension) can be reinstalled in the same positions from which they were removed.

If you are going to install *new side bearings only,* and if the contact pattern was satisfactory, select the shims in the following manner:

1. Measure the new bearing with a micrometer, and compare its thickness with the original bearing.

2. If the new bearing is thicker, subtract the numerical difference between the new and old bearing from the original shim pack.

3. If the new bearing is thinner, add the numerical difference between the old and new bearing to the original shim pack.

If new bearings *and/or* differential case, ring and pinion, or differential carrier are being installed, new shims will have to be selected for installation behind the side bearings for proper ring and pinion gear tooth contact.

1. Install the side bearings to be used in the final assembly onto the differential case. Do not install shims at this time.

2. Mount the case into the carrier bores.

3. Move the ring gear tightly against

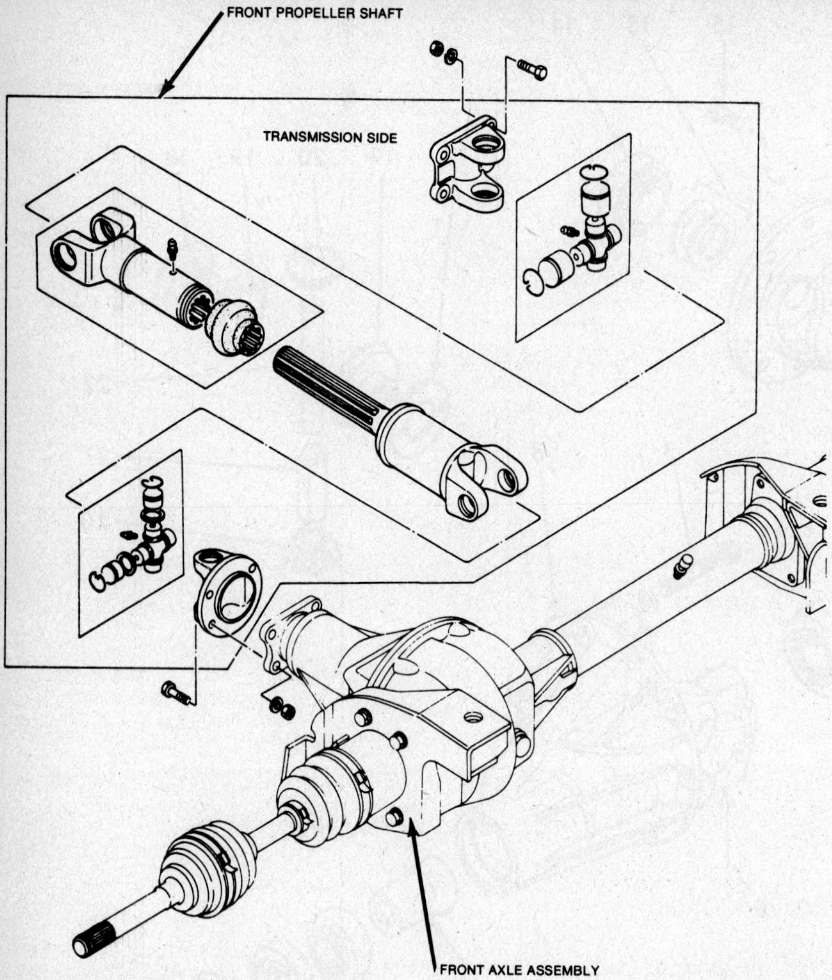

FRONT PROPELLER SHAFT

TRANSMISSION SIDE

FRONT AXLE ASSEMBLY

Four wheel drive front axle assembly

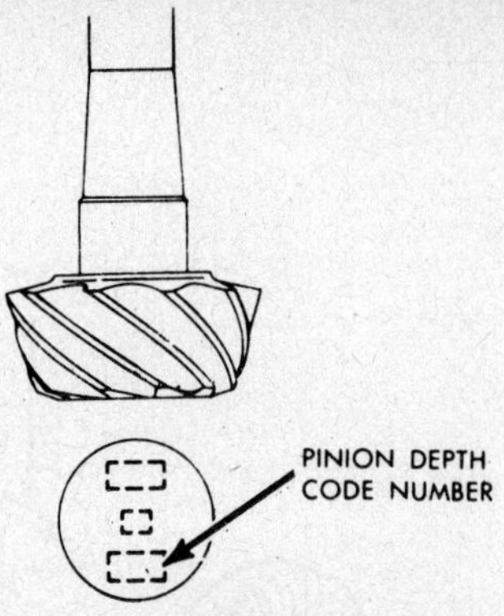

PINION DEPTH CODE NUMBER

Pinion depth code number location

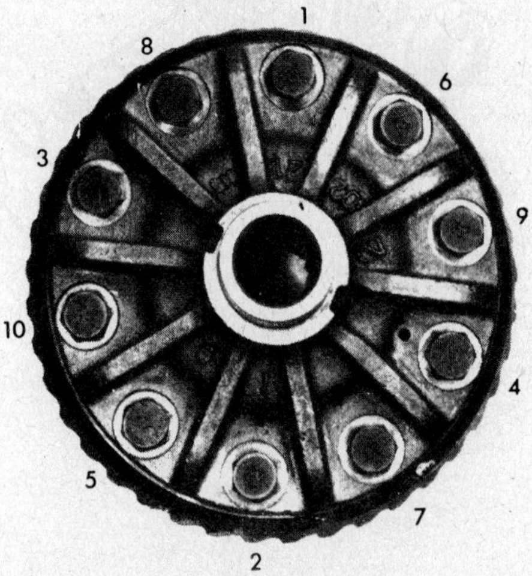

Ring gear tightening sequence

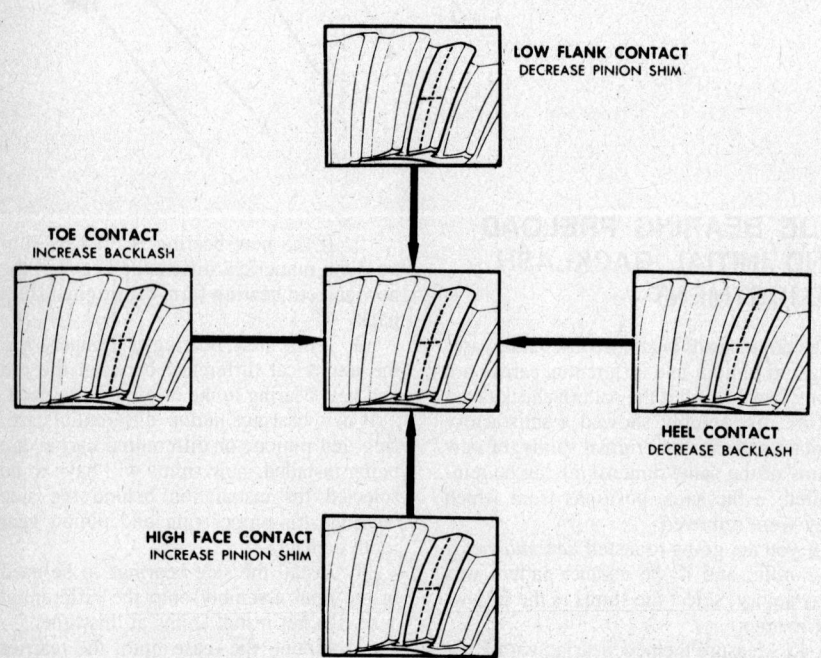

LOW FLANK CONTACT
DECREASE PINION SHIM.

TOE CONTACT
INCREASE BACKLASH

HEEL CONTACT
DECREASE BACKLASH

HIGH FACE CONTACT
INCREASE PINION SHIM

Gear tooth contact patterns

the carrier on the ring gear side, away from the drive pinion, and hold in this position. Using a feeler gauge just thick enough to produce a slight drag, carefully measure the clearance between the bearing and the differential carrier on the side opposite the ring gear. Record this measurement.

4. To determine the proper shims for installation, carry out the following procedure:

a. A predetermined dimension of 0.002 in. is always needed to establish proper preload. Therefore, add 0.002 in. to the clearance measured in Step 3. This will give the necessary combined total thickness of both shim packs.

b. Divide the total dimension into two shim packs, so that the numerical difference between the packs equals the numerical difference between the original shim packs.

5. Remove the case from the carrier. Carefully remove both side bearings. Install the shims as determined in Step 4 behind each bearing.

6. Install the case onto the carrier, tapping carefully into place. Install the side

bearing caps in their original positions and tighten the attaching bolts to 75 ft. lbs.

7. Measure the run-out of the ring gear. If the run-out exceeds 0.002 in., correct by cleaning or replacing parts.

8. Mount a dial indicator against the ring gear teeth with the indicator pin in-line with the direction of tooth travel. Measure the gear backlash in three locations. Backlash should be 0.005–0.007 in.

9. If backlash is not within the limits, the shims behind each side bearing will have to be adjusted.

NOTE: In order to maintain the proper preload on the side bearings, the total thickness of the shim packs must not be changed. Therefore, if the thickness of one shim pack must be increased, the thickness of the opposite shim pack must be decreased by an equal amount.

10. To increase backlash, the right side bearing shim must be increased, and the left side decreased. To decrease backlash, the right side shim must be decreased, while the left side is increased.

NOTE: Backlash changes about 0.002 in. for each 0.003 in. shim change.

GEAR TOOTH CONTACT PATTERN CHECK

A gear tooth contact pattern check before final assembly is necessary to verify whether or not the drive pinion and the ring gear are meshed properly. A tube of red lead gear marking compound is needed.

1. Wipe any oil out of the assembly and carefully clean each tooth of the ring gear with a clean rag soaked in solvent.

2. Apply red lead gear marking compound sparingly to the ring gear teeth.

3. Rotate the drive pinion slowly by hand ¼ of a turn in both directions so as to mark both the drive (convex) side and coast (concave) side of the ring gear teeth. Excessive turning of the ring gear is not needed or recommended.

4. Observe the pattern made on the ring gear teeth and compare it with the illustration. Make the necessary adjustments recommended.

REAR SUSPENSION

The rear suspension consists of semi-elliptical leaf springs with hydraulic double-acting shock absorbers. There is a straight "helper" spring added to the bottom of the spring pack. When the semi-elliptical springs straighten out due to the vehicle being loaded, they come in contact with the helper spring which helps to support any additional weight.

Springs

REMOVAL

1. Jack up the rear of the vehicle and place jackstands under the frame near the rear end of the rear spring brackets.

2. Remove the rear shock absorbers.

3. Remove the parking brake cable clips.

4. Remove the nuts from the U-bolts holding the springs to the axle housing.

5. Jack the rear axle up to remove the weight of the axle housing from the springs.

6. Remove the front and rear shackle pin nuts.

7. Drive out the rear shackle pin by using a hammer and drift and lower the rear end of the leaf spring assembly to the floor.

8. Drive out the front shackle pin and remove the leaf spring assembly rearward.

9. Remove the shackle pin from the rear spring bracket and remove the shackle.

INSPECTION

1. Check the leaf springs for cracks, wear and broken leaves. Replace any leaves found to be cracked, broken, fatigued or seriously worn.

2. Check the shackles for bending and the pins for wear.

3. Check the U-bolts for distortion or other damage.

INSTALLATION

1. Mount the shackle to the bracket.

2. Align the front end of the leaf spring assembly with the front bracket and install the shackle pin.

3. Align the rear end of the leaf spring assembly with the shackle and install the shackle pin.

4. Loosely install the shackle pin nuts and install the U-bolts. Tighten the U-bolt nuts to 40 ft. lbs.

5. Install the shock absorbers.

6. Clip the parking brake cable to the bracket.

7. Remove the jackstands and lower the vehicle so that the vehicle weight is on the left springs.

8. Tighten the shackle pin nuts to 130 ft. lbs.

Shock Absorbers

REMOVAL AND INSTALLATION

Remove the rear shock absorbers by loosening and removing the upper and lower attaching nuts and pulling the shock absorber ends off the mounting studs, together with the washers and rubber brushings. Install the shock absorbers in the reverse order of removal, making sure that you use new rubber bushings and that they are installed correctly in the beveled mounting holes in the end of the shock absorbers.

FRONT SUSPENSION

LUV trucks are equipped with the short and long arm type front suspension. The control arms are attached to the vehicle with bolts and bushings at their inner pivot points and to the steering knuckle, which is part of the front wheel spindle, at their outer points.

The front suspension is an independent type utilizing torsion bar springs. The torsion bar has splines on each end. Height control is provided on the third crossmember of the frame. Both upper and lower control arms are pressed steel and the torsion bar is supported at the ends by forged links. The links are bolted to the third frame crossmember in the rear and the lower control arms in front.

Fore and aft movement of the front suspension is controlled by strut bars bolted to the lower control arms at one end and mounted to the chassis frame using a rubber bumper at the other end. A torsion bar type stabilizer is connected to the lower control arm by shackle rods.

Torsion Bars

REMOVAL AND INSTALLATION

1. Jack up the front of the vehicle and support it with jackstands.

2. Remove the adjusting bolt from the height control arm.

3. Mark the location and remove the height control arm from the torsion bar and the third crossmember.

4. Mark the location and withdraw the torsion bar from the lower control arm.

5. For installation, apply a generous amount of grease to the serrated ends of the torsion bars.

6. Hold the rubber bumpers in contact with the lower control arm. Jack the vehicle up under the lower control arm to accomplish this.

7. Insert the front end of the torsion bar into the control arm.

8. Install the height control arm in position so that its end is reaching the adjusting bolt. Be sure to lubricate the part of the height control arm that fits into the chassis with grease.

9. Install a new cotter pin in the height control arm.

10. Turn the adjusting bolt to the location marked before removal.

11. Lower the vehicle and check the vehicle height and trim attitude.

Shock Absorbers

REMOVAL AND INSTALLATION

1. Raise the vehicle and support it with jackstands.

2. Hold the upper stem of the shock absorber from turning with an open-end wrench, and then, remove the upper stem retaining nut, retainer and rubber grommet.

NOTE: If the vehicle is old, or has frequently been subjected to water or moisture (as is often the case with 4-wheel drive models), the upper stem nut may be rusted beyond even pentrating oil. In this circumstance use a hacksaw to cut the upper stem, and install a new set of front shock absorbers.

3. Remove the bolt retaining the lower shock absorber pivot to the lower control arm and remove the shock absorber from the vehicle.

4. Install the shock absorber by first installing the lower retainer and rubber grommet over the upper stem and then, installing the shock fully extended up through the upper control arm so that the upper stem passes through the mounting hole in the frame bracket.

5. Install the upper rubber grommet, retainer and attaching nut over the shock absorber upper stem.

6. Hold the upper stem of the shock absorber from turning with an open-end wrench and tighten the retaining nut.

7. Install the retainers attaching the shock absorber lower pivot to the lower control arm and tighten them.

Upper Control Arm and Ball Joint

REMOVAL AND INSTALLATION

NOTE: The upper control arm and ball joint are replaced as an assembly.

1. Raise the vehicle and support it on jackstands placed under the lower control arms.

2. Remove the wheel and tire assembly.

3. Remove the cotter pin nut fastening the upper control arm and upper ball joint assembly and disconnect the upper control arm from the steering knuckle.

NOTE: Do not allow the steering knuckle to hang by the flexible brake line. Wire the steering knuckle up to the frame temporarily.

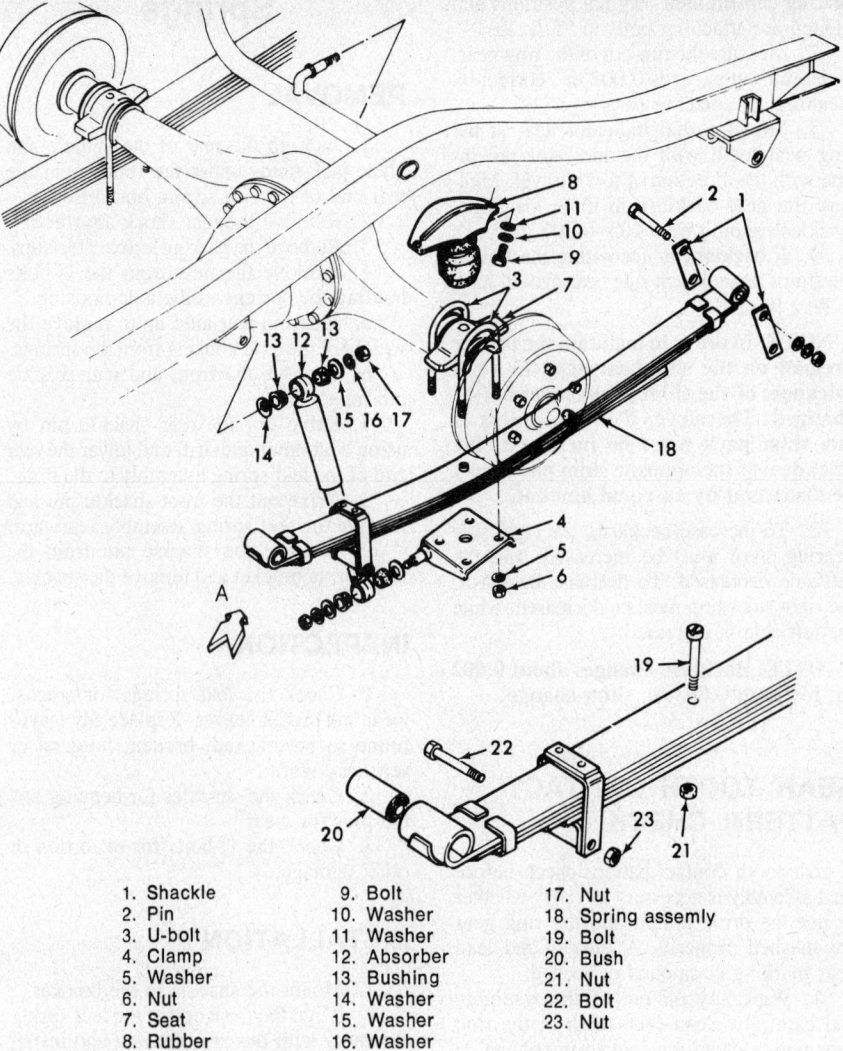

1. Shackle	9. Bolt	17. Nut
2. Pin	10. Washer	18. Spring assembly
3. U-bolt	11. Washer	19. Bolt
4. Clamp	12. Absorber	20. Bush
5. Washer	13. Bushing	21. Nut
6. Nut	14. Washer	22. Bolt
7. Seat	15. Washer	23. Nut
8. Rubber	16. Washer	

Exploded view of the rear suspension

4. Remove the two bolts from the upper pivot shaft and remove the upper control arm from the bracket. Be sure to note the position and number of shims used for adjusting the camber and caster angles when removing the upper control arm. This is to ensure that the shims are reinstalled in their original positions.

5. To remove the pivot shaft and bushings from the upper control arm assembly, remove the bushing nuts from the pivot shaft by loosening them alternately, then remove the pivot shaft.

6. To install the upper control arm and ball joint assembly, first install the pivot shaft boots to the pivot shaft.

7. Fill the internal part of the bushings with grease (molybdenum disulfide) and screw the bushings into the pivot shaft. Be sure to screw the right-side and the left-side bushings alternately into the pivot shafts, carefully avoiding getting grease on the outer face of the bushings. Tighten the nuts to 250 ft. lbs.

NOTE: Be sure that the control arm and bushings are centered properly and that the control arm rotates with resistance but is not binding on the pivot shaft when tightened to the proper torque.

8. Install the grease fittings and lubricate the parts with grease through the grease fittings.

9. Install the ball joint stub through the steering knuckle. Install the castellated nut and tighten it to 75 ft. lbs., applying enough additional torque to line up one of the castellations with the cotter pin hole. Install a new cotter pin.

10. Mount the upper control arm to the chassis frame and install the shims in their original positions between the pivot shaft and bracket. Tighten the pivot shaft attaching nuts to 55 ft. lbs.

NOTE: Tighten the thinner shim pack's nut first for improved shaft-to-frame clamping force and torque retention.

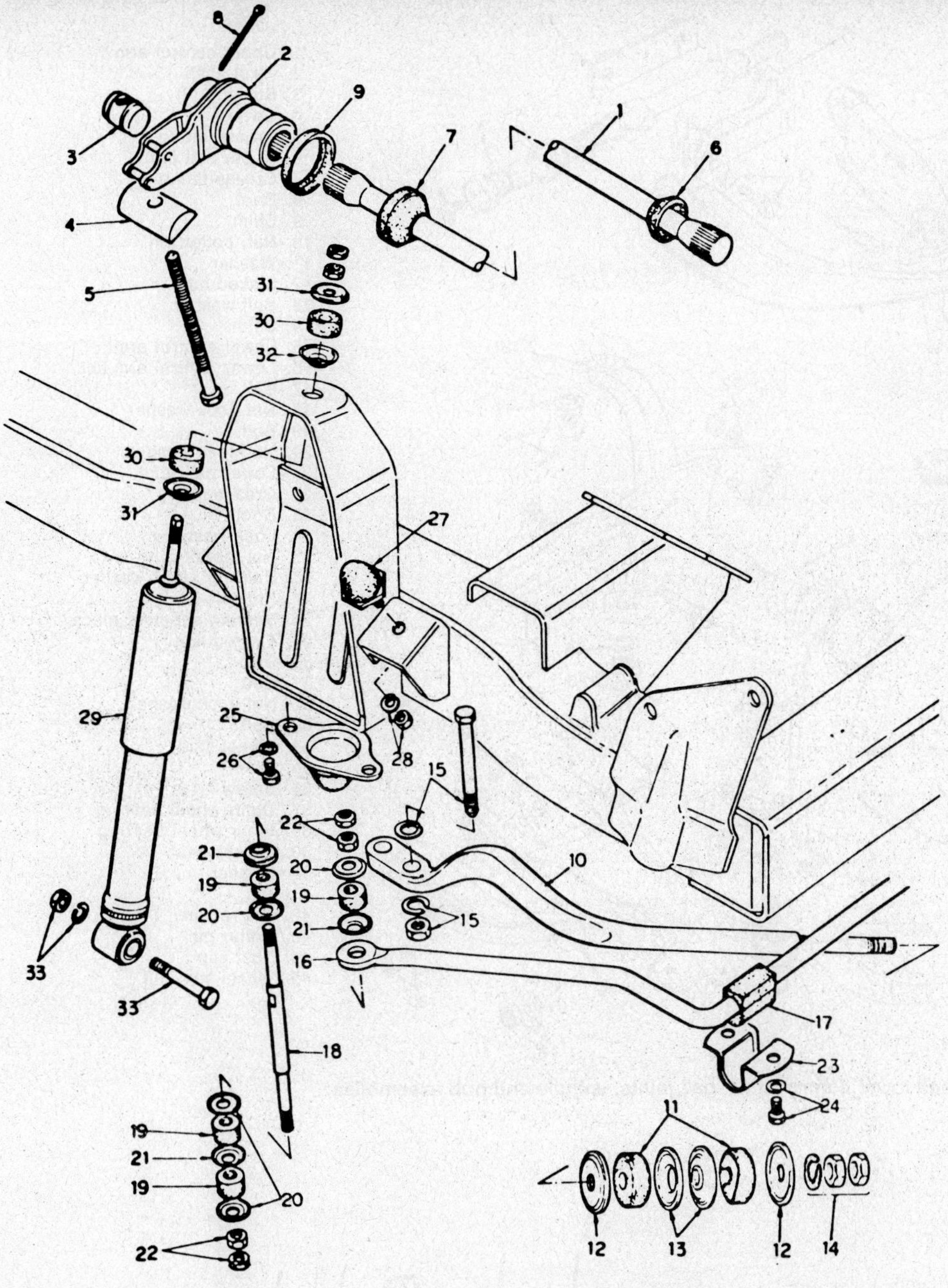

Exploded view of the stabilizer bar, strut rod, shock absorber and torsion bar assemblies

1. Torsion bar
2. Height control arm
3. Pivot nut
4. Height control seat
5. Height control bolt
6. Boot
7. Boot
8. Cotter pin
9. Seal
10. Strut rod assembly
11. Strut rod bushings
12. Strut rod washer
13. Strut rod washer
14. Nut, lock washer
15. Bolt, washer, nut
16. Stabilizer bar
17. Stabilizer bushings
18. Link stud
19. Link stud bushings
20. Stabilizer link stud washers
21. Stabilizer link stud washers
22. Nuts
23. Stabilizer bar bracket
24. Bolt and washer
25. Lower control arm bumper
26. Bolt, washer
27. Upper control arm bumpers (2)
28. Nut, washer
29. Shock absorber
30. Bushing
31. Retainer
32. Retainer
33. Bolt, lock washer, nut

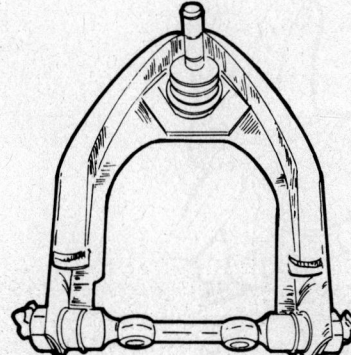

The upper control arm and ball joint assemblies

11. Install the dust cover.
12. Install the wheel and tire assembly and lower the vehicle to the floor.

Lower Ball Joint

REMOVAL AND INSTALLATION

1. Raise the front of the vehicle and support it with jackstands.
2. Remove the wheel and tire assembly.

3. Remove the cotter pin and castellated nut which retains the ball joint to the steering knuckle.
4. Remove the two bolts retaining the lower ball joint and strut rod.
5. Remove the two bolts retaining the strut rod and ball joint to the lower arm. Remove the remaining bolts from the ball joint.
6. Remove the ball joint.
7. Install the lower ball joint by mounting the joint to the lower control arm and tightening the four bolts to 45 ft. lbs.
8. Install the ball joint stud into the

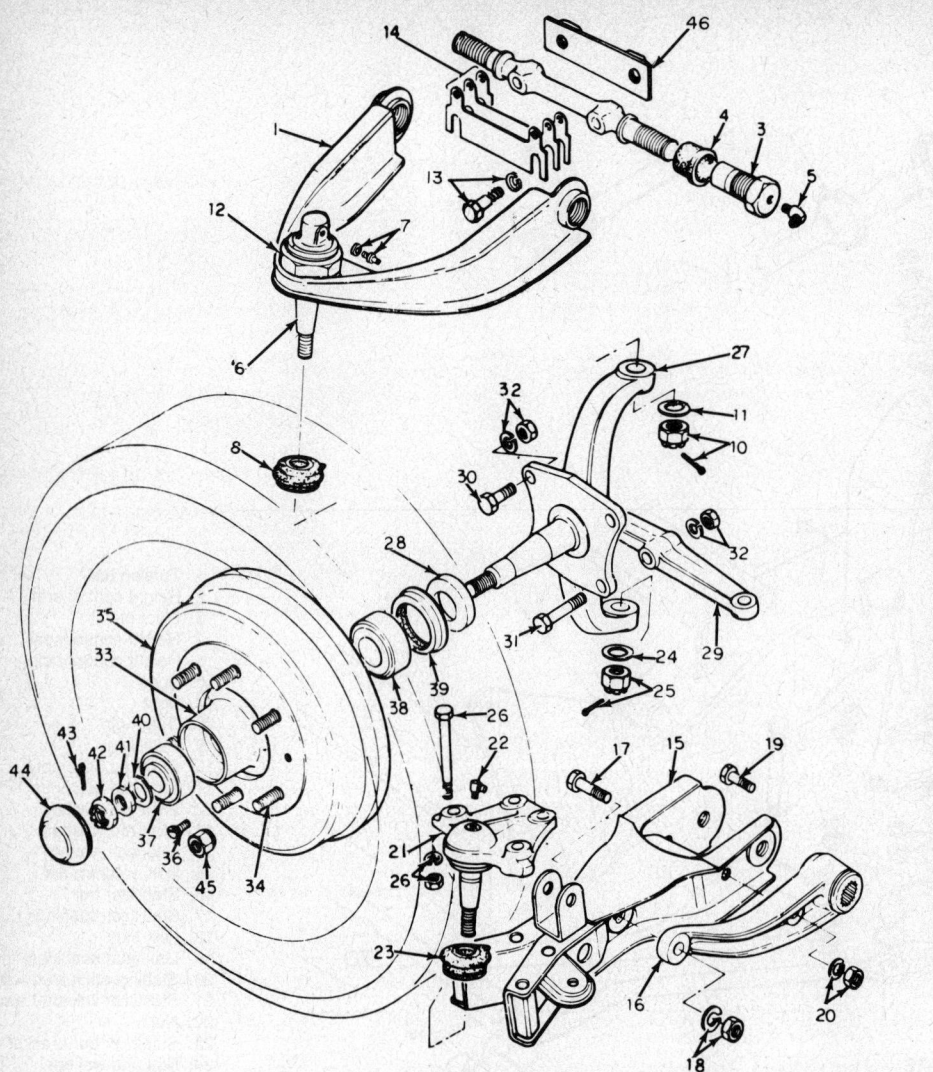

1.	Upper control arm
2.	Pivot shaft
3.	Bushing (2)
4.	Cover
5.	Grease fitting
6.	Upper ball joint
7.	Grease fitting
8.	Boot
9.	Shim
10.	Nut, cotter pin
11.	Washer
12.	Staked nut
13.	Bolt washer
14.	Shims
15.	Lower control arm
16.	Lower control arm link
17.	Bolt
18.	Nut, lock washer
19.	Bolt
20.	Nut, lock washer
21.	Lower ball joint
22.	Grease fitting
23.	Boot
24.	Lock washer
25.	Nut, cotter pin
26.	Bolt, nut, lock washer
27.	Knuckle
28.	Bearing shoulder piece
29.	Tie rod link
30.	Bolt
31.	Bolt
32.	Nut, lock washer
33.	Hub
34.	Wheel stud
35.	Drum
36.	Screw
37.	Outer wheel bearing
38.	Inner wheel bearing
39.	Grease seal
40.	Washer
41.	Nut
42.	Nut retainer
43.	Cotter pin
44.	Dust cap
45.	Wheel stud nut

Exploded view of the upper and lower control arms, ball joints, spindle and hub assemblies

steering knuckle and install the castellated nut and torque it to 75 ft. lbs. and just enough additional torque to align the cotter pin hole with one of the castellations on the nut. Install a new cotter pin.

9. Lubricate the lower ball joint through the grease fitting.

10. Install the wheel and tire assembly and lower the vehicle to the ground.

Lower Control Arm

REMOVAL AND INSTALLATION

1. Jack up the vehicle and support it with jackstands.
2. Remove the wheel and tire.
3. Remove the strut bar by removing

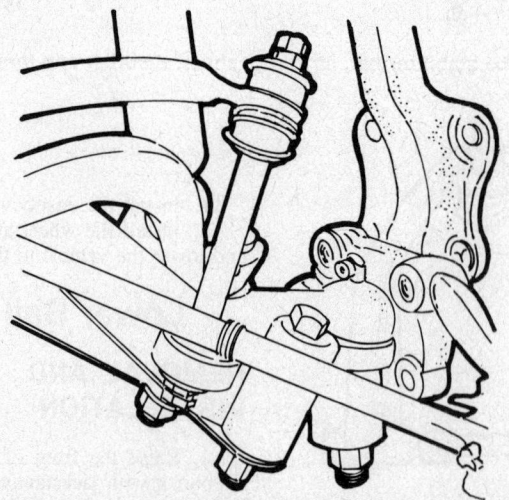

The lower ball joint assembly

the frame side bracket and the double nuts, washer and the rubber bushing from the front side of the strut bar. Next, remove the two bolts fastening the strut bar to the lower control arm and remove the bar.

4. Disconnect the stabilizer bar from the lower control arm.

5. Remove the torsion bar.

6. Disconnect the shock absorber from the lower control arm.

7. If you so desire, remove the lower ball joint from the lower control arm joint at this time.

8. Remove the retaining nut and drive out the bolt holding the lower control arm to the chassis with a soft metal drift. Remove the lower control arm from the vehicle.

9. To install the lower control arm, first, install the lower ball joint to the lower control arm. Tighten the retaining nuts to 45 ft. lbs.

10. Mount the lower control arm to the frame. Drive the bolt into position carefully with a soft metal drift. Use care not to damage the serrated portions. Tighten the nut on the end of the pivot bolt to 135 ft. lbs.

11. Install the stabilizer bar to the lower control arm.

12. Place the washers and bushings on the strut rod and install it through the frame bracket. Install the second set of washers and bushings on the strut rod together with the lockwashers and nut. Leave the nut loose temporarily.

13. Install the strut rod to the lower control arm and tighten the bolts to 45 ft. lbs.

14. Assemble the lower ball joint to the steering knuckle.

15. Install the wheel and tire and lower the vehicle.

16. Tighten the first strut bar-to-chassis frame attaching nut to 175 ft. lbs., and the second locknut to 55 ft. lbs.

Free Wheeling Hub

FOUR WHEEL DRIVE MODELS REMOVAL AND INSTALLATION

1. Jack up your vehicle and support it with jack stands.

2. Place the transfer case in the 2H position.

3. Set the hubs in the free position.

4. Remove the hub cover bolts and remove the hub cover.

COVER ASSEMBLY

1. While pushing the follower toward the knob, turn the clutch assembly clockwise, and then remove the clutch assembly from the knob.

2. Remove the snap-ring and remove the knob from the cover.

NOTE: Do not lose the detent ball.

3. Remove the ball and spring from the knob.

4. Remove the X-ring from the knob, by pressing if off with your fingers.

NOTE: Do not use a screwdriver to remove this ring because it may scratch the ring.

5. Remove the compression spring, retaining spring, and the follower from the clutch assembly.

6. Remove the retaining spring from the clutch assembly by turning it counter-clockwise.

BODY ASSEMBLY

1. Remove the snap-ring, and then remove the inner assembly from the body.

2. Separate the ring, inner, and spacer by removing the snap-ring.

3. Installation is the reverse of removal with the following suggestions:

Apply grease to the X-ring, the inner

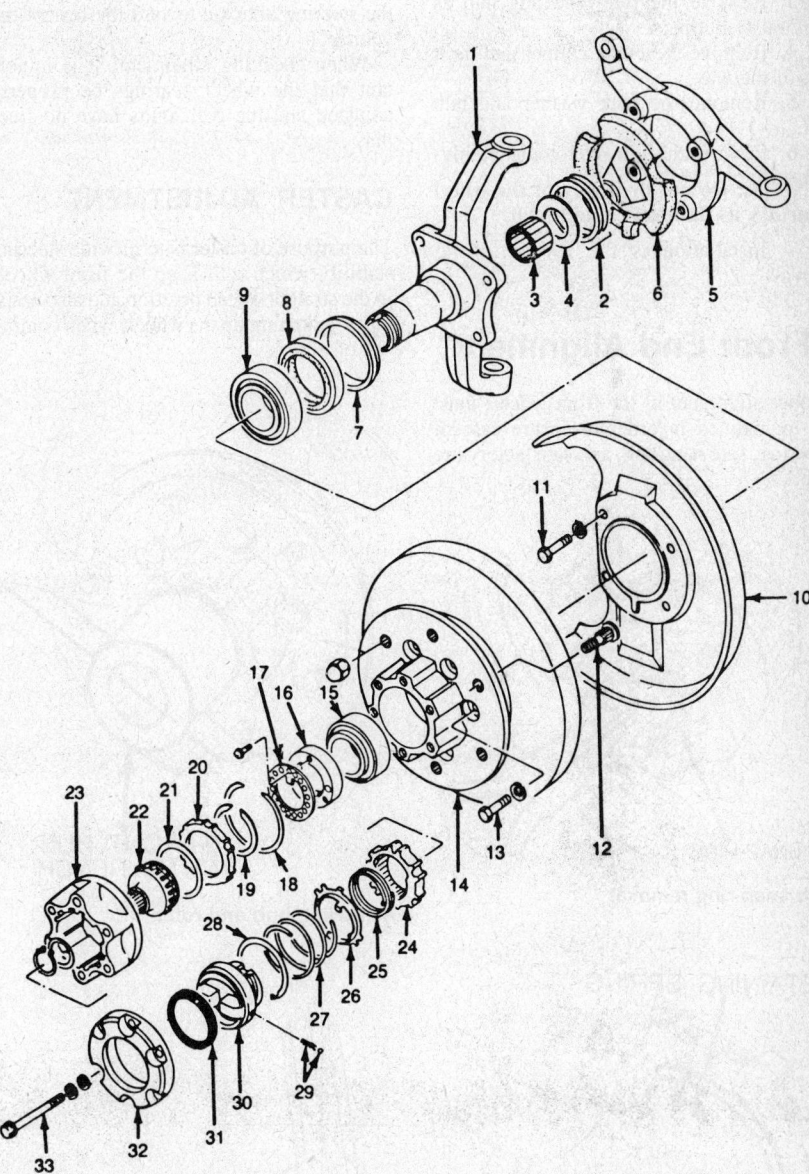

Exploded view 4-wheel drive hub

1. Knuckle	12. Wheel pin	23. Body
2. Oil seal	13. Bolt	24. Clutch
3. Washer	14. Hub and disc	25. Retaining spring
4. Bearing	15. Outer wheel bearing	26. Follower
5. Adapter	16. Hub nut	27. Compression spring
6. Shield	17. Lock washer	28. Snap-ring
7. Retainer ring	18. Shim	29. Detent ball and spring
8. Oil seal	19. Snap-ring	30. Knob
9. Inner hub bearing	20. Ring	31. X-ring
10. Dust shield	21. Spacer	32. Cover
11. Bolt	22. Inner	33. Bolt

cover and the outside circumference of the knob.

Front Wheel Hub

REMOVAL AND INSTALLATION

1. Jack up your vehicle and support it with jack stands.
2. Remove the front wheel.
3. Remove the free wheeling hub as previously outlined.
4. Remove the brake caliper and tie it out of the way.
5. Remove the lock washer and hub nut.
6. Remove the hub and rotor assembly.

NOTE: Do not drop any of the wheel bearings as damage could result.

7. Installation is the reverse of removal.

Front End Alignment

Proper alignment of the front wheels must be maintained in order to ensure ease of steering, safe handling, and satisfactory tire life.

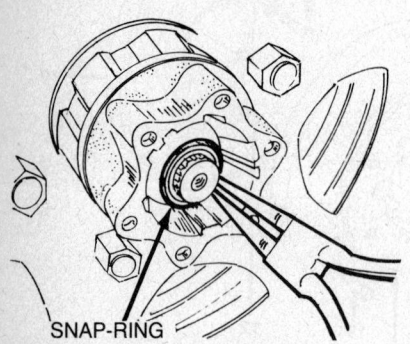

SNAP-RING

Hub snap-ring removal

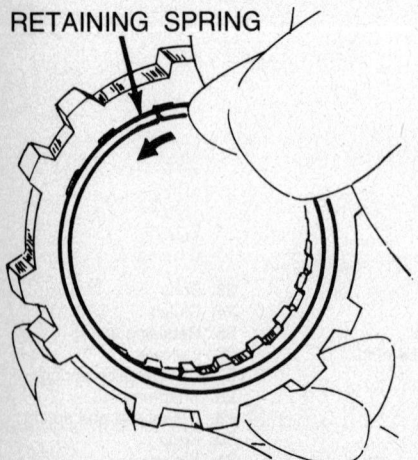

Removing the retaining spring

RETAINING SPRING

The most important factors of front wheel alignment are wheel camber, axle caster, and wheel toe-in.

Wheel toe-in is the distance by which the wheels are closer together at the front than at the rear.

Wheel camber is the amount in which the top of the wheels incline outward from the vertical.

Front axle caster is the amount in degrees which the steering knuckle pivot axis is tilted toward the rear of the vehicle. Positive caster is the inclination of the top of the steering knuckle toward the rear of the vehicle.

When checking alignment, it is important that the wheel bearings be properly adjusted and the ball joints have no free-play.

CASTER ADJUSTMENT

The purpose of caster is to provide steering stability which will keep the front wheels in the straight-ahead position and also assist in straightening up the wheels when coming out of a turn.

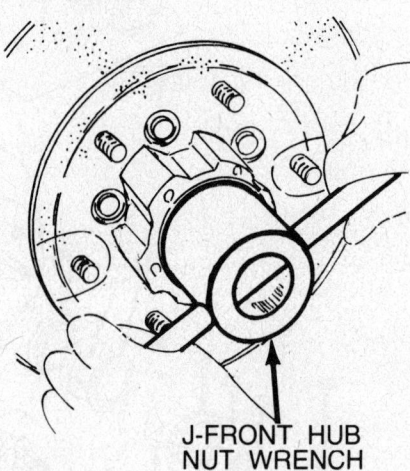

J-FRONT HUB NUT WRENCH

Removing hub and rotor

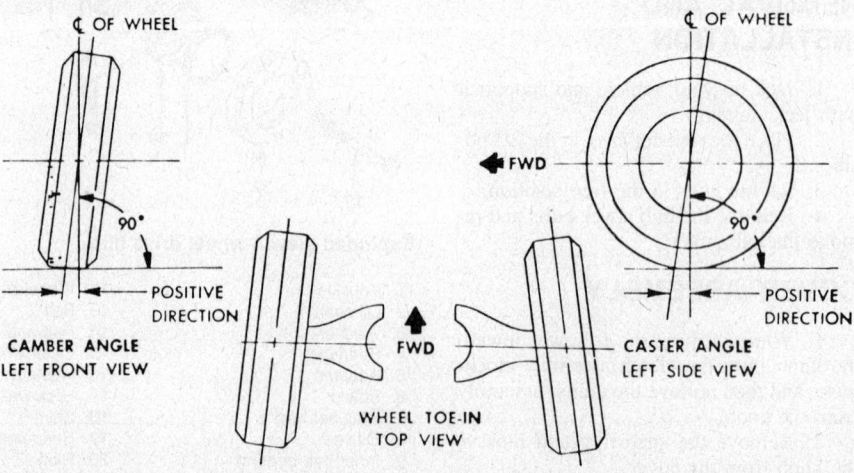

Camber, toe-in and caster

The caster is adjusted by adding or subtracting spacer shims from either the front or rear upper control arm pivot shaft attaching bolts.

CAMBER ADJUSTMENT

The purpose of camber is to more nearly place the weight of the vehicle over the tire contact patch on the road to facilitate ease of steering. The result of excessive camber is irregular wear of the tires on the outside shoulder and is usually caused by bent parts. Excessive negative camber will also cause hard steering and possibly wandering. The tires will wear on the inside shoulders.

The camber angle is adjusted by adding or subtracting spacer shims from both the front and rear upper control arm pivot shaft attaching bolts. The same amount of shims is added or subtracted to both of the bolts at the same time.

TOE-IN

The toe-in measurement is the difference between the distances between the front and rear center of the tread of the two front tires.

The toe-in can be adjusted by turning the intermediate rod after loosening the locknuts on the intermediate rod ends. The locknuts have left-hand and right-hand threads to allow for equal adjustment of both wheels at the same time. Turn the intermediate rod toward the front of the vehicle to reduce the toe-in angle and toward the rear of the vehicle to increase the toe-in angle.

RIDE HEIGHT ADJUSTMENT

NOTE: The ride height should be measured with a full tank of gas, spare tire, jack, no passengers, and with the tires inflated to the correct pressure.

1. Place the vehicle on a smooth level floor and bounce the front end several times.

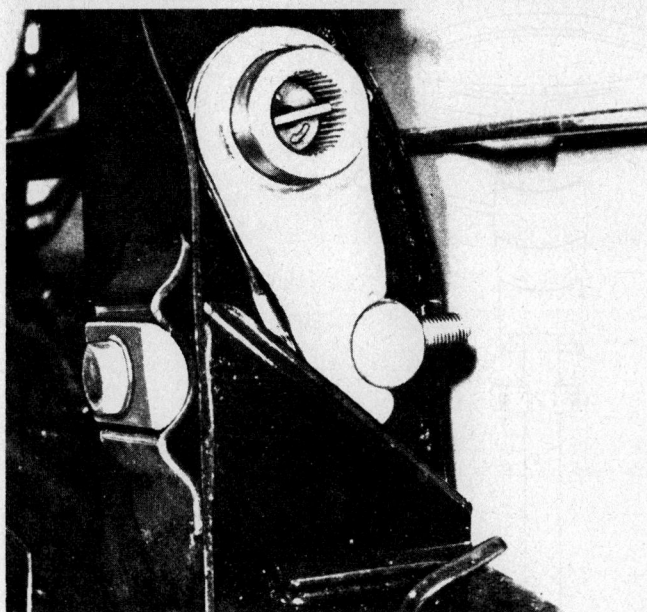

Vehicle ride height adjustment end of the torsion bar

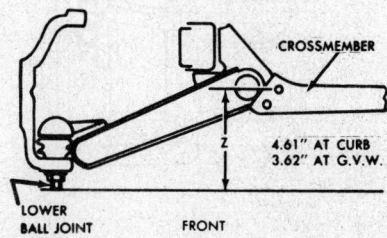

Ride height adjustment at the front of the vehicle

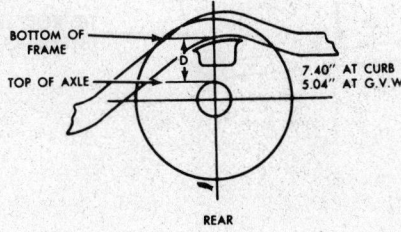

Ride height measurement at the rear of the vehicle

be 7.90 in. (6.26 in. with the vehicle loaded to GVW).

5. After obtaining the correct clearances, securely tighten the strut bar attaching nuts to the proper torque.

STEERING

Steering Wheel

REMOVAL AND INSTALLATION

1. Disconnect the battery ground cable.

2. Remove the horn shroud and spring by pushing and turning it counterclockwise. Remove the horn contact ring and wire.

3. Remove the steering wheel-to-steering shaft retaining nut, washer and lockwasher.

4. Mark the relative position of the steering wheel and shaft to each other with a scribe.

5. Remove the steering column cowling by removing the four attaching screws and washers.

6. Remove the steering wheel from the shaft with a puller.

NOTE: Under no circumstances is the steering shaft to be hammered, jarred, or leaned upon. The steering column is a collapsible, energy-absorbing type and can be easily damaged through mistreatment.

7. Install the steering wheel in the reverse order of removal, aligning the marks made on the steering wheel and the shaft. Draw the steering wheel onto the shaft with the attaching nut.

Turn Signal and Dimmer Switch

REMOVAL AND INSTALLATION

1. Disconnect the battery ground cable.

2. Remove the four screws retaining the steering column cowling and remove the cowling.

3. Remove the wire connectors from the switch.

4. Remove the switch by removing the two screws which retain the switch clamp to the steering column mast jacket.

5. Replace the switch in the reverse order of removal.

Raise the vehicle and then allow it to settle to a normal height.

2. Measure the distance between the bottom of the lower ball joint stud which fits through the steering knuckle and the ground and the distance between the frame crossmember that the lower control arm attaches to and the ground.

The difference between these two measurements should be 2.52 in. (1.54 in. with the vehicle loaded to GVW).

3. Adjust the vehicle height by first loosening the nuts on the front end of the strut bar and then turning the vehicle height adjusting bolt. Turn the bolt clockwise to raise the vehicle. As an additional check, measure the clearance between the rubber bumper and the lower control arm. The clearance should be 7/8 in.

4. Check the ride height at the front of the vehicle as outlined in Step 2 and the ride height at the rear axle by measuring the clearance between the top of the axle and the bottom of the frame where the frame rises to clear the axle. The clearance between the frame and axle at this point should

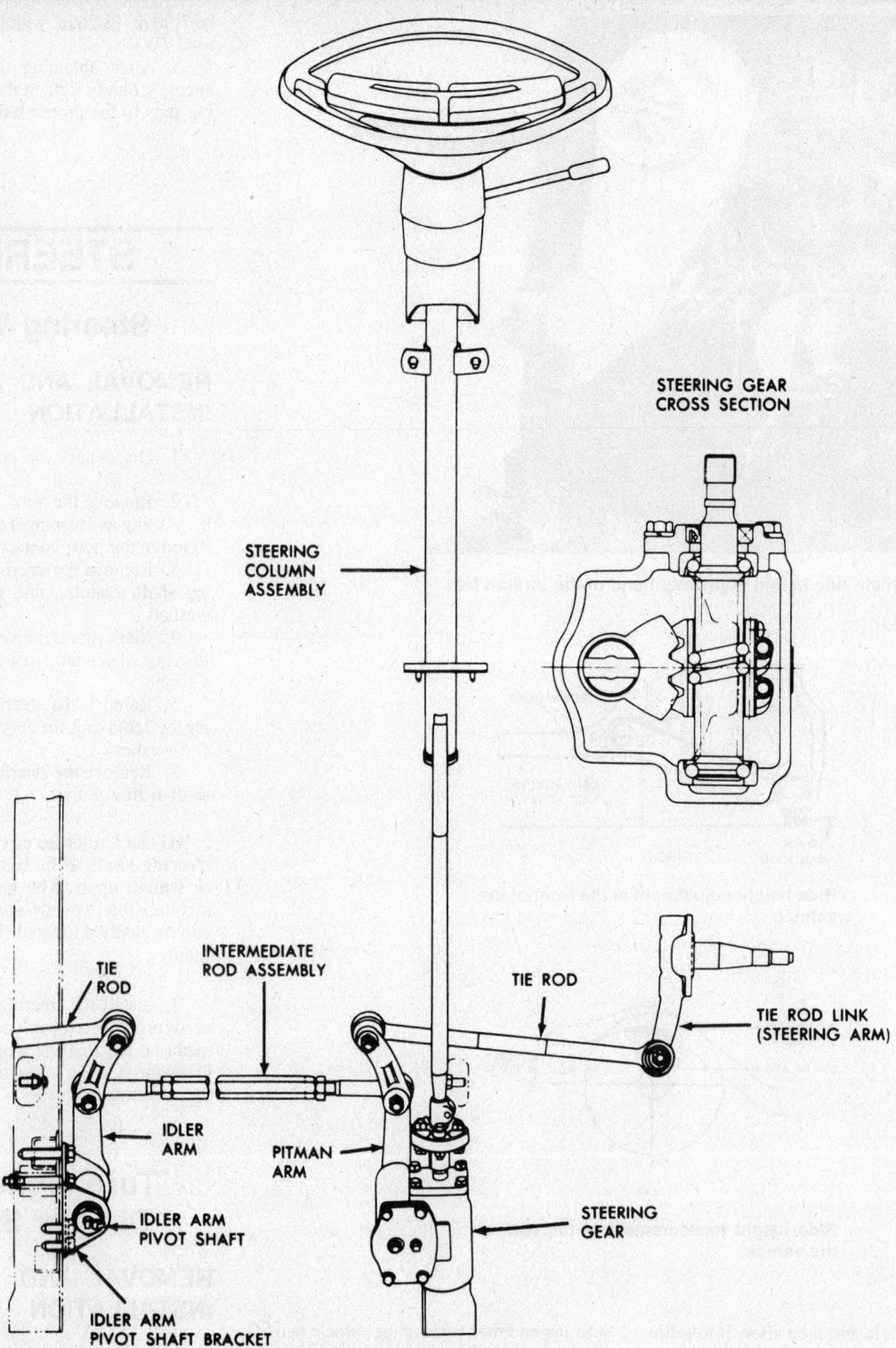

STEERING GEAR CROSS SECTION

STEERING COLUMN ASSEMBLY

TIE ROD

INTERMEDIATE ROD ASSEMBLY

TIE ROD

TIE ROD LINK (STEERING ARM)

IDLER ARM

PITMAN ARM

STEERING GEAR

IDLER ARM PIVOT SHAFT

IDLER ARM PIVOT SHAFT BRACKET

Steering linkage and cross-sectional view of the steering gear

Manual Steering Gear

REMOVAL AND INSTALLATION

1. Raise the vehicle on a hoist.
2. Remove the Pitman arm nut and

washer and mark the relationship of the shaft to the arm. Using a puller, remove the Pitman arm from the Pitman shaft.

3. Remove the engine stone shield.

4. Remove the two lower flexible coupling clamp bolts.

5. Remove the steering gear-to-frame

bolts and remove the steering gear from the vehicle.

6. Install the steering gear in the reverse order of removal, installing the mounting bolts loosely at first and tightening the large bolts to 55 ft. lbs. and the small ones to 20 ft. lbs. only after the flexible coupling bolts have been tightened to 20 ft. lbs.

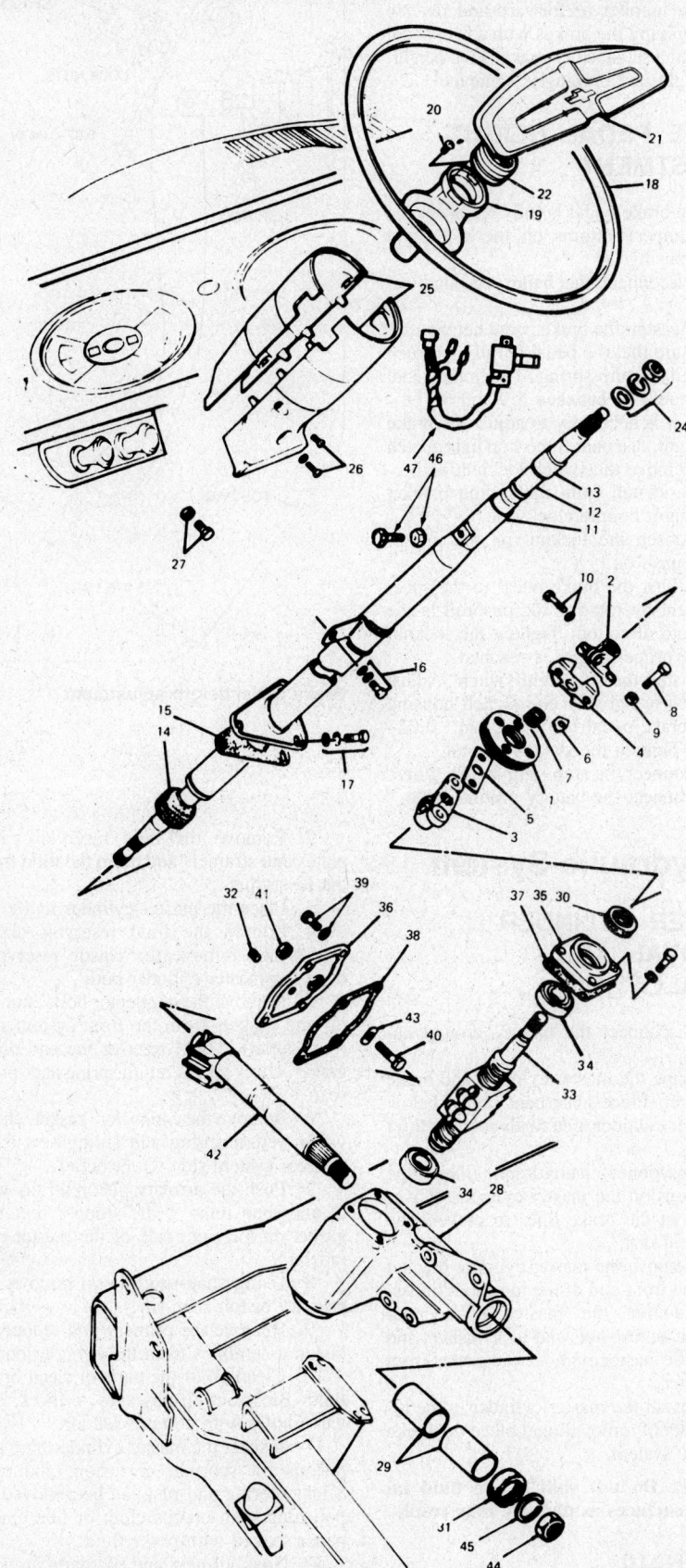

1. Coupling
2. Flange, upper coupling
3. Flange, lower coupling
4. Cross-strap
5. Cross-strap
6. Thrust washer
7. Spring
8. Thru-bolt
9. Lock nut
10. Pinch bolt, lock washer
11. Mast jacket
12. Shaft assembly
13. Bushing
14. Grommet
15. Gasket
16. Bolt and washers
17. Screw and washers
18. Wheel assembly
19. Horn shroud seat
20. Screw
21. Horn shroud
22. Spring
23. Nut
24. Shaft nut and washers
25. Column cowling
26. Cowling screws and washers
27. Bolt, washer
28. Steering gear housing
29. Sector shaft bushings
30. Wormshaft seal
31. Sector (Pitman) shaft seal
32. Filler plug
33. Worm & ball nut assembly
34. Wormshaft bearing
35. End cover
36. Top cover
37. Worm preload shims
38. Gasket
39. Bolt, lock washer
40. Sector adjuster screw
41. Lock nut
42. Sector shaft
43. Adjusting shim
44. Pitman shaft nut
45. Lock washer
46. Bolt, nut (stopper)
47. Hazard warning switch assembly

Exploded view of the steering system components

BRAKE SYSTEMS

On 1975 LUV trucks the front brakes are of the twin-leading shoe type which incorporate two wheel cylinders at each wheel. The front wheel cylinder actuates the lower brake shoe and the rear cylinder the upper brake shoe. The brake linings are molded and bonded to the brake shoes. On 1976 and later models the front brakes are of the floating disc type which incorporates a single piston actuating both inner and outer pads.

The rear brakes are of the duo-servo type with a single wheel cylinder on each wheel. The wheel cylinder has two pistons, actuating both the leading and trailing brake shoes. The brake lining is also molded and bonded to the brake shoes. The leading lining is smaller than the trailing lining.

The hydraulic brakes on all LUV models are vacuum-assisted. The self-adjusters on the 1975 and later front brakes operate during forward stops and the self-adjusters on the rear brakes of all models adjust on rear stops.

The parking brake is actuated by a ratchet-type L-handle mounted to the dash at the right of the steering column. A cable connects the handle to the intermediate cable by means of a lever. The intermediate cable attaches to the two rear cables which operate the rear service brakes. Adjustment of the parking brake is provided at the equalizer.

Adjustment

Disc brakes require no adjustments. Drum brakes, although self-adjusting, may require an initial adjustment after the brakes have been replaced, or whenever the adjuster position has been changed. The final adjustment is made by using the self-adjusting mechanism.

1. With the brake drum removed, disengage the pullback springs from the adjuster plates on the front brakes, or the actuator from the starwheel on the rear brakes.

2. Using the brake drum as an adjustment gauge, adjust the upper and lower shoes an equal number of notches on the front brakes, or turn the starwheel on the rear brakes until the brake drum slides over the brake shoes with a slight drag.

3. Retract the upper and lower shoes of the front brakes two notches, or turn the starwheel the rear brakes 1¼ turns to retract the shoes.

4. Install the brake drums and wheels and lower the vehicle.

NOTE: If the backing plate access plugs were removed on the front brakes, make sure that they are reinstalled before making the final adjustment. Also, the brake drums are to be installed in the same position from which they were removed. Make sure that you can install the drum-to-flange locating screw.

5. Perform the final adjustment by making a number of forward and reverse stops, applying the brakes with a firm pedal effort until a satisfactory brake pedal height, and straight-line braking is achieved.

BRAKE PEDAL HEIGHT ADJUSTMENT

When the brake pedal is fully released, the pedal bumper bottoms on the stop light switch housing.

1. Disconnect the battery ground cable.

2. Measure the brake pedal height after making sure that the pedal is fully returned by the pedal return spring. The brake pedal height should be between 5.9 and 6.3 in.

3. If it is necessary to adjust the brake pedal height, disconnect the stop light switch wiring, remove the switch locknut, and remove the switch from the switch bracket by rotating it counterclockwise.

4. Loosen the locknut on the master cylinder pushrod.

5. Adjust the brake pdeal to the specified height by rotating the pushrod in the appropriate direction. Tighten the locknut when the proper height is reached.

6. Install the stop light switch. Adjust the clearance between the switch housing and the brake pedal tab to 0.03 in., 0.02–0.04 in. Tighten the switch locknut.

7. Connect the stop light switch wires.

8. Connect the battery ground cable.

Hydraulic System

MASTER CYLINDER REMOVAL AND INSTALLATION

1. Disconnect the battery ground cable.

2. Wipe the master cylinder and brake lines clean. Place absorbent cloths below the master cylinder area to absorb any fluid leakage.

3. Disconnect the hydraulic lines at the connections on the master cylinder. Cover the ends of the brake lines to prevent the entrance of dirt.

4. Remove the master cylinder bracket bolt at the front end of the master cylinder.

5. Remove the master cylinder-to-booster attaching nuts and lockwashers and remove the master cylinder and gasket from the booster.

6. Install the master cylinder in the reverse order of removal, and bleed the brake hydraulic system.

NOTE: Do not spill brake fluid on painted surfaces as damage may result.

OVERHAUL

1. Remove the master cylinder from the vehicle.

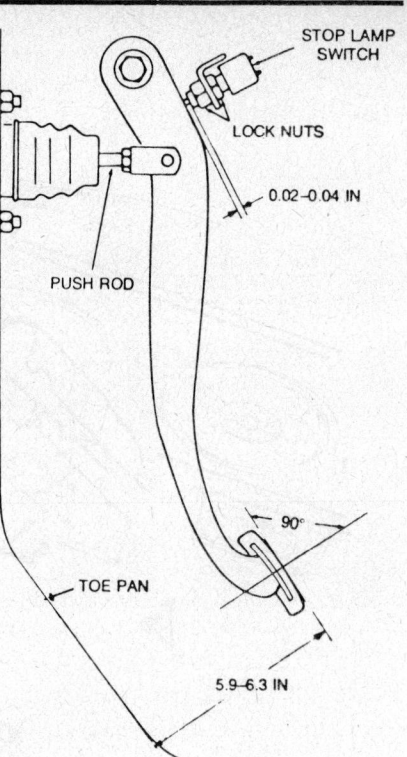

Brake pedal height adjustment

2. Remove the fluid reservoir caps, plates and strainers and drain the fluid from the reservoirs.

3. Place the master cylinder in a vise.

4. Loosen the fluid reservoir clamp screws and remove the plastic reservoirs from the master cylinder body.

5. Remove the connector bolt, connector and gaskets from the front system side (rear outlet). Then, remove the end plug, gasket, check valve, return spring and spring seat.

6. Remove the connector, gasket, check valve, return spring and spring seat from the rear system side (front outlet).

7. Push the primary piston all the way in and then remove the stopper bolt and gasket on the right side of the master cylinder.

8. Using snap-ring pliers, remove the primary piston snap-ring.

9. Remove the primary and secondary piston assemblies from the cylinder bore.

10. Clean all of the parts in clean brake fluid. Blow out all passages, orifices, and valve holes with compressed air.

11. Inspect the master cylinder bore and pistons for scoring, corrosion, and rust. Slight scoring and rust can be removed by polishing with crocus cloth or fine emery paper soaked with brake fluid.

12. Soak all new and old parts in clean brake fluid before reassembling.

13. Insert the secondary piston assembly into the master cylinder bore, so that the

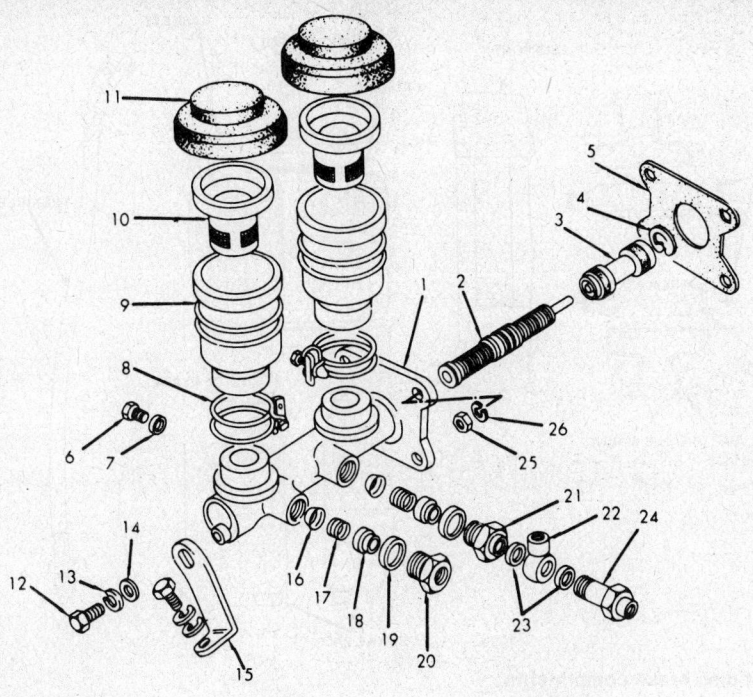

1. Master cylinder
2. Secondary piston
3. Primary piston
4. Snap ring
5. Gasket*
6. Stopper bolt
7. Gasket*
8. Clamp
9. Reservoir
10. Filter
11. Cover
12. Bolt
13. Lock washer
14. Washer
15. Bracket
16. Spring seat
17. Return spring
18. Check valve
19. Gasket*
20. Connector
21. End pulg
22. Connector
23. Gasket*
24. Connector bolt*
25. Nut
26. Washer
NOTE (*) Included in REPAIR KIT

Exploded view of the brake master cylinder

primary stem guide is projected slightly beyond the cylinder bore end.

14. Insert the primary piston into the master cylinder bore so that the secondary piston stem guide enters the hole in the primary piston.

15. Install the snap-ring into the groove in the master cylinder housing.

16. Depress the primary piston and install the piston stopper bolt and new gasket.

17. Install the spring seat, return spring, check valve, new gasket and end plug in the front system side of the master cylinder (rear outlet).

18. Install a new gasket on either side of the connector and secure it into position with the connector bolt.

19. Install the spring seat, return spring, check valve, new gasket and connector in the rear system side of the master cylinder (front outlet).

20. Install the clamps over the lower ends of the fluid reservoirs, place the reservoirs in position on the master cylinder body and then tighten the clamp bolts.

21. Install the reservoir filters, and fill the reservoirs with clean brake fluid. Push in on the primary piston to determine that it returns smoothly. Test the piston assembly two or three times to make sure that fluid comes out of the front and rear outlets.

22. Install the plates and covers.

23. Install plugs in all of the connector outlet ports.

24. Fill the reservoirs to the proper level with clean brake fluid.

25. Insert a rod with a smooth round end to the piston end and press it in to compress the piston return spring.

26. Release the pressure on the rod. Watch for air bubbles in the reservoir fluid.

27. Repeat Steps 25 and 26 as long as bubbles appear in the fluid.

28. Install the master cylinder on the vehicle and bleed the brake hydraulic system.

Power Cylinder

REMOVAL AND INSTALLATION

1. Disconnect the negative battery terminal.

2. Disconnect the brake lines at the master cylinder. Cap them immediately.

3. Remove the bracket connecting the power unit to the fender skirt.

4. Remove the vacuum line from the power unit and move it out of the way.

5. Disconnect the brake pedal return spring, brake pedal-to-pushrod clevis pin, and cotter pin and washer.

6. Remove the power unit-to-firewall nuts and remove the master cylinder and power cylinder as a unit.

7. Installation is reverse of removal.

NOTE: Remember to bleed the brake system upon installation of the power unit. Also, the piston rod height should be checked before the power unit is installed. The height is 0.729 to 0.736 in., measured from the master cylinder mounting face of the power unit to the top of the push rod, when the rod is bottomed in the power cylinder.

Bleeding

The brake hydraulic system must be bled after any line has been disconnected or air has somehow found its way into the system.

The bleeding operation should start with the wheel cylinder nearest the master cylinder and end with the one farthest away.

NOTE: Do not bleed the brakes with the brake drums or calipers removed.

1. Make sure that the master cylinder is full and kept at least ¾ full throughout the entire bleeding process. Check the fluid level in the master cylinder reservoirs frequently during the bleeding operation.

2. Remove the cap from the wheel cylinder or caliper bleeder valve. Position a wrench on the bleeder valve and place a rubber hose over the bleeder valve nipple.

3. Place the other end of the bleeder hose into a clear container containing enough brake fluid to ensure that the end of the bleeder hose will remain submerged.

4. Start the engine and allow it to run during the actual bleeding of each wheel cylinder. This is so vacuum can be applied to the brake booster during the bleeding process.

5. Open the wheel cylinder bleeder valve by turning the wrench counterclockwise about ¾ of a turn. Have an assistant depress the brake pedal. Just before the brake pedal reaches the end of its travel, close the bleeder valve and allow the brake pedal to return slowly to the released position. Repeat this operation until the brake fluid being expelled is free from air bubbles, then close the bleeder valve tightly.

6. Remove the bleeder hose and the wrench from the bleeder valve and install them onto the next wheel cylinder or caliper to be bled. Repeat step 5 on all of the remaining wheel cylinders. Don't forget to check and replenish the brake fluid in the master cylinder reservoirs.

7. After bleeding the brake hydraulic system, check the operation of the brakes. Depress the brake pedal several times then hold it depressed. Notice how far the pedal can be depressed. Release the pedal for about 10 seconds, then depress it again and hold it, taking notice of the distance which it can be depressed before it stops with the same amount of pedal pressure applied as before. If the pedal depresses further or can be

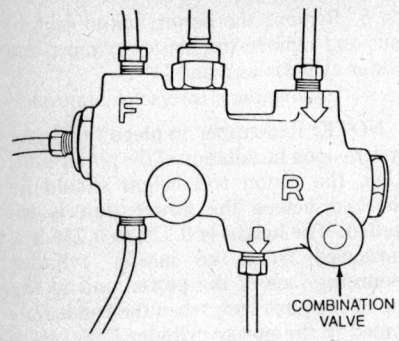

Combination valve

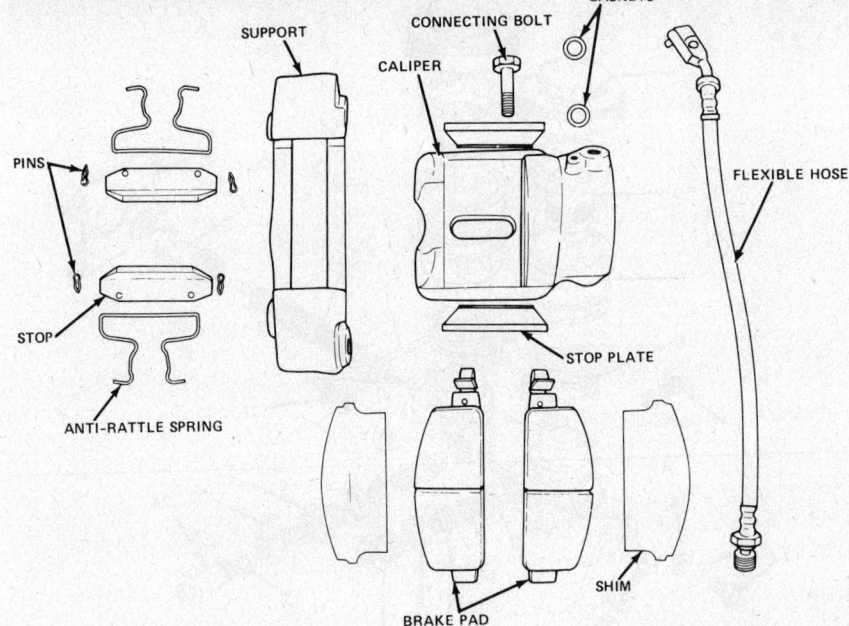

Front disc brake components

COMBINATION VALVE

The combination valve consists of the differential valve (failure indicator) combined with the proportioning valve (pressure control valve). It is mounted on the left side inner fender and is connected to the master cylinder.

The fail indicator incorporates a hydraulic differential switch. A wiring harness connects the electrical terminal of this switch to the brake warning light on the dashboard.

The pressure control valve is a proportioning valve that controls the fluid pressure to the rear brakes to prevent wheel lockup.

This valve cannot be repaired; if found to be defective, it must be replaced.

Front Disc Brakes

DISC BRAKE PADS INSPECTION

Replace the front disc brake pads whenever the wear indicator makes a squeaking noise or when the lining pad is worn to within .039″ of the shoe surface. All four brake pads should always be replaced at the same time (both front wheels together).

REMOVAL AND INSTALLATION

1. Jack up the truck and safely support it with jackstands.
2. Remove the wheel and tire assembly.
3. Remove the pins from the caliper stops and then remove the stops.
4. Remove the caliper from the support, remove the stop plates from the caliper then suspend the caliper assembly from the upper link or frame using a piece of heavy wire.
5. Remove the shoe and lining assem-

"pumped up", then it can be assumed that there is still air in the hydraulic system and further bleeding is required.

blies and shims and mark the locations if to be reinstalled.
6. Remove the anti-rattle springs from the support.
7. Wipe the inside of the caliper clean, including the exterior of the dust seal. Check to see that the dust seal is in good condition.
8. Install the anti-rattle springs, shims and the shoe and lining asemblies to the support.

NOTE: If original linings are being reinstalled, they must be installed in the original position. Also position the wear indicators to the lower side of the support.

9. Install new stop plates to the caliper, then install the caliper, stops and stop pins.
10. Install the wheel and tire assembly.

Disc Brake Calipers

REMOVAL AND INSTALLATION

1. Raise the vehicle on a lift.
2. Remove the wheel and tire assembly.
3. Remove the pins from the caliper stops and then remove the stops.
4. Disconnect the front flexible hose from the brake line.

NOTE: To keep dirt from entering, cap or tape the openings of the flexible hose and brake line.

5. Remove the caliper from the support and remove the stop plates from the caliper.

OVERHAUL

1. Remove the flexible hose from the caliper.
2. Remove the dust seal from the caliper using a small screwdriver.
3. Insert a block of wood into the caliper and force out the piston by applying compressed air into the caliper at the flexible hose attachment. Remove and discard the piston square ring seal.

— CAUTION —
Do not place fingers in front of the piston in an attempt to catch or protect it when applying compressed air.

4. Clean all parts in clean brake fluid. Check the cylinder bore and pistons for wear, scuffing or corrosion and replace as necessary.
5. Apply a silicone lube to the caliper bore and the piston square ring seal and

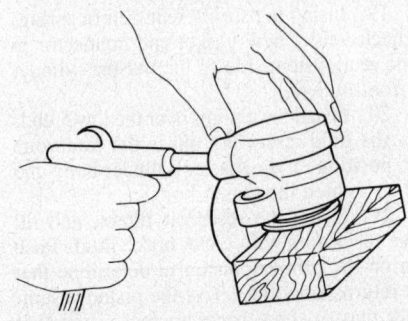

Removing caliper piston with compressed air

insert the piston seal into the caliper bore using finger pressure only.

6. Apply a silicone lubricant to the piston and assemble the dust seal to the piston and caliper. Install the seal ring into the dust seal.

7. Install the flexible hose to the caliper using new gaskets.

8. Lubricate the stop plates and the sliding surfaces of the caliper then install the new stop plates to the caliper, the caliper and the new stop pins.

9. Connect the flexible brake hose to the brake line.

10. Install the wheel and tire assembly.

NOTE: Remember to bleed the brake system following reinstallation.

Brake Disc

REMOVAL AND INSTALLATION

1. Raise the vehicle on a lift.
2. Remove the front tire and wheel assembly.
3. Remove the bolts attaching the caliper support to the adapter and then suspend the caliper and support from the upper link or frame using a piece of heavy wire.
4. Remove the hub grease cap, cotter pin, spindle nut retainer and nut and remove the hub and rotor assembly.
5. Replace the hub and disc as an assembly if either needs replacement.

NOTE: All brake disc have a minimum thickness dimension cast into them. This dimension is the minimum wear dimension and not a refinish dimension.

6. Install the dust shield and adapter to the steering knuckle and torque the long bolts to 55 ft. lbs. and the small bolts to 35 ft. lbs.
7. Install the front hub and disc assembly and adjust the wheel bearings.
8. Assemble the caliper and support assembly to the adapter and torque the bolts to 64 ft. lbs.
9. Install the front wheel and tire assembly.

NOTE: On 4-wheel drive vehicles, see the section on Free Wheel Hub Removal before attempting this procedure.

Front Drum Brakes

BRAKE DRUMS
1975 MODELS ONLY
REMOVAL AND INSTALLATION

1. Jack up the vehicle and support it on jackstands.
2. Remove the wheel cover and remove the wheel and tire assembly.

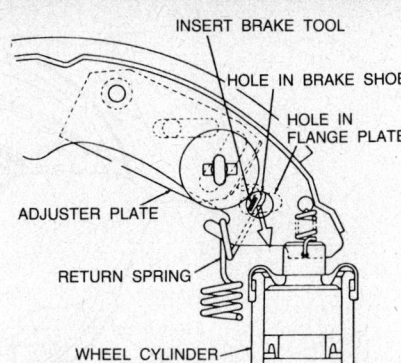

Insert a brake adjusting tool through the hole in the backing plate and the brake shoe. Raise and release the end of the return spring and move the brake in towards the wheel cylinder.

3. Remove the brake drum and hub retaining screws and remove the drum. Identify the drum so that it can be reinstalled in the same position.

If the brake drums are worn considerably, it may be necessary to retract the brake shoes before the drum can be removed. Remove the rubber hole plugs in the backing plate and insert a screwdriver through the hole and into the hole in the brake shoe. Raise the end of the brake shoe return spring to release it from the serration and contact the brake shoe by moving it in toward the wheel cylinder.

NOTE: Never depress the brake pedal when the brake drums are removed.

4. Install the brake drums in the reverse order of removal.

INSPECTION

After removing the brake drum, remove any dirt and inspect the drum for cracks, deep grooves, roughness, scoring, or out-of-roundness. Replace any brake drum which is cracked completely through.

Smooth any slight scores by polishing the friction surface with fine emery paper. Heavy or extensive scoring will cause ex-

cessive brake lining wear and should be removed from the brake drum through resurfacing of the brake drum friction surface. The maximum finished inside diameter of the brake drums must not exceed 10.059 in. The brake drum must be replaced if the diameter is 10.079 in. or greater.

BRAKE SHOES
REMOVAL AND INSTALLATION

The brake linings must be replaced when the lining thickness is 0.059 in. or less.

1. Remove the brake drum.
2. Disconnect the wheel cylinder piston springs from the pistons and shoes with a pair of pliers.
3. Depress and rotate the hold-down spring retainers 90° with a pair of pliers and then remove the springs and retainers.
4. Remove the upper and lower brake shoes.
5. Depress the self-adjusting spring retainers, rotate the shoe 90° while holding the retainer and then separate the self-adjuster retainer, washer, spring, pin, adjuster lever and the brake shoe from each other.

NOTE: If the shoes, adjuster levers and return springs are to be reinstalled, be sure to mark their location so that they will be reinstalled in their original positions.

6. Before you install the brake shoes, make sure that your hands and tools are free from grease and oil that will wet and impair the effectiveness of the brake linings if contact is made.
7. Place the brake shoe in an arbor press or similar tool and install the adjuster pivot pin, adjuster lever, washer, spring and retainers to each brake shoe. Compress the spring and rotate the retainer 90° while compressing the spring, making sure that the pin end is seated in the retainer groove.

NOTE: Install the washer so that its lining side is facing the lever. Also, the left and right-side adjuster levers are not interchangeable and must be reinstalled in their original positions.

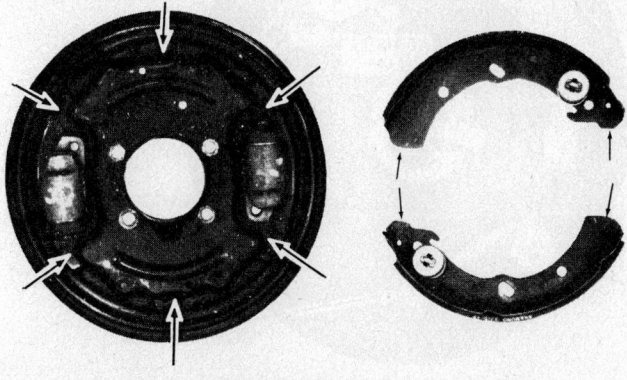

→ LUBRICATION POINTS

Lubrication points for front drum brakes—1975 models

8. Lubricate the brake shoe contact points on the backing plate and the wheel cylinder contact points on the brake shoes with Lubriplate® or similar grease.

9. Hook the return springs to the brake shoes. Be sure to install the left and right springs in their original positions as they are not interchangeable. The left springs are light blue; right springs are black.

10. Fit the grooved portion of the adjuster lever to the guide pin and install the brake shoes in position. Make sure that the shoes are fitted properly to the guide pin. If the end of the brake shoe is not inserted in the groove, it is an indication that the brake shoes are lifted off the ridged portion. Make sure that the return spring end is fitted properly to the adjuster lever.

11. Install the piston springs on the wheel cylinder piston ends.

12. Install the brake shoe hold-down springs and retainers. With a pair of pliers, compress the spring and rotate the retainer 90°, making sure that the pin end is seated in the retainer groove.

13. Using a piece of fine (400 grit) sandpaper, evenly rough the surface of each brake lining before installing the brake drums. Do this to the linings of both wheels.

14. Reinstall the brake drum and adjust the brakes.

WHEEL CYLINDERS REMOVAL AND INSTALLATION

It is not necessary to remove the wheel cylinders from the backing plates to disassemble, inspect, and overhaul the cylinder. Removal is necessary only when the wheel cylinder is damaged beyond repair and must be replaced.

It is a good practice to inspect the wheel cylinders for leakage whenever the brake drums are removed. Simply pull the edge

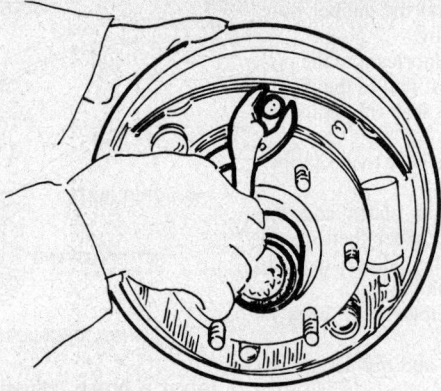

Removing the hold-down spring retainers and springs

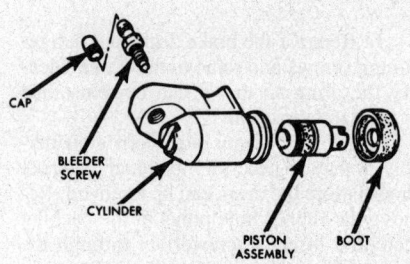

Exploded view of the front wheel cylinder

of the wheel cylinder boot carefully away from the cylinder and note whether or not the interior is wet with brake fluid. Excessive fluid at this point indicates leakage past the piston cup, requiring overhaul or replacement. A slight amount of fluid on the inside of the wheel cylinder is almost always present and acts as a lubricant for the piston.

1. Remove the wheel and tire assembly, the brake drum and the brake shoes.

2. Disconnect the brake system hydraulic line from the wheel cylinder at the rear of the backing plate.

3. Remove the screws securing the wheel cylinder to the backing plate and remove the wheel cylinder from the backing plate.

4. Install the wheel cylinder in the reverse order of removal and bleed the brake hydraulic system.

OVERHAUL

1. Either with the wheel cylinder removed or still on the brake backing plate remove the boot(s) from the cylinder end(s).

2. Remove the piston(s) and cup(s).

NOTE: The front wheel cylinder pistons and cups are serviced as an assembly.

3. Inspect the cylinder bore. Check for staining and corrosion. Discard any wheel cylinder which is excessively corroded. Inspect the piston and discard it if it is excessively pitted, scored or damaged.

4. Polish any stained or slightly scored areas in the cylinder bore with crocus cloth. Move the crocus cloth in a circular motion around the circumference of the cylinder bore, not in a lengthwise manner.

5. Wash the wheel cylinder body thoroughly in clean brake fluid, allowing it to remain lubricated for assembly. Do not lubricate the pistons or cups prior to their installation in the cylinder.

6. On front wheel cylinders, install the piston assembly into the cylinder, being careful not to damage the boot.

7. On rear wheel cylinders, insert the spring-expander into the cylinder bore. Install the new cups with the flat surface toward the outer ends of the cylinder. Be sure that the cups are lint-free. Do not lubricate the cups prior to installation. Install the new pistons into the cylinder with the flat surfaces toward the center of the cylinder. Do not lubricate prior to installation.

8. Press the new boot(s) onto the wheel cylinder.

9. Install the wheel cylinder onto the brake backing plate, if it was removed, assemble the brake shoes to the backing plate,

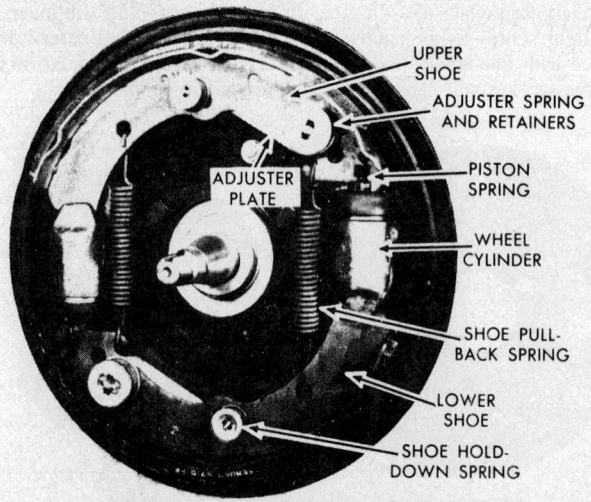

Front drum brake components

Front brake assembly components—1975 models

install the brake drum and bleed the brake hydraulic system.

Front Wheel Bearings—2 Wheel Drive

REMOVAL AND INSTALLATION

1. Remove the hub assembly.
2. Remove the outer roller bearing assembly from the hub. Pry out the inner bearing lip seal and remove the inner bearing assembly.
3. Wash all parts in a cleaning solvent and dry with compressed air.
4. Check the bearings for pitting or scoring. Also check for smooth rotation and lack of noise.
5. Thoroughly lubricate the bearings with new wheel bearing lubricant.
6. Apply a light coat of lubricant to the spindle and inside surface of the hub.
7. Place the inner bearing in the race of the hub and install a new grease seal.
8. Install the hub assembly on the spindle.
9. Install the outer wheel bearing, washer and adjust nut.
10. Adjust the wheel bearings as outlined below.
11. Install the dust cap on the hub.
12. Install the brake caliper and support assembly.
13. Install the wheel and tighten the nuts.

WHEEL BEARING ADJUSTMENT

1. With the wheel raised, remove the hub cap and dust cap and then remove the cotter pin and nut retainer from the end of the spindle.
2. While rotating the wheel, tighten the spindle nut to 22 ft. lbs.
3. Turn the hub 2–3 turns and loosen the nut just enough so that it can be turned with your fingers.
4. Turn the nut all the way in with your fingers and check to be sure the hub has no free play.
5. Measure the starting torque by pulling one of the wheel hub studs with a pull scale. Tighten the spindle nut so that the pull scale reads 1.1–2.6 lbs. when the hub begins to rotate.

NOTE: Make sure that the brake pads are not in contact with the drum when measuring rotating torque.

6. Install the nut retainer, new cotter pin, dust cap and hub cap.
7. Perform the same procedure for each wheel.

Wheel Bearings—4 Wheel Drive

REMOVAL, INSTALLATION AND ADJUSTMENT

1. Raise and support the front end. Place the hub in 2H.
2. Remove the free wheeling hub cover assembly.
3. Remove the snap-ring and shims from the spindle.
4. Remove the free wheeling hub body and lock washer.
5. Remove the outer roller bearing assembly from the hub with your fingers.
6. Using a brass or wood drift, drive out the inner bearing assembly along with the oil seal. Replace the seal.
7. Wash all parts in a non-flammable solvent.
8. Check all parts for cracks or wear. Thoroughly lubricate all bearing parts with a high-temperature (molybdenum-disulfide) wheel bearing grease. Remove any excess. Apply about 2 ounces of the grease to the hub.
9. Lightly coat the spindle with the same grease.
10. Place the inner bearing into the hub race and install a new seal and retaining ring.
11. Carefully install the hub on the spindle and install the outer bearing.
12. Install the spindle nut.
13. While rotating the hub, tighten the hub so that the wheel can just be turned by hand.
14. Turn the hub 2–3 turns and back off the nut just enough so that it can be loosened with the fingers.
15. Finger-tighten the nut so that all play is taken up at the bearing.
16. Attach a pull scale to one of the lugs and check the amount of pull needed to start the wheel turning. Initial pull should be 2.6–4.0 lbs. When performing this test, make sure the brake pads are not touching the rotor. If the rotating torque is not correct, tighten the spindle nut until it is.
17. Install the snap-ring and shims, gasket and cover. Torque the cover bolts to 14 ft. lbs.

Rear Drum Brakes

BRAKE DRUMS REMOVAL AND INSTALLATION

1. Raise the vehicle and support it on jackstands.
2. Remove the hub caps and remove the rear tire and wheel.
3. Loosen the check nuts at the parking brake equalizer sufficiently to remove all tension from the brake cable.

4. Remove the drum-to-hub retaining screws and remove the drum from the vehicle. Identify each brake drum so that it can be reinstalled in its original position. Never depress the brake pedal while any of the brake drums are removed.
5. Install the brake drums in the reverse order of removal.

INSPECTION

Inspect the rear brake drums in the same manner as is outlined for the front brake drums.

BRAKE SHOES REMOVAL AND INSTALLATION

1. Remove the brake drums.
2. Unhook the brake return springs from the anchor pin using a brake tool and remove the springs.
3. Remove the brake shoe hold-down springs using pliers. Depress the spring retainer while rotating it 90° to align the slot in the retainer with the flanged end of the pin.
4. Remove the self-adjuster cable assembly by disconnecting the spring at the adjuster lever and removing the cable end from the anchor pin. Remove the guide plate from the anchor pin.
5. Remove the adjuster lever and the lever hold-down wire from the shoe pivot.

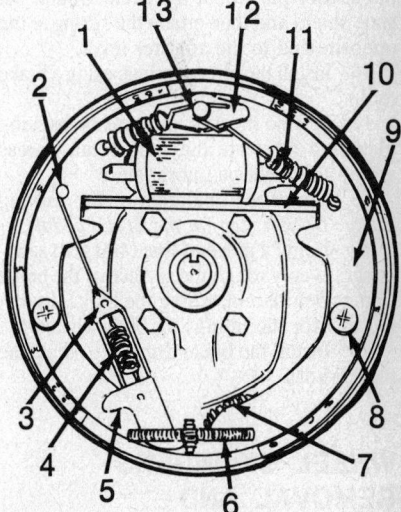

Rear brake assembly components—all models

1. Wheel cylinder	9. Primary shoe
2. Cable guide	10. Parking brake
3. Cable assembly	strut
4. Lever hold down	11. Shoe pull—back
spring	spring
5. Adjuster lever	12. Guide plate
6. Self adjuster	13. Anchor pin
7. Shoe return spring	
8. Shoe hold down	
spring	

6. Separate the shoes from the wheel cylinder pushrods.

7. Separate the primary and secondary brake shoes, adjuster, return spring, and parking brake strut assemblies.

NOTE: If the brake shoes are to be reinstalled, be sure to identify them so that they can be reinstalled in their original positions.

8. Separate the parking brake lever and the rear cable. Remove the clip and washer and remove the parking brake lever from the secondary shoe.

9. Lubricate the parking brake cable with Lubriplate®.

10. Assemble the parking brake lever to the secondary shoe and then assemble the parking brake cable to the lever.

11. Before installation, make sure that the adjusting screw is clean, lubricated and operable.

12. Connect the brake shoes together with bottom return spring and then place the adjuster screw into position. The adjuster screw is installed with the starwheel nearest to the secondary shoe.

13. Assemble the parking brake strut with the spring on the primary shoe end, and assemble the shoes to the wheel cylinder pushrods.

14. Install the shoe hold-down springs using a pair of pliers. Compress the springs and rotate the retainers 90°.

15. Install the guide plate on the anchor pin. Assemble the self-adjuster lever and the lever hold-down wire to the secondary shoe pivot pin. Place the adjuster cable over the anchor pin, route the cable around the shoe shield and then attach the spring at the opposite end to the adjuster lever.

16. Install the return springs using a brake tool.

17. Pry the shoes away from the backing plate and lubricate the shoe contact areas with a thin coat of Lubriplate.®

18. Check the operation of the parking brake. *Do not step on the brake pedal.*

19. Using a piece of fine (400 grit) sandpaper, evenly rough the surface of the brake linings before reinstalling the brake drums. Do this for the linings on both wheels.

20. Install the brake drum and adjust the brake shoes.

WHEEL CYLINDERS REMOVAL AND INSTALLATION

Remove and install the rear wheel cylinders in the same manner as outlined for the front wheel cylinders.

OVERHAUL

Follow the procedure given for overhauling the front wheel cylinders to overhaul the rear wheel cylinders.

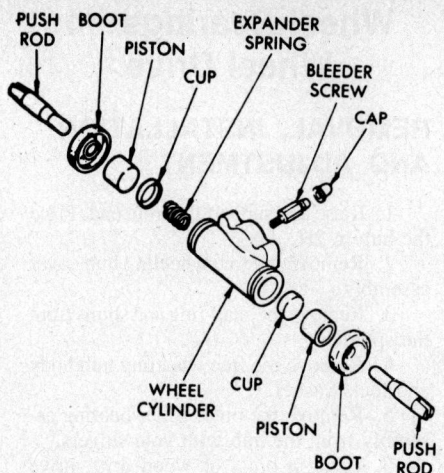

Exploded view of the rear wheel cylinder

Parking Brake

Adjustment

Since the rear brakes are utilized as service brakes and parking brakes, the service brake must be properly adjusted as a base for parking brake adjustment.

1. Jack up the vehicle and safely support it with jackstands.

2. Apply the parking brake two notches from the fully released position.

3. Loosen the equalizer check nut, and tighten or loosen the front jam nut until a light to moderate drag is felt when the rear wheels are rotated frontward.

4. Tighten the nuts securely. Hold the front nut while tightening the jam nut.

5. Fully release the parking brake and rotate the rear wheels. No drag should be present.

6. Lower the vehicle.

FRONT CABLE REMOVAL AND INSTALLATION

1. Disconnect the battery ground cable.

2. Remove the carburetor air cleaner.

3. Drain the cooling system. Disconnect the heater hoses at the heater core out-

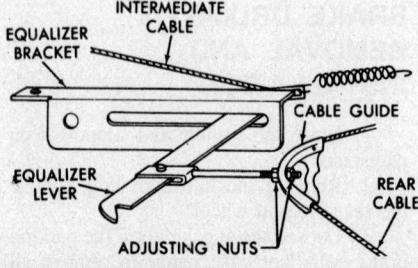

Parking brake adjustment

let tubes at the dash panel and secure the hoses in an upright position to minimize coolant loss.

4. Disconnect the parking brake front cable at the control lever on the rightside of the engine compartment.

5. Remove the right-hand pulley center bolt and remove the pulley.

6. Remove the cable cover nuts at the dash panel and remove the cover.

7. Remove the windshield wiper switch on the instrument panel.

8. Remove the screws attaching the lever assembly to the instrument panel.

9. Pull the assembly rearward and lay it on the floor.

10. Loosen the parking brake light switch bracket screw and rotate the switch and bracket 90°.

11. Manually release the ratchet and then depress the handle all the way in.

12. Remove the cotter pin, washer, pivot pin and the pulley. Remove the cable assembly.

13. To install the cable, install the cable to handle lower end and then pull the handle rearward several notches.

14. Rotate the parking brake light switch and bracket into position and tighten the bracket screw.

15. Install the pulley, pivot pin, washer and cotter pin.

16. For the remainder of the installation procedure follow the removal procedure in reverse starting with step 8.

INTERMEDIATE CABLE REMOVAL AND INSTALLATION

1. Raise the vehicle on a hoist.

2. Disconnect the equalizer lever spring at the lever.

3. Loosen the cable guide nut and remove the cable assembly.

4. Install the intermediate cable in the reverse order of removal and adjust the parking brake.

REAR CABLE REMOVAL AND INSTALLATION

1. Raise the vehicle on a hoist.

2. Remove the rear cable retaining clamps on the left and right-sides.

3. Disconnect the equalizer lever return spring at the lever.

4. Remove the cotter pin, washer and pin and remove the equalizer lever from the front cable and equalizer adjusting bolt clevis.

5. Remove the left and right rear wheel and tire assemblies.

6. Remove the brake drums and shoes, disconnecting the rear cable from the brake lever.

7. Remove the rear cable spring cup using a box wrench.

8. Withdraw the cable ends from the backing plates on either side and remove the cable assembly.

9. Install the cable in reverse order and adjust the parking brake.

CHASSIS ELECTRICAL

Heater Blower

REMOVAL AND INSTALLATION

1. Disconnect the battery ground cable.

2. Disconnect the blower motor electrical leads.

3. Remove the blower-to-heater core screws and remove the blower motor assembly.

4. Install in the reverse order.

Heater Core

REMOVAL AND INSTALLATION

1. Disconnect the battery ground cable.

2. Place a drain pan under the heater hoses at the heater and remove the heater hoses from the core tubes, securing the heater hoses in a raised position to prevent further loss of coolant. Plug or tape the heater core tubes to prevent spillage of coolant in the passenger compartment when removing.

3. Remove the parcel shelf.

4. Loosen the air diverter and defroster door bowden cable clamps at the heater case and disconnect the cables from the doors.

5. Disconnect the blower resistor leads.

6. Remove the control assembly-to-instrument panel screws and swing the control to the left and lay it on the floor. Be careful not to kink the water valve bowden cable.

7. Remove the four heater-to-firewall screws. Pull the heater rearward until the core tubes clear the firewall opening, then remove the heater by moving it to the right and down.

8. Remove the core tube clamp screw and remove the clamp.

9. Remove the seven screws and separate the heater case halves.

10. Remove the core from the case.

11. Install and assemble the heater core and heater case in the reverse order of removal, using new seals around the heater core.

Ignition Switch

REMOVAL AND INSTALLATION

1. Disconnect the battery ground strap.

2. Remove the multi-connector from the rear of the ignition switch.

3. Remove the lock nut from the front of the switch. Remove the switch from the rear of the instrument panel.

4. Installation is the reverse of removal.

NOTE: Align the locating lug on the switch body with the slot in the instrument panel mounting hole during installation.

Radio

REMOVAL AND INSTALLATION

1. Disconnect battery ground cable.

2. Remove the ashtray and ashtray plate.

3. Remove the tuner and volume control knobs, jam nuts, plain washers and face panel.

4. Remove the screws from the front and rear mounting brackets.

5. Disconnect the electrical connections, antenna lead and remove the radio. Remove the front mounting brackets from the radio.

6. Install the radio in the reverse order of removal.

Windshield Wiper Motor and Linkage

REMOVAL AND INSTALLATION

1. Remove the wiper blades and arms.

2. Remove the two bolts attaching the pivot.

3. Remove the four wiper motor mounting bolts and remove the wiper motor and linkage.

4. To remove the motor independently, take out the motor shaft nut and three bolts and then pull off the connector and disconnect the ground cable.

5. Install and assemble in the reverse order of removal. Make sure to install the wiper motor linkage so that it is not twisted or touching any adjacent parts; otherwise, the wiper motor will be loaded and cause poor wiper action.

Removing the rear cable spring cup at the backing plate

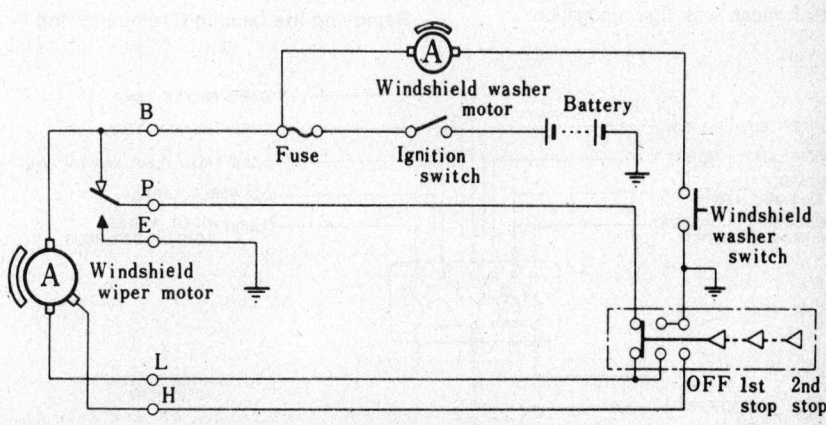

Windshield wiper-washer electrical circuit

Instrument Cluster

REMOVAL AND INSTALLATION

1. Disconnect the speedometer cable.
2. Remove the wing nuts on the rear side of the instrument panel and pull the assembly part way out.
3. Disconnect the wiring harness at the connector and remove the instrument panel.
4. Install the panel in the reverse order of removal.

Fuse Box Location

The fuse box is located under the hood, on the left inner fender panel, near the firewall, adjacent to the master cylinders. The fuse box contains ten fuses in use and four positions for spares.

Lighting

HEADLIGHTS REMOVAL AND INSTALLATION

1. Remove the headlight trim rim.
2. Loosen the three screws attaching the sealed beam unit by turning the retaining ring counterclockwise.
3. Install the headlight by fitting the bosses on the headlight lens into the grooves so that the "TOP" mark is up.
4. Tighten the three attaching screws and install the headlight trim ring.

Horn

If the tone quality of the horn has been altered due to wear in the contact points, check and readjust the point gap with the adjusting screw.

HORN SWITCH INSPECTION

Remove the horn shroud from the steering wheel. Remove the horn button and switch from the shroud. If the contact points are fouled, clean with fine sandpaper.

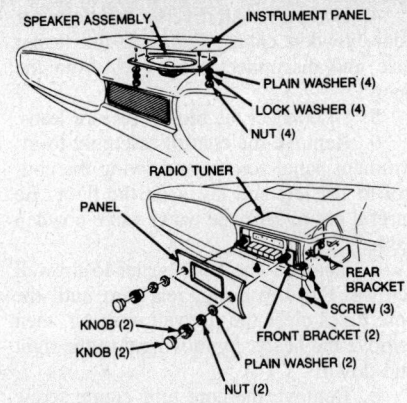

Installation of the radio

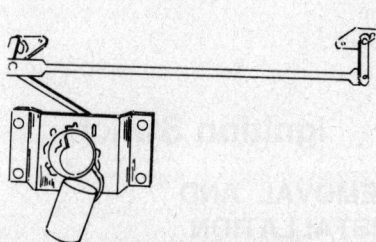

The wiper motor, transmission, and linkage

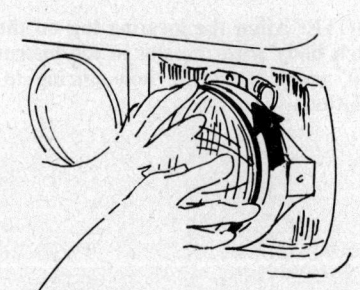

Removing the headlight retaining ring

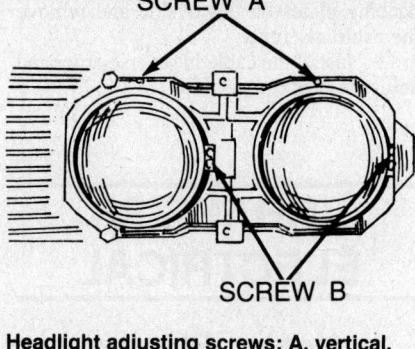

Headlight adjusting screws: A. vertical, B. horizontal—1975–77 models (4-headlights)

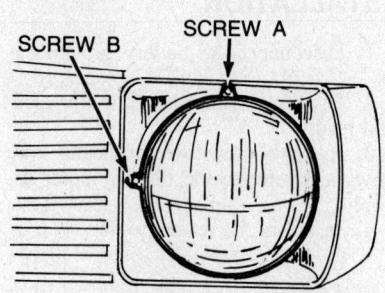

1979–80 headlight adjustment screws

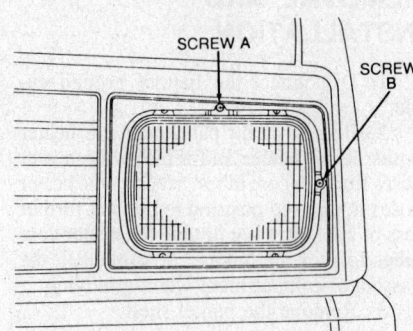

1981–82 headlight adjustment screws: A. vertical, B. horizontal

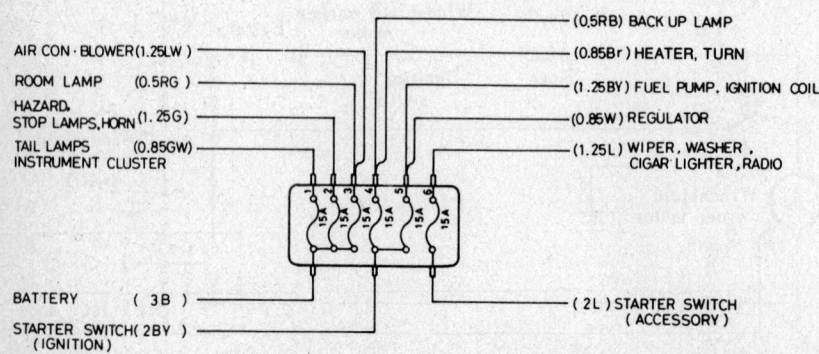

Fuse panel

Horn adjustment

Mazda

INDEX

GENERAL ENGINE SPECIFICATIONS
Piston Engine

Year	Engine Displacement Cu in.	(cc)	Carb Type	Net Horsepower (@ rpm)	Net Torque @ rpm (ft lbs)	Bore and Stroke (in.)	Compression Ratio	Oil Pressure (@ rpm)
'75–'76	96.8	(1586)	2-bbl	70 @ 5000	82 @ 3400	3.07 × 3.27	8.6:1	50–64 @ 3000
'77–'78	109.6	(1796)	2-bbl	66 @ 4500	92 @ 3000	3.07 × 3.07	8.6:1	48–64 @ 3000
'79–'82	120.2	(2000)	2-bbl	NA	NA	3.15 × 3.86	8.6:1	50–64 @ 3000

NA—Not available

GENERAL ENGINE SPECIFICATIONS
Rotary

Model	Engine Displacement Cu in.	(cc)	Carburetor Type	Net Horsepower	Net Torque	Rotor Displacement (cu in.)	Compression Ratio	Oil Pressure @ rpm (psi)
Pick-up	80	(1,308)	4-bbl	110	117	40	9.2:1	71.1 @ 3,000

TUNE-UP SPECIFICATIONS
Piston Engine

Year	Engine Displacement Cu in.	(cc)	Spark Plugs Type	Gap (in.)	Distributor Point Dwell (deg)	Point Gap (in.)	Ignition Timing (deg) MT	AT	Intake Valve Opens (deg)	Fuel Pump Pressure (psi)	Idle Speed (rpm) MT	AT	Valve Clearance (in.)▲ In	Ex
'75–'76	96.8	(1586)	BP-6ES	.031	49–55	0.020	5B②	5B②	13B	2.8–3.6	800–850	650–① 700		.012– .012
'77–'78	109.6	(1796)	BP-6ES	.031	49–55	0.020	8B	8B	18B	2.8–3.6	700–750	—		.012– .012
'79–'82	120.2	(2000)	BPR-6ES	.031	Elec.	Elec.	8B	—	14B	2.8–3.6	600–700	—		.012–③ .012 ③

▲ At the valve (warm engine)
—Not applicable
① Transmission in Drive
② '76 Calif.: 8B
③ 0.009 on the cam side
CO—% at idle: '73–'75—1.5–2.5%
B—BTDC (before top dead center)

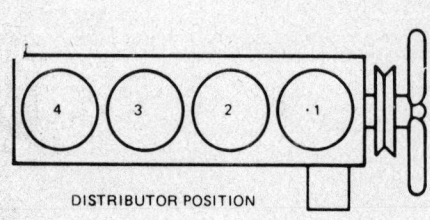

DISTRIBUTOR POSITION

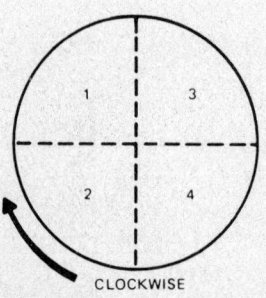

CLOCKWISE

Piston engine firing order

TUNE-UP SPECIFICATIONS
Rotary

Year	Engine Cu in.	Spark Plugs		Distributors (both)▲		Ignition Timing (deg)			Idle Speed (rpm)	
		Type	Gap	Point Gap (in.)	Point Dwell (deg)	Leading Normal	Leading Retarded	Trailing Normal	MT	AT
'75	80	N-80B	0.024–0.028	0.018	58 ± 3	TDC	20A	15A	800–850	750–800①
'76	80	RN 278B	0.039–0.043	0.018	58 ± 3	5A	20A	20A	725–775	725–775①
'77	80	RN 278B	0.039–0.043	0.018	58 ± 3	5A	—	25A	725–775	725–775

▲ '75 models have only one distributor
① Transmission in drive (D)
TDC—Top dead center
A—After top dead center
deg—degrees

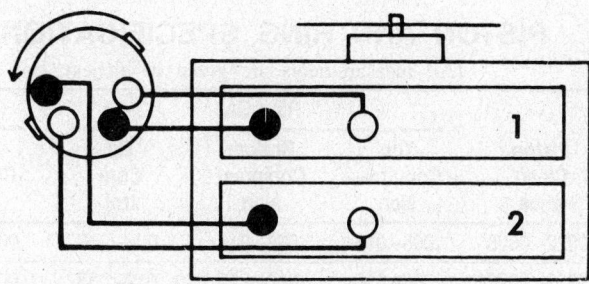

Rotary engine firing order

CAPACITIES

Year	Model	Engine Displacement Cu in.	(cc)	Engine Crankcase (qts) With Filter	Without Filter	Transmission (pts) Manual 4-spd	5-spd	Automatic	Drive Axle (pts)	Gasoline Tank (gals)	Cooling System (qts) W/ AC	W/O AC
'75–'76	B-1600	96.8	(1586)	4.00	3.00	3.00①	—	—	2.80	11.7	—	6.80
'75	Rotary Pick-up	80	(1308)	5.50	4.50	3.60	—	13.20	2.80	20.4	—	10.80
'76–'77	Rotary Pick-up	80	(1308)	6.80	5.30	3.60	4.60	13.20	2.80	20.8	—	10.30
'77–'78	B-1800	109.6	(1796)	3.8	—	3.00	3.8	—	3.0	14.8②	—	7.6
'79–'82	B-2000	120.2	(2000)	4.1	—	3.2	3.6	—	2.8	14.8②	—	7.6③

① After #49825—3.20
② Long body—17.4 gal.
③ 7.0 without heater

CRANKSHAFT AND CONNECTING ROD SPECIFICATIONS
Piston Engine
(All measurements are given in inches)

Year	Engine Displacement Cu in.	(cc)	Crankshaft Main Brg Journal Dia	Main Brg Oil Clearance	Shaft End-Play	Thrust on No.	Connecting Rod Journal Dia	Oil Clearance	Side Clearance
'75–'76	96.8	(1586)	2.4804	.001–.002	.003–.009	4	2.0866	.001–.003	.004–.008
'77–'78	109.6	(1796)	2.4804	.0012–.0019	.003–.009	5	2.0866	.0011–.0030	.004–.008
'79–'82	120.2	(2000)	2.4804	.0012–.0020	.003–.009	5	.7874①	.0011–.0030	.004–.008

① Small end, inner diameter

MAZDA

VALVE SPECIFICATIONS
Piston Engine

Year	Engine Displacement Cu in.	(cc)	Seat Angle (deg)	Face Angle (deg)	Spring Test Pressure (lbs @ in.)	Spring Installed Height (in.)	Stem-to-Guide Clearance (in.) Intake	Exhaust	Stem Diameter (in.) Intake	Exhaust
'75–'76	96.8	(1586)	45	45	①	②	.0007–.0021	.0007–.0023	.3150	.3150
'77–'78	109.6	(1796)	45	45	③	②	.0007–.0021	.0007–.0023	.3150	.3150
'79–'82	120.2	(2000)	45	45	①	②	.0007–.0021	.0007–.0023	.3150	.3150

① Outer: 31.4 @ 1.339
   Inner: 20.9 @1.260
② Outer: 1.339
   Inner: 1.260
③ Outer: 31.4 @ 1.339
   Inner: 20.9 @ 1.260

PISTON AND RING SPECIFICATIONS
(All measurements are given in inches)

Year	Engine Displacement Cu in.	(cc)	Piston Clearance	Ring Gap Top Compression	Bottom Compression	Oil Control	Ring Side Clearance Top Compression	Bottom Compression	Oil Control
'75–'76	96.8	(1586)	.0022–.0028	.008–.016	.008–.016	.008–.016	.0014–.0028	.0012–.0025	.008–.016
'77–'78	109.6	(1796)	.0022–.0028	.008–.016	.008–.016	.012–.035	.0014–.0028	.0012–.0025	—
'79–'82	120.2	(2000)	.0014–.0030	.008–.016	.008–.016	.012–.035	.0012–.0028	.0012–.0025	—

TORQUE SPECIFICATIONS
Piston Engine
(All figures given in ft. lbs.)

Year	Cylinder Head Bolts	Rod Bearing Bolts	Main Bearing Bolts	Crankshaft Pulley Bolt	Flywheel-to-Crankshaft Bolts	Manifold Intake	Exhaust
'75–'78	②	36–40	61–65	101–108	112–118	14–19	12–17①
'79–'82	③	30–33	61–65	101–108	112–118	14–19	16–21

① B1800—16–21
② Cold—56–60
   Hot—69–72
③ Cold—59–64
   Hot—69–72

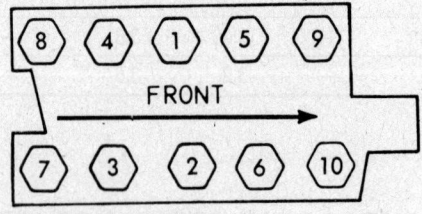

Piston engine cylinder head bolt tightening sequence

TORQUE SPECIFICATIONS
Rotary
(All figures in ft. lbs.)

Engine Displacement Cu In.	(cc)	Front Cover	Bearing Housing	Rear Stationary Gear	Eccentric Shaft Pulley Bolt	Flywheel to Eccentric Shaft Nut	Manifold Intake	Exhaust	Oil Pan	Tension Bolts
80	(1,308)	—	—	—	54–69	289–362	15	32–43	5–7	23–27

Tension bolt loosening sequence

Tension bolt tightening sequence

ECCENTRIC SHAFT SPECIFICATIONS
Rotary
(All measurements are given in inches)

Model	Journal Diameter		Oil Clearance		Eccentric Shaft End-Play		Min. Shaft Runout
	Main Bearing	Rotor Bearing	Main Bearing	Rotor Bearing	Normal	Limit	
Pick-up	1.6929	2.9134	.0016–.0028	.0016–.0031	.0016–.0028	.0035	.0024

SEAL SPECIFICATIONS
Rotary
(All measurements are given in inches)

Model	Apex Seal		Corner Seal Width (OD)	Side Seal		Oil Seal Contact Width of Lip	
	Normal Height	Height Limit		Thickness	Width	Normal	Limit
Pick-up	.33500	.27600	.4331	.0394	.1378	.008	.031

SEAL CLEARANCES
Rotary
(All measurements are given in inches)

Model	Apex Seals				Corner Seal to Rotor Groove		Side Seal			
	To Side Housing		To Rotor Groove				To Rotor Groove		To Corner Seal	
	Normal	Limit	Normal	Limit	Normal	Limit	Normal	Limit	Normal	Limit
Pick-up	.0051–.0067	.012	.0020–.0035	.006	.0008–.0019	.0031	.0016–.0028	.0040	.0020–.0059	.016

ROTOR AND HOUSING SPECIFICATIONS
Rotary
(All measurements are given in inches)

| | Rotor | | | | | Housing | | | | |
| | | | | Front and Rear | | Rotor | | Intermediate | | |
Model	Side Clearance	Standard Protrusion of Land	Limit of Pro-trusion of Land	Distortion Limit	Wear Limit	Width	Distortion Limit	Distortion Limit	Wear Limit
Pick-up	.0047–.0083	.004–.006	.003	.002	.004	3.1438	.002	.002	.004

ALTERNATOR AND REGULATOR SPECIFICATIONS

| | | Alternator | | Regulator | | | | |
Year	Model	Field Current @ 14V	Output (amps)	Air Gap (in.)	Point Gap (in.)	Back Gap (in.)	Volts @ 75°
'75	Rotary Pick-up	40	50	0.028–0.051	0.012–0.018	0.028–0.059	14.5
'75–'76	B1600	28	35	0.028–0.043	0.012–0.016	0.028–0.043	14.5
'76–'77	Rotary Pick-up	56	63	0.028–0.051	0.012–0.018	0.028–0.059	1.40
'77–'78	B1800	—	—	0.028–0.051	0.012–0.018	0.028–0.059	14–15①
'79–'82	B2000	—	—	0.028–0.051	0.012–0.018	0.028–0.059	14–15①

① Alternator @ 4,000 rpm and battery fully charged

BATTERY AND STARTER SPECIFICATIONS
(All trucks use 12 volt, negative ground electrical systems)

| | | | Starter | | | | | | | |
| | | | Lock Test | | | No Load Test | | | Brush Spring Tension (oz) | Min. Brush Length (in.) |
Year	Model	Battery Amp Hour Capacity	Amps	Volts	Torque (ft/lbs)	Amps	Volts	rpm		
'75	Rotary Pick-up	70	1100	5.0	17.0	100	11.5	7800	49–63	0.45
'76–'77	Rotary Pick-up	60MT 70AT	780MT 1100AT	5.0	8.0MT 17.4AT	75MT 100AT	11.5	4900MT 7800AT	49–63	0.45
'75–'76	B1600	60	560	7.5	9.4	60	11.5	6000	35–46	0.45
'77–'78	B1800	45	310	5.0	5.4	53	11.5	6800	49–63	0.45
'79–'82	B2000	45①	310	5.0	5.4	53	11.5	6800	49–63	0.45

① Heavy duty—70

BRAKE SPECIFICATIONS
(All measurements are in. unless noted)

| | | Brake Disc | | | Brake Drum | | | Minimum Lining Thickness | |
Model	Lug Nut Torque (ft. lbs.)	Master Cylinder Bore	Minimum Thick-ness	Maximum Run-Out	Diam-eter	Max. Machine O/S	Max. Wear Limit	Front	Rear
B1600	65–72	0.750	—	—	10.236	10.276	—	0.039	0.039
Rotary Pick-up	65–72	0.875	0.433	0.004	10.236	10.275	—	0.276	0.039
B1800	58–65	0.750	0.433	0.004	10.236	—	10.276	0.276	0.039
B2000	58–65	0.875	0.433	0.0039	10.236	—	10.276	—	0.039

NOTE: Minimum lining thickness is as recommended by the manufacturer. Due to variations in state inspection regulations, the minimum allowable thickness may be different than recommended by the manufacturer.

WHEEL ALIGNMENT SPECIFICATIONS

		Camber		Caster			Steering Axis
Year	Model	Range (deg)	Preferred Setting (deg)	Range (deg)	Preferred Setting (deg)	Toe-in (in.)	Inclination (deg)
'75	Rotary Pick-up	⅔P–1½P	1⅙P	0–½P	¼P	0–0.24	8¾P
'76–'77	Rotary Pick-up	1⅓P–2⅓P	1⅚P	0–½P	¼P	0–0.12	8¾P
'75–'76	B1600	½P–1½P	1P	1P–2P	1½P	0–0.24	7⅓P
'77–'78	B1800	⅜P–1¼P	¾P	⅔P–1⅓P	1P	0–0.24	8°15″
'79–'82	B2000	⅜P–1⅓P	¾P	⅔P–1⅓P	1P	0–0.24	8°15″

TUNE-UP PROCEDURES

Spark Plugs

The spark plugs should be checked and adjusted every 4,000 miles or 4 months for rotary engine-models or every 6,000 miles for piston engine-models. New plugs should be installed every 12,000 miles or 12 months.

The Mazda rotary engine has four spark plugs. Each of the two combustion chambers uses two plugs. The leading bottom spark plug fires first, igniting the fuel/air mixture, as in conventional engines; the trailing top plug fires a short time afterward (10° later), igniting any unburned mixture. This aids in more complete combustion in the long narrow chamber, which helps to reduce exhaust emissions of unburned fuel.

The spark plugs are specially constructed and designed for use only in the Mazda rotary engine.

1. Remove the wire from one of the plugs. Use a spark plug wrench with a rubber insulator to remove the plug.

NOTE: Both the distributor and the engine housing are marked to aid in identification of the spark plug and distributor connections. However, to avoid confusion, it is easier to remove one plug at a time.

2. Check each plug for badly worn electrodes, black deposits, fouling, or cracked porcelain.
3. Clean the plug with a wire brush, if it is dirty.
4. Replace any plug which has a badly worn or burned electrode.
5. Measure the electrode gap with a *wire* gauge.
6. Adjust the gap to the specifications given in the Tune-Up Specifications.
7. If the electrodes show signs of burning white or if the electrodes are burning rapidly, replace the plugs with cold range plugs.

NOTE: When replacing spark plugs be sure all plugs are of the same manufacture and heat range. It is a good idea to replace plugs in sets of four, if possible.

8. Replace the spark plug and torque it to 10 ft. lbs.

Breaker Points

NOTE: 1976 and later 1300 models, 1977 1600 models, and 1979–82 B2000 models have electronic ignition, eliminating the points and condenser. California and Canada models through 1978 have conventional ignition.

1. Release the clips on the distributor cap with a screwdriver. Lift off the cap and move it aside, leaving the wires attached. Pull the rotor from the shaft.
2. Inspect the points. If they are badly pitted or burned, they must be replaced. If they are only slightly burned, they may be filed flat and reused. In either case, they must be removed from the distributor. If the points are in good shape and only require adjustment, proceed to Step 8.
3. Remove the screws securing the points to the distributor breaker plate. Use a magnetic screwdriver to avoid dropping the screws. Remove the points.
4. If the points are slightly burned and are to be reused, clean them with a few strokes of a flat points file. Do this with the points removed from the distributor to avoid getting filings and grit in the works. Do not use an emery board, sandpaper, or the like for this job.
5. Install the new or cleaned points onto the breaker plate, but leave the mounting screws slightly loose. Apply a small dab of grease onto the distributor cam. Do not use oil, which will get onto the points, causing them to burn.
6. The condenser should be replaced whenever the points are replaced. Disconnect the condenser leads and remove the condenser mounting screws. Dual points models have a condenser for each set of points. A smaller condenser, used for radio noise suppression, is mounted next to the other condenser; it need only be replaced if ignition noise (clicking or popping) is heard over the radio. Install and connect the new condenser.

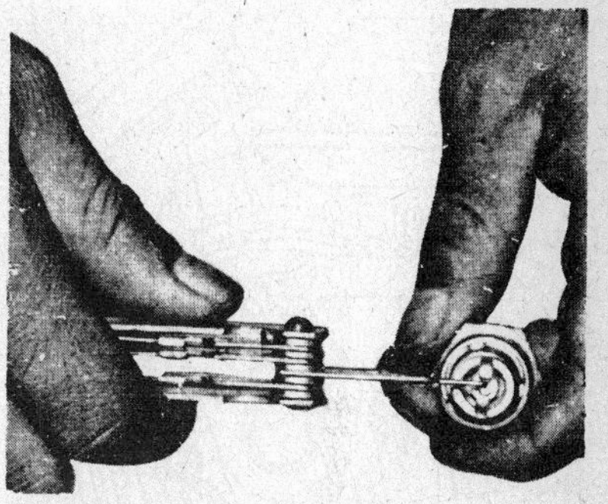

Checking the electrode gap—note the dual electrodes

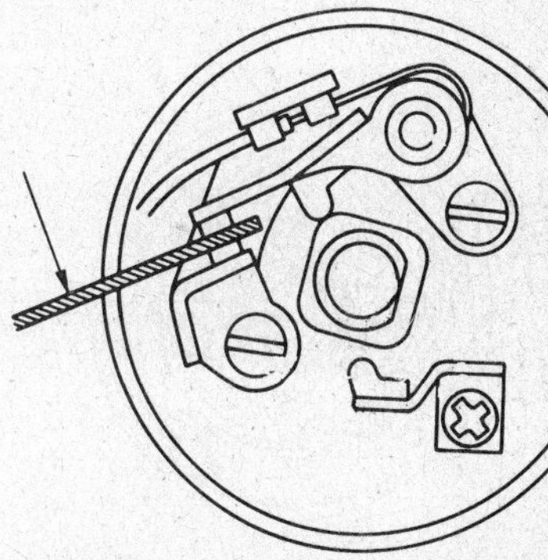

Adjusting the points with the rubbing block on the high point of the cam lobe

7. Check the breaker point alignment. If the points do not meet squarely, gently bend the fixed point slightly. Do not bend the movable point arm to adjust.
8. Rotate the engine until the rubbing block of the points arm is on one of the four high spots (lobes) of the distributor cam. The cam must open the points fully before the gap can be adjusted. The engine can be rotated by cranking it around in short bursts with the starter. You can also rotate the engine by hand with a wrench on the crankshaft (or eccentric shaft) pulley bolt; this is easier with the spark plugs removed. Move the engine only in the direction of normal rotation, to avoid damage to the apex seals (rotary engines).
9. Check the point gap with a flat feeler gauge of the proper thickness (see the Tune-

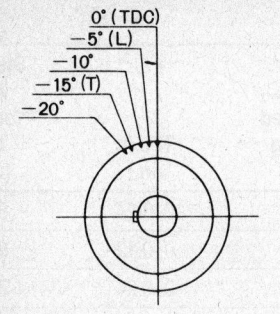

Ignition timing marks—1975 rotary

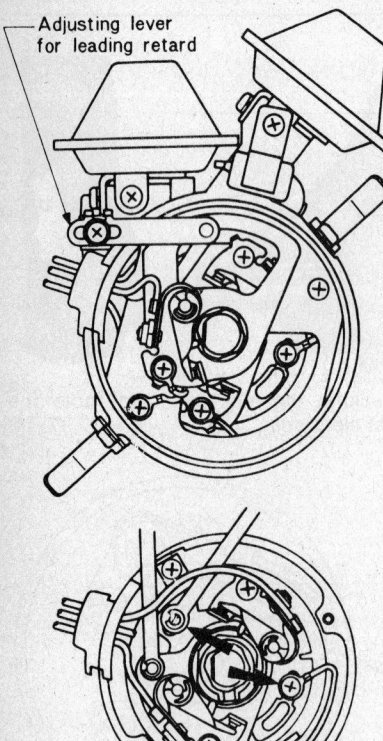

Adjusting the rotary engine ignition timing

Up Specifications). The feeler gauge should move through the points with only a light drag. If there is no drag, or if the gauge cannot be inserted at all, the gap is incorrect.

10. If the gap is incorrect, loosen the point set mounting screws slightly, if they are not already loose. Insert a screwdriver into the adjusting slot and lever the points open or closed until the gap is correct. Tighten the mounting screws and recheck the adjustment.

11. Install the rotor onto the distributor shaft (if the tip is burned or pitted, a new rotor should be used; similarly, if the distributor cap contacts are burned, a new cap should be installed). Install the distributor cap. If a new cap is being installed, hold the new cap next to the old and transfer the wires one at a time to avoid cross-wiring.

After adjusting the point gap, the timing must be checked; any change in the gap (dwell) automatically changes ignition timing.

Dwell Angle

Dwell angle is the number of degrees of crankshaft rotation through which the points remain closed, conducting electricity. It is nothing more than an electric method of measuring point gap. All models are measured and adjusted in the same way.

1. Disconnect and plug the vacuum line(s) at the distributor.
2. Connect the dwell meter in accordance with its manufacturer's instructions.
3. Run the engine at idle, after it has been allowed to warm up.
4. Observe the dwell meter reading. It should be within the specifications in the Tune-Up Specifications.
5. If dwell is not within specifications, shut off the engine, remove the distributor cap and rotor and adjust the point gap. Increasing the gap decreases dwell, and vice-versa.
6. If the dwell angle cannot be brought to within specifications, check for one or more of the following:
   a. Worn distributor cam.
   b. Worn rubbing block.
   c. Bent movable contact arm.
Replace any of the parts, if necessary.
7. When the dwell angle check is completed, disconnect the meter and reconnect the vacuum line(s).

Ignition Timing

1975 ROTARY

1. Connect a tachometer to the engine.
2. Disconnect and plug the vacuum tube on the distributor.
3. Connect a timing light to the wire from the leading (lower) plug of the front rotor housing.
4. Start the engine and run it at idle speed.
5. Shine the timing light on the indicator pin located on the front cover.
6. If the leading timing mark is not correctly aligned with the pointer, stop the engine.
7. Loosen the distributor locknut and rotate the distributor housing (with the engine running) until the timing marks align. Stop the engine and tighten the distributor locknut.
8. Recheck the timing.
9. Change the connection of the timing light to the wire from the trailing (top) plug in the front rotor housing.
10. Start the engine and shine the timing light at the indicator pin. If the trailing timing falls within the specifications, no further adjustments are necessary.
11. Adjust the trailing timing to speci-

fication by rotating the distributor body, as in Step 7.
12. Check the leading timing and record how much it differs from specification.
13. Remove the distributor cap and rotor.
14. Loosen the breaker base setscrews (the ones directly opposite each other near the outside of the distributor body) and turn the distributor base plate until the correct leading plug timing is obtained again.
15. Recheck the timing. The leading and trailing plug timing marks should both be aligned (or within specifications). If not, repeat the procedure until they are.

1976 ROTARY

1. Run the engine at normal operating temperature.
2. Connect a tachometer to the engine.
3. Connect a timing light to the leading spark plug of the front rotor.
4. Run engine at specified idle speed.
5. Aim the timing light at the timing indicator pin on the front cover.
6. If the timing is not correct, loosen the distributor locknut and rotate the distributor housing until the timing mark on the pulley aligns with the indicator pin.
7. Tighten the distributor locknut and recheck the lead timing.
8. Connect the timing light to the trailing spark plug.
9. Check the trailing timing with the timing light.
10. If the trailing timing is not correct, note the amount of error and stop the engine.
11. Remove the distributor cap and rotor.
12. Disconnect the primary wire from the leading point set.
13. Remove the breaker base plate and external lever for the leading set.
14. Slightly loosen the breaker base set screws of the trailing side and turn the base plate as required. Install the leading breaker base assembly, rotor and cap.
15. Check the trailing and leading timing. If they are not correct, repeat the above steps.
16. Leave timing light connected to trailing plug of the front rotor housing.
17. Connect a jumper between both terminals in the coupler of the primary lead wire.
18. Check the leading retard timing. Adjust by moving the external adjusting lever.

1977 ROTARY

1. Check the point gap for both leading and trailing sets. Adjust if necessary.
2. Warm-up engine and run it at specified idle speed.
3. Connect a timing light to the leading spark plug and aim it at the pointer on the front cover. If timing mark and pointer do not align as specified, adjust by loosening and rotating distributor body.

4. Tighten distributor body and switch timing light to trailing plug.

5. Check trailing timing by pointing timing light at pointer on front cover. If not within specifications, adjust by loosening and rotating distributor body.

6. Adjust leading timing by loosening the breaker base set screws in the distributor body and rotating the breaker base. Then, tighten the base, replace the cap and rotor. Start the engine and check the timing. Adjust the timing to specifications by loosening and rotating the distributor body.

7. Recheck the trailing timing and adjust as above, if necessary.

PISTON ENGINE

1. Raise the hood and clean and mark the timing marks. Chalk or fluorescent paint makes a good, visible mark.

2. Disconnect the vacuum line at the distributor and plug the disconnected line.

3. Connect a timing light to the front (no. 1) cylinder, a power source and ground. Follow the manufacturer's instructions.

4. Connect a tachometer to the engine.

5. Start the engine and reduce the idle to 700–750 rpm to be sure that the centrifugal advance mechanism is not working.

6. With the engine running, shine the timing light at the timing pointer and observe the position of the pointer in relation to the timing mark on the crankshaft pulley.

7. If the timing is not as specified, adjust the timing by loosening the distributor hold-down bolt and rotating the distributor in the proper direction. When the proper ignition timing is obtained, tighten the hold-down bolt on the distributor.

8. Check the centrifugal advance mechanism by accelerating the engine to about 2,000 rpm. If the ignition timing advances, the mechanism is working properly.

9. Stop the engine and remove the timing light.

10. Reset the idle to specifications.

11. Remove the tachometer.

Valve Lash

PISTON ENGINE

1. Run the engine until normal operating temperature is reached.

2. Shut off the engine and remove the rocker cover.

3. Torque the cylinder head bolts to 70 ft. lbs.

4. Rotate the crankshaft so that the no. 1 cylinder (front) is in the firing position. This can be determined by removing the spark plug from the no. 1 cylinder and putting your thumb over the spark plug port. When compression is felt, the no. 1 cylinder is on the compression stroke. Rotate the engine with a wrench on the crankshaft pulley and stop it a TDC of the compression stroke on the no. 1 cylinder.

5. Check the valve clearance with a feeler blade. The clearance can be checked at the camshaft or at the valve.

6. If the valve clearance is incorrect, loosen the adjusting screw locknut and adjust the clearance by turning the adjusting screw with the feeler blade inserted. Hold the adjusting screw in the correct position and tighten the locknut.

7. Rotate the crankshaft (in the normal direction of rotation), adjusting the valves for each cylinder at TDC of the compression stroke. Adjust the valves for each cylinder, in the firing order, 1-3-4-2.

8. Install the rocker arm cover and torque the nuts to 18 in. lbs.

Compression

ROTARY ENGINE

Because of the unusual shape of the combustion chamber, the lack of valves, and because there are three chambers for each rotor, a normal gauge is useless for the measurement of rotary engine compression.

Mazda makes a special recording compression tester which produces a separate graph for each of the three chambers. This is an expensive piece of equipment and not one that most mechanics are likely to have. If low compression is suspected, check with your local Mazda dealer.

Carburetor

IDLE SPEED AND MIXTURE

1975 Rotary

Idle speed changes with air temperature. It is suggested by Mazda that the idle adjustment be made indoors with a floor fan blowing through the radiator to assist in cooling. Whenever operating an engine indoors, make certain that provision is made for removal of exhaust gases. Idle speed should be adjusted with the engine at normal operating temperature, all accessories off and fuel tank cap removed.

1. Connect a tachometer to the engine.

2. Set idle speed to specification by turning the adjusting screw.

Mixture can be adjusted by:

3. Check the float level as described in the Fuel System Section.

4. Using a reliable CO meter, check the CO density at idle.

5. If density is not within 0.1%, adjust the idle mixture by turning the mixture screw.

6. Adjust the CO density to 0%, then turn the adjusting screw counterclockwise until the density is 0.5%.

7. Turn the screw clockwise until the density reaches 0.1%. Then turn the screw an additional one quarter turn.

8. Check the idle speed and reset if necessary.

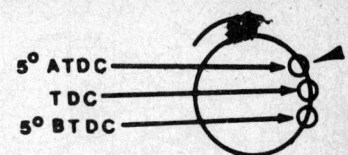

1600 engine timing marks—except California

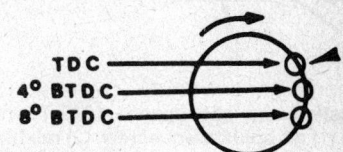

1600 engine timing marks—California

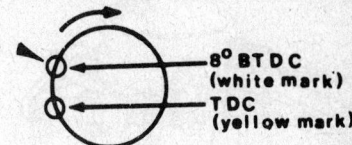

1800 engine timing marks

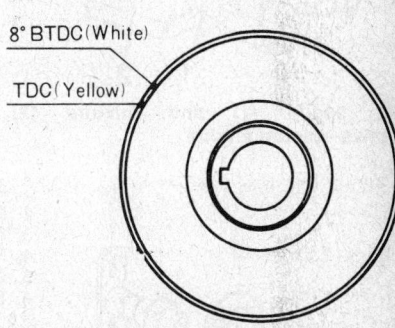

2000 engine timing marks

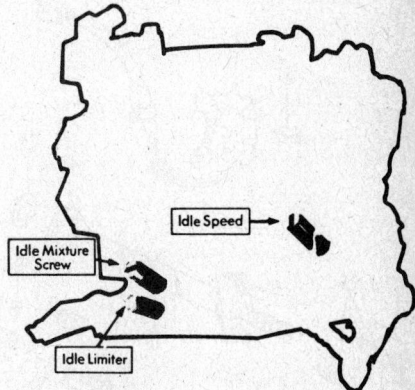

Idle adjustments—rotary engine

1976–77 Rotary

As with 1975 models, the idle speed should be set indoors. See the starting paragraph and steps 1 and 2 under 1975 Rotary.

1. Disconnect the idle compensator tube at the air cleaner.

2. Run the engine at normal operating temperature and make sure that the choke is wide open.

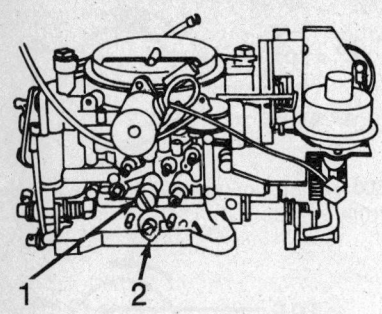

Adjusting the idle speed—1976–77 rotary; (1) air adjustment screw, (2) mixture screw

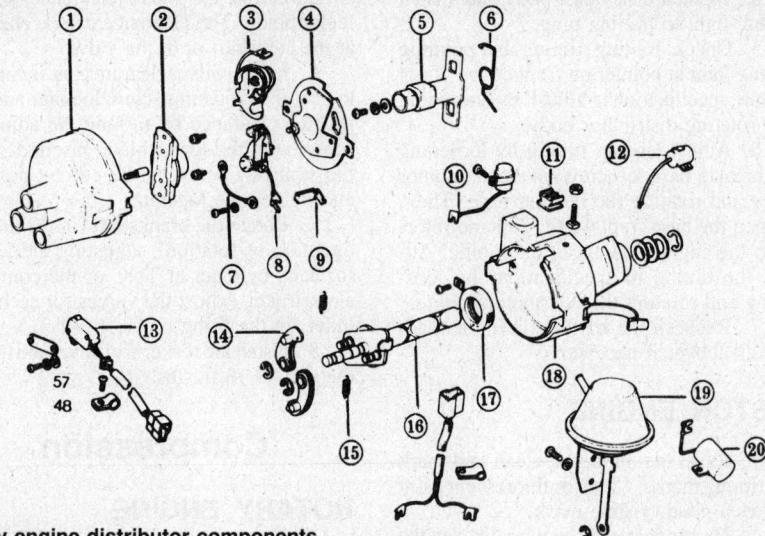

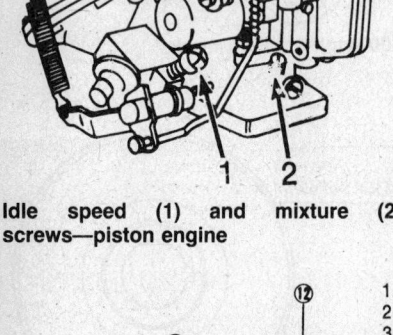

Idle speed (1) and mixture (2) screws—piston engine

Rotary engine distributor components

1. Cap
2. Rotor
3. Point set
4. Breaker plate
5. Cam
6. Spring
7. Ground wire
8. Point set
9. Felt
10. Ignition condenser
11. Terminal
12. Radio supression condenser
13. Vacuum switch—trailing

distributor only
14. Governor
15. Governor spring
16. Shaft
17. Oil seal
18. Distributor housing
19. Vacuum advance unit
20. Ignition condenser

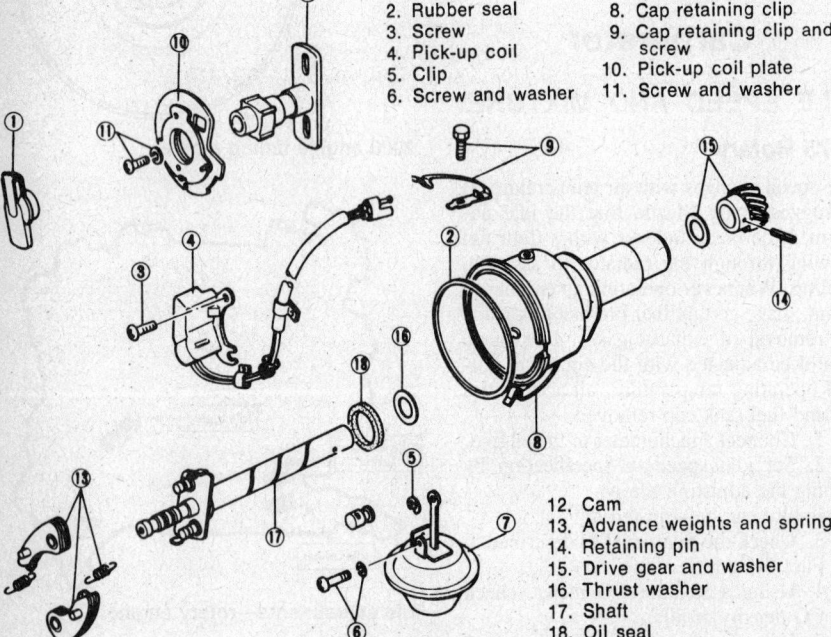

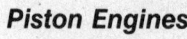

1. Rotor
2. Rubber seal
3. Screw
4. Pick-up coil
5. Clip
6. Screw and washer
7. Vacuum advance unit
8. Cap retaining clip
9. Cap retaining clip and screw
10. Pick-up coil plate
11. Screw and washer

12. Cam
13. Advance weights and springs
14. Retaining pin
15. Drive gear and washer
16. Thrust washer
17. Shaft
18. Oil seal

Exploded view of the electronic ignition distributor

1. Rotor
2. Rubber seal
3. Screw
4. Pick-up coil
5. Clip
6. Screw and washer
7. Vacuum advance unit
8. Cap retaining clip
9. Cap retaining clip and screw
10. Pick-up coil plate
11. Screw and washer
12. Cam
13. Advance weights and springs
14. Retaining pin
15. Drive gear and washer
16. Thrust washer
17. Shaft
18. Oil seal

3. Check the float level as described in the Fuel System Section.

4. Connect an exhaust gas analyzer and tachometer to the engine.

5. With engine at idle, check the CO density.

6. Adjust the idle speed to specification by turning the idle adjusting screw.

7. Turn the mixture adjusting screw clockwise until the engine lopes severely.

8. Turn the screw slowly counterclockwise until the CO density reaches 0.1%, then turn it an additional one quarter turn in the same direction.

Piston Engines

1. Connect a tachometer to the engine. Warm the engine to normal operating temperature.

2. Run the engine (in neutral) to 2,000 rpm for a minute or two.

3. Allow the engine to return to idle. Adjust the idle to specifications by means of the idle speed screw.

4. The mixture can only be adjusted with the aid of an exhaust gas analyzer. Connect the CO meter to the exhaust and note the reading.

5. On models sold in California, disconnect the air hose between the air pump and the check valve, and plug the port of the check valve.

6. Adjust the mixture by means of the mixture screw until the CO concentration meets specifications.

7. If the limiter cap was removed from the mixture screw, reinstall it.

ENGINE ELECTRICAL

Distributor

REMOVAL AND INSTALLATION

Rotary Engine—1975–78

The distributor is located on the right front side of the engine.

1. Open the hood and locate the distributor.
2. Remove the distributor cap.
3. Disconnect the vacuum tube from the advance unit.
4. Disconnect the primary wires from the distributor.
5. Matchmark the distributor body in relation to the engine front housing.
6. Remove the distributor hold-down bolt.
7. Pull the distributor from the front cover.

To install the distributor:

8. Turn the eccentric shaft until the TDC mark on the drive pulley aligns with the indicator pin on the front cover.
9. Align the matchmarks on the distributor housing and drive gear.
10. Install the distributor so that the distributor lockbolt is located in the center of the slot. Engage the gears.
11. Rotate the distributor clockwise until the leading contact point set starts to separate, and tighten the distributor lockbolt.
12. Install the distributor cap and connect the primary wires.
13. Set the ignition timing.
14. Connect the vacuum tube to the vacuum unit on the distributor.

Piston Engine

1. Matchmark the distributor cap and the body of the distributor. Remove the distributor cap.
2. Disconnect the vacuum hose from the diaphragm. Disconnect the electrical wire at the distributor, if so equipped.
3. Scribe matchmarks on the distributor body and the cylinder block to indicate the relative positions.
4. Scribe another mark on the distributor body indicating the position of the rotor.
5. Disconnect the primary wires from the distributor.
6. Remove the distributor hold-down nut, lockwasher and flat washer.
7. Remove the distributor from the engine.

NOTE: Do not crank the engine while the distributor is removed.

To install the distributor:

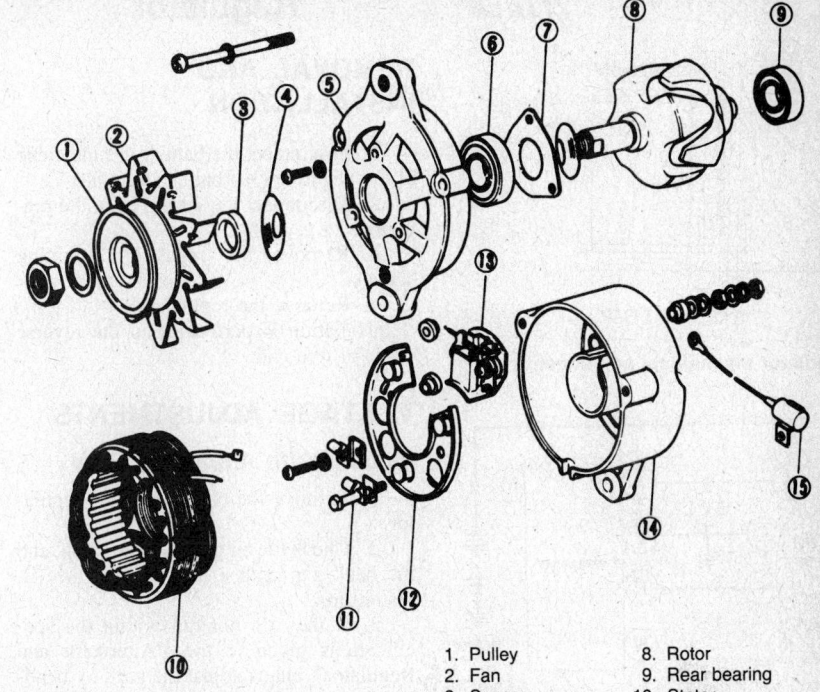

Exploded view of the alternator

1. Pulley
2. Fan
3. Spacer
4. Slinger
5. Front housing
6. Front bearing
7. Bearing retainer
8. Rotor
9. Rear bearing
10. Stator
11. Terminal bolt
12. Diode plate (rectifiers)
13. Brush holder
14. Rear housing
15. Condenser

8. Align the matchmarks on the distributor gear and body.
9. If the engine was cranked while the distributor was removed, turn the crankshaft until the no. 1 cylinder is at the top of the compression stroke. This can be determined by feeling compression with your thumb over the spark plug port. The timing mark on the crankshaft pulley should also be aligned with the timing pointer. Slide the distributor into the engine with the rotor pointing to the no. 1 cylinder firing position (see Firing Order).
10. If the engine has not been cranked while the distributor was removed, slide the distributor (with the O-ring) into the engine, aligning the matchmarks made during removal.
11. Install the flat washer, lockwasher and hold-down nut, but do not tighten the nut.
12. Install the distributor cap and connect the primary wires.
13. Set the ignition timing, and tighten the hold-down nut.
14. Connect the vacuum line wire, it so equipped.

FIRING ORDER

The firing order for the Mazda rotary engine is 1-2, with the trailing spark plugs firing ten degrees after the leading.

The firing order for the piston engine is 1-3-4-2.

Alternator

ALTERNATOR SERVICE PRECAUTIONS

Because of the nature of alternator design, special care must be taken when servicing the charging system.

1. Battery polarity should be checked before making any connections such as jumper cables or battery charger leads. Reversed battery connections will damage the diode rectifiers.
2. The battery must never be disconnected while the alternator is running because the regulator will be ruined.
3. Always disconnect the battery ground cable before replacing the alternator.
4. Do not attempt to polarize an alternator.
5. Do not short across or ground any alternator terminals.
6. Always disconnect the battery ground cable before removing the alternator output cable.
7. If electric arc welding equipment is to be used on the car, first disconnect the battery and alternator cables. Never operate the car with the electric arc welding equipment attached.
8. If the battery is to be "quick charged", disconnect the negative cable from the battery.

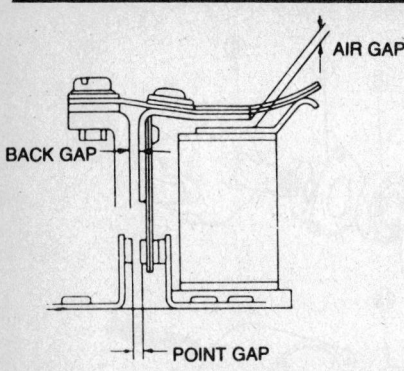

Regulator mechanical adjustments

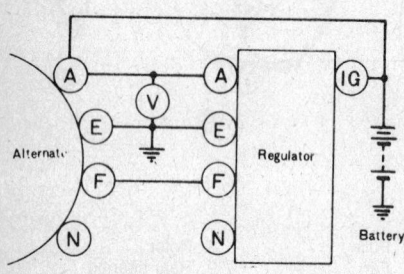

Testing the voltage regulator

REMOVAL AND INSTALLATION

1. Disconnect the battery ground cable at the negative (−) terminal.
2. Disconnect and tag all of the leads from the alternator.
3. Remove the alternator adjusting link bolt. Do not remove the adjusting link.
4. Remove the alternator securing nuts and bolts. Withdraw the drivebelt and remove the alternator.

Installation is performed in the reverse order of removal. Adjust the drivebelt tension as detailed below.

BELT TENSION ADJUSTMENT

1. Check the drivebelt tension by applying about 22 lbs. of thumb pressure to the belt, at the midpoint of the longest span between pulleys. The belt should deflect to the following specifications:
Old belt—0.59–0.67 in.
New belt—0.47–0.55 in.
2. If belt deflection is not within specifications loosen but do not remove the bolt on the adjusting link.
3. Push the alternator in the direction required to obtain proper belt deflection.

—— CAUTION ——
Do not pry or pound the alternator housing.

4. Tighten the adjusting link bolt to 20 ft. lbs.

Regulator

REMOVAL AND INSTALLATION

1. Disconnect the battery ground cable at the negative (−) battery terminal.
2. Disconnect the wiring from the regulator.
3. Remove the regulator mounting screws.
4. Remove the regulator.

Installation is performed in the reverse order of removal.

VOLTAGE ADJUSTMENTS

Models With Ammeters Only

1. Remove the cover from the regulator.
2. Check the air gap, the point gap, and the back gap with a feeler gauge (see illustration).
3. If they do not fall within the specifications given in the "Alternator and Regulator" chart, adjust the gaps by bending the stationary contact bracket.
4. Connect a voltmeter between the "A" and "E" terminal of the regulator.

NOTE: Be sure that the battery is fully charged before proceeding with this test.

5. Start the engine and run it at 2,000 rpm (4,000 alternator rpm). The voltmeter reading should be 13.5–14.5 V.
6. Stop the engine.
7. Bend the upper plate *down* to decrease the voltage setting or *up* to increase the setting, as required.
8. If the regulator cannot be brought within specifications, replace it.
9. When the test is completed, disconnect the voltmeter and replace the regulator cover.

REGULATOR TEST

Models With Warning Light

The alternator regulator is composed of two control units: a constant voltage relay and a pilot lamp relay.

Constant Voltage Relay

1. Use an almost fully charged battery and connect a voltmeter between the "A" and "E" rminals of the regulator.
2. Run the engine at 2,000 rpm and read the voltmeter. It should read from 14–15 volts.
3. If not, adjust the voltage relay.

Pilot Lamp Relay

1. Using a voltmeter and variable resistor, construct a circuit as shown.
2. Light the pilot lamp.
3. Slide the knob of the variable resistor so that the voltage gradually increases.
4. Read the voltage between the "N"

and "E" terminals of the regulator. If the voltage is 3.7–5.7 (4.2–5.2 for 1977 and later) volts, it is operating properly.
5. Slide the knob of the variable resistor to decrease the voltage. Note the point on the voltmeter where the light will light again. If the reading is less than 3.5 volts through 1976 or 3.0 volts for 1977–80, the unit is working properly.
6. Disconnect the test instruments.

REGULATOR

Models With Warning Light

1. Check the air gap, back gap and point gap with a wire gauge. If they are not within specification, adjust the gap by bending the stationary bracket.
2. After the gaps are correctly set, adjust the voltage setting. Bend the upper plate down to decrease the voltage setting, or bend it up to increase the voltage setting.

Constant Voltage Relay

Air Gap .028–.051 in.
Point Gap .012–.018 in.
Back Gap .028–.059 in.

Pilot Lamp Relay

Air Gap .035–.055 in. through 1976, .039–.059 from 1977
Point Gap .028–.043 in. through 1976, .020–.035 in. from 1977
Back Gap .028–.059 in.

Starter

REMOVAL AND INSTALLATION

Rotary Engine

NOTE: There are two possible locations for the starter motor; one is on the lower right-hand side of the engine and the other is on the upper right-hand side.

1. Remove the ground cable from the negative (−) battery terminal.
2. If the car is equipped with the lower mounted starter, remove the gravel shield from underneath the engine.

—— CAUTION ——
Be extremely careful not to contact the hot exhaust pipe while working underneath the car.

3. Remove the battery cable from the starter terminal.
4. Disconnect the solenoid leads from the solenoid terminals.
5. Remove the starter securing bolts and withdraw the starter assembly.

Installation is the reverse.

Piston Engine

1. Raise the hood and disconnect the battery ground cable.

2. Remove the carburetor air cleaner and intake tube for clearance, if necessary.

3. Disconnect the battery cable from the starter solenoid battery terminal.

4. Pull the ignition switch wire from the solenoid terminal.

5. Raise and support the vehicle on jackstands.

6. Working under the vehicle, remove the starter attaching bolts, washers and nuts.

7. Tilt the drive end of the starter and remove the starter.

8. Installation is the reverse of removal.

SOLENOID REPLACEMENT

Perform solenoid replacement with the starter motor removed from the car.

1. Detach the field strap from the solenoid terminals.

2. Remove the solenoid securing screws.

3. Withdraw the solenoid spring and washers from the starter drive housing.

Solenoid installation is performed in the reverse order of removal.

STARTER DRIVE REPLACEMENT

1. Perform the solenoid removal procedure as above.

2. Remove the plunger from the drive engagement fork.

3. Unfasten the nuts from the thru-bolts.

NOTE: Unless further disassembly of the starter is desired, do not remove the thru bolts.

4. Remove the drive housing from the front of the starter.

5. Remove the engagement fork, spring, and spring seat.

6. Withdraw the over-running clutch from the armature shaft.

Assembly is performed in the reverse order of disassembly. Check the clearance between the pinion and the stop collar with the solenoid engaged. It should be 0.02–0.08 in.

ENGINE MECHANICAL

Rotary

NOTE: Because of the unique design of the Mazda rotary engine, some procedures require the use of special factory tools. The text notes where these tools are necessary. If the tools are not available, the job should not be undertaken.

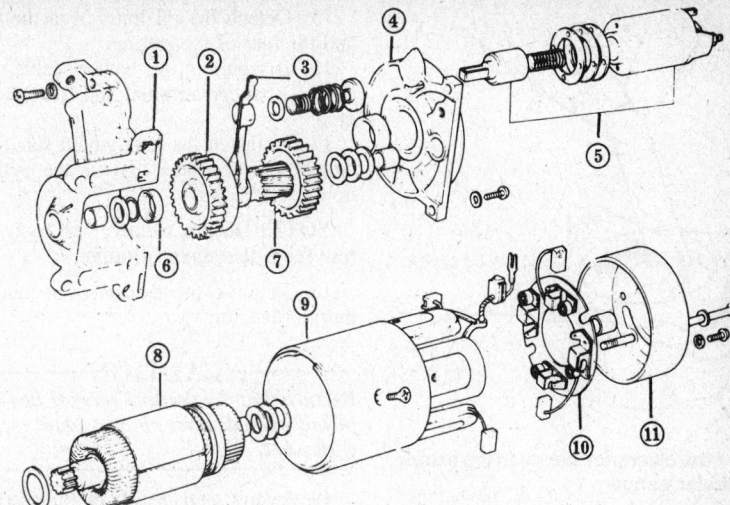

Starter motor components

1. Front housing
2. Overrunning clutch
3. Engagement fork
4. Center frame
5. Solenoid
6. Stop
7. Idler gear
8. Armature
9. Field coil
10. Brush holder
11. End frame

DESIGN

The Mazda rotary engine replaces conventional pistons with three-cornered rotors which have rounded sides. The rotors are mounted on a shaft which has eccentrics rather than crank throws.

The chamber which the rotor travels in is roughly oval-shaped, but with the sides of the oval bowed in slightly. The technical name for this shape is a two-lobe epitrochoid.

As the rotor travels its path in the chamber, it performs the same four functions as the piston in a traditional piston engine: intake, compression, ignition, and exhaust. But all four functions in a rotary engine are happening concurrently, rather than in four separate stages.

Ignition of the compressed fuel/air mixture occurs each time a side of the rotor passes the spark plugs. Since the rotor has three sides, there are three complete power impulses for each complete revolution of the rotor.

As it moves, the rotor exerts pressure on the cam of the eccentric shaft, causing the shaft to turn.

Because there are three power pulses for every revolution of the rotor, the eccentric shaft must make three complete revolutions for every one of the rotor. To maintain this ratio, the rotor has an internal gear that meshes with a fixed gear in a three-to-one ratio. If it were not for this gear arrangement, the rotor would spin freely and timing would be lost.

The Mazda rotary engine has two rotors mounted 60 degrees out of phase. This produces six power impulses for each complete revolution of both rotors and two power impulses for each revolution of the eccentric shaft.

Because of the number of power impulses for each revolution of the rotor, and because all four functions are concurrent, the rotary engine is able to produce a much greater amount of power for its size and weight than a comparable reciprocating piston engine.

Instead of using valves to control the intake and exhaust operations, the rotor uncovers and covers ports on the wall of the chamber as it turns. Thus, a complex valve train is unnecessary. The resulting elimination of parts further reduces the size and weight of the engine, as well as eliminating a major source of mechanical problems.

Spring-loaded carbon seals are used to prevent loss of compression around the rotor apexes and cast iron seals are used to prevent loss of compression around the side faces of the rotor. These seals are equivalent to compression rings on a conventional piston but must be more durable because of the high rotor rpm to which they are exposed.

Oil is controlled by means of circular seals mounted in two grooves on the side face of the rotor. These oil seals function to keep oil out of the combustion chamber and gasoline out of the crankcase, in a similar manner to the oil control ring on a piston.

The rotor housing is made of aluminum and the surfaces of the chamber are chrome plated for durability and the prevention of wear damage.

REMOVAL AND INSTALLATION

— CAUTION —
Be sure that the engine has completely cooled before attempting to remove it.

1. Scribe matchmarks on the hood and hinges. Remove the hood from the hinges.

2. Working from underneath the car, remove the gravel shield; then drain the cooling system and the engine oil.

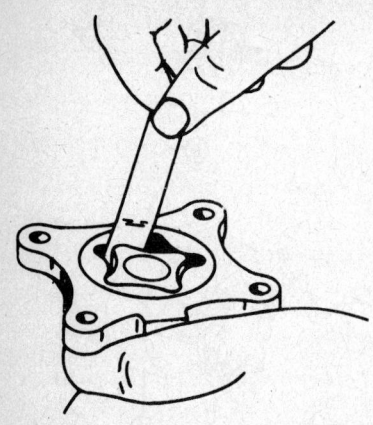

Measure the clearance between the rotors with a feeler gauge

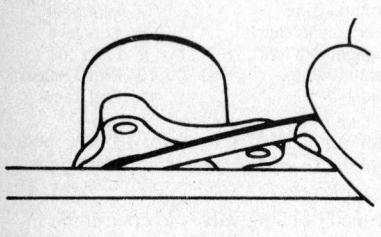

Measure the gap between the straight edge and the housing

3. Disconnect the cable from the negative (−) battery terminal.

4. Remove the air cleaner, its bracket, and its attendant hoses.

5. Detach the accelerator cable, choke cable, and fuel lines from the carburetor.

6. Remove the nuts which secure the thermostat housing. Disconnect the ground cable from the housing and install the housing again after the cable is removed.

7. Disconnect the power brake vacuum line from the intake manifold.

8. Remove the fan shroud securing bolts and then the shroud itself.

9. Remove the bolts which secure the fan clutch to the eccentric shaft pulley.

Withdraw the fan and clutch as a single unit.

NOTE: Keep the fan clutch in an upright position, so that its fluid does not leak out.

10. Unfasten the clamps and remove both of the radiator hoses.

11. Note their respective positions and remove the spark plug cables. Disconnect the primary leads from the distributors and remove both of the distributor caps.

12. Detach all of the leads from the alternator, the water temperature sender, the oil pressure sender, and the starter motor.

13. Disconnect all of the wiring from the emission control system components.

14. Detach the heater hoses at the engine.

15. Detach the oil lines from the front and the rear of the engine.

16. Disconnect the battery cable from the (+) battery terminal and from the engine.

17. Unfasten the nuts which secure the clutch slave cylinder and tie the cylinder up out of the way.

NOTE: Do not remove the hydraulic line from the slave cylinder.

18. Remove the exhaust pipe and the thermal reactor.

───── **CAUTION** ─────

Be sure that the thermal reactor has completely cooled; severe burns could result if it has not.

19. Evenly and in two or three stages, remove the nuts and bolts which secure the clutch housing to the engine.

20. Support the transmission with a jack.

21. Remove the nuts from each of the engine mounts.

22. Attach a lifting sling to the lifting bracket on the rear of the engine housing.

23. Use a hoist to take up the slack on the sling.

───── **CAUTION** ─────

Be sure that the hoist is secure to prevent possible personal injury or damage to the engine.

24. Pull the engine forward until it clears the transmission input shaft. Lift the engine straight up and out of the car.

NOTE: Be careful not to damage any of the components which remain in the car.

25. Remove the heat stove from exhaust manifold.

26. Remove the thermal reactor.

Engine installation is performed in the reverse order of removal.

Rotary Engine Overhaul

ENGINE DISASSEMBLY

1. Mount the engine on a stand.

2. Remove the oil hose support bracket from the front housing.

3. Disconnect the vacuum hoses, air hoses and remove the decel valve.

4. Remove the air pump and drive belt. Remove the air pump adjusting bar.

5. Remove the alternator and drive belt.

6. Disconnect the metering oil pump connecting rod, oil tubes and vacuum sensing tube from the carburetor.

7. Remove the carburetor and intake manifold as an assembly.

8. Remove the gasket and two rubber rings.

9. Remove the thermal reactor and gaskets.

10. Remove the distributor from the front cover.

11. Remove the water pump and gasket.

12. Invert the engine on the stand.

13. Remove the oil pan and gasket.

14. Remove the oil pump screen and gasket.

15. Identify the front and rear rotor housings with a felt tip pen. These are common parts and must be identified to be reassembled in their respective locations.

16. Turn the engine on the stand so that the top of the engine is up.

17. Remove the engine mounting bracket from the front cover.

18. Hold the flywheel with a flywheel holder and remove the eccentric shaft pulley.

19. Turn the engine on a stand so that the front end of the engine is up.

20. Remove the front cover and gasket.

21. Remove the O-ring from the oil passage on the front housing.

22. Remove the oil slinger and distributor drive gear from the shaft.

23. Unbolt and remove the chain adjuster.

24. Remove the locknut and washer from the oil pump driven sprocket.

25. Slide the oil pump drive sprocket and driven sprocket together with the drive chain off the eccentric shaft and oil pump simultaneously.

26. Remove the keys from the eccentric and oil pump shafts.

27. Slide the balance weight, thrust washer and needle bearing from the shaft.

28. Unbolt the bearing housing and slide the bearing housing, needle bearing, spacer and thrust plate off the shaft.

29. Turn the engine on the stand so that the top of the engine is up.

30. If equipped with a manual transmission, remove the clutch pressure plate and clutch disc. Loosen the pressure plate bolts evenly in small stages to prevent distortion and possible injury from the pressure plate flying off. Straighten the tab of the lockwasher and remove the flywheel nut. Remove the flywheel with a puller.

31. If equipped with an automatic transmission, remove the drive plate. Straighten the tab on the lockwasher and remove the counterweight nut, while holding the flywheel with a flywheel holder. Remove the counterweight using a puller.

32. Working at the rear of the engine, loosen the tension bolts in the sequence shown, and remove the tension bolts.

NOTE: Do not loosen the tension bolts one at a time. Loosen the bolts evenly in small stages to prevent distortion.

33. Lift the rear housing off the shaft.

34. Remove any seals that are stuck to the rotor sliding surface of the rear housing and reinstall them in their original locations.

35. Remove all the corner seals, corner seal springs, side seal and side seal springs from the rear side of the rotor. Mazda has

a special tray which holds all the seals and keeps them segregated to prevent mistakes during reassembly. Each seal groove is marked to prevent confusion.

36. Remove the two rubber seals and two O-rings from the rear rotor housing.

37. Remove the dowels from the rear rotor housing.

38. Lift the rear rotor housing away from the rear rotor, being very careful not to drop the apex seals on the rear rotor.

39. Remove each apex seal, side piece and spring from the rear rotor and segregate them.

40. Remove the rear rotor from the eccentric shaft and place it upside down on a clean rag.

41. Remove each seal and spring from the other side of the rotor and segregate these.

42. If some of the seals fall off the rotor, be careful not to change the original position of each seal.

43. Identify the rear rotor with a felt tip pen.

44. Remove the oil seals and the springs. Do not exert heavy pressure at only one place on the seal, since it could be deformed. Replace the O-rings in the oil seal when the engine is overhauled.

45. Hold the intermedidate housing down and remove the dowels from it.

46. Lift off the intermediate housing being careful not to damage the eccentric shaft. It should be removed by sliding it beyond the rear rotor journal on the eccentric shaft while holding the intermediate housing up and, at the same time, pushing the eccentric shaft up.

47. Lift out the eccentric shaft.

48. Repeat the above procedures to remove the front rotor housing and front rotor.

ENGINE ASSEMBLY

1. Place the rotor on a rubber pad or cloth.

2. Install the oil seal rings in their respective grooves in the rotors with the edge of the spring in the stopper hole. The oil seal springs are painted cream or blue in color. The cream colored springs must be installed on the front faces of both rotors. The blue colored springs must be installed on the rear faces of both rotors. When installing each oil seal spring, the painted side (square side) of the spring must face upward (toward the oil seal.)

3. Install a new O-ring in each groove. Place each oil seal in the groove so that the square edge of the spring fits in the stopper hole of the oil seal. Push the head of the oil seal slowly with the fingers, being careful that the seal is not deformed. Be sure that the oil seal moves smoothly in the groove before installing the O-ring.

4. Lubricate each oil seal and groove with engine oil and check the movement of the seal. It should move freely when the head of the seal is pressed.

5. Check the oil seal protrusion and install the seals on the other side of each rotor.

6. Install the apex seals without springs and side pieces into their respective grooves so that each side piece positions on the side of each rotor.

7. Install the corner seal springs and corner seals into their respective grooves.

8. Install the side seal springs and side seals into their respective grooves.

9. Apply engine oil to each spring and check each spring for smooth movement.

10. Check each seal protrusion.

11. Invert the rotor being careful that the seals do not fall out, and install the oil seals on the other side in the same manner.

12. Mount the front housing on a workstand so that the top of the housing is up.

13. Lubricate the internal gear of the rotor with engine oil.

14. Hold the apex seals with used O-rings to keep the apex seals installed and place the rotor on the front housing. Be careful not to drop the seals. Turn the front housing so that the sliding surface faces upward.

15. Mesh the internal and stationary gears and remove the old O-ring which is holding the apex seals in position.

16. Lubricate the front rotor journal of the eccentric shaft with engine oil and lubricate the eccentric shaft main journal.

17. Insert the eccentric shaft. Be careful that you do not damage the rotor bearing and main bearing.

18. Apply sealing agent to the front side of the front rotor housing.

19. Apply a light coat of petroleum jelly onto new O-rings and rubber seals (to prevent them from coming off) and install the O-rings and rubber seals on the front side of the rotor housing.

NOTE: The inner rubber seal is of the square type. The wider white line of the rubber seal should face the combustion chamber and the rubber seal should be positioned as shown. Do not stretch the rubber seal.

20. If the engine is being overhauled, install the seal protector to only the inner rubber seal to improve durability.

21. Invert the front rotor housing, being careful not to let the rubber seals and O-rings fall from their grooves, and mount it on the front housing.

22. Lubricate the dowels with engine oil and insert them through the front rotor housing holes and into the front housing.

23. Apply sealer to the front side of the rotor housing.

24. Install new O-rings and rubber seals on the front rotor housing in the same manner as for the other side.

25. Insert each apex spring seal, making sure that the seal is installed in the proper direction.

26. Install each side piece in its original position and be sure that the springs seat on the side piece.

27. Lubricate the side pieces with en-

Arrow (right) indicates the metering oil pump adjusting screw. The three arrows (left) indicate the connecting rod adjusting holes.

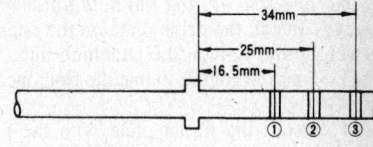

① : 248cc / 6,000rpm / Hr
② : 174cc / 6,000rpm / Hr
③ : 104cc / 6,000rpm / Hr

Connecting rod adjusting holes

gine oil. Make sure that the front rotor housing is free of foreign matter and lubricate the sliding surface of the front housing with engine oil.

28. Turn the front housing assembly with the rotor, so that the top of the housing is up. Pull the eccentric shaft about 1 in.

29. Position the eccentric portion of the eccentric shaft diagonally, to the upper right.

30. Install the intermediate housing over the eccentric shaft onto the front rotor housing. Turn the engine so that the rear of the engine is up.

31. Install the rear rotor and rear rotor housing following the same steps as for the front rotor and the front housing.

32. Turn the engine so that the rear of the engine is up.

33. Lubricate the stationary gear and main bearing.

34. Install the rear housing onto the rear rotor housing. If necessary, turn the rear rotor slightly to mesh the rear housing stationary gear with the rear rotor internal gear.

35. Install a new washer on each tension bolt, and lubricate each bolt with engine oil.

36. Install the tension bolts and tighten them evenly, in several stages in sequence. The specified torque is 23–27 ft. lbs.

37. After tightening the bolts, turn the eccentric shaft to be sure that the shaft and rotors turn smoothly and easily.

38. Lubricate the oil seal in the rear housing.

39. On vehicles with manual transmission, install the flywheel on the rear of the eccentric shaft so that the keyway of the flywheel fits the key on the shaft.

40. Apply sealer to both sides of the flywheel lockwasher and install the lockwasher.

41. Install the flywheel locknut. Hold the flywheel *securely* and tighten the nut to *three hundred and fifty ft. lbs.* (350 ft. lbs.) of torque.

NOTE: 350 ft. lbs is a great deal of torque. In actual practice, it is practically impossible to accurately measure that much torque on the nut. At least a 3 ft. bar will be required to generate sufficient torque. Tighten it as tight as possible, with no longer than 3 ft. of leverage. Be sure the engine is held SECURELY.

42. On vehicles with automatic transmission, install the key, counterweight, lockwasher and nut. Tighten the nut to 350 ft. lbs. *See step 41 and the note following step 41.* Install the drive plate on the counterweight and tighten the attaching nuts.

43. Turn the engine so that the front faces up.

44. Install the thrust plate with the tapered face down, and install the needle bearing on the eccentric shaft. Lubricate with engine oil.

45. Install the bearing housing on the front housing. Tighten the bolts and bend up the lockwasher tabs.

The spacer should be installed so that the center of the needle bearing comes to the center of the eccentric shaft and the spacer should be seated on the thrust plate.

46. Install the needle bearing on the shaft and lubricate it with engine oil.

47. Install the balancer and thrust washer on the eccentric shaft.

48. Install the oil pump drive chain over both of the sprockets. Install the sprocket and chain assembly over the eccentric shaft and oil pump shafts simultaneously. Install the key on the eccentric shaft.

NOTE: Be sure that both of the sprockets are engaged with the chain before installing them over the shafts.

49. Install the distributor drive gear onto the eccentric shaft with the "F" mark on the gear facing the front of the engine. Slide the spacer and oil slinger onto the eccentric shaft.

50. Align the keyway and install the eccentric shaft pulley. Tighten the pulley bolt to 60 ft. lbs.

51. Turn the engine top so the engine faces up.

52. Check eccentric shaft end-play in the following manner:

    a. Attach a dial indicator to the flywheel. Move the flywheel forward and backward.

    b. Note the reading on the dial indicator; it should be 0.0016–0.0028 in.

    c. If the end-play is not within specifications, adjust it by replacing the front spacer. Spacers come in four sizes, ranging from 0.3150–0.3181 in. If necessary, a spacer can be ground on a surface plate with emery paper.

    d. Check the end-play again and, if it is now within specifications, proceed with the next step.

ECCENTRIC SHAFT SPACER THICKNESS CHART

Marking	Thickness
X	8.08 ± 0.01 mm (0.3181 ± 0.0004 in)
Y	8.04 ± 0.01 mm (0.3165 ± 0.0004 in)
V	8.02 ± 0.01 mm (0.3158 ± 0.0004 in)
Z	.800 ± 0.01 mm (0.3150 ± 0.0004 in)

53. Remove the pulley from the front of the eccentric shaft. Tighten the oil pump drive sprocket nut and bend the locktabs on the lockwasher.

54. Fit a new O-ring over the front cover oil passage.

55. Install the chain tensioner and tighten its securing bolts.

56. Position the front cover gasket and the front cover on the front housing, then secure the front cover with its attachment bolts.

57. Install the eccentric shaft pulley again. Tighten its bolt to 60 ft. lbs.

58. Turn the engine so that the bottom faces up.

59. Cut off the excess gasket on the front cover along the mounting surface of the oil pan.

60. Install the oil strainer gasket and strainer on the front housing and tighten the attaching bolts.

61. Apply sealer to the joint surfaces of each housing.

62. Install the gasket and oil pan. Tighten the bolts evenly in two stages to 3.5 ft. lbs.

63. Turn the engine so that the top is up.

64. Install the water pump gasket on the front housing. Tighten the attaching bolts.

65. Rotate the eccentric shaft until the yellow mark (leading side mark) aligns with the pointer on the front cover.

66. Align the marks on the distributor gear and housing and install the distributor so that the lockbolt is in the center of the slot.

67. Rotate the distributor until the leading points start to separate and tighten the distributor locknut.

68. Install the gaskets and thermal reactor and tighten the attaching nuts.

69. Install the hot air duct.

70. Install the carburetor and intake manifold assembly with a new gasket. Tighten the attaching nuts.

71. Connect the oil tubes, vacuum tube and metering oil pump connecting rod to the carburetor.

72. Install the decel valve and connect the vacuum lines, air hoses and wires.

73. Install the alternator bracket, alternator and bolt and check the clearance. If the clearance is more than 0.006 in., adjust the clearance using a shim. Shims are available in three sizes: 0.0059 in., 0.0118 in., and 0.0197 in.

74. Install the alternator drive belt. Attach the alternator to the adjusting brace and adjust the belt tension to specification.

75. Install the air pump with the adjusting brace and install the air pump drive belt. Adjust the air pump drive belt to specifications.

76. Install the engine hanger bracket to the front cover.

77. Remove the engine from the stand.

78. Install the engine in the vehicle.

79. Fill the engine with fresh engine oil and install a new filter. Fill the engine with coolant. Start the engine, check the oil pressure, and warm it to normal operating temperature. Adjust the idle speed, timing and dwell. Recheck all capacities and refill if necessary. Check for leaks.

Intake Manifold

REMOVAL AND INSTALLATION

To remove the intake manifold and carburetor assembly with the engine remaining in the automobile, proceed in the following manner:

1. Perform steps 2, 3, 4, 5, 7, and 13 of Engine Removal and Installation, above. Do not remove the engine. Do not drain the engine oil; merely remove the metering oil pump hose from the carburetor.

2. Perform steps 6 and 7 of the Engine Disassembly procedure.

Install the intake manifold and carburetor assembly in the reverse order of removal. Tighten the manifold securing nuts, working from the inside out, and in two or three stages, to the torque specifications found in the Torque Specifications. Refill the cooling system.

Thermal Reactor

REMOVAL AND INSTALLATION

— CAUTION —
The thermal reactor operates at extremely high temperatures. Allow the engine to cool completely before attempting to remove it.

To remove the thermal reactor, which replaces the exhaust manifold, proceed in the following manner:

1. Remove the air cleaner assembly from the carburetor.

2. Unbolt and remove the air injection

pump as outlined in Emission Controls.

3. Remove the intake manifold assembly, complete with carburetor.

4. Remove the heat stove from the thermal reactor.

5. Unfasten the thermal reactor securing nuts, including those on the exhaust pipe flange.

NOTE: The bottom nut is difficult to reach. Mazda makes a special wrench (part number 49 213 001) to remove it. If the wrench is unavailable, a flexible drive metric socket wrench may be substituted.

6. Lift the thermal reactor away from the engine.

Installation of the thermal reactor is performed in the reverse order of removal.

ENGINE LUBRICATION

Rotary

A conventional pump, which is chain driven, circulates oil through the rotary engine. A full-flow filter is mounted on the top of the rear housing and an oil cooler is used to reduce the temperature of the engine oil.

An unusual feature of the rotary engine lubrication system is a metering oil pump which injects oil into the float chamber of the carburetor. Once there, it is mixed with the fuel which is to be burned, thus providing extra lubrication for the seals. The metering oil pump is designed to work only when the engine is working under a load.

Oil Pan

REMOVAL AND INSTALLATION

1. Raise the front of the car and support it with jackstands.

— CAUTION —
Be sure that the car is supported securely.

2. Remove the drain plug and drain the engine oil.

3. Remove the nuts and bolts which secure the gravel shield and withdraw it from underneath the car.

4. Unfasten the retaining bolts and remove the oil pan with its gasket.

Oil pan installation is performed in the reverse order of removal. Coat both the oil pan flange and its mounting flange with sealer, prior to assembly.

Oil Pump

Removal and Installation

Oil pump removal and installation is con-

tained in the engine overhaul section above. Perform only those steps needed to remove the oil pump.

CHECKING CLEARANCES

1. Separate the havles of the oil pump housing.

2. Measure the clearance between the lobes of the rotors with a feeler gauge. The clearance should be 0.004–0.0035 in. Replace both of the rotors if the clearance exceeds 0.006 in.

3. Check the clearance between the outer rotor and the housing with a feeler gauge. The clearance should be 0.008–0.010 in. If the clearance is greater than 0.012 in., replace both of the rotors.

4. Place a straightedge across the pump housing. Measure the gap between the straightedge and the housing with a feeler gauge. The gap should be 0.001–0.005 in. If the gap exceeds 0.012 in., replace the rotors or the pump housing.

Metering Oil Pump

OPERATION

A metering oil pump, mounted on the top of the engine, is used to provide additional lubrication to the engine when it is operating under a load. The pump provides oil to the carburetor, where it is mixed in the float chamber with the fuel to be burned.

The metering pump is a plunger type and is controlled by throttle opening. A cam arrangement, connected to the carburetor throttle lever, operates a plunger. The plunger, in turn, acts on a differential plunger, the stroke of which determines the amount of oil flow.

When the throttle opening is small, the amount of the plunger stroke is small; as the throttle opening increases, so does the amount of the plunger stroke.

TESTING

1. At the carburetor, disconnect the oil lines which run from the metering oil pump to the carburetor.

2. Use a container which has a scale calibrated in cubic centimeters (cc) on its side to catch the pump discharge from the oil lines.

3. Rum the engine at 2,000 rpm for six minutes.

4. At the end of this time, 2.0–2.5cc's should be collected in the container. If not, adjust the pump as explained below.

ADJUSTMENTS

Rotate the adjusting screw on the metering oil pump to obtain the proper oil flow. Clockwise rotation of the screw *increases* the flow; counterclockwise rotation *decreases* the flow.

If necessary, the oil discharge rate may be further adjusted by changing the position of the cam in the pump connecting rod. The shorter the rod throw, the more oil will be pumped. Adjust the throw by means of the three holes provided.

Oil Cooler

REMOVAL AND INSTALLATION

1. Raise the car and support it with jackstands.

— CAUTION —
Be sure that the car is securely supported.

2. Drain the engine oil.

3. Unfasten the screws which retain the gravel shield and remove the shield.

4. Unfasten the oil lines from the oil cooler.

5. Unfasten the nuts which secure the

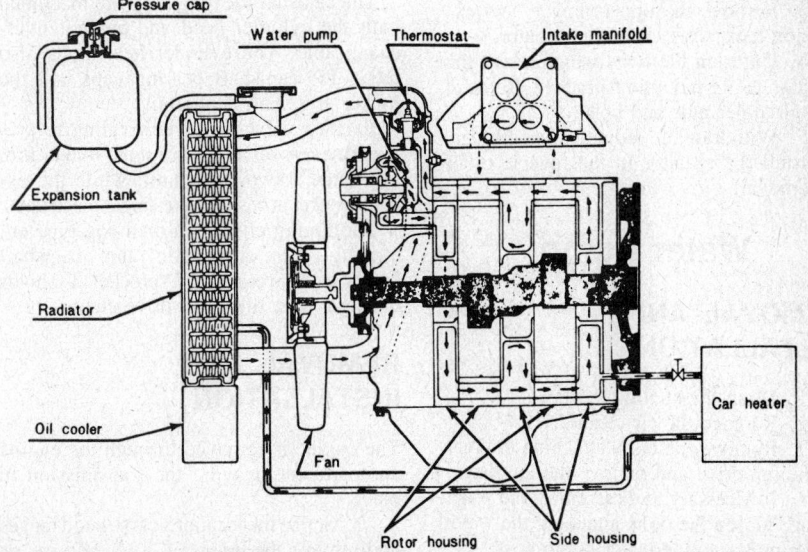

Rotary engine cooling system

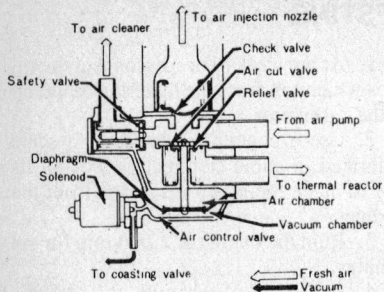

Thermostat installation and by-pass circuit

oil cooler to the radiator.

6. Remove the oil cooler.

Examine the oil cooler for signs of leakage. Blow the cooler fins clean with compressed air. Later models coolers are made from aluminum; they must be repaired by aluminim welding.

Installation is performed in the reverse order of removal.

ENGINE COOLING

Rotary

RADIATOR REMOVAL AND INSTALLATION

— **CAUTION** —
Perform this operation when the engine has cooled completely.

1. Drain the engine coolant into a large, clean container so that it may be reused.

2. Remove the nuts and bolts which attach the shroud to the radiator. Withdraw the shroud.

3. Remove the upper, lower, and expansion tank hoses from the radiator.

4. Unfasten the bolts which attach the radiator to its mounting bracket. Remove the oil cooler nuts and bolts.

5. Withdraw the radiator from the car.

Install the radiator in the reverse order of removal.

Water Pump

REMOVAL AND INSTALLATION

1. Drain the cooling system.

2. Remove the air cleaner.

3. Remove the bolts attaching the rear of the fan drive and remove the fan drive.

4. If necessary to disassemble the water pump, loosen the bolts attaching the water pump pulley to the water pump boss.

5. Remove the air pump and drive belt.

6. Remove the alternator and disconnect the drive belt.

7. If necessary, remove the water pump pulley and bolts.

8. Unbolt and remove the water pump.

9. Installation is the reverse of removal.

Thermostat

REMOVAL AND INSTALLATION

1. Drain the engine coolant into a large, clean container for reuse.

2. Remove the nuts which secure the thermostat housing to the water pump.

3. Lift the thermostat.

Thermostat installation is performed in the reverse order of removal.

— **CAUTION** —
The thermostat is equipped with a plunger which covers and uncovers a by-pass hole at its bottom. Because of this unusual construction, only the specified Mazda thermostat should be used for replacement. A standard thermostat will cause the engine to overheat.

ENGINE MECHANICAL

Piston Engine

Mazda piston engines are single overhead camshaft, four-cylinder engines. Water cools the thin cast iron block and cast aluminum alloy cylinder head with multi-spherical type combustion chambers.

The camshaft bearing caps are machined with the cylinder head and are not interchangeable. The cylinder head bolts also retain the camshaft bearing caps and the rocker arm shaft supports.

Exhaust valves are free rotating to prevent uneven valve wear. Intake rocker arm shafts are a two-piece unit, while the exhaust rocker arm shafts are single piece units.

The timing chain is a dual cog type encircling the crankshaft and camshaft sprockets. The crankshaft sprocket also holds the rotor type oil pump drive chain.

REMOVAL AND INSTALLATION

The engine is removed through the engine compartment, leaving the transmission in place.

1. Scribe the locations of the hood hinges and remove the hood.

2. Remove the engine splash shield.

3. Drain the coolant.

4. Drain the engine oil.

5. Disconnect and remove the battery.

6. Disconnect the primary wire and coil wire from the distributor.

7. Disconnect the wire at the "B" terminal of the alternator and disconnect the plug from the rear of the alternator.

8. Disconnect the wire from the oil pressure switch.

9. Disconnect the engine ground wire.

10. Remove the air cleaner and heat insulator.

11. Disconnect the breather hose from the rocker cover.

12. Disconnect the water temperature gauge wire and solenoid valve wire.

13. Disconnect the coupler for the back-up light switch.

14. Disconnect the vacuum tubes at the intake manifold and the carburetor.

15. Disconnect the starter wires.

16. Remove the upper and lower radiator hoses.

17. Remove the bolts attaching the radiator cowling. The cowling can only be removed after the radiator has been removed.

18. Remove the radiator.

19. Disconnect the heater hoses from the intake manifold.

20. Disconnect the throttle cable from the carburetor and remove the throttle linkage from the rocker cover.

21. Disconnect the choke cable from the carburetor.

22. Disconnect the fuel ventilation hose from the oil separator.

23. Disconnect the fuel line at the carburetor and plug the fuel line.

24. Remove the starter.

25. Disconnect the exhaust pipe from the manifold.

26. Remove the clutch or torque converter cover plate.

27. Support the transmission with a jack and remove the bolts attaching the engine to the transmission.

28. Unbolt the engine mounts.

29. Attach a lifting sling to the engine and pull the engine forward until it clears the transmission shaft.

30. Lift the engine from the vehicle.

31. Installation is the reverse of removal. Be sure to check all fluid levels.

Cylinder Head

REMOVAL AND INSTALLATION

Be sure that the cylinder head is cold before removal. This will prevent warpage.

1. Drain the cooling system. Disconnect the negative battery cable.

2. Scribe alignment marks around the hood hinges and remove the hood.

3. Remove the air cleaner.

4. Disconnect the coil wire and vac-

uum line from the distributor.

5. Rotate the crankshaft to put the no. 1 cylinder at TDC on the compression stroke.

6. Remove the plug wires and distributor cap as a unit.

7. Remove the distributor.

8. Remove the rocker arm cover.

9. Disconnect the exhaust pipe from the manifold.

10. Remove the accelerator linkage.

11. Remove the nut, washer and the distributor gear from the camshaft.

12. Remove the nut, washers, and camshaft gear. Support the timing chain from falling into the timing chain case. Do not remove the cam gear from the timing chain. The relationship between the chain and gear teeth should not be disturbed.

13. Remove the cylinder head bolts and cylinder head-to-front cover bolt.

14. Remove the rocker arm assembly.

15. Remove the camshaft from the camshaft gear.

16. Lift off the cylinder head.

17. Remove all tension from the timing chain.

To install the cylinder head:

18. Clean the rocker cover gasket surface at the head and the cover. Clean the head gasket surface at the head and the block. Clean the water pump gasket surface at the head gasket surface and the front cover.

19. Check the cylinder head flatness with a straightedge and feeler blades. It should not exceed 0.003 in. in any six in. span or 0.006 in. overall. If necessary, the cylinder head can be resurfaced, not to exceed 0.008 in.

20. Clean the cylinder head bolt holes of oil and dirt.

21. Position a new head gasket on the cylinder block.

22. Install the cylinder head on the block using the guides at either end of the block.

23. Install the camshaft on the head and camshaft gear.

24. Install the rocker arm assembly.

25. Install the head bolts. Torque the bolts to specifications in three progressive stages, in the sequence illustrated at the front of this section.

26. Install the camshaft gear washer and nut.

27. Install the distributor gear, washer and nut.

28. Time the engine. Follow the instructions under "Timing Chain and Sprocket Installation."

29. Adjust the timing chain tension. See "Timing Chain Tensioner Adjustment".

30. Connect the exhaust pipe to the exhaust manifold.

31. Install the distributor, distributor cap and plug wires.

32. Install the lower intake bracket bolt.

33. Install the accelerator linkage.

34. Connect the vacuum line and coil wire.

35. Adjust the valve clearance cold.

36. Install the rocker arm cover. Fill the cooling system.

37. Run the engine until normal operating temperature is reached, and check for leaks. Adjust the valve clearance hot.

38. Adjust the carburetor and ignition timing. Install the air cleaner and install the hood.

VALVE GUIDE REMOVAL AND INSTALLATION

Before attempting this, consult the Engine Rebuilding section for general procedures that will apply.

1. Remove the cylinder head.

2. Remove the deposits from the combustion chambers with a stiff wire brush and scraper before removing the valves. Do not scratch the cylinder head surface.

3. Compress the valve springs with a valve spring compressor. Remove the valve spring retainer locks and release the springs.

4. Keep the exhaust and intake valve retainers separate. They should be reassembled to the valve from which they were removed.

5. Remove the spring retainer, springs and valve.

6. Remove the valve stem seals. Identify all parts so that they can be reinstalled in their original locations.

7. Drive out the valve guides.

8. Check the cylinder head flatness as described under Cylinder Head Removal and Installation.

Assemble the cylinder head using new parts where applicable:

a. Lubricate all valves, valve stems, and valve guides with heavy-duty oil (SE). The valve tips should be lubricated with Lubriplate or the equivalent. Apply this before installation.

b. Press new valve guides into each bore until the ring on the guide touches the cylinder head. Note that the intake and exhaust valve guides are different.

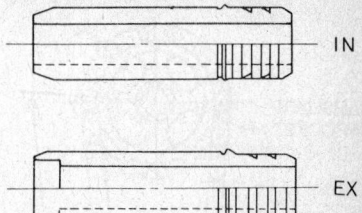

Intake (IN) and exhaust (EX) valve guides

c. Install new valve seals on the valve guides.

d. Install each valve into the valve from which it was removed or fitted.

e. Install the valve springs over the valve. Install the spring retainer.

f. Compress the springs and install the retainer locks. Be sure that the exhaust and intake locks are assembled to the correct valves.

9. Install the cylinder head. See Cylinder Head Installation. Adjust the valves (hot) and set the timing and carburetor.

Rocker Shafts

REMOVAL AND INSTALLATION

This operation should only be performed on a cold engine; the bolts which hold the rocker shafts in place also hold the cylinder head to the block.

1. Raise the hood and cover the fenders.

2. Disconnect the choke cable.

3. If equipped, disconnect the air bypass valve cable.

4. Disconnect the spark plug wires. Remove the wires from the spark wire guides on the rocker covers and position them out of the way.

5. Remove the rocker cover and dis-

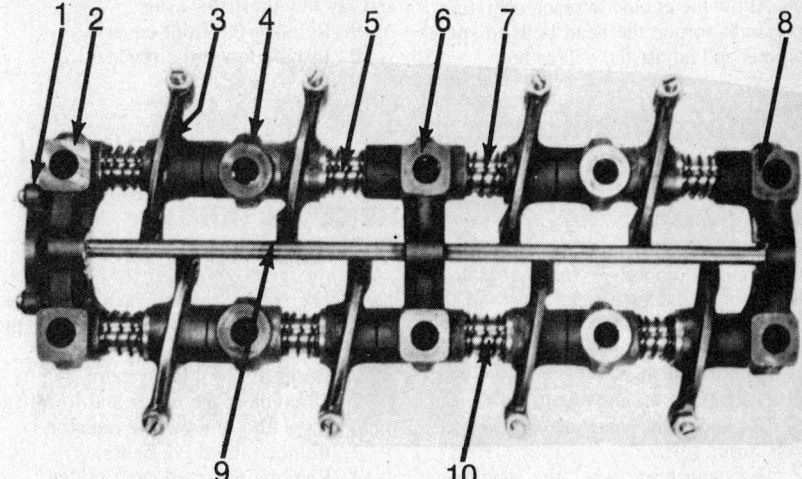

Rocker arm assembly—piston engine

	(exhaust)
1. Thrust plate	6. Center bearing cap
2. Front bearing cap	7. Spring
3. Rocker arm (exhaust)	8. Rear bearing cap
4. Support	9. Oil pipe
5. Rocker arm shaft	10. Rocker arm shaft (intake)

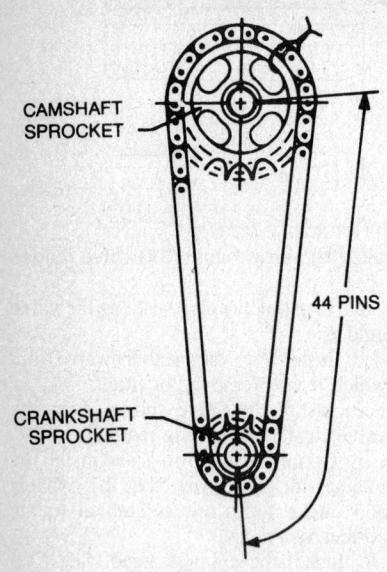

CAMSHAFT SPROCKET

44 PINS

CRANKSHAFT SPROCKET

Installing timing chain—1800 and 2000 engines

card the gasket.

6. Remove the rocker arm shaft attaching bolts evenly and remove the rocker arm shafts.

To install the rocker shafts: Install the rocker arm assemblies on the cylinder head. Temporarily tighten the cylinder head bolts to specifications and offset each rocker arm support 0.04 in., from the valve stem center. Torque the bolts to specifications.

7. Adjust the valves cold.

8. Clean the mating surfaces of the cylinder head and rocker cover.

9. Install the rocker cover with a new gasket.

10. Install the spark plug wires on the plugs. Place the wires in the clips on the rocker cover. Connect the choke and air by-pass valve cable.

11. Start the engine and check for leaks.

12. Allow the engine to reach operating temperature, torque the head bolts to specifications and adjust the valves hot.

Intake Manifold

REMOVAL AND INSTALLATION

1. Drain the cooling system.

2. Remove the air cleaner.

3. Remove the accelerator linkage.

4. Disconnect the choke cable and fuel line. Plug the fuel line.

5. Disconnect the PCV valve hose.

6. Disconnect the heater return hose and by-pass hose.

7. Disconnect and label any attaching vacuum lines.

8. Remove the intake manifold-to-cylinder head attaching nuts.

9. Remove the manifold and carburetor as an assembly.

10. Installation is the reverse of removal.

Exhaust Manifold

REMOVAL AND INSTALLATION

1. Raise and support the vehicle.

2. Remove the two attaching nuts from the exhaust pipe at the manifold.

3. Remove the air pump air injection hose from the check valve or air injection manifold, if equipped. Remove the heat stove and hot air tube to the air cleaner, if equipped.

4. Disconnect the EGR pipe, if so equipped.

5. Remove the exhaust pipe hanger from the bracket on the transmission, if so equipped.

6. Remove the manifold attaching nuts.

7. Remove the manifold.

8. Installation is the reverse of removal.

Front Cover

REMOVAL AND INSTALLATION

1. Drain the cooling system.

2. Disconnect the upper and lower radiator hoses. Remove the radiator.

3. Remove the accessory drive belts.

4. Remove the crankshaft pulley and the water pump.

5. Remove the cylinder head-to-front cover bolt.

6. Drain the oil from the engine.

7. Remove the oil pan-to-front cover bolts.

8. Remove the alternator and bracket and lay the alternator aside.

9. Remove the front cover.

10. Installation is the reverse.

Front Cover Oil Seal

REMOVAL AND INSTALLATION

The front cover oil seal can be removed and a new one installed without removing the front cover.

1. Drain the cooling system.

2. Disconnect the upper and lower radiator hoses and remove the radiator.

3. Remove the drive belt(s).

4. Remove the crankshaft pulley.

5. Pry the front oil seal from the front cover using a wooden or plastic tool to avoid damage to the seal mating surfaces.

To install a new oil seal:

6. Clean the pulley and seal area.

7. Oil the lip of the new seal and the front cover. Press a new front seal into position (flush).

8. Install the crankshaft pulley and torque the bolt to specifications.

9. Install the drive belt(s) and adjust the tension.

10. Install the radiator and connect the upper and lower hoses. Fill the cooling system. Start the engine and check for leaks.

Timing Chain and Tensioner

REMOVAL AND INSTALLATION

1. Remove the cylinder head and front cover. It is not necessary that the intake and exhaust manifolds be removed from the head.

2. Remove the oil pump and chain.

3. Remove the timing chain tensioner.

4. Loosen the timing chain guide strip screws.

5. Remove the oil slinger.

6. Remove the oil pump gear and chain as an assembly.

7. Remove the timing chain, crankshaft gear and camshaft gears from the engine.

To install the timing chain, timing gears and tensioner:

8. Position the crankshaft gear in the timing chain.

9. Position the oil pump chain and gear on the crankshaft and oil pump. Check the oil pump drive chain slack. It should be 0.15 in. Adjusting shims (between and oil pump body and cylinder block) are available in thickness of 0.006 in.

10. Install the oil slinger.

11. Install the oil pump washer and nut. Bend the washer over the nut.

12. Install the timing chain tensioner. Fully compress the snubber spring and wedge a screwdriver into the tensioner release mechanism. Without removing the screwdriver, install the tensioner.

13. Install the cylinder head and camshaft. Be sure that the valve timing is as illustrated. It must be exact. You may have to move the cam gear one or two teeth to obtain the correct alignment.

14. Install the rocker arm shafts and cam bearing caps.

15. Install and torque the cylinder head bolts.

16. Adjust the timing chain tension. Press in on the chain guide strip. Tighten the guide strip attaching screws. Remove the screwdriver from the tensioner, allowing the snubber to take up the chain slack.

17. Replace the front cover.

18. Adjust the valve clearance cold. Run the engine. Torque the cylinder head bolts and adjust the valve clearance hot.

Timing Chain Tensioner

REMOVAL AND INSTALLATION

1. Remove the water pump.
2. Remove the tensioner cover.
3. Remove the attaching bolts from the tensioner. Remove the tensioner.

To install the tensioner:

4. Fully compress the snubber spring. Insert a screwdriver into the tensioner release mechanism.
5. Without removing the screwdriver, insert the tensioner and align the bolt holes. Install and torque the bolts.
6. Adjust the chain tension as follows:
   a. Remove the two blind plugs and aluminum washers from the front cover.
   b. Loosen the guide strip attaching screws.
   c. Press the top of the chain guide strip through the adjusting hole in the cylinder head.
   d. Torque the guide strip screws.
   e. Remove the screwdriver from the tensioner and let the snubber take up the slack in the chain.
   f. Install the blind plugs and aluminum washers.
   g. Install the tensioner cover and gasket.
   h. Install a new gasket and water pump. Install the crankshaft pulley and drive belt and adjust the tension. Check the cooling system level.

TIMING CHAIN TENSIONER ADJUSTMENT

To adjust the tensioner, repeat the above procedure omitting steps 2 and 3.

Camshaft

REMOVAL AND INSTALLATION

Perform this operation on a cold engine only.

1. Disconnect the coil wire and vacuum line from the distributor.
2. Rotate the crankshaft to place the No. 1 cylinder on TDC of the compression stroke. This can be determined by removing the spark plug and feeling compression with your thumb. When compression is felt, rotate the crankshaft until the pointer aligns with the TDC mark on the pulley.
3. Remove the plug wires and distributor cap. Remove the distributor.
4. Remove the valve cover.
5. Release the tension on the timing chain.
6. Remove the cylinder head bolts. Only do this on a *cold* engine.

7. Remove the rocker arm assembly.
8. Remove the nut, washer, and distributor gear from the camshaft.
9. Remove the nut and washer holding the camshaft gear.
10. Remove the camshaft. Do not remove the camshaft gear from the timing chain. Be sure that the gear teeth and chain relationship is not disturbed. Wire the chain and cam gear to a place so that they will not fall into the front cover.

To install the camshaft:

11. Clean all the gasket surfaces.
12. Clean the cylinder head bolt holes.
13. Install the camshaft on the head and install the camshaft gear.
14. Check the valve timing.
15. Install the rocker arm assembly.
16. Install and torque the head bolts.
17. Install the cam gear washer and nut.
18. Install the distributor gear, washer and nut.
19. Adjust the timing chain tension.
20. Check the camshaft end-play. It should be 0.001–0.007 in. If it exceeds 0.008 in., replace the thrust plate with a new one.
21. Install the distributor, distributor cap and plug wires.
22. Connect the vacuum line and coil wire.
23. Adjust the valve clearance cold. Install the valve cover and fill the cooling system.
24. Run the engine and check for leaks. When normal operating temperature is reached, adjust the valve clearance hot.
25. Adjust the carburetor and ignition timing.

Piston and Connecting Rod Positioning

REMOVAL AND INSTALLATION

Refer to the "Engine Rebuilding" section for general engine service.

ENGINE LUBRICATION

Piston Engine Oil Pan

REMOVAL AND INSTALLATION

1. Raise and support the vehicle.
2. Remove the engine skid plate.
3. Drain the engine oil.
4. Remove the clutch release cylinder attaching nuts. Let the cylinder hang.
5. Remove the engine rear brace at-

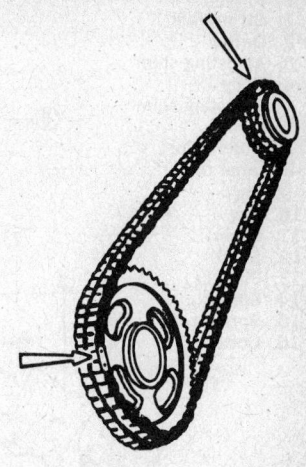

Align the bright links and the marks on the 1600 engine

taching bolts and loosen the bolts on the left side.

6. Disconnect the emission line from the oil pan.
7. Remove the oil pan nuts and bolts and let the oil pan rest on the crossmember.
8. Remove the oil pump pickup tube from the pump.
9. Remove the oil pan.
10. Installation is the reverse of removal.

Rear Main Oil Seal

REPLACEMENT

If the rear main oil seal is being replaced independently of any other parts, it can be done with the engine in place. If the rear main oil seal and the rear main bearing are being replaced, together, the engine must be removed from the vehicle.

1. Remove the transmission.
2. Remove the clutch disc, pressure plate and flywheel.
3. Using an awl, punch two holes in the crankshaft rear oil seal. They should be punched on opposite sides of the crankshaft, just above the bearing cap-to-cylinder block split line.
4. Install a sheet metal screw in each hole. Pry against both screws at the same time to remove the oil seal. Do not scratch the oil seal surface on the crankshaft.
5. Clean the oil recess in the cylinder block and bearing cap. Clean the oil seal surface on the crankshaft.
6. Cost the oil seal surfaces with oil. Coat the oil surface and the seal surface on the crankshaft with Lubriplate. Install the new oil seal and make sure that it is not cocked. Be sure that the seal surface was not damaged.
7. Install the flywheel. Coat the threads of the flywheel attaching bolts to specifications in sequence across from each other.

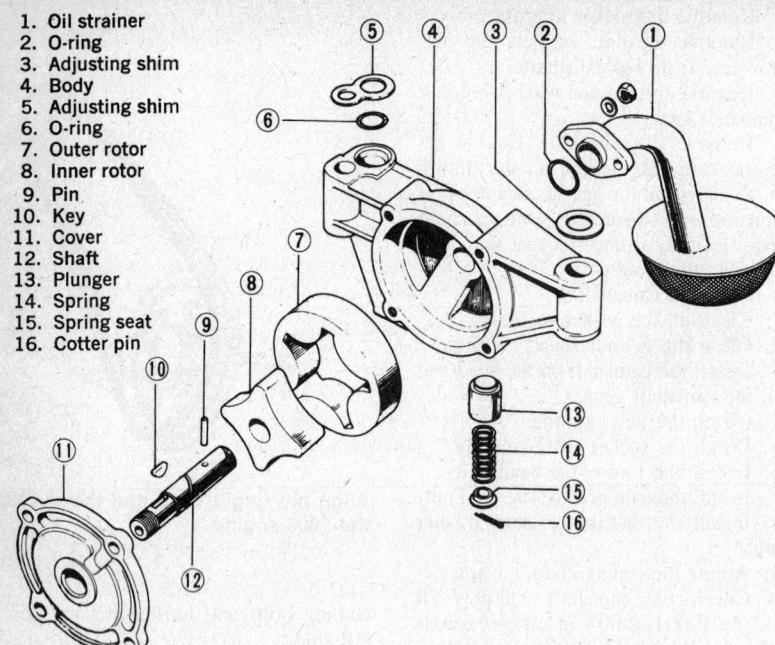

1. Oil strainer
2. O-ring
3. Adjusting shim
4. Body
5. Adjusting shim
6. O-ring
7. Outer rotor
8. Inner rotor
9. Pin
10. Key
11. Cover
12. Shaft
13. Plunger
14. Spring
15. Spring seat
16. Cotter pin

Oil pump components—piston engine

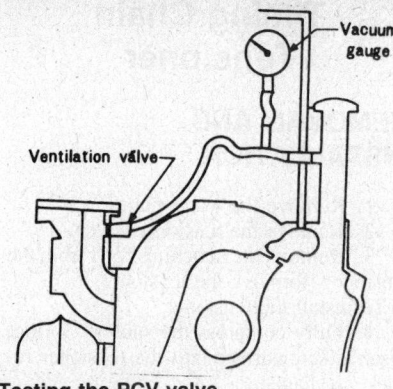

Testing the PCV valve

8. Install the clutch, pressure plate and transmission.

Oil Pump

CHECKING OIL PUMP

1. Measure the clearance between the lobes of the rotors with a feeler gauge. If the clearance exceeds 0.010 in., replace both rotors.

2. Check the clearance between the outer rotor and the pump body with a feeler gauge. Clearance should be 0.006–0.010 in. If it exceeds 0.012 in., replace the pump.

3. Place a straight-edge across the pump body and measure the clearance between the rotor and the straight-edge with a feeler gauge. Then, place a straight-edge across the pump cover and measure the clearance between the straight-edge and the cover. The combined clearances is the rotor end float. If it is 0.006 in. or more, correct it by grinding the cover. End float should be 0.002–0.004 in.

REMOVAL AND INSTALLATION

1. Remove the oil pan.
2. Remove the oil pump gear attaching nut.
3. Remove the bolts attaching the oil pump to the block. Loosen the gear on the pump.
4. Remove the oil pump gear.
To install the oil pump:
5. Install the oil pump gear in the chain.
6. Prime the oil pump and install it on

the gear and cylinder block. Install the bolts and torque them to specifications.

7. Install the washer, gear and nut. Bend the locktab on the washer.

8. Install the oil pan. Fill the engine with oil. Start the engine and check for oil pressure. Check for leaks.

ENGINE COOLING

Piston Engine

The completely sealed cooling system consists of a radiator with pressure cap, centrifugal water pump, thermostat and a fan.

Radiator

REMOVAL AND INSTALLATION

1. Drain the cooling system.
2. If equipped, remove the fan shroud.
3. Remove the fan. On California models, remove the fan clutch.
4. Disconnect the upper and lower radiator hoses.
5. Disconnect and plug the automatic transmmission cooler lines at the base of the radiator, if equipped.
6. Unbolt and remove the radiator.
7. Installation is the reverse of removal.

Water Pump

REMOVAL AND INSTALLATION

1. Drain the cooling system. Remove the fan shroud, if so equipped.
2. Remove the hoses from the water pump.
3. Remove the drive belts.
4. Remove the fan and pulley.
5. Unbolt and remove the water pump.
6. Installation is the reverse of removal. Use sealer or a new gasket upon assembly.

Thermostat

REMOVAL AND INSTALLATION

1. Drain enough coolant to bring the coolant level down below the thermostat housing. The thermostat housing is located on the left front side of the cylinder block. Disconnect the temperature sending unit wire.
2. Remove the coolant outlet elbow.
3. Remove the thermostat from the housing and note the position of the jiggle pin.
4. Install the thermostat with the jiggle pin up.
5. Installation is the reverse of removal. Use sealer or a new gasket upon assembly.

EMISSION CONTROLS

Rotary Engine Positive Crankcase Ventilation (PCV) System

The positive crankcase ventilation valve

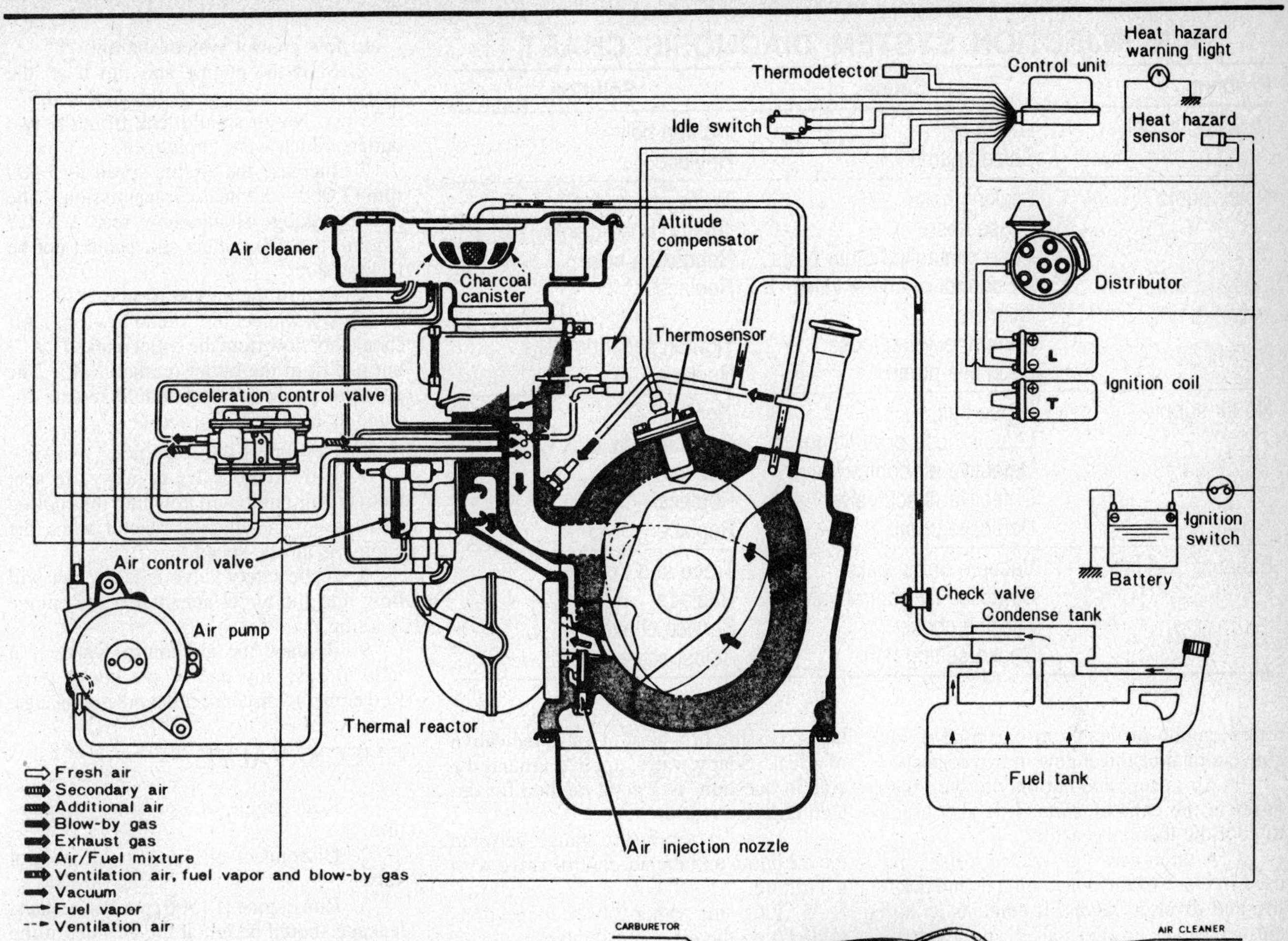

Heat hazard warning light
Control unit
Thermodetector
Idle switch
Heat hazard sensor
Air cleaner
Altitude compensator
Charcoal canister
Distributor
Thermosensor
Ignition coil
Deceleration control valve
Ignition switch
Battery
Air control valve
Check valve
Condense tank
Air pump
Thermal reactor
Fuel tank
Air injection nozzle
Fresh air
Secondary air
Additional air
Blow-by gas
Exhaust gas
Air/Fuel mixture
Ventilation air, fuel vapor and blow-by gas
Vacuum
Fuel vapor
Ventilation air

Typical rotary engine emission control system

(PCV) is located on the intake manifold below the carburetor. The PCV valve, which is operated by intake manifold vacuum, is used to meter the flow of air and fuel vapors through the rotor housing.

TESTING

1. Make sure that the air cleaner element is not clogged.
2. Connect a vacuum gauge into the line which runs between the PCV valve and the oil filler tube, by means of a T-connector.
3. Increase the engine speed to 2,500–3,000 rpm. The vacuum reading should be below 2.4 in. Hg. If it is not, replace the PCV valve.

PCV VALVE REMOVAL AND INSTALLATION

1. Remove the air cleaner.
2. Disconnect the hose at the PCV valve.
3. Unscrew the valve from the manifold.
4. Installation is reverse of removal.

Air Injection System

The air injection system used on the Mazda

CARBURETOR
AIR CLEANER
CHARCOAL (CANISTER)
FUEL VAPOR
(from CONDENSE TANK)
VACUUM SWITCH
ANTI-AFTERBURN VALVE
COASTING VALVE
No. 1 THERMO SENSOR
AIR CONTROL VALVE
CHECK VALVE
VENTILATION VALVE
THERMAL REACTOR
AIR PUMP
FILLER PIPE
CONDENSE TANK
FUEL TANK

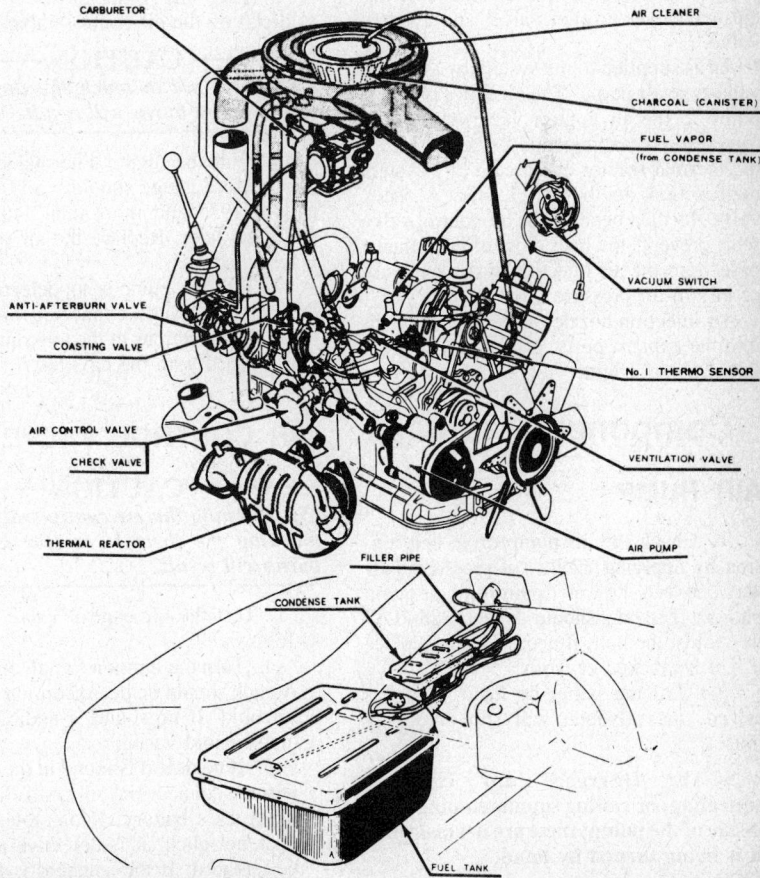

Emission control system components

MAZDA

AIR INJECTION SYSTEM DIAGNOSIS CHART

Problem	Cause	Solution
Noisy drive belt	Loose belt	Tighten belt
	Seized pump	Replace
Noisy pump	Leaking hose	Trace and fix leak
	Loose hose	Tighten hose clamp
	Hose contacting other parts	Reposition hose
	Air control or check valve failure	Replace
	Pump mounting loose	Tighten securing bolts
	Defective pump	Replace
No air supply	Loose belt	Tighten belt
	Leak in hose or at fitting	Trace and fix leak
	Defective air control valve	Replace
	Defective check valve	Replace
	Defective pump	Replace
Exhaust backfire	Vacuum or air leaks	Trace and fix leak
	Defective air control valve	Replace
	Sticking choke	Service choke
	Choke setting rich	Adjust choke

rotary engine differs from one used on a conventional piston engine in two respects:

1. Air is supplied not only to burn the gases in the exhaust ports, it is also used to cool the thermal reactor.

2. A three-way "air control valve" is used in place of the conventional antibackfire and diverter valves. It contains an air cut-out valve, a relief valve, and a safety valve.

Air is supplied to the system by a normal vane-type air pump. The air flows from the pump to the air control valve where it is routed to the air injection nozzles, to cool the thermal reactor or, in case of a system malfunction, to the air cleaner. A check valve, located beneath the air control valve seat, prevents the back-flow of hot exhaust gases into the air injection system, in case of loss of air pressure.

Air injection nozzles are used to feed air into the exhaust ports, just as in a conventional piston engine.

Component Testing

AIR PUMP

1. Check the air pump drive belt tension by applying 22 lbs. of pressure halfway between the water pump and air pump pulleys. The beat should deflect 0.28–0.35 in. Adjust the belt, if necessary, or replace it if it is cracked or worn.

2. Turn the pump by hand. If it has seized, the drivebelt will slip producing noise.

NOTE: Disregard any chirping, squealing, or rolling sounds coming from inside of the pump; these are normal when it is being turned by hand.

3. Check the hoses and connections for leaks. Hissing or a blast of air is indicative of a leak. Soapy water, applied around the area in question, is a good method for detecting leaks.

4. Connect a pressure gauge between the air pump and the air control valve with a T-fitting.

5. Plug the other hose connections (outlets) on the air control valve.

—— CAUTION ——
Be careful not to touch the thermal reactor; severe burns will result.

6. With the engine at normal idle speed, the pressure gauge should read 0.48–0.68 psi for 1975 and more than 1.64 psi for 1976 and later. Replace the air pump if it is less than this.

7. If the air pump is not defective, leave the pressure gauge connected but unplug the two connections at the air control valve and proceed with the next test.

AIR CONTROL VALVE

—— CAUTION ——
When testing the air control valve, avoid touching the thermal reactor as severe burns will result.

1. Test the air control valve solenoid as follows:

a. Turn the ignition switch off and on. A click should be heard coming from the solenoid. If no sound is audible, check the solenoid wiring.

b. If no defect is found in the solenoid wiring, connect the solenoid directly to the truck's battery. If the solenoid still does not click, it is defective and must be replaced. If the solenoid is functioning, then check the components of the

air flow control system, below.

2. Start the engine and run it at idle speed. The pressure gauge should read 0.37–0.75 psi. No air should leak from the two outlets which were unplugged.

3. Increase the engine speed to 3,500 rpm (3,000—automatic transmission). The pressure gauge should now read 1.2–2.8 psi and the two outlets still should not be leaking air.

4. Return the engine to idle.

5. Disconnect the solenoid wiring. Air should not flow from the outlet marked "A", but not from the outlet marked "B". The pressure gauge reading should remain the same as in step 2.

6. Reconnect the solenoid.

7. If the relief valve is faulty, air sent from the air pump will flow into the cooling passages of the thermal reactor when the engine is at idle speed.

8. If the safety valve is faulty, air will flow into the air cleaner when the engine is idling.

9. Replace the air control valve if it fails to pass any one of the above tests. Remember to disconnect the pressure gauge.

CHECK VALVE

1. Run engine at operating temperature.

2. Disconnect air hose at air control valve.

3. Run engine at 1500 rpm. No exhaust leakage should be felt at the air inlet fitting of the air control valve.

Component Removal and Installation

AIR PUMP

1. Remove the air cleaner assembly from the carburetor.

2. Loosen, but do not remove, the adjusting link bolt.

3. Push the pump toward the engine to slacken belt tension and remove the drive belt.

4. Disconnect the air supply hoses from the pump.

5. Unfasten the pump securing bolts and remove the pump.

—— CAUTION ——
Do not pry on the air pump housing during removal and do not clamp the housing in a vise once the pump has been removed. Any type of heavy pressure applied to the housing will cause it to distort.

Installation is performed in the reverse order of removal. Adjust the belt tension by moving the air pump to the specification given in the Testing section.

AIR CONTROL VALVE

── CAUTION ──

Remove the control valve only after the thermal reactor has cooled sufficiently to prevent the danger of a serious burn.

1. Remove the air cleaner assembly.
2. Unfasten the leads from the air control valve solenoid.
3. Disconnect the air hoses from the valve.
4. Loosen the screws which secure the air control valve and remove the valve.

Valve installation is performed in the reverse order of removal.

CHECK VALVE

1. Perform the air control valve removal procedure. Be sure to pay attention to the CAUTION.
2. Remove the check valve seat.
3. Withdraw the valve plate and spring. Install the check valve in the reverse order of removal.

AIR INJECTION NOZZLE

1. Remove the gravel shield from underneath the car.
2. Perform the oil pan removal procedure as detailed in Engine Lubrication.
3. Unbolt the air injection nozzles from both of the rotor housings.

Nozzle installation is performed in the reverse order of removal.

Thermal Reactor

A thermal reactor is used in place of a conventional exhaust manifold. It is used to oxidize unburned hydrocarbons and carbon monozide before they can be released into the atmosphere.

If the engine speed exceeds 4,000 rpm, or if the car is decelerating, the air control valve diverts air into passages in the thermal reactor housing in order to cool the reactor.

A one-way valve prevents hot exhaust gases from flowing back into the air injection system. The valve is located at the reactor air intake.

INSPECTION

── CAUTION ──

Perform thermal reactor inspection only after the reactor has cooled sufficiently to prevent severe burns.

1. Examine the reactor housing for cracks or other signs of damage.
2. Remove the air supply hose from the one-way valve. Insert a screwdriver into the valve and test the butterfly for smooth operation. Replace the valve if necessary.
3. If the valve is functioning properly,

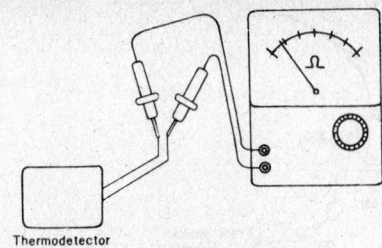

Testing the thermodetector

connect the hose to it again.

NOTE: Remember to check the components of the air injection system which are related to the thermal reactor.

REMOVAL AND INSTALLATION

Thermal reactor removal and installation procedures are given in the Engine Mechanical section.

Air Flow Control System

The control box is located beneath the dash, next to the fuse box and the thermodetector is behind the radiator grille.

COMPONENT TESTING

No. 1 Thermosensor

NOTE: Begin this test procedure with the engine cold.

1. Remove the air cleaner.
2. Examine the no. 1 thermosensor, which is located next to the thermostat housing, for leakage around the boot and for signs of wax leakage.
3. Disconnect the multiconnector from the thermosensor and place the prods of an ohmmeter on the thermosensor terminals.

The ohmmeter should read over 7 k-ohms with the engine cold and less than 2.3 k-ohms after the engine has been warmed up.

4. Replace the thermosensor with a new one, if the reading on the ohmmeter is not within specifications.
5. If the no. 1 thermosensor is functioning properly, proceed with the appropriate test for the thermodetector below.

Thermodetector

1. Unfasten the thermodetector connections.
2. Connect the test prods of an ohmmeter to the leads coming out of the thermodetector.
3. If the ohmmeter reading is below 200 k-ohms, the thermodetector is functioning satisfactorily.
4. Replace the thermodetector if it is defective and proceed with the vacuum switch if it is not.

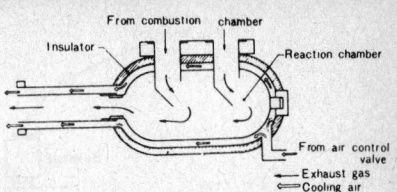

Thermal reactor cooling circuit

Use the following chart to determine the correct ohmmeter reading for the ambient temperature at the time of the test.

THERMODETECTOR RESISTANCE SPECIFICATIONS

Ambient Temperature (°F)	Resistance (k-ohms ± 5%)
−4	10.0
+32	3.0
+68	1.2
+105	0.5

COMPONENT REMOVAL AND INSTALLATION

No. 1 Thermosensor

1. Remove the air cleaner assembly.
2. If necessary, remove the starter motor as detailed under "Engine Electrical" or the deceleration control valve (see below).
3. Unplug the thermosensor multiconnector.
4. Withdraw the boot from the thermosensor.
5. Unfasten its securing nuts and remove the thermosensor.

Installation is performed in the reverse order of removal.

Control Box

── CAUTION ──

Be sure that the ignition switch is turned off to prevent damage to the control box.

1. Working from underneath the instrument panel, locate and disconnect the control box multiconnector.
2. Remove the screws which secure the control box.
3. Remove the control box.

Installation is performed in the reverse order of removal

No. 2 Thermosensor

1. Drain the engine oil into a large, clean container for reuse.
2. Unfasten the connector from the No. 2 thermosensor.

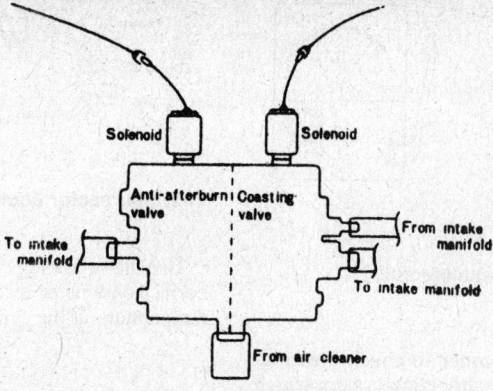

Combination anti-afterburn and coasting valve connections

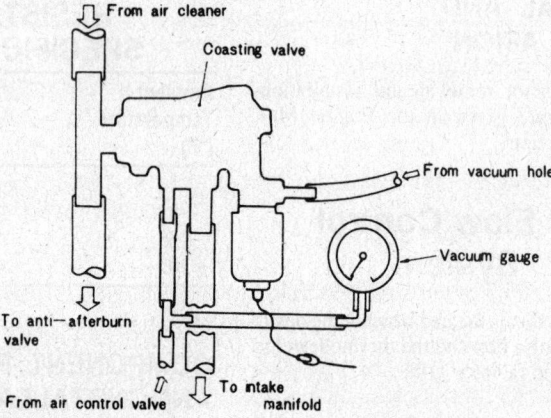

Testing the coasting valve

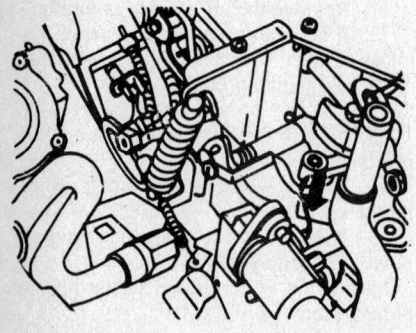

Arrow indicates the position of the anti-afterburn valve

3. Unscrew the thermosensor from the oil pan.

Installation is performed in the reverse order of removal.

No. 2 Control Box

The No. 2 control box is located in the luggage compartment next to the No. 1 control box. Its removal and installation are performed in the same manner as the no. 1 control box.

Other Components

Any of the other components used in the air flow control system are removed by un-fastening their multiconnectors and removing the screws which secure them.

Deceleration Control System

The deceleration control system used an anti-afterburn valve, a coasting valve, and an air supply valve. In addition, an idle sensing switch is fitted to the carburetor. The No. 1 control box is shared with the air flow control system.

The anti-afterburn valve, which is located on the intake manifold, is used to supply fresh air to the manifold during deceleration or when the engine is shut off, in order to prevent afterburning.

A coasting valve, which functions in a similar manner, is used to prevent an overly rich mixture during deceleration. The coasting valve also vents the vacuum chamber of the air control valve during deceleration. The valve is operated by a solenoid which is controlled by the No. 1 control box and the idle sensing switch.

An idle sensing switch is attached to the carburetor. When the throttle closes, its linkage contacts a plunger on the switch which completes the circuit from the No. 1 control box to the coasting valve thus causing the coasting valve to operate. On automatic transmission equipped models, it

also determines trailing distributor operation.

A solenoid-operated air supply valve opens when the ignition is shut off to prevent the engine from dieseling (running on).

In addition to the above components, the truck is equipped with an altitude compensator which provides air to lean out the overly rich mixture that accrues at high altitudes.

On models with an automatic transmission, a kick-down control system is used. Regardless of the gear selected, the transmission will not go above second gear when the choke knob is pulled out.

COMPONENT TESTING

Anti-Afterburn Valve

1. Remove the air cleaner assembly.
2. Remove the hose from the air intake on the anti-afterburn valve.
3. With the engine idling, place your hand over the air intake. If a strong suction is felt, the valve is defective should be replaced.
4. Increase the engine speed to 3,500–3,800 rpm. Release the throttle and allow it to snap shut. Air should be drawn in through the valve air intake for no longer than one second.
5. Keep the engine idling and disconnect the anti-afterburn valve solenoid wiring. Air should flow into the air intake while the solenoid is disconnected.

If the anti-afterburn valve fails to function properly, replace it with a new one. Remember to connect the air supply hose and the solenoid wiring after completing the test.

Combination Anti-Afterburn and Coasting Valve

1. Disconnect the hose which runs from the air cleaner to the combination valve at the air cleaner end.
2. Start the engine and run it at curb idle.
3. There should be no vacuum present at the end of the hose which you disconnected in step 1.
4. Turn the engine off.
5. Disconnect the hose which runs from the coasting valve portion of the combination valve to the intake manifold from the coasting valve end and plug up the port.
6. Operate the engine at idle.
7. Disconnect the anti-afterburn valve solenoid connector.
8. Check for vacuum at the end of the hose which you disconnected in step 1; there should be vacuum present. If not, the anti-afterburn valve is defective.
9. Turn the engine off. Reconnect the anti-afterburn valve electrical leads and the hose to the coasting valve.
10. Disconnect the intake manifold-to-anti-afterburn valve vacuum line at the valve end, and plug the vacuum fitting on the valve.

11. Start the engine and allow it to idle.

12. Disconnect the coasting valve solenoid at the multiconnector.

13. Hold your hand over the end of the vacuum line which you disconnected in step 10. Vacuum should be felt; if not, replace the defective coasting valve.

14. Turn the engine off and reconnect the leads and hoses that were disconnected above.

Altitude Compensator—1975

1. Detach the air intake hose from the altitude compensator.

2. Start the engine and run it at idle.

3. Hold your finger over the altitude compensator air intake; the engine speed should decrease. If it doesn't replace the compensator.

4. Reconnect the air intake hose, if the compensator is in good working order.

Idle Switch

1. Unfasten the idle switch leads.

2. Connect a test meter to the switch terminals.

3. With the engine at idle, the meter should indicate a completed circuit.

4. Depress the plunger on the idle switch; the circuit should be broken (no meter reading).

If the idle switch is not functioning properly, replace it with a new one.

Coolant Temperature Switch

Start this test with the coolant temperature below 68°F.

1. Disconnect the electrical lead from the temperature switch.

2. Connect a test electrical lead from the temperature switch.

3. Connect a test light between one terminal of the switch and a 12 volt battery. Ground the other terminal.

4. The test light should light.

5. Start the engine and allow it to warm up. Once the engine reaches normal operating temperature, the test light should go out.

6. Replace the switch if it doesn't work as outlined.

Choke Switch (Semi-Automatic Choke)

1. Working underneath the instrument panel, disconnect the lead at the back of the choke switch.

2. Connect a ohmmeter to the terminals on the choke switch side of the connector.

3. With the choke knob in (off), the meter should show continuity (resistance reading).

4. Pull the choke knob out, about ½ in. for manual transmission cars or 1 in. for automatics. The meter should show no continuity (read zero).

5. Replace the switch if defective.

COMPONENT REMOVAL AND INSTALLATION

Anti-Afterburn Valve

1. Remove the air cleaner assembly.

2. Disconnect the air hoses and vacuum lines from the valve.

3. Unfasten the solenoid wiring.

4. Remove the securing nuts and withdraw the valve.

Installation is performed in the reverse order of removal.

Coasting Valve

The coasting valve is removed and installed in the same manner as the anti-afterburn valve.

Idle Switch

1. Remove the coasting valve.

2. Remove the carburetor as detailed elsewhere in this section.

3. Disconnect the wiring from the switch.

4. Unfasten the securing screws and remove the siwtch.

Installation is performed in the reverse order of removal. After installing the switch, adjust it as outlined under "Adjustments", below.

Air Supply Valve

1. Remove the air cleaner and the hot air duct.

2. Disconnect the air hose, the vacuum lines, and the solenoid wiring from the valve.

3. Unfasten the screws which secure the valve and remove it.

Air supply valve installation is performed in the reverse order of removal.

Altitude Compensator

1. Disconnect both hoses from the altitude compensator. Be sure to note their positions for correct hook-up.

2. Unfasten the altitude compensator securing bolts.

3. Remove the compensator from its bracket.

Installation is the reverse of removal.

Coolant Temperature Switch

1. Drain the coolant from the radiator enough to bring the coolant level below the temperature switch.

2. Remove the alternator and drive belt if they are in the way.

3. Disconnect the switch multiconnector.

4. Use an open-end wrench to remove the switch.

5. Installation is the reverse of removal.

ADJUSTMENTS

Idle Switch

1. Warm up the engine until the water

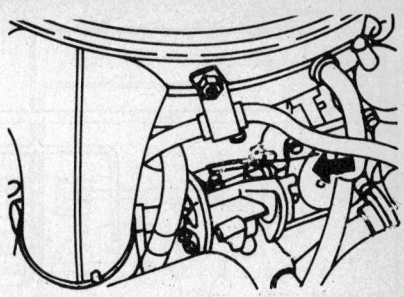

Arrow indicates the position of the coasting valve

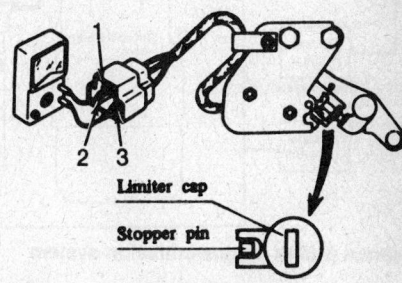

Adjusting the idle switch

temperature is at least 159°F.

2. Make sure that the mixture and idle speed are properly adjusted.

3. Adjust the idle speed to 975–1,100 rpm (1,200–1,300 rpm-automatic transmission) by rotating the throttle adjusting screw.

4. Rotate the idle switch adjusting screw until the switch changes from OFF to ON position.

5. Slowly turn the idle switch adjusting screw back to the point where the switch just changes from ON to OFF.

6. Turn the throttle screw back so that the engine returns to idle.

NOTE: Be sure that the idle switch goes on when the idle speed is still above 1,000 rpm.

Evaporative Emission Control System

The vapors rising from the gasoline in the fuel tank are vented into a separate condensing tank which is located in the luggage compartment. There they condense and return to the fuel tank in liquid form when the engine is not running.

When the engine is running, the fuel vapors are sucked directly into the engine through the PCV valve and are burned along with the air/fuel mixture.

Any additional fuel vapors which are not handled by the condensing tank are stored in a filter which is incorporated into the air cleaner. When the engine is running, the charcoal is purged of its stored fuel vapor.

A check valve vents the fuel vapor into the atmosphere if pressure in the fuel tank becomes excessive.

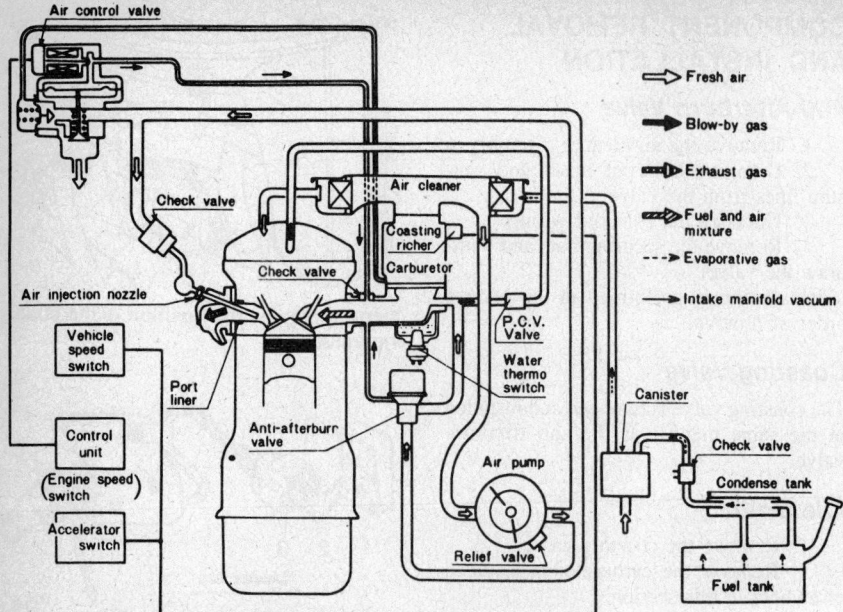

Typical piston engine emission system

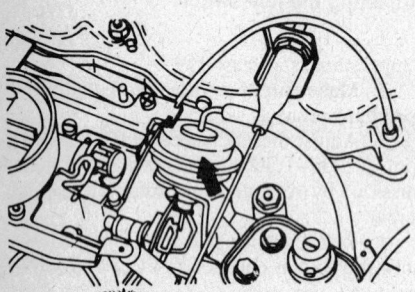

Servo diaphragm

When the vehicle is parked for a short time following a long run, there is a tendency for the fuel in the float chamber to evaporate and enter the intake manifold through the air vent. To prevent this over-rich condition, an air vent solenoid valve is installed on 1977 models to divert the fumes to the canister filter.

SYSTEM TESTING

There are several things to check for if a malfunction of the evaporative emission control system is suspected.

1. Leaks may be traced by using an infrared hydrocarbon tester. Run the test probe along the lines and connections. The meter will indicate the presence of a leak by a high hydrocarbon (HC) reading. This method is much more accurate than a visual inspection which would indicate only the presence of a leak large enough to pass liquid.

2. Leaks may be caused by any of the following, so always check these areas when looking for them:
   a. Defective or worn lines;
   b. Disconnected or pinched lines;
   c. Improperly routed lines;
   d. A defective check valve.

NOTE: If it becomes necessary to replace any of the lines used in the evaporative emission control system, use only those hoses which are fuel resistant or are marked "EVAP."

3. If the fuel tank has collapsed, it may be the fault of clogged or pinched vent lines, a defective vapor separator, or a plugged or incorrect fuel filler cap.

EMISSION CONTROLS

Piston Engine

THROTTLE OPENER

The throttle opener system consists of a servo-diaphragm connected to the throttle lever and a vacuum control valve which controls intake manifold vacuum through the servo-diaphragm.

TESTING THE SYSTEM

Servo-Diaphragm

1. Start the engine and set the idle speed to 800 rpm. Stop the engine.
2. Disconnect the vacuum sensing tube between the servo-diaphragm and the vacuum control valve at the diaphragm.
3. Remove the intake manifold suction hole plug.
4. Connect the intake manifold and the servo-diaphragm with a tube so that the intake manifold vacuum goes directly to the servo-diaphragm.
5. Connect a tachometer and remove the vacuum sensing tube between the carburetor and distributor.
6. Start the engine and read the speed.

If the engine is running 1300–1500 rpm, the servo-diaphragm is operating normally. If the engine speed is 800–1300, adjust the speed with the throttle opening screw. If the engine speed remains normal, about 800 rpm, the servo-diaphragm is defective and should be replaced.

7. Remove the test equipment and reconnect all the lines.

SERVO-DIAPHRAGM

Removal and Installation

1. Remove the air cleaner.
2. Disconnect the vacuum sensing tube from the diaphragm.
3. Remove the cotter pin and link.
4. Loosen the locknut and remove the servo-diaphragm.
5. Installation is the reverse of removal. Adjust the servo-diaphragm.

VACUUM CONTROL VALVE

Removal and Installation

1. Remove the air cleaner.
2. Disconnect the vacuum sensing tubes from the vacuum control valve.
3. Unbolt and remove the vacuum control valve.
4. Installation is the reverse of removal.

Positive Crankcase Ventilation (PCV) System

The function of the PCV valve is to divert blow-by gases from the crankcase to the intake manifold to be burned in the cylinders. The system consists of a PCV valve, an oil separator and the hoses necessary to connect the components.

Ventilating air is routed into the rocker cover from the air cleaner. The air is then moved to the oil separator and from the separator to the PCV valve. The PCV valve is operated by differences in air pressure between the intake manifold and the rocker cover.

PCV VALVE

Standard Test

1. Remove the hose from the PCV valve.
2. Start the engine and run it at approximately 700–1000 rpm.
3. Cover the end of the PCV valve with your finger. A distinct vacuum should be felt. If no vacuum is felt, replace the valve.

Alternate Test

Remove the valve from its fitting. Shake the valve. If a rattle is heard, the valve is probably functioning normally. If no rattle is heard, the valve is probably stuck (open or shut) and should be replaced.

REMOVAL AND INSTALLATION

1. Remove the air cleaner.
2. Disconnect the hose from the PCV valve.
3. Remove the valve from the intake manifold fitting.

To install the valve, reverse the removal procedure.

Evaporative Emission Control System

The evaporative emission control system is designed to control the emission of gasoline vapors into the atmosphere. The system consists of a fuel tank, charcoal canister and a check valve.

When the engine is not running, fuel vapors are channeled to the canister. The fuel returns to the fuel tank as the vapors condense. During periods of engine operation, fuel vapors are removed from the charcoal by fresh air moving through the inlet hole in the bottom of the canister.

CHECK VALVE REMOVAL AND INSTALLATION

The check valve is used only through 1976.
1. Disconnect the hoses from the check valve.
2. Unscrew and remove the valve from the crossmember.

Installation is the reverse of removal.

Air Injection System

CHECKING THE AIR PUMP

1. Disconnect the hose from the air pump outlet.
2. Connect a pressure gauge to the outlet.
3. Check the drive belt for proper tension and run engine at 1500 rpm. Gauge reading should be at least 1 psi. If not, replace the pump.

TESTING THE RELIEF VALVE

1. Run the engine at idle.
2. At idle, no air should be felt at the relief valve. If air flow is felt, replace the valve.
3. Increase the engine speed to 4500 rpm. If air flow is felt, valve is working properly.

PUMP REPLACEMENT

1. Disconnect the inlet and outlet hoses

at the pump.
2. Remove the adjusting bolt and lift off the drive belt.
3. Support the pump and remove the mounting bolts. Lift out the pump.
4. Installation is the reverse of removal. Adjust drive belt to specification. Correct belt adjustment will give a 0.5 in. flex at the mid-point with a 22 lbs. push.

CHECK VALVE REPLACEMENT

Check valve is replaced by disconnecting the hose and unscrewing the valve from the manifold.

AIR CONTROL VALVE TEST

1. Start the engine and run it at idle.
2. Hold a finger over the relief valve port of the air control valve. Discharge air should be felt.
3. Disconnect the vacuum sensing tube from the air control valve and plug the tube. No air should be felt at the relief port.

REPLACING AIR CONTROL VALVE

1. Disconnect the vacuum lines from the valve.
2. Disconnect the wiring from the valve.
3. Disconnect the air hoses from the valve.
4. Unbolt and remove the valve.
5. Install in reverse of removal.

AIR CONTROL VALVE CHECK VALVE TEST

1. Disconnect the vacuum sensing tube from the air control valve solenoid.
2. Blow through the vacuum tube. Air should pass through the valve. Suck on the tube. No air should pass through the valve.

Exhaust Gas Recirculation System

EGR CONTROL VALVE TEST

1. Remove the air cleaner.
2. Run the engine at idle.
3. Disconnect the vacuum sensing tube from the EGR control valve.
4. Disconnect the vacuum sensing tube from the intake manifold vacuum control valve.
5. Connect this vacuum tube to the EGR control valve. The engine should stop. If not, clean or replace the EGR control valve.

REPLACING EGR CONTROL VALVE

1. Remove air cleaner.
2. Disconnect the vacuum sensing tube from the EGR control valve.
3. Disconnect the EGR control valve to exhaust manifold pipe.
4. Disconnect the pipe between the EGR control valve and the intake manifold.
5. Unbolt and remove the EGR control valve.
6. If old valve is to be reused, it should be cleaned with a wire brush before installation.
7. To install, reverse the above procedure.

REPLACING AND/OR TESTING THE WATER TEMPERATURE SWITCH

1. Drain the radiator until the coolant level is below the intake manifold.
2. Disconnect the wires from the switch.
3. Unscrew the switch from the manifold.
4. Suspend the switch in a container of water so that it does not touch the sides or bottom.
5. Heat the water to no more than 113°F and check the switch with an ohmmeter. Continuity should exist between the terminals.
6. Heat the water until the temperature becomes 149°F or more.
7. No continuity should exist. If the switch fails either test, replace it.
8. To replace the switch, reverse the removal procedure.

TESTING THE THREE-WAY SOLENOID VALVE

The valve is located at the top center of the firewall in the engine compartment.
1. Disconnect the wiring to the water thermo switch and connect a jumper wire to the two connectors of the switch.
2. Disconnect the vacuum sensing tube from the EGR valve.
3. Disconnect the vacuum sensing tube which runs to the vacuum amplifier from the three way solenoid valve.
4. Turn the ignition switch on.
5. Blow through the solenoid valve from the tube disconnected from the EGR valve. Air should pass through the valve to the valve air filter.
6. Disconnect the jumper wire from the thermo switch.
7. Blow through the tube disconnected from the EGR valve and make sure the air passes through the opening to the vacuum amplifier tube.
8. If the solenoid valve does not operate properly, replace.

MAZDA

1. Air horn
2. Choke valve lever
3. Clip
4. Choke lever shaft
5. Screw
6. Setscrew
7. Spring
8. Choke valve
9. Connector
10. Connecting rod
11. Spring
12. Fuel return valve
13. Hanger
14. Screw
15. Ring
16. Bolt
17. Carburetor body
18. Bolt
19. Diaphragm cover
20. Screw
21. Diaphragm
22. Accelerator pump arm
23. Float
24. Gasket
25. Connecting rod
26. Spring
27. Spring
28. Small venturi
29. Small venturi
30. Bolt
31. Check ball plug
32. Steel ball
33. Flange
34. Throttle shaft
35. Throttle shaft
36. Throttle lever
37. Spring washer
38. Nut
39. Lock
40. Adjusting arm
41. Starting lever
42. Arm
43. Screw
44. Gasket
45. Valve
46. Screw
47. Throttle valve
48. Throttle lever link
49. Ring
50. Throttle return spring
51. Arm
52. Retainer
53. Metering pump lever
54. Metering pump arm
55. Screw
56. Pin
57. Union bolt
58. Cover
59. Diaphragm spring
60. Diaphragm lever
61. Diaphragm pin
62. Diaphragm chamber
63. Screw
64. Diaphragm
65. Gasket
66. Connecting rod
67. Pin
68. Ring
69. Washer
70. Diaphragm stop ring
71. Diaphragm stop ring
72. Screw
73. Level gauge screw
74. Gasket
75. Gasket
76. Stop ring
77. Float pin
78. Needle valve seat
79. Gasket
80. Collar
81. Throttle adjusting screw
82. Idle adjusting screw
83. Spring
84. Main jet
85. Main jet
86. Gasket
87. Plug
88. Gasket
89. Air bleed
90. Air bleed
91. Slow jet
92. Step jet
93. Air bleed screw
94. Air bleed step
95. Cover
96. Diaphragm
97. Spring
98. Gasket
99. Washer
100. Shim
101. Jet
102. Bleed plug
103. Retainer
104. Pin
105. Screw
106. Gasket
107. Plug
108. Gasket
109. Gasket
110. Bolt
111. Nut
113. Cover
114. Gasket
115. Sight glass
116. Gasket
117. Filter
118. Accelerator
119. Gasket
120. Plug
121. Cover
122. Coasting valve bracket
123. Clip
124. Screw
125. Spring
126. Screw
127. Spring
128. Shim
129. Throttle positioner
130. Nut
131. Rod
132. Collar
133. Shim
134. Collar
135. Arm
136. Plate
137. Retaining spring
138. Lever
139. Setscrew
140. Ring

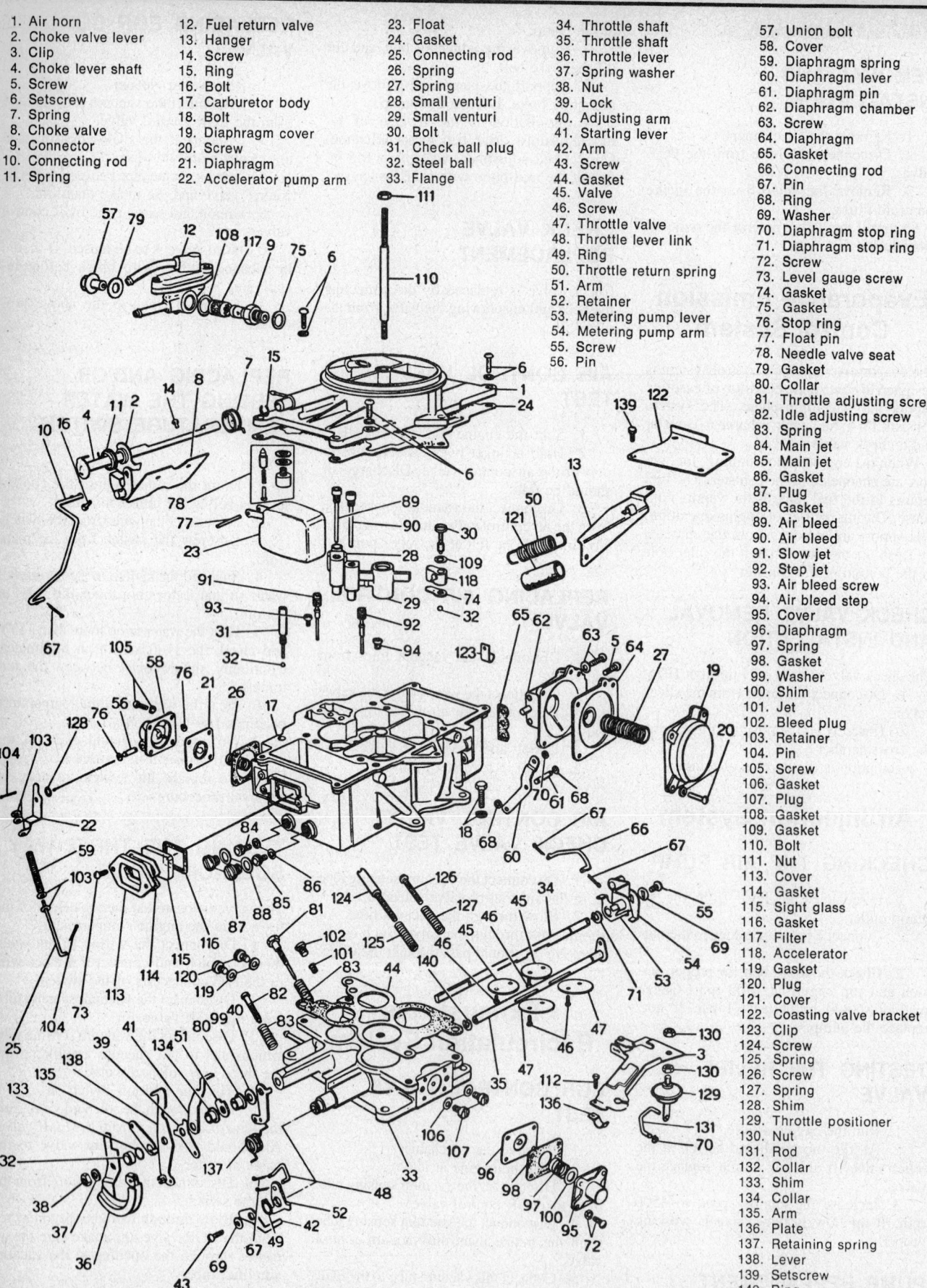

Exploded view of carburetor from a rotary engine

REPLACING THE THREE-WAY SOLENOID VALVE

1. Disconnect the wiring from the valve.
2. Disconnect the hoses from the valve.
3. Remove the screws and replace the valve.

EGR MAINTENANCE WARNING SYSTEM

1976 Only

Every 12,500 miles, the EGR warning light will come on when the ignition switch is turned on. When this occurs the valve should be removed and cleaned and checked for proper operation. When this is done reset the switch by taking off the cover from the switch and sliding the knob in the opposite direction. The switch is located behind the instrument panel, next to the speedometer.

Catalytic Converter

Periodically, the converter should be checked for excessive rust, cracks or corrosion. To replace the converter, raise and support the car and unbolt the converter from the flanges and body. A temperature sensor is located in the right side of the converter. To test its operation, remove a small plate under the floor mat on the passengers side. Remove the coupling and check across the terminals of the coupling with a circuit tester. If there is no current flow, replace the sensor.

Deceleration Control System

CHECKING ANTI-AFTERBURN VALVE

1. Disconnect the outlet hose from the valve.
2. Raise the engine speed and hold your finger over the outlet. Quickly release the accelerator linkage. Air should flow for a few seconds. If air is discharged for longer than three seconds or not at all, replace the valve.

REPLACING THE ANTI-AFTERBURN VALVE

1. Remove the air cleaner.
2. Disconnect all hoses from the valve and unbolt and remove the valve.

FUEL SYSTEM

ELECTRIC FUEL PUMP

Removal and Installation

An external electric fuel pump is mounted on the left frame rail adjacent to the fuel tank. Current is supplied to the pump through the ignition circuit and the pump will operate with the key in the RUN position.

1. Remove the fuel pump shield from the frame. Disconnect the electrical leads from the pump.
2. Disconnect the inlet and outlet lines from the pump. Plug the lines.
3. Unbolt and remove the pump from its mounting bracket.
   To install the fuel pump:
4. Position the fuel pump on the mounting bracket and install the bolts. Be sure that both mounting surfaces are clean.
5. Connect the inlet and outlet hoses.
6. Connect the electrical leads to the pump.
7. Install the fuel pump shield.

Carburetor

REMOVAL AND INSTALLATION

Rotary Engine

1. Remove the air cleaner assembly complete with its hoses and mounting bracket.
2. Detach the choke and accelerator cables from the carburetor.
3. Disconnect the fuel and vacuum lines from the carburetor.
4. Remove the oil line which runs to the metering oil pump, at the carburetor.
5. Remove all electrical wiring from carburetor.
6. Remove the carburetor attaching nuts and/or bolts, gasket or head insulator, and remove the carburetor.

Installation is performed in the reverse order of removal. Use a new gasket.

Piston Engine

1. Remove the air cleaner and duct.
2. Disconnect the accelerator shaft from the throttle lever.
3. Disconnect and plug the fuel supply and fuel return lines and plug these.
4. Disconnect the leads from the throttle solenoid and deceleration valve at the quick-disconnects.

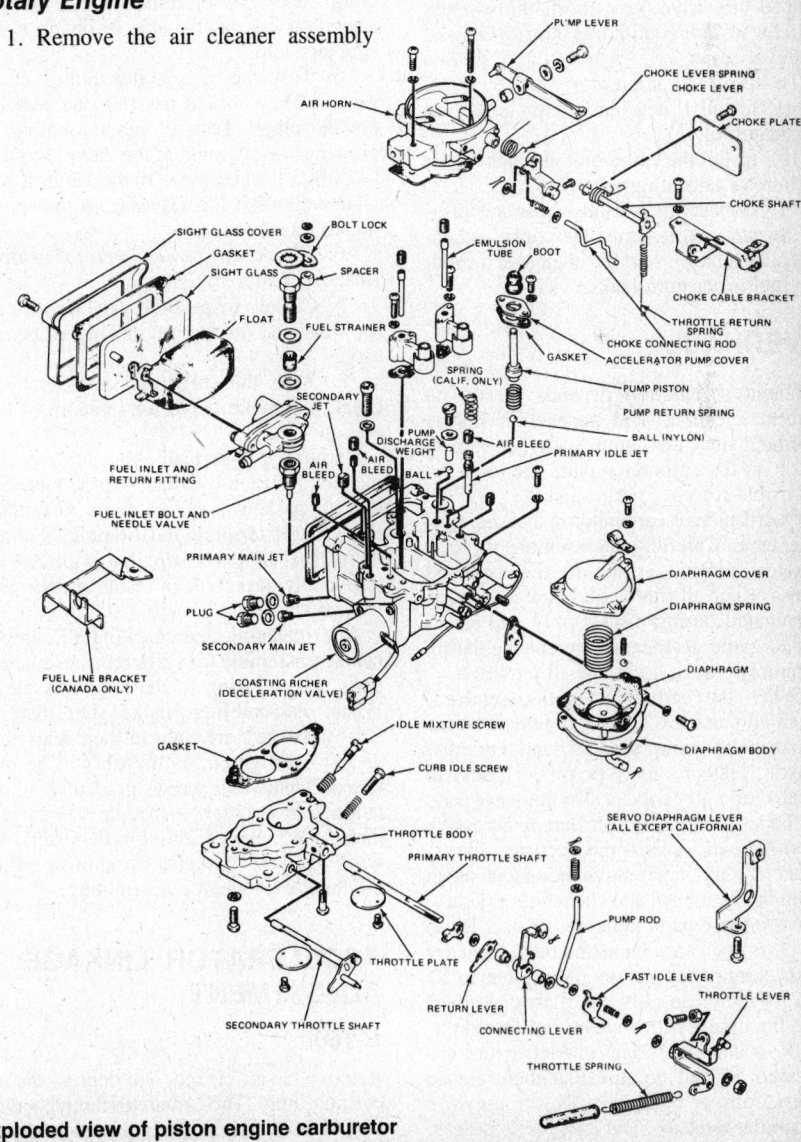

Exploded view of piston engine carburetor

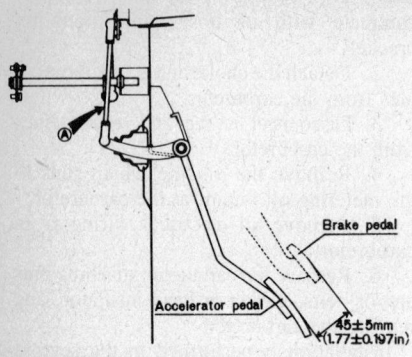

Adjusting the accelerator linkage on piston engine models

5. Disconnect the carburetor-to-distributor vacuum line.
6. Disconnect the throttle return spring.
7. Disconnect the choke cable.
8. Remove the carburetor attaching nuts from the intake manifold studs and remove the carburetor. The attaching nuts are tucked underneath the carburetor body and are difficult to reach; a small socket with an "L" shaped hex drive, or a short, thin wrench sold for work on ignition systems will make removal easier.

To install the carburetor:
9. Install a new carburetor gasket on the manifold.
10. Install the carburetor and tighten the carburetor attaching nuts.
11. Connect the various wires and hoses to the carburetor, adjust the choke and accelerator linkage, start the engine, and check for fuel or vacuum leaks.

OVERHAUL

Efficient carburetion depends greatly on careful cleaning and inspection during overhaul since dirt, gum, water, or varnish in or on the carburetor parts are often responsible for poor performance.

Overhaul your carburetor in a clean, dust-free area. Carefully disassemble the carburetor, referring often to the exploded views. Keep all similar and look-alike parts segregated during disassembly and cleaning to avoid accidental interchange during assembly. Make a note of all jet sizes.

When the carburetor is disassembled, wash all parts (except diaphragms, electric choke units, pump plunger, and any other plastic, leather, fiber, or rubber parts) in clean carburetor solvent. Do not leave parts in the solvent any longer than is necessary to sufficiently loosen the deposits. Excessive cleaning may remove the special finish from the float bowl and choke valve bodies, leaving these parts unfit for service. Rinse all parts in clean solvent and blow them dry with compressed air or allow them to air dry. Wipe clean all cork, plastic, leather, and fiber parts with a clean, lint-free cloth.

Blow out all passages and jets with compressed air and be sure that there are no restrictions or blockages. Never use wire or similar tools to clean jets, fuel passages,

or air bleeds. Clean all jets and valves separately to avoid accidental interchange.

Check all parts for wear or damage. If wear or damage is found, replace the defective parts. Especially check the following:
1. Check the float needle and seat for wear. If wear is found, replace the complete assembly.
2. Check the float hinge pin for wear and the float(s) for dents or distortion. Replace the float if fuel has leaked into it.
3. Check the throttle and choke shaft bores for wear or an out-of-round condition. Damage or wear to the throttle arm, shaft, or shaft bore will often require replacement of the throttle body. These parts require a close tolerance of fit; wear may allow air leakage, which could affect starting and idling.

NOTE: Throttle shafts and bushings are not included in overhaul kits. They can be purchased separately.

4. Inspect the idle mixture adjusting needles for burrs or grooves. Any such condition requires replacement of the needle, since you will not be able to obtain a satisfactory idle.
5. Test the accelerator pump check valves. They should pass air one way but not the other. Test for proper seating by blowing and sucking on the valve. Replace the valve if necessary. If the valve is satisfactory, wash the valve again to remove breath moisture.
6. Check the bowl cover for warped surfaces with a straightedge.
7. Closely inspect the valves and seats for wear and damage, replacing as necessary.
8. After the carburetor is assembled, check the choke valve for freedom of operation.

Carburetor overhaul kits are recommended for each overhaul. These kits contain all gaskets and new parts to replace those that deteriorate most rapidly. Failure to replace all parts supplied with the kit (especially gaskets) can result in poor performance later.

After cleaning and checking all components, reassemble the carburetor, using new parts and referring to the exploded view. When reassembling, make sure that all screws and jets are tight in their seats, but do not overtighten, as the tip will be distorted. Tighten all screws gradually, in rotation. Do not tighten needle valves into their seats; uneven jetting will result. Always use new gaskets. Be sure to adjust the float level when reassembling.

ACCELERATOR LINKAGE ADJUSTMENT

B-1600

Remove the air cleaner and depress the accelerator fully. The carburetor throttle valves should be wide open. If not, check for proper

installation, binding or wear.

Rotary, B1800 and B2000

1. Check the pedal position. The accelerator pedal should be lower than the brake pedal by 2.3" on the rotary pickup and 1.75 inches on the piston engine pick up.
2. If necessary, adjust the nut on the linkage above the pedal to obtain the proper height.
3. Check the free-play of the cable at the carburetor. It should be 0.04–0.12". If not, adjust by turning the clevis nut.

FLOAT AND FUEL LEVEL ADJUSTMENTS—ROTARY ENGINE

1. With the engine running, check the fuel level in the sight glass, using a mirror.
2. If the fuel levels are not within the specified marks on the sight glass, remove the air horn with the floats.
3. Invert the air horn and let the float hang so that it just contacts the needle valve.
4. Measure the clearance between the float and the air horn gasket, which should be 0.10 in. for 1975–1978 models. Bend the float seat lip to adjust the clearance if necessary.
5. Install the air horn and recheck the fuel levels in the sight glass.

FLOAT DROP

Rotary Pick-Up

1. Remove the air horn with the floats and allow the floats to hang free.
2. Measure the clearance between the bottom of the float and the air horn gasket. The clearance should be 2.03–2.07 in.
3. If not, adjust the distance by bending the float stop.
4. Install the air horn and recheck the fuel level in the sight glass.

B-1800 and B-2000

1. Check the fuel level within the float bowl through the sight glass, with the engine running. If the float is not aligned with the level mark, adjustment is necessary.
2. For adjustment, remove the carburetor. Remove the sight glass and invert the carburetor.
3. Measure the distance between the float and the top of the bowl. It should be 0.236 in. on the B1800, and 0.335 in. on the B2000.
4. Adjust by bending the float seat lip.
5. Turn the carburetor upright and allow the float to drip by its own weight.
6. Measure the clearance between the bottom of the float and the bowl. It should be 0.047 in. on the B1800 and 0.039 in. on the B2000. Bend the float stopper to adjust.

FAST IDLE ADJUSTMENT

1. Remove the carburetor.
2. With the choke plate fully closed, adjust the clearance between the primary throttle plate and the wall of the throat by bending the connecting rod between the choke plate linkage and the throttle plate. Clearances are as follows:

B1600—0.070 inch
B1800—0.071 ± 0.008 inch
Rotary Pick-up—0.060 ± 0.008 inch
  (Calif. 0.080 ± 0.006 inch)

MANUAL TRANSMISSION

Removal and Installation

B–1600, B–1800 and B–2000

1. Raise and support the truck. Drain the lubricant from the transmission.
2. Disconnect the ground wire from the battery.
3. Remove the gearshift lever boot.
4. Unbolt the cover plate from the gearshift lever retainer.
5. Pull the gearshift lever, shim and bushing straight up and away from the gearshift lever retainer.
6. Disconnect the wires from the starter motor and back-up light switch.
7. Disconnect the speedometer cable from the extension housing.
8. Remove the driveshaft.
9. Unbolt the exhaust pipe from the bracket on the transmission case.
10. Disconnect the exhaust pipe at the exhaust manifold.
11. Unhook the clutch release fork return spring and remove the clutch release cylinder from the clutch housing.
12. Remove the starter.
13. Support the transmission with a jack.
14. Unbolt the transmission from the rear of the engine.
15. Place a jack under the engine, protecting the oil pan with a block of wood.
16. Unbolt the transmission from the crossmember.
17. Unbolt and remove the crossmember.
18. Lower the jack and slide the transmission rearward until the mainshaft clears the clutch disc.
19. Remove the transmission from under the truck.
20. Installation is the reverse of removal.

ROTARY PICK-UP 4 SPEED OR 5 SPEED

1. Remove the knob from the gearshift lever.
2. Remove the gearshift lever boot.
3. Unbolt the retainer cover from the gearshift lever retainer.
4. Pull the gearshift lever, shim and bushing straight up and away from the gearshift lever retainer.
5. Disconnect the battery ground wire.
6. Remove the belt attaching the power brake vacuum pipe to the clutch housing.
7. Disconnect the ground strap from the transmission case.
8. Remove the clutch release cylinder.
9. Remove the one upper bolt holding the starter and the three bolts and nuts securing the transmission to the engine.
10. Raise and support the truck.
11. Disconnect the wires from the starter motor and the back-up light switch wires.
12. Unbolt and remove the heat insulator from the front exhaust pipe.
13. Disconnect the exhaust pipe from the brackets.
14. Disconnect the exhaust pipe front flange from the exhaust manifold. Remove the front exhaust pipe.
15. Remove the driveshaft.
16. Insert a transmission oil plug into the extension housing.
17. Remove the starter.
18. Install a jack under the engine and support the engine.
19. Unbolt the transmission support from the body.
20. Remove the two lower bolts holding the transmission to the engine.
21. Slide the transmission rearward until the mainshaft clears the clutch disc and remove the transmission from under the truck.
22. Installation is the reverse of removal.

Overhaul

DISASSEMBLY ROTARY PICK-UP

4 Speed

1. Install the transmission in a workstand.
2. Drain the oil from the transmission, if you haven't already done so. Clean any metal chips off the drain plug and reinstall it.
3. Pull outward on the release fork, until it becomes disengaged from the ball stud. Slide the fork and throwout bearing out of the housing.
4. Remove the bellhousing nuts and remove the housing, complete with gasket.
5. Withdraw the adjusting shim from the bellhousing bearing bore.
6. Unfasten the nuts which secure the shift lever tower to the extension housing. Remove the tower and gasket.

Float level adjustment—float bowl inverted and gasket installed

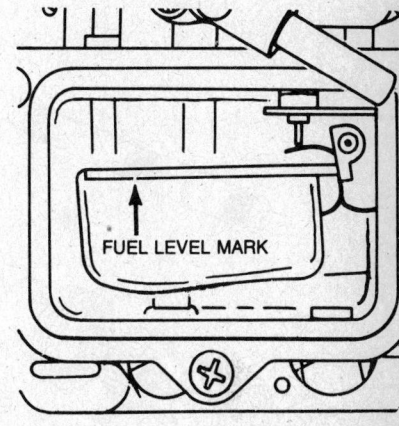

Fuel level mark on the sight glass—piston engine

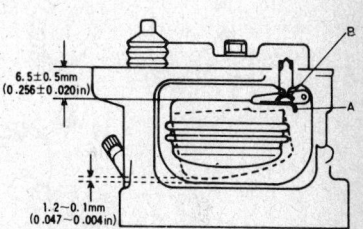

Piston engine float adjustment: bend tab "A" to adjust float drop and bend tab "B" to adjust float level

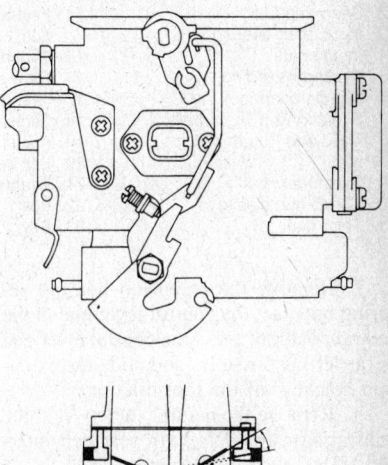

Fast idle adjustments; measure the angle "A" and clearance "B"

14. Remove the blind covers and gaskets from the transmission case.

15. Remove the Reverse shift rod and idler gear from the rear of the transmission case. Unfasten the Reverse shift fork securing bolt and remove the fork.

16. Unfasten Third/Fourth shift fork securing bolt and remove the Third/Fourth shift rod from the rear of the case.

17. Repeat step 16 for the First/Second shift rod.

18. Straighten out the output shaft lockwasher. Hold the output shaft to keep it from turning, and loosen the locknut. Slide the reverse gear and key off the end of the output shaft.

19. Remove the countershaft snap-ring (rear) and remove the Reverse countergear.

20. Unfasten the bearing cover bolts and remove the cover.

22. Remove the reverse idler gear.

22. Hold the fourth synchronizer ring and gear on the output shaft.

23. Remove the countershaft front bearing snap-ring. Using a puller remove the front bearing. Withdraw the adjusting shim from the case bearing bore.

24. Remove the countershaft rear bearing with the puller. Remove the adjusting shim from the case bearing bore.

25. Remove the input shaft bearing snap-ring and remove the bearing with the puller.

26. Lift the countershaft out of the case.

27. Separate the input and output shafts. Remove the input shaft. Remove the fourth synchronizer ring and needle bearing from the input shaft.

28. Lift the output shaft gear assembly out of the case.

29. Remove First/Second and Third/Fourth shift forks from the case. Withdraw the shift interlock pins from the case.

30. Remove the Third/Fourth clutch hub snap-ring, then slide the clutch hub sleeve, third synchronizer ring and Third gear off the front of the output shaft. Be careful not to mix-up the synchronizer rings.

31. Slide the First gear and the synchronizer ring off the rear of the output shaft.

32. Slide the First gear sleeve, Second gear, second synchronizer ring and First/Second clutch hub/sleeve assembly off the output shaft.

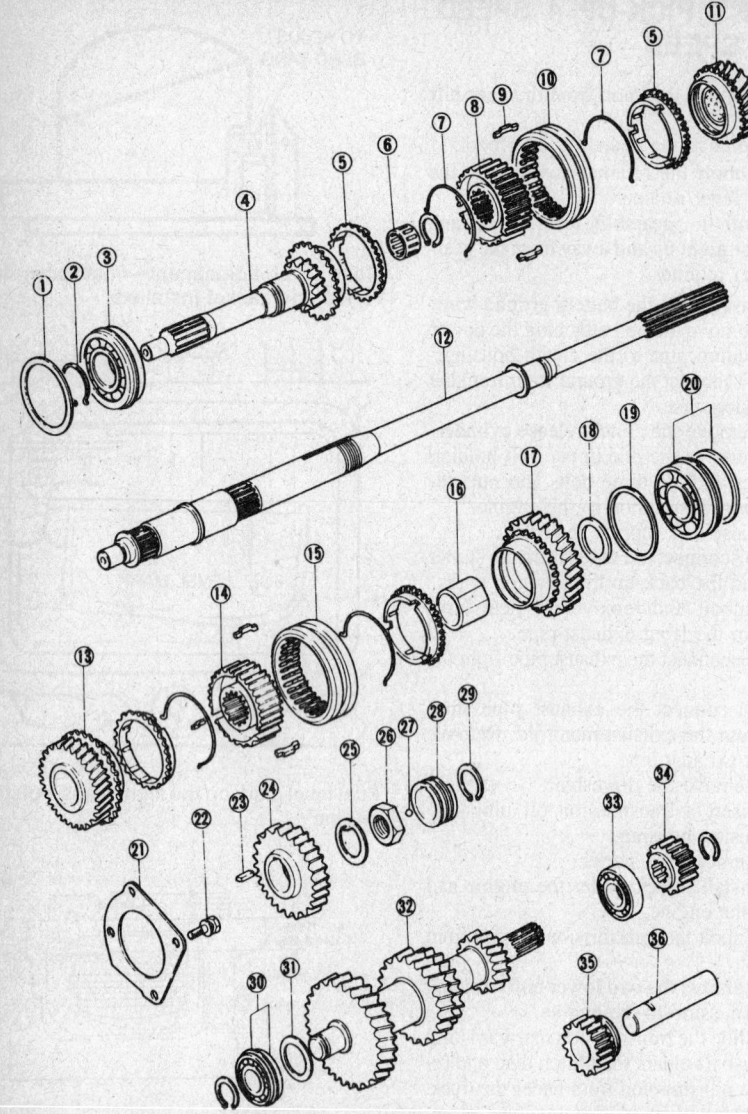

Mainshaft drive train—rotary pickup 4-speed

1. Adjusting shim
2. Snap-ring
3. Input shaft bearing
4. Input shaft
5. Synchronizer ring
6. Needle bearing
7. Synchronizer key spring
8. Third-and-Fourth clutch hub
9. Synchronizer key
10. Clutch hub sleeve
11. Third gear
12. Output shaft
13. Second gear
14. First-and-Second clutch hub
15. Clutch hub sleeve
16. Gear sleeve
17. First gear
18. Thrust washer
19. Adjust shim
20. Ball bearing and clip
21. Bearing stop
22. Bolt
23. Key
24. Reverse gear
25. Lockwasher
26. Locknut
27. Steel ball
28. Speedometer drive gear
29. Snap-ring
30. Ball bearing and clip
31. Adjusting shim
32. Countershaft
33. Needle bearing
34. Reverse countergear
35. Reverse idler gear
36. Reverse idler gear shaft

Inspection

Clean the transmission case thoroughly with solvent and blow it dry with compressed air. Inspect the case for cracks or other signs of damage.

Inspect all of the bearings for wear or roughness.

Examine each of the gears. Replace any gears that have chipped or missing teeth, or gears that show signs of excessive wear.

Check the operation of the synchronizers. Replace any which are worn or damaged.

Place the mainshaft on V-blocks, and measure its runout with a dial indicator. If

7. Remove the extension housing securing nuts, set the control lever end in the neutral position, press the control lever end as far left as possible, and slide the extension housing off the transmission.

8. Remove the neutral switch from the transmission (models with seat belt interlock).

9. Unfasten the gearshift control lever yoke bolt and remove the yoke from the central lever.

10. Remove the speedometer sleeve lockplate. Withdraw the sleeve and driven gear from the extension housing. Remove the back-up light switch, also.

11. Unfasten the speedometer drive gear snap-ring, slide the drive gear off of the output shaft, and remove the lockball.

12. Loosen the bottom cover bolts evenly, and in several stages; then remove the bottom cover and gasket.

13. Remove the cap bolts, the detent springs, and detent balls from the transmission case.

runout exceeds 0.0012 in., replace the mainshaft.

Assembly

1. Install the First/Second clutch hub on its sleeve, place the three shift keys in the clutch hub key slots, and install the key springs. Be sure to keep the open ends of the key springs 120° apart.

2. Perform step 1 for the Third/Fourth synchronizer assembly.

3. Place the synchronizer ring on Second gear and then slide Second gear on the output shaft, so that the synchronizer ring faces the rear of the shaft.

4. Slide the First/Second clutch hub and sleeve on the output shaft so that the clutch oil grooves face forward. Be sure that the three synchronizer keys engage the notches on the Second gear synchronizer ring.

5. Install the First gear sleeve in the output shaft.

6. Fit the synchronizer ring in the First gear and install the gear on the output shaft so that the ring faces the front of the shaft.

7. Install the same thrust washer on the output shaft that you removed during disassembly.

8. Perform step 6 for Third gear.

9. Install the Third/Fourth clutch hub and sleeve on the output shaft, being sure to engage the three synchronizer keys with the notches in the ring.

NOTE: The larger boss on the Third/Fourth clutch hub goes toward the front.

10. Install the snap-ring on the front of the output shaft. Install the output shaft/gear set assembly in the case. Fit the needle bearing on the front of the output shaft.

11. Place the synchronizer ring on the input shaft gear (Fourth) and install the gear on the front of the output shaft. Be sure that the synchronizer keys engage the notches in the synchronizer rings.

12. Position the First/Second and Third/Fourth shift forks in the groove on the clutch hub/sleeve assembly.

13. Install the countergear assembly in the case, being careful to engage each countergear with its respective output shaft gear.

14. Check the output shaft bearing end-play as follows:

    a. Measure the depth of the transmission case output shaft bearing bore.

    b. Measure the height of the bearing.

    c. The difference of these two measurements indicates the correct thickness of the adjusting shim to be used. The amount of end-play permitted is 0–0.0039 in.

    d. Shims are available in thicknesses of 0.0039 or 0.0118 in.

15. Hold the Fourth synchronizer ring off the input shaft synchronizer gear.

16. Install the input and output shaft bearings in their respective bores with a press.

17. Install the input shaft bearing snap-ring.

1. Shift fork
2. Shift fork
3. Shift fork
4. 3rd-and-4th shift rod
5. 1st-and-2nd shift rod

6. Rev.-and-5th shift rod
7. Stop ring
8. Shift rod end
9. Shift rod end
10. Shift rod end

11. Detent ball
12. Detent spring
13. Washer
14. Spring cap bolt
15. Interlock pin

5-speed shift rod and forks

18. Check the countershaft bearing end-play, as outlined in step 14 for the input shaft. The amount of end-play allowed and available shim size are the same for both bearings.

19. Perform step 15 again.

20. Press the countershaft front and rear bearings into their respective bores. Install the snap-ring on the front bearing.

21. Install the Reverse countergear on the rear of the countershaft and secure with its snap-ring.

22. Fit the reverse gear idler shaft in the transmission case.

23. Install the bearing cover on the case.

24. Secure the reverse gear on the output shaft with its key.

25. Hold the output shaft to keep it from turning and tighten its locknut 150–180 ft. lbs. Secure the locknut by bending the tabs on the lockwasher.

26. Fit the first/second shift rod into the case and secure it to the shift fork with the lockbolt. Place the shift rod in Neutral. Drift the interlock pin into its bore.

27. Perform step 26 for the Third/Fourth shift rod.

28. Slide the Reverse shift rod, complete with the Reverse idler gear, in from the rear of the case. Secure the shift rod to the Reverse fork with its lockbolt.

29. Install the detent balls and springs in their bores and secure them with their cap bolts.

30. Check the synchronizer key-to-exposed edge of the synchronizer ring clearance with a feeler gauge; it should be 0.026–0.079 in. If the clearance is greater, the synchronizer key could pop out. If the clearance is greater than specified, replace the selective-fit thrust washer with one of

the three available sizes.

31. Install the blind covers over the gaskets.

32. Fit the lockball, speedometer drive gear, and snap-ring, in that order, on the rear of the output shaft.

33. Install the gearshaft control lever through the holes in the front of the extension housing. Fit the Woodruff key on the control lever and install the yoke over it. Secure the yoke with setbolt.

34. Thread the Neutral switch (for seat belt interlock) into the extension housing.

35. Fit the spring and plunger in the extension housing and secure them with the cap bolt.

36. Install the back-up light switch.

37. Secure the speedometer driven gear in its extension housing bore with the lockplate and bolt.

38. Push the gearshift control lever over to the left as far as possible. Place a gasket on the rear of the transmission case and install the extension housing over it. Secure the extension housing with its bolts. Check the operation of the gearshift control lever.

39. Install the bottom cover on the case. Secure it with its bolts.

40. Insert the select lockpin and spring in the shift tower. Align the slot in the pin with the lockball bore. Drop the lock ball and spring into the bore; secure with cap bolt.

41. Install the shift tower on the extension housing and secure it with its bolts.

42. Perform step 14 for the input shaft bearing and clutch housing bore. The end-play and shim thickness are the same as in step 14.

43. Lubricate the lip of the bellhousing oil seal.

1. Shim
2. Snap ring
3. Main drive shaft bearing
4. Main drive shaft gear
5. Synchronizer ring
6. Sychronizer key
7. Synchronizer key spring
8. 3rd-and-4th clutch hub
9. Clutch sleeve
10. 3rd gear
11. Needle bearing
12. Needle bearing
13. Main shaft
14. Needle bearing
15. 2nd gear
16. 1st-and-2nd clutch hub
17. Clutch sleeve
18. Bearing inner race
19. Needle bearing
20. 1st gear
21. Thrust washer
22. Shim
23. Main shaft front bearing
24. Bearing cover
25. Thrust washer
26. Bearing inner race
27. Needle bearing
28. Reverse gear
29. Stop ring
30. Rev.-and-5th clutch hub
31. Clutch sleeve
32. Main shaft lock nut
33. Needle bearing

34. 5th gear
35. Thrust washer
36. Lock ball
37. Main shaft rear bearing
38. Thrust washer
39. Lock ball
40. Speedometer drive gear
41. Counter shaft front bearing
42. Shim
43. Counter shaft
44. Counter shaft center bearing

45. Counter reverse gear
46. Spacer
47. Reverse gear
48. Counter shaft rear bearing
49. Thrust washer
50. Thrust washer
51. Reverse idler gear

52. Idler gear shaft
53. Thrust washer

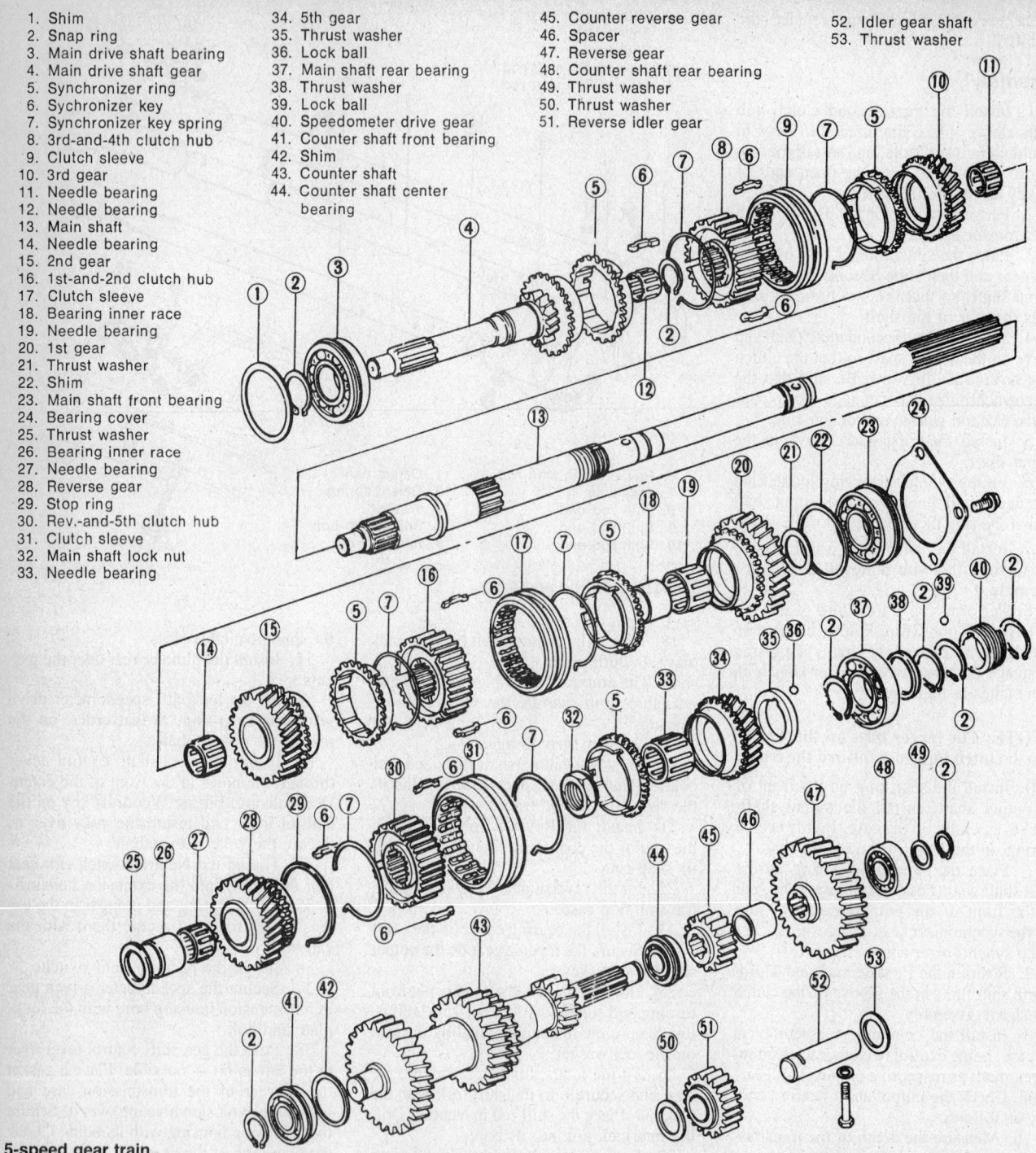

5-speed gear train

44. Put a gasket on the front of the transmission case, install the bellhousing on the case, and secure it with the nuts.

45. Install the throwout bearing, release fork and boot in the bellhousing.

Disassembly—B-1800, B-2000 and Rotary Pick-up 5 Speed

NOTE: The use of special tools is required for the following procedure.

1. Pull the release fork outward until the spring clip of the fork releases from the ball pivot.

2. Remove the fork and release bearing from the clutch housing.

3. Remove the nuts attaching the clutch housing and remove the housing, shim and gasket.

4. Remove the bolts attaching the gearshift lever retainer to the extension housing and remove the retainer and gasket.

5. Remove the spring and steel ball, select lock spindle and spring from the gearshift lever retainer.

6. Unbolt and remove the extension housing with the control lever end down to the left as far as it will go.

7. Unbolt and remove the control lever end, key and control rod.

8. Remove the lockplate and speedometer gear assembly from the extension housing.

9. Remove the back-up light switch from the extension housing.

10. Remove the snap-ring and slide the speedometer drive gear from the mainshaft.

11. Remove the bottom cover and gasket.

12. Unbolt and remove the shift rod ends.

13. Remove the rear bearing housing from the intermediate housing.

14. Remove the snap-ring and remove the mainshaft rear bearing, thrust washer and race. A puller may be necessary.

15. Using the puller, remove the washer and countershaft rear bearing.

16. Remove the counter fifth gear.

17. Remove the intermediate housing from the case.

18. Unbolt and remove the springs and shift locking balls.

19. Remove the two blind covers and gaskets from the case.

20. Unbolt and remove the reverse/fifth shift rod, fork and interlock pin.

21. Unbolt and remove the first/second and third/fourth shift forks, rods and interlock pins.

22. Remove the snap-ring and slide the washer, fifth gear and synchronizer ring from the main shaft. Also, remove the steel ball and needle bearing.

23. Lock the rotation of the mainshaft with second and reverse.

24. Remove the locknut and slide the reverse/fifth clutch hub and sleeve assembly, synchronizer ring, reverse gear and the needle bearing from the mainshaft.

25. Remove the spacer and counter reverse gear from the countershaft.

26. Remove the reverse idler gear, thrust washers and shaft from the transmission case.

27. Remove the bearing rear cover plate.

28. Remove the snap-ring from the front end of the countershaft and install Mazda tool number 49 0839 445 synchronizer ring holder or its equivalent between the fourth synchronizer ring and the synchromesh gear on the main driveshaft.

29. Using a bearing puller, remove the countershaft front bearing.

30. Remove the adjusting shim from the countershaft front bearing bore.

31. With the puller, remove the countershaft center bearing outer race.

32. With a special puller and attachment, remove the mainshaft front bearing, thrust washer, and inner race along with the adjusting shim from the mainshaft front bearing bore.

33. Remove the snap-ring, and using the puller, remove the main drive shaft bearing.

34. Remove the countershaft center bearing inner race with the puller.

35. Separate the input shaft from the mainshaft and remove the input shaft from the case.

36. Remove the synchronizer ring and needle bearing from the input shaft.

37. Remove the mainshaft assembly from the case.

38. Remove the first/second and third/fourth shift forks from the case.

39. Remove the snap-ring and slide the third/fourth clutch hub and sleeve assembly, synchronizer ring and third gear from the mainshaft.

40. Remove the thrust washer, first gear and needle bearing from the rear of the mainshaft.

41. Press out the needle bearing inner

race, synchronizer ring, first and second clutch hub, sleeve assembly, synchronizer ring and second gear from the mainshaft.

Inspection

Inspection of components is carried out in the same manner as described in the Rotary Pick-up 4 Speed section.

Assembly

1. Install the third/fourth clutch hub into the sleeve, place the three keys into the clutch hub slots and install the springs onto the hub.

2. Assemble the first/second and reverse/fifth clutch hub and sleeve as described in step 1.

3. Install the needle bearing, second gear, synchronizer ring, and first/second clutch assembly on the rear section of the mainshaft.

4. Press on the first gear needle bearing inner race.

5. Install the third gear and synchronizer ring onto the front section of the mainshaft.

6. Install the third/fourth clutch assembly onto the mainshaft.

7. Fit the snap ring on the mainshaft.

8. Install the needle bearing, synchronizer ring, first gear and thrust washer on the mainshaft.

9. Install the mainshaft assembly in the case.

10. Install the needle bearing on the front end of the mainshaft.

11. Install the first/second and third/fourth shift forks in their respective clutch sleeves.

12. Press the countershaft center bearing inner race on the countershaft.

13. Position the countershaft in the case.

14. Check the mainshaft bearing end play. Check the depth of the mainshaft bearing bore in the case. Measure the mainshaft bearing height. The difference indicates the required adjusting shim to give a total end-play of less than 0.0039".

15. Install the synchronizer ring holder tool between the fourth synchronizer ring and the synchromesh gear on the input shaft.

16. Position the shims and mainshaft bearing in the bore and install with a press.

17. Install the input shaft bearing on the same way.

18. Check the countershaft front bearing end-play in the same way as the mainshaft bearing end-play.

19. Install the front bearing snap-ring.

20. Press the countershaft center bearing into position.

21. Install the bearing cover plate.

22. Install the reverse idler gear shaft, thrust washers and reverse idler gear in the case.

23. Install the counter reverse gear and spacer on the rear end of the countershaft.

24. Install the thrust washer and press the needle bearing inner race of the reverse gear on the mainshaft.

25. Install the needle bearing, reverse

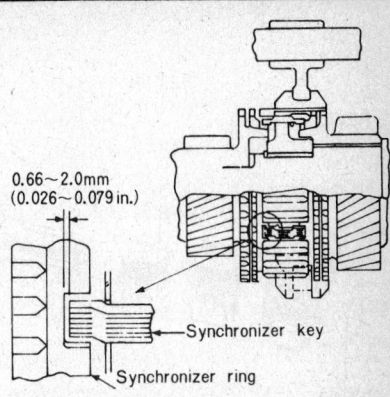

0.66~2.0mm (0.026~0.079 in.)

Synchronizer key

Synchronizer ring

Checking the synchronizer clearance

gear, synchronizer ring, reverse/fifth clutch assembly and new mainshaft lock nut on the mainshaft.

26. Lock the mainshaft with the second and reverse gears. Tighten the locknut to 115–173 ft. lbs. Bend the tabs of the locknut.

27. Install the needle bearing, synchronizer ring and fifth gear on the mainshaft.

28. Install the thrust washer, steel ball and snap-ring on the mainshaft.

29. Check the thrust washer-to-snap-ring clearance. Clearance should be 0.0039–0.0118".

30. Install the first/second shift rod through the holes in the case and fork.

31. Install the interlock pin with a special installer and guide.

32. Install the third/fourth shift rod through the holes in the case and fork.

33. Align the holes and install the lock bolts of each shift fork and rod.

34. Install the interlock pin as above.

35. Position the reverse/fifth shift fork on the clutch sleeve and install the shift rod.

36. Tighten the lock bolt.

37. Install the three shift locking balls, springs and cap bolts.

38. Place the third/fourth clutch sleeve in third gear.

39. Check the clearance between the synchronizer key and the exposed edge of the synchronizer ring with a feeler gauge. The gap should be 0.026–0.079". Adjust by varying thrust washers.

40. Install the two blind covers and gaskets.

41. Install the undercover and gasket. Torque to 4–7 ft. lbs.

42. Apply a thin coat of sealer to the mating edges and install the intermediate housing on the transmission case. Align the lock bolt holes of the housing and reverse idler gear shaft, install and tighten the lock bolt.

43. Position the counter fifth gear and bearing to the rear end of the countershaft and install with a press.

44. Install the thrust washer and snap-ring.

45. Check the clearance between the washer and snap-ring. Clearance should be less than 0.0039".

46. Install the mainshaft rear bearing with

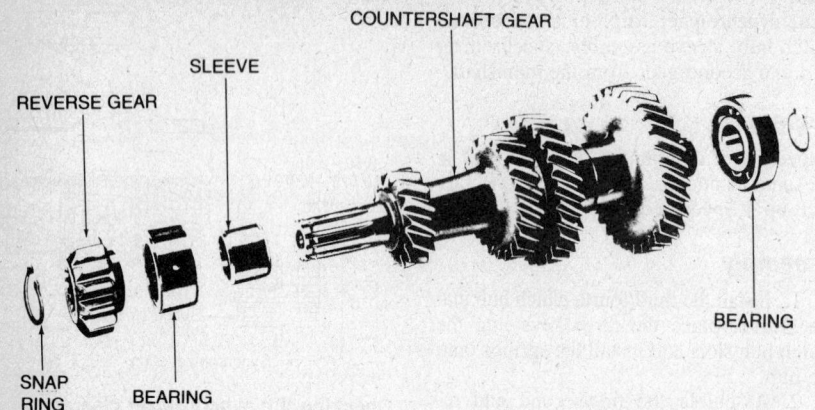

REVERSE GEAR
SLEEVE
COUNTERSHAFT GEAR
BEARING
SNAP RING
BEARING
BEARING

B1600 countershaft

a press.

47. Install the thrust washer and snap-ring.

48. Check the thrust washer-to-snap-ring clearance. Clearance should be less than 0.0059″.

49. Apply a thin coat of sealing agent to the mating surfaces and install the bearing housing on the intermediate housing.

50. Install the shift rod ends on their respective rods.

51. Install the speedometer drive gear and steel ball on the mainshaft. Secure it with a snap-ring.

52. Install the speedometer driven gear assembly on the extension housing and secure it with the bolt and lock plate.

53. Insert the control rod through the holes from the front side of the extension housing.

54. Align the key and insert the control lever end in the control rod.

55. Install the bolt and tighten it to 20–30 ft. lbs.

56. Install the back-up light switch and tighten to 20–30 ft. lbs.

57. Place the gasket on the case and install the extension housing with the control lever end down and as far to the left as it will go.

58. Tighten the bolts.

59. Check the proper operation of the gear shift lever.

60. Insert the select lock spindle and spring from the underside of the shift lever retainer.

61. Install the steel ball and spring in alignment with the spindle groove and install the spring cap bolt.

62. Install the gearshift lever retainer and gasket on the extension housing.

63. Check the bearing end-play. Measure the depth of the bearing bore in the housing. Measure the height of the bearing protrusion. The difference indicates the thickness of the shim needed. The end-play should be less than 0.0039″.

64. Place the gasket on the front side of the case. Apply lubricant to the lip of the oil seal and install the clutch housing on the case.

65. Install the release bearing and fork

on the clutch housing.

Disassembly—B–1600 4 Speed

1. Remove the throwout bearing return spring, throwout bearing, and the release fork.

2. Unfasten the bearing housing, bolts, then remove the housing and gasket.

3. Remove the input shaft and countershaft snap rings.

4. Remove the floorshift lever retainer, complete with gasket from the extension housing.

5. Unfasten the cap bolt and withdraw the spring, steel ball, select lock pin and spring from the retainer.

6. Remove the extension housing securing nuts. Turn the control lever as far left as it will go and slide the extension housing off the output shaft.

7. Remove the spring seat and spring from the end of the shift control lever.

8. Loosen the spring cap and withdraw the spring and plunger from their bore.

9. Unfasten the bolt from the control rod yoke, then remove the control rod and boss from the extension housing.

10. Loosen the setscrew and remove the speedometer driven gear. Remove the back-up light switch.

11. Remove the speedometer drive gear snap-ring, slide the gear off the output shaft and take off the lockball.

12. Tap the front ends of the input shaft and countershaft with a plastic hammer; then remove the intermediate housing assembly from the transmission case.

13. Remove the three cap bolts; then withdraw the springs and lockballs.

14. Unfasten the shift lever securing nut. Remove the reverse shift rod. Reverse idler gear, and shift lever from the intermediate housing.

15. Remove the setscrews from all the shift forks and push the shift rods rearward to remove them. Remove the shift forks as well.

16. Withdraw the Reverse shift rod lockball, spring, and interlock pins from the intermediate housing.

17. Keep the output shaft from turning;

straighten the tabs on its lockwasher, and remove its locknut. Remove reverse gear and key from the output shaft.

18. Remove the snap-ring from the rear of the countershaft and slide the reverse countergear off.

19. Using a plastic hammer, tap the rear of the output shaft and countershaft in turn, being careful not to damage them. Remove both shafts from the intermediate housing.

20. Remove the bearings from the intermediate housing and transmission case.

21. Remove the snap-ring from the output shaft.

22. Slide the Third/Fourth clutch hub, sleeve, synchronizer ring, and Third gear off the output shaft.

23. Remove the thrust washer, First gear, sleeve, synchronizer ring, and second gear from the rear of the output shaft.

Inspection

The inspection procedures for this transmission are identical to those outlined for the Rotary engine 4 speed.

Assembly

1. Install the Third/Fourth synchronizer clutch hub on the sleeve. Place the three synchronizer keys in the clutch hub key slots. Install the key springs with their open ends 120° apart.

2. Install Third gear and the synchronizer ring on the front of the output shaft. Install the Third/Fourth clutch hub assembly on the output shaft. Be sure that the larger boss faces the front of the shaft.

3. Secure the gear and synchronizer with the snap-ring.

4. Perform step 1 to the First/Second synchronizer assembly.

5. Position the synchronizer ring on second gear. Slide Second gear on the output shaft so that the synchronizer ring faces the rear of the shaft.

6. Install the First/Second clutch hub assembly on the output shaft so that its oil grooves face the front of the shaft. Engage the keys in the notches on the Second gear synchronizer ring.

7. Slide the First gear sleeve onto the output shaft. Position the synchronizer ring on First gear. Install the First gear on the output shaft so that the synchronizer ring faces frontward. Rotate the First gear as required to engage the notches in the synchronizer ring with the keys in the clutch hub.

8. Slip the thrust washer on the rear of the output shaft. Install the needle bearing on the front of the output shaft.

9. Install the synchronizer ring on Fourth gear and install the input shaft on the front of the output shaft.

10. Press the countershaft rear bearing and shim into the intermediate housing; then press the countershaft into the rear bearing.

11. Keep the thrust washer and First gear from falling off the output shaft by supporting the shaft. Install the output shaft on

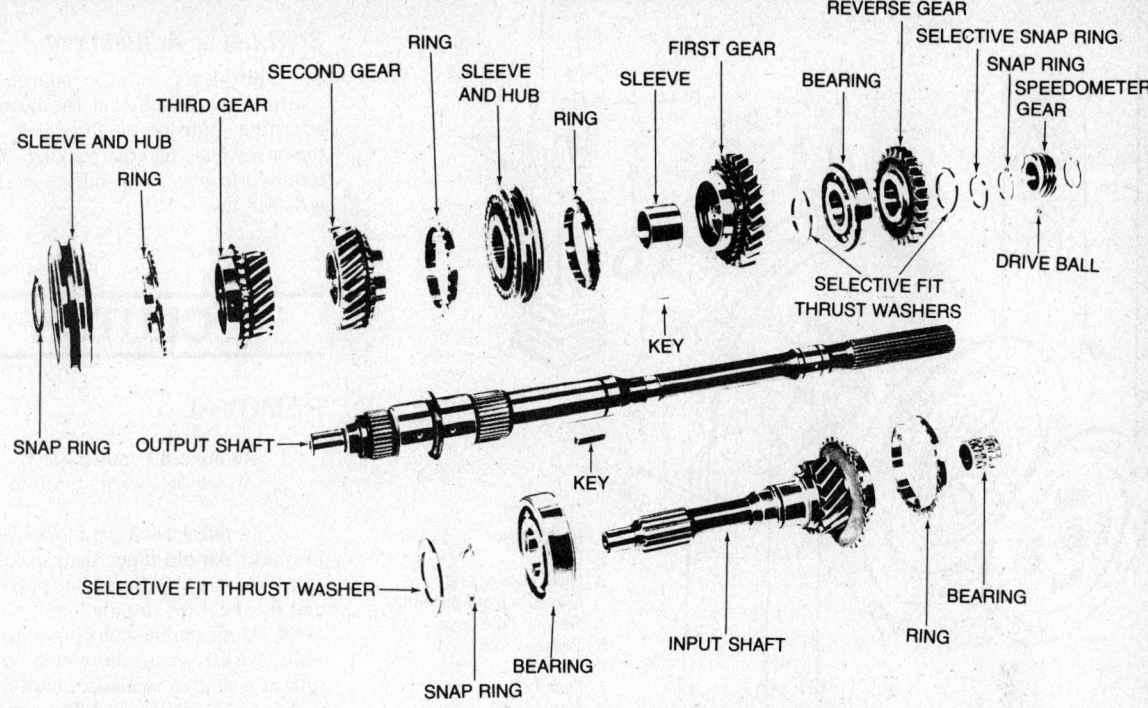

Input and output shafts—B1600

the intermediate housing. Be sure that each output shaft gear engages with its opposite number on the countershaft.

12. Tap the output shaft bearing and shim into the intermediate housing with a plastic hammer. Fit the cover on the housing.

13. Install Reverse gear on the output shaft and secure it with its key. Keep the output shaft from turning while tightening its locknut. Secure the nut by bending the tabs on the lockwasher.

NOTE: The chamfer on the teeth of both the Reverse gear and the Reverse countergear should face rearward.

14. Install the Reverse countergear and secure it with its snap-ring.

15. Install the lockball and spring into the bore in the intermediate housing. Depress the ball with a screwdriver.

16. Install the Reverse shift rod, lever, and idler gear at the same time. Tighten the nut which secures the shift lever to the intermediate housing. Place the Reverse shift rod in the neutral position.

17. Align the bores and insert the shift interlock pin.

18. Install the Third/Fourth shift rod into the intermediate housing end shift bores. Place the shift rod in Neutral.

19. Install the next interlock pin in the bore.

20. Install the First/Second shift rod.

21. Install the lockballs and springs in their bores. Install the cap bolt.

22. Fit the speedometer drive gear and lockball on the output shaft, and install its snap-ring.

Remove the reverse shift lever from the intermediate housing on the B1600

Input shaft, output shaft and countershaft assembled to the intermediate housing—B1600

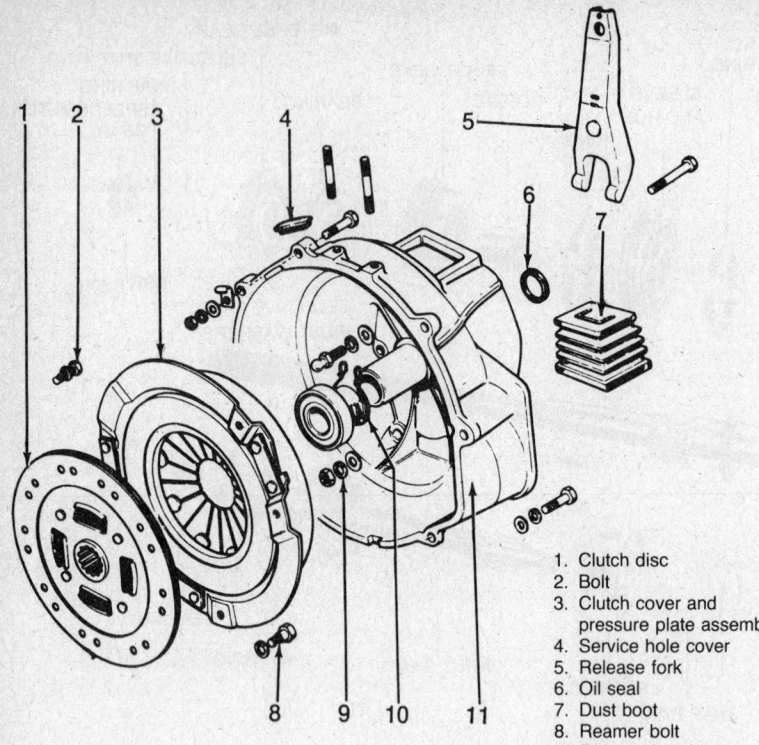

1. Clutch disc
2. Bolt
3. Clutch cover and pressure plate assembly
4. Service hole cover
5. Release fork
6. Oil seal
7. Dust boot
8. Reamer bolt
9. Release bearing
10. Spring
11. Clutch housing

Clutch components

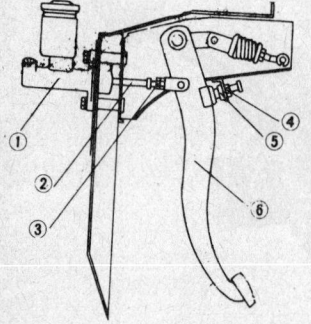

1. Master cylinder
2. Rod
3. Locknut
4. Adjusting bolt
5. Locknut
6. Clutch pedal

Clutch pedal height adjustment

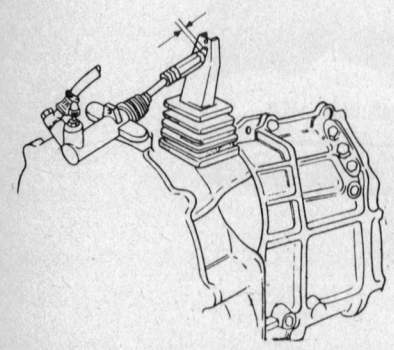

Release fork free play is measured at the arrows

23. Apply sealer to the mating surfaces of the intermediate housing. Install the intermediate housing in the transmission case.

24. Install the input shaft and countershaft front bearings in the transmission case. Fit the snap-ring on the input shaft bearing.

25. Secure the speedometer driven gear to the extension housing with its setscrew.

26. Install the control rod through the holes in the front of the extension housing.

27. Align the key with the keyway and install the yoke on the end of the control rod. Install the yoke lockbolt.

28. Fit the plunger and spring into the extension housing bore and secure with the spring cap.

29. Turn the control rod all the way to the left, install the extension housing on the intermediate housing, and tighten its securing nuts. Check control rod operation.

30. Insert the spring and select lockpin inside the gearshift retainer. Align the steel ball and spring with the lockpin slot, and secure it with the spring cap.

31. Install the spring and spring seat in the control rod yoke.

32. Install the gear shift lever retainer over its gasket on the extension housing.

33. Lubricate the lip of the front bearing cover oil seal and secure the cover on the transmission case.

34. Check the clearance between the front bearing cover and bearing. It should be less than 0.006 in. If it is not within specifications insert additional adjusting shims. The shims are available in 0.006 in. or 0.012 in. sizes.

35. Install the throwout bearing, return

spring and release fork.

Shift Lever Adjustment

The shift lever may be adjusted during transmission installation by means of the adjusting shims on the three bolts between the cover plate and the packing. The force required to move the shift knob should be 4.4–8.8 lbs.

CLUTCH

REMOVAL

1. Remove the transmission.
2. Attach a locking tool to the flywheel.
3. Install a clutch arbor to hold the clutch in place. An old input shaft makes an excellent arbor. Matchmark the pressure plate and flywheel for installation.
4. Unfasten the bolts (4 securing and 2 pilot) which secure the clutch cover, one turn at a time in sequence, until the clutch spring tension is released. Remove the bolts evenly.
5. Remove the clutch disc.

——————— CAUTION ———————
Be careful not to get grease or oil on the surface of the clutch disc.

6. Unfasten the nut which secures the flywheel to the eccentric shaft, using a suitably large wrench.
7. Remove the flywheel with a puller.
8. Unhook the return spring from the throwout bearing and remove the bearing.
9. Pull out the release fork until the retaining spring frees itself from the ball stud. Withdraw the fork from the housing.

INSTALLATION

Clutch installation is performed in the following order:

1. Clean the flywheel and pressure plate surfaces with fine sandpaper. Check the flywheel and pressure plate for warpage, scoring, or signs of heat distortion. If scoring damage is minor, it can usually be cleaned up. Heavy wear or damage warrants replacement of the parts. Be sure there is no oil or grease on them. Grease the eccentric shaft needle bearing.

2. Install the flywheel with its keyway over the key on the eccentric shaft.

3. Apply sealer to both sides of the flywheel lockwasher and position the lockwasher on the eccentric shaft.

4. Install the flywheel locknut(s) and tighten it to 350 ft. lbs. (rotary engines) or 112–118 ft. lbs. (piston engines); then bend the tabs of the lockwasher up around it.

5. Use an arbor to center the clutch disc during installation. Install the clutch disc with the long end of its hub facing the trans-

mission.

NOTE: Use an old input shaft to center the clutch disc, if an arbor is not available.

6. Align the O-mark on the clutch cover with the reamed hole or the O-mark on the flywheel or align the matchmarks made during removal.

7. Tighten the clutch cover bolts evenly, and in two or three stages, to 13–20 ft. lbs.

——— CAUTION ———
Do not tighten the bolts one at a time.

8. Grease the pivot pin. Insert the release fork through its boot so that its retaining spring contacts the pivot pin.

9. Lightly grease the face of the throwout bearing and its clutch housing retainer.

10. Install the throwout bearing and return spring. Check the operation of the release fork and throwout bearing for smoothness.

11. Install the transmission.

PEDAL HEIGHT ADJUSTMENT

Except B–1600

1. Loosen the locknut on the adjusting bolt.

2. Turn the adjusting bolt until the clearance between the pedal pad and the floormat is 8.46 in.

3. Carefully tighten the locknut.

PEDAL FREE-PLAY ADJUSTMENT

The free-play of the clutch pedal before the pushrod contacts the piston in the master cylinder should be 0.02–0.12 in.

To adjust the free-play, loosen the locknut and turn the pushrod until the proper adjustment is obtained. Tighten the locknut after the adjustment is complete.

RELEASE FORK FREE-PLAY ADJUSTMENT

1975 Only

1. Unfasten the return spring from the release fork.

2. Loosen the locknut on the release rod.

3. Turn the adjusting nut on the release rod until the proper release fork free-play is obtained:
   Rotary Pick-Ups—0.14–0.18 in.
   B—1600–0.12–0.14 in.

4. Carefully tighten the locknut and hook the return spring back on the release fork.

Clutch Master Cylinder

REMOVAL AND INSTALLATION

1. Unfasten the hydraulic line from the master cylinder outlet and plug the outlet.

——— CAUTION ———
Use care not to dip any hydraulic fluid on painted surfaces, as it is an excellent paint remover.

2. Remove the nuts which secure the master cylinder assembly to the firewall.

3. Withdraw the master cylinder straight out and away from the firewall.

Installation is performed in the reverse order of removal. Bleed the hydraulic system as detailed below.

OVERHAUL

1. Thoroughly clean the outside of the master cylinder.

2. Drain the hydraulic fluid from the cylinder. Unbolt the reservoir from the cylinder body.

3. Remove the boot from the cylinder.

4. Release the wire piston stop ring with a screwdriver and withdraw the stop washer.

5. Withdraw the piston, piston cups, and return spring from the cylinder bore.

6. Wash all of the parts in clean hydraulic (brake) fluid. Do not use mineral spirits.

7. Examine the piston cups. If they are damaged, softened, or swollen, replace them with new ones.

8. Check the piston and bore for scoring or roughness.

9. Use a wire gauge to check the clearance between the piston and its bore. Replace either the piston or the cylinder if the clearance is greater than 0.006 in.

10. Be sure that the compensating port in the cylinder is not clogged.

ASSEMBLY

Assembly of the master cylinder is performed in the following order:

1. Dip the piston and cups in clean hydraulic (brake) fluid.

2. Bolt the reservoir up to the cylinder body.

3. Fit the return spring into the cylinder.

4. Insert the primary cup in the bore so that its flat side is facing the piston.

5. Place the secondary cup on the piston and insert them in the cylinder bore.

6. Install the stop washer and the wire piston stop.

7. Fill the reservoir half-full of hydraulic fluid. Operate the piston with a screwdriver until fluid spurts out of the cylinder outlet.

8. Fit the boot on the cylinder.

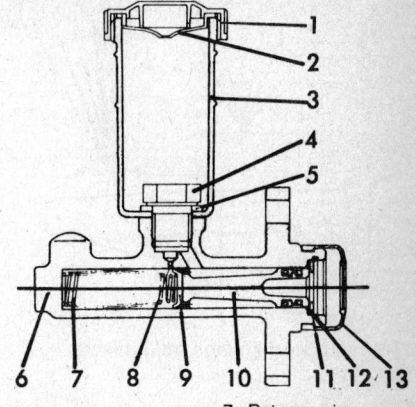

	7. Return spring
1. Cap	8. Compensating port
2. Baffle	9. Primary cup
3. Reservoir	10. Piston
4. Bolt	11. Stop washer
5. Washer	12. Stop wire
6. Cylinder	13. Boot

Cutaway view of the master cylinder

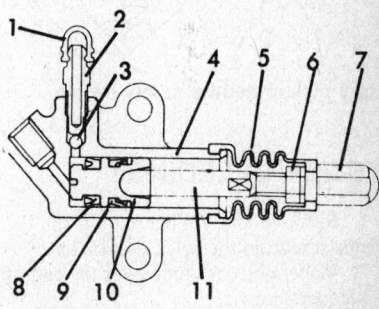

	6. Lock nut
1. Cap	7. Adjusting nut
2. Bleeder screw	8. Primary cup
3. Valve	9. Secondary cup
4. Cylinder	10. Piston
5. Boot	11. Push rod

Cutaway view of the release cylinder

Clutch Release Cylinder

REMOVAL AND INSTALLATION

1. Unscrew the hydraulic line from the release cylinder and plug it.

2. Unhook the release fork return spring from the cylinder.

3. Unfasten the nuts which secure the release cylinder to the transmission.

Installation is performed in the reverse order of removal. Bleed the hydraulic system, as detailed below, and adjust the release fork free-play, as detailed above.

OVERHAUL

Consult the master cylinder overhaul section above for release cylinder overhaul procedures.

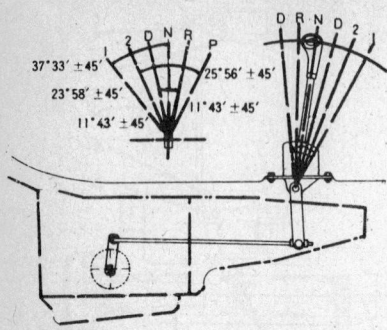

Transmission linkage adjustment

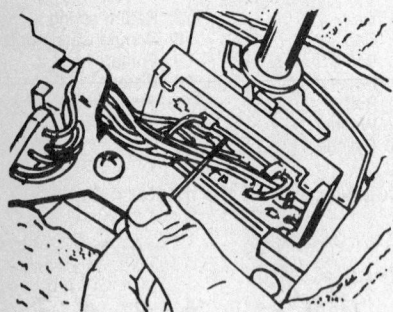

Rotary pickup neutral safety switch

SYSTEM BLEEDING

1. Remove the rubber cap from the bleeder screw on the release cylinder.
2. Place a bleeder tube over the end of the bleeder screw.
3. Submerge the other end of the tube in a jar half-filled with hydraulic (brake) fluid.
4. Depress the clutch pedal fully and allow it to return slowly.
5. Keep repeating step 4, while watching the hydraulic fluid in the jar. As soon as the air bubbles disappear, close the bleeder screw.

NOTE: During the bleeding procedure the reservoir must be kept at least ¾ full.

6. Remove the tube and refit the rubber cap. Fill the reservoir with hydraulic fluid.

AUTOMATIC TRANSMISSION

Removal

ROTARY PICK-UP

1. Disconnect the cable from the negative (−) battery terminal.
2. Remove the power brake vacuum line bracket from the converter housing.

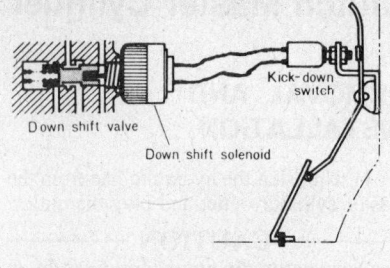

Kickdown switch and downshift solenoid circuit

3. Remove the converter access hole cover. Lock the flex-plate by holding the drive pulley lockbolt with a wrench.
4. Matchmark the converter and flex-plate. Unfasten the four converter-to-flex-plate securing bolts.
5. Jack up the vehicle and securely support it with jackstands.

— CAUTION —

The exhaust system on rotary engine-equipped Mazdas gets considerably hotter than a conventional system; be sure to allow enough time for it to cool before performing steps 6 and 7.

6. Remove the heat shroud. Unfasten the exhaust pipe bracket on the right-hand side of the torque converter housing.
7. Unfasten the bolts which secure the exhaust pipe to the rear side of the front muffler. Detach the exhaust pipe.
8. Unfasten the bolts from the driveshaft flange and center bearing. Push the driveshaft out of the extension housing. Plug the hole in the extension housing, so that fluid doesn't leak out.
9. Detach the speedometer cable at the extension housing.
10. Remove the control rod.
11. Disconnect the starter wiring. Remove the starter from the converter housing.
12. Remove the bottom cover from the converter housing.
13. Support the transmission with a jack.
14. Unfasten the nuts which secure the transmission support member and remove the member.
15. Lower the transmission jack to increase the gap between the transmission and the underbody of the truck.
16. Remove the vacuum fitting from the intake manifold. Unfasten the vacuum line from the converter housing, transmission case, and extension housing. Disconnect the hose from the vacuum modulator and remove the vacuum line.
17. Disconnect the downshift solenoid wiring and separate the wires from the clip.
18. Disconnect the lines which run to the cooler at the left-hand side of the transmission. Remove the clips for these lines from the converter housing and transmission case.

19. Unfasten evenly, and in several stages, the bolts which secure the torque converter housing to the top of the engine.
20. Raise the transmission so that it is level again.
21. Use a small pry bar to carefully apply pressure between the torque converter and the flex-plate.
22. Slide the transmission rearward and lower it from the truck.

— CAUTION —

Do not rest the weight of the transmission on the torque converter splines.

INSTALLATION

Automatic transmission installation is performed in almost the reverse order of removal. There are several points which should be noted, however:

1. Before installing the transmission, use a dial indicator to measure flex-plate runout. Runout should be about 0.012 in. If runout exceeds 0.020 in., the flexplate must be replaced.
2. Hand-tighten the four torque converter installation bolts and then lock the flex-plate with a locking tool. Next, tighten the four bolts evenly, and in several stages, to 27–40 ft. lbs.
3. After completing transmission installation, rotate the eccentric shaft to be sure that there is no interference in the transmission.
4. Fill the transmission with type F transmission fluid. Converter capacity is 6.6 qts.
5. Check and adjust the following items, after completing installation:
    a. Shift linkage.
    b. Neutral safety switch.
    c. Engine idle speed.
    d. Kickdown switch and downshift solenoid.
6. Check the fluid level again and road test the car.

SHIFT LINKAGE ADJUSTMENT

1975

1. Unfasten the T-joint on the intermediate lever.
2. Place the range selector lever, which is mounted on the side of the transmission case, in Neutral (N); i.e., so that the slot in the selector shaft is pointing straight up and down.
3. Adjust the console-mounted gear selector lever by turning the T-joint until it indicates Neutral (N).
4. Reconnect the T-joint. Check the gear selector operation in all other ranges and to see that the linkage has no slack.

1976 and Later

1. Place the transmission selector lever in N.

2. Raise the vehicle and disconnect the clevis from the lower end of the selector arm.

3. Move the manual lever to the N position.

NOTE: The N position is the third detent from the back.

4. Loosen the two clevis retaining nuts and adjust the clevis so that it freely enters the lever hole.

5. Tighten the retaining nuts.

6. Connect the clevis to the lever and secure with the spring washer, flat washer and retaining clip.

NEUTRAL SAFETY SWITCH ADJUSTMENT

Rotary Pick-Up

1. Remove the housing from the shift lever.

2. Adjust the shift lever so that there is 0.–0.12 in. clearance between the pin and the guide plate, when the lever is in neutral.

3. Adjust the neutral safety switch so that the pin hole in the switch body is aligned with the pin hole of the sliding plate when the shift lever is in Neutral.

4. Check the adjustment by trying to start the engine in all gears. It should only start in Park or Neutral.

5. Reinstall the housing on the shift lever.

PAN REMOVAL AND INSTALLATION

1. Raise and support the vehicle.

2. Place a drain pan under the transmission pan.

3. Remove the pan attaching bolts (except the two at the front). Loosen the two at the front slightly. Allow the fluid to drain.

4. Remove the pan.

5. Remove and discard the gasket.

6. Install a new pan gasket and install the pan on the transmission.

7. Lower the vehicle and fill the transmission with fluid. Check the transmission operation.

KICKDOWN SWITCH AND DOWNSHIFT SOLENOID ADJUSTMENT

1. Check the accelerator linkage for smooth operation.

2. Turn the ignition on but do not start the engine.

3. Depress the accelerator pedal fully to the floor. As the pedal nears the end of its travel, a light ''click'' should be heard from the downshift solenoid.

4. If if kickdown switch operates too soon, loosen the locknut on the switch shaft. Adjust the shaft so that the accelerator linkage makes contact with it when the pedal

is depressed ⅞–¹⁵⁄₁₆ of the way to the floor. Tighten the locknut.

5. If no noise comes from the solenoid at all, then check the wiring for the solenoid and the switch.

6. If the wiring is in good condition, then remove the wire from the solenoid and connect it to a 12V power source. If the solenoid does not click when connected, it is defective and should be replaced.

NOTE: When the solenoid is removed, about two pints of transmission fluid will leak out; have a container ready to catch it. Remember to add more fluid to the transmission after installing the new solenoid.

BAND ADJUSTMENT

JATCO Model 3N71B

1. Raise and support the vehicle.

2. Drain the transmission fluid and remove the pan.

3. Loosen the locknut and tighten the servo adjusting bolt to 9–11 ft. lbs.

4. Back off the servo bolt exactly two full turns. Hold the bolt in this position and tighten the locknut securely.

5. Install the pan and refill the transmission.

JATCO Model R3A

1. Raise and support the vehicle.

2. The servo is located on the right side of the transmission case. Remove the servo cover.

3. Loosen the locknut and tighten the servo adjusting bolt to 9–11 ft. lbs.

4. Loosen the servo bolt exactly two full turns. Hold the bolt in this position and tighten the locknut securely.

5. Install the servo cover.

DRIVE AXLES

Driveshaft and U-Joints

REMOVAL AND INSTALLATION

1. Raise the rear end of the car and support it using jackstands.

—— CAUTION ——
Be sure that the car is securely supported. Remember, you will be working underneath it.

2. Matchmark the flanges on the driveshaft and pinion so that they may be installed in their original position.

3. Remove the four bolts which secure the driveshaft to the pinion flange. Unbolt the center bearing.

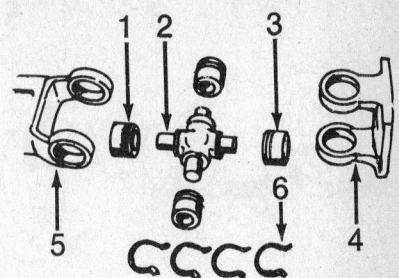

1. Roller bearing (cup)
2. Spider
3. Oil seal
4. Yoke
5. Driveshaft
6. Snap-ring

U-joint components

4. Lower the back end of the driveshaft and slide the front end out of the transmission.

5. Plug up the hole in the transmission to prevent it from leaking.

NOTE: Use an old U-joint yoke; or, if none is available, place a plastic bag, secured with rubber bands, over the hole.

NOTE: Do not remove the oil seals and the center bearing from the support unless they are defective.

Installation is performed in the reverse order of removal. Tighten the center bearing support bolts to 14–21 ft. lbs. and the driveshaft-to-pinion flange bolts to 40–47 ft. lbs.

U-JOINT OVERHAUL

Perform this procedure with the driveshaft removed from the car.

1. Matchmark both the yoke and the driveshaft so that they can be returned to their original balancing position during assembly.

2. Remove the bearing snap-rings from the yoke.

3. Use a hammer and a brass drift to drive in one of the bearing cups. Remove the cup which is protruding from the other side of the yoke.

4. Remove the other bearing cups by pressing them from the spider.

5. Withdraw the spider from the yoke. Examine the spider journals for rusting or wear. Check the bearings for smoothness of pitting.

NOTE: The spider and bearing are replaced as a complete assembly only.

Check the seals and rollers for wear or damage.

Assembly of the U-joint is performed in the following order:

1. Pack the bearing cups with grease.

2. Fit the rollers into the cups and install the dust seals.

3. Place the spider in the yoke and then fit one of the bearing cups into its bore in the yoke.

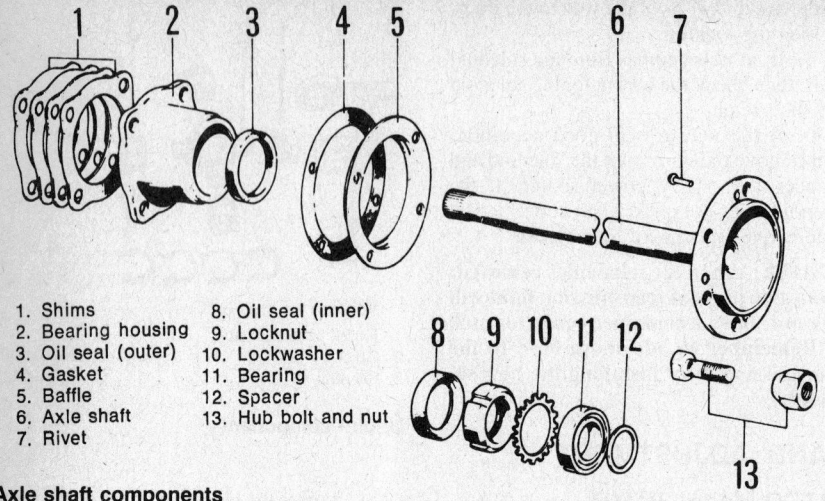

1. Shims
2. Bearing housing
3. Oil seal (outer)
4. Gasket
5. Baffle
6. Axle shaft
7. Rivet
8. Oil seal (inner)
9. Locknut
10. Lockwasher
11. Bearing
12. Spacer
13. Hub bolt and nut

Axle shaft components

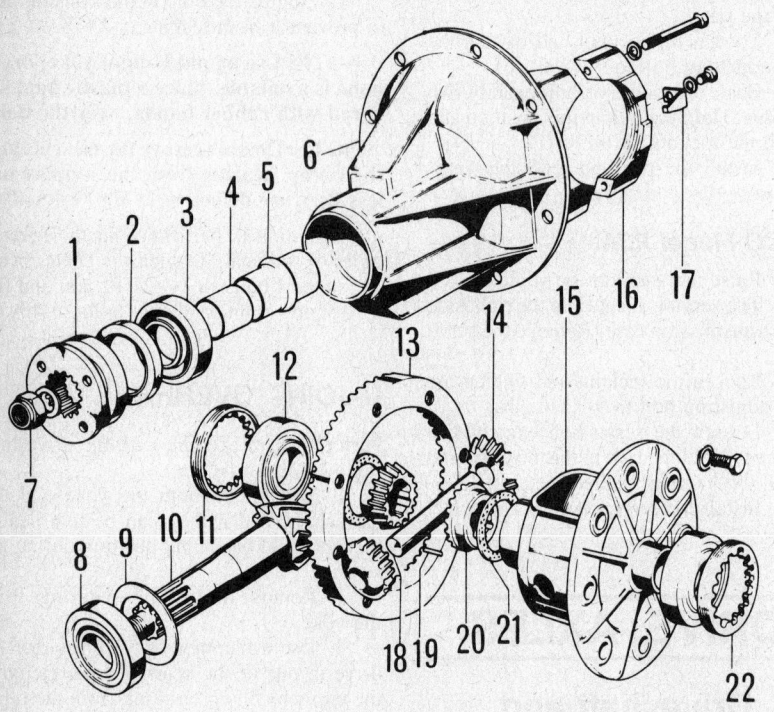

1. Pinion flange
2. Pinion oil seal
3. Pinion front bearing
4. Pinion bearing collar
5. Collapsible pinion bearing spacer
6. Carrier
7. Pinion nut
8. Pinion rear bearing
9. Adjusting washer (adjusting spacer)
10. Drive pinion
11. Pinion side adjusting nut
12. Side bearing
13. Ring gear
14. Pinion gear
15. Differential gear case
16. Bearing cap
17. Adjusting nut lock
18. Pinion shaft
19. Pinion shaft lock pin
20. Side gear
21. Thrust washer
22. Ring gear side adjusting nut

Differential components

4. Press the bearing cup home, while guiding the spider into it so that a snap-ring can be installed.

5. Press-fit the other bearings into the yoke.

6. Select a snap-ring to obtain minimum end-play of the spider. Use snap-rings of the same thickness on both sides to center

the spider.

NOTE: Selective fit snap-rings are available in sizes ranging from 0.048 to 0.054 in.

7. Install the spider/yoke assembly and bearings to the driveshaft in the same manner as the spider was assembled to the yoke.

8. Test the operation of the U-joint assembly. The spider should move freely with no binding.

Axle Shafts

REMOVAL AND INSTALLATION

1. Raise and support the truck.
2. Remove the rear wheel and brake drum.
3. Remove the brake shoes.
4. Remove the parking brake cable retainer.
5. Disconnect and plug the hydraulic brake lines at the wheel cylinders.
6. Unbolt the backing plate and bearing housing.
7. Slide the complete axle shaft from the housing. If necessary, remove the oil seal from the housing.

To install the axle shaft:

8. Install a new axle oil seal in the housing if the old one was removed.
9. Install the axle shaft assembly.
10. Using two bolts and nuts, temporarily install the bearing housing and backing plate to the housing flange.
11. Check the axle shaft end-play with a dial indicator mounted on the backing plate.
12. If only one axle shaft has been removed, the end-play should be 0.002–0.006 in. If both axle shafts have been removed, check the end-play after the first shaft is installed. It should be 0.026–0.033 in. The end-play of the second shaft should then be 0.002–0.006 in. Shims are available to adjust the end-play.
13. After adjusting the end-play, install all bolts and torque them to 12–16 ft. lbs.
14. Install the brake shoes.
15. Install the brake drum and wheel.
16. Connect the brake lines.
17. Bleed the brakes.
18. Lower the truck and road-test it.

BEARING AND SEAL REPLACEMENT

1. Remove the axle shaft.
2. Using a suitable press, press the axle shaft out of the collar and bearing.

NOTE: If the pressure needed to press out the shaft exceeds 10 tons, grind off part of the bearing retaining collar and cut it with a cold chisel, taking care not to damage the shaft surface.

3. Remove the bearing retainer from the shaft.
4. Clean all parts and inspect the condition of the collar, spacer and shaft.
5. Install the retainer and spacer on the shaft.
6. Position the bearing on the shaft with the sealed side toward the shaft flange. Press it on until the spacer comes in contact with the shoulder of the shaft.

7. Press the bearing retaining collar onto the shaft until it contacts the bearing inner race.

NOTE: If the bearing retaining collar can be press fitted with a force less than 2.5 tons, replace the collar.

8. Install the shaft.

Differential

REMOVAL AND INSTALLATION

1. Raise the vehicle and support it with jackstands.

2. Remove the drain (lower) plug from the axle housing and drain the lubricant into a suitable container. Clean and reinstall the plug.

3. Remove the driveshaft as detailed in the appropriate section above.

4. Remove both of the axle shafts as detailed in the section immediately above.

5. Unfasten the nuts which secure the differential carrier to the axle housing and withdraw the carrier assembly from the housing.

Installation is performed in the reverse order of removal. Tighten the carrier-to-housing bolts to 14.5 ft. lbs. Fill the axle housing to the level just below the filler plug with one of the following:

Above 0°F—HP SAE 90
Below 0°F—HP SAE 80

OVERHAUL

NOTE: Differential overhaul requires the use of special tools and equipment. Proper overhaul cannot be performed without them. The following procedures apply to all Mazda differentials as they are all similar in design.

Disassembly

1. Mount the carrier on a workstand.

2. Apply identification marks to the carrier, bearing caps, and adjuster, to aid in installation.

3. Unfasten the bolts which secure adjusting nut lockplates and then remove the lockplates.

4. Loosen, but do not remove, the bearing cap securing nuts and then back off on the adjuster, just enough to remove bearing preload.

5. Remove the differential assembly, complete with the outer bearing races.

——— CAUTION ———
Be sure that each bearing outer race remains with its bearing.

6. Remove the differential bearings from the gear case with a puller.

NOTE: Use care not to mix up the bearings when setting them aside.

7. Unfasten the bolts which secure the ring gear to the gear case and remove their washers. Separate the ring gear from the case.

8. Straighten out the punched portion of the gear case, then drive the pinion gear shaft locking pin of the case with a brass drift.

9. Withdraw the pinion gear shaft.

10. Rotate each of the pinion (spider) gears 90° and remove them, complete with thrust washers.

11. Remove the side gears and thrust washers.

12. Hold the pinion flange by screwing two bolts into it and grabbing them with a pipewrench. Remove the pinion nut.

13. Remove the pinion from the carrier.

NOTE: If the pinion is difficult to remove, tap it with a plastic hammer while guiding it out by hand.

14. Remove the collar, if so equipped, and the collapsible spacer from the pinion.

15. Press out the rear bearing and remove the adjustable shim. Save the shim for later reference.

16. Withdraw the oil seal and the front bearing from the carrier.

17. If necessary, the pinion bearing outer races can be driven out with a brass drift placed in the slots which are provided for this purpose.

NOTE: Do not remove the outer races unless they are worn or damaged. If they are replaced, the bearing cones must be replaced as well.

Inspection

1. Check all of the gears for chipping, broken teeth, wear, or other signs of damage. Replace any gears, as required.

2. Examine the carrier and pinion flange for cracks, wear, and other signs of damage. Replace these parts as necessary.

3. Check the clearance between the splines on the side gears and the rear axle shafts. If it is greater than 0.012 in., replace either the side gears or the axle shafts.

4. Inspect the oil seal for wear and/or damage; replace it if either are present.

ASSEMBLY AND ADJUSTMENT

NOTE: Start out with a handful of collapsible spacers and different sizes of pinion adjusting shims.

1. If the old pinion/ring gear assembly and rear bearing are being used, replace the shim with a new one of the same size (identification marking) as was removed. Use a new collapsible spacer through 1977. On 1978 and later models, use a shim, not a collapsible spacer.

2. If a new pinion/ring gear assembly or rear bearing is being used, determine the correct adjustment shim size in the following manner:

a. Look at the identification markings on the old pinion and shim which were

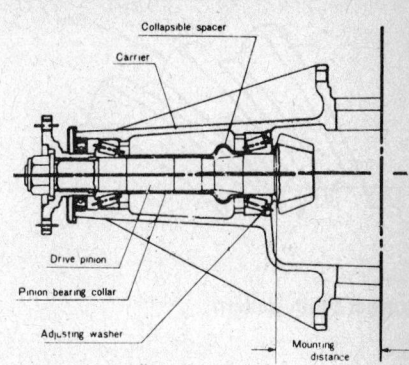

Proper pinion positioning

removed. Record their markings.

NOTE: Pinion markings are given in plus (+) or minus (−) millimeter measurements while the shim has a numbered identification code. Consult the chart below for proper shim identification.

b. Look at the identification measurement stamped on a new pinion and note its value.

c. Calculate the difference between the measurements of the new and old pinions by adding or subtracting, as necessary.

d. If the value on the new pinion is *less* than the value on the old, *add* the difference to the thickness of the old shim (in millimeters). Use a new shim of the total thickness.

e. If the value on the new pinion is *greater* than the value on the old, *subtract* the difference from the thickness of the old shim (in millimeters). Use a new shim having a thickness of the difference.

f. If the rear pinion bearing was replaced, measure the difference (in millimeters) between the new and the old bearing. Add or subtract the difference between the two bearings from the size of the adjusting shim.

g. Select the proper size adjusting shim, as determined in the steps above, from one of the following:

PINION SHIM IDENTIFICATION

Marking	Thickness (mm)	Marking	Thickness (mm)
08	3.08	29	3.29
11	3.11	32	3.32
14	3.14	35	3.35
17	3.17	38	3.38
20	3.20	41	3.41
23	3.23	44	3.44
26	3.26	47	3.47

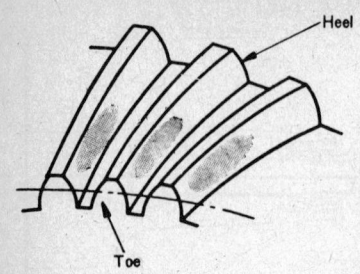

Correct tooth pattern

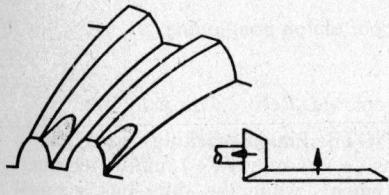

Too much toe contact

3. Position the adjusting shim, of the size as determined in steps 1 or 2, and install the rear pinion bearing on the pinion.

4. If they were removed, install the pinion bearing outer races in the carrier. Be sure that they are properly seated.

5. Place the pinion assembly through the collapsible spacer and into the carrier.

NOTE: Use a new collapsible spacer.

6. Position the front bearing on the pinion. Hold the pinion as far forward as it will go and drive the front bearing on to the pinion until it is fully seated.

7. Coat the lips of the pinion oil seal with grease and fit the seal into the carrier.

8. Tap the pinion flange home on the pinion with a rubber mallet.

9. Install the pinion washer and nut but do not tighten the nut.

10. With the nut still loose, i.e., with no preload on the pinion, check the amount of force required to turn the pinion with a torque wrench that is calibrated in inch pounds; this will measure the amount of drag produced by the oil seal.

11. Install two bolts on the pinion flange and hold it with a spanner or pipe wrench to keep it from rotating. Tighten the pinion nut to the specification shown in the chart.

—————— CAUTION ——————
Use care not to overtighten the pinion, as the spacer will collapse and have to be replaced.

12. Release the pinion flange and measure the amount of preload obtained using the inch/pound torque wrench.

13. Continue tightening the pinion nut, if necessary, a little at a time. Check the preload after each small amount of tightening, until the final preload figure is reached.

—————— CAUTION ——————
If the preload is exceeded, the collapsible

spacer will be compressed too much. A new spacer will have to be installed and the bearing preload adjusted all over again. Proper preload cannot be obtained by simply backing off on the nut.

14. Install thrust washers on both of the side gears and fit the gears into the case.

15. Fit the two pinion (spider) gears into the case, through the opening, so that they are exactly 180° apart.

16. Turn the gears through 90° so that the pinion shaft holes in the case align with the holes in the pinion gears.

17. Insert the pinion gear shaft into the holes in the case and through the holes in the pinion gears.

18. Check the backlash between the side gears and the pinion gears with a dial indicator. The backlash between the gear teeth should be 0–0.004 in. If backlash exceeds 0.008 in., adjust it to specifications by selecting one of the following side gear thrust washers:

NOTE: Use the same thickness thrust washers for both side gears.

19. Install and stake the lockpin onto the pinion shaft.

20. Bolt the ring gear up to the gear case. Torque the bolts evenly, and in sequence, 40–47 ft. lbs. for the B-1600, B-1800 and the rotary pickup, and to 54–61 ft. lbs. for the B-2000. Lock the bolts in place with their lockplates.

21. Install the gear bearings in the gear case hub and fit each of the outer races into its respective bearing.

22. Place the differential gearset in the carrier.

NOTE: Be sure that the marks used for backlash adjustment, which are stamped on the faces of the ring gear and pinion teeth, are aligned.

23. Install the adjusters on their respective sides by consulting the identification marks made during their removal.

24. Install the bearing cups properly by consulting the identification marks made on them during removal.

25. Rotate the adjusters until the bearings are properly positioned in their outer races and their end-play is eliminated.

26. Finger tighten one of the bearing cap bolts on each bearing.

27. Attach a dial indicator to the flange on the carrier so that its plunger comes into contact with the ring gear at right angles to its teeth.

28. Check the backlash between the pinion and the ring gear teeth:

a. If backlash is *more* than specified, loosen the adjusting nut on the pinion side one notch and tighten the ring gear adjusting nut on notch.

b. If the backlash is *less* than specified, loosen the adjusting nut on the ring gear side one notch and tighten the pinion adjusting nut one notch.

c. Repeat the procedure until the specified backlash of 0.0075–0.0083 in. is obtained.

29. Tighten the adjusting nut on the differential bearings to obtain proper preload. Proper preload is determined when the distance between the pilot sections of the bearing caps is 8.0485–8.0513 in. Measure the distance with a vernier caliper.

NOTE: Be careful not to disturb the backlash between the pinion and the ring gear teeth while adjusting the bearing preload.

30. Tighten the bearing cap securing bolts to 47–56 ft. lbs. Install the lockplate on the bearing adjuster so that they cannot loosen.

31. Coat both sides of about six to eight ring gear teeth with red lead. Move the ring gear back and forth several times and then examine the contact pattern made. Compare it to the illustrations. Adjust the preload or backlash, as required to obtain proper tooth contact.

32. Install the carrier in the axle housing, as outlined above.

REAR SUSPENSION

Springs

REMOVAL AND INSTALLATION

1. Raise and support the truck, allowing the spring to hang freely.

2. Support the rear axle with jackstands.

3. Disconnect the rear shock absorber at the lower mount.

4. Remove the spring clip nuts and the spring plate.

5. Remove the spring pin nut and remove the two bolts and nuts attaching the spring pin to the frame bracket.

6. Remove the spring pin and remove the front end of the spring from the truck.

7. Remove the shackle plate nuts and the shackle plate.

8. Remove the spring from the truck.

9. Installation is the reverse of removal.

Shock Absorbers

REMOVAL AND INSTALLATION

1. Remove the nuts, washers and bushings from the upper and lower shock mounts.

2. Remove the shock absorber.

3. To install, reverse the installation procedure. On trucks through 1974, tighten

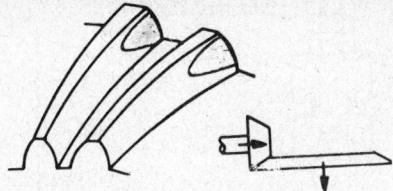

Too much heel contact

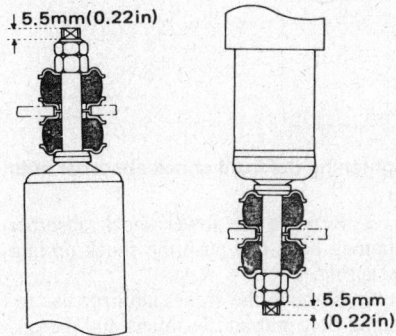

Tightening the rear shock absorber nuts—1976 and later

all mounts to 18–20 ft. lbs. On 1975 and later trucks, both the lower and upper mounts must be tightened to provide 0.138 in. between the end of the rod and the outside nut in 1975, and 0.217 in. 1976 and later.

FRONT SUSPENSION

The Mazda truck front suspension uses a wishbone-type suspension arm with a coil spring. Shock absorbers are hydraulic double-action.

Front Shock Absorber

TESTING

The simplest test for any shock absorber is to bounce the suspect corner of the vehicle until it is bouncing quickly. Let go of the vehicle and count the number of bounces before it comes to rest. A good shock absorber should come to rest in 2–3 bounces at the most.

As an alternative:

1. Remove the shock absorber.
2. Hold the shock in upright position and work it up and down 4–5 times through its full travel.
3. If strong resistance is felt, the shock is functioning properly. If no resistance is felt, or, if there is a sudden free movement in the stroke, replace the shock absorber with a new one. It is also a good idea to

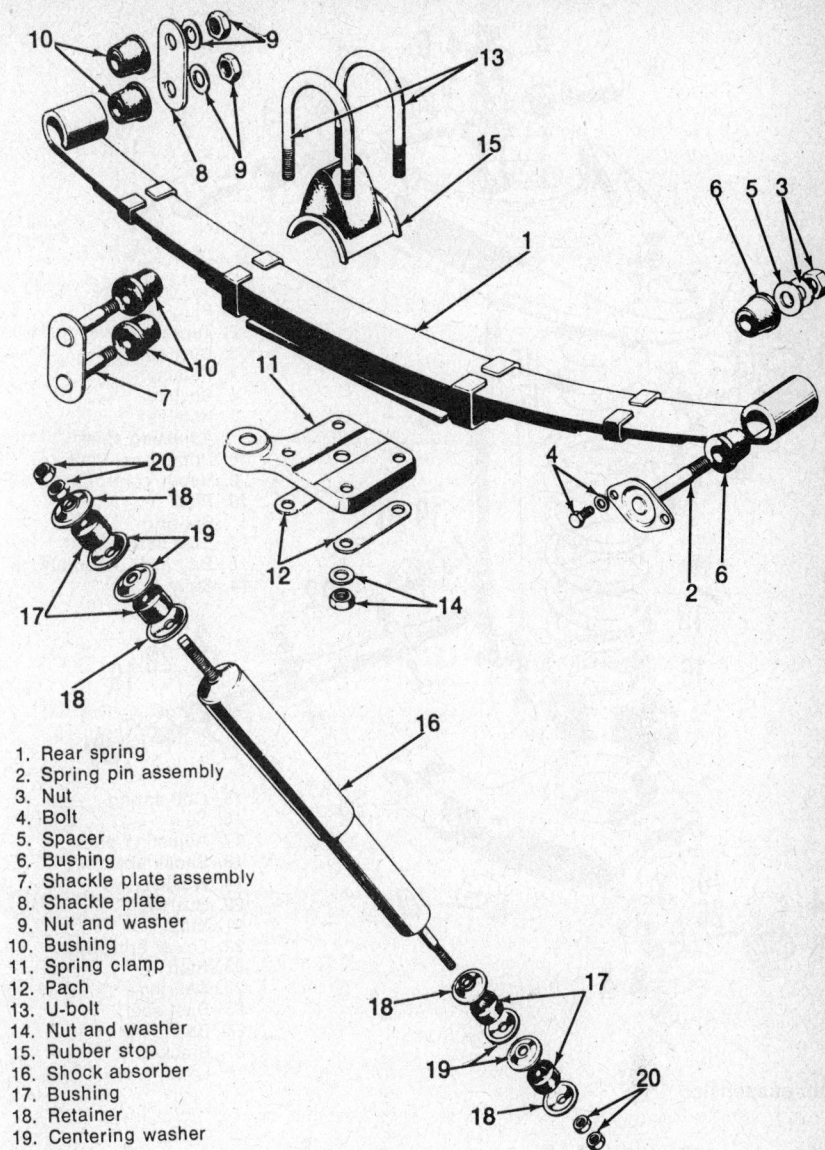

1. Rear spring
2. Spring pin assembly
3. Nut
4. Bolt
5. Spacer
6. Bushing
7. Shackle plate assembly
8. Shackle plate
9. Nut and washer
10. Bushing
11. Spring clamp
12. Pach
13. U-bolt
14. Nut and washer
15. Rubber stop
16. Shock absorber
17. Bushing
18. Retainer
19. Centering washer
20. Nut

Rear suspension

replace a shock absorber if an *excessive* amount of oil is visible on its exterior.

REMOVAL AND INSTALLATION

1. Raise and support the truck.
2. Remove the nuts attaching the upper end of the shock absorber to the cross-member.
3. Remove the rubber bushings and washers.
4. Remove the bolts attaching the lower end of the shock absorber to the lower control arm.
5. Remove the shock from under the lower control arm.
6. Installation is the reverse of removal. Tighten the lower mount to 12–17 ft. lbs. Attach the upper end of the shock

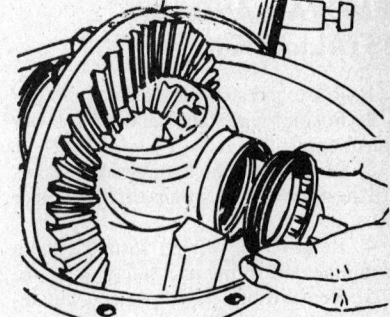

Installing the differential bearing adjuster

to the crossmember and tighten the nuts so that there is 0.256 in. between the top of the shock absorber rod and the top of the upper nut.

7. Lower the truck.

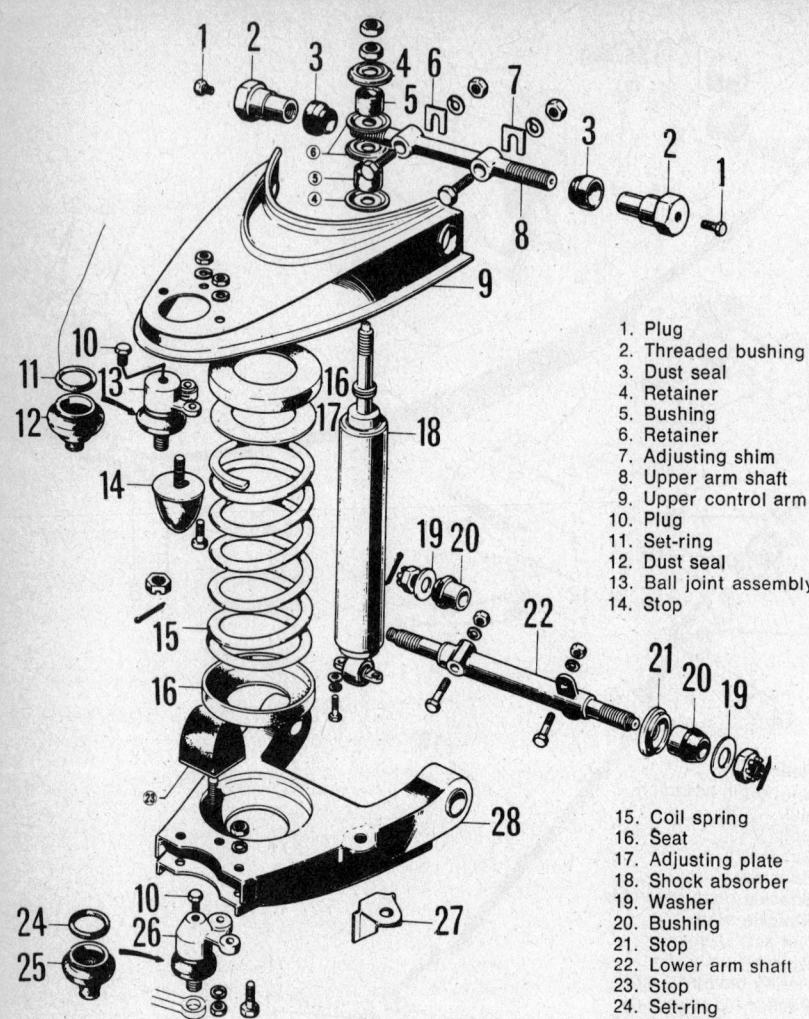

1. Plug
2. Threaded bushing
3. Dust seal
4. Retainer
5. Bushing
6. Retainer
7. Adjusting shim
8. Upper arm shaft
9. Upper control arm
10. Plug
11. Set-ring
12. Dust seal
13. Ball joint assembly
14. Stop

15. Coil spring
16. Seat
17. Adjusting plate
18. Shock absorber
19. Washer
20. Bushing
21. Stop
22. Lower arm shaft
23. Stop
24. Set-ring
25. Dust seal
26. Ball joint
27. Bracket
28. Lower control arm

Front suspension

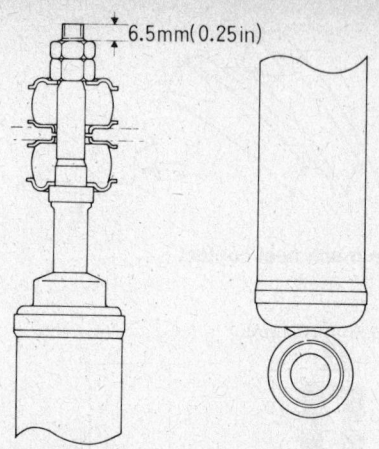

Tightening the front shock absorber nuts

Upper Control Arm

REMOVAL AND INSTALLATION

1. Raise and support the truck.
2. Position jackstands under the lower control arm.
3. Lower the vehicle on the jackstands until the upper control arm is off the bumper stop.
4. Remove the wheel. Install a chain around the coil spring as a safety measure.
5. Remove the cotter pin and nut retaining the upper ball joint.
6. Break the tapered fit loose by striking it with a hammer and separate the ball joint from the spindle.
7. From under the hood, remove the two upper arm retaining bolts and remove the arm from the vehicle. Note the number and position of shims.
8. Remove the three ball joint retaining bolts and remove the ball joint from the upper arm.

To install the upper control arm:
9. Install the ball joint in the upper control arm.
10. Position the upper control arm in the truck and install the alignment shims from where they were removed. Install the retaining nuts and bolts on the shaft and torque them to 62–76 ft. lbs.
11. Position the spindle on the ball joint and install the retaining nut (40–55 ft. lbs.) and a new cotter pin.
12. Remove the safety chain.
13. Install the wheel.
14. Remove the jackstands and lower the truck. Have the front end alignment checked.

Lower Control Arm

REMOVAL AND INSTALLATION

1. Raise the front of the truck and position jackstands under both sides of the frame just behind the lower control arms.
2. Remove the wheel.

3. Remove the lower shock absorber retaining bolts and push the shock up into the spring.
4. Remove the front stabilizer bar retaining bolt, nut and bushings and disconnect the stabilizer bar from the lower control arm.
5. Position a floor jack under the lower control arm and raise the arm to take the spring pressure off. Install a safety chain on the spring.
6. Unbolt the ball joint from the lower control arm.
7. Pull the spindle and ball joint away from the lower arm.
8. If necessary, the lower ball joint can be removed by removing the cotter pin and nut and loosening the ball joint with a hammer.
9. Carefully lower the control arm on the jack, being careful that the spring does not fly out.
10. Remove the three lower control arm retaining bolts and remove the lower control arm.

To install the lower control arm:
11. Position the lower control arm in place and install the three retaining bolts and nuts. Do not tighten. If removed, install the ball joint.
12. Position the spring on the lower control arm and in the upper frame retaining pocket.
13. Use a C-clamp to clamp the spring to the lower control arm.
14. Raise the lower control arm with a floor jack and position the ball joint and spindle in the lower arm.
15. Loosely install the three lower arm-to-ball bolts. Remove the safety chain from the spring, and remove the floor jack and C-clamp.
16. Torque the three ball joint retaining nuts to 60–70 ft. lbs.
17. Pull the shock absorber down and install the bolts and nuts.
18. Install the stabilizer bar on the lower control arm.
19. Install the front wheel. Lower the truck and have the front wheel alignment checked.

Ball Joints

CHECKING

1. Check the ball joint dust seals and replace them if they are defective.

2. Check the end-play of the upper and lower ball joints. If the end-play exceeds 0.039 in., replace the ball joint.

REPLACEMENT

Use the applicable procedures under "Upper Control Arm Removal and Installation", or "Lower Control Arm Removal and Installation".

Front End Alignment

CASTER

Caster is the forward or rearward tilt of the upper ball joint. Rearward tilt is referred to as positive caster, while forward tilt is referred to as negative caster.

Caster is adjusted by changing the shim(s) between the upper arm shaft and the frame, or, by turning the shaft until the correct angle is obtained.

CAMBER

Camber is the outward tilting of the front wheels, at the top, from the vertical.

Camber is adjusted by adding or subtracting the shim(s) between the upper arm shaft and the frame. Shims are available in thicknesses of 0.039 in., 0.063 in., 0.079 in., and 0.126 in.

TOE-IN

Toe-in is the amount, measured in a fraction of an inch, that the wheels are closer together in the front than at the rear.

Toe-in can be increased or decreased by changing the length of the tie-rods. Threaded sleeves on the tie-rods are provided for this purpose. The clamps on the tie rods must be positioned to prevent interference with the center link on the Rotary Pick-Up.

FRONT WHEEL TURNING ANGLE

The turning stop screws are located at the steering knuckle. If necessary, the screws can be adjusted to alter the turning angle.

STEERING

Steering Wheel

REMOVAL AND INSTALLATION

1. Remove the screws which secure the crash pad/horn button assembly to the steering wheel. Remove the assembly. On four-spoke steering wheels, pull the center cap toward the wheel top.

2. Punch matchmarks on the steering wheel and steering shaft.

3. Unfasten the steering wheel hub nut and remove the steering wheel with a puller.

CAUTION

The steering column is collapsible; pounding on it or applying excessive pressure to it may cause it to deform, in which case, the entire column will have to be replaced.

Installation of the steering wheel is performed in the reverse order of removal. Tighten the steering wheel nut to 25 ft. lbs.

COMBINATION (TURN SIGNAL) SWITCH REPLACEMENT

1. Disconnect the ground cable from the battery.

2. Remove the steering wheel, as detailed above.

3. Unfasten the left-hand column shroud securing screws and remove the shroud.

4. Remove the retaining ring from the combination (turn signal) switch.

5. Withdraw the switch over the steering column, after unfastening its multiconnector from underneath the dash panel.

Installation is performed in the reverse order of removal.

Steering Linkage

REMOVAL AND INSTALLATION

Manual or Power Steering

1. Turn the steering wheel so that the front wheels are pointing straight ahead. Then raise the front end of the vehicle and support it with jackstands.

2. Remove the cotter pins and the castellated nuts which secure the ends of the tie-rods to the center link and the steering knuckle.

3. Use a ball joint puller to disconnect the tie rods from the center link and steering knuckle. Remove the tie-rods.

4. Remove the cotter pin and the castellated nut which secure the idler arm to the center link.

5. Use the ball joint puller to detach the idler arm from the center link.

6. Unfasten the nuts at the other end of the idler arm and remove the arm from its bracket.

7. Perform steps 4–5 for the Pitman arm. Remove the center link.

8. Unfasten the nut which secures the Pitman arm to the sector shaft and use a puller to separate them.

Installation is performed in the reverse order of removal. Align the marks on the

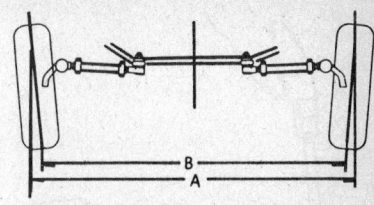

A–B= 0 ～ 6 mm (0 ～ 0.24 in)

Measuring toe-in

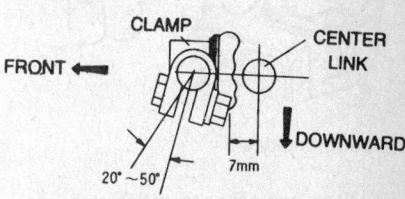

Correct positioning of the tie-rod clamps

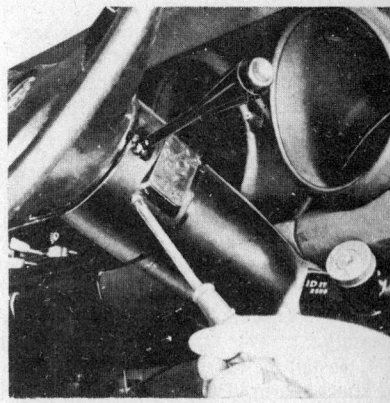

Removing the steering column shroud

pitman arm and the sector shaft to ensure proper steering linkage alignment. Torque the removed nuts and bolts to the specifications given at the end of this section. Check and adjust the toe-in, as outlined above.

IDLER ARM REPLACEMENT

1. Remove the cotter pin and nut from the idler arm. Disconnect the center link from the idler arm with a puller.

2. Unbolt and remove the idler arm from the frame.

3. Remove the cotter pin, nut and washer, and remove the idler arm from the bracket.

4. To install, assemble the arm to the bracket, first lubricating the arm and bushings with lithium grease. Install all parts in the reverse order of removal, using new cotter pins.

REPLACING THE PITMAN ARM

1. Raise and support the front end.
2. Remove the wheels.

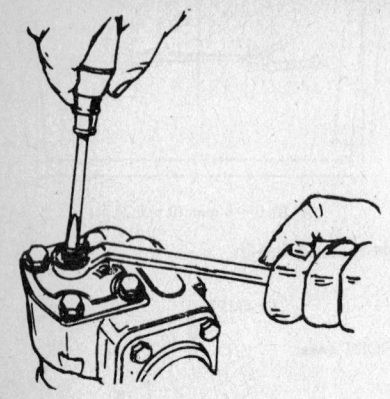

Adjusting backlash

3. Disconnect the center link at the pitman arm.

4. Remove the nut attaching the pitman arm to the sector shaft and remove the arm with a puller.

5. Install the Pitman arm onto the sector shaft, aligning the identification marks. Tighten the nut to 108–130 ft. lbs.

6. Connect the center link to the pitman arm and torque the nut to 22–29 ft. lbs. Install a new cotter pin.

REPLACING THE TIE-ROD

1. Raise and support the front end.
2. Disconnect the tie-rod from the center link and knuckle arm. A puller will be necessary.
3. Install the tie-rod to the center link and knuckle arm. Tighten the nuts to 22–28 ft. lbs. and install new cotter pins.

REPLACING THE CENTER LINK

1. Raise and support the front end.
2. Remove the center link from both tie-rods, pitman arm and idler arm by removing the cotter pins and nuts. A puller will also be necessary.
3. Install the center link and tighten the nuts as follows: center link to pitman arm—22–29 ft. lbs.; center link to idler arm—31–47 ft. lbs. through 1976, 36–58 ft. lbs. for 1977 and later. Install new cotter pins.

Steering Gear

STEERING GEAR ADJUSTMENT

Worm Bearing Preload

1. Remove the gear from the vehicle.
2. Rotate the worm shaft with a torque wrench and check the torque. Rotating torque should be 8–10 in. lbs. for rotary pickup; 5–7 in. lbs. for B–1600, 5–8 in. lbs. for the B–1800 and B–2000. If not adjust as follows on all models:
3. Remove the end cover and shims.

4. If the preload was too light, remove shims; if too heavy, add shims.
5. Install the end cover.

Sector Gear and Ball Nut Backlash

The sector shaft adjusting screw, located in the cover, raises or lowers the sector shaft to provide proper mesh with the sector gear and rack. Adjust as follows:

1. Turn the wormshaft gently and stop it at the center position.
2. Loosen the locknut and turn the adjuster in or out. The standard backlash is zero.
3. Tighten the adjusting screw.

Power Steering Pump

REMOVAL AND INSTALLATION

1. Disconnect the fluid hoses from the pump.
2. Loosen the pump belt adjusting bolt, slide the pump to one side and remove the belt.
3. Support the pump, remove the mounting bolts and lift out the pump.

Installation is the reverse of removal. Adjust belt to give a ½″ deflection at the mid-point of its longest straight stretch. Fill the reservoir and bleed the system.

BRAKE SYSTEMS

Adjustments

FRONT OR REAR DISCS

The front disc brakes are self-adjusting by design. As the brake pads and discs wear, fluid pressure compensates for the amount of wear. Because this action causes the fluid level to go down, the level should be checked and replenished as often as is necessary.

FRONT DRUM BRAKES

B–1600

The brake shoes should be at normal room temperature. Adjust each front brake shoe as follows:

1. Raise and support the truck. The wheels must be free to turn freely.
2. Remove the adjusting slot covers from the brake backing plate.
3. Insert a brake adjusting spoon (a screwdriver will do in a pinch) to grab the starwheel of the wheel cylinder.
4. Rotate the starwheel of one wheel

cylinder toward the inside of the brake drum until the wheel is locked. Then back off the starwheel five notches.

5. Repeat step 4 for each wheel cylinder of each wheel.
6. Install the adjusting slot covers.
7. Check the brake adjustment by spinning the wheel by hand. There should be no drag.
8. Lower the truck.

REAR DRUM BRAKES

1975

1. Block the front wheels, raise the car, and support it with jackstands.
2. Release the parking brake completely. Disconnect the equalizer clevis pin.
3. Remove the adjusting hole plugs from the backing plate.
4. Engage the adjuster with a screwdriver. Turn the adjuster in the direction of the arrow stamped on the backing plate until the brake shoes are fully expanded, i.e., the wheel will not turn.
5. Pump the brake pedal several times to be sure that the brake shoe contracts the drum evenly.

NOTE: If the wheel turns after you remove your foot from the brake pedal, continue turning the adjuster until the wheel will no longer rotate.

6. Back off on the adjuster about five notches. The wheel should rotate freely, without dragging. If it does not, turn the adjuster an additional notch.
7. Pump the brake pedal several times and check wheel rotation again.
8. Fit the plug into the adjusting procedure for the three other rear brake shoes.

BRAKE PEDAL

Rotary Pick-up

1. Detach the wiring from the brake light switch terminals.
2. Loosen the locknut on the switch.
3. Turn the switch until the distance between the pedal and the floor is 7.3 in.
4. Tighten the locknut on switch.
5. Loosen the locknut located on the pushrod.
6. Rotate the pushrod, until a pedal free travel of 0.2–0.6 in. is obtained.
7. Tighten the pushrod locknut.

B–1600, B–1800 and B–2000

There should be 0.02–0.09 in. (0.28–0.35 in. on the B–1800 and B–2000) brake pedal free-travel before the push-rod contacts the piston.

1. Loosen the locknut on the master cylinder pushrod at the clevis, which attaches the pushrod to the pedal.
2. Turn the master cylinder pushrod either in or out to obtain the specified clearance.
3. When the adjustment is complete, tighten the locknut to 8–13 ft. lbs.

Master Cylinder

REMOVAL AND INSTALLATION

1. Detach all of the hydraulic lines from the master cylinder. Detach the fluid level sensor lead if equipped.

NOTE: On models which have a fluid reservoir located separately from the master cylinder, remove the lines which run between the two and plug the lines to prevent leakage.

2. Unfasten the nuts which secure the master cylinder to the power brake unit or firewall.

3. Withdraw the master cylinder assembly straight out and away from the power brake unit or the firewall and pushrod.

—————— CAUTION ——————
Be careful not to spill brake fluid on the painted surfaces of the car, as it makes an excellent paint remover.

Installation of the master cylinder is performed in the reverse order of its removal. Fill up its reservoir and bleed the brake system, as detailed below.

OVERHAUL

1. Clean the outside of the master cylinder and drain any brake fluid remaining in it.

2. Remove the fluid reservoir from the top of the cylinder, if so equipped.

3. Remove the boot from the rear of the cylinder if present; earlier models do not have the boot.

4. Depress the primary piston and withdraw the snap-ring from the rear of the cylinder bore.

5. Withdraw the washers, piston, cups, spacer, seat and return spring from the cylinder bore.

6. Before removing the secondary piston stop bolt and O-ring, and the secondary piston, you must fabricate a guide pin to be inserted into the stop bolt hole. The guide pin will enable the secondary piston to pass over the hole without catching and tearing. The guide pin should be approximately 8.5 mm in length, with a smooth chamfered tip. Depress the secondary piston with a screwdriver. Remove the secondary stop bolt and O-ring and insert the guide pin. Allow the secondary piston to pass over the guide pin and out.

7. Remove the secondary piston assembly from the bore.

NOTE: Blow out the assembly with compressed air, if necessary.

8. Unfasten the hydraulic line fittings from the master cylinder outlet.

9. Withdraw the check valves and springs from the outlets.

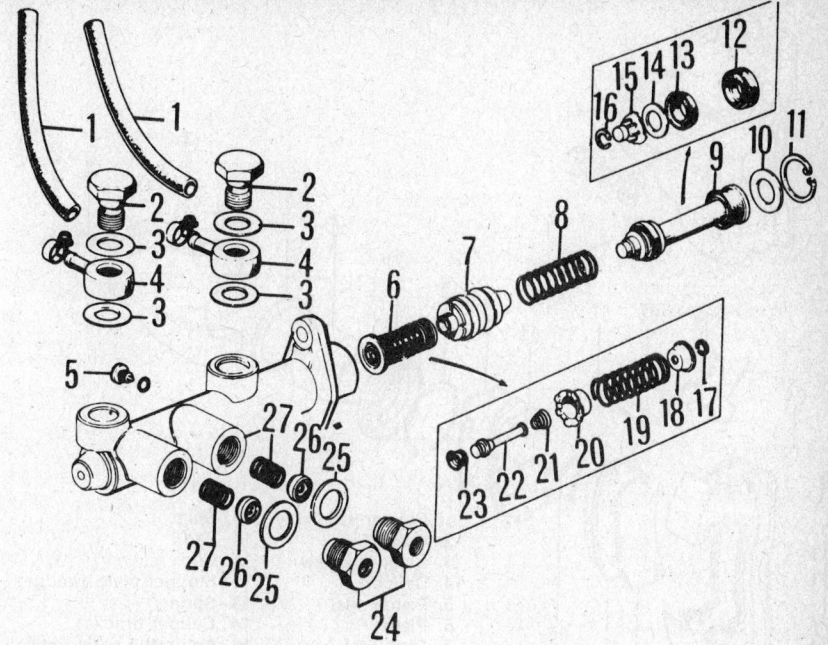

Master cylinder components

1. Hydraulic line	7. Secondary piston
2. Connector bolt	8. Return spring
3. Washer	9. Primary piston
4. Union	10. Washer
5. Stop bolt	11. Retaining ring
6. Valve and spring	12. Secondary cup

13. Primary cup	20. Valve case
14. Spacer	21. Spring
15. Spring seat	22. Valve rod
16. Stop ring	23. Valve
17. Stop ring	24. Outlet fitting
18. Spring seat	25. Washer
19. Return spring	26. Check valve
	27. Spring

10. Wash all of the components in clean brake fluid.

—————— CAUTION ——————
Never use kerosene or gasoline to clean the master cylinder components.

Examine all of the piston cups and replace any that are worn, damaged, or swollen.

Check the cylinder bore for roughness or scoring. Check the clearance between the piston and cylinder bore with a feeler gauge. Replace either the piston or the cylinder if the clearance exceeds 0.006 in.

Blow the dirt and the remaining brake fluid out of the cylinder with compressed air.

Master cylinder assembly is performed in the following order:

1. Dip all of the components, except for the cylinder, in clean brake fluid.

2. Install the check valve assemblies in the master cylinder outlets.

3. Insert the return spring and the valve components into the cylinder bore.

4. Fit the secondary cup and the primary cup over the secondary piston. The flat side of the cups should face the piston.

5. Fit the guide pin into the stop-bolt hole. Place the secondary piston components into the cylinder bore.

6. Depress the secondary piston as far as it will go and withdraw the guide pin. Screw the stop bolt into the hole.

7. Place the primary cups on the primary piston with the flat side of the cups facing the piston.

8. Insert the return spring and the primary piston into the bore.

9. Depress the primary piston, then install the stop-washer and snap-ring.

NOTE: Be sure that the piston cups do not cover up the compensating ports.

10. Install the dust boot on the end of the cylinder.

Brake Failure Warning Valve

CENTRALIZING

1. Turn the ignition switch to the ON position.

2. Make sure that the fluid level in the master cylinder is at the ¾ mark.

3. Depress the brake pedal and the piston will center itself causing the light to go off.

4. Turn the switch to OFF and check the fluid level. Check for a firm pedal.

Bleeding

DISC BRAKES

NOTE: Keep the master cylinder reservoir at least ¾ full during the bleeding operation.

1. Remove the cap from the bleeder screw on that wheel cylinder which is farthest from the master cylinder.

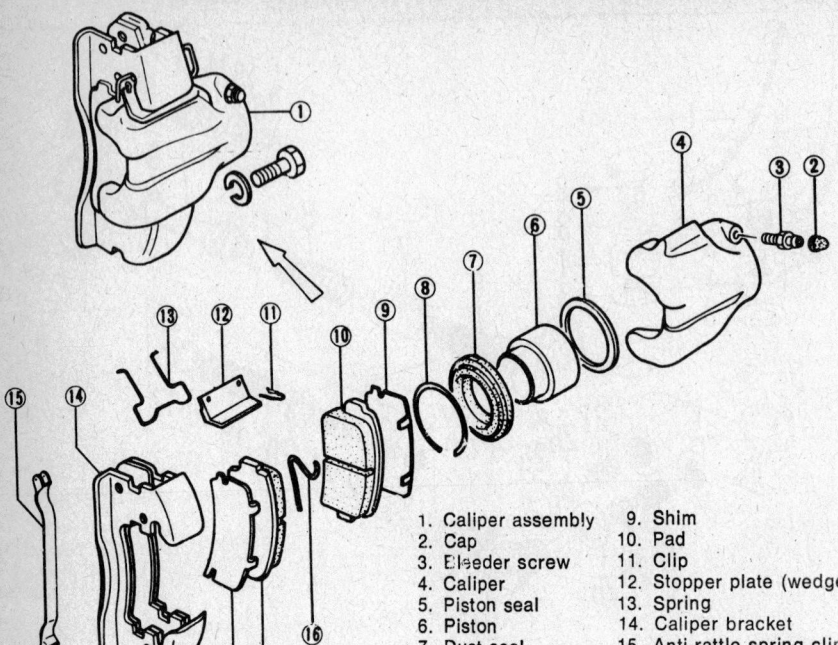

1. Caliper assembly
2. Cap
3. Bleeder screw
4. Caliper
5. Piston seal
6. Piston
7. Dust seal
8. Seal retainer
9. Shim
10. Pad
11. Clip
12. Stopper plate (wedge)
13. Spring
14. Caliper bracket
15. Anti-rattle spring clip
16. Anti-rattle spring

Stopper plate (wedge) disc brake caliper

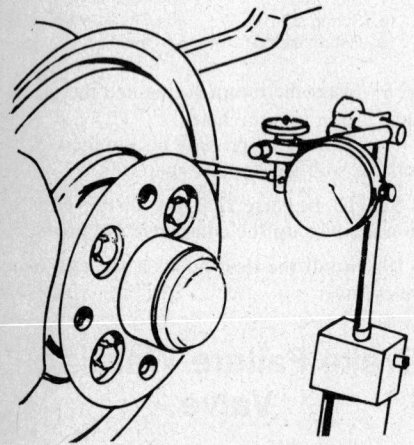

Checking the front brake disc runout

2. Install a vinyl tube over the bleeder screw. Submerge the other end of the tube in a jar half-full of clean brake fluid.

3. Open the bleeder valve. Fully depress the brake pedal and allow it to return slowly.

4. Repeat this operation until air bubbles cease flowing into the jar.

5. Close the valve, remove the tube, and install the cap on the bleeder valve.

DRUM BRAKES (FRONT AND REAR)

1. Repeat steps 1–2 of the disc brake bleeding procedure.

2. Depress the brake pedal rapidly several times.

3. Keep the brake pedal depressed and open the bleeder valve. Close the valve without releasing the pedal.

4. Repeat this operation until bubbles cease to appear in the jar.

5. Remove the tube and install the cap on the bleeder valve.

FRONT DISC BRAKES

Disc Brake Pads

REMOVAL AND INSTALLATION

1. Raise the front of the vehicle and securely support it with jackstands.

2. Remove the hub cap and the wheel.

3. Depending on the type of brake used, either remove the hairpin retainer and withdraw the pad locating pins, or remove the hairpin retainer, the stopper plates (wedges), the caliper assembly and the anti-rattle spring. Support the caliper by a length of wire suspended from the body. Do not allow it to hang by the hydraulic hose.

—————— CAUTION ——————
Do not disconnect the hydraulic line from the caliper when only pad removal is being performed.

4. Remove the return spring and withdraw the pad.

5. Take the rubber cap off of the bleeder screw and fit a vinyl tube over the screw. Submerge the other end of the tube in a jar

half-filled with brake fluid.

6. Open the bleeder screw. Use a screwdriver with its blade wrapped in electrical tape, a C-clamp, or a large pair of locking pliers to depress the piston in the cylinder.

7. Tighten the bleeder screw. Remove the vinyl tube. Fit the rubber cap back on the bleeder screw.

8. Install new pads with shims in the caliper.

9. Install all of the parts which were removed during disassembly.

10. Bleed the brake system, as outlined below.

—————— CAUTION ——————
Replace all of the front brake pads at the same time. Do not use pads of different materials for replacement.

Disc Brake Calipers

REMOVAL AND INSTALLATION

Locating Pin Type Calipers

1. Perform the disc brake pad removal.

2. Detach the hydraulic line from the caliper. Plug the end of the line to prevent the entrance of dirt or the loss of fluid.

3. Unfasten the bolts which secure the caliper to the support and remove the caliper.

Follow the caliper removal procedure in reverse order for installation. Bleed the hydraulic system after completing installation.

Stopper Plate (Wedge) Type Calipers

Perform steps 1–3 of the disc brake pad removal procedure, as outlined. In addition, disconnect and plug the hydraulic line at the caliper.

Caliper installation is performed in the reverse order of removal. Bleed the hydraulic system after completing installation.

OVERHAUL

1. Thoroughly clean the outside of the caliper.

2. Remove the dust boot retainer and the boot.

3. Place a piece of hardwood in front of the piston.

4. Gradually apply compressed air through the hydraulic line fitting and withdraw the piston.

NOTE: If the piston is frozen and cannot be removed from the caliper, tap lightly around it while the air pressure is being applied.

5. Withdraw the piston and seal from the caliper bore.

6. If necessary, remove the bleeder screw.

7. Wash all of the parts in clean brake fluid. Dry them off with compressed air.

———— **CAUTION** ————
Do not wash the parts in kerosene or gasoline.

Examine the caliper bore and piston for scores, scratches, or rust. Replace either part as required. Minor scratches, rust, or scoring can be corrected by dressing with crocus cloth.

NOTE: Discard the old piston seal and dust boot. Replace them with new ones.

Apply clean brake fluid to the piston and bore. Assemble the caliper in the reverse order of disassembly. Install it on the car and bleed the brake system.

Brake Disc

REMOVAL AND INSTALLATION

1. Remove the caliper assembly, as detailed in the appropriate section above.

NOTE: It is unnecessary to completely remove the caliper from the vehicle. Leave the hydraulic line attached and wire the caliper to the underbody of the car so that it is out of the way.

2. Check disc runout, as detailed below, before removing it from the vehicle.

3. Withdraw the grease cap, cotter pin, nut-lock, adjusting nut, and washer from the spindle.

4. Take the thrust washer and outer bearing off the hub.

5. Pull the brake disc/wheel hub assembly off of the spindle.

6. Unbolt and separate the brake disc from the hub after matchmarking them for proper installation.

———— **CAUTION** ————
Do not drive the disc off the hub.

Installation of the disc and hub is performed in the reverse order of removal. Adjust the bearing preload, as detailed below.

INSPECTION

1. With a dial indicator, measure the lateral runout of the disc while the disc is still installed on the spindle.

NOTE: Be sure that the wheel bearings are adjusted properly before checking runout.

2. If runout exceeds more than 0.004 in., replace or resurface the disc.

3. Inspect the surface of the disc for scores or pits and resurface it, if necessary.

4. If the disc is resurfaced, its thickness should be no less than 0.4331 in.

Front Drum Brakes
Brake Drum

REMOVAL AND INSTALLATION

1. Raise and support the truck.

2. Remove the wheel.

3. Remove the brake drum attaching screws and install them in the tapped holes in the brake drum.

4. Turn these screws in evenly to force the brake drum away from the wheel hub.

5. Remove and inspect the brake drum. See "Inspection".

To install the brake drum:

6. Install the brake drum with the attaching screw holes aligned with the holes in the hub.

7. Transfer the attaching screw from the tapped holes in the brake drum to the attaching holes in the hub.

8. Tighten the screws evenly to secure the hub.

9. Install the wheel.

10. Lower the truck and check the brake adjustment.

INSPECTION

1. Brush all dust from the inside of the brake drum.

2. Check the brake drum diameter with a brake gauge. Replace any drums which have a diameter greater than 10.28 in.

3. Inspect the brake drums for cracks. Replace any cracked drums.

4. Look carefully for any scoring of the drums. If the drums are scored, have them reground.

Brake Shoes

INSPECTION

1. Wipe out the accumulated dust and grit.

2. Inspect for excessive lining wear or shoe damage. Replace any cracked shoes.

3. If the lining is worn to within 0.039 in. of the shoe or if the shoes are damaged, they must be replaced.

4. Replace any linings that are contaminated with grease or brake fluid from leaking wheel cylinders. Replace linings in axle sets only.

5. Check the condition of the shoes, retracting springs and hold-down springs for signs of overheating. If the shoes have a slight blue color, this indicates overheating and replacement of the springs as well as the linings is recommended.

6. If signs of overheating are present, the wheel cylinders should be rebuilt as a precaution against future problems.

REMOVAL AND INSTALLATION

1. Raise and support the truck.

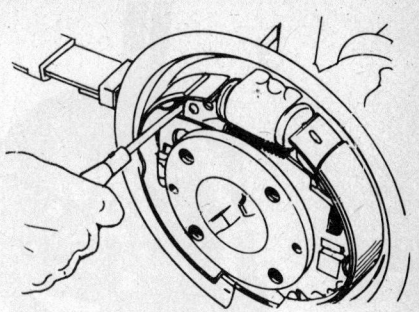
Shoe return spring removal

2. Remove the wheel.

3. Remove the brake drum.

4. Remove the brake shoe retracting springs.

5. Remove the shoe retaining spring guide pin and the retaining spring, by holding the guide pin to the backing plate and compressing and turning the spring 90°. Use a brake spring tool to do this.

6. Remove the brake shoes, noting their positions.

To install new brake shoes:

7. Lubricate the threads of the adjusting screw with brake paste and one or two spots on the adjuster wheel inside threads. Lubricate the backing plate shoe pads.

8. Position each brake shoe on the brake backing plate so that the slot in the shoe web is toward the starwheel in the wheel cylinder.

9. Install the shoe retaining spring guide pin. Install the retaining spring over the guide pin, holding the guide pin in place and depress the retaining spring. Turn it 90° to lock the spring in place.

10. Install the brake shoe retracting spring. Be careful not to bend the springs or stretch the hooks.

11. Install the brake drum.

12. Install the wheel.

13. Adjust the brakes.

14. Bleed the brakes.

15. Lower the truck and check for proper operation.

Wheel Cylinder

REMOVAL AND INSTALLATION

1. Raise and support the truck.

2. Remove the wheel.

3. Remove the brake drum and brake shoes.

4. Disconnect and plug the brake line at the wheel cylinder.

5. Remove the stud nuts and bolt attaching the wheel cylinder to the backing plate and remove the wheel cylinder.

To install the wheel cylinder:

6. Install the wheel cylinder on the backing plate.

7. Clean the end of the brake line and

Checking front wheel bearing preload

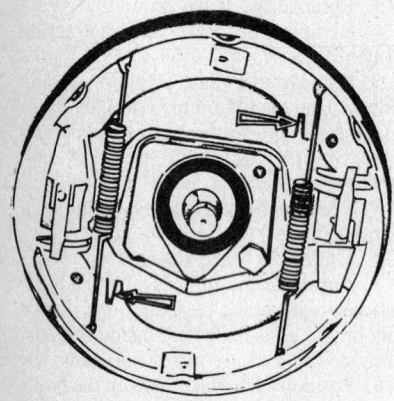

Front brake shoe installation—B1600

attach it to the wheel cylinder. Tighten the tube fitting nut.

8. Install the links in the end of the wheel cylinder.

9. Install the shoes and adjuster assemblies.

10. Install the brake drum and wheel.

11. Adjust the brakes.

12. Bleed the brakes.

13. Lower the truck.

OVERHAUL

1. Remove the wheel cylinder.

2. Remove the piston and adjusting screw with the boot attached to the cylinder. Separate the adjuster and boot from the adjuster.

3. Using compressed air (if possible), remove the piston cup, cup expander and spring. Lay the cylinder face down and apply air pressure to the brake line port.

4. Wash all parts in isopropyl alcohol, except the rubber boot.

5. Examine the cylinder bore, piston and adjuster for wear, roughness or damage. Check the clearance between the piston and cylinder bore. If the clearance is greater than 0.006 in., replace with new parts. Discard the piston cups.

To assemble the wheel cylinder:

6. Lubricate the cylinder bore, adjuster and new piston cup with clean brake fluid.

7. Position the piston return spring in the piston cup expander. Install the return

spring, piston cup expander and piston cup in the cylinder. The flat side of the piston cup goes toward the piston.

8. Install the piston boot to the piston adjuster (smaller lip of the boot in the groove of the piston adjuster.)

9. Insert the piston adjuster into the cylinder and install the larger lip of the boot in the groove on the cylinder body.

10. Install the adjusting screw in the piston adjuster.

11. Install the wheel cylinder.

Front Wheel Bearings

ADJUSTMENT

The front wheel bearings should be adjusted if the wheel is loose on the spindle or if the wheel does not rotate freely.

1. Raise and support the vehicle.

2. Remove the wheel and tire.

3. Attach a spring scale onto a hub bolt.

4. Pull the spring scale squarely and read the pull as the hub begins to turn. It should be 1.3–2.4 lbs. for all pick-ups.

5. If the reading is not correct, remove the grease cap and cotter pin. Adjust the bearings with the large nut on the end of the spindle until the proper reading is obtained.

6. Align the holes of the adjusting nut and spindle and install a new cotter pin.

7. Install the grease cap, wheel and tire.

8. Lower the vehicle.

Alternate Procedure

If a spring scale is not available, the following procedure can be used.

1. Raise and support the vehicle.

2. Remove the wheel and tire and the grease cap.

3. Remove the cotter pin.

4. Rotate the hub and tighten the adjusting nut until the hub binds.

5. Back the adjusting nut off ⅙ turn. Be sure that the hub rotates freely with no side-play.

6. Align the holes of the nut and spindle and install a new cotter pin.

7. Install the grease cap, wheel and tire.

8. Lower the vehicle.

REMOVAL, INSTALLATION AND PACKING

1. Raise and support the vehicle.

2. Remove the wheel cover.

3. Remove the wheel and tire.

4. Remove the grease cap from the hub. Remove the cotter pin, nut lock, adjusting nut and flat washer from the spindle.

5. Remove the hub and drum from the wheel spindle.

6. Remove and discard the old grease retainer. Remove the inner bearing cone and roller from the hub.

7. Clean the grease from the inner and outer bearing cups with solvent and inspect the cups for scratches, pits, or wear.

8. If the cups are worn or damaged, remove them with a drift.

9. Thoroughly clean the inner and outer bearing cones and rollers. *Do not spin the bearings to dry them.* Allow them to air dry.

10. Inspect the cones and rollers for wear and replace as necessary. The cone and roller assembles should be replaced as a set. Do not use new bearings or cups with old bearings or cups.

11. Clean the spindle and the inside of the hub with solvent to remove all of the old grease.

12. Cover the spindle with a cloth and clean the dirt from the dust shield. Remove the cloth carefully. Do not get dirt on the spindle.

13. If the inner or outer bearing cups were removed, install the new replacement cups in the hub. Be sure that they are seated squarely and properly.

14. Pack the inside of the hub with wheel bearing grease. Add grease to the hub until grease is flush with the inside diameter of both bearing cups.

NOTE: It is important that all the old grease is removed, because the more popular lithium base grease is not compatible with the sodium base grease that was originally installed (on earlier models).

15. Pack the bearing cone and roller with wheel bearing grease. Work as much grease as possible between the cone and roller. Lubricate the outside cone surfaced with grease.

16. Install the inner bearing cone and roller in the inner cup. Apply a light film of grease to the grease seal and install the seal. Be sure that the seal is properly seated.

17. Install the hub and drum on the spindle. Keep the hub centered on the spindle to prevent damaging the grease seal.

18. Install the outer bearing cone and roller and the flat washer on the spindle. Install the adjusting nut.

19. Install the wheel and tire.

20. Adjust the wheel bearings.

21. Install the hub cap.

Rear Drum Brakes
Brake Drums

REMOVAL AND INSTALLATION

1. Remove the wheel cover and loosen the lug nuts.
2. Raise the rear of the vehicle and securely support it with jackstands.
3. Remove the lug nuts and the rear wheel.
4. Be sure that the parking brake is fully released.
5. Remove the bolts which secure the drum to the rear axle shaft flange.
6. Pull the brake drum off the flange.

NOTE: If the drum will not come off easily, screw the drum securing bolts into the two tapped holes in the drum. Tighten the bolts evenly in order to force the drum away from the flange.

Rear brake drum installation is performed in the reverse order of removal. Adjust the shoes after installation is completed.

INSPECTION

1. Examine the drum for cracks or overheating spots. Replace the drum if either of these are present.
2. Check the drum for scoring. Light scoring can be corrected with sandpaper.
3. Check the drum with a dial indicator for out-of-roundness; turn the drum if it exceeds 0.0059 in.
4. If the drum must be turned because of excessive scoring or out-of-roundness, the drum's inside diameter should not exceed 10.2758 inches.

NOTE: If one drum is turned, the opposite drum should also be turned to the same size.

Brake Shoes

REMOVAL AND INSTALLATION

1. Perform the brake drum removal procedure, as detailed above.
2. Remove the return springs from the upper side of the shoe with a brake spring removal tool.
3. Remove the return springs from the lower side of the shoes in the same manner, as in step 2.
4. Remove the shoe retaining spring by compressing the retaining spring while turning the pin 90°.
5. Withdraw the primary shoes and the parking brake link.
6. Disengage the parking brake lever from the secondary shoes by unfastening its retaining clip.

7. Remove the secondary shoe.

---------- CAUTION ----------
Be careful not to get oil or grease on the lining material.

Inspect the linings; replace them if they are badly burned or if worn 0.039 in. beyond the specification for a new lining. (See "Brake Specification" chart).
Replace the linings if they are saturated with oil or grease.
Brake shoe installation is performed in the following manner:
1. Lubricate the threads of the adjusting screw, the sliding surfaces of the shoes, and the backing plate flanges with a small quantity of grease.

---------- CAUTION ----------
Be careful not to get grease on the lining surfaces.
----

2. Install the eye of the parking brake cable through the parking brake lever which has previously been installed on the secondary shoe and secured with its retaining clip.
3. Fit the link between the shoes.
4. Engage the shoes with the slots in the anchor (adjusting screw) and the wheel cylinder.
5. Fasten the shoes to the backing plate with the retaining springs and pins.
6. Install the shoe return springs with the tool used during removal.
7. Install the drums and adjust the shoes, as detailed elsewhere.

NOTE: If a slight amount of grease has gotten on the shoes during installation, it may be removed by light sanding.

Wheel Cylinders

REMOVAL AND INSTALLATION

1. Remove the brake drums and shoes.
2. Disconnect the hydraulic line from the wheel cylinder by unfastening the nut on the rear of the backing plate.
3. Plug the line to prevent dirt from entering the system or brake fluid from leaking out.
4. Unfasten the nuts which secure the wheel cylinder to the backing plate and remove the cylinder.

Installation of the wheel cylinder is performed in the reverse order of removal. Bleed the hydraulic system and adjust the brake shoes after installation is completed.

OVERHAUL

1. Remove the wheel cylinder from the backing plate.
2. Remove the piston and adjusting screw with the boot attached to the adjuster.
3. Separate the adjuster screw and boot from the adjuster.

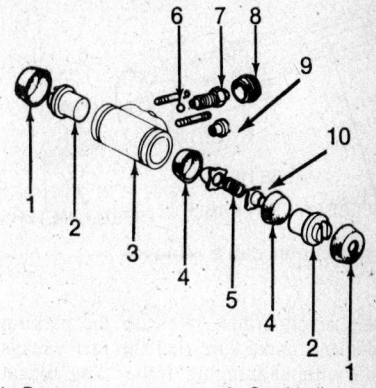

1. Boot
2. Piston
3. Cylinder body
4. Piston cup
5. Return spring
6. Steel ball
7. Bleeder screw
8. Bleeder screw cap
9. Hydraulic line seat
10. Push rod

Rear wheel cylinder components

4. Remove the other piston and boot and separate the boot from the piston.
5. Press in on either piston cup and force the piston cups, cup expanders, and return spring from the cylinder.
6. Wash all parts (except the boots) in clean isopropyl alcohol. Examine the cylinder bore for roughness or scoring.
7. Check the piston-to-cylinder bore clearance. If it exceeds 0.006 in., replace with new parts.
To assemble the wheel cylinder:
8. Lubricate the cylinder bore, adjuster and new piston cups with clean brake fluid, before assembly. Always use new piston cups.
9. Install the piston return spring in a piston cup expander. Place the other piston cup expander and new piston cup on the return spring. Install the return spring, piston cup expanders and piston cups into the cylinder.
10. Install the piston boot to the piston adjuster with the smaller lip of the boot on the groove of the piston adjuster.
11. Insert the piston adjuster into the cylinder assembly and install the larger lip of the boot in the groove of the cylinder.
12. Install the adjusting screw in the piston adjuster.
13. Install the wheel cylinder as detailed above.

PARKING BRAKE

Adjustment

1. Adjust the service brakes before attempting to adjust the parking brake.
2. Use the adjusting nut to adjust the length of the front cable so that the rear brakes are locked when the parking brake lever is pulled out 5–10 notches.
3. After adjustment, apply the parking

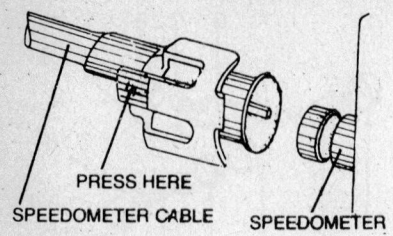

PRESS HERE
SPEEDOMETER CABLE   SPEEDOMETER

Speedometer cable removal

brake several times. Release the parking brake and make sure that the rear wheels rotate without dragging. If they drag, repeat the adjustment.

CHASSIS ELECTRICAL

Wiper Motor

REPLACEMENT

1. Remove the wiper arm attaching screws and remove the wiper arms.

2. Remove the cowl plate screws, move the cowl plate up at the front and disconnect the washer hose. Remove the cowl plate.

3. Disconnect the wires from the wiper motor.

4. Unbolt and remove the motor.

5. Installation is the reverse of removal.

Instrument Cluster

REMOVAL AND INSTALLATION

Rotary Pick-Up

1. Remove the two bolts which secure the steering column bracket to the instrument panel.

2. Unfasten the four instrument cluster securing screws.

3. To disconnect the speedometer cable, reach up under the dash and depress the flat plastic connector tab while pulling the cable away from the head.

4. Unfasten the wiring harness from the instrument cluster.

5. Lift the cluster out.

Installation is performed in the reverse order of removal.

B–1600, B–1800 and B–2000

1. Disconnect the cable from the negative (−) battery terminal.

2. Remove the four instrument cluster securing screws.

3. Move the cluster rearward, so that you can gain access to the back of it.

4. To disconnect the speedometer cable, reach up under the dash and depress the flat plastic connector tab while pulling the cable away from the head.

5. Disconnect the cluster wiring harness from the printed circuit. Note the position of the ammeter leads and disconnect them as well.

6. Remove the screw which secures the ground lead to the cluster. On models with air injection, unfasten the two speedometer sensor lead connectors.

7. Remove the cluster.

Installation is the reverse of removal.

Fuses

FUSE BOX LOCATION

Rotary Pick-Up

The main fuse block is mounted behind the seat at the right side of the cab. Another fuse box is attached to the firewall at the left, rear corner of the engine compartment. Fuse amperage and location are printed on the inside of the fuse box cover.

B–1600 and B–1800

The main fuse is located behind the battery. The fuse box is located at the left, rear corner of the engine compartment. Fuse amperage and location are printed on the inside of the cover.

B–2000

The fuse box is located in the engine compartment at the rear left corner.

FUSIBLE LINKS

On all models except the B–2000, these are located in either one or two boxes next to the battery in the engine compartment. On the B–2000, the fusible link is located on the right fender apron. If these links blow, they must be replaced with the specified parts by disconnecting the battery, disconnecting wiring to each link requiring replacement, removing the attaching screws and the link, and installing the new links or links in the reverse of the removal procedure.

Toyota

INDEX

BEFORE SERVICING, SEE THE SAFETY NOTICE AT THE FRONT OF THE BOOK

TOYOTA

VEHICLE AND ENGINE IDENTIFICATION

Model ①	Series Identification Number	Engine Series Identification	Displacement Cu in. (cc)	Number of Cylinders	Type	Carburetor	Year
P/U—Std. Bed P/U—Long Bed	RN23 RN28	20R	133.6 (2189)	4	OHC	2 bbl	'75–'77
P/U—Std. Bed P/U—Long Bed	RN30 RN40	20R	133.6 (2189)	4	OHC	2 bbl	'78
P/U—Std. Bed P/U—Long Bed	RN36 RN46	20R	133.6 (2189)	4	OHC	2 bbl	'79
P/U—Std. Bed P/U—Long Bed	RN37 RN47	20R	133.6 (2189)	4	OHC	2 bbl	'79
P/U—Std. 2WD P/U—Long 2WD	RN32L RN42L	20R	133.6 (2189)	4	OHC	2 bbl	'80
P/U—Std. 4WD P/U—Long 4WD	RN37L RN47L	20R	133.6 (2189)	4	OHC	2 bbl	'80
P/U—Std. 2WD P/U—Long 2WD	RN34L RN44L	22R	144.4 (2367)	4	OHC	2 bbl	'81
P/U—Std. 4WD P/U—Long 4WD	RN38L RN48L	22R	144.4 (2367)	4	OHC	2 bbl	'81
P/U—Long 2WD	RN44L	"L" type (dies.)	133.5 (2188)	4	OHC	②	'81
P/U—Std. 2WD P/U—Long 2WD	RN34L RN44L	22R	144.4 (2367)	4	OHC	2 bbl	'82
P/U—Std. 4WD P/U—Long 4WD	RN38L RN48L	22R	144.4 (2367)	4	OHC	2 bbl	'82
P/U—Long 2WD	RN44L	"L" type (dies.)	133.5 (2188)	4	OHC	②	'82
L/C—2 door L/C—Wagon	FJ-40 FJ-55	2F	257.9 (4200)	6	OHV	2 bbl	'75–'80
L/C—2 door L/C—Wagon	FJ-40 FJ-60	2F	257.9 (4200)	6	OHV	2 bbl	'81–'82

① P/U—Pick-up Truck
② Fuel Injected
L/C—Land Cruiser

GENERAL ENGINE SPECIFICATIONS

Year	Engine Type	Engine Displacement Cu. In. (cc)	Carburetor Type	Horsepower (@ rpm) ②	Torque @ rpm (ft lbs) ②	Bore × Stroke (in.)	Compression Ratio	Oil Pressure @ rpm (psi)
'75–'78	20R	133.6 (2189)	2-bbl	95 @ 4800	122 @ 2400	3.48 × 3.50	8.4:1	64.0 @ 2500
'75–'82	2F	257.9 (4200)	2-bbl	125 @ 3600	200 @ 1800	3.70 × 4.00	7.8:1	
'79–'80	20R	133.6 (2189)	2-bbl	90 @ 4800	122 @ 2400	3.48 × 3.50	8.4:1	64.0 @ 2500
'81–'82	22R	156.4 (2563)	2-bbl	96 @ 4800	129 @ 2800	3.62 × 3.50	9.0:1	64.0 @ 2500
'81–'82 (dies.)	"L"	133.5 (2188)	①	62 @ 4200	93 @ 2400	3.54 × 3.38	21.5:1	11.4 @ 700

① Fuel Injected
② Figures are SAE net ratings.

TUNE-UP SPECIFICATIONS

Year	Engine Type	Spark Plugs Type	Spark Plugs Gap (in.)	Distributor Point Dwell (deg)	Distributor Point Gap (in.)	Ignition Timing (deg)▲ MT	Ignition Timing (deg)▲ AT	Fuel Pump Pressure (psi)	Manifold Vacuum at Idle* in. Hg	Compression Pressure (psi) @ 250 rpm**	Idle Speed (rpm) MT	Idle Speed (rpm) AT	Valve Clearance (in.) In	Valve Clearance (in.) Ex
'75–'77	2F	W14 EX	0.037	41	0.018	7B	—	3.4–4.7	16.5	149	650	—	0.008	0.014
'75–'78	20R	W16 EP	0.031	52	0.018③	8B②	8B②	2.1–4.3	16.5	156	850①	850	0.008	0.012
'78–'82	2F	⑤	⑥	Electronic		7B	—	3.4–4.7	16.5	149	⑦	—	0.008	0.014
'79–'80	20R	W16 EX-U	0.031	52	0.018	8B	8B	2.1–4.3	15.75	156	850	850	0.008	0.012④
'81–'82	22R	W16 EXR-U	0.031	Electronic		8B	8B	2.1–4.3	15.8	156	700	750	0.008	0.012

NOTE: If these figures do not correspond to information given on the engine compartment decal, use the figures on the decal. They are current for the engine in your truck.

▲ With automatic transmission in D (drive) and manual transmission in Neutral

*These are the minimum readings you must obtain

**Look for uniformity among cylinders rather than specific pressure

① 800—'77–'78 only

② 13B with High Altitude Compensation— see text

③ Distributor air gap 0.008–0.016 in.—'78– '80

④ 1979 20R exhaust valve 0.010 in.

⑤ '78–'79—W14EX '80—W14EX-U '81– '82—W14EXR-U

⑥ '78–'79—0.039 '80–'82—0.031

⑦ '78–'80—800 '81–'82—650

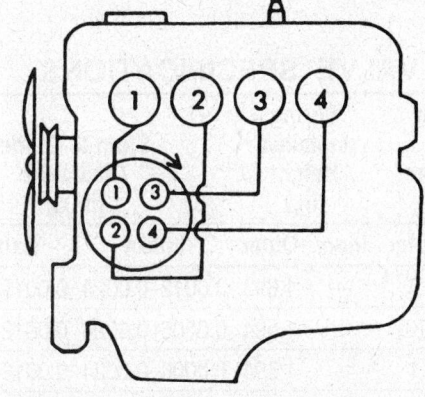

Firing order—20R and 22R engines

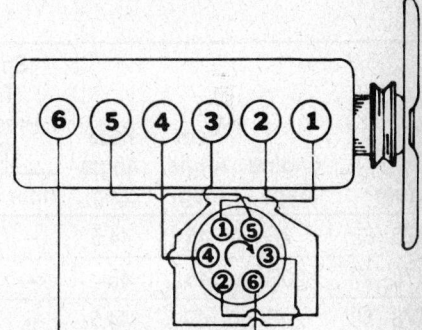

Firing order—2F engines

DIESEL ENGINE TUNE-UP SPECIFICATIONS

Injector Opening Pressure (psi)	Idle Speed (rpm)	Valve Clearance (in.) Intake	Valve Clearance (in.) Exhaust	Cranking Compression Pressure @ 250 rpm	Maximum Compression Variance③	Firing Order
1636–1778① 1493–1777②	700	.010	.014	427 psi maximum 284 psi minimum	71 psi	1-3-4-2

① New

② Used

③ Between highest and lowest cylinder readings

CAPACITIES

Year	Model	Engine Type	Crankcase▲ w/filter	Crankcase▲ wo/filter	Transmission▲ Manual	Transmission▲ Automatic	Trans. Case▲	Differential▲ Front	Differential▲ Rear	Fuel Tank■	Cooling System▲
'75–'79	Pickup 2WD	20R	5.0	4.0	2.0①	7.0④	—	—	1.6	12.1②	8.5③
'79½	Pickup 4WD	20R	5.0	4.0	2.0	6.7	1.7	2.0	2.1	—	7.4
'80	Pickup (all)	20R	5.0	4.0	2.0⑥	6.7④	1.7	2.4	2.3	—	8.9

TOYOTA

CAPACITIES

Year	Model	Engine Type	Crankcase▲		Transmission▲		Trans. Case▲	Differential▲		Fuel Tank■	Cooling System▲
			w/filter	wo/filter	Manual	Automatic		Front	Rear		
'81–'82	Pickup (all)	22R	5.0	4.0	2.1	6.7	1.7	2.4	1.8⑦	13.7⑤	8.9
'81–'82	Pickup (Diesel)	L	6.1	5.1	1.9	—	—	—	1.8	16.0	11.1
'75–'82	Land Cruiser	2F	8.4	7.4	⑧	—	3.6	5.2	5.2	22.2⑨	17.5⑩

▲Measurements in quarts
■ Measurements in gallons
① 5 speed trans.—2.8
② Long bed '76–'78—16.1
③ '78 only—7.4
④ '78 only—6.7
⑤ Long bed—16.1

⑥ 5 speed trans.—2.7
⑦ ¾ Ton—1.9; 4 × 4—2.3
⑧ 3 speed trans.—1.8; 4 speed trans.—3.3
⑨ Station Wagon—21.7
⑩ '78–'82 2-Door—19.9
　 '78–'82 Wagon—18.3

VALVE SPECIFICATIONS

Year	Engine Type	Seat Angle (deg)	Face Angle (deg)	Spring Test Pressure (lbs)		Spring Installed Height (in.)		Stem-to-Guide Clearance (in.)▲		Stem Diameter (in.)	
				Inner	Outer	Inner	Outer	Intake	Exhaust	Intake	Exhaust
'75–'82	2F	45	44.5	—	71.6	—	1.693	0.0012–0.0024	0.0016–0.0028	0.3140	0.3137
'75–'77	20R	45	45	—	60①	—	1.594	0.0006–0.0024	0.0012–0.0026	0.3138–0.3144	0.3136–0.3142
'78–'80	20R	45	44.5	—	55.1	—	1.594	0.0008–0.0024	0.0012–0.0026	0.3138–0.3144	0.3136–0.3142
'81–'82	22R	45	44.5	—	55.1	—	1.594	0.0008–0.0024	0.0012–0.0026	0.3145–0.3188	0.3136–0.3142
'81–'82 (dies.)	L	45③	44.5	—	56②	—	1.547	0.0008–0.0022	0.0016–0.0030	0.3336–0.3342	0.3328–0.3335

▲Valve guides are removable
① Minimum pressure for used spring—54 lbs.
② Minimum pressure for used spring—44 lbs.

③ Blend the seat with 30° and 60° cutters to center the 45° portion on the valve face.

CAMSHAFT SPECIFICATIONS

(All measurements in inches)

Engine	Journal Diameter	Bearing Clearance	Maximum Journal Runout	Lobe Height▲		Maximum Thrust Clearance (End-Play)
				Intake	Exhaust	
20R & 22R	1.2982–1.2984	0.0004–0.0020	0.0080	1.6783–1.6819	1.6806–1.6842	0.0010①
2F	②	0.0010–0.0030	0.0059	1.4960–1.5142	1.4920–1.5098	0.0080③
L (Diesel)	1.3767–1.3774	0.0009–0.0029	0.0020	1.6810–1.6948	1.6900–1.7020	0.0120④

▲Measured from the bottom of the base circle to the top of the lobe (with the cam lobe pointing upward)
① Preferred—0.003–0.007
② Front—1.8880–1.8888

Second—1.8289–1.8297
Third—1.7699–1.7707
Rear—1.7108–1.7116
③ Preferred—0.0035–0.0060
④ Preferred—0.0022–0.0061

CRANKSHAFT AND CONNECTING ROD SPECIFICATIONS

(All measurements in inches)

Year	Engine Type	Engine Displacement Cu. In. (cc)	Crankshaft				Connecting Rod		
			Main Brg Journal Dia	Main Brg Oil Clearance	Shaft End-Play	Thrust on No.	Journal Diameter	Oil Clearance	Side Clearance
'75–'82	2F	257.9 (4200)	①	0.0008–0.0017	0.0024–0.0063	3	2.1252–2.1260	0.0008–0.0024	0.0043–0.0091
'75–'80	20R	133.6 (2189)	2.3614–2.3622	0.0010–0.0022	0.0007–0.0079	3	2.0862–2.0866	0.0010–0.0022	0.0063–0.0102
'81–'82	22R	156.4 (2563)	2.3614–2.3622	0.0006–0.0020	0.0008–0.0089	3	2.0862–2.0866	0.0008–0.0020	0.0008–0.0087
'81–'82 (dies.)	L	133.5 (2188)	2.4402–2.4409	0.0012–0.0028	0.0016–0.0098	3	2.0858–2.0866	0.0012–0.0028	0.0031–0.0079

①No. 1—2.6367–2.6376; No. 2—2.6957–2.6967; No. 3—2.7548–2.7557; No. 4—2.8139–2.8148

TORQUE SPECIFICATIONS

(All readings in ft. lbs.)

Year	Engine Type	Engine Displacement Cu In. (cc)	Cylinder Head Bolts	Rod Bearing Bolts	Main Bearing Bolts	Crankshaft Pulley Bolt	Flywheel-to-Crankshaft Bolts	Manifolds	
								Intake	Exhaust
'75–'82	2F	257.9 (4200)	83–98	35–55	90–108①	116–145	59–62	28–37②	28–37②
'75–'79	20R	133.6 (2189)	52.1–63.7	39.1–47.7	68.7–83.2	79.6–94.0	61.5–68.7	10.6	28.9–36.2
'80	20R	133.6 (2189)	53–63	40–47	69–83	120–130	73–86	13–19	29–36 ②
'81–'82	22R	156.4 (2563)	53–63	40–47	69–83	120–130	73–86	13–19	29–36
'81–'82 (dies.)	L	133.5 (2188)	84–90	37–43	71–81	69–75	84–90	8–11	.11–15

①Rear bearing—76–94 ft. lbs.
②California vehicles—37–51 ft. lbs.

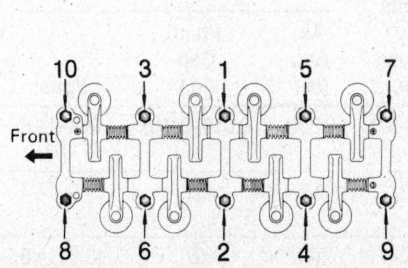

Cylinder head bolt tightening sequence—20R and 22R engines

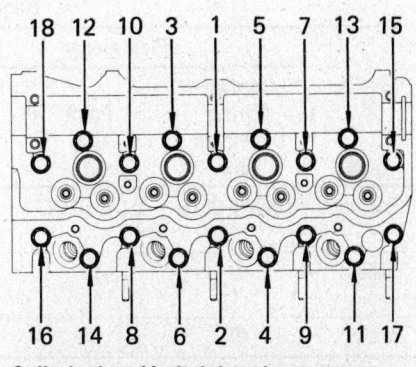

Cylinder head bolt tightening sequence—diesel engine

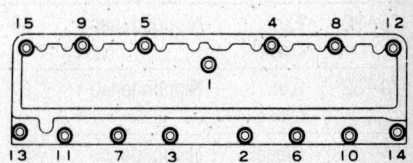

Cylinder head bolt tightening sequence—2F engines

PISTON AND RING SPECIFICATIONS

(All measurements in inches)

| Year | Engine Type | Piston Clearance 68°F | Ring Gap | | | Ring Side Clearance (Ring to Land) | | |
			Top Compression	Bottom Compression	Oil Control	Top Compression	Bottom Compression	Oil Control
'75–'82	2F	0.0012–0.0020	0.0080–0.0160	0.0080–0.0160	—	0.0012–0.0024	0.0008–0.0024	—
'75–'80	20R	0.0012–0.0020	0.0040–0.0120	0.0040–0.0120	0.0040–0.0120	0.0012–0.0028①	0.0012–0.0028①	—
'81–'82	22R	0.0020–0.0028	0.0094–0.0142	0.0071–0.0154	—	0.0080	0.0080	—
'81–'82 (dies.)	L	0.0014–0.0022	0.0780–0.0157	0.0118–0.0197	0.0118–0.0197	0.0024–0.0039	0.0016–0.0031	0.0012–0.0028

① Limit—0.008

WHEEL ALIGNMENT SPECIFICATIONS

| Year | Model | Caster | | Camber | | Toe-in (in.) | Steering Axis Inclination (deg) |
		Range (deg)	Preferred Setting (deg)	Range (deg)	Preferred Setting (deg)		
'75–'78	Pickup	0–1P	½P	½P–1½P	1P	0.24	7¼
'79–'81	Pickup (2WD)	½P–½N	½P	¹/₁₂–½P	1P	0.20(±)0.04① 0.08(±)0.04②	7
'79–'81	Pickup (4WD)	—	③	—	1P	0.16(±)0.04① 0.04(±)0.04②	9½
'75–'78	Land Cruiser	½P–1½P	1P	½P–1½P	1P	0.12–0.20	9½
'79–'82	Land Cruiser	½P–1½P	1P	½P–1½P	1P	0.10–0.20① 0(±)0.04②	9½

N—Negative P—Positive
① Bias Ply Tire
② Radial Ply Tire
③ Vehicle Loaded—3½°P Vehicle Unloaded—4½°P

ALTERNATOR AND REGULATOR SPECIFICATIONS

| Year | Engine | Alternator | | | Regulator | | | | | |
| | | | | | Field Relay | | | Regulator | | |
		Manufacturer	Output (amps)	Type	Contact Spring Deflection (in.)	Point Gap (in.)	Volts to Close (in.)	Air Gap (in.)	Point Gap (in.)	Volts
'75–'82	Exc. Diesel	Nippondenso	40	External	0.008–0.0018	0.016–0.047	4.5–5.8	0.008	0.010–0.018	13.8–14.8
'79–'82	Exc. Diesel	Nippondenso	①	Built-in	②	②	②	②	②	14.0–14.7
'81–'82	Diesel	Nippondenso	55	Built-in	②	②	②	②	②	13.8–14.8

① 40–45 Amp Standard, 55 Amp Optional
② Not Adjustable

STARTER SPECIFICATIONS

| Engine Type | Starter Type/ Rated Voltage | No Load Test | | | Brush Spring Tension | Minimum Brush Length |
		Maximum Amps	Volts	Minimum rpm		
20R	Reduction Gear/12 V	50	11.5	5000	21 ②	0.47
22R	Reduction Gear/12 V	90	12.0	3500	64 ②	0.39
L (dies.)	Reduction Gear/12 V	180	11.0	3500	7.1–8.8 ③	0.47
2F	Direct Drive/12 V	50	11.5	5000	①	0.39

① Not specified by manufacturer   ② Ounces   ③ Pounds

BRAKE SPECIFICATIONS
(All measurements in inches)

| Year | Model | Lug Nut Torque (ft. lbs.) | Front Brake Disc | | Maximum Drum Diameter | | Minimum Lining Thickness | |
			Minimum Thickness	Maximum Run-Out	Front	Rear	Front	Rear
'75–'77	Pick-up	65–86	0.450	0.006	10.10	10.10	0.04	0.04
'78	Pick-up	65–86	0.450 ①	0.006	10.08	10.08	0.04	0.04
'79–'80	Pick-up	65–86	②	0.006	—	10.08	—	0.04
'81–'82	Pick-up	65–86	②	0.006	—	10.08	—	0.04
'75–'79	Land Cruiser	65–86	0.740	0.005	11.70	11.70	③	0.06
'80–'82	Land Cruiser	66–86	0.750	0.005	11.70	11.70	③	0.06

① "K" type disc brake—0.750   ② Except cab and chassis—0.453; cab and chassis—0.748   ③ Drum brakes—0.06; disc brakes—0.04

TUNE-UP PROCEDURES

NOTE: The procedures outlined below are the specific procedures for Toyota vehicles; general tune-up procedures may be found in the section at the end of this book.

Spark Plugs

REPLACEMENT

Check, clean, and adjust the spark plugs every 6,000 miles. Replace them every 12,000 miles.

Clean any foreign material from around the spark plugs before removing them. Use the spark plug wrench supplied in the tool kit.

Clean any plugs which appear to be dirty and file their electrodes flat. Adjust the gap to the figure given in the ''Tune-up Specifications'' chart, above, using a wire feeler gauge.

NOTE: Do not use a flat gauge; an inaccurate reading will result.

Inspect the spark plug hole threads for rust and, if necessary, use a 14 mm plug tap to clean them.

Lightly oil the threads and torque the plugs to 11–14 ft. lbs. Use caution when tightening the plugs, as most Toyota models use aluminum heads.

Breaker Points and Condenser

REPLACEMENT

Loosen the clips which attach the distributor cap to the distributor body and lift the cap straight up. Leave the leads connected to the cap. Remove the rotor and dust cover.

Clean the distributor cap and rotor with alcohol. Inspect them for cracks and other signs of wear or damage. Polish the points with a point file.

NOTE: Do not use emery cloth or sandpaper; these may leave particles on the points, causing them to arc.

If the points are badly pitted or worn, replace them as follows:
1. Unfasten the point lead connector.
2. Remove the point retaining clip and remove the point hold-down screw.

3. Remove the point set.
4. Installation is the reverse of removal.

After replacing the points, or as routine maintenance, adjust the points to the specifications given in the tune-up chart at the beginning of this section as follows:
1. Rotate the engine by hand or by using a remote starter switch, so that the rubbing block is on the high point of the cam lobe.
2. Insert a 0.018 in. feeler gauge between the points; a slight drag should be felt.

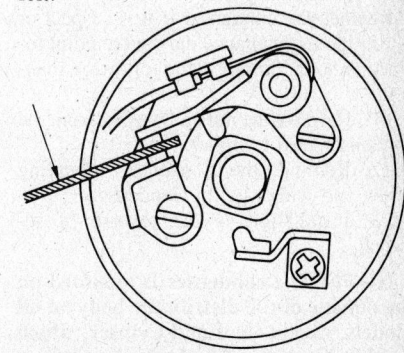

The arrow indicates the feeler gauge used to set the point gap. Make certain that the rubbing block rests on the high spot of the cam, as shown.

NOTE: Some 20R engines with breaker points have a plastic cap over the contact points, making it necessary to adjust the point gap at the rubbing block. Set the rubbing block between two cam lobes and adjust the clearance to 0.018 in. (See illustration). Always check the dwell angle after setting the points.

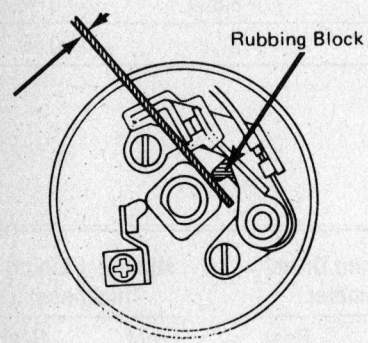

Rubbing Block

Some 20R engines are adjusted at the rubbing block rather than the contact points—see text

3. If no drag is felt or if the feeler gauge cannot be inserted at all, loosen, but do not remove, the point hold-down screw.

4. Insert a screwdriver into the adjustment slot. Rotate the screwdriver until the proper point gap is attained. The point gap is increased by rotating the screwdriver counterclockwise and decreased by rotating it clockwise.

5. Tighten the point hold-down screw. Lubricate the cam lobes, breaker arm, rubbing block, arm pivot, and distributor shaft with special high-temperature distributor grease.

Check the operation of the centrifugal advance mechanism by moving the rotor clockwise. Release the rotor; it should return to its original position. If it does not, check it for binding.

Check the vacuum advance unit by removing the cap and pressing in on the octane selector. Release the octaine selector. It should snap back to its original position. Check for binding if it fails to do so.

Replace the condenser if it is suspect or as routine maintenance during the point replacement operation, in the following manner:

1. Remove the nut and washer from the condenser lead terminal.

2. Remove the condenser mounting screw and withdraw the condenser.

3. Installation is the reverse of removal.

NOTE: The condenser is mounted on the outside of the distributor body on all models, except the Land Cruiser, which has it mounted inside the body.

Install the dust cover, rotor and the distributor cap on the distributor. Adjust the dwell and timing, as outlined below.

ADJUSTMENT

Connect a dwell/tachometer, in accordance with its manufacturer's instructions, between the distributor primary lead and a ground.

——— CAUTION ———

On models with electronic ignition, hook the dwell meter or tachometer to the negative (−) side of the coil, not to the distributor primary lead; damage to the ignition control unit will result.

With the engine warmed up and running at the specified idle speed (see the tune-up chart), take a dwell reading. If the point dwell is not within specifications, shut the engine off and adjust the point gap, as outlined above.

NOTE: Increasing the point gap decreases the dwell angle and vice versa.

Install the dust cover, rotor, and cap. Check the dwell reading again.

Electronic Ignition

NOTE: Two types of electronic ignition systems are used. The first is a semi-transistorized unit (1976–77) which uses conventional breaker points along with a transistorized igniter in lieu of the condensor. The igniter, which contains two transistors and an assortment of resistors, serves as a switching device to control the primary coil circuit. This system reduces the amount of current passing through the breaker points, thereby increasing breaker point life. Breaker points are replaced in the conventional manner. The second type of electronic ignition (1978 and later) is fully transistorized. A stationary magnetic pick-up coil (mounted in the distributor) and a toothed timing rotor (mounted on the distributor shaft) entirely replace the conventional breaker points and condensor. Because no mechanical contact exists between the pick-up coil and the timing rotor, the system is considered to be maintenance-free.

PRECAUTIONS—FULLY TRANSISTORIZED SYSTEM

1. If the engine will not start, do not leave the ignition switch "ON" for more than 10 minutes.

2. Make sure that your test equipment (tachometer, dwell meter, etc.) is compatible to this system before making any connections.

3. Do not connect the tachometer positive lead to the distributor. Connect this lead only to the service connector (yellow) provided in the system.

4. Do not disconnect the battery with the engine running.

5. Do not allow the ignition coil terminals or service connector terminal to touch ground: Damage to the igniter or ignition coil could result.

AIR GAP ADJUSTMENT

1. Remove the distributor cap, ignition rotor and dust cover from the distributor.

2. "Tap" the ignition key to the start position until one of the timing rotor teeth aligns with the pick-up coil. Turn the ignition switch "OFF".

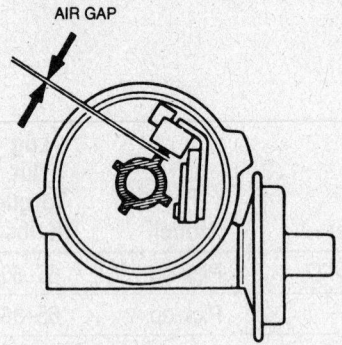

AIR GAP

Check the air gap between the timing rotor and the pick-up coil

3. Using a flat, brass feeler gauge, check the gap between the timing rotor tooth and the pick-up coil. If adjustment is needed, loosen (but do not remove) the pick-up coil attaching screws and move the pick-up coil as necessary to attain the specified clearance. Tighten the pick-up coil attaching screws and recheck the clearance.

4. Reinstall the dust cover, ignition rotor and distributor cap.

IGNITER TROUBLESHOOTING

1975–77

If the igniter in the 1975–77 semi-transistorized ignition is suspected as faulty, it may be checked as follows.

1. Check the coil beforehand, using the methods outlined in the "Troubleshooting" section at the end of this Chapter.

2. Check to see if there is battery voltage at the resistor terminal. Connect a test light between igniter side ballast resistor terminal and the ground bolt at the igniter, or any suitable ground. With the ignition on, the test light should indicate a complete circuit there.

3. Remove the coil primary wire from the distributor and hold it next to a ground. Disconnect the thin secondary wire from the side of the distributor. Make intermittent contacts with a suitable ground point with the secondary distributor wire. You may need an extra length of wire to do this on later models with piggyback coil and igniter assemblies. With the ignition on, sparks should be produced from the coil primary wire.

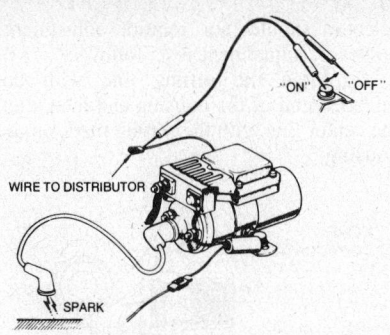

WIRE TO DISTRIBUTOR

"ON"   "OFF"

SPARK

Troubleshooting the igniter: later models have a snap connector in the wire between the igniter and the distributor; on trucks with separate coil and igniter, you will not need the extra wire shown here.

4. If no spark is produced the igniter is probably bad and should be replaced. If a spark is produced, the problem is in the points. Make certain that they are clean and properly adjusted.

FULLY TRANSISTORIZED IGNITION TROUBLESHOOTING

1978 and later

Troubleshooting this system is easy; but you must have an accurate ohmmeter and voltmeter. The numbers in the diagram correspond to the numbers of the following troubleshooting steps. Be sure to perform each step in order.

1. Check for a spark at the spark plugs by hooking up a timing light in the usual manner. If the light flashes, it can be assumed that voltage is reaching the plugs, which should then be inspected, along with the fuel system. If no flash is generated, go on to the following ignition checks.

2. Check all wiring and plastic connectors for tight and proper connections.

3. With an ohmmeter, check between the positive (+) and negative (−) primary terminals of the ignition coil. The resistance (cold) should be 1.3–1.7 ohms. Between the (+) primary terminal and the high tension terminal, the resistance (cold) should be 12–16 kilo-ohms. The insulation resistance between the (+) primary terminal and the ignition coil case should be infinite.

4. The resistor wire (brown and yellow) resistance should be 1.2 ohms (cold). To measure, disconnect the plastic connector at the igniter and connect one wire of the ohmmeter to the yellow wire and one to the brown.

5. Remove the distributor cap and ignition rotor. Check the air gap between the timing rotor spoke and the pick-up coil. When aligned, the air gap should be 0.008–0.016 in. You will probably have to bump the engine around with the starter to line up the timing rotor.

6. Unplug the distributor connector at the distributor. Connect one wire of the

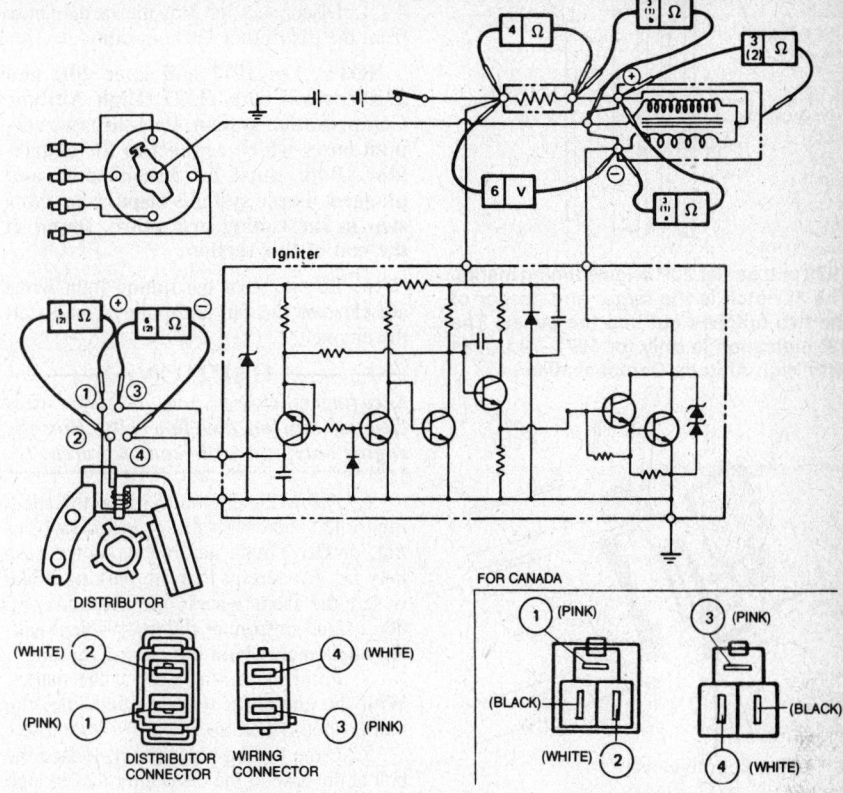

Igniter

DISTRIBUTOR

(WHITE) 2   (WHITE) 4
(PINK) 1   (PINK) 3

DISTRIBUTOR   WIRING
CONNECTOR   CONNECTOR

FOR CANADA

1 (PINK)   3 (PINK)
(BLACK)   (BLACK)
(WHITE) 2   (WHITE) 4

Fully transistorized ignition system troubleshooting

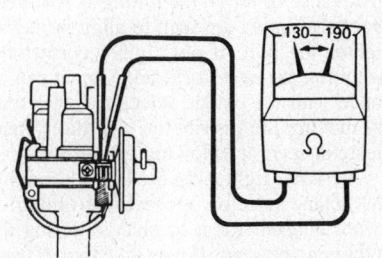

130—190

Ω

Measure the signal generator (pick-up coil) resistance at the pink and white wires

ohmmeter to the white wire, and one wire to the pink wire. The resistance of the signal generator should be 130–190 ohms.

7. Checking the igniter last, connect the (−) voltmeter wire to the (−) ignition coil primary terminal, and the (+) voltmeter wire to the yellow resistor wire at the connector unplugged in step 4. With the ignition switch turned to "On" (not "Start") the voltage should measure 12 volts.

8. Check the voltage between the (−) ignition coil primary terminal and the yellow resistor wire again, but this time use the ohmmeter as resistance. Using the igniter end of the distributor connector unplugged in step 5, connect the positive (+) ohmmeter wire to the pink distributor wire, and the negative (−) ohmmeter wire to the white wire.

—— CAUTION ——
Do not intermix the (+) and (−) terminals of the ohmmeter.

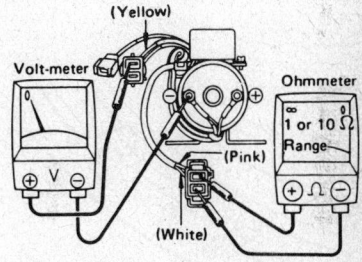

(Yellow)

Volt-meter   Ohmmeter
              1 or 10 Ω
              Range
(Pink)

(White)

Use the ohmmeter as resistance at the igniter end of the distributor connector

Select either the 1 ohm or 10 ohm range of the ohmmeter. With the voltmeter connected as in step 7, and the ignition switch turned on "On" (not "Start"), the voltage should measure nearly zero.

Ignition Timing

NOTE: Timing mark locations differ between the engines used in the Pick-up (20R and 22R) and the Landcruiser (2F). The 20R and 22R timing marks are located on the crankshaft pulley (painted notch) and the timing cover (pointer). The 2F timing marks are located on the flywheel (ball) and the bellhousing (pointer).

1. Clean off the timing marks. You may want to retouch them if they are dark, using chalk or paint. You might have to bump the engine around with the starter to find the marks.

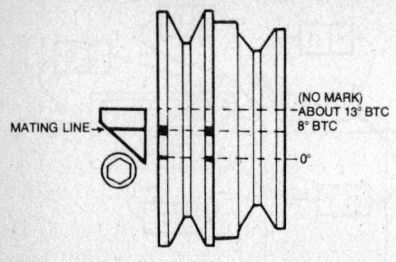

1979 and earlier 20R engine timing marks. The 8° notch is the larger and deeper of the two notches cut into the pulley. The 13° indication is only for 1977–79 trucks with High Altitude Compensation.

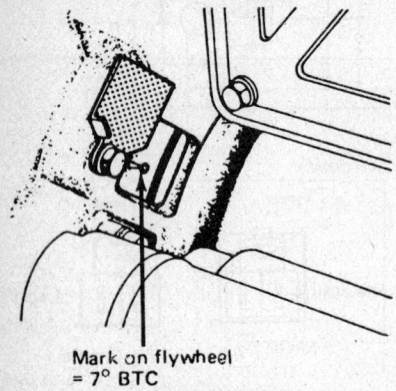

Mark on flywheel = 7° BTC

2F engine timing mark

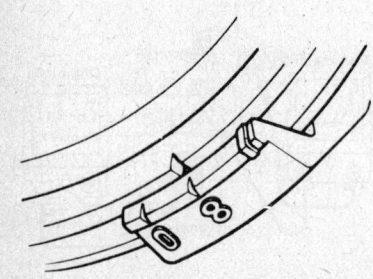

1980 and later 20R and 22R engine timing marks—typical. The "8" mark is 8° before top dead center. Some engines will also have a "5" mark which denotes 5° before top dead center.

2. Warm the engine to operating temperature. Connect a tachometer and check the engine idle speed to see that it is within the range found in the "Tune-Up Specifications" chart. Adjust it, if necessary, according to the procedure found in the Carburetor section.

--- CAUTION ---

On 20R and 22R engines, connect the positive (+) tachometer terminal either to the negative (−) ignition coil terminal or to the yellow service connector, if provided. Do NOT connect it to the distributor side. Improper connections will damage the transistorized igniter.

3. Shut off the engine and connect a timing light according to the manufacturer's directions.

4. Disconnect and plug the vacuum hose from the distributor vacuum unit.

NOTE: On 1977 and later 20R and 22R engines with HAC (High Altitude Compensation system) there are two vacuum hoses which connect to the distributor. Both must be disconnected and plugged. These systems require an extra step in the timing procedure, found at the end of this section.

5. Be sure that the timing light wires are clear of the fan and pulleys, and start the engine.

--- CAUTION ---

Keep fingers, clothes, hair, tools, and wires clear of the fan and fan belts. Run the engine only in a well-ventilated area.

6. Allow the engine to run at the specified idle speed with the gearshift in Neutral, or Drive with automatics as the case may be. Be certain that the parking brake is set, the front wheels are blocked, and don't stand in front of the truck when making adjustments with the engine running.

7. Point the timing light at the marks. With the engine at the specified idle, the marks should line up.

8. If the timing is incorrect, loosen the bolt at the base of the distributor just enough so that the distributor can be turned. Hold the distributor by its base and turn it slightly to advance or retard the timing as required. Once the marks are seen to align properly, tighten the bolt. If only minor corrections in timing are necessary, adjustment can be made with the octane selector, rather than by moving the distributor. See the Octane Selector section following for information.

9. After tightening the bolt, or moving the octane selector, recheck the timing. It is not unusual for it to change during the tightening process. It may take two or three tries to get it perfect. Shut off the engine, disconnect the timing light, and connect the vacuum line at the distributor, except on engines with HAC.

10. On 1977 and later engines with HAC (identified in the Note earlier) after setting the initial timing, reconnect the vacuum hoses at the distributor. Recheck the timing. It should now be about 13° BTC. There is no mark on the pulley to indicate this 13° advance in 1977. It must be estimated according to the illustration found here.

11. If the advance is still about 8° pinch the hose between the HAC valve and the three way connector. It should now be about 13°. If not, the HAC valve should be checked for proper operation.

OCTANE SELECTOR ADJUSTMENT

The octane selector is used as a fine adjustment to match the ignition timing to the grade of gasoline being used. It is located opposite the distributor vacuum advance unit, under a plastic cover. Normally the octane selector should not require adjustment, however, adjustment is as follows:

1. Align the setting line with the threaded end of the housing and then align the center line with the setting mark on the housing.

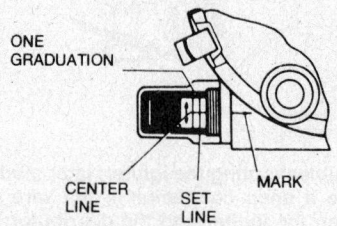

Octane selector setting

2. Drive the truck at 16–22 miles per hour in High gear on a level road.

3. Depress the accelerator pedal all the way to the floor. A slight pinging sound should be heard. As the vehicle accelerates, the sound should go away.

4. If the pinging sound is loud, or if it fails to disappear as the vehicle accelerates, retard the timing by turning the knob toward "R" (retard).

5. If there is no pinging sound at all, advance the timing by turning the knob toward "A" (advance).

6. When the adjustment is completed, replace the dust cover.

NOTE: One graduation of the octane selector is equal to about 10° of crankshaft angle.

Valve Adjustment

20R AND 22R ENGINES

1. Start the engine and allow it to reach normal operating temperature (above 175°F).

2. Stop the engine. Remove the air cleaner assembly, its hoses, and bracket. Remove any other cables, hoses, wires, etc. which are attached to the valve cover. Remove the valve cover.

3. Check the torque of the valve rocker shaft bolts and the camshaft bearing bolts; they should be torqued to 12–17 ft. lbs.

4. Check the torque of the bearing cap union bolts; they should be torqued to 11–16 ft. lbs.

5. Set the no. 1 cylinder to TDC on its compression stroke. To do this, remove the spark plugs and turn the engine with a wrench applied to the crankshaft bolt. Place a finger on the no. 1 spark plug hole. When pressure is felt on your finger and the TDC line on the crankshaft pulley is aligned with the timing pointer (or line), the engine is at TDC. The rocker arms on cylinder no. 1 should be loose, and the rocker arms on cylinder no. 4 should be tight if the engine is at TDC. Note that the timing mark you are watching is not the same one used for engine timing. That notch indicates a certain number of degrees before TDC.

NOTE: Do not start the engine. Valve clearances are checked with the engine stopped to prevent hot oil from being splashed out by the timing chain.

6. Check the clearances (see the "Tune-Up Specifications" chart) and adjust the first set of valves to the proper specifications, if necessary. See the illustrations for the proper adjusting sequence.

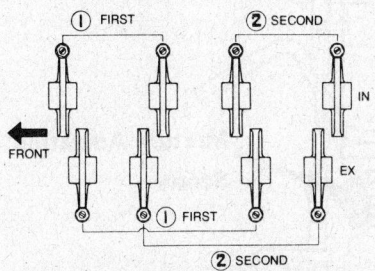

Valve clearance adjustment sequence—20R and 22R engines

NOTE: The clearance is measured with a feeler gauge between the valve stem and the adjusting screw.

7. To adjust the valve clearance, loosen the locknut and turn the adjusting screw until the specified clearance is obtained. Tighten the locknut and check the clearance again.

8. Crank the engine one revolution (360°) and perform steps 6 and 7 for the second set of valves in the illustration. Crank the engine in a clockwise direction (to the right as you face the engine), passing the timing mark just before reaching the TDC mark.

9. Install the spark plug in the no. 1 cylinder. Install the valve cover, air cleaner assembly, and any other components which were removed.

NOTE: If you are assembling the engine after it has been dismantled, the valves must be adjusted with the engine cold. Obtain the valve clearance specification from the beginning of this section and add a minimum of .002″ to these values. Remember: Excess clearance will not damage the engine whereas too little clearance could. After the initial engine start-up, allow the engine to reach normal operating temperature and adjust the valves as previously described to the "Hot" clearances listed in the specification chart.

2F ENGINES

1. Start the engine and allow it to reach normal operating temperature (above 165°F).

2. Stop the engine. Remove the air cleaner assembly with related components. Remove any cables, hoses, wires, etc., which are attached to the valve cover and remove the valve cover.

3. Following the Torque Sequence and Torque Specification charts at the begin-

ning of this section, re-torque the cylinder head bolts. On 2F engines, also torque the manifold attaching nuts (exc. Calif.—28–37 ft. lbs., Calif.—37–51 ft. lbs.) and the rocker support fasteners (8mm bolt—15–21 ft. lbs., 10mm bolt—22–32 ft. lbs.).

4. Start the engine and adjust the idle speed as described in the following procedure.

5. Check the clearance between each of the rocker arms and valve stems using a feeler gauge of the proper size (See the Tune-up Specification chart).

6. If the clearance is incorrect, loosen the locknut and turn the adjusting screw as required. Tighten the locknut and recheck the clearance.

7. After adjusting all of the valves, install the valve cover and any other components which were removed during step 2.

8. Recheck the engine idle speed and adjust if necessary.

DIESEL ENGINE

The valves are adjusted in basically the same manner as the 20R and 22R engines, in that the engine must be off during the adjustment and that the clearance is checked with a feeler gauge between the rocker arm and the valve stem end.

NOTE: The engine must be at normal operating temperature to obtain the proper valve clearances.

1. Remove the valve cover and rotate the crankshaft to align the TDC mark on the crankshaft pulley with the corresponding pointer. The valves of the number one cylinder should be closed (rocker arms should feel loose). If the rocker arms of the number one cylinder are tight, rotate the engine another 360° and again align the TDC marks.

2. Adjust the clearances of the following valves:

Number one cylinder: intake and exhaust

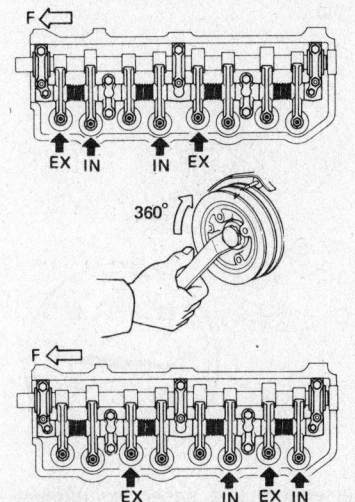

Valve clearance adjustment sequence—diesel engine

Number two cylinder: intake
Number three cylinder: exhaust

3. Rotate the crankshaft 360° and adjust the remaining valves:

Number two cylinder: exhaust
Number three cylinder: intake
Number four cylinder: intake and exhaust

Remember that the cylinder numbering from the front of the engine to the rear is #1 through #4, and that the valve arrangement from the front of the engine is E-I-E-I-E-I-E-I, with E designating each exhaust valve and I designating each intake valve. Choose your specifications from the Diesel Tune-Up Chart accordingly.

Reinstall the valve cover.

——————— CAUTION ———————
Never operate the engine with the valve cover removed.

Carburetor

IDLE SPEED AND MIXTURE—20R AND 2F ENGINES

NOTE: Idle mixture adjustments cannot be performed on 1981 and later carburetors; these adjustments are pre-set at the factory.

The idle speed and mixture should be adjusted under the following conditions: the air cleaner must be installed, the choke fully opened, the transmission should be in Neutral (N), all accessories should be turned off, all vacuum lines should be connected, and the ignition timing should be set to specification.

1. Start the engine and allow it to reach normal operating temperature (180°F).

2. Check the float setting; the fuel level should be just about even with the spot on the sight glass. If the fuel level is too high or low, adjust the float level. (See the Fuel System section)

3. Connect a tachometer in accordance with its manufacturer's instructions. However, connect the tachometer positive (+) lead to the coil Negative (−) terminal or to the yellow service connector, if provided. Do NOT hook it up to the distributor

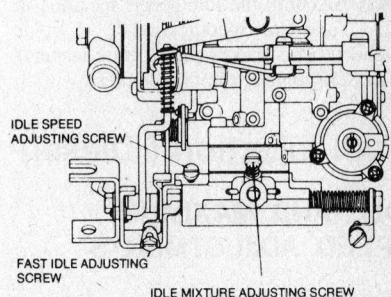

Carburetor adjusting screws—20R engines

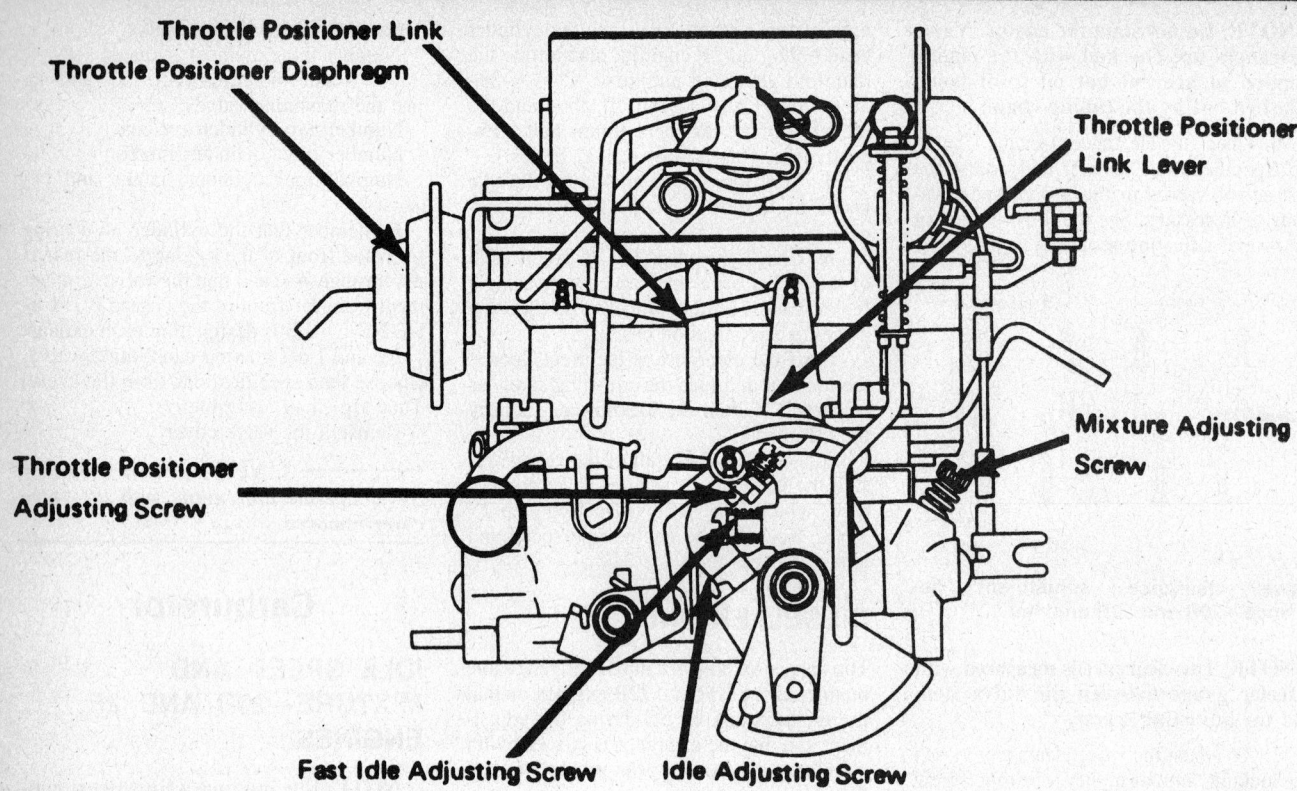

Throttle Positioner Link
Throttle Positioner Diaphragm

Throttle Positioner
Link Lever

Throttle Positioner
Adjusting Screw

Mixture Adjusting
Screw

Fast Idle Adjusting Screw   Idle Adjusting Screw

Carburetor adjusting screws—2F engine

side; damage to the transistorized ignition could result.

4. Turn the idle speed adjusting screw to obtain one of the following initial idle speeds:

   20R—900 rpm
   2F—690 rpm

5. Turn the idle mixture adjusting screw to increase the idle speed as much as is possible.

6. Next, turn the idle speed screw to again obtain the same idle speed figure given in step 4.

7. If possible, turn the idle mixture screw to increase the idle speed again.

8. Keep repeating steps 6 and 7 until the idle mixture adjusting screw will no longer increase the idle speed above the figure specified in step 4.

9. Slowly turn the idle mixture screw *clockwise*, until the idle speed specified in the "Tune-Up Specifications" chart is reached. (This makes the mixture leaner.)

10. Disconnect the tachometer.

Fuel Injection (Diesel)

IDLE AND MAXIMUM SPEED ADJUSTMENTS

NOTE: The following adjustments are made with the transmission in neutral and the parking brake applied fully.

1. Warm the engine to normal operating temperature and allow it to idle.

2. Turn the idle adjustor knob counterclockwise; the knob should return to its unlocked position.

3. Turn the engine off and remove the accelerator connection rod.

4. Connect a tachometer to the engine according to the tachometer manufacturers instructions.

5. Start the engine and check the engine rpm at idle. The idle rpm should be 700 rpm.

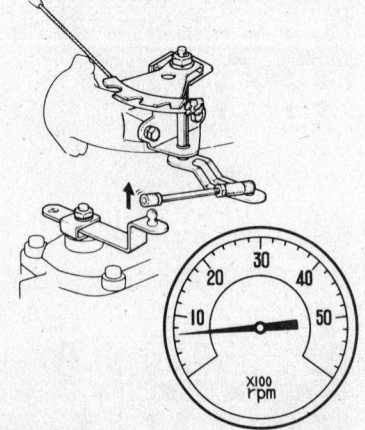

Diesel engine idle speed adjustment—disconnect the accelerator rod at the injection pump lever as shown, prior to adjustment

6. If adjustment is necessary, turn the idle adjusting screw on the fuel injection pump as required to obtain the 700 rpm idle speed.

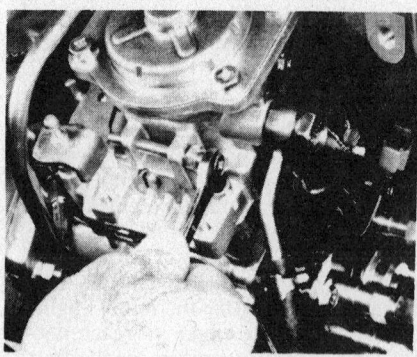

Diesel engine idle speed adjustment screw location

7. Fully depress the injection pump lever, note the maximum engine speed and release the accelerator pedal immediately. The maximum rpm should be 4900.

8. If adjustment is necessary:

   a. Remove the wire seal of the maximum speed adjusting screw, if so equipped.

   b. Using Toyota special service tool #09275-54020 or its equivalent, loosen the locknut of the maximum speed adjusting screw.

Diesel engine maximum speed adjustment—push the lever until it contacts the maximum speed adjusting screw

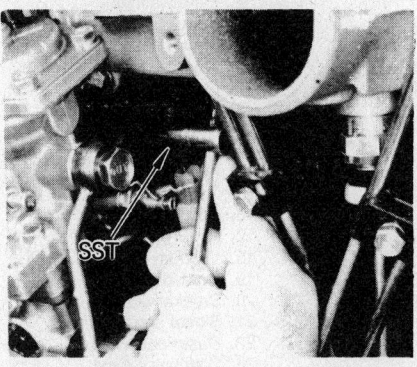

Diesel engine maximum speed adjustment—using the Toyota special service tool to loosen the maximum speed adjusting screw locknut

c. Turn the maximum speed adjusting screw until the proper maximum rpm is obtained.

9. Install the accelerator connecting rod and adjust its length so that there is no slack in the accelerator cable.

After setting the idle and maximum speeds on diesel engines, reinstall the accelerator cable and adjust the cable so that there is no slack

10. Check that the idle speed increases as the idle adjustor knob is pulled outward. Then turn the knob counterclockwise so that the rpm returns to the idle specification.

11. Turn the engine off and disconnect the tachometer from the engine.

ENGINE ELECTRICAL

Distributor

REMOVAL

1. Unfasten the cables from the spark plugs, after marking the wiring order. Remove the high tension cable from the coil.
2. Remove the primary wire and the vacuum line from the distributor. Remove the distributor cap.
3. Match-mark the distributor housing and the engine block; mark the rotor position in the distributor as well. This will aid in correct positioning of the distributor during installation.
4. Remove the clamp from the distributor. Withdraw the distributor from the block.

NOTE: It is easier to install the distributor if the engine timing is not disturbed while it is removed. If the timing has been lost, see "Installation—Timing Disturbed".

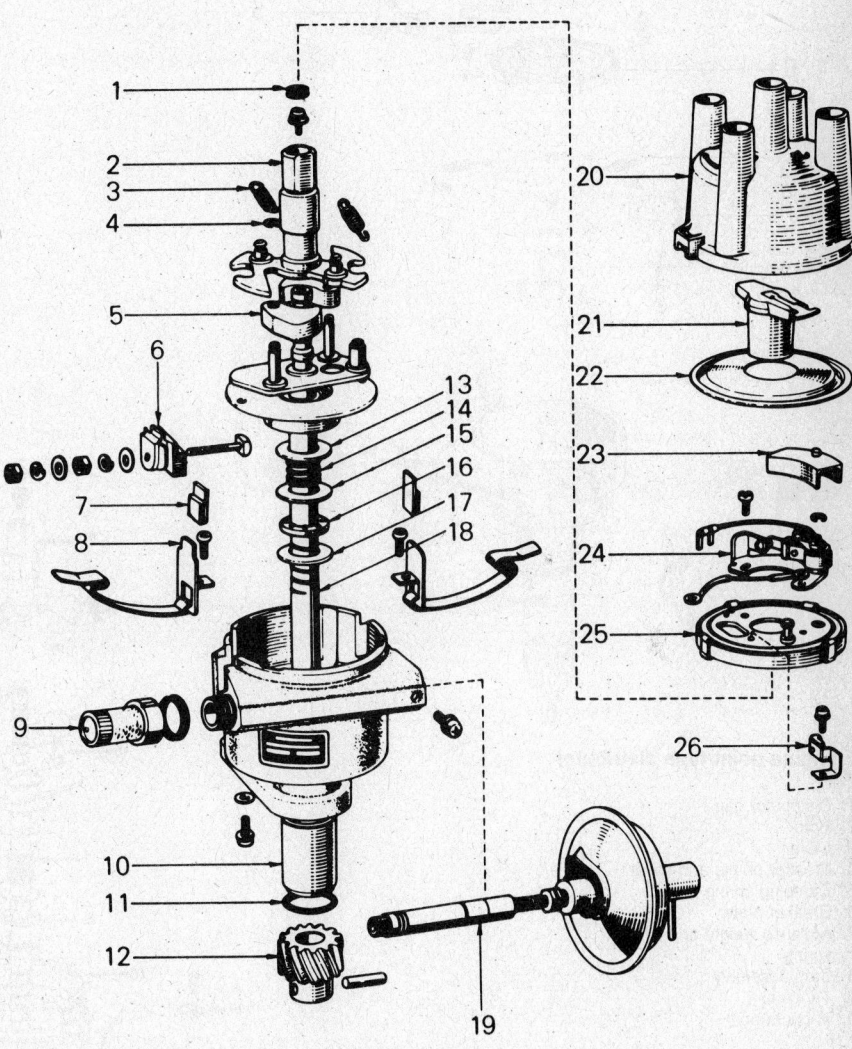

20R engine point type distributor

1. Grease stopper
2. Cam
3. Governor spring
4. E-ring
5. Governor weight
6. Terminal insulator
7. Rubber plug
8. Hold-down clip for cap
9. Octane selector cap
10. Distributor housing
11. O-ring
12. Drive gear
13. Washer
14. Spring
15. Washer
16. Bearing
17. Washer
18. Distributor shaft
19. Vacuum unit and octane selector assembly
20. Distributor cap
21. Rotor
22. Dust cover
23. Points cover
24. Breaker points and ground wire
25. Breaker plate
26. Damping spring

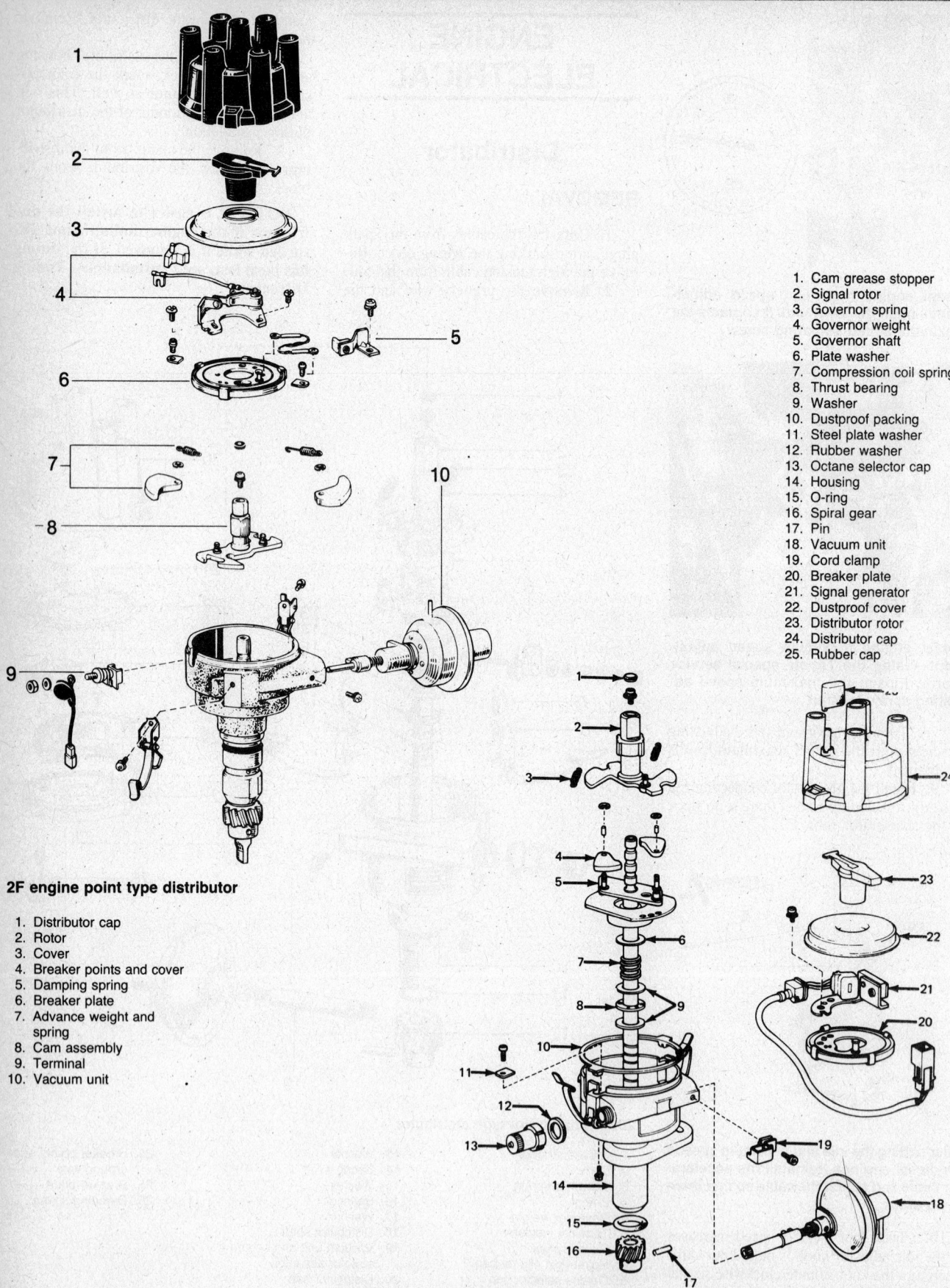

1. Cam grease stopper
2. Signal rotor
3. Governor spring
4. Governor weight
5. Governor shaft
6. Plate washer
7. Compression coil spring
8. Thrust bearing
9. Washer
10. Dustproof packing
11. Steel plate washer
12. Rubber washer
13. Octane selector cap
14. Housing
15. O-ring
16. Spiral gear
17. Pin
18. Vacuum unit
19. Cord clamp
20. Breaker plate
21. Signal generator
22. Dustproof cover
23. Distributor rotor
24. Distributor cap
25. Rubber cap

2F engine point type distributor

1. Distributor cap
2. Rotor
3. Cover
4. Breaker points and cover
5. Damping spring
6. Breaker plate
7. Advance weight and spring
8. Cam assembly
9. Terminal
10. Vacuum unit

20R and 22R engine fully electronic distributor. Some models use a different type of dust cover and/or vacuum unit. No major differences exist between models

INSTALLATION—TIMING NOT DISTURBED

1. Insert the distributor in the block and align the matchmarks made during removal.
2. Engage the distributor drive with the oil pump drive shaft.
3. Install the distributor clamp, cap, high tension wire, primary wire, and vacuum line.
4. Install the wires on the spark plugs.
5. Start the engine, Check the timing and adjust the octane selector.

INSTALLATION—TIMING DISTURBED

If the engine has been cranked, dismantled, or the timing otherwise lost, proceed as follows:

1. Determine the top dead center (TDC) of the number one (no. 1) cylinder's compression stroke by removing the spark plug from the no. 1 cylinder and placing a finger or a compression gauge over the spark plug hole.

Crank the engine until compression pressure starts to build up. Continue cranking the engine until the timing marks indicate TDC (or 0°).

2. Next, align the timing marks to the specifications given in the "Ignition Timing" column of the tune-up chart at the beginning of the Toyota section.
3. Temporarily install the rotor in the distributor shaft so that the rotor is pointing toward the number one terminal in the distributor cap.
4. Use a small screwdriver to align the slot on the distributor drive (oil pump driveshaft) with the key on the bottom of the distributor shaft.

5. Install the distributor in the block by rotating it slightly (no more than one gear tooth in either direction) until the driven gear meshes with the drive.

NOTE: Oil the distributor spiral gear and the oil pump driveshaft end before distributor installation.

6. Temporarily tighten the pinch bolt.
7. Remove the rotor and install the dust cover. Replace the rotor and the distributor cap.
8. Install the primary wire and the vacuum line.
9. Install the no. 1 cylinder spark plug. Connect the cables to the spark plugs in the proper order by using the marks made during removal. Install the high tension wire on the coil.
10. Start the engine. Adjust the ignition timing and the octane selector as previously outlined.

Alternator

PRECAUTIONS

1. Always observe proper polarity of the battery connections; be especially careful when jump-starting the car.
2. Never ground or short out any alternator or alternator regulator terminals.
3. Never operate the alternator with any of its or the battery's leads disconnected.
4. Always remove the battery or disconnect its output lead while charging it.
5. Always disconnect the ground cable when replacing any electrical components.
6. Never subject the alternator to excessive heat or dampness if the engine is being steam-cleaned.
7. Never use arc-welding equipment with the alternator connected.

REMOVAL AND INSTALLATION

NOTE: On some models the alternator is mounted very low on the engine. On these models it may be necessary to remove the gravel shield and work from underneath the car in order to gain access to the alternator.

1. Unfasten the starter-to-battery cable at the battery end.
2. Remove the air cleaner, if necessary, to gain access to the alternator.
3. Unfasten the bolts which attach the adjusting link to the alternator. Remove the alternator drive belt.
4. Unfasten and tag the alternator wiring connection.
5. Remove the alternator attaching bolt and then withdraw the alternator from its bracket.
6. Installation is the reverse order of removal. After installing the alternator, adjust the belt tension.

BELT TENSION ADJUSTMENT

Inspection and adjustment to the alternator drive belt should be performed every 3,000 miles or if the alternator has been removed.

1. Inspect the drive belt to see that it is not cracked or worn. Be sure that its surfaces are free of grease or oil.
2. Push down on the belt halfway between the fan and the alternator pulleys, (or crankshaft pulley) with thumb pressure. Belt deflection should be ⅜–½ in.
3. If the belt tension requires adjustment, loosen the adjusting link bolt and move the alternator until the proper belt tension is obtained.

——— CAUTION ———
Do not overtighten the belt; damage to the alternator bearings could result.

4. Tighten the adjusting link bolt.

Voltage Regulator

REMOVAL AND INSTALLATION

1. Disconnect the negative battery cable.
2. Disconnect the wiring harness.

NOTE: On Land Cruisers disconnect the leads from their screw terminals after noting their position for installation.

3. Remove the retaining hardware and remove the regulator.
4. To install, attach the new regulator to the compartment panel, replace the wiring harness, and connect the battery cable.

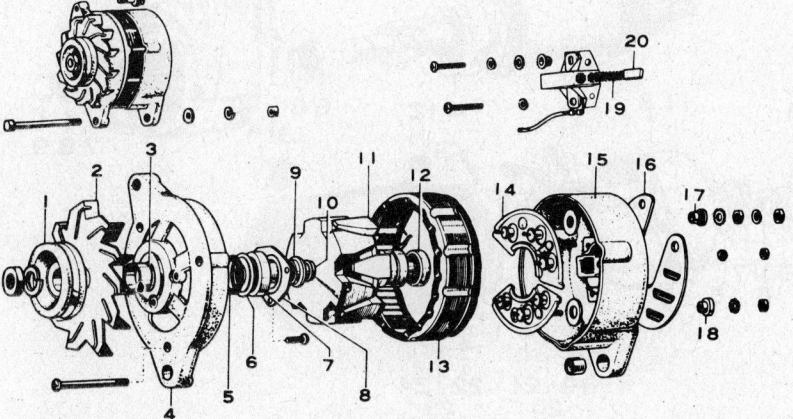

Alternator components—typical

1. Alternator pulley
2. Alternator fan
3. Space collar
4. Drive end frame assembly
5. Felt
6. Felt cover
7. Bearing
8. Bearing retainer plate
9. Space ring
10. Snap-ring
11. Alternator rotor assembly
12. Bearing
13. Alternator stator assembly
14. Holder with rectifiers
15. Rectifier end frame assembly
16. Rear end cover
17. B terminal insulator
18. Insulator
19. Brush spring
20. Alternator brush

VOLTAGE ADJUSTMENT

NOTE: Only external regulators used with gasoline engines are adjustable.

1. Connect a voltmeter to the battery terminals.
2. Start the engine and gradually increase the engine speed to about 1,500 rpm. (2000 rpm for Land Cruisers).
3. At this speed, the voltage reading should be 13.8–14.8 volts.
4. If the voltage does not fall within this range, a minor adjustment may be made to the adjusting arm. Disconnect the ground cable of the battery and remove the regulator cover. Bend the adjusting arm very slightly with a pair of needle nose pliers. Replace the cover and battery cable.

FIELD RELAY ADJUSTMENT

NOTE: Only external regulators used with gasoline engines are adjustable.

NOTE: This adjustment does not apply to Land Cruisers.

1. Remove the cover from the regulator assembly.
2. Use a feeler gauge to check the amount that the contact spring is deflected while the armature is being depressed.
3. If the measurement is not 0.008″–0.018″, adjust the regulator by bending point holder P (See illustration).

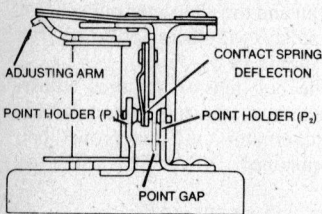

Field relay internal parts—external regulator

4. Check the point gap with a feeler gauge. The gap should be 0.016″–0.047″.
5. Adjust the point gap, as required, by bending the point holder P (See illustration.)
6. Clean off the points with emery cloth if they are dirty and wash them with solvent.

VOLTAGE REGULATOR ADJUSTMENT

NOTE: Only external regulators used with gasoline engines are adjustable.

1. The air (armature) gap must measure 0.008 in. If it does not, adjust by bending the low speed point holder.
2. Measure the point gap with a feeler gauge. It should be 0.010–0.018 in. If it is not, bend the high speed point holder to correct the adjustment. Clean the points with

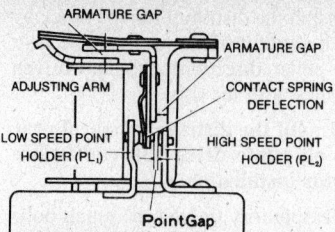

Voltage regulator components—external regulator

emery paper and use a solvent to remove the dust.

3. Check the contact spring deflection with the armature depressed. It should measure between 0.008–0.018 in. as it does on the field relay. If it does not, REPLACE the regulator.
4. Perform the voltage test again. If the voltage reading cannot be brought to specification, replace the voltage regulator. If this fails to correct the situation, the alternator then must be suspected as the defective unit.

Starter

REMOVAL AND INSTALLATION

1. Disconnect the cable which runs from the starter to the battery, at the battery end.
2. Remove the air cleaner assembly, if necessary, to gain access to the starter.

NOTE: On some models with automatic transmissions, it may be necessary to disconnect the throttle linkage connecting rod.

3. Disconnect all the wiring at the starter.
4. Remove the starter toward the front of the vehicle.
5. Installation is the reverse order of removal.

SOLENOID AND BRUSH REPLACEMENT

Direct Drive Type

NOTE: The starter must be removed from the vehicle in order to perform this operation.

1. Remove the field coil lead from the solenoid terminal.
2. Unfasten the solenoid retaining screws. Remove the solenoid by tilting it upward and withdrawing it.
3. Remove the end frame bearing cover screws and remove the cover.
4. Remove the thru-bolts. Remove the commutator end-frame.
5. Withdraw the brushes from their holder if they are to be replaced.
6. Check the brush length against the specification in the Battery and Starter Specifications chart. Replace the brushes with new ones if required.
7. Dress the new brushes with emery cloth so that they will make proper contact.

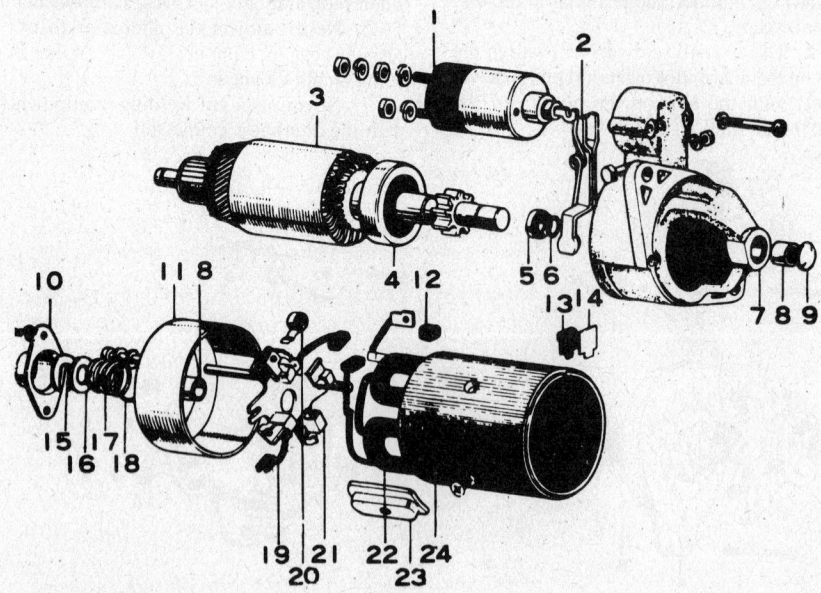

Direct drive starter components

1. Solenoid	9. Bearing cover	17. Brake spring
2. Engagement lever	10. Bearing cover	18. Gasket
3. Armature	11. Commutator end frame	19. Brush
4. Overrunning clutch	12. Rubber bushing	20. Brush spring
5. Clutch stop	13. Rubber grommet	21. Brush holder
6. Snap-ring	14. Plate	22. Field coil
7. Drive housing	15. Lock plate	23. Pole shoes
8. Bushing	16. Washer	24. Field yoke

8. Use a spring scale to check the brush spring tension against the specification in the chart. Replace the springs if they do not meet specification.

Assembly is the reverse of disassembly. Pack the end bearing cover with multipurpose grease before installing it.

Reduction Type

NOTE: The starter must be removed from the vehicle, in order to perform this operation.

1. Disconnect the solenoid lead.
2. Loosen the two bolts on the starter housing and separate the field frame from the solenoid. Remove the O-ring and felt dust seal.
3. Remove the two screws and separate the starter drive from the solenoid.
4. Withdraw the clutch and gears. Remove the ball from the clutch shaft bore or solenoid.
5. Remove the brushes from the holder.
6. Measure brush length and compare it to the specification given in the Battery and Starter Specifications chart. Replace the brushes if they are too short.
7. Check the gears for wear or damage. Replace as required.

Assembly is the reverse of disassembly. Lubricate all bearings and gears with high temperature grease. Grease the ball before inserting in the clutch shaft bore. Align the tab on the brush holder with the notch on the field frame. Check the positive (+) brush

leads to see that they aren't grounded. Align the mark on the solenoid with the bolt anchors on the field frame.

ENGINE MECHANICAL

Design

The 20R gasoline engine is a single overhead camshaft design. The cylinder head is a crossflow aluminum casting with hemispherically shaped combustion chambers. The camshaft is driven by a double-row timing chain.

The 22R gasoline engine is a refined and improved descendent of the 20R engine. The basic design between these engines is virtually identical. Refinements evident in the 22R engine include an increased cylinder bore diameter (though the stroke remains the same), a higher compression ratio, and improved carburetor, intake tract and piston designs. Efficiency, performance and fuel mileage have all been increased due to these changes.

The "L" type diesel engine is a single overhead camshaft design. The camshaft is driven by a single rubber/fabric belt, which makes this engine quieter than many diesels. The engine was designed from the start to be a diesel, as opposed to a few "gasoline converted" engines currently being marketed. This engine bears no resemblance to other Toyota gasoline engines.

Engine Removal and Installation

TWO WHEEL DRIVE PICKUPS

Gasoline Engines

1. Drain the radiator, cooling system, transmission, and engine oil.
2. Disconnect the battery-to-starter cable at the positive battery terminal.
3. Scribe marks on the hood and its hinges to aid in alignment during installation.
4. Remove the hood supports from the body. Remove the hood.

NOTE: Do not remove the supports from the hood.

5. Remove the headlight bezel and the radiator grille.
6. Remove the fan shroud, the hood lock base and the base support.
7. Detach both the upper and lower hoses from the radiator. On cars with automatic transmissions, disconnect the lines from the oil cooler. Remove the radiator.
8. Unfasten the clamps and remove the heater and bypass hoses from the engine. Remove the heater control cable from the water valve.
9. Remove the wiring from the coolant temperature and oil pressure sending units.
10. Remove the air cleaner from its bracket, complete with its attendant hoses.
11. Unfasten the accelerator torque rod from the carburetor. On models equipped with automatic transmissions, remove the transmission linkage as well.
12. Remove the emission control system hoses and wiring, as necessary.
13. Remove the clutch hydraulic line support bracket.
14. Unfasten the high-tension and primary wires from the coil.
15. Mark the spark plug cables and remove them from the distributor.
16. Detach the right-hand front engine mount.
17. Remove the fuel line at the pump.
18. Detach the downpipe from the exhaust manifold.
19. Detach the left-hand front engine mount.
20. Disconnect all the wiring harness multiconnectors.

Perform the following steps on models with manual transmissions:

21. Remove the center console if so equipped.

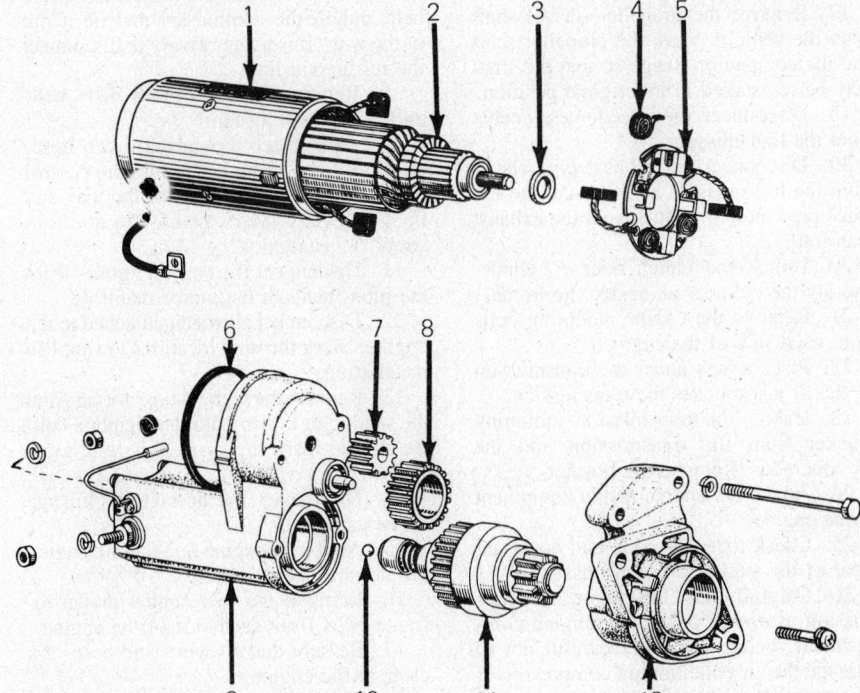

Reduction gear starter components—typical

1. Field frame assembly
2. Armature
3. Felt seal
4. Brush spring
5. Brush holder
6. O-ring
7. Pinion gear
8. Idler gear
9. Magnetic switch assembly
10. Steel ball
11. Clutch assembly
12. Starter housing

22. Remove the shift lever boot(s).

23. Unfasten the four shift lever cap retaining screws. Remove the cap and withdraw the shift lever assembly.

Perform the following steps on models equipped with automatic transmission:

24. Remove the transmission selector linkage:

   a. On models equipped with a floor-mounted selector, disconnect the control rod from the transmission.

   b. On column-mounted gear selector models, remove the shifter rod.

25. Disconnect the neutral safety switch wiring connector.

Perform the following steps on all models:

26. Raise the rear of the vehicle with jacks and support it on jackstands.

27. Remove the retaining screws and remove the parking brake equalizer support bracket. Disconnect the cable which runs between the lever and the equalizer.

28. Remove the speedometer cable from the transmission. Disconnect the back-up wiring.

29. Detach the driveshaft from the rear of the transmission.

NOTE: If oil runs out of the transmission, an old U-joint yoke sleeve makes an excellent plug.

30. Detach the clutch release cylinder assembly, complete with hydraulic lines. Do not disconnect the lines.

31. Unbolt the rear support member mounting insulators.

32. Support the transmission and detach the rear support member retaining bolts. Withdraw the support member from under the car.

33. Install lifting hooks on the engine lifting brackets. Attach a suitable hoist to the engine.

34. Remove the jack from under the transmission.

35. Raise the engine and move it toward the front of the car. Use care to avoid damaging the components which remain on the car.

36. Support the engine on a workstand. Install the engine in the reverse order of removal. Adjust all of the linkages as detailed in the appropriate section. Install the hood and adjust it. Replenish the fluid levels in the engine, radiator, and transmission.

Diesel Engine

1. Make accurate marks on the body to indicate the relationship between the hood supports and the body. Unbolt the hood supports at the body and remove the hood.

2. Disconnect and remove both batteries from the vehicle.

3. Drain the cooling system and remove the radiator, shroud, and radiator hoses.

4. If the vehicle is equipped with air conditioning, remove the compressor drive belt, unbolt the compressor and tie the com-

pressor out of the way. Do not disconnect the refrigerant lines from the compressor.

5. Remove the engine cooling fan, pulley, and drive belt.

6. Disconnect the two heater hoses from the left side of the engine.

7. Disconnect the vacuum reservoir hose from the rear of the alternator.

8. Disconnect the vacuum hose from the "idle-up" unit, if the vehicle is equipped with air conditioning.

9. Disconnect the fuel hoses from the fuel pump return connection and the sedimenter inlet connection.

10. Disconnect the wiring from the following components:

   a. Alternator
   b. Thermo-switch
   c. Oil pressure switch
   d. No. 1 glow plug relay (terminal +B)
   e. Starter

Mark these wires and tie them out of the way.

11. Disconnect the wiring from the left fender and the injection pump (accelerator wire). Also mark and tie these wires out of the way.

12. Using Toyota special service tool #09305-20012 or its equivalent, remove the transmission shift lever from inside the vehicle.

13. Raise the vehicle and support it safely.

14. Drain the engine oil.

15. Remove the engine under-cover and remove the backup light switch wire.

16. Remove the engine shock absorber.

17. Remove the propeller (drive) shaft from the vehicle. Mark the propeller shaft and the companion flange so that the shaft may be reinstalled in its original position.

18. Disconnect the speedometer cable from the transmission.

19. Disconnect the exhaust pipe clamp from the transmission housing and the exhaust pipe mounting nuts from the exhaust manifold.

20. Unbolt the clutch release cylinder and lay the cylinder alongside the frame.

21. Remove the engine mounting bolts from each side of the engine.

22. Place a jack under the transmission so that it just touches the transmission.

23. Unbolt the transmission mounting bracket from the transmission and the crossmember. Remove the bracket.

24. Attach the engine lifting equipment to the engine.

25. Check that all wiring and hoses are clear of the engine and transmission.

26. Carefully raise the engine and transmission assembly out of the engine compartment, being especially careful not to damage the air conditioning compressor, if so equipped.

27. Remove the starter, and with the help of an assistant, disconnect the transmission from the engine. Mount the engine securely in a workstand and service the engine as necessary, according to the appropriate sections of this book.

28. Reverse the previous steps to install the engine. Replenish the fluids in the engine, cooling system, and transmission, if required.

FOUR WHEEL DRIVE PICKUPS

——— **CAUTION** ———

Be sure to support the rear of the engine with a jack to avoid damage to the front motor mounts while performing engine removal procedures!

1. Set the engine to top dead center according to the marks on the vibration damper and timing cover pointer.

2. Remove the transmission and transfer case according to the procedures found in the appropriate sections.

3. Make accurate marks on the body to indicate the relationship between the hood supports and the body. Unbolt the hood supports at the body and remove the hood.

4. Remove the battery and the air cleaner assembly. Mark the hoses from the air cleaner to simplify installation.

5. Drain the cooling system and remove the radiator hoses.

6. Remove the radiator fan shroud and disconnect the heater outlet hose at the radiator.

7. Remove the radiator.

8. If the vehicle is equipped with air conditioning, remove the compressor drive belt, unbolt the compressor and tie it out of the way. It is not necessary to disconnect the refrigerant lines.

9. Remove the water pump drive belt, pulley and cooling fan.

10. Disconnect the heater inlet hose, brake booster hose and emission control hoses. Move the hoses out of the way and tie if necessary. Mark the hose locations to simplify installation.

11. Disconnect the two fuel hoses from the pipes beneath the intake manifold.

12. Disconnect all wiring attached to the engine. Mark the wire locations to simplify installation.

13. Remove the high voltage wiring from the spark plugs, distributor and ignition coil. Be sure to mark the spark plug wire locations.

14. Disconnect the accelerator linkage at the carburetor.

15. Attach an engine hoist to the engine but do not raise the hoist.

16. Remove the two engine mount-to-frame bolts from each side of the engine.

17. Be sure that all wires and hoses are clear of the engine.

18. Carefully raise the engine out of the engine compartment, being especially careful not to damage the air conditioning condensor, if so equipped.

19. Securely mount the engine on a workstand.

20. Perform the necessary service(s) to

the engine according to the appropriate sections of the book.

21. Reverse the previous steps to install the engine. Replenish the fluids in the engine, cooling system, and transmission.

LAND CRUISER AND WAGON

1. Scribe marks on the hood and hinges to aid in alignment during installation. Remove the hinge bolts from the hood and then remove the hood.

2. Drain the cooling system and engine oil.

3. Unfasten the radiator grille mounting bolts and remove the grille.

NOTE: On station wagon models, remove the parking light assembly and wiring first.

4. Remove the hood latch support rod. Detach the hood latch assembly from the radiator upper bracket. Remove the bracket.

5. Disconnect the heater hose from the radiator.

6. Detach the upper radiator hose at the water outlet housing and the lower hose at water pump.

7. Remove the six bolts which secure the radiator and lift the radiator out of the vehicle.

8. Remove the heater hoses from the water valve and heater box. Disconnect the temperature control cable from the water valve.

9. Detach both the the battery cables and remove the battery.

10. Remove the wires from the starter solenoid terminal.

11. Detach the fuel lines from the pump and remove the fuel filter assembly.

12. Disconnect the primary wire from the ignition coil.

13. Detach both of the intermediate rods from the shifter shafts (columnshift models only).

14. Remove the air cleaner assembly complete with hoses, from its bracket.

15. Remove the emission control system cables and hoses as necessary.

16. Disconnect the alternator multiconnector.

17. Disconnect the hand throttle, accelerator, and choke linkages from the carburetor.

18. On models equipped with vacuum assisted 4WD engagement, remove the control unit vacuum hose from its manifold fitting.

19. Disconnect the oil pressure and water temperature gauge sender's wiring.

20. Unfasten the downpipe from the exhaust manifold.

21. Detach the parking brake cable from the intermediate lever.

22. Unbolt the front driveshaft from the flange on the transfer case output shaft.

23. Remove both the left and right engine stone shields. Remove the transmission skid-plate.

24. Remove the cotter pin and disconnect both the high- and low-range shifter rods from their respective inner levers.

25. Remove the high/low range shifter link lever and the high/low shift rod.

26. Disconnect the clutch release fork spring. Remove the clutch release cylinder from its mounting bracket at the rear of the engine.

27. Unfasten the clamp screws and withdraw the vacuum lines from the transfer case control unit vacuum chamber (only on models with vacuum-assisted 4WD engagement).

28. Remove the 4WD indicator switch assembly.

29. Unfasten the speedometer cable from the transmission.

30. Disconnect the rear driveshaft from the transmission.

31. Detach the gearshift rod and gear selector rod from the shift outer lever and the gear selector outer lever, respectively.

32. Unbolt the rear engine mounts from the frame.

33. Perform Step 32 to the front engine mounts.

34. Install lifting hooks on the engine lift-points and connect a hoist.

35. Lift the engine slightly and toward the front, so the engine/transmission assembly clears the front of the vehicle.

Engine removal is performed in the reverse order of its installation. Refill the engine with coolant and lubricant. Check and adjust all linkages, as outlined in the appropriate section. Install the hood and align the matchmarks.

Cylinder Head

CAUTION

Do not perform this operation on a warm engine. Remove the head bolts in the reverse of the tightening sequence. Loosen the head bolts evenly, not one at a time. Keep the pushrods in their original order. Do not attempt to slide the cylinder head off of the block, as it is located with dowel pins. Lift the head straight up and off the block.

REMOVAL AND INSTALLATION

20R and 22R Engines

1. Disconnect the battery, negative cable first.

2. Remove the three exhaust pipe flange nuts and separate the pipe from the manifold.

3. Drain the cooling system, both the radiator and the block. The engine block drain is on the driver's side of the engine. The coolant, if good, may be reused.

4. Remove the air cleaner assembly complete with hoses, from the carburetor.

NOTE: Cover the carburetor with a clean cloth so that nothing can fall into it.

5. Tag all the various vacuum and emission hoses for reassembly and disconnect them at the engine or carburetor. Remove all linkages, fuel lines, coolant lines, etc., from the carburetor, cylinder head, and manifolds. Remove the wire supports.

6. Mark the spark plug leads and disconnect them from the plugs.

7. Matchmark the distributor housing and the engine block. Disconnect the high tension wire and the primary lead and remove the distributor. Installation will be easier if you leave the cap and spark plug wires in place.

8. Remove the four nuts which secure the valve cover.

9. Remove the rubber half circle cam seals. Remove the camshaft sprocket bolt. Slide the distributor drive gear off the camshaft and wire the cam sprocket in place to the timing chain.

10. Remove the timing chain cover bolt at the front of the head. This must be done before the head bolts are loosened.

11. Remove the cylinder head bolts. Loosen the bolts in two or three stages.

NOTE: Improper removal of the cylinder head bolts can cause head warpage.

12. Using pry bars applied evenly at the front and rear of the valve rocker assembly, pry the assembly off its mounting dowels.

13. Lift the head straight up off its dowels. Do NOT pry it off, or attempt to slide it off.

14. Drain the engine oil from the crankcase after the head has been removed, because the oil will become contaminated with coolant when the head is removed.

NOTE: Service procedures are covered in the Unit Repair Section.

Installation is as follows:

1. Clean off the top of the cylinder block and the head, using a scraper or a razor blade. Be careful not to gouge the aluminum head. You may also want to clean off the tops of the pistons, but as this requires rotation of the crankshaft, you must be careful to keep sufficient tension on the cam chain to prevent it from slipping a tooth. Vacuum out any bits which have fallen into the cylinders, being careful not to nick the cylinder walls.

2. Apply a liquid sealer to the front corners of the block and install a new head gasket.

3. Lower the head over the locating dowels. Do not attempt to slide it into place.

4. Rotate the camshaft so that the sprocket aligning pin is at the top. Remove the wire and hold the cam sprocket tight against the chain. Manually rotate the en-

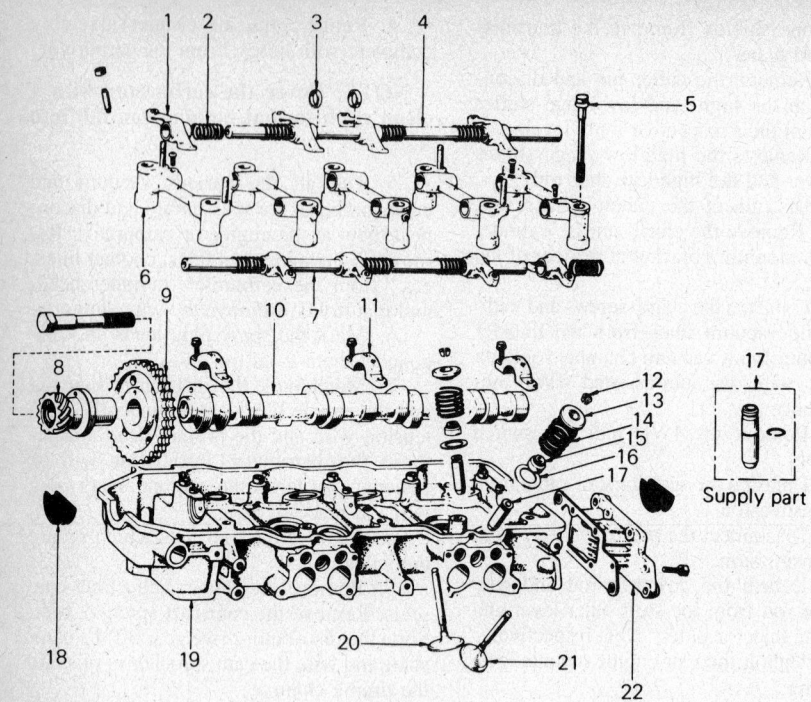

Cylinder head components—20R and 22R engines

1. Rocker arm
2. Spring
3. Spacer
4. Rocker shaft (intake)
5. Head bolt
6. Rocker stand
7. Rocker shaft (exhaust)
8. Distributor drive gear

9. Cam sprocket
10. Camshaft
11. Camshaft bearing cap
12. Valve keeper
13. Spring retainer
14. Valve spring
15. Valve seal
16. Spring seat

17. Valve guide
18. Half circle cam seal
19. Cylinder head
20. Intake valve
21. Exhaust valve
22. Rear cover (EGR cooler)

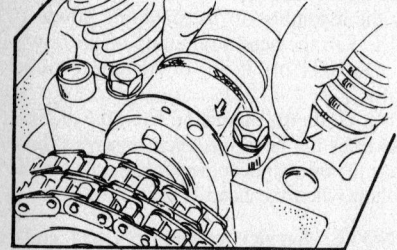

20R and 22R engines—rotate the camshaft so that the pin is at the top. Also note that the arrow on the camshaft bearing cap points to the front of the engine.

gine so that the cam sprocket hole is also at the top. Wire the sprocket in place again.

5. Install the rocker arm assembly over its positioning dowels.

6. Clean the threads of the cylinder head bolts thoroughly and give them a light coat of oil. Install them and tighten evenly, in three stages, in the sequence shown. Torque the bolts to the values located in the Torque Specification Chart.

7. Install the timing chain cover bolt and tighten it to 7–12 ft. lbs.

8. Remove the wire and fit the sprocket over the camshaft dowel. If the chain won't allow the sprocket to reach, rotate the

crankshaft back and forth, while lifting up on the chain and sprocket.

9. Install the distributor drive gear and tighten the sprocket bolt to 51–65 ft. lbs.

10. Adjust the valves as outlined earlier. After completing the adjustment, rotate the crankshaft 352°, so that the 8° BTDC mark on the pulley aligns with the timing mark on the block.

11. Install the distributor, as outlined earlier.

12. Install the spark plugs and leads.

13. Make sure the oil drain plug is installed. Install the rubber half circle cam seals and fill the engine with oil. Pour the oil over the top of the head, onto the distributor drive gear and the valve rockers.

14. Install the rocker cover and tighten the nuts to 7–12 ft. lbs.

15. Connect all the vacuum hoses and electrical leads which were removed during disassembly. Reconnect the fuel line. Install the spark plug lead clips onto the rocker cover. Fill the cooling system. Install the air cleaner.

16. Tighten the exhaust pipe manifold nuts to 25–33 ft. lbs.

17. Reconnect the battery, negative cable last. Start the engine and allow it to reach normal operating temperature. Check the timing and adjust the idle speed and mixture. Shut off the engine and reset the valves.

Diesel Engine

1. Disconnect the cables from both batteries.

2. Remove the air cleaner assembly.

3. Drain the cooling system and remove the radiator, shroud, and radiator hoses.

4. If the vehicle is equipped with air conditioning, remove the compressor drive belt and unbolt the compressor from its mounting brackets. Tie the compressor out of the way. Do not remove the refrigerant lines.

5. Remove the engine cooling fan, pulley, and drive belt.

6. Disconnect the heater hoses at the engine and move the hoses aside.

7. Disconnect the cables which are positioned above the valve cover and move the cables aside.

8. Remove the valve cover and upper front engine cover.

9. Disconnect and remove the glow plugs.

10. Disconnect the fuel injection lines at the injectors and the injection pump. Remove the lines.

11. Remove the fuel injectors. Arrange the injectors so that they may be reinstalled in their original locations.

12. Unbolt and remove the intake manifold assembly. Also remove the water outlet housing from the cylinder head.

13. Unbolt the exhaust manifold from the cylinder head. Secure the manifold in a position away from the cylinder head.

14. Disconnect the fuel feed line at the injection pump and plug the line.

15. Using a wrench on the center crankshaft pulley bolt, rotate the engine (clockwise only) until the TDC mark on the pulley is aligned with the pointer. Check that the valves on the number one cylinder are closed (rocker arms loose). If the valves are not closed, rotate the engine 360° and again align the TDC mark with the pointer.

16. Remove the crankshaft pulley using a puller.

17. Remove the timing belt cover from the front of the engine and the timing belt guide from the front of the crankshaft timing gear.

18. Remove the timing belt idler pulley. If the timing belt is to be reused, mark the belt and all timing gears to indicate their relationships. Remove the timing belt.

19. Remove the timing gear from the camshaft, using a puller.

20. Remove the camshaft oil seal retainer.

21. Gradually loosen the rocker shaft support nuts, working from the ends towards the center. Remove the rocker shaft and arms as an assembly.

22. Gradually remove the cylinder head bolts in the reverse order of the installation torque sequence.

23. Remove the cylinder head from the engine. Refer to the Unit Repair section for cylinder head service information.

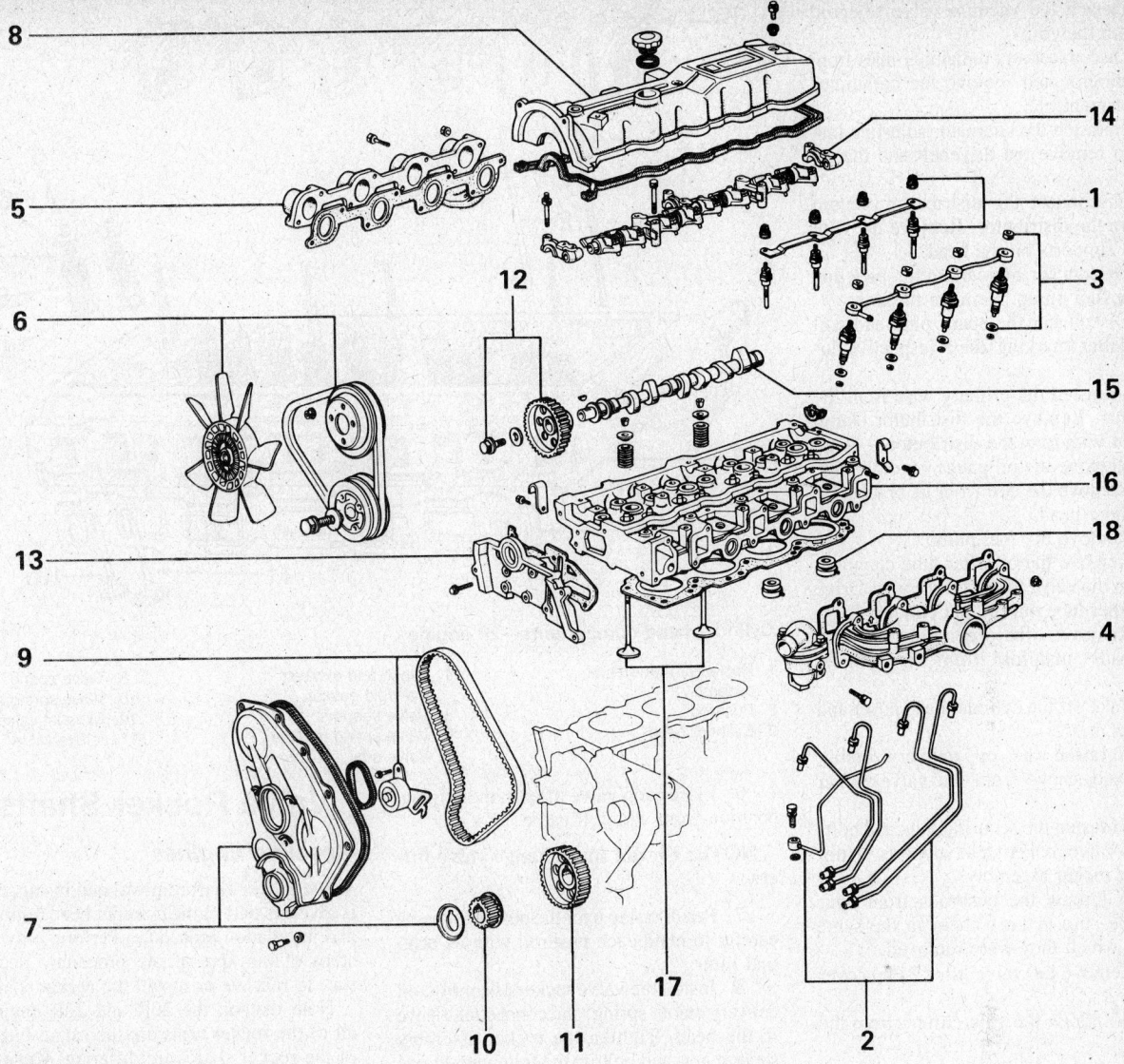

Cylinder head and related components—diesel engine

1. Glow plug
2. Injection pipe and fuel pipe
3. Injection nozzle holder and linkage pipe
4. Intake manifold
5. Exhaust manifold
6. Fan, fan pulley and crankshaft pulley
7. Timing gear cover and belt guide
8. Cylinder head cover
9. Idle pulley and timing belt
10. Crankshaft timing pulley
11. Pump drive pulley
12. Camshaft timing pulley
13. No. 2 oil seal retainer
14. Valve rocker shaft assembly
15. Camshaft
16. Cylinder head
17. Valve and compression spring
18. Combustion chamber subassembly

Installation of the cylinder head is basically the reverse of the previous steps. Note the following points:

a. Clean the mating surfaces of the cylinder block and head, and use a NEW head gasket during installation.

b. DO NOT rotate the engine while the cylinder head is removed.

c. Torque the cylinder head bolts gradually, following the head bolt tightening sequence.

d. Align the timing marks according to the illustration accompanying the Timing Belt Removal and Installation procedure.

e. Replenish the cooling system with the proper type and quantity of coolant.

f. Check for leaks after the engine has been started.

2F Engine

1. Disconnect the battery and drain the cooling system.

2. Remove the air cleaner assembly from its bracket, complete with its attendant hoses.

3. Detach the accelerator cable from its support on the cylinder head cover and also from the carburetor throttle arm.

4. Remove the choke cable and fuel lines from the carburetor.

5. Remove the water hose bracket from the cylinder head cover.

6. Unfasten the water hose clamps and remove the hoses from the water pump and the water valve. Detach the heater temperature control cable from the water valve.

7. Disconnect the PCV line from the cylinder head cover.

8. Disconnect the vacuum lines, which run from the vacuum switching valve, at the various components of the emission control system.

9. Drain the engine oil. Unfasten the oil lines from the oil filter and remove the filter assembly from the manifold.

10. Detach the vacuum valve solenoid wire from the coil.

11. Disconnect any remaining lines from the carburetor and remove the carburetor from the manifold.

12. Unfasten the alternator adjusting link and then remove the drivebelt and the alternator.

13. Disconnect the distributor vacuum line from the distributor. Remove the wire from its supports on the head.

14. Disconnect the carburetor fuel line from the fuel pump. Remove the line.

15. Disconnect the spark plug and coil cables, after marking their respective locations.

16. Unfasten the primary wire from the distributor. Remove the distributor clamp bolts and withdraw the distributor.

17. Remove the oil gauge sending unit.

18. Remove the coil from its bracket on the cylinder head.

19. Remove the fuel pump.

20. Remove the oil filter tube clamping bolt from the valve lifter (side) cover. Drive the oil filler tube out of the cylinder block.

21. Remove the combination intake/exhaust manifold from the cylinder block.

22. Take off the cylinder head cover and its gasket.

23. Unfasten the oil delivery union, spring, and sleeve from the valve rocker shafts.

24. Unfasten the securing nuts and bolts from the valve rocker shaft supports. Withdraw the rocker assembly.

25. Withdraw the pushrods from their bores. Be sure to keep them in the same order in which they were removed.

26. Remove the valve lifter (side) cover and gasket.

27. Withdraw the valve lifters from the block.

NOTE: The valve lifters should be kept, with their respective pushrods, in the sequence in which they were removed.

28. Unfasten the oil delivery union from the oil feed pipe.

29. Loosen the cylinder head bolts in two or three stages and in the order illustrated above.

30. Lift off the cylinder head and the gasket.

NOTE: Service procedures are covered in the Unit Repair Section.

Installation of the cylinder head is performed in the following order:

1. Clean the gasket mounting surfaces of both the cylinder head and block.

2. Place a *new* head gasket over the dowels on the block.

3. Lower the cylinder head on to the block with the air cleaner mounting bracket attached.

4. Tighten the bolts, in stages, and in the sequence illustrated, to the specified torque.

5. Install the oil feed pipe.

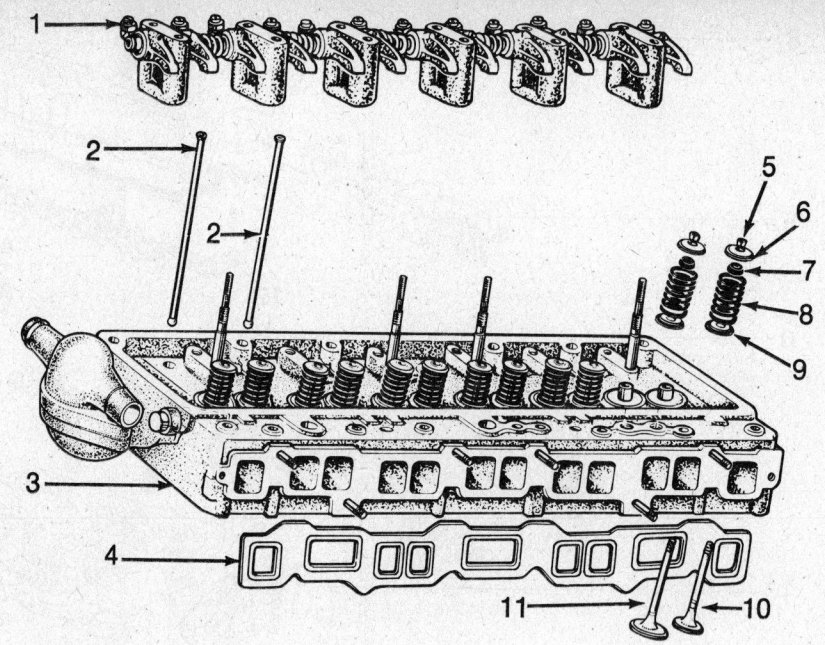

Cylinder head components—2F engine

1. Rocker arm and shaft assembly
2. Pushrods
3. Cylinder head
4. Intake and exhaust manifold gasket
5. Valve keepers
6. Valve spring retainer
7. Valve seal
8. Valve spring
9. Valve spring seat
10. Exhaust valve
11. Intake valve

6. Place each valve lifter in the original position from which it came.

NOTE: Do not interchange valve lifters.

7. Perform step 6 for the pushrods, being careful to mate each pushrod with its original lifter.

8. Install the valve rocker assembly, oil delivery union, spring, and connecting sleeve in the head. Tighten the rocker assembly support nuts and bolts to the following torque specifications, in several stages:

10mm nuts and bolts—25–30 ft. lbs.
8mm bolts—14–22 ft. lbs.

9. Adjust the valves, as outlined above, to the following *cold* specifications (each piston TDC of its compression stroke):

Intake—0.008 in.
Exhaust—0.014 in.

NOTE: Adjust the valve clearance again after the engine is assembled and warmed up.

10. The rest of cylinder head installation is performed in the reverse order of the removal procedure.

Valve Rocker Shafts

Gasoline Engines

Valve rocker shaft removal and installation is given as part of the cylinder head removal and installation procedure. Perform only the steps of the appropriate procedure necessary to remove or install the rocker shafts.

Note that on the 20R and 22R engines all of the rocker arms are the same, but all of the rocker shafts are different. Keep all parts in order so that they may be installed correctly. Lubricate all parts with engine oil prior to assembly.

Diesel Engine

1. Disconnect the cables which are positioned above the valve cover and move the cables aside.

2. Remove the valve cover.

3. Gradually loosen the rocker shaft support fasteners, working from the ends towards the center. Remove the rocker shaft and arms as an assembly. It is not necessary to remove the timing chain or related components.

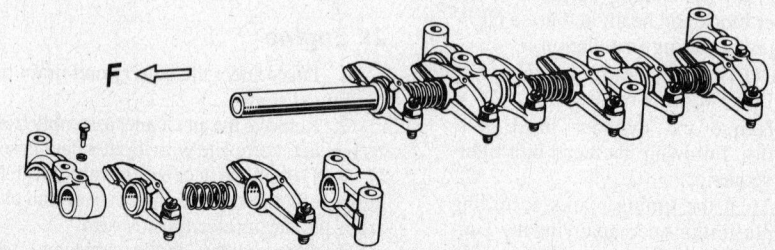

Rocker shaft assembly of the diesel engine

4. To install the rocker shaft assembly, gradually tighten the support bolts, working from the center towards the ends. Finally tighten the bolts to 11–15 ft. lbs.

5. Adjust the valves as previously outlined and install the valve cover. Reposition and connect the cables which were moved during step 1.

Intake Manifold

REMOVAL AND INSTALLATION

20R and 22R Engines

1. Disconnect the battery, negative cable first.

2. Drain the cooling system.

3. Remove the air cleaner assembly, complete with hoses.

4. Disconnect the vacuum lines from the EGR valve and the carburetor. Tag them for assembly.

5. Remove the fuel line, accelerator linkage, electrical leads, and coolant hose from the carburetor.

6. Remove the coolant bypass hose from the manifold.

7. Unbolt and remove the intake manifold, complete with carburetor and EGR valve.

8. Cover the cylinder head intake ports with a clean cloth.

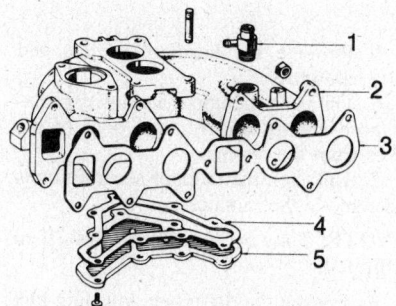

20R and 22R engine intake manifold components

1. Vacuum fitting
2. Intake manifold
3. Gasket
4. Gasket
5. Cover

Installation is the reverse of the removal. Use a new gasket, and torque the mounting nuts to 11–15 ft. lbs. Tighten the bolts in several stages, working from the inside bolts outward. Refill the cooling system.

Combination Manifold

REMOVAL AND INSTALLATION

2F Engines

1. Remove the air cleaner assembly, complete with hoses.

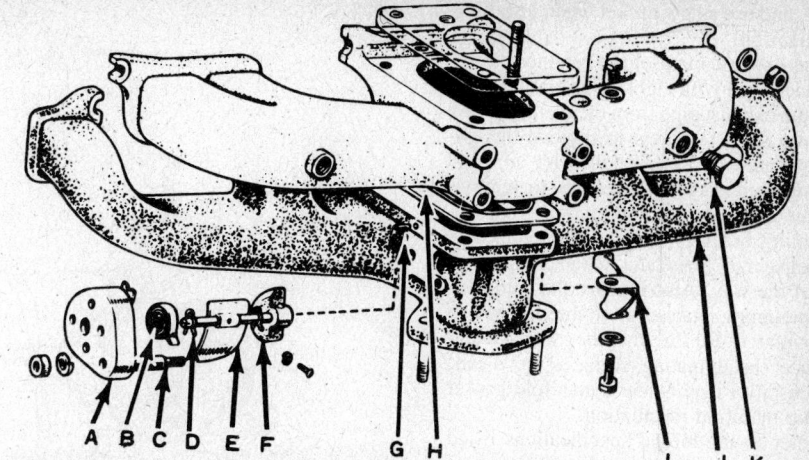

2F engine combination manifold components

a. Heat control valve bimetal case
b. Valve coil
c. Bolt
d. Retaining spring
e. Heat control valve
f. Heat control valve shaft
g. Dowel
h. Manifold gasket
i. Counter weight stop
j. Exhaust manifold
k. Screw plug

2. Disconnect the accelerator and choke linkages from the carburetor, as well as the fuel and vacuum lines. Remove the hand throttle linkage.

3. Remove, or move aside, any of the emission control system components which are in the way.

4. Disconnect the oil filter lines and remove the oil filter assembly from the intake manifold. Unfasten the solenoid valve wire from the ignition coil terminal. Remove the EGR pipes from the exhaust gas cooler, if so equipped.

5. Unfasten the retaining bolts and remove the carburetor from the manifold.

6. Loosen the manifold retaining nuts, working from the inside out, in two or three stages.

7. Remove the intake/exhaust manifold assembly from the cylinder head as a complete unit.

Installation is performed in the reverse order of removal. Always use *new* gaskets. Tighten the bolts, working from the inside out.

NOTE: Tighten the bolts in two or three stages.

Exhaust Manifold

REMOVAL AND INSTALLATION

20R and 22R Engines

1. Remove the three exhaust pipe flange bolts and disconnect the exhaust pipe from the manifold.

2. Disconnect the spark plug leads.

3. Matchmark the distributor rotor, housing and the engine block. Remove the distributor.

4. Remove the air cleaner tube from the heat stove. Remove the outer part of the heat stove.

5. Remove the manifold (14 mm nuts), complete with air injection tubes and the inner portion of the heat stove.

6. Separate the inner portion of the heat stove from the manifold.

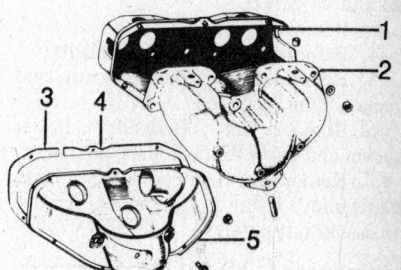

20R and 22R engine exhaust manifold components

1. Inner heat stove
2. Exhaust manifold
3. Gasket
4. Gasket
5. Outer heat stove

Installation is the reverse of removal. Tighten the retaining nuts to 29–36 ft. lbs., working from the inside out. Install the distributor and set the timing. Tighten the exhaust pipe flange nuts to 25–32 ft. lbs.

Diesel Manifolding

Removal of the intake manifold of the diesel engine requires removal of the air cleaner assembly, injection lines, and related hoses and bracketry. If you are in doubt during the disconnection of any item, be sure to mark the item so that it may be properly reinstalled. Before installing the manifold, be sure to clean the cylinder head and manifold mating surfaces of the old gasket material, and use a new gasket when installing the manifold.

The exhaust manifold is retained to the cylinder head with eight fasteners. Disconnect the exhaust pipe from the manifold and remove these fasteners to remove the exhaust manifold. On models with air conditioning, it may be necessary to remove the air conditioning compressor from the mounting brackets (without disconnecting the refrigerant lines) and tie the compressor out of the way. Also remove the compressor mounting bracket(s) if interference is encountered. Be sure that the manifold and cylinder head mating surfaces are clean, and install a new exhaust manifold gasket during manifold installation.

Refer to the torque specifications listed at the beginning of this secion to determine the required tightening torque of the fasteners.

Timing Gear Cover

REMOVAL AND INSTALLATION

20R and 22R Engines

1. Remove the cylinder head as previously outlined.
2. After draining oil, remove the oil pan and its gasket.
3. Remove the radiator.
4. Remove the fan and drive belts.
5. Remove the air pump, hoses, and bracket, if so equipped.
6. Remove the alternator adjuster bracket and move it towards the alternator.
7. Remove the center bolt on the crankshaft pulley. Using a gear puller, remove the crankshaft pulley.

——————— CAUTION ———————
Do not remove the 10 mm bolt from the hole in the pulley, if present. It has been installed to correctly balance the engine.

8. Remove the 2 water bypass tube bolts, the one bolt at the rear of the cover on the left side (behind the coolant inlet pipe), and the six bolts on the front of the timing cover. Gently tap the timing cover off with a plas-

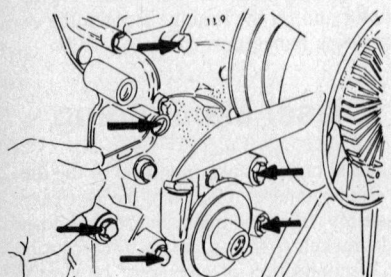

20R and 22R engines—only the six bolts indicated need to be removed to remove the timing cover

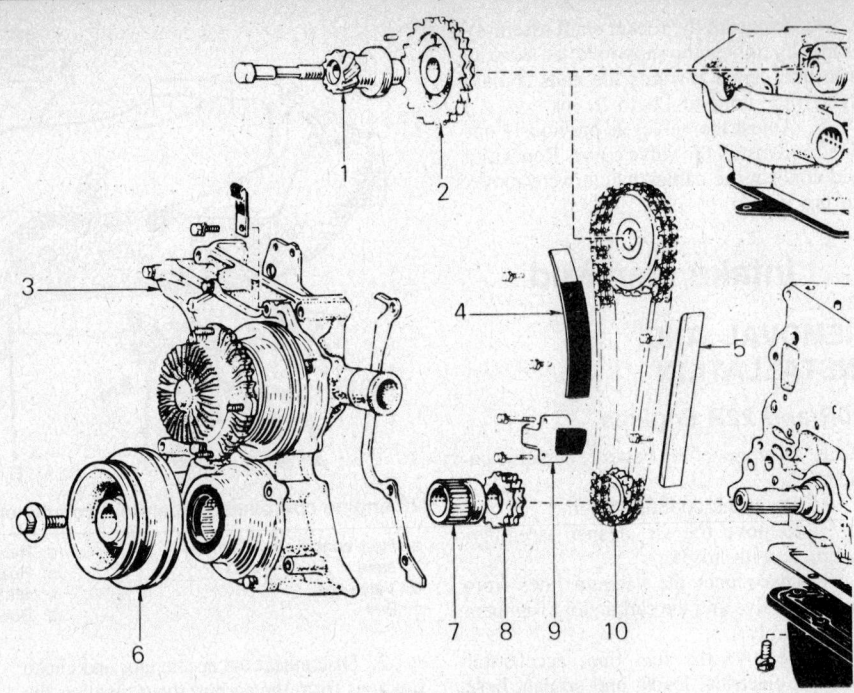

Timing cover and related components—20R and 22R engines

I. Distributor drive gear		6. Crankshaft pulley	
2. Cam sprocket		7. Pump drive spline	
3. Timing chain cover		8. Crankshaft sprocket	
4. Chain damper #2		9. Chain tensioner	
5. Chain damper #1		10. Timing chain	

tic faced hammer. If removal is difficult, there is probably a bolt still in place.
9. When installing, use a new gasket on the timing cover and oil pan. Use sealer at the corners of the oil pan. Tighten the timing cover bolts to 7–12 ft. lbs. Tighten the oil pan bolts to 35–70 in. lbs.
10. Install the crankshaft pulley. Tighten the bolt to 80–94 ft. lbs.

——————— CAUTION ———————
Do not allow the pulley to rotate when tightening the pulley bolt.

11. Further installation is the reverse of removal.

Diesel Engine

Refer to steps 1–8, then 15–17 of the Cylinder Head Removal and Installation procedure. Torque the timing belt cover fasteners to 3–5 ft. lbs., and the crankshaft pulley center bolt to 69–75 ft. lbs.

2F Engines

1. Drain the cooling system and the crankcase.
2. Disconnect the battery.
3. Remove the air cleaner assembly, complete with hoses, from its bracket.
4. Remove the hood latch as well as its brace and support.

5. Remove the headlight bezels and grille assembly.
6. Unfasten the upper and lower radiator hose clamps and remove both of the hoses from the engine.
7. Unfasten the radiator securing bolts and remove the radiator.

NOTE: Take off the shroud first, if so equipped.

8. Loosen the drive belt adjusting link and remove the drive belt. Unfasten the alternator multiconnector, withdraw the retaining bolts, and remove the alternator.
9. Perform step 8 to the air injection pump, if so equipped. Disconnect the hoses from the pump before removing it.
10. Remove the fan and water pump as an assembly.
11. Remove the crankshaft pulley with a gear puller.
12. Remove the gravel shield from underneath the engine.
13. Remove the front driveshaft.
14. Remove the front oil pan bolts, to gain access to the bottom of the timing chain cover.

NOTE: It may be necessary to insert a thin knife between the pan and the gasket in order to break the pan loose. Use care not to damage the gasket.

Installation is the reverse of removal. Be sure to adjust the drive belts.

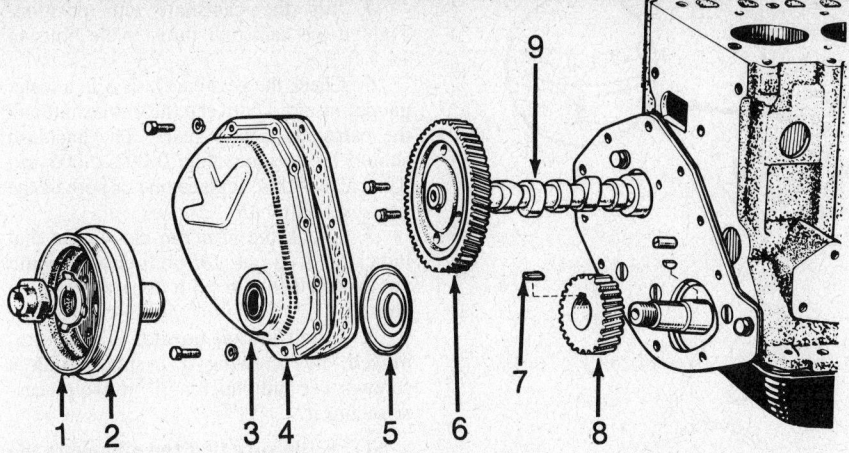

Timing gears, cover and related components—2F engines

1. Crankshaft pulley
2. Balancer
3. Timing cover seal
4. Timing cover
5. Oil slinger
6. Crankshaft
7. Crankshaft key
8. Crankshaft gear
9. Camshaft

Timing Gear Cover Oil Seal

REMOVAL AND INSTALLATION

All Engines

1. Remove the timing chain or belt cover, as previously outlined.
2. Inspect the oil seal for signs of wear, leakage, or damage.
3. If worn, pry the old oil seal out, using a large flat-bladed screwdriver. Remove it toward the *front* of the cover.

NOTE: Once the oil seal has been removed, it must be replaced.

4. Use a socket, pipe, or block of wood and a hammer to drive the oil seal into place. Work from the *front* of the cover.

—— CAUTION ——
Be extremely careful not to damage the seal.

5. Install the timing chain or belt cover as outlined above.

Timing Chain and Tensioner

REMOVAL AND INSTALLATION

20R and 22R Engines

1. Remove the cylinder head and timing chain cover as previously outlined.
2. Remove the chain from the dampers and remove the chain and cam sprocket together.
3. If the chain and sprocket are worn, they will have to be replaced, along with the crankshaft sprocket. Pull the crankshaft sprocket and pump drive spline as a unit, using a gear puller.
4. Measure the chain tensioner for wear. If it is worn below 0.43 in., replace it as a unit.
5. Measure the chain dampers for wear. If either is visibly worn or measures below the limit, replace as a unit.
Damper #1   0.20 in.
Damper #2   0.18 in.
To install:
1. After installing any necessary dampers or a new tensioner, turn the crankshaft by hand until the key is at TDC. If removed, slide the crankshaft sprocket over the key. Place the chain on the sprocket so that the single bright link is over the mark on the sprocket.

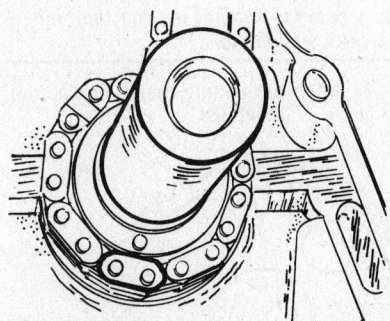

20R and 22R engines—align the crankshaft gear mark with the single bright link of the timing chain

2. Position the cam sprocket in the chain so that the timing mark on the sprocket is located between the two bright links of the chain.
3. Install the oil pump drive spline over the crankshaft key, if removed.
4. After cleaning the old gasket surface thoroughly, install a new cover gasket over the locating dowels.

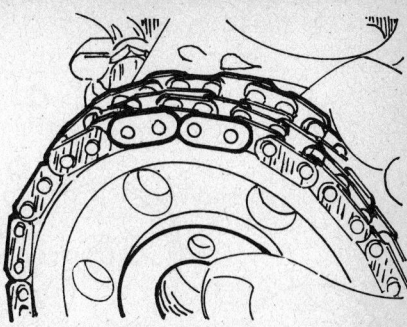

20R and 22R engines—align the camshaft sprocket mark between the two bright links of the timing chain

5. Turn the camshaft sprocket counterclockwise to take any slack out of the chain.
6. Install the timing chain cover and cylinder head as previously outlined.

Timing Belt

REMOVAL AND INSTALLATION

Diesel Engine

The diesel timing belt may be removed by following steps 1–8, then 15–18 of the Cylinder Head Removal and Installation procedure. To install the belt:

1. Temporarily install the idler pulley and check that the pulley bracket can be moved to the left and right by hand.
2. Align each timing gear according to the accompanying illustration. Note that the injection pump gear is positioned in a slightly retarded manner.

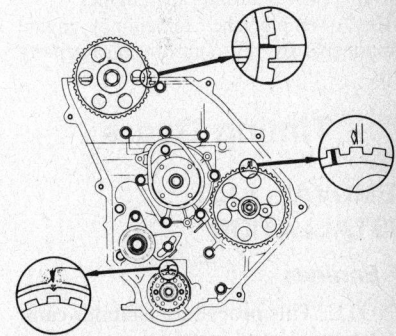

Preliminary timing gear positioning—see text (diesel engine)

3. Install the timing belt without altering the position of any timing gear.
4. Install the idler pulley spring.
5. Temporarily install the crankshaft timing gear center bolt and turn the crankshaft exactly two revolutions (clockwise). As you turn the crankshaft, you should notice movement of the idler pulley bracket.
6. Each timing gear should now align as shown in the accompanying illustration. Note that the injection pump gear marking should now be aligned with the corresponding "diamond" mark on the engine.

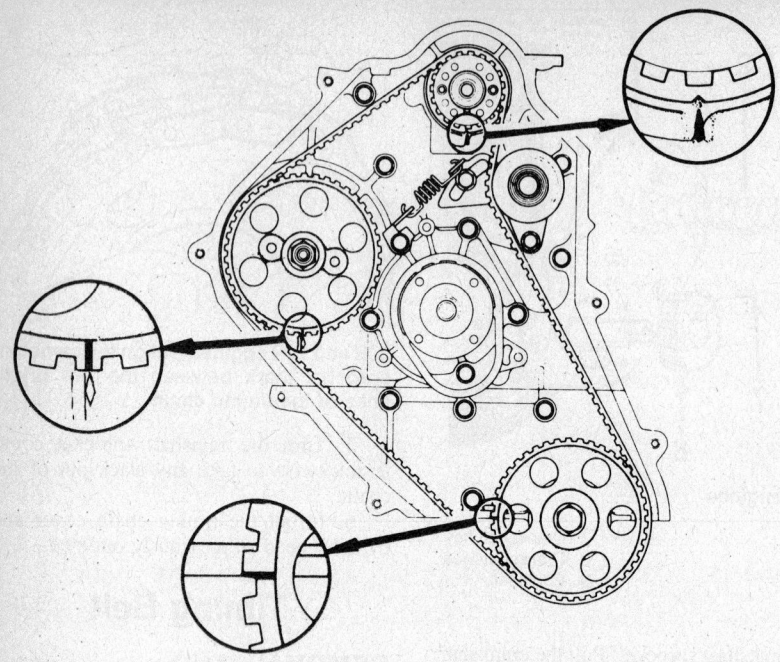

Final view of the timing marks after the crankshaft is turned twice—see text (diesel engine)

7. Tighten the idler pulley bolts to 11–15 ft. lbs.

CAUTION
DO NOT move the idler pulley bracket while tightening the bolts.

8. Install the timing cover and tighten the cover fasteners to 3–5 ft. lbs.

9. Install the crankshaft belt drive pulley. Dip the pulley retaining bolt in engine oil, install the bolt and tighten to 69–75 ft. lbs. WITHOUT turning the engine.

10. Assemble the remaining engine components by reversing the disassembly steps.

Timing Gears

REMOVAL AND INSTALLATION

2F Engines

NOTE: This procedure contains camshaft removal and installation.

1. Perform the cylinder head and timing cover removal procedures, as previously outlined.

2. Slip the oil slinger off the crankshaft.

3. Remove the camshaft thrust plate retaining bolts by working through the holes provided in the camshaft timing gear.

4. Remove the camshaft through the front of the cylinder block. Support the camshaft while removing it, so as not to damage its bearings or lobes.

NOTE: The timing gear is a press-fit and cannot be removed without removing the camshaft.

5. Inspect the crankshaft timing gear. Replace it if it has worn or damaged teeth.

6. To remove it, remove the sliding key from the crankshaft. Withdraw the timing gear with a gear puller.

Installation is performed in the following order:

1. Use a large piece of pipe to press the timing gear onto the crankshaft. Lightly and evenly tap the end of the pipe until the gear is in its original position.

2. Apply a coat of engine oil to the camshaft journals and bearings.

3. Insert the camshaft into the block.

CAUTION
Use care not to damage the camshaft lobes, bearings, or journals.

4. Align the mating marks on each of the gears as illustrated.

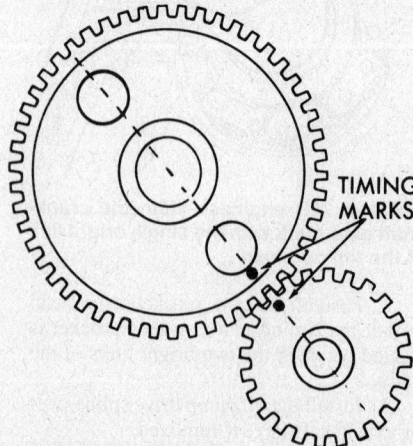

2F engines—align the camshaft and crankshaft gear marks

5. Slip the camshaft into position. Tighten the camshaft thrust plate bolts to 14.5 ft. lbs.

6. Check the gear backlash with a feeler gauge, inserted between the crankshaft and the camshaft timing gears. The backlash should be no more than 0.002–0.005 in.; if it exceeds this, replace one or both of the gears, as required.

7. Check the gear run-out with a dial indicator. Run-out, for both gears, should not exceed 0.008 in.; if it does, replace the gear.

8. Install the oil nozzle, if it was removed, by screwing it in place with a screwdriver and punching it in two places, to secure it.

NOTE: Be sure that the oil hole in the nozzle is pointed toward the timing gear before securing it.

9. Install the oil slinger on the crankshaft.

10. Install the timing gear cover and cylinder head, as outlined above.

Camshaft

REMOVAL AND INSTALLATION

20R and 22R Engines

NOTE: To service the 2F engine camshaft, refer to the previous Timing Gear Removal and Installation procedure.

20R and 22R Engines

1. Disconnect the negative battery cable at the battery.

2. Remove the air cleaner assembly. Mark all of the hose locations to simplify installation.

3. Drain the radiator and remove the upper radiator hose.

4. Disconnect the flexible hoses at the fuel pump and remove the fuel pump. Replace the fuel pump gasket during installation, if necessary.

5. Remove the valve cover. Mark all of the attaching parts to simplify installation.

6. Mark and disconnect the spark plug wires at the spark plugs. Remove the spark plugs.

7. Rotate the engine while holding your finger over the number one spark plug hole. As pressure builds in the number one cylinder, watch the timing marks at the crankshaft damper and align the marks at top dead center.

8. Paint reference marks on both the cam sprocket and the timing chain to indicate their relationship for installation.

9. Remove the distributor cap (with wires intact) and move it out of the way.

10. Mark the position of the distributor rotor on the distributor housing.

11. Mark the position of the distributor housing and the cylinder head, indicating

the relationship between these two components.

12. Disconnect the distributor primary wire and remove the distributor.

13. Remove the half circle seal from the cylinder head.

14. Remove the cam sprocket bolt, the distributor drive gear and the fuel pump eccentric.

15. Remove the rocker shafts as previously outlined.

16. Measure the camshaft thrust clearance using a feeler gauge inserted between the thrust bearing and the cylinder head. If the clearance is greater than 0.0098 in., the cylinder head must be replaced.

17. Remove the camshaft journal caps.

NOTE: The camshaft may now be lifted out of the cylinder head but it is recommended that you continue with the following checking procedures.

18. Check the camshaft journal caps for damage. Clean all of the bearing surfaces, including the caps, cam journal, and the cylinder head.

19. With the camshaft in place on the cylinder head, lay small strips of plastigage on each of the camshaft journals (at the tops of the journals, facing front-to-rear).

20. Reinstall the journal caps in their original locations (arrows facing forward), and torque the caps to 13–16 ft. lbs.

21. Remove the journal caps and gauge the width of the plastigage against the chart on the plastigage package. Maximum journal clearance is 0.004 in. If the journal clearance is greater than specified, measure the cam journal diameters with a micrometer (or have a professional machine shop do so). If the diameter of any cam journal is less than specified, obtain a new camshaft and recheck the journal clearance. If the clearance is still excessive, the cylinder head must be replaced.

To install the camshaft, position it in the cylinder head, install the journal caps (torque to specification), and reverse steps 1–15. Be sure to align all the reference marks made during removal. Replenish the cooling system. If a new cam is installed, use an assembly lube (available at most auto stores) on the cam lobes and engine oil on the journals. If the old cam is damaged excessively (lobes worn round, etc.) change the engine oil and filter.

NOTE: If any of the reference marks made during removal will not align during assembly, remove the timing chain and re-time the engine as previously outlined.

Diesel Engine

Refer to step 1–8, then 15–21 of the Cylinder Head Removal and Installation procedure. The journal clearances are checked in the same manner as the 20R and 22R engines.

During Installation, note the following fastener torque values: rocker shaft supports—11–15 ft. lbs.; camshaft timing gear set bolt—69–75 ft. lbs.; oil seal retainer—8–12 ft. lbs. Refer to the Timing Belt Removal and Installation procedure to properly install the timing belt.

Pistons and Connecting Rods

REMOVAL

1. Remove the following components as outlined in the appropriate sections of this chapter:
   a. Cylinder head
   b. Oil pan
   c. Oil pump (not necessary on 20R and 22R engines)
   d. Oil strainer

NOTE: Details of the following steps can be found in the Engine Rebuilding section.

2. Remove the cylinder ridges with a ridge reamer.

3. Measure the connecting rod side clearance.

4. Mark the connecting rods and caps.

5. Remove the connecting rod cap of the number one cylinder and check the oil clearance with plastigage. Record the clearance and compare with the specification chart. Repeat this step for each connecting rod.

6. With the number one connecting rod cap removed, install a short piece of rubber hose onto each connecting rod bolt (the hose must completely cover the bolt).

7. Using a wooden or plastic handle (an old hammer handle works well), carefully tap the piston/connecting rod assembly out of the cylinder. Do not use excessive force as this could damage the connecting rods. Repeat this step for each cylinder.

8. Refer to the Engine Rebuilding Section for checking the piston/connecting rod assembly and for installing these parts in the cylinder block.

9. Reinstall the oil strainer, oil pump, oil pan and cylinder head following the appropriate procedures.

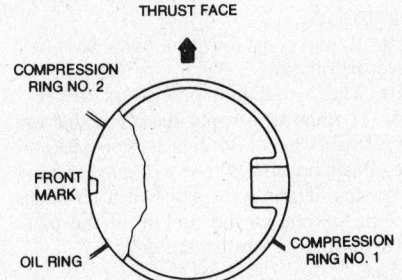

20R and 22R engines—after installing the piston rings, rotate each ring so that the ring gaps are positioned as shown. Failure to stagger the ring gaps will result in excessive oil consumption.

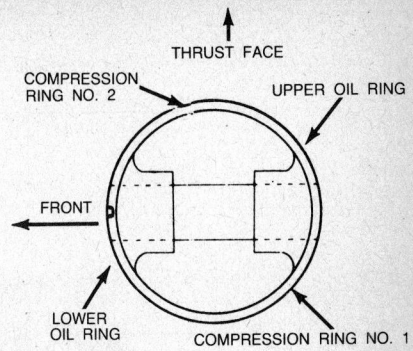

2F engines—after installing the piston rings, rotate each ring so that the ring gaps are positioned as shown. Failure to stagger the ring gaps will result in excessive oil consumption.

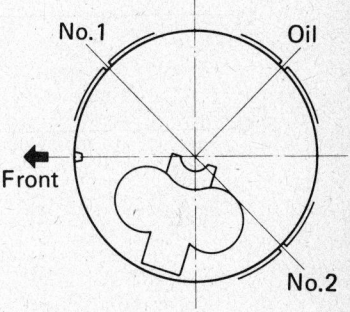

Piston ring gap staggering—diesel engine

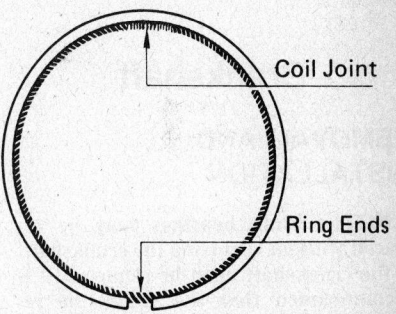

Oil ring installation on the diesel piston—position the ends of the expander opposite the ring gap

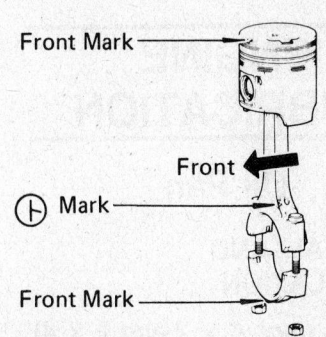

Piston and connecting rod installation—diesel engine

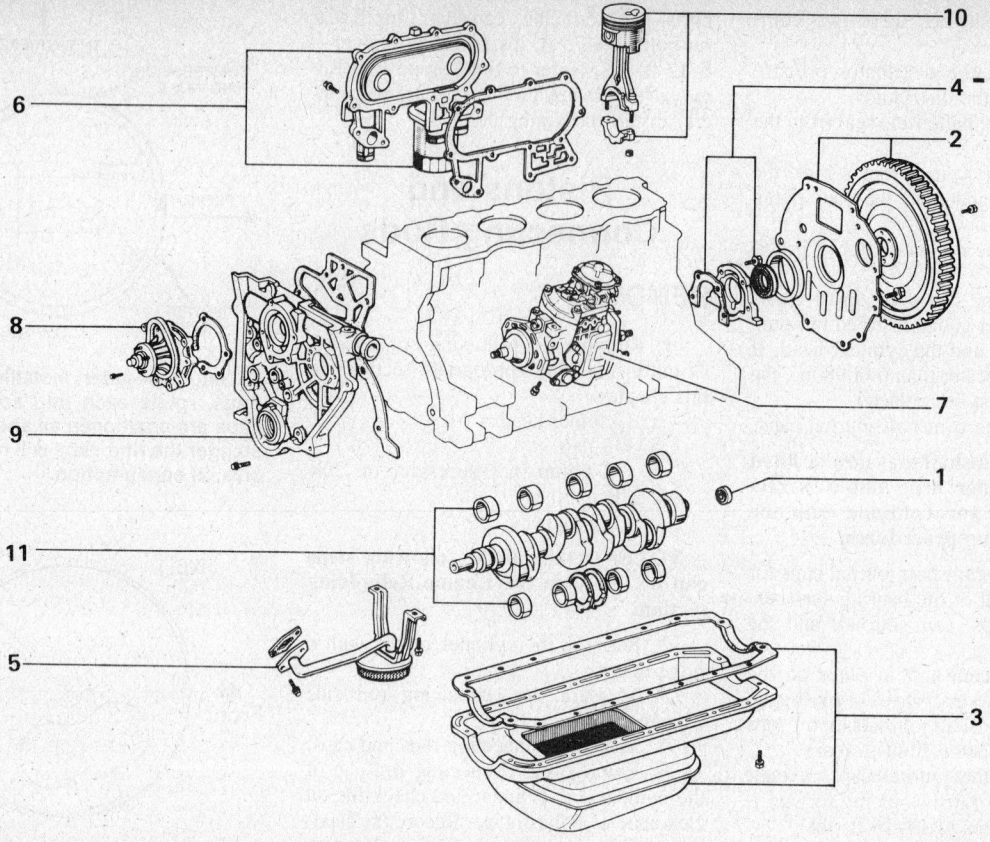

Exploded view of the diesel cylinder block

1. Input shaft bearing
2. Flywheel and rear end plate
3. Oil pan
4. Rear oil seal
5. Oil strainer
6. Oil filter bracket
7. Injection pump
8. Water pump
9. Timing belt case
10. Piston and connecting rod
11. Crankshaft

Crankshaft

REMOVAL AND INSTALLATION

NOTE: Main bearings may be replaced without removing the crankshaft. If the crankshaft must be removed, it is recommended that the engine be removed from the vehicle and mounted in a work stand. Refer to the Engine Rebuilding Section.

ENGINE LUBRICATION

Oil Pan

REMOVAL AND INSTALLATION

Pick-ups (Incl. 4 × 2 and 4 × 4)

1. Raise the hood and leave it open for the duration of this repair.

2. Drain the engine oil.
3. Raise the front end of the truck and support it on jackstands.
4. Remove the steering relay rod and the tie-rods from the idler arm, pitman arm, and steering knuckles as outlined in the Front Suspension section.
5. Remove the engine stiffening plates.
6. Remove the splash pans from under the engine.
7. Support the front of the engine with a jack and remove the front motor mount attaching bolts.
8. Raise the front of the engine slightly with the jack.
9. Remove the oil pan bolts and remove the oil pan.
10. The installation process is the reverse of removal. Apply gasket sealer to the oil pan when installing a new gasket. The oil pan bolts should be tightened to 33–70 in. lbs. Tighten the bolts in a circular pattern, starting in the middle of the pan and working out toward the ends.

Land Cruiser

1. Remove the engine skid plates.
2. Remove the flywheel side cover and skid plate.

3. Disconnect the front driveshaft from the engine.
4. Drain the engine oil.
5. Remove the bolts which secure the oil pan; remove the pan and its gasket.
6. Installation is performed in the reverse order from removal. Always use a new pan gasket.

Oil Pump

REMOVAL AND INSTALLATION

20R and 22R Engines

1. Drain the oil, and remove the oil pan and the oil strainer and pick-up tube.
2. Remove the drive belts from the crankshaft pulley.
3. Remove the crankshaft bolt, and remove the pulley with a gear puller, as outlined in the timing chain cover section.
4. Remove the five bolts from the oil pump and remove the oil pump assembly. Refer to the oil pump specification chart to check the oil pump clearances.

Check the timing chain cover for excessive wear or damage. If necessary, replace the gears or pump body or cover. Unbolt the relief valve (the vertical bolt on the pump body when attached to the engine) and check the piston, oil passages, and sliding surfaces for burrs or scoring. Inspect the crankshaft front oil seal and replace if worn or damaged.

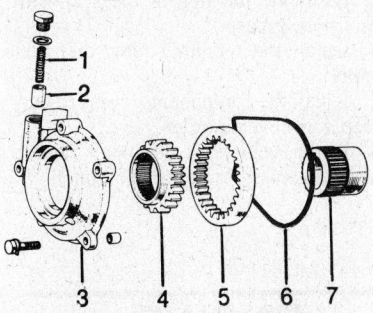

1. Relief valve spring
2. Relief valve
3. Pump body
4. Drive gear
5. Driven gear
6. O-ring
7. Drive spline

Exploded view of the 20R and 22R engine oil pump

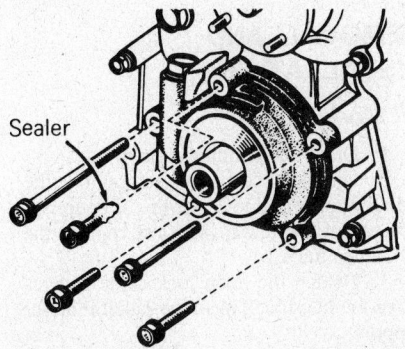

Mounting of the 20R and 22R engine oil pump—apply sealer to the upper mounting bolt as shown

When installing, use a new O-ring if necessary. Apply sealer to the upper bolt and install the five bolts. Install the crankshaft pulley as outlined in the timing cover section, and use a new gasket on the oil strainer and oil pan. Be sure to apply sealer to the

corners of the oil pan gasket before installing the pan. Also, apply sealer to the uppermost oil pump bolt threads before installing this bolt.

Diesel Engine

1. Disconnect the cables which are positioned above the valve cover and move the cables aside. Remove the valve cover.

2. Disconnect the cables from both batteries.

3. Using a wrench on the center crankshaft pulley bolt, rotate the engine (clockwise only) until the TDC mark on the pulley is aligned with the pointer. Check that the valves of the number one cylinder are closed (rocker arms loose). If the valves are not closed, rotate the engine 360° and again align the TDC mark with the pointer.

4. Remove the following components as previously outlined:
   a. Oil pan and pump strainer assembly
   b. Timing cover and belt

5. Disconnect the wiring from the alternator. Remove the alternator and the mounting brackets.

6. If equipped with air conditioning, unbolt the air conditioning compressor and tie it out of the way (without disconnecting the refrigerant hoses). Also remove the compressor bracketry.

7. Refer to the Diesel Fuel System section and remove the fuel injection pump.

8. Remove the crankshaft timing gear, using a puller.

9. Unbolt and remove the water pump.

10. Unbolt and remove the timing case assembly.

11. Remove the oil pump cover plate from the rear of the timing case assembly to gain access to the oil pump. Clearances are checked in the same manner as the pump used in the 20R and 22R engines.

12. Remove the pump gears and check the gears and timing case gear surfaces for damage or excessive wear.

13. Install the gears with the triangular markings of each gear facing the pump plate side of the timing case. Install the pump cover plate.

14. Reverse steps 1–10 to complete the installation. Note that all gasket surfaces must be cleaned, and that damaged gaskets must be replaced. Be sure to follow the

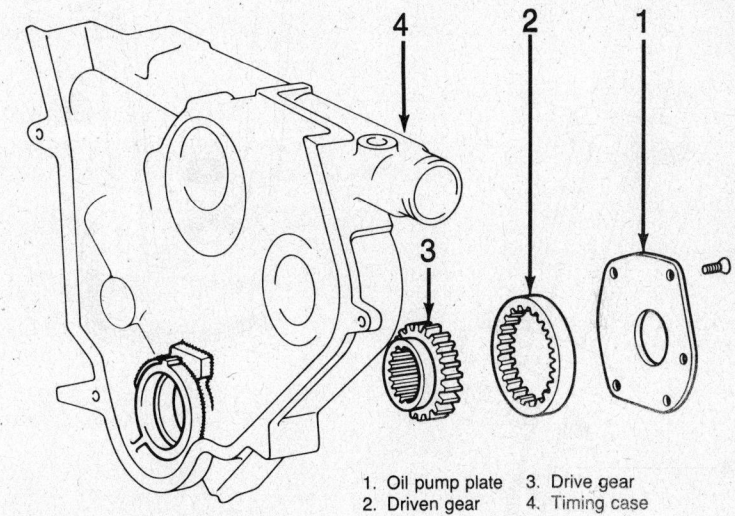

1. Oil pump plate
2. Driven gear
3. Drive gear
4. Timing case

Exploded view of the diesel oil pump

OIL PUMP CLEARANCE SPECIFICATIONS
(All measurements in inches)

Engine	Maximum Gear Tip Clearance①	Maximum Gear Backlash②	Side Clearance③	Cover Wear④	Body Clearance⑤
2F	0.008	0.037	0.006	0.006	—
20R,22R,L	0.012	—	0.006	—	0.008

① 2F Engines: Measured between the gear teeth of each gear and the pump body.
  20R,22R and L Engines: Measured between the gear teeth of each gear and the crescent.

② Measured between the gear teeth with the gears meshed together.
③ Measured between a straightedge positioned across the oil pump body and the gear faces.

④ Measured between a straightedge positioned across the cover and the cover wear (gear contact) surface.
⑤ Measured between the oil pump driven gear and the pump body.

specific procedures concerning timing belt installation and fuel injection pump installation, as outlined previously and in the Diesel Fuel System section.

2F Engines

1. Remove the oil pan as previously outlined.

2. Remove the oil strainer and unfasten the union nuts on the oil pump pipe.

3. Remove the lock wire and the oil pump retaining bolt and pipe from the engine.

4. Remove the oil pump cover and inspect the following parts for nicks, scoring, grooving, etc.:
   a. pump cover
   b. drive and driven gears
   c. pump body.

5. Replace either the damaged parts or the complete pump if damage is excessive. See the Oil Pump Specification chart to check the oil pump clearances.

6. Installation is the reverse of steps 1–3.

NOTE: Be sure to check all of the gaskets and replace if necessary.

Rear Main Seal

REMOVAL AND INSTALLATION

All Engines

1. Remove the following components as outlined in the appropriate sections of this chapter:
   a. Transmission
   b. Torque convertor (auto. trans.)
   c. Clutch cover and disc (manual trans.)
   d. Flywheel
   e. Oil pan

2. Remove the oil seal retaining plate and seal assembly.

3. Carefully pry or drive the old seal from the retaining plate. Be careful not to damage the retaining plate.

4. Install a new seal using either a block of wood or a seal driver (preferred) to firmly seat the new seal.

5. Lubricate the lips of the seal with multipurpose grease.

6. Install the retaining plate and seal assembly.

7. Install the components removed during step 1 in reverse order.

8. If the vehicle is equipped with a manual transmission, adjust the clutch.

ENGINE COOLING

Radiator

REMOVAL AND INSTALLATION

All Models

1. Drain the cooling system.

2. Unfasten the clamps and remove the radiator upper and lower hoses. If equipped with an automatic transmission, remove the oil cooler lines.

3. Detach the hood lock cable and remove the hood lock from the radiator upper support.

NOTE: It may be necessary to remove the grille in order to gain access to the hood lock/radiator support assembly.

4. Remove the fan shroud, if so equipped.

5. On models equipped with a closed cooling system, disconnect the hose from the thermal expansion tank and remove the tank from its bracket.

6. Unbolt and remove the radiator upper support.

7. Unfasten and remove the radiator.

Installation is performed in the reverse order of removal. Remember to check the transmission fluid level on cars with automatic transmissions.

Fill the radiator to the specified level.

Water Pump

REMOVAL AND INSTALLATION

All Engines

1. Drain the cooling system.

2. Unfasten the fan shroud securing bolts and remove the fan shroud, if so equipped.

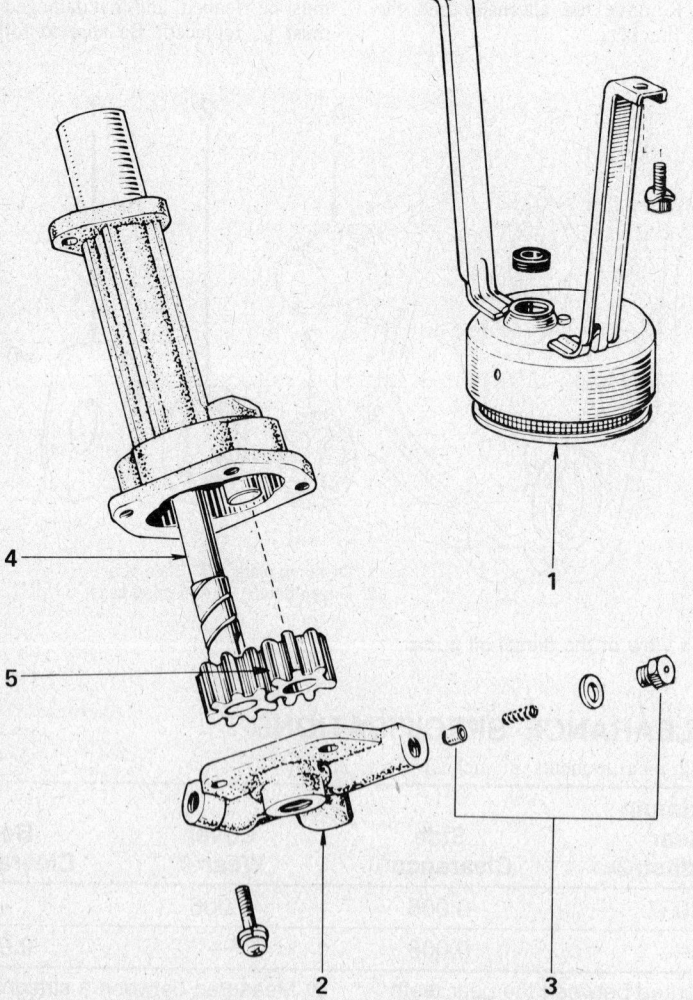

Exploded view of the 2F engine oil pump

1. Strainer
2. Pump cover
3. Pressure relief valve
4. Drive gear
5. Driven gear

3. Loosen the alternator adjusting link bolt and remove the drive belt.

4. Repeat step 3 for the air pump, air conditioning compressor, or power steering pump drive belts, if so equipped.

5. Detach the bypass and radiator hoses from the water pump.

6. Unfasten the water pump retaining bolts and remove the water pump and fan assembly, using care not to damage the radiator with the fan.

— CAUTION —

If the fan is equipped with a fluid coupling, do not tip the fan/pump assembly on its side, as the fluid will run out.

Installation is the reverse of removal. Always use a new gasket between the pump body and its mounting. Check for leaks after installation is completed.

Thermostat

REMOVAL AND INSTALLATION

All Engines

1. Partially drain the cooling system.

2. Unless the upper radiator hose is positioned over one of the thermostat housing (water outlet) bolts, it is not necessary to detach the hose.

3. Remove the bolts and remove the water outlet.

4. When installing a new thermostat always use a new gasket. Be sure that the thermostat is positioned with the spring down.

EMISSION CONTROLS

Positive Crankcase Ventilation System

A positive crankcase ventilation (PCV) system is used on all engines. Blow-by gases are routed from the crankcase to the carburetor where they are combined with the air/fuel mixture and burned in the cylinders.

A valve is used to prevent the gases in the crankcase from being ignited in the event of a backfire. The quantity of blow-by gases is also regulated by the PCV valve which is spring-loaded and has a variable orifice. The valve is mounted on the valve cover of the engine and should be replaced every 24,000 miles, on 1976–78 trucks, and 30,000 miles on 1979 and later trucks.

REMOVAL AND INSTALLATION

To remove the valve simply disconnect the hose from the top of the valve and remove the valve from the rubber grommet in the valve cover.

TESTING

Check the PCV system hoses and connections to determine that there are no leaks, then tighten or replace as necessary.

To check the operation of the valve, remove it and blow through both of its ends. When blowing through the end which goes toward the intake manifold, very little air should pass through the valve. When blowing from the valve cover side, the air should pass freely.

If the valve does not perform in this manner, replace it with a new valve.

NOTE: Toyota does not recommend cleaning of the PCV valve or any adjustments.

Evaporative Emission Control System

Toyota trucks are equipped with evaporative emission control (EEC) systems which prevent hydrocarbon emissions (fuel vapors) originating at the carburetor and the fuel tank from entering the atmosphere. All models use a charcoal canister vapor storage system.

While the engine is off, fuel vapors from the carburetor fuel bowl and the fuel tank are absorbed into the charcoal canister. On some later engines, this occurs even during idling and very low vehicle speeds. When the engine is started, and on some later engines when certain conditions are met (engine temperature, engine speed, vehicle speed), the vapors from the charcoal canister are drawn through the intake manifold to the combustion chambers to be burned with the air/fuel mixture from the carburetor. As the vapors are drawn from the canister, a slight vacuum is created in the canister. This vacuum draws fresh air into the canister through the canister filter. The fresh air purifies the charcoal so that it may be re-used.

Required maintenance for 1978 and earlier vehicles includes replacement of the charcoal canister at 50,000 mile intervals. On 1979 and later models the charcoal canister should be checked at 30,000 and 60,000 miles. Replacement of the charcoal canister is not necessary for these models.

Throttle Positioner (TP)

During rapid deceleration large volumes of fuel/air mixture are drawn into the cylinders due to high manifold vacuum. If the throttle plates close completely there is not sufficient oxygen to permit complete combustion. Therefore a throttle positioner is installed to keep the throttle plates slightly open during deceleration. Vacuum is reduced under the throttle valve which, in turn, acts on the retard chamber of the distributor vacuum unit. This ignition retard compensates for the loss of engine braking caused by the partially-opened throttle.

Once the vehicle drops below a predetermined speed, the vacuum switching valve provides vacuum to the throttle positioner diaphragm. The throttle positioner then retracts allowing the throttle valve to close completely. The distributor also returns to normal operation.

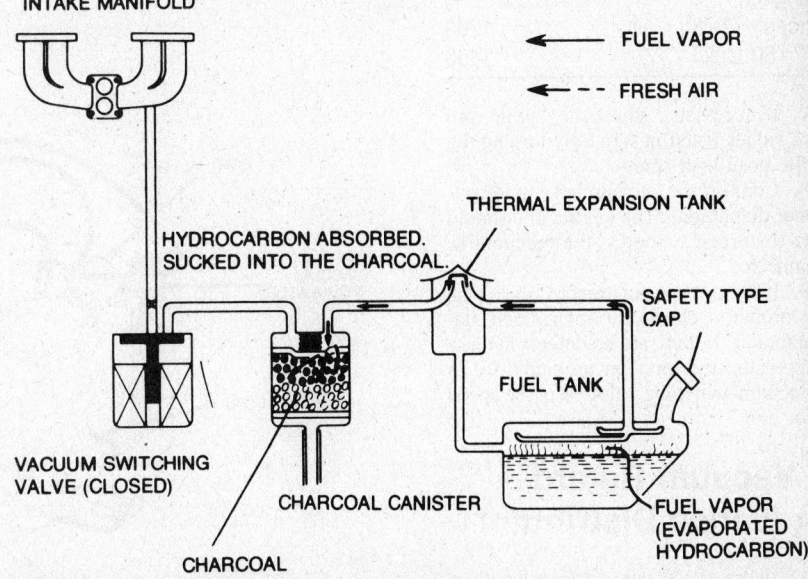

Typical charcoal cannister vapor storage system

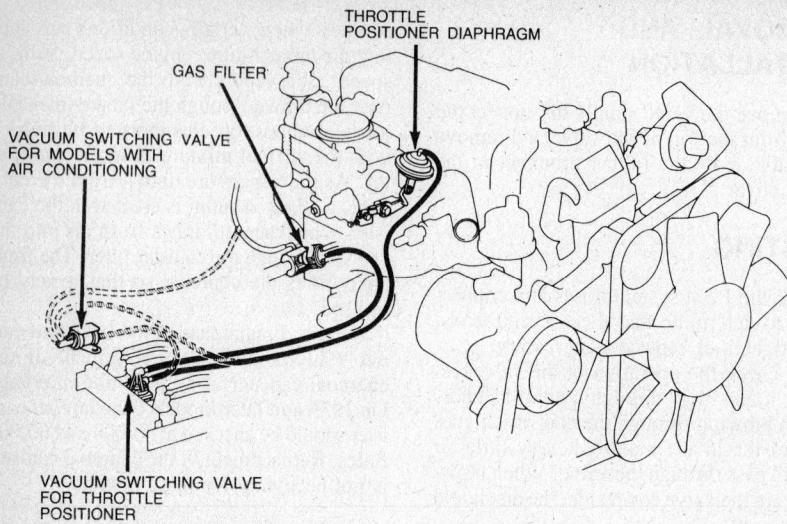

GAS FILTER

THROTTLE POSITIONER DIAPHRAGM

VACUUM SWITCHING VALVE FOR MODELS WITH AIR CONDITIONING

VACUUM SWITCHING VALVE FOR THROTTLE POSITIONER

Typical Throttle Positioner (TP) system

ADJUSTMENT

1. Start the engine and allow it to reach normal operating temperature.

2. Adjust the engine idle speed as previously outlined.

3. Detach the vacuum line from the throttle positioner diaphragm and plug the line.

4. Accelerate the engine slightly to set the throttle positioner.

5. Check the engine speed with a tachometer when the positioner is in place.

6. Check that the engine rpm reads as follows:

20R engine:	
manual transmission	1400
automatic transmission	1050

22R engine:	
all	1050

2F engine	
except '77–'80 Calif	1200
'77–'80 Calif	1400

7. If necessary, adjust the engine rpm to the values listed in step 6 by turning the throttle positioner screw.

8. Connect the vacuum hose to the positioner diaphragm. The engine idle should return to normal as soon as the vacuum line is connected.

9. If the throttle positioner fails to perform properly, check the linkage and diaphragm unit. If there are no defects in these components, the problem probably lies in the vacuum switching valve or in the speed sensor unit.

Vacuum Retard— Advance Distributor

Most Toyota trucks are equipped with a distributor which employs a vacuum spark retard system. Such distributors may be identified by the presence of two vacuum lines connected to the distributor vacuum unit.

Retarding the ignition timing under certain conditions reduces exhaust emissions and helps to compensate for the lack of engine braking due to the activation of the throttle positioner.

TESTING

NOTE: Check all vacuum hoses for leaks, kinks, or improper connections before making any tests. Replace the hose(s) if necessary.

1. Connect a timing light to the engine as previously outlined.

2. Mark and disconnect the vacuum hoses at the distributor vacuum unit.

3. Start the engine and apply vacuum to one of the vacuum unit connections. Note the effect on the ignition timing with the timing light. Release the vacuum at this connection and apply vacuum to the other vacuum unit connection. Note the effect on the ignition timing with the timing light.

4. If the ignition timing advanced and retarded during step 3, the vacuum unit is functioning properly. If the timing did not react in this manner, the distributor vacuum unit is defective.

5. Turn the engine off. Disconnect the timing light and reconnect the vacuum lines to the distributor.

EXHAUST GAS RECIRCULATION SYSTEM

The exhaust gas recirculation (EGR) system is used to reduce the oxides of nitrogen emissions from the engine. Oxides of nitrogen emission levels are highest during periods of high cylinder pressure and high cylinder temperature. The EGR system allows a small amount of engine exhaust gas to be recirculated back to the engine intake system. Since the exhaust gas is unable to be re-burned, its introduction to the combustion chambers results in a cooling effect on the combustion temperature. Consequently, oxides of nitrogen emissions are reduced. An added advantage to this cooling effect is that the engines tendency towards detonation (pinging) is reduced.

The EGR valve is controlled by the same computer and vacuum switching valve which is used to operate other emission control system components. There are several conditions which must be sensed by the computer in order for the computer to permit exhaust gas recirculation:

a. Ignition switch position
b. Vehicle speed
c. Engine speed
d. Engine coolant temperature

Due to the complexity of computer controlled emissions systems and the special

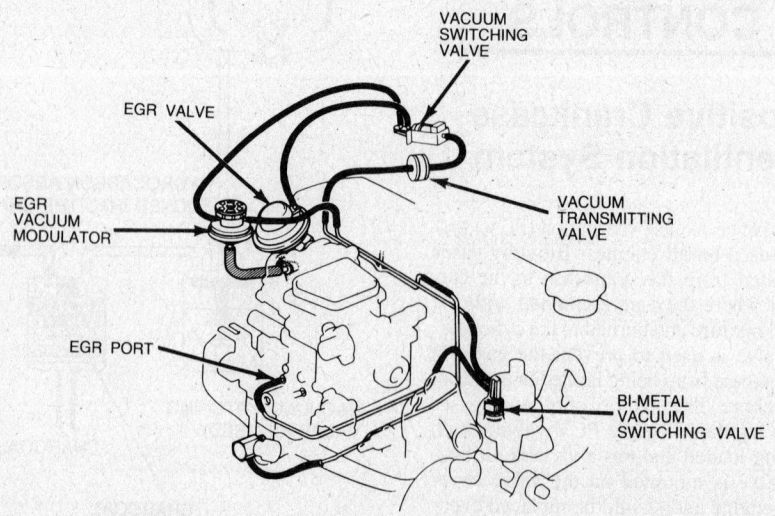

VACUUM SWITCHING VALVE

EGR VALVE

EGR VACUUM MODULATOR

VACUUM TRANSMITTING VALVE

EGR PORT

BI-METAL VACUUM SWITCHING VALVE

Typical exhaust gas recirculation (EGR) system

equipment needed to properly service these systems, only the basic EGR valve tests will be covered here.

EGR VALVE TEST

1977 and Earlier (Except 2F Engines)

1. Allow the engine to reach normal operating temperature and remove the air cleaner lid.

2. Disconnect the hose (coded with white tape) which runs from the vacuum switching valve to the EGR valve at the EGR valve end.

3. Remove the intake manifold hose (coded red) from the vacuum switching valve and connect it to the EGR valve.

4. With the engine idling, a "bubbling" sound should be heard from the carburetor. Disconnect the hose from the EGR valve. The "bubbling" sound should disappear.

5. If the sound does not vary, the EGR valve is defective and should be replaced.

6. Reconnect the vacuum hoses as originally connected and install the air cleaner lid.

1978 and Later (Incl. All 2F Engines)

1. Start the engine and allow it to idle.

2. Apply vacuum directly to the EGR valve. The engine should stall; on 2F engines, the rpm should drop about 50 rpm. If it does, the EGR valve is working properly. If not, the EGR valve is defective and must be replaced.

3. Reconnect the EGR valve vacuum line as originally connected.

Air Injection System

A belt-driven air pump supplies air to an injection manifold which has nozzles in each exhaust port. Injection of air at this point causes combustion of unburned hydrocarbons in the exhaust manifold rather than allowing them to escape into the atmosphere. An anti-backfire valve controls the flow of air from the pump to prevent backfiring which results from an overly rich mixture under closed throttle conditions.

A check valve prevents hot exhaust gas backflow into the pump and hoses, in case of a pump failure, or when the antibackfire valve is working.

In addition newer engines have an air switching valve (ASV). On engines without catalytic converters, the ASV is used to stop air injection under a constant heavy engine load.

On engines with catalytic converters the ASV is used to protect the catalyst from overheating, by blocking the air necessary for the reaction.

On all engines, except the early 2F, the relief valve is built into the ASV.

REMOVAL AND INSTALLATION

Air Pump

1. Disconnect the air hoses from the pump.

2. Loosen the bolt on the adjusting link and remove the drive belt.

3. Remove the pump.

—————— **CAUTION** ——————
Do not pry on the pump housing; it may become distorted.

Installation is in the reverse order of removal. Adjust the drive belt tension to ½–¾ in. under thumb pressure.

Antibackfire Valve and Air Switching Valve

1. Detach the air hoses from the valve.
2. Remove the valve securing bolt.
3. Withdraw the valve.

Installation is performed in the reverse order of removal.

Check Valve

1. Detach the intake hose from the valve.
2. Use an open-end wrench to remove the valve from its mounting.

Installation is the reverse of removal.

Relief Valve (Pump Mounted Type)

1. Remove the air pump from the vehicle.

2. Support the pump so that it cannot rotate.

—————— **CAUTION** ——————
Never clamp the pump in a vise; the aluminum case will be distorted.

3. Use a jaw-type puller to remove the relief valve from the top of the pump.

4. Position the new relief valve over the opening in the pump.

NOTE: The air outlet should be pointing toward the left.

5. Gently tap the relief valve into place using a block of wood and a hammer.

6. Install the pump on the engine, as outlined above.

Air Injection Manifold

1. Remove the check valve, as outlined above.

2. Loosen the air injection manifold attachment nuts and withdraw the manifold.

NOTE: On 20R and 22R engines, it will first be necessary to remove the exhaust manifold as previously outlined.

Installation is the reverse order of removal.

TESTING

—————— **CAUTION** ——————
Do not hammer, pry, or bend the pump housing while tightening the drive belt or testing the pump.

Belt Tension and Air Leaks

1. Before proceeding with the tests, check the pump drive belt tension to see if it is within specifications.

2. Turn the pump by hand. If it has seized, the belt will slip, making a noise. Disregard any chirping, squealing, or rolling sounds from inside the pump; these are normal when it is turned by hand.

3. Check the hoses and connections for leaks. Hissing or a blast of air is indicative of a leak. Soapy water, applied lightly around the area in question, is a good method for detecting leaks.

Air Output

1. Disconnect the air supply hose at the antibackfire valve.

2. Connect a pressure gauge, using a suitable adaptor, to the air supply hose.

NOTE: If there are two hoses, plug the second one.

3. With the engine at normal operating temperature, increase the idle speed to 1,000–1,500 rpm and watch the vacuum gauge.

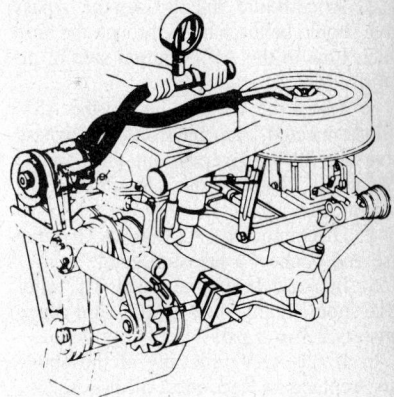

Checking the air pump output

4. The air flow from the pump should be steady and fall between 2 and 6 psi. If it is unsteady or falls below this, the pump is defective and must be replaced.

Pump Noise Diagnosis

The air pump is normally noisy; as engine speed increases, the noise of the pump will rise in pitch. The rolling sound the pump bearings make is normal. But if this sound becomes objectionable at certain speeds, the pump is defective and will have to be replaced.

A continual hissing sound from the air pump pressure relief valve at idle, indicates a defective valve. Replace the relief valves.

If the pump rear bearing fails, a continual knocking sound will be heard.

Bypass Valve

1. Detach the hose which runs from the bypass valve to the check valve, at the bypass valve hose connection.

2. Connect a tachometer to the engine. With the engine running at normal idle speed, check to see that air is flowing from the bypass valve hose connection.

3. Speed up the engine so it is running at 1,500–2,000 rpm. Allow the throttle to snap shut. The flow of air from the bypass valve at the check valve hose connection should stop momentarily and air should then flow from the exhaust port on the valve body or the silencer assembly.

4. Repeat step 3 several times. If the flow of air is not diverted into the atmosphere from the valve exhaust port or if it fails to stop flowing from the hose connection, check the vacuum lines and connections. If these are tight, the valve is defective and requires replacement.

5. A leaking diaphragm will cause the air to flow out both the hose connection and the exhaust port at the same time. If this happens, replace the valve.

Air Switching Valve (ASV) Tests

1. Start the engine and allow it to reach normal operating temperature.

2. At curb idle, the air from the bypass valve should be discharged through the hose which runs to the ASV (output side of air pump).

3. When the vacuum line to the ASV is disconnected, the air from the bypass valve should be diverted out through the ASV-to-air cleaner hose. Reconnect the vacuum line.

4. Disconnect the ASV-to-check valve hose and connect a pressure gauge to it.

5. Increase the engine speed. The relief valve should open when the pressure gauge registers 2.7–6.5 psi.

6. If the ASV fails any of the above tests, replace it. Reconnect all hoses.

Vacuum Delay Valve

The vacuum delay valve is located in the line which runs from the intake manifold to the vacuum surge tank. To check it, proceed as follows:

1. Remove the vacuum delay valve from the vacuum line. Be sure to note which end points toward the intake manifold.

2. When air is blown in from the ASV (surge tank) side, it should pass through the valve freely.

3. When air is blown in from the intake manifold side, a resistance should be felt.

4. Replace the valve if it fails either of the above tests.

5. Install the valve in the vacuum line, being careful not to install it backwards.

Check Valve

1. Before starting the test, check all of the hoses and connections for leaks.

2. Detach the air supply hose from the check valve.

3. Insert a suitable probe into the check valve and depress the plate. Release it; the plate should return to its original position against the valve seat. If binding is evident, replace the valve.

4. With the engine running at normal operating temperature, gradually increase its speed to 1,500 rpm. Check for exhaust gas leakage. If any is present, replace the valve assembly.

NOTE: Vibration and flutter of the check valve at idle speed is at normal condition and does not mean that the valve should be replaced.

Catalytic Converter System

The catalytic converter is a muffler-shaped device, located in the exhaust system between the manifold and the muffler. Its purpose is to oxidize hydrocarbons (HC) and carbon monoxide (CO).

The catalyst is made of noble metals (platinum and palladium) bonded to pellets of granular alumina. These catalysts cause the HC and CO to break down into water and carbon dioxide (CO_2) without taking part in the reaction; thus, it is reasonable to expect a catalyst life of 50,000 miles in normal use. The air pump used in the air injection system also supplies fresh air to the catalyst via the exhaust pipe; this fresh air is used to supply oxygen for the reaction. A thermosensor, inserted into the body of the converter, shuts off the air supply if catalyst temperatures become excessive.

The same sensor circuit also causes an instrument panel warning light labeled ''EXH TEMP'' to come on when the temperature rises beyond the predetermined level.

NOTE: It is normal for the light to come on temporarily if the truck is driven downhill for long periods of time (such as when descending a mountain).

The light will come on and stay on if the air injection system is malfunctioning or if the engine is misfiring, both of which will cause the catalyst temperature to rise.

PRECAUTIONS

1. Use only unleaded fuel.

2. Avoid prolonged idling; the engine should run no longer than 20 minutes at curb idle, nor longer than 10 minutes at fast idle.

3. Reduce fast idle speed, by quickly depressing and releasing the accelerator pedal, as soon as the coolant temperature reaches 120°F.

4. Do not disconnect any spark plug leads while the engine is running.

5. Make engine compression checks as quickly as possible.

6. Do not dispose of the catalyst in a place where anything coated with grease, gas, or oil is present.

CATALYST TESTING

At the present time there is no known way to reliably test catalytic converter operation in the field. The only reliable test is a 12 hour and 40 minute ''soak test'' (CVS) which must be done in a laboratory.

An infrared HC/CO tester is not sensitive enough to measure the higher tailpipe emissions from a partially-failed converter. Thus, a bad converter may allow enough HC and CO emissions to escape, so that the truck is not in compliance with Federal (or state) standards, but still will not cause the needle on the HC/CO tester to move off zero.

A *completely* failed converter should cause the tester to show a slight reading. As a result, it should be possible to spot one of these.

As long as you avoid severe overheating or use of leaded fuels and the truck has less than 50,000 miles on it, it is safe to assume that the converter is working.

If you are in doubt about the converter, take your truck to the diagnostic center which has an infrared tester.

WARNING LIGHT TESTING

NOTE: The warning light will come on when the ignition switch is turned to the Start position, as a means of checking its operation.

1. If the warning light illuminates and remains on, check the components of the air injection system. If these are not defective, check the ignition system for faulty leads, plugs, points, or igniter.

2. If no problems can be found in Step 1, check the warning light wiring for short or open circuits.

3. If nothing can be found in Steps 1 or 2, check the operation of the emission control system vacuum switching valve or the computer, either by substitution of a new unit, or by taking the truck to a service facility which has Toyota's diagnostic emission control system checker.

CONVERTER REMOVAL AND INSTALLATION

———— CAUTION ————
Do not perform this operation on a hot (or even warm) engine. Catalyst temperatures may go as high as 1,700°F, so that any contact with the catalyst could cause severe burns.

1. Disconnect the lead from the converter thermosensor.

2. Remove the wiring shield.

3. Unfasten the pipe clamp securing bolts at either end of the converter. Remove the clamps.

4. Push the tailpipe rearward and remove the converter, complete with thermosensor.

5. Carry the converter with the thermosensor upward to prevent the catalyst from falling out.

6. Unfasten the screws and take out the thermosensor and gasket.

Installation is as follows:

1. Place a new gasket on the thermosensor. Push the thermosensor into the converter and secure it with its two bolts. Be careful not to drop the thermosensor.

NOTE: Service replacement converters are provided with a plastic thermosensor guide. Slide the sensor into the guide to install it. Do not remove the guide.

2. Install new gaskets on the converter mounting flanges.

3. Secure the converter with its mounting clamps.

4. If the converter is attached to the body with rubber O-rings, install the O-rings over the body and converter mounting hooks.

5. Install the wire protector and connect the lead to the thermosensor.

Mixture Control System

The mixture control (MC) system is used on 1980 and later pickup trucks equipped with manual transmissions. The purpose of the MC system is to reduce hydrocarbon and carbon monoxide emissions during sudden engine deceleration. When the throttle is suddenly closed, the intake manifold vacuum increases rapidly. This vacuum, acting on the mixture control valve, causes the valve to open. When the mixture control valve opens, fresh air is admitted into the intake tract of the engine, which effectively lowers the emissions output.

TESTING

1. Start the engine.

2. Disconnect the upper vacuum (sensing) hose from the MC valve.

3. Place your hand over the air inlet of the MC valve. No suction should be felt.

4. Reconnect the upper vacuum (sensing) hose to the MC valve. Suction should be felt at the MC valve air inlet for a moment.

NOTE: At this time, the engine should either idle roughly or stall. This is normal.

5. Replace the valve if either the valve or the engine did not act as previously stated.

Transmission Controlled Spark System

The transmission controlled spark (TCS) is used on vehicles made prior to 1977. The TCS system alters the distributor advance curve under certain operating conditions, thereby reducing emissions of oxides of nitrogen (NO_x).

When the system is operational, the computer closes the vacuum switching valve (VSV) ground circuit. The valve in the VSV closes the passage between the distributor advance side and the carburetor advancer port. In this manner, advance of the engine timing is stopped.

The computer receives its messages from the speed sensor unit and the thermo sensor which only operates when the coolant temperature is between 140–210°F. 1976 trucks use a TVSV (thermostatic vacuum switching valve) in addition to the VSV, computer, and speed sensor, to provide normal vacuum advance at engine temperatures below 122°F.

Spark Control System

A modified TCS system called spark control (SC) is used on 1977 and later trucks. The principle of delayed vacuum advance to minimize HC and NO_x emissions remains the same, but the system is simplified by elimination of the computer control, VSV, and TVSV. Instead, a vacuum transmitting valve (VTV) is placed in the vacuum hose between the distributor diaphragm and the carburetor. Vacuum is delayed to the diaphragm by the closing of a check valve within the VTV. When intake vacuum drops (at wide throttle openings) the check valve opens and faster transmission of vacuum is allowed, thus advancing the distributor timing. The VTV is coded in a dark blue color in automatic transmission trucks, and brown in all manual transmission equipped trucks.

Auxiliary Acceleration Pump System

To reduce emissions, carburetor air/fuel mixtures are calibrated to be as lean as possible. Although a lean mixture will burn readily at hotter temperatures, it is reluctant to ignite when cold—not because of the mixture as such, but because fuel vaporizes less readily when cold. Thus, increasing the amount of fuel in a cold air/fuel mixture increases the amount of vaporized fuel available.

The problem of a poor air/vaporized fuel mixture in a cold engine is accentuated when accelerating. Although the carburetor is equipped with an acceleration pump for normal accelerating engine demands, its capacity is insufficient for a cold engine. The auxiliary acceleration pump (AAP) is designed to send additional fuel into the acceleration nozzle in the carburetor independent of the regular acceleration pump. All 1975 and later trucks are equipped with the AAP system.

The AAP itself is an integral part of the carburetor. It consists of two check valves controlled by springs, and a diaphragm controlled by both a spring and engine vacuum obtained from the intake manifold. At constant speeds, intake manifold vacuum draws the AAP diaphragm back, enlarging the AAP chamber and thus allowing gasoline to enter. When the engine is accelerated, intake manifold vacuum drops, allowing the AAP diaphragm to be pushed back by the spring. The resultant reduction in chamber volume forces the gasoline out through the other check valve, into the acceleration nozzle. Thus, the engine gets a needed squirt of gasoline.

AAP operation is governed by the same

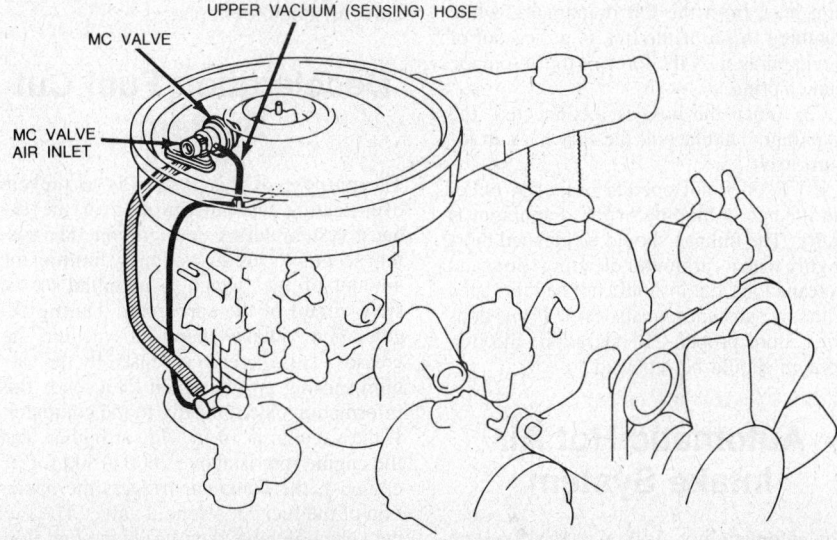

Typical mixture control (MC) system

UPPER VACUUM (SENSING) HOSE

MC VALVE

MC VALVE AIR INLET

TOYOTA

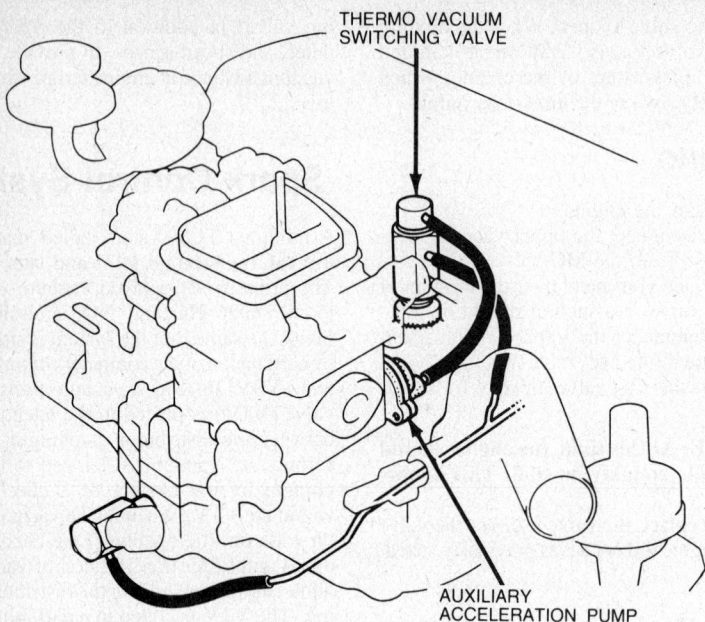

THERMO VACUUM
SWITCHING VALVE

AUXILIARY
ACCELERATION PUMP

Typical Auxiliary Acceleration Pump (AAP) system

TVSV described in the AI section earlier. At cold coolant temperatures, the TVSV allows intake manifold vacuum to reach the AAP diaphragm. At approximately 122°F, the TVSV closes off the passage to vacuum, thus shutting off the AAP.

INSPECTION

The vacuum hose should be checked for leaks, kinks, or improper connections.

1. With the engine cold (below 75°F) and idling (front wheels blocked, parking brake on, transmission in neutral) remove the air cleaner cap and look into the carburetor. At the instant the vacuum hose is removed from the AAP, gasoline should squirt from the nozzle.

2. If it does not, check for vacuum in the hose. If present, the AAP diaphragm may be defective, the nozzle may be blocked, the check valves may be stuck, or gasoline may not be flowing into the chamber.

3. If there is no vacuum in the line, either the line has an air leak or the TVSV is defective.

4. After warming the engine to operating temperature, perform the same test as in Step 1. If gasoline spurts out, the TVSV is defective.

Choke Breaker System

All 20R and 22R engines use an automatic choke, consisting of a thermostatic bimetal spring which expands and contracts in response to cold and heat. This spring is connected by mechanical linkage to the choke plate, and heated by the engine coolant. When the engine is cold, the spring expands and closes the choke. As the engine heats, the spring contracts opening the choke.

The Choke Breaker (CB) system uses a diaphragm which is mechanically connected to the choke linkage and is actuated by intake manifold vacuum. The vacuum causes the diaphragm to pull back on the linkage, opening the choke plate slightly against the force of the automatic choke spring.

The purpose of the CB system is to prevent the cold engine from receiving an over-rich mixture, caused by the closed choke plate, because rich mixtures are higher in HC and CO emissions.

INSPECTION

Check the vacuum hose first for leaks, kinks, and improper connections.

1. With the engine cold and idling (parking brake set, front wheels blocked, and transmission in neutral), remove the lid from the air cleaner. Disconnect the vacuum hose from the CB diaphragm, while watching to see if the link is pulled out of the diaphragm by the force of the automatic choke spring.

2. When the hose is reconnected, the diaphragm should pull the link back in toward itself.

If CB does not operate properly, either the linkage is binding or the diaphragm is faulty. The linkage should be cleaned thoroughly with a carburetor cleaning spray and a clean cloth, but it should not be lubricated with any substance whatsoever. If this does not restore proper CB operation, the diaphragm should be replaced.

Automatic Hot Air Intake System

The automatic hot air intake (HAI) system consists of a heat stove around the exhaust manifold, a thermostatically controlled door (air control valve) in the air cleaner horn, and a length of insulated flexible pipe connecting the two. The purpose of the system is to keep the temperature of the air drawn into the carburetor as constant as possible. It directs a hot air supply to the carburetor in cold weather to provide faster engine warming and to reduce the possibility of carburetor icing. By providing the cold engine with warmer air, the choke stays on for a shorter length of time, thus reducing fuel consumption and the rich mixture condition. Leaner combustion mixtures are inherently lower in HC and CO emissions.

The air control valve in the air cleaner horn is controlled by a vacuum diaphragm. The vacuum hose is connected at one end to the diaphragm, and to both a thermo valve and intake manifold at the other. Initially, when cold, the thermo valve is closed. Intake manifold vacuum therefore causes the diaphragm to rise, opening the door in the air horn to admit preheated air drawn from the heat stove around the exhaust manifold. As the engine temperature rises, the thermo valve opens, thus reducing the level of intake manifold vacuum at the diaphragm. This allows the diaphragm to lower, which in turn closes the door in the air horn to admit cool outside air.

INSPECTION

With the engine idling and warm, connect the diaphragm hose directly to the intake manifold, and plug the thermo valve hose end. The air control valve should rise to admit hot air.

As with all vacuum-operated systems, the hoses should be checked for any kinks, breaks, or improper connections. If none are found and the air valve does not work properly, the diaphragm and the thermo valve must be checked. Suction applied to the vacuum hose should cause the diaphragm to raise the door. If it does, the thermo valve can be considered faulty. If not, the diaphragm should be replaced.

Deceleration Fuel Cut System

The purpose of this system is to prevent over-heating and afterburning in the exhaust system during deceleration. The system accomplishes this action by limiting the amount of fuel which is admitted to the slow circuit of the carburetor. During deceleration, intake manifold vacuum increases. This increase is sensed by the vacuum sensing switch which then sends this information electronically to the computer. If the vacuum is 14 in. Hg. or higher, and the engine rpm is above 2600 (1800 for 2F engines), the computer triggers the operation of the fuel cut solenoid valve. The fuel cut solenoid valve then limits the fuel flow to the carburetor slow circuit.

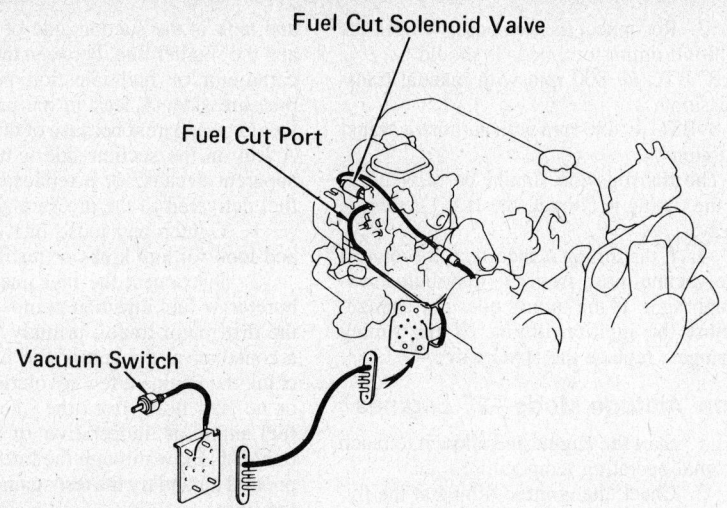

Typical Deceleration Fuel Cut system

TESTING

General System Check

1. Connect a tachometer to the engine.
2. Start the engine and check that it runs normally.
3. Pinch the vacuum hose to the vacuum switch.
4. Gradually increase the engine rpm to 3000 rpm (2000 for 2F engines). The engine should misfire slightly between 2400 and 3000 rpm (1200 and 2000 for 2F engines).

——— CAUTION ———
Perform this procedure quickly to avoid overheating the catalytic converter.

5. Release the hose and gradually increase the engine speed to 3000 rpm (2000 for 2F engines). Check that the engine operation is normal.
6. With the engine at idle unplug the solenoid valve. Check that the engine misfires or stalls.
7. If a problem is found check the switch and solenoid. If everything is normal connect the vacuum line and wiring.

FUEL CUT SOLENOID

1. Disconnect and remove the solenoid.
2. Connect one of the solenoid wires to the positive battery terminal; the other to the negative battery terminal. The solenoid should make a distinct clicking sound. If the solenoid does not click when energized, it is defective and should be replaced.
3. Check the solenoid O-ring for damage and replace if necessary.
4. Install and reconnect the solenoid.

VACUUM SWITCH

1. Disconnect the wire from the vacuum switch.

2. Using an ohmmeter, touch one ohmmeter probe to the body of the switch; the other ohmmeter probe to the terminal of the switch. Continuity should exist between these two points at this time.
3. Start the engine and check the continuity between the same two points (as in step 2). Continuity should NOT exist with the engine running.
4. If the switch performed correctly during steps 2 and 3, turn the engine off and reconnect the switch. If the switch did not perform correctly, replace the switch with a new unit.

High Altitude Compensation System

The piston downstroke (intake) of any engine is fixed, therefore the engine can only ingest a given volume of air in any altitude. There is progressively less oxygen available in air as the altitude changes, but basically, the carburetor will still meter the same amount of fuel. Because of this less oxygen/same amount of fuel condition, the air/fuel mixture available to the engine tends to richen.

The high altitude compensation (HAC) system is designed to perform the following functions as the altitude changes:
  a. Adjust the air/fuel mixture available to the engine
  b. (On some engines) Advance the ignition timing to improve the engines driveability characteristics.

INSPECTION

NOTE: Before checking the HAC system at altitudes near 4000 feet, determine the position of the HAC valve. This can be done by blowing into any one of the three ports on top of the HAC valve when the engine is idling. If the passage is open, the valve is in the high altitude position. If it is closed, the valve is in the low altitude position. Proceed with the appropriate inspection procedure after the position of the valve is determined.

——— CAUTION ———
Before performing any of the following tests, check the vacuum hoses for damage or leaks. Incorrect test results could occur if the vacuum hoses leak or are damaged.

High Altitude Mode—Except 2F Engines

1. Start the engine and allow it to reach normal operating temperature. Check the ignition timing as previously outlined. If it is about 13° BTC, go on with the procedure. If it is only slightly out of adjustment, adjust the timing. If the hose between the HAC valve and the three way connector is pinched, does the ignition timing become about 13° BTC? If so, the HAC valve should be replaced. If not, the check valve must be inspected. It should be possible to blow

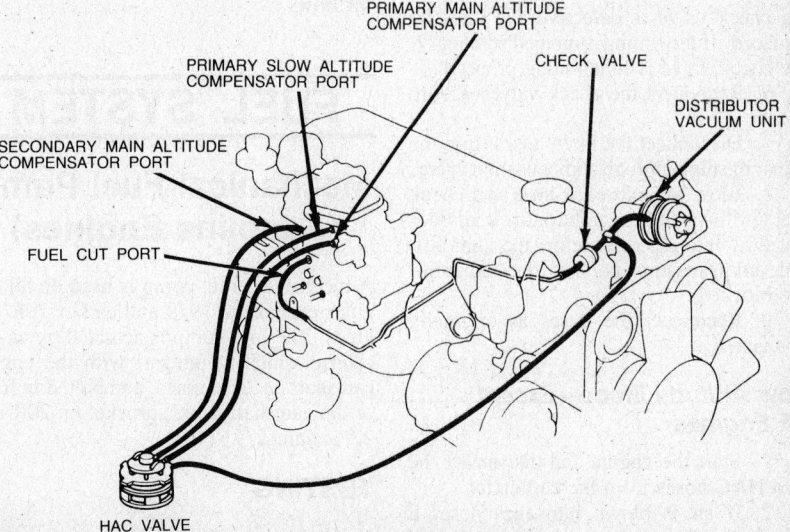

Typical High Altitude Compensation (HAC) system

air through it from the HAC side, and not from the intake manifold side. If faulty, replace. If not, the distributor vacuum advance is faulty and must be repaired or replaced.

2. If the hose between the white side of the check valve and the three way connector is pinched, the ignition timing should stay at 13° BTC for a minute or more. If not, replace the HAC valve.

3. If the hose is disconnected from the black side of the check valve and the hose end blocked, the ignition timing should stay at 13° BTC for one minute or more. If not, replace the check valve.

4. Disconnect the two HAC hoses from the carburetor. If air is blown into each hose, it should flow into the HAC valve. If not, replace the HAC valve.

5. Reconnect the two hoses to the carburetor and disconnect the same hoses from the HAC valve. If air is blown into each hose, it should flow into the carburetor. If not, the carburetor air passages are blocked.

6. If the air does flow into the carburetor, reconnect the hoses. The HAC system is operating correctly.

High Altitude Mode—2F Engines

1. Start the engine and allow it to reach normal operating temperature.

2. Disconnect the outermost hose (furthest from the distributor cap) from the distributor vacuum unit and plug the hose end.

3. Check the ignition timing at the flywheel as previously outlined. The timing should be 7° BTDC.

4. Unplug and reconnect the distributor vacuum unit hose. The ignition timing should advance. If the timing advances, the system is functioning properly. If the timing does not advance, proceed with the following steps.

5. Disconnect the vacuum hose from the black side of the check valve and plug the hose end. The ignition timing should remain stationary for a minimum of one minute. If the timing varies at this time, the check valve is defective and must be replaced. If the timing remained stationary, the check valve is functioning properly.

6. Reconnect the check valve vacuum hose.

7. Disconnect the three hoses from the top of the high altitude compensation valve.

8. Blow air into each hose and check that air flows into the carburetor. If air does not flow into the carburetor, the high altitude compensation ports in the carburetor are blocked.

9. Reconnect the hoses as originally connected.

Low Altitude Mode—Except 2F Engines

1. Start the engine and disconnect the two HAC hoses from the carburetor.

2. If air is blown into each hose, it should not flow in into the HAC valve. If it does, replace the valve.

3. Reconnect the two hoses. Check the ignition timing outlined. It should be:

8° BTC @ 800 rpm with manual transmission

8° BTC @ 850 rpm with automatic transmission

The transmission should be in Neutral. If the timing is correct, the HAC system is okay.

4. If the timing is incorrect, disconnect the vacuum hose from the distributor subdiaphragm. If the timing does not change, adjust the ignition timing. If the timing changes, replace the HAC valve.

Low Altitude Mode—2F Engines

1. Start the engine and allow it to reach normal operating temperature.

2. Check the ignition timing at the flywheel as previously outlined. The timing should be 7° BTDC for engines equipped with HAC.

3. Disconnect the vacuum hose from the bottom of the HAC valve and plug the hose end. The ignition timing should advance approximately 6°. If the timing advances, the system is functioning properly. If the timing does not advance, refer to steps 5–9 of the previous "High Altitude Mode—2F Engines" procedure.

HAC VALVE SERVICE

The only serviceable part of the HAC valve is the filter located in the bottom of the valve. If the filter is clogged, it can be either cleaned or (preferably) replaced.

CHECK VALVE TESTING

The check valve can be tested independent of the system by blowing air into the check valve ports. Air flow should be unrestricted when blowing from the white side to the black side of the valve. When blowing from the black side to the white side of the valve, there should be a noticeable resistance in air flow.

FUEL SYSTEM

Mechanical Fuel Pump (Gasoline Engines)

A mechanical fuel pump is used on all engines except the 1978 and earlier 20R engines. The fuel pump is actuated by an eccentric which is integral with the engine camshaft on 2F engines, and bolted in front of the camshaft drive sprocket on 20R and 22R engines.

TESTING

Fuel pumps should always be tested on the vehicle. The larger line between the pump and tank is the suction side of the system and the smaller line, between the pump and carburetor or fuel injection pump is the pressure side. A leak in the pressure side would be apparent because of dripping fuel. A leak in the suction side is usually only apparent because of a reduced volume of fuel delivered to the pressure side.

1. Tighten any loose line connections and look for any kinks or restrictions.

2. Disconnect the fuel line at the carburetor or fuel injection pump. Disconnect the distributor-to-coil primary wire. Place a container at the end of the fuel line and crank the engine a few revolutions. If little or no fuel flows from the line, either the fuel pump is inoperative or the line is plugged. Blow through the lines with compressed air and try the test again. Reconnect the line.

3. If fuel flows in good volume, check the fuel pump pressure to be sure (pressure tests are possible only on gasoline engines).

4. Attach a pressure gauge to the pressure side of the fuel line. On cars equipped with a vapor return system, squeeze off the return hose.

5. Run the engine at idle and note the reading on the gauge. Stop the engine and compare the reading with the specifications listed in the "Tune-Up Specifications" chart. If the pump is operating properly, the pressure will be as specified and will be constant at idle speed. If pressure varies sporadically or is too high or low, the pump should be repaired or replaced, depending upon the pump type.

6. Remove the pressure gauge.

The following flow test can also be performed:

1. Disconnect the fuel line from the carburetor. Run the fuel line into a suitable measuring container.

2. Run the engine at idle until there is one pint of fuel in the container. One pint should be pumped in 30 seconds or less.

3. If the flow is below minimum, check for a restriction in the line.

The only way to check fuel pump pressure is by connecting an accurate pressure gauge to the fuel line at the carburetor level. Never replace a fuel pump without performing this simple test. If the engine seems to be starving out, check the ignition system first. Also check for a plugged fuel filter or a restricted fuel line before replacing the pump. In rare cases, the fuel pump eccentric will wear to the point of preventing a full fuel pump stroke which will lower the fuel pump output. Keep this in mind, especially on high mileage engines.

REMOVAL AND INSTALLATION

20R and 22R Engines—1979 and Later

1. Disconnect the negative battery terminal.

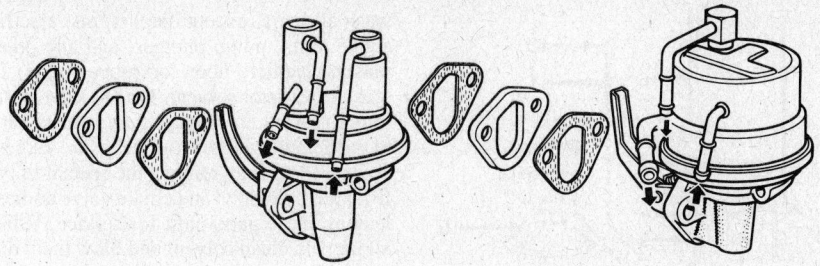

Mechanical fuel pumps used on 20R and 22R engines—arrows indicate the fuel flow in and out of the pump

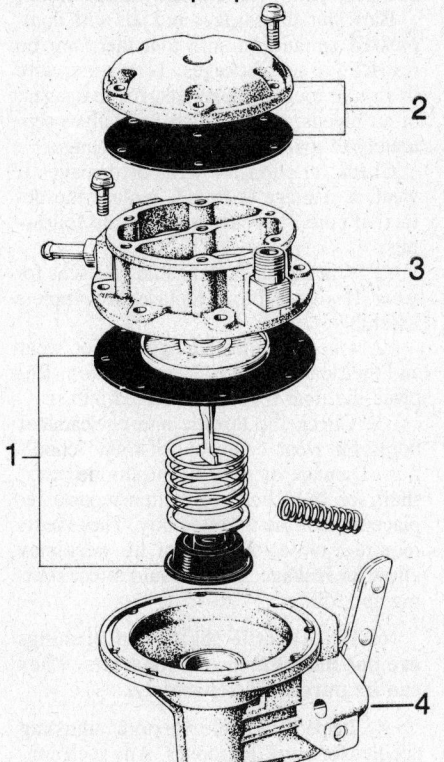

Mechanical fuel pump used on the 2F engine

1. Diaphragm and spring
2. Cover and diaphragm
3. Upper body
4. Lower body

—————— CAUTION ——————
When working on the fuel system, do not smoke or work near any fire hazard. Keep gasoline off rubber or leather parts.

2. Drain the radiator.
3. Remove the upper radiator hose.
4. Remove all three lines from the fuel pump.
5. Remove the two bolts, the fuel pump, and gasket.

NOTE: The fuel pump is not repairable. It must be replaced as a complete unit.

6. Installation is the reverse of removal. On these engines, the fuel pump is serviced as an assembly. If the pump is defective, the entire pump must be replaced.

2F Engines

To remove the fuel pump simply disconnect and plug the fuel lines and remove the two bolts which hold the pump to the block.

When installing a new pump always use a new gasket between the pump and the block to prevent oil leakage. If any new rubber hose must be used to repair the fuel line, be sure that it is gasoline-resistant.

The 2F engine mechanical fuel pump is rebuildable, depending upon parts availability. If you decide to rebuild the fuel pump rather than replace it, follow the instructions supplied with the rebuilding kit.

Electric Fuel Pump (Gasoline Engines)

An electric fuel pump is used on all 1978 and earlier 20R engined pickup trucks. The fuel pump is wired into the ignition switch and oil pressure switch circuits. In the event of an oil pressure loss, the fuel pump is turned off so that the engine will stall, thus preventing engine damage due to the oil pressure loss. The fuel pump will operate only when the ignition switch is turned to the START position and when the oil pressure is normal.

TESTING

1. Disconnect the electrical clip from the oil pressure switch.
2. Turn the ignition switch to On.
3. Check for a smooth flow of gasoline from the fuel filter outlet. If the pump is noisy, it is probably defective. If the pump does not run, check the pump resistor and relay.

With the oil pressure switch electrical clip still off, check the discharge rate of the pump. Connect a line to the outlet of the fuel filter, turn the ignition switch to On, and measure the discharge capacity. It should be over 1.3 quarts per minute.

Turn the key off, and connect a pressure gauge to the filter outlet. Turn the ignition switch to On and measure to fuel pump pressure. It should be between 2.1 and 4.3 psi.

As with the mechanical pump, all tests should be performed, and all lines and the filter should be checked, before replacing the pump.

REMOVAL AND INSTALLATION

1. Remove the negative ($-$) cable from the battery.
2. Remove the fuel tank according to the appropriate procedure.
3. Remove the bolts which secure the access plate to the tank. Remove the plate and its gasket, and remove the pump.

—————— CAUTION ——————
Do not operate the fuel pump unless it is immersed in gasoline and connected to its resistor.

Installation is the reverse of removal. Use a new gasket on the access plate, and check for leaks after installation.

Carburetors

REMOVAL AND INSTALLATION

1. Disconnect the battery ground cable.
2. Remove the air cleaner assembly. Label the disconnected hoses so that they may be correctly reinstalled.
3. On 20R and 22R engines, drain the engine coolant and disconnect the heater hose from the choke unit.
4. Disconnect the fuel line at the carburetor.
5. Label and disconnect the vacuum hoses from the carburetor. Disconnect the choke pipe, if so equipped.
6. Disconnect the accelerator linkage and the automatic transmission throttle rod, if so equipped.
7. On 2F engines, disconnect the magnetic valve wire from the coil terminal and the choke cable from the carburetor.
8. Remove the carburetor-to-manifold attaching nuts and lift the carburetor off of the manifold.
9. Cover the open manifold with a clean cloth to prevent dirt and small objects from entering into the engine.

Installation is performed in the reverse order of removal. After the engine has been started, check for fuel and vacuum leaks.

OVERHAUL

Efficient carburetion depends greatly on careful cleaning and inspection during overhaul since dirt, gum, water, or varnish in or on the carburetor parts are often responsible for poor performance.

Overhaul your carburetor in a clean, dust-free area. Carefully disassemble the carburetor, referring often to the exploded views. Keep all similar and lookalike parts segregated during disassembly and cleaning to avoid accidental interchange during assembly. Make a note of all jet sizes.

When the carburetor is disassembled,

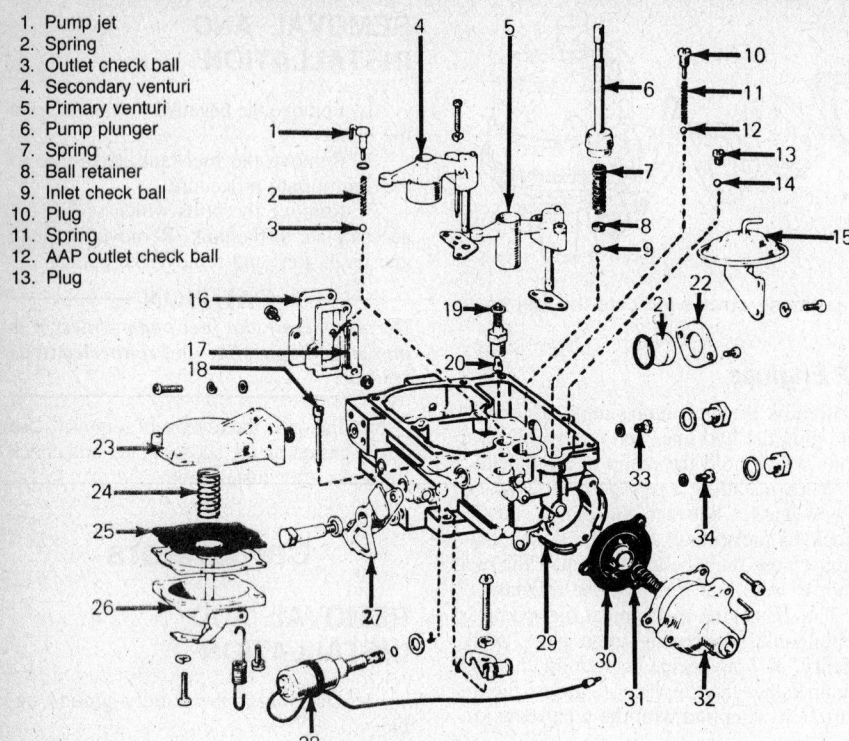

1. Pump jet
2. Spring
3. Outlet check ball
4. Secondary venturi
5. Primary venturi
6. Pump plunger
7. Spring
8. Ball retainer
9. Inlet check ball
10. Plug
11. Spring
12. AAP outlet check ball
13. Plug

14. AAP inlet check ball
15. Throttle positioner
16. Thermostatic valve cover
17. Thermostatic valve
18. Primary slow jet
19. Power valve
20. Power jet

21. Sight glass
22. Glass retainer
23. Diaphragm housing cap
24. Spring
25. Diaphragm
26. Housing
27. Fast idle cam

28. Solenoid valve
29. Carburetor body
30. Diaphragm
31. Spring
32. AAP housing
33. Secondary main jet
34. Primary main jet

Carburetor main body parts—20R engine

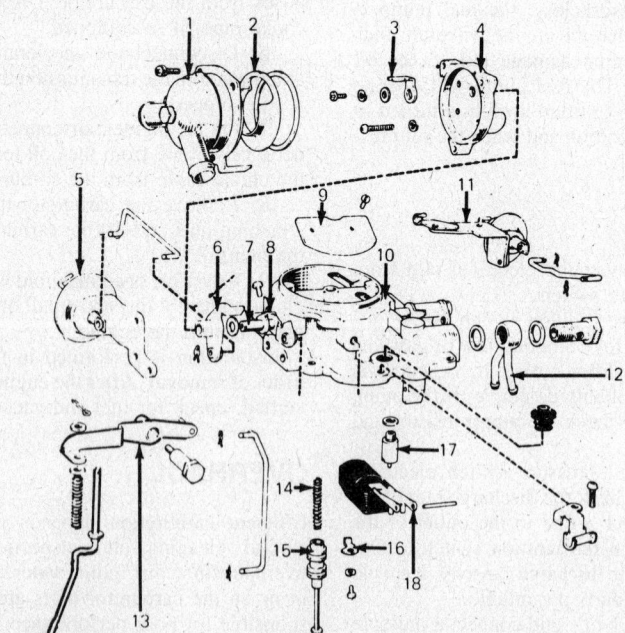

1. Choke coil water housing
2. Choke housing plate
3. Choke lever
4. Choke housing body
5. Choke breaker
6. Relief lever

7. Choke shaft
8. Connecting lever
9. Choke valve
10. Air horn
11. Choke opener
12. Union

13. Pump arm
14. Spring
15. Power piston
16. Piston retainer
17. Needle valve set
18. Float

Carburetor air horn parts—20R engine

wash all parts (except diaphragms, electric choke units, pump plunger, and any other plastic, leather, fiber, or rubber parts) in clean carburetor solvent. Do not leave parts in the solvent any longer than is necessary to sufficiently loosen the deposits. Excessive cleaning may remove the special finish from the float bowl and choke valve bodies, leaving these parts unfit for service. Rinse all parts in clean solvent and blow them dry with compressed air or allow them to air dry. Wipe clean all cork, plastic, leather, and fiber parts with a clean lintfree cloth.

Blow out all passages and jets with compressed air and be sure that there are no restrictions or blockages. Never use wire or similar tools to clean jets, fuel passages, or air bleeds. Clean all jets and valves separately to avoid accidental interchange.

Check all parts for wear or damage. If wear or damage is found, replace the defective parts. Especially check the following:

1. Check the float needle and seat for wear. If wear is found, replace the complete assembly.

2. Check the float hinge pin for wear and the float(s) for dents or distortion. Replace the float if fuel has leaked into it.

3. Check the throttle and choke shaft bores for wear or an out-of-round condition. Damage or wear to the throttle arm, shaft, or shaft bore will often require replacement of the throttle body. These parts require a close tolerance of fit; wear may allow air leakage, which could affect starting and idling.

NOTE: Throttle shafts and bushings are not included in overhaul kits. They can be purchased separately.

4. Inspect the idle mixture adjusting needles for burrs or grooves. Any such condition requires replacement of the needle, since you will not be able to obtain a satisfactory idle.

5. Test the accelerator pump check valves. They should pass air one way but not the other. Test for proper seating by blowing and sucking on the valve. Replace the valve if necessary. If the valve is satisfactory, wash the valve again to remove breath moisture.

6. Check the bowl cover for warped surfaces with a straightedge.

7. Closely inspect the valves and seats for wear and damage, replacing as necessary.

8. After the carburetor is assembled, check the choke valve for freedom of operation.

Carburetor overhaul kits are recommended for each overhaul. These kits contain all gaskets and new parts to replace those that deteriorate most rapidly. Failure to replace all parts supplied with the kit (especially gaskets) can result in poor performance later.

After cleaning and checking all components, reassemble the carburetor, using new parts and referring to the exploded view.

a. Choke valve relief spring
b. Choke lever
c. Choke valve spring
d. Choke level adapter
e. Adapter gasket
f. Choke wire support
g. Choke valve
h. Plug
i. Economizer jet
j. Air bleeder
k. Air horn
l. Main passage plug
m. Plug gasket
n. Strainer
o. Power piston stopper
p. Power piston spring
q. Fitting
r. Needle valve seat gasket
s. Air horn gasket
t. Float pin
u. Needle valve seat
v. Power piston
w. Needle valve
x. Needle valve spring
y. Needle valve push pin
z. Float
aa. Lifter rod
ab. Slow jet
ac. Primary main jet
ad. Gasket
ae. Pump jet screw
af. Pump jet gasket
ag. Pump jet
ah. Spare jet
ai. Power valve
aj. Power jet
ak. Pump discharge weight
al. Level gauge retainer
am. Level gauge glass
an. Level gauge gasket
ao. Primary small venturi
ap. Main body
aq. Discharge check valve
ar. Plug gasket
as. Pump connecting link
at. Choke shaft
au. Plunger washer
av. Fast idle connector
aw. Secondary main jet
ax. Gasket
ay. Gasket
az. Gasket
ba. Pump damping spring
bb. Gasket
bc. Secondary small venturi
bd. Secondary main venturi
be. High speed valve stop lever
bf. Fast idle cam
bg. High speed valve stop
bh. High speed shaft
bi. High speed valve shaft lever
bj. Stop lever attaching screw
bk. High speed valve stop lever spring
bl. Fast idle attaching screw
bm. Throttle adjusting screw
bo. Secondary throttle back spring
bp. Secondary throttle lever
bq. Throttle shaft link
br. Fast idle adjusting screw
bs. Fast idle adjusting screw spring
bt. Primary throttle shaft arm
bu. Throttle lever
bw. Secondary throttle valve
bx. High speed valve
by. Primary throttle valve
bz. Flange
ca. Body to flange gasket
cb. Secondary throttle valve shaft
cd. Idle port plug
ce. Idle adjusting screw spring
cf. Primary throttle valve shaft
cg. Idle adjusting screw

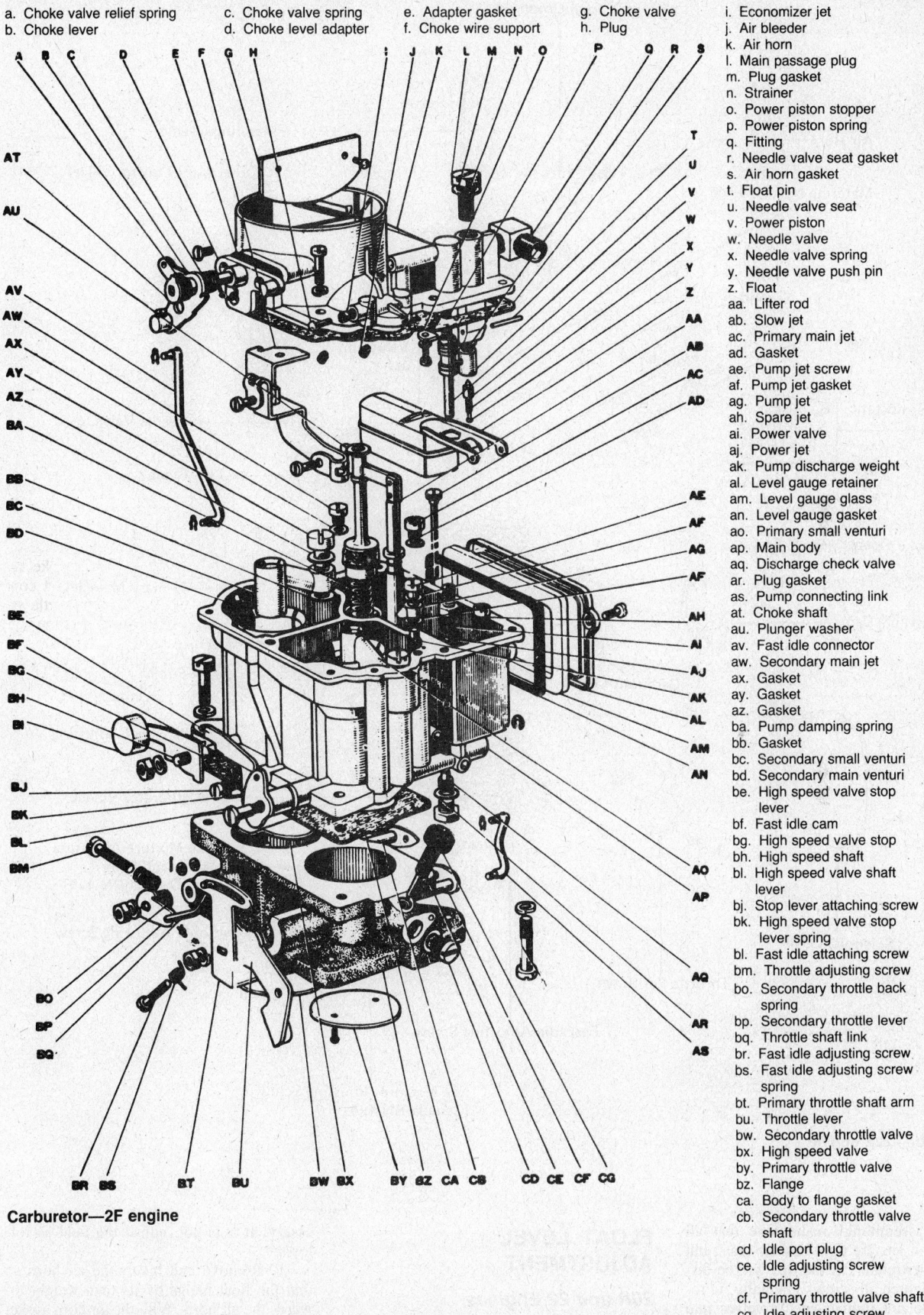

Carburetor—2F engine

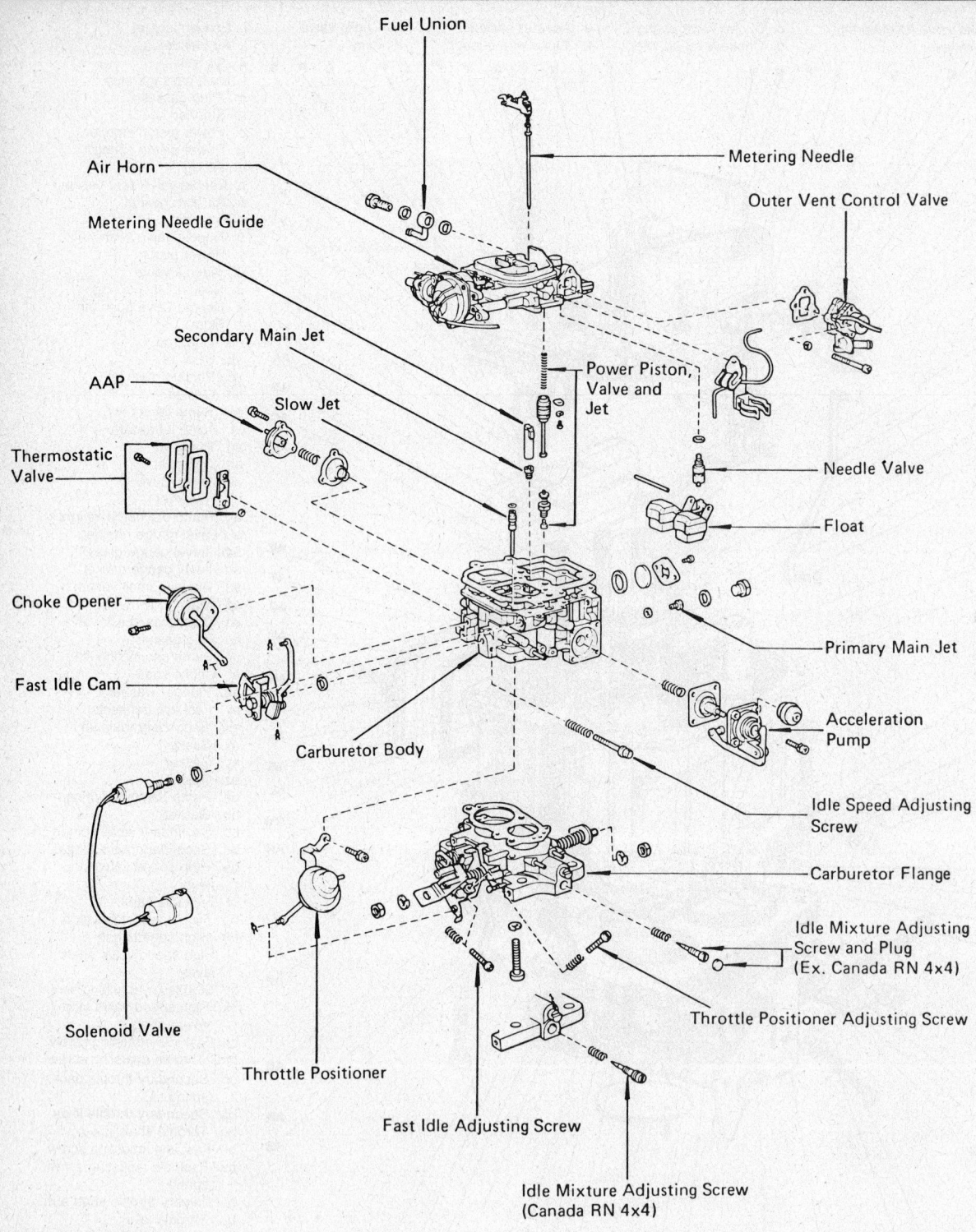

Fuel Union

Metering Needle

Air Horn

Outer Vent Control Valve

Metering Needle Guide

Secondary Main Jet

Power Piston, Valve and Jet

AAP

Slow Jet

Thermostatic Valve

Needle Valve

Float

Choke Opener

Primary Main Jet

Fast Idle Cam

Acceleration Pump

Carburetor Body

Idle Speed Adjusting Screw

Carburetor Flange

Idle Mixture Adjusting Screw and Plug (Ex. Canada RN 4x4)

Solenoid Valve

Throttle Positioner Adjusting Screw

Throttle Positioner

Fast Idle Adjusting Screw

Idle Mixture Adjusting Screw (Canada RN 4x4)

Carburetor—22R engine

When reassembling, make sure that all screws and jets are tight in their seats, but do not overtighten, as the tips will be distorted. Tighten all screws gradually, in rotation. Do not tighten needle valves into their seats; uneven jetting will result. Always use new gaskets. Be sure to adjust the float level when reassembling.

FLOAT LEVEL ADJUSTMENT

20R and 22 Engines

With the engine idling, check the fuel level in the carburetor sight glass. If the fuel level is even with the line, no adjustment is nec-

essary. If it is not, adjust the float as follows:

1. Remove and invert the air horn so that the float hangs by its own weight towards the air horn. With the air horn gasket removed, measure the distance between the tip of the float and the air horn. The distance should be 0.197 for 1977 and earlier en-

CARBURETOR SPECIFICATIONS

Year	Engine	Float Level Adjustment	Fast Idle Adjustment	Choke Unloader	Choke Breaker	Kick Up Adjustment	Accelerator Pump Adjustment
'75–'82	2F	0.295 in. ④	—	50°	38°	28° ⑦	0.374 in.
'75–'78	20R	0.197 in. ①	0.047 in.	50°	40°	0.008 in.	0.177 in.
'79–'80	20R	0.280 in.	0.047 in. ⑤	50°	38°	0.008 in.	0.177 in. ②
'81–'82	22R	0.413 in. ③	24°	45° ⑥	38°	—	—

① '78 20R 0.276 in.
② '80 20R 0.154 in.
③ Raised position; 1.89 lowered position
④ Raised position; 0.043 lowered position
⑤ '79 only. '80: 24°—see text
⑥ Except Canada. Canada: 50°
⑦ Except California. California: 25°

gines, 0.276 for 1978 engines, and 0.413 for 1981 and later (22R) engines. If the distance is incorrect, adjust the float by bending the center tab (marked "A" in the illustration) on all models except 1978. On 1978 models, adjust the float by bending the metal tab across the two slots and one hole right next to where it enters the float.

2. **20R Engines:** Raise the float away from the air horn and measure the distance between the needle valve push pin and the float lip. The distance should be 0.040 in. If adjustment is necessary on 1977 and earlier floats, bend the portion of the float marked "B" in the illustration. If adjustment is necessary on 1978 and later floats, bend the single center tab which resembles the tab marked "A" in the illustration.

3. **22R Engines:** Raise the float away from the air horn and measure the distance between the air horn and the tips of the float furthest away from the air horn. The distance should be 1.89 in. If adjustment is necessary, remove the float from the air horn and bend the tab which is furthest

away from the floats (centered between the hinge points). Recheck the setting after the adjustment has been made.

2F Engines

1. Remove the carburetor air horn. Invert the air horn and allow the float to hang towards the air horn.

2. With the air horn gasket removed, measure the distance between the float and the air horn, at the end of the float opposite the needle valve. The distance should be 0.295 in. If adjustment is necessary, remove the float and bend the tab which is centered between the hinge pivot points. After the adjustment is completed, reinstall the float and recheck the setting.

3. Lift upward on the float and measure the distance between the needle valve push pin and the lip of the float. The distance should be 0.043 in. If adjustment is necessary, remove the float and bend the tabs located just inside of the hinge points. After the adjustment is completed, reinstall the float and recheck the setting.

FAST IDLE ADJUSTMENT— OFF VEHICLE

20R Engines (1979 and Earlier) and 2F Engines

1. Remove the carburetor as previously outlined.

2. Close the choke valve completely and invert the carburetor.

3. Using a wire-type feeler gauge, check the clearance between the upper half of the primary throttle blade and the throttle bore. The clearance should be 0.047 for 20R engines; 0.051 for 2F engines. If necessary, adjust the clearance by turning the fast idle screw.

4. Install the carburetor as previously outlined.

20R Engines (1980) and 22R Engines (1981 and Later)

NOTE: A special blade angle tool must be obtained to properly make this adjustment.

1. Remove the carburetor as previously outlined.

2. Close the choke valve completely and set the throttle shaft lever to the first step of the fast idle cam.

3. Attach the blade angle tool to the primary throttle blade. Adjust the primary throttle blade angle to 24° from horizontal by turning the fast idle screw.

4. Remove the angle tool from the carburetor and install the carburetor as previously outlined.

A (Adjust the raised position)

B (Adjust the lower position)

Float lip

Float adjustment points—20R and 22R engines

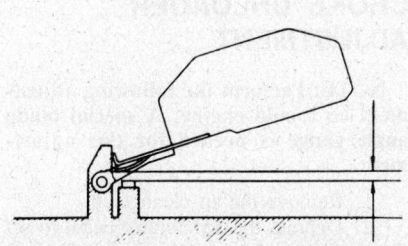

Measuring the float level (raised position)—20R and 22R engines

Measuring the float level (lowered position)—20R engine

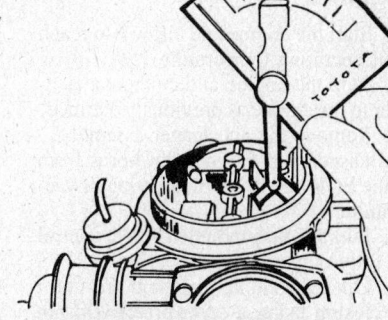

Special blade angle tool used for various carburetor adjustments—shown attached to choke valve

TOYOTA

FAST IDLE ADJUSTMENT— ON VEHICLE

20R Engines (1979 and Earlier)

1. Start the engine and allow it to reach normal operating temperature.
2. Stop the engine and disconnect the vacuum hose from the EGR valve. Connect a tachometer to the engine as previously outlined.
3. Open the throttle valve slightly and close the choke plate, which will set the fast idle cam.
4. Disconnect the vacuum hose(s) from the distributor vacuum unit. Plug the vacuum hose end(s).
5. Without touching the accelerator pedal, start the engine and read the tachometer. If necessary, adjust the fast idle speed to 2400 rpm by turning the fast idle screw.
6. Reconnect the vacuum hoses to both the EGR valve and the distributor vacuum unit. Disconnect the tachometer from the engine.

20R Engines (1980) and 22R Engines (1981 and Later)

1. Start the engine and allow it to reach normal operating temperature.
2. Stop the engine and connect a tachometer to the engine as previously outlined.
3. Remove the air cleaner assembly.
4. Disconnect the vacuum hose at the fast idle cam breaker (if so equipped) and plug the hose end.
5. Disconnect the vacuum hose(s) from the distributor vacuum unit.
6. Disconnect the vacuum hose from the EGR valve.
7. Open the throttle valve slightly and fully pull up on the fast idle linkage. Release the throttle.
8. Without touching the accelerator pedal, start the engine and read the tachometer. If necessary, adjust the fast idle speed to 2400 rpm by turning the fast idle screw.
9. Reconnect the vacuum hoses, disconnect the tachometer and reinstall the air cleaner.

2F Engines

1. Start the engine and allow it to reach normal operating temperature.
2. Stop the engine and connect a tachometer to the engine as previously outlined.
3. Remove the air cleaner assembly.
4. Disconnect the vacuum hoses from both the EGR valve and the distributor vacuum unit.
5. Pull the dash mounted choke control knob fully outward.
6. Open the choke plate and prevent it from closing using a screwdriver. Do not jam the screwdriver into place.
7. Start the engine and read the tachometer. If necessary, adjust the fast idle

speed to 1800 rpm by turning the fast idle screw.
8. Remove the screwdriver from the choke, disconnect the tachometer and reconnect the vacuum hoses.
9. Install the air cleaner assembly.

IDLE MIXTURE PRESET ADJUSTMENT

NOTE: Perform this adjustment on any rebuilt carburetor prior to installation of the carburetor.

1. Carefully turn the idle mixture adjusting screw clockwise (in) until the screw seats lightly.

—————— CAUTION ——————
Do not force the screw! The tip of the screw is easily damaged.

2. Turn the screw counterclockwise (out) 1½ turns for 20R and 2F engines; 2½ turns for 22R engines.
3. Reset the idle mixture adjustment after the engine is running, according to the procedure listed in the tune-up section.

AUTOMATIC CHOKE INSPECTION AND ADJUSTMENT

NOTE: Steps 1–4 must be performed with the engine cold and turned OFF.

1. Remove the air cleaner lid.
2. Depress the accelerator pedal. The choke plate should close. If the choke plate closes, proceed to step 5.
3. If the choke plate does not close, loosen the three screws around the thermostat case.

—————— CAUTION ——————
Do not loosen the center housing screw; coolant leakage will occur.

4. Rotate the case just until the choke plate closes and tighten the case screws.
5. Start the engine and allow it to reach normal operating temperature. If the choke plate opens fully, the choke adjustment is correct. If it does not, loosen the three case screws and rotate the case just until the choke plate is fully open. Tighten the case screws.

CHOKE UNLOADER ADJUSTMENT

NOTE: Perform the following adjustment on a cold engine. A special blade angle gauge is needed for this adjustment.

1. Remove the air cleaner lid.
2. Depress the accelerator pedal to set the choke plate in the fully closed position.
3. Attach the blade angle gauge to the choke plate.

4. Open the primary throttle valve completely. The unloader should open the choke plate to the following angle:
   a. 50° for 2F and 20R engines
   b. 45° for 22R engines, except Canada
   c. 50° for 22R engines, Canada
On 2F and 20R engines, bend the fast idle lever to adjust the angle. On 22R engines, bend the first throttle arm to adjust the angle.
5. Remove the blade angle gauge and reinstall the air cleaner lid.

CHOKE BREAKER ADJUSTMENT

NOTE: A special blade angle gauge is needed for this adjustment.

1. Remove the air cleaner assembly.
2. Attach the blade angle gauge to the choke plate.
3. With the choke blade closed, push the choke breaker link towards the choke breaker until resistance is felt. The choke plate should open to an angle of 40° for 1978 and earlier 20R engines; 38° for all other engines. Bend the choke breaker link to adjust the opening.
4. Detach the blade angle gauge and install the air cleaner assembly.

SECONDARY KICK-UP ADJUSTMENT

This adjustment is not necessary on 22R engines.

20R Engines

1. Remove the carburetor as previously outlined.
2. With the carburetor inverted, open the primary throttle blade fully. Measure the distance between the uppermost portion of the secondary throttle blade and the secondary throttle bore, using a wire-type feeler gauge. The clearance should be 0.008 in. If adjustment is necessary, bend the secondary throttle lever as required to attain the proper clearance.
3. Install the carburetor as previously outlined.

2F Engines

NOTE: A special blade angle gauge is needed for this adjustment.

1. Remove the carburetor as previously outlined.
2. Attach the blade angle gauge to the secondary throttle blade.
3. Open the primary throttle blade fully and read the blade angle gauge. The secondary throttle blade should open slightly to an angle of 28° (except California) or 25° (California). If adjustment is necessary, bend the secondary throttle lever as required to attain the proper angle.
4. Detach the blade angle gauge and

install the carburetor as previously outlined.

ACCELERATOR PUMP ADJUSTMENT

NOTE: This adjustment is not required on 22R engines.

1. Remove the air cleaner assembly.
2. With the choke plate fully open, measure the accelerator pump stroke at the top of the accelerator pump rod by fully opening the throttle from the closed position.
3. The total pump stroke should be 0.177 in. for 1979 and earlier 20R engines; 0.154 in. for 1980 20R engines; and 0.374 in. for 2F engines. Adjust the stroke by bending the linkage (''A'') which is attached to the accelerator pump arm opposite the accelerator pump.
4. Install the air cleaner assembly.

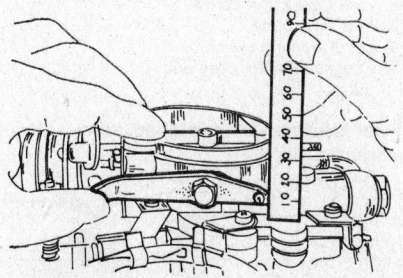

Measuring the accelerator pump stroke at the top of the accelerator pump rod—20R engine shown, others similar

Diesel Fuel System

INJECTION PUMP REMOVAL AND INSTALLATION

1. Disconnect the cables which are positioned above the valve cover and move the cables aside. Remove the valve cover.
2. Disconnect the cables from both batteries.
3. Using a wrench on the center crankshaft pulley bolt, rotate the engine (clockwise only) until the TDC mark on the pulley is aligned with the pointer. Check that the valves of the number one cylinder are closed (rocker arms loose). If the valves are not closed, rotate the engine 360° and again align the TDC mark with the pointer.
4. Disconnect the fuel injection lines at the injection pump and the injectors. Remove the injection lines.
5. Disconnect the fuel feed line at the injection pump and plug the line.
6. Remove the engine cooling fan, belts, and water pump pulley.
7. Remove the crankshaft pulley, using an appropriate puller.
8. Remove the timing belt cover.
9. Using a piece of chalk or a crayon, mark the relationships between each of the timing gears and the timing belt.
10. Remove the timing belt idler pulley, then remove the timing belt.
11. Remove the injection pump drive gear, using an appropriate puller.
12. Note the factory-made alignment mark next to the outer pump fastener. This mark signifies the required relationship between the pump and the timing case assembly. Align this mark during installation.
13. Unbolt and remove the injection pump.

— CAUTION —

DO NOT disassemble the injection pump; only factory-authorized repair centers have the facilities to do so. No adjustments to the pump are possible.

---

14. Installation of the pump is the reverse of the removal procedure. See the Engine Mechanical section for specifics concerning timing belt installation. Make sure all gasket surfaces are clean, and replace any damaged gaskets.

INJECTOR NOZZLE REMOVAL

1. Remove the injection lines.
2. Remove the leakage pipe from the injectors and note the location of each sealing washer.
3. Remove the nozzle(s) from the cylinder head, noting the positions of the nozzle seats and seat gaskets.

— CAUTION —

DO NOT allow dirt to enter the engine through the nozzle holes.

NOTE: Remove accumulations of carbon from the nozzle holes.

4. Keep the injectors in order so that they may be installed in their original positions.

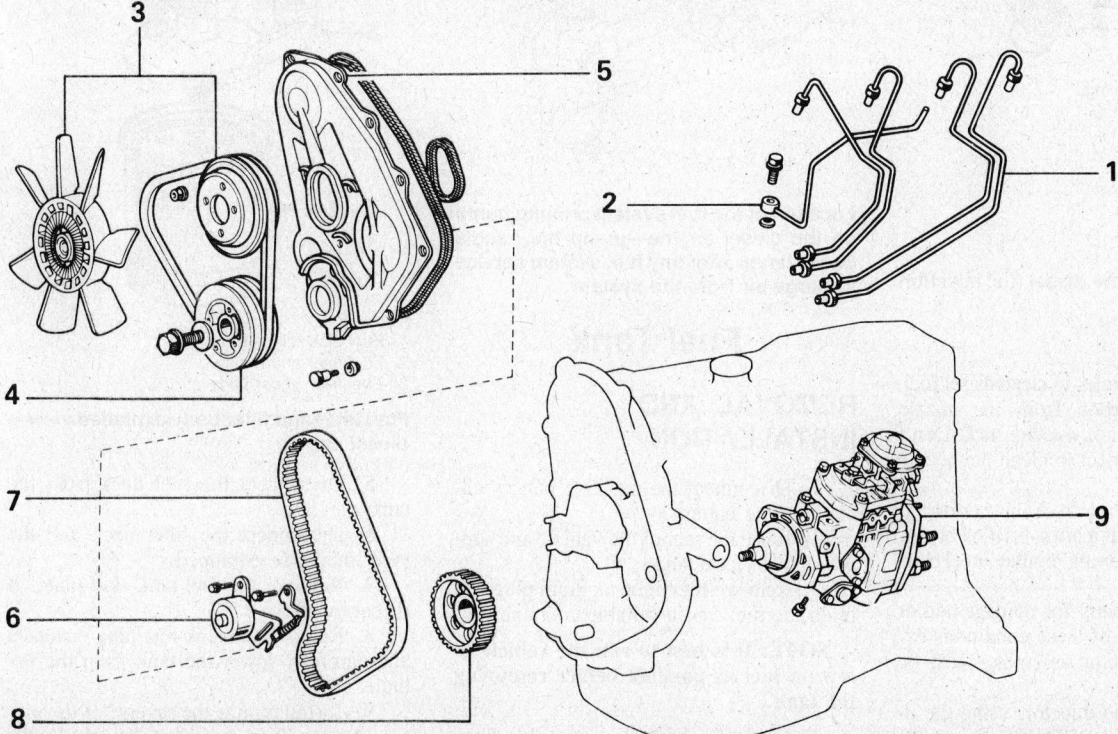

1. Injection pipe
2. Fuel pipe
3. Fan and fan pulley
4. Crankshaft pulley
5. Timing belt cover
6. Idler pulley
7. Timing belt
8. Pump drive pulley
9. Injection pump

Diesel fuel injection pump and related components

5. If the engine exhibited any type of severe miss, excessive smoking, or drastic decrease in power, it is best to have the nozzles professionally tested for opening pressure, leakage, and spray pattern.

INJECTOR NOZZLE CLEANING

1. Remove the nozzle holder retaining nut from the nozzle holder body.
2. Disassemble the injector, following the accompanying illustration.

CAUTION

DO NOT touch the nozzle mating surfaces with your fingers.

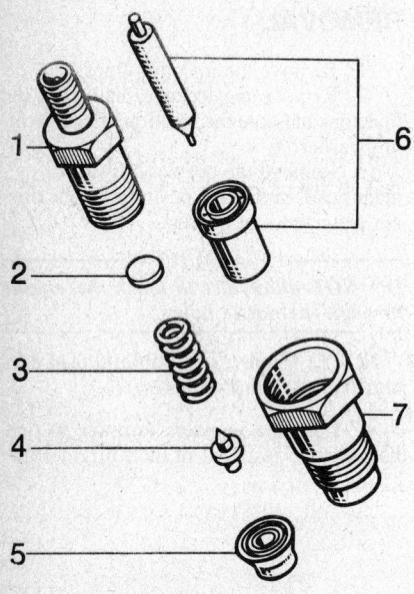

1. Nozzle holder retaining nut
2. Adjusting shim
3. Pressure spring
4. Pressure pin
5. Distance piece
6. Nozzle assembly
7. Nozzle holder body

Exploded view of the diesel fuel injection nozzle

3. Wash the nozzles in clean diesel fuel.
4. Remove carbon from the nozzle needle tip with a small, wooden stick. Don't use any metallic object to clean the nozzle tip.
5. Remove carbon from the exterior of the nozzle body with a brass bristled brush. Don't use a brush having regular, steel bristles.
6. Inspect all parts for damage and/or corrosion. If either of these conditions exist, the entire injector assembly must be replaced.
7. Assemble the injector, using the illustration as a guide. Torque the nozzle holder retaining nut to 44–57 ft. lbs.

INJECTOR NOZZLE INSTALLATION

1. Install the injector assembly, noting that:
 a. the nozzle seat is installed between the injector and the seat gasket, and
 b. the nozzle seat must be positioned with the concave side of the seat towards the injector.

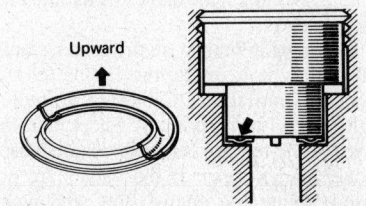

Correct installation of the injector nozzle seat—diesel engine

2. Position a wrench on the hex of the nozzle body (NOT the nozzle retaining nut) and torque to 51–65 ft. lbs.
3. Assemble the remaining lines to the injectors. Torque the injection pipe union nuts to 15–21 ft. lbs.

NOTE: After any service is performed to the diesel fuel system, pump the priming handle on the fuel sedimenter assembly 30–40 times to purge air from the system.

Location of the fuel system priming pump on the diesel engine—pump the handle 30–40 times after any fuel system service to purge air from the system

Fuel Tank

REMOVAL AND INSTALLATION

1. Disconnect the negative battery cable(s) at the battery.
2. Raise the rear of the vehicle and support it with jackstands.
3. Remove the fuel tank drain plug and drain the fuel into a suitable container.

NOTE: It is best to run the vehicle as low on fuel as possible before removing the tank.

4. Disconnect the electrical plug from the sending unit.

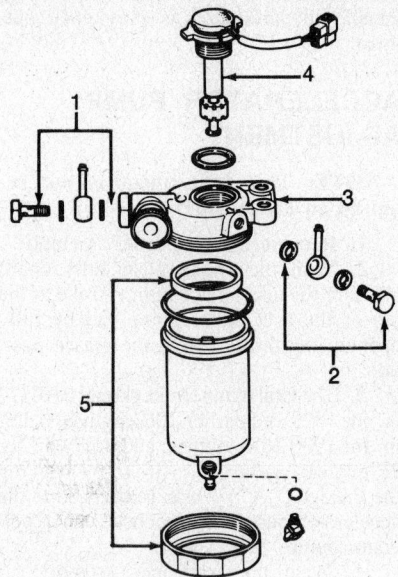

1. Fuel pipe follow screw
2. Fuel pipe follow screw
3. Fuel filter body
4. Level warning switch
5. Fuel sedimenter case and nut

Fuel sedimenter exploded view—diesel engine

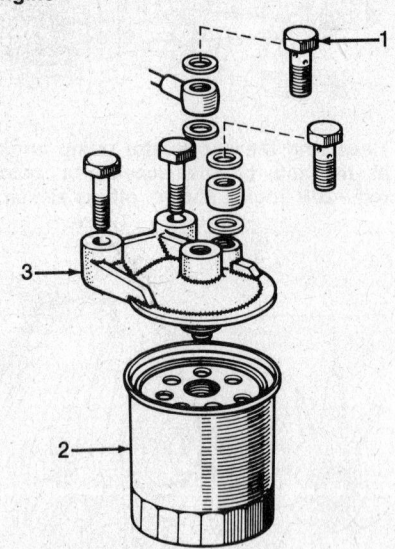

1. Fuel pipe follow screw
2. Fuel filter and O-ring
3. Fuel filter upper body

Fuel filter and filter body exploded view—diesel engine

5. Disconnect the fuel lines from the tank.
6. Disconnect the filler neck and the vent line, if so equipped.
7. Remove the fuel tank skid plate, if so equipped.
8. Remove the tank retaining fasteners and carefully lower the tank from the vehicle.
9. Installation is the reverse of the previous steps. This procedure is basically the same on all models.

CLUTCH

REMOVAL AND INSTALLATION

1. Remove the transmission according to the procedure following the clutch section.

2. Stamp or chalk matchmarks on the clutch cover and flywheel, indicating their relationship.

3. Loosen the clutch cover-to-flywheel retaining bolts one turn at a time. The pressure on the clutch disc must be released GRADUALLY.

4. Remove the clutch cover-to-flywheel bolts. Remove the clutch cover and the clutch disc.

5. If the clutch release bearing is to be replaced, do so at this time as follows:

a. Remove the bearing retaining clip(s) and remove the bearing and hub.

b. Remove the release fork and the boot.

c. The bearing is press fitted to the hub. In some cases, the bearing is available with the hub from automotive suppliers. If this is not the case with your model, contact a machine shop and have the bearing replaced using a hydraulic press. Using other means to replace the bearing could result in personal injury.

d. Clean all parts and lightly grease the input shaft splines and all of the contact points.

e. Install the bearing/hub assembly, fork, boot, and retaining clip(s) in their original locations.

6. Inspect the flywheel surface for cracks, heat scoring (blue marks), and warpage. If oil is present on the flywheel surface, this indicates that either the engine rear oil seal or the transmission front oil seal is leaking. If necessary, refer to the appropriate section for seal replacement. If in doubt concerning the condition of the flywheel, consult an automotive machine shop.

7. Before installing any new parts, make sure that they are clean. During installation, do not get grease or oil on any of the components, as this will shorten clutch life considerably.

8. Position the clutch disc against the flywheel. (Pickups: The short side of the splined section faces the flywheel; Landcruisers—The long side of the splined section faces the flywheel.)

9. Install the clutch cover over the disc and install the bolts loosely. Align the matchmarks made during step 2. If a new or rebuilt clutch cover assembly is installed, use the matchmark on the old cover assembly as a reference.

10. Align the clutch disc with the flywheel using a clutch aligning tool, which is available in most auto stores at a reasonable price.

11. With the clutch aligning tool installed, tighten the clutch cover bolts gradually in a star pattern, as is done with lug nuts. Finally torque the bolts to 11–16 ft. lbs.

12. Install the transmission using the procedure following the clutch section.

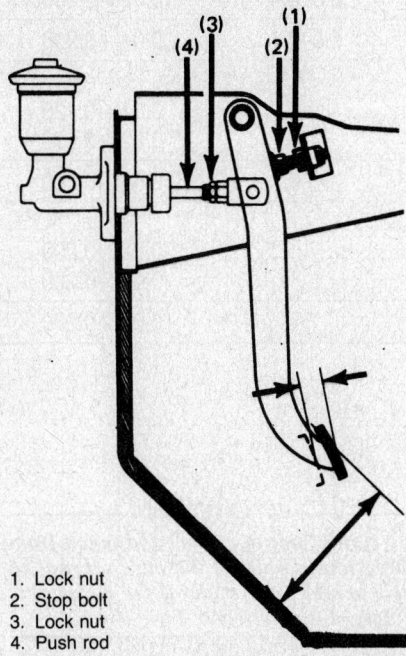

1. Lock nut
2. Stop bolt
3. Lock nut
4. Push rod

Clutch pedal adjustment points—typical. The distance between the ends of the long arrow is the pedal height. The distance between the two short arrows is the pedal free-play. Push rod play is only a small movement of the pedal—see text.

CLUTCH PEDAL HEIGHT ADJUSTMENT

The pedal height measurement is gauged from the angled section of the floorboard to the center of the clutch pedal pad. Refer to the accompanying specification chart to determine the recommended pedal height.

If necessary, adjust the pedal height by loosening the locknut and turning the pedal stop bolt which is located above the pedal towards the drivers seat. Tighten the locknut after the adjustment.

CLUTCH PEDAL PUSH ROD PLAY ADJUSTMENT

The pedal push rod play is the distance between the clutch master cylinder piston and the pedal pushrod located above the pedal towards the firewall. Since it is nearly impossible to measure this distance at the source, it must be measured at the pedal pad, preferably with a dial indicator gauge. Refer to the accompanying specification chart to determine the recommended play.

If necessary, adjust the pedal play by loosening the pedal pushrod locknut and turning the pushrod. Tighten the locknut after the adjustment.

CLUTCH FORK TIP PLAY ADJUSTMENT

The fork tip play is the total amount of travel evident at the outer end of the clutch release fork where the fork comes in contact with the release cylinder pushrod. Refer to the accompanying specification chart to determine the recommended fork tip play.

The fork tip play is adjusted by loosening the release cylinder pushrod locknut and effectively increasing or decreasing the pushrod length as required.

NOTE: Some models do not have adjustable release cylinder pushrods. These models are identified by having no adjustment nuts on the pushrod.

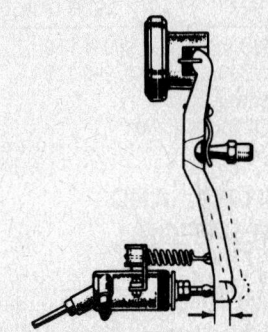

Measuring the fork tip end-play—typical

CLUTCH PEDAL FREE-PLAY ADJUSTMENT

The free-play measurement is the total travel of the clutch pedal from the fully released position to where resistance is felt as the pedal is pushed downward. Refer to the accompanying specification chart to determine the recommended pedal free play.

If the clutch pedal free play is incorrect, perform the previous clutch adjustments then bleed the system accoridng to the procedure which follows. If a pedal free-play dimension is not listed for your model, perform the previous clutch adjustments and disregard the pedal free-play measurement.

Clutch Master Cylinder

REMOVAL

1. Disconnect the master cylinder pushrod from the clutch pedal.

2. Remove the hydraulic line from the master cylinder being careful not to damage the compression fitting.

3. Remove the two bolts holding the master cylinder to the engine compartment.

—————— **CAUTION** ——————
Brake fluid dissolves paint. Do not allow it to drip onto the body when removing the master cylinder.

CLUTCH ADJUSTMENT SPECIFICATIONS

(All measurements in inches)

| Year | Model | Pedal | | | Fork Tip Play |
		Height	Push Rod Play	Free-Play	
'79 and earlier	Pickup	6.0–6.4	0.020–0.200	0.200–0.600	—
'80 and later	Pickup	6.0–6.4	0.040–0.200	0.200–0.600 ①	—②
'79 and earlier	Land Cruiser 2 dr.				
	w/P.B. ③	8.5	0.020–0.120	—	0.120–0.160
	wo/P.B. ④	7.9	0.020–0.120	—	0.120–0.160
'80 and later	Land Cruiser 2 dr.	8.5	0.040–0.200		0.157–0.197
'79 and earlier	Land Cruiser Wagon				
	w/P.B. ③	7.3	0.020–0.200	—	0.120–0.160
	wo/P.B. ④	6.8	0.020–0.200	—	0.120–0.160
'80 and later	Land Cruiser Wagon	7.7	0.040–0.200	—	0.160–0.197

① '80 4WD models—0.980–1.770
② '80 4WD models—0.079–0.118
③ With power brakes
④ Without power brakes

OVERHAUL AND INSTALLATION

1. Disassemble the master cylinder by unscrewing the clutch pedal clevis from the pushrod. Also remove the locknut.

2. Pull off the rubber boot to expose an internal snap-ring. Remove the snap-ring and withdraw the piston and compression spring.

3. Take a clean rag and wipe out the inside of the cylinder. Inspect the inside of the cylinder for scoring and deposits. Use crocus cloth or a small hone to refinish the inside of the cylinder. If light honing will not remove score marks replace the cylinder.

> ——— CAUTION ———
> *Be careful not to remove too much from the cylinder walls as the cups will not be able to seal the cylinder if the diameter is enlarged excessively.*

4. Wash all metal parts in solvent.

5. Further disassembly should be avoided unless the reservoir is leaking. If the reservoir needs to be replaced, remove the cap and remove the master cylinder reservoir bolt located at the bottom of the reservoir. Tighten the bolt upon reassembly.

6. With new parts from a rebuilding kit assemble the master cylinder. Coat the cylinder wall with brake fluid so that the edges of the new cups will not be damaged.

7. Reinstall the master cylinder. Partially tighten the hydraulic line before tightening the master cylinder mounting bolts. Adjust the push rod play clearance as outlined earlier, after bleeding the system.

Clutch Release Cylinder

REMOVAL

1. Jack up the front of the truck and support it on jackstands.

2. Remove the tension spring on the clutch fork.

3. Remove the hydraulic line from the release cylinder. Be careful not to damage the fitting.

4. Turn the release cylinder pushrod in sufficiently to gain clearance from the fork.

5. Remove the mounting bolts and withdraw the cylinder.

OVERHAUL

1. Remove the pushrod, rubber boot, piston and cups from the cylinder.

2. Clean the inside of the cylinder with a rag and inspect for scoring. If there is no serious damage, hone the cylinder just enough to remove deposits. Replace the cylinder if light honing does not remove the score marks. Wash all the parts in brake fluid before assembly.

3. Coat the new rubber parts in brake fluid and reassemble.

INSTALLATION

1. Install the hydraulic line from the master cylinder.

2. Position the cylinder on the clutch

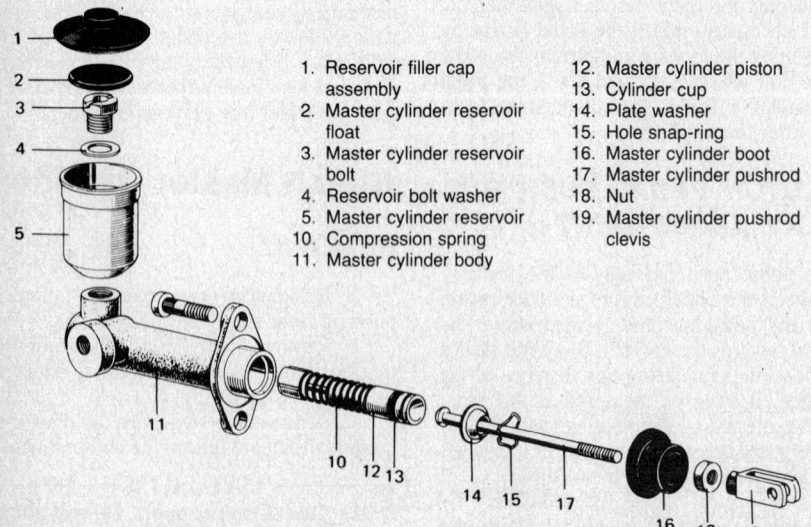

1. Reservoir filler cap assembly
2. Master cylinder reservoir float
3. Master cylinder reservoir bolt
4. Reservoir bolt washer
5. Master cylinder reservoir
10. Compression spring
11. Master cylinder body
12. Master cylinder piston
13. Cylinder cup
14. Plate washer
15. Hole snap-ring
16. Master cylinder boot
17. Master cylinder pushrod
18. Nut
19. Master cylinder pushrod clevis

Clutch master cylinder exploded view—typical

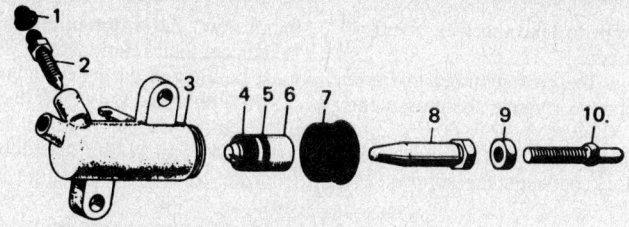

Clutch slave cylinder exploded view—typical

1. Bleeder plug cap
2. Bleeder plug
3. Slave cylinder body
4. Cylinder cup
5. Cylinder cup
6. Slave cylinder piston
7. Slave cylinder boot
8. Slave cylinder pushrod No. 1
9. Nut
10. Slave cylinder pushrod No. 2

housing and install the clamp and retaining screws.

3. Adjust the fork tip clearance as previously outlined.

NOTE: The system must be bled after the cylinder is reinstalled.

Hydraulic System Bleeding

NOTE: This procedure may be utilized when either the clutch master or release cylinder has been removed or if any of the hydraulic lines have been disturbed.

CAUTION
Do not spill brake fluid on the body of the vehicle as it will destroy the paint.

1. Fill the master cylinder reservoir with brake fluid.
2. Remove the cap and loosen the bleeder screw on the clutch release cylinder. Cover the hole with your finger.
3. Have an assistant pump the clutch pedal several times. Take your finger off the hole while the pedal is being depressed so that the air in the system can be released. Put your finger back on the hole and release the pedal.
4. After fluid pressure can be felt (with your finger) tighten the bleeder screw.
5. Put a short length of hose over the bleeder screw and place the other end into a jar half full of clean brake fluid.
6. Depress the clutch pedal and loosen the bleeder screw. Allow the fluid to flow into the jar.
7. Tighten the plug and then release the clutch pedal.
8. Repeat steps 6 and 7 until no air bubbles are visible in the bleeder tube.
9. When there are no more air bubbles in the system, tighten the plug fully with the pedal depressed. Replace the plastic cap.
10. Fill the master cylinder to the correct level with brake fluid.
11. Check the system for leaks.

MANUAL TRANSMISSION

REMOVAL AND INSTALLATION

2WD Pickup

NOTE: A special service tool is needed for removal of the transmission shift lever on floorshift models: Toyota #09305-20011 is used on 1979 and earlier models; #09305-20012 is used on 1980 and later models. Equivalents of these special tools may also be used.

1. Disconnect the battery cables at the battery.

NOTE: Steps 2–4 apply to floorshift equipped models.

2. Remove the center floor console, if so equipped.
3. Remove the shift lever handle. Remove the floor mat or carpet along with the shift lever boot in order to gain access to the shift lever.
4. Using the proper shift lever removal tool mentioned previously, remove the shift lever.
5. Raise the vehicle and support it safely with jack stands.
6. Drain the transmission fluid.
7. Chalk matchmarks on the driveshaft flange and the differential pinion flange to indicate their relationships. These marks must be aligned during installation.
8. Remove the driveshaft flange bolts and the center support bearing-to-frame bolts (if equipped with a 2-piece driveshaft). Lower the driveshaft out of the vehicle.
9. Disconnect the wiring at the back-up lamp switch.
10. Disconnect the speedometer cable at the transmission and tie the cable out of the way.
11. Disconnect the wiring at the starter. Remove the starter mounting bolts and lower the starter out of the vehicle.

12. If the hydraulic line from the clutch release cylinder is clamped to the frame, remove the clamp retaining bolt. Remove the release cylinder mounting bolts and the fork spring (if so equipped). Tie the release cylinder out of the way.

NOTE: It is not necessary to disconnect the hydraulic line from the release cylinder.

13. On column shift vehicles, disconnect the shift selector linkage at the transmission.
14. On column shift vehicles, remove the transmission cross shafts.
15. Support the rear of the transmission with a jack and remove the transmission-to-transmission mounting bolts.
16. Raise the rear of the transmission SLIGHTLY; just enough to take the weight off of the crossmember.
17. Remove the crossmember-to-frame attaching bolts and remove the crossmember from the vehicle.
18. Place a support under the engine with a wooden block between the support and the engine.

CAUTION
The wooden block and support should be no more than about ¼ away from the engine so that when the engine is lowered, damage will not occur to any underhood components. If possible, shim the support so that the wooden block touches the engine.

19. Lower the jack until the engine rests on the support and block.

NOTE: For the next step, it is recommended that you have an assistant help you guide the transmission out of the vehicle.

20. Remove the transmission-to-engine attaching bolts and draw the transmission rearward and down away from the engine.
21. Refer to the Unit Repair Section for overhaul procedures.
Installation is the reverse of removal. Observe the following points:
1. If the clutch has been replaced, make sure that the clutch disc is aligned properly. Refer to the clutch section.
2. Lightly lubricate the following parts with multi-purpose grease:
   a. End of the input shaft
   b. Splines of the input shaft
   c. Inner surface of the release bearing
   d. Release fork contact points
   e. Driveshaft splines
3. Replenish the transmission (and transfer case) fluid levels.
4. If the clutch has been replaced, make the necessary adjustments as previously outlined in the clutch section.
5. Align the matchmarks made during disassembly.
6. Check the back-up lamp and indicator (4WD) operation.

TOYOTA

4WD Pickup

NOTE: A special service tool, Toyota #09305-20012 or its equivalent, is needed to remove the transmission shift lever.

1. Disconnect the battery cables at the battery.
2. Remove the shift lever handles. Remove the front floor mat or carpet along with both shift lever boots to gain access to the shift levers.
3. Using the special shift lever removal tool mentioned previously, remove the transmission shift lever.
4. Using needle nose pliers, remove the transfer case shift lever retainer, then remove the shift lever.
5. Raise the vehicle and support it securely with jackstands.

NOTE: Because of space limitations, it may be necessary to raise both the front and rear of the vehicle. If this is done, place jackstands under both axles as follows: On the outside of the U-bolts at the front axle; on the inside of the U-bolts at the rear axle.

6. Drain the lubricant from both the transmission and the transfer case.
7. Chalk matchmarks on the driveshaft flanges and the differential pinion flanges to indicate their relationships. These marks must be aligned during installation.
8. Remove the four bolts from each end of the front driveshaft and remove the driveshaft assembly.

NOTE: Do not disassemble the front driveshaft to remove it.

9. Chalk matchmarks on the rear driveshaft and the slip yoke to indicate their relationships. These marks must be aligned during installation.
10. Remove the four bolts from the rearward flange of the rear driveshaft. Lower the driveshaft out of the vehicle. Remove the four bolts from the slip yoke flange then remove the flange and yoke assembly.
11. Unbolt the clutch release cylinder and tie it out of the way.

NOTE: It is not necessary to disconnect the hydraulic line from the clutch release cylinder.

12. Disconnect the positive battery cable at the starter motor switch.
13. Disconnect the remaining wire at the starter.
14. Remove the two starter retaining bolts and lower the starter out of the vehicle.
15. Disconnect the speedometer cable at the transfer case and tie it out of the way.
16. Disconnect the exhaust pipe clamp at the transmission housing.
17. Disconnect the wiring for the back-up lamp switch and the 4WD indicator switch.
18. Remove the crossmember-to-transfer case adaptor mounting bolts. Using a jack, raise the transmission and transfer case assembly SLIGHTLY off of the crossmem-

ber; just enough to take the weight off of the crossmember.
19. Remove the crossmember-to-frame attaching bolts and remove the crossmember.
20. Place a support under the engine with a wooden block between the support and the engine.

CAUTION

The wooden block and support should be no more than about ¼" away from the engine so that when the engine is lowered, damage will not occur to any underhood components. If possible, shim the support so that the wooden block touches the engine.

---

21. Lower the jack until the engine rests on the support.

NOTE: For the next step, it is recommended that you have an assistant help you guide the transmission and transfer case assembly out of the vehicle.

22. Remove the transmission-to-engine attaching bolts and draw the transmission and transfer case assembly rearward and down away from the engine.
23. To separate the transmission and transfer case, stand the transmission on its front face with the tailshaft pointing upward. Remove the transfer case-to-adapter mounting bolts and lift the transfer case off of the transmission assembly.
24. Refer to the Unit Repair Section for overhaul procedures.

To install the transmission, reverse the previous steps. Refer to the end of the 2WD procedure for installation points.

Land Cruiser

1979 AND EARLIER MODELS

NOTE: Steps 2–4 pertain to 2 door models.

1. Disconnect the battery cables at the battery.
2. Remove the front seats, seat tracks, and the console box, if so equipped.
3. Remove the heater pipe clamp which is located on the transmission tunnel to the right of the transfer case shift lever.
4. If the fuel tank is mounted beneath the passenger seat, drain the fuel, remove the fuel tank cover, disconnect the lines, etc., and remove the fuel tank.
5. Remove the shift lever knobs and the shift lever boots.
6. Using Toyota special service tool #09305-60010 or its equivalent, remove the transmission shift lever.
7. Remove the transmission tunnel cover.
8. Raise the vehicle and support it safely with jack stands.
9. Drain the lubricant from both the transmission and the transfer case.
10. Remove the undercover located beneath the front driveshaft.
11. Chalk matchmarks on the driveshaft

flanges and the differential pinion flanges to indicate their relationships. These marks must be aligned during installation.
12. Unbolt the driveshaft flanges and remove both the front and rear driveshafts.
13. Disconnect the speedometer cable from the transfer case and tie it out of the way.
14. Disconnect the parking brake cable at the parking brake lever. Leave the cable attached at the drum end; the cable will be removed with the transmission and transfer case assembly.
15. If the vehicle is equipped with a vacuum 4WD engagement system, mark and disconnect the following items at the transfer case:
    a. Wiring for the indicator
    b. Wiring for the transfer switch
    c. Vacuum hoses
16. Disconnect the wiring for the back-up lamp switch. Unbolt the back-up lamp wiring harness clamp from the transfer case, if so equipped.
17. On column shift models, disconnect the shift linkage at the transmission.
18. Remove the power take-off (PTO) lever, if so equipped.
19. Follow steps 18–22 of the 4WD Pickup procedure to remove the transmission and transfer case assembly.
20. To separate the transmission from the transfer case:
    a. Remove the 4WD engagement lever guide.
    b. Remove the 4WD lever and rod as an assembly. ,
    c. Remove the back-up lamp switch.
    d. If the vehicle is equipped with a PTO, remove the PTO unit from the transmission. If the vehicle does not have a PTO, remove the cover from the left side of the transfer case.
    e. Remove the rear transfer case cover (six bolts) from the transfer case. Remove the shaft nut located behind the cover.

NOTE: This nut is staked at the factory; to remove it, you must tap the staked portions outward to clear the shaft. Restake the nut after installation.

    f. Remove the five transfer case-to-transmission bolts.

NOTE: Two of these bolts are located inside the left side of the transfer case, where the PTO or cover was previously removed.

    g. Using a puller assembled to the transfer case and the transmission output shaft, separate the transfer case from the transmission.
21. Refer to the Unit Repair Section for overhaul procedures.
22. Installation is the reverse of the previous steps. Refer to the installation points at the end of the 2WD Pickup procedure.

1980 AND LATER

1. Disconnect the battery cables at the battery.

2. Remove the entrance scuff plates from the floor of the interior.

3. Remove both side trim panels from beneath the instrument panel.

4. Remove the center heater duct.

5. Remove the front floor mat or carpet.

6. Remove the handles from both shift levers.

7. Remove the transmission tunnel cover along with the shift lever boots.

8. Disconnect the wiring from both the back-up lamp switch and the 4WD indicator (if so equipped).

9. Using Toyota special service tool #09305-55010 or its equivalent, remove the transmission shift lever.

10. Raise the vehicle and support it safely with jack stands.

11. Remove the transfer case skid plate.

12. Disconnect the speedometer cable at the transfer case and tie it out of the way.

13. Chalk matchmarks on the driveshaft flanges and the differential pinion flanges to indicate their relationships. These marks must be aligned during installation.

14. Remove the mounting bolts from the driveshaft flanges and remove the driveshaft assemblies.

15. Disconnect the starter wiring. Remove the starter mounting bolts and remove the starter from the vehicle.

16. Unbolt the clutch release cylinder and move it out of the way.

NOTE: It is not necessary to disconnect the hydraulic line from the release cylinder.

17. Drain the lubricant from both the transmission and the transfer case.

18. Remove the tachometer sensor, if so equipped.

19. Follow steps 18–22 of the 4WD Pickup procedure to remove the transmission and transfer case assembly.

20. To separate the transfer case from the transmission, remove the transfer case mounting bolts and slide the transfer case off of the transmission.

21. Refer to the Unit Repair Section for overhaul procedures.

22. Installation is the reverse of the previous steps. Refer to the installation points at the end of the 2WD Pickup procedure.

SHIFT LINKAGE ADJUSTMENT

Column Shifter

Shift lever adjustment:
The only adjustments which may be performed on the column shift linkages are for the length of the column-to-transmission rods. Adjust these so that the transmission operates smoothly.

Floor Shifter

All Toyota models equipped with a floor shifter have internally-mounted shift linkages. On older models, the linkage is contained in the side cover which is bolted on the transmission case.

No external adjustment is needed or possible.

AUTOMATIC TRANSMISSION

Description

The A-30 Toyoglide transmission is used in all 1977 and earlier models. The A-30 is a fully automatic three-speed transmission using a combination of multiple disc clutches and front and rear bands to accomplish gear ratio changes. Internal adjustments necessary on this transmission include only the front and rear bands.

The A-40 transmission is used in 1978–79 models. The A-40 is also a fully automatic three-speed, but it does not use bands for gear changes, thus internal adjustments are not possible.

In 1980, the A-40 was replaced by the A-43 three-speed, which is used through the current model year. Internal adjustments are not required on this transmission.

The A-43D is a fully automatic four-speed transmission first offered as an option on 1981 models and is available through the current model year. The fourth speed of this transmission is an overdrive ratio of 0.688 to 1, which offers improved gasoline mileage by lowering the engine rpm at highway speeds. The hydraulic circuit of the overdrive mode is electrically controlled. The main electrical components include the following:

1. A dash mounted overdrive control switch

2. A dash mounted ''OVERDRIVE-OFF'' indicator lamp

3. A transmission mounted solenoid

4. An engine mounted thermo-switch which prevents overdrive engagement until the engine coolant temperature reaches 131°F.

REMOVAL

A-30 and A-40 Transmissions

1. Disconnect the battery cables at the battery.

2. Disconnect the transmission throttle linkage at the carburetor.

3. Raise the vehicle and support it with jack stands.

4. Drain the transmission fluid.

5. Disconnect the wiring from the starter.

6. Unbolt the starter and lower it out of the vehicle.

7. Disconnect the exhaust pipe from the exhaust manifold. Remove the exhaust clamp from the exhaust pipe.

8. Disconnect the linkage from the drivers side of the transmission.

9. Disconnect the speedometer cable and tie it out of the way.

10. Disconnect the parking brake cable from the parking brake control lever.

11. Chalk matchmarks on the rear driveshaft flange and the differential pinion flange. These marks must be aligned during installation.

12. Unbolt the rear driveshaft flange. If the vehicle has a two-piece driveshaft, remove the center bearing bracket-to-frame bolts. Remove the driveshaft from the vehicle.

13. Support the transmission using a jack with a wooden block placed between the jack and the transmission pan. Do not raise the transmission—just raise the jack until the wooden block touches the transmission pan.

14. Place a support under the engine with a wooden block between the support and the engine.

— CAUTION —
The wooden block and support should be no more than about ¼" away from the engine so that when the engine is lowered, damage will not occur to any underhood components.

15. Remove the transmission mount-to-crossmember bolts.

16. Raise the transmission SLIGHTLY, just enough to take the weight of the transmission off of the crossmember. Remove the crossmember-to-frame mounting bolts and remove the crossmember from the vehicle.

17. Slowly lower the transmission until the engine rests on the support placed during step 14.

18. Disconnect the two fluid cooler lines at the transmission. Plug the lines and the holes in the transmission to prevent the entry of dirt.

— CAUTION —
Before performing step 19, place a drain pan under the torque convertor area of the transmission. Fluid leakage will occur as the transmission is uncoupled.

19. Remove the transmission-to-engine mounting bolts. Carefully pull the transmission to the rear and after the transmission uncouples from the engine, lower the transmission out of the vehicle.

20. Remove the torque convertor from the flywheel.

A-43 and A-43D Transmissions

1. Disconnect the battery cables at the battery.

2. Remove the air cleaner assembly.

3. Disconnect the transmission throttle cable at the carburetor.

4. Raise the vehicle and support it safely with jack stands.

5. Disconnect the wiring connectors (near the starter) for the neutral start switch and the back-up light switch. Also, on A-43D transmission equipped models, dis-

connect the solenoid switch wiring at the same location.

6. Disconnect the starter wiring at the starter. Unbolt the starter and remove it from the vehicle.

7. Drain the transmission fluid.

8. Chalk matchmarks on the rear driveshaft flange and the differential pinion flange. These marks must be aligned during installation.

9. Unbolt the rear driveshaft flange. If the vehicle has a two-piece driveshaft, remove the center bearing bracket-to-frame bolts. Remove the driveshaft from the vehicle.

10. Disconnect the speedometer cable from the transmission and tie it out of the way.

11. Disconnect the shift linkage at the transmission.

12. Disconnect the exhaust pipe clamp at the bellhousing and remove the oil filler tube.

13. Disconnect the transmission oil cooler lines at the transmission.

14. Support the transmission using a jack with a wooden block placed between the jack and the transmission pan. Do not raise the transmission—just raise the jack until the wooden block touches the transmission pan.

15. Place a wooden block (or blocks) between the engine oil pan and the front frame crossmember.

--- CAUTION ---

The wooden block(s) should be no more than about 1/4" away from the engine so that when the engine is lowered, damage will not occur to any underhood components.

16. Remove the transmission mount-to-crossmember bolts.

17. Raise the transmission SLIGHTLY—just enough to take the weight of the transmission off of the crossmember. Remove the crossmember-to-frame mounting bolts and remove the crossmember from the vehicle.

18. Slowly lower the transmission until the engine rests on the wooden block placed during step 15.

19. Remove the engine undercover in order to gain access to the engine crankshaft pulley.

20. Remove the two rubber plugs from the service holes located at the rear of the engine in order to gain access to the torque convertor bolts.

21. Rotate the crankshaft as necessary to remove the torque convertor bolts (6). Access to these bolts is through the service holes mentioned in step 20.

22. Obtain a bolt of the same dimensions as the torque convertor bolts. Cut the head off of the bolt and hacksaw a screwdriver slot in the bolt opposite the threaded end.

NOTE: This modified bolt is used as a guidepin. Two guides pins are needed to properly install the transmission.

23. Thread the guide pin into one of the torque convertor bolt holes. The guide pin will help keep the convertor with the transmission.

24. Remove the transmission-to-engine mounting bolts.

25. Carefully move the transmission rearward by prying on the guide pin through the service hole.

--- CAUTION ---

As soon as the transmission is away from the engine about 1/8", feed wire through the front of the transmission and secure the wire in order to keep the convertor attached to the transmission. Also, try to keep the nose of the transmission pointed upward SLIGHTLY to help keep the convertor in place.

26. Pull the transmission rearward and lower it out of the vehicle.

--- CAUTION ---

Do not allow the attached cables to catch on any components during removal.

27. With the transmission out of the vehicle, remove the torque convertor as follows:

a. Place a drain pan under the front of the transmission.

b. Pull the convertor straight off of the transmission and allow the fluid to drain.

Torque Convertor and Flywheel Run-out

TESTING

Prior to installation of the transmission, Toyota recommends to check the torque convertor and flywheel run-out dimensions. If either of these run-out limits are beyond the maximum allowable limits, excessive wear of the front transmission seal will occur.

Refer to the accompanying chart to assist in performing and interpreting this procedure. A dial indicator gauge is needed to perform the run-out checks.

1. Mount the torque convertor on the flywheel and torque the convertor bolts to 11–16 ft. lbs.

2. Mount the dial indicator so that the indicator probe touches the outer surface of the convertor extension sleeve (90° to the convertor centerline).

3. Adjust the dial indicator to zero.

4. Slowly rotate the convertor and read the dial indicator. The indicator needle should not deviate more than the following amounts:

1980 and earlier transmissions—0.008 in.

1981 and later transmissions—0.012 in.

5. Remove the torque convertor from the flywheel.

6. Except A-43 and A-43D transmis-

sions: Mount the dial indicator so that the indicator probe touches the flywheel drive plate (convertor mounting) surface. A-43 and A-43D transmissions: Mount the dial indicator so that the indicator probe touches the flywheel ring gear just inside of the gear teeth (surface faces the rear of the vehicle).

7. Zero the indicator needle and slowly rotate the flywheel. The indicator needle should not deviate more than the following amounts:

A-30 transmissions: 0.005 in.

A-40 transmissions: 0.012 in.

A-43 and A-43D trans: 0.008 in.

INSTALLATION

A-30 and A-40 Transmissions

1. Apply a coat of multipurpose grease to the torque converter stub shaft and the pilot hole of the flywheel.

2. Assemble the torque converter into the transmission, so that its output shaft and the transmission input shaft are aligned. Rotate the torque converter until the dowel pin is at the bottom.

3. Install a guide pin into the bottom bolt hole next to the dowel pin. Align the flywheel and the torque converter.

4. Tighten the torque converter bolts to 11–16 ft. lbs. Rotate the crankshaft half a turn to reach all the bolts, and tighten them evenly.

5. Bolt the transmission to the engine. Tighten the bolts to 37–51 ft. lbs.

6. Replace the frame crossmember and the driveshaft. Attach the parking brake cable.

7. Replace the starter and its wiring. Attach the transmission cooler lines. Attach the speedometer cable.

8. Replace the exhaust pipe clamp and bolt the exhaust pipe to the manifold.

9. Install and adjust the throttle linkage rod. Attach the connecting rod to the transmission and adjust the shift lever linkage.

10. Fill the transmission with the specified type fluid. If the torque converter was completely drained, the transmission will need about 7 quarts of fluid.

11. Connect the battery cables. Road test and check for leaks.

A-43 and A-43D Transmissions

1. Apply a coat of multi-purpose grease to the torque convertor stub shaft and the corresponding pilot hole in the flywheel.

2. Install the torque convertor into the front of the transmission. Push inward on the torque convertor while rotating it to completely couple the torque convertor to the transmission.

3. To make sure that the convertor is properly installed, measure the distance between the torque convertor mounting lugs and the front mounting face of the transmission. The proper distance is 0.080 in.

4. Install guide pins into two opposite mounting lugs of the torque convertor.

5. Raise the transmission to the engine

TORQUE CONVERTOR AND FLYWHEEL
RUN-OUT TESTING

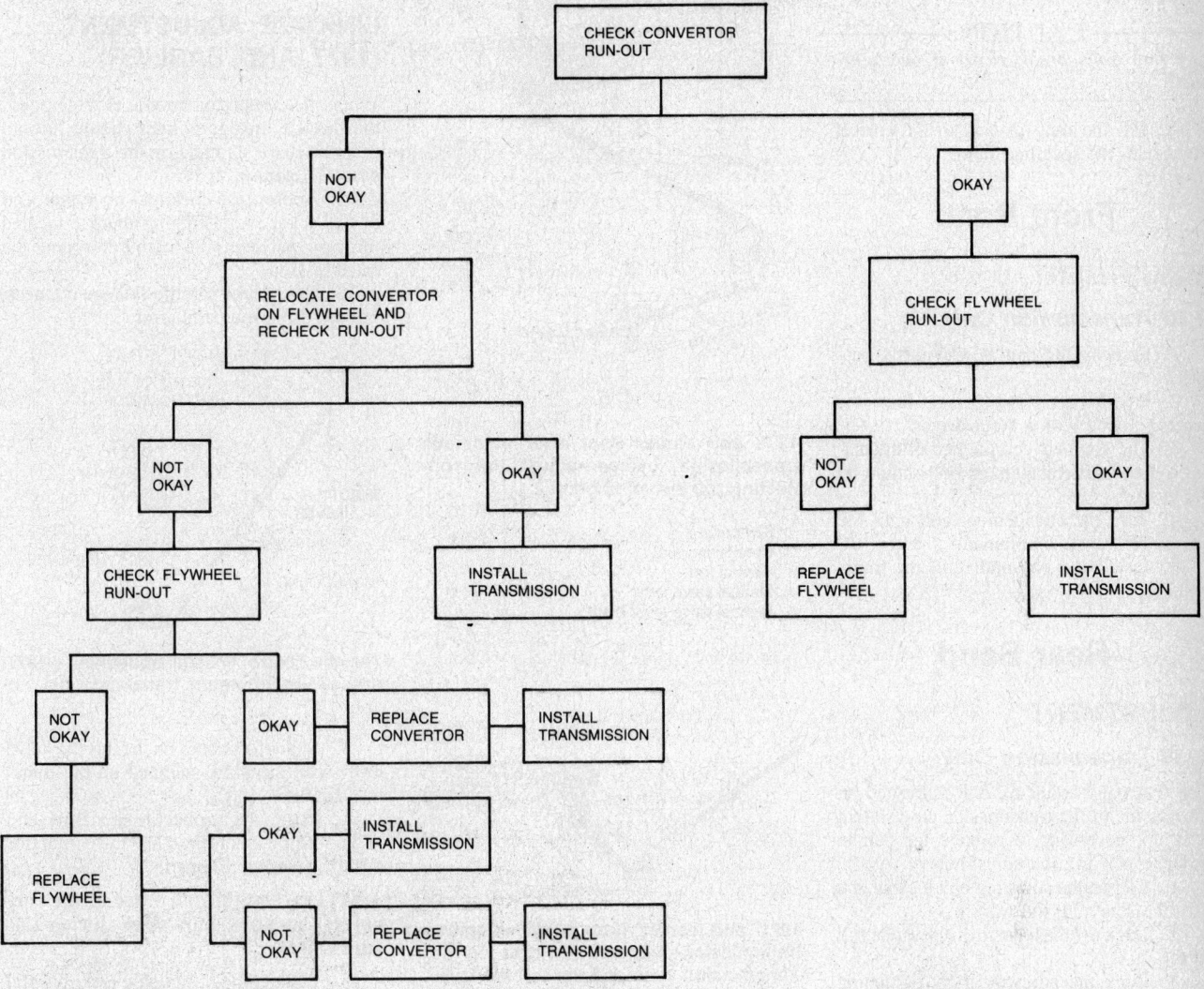

and align the transmission with the engine alignment dowels. Also, position the convertor guide pins into the mounting holes of the flywheel.

6. Install and tighten the transmission-to-engine mounting bolts. Torque the bolts to 37–57 ft. lbs.

7. Remove the convertor guide pins and install the convertor mounting bolts. Rotate the crankshaft as necessary to gain access to the guide pins and bolts through the service holes.

8. Evenly tighten the convertor mounting bolts to 11–15 ft. lbs. Install the rubber plugs into the access holes.

9. Install the engine undercover.

10. Raise the transmission slightly and remove the wood block(s) from beneath the engine oil pan.

11. Install the transmission crossmember. Torque the crossmember-to-frame bolts to 26–36 ft. lbs.

12. Lower the transmission onto the crossmember and install the transmission

mounting bolts. Torque the bolts to 14–22 ft. lbs.

13. Install the oil filler tube and connect the exhaust pipe clamp.

14. Connect the oil cooler lines to the transmission and torque the fittings to 15–21 ft. lbs.

15. Connect the shift linkage and the speedometer cable.

16. Install the driveshaft and the starter.

17. Connect the wiring which was disconnected during removal of the transmission.

18. Connect and adjust the transmission throttle cable (adjustment covered in a later procedure).

19. Install the air cleaner assembly and connect the battery cables.

20. Fill the transmission with the specified type of fluid. If the torque convertor was completely drained, the transmission will need about 7 quarts of fluid.

21. Road test the vehicle and check for leaks.

Transmission Pan and Filter

REMOVAL AND INSTALLATION

1. Jack up the front end of the vehicle and support it on jackstands.

2. Place a container under the transmission drain plug and drain the transmission fluid.

3. Remove the pan securing bolts and remove the pan and gasket.

4. The pan may be washed in solvent for cleaning but must be absolutely dry when it is reinstalled. Do not wipe it out with a rag, or you will risk leaving bits of lint inside the transmission.

5. Remove all traces of the old gasket from the pan and from the transmission. Install a new gasket on the pan using small quantities of sealer around the bolt holes.

6. Replace the transmission filter at this time, if necessary.

7. Install the pan, tightening the securing bolts to 11–14 ft. lbs.

──── CAUTION ────
The pan bolts break easily if overtightened.

8. Fill the transmission to the correct level with the specified fluid.

Front Band

ADJUSTMENT

A-30 Transmission Only

1. Remove the pan as previously outlined.

2. Pry the band engagement lever toward the band with a screwdriver.

3. The gap between the end of the piston rod and the engagement bolt should be 0.118 in.

4. Turn the engagement bolt until the proper clearance is obtained.

5. Install the pan and refill the transmission.

Rear Band

ADJUSTMENT

A-30 Transmission Only

The rear band adjusting bolt is located on the outside of the transmission case so that it is not necessary to remove the pan in order to perform the adjustment.

1. Loosen the adjusting bolt locknut and turn the screw all the way in.

2. Back off the adjusting screw one full turn.

3. Lock the adjustment by tightening the adjusting screw locknut.

Shift Linkage

ADJUSTMENT

1979 AND EARLIER TRANSMISSION

1. Check all of the shift linkage bushings for wear. Replace any that are excessively worn.

2. Set the manual valve lever on the transmission in the Neutral position.

3. Lock the connecting rod swivel with the locknut so that the pointer, selector, and manual valve lever are all in the Neutral position.

4. Check the operation by moving the selector through all the gears.

1980 AND LATER TRANSMISSIONS

1. Loosen the adjustment nut on the transmission connecting rod.

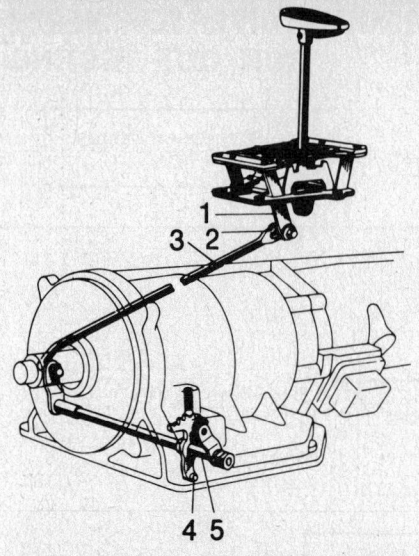

1979 and earlier floor shift automatic transmission linkage—adjust the connecting rod swivel at point 2.

1. Shift lever
2. Connecting rod
3. Control rod
4. Manual valve lever
5. Manual valve lever shaft

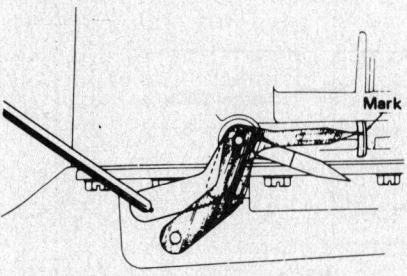

1979 and earlier floor shift automatic transmission—alignment marks on the transmission case and the throttle lever

2. Push the manual lever of the transmission fully forward.

3. Move the manual lever back three notches, which is the NEUTRAL position.

4. Set the gearshift selector lever in its NEUTRAL position.

5. Apply a slight amount of forward pressure on the selector lever (towards the reverse position) and tighten the connecting rod adjustment nut.

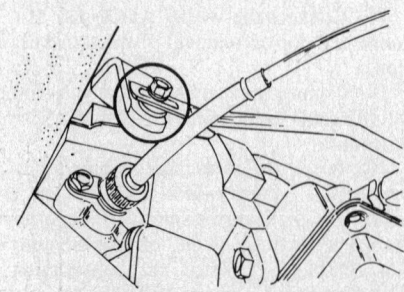

On 1980 and later automatics, loosen this nut to adjust the shift linkage

Transmission Throttle Control

LINKAGE ADJUSTMENT (1977 AND EARLIER)

When the carburetor throttle is wide open, the throttle linkage pointer should line up with the mark stamped on the transmission case. To adjust:

1. Loosen the locknuts on either end of the linkage adjusting turnbuckle located midway between the carburetor and the transmission.

2. Detach the throttle linkage connecting rod from the carburetor.

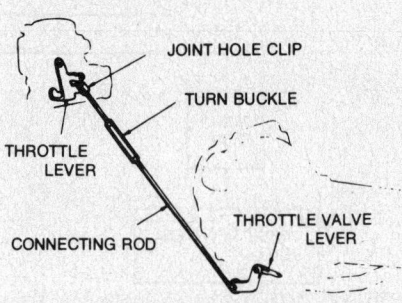

Throttle control linkage adjustment—1977 and earlier automatic transmissions

3. Align the pointer on the throttle valve lever with the mark stamped on the transmission case.

4. Rotate the turnbuckle so that the end of the throttle linkage rod and the carburetor throttle lever are aligned.

NOTE: The throttle valve of the carburetor must be fully open during this adjustment.

5. Tighten the turnbuckle locknuts and connect the throttle rod to the carburetor.

6. Open the throttle valve and check to see that the pointer and the mark are aligned on the transmission.

7. Road-test the truck. If the transmission keeps shifting rapidly back and forth between gears at certain speeds or if it fails to down-shift properly when going up hills, repeat the throttle linkage adjustment.

CABLE ADJUSTMENT (1978 AND LATER)

1. Remove the air cleaner assembly.

2. Push the accelerator to the floor and check that the throttle opens fully. If not, adjust the accelerator link so that it does.

3. Push back the rubber boot from the throttle cable which runs down to the transmission. Loosen the throttle cable adjustment nuts so that the cable housing can be adjusted.

4. Fully open the carburetor throttle by having an assistant press the accelerator all the way to the floor.

5. Adjust the cable housing so that, with the throttle wide open, the distance between the outer cable end rubber cap to the inner cable stopper is 2.05 in.

NOTE: 1979 and later distance is 0–0.04 in.

6. Tighten the nuts and double check the adjustment. Install the rubber boot and the air cleaner.

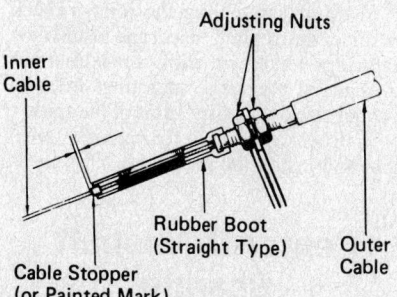

Throttle control cable adjustment—1978 and later automatic transmissions

Neutral Safety Switch

The neutral safety switch prevents the vehicle from starting unless the gearshift selector is in either the PARK or NEUTRAL positions. If the vehicle will start in these positions, adjustment of the switch is required.

ADJUSTMENT

1979 and Earlier Transmissions

1. Remove the screws which hold the center console in place.
2. Remove the electrical connector and remove the console from the vehicle.
3. Loosen the switch securing bolts.
4. Set the selector in the Drive position.
5. Move the switch so that the arm just contacts the control shaft lever.
6. Tighten the switch retaining bolts.
7. Check the operation of the switch; the truck should start only in Neutral or in Park. The back-up lamps should only operate in the Reverse position.
8. If the switch cannot be adjusted so that it functions properly, replace it with a new one.
9. Reinstall the console.

1980 and Later Transmissions

1. Loosen the neutral start switch bolt.
2. Place the gearshift selector lever in the Neutral position.
3. Align the shaft groove of the switch with the neutral Basic line. Hold the switch in this position and tighten the switch bolt to 35–60 in. lbs.

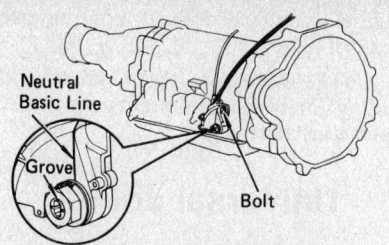

Neutral safety switch adjustment—1980 and later automatic transmissions

TRANSFER CASE

REMOVAL, OVERHAUL, AND INSTALLATION

On all models, the transfer case is removed from the vehicle along with the transmission. Refer to the following:

1. Transmission removal and installation procedure
2. Unit Repair Section for overhaul

DRIVE TRAIN

Driveshaft

REMOVAL AND INSTALLATION

2WD Standard Bed Pickup

1. Jack up the rear of the truck and support the rear axle housing with jack stands.
2. Paint a mating mark on the two halves of the rear universal joint flange.
3. Remove the bolts which hold the rear flange together.
4. Remove the splined end of the driveshaft from the transmission.

NOTE: Plug the end of the transmission with a rag or dummy flange to avoid losing transmission oil.

5. Remove the driveshaft from under the truck.

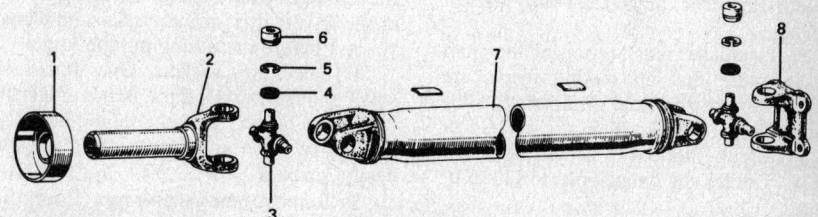

1. Sliding shaft dust cover
2. Universal joint yoke sleeve
3. Universal joint spider
4. Spider bearing seal
5. Snap-ring
6. Spider bearing
7. Driveshaft
8. Universal joint yoke falnge

Exploded view of a one-piece driveshaft assembly—typical

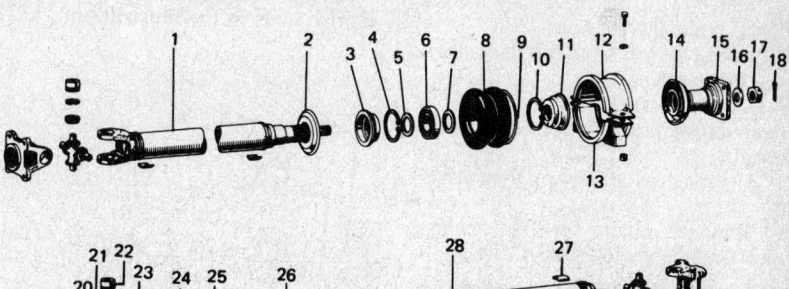

Exploded view of a two-piece driveshaft assembly—typical

1. Intermediate driveshaft
2. Dust deflector No. 1
3. Dust deflector No. 2
4. Hole snap-ring
5. Dust deflector No. 3
6. Radial ball bearing
7. Dust deflector No. 4
8. Center support bearing cushion
9. Set ring
10. Hole snap-ring
11. Dust deflector No. 2
12. Center support bearing housing No. 1
13. Center support bearing housing No. 2
14. Dust deflector No. 1
15. Universal joint flange
16. Plate washer
17. Castle nut
18. Cotter pin
19. Universal joint flange yoke
20. Universal joint spider
21. Universal joint spider bearing seal
22. Universal joint spider bearing
23. Hole snap-ring
24. Grease fitting
25. Universal joint sleeve yoke
26. Sliding shaft dust cover
27. Balance piece
28. Driveshaft

Installation is the reverse of removal. Grease the splined end of the shaft before installing. Tighten bolts to 11–16 ft. lbs.

2WD Long Bed Pickup

1. Jack up the rear of the truck and support the rear axle housing with jack-stands.

2. Paint mating marks on all six flange halves.

3. Remove the bolts attaching the rear universal joint flange to the drive pinion flange.

4. Drop the rear section of the shaft slightly and pull the unit out of the center bearing sleeve yoke.

5. Remove the center bearing support from the crossmember.

6. Unbolt the driveshaft flange from the rear of the transmission and remove drive-shaft along with center bearing support.

To install:

1. Connect the output flange of the transmission to the flange on the front half of the shaft.

2. Install the center bearing support to the crossmember, but do not fully tighten the bolts.

3. Install the rear section of the shaft making sure that all mating marks are aligned. Make sure line on bearing in center support mount is in the middle of the hole at the bottom of center mount.

4. Tighten the flange bolts to 11–16 ft. lbs.

4WD Pickup—All

1. Jack the truck off the ground and place support stands under both the front and rear axles.

2. Match-mark all driveshaft flanges BEFORE removing the bolts.

3. Unbolt the rear driveshaft flange from the rear pinion flange.

4. Unbolt the rear driveshaft flange from the rear transfer case flange and remove driveshaft.

5. Repeat steps 3 and 4 on front drive-shaft.

6. Reverse order for reassembly. Tighten flange bolts to 29–43 ft. lbs.

NOTE: For 4 × 4 Long Bed Pickups, see above for rear driveshaft removal and installation.

Land Cruiser

1. Raise the vehicle and support it with jackstands.

2. Match-mark all driveshaft flanges BEFORE removing the bolts.

3. Unfasten the bolts which secure the universal joint flange to the differential pinion flange.

4. Perform step 2 for the U-joint-to-transfer case flange bolts.

5. Withdraw the driveshaft from beneath the vehicle.

6. Repeat steps 3–5 on the front drive-shaft.

Installation is performed in the reverse order of removal.

NOTE: Lubricate the U-joints and sliding joints with multipurpose grease before installation.

Universal Joints

OVERHAUL

Universal joints are marked at the factory if oversize parts have been used during assembly. Before buying a rebuilding kit for your truck, note any ''V'' punch marks on the sleeve yoke, drilled marks, or red painted marks on the bearing caps. These marks will correspond to the oversize parts you will have to get from your dealer. The rebuilding kit or parts you buy should include new bearing seals, snap-rings, spiders, and spider bearings.

Although there are special tools available for rebuilding universal joints, you should be able to do the job easily with the assortment of sockets noted in this procedure. Be certain to paint or scratch mating marks on the driveshaft(s) and universal joint flange yoke(s) before disassembling the joints.

1. Select two sockets. One should be small enough to pass through the universal joint yoke hole. The other should be large enough so that the spider bearing cap fits easily inside it.

2. Remove the snap-rings from the bearing holes of the yoke.

3. Position the yoke in a vise so that one socket is centered against a bearing cap and the other socket aligned so that the bearing cap may pass inside of it.

NOTE: Refer to the positions of the service tools in the illustration.

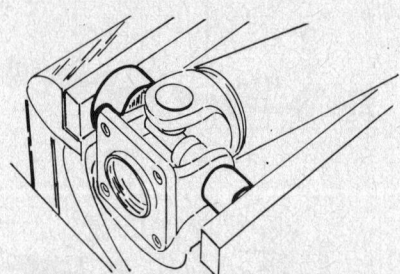

Removing the universal joint spider from the driveshaft flange—note the size and positions of the service tools

4. Tighten the vise just enough to hold the sockets and yoke in position. Check to see that they are positioned correctly.

5. As you tighten the vise, one bearing cap will be pressed against the cross of the U-joint forcing the other cap out of the yoke.

6. Proceed in this manner to remove all caps and then remove the cross.

To assemble:

1. Note any markings and use oversize parts as necessary.

2. Repack the spider bearing cups with grease, and assemble the needle bearing rollers into the cups.

3. Position the spider in the driveshaft yoke. Place the bearing cups inside the lip of the yoke, so that they are held in place by the ends of the spider.

4. Position two sockets of equal size on either side of the bearings, and slip this assembly between the jaws of the vise.

5. As you close the vise, the sockets should force the bearing caps into the holes of the yoke and onto the arms of the spider.

6. After assembling the joints, check the spider thrust play. Select and install new snap-rings which will allow a maximum of 0.002 in. of play. The snap-rings must be of equal size on opposite arms of the spider.

7. Check the joints for smooth movement and install the driveshaft.

Center Driveshaft Bearing

REPLACEMENT

The center support bearing is a sealed unit which requires no periodic maintenance. The following procedure should be used if it should become necessary to replace the bearing.

1. Remove the intermediate driveshaft and the center support bearing assembly.

2. Paint mating marks on the universal joint flange and the intermediate driveshaft.

3. Remove the cotter pin and castle nut from the intermediate driveshaft. Remove the universal joint flange from the drive-shaft using a press.

4. Remove the center support bearing assembly from the driveshaft.

5. Remove the two bolts from the bearing housing and remove the housing.

6. Remove the dust deflectors (type #2) from both sides of the bearing cushion. Remove the dust deflectors type #3 and #4 from either side of the bearing.

7. Remove the snap-rings from each side of the bearing. This is easy to do if you have a snap-ring tool which fits the holes in the ring, and very difficult otherwise. Remove the bearing.

To assemble:

1. Install the new bearing into the cushion and fit a snap-ring on each side.

2. Apply a coat of multipurpose grease to the dust deflectors type #3 and #4, and put them in their respective places on each side of the bearing. Type #4, which has a slightly larger outside diameter, goes on the rear of the bearing.

3. Press the type #2 dust deflectors onto each side of the cushion. The water drain holes in the deflectors should be in the same position on each side of the cushion.

4. Assemble the two halves of the housing around the cushion. The water drain holes should face the bottom of the housing.

5. Press the support bearing assembly firmly onto the intermediate driveshaft, with the #3 type seal facing the front.

6. Match the mating marks painted earlier, and install the universal joint flange to the driveshaft. Tighten the castle nut to about 130 ft. lbs., and use a new cotter pin to lock it in place. Tighten the nut to align the holes for the cotter pin, but do not loosen it. It is okay to tighten it up to 150 ft. lbs.

NOTE: Check to see if the center support bearing assembly will rotate smoothly around the driveshaft.

7. When reinstalling the driveshaft, be certain to match up the marks on both the front transmission flange and the flange on the sleeve yoke of the rear driveshaft.

FRONT DRIVE AXLE

Axle Shaft

REMOVAL AND INSTALLATION

4WD Pickup

1. Set the control handle in the free position.

2. Remove the bolts in the hub and remove the hub and gasket.

3. Remove the nuts, spring washers and cone washers.

NOTE: Cone washers can be removed by using a tapered punch.

4. Remove hub body and gasket.

5. Remove snap-ring from free wheel hub body.

6. Remove hub ring, spacer and inner hub.

7. Remove compression spring, follower, tension spring, and clutch.

8. Remove snap-ring, free wheel hub cover ball and spring, seal, and control handle.

NOTE: Check inner hub and free wheel hub ring oil clearance. Clearance should be 0.012 in.

9. Disconnect the brake line and the two bolts holding the brake caliper.

10. Remove the dust cap and snap-ring.

11. Remove the cone washers with a tapered punch.

12. Remove the flange by installing two bolts in the special holes for flange removal. Tighten these bolts until the flange comes loose. Remove the bolts by loosening them and remove the flange.

13. Remove the locknut, washer, and adjusting nut. Pull the rotor assembly off the spindle. The outer and inner bearings and seal will come apart as a unit.

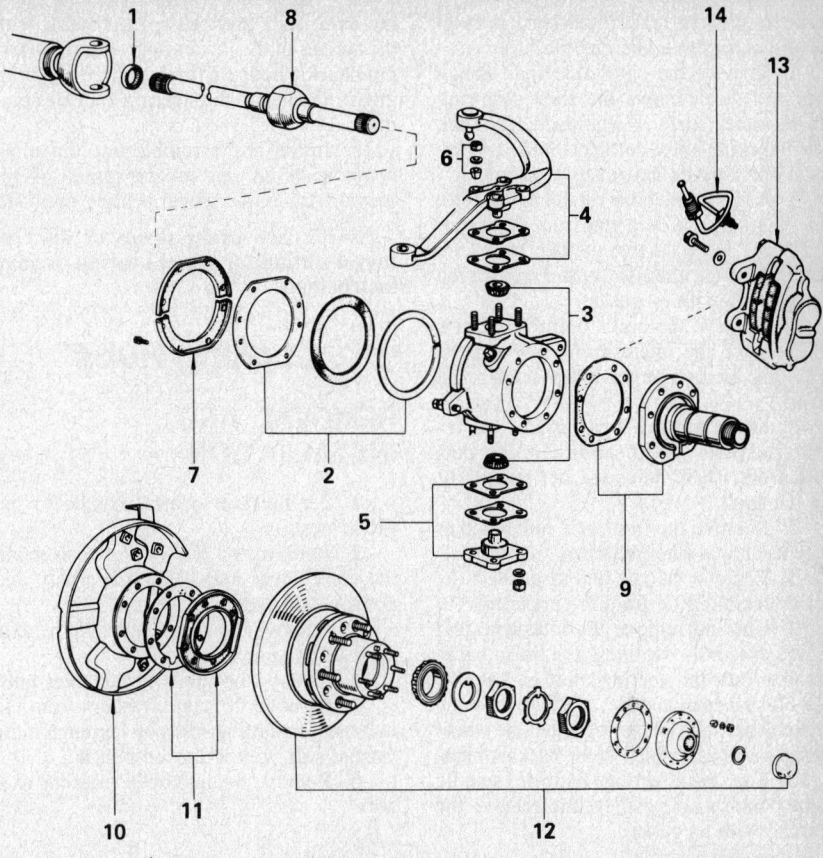

Front axle and steering knuckle (4WD)—pick-up illustrated, Land Cruiser similar

1. Oil seal	6. Nut, washer dowel	10. Dust cover
2. Oil seal set	7. Oil seal retainer	11. Dust seal and gasket
3. Bearings	8. Front axle shaft	12. Front axle hub with disc
4. Steering knuckle	9. Knuckle spindle and	13. Brake caliper
5. Bearing cup and shim	gasket	14. Brake line

14. Set the rotor on two blocks of wood. Using a drift pin drive the seal out. The inner bearing will drop out at this time. Using this pin drive the front and rear race from the rotor.

15. Place the rotor in a vice and remove the front axle hub.

16. Inspect the rotor, spindle, and hub for damage.

17. Remove the dust seal, gasket, and dust cover.

18. Remove the spindle and gasket.

19. Position the flat part of the outer shaft up and pull out the shaft.

20. Remove the oil seal retainer.

21. Remove the cone type washers from the drag link with a tapered punch.

22. Remove the drag link and tie rod.

23. Remove the bottom bearing cap and shim.

24. Remove the upper and lower bearings with the proper tool.

NOTE: The steering knuckle bearing remover is available from your Toyota dealer. Part #09606-60010. Remember to mark the bearings in order to reassemble them in their proper place:

25. Remove the upper and lower races with a brass drift pin.

26. Remove the steering knuckle and inspect for damage or wear.

27. Place the inner shaft in a vice. Using a drift pin drive the outer shaft apart and remove six ball bearings.

NOTE: Tilt the inner race and cage. Take the balls out one at a time.

28. Remove the cage and race from the shaft.

NOTE: Turn the large opening in the cage against the protruding portion of the shaft, pull the race and cage out.

29. Remove the inner race from the cage through the large opening.

30. Remove the inner oil seal. Thoroughly wash and inspect all parts for wear or damage.

31. Installation is the reversal of removal with the following suggestions:
   a. Replace all oil and grease seals.
   b. Pack the hub interior, inner and outer bearings with a multipurpose grease.

Land Cruiser

1. Raise and support the vehicle securely and remove the wheel/tire assembly.

2. Plug the brake master cylinder res-

ervoir to prevent brake fluid leakage from the disconnected brake flexible hose.

3. Remove the outer axle shaft flange cap, and then remove the shaft snap-ring on the outer shaft. If equipped with free wheel locking hubs, complete steps 1–4 under 4WD Pick-up axle shaft removal.

4. Remove the bolts retaining the outer axle shaft flange onto the front axle hub, and then, screw in two service bolts into the shaft flange alternately, and remove the shaft flange with its gasket.

5. Remove the brake drum set screws and remove the brake drum. If equipped with disc brakes, remove the caliper and disc.

6. Straighten the lockwasher, and remove the front wheel bearing adjusting nuts with front wheel adjusting nut wrench or similar tool.

7. Remove the front axle hub together with its claw washer, bearings, and oil seal.

8. Remove the clip and disconnect the brake flexible hose from the brake tube.

9. Cut and remove the lock wire and remove the bolts retaining the brake backing plate onto the steering knuckle. Remove the brake backing plate together with the brake shoes, tension springs, and the wheel cylinder still assembled to the backing plate.

10. Tap the steering knuckle spindle lightly with a soft mallet, and remove the spindle with its gasket.

NOTE: When removing the steering knuckle spindle on a vehicle equipped with the ball joint type axle shaft joint, be prepared for the disconnection of the outer axle shaft from the joint. The joint ball will fall from the joint. Try to cushion its fall or catch it if you can.

11. On those models equipped with the ball type axle shaft joint, slide the inner front axle shaft out of the axle housing. On those models equipped with the Birfield constant velocity joint type of axle joint, remove the entire axle shaft assembly from the axle housing.

12. Remove bushing from inside of knuckle spindle with a bearing puller. Install new bushing using a metal tube as a seating tool.

13. Remove axle housing oil seal with a bearing puller. To install, use a metal tube as a seating tool.

Install the axle shaft in the reverse order of removal.

14. On those models equipped with the ball joint type axle joint, install the inner axle with its proper spacer in position until the splines are fully meshed with the differential side gear splines. Next, fill the steering knuckle three quarters full with grease and place the joint ball on the inner shaft end. Install the outer shaft and the front axle shaft spacer into the steering knuckle spindle and install the spindle with its gasket onto the steering knuckle.

15. On those models equipped with the Birfield constant velocity joint axle joint, install the axle into the housing and rotate

the axle shaft until its splines mesh with the splines in the differential. Fill the steering knuckle housing three quarters full with grease and install the steering knuckle spindle.

16. Install and assemble the remaining components in the reverse order of removal. Adjust the wheel bearing preload.

NOTE: See brake drum or disc removal section for wheel bearing preload instructions.

Locking Hubs

REMOVAL AND INSTALLATION

1. Set the hub control handle to the FREE position.

2. Remove the hub bolts which retain the front cover and handle assembly and remove the assembly.

3. Remove the snap-ring from the axle shaft using snap-ring pliers.

4. Remove the hub body mounting nuts.

5. Remove the cone washers from the hub body mounting studs by tapping on the washer slits with a tapered punch.

6. Remove the hub body from the axle hub.

7. Installation is the reverse of the previous steps. Use a new gasket when installing the hub.

DISASSEMBLY

1. Remove the snap-ring which attaches the control handle to the hub cover. Remove the control handle.

2. Remove the ball and spring from the control handle.

3. Remove the snap-ring which holds the free wheel hub ring and the inner hub into the hub body.

4. Remove the inner hub and the free wheel hub ring from the hub body.

5. Remove the snap-ring from the inner hub and remove the free wheel hub and spacer from the inner hub.

INSPECTION

1. Check all parts for damage or excessive wear.

2. Temporarily install the control handle into the hub cover and make sure the handle operates freely.

3. Check that the clutch slides freely within the hub body.

4. Measure the inner diameter of the hub ring and the outer diameter (smooth

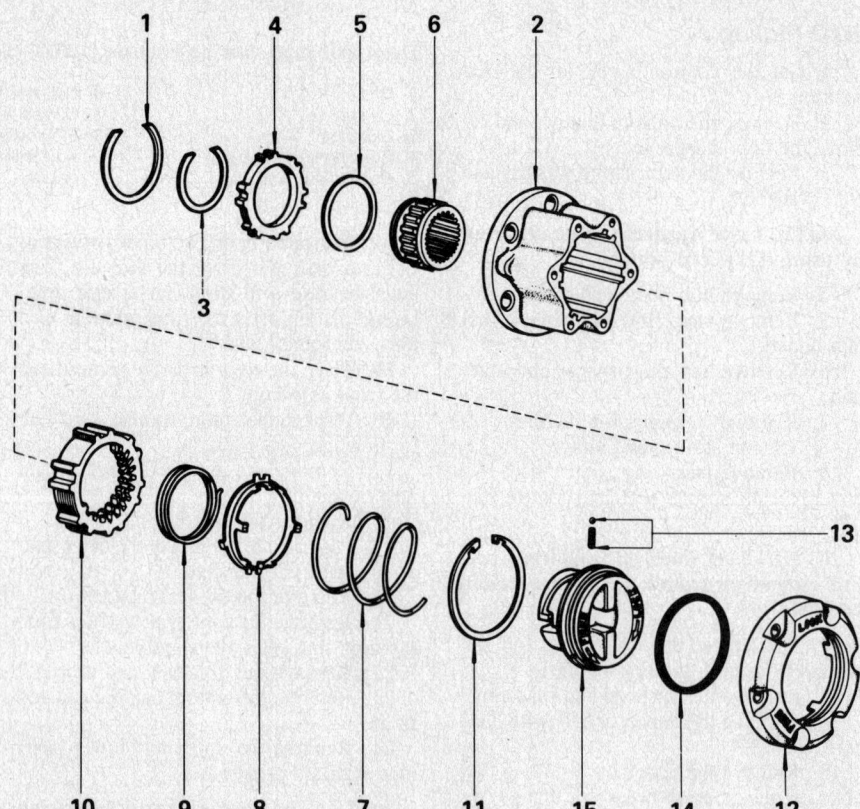

Exploded view of a free-wheeling hub assembly

1. Snap-ring
2. Free wheel hub body
3. Snap-ring
4. Free wheel hub ring
5. Spacer
6. Inner hub
7. Spring
8. Pawl
9. Spring
10. Clutch
11. Snap-ring
12. Free wheel hub cover
13. Steel ball and spring
14. Seal
15. Control handle

surface) of the inner hub. The difference between these measurements should be no greater than 0.012 in.

Assembly

1. Apply a coat of multipurpose grease to the sliding service of each part.

2. Install the seal, spring, and ball into the control handle.

3. Install the control handle and snap-ring.

4. Install the tension spring into the clutch with the end of the spring aligned with the initial groove of the clutch.

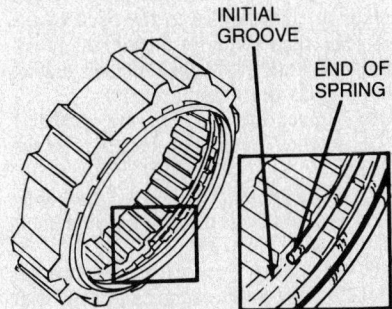

Aligning the end of the tension spring with the initial groove of the clutch—see text

5. Install the follower pawl as follows:

a. Place the pawl on the tension spring with one of the large tabs (of the pawl) against the bent end of the tension spring.

b. Place the top ring of the tension spring on the small tabs of the pawl.

6. Position the hub cover into the large end of the tension spring. Compress the spring and install the clutch with the pawl tab of the clutch fit to the control handle.

7. Install the inner hub and hub ring into the hub body. Install the snap-ring.

8. Temporarily install the cover and handle assembly into the hub body. Adjust the control handle to the FREE position and check that the inner hub turns smoothly.

9. Remove the cover and handle assembly from the hub body and install these components as previously outlined.

Differential

Overhaul of the differential carrier is a complex operation requiring special tools and technical knowledge. If either of these is not available, it may be wise (economically) to remove the carrier yourself and have a professional perform the overhaul, rather then purchase special (and expensive) tools or take the vehicle to a shop.

REMOVAL AND INSTALLATION

1. Drain the lubricant from the differential.

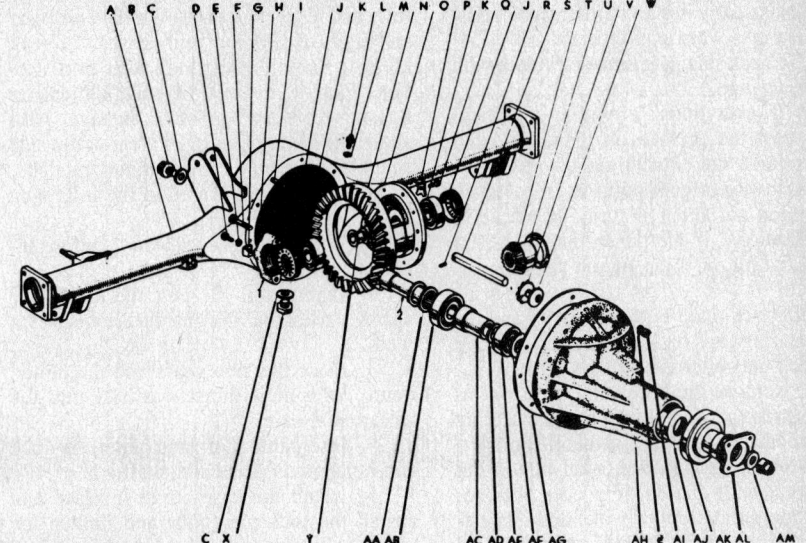

Differential components

a.	Housing assembly	n.	Ring gear and drive pinion 1 and 2	aa.	Shim
b.	Filler plug			ab.	Bearing
c.	Gasket	o.	Case	ac.	Spacer
d.	Bolt	p.	Lockplate	ad.	Shim
e.	Lock washer	q.	Bolt	ae.	Bearing
f.	Hexagon bolt	r.	Lockpin	af.	Oil slinger
g.	Bearing adjusting nut lock	s.	Pinion shaft	ag.	Gasket
h.	Lockwasher	t.	Side gear	ah.	Carrier
i.	Stud	u.	Thrust washer	ai.	Nut
j.	Bearing adjusting nut	v.	Pinion	aj.	Oil seal
k.	Bearing	w.	Thrust washer	ak.	Dust deflector
l.	Breather plug	x.	Drain plug	al.	Universal joint flange
m.	Lockwasher	y.	Oil reservoir	am.	Flat washer

2. Remove the axle shafts as previously outlined.

3. Remove the driveshaft as previously outlined.

4. Remove the carrier retaining nuts and pull the carrier assembly out of the differential housing.

5. Installation is performed in the reverse of the previous steps. Apply a thin coat of liquid or silicone sealer to the new carrier to housing gasket before installing the carrier. Also apply sealer to the carrier side face of each carrier retaining nut before installing these nuts.

OVERHAUL

1. Thoroughly wash and rinse the carrier and blow dry with compressed air.

2. Securely clamp the carrier in a vise or suitable stand.

3. Apply a light coating of mechanic's blue to the teeth of the ring gear.

4. Applying a slight drag on the ring gear to avoid backlash, rotate the pinion in a smooth and continuous manner to obtain a good tooth pattern on the ring gear.

5. Next, attach a dial indicator gauge to the carrier base and check the ring gear backlash.

6. Also check ring gear runout at this time. If the tooth pattern obtained is correct, and the backlash and runout are within limits, any gear noise must come from the side gear.

7. With the dial indicator gauge set up on the carrier, check the backlash between the pinion gears and side gears. Excessive

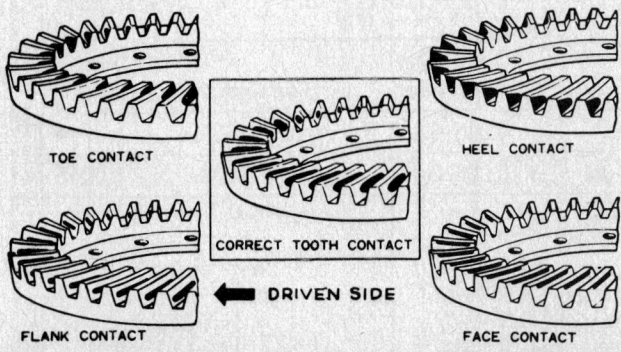

Ring gear tooth contact patterns

backlash usually is due to either worn thrust washers or a worn pinion shaft.

8. Check side gear thrust clearance with a feeler gauge.

9. If everything is within specifications, test the preload on the differential drive pinion nut. Punch mark both pinion and nut in their original positions, then loosen the pinion nut about ½ turn and torque to specifications. If the punch marks line up again (within 60°) the pinion preload was correct.

10. Punch mark both the carrier and the side bearing caps for identification, remove the lock-nuts and take off the caps.

11. Remove the differential case assembly from the carrier. Do not mix the bearing cups; paint mark them for identification.

12. Remove the differential pinion nut (do not let the pinion drop out), then remove the pinion spacer, yoke and oil seal.

13. With a brass punch, drive out the pinion bearing cups.

NOTE: This should be done only when the bearings are to be replaced.

14. Press or pull off the drive pinion rear bearing. Avoid damaging the flat spacer behind the bearing.

15. Measure the spacer thickness and note the measurement for future use. Remove both side bearings from the differential case and mark them "L" and "R" for identification.

NOTE: Remove side bearings only if they must be replaced.

16. Punch mark the differential case and cover, then remove the cover bolts and the cover (where fitted).

17. Remove the shaft and pinions, the side gears and all thrust washers.

NOTE: Some differential types have four spider pinion gears; punch mark the gears before removal so they can be correctly reinstalled.

Check all bearing cones and cups for wear. Inspect the tooth surfaces of all gears carefully and inspect all thrust washers for wear and signs of slipping in their seats. Check all gear shafts for scoring, wear or distortion. Finally, inspect the case and carrier housing for cracks or other damage. Also check the case for signs of wear at the side gear bores, bearing cap and mounting hubs.

Assembly is performed in the following order:

1. Wash and clean all parts before installation.

2. Lightly oil all bearings and gear shafts, except the ring gear and drive pinion teeth.

3. Place the side gears and the pinion gears, with their thrust washers, into the differential case.

4. Insert the shaft and align the lock pin holes in the case and shaft.

5. Install the case cover in place and install the lock pin (bolt) and tighten the cover bolts to specification; check the play.

6. If the side bearings were removed, install them now. If the ring gear was removed, install it now. Tighten the bolts in symmetrical sequence to avoid distortion and runout.

7. Install the drive pinion bearing cups into the carrier housing, using a suitable installing tool. Make sure the cups are seated solidly.

8. Assemble the drive pinion rear bearing to the drive pinion and insert it into the carrier housing. Install the spacer and front bearing to the drive pinion; install the yoke and tighten the nut to specifications.

———— CAUTION ————
The drive pinion oil seal is NOT installed at this point.

9. The drive pinion preload is measured in in. lbs. (not ft. lbs.). Adjust the preload by changing the length of the bearing spacer (between the front and rear bearings) until the required preload is obtained.

10. Place the previously assembled differential case into position in the bearing hubs and put the caps into position as marked (L and R).

11. Set the case so that there will be the least amount of backlash between the ring gear and pinion (in order to save time adjusting).

12. Install the adjusting nuts (also marked L and R) and take care not to cross-thread them.

13. Finger-tighten the bearing caps until the threads are lined up correctly, then tighten slowly.

14. Back off the right-hand adjusting nut (ring gear teeth side) and screw in the other nut until almost no backlash is felt.

15. Attach a dial indicator gauge so that it reads at right angles to the back of the ring gear, then screw in the righthand adjusting nut until the gauge indicates that all side play has been eliminated.

16. Tighten the adjusting nut another 1 or 1½ notches (depending on the fit of the lock tabs).

17. Recheck the preload on the drive pinion as before; this time the specifications are different.

18. If too loose, readjust the side bearing preload; if too tight, adjust the ring gear backlash.

19. Install the dial indicator gauge so that it contacts the ring gear teeth at right angles. Adjust the backlash to specifications.

20. If too great, adjust by loosening the bearing cap bolts slightly and screwing the right-hand adjusting nut (ring gear teeth side) out about two notches.

21. Tighten the left-hand adjusting nut the same amount.

NOTE: One notch of the adjusting nut equals about 0.002 in. of backlash.

22. Recheck the backlash, then tighten the bearing cap nuts.

23. Using a dial indicator recheck all runout dimensions (ring gear back, ring gear outer circumference and differential case).

24. Apply a thin coat of mechanic's blue, red lead or even lipstick to the ring gear

DIFFERENTIAL SPECIFICATIONS

Model	Backlash (in.)		Runout (in.) Ring Gear	Torque (ft. lbs.)		Pinion Bearing Preload ④ (in. lbs.)	
	Ring Gear and Pinion	Side Gears		Side Bearing Cap	Differential Pinion Nut	New	Used
Pick-up (all)	0.005–0.007	0.002–0.008	①	51–65	②	③	③
Land Cruiser (all)	0.006–0.008	0.001–0.008	0.004	65–80	145–175	16–23	8–11

① '75—0.002 in.
  '76–'77—0.004 in.
  '78–82:
    w/7½" ring gear—0.003 in.
    w/8" ring gear—0.004 in.
② w/7.5" ring gear—80–173 ft. lbs.
  w/8.0" ring gear—123–151 ft. lbs.

③ '75—8.5–11.5 new
    2.2–6.6 used
  '76–82 except '81–'82 2WD w/7.5" ring gear:
    16.5–22.5 new
    7.8–11.3 used

'81–'82 2WD w/7.5" ring gear:
    10.4–16.5 new
    5.2–8.7 used
④ Without oil seal or differential gears installed

teeth. Rotate the gear several times, applying a light drag to the ring gear. Rotate the gear in both directions.

25. Inspect the tooth pattern. There are four basic tooth patterns: heel, toe, flank and face. Most often the tooth pattern obtained will be a combination of two of these patterns and the adjustments must be made accordingly.

Heel contact Move the drive pinion, in by increasing the thickness of the spacer (between the pinion head and rear bearing). Readjust backlash by moving the ring gear away from the pinion.

Face contact Adjust same as above.

Toe contact Adjust by moving the drive pinion out by reducing the thickness of the spacer. Readjust backlash.

Flank contact Adjust same as toe contact.

Continue assembling as follows:

26. Remove the drive pinion nut and install the seal into the differential carrier housing, then install the oil slinger, dust shield and yoke and retorque the pinion nut as specified.

27. Install the differential carrier assembly into the axle housing.

Steering Knuckle

REMOVAL AND INSTALLATION

2WD Pick-up

NOTE: On Pickups with coil springs, it will be necessary to obtain a spring compressor for installation.

1. Jack up front of vehicle and support on stands.
2. Remove wheel.
3. If vehicle has front disc brakes, remove brake caliper.
4. Remove axle hub dust cap. Remove cotter key, lock, front nut and front nut washer from axle hub. Remove front bearing and remove brake disk or drum.
5. On drum brakes, remove brake line and plug.
6. Remove cotter keys and four bolts holding the brake backing plate and brake shoes on drum and the rotor dust cover on disk brakes. Remove the plate or cover.
7. Remove steering link from back of knuckle.
8. Support the lower arm with a jack and raise to put pressure on spring.

——— CAUTION ———
Be careful not to unbalance vehicle support stands when jacking up lower arm!

9. Remove cotter key and large lower ball joint nut and separate the ball joint from the steering knuckle with a gear puller
10. Repeat step 9 on upper ball joint.

NOTE: Do not let the steering knuckle fall after removing upper ball joint.

Installation is the reverse of removal.

11. On Pickups with coil springs, use a spring compressor when reassembling. Observe the following torques:

Large nut on upper ball joint: 66–94 ft. lbs.

Large nut on lower ball joint: 87–123 ft. lbs.

Rotor dust cover or drum backing plate to steering knuckle: 66–94 ft. lbs.

NOTE: See brake section for hub nut installation procedures.

——— CAUTION ———
Be sure to bleed brakes.

4WD Pickup and Land Cruiser

1. Complete front axle shaft removal procedures in drive axle section, above.
2. Unbolt and remove the tie rod from the knuckle arm with a gear puller. On the Pickup, if removing the driver's side knuckle see section on steering adjustment below for removal of the steering drag link.
3. Remove the oil seal retainer at the back of the steering knuckle.
4. Remove the four nuts on the top steering knuckle cap along with the cone washers. See section on axle shaft removal for procedures in removing cone washers.
5. Remove the four nuts on the bottom steering knuckle cap along with cone washers.
6. Using a small drift and hammer, tap the knuckle bearing caps out from inside the steering knuckle.

——— CAUTION ———
Do not tap on the bearings!

NOTE: Do not mix or lose the upper and lower bearing cap shims.

Installation is the reverse of removal.

To test the knuckle bearing preload, attach a spring scale to the end hole in the steering knuckle at a right angle to the arm. The force required to move the knuckle from side to side should be 4–8 lbs. 4WD Pickup; 4–5 lbs. (Land Cruiser). If the preload is not correct, adjust by replacing shims.

REAR DRIVE AXLE

Axle Shaft

REMOVAL AND INSTALLATION

Pick-Ups

1. Loosen the lug nuts on the wheel, then raise the truck and support it on jackstands.

2. Drain the axle housing.
3. Remove the lug nuts and remove the wheel.
4. Remove the brake drum securing screw and remove the drum.
5. Remove the brake springs and the retracting spring clamp bolt. Remove the lower springs and shoe strut. Remove the brake shoes, screws, and the parking brake lever. Disengage the parking brake cable from the lever and the backing plate.
6. Plug the master cylinder reservoir inlet to prevent the fluid from running out. Disconnect the brake line from the wheel cylinder, being careful not to damage the fitting. Plug the brake line.
7. Remove the four nuts retaining the brake backing plate to the axle housing.
8. Pull the backing plate and axle from the axle housing.

Install the Axle in the Following Manner:

1. Install a new O-ring onto the axle housing.
2. Install the axle shaft and brake backing plate assembly into the axle housing. Be careful not to damage the oil seal with the axle splines. Rotate the axle back and forth until the shaft splines mesh with the differential gear splines.
3. Install the brake backing plate nuts and tighten to 44–58 ft. lbs.
4. Install the brake shoes and lever assembly. Connect the parking brake cable and the brake shoe springs. Connect the brake line to the wheel cylinder.
5. After installing the brake drum, bleed the brakes and adjust the brake shoe clearance. Refill the axle housing with SAE 90W GL5 gear oil.

Land Cruiser

SEMI-FLOATING TYPE DIFFERENTIAL

1. Remove the hub cap and loosen the wheel nuts.
2. Raise the rear axle housing with a jack and support the rear of the vehicle with jackstands.
3. Drain the oil from the differential.
4. Remove the wheel nuts and take off the wheels.
5. Remove the brake drum and related parts, as detailed below.
6. Remove the cover from the back of the differential housing.
7. Remove the pin from the differential pinion shaft.
8. Withdraw the pinion shaft and its spacer from the case.
9. Use a mallet to tap the rear axle shaft toward the differential, to aid in removal of the axle shaft C-lock.
10. Remove the C-lock.
11. Withdraw the axle shaft from the housing.
12. Repeat the removal procedure for the opposite side.
13. To remove oil seal and bearing, use a bearing puller and remove axle bearing

and oil seal together. To replace, use a metal tube to drive bearing and seal into seat.

— CAUTION —

Do not mix the parts of the left and right axle shaft assemblies.

Installation is performed in the reverse order of removal. After installing the axle shaft, C-lock, spacer, and pinion shaft, measure the clearance between the axle shaft and the pinion shaft spacer with a feeler gauge. The clearance should fall between 0.0024–0.0181 in. If the clearance is not within specifications, use one of the following spacers to adjust it:

1.172–1.173 in.
1.188–1.189 in.
1.204–1.205 in.

The rest of the axle shaft installation is the reverse of removal. Remember to fill the axle with lubricant.

FULL FLOATING TYPE DIFFERENTIAL

1. Remove the nuts from the rear axle shaft plate.
2. Remove the cone washers from the mounting studs by tapping the slits of the washers with a tapered punch.
3. Install bolts into the two unused holes of the axle shaft plate.
4. Tighten the bolts to draw the axle shaft assembly out of the housing.
5. Installation is the reverse of the previous steps. Install the axle using a new gasket and torque the axle shaft nuts to 21–25 ft. lbs.

Rear Axle Hub

REMOVAL AND INSTALLATION

Land Cruiser

FULL FLOATING TYPE DIFFERENTIAL

1. Raise the vehicle and support it safely with jack stands.
2. Remove the rear wheels.
3. Remove the rear axle shaft as previously outlined.
4. Loosen the lock screws and remove the adjusting nut from inside the hub using Toyota special tool #09509-25011 or its equivalent.
5. Remove the hub from the axle housing. Inspect all parts for damage or excessive wear. If the seal needs to be replaced, pry the seal out of the hub with an appropriate tool. The seal is installed by tapping it into the hub until it is firmly seated. If the bearing race(s) needs replacement, drive the race(s) from the hub using a brass drift. Use the brass drift to install the new race(s). Drive the new race(s) into the hub until firmly seated.
Install the hub in the following manner:

1. Place the hub on the axle housing and install the outer bearing.
2. Install the lock plate with the lock plate tab positioned into the groove of the axle housing.
3. Install and tighten the adjusting nut with the special tool used during removal.
4. Torque the nut to 43 ft. lbs. Rotate the hub a few times and retorque the adjusting nut to 43 ft. lbs.
5. Loosen the adjusting nut until the hub can be turned by hand.
6. Tighten the nut a small amount and check the amount of pressure required to rotate the hub using a spring tension gauge.
7. The recommended rotational torque is 5.7–12.6 ft. lbs. Tighten or loosen the adjusting nut as required to obtain this reading.
8. Align one of the axle housing slots with one of the adjusting nut slots. Install the lock screws into the holes of the adjusting nut which are at right angles to the aligned slots. Torque the lock screws to 35–60 in. lbs.
9. Recheck the rotational torque and install the axle shaft using a new gasket. Tighten the axle shaft nuts to 21–25 ft. lbs.
10. Install the wheels and lower the vehicle.

Differential

REMOVAL, INSTALLATION, AND OVERHAUL

Refer to the procedures listed with the Front Drive Axle section.

STEERING

Steering Wheel

REMOVAL AND INSTALLATION

Three-Spoke

— CAUTION —

Do not attempt to remove or install the steering wheel by hammering on it. Damage to the energy-absorbing steering column could result.

---

1. Unfasten the horn and turn signal multiconnector(s) at the base of the steering column shroud.
2. Loosen the trim pad retaining screws from the back side of the steering wheel.
3. Lift the trim pad and horn button assembly(ies) from the wheel.
4. Remove the steering wheel hub retaining nut.
5. Scratch matchmarks on the hub and shaft to aid in correct installation.

6. Use a steering wheel puller to remove the steering wheel.

Installation is the reverse of removal. Tighten the wheel retaining nut to 22–29 ft. lbs.

Two-Spoke

The two-spoke steering wheel is removed in the same manner as the three-spoke, except that the trim pad should be pried off with a screwdriver. Remove the pad by lifting it toward the top of the wheel.

Four-Spoke

— CAUTION —

Do not attempt to remove or install the steering wheel by hammering on it. Damage to the energy absorbing steering column could result.

---

1. Unfasten the horn and turn signal connectors at the base of the steering column shroud, underneath the instrument panel.
2. Gently pry the center emblem off the front of the steering wheel.
3. Insert a wrench through the hole and remove the steering wheel retaining nut.
4. Scratch matchmarks on the hub and shaft to aid installation.
5. Use a steering wheel puller to remove the steering wheel.

Installation is the reverse of removal. Tighten the steering wheel retaining nut to 15–22 ft. lbs.

Turn Signal Switch

REMOVAL AND INSTALLATION

1. Disconnect negative (−) battery cable at the battery.
2. Remove the steering wheel, as outlined in the appropriate section above.
3. Unfasten the screws which secure the upper and lower steering column shroud halves.
4. Unfasten the screws which retain the turn signal switch and remove the switch from the column. On 1979 and later Pickups, the windshield wiper switch is part of the assembly, and will be removed as well.

Installation is performed in the reverse order of removal.

Ignition Lock/Switch

REMOVAL AND INSTALLATION

1. Disconnect the negative (−) battery cable.
2. Unfasten the ignition switch connector underneath the instrument panel.
3. Remove the screws which secure the upper and lower halves of the steering column cover.

4. Turn the lock cylinder to the "ACC" position with the ignition key.

5. Push the lock cylinder stop in with a small, round object (cotter pin, punch, etc.)

NOTE: On some models it may be necessary to remove the steering wheel and turn signal switch first.

6. Withdraw the lock cylinder from the lock housing while depressing the stop tab.

7. To remove the ignition switch, unfasten its securing screws and withdraw the switch from the lock housing.

Installation is performed in the following order:

1. Align the locking cam with the hole in the ignition switch and insert the switch in the lock housing.

2. Secure the switch with its screw(s).

3. Make sure that both the lock cylinder and the column lock are in the "ACC" position. Slide the cylinder into the lock housing until the stop tab engages the hole in the lock.

4. The rest of installation is performed in the reverse order of removal.

Power Steering Pump

REMOVAL AND INSTALLATION

1. Remove the fan shroud.

2. Unfasten the nut from the center of the pump pulley.

NOTE: Use the drive belt as a brake to keep the pulley from rotating.

3. Withdraw the drive belt.

4. Remove the pulley and the Woodruff key from the pump shaft.

5. Detach the intake and outlet hoses from the pump reservoir.

NOTE: Tie the hose ends up high so the fluid cannot flow out of them. Drain or plug the pump to prevent fluid leakage.

6. Remove the bolt from the rear mounting brace.

7. Remove the front bracket bolts and withdraw the pump.

Installation is performed in the reverse order of removal. Note the following, however:

1. Tighten the pump pulley mounting bolt to 25–39 ft. lbs.

2. Adjust the pump drive belt tension. The belt should deflect 0.31–0.39 in. under thumb pressure applied midway between the air pump and the power steering pump.

3. Fill the reservoir with "Dexron" automatic transmission fluid. Bleed the air from the system.

BLEEDING

1. Raise the front of the car and support it securely with jackstands.

2. Fill the pump reservoir with "Dexron" automatic transmission fluid.

3. Rotate the steering wheel from lock to lock several times. Add fluid as necessary.

4. With the steering wheel turned fully to one lock, crank the starter while watching the fluid level in the reservoir.

NOTE: Do not start the engine. Operate the starter with a remove starter switch or have an assistant do it from inside of the car. Do not run the starter for prolonged periods.

5. Repeat step 4 with the steering wheel turned to the opposite lock.

6. Start the engine. With the engine idling, turn the steering wheel from lock to lock two or three times.

7. Lower the front of the car and repeat step 6.

8. Center the wheel at the midpoint of its travel. Stop the engine.

9. The fluid level should not have risen more than 0.2 in. If it does, repeat step 7.

10. Check for fluid leakage.

Manual Steering Gear

REMOVAL AND INSTALLATION

2WD Pick-Up

1. Remove the pitman arm from the sector shaft with a puller.

2. Match mark the flexible coupling and worm-shaft and remove the lock bolt.

3. Unbolt and remove the steering gear housing.

4. Install in reverse of removal. Torque the housing bolts to 26–36 ft. lbs., and the pitman arm to 80–90 ft. lbs. Tighten the coupling yoke to 15–20 ft. lbs.

4WD Pick-up

1. Remove the pitman arm from the sector shaft with a puller.

2. Match mark and then loosen the intermediate shaft coupling at the steering gear worm shaft.

3. Loosen the bolt holding the intermediate shaft at the coupling near the fire wall and slide the shaft up off the steering gear worm shaft.

4. Remove the four bolts on the steering gear base and remove the steering gear.

5. Installation is the reverse of removal.

Observe the following torques:

Steering gear housing to frame: 37–47 ft. lbs. Pitman arm to sector shaft: 116–137 ft. lbs. Worm shaft coupling lock bolt: 22–32 ft. lbs.

Land Cruiser

55 SERIES

1. Remove the worm yokes from the worm and main shaft.

2. Remove the intermediate shaft assembly.

3. Remove the Pitman arm from the sector shaft.

4. Unbolt and remove the gear housing.

5. Install in reverse of removal. Torque the Pitman arm to 119–141 ft. lb.

NOTE: The intermediate shaft must be installed with the wheels in a straight ahead position and the steering wheel straight ahead.

40 SERIES

1. Remove the horn button assembly and, using a puller, remove the steering wheel.

2. Remove the steering column jacket lower clamp.

3. Remove the turn signal switch assembly.

4. Remove the steering column access plate.

5. Remove the carburetor and oil filter. (not necessary on 1975–76)

6. Disconnect the # 1 shift rod and select rod at the ends of the shift control and select levers.

7. Remove the lower shift control bracket clamp.

8. Remove the shift control lever, select lever, control shaft lower bracket, control shaft low speed lever, and control shaft lower bracket.

9. Pull the control shaft out toward the driver's side.

10. Remove the pitman arm with a puller.

11. Remove the steering gear box bracket cap and lift out the gear box.

12. Installation is the reverse of removal. Torque the gear box bracket cap to 75–90 ft. lbs. (30–40 for 1975–76); the pitman arm to 120–140 ft. lbs., the steering wheel nut to 30–50 ft. lbs.

ADJUSTMENTS

Adjustments to the manual steering gear are not necessary during normal service. Adjustments are performed only as part of overhaul, which is covered in the General Repair Section.

Power Steering Gear

REMOVAL AND INSTALLATION

Pick-ups

1. Disconnect the hydraulic lines from the steering gear.

2. Mark the relationship between the intermediate shaft U-joint yoke and the steering gear worm shaft.

3. Loosen the set bolt of the intermediate shaft U-joint yoke and disconnect the intermediate shaft from the steering gear worm shaft.

4. Using a puller, remove the Pitman arm from the steering gear.

5. Remove the steering gear mounting bolts and remove the steering gear through the engine compartment.

6. Installation is the reverse of the previous steps. Be sure to align the marks made during step 2. Torque the steering gear mounting bolts to 37–47 ft. lbs., the pitman arm nut to 116–137 ft. lbs.; the U-joint yoke bolt to 22–32 ft. lbs.; the pressure hose fitting to 29–36 ft. lbs.; and the return line fitting to 24–30 ft. lbs.

NOTE: During installation of the hydraulic lines, position each line clear of any surrounding components then tighten the fittings.

Land Cruiser

1. Disconnect the hydraulic lines from the steering gear.

2. Remove the steering shaft coupling set bolt.

3. Remove the steering column-to-firewall bolts.

4. Loosen the steering column-to-dash bolts.

5. Using a puller, disconnect the relay rod from the Pitman shaft.

6. Using a puller, remove the Pitman arm from the steering gear.

7. Pull the steering column towards the passenger compartment to uncouple the steering shaft from the steering gear.

8. Remove the steering gear mounting fasteners and remove the steering gear from the vehicle.

9. Installation is the reverse of the previous steps. Be sure to align the marks on the pitman arm with the corresponding marks on the pitman shaft. Torque the steering gear mounting fasteners to 40–63 ft. lbs.; the Pitman arm nut to 120–141 ft. lbs.; the coupling set bolt to 22–32 ft. lbs.; the pressure hose fitting to 29–36 ft. lbs.; and the return hose fitting to 24–30 ft. lbs.

NOTE: During installation of the hydraulic lines, position each line clear of any surrounding components then tighten the fittings.

Steering Linkage

REMOVAL AND INSTALLATION

2WD Pick-up

1. Raise the front of the vehicle and support it with jack stands.

2. Remove the front wheels.

3. Remove the nut on the pitman arm and using a puller remove it from the steering sector shaft.

4. Unfasten the idler arm support securing bolts and remove the support from the frame.

5. Remove the castle nuts and cotter pins from the tie-rod ends and separate them

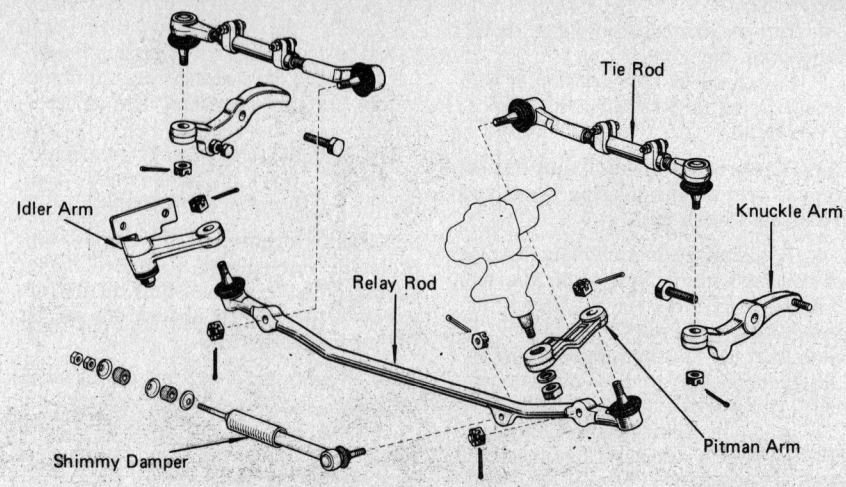

2WD Pick-up steering linkage—1979 and later shown, earlier models similar

from the steering knuckle arms with a puller.

6. Remove the relay rod complete with the tie-rods, Pitman arm and idler arm.

Installation is the reverse of removal with the following notes.

7. Align the marks on the Pitman arm and sector shaft before installing the Pitman arm.

8. Torque all of the following to 55–79 ft. lbs.: tie-rod ends to steering knuckles and relay rod; relay rod to Pitman arm. Torque the relay rod to the idler arm at 37–50 ft. lbs. Torque the Pitman arm to the sector shaft at 80–90 ft. lbs.

4WD Pick-up

1. Jack up the vehicle and support it on stands.

2. Remove the front wheels.

3. Remove cotter pin and nut from the shimmy damper at the tie-rod and remove

shimmy damper from the tie-rod with a puller. Remove the lock nut from other end of the damper. Be sure to note the order of the rubber spacers and washers, and remove damper.

4. Repeat the above procedure where the tie-rod ends connect to the steering knuckles. Remove the tie-rod.

5. To remove the drag link, remove the cotter pin from the steering knuckle end of the drag, and, using a screw driver, unscrew the cap at the end of the drag link.

NOTE: The cap may be tight, so you may have to use a wrench or pliers to turn the screw driver.

6. When the cap is removed, you should be able to dislodge the spring seat, spring and outer socket holder inside the drag link by working the steering knuckle back and forth. The steering knuckle socket in the drag link can now be removed.

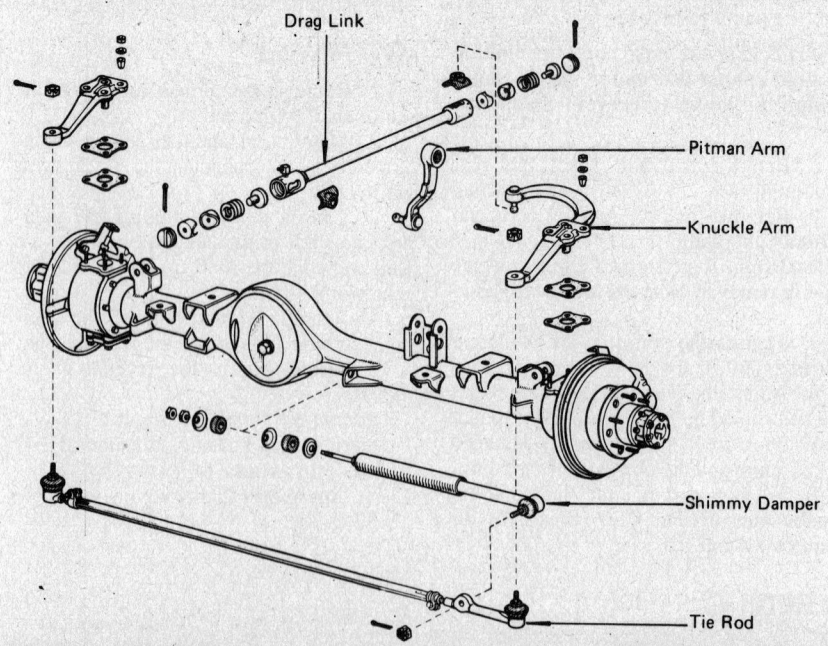

4WD Pick-up steering linkage

NOTE: Be sure to note the order in which the spring seat, spring and outer socket come out of the drag link. Their order will be reversed on the side of the drag link that attaches to the Pitman arm.

7. Repeat steps 5 and 6 on the Pitman arm side of the drag link.

Installation is the reverse of removal. Be sure to insert assemblies in drag link in their correct orders. On drag link, screw in caps completely then loosen 1–⅓ turns.

Observe the following torques:

Shimmy damper to axle housing mount: 8–11 ft. lbs.

Tie-rod end to steering knuckle arm: 55–79 ft. lbs.

Shimmy damper to tie-rod end: 37–50 ft. lbs.

NOTE: Be sure to grease drag link ends at their grease nipples, and, when installing drag link end caps, you tighten them completely and then loosen them 1⅓ turns.

Land Cruiser

1. Remove the hubcaps and loosen the lug nuts.

2. Jack up the front of the vehicle and support it on stands. Remove the wheels.

3. Unfasten the Pitman arm retaining nut.

4. Punch matchmarks on the Pitman arm and the sector shaft to aid reinstallation.

5. Remove the Pitman arm from the sector shaft with a puller.

6. Detach the drag link from the center arm with a tie-rod puller. Remove the link together with the Pitman arm.

7. Detach the tie rod ends from the steering knuckle arm with a puller.

8. Detach the relay rod ends from the center arm. Remove the tie rod/relay rod assembly.

9. Disconnect the end of the steering damper from its bracket on the front crossmember.

10. Remove the center arm attaching nut and use a puller to remove the arm, complete with damper.

11. Remove the skid plate and then remove the center arm bracket from the frame.

Installation is the reverse of removal.

12. Be sure to align the matchmarks, which were made during removal, on the Pitman arm and the sector shaft. Tighten the mounting bolt to 120–140 ft. lbs.

13. Lubricate all of the rod ends and damper ends with multipurpose grease.

14. After the linkage is installed, adjust the toe-in to the proper specifications.

FRONT SUSPENSION

Springs

REMOVAL AND INSTALLATION

2WD Pick-up

1978 AND EARLIER

1. Remove the hubcap and loosen the lug nuts.

2. Raise the front end of the truck and support the front suspension crossmember with jackstands.

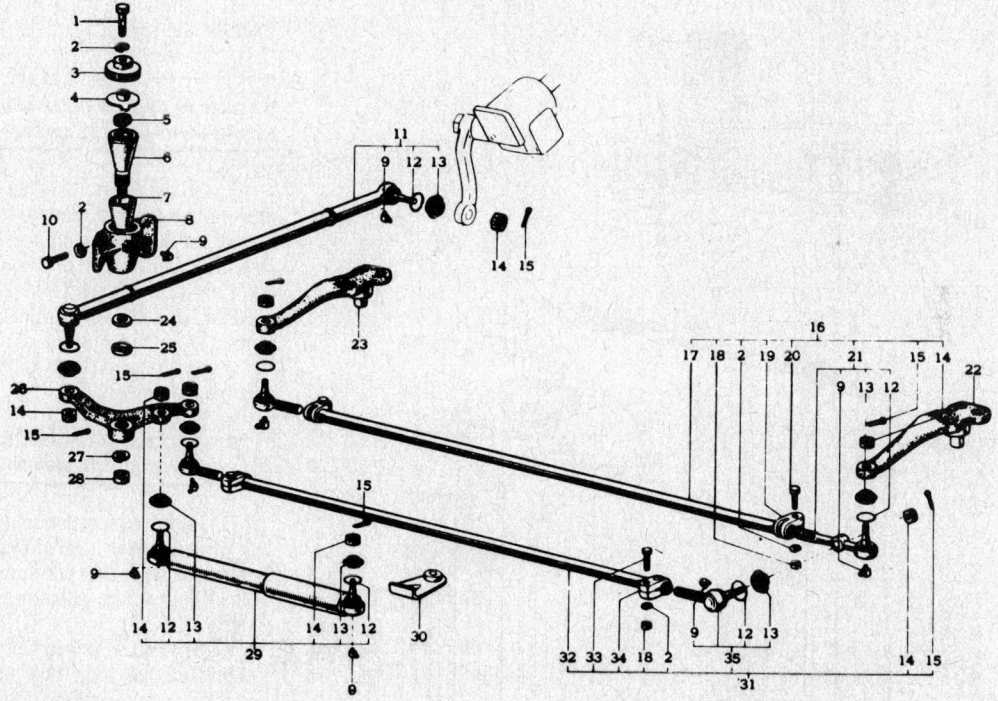

Land Cruiser steering linkage

1. Bolt
2. Lockwasher
3. Center arm shaft nut
4. Center arm nut lock plate
5. Compression spring
6. Center arm shaft
7. Shaft bushing
8. Center arm bracket
9. Grease fitting
10. Bolt
11. Steering drag link assembly
12. Set ring

13. Joint dust seal
14. Lock nut
15. Cotter pin
16. Tie-rod assembly
17. Steering tie-rod
18. Lock nut
19. Tie-rod end clamp
20. Bolt
21. Tie-rod end assembly
22. Steering knuckle arm
23. Steering knuckle arm
24. Dust seal

25. Center arm dust lower seal
26. Steering center arm
27. Lock washer
28. Nut
29. Steering damper
30. Damper bracket
31. Steering relay rod assembly
32. Steering relay rod
33. Bolt
34. Tie-rod end clamp
35. Relay rod end assembly

3. Remove the lug nuts and the wheel.

4. Remove the stabilizer bar connecting bolts and remove the bracket parts, being careful to note their removal sequence in order to aid in installation.

5. Remove the tie rod cotter pin and nut. Use a puller to remove the end of the tie rod from the knuckle arm.

6. Remove the shock absorber, as detailed in the appropriate section. Detach the brake hose.

7. Raise the lower control arm, using a jack, so that the arm is free of the steering knuckle.

8. Loosen the ball joint attachment nut and remove the ball joint puller.

9. Slowly lower the jack underneath the control arm.

— CAUTION —

If the jack is lowered too fast, the spring could suddenly release, causing damage or injury.

---

10. Remove the coil spring and its insulator from underneath the truck.

Inspect the coil spring, its insulator; and bumper for cracks, wear, or damage. Replace parts as necessary.

Installation is basically performed in the reverse order of removal. However, a coil spring compressor should be used to install the spring, rather than the method used for removing it.

Torque the suspension components to the following specifications:

Lower control arm—51–65 ft. lbs. (1976–78 33–43 ft. lbs.)

Ball joint—87–123 ft. lbs.

1979 AND LATER

1979 and later models are equipped with torsion bar front springs.

— CAUTION —

Great care must be taken to make sure springs are not mixed after removal. It is strongly suggested that before removal, each spring be marked with paint, showing front and rear of spring and from which side of the truck it was taken. If springs are installed backwards or on the wrong sides of the truck, they could fracture. If replacing springs, it is not necessary to mark them.

---

1. Jack up truck and support the frame on stands. Remove the wheel.

2. Slide the boot from the rear of torsion bar spring and paint an exact mark from spring housing onto spring.

3. Follow the same procedure on the front of the spring.

— CAUTION —

Be sure to make a mark showing front of spring from back of spring.

---

4. On the rear torsion bar spring holder, there is a long bolt that passes through the arm of the holder and up through the frame crossmember. REMOVE THE LOCKING NUT ONLY FROM THIS BOLT.

5. Using a small ruler, measure the length from the bottom of the remaining nut to the threaded tip of the bolt and record this measurement.

— CAUTION —

Be sure to complete step five accurately.

---

6. Place a jack under the rear torsion bar spring holder arm and jack up the arm to remove the spring pressure from the long bolt. Remove the adjusting nut from the long bolt.

7. SLOWLY lower jack.

8. Remove long bolt and its spacers and remove rear holder. You should be able to pull the torsion bar out of the front and rear holders.

Inspect all parts for wear damage or cracks. Check the boots for rips and wear. Inspect the splined ends of the torsion bar spring and the splined holes in the rear holder and the front torque arm for damage. Replace as necessary.

On the rear ends of the torsion bar springs, there are markings to show which is right and which is the left bar. Do not confuse them.

To install:

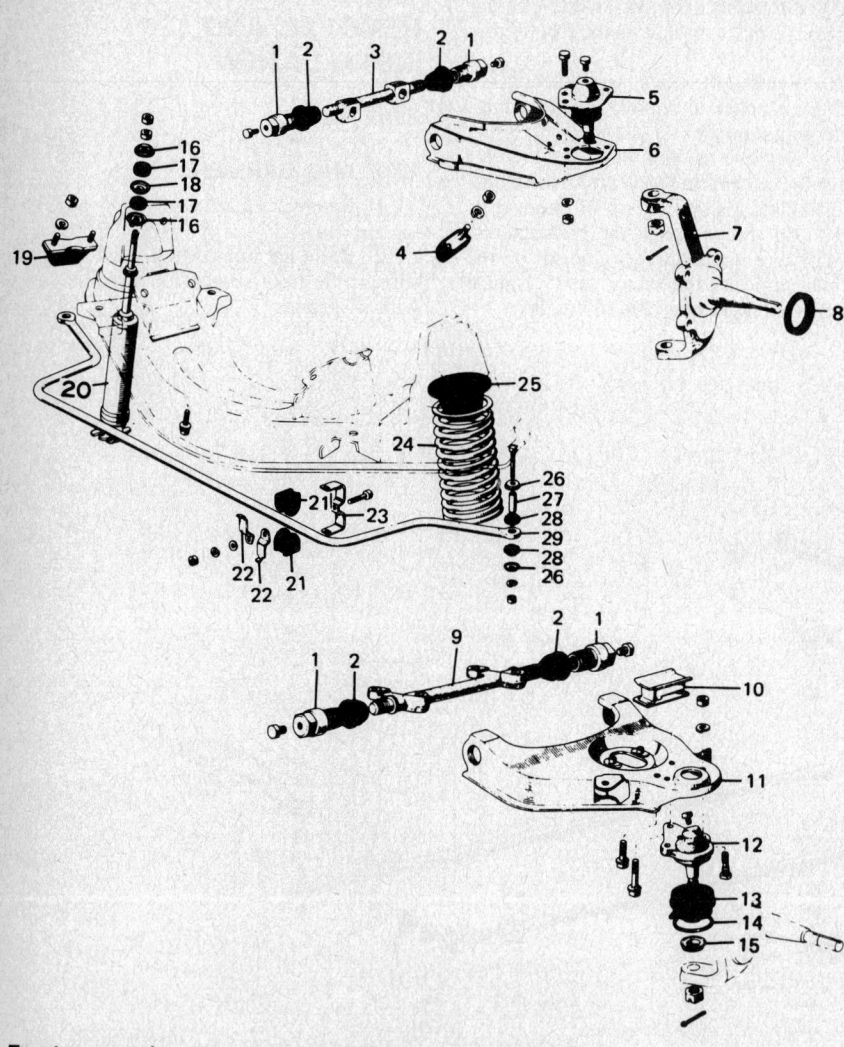

Front suspension components—1978 and earlier 2WD pick-up

1. Arm pivot bushing
2. Arm pivot dust seal
3. Upper suspension arm shaft
4. Front spring bumper No. 2
5. Upper ball joint assembly
6. Suspension upper arm subassembly
7. Steering knuckle
8. Steering knuckle grease retainer
9. Lower suspension arm shaft
10. Lower arm bumper stop plate
11. Suspension lower arm subassembly
12. Lower ball joint
13. Lower ball joint dust cover
14. Set ring
15. Lower ball joint dust cover plate
16. Cushion retainer
17. Shock absorber cushion
18. Cushion retainer
19. Front spring bumper No. 1
20. Front shock absorber
21. Stablizer bushing
22. Stablizer link cover
23. Stablizer link
24. Front coil spring
25. Front coil spring insulator
26. Cushion retainer
27. Collar
28. Stablizer cushion
29. Stablizer bar

9. Coat the splined ends of the torsion bar with multipurpose grease.

10. If refitting old torsion bars:

a. Slide the front of the bar into the opening on the torque arm, making sure you line up the marks you made earlier on the torsion bar spring and the torque arm.

b. Repeat the above step with the rear spring holder and replace the long bolt and its spacers.

c. Place a pipe that will fit in the notch on the rear holder arm on a jack and jack up the arm.

d. Tighten the adjusting nut so that it is the same length as it was before removal.

NOTE: Do not replace the lock nut yet.

11. When installing a new torsion bar spring:

a. Slide the front of the torsion bar into the opening on the torque arm.

b. Fit the rear holder in place and install the rear of the torsion in it so that when the long bolt and spacers are installed, the distance from the top of the upper spacer to the tip of the threaded end of bolt is 0.7–1.0 in.

NOTE: Make sure the bolt and bottom spacer are snuggly in the holder arm while measuring.

c. When the correct measurement is achieved, fit a pipe or round bar in the notch on the rear holder arm. Jack up arm on pipe.

d. Replace the adjusting nut and tighten until the distance from the bottom of the nut to the tip of the threaded end of bolt is 71–89 mm (2.8–3.5 in.).

NOTE: Do not install the lock nut yet.

12. Apply multipurpose grease to the boot lips and refit the boots over splines.

13. Replace the wheel and lower the truck.

14. With the wheels on the ground, measure the distance from the ground to the center of the lower arm shaft (See chart). Adjust vehicle height with the adjusting nut on the rear spring holder.

NOTE: If, after achieving the correct vehicle height, the distance from the bottom of the adjusting nut to the top of the threaded end of the long bolt is more than 3.8 in., change the position of the rear spring holder arm spline and reassemble.

15. Replace and tighten the lock nut on the long bolt.

——— **CAUTION** ———
Make sure the adjusting nut does not move when tightening lock nut.

4WD Pick-up

1. Jack up the front of vehicle and place support stands under the chassis frame.

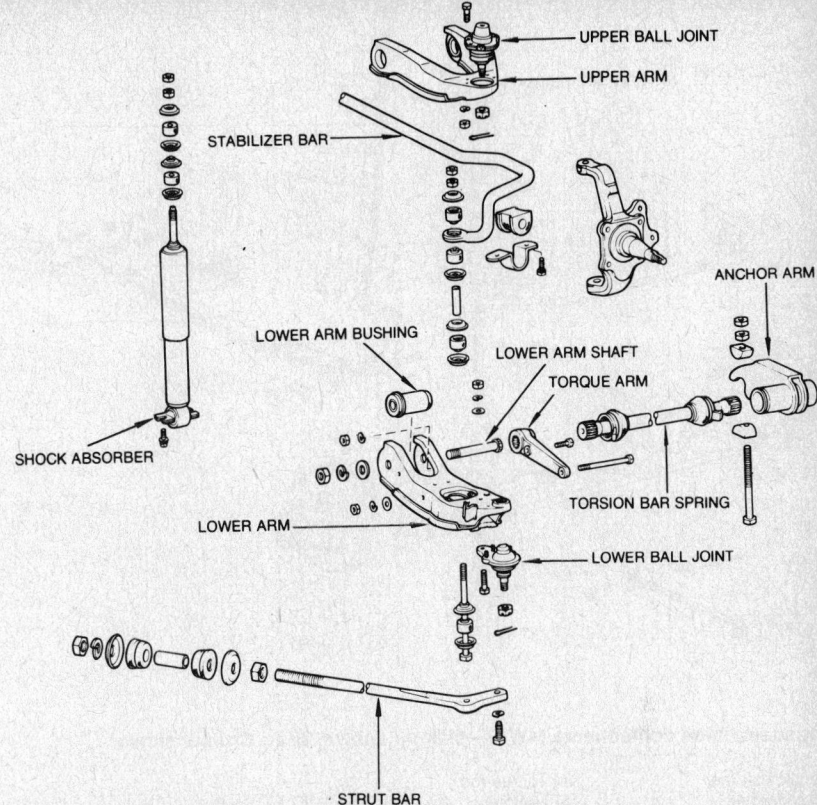

Front suspension components—1979 and later 2WD pick-up

NOTE: Do not place supports under front axle housing.

2. Remove wheel.

3. Remove the bolt from the bottom of the shock absorber and raise shock up out of the way.

4. If removing driver's side front leaf spring, remove the cotter pin from the end of the steering drag link at the axle housing. Unscrew the slitted bolt in the end of the drag link and remove the bolt, spring holder, spring, and outer socket holder. Remove drag link from steering knuckle arm.

NOTE: Be careful not to lose inner socket holder.

5. Remove stabilizer bar bolt and spacer and washer assembly.

6. Disconnect brake line at the holder behind the brake assembly. Drive out shim holding brake line to holder and withdraw brake line. Plug end of brake line running to master cylinder to prevent fluid loss.

7. Place a jack under the front axle housing and raise to put pressure on the leaf spring. Remove the four nuts holding the two U-bolts to the axle housing and remove the U-bolts.

8. Lower the jack enough to take the pressure off the leaf spring but so it still supports the axle housing.

9. Remove the bolts holding the leaf spring to its hangers and carefully pry the spring from its holders.

NOTE: It may be necessary to lower the jack under the axle housing to remove spring.

Installation is the reverse of removal.

——— **CAUTION** ———
Be sure to refill brake master cylinder reservoir and bleed brakes!

NOTE: Finger tighten the front and rear leaf spring hanger pin nuts. After the spring is attached to the axle housing and chassis, jack up the axle housing until the vehicle clears its support stands and then torque pin nuts.

Observe the following torques:
U-bolt nuts: 73–108 ft. lbs.
Front hanger pin placer bolts: 8–11 ft. lbs.
Front hanger pin nut: 55–79 ft. lbs.
Rear shackle pin nuts: 55–79 ft. lbs.

Land Cruiser

Land Cruiser models are equipped with leaf springs in the front and rear. Thus, front spring removal is performed in almost the same manner as rear spring removal. Follow the procedure outlined in the rear suspension section, below.

——— **CAUTION** ———
Be careful when raising or lowering the front suspension with a jack so as not to damage any of the steering system components.

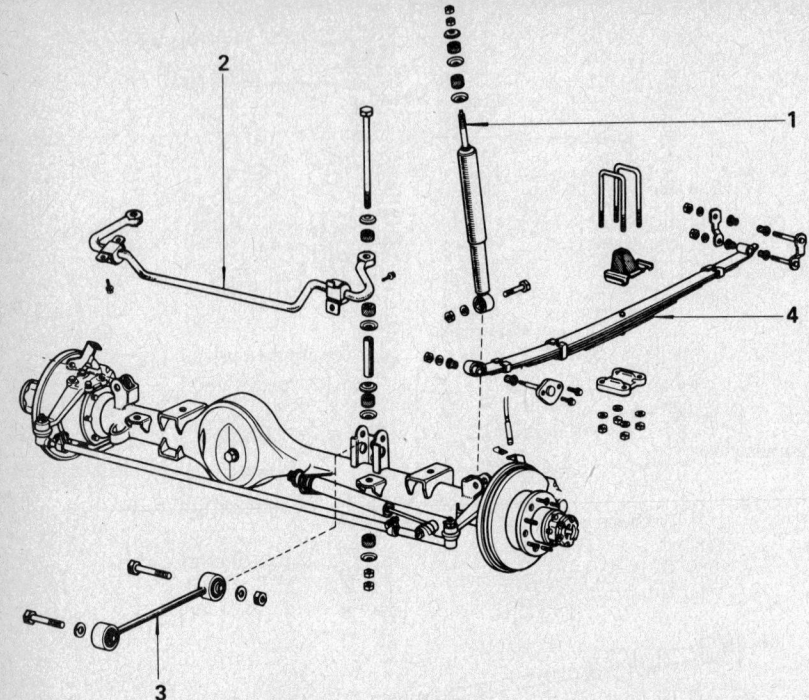

Front suspension components (4WD)—pick-up shown, Land Cruiser similar

1. Shock absorber
2. Stablizer bar
3. Torque rod
4. Leaf spring

Front Shock Absorber

REMOVAL AND INSTALLATION

2WD Pick-up

1. Remove the hubcap and loosen the lug nuts.
2. Raise the front of the truck and support it with jack stands.
3. Remove the lug nuts and the wheel.
4. Unfasten the double nuts at the top end of the shock absorber. Remove the cushions and cushion retainers.
5. Remove the two bolts which secure the lower end of the shock absorber to the lower control arm.
6. Remove the shock absorber. Installation is the reverse of removal.

4WD Pick-up

Removal and installation is the same as the 2WD Pick-up, except there is only one through-bolt holding the bottom of the shock in place.

Land Cruiser

Complete steps 1–3 of the 2WD Pick-up shock absorber removal.

— CAUTION —
Be careful not to damage steering assembly when jacking up front of vehicle.

Remove bolts holding the top and bottom of the shock in place and remove shock. Installation is the reverse of removal.

Stabilizer Bar

REMOVAL AND INSTALLATION

2WD Pick-up

1. Remove one torsion bar spring according to the previous spring removal and installation procedure.
2. Remove the stabilizer bar attachment hardware from the ends of the stabilizer bar. During installation, be sure to arrange the spacers, bushings, and washers as originally installed.
3. Remove the stabilizer bar-to-frame brackets and bushings and lower the stabilizer bar from the vehicle.
4. Installation is the reverse of the previous steps. Be sure to carefully inspect each bushing for damage and replace the bushing(s) if necessary. Torque all stabilizer bar fasteners to 8–11 ft. lbs.

4WD Pick-up and Land Cruiser

Follow steps 2–4 of the previous 2WD Pick-up procedure. Removal of a spring is not necessary on these models.

Upper Control Arm

REMOVAL AND INSTALLATION

2WD Pick-up

1. Raise and support the truck under the frame.
2. Remove the wheel.
3. Raise the lower control arm with a jack.
4. Remove the nut from the upper ball joint stud.
5. Separate the ball joint from the steering knuckle.
6. Unbolt and remove the upper arm at the two bolts holding the inner shaft to the frame, taking note of the number and size of the aligning shims.
7. Installation is the reverse of removal. Replace the shims as found. Tighten fasteners, but do not torque them until the truck is on the ground.
8. Lower the truck and torque the upper arm mounting bolts to 95–153 ft. lbs.

Lower Control Arm

REMOVAL AND INSTALLATION

2WD Pick-up

1. Raise and support the front end.
2. On 1978 and earlier Pick-ups, remove the coil spring as previously outlined. On 1979 and later Pick-ups, remove the torsion bar spring as previously outlined.
3. Remove the stabilizer bar and the strut bar from the lower arm, if so equipped.
4. On 1979 and later Pick-ups, remove the bottom of the shock absorber from the lower arm.
5. Unbolt and remove lower ball joint.

NOTE: If the lower ball joint is not to be replaced, simply unbolt it from the lower control arm. It is not necessary to separate the ball joint from the steering knuckle.

6. On 1978 and earler Pick-ups, unbolt and remove the lower control arm at the four bolts mounting the lower control arm on the frame. On 1979 and later Pick-ups, unbolt and remove the nut from the lower arm shaft. Remove the spring torque arm from the other side of the lower control arm and remove the lower arm shaft bolt and the lower arm.

Installation is the reverse of removal. Tighten the bolt(s) holding the lower control arm to the frame but do not torque them until the vehicle is on the ground. Observe the following torques during installation:

	Ft. Lbs.
Ball joint retainer bolts (1978 and earlier):	
Large bolts	21–32
Small bolts	21–28
Ball joint retainer bolts (1979 and later):	
Large bolts	29–39
Small bolts	15–21
Strut bar (1979 and later):	55–75
Torque arm (1979 and later):	29–39

7. Lower the truck and torque the lower arm mounting bolt(s) to the following values:

   a. 1978 and earlier: 33–43 ft. lbs.
   b. 1979 and later: 145–217 ft. lbs.

--------- CAUTION ---------
Do not tighten the control arm bolts fully until the vehicle is lowered; if the bolts are tightened with the control arm(s) hanging, excessive bushing wear will result.

Ball Joints

INSPECTION

To check the lower ball joint for wear, jack up the lower suspension arm, after removing all excess play from the other suspension parts (wheel bearings, tie-rods, etc.). The bottom of the tire should not move more than 0.2 in. when the tire is pushed and pulled inward and outward. The tire should not move more than 0.09 in. up and down. If the play is greater than these figures, replace the ball joint. The upper ball joint should be replaced if a distinct looseness is felt when turning the ball joint stud with the steering knuckle removed.

REMOVAL AND INSTALLATION

1978 AND EARLIER

1. Remove the wheel and tire.
2. Support the front suspension cross-member with jackstands.
3. Place a jack under the lower control arm and raise the control arm until the spring bumper is off the frame.
4. Disconnect the flexible brake hose.
5. Disconnect the tie-rod end from the steering knuckle using a puller.
6. Using a suitable puller remove the ball joint from the steering knuckle.
7. Remove the ball joint from the lower arm.
8. From this position the upper ball joint may also be removed in a similar manner. Removal and installation will be easier if the lower is removed first.
9. Install the new ball joints and reassemble the steering components. Due to the fact that the shock absorber is not removed

in this procedure the coil spring may be positioned with the jack and no compressor is necessary.

NOTE: Be sure to grease the new ball joints before using the vehicle.

10. Tighten the upper ball joint nuts to 15–22 ft. lbs., the lower to 22–29 ft. lbs. Tighten the steering knuckle to the upper joint to 65–94 ft. lbs.; the knuckle to the lower joint to 87–123 ft. lbs. Bleed the brakes before driving the truck.

1979 AND LATER

1. Jack up the vehicle and support it with jackstands.
2. Remove the front wheel.
3. Support the lower control arm with a jack.
4. Remove the brake caliper and tie it out of the way, as outlined later in this section.
5. Remove the tie rod end.
6. Remove the ball joint from the steering knuckle.

NOTE: You can also remove the upper ball joint now if needed. Removal and installation will be easier if the bottom joint is removed first.

7. Installation is the reverse of removal.

NOTE: Be sure to grease the ball joints before moving the vehicle.

The following torque figures are needed. Upper mounting bolts 15–21 ft. lbs. Upper ball joint 66–94 ft. lbs. lower mounting bolts 15–39 ft. lbs. lower ball joint 87–122 ft. lbs.

Front-End Alignment

Front-end alignment measurements require the use of special equipment. Before measuring alignment or attempting to adjust it, always check the following points:

1. Be sure that the tires are properly inflated.
2. See that the wheels are properly balanced.
3. Check the ball joints to determine if they are worn or loose.
4. Check front wheel bearing adjustment.
5. Be sure that the car is on a level surface.
6. Check all suspension parts for tightness.

CASTER AND CAMBER ADJUSTMENTS

Measure the caster and camber angles. If they are not within specifications, adjust them by adding or subtracting the shims on the mounting bolts between the upper control arm and the suspension member:

1. To increase camber, remove shims equally from both of the control shaft

mounting bolts. Do the reverse to decrease camber.

2. To increase caster, add camber adjusting shims to the rear mounting bolt, or remove them from the front mounting bolt. Do the reverses to decrease caster.

NOTE: Caster and camber adjustments should always be performed in a single operation.

TOE-IN ADJUSTMENT

Measure the toe-in. Adjust it, if necessary, by loosening the tie rod end clamping bolts and rotating the tie rod adjusting tubes. Tighten the clamping bolts when finished.

NOTE: Both tie rod ends should be the same length. If they are not, perform the adjustment until the toe-in is within specifications and the tie rod ends are equal in length.

REAR SUSPENSION

Springs

REMOVAL AND INSTALLATION

1. Loosen the rear wheel lug nuts.
2. Raise the rear of the vehicle. Support the frame and rear axle housing with stands.
3. Remove the lug nuts and the wheel.
4. Remove the cotter pin, nut, and washer from the lower end of the shock absorber.
5. On Land Cruiser models, perform the following:
   a. Remove the cotter pins and nuts from the lower end of the stabilizer link.
   b. Detach the link from the axle housing.
6. Detach the shock absorber from the spring seat pivot pin.
7. Remove the parking brake cable clamp (except Land Cruiser).

NOTE: Remove the parking brake equalizer, if necessary.

8. Unfasten the U-bolt nuts and remove the spring seat assemblies.
9. Adjust the height of the rear axle housing so that the weight of the rear axle is removed from the rear springs.
10. Unfasten the spring shackle retaining nuts. Withdraw the spring shackle inner plate. Carefully pry out the spring shackle with a bar.
11. Remove the spring bracket pin from the front end of the spring hanger and remove the rubber bushings.
12. Remove the spring.

—————— CAUTION ——————
Use care not to damage the hydraulic brake line or the parking brake cable.

Installation is performed in the following order:

1. Install the rubber bushings in the eye of the spring.

2. Align the eye of the spring with the spring hanger bracket and drive the pin through the bracket holes and rubber bushings.

NOTE: Use soapy water as lubricant, if necessary, to aid in pin installation. Never use oil or grease.

3. Finger-tighten the spring hanger nuts and/or bolts.

4. Install the rubber bushings in the spring eye at the opposite end of the spring.

5. Raise the free end of the spring. Install the spring shackle through the bushings and the bracket.

6. Install the shackle inner plate and finger-tighten the retaining nuts.

7. Center the bolt head in the hole which is provided in the spring seat on the axle housing.

8. Fit the U-bolts over the axle housing. Install the lower spring seat.

9. Tighten the U-bolt nuts.

NOTE: Some models have two sets of nuts, while others have a nut and lockwasher.

10. Install the parking brake cable clamp. Install the equalizer, if it was removed.

11. Pick-up and Land cruiser:

a. Raise the rear axle with the jack so that the stands no longer support the frame.

b. Tighten the hanger pin and shackle nuts.

c. Install the shock absorber bushings and washers. Tighten and install the cotter pins.

d. Install the stablizer link and hand-tighten its retaining nuts (Land Cruiser).

e. Install the wheels, remove the stands, and lower the vehicle to the ground.

f. Tighten the stabilizer link bolts, bounce the vehicle, and tighten them again (Land Cruiser).

Shock Absorbers

REMOVAL AND INSTALLATION

1. Jack up the rear of the vehicle.

2. Support the rear axle housing with jackstands.

3. Unfasten the upper shock absorber retaining nuts and/or bolts from the upper frame member.

4. Depending upon the type of rear springs used, either disconnect the lower end of the shock absorber from the spring seat, or the rear axle housing, by removing its cotter pins, nuts, and/or bolts.

5. Remove the shock absorber.

Inspect the shock for wear, leaks, or other signs of damage.

Installation is performed in the reverse order from removal.

HYDRAULIC BRAKE SYSTEM

Adjustments

FRONT DRUM BRAKE

Land Cruiser

These models are equipped with rear drum brakes which require manual adjustment. Perform the adjustment in the following order.

1. Chock the front wheels and fully release the parking brake.

2. Raise the rear of the vehicle and support it with jackstands.

3. Remove the adjusting hole plug from the backing plate.

4. Expand the brake shoes by turning the adjusting wheel with a star-wheel adjuster or a thin-bladed screw driver.

5. Pump the brake pedal several times, while expanding the shoes, so that the shoe contacts the drum evenly.

NOTE: If the wheel still turns when your foot is removed from the brake pedal, continue expanding the shoes until the wheel locks.

6. Back off on the adjuster, just enough so that the wheel rotates without dragging.

7. After this point is reached, continue backing off for five additional notches.

NOTE: On models which have two wheel cylinders at each wheel, adjust each set of brakes separately; never adjust both at once.

8. If the wheel still does not turn freely, back off one or two more notches. If after this, it still drags, check for worn or defective parts.

9. Pump the brake pedal again, and check wheel rotation.

10. Reverse steps 1–3.

Pick-up, 4 × 4 Pick-up

These models are equipped with self-adjusting rear drum brakes. No adjustment is necessary.

FRONT DRUM BRAKE

Perform the adjustments in the same manner as detailed for the rear drum brakes.

FRONT DISC BRAKE

Front disc brakes require no adjustment. Hydraulic pressure maintains the proper brake pad-to-disc contact at all times.

NOTE: Because of this, the brake fluid level should be checked regularly.

Master Cylinder

REMOVAL AND INSTALLATION

Be careful not to spill brake fluid on the painted surfaces of the vehicle; it will damage the paint.

1. Unfasten the hydraulic line from the master cylinder.

2. Detach the hydraulic fluid pressure differential switch wiring connectors.

3. Loosen the master cylinder reservoir mounting bolt.

4. Then do one of the following:

a. On models with manual brakes, remove the master cylinder securing bolts and the clevis pin from the brake pedal. Remove the master cylinder.

b. On other models with power brakes, unfasten the nuts and remove the master cylinder assembly from the power brake unit.

Installation is performed in the reverse order of removal. Note the following however:

1. Before tightening the master cylinder mounting nuts or bolts, screw the hydraulic line into the cylinder body, a few turns.

2. After installation is completed, bleed the master cylinder and the brake system.

OVERHAUL

1. Remove the reservoir caps and floats and unscrew the bolts that hold the reservoir to the main body.

2. Remove warning switches (where fitted), then remove from the rear of the cylinder, in order: boot and snap-ring, stop plate (washer), piston No. 1 with spacer, cylinder cup, spring retainer and spring.

3. Remove the end plug and gasket from the front of the cylinder, then remove the front piston stop bolt from underneath. Pull out the spring and its retainer, piston no. 2, the spacer and the cylinder cup.

4. Remove the two outlet fittings, washers, check valves and springs.

5. Remove the piston cups from their seats on the pistons only if they are to be replaced.

After washing all parts in clean brake fluid, dry with compressed air. Inspect the cylinder bore for wear, scuff marks or nicks. Cylinders may be honed slightly, but the limit is 0.006 in. It is recommended that it be replaced rather than overhauled.

Reverse the sequence of disassembly. Absolute cleanliness is important, and all parts must be coated with clean brake fluid. Bleed the master cylinder and make sure all lines are tightened correctly and do not leak. Use fluid that meets specifications (for standard brakes) and use the special disc brake fluid (DOT-3) for disc brake equipped cars.

Proportioning Valve

A proportioning valve is used on all models to reduce the hydraulic pressure to the rear brakes because of weight transfer during high speed stops. This helps to keep the rear brakes from locking up by improving front to rear brake balance.

REMOVAL AND INSTALLATION

1. Disconnect the brake lines from the valve unions.
2. Remove the valve mounting bolt, if used, and remove the valve.

NOTE: If the proportioning valve is defective, it must be replaced as an assembly; it cannot be rebuilt.

Installation is the reverse of removal. Bleed the brake system after it is completed.

Power Brake Booster

REMOVAL AND INSTALLATION

1. Remove brake master cylinder. See above for instructions.
2. Remove the air line running from the brake booster to the manifold.
3. Working inside the driver's compartment, remove the clevis pin that connects the brake pedal to the booster rod. Remove the four nuts holding the booster assembly to the fire wall and remove the assembly.

Installation is the reverse of removal.

NOTE: When installing a new booster, make sure there is a little clearance between the push rod end and the master cylinder piston.

Bleeding the System

—————— CAUTION ——————
Do not reuse brake fluid which has been bled from the brake system.

1. Insert a clear vinyl tube into the bleeder plug on the master cylinder or the wheel cylinders.

NOTE: If the master cylinder has been overhauled or if air is present in it, start the bleeding procedure with the master cylinder. Otherwise, (and after bleeding the master cylinder) start with the wheel cylinder which is furthest from the master cylinder.

2. Insert the other end of the tube into a jar which is half filled with brake fluid.
3. Slowly depress the brake pedal (have an assistant do it) and turn the bleeder plug 1/3–1/2 of a turn at the same time.

NOTE: If the brake pedal is depressed too fast, small air bubbles will form in the brake fluid which will be very difficult to remove.

4. Close the bleeder plug before hydraulic pressure decreases in the cylinder.
5. Repeat this procedure until the air bubbles are removed and then go on to the next wheel cylinder.

—————— CAUTION ——————
Replenish the brake fluid in the master cylinder reservoir, so that it does not run out during bleeding.

Front Disc Brakes

PADS

Removal and Installation

1. Remove the hub cap and loosen the lug nuts.
2. Raise the front of the vehicle with a jack and support it with stands on the chassis pads provided.
3. Remove the lug nuts and the wheel.
4. Remove the clips, springs, and the pins (which have the holes).
5. Withdraw the anti-squeal shims and the pads.

6. Check pad thickness against the specifications.

Install the pads in the following order:

1. Clean the back of the pistons, cylinder boots and the caliper surfaces which contact the brake pads.
2. Fit the pads and anti-squeal shims into the caliper.

NOTE: Install the shims with their arrows pointing toward the rotational direction of the disc.

3. Install the spring so that it presses correctly against the pads.
4. After completing installation, depress the brake pedal several times before lowering the car. This will provide proper operating clearance for the wheel cylinder components.
5. Install the wheel and lower the vehicle.

CALIPERS

Removal and Installation

—————— CAUTION ——————
Do not unfasten the bridge bolt and separate the caliper halves.

1. Remove the wheel covers and loosen the lug nuts.
2. Raise the front of the vehicle and support it with jackstands.
3. Remove the lug nuts and the wheel.
4. Plug the master cylinder inlet, so that the brake fluid will not run out when the hydraulic line is disconnected.

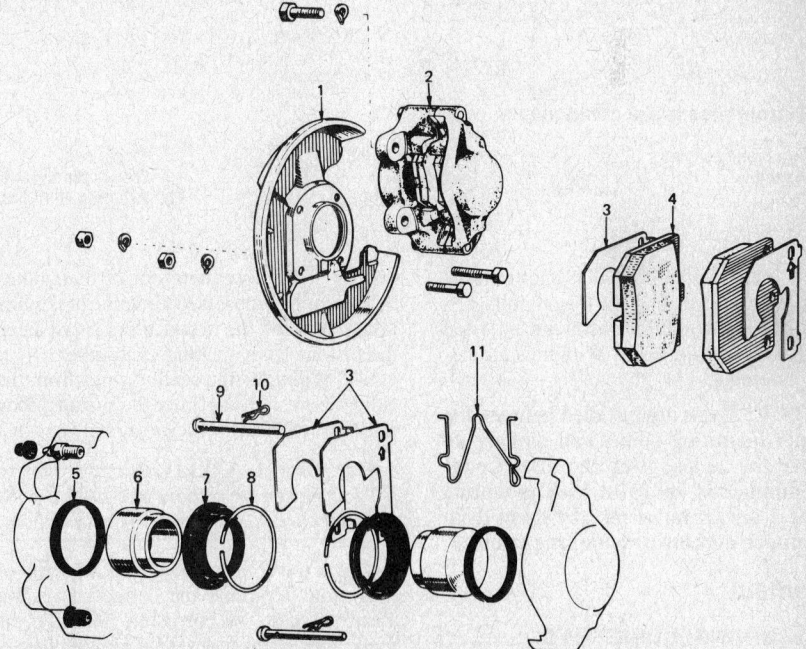

2WD front disc brake components

1. Brake backing plate
2. Caliper
3. Anti-squeal shim
4. Brake pad
5. Seal ring
6. Piston
7. Piston boot
8. Set ring
9. Pad pin
10. Anti-rattle spring

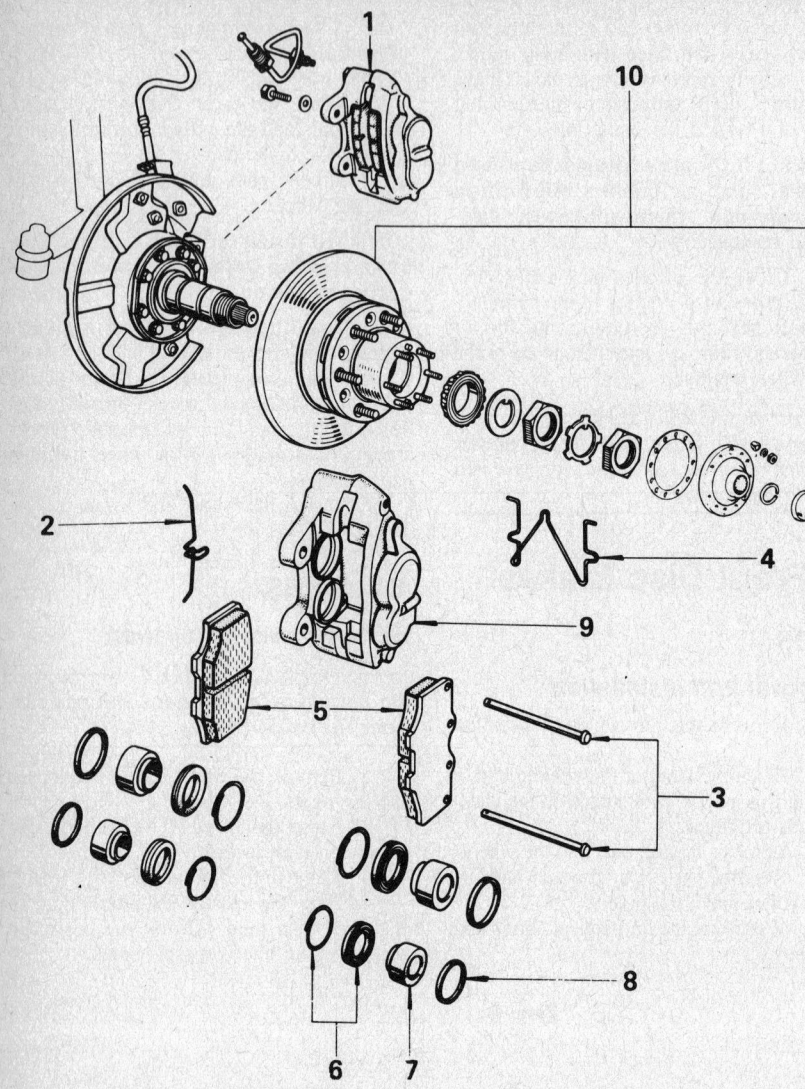

4WD front disc brake components

1. Disc brake cylinder
   assembly
2. Clip
3. Hole pin
4. Anti-rattle spring
5. Pad
6. Ring and boot
7. Piston
8. Piston seal
9. Disc brake cylinder
10. Axle hub with disc

5. Remove the hydraulic line from the caliper by unfastening the union bolt.

6. Remove the lockwire and unfasten the caliper securint bolts. Withdraw the caliper assembly.

NOTE: Shims are installed between the caliper mounting points and its body to center the caliper over the disc. Count the number of shims at each mounting point. Use care not to mix the shims from the upper and lower mounting points.

Overhaul

PICK-UP INCLUDING 4WD

1. Remove the caliper assembly from the vehicle, and separate the pads from the caliper.

2. Remove the snap-ring and the dust boot from caliper bores.

3. Place a block of wood between the pistons and below them out of their bores by applying compressed air to the brake line union. Use of the wood block is to keep the pistons from striking each other.

4. Withdraw the sealing rings from the caliper bores. Do not mix the pistons; they must be returned to their original bores.

CAUTION

Do not loosen or remove the bridge bolts which secure the halves of the caliper body.

Check the caliper body for cracks and/or distortion. Examine the caliper bores for wear, damage, or corrosion. Replace the guide pins (with holes) if they are bent.

Assembly is performed in the following order:

1. Replace all rubber parts with new ones.

2. Coat the sealing rings and the caliper bore with the rubber grease supplied in the rebuilding kit; do not use any other type of lubricant.

3. Fit the sealing rings into the grooves in the caliper bores.

4. Install the O-rings and spacers (if used) on the pistons and carefully insert each piston into its original bore. Use only finger-pressure to seat the pistons.

5. Install the boots over the bores and secure them with the snap-rings.

6. Install the calipers and the brake pads, then bleed the brake system.

LAND CRUISER

NOTE: Do not separate the caliper halves.

1. Remove the caliper.

2. Remove the retaining pin and anti-rattle spring.

3. Remove the brake pads.

4. Remove the piston retaining ring.

5. Remove the piston boot and piston.

6. Remove the piston seal.

7. Assembly is the reverse of disassembly.

ROTOR

Removal and Installation

PICK-UP

1. Remove the brake pads and the caliper.

2. Check the disc run-out, as detailed under Inspection, below, at this point. Make a note of the results for use during installation.

3. Remove the grease cap from the hub. Remove the cotter pin and castle nut.

4. Remove the wheel hub with the brake rotor attached, inspect the rotor.

5. Installation is performed in the following order:

6. Coat the hub seal lip with multipurpose grease and install the rotor/hub assembly.

7. Adjust the wheel bearing preload as detailed below.

8. Measure rotor run-out. Check it against specifications.

NOTE: If the wheel bearing nut is improperly tightened, rotor run-out will be affected.

9. Tighten the caliper securing bolts to 65-87 ft. lbs.

10. Install the remainder of the components.

11. Bleed the brake system.

12. Road test the vehicle. Check the rolling resistance of the wheel.

4WD PICK-UP, LAND CRUISER

1. For 4WD Pick-up, complete steps 1–8 under front drive axle removal, above. Be sure to check rotor run-out, as described in Inspection section, below.

2. For Land Cruiser, complete steps 1–7 under front drive axle removal, above. Be sure to check rotor run-out, as described in Inspection section, below.

NOTE: Run-out limit for Land Cruiser is 0.005 in.

3. For both vehicles, complete steps 5–12 under Pick-up Rotor Removal and Installation, above, with the following notes:

4. When replacing the adjusting nut on the 4WD Pick-up, tighten the nut to 43 ft. lbs. and then loosen it again. Tighten the nut to 3–5 ft. lbs. and test preload. Lock the adjusting nut and tighten the lock nut over it to 58–72 ft. lbs.

NOTE: Reverse steps taken from other sections to complete assembly procedures.

NOTE: Tighten Land Cruiser caliper securing bolts to 54–76 ft. lbs.

Front Drum Brakes

DRUMS

Removal and Installation

1. Remove the hub cap and loosen the lug nuts.
2. Raise the front of the vehicle and support it with jackstands.
3. Remove the lug nuts and the wheel.
4. On Pick-up models:
   a. Remove the axle hub grease cap.
   b. Remove the cotter pin and claw washer.
   c. Unfasten the nut and withdraw the drum, complete with the hub.
5. On Land Cruiser models:
   a. Unfasten the brake drum retaining screws.
   b. Tap the drum lightly with a mallet to free it.

——————— CAUTION ———————
Do not depress the brake pedal once the drum has been removed.

Inspect the brake drum as detailed in the section below.

Installation is performed in the reverse order of removal. On Pick-up models adjust the wheel bearing preload.

Inspection

1. Clean the drum.
2. Inspect the drum for scoring, cracks, grooves, and out of roundness. Replace or turn the drum, as required.
3. Light scoring may be removed by dressing the drum with *fine* emery cloth.
4. Heavy scoring will require the use of a brake drum lathe to turn the drum.

BRAKE SHOES

REMOVAL AND INSTALLATION

PICK-UP

1. Remove the drum.
2. Remove the following parts in the order listed:

   a. Shoe retaining spring pins.
   b. Shoe retaining springs.
   c. Shoe tension (return) springs.
   d. Shoes.

NOTE: Use a brake shoe removal tool to aid in removal of the tension springs.

3. After removal, keep the brake shoes in their proper order.

——————— CAUTION ———————
Be careful to keep oil or grease from contacting the lining surface.

Inspect the brake shoes for wear, rust or damage. Inspect the brake linings for wear.
Inspect the tension spring for deformation or weakness.
Installation is performed in the following order:

1. Coat all of the points where the brake shoes make contact with other brake assembly parts, with grease.

——————— CAUTION ———————
Be careful not to get grease on the surface of the lining.

2. Fit the upper and lower shoes into the grooves on the wheel cylinders and adjusting bolts. Install the spring pins in the shoes and then attach the retaining springs.
3. Hook the brake shoe tension springs on the upper and lower shoes with the aid of the tool used during removal.
4. Install the drum.

LAND CRUISER

1. Remove the brake drum.
2. Remove the upper shoe by pulling out the end, while applying an upward force on it.
3. Depress the lower shoe and repeat the removal procedure for it.

——————— CAUTION ———————
Do not interchange the upper and lower shoes. Do not allow grease to contact the lining surface.

Inspect the shoes for wear, rust or damage. Check the linings for wear.
Inspect the springs for weakness and deformation.
Installation is performed in the following order:

1. Grease all points at which the brake shoes makes contact with other brake components.

——————— CAUTION ———————
Do not allow grease to contact the lining surface.

2. Fit the ends of the lower brake shoe into the grooves on the wheel cylinder piston and the adjusting bolt.
3. Push up on the upper brake shoe and fit it into the grooves on the piston and the adjusting bolt.
4. Hook the return springs on the brake shoes.
5. Install the brake drum.

WHEEL CYLINDERS

Removal and Installation

1. Perform the brake drum and brake shoe removal procedures.
2. Plug the master cylinder reservoir inlet, to prevent fluid from leaking out.
3. Remove the hydraulic lines from the wheel cylinders by unfastening the union bolt.
4. Remove the wheel cylinder attachment screws and withdraw the wheel cylinders.

——————— CAUTION ———————
Do not mix the right and left wheel cylinders.

To install the wheel cylinders, proceed in the following manner:
1. Use the attaching screws to install the wheel cylinder to the backing plate.

NOTE: The wheel cylinder adjusting nut and bolt on the right side of the brake have left-hand threads; while those on the left side have right-hand threads. Be careful not to mix them.

2. Connect the hydraulic line to the wheel cylinders.

——————— CAUTION ———————
Use care to see that the hydraulic line is not twisted.

3. Install the brake drum and shoes. Bleed the brake system.

General Overhaul

Remove the boots, pistons and the cups and closely inspect the bores for signs of wear, scoring and/or scuffing. When in doubt, replace or hone the wheel cylinders with a special brake hone, using clean brake fluid as lubricant. Wash residue from the bores using clean fluid; never use oil or any other solvent on any brake components. Blow dry with air and install with fresh brake fluid. The general limit for a honed cylinder is 0.005 in. oversize (Do not try to save money by reusing brake components such as cylinders and cups.) The self-adjuster screws should be taken apart and all dirt and rust removed with a wire brush. Lightly coat with Lubriplate before assembly; components should turn freely.

Rear Drum Brakes

DRUMS

Removal and Installation

The rear brake drum removal and installation procedure for all models is performed in the same manner as that for the front brake drum.

NOTE: Release the parking brake before attempting rear drum removal. Do not depress the brake pedal, once the drum has been removed.

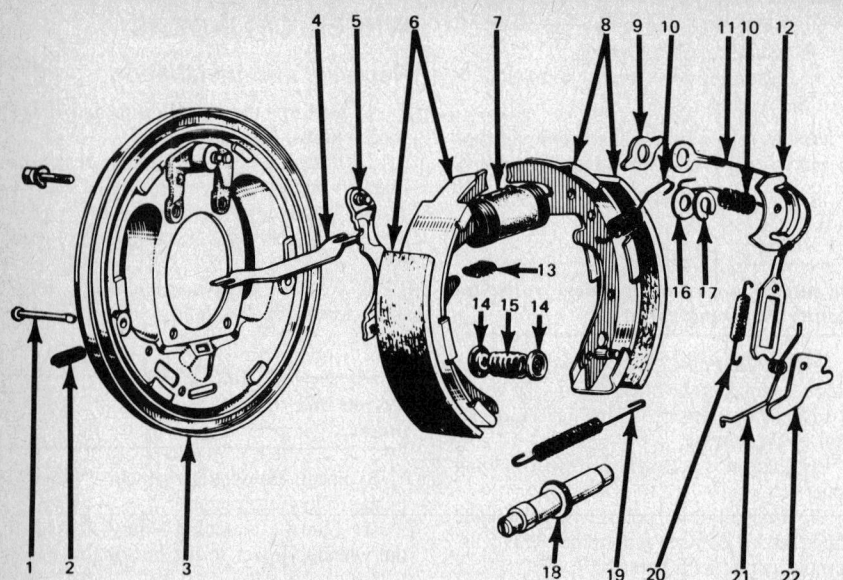

Rear drum brakes—pick-up

1. Shoe hold down spring
   pin
2. Adjusting hole plug
3. Backing plate
4. Parking brake shoe strut
5. Parking brake shoe lever
6. Front brake shoe
7. Wheel cylinder
8. Rear brake shoe
9. Shoe guide plate
10. Return spring
11. Automatic adjuster cable

12. Cable guide
13. Parking brake strut spring
14. Hold down spring seat
15. Shoe hold down spring
16. Washer
17. C washer
18. Adjusting screw set
19. Retracing spring
20. Adjusting cable spring
21. Adjusting lever spring
22. Adjusting lever

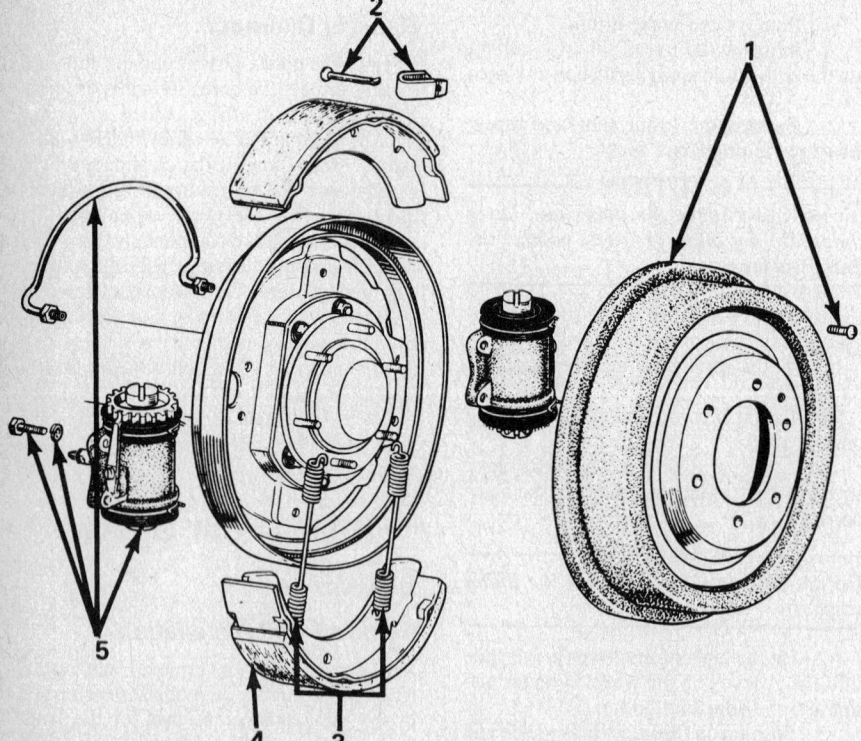

Rear drum brakes—Land Cruiser

1. Brake drum
2. Shoe hold down springs
   and pins

3. Shoe return springs
4. Shoe assemblies
5. Wheel cylinders

Inspection

Inspection for the rear brake drum is performed in the same way as that for the front brake drum (see above).

BRAKE SHOES

Removal and Installation

PICK-UP, 4WD PICK-UP, LAND CRUISER

Land Cruiser rear brake shoe removal and installation procedures are identical to those for the Land Cruiser front brake shoes.

The procedures for the Pick-up and the 4WD Pick-up are also similar to the Land Cruiser front shoe removal procedure, except for the following points:

Check to see if your vehicle has front drum or disc brakes.

On vehicles with front drum brakes, remove and install the parking, brake strut and springs along with the front shoe.

On vehicles with front disc brakes, release the spring on the self adjusting cable where it fastens to the self adjusting rachet arm at the bottom of the brake assembly. Remove the rachet arm and its spring. Remove the top of the cable and remove the parking brake strut in the same manner as described on the vehicle with front drum brakes.

On 2WD and 4WD Pick-ups:

1. Disconnect the parking brake cable from the shoe lever. Remember to connect it during installation.

2. Remove and install the rear shoe complete with the parking shoe lever.

WHEEL CYLINDERS

Removal and Installation

PICK-UP AND 4WD PICK-UP

1. Plug the master cylinder inlet to prevent hydraulic fluid from leaking.

2. Remove the brake drums and shoes as detailed in the appropriate section above.

3. Working from behind the backing plate, disconnect the hydraulic line from the wheel cylinder.

4. Unfasten the screws retaining the wheel cylinder and withdraw the cylinder.

Installation is performed in the reverse order of removal.

Remember to bleed the brake system after completing wheel cylinder, brake shoe and drum installation.

LAND CRUISER

The front brake wheel cylinder removal procedure is performed in the same manner as the procedure for the Pick-up and Land Cruiser rear brakes. For details see the section dealing with these vehicles.

Overhaul

See ''General Overhaul'' for a description of wheel cylinder overhaul procedures.

PICK-UP, 4WD PICK-UP

NOTE: Adjust the rear brake shoes, as detailed at the beginning of this chapter, before attempting to adjust the parking brake.

1. Loosen the parking brake warning light switch bracket.

2. Push the parking brake lever in until it is stopped by the pawl.

3. Move the switch so that it will be "off" at this position but "on" when the handle is pulled out.

4. Tighten the switch bracket and push the brake lever in again.

5. Working from underneath the vehicle, loosen the locknut on the parking brake cable equalizer.

6. Screw the adjusting nut *in,* just enough so that the brake cables have no slack.

7. Hold the adjusting nut in this position while tightening the locknut.

8. Check the rotation of the rear wheels to make sure that the brakes are not dragging.

9. Pull out on the parking brake lever, and count the number of notches needed to apply the parking brake. Check the number against the figures given in the chart.

LAND CRUISER

Land Cruiser models use a separate drum brake assembly, operating on the driveshaft, to serve as a parking brake. Adjust it as follows:

1. Push the parking brake lever all the way in, so that the brake is released.

2. Raise the rear of the vehicle and support it with jackstands.

3. Turn the parking brake adjustment shaft, which is located at the bottom of the parking brake backing plate, counterclockwise until the shoes seat against the drum.

4. Back the adjuster off one notch.

5. Apply the parking brake; the drum should be locked. Release the brake; the drum should rotate freely.

NOTE: If the drum does not rotate freely with the brake off, loosen the adjuster one more notch.

6. Adjust the turnbuckles on the parking brake intermediate levers and the adjusting nuts on the end of the parking brake cables, so that 6–9 notches are required to apply the parking brake (1975). Set for 7–12 notches for 1976 and later.

CHASSIS ELECTRICAL

Heater

NOTE: On models equipped with air conditioning, the heater and air conditioner are completely separate units. The
heater removal procedure is the same as outlined here. However, be certain when working under the dashboard that only the heater hoses are disconnected. The air conditioning hoses are under pressure; if disconnected, the escaping refrigerant will freeze any surface with which it comes in contact, including your skin and eyes. Refer all air conditioning work to a qualified mechanic.

REMOVAL AND INSTALLATION

Pick-up

1978 AND EARLIER

The heater core and blower motor are assembled into one unit which is centrally located in the passenger compartment. To effect repairs on either the core or blower motor, remove the entire assembly from the truck and separate the components with the unit removed.

1. Drain the cooling system completely.

2. Remove the package tray from under the dashboard.

3. Unfasten the hose clamps holding the heater hoses to the core.

NOTE: Hold a shallow pan under the hoses so that any water left in them will not run on the floor of the truck.

4. Remove the defroster hoses from the heater case.

5. Disconnect the heater control cables from the heater case.

6. Remove the fresh air intake duct.

7. Remove the electrical connector feeding the heater blower motor.

8. There are four bolts holding the assembly in the inside of the cowl. Remove the bolts and withdraw the heater assembly from the passenger compartment.

9. To remove the blower motor, tap the fan retaining nut slightly and then remove the nut from the shaft. Withdraw the fan. Remove the blower motor-to-heater case attaching screws and remove the motor.

10. To remove the core, remove the heater control panel and heater lower case cover as a unit. The core may then be taken out of the heater case.

11. Upon reassembly of the unit be sure to tighten all clamps to prevent leaks. Fill the cooling system with the correct mixture of coolant. With the heater off, run the engine to operating temperature. Open the heater control valve and see if the system is functioning properly.

1979 AND LATER

The heater removal is basically the same with the following exceptions.

1. Remove the glove box from the dashboard.

2. Remove the heater controls from the dashboard.

3. Remove the 3 bolts holding the unit in place.

4. To remove the blower motor, remove the three screws on the blower housing and remove the motor.

screw and clips from the heater unit. The core may then be removed from the case.

Front Heater Core

NOTE: To service the heater core of Pick-up models, refer to the previous Heater Removal and Installation procedure.

REMOVAL AND INSTALLATION

Land Cruiser

1979 AND EARLIER

1. Turn off the water valve.

2. Detach both hoses from the heater core.

3. Unfasten the air duct clamp.

4. Detach the defroster hoses from the heater box.

5. Unfasten its attachment bolts and withdraw the core.

Installation is the reverse of removal.

1980 AND LATER

NOTE: The entire heater unit must be removed to gain access to the heater core. This procedure requires almost complete disassembly of the instrument panel and lowering of the steering column. If you decide to perform this operation, note the following points before proceeding:

a. Be sure to tag any wiring which must be disconnected so that it may be correctly installed.

b. As fasteners are removed, arrange them so that they may be installed in their original locations.

c. Do not force any parts to remove them; if a part cannot easily be removed, remove any additional fasteners which may have been initially overlooked.

d. When disconnecting coolant hoses, be careful not to damage the heater core tubes. Place a drain pan under the coolant hose connections before disconnecting the hoses.

1. Disconnect the negative battery cable at the battery.

2. Remove the glove box and the glove box door.

3. Remove the lower heater ducts (#2 in the accompanying illustration).

4. Remove the large heater duct from the passenger side of the heater unit (#3 in the accompanying illustration).

5. Remove the ductwork from behind the istrument panel (#4 in the accompanying illustration).

6. Remove the radio, if so equipped.

7. Disconnect the wiring connector from the right side inner portion of the glove opening.

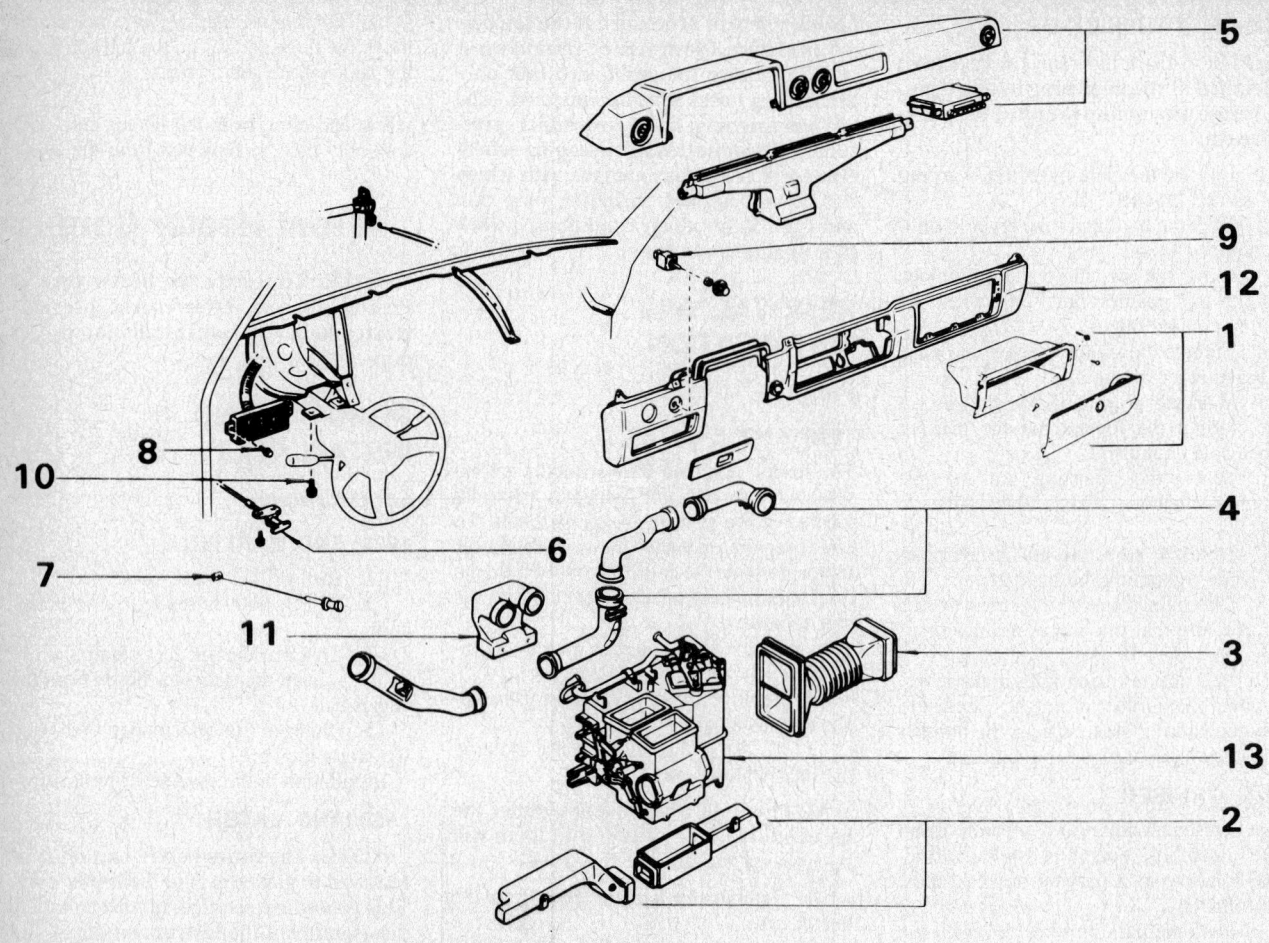

Heater unit—1980 and later Land Cruiser

1. Glove compartment
2. Duct
3. Duct
4. Duct
5. Safety pad
6. Hood release lever
7. Throttle cable
8. Fuse block setting screw
9. Rheostat connector
10. Steering column mounting nut
11. Center duct
12. Lower instrument panel
13. Heater unit

8. Remove the instrument panel pad (8 fasteners).

9. Remove the hood release lever.

10. Disconnect the hand throttle control cable.

11. Remove the retaining screw from the left side of the fuse block.

12. Remove the steering column-to-instrument panel attaching nuts and carefully lower the steering column. Tag and disconnect the wiring as necessary in order to lower the column assembly.

13. Disconnect the electrical connector from the rheostat located to the left of the steering column opening.

14. Remove the center dual outlet duct which is attached to the upper portion of the heater unit (#11 in the accompanying illustration).

15. Remove the lower instrument panel. The fasteners are located in the following places:

   a. Left side of the instrument panel: two at the left side end and two at the left lower end.

   b. Above the steering column: two.

   c. To the right of the steering column opening: two.

   d. Left upper corner of the glove box opening: two.

   e. Left lower corner of the glove box opening: one.

   f. Right side of the instrument panel: two at the right side end and two at the right lower end.

16. Tag and disconnect the hoses from the heater unit.

17. Remove the heater unit-to-firewall fasteners and remove the heater unit.

18. Remove the heater core pipe clamps from the heater unit. Also remove the heater core retaining clamp.

19. Withdraw the heater core from the heater unit.

Installation of the heater core and heater unit is the reverse of the previous steps. Torque the steering column-to-instrument panel fasteners to 14–15 ft. lbs. Replenish the cooling system and check for leaks.

Rear Heater Core

REMOVAL AND INSTALLATION

Land Cruiser

1. Shut the water valve.

2. Detach both of the hoses from the rear heater core.

3. Detach the wiring from the rear heater.

4. Unfasten the bolts and lift out the core.

Installation is the reverse of removal.

Heater Blower Motor

NOTE: To service the blower motor of Pick-up Models, refer to the previous Heater Removal and Installation procedure.

REMOVAL AND INSTALLATION

Land Cruiser

1979 AND EARLIER

1. Loosen the air duct clamping screws and remove the ducts.
2. Remove the air duct screen.
3. Unfasten the mounting bolts and remove the blower motor complete with fan.
Installation is the reverse of removal.

1980 AND LATER

1. Disconnect the electrical connector from the blower motor.
2. Disconnect the flexible tube from the side of the blower motor.
3. Remove the blower motor fasteners and lower the blower motor out of the air inlet duct.
Installation is the reverse of the previous steps. During installation, be sure to position the motor so that the flexible tube can be attached to the motor.

Radio

——————— CAUTION ———————
Never operate the radio without a speaker; severe damage to the output transistors will result. If the speaker must be replaced, use a speaker of the correct impedance (ohms) or else the output transistors will be damaged and require replacement.

REMOVAL AND INSTALLATION

Pick-up

1978 AND EARLIER

1. Remove the knobs from the radio.
2. Remove the nuts from the radio control shafts.
3. Detach the antenna lead from the jack on the radio case.
4. Detach the power and speaker leads.
5. Remove the radio support nuts and bolts.
6. Remove the radio from beneath the dashboard.
Installation is the reverse of removal.

1979 AND LATER

1. Disconnect the negative battery cable from the battery.
2. Remove steering column upper and lower covers.
3. Remove the five screws holding the instrument cluster trim panel and remove trim panel.
4. Remove the knobs from the radio and remove the securing nuts from the control shafts.
5. Remove the heater/air conditioner knobs from their control arms. Do not remove the blower fan control knob.

6. Remove the two screws holding the heater control dash light. Remove the ashtray and remove all of the screws holding the center dash facade onto the dash.
7. Pull the facade out, and carefully disconnect the cigarette lighter and the blower fan control at their plugs.
8. Unscrew any remaining screws holding the radio and pull it out part way. Disconnect the power source, speaker coupling and antenna from the radio and remove through the dash.
Installation is the reverse of removal.

Windshield Wipers

MOTOR REMOVAL AND INSTALLATION

Pick-up

1. Disconnect the wiring from the wiper motor and unbolt it from the fire wall.
2. On 1978 and earlier models, remove the arm nut and crank arm from the wiper motor. On 1979 and later models, pry the wiper link from the crank arm.
3. Remove the motor.
Installation is the reverse of removal.

Land Cruiser

EXCEPT 1980 AND LATER STATION WAGON

1. Detach the wiper link from the motor with a screwdriver.
2. Unfasten the two bracket bolts at the rear of the motor.
3. Disconnect the wiper motor wiring.
4. Unfasten the wiper motor screws and withdraw the motor.
Installation is the reverse of removal.

1980 AND LATER STATION WAGON

NOTE: On these models, the wiper motor is removed with the linkage assembly.

1. Remove the wiper arm retaining nuts and remove the wiper arm and blade assemblies.
2. Remove both wiper arm pivot covers.
3. Remove the pivot-to-cowl attaching screws.
4. Remove the two service hole covers from the cowl area of the engine compartment.
5. Disconnect the wiring from the wiper motor.
6. From the engine compartment, remove the wiper motor plate-to-cowl retaining screws.
7. Withdraw the wiper motor and linkage from the cowl panel as an assembly.
8. Pry the linkage off of the wiper motor and disconnect the linkage from the motor.

Installation is the reverse of the previous steps.

LINKAGE REMOVAL AND INSTALLATION

Pick-up

1. Remove the wiper motor as described above.
2. Remove the wiper arms by removing their retaining nuts and working them off their shafts.
3. Remove the nuts and spacers holding the wiper shafts and push the shafts down into the body cavity. Pull the linkage out of the cavity through the wiper motor hole.
Installation is the reverse of removal.

Land Cruiser—2 Door

1. Remove the wiper arm assemblies.
2. Remove the end plate from the pivot housing.
3. Remove the wiper motor complete with the linkage cable.
4. Separate the wiper motor and transmission.
5. Remove the linkage cable.
Installation is performed in the reverse order of removal.

Land Cruiser—Station Wagon

1979 AND EARLIER

1. Perform the wiper motor removal procedures above.
2. Remove the wiper arm assemblies.
3. Remove the instrument cluster, as detailed below.
4. Loosen the throttle cable to improve access to the wiper linkage.
5. Remove the linkage attachment bolts and withdraw the linkage.
Installation is the reverse of removal.

1980 AND LATER

Refer to the Motor Removal and Installation procedure.

Instrument Cluster

REMOVAL AND INSTALLATION

Pick-up

1978 AND EARLIER

1. Loosen the steering column clamp bolts at the base of the instrument panel. This will allow the steering column to drop slightly.
2. Remove the three retaining screws on the instrument group and pull out gently on the hood of the cluster.
3. Disconnect the speedometer cable and the wiring connector and withdraw the cluster.
Installation is the reverse of removal.

TOYOTA

1980 AND LATER

1. Disconnect the negative battery cable at the battery.

2. Remove the upper and lower steering column covers.

3. Remove the five screws holding the instrument trim panel and remove the panel.

4. Disconnect the speedometer cable from the back of the speedometer.

5. Remove the four screws holding the instrument panel in place and pull the panel forward. Unplug the two connectors from the back of the panel and remove the panel. Installation is the reverse of removal.

Land Cruiser

1. Disconnect the speedometer cable.

2. Remove the instrument panel attaching screws.

3. Loosen the steering column clamp by removing the attaching bolts.

4. Pull out the instrument panel and the speedometer, disconnect the wiring connectors, and remove the panel.

Install the panel in the reverse order from removal.

Fuses and Fusible Links

The fuse box is located on the lefthand side, underneath the dashboard, on all models. All models are equipped with fusible links on the battery cables running from the positive (+) battery terminal.

Volkswagen

INDEX

BEFORE SERVICING, SEE THE SAFETY NOTICE AT THE FRONT OF THE BOOK

VOLKSWAGEN

INTRODUCTION

The Volkswagen pick-up was introduced in 1980. It is the first VW ever to be both designed and built by Volkswagen of America.

The pick-up is based on the Rabbit, and like the Rabbit is available with either a fuel injected gasoline or a diesel engine. The available transmissions are a four or five-speed manual, or a three-speed automatic (1980).

The engines are all water cooled, transversely mounted units. The truck has an independent front suspension, rack and pinion steering and power assisted brakes (disc in the front, self-adjusting drums in the rear).

MODEL IDENTIFICATION

Vehicle Identification Plate

On the Rabbit pick-up, the plate is on top of the body crossmember above the grille. On the plate are the date of manufacture and the chassis number.

Chassis Number

The chassis number is located on the left front corner of the instrument panel on the Rabbit pick-up, and is visible through the windshield. The chassis number is also on top of the right suspension strut mounting. It also appears on the vehicle identification plate.

Engine Number

The Engine number is stamped on the front of the engine block between the fuel pump and the distributor.

Vehicle identification plate

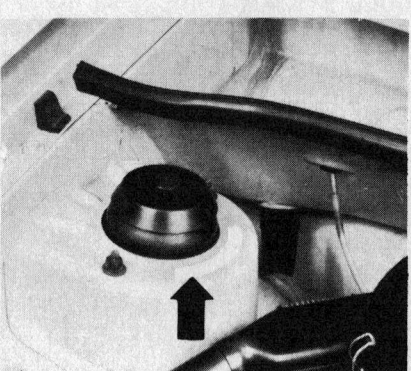
Chassis number

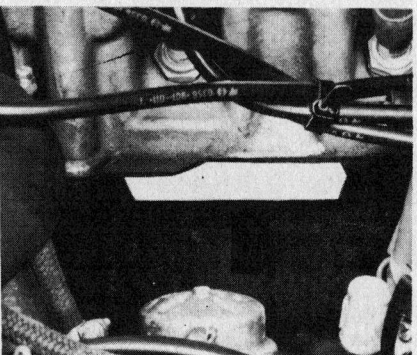
Engine number

GENERAL ENGINE SPECIFICATIONS

Year	Engine Displacement cu in. (cc)	Carburetor Type	Horsepower @ rpm (SAE)	Torque @ rpm (ft lbs) (SAE)	Bore × Stroke (in.)	Compression Ratio	Oil Pressure @ rpm (psi)
'80	88.9 (1457)	Fuel inj.	71 @ 5800	73 @ 3500	3.13 × 2.89	8:1	28 @ 2000
	89.7 (1471)	Diesel	48 @ 5000	56.5 @ 3000	3.01 × 3.15	23.5:1	27 @ 2000
'81–'82	105.0 (1715)	Fuel inj.	78 @ 5500①	88.2 @ 3100②	3.13 × 3.40	8.2:1	28 @ 2000
	97.1 (1588)	Diesel	52 @ 4800	71.5 @ 3000	3.01 × 3.40	23:1	28 @ 2000

① 74 @ 5000—California
② 89.6 @ 3000—California

GASOLINE TUNE-UP SPECIFICATIONS

Year	Engine Displacement cm³	Spark Plugs Type	Gap (in.)	Distributor Point Dwell (deg)	Distributor Point Gap (in.)	Ignition Timing (deg)	Intake Valve Opens (deg)	Compression Pressure (psi)	Idle Speed (rpm)	Valve Clearance (in.) In	Valve Clearance (in.) Ex
'80	1457	W7D N8Y	.024–.028	44–50	.016	3A @ idle	4B	142–184	850–1000	.008–.012	.016–.020
'81–'82	1715	W7D N8Y	.028	Electronic	—	3A @ idle	4B	142–184	850–1000①	.008–.012	.016–.020

NOTE: The underhood specifications sticker often reflects tune-up specification changes made in production. Sticker figures must be used if they disagree with those in this chart.
A—After Top Dead Center
B—Before Top Dead Center
① w/o idle stabilizer

DIESEL TUNE-UP SPECIFICATIONS

Year	Valve Clearance (cold) Intake (in.)	Valve Clearance (cold) Exhaust (in.)	Intake Valve Opens (deg)	Injection Pump Setting (deg)	Injection Nozzle Pressure (psi) New	Injection Nozzle Pressure (psi) Used	Idle Speed (rpm)	Cranking Compression Pressure (psi)
'80	.008–.012	.016–.020	NA	Align marks	1849	1706	770–870	398 minimum
'81–'82	.008–.0012	.016–.020	NA	Align marks	1849	1706	800–850	398 minimum

NOTE: Valve clearance need not be adjusted unless it varies more than 0.002 in. from specification.
NA: Information not available

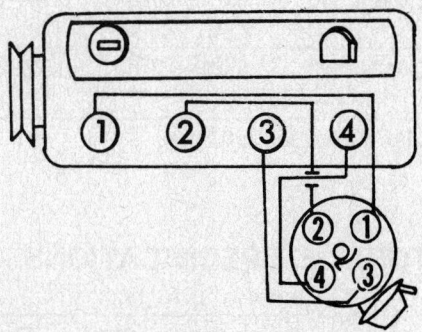

Firing order; 1-3-4-2

CAPACITIES

Year	Engine Displacement cu in. (cc)	Engine Crankcase (qts) With Filter	Engine Crankcase (qts) Without Filter	Transmission (pts) Manual	Transmission (pts) Automatic	Drive Axle (pts)	Gasoline Tank (gals)	Cooling System (pts)
'80	Gasoline	3.7	3.2	3.2①	6.4	1.6	15	9.8
	Diesel	3.7	3.2	2.6	—	1.6	15	12.6
'81–'82	Gasoline Diesel	4.7	4.2	3.2①	—	1.6	15	14.6

① 5-speed—4.2

VOLKSWAGEN

CRANKSHAFT AND CONNECTING ROD SPECIFICATIONS
(All measurements are given in inches)

| Year | Crankshaft | | | | Connecting Rod | | |
	Main Brg. Journal Dia.	Main Brg. Oil Clearance	Shaft End-Play	Thrust on No.	Journal Diameter	Oil Clearance	Side Clearance (max.)
'80–'82	2.126	0.001–0.003	0.003–0.007	3	1.811	0.001–0.003	0.015

NOTE: Main and connecting rod bearings are available in three undersizes.

VALVE SPECIFICATIONS

| Year | Seat Angle (deg) | Spring Test Pressure (lbs. @ in.) | Stem to Guide Clearance (in.) | | Stem Diameter (in.) | |
			Intake	Exhaust	Intake	Exhaust
'80–'82	45	96–106① @ 0.92 in.	0.001–0.002	0.001–0.002	0.314	0.314

NOTE: Exhaust valves must be grounded by hand.
① Outer spring, inner spring test pressure is 46–51 lbs. @ 0.72 in.

PISTON AND RING SPECIFICATIONS
(All measurements in inches)

| Year, Model | Piston Clearance | Ring Gap | | | Ring Side Clearance | | |
		Top Compression	Bottom Compression	Oil Control	Top Compression	Bottom Compression	Oil Control
Gasoline Engine	0.001–0.003	0.012–0.018	0.012–0.018	0.010–0.016	0.001–0.002	0.001–0.002	0.001–0.002
Diesel Engine	0.001–0.003	0.012–0.020	0.012–0.020	0.010–0.016	0.002–0.400	0.002–0.003	0.001–0.002

NOTE: Three piston sizes are available to accommodate overbores up to 0.040 in.

TORQUE SPECIFICATIONS
(All readings in ft. lbs.)

| Year | Cylinder Head Bolts | Rod Bearing Bolts | Main Bearing Bolts | Crankshaft Pulley Bolt | Flywheel To Crankshaft Bolts | Manifold | |
						Intake	Exhaust
'80–'82	61①	33	47	56	54②	18	18

① 69 ft. lbs. warm
② Pressure plate to crankshaft bolts

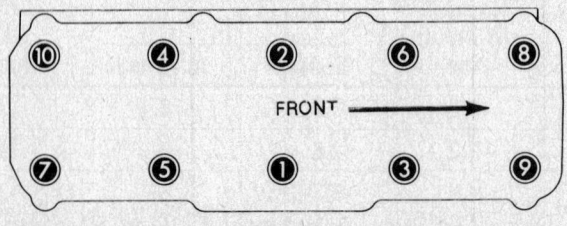

Cylinder head torque sequence

BATTERY AND STARTER SPECIFICATIONS

(All models use 12 volt, negative ground system)

Year	Battery Amp Hour Capacity	Lock Test			No Load Test			Brush Spring Tension (oz.)	Minimum Brush Length (in.)
		Amps	Volts	Torque (ft. lbs.)	Amps	Volts	RPM		
'80–'82	45/54①	280–370	7.5	2.42	33–55	11.5	6000–8000	35.5	0.5

① w/AC

WHEEL ALIGNMENT

Year	CASTER		CAMBER		Toe-in (in.)	Steering Axis Inclination (deg)
	Range (deg)	Pref Setting (deg)	Range (deg)	Pref Setting (deg)		
'80–'82	+1°20'–2°20'	+1°50'	−10'–+50'	+20'	0.08	10°30'

TUNE-UP PROCEDURES

VW recommends a tune-up, including new points and plugs, at 15,000 mile intervals. The only procedure required for diesel engines in this section is the valve lash adjustment and minimum/maximum engine speed checking and adjustment.

Spark Plugs

The firing order is 1-3-4-2, with no. 1 cylinder at the right of the engine.

1. Grasp the spark plug boot and pull it straight out. Don't pull on the wire. Either number the wires or remove them one at a time to avoid mixups.

2. Place the spark plug socket firmly on the plug and screw the spark plug out.

NOTE: The cylinder head is aluminum alloy, which is easily stripped of threads. Remove the plugs only when the engine is cold.

If removal is difficult, loosen the plug only slightly and drip penetrating oil onto the threads.

3. Inspect the plugs and clean or discard them. The recommended spark plug gap is listed in the "Tune-Up Specifications" chart. Use a round wire feeler gauge to check the gap between the plug electrodes. If the gap is incorrect, gently bend the side electrode to correct. Do not bend the center electrode.

4. Torque the new spark plugs to 22 ft. lbs. Install the ignition wire boots firmly.

Breaker Points and Condenser

Snap off the two retaining clips on the dis-

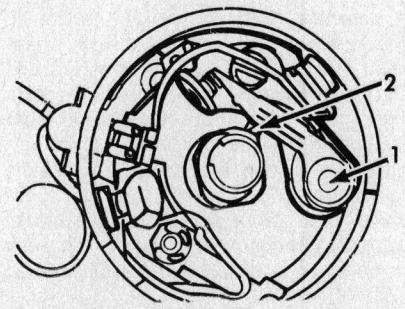

Breaker points and condenser. Lubricate at (1) with a drop of engine oil and at (2) with high melting point grease

tributor cap. Remove the cap and examine it for cracks, deterioration, or carbon tracking. Replace the cap, if necessary, by transferring one wire at a time from the old cap to the new one. Examine the rotor for corrosion or wear and replace it if questionable. Remove the dust shield. Check the points for pitting and burning. Slight imperfections on the contact surface may be filed off with a point file. It is best to replace the breaker point set. Always replace the condenser when you replace the point set.

To replace the breaker points:

1. Remove the rotor.

2. Unsnap the point connector from the terminal at the side of the distributor. Remove the retaining screw, and lift out the point set.

3. Install the new point set, making sure that the pin on the bottom engages the hole in the breaker plate.

4. Install the wire connector and the retaining screws (hand-tight).

5. Turn the engine with a wrench on the crankshaft pulley until the breaker arm rubbing block is in the high point of one of the cam lobes. Turn the engine only in the direction of normal rotation to avoid damage to the timing belt.

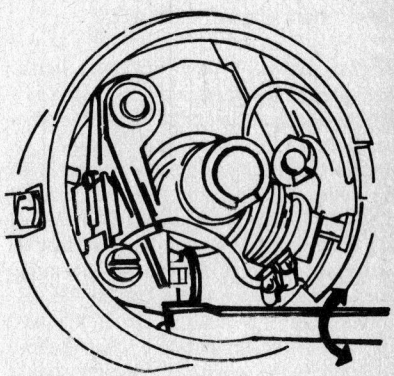

Adjusting the point gap

6. A 0.016 in. feeler gauge should just slip through the points. If the gap is incorrect, pivot a screwdriver in the point set notch and the two projections on the breaker plate to bring it within specifications.

7. When the gap is correct, tighten the retaining screw. Recheck the adjustment.

8. Lubricate the distributor cam with silicone grease.

9. Install the dust cover, rotor and distributor cap.

10. Check the dwell angle and the ignition timing.

11. The condenser is mounted on the outside of the distributor. Undo the mounting screw and the terminal block to replace.

Dwell Angle (Breaker-Point Gasoline Engines Only)

The dwell angle or cam angle is the number of degrees that the distributor cam rotates while the points are closed. There is an inverse relationship between dwell angle and point gap. Increasing the point gap will

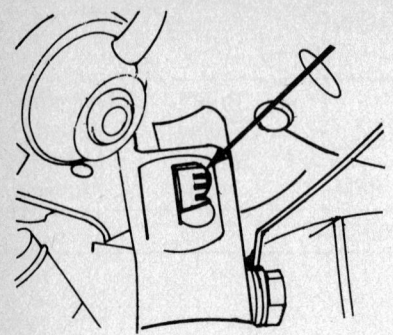

Timing window

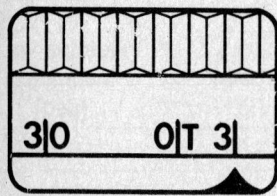

Timing mark aligned at 3° ATDC

decrease the dwell angle and vice versa. Checking the dwell angle with a meter is a far more accurate method of measuring point opening than the feller gauge method.

After setting the point gap to specification with a feeler gauge, check the dwell angle. Attach the dwell meter. The negative lead is grounded and the positive lead is connected to the primary wire, Terminal No. 1 that runs from the coil to the distributor. Start the engine, let it idle and reach operating temperature, and observe the dwell on the meter. The reading should fall within the allowable range. If it does not, the gap will have to be reset. Dwell can also be checked with the engine cranking. In this case, dwell will vary between 0° and the dwell figure for that setting.

Hall Effect Electronic Ignition System

1981 and later trucks are equipped with the Hall effect electronic ignition system.

The distributor contains the Hall Effect pickup assembly which replaces the breaker points assembly in conventional systems.

The "Hall Effect" is a shift in magnetic field caused when one of the rotors on the distributor shaft passes the sensors mounted in the distributor. This shift performs the same function as breaker points, which is to allow the current (coil field) stored in the coil to collapse, causing a spark to run from the coil to the distributor and down to the spark plugs which make the current jump a gap between the two spark plug electrodes, causing a spark which ignites the air-fuel mixture in the combustion chamber. Since there are no breaker points and condenser to replace, the system should be maintenance free.

ELECTRONIC IGNITION PRECAUTIONS

When working on the Hall ignition, observe the following precautions to prevent damage to the ignition system.

1. Connect and disconnect test equipment only when the ignition switch is OFF.

2. Do not crank the engine with the starter for compression tests, etc., until the high tension coil wire is grounded.

3. Do not replace the original equipment coil with a conventional coil.

4. Do not install any kind of condenser to coil terminal.

5. Do not use a battery booster for longer than 1 (one) minute.

6. Do not tow cars with defective ignitions systems without disconnecting the plugs on the idle stabilizer (if equipped) at the ignition control unit.

IGNITION COIL TEST

A defective Hall ignition coil cannot be checked with standard coil testing equipment. If there is no high tension current and all other components of the ignition system check out, see if you're getting a spark from the coil wire to the distributor cap by unplugging the coil wire at the distributor, holding the end of it with insulated pliers about ½ in. from ground (engine block, etc.) and turning over the engine. If a weak or no spark is obtained, try replacing the coil.

HALL PICKUP UNIT TEST

1. Check for voltage on positive terminal (15) of the ignition coil. There should be voltage with the ignition ON.

2. Ground a high tension coil wire.

3. Connect a test light (4 to 24 volts) between positive terminal (15) and negative terminal (1).

4. Crank the engine with the starter for approximately 5 seconds. The test light should flicker. If not, replace the ignition distributor.

IGNITION CONTROL UNIT TEST

1. Disconnect the plugs at the control unit and connect the plugs to each other.

2. Turn the ignition switch on and make sure there is current at positive terminal (15) of the ignition coil. Turn the ignition OFF.

3. Disconnect the high tension wire between the ignition coil and the distributor at the distributor.

4. Disconnect the wire (plug) between the control unit and the distributor at the distributor.

5. Connect the positive (+) terminal of the voltmeter to negative terminal (1) of the ignition coil and the negative (−) terminal to ground.

6. Turn the ignition ON. There must be a voltage reading of at least 12 volts. If voltage drops below 12 volts in one second, turn off the ignition. The control unit is defective and will have to be replaced.

7. Disconnect the green wire where it connects to the distributor and ground the wire. Turn the ignition switch ON. The voltmeter should read about 12 volts. Disconnect the ground wire. The voltage should drop to 6 volts. If not, replace the control unit. Turn off the ignition.

8. Connect the terminals of the voltmeter to the outer connector of the control unit. Connect the positive (+) lead to the red wire and the negative (−) lead to the brown wire. Switch on the ignition. The voltmeter should read about 10 volts. If not, replace the control unit.

IDLE STABILIZER

The idle stabilizer is located on top of the ignition control unit. The idle stabilizer controls idle speed by either advancing or retarding the distributor timing in accordance with engine load (air conditioner on, lights on, etc.) If idle speed is erratic or if the engine fails to start, try bypassing the idle stabilizer by disconnecting the two plugs at the idle stabilizer and plugging them together. If idle improves, the idle stabilizer should probably be replaced.

Ignition Timing

BREAKER-POINT IGNITION SYSTEMS

1. Attach the timing light according to the manufacturer's instructions. Hook-up a dwell/tachometer since you'll need an rpm indication for correct timing.

2. Locate the timing mark opening in the clutch or torque converter housing at the rear of the engine directly behind the distributor. The OT mark stands for TDC or 0° advance. The other mark(s) identify advance and correct timing position. Mark them with chalk so that they will be more visible. Don't disconnect the vacuum line(s).

3. Start the engine and allow it to reach the normal operating temperature. The engine should be running at normal idle speed.

4. Shine the timing light at the marks.

5. The light should now be flashing when the timing mark and the V-shaped pointer are aligned.

6. If not, loosen the distributor hold-down bolt and rotate the distributor very slowly to align the marks.

7. Tighten the mounting nut when the ignition timing is correct.

8. Recheck the timing when the distributor is secured.

With ignition timing correctly adjusted, the spark plugs will fire at the exact instant in which the piston is nearing the top of the compression stroke, thus providing maximum power and economy.

ELECTRONIC IGNITION SYSTEMS

1. Run the engine to operating temperature. Connect tachometer. See Electronic Ignition Precautions.

2. Stop the engine. Disconnect the plugs on the idle stabilizer (if equipped) at the control unit and plug them together.

3. Check the idle speed. It should be between 800 and 1000 rpm.

4. Attach the timing light according to its manufacturer's instruction. Shine the light at the timing marks (located on the flywheel; see step 2 of Point Ignition Systems). The pointer in the hole must line up with the timing mark on the flywheel. To adjust the timing, loosen the distributor at its base and turn it until the marks are aligned.

5. Stop the engine and reconnect the plugs at the control unit.

Valve Lash

Check the valve clearance every 20,000 miles, with the engine at normal operating temperature.

1. Remove the camshaft cover and the distributor cap.

2. Set the engine at TDC on no. 1 cylinder by aligning the 0° T mark on the flywheel with the pointer and aligning the distributor rotor with the no. 1 cylinder mark on the rim of the distributor body.

NOTE: Always turn the crankshaft in the normal direction of rotation. Do not turn the engine by means of the timing belt (or camshaft bolt), because the belt will stretch or lose teeth.

3. The valve clearances of cylinder no. 1 should be checked when the valves of no. 4 cylinder overlap, i.e., when both no. 4 cylinder valves move in opposite directions simultaneously. It may be necessary to move the crankshaft slightly to find this position. When this happens, the exhaust valve is closing and the intake opening. Check and note the clearance of both the intake and exhaust valves for no. 1 cylinder.

4. Turn the crankshaft 180° (90° at the distributor rotor) in the normal direction of rotation. Check and note the valve clearances of cylinder no. 3 at the overlap position of cylinder no. 2.

5. Turn the crankshaft 180°. Check and note the valve clearances of cylinder no. 4 at the overlap position of cylinder no. 1.

6. Turn the crankshaft 180°. Check and note the valve clearances of cylinder no. 2 at the overlap position of cylinder no. 3.

7. Compare the noted clearances with those listed in the Tune-Up Specifications. Adjustment is made by replacing the tappet clearance disc in the top of each tappet. These are available in 26 sizes ranging from

ELECTRONIC IGNITION TESTING SPECIFICATIONS

Component Tested	Specification
Rotor resistance	5000 ohms
Plug wire resistance	
With radio	800–1200 ohms
W/O radio	0 ohms
Spark Plug Connector resistance	
Suppressed	4000–6000 ohms
Not suppressed	800–1200 ohms
Air gap①	0.25 mm (0.010 in.)
Inductive signal resistance②	890–1285 ohms
Resistance from the coil tower to the negative coil terminal	5500–8000 ohms
Resistance from the coil positive terminal to the coil negative terminal	0.95–1.50 ohms
Vacuum retard	8°–10°
Vacuum advance	4°–8°
Centrifugal advance	6°–12°

① Air gap is adjustable by bending the teeth on the stator (reluctor)
② Measure resistance between the connectors to the control unit on the distributor (connects to the green and white wires)

3.0 mm (0.119 in.) to 4.25 mm (0.166 in.) in increments of 0.05 mm (0.002 in.). The thickness of each disc is marked on the bottom.

NOTE: If a valve clearance deviates 0.002 in. or less from the specified clearance, it need not be adjusted.

8. To remove a tappet clearance disc, turn the cylinder to TDC and press down the tappet so that the disc can be lifted out.

NOTE: When adjusting clearances on a diesel, the pistons must not be at TDC. Turn the crankshaft ¼ turn past TDC, so that the valves do not contact the pistons when the tappets are depressed.

A special tool is available from VW for this operation. Once the disc is removed, check its size and determine what size will be needed to produce the required adjustment.

9. Install the required disc. When all the clearances have been corrected, recheck valve clearances.

CIS Fuel Injection

IDLE AND CO ADJUSTMENT

All Except 1980 California And 1981–82 Models

The following adjustments can be made *only*

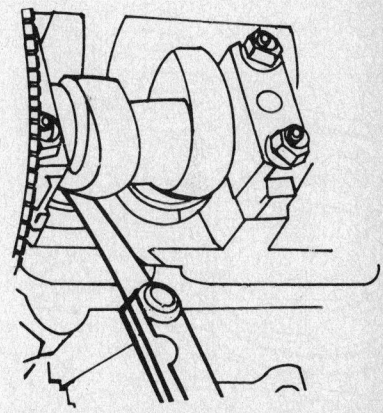

Checking valve clearance with a feeler guage

with a CO meter and the CO adjusting tool (VW-P377).

1. Run the engine until it reaches normal operating temperature.

2. Adjust the ignition timing to specification with the vacuum hoses connected and the engine at idle.

3. Adjust the idle speed to specification.

4. Remove the charcoal filter hose from the air cleaner except on Canadian models.

5. Turn on the headlight high beams.

6. Remove the plug from the CO adjusting hole and insert adjustment tool VW-P377. Turn the adjustment screw clockwise

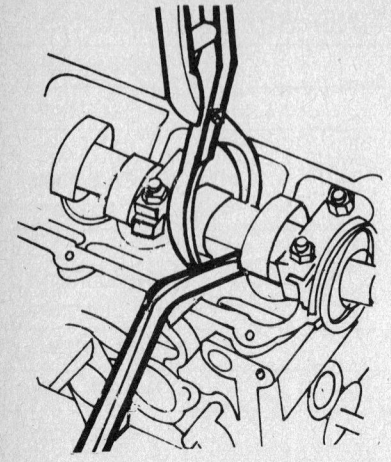

Using special tools to depress the tappet and remove the tappet clearance disc

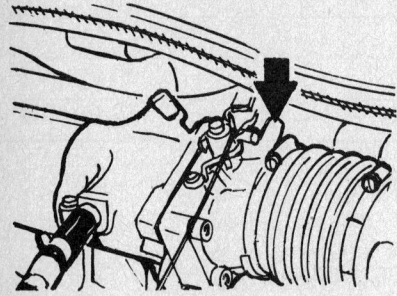

Fuel injection idle adjustment screw

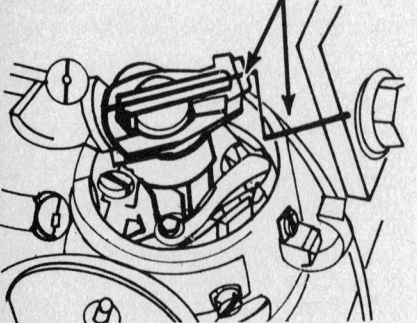

CO-adjusting tool installed—CIS fuel injection

Rotor adjustment with notch for cylinder no. 1

Special adapter VW 1324 is necessary to use an external techometer on diesel engines

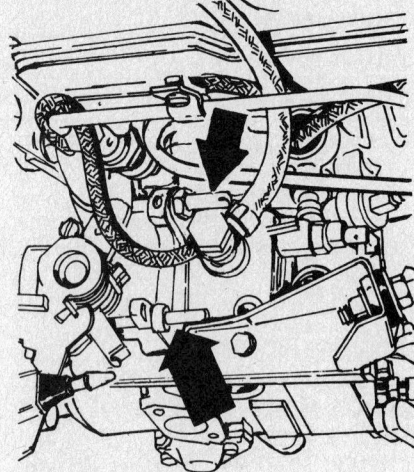

Diesel engine idle speed (upper) and maximum speed (lower) adjustment screws

to raise the percentage of CO and counterclockwise to lower the percentage of CO.

> **CAUTION**
> *Do not push the adjustment tool down or accelerate the engine with the tool in place.*

7. Remove the tool after each adjustment and accelerate the engine briefly before reading the percentage of CO. The correct CO values are as follows:

49 States: 1.5% M/T; 0.1% A/T 0.6 + 0.4%

1980 California, 1981–82 Models

1. The engine must be at operating temperature.
2. Disconnect crankcase breather hose at the cylinder head and plug the hose.
3. Disconnect the two plugs on the idle stabilizer at the control unit and plug them together.
4. Do not have any electrical accessories (air conditioner, lights, etc.) on.
5. Connect a tachometer and timing light. Check the timing. Adjust if necessary.

6. Check the idle speed against the specifications chart or your underhood sticker. Adjust the idle at the idle adjustment screw on the throttle chamber (880–1000 rpm).

NOTE: Only adjust the idle when the radiator fan is not on.

The only way CO levels can be adjusted on these models is with special dealer tools (frequency counter, CO tester, etc.) which are usually not available to the general public.

Diesel Fuel Injection

IDLE SPEED/MAXIMUM SPEED ADJUSTMENTS

Volkswagen diesel engines have both an idle speed and a maximum speed adjustment. The maximum engine speed adjustment prevents the engine from over-revving and swallowing itself whole. The adjusters are located side by side on top of the injection pump. The screw closest to the engine is the idle speed adjuster, while the outer screw is the maximum speed adjuster.

The idle and maximum speed must be adjusted with the engine warm (normal operating temperature). Because the diesel engine has no conventional ignition, you will need a special adaptor (VW 1324) to connect your tachometer, or use the tachometer in the instrument panel, if equipped. You should check with the manufacturer of your tachometer to see if it will work with diesel engines. Adjust all engines to 770–870 rpm (through 1980) or 800–850 rpm (from 1981).

When adjustment is correct, lock the locknut on the screw and apply a dab of paint of non-hardening thread sealer to prevent the screw from vibrating loose.

The maximum speed for all engines is between 5500 and 5600 rpm (through 1980) or 5300–5400 rpm (from 1981). If it is not in this range, loosen the screw and correct the speed (turning the screw clockwise decreases rpm). Lock the nut on the adjusting screw and apply a dab of paint in the same manner as you did on the idle screw.

> **CAUTION**
> *Do not attempt to squeeze more power out of your engine by raising the maximum speed. If you do, you'll probably be in for a major overhaul in the not too distant future.*

ENGINE ELECTRICAL

Distributor

The distributor is a single breaker point unit

on some 1980 models. Electronic ignition is used on all models since 1981. It has both centrifugal and vacuum advance mechanisms. A vacuum retard system works only at idle.

The distributor is gear driven by an intermediate shaft which also drives the fuel pump. The distributor shaft also turns the oil pump.

REMOVAL AND INSTALLATION

1. Disconnect the coil high tension wire.
2. Detach the primary wire.
3. Remove the distributor cap.
4. Turn the engine until the rotor aligns with the index mark on the outer edge of the distributor. This is the No. 1 position. Mark the bottom of the distributor housing and its mounting flange on the engine.
5. Remove the bolt and lift off the retaining flange. Lift the distributor straight out of the engine.

If the engine has not been disturbed while the distributor was out, i.e., the crankshaft was not turned, then reinstall the distributor in the reverse order of removal. Carefully align the marks.

If the engine has been rotated while the distributor was out, then proceed as follows:

1. Turn the crankshaft so that no. 1 piston is on its compression stroke and the O°T timing mark is aligned with the V-shaped pointer.
2. Turn the distributor so that the rotor points approximately 15° before the No. 1 cylinder position on the distributor.
3. Insert the distributor into the engine block. If the oil pump drive doesn't engage, remove the distributor and, using a long screwdriver turn the pump shaft so that it is parallel to the centerline of the crankshaft.
4. Install the distributor, aligning the marks. Tighten the retaining nut.
5. Install the cap. Adjust the ignition timing.

Alternator

ALTERNATOR PRECAUTIONS

An alternating current (AC) generator (alternator) is used. Unlike the direct current (DC) generators, there are several precautions which must be strictly observed in order to avoid damaging the unit.

1. Reversing the battery connections will result in damage to the diodes.
2. Booster batteries should be connected from negative to ground, and positive to positive.
3. Never use a fast charger as a booster to start cars with AC circuits.
4. When servicing the battery with a fast charger, always disconnect the car battery cables.
5. Never attempt to polarize an AC generator.
6. Avoid long soldering times when replacing diodes or transistors. Prolonged heat is damaging to AC generators.
7. Do not use test lamps of more than 12 volts (V) for checking diode continuity.
8. Do not short across or ground any of the terminals on the AC generator.
9. The polarity of the battery, generator, and regulator must be matched and considered before making any electrical connections within the system.
10. Never operate the AC generator on an open circuit. Make sure that all connections within the circuit are clean and tight.
11. Disconnect the battery terminals when performing any service on the electrical system. This will eliminate the possibility of accidental reversal of polarity.
12. Disconnect the battery ground cable if arc welding is to be done on any part of the car.

REMOVAL AND INSTALLATION

The alternator and voltage regulator are combined in one housing. No voltage adjustment can be made with this unit. The regulator can be replaced without removing the alternator. Unbolt the regulator and remove from the rear.

1. Disconnect the battery cables.
2. Remove the multi-connector retaining bracket and unplug the connector from the rear of the alternator.
3. Loosen and remove the top mounting nut and bolt.
4. Using a socket inserted through the timing belt cover (it is not necessary to remove the cover), loosen the lower mounting bolt.
5. Swing the alternator over and remove the alternator belt.
6. Remove the lower nut and bolt.
7. Remove the alternator.
8. Install the alternator with the lower bolt. *Do not* tighten it at this point.
9. Install the alternator belt over the pulleys.
10. Loosely install the top mounting bolt and pivot the alternator until the belt is correctly tensioned.
11. Tighten the top and bottom bolts to 14 ft. lbs.
12. Connect the alternator and battery wires.

BELT REPLACEMENT AND TENSIONING

1. Loosen the top alternator mounting bolt.
2. Using a socket inserted through the timing belt cover loosen the lower mounting bolt.
3. Use a wooden hammer handle or a broomstick to lever the alternator over and

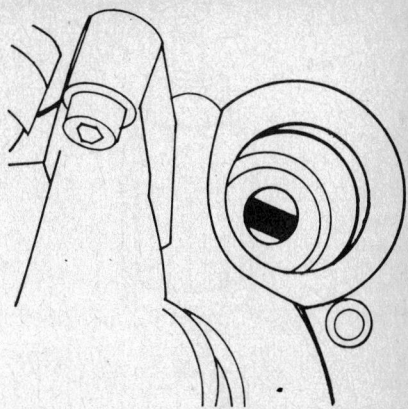

The oil pump drive should be parallel to the crankshaft

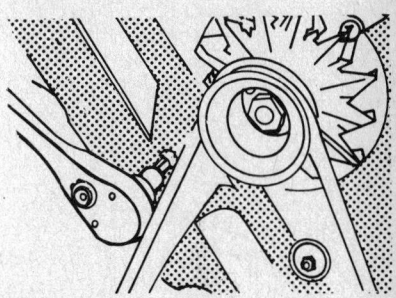

Removing the lower alternator bolt through the timing cover

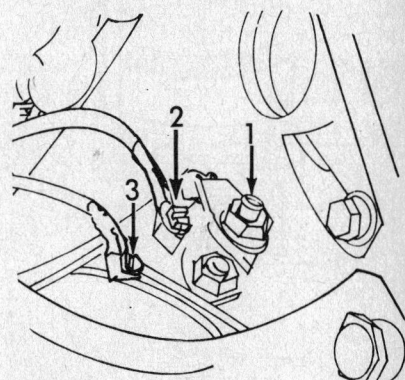

Starter electrical connections: (1) solenoid, (2) coil, (3) positive battery cable

remove the belt.
4. Slip the new belt over the pulleys.
5. Pry the alternator over until the belt deflection midway between the crankshaft pulley and the alternator pulley is $3/8$–$9/16$ in. (10–15 mm).
6. Securely tighten the mounting bolts.

Starter

A new type of starter has been installed on some models that are equipped with a manual transmission. The new style starter is not interchangeable with the old design. The new starter does not need a rear support bracket.

VOLKSWAGEN

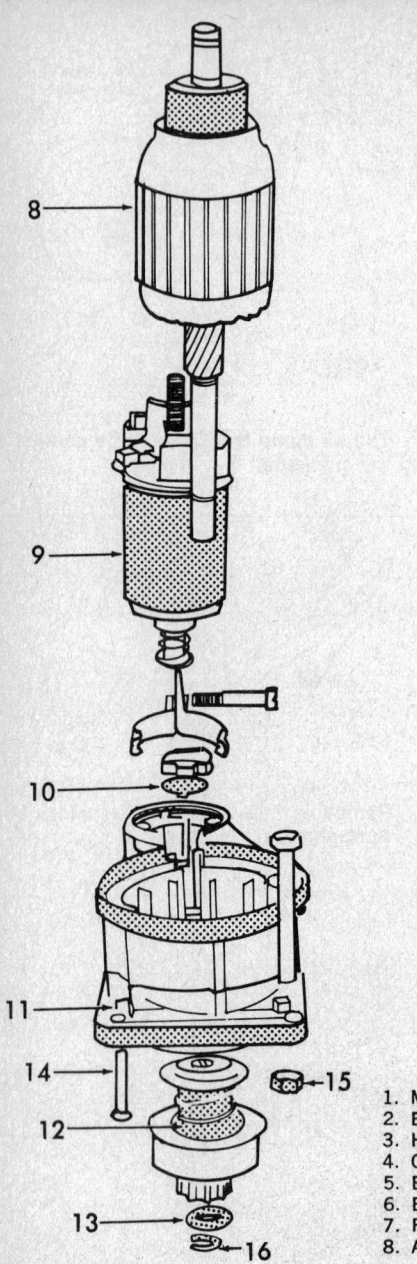

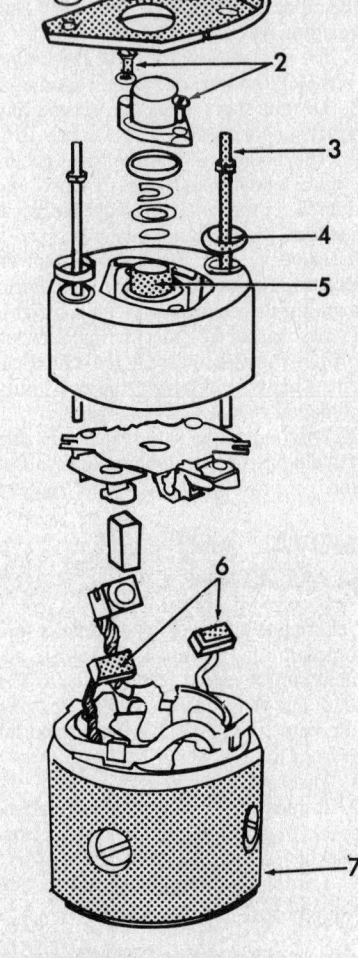

1. Mounting bracket
2. End cap screws
3. Housing screws
4. Cupped washer
5. End plate bushing
6. Brushes
7. Field coil housing
8. Armature
9. Solenoid
10. Disc
11. Mounting housing
12. Drive pinion
13. Stop ring
14. Solenoid bolt
15. Starter bolt and nut
16. Circlip

Exploded view of new type starter

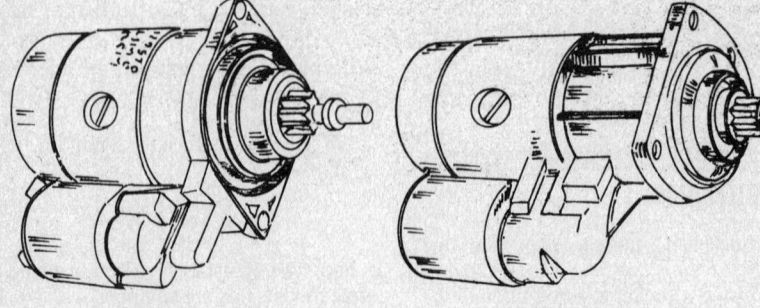

NEW TYPE   OLD TYPE

New and old type starters are not interchangeable

REMOVAL AND INSTALLATION

Old Style

1. Disconnect the battery ground cable.
2. Raise the front of the car.
3. Mark with tape and then disconnect the wires from the starter solenoid.
4. Disconnect the large cable.
5. Remove the starter retaining nuts.
6. Unscrew the bolt. Remove the starter.
7. Installation of the starter is carried out in reverse order of removal.

New Style

1. Disconnect the battery ground cable.
2. Support the weight of the engine with either Volkswagen special tool 10-222 or use a jack with a block of wood under the oil pan. Don't jack the engine too high, just take the weight off the motor mounts. Be careful not to bend the oil pan.
3. Remove the engine/transmission cover plate.
4. Unbolt and remove the starter side motor mount and carrier.
5. Disconnect and mark the starter wiring.
6. Remove the bolts holding the starter and remove the starter.
7. Install the starter and tighten the nuts and bolts to 14 ft. lbs.
8. Install the engine mount and carrier.
9. Install and attach remaining components. Don't forget to reconnect the battery cable.

OVERHAUL

Use the following procedure to replace brushes or starter drive.

1. Remove the solenoid.
2. Remove the end bearing cap.
3. Loosen both of the long housing screws.
4. Remove the lockwasher and spacer washers.
5. Remove the long housing screws and remove the end cover.
6. Pull the two field coil brushes out of the brush housing.
7. Remove the brush housing assembly.
8. Loosen the nut on the solenoid housing, remove the sealing disc, and remove the solenoid operating lever.
9. Loosen the large screws on the side of the starter body and remove the field coil along with the brushes.

NOTE: If the brushes require replacement, the field coil and brushes and/or the brush housing and its brushes must be replaced as a unit.

10. If the starter drive is being replaced on the new type starter, push the stop-ring down and remove the circlip on the end of the shaft. Remove the stop-ring and remove

the drive.

11. To remove the starter drive on old type starters, remove the armature and pull the drive unit off the end.

12. Assembly of the starter is carried out in the reverse order of disassembly. Use a gear puller to install the stop-ring in its groove (on models so equipped). Use a new circlip on the shaft.

SOLENOID REPLACEMENT

1. Remove the starter.

2. Remove the nut which secures the connector strip on the end of the solenoid.

3. Take out the two retaining screws on the mounting bracket and pull out the solenoid after it has been unhooked from the operating lever.

4. Installation is the reverse of removal. In order to facilitate engagement of the lever, the pinion should be pulled out as far as possible when inserting the solenoid.

ENGINE MECHANICAL

The engine is an inline four cylinder unit with single overhead camshaft. It is inclined 30° to the rear. The crankshaft runs in five bearings with thrust taken on the center bearing. The cylinder block is cast iron. A steel reinforced rubber belt drives the intermediate shaft and camshaft. The intermediate shaft drives the oil pump, distributor and fuel pump.

The cylinder head is lightweight aluminum alloy. The intake and exhaust manifolds are mounted on the same side of the cylinder head. The valves are opened and closed by camshaft lobes operating on cupped cam followers which fit over the valves and springs. This design results in lighter valve train weight and fewer moving parts.

The key difference between the gasoline and diesel engine is that the diesel has no carburetor and no electrical ignition system. There are no plugs, points or coil to replace. Combustion occurs when a fine mist of diesel fuel is sprayed into hot compressed air (1650°F) under high pressure (850 psi). The air is heated by the compression as the piston moves up on the compression stroke. The diesel engine has a compression ratio of 23.5:1 compared to the gasoline engine's compression ratio of 8.2:1.

VW's diesel block, flywheel, bearings and crankshaft are identical to those in the Rabbit gasoline engine. The connecting rod wrist pins were strengthened and new pistons and cylinder head, made of aluminum for lightness, were designed.

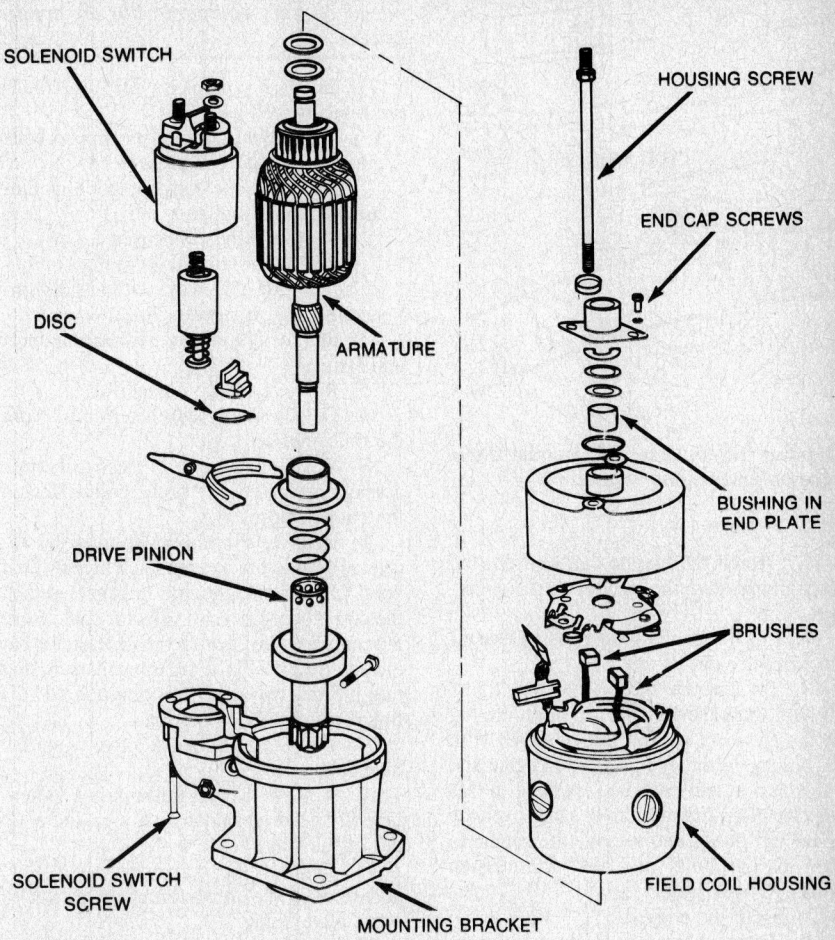

Exploded view of the old type starter

SOLENOID SWITCH · **DISC** · **DRIVE PINION** · **ARMATURE** · **SOLENOID SWITCH SCREW** · **MOUNTING BRACKET** · **HOUSING SCREW** · **END CAP SCREWS** · **BUSHING IN END PLATE** · **BRUSHES** · **FIELD COIL HOUSING**

Removal and Installation

MANUAL TRANSMISSION

Gasoline Engines

The engine and transmission are removed as an assembly.

1. Disconnect the battery ground cable.

2. Drain the coolant by unbolting the lower water pump flange or by removing the hoses.

─── CAUTION ───
Do not disconnect or loosen any refrigerant hose connections during engine removal on cars equipped with air conditioning.

3. On cars equipped with air conditioning:

a. Loosen the compressor support bolts and remove the compressor.

b. Remove the radiator cooling fan, air ducts and radiator.

c. Remove the condenser.

d. Place the air conditioning compressor and condenser out of the way

without disconnecting any refrigerant lines.

4. Remove the radiator with the air ducts and fan.

5. Detach and label all the electrical wires connecting the engine to the body.

6. Disconnect and plug the fuel line at the fuel pump. Detach the coolant hoses at the left end of the engine. Disconnect the accelerator cable and remove the air cleaner.

7. Disconnect the speedometer cable from the transmission. Detach the clutch cable.

8. Remove the engine support to the right of the starter.

9. Remove the headlight caps inside the engine compartment.

10. Unbolt the driveshafts from the transmission and wire them up.

11. Unbolt the exhaust pipe from the manifold and unbolt the exhaust pipe brace.

12. Unbolt the transmission rear mount from the body (alongside the tunnel).

13. Detach the ground strap from the transmission and body.

14. Remove the shift linkage.

15. Attach a chain sling to the alternator bracket and the lifting eye at the left end of the engine. Lift the engine and transmission slightly.

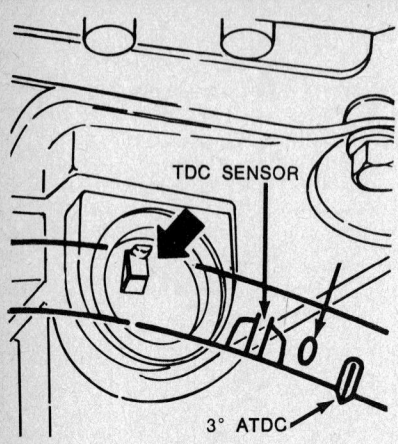

Aligning the flywheel for manual transmission and engine separation

16. Detach the engine carrier from the body and remove the left transmission carrier.

17. Lift the engine/transmission assembly carefully out of the car.

18. To separate the engine and transmission, turn the flywheel to align the lug on the flywheel (to the left of TDC) with the pointer in the opening. The engine and transmission can only be separated in this position. Remove the cover plate over the driveshaft flange and remove the engine to transmission bolts and the transmission housing cover plate.

To install the engine:

19. To attach the transmission to the engine, the recess in the flywheel edge must be at 3:00 o'clock (facing the left end of the engine). Torque the engine to transmission bolts to 40 ft. lbs. Lift the engine/transmission assembly into place. Loosen the bolts for the engine and transmission mounts. Move the engine assembly from side to side until the rear transmission mount is straight. Center the left and right transmission mounts and tighten all transmission bolts. Push the front mount upward to center the rubber cone, then tighten the mount. Loosen the exhaust pipe clamps, release any strain, then tighten the clamps. Torque the 10 mm bolts to 29 ft. lbs. Torque the driveshaft flange bolts to 32 ft. lbs. Refill the cooling system.

AUTOMATIC TRANSMISSION

Gasoline Engines

The engine and transmission are removed as an assembly.

1. Shift the transmission into "Park." Disconnect both battery cables.

2. Drain the coolant by unbolting the lower water pump flange or by removing the hoses.

— **CAUTION** —
Do not disconnect or loosen any refrigerant hose connections during engine re-

moval on cars equipped with air conditioning.

3. On cars equipped with air conditioning, proceed as follows:

a. Loosen the compressor support bolts and remove the compressor.

b. Remove the radiator cooling fan, air ducts, and radiator.

c. Remove the condenser.

d. Place the air conditioning components out of the way without disconnecting any refrigerant lines.

4. Remove the radiator with the air ducts and fan.

5. Remove the air cleaner.

6. Detach the speedometer cable from the transmission.

7. Detach and label all electrical wires connecting the engine to the body. Detach the coolant hoses.

8. Remove the screws holding the accelerator cable bracket to the carburetor float bowl (do not disassemble linkage), detach the end of the gearshaft selector cable from the transmission, detach the accelerator cable and pedal cable at the transmission, and remove the two bracket bolts behind this linkage on the transmission.

9. Unbolt the exhaust pipe from the manifold.

10. Remove the rear transmission mount. Unbolt the driveshafts and wire them up out of the way.

11. Remove the converter cover plate and remove the three torque converter to drive plate bolts.

12. Attach a chain sling to the alternator bracket and the lifting eye at the left end of the engine. It may be necessary to remove the alternator. Lift the engine and transmission slightly.

13. Detach the engine front mounting support; remove the left transmission carrier and the right engine carrier.

14. Lift the engine/transmission assembly carefully out of the car.

15. The transmission can now be detached from the engine.

To install the engine:

16. The engine to transmission bolts should be torqued to 40 ft. lbs. Lift the engine/transmission assembly into place and install the left transmission carrier, tightening first the body, then the transmission bolts. Lower the assembly to attach the engine carrier to the body, tightening the bolts to 40 ft. lbs. Install the engine mounting support. Check that all mounts and clamps are free of strain. Torque converter bolts should be torqued to 21 ft. lbs. and driveshaft bolts to 32 ft. lbs. Refill the cooling system. Check the adjustment of transmission and carburetor linkages.

DIESEL ENGINES

The diesel engine is removed with the transmission attached.

1. Disconnect the battery.

2. Disconnect the radiator hoses and

drain the coolant. It can be saved for reuse, if it's not too old.

3. Remove the radiator complete with fan.

4. Remove the alternator.

5. Disconnect the fuel filter and set it aside near the windshield washer reservoir.

6. Detach the supply and return lines from the injection pump.

7. Disconnect the accelerator cable from the lever on the injection pump and remove the injection pump complete with bracket.

8. Disconnect the cold start cable from the pump.

9. Disconnect and label all electrical wires and leads.

10. Remove the front transmission mount.

11. Disconnect the clutch cable.

12. Remove the relay rod and connecting rod from the transmission and turn the relay lever shaft to the rear.

13. Disconnect the selector rod.

14. Unbolt the driveshafts and wire them up out of the way. Remove the rear support.

15. Disconnect the exhaust pipe at the manifold and remove the rear transmission mount.

16. Attach a lifting sling to the engine and take the weight from the engine mounts. Remove the left and right transmission mounts.

17. Carefully guide the engine out of the car while turning it slightly.

18. To separate the engine from the transmission, unscrew the plug from the TDC sensor opening and turn the flywheel to align the mark on the flywheel with the pointer. The engine/transmission can only be separated in this position.

19. Remove the cover plate over the driveshaft flange and remove the engine-to-transmission bolts.

20. Press the engine off the transmission.

21. Installation is the reverse of removal. Turn the flywheel so that the recess in the flywheel is level with the driveshaft flange. Lower the engine into the car and attach the left transmission mount to the transmission first. Align the rear transmission mount, center the engine/transmission and center the front transmission mount. Adjust the accelerator and cold start cables and bleed the injection system.

Cylinder Head

REMOVAL AND INSTALLATION

The engine should be cold before the cylinder head can be removed. The head is retained by 10 socket head bolts. It can be removed without removing the intake and exhaust manifolds.

NOTE: 12 point socket head bolts are used. These should be used in complete sets only and need not be retorqued.

Gas Engines

1. Disconnect the battery ground cable.
2. Drain the cooling system.
3. Disconnect the air duct from the throttle valve assembly.
4. Disconnect the throttle valve assembly.
5. Remove the injectors and disconnect the line from the cold start valve.
6. Disconnect the radiator and heater hoses.
7. Disconnect the vacuum and PCV lines (label lines for installation).
8. Remove the auxiliary air regulator from the intake manifold.
9. Disconnect all electrical lines and remove the spark plugs (label all lines·and wires for installation).
10. Separate the exhaust pipe from the exhaust manifold.
11. Remove the EGR line from the exhaust manifold.
12. Remove the intake manifold.
13. Remove the timing belt cover and belt.
14. Loosen the cylinder head bolts in the reverse of the tightening sequence.
15. Remove the bolts and lift the head straight off.
16. Check the flatness of the cylinder block.
17. Install the new cylinder head gasket with the word TOP or OBEN facing upward.
18. Install bolts no. 10 and 8 first; these holes are smaller and will properly locate the gasket and cylinder head.
19. Install the remaining bolts. Tighten them in three stages using the sequence shown in the illustration. Cylinder head bolts must be torqued cold to 55 ft. lbs., then tightened ¼ turn more.
20. Install the remaining components in the reverse order of removal.

Diesel Engines

The head is retained by Allen bolts. The engine should be cold when the head is removed. The word TOP or OBEN on the new gasket should face up.

1. Disconnect the battery ground cable.
2. Drain the cooling system.
3. Remove the air cleaner.
4. Disconnect the fuel lines. Disconnect and tag all electrical wires and leads.
5. Separate the exhaust pipe from the manifold. Disconnect the radiator and heater hoses.
6. Remove the timing cover and belt (See timing belt replacement).
7. Loosen the cylinder head bolts in the reverse order of the tightening sequence.
8. Remove the head. Do not lay the head on the gasket surface with the injectors installed. Support it at the ends on strips of wood.
9. Install the cylinder head with a new gasket. Be sure the new gasket has the same

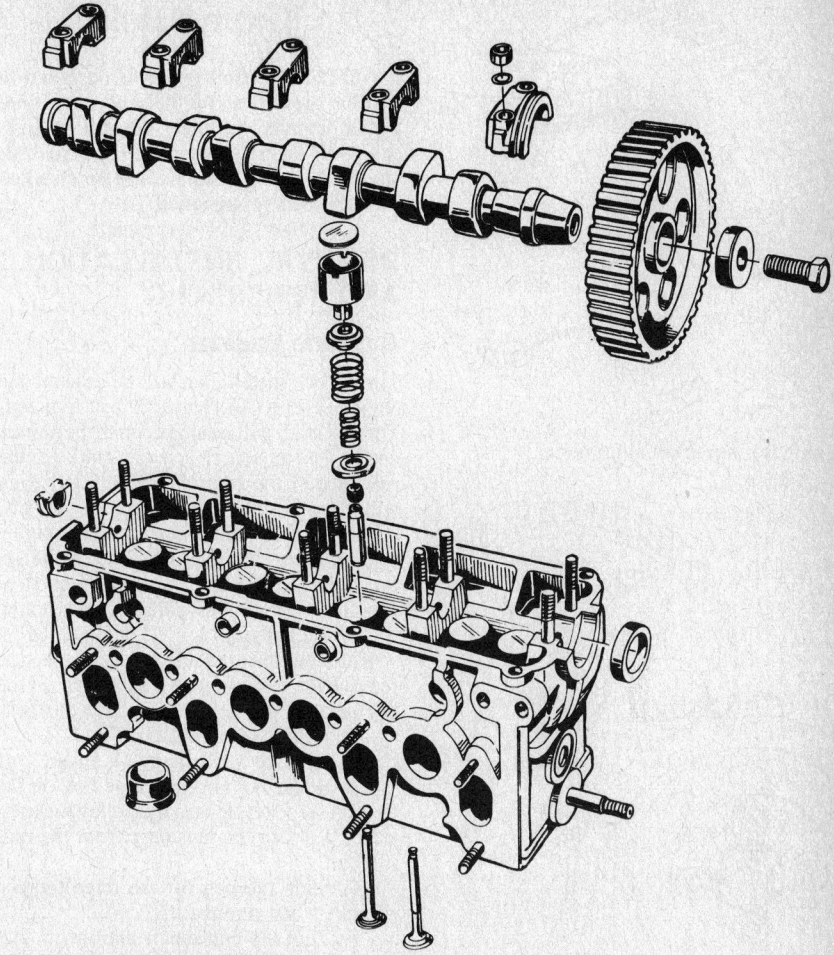

Exploded view of the cylinder showing valve train components

number of notches and the same identifying number as the old one, unless the pistons were also replaced.

Install bolts 8 and 10 first and torque the bolts to the specification in the proper sequence.

OVERHAUL

Valve guides are a shrink fit. Always install new valve seals when doing a valve job. Valve seats are not replaceable; the cylinder head should be replaced if the seat width and face angle cannot be maintained.

Refer to the general information section under Engine Overhaul.

Intake Manifold

REMOVAL AND INSTALLATION

1. Disconnect the air duct from the throttle valve body. Drain the cooling system.
2. Disconnect the accelerator cable.
3. Remove the injectors and disconnect the line from the cold start valve.

4. Disconnect all coolant hoses.
5. Disconnect all vacuum and emission control hoses (label all hoses for installation).
6. Remove the auxiliary air regulator.
7. Disconnect all electrical lines (label all wires for installation).
8. Disconnect the EGR line from the exhaust manifold.
9. Loosen and remove the retaining bolts and lift off the manifold.
10. Install a new gasket. Install the manifold and tighten the bolts to 18 ft. lbs.
11. Install the remaining components in the reverse order of removal.

Exhaust Manifold

REMOVAL AND INSTALLATION

1. Disconnect the EGR tube from the exhaust manifold.
2. Remove the interfering air pump components if so equipped.
3. Remove the air cleaner hose from the exhaust manifold.
4. Disconnect the intake manifold support.

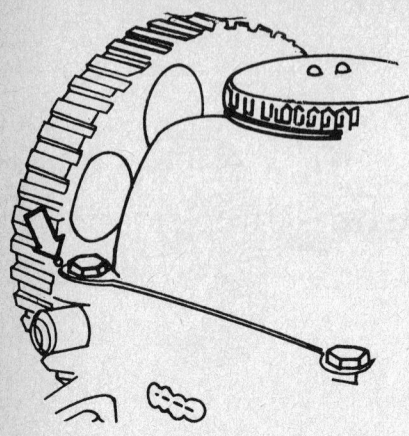

Camshaft sprocket alignment

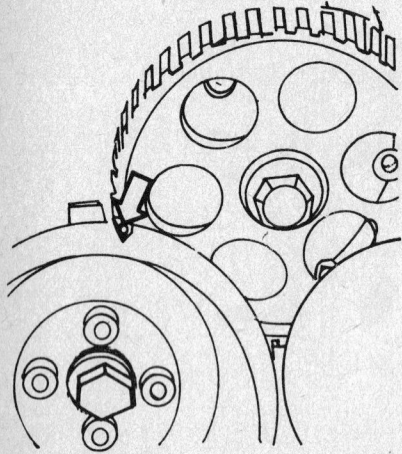

Crankshaft pulley and intermediate shaft alignment

5. Separate the exhaust pipe from the manifold.

6. Remove the retaining nuts and remove the manifold.

7. Clean the cylinder head and manifold mating surfaces.

8. Install the exhaust manifold using a new gasket.

9. Tighten the nuts to 18 ft. lbs. Work from the inside out.

10. Install the remaining components in the reverse order of removal. Use a new manifold flange gasket.

Timing Belt Cover

REMOVAL AND INSTALLATION

1. Loosen the alternator mounting bolts.

2. Pivot the alternator and slip the drive belt off the sprockets.

3. Unscrew the cover retaining nuts and remove the cover.

4. Reposition the spacers on the studs and then install the washers and nuts.

5. Install the alternator belt and adjust its tension.

Timing Belt

NOTE: The timing belt is designed to last for more than 60,000 miles and does not normally require tension adjustments. If the belt is removed or replaced, the basic valve timing must be checked and the belt retensioned.

REMOVAL, INSTALLATION, AND TENSIONING

Gasoline Engines

Timing belt installation will be easier if the engine is set to TDC prior to belt removal. The 0°T mark will be aligned with the pointer on the bell housing, and the mark on the rear face of the camshaft pulley will align with the camshaft cover gasket on the left. Also, the V-notch in the crankshaft pulley should align with the dot mark on the intermediate shaft, and the distributor rotor should be pointing toward the mark on the rim of the housing.

If the belt has broken and timing is off, remove the belt cover and belt, then set the engine to TDC before installing the belt, as outlined in steps 5, 6 and 7.

1. Remove the timing belt cover.

2. While holding the large hex on the tension sprocket, loosen the pulley locknut.

3. Release the tensioner from the timing belt.

4. Slide the belt off the three toothed sprockets and remove it.

5. Turn the crankshaft until no. 1 cylinder is at TDC. At this point, the 0°T mark will be aligned with the pointer on the bell housing.

6. Align the timing mark on the rear face of the camshaft pulley with the camshaft cover gasket on the left.

7. Align the V-notch in the crankshaft pulley with the dot mark on the intermediate shaft. The distributor rotor should be pointing to the no. 1 cylinder mark on the rim of the distributor.

—————— CAUTION ——————

If the timing marks are not correctly aligned, valve timing will be incorrect. Poor performance and serious engine damage can result from improper valve timing. Steps 5, 6 and 7 should not be necessary if the engine was in time and set to TDC prior to belt removal.

8. Install the belt on the sprockets.

9. Adjust the tensioner by turning the large tensioner hex to the right. Tension is correct when you can just twist the belt 90° with two fingers at the midpoint. Tighten the locknut to 32 ft. lbs.

10. Install the timing belt cover and check the ignition timing.

Diesel Engine

The drive belt on the diesel also drives the injection pump. It is necessary that this procedure be followed exactly to ensure proper valve timing and injection pump timing. You will also need special tool VW 210 to properly tension the belt.

1. Remove the alternator belt.

2. Remove the timing belt cover and rocker cover.

3. Set the engine at TDC on no. 1 cylinder. In this position both valves of no. 1 cylinder will be closed and the OT mark on the flywheel will be aligned with the pointer on the bell housing.

4. Use a pin (VW special tool 2064) or suitable bolt to hold the injection pump sprocket and camshaft sprocket in position. The pin or bolt must be exactly the size of the hole. There can be no "slop" in the gears.

5. Loosen the tensioner. Remove the fan belt pulley from the crankshaft.

6. Remove the belt and belt shield from the drive gears.

To install the belt:

7. Check that the TDC mark is aligned with the flywheel mark.

8. Loosen the camshaft sprocket bolt ½ turn and tap the gear loose from the camshaft with a rubber mallet.

9. Install the drive belt and remove the pin from the camshaft and injection pump gears.

10. Tension the belt by turning the tensioner to the right.

11. Check the belt tension between the camshaft and injection pump sprockets. On VW 210 special tool, the scale should read 12–13.

12. Tighten the camshaft sprocket bolt to 32 ft. lbs.

13. Turn the crankshaft 2 complete turns in the direction of normal rotation and check the belt tension again.

Timing Sprockets

REMOVAL AND INSTALLATION

The camshaft, intermediate shaft, and crankshaft sprockets are located by keys on their respective shafts and each is retained by a bolt. To remove any or all of the pulleys, first remove the timing belt cover and belt.

NOTE: When removing the crankshaft pulley, don't remove the four allen head bolts which hold the outer belt pulley to the timing belt sprocket.

1. Remove the center bolt.

2. Gently pry the sprocket off the shaft. If the gear does not come off easily, use a gear puller. Don't hammer on the sprocket.

3. Remove the sprocket and key.

4. Install in the reverse order of removal.

5. Tighten the center bolt to 58 ft. lbs.

6. Install the timing belt, check the valve timing, tension the belt, and install the cover.

Camshaft

REMOVAL AND INSTALLATION

1. Remove the timing belt.
2. Remove the camshaft sprocket.
3. Remove the air cleaner.
4. Remove the camshaft cover.
5. Unscrew and remove the no. 1, 3 and 5 bearing caps.
6. Unscrew the no. 2 and 4 bearing caps, diagonally and in increments.
7. Lift the camshaft out of the cylinder head.
8. Lubricate the camshaft journals and lobes with assembly lube or gear oil before installing it in the cylinder head.
9. Replace the camshaft oil seal with a new one whenever the cam is removed.
10. Install the no. 1, 3 and 5 bearing caps and tighten the nuts to 14 ft. lbs. Note that the bores are offset, and the numbers are not always on the same side.
11. Install the no. 2 and 4 bearing caps and diagonally tighten the nuts to 14 ft. lbs.

NOTE: If checking end-play, install a dial indicator so that the feeler touches the camshaft snout. End-play should be no more than 0.006 in. (0.15 mm)

12. Replace the seal in the no. 1 bearing cap. If necessary, replace the end plug in the cylinder head.
13. Install the camshaft cover.

1. Alternator belt
2. Belt pulleys
3. Timing gear cover
4. Crankshaft sprocket
5. Intermediate sprocket
6. Drive belt
7. Tensioner
8. Camshaft sprocket

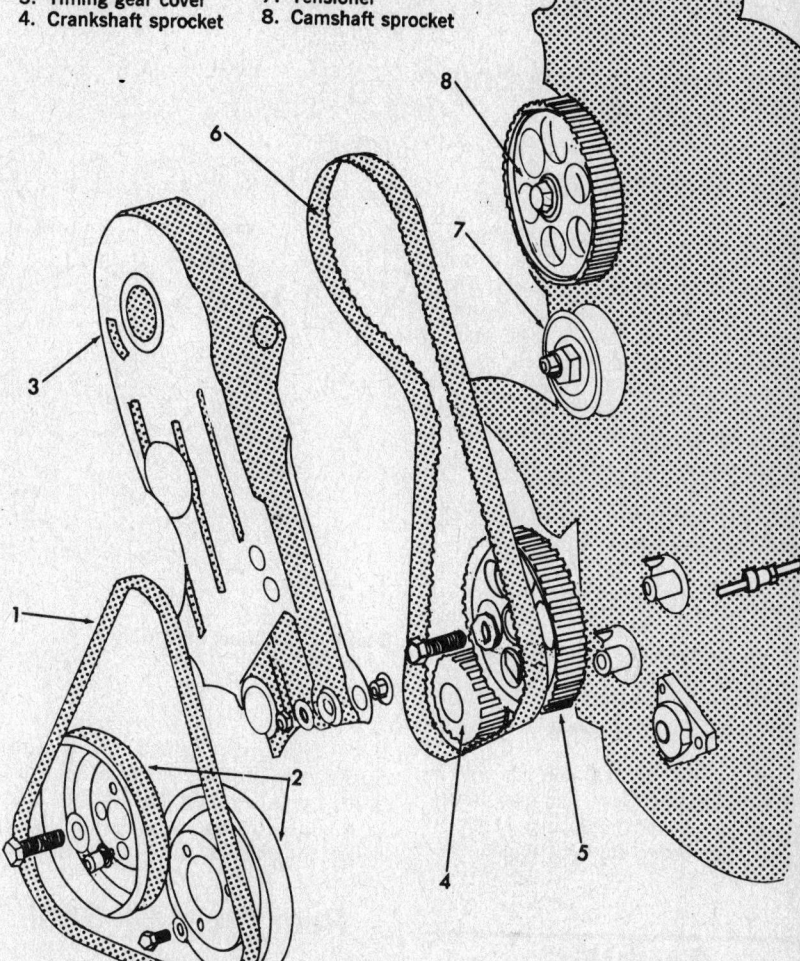

Exploded view of camshaft drive arrangement

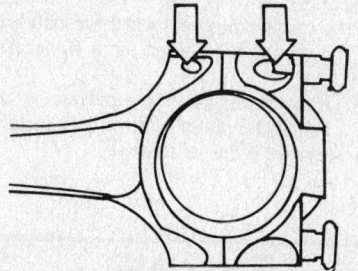

The connecting rod and cap alignment casting grooves must face the intermediate shaft

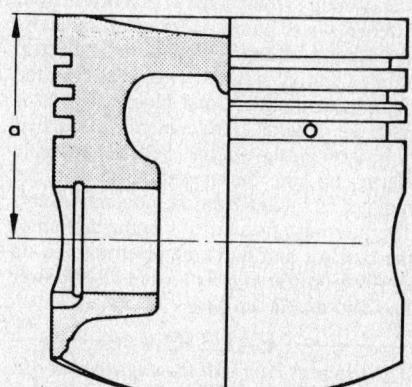

Piston height measurement, diesel engine

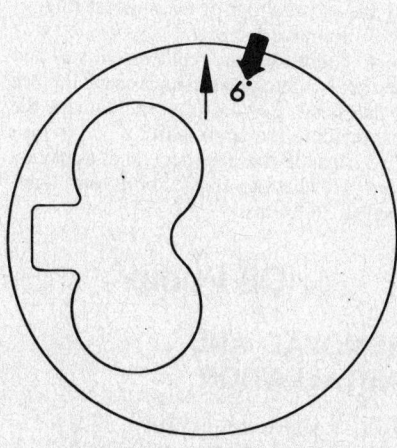

Diesel pistons are identified by the number "9" next to the arrow denoting installation direction

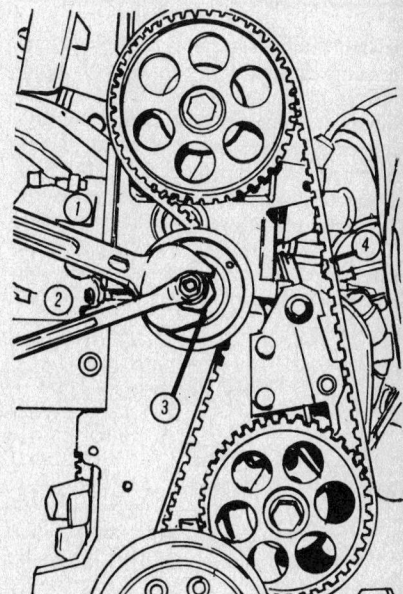

Turn the tensioner (3) toward (1) to tighten belt and toward (2) to loosen. Check tension at (4)

14. Install the camshaft pulley and the timing belt.

15. Check the valve clearance.

Piston and Connecting Rods

GASOLINE ENGINES

The pistons must be installed in the block with the arrow at the edge of the crown facing toward the right front wheel. The connecting rod and cap alignment casting grooves must face the intermediate shaft. New connecting rod bolts must always be used. The pistons must be heated to 140°F in an oven before the piston pins can be pressed in. Three piston oversizes are available to accommodate overbores up to 0.040 in.

There is a piston size code stamped on the cylinder block above the water pump.

DIESEL ENGINES

The same installation procedures apply to the diesel as to the gas engine. However, whenever new pistons or a short block are installed, the piston projection must be checked.

A spacer (VW 385/17) and bar with a micrometer are necessary, and must be set up to measure the maximum amount of piston projection above the deck height.

ENGINE LUBRICATION

The lubrication system is a conventional wet-sump design. The gear type oil pump is driven by the intermediate shaft. A pressure relief valve limits pressure and prevents extreme pressure from developing in the system. All oil is filtered by a full flow replaceable filter. A bypass valve assures lubrication in the event the filter becomes plugged. The oil pressure switch is located at the end of the cylinder head gallery (the end of the system) to assure accurate pressure readings.

Oil Pan

REMOVAL AND INSTALLATION

1. Drain the engine oil.
2. Loosen and remove the bolts retaining the oil pan.
3. Lower the pan from the car.
4. Install the pan using a new oil pan gasket.

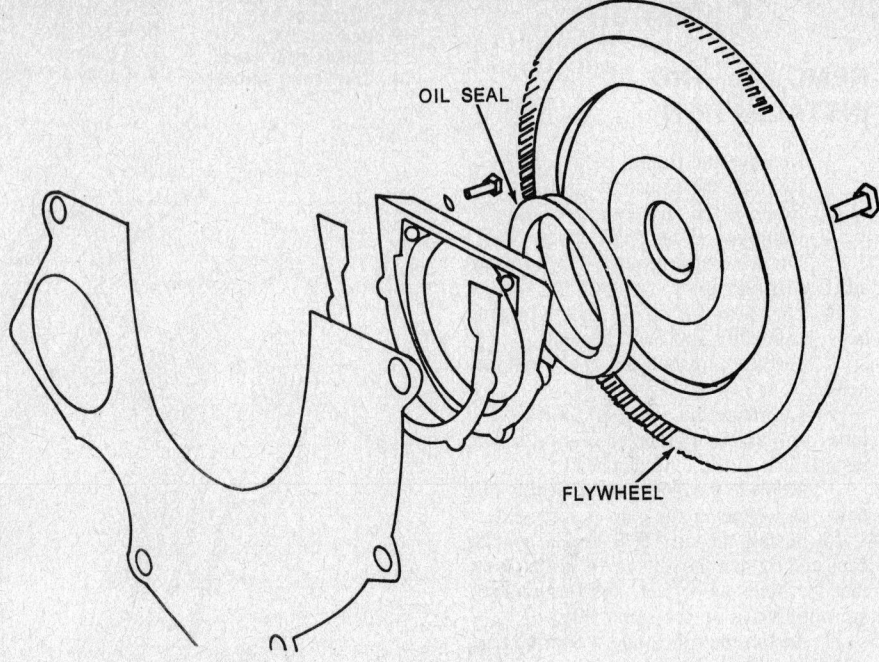

Rear main oil seal assembly

5. Tighten the retaining bolts in a criss-cross pattern. Tighten hex head bolts to 14 ft. lbs., or Allen head bolts to 7 ft. lbs.
6. Refill the engine with oil. Start the engine and examine the pan for leaks.

Rear Main Oil Seal

REPLACEMENT

The engine should be removed from the car. See Transmission Removal and Installation.

1. Remove the transmission and flywheel.
2. Using a small prybar, very carefully pry the old seal out of the support ring.
3. Remove the seal.
4. Lightly oil the replacement seal and then press it into place using a circular piece of flat metal. Be careful not to damage the seal or score the crankshaft.
5. Install the flywheel and transmission. Flywheel-to-engine bolts are tightened to 36 ft. lbs.

Oil Pump

REMOVAL AND INSTALLATION

1. Remove the oil pan.
2. Remove the two mounting bolts.
3. Pull the oil pump down and out of the engine.
4. Unscrew the two bolts and separate

the pump halves.
5. Remove the driveshaft and gear from the upper body.
6. Clean the bottom half in solvent. Pry up the metal edges to remove the filter screen for cleaning.
7. Examine the gears and driveshaft for wear or damage. Replace them if necessary.
8. Reassemble the pump halves.
9. Prime the pump with oil and install in the reverse order of removal.

ENGINE COOLING

The cooling system consists of a belt driven, external water pump, thermostat, radiator, and thermostatically controlled electric cooling fan. When the engine is cold the thermostat is closed and blocks the water from the radiator so the coolant is circulated only through the engine. When the engine warms up, the thermostat opens and the radiator is included in the coolant circuit. The thermostatic switch is in the bottom of the radiator and turns the electrical fan on at 199°F, off at 186°F. This reduces power loss and engine noise.

——— **CAUTION** ———
The fan may run with the engine shut off. Keep fingers out of the way when the engine is warm.

Radiator and Fan

REMOVAL AND INSTALLATION

1. Drain the cooling system.
2. Remove the inner shroud mounting bolts.
3. Disconnect the lower radiator hose.
4. Disconnect the thermostatic switch lead.
5. Remove the lower radiator shroud.
6. Remove the lower radiator mounting units.
7. Disconnect the upper radiator hose.
8. Detach the upper radiator shroud.
9. Disconnect the heater and intake manifold hoses.
10. Remove the side mounting bolts and lift the radiator and fan out as an assembly.
11. Installation is the reverse of removal.

Thermostat

REMOVAL AND INSTALLATION

The thermostat is located in the bottom radiator hose neck on the water pump.
1. Drain the cooling system.
2. Remove the two retaining bolts from the lower water pump neck.

NOTE: It isn't necessary to disconnect the hose.

3. Move the neck, with the hoses attached, out of the way.
4. Remove the thermostat.
5. Install a new seal on the water pump neck.
6. Install the thermostat with the spring end up.
7. Replace the water pump neck and tighten the two retaining bolts.

Water Pump

REMOVAL AND INSTALLATION

1. Drain the cooling system.
2. Remove the alternator and drive belt.
3. Remove the timing belt cover.
4. Disconnect the lower radiator hose, engine hose, and heater hose from the water pump.
5. Remove the four pump retaining bolts. Notice where the different length bolts are located.
6. Turn the pump slightly and lift it out of the engine block.
7. Installation is the reverse of removal. Use a new seal on the mating surface with the engine.

EMISSION CONTROLS

Crankcase Ventilation

The crankcase ventilation system keeps harmful vapor byproducts of combustion from escaping into the atmosphere and prevents the building of crankcase pressure which can lead to oil leaking. Crankcase vapors are recirculated from the camshaft cover through a hose to the air cleaner. Here they are mixed with the air/fuel mixture and burned in the combustion chamber.

SERVICE

The only maintenance required on the crankcase ventilation system is a periodic check. At every tune up, examine the hoses for clogging or deterioration. Clean or replace the hoses as necessary.

Evaporation Emission Control System

This system prevents the escape of raw fuel vapors (unburned hydrocarbons or HC) into the atmosphere. The system consists of a sealed carburetor, unvented fuel tank filler cap, fuel tank expansion chamber, an activated charcoal filter canister and connector hoses. Fuel vapors which reach the filter deposit hydrocarbons on the surface of the charcoal filter element. Fresh air enters the filter when the engine is running and forces the hydrocarbons to the air cleaner where they join the air/fuel mixture and are burned.

Many models are equipped with a charcoal filter valve which prevents vapors from escaping from the canister when the engine is not running.

SERVICE

Maintenance of the system requires checking the condition of the various connector hoses and the charcoal filter at 10,000 mile intervals. The charcoal filter should be replaced at 50,000 mile intervals.

Dual Diaphragm Distributors

The purpose of the dual diaphragm distributor is to improve exhaust emissions during one of the engine's dirtier operating modes—idling. The distributor has a vacuum retard diaphragm, in addition to a vacuum advance diaphragm. A temperature valve shuts off vacuum from the carburetor when coolant temperatures are below 130°F.

TESTING

Advance Diaphragm

1. Connect a timing light to the engine. Check the ignition timing.
2. Remove the retard hose from the distributor and plug it. Increase the engine speed. The ignition timing should advance. If it doesn't, then the vacuum unit is faulty and must be replaced.

Temperature Valve

1. Remove the temperature valve and place the threaded portion in hot water.
2. Create a vacuum by sucking on the angled connection.
3. The valve must be open above approximately 130°F.

Exhaust Gas Recirculation (EGR)

To reduce NOx (oxides of nitrogen) emissions, metered amounts of exhaust gases are added to the air/fuel mixture. The recirculated exhaust gas lowers the peak flame temperature during combustion. Exhaust gas from the manifold passes through a filter where it is cleaned. The vacuum operated EGR valve controls the volume of this exhaust gas which is allowed into the intake manifold. There is no EGR at idle, partial at slight throttle and full EGR at mid-throttle.

The EGR valve on fuel injected models is controlled by a temperature valve and a vacuum amplifier. The valve is located at the front of the intake manifold.

TESTING

EGR Valve—Fuel Injected Models

Be sure the vacuum lines are not leaking. Replace any that are leaking or cracked.
1. Warm the engine to normal operating temperature.
2. Run the engine at idle.
3. Remove the vacuum hose from the EGR valve.
4. Connect the line from the brake booster to the EGR valve (this can be done

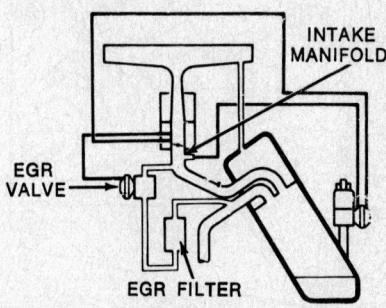

EGR system schematic

by installing a Tee in the vacuum line to the retard side of the distributor diaphragm and running a separate hose from there to the EGR valve).

5. If the engine speed does not change, the EGR valve is clogged or damaged.

EGR Temperature Valve

Warm the engine to normal operating temperature.

1. With the engine at idle, attach a vacuum gauge between the EGR temperature control valve and the EGR valve. The valve should be replaced if the gauge shows less than 2 in. Hg.

EGR Deceleration Valve

1. Remove the hose from the deceleration valve. Plug the hose.

2. Run the engine for a few seconds at 3000 rpm.

3. Snap the throttle valve closed.

4. With your finger, check for suction at the hose connection.

5. Remove the hose from the connector.

6. Run the engine at about 3000 rpm. No suction should be felt.

EGR Vacuum Amplifier

1. Run the engine at idle.

2. Connect a vacuum gauge between the vacuum amplifier and the throttle valve port.

3. The gauge should read 0.2–0.3 in. Hg. If not, check the throttle plate for correct position or check the port for obstruction.

4. Connect a vacuum gauge between the vacuum amplifier and the temperature valve.

5. Replace the vacuum amplifier if the gauge reads less than 2 in. Hg.

MAINTENANCE

The only maintenance to is reset the EGR elapsed mileage switch.

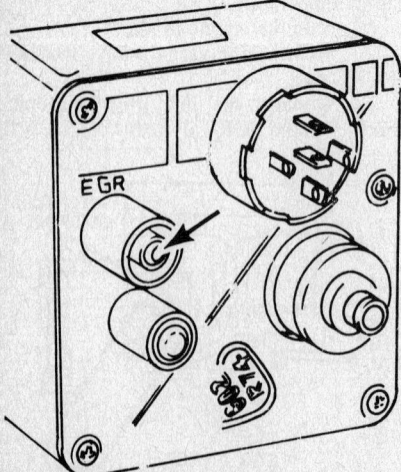

Resetting the EGR elapsed mileage odometer

Resetting the Elapsed Mileage Switch

The EGR reminder light in the speedometer should light up every 15,000 miles as a reminder for maintenance.

To reset the light switch, press the white button. The speedometer light should go out.

REMOVAL AND INSTALLATION

EGR Valve

1. Disconnect the vacuum hose from the EGR valve.

2. Unbolt the EGR line fitting on the opposite side of the valve.

3. Remove the two remaining bolts and lift the EGR valve from the intake manifold.

4. Install the EGR valve in the reverse order of removal. Use a new gasket at the intake manifold.

Catalytic Converter

MAINTENANCE

Required maintenance on the catalytic converter involves checking the condition of the ceramic insert every 30,000 miles. As this interval is reached, an indicator light on the dash will glow. Once service to the converter is performed, the odometer must be reset.

TESTING AND SERVICE

———— CAUTION ————

Do not drop or strike the converter assembly or damage to the ceramic insert will result.

Damage and overheating of the catalytic converter, indicated by the flickering of the "CAT" warning light, can be caused by the following:

1. Engine misfire caused by faulty spark plug, ignition wires and so on.

2. Improper ignition timing.

3. CO valve set too high.

4. Faulty air pump diverter valve.

5. Faulty temperature sensor.

6. Engine under strain caused by trailer hauling high speed driving in hot weather, etc.

A faulty converter is indicated by one of the following symptoms:

1. Poor engine performance.

2. The engine stalls.

3. Rattling in the exhaust system.

4. A CO reading greater than 0.4% at the tail pipe.

Check or replace the converter as follows:

1. Disconnect the temperature sensor.

2. Loosen and remove the bolts holding the converter to the exhaust system and

the chassis.

3. Remove the converter.

4. Hold the converter up to a strong light and look through both ends, checking for blockages. If the converter is blocked, replace it.

5. Install the converter in the reverse order of removal.

6. Reset the elapsed mileage odometer by pushing the white button marked "CAT".

Oxygen Sensor System

Many models are equipped with an oxygen sensor system which lowers toxic exhaust emissions while increasing fuel economy. In effect, the sensor system monitors the oxygen content in the exhaust system and, through a control unit and frequency valve, makes adjustments to the air/fuel mixture to achieve maximum fuel efficiency over a wide range of operating conditions. The system consists of the following:

1. **Oxygen Sensor:** located in the exhaust manifold. Unscrew to replace.

Resetting the catalytic converter elapsed mileage odometer

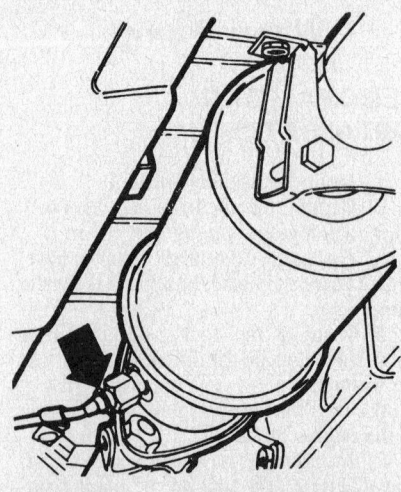

Checking the catalytic converter—the arrow indicates the temperature sensor

2. **Control Unit:** located behind the glove compartment cover.

Frequency Valve: located next to the fuel distributor.

3. **Thermoswitch:** located in the coolant system.

4. **Oxygen Sensor System Relay:** white colored relay located in the fuse/relay panel.

5. **Elapsed Mileage Switch:** located on the firewall.

6. **Warning Light:** marked OXS and located in the instrument panel. Comes on when the oxygen sensor must be replaced (every 30,000 miles).

RESETTING THE ELAPSED MILEAGE SWITCH

After replacing the oxygen sensor, reset the elapsed mileage switch by pushing the white button on the front of the switch.

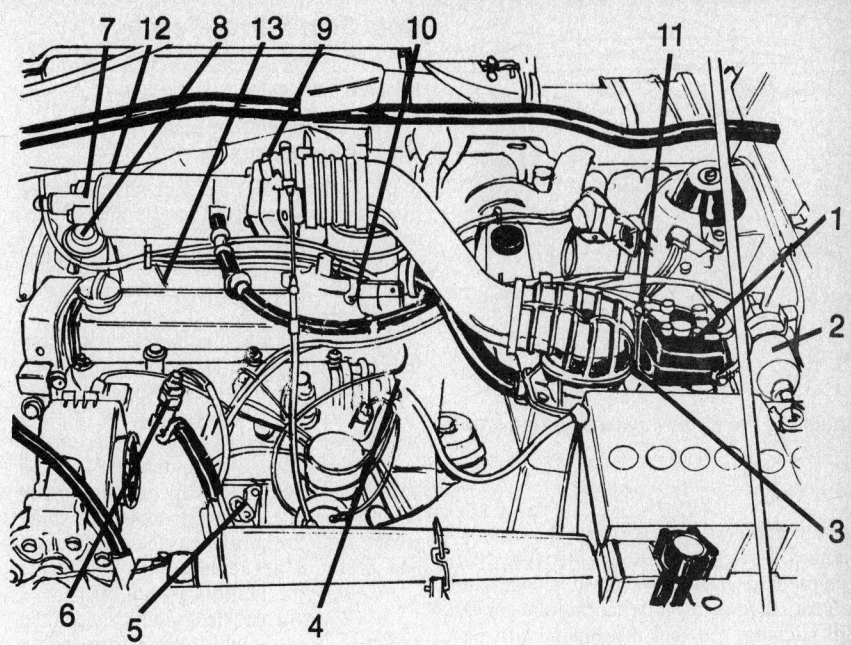

1. Fuel distributor
2. Fuel filter
3. Air flow sensor
4. EGR temperature control valve (not shown)
5. Control pressure regulator
6. Thermo-time switch
7. Cold start valve
8. EGR valve
9. Idle adjust
10. Deceleration valve
11. Plug for CO adjustment
12. Auxiliary air regulator (not shown)
13. Fuel injector

CIS fuel injection components

FUEL SYSTEM

Fuel Pump

TESTING—ELECTRICAL

1. Have a helper operate the starter. Listen at the rear wheel to determine if the pump is running.

2. If the pump is not running, check the fuse on the front of the fuel pump relay.

3. If the fuse is good, replace the fuel pump relay.

4. If the fuel pump still does not operate, the fuel pump is faulty and must be replaced.

TESTING—FUEL PUMP DELIVERY

1. Check the condition of the fuel filter, make sure it is clean.

2. Connect a jumper wire between the #1 terminal on the ignition coil and ground.

3. Disconnect the return fuel line and hold it in a measuring container with a capacity of 1 quart or 1000 cc.

4. Have a helper run the starter for 30 seconds while watching the quantity of fuel delivered.

The minimum allowable flow is 900 cc (⁹⁄₁₀ of a quart) in 30 seconds.

NOTE: For the above test, the battery must be fully charged. Also, make sure you have plenty of fuel in the tank.

If the pump fails its specific test, check for a dirty fuel filter, blocked lines or blocked fuel tank strainer (if so equipped). If all of these are in good condition, replace the pump.

REMOVAL AND INSTALLATION

1. Raise the vehicle and support it on jack stands. Disconnect the battery ground cable.

2. Remove the right rear wheel on all cars.

3. Remove the gas tank filler cap to release the fuel pressure.

4. Clamp off the line between the fuel pump and the fuel tank with a pair of soft jawed vise grips or other suitable lock pliers. Don't clamp the line too tightly or you may damage it.

5. Disconnect the clamped line from the fuel pump. There's bound to be a little gas in the line, so be careful.

6. If your vehicle has an accumulator mounted next to the fuel pump, disconnect the fuel lines from the accumulator. Disconnect the wiring from the fuel pump and remove all other lines after marking them for assembly.

7. Remove the nuts on the lower bracket, loosen the nut on the upper slotted bracket where it connects to the body and slide the pump out.

8. Install the new fuel pump in the reverse order of removal. Make sure that the new seal washers are installed on the fuel discharge line.

CIS Fuel Injection

AIR FLOW SENSOR-TESTING AND ADJUSTMENT

Sensor Plate Lever and Control Plunger

1. Run the engine for a short time at idle.

2. Remove the air duct from the air flow sensor assembly.

3. Using a magnet, lift the sensor plate. A light even resistance must be felt over the sensor plate entire travel.

NOTE: Make certain that the air sensor plate is centered in the air cone. If adjustment is necessary, proceed as follows:

a. Loosen the centering bolt slightly.

b. Run a 0.004 in. (0.10 mm) feeler gauge around the perimeter of the air gap.

c. Tighten the centering bolt.

4. No resistance must be felt when the sensor plate is moved rapidly up and down. If resistance is felt, the air sensor must be replaced.

5. If the sensor plate is hard to move

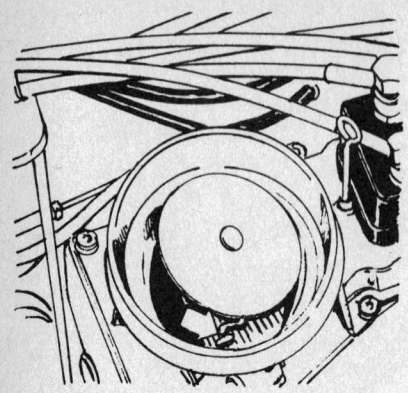

Adjusting the air flow sensor spring stop

upward but moves freely down, the control plunger is sticking. Remove the fuel distributor and clean the control plunger in solvent. If after installation the plunger is still sticking, the fuel distributor must be replaced.

Sensor Plate Height Adjustment

The height adjustment of the sensor plate must be checked under fuel pressure. You will also need a bridging adaptor (US 4480/3).

1. Install a pressure gauge in the line between the fuel distributor and control pressure regulator.
2. Remove the rubber elbow from the air flow sensor housing.
3. Remove the fuel pump relay from the fuse panel and install a bridging adapter (US 4480/3).
4. Switch the adapter ON and wait until pressure reads 49–54 psi.
5. Switch the bridging adapter OFF; the pressure should fall to 28–37 psi.
6. The upper edge of the sensor plate must be even with the bottom of the air cone taper or no more than 0.020 in. below the bottom of the taper.
7. Bend the clip to adjust the height.
8. Recheck the pressure readings after adjusting.
9. Remove the pressure gauge, reconnect the fuel lines and install the fuel pump relay.

Thermo-Time Switch—Testing

NOTE: To properly perform the following tests, the engine must be cold with the water temperature below 95°F (35°C).

1. Disconnect the electrical connector from the cold start valve on the end of the intake manifold.
2. Connect a test light across the cold start valve terminals.
3. Connect a jumper wire from the #1 terminal on the ignition coil to a good ground.
4. Have an assistant operate the starter. If the test light fails to light after 8 seconds, the thermo-time switch is defective and should be replaced.

Cold Start Valve—Testing

1. Remove the electrical connector from the cold start valve.

NOTE: Do not remove the fuel line from the cold start valve.

2. Remove the cold start valve from the manifold and point the nozzle into a measuring container.
3. Connect a jumper wire from one terminal of the cold start valve to terminal #15 on the ignition coil.
4. Connect a second jumper wire from the other cold start valve terminal to ground.
5. Remove the fuel pump relay and bridge the relay plate terminals #L13 and #L14 with a fused (8 amp) jumper wire.
6. Have an assistant turn the ignition switch on while observing the fuel spray pattern from the cold start valve. The spray pattern from the nozzle must be cone-shaped and steady, if not replace the valve.
7. Turn the ignition switch off.
8. Wipe the nozzle dry with a clean rag and check for leakage. If drops form within one minute, the valve is defective and must be replaced.

Auxiliary Air Regulator—Testing

NOTE: The engine must be cold to perform this test.

1. Unplug the electrical connector from the auxiliary air regulator.
2. Start the engine and check the idle.
3. Pinch the hose between the auxiliary air regulator and the intake manifold. The engine idle should drop. Reconnect the electrical connector.
4. Repeat the test on the engine at operating temperature. The idle speed should remain constant when the hose is pinched. If not, replace the auxiliary air regulator.

Control Pressure Regulator—Testing

The system is under considerable constant pressure. The only practical test that should be attempted by the owner is one using an ohmmeter.

Be sure the engine is at normal operating temperature. There should be no loose fuel fittings or other fire hazards when the electrical connections are disengaged.

1. Remove the electrical connector from the control pressure regulator and auxiliary air regulator.
2. Start the engine and run it at idle.
3. Check the terminals of the control pressure regulator wiring harness for voltage. It should be at least 11.5 volts.
4. Connect an ohmmeter across the terminals of the control pressure regulator socket. Resistance should be between 16 and 22 ohms. If there is no resistance, replace the control pressure regulator.

Fuel Injectors—Testing

1. Remove the injector but leave it connected to the fuel line.

2. Point the injector into a measuring container.
3. Remove the fuel pump relay and bridge the relay plate terminals #L13 and L14 with a fused (8 amp) jumper wire.
4. Remove the air duct from the air flow sensor.
5. Have an assistant turn the ignition switch on.
6. Lift the air flow sensor plate with a magnet and observe the injector nozzle spray pattern. The spray pattern must be cone-shaped and even, if not replace the injector.
7. Turn the ignition off and hold the injector horizontally. It should not drip.

NOTE: One or more injectors may be checked at the same time.

8. Moisten the rubber seals on the injectors with fuel before installing.
9. Press the injectors firmly into place.

Fuel Distributor—Removal and Installation

1. Release the pressure in the system by loosening the fuel line on the control pressure regulator (large connector). Have a rag ready to catch the fuel that escapes.
2. Mark the fuel lines in the top of the distributor so that you will be able to put them back in their correct positions.

NOTE: Using different colored paints is usually a good marking device. When you mark each line, be sure to mark the spot where it connects to the distributor.

3. Clean the fuel lines, then remove them from the distributor. Remove the little looped wire plug (the CO adjusting screw plug). Remove the two retaining screws in the top of the distributor.

NOTE: When removing the fuel distributor be sure the control plunger does not fall out from underneath.

4. If the control plunger has been removed, moisten it with gasoline before installing. The small shoulder on the plunger is inserted first.

NOTE: Always use new gaskets and O-ring when removing and installing fuel distributor. Lock all retaining screws with Loctite or its equivalent.

System Pressure Adjustments

The fuel system pressure is present at the factory and is adjusted by either adding or subtracting shims to or from the back of the pressure relief valve spring located in the fuel distributor.

Since special pressure and measuring gauges are needed to adjust system pressure, this job should be left to your Volkswagen dealer.

Substitute for Bridging Adapter 4480/3

The bridging adapter simply connects two terminals of the fuel pump relay socket. To fashion a homemade adapter, attach an 8 amp in-line fuse (the kind commonly used in radios; make sure it's 8 amp, though) between term1nals L13 and L14 of the fuel pump relay socket in the fuse/relay panel.

Diesel Fuel Injection

The diesel fuel system is an extremely complex and sensitive system. Very few repairs or adjustments are possible by the owner. Any service other than that listed here should be referred to an authorized VW dealer or diesel specialist. The injection pump itself is not repairable, it can only be replaced.

Any work done to the diesel fuel injection should be done with absolute cleanliness. Even the smallest specks of dirt will have a disastrous effect on the injection system.

Do not attempt to remove the fuel injectors. They are very delicate and must be removed with a special tool to prevent damage. The fuel in the system is also under tremendous pressure (1700–1850 psi), so it's not wise to loosen any lines with the engine running. Exposing your skin to the spray from the injector at working pressure can cause fuel to penetrate the skin.

CHECKING INJECTION PUMP TIMING

Checking the injection pump timing also involves checking the valve timing. To alter the injection pump timing, the camshaft gear must be removed and repositioned. This also changes the valve timing. Special tool (VW 210) is necessary to properly tension the injection pump drive belt on the diesel engine.

1. Set the engine at TDC on no. 1 cylinder. In this position, the TDC mark on the flywheel should be aligned with boss on the bell housing and both valves of no. 1 cylinder should be closed.
2. The marks on the pump and mounting plate should also be aligned.
3. If the valve timing is incorrect, set the valve timing as detailed in the engine section.

ACCELERATOR CABLE ADJUSTMENT

The ball pin on the pump lever should be pointing up and be aligned with the mark in the slot. The accelerator cable should be attached at the upper hole in the bracket. With the pedal in the full throttle position, adjust the cable so that the pump lever contacts the stop with no binding or strain.

COLD START CABLE ADJUSTMENT

When the cold start knob on the dash is pulled out, the fuel injection pump timing is advanced 2.5°. This improves cold start-

ing and running until the engine warms up.

1. Insert the washer on the cable.
2. Insert the cable in the bracket with the rubber housing. Install the cable in the pin.
3. Install the lockwasher.
4. Move the lever to the zero position (direction of arrow). Pull the inner cable tight and tighten the clamp screw.

CHECKING GLOW PLUGS CURRENT SUPPLY

1. Connect a test light between No. 4 cylinder glow plug and ground.
2. Turn the key to the heat position. The test light should light up.
3. If not, check the glow plug relay, ignition switch, or fuse box relay plate.

CHECKING GLOW PLUGS

Make this check after establishing that there is current to the glow plugs.

1. Remove the wire and glow plug bus bar.
2. Connect the test light between the battery positive terminal and each glow plug in turn.
3. If the light lights, the glow plug is OK. If not, the glow plug is defective and must be replaced.

MANUAL TRANSMISSION

Transaxle

REMOVAL AND INSTALLATION

The engine and transaxle may be removed together as explained under Engine Removal and Installation or the transaxle may be removed alone, as explained here.

1. Disconnect the battery ground cable.
2. Support the left end of the engine at the lifting eye.
3. Remove the left transmission mount (between the transmission and the firewall).
4. Turn the engine until the lug on the flywheel (to the left of the TDC mark) aligns with the flywheel timing pointer.
5. Detach the speedometer drive cable, backup light wire, and clutch cable.
6. Remove the engine to transmission bolts.
7. Disconnect the shift linkage.
8. Detach the transmission ground strap.
9. Remove the starter.
10. Remove the engine mounting support near the starter.
11. Remove the rear transmission mount.

12. Unbolt and wire up the driveshafts.
13. From underneath, remove the bolts for the large cover plate, but don't remove it. Unbolt the small cover plate on the firewall side of the engine. Remove the engine to transmission nut immediately below the small plate.
14. Press the transmission off the dowels and remove it from below the car.

To install the transaxle:

15. The recess in the flywheel edge must be at 3:00 o'clock. Tighten the engine to transmission bolts to 47 ft. lbs. Tighten the engine mounting support bolts to 47 ft. lbs. Tighten the driveshaft bolts to 32 ft. lbs.
16. Check the adjustment of the shift linkage.

SHIFT LINKAGE ADJUSTMENT

1. Align the holes of the lever housing plate with the holes of the lever bearing plate.
2. Loosen the shift rod clamp. Pull the boot off the lever housing and push it out of the way. It may be necessary to loosen the screws in the cover plate to free the boot.
3. Check that the shift finger is in the center of the stopping plate.
4. Adjust the shift rod end so that it is ¾ in. (⁹⁄₃₂ in. for five speed transmissions) from the right side of the lever housing. Tighten the shift rod clamp and check the shifter operation.

SELECTOR SHAFT LOCKBOLT ADJUSTMENT

Make this adjustment after linkage adjustment, if the linkage still feels spongy or jams.

1. Disconnect the shift linkage and put the transmission in Neutral.
2. Loosen the locknut and turn the adjusting sleeve in until the lockring lifts off the sleeve.
3. Turn the adjusting sleeve back until the lockring just contacts the sleeve. Tighten the locknut.
4. Turn the shaft slightly. The lockring should lift as soon as the shaft is turned.
5. Reconnect the linkage.

FIFTH GEAR LOCKBOLT ADJUSTMENT

This adjustment is made with the transmission in neutral. The fifth gear lockbolt is located on top of the transmission next to the selector shaft lockbolt. It has a large protective cap over it.

1. Remove the protective cap.
2. Loosen the locknut and tighten the adjusting sleeve until the detent plunger in the center of the sleeve just begins to move up.
3. Loosen the adjusting sleeve ⅓ of a

VOLKSWAGEN

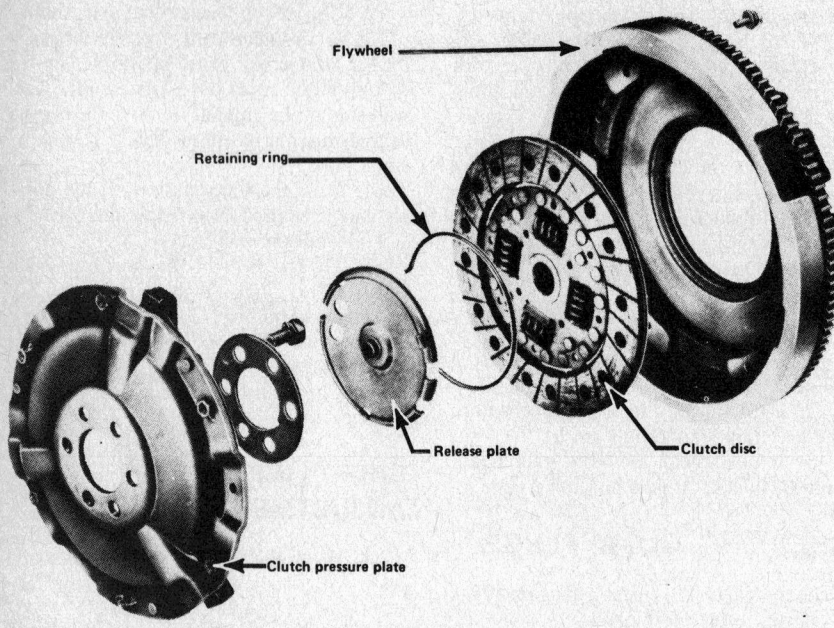

Clutch assembly: the pressure plate is bolted to the crankshaft and the clutch is actuated by a pushrod working on the release plate

turn and tighten the locknut. Make sure the transmission shifts in and out of fifth gear easily. Replace the protective cap.

Clutch

PEDAL FREE PLAY ADJUSTMENT

The clutch should have 9/16 in. free play at the pedal. Pedal free play is the distance the pedal can be depressed before the linkage starts to act on the throwout bearing.

1. Adjust the clutch pedal free play by loosening the two nuts on the cable near the front of the transmission.

2. After obtaining the correct free play, tighten the adjusting nuts.

REMOVAL AND INSTALLATION

1. Remove the transmission.

2. Attach a toothed flywheel holder and gradually loosen the flywheel to pressure plate bolts one or two turns at a time in a crisscross pattern to prevent distortion.

3. Remove the flywheel and the clutch disc.

4. Use a screwdriver to remove the release plate retaining ring. Remove the release plate.

5. Lock the pressure plate in place and unbolt it from the crankshaft. Loosen the bolts one or two turns at a time in a crisscross pattern to prevent distortion.

6. On installation, use new bolts to attach the pressure plate to the crankshaft. Use a thread locking compound and torque the bolts in a diagonal pattern to 54 ft. lbs.

7. Lubricate the clutch disc splines with multi-purpose grease. Lubricate the release plate contact surface and pushrod socket with multi-purpose grease. Install the release plate, retaining ring, and clutch disc.

8. Install a dummy shaft to align the clutch disc.

9. Install the flywheel, tightening the bolts one or two turns at a time in a crisscross pattern to prevent distortion. Torque the bolts to 14 ft. lbs.

10. Replace the transmission.

AUTOMATIC TRANSMISSION

Transaxle

REMOVAL AND INSTALLATION

The engine and transaxle may be removed together as explained under Engine Removal and Installation or the transaxle may be removed alone, as explained here.

1. Disconnect both battery cables.

2. Disconnect the speedometer cable at the transmission.

3. Support the left end of the engine at the lifting eye. Attach a hoist to the transaxle.

4. Unbolt the rear transmission carrier from the body then from the transaxle. Unbolt the left side carrier from the body.

5. Unbolt the driveshafts and wire them up.

6. Remove the starter.

7. Remove the three converter to drive plate bolts.

8. Shift into P and disconnect the floor-shift linkage at the transmission.

9. Remove the accelerator and carburetor cable bracket at the transmission.

10. Unbolt the left side transmission carrier from the transmission.

11. Unbolt the front transmission mount from the transmission.

12. Unbolt the bottom of the engine from the transmission. Lift the transaxle slightly, remove the rest of the bolts, pull the transmission off the mounting dowels, and lower the transaxle out of the car. Secure the converter so it doesn't fall out.

—————— CAUTION ——————
Don't tilt the torque converter.

To install:

1. Be sure the torque converter is fully seated on the one-way clutch support. Push the transmission onto the mounting dowels and install two bolts. Lift the unit until the left driveshaft can be installed and install the rest of the bolts. Torque them to 39 ft. lbs.

2. Tighten the front transmission mount bolts to 39 ft. lbs. Install the left side transmission carrier to the transmission.

3. Connect the accelerator and carburetor cable bracket. Connect the floor-shift linkage.

4. Tighten the torque converter to drive plate bolts to 22 ft. lbs. Torque the driveshaft bolts to 32 ft. lbs.

5. Install the rear transmission carrier and make sure that the left side carrier is aligned in the center of the body mount. Bolt the left side carrier to the body.

6. Connect the speedometer cable and the battery cables.

PAN REMOVAL AND INSTALLATION, STRAINER SERVICE

1. Remove the drain plug and let the fluid drain into a pan. If the pan has no drain plug, loosen the pan bolts until a corner of the pan can be lowered to drain the fluid.

2. Remove the pan bolts and take off the pan.

3. Discard the old gasket and clean the pan out. Be very careful not to get any threads or lint from rags into the pan.

4. The filter needn't be replaced unless the fluid is dirty or smells burnt. The specified torque for the strainer screws is 2 ft. lbs.

5. Replace the pan with a new gasket and tighten the bolts, in a crisscross pattern, to 14 ft. lbs.

6. Using a long-necked funnel, pour in 2½ qts. of Dextron automatic transmission fluid through the dipstick tube. Start the engine and shift through all the transmis-

sion ranges with the car stationary. Check the level on the dipstick with the lever in Neutral. It should be up to the lower end of the dipstick. Drive the car until it is warmed up and recheck the level.

LINKAGE ADJUSTMENT

Check the cable adjustment as follows:

1. Run the engine at 1000—1200 rpm with the parking brake on.

2. Select Reverse. A drop in engine speed should be noticed.

3. Select Park. Engine speed should increase. Pull the shift lever against Reverse, the engine speed shouldn't drop (because reverse gear has not been engaged).

4. Move the shift lever to engage Reverse. Engine speed should drop as the gear engages.

5. Move the shift lever to Neutral. An increase in engine speed should be noticed.

6. Shift the lever into Drive. A noticeable drop in engine speed should result.

7. Shift into 1. The lever must engage without having to overcome any resistance.

8. To adjust the cable, shift into Park. Loosen the cable clamp at the transmission end of the cable, press the transmission lever all the way to the left and tighten the cable clamp.

TRANSMISSION CABLE ADJUSTMENT

Make sure the throttle is closed, and the choke and fast idle cam are off (carbureted models).

1. Detach the cable end at the transmission.

2. Press the lever at the transmission into its closed throttle position.

3. You should be able to attach the cable end onto the transmission lever without moving the lever.

4. Adjust the cable length to the correct setting.

SECOND GEAR (REAR) BAND ADJUSTMENT

NOTE: The transmission must be horizontal when band adjustments are performed.

1. Loosen the locknut on the adjusting screw, which is located on the front of the transmission.

2. Tighten the adjusting screw to 7 ft. lbs.

3. Loosen the screw and tighten it again to 4 ft. lbs.

4. Turn the screw out exactly 2½ turns and then tighten the locknut.

NEUTRAL START/BACKUP LIGHT SWITCH

The combination neutral start and backup light switch is mounted inside the shifter

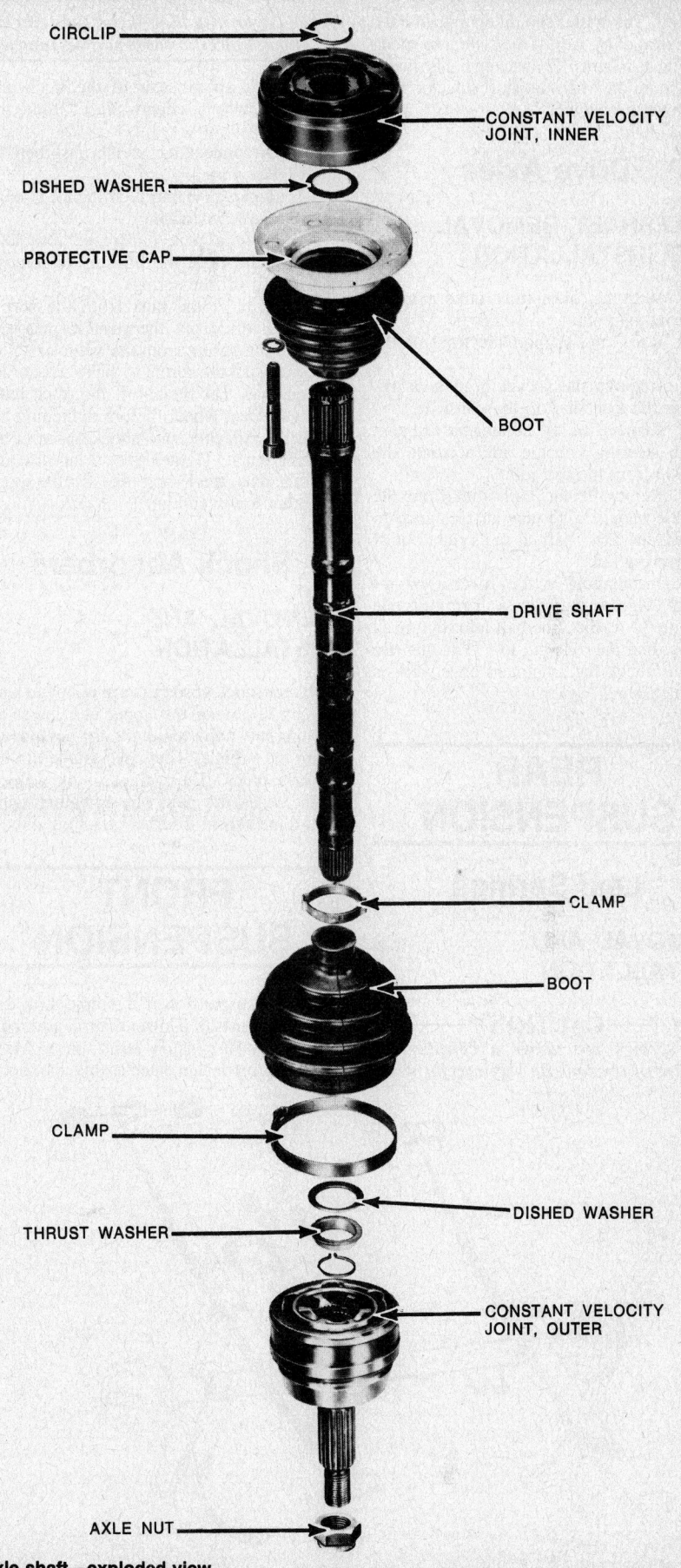

CIRCLIP

CONSTANT VELOCITY JOINT, INNER

DISHED WASHER

PROTECTIVE CAP

BOOT

DRIVE SHAFT

CLAMP

BOOT

CLAMP

DISHED WASHER

THRUST WASHER

CONSTANT VELOCITY JOINT, OUTER

AXLE NUT

Axle shaft—exploded view

VOLKSWAGEN

housing. The starter should operate in Park or Neutral only. Adjust the switch by moving it on its mounts. The backup lights should only come on when the shift selector is in the Reverse position.

Drive Axles

HALFSHAFT REMOVAL AND INSTALLATION

1. With the car on the ground, remove the front axle nut.
2. Raise and support the front of the vehicle.
3. Remove the socket head bolts retaining the axle shaft to the transaxle.
4. Remove the bolt holding the ball joint to the steering knuckle and separate the knuckle from the ball joint.
5. Removing the ball joint from the knuckle should give enough clearance to remove the axle shaft. It pulls right out of the steering hub.
6. Installation is the reverse of removal. Tighten the axle shaft to transaxle bolts to 32 ft. lbs., the ball joint bolt to 21 ft. lbs. and the axle nut to 173 ft. lbs. Be sure to check the alignment after work is completed.

REAR SUSPENSION

Leaf Springs

REMOVAL AND INSTALLATION

—————— CAUTION ——————
The springs are under a considerable amount of tension. Be very careful when

removing or installing them; they can exert enough force to cause serious injuries.

1. Jack up the rear of the truck and support it with jackstands placed under the frame.
2. Disconnect the shock absorbers at their lower end.
3. Remove the nuts securing the U-bolts around the axle housing.
4. Place a jack under the rear axle housing and raise the housing to remove the weight off the springs.
5. Remove the nuts from the spring shackles, drive out the shackle pins and remove the spring from the vehicle.
6. Install the spring in the reverse order of removal. The weight of the truck must be on the rear wheels before tightening the front pin, shackle, and shock absorber attaching nuts. Tighten the front pin and shackle nuts, the U-bolt nuts and the shock absorber lower end nut.

Shock Absorbers

REMOVAL AND INSTALLATION

The rear shock absorbers are removed simply by removing the upper and lower attaching nuts, and removing the component from the vehicle. They are installed in the reverse order. The weight of the vehicle must be on the rear wheels before tightening the shock absorber attaching nuts.

FRONT SUSPENSION

The front suspension is a simple strut design. It consists of a lower control arm, ball joint, and suspension strut. In a MacPherson strut design, such as this, the shock

absorber strut serves as a locating member of the suspension as well as a damper. A shock absorber insert is located inside the strut. A coil spring is used.

Ball Joint

REMOVAL AND INSTALLATION

1. Jack up the front of the truck and support it on stands.
2. Remove the retaining bolt and nut.
3. Pry the lower control arm and ball joint down and out of the strut.
4. Drill out the rivets; enlarge the holes to 21/64 in.
5. Remove the ball joint assembly.
6. Bolt the new ball joint in place. Torque the bolts to 18 ft. lbs. Tighten the retaining bolt for the ball joint stud to 21 ft. lbs.

Shock Absorber

REMOVAL AND INSTALLATION

Since the shock absorber cartridge is con-

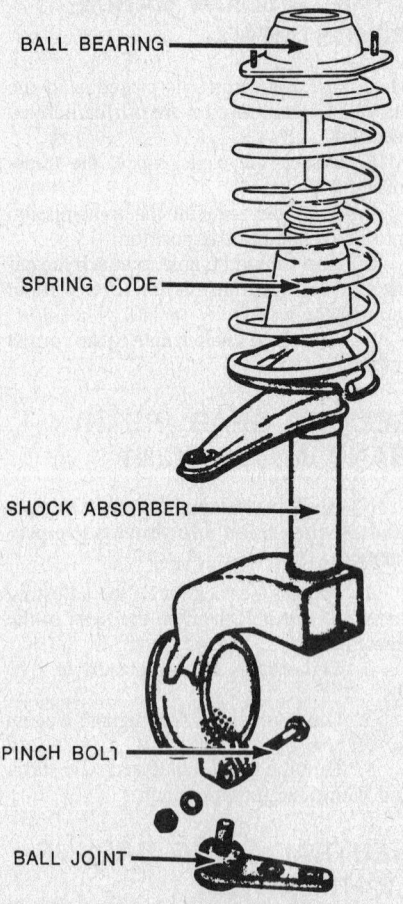

A pinch bolt holds the ball joint to the combination strut and steering knuckle

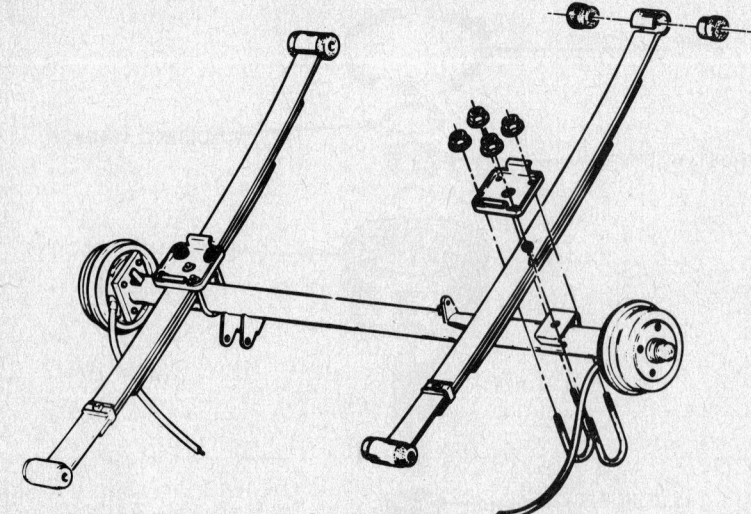

Rear suspension

tained within the strut assembly, it is necessary to remove the strut and then compress the coil spring in order to remove the shock.

Strut

REMOVAL AND INSTALLATION

1. Remove the brake hose from the strut clip.
2. Mark the position of the camber adjustment bolts before removing them from the hub (wheel bearing housing).
3. Remove the upper mounting nuts and remove the strut from the car.
4. Installation is the reverse. The upper nuts are tightened to 14 ft. lbs., and the lower strut-to-hub bolts to 58 ft. lbs. Use new washers on the lower bolts. If the shock absorber was replaced, camber will have to be adjusted.

Coil Spring

REMOVAL AND INSTALLATION

To remove the spring, the strut must be mounted in a large vise, the spring compressed, the retaining nut and cover removed, and the spring slowly released. A special tool is needed to remove the shock absorber retainer, after which the shock absorber is easily removed. Assembly is the reverse of removal.

Front End Alignment

CAMBER ADJUSTMENT

Camber is adjusted by loosening the nuts of the two bolts holding the top of the wheel bearing housing to the bottom of the strut, and turning the top eccentric bolt. The range of adjustment is 2°.

CASTER

Other than the replacement of damaged suspension components, caster is not adjustable.

TOE-IN ADJUSTMENT

Toe-in is checked with the wheels straight ahead. Only the right tie-rod is adjustable, but replacement left tie-rods are adjustable. Replacement left tie-rods should be set to the same length as the original. Toe-in should be adjusted only with the right tie-rod. If the steering wheel is crooked, remove and align it.

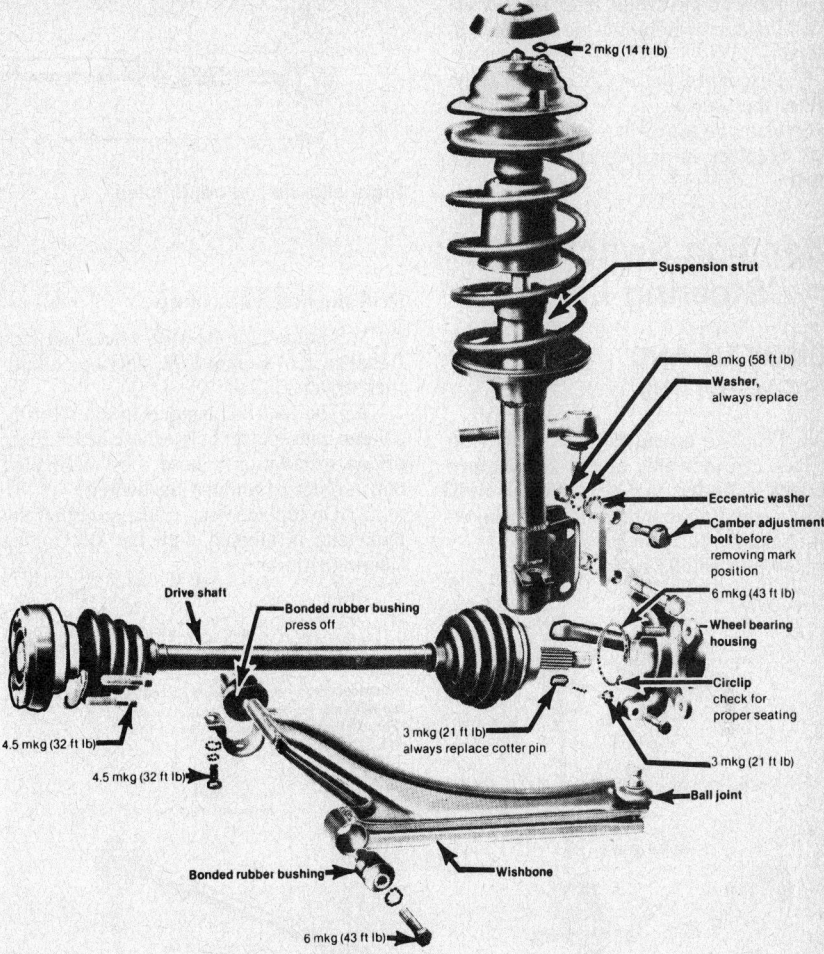

Exploded view of the front suspension

STEERING

The Rabbit pick-up has rack and pinion steering with end-mounted tie-rods. No periodic maintenance is required on either rack and pinion steering system.

Steering Wheel

REMOVAL AND INSTALLATION

1. Grasp the center cover pad and pull it from the wheel.
2. Loosen and remove the steering shaft nut.
3. Pull the wheel off the shaft. A puller isn't normally needed.
4. Disconnect the horn wire.
5. Replace the wheel in the reverse order of removal. Tighten the nut to 36 ft. lbs.

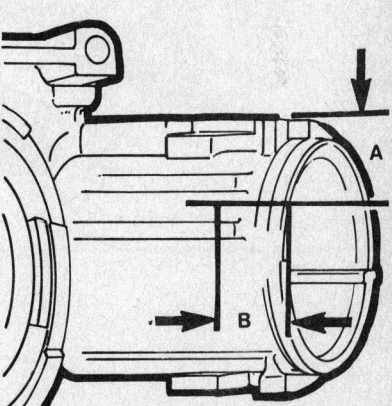

Dimensions for drilling the ignition lock cylinder hole (if not equipped)

Turn Signal and Headlight Dimmer Switch

REPLACEMENT

1. Disconnect the battery ground cable.
2. Remove the steering wheel.

3. Remove the switch retaining screws.

4. Pry the switch housing off the column.

5. Disconnect the electrical plugs at the back of the switch.

6. Remove the switch housing.

7. Replace in the reverse order of removal.

Ignition Switch and Steering Lock

REMOVAL AND INSTALLATION

NOTE: The access hole for removing the lock cylinder may be missing. Before the lock cylinder can be removed, drill a hole according to following dimensions:

a = 12 mm (0.472 in.)
b = 10 mm (0.393 in.)

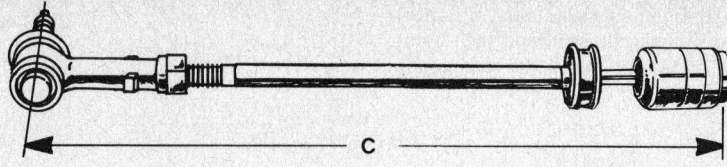

Right side tie rod adjustment

Drill the hole ⅛ in. deep.

1. Remove the steering wheel and turn signal switch. Remove the steering column shaft covers.

2. The lock is clamped to the steering column with special bolts whose heads shear off on installation. These must be drilled out in order to remove the switch.

3. On replacement, make sure that the lock tang is aligned with the slot in the steering column.

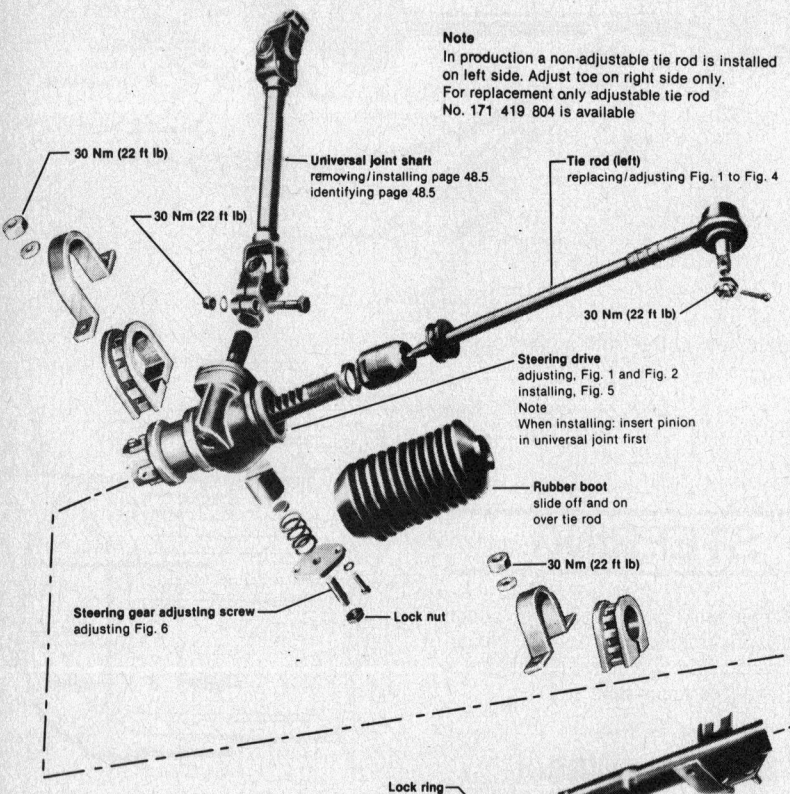

Note
In production a non-adjustable tie rod is installed on left side. Adjust toe on right side only. For replacement only adjustable tie rod No. 171 419 804 is available

30 Nm (22 ft lb)

30 Nm (22 ft lb)

Universal joint shaft
removing/installing page 48.5
identifying page 48.5

Tie rod (left)
replacing/adjusting Fig. 1 to Fig. 4

30 Nm (22 ft lb)

Steering drive
adjusting, Fig. 1 and Fig. 2
installing, Fig. 5
Note
When installing: insert pinion
in universal joint first

Rubber boot
slide off and on
over tie rod

30 Nm (22 ft lb)

Steering gear adjusting screw
adjusting Fig. 6

Lock nut

Lock ring

Spring clamp
always replace
remove to adjust toe
installing: ends of clamp
point upward

30 Nm (22 ft lb)

Tie rod (right)
replacing/adjusting
Fig. 1 to Fig. 2

Rubber boot
slide off and
on over tie rod

30 Nm (22 ft lb)

Steering gear components

Steering Gear

REMOVAL AND INSTALLATION

1. Disconnect the steering shaft universal joint and wire up out of the way.

2. Disconnect the tie rods at the steering rack and wire up and out of the way.

3. Remove the steering rack and drive.

4. Install the steering rack and drive and torque the attaching hardware to 14 ft. lbs.

5. Set the steering rack with equal distances between the housing on the right side and left side.

6. Install the tie rods and screw both sides in until an equal distance is reached on both rods.

7. Tighten the steering gear adjusting screw until it touches the thrust washer. Tighten the lock nut.

8. Install the steering shaft.

9. Check the front end alignment.

Steering Linkage

TIE-ROD REMOVAL AND INSTALLATION

1. Center the steering rack.

2. Remove the cotter pin and nut from the tie rod end.

3. Disconnect the tie rod from the steering rack.

4. If the left side tie rod is being replaced, adjust it to 14.92 in. (379 mm).

5. Adjust the steering rack and tie rods as outlined in steps 5 and 6 of the "Steering Gear Removal and Installation".

6. Tighten the tie rod end retaining nut to 21 ft. lbs. and install a new cotter pin.

BRAKE SYSTEMS

The hydraulic system is a dual circuit type that has the advantage of retaining 50% braking effectiveness in the event of failure in one system. The circuits are arranged so that you always have one front and one rear brake for a more controlled emergency stop.

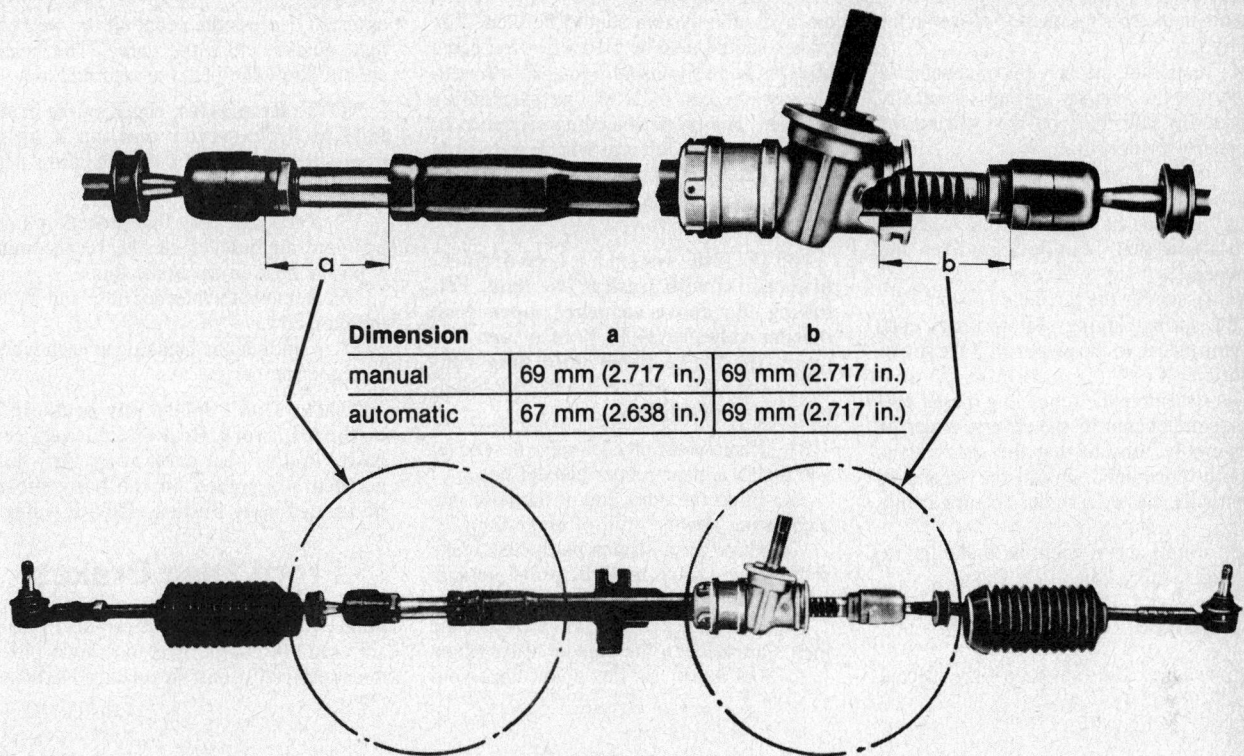

Dimension	a	b
manual	69 mm (2.717 in.)	69 mm (2.717 in.)
automatic	67 mm (2.638 in.)	69 mm (2.717 in.)

Adjusting the tie rod position

The right front and left rear are in one circuit; the left front and right rear are in the second circuit.

There is also a brake failure switch and a proportioning valve.

The brake failure unit is a hydraulic valve/electrical switch which warns of brake problems by the warning light on the instrument panel. A piston inside the switch is kept centered by one brake system pressure on one side and the other system pressure on the opposite side. Should a failure occur in one system, the piston would go to the "failed" side and complete an electrical circuit to the warning lamp. This switch also functions as a parking brake reminder light and will go out when the parking brake is released. The proportioning valve provides balanced front-to-rear braking during hard stops.

Extreme brake line pressure will overcome the spring pressure on the piston within the valve causing it to proportionally restrict pressure to the rear brakes. In this manner, the rear brakes are kept from locking. The proportioner doesn't operate under normal braking conditions.

ADJUSTMENT

The front disc brakes require no adjustment, as disc brakes automatically adjust themselves to compensate for pad wear. The VW pick-up has self-adjusting rear drum brakes.

Master Cylinder

REMOVAL AND INSTALLATION

1. Disconnect and plug the brake lines.
2. Disconnect the electrical plug from the sending unit for the brake failure switch.
3. Remove the two master cylinder mounting nuts.
4. Lift the master cylinder and reservoir out of the engine compartment being careful not to spill any fluid on the fender. Empty out and discard the brake fluid.

CAUTION
Do not depress the brake pedal while the master cylinder is removed.

---

5. Position the master cylinder and reservoir assembly onto the studs for the booster and install the washers and nuts. Tighten the nuts to no more than 9 ft. lbs.
6. Remove the plugs and connect the brake lines.
7. Bleed the entire brake system.

OVERHAUL

1. Remove the master cylinder from the booster.
2. Firmly mount the master cylinder in a vise. Use clean rags to protect the cylinder from the vise jaws.

3. Grasp the plastic reservoir and pull it out of the rubber plugs. Remove the plugs.
4. In the center of the cylinder there is a stop screw; remove it. Discard the stop screw seal; there should be a new one in the rebuilding kit.
5. At the end of the master cylinder is a snap-ring (circlip). Remove it, using snap-ring pliers.
6. Shake out the secondary piston assembly. If the primary piston remains lodged in the bore, it can be forced out by applying compressed air to the open line fitting.
7. Disassemble the secondary piston. The two secondary springs will be replaced with those in the rebuilding kit. Save the washers and spacers.
8. Carefully clamp the secondary piston. Slightly compress the spring and screw out the stroke limiting bolt.
9. Remove the secondary piston stop sleeve bolt, spring, spring seat, and support washer.
10. Replace all the parts with those supplied in the overhaul kit. Be careful not to interchange the piston cups and the piston seals.
11. Clean all metal parts in alcohol and dry them with compressed air.
12. Check every part you are reusing. Pay close attention to the cylinder bores. If there is any scoring or rust, have the master cylinder honed or replace it.
13. Lightly coat the bores and cups with brake fluid. Assemble the cylinder com-

ponents in the exact sequence shown in the illustration.

14. Install the primary piston assembly; notice that the primary spring is conically shaped. Be sure that you aren't using the secondary spring.

15. Using a plastic rod or other non-metallic tool, push the primary piston assembly into the housing until the stop bolt (with a new seal), can be screwed in and tightened.

16. Assemble the secondary piston. Fasten the spring, spring seat, primary cup, and stop sleeve to the piston with the stroke limiting bolt.

17. Assemble the remaining master cylinder components in the reverse order of disassembly. Ensure that the snap-ring is properly positioned. Install the secondary piston with master cylinder opening facing down.

18. Install and tighten the brake failure warning sending unit.

BLEEDING

Anytime a brake line has been disconnected

the hydraulic system should be bled. The brakes should also be bled when the pedal travel becomes unusually long ("soft pedal") or the car pulls to one side during braking. The proper bleeding sequence is: right rear wheel, left rear wheel, right front caliper, and left front caliper. You'll need a helper to pump the brake pedal while you open the bleeder valves.

NOTE: If the system has been drained, first refill it with fresh brake fluid. Following the above sequence, open each bleeder valve by ½ to ¾ of a turn and pump the brake pedal until fluid runs out of the valve. Proceed with the bleeding as outlined below.

1. Remove the bleeder valve dust cover and install a clear rubber bleeder hose.

2. Insert the other end of the hose into a container about ⅓ full of brake fluid.

3. Have an assistant pump the brake pedal several times until the pedal pressure increases.

4. Hold the pedal under pressure and then start to open the bleeder valve about ½ to ¾ of a turn. At this point, have your

assistant depress the pedal all the way and then quickly close the valve. The helper should allow the pedal to return slowly.

NOTE: Keep a close check on the brake fluid in the reservoir and top it up as necessary throughout the bleeding process.

5. Keep repeating this procedure until no more·air bubbles can be seen coming from the hose in the brake fluid.

6. Remove the bleeder hose and install the dust cover.

7. Continue the bleeding at each wheel in sequence.

NOTE: Don't splash any brake fluid on the paintwork. Brake fluid is very corrosive and will eat paint away. Any fluid accidentally spilled on the body should be immediately flushed off with water.

Front Disc Brakes

Single piston floating caliper disc brakes are used. In this design, the single piston forces one pad against the rotating disc brake.

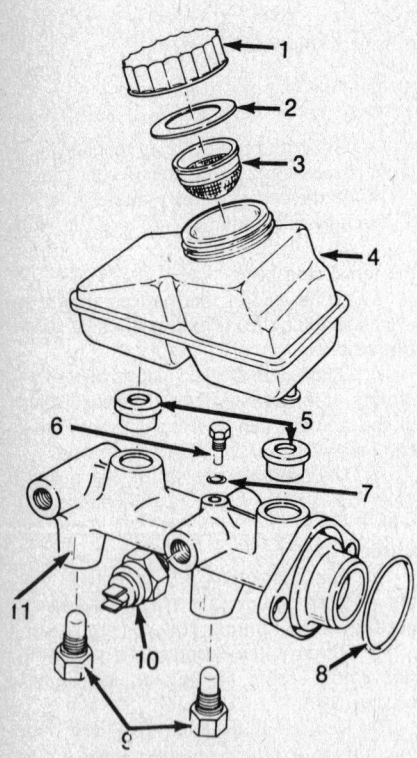

1. Reservoir cap
2. Washer
3. Filter screen
4. Reservoir
5. Master cylinder plugs
6. Stop screw
7. Stop screw seal
8. Master cylinder seal
9. Residual pressure valves
10. Warning light sender unit
11. Brake master cylinder housing

Master cylinder body and reservoir

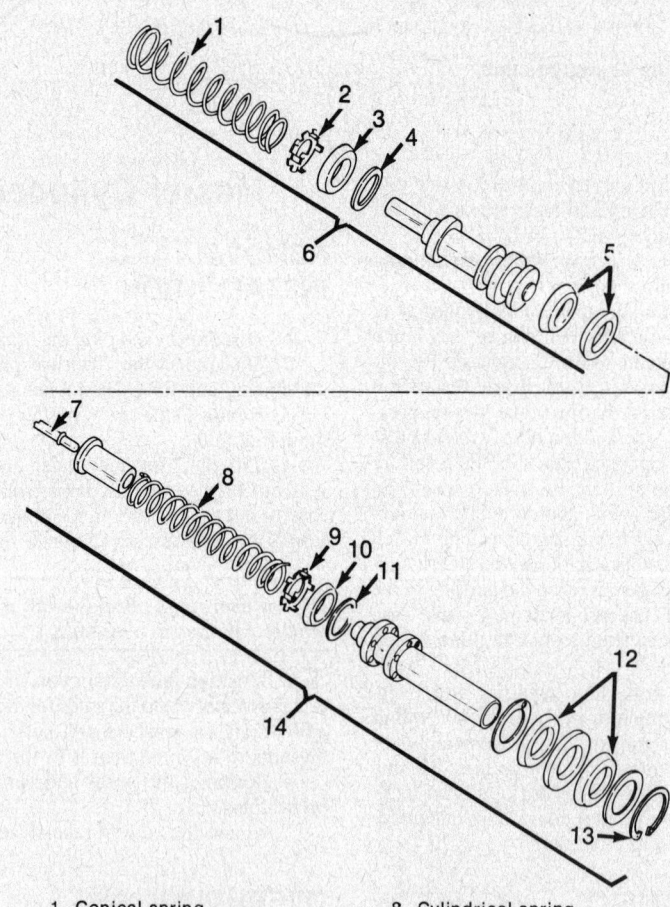

1. Conical spring
2. Spring seat
3. Primary cup
4. Washer
5. Secondary cups
6. Primary piston assembly
7. Stroke limiting screw

8. Cylindrical spring
9. Spring seat
10. Primary cup
11. Washer
12. Secondary cups
13. Circlip
14. Secondary piston assembly

Exploded view of the master cylinder components

Counter pressure forces against the floating frame and the frame then pushes the second pad into the disc. The advantages of the floating caliper are better heat dissipation, simpler repair, fewer leaks, and less sensitivity to variance in disc thickness and parallelism.

Brake Pads

REMOVAL AND INSTALLATION

Brake pads should be replaced when there is no visible clearance between the pads and the cross-spring or when they are worn to a thickness of ¼ in.

1. Jack up the front of the truck and support it on stands. Remove the wheels.
2. Pry the clip out of both retaining pins.
3. While pressing down on the cross-spring, push the pad retaining pins out with a drift or small screwdriver.
4. Reference mark positions of the brake pads if they are being reused.
5. Remove the cross-spring from the caliper.
6. Remove the inner brake pad. VW has a special tool for this purpose, but by using a small drift or punch you can pry the pad out of the caliper until it can be gripped by a pair of pliers and removed.
7. The outer brake pad is positioned in a notch. Use a flat, smooth piece of hardwood or metal to press the floating caliper frame and piston cylinder outward.
8. Grip the outer pad and remove it.
9. Siphon out about half of the brake fluid in the reservoir to prevent it from overflowing when the piston is pushed in and new thicker pads are inserted. Press the piston back into the cylinder with the flat piece of wood or metal. *Do not apply the brakes with the pads removed.*
10. Check that piston is at the proper 20° angle. You can make a gauge out of stiff cardboard.
11. Install the brake pads into the caliper.

NOTE: Replace used pads in the side of the caliper from which they were removed. When installing new pads always replace the pads on the opposite wheel at the same time.

12. Position the cross-spring in the caliper and then carefully tap the pad retaining pins into place with a small hammer. Install the pin clip.

Calipers

REMOVAL AND INSTALLATION

1. Jack up and support the front of the truck.
2. Remove the brake pads.

3. If you are removing the caliper for overhaul, disconnect and plug the brake line at the caliper. If not, do not remove the hose—hang the caliper by a wire.
4. Remove the two caliper-to-strut retaining bolts and remove the caliper.
5. Install the caliper using the reverse of the removal procedure. Tighten the two retaining bolts to 43 ft. lbs.
6. Bleed the brakes.

OVERHAUL

1. Remove the caliper.
2. Mount the caliper in a soft-jawed vise or place cloths over the jaws to protect the caliper.

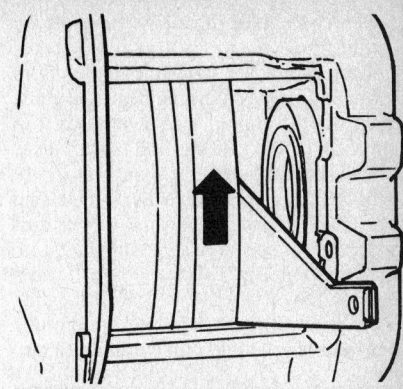

Checking that the piston is at the correct 20° angle

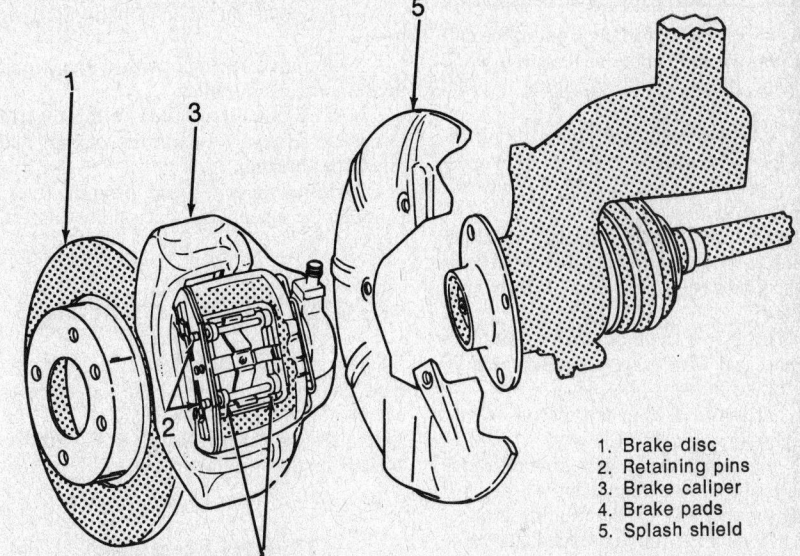

1. Brake disc
2. Retaining pins
3. Brake caliper
4. Brake pads
5. Splash shield

Caliper and disc mounting

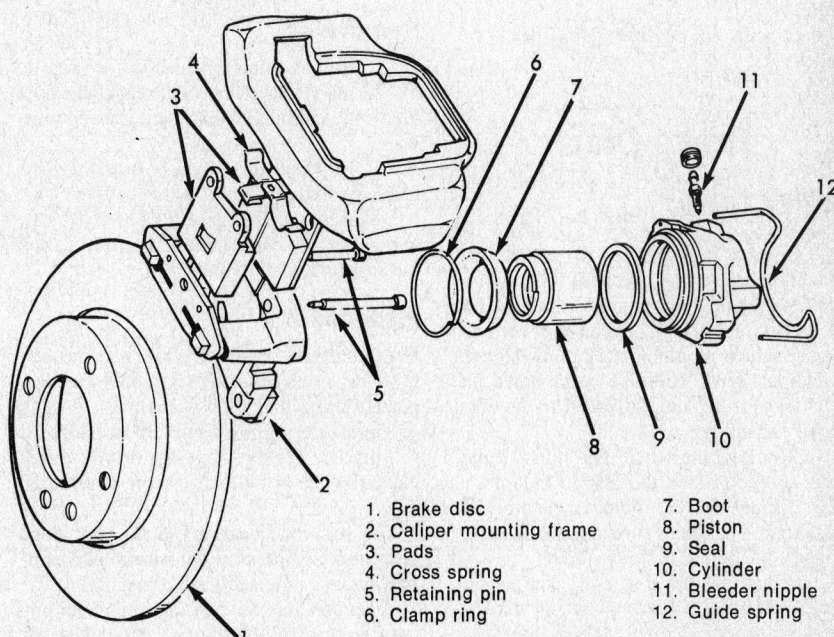

1. Brake disc
2. Caliper mounting frame
3. Pads
4. Cross spring
5. Retaining pin
6. Clamp ring
7. Boot
8. Piston
9. Seal
10. Cylinder
11. Bleeder nipple
12. Guide spring

Exploded view of the caliper

3. Pry the fixed mounting frame off the floating frame.

4. Separate the caliper cylinder from the floating frame by prying it and the guide spring off the frame. Use a brass drift to lightly tap on the cylinder and place a piece of wood under the piston to protect it.

5. Using pliers remove the piston clamp ring. Remove and discard the rubber dust cover, a new one should be supplied with the rebuilding kit.

6. Remove the piston from the cylinder. If it is stubborn, remove the bleeder screw and blow it out with compressed air.

--- CAUTION ---

Hold the piston over a block of wood when doing this as the piston will fly out with considerable force.

7. When the piston pops out of the caliper, remove the rubber seal with a wood or plastic pin to avoid damaging the seal groove.

8. Clean all metal parts in alcohol. Inspect the pistons and their bores, they must be free of scoring and pitting. Replace the cylinder if there is any damage.

9. Discard all rubber parts. The caliper rebuilding kit includes new boots and seals which should be used as the caliper is reassembled.

10. Lightly coat the cylinder bore, piston, and seal with brake assembly paste or fresh brake fluid.

11. Using a vise, install the piston into the cylinder.

12. Piston the guide spring in the groove of the brake cylinder and using a brass drift install the cylinder on the floating frame.

13. Place the mounting frame in the guide spring and slip it onto the floating frame. The fixed frame has two grooves which position it over the raised ribs of the floating frame.

14. Install the caliper and bleed the brakes.

Brake Disc

INSPECTION

Brake discs may be checked for lateral runout while on the car. This check will require a dial indicator and stand to mount it on the caliper. VW has a special tool for this purpose which mounts the dial indicator to the caliper, but it can also be mounted on the shaft of a C-clamp attached to the outside of the caliper.

1. Remove the wheel and reinstall the wheel bolts to retain the disc to the hub.

2. Mount the dial indicator securely to the caliper. The feeler should touch the disc about ½-in. below the outer edge.

3. Rotate the disc and observe the gauge. Radial run-out (wobble) must not exceed 0.004 in. A disc which exceeds this specification must be replaced or refinished.

4. Brake discs which have excessive radial runout, sharp ridges, or scoring can be refinished. Finish grinding must be done on both sides of discs to prevent squeaking and vibrating. Discs which have only light grooves and are otherwise acceptable can be used without refinishing.

The standard disc is 0.47 in. thick. It should not be ground to less than 0.41 in.

REMOVAL AND INSTALLATION

1. Loosen the wheel bolts. Remove the hub cap.

2. Jack up the front of the truck and place it on stands. Remove the wheel(s).

3. Remove the caliper.

4. Remove the disc-to-hub retaining screw.

5. Remove the disc with a sharp pull by hand or use a puller.

6. The disc is installed in the reverse order of removal. Install the caliper and bleed the brakes.

7. Install the wheel and lower the truck. Tighten the wheel bolts diagonally to 65 ft. lbs.

Front Wheel Bearings

There is no front wheel bearing adjustment. The bearing is pressed into the steering knuckle. Axle nut torque is 175 ft. lbs. The axle nut should be tightened only with the wheels resting on the ground.

Drum Brakes

BRAKE DRUMS

Removal

1. Remove one wheel bolt.

2. Insert a screwdriver through the wheel bolt hole and push the adjusting wedge upward.

3. Reinstall the wheel bolt and tighten to 65 ft. lbs.

4. Remove the grease cap, axle nut, and cotter pin, and remove the drum. See the inspection procedure.

Inspection

Check the brake drum for any cracks, scores, grooves, or an out-of-round condition. Replace a drum that shows cracking. Smooth out light scoring with fine emery cloth. If scoring is extensive have the drum turned. Never have a drum turned more than 0.020 in.

The stub axle bearings in the rear brake drum must be pressed out for replacement. Always use new seals on reassembly.

After greasing the bearings and installing them in the drum with new seals, place the drum onto the stub axle.

Installation

1. Install the washer and the hex nut. Tighten the nut and then loosen it. Retighten the nut slightly so that the washer between the nut and the bearing can just be moved with a screwdriver. Correct bearing play is 0.001–.003 in.

2. Install the castellated nut and insert a new cotter pin. Fill the hub cap with grease and install it.

3. Install the wheel and adjust the brakes.

Brake Shoes

REMOVAL AND INSTALLATION

1. Remove the drum.

2. Remove the spring retainers by pressing in and turning ¼ turn.

3. Remove the brake shoes from the supports and the lower return spring.

4. Unhook the parking brake cable on the lever.

5. Use pliers to unhook the spring for the adjusting wedge and the upper return spring.

6. Remove the brake shoes.

7. To remove the self-adjuster push rod, place the push rod in a vise and unhook the tensioning spring.

8. To install, place the push rod in a vise, attach the brake shoe to the push rod to install the tension spring on the rod and shoe.

9. Install the adjusting wedge with the lug toward the backing plate.

10. Attach the brake shoe with the lever to the push rod. Install the upper return spring.

11. Hook the parking brake cable on the lever. Place the shoes on the cylinder pistons and hook the lower return spring into the shoes.

12. Mount the brake shoes on the support and hook the spring for the adjusting wedge into the wedge and shoe.

13. Install the retaining springs and retainers. Install the drum and adjust the wheel bearings. Apply the brakes firmly to set the self-adjuster.

Wheel Cylinders

REMOVAL AND INSTALLATION

1. Remove the brake shoes.

2. Loosen the brake line on the rear of the cylinder, but do not pull the line away from the cylinder or it may bend.

3. Remove the bolts and lockwashers that attach the wheel cylinder to the backing plate and remove the cylinder.

4. Position the new wheel cylinder on

the backing plate and install the cylinder attaching bolts and lockwashers.

5. Attach the brake line.

6. Install the brakes and bleed the system.

OVERHAUL

1. Remove the brakes.

2. Place the bucket or some newspapers under the brake backing plate to catch the brake fluid that will run out to the wheel cylinder.

3. Remove the boots from the ends of the wheel cylinders.

4. Push one piston toward the center of the cylinder to force the opposite piston and cup out the other end of the cylinder. Reach in the open end of the cylinder and push the spring, cup, and piston out of the cylinder.

5. Remove the bleeder screw from the rear of the cylinder, on the back of the backing plate.

6. Inspect the inside of the wheel cylinder. If it is scored in any way, the cylinder must be honed with a wheel cylinder hone or fine emery paper, and finished with crocus cloth if emery paper is used. If the inside of the cylinder is excessively worn the cylinder will have to be replaced, as only 0.003 in. of material can be removed from the cylinder walls. Whenever honing or cleaning wheel cylinders, keep a small amount of brake fluid in the cylinder to serve as a lubricant.

7. Clean any foreign matter from the pistons. The sides of the pistons must be smooth for the wheel cylinders to operate properly.

8. Clean the cylinder bore with alcohol and a lint-free rag. Pull the rag through the bore several times to remove all foreign matter and dry the cylinder.

9. Install the bleeder screw and the return spring in the cylinder.

10. Coat new cylinder cups with new brake fluid and install them in the cylinder. Make sure they are square in the bore or they will leak.

11. Install the pistons in the cylinder after coating them with new brake fluid.

12. Coat the insides of the boots with new brake fluid and install them on the cylinder. Install and bleed the brakes.

REAR WHEEL BEARINGS

Rear wheel bearing adjustment is covered under Brake Drum Removal and Installation.

Parking Brake

CABLE

Adjustment

On the Rabbit pick-up, adjustment is made

at the cable end nuts on top of the handbrake lever.

1. Block the front wheels. Raise the rear of the car.

2. Apply the parking brake so that the lever is on the second notch.

3. Tighten the compensator nut or adjusting nuts until both rear wheels cannot be turned by hand.

4. Release the parking brake lever and check that both wheels can be easily turned.

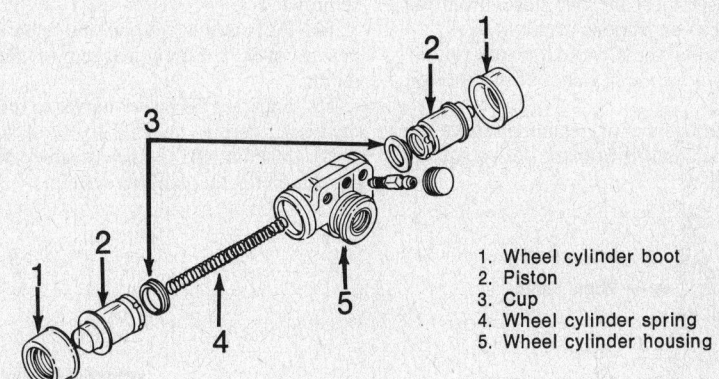

Exploded view of the brake wheel cylinder

1. Wheel cylinder boot
2. Piston
3. Cup
4. Wheel cylinder spring
5. Wheel cylinder housing

CHASSIS ELECTRICAL

Heater

The heater core and blower are contained in the heater assembly which is located in

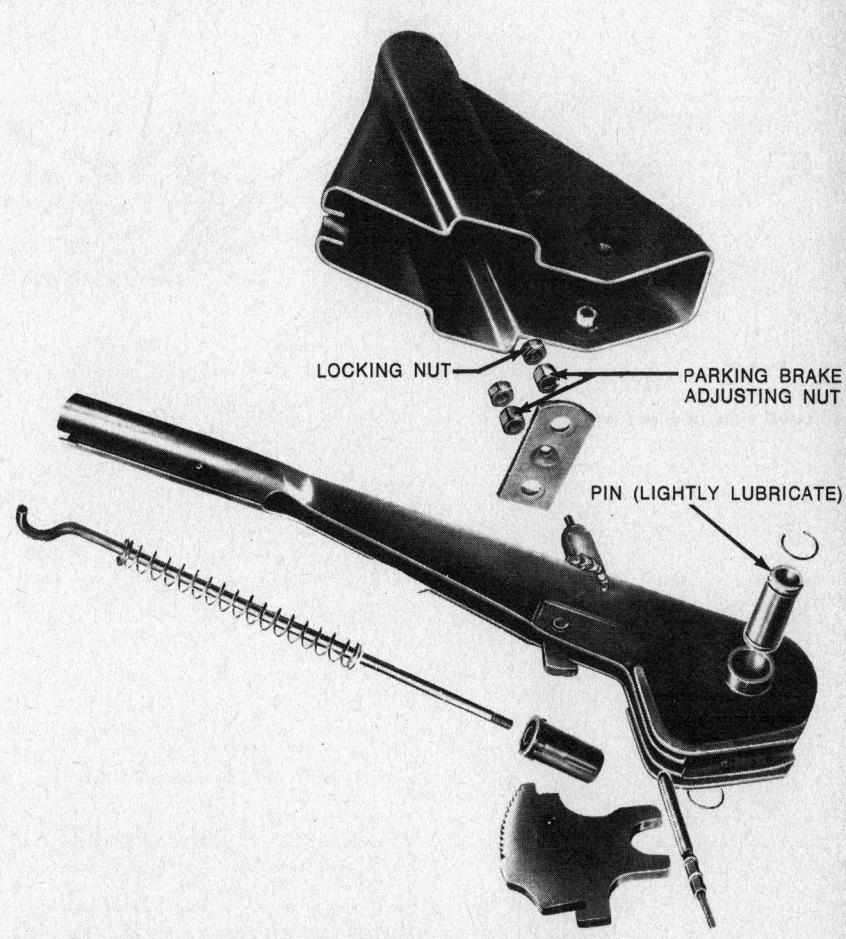

LOCKING NUT

PARKING BRAKE ADJUSTING NUT

PIN (LIGHTLY LUBRICATE)

Parking brakes: only one of the two cables is shown

VOLKSWAGEN

the passenger compartment under the center of the dash.

REMOVAL AND INSTALLATION

1. Disconnect the battery ground cable.

2. Drain the cooling system.

3. Remove the windshield washer container from its mounts. Remove the ignition coil.

4. Disconnect the two hoses from the heater core connections at the firewall.

5. Unplug the electrical connector.

6. Remove the heater control knobs on the dash.

7. Remove the two retaining screws and remove the controls from the dash complete with brackets.

8. Pull the cable connection off the electric motor.

9. Disconnect the cable from the lever on the round knob.

10. Using a screwdriver, pry the retaining clip off the fresh air housing (the front portion of the heater).

11. Remove the fresh air housing complete with the controls.

12. Detach the left and right air hoses.

13. Remove the heater-to-dash panel mounting screws and lower the heater assembly.

14. Pull out the two pins and remove the heater cover. Unscrew and remove the fan motor.

15. Separate the heater halves to remove the heater core.

16. Installation is the reverse of removal. Refill the cooling system.

Windshield Wiper Motor

REMOVAL AND INSTALLATION

When removing the wiper motor, leave the mounting frame in place. Do not remove the wiper drive crank from the motor shaft—if it must be removed for any reason, matchmark the shaft, motor, and crank for reinstallation.

1. Access is with the hood open. Disconnect the battery ground cable.

2. Detach the connecting rods from the motor crank arm.

3. Pull off the wiring plug.

4. Remove the 4 mounting bolts. You may have to energize the motor for access to the top bolt.

5. Remove the motor. Reverse the procedure for installation.

Instrument Cluster

REMOVAL AND INSTALLATION

1. Disconnect the battery ground cable.

2. Remove the fresh air controls trim plate.

3. Remove the radio or glove box.

4. Unscrew the speedometer drive cable from the back of the speedometer. Detach the electrical plug.

5. Remove the attaching screw inside the radio/glove box opening.

6. Remove the instrument cluster. Reverse the procedure for installation.

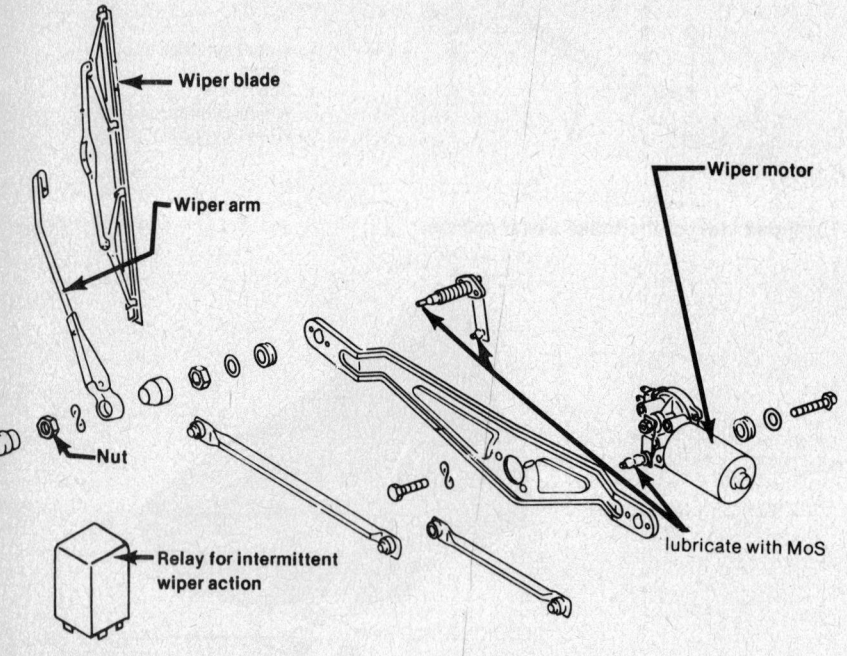

Wiper blade

Wiper arm

Nut

Relay for intermittent wiper action

Wiper motor

lubricate with MoS

Exploded view of wiper linkage

AMERICAN TRUCK UNIT REPAIR SECTION

Electrical Sections

INDEX

BEFORE SERVICING, SEE THE SAFETY NOTICE AT THE FRONT OF THE BOOK

ELECTRICAL DIAGNOSIS

To satisfy the growing trend toward organized engine diagnosis and tune-up, the following gauge and meter hook-ups, as well as diagnosis procedures are covered. The most sophisticated tune-up and diagnostic facilities are no more than a complex of the basic gauges and meters in common, everyday use. Therefore, to understand gauge and meter hook-ups, their applications and procedures, is to be equipped with the know-how to perform the most exacting diagnosis.

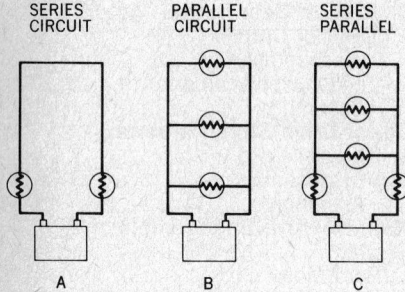

Basic electrical circuits

KNOW YOUR INSTRUMENTS

Ohmmeter

An ohmmeter is used to measure electrical resistance in a unit or circuit. The ohmmeter has a self-contained power supply. In use, it is connected across (or in parallel with) the terminals of the unit being tested.

Ammeter

An ammeter is used to measure current (amount of electricity) flowing through a unit, or circuit. Ammeters are always connected in the line (in series) with the unit or circuit being tested.

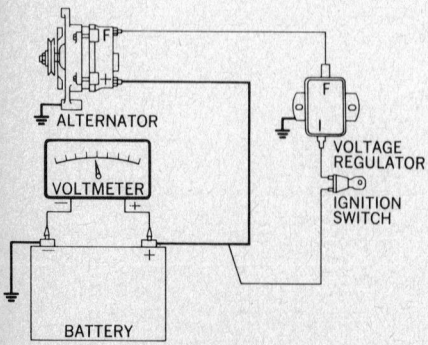

Voltmeter connected in parallel circuit

Voltmeter

A voltmeter is used to measure voltage (electrical pressure) pushing the current through a unit, or circuit. The meter is connected across the terminals of the unit being tested.

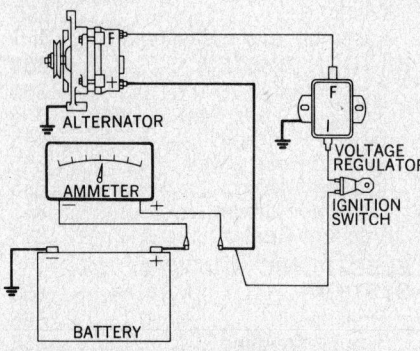

Ammeter connected to test wire

Testing the Starting Motor

TESTING THE STARTER CIRCUIT

The starter circuit should be divided and tested in four separate phases:
1. Cranking voltage check
2. Amperage draw
3. Voltage drop—grounded side
4. Voltage drop—battery side

NOTE: The battery must be in good condition for this test to have significance. To accurately check battery condition, use equipment designed to measure its capacity under a load. Instructions accompanying the equipment should be followed.

Cranking Voltage

Connect voltmeter leads to prods tapped into the battery posts (observe polarity and reverse meter leads if necessary). Remove the high tension wire from the distributor cap and ground it to prevent starting. With electronic ignition, disconnect the control box harness from the distributor. Now, turn the key. Observe both voltmeter reading and cranking speed. The cranking speed should be even, and at a satisfactory rate of speed, with a voltmeter reading of at least 9.6 volts for 12-volt systems.

Amperage Draw

The amount of current the starter motor draws is usually (but not always) associated with the mechanical problems involved in cranking the engine. (Mechanical trouble in the engine, frozen or worn starter parts, misaligned starter or starter components, etc.) Because starter motor amperage draw is directly influenced by anything restricting the free turning of the engine, or starter,

it is important that the engine and all components be at operating temperatures.

To measure starter current draw, remove the high tension wire from the center of the distributor cap and ground it. With electronic ignition, disconnect the control box harness from the distributor. A very simple and inexpensive starter current indicator is available at auto stores. This indicator is an induction type gauge and shows, without disconnecting any wires, starter current draw.

Place the yoke of the meter directly over the insulated starter supply cable (cable must be straight for a minimum of 2 in.). Close the starter switch for about 20 seconds, watch the meter dial and record the average reading. If the indicator swings in the wrong direction, reverse the position of the meter.

The cranking amperage draw can vary from 150 to 400 amperes, depending on the engine size, engine compression, and starter type.

NOTE: When starter specifications are not available, average starter draw amperage can be derived from testing a like starter unit, known to be operating satisfactorily.

More accurate but complex equipment is available from many manufacturers. This equipment consists of a combination voltmeter, ammeter, and carbon pile rheostat. When using this equipment, follow the equipment manufacturer's procedures and recommendations.

High amperage and lazy performance would suggest an excessively tight engine, friction in the starter or starter drive, grounded starter field or armature.

Normal amperage and lazy performance suggest high resistance, or possibly poor connections somewhere in the starter circuit.

Low amperage and lazy or no performance suggest battery condition poor, bad cables or connections along the line.

Voltage Drop—Grounded Side

With a voltmeter on the 3-volt scale, without disconnecting any wires, connect negative test lead of the voltmeter to a prod

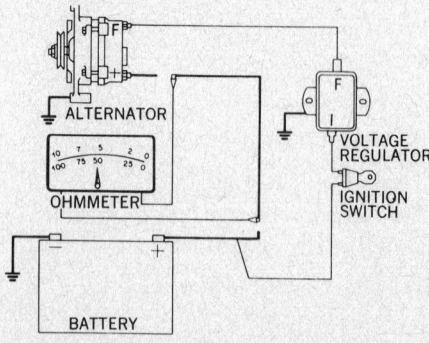

Ohmmeter connected to test wire resistance

secured in the grounded battery post. The positive test lead is connected to a cleaned, bare metal portion of the starter motor housing. Close the starter switch and note the voltmeter reading. If the reading is the same as battery reading, the ground circuit is open somewhere between the battery and the starter. In many cases the reading will be very small. The reading shown will indicate voltage drop (loss) between battery ground post and starter housing. The drop should not exceed 0.2 volt. If the voltage drop is above the specified amount, the next step is to isolate and correct the cause. It can be a bad cable or connection anywhere in the battery-to-starter ground circuit. A check of this type should progress along the various points of possible trouble, between the battery ground post and the starter motor housing, until the trouble spot has been located.

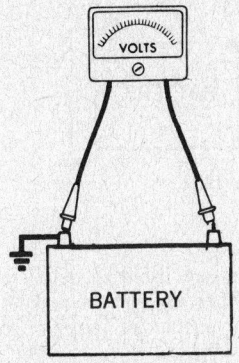

Voltmeter connected to battery for cranking voltage test

Voltage Drop—Battery Side

Bad starter cranking may result from poor connections or faulty components of the battery or hot phase of the starter motor circuit. To check this phase of the circuit, without disconnecting any wires, connect one lead of a voltmeter to a prod secured in the hot post of the battery and the other voltmeter lead to the field terminal of the starting motor. The meter should be set to the 16–20 volt scale. Before closing the starter switch, the voltmeter reading will be that of the battery. After closing the starter switch, change the selector on the voltmeter to the 3-volt scale. With a jumper wire between the relay battery terminal and the relay starter switch terminal, crank the engine. If the starting motor cranks the engine, the relay (solenoid) is operating.

While the engine is being cranked, watch the voltmeter. It should not register more than 0.5 volt. If more than this, check each part of the circuit for voltage drop to isolate the trouble, (high resistance).

Without disturbing the voltmeter-to-battery hook-up, move the free voltmeter lead to the battery terminal of the relay (solenoid), and crank the engine. The voltmeter should show no more than 0.1 volt.

If this reading is correct, move the same voltmeter lead to the starting motor terminal of the relay (solenoid). While the engine is being cranked, the voltmeter should show no more than 0.3 volt. If it does, the trouble lies in the relay.

If the reading is correct, the trouble is in the cable or connections between the relay and the starting motor.

Diagnosis

Starter Won't Crank the Engine

1. Dead battery.
2. Open starter circuit, such as:
   a. Broken or loose battery cables.
   b. Inoperative starter motor solenoid.

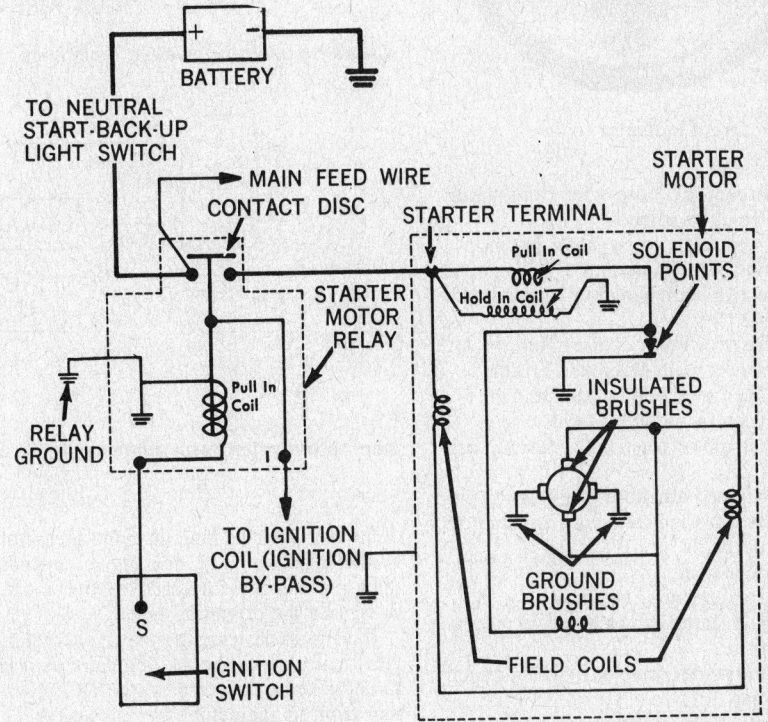

Positive engagement starter circuits

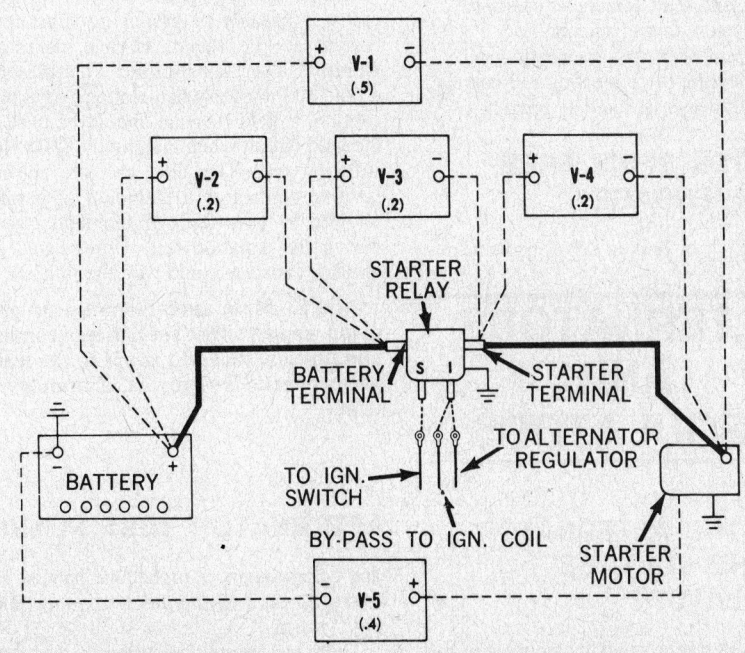

Starter cable resistance tests

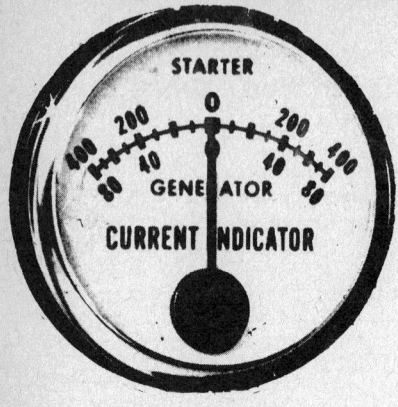

Starter current indicator

c. Broken or loose wire from starter switch to solenoid.
d. Poor solenoid or starter ground.
e. Bad starter switch.
3. Defective starter internal circuit, such as:
a. Dirty or burnt commutator.
b. Stuck, worn or broken brushes.
c. Open or shorted armature.
d. Open or grounded fields.
4. Starter motor mechanical faults, such as:
a. Jammed armature end bearings.
b. Bad bearing, allowing armature to rub fields.
c. Bent shaft.
d. Broken starter housing.
e. Bad starter worm or drive mechanism.
f. Bad starter drive or flywheel driven gear.
5. Engine hard or impossible to crank such as:
a. Hydrostatic lock, water in combustion chamber.
b. Crankshaft seizing in bearings.
c. Piston or ring seizing.
d. Bent or broken connecting rod.
e. Seizing of connecting rod bearing.
f. Flywheel jammed or broken.

STARTER SPINS FREE, WON'T ENGAGE

1. Sticking or broken drive mechanism.

ALTERNATORS AND REGULATORS

IS IT THE ALTERNATOR OR THE VOLTAGE REGULATOR?

The first step in diagnosing troubles of the charging system, is to identify the source

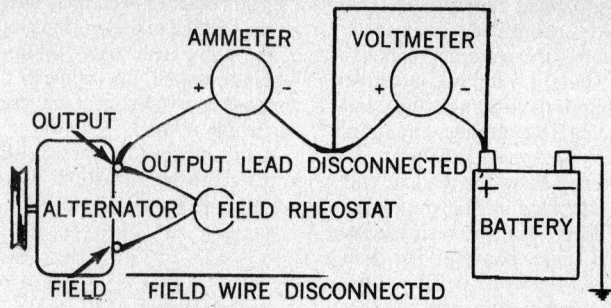

Checking charging system resistance

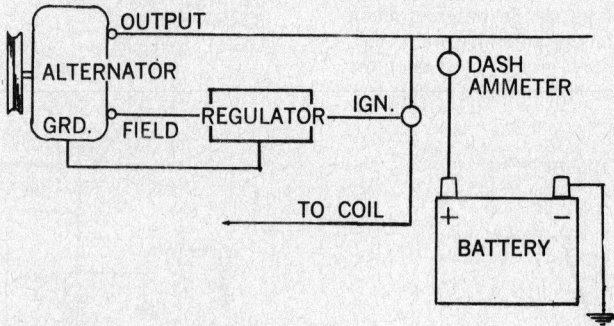

Alternator system with ammeter in the circuit

of failure. Does the fault lie in the alternator or the regulator? The next move depends upon preference or necessity; either repair or replace the offending unit.

It is just as easy to separate an alternator, electrically, from the AC regulator as it is to separate its counterpart, the DC generator from its regulator.

AC generator output is controlled by the amount of current supplied to the field circuit of the system.

Unlike the DC generator, an AC generator is capable of producing substantial current at idle speed. Higher maximum output is also a possibility. This presents a potential danger when testing. As a precaution, a field rheostat should be used in the field circuit when making the following isolation test. The field rheostat permits positive control of the amount of current allowed to pass through the field circuit during the isolation test. Unregulated alternator capacity could ruin the unit.

NOTE: Most manufacturers of precision gauges offer special test connectors, in sets, that will adapt to the leads and connections of any AC charging system.

ALTERNATOR TEST PLANS

The following is a procedure pattern for testing the various alternators and their control systems.

There are certain precautionary measures that apply to alternator tests in general.

These items are listed in detail to avoid repetition when testing each make of alternator, and to encourage a habit of good test procedure.

1. Check alternator drive belt for condition and tension.
2. Disconnect battery cables, check physical, chemical, and electrical condition of battery.
3. Be absolutely sure of polarity before connecting any battery in the circuit. Reversed polarity will ruin the diodes.
4. Never use a battery charger to start the engine.
5. Disconnect both battery cables when making a battery recharge hook-up.
6. Be sure of polarity hook-up when using a booster battery for starting.
7. Never ground the alternator output or battery terminal.
8. Never ground the field circuit between alternator and regulator.
9. Never run any alternator on an open circuit with the field energized.
10. Never try to polarize an alternator.
11. Do not attempt to motor an alternator.
12. The regulator cover must be in place when taking voltage limiter readings.
13. The ignition switch must be in off position when removing or installing the regulator cover.
14. Use insulated tools only to make adjustments to the regulator.
15. When making engine idle speed adjustments, always consider potential load factors that influence engine rpm. To compensate for electrical load, switch on the lights, radio, heater, air conditioner, etc.

Diagnosis

LOW OR NO CHARGING

1. Blown fuse.
2. Broken or loose fan belt.
3. Voltage regulator not working.
4. Brushes sticking.
5. Slip ring dirty.
6. Open circuit.
7. Bad wiring connections.
8. Bad diode rectifier.
9. High resistance in charging circuit.
10. Voltage regulator needs adjusting.
11. Grounded stator.
12. May be open rectifiers (check all three phases).
13. If rectifiers are found blown or open, check capacitor.

NOISY UNIT

1. Damaged rotor bearings.
2. Poor alignment of unit.
3. Broken or loose belt.
4. Open diode rectifiers.

REGULATOR POINTS BURNT OR STUCK

1. Regulator set too high.
2. Poor ground connections.
3. Shorted generator field.
4. Regulator air gap incorrect.

Chrysler Isolated Field Alternator (Electronic Regulator)

The Chrysler isolated field alternator derives its name from its construction. Both of the brushes are insulated from ground and there is no heat sink connection, thereby isolating the internal field.

TROUBLESHOOTING

Fusible Links

Chrysler Corporation trucks have a single fusible link which is connected between the starter relay and the junction block. Failure of this link will cause all electrical systems to stop functioning.

Charging System Operation

NOTE: If the current indicator is to give an accurate reading, the battery cables must be of the same gauge and length as the original equipment.

1. With the engine running and all electrical systems off, place a current indicator over the positive battery cable.
2. If a charge of about 5 amps is recorded, the charging system is working. If a draw of about 5 amps is recorded the

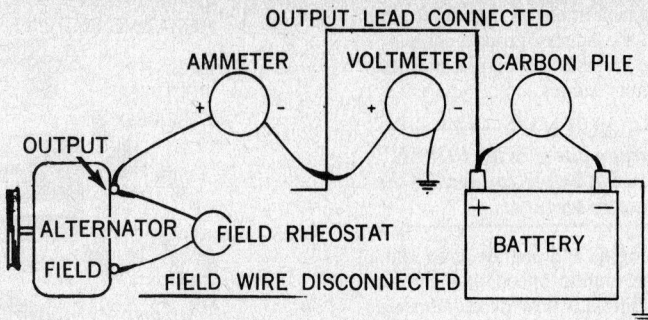

Checking current output of the charging system

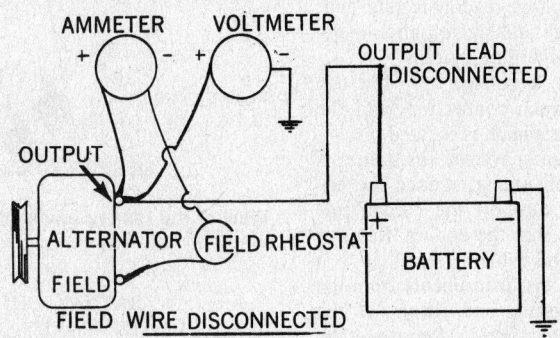

Checking field current draw

system is not working. The needle moves toward the battery when a charge condition is indicated and away from the battery when a draw condition is indicated. If a draw is indicated, proceed to the next testing procedure. If an overcharge of 10–15 amps is indicated, check for a faulty regulator.

Ignition Switch-to-Regulator Circuit Check

1. Disconnect the regulator wires at the regulator.
2. Turn the key on but do not start the engine.
3. Using a voltmeter or test light, check for voltage across the I and F terminals. If there is current present, the circuit is good. If there is no current, check for bad connections, a bad ballast resistor, a bad ammeter, broken wires, or bad ground at the alternator or voltage regulator. Also, check for voltage from the I wire to ground; current should be present. Check for voltage from the F terminal to ground; current should not be present.

Isolation Test

This test determines whether the regulator or alternator is bad if everything else in the circuit was OK.

1. Disconnect, at the alternator, the wire that runs between one of the alternator field connections and the voltage regulator.
2. Run a jumper wire from the disconnected alternator terminal to ground.

3. Connect a voltmeter to the battery. The positive voltmeter lead connects to the positive battery terminal, and the negative lead goes to the negative terminal. Record the reading.
4. Make sure that all electrical systems are turned off. Start the engine. Do not race the engine.
5. Gradually raise engine speed to 1500–2000 rpm. There should be an increase of one to two volts on the voltmeter. If this is true, the alternator is good and the voltage regulator should be repaired. If there is no voltage increase, the alternator is faulty.

Charging Circuit Resistance Test

The purpose of this test is to determine the amount of "voltage drop" between the alternator output terminal wire and the battery.

1. Disconnect the battery ground cable and the "BAT" lead at the alternator output terminal.
2. Connect an ammeter with a scale to 100 amps in series between the alternator "BAT" terminal and the disconnected "BAT" wire.
3. Connect the positive lead of a voltmeter to the disconnected "BAT" wire. Connect the negative lead of the voltmeter to the negative post of the battery.
4. Disconnect the green colored regulator field wire from the alternator. Connect a jumper lead from the alternator field terminal to ground.

5. Connect a tachometer to the engine and reconnect the battery ground cable.
6. Connect a variable carbon pile rheostat to the battery cables.

——— CAUTION ———

Be sure the carbon pile is in the "OPEN" or "OFF" position before connecting the leads to the battery terminals.

7. Start the engine and operate at an idle.
8. Adjust the engine speed and carbon pile to maintain a flow of 20 amperes in the circuit. Observe the voltmeter reading which should not exceed .7 volts.
9. If a higher voltage reading is indicated, inspect, clean and tighten all connections in the charging system.
10. If necessary, a voltage drop test can be done at each connection until the excessive resistance is located.
11. If the charging system resistance is within specifications, reduce the engine speed, turn off the carbon pile rheostat and stop the engine. Remove battery ground cable.
12. Remove the test instruments from the electrical system and reconnect the charging system wiring. Reconnect the battery ground cable.

Current Output Test

This test determines if the alternator is capable of delivering its rated current output.
1. Disconnect the battery ground cable and the "BAT" lead wire at the alternator output terminal.
2. Connect an ammeter in series between the alternator output terminal and the disconnected "BAT" lead wire.

NOTE: The ammeter must have a scale of 100 amps.

3. Connect the positive lead of a voltmeter to the output terminal of the alternator and the negative lead to a good ground.
4. Disconnect the green colored wire at the voltage regulator and connect a jumper wire from the alternator field terminal to ground.
5. Connect a tachometer to the engine and reconnect the battery ground wire.
6. Connect a variable carbon pile rheostat between the positive and negative battery cables.

——— CAUTION ———

Be sure the rheostat control is in the "OPEN" or "OFF" position before connecting the leads to the battery cables.

7. Start the engine and operate at idle. Adjust the carbon pile rheostat control and the engine speed in increments until the voltmeter reading is 15 volts (13 volts for the 100 and 117 amp alternators) and the engine speed is 1250 rpm (900 rpm for the 100 and 117 amp Chryslers).

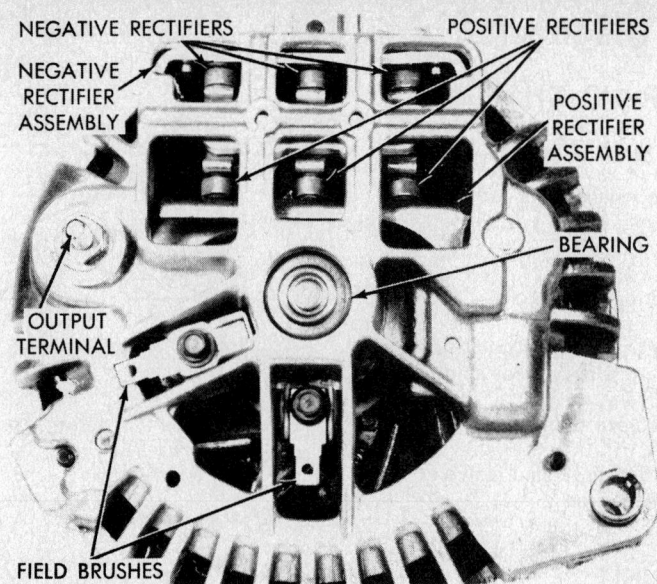

View of the rear housing of the 100 amp Chrysler alternator

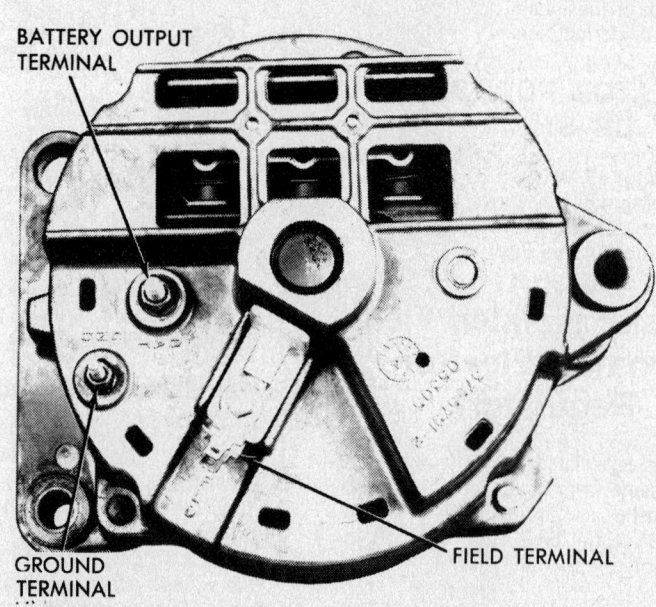

View of the rear housing on all but 100 amp Chrysler alternator

——— CAUTION ———

Do not allow the voltage to rise above 16 volts.

8. The ammeter readings must be within the following specifications.

Current Rating	Identification	Current Output
41 amp	Red or violet tag	40 amps min.
60 amp	Blue, natural or yellow	57 amps min.
100, 117 amp	Yellow	72 amps min.

NOTE: If measured at the battery, current output will be approximately 5 amperes lower than specified.

9. If the readings are less than specified, the alternator should be removed and checked during a bench test.
10. After the current output test is completed, reduce the engine speed, turn the carbon pile rheostat off and then stop the engine.
11. Disconnect the battery ground cable, remove the ammeter, voltmeter and carbon pile. Remove the jumper wire from the field terminal and reconnect the green colored wire to the alternator field terminal.

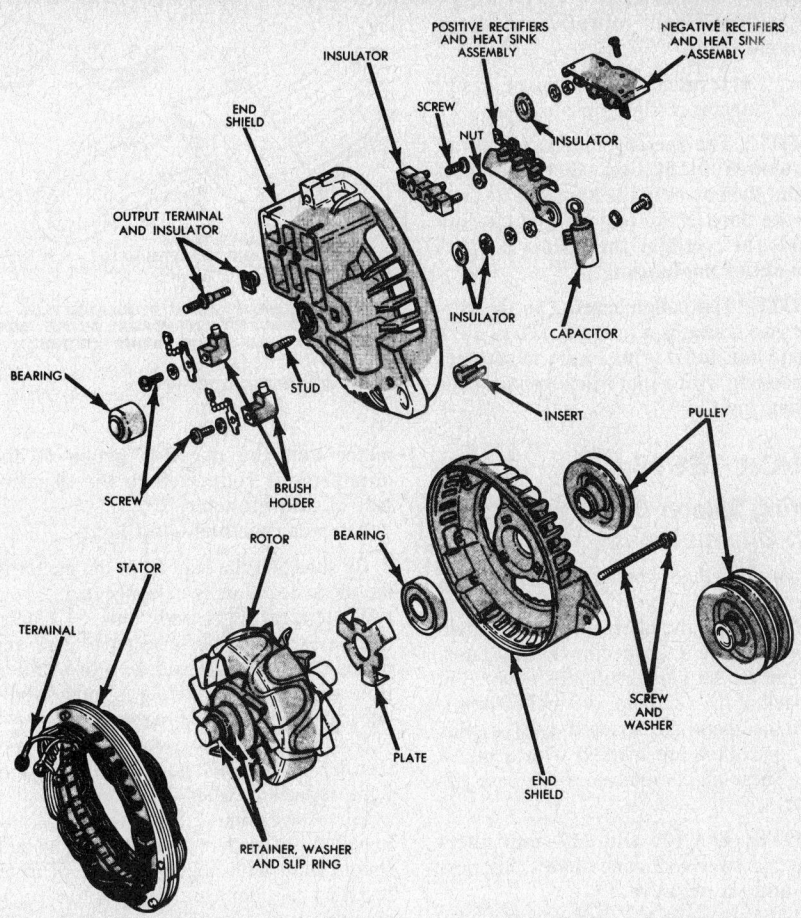

Typical Chrysler alternator

meter to ignition Terminal No. 1 of the ballast resistor.

3. Connect the negative voltmeter lead to a good *body* ground.
4. Start engine and allow it to idle at 1250 rpm, all lights and accessories turned off. Voltage should be as follows:

Ambient Temp. ¼ in. from Regulator	Voltage
20°F.	14.9 to 15.9
80°F.	13.9 to 14.6
140°F.	13.3 to 13.9
Above 140°F.	Less Than 13.6

5. If the voltage is *below* specifications, check the following:
   a. Voltage regulator ground—check voltage drop between regulator cover and ground.
   b. Harness wiring—disconnect regulator plug (ign. switch off), then turn on ign. switch and check for battery voltage at the terminals having the red and green leads. *Wiring harness must be disconnected from the regulator when checking individual leads*. If no voltage is present in either lead, the problem is in the truck wiring or alternator field.
6. If Step 5 tests showed no malfunctions, install a new regulator and repeat Step 4.
7. If voltage is *above* specifications (Step 4), or fluctuates, check the following:
   a. Ground between regulator and body, and between body and engine.
   b. Ignition switch circuit between switch and regulator.
8. If voltage is still more than ½ volt above specifications, install a new regulator and repeat Step 4.

12. Reconnect the battery cable, if no further testing is to be done to the charging circuit.

Rotor Field Coil Draw Test

The rotor field coil can be tested on or off the vehicle.
1. If on the vehicle, remove the drive belt and wiring connections from the alternator.
2. Connect a jumper wire from the negative terminal of the battery to one of the field terminals of the alternator.
3. Connect the test ammeter positive lead to the other field terminal of the alternator and the negative ammeter lead to the positive battery terminal.
4. Connect a jumper wire between the alternator end shield and the battery negative terminal.
5. Slowly rotate the alternator pulley by hand and observe the ammeter reading.
6. The field coil draw should be 4.5 to 6.5 amperes at 12 volts. (4.75 to 6.0 amperes at 12 volts—100 and 117 amp alternators).
7. A low rotor coil draw is an indication of high resistance in the field coil circuit (brushes, slip rings or rotor coil). A higher rotor coil draw indicates possible shorted rotor coil or grounded

rotor. No reading indicates an open rotor or defective brushes.
8. Remove the test equipment and jumper leads.

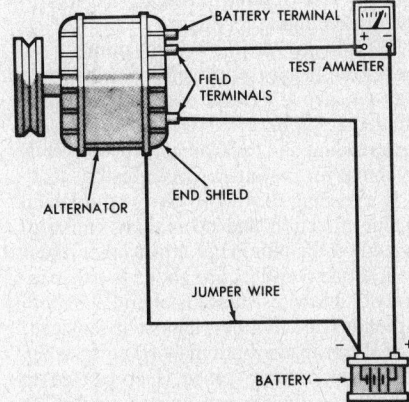

Rotor field coil current draw test

Electronic Voltage Regulator Test

1. Make sure battery terminals are clean and battery is charged.
2. Connect the positive lead of a test volt-

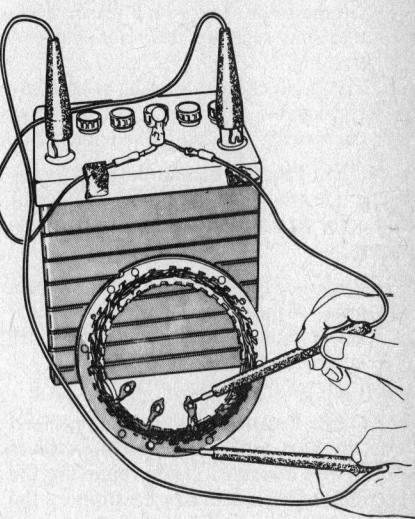

Stator test for ground on Chrysler systems

835

Chrysler Overhaul and Internal Testing

Alternator disassembly, repair and assembly procedures are basically the same for all Chrysler alternators. Certain variations in design, or production modifications, could require slightly different procedures that should be obvious upon inspection of the unit being serviced.

Disassembly

To prevent damage to the brush assemblies (100 and 117 amp), they should be removed before proceeding with the disassembly of the alternator. The brushes are mounted in a plastic holder that positions the brushes vertically against the slip rings.

1. Remove the retaining screw, flat washer, nylon washer and field terminal and carefully lift the plastic holder containing the spring and brush assembly from the end housing.
2. The ground brush (40 and 60 amp) is positioned horizontally against the slip ring and is retained in the holder that is integral with the end housing. Remove the retaining screw and lift the clip, spring and brush assembly from the end housing.

----- CAUTION -----

The stator is laminated, don't burr the stator or end housings.

3. Remove the through bolts and pry between the stator and drive end housing with a thin blade screwdriver. Carefully separate the drive end housing, pulley and rotor assembly from the stator and rectifier housing assembly.
4. The pulley is an interference fit on the rotor shaft. Remove with a puller and special adapters.
5. Remove the three nuts and washers and, while supporting the end frame, tap the rotor shaft with a plastic hammer and separate the rotor and end housing.
6. The drive end ball bearing is an interference fit with the rotor shaft. Remove the bearing with puller and adapters.

NOTE: Further dismantling of the rotor is not advisable, as the remainder of the rotor assembly is not serviced separately.

7. Remove the DC output terminal nuts and washers and remove terminal screw and inside capacitor (on units so equipped).
8. Remove the insulator.

NOTE: Positive rectifiers are pressed into the heat sink and negative rectifiers in the end housing. When removing the rectifiers, it is necessary to support the end housing and/or heat sink to prevent damage to these castings. Another caution is in order relative to the diode rectifiers. Don't subject them to unneces-

sary jolting. Heavy vibration or shock may ruin them.

a. Cut rectifier wire at point of crimp.
b. Support rectifier housing.

NOTE: The factory tool is cut away and slotted to fit over the wires and around the bosses in the housing. Be sure that the bore of the tool completely surrounds the rectifier, then press the rectifier out of the housing.

NOTE: The roller bearing in the rectifier end frame is a press fit. To protect the end housing it is necessary to support the housing with a tool when pressing out the bearing.

BENCH TESTS

Testing Silicon Diode Rectifiers With Ohmmeter

Preferred method—rectifiers open in all three phases.

Disassemble the alternator and separate the wires at the Y-connection of the stator.

There are six diode rectifiers mounted in the back of the alternator (40 and 60 amp). Three of them are marked with a plus (+), and three are marked with a minus (−). These marks indicate diode case polarity.

NOTE: The 100 and 117 amp alternator has twelve silicone diodes. Six positive and six negative.

To test, set ohmmeter to its lowest range. If case is marked positive (+), place positive meter probe to case and negative probe to the diode lead. Meter should read between 4 and 10 ohms. Now, reverse leads of ohmmeter, connecting negative meter probe to positive case and positive meter probe to wire of rectifier. Set meter on a high range. Meter needle should move very little, if any (infinite reading). Do this to all positive diode rectifiers.

The diode rectifiers with minus (−) marks on their cases are checked the same way as above. Only now the negative ohmmeter probe is connected to the case for a reading of 4 to 10 ohms. Reverse leads as above for the other part to test.

If a reading of 4 to 10 ohms is obtained in one direction and no reading (infinity) is read on the ohmmeter in the other direction, diode rectifiers are good. If either infinity or a low resistance is obtained in both directions on a rectifier, it must be replaced.

If meter reads more than 10 ohms when ohmmeter positive probe is connected to positive on diode, and negative probe to negative, replace diode rectifier.

NOTE: With this test, it is necessary to determine the polarity of the ohmmeter probes. This can be done by connecting the ohmmeter to a DC voltmeter. The voltmeter will read up-scale when the positive probe of the ohmmeter is connected to the positive side of the volt-

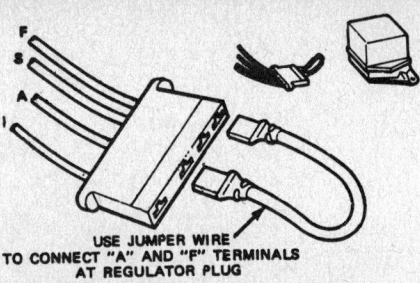

USE JUMPER WIRE
TO CONNECT "A" AND "F" TERMINALS
AT REGULATOR PLUG

USE OF JUMPER WIRE AT REGULATOR PLUG
TO TEST ALTERNATOR FOR NORMAL OUTPUT AMPS
AND FOR FIELD CIRCUIT WIRING CONTINUITY

Isolation test jumper wire

meter and the negative probe of the ohmmeter is connected to the negative side of the voltmeter.

Alternate method—test light.

Be sure that the lead from the center of the diode rectifiers is disconnected.

To test rectifiers with plus (+) case, touch positive probe of tester to case and minus (−) probe to lead wire of rectifier. Bulb should light if rectifier is good. If bulb does not light, replace rectifier.

Now reverse tester probe connections to rectifier. Bulb should not light. If bulb does light, replace rectifier.

For testing minus (−) marked cases, follow above procedure, except that now bulb should light with negative probe of tester touching rectifier case and positive probe touching lead wire.

Rectifier is good if the bulb lights when tester probes are connected one way, and does not light when tester connections are reversed.

Rectifier must be replaced if the bulb does not light either way. Also, replace rectifier if bulb lights both ways.

NOTE: The usual cause of an open or blown diode or rectifier is a defective capacitor or a battery that has been installed in reverse polarity. If the battery is installed properly and the diodes are open, test the capacitor.

Capacitor capacities:
Int. installed ..... 158 microfarad. min.
Ext. installed .... 5 microfarad. min.

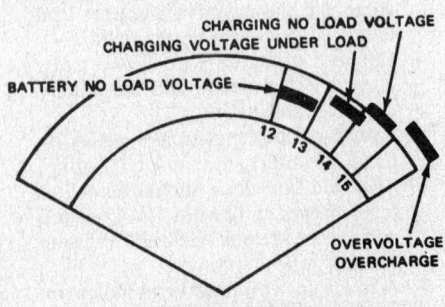

CHARGING NO LOAD VOLTAGE
CHARGING VOLTAGE UNDER LOAD
BATTERY NO LOAD VOLTAGE
12 13 14 15
OVERVOLTAGE
OVERCHARGE

VOLTMETER TEST
TYPICAL VOLTAGE BANDS SHOWN

Voltmeter reading during isolation test

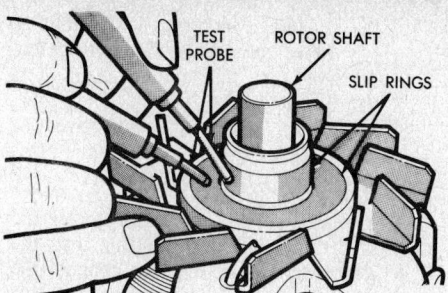

Rotor tests for short or open circuits on Chrysler systems

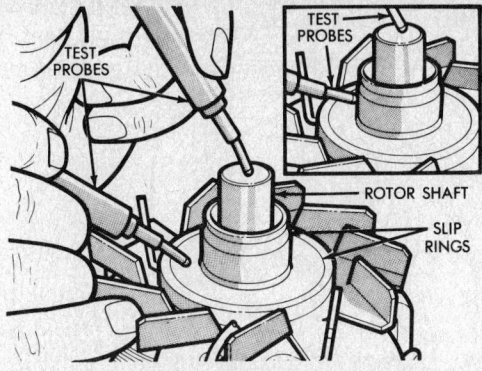

Rotor tests for ground on Chrysler systems

ALTERNATOR BENCH TESTS

FIELD COIL DRAW

1. Connect a jumper between one FLD terminal and the positive terminal of a fully charged 12 volt battery.
2. Connect the positive lead of a test ammeter to the other field (FLD) terminal and the negative test lead to the negative battery terminal.
3. Slowly rotate the rotor by hand and observe the ammeter. The proper field coil draw is 2.3–2.7 amps at 12 volts.

NOTE: Field coil draw for the 100 and 117 ampere alternators should be 4.75 amperes to 6.0 amperes at 12 volts.

Field Circuit Ground Test

1. Touch one test lead of a 110 volt AC test bulb to one of the alternator brush (field) terminals and the other test lead to the end shield.
2. If the lamp lights, remove the field brush assemblies and separate the end housing by removing the three through-bolts.
3. Place one test lead on a slip ring and the other on the end shield.
4. If the lamp lights, the rotor assembly is grounded internally and must be replaced.
5. If the lamp does not light, the cause of the problem was a grounded brush.

Grounded Stator

1. Disconnect the diode rectifiers from the stator leads.
2. Test from stator leads to stator core, using a 110-volt test lamp. Test lamp should not light. If it does, stator is grounded and must be replaced.

Low Output

(About 50% output accompanied with a growl-hum caused by a shorted phase or a shorted rectifier.)

Perform steps 1, 2 and 3 (rectifier open in all three phases). If the rectifiers are found to be within specifications, replace the stator assembly.

Current Output Too High (No Control) Caused by Open Rectifier or Open Phase

Perform steps 1, 2 and 3 (rectifier open in all three phases). If the rectifier tests satisfactorily, inspect the stator connections before replacing the stator.

Assembly

1. Support the heat sink or rectifier end housing on circular plate.
2. Check rectifier identification to be sure the correct rectifier is being used. The part numbers are stamped on the case of the rectifier. They are also marked, red for positive and black for negative.
3. Start the new rectifier into the casting and press it in squarely.

--- CAUTION ---

Do not start rectifier with a hammer or it will be ruined.

4. Crimp the new rectifier wire to the wires disconnected at removal, or solder (using a heat sink with rosin core solder).
5. Support the end housing on tool so that the notch in the support tool will clear the raised section of the heat sink, then press the bearing into position with tool SP-3381, or equivalent.

NOTE: New bearings are pre-lubricated, additional lubrication is not required.

6. Insert the drive end bearing in the drive end housing and install the bearing plate, washers and nuts to hold the bearing in place.
7. Position the bearing and drive end housing on the rotor shaft and, while supporting the base of the rotor shaft, press the bearing and housing in position on the rotor shaft with an arbor press and arbor tool.

--- CAUTION ---

Be careful that there is no cocking of the bearing at installation; or damage will result. Press the bearing on the rotor shaft until the bearing contacts the shoulder on the rotor shaft.

8. Install pulley on rotor shaft. Shaft of rotor must be supported so that all pressing force is on the pulley hub and rotor shaft.

NOTE: Do not exceed 6,800 lbs. pressure. Pulley hub should just contact bearing inner race.

9. Some alternators will be found to have the capacitor mounted internally. Be sure the heat sink insulator is in place.
10. Install the output terminal screw with the capacitor attached through the heat sink and end housing.
11. Install insulating washers, lockwashers and locknuts.
12. Make sure the heat sink and insulator are in place and tighten the locknut.
13. Position the stator on the rectifier end housing. Be sure that all of the rectifier connectors and phase leads are free of interference with the rotor fan blades and that the capacitor (internally mounted) lead has clearance.
14. Position the rotor assembly in the rectifier end housing. Align the through bolt holes in the stator with both end housings.
15. Enter stator shaft in the rectifier end housing bearing, compress stator and both end housings manually and install through-bolts, washers and nuts.
16. Install the insulated brush and terminal attaching screw.
17. Install the ground screw and attaching screw.
18. Rotate pulley slowly to be sure the rotor fan blades do not hit the rectifier and stator connectors.

Delcotron 10-SI, 15-SI and 27-SI, Type 100 (General Motors Corp.)

NOTE: The internal alternator wiring is identical between the 10-SI, 15-SI and the 27-SI units, except the 10-SI uses a Wye stator winding while a Delta stator winding is used in the 15-SI and 27-SI alternators. The disassembly and assembly of the units remain basically the same.

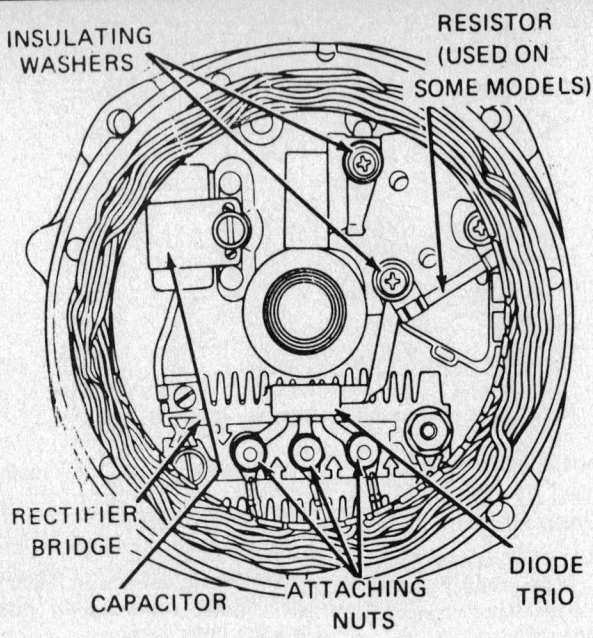

INSULATING WASHERS

RESISTOR (USED ON SOME MODELS)

RECTIFIER BRIDGE

CAPACITOR

ATTACHING NUTS

DIODE TRIO

Delcotron end-frame view

Delcotron 10-SI and 15-SI

This system is an integrated AC generating system containing a built-in voltage regulator. Removal and replacement is essentially the same as for the standard AC generator.

The regulator is mounted inside the slip ring end frame. All regulator components are enclosed in an epoxy molding, and the regulator cannot be adjusted.

Troubleshooting

NOTE: See the "Alternator Test Plans" section before proceeding further. Make sure that the continuous running blower, if equipped, is disconnected. This blower will run with the key on even if the blower control is off, unless disconnected.

CHARGING SYSTEM TEST

Low Charging Rate

1. After battery condition, drive belt tension, and wiring terminals and connections have been checked, charge the battery fully and perform the following test:
2. Connect a test voltmeter between the alternator BAT. terminal and ground, ignition switch on. Connect the voltmeter in turn to alternator terminals No. 1 and No. 2, the other voltmeter lead being grounded as before. A zero reading indicates an open circuit between the battery and each connection at the alternator. If this test discloses no faults in the wiring, proceed to Step 3.

3. Connect the test voltmeter to the alternator BAT. terminal (the other test lead to ground), start the engine and run at 1,500–2,000 rpm with all lights and electrical accessories turned on. If the voltmeter reads 12.8 volts or greater, the alternator is good and no further checks need be made. If the voltmeter reads less than 12.8 volts, ground the field winding by inserting a screwdriver into the test hole in the end frame.

—————— CAUTION ——————
Do not force tab more than 3/4 in. into end frame.

a. If voltage increases to 13 volts or more, the regulator unit is defective.
b. If voltage does not increase significantly, alternator is defective.

Alternator Output Test

1. Connect a test voltmeter, ammeter and a 10 ohm, 6 watt resistor into the charging circuit. Do not connect the carbon pile to the battery posts at this time.
2. Increase alternator speed and observe voltmeter—if voltage is uncontrolled with speed and increases to 15.5 volts or more, check for a grounded brush lead clip as covered previously. If brush lead clip is not grounded, the voltage regulator is faulty and must be replaced.
3. Connect the carbon pile load to the battery terminals.
4. Operate the alternator at moderate speed and adjust the carbon pile to obtain maximum alternator output as indicated on the ammeter. If output is within 10 amperes of rated output as stamped on the alternator frame, alternator is O.K. If output is not within specifications, ground the alternator field by inserting a screwdriver into the test hole in the end frame. If output now is within 10 amperes of rating, replace the voltage regulator; if still not within specifications, check field winding, diode trio, rectifier bridge and stator, as described later.

Disassembly and Assembly

1. Hold generator in a vice, clamping the mounting flange lengthwise.
2. Make a scribe mark to help locate frame end parts in the same position during assembly.

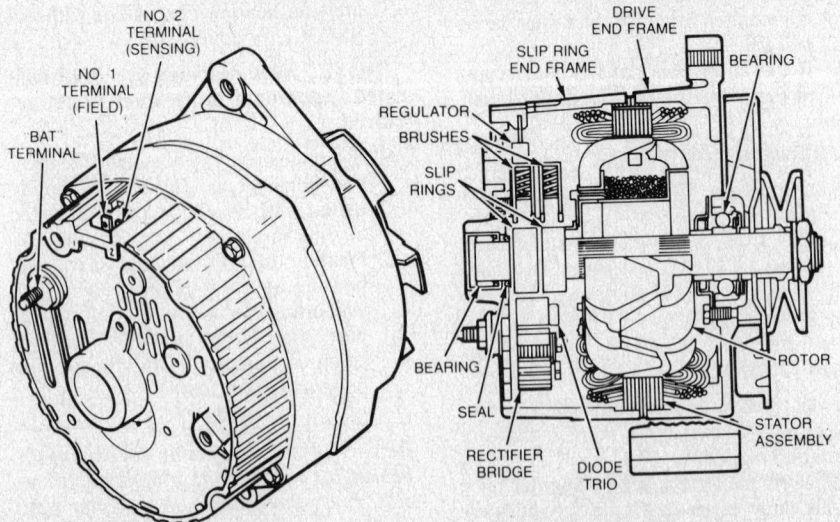

NO. 2 TERMINAL (SENSING)

NO. 1 TERMINAL (FIELD)

BAT TERMINAL

DRIVE END FRAME

SLIP RING END FRAME

BEARING

REGULATOR

BRUSHES

SLIP RINGS

BEARING

SEAL

RECTIFIER BRIDGE

DIODE TRIO

ROTOR

STATOR ASSEMBLY

10-SI Delcotron

3. Remove 4 through-bolts and separate the slip ring end frame from the drive end frame and rotor assembly.

NOTE: Prying with a screwdriver at stator slot will aid disassembly.

4. Remove 3 stator lead attaching nuts and separate stator from end frame.
5. Remove insulated screws and ground screw from brush holder.
   Remove diode trio, resistor, brush holder, and regulator from end frame.
6. Remove screws attaching capacitor to end frame and diode bridge; remove capacitor.
7. **10-SI Series**
   Remove ground screw and battery terminal stud nut from rectifier bridge. Remove rectifier bridge, terminal stud, and insulating washer from end frame.
   27-SI Series
   Remove 2 ground screws, a connector strap screw, and the battery terminal stud nut. Remove rectifier bridge, connector, terminal stud, and insulating washers from end frame.
8. Press bearing from end frame using a tube slightly smaller OD than the bearing. Support the end frame from inside and press bearing from outside toward the inside.

NOTE: Some models may have a seal separate and in front of bearing. Discard the seal when replacing the bearing as the new bearing has an integral seal.

9. Separate drive end frame from rotor as follows:
   a. Place rotor in a vise and tighten only enough to permit pulley nut removal.

NOTE: Rotor may be distorted if vise is over tightened.

b. Remove pulley nut, washer, pulley, fan, and collar from rotor shaft.
c. Remove drive end frame from rotor shaft and remove rotor from vise.
10. Press bearing from drive end frame after removing bearing retainer plate:
   a. Remove screws attaching bearing seal and retainer assembly to housing.
   b. Support end frame from inside the housing on a metal tube with a slightly larger ID than the OD of the bearing.
   c. Press bearing and grease slinger (or flat washer used on some models) from end frame using a metal tube or collar against the grease slinger.
11. To assemble, reverse the order of the disassembly procedure. Torque the pulley nut to 50 ft. lbs.

CAUTION

During the assembly, do not interchange the ground screw (without insulator) for an insulated screw as this would cause uncontrolled or no alternator output.

Cleaning and Inspection

1. Clean all metal parts, except stator and rotor assemblies, in solvent.
2. Wipe off bearings and inspect them for pitting or roughness.
3. Inspect rotor slip-rings for scoring. They may be cleaned with 400 grit sandpaper (not emery), rotating the rotor to make the rings concentric. Maximum out-of-true is 0.001 in. If slip-rings are deeply scored, the entire rotor must be replaced as a unit.
4. Inspect brushes for wear; minimum length is ¼ in.

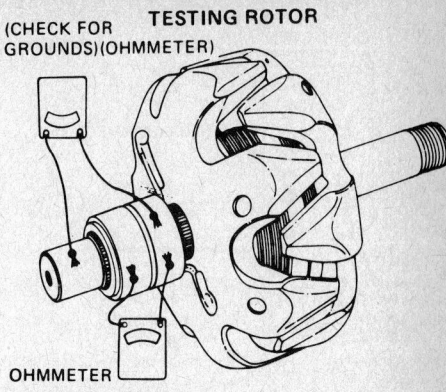

Checking Delcotron rotor for grounds or open circuits

CHARGING SYSTEM TEST

High Charging Rate

1. With the battery fully charged, connect a voltmeter between alternator terminal no. 2 and ground. If the reading is zero, no. 2 circuit from the battery is open.
2. If no. 2 circuit is OK, but an obvious overcharging condition still exists, proceed as follows:
   a. Remove the alternator and separate the end frames.
   b. Connect a low-range ohmmeter between the brush lead clip and the end frame, as illustrated (test no. 1), then reverse the lead connections. If both readings are zero, either the brush lead clip is grounded or the regulator is defective. A grounded brush lead clip can be due to a damaged insulating sleeve or omission of the insulating washer.

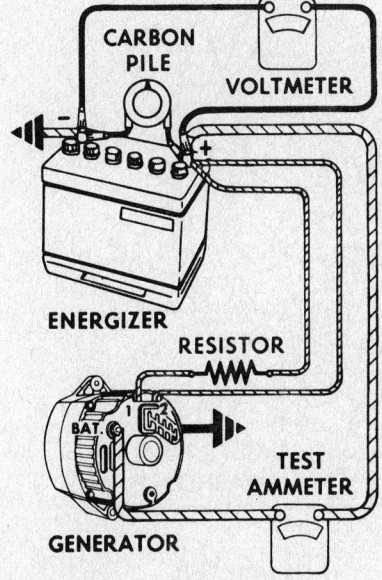

10-SI output test

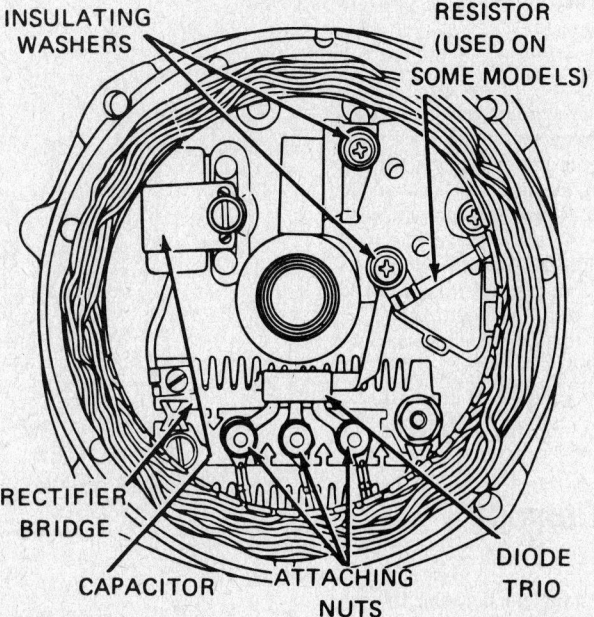

END FRAME VIEW

10-SI brush lead clip ground test

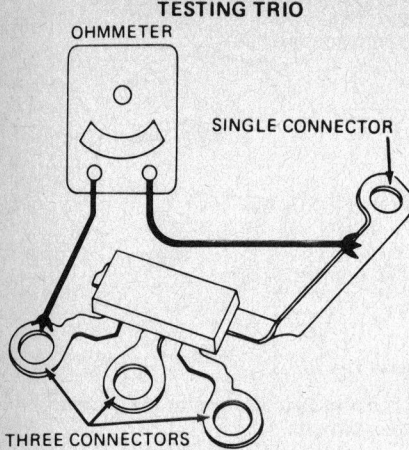

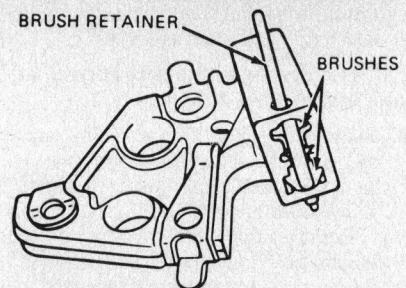

TESTING TRIO

OHMMETER

SINGLE CONNECTOR

THREE CONNECTORS

Testing the 10-SI diode trio

DIODE TRIP

Initial Testing

1. Before removing this unit, connect an ohmmeter between the brush lead clip and the end frame. The lowest reading scale should be used for this test.
2. After taking a reading, reverse the lead connections. If the meter reads zero, the brush lead clip is probably grounded, due to omission of the insulating sleeve or insulating washer.

Removal

1. Remove the three nuts which secure the stator.
2. Remove stator.
3. Remove the screw which secures the diode trio lead clip, then remove diode trio.

   NOTE: The position of the insulating washer on the screw is critical; make sure it is returned to the same position on reassembly.

Testing

1. Connect an ohmmeter, on lowest range, between the single brush connector and one stator lead connector.
2. Observe the reading, then reverse the meter leads. Repeat this test with each of the other two stator lead connectors. The readings on each of these tests should NOT be identical, there should be one low and one high reading for each test. If this is not the case, replace the diode trio.

─── **CAUTION** ───
Do not use high voltage on the diode trio.

RECTIFIER BRIDGE

Testing

1. Connect an ohmmeter between the heat sink (ground) and the base of one of the three terminals. Then, reverse the

meter leads and take a reading. If both readings are identical, the bridge is defective and must be replaced.
2. Repeat this test with the remaining two terminals, then between the INSULATED heat sink (as opposed to the GROUNDED heat sink in previous test) and each of the three terminals. As before, if any two readings are identical, on reversing the meter leads, the rectifier bridge must be replaced.

Removal

1. Remove the attaching screw and the BAT. terminal screw.
2. Disconnect the condenser lead.
3. Remove the rectifier bridge.

   NOTE: The insulator between the insulated heat sink and the end frame is extremely important to the operation of the unit. It must be replaced in exactly the same position on reassembly.

BRUSH AND/OR VOLTAGE REGULATOR R & R

1. Remove two brush holder screws and stator lead to strap nut and washer, brush holder screws and one of the diode trio lead strap attaching screws.

   NOTE: The insulating washers must be replaced in the same position on reassembly.

2. Remove brush holder and brushes. The voltage regulator may also be removed at this time, if desired.
3. Brushes and brush spring must be free

BRUSHES RETAINED IN HOLDER

BRUSH RETAINER

BRUSHES

10-SI brush holder

of corrosion and must be undamaged and completely free of oil or grease.
4. Insert spring and brushes into holder, noting whether they slide freely without binding. Insert wooden or plastic toothpick into bottom hole in holder to retain brushes.

   NOTE: The brush holder is serviced as a unit; individual parts are not available.

5. Reassemble in reverse order of disassembly.

Delcotron 27-SI Series, Type 200

The 27-SI Series, type 200 alternator features a solid state voltage regulator that is mounted inside the slip ring end frame. The regulated voltage can be adjusted externally by repositioning a voltage adjustment cap,

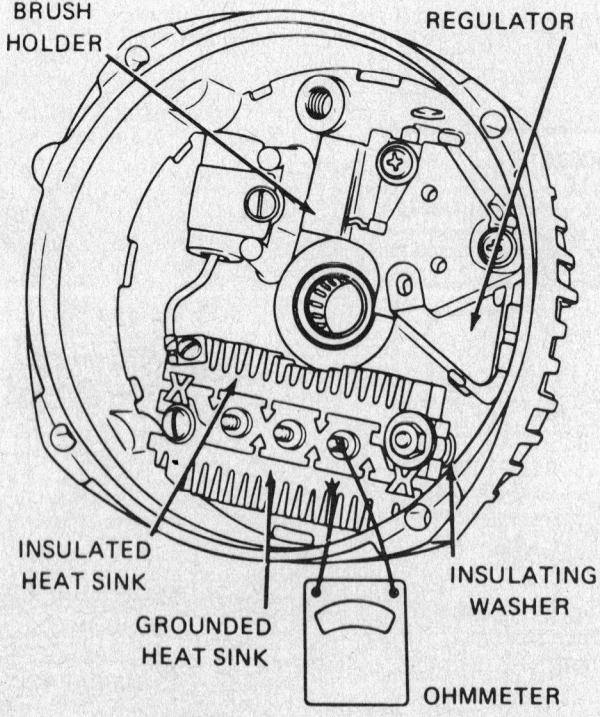

BRUSH HOLDER

REGULATOR

INSULATED HEAT SINK

GROUNDED HEAT SINK

INSULATING WASHER

OHMMETER

Testing the 10-SI rectifier bridge

located on the slip ring end frame. Two brushes carry current through the two slip rings to the field coil, mounted on the rotor. The stator windings are assembled on the inside of a laminated core that forms part of the frame. A rectifier bridge connected to the stator windings contains six diodes, their main function is to change the stator A.C. current to a D.C. current which is present at the output terminal. Field current is supplied through residual magnetism and a diode trio, which is also connected to the stator windings. A capacitor (or condensor) is mounted in the end frame to protect the rectifier bridge and diode trio from high voltages and also suppresses radio noise. An "R" terminal is provided to operate auxiliary equipment in some circuits.

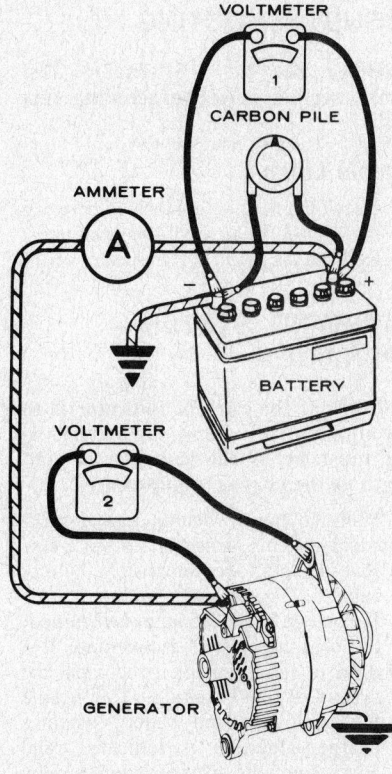

Alternator bench test connections

Alternator Output Test

To test the output of the alternator in a bench test stand, have a fully charged battery and connect an ammeter between the battery positive post (on negative grounded units) and the battery terminal of the alternator. Connect a voltmeter to the positive and negative posts of the battery. Ground the battery negative post to the alternator frame or to a common ground.

—— IMPORTANT ——
Rotor magnetism must be present in this alternator to perform properly. If the alternator has been disassembled for service, it may be necessary to induce magnetism back into the rotor to provide

voltage build-up when the engine is started. To magnetize the rotor, connect the Integral Charging System to the battery in a normal manner, then momentarily connect a jumper lead from the battery positive post to the Integral Charging System relay terminal. This procedure will restore normal residual magnetism in the rotor.

After making the required meter connections between the alternator and the battery on the test stand, proceed as follows:
1. Slowly increase the alternator speed and observe the voltage.
2. If the voltage is uncontrolled with speed and increases over 15.5 volts on a 12 volt system, test the regulator.

   NOTE: The regulator can be tested on a commercial tester. If a tester is not available, replace the voltage regulator.
3. If the voltage is below 15.5 volts on a 12 volt system, connect a carbon pile rheostat to the battery.
4. Operate the alternator at a moderate speed and adjust the rheostat as required to obtain the maximum current output.
5. If the output is within 10 amperes of the rated output as stamped on the alternator frame, the alternator is good.
6. If the output is not within 10 amperes of the rated output, keep the battery loaded with the carbon pile and ground the tab in the end frame hole.

—— CAUTION ——
The tab is within ¾ inch of the casting surface. Do not force the probe tool deeper than one inch into the end frame.

7. Operate the alternator at moderate speed and adjust the carbon pile rheostat as required to obtain maximum output, with the tab pushed in to ground.
8. If the output is within 10 amperes of the rated output, check field winding and regulator.
9. If the output is not within 10 amperes of the rated output, check the field winding, diode trio, rectifier bridge and stator.
10. Stop the unit and disconnect the various test meters from the alternator and make necessary repairs or tests.

ELECTRICAL TESTS

The electrical tests are made in the same manner as the tests for the 10-SI and 27-SI, type 100 alternators with the exception of the following:
1. The Delta windings of the stator cannot be checked for open circuits.
2. The regulator can be checked with a commercial tester and the connector cap can be checked with an ohmmeter. Check the connector body with the ohmmeter in the middle range scale.

Connect the ohmmeter to each adjacent pair of terminals, making four checks in all. If any one check is infinite, replace the connector body.

Voltage Adjustment

A four positioned cap (connector body), is used to regulate the desired increase or decrease of voltage by removing the cap from its seat and rotating in 90 degree increments. Reposition the cap in its seat and align the proper marking on the cap with the indicator arrow on the alternator housing. The cap is marked "LO", "2", "3" and "HI".

Disassembly and Assembly

1. Hold generator in a vice, clamping the mounting flange lengthwise.
2. Make a scribe mark to help locate frame end parts in the same position during assembly.
3. Remove 4 through-bolts and separate the slip ring end frame from the drive end frame and rotor assembly.

   NOTE: Prying with a screwdriver at stator slot will aid disassembly.
4. Remove 3 stator lead attaching nuts and separate stator from end frame.
5. Remove 3 screws from brush holder and disconnect regulator lead from regulator.
   Remove diode trio and brush holder. Then lift regulator and unplug it from the voltage adjustment connector body.
6. Remove screw and clip attaching the connector body to the end frame. Pull connector body from end frame.
7. Remove screws attaching capacitor to end frame and diode rectifier bridge.
8. Remove 2 ground screws attaching diode bridge to end frame. Then disconnect the "R" terminal and battery terminal connectors from the bridge and end frame. Remove rectifier bridge from end frame.
9. Press bearing from end frame using a tube with a slightly smaller OD than

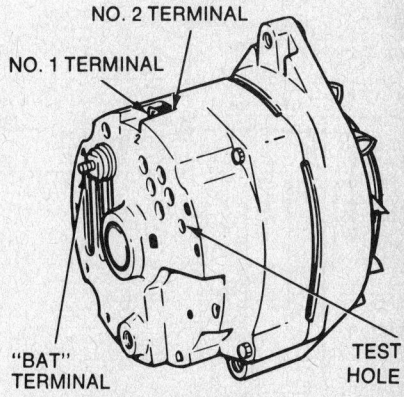

15-SI test connectors

the bearing. Support the end frame from inside and press bearing from outside toward the inside.

NOTE: Some models have a seal separate and in front of bearing. Discard the seal when replacing the bearing as the new bearing has an integral seal.

10. Separate drive end frame from rotor as follows:
   a. Place rotor in a vise and tighten only enough to permit pulley nut removal.

NOTE: Rotor may be distorted if vise is over tightened.

   b. Remove pulley nut, washer, pulley, fan, and slinger collar from rotor shaft.
   c. Remove drive end frame and rear collar from rotor shaft and remove rotor from vise.
11. Press bearing from drive end frame after removing bearing retainer plate:
   a. Remove screws attaching bearing seal and retainer assembly to housing.
   b. Support end frame from inside the housing on a metal tube slightly larger ID than the OD of the bearing.
   c. Press bearing from end frame using a metal tube or collar against the bearing inner race.
12. The assembly is in the reverse order of the disassembly. Tighten the pulley nut to 75 ft. lbs.

--- **CAUTION** ---
Do not interchange the ground screw (without insulator) for an insulated screw as this may cause uncontrolled or no alternator output.

Delcotron 27-SI Series, Type 205

The type 205, 27-SI series is basically the same as the type 200, but with internal

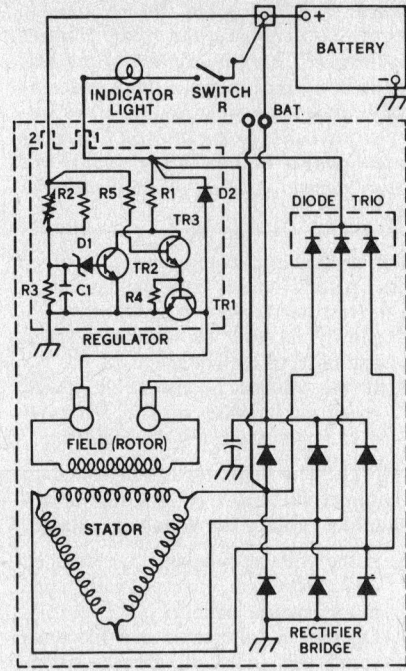

27-SI schematic

wiring changes. A recognizable feature of this alternator from the outside is the splined rotor shaft extending from the rear of the end housing. The regulator voltage setting is not adjustable and the rotor field windings do not rely on residual magnetism to excite the field circuit to begin the charging cycle. The initial field current is supplied through an indicator light circuit with connectors engaging their respective terminals at the end frame housing.

ELECTRICAL TESTS

The electrical tests of the internal components are basically the same as the tests performed on the type 200 components.

Disassembly and Assembly

The disassembly and assembly is typical of the 27-SI series.

Ford-Autolite (Ford Motor Co.)

The Ford-Autolite charging system is a negative ground system. It includes an alternator, an electro-mechanical regulator or an electronic regulator, a charge indicator or an ammeter and a storage battery.

NOTE: Late model Ford systems have replaced the electro-mechanical regulator with either a non-adjustable transistorized regulator or an adjustable transistorized regulator. The adjustable transistorized unit used with high output systems has a single, voltage limit adjusting screw under the cover. Do not use a metal screwdriver for adjustment.

TROUBLESHOOTING

NOTE: See the "Alternator Test Plans" section before proceeding further.

Fusible Links

1. Check the fusible link located between the starter relay and the alternator. Replace the link if it is burned or open.

CHARGING SYSTEM OPERATION

NOTE: If the current indicator is to give an accurate reading, the battery cables must be of the same gauge and length as the original equipment.

1. With the engine running, and all electrical systems turned off, place a current indicator over the positive battery cable.
2. If a charge of about 5 amps is recorded, the charging system is working. If a draw of about 5 amps is recorded, the system is not working. The needle moves toward the battery when a charge condition is indicated, and away from the battery when a draw

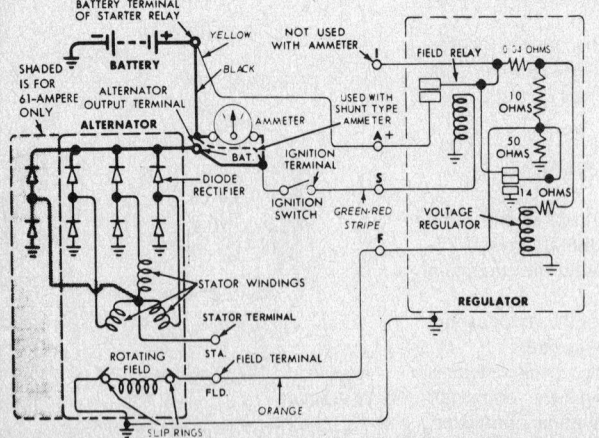

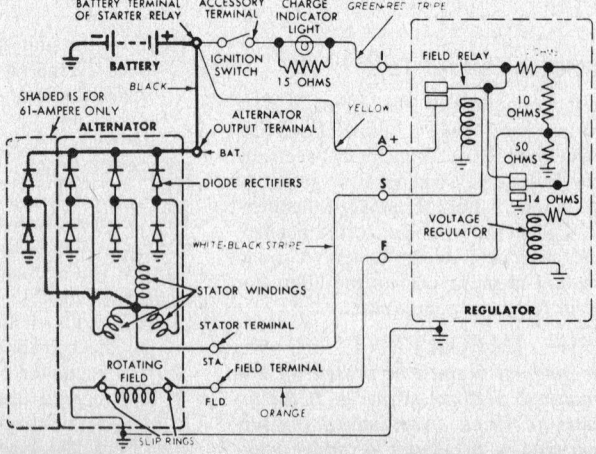

Charging system schematic with electro-mechanical regulator and charging light

condition is indicated. If a draw is indicated, continue to the next testing procedure. If an overcharge of 10–15 amps is indicated, check for a faulty regulator or a bad ground at the regulator or the alternator.

Testing the Ignition Switch to Regulator Circuit

1. Disconnect the regulator wiring harness from the regulator.
2. Turn on the key. Using a test light or voltmeter, check for voltage between the I wire and ground. Check for voltage between the A wire and ground. If voltage is present at this part of the system, the circuit is OK. If there is no voltage at the I wire, check for a burned-out charge indicator bulb, a burned-out resistor, or a break or short in the wiring. If there is no voltage present at the A wire, check for a bad connection at the starter relay or a break or short in the wire.

Isolation Test

This test determines whether the regulator or the alternator is faulty, after the rest of the circuit is found to be in good working order.

1. Disconnect the regulator wiring harness from the regulator.
2. Connect a jumper wire from the A wire to the F wire in the wiring harness plug.
3. Connect a voltmeter to the battery. The positive voltmeter lead goes to the positive terminal and the negative lead to the negative terminal. Record the reading on the voltmeter.
4. Turn off all of the electrical systems and start the engine. Do not race the engine.
5. Gradually increase engine speed to 1500–2000 rpm. The voltmeter reading should increase above the previously recorded battery voltage reading by at least one to two volts. If there is no increase, the alternator is not working correctly. If there is an increase, the voltage regulator needs to be replaced.

OVERHAUL

Disassembly—Except 65, 70, 90 Amp Alternators

1. Mark both end housings with a scribe mark for assembly.
2. Remove the three housing through-bolts.
3. Separate the front housing and rotor from the stator and rear housing.
4. Remove the nuts from the rectifier to rear housing mounting studs, and remove the rear housing.
5. Remove the brush holder mounting screws and the holder, brushes, springs, insulator, and terminal.

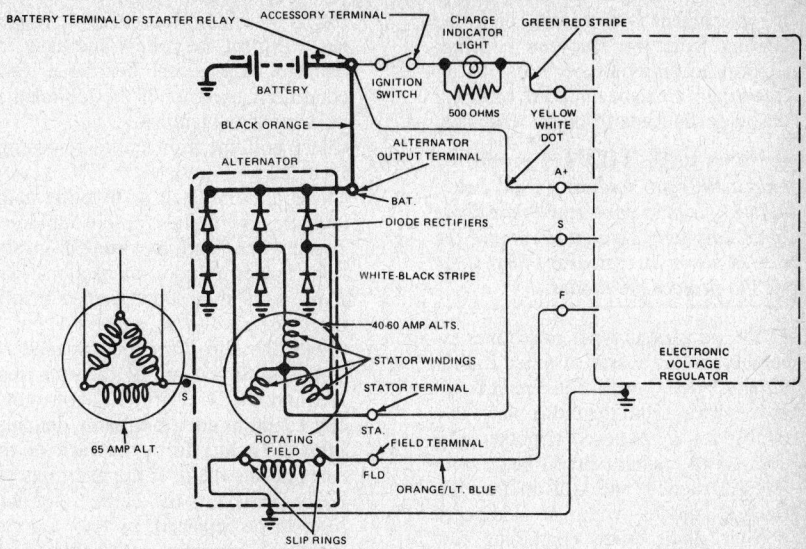

Alternator charging system with indicator lamp

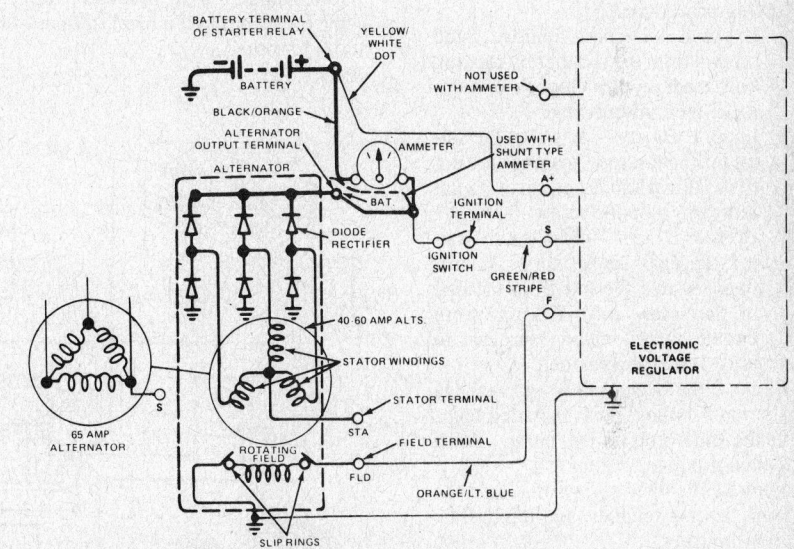

Alternator charging system with ammeter

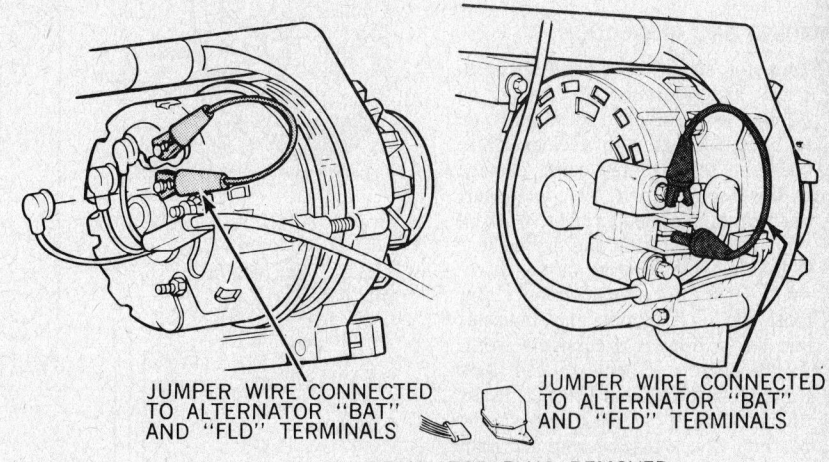

Location of jumper wire for circuit tests on rear and side terminal alternators

6. If replacement is necessary, press the bearing from the rear end housing, support housing on inner boss.

7. If rectifiers are to be replaced, carefully unsolder the leads from the terminals.

——————— CAUTION ———————

Use only a 100-watt soldering iron. Leave the soldering iron in contact with the diode terminals only long enough to remove the wires. Use pliers as temporary heat sinks in order to protect the diodes.

8. There are various types of rectifier assembly circuit boards installed in production. One type has the circuit board spaced away from the diode plates and the diodes are exposed. Another type consists of a single circuit board with integral diodes; and still another has integral diodes with an additional booster diode plate containing two diodes. This last type is used only on the eight-diode, 61-amp. Autolite alternator. To disassemble, use the following procedures:

   a. Exposed Diodes—remove the screws from the rectifier by rotating bolt heads ¼ turn clockwise to unlock, then unscrewing.

   b. Integral Diodes—press out the stator terminal screw, making sure not to twist it while doing this. Do not remove grounded screw.

   c. Booster Diodes—press out the stator terminal screw about ¼ in., then remove the nut from the end of the screw and lift screw from circuit board, making sure not to twist it as it comes out.

9. Remove the drive pulley and fan. On alternator pulleys with threaded holes in the outer end of the pulley, use a standard puller for removal.

10. Remove the three screws that hold the front bearing retainer, and remove the front housing.

11. If the bearing is to be replaced, press from housing.

Cleaning and Inspection

1. The rotor, stator, diode rectifier assemblies, and bearings are not to be cleaned with solvent. These parts are to be wiped off with a clean cloth. Cleaning solvent may cause damage to the electrical parts or contaminate the bearing internal lubricant. Wash all other parts in solvent and dry them.

2. Rotate the front bearing on the driveshaft. Check for any scraping noise, looseness or roughness that indicates that the bearing is excessively worn. As the bearing is being rotated, look for excessive lubricant leakage. If any of these conditions exist, replace the bearing. Check rear bearing and rotor shaft.

3. Place the rear end housing on the slip ring end of the shaft and rotate the bearing on the shaft. Make a similar check for noise, looseness or roughness. Inspect the rollers and cage for damage. Replace the bearing if these conditions exist, or if the lubricant is missing or contaminated.

4. Check both the front and rear housings for cracks.

5. Check all wire leads on both the stator and rotor assemblies for loose soldered connections, and for burned insulation. Solder all poor connections. Replace parts that show burned insulation.

6. Check the slip rings for damaged insulation and runout. If the slip rings are more than 0.0005 in. out of round, take a light cut (minimum diameter limit 1.22 in.) from the face of the rings to true them. If the slip rings are badly damaged, the entire rotor will have to be replaced, as they are serviced as a complete assembly.

7. Replace any parts that are burned or cracked. Replace brushes that are worn to less than ⁵⁄₁₆ in. in length. Replace the brush spring if it had less than 7–12 oz. tension.

Field Current Draw Test

NOTE: Alternator must be removed from the truck.

1. Connect a test ammeter between the alternator frame and the positive post of a 12-volt test battery.

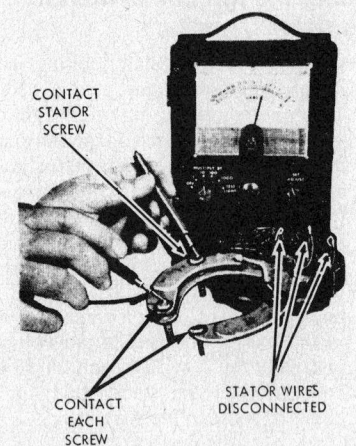

Testing the diodes on a 65 amp alternator

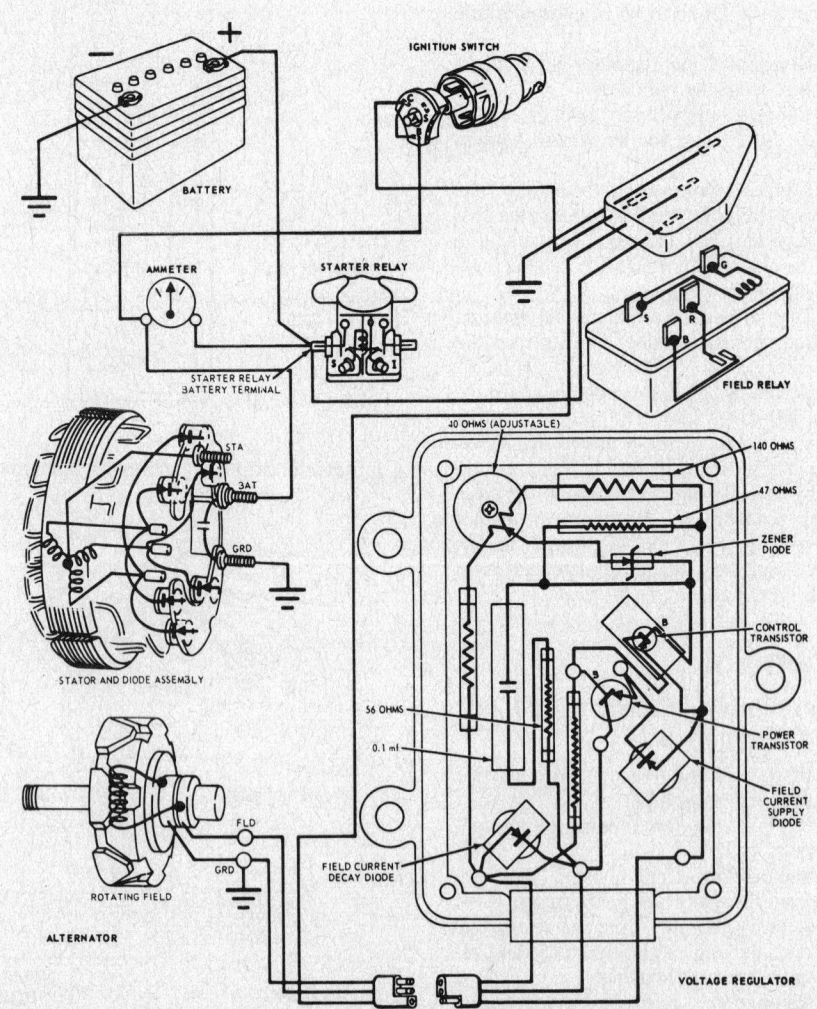

Charging system schematic with transistor regulator and ammeter

2. Connect a jumper wire between the negative test battery post and the alternator field terminal.
3. Observe the ammeter:
   a. Little or no current flow indicates high brush resistance, open field windings, or high winding resistance.
   b. Current in excess of specifications (approximately 2.9 amps. for most models) indicates shorted or grounded field windings, or brush leads touching.

NOTE: Sometimes the alternator produces current output at low engine speeds, but ceases to put out at higher speeds. This can be caused by centrifugal force expanding the rotor windings to the point where they short to ground. Place in a test stand and check field current draw while spinning alternator.

Diode Tests

Disassemble the alternator. Disconnect diode assembly from stator and make tests.

To test one set of diodes, contact one ohmmeter probe to the diode plate and contact each of the three stator lead terminals with the other probe. Reverse the probes and repeat the test. All six tests (eight for 61 amp. Autolite eight-diode models) should show a reading of about 60 ohms in one direction and infinite ohms in the other. If two high readings, or two low readings, are obtained after reversing probes the diode is faulty and must be replaced.

Stator Tests

Disassemble the stator from the alternator assembly and rectifiers. Connect test ohmmeter probes between each pair of stator leads. If the ohmmeter does not indicate equally between each pair of leads, the stator coil is open and must be replaced.

Connect test ohmmeter probes between one of the stator leads and the stator core. The ohmmeter should not show any reading. If it does show continuity, the stator winding is grounded and must be replaced.

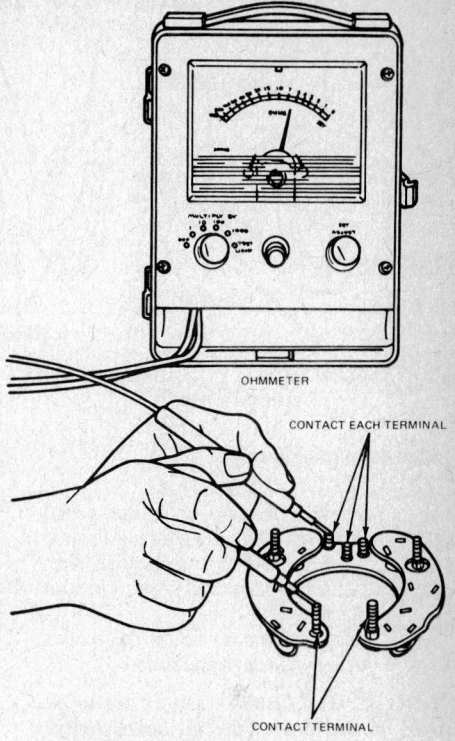

OHMMETER

CONTACT EACH TERMINAL

CONTACT TERMINAL

Testing the diodes on all but 65 amp alternators

Assembly—Except 65, 70, 90 Amp Alternators

1. Press the front bearing into the front housing boss, putting pressure on outer race only. Install bearing retainer.
2. If the stop ring on the driveshaft was damaged, install a new stop ring. Push the new ring onto the shaft and into the groove.
3. Position the front bearing spacer on the driveshaft against the stop ring.
4. Place the front housing over the shaft, with the bearing positioned in the front housing cavity.
5. Install fan spacer, fan, pulley, lockwasher and retaining nut and tighten nut to 60–100 ft. lbs. holding the drive shaft with an Allen key.
6. If rear bearing was removed, press a new one into rear housing.
7. Assemble brushes, springs, terminal and insulator in the brush holder, retract the brushes and insert a short length of 1/8 in. rod or stiff wire through the hole in the holder to hold the brushes in the retracted position.
8. Position the brush holder assembly in the rear housing and install mounting screws. Position brush leads to prevent shorting.
9. Wrap the three stator winding leads around the circuit board terminals and solder them using only rosin core solder and a 100-watt iron. Position the stator neutral lead eyelet on the stator terminal screw and install the screw in the rectifier assembly.

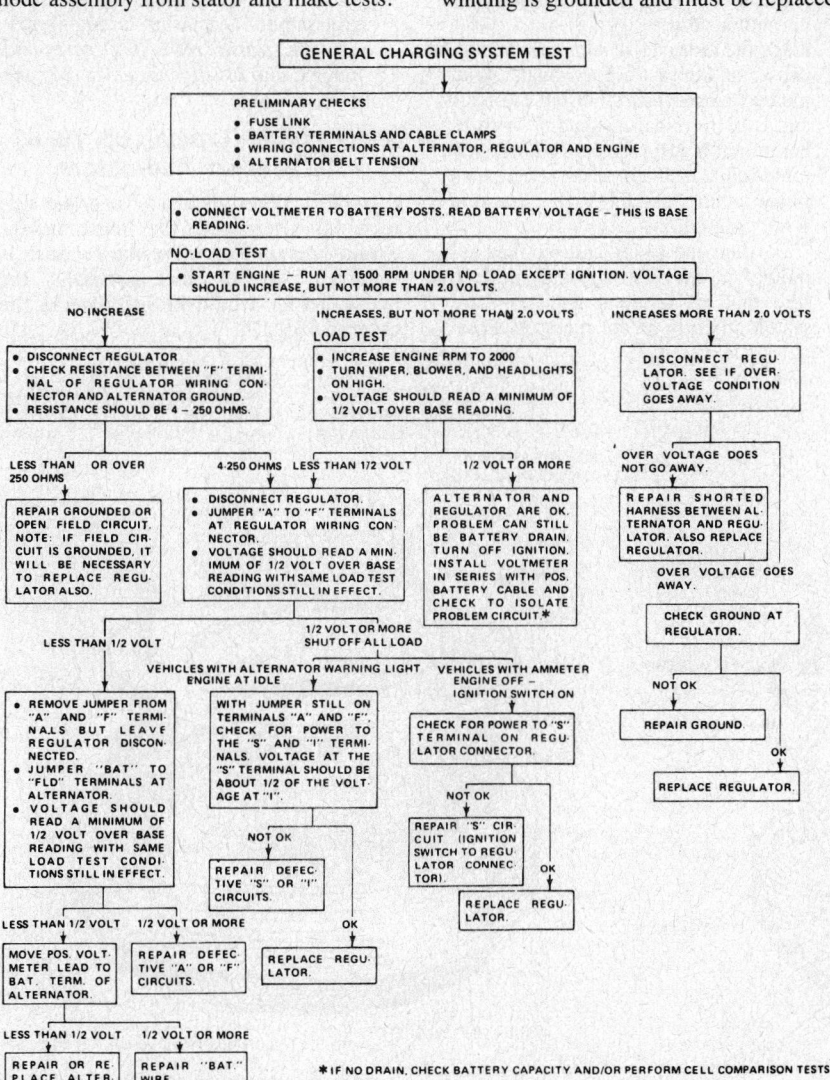

General charging system tests with ohmmeter and voltmeter

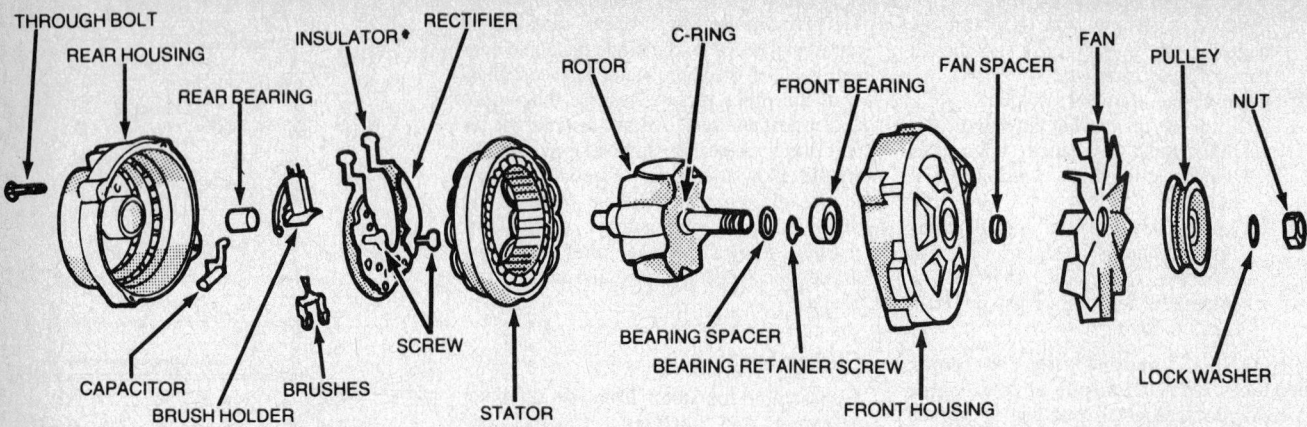

THROUGH BOLT
REAR HOUSING
REAR BEARING
INSULATOR
RECTIFIER
ROTOR
C-RING
FRONT BEARING
FAN SPACER
FAN
PULLEY
NUT
CAPACITOR
BRUSH HOLDER
BRUSHES
SCREW
STATOR
BEARING SPACER
BEARING RETAINER SCREW
FRONT HOUSING
LOCK WASHER

Side terminal alternator

10. a. Exposed Diodes—insert the special screws through the wire lug, dished washers and circuit board. Turn ¼ turn counterclockwise to lock in place.
    b. Integral Diodes—insert the screws straight through the holes.

NOTE: The dished washers are to be used on the molded circuit boards only. Using these washers on a fiber board will result in a serious short circuit, as only a flat insulating washer between the stator terminal and the board is used on fiber circuit boards.

    c. Booster Diodes—position the stator wire terminal on the stator terminal screw, then position screw on rectifier. Position square insulator over the screw and into the square hole in the rectifier, rotate terminal screw until it locks, then press it in fingertight. Position the stator wire, then press the terminal screw into the rectifier and insulator with a vise.

11. Place the radio noise suppression condenser on the rectifier terminals. With molded circuit board, install the STA and BAT terminal insulators. With fiber circuit board, place the square stator terminal insulator in the square hole in the rectifier assembly, then position BAT terminal insulator.

Position the stator and rectifier assembly in the rear housing, making sure that all terminal insulators are seated properly in the recesses. Position STA, BAT and FLD insulators on terminal bolts; install nuts.

12. Clean the rear bearing surface of the rotor shaft with a rag, then position rear housing and stator assembly over rotor. Align matchmarks made during disassembly and install through-bolts. *Remove brush retracting wire and place a dab of silicone sealer over the hole.*

Disassembly (Typical) 65, 70, 90 and 100 Ampere Alternators

NOTE: When disassembling the side terminal alternator, the brush holder would be removed after the rectifier is removed. During the assembly, the brush holder would be installed in the reverse order.

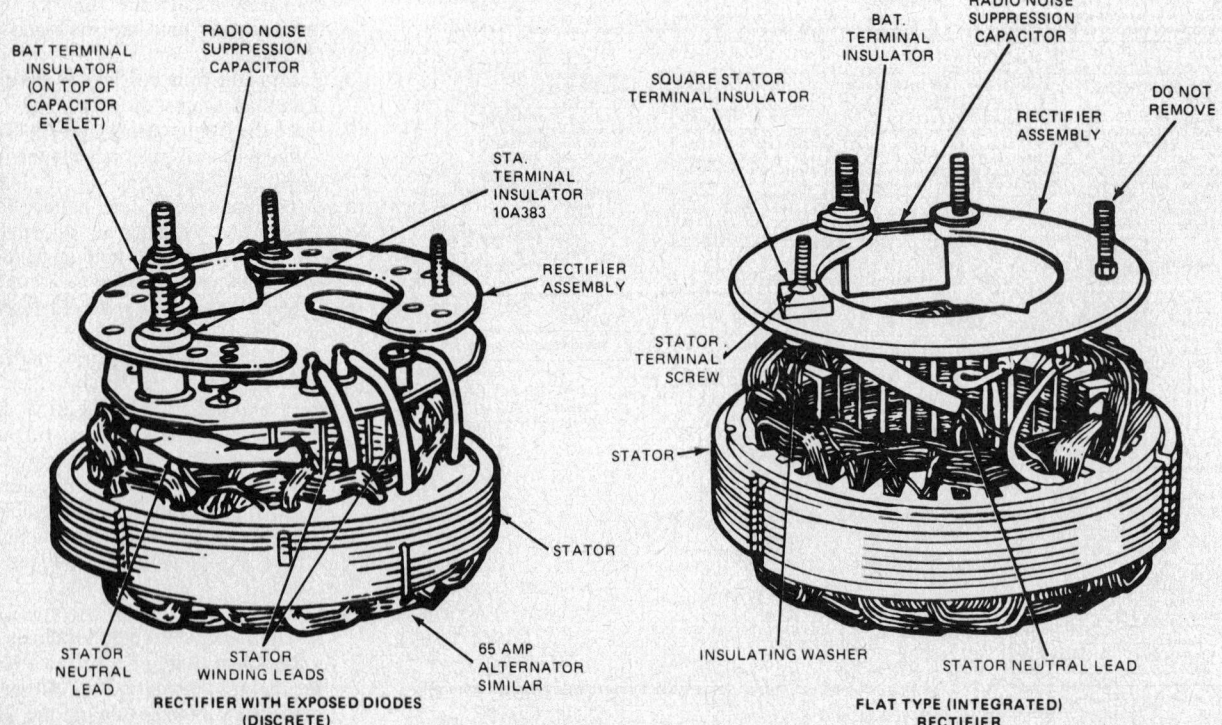

BAT TERMINAL INSULATOR (ON TOP OF CAPACITOR EYELET)
RADIO NOISE SUPPRESSION CAPACITOR
STA. TERMINAL INSULATOR 10A383
RECTIFIER ASSEMBLY
STATOR NEUTRAL LEAD
STATOR WINDING LEADS
STATOR
65 AMP ALTERNATOR SIMILAR

RECTIFIER WITH EXPOSED DIODES (DISCRETE)

BAT. TERMINAL INSULATOR
RADIO NOISE SUPPRESSION CAPACITOR
SQUARE STATOR TERMINAL INSULATOR
RECTIFIER ASSEMBLY
DO NOT REMOVE
STATOR TERMINAL SCREW
STATOR
INSULATING WASHER
STATOR NEUTRAL LEAD

FLAT TYPE (INTEGRATED) RECTIFIER

Stator and rectifier assemblies

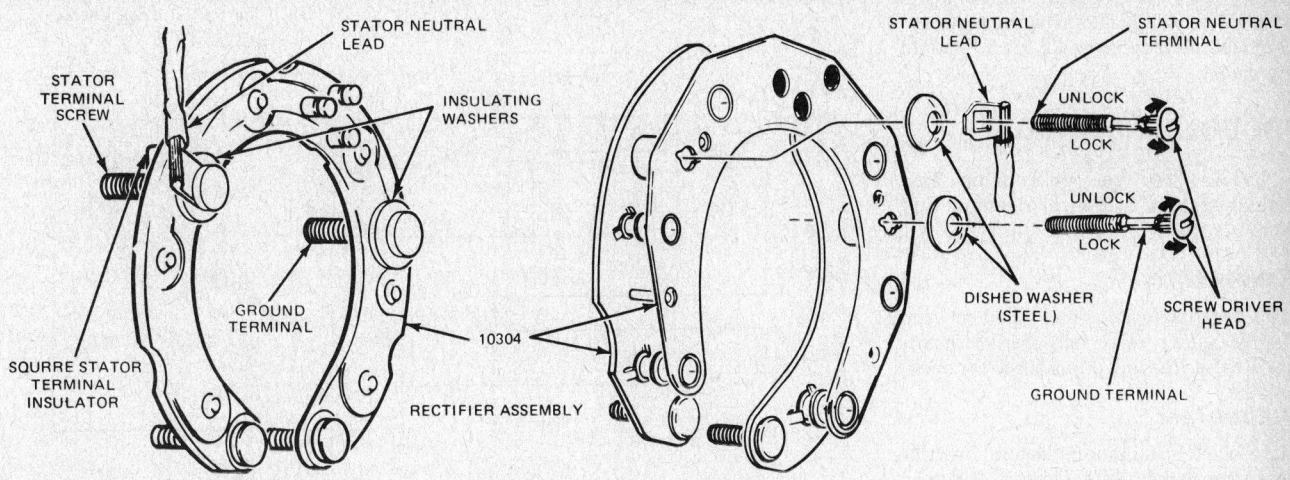

FLAT TYPE (INTEGRATED) RECTIFIER   RECTIFIER (DISCRETE) WITH EXPOSED DIODES

Rectifier assembly exploded view

1. Remove the brush holder and cover assembly from the rear housing.
2. Mark both end housings and the stator.
3. Remove the three housing through-bolts.
4. Separate the front housing and rotor from the stator and rear housing.
5. Remove the drive pulley nut, lock-washer, flat washer, pulley, fan, fan spacer and rotor from the front housing.
6. Remove the three screws that hold the front bearing retainer and remove the retainer. If the bearing is damaged or has lost its lubricant, support the housing close to the bearing boss and press out the bearing.
7. Remove all the nut and washer assemblies and insulators from the rear housing and remove the rear housing from the stator and rectifier assembly.
8. If necessary, press the rear bearing from the housing, supporting the housing on the inner boss.
9. Unsolder the three stator leads from the rectifier assembly, and separate the stator from the assembly. Use a 200-watt soldering iron.
10. Perform a diode test and an open and grounded stator coil test.

Cleaning and Inspection

Nicks and scratches may be removed from the rotor slip rings by turning down the slip rings. Do not go beyond the minimum diameter limit of 1.22 in. If the slip rings are badly damaged, the entire rotor must be replaced. The rectifier also is serviced as an assembly. See "Lower Ampere Alternator" Section for test procedures.

Assembly—65, 70, 90 and 100 Amp

1. If the front bearing is being replaced,

press the new bearing into the bearing boss, putting pressure on the outer race only. Install the bearing retainer and tighten the retainer screws until the tips of the retainer touch the housing.
2. Position the rectifier assembly to the stator, wrap the three stator leads around the diode plate terminals and solder them using a 200-watt soldering iron.
3. If the rear housing bearing was removed, press in a new bearing from the inside of the housing, putting pressure on the outer race only.
4. Install the BAT-GRD insulator, and position the stator and rectifier assembly in the rear housing.
5. Install the STA (purple) and BAT (red) terminal insulators on the terminal bolts and install the nut and washer assemblies. *Make certain that the shoulders on all insulators, both inside and outside of the housing, are seated properly before tightening the nuts.*
6. Position the front housing over the rotor and install the an spacer, fan, pulley, flat and lockwasher and nut on the rotor shaft.
7. Wipe the rear bearing surface of the rotor shaft with a clean rag.
8. Position the rotor with the front housing into the stator and rear housing assembly, and align the matchmarks made during disassembly. Seat the machined portion of the stator core into the step in both housings and install the through-bolts.
9. If the field brushes have worn to less than ⅜ in., replace both brushes. Hold the brushes in position by inserting a stiff wire into the brush holder.
10. Position the brush holder assembly into the rear housing and install the three mounting screws. Remove the brush retracting wire and put a dab of silicone cement over the hole.

Brush Replacement
65, 70, 90 and 100 Amp

1. Remove the brush holder and cover assembly from the rear housing.
2. Remove the terminal bolts from the brush holder and cover assembly, then remove the brush assemblies.
3. Position the new brush terminals on the terminal bolts and assemble the terminals, bolts, brush holder washers and nuts. The insulating washer mounts under the FLD terminal nut. The entire brush and cover assembly also is available for service.
4. Depress the brush springs in the brush holder cavities and insert the brushes on top of the springs. Hold the brushes in position by inserting a stiff wire in the brush holder as shown. Position the brush leads as shown.
5. Install the brush holder and cover assembly into the rear housing. Remove the brush retracting wire and put a dab of silicone cement over the hole.

Autolite Alternator with Integral Regulator

Some vehicles are equipped with an Autolite alternator having an integral regulator mounted to the rear end housing. The regulator is a hybrid unit featuring use of solid state integrated circuits. These circuits may consist of transistors, diodes and resistors. The unusual feature of this type of micro-electronic circuit is that the entire circuit is within a silicone crystal approximately ⅛ in. square. Because of the small size of the circuit, it is not repairable or adjustable and must be replaced as a unit if found to be defective. It should be noted that the size of the regulator housing is dictated only by the fact that some means of connecting the regulator to the alternator is necessary. Overhaul is the same as for other Autolite alternators.

TROUBLESHOOTING

NOTE: See the ''Alternator Test Plans'' section before proceeding further.

Fusible Links

1. Check the fusible link located between the starter relay and the alternator. Replace the link if it is burned or open.

Output Test

1. Place transmission in Neutral or Park.
2. Remove the positive battery cable and install a battery adapter switch in the line.
3. Attach one lead of a test voltmeter to the negative battery post and the other test lead to the circuit side of the adapter switch.
4. Connect a test ammeter to each side of the adapter switch, so that charging current will go through the ammeter when the switch is opened.

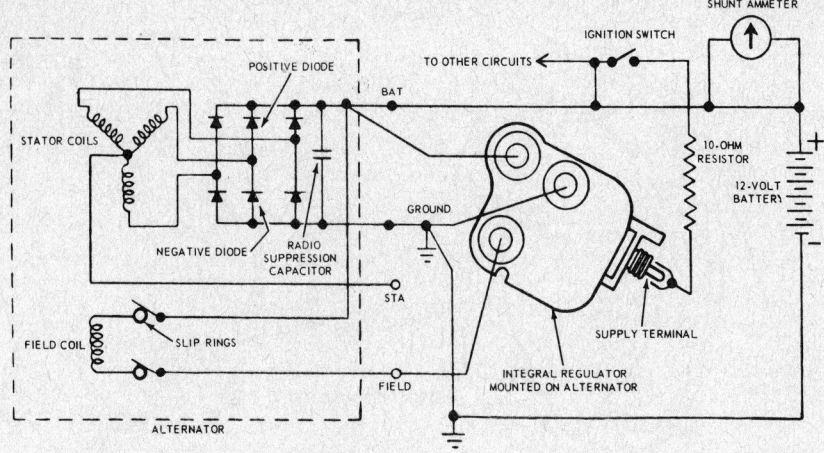

Charging system schematic with integral regulator

5. Connect a jumper wire between the alternator frame and the integral regulator field terminal (cover plug removed).
6. Close adapter switch, start engine and open adapter switch.
7. Running engine at 2,000 rpm, observe voltmeter and ammeter. At 15 volts indicated, the ammeter should read 50–57 amps. If so, and there is still a no-charge condition, the regulator is probably faulty and must be replaced. An output 2–8 amps. below 50 amps. usually indicates an open diode recti-

fier, while an output 10–15 amps. below minimum specifications usually indicates a shorted diode. An alternator with a shorted diode usually will whine at idle speed.

Field Test (Voltmeter)

1. Turn ignition switch to OFF position.
2. Remove wire from regulator supply terminal.
3. Remove cover plug from regulator field terminal and connect one test voltmeter lead to this terminal. A ¼ ohm resistor should be in the circuit.

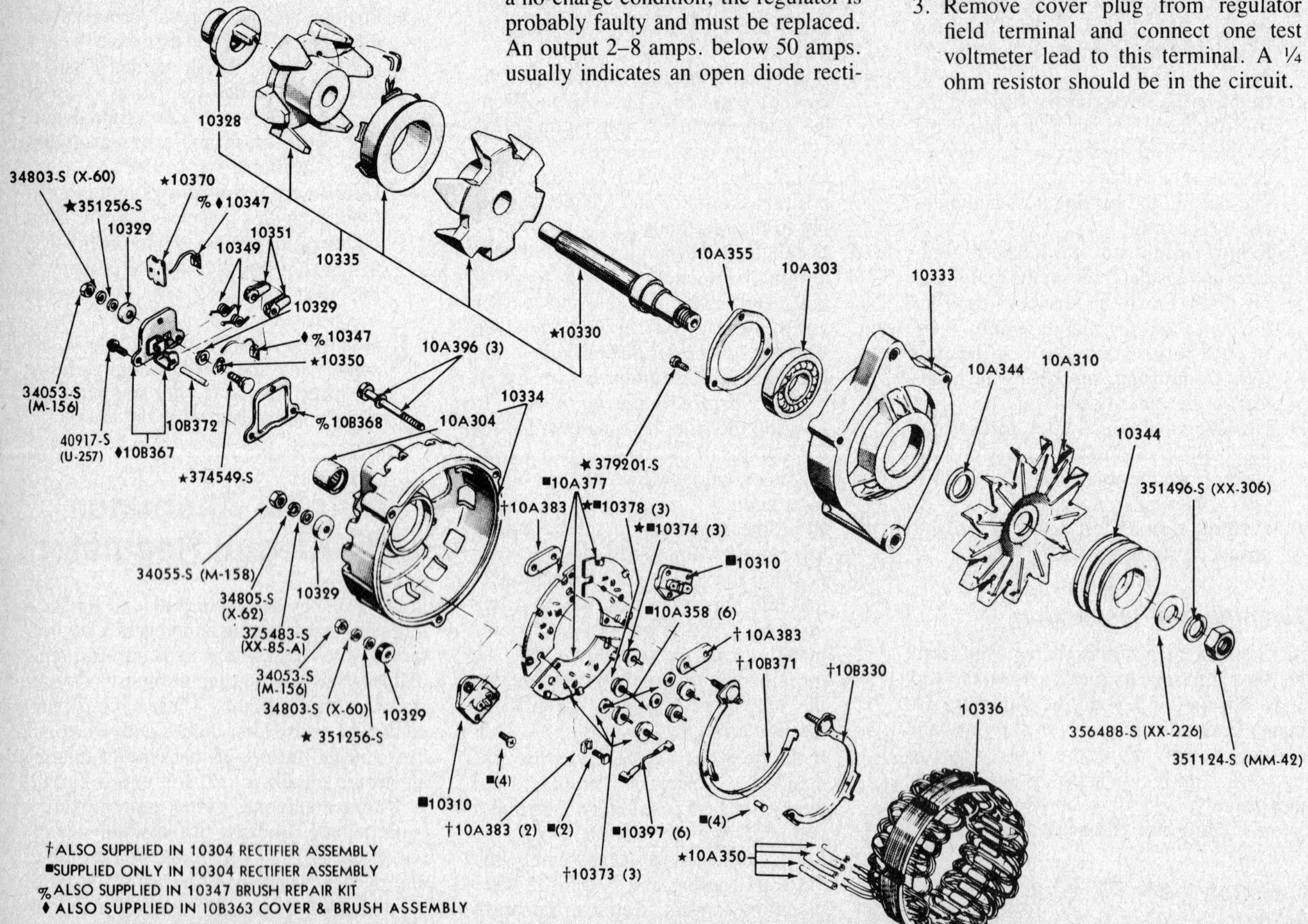

† ALSO SUPPLIED IN 10304 RECTIFIER ASSEMBLY
■ SUPPLIED ONLY IN 10304 RECTIFIER ASSEMBLY
% ALSO SUPPLIED IN 10347 BRUSH REPAIR KIT
♦ ALSO SUPPLIED IN 10B363 COVER & BRUSH ASSEMBLY

70 and 90 amp rear terminal alternators

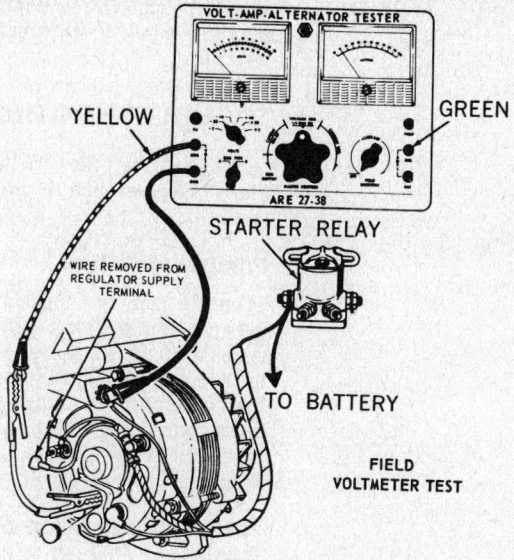

Output test

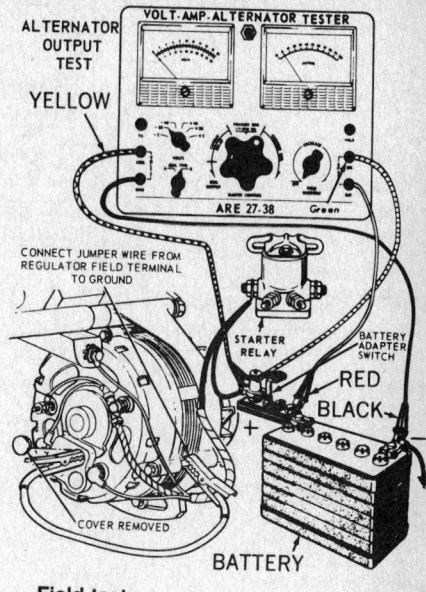

Field test

4. Connect the other test voltmeter lead to a good engine ground.
5. The voltmeter should read 12 volts. If *no* voltage is present, the field circuit is open or grounded.
6. If voltmeter reads more than I volt, but still less than battery voltage, there is probably a partial ground in the alternator field circuit and the circuit should be checked with an ohmmeter.

Field Test (Ohmmeter)

1. Disconnect battery ground cable; remove alternator from truck.
2. Remove the regulator from the alternator (covered later).
3. Make the ohmmeter tests as illustrated. If any of the tests indicates a field circuit problem, disassemble the alternator to further isolate the trouble.
   a. Contact each ohmmeter probe to a slip ring. Resistance should be 4–5 ohms. A higher reading indicates a damaged slip ring soldered connection or a broken wire. A lower reading indicates a shorted wire or slip ring assembly.
   b. Contact one ohmmeter probe to a slip ring and the other probe to the rotor shaft. Any reading other than infinite ohms indicates a short to ground. If neither of these tests (A and B) isolates the trouble, the brushes or brush assembly are the probable cause.

Voltage Limiter Test

1. Check the battery specific gravity. If it is not at least 1.230, charge the battery or install a charged battery for the test.

2. Make sure all lights and accessories are turned off, including such items as dome lights.
3. Make the test connections as illustrated.
4. Place transmission in Neutral or Park, close battery adapter switch and start the engine.
5. Open the battery adapter switch and operate engine at 2,000 rpm for 5 minutes. The voltmeter should read 13.3–15.3 volts.
6. If voltage does not rise above 12 volts, perform a regulator supply voltage test to determine whether or not the regulator is getting voltage from the battery. Before replacing a regulator, check the wiring of the entire charging system for shorts, opens, or high resistance connections.

Regulator Supply Voltage Test

The regulator is "turned on" by the application of battery voltage through a 10 ohm resistor wire. If the supply circuit is defective, the regulator will not function and the alternator will not put out current.

1. Connect a 12-volt test light or voltmeter between the regulator supply lead and ground.
2. Turn on the ignition switch. The test light should glow or the voltmeter indicate. If not, the supply circuit should be checked back to the battery, especially the resistance wire.

Overhaul

The overhaul procedures for the alternator are the same as for the Ford Autolite electro-mechanical alternator.

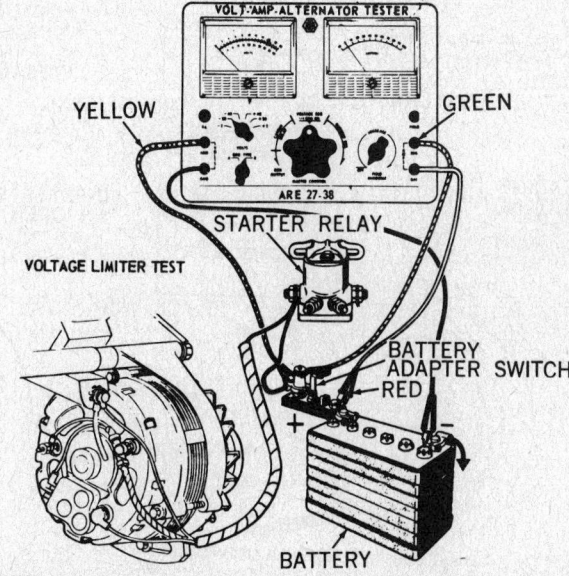

Voltage limiter test

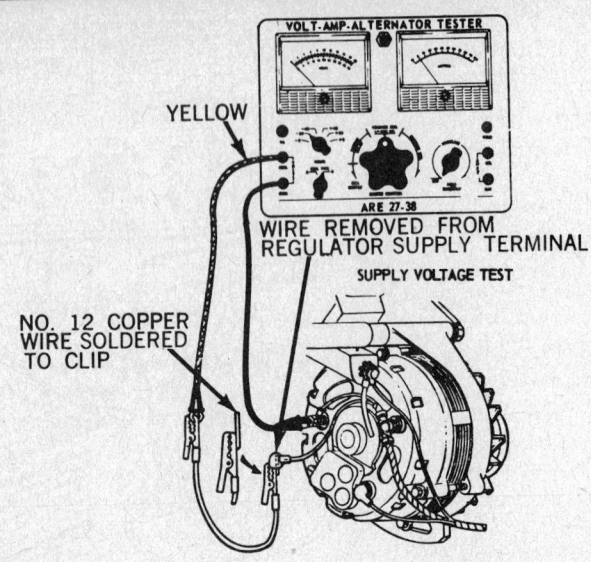

Supply voltage test

Motorola System

The Motorola alternator is an electro-mechanical device producing alternating current, which is changed to direct current by the rectifier diodes, accomplished by the characteristics of the diodes to allow current to flow in one direction only.

A three phase stator winding is used, a "Wye" type for the 37 ampere rated alternator, and a "Delta" type for the 51 and 55 ampere rated alternators.

A field diode assembly is used to provide the excitation current to the rotor (field) windings when the alternator is operating and is sensed and regulated by the voltage regulator to control the output of the alternator.

The field diode assembly is either mounted on a circuit board or encased within a epoxy "pot" with the leads attached in parallel to the positive rectifier diodes. If one or more of the field diodes become open, shorted, or downgraded, the alternator output will be affected.

NOTE: Do not use the regulator terminal for a source of current for any reason. To do so would adversely affect the operation of the voltage regulator.

CAUTION

Some alternators are equipped with a 7 volt terminal for the supply of current to the electric automatic choke. This terminal is located on the negative rectifier assembly. Do not interchange the wires between the regulator terminal and this terminal.

The voltage regulator is a sealed unit and requires no adjustment. Replacement of the unit is required if the regulator becomes defective.

TROUBLESHOOTING

NOTE: See the "Alternator Test Plans" section before proceeding further.

Fusible Link Test

There are many fuse links in the truck however the fuse link located in the wiring between the battery terminal of the horn relay to the main wire harness is the only one that concerns the charging system. This link protects the entire wiring harness. If it fails, all the electrical systems will fail to function.

Testing the Ignition Switch to Regulator Circuit

1. Disconnect the regulator wires from the regulator.
2. Turn on the key. Using a test light or voltmeter, check for current between the voltage supply wire and ground. This wire is usually orange and has another wire connected to it, usually blue or orange with a tracer.
3. If current is present, this part of the system is OK. If no voltage is present, check for broken or shorted wiring, a bad indicator bulb, a bad fuse in the fuse panel, or a bad connection at the ignition switch or on the battery side of the starter relay.

ALTERNATOR TESTS (IN VEHICLE)

NOTE: Various types of charging system testers are available to perform the tests necessary to determine if the system

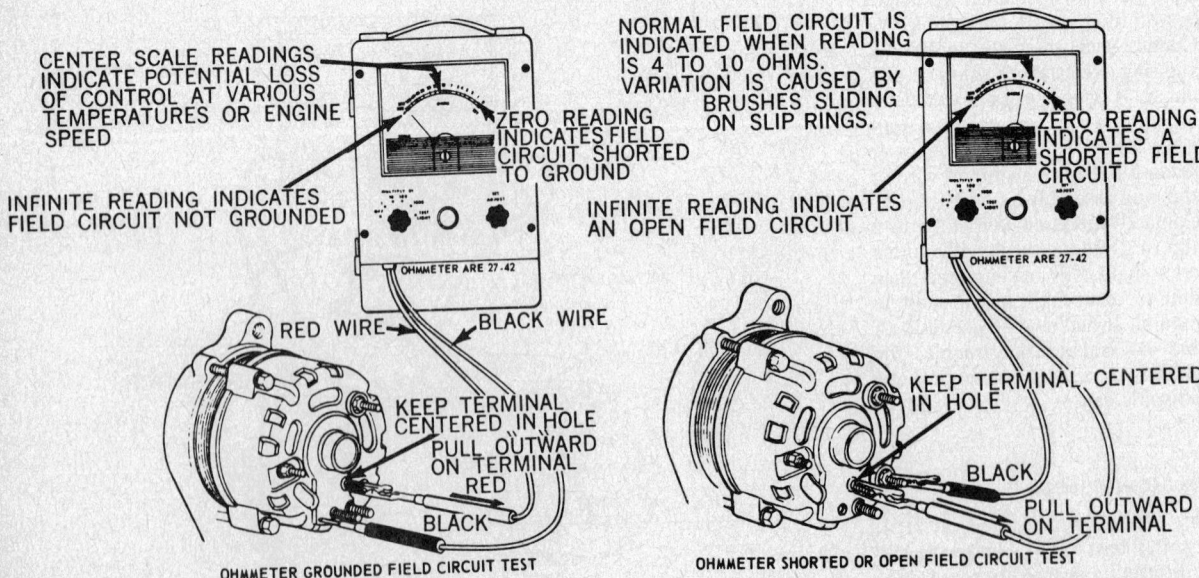

Field circuit test with ohmmeter

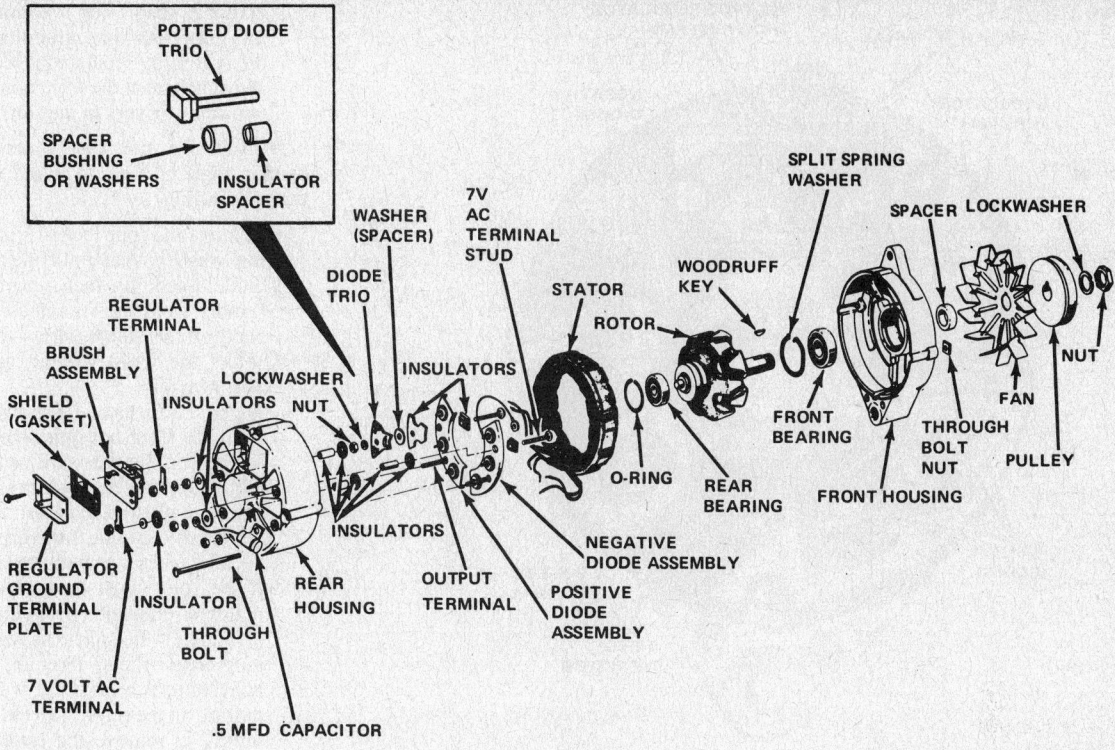

Motorola alternator

or components are defective. Follow the manufactures instructions for the tester being used, as the following charging system tests are generalized.

——— CAUTION ———

Do not disconnect the output lead or the voltage regulator, other than as directed, while the alternator is being operated. Do not ground the field terminal. Severe charging system damage could result.

Alternator Output Test

1. Connect voltmeter to battery, observing proper polarity.
2. Start the engine and operate at 1000 RPMs for two minutes with the headlamps on low beam.
3. Observe the voltage reading. If the voltage remains above 13 volts and below 15 volts, the alternator and the regulator are working satisfactorily.
4. If the voltage is registering out of the above range, further testing will have to be done.

Field Draw Test

1. Loosen the alternator belt so that the rotor can be turned by hand.
2. Connect ammeter leads between the positive battery post and the positive brush post on the alternator.
3. The ammeter should register a reading within a range of 1½ to 3 amperes and if by turning the rotor by hand, the reading varies within the scale, the

brushes and the slip rings require cleaning or repairs.
4. If the readings are too high or too low, the alternator should be removed and disassembled for further tests and repairs.

Regulator Bypass Test

1. Connect a voltmeter to the battery, observing the proper polarity. Disconnect the voltage regulator.
2. Start the engine and allow to idle.
3. Connect an ammeter lead between the positive battery post to the alternator positive brush terminal.
4. Increase the engine speed while observing the voltage reading. A reading of 16 volts should be obtained, if the alternator is not defective.

NOTE: Do not allow the voltage to increase over 16 volts, as damage to the charging system can result.

Field Diode Assembly Test

NOTE: A shorted or open field diode assembly will cause reduced alternator output and require unit disassembly and removal of the diode assembly for testing. A downgrading of one or more of the diodes will cause the dash indicator bulb to glow dimly, but will normally not effect the alternator output.

1. Start the engine and operate at idle speed.
2. With the voltmeter adjusted to the low scale, connect the leads to the alter-

nator output terminal and the negative lead to the regulator terminal.
3. Turn the blower motor to the high position and turn the headlamps to the high beam position for approximately two minutes of operation. This causes the diode assembly to heat up due to the electrical load.
4. Observe the reading on the voltmeter. A range of 0 to 0.2 volts indicates the diode assembly is good. A reading above 0.2 volts indicates the downgrading of the diode assembly although it is not necessary to replace the assembly unless the reading is over 0.6 volts.

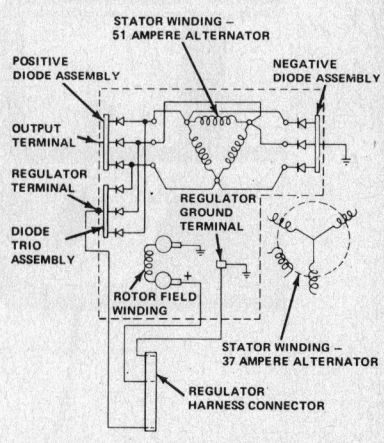

51 and 55 amp Motorola alternator internal circuit

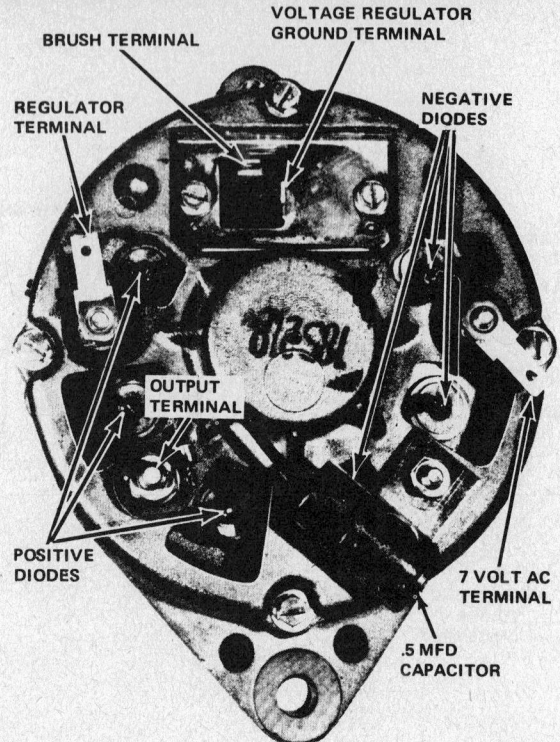

REGULATOR TERMINAL

BRUSH TERMINAL

VOLTAGE REGULATOR GROUND TERMINAL

NEGATIVE DIODES

OUTPUT TERMINAL

POSITIVE DIODES

7 VOLT AC TERMINAL

.5 MFD CAPACITOR

Motorola terminal locations

5. A pulsating reading on the meter indicates a positive diode of the rectifier or a soldered connection is breaking down under heat, and the alternator will have to be disassembled for testing repairs.

6. If the reading is over 0.6 volts and the alternator output was deemed satisfactory in the earlier tests, a bench test of the diode assembly will have to be made.

7. If the dash indicator bulb remains on dimly after a satisfactory diode assembly test has been made, inspect the following locations for loose or corroded connections.
   a. Alternator output terminal
   b. Starter relay battery terminal
   c. Ignition switch
   d. Fuse panel
   e. Instrument harness connections
   f. Instrument cluster printed circuits
   g. Indicator bulb socket
   h. Main wiring harness connectors

ALTERNATOR

Disassembly

1. Remove the two self-tapping screws and the cover. Pull the brush assembly straight up to clear the locating pins, then lift out the brush assembly.

2. Scribe a matchmark across the front

housing, stator, and rear housing. Remove the four through-bolts and nuts, then carefully separate the rear housing and stator from the front housing using two screwdrivers in the slots provided.

NOTE: Do not insert screwdrivers deeper than 1/16 in., to avoid damaging stator winding.

3. Remove the four locknuts and insulating washers that hold the stator and diode assembly, then separate the assembly from the rear housing. Avoid bending the stator wires—do not unsolder the wires without using pliers as a heat sink.

4. There is no reason to remove the rotor from the front housing unless there is a defect in the field coil or front bearing. Front and rear bearings are lubricated for life and sealed and, as a rule, do not go bad unless the drive belt has been adjusted witrh too much tension. If the rotor must be removed, use a puller to remove the front drive pulley, then unseat the split-ring washer using long-nose pliers through the front housing to compress the washer while pulling on the rotor. Tap the rotor shaft lightly to remove the rotor and front bearing, then reach in and remove the split-ring washer. Bearings must be removed using a puller and new bearings must be pressed into place.

Assembly

1. Clean the bearing and the inside of the bearing hub in the front housing, then gently seat the bearing using a socket of appropriate size and a small hammer.

2. Insert the split-ring washer into the hub of the front housing and seat the washer in its groove. Be extremely careful doing this, because the bearing seal is easily damaged.

3. The front bearing now must be seated against the shoulder on the rotor shaft. Install the fan and pulley spacer, then the Woodruff key, fan and pulley. Using a 7/16 in. socket or equivalent tool to fit inside the rear bearing race, apply pressure to drive the bearing against the shoulder of the rotor shaft.

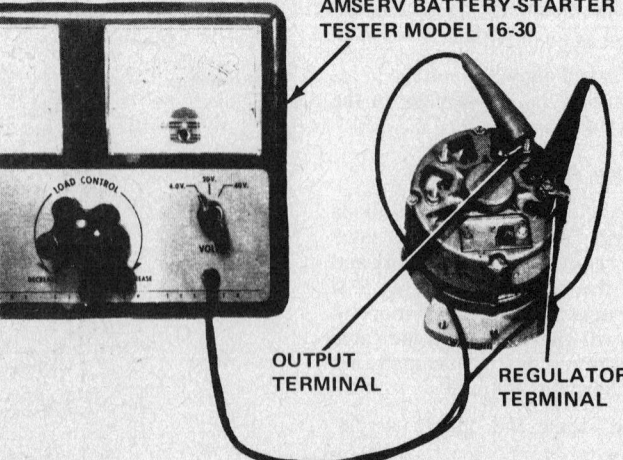

AMSERV BATTERY-STARTER TESTER MODEL 16-30

OUTPUT TERMINAL

REGULATOR TERMINAL

Motorola field diode test

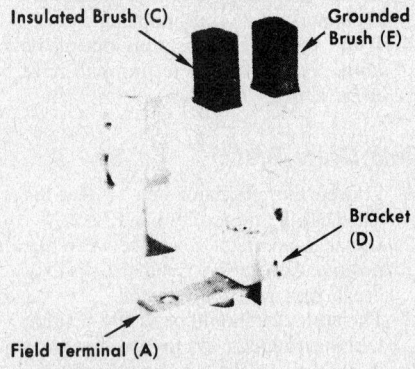

Insulated Brush (C)

Grounded Brush (E)

Bracket (D)

Field Terminal (A)

Motorola brush assembly

4. Assemble the front and rear housing assemblies by hand, making certain that the rear bearing is properly seated in the rear housing hub and that the diode wires are not touching the rotor at any point.

5. Align the matchmarks made during disassembly, then spin the rotor to make sure sufficient clearance exists between it and the diode wires. Install the through-bolts and tighten them evenly, using only a hand wrench. Continue assembly in reverse of disassembly.

STATOR

In-Circuit Test

NOTE: When making the in-circuit test, consideration must be given to the rectifier diodes, which are connected to the stator windings. When properly polarized, the diode will conduct current in one direction only. A shorted diode would make the stator appear to be shorted also, so if during this test, a defect is noted, the stator windings and the rectifier diodes must be tested individually. Do not use a 120 volt test lamp as the diodes will be damaged.

1. With the use of a diode continuity light tool or a dc test lamp, connect one test lead to a diode terminal and the second lead to ground. Observe the test lamp and reverse the test leads.

2. The test lamp should light in one direction and not in the other with the leads reversed.
   a. If the test lamp lights in both directions, the stator windings are shorted or one of the negative diodes are shorted. Disassemble, unsolder, and test.
   b. If the test lamp does not light in either direction, all three rectifiers in the negative assembly are indicated to be open. Disassemble, unsolder, and test.

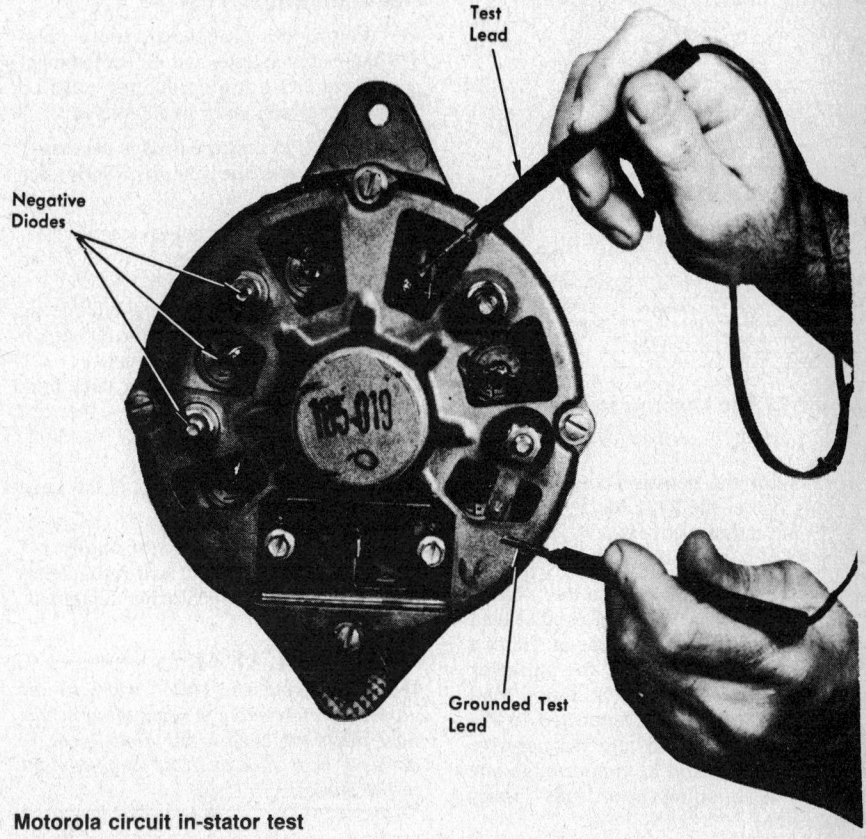

Motorola circuit in-stator test

Out of Circuit Tests

To prepare for out of the circuit tests, the stator and diode assembly must be removed from the rear housing. Unsolder the stator leads from the diode stems. Upon reassembly, be certain that the same leads are soldered to the diodes in the same location as removed.

Stator Short Test

1. With the use of a test lamp or ohmmeter, test the windings of the stator by attaching one lead to the stator core and probing the stator leads with the other test lead.

2. The test lamp will light and the ohmmeter will register if a short circuit exists between the windings and the core. The short circuit must be found or the stator unit be replaced.

Stator Load Test

To test the stator coil windings for short circuits or high resistance, the following tools are needed. A fully charged 12 volt battery, a voltmeter, an ammeter, and a variable load control.

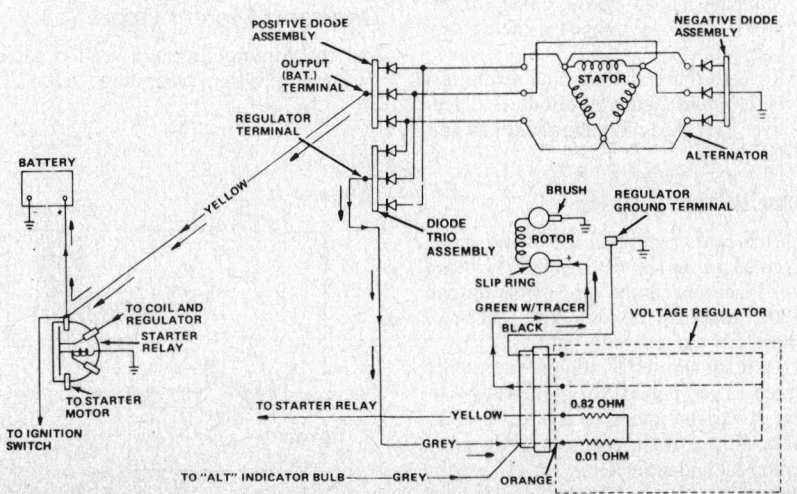

Motorola charging system

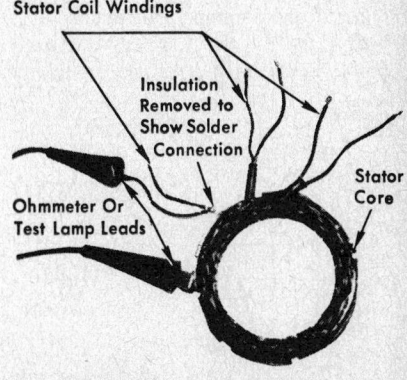

Motorola stator winding short test

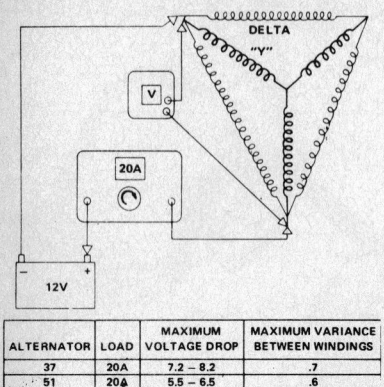

ALTERNATOR	LOAD	MAXIMUM VOLTAGE DROP	MAXIMUM VARIANCE BETWEEN WINDINGS
37	20A	7.2 – 8.2	.7
51	20A	5.5 – 6.5	.6

51 and 55 amp Motorola stator load test

1. Connect the negative battery lead to any one of the three stator leads.
2. Connect the positive battery lead to one lead of the variable load control.

NOTE: If the load control has a built-in ammeter, the other load control lead would be connected to either of the two remaining stator leads. If the ammeter is a separate unit, the remaining load control lead would be connected to the positive ammeter lead and the negative ammeter lead would be connected to one of the two remaining stator leads. (series connection)

3. Connect the voltmeter leads between the two stator leads being tested, (parallel connection) and adjust the variable load control to draw 20 amperes. Allow the windings to warm up for 15 seconds and note the reading on the voltmeter scale. The reading should not exceed 8.2 volts for a 37 ampere rated alternator, or exceed 6.5 volts for the 51 and 55 ampere rated alternators.
4. Stop the current flow to the coil and disconnect the test leads from the stator leads and reconnect them to the remaining stator leads and test the circuits as outlined in paragraph 3. Continue with the test for the third set of windings.
5. Note the variance between the windings. It should not exceed 0.7 volt for the 37 ampere alternator or 0.6 volt for the 51 and 55 ampere alternator.

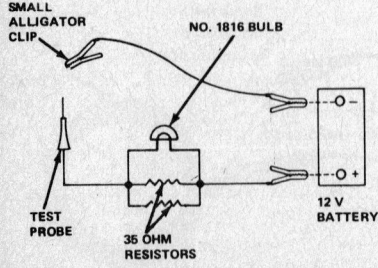

Rectifier diode test producing a 15 amp load

Rectifier Diode Test

1. With diodes unsoldered, use a commercial type tester and follow the manufacturer's test procedure or make up a heavy load tester as illustrated.

NOTE: A 15 ampere load is necessary to properly test the rectifier diodes for heat related defects.

2. With the use of the heavy load tester probes, connect them to the diode so the test bulb is lighted.
3. Maintain the test load on the diode for 1 to 3 minutes. If the light flickers or goes out, the diode is defective.
4. If the light remains on after three minutes, immediately reverse the test leads. If the test bulb lights, the diode is defective.
5. Test the remaining diodes in the same manner.

NOTE: The diodes are normally not replaced separately, but are replaced as a positive or negative rectifier bridge assembly.

--- CAUTION ---

When soldering the stator wires to the diodes, it is advisable to use a set of needle nose pliers attached to the diode stem, to act as a heat sink to avoid heat damage to the diodes.

Field Diode Assembly (Diode Trio)

Two types of diode assemblies are used. The board and the potted type and both are tested with the same procedure.

1. With the diode assembly removed, use a commercial type tester and follow the manufacturer's test procedures or make a load tester as illustrated.
2. Connect the test leads to one of the diodes so that the test bulb is lighted.

NOTE: A one ampere load is needed to properly test the field diode assembly for heat related defects.

3. Maintain a load on the diode for approximately one minute to detect any heat failure.
4. Reverse the test leads and if the test bulb would light, the diode is defective. Test the remaining diodes as outlined.

Rotor Winding Tests

With the rotor removed, use a test probe connected in series with a 110 volt test lamp. Place one probe on a slip ring and the other probe on the rotor core. The rotor is shorted if the test bulb lights.

To test for shorted windings, use a fully charged 12 volt battery, an ammeter, a voltmeter, a variable rheostat, and test probes.

With the use of the test probe leads, place the rheostat and ammeter in series with the battery. Connect one test probe to one slip ring and the other test probe to the other

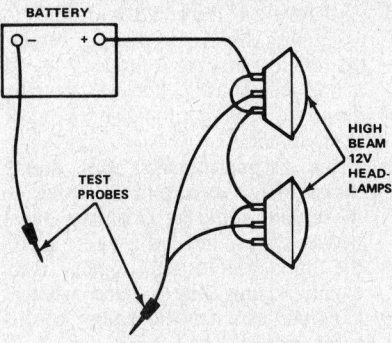

Field diode test producing a 1 amp load

slip ring. Place the voltmeter in parallel with the slip rings.

Slowly reduce the resistance of the rheostat to zero and with full battery voltage, (12.6 ± 0.2 volt), applied to the rotor coil, the field current should register between 1.8 to 2.5 amperes. Excessive ampere draw would indicate shorted windings and low ampere draw would indicate open windings of the rotor.

The Prestolite System

Prestolite alternators incorporate an *isolation diode*, mounted as a component part of the internal positive heat sink assembly. Such alternators are almost identical to late model Motorola units in operation. Test procedures for the Motorola alternator also apply to the diode-equipped Prestolite.

TROUBLESHOOTING

NOTE: See the "Alternator Test Plans" section before proceeding further.

Fusible Link Test

See the Motorola system section for the fuse link test.

Charging System Operation

See the Motorola system section for the "Charging System Operation" tests.

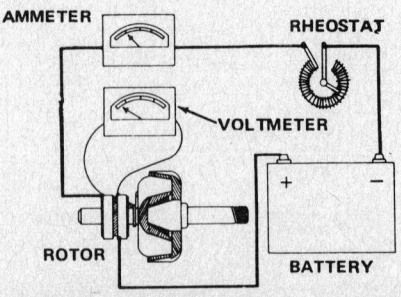

Motorola rotor winding test

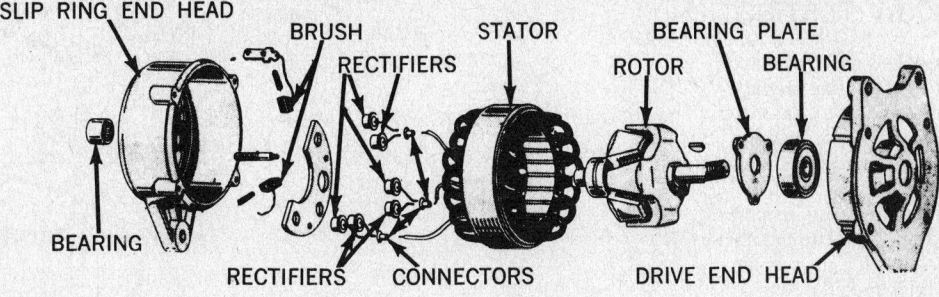

Prestolite alternator

Testing the Ignition Switch-to-Regulator Circuit

1. Disconnect the regulator wires from the regulator.
2. Turn on the key. Using a test light or voltmeter, check for current between the I terminal and ground and the L terminal ground. If voltage is present, this part of the system is OK. If no voltage is present, check for broken or shorted wires, a bad indicator bulb, a bad ammeter (if so equipped), or bad connections.

Alternator Disassembly

1. Remove the two brush mounting screws and cover, then tip the brush assembly away from the alternator and remove.
2. Matchmark the rear housing, stator and drive end housing, then remove the four retaining screws. The stator and rear housing are removed as a unit by tapping lightly with a fiber hammer to separate them from the front housing.
3. The rotor should not be removed unless it or the front bearing is defective. To remove the rotor under these conditions, first remove the pulley nut and pulley (using a two-jaw puller), then remove the fan, Woodruff key and spacer. The rotor is removed from the front housing using a three-paw puller.
4. The front bearing is easily removed, after taking out the retaining ring, by pressing it out in a large vise using sockets to support the housing from the rear.

Stator Coil Test—Diode Type

1. Using a No. 57 bulb, connected in series with a 12-volt battery, as a test light, touch one test lead to the connection of the three stator windings and the other test lead to each stator lead that is connected to the diodes. If the bulb does not light, the winding is open.
2. To test for a grounded stator, use a 110-volt test lamp. First disconnect the diodes from the stator leads, then touch one test lead to the stator core and the other test lead to each of the three stator leads. If the test lamp lights, the winding is grounded.

NOTE: If all other components are O.K. and alternator still does not work, it can be assumed that the stator windings are internally shorted. This type of short is impossible to detect by using the previous test. Diode tests are the same as for the Motorola alternator.

Alternator Assembly

1. Press the front bearing into the front housing, making sure the dust seal faces the rotor. Install the bearing retaining snap-ring, then press the shoulder of the shaft against the inner bearing race using a tool that fits over the shaft and against the race. Install the spacer, Woodruff key, fan and pulley, then install lockwasher and pulley nut.
2. Install the diode heat sink, negative diodes and stator. Solder any stator to diode connections that were unsoldered, using pliers as a heat sink to prevent overheating.
3. Install the rotor and front drive housing to stator and rear housing, aligning matchmarks made during disassembly. Install the four retaining screws, then the brush holder assembly and retaining screws.
4. Make sure the stator leads and brush holder assembly clear the rotor and that the rotor can be spun by hand without binding.

ELECTRONIC IGNITION SYSTEM

Ford-Motorcraft Solid-State Ignition System (SSI)

The Ford-Motorcraft Solid-State Ignition System is a pulse triggered, breakerless, transistor controlled ignition system. The system utilizes most of the standard ignition components, but substitutes an amplifier module and magnetic pickup assembly for the conventional ignition contact points.

OPERATION

With the ignition switch "on", the primary circuit is on and the ignition coil is energized. When the armature "spokes" approach the magnetic pick-up coil assembly, they induce a voltage which tells the amplifier to turn the coil primary current off. A timing circuit in the amplifier module will turn the current on again after the coil field has collapsed. When the current is "on", it flows from the battery through the ignition switch, the primary windings of the ignition coil, and through the amplifier module circuits to ground. When the current is off, the magnetic field built up in the ignition coil is allowed to collapse, inducing a high voltage into the secondary windings of the coil. High voltage is produced each time the field is thus built up and collapsed.

The high voltage flows through the coil high tension lead to the distributor cap where the rotor distributes it to one of the spark plug terminals in the distributor cap. This process is repeated for every power stroke of the engine.

Ignition system troubles are caused by a failure in the primary and/or the secondary circuit; incorrect ignition timing; or incorrect distributor advance. Circuit failures may be caused by shorts, corroded or dirty terminals, loose connections, defective wire insulation, cracked distributor cap or rotor, defective pick-up coil assembly or amplifier module, defective distributor points, fouled spark plugs, or by improper dwell angle.

If an engine starting or operating trouble is attributed to the ignition system, start the engine and verify the complaint. On engines that will not start, be sure that there is gasoline in the fuel tank and that fuel is reaching the carburetor. Then locate the ignition system problem by an oscilloscope test or by a spark intensity test.

IGNITION SYSTEMS
ELECTRONIC

PRIMARY CIRCUIT TESTING

A breakdown or energy loss in the primary circuit can be caused by: defective primary wiring, loose or corroded connections, inoperative or defective magnetic pick-up coil assembly, or defective amplifier module.

A complete test of the primary circuit consists of checking the circuits in the ignition coil, the magnetic pick-up coil assembly and the amplifier module. Wiring harness checks will be included as a part of basic component circuit tests.

Always inspect connectors for dirt, corrosion or poor fit before assuming you have spotted a possible problem.

Dura Spark II Ignition System

The Dura Spark II is a solid state ignition system incorporating high energy secondary components. The distributor, coil and module are the same as the units used in the regular Solid State Ignition system (SSI). The system incorporates an adapter on the distributor to accomodate the larger cap and larger rotor used with the higher voltage. The high voltage and wide spark plug gap increases the spark plug life and overall engine performance. The higher voltage is accomplished through the use of a 1.10 ohm ballast resistor, integral with the primary wire harness, which increases the energy input to the coil and in turn, the secondary energy level. The system is easily identified by the large blue adapter and distributor cap.

DUAL MODE TIMING IGNITION MODULE

On some applications, a special Dura Spark II ignition module is used with altitude compensation. This special module plus the barometric pressure switch, allows the base engine timing to be modified to suit altitude conditions. All other elements and performance characteristics of this module are identical in both modes of operation to the basic Dura Spark II system. All Dura Spark II modules equipped with altitude features, have three connectors instead of the normal two. A barometric switch provides an automatic retard signal to the module at different altitudes, giving appropriate advanced timing at higher altitude and retard mode for spark knock control at lower altitudes.

DISTRIBUTOR

The distributors are equipped with both vacuum and centrifugal spark advances which operate the same regardless of the type of ignition system used. A dual vacuum advance is used on certain engines to

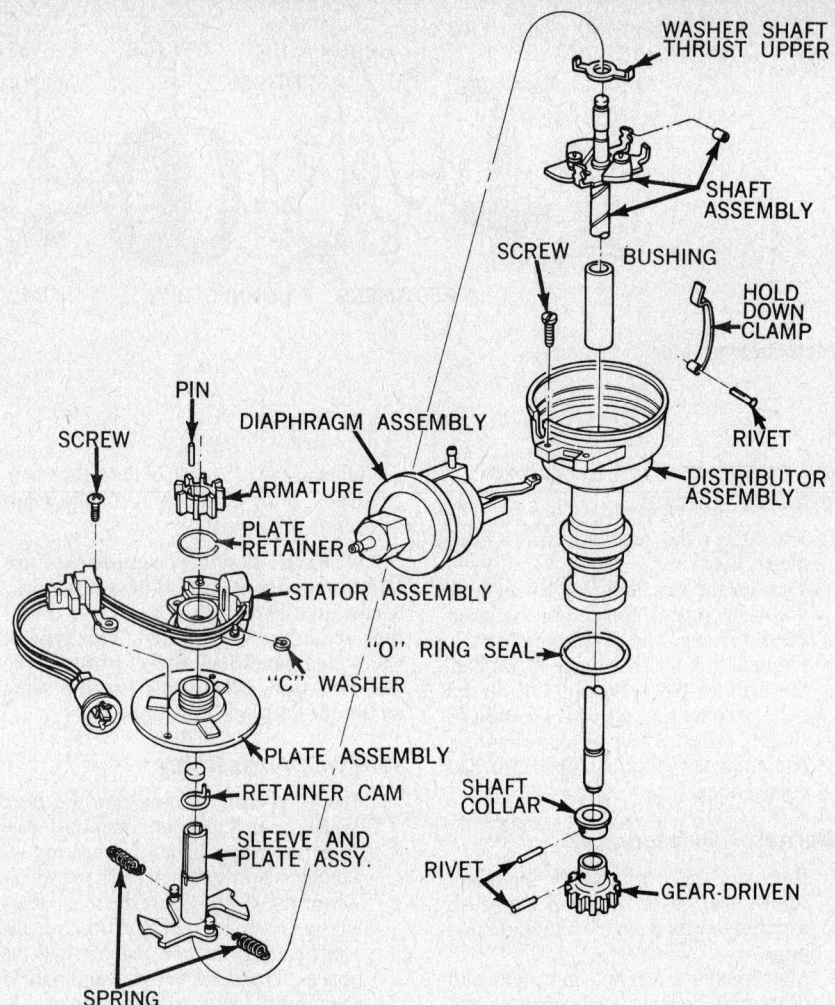

8-cylinder breakerless distributor

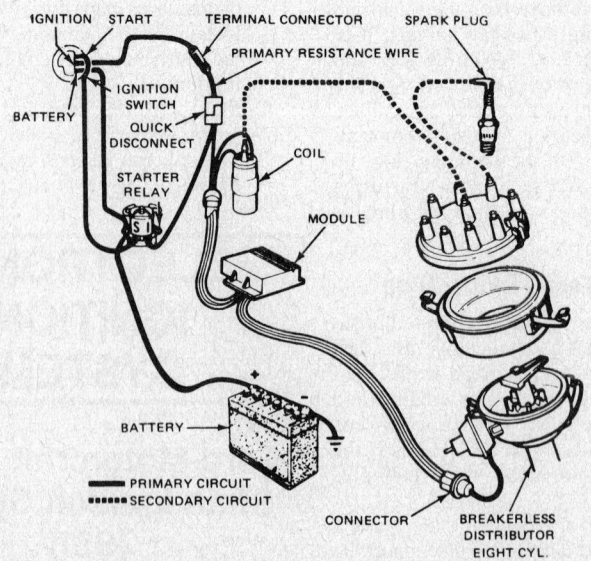

Breakerless ignition circuit routings

provide ignition retard during engine closed throttle operation, to help control engine exhaust emissions.

CIRCUIT OPERATION

All systems consist of a primary (low voltage) and a secondary (high voltage) circuit.
The Primary Circuit—The components involved in the primary circuit are:
1. Battery
2. Ignition switch
3. Primary circuit resistance wire (integral wire in the SSI and Dura Spark II systems)
4. Primary windings of the ignition coil
5. Magnetic pickup coil assembly in the distributor
6. Ignition module.

The Secondary Circuit—The components of the secondary circuit are:
1. Secondary windings of the ignition coil
2. Distributor rotor
3. Distributor cap and adapter (Dura Spark II)
4. Secondary spark plug wires
5. Spark plugs

Operation

With the ignition switch in the "ON" position, the primary circuit is energized and the magnetic field is built up by the current flowing through the primary windings of the ignition coil. When the armature spokes align with the center of the magnetic pickup coil, the module turns off the coil primary current and the high voltage is produced in the secondary circuit by the collapsing magnetic field. High voltage is produced each time the magnetic field is caused to collapse due to a timing circuit in the module, which starts and stops the primary circuit through the coil. The high voltage flows through the coil secondary lead to the distributor cap, where the rotor distributes the spark to the proper spark plug terminal in the distributor cap. The secondary current then flows through the secondary wire to the spark plug.

System Adjustments

No adjustments are made to the Dura Spark II ignition system except the initial timing and spark plug gap.

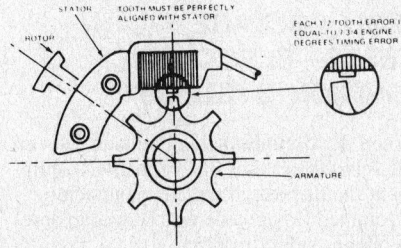

Armature alignment

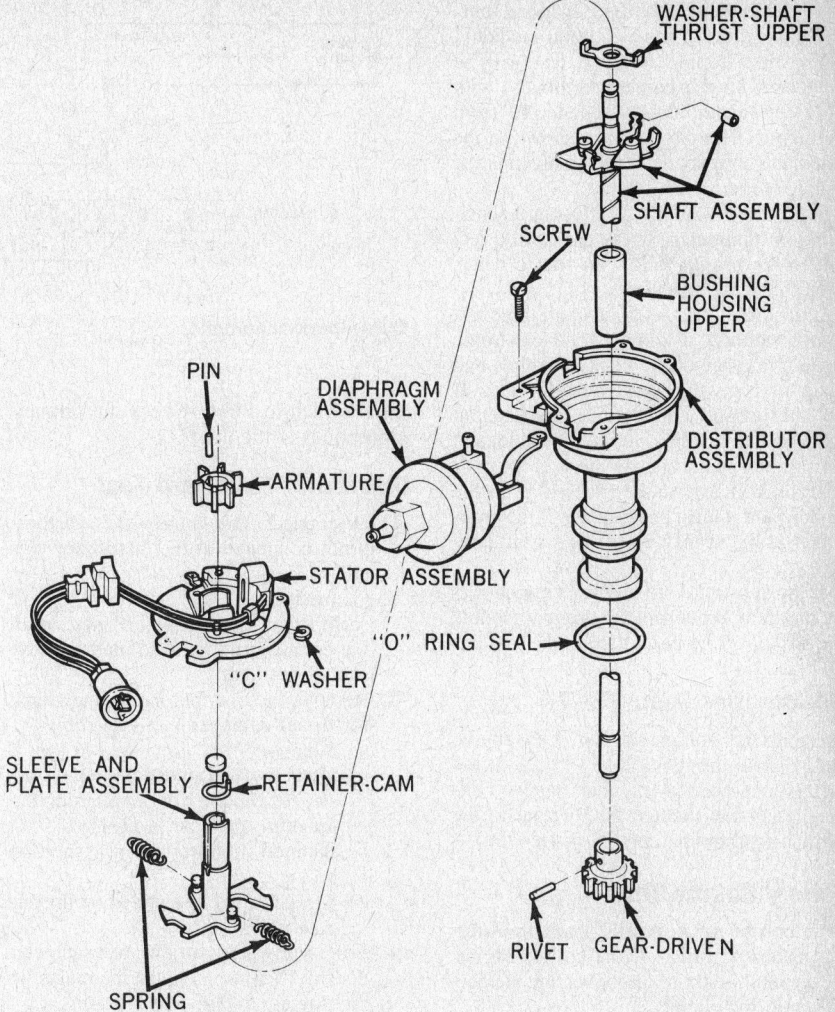

6-cylinder breakerless distributor

SECONDARY WIRE USAGE

Dura Spark II

Spark plug wires that are used with the Dura Spark II system are 8mm in size, to contain the higher output voltage. Two types of wires are used in this system and some engines will have both types. It is important to identify the type of wire to a cylinder before a replacement is obtained and installed. Both types are blue in color and have silicone jacketing. The insulation material underneath the jacketing can be a EPDM or have another silicone layer, separated by glass braid. EPDM wires are used where the engine temperatures are cooler and are identified by the letters "SE". The silicone jacket type are used where the engine temperatures are high and are identified by the letters "SS".

NOTE: Whenever a Dura Spark II high tension wire is removed for any purpose from a spark plug, coil or distributor cap, silicone grease must be applied to the boot before it is reconnected.

The spark plug wires are marked with the cylinder number, model year and date of cable manufacture (quarter and year). Service replacement wires do not have this information.

Solid State Ignition System (SSI)

The SSI system uses 7mm secondary wires and should not be interchanged with the Dura Spark II secondary wires.

Troubleshooting

BREAKERLESS—'75–'77
DURA SPARK II—1977

TROUBLESHOOTING

Make sure that the battery is fully charged before beginning tests. Perform a Spark Intensity Test. If no spark is observed, make sure that the high tension coil wire is good. Disconnect the three-way and four-way connectors at the electronic module.

The first trouble isolation test will be conducted on the harness terminals, with the electronic module disconnected from the circuit. The pin numbers shown in the schematic correspond to those shown in the trouble isolation test table.

Make the following tests using a sensitive volt-ohmmeter. These tests will direct you to the proper follow-up test to determine the actual problem.

If the circuit checks good at all these test points, connect a known good electronic module in place of the vehicle module and again perform the spark intensity test. If the substitution corrects the malfunction again reconnect the vehicle module and perform the spark intensity test. If the malfunction still exists, the problem is in the module and it must be replaced. If the problem is gone, it may be in the wiring connectors.

If the substitute module does not correct the problem, reconnect the original module and make repairs elsewhere in the system.

Module Bias Test, '75–'77

Measure the voltage at Pin 3 to engine ground with the ignition key "on". If the voltage observed is less than battery voltage, repair the voltage feed wiring to the module for running conditions (re-wire).

Battery Source Test

1. Connect the voltmeter leads from the battery terminal at the coil to engine ground, without disconnecting the coil from the circuit.
2. Install a jumper wire from the DEC terminal of the coil to a good engine ground.
3. Turn the lights and all accessories off.
4. Turn the ignition switch "on".
5. If the voltmeter reading is between 4.9 and 7.9 volts, the primary circuit from the battery is satisfactory.
6. If the voltmeter reading is less than 4.9 volts, check the following:
   a. The primary wiring for worn insulation, broken strands, and loose or corroded terminals.
   b. The resistance wiring for defects.
7. If the voltmeter reading is greater than 7.9 volts, the resistance wire should be replaced after verifying a defect.

Cranking Test

Measure the voltage at Pin 1 to engine ground with the engine cranking. If the voltage observed is not 8 to 12 volts, repair the voltage feed to the module for starting conditions (white wire).

Starting Circuit Test

If the reading is not more than 6 volts, the ignition by-pass circuit is open or grounded from either the starter solenoid or the ig-

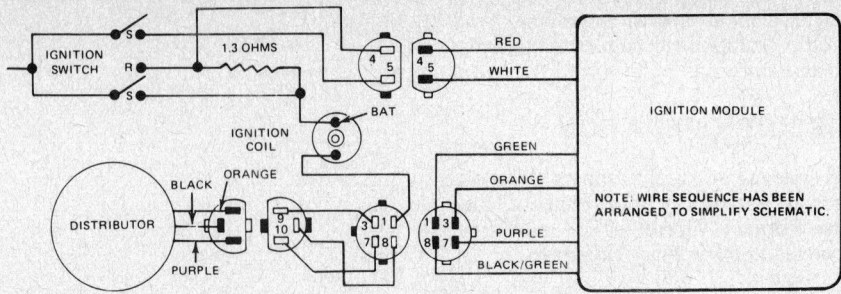

Dura-Spark schematic

nition switch to Pin 5. Check the primary connections at the coil.

Distributor Hardware Test

1. Disconnect the three-wire weather-proof connector at the distributor pigtail.
2. Connect a D.C. voltmeter on a 2.5 volt scale to the two parallel blades. With the engine cranking, the meter needle should oscillate.
3. Remove the distributor cap and check for visual damage or misassembly.
   a. Sintered iron armature (6 or 8 toothed wheel) must be tight on the sleeve, and the roll pin aligning the armature must be in position.
   b. Sintered iron stator must not be broken.
   c. Armature must rotate when the engine is cranked.
4. If the hardware is alright, but the meter doesn't oscillate, replace the magnetic pick-up assembly.

Magnetic Pick-up Tests

1. Resistance of pick-up coil measured between two parallel pins in the distributor connector must be 400–800 ohms.
2. Resistance between the third blade (ground) and the distributor bowl must be zero ohms.
3. Resistance between either parallel blade and engine ground must be greater than 70,000 ohms.
4. If any test fails, the distributor stator assembly is defective and must be replaced.
5. If the above readings are not the same as measured in the original test, check for a defective harness. If the readings are the same, proceed.
6. If these tests check alright, the signal generator portion of the distributor is working properly.

Ignition Coil Test

The breakerless ignition coil must be diagnosed separately from the rest of the ignition system.

1. Primary resistance must be 1.0–2.0 ohms, measured from the BAT to the DEC terminals.

2. Secondary resistance must be 7,000–13,000 ohms, measured from the BAT or DEC terminal to the center tower of the coil.
3. If resistance tests are alright, but the coil is still suspected, test the coil on a coil tester by following the test equipment manufacturer's instructions for a standard coil. If the reading differs from the original test, check for a defective harness.

Module Test

1. Unplug the electronic module connector, but don't remove the existing module from the car.
2. Connect a module which is known to be good to the connector. There is no need to attach the module to the car in order to have it work.
3. Start the engine; if it starts and operates correctly go on to the next step. If it won't start and run, the trouble is somewhere else. Check and repair the wiring and other systems, as required.
4. If the engine started in step 3, reconnect the original module and try to start the engine again. If the engine won't start, replace the module.
5. If the engine starts in step 4, the original module is not defective. Check all the wiring and connections in the ignition system.

Short Test

If the resistance from Pin 5 to ground is less than 4 ohms, check for a short to ground at the DEC terminal of the ignition coil or in the connection wiring to that terminal.

HIGH VOLTAGE TESTS—ELECTRONIC IGNITION SYSTEMS

When performing the high voltage tests on the ignition systems, the proper test equipment should be used and the manufacturer's recommended procedures followed in order to obtain correct results.

1. Connecting the test equipment to the ignition system in the proper order,

measure the coil reserve voltage, which should be 28 KV minimum.

2. Measure the spark plug required voltage of each spark plug. The required voltage is 8-20 KV.

—————— CAUTION ——————

Do not remove the following spark plug wires when performing these tests.

No. 1 or No. 8 wires on V-8 engines.
No. 3 or No. 5 wires on I-6 engines.
No. 1 or No. 4 wires on V-6 engines.
No. 1 or No. 3 wires on 4 cylinder engines.

3. Check the coil to distributor cap, distributor cap to spark plug wires with an ohmmeter. The reading should be 5 K ohms per inch maximum.

—————— CAUTION ——————

Unless specified, all high voltage measurements are to be made with a "clampon" probe. Never attempt to puncture the high voltage insulation to perform tests. A spark plug wire should never be removed for longer than 30 seconds on catalytic converter equipped vehicles.

NOTE: When removing any Dura Spark II high tension lead, the interior of the terminal boot must be greased with a silicone grease, meeting Ford Motor Co. specifications.

Adjustments

The air gap between the armature and magnetic pick-up coil in the distributor is not adjustable, nor are there any adjustments for the amplifier module. Inoperative components are simply replaced. Any attempt to connect components outside the vehicle may result in component failure.

Dura Spark II
Solid State Ignition
(SSI)

1978 and Later

To properly diagnose the ignition system, a starting place must be established and an order of inspection followed until the fault is found and repaired. A recheck should be made, again in its order of inspection, to verify the repairs and to assure trouble-free operation.

Run Mode Test

1. If no spark is available at the spark plug, remove the coil high tension lead at the distributor and either place it ¼ inch from the engine block or place a modified spark plug into the coil wire and ground the spark plug body.

2. Turn the ignition switch to the "RUN" position and tap the distributor body with a screwdriver type tool handle.

Check for spark while tapping.

3. If spark is available, crank the engine with the starter and check for spark. If spark occurs, the primary ignition system is OK.

4. If no spark occurs, turn the key to the "OFF" position and crank the engine to align the engine timing pointer with the initial timing degree line on the damper pulley. Turn the key to the "RUN" position and again tap the distributor and check for spark.

5. If no spark occurs, measure battery voltage and measure the battery voltage on the module's red wire without disconnecting any connectors. The voltage in the red wire should equal battery voltage.

6. If battery voltage is not present in the module red wire, repair the circuit between the battery and the module connector. Recheck the voltage supply.

7. With the voltage present in the module's red wire, cycle the ignition switch between the "RUN" and "OFF" position. A spark should be seen each time the switch is turned to the "OFF" position.

8. If no spark occurs, measure the voltage on the battery side of the coil.
   a. Less than 6 volts—Repair the wire carrying current to the battery terminal of the coil and repeat test.
   b. If voltage is 6–8 volts—Substitute, but do not install, a known good module and repeat the test. If spark then occurs, reconnect the original module to verify its being defective. Replace as required. Refer to step 10 if the battery voltage is present.

9. If a spark occurs from step 7, substitute, but do not install, and ground a good distributor of any calibration 4, 6 or 8 cylinder. Spin the distributor shaft and check for high tension spark.
   a. If a spark occurs, reconnect the old distributor and verify its being defective. Replace as required.
   b. If no spark occurs, disconnect the distributor connector and 4 post connector at the module. Check the harness wires that mate with the module and distributor orange and purple wires for continuity between the module and distributor end of the harness. Check to be sure there is no short between the two wires and there is an open circuit to ground. If not OK, repair the wiring and repeat the test to verify repairs.
   c. If no spark occurs after completing step 9b, reconnect the distributor connector and substitute, but do not install, a known good module and repeat the test. If a spark occurs, reconnect the original module and verify it is defective. Repair as required.

10. If battery voltage is present at the battery terminal of the coil,

   a. Disconnect the 4 wire connector at the module. Insert a paper clip between the green and black wires of the module and remeasure the voltage at the battery terminal of the coil.
   b. If the voltage is between 6 to 8 volts, substitute, but do not install, a known good module and repeat the tests. If spark occurs, reconnect the old module and verify its being defective. Replace as required.
   c. If battery voltage is still present at the battery terminal of the coil, be sure the coil connector remains in place on the coil and ground the negative terminal of the coil. Remeasure the voltage on the coil battery terminal. If battery voltage still is present, remove the paper clip from the 4 wire connector and reconnect the module. Substitute, but do not install, a known good coil and repeat the test. If a spark does not occur, connect the original coil and substitute a known good module, but do not install, and repeat the test. If a spark occurs, replace the module as required. If 4 to 7 volts is measured at the coil positive terminal, remove the ground from the coil negative terminal and ground the paper clip connector in the 4 wire connector. Remeasure the voltage at the coil battery terminal. The voltage should be 4 to 7 volts. If the 4 to 7 volts are present, repair the ground circuit mating with the module black wire. Remove the paper clip from the 4 wire connector and reconnect the module. Repeat the test. If no voltage is present, repair the module to coil wire that mates with the module green wire. Remove the paper clip from the connector and reconnect the module. Repeat the test.

Cranking Test

1. Measure the voltage at the battery terminal of the ignition coil while cranking the engine. The reading should be within 1.0 volt of battery voltage. If not with-in specifications, repair the wire or circuit to the coil terminal.

2. While cranking the engine, check for spark from the high tension leads.

3. If no spark occurs, check the battery voltage on the white wire, while cranking the engine without disconnecting the module's two wire connectors. The voltage should be within 1.0 volt of battery voltage. If not, repair the white feed wire to the module.

4. Substitute, but do not install, a known good module and repeat the test. If a spark occurs, reconnect the original module and verify its being defective. Replace as required.

INTERMITTENT OPERATION DIAGNOSIS

Should the ignition system become operative during the tests and a repair has not been made to the system, it is likely an intermittent connection or component has become functional. Try to duplicate the problem with the engine running, by wiggling the wires at the coil, module, distributor and other harness connections, preferrably the connections that have been disturbed during the test proceedings. Check all ground connections, especially with-in the distributor. Disconnecting and connecting connectors may also help.

Heating Components for Tests
PICK-UP COIL

Using a 250 watt heat lamp, approximately 1 to 2 inches from the pick-up coil, apply heat for 4 to 6 minutes while monitoring the pick-up coil continuity between the parallel blades of the disconnected distributor connector. The resistance should be 400 to 1000 ohms. Tapping with a screwdriver type handle may also be helpful to locate problem. If specifications cannot be met or held, replace the pick-up coil.

IGNITION MODULE

With the engine running, heat the module by placing a 250 watt heat lamp bulb approximately 1 to 2 inches from the module top surface.

----------- CAUTION -----------
This procedure should not heat the module over 212 degrees F. After the first 10 minutes of heating, check the temperature by applying a few drops of water on the module housing. Repeat the check every one to two minutes until the water droplets boil.

Tapping the module may be helpful, but do not tap hard enough to damage or distort the housing. If this procedure results in an ignition malfunction, substitute, but do not install, a known good module. If the ignition malfunction is corrected by the substitution, reinstall the original module and recheck. Replace the module as required.

Delco-Remy High Energy Ignition (HEI) System

COMPONENTS

The Delco-Remy High Energy Ignition (HEI) System is a breakerless, pulse triggered, transistor controlled, inductive discharge ignition system.

There are only nine external electrical connections; the ignition switch feed wire, and the eight spark plug leads. On V8 engines, the ignition coil is located within the

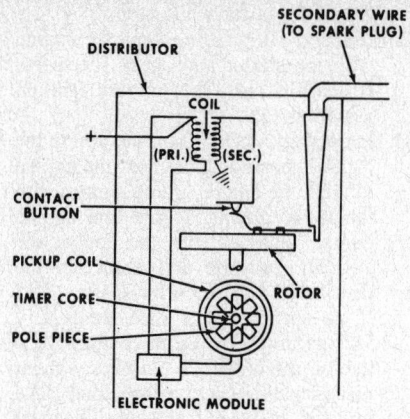

HEI schematic

distributor cap, connecting directly to the rotor.

OPERATION

The magnetic pick-up assembly located inside the distributor contains a permanent magnet, a pole piece with internal teeth, and a pick-up coil. When the teeth of the rotating timer core and pole piece align, an induced voltage in the pick-up coil signals the electronic module to open the coil primary circuit. As the primary current decreases, a high voltage is induced in the secondary windings of the ignition coil, directing a spark through the rotor and high voltage leads to fire the spark plugs. The dwell period is automatically controlled by the electronic module and is increased with increasing engine rpm. The HEI System features a longer spark duration which is instrumental in firing lean and EGR diluted fuel/air mixtures. The condenser (capacitor) located within the HEI distributor is provided for noise (static) suppression purposes only and is not a regularly replaced ignition system component.

MAJOR REPAIR OPERATIONS (DISTRIBUTOR IN ENGINE)

Ignition Coil Replacement V8 Engines

1. Disconnect the feed and module wire terminal connectors from the distributor cap.
2. Remove the ignition set retainer.
3. Remove the 4 coil cover-to-distributor cap screws and the coil cover.
4. Remove the 4 coil-to-distributor cap screws.
5. Using a blunt drift, press the coil wire spade terminals up out of distributor cap.
6. Lift the coil up out of the distributor cap.
7. Remove and clean the coil spring, rubber seal washer and coil cavity of the distributor cap.
8. Reverse the above procedures to install.

Six Cylinder Engines

On 6 cylinder engines, a separate ignition

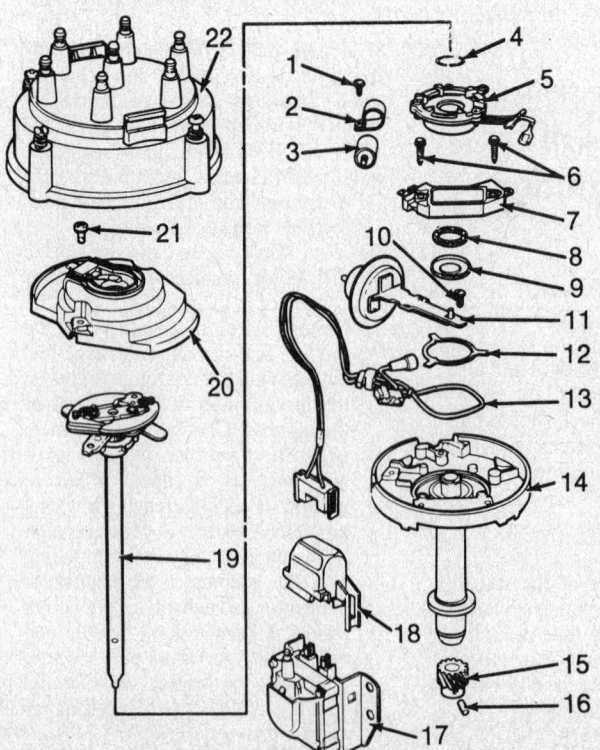

1. Screw
2. Bracket
3. Capacitor
4. Thin C-washer (retainer)
5. Pole piece and plate assembly (pick up coil)
6. Screw
7. Module assembly
8. Felt washer
9. Plastic grease retainer seal
10. Screw
11. Vacuum control assembly
12. Retainer (wire harness)
13. Wire harness assembly
14. Housing assembly
15. Gear
16. Roll pin
17. Ignition coil
18. Cover
19. Distributor shaft assembly
20. Rotor
21. Screw
22. Distributor cap

6-cylinder HEI distributor

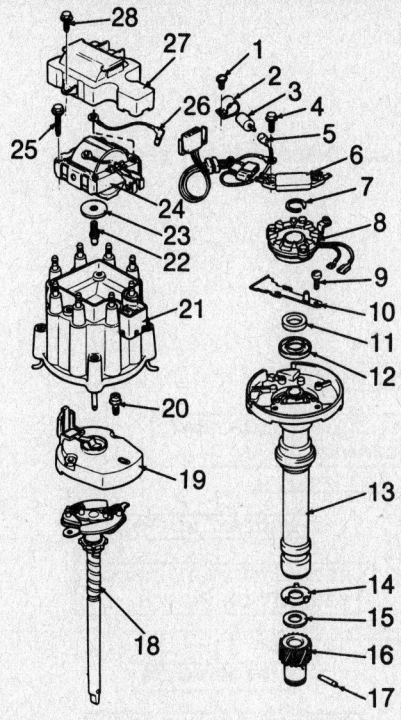

V8 HEI distributor

1. Screw
2. Bracket
3. Capacitor
4. Screw
5. Wiring harness assembly
6. Module assembly
7. Thin C-washer (retainer)
8. Pole piece and plate assembly (pick up coil)
9. Screw
10. Plastic retainer
11. Felt washer
12. Plastic grease retainer seal
13. Housing assembly
14. Thrust washer
15. Shim
16. Gear
17. Roll pin
18. Distributor shaft assembly
19. Rotor
20. Screw
21. Distributor cap
22. Resistor brush and spring
23. Seal
24. Ignition coil
25. Screw
26. Ground lead
27. Cover
28. Screw

coil is used. To remove and install it, proceed as follows:

1. Remove the ignition switch-to-coil lead from the coil.
2. Unfasten the distributor leads from the coil.
3. Remove the screws which secure the coil to the engine and lift it off.

Installation is the reverse of removal.

Distributor Cap Replacement

1. Remove the feed and module wire terminal connectors from the distributor cap.
2. Remove the retainer and spark plug wires from the cap.
3. Depress and release the 4 distributor cap-to-housing retainers and lift off the cap assembly.
4. Remove the 4 coil cover screws and cover (V8 only).
5. Using a finger or a blunt drift, push the spade terminals up out of the distributor cap (V8 only).
6. Remove all 4 coil screws and lift the coil, coil spring and rubber seal washer out of the cap coil cavity (V8 only).
7. Using a new distributor cap, reverse the above procedures to assemble.

Rotor Replacement

1. Disconnect the feed and module wire connectors from the distributor.
2. Depress and release the 4 distributor cap-to-housing retainers and lift off the cap assembly.
3. Remove the two rotor attaching screws and rotor.

4. Reverse the above procedure to install.

Vacuum Advance Unit Replacement

1. Remove the distributor cap and rotor as previously described.
2. Disconnect the vacuum hose from the vacuum advance unit. Remove the module.
3. Remove the two vacuum advance retaining screws, pull the advance unit outward, rotate and disengage the operating rod from its tang.
4. Reverse the above procedure to install.

Module Replacement

1. Remove the distributor cap and rotor as previously described.
2. Disconnect the harness connector and pick-up coil spade connectors from the module (note their positions).
3. Remove the two screws and module from the distributor housing.
4. Coat the bottom of the new module with dielectric lubricant. Reverse the above procedure to install. Be sure that the leads are installed correctly.

Distributor Removal

1. Disconnect the ground cable from the battery.
2. Disconnect the feed and module terminal connectors from the distributor cap. (Don't use a screwdriver).
3. Disconnect the hose at the vacuum advance.
4. Depress and release the 4 distributor

cap-to-housing retainers and lift off the cap assembly.
5. Using crayon or chalk, make locating marks on the rotor and module and on the distributor housing and engine for installation purposes.
6. Loosen and remove the distributor clamp bolt and clamp, and lift distributor out of the engine. Noting the relative position of the rotor and module alignment marks, make a second mark on the rotor to align it with the one mark on the module.

Distributor Installation

1. With a new O-ring on the distributor housing and the second mark on the rotor aligned with the mark on the module, install the distributor, taking care to align the mark on the housing with the one on the engine. It may be necessary to lift the distributor and turn the rotor slightly to align the gears and the oil pump driveshaft.
2. With the respective marks aligned, install the clamp and bolt finger tight.
3. Install and secure the distributor cap.
4. Connect the feed and module connectors to the distributor cap.
5. Connect a timing light to the engine and plug the vacuum hose.
6. Connect the ground cable to the battery.
7. Start the engine and set the timing.
8. Turn the engine off and tighten the distributor clamp bolt. Disconnect the timing light and unplug and connect the hose to the vacuum advance.

SERVICE PROCEDURES (DISTRIBUTOR REMOVED)

Driven Gear Replacement

1. With the distributor removed, use a 1/8 in. pin punch and tap out the driven gear roll pin.
2. Hold the rotor end of shaft and rotate the driven gear to shear any burrs in the roll pin hole.
3. Remove the driven gear from the shaft.
4. Reverse the above procedure to install.

Mainshaft Replacement

1. With the driven gear and rotor removed, gently pull the mainshaft out of the housing.
2. Remove the advance springs, weights and slide the weight base plate off the mainshaft.
3. Reverse the above procedure to install.

Pole Piece, Magnet or Pick-up Coil Replacement

1. With the mainshaft out of its housing, remove the 3 retaining screws, pole piece and magnet and/or pick-up coil.
2. Reverse the removal procedure to install making sure that the pole piece teeth do not contact the timer core teeth

IGNITION SYSTEMS
ELECTRONIC

ENGINE CRANKS, BUT WILL NOT START

NOTE: IF A TACHOMETER IS CONNECTED TO THE TACHOMETER TERMINAL, DISCONNECT IT BEFORE PROCEEDING WITH THE TEST.

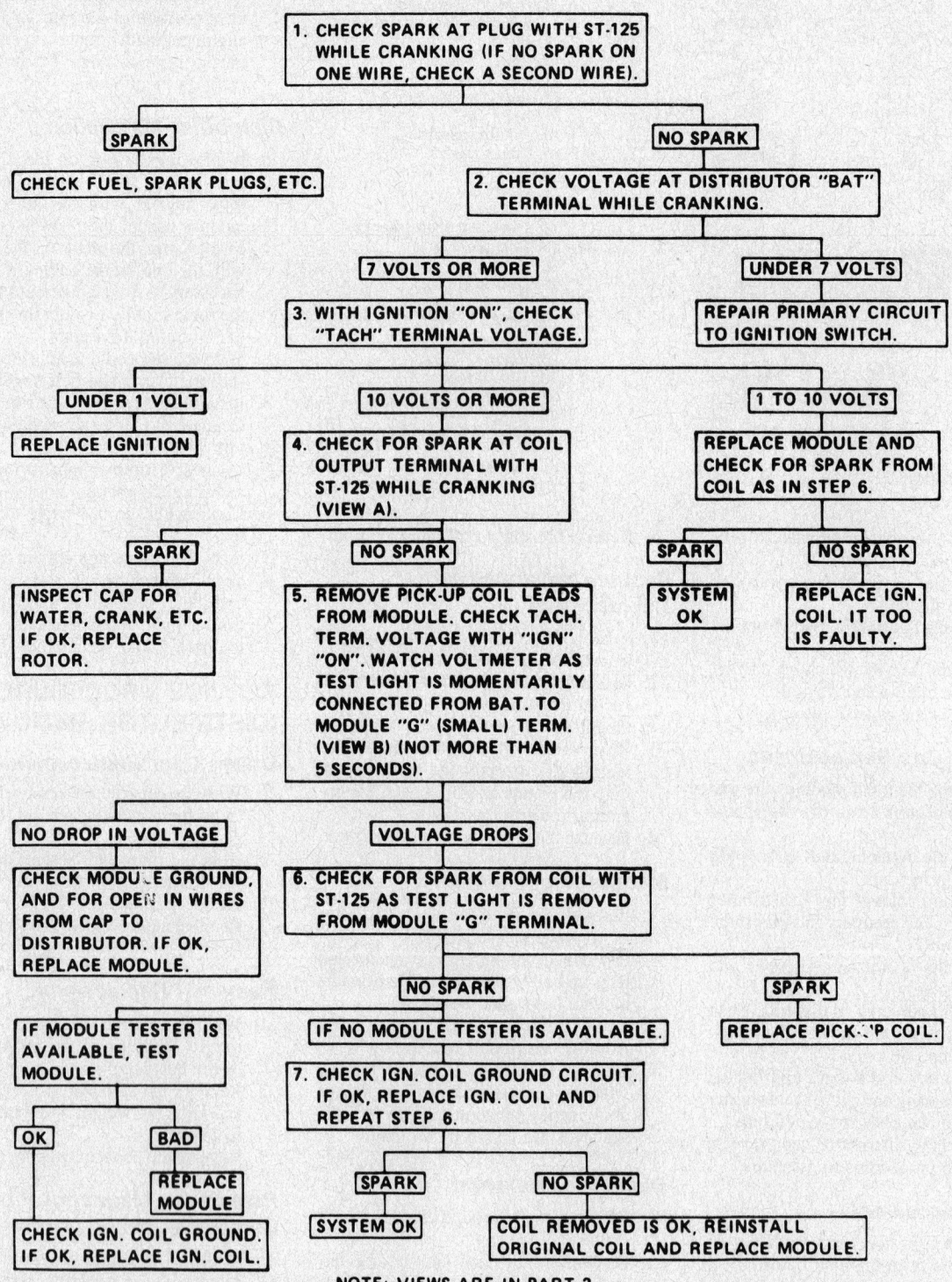

NOTE: VIEWS ARE IN PART 2.

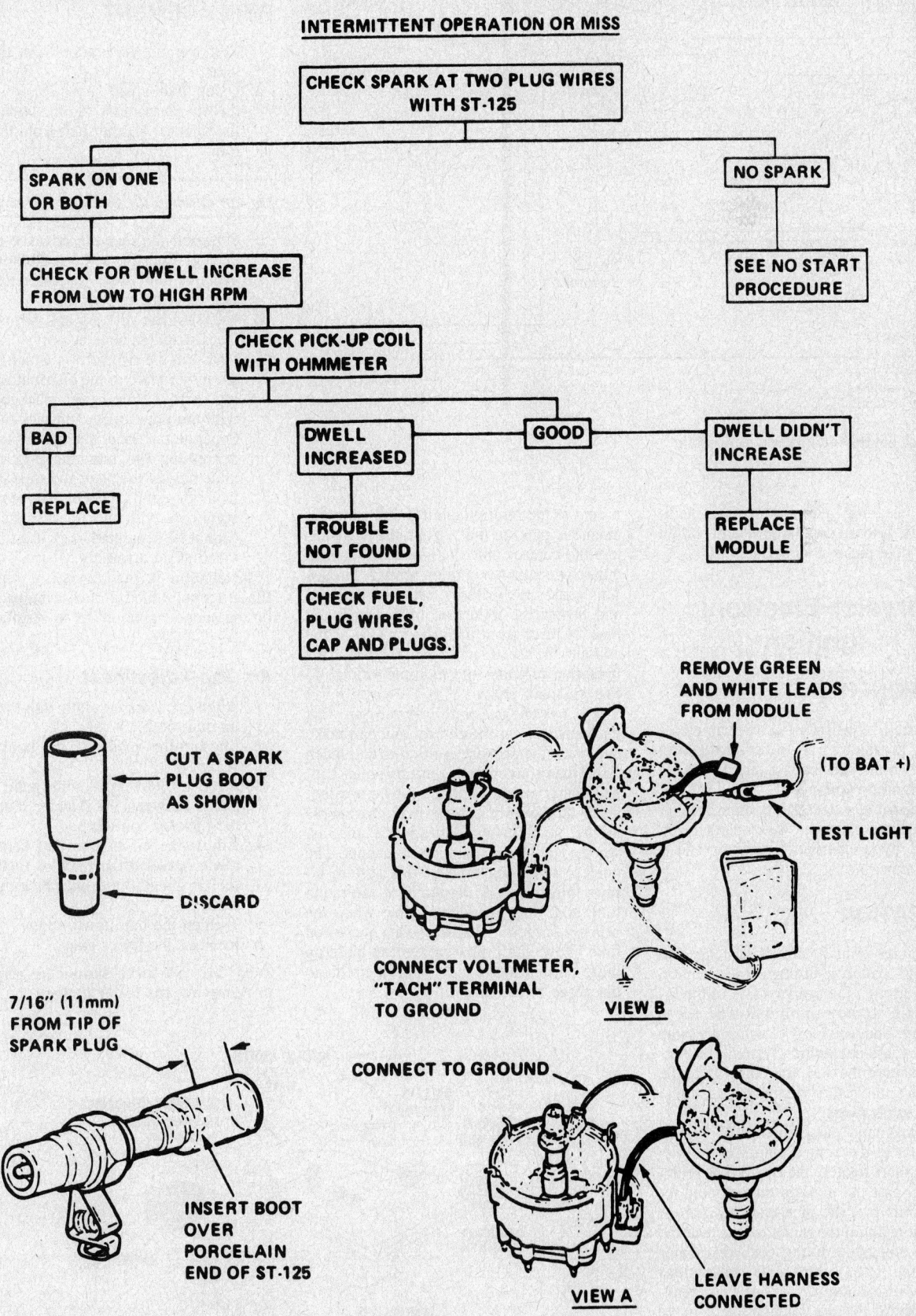

INTERMITTENT OPERATION OR MISS

CHECK SPARK AT TWO PLUG WIRES WITH ST-125

SPARK ON ONE OR BOTH

NO SPARK

CHECK FOR DWELL INCREASE FROM LOW TO HIGH RPM

SEE NO START PROCEDURE

CHECK PICK-UP COIL WITH OHMMETER

BAD

REPLACE

DWELL INCREASED

GOOD

DWELL DIDN'T INCREASE

TROUBLE NOT FOUND

REPLACE MODULE

CHECK FUEL, PLUG WIRES, CAP AND PLUGS.

CUT A SPARK PLUG BOOT AS SHOWN

DISCARD

REMOVE GREEN AND WHITE LEADS FROM MODULE

(TO BAT +)

TEST LIGHT

CONNECT VOLTMETER, "TACH" TERMINAL TO GROUND

VIEW B

7/16" (11mm) FROM TIP OF SPARK PLUG

CONNECT TO GROUND

INSERT BOOT OVER PORCELAIN END OF ST-125

LEAVE HARNESS CONNECTED

VIEW A

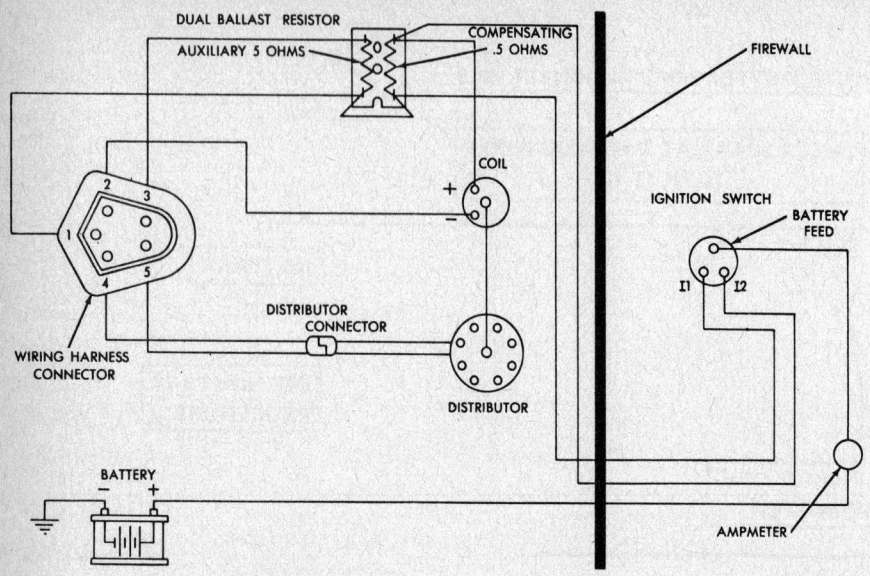

Chrysler electronic ignition schematic

PICK-UP COIL REPLACEMENT

1. Remove the distributor from the engine.
2. Using two small pry-bars or screwdrivers (maximum 7/16 in. wide), pry the reluctor off the shaft from the bottom.

——————— CAUTION ———————
Do not damage the teeth on the reluctor.

3. Unfasten the vacuum advance-to-distributor housing screws. Remove the vacuum unit, after disconnecting the arm from the upper plate.
4. Unfasten the pick-up coil wires from the distributor housing.
5. Unfasten the two screws which secure the lower plate to the distributor housing. Lift out the lower plate together with the upper plate and pick-up coil.
6. Separate the upper and lower plates by depressing the retaining clip on the underside of the plate and slide it away from the stud. The pick-up coil will come off with the upper plate; they cannot be separated; they must be serviced as an assembly.

Installation is the reverse of removal. Place a small amount of distributor grease on the support pins on the lower plate.

Air Gap Adjustment

1. Align one reluctor tooth with the pick-up coil tooth.
2. Loosen the pick-up coil hold-down screw.
3. Insert a 0.008 in. nonmagnetic feeler gauge between the reluctor tooth and the pick-up coil tooth.
4. Adjust the air gap so that contact is made between the reluctor tooth, the feeler gauge, and the pick-up coil tooth.
5. Tighten the hold-down screw.
6. Remove the feeler gauge.

NOTE: No force should be required in removing the feeler gauge.

by installing and rotating the mainshaft. Loosen the 3 screws and realign the pole piece as necessary.

Chrysler Electronic Ignition

COMPONENTS

This system consists of a special pulse-sending distributor, an electronic control unit, a two-element ballast resistor, and a special ignition coil.

The distributor does not contain breaker points or a condenser, these parts being replaced by a distributor reluctor and a pick-up unit.

OPERATION

The ignition primary circuit is connected from the battery, through the ignition switch, through the primary side of the ignition coil, to the control unit where it is grounded. The secondary circuit is the same as in conventional ignition systems: the secondary side of the coil, the coil wire to the distributor, the rotor, the spark plug wires, and the spark plugs.

The magnetic pulse distributor is also connected to the control unit. As the distributor shaft rotates, the distributor reluctor turns past the pick-up unit. As the reluctor turns past the pick-up unit, each of the eight teeth on the reluctor pass near the pick-up unit once during each distributor revolution (two crankshaft revolutions since the distributor runs at one-half crankshaft speed). As the reluctor teeth move close to the pick-up unit, the magnetic rotating reluctor induces voltage into the magnetic pick-up unit. This voltage pulse

is sent to the ignition control unit from the magnetic pick-up unit. When the pulse enters the control unit, it signals the control unit to interrupt the ignition primary circuit. This causes the primary circuit to collapse and begins the induction of the magnetic lines of force from the primary side of the coil into the secondary side of the coil. This induction provides the required voltage to fire the spark plugs.

The advantages of this system are that the transistors in the control unit can make and break the primary ignition circuit much faster than conventional ignition points can, and higher primary voltage can be utilized, since this system can be made to handle higher voltage without adverse effects, whereas ignition breaker points cannot. The quicker switching time of this system allows longer coil primary circuit saturation time and longer induction time when the primary circuit collapses. This increased time allows the primary circuit to build up more current and the secondary circuit to discharge more current.

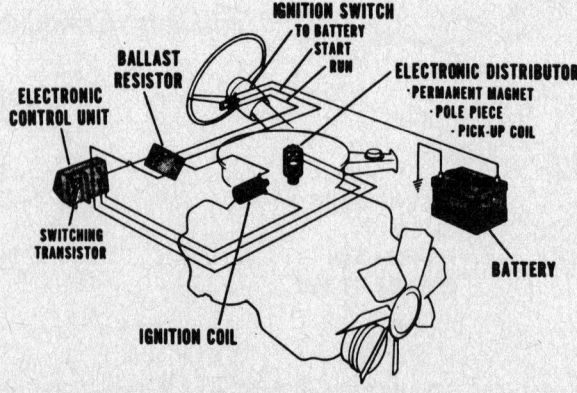

Chrysler electronic ignition underhood layout

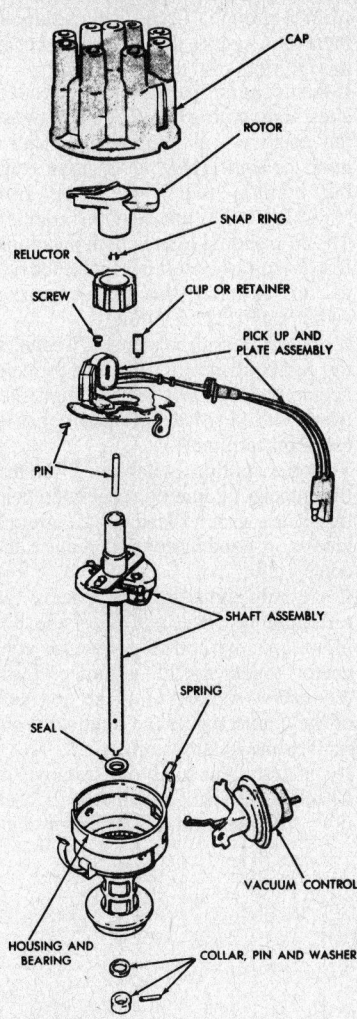

V8 distributor

7. Check the air gap with a 0.008 in. feeler gauge. A 0.008 in. feeler gauge should not fit into the air gap.

--- CAUTION ---

A 0.008 in. feeler gauge can be forced into the air gap. Do not force the gauge into the air gap.

8. Apply vacuum to the vacuum unit and rotate the governor shaft. The pick-up pole should not hit the reluctor teeth. The gap was not properly adjusted if any hitting occurs. If hitting occurs on only one side of the reluctor, the distributor shaft is probably bent, and the governor and shaft assembly should be replaced.

TROUBLESHOOTING ELECTRONIC IGNITION SYSTEM

Chrysler Corporation has an Electronic Ignition System Tester to be used when checking the system. However, many shops are not able to obtain this equipment,

so an alternate method has been developed. The system may be tested using a voltmeter with a scale of 20 volts and an ohmmeter with a scale of 20,000 ohms.

When the ignition system is suspected of malfunctions, the following procedure should be used.

1. Inspect the secondary wires for cracks and tightness.
2. Check all primary wires and connections at the components for tightness.
3. Check and note the battery voltage.
4. Be sure the ignition switch is in the "OFF" position and remove the multi-wiring connector from the control unit.
5. Turn the ignition switch to the "ON" position and connect the negative lead of the voltmeter to a good ground.
6. Connect the positive lead of the voltmeter to the number 1 terminal of the wiring harness connector. The voltage should be within 1 volt of battery voltage. If more than 1 volt, the circuit must be checked for high resistance.
7. Connect the positive lead of the voltmeter to the wiring harness connector number 2 terminal. Available voltage should be within 1 volt of battery voltage. If more than 1 volt, the circuit should be checked for high resistance.
8. Connect the positive lead of the volt-

meter to the wiring harness connector terminal number 3. Available voltage should be within 1 volt of battery voltage. If more than 1 volt, the circuit must be checked for high resistance.

9. Turn the ignition switch to the "OFF" position.
10. Connect an ohmmeter to the wiring harness connector terminal numbers 4 and 5. This checks the distributor pick-up coil. The ohmmeter resistance reading should be between 150 and 900 ohms. If the readings are higher or lower than specified, disconnect the dual lead connector coming from the distributor. Using the ohmmeter leads, check the resistance at the dual lead connector. If the reading is not between 150 and 900 ohms, replace the pick-up coil assembly in the distributor. If the reading is within specifications at the dual lead connector, check the wiring harness between the control unit and the dual lead connector.
11. Connect one ohmmeter lead to a good ground and the other lead to either connector of the distributor. The ohmmeter should show an open circuit. If the ohmmeter shows a reading, the pickup coil in the distributor must be replaced.
12. When checking the electronic control

TROUBLESHOOTING CHRYSLER ELECTRONIC IGNITION

Condition	Possible Cause	Correction
ENGINE WILL NOT START (Fuel and carburetion known to be OK)	a) Dual Ballast	Check resistance of each section: Compensating resistance: .50-.60 ohms @ 70°-80°F Auxiliary Ballast: 4.75-5.75 ohms Replace if faulty. Check wire positions.
	b) Faulty Ignition Coil	Check for carbonized tower. Check primary and secondary resistances: Primary: 1.41-1.79 ohms @ 70°-80°F Secondary: 9,200-11,700 ohms @ 70°-80°F Check in coil tester.
	c) Faulty Pickup or Improper Pickup Air Gap	Check pickup coil resistance: 400-600 ohms Check pickup gap: .010 in. feeler gauge should not slip between pickup coil core and an aligned reluctor blade. No evidence of pickup core striking reluctor blades should be visible. To reset gap, tighten pickup adjustment screw with a .008 in. feeler gauge held between pickup core and an aligned reluctor blade. After resetting gap, run distributor on test stand and apply vacuum advance, making sure that the pickup core does not strike the reluctor blades.
	d) Faulty Wiring	Visually inspect wiring for brittle insulation. Inspect connectors. Molded connectors should be inspected for rubber inside female terminals.
	e) Faulty Control Unit	Replace if all of the above checks are negative. Whenever the control unit or dual ballast is replaced, make sure the dual ballast wires are correctly inserted in the keyed molded connector.
ENGINE SURGES	a) Wiring	Inspect for loose connection and/or broken conductors in harness.
SEVERELY (Not Lean Carburetor)	b) Faulty Pickup Leads	Disconnect vacuum advance. If surging stops, replace pickup.
	c) Ignition Coil	Check for intermittent primary.
ENGINE MISSES (Carburetion OK)	a) Spark Plugs	Check plugs. Clean and regap if necessary.
	b) Secondary Cable	Check cables with an ohmmeter, or observe secondary circuit performance with an oscilloscope.
	c) Ignition Coil	Check for carbonized tower. Check in coil tester.
	d) Wiring	Check for loose or dirty connections.
	e) Faulty Pickup Lead	Disconnect vacuum advance. If miss stops, replace pickup.
	f) Control Unit	Replace if the above checks are negative.

unit, connect one ohmmeter lead to a good ground and the other lead to the control unit connector pin number 5. The ohmmeter should show continuity between the ground and the connector pin. If continuity does not exist, tighten the bolts holding the control unit to the vehicle panel and recheck. If continuity does not exist, the control unit must be replaced.

13. Reconnect the wiring harness at the control unit and distributor.

CAUTION

Whenever removing or replacing the wiring harness connector to the control unit or the distributor, the ignition switch must be in the "OFF" position.

14. Check the reluctor tooth and pick-up coil air gaps, specifications of 0.008 inch.
15. To check the secondary ignition system, remove the high voltage cable from the center tower of the distributor cap and hold approximately ³⁄₁₆ inch from the engine block and crank the engine with the ignition switch in the "START" position.
16. If arcing does not occur, replace the control unit. Recheck by cranking the engine. If arcing still does not occur, replace the ignition coil.

AMC Breakerless Inductive Discharge (BID) Ignition

COMPONENTS

The AMC breakerless inductive discharge (BID) ignition system consists of five components:

1. Control unit
2. Coil
3. Breakerless distributor
4. Ignition cables
5. Spark plugs

The control unit is a solid-state, epoxy-sealed module with waterproof connectors. The control unit has a built-in current regulator, so no separate ballast resistor or resistance wire is needed in the primary circuit. Battery voltage is supplied to the ignition coil positive (+) terminal when the ignition key is turned to the "ON" or "START" position; low voltage is also supplied by the control unit.

The coil used with the BID system requires no special service. It works just like the coil in a conventional ignition system.

The distributor is conventional, except for the lack of points, condenser and cam. Advance is supplied by both a vacuum unit and a centrifugal advance mechanism. A standard cap, rotor, and dust shield are used.

In place of the points, cam, and condenser, the distributor has a sensor and trigger wheel. The sensor is a small coil which generates an electromagnetic field when excited by the oscillator in the control unit.

Standard spark plugs and ignition cables are used.

OPERATION

When the ignition switch is turned on, the control unit is activated. The control unit then sends an oscillating signal to the sensor which causes the sensor to generate a magnetic field. When one of the trigger wheel teeth enters this field, the strength of the oscillation in the sensor is reduced. Once the strength drops to a predetermined level, a demodulator circuit operates the control unit's switching transistor. The switching transistor is wired in series with the coil primary circuit; it switches the circuit off when it gets the demodulator signal.

From this point on, the BID ignition system works in the same manner as a conventional ignition system.

TROUBLESHOOTING

1. Check all of the BID ignition system electrical connections.
2. Disconnect the coil-to-distributor high tension lead.
3. Hold the end of the lead ½ in. away from a ground. Crank the engine. If there is a spark, the trouble is not in the ignition system.
4. If there was no spark in step 3, connect a test light with a No. 57 bulb between the positive coil terminal (+) and a good ground. Have an assistant turn the ignition switch to "ON" and "START" (Do not start the engine). The bulb should light in both positions; if it doesn't, the fault lies in the battery-to-coil circuit. Check the ignition switch and related wiring.
5. If the test light lit in step 4, disconnect the coil-to-distributor leads at the connector and connect the test light between the positive (+) and negative (−) coil terminals.
6. Turn the ignition switch on. If the test light doesn't come on, check the control unit's ground lead. If the ground lead is in good condition, replace the control unit.
7. If the bulb lights in step 6, leave the test light in place and short the terminals on the coil-to-distributor connector together with a jumper lead, (connector separated) at the coil side of the connector. If the light stays on, replace the control unit.
8. If the test light goes out, remove it. Check for a spark, as in step 2, each time that the coil-to-distributor con-

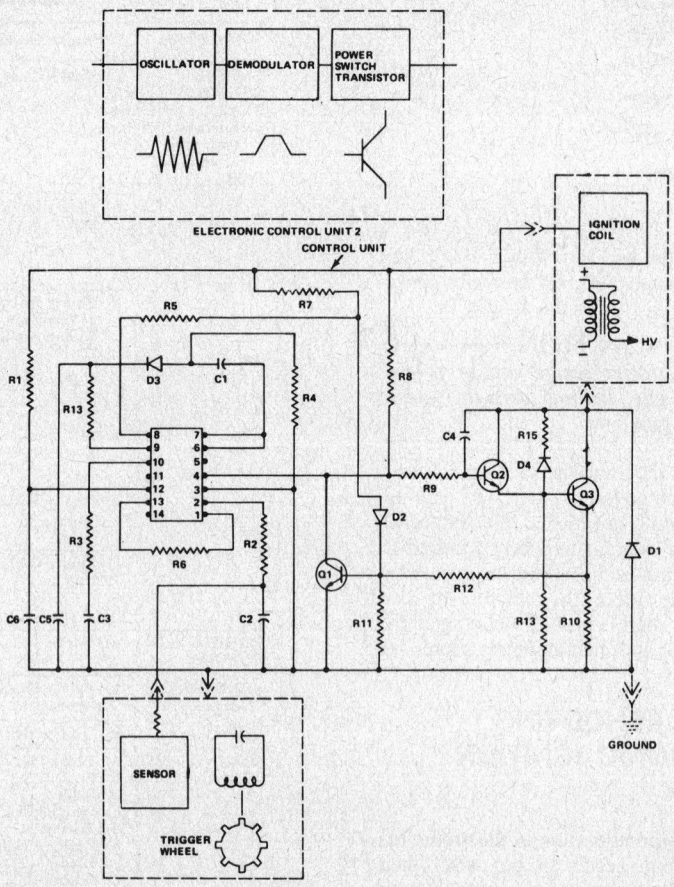

BID schematic

nector terminals are shorted together with the jumper lead. If there is a spark, replace the control unit; if there is no spark, replace the coil.

Coil Testing

Test the coil with a conventional coil checker or an ohmmeter. Primary resistance should be 1–2 ohms and secondary resistance should be 8–12 kilohms. The open output circuit should be more than 20 kilovolts. Replace the coil if it doesn't meet specifications.

Sensor Testing

Check the sensor resistance by connecting an ohmmeter to its leads. Resistance should be 1.8 ohms (±10%) at 77° F. Replace the sensor if it doesn't meet these specifications.

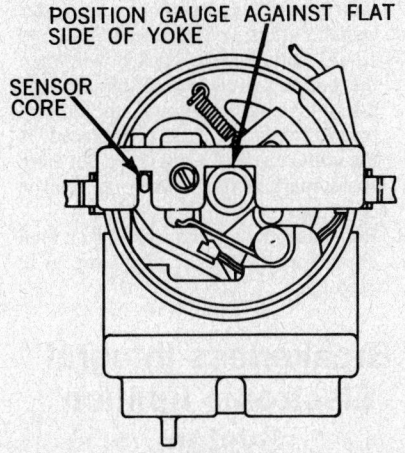

Using a special gauge to align the BID sensor coil

DISTRIBUTOR OVERHAUL

NOTE: If you must remove the sensor from the distributor for any reason, it will be necessary to have the special sensor positioning gauge in order to align it properly during installation.

1. Scribe matchmarks on the distributor housing, rotor, and engine block. Disconnect the leads and vacuum lines from the distributor. Remove the distributor. Unless the cap is to be replaced, leave it connected to the spark plug cables and position it out of the way.
2. Remove the rotor and dust cap.
3. Place a small gear puller over the trigger wheel, so that its jaws grip the inner shoulders of the wheel and not its arms. Place a thick washer between the gear puller and the distributor shaft to act as a spacer; do not press against the smaller inner shaft.
4. Loosen the sensor hold-down screw with a small pair of needle-nosed pliers; it has a tamperproof head. Pull

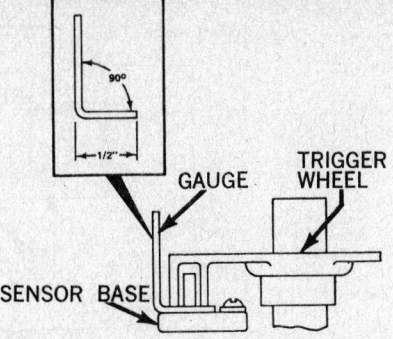

Fabricating a BID wheel clearance gauge

the sensor lead grommet out of the distributor body and pull out the leads from around the spring pivot pin.

5. Release the sensor securing spring by lifting it. Make sure that it clears the leads. Slide the sensor off the bracket.

NOTE: A special gauge is required for sensor installation.

6. Remove the vacuum advance unit securing screw. Slide the vacuum unit out of the distributor. Remove it only if it is to be replaced.
7. Clean and dry the vacuum unit and sensor brackets. Lubrication of these parts is not necessary.

BID distributor assembly is as follows:

1. Install the vacuum unit, if it was removed.
2. Assemble the sensor, sensor guide, flat washer, and retaining screw. Tighten the screw only far enough to keep the assembly together; don't allow the screw to project below the bottom of the sensor.

NOTE: Replacement sensors come with a slotted-head screw to aid in assembly. If the original sensor is being used, replace the tamper-proof screw with a conventional one. Use the original washer.

3. Secure the sensor on the vacuum advance unit bracket, making sure that the tip of the sensor is placed in the notch on the summing bar.
4. Position the spring on the sensor and

route the leads around the spring pivot pin. Fit the sensor lead grommet into the slot on the distributor body. Be sure that the lead can't get caught in the trigger wheel.

5. Place the special sensor positioning gauge over the distributor shaft, so that the flat on the shaft is against the large notch on the gauge. Move the sensor until the sensor core fits into the small notch on the gauge. Tighten the sensor securing screw with the gauge in place (through the round hole in the gauge).
6. It should be possible to remove and install the gauge without any side movement of the sensor. Check this and remove the gauge.
7. Position the trigger wheel on the shaft. Check to see that the sensor core is

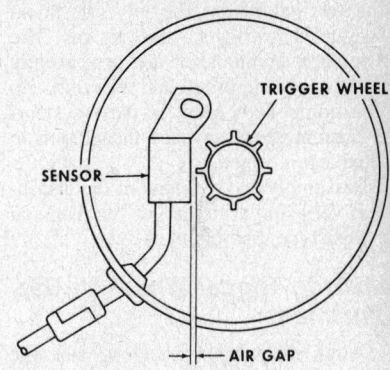

Sensor-to-trigger wheel gap

centered between the trigger wheel legs and that the legs don't touch the core.

8. Bend a piece of 0.050 in. gauge wire, so that it has a 90° angle and one leg ½ in. long. Use the gauge to measure the clearance between the trigger wheel legs and the sensor boss. Press the trigger wheel on the shaft until it just touches the gauge. Support the shaft during this operation.
9. Place 3 to 5 drops of SAE 20 oil on the felt lubricator wick.
10. Install the dust shield and rotor on the shaft.

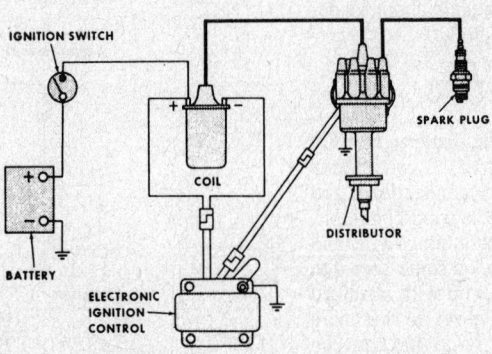

IHC electronic ignition system

11. Install the distributor on the engine using the matchmarks made during removal and adjust the timing. Use a new distributor mounting gasket.

IH Electronic Ignition

HOLLEY MODEL 1530 '75–'78 (EARLY PRODUCTION)

The system uses a standard ignition coil with no ballast resistor or resistance wire, since the control box regulates the primary, low-voltage, current. The distributor part of the system consists of a metal detecting sensor and a toothed trigger wheel in place of the distributor cam. The only adjustment is for sensor to trigger wheel air gap. The control box components are permanently sealed in a waterproof and vibration resistant compound. Most of these systems use vacuum spark advance in addition to mechanical advance.

Disassembly and overhaul of the distributor is very similar to that for International V8 point-type distributors.

Sensor to Trigger Wheel Air Gap Adjustment

1. Align the trigger wheel so that one tooth is aligned with the centerline of the sensor. The tooth should be at right angles to the flat side of the sensor.
2. The gap should be .008 in. for 1975 and later models.
3. A distributor machine or a dwell/tachometer calibrated for electronic ignition systems can be used to measure dwell.

NOTE: Most ordinary dwell/tachometers will give a reading, but this will not be accurate.

On 1975 and later models, dwell should be 26–32 degrees at curb idle and also at 300 distributor rpm with 12–13 volts primary input.

4. Adjust the gap and dwell by moving the sensor. Move the sensor toward the trigger wheel to decrease dwell or away to increase dwell. .001 in. of sensor movement equals about ½ degree of dwell change.

TROUBLESHOOTING

1. Make sure that the battery is fully charged, delivering 12–13 volts. Make sure that all wiring, connections, and mounting bolts are in good condition.
2. Disconnect one spark plug wire and insert an extension of some sort into the boot. Hold the wire with insulated pliers and a heavy glove so that there is a gap of about ¼–½ in. between the extension and a ground. If the spark jumps the gap when the engine is

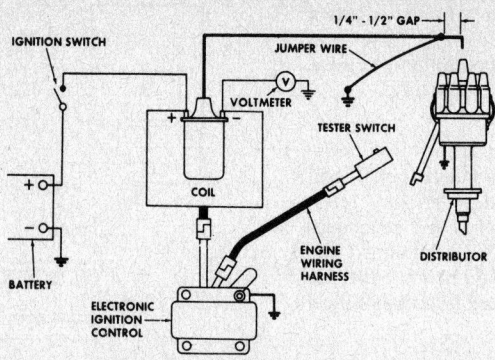

Voltmeter connected to coil negative terminal

cranked with the starter, the system is in good condition. If not, replace the wire and go on.
3. Detach the coil wire from the center of the distributor cap. Attach one end of a jumper wire to a ground and the other around the coil wire (don't pierce the insulation) ¼–½ in. from the metal tip. If there is a spark when the engine is cranked, the distributor cap, rotor, or spark plug and coil wires may be faulty. If not, keep the jumper in place and go on.
4. Disconnect the primary wiring plug near the distributor and plug a tester switch, part no. SE-2503, into the wiring harness. The switch replaces the distributor sensor in the circuit. Turn the ignition switch on and press the tester switch button. If there is a spark at the jumper, the sensor is defective and must be replaced. If not, go on.
5. Disconnect the primary wiring plug near the control box and install the tester switch. Turn the ignition switch on and press the tester switch button. If there is a spark at the jumper now, the primary wiring harness is defective. If not, go on.
6. Connect a voltmeter between the coil negative terminal and a ground. Voltage should be 12–13 volts. A low reading indicates high resistance between the battery and the coil, probably due to defective wires or ignition switch.

7. Connect the voltmeter between the coil negative terminal and a ground. With the ignition switch on, voltage should be 5–8 volts. A lower or higher reading indicates a bad coil. Press the tester switch button; voltage should go up to 12–13 volts and go back down when the button is released. If the voltage doesn't go up and down, the control box is faulty and must be replaced. If the voltage goes up and down but there is no spark at the jumper, the coil is defective.
8. Reconnect the system and make a final check for spark at the plug wire, as in Step 2.

Breakerless Integral Electronic Ignition System

PRESTOLITE IDN-4000 SERIES 1978 AND LATER

The Breakerless Integral Electronic Ignition system is available for both the four cylinder and V-8 engines. The system consists of two major components, the ignition coil and the distributor. The electronic control unit, consisting of a circuit board and sensor, is located within the distributor and is replaced as a complete unit, should service be required. Either a four or eight

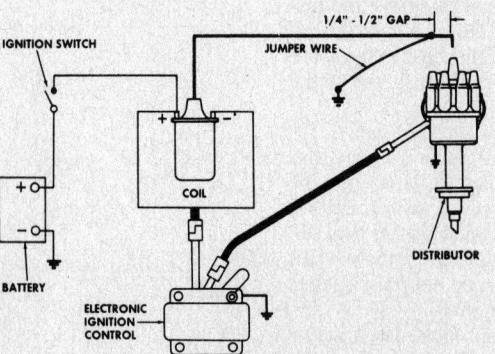

Spark gap test

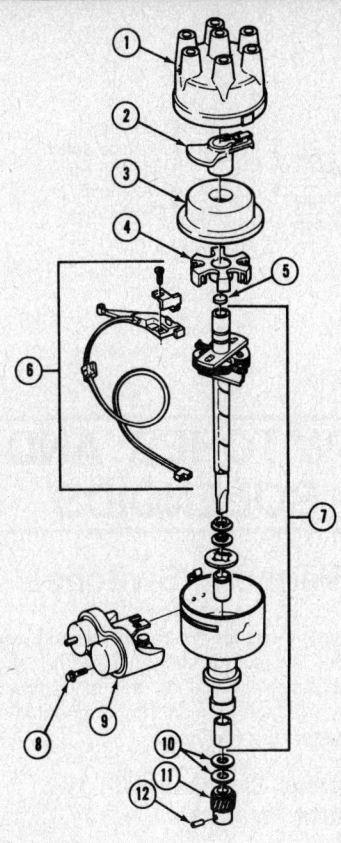

BID distributor

1. Cap	7. Distributor body
2. Rotor	8. Vacuum unit screw
3. Dust shield	9. Vacuum advance unit
4. Trigger wheel	10. Shim
5. Felt lubricator	11. Drive gear
6. Sensor assembly	12. Pin

toothed trigger wheel is located on the distributor shaft, depending upon the engine in which it is to be used.

The distributor is easily identified by the male type terminal on the distributor cap secondary system. The distributor incorporates a mechanical (centrifugal) spark advance system. Most distributors will have a vacuum operated advance system to automatically provide the correct spark advance timing for the various engine speed and load conditions.

The sensor mounting plate configuration and vacuum advance unit location varies between distributors with clockwise and counterclockwise rotation.

Disassembly and Overhaul

The disassembly and overhaul of the distributor is similar to that of the conventional point type distributor. Certain specifications should be adhered to during the overhaul of the distributor. The distributor shaft side play should be between 0.002 and 0.004 inch with a maximum of 0.006 inch. The distributor shaft end play should be 0.035 to 0.040 inch, except distributors with left hand (counterclockwise) rotation,

which should be 0.004 to 0.018 inch. The distributor dwell should be 26 to 32 degrees, except distributors numbered IDN-4001B, IDN-4002R, IDN-4001, IDN-4010 and IDN-4001A, which have a dwell of 28 to 34 degrees.

All distributors should have an air gap between the end of the trigger wheel tooth and the sensor of 0.008 inch.

Sensor to Trigger Wheel Air Gap Adjustment

1. Rotate the distributor shaft until one tooth of the trigger wheel is aligned with the center of the sensor.

NOTE: The trigger wheel tooth should be perpendicular to the flat surface of the sensor when properly aligned.

2. Using an appropriate feeler gauge, measure the air gap between the sensor and the end of the trigger wheel tooth.
3. Loosen and move the sensor as needed to obtain the specified air gap. Tighten the sensor mounting screw and recheck the air gap.
4. The dwell can be checked by installing the distributor in a test stand or in the vehicle engine. Use the appropriate dwell meter to check the dwell.
5. Should the dwell need to be changed, move the sensor towards the trigger wheel to decrease dwell or away from the trigger wheel to increase dwell. Dwell is affected approximately ½ degree per 0.001 inch of sensor movement.

TROUBLESHOOTING

Engine Not Starting

1. Battery voltage should be 12–13 volts before starting the tests.
2. Disconnect spark plug wire at the spark plug and hold the end terminal with an adapter, approximately ½ inch from a ground on the engine. Have an assistant crank the engine and observe for a spark from the wire and adapter to ground. Test at least two wires.
3. If a spark occurs, the electrical system is functioning and the no-start problem is elsewhere.

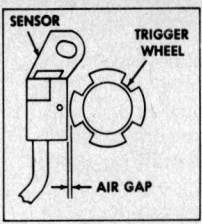
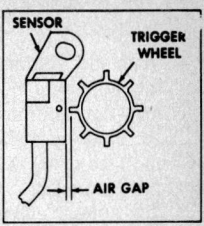

Air gap adjustments

4. If no spark occurs, check for spark at the coil lead by disconnecting it from the distributor cap and holding it approximately ½ inch from a ground and again, have an assistant crank the engine.
5. If a spark occurs, the problem is in the distributor cap, rotor or spark plug cables.
6. If no spark occurs, check the distributor trigger wheel tooth to sensor air gap as previously outlined.
7. If the air gap is out of specifications, adjust and retest for spark. If still no spark occurs, "bump" the starter to position two trigger wheel teeth to straddle the sensor.
8. Connect a voltmeter between the coil positive (+) terminal and ground. Turn the ignition on and the voltage should read battery voltage (12–13 volts).
9. Should the voltage be noticeably lower than battery voltage, a high resistance exists between the battery and the coil. This resistance must be found and repaired before proceeding.

NOTE: Refer to the Primary Voltage Drop Test at the end of this troubleshooting outline.

10. If battery voltage is present at the coil positive (+) terminal, move the clip of the voltmeter lead to the negative (−) coil terminal and check the voltage present with the ignition switch on. The voltage obtained will be one of the following:
    a. 5–8 volts—Normal
    b. 12–13 volts—Problem
    c. 0–5 volts—Problem

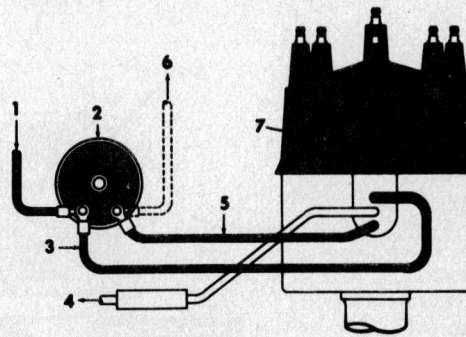

1. From ignition switch
2. Ignition coil
3. Red wire
4. To decelerate throttle modulator (where used)
5. Brown wire
6. To governor control unit (where used)
7. Distributor

Distributor primary wiring

If Voltage Is 5 To 8 Volts—(A)

1. With the voltmeter still connected to the negative (−) terminal of the coil, turn the ignition switch on and place the blade of a flat screwdriver against the face of the sensor while observing the voltmeter.
2. The voltage should increase to 12–13 volts.
3. Remove the screwdriver and the voltage should drop to 5–8 volts.
4. The voltage should switch up and down when the screwdriver blade is placed against and then removed from the sensor surface.
5. If the voltage does not switch up or down, the electronic control unit is defective and must be replaced.
6. To verify the secondary spark from the coil to ground as the voltage moves up or down, re-establish the ½ inch gap between the coil lead and engine ground.
7. With the ignition switch on, place the screwdriver blade against the face of the sensor and a spark should occur across the gap. If no spark occurs, the coil is defective and must be replaced.
8. After replacing the defective component(s), reassemble the shield, rotor, distributor cap and wiring. Recheck for spark at the spark plugs.
9. Check the dwell and the ignition timing. Adjust as required in this order. When the distributor is equipped with a vacuum advance, disconnect the vacuum hose before adjusting the timing.

If Voltage Reading Is 12–13 Volts (B)

1. Connect a jumper wire between the distributor housing and the battery negative (−) terminal.
2. Observe the voltage reading. If the voltage remains at 12–13 volts, the electronic control unit is defective and must be replaced.
3. Should the voltage change to 5–8 volts with the jumper wire connected, a poor ground circuit exists between the distributor and the battery. All grounding straps should be examined, cleaned and tightened as required.

If The Voltage Is Between 0–5 Volts (C)

1. Disconnect the voltmeter lead from the coil and disconnect the brown wire from the coil negative (−) terminal.
2. Reconnect the voltmeter lead to the coil negative (−) terminal, with the other voltmeter lead still connected to a ground.
3. With the ignition switch on, observe the voltage reading. If the voltage is still 0–5 volts, the coil is faulty and must be replaced.
4. If the voltage increases to 12–13 volts,

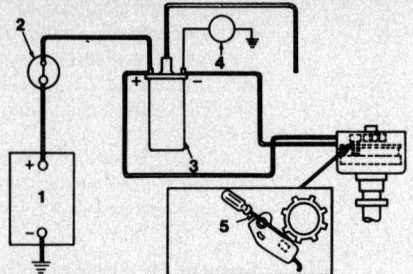

Testing the electronic control unit

1. Battery
2. Ignition switch
3. Ignition coil
4. Voltmeter
5. Screwdriver

the electronic control unit is defective and must be replaced.
5. After the necessary repairs are made, be sure to reconnect the brown wire to the coil negative (−) terminal.

PRIMARY VOLTAGE DROP TEST

1. Remove the distributor cap, rotor and shield. "Bump" the starter to position two teeth of the trigger wheel, straddling the sensor.
2. Connect the voltmeter positive (+) lead to the battery positive (+) post and connect the voltmeter negative (−) lead to the coil positive (+) terminal.
3. Turn the ignition on and observe the voltmeter reading. A reading of less than one volt should be obtained.
4. If a voltage reading higher than one volt exists, move the following components while observing the voltmeter scale.
   a. Battery cables
   b. Starter solenoid battery terminal
   c. Dash panel connector at the firewall (if used)
   d. Ammeter terminals
   e. Ignition switch connectors
5. If a fluctuation or upswing of the voltmeter is noted while flexing the connectors and cables, a poor connection or defective cable exists and must be corrected.

SWITCHES AND SOLENOIDS

Magnetic Switches

Magnetic switches serve only to make contact for the starter motor. Usually, such switches are located on the inner fender panel, although they are found mounted on the starter in a few cases.

Magnetic Switches with Two Control Terminals

On this type of magnetic switch current is supplied from the ignition switch or transmission neutral button to one of the magnetic switch control terminals. The other control terminal is connected to the transmission neutral safety switch (on the transmission) where it is grounded.

Magnetic Switches with Ignition Resistor By-Pass Terminals

All normally use a magnetic switch with a single control terminal. The second terminal is an ignition resistor by-pass terminal.

SOLENOIDS WITHOUT RELAYS

This type of starter solenoid is always mounted on the starter. Makes electrical

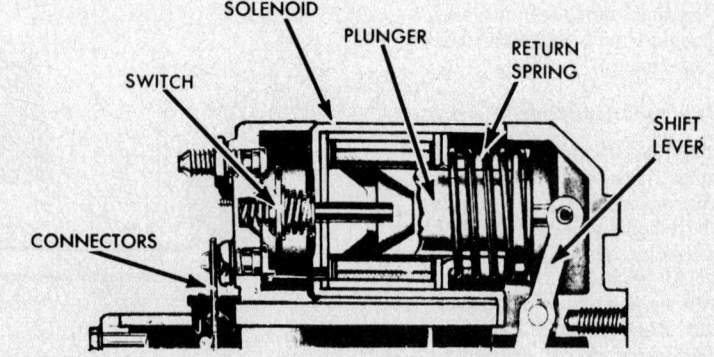

Starter solenoid mounted on starter motor

contact for the starter and pulls the starter and drive clutch into mesh with the flywheel. The Chrysler reduction gear starter has this solenoid embodied in the starter housing.

There is only one control terminal on the solenoid.

The ignition by-pass terminal is usually marked R or IGN, if it is used.

SOLENOIDS WITH SEPARATE RELAYS

The solenoid itself is always mounted on the starter. In addition to making contact for the starter, it also pulls the starter drive clutch gear into mesh with the flywheel. A single control terminal is used on the solenoid itself. The relay is usually found mounted to the inner fender panel or on the firewall.

SOLENOIDS WITH BUILT-IN RELAYS

These units are always mounted on the starter and are connected, through linkage, to the starter drive clutch. The relay portion is a square box built into and integral with the front end of the solenoid assembly.

NEUTRAL SAFETY SWITCHES

The purpose of the neutral safety switch is to prevent the starter from cranking the engine except when the transmission is in neutral or park.

On some trucks the neutral safety switch is located on the transmission. It serves to ground the solenoid or magnetic switch, whichever is used.

On other trucks the neutral safety switch is located either at the bottom of the steering column, where it contacts the shift mechanism, on the steering column, underneath the dash, or on the shift linkage (console).

Some manual transmission models have a clutch linkage safety switch to prevent starter operation unless the clutch pedal is depressed.

On most trucks the neutral safety switch and the backup light switch are combined into a single switch mechanism.

Troubleshooting Neutral Safety Switches—Quick Test

If the starter fails to function and the neutral safety switch is to be checked, a jumper can be placed across its terminals. If the starter then functions the safety switch is defective.

In the case of neutral safety switches with one wire, this wire must be grounded for testing purposes. If the starter works with the wire grounded, the switch is defective.

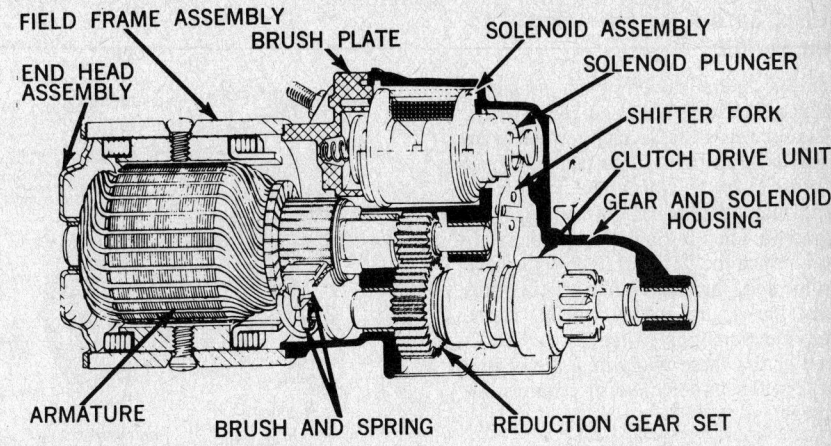

Reduction gear starter motor

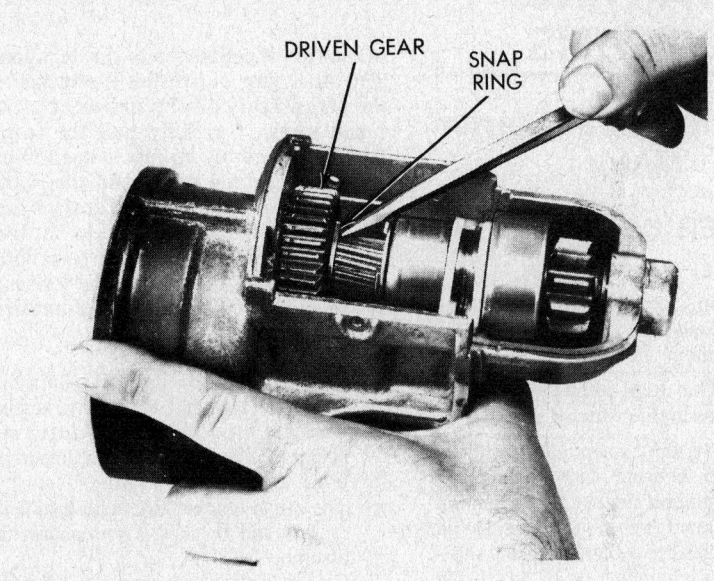

Removing the drive gear snap-ring on reduction gear starter motors

Removing the terminal screw on reduction gear starter motors

Neutral Safety Switch—Back-Up Light Switch

When the neutral safety switch is built in combination with the back-up light switch, the easiest way to tell which terminals are for the back-up lights is to take a jumper and cross every pair of wires. The pair of wires which light the back-up lamps should be ignored when testing the neutral safety switch. Once the back-up light wires have been located, jump the other pair of wires to test the neutral safety switch. If the starter functions only when the jumper is placed across these two wires, the neutral safety switch is defective or requires adjustment.

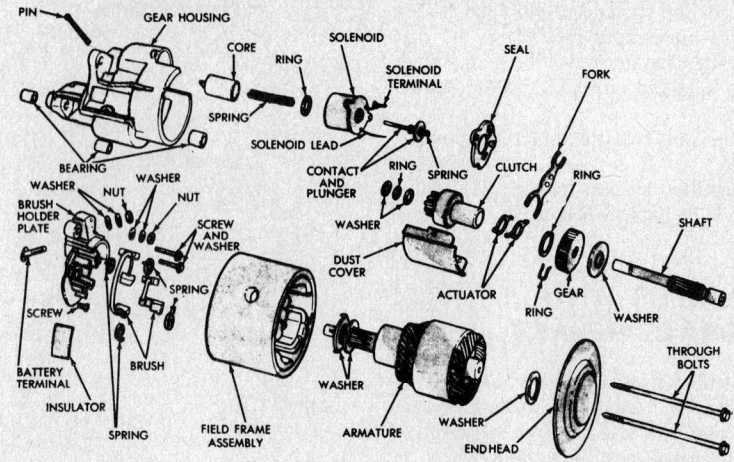

Reduction gear starter

STARTING SYSTEMS

Reduction-Gear Starter Motor

CHRYSLER CORPORATION

The housing is die-cast aluminum. A 3.5 to 1 reduction, combined with the starter to ring gear ratio, results in a total gear reduction of about 45 to 1.

NOTE: The high-pitched sound is caused by the higher starter speed.

The positive shift solenoid is enclosed in the starter housing and is energized through the ignition switch. When ignition switch is turned to start, the solenoid plunger engages drive gear through a shifting fork. At the completion of travel, the plunger closes a switch to revolve the starter.

The tension of the spring-type shifting prevents a butt-tooth lock up and motor will not start before total shift.

An overrunning clutch prevents motor damage if key is held on after engine starts.

No lubrication is required due to Oilite bearings.

Disassembly

1. Support assembly in a vise equipped with soft jaws. Do not clamp. Care must be used not to distort or damage the die cast aluminum.
2. Remove the through-bolts and the end housing.
3. Carefully pull the armature up and out of the gear housing, and the starter frame and field assembly. Remove the steel and fiber thrust washer.

NOTE: On eight cylinder engines the starting motors have the wire of the shunt field coil soldered to the brush terminal. Six cylinder engines have the four coils in series and do not have a wire soldered to the brush terminal. One pair

of brushes is connected to this terminal. The other pair of brushes is attached to the series field coils by means of a terminal screw. Carefully pull the frame and field assembly up just enough to expose the terminal screw and the solder connection of the shunt field at the brush terminal. Place two wood blocks between the starter frame and starter gear housing to facilitate removal of the terminal screw and unsoldering of the shunt field wire at the brush terminal.

4. Support the brush terminal with a finger behind terminal and remove screw.
5. On eight cylinder engine starters unsolder the shunt field coil lead from the brush terminal and housing.
6. The brush holder plate with terminal, contact and brushes is serviced as an assembly.
7. Clean all old sealer from around plate and housing.
8. Remove the brush holder attaching screw.
9. On the shunt type, unsolder the solenoid winding from the brush terminal.
10. Remove $1\frac{1}{32}$ in. nut, washer and insulator from solenoid terminal.
11. Remove brush holder plate with brushes as an assembly.
12. Remove gear housing ground screw.
13. The solenoid assembly can be removed from the well.
14. Remove nut, washer and seal from starter battery terminal and remove terminal from plate.
15. Remove solenoid contact and plunger from solenoid and remove the coil sleeve.
16. Remove the solenoid return spring, coil retaining washer, retainer and the dust cover from the gear housing.
17. Release the snap-ring that locates the driven gear on pinion shaft.
18. Release front retaining ring.
19. Push pinion shaft toward the rear and remove snap-ring, thrust washers, clutch and pinion, and two shift fork nylon actuators.
20. Remove driven gear and friction washer.
21. Pull shifting fork forward and remove moving core.

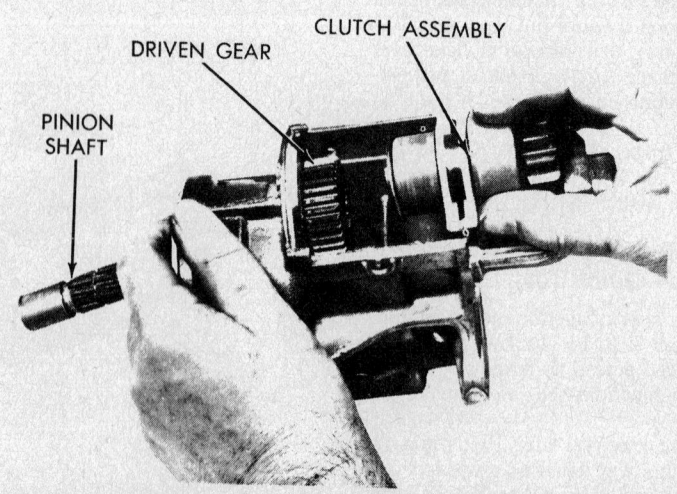

Removing the clutch assembly from a reduction gear starter

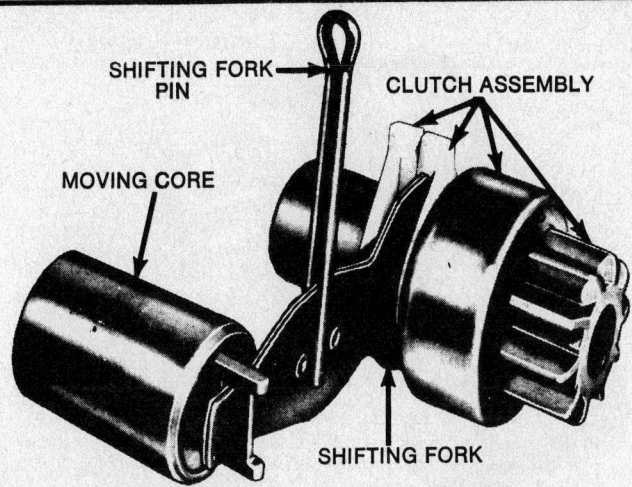

Shift fork and clutch arrangement on a reduction gear starter

22. Remove fork retainer pin and shifting fork assembly. The gear housing with bushings is serviced as an assembly.

Replacement of Brushes

1. Brushes that are worn more than one-half the length of new brushes, or are oil-soaked, should be replaced.
2. When resoldering the shunt field and solenoid lead, make a strong, low-resistance connection using a high-temperature solder and resin flux. Do not use acid or acid-core solder. Do not break the shunt field wire units when removing and installing the brushes.

Starter Clutch and Pinion Gear Inspection

1. Do not immerse the starter clutch unit in a cleaning solvent. The outside of the clutch and pinion must be cleaned with a cloth so as not to wash the lubricant from the inside of the clutch.
2. Rotate the pinion. The pinion gear should rotate smoothly and in one direction only. If the starter clutch unit does not function properly, or if the pinion is worn, chipped, or burred, replace the starter clutch unit.

Commutator Inspection

1. Inspect the commutator and the surface contacted by the brushes when the starter is assembled, for flat spots, out-of-roundness, or excessive wear.
2. Reface the commutator if necessary, removing only a sufficient amount of metal to provide a smooth, even surface.
3. Using light pressure, clean the grooves of the face of the commutator with a pointed tool. Neither remove any metal or widen the grooves.

Assembly

1. The shifter fork consists of two spring steel plates held together by two rivets.

Before assembling the starter, check the plates for side movement. After lubricating between the plates with a small amount of SAE 10 engine oil, they should have about $1/16$ in. side movement to insure proper pinion gear engagement.
2. Position the shift fork in the drive housing and install the shifting fork retainer pin. One tip of the pin should be straight and the other bent at a 15 degree angle away from the housing. The fork and retainer pin should operate freely after bending the tip of the pin.
3. Install the solenoid moving core and engage the shifting fork.
4. Place the pinion shaft into the drive housing and install the friction washer and drive gear.
5. Install the clutch and pinion assembly, thrust washer, and retaining washer.
6. Engage the shifting fork with the clutch actuators.

--- CAUTION ---

The friction washer must be positioned on the shoulder of the splines of the pinion shaft before the driven gear is positioned.

7. Install the driven gear snap-ring.
8. Install the pinion shaft retaining ring.
9. The starter solenoid return spring can now be inserted in the moveable core.
10. Install the solenoid contact plunger assembly into the solenoid and reform the double wires so they can be curved around the contactor. This will allow the terminal stud to enter the brush holder properly.

--- CAUTION ---

The contactor must not touch these double wires after assembly is complete.

11. Assemble the battery terminal stud in the brush holder.
12. Position the seal on the brush holder plate.
13. Run the solenoid lead wire through the hole in the brush holder and attach the solenoid stud, insulating washers, flat washer, and nut.
14. Wrap the solenoid lead wire tightly around the brush terminal post and solder it.
15. Fix the brush holder to the solenoid attaching screws.

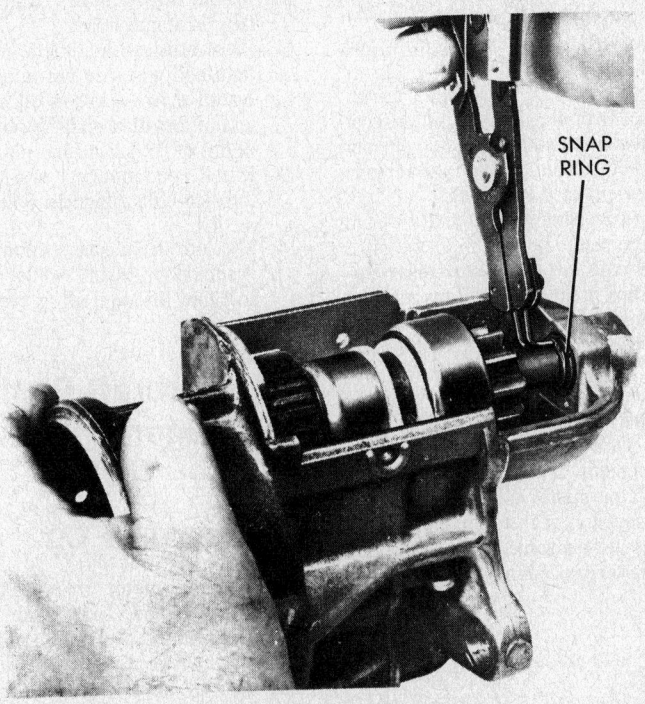

Removing the retaining ring from a reduction gear starter

16. Gently lower the solenoid coil and brush plate into the gear housing.
17. Position the brush plate assembly into the starter gear housing, install the nuts, and tighten.
18. Solder the shunt coil lead wire to the starter brush terminal.
19. Install the brush terminal screw.
20. Position the field frame on the gear housing and start the armature into the housing, carefully engaging the splines on the shaft with the reduction gear by rotating the armature.
21. Install the fiber thrust washer and the steel washer on the armature shaft.
22. Replace the starter end housing and starter through-bolts; tighten securely.

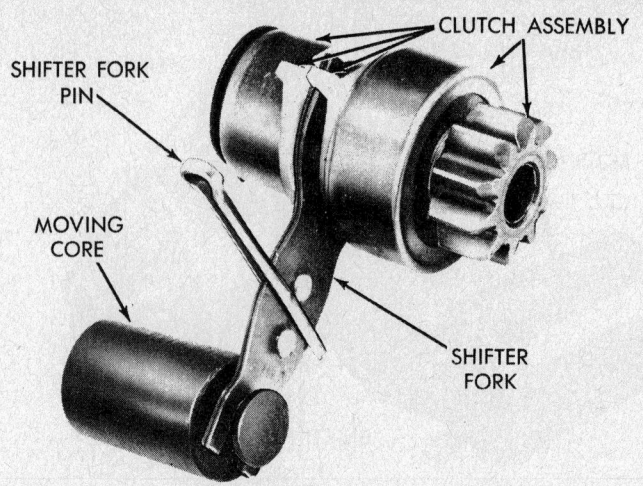

Removing the shift fork from a direct drive starter

Direct Drive Starter Motor

CHRYSLER CORPORATION

This starter can be identified by the externally mounted solenoid bolted to the case.

Disassembly

1. Remove through-bolts and tap commutator end head from frame.
2. Remove thrust washers from armature shaft.
3. Lift brush holder springs and remove brushes from holders.
4. Remove brush holder plate.
5. Disconnect the field coil wires at the solenoid connector, and remove the solenoid screws.
6. Remove solenoid and boot.
7. Drive out shift fork pivot pin.
8. Remove drive end pinion housing and spacer washer.
9. Remove shift fork from starter drive.
10. Slide overrunning clutch pinion gear toward commutator, drive stop retainer toward clutch pinion gear and remove the now-exposed snap-ring.
11. Remove overrunning clutch drive from armature shaft.
12. If field coils are good, stop disassembly at this point. If field coils must be replaced, remove ground brushes terminal screw and remove brushes, terminal and shunt wire. Remove pole shoe screws, using a ratchet-type impact driver and special wide screwdriver blade, then remove field coils.
13. Replacement of the brushes, inspection of the starter clutch and pinion, and inspection of the commutator procedures are the same as the reduction-gear starter procedures.

Assembly

1. Install field coils into frame, if removed.
2. Lubricate armature shaft and splines with engine oil.

3. Install starter drive, stop retainer, lock ring and spacer washer.
4. Install shift fork, with *narrow* leg of fork toward commutator.
5. Install pinion housing onto armature shaft, indexing shift fork with slot in housing.
6. Install shift fork pivot pin.
7. With clutch drive, shift fork, and pinion housing assembled onto the armature, slide armature into frame until pinion housing indexes with slot.
8. Install solenoid and boot, tightening bolts to 60–70 in. lbs.
9. Connect field coil wires to solenoid connector, making sure they do not touch frame.
10. Install brush holder plate, indexing tang in frame hole.
11. Place brushes in holders, making sure field coil wires do not interfere.
12. Install thrust washers on commutator end of armature shaft to obtain a maximum of 0.010 in. end-play.
13. Install commutator end head and through-bolts. Tighten bolts to 40–50 in. lbs.
14. Measure drive gear pinion clearance; it should be ⅛ in. Adjust by moving solenoid fore and aft as required.

Motorcraft Positive Engagement Starter Motor

FORD MOTOR CO.

This starting motor is a series-parallel wound, four pole, four brush unit. It is equipped with an overrunning clutch drive pinion, which is engaged with the flywheel ring gear by an actuating lever, operated by a movable pole piece. This pole piece is hinged to the starter frame and can drop into position through an opening in the frame.

Three conventional field coils are located at three pole piece positions. The fourth field coil is designed to serve also as an engaging coil and a hold-in coil for the operation of the drive pinion.

When the ignition switch is turned to the start position, the starter relay is energized and current flows from the battery to the starter motor terminal. This prime surge of current first flows through the starter engaging coil, creating a very strong magnetic field. This magnetism draws the movable pole piece down toward the starter frame, which then causes the lever attached to it to move the starter pinion into engagement with the flywheel ring gear.

When the movable pole shoe is fully seated, it opens the field coil, grounding contacts, and the starter is then in normal operation. A holding coil is used to hold the movable pole shoe in the fully seated position during the engine cranking operation.

Trucks, equipped with automatic transmissions have a starter neutral switch circuit control. This is to prevent operation of the starter if the selector lever is not in Neutral or Park.

Disassembly

1. Remove brush cover band and starter drive gear actuating lever cover. Observe the brush lead locations for reassembly, then remove the brushes from their holders.

   NOTE: Factory brush length is ½ in.; wear limit is ¼ in.

2. Remove the through-bolts, starter drive gear housing and the drive gear actuating lever return spring.
3. Remove the pivot pin retaining the starter gear actuating lever and remove the lever and the armature.
4. Remove the stop ring retainer. Remove

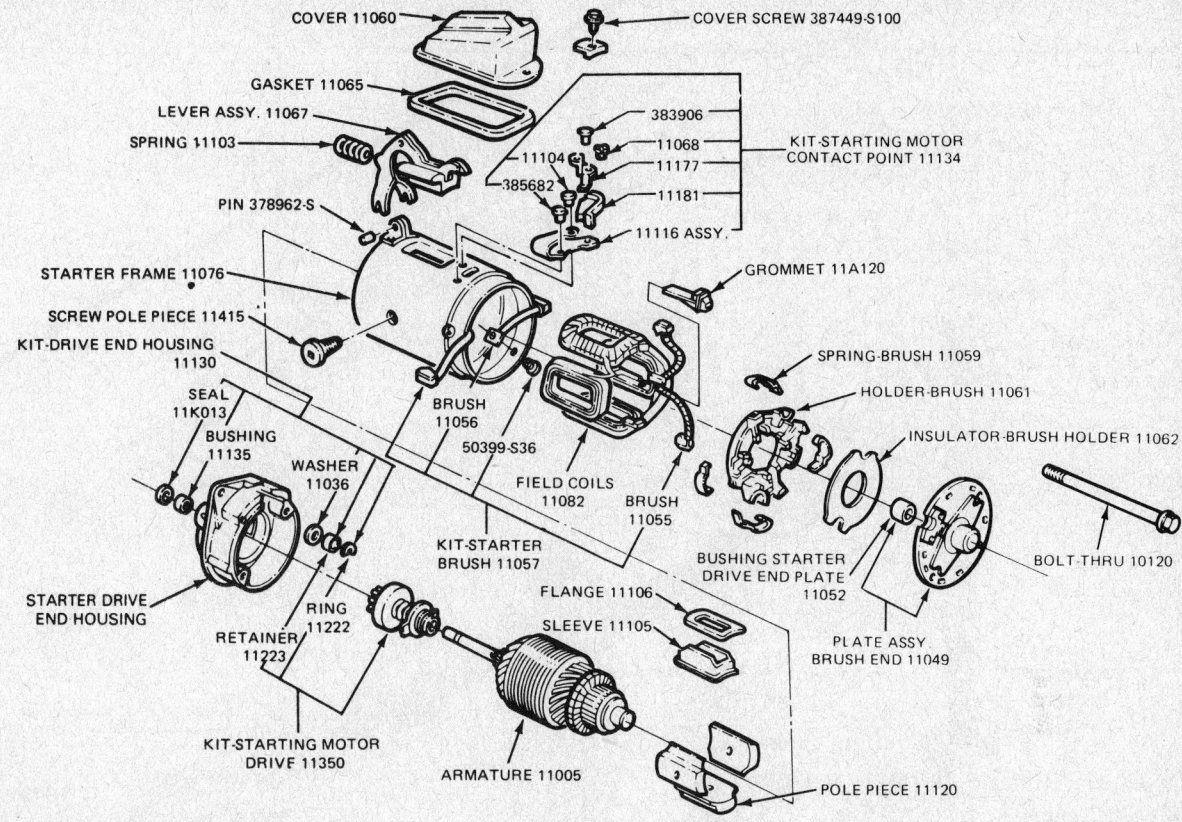

COVER 11060 — COVER SCREW 387449-S100

GASKET 11065

LEVER ASSY. 11067

SPRING 11103

383906

11068

11177

11181

KIT-STARTING MOTOR CONTACT POINT 11134

PIN 378962-S

11104

385682

11116 ASSY.

STARTER FRAME 11076

GROMMET 11A120

SCREW POLE PIECE 11415

KIT-DRIVE END HOUSING 11130

SPRING-BRUSH 11059

HOLDER-BRUSH 11061

SEAL 11K013

INSULATOR-BRUSH HOLDER 11062

BUSHING 11135

WASHER 11036

BRUSH 11056

50399-S36

FIELD COILS 11082

BRUSH 11055

BUSHING STARTER DRIVE END PLATE 11052

BOLT-THRU 10120

KIT-STARTER BRUSH 11057

STARTER DRIVE END HOUSING

RING 11222

RETAINER 11223

FLANGE 11106

SLEEVE 11105

PLATE ASSY. BRUSH END 11049

KIT-STARTING MOTOR DRIVE 11350

ARMATURE 11005

POLE PIECE 11120

Ford starter

and discard the stop ring holding the drive gear to the armature shaft; then remove the drive gear assembly.

5. Remove the brush end plate.
6. Remove the two screws holding the ground brushes to the frame.
7. On the field coil that operates the starter drive gear actuating lever, bend the tab up on the field retainer and remove the field coil retainer.
8. Remove the three coil retaining screws. Unsolder the field coil leads from the terminal screw, then remove the pole shoes and coils from the frame (use a 300 watt iron).
9. Remove the starter terminal nut, washer, insulator and terminal from the starter frame.
10. Check the commutator for runout. If the commutator is rough, has flat spots, or is more than 0.005 in. out of round, reface the commutator. Clean the grooves in the commutator face.
11. Inspect the armature shaft and the two bearings for scoring and excessive wear. Replace if necessary.
12. Inspect the starter drive. If the gear teeth are pitted, broken, or excessively worn, replace the starter drive.

Assembly

1. Install starter terminal, insulator, washers and retaining nut in the frame. (Be sure to position the slot in the screw perpendicular to the frame end surface.)
2. Position coils and pole pieces, with the coil leads in the terminal screw slot, then install the retaining screws. As the pole screws are tightened, strike the frame several sharp hammer blows to align the pole shoes. Tighten, then stake the screws.
3. Install solenoid coil and retainer and bend the tabs to hold the coils to the frame.
4. Solder the field coils and solenoid wire to the starter terminal, using rosin-core solder and a 300 watt iron.
5. Check for continuity and ground connections in the assembled coils.
6. Position the solenoid coil ground terminal over the nearest ground screw hole.
7. Position the ground brushes to the starter frame and install retaining screws.
8. Position the brush end plate to the frame, with the end plate boss in the frame slot.

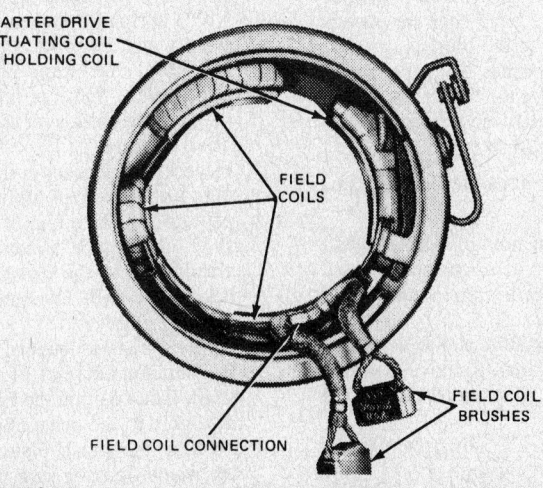

STARTER DRIVE ACTUATING COIL AND HOLDING COIL

FIELD COILS

FIELD COIL CONNECTION

FIELD COIL BRUSHES

Field coil assembly

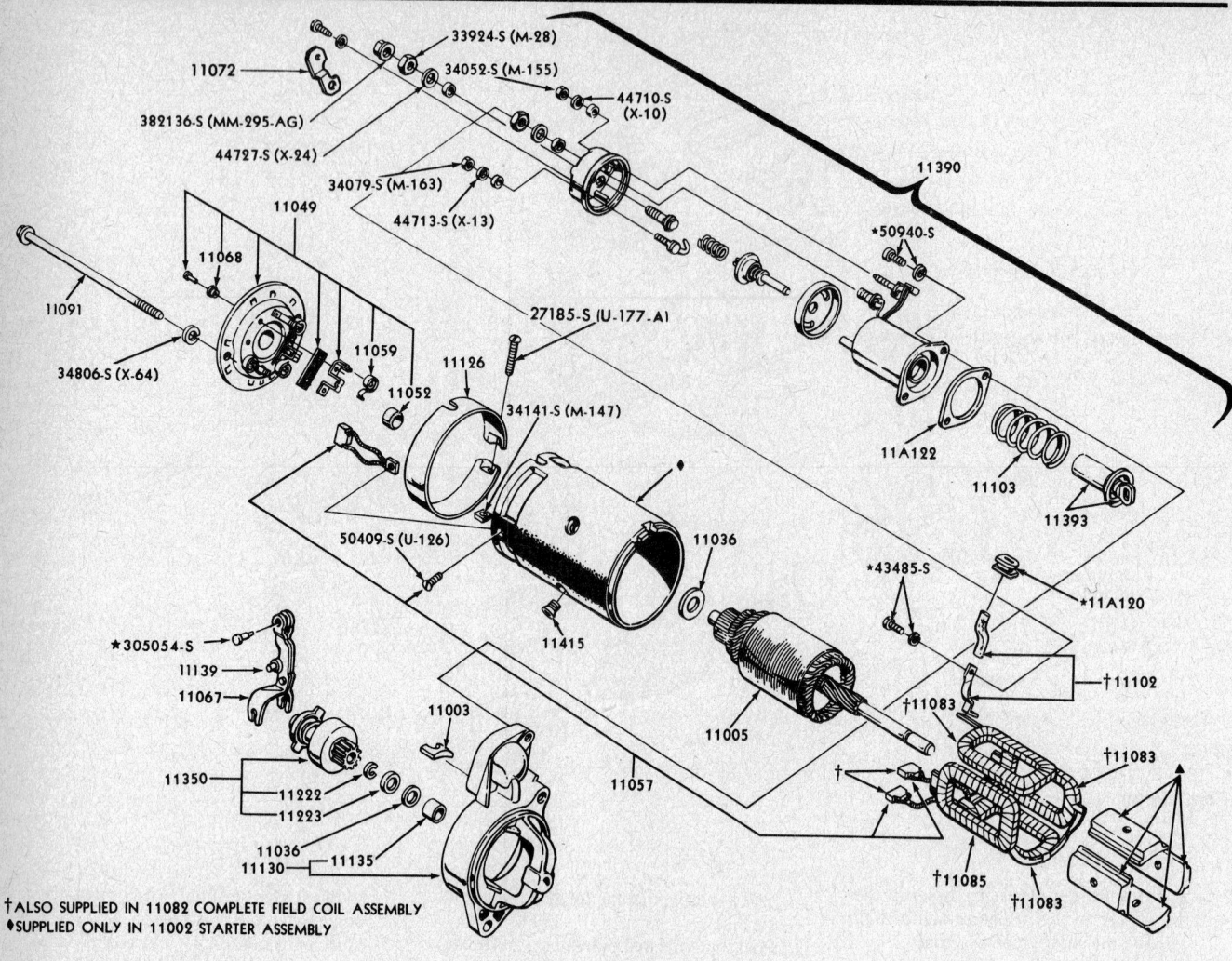

33924-S (M-28)
11072
34052-S (M-155)
382136-S (MM-295-AG)
44710-S (X-10)
44727-S (X-24)
34079-S (M-163)
11049
44713-S (X-13)
11390
11068
*50940-S
11091
27185-S (U-177-A)
34806-S (X-64)
11059
11126
11A122
11052
34141-S (M-147)
11103
11393
50409-S (U-126)
11036
11415
*43485-S
*11A120
*305054-S
11139
†11102
11067
†11083
11350
11003
11222
11223
11005
†11085
11036
11130
11135
11057
†11083
†11083

†ALSO SUPPLIED IN 11082 COMPLETE FIELD COIL ASSEMBLY
♦SUPPLIED ONLY IN 11002 STARTER ASSEMBLY

Ford solenoid type starter

Disassembly

1. Disconnect the copper strap from the solenoid starter terminal, remove the remaining screws and remove the solenoid.
2. Loosen the retaining screw and slide the brush cover band back far enough to gain access to the brushes.
3. Remove the brushes from their holders, then remove the through-bolts and separate the drive end housing from the frame and brush end plate.

   NOTE: Factory brush length is ½ in., wear limit ¼ in.

4. Remove the solenoid plunger and shift fork. These two items can be separated from each other by removing the roll pin.
5. Remove the armature and drive assembly from the frame. Remove the drive stop ring and slide the drive off the armature shaft.
6. Remove the drive stop ring retainer from the drive housing.
7. Inspection of the commutator, arma-ture and bearings, and pinion gear procedures is the same as the positive engagement starter procedures.

Assembly

1. Lubricate the armature shaft splines with Lubriplate, then install drive assembly and a new stop ring.
2. Lubricate shift lever pivot pin with Lubriplate, then position solenoid plunger and shift lever assembly in the drive housing.
3. Place a new retainer in the drive housing. Apply a small amount of Lubriplate to the drive end of the armature shaft, then place armature and drive assembly into the drive housing, indexing the shift lever tangs with the drive assembly.
4. Apply a small amount of Lubriplate to the commutator end of the armature shaft, then position the frame and field assembly to the drive housing.
5. Position the brush plate assembly to the frame, making sure it properly indexes. Install through-bolts and tighten to 45–85 in. lbs.
6. Install brushes into their holders and make sure leads are not touching any interior starter components.
7. Place the rubber gasket between the solenoid mount and the frame surface.
8. Place the starter solenoid in position with metal gasket and spring, install heat shield (if so equipped) and install solenoid screws.
9. Connect copper strap and install cover band.

Delco-Remy Starter Motor

GENERAL MOTORS CORP.

There are many different versions of the Delco-Remy starter, depending upon application. In general, six-cylinder engines use a unit having four field coils in series between the terminal and armature. Standard V8 engines use, depending on dis-

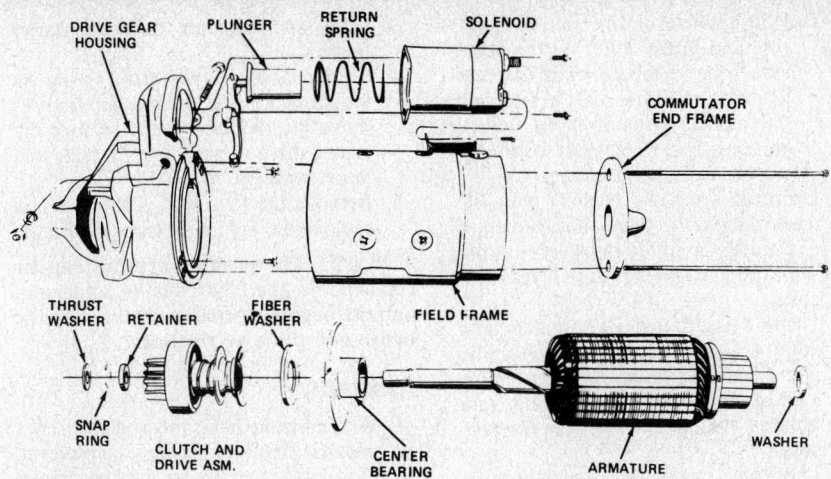

DRIVE GEAR HOUSING · PLUNGER · RETURN SPRING · SOLENOID · COMMUTATOR END FRAME · THRUST WASHER · RETAINER · FIBER WASHER · FIELD FRAME · SNAP RING · CLUTCH AND DRIVE ASM. · CENTER BEARING · ARMATURE · WASHER

Delco starter

placement, one of three types: one has two field coils in series with the armature and parallel to each other; another has two field coils in parallel between the field terminal and ground, and another has three field coils in series with the armature and one field connected between the motor terminal and ground. Heavy-duty starter motors, such as used on some of the largest G.M. high-output engines (over 400 cu. in.) have series compound windings.

9. Lightly Lubricate the armature shaft splines and install the starter drive gear assembly in the shaft. Install a new retaining stop ring and stop ring retainer.

10. Position the fiber thrust washer on the commutator end of the armature shaft, then position the armature in the starter frame.

11. Position the starter drive gear actuating lever to the frame and starter drive assembly, and install the pivot pin.

   NOTE: Fill drive gear housing bore ¼ full of grease.

12. Position the drive actuating lever return spring and the drive gear housing to the frame, then install and tighten the through-bolts. Do not pinch brush

leads between brush plate and frame. Be sure that the stop ring retainer is properly seated in the drive housing.

13. Install the brushes in the brush holders and center the brush springs on the brushes.

14. Position the drive gear actuating lever cover on the starter and install the brush cover band with a new gasket.

15. Check starter no-load amperage draw.

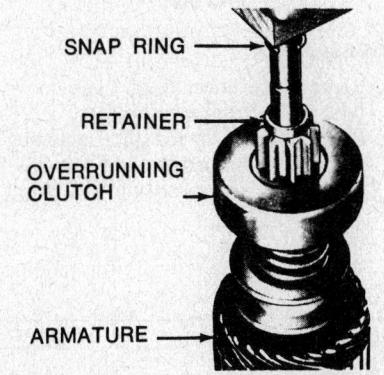

SNAP RING · RETAINER · OVERRUNNING CLUTCH · ARMATURE

Forcing the snap-ring over the armature shaft

Motorcraft Solenoid Actuated Starter Motor

FORD MOTOR CO.

This starter motor is a four-brush, four-field, four-pole wound unit. The frame encloses a wound armature, which is supported at the drive end by caged needle bearings and at the commutator end by a sintered copper bushing. The four pole shoes are retained to the frame by one pole screw apiece, and on each pole shoe is wound a ribbon-type field coil connected in series-parallel.

The solenoid is mounted to a flange on

the starter drive housing, which encloses the entire shift mechanism and solenoid plunger. The solenoid utilizes two windings—a pull-in winding and a hold-in winding.

In spite of these differences, all Delco-Remy starters are disassembled and assembled in essentially the same manner.

Disassembly

1. Disconnect the field coil connectors from the motor solenoid terminal.

   NOTE: On models so equipped, remove solenoid mounting screws.

2. Remove the through-bolts.

3. Remove commutator end frame, field frame and armature assembly from drive housing.

4. Remove the overrunning clutch from the armature shaft as follows:
   a. Slide the two-piece thrust collar off the end of the armature shaft.
   b. Slide a standard ½ in. pipe coupling or other spacer onto the shaft so that the end of the coupling butts against the edge of the retainer.
   c. Tap the end of the coupling with a hammer, driving retainer towards armature end of snap-ring.
   d. Remove snap-ring from its groove in the shaft using pliers. Slide retainer and clutch from armature shaft.

5. Disassemble brush assembly from field frame by releasing the V-spring and removing the support pin. The brush holders, brushes and springs now can be pulled out as a unit and the leads disconnected.

6. On models so equipped, separate solenoid from lever housing.

Cleaning and Inspection

1. Clean parts with a rag, but do not immerse the parts in a solvent. Immersion in a solvent will dissolve the grease that is packed in the clutch mechanism and damage the armature and field coil insulation.

2. Test overrunning clutch action. The pinion should turn freely in the overrunning direction and must not slip in

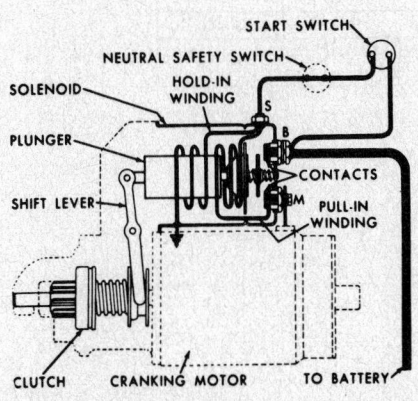

START SWITCH · NEUTRAL SAFETY SWITCH · SOLENOID · HOLD-IN WINDING · PLUNGER · SHIFT LEVER · CONTACTS · PULL-IN WINDING · CLUTCH · CRANKING MOTOR · TO BATTERY

Solenoid windings

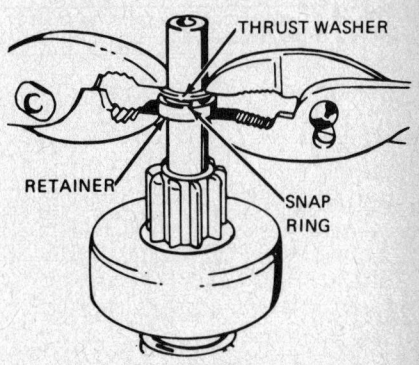

THRUST WASHER · RETAINER · SNAP RING

Forcing the snap-ring into the retainer

the cranking direction. Check pinion teeth to see that they have not been chipped, cracked, or excessively worn. Replace the unit if necessary.

3. Inspect the armature commutator. If the commutator is rough or out of round, it should be turned down.

Some starter motor models use a molded armature commutator design and no attempt to undercut the insulation should be made or serious damage may result to the commutator.

Assembly

1. Install brushes into holders. Install solenoid, if so equipped.
2. Assemble insulated and grounded brush holder together using the V-spring and position the assembled unit on the support pin. Push holders and spring to bottom of support and rotate spring to engage the slot in support. Attach ground wire to grounded brush and field lead wire to insulated brush, then repeat for other brush sets.
3. Assemble overrunning clutch to armature shaft as follows:
   a. Lubricate drive end of shaft with silicone lubricant.
   b. Slide clutch assembly onto shaft with pinion outward.
   c. Slide retainer onto shaft with cupped surface facing away from pinion.
   d. Stand armature up on a wood surface, commutator downwards. Position snap-ring on upper end of shaft and drive it onto shaft with a small block of wood and a hammer. Slide snap-ring into groove.
   e. Install thrust collar onto shaft with shoulder next to snap-ring.
   f. With retainer on one side of snap-ring and thrust collar on the other side, squeeze together with two sets of pliers until ring seats in retainer. On models without thrust collar, use a washer. Remember to remove washer before continuing.
4. Lubricate drive end bushing with silicone lubricant, then slide armature and clutch assembly into place, at the same time engaging shift lever with clutch.
5. Position field frame over armature and apply sealer (silicone) between frame and solenoid case. Position frame against drive housing, making sure brushes are not damaged in the process.
6. Lubricate commutator end bushing with silicone lubricant, place a leather brake washer on the armature shaft and slide commutator end frame onto shaft. Install through-bolts and tighten to 65 in. lbs.
7. Reconnect field coil connector/s to the solenoid motor terminal. Install solenoid mounting screws, if so equipped.
8. Check pinion clearance; it should be 0.010–0.140 in. on all models.

Prestolite Starter Motor

Disassembly

1. Remove the cover band and remove the brushes from their holders.
2. Remove the brush end plate mounting screws and the two through-bolts.
3. Remove the drive housing, end brush plate, and armature from the starter frame.
4. Compress the starter drive spring on the armature side of the shaft and remove the lock screw and remove the starter drive, center bearing plate and thrust washers.
5. Remove the four field pole shoes and remove the field coils from the frame.

NOTE: The positive brushes can be replaced on the field coils by soldering, and the negative brushes replaced on the brush end plate by riveting.

Assembly

1. Assemble the field coils and pole shoes into the frame and secure with screws.
2. Assemble the center bearing plate, thrust washers, and starter drive on the armature shaft and secure with the locking screw.
3. Place the armature assembly into the drive housing aligning the slot in the shaft center bearing support with the pin in the drive housing.
4. Install the end frame to the frame housing and install the six mounting screws.
5. Position the armature assembly into the frame housing and engage the frame dowel with the bolt of the drive frame. Install the two through-bolts and secure.
6. Install the brushes into the holders. Center the brush springs on the brushes and locate the insulated brush leads clear of the armature. Install the cover band.

SPECIFICATIONS

PRESTOLITE STARTER

Vendor	Current Draw Under Normal Load (Amperes)	Minimum Stall Torque		Maximum Load (Amperes)	No-Load (Amperes)	Brushes			Through Bolt Torque (In-Lbs)	Mounting Bolt Torque (Ft-Lbs)
		(Ft-Lbs)	Volts			Mfg. Length (Inches)	Wear Limit (Inches)	Brush Spring Tension (Ounces)		
Prestolite	200	17.2	5	525	60	0.46–0.48	0.25	45–53	72–96	23–28

Maximum commutator runout in inches is 0.005. Maximum starting circuit voltage drop (battery + terminal to starter terminal) at normal engine temperature 0.5 volt.

Emission Control Systems

INDEX

EMISSION CONTROL

Gasoline Engines

INTRODUCTION

The emission control devices required by law on trucks are determined by weight classification and were considered either "light duty" or "heavy duty" applications, with the Gross Vehicle Weight (GVW) of 6000 lbs. as the dividing line. State and Federal Government regulations have now mandated a new weight standard from the 6000 lbs. GVW to a new GVW of 8500 lbs. or less as "light duty" and a GVW of 8500 lbs. or more as "heavy duty" applications.

The light duty emission devices are normally the same as used on the passenger cars.

During certain model years, passenger carrying vehicles, such as window vans with greater GVW of 6000 lbs. were also considered to be light duty models and must comply with the light duty emission control requirements.

Heavy duty truck models use fewer emission control devices than the light duty models, although more emission controls are being required in each succeeding year to comply with the changing emission control regulations and requirements.

The State of California remains stringent in their emission control standards and through out this section, reference will be made to either the California, High Altitude or to the Federal engines. (Federal referring to the remaining 49 states, High Altitude referring to areas above 4000 ft. (1,219 meters)).

ENGINE MODIFICATIONS

Internal engine modifications have been made from year to year by redesigning the following:

1. Lowering the compression ratios to allow the use of low or nonleaded fuels.
2. Combustion chambers and piston modifications for a more efficient air/fuel flow rate and burning time.
3. Camshaft modification to improve valve timing and to increase valve overlap periods.
4. Higher engine operating temperatures and increased cooling areas.
5. Balanced fuel induction manifolds to properly balance the air/fuel flow to the cylinders.
6. Other modifications include changes in metals used in the construction of the engines and components to allow the operation of the engine with non-leaded, non-lubricating fuels.

External engine modifications have been made to the carburetors and distributors to provide the proper air/fuel mixture and to provide the proper timing of the ignition spark to insure the engine emission levels remain within the legislated limits, while providing the best engine performance and fuel economy at varying speeds and loads.

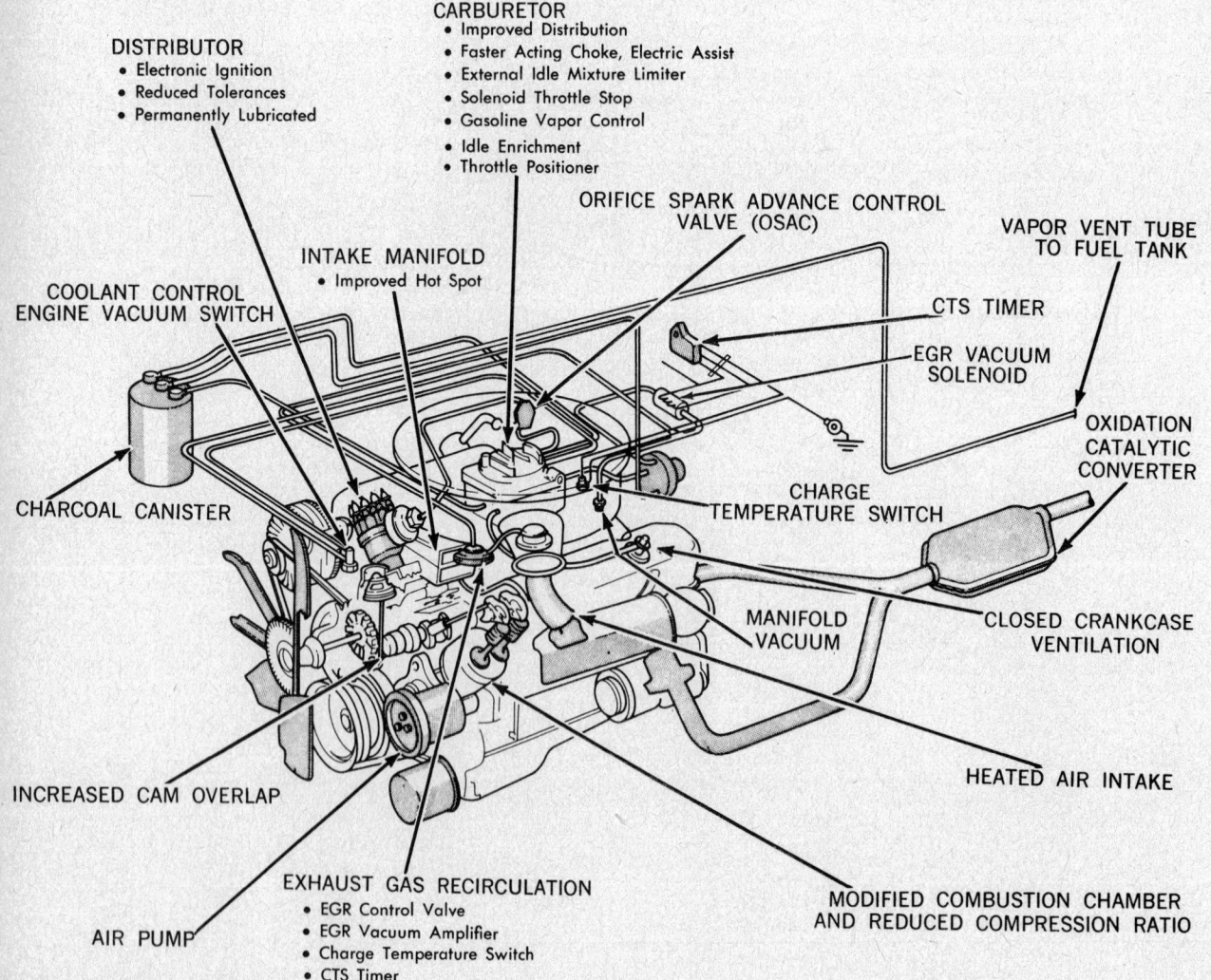

DISTRIBUTOR
• Electronic Ignition
• Reduced Tolerances
• Permanently Lubricated

CARBURETOR
• Improved Distribution
• Faster Acting Choke, Electric Assist
• External Idle Mixture Limiter
• Solenoid Throttle Stop
• Gasoline Vapor Control
• Idle Enrichment
• Throttle Positioner

ORIFICE SPARK ADVANCE CONTROL VALVE (OSAC)

VAPOR VENT TUBE TO FUEL TANK

INTAKE MANIFOLD
• Improved Hot Spot

CTS TIMER

COOLANT CONTROL ENGINE VACUUM SWITCH

EGR VACUUM SOLENOID

OXIDATION CATALYTIC CONVERTER

CHARCOAL CANISTER

CHARGE TEMPERATURE SWITCH

MANIFOLD VACUUM

CLOSED CRANKCASE VENTILATION

INCREASED CAM OVERLAP

HEATED AIR INTAKE

EXHAUST GAS RECIRCULATION
• EGR Control Valve
• EGR Vacuum Amplifier
• Charge Temperature Switch
• CTS Timer

AIR PUMP

MODIFIED COMBUSTION CHAMBER AND REDUCED COMPRESSION RATIO

Typical Emission Control System

EMISSION CONTROL SYSTEMS

In order to control the engine crankcase, fuel and exhaust emissions, three major systems have been designated.

1. Crankcase controls are used to provide a more complete scavenging of the crankcase vapors and to route the vapors to the engine fuel induction system for burning with the air/fuel mixture.

2. Evaporation controls are used to prevent the emission of gasoline vapors from the fuel tank and carburetor, into the atmosphere. Charcoal canisters are used to store the gasoline vapors during periods of engine shutdown and during periods of engine operation, the gasoline vapors are drawn into the fuel induction system and burned with the air/fuel mixture.

3. Exhaust controls are used to limit the emission of Carbon Monoxide (CO), Hydrocarbons (HC) and Oxides of Nitrogen (NOx) from the engine exhaust. Numerous controls are used on the engines and the exhaust systems to perform this removal of pollutants.

Maintenance

In order for the emission controls to function properly, maintenance must be performed at regular intervals, either by time or mileage increments. Owner manuals will normally contain a maintenance schedule for services to be done and should be followed for longer emission systems and vehicle life.

EMISSION CERTIFICATION LABEL

An Emission Certification label is attached to either the engine or engine compartment

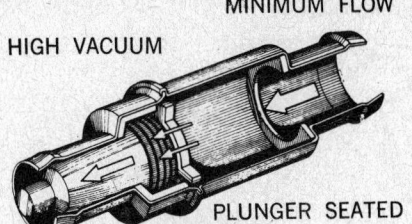

PCV valve at low engine speed or during idle

sheet metal and should be consulted before any adjustments are made to the engine.

NOTE: It is a good practice to copy the information from the Emission Certification label and keep with the owners manual, in case the label becomes mutilated or lost.

Emission Control Systems and Components

CRANKCASE CONTROL SYSTEM

Positive Crankcase Ventilation (PCV)

With the engine operating, crankcase ventilation air is drawn through an air cleaner mounted filter assembly, through a hose to the crankcase air inlet, down into the crankcase and up to the rocker arm chamber, out through a flow control valve and into a hose connected to the base of the carburetor or to the intake manifold. The crankcase vapors are then mixed with the air/fuel mix-

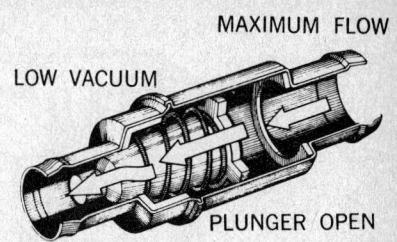

PCV valve operation at high engine speed

ture and burned through the normal combustion process. The purpose of the flow control valve is to restrict the flow of crankcase vapors when the intake manifold is high (such as idle or coast modes), to avoid upsetting the air/fuel mixture at idle and causing roughness of the engine at low speeds or while idling.

With the flow control valve open at times of low engine vacuum and high air flow through the carburetor (such as having the throttle valves open as in the drive mode), the added crankcase vapor flow has no noticable effect on the engine operation.

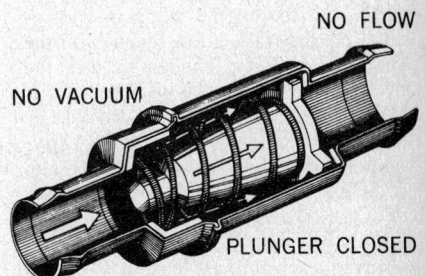

PCV valve operation with engine off or during backfire

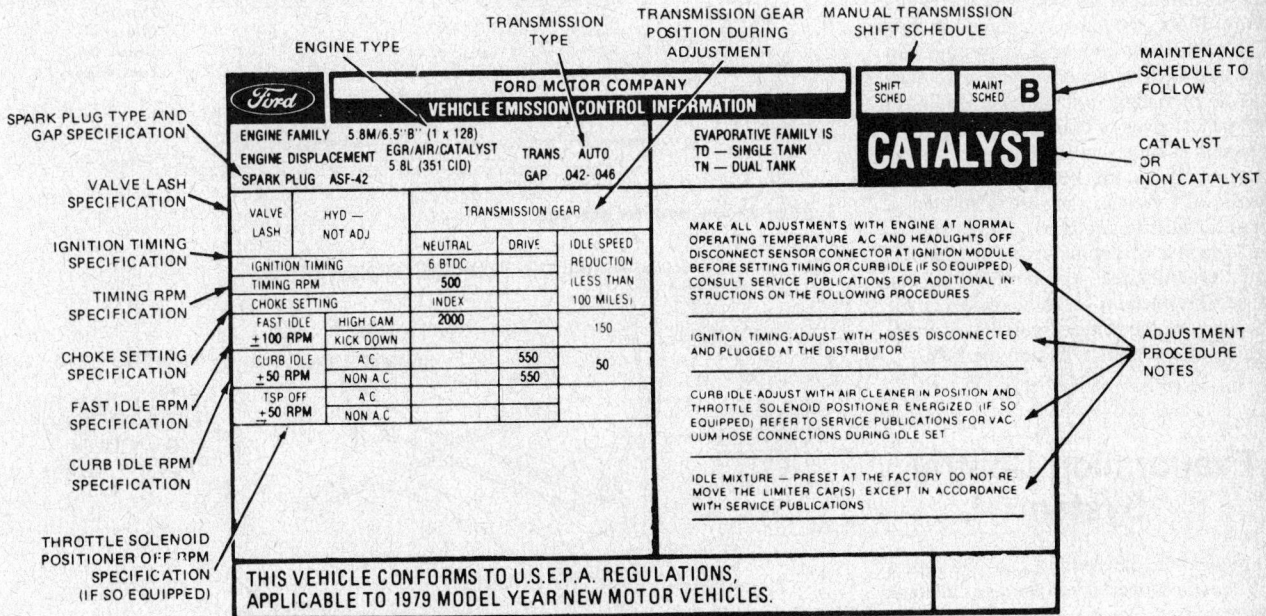

Emission Certification Label (typical)

EMISSION CONTROL SYSTEMS

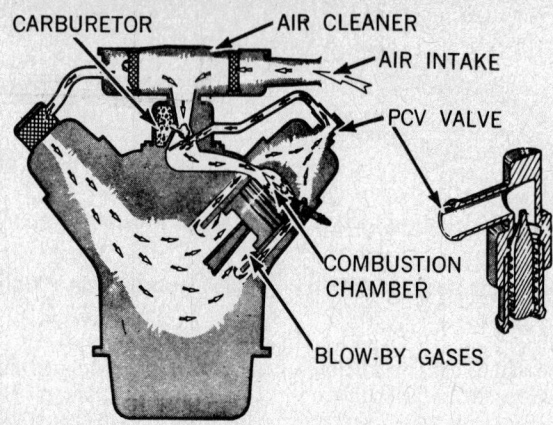

Closed crankcase ventilation system

stopped and are routed from and/or through the canister(s) to the engine fuel induction system, when the engine is operating.

On single canister arrangements, the throttle valve is normally used as purge valve, with the vapor hoses routed to the intake manifold or to the carburetor base. On some vehicle models, the purging of the canister is accomplished by air movement through the air cleaner snorkel and into the engine, by having the purge hose connected from the canister to the snorkel.

On dual canister arrangements, the purging action of the secondary canister is triggered by a vacuum signal from the distributor vacuum hose to open the canister purge switch, which allows the vapors to purge through the PC system and into the engine.

Crankcase Control Testing

Checking crankcase vacuum is the most effective way to test any PCV system. If there is vacuum in the crankcase, then the major part of the system has to be working.

On all models, use a piece of paper or a PCV test to measure the crankcase vacuum at the oil filler cap, with the cap removed, and the engine idling in Park or Neutral. It may take a few seconds for the vacuum to build up enough to suck the piece of paper against the oil filler hole. If the vacuum does not build up, check to be sure you have plugged the fresh air entry. An alternate method on some models is to use the piece of paper or PCV tester on the end of the fresh air entry hose. When you do it that way, the oil filler cap must be the solid type and you must leave it in place.

If there is no crankcase vacuum, pull the PCV valve from the crankcase and hold your finger over the end of it. You should feel full manifold vacuum with the engine idling. If not, the valve is plugged or there is an obstruction in a hose or passageway. On some designs the valve may be screwed into its mounting, with a hose leading to the rocker cover or crankcase. If the valve has good suction, but there is no crankcase vacuum, check the hose to be sure it is open. PCV valves that are restricted or plugged must be replaced, unless they are the type that will come apart for cleaning. Lack of crankcase vacuum can also be caused by vacuum leaks at rocker cover, oil pan, or other engine gaskets. Usually, tightening the bolts will stop the leak.

Evaporation Control System

To prevent the emission of gasoline vapors into the atmosphere from the gasoline tank and carburetor vents, vapors are routed by hoses to one or more charcoal filled canisters for storage while the engine is

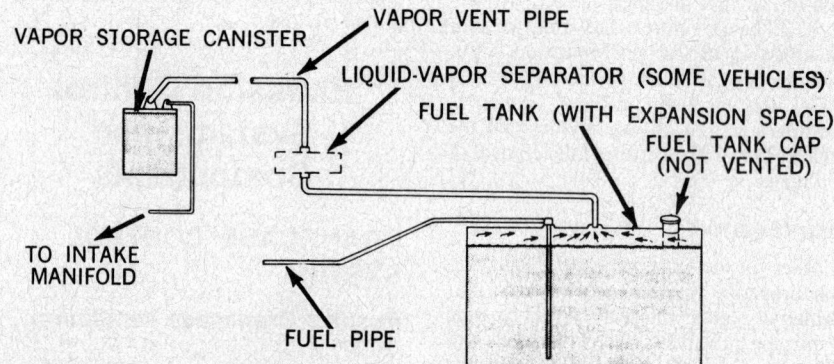

Typical gasoline evaporation system

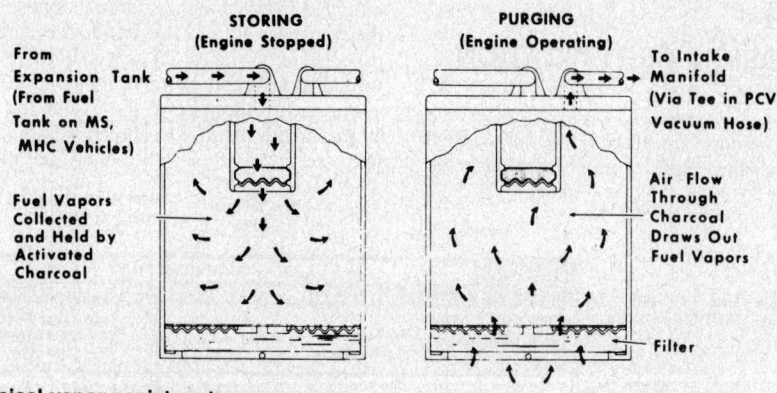

Typical vapor canister storage

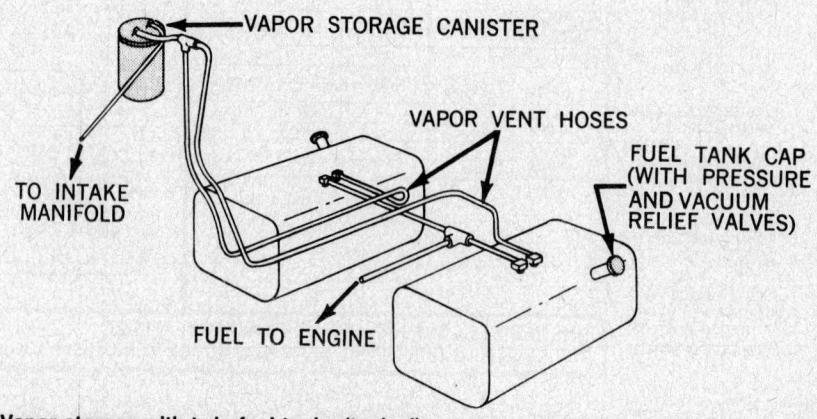

Vapor storage with twin fuel tanks (typical)

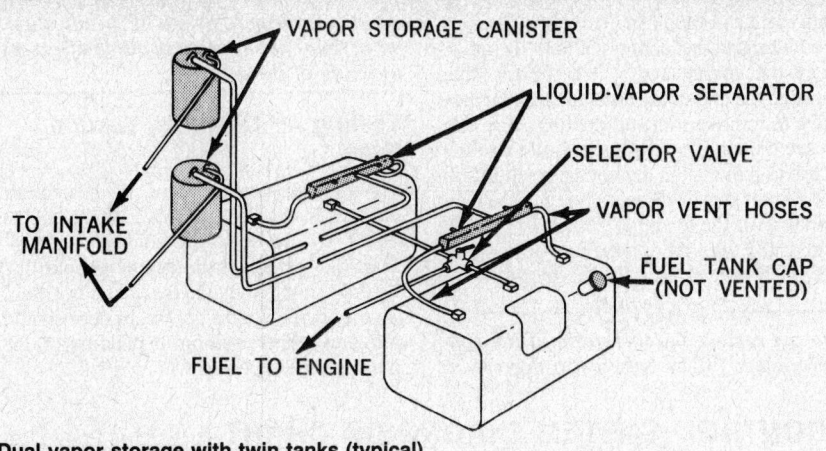

Dual vapor storage with twin tanks (typical)

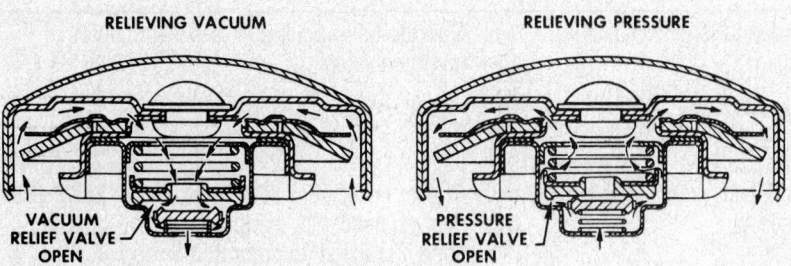

Pressure-vacuum type fuel filler type cap operation

Fuel filler caps that are used with the vapor Emission Control System, normally have a pressure-vacuum valve assembly as part of the cap, to allow air to enter the tank as the fuel is consumed to avoid fuel tank collapse, when the vacuum is between 15 to 25 in. Hg. When the fuel tank internal pressure builds up from .75 to 2.0 psi (nominal) over atmospheric pressure, the pressure valve opens to relieve the excess internal pressures.

Larger trucks will normally have fuel caps with anti-surge mechanisms built into the caps to prevent fuel spillage during truck operation or will have non-vented caps with the fuel tanks vented through vapor storage canisters.

Vapor separators and anti-rollover valves are used with the vapor control systems, to avoid having raw fuel collect in the charcoal canister or to have fuel leakage in case of a vehicle rollover.

Evaporation Control System Inspection

The system inspection consists of examining the fuel resistance hoses, connections, metal lines, nylon lines, valves, separators and canisters. The only needed replacement is the canister air filter.

Exhaust Control System

Exhaust controls vary considerably in design. There are many different systems or devices used on the domestic makes to control exhaust emissions. Following are basic descriptions of the common systems.

THERMOSTATIC AIR CLEANER

Fresh air supplied to the air cleaner comes either from the normal snorkel, or from a tube connected to an exhaust manifold stove. A door in the snorkel regulates the source of incoming air so that a warm engine always takes in warm air, approximately 100°F. The door may be controlled by a thermostatic spring or expansion bulb, or it may be vacuum operated. The vacuum operated designs use a thermostatic bimetal switch inside the air cleaner that bleeds off vacuum as the engine warms up, and regulates the position of the air door. On all late models, the snorkel is connected to a long tube so it takes in cooler air from outside the engine compartment. In hot climates the cool air tube is necessary because underhood air can easily reach 200°F.

Vacuum operated air doors are all designed so that the air cleaner takes in cold air when there is no vacuum. This means that an air door in the hot air position will switch to the cold position at wide open throttle because of the loss of manifold vacuum. The sudden switching of the door from hot to cold may cause a stumble or misfire in the engine, so some designs include a modulator valve mounted on the side of the air cleaner to block the vacuum

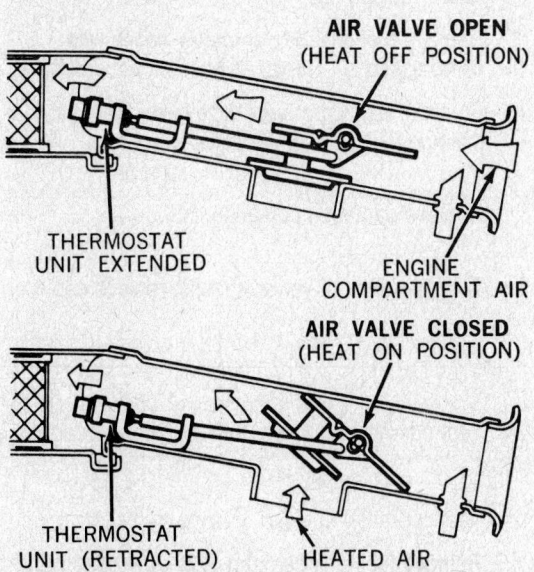

Thermostatic controlled air cleaner operation

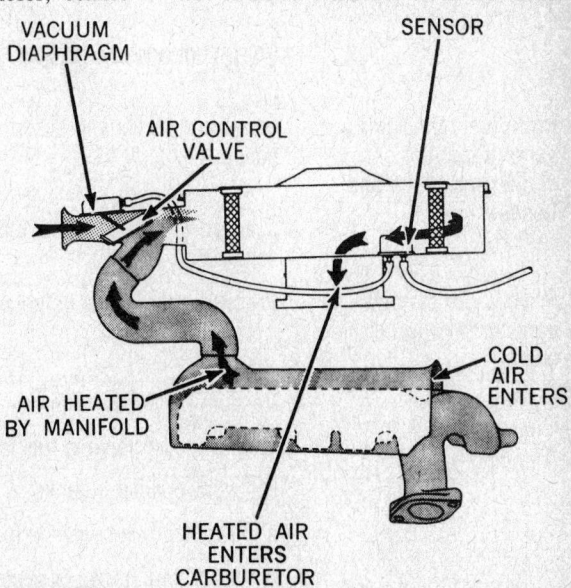

Vacuum operated air cleaner operation

and hold the door in the hot air position. A small thermostat inside the modulator opens it when the underhood temperatures reach normal. Other designs use a delay valve that allows the air door to move to the cold position slowly, to prevent stumble.

Testing Air Cleaners, Non-Vacuum Type

To test the non-vacuum type of heated air cleaner, start with an engine that is cold enough to have the air door in the hot air position. Remove the top of the air cleaner

and put a thermometer inside the cleaner, then replace the cover without the nuts. Start the engine and watch the air door through the end of the air cleaner. You may have to remove some air ducting to be able to see the air door. As soon as the air door starts to move from the hot air position, lift the top off the air cleaner and read the temperature. If the temperature is between 130 and 150°F. the thermostat is working correctly. If not, replace the thermostat.

—————— CAUTION ——————
Do not replace the thermostat if the temperature is off by only a few degrees. It

must be considerably out of specification, or perhaps not opening at all, to affect the running of the vehicle.

Testing Air Cleaners, Vacuum Type

To test the vacuum type of heated air cleaner, inspect the air door with the engine off. It should be in the cold air position. Start the engine. If the engine is cold, the air door should move to the hot air position. As the engine warms up, the air door should move to a mid position, depending on the outside air temperature.

EVAPORATION CONTROL SYSTEM DIAGNOSIS CHART

Problem	Cause	Remedy
Persistent odor of fuel vapors	Canister saturated due to extend parking of vehicle.	Operate (idle) engine for several minutes to purge canister.
	Fuel tank cap not sealing.	Replace cap.
	Canister not purging:	
	a. Vacuum hose to intake manifold or tee obstructed or leaking.	Check for vacuum at canister end of hose. Blow through hose with compressed air. Replace hose if cracked, deteriorated or obstruction cannot be removed.
	b. Vacuum orifice in manifold fitting or tee obstructed.	Remove manifold fitting or tee and blow orally through fitting to check for obstruction. If orifice is plugged, soak fitting in solvent and blow out with compressed air.
	Loose vent hose connections or loose filler neck connections.	Pressure test vapor vent system for leakage. If leakage is indicated, visually inspect for damaged hoses or tubes, loose, damaged or missing clamps. Repair is needed.
Fuel leakage:		
a. From fuel tank cap	Fuel tank cap seal faulty.	Replace cap.
	Pressure relief valve in fuel tank cap faulty.	Test operation of pressure relief valve. If valve is faulty, replace cap.
	Valve vent hoses obstructed.	Remove fuel tank cap and blow hoses with compressed air. Replaced hoses if necessary.
b. From fuel tank liquid vapor separator or connecting tubes and hoses	Loose connections, cracked or broke tube or hose.	Pressure test vapor vent system for leakage. If leakage is indicated, repair as needed.
	Cracked or damaged fuel tank or liquid/vapor separator	Replace damaged components.
c. From vapor storage canister (through air flow filter)	Pressure relief valve in fuel tank cap faulty.	Test operation of valve. If faulty, replace cap.
Noisy fuel tank— wall fluctuation ("oilcanning")	Vacuum buildup in tank:	
	Vacuum relief valve in fuel tank cap faulty.	Test operation of valve. If faulty, replace cap.
	Pressure buildup in tank:	
	a. Pressure relief valve in fuel tank cap faulty.	Test operation of valve. If faulty, replace cap.
	b. Vapor vent hoses obstructed.	Remove fuel tank cap and blow out hoses with compressed air. Replace hoses if necessary.

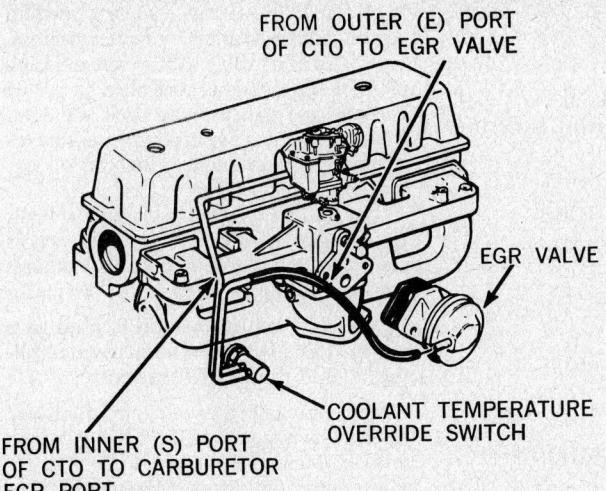

Typical 6 cylinder engine EGR system

FROM OUTER (E) PORT OF CTO TO EGR VALVE

EGR VALVE

COOLANT TEMPERATURE OVERRIDE SWITCH

FROM INNER (S) PORT OF CTO TO CARBURETOR EGR PORT

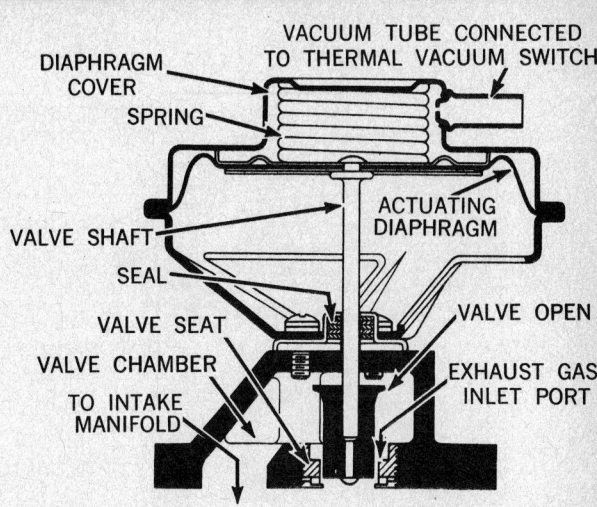

Cross section—ported vacuum signal EGR valve (typical)

VACUUM TUBE CONNECTED TO THERMAL VACUUM SWITCH

DIAPHRAGM COVER

SPRING

ACTUATING DIAPHRAGM

VALVE SHAFT

SEAL

VALVE OPEN

VALVE SEAT

VALVE CHAMBER

EXHAUST GAS INLET PORT

TO INTAKE MANIFOLD

If the outside air is extremely cold, the air door may stay in the hot air position indefinitely. On a warm day, after the engine warms up the air door should move to the cold air position. If it doesn't, the temperature sensor inside the air cleaner might be faulty, or the air door itself might be hanging up. Check the air door by running a hose from manifold vacuum to the vacuum motor. Connect and disconnect the hose to see if the air door moves freely. If the air door is free, check out the hoses for leaks or blockage. If the hoses are okay, the trouble must be in the temperature sensor, and it should be replaced.

Modulators are used in the air cleaner vacuum line on some engines. The modulator mounts on the side of the air cleaner and has two hose connections, one to the air cleaner temperature sensor, and the other to the vacuum motor. Below 50–80°F. the modulator is a one-way check valve, which allows vacuum to move the air door to the hot air position, but traps the vacuum so the door will not jump back to the cold air position during acceleration. This prevents a stumble.

After the modulator warms up, the check valve unseats so that the vacuum can pass freely in either direction, and the air door then operates normally. The connections for the modulator are important. The connection in the center goes to the vacuum motor, and the connection on the edge goes to the vacuum source, which is the temperature sensor.

To test the modulator on a cold engine, apply enough vacuum to the edge port to move the air door to the hot position. Then remove the hose from the port, and the air

door should stay in the hot position. Make the same test when the engine is warmed up, and the air door should move to the cold position when you pull off the hose.

EXHAUST GAS RECIRCULATION

NOx (oxides of nitrogen) is a tailpipe emission caused by the oxidation of nitrogen in the combustion chamber. When the peak combustion temperatures go over 2500°F. NOx is formed in excessive amounts. To keep the combustion temperatures down, exhaust gas is recirculated.

Recirculation of the exhaust gases is accomplished by having a movable valve between the exhaust and intake manifolds, and upon a predetermined demand, route engine vacuum to the valve and open the connecting port to allow the exhaust gases to flow into the intake manifold and mix with the air/fuel mixture.

Three types of EGR valves are used, with the major differences in the method used to control the valve opening. The three types are as follows:

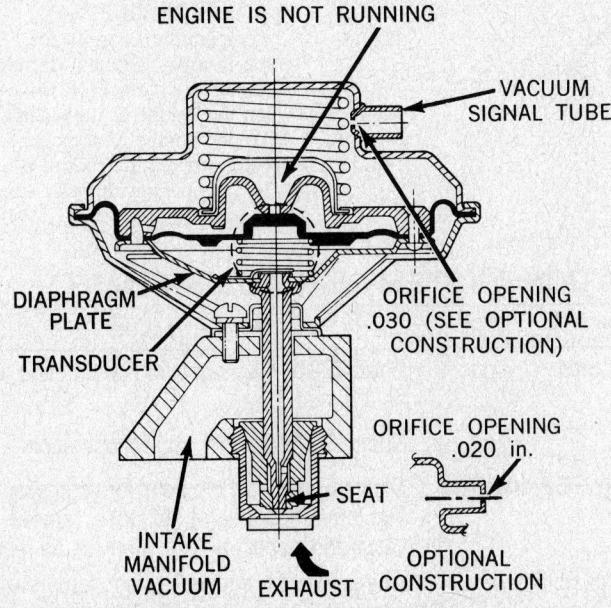

DIAPHRAGM IS SEATED WHEN ENGINE IS NOT RUNNING

VACUUM SIGNAL TUBE

DIAPHRAGM PLATE

TRANSDUCER

ORIFICE OPENING .030 (SEE OPTIONAL CONSTRUCTION)

ORIFICE OPENING .020 in.

SEAT

INTAKE MANIFOLD VACUUM

EXHAUST

OPTIONAL CONSTRUCTION

Cross section—typical negative back pressure EGR valve

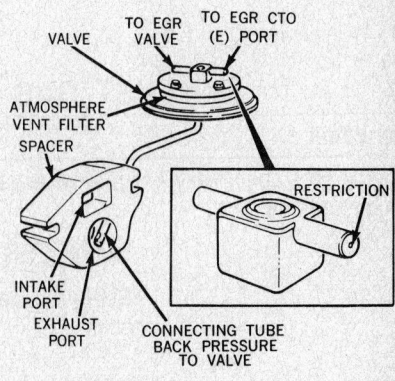

TO EGR VALVE

TO EGR CTO (E) PORT

VALVE

ATMOSPHERE VENT FILTER

SPACER

RESTRICTION

INTAKE PORT

EXHAUST PORT

CONNECTING TUBE BACK PRESSURE TO VALVE

EGR valve with external, non-integral back pressure sensor

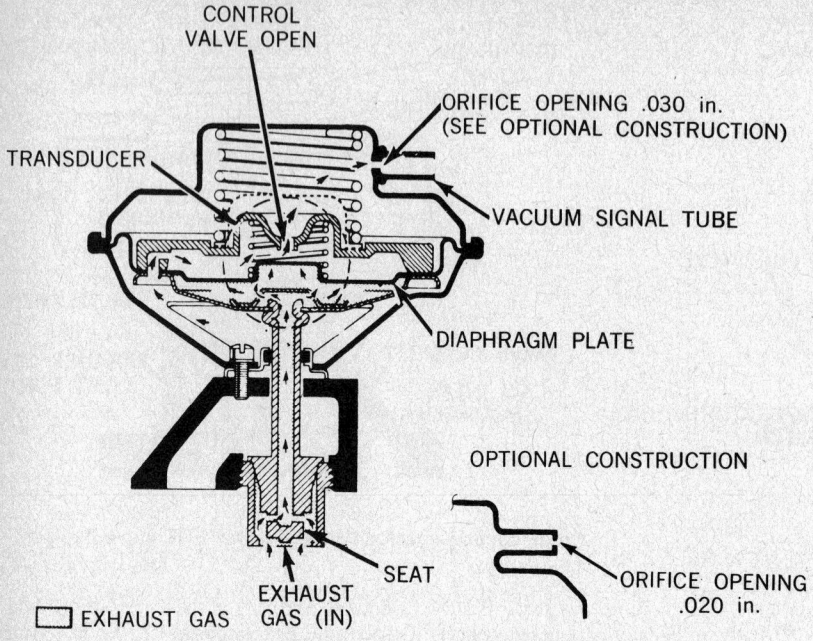

Cross section—typical positive back pressure EGR valve

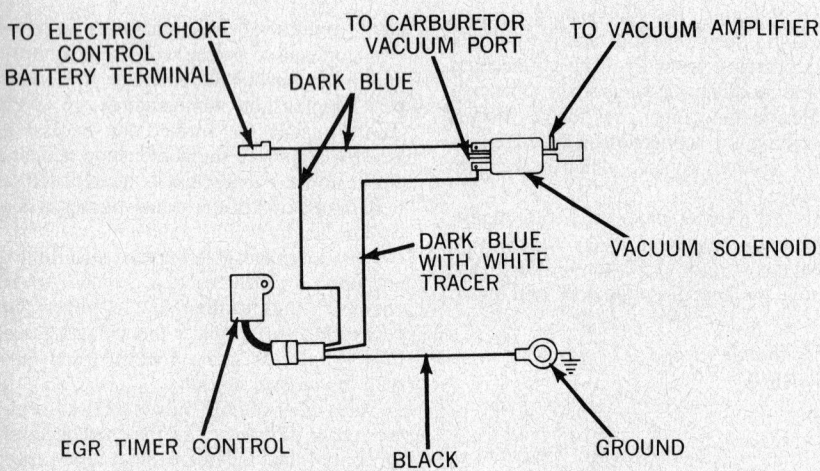

Typical time delay circuitry—EGR valve

1. An EGR valve with no back pressure sensor and is controlled by ported vacuum.

2. An EGR valve with an integral back pressure sensor and is controlled by ported vacuum and exhaust gas back pressure. Both positive and negative type transducers are used to react to either high or low exhaust gas back pressures.

3. An EGR valve with an external, non-integral back pressure sensor and is controlled by ported vacuum and exhaust gas back pressure.

NOTE: Venturi vacuum is used as a triggering agent when a vacuum amplifier is used in the EGR system.

Several different types of controls are used to turn the vacuum to the EGR valve on and off. Most of them have to do with engine temperature, as described later.

When the EGR valve hose is connected to the base of the carburetor, without a separate amplifier, the system is operated by ported vacuum. The hose may not run directly from the EGR valve to the carburetor, but may go through a temperature control valve of some sort. In a ported vacuum system, the vacuum to operate the EGR valve is taken from a port that is above the throttle plate at idle, and thus not subject to vacuum. Because there is no vacuum, the spring in the EGR valve closes it, and the exhaust gas does not recirculate. As the throttle is opened, the port is exposed to vacuum, and the EGR valve opens.

Vacuum systems, with an amplifier, are the most complicated, because of the number of hoses. Manifold vacuum is connected to the amplifier by a hose, and then connects to the EGR valve. The amplifier also connects to venturi vacuum. At idle there is no venturi vacuum, but above idle the air moves through the carburetor venturi fast enough to create a vacuum. This slight amount of vacuum opens the amplifier, which then allows manifold vacuum to open the EGR valve.

Temperature controls for EGR systems come in many different designs. They are all made so that the EGR valve stays closed when the engine or the outside air is cold. After the engine or the outside air warms up, the temperature control allows the EGR valve to operate normally. Before March

EXHAUST GAS RECIRCULATION SYSTEM DIAGNOSIS CHART

Condition	Possible Cause	Correction
Engine idles abnormally rough and/or stalls.	EGR valve vacuum hoses misrouted.	Check EGR valve vacuum hose routing. Correct as required.
	Leaking EGR valve.	Check EGR valve for correct operation.
	EGR valve gasket failed or loose EGR attaching bolts.	Check EGR attaching bolts for tightness. Tighten as required. If not loose, remove EGR valve and inspect gasket. Replace as required.
	EGR thermal control valve and/or EGR-TVS.	Check vacuum into valve from carburetor EGR port with engine at normal operating

EXHAUST GAS RECIRCULATION SYSTEM DIAGNOSIS CHART

Condition	Possible Cause	Correction
Engine idles abnormally rough and/or stalls.		temperature and at curb idle speed. Then check the vacuum out of the EGR thermal control valve to EGR valve. If the two vacuum readings are not equal within ± ½ in. Hg. (1.7 kPa), then proceed to EGR vacuum control diagnosis.
	Improper vacuum to EGR valve at idle.	Check vaccum from carburetor EGR port with engine at stabilized operating temperature and at curb idle speed. If vacuum is more than 1.0 in. Hg., refer to carburetor idle diagnosis.
Engine runs rough on light throttle acceleration, poor part load performance and poor fuel economy.	EGR valve vacuum hose misrouted.	Check EGR valve vacuum hose routing. Correct as required.
	Failed EGR vacuum control valve.	Same as listing in "Engine Idles Rough" condition.
	EGR flow unbalanced due to deposit accumulation in EGR passages or under carburetor.	Clean EGR passages of all deposits.
	Sticky or binding EGR valve.	Remove EGR valve and inspect. Clean or replace as required.
	Wrong or no EGR gaskets.	Check and correct as required.
Vehicle with back pressure EGR valve.	Control valve blocked or air flow restricted.	Check internal control valve function per service procedure.
Engine stalls on decelerations.	Restriction in EGR vacuum line.	Check EGR vacuum lines for kinks, bends, etc. Remove or replace hoses as required. Check EGR vacuum control valve function.
		Check EGR valve for excessive deposits causing sticky or binding operation. Clean or repair as required.
	Sticking or binding EGR valve.	Remove EGR valve and inspect, clean or repair as required.
Vehicle with a back pressure EGR valve.	Control valve blocked or air flow restricted.	Check internal control valve function per service procedure.
Part throttle engine detonation.	Insufficient exhaust gas recirculation flow during part throttle accelerations.	Check EGR valve hose routing. Check EGR valve operation. Repair or replace as required. Check EGR thermal control valve and/or EGR-TVS as listed in "Engine Idles Rough" section. Replace valve as required. Check EGR passage and valve for excessive deposit. Clean as required.
Vehicle with a back pressure EGR valve.	Control valve blocked or air flow restricted.	Check internal control valve function per service procedure.
Engine starts but immediately stalls when cold.	EGR valve hoses misrouted.	Check EGR valve hose routing.
	EGR system malfunctioning when engine is cold.	Perform check to determine if the EGR thermal control valve and/or EGR-TVS are operational. Replace as required.
Vehicle with a back pressure EGR valve.	Control valve blocked or air flow restricted.	Check internal control valve function per service procedure.

① Detonation can be caused by several other engine variables. Perform ignition and carburetor related diagnosis.

EMISSION CONTROL SYSTEMS

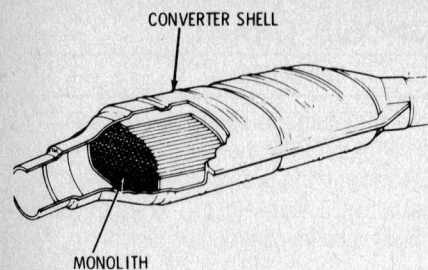

CONVERTER SHELL

MONOLITH

Cutaway of a monolith converter

15, 1973, many EGR systems used a temperature control that was sensitive to outside air temperature. Even with a fully warmed up engine, the EGR system would stay off if the outside temperature was cold enough. On vehicles made after March 15, 1973, the temperature controls were all sensitive to engine coolant temperature, or engine compartment temperature.

Testing EGR Systems

Testing of the EGR systems should verify that the EGR valve is closed at idle, open above idle, and that the exhaust gas is actually recirculating. If the EGR valve sticks open at idle, the engine will run very rough, or may not even start. If this happens the valve should be removed and cleaned, or replaced. To check for valve opening above idle, check with a mirror or your fingers to see if the diaphragm or stem moves when the engine is at a fast idle in Park or Neutral. If the diaphragm does not move when the throttle is opened, there is either a problem with vacuum, or the valve is stuck closed. With a vacuum gauge connected to the EGR port, you should see vacuum on the gauge when the throttle is opened. EGR valves should not leak when tested with a hand vacuum pump. If they do they must be replaced.

To find out if the exhaust gas is actually recirculating, use a hand vacuum pump or mouth suction through a hose to open the EGR valve with the engine idling. If the engine runs rough or dies, you know the exhaust gas is recirculating. If the engine does not run rough, make a second test at 2500 rpm. Opening the EGR valve at that

rpm should cause a change in engine speed. If it does, you know the exhaust gas is recirculating. To make the 2500 rpm test, remove and plug the hose from the EGR port. Attach your suction hose to the EGR valve before running the engine at 2500 rpm. Simply pulling off the EGR hose at 2500 rpm is not a valid test, because the extra air entering the engine through the hose could cause a speed change all by itself. On most engines you won't have to go this far, because opening the EGR valve at idle will prove that the exhaust is recirculating.

If the exhaust is not recirculating, it means that a passageway or the valve itself is clogged up. The only way to fix it is to scrape out the clogging as best you can, or replace the valve.

The back-pressure sensor is a pressure-operated bleed that disables the EGR valve and keeps it closed when there is no exhaust pressure. This type of valve cannot be tested with a hand vacuum pump with the engine off because the bleed is open. The only practical way to test these new valves is by substitution of a known good valve. If a valve is not available, the suspected valve can be removed, and the holes temporarily taped shut. If this corrects the problem, then a new valve should be installed.

EGR delay systems are used on some vehicles to prevent the recirculation of the exhaust gases for approximately 60 seconds after the ignition switch is turned on by an electrical timer, connected to an engine mounted solenoid switch. The solenoid is connected in the vacuum line between the carburetor venturi nipple and the vacuum amplifier.

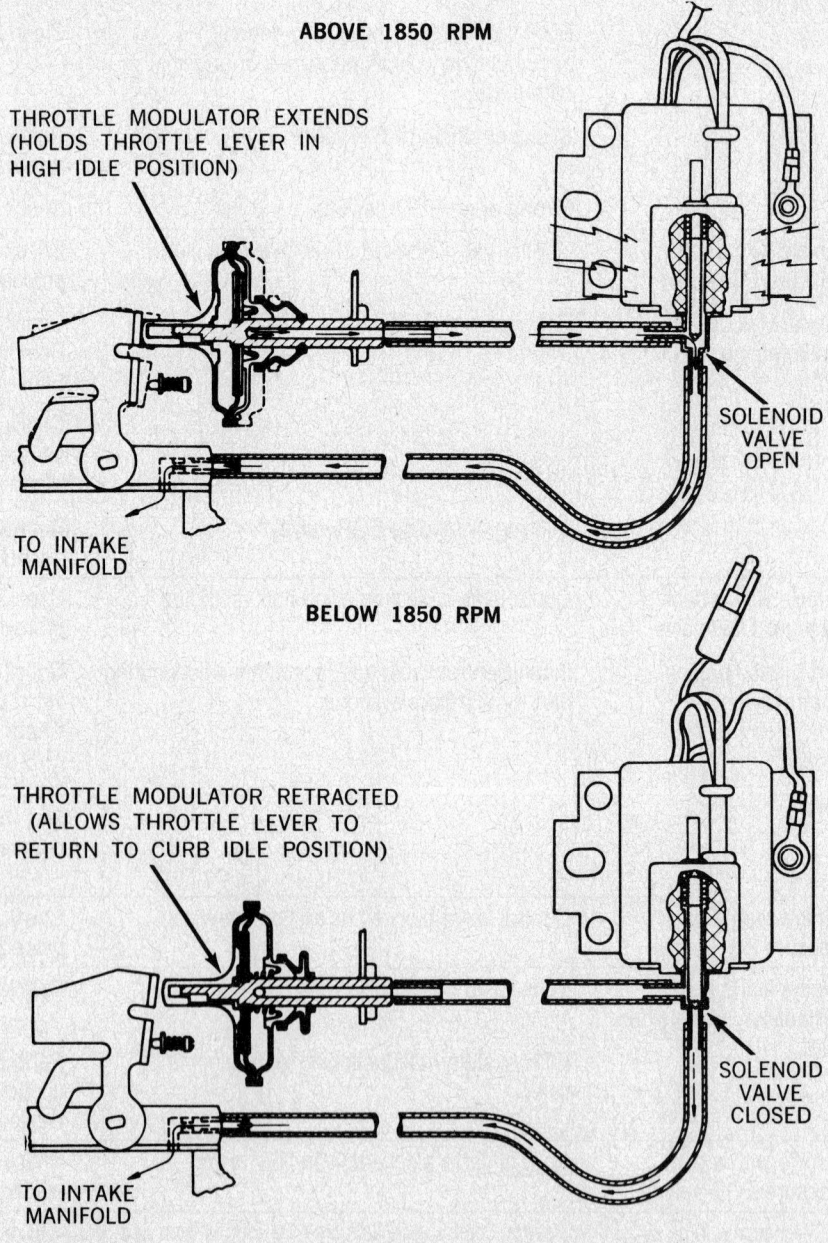

ABOVE 1850 RPM

THROTTLE MODULATOR EXTENDS (HOLDS THROTTLE LEVER IN HIGH IDLE POSITION)

TO INTAKE MANIFOLD

SOLENOID VALVE OPEN

BELOW 1850 RPM

THROTTLE MODULATOR RETRACTED (ALLOWS THROTTLE LEVER TO RETURN TO CURB IDLE POSITION)

TO INTAKE MANIFOLD

SOLENOID VALVE CLOSED

Typical throttle modulator operation used on IHC vehicles

CONVERTER SHELL

OUTER WRAP

INSULATION

FILL PLUG · INSULATION · BED SUPPORT · CATALYST

INLET GAS · CATALYTIC PELLET COMPOUND · OUTLET GAS

Underfloor converter—showing replaceable pellets

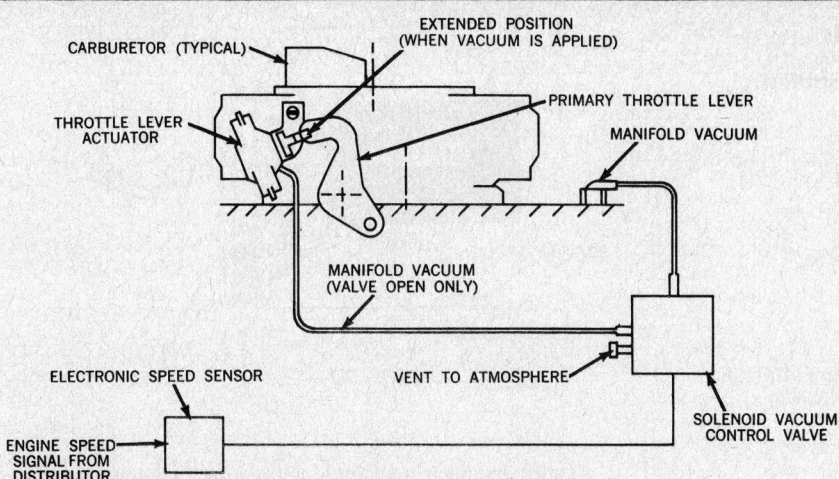

Typical throttle return control system used on G.M. vehicles

A charge temperature switch is used on some models by being installed in the intake manifold on the number 6 branch, 6 cyl., and on the number 8 branch on the V8 engine. No EGR timer on EGR valve operation is permitted when the air/fuel mixture temperature is below 60°F. (16°C).

CATALYTIC CONVERTER

A catalytic converter is a chamber in the exhaust system that contains a catalyst. When hydrocarbons or carbon monoxide pass over the catalyst they react with the oxygen in the exhaust and are converted into harmless water and carbon dioxide. The catalyst inside the converter is made in two forms. General Motors, and Jeep use the pellet form, in which loose pellets are packaged into the converter and can be emptied out and changed, if necessary. Ford, International and Chrysler use the honeycomb catalyst, which is built into the converter shell and is not replaceable. On Ford, International and Chrysler products the entire converter must be replaced if it goes bad.

There is no way to test a converter in the field to see if it is actually working. Tailpipe readings may be used to set carburetor idle mixtures, when the car maker requires it, but taking a tailpipe reading to determine if the converter is working is not possible.

The one field check that is recommended in all cases is to inspect for mechanical damage. If a converter gets overheated, the catalyst can melt and block the exhaust. Pellets or pieces of the catalyst may even come flying out the tailpipe while the engine is running. If this happens, the pellets or the entire converter must be changed.

Checking for a melted converter that restricts the exhaust can be done with a vacuum gauge connected to the engine. Run the engine at about 2500 rpm in Park or Neutral. If the vacuum reading is steady, the exhaust is okay. If the vacuum reading slowly drops, it indicates a buildup of pressure in the exhaust.

The use of leaded fuel will slowly destroy the efficiency of the catalyst until finally, after several tanks full, it won't do its job any more. If used long enough, leaded fuel can even cause catalyst plugging to the point that the engine will not run. If you know that a vehicle has been run on several tanks of leaded fuel, then you can be sure that the catalyst has lost its ability to convert. But there is no way to test for this condition in the field.

Do not change the catalyst if the vehicle has been run on only one tank or less of leaded fuel. Switching back to lead free fuel will allow the catalyst to recover and be almost as efficient as it was.

Converter Overheat Protection

Engine controls are used to prevent the converter from being damaged by overheating due to overly rich fuel mixtures during periods of deceleration.

The controls are named differently by the manufacturers, but are all designed to accomplish the same purpose and to operate basically in the same manner. To prevent the engine from operating at a rich mode when the throttle plates are closed during deceleration, electrical and/or mechanical means are provided to hold the throttle plates open at predetermined engine speeds, in order to lean the air/fuel mixture as necessary to control the exhaust emissions. The engine control should be inoperative under engine speeds of 1800 to 2000 RPMs to avoid engine overrun or vehicle overspeed in slow traffic.

The various parts are as follows:

1. The throttle level actuator is mounted as part of the carburetor assembly and operates when vacuum is applied to it from a separate solenoid vacuum control valve.

2. The solenoid vacuum control valve is controlled by a signal from the electronic speed sensor or a throttle modulator deceleration valve vacuum signal to allow vacuum to be routed to the throttle lever actuator.

3. Electronic speed sensor is mounted near or included with the distributor and senses the engine speed and sends a signal to the solenoid vacuum control valve as long as the preset speed is exceeded.

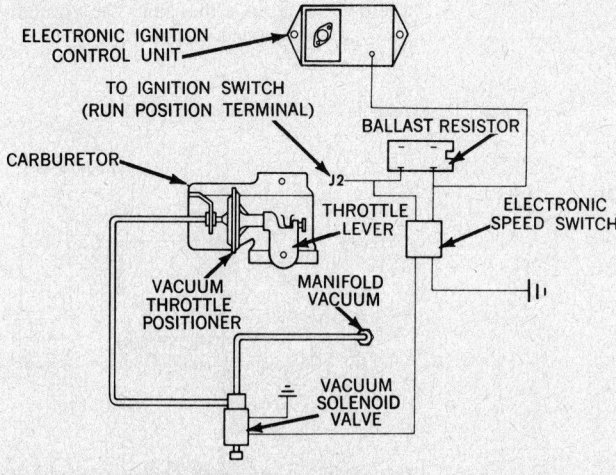

Typical throttle positioner system used on Chrysler Corp. vehicles having California Emission requirements

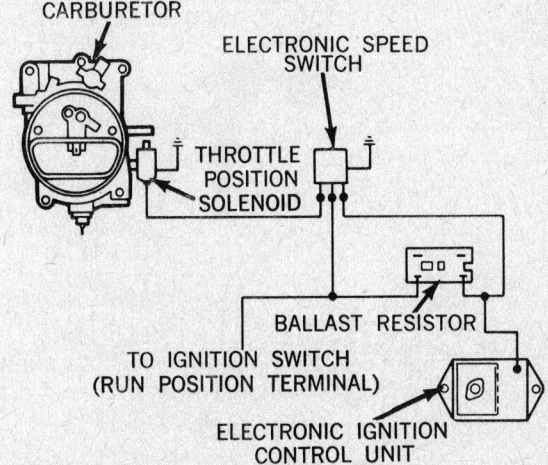

Typical throttle positioner electrical circuitry used on Chrysler Corp. vehicles

EMISSION CONTROL SYSTEMS

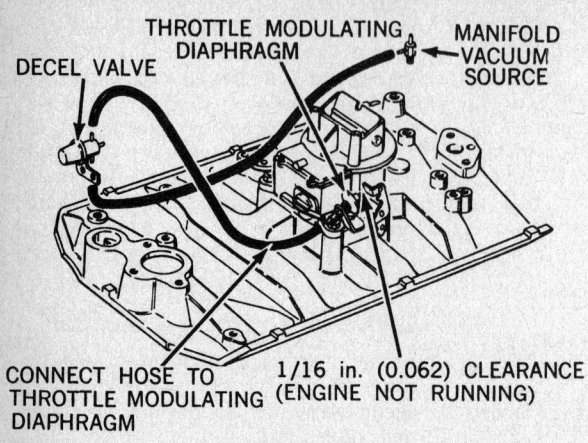

Typical vacuum throttle modulating system

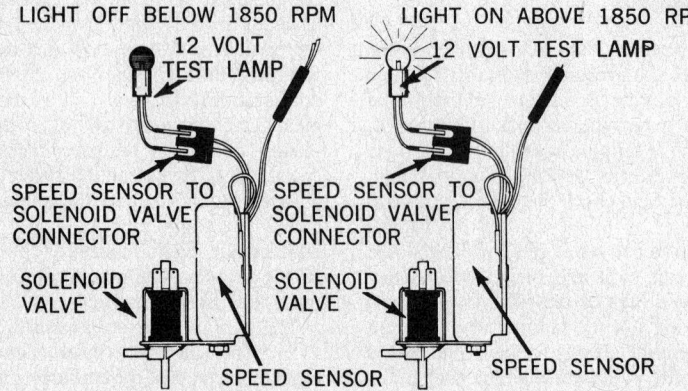

Testing an electric speed sensor switch

Testing the System

To test the electrical speed sensor system, place the transmission in neutral or park and set the hand brake. With a tachometer attached to the engine, increase the engine speed to approximately 2000 RPM. The solenoid or modulator stem should extend to hold the carburetor throttle lever off curb idle setting. As the engine speed is reduced to below 1800 RPM, the solenoid or modulator stem should retract to the off position. A hand held vacuum pump and test lamp can be used to test the individual components of the system.

To test the vacuum operated system, without an electrical sensor, 21 to 22 in. Hg. must be directed to the decel valve to open the port to direct vacuum to the throttle modulating diaphragm, located on the carburetor base. With the vacuum present, the stem of the modulating diaphragm will be extended. Release of the vacuum should allow the stem of the modulating diaphragm to retract.

VACUUM OPERATED EXHAUST HEAT RISER VALVES

Exhaust heat riser valves have been used for many years to force part of the engine exhaust through a passageway under the intake manifold and preheat the fuel mixture. The heat valve was spring loaded into the closed position, but heat would make the spring relax so that during high speed operation or after warmup the exhaust would push it open.

Now, many engines use vacuum operated heat valves, controlled by a vacuum switch that is sensitive to engine temperature.

On these systems, manifold vacuum is used to close the valve, and force the exhaust gases through the crossover passage in the intake manifold. All the systems have a temperature valve that shuts the vacuum off when the engine warms up.

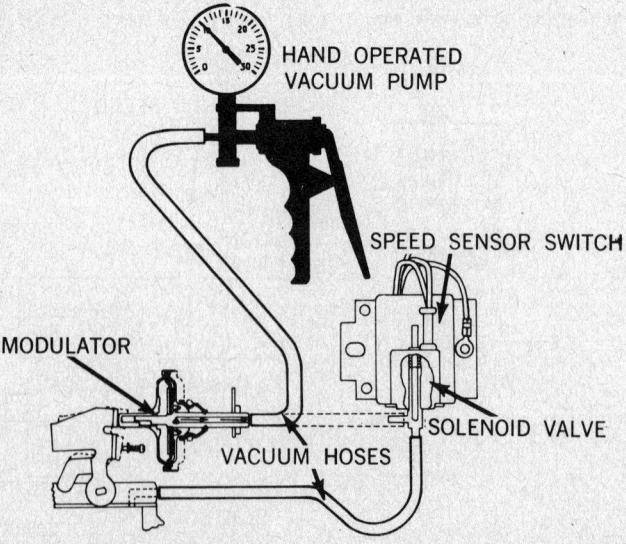

Typical vacuum modulator testing

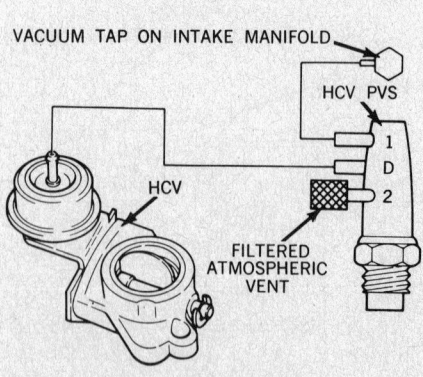

Typical exhaust heated control valve vacuum circuit using a ported vacuum coolant switch

Testing an electric solenoid valve with the engine running

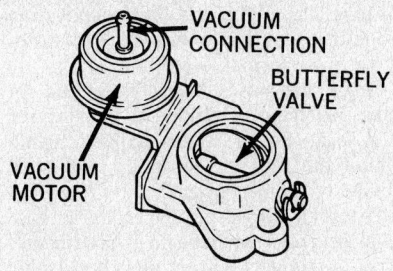

Typical vacuum operated exhaust heat control valve

A simple coolant temperature-sensitive vacuum switch is mounted on the intake manifold coolant passage and has two hose connections. It actually does triple duty because it also controls the vacuum supply to the idle enrichment system and the air switching valve.

A second type vacuum switch has three hose connections, but one of them is a vent with a filter to keep the dirt out.

A third control uses either a coolant vacuum switch, or a vacuum solenoid connected to an oil temperature switch. The coolant vacuum switch has two hose connections and a vent when it controls the

heat valve only. When it is tied into other emission control systems, it can have as many as five hose connections, and a vent. Some models also have a check valve in the hose so that vacuum will be trapped in the heat valve actuator when the engine is accelerated. This keeps the heat valve in the closed position and prevents a rattle.

Testing Vacuum Operated Exhaust Heat Riser Valves

Testing the vacuum operated heat riser valve is a matter of making sure it closes and opens freely. You can move it to see if it works, on a warm engine. On a cold engine, the valve should be closed, and disconnecting the hose should allow it to open. On a cold engine, there should be vacuum at the vacuum actuator, and on a warm engine the vacuum should be shut off.

AIR INJECTION SYSTEMS

A belt-driven air pump supplies air to small tubes positioned in the exhaust port near each exhaust valve. The air mixes with unburned hydrocarbons in the exhaust and the hydrocarbons actually burn up in the

exhaust system. Air injection systems are used on engines with catalytic converters, so that the converter gets enough air to keep the reaction going.

Plumbing on air injection systems varies considerably.

A check valve is used between the pump and the exhaust port nozzle to keep hot exhaust gases from traveling up the plumbing and destroying the pump. V8s use two check valves.

An anti-backfire valve, also called by-

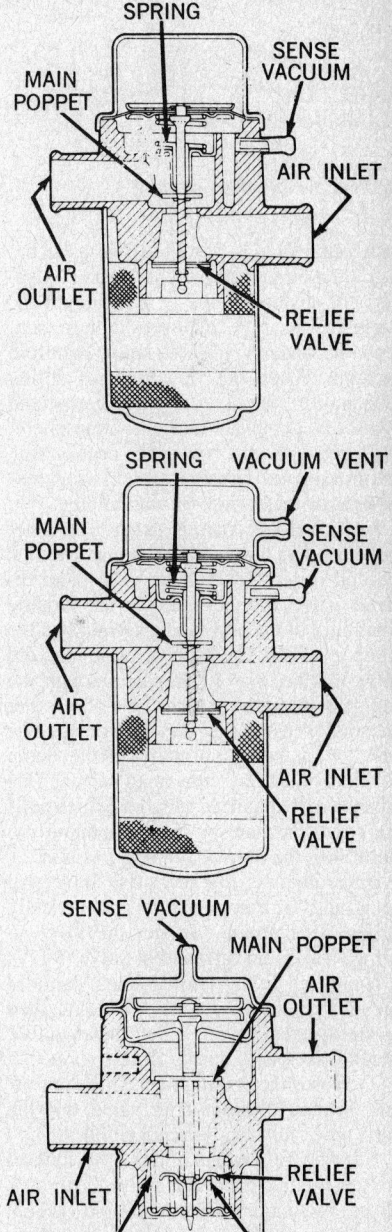

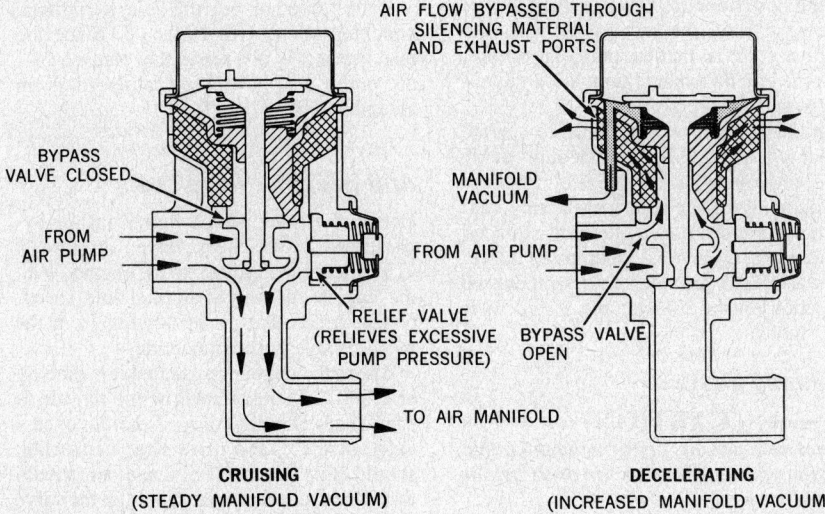

Diverter valve operation

CRUISING (STEADY MANIFOLD VACUUM)

DECELERATING (INCREASED MANIFOLD VACUUM)

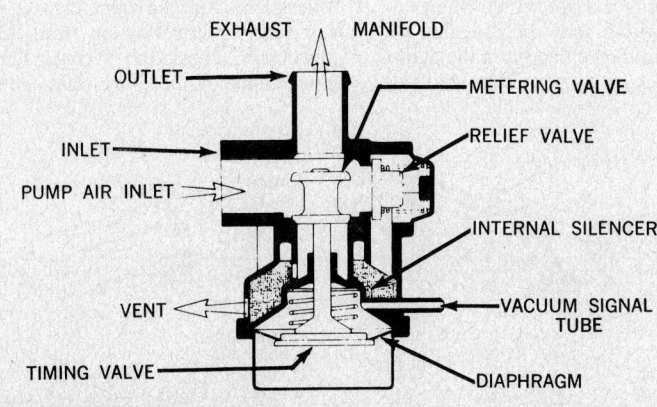

Diverter valve with internal muffler

Three types of diverter valves: A. Air by-pass valve; B. Closed air by-pass valve; C. Timed air by-pass valve with vacuum vent

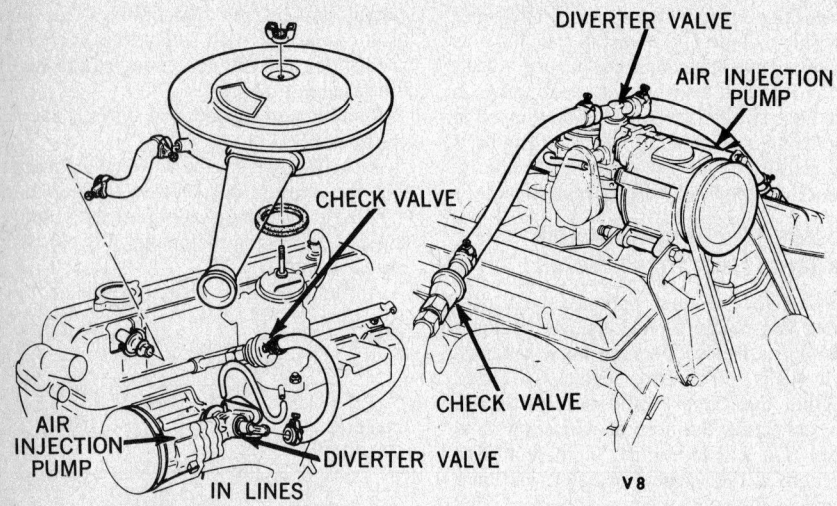

Typical air injection system

pass valve or diverter valve, is used between the pump and the check valve. Usually, the diverter valve is mounted on the pump or near it. A small sensing hose connects the diverter valve to intake manifold vacuum. When the vacuum rises during deceleration, the diverter valve opens, and sends the pump air into the atmosphere. This prevents the overrich deceleration mixture in the exhaust system from exploding or backfiring out the tailpipe.

Some models started using a diverter valve that has the small hose connection on the end instead of the side. The older diverter valve was normally in the running position, but the new one is normally in the dump position. In other words, the old valve allowed the air to pass through the engine exhaust ports regardless of whether the small sensing line was hooked up. The new valve, being normally in the dump position, must have the small sensing line hooked up to manifold vacuum, which pulls the valve mechanism from the dump position into the normal running position.

Unfortunately, the new style valve will not go into the dump position automatically during deceleration. To get the valve to dump, a vacuum differential valve (VDV) is connected in the sensing line. Manifold vacuum goes through the VDV and then to the diverter valve. When the manifold vacuum increases during deceleration, the VDV closes the sensing line. This shuts off the vacuum to the diverter valve, and the valve goes into the dump position.

A further refinement of this, is to connect the sensing line to ported (above the throttle plates) vacuum instead of manifold vacuum and eliminate the VDV. In this situation, the diverter valve only receives vacuum above idle, because the vacuum port in the carburetor throat is above the throttle plate at idle. So whenever the engine idles, the diverter valve goes to the dump position. It also dumps during deceleration, because the throttle at that time is in the idle position.

Some systems have a delay valve, similar to a spark delay valve, in the sensing hose. This delays for a few seconds the drop in vacuum when the throttle closes, so that the air is not dumped every time the driver takes his foot off the throttle in traffic.

Temperature controls are also used in the sensing hose hookup. Usually, the temperature valve shuts the vacuum off when the engine is cold, so that the pump air doesn't go to the engine exhaust ports until the engine warms up.

An idle vacuum valve is used to operate in conjunction with the vacuum delay valve, to provide backfire control, full time idle dumping of secondary air during cold engine operation, deceleration or extended idle periods of ½ to 2 minutes or more. The valve also provides cold temperature protection for the catalyst and a cold EGR valve lockout.

Air Pump Tests

CAUTION

Do not hammer on, pry or bend the pump housing while tightening the drive belt or testing the pump.

Before proceeding with the tests, check the pump drive belt tension.

If the belt squeals when the engine is running, the pump may be dragging or seized. Remove the belt and turn the pump by hand to check for seizure. Disregard any chirping, squealing, or rolling sounds from inside the pump when turning it by hand, as these are normal.

Check the hoses and connections for leaks. Hissing or a blast of air is indicative of a leak. Soapy water, applied lightly around the area in question, is a good method for detecting leaks.

To test air output, disconnect the air hose from the pump wherever it is convenient. If you disconnect it from one check valve on a V8, the other hose should also be disconnected and plugged for the test. Run the engine at idle and feel the blast of air from the hose with your hand. Increase the engine speed to 1500 rpm and feel the blast of air again. If the blast increases, and is steady, the pump is okay.

Pump Noise Diagnosis

The air pump is normally noisy; as engine speed increases, the noise of the pump will rise in pitch. The rolling sound the pump bearings make is normal. However, if this sound becomes objectionable at certain speeds, the pump may be defective and will have to be replaced.

A continual hissing sound from the air pump pressure relief valve at idle indicates a defective valve. Replace the relief valve.

If the pump rear bearing fails, a continual knocking sound will be heard. Since the rear bearing is not separately replaceable, the pump will have to be replaced as an assembly.

Anti-backfire Valve Tests

Detach the hose, which runs from the bypass valve to the check valve.

Connect a tachometer to the engine. With the engine running at normal idle speed, check to see that air is flowing from the bypass valve hose connection.

Speed the engine up, so that it is running at 1,500–2,000 rpm. Allow the throttle to snap shut. The flow of air from the bypass valve at the check valve hose connection should stop momentarily and air should then flow from the exhaust port on the valve body or the silencer assembly.

Let the throttle snap shut several times. If the flow of air is not diverted into the atmosphere from the valve exhaust port or if it fails to stop flowing from the hose connection, check the vacuum lines and connections. If these are tight, either the

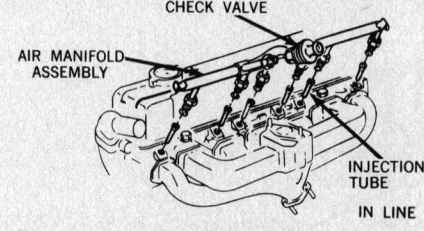

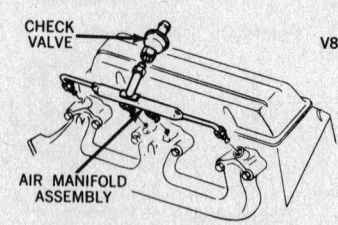

Typical air injection tubes

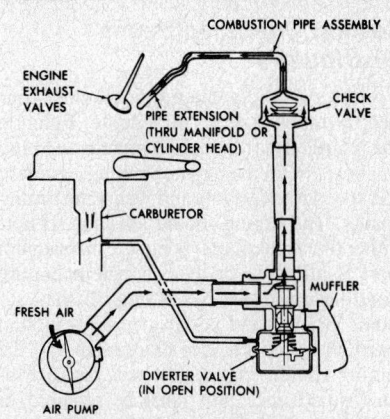

Typical air injection system operation

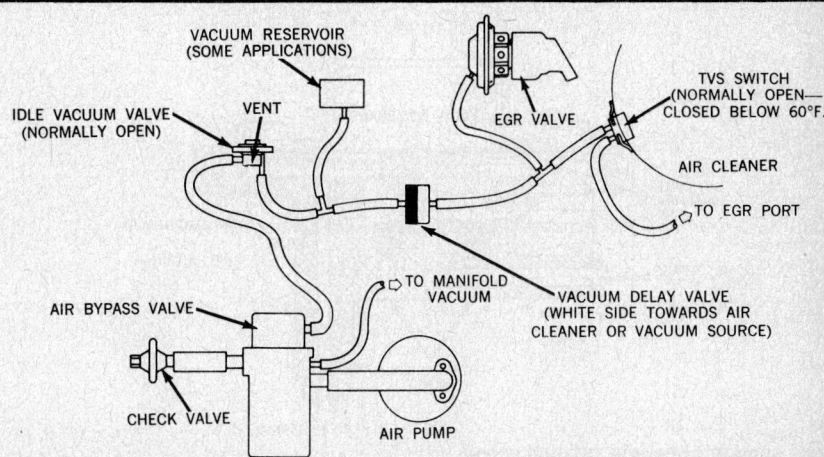

Typical air injection system with an idle vacuum valve used to control converter overheating

bypass valve or one of the accessory valves in the small sensing hose is defective and must be replaced.

A leaking diaphragm will cause the air to flow out both the hose connection and the exhaust port at the same valve.

Late model systems should stop flowing at idle, as described earlier. If not, the bypass valve or accessory valve is defective.

Check Valve Test

Remove the hose from the check valve. With the engine running at 1,500 rpm in Park or Neutral, hold the back of your hand near the check valve to test for exhaust gas leakage. If the valve leaks, it must be replaced.

NOTE: Vibration and flutter of the valve at idle is a normal condition caused by exhaust pulsations. It does not mean that the valve is defective.

Vacuum Differential Valve Test

Disconnect the small sensing hose at the bypass valve and connect a vacuum gauge to the hose. With the engine idling in Park or Neutral, the gauge should read full manifold vacuum.

Run the engine at a steady 2500 rpm in Park or Neutral, and release the throttle. As the engine decelerates, the vacuum gauge should drop close to zero, then return to full manifold vacuum as the engine speed drops to idle. If not, the VDV is defective and must be replaced.

NOTE: The small hose nozzle should be connected to manifold vacuum.

PULSE AIR INJECTION REACTOR SYSTEM

The Pulse Air Injection Reactor (PAIR) system is installed on the small inline 6 cylinder engine, used in General Motors light duty trucks, beginning in 1979. The PAIR system uses no air pump, but relies on the negative and positive exhaust gas impulses to draw fresh air into the exhaust manifold to assist in the further burning of the hydrocarbons (HC) before leaving the tailpipe.

Four individual check valves are used to prevent the exhaust gases from entering the fresh air intake chamber plenums. Two sets of pipes are used, one set in the front section

of the exhaust manifold and the second set in the rear section of the exhaust manifold.

Two sets of plenum chambers are used and connected to the carburetor air cleaner by a common hose, for the fresh air intake.

During periods of high engine rpm, the check valves will remain closed to prevent the flow of exhaust gases to the engine air cleaner.

Failure Diagnosis

1. Inspect the pulse air valve and pipes for leakage or defective operation, if a hissing noise is heard.

2. If one or more of the check valves are defective, exhaust gases will enter the carburetor area and cause poor drive-ability such as stalling, surge, or poor performance.

Inspection of Pulse Air Injection Reactor System

1. Burned off paint on the rocker arm plenum chambers indicates a defective pulse air valve. Rubber grommets and hoses will deteriorate and can cause a hissing noise.

2. Inspect the carburetor for pieces of rubber hoses or grommets, indicating an overheating of the components.

3. Inspect the operation of the pulse air valve by applying at least 17 in. Hg at the grommet end of the valve. A drop of 6 in. Hg in two seconds is allowed.

Electronic Ignition System

A change has been made through the model years from the conventional distributors to the electronic ignition systems for more precise ignition control.

Different types are available from the manufacturers, but the operation of the systems are basically the same. Greater dependability, higher secondary voltages and less need for adjustments are the important

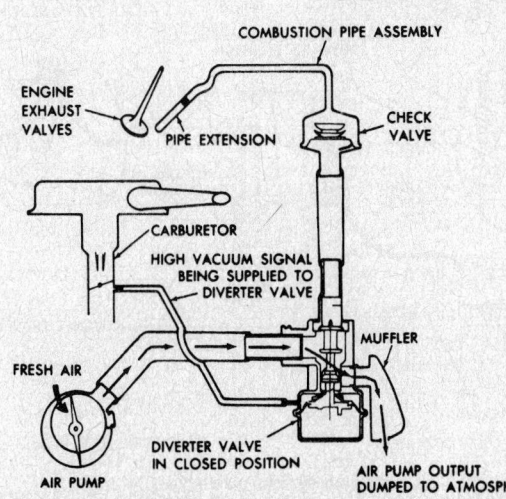

Typical air diverter valve operation

EMISSION CONTROL SYSTEMS

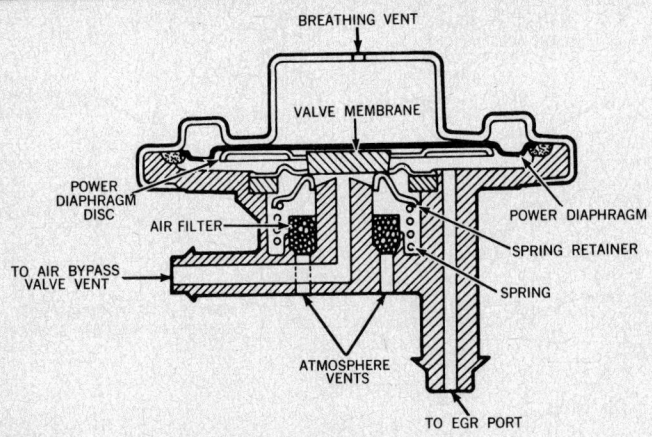

Cross section of an idle vacuum valve

factors considered in using this system for emission control.

Refer to the individual truck sections and to the Electrical section for expanded information.

DISTRIBUTOR CONTROLS

All distributor controls act in some way to change or eliminate vacuum advance during certain operating conditions. Usually, the control cuts down on the amount of vacuum advance, in effect retarding the spark, so that the exhaust will get hotter and burn up hydrocarbon and carbon monoxide emissions before they go out the tailpipe.

The distributor vacuum advance unit might be connected, according to factory design, to either manifold vacuum or ported (above the throttle plates) carburetor vacuum. Either way, the vacuum spark advance curve is approximately the same for all running conditions above idle. At idle, however, the manifold vacuum hookup results in full advance, while the ported hookup gives zero advance. If the hoses are hooked up the wrong way, the addition or lack of advance will affect idle speed, requiring a readjustment of the throttle position to bring the idle speed back to specifications. When this is done, emissions will usually be high, so it is important to keep the hoses hooked up correctly.

DUAL DIAPHRAGM DISTRIBUTORS

These distributors have two hose connections, one in the normal position, and the other closer to the distributor body. The hose fitting next to the body is for the retard diaphragm, and is connected to manifold vacuum. The retard diaphragm affects the spark only at idle, when there is no vacuum on the advance diaphragm. In effect, the retard diaphragm provides a movable resting place for the advance diaphragm. When ported vacuum is not acting on the advance

diaphragm, it returns to the neutral or no-advance position against the retard diaphragm. At idle, manifold vacuum pulls the retard diaphragm to the retard position, and the advance diaphragm follows along to retard the spark.

Testing Dual Diaphragm Distributors

To test a dual diaphragm distributor, connect a timing light to the engine. Remove the retard hose from the distributor and plug the hose. With the engine running, increase the speed to a fast idle and watch the timing marks. The timing should advance. If not, either the vacuum unit is faulty, the vacuum port is plugged, or there is a temperature control device that is shutting off the vacuum. Apply hand pump or mouth suction vacuum to the advance diaphragm and the timing should advance. If not, the distributor or advance unit must be repaired or replaced. Failure to advance could be caused by a faulty diaphragm or a sticky advance plate.

Remove the advance hose from the vacuum unit and read the timing at normal idle speed. Remove the plug that was inserted in the retard hose, and check for full manifold vacuum at the end of it. If there is no vacuum, temperature controls may be shutting it off.

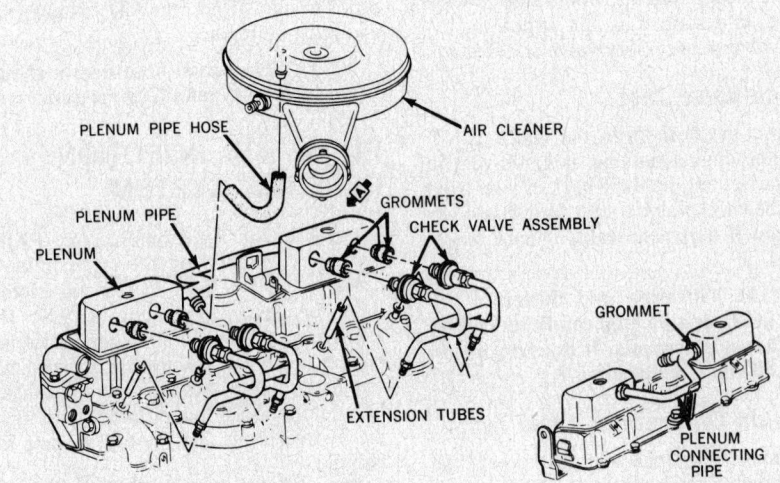

Pulse Air Injection System (PAIR)

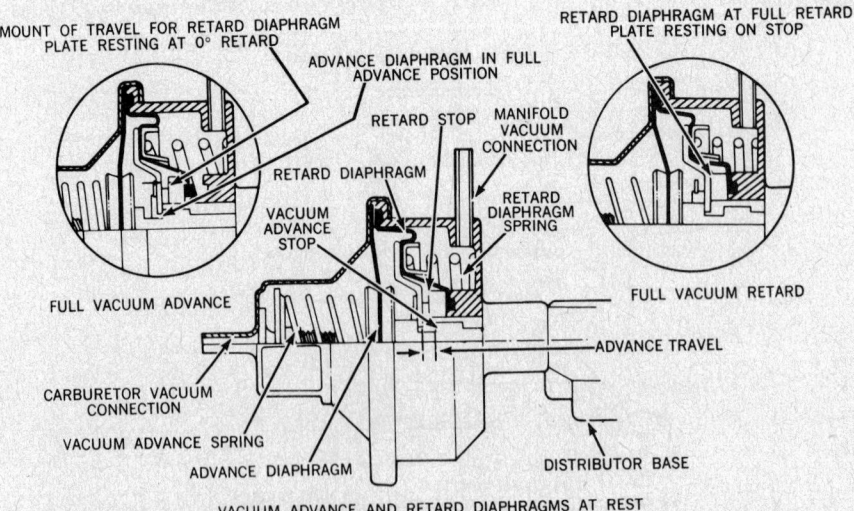

Dual diaphragm vacuum control

Connect the hose to the retard diaphragm, or apply vacuum from another source. The timing should immediately retard several degrees. If not, the diaphragm is not working, and the unit must be replaced. Reconnect all hoses as they were originally.

DISTRIBUTOR VACUUM DECELERATION VALVE

Its purpose is to advance the spark during deceleration, by sending full manifold vacuum to the vacuum advance unit. At all other times the vacuum advance unit receives ported (above the throttle plates) carburetor vacuum.

Three checks should be made on the valve: the amount of vacuum at the distributor, any valve leaks, and the adjustment. To check the amount of vacuum at the distributor, use a T-fitting and a short length of vacuum hose to connect a vacuum gauge into the distributor vacuum line near the distributor. At idle, with the engine fully warmed up, the vacuum on the gauge should be less than 1 Hg. If the gauge shows more than 1 Hg. the idle speed is too fast, or the valve is leaking. To check for a leak,

remove the large manifold vacuum hose on the side of the valve. If the vacuum drops, the valve is leaking and must be replaced. If the vacuum stays high, reduce the engine idle speed so that the port in the carburetor is covered.

To check the valve adjustment, connect the manifold vacuum hose and run the engine at 2000 rpm for 5 seconds. Then release the throttle. The distributor vacuum should go over 16 in. Hg. and stay there for about one second. Within about three seconds after you release the throttle, the distributor vacuum should drop to below 6 in. Hg. If the carburetor is equipped with

AIR INJECTION REACTOR SYSTEM DIAGNOSIS CHART

Condition	Possible Cause	Correction
No air supply—accelerate engine to 1500 rpm and observe air flow from hoses. If the flow increases as the rpm's increase, the pump is functioning normally. If not, check possible cause.	Loose drive belt.	Tighten to specifications.
	Leaks in supply hose.	Locate leak and repair.
	Leak at fittings.	Tighten or replace clamps.
	Air expelled through by-pass valve:	
	a. Connect a vacuum line directly from engine manifold vacuum to by-pass valve	If this corrects the problem, go to step b. If not, replace air by-pass valve.
	b. Connect vacuum line from engine manifold vacuum source to by-pass valve through vacuum diffential valve directly, by passing the differential vacuum delay and separator valve.	If this corrects the problem, check differential vacuum, delay and separator valve and vacuum source line for plugging. Replace as required. If it doesn't, replace vacuum differential valve.
	Check valve inoperative.	Disconnect hose and blow through hose toward check valve. If air passes, function is normal. If air can be sucked from check valve, replace check valve.
	Pump failure.	Replace pump.
Excessive pump noise, chirping, rumbling, knocking, loss of engine performance.	Leak in hose.	Locate source of leak using soap solution and correct.
	Loose hose	Reassemble and replace or tighten hose clamp.
	Hose touching other engine parts.	Adjust hose position.
	Vacuum differential valve inoperative.	Replace vacuum differential valve.
	By-pass valve inoperative.	Replace by-pass valve.
	Pump mounting fasteners loose.	Tighten mounting screws as specified.
	Pump failure.	Replace pump.
	Check valve inoperative.	Replace check valve.
Excessive belt noise.	Loose belt.	Tighten to spec.
	Seized pump.	Replace pump.
Excessive pump noise. Chirping.	Insufficient break-in.	Run vehicle 10–15 miles at interstate speeds. Recheck.
Centrifugal filter fan damaged or broken.	Mechanical damage.	Replace centrifugal filter fan.
Exhaust tube bent or damaged.	Mechanical damage.	Replace exhaust tube.
Poor idle or driveability.	A defective A.I.R. system cannot cause poor idle or driveability.	Do not replace A.I.R. system.

EMISSION CONTROL SYSTEMS

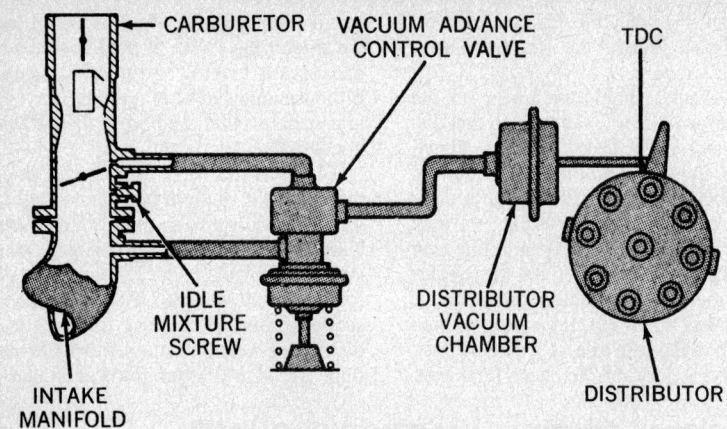

Carburetor-control valve-distributor relationship

a dashpot to make the throttle close slowly, the time may be about one second longer. If the time is too long, remove the cover on the valve and turn the screw clockwise to reduce the time. To increase the time, turn the screw counterclockwise. If the valve will not adjust properly, it must be replaced, and the new valve adjusted to specifications.

SPARK DELAY VALVE

This small valve is connected between the carburetor and the distributor vacuum advance, so that the ported (above the throttle plates) vacuum to the distributor must pass through the valve. A restriction in the valve delays the vacuum applied to the vacuum advance unit so that the advance comes in slowly. When there is no vacuum at the carburetor port, as during idle or wide open throttle a check valve inside the spark delay valve opens and dumps the vacuum so that the vacuum advance unit returns to the no-advance position without any delay.

Spark delay valves can be tested for correct operation and leaks with a source of vacuum such as a hand vacuum pump or a running engine, and a vacuum gauge. Connect the vacuum gauge to the distributor side of the valve, and the vacuum source to the other side. The gauge should rise slowly until it reads the amount of vacuum available. The time to rise to the maximum reading should be from one to 28 seconds. If the vacuum gauge does not read anything, the valve is plugged. If the vacuum reads instantly, without any delay, the valve is open. In either case, the spark delay valve must be replaced. To test the check valve part of the spark delay valve, remove the vacuum source and the vacuum gauge should drop instantly to zero without any delay. If there is any delay, the spark delay valve is defective and must be replaced.

TRANSMISSION CONTROLLED SPARK

The purpose of the transmission controlled

spark is to eliminate vacuum spark advance in the lower gears. When the transmission is in high gear, vacuum spark advance is allowed for better gasoline milage and part throttle response. This system was used during the 1975–1976 model years on most light duty models and continued on some California and High Altitude vehicles in later years.

Testing TCS Systems

Testing the system is done by connecting a vacuum gauge to the distributor vacuum line with a long hose so you can put it through the window into the front seat and see it while driving. There should be no vacuum in the lower gears on a warm engine, but after the transmission shifts into a gear that allows vacuum advance, you should see vacuum on the gauge. Engines that run their distributors on manifold vacuum will show vacuum at all times when in the proper gear. Engines that use ported (above the throttle plates) vacuum will show vacuum in the proper gear only when the throttle is open. If you don't get vacuum when you should, test the individual units in the system.

Vacuum solenoids can be tested by disconnecting all wiring and connecting hot and ground wires to the solenoid terminals, to make it open or close. You should be able to blow through the solenoid when it is open, but not when it's closed. Because

solenoids exist in both normally open and normally closed designs, it is important to use the right solenoid. If the wrong solenoid is used, the system will work backwards, giving advance in the lower gears but not in high. The same goes for the transmission switch, which exists in both normally open and normally closed designs. The term "normally open" means that the solenoid or switch is open when it is not energized or activated. In the case of a vacuum solenoid, normally open means that if you were holding the solenoid in your hand without any wires connected to it, the vacuum passages would be open, allowing vacuum to pass. In the case of a transmission switch, the term "normally open" refers to the electrical path, which is "open" or "off" so that it will not conduct electricity. Normally closed, of course, means that the electric contacts are closed so that the current can pass. But normally closed on a vacuum solenoid means that the vacuum passage is blocked so the vacuum can't get through.

TEMPERATURE ACTIVATED VACUUM (TAV) AND COLD TEMPERATURE ACTIVATED VACUUM (CTAV) SYSTEMS

This system switches the vacuum source back and forth between the carburetor spark port and EGR port, according to the air temperature. A 3-nozzle vacuum solenoid is used. Below approximately 55°F. outside air temperature, the temperature switch is open, and the solenoid is not energized. In this position, the solenoid connects the spark port to the vacuum advance unit. Above 55°F. the temperature switch closes, and energizes the solenoid. In this position, the solenoid connects the EGR port to the vacuum advance unit.

The temperature switch is located in the air cleaner, and a latching relay is on the firewall. Once the temperature switch has closed, the relay latches so that any sudden rush of cold air through the air cleaner will not cycle the solenoid on and off. The latching relay keeps the solenoid energized as long as the ignition switch is on. When the ignition switch is turned off, the relay un-

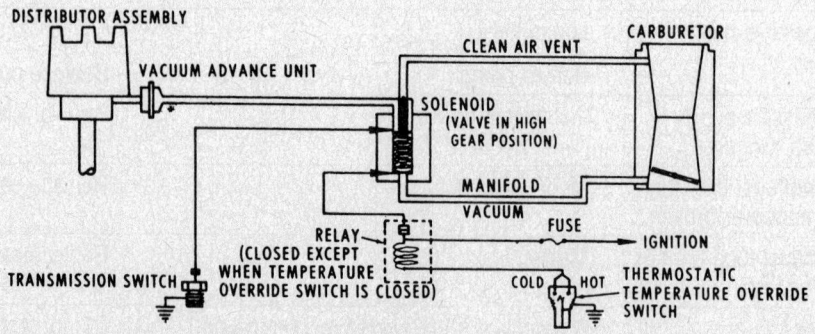

Typical transmission controlled spark system

latches and the system is ready for the next start, whether the air temperature is hot or cold. If the air at the temperature switch is over 55°F. the latching relay will come on when the ignition switch is turned on.

Testing

Test the system with a vacuum gauge connected to the vacuum advance hose at the distributor. With the temperature above 65°F. (to be sure the temperature switch has closed) you should be getting vacuum from the EGR port. If you disconnect the EGR port hose and the vacuum drops, you know the system is working. When making a cold test, the vacuum should come from the spark port hose, so disconnecting that hose should make the vacuum drop. Because both ports are above the throttle plate, the throttle must be opened slightly to get vacuum at the hose.

Identifying the spark port and EGR ports on the carburetor is easy if they are marked. If there is no marking on the carburetor, connect two vacuum gauges, one to each port. At idle you should not have any vacuum. If you do have vacuum, it usually means the engine is idling too fast. Close the throttle slightly to slow down the idle and the vacuum should drop to almost zero.

When you open the throttle, you will see vacuum on one gauge before the other. The gauge that gets vacuum first is connected to the spark port.

ORIFICE SPARK ADVANCE CONTROL (OSAC)

It is a mechanism that delays the application of vacuum to the distributor vacuum advance unit. When the throttle is opened, the carburetor port is exposed to vacuum. This vacuum goes through a hose to the OSAC valve, and then to the distributor vacuum advance. The OSAC valve is sometimes mounted on the firewall, and sometimes on the air cleaner. Inside the OSAC valve is a calibrated orifice that delays the vacuum as much as 27 seconds, depending on the calibration of the valve.

Some OSAC valves have temperature control that senses the temperature inside the air cleaner or inside the plenum chamber behind the firewall, depending on where the valve is mounted. If the valve contains temperature control, it will be wide open below 60°F. bypassing the orifice and allowing vacuum advance without any delay. Above 60°F. the bypass closes and the delay takes over.

Testing

To test the valve, connect a vacuum gauge to the DIST connection on the valve. With the engine idling, you should have no reading on the gauge. If there is a reading, the engine is idling too fast. With the engine idling, open the throttle to a fast idle, and hold it steady. The vacuum on the gauge

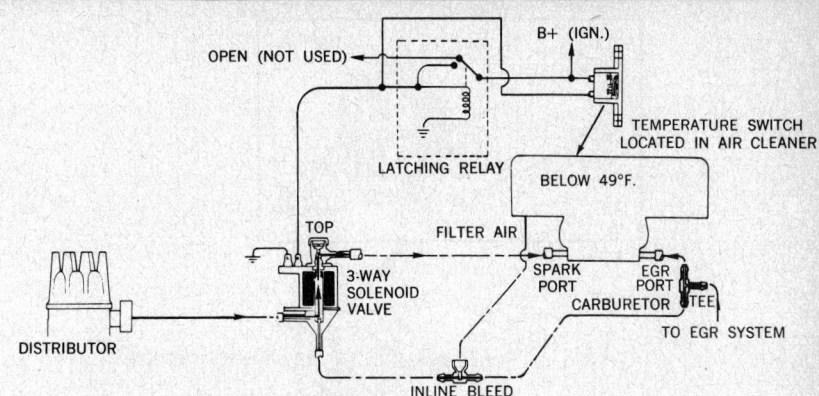

Cold temperature activated vacuum system

will rise slowly until it reaches a maximum reading. If not, there is something wrong with the system, and you should check out the hoses and the carburetor port, or replace the valve is necessary.

VACUUM REDUCER VALVE

Inserted between the manifold vacuum source and the distributor, this valve reduces the vacuum acting on the advance diaphragm by about 3 in. Hg. This valve is always used on a system that includes a distributor thermal vacuum switch. The vacuum advance unit operates on ported (above the throttle plates) vacuum, except when the engine overheats above 225°F. This opens the thermal vacuum switch and sends full manifold vacuum through the vacuum reducer valve to the advance unit. Thus, the vacuum reducer valve is only operating when the engine is overheated.

To test the valve, connect a vacuum gauge to the TVS nozzle, and a hand vacuum pump to the MAN nozzle. When you pump up 15 in. Hg. vacuum on the hand pump, the vacuum on the separate gauge should be 3 to 4 in. Hg. lower. Both gauges should hold the vacuum without leakdown. If not, the valve is defective and must be replaced.

RETARD DELAY VALVE

When the throttle is suddenly opened, engine vacuum drops immediately, and this causes the vacuum advance to move quickly from the advance position to the neutral or no-advance position. A retard delay valve is a restriction with a one-way check valve. It allows the vacuum to act on the vacuum advance unit normally, but when the vacuum drops, the delay valve traps the vacuum in the advance unit and lets it out slowly. It takes several seconds for the advance unit to return to the neutral position.

Some models have the retard delay valve hooked up so that it only operates when the engine is cold. At normal operating temperature the delay is bypassed.

Testing of the delay valve can be done

with a hand vacuum pump. Connect the pump to the MAN side of the valve, or the side that connects to the vacuum source on the engine. Connect a separate vacuum gauge to the other side of the valve. When the hand pump is operated, the vacuum will rise on both the pump gauge and the separate gauge equally. When the release is pulled, the pump gauge will drop to zero immediately, but the separate gauge will take several seconds to drop to zero. If it doesn't work that way, the delay valve is defective, and must be replaced.

COLD START SPARK ADVANCE

A coolant sensitive vacuum switch (PVS) is combined with a delay valve (distributor retard control valve) to provide retard delay when the engine coolant is below 128°F. The hose routing is set up so that the vacuum advance unit operates on manifold vacuum through the retard delay valve when the engine is cold, and on ported vacuum through a spark delay valve when the engine is warm. The system also has an overheat PVS that switches the vacuum advance over to manifold vacuum (through the spark delay valve) when the engine coolant gets over 235°F.

Testing the spark delay valve is covered in this section under Spark Delay Valve. Testing for the distributor retard control valve is the same as for the retard delay valve in this section.

When the 128° PVS is cold, connection No. 2 is blocked and D and 1 are connected. When it is over 128°F No. 1 is blocked and D and 2 are connected.

Carburetor Choke Controls

NON-ELECTRIC CHOKE

A non-electric choke uses a "stove" on the exhaust manifold or a well on the intake manifold to provide heat. When the well

EMISSION CONTROL SYSTEMS

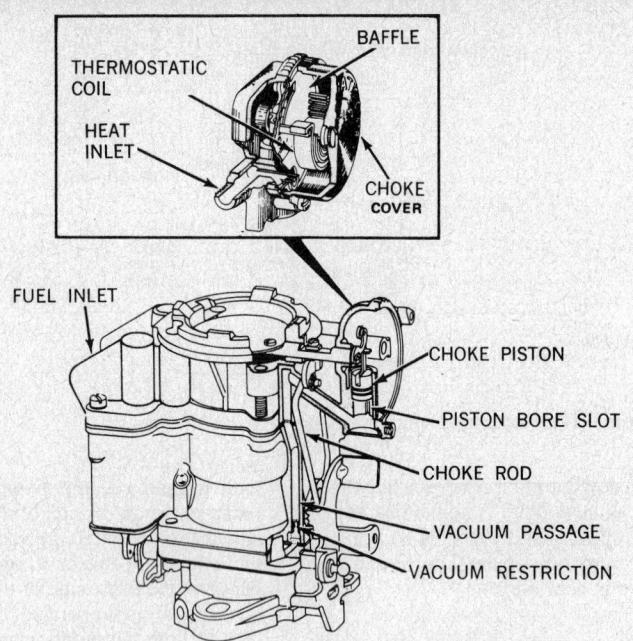

Non-electric choke assembly using a manifold heated choke stove

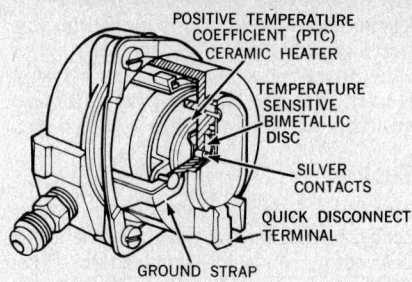

Electric choke assembly—Used with a choke stove

is used, the choke coil is surrounded by the warm intake manifold, heated by the exhaust crossover passage. When the stove is used, the choke housing is connected to engine vacuum, and a long tube pulls the heated air from the stove into the choke housing to heat up the choke coil and cause the choke to open as the engine warms up. When an electric choke is used, it can be in addition to all the above, or it can be the only source of choke heat, depending on the design.

ELECTRIC CHOKE

The electric choke has a small heater next to the choke coil. This heater receives its current from different sources, depending on the car maker.

Ford Motor Company and Jeep chokes are powered from the alternator "center tap," which produces about 7 volts. As the alternator is only putting out voltage when the engine is running, the electric choke is automatically shut off when the engine is off. It is important that the choke is connected only to the special "center tap" provided on the alternator. The description "center tap" refers to the construction of the alternator wiring, and not to the location of the connection.

Inside is a thermostatic switch that turns on the heating element at approximately 80°F. Above that, the element stays on as long as the engine is running. The 80°F. figure was selected because the engine is warm enough at that temperature to keep running without the choke. When the heater comes on, the choke opens very quickly. When the engine is shut off and cools

down, the choke switch may stay on to as low as 65°F. at the choke housing. On a warm restart, where the choke switch was still on, the heating element would heat up the choke and open it shortly after the engine started.

Chrysler Corporation vehicles with an electric choke use a well type choke, which receives heat both from the intake manifold and the electric choke heater. A separate choke control unit is mounted on top of the intake manifold and connected to the heater with a wire. This wire disconnects at the choke control unit only, not at the heater.

Choke control units may be single and double stage. The double stage is recog-

nized by the external resistor alongside the unit. The single stage unit turns on the choke heater at approximately 60°F. and off at 110°F. The double stage unit keeps the heater on below 60°F. but the current runs through the resistor. At approximately 60°F. the resistor is taken out of the circuit and the heater gets full current. At 110°F. the control unit turns the heater off.

Testing can be done with a non-powered test light on the choke terminal to find out if the heater is on or off. The ignition switch must be on. If the light glows, you know the control unit is on. On two-stage units, the light will glow dimly when the resistor is in the circuit, and brightly when the resistor is out. The current to the control unit comes from the ignition switch, and there is no fuse.

Chevrolet and GMC use an electric choke that is mounted on the carburetor. The choke has a dual element behind the coil spring. Whenever the engine is running, the choke heater is in operation. Below 50–70°F. a bimetal snap disc in the choke cover turns off the large section of the heating element so that only the small section gives off heat. Above 50–70°F. the disc switches on the large heating element for faster choke opening.

Current to the choke is controlled by a

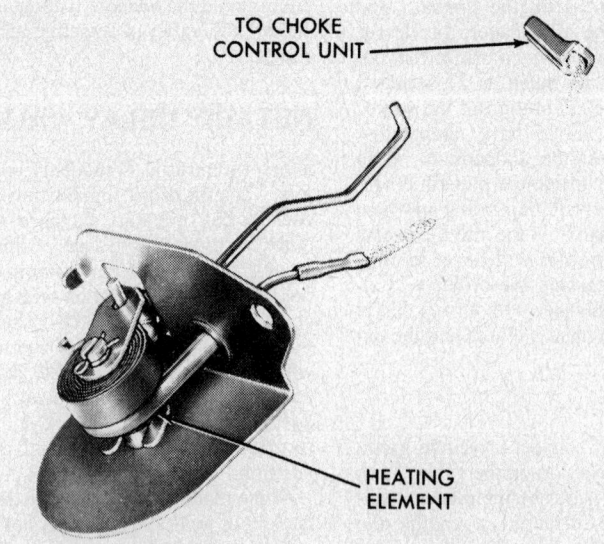

Manifold heat type choke assembly

three-terminal oil pressure switch. One of the terminals is a ground for the red oil pressure light on the instrument panel. The other two terminals are a switch in series between the ignition switch and the choke heater. Oil pressure operates the switch so that the choke gets current only when the engine is running. The circuit is fused through the backup light or transmission fuse in the fuse block.

NOTE: Failure of the choke heater circuit will cause the oil pressure light to go on.

IDLE ENRICHMENT SYSTEM

In order to reduce the cold engine stalling, a metering system is used to relate to the carburetor, rather than to the choke. The system enriches the carburetor mixtures in the curb idle and fast idle modes. The car-

buretor will have the complete idle system enriched during periods of cold to semi-cold operating conditions. The idle enrichment valve is manifold vacuum controlled and opens or closes a passageway that admits extra air to the idle circuit.

Some models have a coolant temperature control valve, mounted on a coolant passage and connected by hose between the manifold vacuum source and the idle enrichment valve. When the engine is cold, the valve is open and allows vacuum to operate the idle enrichment valve to richen the idle fuel mixture. When the engine warms up, the valve closes and cuts off the vacuum to the coolant temperature valve.

A vacuum solenoid may be included in the vacuum hose arrangement to provide EGR valve delay while the engine is cold.

Testing

Testing the system can be done on a cold

engine by disconnecting the hose at the carburetor and connecting a vacuum gauge to the hose. Start the engine and note the length of time that vacuum appears on the gauge. At the end of the timed period, the gauge should drop to zero. Allow the engine to warm up to operating temperature and make the test again. This time you should not see any vacuum on the gauge, because the CCIE (coolant control idle enrichment), valve should be closed. If there is no timer, you will see vacuum for several minutes after a cold start, until the engine warms up.

To check the effect of the idle enrichment use a hand vacuum pump on the idle enrichment valve on the carburetor. With vacuum applied, the valve will be closed, richening the idle, and changing the idle speed. Release the vacuum and the speed should go back where it was. If there is no speed change, either the valve is not working, or

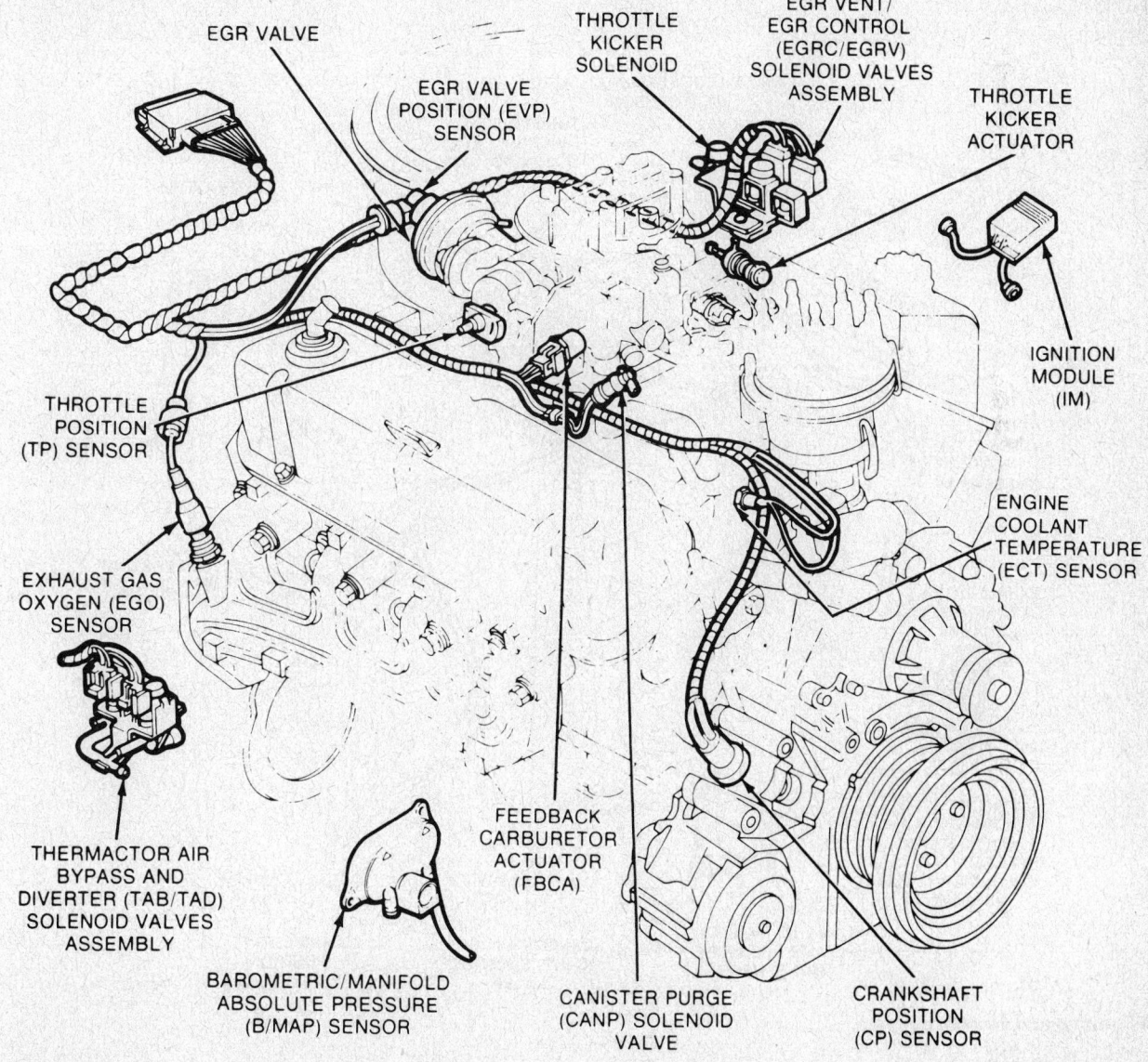

Typical feedback carburetor and electronic control system

EMISSION CONTROL SYSTEMS

a carburetor passage is blocked with dirt. The valve should also hold vacuum without leaking down.

ELECTRONIC FUEL MIXTURE CONTROL SYSTEMS

The control of air fuel mixtures to exacting specifications through all ranges of engine operation from idle to fast acceleration is monitored by this system. A central control module, receives input from a number of sensors. The module sends signals to fuel and EGR control components.

Typical Sensor Units

1. Throttle position sensor
2. Barometric/manifold absolute pressure sensor

3. Exhaust gas oxygen sensor
4. Crankshaft position sensor (timing sensor)
5. Engine coolant temperature sensor
6. Air intake temperature sensor
7. EGR valve position sensor

EMISSION CONTROLS

Diesel Engines

Because the diesel engine has inherently low air pollution characteristics due to its combustion system, exhaust emissions are controlled by engine modifications.

Crankcase and fuel vapors are negligible so that no special systems are required to control them, but a PCV crankcase system is used to purge the crankcase of unwanted fumes.

The State and Federal governments are devising pollution standards for the engine, but have not as yet developed the proper regulations.

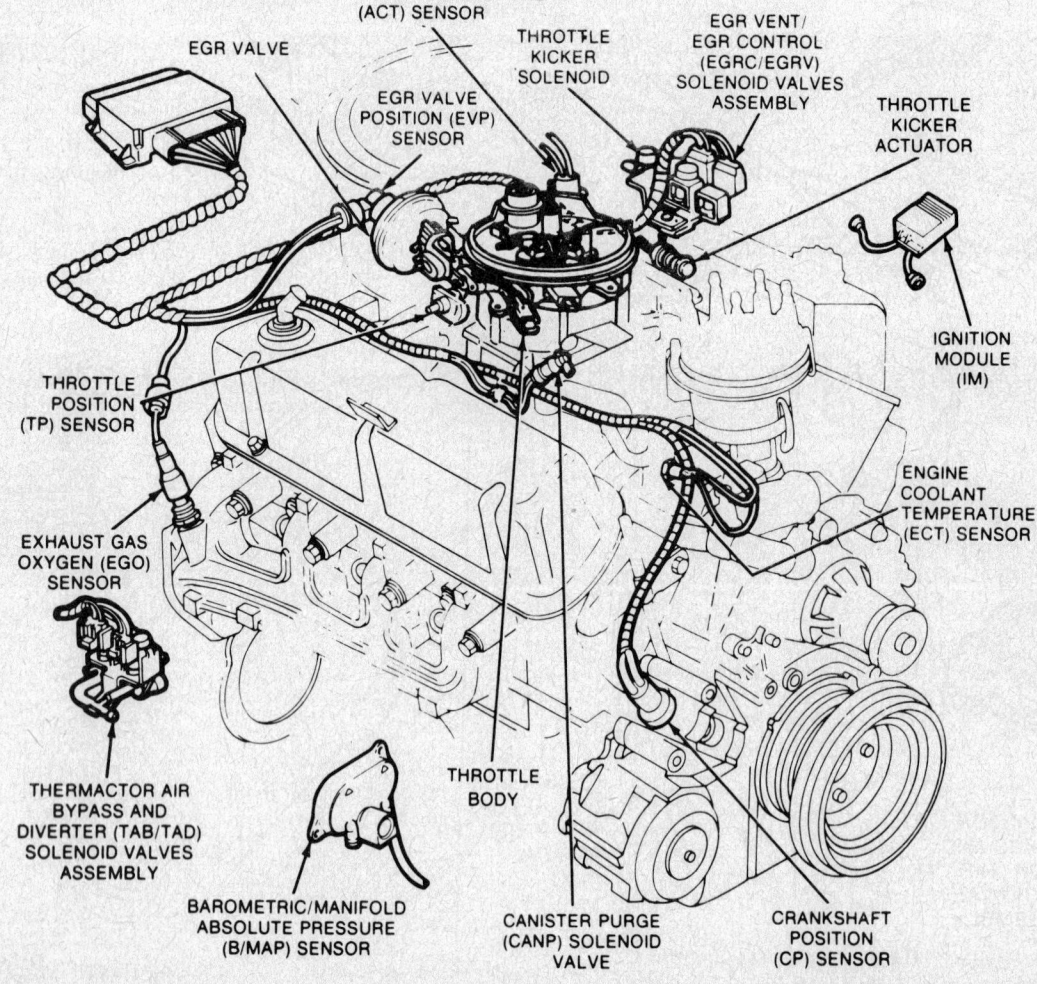

EFI wiring and vacuum diagram

Carburetors

INDEX

BEFORE SERVICING, SEE THE SAFETY NOTICE AT THE FRONT OF THE BOOK

Carburetor Identification

All carburetors are identified by code numbers, either stamped on the attaching flange side, the main body or on a metal tag, retained by a bowl cover screw. This identifying number is most important to the repairman in order to obtain the correct carburetor replacement or parts and to properly adjust the carburetor when matched to a specific engine.

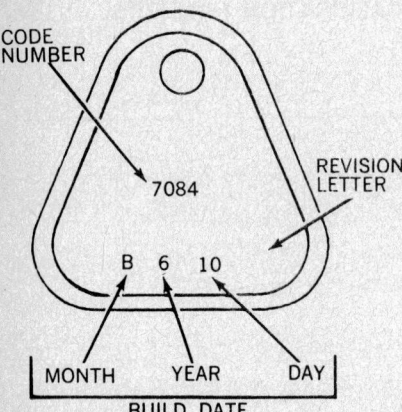

Carter carburetors for Jeep usage—typical (© Jeep Corp.)

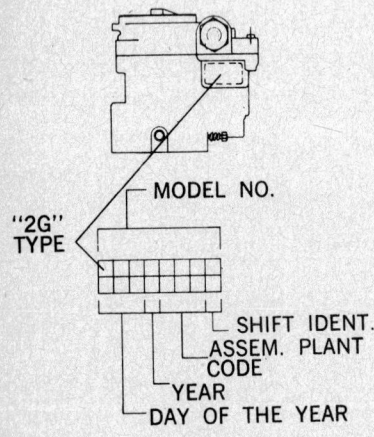

Rochester two barrel models—typical (© General Motors Corp.)

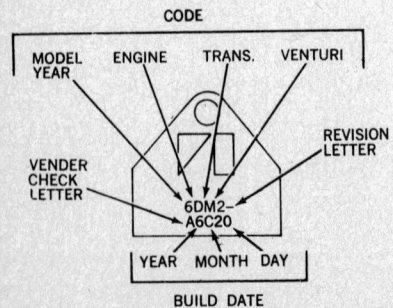

Motorcraft carburetors for Jeep usage—typical (© Jeep Corp.)

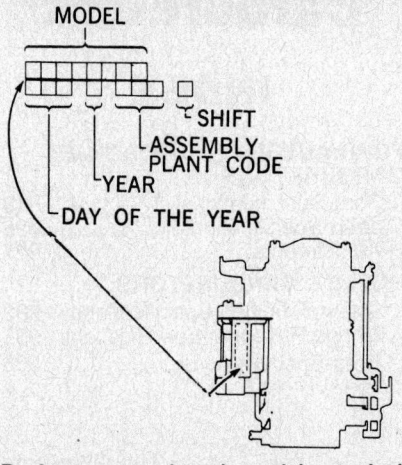

Rochester one barrel models—typical (© General Motors Corp.)

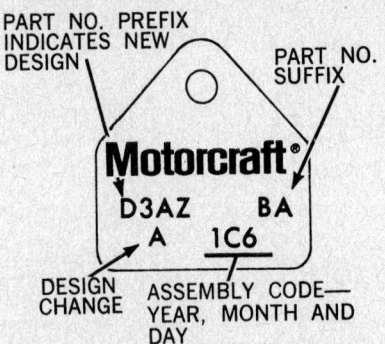

Motorcraft carburetors for Ford usage—typical (© Ford Motor Co.)

Angle Degree Tool

An angle degree tool is recommended by Rochester Products Division, for use to confirm adjustments to the choke valve and related linkages on their late model two and four barrel carburetors, in place of the plug type gauges.

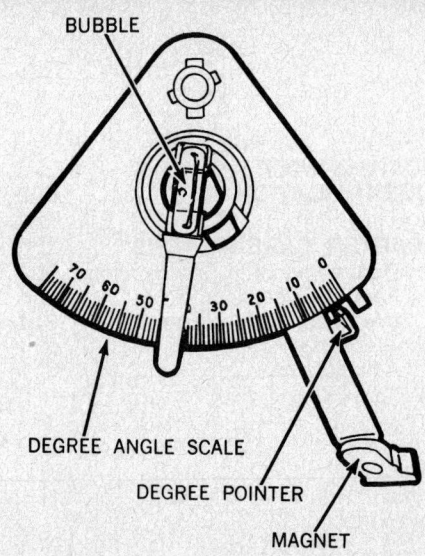

Degree angle tool—typical (© Kent-Moore Tools)

Decimal and degree conversion charts are provided for use by technicians who have access to an angle gauge and not plug gauges. It must be remembered that the relationship between the decimal and the angle readings are not exact, due to manufacturers tolerances.

To use the angle gauge, rotate the degree scale until zero (0) is opposite the pointer. With the choke valve completely closed, place the gauge magnet squarely on top of the choke valve and rotate the bubble until it is centered. Make the necessary adjustments to have the choke valve at the specified degree angle opening as read from the degree angle tool.

NOTE: The carburetor may be off the engine for adjustments. Be sure the carburetor is held firmly during the use of the angle gauge.

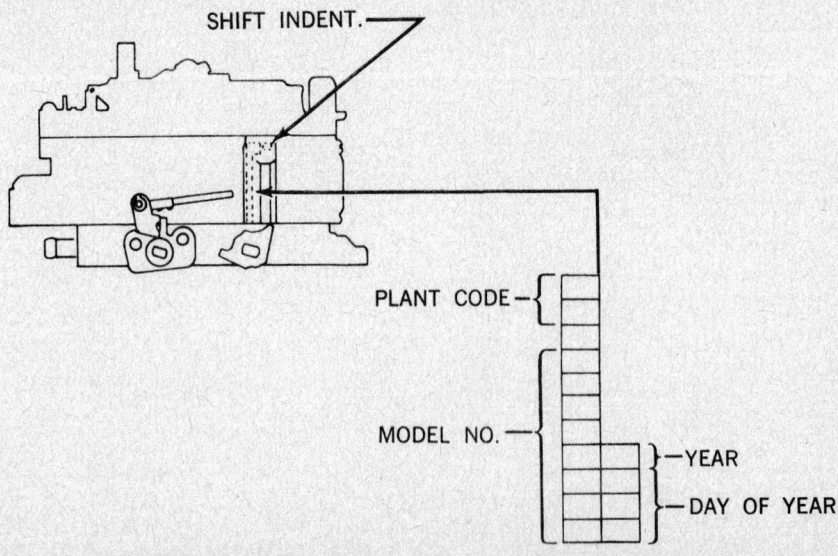

Rochester four barrel models—typical (© General Motors Corp.)

MODEL BBD
Dodge/Plymouth
(All measurements in inches)

Year	Carburetor List Number	Float Level①	Choke Unloader	Fast Idle Cam Setting	Choke Valve Initial Opening w/Vacuum Kick	Fast Idle Speed (RPM)	Choke Setting	Accelerator Pump Setting	Step-up Piston Gap
'75	8019S	.250	.280	.070	.130	1500	Fixed	.500	.035
	8020S	.250	.280	.070	.130	1500	Fixed	.500	.035
	8022S	.250	.310	.070	.070	1500	Fixed	.500	.035
	8024S	.250	.280	.070	.130	1500	Fixed	.500	.035
	8025S	.250	.310	.070	.070	1500	Fixed	.500	.035
	6536S	.250	.280	.095	.150	1700	Fixed	.500	.035
	6537S	.250	.310	.095	.110	1500	Fixed	.500	.035
	8013S	.250	.310	.070	.130	1500	Fixed	.500	.035
	8014S	.250	.310	.070	.110	1500	Fixed	.500	.035
'76	8081S	.250	.310	.070	.150	1500	Fixed	.500	—
	8108S	.250	.310	.070	.150	1500	Fixed	.500	—
	8082S	.250	.280	.070	.130	1500	Fixed	.500	—
	8085S	.250	.280	.070	.130	1500	Fixed	.500	—
	6536S	.250	.280	.095	.150	1700	Fixed	.500	—
	6537S	.250	.280	.095	.110	1500	Fixed	.500	—
	8013S	.250	.310	.070	.130	1500	Fixed	.500	—
	8014S	.250	.310	.070	.110	1500	Fixed	.500	—
'77	8081S	.250	.280	.070	.150	1500	Fixed	.500	—
	8082S	.250	.280	.070	.130	1500	Fixed	.500	—
	8085S	.250	.280	.070	.130	1500	Fixed	.500	—
	8147S	.250	.310	.070	.070	1500	Fixed	.500	—
	8146S	.250	.280	.070	.070	1600	Fixed	.500	—
	8113S	.250	.310	.070	.130	1500	Fixed	.500	—
	8110S	.250	.280	.070	.095	1500	Fixed	.500	—
'78	8149S	.250	.280	.070	.130	1500	Fixed	.500	.035
	8151S	.250	.280	.070	.130	1500	Fixed	.500	.035
	8180S	.250	.280	.070	.150	1600	Fixed	.500	.035
	8152S	.250	.280	.070	.130	1500	Fixed	.500	.035
	8147S	.250	.310	.070	.070	1500	Fixed	.500	.035
	8154S	.250	.310	.070	.130	1500	Fixed	.500	.035
	8156S	.250	.310	.070	.110	1500	Fixed	.500	.035
	8146S	.250	.280	.070	.070	1500	Fixed	.500	.035

CARBURETORS
CARTER

MODEL BBD
Dodge/Plymouth
(All measurements in inches)

Year	Carburetor List Number	Float Level①	Choke Unloader	Fast Idle Cam Setting	Choke Valve Initial Opening w/Vacuum Kick	Fast Idle Speed (RPM)	Choke Setting	Accelerator Pump Setting	Step-up Piston Gap
'79	8214S	.250	.280	.070	.110	1400	Fixed	.500	—
	8215S	.250	.280	.070	.110	1600	Fixed	.500	—
	8249S	.250	.280	.070	.110	1400	Fixed	.500	—
	8232S	.250	.280	.070	.110	1500	Fixed	.500	—
	8210S	.250	.280	.070	.110	1400	Fixed	.500	—
	8211S	.250	.280	.070	.110	1500	Fixed	.500	—
'80–'81	8146S	—	.310	.070	.070	1500	Fixed	.500	.035
	8147S	—	.310	.110	.150	1500	Fixed	.500	.035

① Carburetor bowl inverted

MODEL TQ
Dodge/Plymouth
(All measurements in inches)

Year	Carburetor List Number	Float Level	Fast Idle Speed (RPM)	Auto Choke Setting	Fuel Bowl Vent Adjustment	Accelerator Pump Stroke Adjustment①	Secondary Throttle Lock-Out Adjustment	Metering Rod Adjustment	Vacuum Kick Adjustment	Vacuum Choke Pull-off Adjustment	Fast Idle Cam and Linkage Adjustment③	Choke Unloader Adjustment②
'75	9034S	1.0	—	—	—	—	—	—	—	—	—	—
	9035S	1.0	—	—	—	—	—	—	—	—	—	—
	6545S	²⁹/₃₂	1700	Fixed	—	³¹/₆₄ (²³/₆₄)	.060–.090	—	.160	.040	.100	.310
	9036S	²⁹/₃₂	1700	Fixed	—	³¹/₆₄ (²³/₆₄)	.060–.090	—	.160	.040	.100	.310
'76	6545S	²⁹/₃₂	1700	Fixed	—	³¹/₆₄ (²³/₆₄)	.060–.090	—	.160	.040	.100	.310
	9036S	²⁹/₃₂	1700	Fixed	—	³¹/₆₄ (²³/₆₄)	.060–.090	—	.160	.040	.100	.310
'77	6545S	²⁷/₃₂	1700	Fixed	—	½ (⁵/₁₆)	.060–.090	—	.160	.040	.100	.310
	9096S	²⁷/₃₂	1700	Fixed	—	½ (⁵/₁₆)	.060–.090	—	.160	.040	.100	.310
'78	9118S	²⁷/₃₂	1700	Fixed	—	½ (⁵/₁₆)	.060–.090	—	.160	.040	.100	.310
	9151S	²⁷/₃₂	1700	Fixed	—	½ (⁵/₁₆)	.060–.090	—	.160	.040	.100	.310
	9116S	²⁹/₃₂	1600	Fixed	—	¹¹/₃₂ (⁹/₆₄)	.060–.090	—	.100	.040	.100	½
	9149S	²⁹/₃₂	1600	Fixed	—	¹¹/₃₂ (⁹/₆₄)	.060–.090	—	.100	.040	.100	½
	9117S	²⁷/₃₂	1700	Fixed	—	½ (⁵/₁₆)	.060–.090	—	.100	.040	.100	.310
	9150S	²⁷/₃₂	1700	Fixed	—	½ (⁵/₁₆)	.060–.090	—	.100	.040	.100	.310
	9173S	²⁹/₃₂	1500	Fixed	—	⁵/₁₆ (³/₁₆)	.060–.090	—	.150	.040	.100	.310
	9123S	²⁹/₃₂	1600	Fixed	—	³³/₆₄ (⁵/₁₆)	.060–.090	—	.150	.040	.100	½
	9124S	²⁹/₃₂	1600	Fixed	—	³³/₆₄ (⁵/₁₆)	.060–.090	—	.100	.040	.100	½
	9152S	²⁹/₃₂	1600	Fixed	—	³³/₆₄ (⁵/₁₆)	.060–.090	—	.100	.040	.100	½
	9175S	²⁹/₃₂	1700	Fixed	—	³³/₆₄ (⁵/₁₆)	.060–.090	—	.150	.040	.100	½

MODEL TQ
Dodge/Plymouth
(All measurements in inches)

Year	Carburetor List Number	Float Level	Fast Idle Speed (RPM)	Auto Choke Setting	Fuel Bowl Vent Adjustment	Accelerator Pump Stroke Adjustment①	Secondary Throttle Lock-Out Adjustment	Metering Rod Adjustment	Vacuum Kick Adjustment	Vacuum Choke Pull-off Adjustment	Fast Idle Cam and Linkage Adjustment③	Choke Unloader Adjustment②
	9126S	²⁹⁄₃₂	1600	Fixed	—	³³⁄₆₄ (⁵⁄₁₆)	.060–.090	—	.100	.040	.100	½
	9151S	²⁹⁄₃₂	1400	Fixed	—	³³⁄₆₄ (⁵⁄₁₆)	.060–.090	—	.160	.040	.100	½
	9150S	²⁹⁄₃₂	1400	Fixed	—	³³⁄₆₄ (⁵⁄₁₆)	.060–.090	—	.100	.040	.100	½
'79	9228S	²⁹⁄₃₂	1600	Fixed	—	¹¹⁄₃₂ (⁹⁄₆₄)	.060–.090	—	.100	.040	.100	.500
	9229S	²⁹⁄₃₂	1600	Fixed	—	¹¹⁄₃₂ (⁹⁄₆₄)	.060–.090	—	.100	.040	.100	.500
	9223S	²⁹⁄₃₂	1600	Fixed	—	¹¹⁄₃₂ (⁹⁄₆₄)	.060–.090	—	.100	.040	.100	.500
	9227S	²⁹⁄₃₂	1600	Fixed	—	¹¹⁄₃₂ (⁹⁄₆₄)	.060–.090	—	.100	.040	.100	.500
	9224S	²⁹⁄₃₂	1600	Fixed	—	⁵⁄₁₆ (³⁄₁₆)	.060–.090	—	.100	.040	.100	.500
	9225S	²⁹⁄₃₂	1600	Fixed	—	⁵⁄₁₆ (³⁄₁₆)	.060–.090	—	.100	.040	.100	.500
	9207S	²⁹⁄₃₂	1600	Fixed	—	³¹⁄₆₄ (²³⁄₆₄)	.060–.090	—	.150	.040	.100	.310
	9208S	²⁹⁄₃₂	1600	Fixed	—	³¹⁄₆₄ (²³⁄₆₄)	.060–.090	—	.150	.040	.100	.310
	9209S	²⁹⁄₃₂	1600	Fixed	—	³¹⁄₆₄ (²³⁄₆₄)	.060–.090	—	.150	.040	.100	.310
	9210S	²⁹⁄₃₂	1600	Fixed	—	³¹⁄₆₄ (²³⁄₆₄)	.060–.090	—	.150	.040	.100	.310
	9211S	²⁹⁄₃₂	1400	Fixed	—	³¹⁄₆₄ (²³⁄₆₄)	.060–.090	—	.100	.040	.100	.500
	9212S	²⁹⁄₃₂	1400	Fixed	—	³¹⁄₆₄ (²³⁄₆₄)	.060–.090	—	.100	.040	.100	.500
	9247S	²⁹⁄₃₂	1400	Fixed	—	³¹⁄₆₄ (²³⁄₆₄)	.060–.090	—	.100	.040	.100	.500
	9248S	²⁹⁄₃₂	1400	Fixed	—	³¹⁄₆₄ (²³⁄₆₄)	.060–.090	—	.100	.040	.100	.500
'80	9279S	²⁹⁄₃₂	1600	Fixed	—	.340(.190)	.060–.090	—	.130	.040	.130	.310
	9288S	²⁹⁄₃₂	1600	Fixed	—	.340(.190)	.060–.090	—	.120	.040	.120	.310
	9296S	²⁹⁄₃₂	1500	Fixed	—	.340(.140)	.060–.090	—	.100	.040	.100	.310
	9254S	²⁹⁄₃₂	1500	Fixed	—	.340(.190)	.060–.090	—	.130	.040	.100	.310
	9265S	²⁹⁄₃₂	1600	Fixed	—	.340(.140)	.060–.090	—	.150	.040	.100	.310
	9255S	²⁹⁄₃₂	1600	Fixed	—	.340(.190)	.060–.090	—	.120	.040	.100	.310
	9252S	²⁹⁄₃₂	1600	Fixed	—	.340(.190)	.060–.090	—	.120	.040	.120	.310
	9251S	²⁹⁄₃₂	1600	Fixed	—	.340(.190)	.060–.090	—	.120	.040	.120	.310
	9292S	²⁹⁄₃₂	1600	Fixed	—	.340(.190)	.060–.090	—	.150	.040	.130	.310
	9298S	²⁹⁄₃₂	1600	Fixed	—	.340(.140)	.060–.090	—	.150	.040	.100	.310
	9299S	²⁹⁄₃₂	1600	Fixed	—	.340(.140)	.060–.090	—	.150	.040	.100	.310
	9281S	²⁹⁄₃₂	1600	Fixed	—	.340(.190)	.060–.090	—	.180	.040	.130	.310
	9261S	²⁹⁄₃₂	1600	Fixed	—	.340(.190)	.060–.090	—	.130	.040	.130	.310
'81	9311S	²⁹⁄₃₂	1500	.040	—	.340	.060–.090	—	.150	.040	.100	.310
	9314S	²⁹⁄₃₂	1500	.040	—	.340	.060–.090	—	.150	.040	.100	.310
	9325S	²⁹⁄₃₂	1500	.040	—	.340	.060–.090	—	.120	.040	.100	.310
	9329S	²⁹⁄₃₂	1600	.040	—	.340	.060–.090	—	.130	.040	.100	.310
	9330S	²⁹⁄₃₂	1500	.040	—	.340	.060–.090	—	.130	.040	.100	.310
	9331S	²⁹⁄₃₂	1700	.040	—	.340	.060–.090	—	.110	.040	.100	.310

CARBURETORS
CARTER

MODEL TQ
Dodge/Plymouth
(All measurements in inches)

Year	Carburetor List Number	Float Level	Fast Idle Speed (RPM)	Auto Choke Setting	Fuel Bowl Vent Adjustment	Accelerator Pump Stroke Adjustment①	Secondary Throttle Lock-Out Adjustment	Metering Rod Adjustment	Vacuum Kick Adjustment	Vacuum Choke Pull-off Adjustment	Fast Idle Cam and Linkage Adjustment③	Choke Unloader Adjustment②
	9332S	29/32	1700	.040	—	.340	.060–.090	—	.110	.040	.100	.310
	9357S	29/32	1800	.040	—	.340	.060–.090	—	.130	.040	.100	.310
	9358S	29/32	1700	.040	—	.340	.060–.090	—	.180	.040	.100	.310
	9359S	29/32	1500	.040	—	.340	.060–.090	—	.130	.040	.100	.310

① Stage I (Stage II)
② Measure at the lowest edge of the choke valve on the throttle lever side
③ Set the linkage with idle on the second highest step of the cam

MODEL YF
Ford
(All measurements in inches)

Year	Carburetor List Number	Float Level	Float Drop	Choke Unloader Setting	Choke Setting	Dash Pot Plunger	Initial Choke Opening
'75	D4TE						
	ACA	3/8	—	—	Manual	—	—
	AGA	3/8	—	—	Manual	—	—
	AVA	3/8	—	—	Manual	—	—
	AUA	3/8	—	—	Manual	—	—
	D5TE						
	ADA	3/8	—	.280	Index	—	.290
	ADB	3/8	—	.280	Index	—	.290
	AKA	3/8	—	.280	Index	—	.290
	AKB	3/8	—	.280	Index	—	.290
	AMA	3/8	—	.280	1 Rich	—	.230
	AGA	3/8	—	.280	1 Rich	—	.230
	AGB	3/8	—	.280	1 Rich	—	.230
	ANA	3/8	—	.280	1 Rich	—	.230
	AHA	3/8	—	.280	Index	—	.290
	APA	3/8	—	.280	Index	—	.290
	APB	23/32	—	.280	Index	—	.290
	AJA	3/8	—	—	Manual	—	—
	AJB	3/8	—	—	Manual	—	—
	AFA	3/8	—	—	Manual	—	—
	AFB	3/8	—	—	Manual	—	—
	ALA	3/8	—	.280	Index	—	.290
	ALB	3/8	—	.280	Index	—	.290
	CAA	3/8	—	.280	Index	—	.290

MODEL YF
Ford
(All measurements in inches)

Year	Carburetor List Number	Float Level	Float Drop	Choke Unloader Setting	Choke Setting	Dash Pot Plunger	Initial Choke Opening
	CAB	23/32	—	.280	Index	—	.290
	CBA	3/8	—	.280	Index	—	.290
	D5PE ANA	3/8	—	.280	—	—	—
	AVA	3/8	—	—	—	—	—
	D4HE AA	3/8	—	—	Manual	—	—
	D5UE HA	23/32	—	.280	Index	—	.290
	HB	23/32	—	—	—	—	—
	GA	23/32	—	—	—	—	—
	GB	23/32	—	.280	Index	—	.290
	EA	23/32	—	.280	Index	—	.290
	EB	23/32	—	—	—	—	—
	FA	23/32	—	.280	Index	—	.290
	FB	23/32	—	.280	Index	—	.290
	RA	23/32	—	—	—	—	—
	RB	23/32	—	—	—	—	—
	AAA	23/32	—	.280	Index	—	.290
	AAB	23/32	—	.280	Index	—	.290
'76	D5TE AGA	3/8	—	.280	1 Rich	—	.230
	APA	3/8	—	.280	Index	—	.290
	APB	23/32	—	.280	Index	—	.290
	AJA	3/8	—	—	Manual	—	—
	AJB	3/8	—	—	Manual	—	—
	AFA	3/8	—	—	Manual	—	—
	AFB	3/8	—	—	Manual	—	—
	CAA	3/8	—	.280	Index	—	.290
	CAB	23/32	—	.280	Index	—	.290
	CBA	3/8	—	.280	Index	—	.290
	CBB	3/8	—	.280	Index	—	.290
	D5PE ANA	3/8	—	.280	Index	—	.290
	D6UE FA	23/32	—	.280	Index	—	.290
	MA	23/32	—	.280	Index	—	.290
	D6TE ZA	23/32	—	.280	Index	—	.290

MODEL YF
Ford
(All measurements in inches)

Year	Carburetor List Number	Float Level	Float Drop	Choke Unloader Setting	Choke Setting	Dash Pot Plunger	Initial Choke Opening
	KA	23/32	—	.280	Index	—	.290
	DA	23/32	—	.280	Index	—	.290
	HA	23/32	—	.280	Index	—	.290
	D5UE						
	EA	3/8	—	.280	Index	—	.290
	EB	23/32	—	.280	Index	—	.290
	FA	3/8	—	.280	Index	—	.290
	FB	23/32	—	.280	Index	—	.290
	RA	23/32	—	—	—	—	—
	RB	23/32	—	—	—	—	—
	AAA	23/32	—	—	—	—	—
	AAB	23/32	—	.280	Index	—	.290
'77	D5TE						
	AGA	3/8	—	.280	1 Rich	—	.230
	AGB	23/32	—	.280	1 Rich	—	.230
	AJA	3/8	—	—	Manual	—	—
	AJB	3/8	—	—	Manual	—	—
	AFA	3/8	—	—	Manual	—	—
	AFB	3/8	—	—	Manual	—	—
	D5PF						
	ANA	3/8	—	.280	—	—	—
	D7PE						
	LA	3/8	—	—	—	—	—
	KA	3/8	—	—	—	—	—
	SA	3/8	—	—	—	—	—
	RA	3/8	—	—	—	—	—
	NA	3/8	—	—	—	—	—
	D7TE						
	CAA	25/32	—	—	—	—	—
	CBA	25/32	—	—	—	—	—
	CCA	25/32	—	—	—	—	—
	PA	25/32	—	.280	Index	—	.290
	CFA	25/32	—	—	—	—	—
	CFB	25/32	—	—	—	—	—
	MA	25/32	—	.280	Index	—	.290
	CDA	25/32	—	—	—	—	—
	CEA	25/32	—	—	—	—	—
	D6TE						
	ZA	23/32	—	.280	Index	—	.290

MODEL YF
Ford
(All measurements in inches)

Year	Carburetor List Number	Float Level	Float Drop	Choke Unloader Setting	Choke Setting	Dash Pot Plunger	Initial Choke Opening
	HA	23/32	—	.280	Index	—	.290
	D6UE MA	23/32	—	.280	Index	—	.290
'78	D8TE BVA	25/32	1 19/32	.280	Index	—	.230
	CKB	25/32	1 19/32	.280	Index	.070	.230
	BWA	25/32	1 19/32	.280	Index	.070	.230
	BUA	25/32	1 19/32	.280	Index	.070	.230
	BUB	25/32	—	—	—	—	—
	CNA	25/32	1 19/32	.280	Index	.070	.230
	AAA	25/32	1 19/32	.280	Index	.070	.230
	UA	23/32	1½	—	Manual	—	—
	CDA	23/32	1½	—	Manual	—	—
	D8UE AAA	—	—	—	—	—	—
	ZA	25/32	1 19/32	.280	Index	.070	.230
	D6TE ZA	23/32	—	.280	Index	—	.290
	D6UE MA	23/32	—	.280	Index	—	.290
	D2UE EA	25/32	1 19/32	—	—	—	—
'80	EOTE–9510 ABA,FA, LA,KA	.69	1.53	.28	①	—	.290
	ACA,ARA	.69	1.53	.28	①	—	.320
	AEA,AFA, ALA,AKA, ATA,CA, GA	.69	1.53	.28	①	—	.230
'81	EOTE–9510 AMA,FA	.69	—	.28	Index	—	.290
	D5TE–9510 CA,VA	.69	—	.28	Index	—	.290
	AGB	3/8	—	.28	1 Rich	—	.230
	E1TE–9510 UA,ARA, ARB	.78	—	.28	Index	—	.230
	AUA,VA	.78	—	.28	2 Rich	—	.300
	AZA,GA	.78	—	.330	2 Rich	—	.320

① See Ford calibration specifications

909

CARBURETORS
CARTER

MODEL TQ
International
(All measurements in inches)

Year	Carburetor List Number	Float Level	Fast Idle Speed (RPM)	Auto Choke Setting	Fuel Bowl Vent Clearance	Accelerator Pump Stroke Adjustment	Secondary Throttle Lock-Out Adjustment	Metering Rod Adjustment	Vacuum Kick Adjustment	Vacuum Pull-off Choke Adjustment	Fast Idle Cam and Linkage Adjustment	Choke Unloader Adjustment
'79	TQ91285	.91 ± .030 (Old Needles) .88 ± .030 (New Needles)	1600	¼ Rod	.800–.830	Primary① .328–.358 Secondary① .120–.260	.060–.090	.468 ± .031	Vac. High .440–.460 Vac. Low .235–.255	.840–.880	.089–.109	.280–.320
	TQ6591S, 6550S	1.06	1550–1600	1 Rich	.800–.830	Primary .328–.358 Secondary .120–.260	.060–.090	¹⁵⁄₃₂	Vac. High .335–.355 Vac. Low .250–.270	.840–.880 (6550S only)	.089–.109	.280–.320
	TQ6590S, 6552S, 6551S	1.06	1550–1600	1 Rich	.800–.830	Primary .328–.358	.060–.090	¹⁵⁄₃₂	Vac. High .335–.355 Vac. Low .250–.270	.840–.880 (6551S only)	.089–.109	.280–.320

① Rod in inner hole

MODEL BBD–2
Jeep
(All measurements in inches)

Year	Carburetor Number	Float Level (in.)	Step-up Piston Gap (in.)	Initial Choke Clearance (in.)	Fast Idle Cam Setting (in.)	Choke Cover Setting	Choke Unloader (Min.) (in.)	Fast Idle Speed (RPM)①
'77	8107	.250	.040	.128	.095	2 Rich	.280	1700
'78	8107	.250	.040	.128	.095	2 Rich	.280	1700
'79	8185	.250	.035	.140	.110	1 Rich	.280	1600
	8186	.250	.035	.150	.110	1 Rich	.280	1500
	8187	.250	.035	.140	.110	1 Rich	.280	1600
	8188	.250	.035	.150	.110	1 Rich	.280	1500
	8195	.250	.035	.140	.110	1 Rich	.280	1500(M) 1600(A)
	8229	.250	.035	.128	.095	1 Rich	.280	1500
'80	8256	.250	.035	.128	.093	2 Rich	.280	1850
	8257	.250	.035	.128	.095	2 Rich	.280	1700
	8253	.250	.035	.128	.095	2 Rich	.280	1850
	8254	.250	.035	.120	.086	2 Rich	.280	1700
	8255	.250	.035	.140	.093	2 Rich	.280	②
	8277	.250	.035	.116	.081	1 Rich	.280	1700
'81	8302	.250	.035	.140	.095	1 Rich	.280	1850
	8303	.250	.035	.140	.095	1 Rich	.280	1700
	8311	.250	.035	.120	.085	1 Rich	.280	1700
	8306	.250	.035	.140	.095	1 Rich	.280	1700
	8312	.250	.035	.140	.095	1 Rich	.280	②
	8307	.250	.035	.140	.095	1 Rich	.280	1700

① On second step of fast idle cam with TCS solenoid and EGR disconnected.
② Manual transmission 1700 rpm and automatic transmission 1850 rpm

MODEL YF
Jeep
(All measurements in inches)

Year	Carburetor Number	Float Level	Float Drop	Initial Choke Clearance	Fast Idle Cam Setting	Choke Cover Setting	Choke Unloader (Min.)	Fast Idle Speed (RPM)①	Dash Pot
'75	7043	.476	1.38	.215	.190	1 Rich	.275	1600	—
	7041	.476	1.38	.215	.190	1 Rich	.275	1600	.075
	7040	.476	1.38	.215	.190	1 Rich	.275	1600	.075
'76	7088	.476	1⅜	.215	.195	1 Rich	.275	1600	.075
	7084	.476	1⅜	.215	.195	2 Rich	.275	1600	.075
	7109	.476	1⅜	.215	.195	2 Rich	.275	1600	.075
	7083	.476	1⅜	.215	.195	1 Rich	.275	1600	.075
	7085	.476	1⅜	.215	.195	1 Rich	.275	1600	.075
'77	7154	.476	1⅜	.215	.195	1 Rich	.275	1600	—
	7151	.476	1⅜	.215	.195	1 Rich	.275	1600	—
	7153	.476	1⅜	.215	.195	1 Rich	.275	1600	—
	7110, 7111 (Alt.)	.476	1⅜	.221	.201	2 Rich	.275	1800	—
'78	7201	.476	1⅜	.215	.195	Index	.275	1600	—
	7228	.476	1⅜	.215	.195	1 Rich	.275	1600	—
	7230	.476	1⅜	.215	.195	1 Rich	.275	1600	—
	7231 (Alt.)	.476	1⅜	.221	.201	2 Rich	.275	1500	—

① On 2nd step of fast idle cam with TCS solenoid and EGR disconnected
② Without Air Guard

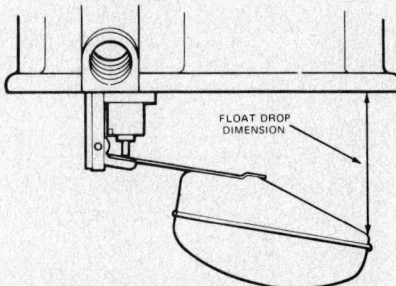

Measurement of float drop—YF carburetor
(© Jeep Corp.)

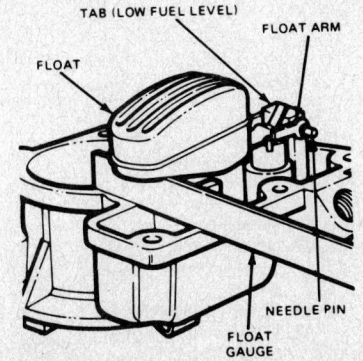

Float level measurement—YF carburetor
(© Jeep Corp.)

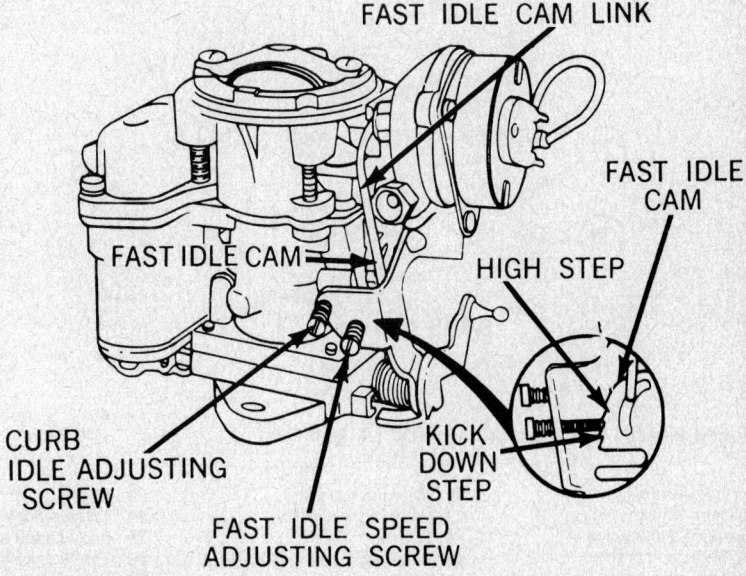

Typical adjustment points—YF carburetor with electric choke
(© Ford Motor Co.)

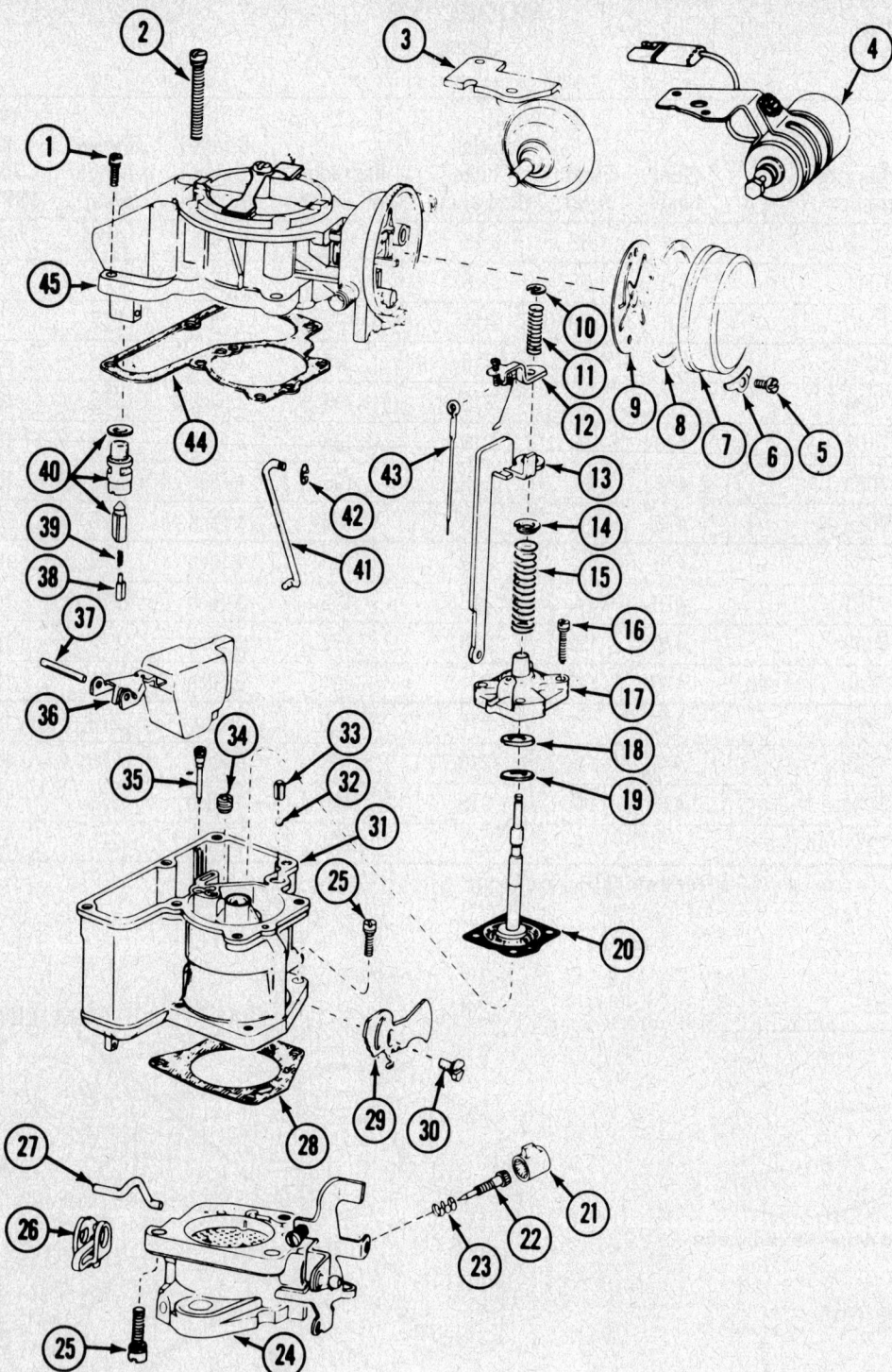

Exploded view of YF carburetor—typical (© Jeep Corp.)

1. Air horn screw (short)	12. Metering rod arm	23. Spring	35. Low speed jet
2. Air horn screw (long)	13. Diaphragm lifter link	24. Throttle body	36. Float
3. Dashpot and bracket	14. Washer	25. Body flange screw (3)	37. Float pin
4. Solenoid and bracket	15. Diaphragm spring	26. Throttle shaft arm	38. Needle pin
5. Coil housing screw	16. Diaphragm housing screw	27. Pump connector link	39. Needle spring
6. Coil housing retainer	(4)	28. Body gasket	40. Needle, needle seat,
7. Choke cover	17. Diaphragm housing	29. Fast idle cam	gasket
8. Coil housing gasket	18. Washer	30. Fast idle cam screw	41. Choke connector rod
9. Coil housing baffle plate	19. Spacer	31. Main body	42. Choke connector rod
10. Upper pump spring	20. Diaphragm	32. Discharge ball	retainer
retainer	21. Idle screw limiter cap	33. Discharge ball weight	43. Metering rod
11. Upper pump spring	22. Idle mixture screw	34. Metering jet	44. Air horn gasket
			45. Air horn

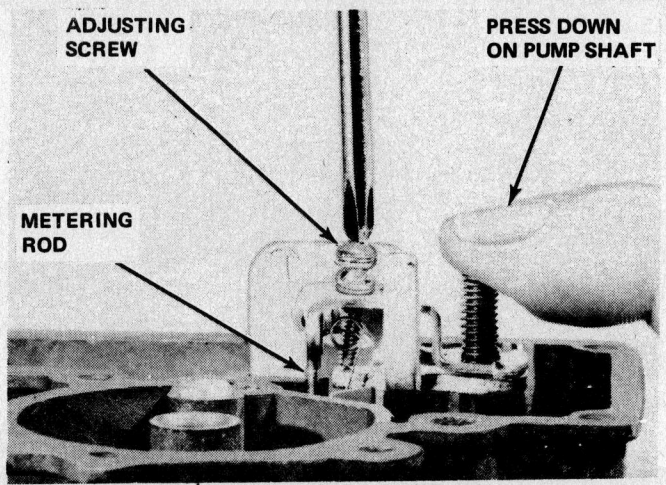

Metering rod adjustment—YF carburetor with electric choke
(© Jeep Corp.)

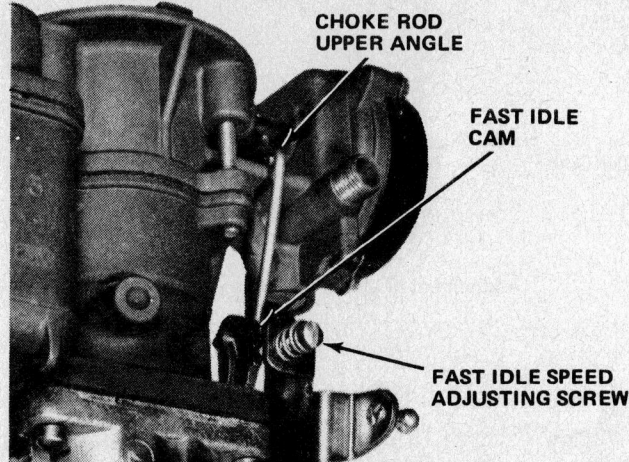

Fast idle cam and linkage adjustment—YF carburetor
(© Jeep Corp.)

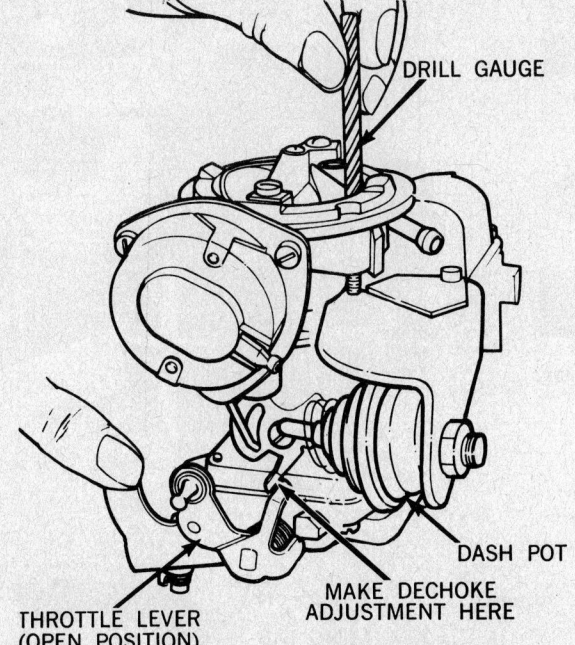

Choke plate unloader (dechoke) adjustment—typical YFA carburetor (© Ford Motor Co.)

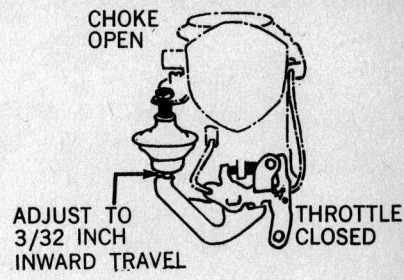

BBS dashpot adjustment

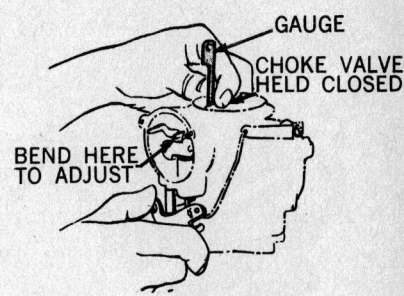

BBS unloader adjustment

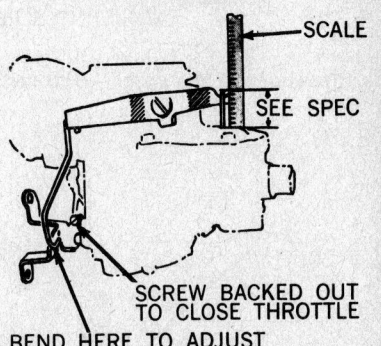

BBS pump adjustment

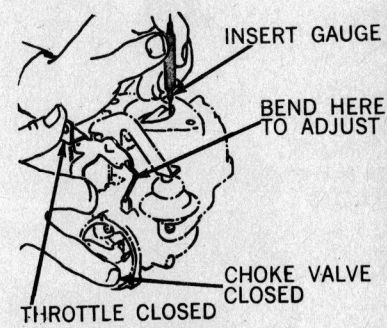

BBS fast idle adjustment

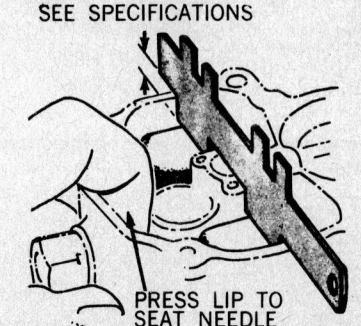

BBS float adjustment (invert fuel bowl)

913

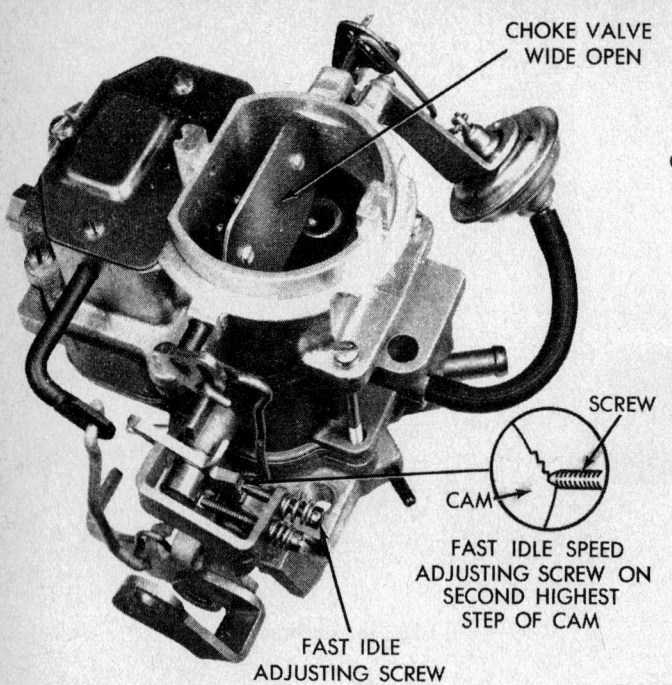

CHOKE VALVE
WIDE OPEN

SCREW

CAM

FAST IDLE SPEED
ADJUSTING SCREW ON
SECOND HIGHEST
STEP OF CAM

FAST IDLE
ADJUSTING SCREW

Adjustment of fast idle speed—BBD carburetor (© Chrysler Corp.)

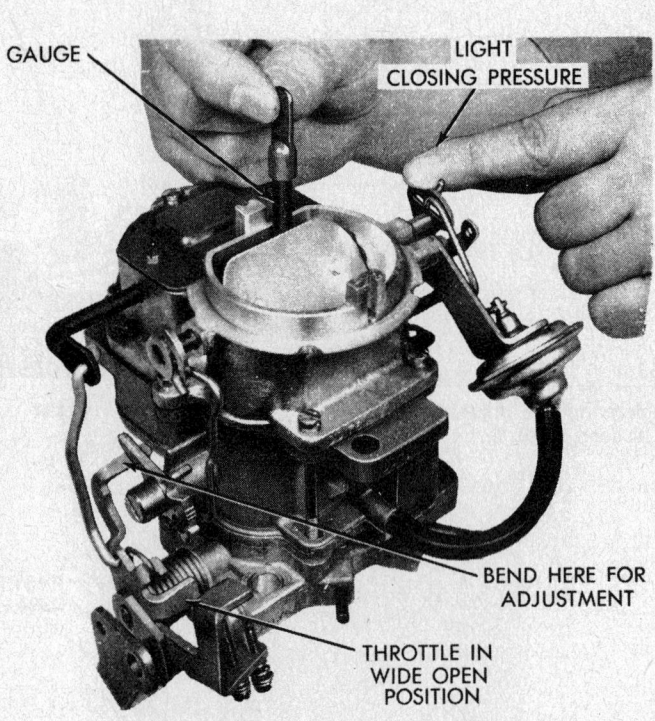

GAUGE

LIGHT
CLOSING PRESSURE

BEND HERE FOR
ADJUSTMENT

THROTTLE IN
WIDE OPEN
POSITION

Adjustment of choke unloader—BBD carburetor (© Chrysler Corp.)

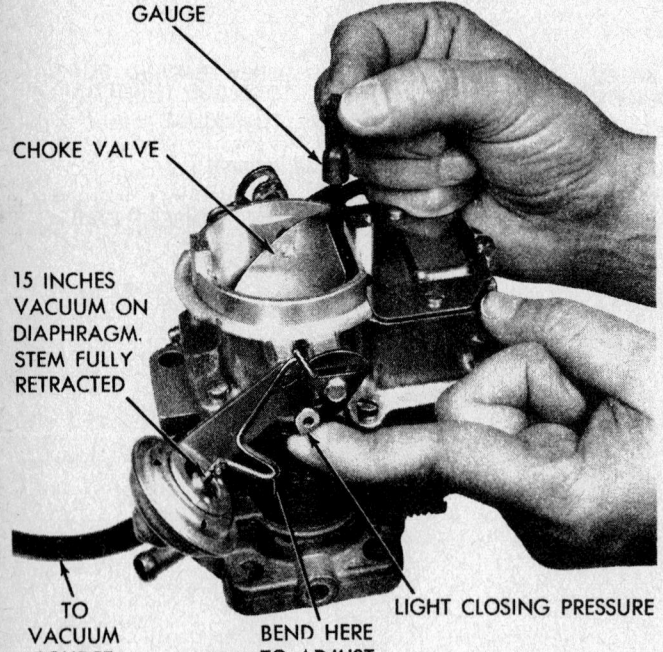

GAUGE

CHOKE VALVE

15 INCHES
VACUUM ON
DIAPHRAGM.
STEM FULLY
RETRACTED

TO
VACUUM
SOURCE

BEND HERE
TO ADJUST

LIGHT CLOSING PRESSURE

Adjustment of initial choke opening (vacuum kick)—BBD carburetor (© Chrysler Corp.)

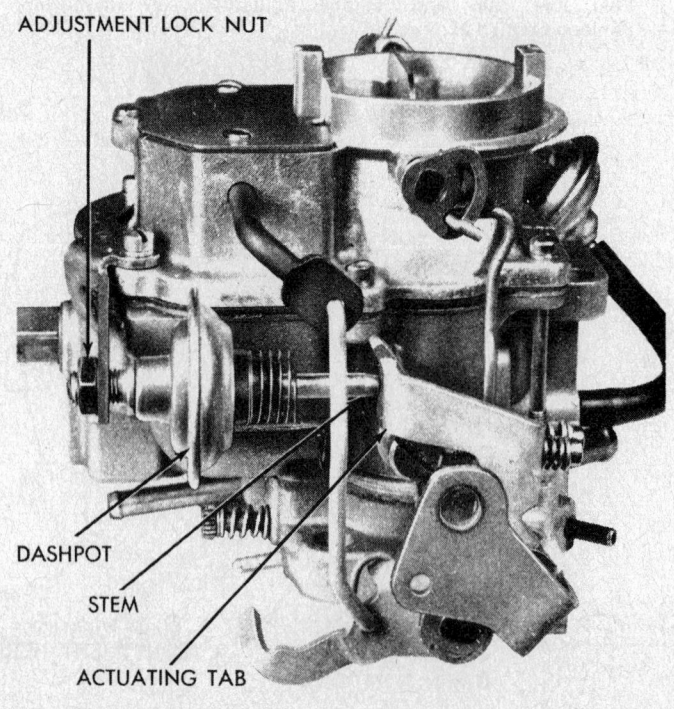

ADJUSTMENT LOCK NUT

DASHPOT

STEM

ACTUATING TAB

Dashpot installation—typical BBD carburetor (© Chrysler Corp.)

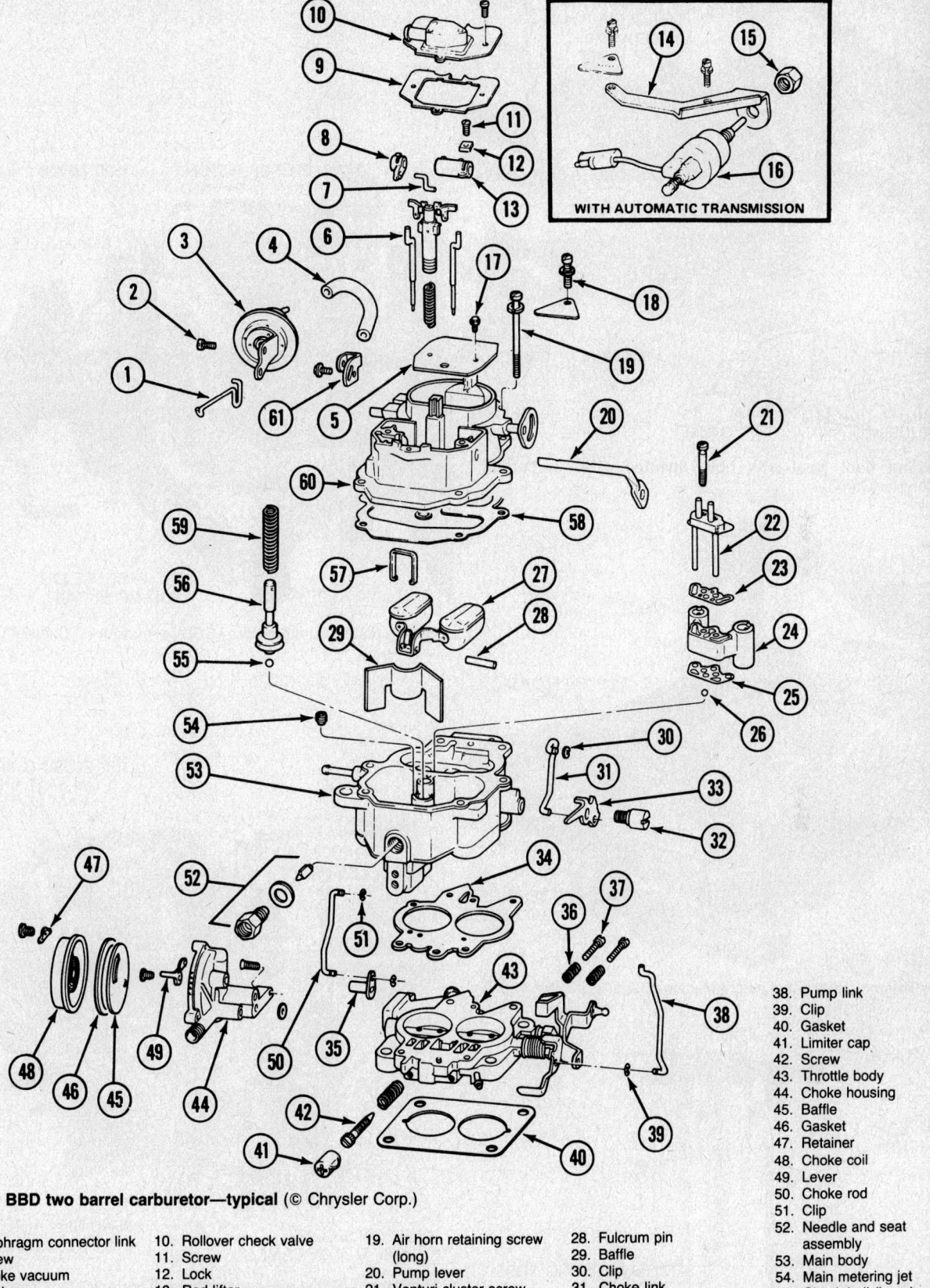

WITH AUTOMATIC TRANSMISSION

Carter BBD two barrel carburetor—typical (© Chrysler Corp.)

1. Diaphragm connector link
2. Screw
3. Choke vacuum diaphragm
4. Hose
5. Valve
6. Metering rod
7. S-Link
8. Pump arm
9. Gasket
10. Rollover check valve
11. Screw
12. Lock
13. Rod lifter
14. Bracket
15. Nut
16. Solenoid
17. Screw
18. Air horn retaining screw (short)
19. Air horn retaining screw (long)
20. Pump lever
21. Venturi cluster screw
22. Idle fuel pick-up tube
23. Gasket
24. Venturi cluster
25. Gasket
26. Check ball (small)
27. Float
28. Fulcrum pin
29. Baffle
30. Clip
31. Choke link
32. Screw
33. Fast idle cam
34. Gasket
35. Thermostatic choke shaft
36. Spring
37. Screw
38. Pump link
39. Clip
40. Gasket
41. Limiter cap
42. Screw
43. Throttle body
44. Choke housing
45. Baffle
46. Gasket
47. Retainer
48. Choke coil
49. Lever
50. Choke rod
51. Clip
52. Needle and seat assembly
53. Main body
54. Main metering jet
55. Check ball (large)
56. Accelerator pump plunger
57. Fulcrum pin retainer
58. Gasket
59. Spring
60. Air horn
61. Lever

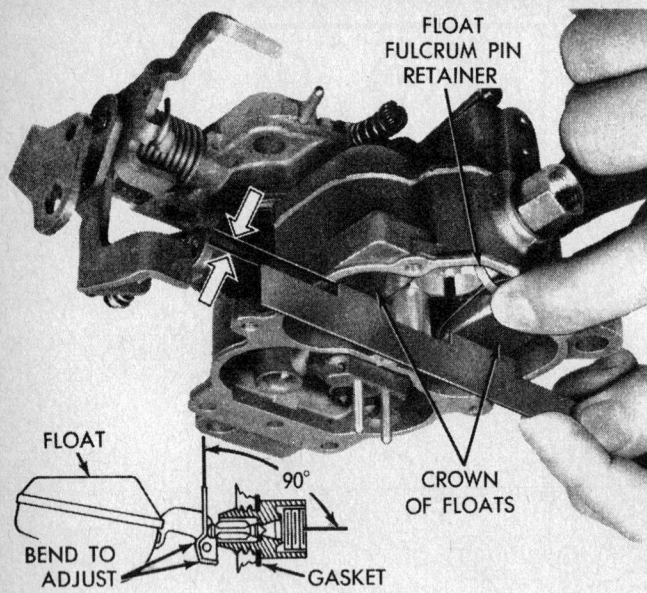

Adjusting float level with bowl inverted—BBD carburetor (© Chrysler Corp.)

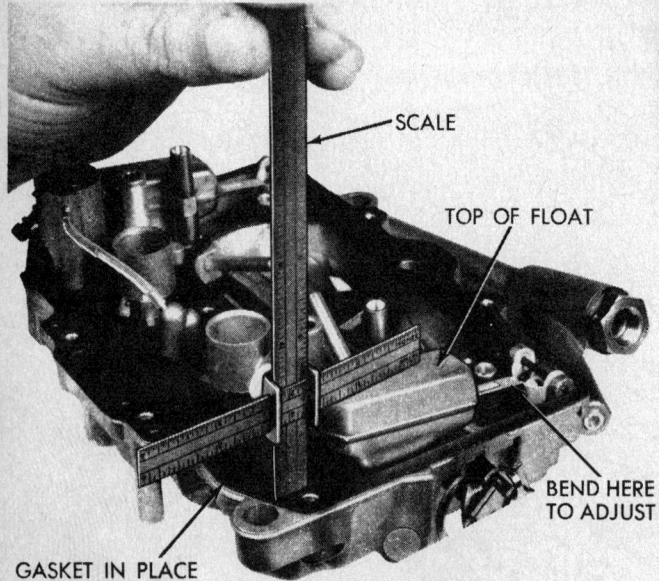

Carter Thermo-Quad® float height measurement (© Chrysler Corp.)

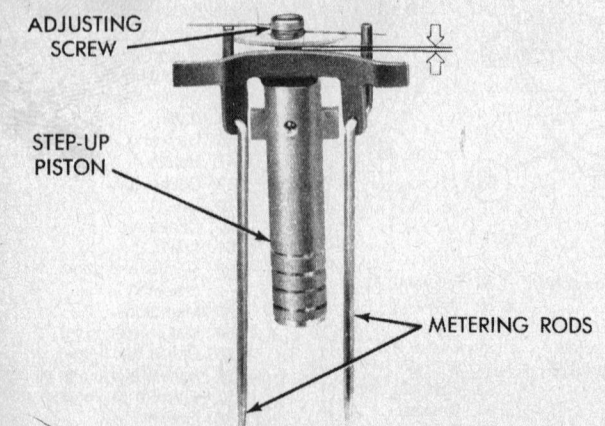

Step-up piston clearance adjustment—BBD carburetor (© Chrysler Corp.)

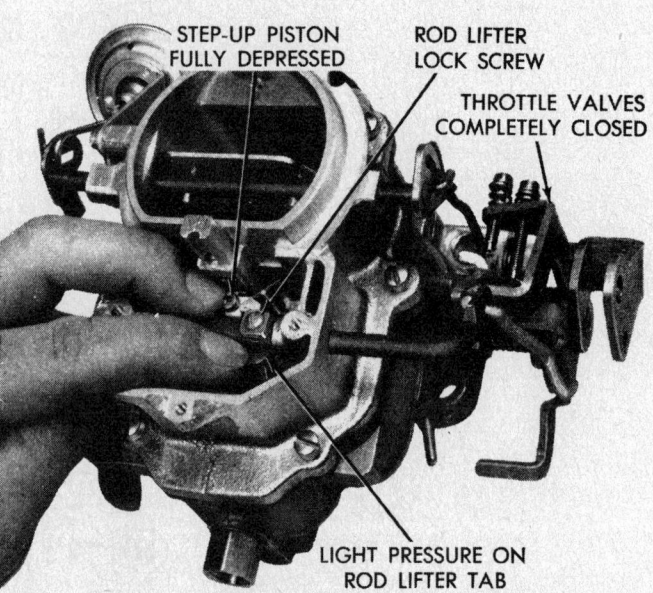

Step-up piston qualification—BBD carburetor (© Chrysler Corp.)

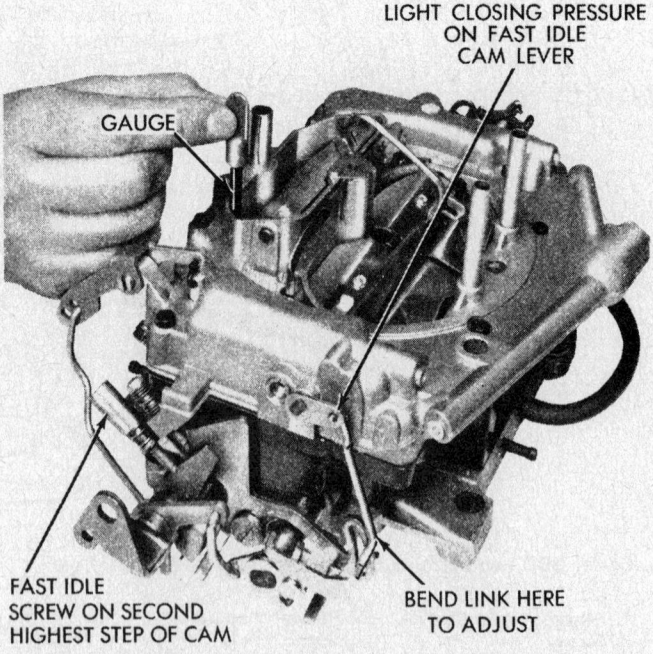

Adjustment of fast idle cam setting—Thermo-Quad® carburetor (© Chrysler Corp.)

1. Fuel inlet nut and gasket
2. Idle compensator screw
3. Idle compensator
4. Idle compensator gasket
5. "E" retainer
6. Primary diaphragm choke pull-off rod washer
7. Primary diaphragm choke pull-off rod
8. Auxiliary diaphragm choke pull-off rod (if equipped)
9. Choke lever screw
10. Choke lever
11. Choke connector rod
12. Countershaft lever screw
13. Countershaft, lever, outer
14. Countershaft lever spring
15. Countershaft lever, inner
16. Fast idle cam rod
17. Throttle connector rod
18. Cover plate screw
19. Metering rod cover plate (opposite pump)
20. Metering rod cover plate (pump side)
21. Step-up piston cover plate
22. Step-up piston and hanger assembly
23. Metering rod
24. Step-up piston spring
25. Bowl cover screw
26. IH part number location
27. Bowl cover assembly
28. Float pin
29. Float assembly
30. Needle, seat, and gasket
31. Pump passage tube
32. Bowl cover gasket
33. Secondary metering jet
34. Primary metering jet
35. Quad rings

36. Pin spring retainer
37. Bowl vent valve lever, upper
38. Bowl vent valve lever spring
39. Bowl vent valve arm
40. Bowl vent valve grommet
41. Rivet plug
42. Pump housing screw
43. Pump housing
44. Pump housing gasket
45. Discharge check needle
46. Pump arm screw
47. Pump arm

48. Pump "S" link
49. Air valve lock plug
50. Air valve adjustment plug
51. Air valve spring
52. Pump intake check assembly
53. Plunger assembly
54. Plunger spring
55. Main body
56. Main body gasket
57. Step-up piston lifter
58. Step-up piston lifter lever pin
59. Solenoid and diaphragm choke pull-off bracket screw
60. Solenoid
61. Solenoid operating lever screw
62. Curb idle speed screw and lever
63. Bowl vent lever, lower
64. Throttle shaft washer
65. Hose
66. Primary diaphragm choke pull-off bracket
67. Auxiliary choke pull-off and dashpot
68. Auxiliary choke pull-off and bracket (if equipped)
69. Dashpot and bracket
70. Limiter cap
71. Idle mixture screw
72. Idle mixture screw spring
73. Throttle body assembly
74. Carter part number location
75. Low idle speed screw

Exploded view of a typical late-model Thermo-Quad® (© Chrysler Corp.)

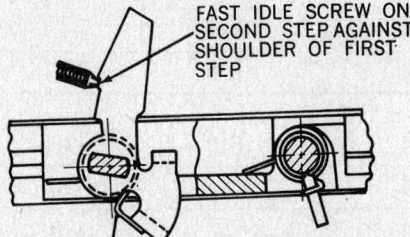

FAST IDLE SCREW ON SECOND STEP AGAINST SHOULDER OF FIRST STEP

Carter Thermo-Quad® fast idle speed adjustment cam position (© Chrysler Corp.)

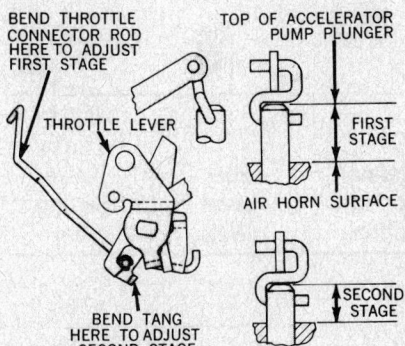

BEND THROTTLE CONNECTOR ROD HERE TO ADJUST FIRST STAGE

THROTTLE LEVER

BEND TANG HERE TO ADJUST SECOND STAGE

TOP OF ACCELERATOR PUMP PLUNGER

FIRST STAGE

AIR HORN SURFACE

SECOND STAGE

Adjustment of the primary and secondary accelerator pump— Thermo-Quad® carburetor (© Chrysler Corp.)

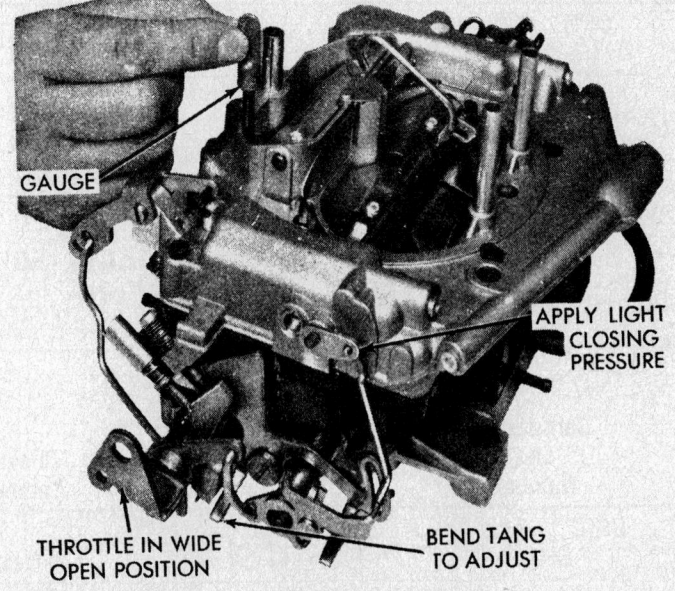

GAUGE

APPLY LIGHT CLOSING PRESSURE

THROTTLE IN WIDE OPEN POSITION

BEND TANG TO ADJUST

Choke unloader adjustment—Thermo-Quad® carburetor (© Chrysler Corp.)

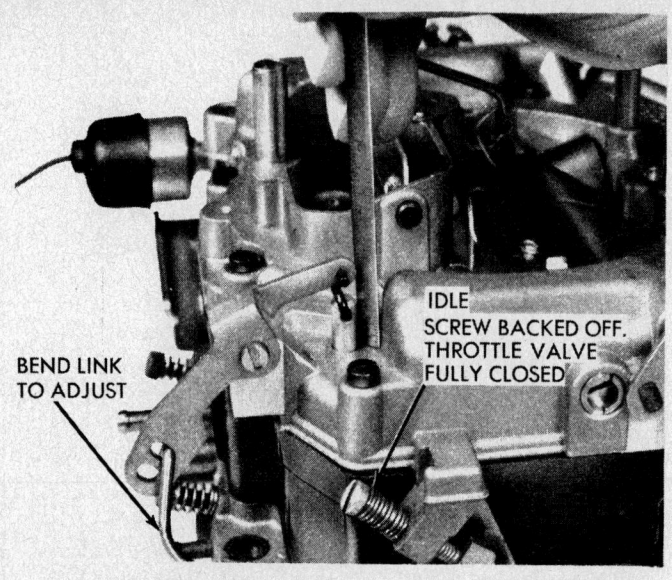

Accelerator pump stroke adjustment—Thermo-Quad® carburetor
(© Chrysler Corp.)

MODEL 2100
Ford
(All measurements in inches)

Year	Carburetor List Number	Float Level (Dry)	Choke Unloader Setting	Choke Setting	Accelerator Pump Rod Location	Fuel Level (Wet)	Initial Choke Valve Setting (Min)
'75	D5TE						
	ABA	$7/16$	—	Manual	4	.810	—
	ASA	$31/64$	—	Index	4	.875	—
	ATA	$31/64$	—	Index	4	.875	—
'76	D5TE						
	ABA	$7/16$	—	Manual	4	.810	—
	ASA	$31/64$	—	Index	4	$7/8$	.179
	ATA	$31/64$	—	Index	4	$7/8$	.179

MODEL 2150
Ford
(All measurements in inches)

Year	Carburetor List Number	Float Level (Dry)	Choke Unloader Setting	Choke Setting	Accelerator Pump Rod Location	Fuel Level (Wet)	Initial Choke Valve Setting (Min)
'75	D5TE						
	BHA	$31/64$	—	Index	2	$7/8$	.135
	BJA	$31/64$	—	2 Rich	2	$7/8$	.160
	LA	$31/64$	—	Index	2	$7/8$	.135
	PA	$31/64$	—	3 Rich	2	$7/8$	.160

MODEL 2150
Ford
(All measurements in inches)

Year	Carburetor List Number	Float Level (Dry)	Choke Unloader Setting	Choke Setting	Accelerator Pump Rod Location	Fuel Level (Wet)	Initial Choke Valve Setting (Min)
	AAD	31/64	—	3 Rich	3	.875	.179
	ACB	7/16	—	Manual	4	.810	—
	YD	31/64	—	3 Rich	3	.875	.179
	BCA	31/64	—	2 Rich	2	7/8	.179
	BCB	31/64	—	2 Rich	2	7/8	.179
	BFA	31/64	—	2 Rich	3	7/8	.179
	BFB	31/64	—	2 Rich	3	7/8	.179
	AUB	31/64	—	2 Rich	3	7/8	.179
	BGA	31/64	—	3 Rich	3	7/8	.179
	VA	31/64	—	2 Rich	3	7/8	.179
	ZA	31/64	—	3 Rich	4	7/8	.179
	BDA	31/64	—	2 Rich	2	7/8	.179
	BDB	31/64	—	2 Rich	2	7/8	.179
	BEA	31/64	—	2 Rich	3	7/8	.179
	D5UE						
	BA	31/64	—	1 Rich	3	.875	.153
	CA	1/2	—	3 Rich	2	.875	.145–.175
	DC	31/64	—	3 Rich	3	.875	.153
	JD	31/64	—	3 Rich	3	.875	.160
	KD	31/64	—	3 Rich	3	.875	.160
	ZA	31/64	—	1 Rich	3	.875	.153
'76	D5TE						
	BMA	31/64	—	Index	2	7/8	.140
	PA	31/64	—	2 Rich	2	7/8	.160
	AAF	31/64	—	3 Rich	3	7/8	.140
	AUB	31/64	—	2 Rich	3	7/8	.179
	BCA	31/64	—	2 Rich	2	7/8	.179
	BCB	31/64	—	2 Rich	2	7/8	.179
	BFA	31/64	—	2 Rich	3	7/8	.179
	BFB	31/64	—	2 Rich	3	7/8	.179
	BGA	31/64	—	3 Rich	3	7/8	.179
	BYA	31/64	—	2 Rich	3	7/8	.140
	VA	31/64	—	2 Rich	3	7/8	.179
	YF	31/64	—	2 Rich	3	7/8	.140
	ZA	31/64	—	3 Rich	3	7/8	—
	ZB	31/64	—	2 Rich	3	7/8	—

CARBURETORS
AUTOLITE/FORD/MOTORCRAFT

MODEL 2150
Ford
(All measurements in inches)

Year	Carburetor List Number	Float Level (Dry)	Choke Unloader Setting	Choke Setting	Accelerator Pump Rod Location	Fuel Level (Wet)	Initial Choke Valve Setting (Min)
	BEA	31/64	—	2 Rich	3	7/8	—
	BEB	31/64	—	2 Rich	3	7/8	—
	BDA	31/64	—	2 Rich	2	7/8	—
	BDB	31/64	—	2 Rich	2	7/8	—
	ACB	7/16	—	Manual	4	.810	—
	D5UE						
	AA	31/64	—	3 Rich	2	7/8	.160
	CA	1/2	—	3 Rich	2	7/8	.145–.175
	LA	31/64	—	3 Rich	2	7/8	.160
	MA	31/64	—	3 Rich	2	7/8	.160
	BA	31/64	—	1 Rich	3	7/8	.153
	DC	31/64	—	3 Rich	3	7/8	.153
	JD	31/64	—	3 Rich	3	7/8	.160
	KD	31/64	—	3 Rich	3	7/8	.160
	ZA	31/64	—	1 Rich	3	7/8	.153
	D6TE						
	FA	31/64	—	Index	2	7/8	.140
	GA	31/64	—	3 Rich	2	7/8	.140
	JA	31/64	—	3 Rich	2	7/8	.135
	MA	31/64	—	3 Rich	2	7/8	.135
	VA	31/64	—	2 Rich	2	7/8	.135
	YB, YA	31/64	—	3 Rich	2	7/8	.135
	RA	31/64	—	2 Rich	2	7/8	.179
	SA, TA	31/64	—	2 Rich	3	7/8	.179
	AAC	31/64	—	3 Rich	4	7/8	.160
	D6UE						
	JA	31/64	—	3 Rich	2	7/8	.180
'77	D7TE						
	AHA	31/64	—	Index	3	7/8	.160
	ALA	31/64	—	Index	3	7/8	.160
	AKA	31/64	—	Index	3	7/8	.160
	BEA	31/64	—	Index	3	7/8	.160
	BZA	31/64	—	Index	3	7/8	.160
	BZB	31/64	—	Index	3	7/8	.160
	ANA	31/64	—	3 Rich	4	7/8	.160
	CJA	31/64	—	3 Rich	4	7/8	.160
	CZA	31/64	—	3 Rich	4	7/8	.160

MODEL 2150
Ford
(All measurements in inches)

Year	Carburetor List Number	Float Level (Dry)	Choke Unloader Setting	Choke Setting	Accelerator Pump Rod Location	Fuel Level (Wet)	Initial Choke Valve Setting (Min)
	AMA	31/64	—	3 Rich	4	7/8	.160
	DBA	31/64	—	3 Rich	4	7/8	.160
	ARA	31/64	—	3 Rich	4	7/8	.160
	AUA, CKA	31/64	—	3 Rich	4	7/8	.160
	AYA, DAA	31/64	—	3 Rich	4	7/8	.160
	AZA, APA	31/64	—	3 Rich	4	7/8	.160
	CUA	31/64	—	3 Rich	4	7/8	.160
	D7PE						
	AGA	31/64	—	2 Rich	3	7/8	.145
	D7UE						
	ADA	31/64	—	2 Rich	4	7/8	.170
	TA	7/16	—	3 Rich	3	13/16	.170
	ZC	7/16	—	Index	3	13/16	.170
	YA	7/16	—	3 Rich	2	13/16	.170
	AAA	31/64	—	1 Rich	2	13/16	.170
	ACA	31/64	—	1 Rich	3	7/8	.170
	AEA	31/64	—	1 Rich	4	7/8	.170
	ABA	31/64	—	1 Rich	4	7/8	.170
	ARB	31/64	—	1 Rich	4	7/8	.170
	ANA	31/64	—	2 Rich	3	7/8	.170
	APA	31/64	—	2 Rich	3	7/8	.170
'78	**D8TE**						
	LA	31/64	—	Index	3	7/8	.130
	ARA	31/64	—	Index	3	7/8	.145
	DA	31/64	—	Index	4	7/8	.130
	CTA	31/64	—	Index	4	7/8	.130
	DBA	31/64	—	2 Rich	4	7/8	.130
	BLA	31/64	—	2 Rich	4	7/8	.130
	CRA	31/64	—	2 Rich	4	7/8	.130
	BJA	31/64	—	3 Rich	3	7/8	.175
	ATA	31/64	—	2 Rich	3	7/8	.145
	BEA	31/64	—	3 Rich	2	7/8	.200
	BA	31/64	—	Index	3	7/8	.140
	DP7E						
	AGA	31/64	—	2 Rich	3	7/8	.145
	D7UE						
	APA	31/64	—	2 Rich	3	7/8	.170

MODEL 2150
Ford
(All measurements in inches)

Year	Carburetor List Number	Float Level (Dry)	Choke Unloader Setting	Choke Setting	Accelerator Pump Rod Location	Fuel Level (Wet)	Initial Choke Valve Setting (Min)
	D8UE						
	VA	31/64	—	Index	4	7/8	.145
	DA	31/64	—	3 Rich	3	7/8	.185
	KA	7/16	—	Index	3	13/16	.185
	GA	31/64	—	1 Rich	2	7/8	.205
	HA	31/64	—	Index	2	7/8	.215
	MA	31/64	—	Index	2	7/8	.215
	MB	31/64	—	Index	2	7/8	.215
	SA	31/64	—	3 Rich	3	7/8	.180
'80	EOTE-9510						
	BGA, CYA, GZA, ABA, BEA	.810	—	.20	—	—	.140
	BHA	.810	—	.20	—	—	.135
	BRA, DDA	.810	—	.20	—	—	.128
	CFA, EAA	.810	—	.25	—	—	.128
	CVA, NA	.875	—	.20	—	—	.105
	BYA	.875	—	.115	—	—	.140
	BSA Calibration Number: 0-59J-R0 0-59G-R10	.875	—	.115	—	—	.140
	0-59J-R10 0-59H-R10	.875	—	.20	—	—	.140
	DCA	.875	—	.25	—	—	.140
	AAA, PA, SA, TA, VA	.810	—	.25	—	—	.185
	AA	.810	—	.25	—	—	.105
	CLA	.875	—	.20	—	—	.140
	BLA, BFA, BZA	.875	—	.25	—	—	.148
	CCA, CBA	.875	—	.25	—	—	.159
	EDA, DGA	.875	—	.25	—	—	.155
	EEA, EFA	.875	—	.20	—	—	.160
	DEA, ECA	.875	—	.25	—	—	.175
	DFA	.875	—	.25	—	—	.185
'81	E1TE-9510 BJA, CHA, BCA	31/64	—	.250	V notch	—	.148

MODEL 2150
Ford
(All measurements in inches)

Year	Carburetor List Number	Float Level (Dry)	Choke Unloader Setting	Choke Setting	Accelerator Pump Rod Location	Fuel Level (Wet)	Initial Choke Valve Setting (Min)
	BTA	31/64	—	.250	V notch	—	.130
	BVA	7/16	—	.200	V notch	—	.130
	CEA, CFA	31/64	—	.200	V notch	—	.160
	CAA, BYA	31/64	—	.250	V notch	—	.175
	BSA	31/64	—	.250	V notch	—	.130
	CCA	31/64	—	.250	V notch	—	.155
	BZA, CBA	31/64	—	.250	V notch	—	.180
	CNA, CMA, CPA, CRA, CSA, CKA, CLA	7/16	—	.200	V notch	—	.125
	E1UE-9510 KA	31/64	—	.250	V notch	—	.180
	GA	7/16	—	.200	V notch	—	.130
	HA	31/64	—	.200	V notch	—	.125

① Wet float setting 1980 only
② For choke settings see the Ford Calibration Specifications 1980 only
③ For 1979 carburetor specifications see Ford Calibration Specifications

MODEL 7200
Ford
(All measurements in inches)

Year	Carburetor List Number	Float Level (Dry)	Float Drop	Choke Unloader Setting	Choke Setting	Dash Pot Plunger	Initial Choke Setting
'81	E1TE-9510 YA, AHA	1.455①	—	—	Index	—	—
	ZA	1.040①	—	—	Index	—	—

① ± .025 inches

MODEL 4350
Ford
(All measurements in inches)

Year	Carburetor List Number	Float Level (Dry)	Choke Unloader Setting	Choke Setting	Accelerator Pump Rod Location	Fuel Level (Wet)	Initial Choke Valve Setting (Min)
'75	D5TE ARC	15/16	.300	Index	3	—	.160
	ARD	1.0	.300	Index	3	—	.160

MODEL 4350
Ford
(All measurements in inches)

Year	Carburetor List Number	Float Level (Dry)	Choke Unloader Setting	Choke Setting	Accelerator Pump Rod Location	Fuel Level (Wet)	Initial Choke Valve Setting (Min)
	BBA	15/16	—	Index	3	—	.160
	BBB	.92	.300	Index	3	—	.160
	BBC	1.0	.300	Index	3	—	.160
	D5UE						
	SA	15/16	.300	Index	3	—	.160
	SB	1.0	.300	Index	3	—	.160
	NA	15/16	.300	Index	3	—	.160
	NB	.92	.300	Index	3	—	.160
	NC	1.00	.300	Index	3	—	.160
'76	D5TE						
	ARC	15/16	.300	Index	3	—	.160
	ARD	1.0	.300	Index	3	—	.160
	BBA	15/16	.300	Index	3	—	.160
	BBB	.92	.300	Index	3	—	.160
	BBC	1.0	.300	Index	3	—	.160
	D6TE						
	NA	1.0	.300	Index	3	—	.160
	UA	1.0	.300	Index	3	—	.160
	D5UE						
	NA	15/16	.300	Index	3	—	.160
	NB	.92	.300	Index	3	—	.160
	NC	1.0	.300	Index	3	—	.160
	SA	15/16	.300	Index	3	—	.160
	SB	1.0	.300	Index	3	—	.160
	D6UE						
	KA	1.0	.300	Index	3	—	.160
	LA	1.0	.300	Index	3	—	.160
'77	D7TE						
	BLA	1.0	.300	Index	3	—	.160
	BJA	1.0	.300	Index	3	—	.160
	D7UE						
	AGA	1.0	.300	Index	3	—	.160
	AFA	1.0	.300	Index	3	—	.160
'78	D8TE						
	AKA	1.0	.300	Index	3	①	.160
	AMA	1.0	.300	Index	3	①	.160
	D7UE						
	ASA	1.0	.300	Index	3	①	.160

MODEL 4350
Ford
(All measurements in inches)

Year	Carburetor List Number	Float Level (Dry)	Choke Unloader Setting	Choke Setting	Accelerator Pump Rod Location	Fuel Level (Wet)	Initial Choke Valve Setting (Min)
	D8UE						
	AA	1.0	.300	Index	3	①	.160
	CA	1.0	.300	Index	3	①	.160

① Fuel level between 4 and 6 on special gauge

MODEL 2100
Jeep
(All measurements in inches)

Year	Carburetor List Number	Float Level (Dry)	Fuel Level (Wet)	Initial Choke Valve Clearance	Fast Idle Cam Setting ②	Choke Cover Setting	Choke Unloader Valve Clearance	Fast Idle Speed ①	Dash Pot Clearance	Bowl Vent Clearance	Rod Pump Location Hole
'75	5RHM2	.555	.930	.140	.130	2 Rich	.250	1600	—	—	3
	5RHA2	.555	.930	.140	.130	2 Rich	.250	1600	—	—	3
	5DM2	.400	.780	.130	.130	2 Rich	.250	1600	.095	—	3
	5DM2J	.400	.780	.130	.130	2 Rich	.250	1600	.095	—	3
'76	6RHM2	.555	.930	.136	.115	2 Rich	.250	1600	—	—	—
	6RHA2	.555	.930	.136	.115	2 Rich	.250	1600	—	—	—
	6DM2	.555	.930	.132	.120	2 Rich	.250	1600	.075	—	—
	6DA2J	.555	.930	.136	.126	1 Rich	.250	1600	.075	—	—
	6DM2J	.555	.930	.136	.126	1 Rich	.250	1600	.075	—	—
'77	6RHM2	.555	.930	.136	.115	2 Rich	.250	1600	—	—	3
	6RHA2	.555	.930	.136	.115	2 Rich	.250	1600	—	—	3
	6DM2	.555	.930	.132	.120	2 Rich	.250	1600	.093	—	3
	6DA2J	.555	.930	.136	.120	1 Rich	.250	1600	—	—	3
	6DM2J	.555	.930	.132	.126	1 Rich	.250	1600	.093	—	3
'78	8DM2	.555	.930	.132	.120	2 Rich	.250	1500	—	.120	3
	8DM2C	.555	.930	.132	.120	1 Rich	.250	1500	—	.120	3
	8DA2J	.555	.930	.136	.126	1 Rich	.250	1600	—	.120	3
	8DA2JC	.555	.930	.136	.126	1 Rich	.250	1600	—	.120	3
	6RHA2	.555	.930	.136	.115	2 Rich	.250	1600	—	.120	3
	6RHM2	.555	.930	.136	.115	2 Rich	.250	1600	—	.120	3
'79	9DM2	.555	.930	.125	.120	2 Rich	.250	1500	—	.120	—
	9DM2C	.555	.930	.132	.120	1 Rich	.250	1500	—	.120	—
	9DA2J	.555	.930	.128	.113	1 Rich	.250	1600	—	.120	—
	9DM2H	.555	.930	.140	.125	Index	.250	1500	—	.120	—

CARBURETORS
AUTOLITE/FORD/MOTORCRAFT

MODEL 2100
Jeep
(All measurements in inches)

Year	Carburetor List Number	Float Level (Dry)	Fuel Level (Wet)	Initial Choke Valve Clearance	Fast Idle Cam Setting ②	Choke Cover Setting	Choke Unloader Valve Clearance	Fast Idle Speed ①	Dash Pot Clearance	Bowl Vent Clearance	Rod Pump Location Hole
'80	ODMJ12	.375	.093	.125	.113	2 Rich	.300	1500	—	.120	3
	ODM2JC	.375	.093	.120	.106	2 Rich	.300	1500	—	.120	3
	ODA2J2	.375	.093	.120	.106	2 Rich	.300	1600	—	.120	3
	ODA2J	.375	.093	.128	.113	2 Rich	.300	1600	—	.120	3
	ODM2A	.375	.093	.128	.113	2 Rich	.360	1500	—	.120	3

①TCS solenoid and EGR disconnected, fast idle screw on 2nd cam step.
②Measured between choke valve and air horn, fast idle screw on 2nd cam step.

MODEL 2150
Jeep
(All measurements in inches)

Year	Carburetor List Number	Float Level (Dry)	Fuel Level (Wet)	Initial Choke Valve Clearance	Fast Idle Cam Setting ②	Choke Cover Setting	Choke Unloader Valve Clearance	Fast Idle Speed ①	Dash Pot Clearance	Bowl Vent Clearance	Rod Pump Location Hole
'77	7DM2A	.555	.930	.110	.089	2 Rich	.290	1600	—	—	3
	7DA2A	.555	.930	.104	.089	1 Rich	.290	1600	—	—	3
'78	8DA2A	.555	.930	.089	.078	2 Rich	.290	1600	—	—	3
	8DM2A	.555	.930	.093	.078	2 Rich	.290	1600	—	—	3
'79	9RHM2	.555	.930	.104	.086	2 Rich	.348	1500	—	—	3
	9RHA2	.555	.930	.113	.093	2 Rich	.350	1600	—	—	3
'80	ORHM2	.575	.930	.104	.081	2 Rich	.348	1500		.120	3
	ORHA2	.575	.930	.104	.081	2 Rich	.350	1600		.120	3
'81	DMJ2	.375	.930	.125	.113	2 Rich	.300	1500		.120	3
	DA2J	.375	.930	.128	.113	1 Rich	.300	1600		.120	3
	DM2A	.375	.930	.128	.113	1 Rich	.360	1500		.120	3
	RHM2	.575	.930	.104	.081	2 Rich	.348	1500		.120	3
	RHA2	.575	.930	.113	.086	2 Rich	.350	1600		.120	3

①TCS solenoid and EGR disconnected, fast idle screw on 2nd cam step
②Measured between choke valve and air horn fast idle screw on 2nd cam step
③Measured from machined bowl surface to a point ⅛ inch from float tip with the needle seated

MODEL 4350
Jeep
(All measurements in inches)

Year	Carburetor List Number	Float Level (Dry)	Fuel Level (Wet)	Initial Choke Valve Clearance	Fast Idle Cam Setting ②	Choke Cover Setting	Choke Unloader Valve Clearance	Fast Idle Speed ①	Dash Pot Clearance	Bowl Vent Clearance	Rod Pump Location Hole
'75	5THA4	.900	—	.140	.160	2 Rich	.325	1600	—	—	—
	5THM4	.900	—	.140	.160	2 Rich	.325	1600	—	—	Lower

MODEL 4350
Jeep
(All measurements in inches)

Year	Carburetor List Number	Float Level (Dry)	Fuel Level (Wet)	Initial Choke Valve Clearance	Fast Idle Cam Setting ②	Choke Cover Setting	Choke Unloader Valve Clearance	Fast Idle Speed ①	Dash Pot Clearance	Bowl Vent Clearance	Rod Pump Location Hole
'76	6THA4	.900	—	.135	.135	2 Rich	.325	1600	—	—	Lower
	6THMA	.900	—	.135	.135	2 Rich	.325	1600	—	—	—
	6THA4C	.900	—	.135	.135	2 Rich	.325	1600	—	—	—
'77	6THA4	.900	—	.135	.135	2 Rich	.325	1600	—	—	—
	6THM4	.900	—	.135	.135	2 Rich	.325	1600	—	—	—
	6THA4C	.900	—	.135	.135	2 Rich	.325	1600	—	—	—
'78	6THA4	.900	—	.135	.135	2 Rich	.325	1600	—	—	—
	6THM4	.900	—	.135	.135	2 Rich	.325	1600	—	—	—

① TCS solenoid and EGR disconnected, fast idle screw on 2nd cam step.
② Measured between choke valve and air horn, fast idle screw on 2nd cam step.

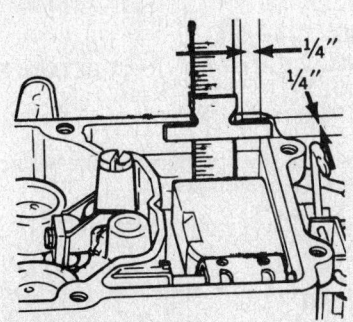

Fuel level adjustment (wet)—models 2100 and 2150 carburetors (© Ford Motor Co.)

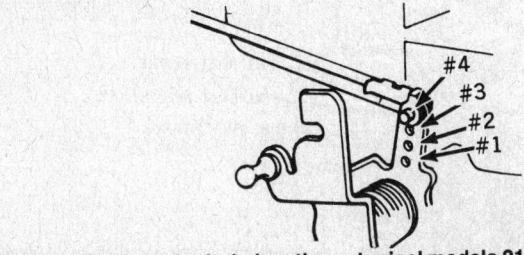

Accelerator pump stroke hole location— typical models 2100 and 2150 carburetors
(© Ford Motor Co.)

Indexing marks for automatic choke thermostatic spring housing and choke housing—typical models 2100 and 2150 carburetors (© Ford Motor Co.)

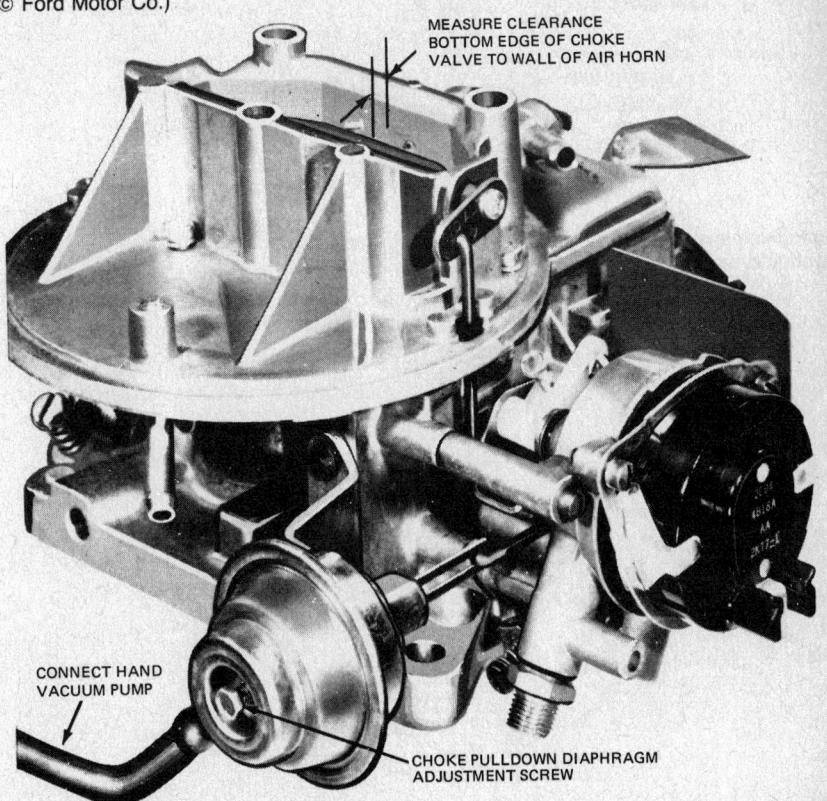

Adjustment of choke plate initial setting—typical models 2100 and 2150 carburetors
(© Ford Motor Co.)

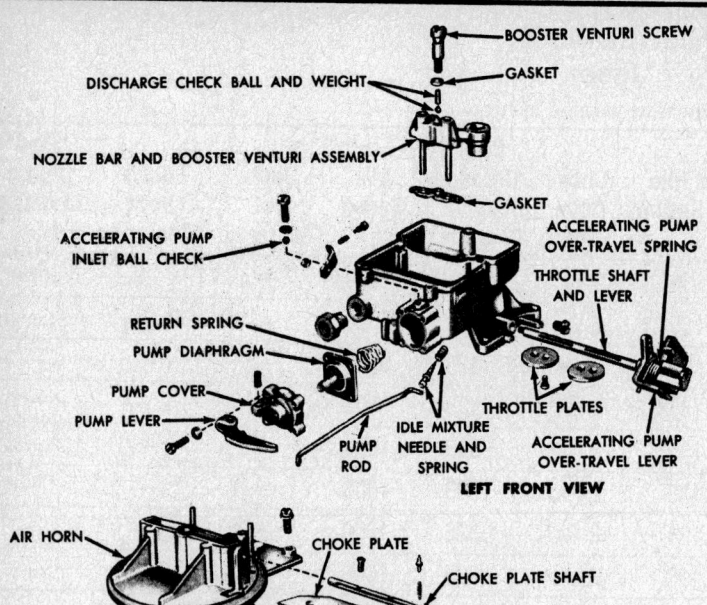

LEFT FRONT VIEW

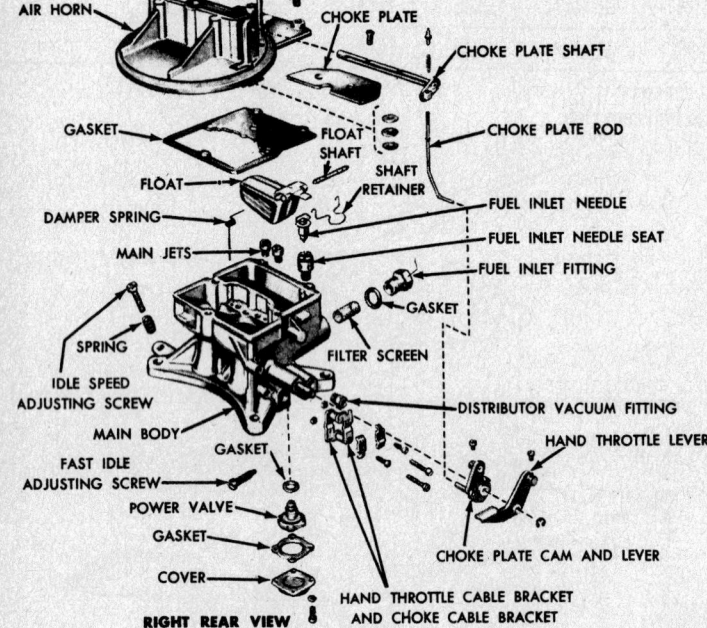

RIGHT REAR VIEW

Exploded view of model 2100 carburetor (with manual choke, manual throttle, and automatic choke mechanisms shown) (© Ford Motor Co.)

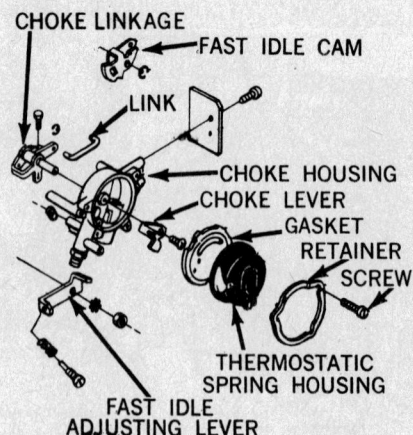

Automatic choke assembly (typical)—model 2100 carburetor

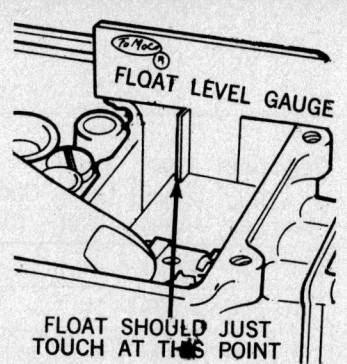

Float level adjustment (dry)—models 2100 and 2150 carburetors (© Ford Motor Co.)

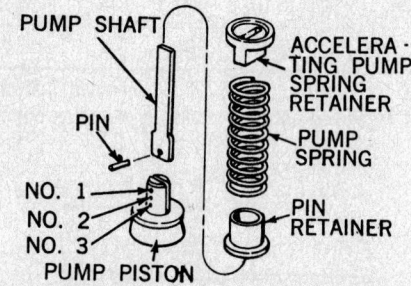

Setting accelerator pump stroke—Motorcraft 4350 carburetor

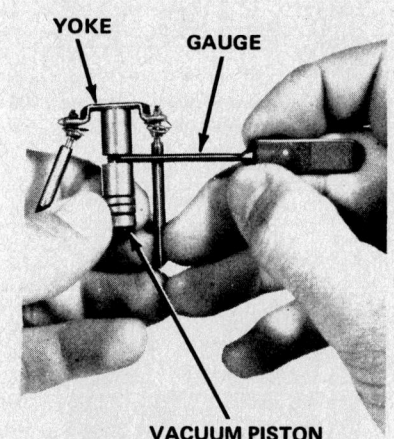

Metering rod vacuum piston adjustment to a clearance of .120 inches (© Jeep Corp.)

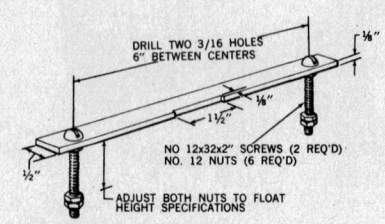

Fabrication of the float gauge—models 4300 and 4350 carburetors

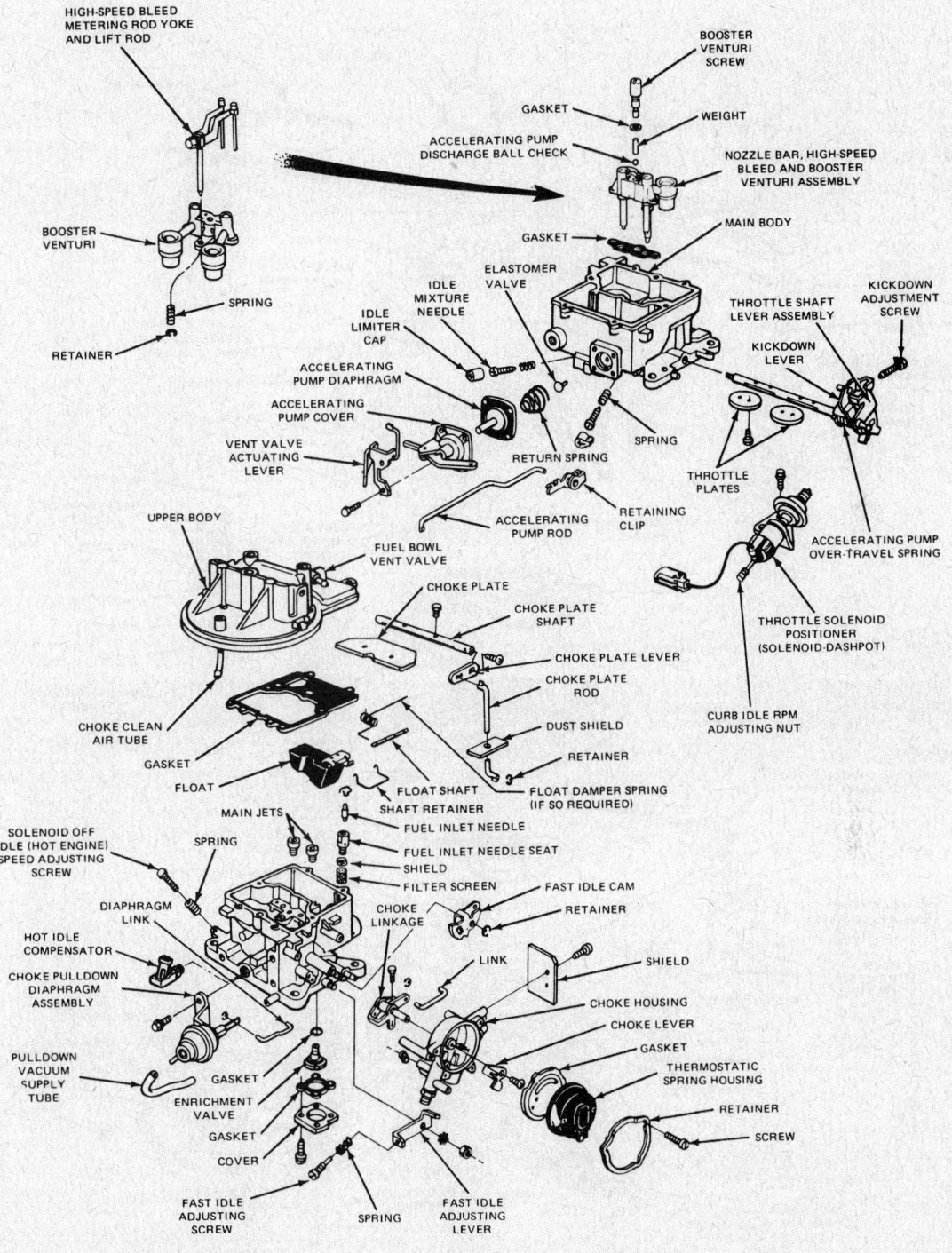

HIGH-SPEED BLEED
METERING ROD YOKE
AND LIFT ROD

BOOSTER
VENTURI
SCREW

GASKET

WEIGHT

ACCELERATING PUMP
DISCHARGE BALL CHECK

NOZZLE BAR, HIGH-SPEED
BLEED AND BOOSTER
VENTURI ASSEMBLY

BOOSTER
VENTURI

GASKET

MAIN BODY

SPRING

RETAINER

IDLE
MIXTURE
NEEDLE

ELASTOMER
VALVE

THROTTLE SHAFT
LEVER ASSEMBLY

KICKDOWN
ADJUSTMENT
SCREW

IDLE
LIMITER
CAP

KICKDOWN
LEVER

ACCELERATING
PUMP DIAPHRAGM

ACCELERATING
PUMP COVER

VENT VALVE
ACTUATING
LEVER

RETURN SPRING

SPRING

THROTTLE
PLATES

UPPER BODY

FUEL BOWL
VENT VALVE

ACCELERATING
PUMP ROD

RETAINING
CLIP

ACCELERATING PUMP
OVER-TRAVEL SPRING

CHOKE PLATE

CHOKE PLATE
SHAFT

THROTTLE SOLENOID
POSITIONER
(SOLENOID-DASHPOT)

CHOKE PLATE LEVER

CHOKE PLATE
ROD

CHOKE CLEAN
AIR TUBE

DUST SHIELD

CURB IDLE RPM
ADJUSTING NUT

GASKET

RETAINER

FLOAT

FLOAT SHAFT

SHAFT RETAINER

FLOAT DAMPER SPRING
(IF SO REQUIRED)

MAIN JETS

FUEL INLET NEEDLE

SOLENOID OFF
IDLE (HOT ENGINE)
SPEED ADJUSTING
SCREW

SPRING

FUEL INLET NEEDLE SEAT

SHIELD

FILTER SCREEN

FAST IDLE CAM

DIAPHRAGM
LINK

CHOKE
LINKAGE

RETAINER

HOT IDLE
COMPENSATOR

LINK

SHIELD

CHOKE PULLDOWN
DIAPHRAGM
ASSEMBLY

CHOKE HOUSING

CHOKE LEVER

PULLDOWN
VACUUM
SUPPLY
TUBE

GASKET

GASKET

THERMOSTATIC
SPRING HOUSING

ENRICHMENT
VALVE

RETAINER

GASKET

SCREW

COVER

FAST IDLE
ADJUSTING
SCREW

SPRING

FAST IDLE
ADJUSTING
LEVER

Exploded view of Motorcraft 2150 carburetor—typical

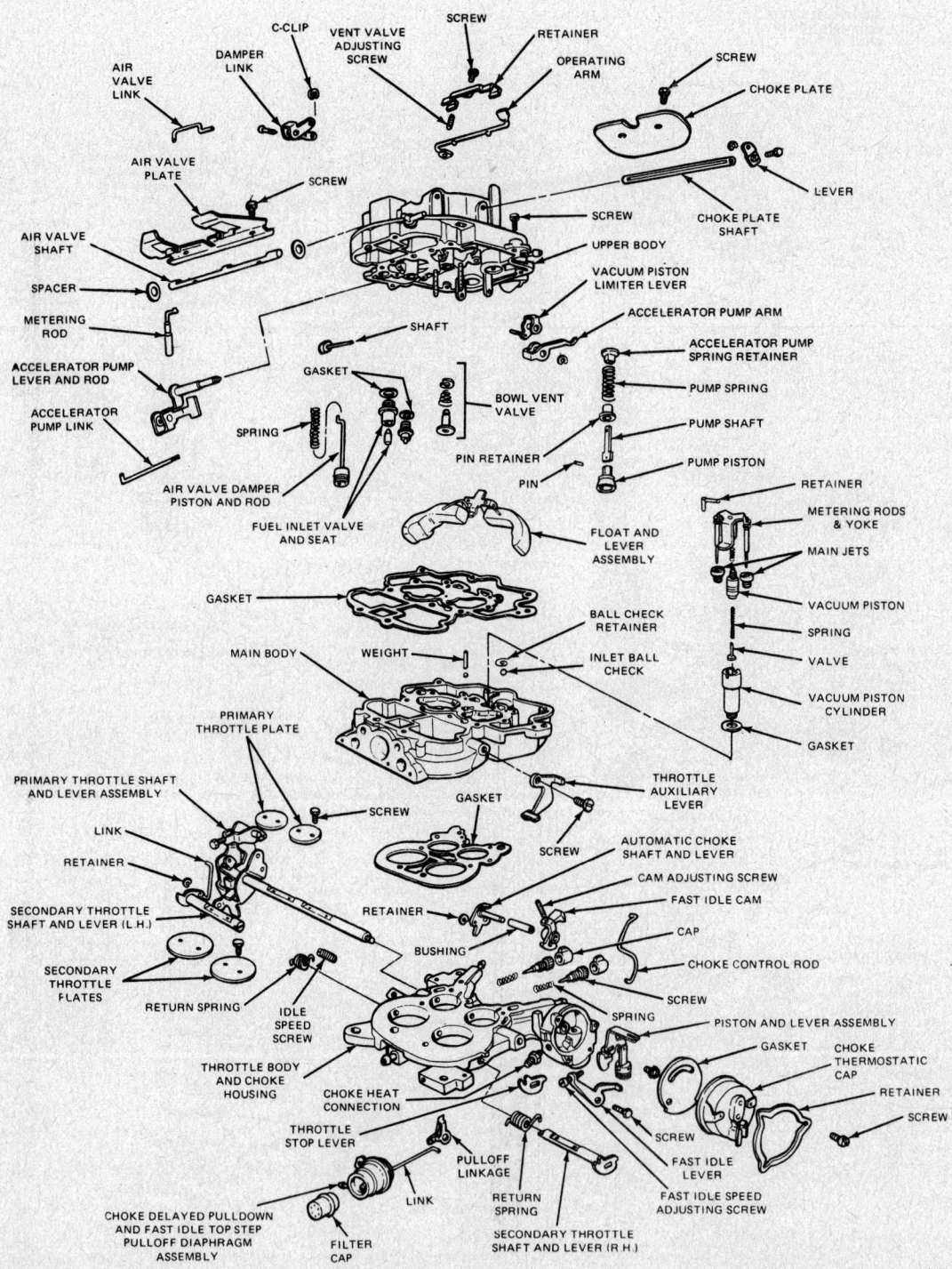

Exploded view of Motorcraft 4350—typical of 4300 series carburetors

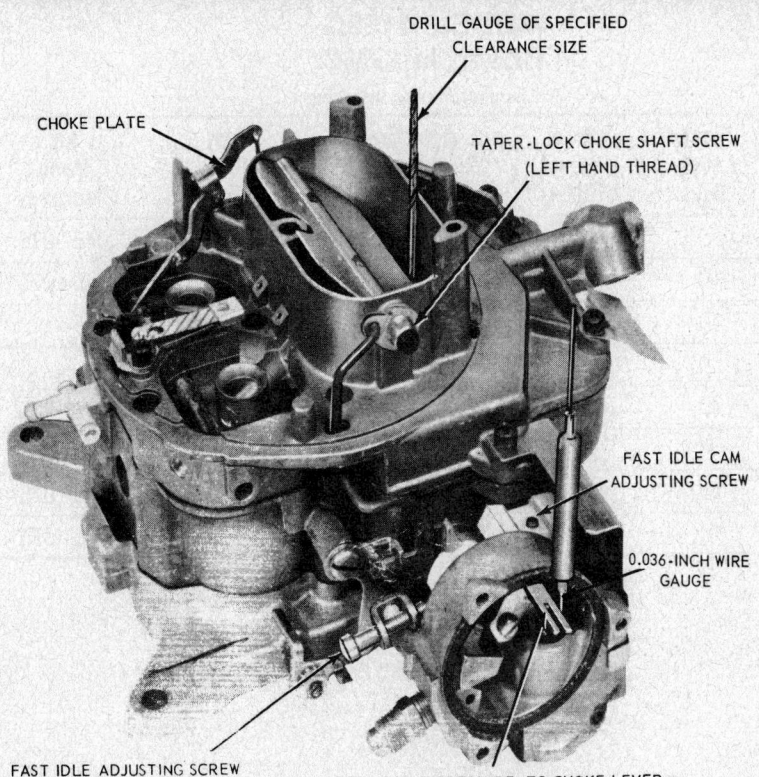

DRILL GAUGE OF SPECIFIED
CLEARANCE SIZE

CHOKE PLATE

TAPER-LOCK CHOKE SHAFT SCREW
(LEFT HAND THREAD)

FAST IDLE CAM
ADJUSTING SCREW

0.036-INCH WIRE
GAUGE

FAST IDLE ADJUSTING SCREW

APPLY LIGHT PRESSURE TO CHOKE LEVER

Choke plate initial setting (pull-down) and fast idle cam adjustment—models 4300 and 4350 carburetors (© Ford Motor Co.)

FLOATS SHOULD JUST CONTACT GAUGE

BEND TAB TO RAISE OR LOWER FLOAT

SET GAUGE TO
SPECIFICATIONS

INSTALL FLOAT PIN
FROM THIS SIDE

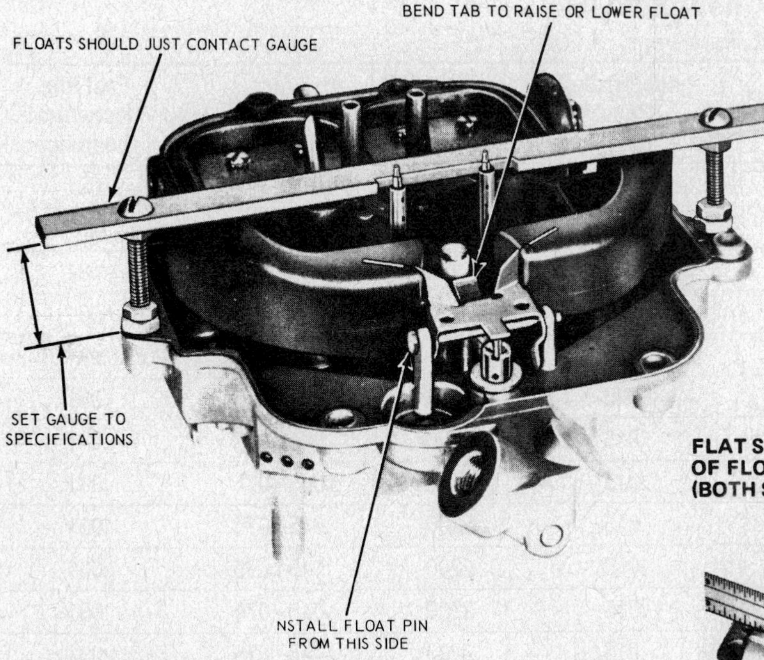

Checking the float level with a fabricated gauge—models 4300 and 4350 carburetors (© Ford Motor Co.)

**FLAT SURFACE
OF FLOAT PONTOON
(BOTH SIDES)**

**FLOAT LEVEL
ADJUSTING TAB**

**SMOOTH AREA
OF CASTING**

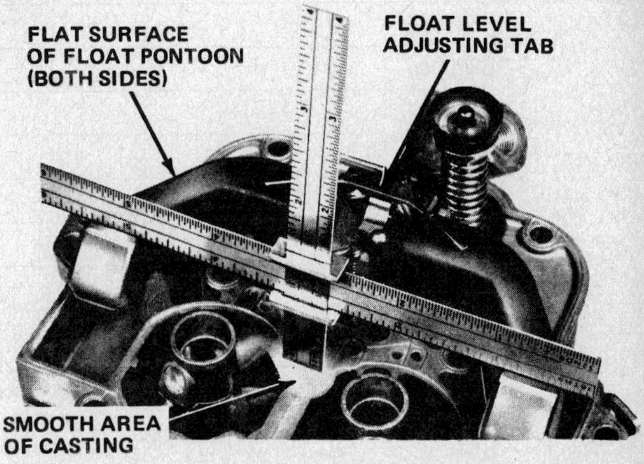

Adjustment of the float level with a "T" scale—models 4300 and 4350 carburetors (© Jeep Corp.)

MODEL 4150G
Chevrolet/GMC
(All measurements in inches)

Year	Carburetor List No.	Float Level (Dry)	Fuel Level (Wet)	Accelerator Pump (Min.)	Fast Idle (RPM)	Air Vent Clearance	Fast Idle Mechanical Clearance
'75–'76	R6928A	①	—	.015	2200	.045–.075	.038
	R6929A	①	—	.015	2200	.045–.075	.038
	R6930A	①	—	.015	2200	—	.031
	R6931A	①	—	.015	2200	—	.031
	R7264A	①	—	.015	2200	.045–.075	.038
	R7266A	①	—	.015	2200	.045–.075	.038
'77	R7703A	②	—	.015	2200	.045–.075	.038
	R7704A	②	—	.015	2200	.045–.075	.031

① Primary bowl—.197
  Secondary bowl—.166
② Primary bowl—.194
  Secondary bowl—.213

MODEL 4150EG
Chevrolet/GMC
(All measurements in inches)

Year	Carburetor List No.	Float Level (Dry)	Fuel Level (Wet)	Accelerator Pump (Min.)	Fast Idle (RPM)	Air Vent Clearance	Fast Idle Mechanical Clearance
'78	R7923A	②	—	.015	2200	.045–.075	.031
	R7927A	②	—	.015	2200	.045–.075	.031
	R7925A	②	—	.015	2200	—	.031
	R7928A	②	—	.015	2200	—	.031
	R7924A	②	—	.015	2200	.045–.075	.031
	R7926A	②	—	.015	2200	—	.031
'79	R8278A	②	—	.015	2200	.045–.075	.031
	R8280A	②	—	.015	2200	.045–.075	.031
	R8282A	②	—	.015	2200	.045–.075	.031
	R8283A	②	—	.015	2200	.045–.075	.031
	R8444A	②	—	.015	2200	.045–.075	.031
	R8279A	②	—	.015	2200	.045–.075	.031
	R8281A	②	—	.015	2200	.045–.075	.031
'80	R8848A	②	—	.015	2200	.045–.075	.031
	R8849A	②	—	.015	2200	.045–.075	.031
	R8852A	②	—	.015	2200	.045–.075	.031
	R8853A	②	—	.015	2200	.045–.075	.031
	R8856A	②	—	.015	2200	.045–.075	.031

MODEL 4150EG
Chevrolet/GMC
(All measurements in inches)

Year	Carburetor List No.	Float Level (Dry)	Fuel Level (Wet)	Accelerator Pump (Min.)	Fast Idle (RPM)	Air Vent Clearance	Fast Idle Mechanical Clearance
	R8850A	②	—	.015	2200	—	.031
	R8851A	②	—	.015	2200	—	.031
	R8854A	②	—	.015	2200	—	.031
	R8855A	②	—	.015	2200	—	.031
	R8857A	②	—	.015	2200	—	.031

① Primary bowl—.197
   Secondary bowl—.166
② Primary bowl—.194
   Secondary bowl—.213

MODEL 1945 1–bbl
Dodge/Plymouth
(All measurements in inches)

Year	Carburetor List No.	Float Level (Dry)	Vacuum Kick Choke (Unloader)	Choke Setting	Pump Rod Adjustment (Hole)	Fast Idle Cam Position	Fast Idle Speed	Vacuum Kick (Initial Choke Opening)
'75	R7074A	3/64	.250	②	2⁷/₃₂	.080	1600	.110
	R7209A	3/64	.250	②	2⁷/₃₂	.080	1600	.130
	R7076A	3/64	.250	②	2²¹/₆₄	.080	1700	.090
	R7210A	3/64	.250	②	2²¹/₆₄	.080	1700	.090
	R7078A	3/64	.250	②	2⁷/₃₂	.080	1600	.110
	R7079A	3/64	.250	②	2²¹/₆₄	.080	1700	.090
	R7080A	3/64	.250	②	2⁷/₃₂	.080	1600	.110
	R7081A	3/64	.250	②	2²¹/₆₄	.080	1700	.090
	R7082A	3/64	.250	②	2⁷/₃₂	.080	1600	.110
	R7083A	3/64	.250	②	2²¹/₆₄	.080	1700	.090
'76	R7428A	①	.250	②	2⁷/₃₂(2)	.080	1600	.110
	R7429A	①	.250	②	2²¹/₆₄(3)	.080	1700	.110
	R7401A	①	.250	②	2⁷/₃₂(2)	.080	1600	.110
	R7080A	①	.250	②	2⁷/₃₂(2)	.080	1600	.110
	R7081A	①	.250	②	2²¹/₆₄(3)	.080	1700	.090
	R7082A	①	.250	②	2⁷/₃₂(2)	.080	1600	.110
	R7083A	①	.250	②	2²¹/₆₄(3)	.080	1700	.090
'77	R7815A	①	.250	②	2²¹/₆₄(3)	.080	1600	.110
	R7816A	①	.250	②	2²¹/₆₄(3)	.080	1700	.110
	R7847A	①	.250	②	2⁷/₃₂(2)	.080	1600	.110
	R7848A	①	.250	②	2²¹/₆₄(3)	.080	1700	.110

MODEL 1945 1–bbl
Dodge/Plymouth
(All measurements in inches)

Year	Carburetor List No.	Float Level (Dry)	Vacuum Kick Choke (Unloader)	Choke Setting	Pump Rod Adjustment (Hole)	Fast Idle Cam Position	Fast Idle Speed	Vacuum Kick (Initial Choke Opening)
'78	—	—	—	—	—	—	—	—
'79	R8593A	①	.250	②	2⁷/₃₂(1)	.080	1600	.100
	R8594A	①	.250	②	2²¹/₆₄(2)	.080	1600	.100
	R8799A	①	.250	②	2⁷/₃₂(1)	.080	1600	.100
	R8800A	①	.250	②	2²¹/₆₄(2)	.080	1600	.100
'80	R8978A	①	.250	②	1.70(1)	.080	1600	.130
	R8720A	①	.250	②	1.61(2)	.090	1600	.130
	R9107A	①	.250	②	1.70(1)	.080	1600	.100
	R9106A	①	.250	②	1.61(2)	.080	1600	.100
	R8979A	①	.250	②	1.70(1)	.080	1600	.130
	R8721A	①	.250	②	1.61(2)	.080	1600	.130
'81	R9131A	①	.250	②	1.615(2)	.090	1600	.130
	R9132A	①	.250	②	1.615(2)	.090	1600	.130
	R9134A	①	.250	②	1.615(2)	.090	1600	.130
	R9152A	①	.250	②	1.615(2)	.080	1800	.130
	R9153A	①	.250	②	1.615(2)	.080	1800	.130
	R9399A	①	.250	②	1.615(2)	.080	1800	.130

① Flush with top of bowl cover gasket, carb inverted
② Fixed setting

MODEL 2210 2–bbl
Dodge/Plymouth
(All measurements in inches)

Year	Carburetor List No.	Float Level (Dry)	Vacuum Kick Choke (Unloader)	Choke Setting	Pump Rod Location	Fast Idle Cam Position	Fast Idle Speed	Vacuum Kick (Initial Choke Opening)
'75	R6764A	.180	.170	①	②	.110	1700	.150
	R6765A	.180	.170	①	②	.110	1800	.150
'76	R6764A	.180	.170	①	②	.110	1700	.150
	R6765A	.180	.170	①	②	.110	1800	.150
	R6886–1A	.180	.170	①	②	.110	1400	.150
'77	R7676A	³/₁₆ ③	.170	①	⑤	.110	1700	.150
	R7870A	³/₁₆ ③	.170	①	④	.110	1800	.150
	R6886–1A	³/₁₆ ③	.170	①	④	.110	1600	.90

① Fixed setting
② Accelerator pump setting: At curb idle—.260 in. (R6764A—.270) At closed throttle—.310 in.
③ Bottom of float to be parallel with air horn bottom
④ At curb idle—slot #1—.310 in.
⑤ At curb idle—slot #2—.320 in.

MODEL 2245
Dodge/Plymouth
(All measurements in inches)

Year	Carburetor List No.	Float Level (Dry)	Vacuum Kick Choke (Unloader)	Choke Setting	Pump Rod Location (Hole)	Fast Idle Cam Position	Fast Idle Speed (RPM)	Vacuum Kick (Initial Choke Opening)
'75	R7187A	.180	.170	①	②	.110	1600	.150
	R7188A	.180	.170	①	②	.110	1600	.150
'76	R7403A	.180	.170	①	②	.110	1600	.150
	R7188A	.180	.170	①	②	.110	1600	.150
'77	R7697A	³⁄₁₆③	.170	①	④	.110	1600	.150
	R7871A	³⁄₁₆③	.170	①	⑤	.110	1600	.150
	R8036A	³⁄₁₆③	.170	①	④	.110	1600	.150
	R8182A	³⁄₁₆③	.170	①	④	.110	1600	.150
'78	R8453A	.180	.170	①	⑥	.110	1600	.150
	R8135A	.180	.170	①	⑦	.110	1600	.90
	R6886A	.180	.170	①	⑦	.110	1600	.150
	R7756A	.180	.170	①	⑦	.110	1600	.150
	R8484A	.180	.170	①	⑥	.110	1600	.150
	R7088A	.180	.170	①	⑦	.110	1600	.150
	R8028A	.180	.170	①	⑥	.110	1600	.150
	R7871A	.180	.170	①	⑥	.110	1600	.130
	R8026A	.180	.170	①	⑥	.110	1600	.150
'79	R8597A	.200③	.170	①	.290(1)	.110	1600	.110
	R8598A	.200③	.170	①	.290(1)	.110	1600	.110
	R8925A	.200③	.170	①	.290(1)	.110	1600	.110
'80	R7871A	³⁄₁₆	.170	Fixed	Slot #1	.110	1700	.150

NOTE: Number in Parenthesis is number of slot
① Fixed setting
② Accelerator pump setting:
  Curb idle—.260 in.
  Closed throttle—.310 in.
  #1 Slot
③ Float drop—bottom of float to be parallel with air horn bottom
④ At idle—slot #1—.310 in.
⑤ At idle—slot #2—.320 in.
⑥ At idle—slot #2—.260 in.
⑦ At idle—slot #2—.260 in.

MODEL 2280G
Dodge/Plymouth
(All measurements in inches)

Year	Carburetor List Number	Float Level	Choke Vacuum Kick	Fast Idle Cam	Fast Idle (rpm)	Choke Unloader	Bowl Vent Valve
'80	R8999A	⁵⁄₁₆	.130	.070	1600	.310	.030
	R9000A	⁵⁄₁₆	.130	.070	1600	.310	.030
	R9001A	⁵⁄₁₆	.150	.070	1600	.310	.030
	R9209A	⁵⁄₁₆	.150	.070	1600	.310	.030
	R9224A	⁵⁄₁₆	.150	.070	1600	.310	.030

MODEL 2280
Dodge/Plymouth
(All measurements in inches)

Year	Carburetor List Number	Float Level	Choke Vacuum Kick	Fast Idle Cam	Fast Idle (rpm)	Choke Unloader	Vent Valve
'81	R9135A	9/32	.110	.070	1500	.310	—
	R9136A	9/32	.130	.070	1500	.310	—
	R9151A	9/32	.110	.070	1500	.310	—
	R9437A	9/32	.130	.070	1500	.310	—

MODEL 2300G
Dodge/Plymouth
(All measurements in inches)

Year	Carburetor List Number	Float Level	Choke Unloader	Pump Rod Location	Fast Idle Cam Position	Fast Idle (rpm)	Vacuum Kick Initial Choke Opening
'75	R6769–1A	①	—	—	.035	—	—
	R7137A	①	—	—	.035	—	—
'76	R6769–1A	①	—	—	.035	—	—
	R7137A	①	—	—	.035	—	—
'77	R6769–1A	①	—	—	.035	—	—
	R7137A	①	—	—	.035	—	—

① Check the float level to the bottom of the sight plug on the carburetor

MODELS 2300, 2300G
Ford
(All measurements in inches)

Year	Carburetor List No.	Float Level	Choke Unloader Setting	Choke Setting	Accelerator Pump Rod Location	Fuel Level (Wet)	Initial Choke Valve Setting
'75–'76	D4TE						
	AKA	②	—	Manual	#2 hole	①	—
	AKA	②	—	Manual	#2 hole	①	—
	AMA	②	—	Manual	#2 hole	①	—
	ALA	②	—	Manual	#2 hole	①	—
'75–'78	D4TE						
	AJA	②	—	Manual	#2 hole	①	—
'78	D8TE						
	BPA	②	—	Manual	#2 hole	①	—
	CEA	②	—	Manual	#2 hole	①	—
	AJA	②	—	Manual	#2 hole	①	—

MODEL 2300 EG
Ford
(All measurements in inches)

Year	Carburetor List Number	Float Level (Dry)	Float Drop	Choke Unloader Setting	Choke Setting	Dash Pot Plunger	Initial Choke Setting
'80	EOTE–9510 PA, PB, BCA, BCB, EVA, EYA	①	—	—	—	—	.375
'81	D9TE–9510 ABC, APA	①	—	—	Manual	—	.350–.400

① Check float level to the bottom of the sight plug in the carburetor

MODEL 4150G
Ford
(All measurements in inches)

Year	Carburetor List No.	Float Level	Choke Unloader Setting	Choke Setting	Accelerator Pump Rod Location	Fuel Level (Wet)	Initial Choke Valve Setting
'75–'78	D5TE CB	②	—	Manual	#2 hole	①	—
	CA	②	—	Manual	#1 hole	①	—
	CB	②	—	Manual	#2 hole	①	—
'75–'77	D5TE BA	②	—	Manual	#2 hole	①	—
	AA	②	—	Manual	#2 hole	①	—
'75–'78	D5TE BRA	②	—	Manual	#2 hole	①	—
'75	D5TE AA	②	—	Manual	#2 hole	①	—
'76	D5TE BA	②	—	Manual	#2 hole	①	—
	BRA	②	—	Manual	#2 hole	①	—
'78	D8TE AHA	②	—	Manual	—	①	—
	BZA	②	—	Manual	—	①	—
	AGA	②	—	Manual	—	①	—
	BRA	②	—	Manual	—	①	—
	CBA	②	—	Manual	—	①	—
	BSA	②	—	Manual	—	①	—

CARBURETORS
HOLLEY

MODEL 4150EG
Ford
(All measurements in inches)

Year	Carburetor List Number	Float Level (Dry)	Float Drop	Choke Unloader Setting	Choke Setting	Dash Pot Plunger	Initial Choke Setting
'80	D9HE–9510 CA, DA, EA, FA	①	—	—	—	—	—
	EOHE–9510 CA,EA	①	—	—	—	—	—
'81	D9HE–9510 CA,EA	①	—	—	Manual	—	—

① Check float level to the bottom of the sight plug in the carburetor

MODEL 4150MG
Ford

Year	Carburetor List Number	Float Level	Choke Unloader Setting	Choke Setting	Accelerator Pump Rod Location	Fuel Level (Wet)	Initial Choke Valve Setting
'75	D4HE CA	②	—	Manual	#1 hole	①	—
	DA	②	—	Manual	#1 hole	①	—
'75–'77	D5HE CA	②	—	Manual	#1 hole	①	—
	BA	②	—	Manual	#1 hole	①	—
'76	D4HE CA	②	—	Manual	#1 hole	①	—
	DA	②	—	Manual	#1 hole	①	—
'76	D5HE CA	②	—	Manual	#1 hole	①	—
	BA	②	—	Manual	#1 hole	①	—
'76	D6HE CB	②	—	Manual	#1 hole	①	—
	DB	②	—	Manual	#1 hole	①	—
'77	D7HE AA	②	—	Manual	#1 hole	①	—
	CA	②	—	Manual	#1 hole	①	—
'78	D8HE AA	②	—	Manual	#1 hole	①	—
	EA	②	—	Manual	#1 hole	①	—
	CA	②	—	Manual	#1 hole	①	—
	BA	②	—	Manual	#1 hole	①	—
	FA	②	—	Manual	#1 hole	①	—
	DA	②	—	Manual	#1 hole	①	—

MODEL 4160C
Ford

Year	Carburetor List Number	Float Level (Dry)	Float Drop	Choke Unloader Setting	Choke Setting	Dash Pot Plunger	Initial Choke Setting
'75	D4TE						
	ARA	②	.315	Index	#1 hole	①	.180
	ASA	②	.315	Index	#1 hole	①	.180
	ANA	②	.315	Index	#1 hole	①	.180
	EAA	②	.315	Index	#1 hole	①	.180
	D5TE						
	DA	②	.315	Index	#1 hole	①	.180
	EA	②	.315	Index	#1 hole	①	.180
	FA	②	.315	Index	#1 hole	①	.180
	GA	②	.315	Index	#1 hole	①	.180
	DB	②	.315	Index	#1 hole	①	.180
'76	D5TE						
	EA	②	.315	Index	#1 hole	①	.180
	DA	②	.315	Index	#1 hole	①	.180
	AB	②	.315	Index	#1 hole	①	.180
	GA	②	.315	Index	#1 hole	①	.180
	GB	②	.315	2 Lean	#1 hole	①	.190
	FA	②	.315	Index	#1 hole	①	.180
	FB	②	.315	2 Lean	#1 hole	①	.200
	DB	②	.315	Index	#1 hole	①	.180

① Fuel level to lower edge of sight plug hole
② With fuel bowl inverted, float should be parallel with float bowl floor

MODEL 4180C
Ford
(All measurements in inches)

Year	Carburetor List Number	Float Level (Dry)	Float Drop	Choke Unloader Setting	Choke Setting	Dash Pot Plunger	Initial Choke Setting
'80	D9TE-9510						
	DKA	①	—	.315②	—	—	.210
'81	D9TE-9510						
	BKA	①	—	—	5 Rich	—	.195-.225

① Check float level to the bottom of the sight plug in the carburetor
② ± .015 inch

MODEL 4180EG
Ford
(All measurements in inches)

Year	Carburetor List Number	Float Level (Dry)	Float Drop	Choke Unloader Setting	Choke Setting	Dash Pot Plunger	Initial Choke Setting
'80	EOTE-9510 ETA, JB, EUA, RB, JA, RA, ERA, MB, SB, SA, ESA, MA	①	—	—	—	—	.210
	D9TE-9510 AHE, EBA, ETA, EUA	①	—	—	—	—	.210
'81	D9TE-9510 EBA, AHE, ETA, EUA	①	—	—	Manual	—	.185-.235
	EOTE-9510 RA, JA, MA, SA	①	—	—	Manual	—	.185-.235

① Check float level to the bottom of the sight plug in the carburetor

MODEL 1920
International
(All measurements in inches)

Year	Carburetor List No. (49 States)	Carburetor List No. (Calif.)	Float Level	Fuel Level	Fast Idle Speed (RPM)	Auto Choke Setting	Dash-Post Setting	Fuel Bowl Vent Clearance	Pump Piston Stroke Adjustment	Fast Idle Cam Pos. Adjustment (Top Step—Hot)	Choke Vac. Pulldown (Kick) Adjustment	Choke Unloader Adjustment	Choke qualification Adjustment
'75-'76	7161	7161	①	$11/16 \pm 1/32$	2000	1 Rich	—	—	$25/32$	—	—	.345-.295	.100-.130
'77-'78	7161, 7161-1	7576 8238	①	$11/16 \pm 1/32$	2000	1 Rich	—	—	$25/32$	—	—	.235-.295	.100-.130
'79-'80	7771	7771	①	$11/16 \pm 1/32$	2200	1 Lean	—	—	$25/32$	—	—	.235-.295	.150-.180

① Flush with top edge of bowl and with fuel inlet valve held closed

MODEL 1940C
International
(All measurements in inches)

Year	Carburetor List Number	Float Level	Fuel Level	Automatic Choke	Dash Pot Setting	Choke Unloader	Fast Idle (rpm)	Curb Idle (rpm)	Pump Stroke	Idle CO %
'75-'76	7161	①	$11/16 \pm 1/32$	1 Rich	.100-.130	.235-.295	2000	525-575	$25/32$	0.5-2.0
'77-'78	7161 7161-1 7576	①	$11/16 \pm 1/32$	1 Rich	.100-.130	.235-.295	2000	525-575	$25/32$	0.5-2.0
'79	7771	①	$11/16 \pm 1/32$	1 Rich	.100-.130	.235-.295	2200	675-725	$25/32$	0.3-1.5

① Flush with top edge of bowl, with fuel inlet valve held closed

MODEL 2210C
International
(All measurements in inches)

Year	Carb. List No. (48 States)	Carb. List No. (Calif.)	Float Level	Fuel Level	Fast Idle Speed	Auto Choke Setting	Dash Pot Setting	Fuel Bowl Vent Clearance	Pump Piston Stroke Adjustment	Fast Idle Cam Position Adjustment (Top Step—Hot)	Choke Vac. Pulldown (Kick) Adjustment	Choke Unloader Adjustment	Choke Qualification Adjustment
'75–'80	6620-1	—	.180	½①	2000	②	—	—	—	—	—	.198–	.040–
	7309											.258	.070
	7214, 7214-1	—	.180	½①	1800	Preset	—	—	—	—	—	.228 ± .030	.135 ± .015
	—	7309, 6620-2, 7133, 7940 8241	.180	½①	2200	②	—	—	—	—	—	.198– .258	.040– .070
	—	7657, 7217, 8244	.180	½①	1800	Preset	—	—	—	—	—	.198– .258	.120– .150

① @ 5.5 PSI
② Choke with index marks—1 notch lean (restrained)
  Choke without index marks—preset (unrestrained)

MODEL 2245C
International
(All measurements in inches)

Year	Carburetor Number	Float Level	Fuel① Level	Automatic Choke	Dash Pot Setting	Choke Unloader	Fast Idle (rpm)	Curb② Idle (rpm)	Idle CO %
'79	7773	.180	½	Pre-set	.105–.135	.198–.258	2200	675–725	0.1–0.8

① 5.5 psi of fuel pressure
② Transmission in neutral and air conditioning off

MODEL 2300, 2300C, 2300G, 2300EG
International
(All measurements in inches)

Year	Carburetor List Number	Fuel Level	Fast Idle (rpm)	Automatic Choke Setting	Dash Pot Setting	Governor No load (rpm)	Governor Full load (rpm)	High Idle (rpm)	Curb Idle (rpm)	Idle CO %
'75–'76	6899	⅜	2000	—	—	4000	3800	1450 ± 50	625–675	0.5–1.5
	7216	⅜	2400	—	—	3800	3600	1350 ± 50	525–575	0.5–2.5
	7198	⅜	2000	—	—	3400	3200	1350 ± 50	500–550	1.0–2.0
'75–'78	6801-1	⅜	2200	—	—	4000	3800	1350 ± 50	650–700	2.0
	8232	⅜	2200	—	—	4000	3800	1350 ± 50	650–700	1.5
	7213	⅜	2400	—	—	3800	3600	1350 ± 50	525–575	0.5–2.5
	8235	⅜	2400	—	—	3800	3600	1350 ± 50	525–575	0.5–2.5
	6908	⅜	2000	—	—	3400	3200	1350 ± 50	500–550	1.5–3.0
	8238	⅜	2000	—	—	3400	3200	1350 ± 50	500–550	1.5–3.0

CARBURETORS
HOLLEY

MODEL 2300, 2300C, 2300G, 2300EG
International
(All measurements in inches)

Year	Carburetor List Number	Fuel Level	Fast Idle (rpm)	Automatic Choke Setting	Dash Pot Setting	Governor No load (rpm)	Governor Full load (rpm)	High Idle (rpm)	Curb Idle (rpm)	Idle CO %
'77–'78	7656	⅜	2000	—	—	4000	3800	1450 ± 50	625–675	1.0–3.0
	8242	⅜	2000	—	—	4000	3800	1450 ± 50	625–675	1.0–3.0
	7580	⅜	2400	—	—	3800	3600	1350 ± 50	525–575	0.5–2.0
	7922	⅜	2400	—	—	3800	3600	1350 ± 50	525–575	0.5–2.0
	8245	⅜	2400	—	—	3800	3600	1350 ± 50	525–575	0.5–2.0
	7198	⅜	2000	—	—	3400	3400	1350 ± 50	500–550	1.0–2.0
	8248	⅜	2000	—	—	3400	3400	1350 ± 50	500–550	1.0–2.0
'79–'81	8736	⅜	2200	—	—	4000	3800	1450 ± 50	625–675	1.0–3.0
	7922	⅜	2400	—	—	3800	3600	1350 ± 50	525–575	0.5–2.5
	8741	⅜	2000	—	—	3400	3200	1350 ± 50	500–550	1.0–2.0
	9072	⅜	2000	—	—	3800	3600	1350 ± 50	625–675	1.0–3.0
	8242	⅜	2000	—	—	4000	3800	1450 ± 50	625–675	1.0–3.0
	9076	⅜	2400	—	—	3800	3600	1350 ± 50	525–575	0.5–2.0
	8245	⅜	2400	—	—	3800	3600	1350 ± 50	525–575	0.5–2.0
	8248	⅜	2000	—	—	3400	3200	1350 ± 50	500–550	1.0–2.0
	8232	⅜	2200	—	—	4000	3800	1350 ± 50	650–700	2.0
	8180	⅜	2200	—	—	4000	3800	1300 ± 50	650–700	1.5
	8236	⅜	2400	—	—	3800	3600	1350 ± 50	525–575	0.5–2.5
	8235	⅜	2400	—	—	3800	3600	1350 ± 50	525–575	0.5–2.5
	8238	⅜	2000	—	—	3400	3200	1350 ± 50	500–550	1.5–3.0

MODELS 4150G, 4150EG
International
(All measurements in inches)

Year	Carburetor List No.	Fuel Valve Seal	Fuel Level	Fast Idle Setting (in. or RPM)	Governor Speed No-Load (RPM)	Governor Speed Full-Load (RPM)	Curb Idle Speed (RPM)	Idle Mixture Setting % CO
'75–'80 (Federal)	6803-3	—	①	2000	3800	3600	650-700	2.0 Max
	7215	—	①	2400	3800	3600	525-575	0.5-2.5
	7251	—	①	2400	3800	3600	525-575	0.5-2.5
	6911	—	①	2000	3400	3200	500-550	1.5-3.0
'75–'80 (Calif)	7028, 7529	—	①	.015-.020	3800	3600	625-675	0.5-1.5
	7218, 7218-1	—	①	2400	3800	3600	525-575	0.5-2.5
	7581	—	①	2400	3800	3600	525-575	0.5-2.5
	7921	—	①	2400	3800 ± 50	—	525-575	0.5-2.5
'75–'80 (50 States)	7029, 7029-1	—	①	2400	3800	3600	525-575	0.5-2.5
	6974	—	①	2000	3400	3200	500-550	1.0-2.0

①Primary ⅜ in., Secondary ⅝ in.

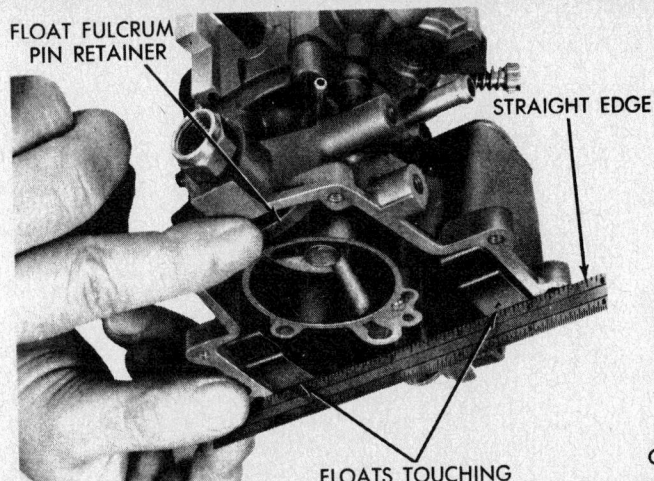

FLOAT FULCRUM PIN RETAINER

STRAIGHT EDGE

FLOATS TOUCHING

Adjusting the fuel level with the fuel bowl inverted—model 1945 carburetor (© Chrysler Corp.)

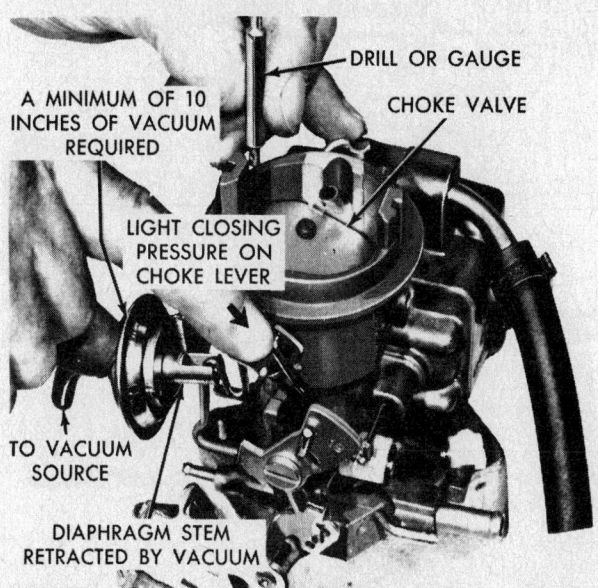

DRILL OR GAUGE

CHOKE VALVE

A MINIMUM OF 10 INCHES OF VACUUM REQUIRED

LIGHT CLOSING PRESSURE ON CHOKE LEVER

TO VACUUM SOURCE

DIAPHRAGM STEM RETRACTED BY VACUUM

Choke vacuum kick setting—model 1920 one barrel (© Chrysler Corp.)

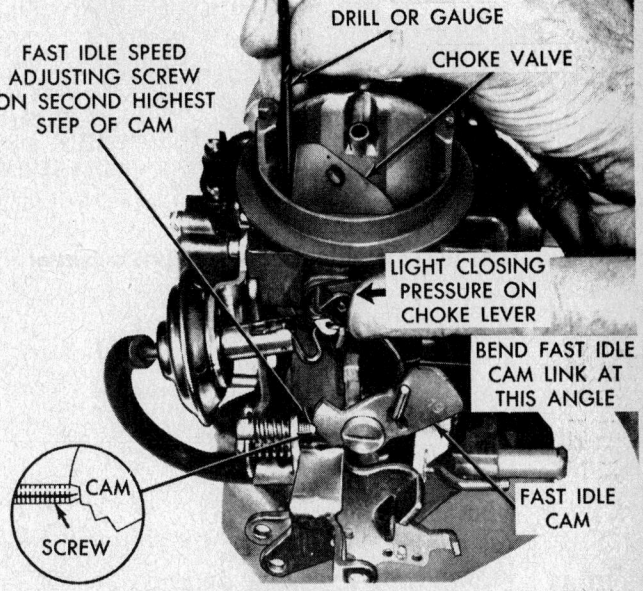

DRILL OR GAUGE

CHOKE VALVE

FAST IDLE SPEED ADJUSTING SCREW ON SECOND HIGHEST STEP OF CAM

LIGHT CLOSING PRESSURE ON CHOKE LEVER

BEND FAST IDLE CAM LINK AT THIS ANGLE

CAM

SCREW

FAST IDLE CAM

Fast idle cam adjustment—model 1920 one barrel (© Chrysler Corp.)

FLOAT SPRING

CARBURETOR INVERTED

FLOAT GAUGE

FLOAT

FLOAT TAB

Checking float setting—model 1920 one barrel (© Chrysler Corp.)

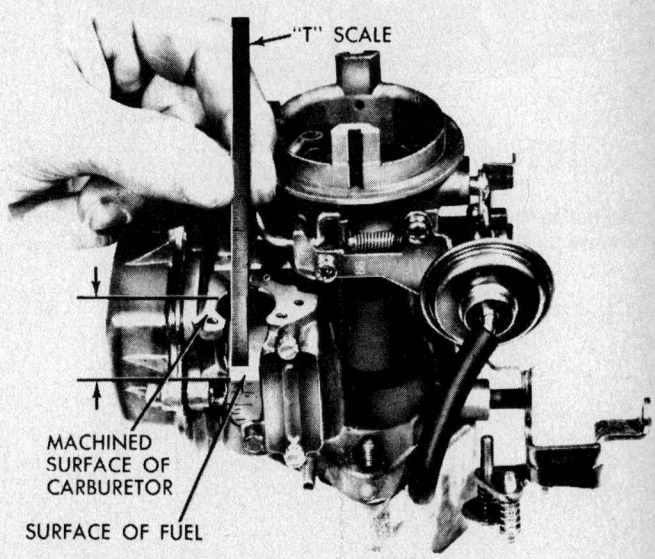

"T" SCALE

MACHINED SURFACE OF CARBURETOR

SURFACE OF FUEL

Measuring wet fuel level—model 1920 one barrel (© Chrysler Corp.)

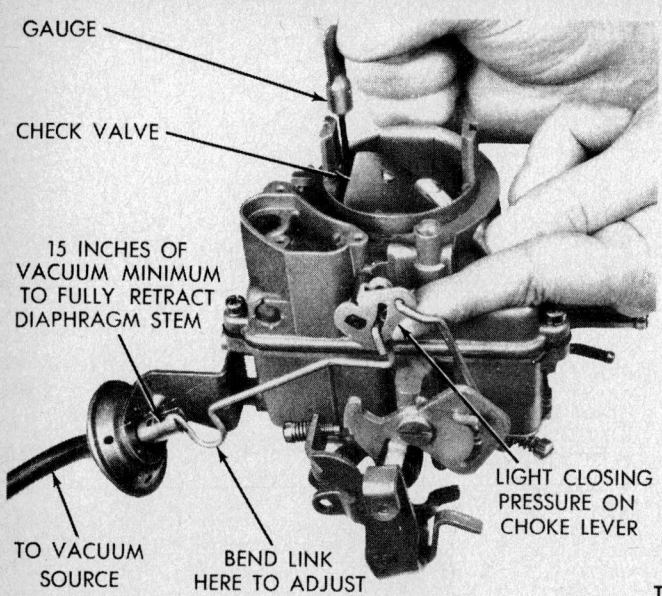

GAUGE

CHECK VALVE

15 INCHES OF VACUUM MINIMUM TO FULLY RETRACT DIAPHRAGM STEM

TO VACUUM SOURCE

BEND LINK HERE TO ADJUST

LIGHT CLOSING PRESSURE ON CHOKE LEVER

Choke valve initial setting (vacuum kick)—model 1945 carburetor (© Chrysler Corp.)

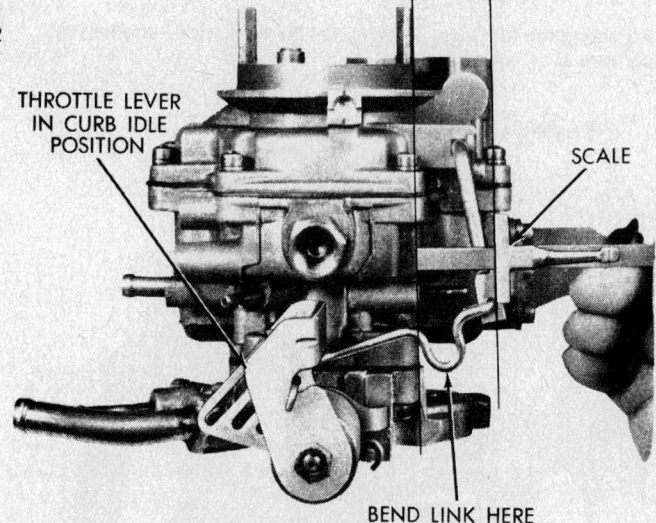

THROTTLE LEVER IN CURB IDLE POSITION

SCALE

BEND LINK HERE FOR ADJUSTMENT

Accelerator pump piston stroke adjustment—model 1945 carburetor (© Chrysler Corp.)

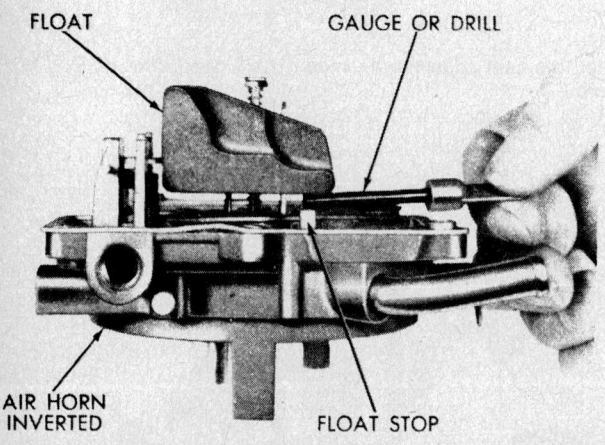

FLOAT

GAUGE OR DRILL

AIR HORN INVERTED

FLOAT STOP

Adjusting the float level—models 2210, 2210C and 2245 carburetors (© Chrysler Corp.)

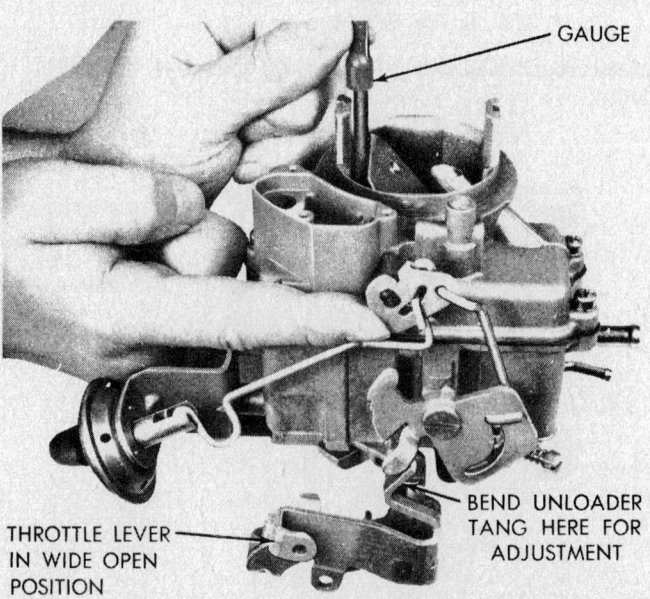

GAUGE

BEND UNLOADER TANG HERE FOR ADJUSTMENT

THROTTLE LEVER IN WIDE OPEN POSITION

Choke valve unloader adjustment—model 1945 carburetor (© Chrysler Corp.)

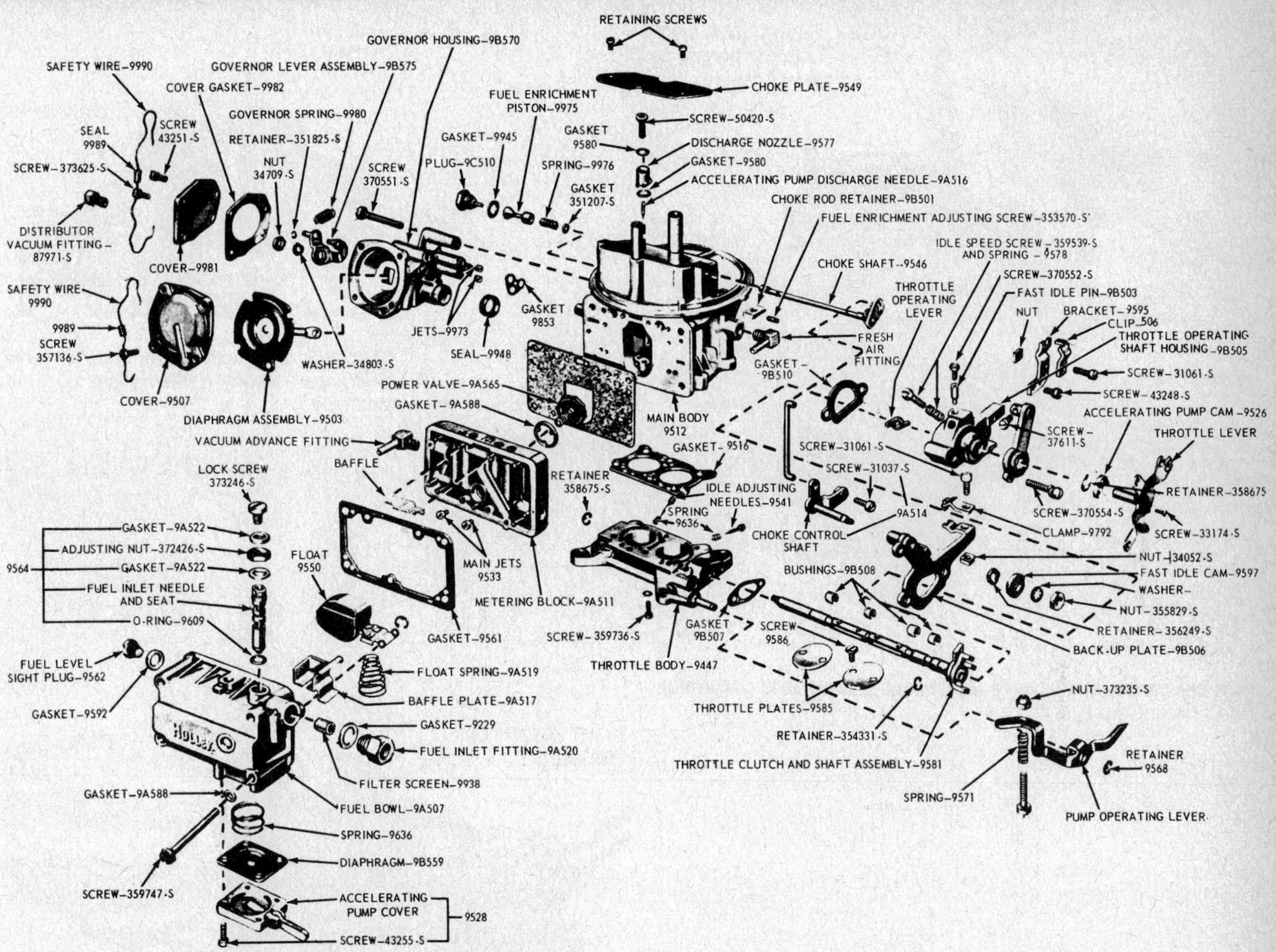

Holley two barrel—typical

RETAINING SCREWS

SAFETY WIRE-9990
GOVERNOR LEVER ASSEMBLY-9B575
COVER GASKET-9982
GOVERNOR HOUSING-9B570
CHOKE PLATE-9549
SEAL 9989
GOVERNOR SPRING-9980
FUEL ENRICHMENT PISTON-9975
SCREW 43251-S
RETAINER-351825-S
SCREW-50420-S
SCREW-373625-S
NUT 34709-S
GASKET-9945
GASKET 9580
DISCHARGE NOZZLE-9577
DISTRIBUTOR VACUUM FITTING- 87971-S
SCREW 370551-S
PLUG-9C510
SPRING-9976
GASKET-9580
ACCELERATING PUMP DISCHARGE NEEDLE-9A516
COVER-9981
GASKET 351207-S
CHOKE ROD RETAINER-9B501
FUEL ENRICHMENT ADJUSTING SCREW-353570-S
SAFETY WIRE 9990
CHOKE SHAFT-9546
IDLE SPEED SCREW-359539-S AND SPRING- 9578
9989 SCREW 357136-S
JETS-9973
GASKET 9853
THROTTLE OPERATING LEVER
SCREW-370552-S
FAST IDLE PIN-9B503
COVER-9507
SEAL-9948
FRESH AIR FITTING
NUT
BRACKET- 9595
CLIP- 506
THROTTLE OPERATING SHAFT HOUSING-9B505
DIAPHRAGM ASSEMBLY-9503
POWER VALVE-9A565
GASKET- 9B510
SCREW-31061-S
VACUUM ADVANCE FITTING
GASKET- 9A588
MAIN BODY 9512
SCREW-43248-S
LOCK SCREW 373246-S
BAFFLE
GASKET- 9516
SCREW-31061-S
ACCELERATING PUMP CAM-9526
THROTTLE LEVER
RETAINER 358675-S
IDLE ADJUSTING NEEDLES-9541
SCREW-31037-S
SCREW-37611-S
GASKET-9A522
ADJUSTING NUT-372426-S
SPRING 9636
9A514
SCREW-370554-S
RETAINER-358675
GASKET-9A522
FLOAT 9550
CHOKE CONTROL SHAFT
CLAMP-9792
SCREW-33174-S
9564
FUEL INLET NEEDLE AND SEAT
MAIN JETS 9533
BUSHINGS-9B508
NUT- 34052-S
FAST IDLE CAM-9597
O-RING-9609
METERING BLOCK-9A511
WASHER-
NUT- 355829-S
FUEL LEVEL SIGHT PLUG-9562
GASKET-9561
SCREW-359736-S
GASKET 9B507
SCREW 9586
RETAINER 356249-S
BACK-UP PLATE-9B506
GASKET-9592
THROTTLE BODY-9447
FLOAT SPRING-9A519
NUT-373235-S
BAFFLE PLATE-9A517
GASKET-9A588
GASKET-9229
THROTTLE PLATES-9585
FUEL INLET FITTING-9A520
RETAINER-354331-S
RETAINER 9568
FILTER SCREEN-9938
THROTTLE CLUTCH AND SHAFT ASSEMBLY-9581
SCREW-359747-S
FUEL BOWL-9A507
SPRING-9636
SPRING-9571
DIAPHRAGM-9B559
PUMP OPERATING LEVER
ACCELERATING PUMP COVER
9528
SCREW-43255-S

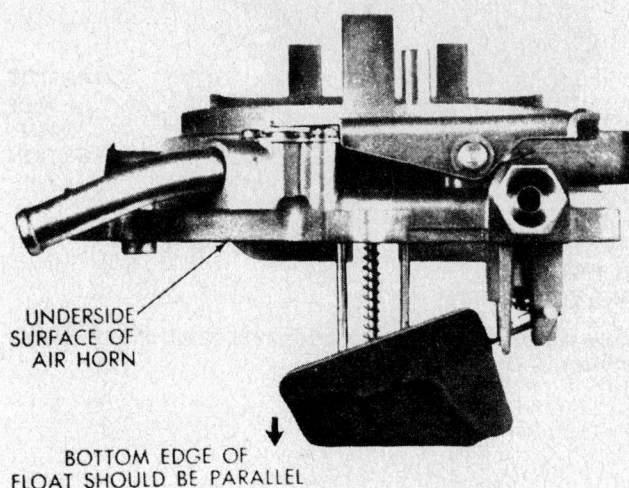

UNDERSIDE SURFACE OF AIR HORN

BOTTOM EDGE OF FLOAT SHOULD BE PARALLEL

Adjusting the float drop—models 2210, 2210C and 2245 carburetors (© Chrysler Corp.)

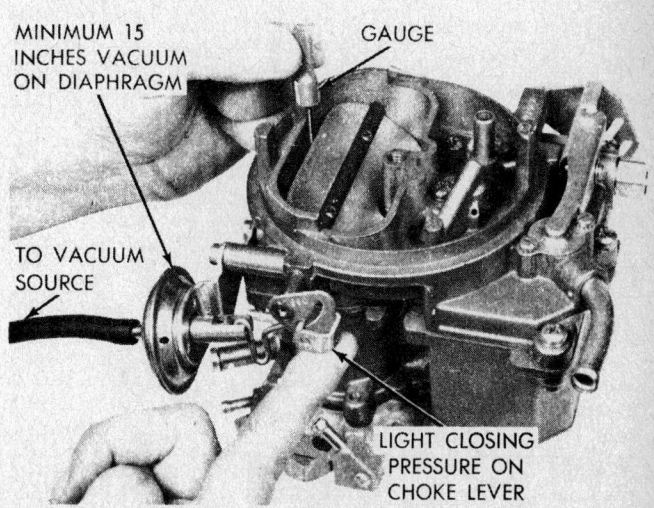

MINIMUM 15 INCHES VACUUM ON DIAPHRAGM

GAUGE

TO VACUUM SOURCE

LIGHT CLOSING PRESSURE ON CHOKE LEVER

Adjusting the initial choke valve setting—models 2210, 2210C and 2245 carburetors (© Chrysler Corp.)

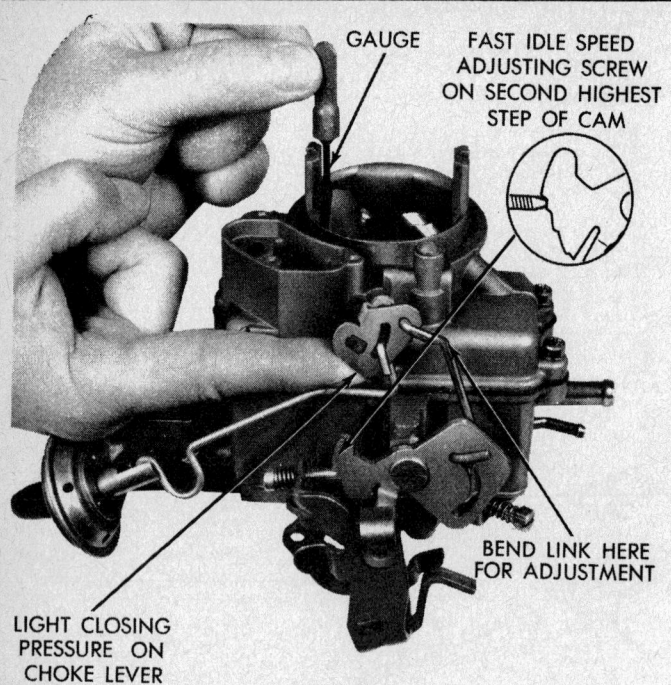

GAUGE

FAST IDLE SPEED
ADJUSTING SCREW
ON SECOND HIGHEST
STEP OF CAM

BEND LINK HERE
FOR ADJUSTMENT

LIGHT CLOSING
PRESSURE ON
CHOKE LEVER

Fast idle cam-to-choke valve adjustment—model 1945 carburetor
(© Chrysler Corp.)

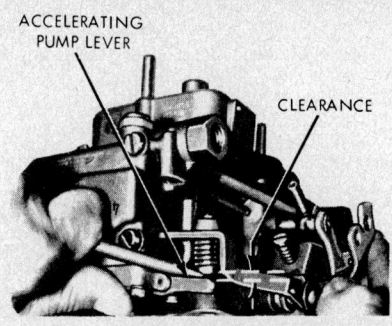

ACCELERATING
PUMP LEVER

CLEARANCE

Checking the accelerator pump lever clearance—Holley 4150 typical (© Ford Motor Co.)

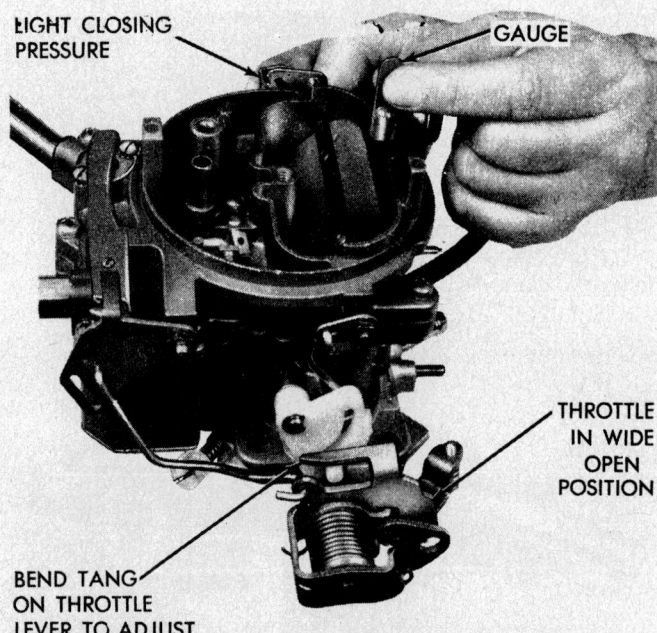

LIGHT CLOSING
PRESSURE

GAUGE

THROTTLE
IN WIDE
OPEN
POSITION

BEND TANG
ON THROTTLE
LEVER TO ADJUST

Choke unloader adjustment—models 2210, 2210C and 2245 carburetors (© Chrysler Corp.)

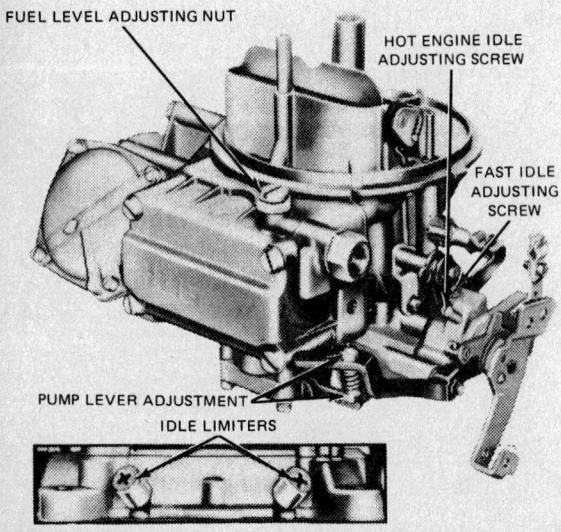

FUEL LEVEL ADJUSTING NUT

HOT ENGINE IDLE
ADJUSTING SCREW

FAST IDLE
ADJUSTING
SCREW

PUMP LEVER ADJUSTMENT

IDLE LIMITERS

Adjustment locations—model 2300 carburetor (© Chrysler Corp.)

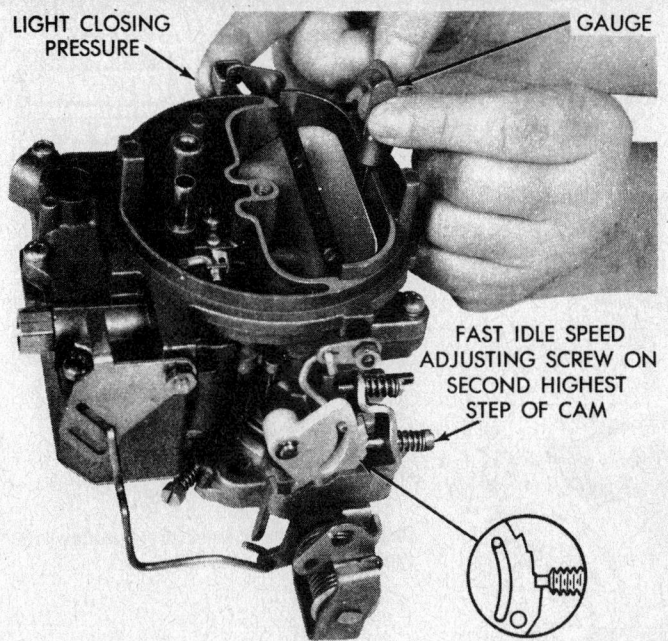

Fast idle cam position—models 2210, 2210C and 2245 carburetors (© Chrysler Corp.)

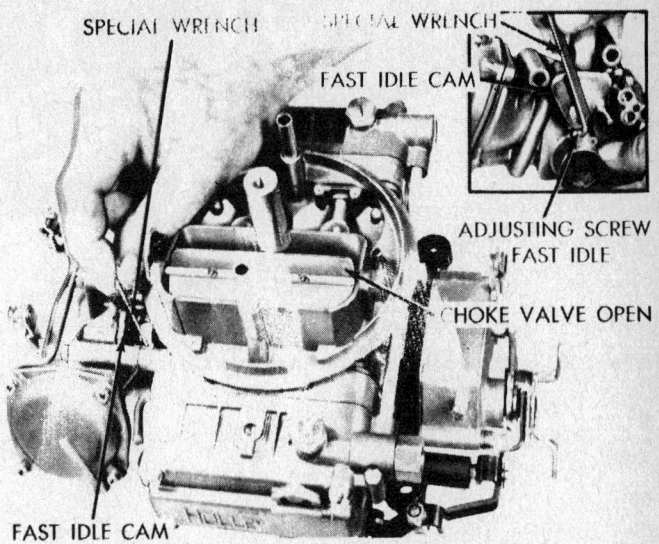

Fast idle speed adjustment—Holley 4150 typical (© Chrysler Corp.)

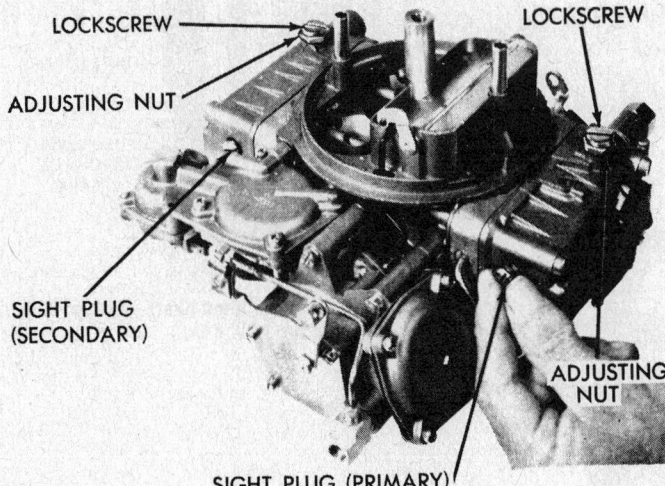

Fuel level sight plug location—Holley 4150 typical (© Chrysler Corp.)

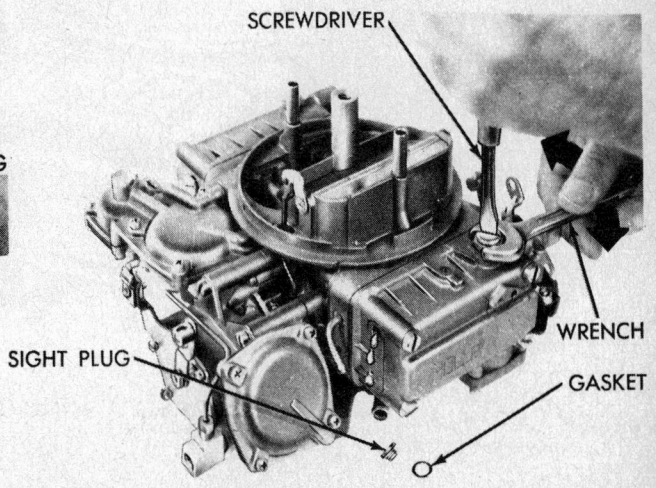

Adjusting the fuel level—Holley 4150 typical (© Chrysler Corp.)

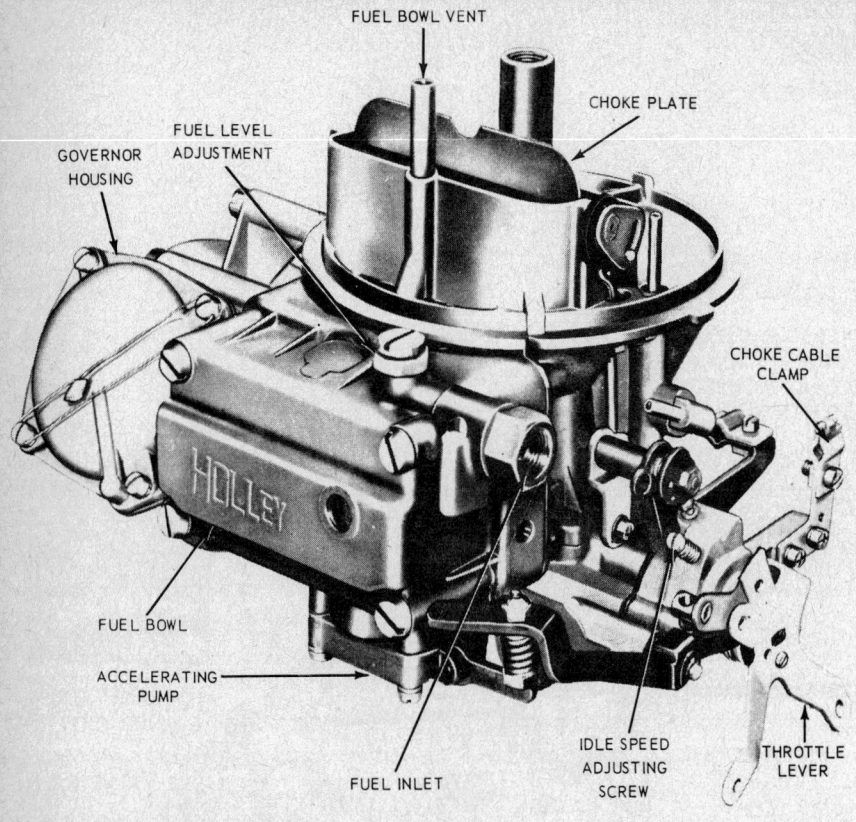

FUEL BOWL VENT

CHOKE PLATE

FUEL LEVEL ADJUSTMENT

GOVERNOR HOUSING

CHOKE CABLE CLAMP

FUEL BOWL

ACCELERATING PUMP

FUEL INLET

IDLE SPEED ADJUSTING SCREW

THROTTLE LEVER

Holley 2300 carburetor—typical (© Ford Motor Co.)

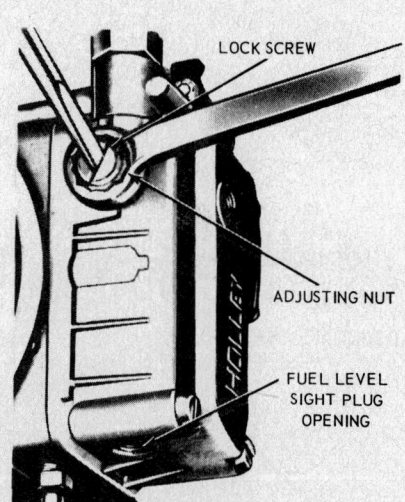

TURN ADJUSTING NUT UNTIL FLOAT IS PARALLEL WITH TOP OF BOWL (HOLDING BOWL UPSIDE DOWN)

Adjusting the float level (dry)—Holley 4150 typical (© Ford Motor Co.)

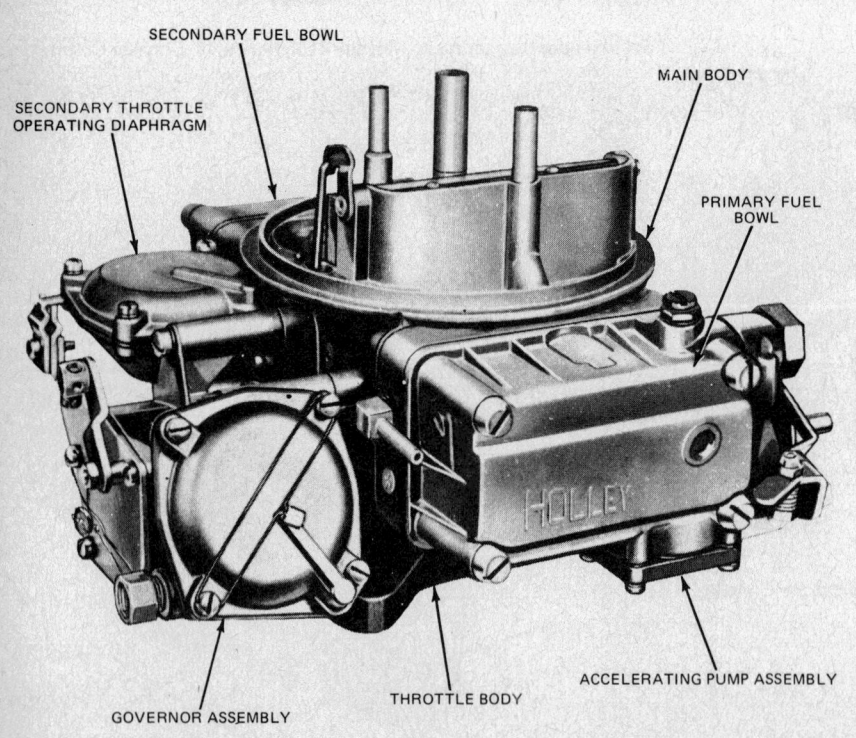

SECONDARY FUEL BOWL

SECONDARY THROTTLE OPERATING DIAPHRAGM

MAIN BODY

PRIMARY FUEL BOWL

GOVERNOR ASSEMBLY

THROTTLE BODY

ACCELERATING PUMP ASSEMBLY

Holley 4150 carburetor—typical (© Ford Motor Co.)

LOCK SCREW

ADJUSTING NUT

FUEL LEVEL SIGHT PLUG OPENING

Adjusting the fuel level (wet)—Holley 4150 typical (© Ford Motor Co.)

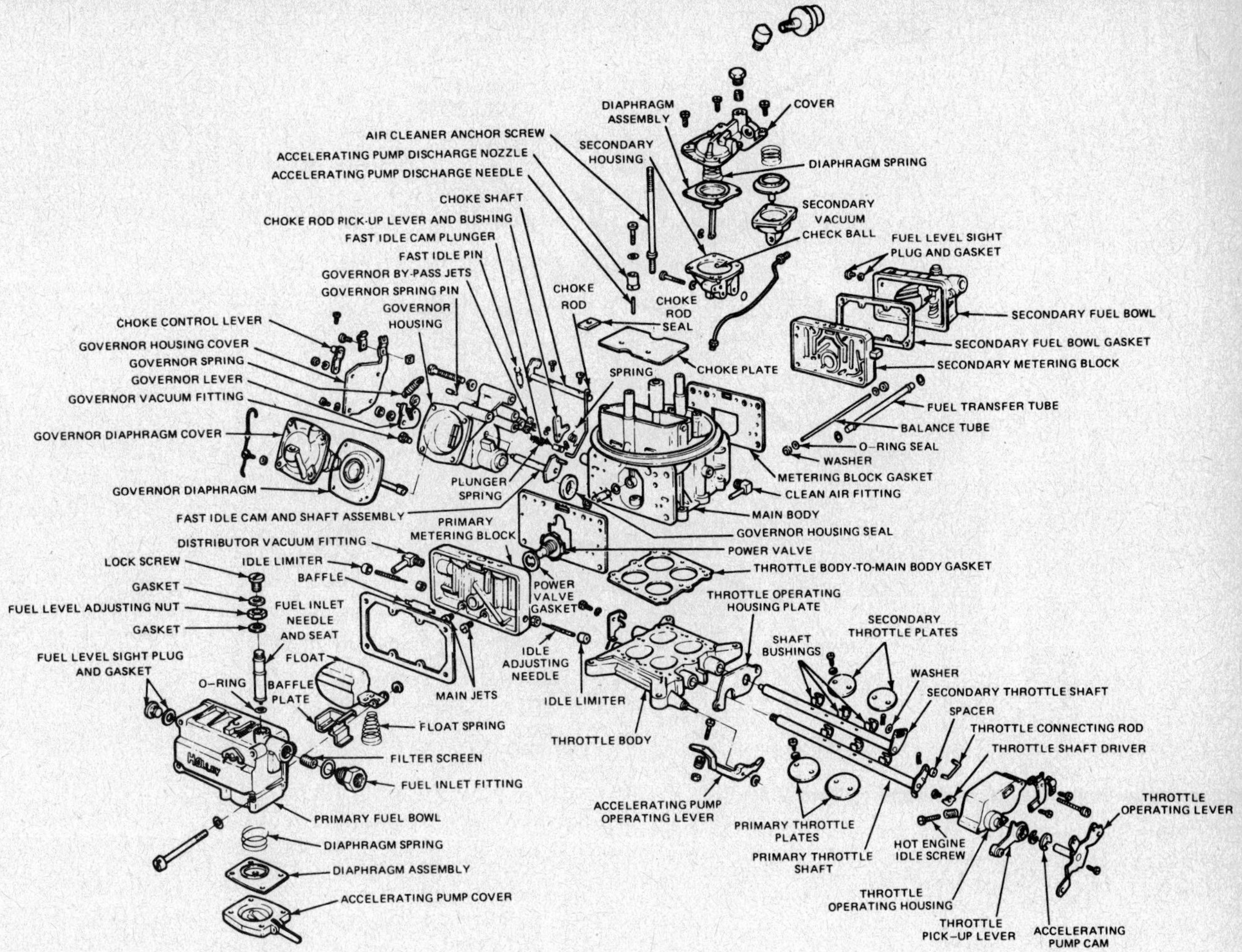

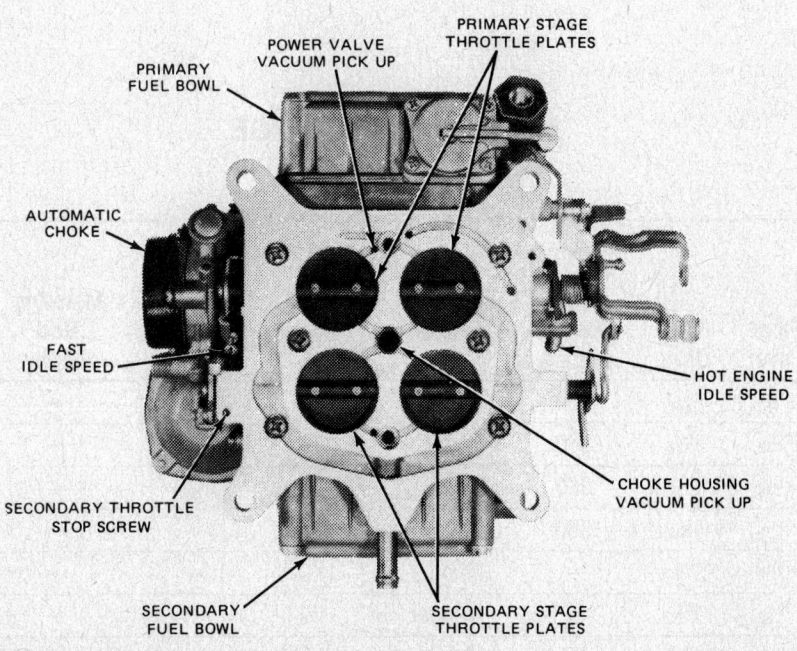

Holley four barrel—typical

- DIAPHRAGM ASSEMBLY
- COVER
- AIR CLEANER ANCHOR SCREW
- ACCELERATING PUMP DISCHARGE NOZZLE
- ACCELERATING PUMP DISCHARGE NEEDLE
- SECONDARY HOUSING
- DIAPHRAGM SPRING
- CHOKE SHAFT
- CHOKE ROD PICK-UP LEVER AND BUSHING
- FAST IDLE CAM PLUNGER
- FAST IDLE PIN
- SECONDARY VACUUM CHECK BALL
- FUEL LEVEL SIGHT PLUG AND GASKET
- GOVERNOR BY-PASS JETS
- GOVERNOR SPRING PIN
- GOVERNOR HOUSING
- CHOKE ROD
- CHOKE ROD SEAL
- SECONDARY FUEL BOWL
- CHOKE CONTROL LEVER
- GOVERNOR HOUSING COVER
- GOVERNOR SPRING
- GOVERNOR LEVER
- GOVERNOR VACUUM FITTING
- GOVERNOR DIAPHRAGM COVER
- SPRING
- CHOKE PLATE
- SECONDARY FUEL BOWL GASKET
- SECONDARY METERING BLOCK
- FUEL TRANSFER TUBE
- BALANCE TUBE
- O-RING SEAL
- WASHER
- METERING BLOCK GASKET
- CLEAN AIR FITTING
- GOVERNOR DIAPHRAGM
- PLUNGER SPRING
- FAST IDLE CAM AND SHAFT ASSEMBLY
- PRIMARY METERING BLOCK
- MAIN BODY
- GOVERNOR HOUSING SEAL
- POWER VALVE
- THROTTLE BODY-TO-MAIN BODY GASKET
- DISTRIBUTOR VACUUM FITTING
- LOCK SCREW
- GASKET
- IDLE LIMITER
- BAFFLE
- POWER VALVE GASKET
- THROTTLE OPERATING HOUSING PLATE
- SECONDARY THROTTLE PLATES
- SHAFT BUSHINGS
- FUEL LEVEL ADJUSTING NUT
- GASKET
- FUEL INLET NEEDLE AND SEAT
- IDLE ADJUSTING NEEDLE
- WASHER
- SECONDARY THROTTLE SHAFT
- SPACER
- THROTTLE CONNECTING ROD
- THROTTLE SHAFT DRIVER
- FUEL LEVEL SIGHT PLUG AND GASKET
- O-RING
- FLOAT
- BAFFLE PLATE
- MAIN JETS
- IDLE LIMITER
- FLOAT SPRING
- THROTTLE BODY
- ACCELERATING PUMP OPERATING LEVER
- PRIMARY THROTTLE PLATES
- PRIMARY THROTTLE SHAFT
- HOT ENGINE IDLE SCREW
- THROTTLE OPERATING LEVER
- FILTER SCREEN
- FUEL INLET FITTING
- PRIMARY FUEL BOWL
- DIAPHRAGM SPRING
- DIAPHRAGM ASSEMBLY
- ACCELERATING PUMP COVER
- THROTTLE OPERATING HOUSING
- THROTTLE PICK-UP LEVER
- ACCELERATING PUMP CAM

- PRIMARY FUEL BOWL
- POWER VALVE VACUUM PICK UP
- PRIMARY STAGE THROTTLE PLATES
- AUTOMATIC CHOKE
- FAST IDLE SPEED
- HOT ENGINE IDLE SPEED
- SECONDARY THROTTLE STOP SCREW
- CHOKE HOUSING VACUUM PICK UP
- SECONDARY FUEL BOWL
- SECONDARY STAGE THROTTLE PLATES

Bottom view—Holley 4160C carburetor (© Ford Motor Co.)

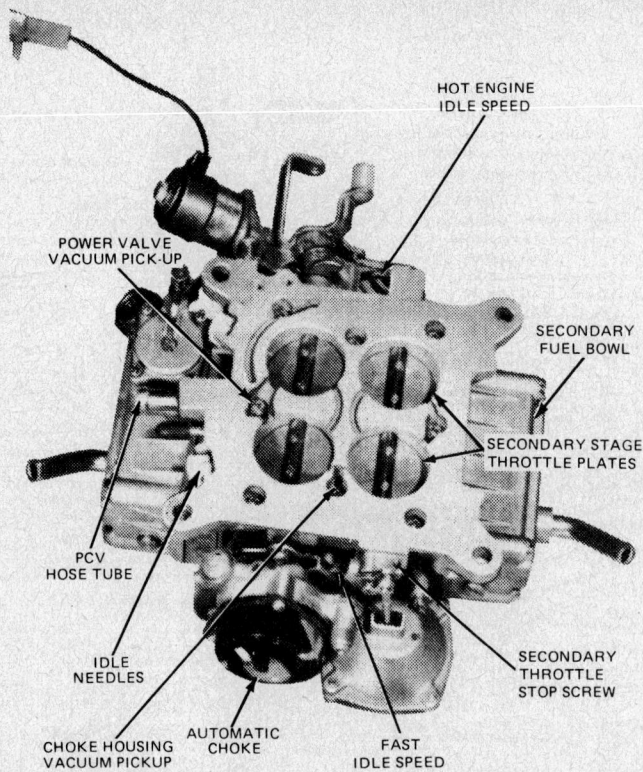

POWER VALVE
VACUUM PICK-UP

HOT ENGINE
IDLE SPEED

SECONDARY
FUEL BOWL

SECONDARY STAGE
THROTTLE PLATES

PCV
HOSE TUBE

IDLE
NEEDLES

CHOKE HOUSING
VACUUM PICKUP

AUTOMATIC
CHOKE

FAST
IDLE SPEED

SECONDARY
THROTTLE
STOP SCREW

Bottom view—Holley 4180C carburetor (© Ford Motor Co.)

MODEL 2GV/2GC/2GE
Chevrolet/GMC
(All measurements in inches)

Year	Carburetor Number	Float Level	Float Drop	Choke Unloader Setting	Choke Setting	Pump Rod Location	Fast Idle Speed (RPM)	Metering Rod Setting	Fast Idle Cam 2nd Step	Choke Vacuum Break
'75	7045115	$^{21}/_{32}$	$^{31}/_{32}$	.350	Index	$1^{5}/_{8}$	—	—	.400	.130
	7045116	$^{21}/_{32}$	$^{31}/_{32}$	.350	Index	$1^{5}/_{8}$	—	—	.400	.130
	7045123	$^{21}/_{32}$	$^{31}/_{32}$	.350	Index	$1^{5}/_{8}$	—	—	.400	.130
	7045124	$^{21}/_{32}$	$^{31}/_{32}$	.350	Index	$1^{5}/_{8}$	—	—	.400	.130
	7044133	$^{19}/_{32}$	$1^{9}/_{32}$	—	Manual	$1^{9}/_{16}$	—	—	—	—
	7044134	$^{19}/_{32}$	$1^{9}/_{32}$	—	Manual	$1^{7}/_{16}$	—	—	—	—
	7044434	$^{19}/_{32}$	$1^{9}/_{32}$	—	Manual	$1^{7}/_{16}$	—	—	—	—

MODEL 2GV/2GC/2GE
Chevrolet/GMC
(All measurements in inches)

Year	Carburetor Number	Float Level	Float Drop	Choke Unloader Setting	Choke Setting	Pump Rod Location	Fast Idle Speed (RPM)	Metering Rod Setting	Fast Idle Cam 2nd Step	Choke Vacuum Break
'76	7044133	$^{19}/_{32}$	$1^9/_{32}$	—	—	$1^9/_{16}$	—	—	—	—
	7044134	$^{19}/_{32}$	$1^9/_{32}$	—	—	$1^7/_{16}$	—	—	—	—
	704434	$^{19}/_{32}$	$1^9/_{32}$	—	—	$1^7/_{16}$	—	—	—	—
	17056115	$^{21}/_{32}$	$1^9/_{32}$	.325	Index	$1^{11}/_{16}$	—	—	.260	.130
	17056116	$^{21}/_{32}$	$1^9/_{32}$	.325	1 Rich	$1^{11}/_{16}$	—	—	.260	.130
	17056123	$^{21}/_{32}$	$1^9/_{32}$	.325	Index	$1^{11}/_{16}$	—	—	.260	.130
	17056124	$^{21}/_{32}$	$1^9/_{32}$	.325	1 Rich	$1^{11}/_{16}$	—	—	.260	.130
'77	7044133	$^{19}/_{32}$	$1^9/_{32}$	.325	Index	$1^{21}/_{32}$	—	—	.260	.130
	7044134	$^{19}/_{32}$	$1^9/_{32}$	.325	Index	$1^{21}/_{32}$	—	—	.260	.130
	17056433	$^{19}/_{32}$	$1^9/_{32}$	.325	Index	$1^{21}/_{32}$	—	—	.260	.130
	17056434	$^{19}/_{32}$	$1^9/_{32}$	.325	Index	$1^{21}/_{32}$	—	—	.260	.130
	17056137	$^{19}/_{32}$	$1^9/_{32}$	.325	Index	$1^{21}/_{32}$	—	—	.260	.190
'78	7044133	$^{19}/_{32}$	$1^9/_{32}$	—	Manual	$1^9/_{16}$	—	—	—	—
	7044134	$^{19}/_{32}$	$1^9/_{32}$	—	Manual	$1^7/_{16}$	—	—	—	—
	17058423	$^{19}/_{32}$	$1^9/_{32}$	—	Manual	$1^9/_{16}$	—	—	—	—
	17058424	$^{19}/_{32}$	$1^9/_{32}$	—	Manual	$1^7/_{16}$	—	—	—	—
	17058104	$^{15}/_{32}$	$1^9/_{32}$	.325	Index	$1^{21}/_{32}$	—	—	.260	.130
	17058105	$^{15}/_{32}$	$1^9/_{32}$	.325	Index	$1^{21}/_{32}$	—	—	.260	.130
	17058107	$^{15}/_{32}$	$1^9/_{32}$	.325	Index	$1^{17}/_{32}$	—	—	.260	.130
	17058109	$^{15}/_{32}$	$1^9/_{32}$	.325	Index	$1^{17}/_{32}$	—	—	.260	.130
	17058102	$^{15}/_{32}$	$1^9/_{32}$	.325	Index	$1^{17}/_{32}$	—	—	.260	.130
	17058103	$^{15}/_{32}$	$1^9/_{32}$	.325	Index	$1^{17}/_{32}$	—	—	.260	.130
	17058405	$^{1}/_{2}$	$1^9/_{32}$	.325	½ Lean	$1^{21}/_{32}$	—	—	.260	.140
	17058405	$^{1}/_{2}$	$1^9/_{32}$	.325	½ Lean	$1^{21}/_{32}$	—	—	.260	.140
	17058447	$^{7}/_{16}$	$1^5/_{32}$	.140	1 Rich	$1^5/_{8}$	—	—	.080	.110
	17058143	$^{7}/_{16}$	$1^5/_{32}$	.140	1 Rich	$1^5/_{8}$	—	—	.080	.040
	17058147	$^{7}/_{16}$	$1^5/_{32}$	.140	1 Rich	$1^5/_{8}$	—	—	.080	.100
	17058144	$^{7}/_{16}$	$1^5/_{32}$	.140	1 Rich	$1^5/_{8}$	—	—	.080	.060
'79	7044133	$^{19}/_{32}$	$1^9/_{32}$	—	Index	$1^9/_{16}$	—	—	—	—
	7044134	$^{19}/_{32}$	$1^9/_{32}$	—	Index	$1^7/_{16}$	—	—	—	—
	17059126	$^{5}/_{8}$	$1^9/_{32}$	—	Index	$1^{15}/_{32}$	—	—	—	—
	17059127	$^{17}/_{32}$	$1^9/_{32}$	—	Index	$1^{15}/_{32}$	—	—	—	—
	17059423	$^{5}/_{8}$	$1^9/_{32}$	—	Index	$1^{21}/_{32}$	—	—	—	—
	17059424	$^{17}/_{32}$	$1^9/_{32}$	—	Index	$1^{15}/_{32}$	—	—	—	—
	17059420	$^{17}/_{32}$	$1^9/_{32}$	—	Index	$1^{15}/_{32}$	—	—	—	—

MODEL 2G/2GV
Chevrolet/GMC
(All measurements in inches)

Year	Carburetor Number	Float Level	Float Drop	Choke Unloader	Choke Setting	Pump Rod Adj.	Fast Idle (rpm)	Metering Rod Setting	Fast Idle Cam 2nd step	Choke Vacuum Break
'80	7044133	$^{11}/_{16}$	$1^9/_{32}$	—	Manual	$1^9/_{16}$	—	—	—	—
	7044134	$^{11}/_{16}$	$1^9/_{32}$	—	Manual	$1^7/_{16}$	—	—	—	—
	17058120	$^{11}/_{16}$	$1^9/_{32}$	—	Manual	$1^{21}/_{32}$	—	—	—	—
	17080120	$^5/_8$	$1^9/_{32}$	—	Manual	$1^{21}/_{32}$	—	—	—	—
	17080126	$^5/_8$	$1^9/_{32}$	—	Manual	$1^{21}/_{32}$	—	—	—	—
	17080127	$^5/_8$	$1^9/_{32}$	—	Manual	$1^{21}/_{32}$	—	—	—	—
	17080129	$^5/_8$	$1^9/_{32}$	—	Index	$1^{21}/_{32}$	—	—	—	.130
	17080420	$^5/_8$	$1^9/_{32}$	—	Manual	$1^{21}/_{32}$	—	—	—	—
	17080423	$^5/_8$	$1^9/_{32}$	—	Manual	$1^{21}/_{32}$	—	—	—	—
	17080424	$^5/_8$	$1^9/_{32}$	—	Manual	$1^{21}/_{32}$	—	—	—	—

MODEL M2MC/M2ME
Chevrolet/GMC
(All measurements in inches)

Year	Carburetor Number	Float Level	Float Drop	Choke Unloader	Choke Setting	Pump① Rod Adj.	Fast② Idle (rpm)	Metering Rod Setting	Fast Idle Cam Setting	Choke Vacuum Break
'79	17059100	$^{15}/_{32}$	—	—	1 Lean	$^{13}/_{32}$	1600	—	38°	29°
	17059101	$^{15}/_{32}$	—	—	1 Lean	$^{13}/_{32}$	1600	—	38°	29°
	17059102	$^{15}/_{32}$	—	—	1 Lean	$^{13}/_{32}$	1600	—	38°	29°
	17059103	$^{15}/_{32}$	—	—	1 Lean	$^{13}/_{32}$	1600	—	38°	29°
	17059142	$^{15}/_{32}$	—	—	1 Lean	$^{13}/_{32}$	1600	—	38°	29°
	17059143	$^{15}/_{32}$	—	—	1 Lean	$^{13}/_{32}$	1600	—	38°	29°
	17059144	$^{15}/_{32}$	—	—	1 Lean	$^{13}/_{32}$	1600	—	38°	29°
	17059145	$^{15}/_{32}$	—	—	1 Lean	$^{13}/_{32}$	1600	—	38°	29°
'80	17080100	$^7/_{16}$	—	38°	—	$^9/_{32}$	③	—	38°	29°
	17080102	$^7/_{16}$	—	38°	—	$^9/_{32}$	③	—	38°	29°
	17080142	$^7/_{16}$	—	38°	—	$^9/_{32}$	③	—	38°	29°
	17080143	$^7/_{16}$	—	38°	—	$^9/_{32}$	③	—	38°	29°
	17080145	$^7/_{16}$	—	38°	—	$^9/_{32}$	③	—	38°	29°
'81	17081101	$^{13}/_{32}$	—	38°	—	$^5/_{16}$	③	—	38°	29°
	17081103	$^{13}/_{32}$	—	38°	—	$^5/_{16}$	③	—	38°	29°
	17081142	$^{13}/_{32}$	—	38°	—	$^5/_{16}$	③	—	38°	29°
	17081143	$^{13}/_{32}$	—	38°	—	$^5/_{16}$	③	—	38°	29°
	17081144	$^{13}/_{32}$	—	38°	—	$^5/_{16}$	③	—	38°	29°
	17081145	$^{13}/_{32}$	—	38°	—	$^5/_{16}$	③	—	38°	29°

① Rod installed in the inner hole of the pump lever (nearest the carburetor)
② Manual transmission—1300 rpm in neutral
③ See underhood emissions label for idle speed specifications

MODEL IMV
Chevrolet/GMC
(All measurements in inches)

Year	Carburetor Number	Float Level	Float Drop	Choke Unloader Setting	Choke Setting	Pump Rod Location	Fast Idle Speed (RPM)	Metering Rod Setting	Fast Idle Cam 2nd Step	Choke Vacuum Break
'75	7045002	11/32	—	.325	Fixed	—	1800	.080	.260	①
	7045003	11/32	—	.325	Fixed	—	1800	.080	.275	①
	7045004	11/32	—	.325	Fixed	—	1800	.080	.245	①
	7045005	11/32	—	.325	Fixed	—	1800	.080	.275	②
	7045302	11/32	—	.275	Fixed	—	1800	.080	.245	①
	7045303	11/32	—	.275	Fixed	—	1800	.080	.275	②
	7045304	11/32	—	.325	Fixed	—	1800	.080	.245	①
	7045305	11/32	—	.325	Fixed	—	1800	.080	.275	②
'76	17056002	11/32	—	.335	Fixed	—	2100	.080	.130	③
	17056003	11/32	—	.335	Fixed	—	2100	.080	.145	.180
	17056004	11/32	—	.335	Fixed	—	2100	.080	.130	③
	17056006	1/4	—	.270	Fixed	—	2100	.080	.130	.165
	17056007	1/4	—	.275	Fixed	—	2100	.070	.130	.165
	17056008	1/4	—	.275	Fixed	—	2100	.070	.150	.190
	17056009	1/4	—	.275	Fixed	—	2100	.080	.150	.190
	17056302	11/32	—	.325	Fixed	—	2100	.080	.155	.190
	17056303	11/32	—	.325	Fixed	—	2100	.080	.180	.225
	17056308	1/4	—	.275	Fixed	—	2100	.070	.150	.190
	17056309	1/4	—	.275	Fixed	—	2100	.070	.150	.190

① Primary—.300 Secondary—.325 ② Primary—.350 Secondary—.325 ③ Primary—.165 Auxiliary—.265

MODEL IME/IM
Chevrolet/GMC
(All measurements in inches)

Year	Carburetor Number	Float Level	Float Drop	Choke Unloader Setting	Choke Setting	Pump Rod Location	Fast Idle Speed (RPM)	Metering Rod Setting	Fast Idle Cam 2nd Step	Choke Vacuum Break
'77	17057001	3/8	—	.325	Index	—	2100	.080	.125	.150
	17057002	3/8	—	.325	Index	—	2100	.080	.110	.135
	17057004	3/8	—	.325	Index	—	2100	.080	.110	.135
	17057005	3/8	—	.325	Index	—	2100	.080	.125	.180
	17057010	3/8	—	.325	Index	—	2100	.080	.110	.180
	17057302	3/8	—	.325	Index	—	2100	.080	.150	.135
	17057303	3/8	—	.325	Index	—	2100	.090	.125	.150

CARBURETORS
ROCHESTER

MODEL IME/IM
Chevrolet/GMC
(All measurements in inches)

Year	Carburetor Number	Float Level	Float Drop	Choke Unloader Setting	Choke Setting	Pump Rod Location	Fast Idle Speed (RPM)	Metering Rod Setting	Fast Idle Cam 2nd Step	Choke Vacuum Break
	17057006	5/16	—	.275	Index	—	2400	.070	.150	.180
	17057007	5/16	—	.275	Index	—	2400	.070	.150	.180
	17057008	5/16	—	.275	Index	—	2400	.065	.150	.180
	17057009	5/16	—	.275	Index	—	2400	②.065		
	17057308	5/16	—	.275	Index	—	2400	.065	.150	.180
	17057309	5/16	—	.275	Index	—	2400	.065	.150	.180
'78	17058009	1/4	—	—	Index	—	2400①	.065	—	—
	17058011	1/4	—	—	Index	—	2400①	.065	—	—
	17058423	19/32	1 9/32	—	Index	1 9/16	—	—	—	—
	17058434	19/32	1 9/32	—	Index	1 7/16	—	—	—	—
	7044133	19/32	1 9/32	—	Index	1 9/16	—	—	—	—
	7044134	19/32	1 9/32	—	Index	1 7/16	—	—	—	—
	17058013	3/8	—	.500	Index	—	2000①	.080	.180	.200
	17058014	5/16	—	.500	Index	—	2100①	.100	.180	.200
	17058020	5/16	—	.500	Index	—	2100①	.100	.180	.200
	17058314	3/8	—	.400	Index	—	2000①	.100	.190	.245
'79	17058009	1/4	—	—	Index	—	2400	.065	—	—
	17058011	1/4	—	—	Index	—	2400	.065	—	—
	17059009	5/16	—	.520	2 Rich	—	2400	.065②	.275	.400
	17059309	5/16	—	.521	2 Rich	—	2400	.065	.275	.400
	17059359	5/16	—	.521	2 Rich	—	2400	.065	.275	.400
'80	17080009	11/32	—	.520	③	—	2400	.090	.275	.400
	17080309	11/32	—	.520	③	—	2400	.090	.275	.400
	17080359	11/32	—	.520	③	—	2400	.090	.275	.400
'81	17081009	11/32	—	.520	③	—	④	.090	.275	.400
	17081309	11/32	—	.520	③	—	④	.090	.275	.400
	17081329	11/32	—	.520	③	—	④	.090	.275	.400

① In neutral
② .090 inches on medium duty truck applications
③ Not adjustable
④ See emission label under hood of vehicle

MODEL 2SE
Chevrolet/GMC
(All measurements in inches)

Year	Carburetor Number	Float Level	Float Drop	Choke① Unloader	Choke Setting	Pump③ Rod Adj.	Fast Idle (rpm)	Metering Rod Setting	Fast Idle① Cam 2nd step	Choke① Vacuum Break
'79	17059640	⅛	—	49°	②	9/16	2000	—	—	20°
	17059641	⅛	—	49°	②	9/16	1800	—	—	23.5°
	17059643	⅛	—	49°	②	9/16	1800	—	—	23.5°
	17059740	⅛	—	49°	②	9/16	2000	—	—	20°
	17059741	⅛	—	49°	②	9/16	2100	—	—	20°
	17059764	⅛	—	49°	②	9/16	2100	—	—	20°
	17059765	⅛	—	49°	②	9/16	2100	—	—	23.5°
	17059767	⅛	—	49°	②	9/16	2100	—	—	23.5°
'80	17080621	⅛	—	41°	⑤	9/16	④	—	17°	22°
	17080622	⅛	—	41°	⑤	9/16	④	—	17°	22°
	17080623	⅛	—	41°	⑤	9/16	④	—	17°	22°
	17080626	⅛	—	41°	⑤	9/16	④	—	17°	22°
	17080720	⅛	—	41°	⑤	9/16	④	—	17°	22°
	17080721	⅛	—	41°	⑤	9/16	④	—	17°	23.5°
	17080722	⅛	—	41°	⑤	9/16	④	—	17°	20°
	17080723	⅛	—	41°	⑤	9/16	④	—	17°	23.5°
'81	17081621	3/16	—	38°	⑤	⅝	④	—	15°	38°
	17081622	3/16	—	38°	⑤	⅝	④	—	15°	38°
	17081623	3/16	—	38°	⑤	⅝	④	—	15°	38°
	17081624	3/16	—	38°	⑤	⅝	④	—	15°	38°
	17081625	3/16	—	38°	⑤	⅝	④	—	15°	38°
	17081626	3/16	—	38°	⑤	⅝	④	—	15°	38°
	17081627	3/16	—	38°	⑤	⅝	④	—	15°	38°
	17081629	3/16	—	41°	⑤	⅝	④	—	15°	38°
	17081630	3/16	—	38°	⑤	⅝	④	—	15°	38°
	17081633	3/16	—	38°	⑤	⅝	④	—	15°	38°
	17081720	3/16	—	41°	⑤	⅝	④	—	15°	38°
	17081721	3/16	—	41°	⑤	⅝	④	—	15°	38°
	17081725	3/16	—	41°	⑤	⅝	④	—	15°	38°
	17081726	3/16	—	41°	⑤	⅝	④	—	15°	38°
	17081727	3/16	—	41°	⑤	⅝	④	—	15°	38°

① Use angle degree tool or change over to decimal equivalent on the conversion chart at the end of this section
② 1 notch counterclockwise
③ Measure distance from air horn casting
④ See emissions label underhood for exact rpm specification
⑤ Riveted choke cap is not adjustable under normal circumstances

MODEL M4MC/4MV
QUADRAJET FOUR BARREL
Chevrolet/GMC
(All measurements in inches)

Year	Model or Type	Float Level	Air Valve Dashpot	PUMP ROD Adj.	PUMP ROD Hole	Initial Choke Valve Opening	Vacuum Break	Choke Unloader	Air Valve Spring Wind-up
'75	7045212	3/8	.015	.275	Inner	.430	.225	.450	7/16
	7045213	11/32	.015	.275	Inner	.430	.210	.450	7/8
	7045214	11/32	.015	.275	Inner	.430	.215	.450	7/8
	7045215	11/32	.015	.275	Inner	.430	.215	.450	7/8
	7045216	11/32	.015	.275	Inner	.430	.210	.450	7/8
	7045217	3/8	.015	.275	Inner	.430	.225	.450	7/16
	7045225	11/32	.015	.275	Inner	.430	.200	.450	3/4
	7045229	15/32	.015	.275	Inner	.430	.200	.450	3/4
	7045583	11/32	.015	.275	Inner	.430	.230	.450	7/8
	7045584	11/32	.015	.275	Inner	.430	.230	.450	7/8
	7045585	11/32	.015	.275	Inner	.430	.230	.450	7/8
	7045586	11/32	.015	.275	Inner	.430	.230	.450	7/8
	7045588	11/32	.015	.275	Inner	.430	.230	.450	3/4
	7045589	11/32	.015	.275	Inner	.430	.230	.450	3/4
	7045202	15/32	.015	.275	Inner	.300	.180/.170	.325	7/8
	7045203	15/32	.015	.275	Inner	.300	.180/.170	.325	7/8
	7045218	15/32	.015	.275	Inner	.325	.180/.170	.352	3/4
	7045219	15/32	.015	.275	Inner	.325	.180/.170	.352	3/4
	7045220	17/32	.015	.275	Inner	.300	.200/.550	.325	9/16
	7045512	17/32	.015	.275	Inner	.300	.180/.550	.325	9/16
	7045517	17/32	.015	.275	Inner	.300	.180/.550	.325	9/16
'76	7045213	11/32	.015	9/32	Inner	.290	.145	.295	7/8
	7045214	11/32	.015	9/32	Inner	.290	.145	.295	7/8
	7045215	11/32	.015	9/32	Inner	.290	.145	.295	7/8
	7045216	11/32	.015	9/32	Inner	.290	.145	.295	7/8
	7045225	11/32	.015	9/32	Inner	.290	.138	.295	3/4
	7045229	11/32	.015	9/32	Inner	.290	.138	.295	3/4
	7045583	11/32	.015	9/32	Inner	.290	.155	.295	7/8
	7045584	11/32	.015	9/32	Inner	.290	.155	.295	7/8
	7045585	11/32	.015	9/32	Inner	.290	.155	.295	7/8
	7045586	11/32	.015	9/32	Inner	.290	.155	.295	7/8
	7045588	11/32	.015	9/32	Inner	.290	.155	.295	3/4
	7045589	11/32	.015	9/32	Inner	.290	.155	.295	3/4
	17056212	3/8	.015	9/32	Inner	.290	.155	.295	7/16
	17056217	3/8	.015	9/32	Inner	.290	.155	.295	7/16
	17056208	7/16	.015	9/32	Inner	.325	.185	.325	7/8

MODEL M4MC/4MV
QUADRAJET FOUR BARREL
Chevrolet/GMC

(All measurements in inches)

Year	Model or Type	Float Level	Air Valve Dashpot	PUMP ROD Adj.	PUMP ROD Hole	Initial Choke Valve Opening	Vacuum Break	Choke Unloader	Air Valve Spring Wind-up
	17056209	7/16	.015	9/32	Inner	.325	.185	.325	7/8
	17056218	5/16	.015	9/32	Inner	.325	.185	.325	7/8
	17056219	5/16	.015	9/32	Inner	.325	.185	.325	7/8
	17056508	7/16	.015	9/32	Inner	.325	.185	.325	7/8
	17056509	7/16	.015	9/32	Inner	.325	.185	.325	7/8
	17056512	7/16	.015	9/32	Inner	.325	.185	.275	7/8
	17056517	7/16	.015	9/32	Inner	.325	.185	.275	7/8
	17056518	5/16	.015	9/32	Inner	.325	.185	.325	7/8
	17056519	5/16	.015	9/32	Inner	.325	.185	.325	7/8
'77	17057202	15/32	.015	9/32	Inner	.325	.160	.280	7/8
	17057204	15/32	.015	9/32	Inner	.325	.160	.280	7/8
	17057502	15/32	.015	9/32	Inner	.325	.165	.280	7/8
	17057582	15/32	.015	3/8	Outer	.325	.182	.280	7/8
	17057584	15/32	.015	3/8	Outer	.325	.180	.280	7/8
	17057503	15/32	.015	9/32	Inner	.325	.165	.280	7/8
	17057504	15/32	.015	9/32	Inner	.325	.165	.280	7/8
	17057209	7/16	.015	9/32	Inner	.325	—	.325	7/8
	17057218	7/16	.015	9/32	Inner	.325	.160	.280	7/8
	17057222	7/16	.015	9/32	Inner	.325	.160	.280	7/8
	17057518	7/16	.015	9/32	Inner	.325	.165	.280	7/8
	17057522	7/16	.015	9/32	Inner	.325	.165	.280	7/8
	17057586	7/16	.015	3/8	Outer	.325	.180	.295	7/8
	17057588	7/16	.015	3/8	Outer	.325	.180	.280	7/8
	17057219	7/16	.015	9/32	Inner	.325	.165	.280	7/8
	17057519	7/16	.015	9/32	Inner	.325	.165	.280	7/8
	17057512	7/16	.015	9/32	Inner	.325	.165	.240	7/8
	17057517	7/16	.015	9/32	Inner	.325	.165	.240	7/16
	17056212	3/8	.015	9/32	Inner	.290	.120	.295	7/16
	17057221	3/8	.015	9/32	Inner	.325	.160	.325	7/8
	17056217	3/8	.015	9/32	Inner	.290	.120	.295	7/16
	17057213	11/32	.015	9/32	Inner	.285	.115	.205	7/8
	17057215	11/32	.015	9/32	Inner	.285	.115	.205	7/8
	17057216	11/32	.015	9/32	Inner	.285	.115	.205	7/8
	17057525	11/32	.015	9/32	Inner	.285	.120	.225	3/4
	17057514	11/32	.015	9/32	Inner	.285	.120	.280	7/8
	17507529	11/32	.015	9/32	Inner	.285	.110	.205	7/8

MODEL M4MC/4MV
QUADRAJET FOUR BARREL
Chevrolet/GMC
(All measurements in inches)

Year	Model or Type	Float Level	Air Valve Dashpot	PUMP ROD Adj.	PUMP ROD Hole	Initial Choke Valve Opening	Vacuum Break	Choke Unloader	Air Valve Spring Wind-up
	17057229	11/32	.015	9/32	Inner	.285	.110	.205	7/8
	7045583	11/32	.015	9/32	Inner	.285	.120	.295	7/8
	7045585	11/32	.015	9/32	Inner	.285	.120	.295	7/8
	7045586	11/32	.015	3/8	Outer	.285	.120	.295	7/8
'78	17058201	15/32	.015	9/32	Inner	.314	.168	.277	7/8
	17058213	15/32	.015	9/32	Inner	.217	.095	.204	7/8
	17058215	15/32	.015	9/32	Inner	.217	.095	.204	7/8
	17058229	15/32	.015	9/32	Inner	.217	.095	.204	7/8
	17058503	15/32	.015	9/32	Inner	.217	.179	.277	7/8
	17058506	15/32	.015	9/32	Inner	.314	.179	.277	7/8
	17058508	15/32	.015	9/32	Inner	.314	.179	.277	7/8
	17058509	15/32	.015	11/32	Outer	.314	.179	.277	7/8
	17058510	15/32	.015	11/32	Outer	.314	.179	.277	7/8
	17058513	15/32	.015	9/32	Inner	.314	.120	.225	7/8
	17058514	15/32	.015	9/32	Inner	.217	.120	.225	7/8
	17058515	15/32	.015	9/32	Inner	.217	.120	.225	7/8
	17058518	15/32	.015	9/32	Inner	.217	.179	.277	7/8
	17058519	15/32	.015	9/32	Inner	.314	.179	.277	7/8
	17058522	15/32	.015	9/32	Inner	.314	.179	.277	7/8
	17058523	15/32	.015	9/32	Inner	.314	.179	.277	7/8
	17058524	15/32	.015	9/32	Inner	.314	.179	.277	7/8
	17058527	15/32	.015	9/32	Inner	.314	.179	.277	7/8
	17058528	15/32	.015	9/32	Inner	.314	.179	.277	7/8
	17058529	15/32	.015	9/32	Inner	.314	.112	.277	7/8
	17058586	15/32	.015	11/32	Outer	.314	.179	.277	7/8
	17058588	15/32	.015	11/32	Outer	.314	.179	.277	7/8
	17058212	7/16	.015	9/32	Inner	.217	.120	.225	7/8
	17058218	7/16	.015	9/32	Inner	.314	.157	.277	7/8
	17058219	7/16	.015	9/32	Inner	.314	.168	.277	7/8
	17058222	7/16	.015	9/32	Inner	.314	.157	.277	7/8
	17058525	7/16	.015	9/32	Inner	.314	.120	.277	3/4
	17058501	3/8	.015	9/32	Inner	.314	.164	.277	7/8
	17058520	3/8	.015	9/32	Inner	.314	.164	.277	7/8
	17058521	3/8	.015	9/32	Inner	.314	.164	.277	7/8
	17058512	13/32	.015	9/32	Index	.314	.168	.260	7/8
'79	17059212	7/16	.015	9/32	Inner	.314	.136	.260	3/4

MODEL M4MC/4MV
QUADRAJET FOUR BARREL
Chevrolet/GMC
(All measurements in inches)

Year	Model or Type	Float Level	Air Valve Dashpot	PUMP ROD Adj.	PUMP ROD Hole	Initial Choke Valve Opening	Vacuum Break	Choke Unloader	Air Valve Spring Wind-up
	17059512	¹³⁄₃₂	.015	⁹⁄₃₂	Inner	.314	.136	.260	¾
	17059061	¹⁵⁄₃₂	.015	¹³⁄₃₂	Inner	.314	.129	.277	⅞
	17059201	¹⁵⁄₃₂	.015	¹³⁄₃₂	Inner	.314	.129	.277	⅞
	17059065	¹⁵⁄₃₂	.015	¹³⁄₃₂	Inner	.314	.129	.277	⅞
	17059205	¹⁵⁄₃₂	.015	¹³⁄₃₂	Inner	.314	.129	.277	⅞
	17059066	¹⁵⁄₃₂	.015	¹³⁄₃₂	Inner	.314	.129	.277	⅞
	17059206	¹⁵⁄₃₂	.015	¹³⁄₃₂	Inner	.314	.129	.277	⅞
	17059068	¹⁵⁄₃₂	.015	¹³⁄₃₂	Inner	.314	.129	.277	⅞
	17059208	¹⁵⁄₃₂	.015	¹³⁄₃₂	Inner	.314	.129	.277	⅞
	17059069	¹⁵⁄₃₂	.015	¹³⁄₃₂	Inner	.314	.129	.277	⅞
	17059209	¹⁵⁄₃₂	.015	¹³⁄₃₂	Inner	.314	.129	.277	⅞
	17059076	¹⁵⁄₃₂	.015	¹³⁄₃₂	Inner	.314	.129	.277	⅞
	17059226	¹⁵⁄₃₂	.015	¹³⁄₃₂	Inner	.314	.129	.277	⅞
	17059077	¹⁵⁄₃₂	.015	¹³⁄₃₂	Inner	.314	.129	.277	⅞
	17059227	¹⁵⁄₃₂	.015	¹³⁄₃₂	Inner	.314	.129	.277	⅞
	17059213	¹⁵⁄₃₂	.015	⁹⁄₃₂	Inner	.234	.129	.260	1
	17059215	¹⁵⁄₃₂	.015	⁹⁄₃₂	Inner	.234	.129	.260	1
	17059363	¹⁵⁄₃₂	.015	¹³⁄₃₂	Inner	.314	.149	.277	⅞
	17059503	¹⁵⁄₃₂	.015	¹³⁄₃₂	Inner	.314	.149	.277	⅞
	17059506	¹⁵⁄₃₂	.015	¹³⁄₃₂	Inner	.314	.149	.277	⅞
	17059368	¹⁵⁄₃₂	.015	¹³⁄₃₂	Inner	.314	.149	.277	⅞
	17059508	¹⁵⁄₃₂	.015	¹³⁄₃₂	Inner	.314	.149	.277	⅞
	17059377	¹⁵⁄₃₂	.015	⁹⁄₃₂	Outer	.314	.149	.277	⅞
	17059527	¹⁵⁄₃₂	.015	⁹⁄₃₂	Outer	.314	.149	.277	⅞
	17059378	¹⁵⁄₃₂	.015	⁹⁄₃₂	Outer	.314	.149	.277	⅞
	17059528	¹⁵⁄₃₂	.015	⁹⁄₃₂	Outer	.314	.149	.277	⅞
	17059509	¹⁵⁄₃₂	.015	¹³⁄₃₂	Inner	.314	.179	.277	⅞
	17059515	¹⁵⁄₃₂	.015	⁹⁄₃₂	Inner	.234	.129	.260	1
	17059510	¹⁵⁄₃₂	.015	⁹⁄₃₂	Inner	.314	.179	.277	⅞
	17059529	¹⁵⁄₃₂	.015	⁹⁄₃₂	Inner	.234	.129	.260	1
	17059513	¹⁵⁄₃₂	.015	⁹⁄₃₂	Inner	.234	.129	.260	1
	17059586	¹⁵⁄₃₂	.015	¹³⁄₃₂	Inner	.314	.179	.277	⅞
	17059588	¹⁵⁄₃₂	.015	¹³⁄₃₂	Inner	.314	.179	.277	⅞
	17059229	¹⁵⁄₃₂	.015	⁹⁄₃₂	Inner	.234	.129	.260	1
	17059520	⅜	.015	⁹⁄₃₂	Inner	.324	.164	.277	⅞
	17059521	⅜	.015	⁹⁄₃₂	Inner	.314	.164	.277	⅞

MODEL M4MC/4MV
Chevrolet/GMC
(All measurements in inches)

Year	Carburetor Number	Float Level	Float Drop	Choke Unloader	Choke Setting	Pump① Rod Adj.	Fast Idle (rpm)	Metering Rod Setting	Fast Idle Cam 2nd Step	Choke Vacuum Break
'80	17080201	$^{15}/_{32}$	—	42°	②	$^{9}/_{32}$	—	—	46°	23°
	17080205	$^{15}/_{32}$	—	42°	②	$^{9}/_{32}$	—	—	46°	23°
	17080206	$^{15}/_{32}$	—	42°	②	$^{9}/_{32}$	—	—	46°	23°
	17080224	$^{15}/_{32}$	—	42°	②	$^{9}/_{32}$	—	—	46°	23°
	17080290	$^{15}/_{32}$	—	42°	②	$^{9}/_{32}$	—	—	46°	26°
	17080291	$^{15}/_{32}$	—	42°	②	$^{9}/_{32}$	—	—	46°	26°
	17080292	$^{15}/_{32}$	—	42°	②	$^{9}/_{32}$	—	—	46°	26°
	17080295	$^{15}/_{32}$	—	42°	②	$^{9}/_{32}$	—	—	46°	23°
	17080297	$^{15}/_{32}$	—	42°	②	$^{9}/_{32}$	—	—	46°	23°
	17080503	$^{15}/_{32}$	—	42°	②	$^{9}/_{32}$	—	—	46°	26°
	17080506	$^{15}/_{32}$	—	42°	②	$^{9}/_{32}$	—	—	46°	26°
	17080508	$^{15}/_{32}$	—	42°	②	$^{9}/_{32}$	—	—	46°	26°
	17080523	$^{15}/_{32}$	—	42°	②	$^{9}/_{32}$	—	—	26°	23°
	17080524	$^{15}/_{32}$	—	42°	②	$^{9}/_{32}$	—	—	46°	23°
	17080525	$^{15}/_{32}$	—	42°	②	$^{9}/_{32}$	—	—	46°	23°
	17080526	$^{15}/_{32}$	—	42°	②	$^{9}/_{32}$	—	—	46°	23°
	17080226	$^{15}/_{32}$	—	42°	②	$^{9}/_{32}$	—	—	46°	23°
	17080227	$^{15}/_{32}$	—	42°	②	$^{9}/_{32}$	—	—	46°	23°
	17080527	$^{15}/_{32}$	—	42°	②	$^{9}/_{32}$	—	—	46°	23°
	17080528	$^{15}/_{32}$	—	42°	②	$^{9}/_{32}$	—	—	46°	23°
	17080213	$^{3}/_{8}$	—	40°	②	$^{9}/_{32}$	—	—	37°	30°
	17080215	$^{3}/_{8}$	—	40°	②	$^{9}/_{32}$	—	—	37°	30°
	17080513	$^{3}/_{8}$	—	40°	②	$^{9}/_{32}$	—	—	37°	30°
	17080515	$^{3}/_{8}$	—	40°	②	$^{9}/_{32}$	—	—	37°	30°
	17080229	$^{3}/_{8}$	—	40°	②	$^{9}/_{32}$	—	—	37°	30°
	17080529	$^{3}/_{8}$	—	40°	②	$^{9}/_{32}$	—	—	37°	30°
	17080225	$^{15}/_{32}$	—	42°	②	$^{9}/_{32}$	—	—	46°	23°
	17080212	$^{3}/_{8}$	—	40°	②	$^{9}/_{32}$	—	—	30°	24°
	17080512	$^{3}/_{8}$	—	40°	②	$^{9}/_{32}$	—	—	30°	24°
'81	17080212	$^{3}/_{8}$	—	40°	②	$^{9}/_{32}$	—	—	30°	24°
	17080213	$^{3}/_{8}$	—	40°	②	$^{9}/_{32}$	—	—	30°	23°
	17080215	$^{3}/_{8}$	—	40°	②	$^{9}/_{32}$	—	—	30°	23°
	17080298	$^{3}/_{8}$	—	40°	②	$^{9}/_{32}$	—	—	30°	23°
	17080507	$^{3}/_{8}$	—	40°	②	$^{9}/_{32}$	—	—	30°	23°
	17080512	$^{3}/_{8}$	—	40°	②	$^{9}/_{32}$	—	—	30°	24°
	17080513	$^{3}/_{8}$	—	40°	②	$^{9}/_{32}$	—	—	30°	23°
	17081200	$^{15}/_{32}$	—	42°	②	$^{9}/_{32}$	—	—	23°	24°

MODEL M4MC/4MV
Chevrolet/GMC
(All measurements in inches)

Year	Carburetor Number	Float Level	Float Drop	Choke Unloader	Choke Setting	Pump① Rod Adj.	Fast Idle (rpm)	Metering Rod Setting	Fast Idle Cam 2nd Step	Choke Vacuum Break
	17081201	15/32	—	42°	②	9/32	—	—	23°	23°
	17081205	15/32	—	42°	②	9/32	—	—	23°	23°
	17081206	15/32	—	42°	②	9/32	—	—	23°	23°
	17081220	15/32	—	42°	②	9/32	—	—	23°	23°
	17081226	15/32	—	42°	②	9/32	—	—	23°	24°
	17081227	15/32	—	42°	②	9/32	—	—	—	24°
	17081290	13/32	—	42°	②	9/32	—	—	24°	23°
	17081291	13/32	—	42°	②	9/32	—	—	24°	23°
	17081292	13/32	—	42°	②	9/32	—	—	24°	23°
	17081506	13/32	—	36°	②	9/32	—	—	36°	23°
	17081508	13/32	—	36°	②	9/32	—	—	36°	23°
	17081524	13/32	—	36°	②	5/16③	—	—	36°	25°
	17081526	13/32	—	36°	②	5/16③	—	—	36°	25°

① Place the pump arm linkage in the inner hole of the arm, except on carburetors with a 5/16 pump rod height (see ③)
② 1980 and 1981 choke cover are riveted in position and are not adjustable under normal conditions
③ On carburetors with 5/16 pump rod height, place the pump arm linkage in the outer hole of the arm

MODEL 2SE
Jeep
(All measurements in inches)

Year	Carburetor Number	Float Level	Pump Stem Height	Fast② Idle Cam	Fast Idle (rpm)	Air① Valve Link	Primary Vacuum Break	Choke Unloader	Choke Setting
'81	17081790	.208	.128	25°	2400	2°	19°	32°	③
	17081791	.256	.128	25°	2600	2°	19°	32°	③

① Maximum degree setting
② 2nd step on cam
③ Tamper resistant—riveted cover

MODEL E2SE
Jeep
(All measurements in inches)

Year	Carburetor Number	Float Level	Pump Stem Height	Fast Idle Cam 2nd step	Fast Idle (rpm)	Air① Valve Link	Choke Unloader	Choke Setting
'81	170811796	.208	.128	25°	2400	2°	19°	②
	170811797	.208	.128	25°	2600	2°	19°	②

① Maximum degree setting
② Tamper resistant—Riveted choke cover

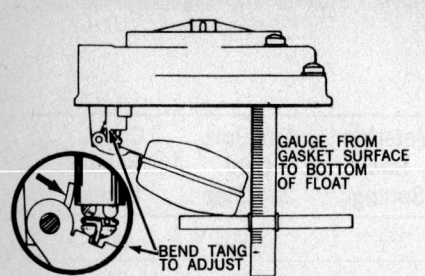

Float drop adjustment—Rochester model 2G (© General Motors Corp.)

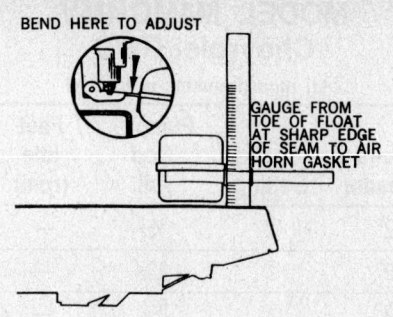

Float level adjustment—Rochester model 2G (© General Motors Corp.)

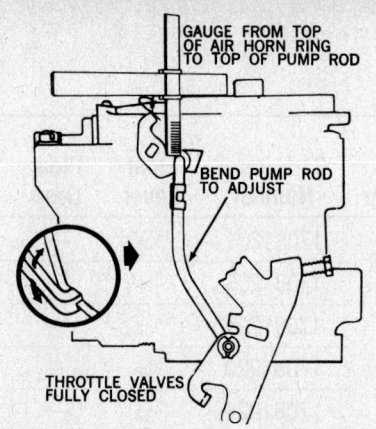

Accelerator pump rod adjustment— Rochester model 2G (© General Motors Corp.)

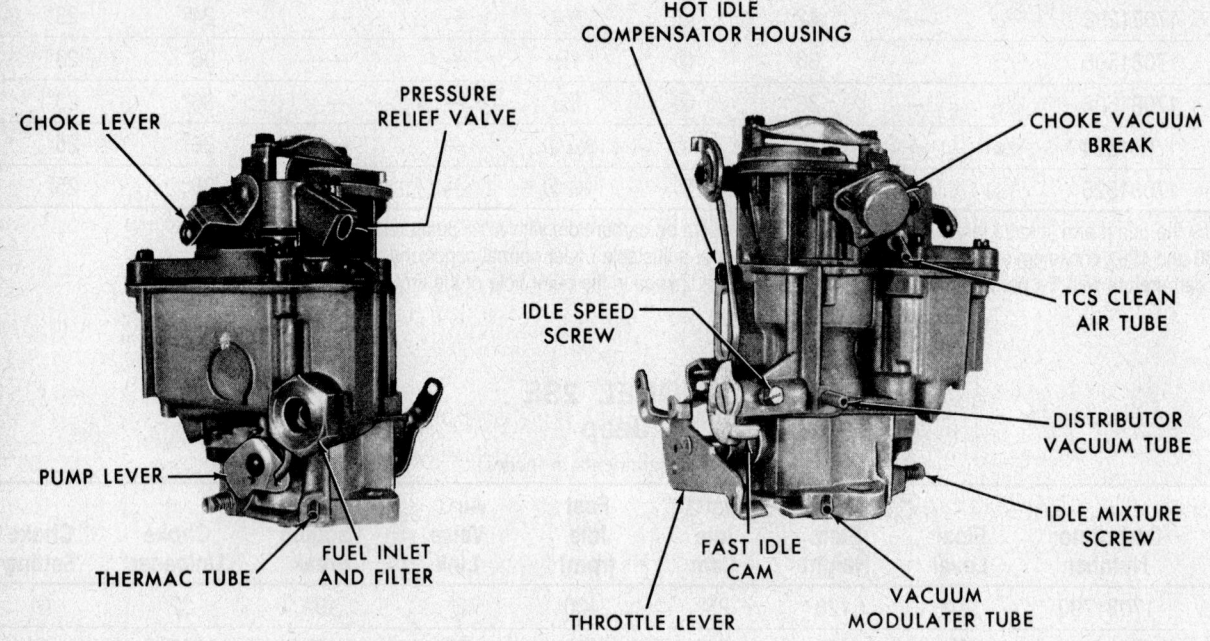

Rochester Monojet® carburetor—typical (© General Motors Corp.)

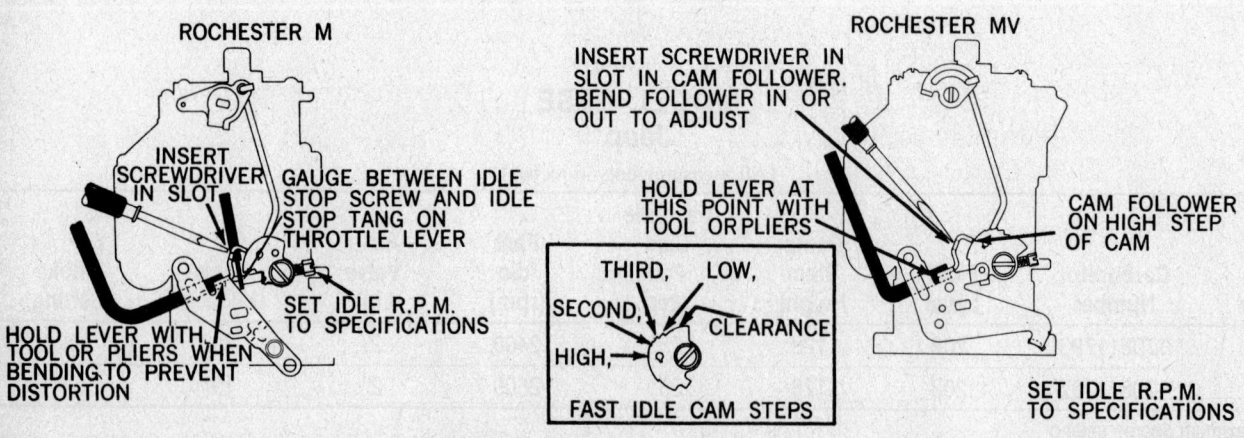

Fast idle adjustment—Monojet® carburetor (© General Motors Corp.)

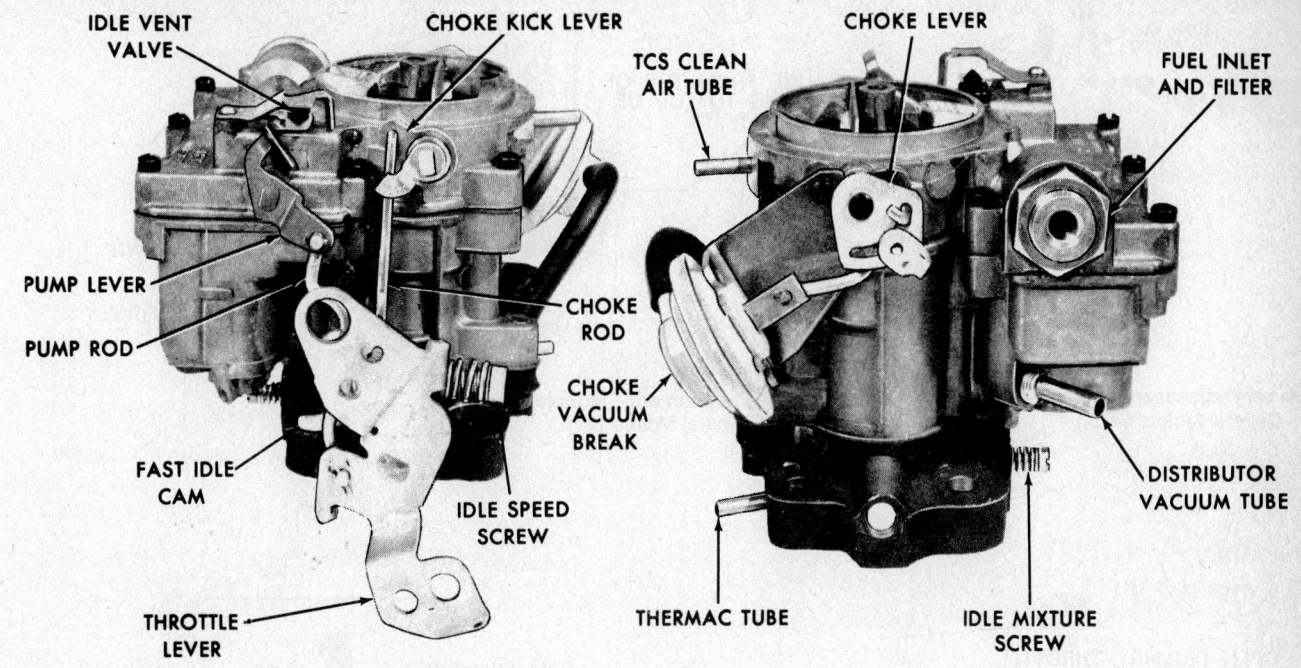

IDLE VENT VALVE

CHOKE KICK LEVER

CHOKE LEVER

TCS CLEAN AIR TUBE

FUEL INLET AND FILTER

PUMP LEVER

PUMP ROD

CHOKE ROD

CHOKE VACUUM BREAK

FAST IDLE CAM

IDLE SPEED SCREW

DISTRIBUTOR VACUUM TUBE

THROTTLE LEVER

THERMAC TUBE

IDLE MIXTURE SCREW

Rochester model 2GV—typical (© General Motors Corp.)

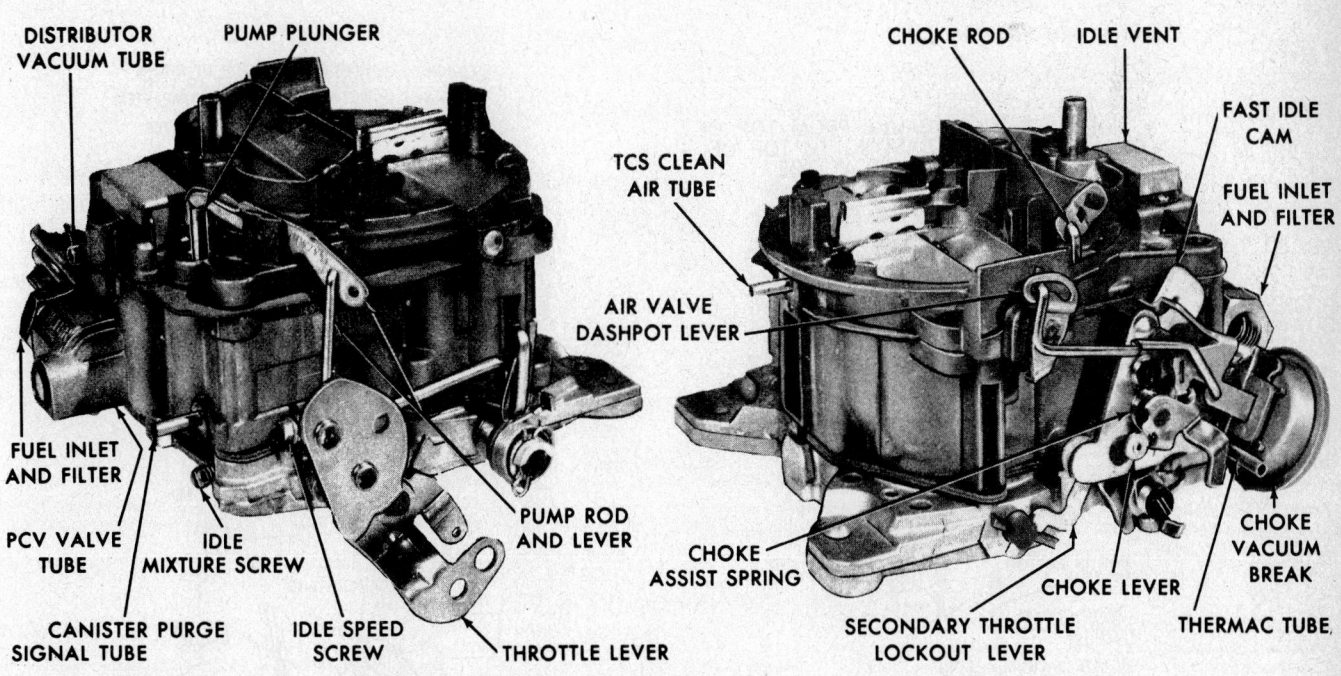

DISTRIBUTOR VACUUM TUBE

PUMP PLUNGER

CHOKE ROD

IDLE VENT

FAST IDLE CAM

TCS CLEAN AIR TUBE

FUEL INLET AND FILTER

AIR VALVE DASHPOT LEVER

FUEL INLET AND FILTER

PCV VALVE TUBE

IDLE MIXTURE SCREW

PUMP ROD AND LEVER

CHOKE VACUUM BREAK

CANISTER PURGE SIGNAL TUBE

IDLE SPEED SCREW

THROTTLE LEVER

CHOKE ASSIST SPRING

SECONDARY THROTTLE LOCKOUT LEVER

CHOKE LEVER

THERMAC TUBE

Rochester Quadrajet® carburetor (4MV shown)—typical (© General Motors Corp.)

CARBURETORS
ROCHESTER

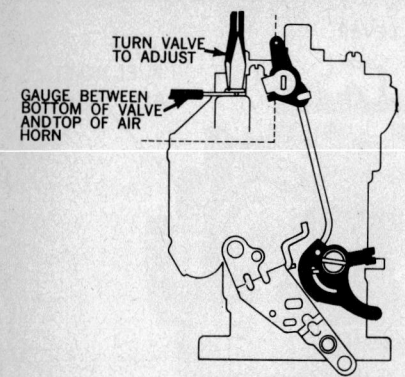

Idle vent adjustment—Monojet® carburetor (© General Motors Corp.)

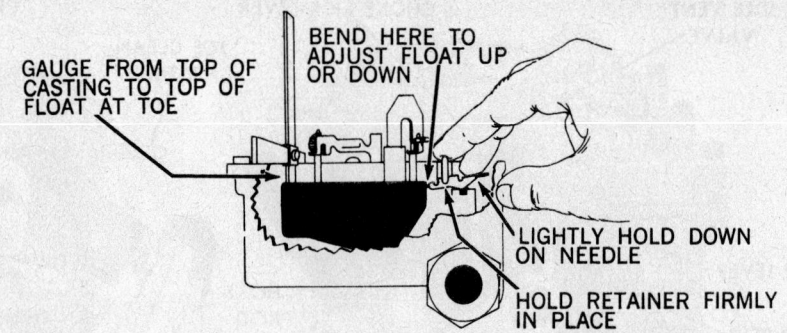

Float level adjustment—Monojet® carburetor (© General Motors Corp.)

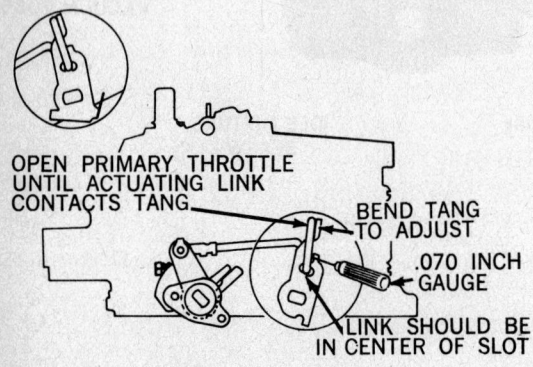

Secondary opening adjustment—typical Quadrajet® carburetor (© General Motors Corp.)

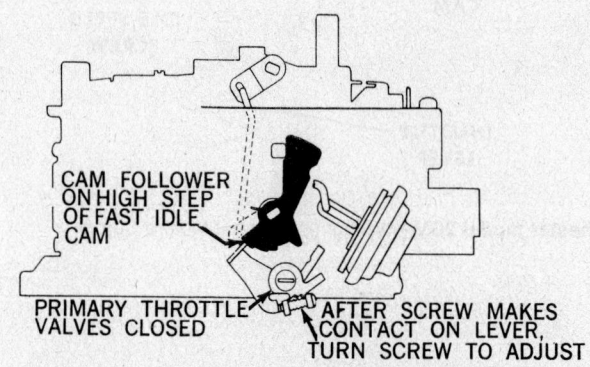

Fast idle adjustment—typical Quadrajet® carburetor (© General Motors Corp.)

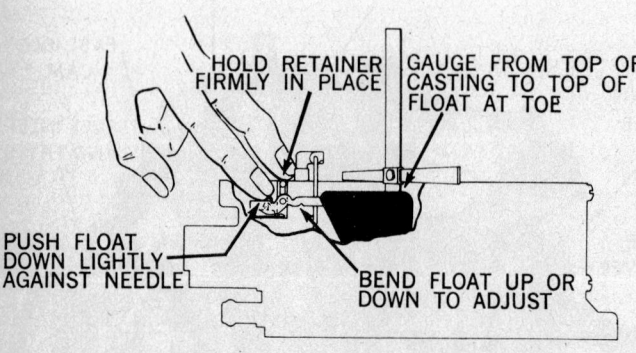

Float level adjustment—typical Quadrajet® carburetor (© General Motors Corp.)

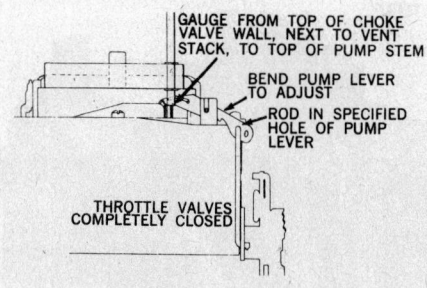

Pump rod adjustment—typical Quadrajet® carburetor (© General Motors Corp.)

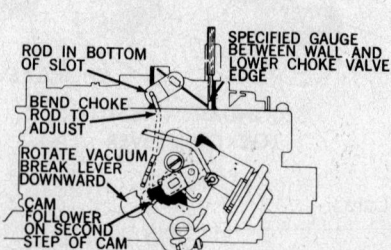

Choke rod adjustment—typical Quadrajet® carburetor (© General Motors Corp.)

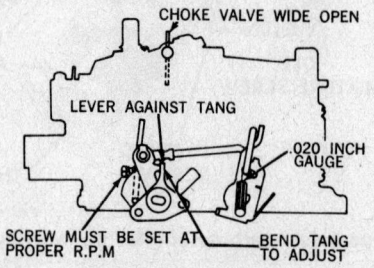

Secondary closing adjustment—typical Quadrajet® carburetor (© General Motors Corp.)

964

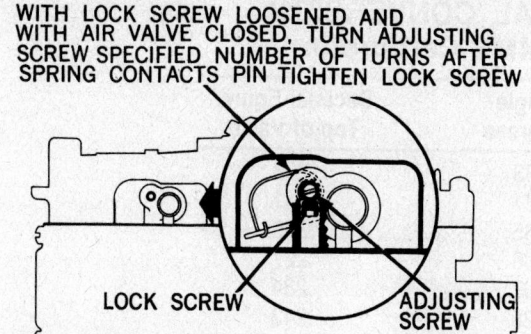

WITH LOCK SCREW LOOSENED AND
WITH AIR VALVE CLOSED, TURN ADJUSTING
SCREW SPECIFIED NUMBER OF TURNS AFTER
SPRING CONTACTS PIN TIGHTEN LOCK SCREW

LOCK SCREW

ADJUSTING SCREW

Air valve spring adjustment—typical Quadrajet® carburetor
(© General Motors Corp.)

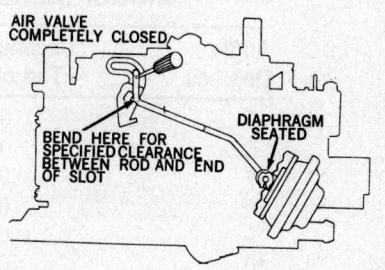

AIR VALVE COMPLETELY CLOSED

BEND HERE FOR SPECIFIED CLEARANCE BETWEEN ROD AND END OF SLOT

DIAPHRAGM SEATED

Air valve dashpot adjustment—typical Quadrajet® carburetor (© General Motors Corp.)

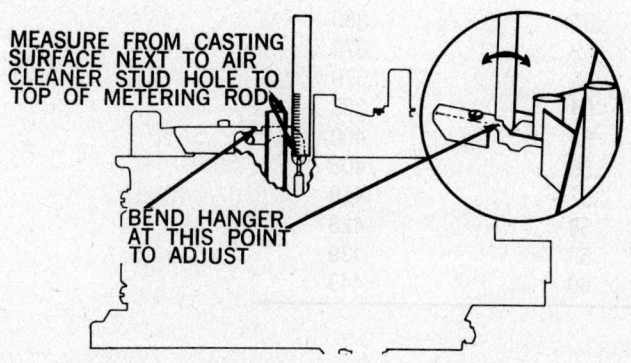

MEASURE FROM CASTING SURFACE NEXT TO AIR CLEANER STUD HOLE TO TOP OF METERING ROD

BEND HANGER AT THIS POINT TO ADJUST

Secondary metering adjustment—typical Quadrajet® carburetor
(© General Motors Corp.)

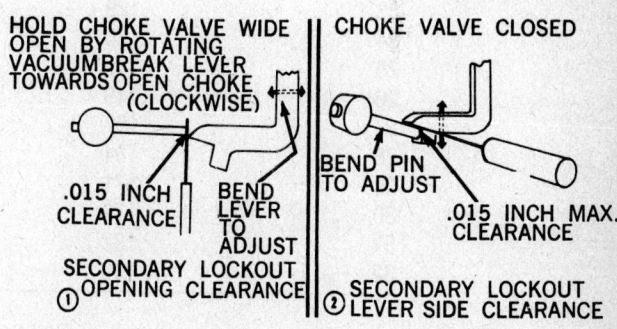

HOLD CHOKE VALVE WIDE OPEN BY ROTATING VACUUMBREAK LEVER TOWARDS OPEN CHOKE (CLOCKWISE)

CHOKE VALVE CLOSED

.015 INCH CLEARANCE

BEND LEVER TO ADJUST

BEND PIN TO ADJUST

.015 INCH MAX. CLEARANCE

① SECONDARY LOCKOUT OPENING CLEARANCE

② SECONDARY LOCKOUT LEVER SIDE CLEARANCE

Secondary lockout adjustment—typical Quadrajet® carburetor
(© General Motors Corp.)

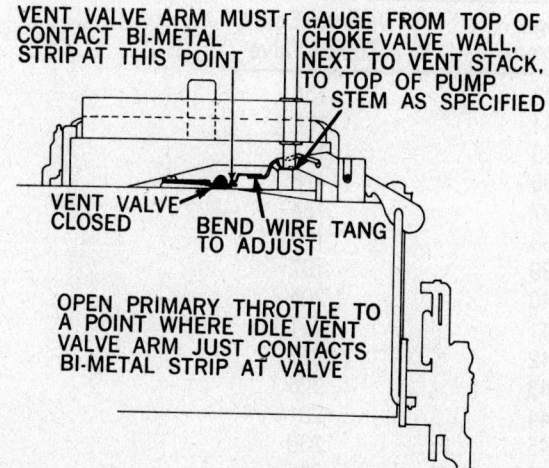

VENT VALVE ARM MUST CONTACT BI-METAL STRIP AT THIS POINT

GAUGE FROM TOP OF CHOKE VALVE WALL, NEXT TO VENT STACK, TO TOP OF PUMP STEM AS SPECIFIED

VENT VALVE CLOSED

BEND WIRE TANG TO ADJUST

OPEN PRIMARY THROTTLE TO A POINT WHERE IDLE VENT VALVE ARM JUST CONTACTS BI-METAL STRIP AT VALVE

Idle vent adjustment—typical Quadrajet® carburetor (© General Motors Corp.)

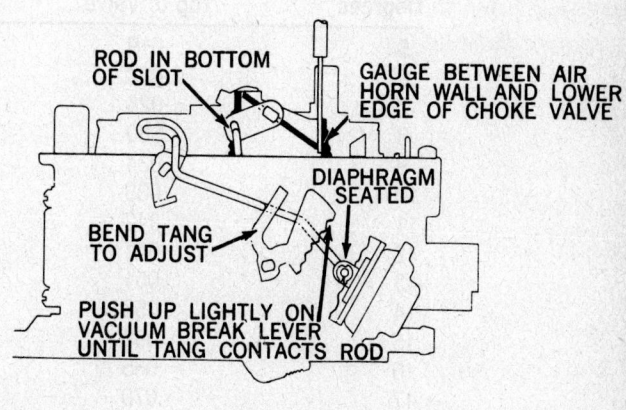

ROD IN BOTTOM OF SLOT

GAUGE BETWEEN AIR HORN WALL AND LOWER EDGE OF CHOKE VALVE

DIAPHRAGM SEATED

BEND TANG TO ADJUST

PUSH UP LIGHTLY ON VACUUM BREAK LEVER UNTIL TANG CONTACTS ROD

Vacuum break adjustment—typical Quadrajet® carburetor
(© General Motors Corp.)

ANGLE DEGREE TO DECIMAL CONVERSION
Model M2MC, M2ME and M4MC Carburetor

Angle Degrees	Decimal Equiv. Top of Valve	Angle Degrees	Decimal Equiv. Top of Valve
5	.023	33	.203
6	.028	34	.211
7	.033	35	.220
8	.038	36	.227
9	.043	37	.234
10	.049	38	.243
11	.054	39	.251
12	.060	40	.260
13	.066	41	.269
14	.071	42	.277
15	.077	43	.287
16	.083	44	.295
17	.090	45	.304
18	.096	46	.314
19	.103	47	.322
20	.110	48	.332
21	.117	49	.341
22	.123	50	.350
23	.129	51	.360
24	.136	52	.370
25	.142	53	.379
26	.149	54	.388
27	.157	55	.400
28	.164	56	.408
29	.171	57	.418
30	.179	58	.428
31	.187	59	.439
32	.195	60	.449

ANGLE DEGREE TO DECIMAL CONVERSION
Model 4MV Carburetor

Angle Degrees	Decimal Equiv. Top of Valve	Angle Degrees	Decimal Equiv. Top of Valve
5	.019	33	.158
6	.022	34	.164
7	.026	35	.171
8	.030	36	.178
9	.034	37	.184
10	.038	38	.190
11	.042	39	.197
12	.047	40	.204
13	.051	41	.211
14	.056	42	.217
15	.060	43	.225
16	.065	44	.231
17	.070	45	.239
18	.075	46	.246
19	.080	47	.253
20	.085	48	.260

ANGLE DEGREE TO DECIMAL CONVERSION
Model 4MV Carburetor

Angle Degrees	Decimal Equiv. Top of Valve	Angle Degrees	Decimal Equiv. Top of Valve
21	.090	49	.268
22	.095	50	.275
23	.101	51	.283
24	.106	52	.291
25	.112	53	.299
26	.117	54	.306
27	.123	55	.314
28	.128	56	.322
29	.134	57	.329
30	.140	58	.337
31	.146	59	.345
32	.152	60	.353

Emission Calibration Numbers

Emission calibration numbers are used by Ford Motor Company to provide the technician with the necessary specifications to adjust a specific engine to the proper emission control levels.

The calibration numbers are listed on the lower right of the Vehicle Emission Control Information label, which is attached to the engine valve cover.

The information on the decal must be used when differences exist between the decal and other specification tables, unless otherwise noted by Ford Motor Company.

Year	Emission Calibration Number	Choke Setting	Fast Idle (RPM) High Cam	Fast Idle (RPM) Kick Down①	Choke Valve Pull Down
'77	7-53G-RO	3 Rich	2000	—	—
	7-53H-RO	3 Rich	2000	—	—
	7-53S-RO	3 Rich	2000	—	—
	7-54K-RO	3 Rich	2100	—	—
	7-54S-RO	3 Rich	2100	—	—
	7-54T-RO	3 Rich	2100	—	—
	7-59G-RO	Index	1900	—	—
	7-60G-RO	Index	1900	—	—
	7-62G-RO	Index	1900	—	—
	7-64U-RO	3 Rich	—	1500	—

Year	Emission Calibration Number	Choke Setting	Fast Idle (RPM) High Cam	Kick Down ①	Choke Valve Pull Down
	7-65G-RO	3 Rich	—	1500	—
	7-65H-RO	3 Rich	—	1500	—
	7-65U-RO	Index	—	1500	—
	7-71-RO	3 Rich	—	1250	—
	7-71J-RO	3 Rich	—	1250	—
	7-72-RO	3 Rich	—	1500	—
	7-72J-RO	3 Rich	—	1500	—
	7-73-RO	3 Rich	—	1200	—
	7-74-RO	3 Rich	—	1500	—
'78	5-81A-RO	None	—	—	—
	5-81B-RO	None	2200	—	—
	5-82-RO	None	2200	—	—
	5-82A-RO	None	2200	—	—
	5-85A-R1	None	2200	—	—
	5-85J-R6	None	—	—	—
	5-86A-RO	None	2200	—	—
	5-86J-R3	None	2500	—	—
	5-89-R2	None	2000	—	—
	5-89J-R3	None	2200	—	—
	5-90A-R1	None	2200	—	—
	5-90B-R1	None	2200	—	—
	5-90J-R3	None	2200	—	—
	6-51A-RO	Index	—	1600	—
	6-51E-RO	Index	—	1600	—
	6-93-R7	None	2500	—	—
	6-94-R4	None	2500	—	—
	6-95-R6	None	2500	—	—
	6-95-95	None	2500	—	—
	7-60E-R11	Index	1900	—	—
	7-71-R10	2 Rich	—	1250	—
	7-71J-R10	2 Rich	—	1450	—
	7-72-R11	3 Rich	—	1500	—
	7-72J-R11	3 Rich	—	1500	—
	7-73-R10	2 Rich	—	1250	—
	7-74-R10	3 Rich	—	1500	—
	7-74J-R11	3 Rich	—	1500	—
	7-75A-R16	1 Rich	—	1250	—
	7-76A-R10	2 Rich	—	1500	—
	7-76J-R11	3 Rich	—	1700	—

Year	Emission Calibration Number	Choke Setting	Fast Idle (RPM) High Cam	Kick Down [1]	Choke Valve Pull Down
	7-77-R10	1 Rich	—	1500	—
	7-77A-R10	None	—	1500	—
	7-77J-R10	1 Rich	—	1500	—
	7-77M-R10	None	—	1500	—
	7-78-R10	1 Rich	—	1500	—
	7-78J-R10	1 Rich	—	1500	—
	7-79-R1	3 Rich	—	1250	—
	7-80-RO	3 Rich	—	1500	—
	7-81K-RO	None	1400	—	—
	7-93J-RO	None	2500	—	—
	7-95J-RO	None	2500	—	—
	7-96J-90	None	2500	—	—
	8-51J-RO	Index	—	1600	—
	8-51K-RO	Index	—	1600	—
	8-51L-RO	Index	—	1600	—
	8-51M-RO	Index	—	1600	—
	8-51S-RO	Index	—	1600	—
	8-51T-RO	Index	—	1600	—
	8-52K-RO	Index	—	1600	—
	8-52L-R10	Index	—	1600	—
	8-52U-RO	Index	—	1600	—
	8-53A-RO	1 Rich	2000	—	—
	8-53G-RO	3 Rich	2000	—	—
	8-53S-RO	3 Rich	2000	—	—
	8-54A-RO	3 Rich	2000	—	—
	8-54G-RO	3 Rich	2000	—	—
	8-54S-RO	3 Rich	2100	—	—
	8-54T-R10	3 Rich	2100	—	—
	8-59G-RO	Index	2100	—	—
	8-59T-R2	Index	2100	—	—
	8-60A-RO	2 Rich	2200	—	—
	8-60J-RO	Index	2100	—	—
	8-60S-R11	Index	1900	—	—
	8-60S-R12	Index	1900	—	—
	8-62T-RO	—	—	—	—
	8-62J-RO	Index	2100	—	—
	8-64G-RO	3 Rich	—	1750	—
	8-64S-RO	Index	—	1500	—
	8-65A-RO	Index	2100	—	—

Year	Emission Calibration Number	Choke Setting	Fast Idle (RPM) High Cam	Kick Down①	Choke Valve Pull Down
	8-65G-RO	1 Rich	2000	—	—
	8-65S-RO	Index	—	1500	—
	8-65U-RO	Index	—	1500	—
	R-66U-RO	Index	—	1500	—
	8-97-RO	Index	—	1200	—
	7-97J-RO	Index	—	1200	—
'79	9-51G-RO	Index	—	1600	.230
	9-51J-RO	Index	—	1600	.230
	9-51K-RO	Index	—	1600	.230
	9-51L-RO	Index	—	1600	.230
	9-51M-RO	Index	—	1600	.230
	9-51S-RO	Index	—	1600	.230
	9-51T-RO	Index	—	1600	.230
	9-52G-RO	Index	—	1600	.230
	9-52J-RO	Index	—	1600	.230
	9-52L-RO	Index	—	1600	.230
	9-52M-RO	Index	—	1600	.230
	9-53G-RO	3 Rich	2000	—	.140
	9-53H-RO	3 Rich	2000	—	.140
	9-54A-RO	—	—	—	.145
	9-54G-RO	3 Rich	2000	—	.145
	9-54H-RO	3 Rich	2000	—	.145
	9-54J-RO	2 Rich	2000	—	.145
	9-54R-RO	3 Rich	2000	—	.145
	9-54S-RO	1 Rich	2400	—	.136
	9-54T-RO	3 Rich	2000	—	.145
	9-54U-RO	1 Rich	2400	—	.136
	9-59H-RO	Index	2000	—	.135
	9-59J-RO	Index	2000	—	.145
	9-59K-RO	Index	2000	—	.145
	9-59S-RO	Index	2000	—	.135
	9-60T-RO	—	—	—	.150
	9-60G-RO	Index	2000	—	.145
	9-60H-RO	Index	2000	—	.150
	9-60J-RO	Index	2000	—	.140
	9-60L-RO	Index	2000	—	.150
	9-60M-RO	Index	2000	—	.150
	9-60S-RO	3 Rich	2100	—	.150
	9-61G-RO	Index	2000	—	.145

Year	Emission Calibration Number	Choke Setting	Fast Idle (RPM) High Cam	Kick Down ①	Choke Valve Pull Down
	9-61H-RO	Index	2000	—	.135
	9-62A-RO	—	—	—	.145
	9-62B-RO	—	—	—	.145
	9-62J-RO	Index	1900	—	.145
	9-62M-RO	Index	1900	—	.145
	9-63H-RO	Index	—	1500	.190
	9-64G-RO	Index	2200	—	.200
	9-64H-RO	Index	2200	—	.200
	9-64S-RO	Index	2200	—	.200
	9-66G-RO	5 Rich	—	1600	.210
	9-72J-RO	3 Rich	2000	—	.150
	9-77J-RO	Index	—	1600	.290
	9-77M-RO	Manual	2550	—	—
	9-78J-RO	Index	—	1600	.290
	9-83G-RO	Manual	2200	—	—
	9-83H-RO2	Manual	2500	—	—
	9-87G-RO	Manual	2700	—	—
	9-97J-RO	5 Rich	—	1600	.210
	7-76J-R11	3 Rich	—	1700	.180
	7-93J-RO	Manual	2500	—	—
	7-95J-RO	Manual	2500	—	—
	9-71J-RO	3 Rich	1750	—	—
	9-73J-RO	2 Rich	1750	—	—
	9-74J-RO	3 Rich	2000	—	—
	9-97J-R11	5 Rich	—	1600	—
'80	0-51F-RO	Index	—	1600	—
	0-51G-RO	2 Rich	—	1400	—
	0-51H-RO	2 Rich	—	1400	—
	0-51L-RO	Index	—	1400	—
	0-51M-RO	Index	—	1400	—
	0-51S-RO	Index	—	1600	—
	0-51T-RO	Index	—	1600	—
	0-52H-RO	2 Rich	—	1400	—
	0-52J-RO	2 Rich	—	1400	—
	0-52L-RO	2 Rich	—	1400	—
	0-52M-RO	2 Rich	—	1400	—
	0-52S-RO	Index	—	1600	—
	0-53D-RO	3 Rich	2000	—	—
	0-53G-RO	3 Rich	2000	—	—

Year	Emission Calibration Number	Choke Setting	Fast Idle (RPM) High Cam	Kick Down ①	Choke Valve Pull Down
	0-53H-RO	3 Rich	2000	—	—
	0-53K-RO	3 Rich	2000	—	—
	0-53L-RO	3 Rich	2000	—	—
	0-53N-RO	3 Rich	2500	—	—
	0-53Q-RO	3 Rich	2500	—	—
	0-53S-RO	3 Rich	2500	—	—
	0-54D-RO	3 Rich	2000	—	—
	0-54F-RO	3 Rich	2000	—	—
	0-54G-RO	Index	2000	—	—
	0-54H-RO	3 Rich	2000	—	—
	0-54K-RO	Index	2000	—	—
	0-54L-RO	3 Rich	2000	—	—
	0-54M-RO	3 Rich	2100	—	—
	0-54N-RO	1 Rich	2400	—	—
	0-54P-RO	3 Rich	2000	—	—
	0-54Q-RO	1 Rich	2400	—	—
	0-54R-RO	3 Rich	2100	—	—
	0-54T-RO	3 Rich	2000	—	—
	0-54V-RO	3 Rich	2100	—	—
	0-60A-RO	3 Rich	2000	—	—
	0-59C-RO	3 Rich	2000	—	—
	0-59G-RO	3 Rich	2000	—	—
	0-59G-R10	3 Rich	2000	—	—
	0-59H-RO	3 Rich	2000	—	—
	0-59H-R10	3 Rich	2000	—	—
	0-59J-RO	3 Rich	2000	—	—
	0-59J-R10	3 Rich	2000	—	—
	0-59S-RO	3 Rich	2000	—	—
	0-60B-RO	3 Rich	2000	—	—
'81	1-57G-R1	—	2200	—	—
	1-58G-RO	—	2000	—	—
	1-51D-RO	—	—	1400	—
	1-51D-R10	—	—	1400	—
	1-51E-RO	—	—	1400	—
	1-51F-RO	—	—	1400	—
	1-51G-RO	—	—	1400	—
	1-51H-RO	—	—	1400	—
	1-51K-RO	—	—	1400	—

Year	Emission Calibration Number	Choke Setting	Fast Idle (RPM) High Cam	Kick Down①	Choke Valve Pull Down
	1-51L-RO	—	—	1400	—
	1-51E-R10	—	—	1400	—
	1-51F-R10	—	—	1400	—
	1-51G-R10	—	—	1400	—
	1-51H-R10	—	—	1400	—
	1-51K-R10	—	—	1400	—
	1-51L-R10	—	—	1400	—
	1-51S-RO	—	—	1400	—
	1-51S-R10	—	—	1400	—
	1-51T-RO	—	—	1400	—
	1-52G-RO	—	—	1400	—
	1-52H-RO	—	—	1400	—
	1-52K-RO	—	—	1400	—
	1-52L-RO	—	—	1400	—
	1-52G-R10	—	—	1400	—
	1-52H-R10	—	—	1400	—
	1-52K-R10	—	—	1400	—
	1-52L-R10	—	—	1400	—
	1-52S-RO	—	—	1400	—
	1-52T-RO	—	—	1400	—
	1-53D-RO	—	2200	—	—
	1-53F-RO	—	2200	—	—
	1-53G-RO	—	2200	—	—
	1-53H-RO	—	2200	—	—
	1-53K-RO	—	2200	—	—
	1-53D-R10	—	2200	—	—
	1-53G-R10	—	2200	—	—
	1-53K-R10	—	2200	—	—
	1-59A-RO	—	2000	—	—
	1-59B-RO	—	2000	—	—
	1-59H-RO	—	2000	—	—
	1-59K-RO	—	2000	—	—
	1-60A-RO	—	2200	—	—
	1-60B-RO	—	2200	—	—
	1-60H-R1	—	2000	—	—
	1-60J-RO	—	2000	—	—
	1-60K-RO	—	2000	—	—

Year	Emission Calibration Number	Choke Setting	Fast Idle (RPM) High Cam	Fast Idle (RPM) Kick Down ①	Choke Valve Pull Down
	1-63T-RO	—	1700	—	—
	1-64A-RO	—	2000	—	—
	1-64G-R1	—	2000	—	—
	1-64H-R2	—	2000	—	—
	1-64R-R1	—	1650	—	—
	1-64S-RO	—	1650	—	—
	1-64T-RO	—	1650	—	—

① Kickdown—2nd step of fast idle cam

Engine Rebuilding

INDEX

ENGINE REBUILDING

This section describes, in detail, the procedures involved in rebuilding a typical engine. The procedures are basically identical to those used in rebuilding engines of nearly all design and configurations.

The section is divided into two parts. The first, Cylinder Head Reconditioning, assumes that the cylinder head is removed from the engine, all manifolds are removed, and the cylinder head is on a workbench. The camshaft should be removed from overhead cam cylinder heads. The second section, Cylinder Block Reconditioning, covers the block, pistons, connecting rods and crankshaft. It is assumed that the engine is mounted on a work stand, and the cylinder head and all accessories are removed.

Procedures are identified as follows:

Unmarked—Basic procedures that must be performed in order to successfully complete the rebuilding process.

Starred (*)—Procedures that should be performed to ensure maximum performance and engine life.

Double starred (**)—Procedures that may be performed to increase engine performance and reliability.

In many cases, a choice of methods is also provided. Methods are identified in the same manner as procedures. The choice of method for a procedure is at the discretion of the user.

The tools required for the basic rebuilding procedure should, with minor exceptions, be those included in a mechanic's tool kit. An accurate torque wrench, and a dial indicator (reading in thousandths) mounted on a universal base should be available. Special tools, where required, all are readily available from the major tool suppliers. The services of a competent automotive machine shop must also be readily available.

When assembling the engine, any parts that will be in frictional contact must be prelubricated, to provide protection on initial start-up. Any product specifically formulated for this purpose may be used. NOTE: *Do not use engine oil.* Where semi-permanent (locked but removable) installation of bolts or nuts is desired, threads should be cleaned and coated with Loctite® or a similar product (non-hardening).

Aluminum has become increasingly popular for use in engines, due to its low weight and excellent heat transfer characteristics. The following precautions must be observed when handling aluminum engine parts:

—Never hot-tank aluminum parts.

—Remove all aluminum parts (identification tags, etc.) from engine parts before hot-tanking (otherwise they will be removed during the process).

—Always coat threads lightly with engine oil or anti-seize compounds before installation, to prevent seizure.

—Never over-torque bolts or spark plugs in aluminum threads. Should stripping occur, threads can be restored using any of a number of thread repair kits available (see next section).

Magnaflux and Zyglo are inspection techniques used to locate material flaws, such as stress cracks. Magnafluxing coats the part with fine magnetic particles, and subjects the part to a magnetic field. Cracks cause breaks in the magnetic field, which are outlined by the particles. Since Magnaflux is a magnetic process, it is applicable only to ferrous materials. The Zyglo process coats the material with a fluorescent dye penetrant, and then subjects it to blacklight inspection, under which cracks glow brightly. Parts made of any material may be tested using Zyglo. While Magnaflux and Zyglo are excellent for general inspection, and locating hidden defects, specific checks of suspected cracks may be made at lower cost and more readily using spot check dye. The dye is sprayed onto the suspected area, wiped off, and the area is then sprayed with a developer. Cracks then will show up brightly. Spot check dyes will only indicate surface cracks; therefore, structural cracks below the surface may escape detection. When questionable, the part should be tested using Magnaflux or Zyglo.

REPAIRING DAMAGED THREADS

Several methods of repairing damaged threads are available. Heli-Coil® (shown here), Keenserts® and Microdot® are among the most widely used. All involve basically the same principle—drilling out stripped threads, tapping the hole and installing a prewound insert— making welding, plugging and oversize fasteners unnecessary.

Two types of thread repair inserts are usually supplied—a standard type for most Inch Coarse, Inch Fine, Metric Coarse and Metric Fine thread sizes and a spark plug type to fit most spark plug port sizes. Consult the individual manufacturer's catalog to determine exact applications. Typical thread repair kits will contain a selection of prewound threaded inserts, a tap (corresponding to the outside diameter threads of the insert) and an installation tool. Most manufacturers also supply blister-packed thread repair inserts separately and a master kit with a variety of taps and inserts plus installation tools.

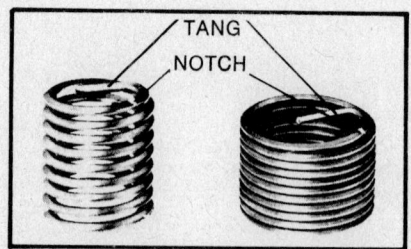

Standard thread repair insert (left) and spark plug thread insert (right)

Before effecting a repair to a threaded hole, remove any snapped, broken or damaged bolts or studs. Penetrating oil can be used to free frozen threads; the offending item can be removed with locking pliers or with a screw or stud extractor. After the hole is clear, the thread can be repaired as follows.

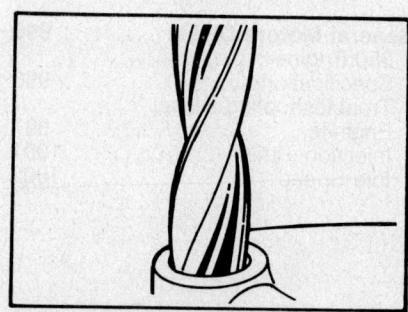

Drill out the damaged threads with the specified drill. Drill completely through the hole or to the bottom of a blind hole.

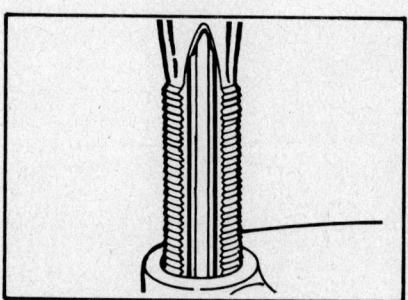

With the tap supplied, tap the hole to receive the threaded insert. Keep the tap well oiled and back it out frequently to avoid clogging the threads.

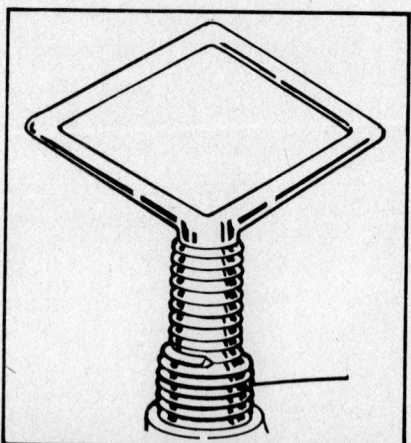

Screw the threaded insert onto the installation tool until the tang engages the slot. Screw the insert into the tapped hole until it is ¼-½ turn below the top surface. After installation, break the tang off with a hammer and punch.

NOTE: This engine rebuilding section is a guide to accepted rebuilding procedures. Typical examples of standard rebuilding procedures are illustrated.

CYLINDER HEAD RECONDITIONING

Procedure	Method
Identify the valves:	Invert the cylinder head, and number the valve faces front to rear, using a permanent felt-tip marker.
Remove the rocker arms (OHV engines only):	Remove the rocker arms with shaft(s) or balls and nuts. Wire the sets of rockers, balls and nuts together, and identify according to the corresponding valve.
Remove the camshaft (OHC engines only):	See the engine service procedures earlier in this book for details concerning specific engines.
Remove the valves and springs:	Using an appropriate valve spring compressor (depending on the configuration of the cylinder head), compress the valve springs. Lift out the keepers with needlenose pliers, release the compressor, and remove the valve, spring, and spring retainer.
Remove glow plugs and fuel injectors (Diesel engines only):	Label and remove all fuel injectors and glow plugs from the head. Glow plugs unscrew. See the appropriate car section for injector removal. Inspect glow plugs for bulges, cracks or signs of melting. Clean injector tips with a steel brush, then inspect for evidence of melting.
**Remove pre-combustion chamber inserts (Diesel engines only): 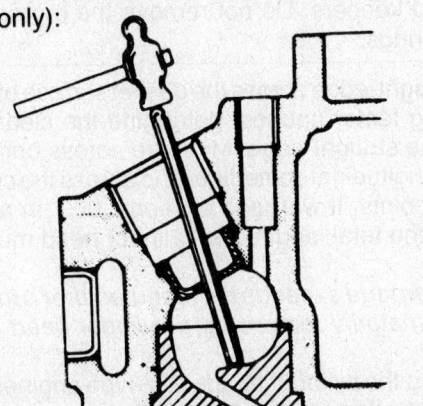	**Remove the pre-combustion chambers using a hammer and a thin, blunt brass drift, inserted through the injector hole (or glow plug hole, whichever is more convenient). If chamber is to be reused, carefully remove all carbon from it. NOTE: *Remove chamber only if being replaced, if a glow plug tip has broken off and must be removed, or if chamber is obviously damaged or loose.*

Removing pre-combustion chamber with a drift (© G.M. Corp.)

| Check the valve stem-to-guide clearance: 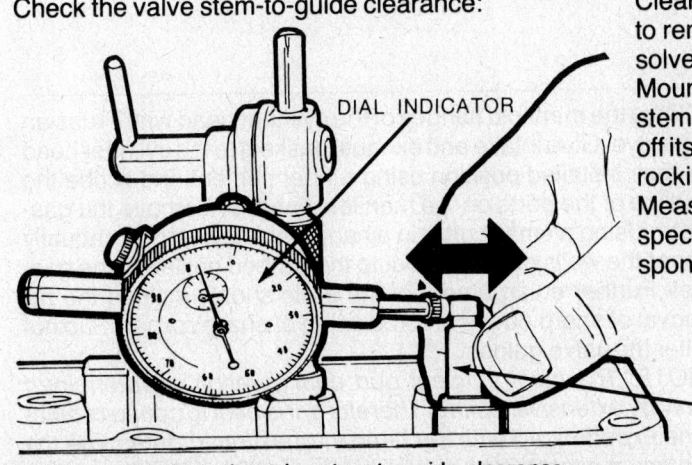 | Clean the valve stem with lacquer thinner or a similar solvent to remove all gum and varnish. Clean the valve guides using solvent and an expanding wire-type valve guide cleaner. Mount a dial indicator so that the stem is at 90° to the valve stem, as close to the valve guide as possible. Move the valve off its seat, and measure the valve guide-to-stem clearance by rocking the stem back and forth to actuate the dial indicator. Measure the valve stems using a micrometer, and compare to specifications, to determine whether stem or guide wear is responsible for excessive clearance. |

DIAL INDICATOR

VALVE STEM

Checking the valve stem-to-guide clearance

ENGINE REBUILDING

CYLINDER HEAD RECONDITIONING

Procedure	Method

De-carbon the cylinder head and valves:

Chip carbon away from the valve heads, combustion chambers, and ports, using a chisel made of hardwood. Remove the remaining deposits with a stiff wire brush.
NOTE: *Ensure that the deposits are actually removed, rather than burnished.*

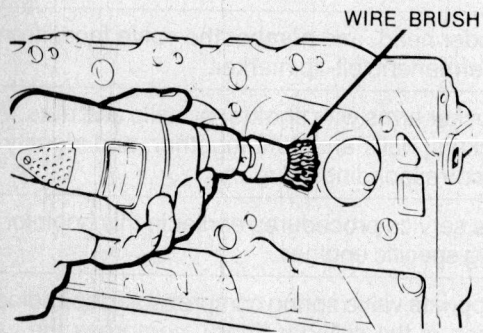

WIRE BRUSH

Removing carbon from the cylinder head

Hot-tank the cylinder head (cast iron heads only):
CAUTION: *Do not hot-tank aluminum parts.*

Have the cylinder head hot-tanked to remove grease, corrosion, and scale from the water passages.
NOTE: *In the case of overhead cam cylinder heads, consult the operator to determine whether the camshaft bearings will be damaged by the caustic solution.*

Degrease the remaining cylinder head parts:

Using solvent (i.e., Gunk), clean the rockers, rocker shaft(s) (where applicable), rocker balls and nuts, springs, spring retainers, and keepers. Do not remove the protective coating from the springs.

Check the cylinder head for warpage:

Place a straight-edge across the gasket surface of the cylinder head. Using feeler gauges, determine the clearance at the center of the straight-edge. Measure across both diagonals, along the longitudinal centerline, and across the cylinder head at several points. If warpage exceeds .003' in a 6' span, or .006' over the total length, the cylinder head must be resurfaced.
NOTE: *If warpage exceeds the manufacturer's maximum tolerance for material removal, the cylinder head must be replaced.*
When milling the cylinder heads of V-type engines, the intake manifold mounting position is altered, and must be corrected by milling the manifold flange a proportionate amount.

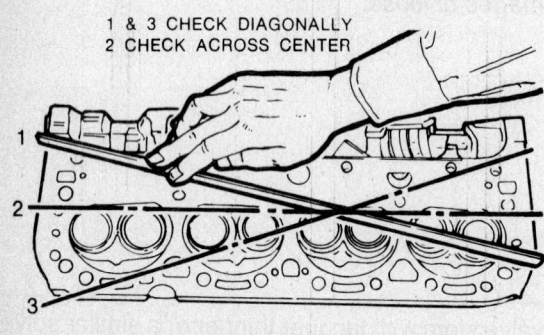

1 & 3 CHECK DIAGONALLY
2 CHECK ACROSS CENTER

Checking cylinder head for warpage

**Porting and gasket matching:

**Coat the manifold flanges of the cylinder head with Prussian blue dye. Glue intake and exhaust gaskets to the cylinder head in their installed position using rubber cement and scribe the outline of the ports on the manifold flanges. Remove the gaskets. Using a small cutter in a hand-held power tool gradually taper the walls of the port out to the scribed outline of the gasket. Further enlargement of the ports should include the removal of sharp edges and radiusing of sharp corners. Do not alter the valve guides.
NOTE: *The most efficient port configuration is determined only by extensive testing. Therefore, it is best to consult someone experienced with the head in question to determine the optimum alterations.*

CYLINDER HEAD RECONDITIONING

Procedure	Method

*Knurling the valve guides:

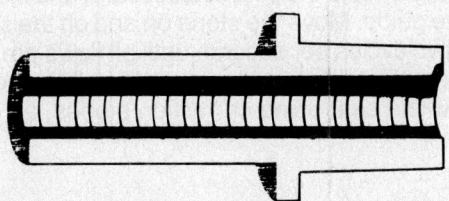

Cut-away view of a knurled valve guide

*Valve guides which are not excessively worn or distorted may, in some cases, be knurled rather than replaced. Knurling is a process in which metal is displaced and raised, thereby reducing clearance. Knurling also provides excellent oil control. The possibility of knurling rather than replacing valve guides should be discussed with a machinist.

Replacing the valve guides:
NOTE: *Valve guides should only be replaced if damaged or if an oversize valve stem is not available.*

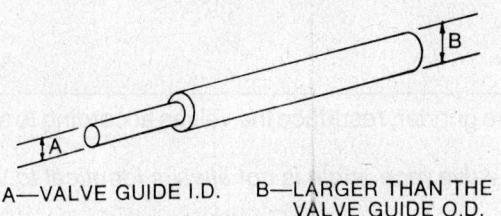

A—VALVE GUIDE I.D.   B—LARGER THAN THE VALVE GUIDE O.D.
Valve guide removal tool

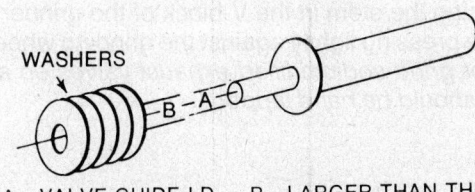

WASHERS

A—VALVE GUIDE I.D.   B—LARGER THAN THE VALVE GUIDE O.D.

Valve guide installation tool (with washers used for installation)

Depending on the type of cylinder head, valve guides may be pressed, hammered, or shrunk in. In cases where the guides are shrunk into the head, replacement should be left to an equipped machine shop. In other cases, the guides are replaced as follows: Press or tap the valve guides out of the head using a stepped drift (see illustration). Determine the height above the boss that the guide must extend, and obtain a stack of washers, their I.D. similar to the guide's O.D., of that height. Place the stack of washers on the guide, and insert the guide into the boss.
NOTE: *Valve guides are often tapered or beveled for installation.*
Using the stepped installation tool (see illustration), press or tap the guides into position. Ream the guides according to the size of the valve stem.

Replacing valve seat inserts:

Replacement of valve seat inserts which are worn beyond resurfacing or broken, if feasible, must be done by a machine shop.

Resurfacing the valve seats using reamers:

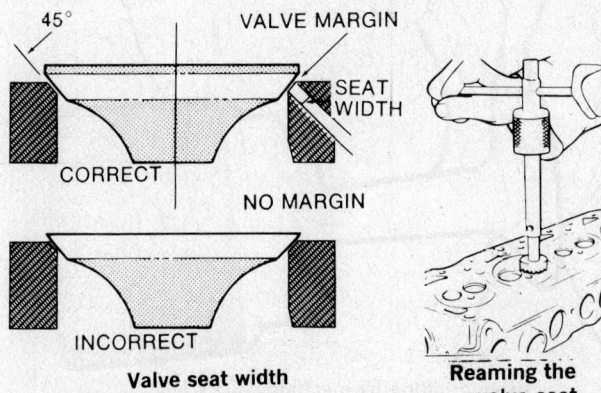

Valve seat width and centering

Reaming the valve seat

Select a reamer of the correct seat angle, slightly larger than the diameter of the valve seat, and assemble it with a pilot of the correct size. Install the pilot into the valve guide, and using steady pressure, turn the reamer clockwise.
CAUTION: *Do not turn the reamer counterclockwise.*
Remove only as much material as necessary to clean the seat. Check the concentricity of the seat (see below). If the dye method is not used, coat the valve face with Prussian blue dye, install and rotate it on the valve seat. Using the dye marked area as a centering guide, center and narrow the valve seat to specifications with correction cutters.
NOTE: *When no specifications are available, minimum seat width for exhaust valves should be* $5/64''$, *intake valves* $1/16''$.
After making correction cuts, check the position of the valve seat on the valve face using Prussian blue dye.
NOTE: *Do not cut induction hardened seats; they must be ground.*

ENGINE REBUILDING

CYLINDER HEAD RECONDITIONING

Procedure	Method

*Resurfacing the valve seats using a grinder:

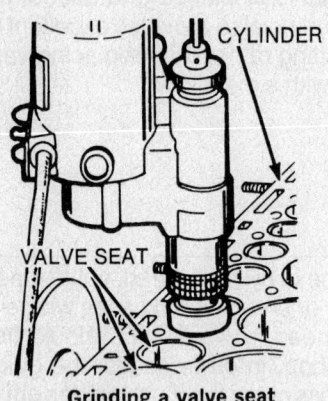

Grinding a valve seat

*Select a pilot of the correct size, and a coarse stone of the correct seat angle. Lubricate the pilot if necessary, and install the tool in the valve guide. Move the stone on and off the seat at approximately two cycles per second, until all flaws are removed from the seat. Install a fine stone, and finish the seat. Center and narrow the seat using correction stones, as described above.

Resurfacing (grinding) the valve face:

Using a valve grinder, resurface the valves according to specifications.

CAUTION: *Valve face angle is not always identical to valve seat angle.*

A minimum margin of $1/32''$ should remain after grinding the valve. The valve stem top should also be squared and resurfaced, by placing the stem in the V-block of the grinder, and turning it while pressing lightly against the grinding wheel.

NOTE: *Do not grind sodium filled exhaust valves on a machine. These should be hand lapped.*

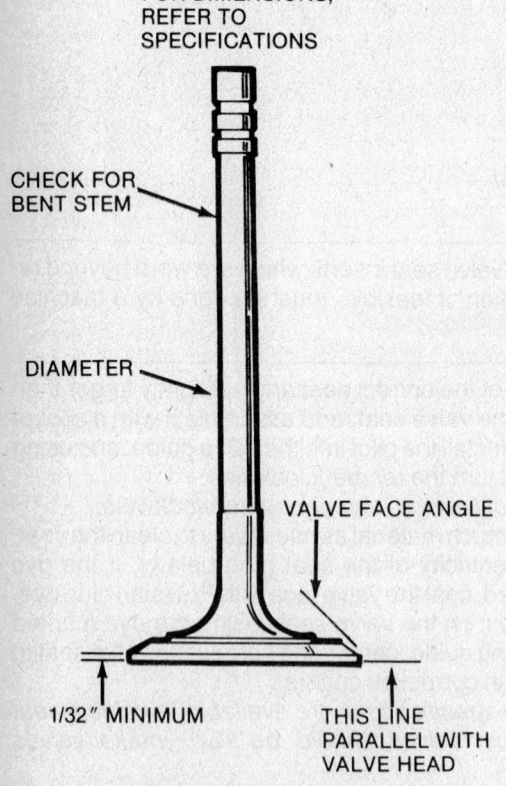

FOR DIMENSIONS, REFER TO SPECIFICATIONS

CHECK FOR BENT STEM

DIAMETER

VALVE FACE ANGLE

1/32" MINIMUM

THIS LINE PARALLEL WITH VALVE HEAD

Critical valve dimensions

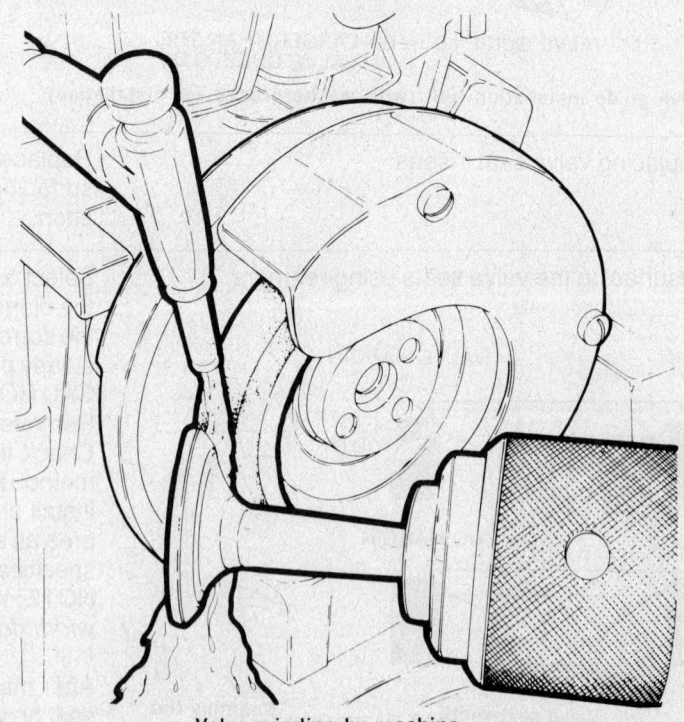

Valve grinding by machine

CYLINDER HEAD RECONDITIONING

Procedure	Method

Checking the valve seat concentricity:

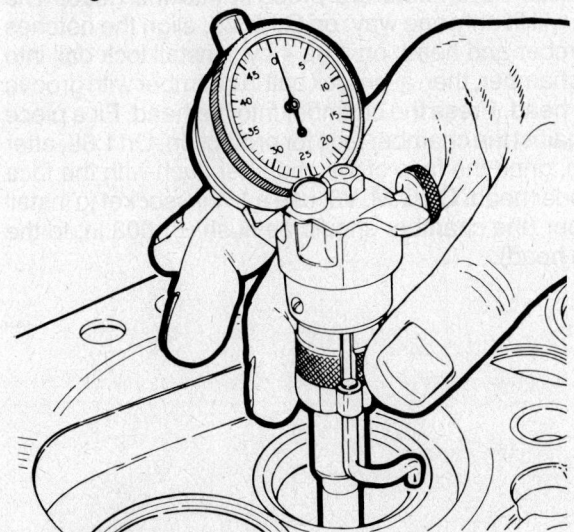

Checking valve seat concentricity using a dial gauge

Coat the valve face with Prussian blue dye, install the valve, and rotate it on the valve seat. If the entire seat becomes coated, and the valve is known to be concentric, the seat is concentric.
*Install the dial gauge pilot into the guide, and rest the arm on the valve seat. Zero the gauge, and rotate the arm around the seat. Run-out should not exceed .002″.

---

*Lapping the valves:
NOTE: *Valve lapping is done to ensure efficient sealing of resurfaced valves and seats.*

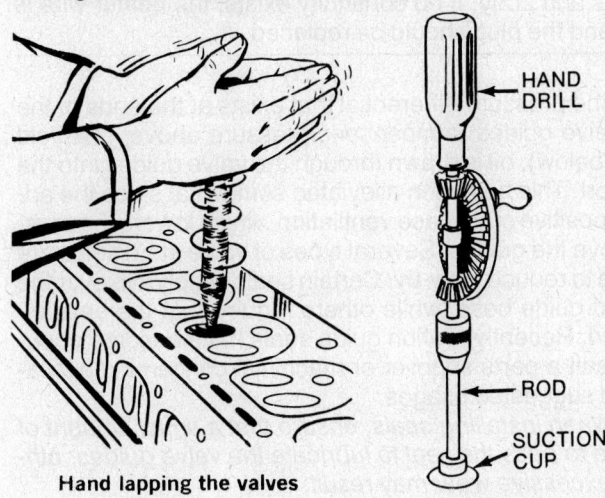

HAND DRILL

ROD

SUCTION CUP

Hand lapping the valves

*Invert the cylinder head, lightly lubricate the valve stems, and install the valves in the head as numbered. Coat valve seats with fine grinding compound, and attach the lapping tool suction cup to a valve head.
NOTE: *Moisten the suction cup.*
Rotate the tool between the palms, changing position and lifting the tool often to prevent grooving. Lap the valve until a smooth, polished seat is evident. Remove the valve and tool, and rinse away all traces of grinding compound.
**Fasten a suction cup to a piece of drill rod, and mount the rod in a hand drill. Proceed as above, using the hand drill as a lapping tool.
CAUTION: *Due to the higher speeds involved when using the hand drill, care must be exercised to avoid grooving the seat.* Lift the tool and change direction of rotation often.

Home made mechanical valve lapping tool

Check the valve springs:

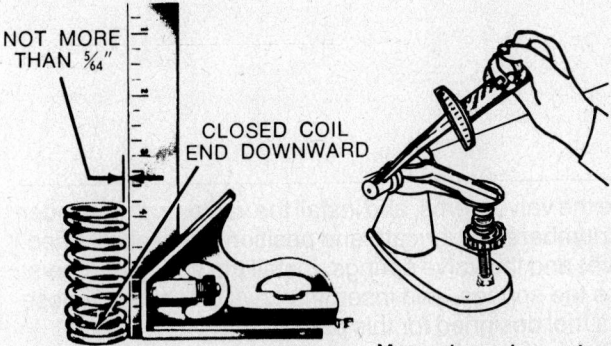

NOT MORE THAN 5⁄64″

CLOSED COIL END DOWNWARD

Checking valve spring free length and squareness

Measuring valve spring test pressure

Place the spring on a flat surface next to a square. Measure the height of the spring, and rotate it against the edge of the square to measure distortion. If spring height varies (by comparison) by more than 1⁄16″ or if distortion exceeds 1⁄16″, replace the spring.
**In addition to evaluating the spring as above, test the spring pressure at the installed and compressed (installed height minus valve lift) height using a valve spring tester. Springs used on small displacement engines (up to 3 liters) should be ∓ 1 lb. of all other springs in either position. A tolerance of ∓ 5 lbs. is permissible on larger engines.

CYLINDER HEAD RECONDITIONING

Procedure	Method

Install pre-combustion chambers (Diesel engines only)

Pre-combustion chambers are press-fit into the head. The chambers will fit only one way: on G.M. V8, align the notches in the chamber and head; on 1.8L 4 cyl., install lock ball into groove in chamber, then align lock ball in chamber with groove in cylinder head. Press the chamber into the head. Fit a piece of metal against the chamber face for protection. On 1.8L, after installation, grind the face of the chamber flush with the face of the cylinder head. On G.M. V8, use a 1¼ in. socket to install the chamber (the chamber should be flush ± .003 in. to the face of the head).

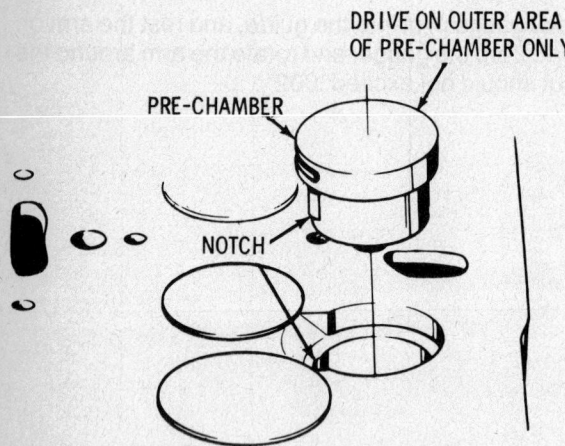

DRIVE ON OUTER AREA OF PRE-CHAMBER ONLY

PRE-CHAMBER

NOTCH

Align the notches to install the pre-combustion chamber (© G.M. Corp.)

Install fuel injectors and glow plugs (Diesel engines)

Before installing glow plugs, check for continuity across plug terminals and body. If no continuity exists, the heater wire is broken and the plug should be replaced.

---

*Install valve stem seals:

*Due to the pressure differential that exists at the ends of the intake valve guides (atmospheric pressure above, manifold vacuum below), oil is drawn through the valve guides into the intake port. This has been alleviated somewhat since the addition of positive crankcase ventilation, which lowers the pressure above the guides. Several types of valve stem seals are available to reduce blow-by. Certain seals simply slip over the stem and guide boss, while others require that the boss be machined. Recently, Teflon guide seals have become popular. Consult a parts supplier or machinist concerning availability and suggested usages.

NOTE: *When installing seals, ensure that a small amount of oil is able to pass the seal to lubricate the valve guides; otherwise, excessive wear may result.*

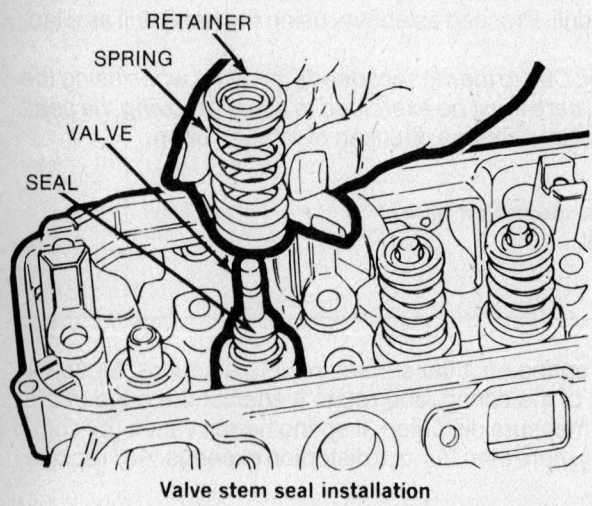

RETAINER

SPRING

VALVE

SEAL

Valve stem seal installation

Install the valves:

Lubricate the valve stems, and install the valves in the cylinder head as numbered. Lubricate and position the seals (if used, see above) and the valve springs. Install the spring retainers, compress the springs, and insert the keys using needlenose pliers or a tool designed for this purpose.

NOTE: *Retain the keys with wheel bearing grease during installation.*

CYLINDER HEAD RECONDITIONING

Procedure	Method

Check valve spring installed height:

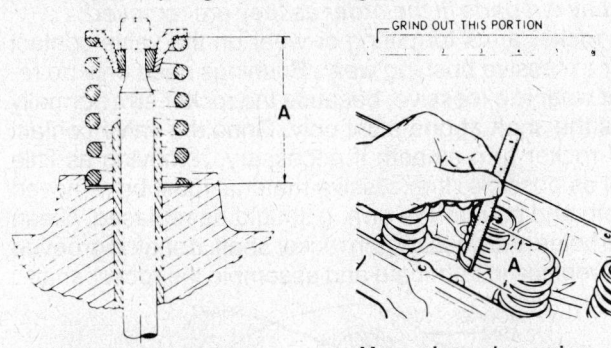

GRIND OUT THIS PORTION

Valve spring installed
height dimension

Measuring valve spring
installed height

Measure the distance between the spring pad and the lower edge of the spring retainer, and compare to specifications. If the installed height is incorrect, add shim washers between the spring pad and the spring.
CAUTION: *Use only washers designed for this purpose.*

Install the camshaft (OHC engines only) and check end play:

See the engine service procedures earlier in this book for details concerning specific engines.

Inspect the rocker arms, balls, studs, and nuts (OHV engines only):

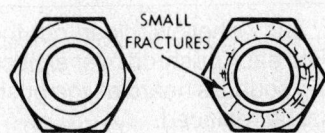

SMALL
FRACTURES

Stress cracks in the rocker nuts

Visually inspect the rocker arms, balls, studs, and nuts for cracks, galling, burning, scoring or wear. If all parts are intact, liberally lubricate the rocker arms and balls, and install them on the cylinder head. If wear is noted on a rocker arm at the point of valve contact, grind it smooth and square, removing as little material as possible. Replace the rocker arm if excessively worn. If a rocker stud shows signs of wear, it must be replaced (see below). If a rocker nut shows stress cracks, replace it. If an exhaust ball is galled or burned, substitute the intake ball from the same cylinder (if it is intact), and install a new intake ball.
NOTE: *Avoid using new rocker balls on exhaust valves.*

Replacing rocker studs (OHV engines only):

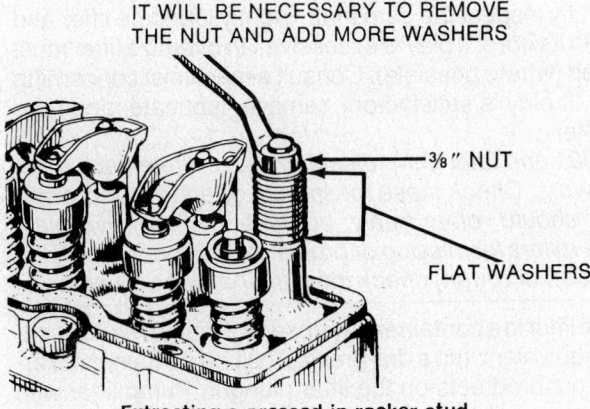

AS STUB BEGINS TO PULL UP,
IT WILL BE NECESSARY TO REMOVE
THE NUT AND ADD MORE WASHERS

⅜" NUT

FLAT WASHERS

Extracting a pressed-in rocker stud

In order to remove a threaded stud, lock two nuts on the stud, and unscrew the stud using the lower nut. Coat the lower threads of the new stud with Loctite®, and install.
Two alternative methods are available for replacing pressed in studs. Remove the damaged stud using a stack of washers and a nut (see illustration). In the first, the boss is reamed .005–.006" oversize, and an oversize stud pressed in. Control the stud extension over the boss using washers, in the same manner as valve guides. Before installing the stud, coat it with white lead and grease. To retain the stud more positively drill a hole through the stud and boss, and install a roll pin. In the second method, the boss is tapped, and a threaded stud installed. Retain the stud using Loctite® Stud and Bearing Mount.

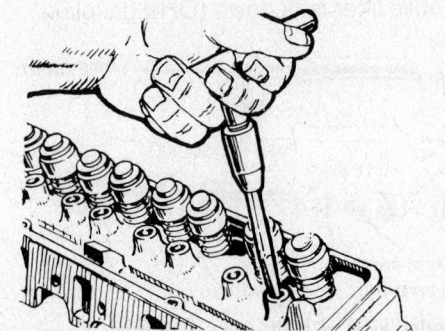

Reaming the stud bore for oversize rocker studs

CYLINDER HEAD RECONDITIONING

Procedure	Method

Inspect the rocker shaft(s) and rocker arms (OHV engines only):

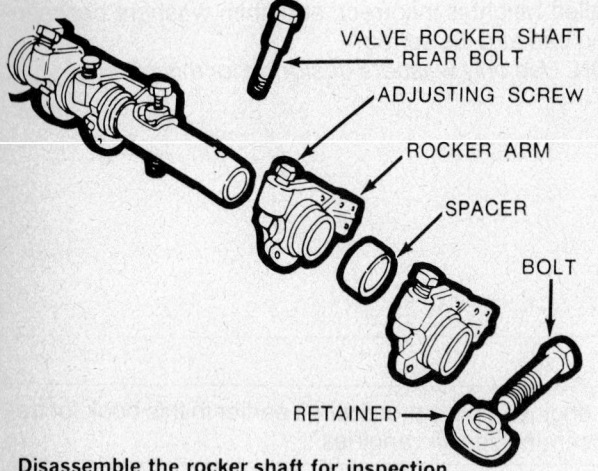

Disassemble the rocker shaft for inspection

Remove rocker arms, springs and washers from rocker shaft. NOTE: *Lay out parts in the order as they are removed.* Inspect rocker arms for pitting or wear on the valve contact point, or excessive bushing wear. Bushings need only be replaced if wear is excessive, because the rocker arm normally contacts the shaft at one point only. Grind the valve contact point of rocker arm smooth if necessary, removing as little material as possible. If excessive material must be removed to smooth and square the arm, it should be replaced. Clean out all oil holes and passages in rocker shaft. If shaft is grooved or worn, replace it. Lubricate and assemble the rocker shaft.

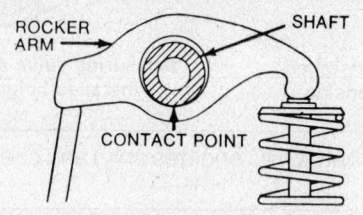

Rocker arm-to-rocker shaft contact area

Inspect the camshaft bushings and the camshaft (OHC engines):

See next section.

Inspect the pushrods (OHV engines only):

Remove the pushrods, and, if hollow, clean out the oil passages using fine wire. Roll each pushrod over a piece of clean glass. If a distinct clicking sound is heard as the pushrod rolls, the rod is bent, and must be replaced.

*The length of all pushrods must be equal. Measure the length of the pushrods, compare to specifications, and replace as necessary.

Inspect the valve lifters (OHV engines only):

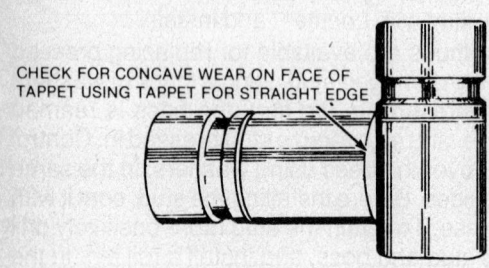

CHECK FOR CONCAVE WEAR ON FACE OF TAPPET USING TAPPET FOR STRAIGHT EDGE

Checking the lifter face

Remove lifters from their bores, and remove gum and varnish, using solvent. Clean walls of lifter bores. Check lifters for concave wear as illustrated. If face is worn concave, replace lifter, and carefully inspect the camshaft. Lightly lubricate lifter and insert it into its bore. If play is excessive, an oversize lifter must be installed (where possible). Consult a machinist concerning feasibility. If play is satisfactory, remove, lubricate, and reinstall the lifter.
NOTE: *1981 and later G.M. diesel V8 valve lifters have roller cam followers. Check these for smooth operation and wear. The roller should rotate freely, but without excessive play. Check the rollers for missing or broken needle bearings. If the roller is pitted or rough, check the camshaft lobe for wear.*

*Testing hydraulic lifter leak down (OHV gasoline engines only):

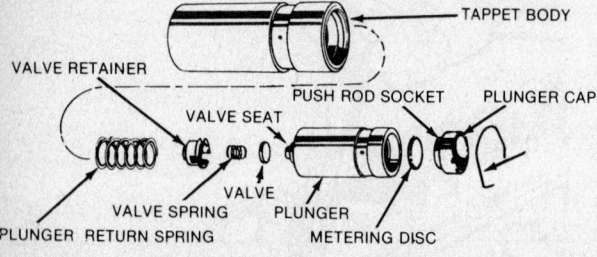

Typical exploded view of hydraulic valve lifter

Submerge lifter in a container of kerosene. Chuck a used pushrod or its equivalent into a drill press. Position container of kerosene so pushrod acts on the lifter plunger. Pump lifter with the drill press, until resistance increases. Pump several more times to bleed any air out of lifter. Apply very firm, constant pressure to the lifter, and observe rate at which fluid bleeds out of lifter. If the fluid bleeds very quickly (less than 15 seconds), lifter is defective. If the time exceeds 60 seconds, lifter is sticking. In either case, recondition or replace lifter. If lifter is operating properly (leak down time 15–60 seconds), lubricate and install it.

CYLINDER HEAD RECONDITIONING

Procedure	Method
Bleed the hydraulic lifters (diesel engines only):	After the cylinder heads are installed on G.M. V8 diesels, the valve lifters must be bled down before the crankshaft is turned. Failure to bleed down the lifters will cause damage to the valve train. See diesel engine rocker arm replacement procedure in Oldsmobile 88, 98, etc. car section for procedures. NOTE: *When installing new lifters, prime by working the lifter plunger while submerged in clean kerosene or diesel fuel.*

CYLINDER BLOCK RECONDITIONING

Procedure	Method
Checking the main bearing clearance: 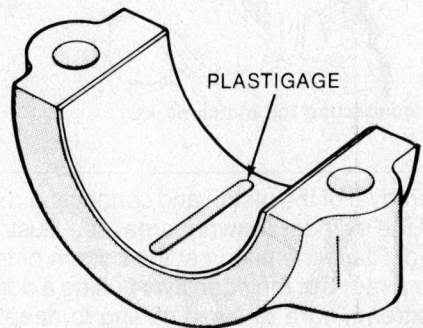 **Plastigage® installed on the lower bearing shell** 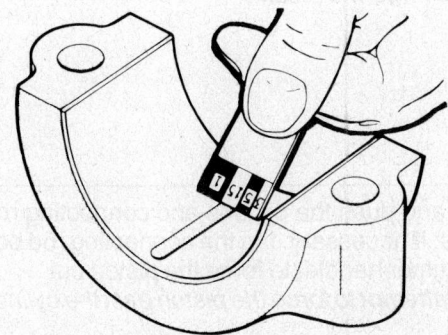 **Measuring Plastigage® to determine bearing clearance**	Invert engine, and remove cap from the bearing to be checked. Using a clean, dry rag, thoroughly clean all oil from crankshaft journal and bearing insert. NOTE: *Plastigage is soluble in oil; therefore, oil on the journal or bearing could result in erroneous readings.* Place a piece of Plastigage along the full length of journal, reinstall cap, and torque to specifications. Remove bearing cap, and determine bearing clearance by comparing width of Plastigage to the scale on Plastigage envelope. Journal taper is determined by comparing width of the Plastigage strip near its ends. Rotate crankshaft 90° and retest, to determine journal eccentricity. NOTE: *Do not rotate crankshaft with Plastigage installed.* If bearing insert and journal appear intact, and are within tolerances, no further main bearing service is required. If bearing or journal appear defective, cause of failure should be determined before replacement. *Remove crankshaft from block (see below). Measure the main bearing journals at each end twice (90° apart) using a micrometer, to determine diameter, journal taper and eccentricity. If journals are within tolerances, reinstall bearing caps at their specified torque. Using a telescope gauge and micrometer, measure bearing I.D. parallel to piston axis and at 30° on each side of piston axis. Subtract journal O.D. from bearing I.D. to determine oil clearance. If crankshaft journals appear defective, or do no meet tolerances, there is no need to measure bearings; for the crankshaft will require grinding and/or undersize bearings will be required. If bearing appears defective, cause for failure should be determined prior to replacement.
Checking the connecting rod bearing clearance:	Connecting rod bearing clearance is checked in the same manner as main bearing clearance, using Plastigage. Before removing the crankshaft, connecting rod side clearance also should be measured and recorded. *Checking connecting rod bearing clearance, using a micrometer, is identical to checking main bearing clearance. If no other service is required, the piston and rod assemblies need not be removed.

ENGINE REBUILDING

CYLINDER BLOCK RECONDITIONING

Procedure	Method

Removing the crankshaft:

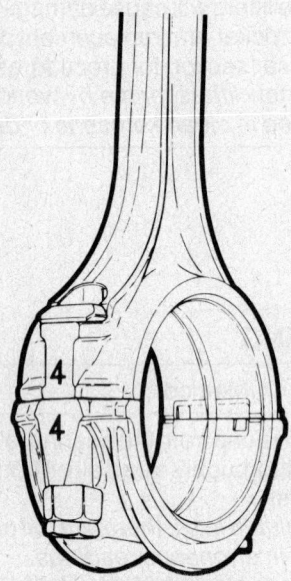

Connecting rod matched to cylinder with a number stamp

Using a punch, mark the corresponding main bearing caps and saddles according to position (i.e., one punch on the front main cap and saddle, two on the second, three on the third, etc.). Using number stamps, identify the corresponding connecting rods and caps, according to cylinder (if no numbers are present). Remove the main and connecting rod caps, and place sleeves of plastic tubing over the connecting rod bolts, to protect the journals as the crankshaft is removed. Lift the crankshaft out of the block.

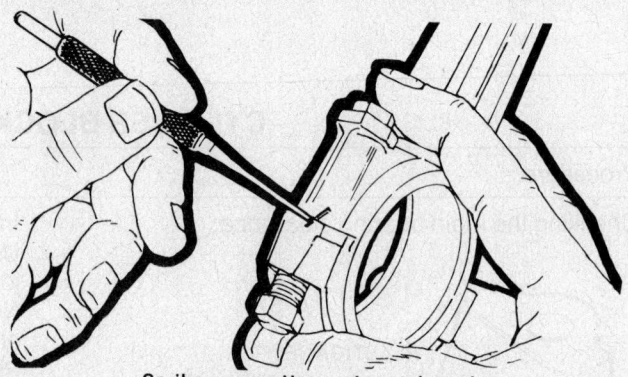

Scribe connecting rod matchmarks

Remove the ridge from the top of the cylinder:

RIDGE CAUSED BY CYLINDER WEAR

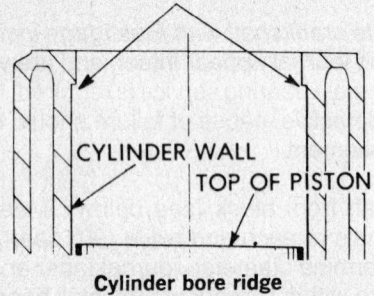

CYLINDER WALL
TOP OF PISTON

Cylinder bore ridge

In order to facilitate removal of the piston and connecting rod, the ridge at the top of the cylinder (unworn area; see illustration) must be removed. Place the piston at the bottom of the bore, and cover it with a rag. Cut the ridge away using a ridge reamer, exercising extreme care to avoid cutting to deeply. Remove the rag, and remove cuttings that remain on the piston.

CAUTION: *If the ridge is not removed, and new rings are installed, damage to rings will result.*

Removing the piston and connecting rod:

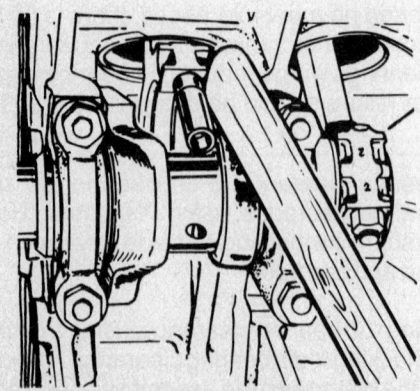

Removing the piston

Invert the engine, and push the pistons and connecting rods out of the cylinders. If necessary, tap the connecting rod boss with a wooden hammer handle, to force the piston out.

CAUTION: *Do not attempt to force the piston past the cylinder ridge* (see above).

CYLINDER BLOCK RECONDITIONING

Procedure	Method
Service the crankshaft:	Ensure that all oil holes and passages in the crankshaft are open and free of sludge. If necessary, have the crankshaft ground to the largest possible undersize. **Have the crankshaft Magnafluxed, to locate stress cracks. Consult a machinist concerning additional service procedures, such as surface hardening (e.g., nitriding, Tuftriding) to improve wear characteristics, cross drilling and chamfering the oil holes to improve lubrication, and balancing.
Removing freeze plugs:	Drill a small hole in the middle of the freeze plugs. Thread a large sheet metal screw into the hole and remove the plug with a slide hammer.
Remove the oil gallery plugs:	Threaded plugs should be removed using an appropriate (usually square) wrench. To remove soft, pressed in plugs, drill a hole in the plug, and thread in a sheet metal screw. Pull the plug out by the screw using pliers.
Hot-tank the block: NOTE: *Do not hot-tank aluminum parts.*	Have the block hot-tanked to remove grease, corrosion, and scale from the water jackets. NOTE: *Consult the operator to determine whether the camshaft bearings will be damaged during the hot-tank process.*

Check the block for cracks:	Visually inspect the block for cracks or chips. The most common locations are as follows:
	    Adjacent to freeze plugs.
	    Between the cylinders and water jackets.
	    Adjacent to the main bearing saddles.
	    At the extreme bottom of the cylinders.
	Check only suspected cracks using spot check dye (see introduction). If a crack is located, consult a machinist concerning possible repairs.
	
	**Magnaflux the block to locate hidden cracks. If cracks are located, consult a machinist about feasibility of repair.

Install the oil gallery plugs and freeze plugs:	Coat freeze plugs with sealer and tap into position using a piece of pipe, slightly smaller than the plug, as a driver. To ensure retention, stake the edges of the plugs. Coat threaded oil gallery plugs with sealer and install. Drive replacement soft plugs into block using a large drift as a driver. *Rather than reinstalling lead plugs, drill and tap the holes, and install threaded plugs.
*Check the deck height:	*The deck height is the distance from the crankshaft centerline to the block deck. To measure, invert the engine, and install the crankshaft, retaining it with the center main cap. Measure the distance from the crankshaft journal to the block deck, parallel to the cylinder centerline. Measure the diameter of the end (front and rear) main journals, parallel to the centerline of the cylinders, divide the diameter in half, and subtract it from the previous measurement. The results of the front and rear measurements should be identical. If the difference exceeds .005″, the deck height should be corrected. NOTE: *Block deck height and warpage should be corrected at the same time.*

CYLINDER BLOCK RECONDITIONING

Procedure	Method

Check the block deck for warpage:

Using a straightedge and feeler gauges, check the block deck for warpage in the same manner that the cylinder head is checked (see Cylinder Head Reconditioning). If warpage exceeds specifications, have the deck resurfaced.

NOTE: *In certain cases a specification for total material removal (Cylinder head and block deck) is provided. This specification must not be exceeded.*

Check the bore diameter and surface:

Measuring the cylinder bore with a dial gauge

Visually inspect the cylinder bores for roughness, scoring, or scuffing. If evident, the cylinder bore must be bored or honed oversize to eliminate imperfections, and the smallest possible oversize piston used. The new pistons should be given to the machinist with the block, so that the cylinders can be bored or honed exactly to the piston size (plus clearance). If no flaws are evident, measure the bore diameter using a telescope gauge and micrometer, or dial guage, parallel and perpendicular to the engine centerline, at the top (below the ridge) and bottom of the bore. Subtract the bottom measurements from the top to determine taper, and the parallel to the centerline measurements from the perpendicular measurements to determine eccentricity. If the measurements are not within specifications, the cylinder must be bored or honed, and an oversize piston installed. If the measurements are within specifications the cylinder may be used as is, with only finish honing (see below).

NOTE: *Prior to boring, check the block deck warpage, height and bearing alignment.*

CAUTION: *The 4 cyl. 140 G.M. engine cylinder walls are impregnated with silicone. Boring or honing can be done only by a shop with the proper equipment.*

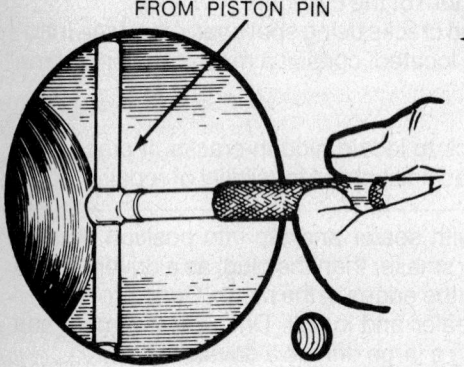

TELESCOPE GAUGE 90° FROM PISTON PIN

Measuring cylinder bore with a telescope gauge

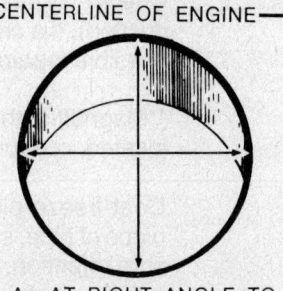

←—CENTERLINE OF ENGINE—→

A—AT RIGHT ANGLE TO CENTERLINE OF ENGINE
B—PARALLEL TO CENTERLINE OF ENGINE

Cylinder bore measuring points

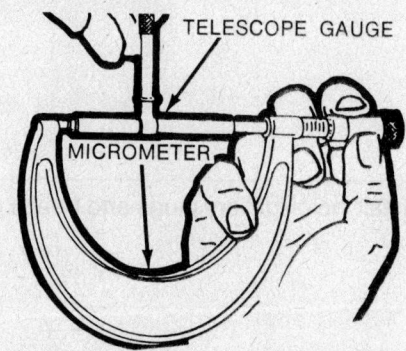

TELESCOPE GAUGE
MICROMETER

Determining cylinder bore by measuring telescope gauge with a micrometer

Check the cylinder block bearing alignment:

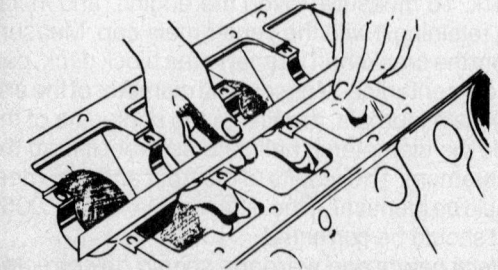

Checking main bearing saddle alignment

Remove the upper bearing inserts. Place a straightedge in the bearing saddles along the centerline of the crankshaft. If clearance exists between the straightedge and the center saddle, the block must be alignbored.

CYLINDER BLOCK RECONDITIONING

Procedure	Method

Clean and inspect the pistons and connecting rods:

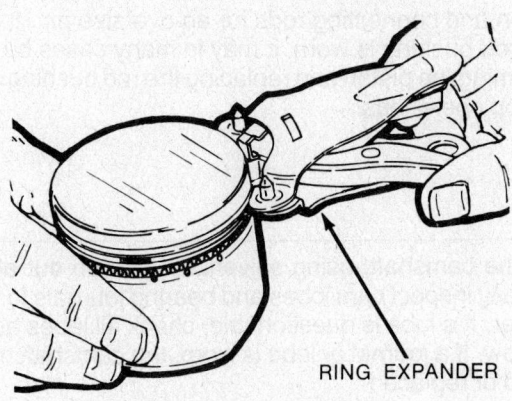

RING EXPANDER

Removing the piston rings

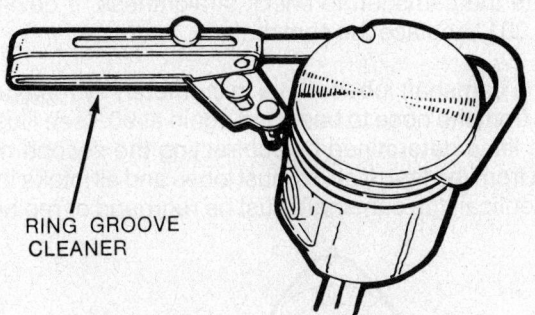

RING GROOVE CLEANER

Cleaning the piston ring grooves

Using a ring expander, remove the rings from the piston. Remove the retaining rings (if so equipped) and remove piston pin.

NOTE: *If the piston pin must be pressed out, determine the proper method and use the proper tools; otherwise the piston will distort.*

Clean the ring grooves using an appropriate tool, exercising care to avoid cutting too deeply. Thoroughly clean all carbon and varnish from the piston with solvent.

CAUTION: *Do not use a wire brush or caustic solvent on pistons.*

Inspect the pistons for scuffing, scoring, cracks, pitting, or excessive ring groove wear. If wear is evident, the piston must be replaced. Check the connecting rod length by measuring the rod from the inside of the large end to the inside of the small end using calipers (see illustration). All connecting rods should be equal length. Replace any rod that differs from the others in the engine.

*Have the connecting rod alignment checked in an alignment fixture by a machinist. Replace any twisted or bent rods.

*Magnaflux the connecting rods to locate stress cracks. If cracks are found, replace the connecting rod.

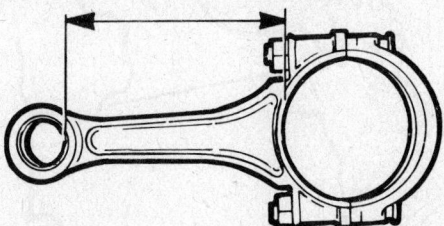

Check the connecting rod length (arrow)

Fit the pistons to the cylinders:

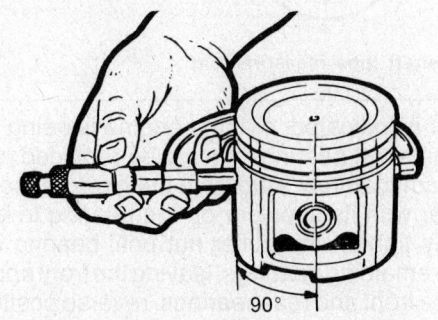

90°

Measuring the piston prior to fitting

Using a telescope gauge and micrometer, or a dial gauge, measure the cylinder bore diameter perpendicular to the piston pin, 2½° below the deck. Measure the piston perpendicular to its pin on the skirt. The difference between the two measurements is the piston clearance. If the clearance is within specifications or slightly below (after boring or honing), finish honing is all that is required. If the clearance is excessive, try to obtain a slightly larger piston to bring clearance within specifications. Where this is not possible, obtain the first oversize piston, and hone (or if necessary, bore) the cylinder to size.

Assemble the pistons and connecting rods:

Inspect piston pin, connecting rod small end bushing, and piston bore for galling, scoring, or excessive wear. If evident, replace defective part(s). Measure the I.D. of the piston boss and connecting rod small end, and the O.D. of the piston pin. If within specifications, assemble piston pin and rod.

CAUTION: *If piston pin must be pressed in, determine the proper method and use the proper tools; otherwise the piston will distort.*

ENGINE REBUILDING

CYLINDER BLOCK RECONDITIONING

Procedure	Method

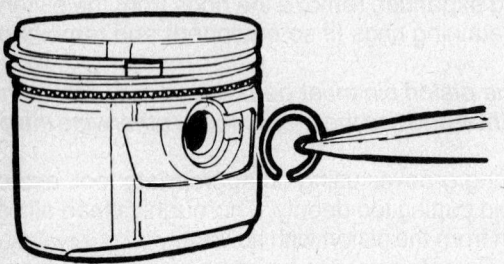

Installing piston pin lock rings

Install the lock rings; ensure that they seat properly. If the parts are not within specifications, determine the service method for the type of engine. In some cases, piston and pin are serviced as an assembly when either is defective. Others specify reaming the piston and connecting rods for an oversize pin. If the connecting rod bushing is worn, it may in many cases be replaced. Reaming the piston and replacing the rod bushing are machine shop operations.

Clean and inspect the camshaft:

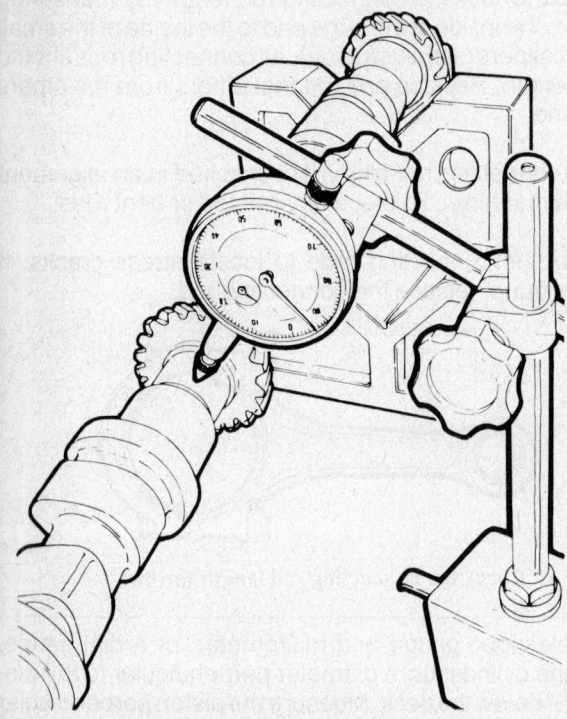

Checking the camshaft for straightness

Degrease the camshaft, using solvent, and clean out all oil holes. Visually inspect cam lobes and bearing journals for excessive wear. If a lobe is questionable, check all lobes as indicated below. If a journal or lobe is worn, the camshaft must be reground or replaced.

NOTE: *If a journal is worn, there is a good chance that the bushings are worn.*

If lobes and journals appear intact, place the front and rear journals in V-blocks, and rest a dial indicator on the center journal. Rotate the camshaft to check straightness. If deviation exceeds .001°, replace the camshaft.

*Check the camshaft lobes with a micrometer, by measuring the lobes from the nose to base and again at 90° (see illustration). The lift is determined by subtracting the second measurement from the first. If all exhaust lobes and all intake lobes are not identical, the camshaft must be reground or replaced.

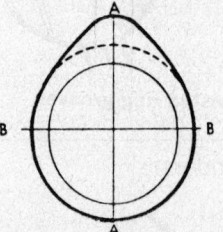

Camshaft lobe measurement

Replace the camshaft bearings (OHV engines only):

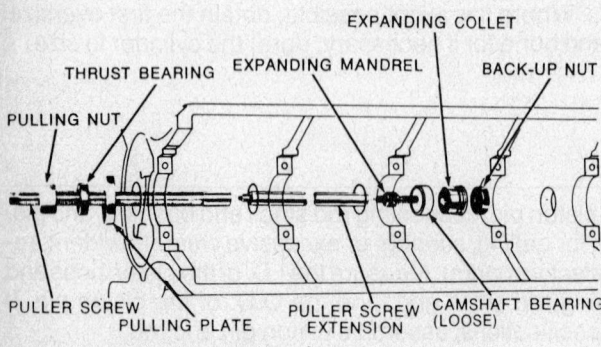

Camshaft removal and installation tool (typical)

If excessive wear is indicated, or if the engine is being completely rebuilt, camshaft bearings should be replaced as follows: Drive the camshaft rear plug from the block. Assemble the removal puller with its shoulder on the bearing to be removed. Gradually tighten the puller nut until bearing is removed. Remove remaining bearings, leaving the front and rear for last. To remove front and rear bearings, reverse position of the tool, so as to pull the bearings in toward the center of the block. Leave the tool in this position, pilot the new front and rear bearings on the installer, and pull them into position: Return the tool to its original position and pull remaining bearings into postion.

NOTE: *Ensure that oil holes align when installing bearings.*

Replace camshaft rear plug, and stake it into position to aid retention.

CYLINDER BLOCK RECONDITIONING

Procedure	Method

Finish hone the cylinders:

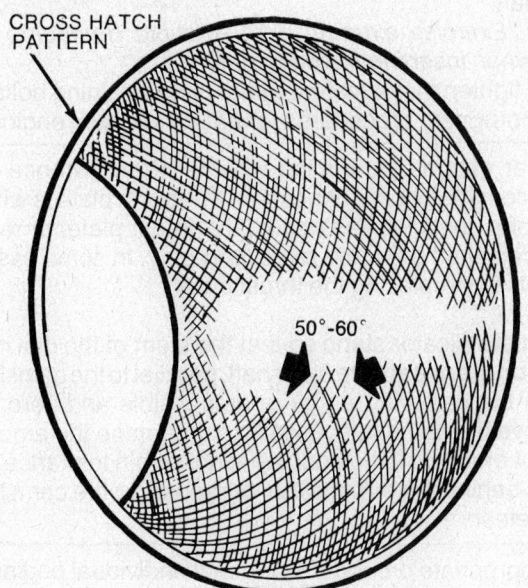

CROSS HATCH PATTERN

50°-60°

Chuck a flexible drive hone into a power drill, and insert it into the cylinder. Start the hone, and move it up and down the cylinder at a rate which will produce approximately a 60° cross-hatch pattern (see illustration).
NOTE: *Do not extend the hone below the cylinder bore.*
After developing the pattern, remove the hone and recheck piston fit. Wash the cylinders with a detergent and water solution to remove abrasive dust, dry, and wipe several times with a rag soaked in engine oil.

Check piston ring end-gap:

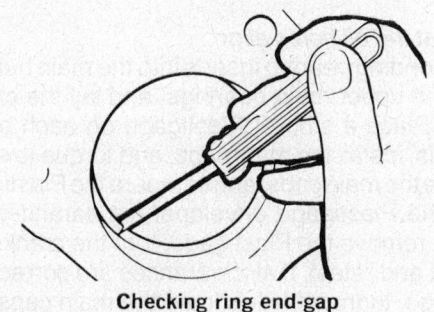

Checking ring end-gap

Compress the piston rings to be used in a cylinder, one at a time, into that cylinder, and press them approximately 1″ below the deck with an inverted piston. Using feeler gauges, measure the ring end-gap, and compare to specifications. Pull the ring out of the cylinder and file the ends with a fine file to obtain proper clearance.
CAUTION: *If inadequate ring end-gap is utilized, ring breakage will result.*

Install the piston rings:

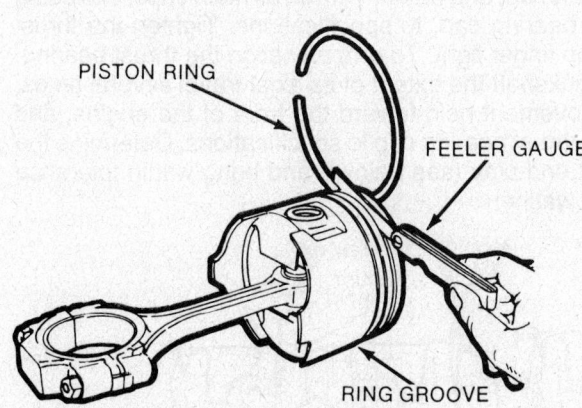

PISTON RING

FEELER GAUGE

RING GROOVE

Checking ring side clearance

Inspect the ring grooves in the piston for excessive wear or taper. If necessary, recut the groove(s) for use with an over-width ring or a standard ring and spacer. If the groove is worn uniformly, overwidth rings, or standard rings and spacers may be installed without recutting. Roll the outside of the ring around the groove to check for burrs or deposits. If any are found, remove with a fine file. Hold the ring in the groove, and measure side clearance. If necessary, correct as indicated above.
NOTE: *Always install any additional spacers above the piston ring.*
The ring groove must be deep enough to allow the ring to seat below the lands (see illustration). In many cases, a "go-no-go" depth gauge will be provided with the piston rings. Shallow grooves may be corrected by recutting, while deep grooves require some type of filler or expander behind the piston. Consult the piston ring supplier concerning the suggested method. Install the rings on the piston, lowest ring first, using a ring expander.
NOTE: *Position the ring markings as specified by the manufacturer (see car section).*

ENGINE REBUILDING

CYLINDER BLOCK RECONDITIONING

Procedure	Method
Install the camshaft (OHV engines only):	Liberally lubricate the camshaft lobes and journals, and install the camshaft. CAUTION: *Exercise extreme care to avoid damaging the bearings when inserting the camshaft.* Install and tighten the camshaft thrust plate retaining bolts. See the appropriate procedures for each individual engine.
Check camshaft end-play (OHV engines only): 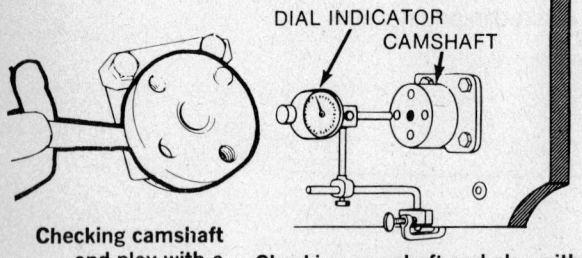 **Checking camshaft end-play with a feeler gauge** **Checking camshaft end-play with a dial indicator**	Using feeler gauges, determine whether the clearance between the camshaft boss (or gear) and backing plate is within specifications. Install shims behind the thrust plate, or reposition the camshaft gear and retest end-play. In some cases, adjustment is by replacing the thrust plate. *Mount a dial indicator stand so that the stem of the dial indicator rests on the nose of the camshaft, parallel to the camshaft axis. Push the camshaft as far in as possible and zero the gauge. Move the camshaft outward to determine the amount of camshaft endplay. If the endplay is not within tolerance, install shims behind the thrust plate, or reposition the camshaft gear and retest.
Install the rear main seal (where applicable):	See the appropriate procedures for each individual engine.
Install the crankshaft: 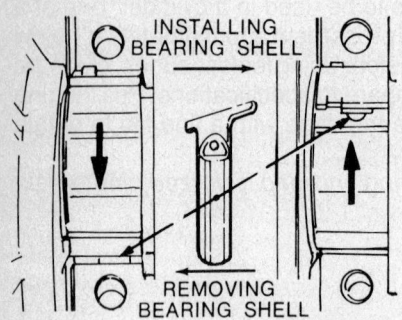 **Removal and installation of upper bearing insert using a roll-out pin** 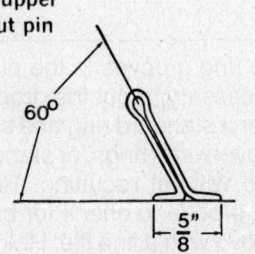 **Home-made bearing roll-out pin**	Thoroughly clean the main bearing saddles and caps. Place the upper halves of the bearing inserts on the saddles and press into position. NOTE: *Ensure that the oil holes align.* Press the corresponding bearing inserts into the main bearing caps. Lubricate the upper main bearings, and lay the crankshaft in position. Place a strip of Plastigage on each of the crankshaft journals, install the main caps, and torque to specifications. Remove the main caps, and compare the Plastigage to the scale on the Plastigage envelope. If clearances are within tolerances, remove the Plastigage, turn the crankshaft 90°, wipe off all oil and retest. If all clearances are correct, remove all Plastigage, thoroughly lubricate the main caps and bearing journals, and install the main caps. If clearances are not within tolerance, the upper bearing inserts may be removed, without removing the crankshaft, using a bearing roll out pin (see illustration). Roll in a bearing that will provide proper clearance, and retest. Torque all main caps, excluding the thrust bearing cap, to specifications. Tighten the thrust bearing cap finger tight. To properly align the thrust bearing, pry the crankshaft the extent of its axial travel several times, the last movement held toward the front of the engine, and torque the thrust bearing cap to specifications. Determine the crankshaft end-play (see below), and bring within tolerance with thrust washers.

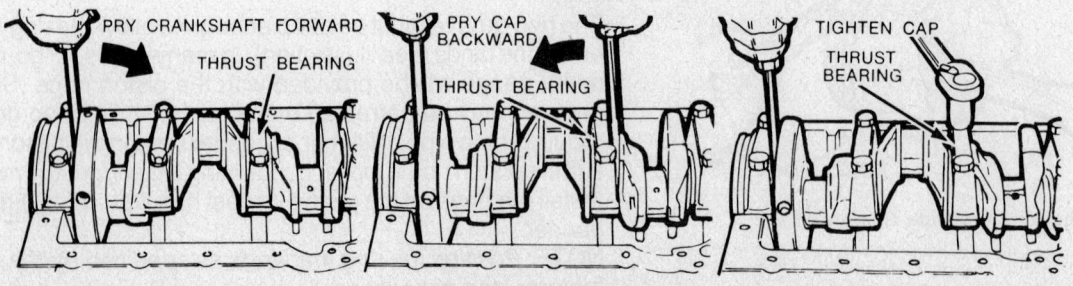

Aligning the thrust bearing

CYLINDER BLOCK RECONDITIONING

Procedure	Method

Measure crankshaft end-play:

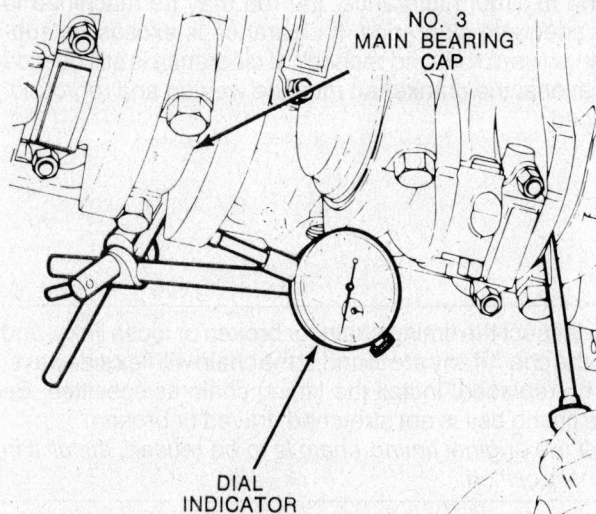

Checking crankshaft end-play with a dial indicator

Mount a dial indicator stand on the front of the block, with the dial indicator stem resting on the nose of the crankshaft, parallel to the crankshaft axis. Pry the crankshaft the extent of its travel rearward, and zero the indicator. Pry the crankshaft forward and record crankshaft end-play.

NOTE: *Crankshaft end-play also may be measured at the thrust bearing, using feeler gauges* (see illustration).

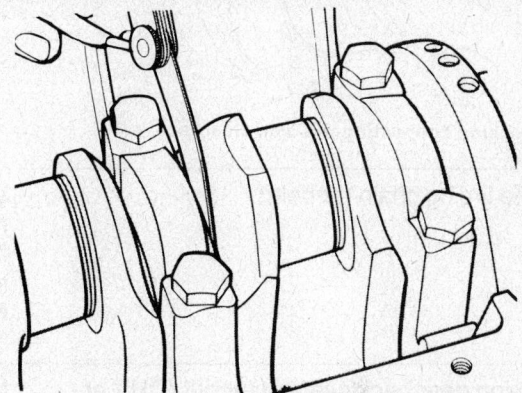

Checking crankshaft end-play with a feeler gauge

Install the pistons:

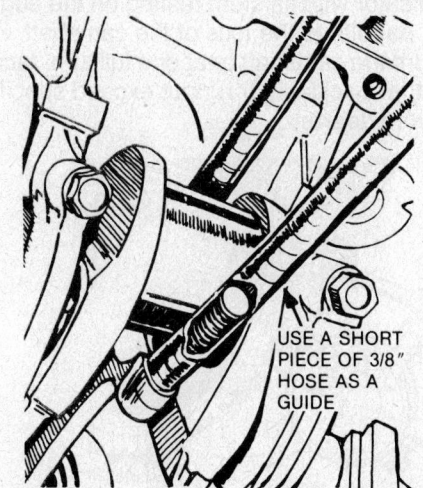

Tubing used to protect crankshaft journals and cylinder walls during piston installation

Press the upper connecting rod bearing halves into the connecting rods, and the lower halves into the connecting rod caps. Position the piston ring gaps according to specifications (see car section), and lubricate the pistons. Install a ring compressor on a piston, and press two long (8") pieces of plastic tubing over the rod bolts. Using the tubes as a guide, press the pistons into the bores and onto the crankshaft with a wooden hammer handle. After seating the rod on the crankshaft journal, remove the tubes and install the cap finger tight. Install the remaining pistons in the same manner. Invert the engine and check the bearing clearance at two points (90° apart) on each journal with Plastigage.

NOTE: *Do not turn the crankshaft with Plastigage installed.*

If clearance is within tolerances, remove *all* Plastigage, thoroughly lubricate the journals, and torque the rod caps to specifications. If clearance is not within specifications, install different thickness bearing inserts and recheck.

CAUTION: *Never shim or file the connecting rods or caps.* Always install plastic tube sleeves over the rod bolts when the caps are not installed, to protect the crankshaft journals.

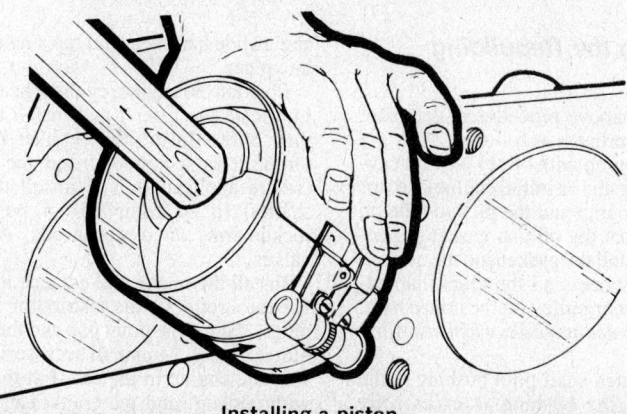

Installing a piston

ENGINE REBUILDING

CYLINDER BLOCK RECONDITIONING

Procedure	Method
Check connecting rod side clearance: 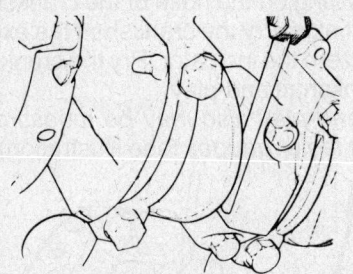 **Checking connecting rod side clearance**	Determine the clearance between the sides of the connecting rods and the crankshaft, using feeler gauges. If clearance is below the minimum tolerance, the rod may be machined to provide adequate clearance. If clearance is excessive, substitute an unworn rod, and recheck. If clearance is still outside specifications, the crankshaft must be welded and reground, or replaced.
Inspect the timing chain (or belt):	Visually inspect the timing chain for broken or loose links, and replace the chain if any are found. If the chain will flex sideways, it must be replaced. Install the timing chain as specified. Be sure the timing belt is not stretched, frayed or broken. NOTE: *If the original timing chain is to be reused, install it in its original position.*
Check timing gear backlash and runout (OHV engines):	Mount a dial indicator with its stem resting on a tooth of the camshaft gear (as illustrated). Rotate the gear until all slack is removed, and zero the indicator. Rotate the gear in the opposite direction until slack is removed, and record gear backlash. Mount the indicator with its stem resting on the edge of the camshaft gear, parallel to the axis of the camshaft. Zero the indicator, and turn the camshaft gear one full turn, recording the runout. If either backlash or runout exceed specifications, replace the worn gear(s).

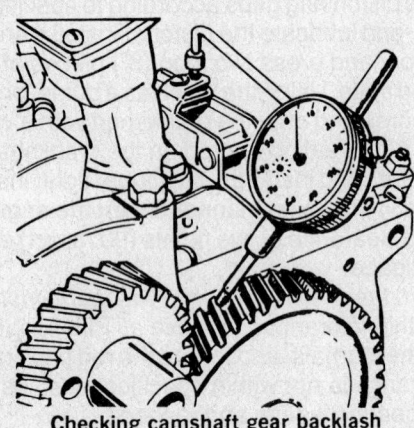

Checking camshaft gear backlash

Checking camshaft gear runout

Completing the Rebuilding Process

Following the above procedures, complete the rebuilding process as follows:

Fill the oil pump with oil, to prevent cavitating (sucking air) on initial engine start up. Install the oil pump and the pickup tube on the engine. Coat the oil pan gasket as necessary, and install the gasket and the oil pan. Mount the flywheel and the crankshaft vibration damper or pulley on the crankshaft. NOTE: *Always use new bolts when installing the flywheel.*

Inspect the clutch shaft pilot bushing in the crankshaft. If the bushing is excessively worn, remove it with an expanding puller and a slide hammer, and tap a new bushing into place.

Position the engine, cylinder head side up. Lubricate the lifters, and install them into their bores. Install the cylinder head, and torque it as specified. Insert the pushrods (where applicable), and install the rocker shaft(s) (if so equipped) or position the rocker arms on the pushrods. Adjust the valves.

Install the intake and exhaust manifolds, the carburetor(s), the distributor and spark plugs. Adjust the point gap and the static ignition timing. Mount all accessories and install the engine in the car. Fill the radiator with coolant, and the crankcase with high quality engine oil.

Break-in Procedure

Start the engine, and allow it to run at low speed for a few minutes, while checking for leaks. Stop the engine, check the oil level, and fill as necessary. Restart the engine, and fill the cooling system to capacity. Check the point dwell angle and adjust the ignition timing and the valves. Run the engine at low to medium speed (800–2500 rpm) for approximately ½ hour, and retorque the cylinder head bolts. Road test the car, and check again for leaks.

Follow the manufacturer's recommended engine break-in procedure and maintenance schedule for new engines.

STANDARD TORQUE SPECIFICATIONS AND CAPSCREW MARKINGS

Newton-Meter has been designated as the world standard for measuring torque and will gradually replace the foot-pound and kilogram-meter torque measuring standard. Torquing tools are still being manufactured with foot-pounds and kilogram-meter scales, along with the new Newton-Meter standard. To assist the repairman, foot-pounds, kilogram-meter and Newton-Meter are listed in the following charts, and should be followed as applicable.

U.S. BOLTS

SAE Grade Number	1 or 2			5			6 or 7			8		
Capscrew Head Markings (Manufacturer's marks may vary. Three-line markings on heads below indicate SAE Grade 5.) 	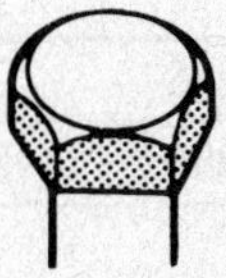						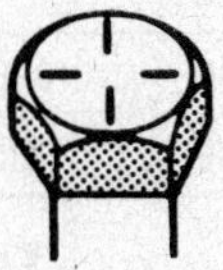			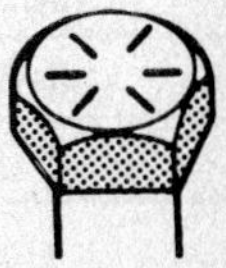		
Usage	Used Frequently			Used Frequently			Used at Times			Used at Times		
Quality of Material	Indeterminate			Minimum Commercial			Medium Commercial			Best Commercial		
Capacity Body Size	Torque			Torque			Torque			Torque		
(inches)–(thread)	Ft-Lb	kgm	Nm	Ft-Lb	kgm	Nm	Ft-Lb	kgm	Nm	Ft-Lb	kgm	Nm
1/4–20	5	0.6915	6.7791	8	1.1064	10.8465	10	1.3630	13.5582	12	1.6596	16.2698
–28	6	0.8298	8.1349	10	1.3830	13.5582				14	1.9362	18.9815
5/16–18	11	1.5213	14.9140	17	2.3511	23.0489	19	2.6277	25.7605	24	3.3192	32.5396
–24	13	1.7979	17.6256	19	2.6277	25.7605				27	3.7341	36.6071
3/8–16	18	2.4894	24.4047	31	4.2873	42.0304	34	4.7022	46.0978	44	6.0852	59.6560
–24	20	2.7660	27.1164	35	4.8405	47.4536				49	6.7767	66.4351
7/16–14	28	3.8132	37.9629	49	6.7767	66.4351	55	7.6065	74.5700	70	9.6810	94.9073
–20	30	4.1490	40.6745	55	7.6065	74.5700				78	10.7874	105.7538
1/2–13	39	5.3937	52.8769	75	10.3725	101.6863	85	11.7555	115.2445	105	14.5215	142.3609
–20	41	5.6703	55.5885	85	11.7555	115.2445				120	16.5860	162.6960
9/16–12	51	7.0533	69.1467	110	15.2130	149.1380	120	16.5960	162.6960	155	21.4365	210.1490
–18	55	7.6065	74.5700	120	16.5960	162.6960				170	23.5110	230.4860
5/8–11	83	11.4789	112.5329	150	20.7450	203.3700	167	23.0961	226.4186	210	29.0430	284.7180
–18	95	13.1385	128.8027	170	23.5110	230.4860				240	33.1920	325.3920
3/4–10	105	14.5215	142.3609	270	37.3410	366.0660	280	38.7240	379.6240	375	51.8625	508.4250
–16	115	15.9045	155.9170	295	40.7985	399.9610				420	58.0860	568.4360
7/8–9	160	22.1280	216.9280	395	54.6285	535.5410	440	60.8520	596.5520	605	83.6715	820.2590
–14	175	24.2025	237.2650	435	60.1605	589.7730				675	93.3525	915.1650
1–8	236	32.5005	318.6130	590	81.5970	799.9220	660	91.2780	894.8280	910	125.8530	1233.7780
–14	250	34.5750	338.9500	660	91.2780	849.8280				990	136.9170	1342.2420

METRIC BOLTS

Description	Torque ft-lbs. (Nm)			
Thread for general purposes (size x pitch (mm))	Head Mark 4		Head Mark 7	
6 x 1.0	2.2 to 2.9	(3.0 to 3.9)	3.6 to 5.8	(4.9 to 7.8)
8 x 1.25	5.8 to 8.7	(7.9 to 12)	9.4 to 14	(13 to 19)
10 x 1.25	12 to 17	(16 to 23)	20 to 29	(27 to 39)
12 x 1.25	21 to 32	(29 to 43)	35 to 53	(47 to 72)
14 x 1.5	35 to 52	(48 to 70)	57 to 85	(77 to 110)
16 x 1.5	51 to 77	(67 to 100)	90 to 120	(130 to 160)
18 x 1.5	74 tc 110	(100 to 150)	130 to 170	(180 to 230)
20 x 1.5	110 to 140	(150 to 190)	190 to 240	(160 to 320)
22 x 1.5	150 to 190	(200 to 260)	250 to 320	(340 to 430)
24 x 1.5	190 to 240	(260 to 320)	310 to 410	(420 to 550)

CAUTION: Bolts threaded into aluminum require much less torque

GENERAL MOTORS DIESEL

GENERAL ENGINE SPECIFICATIONS

Year	Engine No. Cyl. Displacement (cu. in.)	Carburetor Type	Horsepower @ rpm	Torque @ rpm (ft. lbs.)	Bore × Stroke (in.)	Compression Ratio	Oil Pressure @ 2000 rpm
'78	8–350	Diesel	120 @ 3600	220 @ 1600	4.057 × 3.385	22.5:1	40
'79–'81	8–350	Diesel	125 @ 3600	225 @ 1600	4.057 × 3.385	22.5:1	40

TUNE-UP SPECIFICATIONS

Year	Engine No. Cyl. Displacement (cu. in.)	Ignition Timing (deg)① Man Trans.	Ignition Timing (deg)① Auto. Trans.	Compression (lbs.)	Valves Intake Opens (deg)	Fuel Pump Pressure (psi)	Idle Speed (rpm)① Man. Trans.	Idle Speed (rpm)① Auto. Trans.
'78	8–350	—	5B	275 min.	16	5.5–6.5	—	575
'79	8–350	—	4.5B	275 min.	16	5.5–6.5	—	575
'80	8–350	—	5B	275 min.	16	5.5–6.5	—	600
'81	8–350	—	8B/5B	275 min.	16	5.5–6.5	—	575/600

NOTE: The underhood specifications sticker often reflects tune-up specification changes made in production. Sticker figures must be used if they disagree with those in this chart.

① Where two figures are separated by a slash, the first is for Federal cars, the second is for California cars.

FIRING ORDER

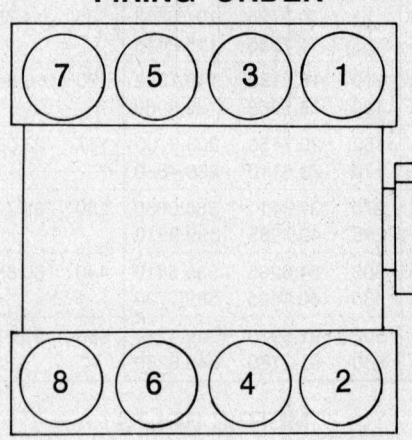

Engine firing order: 1-8-4-3-6-5-7-2
(© General Motors Corp.)

VALVE SPECIFICATIONS

Year	Engine No. Cyl. Displacement (cu. in.)	Seat Angle (deg)	Face Angle (deg)	Spring Test Pressure③ (lbs. @ in.)	Spring Installed Height (in.)	Stem to Guide Clearance (in.) Intake	Stem to Guide Clearance (in.) Exhaust	Stem Diameter (in.) Intake	Stem Diameter (in.) Exhaust
'78	8–350	45①	44②	151 @ 1.336	1⁴⁷⁄₆₄	.0010–.0027	.0015–.0032	.3425–.3432	.3420–.3427
'79–'80	8–350	45①	44②	151 @ 1.300	1⁴³⁄₆₄	.0010–.0027	.0015–.0032	.3425–.3432	.3420–.3427
'81	8–350	45①	44②	205 @ 1.300	1⁴³⁄₆₄	.0010–.0027	.0015–.0032	.3425–.3432	.3420–.3427

① Figure is for intake valve; for exhaust—31°   ② Figure is for intake valve; for exhaust—30°   ③ Valve open

CRANKSHAFT AND CONNECTING ROD SPECIFICATIONS

All measurements are given in inches

Year	Engine No. Cyl. Displacement (cu in.)	Crankshaft				Connecting Rod		
		Main Brg. Journal Dia.	Main Brg. Oil Clearance	Shaft End-Play	Thrust on No.	Journal Diameter	Oil Clearance	Side Clearance
'78–'81	8–350	2.9993–3.0003	.0005–.0021①	.0035–.0135	3	2.1238–2.1248	.0005–.0026	.006–.020

① #5: .0015–.0031

PISTON AND RING SPECIFICATIONS

All measurements are given in inches.

Year	Engine No. Cyl. Displacement (cu. in.)	Ring Gap			Ring Side Clearance			Piston Clearance
		Top Compression	Bottom Compression	Oil Control	Top Compression	Bottom Compression	Oil Control	
'78–'81	8–350	015–.025	.015–.025	.015–.055	.005–.007	.0018–.0038	.001–.005	.005–.006

PISTON PIN SPECIFICATIONS

All measurements in inches

Year	Engine	Diameter	Pin to Rod Clearance	Pin to Piston Clearance
'78–'81	350	1.0949–1.0953	.0003–.0013	.0003–.0005

TORQUE SPECIFICATIONS

All readings in ft. lbs.

Year	Engine	Cylinder Head Bolts	Rod Bearing Bolts	Main Bearing Bolts	Crankshaft Bolt	Flywheel to Crankshaft Bolts	Manifold Intake	Manifold Exhaust
'78–'81	350	130①	42	120	200–310	60	40①	25

① Clean and dip entire bolt in engine oil before tightening to obtain a correct torque reading.

TROUBLESHOOTING

Condition	Cause	Correction
Engine will not crank	1. Loose or corroded battery cables	1. Check connections at batteries, engine block and starter solenoid.
	2. Discharged batteries	2. Check generator output and generator belt adjustment.
	3. Starter inoperative	3. Check voltage to starter and starter solenoid. If okay, remove starter for repair.
Engines cranks slowly, will not start (minimum engine cranking speed 100 rpm cold, 240 rpm hot)	1. Battery cable connections loose or corroded	1. Check connections at batteries, engine block and starter.
	2. Batteries undercharged	2. Check charging system.
	3. Wrong engine oil	3. Drain and refill with oil of recommended viscosity.
Engine cranks normally, will not start	1. Incorrect starting procedure	1. Use recommended starting procedure.
	2. No voltage to fuel solenoid	2. Connect a 12 volt test lamp from wire at injection pump solenoid to ground, turn ignition to "ON", lamp should light. If lamp lights, remove test light, connect and disconnect solenoid connector and listen for solenoid operation. If solenoid does not operate, remove injection pump for repair.

TROUBLESHOOTING

Condition	Cause	Correction
	3. Plugged fuel return system	3. Disconnect fuel return line at injection pump and route hose to a metal container. Connect a hose to the injection pump connection, route it to the metal container. Crank the engine, if it starts and runs, correct restriction in fuel return lines.
	4. No fuel to nozzles	4. Loosen injection line at a nozzle, do not disconnect. Use care to direct fuel away from sources of ignition. Wipe connection to be sure it is dry. Crank 5 seconds. Fuel should seep from injection line. Tighten connection. If fuel seeps, go to step 8.
	5. No fuel to injection pump	5. Remove line at inlet to injection pump fuel filter. Connect hose from line to metal container. Crank engine. If no fuel is discharged, test the engine fuel pump. (If fuel does not flow from pump outlet, go to step 6.) If the fuel pump is okay, check the injection pump fuel filter and, if plugged, replace it. If fuel filter and line to injection pump are okay, remove injection pump for repair.
	6. Restricted fuel tank filter	6. Remove fuel tank and check filter. Filter for diesel fuel is blue.
	7. Incorrect or contaminated fuel	7. Flush fuel system and install correct fuel.
	8. Pump timing incorrect	8. Make certain that pump timing mark is aligned with mark on adapter.
	9. Low compression	9. Check compression to determine cause.
Engine starts but will not continue to run at idle	1. Slow idle incorrectly adjusted	1. Adjust idle screw to specification.
	2. Fast idle solenoid inoperative	2. With engine cold, start engine; solenoid should move to hold injection pump lever in fast idle position.
	3. Restricted fuel return system	3. Disconnect fuel return line at injection pump and route hose to a metal container. Connect a hose to the injection pump connection, route it to the metal container. Crank the engine and allow it to idle. If engine idles normally, correct restriction in fuel return lines.
	4. Pump timing incorrect	4. Make certain that timing mark on injection pump is aligned with mark on adapter.
	5. Limited fuel to injection pump	5. Test the engine fuel pump, check fuel lines. Replace or repair as necessary.
Engine starts but will not continue to run at idle	6. Air in injection lines to nozzles	6. Loosen injection line at nozzle(s) and bleed air. Use care to direct fuel away from sources of ignition.
	7. Incorrect or contaminated fuel	7. Flush fuel system and install correct fuel.
	8. Injection pump malfunction	8. Remove injection pump for repair.
	9. Low compression	9. Check compression to determine cause.
	10. Fuel solenoid closes in run position	10. Ignition switch out of adjustment.

TROUBLESHOOTING

Condition	Cause	Correction
Engine starts and idles rough without abnormal noise or smoke	1. Slow idle incorrectly adjusted	1. Adjust slow idle screw to specification.
	2. Injection line leaks	2. Wipe off injection lines and connections. Run engine and check for leaks. Correct leaks.
	3. Restricted fuel return system	3. Disconnect fuel return line at injection pump and route hose to a metal container. Connect a hose to the injection pump connection, route it to the metal container. Start the engine and allow it to idle. If engine idles normally, correct restriction in fuel return lines.
	4. Air in injection lines to nozzles	4. Loosen injection line at nozzle(s) and bleed air. Use care to direct fuel away from sources of ignition.
	5. Internal fuel leak at nozzle(s)	5. Disconnect fuel return system from nozzles on one bank at a time. Connect a hose to the injection pump fuel return line connection, route it to a metal container. Start engine and allow it to idle. Watch for normal fuel leakage at the nozzles. Replace any nozzle with excessive fuel leakage.
	6. Nozzle(s) malfunction	6. With engine running, loosen injection line fitting at each nozzle in turn. Use care to direct fuel away from sources of ignition. Each good nozzle should change engine idle quality when fuel is allowed to leak. It is possible for a nozzle to have an internal defect that allows too much fuel into the return fuel line. If this happens, the fuel delivery for the next nozzle in the firing order may be inadequate. This may result in a miss at idle. If a miss is isolated to a specific cylinder, it may be the previous nozzle in the firing order that contains a defect. If nozzle is found that does not change idle quality, it should be replaced.
	7. Incorrect or contaminated fuel	7. Flush fuel system and install correct fuel.
	8. Uneven fuel distribution to cylinders	8. Install new or reconditioned nozzles, one at a time, until condition is corrected as indicated by normal idle.
Engine starts and idles rough with excessive noise and/or smoke	1. Injection pump timing incorrect	1. Be sure timing mark on injection pump is aligned with mark on adapter.
	2. Air in injection lines to nozzles	2. Loosen injection line at nozzle(s) and bleed air. Use care to direct fuel away from sources of ignition.
Engine starts and idles rough with excessive noise and/or smoke	3. Nozzle(s) malfunction	3. With engine running, loosen injection line at each nozzle, one at a time. Use care to direct fuel away from sources of ignition. Each good nozzle should change engine idle quality when fuel is allowed to leak. If a nozzle is found that does not affect idle quality or changes noise and/or smoke, it should be replaced.
	4. High pressure lines incorrectly installed	4. Check routing of each line, correct as required. Firing order is 1-8-4-3-6-5-7-2.

ENGINE REBUILDING

TROUBLESHOOTING

Condition	Cause	Correction
Engine misfires above idle but idles correctly	1. Plugged fuel filter	1. Replace filter.
	2. Incorrect injection pump timing	2. Be sure that timing mark on injection pump and adapter are aligned.
	3. Incorrect or contaminated fuel	3. Flush fuel system and install correct fuel.
Engine will not return to idle	1. External linkage binding or misadjusted	1. Free up linkage. Adjust or replace as required.
	2. Internal injection pump malfunction	2. Remove injection pump for repair.
Fuel leaks on ground, no engine malfunction	1. Loose or broken fuel line or connection	1. Examine complete fuel system, including tank, lines, injection and fuel return lines. Determine source and cause of leak and repair.
	2. Injection pump internal seal leak	2. Remove injection pump for repair.
Noticeable loss of power	1. Restricted air intake	1. Check air cleaner element.
	2. Restricted or damaged exhaust system	2. Check system and replace as necessary.
	3. Plugged fuel filter	3. Replace filter.
	4. Plugged fuel tank vacuum vent in fuel cap	4. Remove fuel cap. If loud hissing noise is heard, vacuum vent in fuel cap is plugged. Replace cap. (Slight hissing sound is normal.)
	5. Pinched or otherwise restricted return system	5. Examine system for restriction and correct as required.
	6. Restricted fuel supply from fuel tank to injection pump	6. Examine fuel supply system to determine cause of restriction. Repair as required.
	7. Incorrect or contaminated fuel	7. Flush fuel system and install correct fuel.
	8. Restricted fuel tank filter	8. Remove fuel tank and check filter. Filter for diesel fuel is blue.
	9. External compression leaks	9. Check for compression leaks at all nozzles and glow plugs. If leak is found, tighten nozzle clamp or glow plug. If leak does not stop at a nozzle, remove it and install a new carbon stop seal and compression seal.
	10. Plugged nozzle(s)	10. Remove nozzles. Have them checked by plugging and repair or replace.
	11. Low compression	11. Check compression to determine cause.
Rap from one or more cylinders (sounds like rod bearing knock)	1. Air in fuel system	1. Check for air leaks in fuel line and correct.
	2. Air in high pressure line(s)	2. Loosen injection line at nozzle(s) and bleed air at each cylinder determined to be causing noise. Use care to direct fuel away from sources of ignition.
Rap from one or more cylinders (sounds like rod bearing knock)	3. Nozzle(s) sticking open or with very low nozzle opening pressure	3. Loosen injection lines at nozzles one at a time. Noise will stop or change when line is loosened at bad nozzle. Remove nozzle for repair.
Objectionable overall combustion noise over normal noise level with excessive black smoke	1. Timing not set to specification	1. Make certain that timing mark on injection pump is aligned with mark on adapter.
	2. Internal engine problem	2. Check for presence of an excessive amount of oil in the air crossover. If present, determine cause and correct.

TROUBLESHOOTING

Condition	Cause	Correction
	3. Injection pump housing pressure out of specifications	3. Check housing pressure. If incorrect, replace fuel return line connector assembly.
	4. Injection pump internal problem	4. Remove injection pump for repair.
Internal or external engine noise	1. Engine fuel pump, generator, water pump, valve train, vacuum pump, bearings, etc.	1. Repair or replace as necessary. If noise is internal, see diagnosis for "Rap from one or more cylinders" and "Engine starts and idles rough with excessive noise and/or smoke."
Engine overheats	1. Coolant system leak, oil cooler system leak or coolant recovery system not operating	1. Check for leaks and correct as required. Check coolant recovery jar, hose and radiator cap.
	2. Belt slipping or damaged	2. Replace or adjust as required.
	3. Thermostat stuck closed	3. Check and replace if required.
	4. Head gasket leaking	4. Check and repair as required.
Instrument panel oil warning lamp on at idle	1. Oil ooler or oil cooler line restricted	1. Remove restriction in cooler or cooler line.
	2. Oil pump pressure low	2. Check and repair oil pump.

DESCRIPTION OF 350 V8

The 5.7 liter, 350 cu.in. V8, 4 cycle diesel is the first factory-built diesel engine to be installed in a G.M. truck. The base of the engine (short block) is very similar in design to a V8 gasoline engine; the major differences being the cylinder heads, combustion chamber, fuel distribution system, air intake manifold and the method of ignition. The cylinder block, crankshaft, main bearings, connecting rods and pistons look much the same as their gasoline engine counterparts, although they are of much heavier construction due to the higher compression ratio required to ignite diesel fuel. The cylinder heads are also designed for much higher compression. The intake and exhaust valves are of special design and construction.

TUNE-UP

COMPRESSION TEST

When checking the compression, always make sure that the batteries are at or near full charge. The total reading for any given cylinder is not as important as the difference between all cylinders. The cylinder with the lowest reading should not be less than 70% of the one with the highest reading and no cylinder should be less than 275 psi.

1. Remove the air cleaner and cover the air crossover.

2. Disconnect the wire from the fuel solenoid terminal on the injection pump.

3. Tag and disconnect all glow plug wiring and then remove the glow plugs.

4. Screw a compression gauge into the hole of the cylinder that is being checked.

5. Crank the engine. Six "puffs" per cylinder should be enough for an accurate reading. Normal compression will build up quickly and evenly if the cylinder is OK.

NOTE: Never add oil to any cylinder during a compression test, as extensive damage may result.

6. Installation is in the reverse order.

VALVE ADJUSTMENT

This engine uses hydraulic valve lifters; no adjustment is necessary or possible.

INJECTION TIMING

Adjustment

For the engine to be properly timed, the marks on the top of the injection pump adapter and the flange of the injection pump must be in alignment. This is done with the engine turned off.

1. Loosen the three pump retaining nuts with the proper tool.

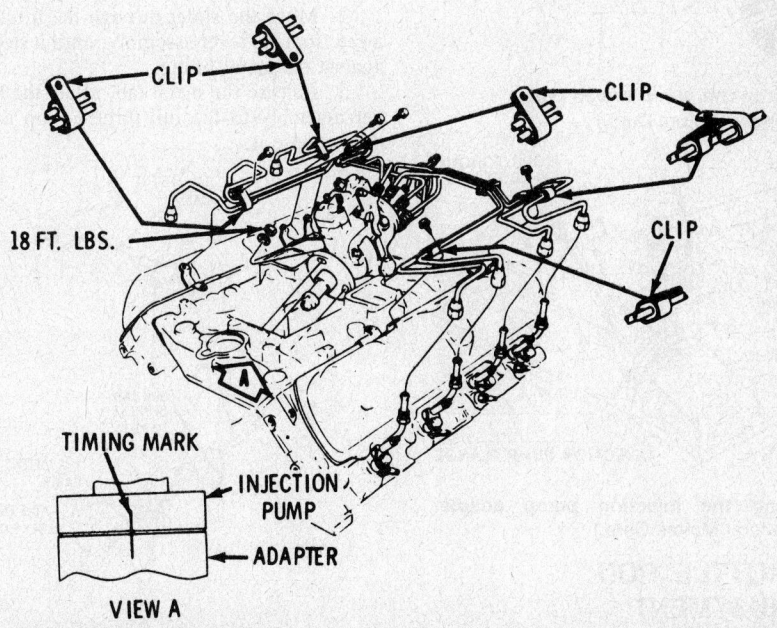

Injection pump timing marks (© General Motors Corp.)

2. Use a ¾ in. open end wrench on the boss at the front of the injection pump and rotate the pump until the two timing marks align.

3. Tighten the retaining nuts to 35 ft. lbs. and then adjust the throttle rod.

Establishing A New Timing Mark

When a new injection pump adapter has been installed you will need to make a new timing mark also.

1. File off the original mark on the adapter. DO NOT file off the mark on the pump flange.

2. Position the no. 1 cylinder at TDC of the compression stroke.

3. Align the mark on the vibration balancer with the zero mark on the indicator. The position of the injection pump driven gear should be offset to the right when the No. 1 cylinder is at TDC.

4. Install a special timing tool into the pump adapter. Torque the tool, toward the no. 1 cylinder, to 50 ft. lbs.

5. Mark the pump adapter, remove the special tool and install the injection pump.

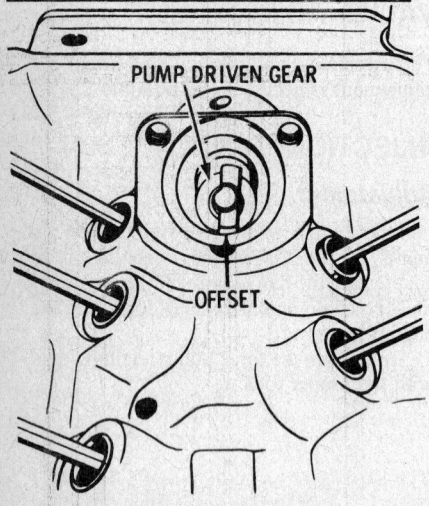

Offset on the pump driven gear
(© General Motors Corp.)

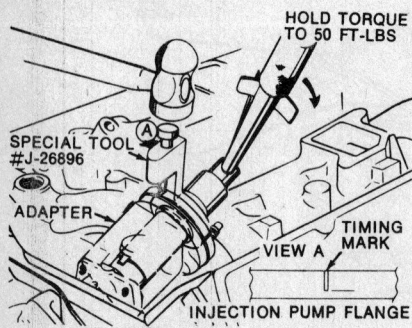

Marking the injection pump adapter
(© General Motors Corp.)

THROTTLE ROD ADJUSTMENT

1. Check timing.

2. Remove the clip from the cruise control rod (if so equipped) and disconnect the rod from the throttle lever assembly.

3. Disconnect the detent cable from the throttle assembly.

4. Loosen the lock nut on the pump rod and shorten it several turns.

5. Rotate the lever assembly to the full throttle position and hold it there.

6. Lengthen the pump rod until the injection pump lever just contacts the full throttle stop.

7. Release the lever assembly and tighten the pump rod lock nut.

8. Remove the pump rod from the lever assembly and reconnect the detent cable.

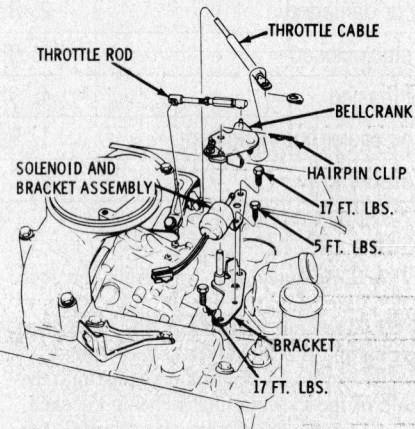

Throttle linkage (© General Motors Corp.)

DETENT CABLE ADJUSTMENT

NOTE: The throttle rod must be adjusted before adjusting the detent cable.

1. Depress and hold the metal lock tab on the cable upper end.

2. Move the slider through the fitting, away from the lever assembly, until it stops against the metal fitting.

3. Release the metal tab, rotate the lever assembly to the full throttle stop and then release it.

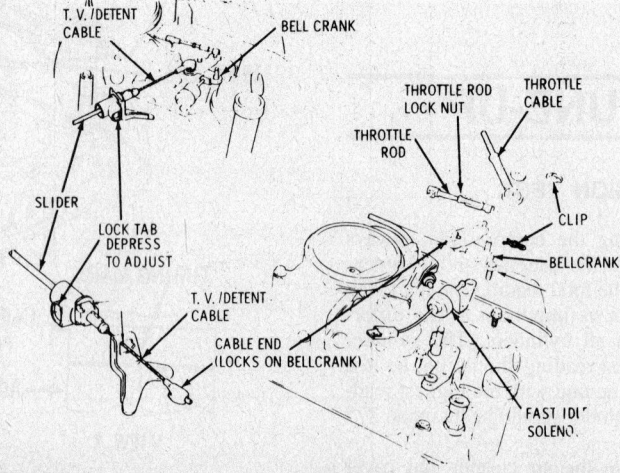

Detent cable adjustment (© General Motors Corp.)

4. Reconnect the pump rod and the cruise control rod if necessary.

IDLE SPEED

Slow Idle Adjustment

1. Run the engine until it reaches normal operating temperature.

2. Insert the probe of a magnetic pickup tachometer into the timing indicator hole.

3. Set the parking brake and block the drive wheels.

4. Place the transmission in Drive and turn the A/C off (if so equipped).

5. Turn the slow idle adjustment screw on the injection pump to obtain the idle speed specified on the emission control label.

Fast Idle Solenoid Adjustment

'78–'79

1. Set the parking brake and block the drive wheels.

2. Run the engine until it reaches normal operating temperature.

3. Place the transmission in Drive and disconnect the compressor clutch wire.

4. Turn the A/C on. On cars without A/C, disconnect the solenoid wire and then connect jumper wires to the solenoid terminals. Ground one wire and connect the other to the battery, this will activate the solenoid.

5. Adjust the fast idle solenoid plunger to obtain 650 rpm.

'80–'81

1. With the ignition off, disconnect the single green wire from the fast idle relay located on the firewall.

2. Set the parking brake and block the drive wheels.

3. Start the engine and adjust the solenoid (energized) to the specifications on the underhood emission control label.

4. Turn off the engine and reconnect the green wire.

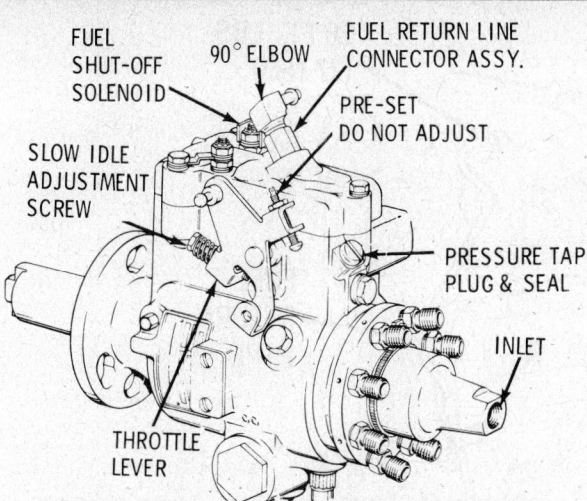

Slow idle adjustment screw (© General Motors Corp.)

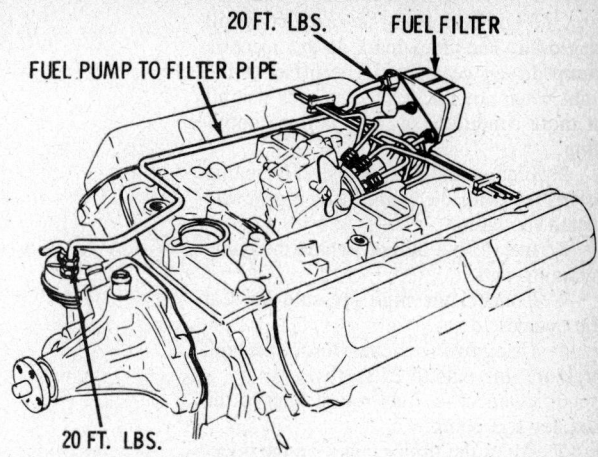

Fuel supply pump, filter and lines (© General Motors Corp.)

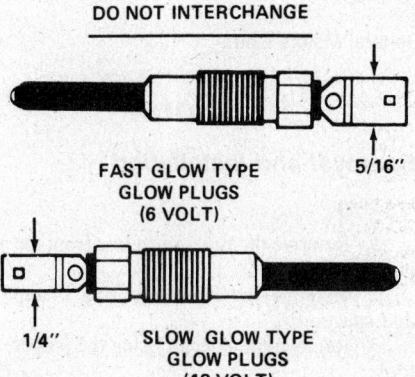

Glow plug identification (© General Motors Corp.)

GLOW PLUGS

Eight glow plugs are used to heat the pre-chamber to aid in starting. They are essentially small heaters that turn on when the ignition switch is turned to the "RUN" position prior to starting the engine. They remain on for a short time after starting and then automatically shut off.

There are two types of glow plugs used on G.M. diesels; the "fast-glow" type and the "slow-glow" type. The fast-glow type use pulsing current applied to 6 volt glow plugs, while the slow-glow type use a continuous current applied to 12 volt glow plugs.

An easy way to tell the plugs apart is that the fast-glow (6V) plugs have a 5/16 in. wide electrical connector plug, while the slow glow (12V) connector is 1/4 in. wide. Do not attempt to interchange any parts of these two glow plug systems.

Removal and Installation

NOTE: Use extreme care when removing a glow plug as the tip may break off; requiring cylinder head removal.

1. Tag and disconnect the electrical connectors.
2. Using the large hex nut, loosen the

glow plug and carefully lift it out of the cylinder head.
3. Installation is in the reverse order.

FUEL SYSTEM

Fuel Supply Pump

These engines use a small, mechanical fuel pump to deliver fuel from the lines to the injection pump.

Removal

1. Disconnect and plug the two fuel lines. Disconnect the vapor return hose (if so equipped).
2. Remove the two mounting bolts.
3. Remove the pump and gasket.

Installation

1. Install pump and gasket. Tighten mounting bolts to 27 ft. lbs.
2. Install both fuel lines and the vapor return hose.
3. Start engine and check for leaks.

Fuel Filter

Removal and Installation

The fuel filter is a square assembly located at the back of the engine, above the intake manifold. Disconnect the fuel lines, remove the mounting bolt and remove the filter. Install a new filter in the reverse.

Injection Pump

Removal

1. Remove the air cleaner.
2. Remove the filters and pipes from the valve covers and air crossover.

3. Remove the air crossover and cap the intake manifold with screened covers or tape.
4. Disconnect the throttle rod and return spring.
5. Remove the bellcrank.
6. Remove the throttle and detent cables from the intake manifold brackets.
7. Disconnect the fuel lines from the filter and remove the filter.
8. Disconnect the fuel inlet line at the pump.
9. Remove the rear A/C compressor (if so equipped) and remove the fuel line.
10. Disconnect the fuel return line from the injection pump.
11. Remove the clamps and pull the fuel return lines from each injection nozzle.
12. Using two wrenches, disconnect the high pressure lines at the nozzles.
13. Remove the three injection pump retaining nuts.
14. Remove the pump and cap all lines and nozzles.

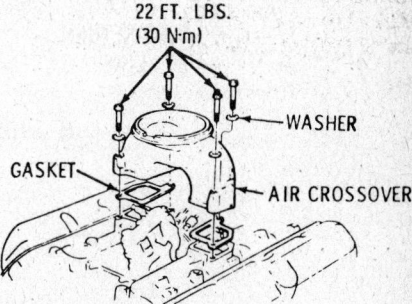

Typical air crossover (© General Motors Corp.)

Installation

1. Remove the protective caps from all lines and nozzles. Place the engine on TDC for the no. 1 cylinder. The mark on the harmonic balancer on the crankshaft will be aligned with the zero mark on the timing

tab, and both valves for no. 1 cylinder will be closed. The index mark on the injection pump driven gear should be offset to the right when no. 1 is at TDC. Check that all of these conditions are met before continuing.

2. Line up the offset tang on the pump driveshaft with the pump driven gear and install the pump.

3. Install, but do not tighten the pump retaining nuts.

4. Connect the high pressure lines at the nozzles.

5. Using two wrenches, torque the high pressure line nuts to 25 ft. lbs.

6. Connect the fuel return lines to the nozzles and pump.

7. Align the timing mark on the injection pump with the line on the pump adaptor and torque the mounting nuts to 35 ft. lbs.

NOTE: A ¾ in. open end wrench on the boss at the front of the injection pump will aid in rotating the pump to align the marks.

8. Adjust the throttle rod.

9. Install the fuel inlet line between the transfer pump and the filter.

10. Install the rear A/C compressor brace (if so equipped).

11. Install the bellcrank and clip.

12. Connect the throttle rod and return spring.

13. Adjust the transmission cable.

14. Start the engine and check for fuel leaks.

15. Remove the screened covers or tape and install the air crossover.

16. Install the tubes in the airflow control valve in the air crossover and install the ventilation filters in the valve covers.

17. Install the air cleaner.

18. Start the engine and allow it to run for two minutes. Stop the engine, let it stand for two minutes, then restart. This permits the air to bleed off within the pump.

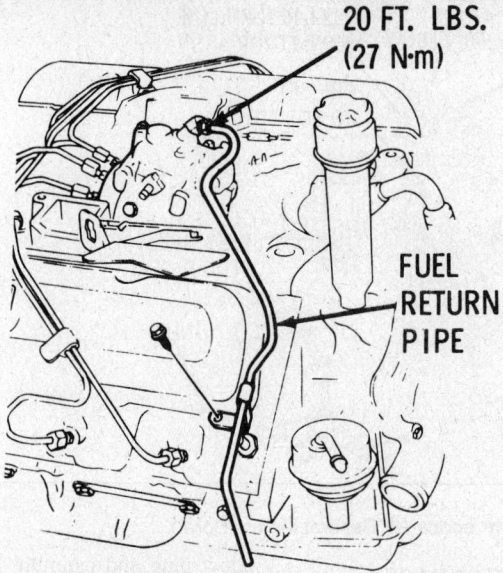

Fuel return pipe—Calif. (© General Motors Corp.)

Injectors

Removal and Installation

'78–'79

1. Remove the fuel return line from the nozzle.

2. Remove the injector spring clamp and spacer.

3. Remove the injector using the proper tool.

4. Cap the high pressure line and the injector tip.

NOTE: The injector tip is highly susceptible to damage and must be protected at all times.

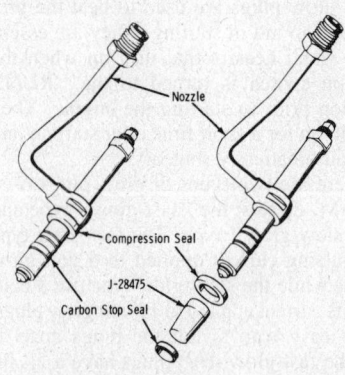

Nozzle seal installation—1978–79 (© General Motors Corp.)

5. If an old nozzle is being installed, a new compression seal and carbon stop seal must be installed after removal of the used ones.

6. Remove the caps and install the injector, spacer and clamps. Tighten to 25 ft. lbs.

7. Replace the return line, start the engine and check for leaks.

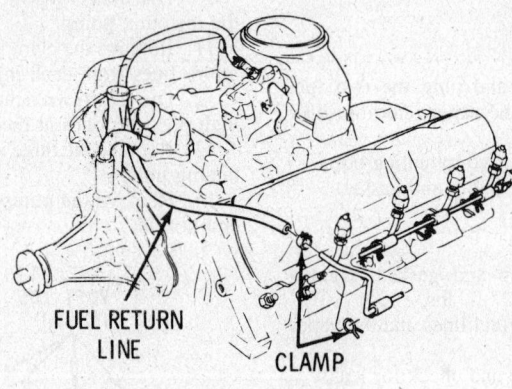

L. H. SIDE OF ENGINE

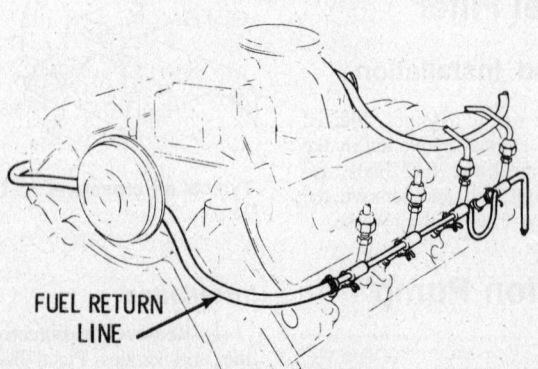

R. H. SIDE OF ENGINE

Fuel return lines—except Calif. (© General Motors Corp.)

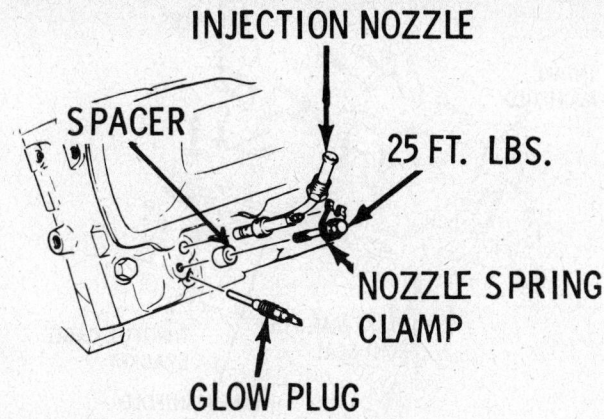

Injector nozzle installation—1978–79 (© General Motors Corp.)

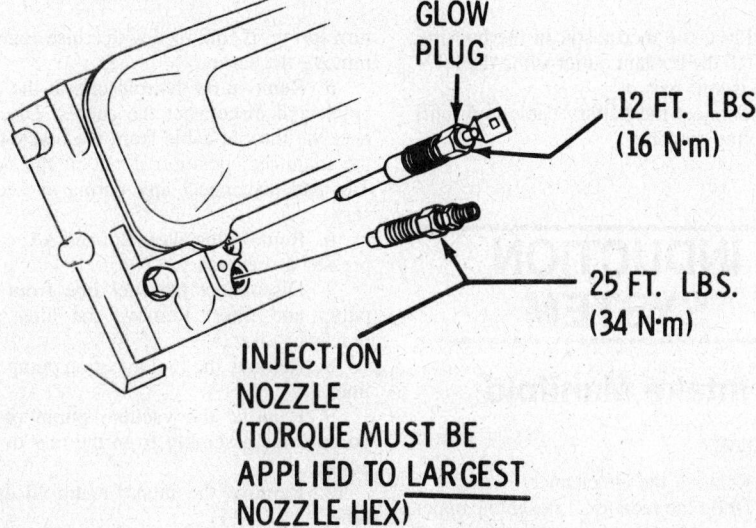

Injector nozzle installation—1980–81 (© General Motors Corp.)

'80–'81

The injectors on these engines are simply unscrewed from the cylinder head, after the fuel lines have been removed, much like a spark plug. Be careful not to damage the injector tip and make sure that the copper gasket is removed from the cylinder head if it does not come off with the injector.

Clean the carbon build-up from the tip of the injector with a soft brass wire brush. Installation is in the reverse.

NOTE: '81 engines use two types of injectors; CAV Lucas and Diesel Equipment. When installing the inlet fittings, tighten to 45 ft. lbs. on the Diesel Equipment injector and to 25 ft. lbs. on the CAV injector.

Injection Pump Fuel Lines

When any fuel lines are to be removed, clean all the fittings before loosening. Immediately cap all lines, nozzles and fittings to maintain system cleanliness.

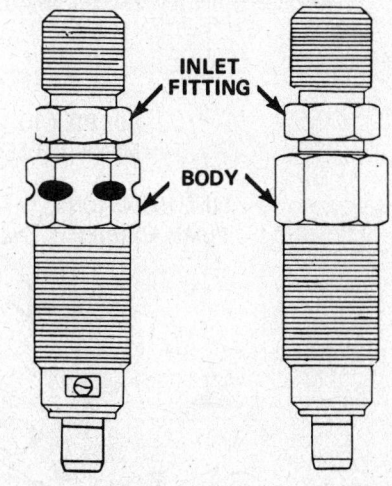

INLET FITTING TO BODY TORQUE DIESEL EQUIPMENT — 45 FT. LBS. C.A.V. LUCAS — 25 FT. LBS.

INLET FITTING

BODY

DIESEL EQUIPMENT   C.A.V. LUCAS

Injector identification—1981 (© General Motors Corp.)

Removal and Installation

All lines may be removed without removing the injection pump. No back-up wrench is necessary when removing a line from the pump fitting.

1. Remove the air cleaner.
2. Disconnect and remove all filters and pipes from the valve covers and the air crossover.
3. Remove the air crossover and cap the openings with screened covers or tape.
4. Remove the injection pump line clamps. Cap all open lines, nozzles or fittings. Use a back-up wrench on the upper hex nut of the injector to prevent a fuel leak.
5. Loosely install the new fuel lines. Check that routing is correct and then tighten the pump end to 35 ft. lbs. and the nozzle end to 25 ft. lbs. Use a back-up wrench on the upper hex nut of the injector to prevent nozzle damage.

NOTE: If more than one line is being replaced, always start with the bottom line.

6. Install the clamps. Installation of remaining components is the reverse.
7. Start the engine and check for leaks.

COOLING SYSTEM

Water Pump

Removal

1. Drain the radiator. Disconnect the lower radiator hose at the water pump.
2. Disconnect the heater and by-pass hoses at the water pump.
3. Remove the fan assembly and all accessory drive belts.
4. Remove the water pump pulley.
5. Disconnect the alternator, power steering pump bracket and, if so equipped, the A/C compressor bracket.
6. Unscrew the mounting bolts and remove the water pump.

Installation

1. Transfer studs from old pump to new one (if pump is being replaced).
2. Clean all old gasket material from the engine block.
3. Apply a thin coat of RTV sealant to the pump housing and then position the new gasket on housing.
4. Remaining installation is in the reverse. Adjust all drive belts and refill the cooling system.

Fan and Hub

Removal

1. Disconnect the negative battery cable.

2. Remove the radiator fan shroud as necessary.

3. Matchmark the fan clutch hub and the water pump hub and then unscrew the fan clutch hub-to-water pump hub mounting nuts and remove the entire fan clutch assembly.

4. Remove mounting screws and separate fan from fan clutch.

Installation

NOTE: No attempt should be made to repair a bent or damaged fan blade. A damaged fan assembly should always be replaced with a new one.

1. Attach the fan to the fan clutch hub.

2. Install the fan clutch assembly to the water pump hub and tighten the bolts to 20 ft. lbs. Be sure to align the matchmarks made earlier.

3. Reinstall the radiator shroud if removed.

4. Reconnect the negative battery cable.

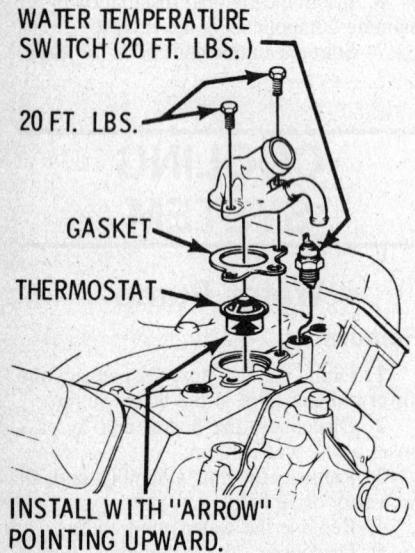

INSTALL WITH "ARROW" POINTING UPWARD.

Typical thermostat installation (© General Motors Corp.)

Thermostat

Removal

1. Disconnect the negative battery cable.

2. Drain the cooling system until the coolant level is below that of the thermostat.

3. Remove the water outlet attaching bolts and remove the outlet.

4. Remove the thermostat.

Installation

1. Make sure the sealing surfaces are clean and then place a ⅛ in. bead of RTV sealant around the coolant outlet sealing surface on the thermostat housing.

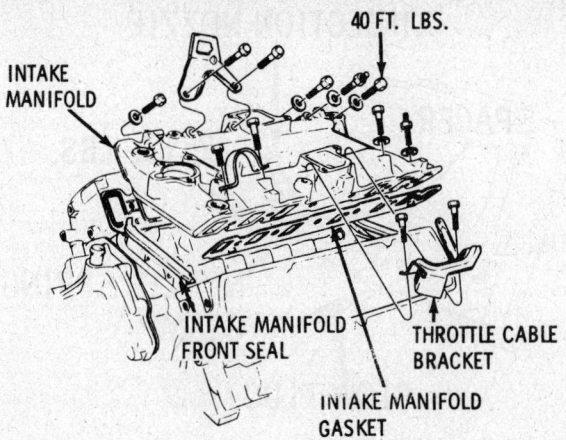

Intake manifold (© General Motors Corp.)

2. Place the thermostat in the housing and install the coolant outlet while the RTV sealant is still wet.

3. Connect the battery cable and refill the cooling system.

INDUCTION SYSTEM

Intake Manifold

Removal

1. Remove the air cleaner.

2. Drain the radiator. Loosen the upper bypass hose clamp, remove the thermostat housing bolts and remove the housing and thermostat.

3. Remove the breather pipes from the valve covers and the air cross over. Remove the air crossover and cap the holes with screened covers or tape.

4. Disconnect the throttle rod and return spring. If equipped with cruise control, remove the servo.

5. Remove the hairpin clip at the bell crank and disconnect the cables. Disconnect the throttle cable from the bracket on the manifold; position it out of the way. Tag and disconnect any wiring as necessary.

6. Remove the alternator and A/C compressor as necessary.

7. Disconnect the fuel line from the pump and filter. Remove the filter and bracket.

8. Remove the fuel injection pump and lines.

9. Remove the vacuum pump or oil pump drive assembly from the rear of the engine.

10. Remove the intake manifold drain tube.

11. Unscrew the mounting bolts and remove the intake manifold. Remove the adapter seal and the injection pump adapter.

Installation

1. Clean the mating surfaces and coat all with sealer. Position the manifold gasket

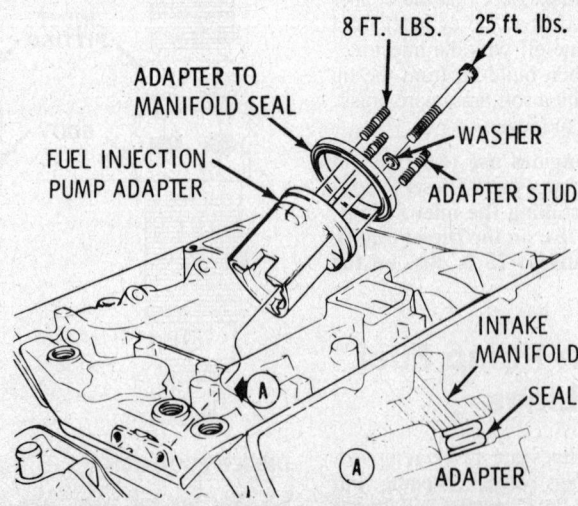

Injection pump adapter and seal (© General Motors Corp.)

on the heads and install the end seals; make sure the ends are positioned under the heads.

2. Carefully lower the manifold into position on the engine.

3. Clean the mounting bolts thoroughly and then dip them in clean engine oil. Install the bolts and tighten them in sequence to 15 ft. lbs. Next, tighten all bolts to 30 ft. lbs., and finally to 40 ft. lbs., always in sequence.

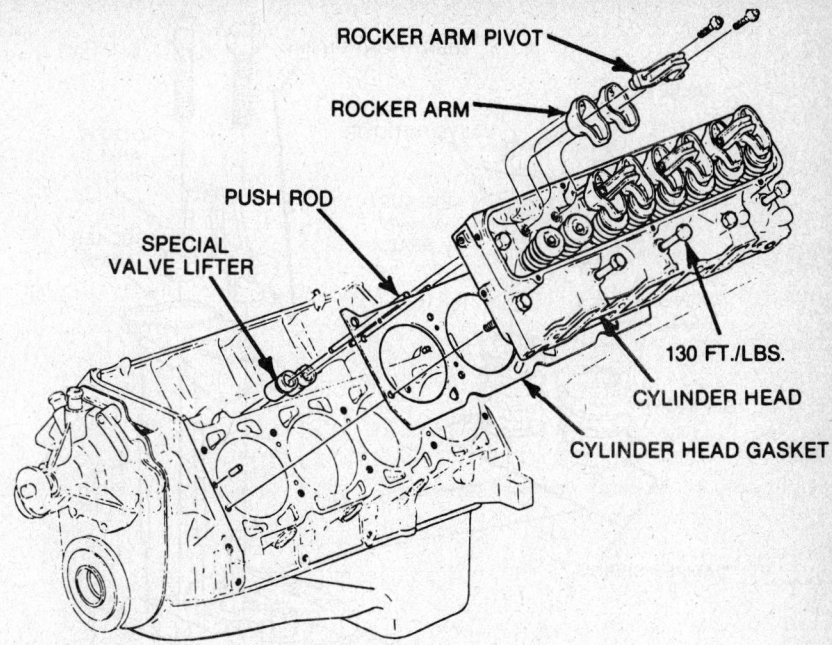

Cylinder head and components (© General Motors Corp.)

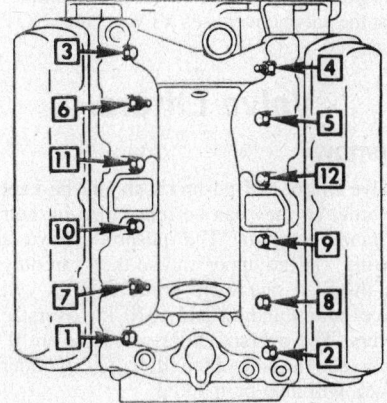

Intake manifold torque sequence (© General Motors Corp.)

4. Install the drain tube and clamp.

5. Apply chassis lube to the adapter and the seal, install the seal on the adapter with the proper tool and then install the adapter.

6. Align the offset tang on the pump drive shaft with the offset in the pump driven gear and install the pump. Connect the fuel lines to the injectors. Align the mark on the injection pump with the one on the adapter. A ¾ in. open end wrench can be used on the boss at the front of the pump to aid in rotating the pump to align the marks.

7. Installation of the remaining components is in the reverse order.

CYLINDER HEAD AND VALVE TRAIN

Cylinder Head

Removal

1. Remove the intake manifold.

2. Remove the rocker arm cover(s), after removing any accessory brackets that are in the way.

3. Tag and disconnect the glow plug wiring.

4. If the right cylinder head is being removed, disconnect the ground strap from the head.

5. Remove the rocker arm bolts, the bridged pivots, the rocker arms and the pushrods. Make sure to keep all parts in order so they can be returned to their original position.

6. Remove the fuel return lines from the injectors.

7. Remove the exhaust manifold(s).

8. Remove the engine block drain plug on the side of the engine that the head is being removed from.

9. Unscrew the head bolts and carefully lift off the cylinder head.

Installation

1. Clean the cylinder head-to-engine block mating surfaces thoroughly. Install new head gaskets on the engine block. Do NOT coat the gaskets with any kind of sealer. The gaskets have a special coating that eliminates the need for sealer. The use of any additional sealer will interfere with this coating and lead to leakage.

2. Carefully position the cylinder head on the block.

3. Clean the head bolts thoroughly and then dip them in clean engine oil. Install them into the cylinder head until the heads of the bolts are in light contact with the top of the cylinder head.

4. Tighten all bolts (in sequence illustrated) to 100 ft. lbs. When this is done, retighten all bolts to 130 ft. lbs.

5. Installation of the remaining components is in the reverse. Use RTV silicone sealant when installing the rocker arm covers.

NOTE: Never install the rocker arms without first following the valve lifter bleed down procedure detailed later in this section.

Rocker Arm

Removal and Installation

NOTE: When the rocker arms are loosened or removed, the lifters must be bled down to prevent the buildup of oil pressure inside each lifter. If this pressure is not eliminated, the lifter could raise higher than normal and bring the valves within striking distance of the piston. Valve lifter bleed-down procedures are detailed later in this section.

1. Remove the air cleaner.

2. Remove the high pressure fuel lines from the injectors.

3. Remove the valve cover.

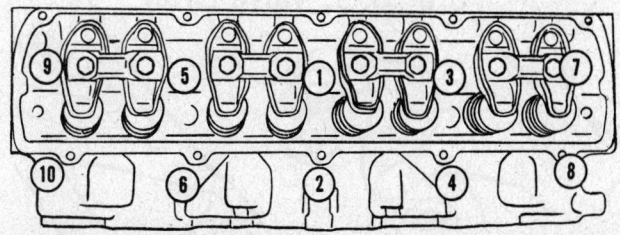

Cylinder head torque sequence (© General Motors Corp.)

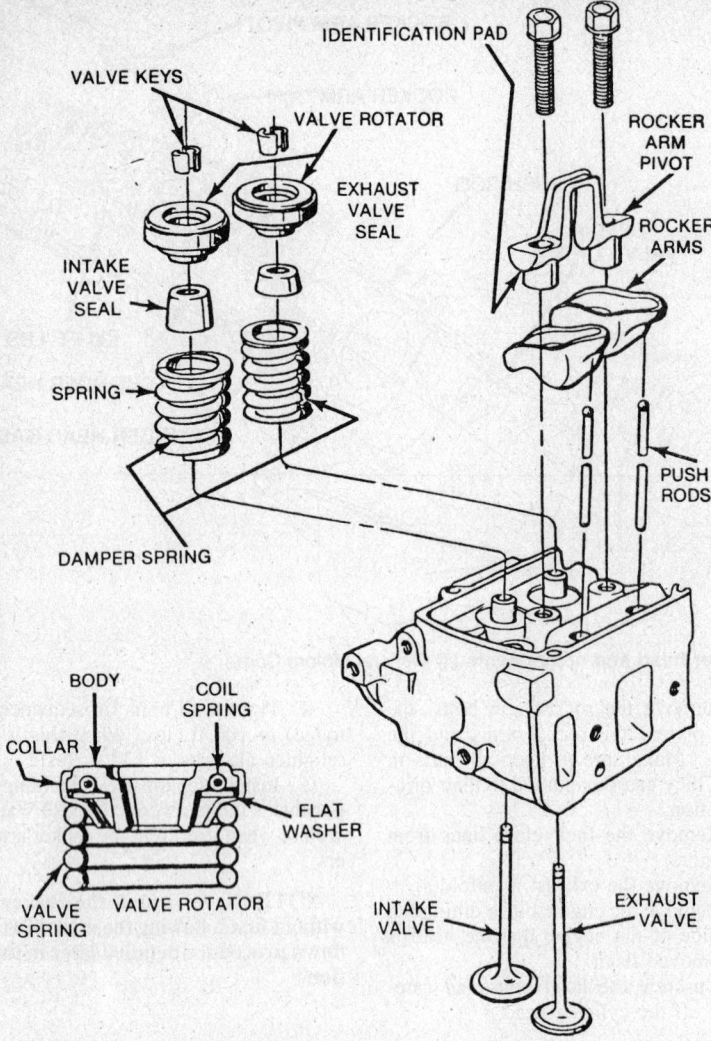

Exploded view of the cylinder head (© General Motors Corp.)

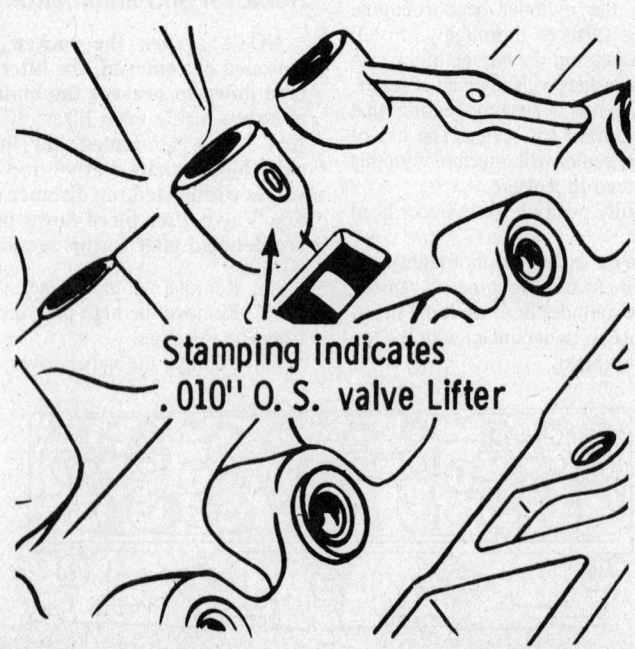

Oversize valve lifters are marked (© General Motors Corp.)

4. Remove the rocker arm pivot bolts, the bridged pivot and the rocker arms. Each rocker set (one set to a cylinder) is removed as a unit.

5. Lubricate the pivot wear points and position each set of rocker arms in its proper location. Do not tighten the pivot bolts.

6. Bleed the lifters as detailed later in this section.

7. Tighten the pivot bolts alternately to 25 ft. lbs. Installation of the remaining components is in the reverse. Remember that the valve cover uses RTV sealant, NOT a gasket.

Valve Lifters

Removal

Valve lifters and pushrods should be kept in order so they can be reinstalled in their original position. The pushrods have a "wing" at the upper end so they can only be installed one way. Some engines will have both standard and .010 in. oversize lifters. The oversize lifter will have an '0' etched on the side of the lifter. The cylinder block will also be marked.

1. Remove the intake manifold.

2. Remove the valve covers and the rocker arm assemblies. Lift out the pushrods.

3. Remove the valve lifter guide retainer bolts and then remove the retainer guides.

4. Remove the valve lifters.

Disassembly

1. Pry out the retainer ring with a small screwdriver.

2. Remove the pushrod seat and the oil metering valve.

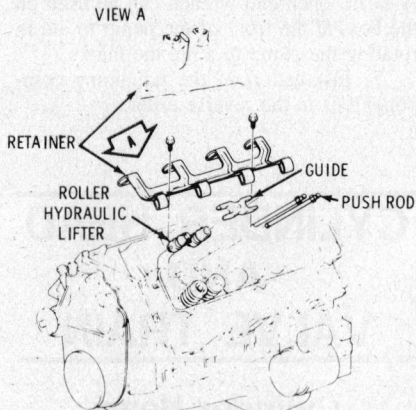

Valve lifter retainer guides
(© General Motors Corp.)

3. Remove the plunger and the plunger spring.

4. Remove the check valve retainer from the plunger and then remove the valve and spring.

Cleaning and Inspection

After the lifters are disassembled, all parts

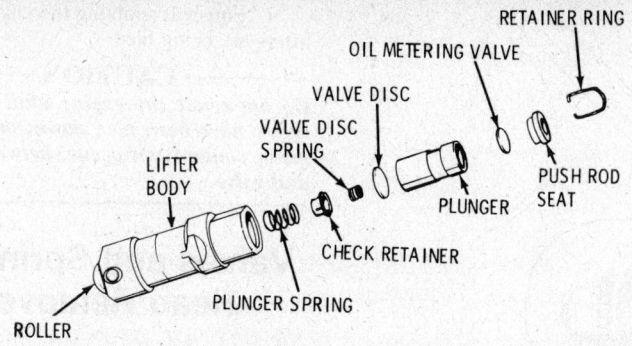

Exploded view of the valve lifter (© General Motors Corp.)

should be cleaned in solvent. A small particle under the check valve will cause malfunctioning of the lifter. Inspect all parts for nicks, burrs or scoring. If the roller body or the plunger are found to be defective in any way, the entire lifter assembly should be replaced. Whenever the lifters are removed, check as follows:

1. The roller should rotate freely, but without excessive play.

2. Check that the needle bearing is not missing or broken.

3. The roller should be free of pitting or roughness. If either of these conditions are present, check the camshaft for a similiar condition. Replace the lifter or the camshaft if necessary.

Assembly

1. Coat all parts with a light coating of clean engine oil.

2. Assemble the valve disc spring and retainer into the plunger. Make sure the retainer flange is pressed tight against the bottom of the recess in the plunger.

3. Install the plunger spring over the check retainer.

4. Hold the plunger with the spring facing up and insert it into the lifter body. Hold it vertically to prevent cocking the spring.

5. Install the oil metering valve and the pushrod seat into the lifter. Install the retaining ring.

Installation

Prime the new lifter by working the lifter plunger while the assembly is submerged in new kerosene or diesel fuel. A dry lifter can be damaged when starting the engine.

1. When a rocker arm is loosened or removed, valve lifter bleed down is required.

2. Install the lifters and pushrods into their original position in the cylinder block.

3. Install the intake manifold.

4. Installation of the remaining components is the reverse.

VALVE LIFTER DIAGNOSIS

1. **Momentarily Noisy When Car is Started:** This condition is normal. Oil drains from the lifters which are holding the valves open when the engine is not running. It will take a few seconds for the lifter to fill after the engine is started.

2. **Intermittently Noisy On Idle Only, Disappearing When Engine Speed Is Increased:** Intermittent clicking may be an indication of a pitted check valve disc, or it may be caused by dirt.

To correct, clean the lifter and inspect. If check valve disc is defective, replace lifter.

3. **Noisy At Slow Idle Or With Hot Oil, Quiet With Cold Oil Or As Engine**

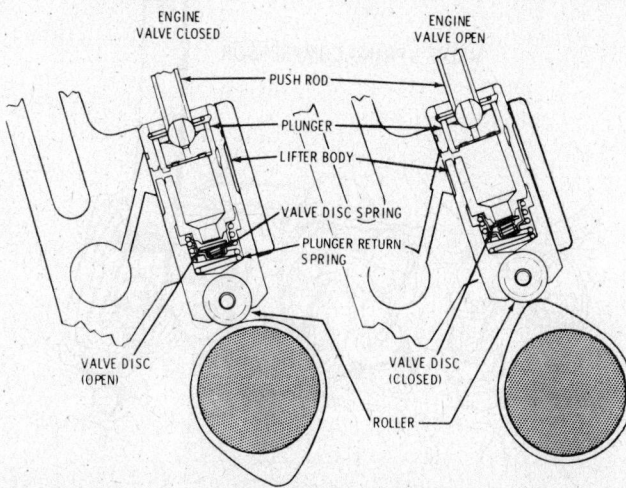

Cross section of a valve lifter (© General Motors Corp.)

Speed Is Increased: Leak check the suspected lifters and replace any lifters that do not need specifications.

4. **Noisy At High Car Speeds And Quiet At Low Speeds:**

a. **High oil level:** Oil level above the "Full" mark allows crankshaft counterweights to churn the oil into foam. When foam is pumped into the lifters, they will become noisy since a solid column of oil is required for proper operation.

b. **Low oil level:** Oil level below the "Add" mark allows the pump to pump air at high speeds which results in noisy lifters.

To correct, fill until proper oil level is obtained.

c. Oil pan bent on bottom or pump screen cocked, replace or repair as necessary.

5. **Noisy At Idle Becoming Louder As Engine Speed Is Increased To 1500 rpm:** This noise is not connected with lifter malfunction. It becomes most noticeable in the car at 10 to 15 mph "L" range, or 30 to 35 mph "D" range and is best described as a hashy sound. At slow idle, it may be entirely gone or appear as a light ticking noise in one or more valves. It is caused by one or more of the following:

a. Badly worn or scuffed valve tip and rocker arm pad.

b. Excessive valve stem to guide clearance.

c. Excessive valve seat runout.

d. Off square valve spring.

e. Excessive valve face runout.

f. Valve spring damper clicking on rotator.

To check valve spring and valve guide clearance remove the valve covers:

a. Occasionally this noise can be eliminated by rotating the valve spring and valve. Crank engine until noisy valve is off its seat. Rotate spring. This will also rotate valve. Repeat until valve becomes quiet. If correction is obtained, check for an off square valve spring. If spring is off square more than $1/16$ in free position, replace spring.

b. Check for excessive valve stem to guide clearance. If necessary, correct as required.

6. **Valves Noisy Regardless of Engine Speed:** This condition can be caused by foreign particles or excessive valve lash.

Check for valve lash by turning engine so the piston in that cylinder is on top dead center of firing stroke. If valve lash is present, the push-rod can be freely moved up and down a certain amount with rocker arm held against valve. If OK, clean suspected valve lifters.

Valve lash indicates one of the following:

a. Worn push-rod.

b. Worn rocker arm.

c. Lifter plunger stuck in down position due to dirt or carbon.

d. Defective lifter

Checking of the above four items:

1. Look at the upper end of push-rod.

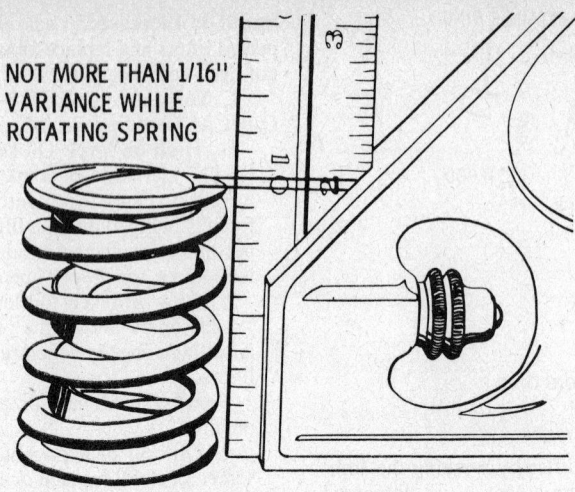

NOT MORE THAN 1/16''
VARIANCE WHILE
ROTATING SPRING

Checking the valve spring (© General Motors Corp.)

Excessive wear of the spherical surface indicates one of the following conditions.

    a. Improper hardness of the push-rod ball. The push-rod and rocker arm must be replaced.

    b. Improper lubrication of the push-rod. The push-rod and rocker arm must be replaced. The oiling system to the push-rod should be checked.

    2. If push-rod appears in good condition and has been properly lubricated, replace rocker arm and recheck valve lash.

    3. If valve lash exists and push-rod and rocker arm are okay, trouble is in the lifter. Lifter should be replaced.

Any time the valves are removed for service the tips should be inspected for improper pattern which could indicate valve rotator malfunction.

VALVE LIFTER BLEED DOWN

If the intake manifold has been removed and if any rocker arms have been loosened or removed; it will be necessary to remove those valve lifters, disassemble them, drain the oil from them and then reassemble them.

If the intake manifold has not been removed, but the rocker arms have been loosened or removed, the valve lifters must be bled down by the following procedure:

    1. Before installing any removed rocker arms, rotate the engine crankshaft so that no. 1 cylinder is 32° before top dead center. This is ½ in. counterclockwise from the 0° pointer. To verify that no. 1 cylinder TDC is coming up, remove the no. 1 cylinder glow plug, then turn the engine: compression pressure will force air out the glow plug hole.

NOTE: Use only hand wrenches to torque the rocker arm pivot bolts to avoid engine damage.

    2. If removed, install the no. 5 cylinder pivot and rocker arms, then torque the bolts alternately between the intake and exhaust valves until the intake valve begins to open, then stop.

    3. Install the remaining rocker arms except no. 3 and no. 8 intake valves (if these rocker arms were removed).

    4. If removed, install the no. 3 and no. 8 intake valve pivots, but do not torque beyond the point that the valve would be fully open. This is indicated by strong resistance while still turning the pivot retaining bolts. Going beyond this point will bend the push-rod. Torque the bolts SLOWLY, allowing the lifter to bleed down.

    5. Finish torquing no. 5 cylinder rocker arm pivot bolt slowly. Do not go beyond the point that the valve would be fully open, as in step 4.

    6. Do not turn the engine for at least 45 minutes.

    7. Finish assembling the engine as the lifters are being bled.

CAUTION

Do not rotate the engine until the valve lifters have been bled down, or metal to metal contact can occur, between piston and valve.

Valves and Springs— Head Removed

NOTE: If only the valve springs are being removed, the cylinder head need not be removed.

Removal and Installation

    1. Remove the valve keys by compressing the valve springs with a valve spring compressor.

    2. Remove the valve spring rotators or the retainers and springs.

    3. Remove the oil seals from the valve stems.

    4. Remove the valves. Keep them separated so they can be installed in their original locations.

    5. Install the valves in the respective guides.

    6. Install new seals over the valve stem. Position them as far down the stem as possible, they will position themselves correctly when the engine is started.

    7. Position the valve springs over the valve stems.

    8. Install the valve rotators, compress the springs and install the valve stem keys. Check the springs and keys to make sure they are properly seated.

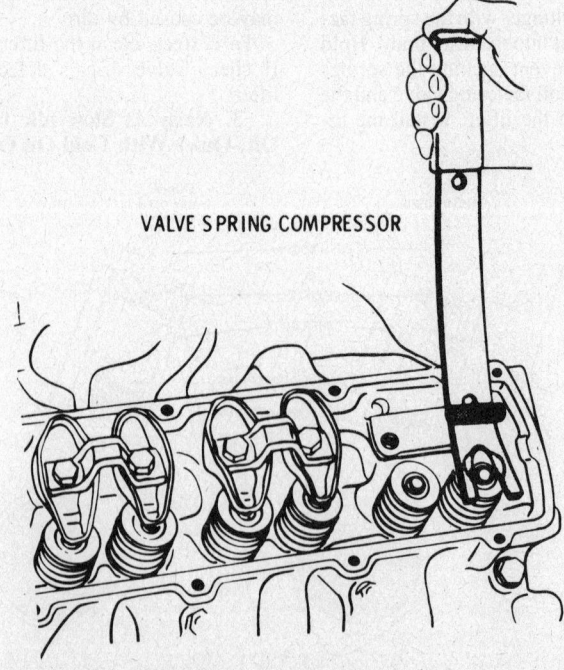

VALVE SPRING COMPRESSOR

Removing the valve spring (© General Motors Corp.)

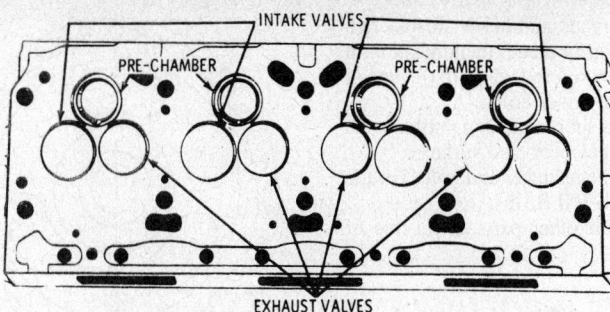

Valve locations (© General Motors Corp.)

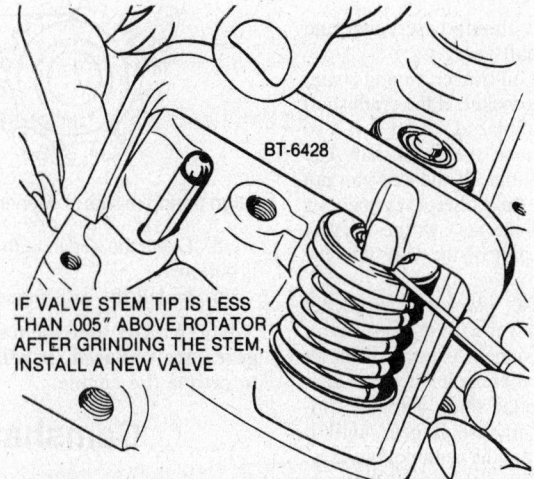

IF VALVE STEM TIP IS LESS
THAN .005″ ABOVE ROTATOR
AFTER GRINDING THE STEM,
INSTALL A NEW VALVE

Checking rotator height (© General Motors Corp.)

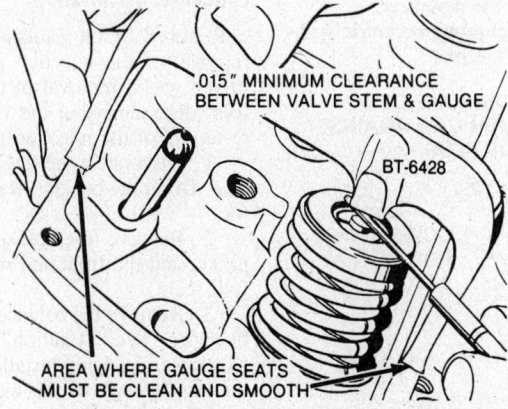

.015″ MINIMUM CLEARANCE
BETWEEN VALVE STEM & GAUGE

BT-6428

AREA WHERE GAUGE SEATS
MUST BE CLEAN AND SMOOTH

Checking valve height (© General Motors Corp.)

MEASURING VALVE STEM HEIGHT

Whenever a new valve is installed, or after grinding valves, it will be necessary to measure valve stem height as follows:

There should be at least .015″ clearance on all valves between gauge surface and end of valve stem. (Valve stem can be gauged with or without the valve rotator on the valve). If clearance is less than .015″, re-

move valve and grind tip of valve stems as required on a valve refacing machine, using the "Vee" block attachment to insure a smooth 90° end. Also be certain to break sharp edge on ground valve tip. Observe an original valve to determine chamfer.

After all valve keys have been installed on valves, tap each valve stem end with a mallet to seat valve rotators and keys. Regauge all valves between valve stem and

gauge (.015″ minimum) and valve rotator and gauge(.030″ minimum). If any valve stem end is less than .005″ above rotator, the valve is too short and a new valve must be installed.
EXAMPLE:
Valve rotator to
gauge clearance   .038″
Minus valve stem-
to-gauge clearance   − .035″
                                      = .003″

This is less than .005″ and a new valve should be installed.

NOTE: There must be a minimum of .030″ clearance between valve rotator and gauge. Failure to maintain this clearance will cause rocker arm and valve rotator interference.

ENGINE BLOCK

Engine

Removal and Installation

1. Drain the cooling system.
2. Remove the air cleaner.
3. Mark the hood-to-hinge position and remove the hood.
4. Disconnect the ground cables from the batteries.
5. Disconnect the ground wires at the fender panels and the ground strap at the cowl.
6. Disconnect the radiator hoses, cooler lines, heater hoses, vacuum hoses, power steering pump hoses, air conditioning compressor (hoses attached), fuel inlet hose and all attached wiring.
7. Remove the bellcrank clip.
8. Disconnect the throttle and transmission cables.
9. Remove the radiator.
10. Raise and support the car.
11. Disconnect the exhaust pipes at the manifold.
12. Remove the torque converter cover and the three bolts holding the converter to the flywheel.
13. Remove the engine mount bolts.
14. Remove the three right side transmission-to-engine bolts. Remove the starter.
15. Lower the car and attach a hoist to the engine.
16. Slightly raise the transmission with a jack.
17. Remove the three left side transmission-to-engine bolts and remove the engine.
18. Installation is the reverse of removal. Converter cover bolts are torqued to 40 ft. lbs.

Front Cover

Removal

1. Drain the cooling system and disconnect the radiator hoses.

ENGINE REBUILDING

2. Remove all belts, fan and pulley, crankshaft pulley and balancer, using a balancer puller.

> **CAUTION**
> *The use of any other type of puller, such as a universal claw type which pulls on the outside of the hub, can destroy the balancer. The outside ring of the balancer is bonded in rubber to the hub. Pulling on the outside will break the bond. The timing mark is on the outside ring. If it is suspected that the bond is broken, check that the center of the keyway is 16° from the center of the timing slot. In addition, there are chiseled aligning marks between the weight and the hub.*

3. Unbolt and remove the cover, timing indicator and water pump.

4. It may be necessary to grind a flat on the cover for gripping purposes.

Installation

1. Grind a chamfer on one end of each dowel pin.

2. Cut the excess material from the front end of the oil pan gasket on each side of the block.

3. Clean the block, oil pan and front cover mating surfaces with solvent.

4. Trim about ⅛ in. off each end of a new front pan seal.

5. Install a new front cover gasket on the block and a new seal in the front cover.

6. Apply sealer to the gasket around the coolant holes.

7. Apply RTV sealer to the block at the junction of the pan and front cover.

8. Place the cover on the block and press down to compress the seal. Rotate the cover left and right and guide the pan seal into the cavity using a small screwdriver.

Oil the bolt threads and heads, install two to hold the cover in place, then install both dowel pins (chamfered end first). Install remaining front cover bolts.

9. Apply a lubricant, compatible with rubber on the balancer seal surface.

10. Install the balancer and bolt. Torque the bolt to 200–300 ft. lbs.

11. Install all other parts in reverse of removal.

Timing Chain and Sprockets

Removal and Installation

1. Remove the timing case cover and take off the camshaft gear.

2. Remove the oil slinger, timing chain, and the camshaft sprocket. If the crankshaft sprocket is to be replaced, remove it also at this time. Remove the crankshaft key before using the puller. If the key can not be removed, align the puller so it does not overlap the end of the key, as the keyway is only machined part of the way into the crankshaft gear.

3. Reinstall the crankshaft sprocket being careful to start it with the keyway in perfect alignment since it is rather difficult to correct for misalignment after the gear has been started on the shaft. Turn the timing mark on the crankshaft gear until it points directly toward the center of the camshaft. Mount the timing chain over the camshaft gear and start the camshaft gear up on to its shaft with the timing marks as close as possible to each other and in line between the shaft centers. Rotate the camshaft to align the shaft with the new gear.

4. Install the fuel pump eccentric with the flat side toward the rear.

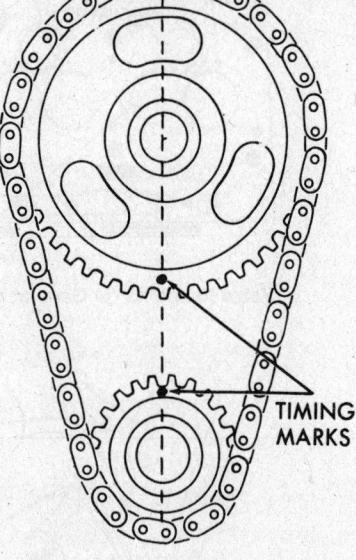

Align timing marks (© General Motors Corp.)

5. Drive the key in with a hammer until it bottoms.

6. Install the oil slinger.

NOTE: Any time the timing chain and gears are replaced, it will be necessary to retime the engine.

Camshaft

Removal

NOTE: If camshaft is to be removed, the air conditioning, if equipped, must be discharged by a professional and the condenser removed.

Removal of the camshaft also requires removal of the injection pump drive and driven gears, removal of the intake manifold, disassembly of the valve lifters, and re-timing of the injection pump.

1. Disconnect the negative battery cables. Drain the coolant. Remove the radiator.

2. Remove the intake manifold and gasket and the front and rear intake manifold seals.

3. Remove the balancer pulley and the balancer. See "Caution" under "Front Cover Removal and Installation." Remove the engine front cover using the appropriate procedure.

4. Remove the valve covers. Remove the rocker arms, pushrods and valve lifters; see the procedure earlier in this section. Be sure to keep the parts in order so that they may be returned to their original positions.

5. If equipped with air conditioning, the condenser must be discharged and removed from the car.

> **CAUTION**
> *Compressed refrigerant expands (boils) into the atmosphere at a temperature of -21°F or less. It will freeze any surface it contacts, including your skin or eyes.*

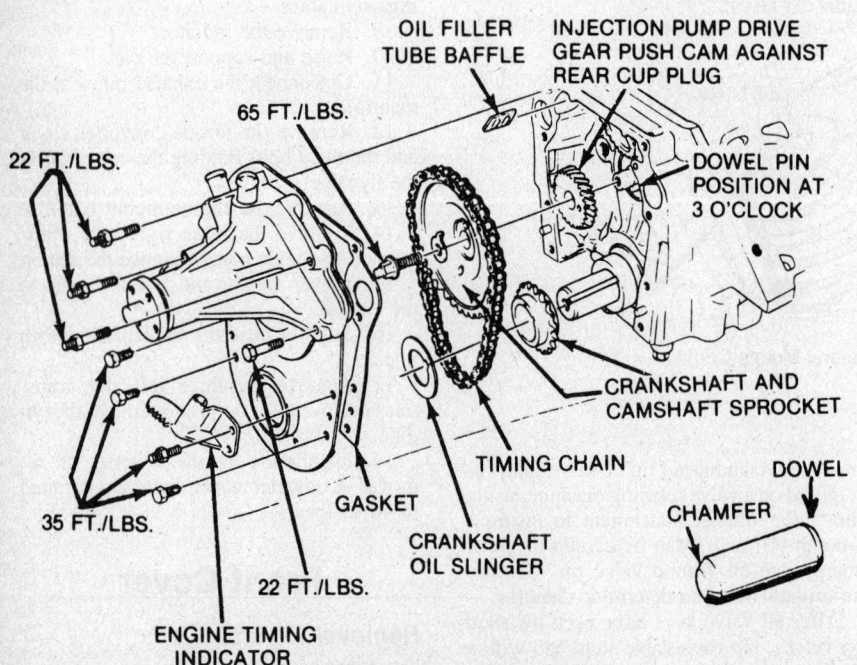

OIL FILLER TUBE BAFFLE

INJECTION PUMP DRIVE GEAR PUSH CAM AGAINST REAR CUP PLUG

65 FT./LBS.

22 FT./LBS.

DOWEL PIN POSITION AT 3 O'CLOCK

CRANKSHAFT AND CAMSHAFT SPROCKET

TIMING CHAIN

DOWEL

35 FT./LBS.

GASKET

CHAMFER

CRANKSHAFT OIL SLINGER

22 FT./LBS.

ENGINE TIMING INDICATOR

Front cover, timing chain and sprockets (© General Motors Corp.)

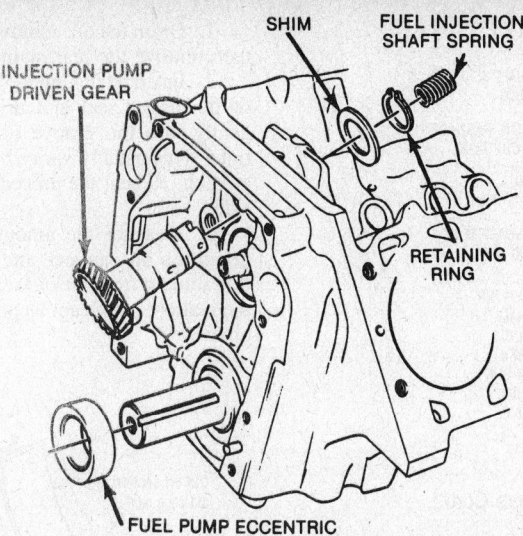

Injection pump driven gear (© General Motors Corp.)

6. Remove the camshaft sprocket retaining bolt, and remove the timing chain and sprockets, using the procedure outlined earlier.

7. Position the camshaft dowel pin at the 3 o'clock position.

8. Push the camshaft rearward and hold it there, being careful not to dislodge the oil gallery plug at the rear of the engine. Remove the injection pump drive gear by sliding it from the camshaft while rocking the pump driven gear.

9. To remove the fuel injection pump driven gear, remove the pump adapter, remove the snap ring, and remove the selective washer. Remove the driven gear and spring.

10. Remove the camshaft by sliding it out the front of the engine. Be extremely careful not to allow the cam lobes to contact any of the bearings, or the journals to dislodge the bearings during camshaft removal. Do not force the camshaft, or bearing damage will result.

Installation

1. If either the injection pump drive or driven gears are to be replaced, replace both gears.

2. Coat the camshaft and the cam bearings with GM lubricant #1052365 or the equivalent.

3. Carefully slide the camshaft into position in the engine.

4. Fit the crankshaft and camshaft sprockets, aligning the timing marks as shown in the timing chain removal and installation procedure. Remove the sprockets without disturbing the timing.

5. Install the injection pump driven gear, spring, shim, and snap ring. Check the gear end play. If the end play is not within 0.002–0.006 in. replace the shim to obtain the specified clearance. Shims are available in 0.003 in. increments, from 0.080 to 0.115 in.

6. Position the camshaft dowel pin at

3 o'clock position. Align the zero marks on the pump drive gear and pump driven gear. Hold the camshaft in the rearward position and slide the pump drive gear onto the camshaft. Install the camshaft bearing retainer.

7. Install the timing chain and sprockets, making sure the timing marks are aligned.

8. Install the lifters, pushrods and rocker arms. Make sure you follow the Valve Lifter Bleed Down procedure. Failure to bleed down the lifters could bend valves when the engine is turned over.

9. Install the injection pump adapter and

injection pump. See the appropriate sections for procedures.

10. Install the remaining components in the reverse order of removal.

Crankshaft

Removal

1. Remove the oil pan, the oil pump and the front cover.

2. Rotate the crankshaft to a position where the connecting rod nuts are most accessible. Unscrew the nuts and remove the connecting rod caps. Install thread protectors.

3. Remove the fuel pump eccentric from the crankshaft.

4. Remove the main bearing caps.

5. Note the position of the keyway in the crankshaft so it can be installed in the same position.

6. Lift the crankshaft out of the block. The connecting rods will pivot to the center of the engine during removal. Do not allow them to move in their bore any more them that.

Installation

1. Install enough oil pan bolts into the pan rails so that rubber bands can be stretched between them and the connecting rods. Align the rods so that the inner thread protectors of adjacent rods overlap approximately one inch. Connecting rod alignment can be adjusted by increasing the tension on a rubber band with additional turns around the pan bolts.

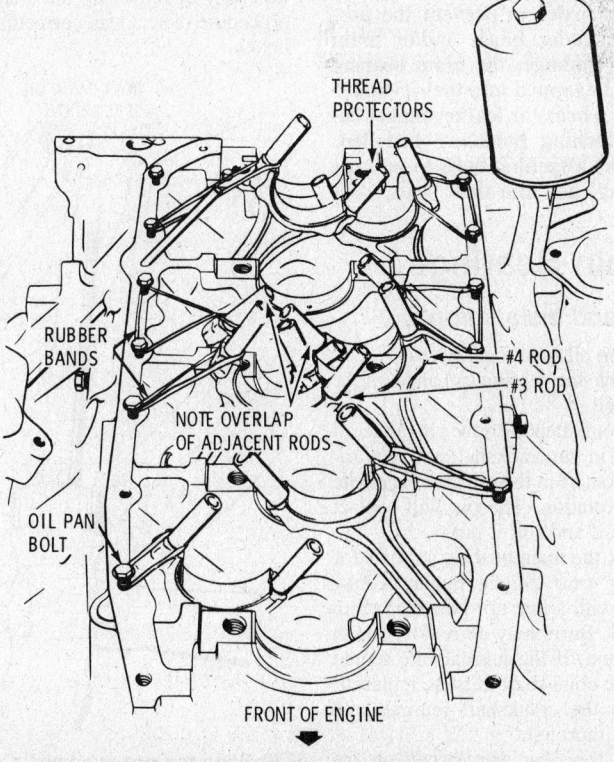

Crankshaft installation (© General Motors Corp.)

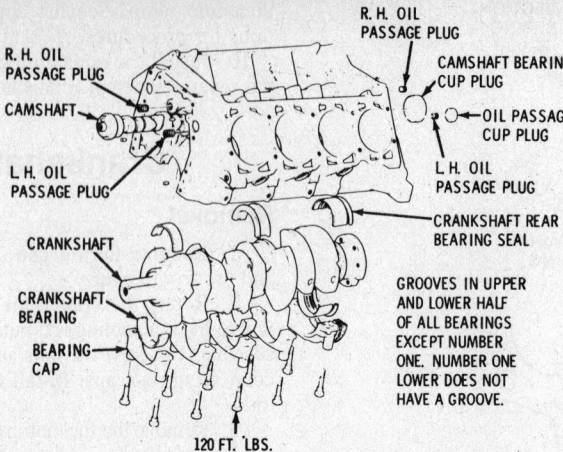

Exploded view of the short block (© General Motors Corp.)

2. Measure the crankshaft journals and crankpins with a micrometer to determine the correct size rod and main bearings to be used.

NOTE: **Whenever a new or reconditioned crankshaft is installed, new connecting rod bearings and main bearings should be used.**

3. Position the crankshaft keyway in the same position as removed and lower the crankshaft into the block. The connecting rods will follow the crankpins into the correct position as the crankshaft is lowered.

4. Remove the rubber bands, thread protectors and pan bolts and assemble the remaining components in the reverse order of removal.

NOTE: **In order to prevent the possibility of cylinder block and/or main bearing cap damage, the main bearing caps should be tapped into their cylinder cavity using a brass or leather mallet before the attaching bolts are installed. Never use the attaching bolts to pull the main bearing caps into their seats.**

Main Bearings

Removal and Installation

1. Loosen all main bearing caps.
2. Remove the bearing cap and remove the lower shell.
3. Insert a flattened cotter pin in the oil passage hole in the crankshaft and then rotate the crankshaft in the direction opposite of cranking rotation. The pin will contact the upper shell and roll it out.
4. Check the main bearing journals for roughness or wear. Slight roughness may be removed with a fine grit polishing cloth dipped in oil. Burrs may be removed with a fine oil stone. If the journals are scored or ridged, the crankshaft must be replaced.
5. Clean the crankshaft journals and bearing caps thoroughly.
6. Place the new upper shell on the crankshaft journal with the locating tang in

the correct position and rotate the shaft to turn it into position using a cotter pin.

7. Place a new shell in the bearing cap and install the cap. Lubricate the bolt threads with engine oil and tighten to 120 ft. lbs.

NOTE: **Always install new rear main oil seal when replacing the #5 bearing.**

Rear Main Bearing Oil Seal

UPPER OIL SEAL

Repair

Tools have been released to provide a means of correcting upper seal leaks without the necessity of removing the crankshaft. The procedure of seal leak correction is detailed below.

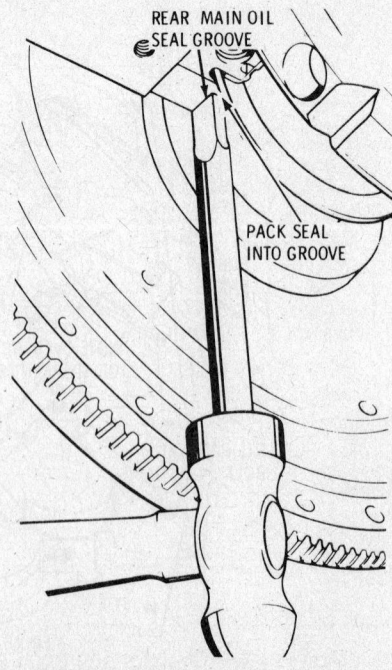

Packing the upper oil seal (© General Motors Corp.)

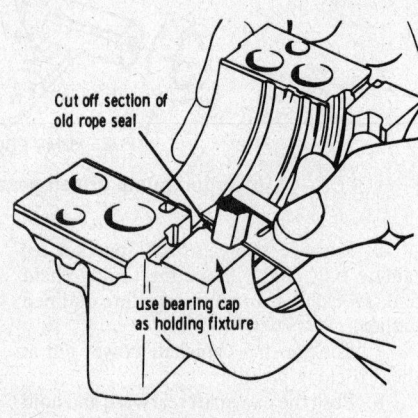

Cutting off the lower seal ends (© General Motors Corp.)

4. Place a drop of sealer on each end of the seal and cap.
5. Using two screwdrivers, work these two pieces of seal into the cylinder block. Use the packing tool and pack each piece up into the block.
6. Replace the lower seal and replace the cap.
7. Installation of the remaining components is in the reverse order.

LOWER OIL SEAL

REMOVAL

1. Drain the oil and remove the oil pan.
2. Remove the rear main bearing insert and oil seal.
4. Clean the bearing cap and seal grooves. Check for cracks.

Installation

1. Install the seal into the bearing cap by hand.
2. Use a seal installer and hammer the seal into the groove. To check if the seal is fully seated in the cap, slide the tool away from the seal. With the tool fully seated in the cap, slide the tool against the seal. If the tool butts against the seal, it must be driven further into the groove. If the undercut area of the tool slides over the seal, it's fully seated.
3. With the tool slightly rotated, cut the seal flush with the mating surface of the cap. Use a small screwdriver and pack the

Also within the first column, near the top right:

1. Drain the oil, remove the oil pan and then remove the rear main bearing cap.
2. Insert a packing tool against one end of the upper seal and drive the old seal gently into the groove until it is packed tight. This usually varies between ¼–¾ of an inch. Repeat the procedure on the other side.
3. Measure the amount the seal was driven up on one side and add ⅟₁₆ in. Cut this amount from the old seal removed from the main bearing cap. Repeat procedure for other side.

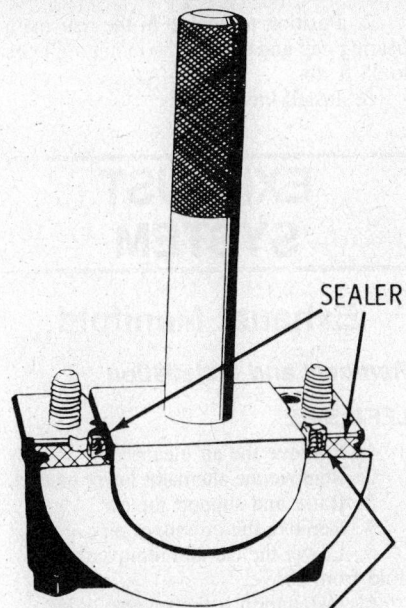

AFTER CORRECTLY POSITIONING SEAL, ROTATE TOOL SLIGHTLY AND CUT OFF EACH END OF SEAL FLUSH WITH CAP.

Installing the lower oil seal (© General Motors Corp.)

seal end fibers toward the center, away from the edges.

4. Clean and install the bearing insert.

5. Install the bearing caps, lubricate the bolt threads with oil and tighten to 120 ft.lbs.

6. Installation of remaining components is the reverse.

Connecting Rods and Pistons

Removal

1. Remove the intake manifold and cylinder head(s).

2. Remove the oil pan and oil pump assembly.

3. Stamp the cylinder number on the machined surfaces of the bolt bosses of the connecting rod and cap to aid in installation.

4. Examine the cylinder bore. If a ridge exsists, remove it with a ridge reamer before attempting to remove the piston and rod assembly.

5. Remove the connecting rod bearing cap and bearing. Use a short piece of ⅜ in. hose to cover the bolt threads. This will prevent damage to the threads themselves and to the bearing journal.

6. Remove the rod and piston assembly through the top of the cylinder bore. Repeat this procedure on the other cylinders.

Installation

1. Make sure that the thread covers are still on all of the rod bolts.

2. Coat the rings and piston with clean engine oil and then install a ring compressing tool onto the piston.

3. Install each rod and piston into its respective cylinder bore so that the curved edge of the valve depression in top of the piston is toward the inner side of the engine.

NOTE: When installing a piston in the forward two cylinders on either side of the engine, the larger valve depression goes toward the front. On the rear half of the engine, the large depression faces the rear.

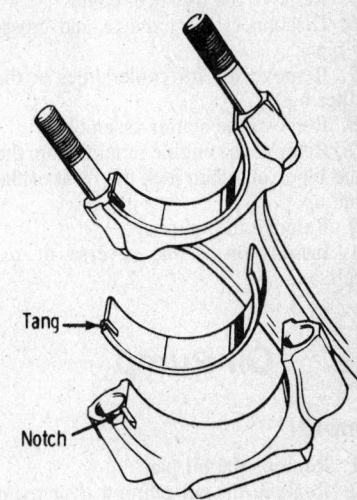

Connecting rod bearing (© General Motors Corp.)

4. Lubricate the crankpin with clean engine oil and install the connecting rod bearing and cap, with the bearing index tang in the rod and cap on the same side.

5. When all pistons have been correctly installed in their cylinders, tighten the connecting rod bolt nuts to 42 ft. lbs.

LUBRICATION SYSTEM

Oil Pan

Removal and Installation

1. Remove the oil pump drive and the vacuum pump (A/C only).

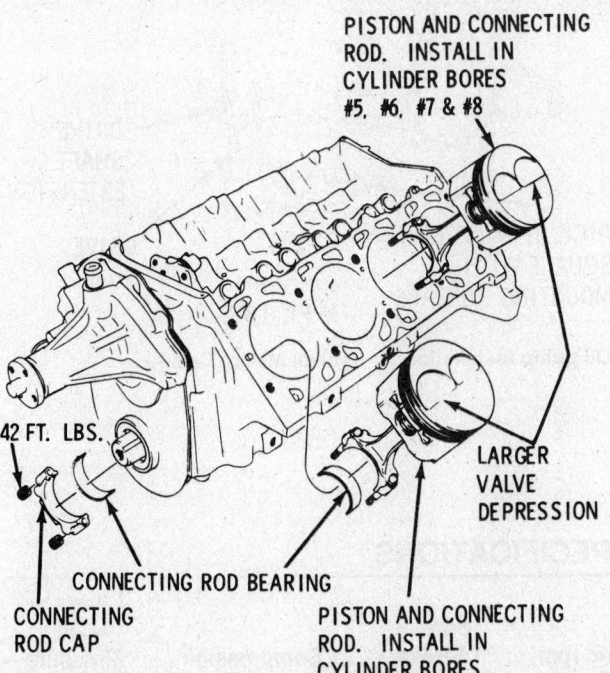

Piston locations in the block (© General Motors Corp.)

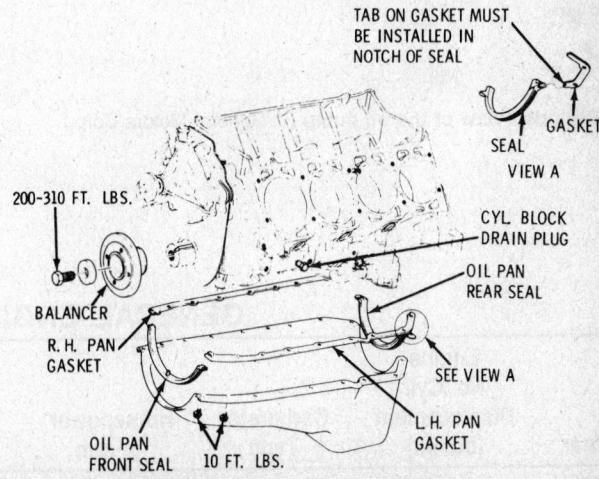

Oil pan installation (© General Motors Corp.)

2. Disconnect the battery cables. Remove the dipstick.

3. Remove the upper radiator support and the fan shroud attaching screws.

4. Raise and support the car. Drain the oil.

5. Remove the flywheel cover.

6. Disconnect the exhaust and crossover pipes.

7. Remove the oil cooler lines at the oil filter base.

8. Remove the starter assembly.

9. Remove the engine mounts from the engine block and then jack the front of the engine up.

10. Remove the oil pan.

11. Installation is the reverse of removal.

Oil Pump

Removal

1. Remove the oil pan.

2. Remove the oil pump-to-rear main bearing bolts and remove the pump and drive shaft extension.

Disassembly

1. Remove the oil pump drive shaft extension.

2. Remove the cotter pin, spring and the pressure regulator valve. Place your thumb over the pressure regulator bore as the spring is under pressure.

3. Remove the oil pump cover and gasket.

4. Remove the drive gear and idler gear from the pump body.

Assembly

1. Install the gear and shaft in the pump body and check the gear end clearance. Place a straight edge over the gears and measure the clearance between the straight edge and the gasket surface. Clearance should be between 0.0005 and 0.0075 in. If the end clearance is near the upper limit, check for scores in the cover that would bring the total clearance over the limit.

2. Install the cover screws and tighten alternately and evenly.

3. Position the pressure regulator valve in the pump cover, closed end first, then install the spring and the retaining pin.

4. Connect the drive shaft extension to the driveshaft.

Installation

1. Insert the drive shaft extension through the opening in the main bearing cap and block until the shaft mates with the vacuum pump driven gear.

2. Position the pump in the rear main bearing cap and tighten the mounting bolts to 35 ft. lbs.

3. Install the oil pan.

EXHAUST SYSTEM

Exhaust Manifold

Removal and Installation

LEFT SIDE

1. Remove the air cleaner.

2. Remove the alternator lower bracket.

3. Raise and support the car.

4. Remove the crossover pipe.

5. Lower the car and remove the manifold from above.

6. Installation is the reverse order.

RIGHT SIDE

1. Raise and support the car.

2. Remove the crossover pipe.

3. Disconnect the exhaust pipe.

4. Remove the right front wheel.

5. Remove the manifold from under the car.

6. Installation is in the reverse order.

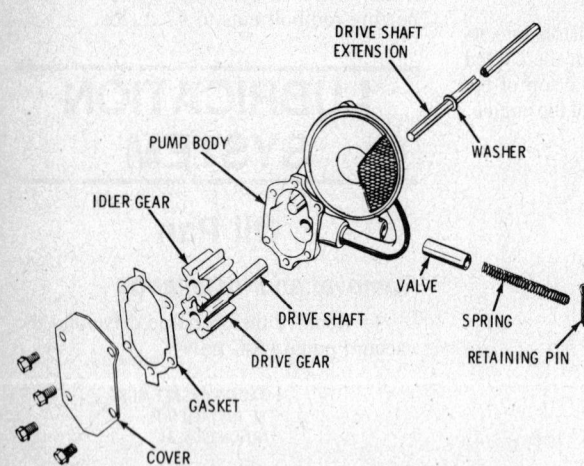

Exploded view of the oil pump (© General Motors Corp.)

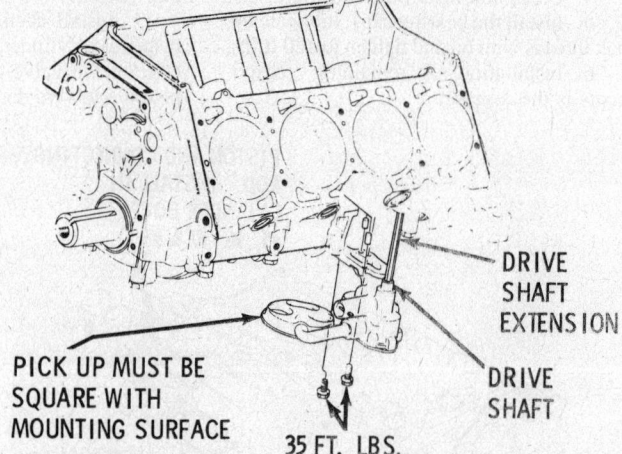

Oil pump installation (© General Motors Corp.)

GENERAL ENGINE SPECIFICATIONS

Year	Engine No. Cyl. Displacement (cu. in.)	Carburetor Type	Horsepower @ rpm	Torque @ rpm (ft lbs)	Bore × Stroke (in.)	Compression Ratio	Oil Pressure @ 2000 rpm
'82	8–379	Diesel	130 @ 3600	240 @ 2000	3.98 × 3.80	21.5:1	45

TUNE-UP SPECIFICATIONS

Year	Engine No. Cyl. Displacement (cu. in.)	Ignition Timing (deg)①		Compression (lbs)	Valves Intake Opens (deg)	Fuel Pump Pressure (psi)	Idle Speed (rpm)①	
		Man Trans.	Auto. Trans.				Slow	Fast
'82	8–379	NA	NA	275	NA	5.5–6.5	575/550	700

NOTE: The underhood specifications sticker often reflects tune-up specification changes made in the production run. Sticker figures must be used if they differ with those in this chart.

① Where two figures are separated by a slash, the first is for manual trans, the second is for auto trans

NA—Not available

FIRING ORDER

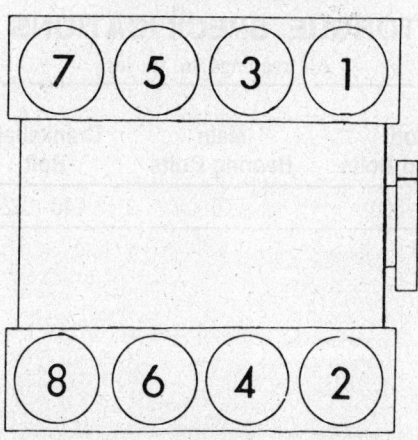

Engine firing order: 1-8-7-2-6-5-4-3
(© General Motors Corp.)

VALVE SPECIFICATIONS

Year	Engine No. Cyl. Displacement (cu in.)	Seat Angle (deg)	Face Angle (deg)	Spring Test Pressure① (lbs. @ in.)	Spring Installed Height (in.)	Stem to Guide Clearance (in.)		Stem Diameter (in.)	
						Intake	Exhaust	Intake	Exhaust
'82	8–379	46	45	230 @ 1.389	1.81	.0010–.0027	.0010–.0027	.3414	.3414

① Valve open

CRANKSHAFT AND CONNECTING ROD SPECIFICATIONS

All measurements are given in inches

Year	Engine No. Cyl. Displacement (cu in.)	Crankshaft				Connecting Rod		
		Main Brg. Journal Dia.	Main Brg. Oil Clearance	Shaft End-Play	Thrust on No.	Journal Diameter	Oil Clearance	Side Clearance
'82	8–379	2.9494–2.9504①	.0017–.0032②	.0019–.0070	3	2.3981–2.3991	.0018–.0039	.007–.025

① Figure is for #1,2,3,4. #5: 2.9492–2.9502 in.
② Figure is for #1,2,3,4. #5: .0021–.0036 in.

PISTON AND RING SPECIFICATIONS

All measurements are given in inches

Year	Engine No. Cyl. Displacement (cu. in.)	Ring Gap			Ring Side Clearance			Piston Clearance
		Top Compression	Bottom Compression	Oil Control	Top Compression	Bottom Compression	Oil Control	
'82	8–379	.0118–.0216	.0295–.0394	.0098–.0200	.0029–.0070	.0015–.0031	.0015–.0037	.0040–.0110

PISTON PIN SPECIFICATIONS

All measurements in inches

Year	Engine	Diameter	Pin to Rod Clearance	Pin to Piston Clearance
'82	379	1.2203–1.2206	.0003–.0012	.0004–.0006

TORQUE SPECIFICATIONS

All readings in ft. lbs.

Year	Engine	Cylinder Head Bolts	Rod Bearing Bolts	Main Bearing Bolts	Crankshaft Bolt	Flywheel to Crankshaft Bolts	Manifold	
							Intake	Exhaust
'82	379	88–103	44–52	①	140–162	NA	25–37	18–25

NA Not available
① Inner: 105–117
    Outer: 94–105

DESCRIPTION OF 379 V8

The 6.2 liter, 379 cu. in. V8, 4 cycle diesel is developed and produced by Chevrolet. It is a totally new engine designed specifically for truck application with heavy duty usage in mind.

The base of the engine (short block) is very similar in design to a V8 gasoline engine; the major difference being the cylinder heads, combustion chamber, fuel distribution system, air intake manifold and the method of ignition. The cylinder block, crankshaft, main bearings, connecting rods and pistons look much the same as their gasoline engine counterparts, although they are of much heavier construction due to the higher compression ratio required to ignite diesel fuel. The intake and exhaust manifolds are of special design and construction.

The cylinder head incorporates a 17 bolt head design which locates 5 bolts around each cylinder. This helps gasket durability. It also includes a high swirl pre-combustion chamber which mixes fuel and air to provide an efficient fuel burn and low emissions. A special cavity in the piston top further assists in mixing the combustion products for complete burning.

Main bearing caps all use 4 bolts instead of the normal 2 to provide rigid support for the crankshaft and minimize stress. The rolled fillet nodular iron crankshaft utilizes a torsional damper, tuned to reduce vibrations.

The engine also uses 3 roller hydraulic lifters running on a forged steel camshaft.

TUNE-UP

COMPRESSION TEST

When checking the compression, always make sure that the batteries are at or near full charge. The total reading for any given cylinder is not as important as the difference between all cylinders. The cylinder with the lowest reading should not be less than 70% of the one with the highest reading and no cylinder should be less than 275 psi.

1. Remove the air cleaner and cover the air crossover.
2. Disconnect the wire from the fuel solenoid terminal on the injection pump.
3. Tag and disconnect all glow plug wiring and then remove the glow plugs.
4. Screw a compression gauge into the hole of the cylinder that is being checked.
5. Crank the engine. Six "puffs" per cylinder should be enough for an accurate reading. Normal compression will build up quickly and evenly if the cylinder is OK.

NOTE: Never add oil to any cylinder during a compression test, as extensive damage may result.

6. Installation is in the reverse order.

VALVE ADJUSTMENT

This engine uses hydraulic valve lifters; no adjustment is necessary or possible.

INJECTION TIMING

Adjustment

For the engine to be properly timed, the marks on top of the engine front cover and the injection pump flange must be aligned. This is done with the engine turned off.

1. Loosen the three pump retaining nuts.
2. Use the proper tool and rotate the pump until the two timing marks are in alignment.
3. Tighten the retaining nuts to 30 ft. lbs. and then adjust the throttle rod.

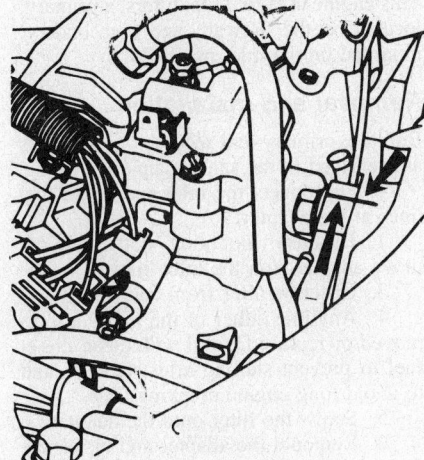

Injection pump timing marks
(© General Motors Corp.)

Establishing a New Timing Mark

When a new front cover has been installed, a new timing mark will also be required.
1. Remove the injection pump and then position the No. 1 cylinder at TDC of the compression stroke.
2. Install a special timing tool into the injection pump. Do not use a gasket.
3. The slot on the injection pump gear should be in the vertical 6 o'clock position and the timing marks on the gears will be aligned. If not, remove the tool and rotate the engine 360°.
4. Fasten the gear to the fixture and tighten.
5. Install a 10mm nut to the upper housing stud to hold the fixture flange nut finger tight.
6. Torque the large bolt (18mm) counterclockwise (toward left bank) to 50 ft. lbs. Tighten the 10mm nut.
7. Make sure that the crankshaft has not rotated and the fixture did not bind on the 10mm nut.
8. Strike a scriber with a mallet to mark the TDC position on the front cover.
9. Remove the tool, install the injection pump and attach the gear to the pump hub.
10. Adjust injection timing.

THROTTLE POSITION SWITCH ADJUSTMENT

1. Loose assemble throttle position switch to the injection pump with the throttle lever in the closed position.
2. Attach an ohmmeter across the IGN (pink) and EGR (yellow) terminals or wires.
3. Insert the proper "switch-closed" gage block between the gage boss on the injection pump and the wide open stop screw on the throttle shaft.
4. Rotate and hold the throttle lever against the gage block.
5. Rotate the throttle switch clockwise (facing throttle switch) until continuity just occurs (high meter reading) across the IGN and EGR terminals or wires. Hold the switch body in this position and tighten the mounting screws.

NOTE: The switch point must only be set while rotating the switch body in the clockwise direction.

6. Release the throttle lever and allow it to return to the idle position. Remove the "switch-closed" gage bar and insert a "switch-open" gage bar.
7. Rotate the throttle lever against the "switch-open" gage bar. There should be no continuity accross the IGN and EGR terminals or wires.
8. If no continuity exsists, the switch is set properly. If there is continuity, the switch must be reset by repeating the entire procedure again.
9. Remove the gage bar and the ohmmeter.

TRANSMISSION VACUUM REGULATOR VALVE ADJUSTMENT

1. Attach the vacuum regulator valve snugly, but loosely, to the injection pump. The switch body must be free to rotate on the pump.
2. Apply approximately 9–10 psi of vacuum to the inboard nipple. Attach a vacuum gauge to the outboard nipple.
3. Insert a vacuum regulator valve gage bar between the gage boss on the injection pump and the wide open stop screw on the throttle lever.
4. Rotate and hold the throttle shaft against the gage bar.
5. Slowly rotate the vacuum regulator valve body clockwise (facing the valve) until the vacuum gauge reads 5.6 psi. Hold the valve at this position and tighten the mounting screws.

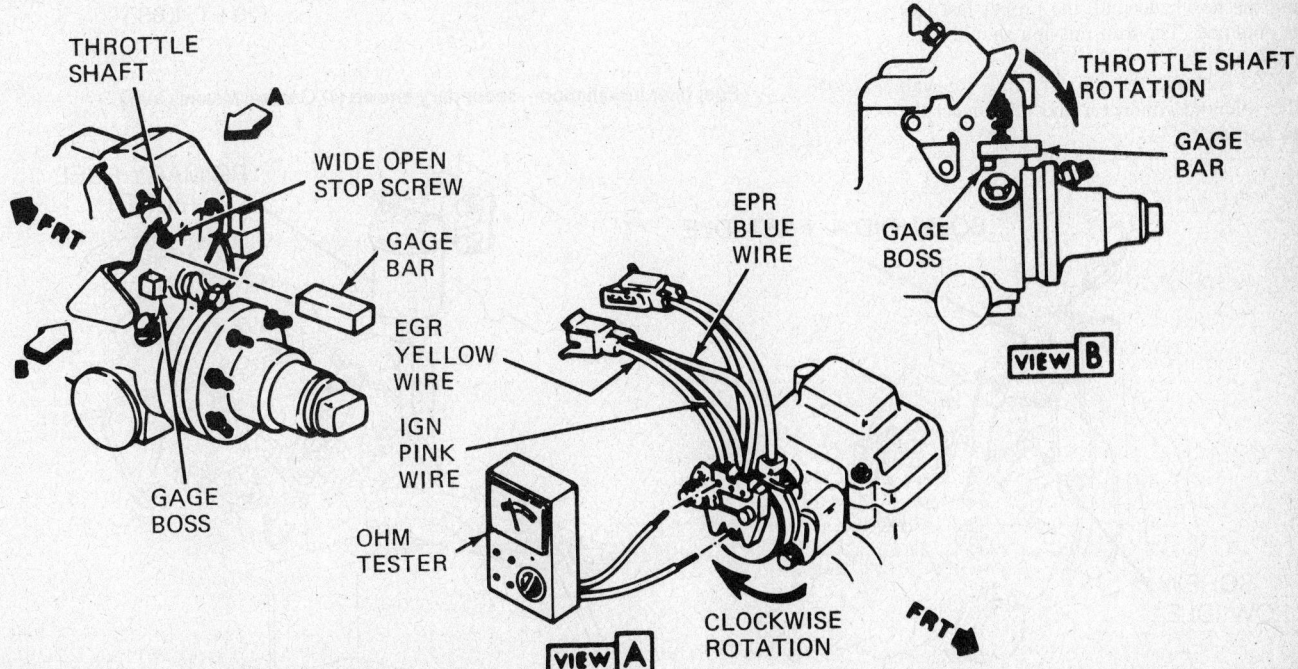

Throttle position switch adjustment (© General Motors Corp.)

ENGINE REBUILDING

NOTE: The valve must only be set while rotating in the clockwise direction.

6. Check by releasing the throttle shaft and allowing it to return to the idle stop position. Rotate the throttle shaft back against the gage bar and check that the vacuum gauge still reads 5.6 psi. If not, the valve must be reset again.

IDLE SPEED

Slow Idle Adjustment

1. Run the engine until it reaches normal operating temperature.
2. Set the parking brake and block the drive wheels.
3. Remove the air cleaner and turn all accessories off.
4. Install a diesel tachometer.
5. Turn the low idle speed screw on the injection pump until the proper idle is obtained. Automatic transmissions should be in Drive and manual transmissions should be in Neutral.
6. Disconnect the tachometer and install the air cleaner.

Fast Idle Speed Adjustment

1. Run the engine until it reaches normal operating temperature.
2. Set the parking brake and block the drive wheels.
3. Disconnect the connector from the fast idle solenoid. Connect an insulated jumper wire between the positive battery terminal and the solenoid terminal. This will energize the terminal.
4. Open the throttle momentarily to ensure that the fast idle solenoid plunger is energized and fully extended.
5. Adjust the extended plunger by turning the hex head until the proper fast idle is obtained. The transmission should be in Neutral.
6. Remove the jumper wire, reinstall the solenoid connector and disconnect the tachometer.

GLOW PLUGS

Eight glow plugs are used to preheat the chamber as an aid to starting. They are essentially small 12 volt heaters that turn on when the ignition switch is turned to the ''Run'' position prior to starting the engine. They remain on for a short time after starting and then automatically shut off.

Removal and Installation

NOTE: Use extreme care when removing the glow plugs as the tip may break off; requiring cylinder head removal to retrieve it.

1. Tag and disconnect the electrical connectors.
2. Using the large hex nut, loosen the plug and carefully pull it out of the cylinder head.
3. Installation is in the reverse order.

FUEL SYSTEM

Fuel Filter

This engine uses two fuel filters; a primary, located on the firewall, and a secondary, mounted on the inlet manifold.

Removal and Installation

Both the primary and secondary fuel filters are serviced in the same manner.
1. Disconnect the inlet and outlet fuel lines at the adapter.
2. Unscrew mounting bolts and remove adapter from the inlet/firewall.
3. Unscrew filter from adapter.
4. Anytime either of the filters are removed or replaced, refill with clean diesel fuel to prevent stalling after start up, and to avoid long engine cranking time.
5. Screw the filter onto the adapter.
6. Remount the adapter and install the fuel lines.
7. Run engine and check for leaks.

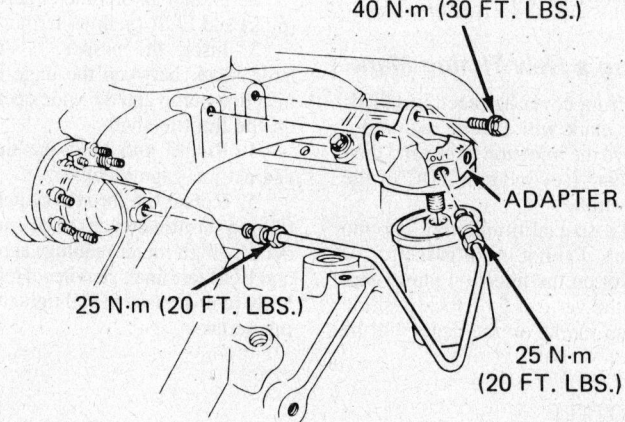

Fuel filter installation—secondary shown (© General Motors Corp.)

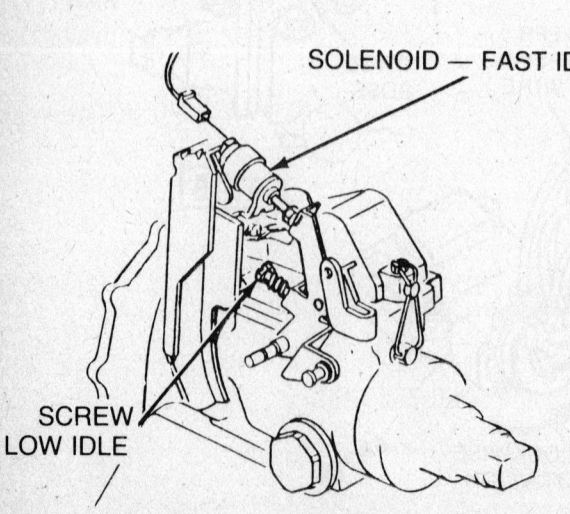

Idle speed adjustment (© General Motors Corp.)

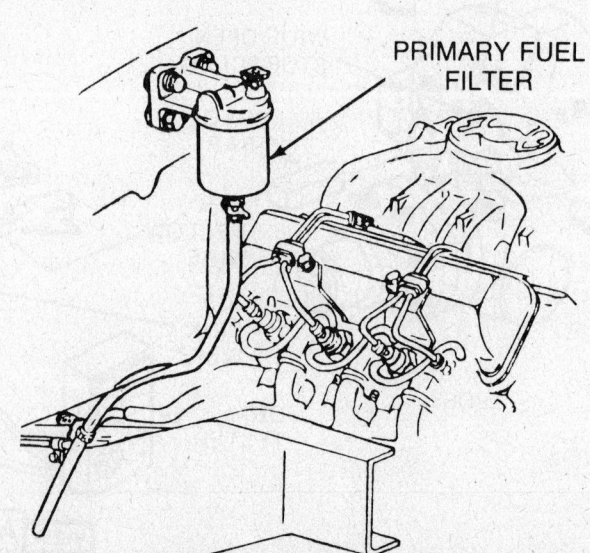

Draining water from the primary filter (© General Motors Corp.)

Water Drain

Water can be drained from the primary fuel filter only.

1. Open the petcock on top of the primary filter housing.

2. Place a drain pan below the filter and open the petcock on the bottom of the filter.

NOTE: A length of hose can be attached to the petcock to direct the drained fuel below the frame.

3. When all water is drained, close both petcocks tightly. If all fuel in the filter has been drained, remove the filter and fill it with clean diesel fuel.

4. Start the engine and let it run briefly. It may run rough at first until all air is purged from the system. If roughness continues, check that both petcocks are closed tightly.

Fuel Line Heater

Removal and Installation

1. Disconnect the batteries and remove the air cleaner.

2. Remove the crankcase ventilator bracket from the intake manifold and position it out of the way.

3. Disconnect the fuel lines to the secondary fuel filter and then remove the filter.

4. Loosen the vacuum pump hold-down clamp and rotate the pump to gain access to the manifold bolts.

5. Remove the intake manifold. Install screened covers or tape over the openings.

6. Remove all but #5 and #7 fuel injection lines. Cap all lines, nozzles and fittings.

7. Disconnect the fuel line at the fuel supply pump.

8. Disconnect the fuel line clip and the wire connector.

9. Remove the fuel line heater and the fuel line to the primary filter.

10. Installation is in the reverse order.

Fuel Supply Pump

These engines use a small mechanical fuel pump (much like the ones on gasoline engines) to deliver fuel from the tank and lines to the injection pump. See the preceding section for illustration.

Removal and Installation

1. Disconnect and plug the two fuel lines.

2. Remove the two mounting bolts.

3. Remove the pump and gasket.

4. Install the pump and gasket. Tighten the mounting bolts to 27 ft. lbs.

5. Install both fuel lines.

6. Start the engine and check for leaks.

Injection Pump

Removal

1. Disconnect the batteries.

2. Remove the fan and the fan shroud.

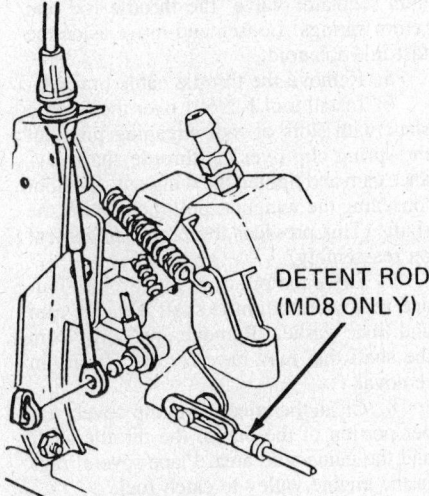

DETENT ROD (MD8 ONLY)

Accelerator linkage
(© General Motors Corp.)

3. Remove the intake manifold.

4. Remove all fuel lines. Cap all lines, nozzles and fittings.

5. Disconnect the accelerator cables at the injection pump. Disconnect the detent cable if applicable.

6. Tag and disconnect all necessary wires and hoses at the injection pump.

7. Disconnect the fuel return line and the line at the pump.

8. If equipped with AC, remove the AC hose retainer bracket.

9. Remove the oil filler tube complete with PCV vent hose assembly.

10. Scribe or paint a mark on the front cover and align, alignment mark on pump and front cover.

11. It will be necessary to rotate the engine in order to gain access to the injection pump retaining bolts through the oil filler neck hole.

12. Remove the pump-to-front cover nuts, remove the pump and cap all lines and fittings.

Testing

1. Drain all fuel from the pump.

2. Connect an air line to the pump inlet connection. Make sure that the air supply is clean and dry.

3. Seal off the return line fitting and completely immerse the pump in a bath of clean test oil.

4. Raise the air pressure in the pump to 20 psi. Leave the pump immersed in the oil for 10 min. to allow any trapped air to escape.

5. Watch for leaks after the 10 min. period. If the pump is not leaking, reduce the pressure to 2 psi for 30 sec. If there is still no leak, increase the pressure to 20 psi again. If still no leaks are seen, the pump is OK.

Installation

1. Replace the gasket.

2. Align the locating pin on the pump

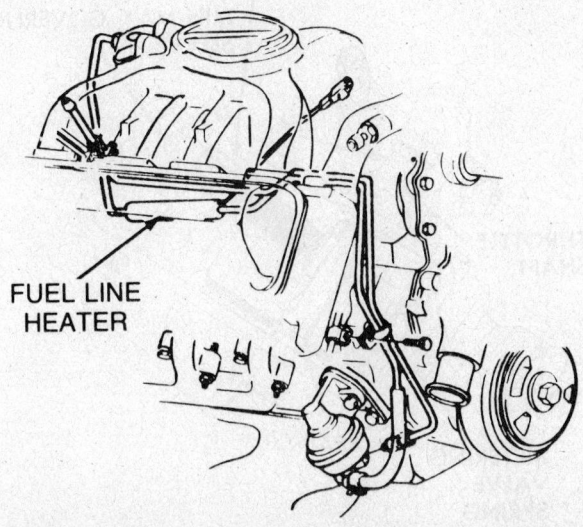

FUEL LINE HEATER

Fuel line heater (© General Motors Corp.)

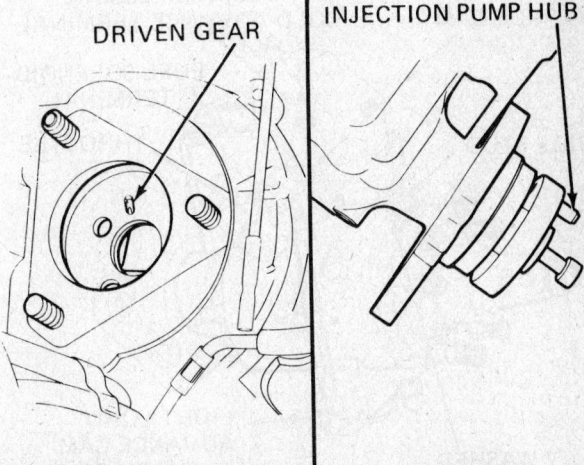

DRIVEN GEAR   INJECTION PUMP HUB

Injection pump locating pin (© General Motors Corp.)

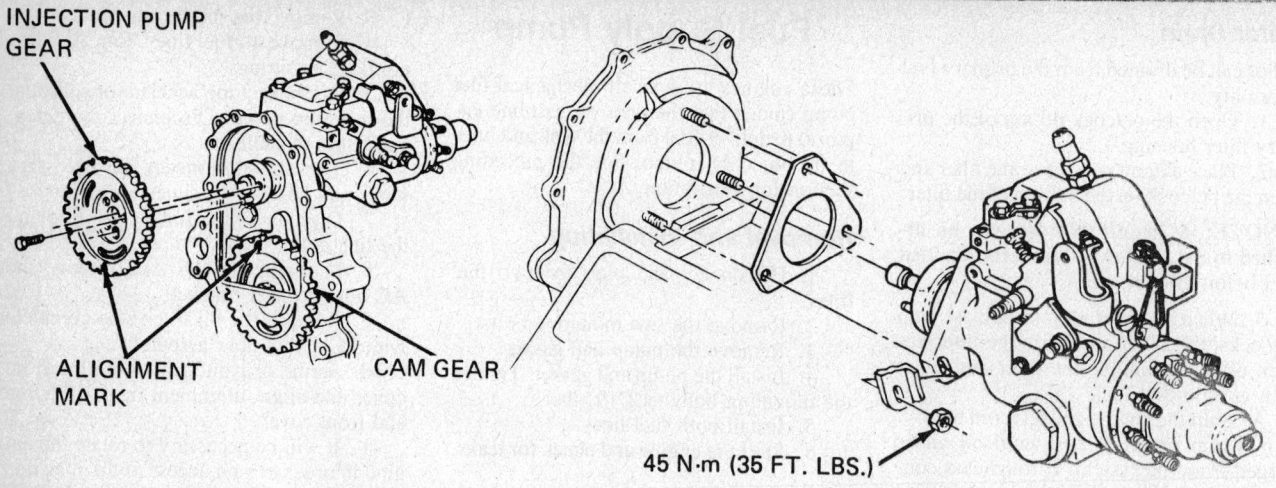

Injection pump installation (© General Motors Corp.)

hub with the slot in the injection pump gear. At the same time, align the timing marks.

3. Attach the pump to the front cover and tighten the mounting nuts to 30 ft. lbs.

4. Attach pump-to-drive gear and tighten the bolts to 20 ft. lbs.

5. Install the oil filler tube along with the PCV vent hose assembly.

6. Install the AC hose retainer bracket if removed.

7. Install the fuel line at the pump and tighten to 20 ft. lbs. Install the fuel return line.

8. Connect all wires and hoses. Connect the accelerator cable.

9. Connect the injection lines.

10. Install the intake manifold.

11. Install the fan shroud, the fan and connect the batteries.

THROTTLE SHAFT SEAL REPLACEMENT

1. Disconnect the batteries.

2. Remove the air cleaner and the intake manifold. Cover the holes with screened covers or tape.

3. Disconnect the injection pump fuel solenoid, the housing pressure cold advance wires and the fuel return pipe.

4. Remove the T.P.S. switch or vacuum regulator valve, the throttle rod and return springs. Loosen and move aside the fast idle solenoid.

5. Remove the throttle cable bracket.

6. Install tool J-29601 over the throttle shaft with slots of tool engaging pin. Put the spring clip over the throttle shaft advance cam and tighten the wing nut. Without loosening the wingnut, pull the tool off the shaft. (This provides the proper alignment on reassembly).

7. Drive the pin from the throttle shaft and remove the throttle shaft advance cam and fiber washer. Remove any burrs from the shaft that may have resulted from pin removal.

8. Clean the injection pump cover, upper portion of the pump, the throttle shaft and the guide stud area. Place several rags in the engine valley to catch fuel.

9. Remove injection pump cover and remove screws from the cover.

NOTE: Extreme care must be exercised to keep foreign material out of the pump when the cover is off.

If any objects are dropped into the pump, they must be removed before the engine is started or injection pump damage or engine damage could occur.

10. Observe position at metering valve spring over the top of the guide stud. This position must be exactly duplicated during reassembly.

11. Remove the guide stud and washer. Note location of parts prior to removal.

12. Rotate the min-max governor assembly up to provide clearance and remove from the throttle shaft. If idle governor spring becomes disengaged from throttle block, it must be reinstalled with tightly wound coils toward throttle block.

13. Remove the throttle shaft assembly

Injection pump housing—right side (© General Motors Corp.)

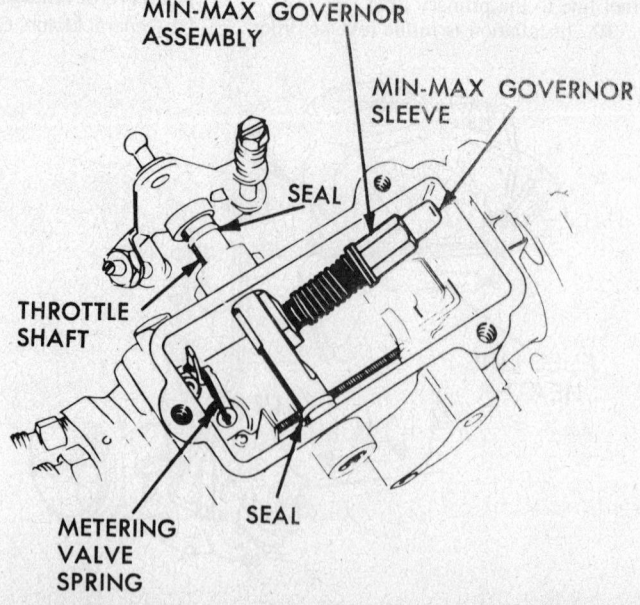

Injection pump cover removed (© General Motors Corp.)

and examine the shaft for unusual wear or damage, replace if required.

14. Examine the throttle shaft bushings in the pump housing for any evidence of damage or unusual wear and leaks. Remove the pump and send to the local Roosa Master dealer if bushing replacement is necessary.

15. Remove the throttle shaft seals. Do not attempt to cut the seals to remove, as any nicks in the seal seat will cause leakage.

16. Install new shaft seals using care not to cut the seals on the sharp edges of the shaft. Apply a light coating of clean chassis grease on the seals.

17. Carefully slide the throttle shaft back into the pump to the point where the min-max governor assembly will slide back onto the throttle shaft.

18. Rotate the min-max governor assembly downward, hold in position and slide the throttle shaft and governor into position.

19. Install a new mylar washer, the throttle shaft advance cam, (do not tighten cam screw at this time), and a new throttle shaft drive pin.

20. Align the throttle shaft advance cam so tool J-29601 can be reinstalled over the throttle shaft, pin in the slots and the spring clip over the advance cam.

21. Put a .005″ feeler gage between the cam and the mylar washer. Tighten the cam screw and remove tool J-29601.

22. Reinstall the guide stud with a new washer, making certain that the upper extension of the metering valve spring rides on top of the guide stud. Torque the guide stud to 85 in. lbs. Overtorquing the guide stud may strip the aluminum threads in the housing.

23. Hold the throttle in the idle position.

24. Install new pump cover seal. Make sure the screws are not in the cover and position the cover about ¼ inch forward (toward shaft end) and about ⅛ inch above the pump.

25. Move the cover rearward and downward into position, being careful not to cut

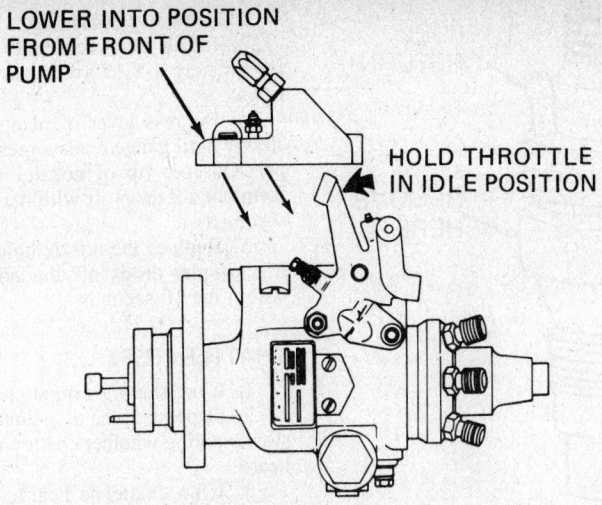

Pump cover installation (© General Motors Corp.)

the seal. Reinstall the cover screws. Be careful not to drop and lose the flat washer and internal lock washer with each screw. Flat washer must be against pump cover. Torque to 33 in. lbs. Install vacuum regulator valve or T.P.S. switch as outlined.

26. Reconnect the negative cables to both batteries.

27. Turn the ignition switch to the run position and touch the pink solenoid wire to the solenoid. A clicking noise should be heard as the wire is connected and disconnected. If this clicking is not observed, the linkage may be jammed in a wide open throttle position and the engine MUST NOT be started. If clicking is observed, connect the pump solenoid and housing pressure cold advance wires, then proceed to Step 30.

28. Remove the cover. Ground the solenoid lead (opposite the hot lead) and connect the pink wire. With the ignition switch in the run position, the solenoid in the cover should move the linkage. If not, the solenoid must be replaced. Minimum voltage across the solenoid terminals must be 12.0.

29. Reinstall the cover and repeat Step 27.

30. Reinstall throttle cable bracket, detent cable and fast idle solenoid.

31. Reinstall the throttle cable and return springs. Make sure the timing mark on the pump and housing are aligned and make sure the nuts attaching the pump to the housing are tight. Install fuel return pipe.

32. Start the engine and check for leaks.

33. Idle roughness may be observed due to the air in the pump, give it plenty of time to purge by allowing the engine to idle. It may be necessary to shut the engine down for several minutes to allow air bubbles to rise to the top of the pump where they will be purged.

34. Adjust vacuum regulator valve.

35. Remove the screened covers or tape, then reinstall the intake and air cleaner.

Injection Nozzle

Removal

1. Disconnect the batteries.
2. Disconnect the fuel line clip and remove the fuel return hose.
3. Remove the fuel injection line.
4. Remove the injection nozzle using the special tool if possible. If not, use a 30mm open end wrench. Be sure to remove the nozzle using the large 30 mm hex nut. Failure to do this will result in damage to the injection nozzle. Always cap the nozzle and lines to prevent damage and contamination.

Testing

If all of the following tests are satisfied, the nozzle holder can be installed in the engine without any changes. If any one of the tests is not satisfied, the complete nozzle holder assembly must be replaced.

PREPARATION

1. Connect the nozzle holder assembly to the test line.

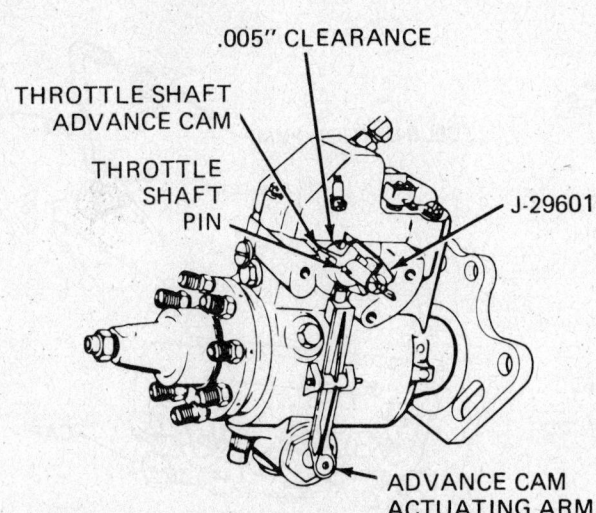

Injection pump with tool installed (© General Motors Corp.)

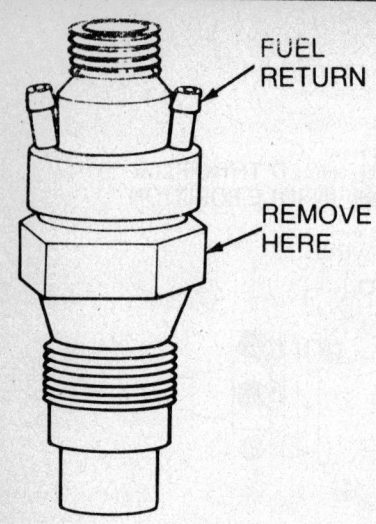

Injection nozzle (© General Motors Corp.)

2. Close the shutoff valve to the pressure gauge.

3. Fill and flush the nozzle holder assembly with test oil by activating the lever repeatedly and briskly. This will apply test oil to all functionally important areas of the nozzle and purge it of air.

OBTAINING PRESSURE CHECK

1. Open shutoff valve at pressure gauge ¼ turn.

2. Depress lever of tester slowly. Note at what pressure the needle of the pressure gauge stopped, indicating an increase in pressure (nozzle does not chatter) or at which pressure the pressure dropped substantially (nozzle chatters). The maximum observed pressure is the opening pressure.

3. The opening pressure should not fall below the lower limit of 1600 psi.

4. Replace nozzles which fall below the lower limit.

LEAKAGE TEST

1. Further open shutoff valve at pressure gauge (½ to 1-½ turns).

2. Blow-dry nozzle tip.

3. Install two clear plastic lines (approximately 1-1 ½")over leak-off connections.

4. Depress lever of manual test stand slowly until gauge reads a pressure of 1380 psi. Observe tip of nozzle. A drop may form but not drop off within a period of 10 seconds.

5. Replace the nozzle holder assembly if a droplet drops off the nozzle bottom within the 10 seconds.

CHATTER TEST

1. Close shutoff lever at pressure gauge.

2. Depress lever of manual test stand slowly noting whether chatter noises can be heard.

3. If no chatter is heard, increase the speed of lever movement until it reaches a point where the nozzle chatters.

4. The chatter indicates that the nozzle needle moves freely and that the nozzle seat, guide, as well as the pintle, have no mechanical defects.

5. Replace nozzles which do not chatter.

SPRAY PATTERN

1. Close shutoff valve at pressure gauge.

2. Depress lever of manual test stand downward abruptly and quickly. The spray should have a tight, evenly shaped conical pattern which is well atomized. This pattern should be concentric to the nozzle axis. Streamlike injections indicate a defect.

Installation

1. Remove protective caps from the nozzle.

2. Install nozzle and torque to 50 ft. lbs.

3. Connect fuel injection line, torque nut to 20 ft. lbs.

4. Install fuel return hose.

5. Install fuel line clip.

6. Connect battery.

Injection Pump Fuel Lines

Removal

1. Disconnect the batteries.

2. Disconnect the air cleaner bracket at the valve cover.

3. Remove the crankcase ventilator bracket and position it out of the way.

4. Disconnect the fuel lines and remove the secondary fuel filter.

5. Loosen the vacuum pump hold-down clamp and then rotate the pump to gain access to the mainfold bolt.

6. Remove the intake manifold bolts. The injection line clips are retained by the same bolts.

7. Remove the intake manifold and cover the holes with screened covers or tape.

8. Remove the injection line clips at the loom brackets.

9. Remove the injection lines at the nozzles and cover the nozzles with protective caps.

10. Tag and disconnect injection lines at the injection pump.

11. Remove fuel line from injection pump.

Installation

1. Install the injection lines as shown in the illustrations.

2. Remove the covers or tape and install the intake manifold.

3. Install the secondary fuel filter and lines.

4. Tighten the vacuum pump hold-down clamp and then install the crankcase ventilator.

5. Connect the air cleaner and the batteries.

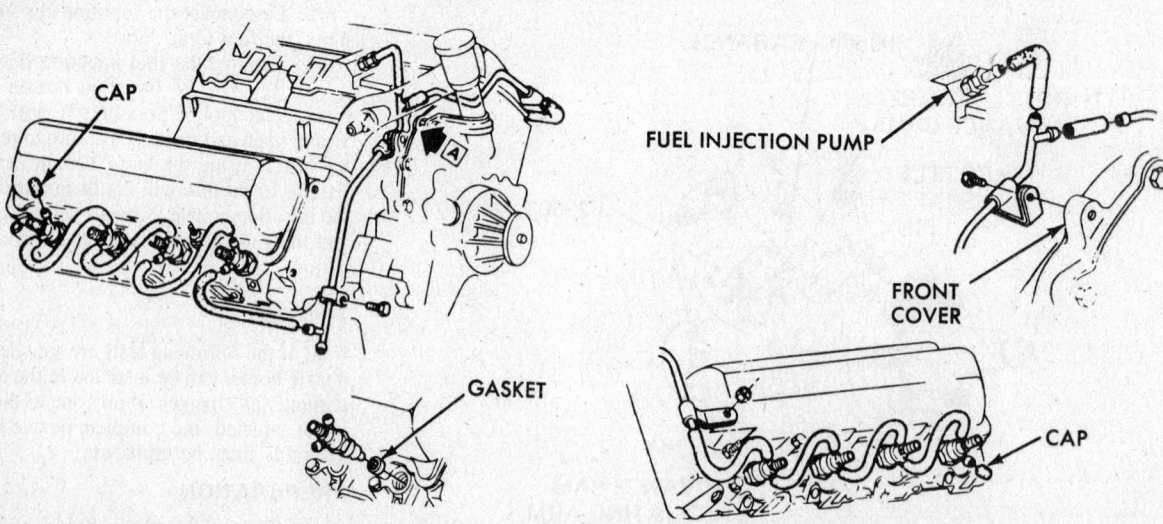

Nozzle installation (© General Motors Corp.)

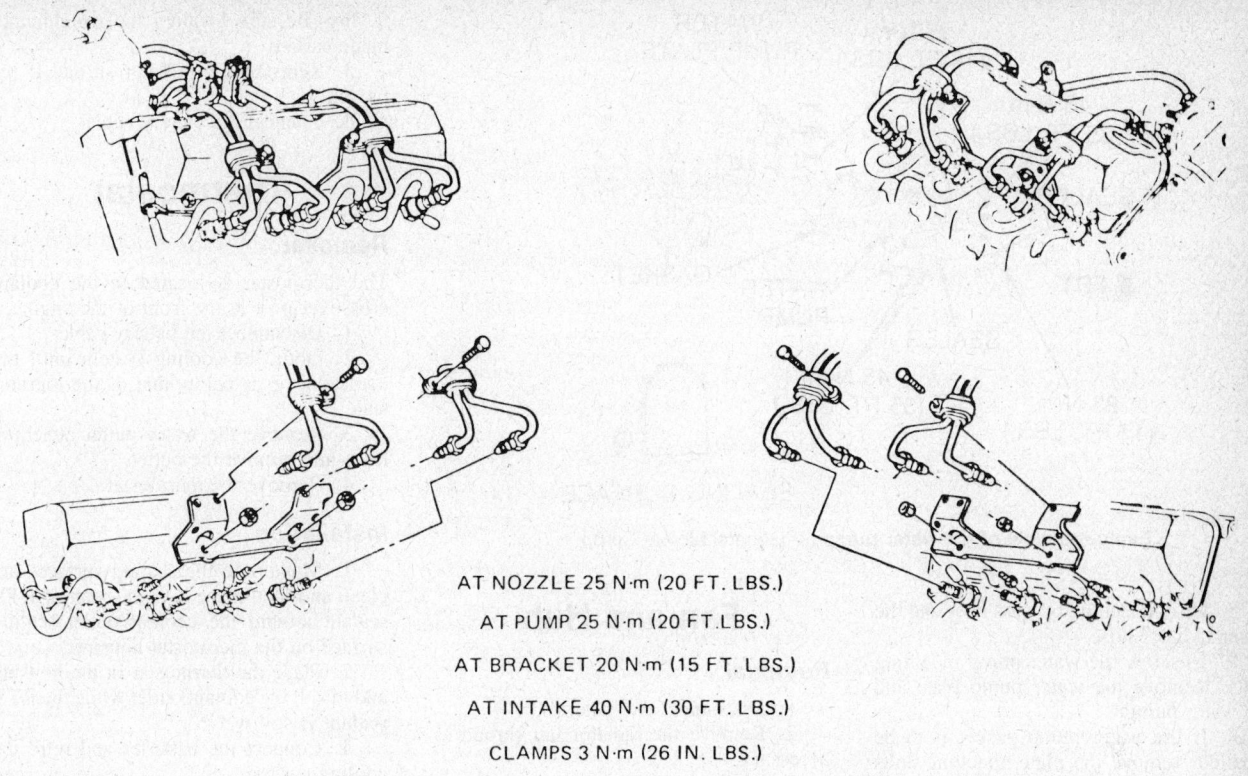

AT NOZZLE 25 N·m (20 FT. LBS.)

AT PUMP 25 N·m (20 FT. LBS.)

AT BRACKET 20 N·m (15 FT. LBS.)

AT INTAKE 40 N·m (30 FT. LBS.)

CLAMPS 3 N·m (26 IN. LBS.)

2 PLACES

L.H.

R.H.

Injection line installation (© General Motors Corp.)

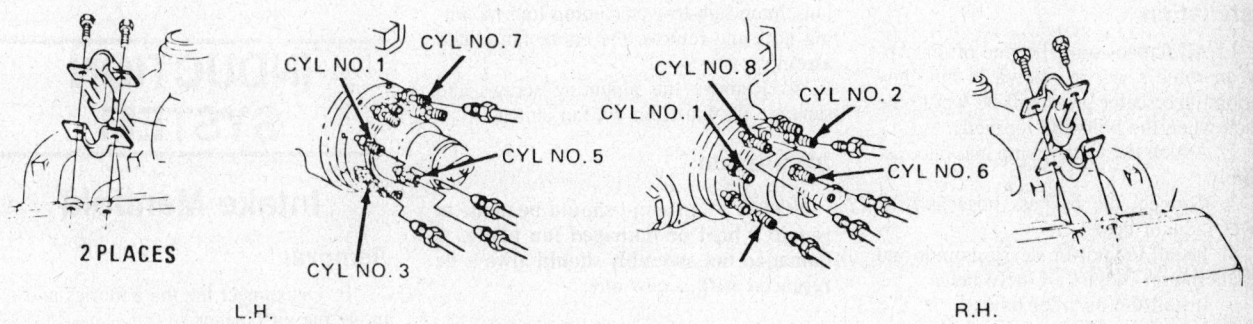

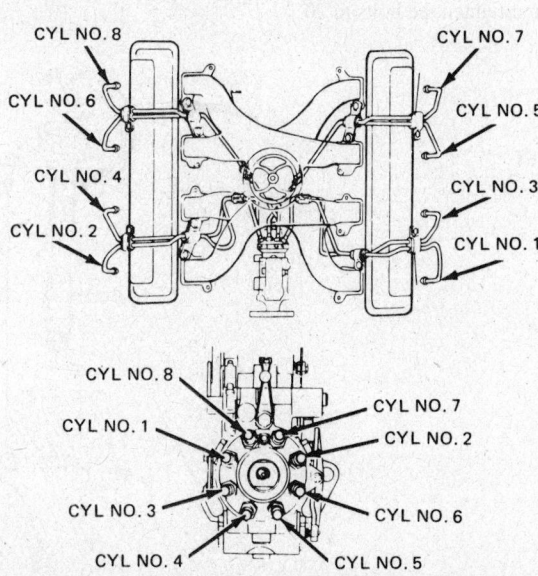

Injection line routing (© General Motors Corp.)

COOLING SYSTEM

Water Pump

Removal

1. Disconnect the batteries.
2. Remove the fan and the fan shroud.
3. Drain the radiator. If equipped with A/C, remove the A/C hose bracket nuts.
4. Remove the oil filler tube.
5. Remove the alternator pivot bolt and then remove the drive belt. Remove the lower bracket.
6. Remove the power steering belt. Remove the power steering pump and position it out of the way.
7. Remove the AC belt if so equipped.

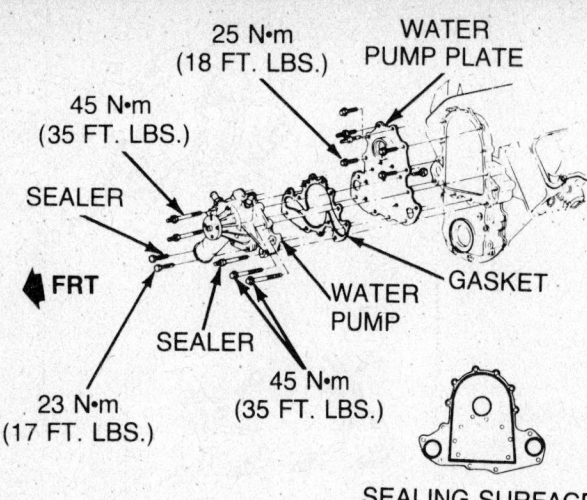

Exploded view of the water pump (© General Motors Corp.)

8. Disconnect the by-pass hose and the lower radiator hose.

9. Unscrew the water pump mounting bolts. Remove the water pump plate and the water pump.

10. If the water pump gasket is to be repaired, remove the plate attaching bolts to the water pump and replace the gasket.

Installation

1. All flanges must be free of oil. Apply anarobic sealer as shown in the illustration. The sealer must still be wet to the touch when the bolts are torqued.

2. Attach the water pump and plate assembly.

3. Connect the by-pass hose and the lower radiator hose.

4. Install the power steering pump and the alternator. Adjust all drive belts.

5. Install the oil filler tube.

6. Install the fan shroud and the fan.

7. Fill system with coolant, connect batteries start the engine and check for leaks.

Fan and Hub

Removal

1. Disconnect the batteries.

2. Remove the radiator fan shroud as necessary.

3. Matchmark the fan clutch hub and the water pump hub and then unscrew the fan clutch hub-to-water pump hub mounting nuts and remove the entire fan clutch assembly.

4. Remove the mounting screws and separate the fan from the fan clutch.

Installation

NOTE: No attempt should be made to repair a bent or damaged fan blade. A damaged fan assembly should always be replaced with a new one.

1. Attach the fan to the fan clutch hub.

2. Install the fan clutch assembly to the water pump hub and tighten the bolts to 20 ft. lbs. Be sure to align the matchmarks made earlier.

3. Reinstall the radiator shroud if removed.

4. Connect the battery cables.

Thermostat

Removal

The thermostat is located in the coolant crossover pipe at the front of the engine.

1. Disconnect the battery cables.

2. Drain the cooling system until the coolant level is below that of the thermostat.

3. Remove the water outlet attaching bolts and remove the outlet.

4. Remove the thermostat.

Installation

1. Make sure the sealing surfaces are clean and then place a 1/8 in. bead of RTV sealant around the coolant outlet sealing surface on the thermostat housing.

2. Place the thermostat in the housing and install the coolant outlet while the RTV sealant is still wet.

3. Connect the batteries and refill the cooling system.

INDUCTION SYSTEM

Intake Manifold

Removal

1. Disconnect the the batteries and remove the air cleaner.

2. Remove the crankcase ventilator tubes.

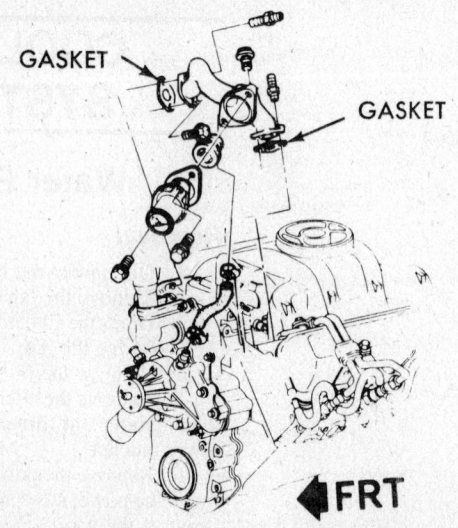

Thermostat and housing (© General Motors Corp.)

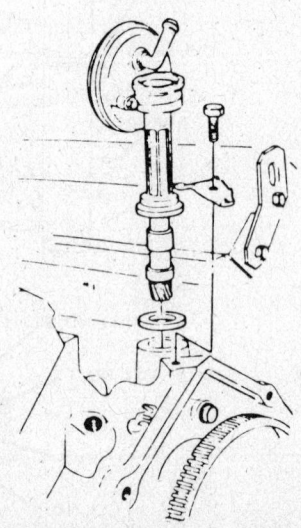

Vacuum pump (© General Motors Corp.)

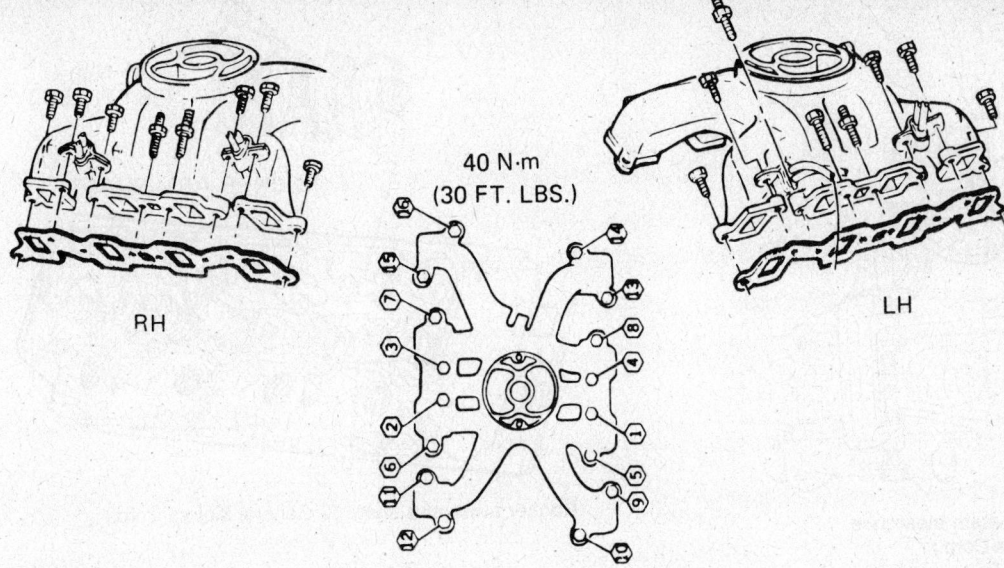

Intake manifold torque sequence (© General Motors Corp.)

3. Disconnect the fuel lines and remove the secondary fuel filter.

4. Loosen the vacuum pump hold-down clamp and then rotate the pump in order to gain access to the manifold bolt.

5. Remove the intake manifold bolts. The injection line clips are retained by the same bolts.

6. Remove the intake manifold.

7. If any further operations are to be performed while the manifold is off, install screened covers or tape over the holes.

Installation

1. Remove the tape or screened cover if installed.

2. Make sure that the gasket surfaces are clean and install a new gasket.

NOTE: The gasket has an opening for the EGR on light duty applications. On heavy duty applications it has an insert covering the opening.

3. Install the intake manifold and tighten the bolts in the sequence shown.

4. Install the secondary fuel filter.

5. Install the fuel lines.

6. Installation of the remaining components is in the reverse order.

CYLINDER HEAD AND VALVE TRAIN

Cylinder Head

Removal

1. Remove the fuel injection lines. Cap all lines, nozzles and fittings.

2. Remove the intake manifold.

3. Remove the rocker arm covers, after removing any accessory brackets that are in the way.

4. Drain the radiator and remove the dipstick tube.

5. Disconnect the ground wire at the cowl.

6. Raise and support the car, disconnect the exhaust pipe from the manifold and then lower the car.

7. If equipped with AC, remove the compressor and position it out of the way.

8. Remove the alternator.

9. Tag and disconnect the glow plug wires.

10. Remove the rocker arm assemblies and then remove the push rods. Mark the push rods for reinstallation. Keep the rocker arms and push rods in order so they can be installed in the same location.

11. Disconnect the radiator, by-pass and heater hoses.

12. Disconnect the ground strap.

13. Remove the thermostat housing/crossover at the head.

14. Remove the cylinder head bolts (17 on each side). The rear left head bolt may have to remain in the head upon removal.

15. Carefully lift off the cylinder head.

Inspection

1. Check for cracks in the exhaust ports, combustion chambers, or external cracks to the coolant chamber.

2. Check the valves for burned heads, cracked faces or damaged stems. Check the deck face for scratches or dents across the gasket fire-ring area. Marks across the coolant seal surfaces can be no deeper than .003 in.

NOTE: Excessive valve stem to bore clearance will cause excessive oil combustion and may cause valve breakage. Insufficient clearance will result in noisy and sticky functioning of the valve and disturb engine smoothness.

3. Measure valve stem clearance as follows:

a. Clamp a dial indicator on one side

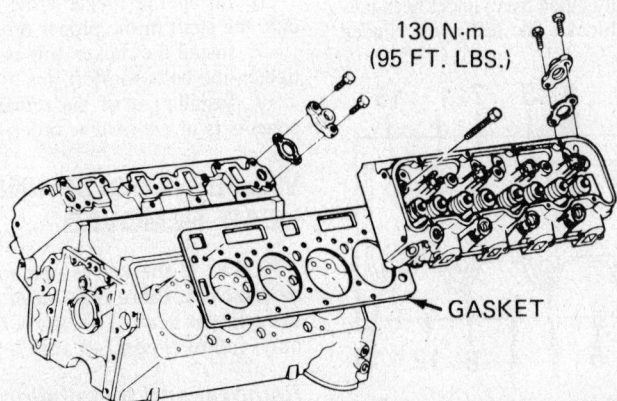

Cylinder head removal (© General Motors Corp.)

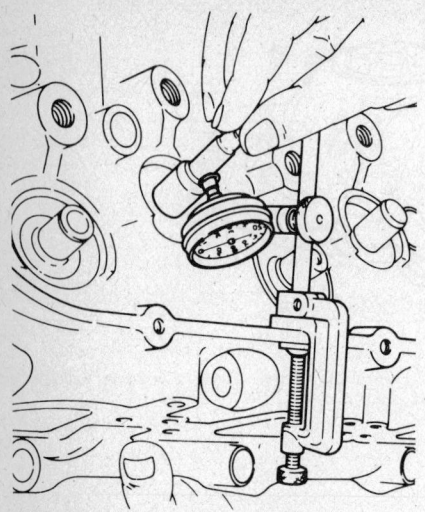

Measuring valve stem clearance
(© General Motors Corp.)

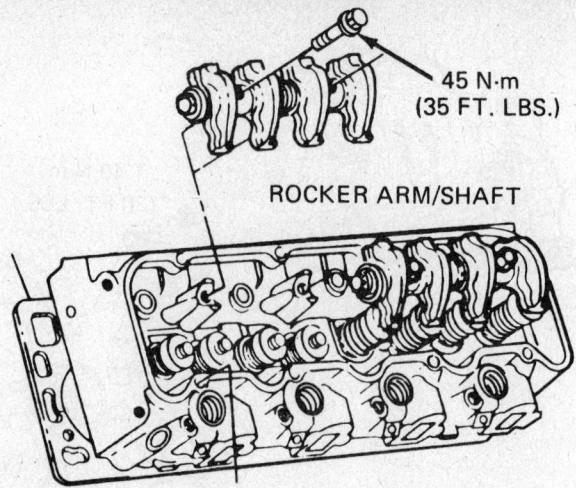

45 N·m
(35 FT. LBS.)

ROCKER ARM/SHAFT

Rocker arms and shaft (© General Motors Corp.)

of the cylinder head rocker arm cover gasket rail.

b. Position the indicator so that the movement of the valve stem from side to side (crosswise to the head) will cause a direct movement of the indicator stem. The indicator stem must contact the valve stem just above the valve guide.

c. Drop the valve head about 1/16 in. off the valve seat.

d. Move the stem from side to side using light pressure to obtain a clearance reading. If the clearance exceeds specifications, it will be necessary to ream the valve guides for oversize valves.

4. Use a spring tester and check the valve spring tension. Springs should be replaced if they are not within 10 lbs. of the specified load (without dampers).

Installation

1. Clean the cylinder head-to-engine block mating surfaces thoroughly. Install new head gaskets on the engine block. Do NOT coat the gaskets with any kind of sealer. The gaskets come with a special coating that eliminates the need for sealer. The use of any additional sealer will interfere with this coating and lead to leakage.

2. Carefully guide the cylinder head into place on the block. The left rear cylinder

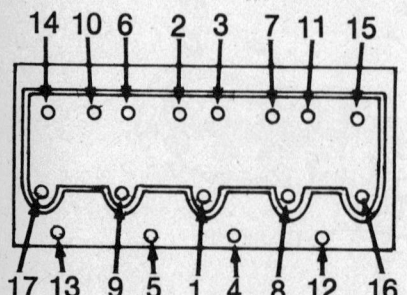

14 10 6 2 3 7 11 15

17 13 9 5 1 4 8 12 16

Cylinder head torque sequence (© General Motors Corp.)

head bolt must be installed in the head prior to installation.

3. Coat the threads of the head bolts with sealing compound and then install them finger tight.

4. Tighten each bolt a little at a time (in the sequence illustrated) until the specified torque is achieved.

5. Installation of the remaining components is in the reverse order. Use RTV silicone sealant when installing the rocker arm covers.

ROCKER ARMS AND PUSH RODS

Removal and Installation

1. Remove the rocker arm covers.

2. Remove the rocker arm and shaft.

3. If the rocker arm is to be removed, remove the cotter pin and then remove the rocker arm from the shaft.

4. Lift out the push rods. The push rod upper end must be marked for reinstallation.

5. Install the push rods if removed. Make sure that the marked end is up, failure to do so could cause premature wear or damage.

6. Install the rocker arms and spring onto the shaft in the proper order.

7. Install the rocker arm assembly and tighten the bolts to 35 ft. lbs.

8. Installation of the remaining components is in the reverse order.

VALVES AND SPRINGS— HEAD REMOVED

NOTE: If the valves are not going to be removed, there is no need to remove the cylinder head. To remove the springs only, follow Steps 1–3 and 7–9.

Removal and Installation

1. Remove the valve keys by com-

pressing the valve springs with a valve spring compressor.

2. Release the compressor and remove the rotators or spring caps, the springs and the spring damper.

3. Remove the oil seal and the valve spring shims.

4. Remove the valves from the cylinder head and place them in a rack in their proper sequence so they can be assembled in their original positions.

5. If necessary to remove the pre-chamber, remove the glow plug and injection nozzle and then tap out the pre-chamber with a blunt nylon drift.

6. Insert the valve into its proper port.

7. Install the valve spring shim on the valve spring seat and then install a new oil seal.

8. Set the valve spring (with damper) and valve cap in position.

9. Compress the spring, install the valve locks and make sure the locks seat properly in the groove of the valve stem. Grease can be used to hold the locks in place while releasing the compressor.

10. Install the remaining valves.

11. Check the installed height of the valve springs using a narrow thin scale. Measure from the top of the spring or shim to the top of the valve spring shield or valve spring. If this measurement exceeds the specified height, install a valve spring seat shim approximately 1/16 in. thick. At no time should the spring be shimmed to give an installed height under the minimum specified.

12. Install the pre-chamber if removed. It can only be installed in one position. Use a 1¼ in. socket to reinstall the pre-chamber. It should be flush to .002 in. above the face of the head.

VALVE LIFTERS

Removal

Valve lifters and push rods should be kept in order so they can be installed in their

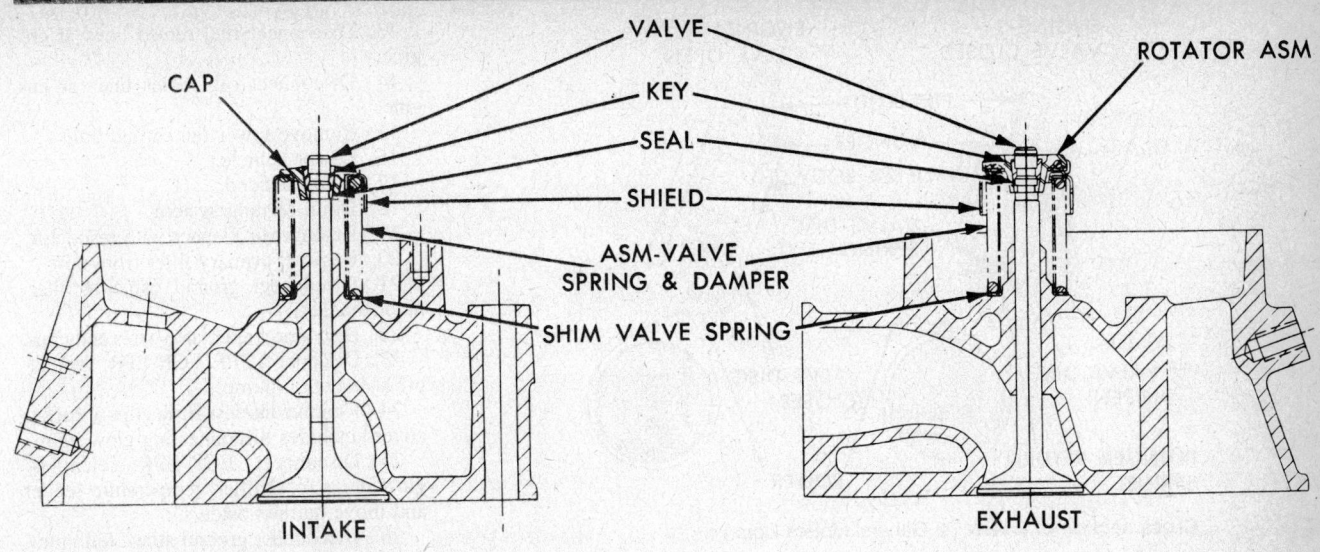

Cross section of the valves (© General Motors Corp.)

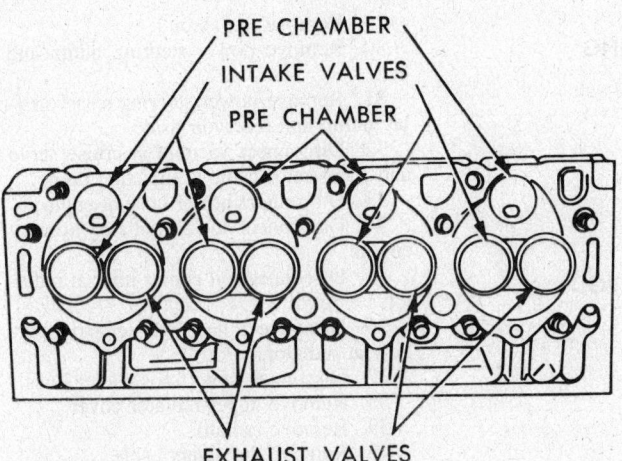

Valve location (© General Motors Corp.)

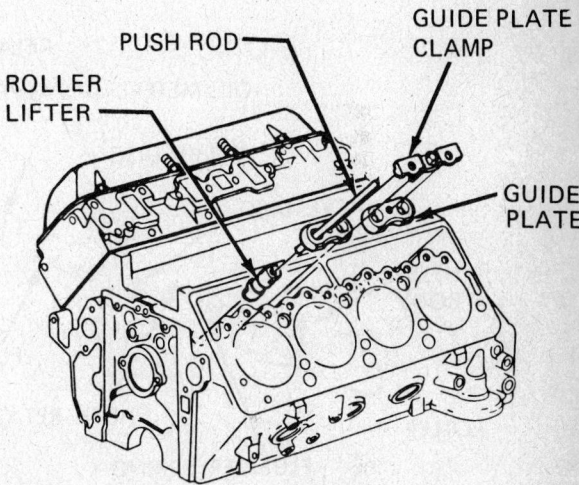

Valve lifter removal (© General Motors Corp.)

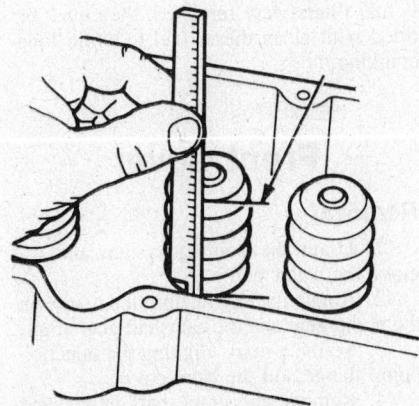

Measuring valve installed height
(© General Motors Corp.)

original position. The pushrods must be installed with the painted or marked end up because the premium ball is located on the upper end only.

1. Remove the rocker arm covers and the rocker arms.

2. Remove the guide clamps and the guide plates. It may be necessary to use mechanical fingers to remove the guide plates.

3. Remove the lifters through the access hole in the cylinder head using the proper tool and a magnet.

Disassembly

1. Pry out the retainer ring with a small screwdriver.

2. Remove the pushrod seat and the oil metering valve.

3. Remove the plunger and the plunger spring.

4. Remove the check valve retainer from the plunger and then remove the valve and spring.

Cleaning and Inspection

After the lifters are disassembled, all parts should be cleaned in solvent. A small particle under the check valve will cause malfunctioning of the lifter. Inspect all parts

for nicks, burrs or scoring. If the roller body or the plunger are found to be defective in any way, the entire lifter assembly should be replaced. Whenever the lifters are removed, check as follows:

1. The roller should rotate freely, but without excessive play.

2. Check that the needle bearing is not missing or broken.

3. The roller should be free of pitting or roughness. If either of these conditions are present, check the camshaft for a similiar condition. Replace the lifter or the camshaft if necessary.

Assembly

1. Coat all parts with a light coating of clean engine oil.

2. Assemble the valve disc spring and retainer into the plunger. Make sure the retainer flange is pressed tight against the bottom of the recess in the plunger.

3. Install the plunger spring over the check retainer.

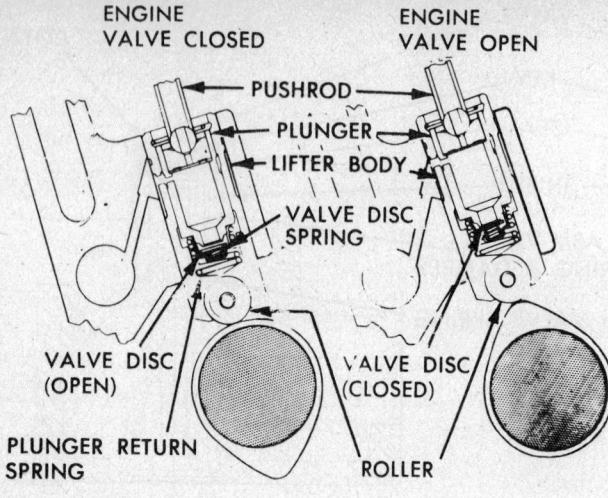

Cross section of a lifter (© General Motors Corp.)

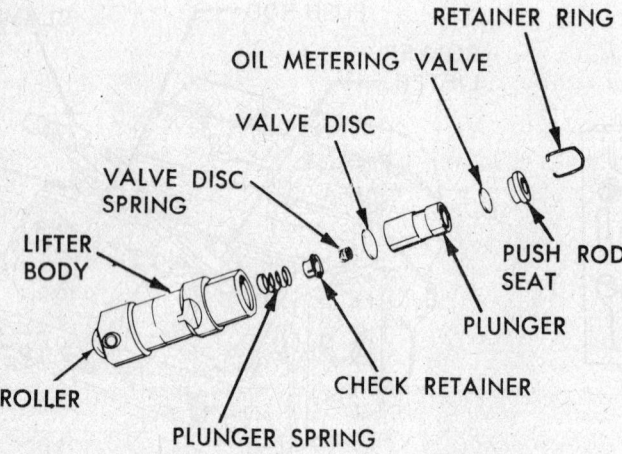

Exploded view of a valve lifter (© General Motors Corp.)

4. Hold the plunger with the spring facing up and insert it into the lifter body. Hold it vertically to prevent cocking the spring.

5. Install the oil metering valve and the pushrod seat into the lifter. Install the retaining ring.

Installation

Prime the new lifter by working the lifter plunger while the assembly is submerged in new kerosene or diesel fuel. A dry lifter can be damaged when starting the engine.

1. Install the lifter into its original position in the cylinder block. Use rigid mechanic's wire or a welding rod and fabricate a lifter installing tool.

2. Install the valve lifter guide plate.

3. Install the guide plate clamp. The crankshaft must be rotated 720° after assembly of the lifter guide plate clamp to insure free movement of the lifters in the guide plates.

ENGINE BLOCK

Engine

Removal and Installation

1. Disconnect batteries.
2. Raise vehicle.
3. Remove transmission dust cover.
4. Disconnect torque converter.
5. Disconnect exhaust.
6. Remove starter bolts.
7. Disconnect wires and remove starter.
8. Remove transmission bell housing bolts.
9. Remove left motor mount bolts.
10. Remove right motor mount bolts.
11. Disconnect block heaters.
12. Remove wire harness, trans cooler lines and front battery cable clamp at oil pan.
13. Disconnect fuel return lines at engine.
14. Disconnect oil cooler lines at engine.
15. Remove lower fan shroud bolts.
16. Lower vehicle.
17. Remove hood.
18. Drain cooling system.
19. Remove air cleaner with resonator.
20. Remove primary filter from cowl.
21. Disconnect ground cable at alternator bracket.
22. Disconnect alternator wires and clips.
23. Disconnect TPS, EGR-EPR, fuel cut-off at injection pump.
24. Remove harness from clips at rocker covers includes disconnecting glow plugs.
25. Disconnect EGR-EPR solenoids, glow plugs, controller, temperature sender and move harness aside.
26. Disconnect ground strap, left side.
27. Remove fan.
28. Remove upper radiator hoses at engine.
29. Remove fan shroud.
30. Remove power steering pump and belt.
31. Remove power steering reservoir—lay pump and reservoir aside.
32. Disconnect vacuum at cruise servo and accelerator cable at injection pump.
33. Disconnect heater hose at engine.
34. Disconnect lower radiator hose at engine.
35. Disconnect oil cooler lines at radiator.
36. Disconnect heater hose and overflow at radiator.
37. Disconnect auto trans cooler lines.
38. Remove upper radiator cover.
39. Remove radiator.
40. Remove the detent cable.
41. Remove engine and support transmission.
42. Installation is in the reverse order. If fuel filters were removed, they must be filled with clean diesel fuel to avoid long cranking.

Front Cover

Removal

1. Drain the cooling system and remove the water pump.
2. Rotate the engine until the marks on the pump gear and the camshaft gear align.
3. Scribe a mark aligning the injection pump flange and the front cover.
4. Remove the crankshaft pulley and the torsional damper.
5. Remove the 4 front cover-to-oil pan bolts.
6. Remove the fuel return line clips.
7. Remove the injection pump driven gear and then remove the injection pump retaining bolts from the front cover.
8. Remove the baffle. Remove the remaining front cover bolts and remove the front cover.

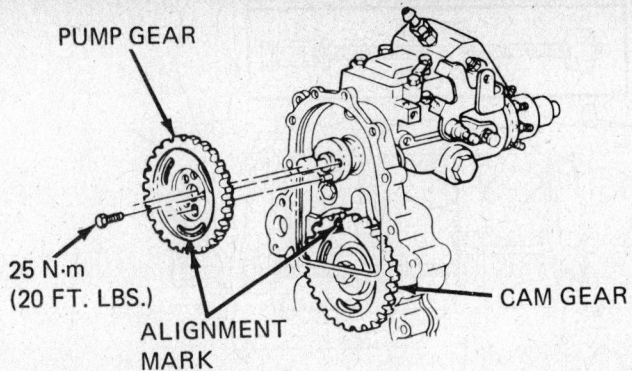

Gear alignment (© General Motors Corp.)

Installation

1. Clean all sealing surfaces and place a 1/16 in. bead of sealant as shown in the illustration. Apply RTV sealer to the bottom portion of the front cover where it attaches to the oil pan.

2. Install the front cover and then install the baffle.

3. Install the injection pump making sure the scribe marks on the pump and the front cover align.

4. Install the injection pump driven gear making sure that the marks on the pump gear and the cam gear align.

5. Installation of the remaining components is in the reverse order.

Timing Chain and Sprockets

Removal and Installation

1. Remove the front cover.

2. Remove the bolt and washer attaching the camshaft gear to the camshaft sprocket.

3. Remove the injection pump gear.

4. Slide the cam sprocket and timing chain off the shaft and then remove the crankshaft sprocket.

5. Install the crank sprocket, the cam sprocket and the timing chain together. Make sure the timing marks on the sprockets are aligned.

6. Rotate the crankshaft 360° so that the camshaft gear and the injection pump gear are aligned.

7. Install the front cover. Anytime the timing chain, gears or sprockets are removed it will be necessary to retime the engine.

Camshaft

Removal

1. Disconnect the batteries, raise the car and drain the cooling system.

2. Disconnect the exhaust pipe at the manifolds.

3. Remove the fan shroud, the fan and the radiator. Lower the car.

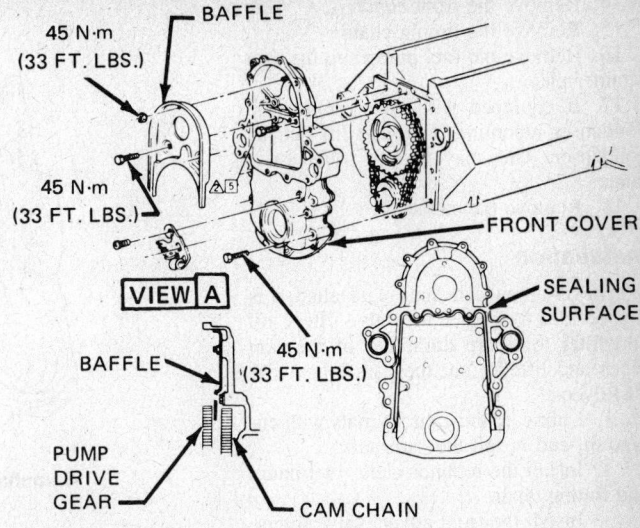

Front cover installation (© General Motors Corp.)

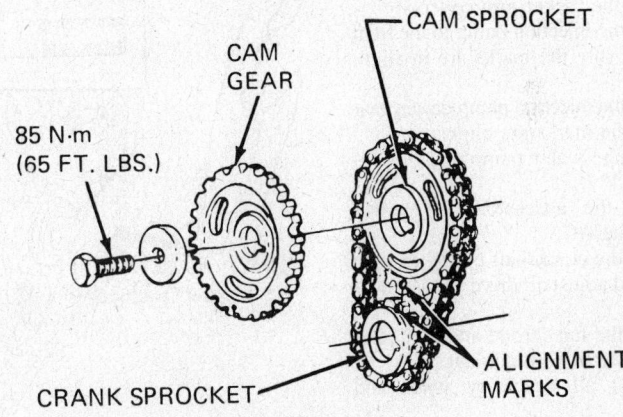

Timing chain (© General Motors Corp.)

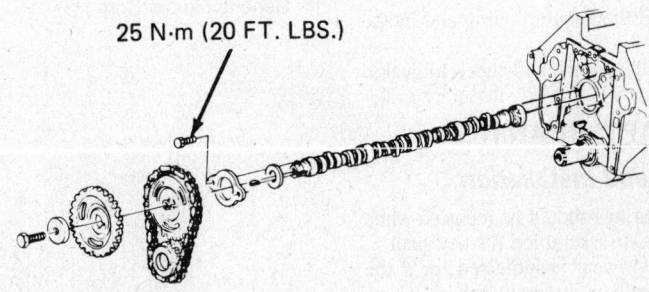

Camshaft (© General Motors Corp.)

4. Remove the vacuum pump and the intake manifold.

5. Remove the injection lines. Cap all lines, nozzles and fittings.

6. Remove the water pump and then remove the injection pump gear.

7. Scribe a mark on the front cover aligning the pump flange and the cover.

8. Remove the injection pump, the power steering pump and the alternator.

9. If equipped with AC, remove the compressor and position it out of the way.

10. Remove the rocker arm covers, the rocker arm shaft assembly and the push rods. Place parts in a rack so they may be installed in the original location.

11. Remove the thermostat housing/crossover from the cylinder heads.

12. Remove the cylinder head with the exhaust manifolds attached.

13. Remove the valve lifter clamps, guide plates and valve lifters. Keep parts in order so they may be installed in the original location.

14. Remove the front cover.
15. Remove the timing chain.
16. Remove the fuel pump and the cam retainer plate.
17. If equipped with AC, remove the condenser mounting bolts and lift out the condenser. This may require some assistance.
18. Remove the camshaft.

Installation

Whenever a new camshaft is installed, it is a good idea to replace the valve lifters, oil and filter to insure durability of the cam lobes and lifters. Coat the cam lobes with "Molycote".

1. Lubricate the cam journals with engine oil and install the camshaft.
2. Install the retainer plate, fuel pump and timing chain.
3. Install the front cover, valve lifters, guide plates and clamps.
4. Install the cylinder head, push rods and rocker arm shaft assemblies.
5. Install the rocker arm covers.
6. Install the injection pump to the front cover making sure the marks are in alignment.
7. Install the injection pump driven gear making sure the marks are aligned.
8. Install the water pump and fuel injection lines.
9. Install the alternator, the power steering and the AC.
10. Install the crankshaft pulley and the fan. Install and adjust all drive belts as necessary.
11. Install the fan shroud and the radiator. Fill the system with coolant.
12. Connect all necessary wires and hoses.
13. Raise the car, connect the exhaust pipes to the manifolds and then lower the car.
14. Install the vacuum pump and intake manifold.
15. Start the engine and check for leaks.

CAMSHAFT BEARINGS

Removal and Installation

Camshaft bearings should be replaced while the engine is disassembled for overhaul.

If excessive wear is indicated, or if the engine is being completely rebuilt, camshaft bearings should be replaced as follows: Drive the camshaft rear plug from the block. Assemble the removal puller with its shoulder on the bearing to be removed. Gradually tighten the puller nut until bearing is removed. Remove remaining bearings, leaving the front and rear for last. To remove front and rear bearings, reverse position of the tool, so as to pull the bearings in toward the center of the block. Leave the tool in this position, pilot the new front and rear bearings on the installer, and pull them into position. Return the tool to its original position and pull remaining bearings into position.

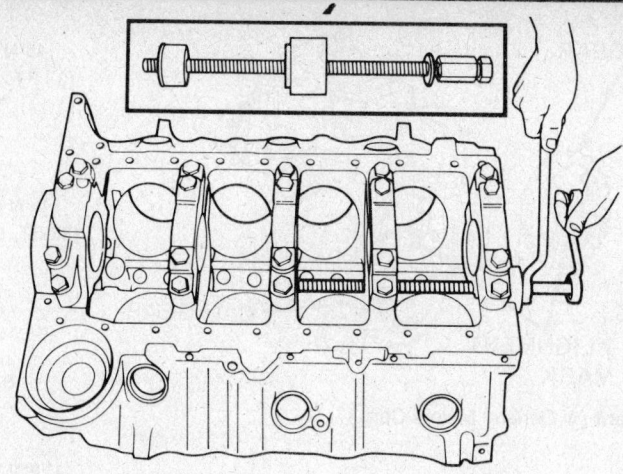

Camshaft bearing removal (© General Motors Corp.)

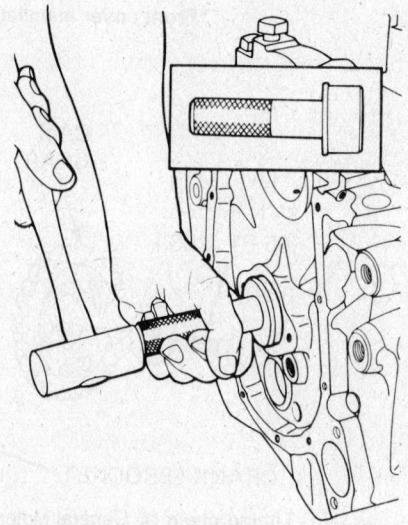

Replacing the camshaft front bearing (© General Motors Corp.)

NOTE: Ensure that oil holes align when installing bearings.

Replace camshaft rear plug, and stake it into position to aid retention.

Crankshaft

Removal and Installation

1. Remove the engine. Remove the flywheel.
2. Mount the engine in a stand and secure.
3. Remove the oil dipstick and tube.
4. Remove the glow plugs. Remove the front cover.
5. Remove the oil pan and oil pump.
6. Remove the connecting rod caps. Install protective hose on the connecting rod studs. Keep the bearings in order so they can be installed in their original location.
7. Remove the main bearing caps. Keep

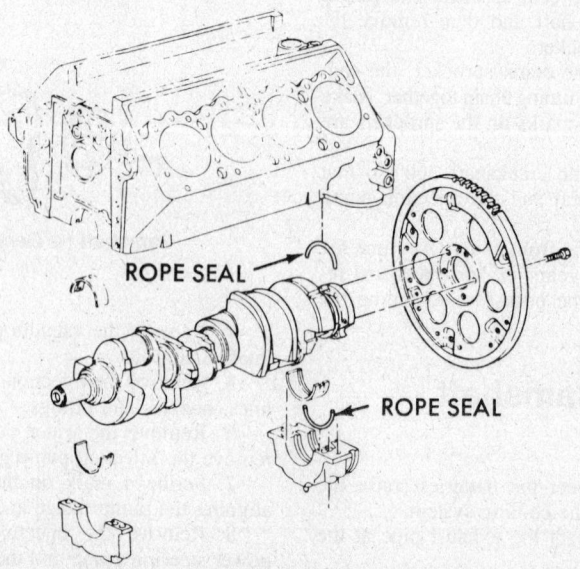

Crankshaft (© General Motors Corp.)

them in order so they can be installed in their original location.

8. Lift the crankshaft out of the block. The connecting rods will pivot to the center of the engine during removal. Do not allow them to move in their bore any more than that.

9. Installation is in the reverse order.

Main Bearings

Removal and Installation

1. Loosen all main bearing caps.

2. Remove the bearing cap and remove the lower shell.

3. Insert a flattened cotter pin in the oil passage hole in the crankshaft and then rotate the crankshaft in the direction opposite of cranking rotation. The pin will contact the upper shell and roll it out.

4. Check the main bearing journals for roughness or wear. Slight roughness may be removed with a fine grit polishing cloth dipped in oil. Burrs may be removed with a fine oil stone. If the journals are scored or ridged, the crankshaft must be replaced.

5. Clean the crankshaft journals and bearing caps thoroughly.

6. Place the new upper shell on the crankshaft journal with the locating tang in the correct position and rotate the shaft to turn it into position using a cotter pin.

7. Place a new shell in the bearing cap and install the cap. Torque all main bearing caps EXCEPT the rear main cap to 105–117 ft. lbs. for the inner bolts and 94–105 ft. lbs. for the outer bolts. Torque the rear main bearing cap to 10–12 ft. lbs. and then tap the end of the crankshaft, first rearward and then forward, with a lead hammer. This will line up the rear main bearing and crankshaft thrust faces. Retorque all main bearing caps to the original specifications.

NOTE: Always install a new rear main oil seal when replacing the #5 bearing.

Rear Main Bearing Oil Seal

UPPER OIL SEAL

Repair

Tools have been released to provide a means of correcting upper seal leaks without the necessity of removing the crankshaft. The procedure of seal leak correction is detailed below.

1. Drain the oil, remove the oil pan and then remove the rear main bearing cap.

2. Insert a packing tool against one end of the upper seal and drive the old seal gently into the groove until it is packed tight. This usually varies between ¼–¾ of an inch. Repeat the procedure on the other side.

3. Measure the amount the seal was driven up on one side and add ¹⁄₁₆ min. Cut this amount from the old seal removed from the main bearing cap. Repeat procedure for other side.

4. Place a drop of sealer on each end of the seal and cap.

5. Using two screwdrivers, work these two pieces of seal into the cylinder block. Use the packing tool and pack each piece up into the block.

6. Replace the lower seal and replace the cap.

7. Installation of the remaining components is in the reverse order.

LOWER OIL SEAL

Removal

1. Drain the oil and remove the oil pan and pump.

2. Remove the rear main bearing cap.

3. Remove the rear main bearing insert and oil seal.

4. Clean the bearing cap and seal grooves. Check for cracks.

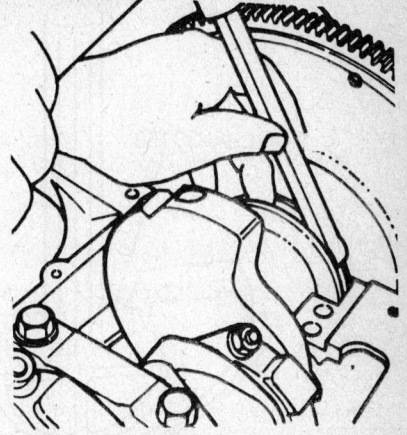

Packing the upper oil seal (© General Motors Corp.)

Installation

1. Apply Loctite® 496 or the equivalent and install the seal into the cap by hand.

2. Use a seal installer and hammer the seal into the groove. To check if the seal is fully seated in the cap, slide the tool away from the seal. With the tool fully seated in the cap, slide the tool against the seal. If the tool butts against the seal, it must be driven further into the groove. If the undercut area of the tool slides over the seal, it's fully seated.

3. With the tool slightly rotated, cut the seal flush with the mating surface of the cap. Use a small screwdriver and pack the seal end fibers toward the center, away from the edges.

4. Clean and install the bearing insert.

5. Apply a thin film of anarobic sealant to the cap. Keep the sealant off the seal and bearing.

6. Just prior to assembly apply a light coating of oil to the crankshaft surface that will contact the seal.

7. Install the bearing cap and tighten to specifications.

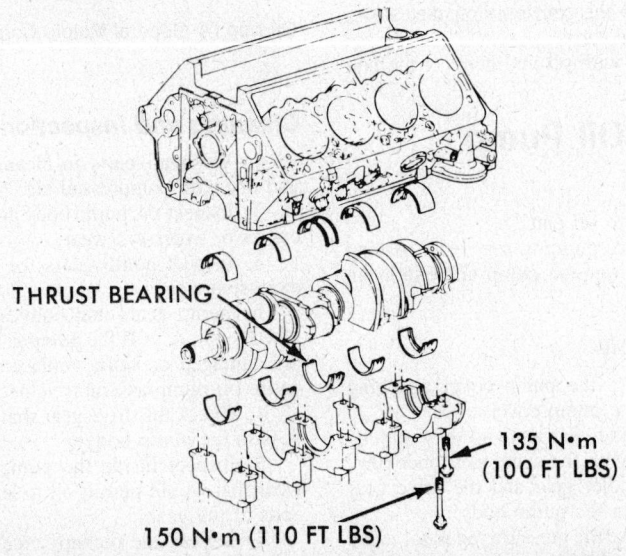

THRUST BEARING

135 N•m (100 FT LBS)

150 N•m (110 FT LBS)

Main bearings (© General Motors Corp.)

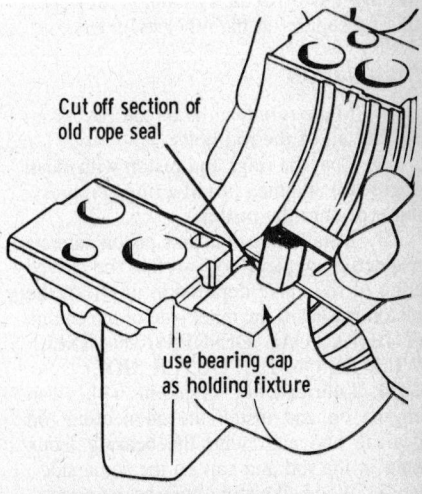

Cut off section of old rope seal

use bearing cap as holding fixture

Cutting off the lower seal ends (© General Motors Corp.)

ENGINE REBUILDING

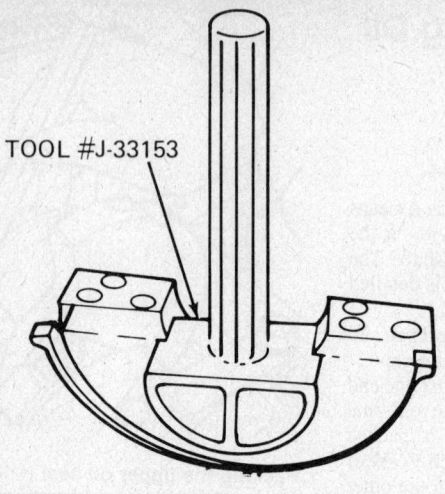

TOOL #J-33153

Installing lower oil seal (© General Motors Corp.)

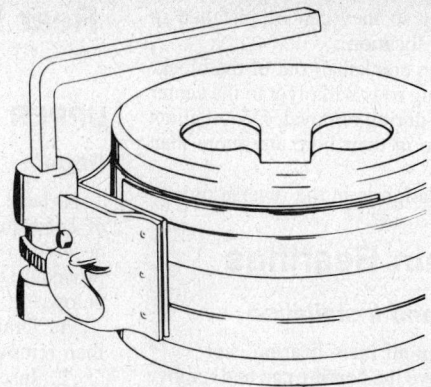

Piston ring compressor (© General Motors Corp.)

8. Installation of the remaining components is in the reverse order.

Connecting Rods and Pistons

Removal

1. Remove the intake manifold and cylinder head(s).

2. Remove the oil pan and oil pump assembly.

3. Stamp the cylinder number on the machined surfaces of the bolt bosses of the connecting rod and cap to aid in installation.

4. Examine the cylinder bore. If a ridge exists, remove it with a ridge reamer before attempting to remove the piston and rod assembly.

5. Remove the connecting rod bearing cap and bearing. Use a short piece of 3/8 in. hose to cover the bolt threads. This will prevent damage to the threads themselves and to the bearing journal.

6. Remove the rod and piston assembly through the top of the cylinder bore. Repeat this procedure on the other cylinders.

Installation

1. Make sure that the thread covers are still on all of the rod bolts.

2. Coat the rings and piston with clean engine oil and then install a ring compressing tool onto the piston.

3. Install each rod and piston into its respective cylinder bore so that the curved edge of the valve depression in top of the piston is toward the inner side of the engine (THE ACTUAL DEPRESSION ITSELF WILL BE ON THE OUTER SIDE).

4. Lubricate the crankpin with clean engine oil and install the connecting rod bearing and cap, with the bearing index tang in the rod and cap on the same side.

5. When all pistons have been correctly installed in their cylinders, tighten the connecting rod bolt nuts to 45 ft. lbs.

LUBRICATION SYSTEM

Oil Pan

Removal and Installation

1. Disconnect the batteries, raise the car and drain the oil.

2. Remove the transmission dust cover.

3. Remove the oil pan bolts.

4. Remove the left side engine mount thru-bolt.

5. Raise the engine and remove the oil pan.

6. Clean the entire sealing surface and apply a 3/32 in. bead of sealer. The sealer must be wet to the touch when the pan bolts are tightened down.

7. Install the oil pan and tighten the bolts to 15 ft. lbs.

8. Lower the engine and install the engine mount thru-bolt.

9. Install the transmission dust cover and lower the car.

10. Refill with oil and connect the batteries.

Oil Pump

Removal

1. Remove oil pan.

2. Remove pump-to-rear main bearing cap bolt and remove pump and extension shaft.

Disassembly

1. Remove the pump cover attaching screws and the pump cover.

2. Mark the gear teeth so they may be reassembled with the same teeth indexing. Remove the idler gear and the drive gear and shaft from the pump body.

3. Remove the pressure regulator valve retaining pin, the pressure regulator valve and all related parts.

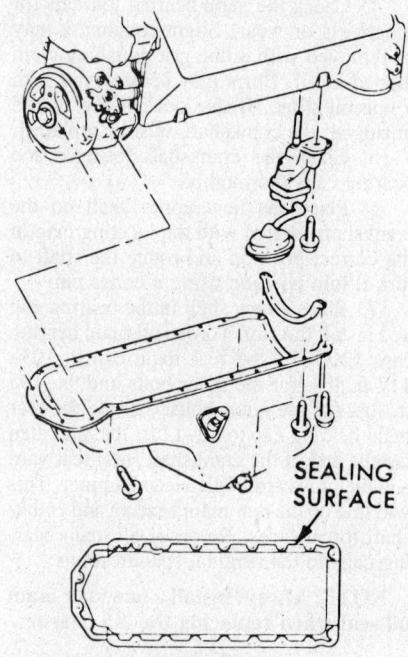

SEALING SURFACE

Oil pan (© General Motors Corp.)

Cleaning and Inspection

1. Wash all parts in cleaning solvent and dry with compressed air.

2. Inspect the pump body and cover for cracks or excessive wear.

3. Inspect pump gears for damage or excessive wear.

The pump gears and body are not serviced separately. If the pump gears or body are damaged or worn, replacement of the entire oil pump assembly is necessary.

4. Check the drive gear shaft for looseness in the pump body.

5. Inspect inside the pump cover for wear that would permit oil to leak past the ends of the gears.

6. Inspect the pickup screen and pipe assembly for damage to the screen, pipe or relief grommet.

7. Check the pressure regulator valve for fit.

Assembly

1. Install the pressure regulator valve and related parts.
2. Install the drive gear and shaft in the pump body.
3. Install the idler gear in the pump body with the smooth side of gear towards pump cover opening.
4. Install the pump cover and torque attaching screws to specifications.
5. Turn driveshaft by hand to check for smooth operation.

Installation

1. Assemble pump and extension shaft to rear main bearing cap, aligning hex on top end of extension shaft with drive hex on lower end of vacuum pump drive shaft.
2. Install pump to rear bearing cap bolt and torque to specifications.
3. Install oil pan.

EXHAUST SYSTEM

Exhaust Manifold

Removal and Installation

RIGHT SIDE

1. Disconnect the batteries.
2. Raise the car and disconnect the exhaust pipe from the manifold. Lower the car.

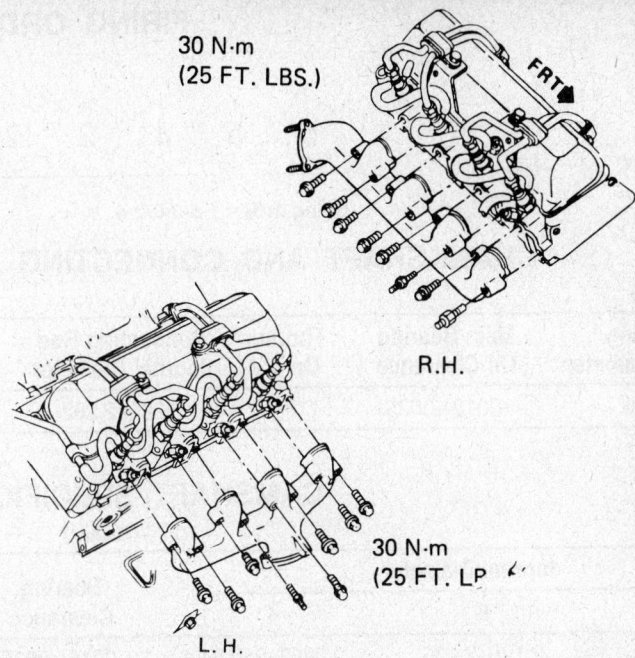

30 N·m (25 FT. LBS.)

R.H.

30 N·m (25 FT. LP

L. H.

Exhaust manifold torque sequence (© General Motors Corp.)

3. Tag and disconnect the glow plug wires. Remove the air cleaner duct bracket.
4. Remove the glow plugs, unscrew the manifold bolts and remove the manifold.
5. Installation is in the reverse order.

LEFT SIDE

1. Disconnect the batteries.
2. Remove the dipstick tube nut. Remove the dipstick tube.

3. Tag and disconnect the glow plug wires and remove the glow plugs.
4. Remove the manifold bolts. Raise the car and disconnect the exhaust pipe at the manifold.
5. Remove the manifold from the bottom.
6. Start the manifold bolts while the car is still raised, lower the car and then install the remaining components in the reverse order.

MITSUBISHI DIESEL

GENERAL ENGINE SPECIFICATIONS

No. Cyl.— Cu. In.	Bore × Stroke (in.)	Horsepower @ rpm	Torque @ rpm	Compression Ratio	Compression Pressure (psi)	Oil Pressure @ 2000 rpm (psi)	Firing Order
6-243	3.62 × 3.94	100 @ 3700	163 @ 2200	20:1	425	42–71	153624

TUNE-UP SPECIFICATIONS

Injection Pressure (psi)	Idle Speed (rpm)	Injection Timing (deg.)①	Valve Clearance② (in.) Intake	Valve Clearance② (in.) Exhaust	Intake Valve Opens (deg.)①	Injection Pump Type	Maximum Speed (rmp)
1777.5	550–600	18	.012	.012	29–35	PES6A65B	3950–4050

① Before top dead center
② Cold

ENGINE REBUILDING

FIRING ORDER

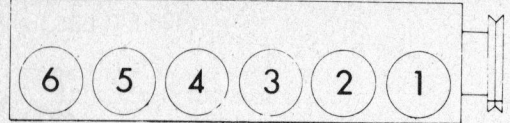

Firing order: 1-5-3-6-2-4

CRANKSHAFT AND CONNECTING ROD SPECIFICATIONS

(Inches)

Main Bearing Journal Diameter	Main Bearing Oil Clearance	Thrust On #	Connecting Rod Journal Diameter	Rod Bearing Oil Clearance	Connecting Rod Side Clearance	Crankshaft End-Play
2.754–2.755	.0012–.0035	7	2.281–2.282	.0015–.0044	.006–.018	.004–.010

CAMSHAFT SPECIFICATIONS

(Inches)

Journal Diameter			Bearing Clearance	Cam Lobe Height	End-Play	Valve Lift
1–2	3	4				
2.145–2.146	2.125–2.126	2.0863–2.0864	.0016–.0035	1.835	.002–.008	.408

VALVE SPECIFICATIONS

(Inches)

Face Angle (deg.)	Seat Angle (deg.)	Stem Diameter	Stem-To-Guide Clearance		Spring Tension (lbs. @ in.)		Spring Free Length	
			Intake	Exhaust	Inner	Outer	Inner	Outer
45	45	.314	.002–.003	.003–.004	16 @ 1.53	37 @ 1.77	1.71	2.01

PISTON AND RING SPECIFICATIONS

(Inches)

Piston to Bore Clearance	Ring End Gap	Ring to Groove Clearance	Piston Pin Diameter	Piston Pin to Bushing Clearance
.006–.008	.012–.020	.001–.002	1.1021–1.1023	.0008–.0020

TORQUE SPECIFICATIONS

(Ft. Lbs.)

Cylinder Head	Main Bearing Caps	Connecting Rod Caps	Crankshaft Pulley	Flywheel	Injection Nozzle	Injection Pump
90	65–72 oiled ①	62–68 oiled	289	76–83	43–58	18–25

① With "H" mark: 77–85 oiled

FUEL SYSTEM

Injection Pump

Timing

1. Disconnect the battery ground cable.
2. Disconnect the fuel shutoff rod at the injection pump lever. The rod snaps over the ball stud.
3. Clean all foreign matter away from the #1 delivery valve, pipe and pump area.
4. Turn the engine in the direction of rotation until the #1 piston is at TDC compression.
5. Continue turning the engine 1¾ turns more.
6. Disconnect the #1 injection pipe from the delivery valve.

— CAUTION —

When disconnecting the injection pipe(s) at the delivery valve(s), hold the delivery valve holder(s) stationary and loosen the injection pipe fitting. Do not turn the delivery valve holder as this will disturb the delivery valve calibration.

7. Turn the engine in rotation direction in very small increments. Stop when fuel

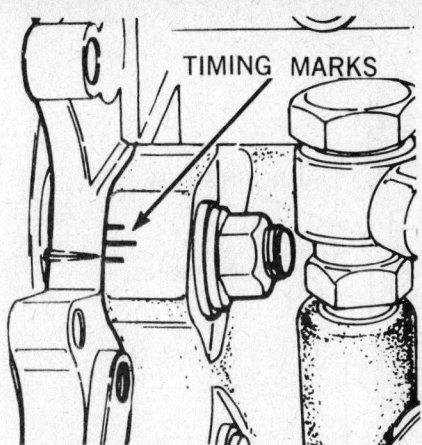

Injection pump timing marks

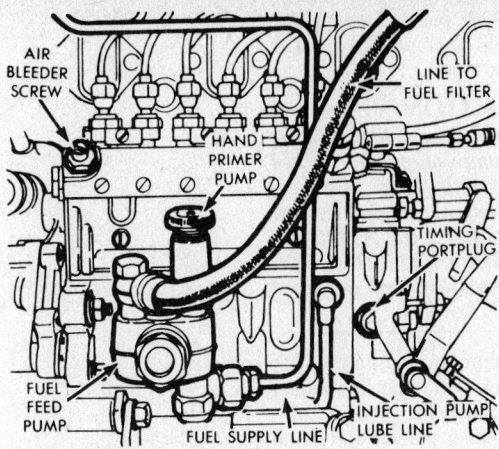

Inject pump components

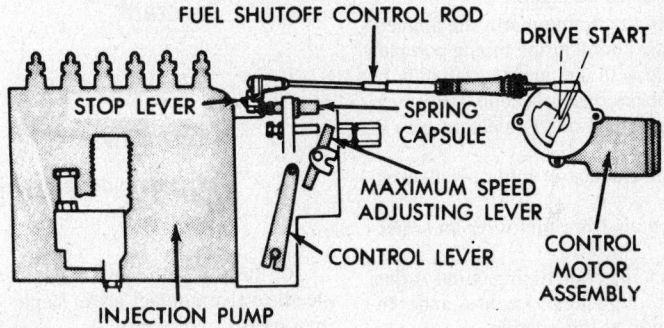

Injection linkage components

emerges from the delivery valve holder. This is the point at which injection begins.

8. Check the injection timing point on the scale on the back of the crankshaft damper. If the timing is correct, the mark should be at the standard valve shown on the Vehicle Emission Control Information Label on the valve cover, minus 2 degrees.

9. If the timing is not at the standard mark, minus 2 degrees, loosen the four pump-to-flange plate nuts and rotate the pump to advance or retard the timing. The crankshaft angle varies by 6 degrees per division on the pump flange scale.

10. Tighten the pump flange nuts.

Removal

1. Disconnect battery negative cable at battery.

2. Disconnect fuel shutoff rod at stop lever. Rod end snaps over stop lever ball stud.

3. Remove steering pump and mounting bracket assembly from engine and set aside.

4. Clean dirt, paint, and any other foreign material from fuel line, hose fittings, and injection pipes at injection pump.

5. Drain engine oil. Remove dipstick and dipstick tube.

6. Disconnect throttle cable and linkage from injection pump control lever.

7. Remove throttle control bracket assembly from block, injection pump, and control motor bracket. Set to one side.

8. Disconnect fuel supply line to fuel feed pump, loosening anchor clamps as necessary.

9. Disconnect fuel filter hoses from fuel feed pump and injection pump. Replace hollow bolts with seals into pumps to prevent dirt entry.

10. Turn engine crankshaft until No. 1 piston is positioned between 7 degrees BTDC and TDC on the compression stroke. Check pointer. It should be about midway between TDC and the 14 degree line on the crankshaft damper.

11. Disconnect injection pipes from delivery valves and move away from block.

CAUTION

When disconnecting the injection pipe(s) at the delivery valve(s), hold the delivery valve holder(s) stationary and loosen the injection pipe fitting. Do not turn the delivery valve holder as this will disturb the delivery valve calibration.

Cap open delivery valves to prevent dirt from entering.

12. Disconnect injection pump lube line at block fitting near starter motor forward end.

13. Injection pump assembly is attached to engine by five screws and one bolt. Front screws extend through timing case and engine front plate into pump flange plate. Rear bolt fastens flange plate to engine front plate. Remove these six fasteners.

14. Pull injection pump rearward to disengage from engine front plate and timing gear case. Twist pump toward block and continue pulling rearward until automatic timer is free of case.

Disassembly

1. Mount injection pump securely in soft-jawed vise.

2. Remove nut front of injection pump shaft.

3. Position a timer remover and installer, such as tool MH-069097, over timer.

4. Pull drive gear and automatic timer from injection pump shaft. Disassemble automatic timer.

NOTE: The injection pump is serviced as an assembly. If diagnosis and tests indicate injection pump malfunction, install replacement pump.

Assembly

1. Install drive gear and automatic timer assembly with gear mark aligned with drive gear keyway and plate notch aligned with "3" on gear. Use a timer remover and installer, such as tool MH-061097.

Installation

1. Loosen four nuts attaching injection pump to mounting flange plate. Align center timing mark on pump flange with pointer on plate.

2. Be sure O-ring seal is in place on forward face of pump mounting flange.

3. Remove threaded timing port plug on governor housing behind control lever to expose pump camshaft bushing timing mark. Turn pump drive gear to align timing mark on camshaft bushing with pointer on governor. Guide plate notch on drive gear will be at approximately 8 o'clock point as viewed from front.

4. Be sure that crankshaft is still positioned between TDC and 7 degrees BTDC. See Removal, step 10, with no. 1 piston on compression stroke.

5. Insert automatic timer into timing gear case. Turn injection pump in until against block. Then turn pump drive gear clockwise or counterclockwise to mesh drive

and idler gears. Push pump forward into timing gear case and turn away from block to align attachment holes.

— **CAUTION** —

Correct gear mesh is assured by drive gear guide plate. If pump cannot be pushed forward manually until flange plate seal diameter contacts engine front plate, gear mesh is incorrect. DO NOT ATTEMPT TO FORCE PUMP INTO POSITION. Retract pump and turn drive gear as needed to achieve correct gear mesh.

6. Attach the pump to the timing gear case. Turn the crankshaft opposite rotation direction until it reaches the specified timing mark. The governor pointer and pump camshaft bushing timing marks should now be aligned. If not, the pump must be removed and installed again.

7. When the timing marks are aligned, install the governor housing timing port plug and continue with the pump installation by reversing the removal procedure. However, do not yet connect no. 1 injection pipe or battery cable.

8. Refill crankcase with specified engine oi.

9. Bleed air from fuel filter and injection pump.

10. Check injection timing point. Adjust as required, following procedures under Injection Timing in this section.

Injection Nozzles

Removal

1. Disconnect the injector line from the nozzle holder at the cylinder.

2. Remove the nozzle holder and nozzle assembly.

Disassembly

1. Place the nozzle holder in a vise. Tighten vise against retaining nut.

2. Remove the nozzle holder body from the retaining nut. Lift the pressure pin, spring, washer, spacer, and nozzle tip from the nozzle holder.

Inspection

1. Immerse the nozzle tip in clean fuel oil and operate the needle valve manually. If the needle valve binds in the nozzle tip, replace the tip.

2. Inspect nozzle tip under magnifying glass. Look for roughness or irregularities.

3. Check clearance between needle valve and nozzle tip orifice. If clearance is asymmetrical, replace nozzle tip.

4. Inspect needle valve tip and pressure pin contact area. Replace the nozzle if the needle valve tip is deformed or if pressure pin contact areas are unevenly worn.

5. Visually inspect pressure spring for squareness, cracks, or breakage. Replace spring if defective.

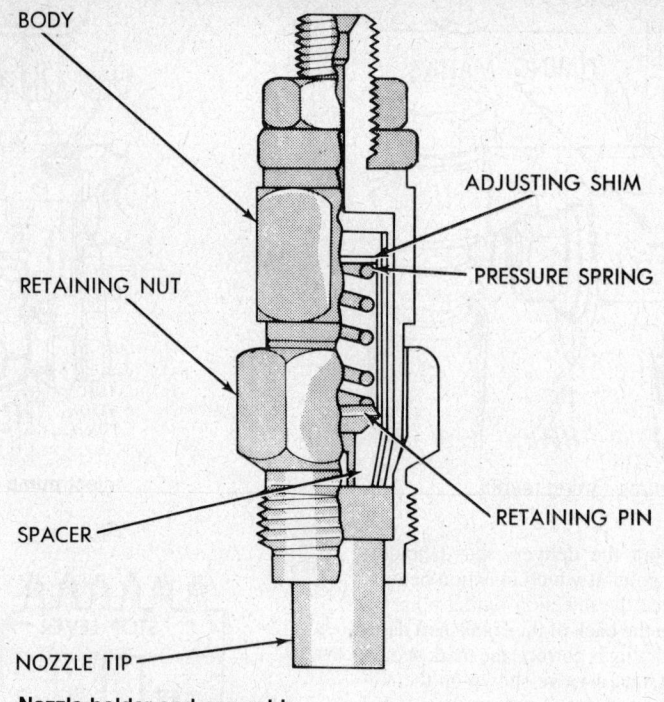

Nozzle holder and assembly

6. Inspect pressure spring seat and needle valve contact area. Replace defective parts.

Assembly

1. Mount nozzle holder retaining nut in vise.

2. Wash nozzle tip and needle valve assembly in clean fuel oil.

3. Assemble spacer, pressure pin, and pressure spring onto nozzle tip.

4. Install adjusting shim into nozzle holder body. Assemble nozzle holder and tip to retaining nut and torque nozzle holder to between 59 and 78.5 Nm (43.4 and 57.9 ft. lbs.).

Injection Pressure Adjustment

1. Install nozzle holder and tip assembly on nozzle tester.

2. Operate nozzle tester handle several times to bleed nozzle under test and connecting line.

3. Operate nozzle tester lever while watching tester pressure gauge. As lever is operated, pressure should rise steadily. At some point, pressure will reach a maximum and drop off suddenly. The maximum pressure reading is the injection pressure.

4. Standard injection pressure is between 11,756 kPa (1705 psi) and 12,756 kPa (1850 psi). If injection pressure does not meet specifications, it must be adjusted. Pressure is adjusted by installing or removing shims between the nozzle body and the pressure spring. Changing thickness of the shim pack by 0.1 mm (0.004 inch) varies injection pressure by 979 kPa (142 psi). Shims are available in thicknesses from 1

to 1.95 mm (0.04 to 0.077 inch) at 0.05 mm (0.002 inch) intervals.

5. Install shim pack of required thickness to ensure injection pressure is within specifications. Reassemble nozzle holder and nozzle assembly.

Fuel Control Motor

Removal

1. Disconnect motor connector.

2. Disconnect capsule rod at control motor and injection pump stop lever and remove.

3. Remove three motor mounting bolts.

4. Remove motor from side of block.

Installation

Install the motor by reversing removal procedure.

— **CAUTION** —

Do not crank the motor before installing capsule rod.

Capsule Rod

Adjustment

1. Check capsule rod installation at motor drive lever. With the injection pump lever in the DRIVE position, the drive lever at the motor should be between the two marks.

2. Turn the drive lever with a screwdriver until it is nearly straight up and down, pointing upward.

3. Disconnect the capsule rod. Be sure

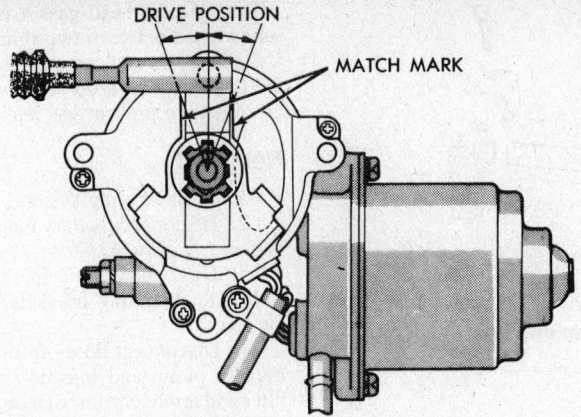

Capsule rod adjustment

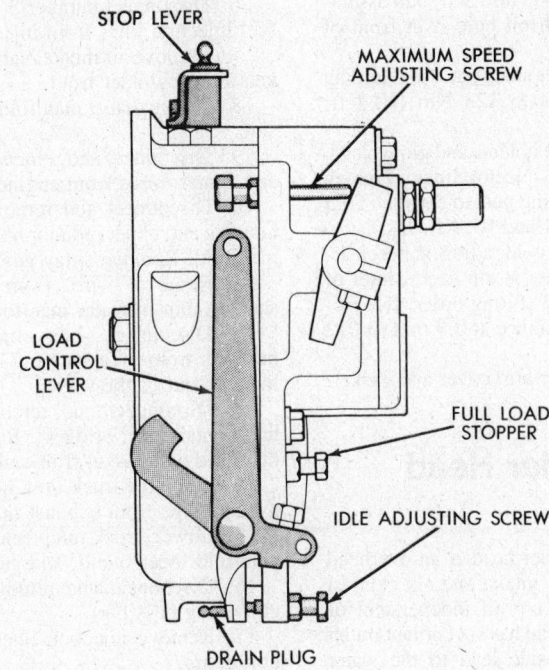

Idling control

that the injection pump stop lever is in the DRIVE position.

4. Loosen the capsule rod lock nut and adjust rod length until the drive lever is properly positioned between the match marks.

5. Tighten the lock nut and install the capsule rod to the drive lever. The nominal length of the capsule rod is 322.6 mm (12.7 inches).

Idle Speed

Adjustment

1. Remove cover and gasket from tachometer takeoff on right side of engine in front of oil filter assembly. Install mechanical tachometer adapter and attach mechanical tachometer and drive cable.

2. Turn hand throttle counterclockwise and pull all the way out. Depress accelerator to floor and crank engine. Hold accelerator to floor after engine starts. Allow engine to warm up until some speed is attained (1250–1500 rpm). Release accelerator slowly until engine runs smoothly. When engine begins to warm, turn hand throttle clockwise to reduce engine speed to idle.

— CAUTION —

If a new accelerator pump has been installed, do not allow engine speed to rise above 1300 rpm. If engine overspeeds, it may run away and damage or destroy itself.

3. Be sure that governor control lever is at idling position before attempting to adjust idle speed.

4. Check tachometer. If idle speed is not between 550 and 600 rpm, adjust idle speed.

5. Loosen idle adjusting screw locknut. Adjust screw as necessary to set idle to specifications. Turn adjusting screw IN

to increase idle speed: OUT to decrease idle speed.

6. When idle speed is as specified, tighten idle adjusting screw locknut. Recheck idle speed to be sure it has not shifted.

COOLING SYSTEM

Water Pump

Description

The water pump is a centrifugal impeller type mounted to the front of the engine block. It forces coolant through the water jacket passages in block and head.

The pump shaft is supported by ball bearing assemblies at front and rear. The bearings are packed in multi-purpose grease. The drive pulley flange is pressed onto the front of the shaft. The impeller is threaded onto the rear of the shaft. The pump housing is enclosed by a rear cover and a water seal between impeller and housing prevents water leaks. The ratio between the crankshaft pulley and the pump drive pulley is 1:1.31.

Removal

1. Drain coolant and remove radiator hoses and bypass hose.

2. Loosen alternator mounting bolts and remove fan drive belt.

3. Remove cooling fan, spacer, and drive pulley.

4. Remove water pump mounting bolts and lift pump off front of engine block.

Installation

1. Mount water pump to front of block.

2. Install drive pulley, spacer, and cooling fan. Torque bolts to 30 ft. lbs.

3. Install fan drive belt and tighten to specified tension. (See Accessory Belt Drive.) Tighten alternator bolts to 30 ft. lbs.

4. Fill cooling system with specified coolant.

ENGINE MECHANICAL

Rocker Arm and Shaft Assembly

Removal

1. Remove cylinder head cover and gasket (6 Phillips-head screws).

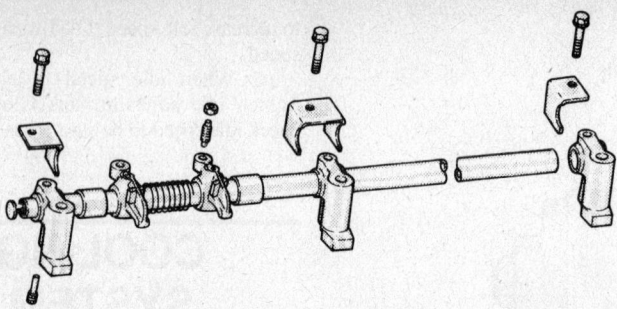

Exploded view of the rocker arm and shaft assembly

2. Remove nozzle holders and glow plugs.

3. Remove rocker shaft bracket retaining bolts.

4. Remove rocker arm shaft assembly.

Disassembly

1. Remove shaft retainer screws and shaft retainers from bracket assemblies.

2. Slide rocker shaft out of mounting brackets and remove spacers, rocker arms, and springs. Number rocker arms from front to rear to entire assembly in original order.

Inspection

1. Inspect components and replace those with excessive wear.

2. Inspect rocker arms for excessive wear. Replace as required.

3. Inspect adjusting screws for wear at push rod contact. Replace if excessively worn or if threads are damaged.

4. Measure rocker bushing I.D. Bushing I.D. should be between 20 and 20.021 mm (0.786 and 0.787 inch).

5. Measure rocker shaft O.D. Rocker shaft O.D. should be between 19.966 and 19.984 mm (0.784 and 0.785 inch). Rocker bushing-to-shaft clearance should be between 0.016 and 0.055 mm (0.0006 and 0.0021 inch). If clearance exceeds 0.07 mm (0.003 inch), replace the rocker bushing. Replace the bushing with a rocker shaft bushing remover and installer, such as tool MH-061060.

6. Be sure rocker and rocker shaft oil holes are clear. Check oil intake in front rocker shaft bracket.

7. Check both ends of push rods for wear. If ends are worn, replace push rods.

8. Check push rods for bend on surface plate. Push rod bend should be 0.4 mm (0.016 inch) or less. Replace push rods with excessive bend.

Assembly

1. Install push rods in block in original position.

2. Install brackets, spacers, rocker arms, and springs in proper order.

3. Install shaft retainers to brackets and tighten mounting screws. Be sure rocker arms move freely on shaft.

Installation

1. Position rocker arm and shaft assembly so bracket with oil hole is at front of engine.

2. Install rocker shaft bracket retaining bolts. Torque bolts to 123 Nm (90.4 ft. lbs.).

3. Install nozzle holders and glow plugs. Install and tighten injector lines. Tighten nozzle holder retaining nuts to between 59.5 and 78.5 Nm (43.4 and 57.9 ft. lbs.).

4. With engine cold, adjust valve clearance at each cylinder at top dead center of compression stroke. (Firing order: 1-5-3-6-2-4). Set valve clearance at 0.3 mm (0.012 inch).

5. Install rocker arm cover and gasket.

Cylinder Head

Description

The cast iron cylinder head is an overhead valve type with six intake and six exhaust ports. These ports are all independent of one another. The head has six coolant outlet holes in the right side lead to the water jacket. A coolant guide (director) pressed into the bottom of the head directs the coolant to each cylinder. Each of the intake and exhaust valves seats in a special steel insert pressed into the head.

The cylinder head mounts to the block with 25 bolts, 7 of which secure the rocker arm and shaft assembly mounting brackets. The combustion chamber is cast into the head. It is of the swirl chamber type. A combustion chamber jet is pressed in from below. Glow plugs are installed in the upper part of the combustion chambers to facilitate starting.

The cylinder head gasket is of asbestos sandwiched between two thin steel sheets. Cylinder bores and combustion chamber jets are covered with apron-type stainless steel grommets to prevent gas leakage.

Removal

1. Drain cooling system.

2. Disconnect battery negative cable at battery.

3. Disconnect air cleaner from air manifold and mounting brackets. Remove air cleaner.

4. Disconnect hoses from fuel filter at transfer pump and injection pump. Drain filter and remove from back of air manifold.

5. Remove nuts securing air manifold and air cleaner mounting brackets.

6. Disconnect number 3 and number 6 fuel injection lines from injection pump.

7. Remove air intake manifold and gaskets from cylinder head.

8. Push exhaust manifold shield to one side.

9. Disconnect and remove bypass hose and heater hoses from engine.

10. Disconnect and remove thermostat housing and upper radiator hose from water manifold. Remove spray gasket.

11. Remove wire from temperature sending unit in water manifold.

12. Disconnect fuel line mounting brackets from cylinder head and push fuel lines up out of the way.

13. Disconnect and remove three exhaust manifold bridges. Remove water manifold and gasket from cylinder head.

14. Raise the truck on a hoist. Remove exhaust pipe from exhaust manifold.

15. Lower truck and remove exhaust manifold, heat shield, and gasket.

16. Disconnect and remove wire from glow plug buss bar.

17. Remove injection lines from injection pump.

18. Disconnect fuel injection line and remove fuel injection line bracket and ground strap from cylinder head.

19. Disconnect alternator bracket and engine lifting fixture and push to one side.

20. Remove cylinder head cover and gasket.

21. Loosen and remove cylinder head bolts in the sequence shown.

22. Lift out rocker arm and shaft assembly.

23. Remove push rods. Mark for identification to ensure installation in original location.

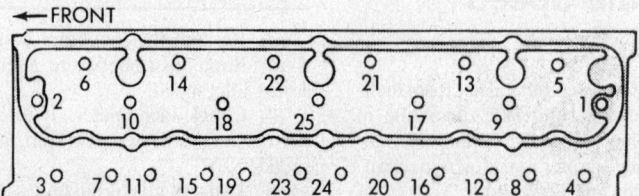

Cylinder head bolt removal sequence

24. Remove injector tubes, injector holders, and injectors.

25. Disconnect and remove glow plug buss bar.

26. Remove six glow plugs from cylinder head.

27. Lift the cylinder head from engine and install in holding fixture. Remove head gasket.

Cleaning and Inspection

1. Check the head for cracks, damage, and evidence of water leaks. Clean oil, grease, scale, sealant, and carbon from head. Remove all burrs. Clean gasket surfaces of cylinder block.

2. Inspect all cylinder head surfaces with a straightedge. Out-of-flatness should not exceed 0.25 mm (0.010 inch). If it does, a surface grinder should be used to correct the head out-of-flatness to less than 0.15 mm (0.006 inch).

3. Check each combustion chamber jet for cracks or melting. If a jet is seriously cracked or melted, remove with a push rod inserted in the glow plug bore.

Installation

1. Install glow plugs in cylinder head. Tighten firmly. Install glow plug buss bar, be sure connections at each glow plug are tight.

2. Replace injectors, injector tubes, and injector holders in cylinder head. Tighten nozzle holder retaining nuts to 50 Nm (37 ft. lbs.).

3. Coat new head gasket lightly with Chrysler sealer, part no. 3419115, or equivalent. Place gasket on cylinder block and install cylinder head over dowels.

4. Install cylinder head bolts and tighten in the sequence shown. Do not install head bolts which retain rocker arm and shaft assembly. Tighten to 12 Nm (90.4 ft. lbs.)

5. Install push rods. Be sure to install in original location.

6. Install rocker arm and shaft assembly. Remember—bracket mounting bolts are cylinder head bolts. Torque to 123 Nm (90.4 ft. lbs.).

7. Adjust valve clearance to 0.3 mm (0.012 inch) at the top dead center of compression stroke of each cylinder.

8. Install cylinder head cover and gasket.

9. Position and install alternator mounting bracket and engine lifting fixture.

10. Connect fuel injection lines to injection pump. (Except numbers 3 and 6). Install bracket and ground strap. Install fuel line to transfer pump.

11. Install exhaust manifold and shield assembly using new gasket.

12. Raise vehicle on hoist and install exhaust pipe to exhaust manifold.

13. Lower vehicle. Install water manifold on cylinder head using new gasket. Install three exhaust manifold bridges.

14. Install fuel lines in bracket.

15. Connect wire to temperature sending unit on water manifold.

16. Install thermostat housing to water manifold using new gasket. Install upper radiator hose to thermostat housing.

17. Install bypass and heater hoses to engine.

18. Install exhaust manifold shield to exhaust manifold.

19. Install air intake manifold with new gaskets and spray shield.

20. Connect number 3 and number 6 fuel injection lints to injection pump.

21. Install fuel filter to back of air manifold. Connect transfer pump-to-fuel filter hose and fuel filter-to-injection pump hose.

22. Install nuts securing air cleaner mounting brackets and air manifold.

23. Install air cleaner to air cleaner mounting brackets and air manifold intake. Tighten firmly.

24. Close all drain cocks. Be sure all cylinder block plugs are installed and tightened to specifications. Fill cooling system with specified coolant.

25. Connect battery negative cable at battery.

Valves

Description

Valves are arranged in line in the cylinder head. They operate in valve guides pressed into the cylinder head. Valve seats are replaceable inserts.

Removal

1. Remove the cylinder head from the engine and place on bench.

2. Compress valve springs.

3. Remove valve retaining locks, valve spring retainers, inner and outer valve springs, and valve stem cup seals.

4. Before removing valves from valve guides, remove any burrs from valve stem lock grooves to prevent damage to the valve guides. Identify valves to ensure installation in original location.

Inspection

1. Clean valves thoroughly. Discard burned, warped, or cracked valves.

2. Measure valve stems for wear. Intake valve stem diameter should measure 8.0 mm (0.314 inch). If wear exceeds 0.1 mm (0.004 inch), replace the valve. Exhaust valve stem diameter should measure 8.0 mm (0.314 inch). If wear exceeds 0.15 mm (0.006 inch), replace the valve. If the top of the valve cap is excessively worn or pitted, replace the valve.

3. Remove carbon and varnish deposits from inside of valve guides.

4. Measure valve stem-to-guide clearance as follows:

   a. Install tool C-3973 or equivalent over the valve and install valve in guide.

   b. Attach dial indicator to the cylinder head and set it at right angles to the valve stem being measured.

   c. Move valve stem toward and away from indicator. Intake valve stem-to-guide clearance should be between 0.005 and 0.085 mm (0.0002 and 0.003 inch). If intake valve stem-to-guide clearance exceeds 0.15 mm (0.006 inch), replace both valve and valve guide. Exhaust valve stem-to-guide clearance should be between 0.070 and 0.100 mm (0.003 and 0.004 inch). If exhaust valve stem-to-guide clearance exceeds 0.20 mm (0.008 inch), replace both valve and valve guide.

Valve Guides

Replacement

1. Remove the old valve guide using a valve guide remover, such as Tool 31691-10500.

2. Press new valve guide into cylinder head using a valve guide installer, Tool 31691-10600. The valve guide installed length is between 19.7 and 20.3 mm (0.7583 and 0.791 inch).

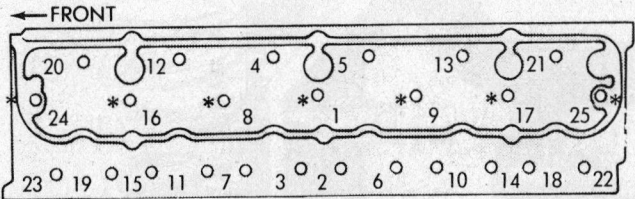
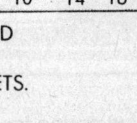

Cylinder head bolt tightening sequence

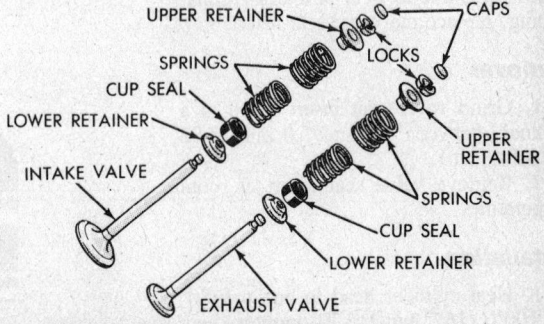

Exploded view of the valve assemblies

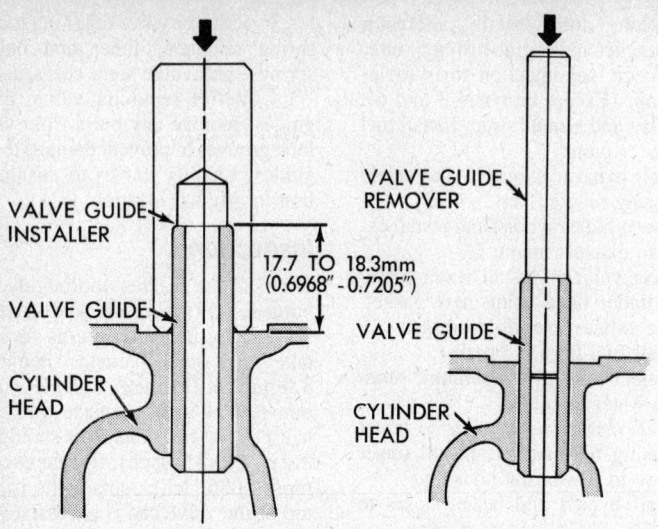

VALVE GUIDE INSTALLER

VALVE GUIDE

CYLINDER HEAD

17.7 TO 18.3mm (0.6968" - 0.7205")

VALVE GUIDE REMOVER

VALVE GUIDE

CYLINDER HEAD

Valve guide removal and installation

Valve Seats

Inspection

Valve seats and valve faces have an angle of 45 degrees. Check each valve seat for evidence of burning and defective contact. If necessary, correct the seat with a valve seat cutter. Be sure to use the proper size valve guide pilot for reseating stones. Apply even cutting pressure. Polish seat surface with No. 400 emery paper between cutter and seat after correction. A true and complete surface must be obtained.

1. Measure valve seat concentricity with a dial indicator. Runout should not exceed 0.1 mm (0.004 inch) total indicator reading.

2. Check remaining margin after valves are refaced. Discard valves if margin is less than 1.5 mm (0.059 inch).

3. Check valve seat with Prussian blue to determine where valve contacts seat. Coat valve seat lightly with Prussian blue. Set valve in place and rotate with slight pressure. If blue is transferred to center of valve face, contact is satisfactory. If blue is transferred to top edge of valve face, lower the valve seat with a 30-degree stone. If blue is transferred to bottom edge of valve face, raise valve seat with a 60-degree stone.

4. If valve seat width exceeds 2.0 mm (0.079 inch) due to wear or excessive machining, replace the valve seat insert.

Removal

1. Grind valve seat insert down to a thickness between 0.5 and 1.0 mm (0.02 and 0.04 inch).

2. Remove valve seat insert at room temperature.

Installation

1. Heat cylinder head to between 80° and 100°C (167° and 212°F). Immerse new insert in ether or alcohol with dry ice.

2. Press insert into heated head. Install intake and exhaust valve inserts with Insert Caulking Tool.

3. Allow head to cool to room temperature.

4. Caulk valve seat insert circumference with appropriate caulking tool and machine seat width to less than 2.0 mm (0.0787 inch).

Valve Springs

Removal

1. Remove the cylinder head as previously outlined.

2. Compress the valve springs with tool C-3422A or its equivalent.

3. Remove the valve retaining locks, valve spring retainers, and the inner and outer valve springs.

4. Inspect the valve stem lock grooves for burrs. Deburr if necessary, to prevent

damage to the valve guides when the valves are removed from the cylinder head.

5. Withdraw the valves from the cylinder head. Mark the valves so that they may be reinstalled in their original locations.

Inspection

1. Inspect each spring for breakage or damage.

2. Measure the free length of inner and outer valve springs. The standard dimension of the inner spring (free length) is 43.5 mm (1.690 inch). The standard dimension of the outer spring (free length) is 51.17 mm (1.996 inch). Replace inner springs with a free length of 42.5 mm (1.650 inch) or less; replace outer springs with a free length of 50 mm (1.965 inch) or less.

3. Set up a valve spring tester, such as tool C-647, to test inner and outer valve springs as follows:

INNER SPRING

a. Inner valve spring installed length is 39 mm (1.533 inch). Turn the table of the valve spring tester until the surface is in line with the 1.533 inch mark on the threaded stud with the zero mark to the front.

b. Place spring on stud over table and raise compressing lever to set tone device.

c. Pull down on torque wrench until "ping" is heard. Take torque reading. Multiply torque reading by two to obtain spring load at test length. Spring load should be 70.6 N (15.9 lbs.). If spring load is less than 56.9 N (12.8 lbs.), replace the spring.

OUTER SPRING

a. Outer valve spring installed length is 45 mm (1.769 inch). Turn the table of the valve spring tester until the surface is in line with the 1.769 inch mark on the threaded stud with the zero mark to the front.

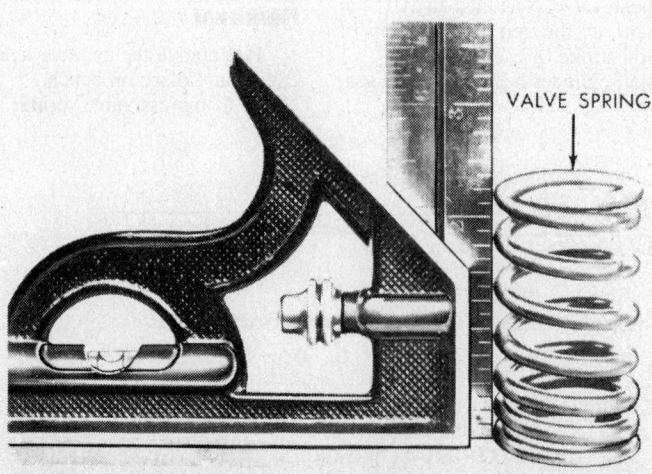

VALVE SPRING

Checking the valve spring for squareness

b. Place spring on stud over table and raise compression lever to set tone device.

c. Pull on torque wrench until "ping" is heard. Take torque reading. Multiply reading by two to obtain spring load at test length. Spring load should be 156.9 N (35.28 lbs.). If spring load at test length is 132.4 N (29 lbs.) or less, replace the outer spring.

4. Check each valve spring for squareness with a mechanic's square and a surface plate. Test each spring from both ends. Springs should be square within 1.5 degrees. If springs are more than 2 degrees out of square, install a new spring.

Installation

1. Lubricate valve stems and insert them in valve guides in cylinder head.

2. Install new valve stem cup seals on all valve stems. Install inner and outer valve springs and retainers.

3. Compress valve springs. Install valve stem locks and release too.

If valves and/or seats have been reground, measure installed height of valve springs. Measure from bottom of cylinder head spring seat to bottom surface of spring retainer. (If spacers are used, measure from top of spacer.) If spring height is greater than specified, inner spring: 39 mm (1.533 inch)—outer spring: 45 mm (1.769 inch), install appropriate spacer in head counterbore to bring spring height back to specification.

Timing

Intake and exhaust valves are timed by the gear set to operate as shown when the engine is cold and valve clearance is adjusted to 0.3 mm (0.012 inch).

Valve	Open	Closed
Intake	32 BTDC	64 ABDC
Exhaust	68 BBDC	28 ATDC

BTDC: before top dead center
ABDC: after bottom dead center
BBDC: before bottom dead center
ATDC: after top dead center

Timing Gear Case

Description

The front plate and aluminum alloy gear case are attached to the front of the block. The gear case contains the timing gear assembly. The front plate and timing gear case are positioned on the block by two locating dowels. The timing gear case oil seal and gasket prevent oil leakage from the front of the crankcase.

Removal

1. Disconnect battery negative cable.
2. Drain cooling system.
3. Remove upper and lower radiator

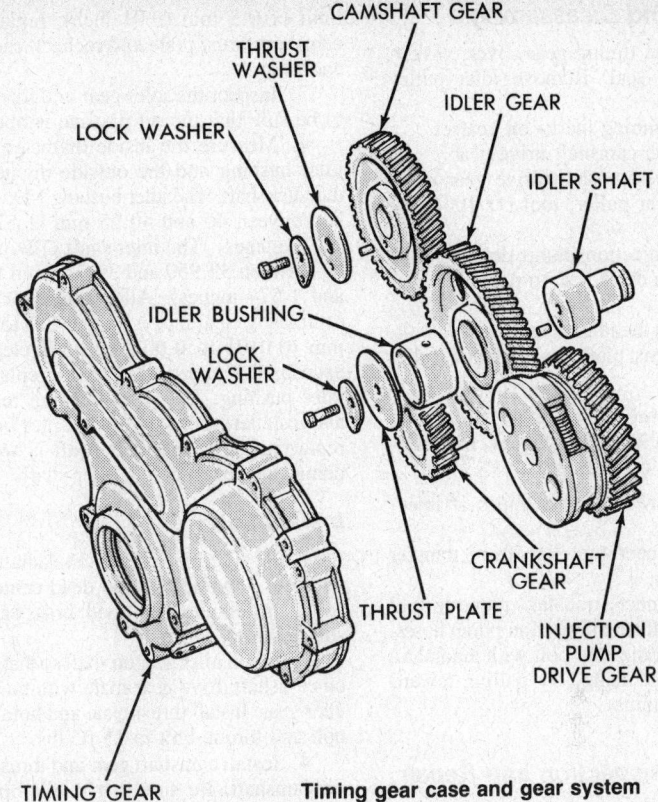

Timing gear case and gear system

hoses from radiator. Disconnect overflow lines from coolant reserve tank.

4. Raise truck on hoist. Disconnect and remove two transmission oil cooler lines and bracket from radiator bottom tank (automatic transmission). Lower truck to shop floor).

5. Loosen radiator mounting bolts.

6. Remove cooling fan.

7. Remove rubber shield between radiator and grille. Remove radiator and fan shroud.

8. Remove all drive belts. Remove idler pulley.

9. Remove crankshaft pulley retaining nut.

10. Turn crankshaft until keyway is at 12 o'clock. Remove crankshaft pulley and damper assembly with a crankshaft pulley puller, such as tool MH-061101.

11. Remove timing gear case, gasket, and idler pulley bracket.

12. Remove front oil seal.

Installation

1. Install new front oil seal.

2. Clean all gasket surfaces on timing gear case and front of block. Coat timing gear case gasket with sealing compound and position over dowels on engine front plate.

3. Position timing gear case over gear assembly. Install gear case and idler pulley bracket. Torque bolts to 7 ft. lbs.

4. Install crankshaft pulley over key in crankshaft. Be careful not to damage front

oil seal lip. Install crankshaft pulley retaining nut and torque to specifications.

5. Install idler pulley.

6. Install all drive bolts. Set belt tension to specifications with belt tension gauge.

7. Position fan shroud inside engine compartment. Install radiator. Tighten lower radiator mounting bolts finger-tight. Install rubber shield between radiator and grille.

8. Install cooling fan. Align radiator and tighten radiator mounting bolts to 30 ft. lbs.

9. Raise truck on hoist. Connect two oil cooler lines and bracket to radiator bottom tank. Tighten bolts to specifications (automatic transmission). Lower truck to shop floor.

10. Connect fan shroud to back of radiator. Connect radiator overflow line to coolant reserve tank. Connect upper and lower radiator hoses to radiator. Tighten hose clamps securely.

11. Fill cooling system with specified coolant.

12. Connect battery negative cable.

Timing Gear Assembly

Description

The timing gear assembly consists of the crankshaft gear, idler gear, camshaft gear, and the injection pump drive gear. Each gear is a helical gear of high-carbon steel. Gear engagement and tooth number for the assembly are shown.

1043

ENGINE REBUILDING

Removal and Disassembly

1. Remove timing gear cover, gasket, and front oil seal. Remove idler pulley bracket.

2. Align timing marks on gearset.

3. Remove camshaft drive gear.

3. Remove camshaft drive gear using a camshaft gear puller, tool DT-1001A or its equivalent.

4. Turn injection pump drive gear to allow notch in drive gear to pass idler gear teeth.

5. Loosen the idler gear mounting bolt, remove the thrust plate, and extract the idler gear.

NOTE: If the idler shaft requires removal, use an idler shaft puller, tool MH-061077 or its equivalent.

6. Disconnect injector pipes at injection pump.

7. Disconnect fuel line from transfer pump and cap.

8. Disconnect transfer pump-to-fuel filter and fuel filter-to-injection pump hoses.

9. Loosen the stay bolt with automatic timer gear, and flange by pulling toward the back of engine.

Cleaning, Inspection and Repair

1. Inspect the camshaft gear, idler gear, and injection pump drive gear for tooth surface spalling and wear. Replace gears if damaged.

2. Install camshaft gear on camshaft and check for camshaft end play with a dial indicator. Camshaft end play between 0.05 and 0.20 mm (0.002 and 0.008 inch) is acceptable. If end play exceeds the repair limit of 0.3 mm (0.01 inch), replace the camshaft thrust plate and recheck camshaft end-play.

3. Inspect the idler gear and idler shaft to be sure that the oil passage is open.

4. Measure the inside diameter of the idler bushing and the outside diameter of the idler shaft. The idler bushing I.D. should be between 40 and 40.25 mm (1.575 and 1.576 inches). The idler shaft O.D. should be between 39.950 and 39.975 mm (1.573 and 1.574 inches). Allowable idler shaft-to-bushing clearance is from 0.025 to 0.075 mm (0.0101 to 0.003 inch). If clearance exceeds 0.1 mm (0.004 inch), replace the idler bushing. Use idler bushing remover and installer, tool MH-061228, for bushing replacement. If the idler shaft is worn or damaged, install a new idler shaft.

Installation

1. Be sure that engine crankshaft is set with no. 1 cylinder at top dead center.

2. Install idler shaft with brass drift and soft hammer.

3. Install idler gear on shaft so that marks on camshaft drive gear mate with marks on idler gear. Install thrust plate and hold-down bolt and torque bolt to 15 ft. lbs.

4. Install camshaft gear and thrust plate on camshaft. Be sure that marks on camshaft gear mate properly with marks on idler gear. Tighten hold-down bolt to 28 ft. lbs.

5. Place injection pump assembly in position. Mesh pump drive gear with idler gear so that marks on gear mate properly with marks on idler gear. Be sure pump mounting flange scale is set at proper injection timing point.

6. Install mounting bolts to timing gear case and flange mount, and tighten nuts to 9 ft. lbs.

7. Connect fuel feed pipe and filter hoses to pump assembly.

8. Operate primer pump and bleed air from fuel filter and injection pump.

9. Connect injector pipes at injection pump outlets.

10. Check the idler gear for end play with a feeler gauge between gear and thrust plate. End play between 0.05 and 0.15 mm (0.002 and 0.006 inch) is standard. If play exceeds the repair limit of 0.035 mm (0.014 inch), replace the thrust plate and recheck.

11. Check gears for backlash by mounting a dial indicator so that lash is measured from the gear tooth profile at right angles to the gear shaft. When checking lash between idler gear and injection pump drive gear, be sure stay bolt at rear of pump is tightened to specifications. Backlash should measure between 0.11 and 0.24 mm (0.004 and 0.009 inch). Replace the gear if backlash exceeds the repair limit of 0.3 mm (0.01 inch).

12. Install new front oil seal, timing gear cover (use new gasket), and crankshaft drive pulley.

13. Check crankshaft pulley oil seal and cone contact surfaces. Measure damper for circumferential runout. Runout should not exceed 0.5 mm (0.02 inch). Replace crankshaft pulley if contact surfaces are damaged or if runout is out of specifications.

Pistons, Pins, and Rings

Description

The 243 Diesel engine uses an aluminum alloy piston with a top recess which forms a combustion chamber. This oval recess is tapered upward slightly from edge to center to compensate for thermal expansion during operation. The piston pin bore is off-set from the piston centerline 1.5 mm (0.059 inch). A piston weight classification symbol is stamped on the piston head. This symbol is a guide for equalizing the weight of the pistons in a given engine to minimize vibration. Piston weight classifications are shown in the accompanying tale.

Four piston rings are used. The three top rings are compression rings. The fourth ring is an oil ring with an expander. The top compression ring is chrome-plated and semi-keystone in cross-section to minimize ring stick. The no. 2 and no. 3 compression rings are tapered.

The full-floating piston pin is hollow and secured in the piston pin bore with snap-rings.

Removal

1. Disconnect battery negative cable at battery.

2. Raise truck on hoist.

3. Drain engine oil. Remove dipstick

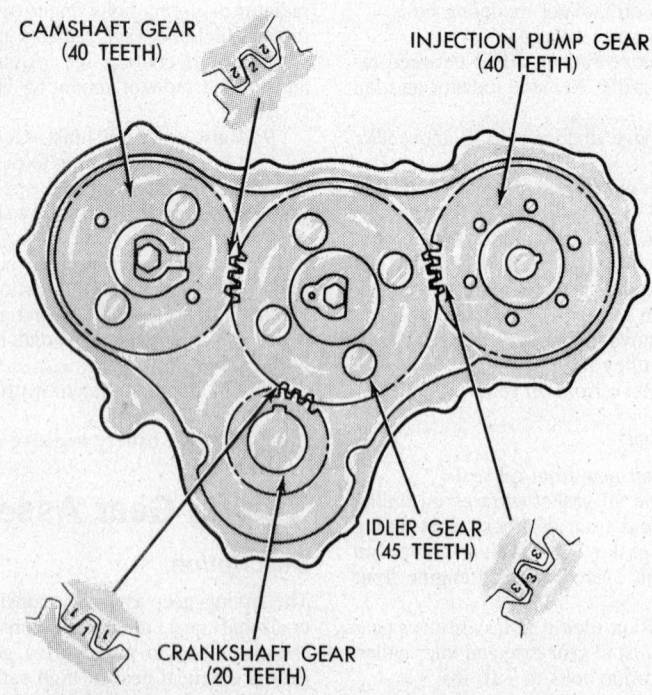

CAMSHAFT GEAR
(40 TEETH)

INJECTION PUMP GEAR
(40 TEETH)

IDLER GEAR
(45 TEETH)

CRANKSHAFT GEAR
(20 TEETH)

Gear engagement and tooth numbers for timing

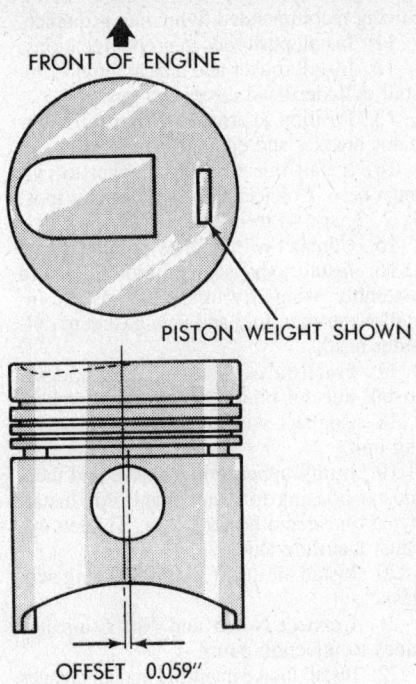

FRONT OF ENGINE

PISTON WEIGHT SHOWN

OFFSET 0.059"

Piston

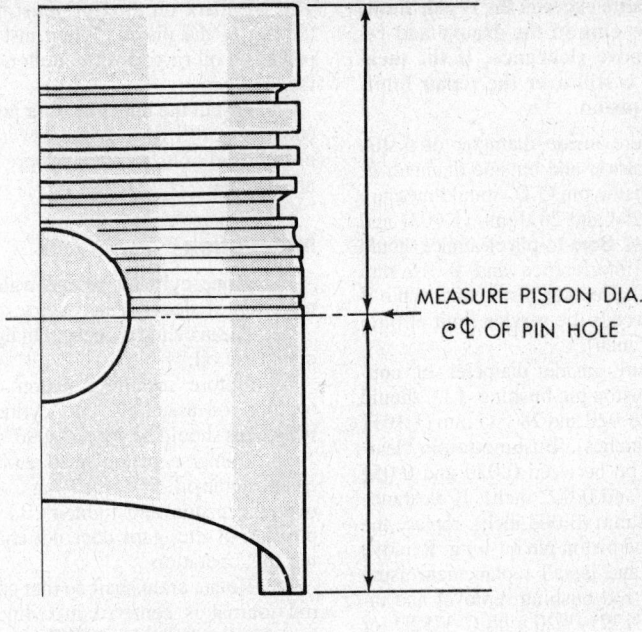

MEASURE PISTON DIA.
℄ OF PIN HOLE

Piston measuring point

tube from oil pan. On automatic transmission models, disconnect and remove two transmission cooling lines and bracket. Remove oil pan bolts.

4. Lower truck to shop floor and remove nuts from engine mounts.

5. Raise truck on hoist and install stand under compressor bracket (if so equipped).

6. Remove transmission inspection plate and oil pan. Remove stand from under compressor bracket.

7. Remove oil pickup tube, filter, and gasket.

8. Turn crankshaft until connecting rod journal of piston to be removed is at bottom center. Remove connecting rod cap nuts. Install bolt covers to prevent crankshaft journal damage. Mark rod and cap to ensure proper orientation on assembly. Remove cap and bearing inserts from cap and rod.

9. Push rod and piston assembly out of the way and measure rod journal O.D. with micrometer. It should measure between 57.945 and 57.965 mm (2.281 and 2.282 inches). The crankpin repair limit is −0.15 mm (−0.006 inch). If the crankpin O.D. measures −0.9 mm (−0.035 inch) or more, the crankshaft must be replaced.

10. Oil bearing inserts and retain for reassembly.

11. Lower truck to shop floor.

12. Remove air cleaner from manifold connection and brackets. Disconnect fuel filter from air manifold and push to one side.

13. Disconnect fuel line from transfer pump and return line from injector pipe outside.

13. Disconnect fuel line from transfer pump and return line from injector pipe outlet.

14. Remove air intake manifold bolts and air cleaner brackets.

15. Disconnect no. 3 and no. 6 fuel injector pipes at injection pump.

16. Remove air intake manifold and gaskets. Discard gaskets. Remove exhaust manifold shield and set aside.

17. Drain cooling system. Disconnect and remove bypass hose and heater hoses.

18. Remove thermostat housing and upper radiator hose from water manifold. Disconnect wire from temperature sending unit on water manifold.

19. Relelease injector pipes from support bracket. Remove three exhaust manifold bridges. Remove water manifold from cylinder head.

20. Raise truck on hoist. Remove exhaust pipe from exhaust manifold. Lower truck to shop floor.

21. Remove exhaust manifold and shield assembly. Disconnect wire from glow plug buss bar.

22. Disconnect four remaining fuel injector pipes from injection pump. Remove fuel line bracket from cylinder head.

23. Disconnect alternator bracket and engine lifting fixture. Push alternator out of the way.

24. Remove rocker shaft assembly. Remove push rods and keep in order for reassembly.

25. Remove cylinder head bolts in recommended sequence. Remove cylinder head and head gasket and place on bench.

26. Raise truck on hoist. Using a hardwood block, drive connecting rod up until piston clears cylinder bore. Lower truck to shop floor.

27. Remove piston and rod assembly from top of cylinder bore.

Disassembly

1. Remove piston rings from piston.

2. Remove piston pin snap-rings. Press piston pin out of piston and rod assembly using a piston pin remover and installer, tool C-3724 or its equivalent.

Inspection

1. Measure piston diameter at skirt with micrometer. Make measurement at point shown.

Dimensions for standard and oversize pistons are shown in the accompanying table.

2. Proceed as follows to fit the piston rings:

a. Measure piston ring gap about 2 inches from bottom of cylinder bore into which piston is to be fitted. Push rings into bore with inverted piston to ensure positioning them squarely in bore.

b. Insert feeler gauge in ring gap. Gap should be between 0.30 to 0.50 mm (0.012 to 0.020 inch). If the ring gap is 1.5 mm (0.059 inch) or more, replace ring.

c. Install rings in piston is specified position. Measure side clearance as shown. Measure clearance with straightedge holding ring flush with piston surface. Ring-to-groove clearance should be as follows:

	MM	Inches
No. 1 (top ring)	0.028–0.059	0.0011–0.002
Nos. 2, 3, and 4	0.025–0.060	0.00098–0.0023

NOTE: Repair limits on no. 1 rings are 0.2 mm (0.008 inch) and on nos. 2, 3, and 4, 0.15 mm (0.006 inch). If the

measured value exceeds the repair limit, install a new ring in the groove and re-measure groove clearance. If the measured valve is still over the repair limit, replace the piston.

3. Measure inside diameter of piston pin bore in piston and outside diameter of piston pin. Piston pin O.D. should measure between 27.994 and 28.0 mm (1.1021 and 1.1023 inches). Bore-to-pin clearance should be between interference and 0.016 mm (0.0006 inch). Replace piston and/or pin if clearance exceeds the service limit of 0.05 mm (o.0002 inch).

4. Measure inside diameter of connecting rod piston pin bushing. I.D. should be between 28.020 and 28.045 mm (1.1031 and 1.1041 inches). Bushing-to-pin clearance should be between 0.020 and 0.051 mm (0.0008 and 0.002 inch). If clearance exceeds 0.08 mm (0.003 inch), replace the connecting rod piston pin bushing. Remove old bushing and install replacement using a connecting rod bushing remover and installer, tool 31391-0220 with C-3752D (or equivalents).

Assembly

1. Assemble piston to connecting rod and combustion chamber side of piston on side of connecting rod with weight stamping. The piston pin should press into piston and bushing with a push fit at room temperature. If assembly is difficult, heat piston to between 104°F and 122°F in a piston heater. Then install piston to connecting rod using a piston pin remover and installer tool C-3724 or its equivalent.

2. Install snap-rings in piston pin bore as shown.

3. Install piston rings in ring grooves.

The UP mark on the ring must be toward the top of the piston. When installing expander in oil ring, position teflon tape over the ring gap.

4. Install the upper bearing insert in the connecting rod. Install bolt covers on connecting rod bolts to prevent bore and journal damage.

Installation

1. Hone cylinder sleeve walls. Ridge ream top of sleeve if necessary.

2. Clean cylinder sleeve. Oil lightly with crankcase oil.

3. Before installing piston and connecting rod assembly into cylinder bore. Ring gaps should be spaced at 90° intervals.

4. Immerse piston head and rings in clean engine oil. Slide the Ring Compressor over the piston and tighten. Be sure that position of ring gaps does not change during this operation.

5. Rotate crankshaft so that connecting rod journal is centered in cylinder bore. Insert rod and piston assembly so that combustion chamber side of piston is opposite camshaft side of engine.

6. Tap piston down in cylinder sleeve with hammer handle. Guide connecting rod into position over rod journal.

7. Install lower bearing insert and rod cap. Tighten cap bolts to 68 ft. lbs.

8. Check connecting rod for side play with feeler gauge. End play should be between 0.15 and 0.45 mm (0.006 and 0.018 inch).

9. Measure protrusion of piston from top of engine block. Piston should protrude from 0.3 to 0.7 mm (0.01 to 0.028 inch).

10. Install head gasket and cylinder head. Install head bolts. Torque to 90 ft. lbs. fol-

lowing recommended tightening sequence.

11. Install push rods in proper locations.

12. Install rocker and arm assembly. Install cylinder head cover and gasket.

13. Position alternator and install alternator bracket and engine lifting fixture.

14. Install injector pipe bracket to cylinder head. Connect four injector pipes (nos. 1, 2, 3, and 4) to injection pump.

15. Connect wire to glow plug buss bar.

16. Install exhaust manifold and shield assembly using new manifold gasket. Install water manifold and new gasket to cylinder head.

17. Install three exhaust manifold bridges. Install injector pipes to mounting bracket.

18. Connect wire to temperature sending unit.

19. Install upper radiator hose and thermostat housing to water manifold. Install bypass hose and heater hoses. Tighten exhaust manifold shield.

20. Install air intake manifold using new gasket.

21. Connect No. 3 and No. 6 injector pipes to injection pump.

22. Install intake manifold and air cleaner bracket mounting bolts. Connect air cleaner to air intake manifold.

23. Install fuel hoses from filter assembly to transfer pump and injection pump. Install fuel filter to end or air intake manifold.

24. Raise truck on hoist. Install exhaust pipe to exhaust manifold.

25. Install oil pickup tube, strainer, and new gasket to oil pump.

26. Install new oil pan gasket and position oil pan to block. Install transmission inspection plate and oil pan bolts. Tighten bolts to 15 ft. lbs.

27. Install oil dipstick tube to oil pan. Install transmission oil cooler lines and bracket on models with automatic transmission.

28. Lower truck to shop floor. Tighten engine mount nuts. Connect fuel line to transfer pump and return line to injector line connection.

29. Fill crankcase with specified engine oil.

30. Fill cooling system with specified coolant.

31. Connect battery negative cable.

Connecting Rods and Connecting Rod Bearings

Description

Connecting rods for the 243 Diesel engine are classified by weight range in the same manner as the pistons. When selecting a replacement connecting rod, it should be in the same weight range as the original. If a replacement rod in the same weight range is not available, use a rod within three adjacent weight ranges. Connecting rod as-

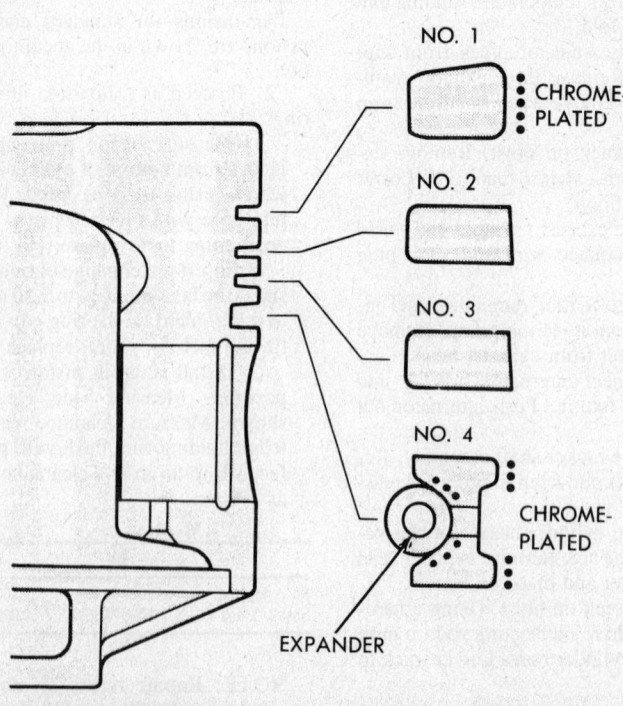

Piston ring installation

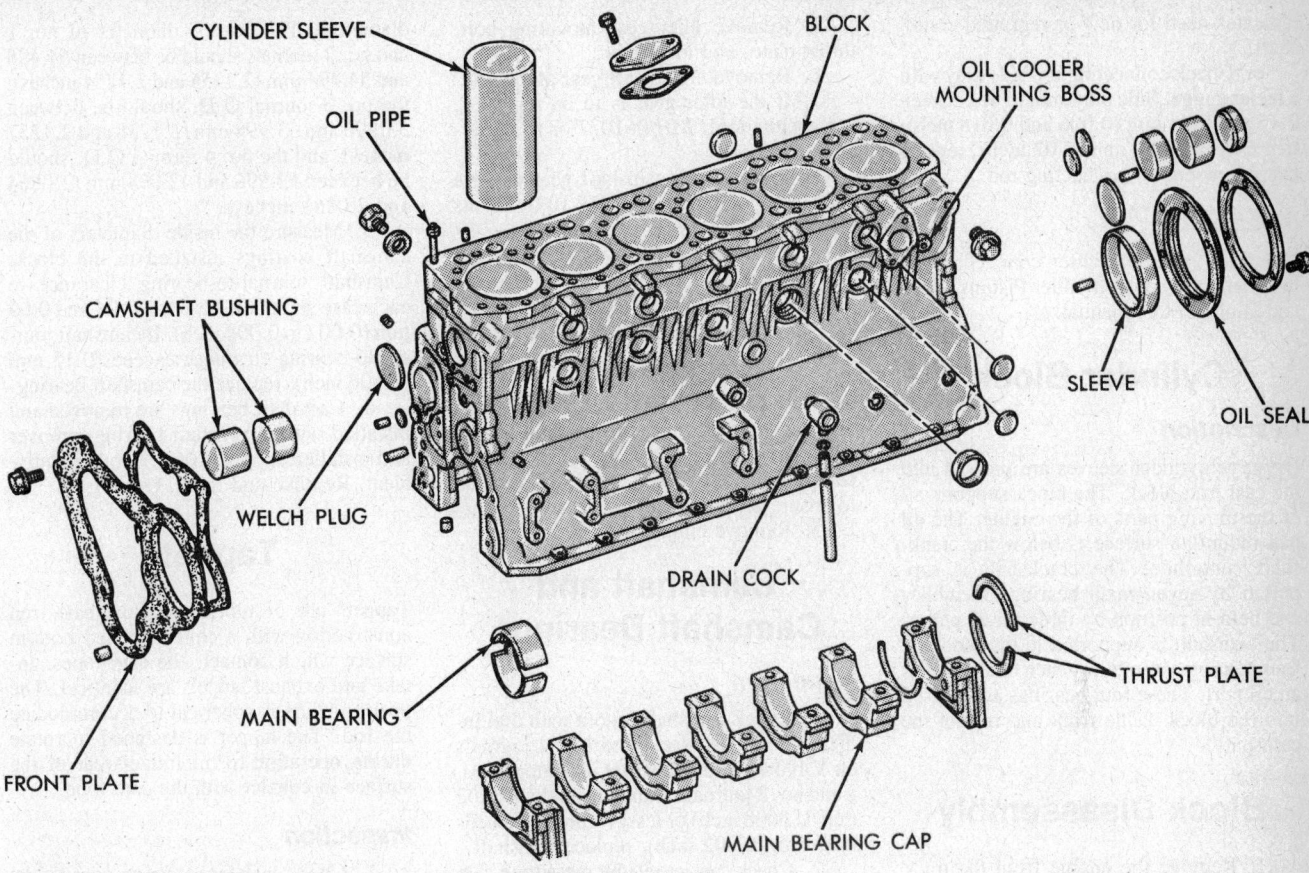

Cylinder block assembly

semblies, including bolts, nuts, and piston pin bushing, are classified in 13 weight ranges. The weight range mark is stamped into the rod near the rod bearing end. Connecting rod weight ranges are as shown in the accompanying table.

Removal

Removal and disassembly of the connecting rod assembly is covered under Pistons, Pins, and Rings in this manual.

Inspection

1. Visually inspect the connecting rod for cracks or other damage. Carefully check boundary areas dividing curved and straight portions at the bearing end and at the piston pin end. Check the oil orifice at the piston pin end.

2. Check connecting rod for bend or distortion. The connecting rod should be straight within 0.05 mm (0.002 inch). If the bend or distortion exceeds 0.15 mm (0.006 inch) replace the connecting rod.

3. Inspect connecting rod journal (crankpin) for roughness, spalling, uneven wear, or overheating. The crankpin may be reground or the crankshaft may require replacement, depending on the degree of damage.

4. Measure crankpin dimensions at two points, front and rear, and in two sections, A and B, as shown. Measure diameter, out-of-round, and taper.

Standard crankpin diameter is 57.945 to 57.965 mm (2.281 to 2.282 inches). The crankpin may be ground to an undersize as long as the diameter measures within 0.15 mm (0.005 inch) of the standard dimension. If the crankpin measures −0.90 mm (0.035 inch), the crankshaft must be replaced. Taper and out-of-round should be within 0.01 mm (0.004 inch), or less. If neither exceed 0.03 mm (0.001 inch), grind the crankpin to an undersize.

Maintain the crankshaft journal and crankpin centerlines at 49.95 to 50.05 mm (1.966 to 1.970 inches) when regrinding the crankpin. Maintain the fillet R at the dimension shown.

5. Install the connecting rod bearing inserts in the connecting rod in correct orientation. Tighten to specified torque of 83.4 to 93.1 Nm (61.5 to 68.7 ft. lbs.).

6. Measure the inside diameter of the connecting rod bearing with an inside micrometer or telescoping gauge.

Proper bearing-to-crankpin clearance is from 0.039 to 0.113 mm (0.0015 to 0.0044 inch). If clearance exceeds 0.15 mm (0.006 inch), new bearing inserts should be installed. If the crankpin required regrinding, undersize bearing inserts are available in the following dimensions: −0.25, −0.50, and −0.75 mm (−0.01, −0.02, and −0.03 inch).

7. Install connecting rod bearing inserts in pairs. Do not use a new bearing

insert with an old bearing insert. Do not file rods or bearing caps.

Bearing Fitting

SHIM STOCK METHOD

1. Place a piece of oiled brass shim stock ½-inch wide, ¾-inch long, and 0.001-inch thick between the lower bearing insert and the connecting rod journal.

2. Install bearing cap and tighten to specified torque of 83.4 to 93.1 Nm (61.5 to 68.7 ft. lbs.).

3. Turn crankshaft ¼ turn in each direction. If clearance is satisfactory, a slight drag should be felt.

4. When clearance is satisfactory, remove shim stock and torque connecting rod bolts to specifications.

PLASTIC GAUGE METHOD

1. Remove cap and lower bearing insert and wipe insert and journal clean.

2. Place a strip of plastic gauge across full width of bearing insert at cap center, parallel to crankshaft centerline.

3. Install cap and bearing insert to connecting rod and torque to specifications.

4. Remove bearing cap and determine amount of clearance by measuring width of plastic gauge with envelope scale.

5. If clearance is not within specifications, install undersize bearing inserts and recheck. Excessive taper of plastic gauge

indicates need for new or reground crankshaft.

6. Check connecting rod side play with a feeler gauge. Side play should be between 0.15 and 0.45 mm (0.006 and 0.018 inch). If it exceeds 0.50 mm (0.02 inch), replace bearing inserts or connecting rod.

Reassembly

Assembly of engine after connecting rod installation is covered under Pistons, Pins, and Rings in this manual.

Cylinder Block

Description

Dry-type cylinder sleeves are pressed into the cast iron block. The block supports all of the moving parts of the engine. The oil pan mounting surface is below the crankshaft centerline. The crankshaft is supported by seven main bearing assemblies and held in position by three thrust plates. The camshaft is supported in the block by four bearing assemblies, each of which has an oil port. These four bearings are pressed into the block at the front and rear of the camshaft.

Block Disassembly

1. Remove the engine from the truck and place it in a workstand.
2. Remove the cylinder head and head gasket and place on bench.
3. Remove the crankshaft pulley retaining nut. Install a Crankshaft Pulley Puller over pulley and damper assembly. Remove assembly.
4. Remove flywheel housing and flywheel.
5. Remove timing gear case.
6. Turn the crankshaft until No. 1 cylinder is at top dead center. Remove injection pump assembly.

7. Remove idler gear mounting bolt, thrust plate, and idler gear.
8. Remove crankshaft gear and baffle.
9. If the idler gear is to be removed, use special tool, MH 061077 or its equivalent.
10. Remove the camshaft gear using a camshaft gear puller, tool DT 1001A or its equivalent.
11. Turn the engine over in the workstand and remove the oil pan.
12. Remove oil pickup tube and strainer. Loosen joint bolt and remove oil pump from block.
13. Remove thrust plate and extract camshaft from front of block. Do not damage camshaft bearings during removal.
14. Remove tappets from recesses above camshaft. Identify each tappet on removal to ensure proper installation.
15. Remove engine front plate.

Camshaft and Camshaft Bearings

Inspection

1. Check camshaft runout with dial indicator. Support No. 1 and No. 4 journals on V-blocks and apply dial indicator to no. 2 and no. 3 journals. Runout should be 0.02 mm (0.0008 inch) or less. If runout exceeds 0.05 mm (0.002 inch), replace camshaft.
2. Check cam profile by measuring cam long and short diameters with micrometer. Inspect cam profile for wear or damage. The long diameter should measure 46.615 mm (1.835 inches); the short diameter should measure 39.426 mm (1.552 inches). If cam profile is worn or damaged, or diameters differ from standard by 0.5 mm (0.02 inch) or more, replace the camshaft.
3. Check camshaft journals for damage and uneven wear. If journals are excessively worn or damaged, the camshaft must be replaced.
4. Measure camshaft journal outside

diameters. The outside diameter of no. 1 and no. 2 journals should be between 54.496 and 54.494 mm (2.1455 and 2.1454 inches); the no. 3 journal O.D. should be between 53.996 and 53.994 mm (2.1258 and 2.1257 inches); and the no. 4 journal O.D. should be between 52.996 and 42.994 mm (2.0864 and 2.0863 inches).
5. Measure the inside diameters of the camshaft bearings installed in the block. Camshaft journal-to-bearing clearance in each case should be between 0.04 and 0.09 mm (0.002 to 0.004 inch). If camshaft journal-to-bearing clearance exceeds 0.15 mm (0.006 inch), replace the camshaft bearing.
6. Camshaft bearings are removed and installed with a camshaft bearing remover and installer, tool MH 061070 or its equivalent. Remove and install bearings.

Tappets

Tappets are of tubular, hollow cast iron construction with a chill-hardened bottom surface which contacts the cam lobes. Intake and exhaust tappets are identical. The push rod side is spherical to accommodate the rod. The tappet is designed to rotate during operation to minimize wear of the surface in contact with the cam lobe.

Inspection

1. Check each tappet for wear or cracks in the structure or in the cam lobe contacting surface. Replace defective tappets.
2. Measure the tappet outside diameter above the shoulder. Tappet O.D. should measure between 22.035 and 22.086 mm (0.8675 and 0.8695 inch).
3. Measure inside diameters of tappet openings in block. Nominal I.D. for tappet openings is 22 mm (0.866 inch). If clearance between tappet and tappet opening exceeds 0.1 mm (0.004 inch) the tappet and/or the block should be replaced.

Crankshaft

Removal

1. Remove pistons and rod assemblies from the cylinder block as follows:
   a. Before attempting to remove piston and rod assemblies from the top of block, turn engine up in workstand and remove top ridge from cylinder sleeve with a Ridge Reamer. Keep tops of pistons covered during this operation.
   b. As each piston and rod assembly is pushed out of bore, match cap and rod assemblies by cylinder.
   c. Rotate crankshaft to center each connecting rod in bore. Remove cap.
   d. Turn block sideways in workstand and remove piston and rod assemblies through top of block. Use bolt covers to protect journal surfaces. Push on upper bearing inserts with hardwood block to remove assemblies.
2. Remove main bearing caps from no.

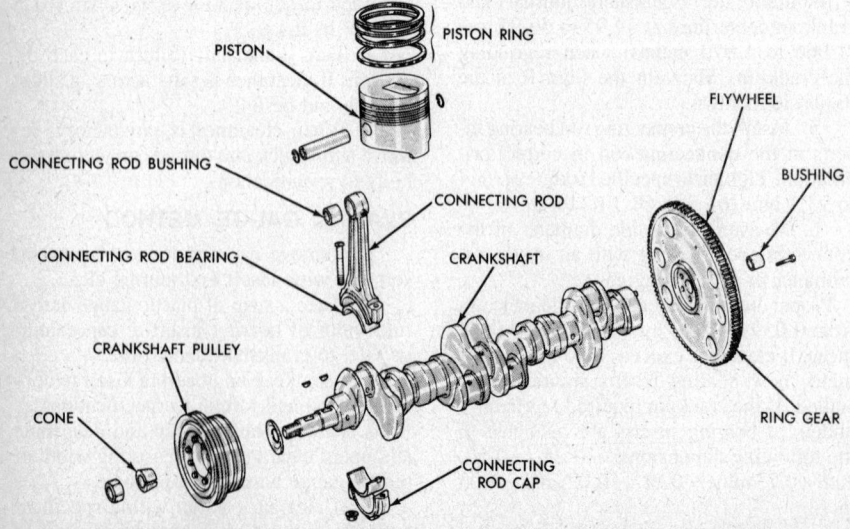

PISTON RING · PISTON · CONNECTING ROD BUSHING · CONNECTING ROD · CONNECTING ROD BEARING · CRANKSHAFT · CRANKSHAFT PULLEY · CONE · CONNECTING ROD CAP · FLYWHEEL · BUSHING · RING GEAR

Moving parts of the engine

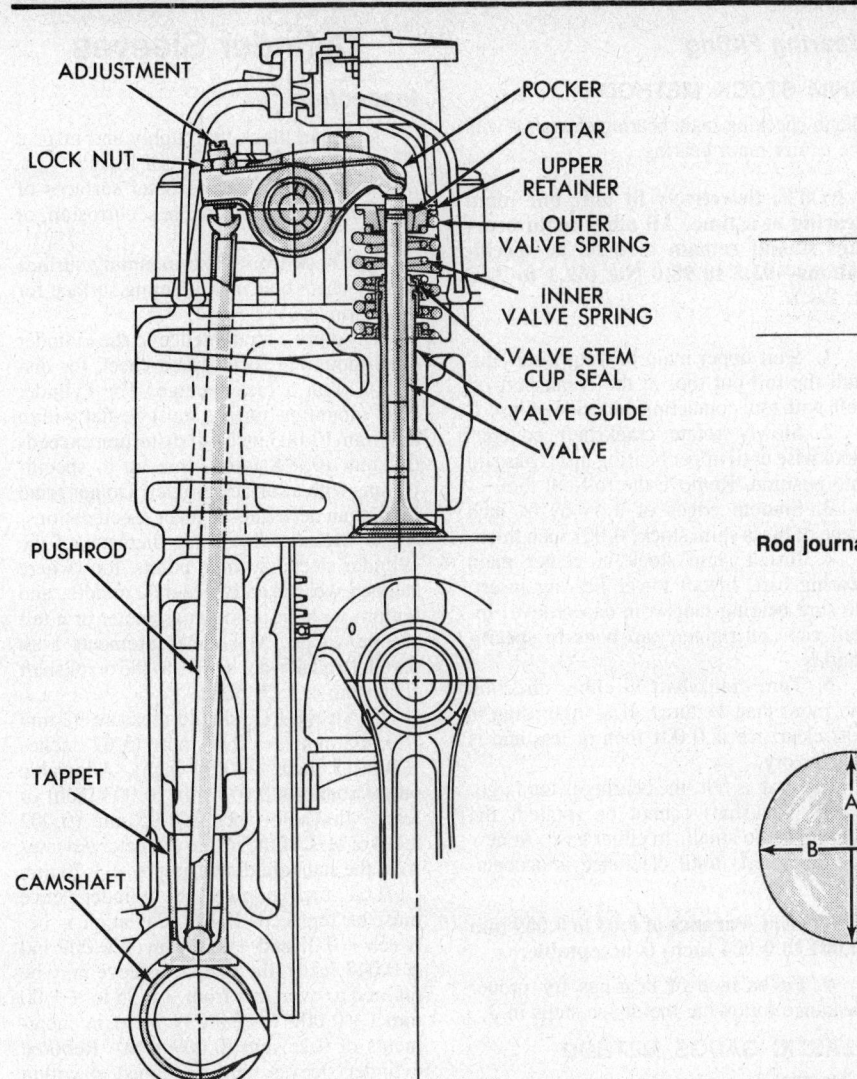

Camshaft, tappets and pushrods

ADJUSTMENT

LOCK NUT

PUSHROD

TAPPET

CAMSHAFT

ROCKER

COTTAR

UPPER RETAINER

OUTER VALVE SPRING

INNER VALVE SPRING

VALVE STEM CUP SEAL

VALVE GUIDE

VALVE

Rod journal measuring points

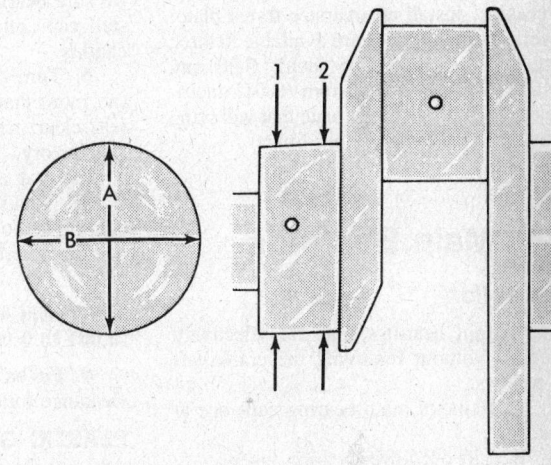

Main bearing journal measuring points

1 (front) and no. 7 (rear) main bearings. Use puller C-3752D, or its equivalent, and appropriate adapters. Remove lower main bearing inserts and identify as to cap number.

3. Remove bearing caps from intermediate main bearings, nos. 2 through 6. Use puller C-3752 D or its equivalent and appropriate adapters. Remove lower main bearing inserts and identify as to cap number.

4. Remove the crankshaft. Remove and identify the upper main bearing inserts. Mate with corresponding lower main bearing inserts. Identify bearing pairs as to cap number.

5. Remove thrust bearing plates from no. 7 main bearing journal.

Inspection

1. Support the crankcase on V-blocks under no. 1 and no. 7 journals. Mount a dial indicator to contact center main bearing journal.

2. Rotate crankshaft and note total in-dicator reading. This is crankshaft runout. One-half the runout reading is crankshaft bend. Bend should be 0.03 mm (0.001 inch) or less. If bend exceeds 0.07 mm (0.003 inch), replace the crankshaft.

3. Inspect crankshaft journal surfaces for roughness, spalling, or overheating. If necessary, the journal surfaces should be reground.

4. Measure outside diameter of each journal at two points, front and rear. Make measurements in two directions, A and B, as shown. Check O.D., out-of-round, and taper. Journal outside diameter should be between 69.950 and 69.970 mm (2.754 and 2.755 inches). Journals may be reground to an undersize as long as the O.D. measures between 69.800 and 69.820 mm (2.748 and 2.749 inches). If the crankshaft must be ground to an undersize less than 69.050 to 69.070 mm (2.719 to 2.720 inches) to clean it up, replace the crankshaft. Journal taper and out-of-round should not exceed 0.01 mm (0.0004 inch). If either exceeds 0.03 mm (0.001 inch), replace the crank-shaft.

NOTE: If journals are ground to an undersize, they should be finished to the dimensions shown in the accompanying table.

5. Inspect main bearing inserts for evidence of improper surface contact, foreign matter, scratches, spalling, and improper contact of bearing back with block or cap. Replace damaged or defective bearings.

6. Install bearings and caps on block in original positions. Tighten cap bolts to specified torque.

7. Measure bearing inside diameters at two points front and rear, and in two directions A and B, as shown. Obtain the difference between the bearing I.D. and the corresponding journal O.D. to determine clearance. Standard clearance is between 0.03 and 0.089 mm (0.001 and 0.004 inch). If clearance exceeds 0.20 mm (0.008 inch), replace the bearing inserts or grind the crankshaft to an undersize. Main bearing inserts are available in three under-sizes: −0.25 mm (−0.01 inch), −0.50 mm (−0.02 inch), and −0.75 mm (−0.03 inch).

8. Measure the thickness of the crankshaft thrust plate. It should measure between 34 and 34.025 mm (1.339 and 1.341 inches).

9. Inspect keyway and thread on front of crankshaft. Correct any defects.

10. Check oil seal for uneven wear, damage or deterioration. Replace defective oil seals. Remove oil seal sleeve with a chisel around its circumference. Be careful not to damage crankshaft rear journal when removing oil seal sleeve.

11. Install new oil seal. Press in oil seal sleeve with a crankshaft rear oil seal sleeve installer, tool 31691-00070 or its equivalent.

12. Install dial indicator to measure crankshaft end play. End play should be between 0.10 and 0.25 mm (0.004 and 0.01 inch) with crankshaft installed and bearing caps torqued to specifications. If end play exceeds 0.40 mm (0.016 inch), install new thrust plates and recheck. If end play is still excessive, install an oversize thrust plate. Oversize thrust plates are available in three sizes: 0.15 mm (0.006 inch), 0.30 mm (0.012 inch), and 0.45 mm (0.018 inch). Select an oversize thrust plate that will bring crankshaft end play within limits.

Main Bearings

Inspection

1. Main bearings may be selectively checked without removing the crankshaft as follows:

   a. Remove main bearing caps one at a time.

   b. Lift out lower bearing insert.

   c. Remove upper bearing insert by installing a roll-out tool (C-3059 or its equivalent) into crankshaft oil hole. Tool should contact upper bearing insert on side opposite tang.

   d. Slowly rotate crankshaft until upper bearing insert is forced out.

2. Inspect main bearing inserts for improper surface contact, corrosion, spalling, scratches, improper contact of insert back with block or cap, and evidence of a spun bearing. Replace defective inserts in pairs.

3. If bearing inserts appear to be in good condition or replacements have been obtained for defective bearings, they may be fitted either by the shim stock method or the plastic gauge method.

4. Install new bearings if clearance is not within specifications. Undersize bearing inserts are available in three sizes: −0.25 mm (−0.010 inch), −0.50 mm (−0.020 inch), and −0.75 mm (−0.030 inch).

NOTE: If a new or reground crankshaft must be installed, all bearing clearances must be checked either by the shim stock method or by the plastic gauge method. Do not simply install new standard bearing inserts and assume that clearances will be correct.

Bearing Fitting

SHIM STOCK METHOD

Begin checking main bearing clearance with the center main bearing.

NOTE: Selectively fit only one main bearing at a time. All other main bearings should remain torqued at specifications—93.5 to 98.0 Nm (69.1 to 72.3 ft. lbs.).

1. Start upper main bearing insert. Install the roll-out tool in the crankshaft oil hole with tool contacting tang side of insert.

2. Slowly rotate crankshaft counterclockwise until upper bearing insert has slid into position. Remove the roll-out tool.

3. Smooth edges of a ½ by ¾ inch piece of brass shim stock, 0.001 inch thick.

4. Install shim stock in center main bearing cap. Install lower bearing insert. Be sure bearing tang is in cap groove. Install cap and tighten cap bolts to specifications.

5. Turn crankshaft in either direction (no more than ¼ turn). If a slight drag is felt, clearance is 0.001 inch or less and is satisfactory.

If no drag is felt, the bearing is too large. If the crankshaft cannot be rotated, the bearing is too small. In either case, fit new bearing inserts until clearance is acceptable.

NOTE: Clearance of 0.03 to 0.089 mm (0.001 to 0.004 inch) is acceptable.

6. Fit balance of bearings for proper clearance following the above steps in 3.

PLASTIC GAUGE METHOD

NOTE: As in the shim stock method, check clearances one bearing at a time.

1. Support crankshaft weight with jack or stand under counterweight adjacent to bearing being checked. Support crankshaft at vibration damper when fitting No. 1 (front) bearing. All bearing caps except the one being checked should be torqued to specifications.

2. Remove main bearing cap and lower bearing insert.

3. Clean insert and exposed portion of journal.

4. Place strip of plastic gauge across full width of bearing insert parallel to crankshaft centerline.

5. Install bearing cap and insert and torque cap bolts to specifications.

6. Remove bearing cap and insert and determine bearing clearance by measuring width of compressed plastic gauge material with envelope scale. Acceptable clearance is from 0.03 to 0.089 mm (0.001 to 0.004 inch).

7. Check clearances on balance of bearings following above steps.

NOTE: Excessive taper of compressed plastic gauge indicates that a new or reground crankshaft is needed.

Cylinder Sleeves

Inspection

1. Clean block thoroughly and inspect all core hole welch plugs for leaks.

2. Inspect inner and outer surfaces of cylinder sleeves for scratches, corrosion, or rust.

3. Check front plate mounting surface and flywheel housing mounting surface for distortion.

4. Apply a straightedge to the cylinder head mounting surface and check for distortion with a feeler gauge. The cylinder head mounting surface must be flat within 0.07 mm (0.003 inch). If distortion exceeds 0.2 mm (0.008 inch), true up to specifications with a surface grinder. Do not grind more than necessary to meet specifications.

5. Measure the inside diameter of the cylinder sleeve at three points: top (where stepped wear usually occurs), middle, and bottom with an inside micrometer or a telescope gauge. Make measurements both parallel and at right angles to the crankshaft centerline at each point.

6. Sleeve I.D. should measure 92 mm +0.035 mm − 0.00 mm (3.62 inches +0.0013 inch − 0.00 inch). Allowable out-of-round is 0.075 mm (0.003 inch) or less. Allowable taper is 0.05 mm (0.002 inch) or less. If the inside diameter deviates from the standard dimension by +1.20 mm (+0.047 inch) or more, the cylinder sleeve must be replaced. If I.D. deviation is between +0.25 and +1.20 mm (+0.009 and +0.047 inch), the cylinder sleeve may be rebored to oversizes from +0.25 to +1.00 mm (+0.009 to +0.039 inch) in increments of 0.25 mm (0.009 inch). Rebored cylinder sleeves must be honed to within −0.00 and +0.035 mm (0.001 inch). Oversized pistons and piston rings must be used with oversize cylinder sleeves. If the I.D. deviates from the standard dimension by less than +0.25 mm (0.009 inch), hone out the cylinder sleeve and replace the piston rings.

If sleeve wear is uneven, the amount of oversize is determined on maximum war. If maximum uneven wear is 0.4 mm (0.016 inch), the sleeve must be rebored to +1.00 mm (+0.39 inch) to ensure compliance with taper and out-ofround specifications.

NOTE: If one cylinder sleeve is rebored to a given oversize, all other cylinder sleeves must be rebored to the same oversize.

Removal

1. Mount portable boring bar to top of block. Align boring bar with center of cylinder sleeve at bottom where eccentric wear is minimum.

2. Bore sleeve wall out to thickness of 0.5 mm (0.02 inch).

3. Extract sleeve. Take care not to damage block inner surface.

4. Check block bottom hole condition

after sleeve has been extracted. Bottom hole must be rebored before installing new cylinder sleeve if damage or other defects are noted.

Installation (If Bottom Hole Is Not Rebored)

1. Measure inside diameter of bottom hole in block and outside diameter of sleeve to be installed. Sleeve-to-bottom hole clearance must be from 0.08 to 0.145 mm (0.003 to 0.006 inch) after installation.

2. Press cylinder sleeve into block with a hydraulic press. Use a cylinder sleeve installer. Press sleeve into block until top surface of sleeve is flush.

3. After press-fitting is complete, bore sleeve and finish to an I.D. of 92 to 92.035 mm (3.620 to 3.623 inches) by honing.

NOTE: Before honing or boring, place rags under the bores to prevent abrasive material and metal chips from entering crankcase area.

Installation (If Bottom Hole Must Be Rebored)

1. The standard bottom hole in the block is between 94.955 and 94.990 mm (3.738 and 3.739 inches). Select an oversize sleeve with an O.D. 0.5 mm (0.02 inch) larger.

2. Bore hole in bottom of block with a diameter of between 94.955 and 94.990 mm (3.738 and 3.739 inches) if a standard sleeve is to be used. If an oversize sleeve is to be used, the bottom hole should have an O.D. of between 95.455 and 95.490 mm (3.758 and 3.759 inches). This will ensure clearance between the bottom hole and sleeve outside diameter of between 0.08 and 0.145 mm (0.003 and 0.006 inch).

3. Press-fit cylinder sleeve into block as described above.

4. After the sleeve has been fitted, bore the sleeve and finish to an I.D. of 92 to 92.035 mm (3.620 and 3.623 inches) by honing.

Resizing

1. Used carefully, a cylinder bore resizing hone, tool C-823 or its equivalent, equipped with 220 grit stones, is the best tool for resizing sleeves to a specific oversize. This tool will reduce taper and out-of-round as well as deglaze the sleeve surface. It will also remove light scoring, scuffing, or scratches.

2. If resizing is unnecessary, cylinder walls can be deglazed with a cylinder surface hone, tool C-3501 or its equivalent, with 280 grit stones. If bore is straight and round, 20 to 60 strokes will be sufficient to provide a satisfactory surface depending on conditions. After each 20 strokes, inspect cylinder walls. Use an appropriate honing oil. Do not use engine or transmission oil, mineral spirits, or kerosene.

3. Move hone up and down fast enough to get a cross-hatch pattern. When hone marks intersect at 50 to 60 degrees, cross-

hatch angle is most satisfactory for proper ring seating.

4. After resizing and honing, reclean block thoroughly to remove all traces of abrasives.

--- CAUTION ---

Be sure all abrasives are removed from engine parts after honing. Use of soap and water solution applied with a brush is recommended. Part should then be thoroughly dried. Cleaning is complete when the bore can be wiped with a white cloth and the cloth remains clean. After cleaning, oil bore to prevent rust formation.

Block Reassembly

NOTE: When reassembling the engine after complete disassembly and cylinder sleeve reconditioning or replacement, observe the following.

1. Clean all parts prior to installation. Pay special attention to bottom holes, bearing oil holes, and sleeve inner walls.

2. Install new gaskets and oil seals throughout.

3. Apply engine oil to moving parts before installation.

4. Use sealing compounds specified for gaskets and packing.

5. Follow torque and tightening specifications.

To reassemble:

1. Install upper main bearing inserts in block. Be sure that inserts are in original position if reused.

2. Install thrust plate to rear of No. 7 (rear) bearing.

3. Install crankshaft and make sure it rotates freely.

4. Install lower bearing inserts in No. 1 (front) and No. 7 (rear) bearing caps. Attach thrust plates to front and rear of No. 7 bearing cap. Be sure that caps are installed so that lettering on the caps faces the front of the block. Torque cap bolts to specifications.

5. Insert side seal. Apply sealing compound, Super-Bond No. 10 or equivalent, to cap groove of no. 7 main bearing and side seal. Insert side seal so that seal conforms to corner of block.

6. Measure crankshaft end-play.

7. Fit lower bearing inserts in intermediate bearing caps (nos. 2 through 6). Install caps to block and torque bolts to specifications.

8. Insert piston and rod assemblies for each cylinder in the corresponding sleeve from the top of the block. The combustion chamber side of the piston must be opposite to the camshaft side of the block.

9. Install rod bearing inserts and rod caps and torque bolts to 68 ft. lbs. Check each rod assembly for side play.

10. Invert the block in the workstand and install tappets in tappet openings. Be sure that tappets are returned to original positions.

11. Apply sealing compound to both sides of new front plate gasket and position it on front face of block.

12. Install front plate over dowel pins and bolt in place. Torque bolts to 9 ft. lbs.

13. Insert camshaft and install thrust plate. Be careful not to damage camshaft bearings.

14. Insert oil pump assembly from bottom of block and tighten joint bolt to 40 ft. lbs.

15. Apply sealing compound to bottom and install oil gasket.

16. Install oil pickup tube and strainer. Apply sealing compound to oil pan contact surface and install oil pan bolts. Torque bolts to 15 ft. lbs.

NOTE: Install bracket for water drain pipe under fifth oil pan bolt from rear on left.

17. Install crankshaft drive gear.

18. Be sure that No. 1 cylinder is at top dead center on compression stroke. Rotate crankshaft if necessary.

19. Install idler gear so that timing marks match with crankshaft gear.

20. Install camshaft gear. Make sure timing marks on camshaft gear mate with marks on idler gear. Tighten retaining bolts to 28 ft. lbs. and lock in place.

21. Install injection pump assembly. Make sure timing marks mate with marks on idler gear. Tighten mounting bolts and stay bolt.

22. Make sure that all timing gears mate with the timing marks as specified.

23. Apply sealing compound to front plate side of timing gear case gasket and position on front plate.

24. Install timing gear case over dowels and tighten mounting bolts to 9 ft. lbs.

25. Install crankshaft pulley and damper assembly with cone. Torque retaining nut to 289 ft. lbs. Be sure that the oil seal lip is not damaged during installation.

26. Install rear oil seal, rear oil seal sleeve and mounting bolts. Torque bolts to 36 in. lbs.

27. Insert welch plug at rear end of camshaft in hole in block.

28. Install flywheel housing. Torque bolts to 28 ft. lbs.

29. Install flywheel. Torque bolts to 83 ft. lbs. and lock in place by bonding washer tabs.

30. Install head gasket, cylinder head, rocker arm and shaft assembly, and cylinder head cover.

At this point, the engine may be reinstalled in truck.

ENGINE OILING

Description

The engine oiling system is a full-pressure type with a trochoid gear pump and two

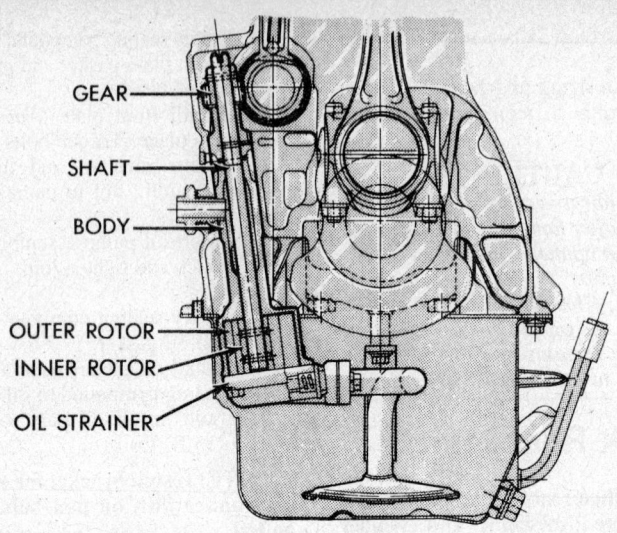

GEAR

SHAFT

BODY

OUTER ROTOR

INNER ROTOR

OIL STRAINER

Cross section of the oil pump

throwaway oil filters. Oil from the camshaft-driven oil pump is forced into a series of oil passages in the engine.

If the oil filter elements become clogged, the pressure difference between the oil filter inlet and outlet will increase and open the pressure relief valve (oil bypass valve), allowing oil to flow directly into the engine oil passages, not through the filter. This will prevent engine seizure. An alarm switch on the filter head warns the operator that the engine is lubricated with unfiltered oil.

Oil Pan

Removal (On Vehicle)

1. Disconnect battery negative cable at battery and remove oil dipstick.
2. Raise truck on hoist and drain oil.
3. Disconnect and remove dipstick tube from oil pan.
4. Disconnect transmission oil cooler lines (automatic transmission).
5. Remove oil pan bolts and lower truck to shop floor.
6. Remove nuts from engine mounts.
7. Raise truck on hoist. Install stand under compressor bracket (if so equipped).
8. Remove transmission inspection plate.
9. Remove oil pan and discard oil pan gasket.

Installation

1. Clean block and oil pan gasket surfaces. Install new pan gasket with sealing compound.
2. Position oil pan to bottom of block. Install transmission inspection plate.
3. Install oil pan bolts and torque to 15 ft. lbs.
4. Install oil dipstick tube. Install trans-

mission oil cooler lines (automatic transmission). Remove stand from under compressor bracket (if so equipped).
5. Lower truck to shop floor.
6. Install engine mount nuts and torque to specifications.
7. Refill crankcase with specified oil.
8. Connect battery negative cable to battery. Insert oil dipstick.

Oil Pump

Removal

1. Remove oil pan and gasket.
2. Remove oil pickup tube, strainer, and gasket.
3. Remove oil pump joint bolt with Tool C-4532 or its equivalent.
4. Remove filter assembly-to-oil pump tube. Remove joint bolt and oil pump, including gasket.
5. Clean block surfaces for oil pump and oil pan mounting. Discard oil pan gasket and clean pan gasket surfaces. Discard oil pump gasket. Clean oil pump gasket surfaces.

Disassembly

1. Loosen bolts and remove strainer (cover) from oil pump.
2. Remove inner rotor and shaft and lift out outer rotor.

Inspection

1. Clean all parts thoroughly. Mating face of oil pump cover should be smooth. Replace cover if scratched or grooved.
2. Install outer rotor into pump body. Install inner rotor into outer rotor and seat in pump body.
3. Place straightedge across pump body face. Insert feeler gauge. Clearance should

be between 0.035 and 0.095 mm (0.0014 and 0.004 inch). If clearance exceeds 0.15 mm (0.006 inch), replace both inner and outer rotors as an assembly.
4. Check clearance between inner and outer rotors with feeler gauge. Clearance should be 0.17 mm (0.007 inch) or less. If clearance exceeds 0.25 mm (0.01 inch), replace both inner and outer rotors as an assembly.
5. Measure the clearance between the outer rotor and the pump body with a feeler gauge. Clearance should be between 0.2 and 0.3 mm (0.008 and 0.01 inch). If clearance exceeds 0.5 mm (0.02 inch) replace the outer rotor.
6. Measure rotor shaft O.D. and pump body I.D. Clearance between shaft and body should be between 0.032 and 0.074 mm (0.001 and 0.003 inch). If clearance, exceeds 0.15 mm (0.006 inch), replace inner rotor and shaft and/or pump body. Replace all parts that show signs of excessive wear.
7. If oil pressure is lower than specified, look for worn parts or other causes of pressure loss.

Assembly

1. Install outer rotor in pump body. Install inner rotor and shaft in outer rotor.
2. Install strainer (cover) on oil pump body. Torque bolts to specifications.

Installation

1. Install new oil pump gasket. Position joint bolt and oil pump to block.
2. Install pick-up tube and filter to oil pump. Tighten joint bolt to 43 ft. lbs. with an oil pump joint bolt wrench, Tool C-4532 or its equivalent.
3. Install new oil pan gasket with sealing compound. Install oil pan and torque bolts to 15 ft. lbs.

Compression Test

Engine Compression should be tested whenever engine performance indicates internal engine problems.

1. Remove glow plug from no. 1 cylinder and install cylinder compression pressure adapter in its place.
2. Install compression gauge to adapter.
3. Disconnect the fuel control motor to cut off fuel input.
4. Crank engine and read compression at no. 1 cylinder.
5. At cranking speed of 170 rpm, compression pressure should measure between 2937 and 1965 kPa (426 and 285 psi). If compression pressure is below 1568.6 kPa (227.5 psi) the need for engine repair is indicated.
6. Test compression on no. 2 through no. 6 cylinders following steps 1 through 5 above.

NISSAN DIESEL

ENGINE TUNE-UP SPECIFICATIONS

| Injector Opening Pressure (psi) | Low Idle | Valve Clearance① (in.) | | Intake Valve Opens (deg.) | Injection Timing (rpm) | Firing Order |
		Intake	Exhaust			
1422	700	.014	.014	28B	20B @ 1000	1-4-2-6-3-5

① Hot or cold

FIRING ORDER

Firing order: 1-3-4-2

CRANKSHAFT AND CONNECTING ROD

Main Bearing Journal Diameter (in.)	Main Bearing Oil Clearance (in.)	Thrust On	Connecting Rod Journal Diameter (in.)	Connecting Rod Bearing Oil Clearance (in.)	Connecting Rod Side Clearance (in.)	Crankshaft End-Play (in.)
2.7918–2.7988	.0013–.0038	3	2.0840–2.0906	.0013–.0038	.0039–.0079	.0024–.0094

CAMSHAFT SPECIFICATIONS
(Inches)

| Journal Diameter | | | Journal-to-Bearing Clearance | | | Cam Lobe Height | Lift | Crankshaft End-Play |
1	2 and 3	4	1	2 and 3	4			
1.774–1.789	1.714–1.729	1.608–1.624	.0012–.0043	.0015–.0049	.0059–.0079	1.468–1.469	.248	.0032–.0102

VALVE SPECIFICATIONS

| Face Angle (deg.) | Seat Angle (deg.) | Stem Diameter (in.) | Stem-to-Guide Clearance (in.) | | Spring Tension Lb. @ Inches | Spring Free Length (in.) |
			Intake	Exhaust		
45	45	.3137–.3143	.0006–.0018	.0016–.0028	33 @ 1.634	1.929

PISTON, RING, AND PIN SPECIFICATIONS
(Inches)

| Piston Diameter | Piston Clearance | Ring-to-Groove Clearance | | | Ring End Gap | Piston Pin Clearance |
		1	2 and 3	4		
3.2617–3.2723	.0047–.0067	.0024–.0039	.0016–.0032	.0008–.0024	.0118–.0197	.00012

GENERAL ENGINE SPECIFICATIONS

No. Cyl.-Cu. In.	Bore × Stroke	HP @ rpm	Torque @ rpm	Compression Ratio	Compression Press (psi)①	Oil Pressure (psi) @ 2000 rpm	Weight Dry (lb.)
6-198	3.27 × 3.94	73 @ 3200	133 @ 1600	22:1	426	50	662

① At 200 rpm

TORQUE SPECIFICATIONS
(Ft. Lbs.)

Cylinder Head	Main Bearings	Connecting Rod Caps	Int. and Exh. Manifolds	Crankshaft Damper	Flywheel	Injector Nozzle Holder	Injection Pump
94 large 36 small	109–116	36–40	11–13	217–239	33–36	50–65	15–18

FUEL SYSTEM

Injection Pump

REMOVAL AND INSTALLATION

NOTE: In some applications, this procedure is best done with the engine removed from the vehicle.

1. Remove the inlet and outlet lines from the oil cooler.
2. Remove the bolts (4) and separate the oil filter and lines from the cooler.

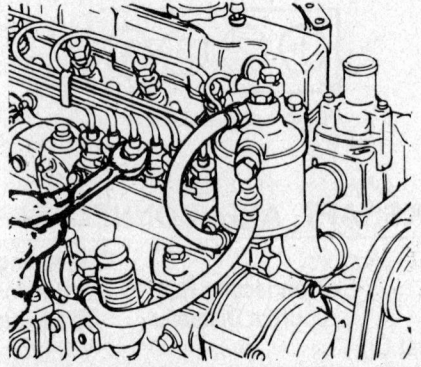
Injection line removal

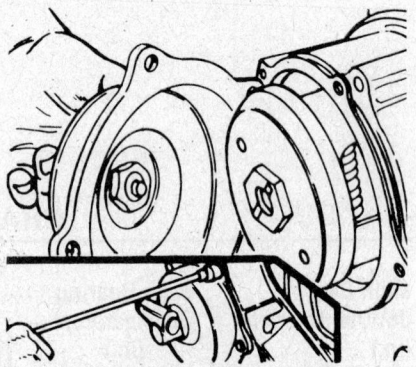
Timing cover removal

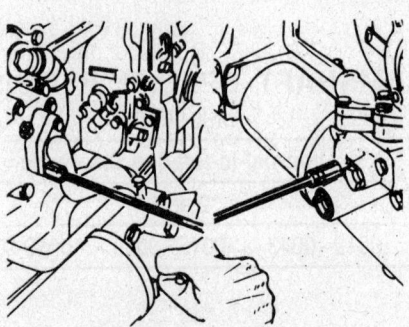
Water passage removal

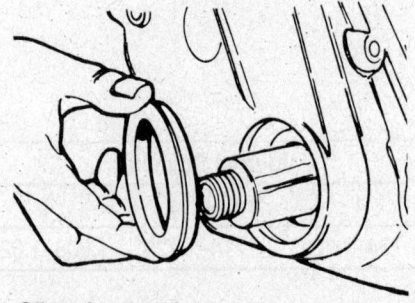
Oil seal removal

3. Remove the coolant hose between the oil cooler and the head.
4. Remove the bolts (10) and separate the cooler from the block.
5. Disconnect the fuel lines and remove the fuel filter from the bracket.
6. Remove the injection lines from the nozzles and pump. Cover all openings immediately.
7. Remove the fan, spacer and pulley from the water pump.
8. Remove the bypass hose from the pump and thermostat housing.
9. Remove the three bolts and lift off the water pump and gasket.
10. Remove the inspection cover and pointer from the flywheel housing and lock the flywheel in place with a locking tool.

11. Flatten the lockwasher and remove the crankshaft pulley nut.
12. Tap evenly around the edge of the pulley using a brass drift, until the cone protrudes from the pulley. Remove the cone.
13. Drive the pulley and damper from the crankshaft with a soft mallet.
14. Remove the inner cover from the timing gear case.
15. Pry out the oil seal.
16. Remove the mounting bolts and tap the case loose with a soft mallet.
17. Remove the tachometer drive supports nuts.
18. Remove the timer round nut.
19. Thread the timer extractor, special tool # 57926-581 into the timer weight holder. Remove the timer assembly by tightening the extractor bolt.
20. Unbolt and separate the injection pump from the front end plate.

Fuel filter removal

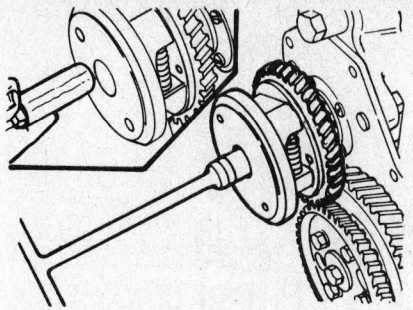

Removing timer round nut

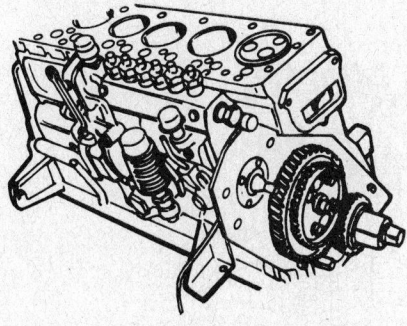

Injection pump and endplate assembly

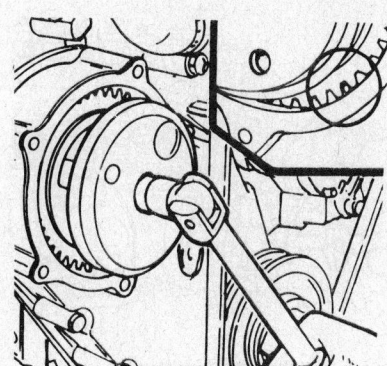

Timer installation

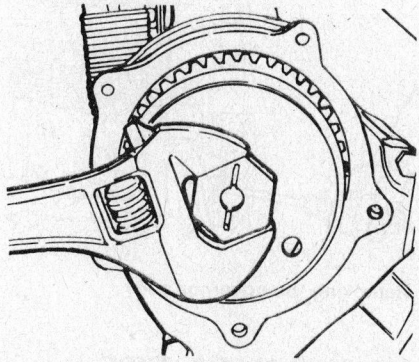

Tachometer drive coupling installation

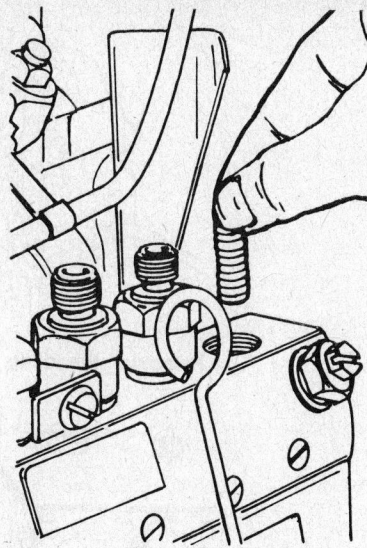

Delivery valve spring removal

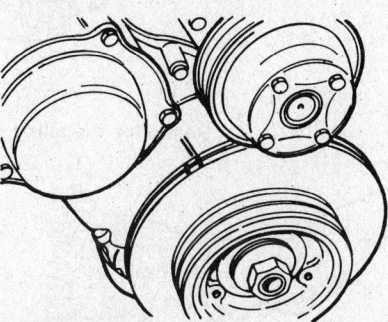

#1 piston at 20° BTDC

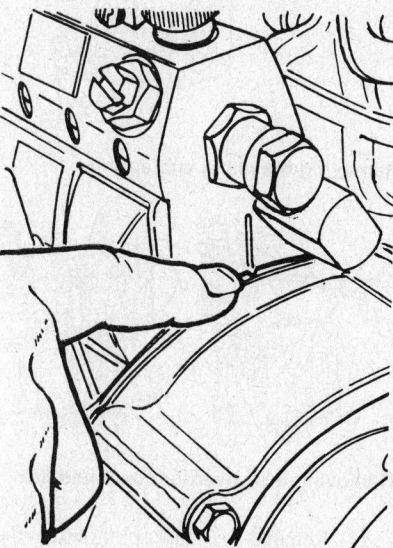

Lock the pump at this point, which is the beginning of injection

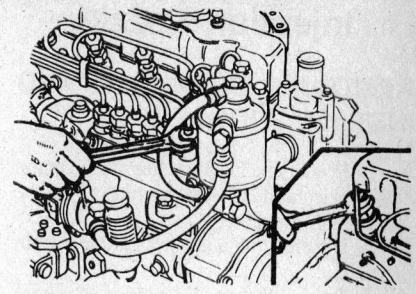

Connecting injection lines

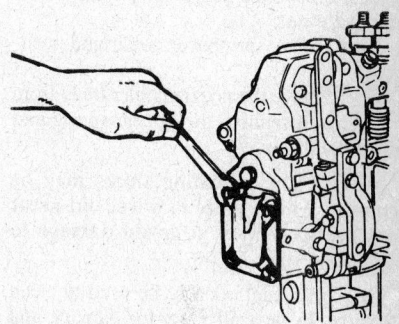

Removing the cam cover

Feed pump removal

21. Temporarily install the injection pump and gasket on the front plate.

22. Check the timing marks and bring the #1 piston to TDC.

23. Mesh the injection pump drive gear and idler gear at the timing marks.

24. After aligning the injection pump keyway, install the lockwasher and round nut and torque to 50–58 ft. lbs.

25. Install the tachometer drive coupling.

26. Check the backlash between the pump drive gear and the idler gear. Backlash should be .0028–.0079". Adjust if necessary.

27. Remove the #1 cylinder holder clamp, loosen the delivery valve and pull out the delivery spring. Tighten the valve holder to 22–25 ft. lbs.

28. Connect the fuel supply lines.

29. Bring the #1 piston to 20° BTDC. This can be done by aligning the first mark, in normal rotation, on the crankshaft pulley with the raised line on the gear case.

30. Hand prime the pump. Push the pump in all the way toward the block. Move the pump slowly away from the block until the fuel just stops flowing from the valve holder. Lock the pump in place.

31. Remove the delivery holder and assemble the spring. Torque the holder to 22–25 ft. lbs.

32. Install remaining parts in reverse order of removal.

NOTE: Oil filter bolt torque is 15–18 ft. lbs.

ENGINE REBUILDING

Injection Nozzle

REMOVAL, OVERHAUL AND INSTALLATION

1. Loosen the injection lines at the pump and nozzles and remove the lines. Cap the openings immediately.
2. Unscrew the injector and holder from the head.
3. Secure the nozzle holder in a vise and remove the lock nut.
4. Remove the nipple.
5. Remove the nozzle holder body from the nozzle nut.
6. Remove the spacer collar and push-rod.
7. Remove the nozzle holder body from the vise and remove the nozzle spring and adjusting shims.

NOTE: The adjusting shims may be removed with a piece of wire, but great care must be taken to avoid damage to the nozzle tip.

8. Clean fuel oil may be used to clean all parts. Inspect all parts for damage and good fit.
9. Assemble the nozzle in reverse order of disassembly.
10. Install the nozzle in a tester.
11. Operate the tester lever at 1 stroke per second and read the pressure at injection. The pointer will oscillate slightly during injection.
12. Increase or decrease the thickness of the nozzle spring adjusting shims until opening pressure is 1,422.3 psi. A total of 31 different shims are available. A shim thickness of .05 mm equals a difference of 85.338 psi.
13. Install the nozzles and lines. Torque the nozzles to 50–65 ft. lbs.

Governor

RSV MECHANICAL TYPE

Removal

1. Remove the injection pump and place it in a holding fixture.
2. Install the timer.
3. Drain the cam and governor chambers.
4. Remove the supply pump.
5. Remove the cam cover.
6. Using a special wrench, ST-57916-432, on the timer, turn the camshaft until all the tappets are raised to TDC. Place a tappet holder, 57931-210, between the tappet adjusting bolt and nut for each cylinder.
7. Remove the rear cover and dipstick.
8. Loosen the balance idler spring and the auxiliary idler spring lock nut.
9. Loosen the governor cover lock screw.
10. Unbolt and remove the governor cover from the governor body. Remove the link from the control rack.

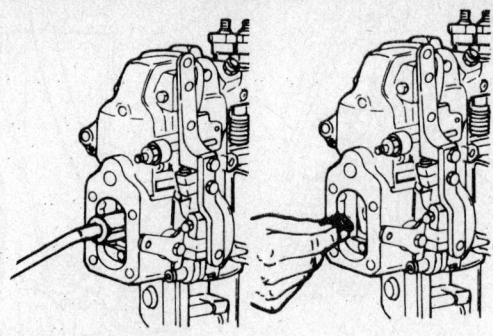

Removing the idling spring, type RSV

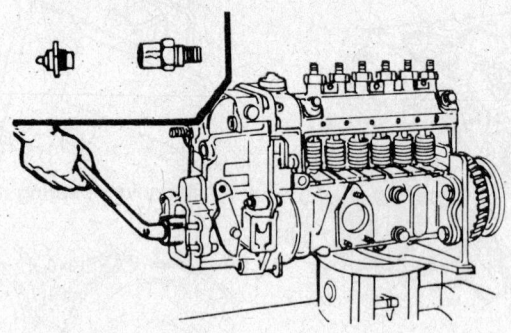

Removing the idling spring, type RAD

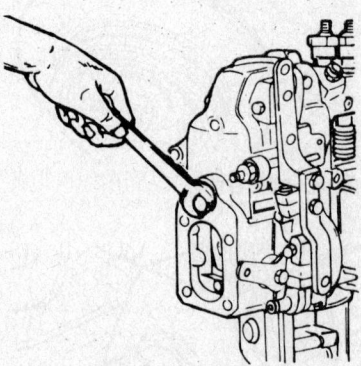

Removing the idling sub spring

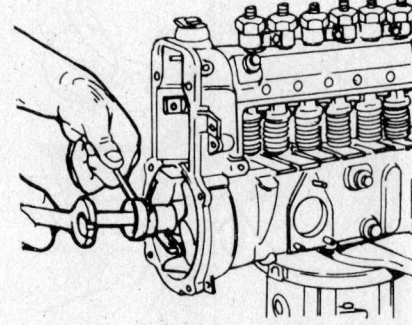

Removing the counterweights

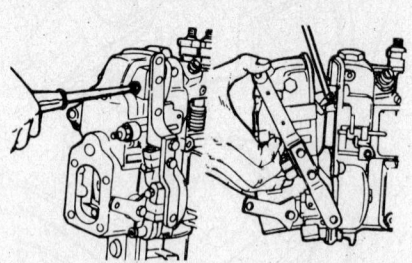

Removing the governor cover and link

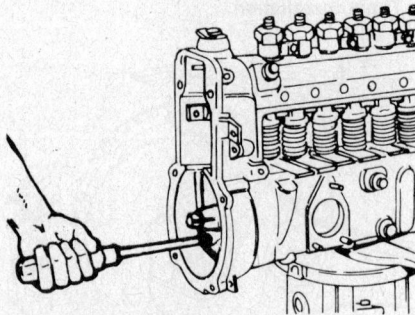

Removing the governor body

11. Remove the start spring from the spring eye.
12. Remove the counterweights from the camshaft.
13. Hold the timer and remove the slotted nuts and lockwashers.
14. Using a puller, ST57926-512, remove the flyweight assembly.
15. Remove the timer.
16. Unbolt and remove the governor body.

MZ PNEUMATIC TYPE

Removal

1. Follow steps 1 through 6 of RSV Type Removal.
2. Unbolt and remove the diaphragm housing and main spring.
3. Remove the diaphragm ring with a screwdriver.

Removing the timer

4. Remove the cotter pin from the connecting rod bolt with a needle-nosed pliers.

5. Remove the diaphragm assembly from the control rack.

6. Remove the five set screws and remove the governor body by applying force with a screwdriver blade in the slit between the governor and pump housings.

7. Remove the timer.

RSV TYPE

Installation

1. Apply RTV silicone gasket material to the governor body and install the governor on the injection pump.

2. Tighten the upper spring eye screw holding the starting spring.

3. Install the timer.

4. Install the flyweight assembly.

5. Apply RTV silicone gasket material to the governor cover and install the starting spring on the housing side of the spring eye.

6. Install the link leaf spring in the hole in the end of the control rack.

7. Install the cover and set screws.

MZ TYPE

Installation

1. Apply RTV silicone gasket material to the governor body, position it on the pump body and tap it into position with a plastic mallet. Install the set screws.

2. Install the diaphragm and balance spring on the control rack connecting bolt and lock with a new cotter pin. Apply chassis lube to the diaphragm ring.

3. Insert the main spring and install diaphragm housing with the four bolts.

INJECTION PUMP SERVICE

Replacing the Delivery Valve

1. Thoroughly clean the area around the nozzle tube and delivery valve.

2. Remove the nozzle tube.

3. Remove the delivery valve holder lock plate.

4. Remove the delivery valve holder and spring.

5. Using ST57930-032, remove the delivery valve.

6. Position the delivery valve in the pump housing making sure no dirt gets be-

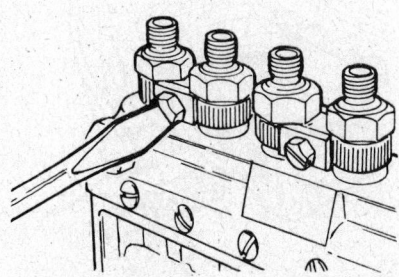

Removing delivery valve holder lock plate

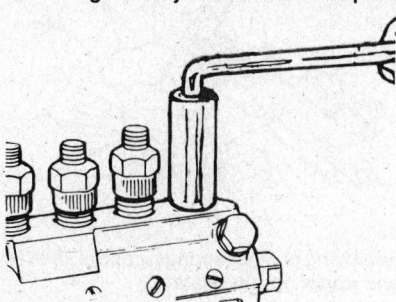

Loosening the delivery valve holder

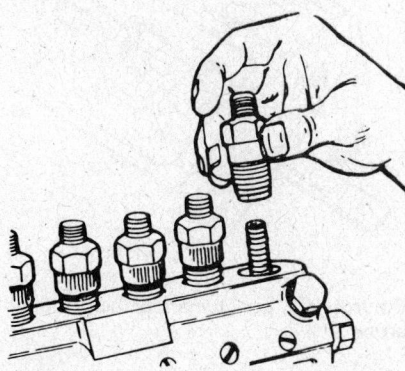

Removing the delivery valve holder and spring

tween the top of the plunger barrel and the delivery valve.

7. Install a new delivery valve gasket. The gasket is installed with the larger face downward and may be tapped into place through the extractor.

8. Install the delivery valve spring.

9. Install the delivery valve holder and torque it to 22–25 ft. lbs.

10. Loosen the holder and retorque it.

11. Install the lock plate, nozzle tube and nozzle clamp.

Replacing the Plunger.

1. Remove the delivery valve.

2. Push the plunger spring up with two screwdrivers and remove the lower spring seat from the plunger.

3. Insert a hooked wire through the top of the pump housing, down through the plunger opening and hook it on the lead unit of the plunger. Pull up to remove the plunger and barrel.

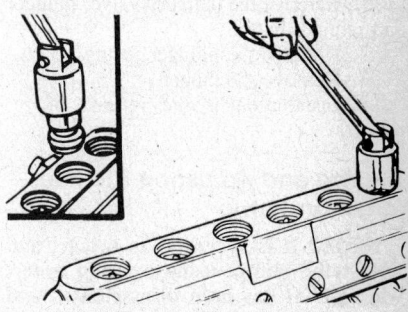

Removing the delivery valve with tool 57930-032

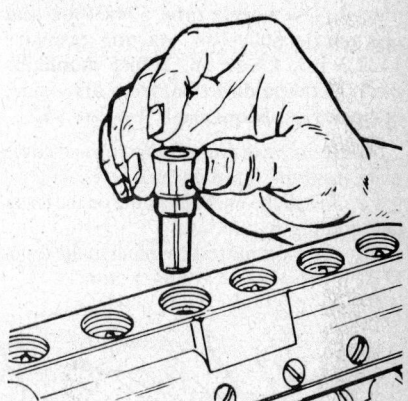

Plunger barrel removal, with delivery valves removed

Inserting the plunger spring holder

4. Immerse a new plunger in clean fuel oil and thoroughly wash off the rust preventive.

NOTE: The plunger was lapped at the factory. Do not hold it by the lapped section.

5. Operate the plunger in clean fuel oil to check its operation.

6. Slowly insert the plunger and barrel

into the pump with the barrel groove and plunger notch facing forward. Make certain the plunger piston pin is properly seated in the groove in the control sleeve.

7. Push the plunger spring up with two screwdrivers and insert the lower spring seat.

8. Install the remaining parts in reverse of disassembly.

Replacing the Tappets

1. Remove the delivery valve, plunger and plunger barrel.

2. Remove the plunger spring.

3. Remove the tappet.

4. Installation is the reverse of removal.

Testing and Adjusting the Fuel Injection Pump

NOTE: It is necessary to inspect and adjust the pump, using a pump tester, whenever it has been disassembled and assembled, when the plunger or plunger barrel have been replaced or when any of the component parts have been replaced. Use nozzle tube 57805-002 and test nozzle 5000-101, starting pressure 1422.3 psi. Clean no. 2 fuel should be used. Rotating direction, from drive side, is clockwise. Sequence is 1-4-2-6-3-5.

1. Remove the fuel feed pump and cover plate from the injection pump.

2. Install the injection pump on the tester and holding fixture.

3. Connect the test coupling to the tester drive shaft with the coupling disc.

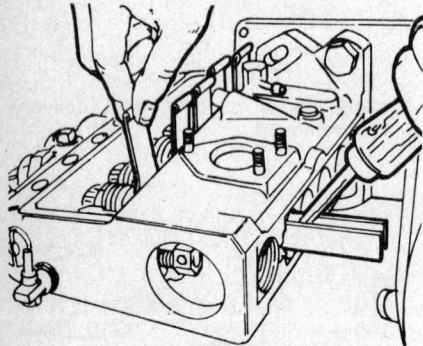

Inserting tappet holder and insert tool

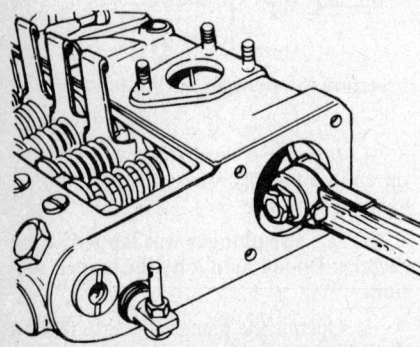

Removing tappet with tappet clamp

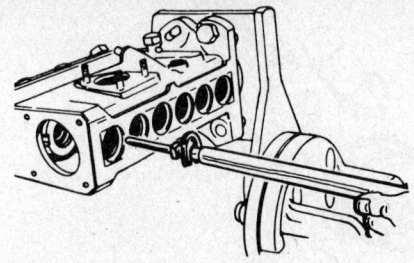

Removing plungers with tool 57921-412

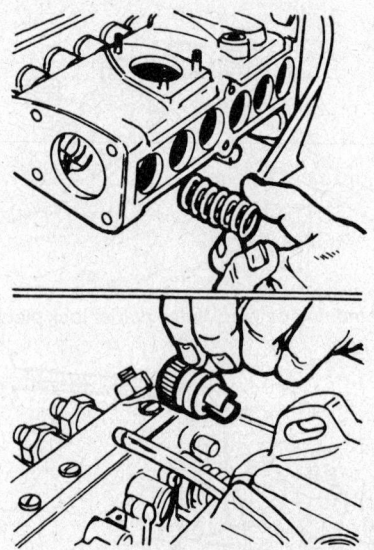

Removing plunger springs, control sleeves and upper spring seats

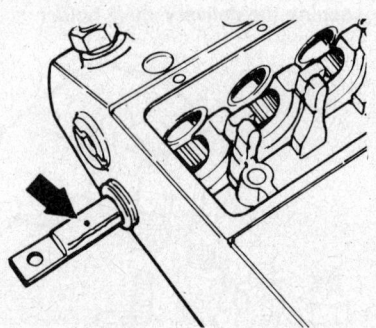

Control rack; punch mark is indicated by arrow

4. Remove the cap and position the tester dial to measure the camshaft rotating angle.

5. Install a tappet lift gauge on the #1 tappet.

6. Bottom the tappet and set the dial gauge to 0.

7. Bleed the pump at the bleeder screw.

8. Loosen the nozzle holder ball valve.

9. Feed fuel to the pump inlet while slowly turning the pump tester by hand in the normal engine rotation direction. Fuel will flow from the test nozzle. When the fuel stops flowing the injection point has been reached. The tappet, at this precise point, must be .08858–.09251″ above BDC.

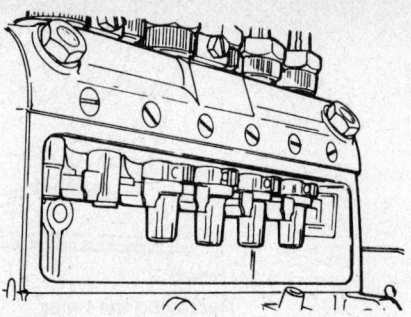

Control sleeves installed

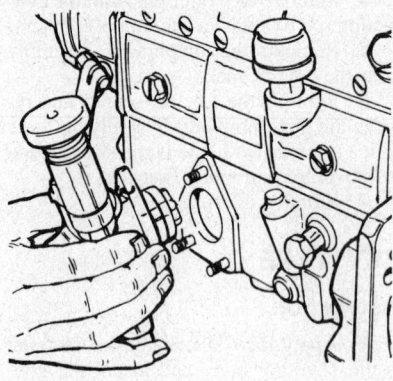

Fuel feed pump removal

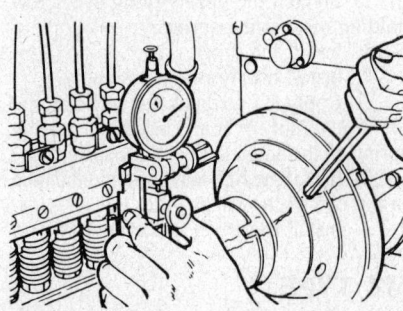

Checking injection start timing with a lift gauge

10. If the fuel does not stop flowing after .0926″, turn the adjusting bolt counterclockwise to raise the position of the plunger.

11. If the fuel stops flowing before .0886″, turn the adjusting bolt clockwise to lower the plunger position.

12. When adjustment is made, torque the locknut to 43–50 ft. lbs.

13. With the pump set at initial injection, set the angle scale mark on the tester flywheel at 0 or 180°.

14. If adjustment is correct, fuel should stop flowing at #4 cylinder when the tester has been turned 60° in normal rotation. If fuel does not stop flowing at the correct time, adjust as above.

15. Check and adjust each cylinder in turn.

16. When timing for each cylinder is correct, position the cam at TDC, check the plunger piston pin-to-plunger barrel clearance and make sure that the tappet vertical clearance is at least .0118″ for each tappet.

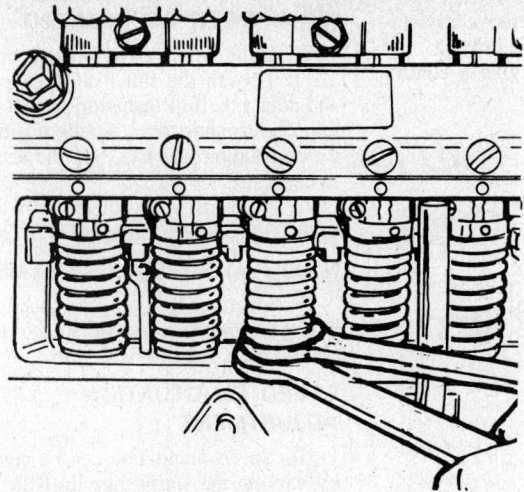

Turning the adjusting bolt

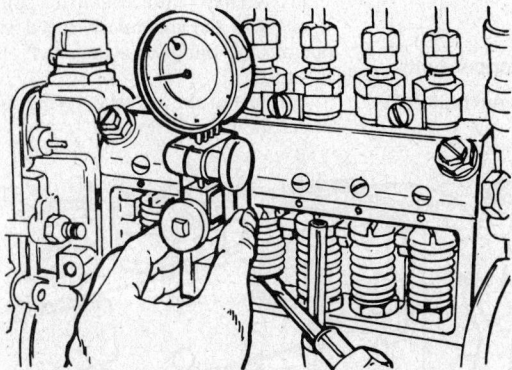

Checking tappet clearance

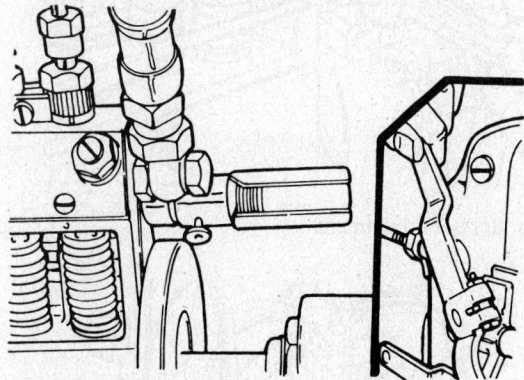

Attaching a measuring device to the pump

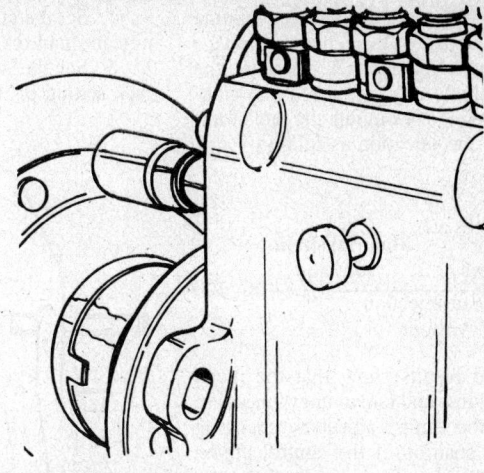

Installing the tester lock screw

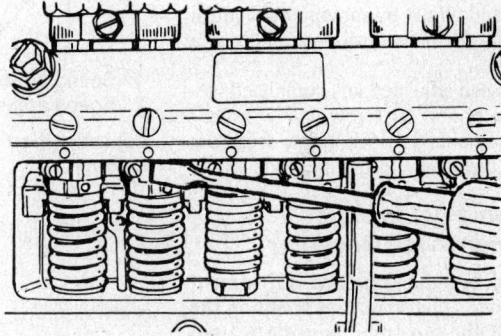

Loosening the pinion set screw

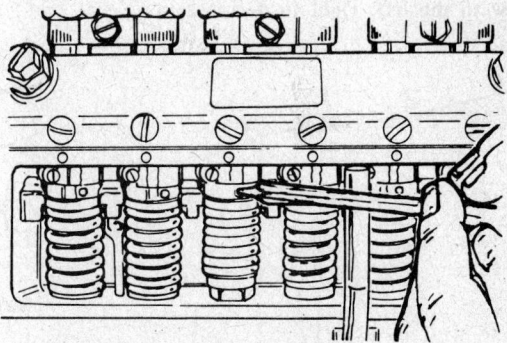

Installing the appropriate sized pin

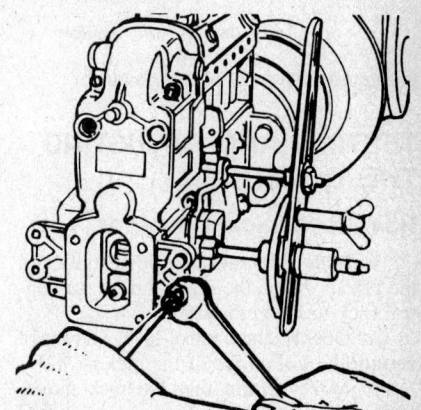

Adjusting the full load stopper bolt (RAD shown)

Standard Fuel Injection Volume Adjustment

1. Determine the zero position of the control by attaching the measuring device to the pump and pushing the index all the way to governor side. Match the scale on the left end of the index and set the 0 (zero) position of the scale at the position at which the measuring device index stops. On RSV mechanical governors, loosen the stop bolt to align this index.

2. Remove the rack guide screw from the rear of the pump housing and apply the lock screw attached to the tester. Secure the control rack in the standard position for adjustment.

NOTE: The lock screw should be tightened by hand; overtightening will bend the rack.

3. Start the tester and run the pump at rated speed.

4. Set the pump feed pressure at 21.3–

22.75 psi and measure the injection volume at the rated stroke of the female cylinder.

5. In the same manner, measure the injection volume at rated speed and standard rack position. Compute the rate of unevenness of the injection as follows:

$$\frac{\text{Max. or min. injection volume for each plunger} - \text{Main injection volume}}{\text{Mean injection volume}} \times 100$$

6. If the results show that the mean injection volume and rate of unevenness are not within the limits, adjust by changing the relative position of the control pinion and control sleeve. This may be done by:

a. Loosen the pinion set screw.

b. Place a pin in the hole in the control sleeve and adjust by moving the control sleeve along the control rack a little at a time.

c. When adjustment is completed, secure the pinion set screw.

d. Remove the lock screw from the control rack and reinstall the guide screw.

Maximum Fuel Injection Adjustment—MZ Governor

NOTE: See the standard adjustment tables above. The stroke set screw on the bottom of the governor housing is used to adjust the maximum injection volume. To increase the volume, turn the stroke set screw to the left; right to decrease volume.

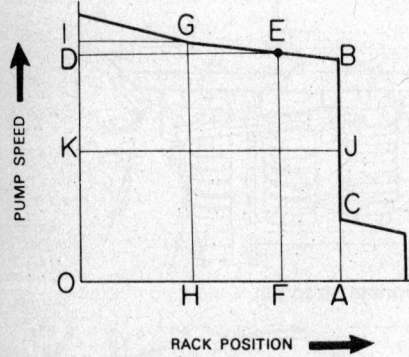

Schematic diagram of the governor

TESTING AND ADJUSTING THE GOVERNOR

RSV Mechanical Governor

1. Match the adjusting device index to the zero point on the scale and set the control rack to the zero position.

2. Operate the control lever and make certain the full stroke of the rack is .827".

3. Make certain that the rack moves freely in the direction for maximum fuel injection by the spring force of the starting spring.

4. Set the stop bolt to remove any significant load on the governor linkage.

5. Set the stop bolt to give a control rack setting of .0917–.03937".

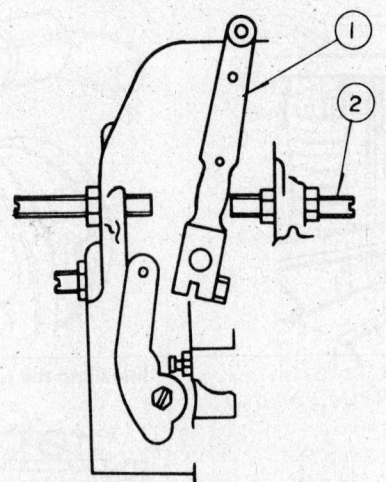

1. Speed control lever
2. Speed adjusting bolt (stopper bolt)

Adjusting the speed adjustment bolt (RSV shown)

HIGH SPEED ADJUSTMENT

6. Remove the governor rear cover.

7. Loosen the full load stop lock nut and adjust the full load stop so that its setting corresponds to an A rack position between rotation and BC. See the accompanying chart.

8. To increase the volume, turn the stop to the right; left to decrease.

MAXIMUM SPEED ADJUSTMENT

9. Operate the pump at speed G and adjust the maximum speed stop so that the control rack position is G mm.

SPEED FLUCTUATION ADJUSTMENT

10. Speed fluctuation can be controlled by varying the spring rate on RSV governors.

BALANCE SPRING ADJUSTMENT

11. Set the control lever to the point where it contacts the maximum speed stop and operate the pump at a rate of F, between A and B.

12. Install the balance spring assembly under the tension lever.

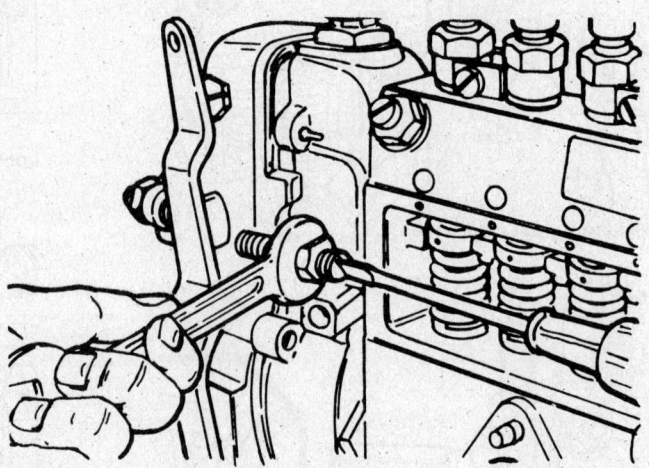

Maximum speed stopper adjustment

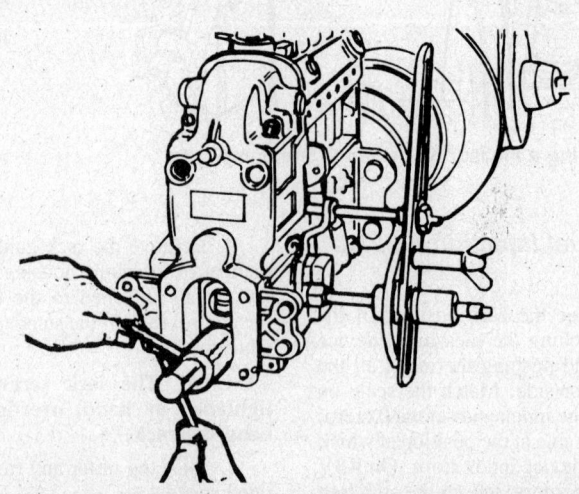

Adjusting the idling spring

13. Tighten the balance spring assembly with tool 57916-212 until the control rack position G is H mm and secure with the lock nut.

14. Gradually accelerate the engine from speed D and make certain that the control rack is at G mm when the action of the spring ends at speed E.

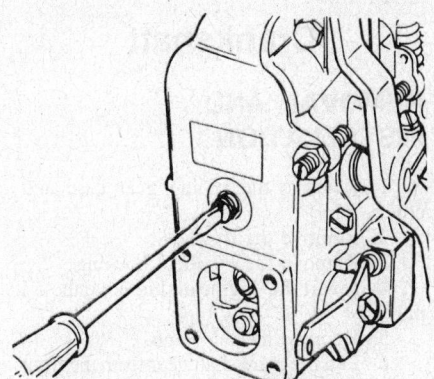

Auxiliary idle spring adjustment

IDLE SPEED ADJUSTMENT

15. Set the control lever at the stop position so that the control rack is at point B.

16. Set the speed to D and tighten the idle auxiliary spring so that the position of the rack is C mm. Secure with the lock nut.

NOTE: Do not tighten the auxiliary idle spring too much or overspeeding will result.

MZ Pneumatic Governor

1. Set the measuring device index at the zero point on the scale and set the control rack at the zero position.

2. Operate the control lever and make certain the full stroke of the control rack is .827".

3. Connect a hose between the vacuum pump of the tester and the negative pressure chamber of the governor. Apply negative pressure equal to engine operation.

4. Operate the pump at 500 rpm and adjust the governor.

5. Tighten the stroke set screw so that the control rack is set at a position equal to zero.

6. Adjust the stroke of the balance spring to .236".

7. If movement of the control rack deviates considerably from the performance curve, adjust by increasing or decreasing the thickness of the adjusting shims.

8. Operate the tester vacuum pump and check the control rack position and movement in relation to the pressure shown on the gauge. If the movement of the control rack for pressure variations does not conform to the performance curve, the idle speed is either too high or too low. Turn the auxiliary idle spring right to increase and left to decrease speed.

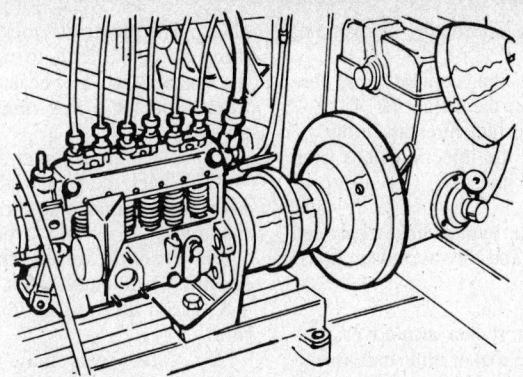

Pump installed on tester, with synchronizer and strobe light

Testing and Adjusting the Timer

1. Install a timing light, such as tool 5783-001 on the tester using the cover plate attaching bolts, so that the synchronizer lever attachment is applied to the tappet.

2. Start the pump and turn on the timing light.

3. Direct the light at the angle scale on the flywheel and measure the angular change based on variations in pump speed.

4. If the tester does not have an angle scale:

   a. Attach an angle scale to the timer coupling and mount a pointer on the tester drive shaft.

   b. Operate the pump and direct the light on the scale.

5. If the angular change is not within limits, disassemble the timer and adjust the spring force by increasing or decreasing the shims, or if necessary, replace the spring.

ENGINE MECHANICAL

NOTE: Disassembly of major components is best done with the engine out of the vehicle and mounted on a rotary work stand.

Cylinder Head

REMOVAL, OVERHAUL AND INSTALLATION

1. Remove the air cleaner.

2. Remove the crankcase vent hose and remove the intake and exhaust manifolds. These are bolted together.

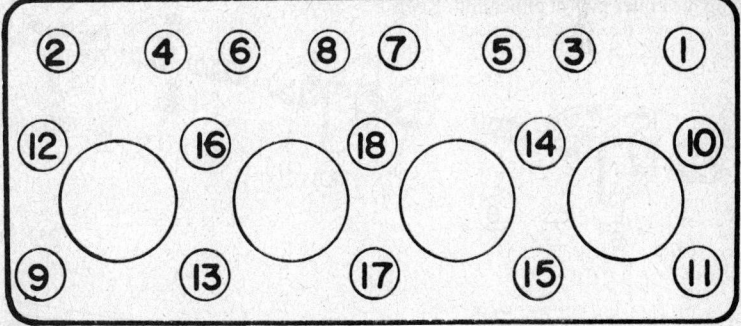

Cylinder head bolt loosening sequence

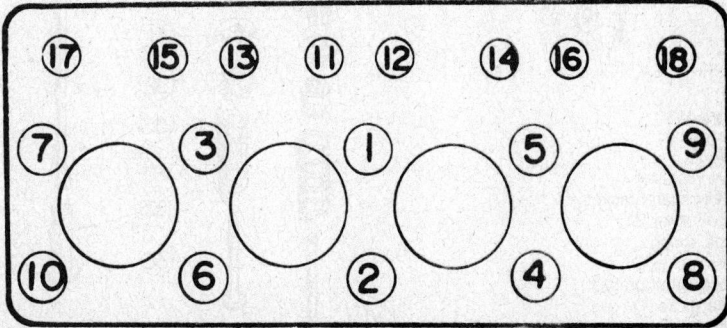

Cylinder head bolt tightening sequence

3. Remove the alternator, bracket and belts.

4. Disconnect the coolant hose between the head and the oil cooler.

5. Remove the fuel filter assembly.

6. Disconnect the injection lines from the pump and the injectors. Cap all openings at once.

7. Remove the bypass hoses between the coolant pump and the thermostat housing.

8. Remove the fan.

9. Remove the rocker arm cover.

10. Remove the rocker arm shaft assembly.

11. Remove the pushrods and keep them in order.

12. Remove the fuel return lines.

13. Remove the nozzles from the head.

14. Remove the cylinder head bolts in the sequence shown.

15. Attach a hoist to the head and lift it clear of the block. On occasion, the precombustion chambers may fall out, especially if the head is bumped or handled roughly. Take care that they are returned to their original positions if this occurs.

16. Remove the head gasket and O-rings.

NOTE: Before disassembling the head, make all necessary valve train measurements.

17. Place the head in a holding fixture.

18. Disassemble the valves. Mark all parts for assembly in their original positions.

19. Remove the retaining wire and lift off the valve stem seals.

20. Unscrew the glow plugs.

21. Disassemble the rocker arm shaft by removing the cotter pins at either end. Keep

all parts in order. If rocker arm brackets prove to be difficult to remove, immerse the assembly in water heated to about 160°F. Immersion for a few minutes will loosen the parts.

22. Clean and inspect all parts.

23. Check the head with a straightedge. Maximum warpage is .0079″. Do not remove more than .011″ from the head.

24. Check the valve springs for free length and tilt. Free length must not be less than 1.850″ and tilt must not exceed .03937″ (1 mm).

25. Valve seats may be removed by cracking with a cold chisel or with a valve seat remover. New valve seats should be cooled in dry ice for five minutes prior to installation, at the same time the head should be immersed in 175°F water.

26. Assemble the head in reverse order of disassembly.

27. Place a new cylinder head gasket on the block with the stainless steel inset side facing up.

28. Install the O-rings around the water and oil passages.

29. Position the head on the block.

30. Coat the head bolts with clean engine oil and torque them in sequence, in stages as follows:
   a. Large: 43, 94
   b. Small: 21, 36

31. Install the pushrods, pressing down and turning them to be sure of proper seating.

32. Install the rocker arm shaft assembly, torquing the bolts to 18 ft. lbs. in sequence from the center to each end.

33. Install the injection nozzles.

34. Install all other parts in reverse order of removal.

Crankshaft

REMOVAL AND INSTALLATION

1. Remove the timing gear case and cover.

2. Remove the flywheel.

3. Remove the flywheel housing.

4. Invert the engine and remove the oil pan.

5. Remove the oil pump.

6. Pull the crankshaft gear from the front end of the shaft.

7. Remove the connecting rod bearing caps.

8. Remove the main bearing caps.

NOTE: Loosen the cap bolts alternately and evenly. A puller, tool #ST16660000 may be necessary to remove the caps.

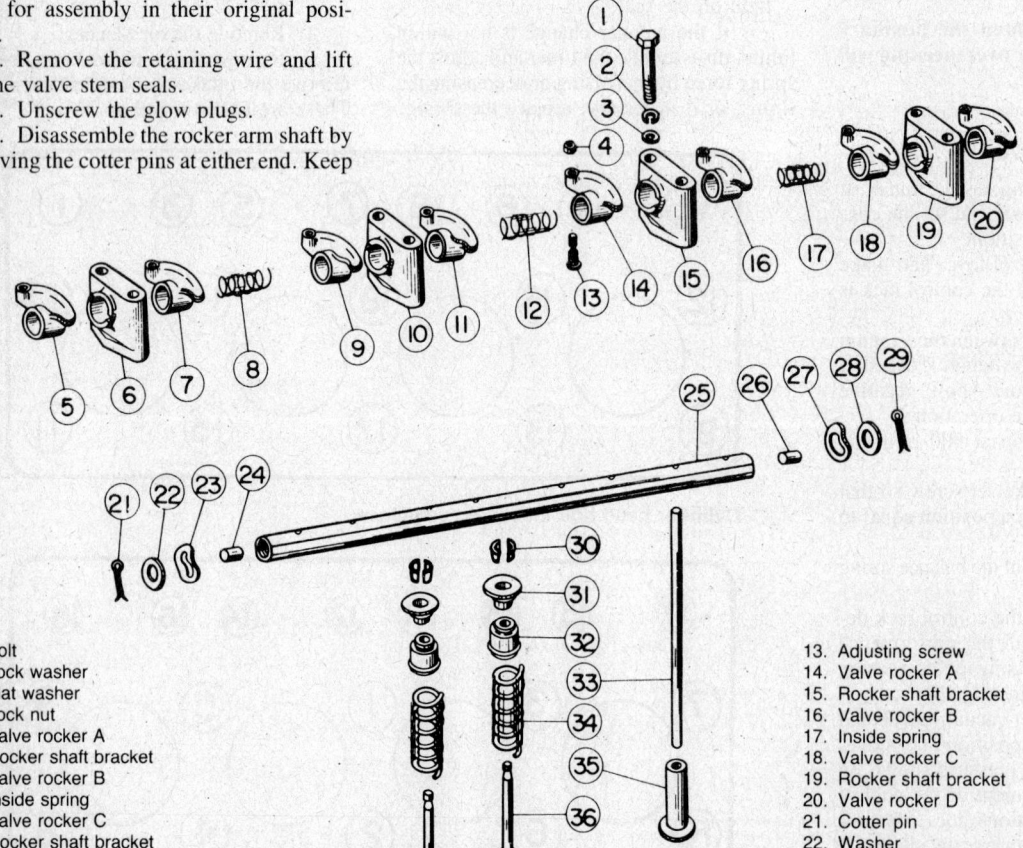

1. Bolt
2. Lock washer
3. Flat washer
4. Lock nut
5. Valve rocker A
6. Rocker shaft bracket
7. Valve rocker B
8. Inside spring
9. Valve rocker C
10. Rocker shaft bracket
11. Valve rocker D
12. Inside spring
13. Adjusting screw
14. Valve rocker A
15. Rocker shaft bracket
16. Valve rocker B
17. Inside spring
18. Valve rocker C
19. Rocker shaft bracket
20. Valve rocker D
21. Cotter pin
22. Washer
23. Outside spring
24. Plug
25. Rocker shaft
26. Plug
27. Outside spring
28. Washer
29. Cotter pin
30. Split collar
31. Spring seat
32. Valve stem seal
33. Push rod
34. Valve spring
35. Valve lifter
36. Valve

Rocker arm assembly

9. Remove the crankshaft with a hoist.

NOTE: The #3 bearing contains a thrust washer. Avoid mix-ups.

10. Lift out the upper bearing halves. Mark them for reassembly.

11. Coat all parts with clean engine oil. Assembly is the reverse of disassembly. Oil groove on the thrust bearing faces away from the journal. Bearing caps have an F which faces front. Guide tool ST16490000 is available for installation of bearing caps. Rear main seal is replaced at this time.

Piston

REMOVAL AND INSTALLATION

1. Remove the head as described previously.
2. Remove the oil pan.
3. Remove the ridge at the top of each cylinder.
4. Remove the connecting rod bearing caps.
5. Remove the upper bearing halves.
6. Apply force to the bottom end of the rods and push the pistons out through the block.
7. Coat all parts and the cylinder liner with clean engine oil.
8. Stagger the piston ring gaps.
9. Bring the crank pins, one at a time, to top dead center and install the piston. Push down on the piston while slowly turning the crankshaft journal to bottom dead center.

NOTE: The stamped side of the connecting rod is on the exhaust side of the engine.

10. Install each rod cap as the piston reaches bottom dead center.
11. Install all other parts in reverse order of removal.

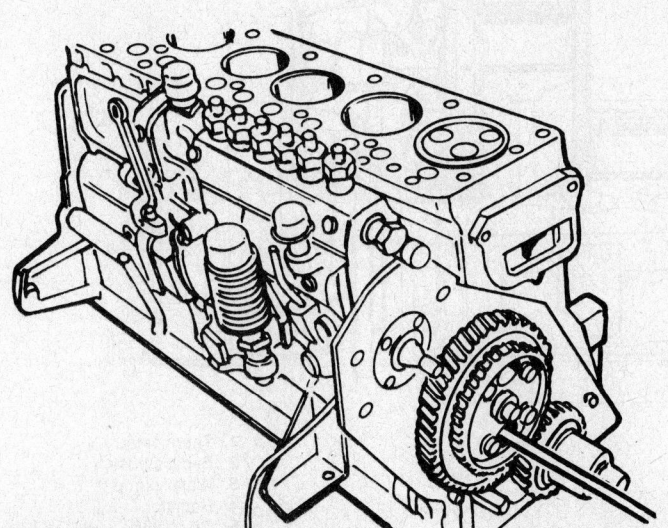

Removing the camshaft locating bolts

Camshaft

REMOVAL AND INSTALLATION

1. Remove the head as previously described.
2. Remove the lifters and mark them for reassembly.
3. Remove the front case and cover.
4. Remove the tachometer drive support nuts.
5. Remove the timer round nut.
6. Thread the timer extractor, ST 57926-581, into the timer weight holder. Remove the timer assembly by tightening the extractor bolt.
7. Remove the oil pump drive spindle.
8. Remove the camshaft locating plate bolts and carefully slide the camshaft from the engine.
9. Coat the camshaft with clean engine oil and carefully slide it into the block. Install the locating plate.
10. Install the oil pump drive spindle by aligning the oil pump drive shaft groove and the camshaft oil pump drive gear with the spindle.
11. Install all other parts in reverse order, following previously given instructions.

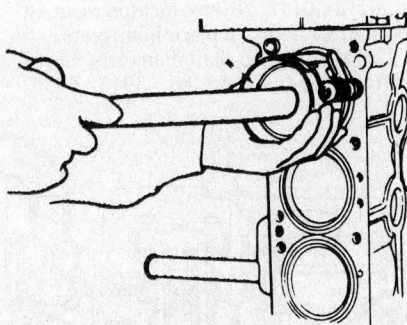

Installing the piston and rod assembly

Piston and Ring

OVERHAUL

1. Remove the old rings.
2. Heat the piston in clean 140°F engine oil, remove the snap-ring and slide out the piston pin.
3. Visually check all parts for wear and damage.
4. Measure 2″ down from the top of the piston on a side opposite the pin hole, and measure piston diameter. Replace the piston if wear exceeds .0059″.
5. Remove carbon from the ring grooves and check ring clearance at five points around the piston.

REPAIR LIMITS

#1	.0197″
#2	.0118″
Oil	.0059″

6. Place a ring in the cylinder and square it by pushing it in with a piston. Measure the end gap. Replace the rings if end gap exceeds .0059″.
7. Check piston pin-to-piston clearance. Clearance should not exceed .0039″.
8. Measure bearing-to-crankpin clearance. Clearance should not exceed .0059″.
9. Check connecting rod straightness. Deviation should not exceed .0012″ per 100 mm.
10. When all specifications are acceptable, assemble and install the pistons.

Cylinder Liner

REPLACEMENT

1. The nominal size for a liner is 3.268″. If the liner wear exceeds .0079″, replace the liner.
2. Install a puller such as ST-1030000 over the liner and tighten the extractor bolt, pulling the liner from the block.
3. Carefully clean the new cylinder liner and block surfaces with clean engine oil and install the liner using ST1030000. Make sure the liner is fully seated.
4. Check the following liner dimensions:

	Inches
Height above block	.00078–.00360
Block-to-liner	.0004–.0012
Nominal bore	3.268

ENGINE REBUILDING

Camshaft Bushing

REPLACEMENT

1. Using a suitable puller, remove the bushings one-by-one starting from the front. The rear bushing, however, must be pulled from the rear.

2. The bushings are driven in, in order, from the rear. Make sure that the beveled side faces the front in all cases. Make certain that oil passages are aligned and the bushings are flush-fit.

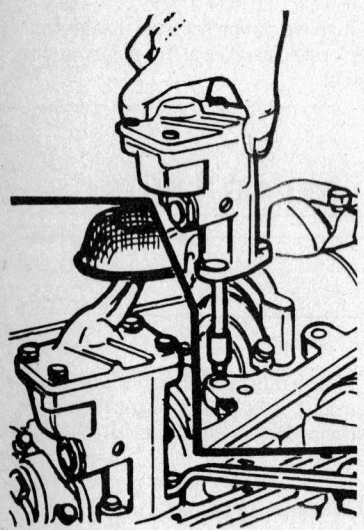

Removing the oil pump

LUBRICATING SYSTEM

Oil Pump

OVERHAUL

1. Remove the oil pump.
2. Remove the pump cover plate.
3. Measure the distance between the gear face and the case gasket surface.
4. Measure the gear tip-to-bore clearance.
5. Measure the gear backlash.
6. Remove the pin from the pump driveshaft and pull the gear from the shaft.
7. Remove the driven gear from the idler shaft.
8. Press the idler shaft from the pump body.
9. Face the relief valve away from you and remove the cotter pin. The plug and valve will pop out.
10. Wash all parts in solvent and visually check for wear and damage.
11. Check measurements. Gear face to case surface should be .008–.0032″. Clearance between the teeth tip and the case bore should be .0029–0059″. Backlash should be .0118–.0157″. If any measurement exceeds these limits, replace both gears.
12. Measure the shaft diameters. Driveshaft tip end should be .5943–.5950″.

Driveshaft gear end should be .5148–.5155″. Idler shaft should be .5158–.5182″. Driveshaft-to-bore clearance should be .00945–.00272″.

13. Coat all parts in clean engine oil. Assembly is the reverse of disassembly.

NOTE: Place the beveled side of the gears toward the oil pump body. Check clearances during assembly. Check operation after assembly.

COOLING SYSTEM

Water Pump

OVERHAUL

1. Remove the water pump from the engine.
2. Remove the snap-ring and, using a suitable puller, remove the hub.
3. Remove the bearing lockwire.
4. Remove the back plate and gasket.
5. Place a tube with a slightly larger diameter than the bearing over the bearing and onto the impeller. Place the pump body, nose down, in a press and press off the impeller and bearing.

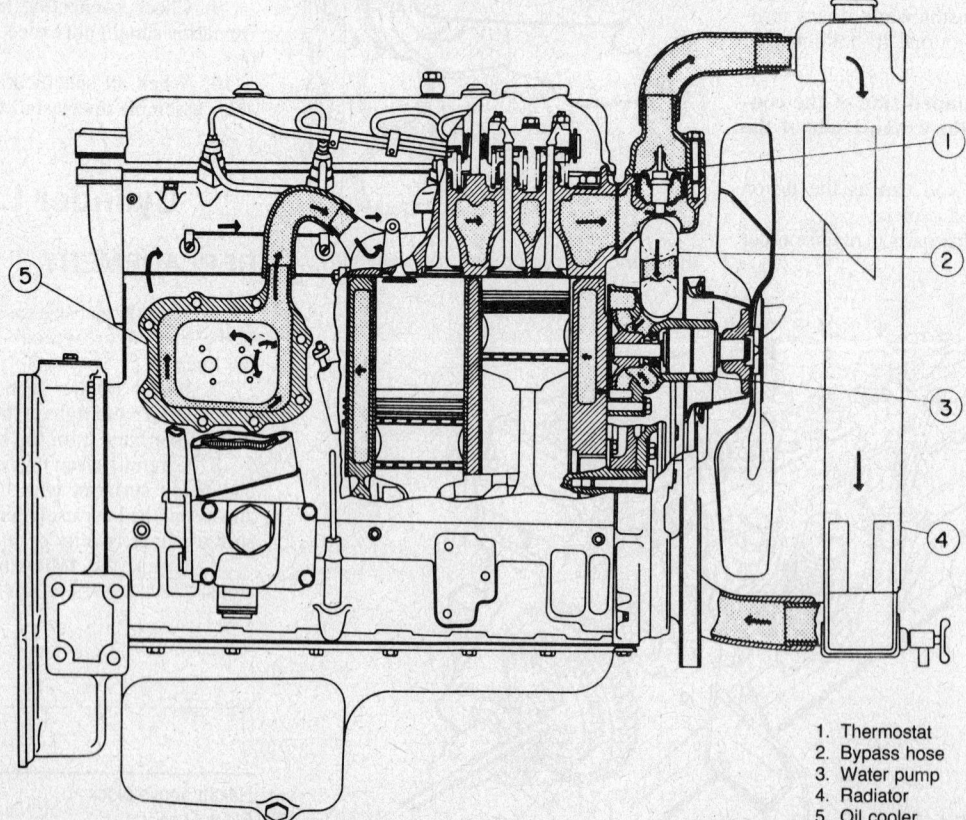

1. Thermostat
2. Bypass hose
3. Water pump
4. Radiator
5. Oil cooler

Cutaway view of the cooling system

6. Drive the seal from the housing with a brass drift.

7. Clean and check all parts for wear and damage.

8. Coat the underside of a new seal with non-hardening sealer and drive it into place in the pump body using a brass drift.

9. Force the bearing into place from the outside using a press. Install the lockwire. Leave the end of the lockwire protruding for easy removal.

10. Force the pulley hub into position with a press. The distance between the front surface of the hub and the back surface of the pump body should be 5.63″.

11. Install the snap-ring.

12. Place a .028″ feeler gauge between the impeller and the pump body and press the impeller into place.

13. Install the back plate and new gasket.

14. Install the pump on the engine.

ELECTRICAL SYSTEM

Starter

DISASSEMBLY, OVERHAUL AND ASSEMBLY

1. Separate the starter solenoid terminal-to-case connection.

2. Remove the drive pinion lever pin.

3. Remove the solenoid.

4. Remove the rear cover.

5. Remove the field coil terminal screws.

6. Using a small piece of bent wire, remove the brushes and springs.

7. Remove the brush holder and thrust washer.

8. Separate the yoke and gear case.

9. Using a wooden mallet, tap the gear case off the armature.

10. Remove the drive pinion lever.

11. Pry the pinion stop washer off the armature.

12. Remove the pinion stop and pinion assembly.

13. Remove the center bearing from the armature shaft.

14. Remove the thrust washer from the armature shaft.

15. Observe the following specifications:
Commutator undercut: .008″
Brush wear limit: .512″
Brush spring tension limit: 2.07 lbs.

16. Assembly is the reverse of disassembly. After assembly, adjust the pinion plunger gap. Gap should be .008–.059″ measured between the pinion and pinion stopper. Gap is adjusted by turning the adjusting screw on the end of the plunger.

Alternator

DISASSEMBLY, OVERHAUL AND ASSEMBLY

1. Remove pulley nut, pulley, fan, fan base, key and spacer.

2. Remove brush cover and brushes.

3. Remove the three through-bolts and separate the alternator halves.

4. Remove the bearing retainer screws and front cover.

5. Remove the felt seal.

6. Unsolder the diode connections without allowing the diodes to become excessively hot.

7. Separate the stator and rear cover.

8. Remove the SR holder from the rear cover.

9. Remove the brush holder.

10. Note the following specifications:
Rotor coil resistance: 5 ohms
Slip ring deflection limit: .012
Slip ring O.D.: 1.26″
Brush wear limit: .295″
Brush spring limit: .436 lb.

11. Assembly is the reverse of disassembly.

TURBOCHARGER

Inspection

BEARING CLEARANCE INSPECTION PROCEDURE

Whenever there is any reason to suspect that the turbocharger bearings are sufficiently worn to permit either the compressor or the turbine wheel to rub on its housing, such as when rubbing can be heard, make the following bearing clearance inspection.

— CAUTION —

Operation of a turbocharger having an excessive amount of bearing axial or radial clearance will very quickly result in irreparable damage to the turbocharger compressor, turbine, or both.

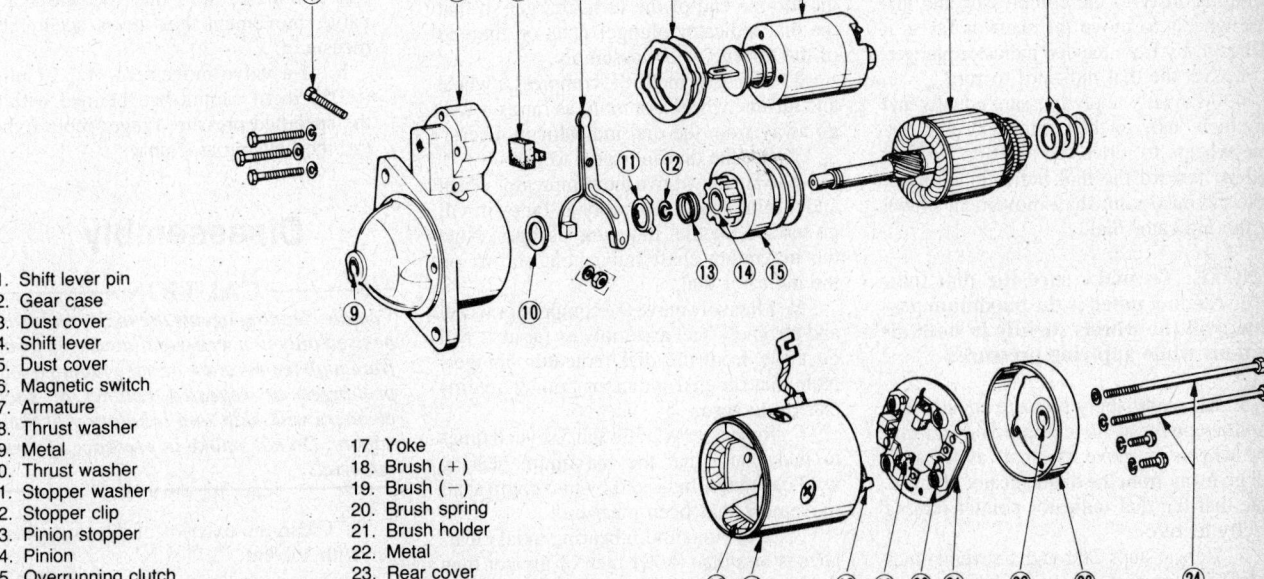

1. Shift lever pin
2. Gear case
3. Dust cover
4. Shift lever
5. Dust cover
6. Magnetic switch
7. Armature
8. Thrust washer
9. Metal
10. Thrust washer
11. Stopper washer
12. Stopper clip
13. Pinion stopper
14. Pinion
15. Overrunning clutch
16. Field coil
17. Yoke
18. Brush (+)
19. Brush (−)
20. Brush spring
21. Brush holder
22. Metal
23. Rear cover
24. Through-bolt

Typical direct drive starter motor

ENGINE REBUILDING

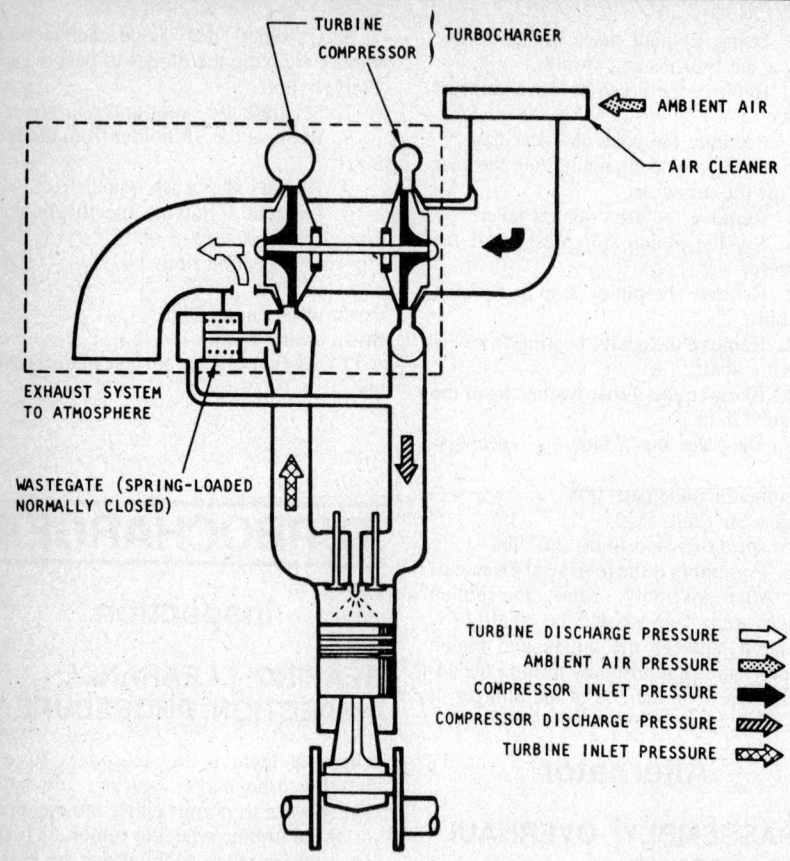

Airflow through the turbocharger

TURBINE DISCHARGE PRESSURE ⇨
AMBIENT AIR PRESSURE ▨
COMPRESSOR INLET PRESSURE ➡
COMPRESSOR DISCHARGE PRESSURE ▥
TURBINE INLET PRESSURE ⤃

With the turbocharger removed from the engine, check the journal bearings for radial clearance as follows:

1. Attach a turbocharger gauge set to the center housing so that the indicator plunger extends through the oil outlet port and contacts the shaft of the turbine wheel assembly.

2. Manually apply pressure equally and simultaneously to the compressor and turbine wheels to move the shaft as far as it will go away from the dial indicator plunger.

3. Set the dial indicator to zero.

4. Manually apply pressure equally and simultaneously to the compressor and turbine wheels to move the shaft as far as it will go toward the dial indicator plunger. Note the maximum shaft movement shown on the indicator dial.

NOTE: To make sure the dial indicator reading noted is the maximum possible, roll the wheels slightly in both directions while applying pressure.

5. Manually apply pressure equally and simultaneously to the compressor and turbine wheels to move the shaft as far as it will go away from the dial indicator plunger. Note that the dial indicator pointer returns exactly to zero.

6. Repeat steps 2 through 5 several times to make sure that the maximum bearing radial clearance, indicated by maximum shaft movement, has been measured.

7. If the maximum bearing radial clearance is less than 0.003 inch or greater than 0.006 inch, replace the CHRA. Before starting the engine, find the cause of CHRA failure by troubleshooting the engine.

With the turbocharger removed from the engine, check the thrust bearing for axial clearance as follows:

1. Attach a turbocharger gauge set at the turbine end of the turbocharger so that the dial indicator plunger rests on the end of the turbine wheel assembly.

2. Manually move the compressor wheel and turbine wheel assembly as far as it will go away from the dial indicator plunger.

3. Set the dial indicator to zero.

4. Manually move the compressor wheel and turbine wheel assembly as far as it will go toward the dial indicator plunger. Note the maximum shaft movement shown on the indicator dial.

5. Manually move the compressor wheel and turbine wheel assembly as far as it will go away from the dial indicator plunger. Note that the dial indicator pointer returns exactly to zero.

6. Repeat steps 2 through 5 several times to make sure that the maximum bearing axial clearance, indicated by maximum shaft movement, has been measured.

7. If the maximum bearing axial clearance is less than 0.001 inch or greater than 0.003 inch, replace the CHRA. Before starting the engine, find the cause of CHRA failure by troubleshooting the engine.

WASTEGATE INSPECTION AND FUNCTIONAL TEST

Whenever there is reason to think that the wastegate may not be operating properly, inspect and test it as follows:

1. Clean the exterior of the turbocharger with solvent.

2. Flatten tabs on lockplates (11), and remove nuts (10), lockplates, cover (12), and gasket (13).

3. Inspect the wastegate poppet valve and seat for scoring, wear, or erosion. Use solvent and a wire brush to remove any carbon build-up at the valve. Do not immerse the turbine housing assembly in solvent.

4. Inspect the sensing hose (2) for proper routing, connections, and condition.

5. Test wastegate operation as follows:

a. Remove hose clamps (1) and hose (2) from turbocharger.

b. Attach a turbocharger gauge set at the turbine end of the turbocharger so that the dial indicator plunger rests on the flat face of the wastegate poppet valve.

c. Set the dial indicator to zero.

d. While gently tapping the turbine housing with a soft mallet, apply calibration air pressure 8.32–8.89 psi to the wastegate sensing port.

— CAUTION —
The wastegate is designed to allow a small bleed-off of pressure. Make sure the specified pressure is maintained at the sensing port during this test.

e. Note the valve movement shown on the indicator dial.

f. Release the air pressure at the sensing port. Note that the dial indicator pointer returns exactly to zero.

g. Repeat steps c through f several times to make sure that the wastegate valve movement has been accurately measured.

h. If a valve movement of 1.27 mm (0.050 inch) cannot be obtained within the specified pressure range, replace the turbine housing assembly.

Disassembly

— CAUTION —
Volatile cleaning agents are toxic, and must be used only in a well-ventilated area away from high temperature or open flame. Avoid prolonged or repeated contact of such cleaners with skin and inhalation of their vapors. Do not smoke in presence of these materials.

1. Clean the exterior of the turbocharger with solvent.

NOTE: Scribe a matchmark on the compressor housing and the center housing for orientation during reassembly.

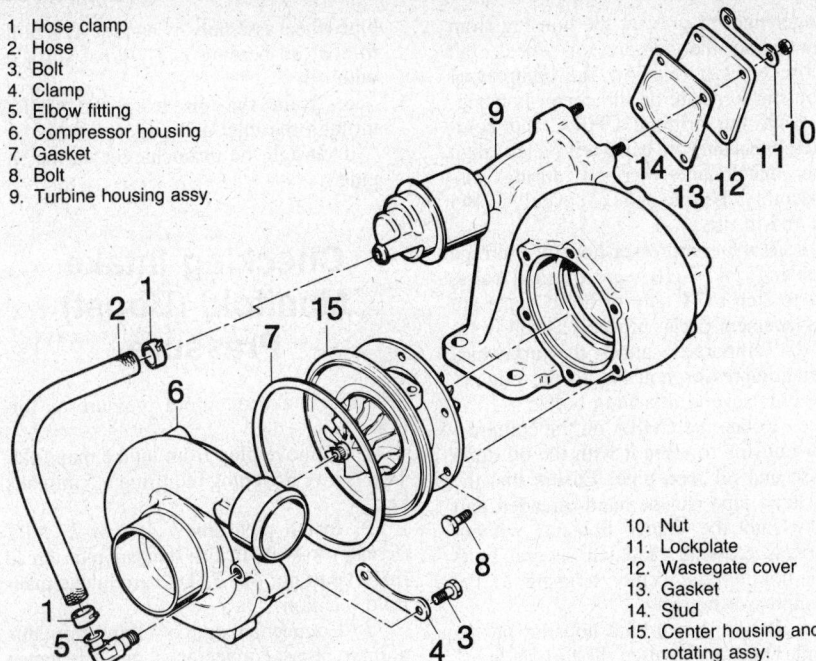

1. Hose clamp
2. Hose
3. Bolt
4. Clamp
5. Elbow fitting
6. Compressor housing
7. Gasket
8. Bolt
9. Turbine housing assy.

10. Nut
11. Lockplate
12. Wastegate cover
13. Gasket
14. Stud
15. Center housing and rotating assy.

Exploded view of the turbocharger

2. Remove hose clamps (1) and hose (2) from turbocharger.

3. Hold compressor housing assembly (6) in a vise with the housing inlet down. Remove bolts (3) and clamps (4).

———— **CAUTION** ————
When removing the compressor housing, avoid damaging the compressor wheel blades.

4. Carefully lift the CHRA and turbine housing straight up. If the housings are frozen together, rotate the CHRA and turbine housing using a pipe wrench or similar tool.

5. If elbow fitting (5) is damaged, remove it from the compressor housing.

6. Remove gasket (7) from the center housing.

NOTE: Scribe a matchmark on the turbine housing and the center housing for orientation during reassembly.

7. Hold the turbine housing assembly (9) in a vise with the housing outlet down. Remove bolts (8).

NOTE: When removing the turbine housing assembly, avoid damaging the turbine wheel blades.

8. Carefully lift CHRA (15) straight up.

NOTE: Clamp ring remains assembled to CHRA.

9. Flatten tabs of lockplates (11) and remove nuts (10), lockplates, cover (12), and gasket (13) from turbine housing assembly (9).

10. If studs (14) are damaged, remove from turbine housing assembly.

Cleaning

———— **CAUTION** ————
Volatile cleaning agents are toxic, and must be used only in a well-ventilated area away from high temperature or open flame. Avoid prolonged or repeated contact of such cleaners with skin and inhalation of their vapors. Do not smoke in presence of these materials. Do not use abrasive cleaning methods that could damage machined surfaces. Before cleaning, inspect all parts for burning, rubbing, or impact damage that might not be evident after cleaning.

Clean all parts in a non-caustic cleaning solution. Use a soft bristle brush, a plastic-blade scraper, and low-pressure filtered compressed air to remove all residue. Do not immerse the CHRA or the turbine housing assembly in solvent.

Inspection

Inspect the compressor housing assembly for the following defects:

1. Rubbing of the compressor wheel.

2. Worn, stripped, or crossed threads and corrosion in tapped holes.

3. Nicks, dents, or warpage that could prevent proper sealing between the counterbore and the backplate assembly.

Inspect the turbine housing and wastegate assembly for the following defects:

1. Rubbing of the turbine wheel.

2. Worn, stripped, or crossed threads and corrosion in tapped holes.

3. Nicks, dents, or warpage that could prevent proper sealing between the counterbore and the center housing.

4. Scoring, wear, or erosion on the face or seat of the wastegate valve.

5. Nicks, dents, or warpage on the wastegate cover sealing surface.

6. Damage to the wastegate cover locating studs.

Check the compressor wheel for the following defects:

1. Blade damage due to rubbing on the compressor housing.

2. Blade damage due to impact with ingested objects.

3. Blade tip erosion from ingested sand and dirt.

Check the turbine wheel assembly for the following defects:

1. Blade damage due to rubbing on the turbine housing.

2. Blade damage due to impact with objects expelled from the engine.

3. Blade tip erosion.

Check the center housing (15) for the following defects:

1. Surface defects, warpage, or corrosion of the oil inlet and outlet ports.

2. Worn, stripped, or crossed threads in tapped holes.

3. Damage to the ring clamp that would prevent proper sealing between the center housing and the turbine housing assembly.

Repair and Replacement

IH recommends 100 percent replacement of the parts listed at each overhaul or whenever the turbocharger is disassembled and these parts are removed.

Repair or replace all other parts and assemblies as follows:

1. Clean up light wheel rub on the compressor housing with silicone carbide abrasive cloth. If more than light clean-up is required, replace the housing.

2. Clean the turbine housing wastegate valve and seat with solvent and a wire brush. If heavy carbon build-up cannot be removed, replace the turbine housing assembly.

3. Replace all parts that do not meet inspection requirements.

Assembly

Reassemble the turbocharger as follows:

1. If studs (14) were removed, lightly coat tapped threads in turbine housing (9) with Fel-Pro or equivalent high-temperature antiseize compound and install new studs. Torque to 150 to 190 inch-pounds.

2. Apply a coat of Fel-Pro or equivalent high-temperature antiseize compound to the threads of studs (14) and nuts (10) before reassembly.

3. Install gasket (13) with raised side of bead against turbine housing assembly (9).

4. Install cover (12), lockplates (11),

and nuts (10). Torque nuts to 80 to 100 inch-pounds. Bend up tabs of lockplates.

5. Hold the turbine housing assembly in a vise with the housing outlet down.

6. Apply a coat of Fel-Pro or equivalent high-temperature antiseize compound to the threads of bolts (8) before installation.

CAUTION

Excessive looseness of the turbine housing can damage the turbine wheel and ruin the CHRA.

---

7. Carefully lower CHRA (15) onto turbine housing. Install bolts (8):

a. If either the CHRA or the turbine housing is new, tighten bolts finger-tight so that the turbine housing cannot contact the turbine wheel, but loose enough to allow the turbine housing to rotate on the center housing.

b. If the original CHRA and turbine housing assembly are being reinstalled, align the matchmarks scribed during disassembly. Torque bolts (8) evenly to 164 to 181 inch-pounds.

8. If removed, install new elbow fitting (5) in compressor housing (6). Coat fitting threads with Loctite® or equivalent pipe thread sealant and install fitting 5½ to 6½ turns into housing.

9. Place gasket (7) on CHRA.

CAUTION

Excessive looseness of the compressor housing can damage the compressor wheel and ruin the CHRA. Excessive rotation of the compressor housing can ruin the gasket.

---

10. Lower compressor housing (6) onto CHRA and turbine housing assembly as close to the original alignment as possible. Make sure the gasket stays in place.

11. Install clamps (4) and bolts (3):

a. If either the CHRA or the compressor housing is new, tighten the bolts

finger-tight to prevent the housing from contacting the compressor wheel, but loose enough to allow the compressor housing to rotate on the center housing.

b. If the original CHRA and compressor housing are being reinstalled, align the matchmarks scribed during disassembly. Torque bolts (3) evenly to 145 to 165 in. lbs.

c. If the compressor housing, turbine housing, and CHRA are original parts, go to step m. If any of these items are replacement parts, proceed as follows:

d. Temporarily attach the turbocharger compressor housing to the engine. Tighten several attaching bolts.

e. Rotate the CHRA on the compressor housing to align it with the oil drain hose and oil feed pipe. Ensure that the oil feed pipe can be hand-threaded part way into the center housing without threads crossing. Tighten several bolts (3) holding the center housing to the compressor housing.

f. Rotate the turbine housing on the center housing to align the turbine housing mounting holes with the holes of the support bracket on the engine. Connect turbocharger exhaust inlet pipe to the turbine housing. Tighten several bolts (8) holding the turbine housing to the center housing.

g. Remove the turbocharger from the engine.

h. Torque all turbine housing attaching bolts (8) to 164 to 181 in. lbs. Torque all compressor housing attaching bolts (3) to 145 to 165 in. lbs.

NOTE: Scribe matchmarks on new housings for future reference.

12. Install hose (2) and secure with hose clamps (1).

13. If a new CHRA was installed, preoil the turbocharger as follows before mounting the unit on the engine:

a. Fill the oil inlet port with clean engine oil.

b. Turn the compressor wheel and tur-

bine wheel assembly by hand several turns to coat all bearing and journal surfaces with oil.

c. Drain the oil from the CHRA through the inlet and outlet ports.

d. Install the turbocharger on the engine.

Checking Intake Manifold (Boost) Pressure

Measure intake manifold pressure as follows:

1. Remove plug from intake manifold. This is a ⅛ BSP plug requiring a 5 mm hex key.

2. Install pipe elbow 45°, ⅛-27 NPT (female) × ⅛-28 British standard pipe thread (male) part no. 477 754-C1, to intake manifold location.

3. Connect a length of tubing from this point to 30 psi connector on pressure gauge kit panel (SE-2239).

In view of the limited availability of tachometers for diesel adaptation and the absence of a mechanical drive on this engine, the rpm versus mph for all tire sizes, axle ratios and transmission ratios is being provided. They are as follows:

MPH (Miles Per Hour)	RPM Range Due to Tire Size And Axle Ratio
56 High Gear	2450–2800
35 3rd Gear, T-427	2475–2650
40 3rd Gear, T-428	2450–2650

4. Normal turbocharger (boost) pressure should be 365 mm Hg (5.8–7.3 psi) at full load from 2400 to 2800 rpm.

5. Should (boost) pressure be below 4.9 psi, inspect induction system, i.e., air cleaner element, hoses, pipes, turbocharger, etc.

Brakes

INDEX

BEFORE SERVICING, SEE THE SAFETY NOTICE AT THE FRONT OF THE BOOK

BRAKES

HYDRAULIC BRAKE SYSTEM TROUBLE DIAGNOSIS

Condition	Possible Cause	Correction
Insufficient brakes	1. Improper brake adjustment. 2. Worn lining. 3. Sticking brakes. 4. Brake valve pressure low. 5. Slack adjuster to diaphragm rod not adjusted properly. 6. Master cylinder low on brake fluid.	1. Adjust brakes. 2. Replace brake lining and adjust brakes. 3. Lubricate brake pivots and support platforms. 4. Inspect for leaks and obstructed brake lines. 5. Adjust slack adjuster. 6. Fill master cylinder and inspect for leaks.
Brakes apply slowly	1. Improper brake adjustment or lack of lubrication. 2. Low air pressure. 3. Brake valve delivery pressure low. 4. Excessive leakage with brakes applied. 5. Restriction in brake line or hose.	1. Adjust brakes and lubricate linkage. 2. Check belt tension and compressor for output. Adjust as necessary. 3. Check valve pressure and clean or replace as necessary. 4. Inspect all fittings and lines for leaks and repair as necessary. 5. Clean or replace brake line or hose.
Spongy pedal	1. Air in hydraulic system. 2. Swollen rubber parts due to contaminated brake fluid. 3. Improper brake shoe adjustment. 4. Brake fluid with low boiling point. 5. Brake drums ground excessively.	1. Fill and bleed hydraulic system. 2. Clean hydraulic system and recondition wheel cylinders and master cylinder. 3. Adjust brakes. 4. Flush hydraulic system and refill with proper brake fluid. 5. Replace brake drums.
Erratic brakes	1. Linings soaked with grease or brake fluid. 2. Primary and secondary shoes mounted in wrong position.	1. Correct the leak and replace brake lining. 2. Match the primary and secondary shoes and mount in proper position.
Chattering brakes	1. Improper adjustment of brake shoes. 2. Loose front wheel bearings. 3. Hard spots in brake drums. 4. Out-of-round brake drums. 5. Grease or brake fluid on lining.	1. Adjust brakes. 2. Clean, pack and adjust wheel bearings. 3. Grind or replace brake drums. 4. Grind or replace brake drums. 5. Correct leak and replace brake lining.
Squealing brakes	1. Incorrect lining. 2. Distorted brakedrum. 3. Bent brake support plate. 4. Bent brake shoes. 5. Foreign material embedded in brake lining. 6. Dust or dirt in brake drum. 7. Shoes dragging on support plate. 8. Loose support plate. 9. Loose anchor bolts. 10. Loose lining on brake shoes or improperly ground lining.	1. Install correct lining. 2. Grind or replace brake drum. 3. Replace brake support plate. 4. Replace brake shoes. 5. Replace brake shoes. 6. Use compressed air and blow out drums and support plate and shoes. 7. Sand support plate platforms and lubricate. 8. Tighten support plate attaching nuts. 9. Tighten anchor bolts. 10. Replace brake shoes and cam-grind lining.
Brakes fading	1. Improper brake adjustment. 2. Improper brake lining. 3. Improper type of brake fluid. 4. Brake drums ground excessively.	1. Adjust brakes correctly. 2. Replace brake lining. 3. Drain, flush and refill hydraulic system. 4. Replace brake drums.
Dragging brakes	1. Improper brake adjustment. 2. Distorted cylinder cups. 3. Brake shoe seized on anchor bolt. 4. Broken brake shoe return spring. 5. Loose anchor bolt. 6. Distorted brake shoe. 7. Loose wheel bearings.	1. Correct adjust brakes. 2. Recondition or replace cylinder. 3. Clean and lubricate anchor bolt. 4. Replace brake shoe return spring. 5. Adjust and tighten anchor bolt. 6. Replace defective brake shoes. 7. Lubricate and adjust wheel bearings.

HYDRAULIC BRAKE SYSTEM TROUBLE DIAGNOSIS

Condition	Possible Cause	Correction
	8. Obstruction in brake line.	8. Clean or replace brake line.
	9. Swollen cups in wheel cylinder or master cylinder.	9. Recondition wheel or master cylinder.
	10. Master cylinder linkage improperly adjusted.	10. Correctly adjust master cylinder linkage.
Hard pedal	1. Incorrect brake lining.	1. Install matched brake lining.
	2. Incorrect brake adjustment.	2. Adjust brakes and check fluid.
	3. Frozen brake pedal linkage.	3. Free up and lubricate brake linkage.
	4. Restricted brake line or hose.	4. Clean out or replace brake line hose.
Wheel locks	1. Loose or torn brake lining.	1. Replace brake lining.
	2. Incorrect wheel bearing adjustment.	2. Clean, pack and adjust wheel bearings.
	3. Wheel cylinder cups sticking.	3. Recondition or replace the wheel cylinder.
	4. Saturated brake lining.	4. Reline front, rear or all four brakes.
Brakes fade (high speed)	1. Improper brake adjustment.	1. Adjust brakes and check fluid.
	2. Distorted or out of round brake drums.	2. Grind or replace the drums.
	3. Overheated brake drums.	3. Inspect for dragging brakes.
	4. Incorrect brake fluid (low boiling temperature).	4. Drain flush and refill and bleed the hydraulic brake system.
	5. Saturated brake lining.	5. Reline brakes as necessary.

HYDRAULIC BRAKES

General Information

Servicing the hydraulic system is chiefly a matter of adjustments, replacement of worn or damaged parts and correcting the damage caused by grit, dirt or contaminated brake fluid. It is highly important to make sure the brake system is clean and tightly sealed when a brake job is completed and that only approved heavy duty brake fluid is used.

The approved heavy duty type brake fluid retains the correct consistency throughout the widest range of temperature variation, will not affect rubber cups, helps protect the metal parts of the brake system against failure and assures long trouble-free brake operation.

Never use brake fluid from a container that has been used for any other liquid. Mineral oil, alcohol, anti-freeze, or cleaning solvents, even in very small quantities, will contaminate brake fluid. Contaminated brake fluid will cause piston cups and the valve in the master cylinder to swell or deteriorate.

Brake adjustment is required after installation of new or relined brake shoes. Adjustment is also necessary whenever excessive travel of pedal is needed to start braking action.

LOW PEDAL

Normal brake lining wear reduces pedal reserve. Low pedal reserve may also be caused by the lack of brake fluid in the master cylinder. The wear condition may be compensated for by a minor brake adjustment. Check fluid level in master cylinder and add as required.

FLUID LOSS

If the master cylinder requires constant addition of hydraulic fluid, fluid may be leaking past the piston cups in the master cylinder or brake cylinders, the hydraulic lines; hoses or connections may be loose or broken. Loose connections should be tightened, or other necessary repairs or parts replacement made and the hydraulic brake system bled.

FLUID CONTAMINATION

To determine if contamination exists in the brake fluid, as indicated by swollen, deteriorated rubber cups, the following tests can be made.

Place a small amount of the drained brake fluid into a small clear glass bottle. Separation of the fluid into distinct layers will indicate mineral oil content. Be safe and discard old brake fluid that has been bled from the system. Fluid drained from the bleeding operation may contain dirt particles or other contamination and should not be reused.

BRAKE ADJUSTMENT

Normally self adjusting brakes will not require manual adjustment but in the event of a brake reline it may be advisable to make the initial adjustment manually to speed up adjusting time.

AUTOMATIC ADJUSTER CHECK

Place vehicle on a hoist, with a helper in the driver's seat to apply brakes. Remove plug from rear adjustment to observe adjuster star wheel. Then, to exclude possibility of maximum adjustment; that is, the adjuster refuses to operate because the closest possible adjustment has been reached; the star wheel should be backed off approximately 30 notches. It will be necessary to hold adjuster lever away from star wheel to allow backing off of the adjustment.

Spin the wheel and brake drum in reverse direction and apply brakes vigorously. This will provide the necessary inertia to cause the secondary brake shoe to leave the anchor. The wrap up effect will move the secondary shoe, and cable will pull the adjuster lever up. Upon release of brake pedal, the lever should snap downward, turning star wheel. Thus, a definite rotation of adjuster star wheel can be observed if automatic adjuster is working properly. If by the described procedure one or more automatic adjusters do not function properly, the respective drum must be removed for adjuster servicing.

HYDRAULIC LINE REPAIR

Steel tubing is used in the hydraulic lines between the master cylinder and the front brake tube connector, and between the rear brake tube connector and the rear brake cylinders. Flexible hoses connect the brake tube to the front brake cylinders and to the rear brake tube connector.

When replacing hydraulic brake tubing, hoses, or connectors, tighten all connections securely. After replacement, bleed the

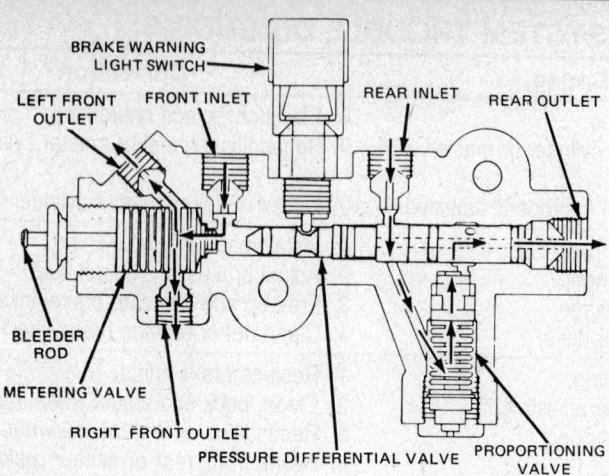

Typical light duty pressure differential valve

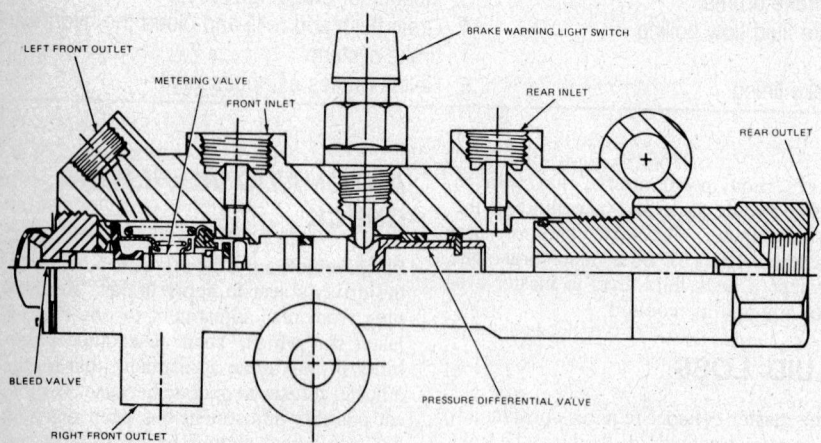

Typical heavy duty pressure differential valve

brake system at the wheel cylinders and at the booster, if so equipped.

BRAKE TUBE

If a section of the brake tube becomes damaged, the entire section should be replaced with tubing of the same type, size, shape, and length. Copper tubing should not be used in the hydraulic system. When bending brake tubing to fit the frame or rear-axle contours, be careful not to kink or crack the tube.

All brake tubing should be double flared to provide good leak-proof connections. Always clean the inside of a new brake tube with clean isopropyl alcohol.

BRAKE HOSE

A flexible brake hose should be replaced if it shows signs of softening, cracking, or other damage.

When installing a new brake hose, position the hose to avoid contact with other truck parts.

Pressure Differential Switch

The hydraulic system safety switch is used to warn vehicle operator that one of the hydraulic systems has failed. A failure in one part of the brake system does not result in failure of the entire hydraulic brake system.

As an example, failure of rear brake system will leave front brake system still operative.

As pressure falls in one system the other system's normal pressure forces piston to inoperative side contacting switch terminal, causing a red warning light to come on in instrument panel, thus, warning operator of vehicle that one of the systems has failed and should be repaired.

The safety switch body is mounted in a vertical position, with the brake tubes connected to opposite sides.

The component parts of the switch body are not serviced. However, terminal unit can be removed if a malfunction occurs and a new terminal unit installed.

CENTRALIZING THE PRESSURE DIFFERENTIAL VALVE

1. Turn the ignition switch to the ACC or ON position. Loosen the pressure differential valve inlet tube nut of the system that remained operative, or the side opposite the system that was bled last. Operate the brake pedal carefully and gradually until the pressure differential valve is returned to a centralized position and the brake warning light goes out. Tighten the tube nut.

2. Check the fluid level in the master cylinder reservoirs and fill them to within ¼" of the top with the specified brake fluid.

3. Turn the ignition switch to the OFF position.

WITH SPLIT HYDRAULIC BRAKES

The pressure differential valve used with the split hydraulic brake system has a self-centering spring. Use the following procedure to reset the valve:

1. Remove the switch connector wire.

2. Remove the threaded hex-shaped electrical switch body from the center of the valve. This allows the valve centering springs to re-position the valve.

3. Install the electrical switch and connect the wire.

4. Apply the brakes a few times and check the operation of the warning light. The light should go on with the ignition switch in the START position only.

Bleeding Brakes

MANUAL BLEEDING
Dual-Brake System

HYDRAULIC MASTER CYLINDER

The primary and secondary hydraulic brake systems are individual systems and are bled separately. Bleed the longest line first on the individual system being serviced. *During the complete bleeding operation, do not allow the reservoir to run dry. Keep the master cylinder reservoirs filled with the specified brake fluid. Never use brake fluid that has been drained from the hydraulic system.*

1. Bleed the master cylinder at the outlet port side of the system being serviced.

NOTE: On a master cylinder without bleed screws, loosen the master cylinder to hydraulic line nut. Operate the brake pedal slowly until the brake fluid at the outlet connection is free of bubbles, then tighten the tube nut to the specified torque. Do not use the secondary piston stop screw located on the bottom of the master cylinder to bleed the brake system. Loosening or removing this screw

could result in damage to the secondary piston or stop screw. Operate the brake pedal slowly until the brake fluid at the outlet connection is free of air bubbles, then tighten the bleed screw.

2. Position a suitable ⅜" box wrench on the bleeder fitting on the brake wheel cylinder. Attach a rubber drain tube to the bleeder fitting. The end of the tube should fit snugly around the bleeder fitting.

3. Submerge the free end of the tube in a container partially filled with clean brake fluid, and loosen the bleeder fitting approximately ¾ turn.

4. Push the brake pdeal down slowly thru its full travel. Close the bleeder fitting, then return the pedal to the fully-released position. Repeat this operation until air bubbles cease to appear at the submerged end of the bleeder tube.

5. When the fluid is completely free of air bubbles, close the bleeder fitting and remove the bleeder tube.

6. Repeat this procedure at the brake wheel cyliinder on the opposite side. Refill the master cylinder reservoir after each wheel cylinder is bled.

When the bleeding operation is complete, the master cylinder fluid level should be filled to within ¼" from the top of the reservoirs.

7. Centralize the pressure differential valve.

Master Cylinder Service

BENDIX TANDEM

Diassembly

1. Clean the outside of the master cylinder assembly. Remove the residual pressure valves.

2. Remove the tube seats by installing "easy outs" firmly into the seats. Tap lightly with a hammer to loosen, remove seats.

3. Slide clamp off master cylinder cover and remove the cover and its gasket. Drain the brake fluid from the master cylinder.

4. Remove the snap-ring from the open end of the cylinder with snap ring pliers. Remove the washer from cylinder bore.

5. Remove the front piston retaining screw. Carefully remove the rear piston assembly.

6. Remove the front piston assembly.

Cleaning and Inspection

1. Clean all parts with a suitable solvent and dry with filtered compressed air. Wash cylinder bore with clean brake fluid and check for damage or wear.

2. If cylinder bore is lightly scratched or shows slight corrosion it can be cleaned with crocus cloth. Heavier scratches or corrosion can be removed by honing, provid-

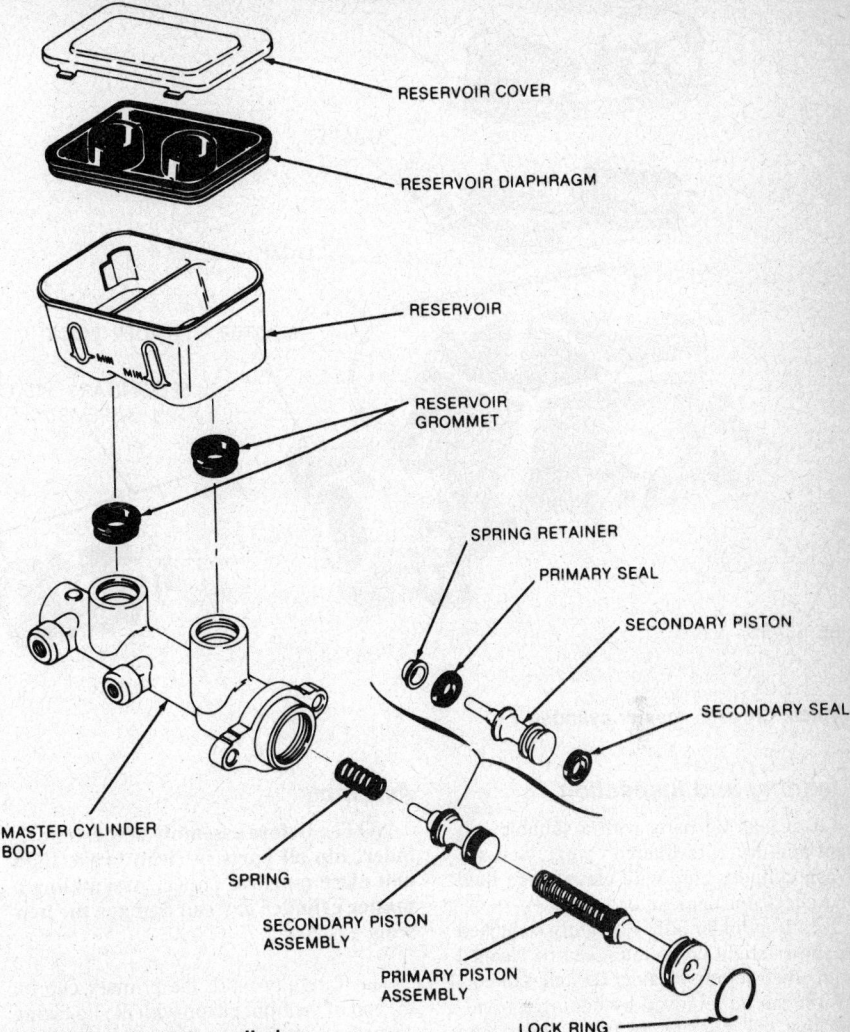

RESERVOIR COVER

RESERVOIR DIAPHRAGM

RESERVOIR

RESERVOIR GROMMET

SPRING RETAINER

PRIMARY SEAL

SECONDARY PISTON

SECONDARY SEAL

MASTER CYLINDER BODY

SPRING

SECONDARY PISTON ASSEMBLY

PRIMARY PISTON ASSEMBLY

LOCK RING

Typical Delco master cylinder

ing that diameter of cylinder bore is not increased by more than .002 inch. If master cylinder bore does not clean up at .002 inch when honed, the master cylinder should be replaced.

3. If master cylinder pistons are badly scored or corroded, replace them with new ones. All caps and seals should be replaced when rebuilding a master cylinder.

Assembly

NOTE: Before assembly of master cylinder, dip all parts in clean brake fluid and place on clean paper. Assembling master cylinder dry can damage rubber seals.

1. Coat master cylinder bore with brake fluid and carefully slide the front piston into cylinder body.

2. Slide the rear piston assembly into the cylinder bore. Compress pistons and install the front piston retaining screw.

3. Position washer in cylinder bore and secure with snap-ring.

4. Install the residual pressure valve and spring in the outlet port and install tube seats firmly.

CHRYSLER TANDEM

Disassembly

1. Clean the outside of the master cylinder assembly. Remove the master cylinder cover and drain the brake fluid.

2. Remove the front piston retainer screw from inside reservoir and the snapring from the outer end of cylinder bore. Slide the rear piston assembly out of cylinder bore.

3. Tamp the master cylinder assembly lightly on bench, open end down, to remove the front piston and spring. If the front piston sticks in cylinder bore, use air pressure to force it out.

4. Remove the front piston compression spring from the cylinder bore.

5. Remove the tube seats by installing "easy outs" firmly into the seats. Tap lightly with a hammer to loosen, remove the seats.

6. Take note of the position of cup lips and remove them from pistons. DO NOT remove the center cup of the rear piston. If this cup is damaged or worn, install a new rear piston assembly.

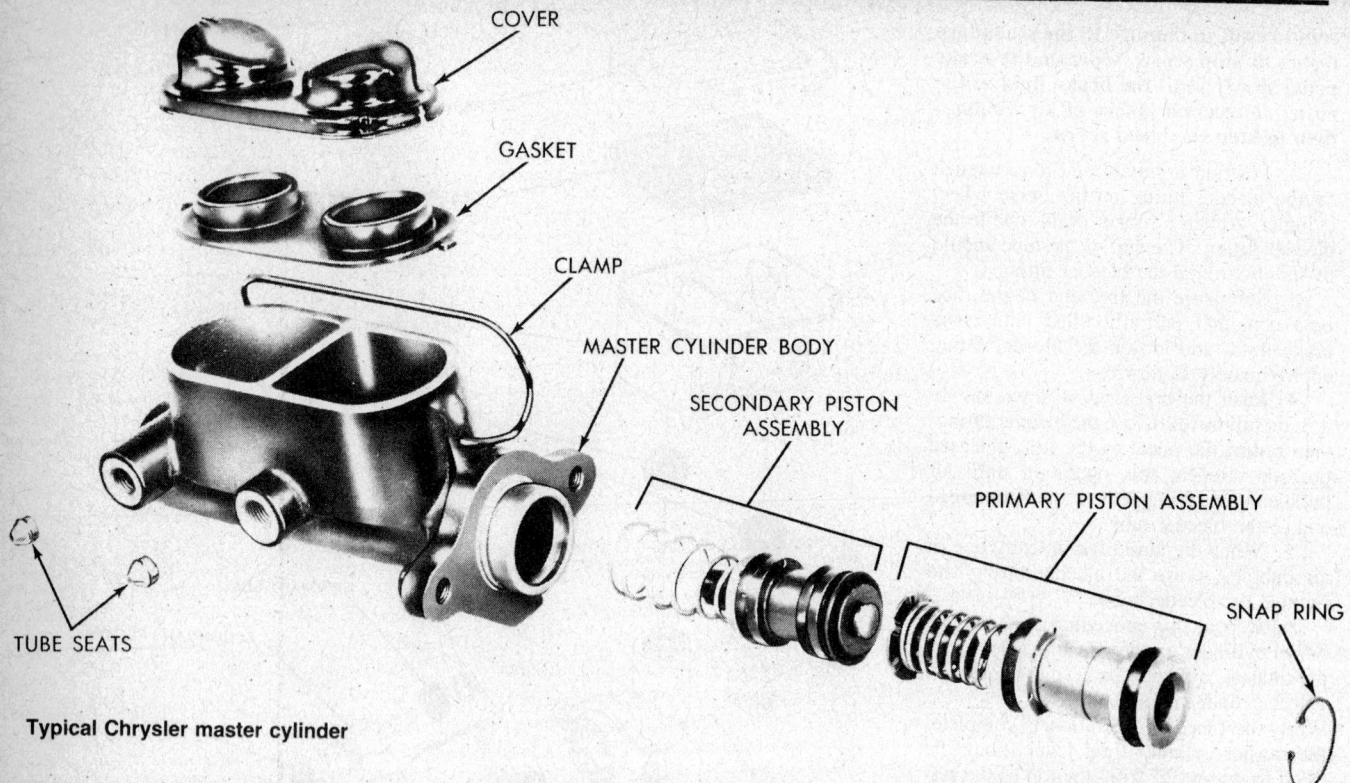

Typical Chrysler master cylinder

Typical Ford master cylinder

Cleaning and Inspection

1. Clean all parts with a suitable solvent and dry with filtered compressed air. Wash cylinder bore with clean brake fluid and check for damage or wear.

2. If cylinder bore is slightly scratched or shows slight corrosion it can be cleaned with crocus cloth. Heavier scratches or corrosion can be removed by honing, providing that the diameter of the cylinder bore is not increased by more than .002 inch. If master cylinder bore does not clean up at .002 inch when honed, the master cylinder should be replaced.

3. If master cylinder pistons are badly scored or corroded, replace them with new ones. All caps and seals should be replaced when rebuilding a master cylinder.

Assembly

NOTE: Before assembly of master cylinder, dip all parts in clean brake fluid and place on clean paper. Assembling a master cylinder dry can damage the new seals.

1. Carefully work the primary cup on the end of the front piston with the lip facing away from the piston.

2. Carefully work the second seal cup over the rear end of the piston and into the second land. Be sure that the lip of the cup is facing the front of piston.

3. Carefully work the rear secondary cup over the piston and into the rear land. The lip must face the rear of the piston.

4. Slide the cup retainer over the stem of the front piston with the beveled side away from the piston cup.

5. Position the small end of the pressure spring into the retainer, then slide the assembly into the master cylinder bore.

CAUTION

Be sure that the cups enter the cylinder bore evenly in order that the sealing quality of the cups is not damaged, keep the seals and cylinder bore well lubricated with brake fluid.

6. Carefully work the secondary cup over the rear end of the rear piston with the lip facing towards the front.

7. Center the spring retainer of the rear piston assembly over the shoulder of the front piston. Push the piston assemblies into the cylinder bore. Carefully work the cup lips into bore, then seat piston assemblies.

8. Holding the pistons in their seated position, install the piston retaining screw and tighten securely.

9. Install new tube seats. (When bench bleeding is performed, the tube seats will be correctly positioned.)

WAGNER TANDEM

Disassembly

1. Clean the outside of the master cylinder. Remove the cylinder cover screw or spring retaining clip. Lift off the cover and the diaphragm gasket and pour off excess brake fluid. Use the push rod to stroke the cylinder forcing fluid from the cylinder through the outlet ports.

2. Loosen and remove the piston stop screw and gasket from the right hand side

of the cylinder.

3. Pull back the push rod boot and remove the snap-ring from the groove in the end of the cylinder bore.

4. Remove the push rod and stop plate from the internal parts from the master cylinder. Remove the internal parts from the master cylinder. If the parts will not slide out apply air pressure at the secondary outlet port. If after applying air, parts still do not move easily, check bore carefully for extensive damage which may eliminate possibility of rebuilding master cylinder.

Inspection and Repair

1. Clean all parts in clean brake fluid. Inspect the parts for chipping, excessive wear or damage. Replace them as required. When using a master cylinder repair kit, install all the parts supplied.

2. Check all recesses, openings and internal passages to be sure they are open and free of foreign matter. Passages may be probed with soft copper wire, 0.020″ OD, or smaller.

3. Minor scratches or blemishes in the cylinder bore can be removed with crocus cloth or a clean up hone. Do not oversize the bore more than 0.007″.

Assembly

1. Dip all parts except the master cylinder in clean hydraulic brake fluid of the specified type.

2. Install the rear rubber cup on the secondary piston with the cup lip facing the rear. All other cups face the front or closed end of the cylinder.

3. Assemble and install the secondary piston spring, front cup, and the secondary piston.

4. Install the piston stop screw and gasket, making sure the screw enters the cylinder behind the rear of the secondary piston.

5. Assemble and install the primary piston and push rod parts.

6. Locate the stop plate in the seat in the bore and engage the snap ring into the groove at the rear of the cylinder.

7. Install the push rod boot onto the push rod and the groove of the cylinder housing.

8. Bleed the master cylinder.

Bench Bleeding the Master Cylinder

Before the master cylinder is installed on the vehicle, the unit should be bled.

1. Support the master cylinder body in a vise, and fill both fluid reservoirs with the specified brake fluid.

─────── CAUTION ───────
Do not tighten the vise too tightly on the master cylinder as this can cause damage to the cylinder which can not be repaired.

2. Loosely install plugs in the front and rear brake outlet bores. Depress the primary piston several times until air bubbles cease to appear in the brake fluid.

3. Tighten the plugs and attempt to depress the piston. The piston travel should be restricted after all air is expelled.

4. Remove the plugs. Install the cover and diaphragm gasket assembly, and make sure the cover screw is tightened securely.

SPLIT SYSTEM—GMC (TANDEM)

Disassembly

1. Remove the cover and reservoir seal.

2. Remove the retaining ring from the groove in the end of the cylinder of the cylinder bore.

3. Remove all parts from the cylinder bore.

4. Remove the bleeder screw valves.

Assembly

1. Clean all parts in clean brake fluid.

2. Leave a coating of brake fluid on all internal parts and install parts in the cylinder bore using new rubber seals.

3. Install retainer ring and bleeder screws.

QUICK TAKE UP—GMC

1. Depress the primary piston and remove the snap-ring.

2. Remove the primary and secondary pistons and return springs from the cylinder bore.

3. Disassemble the secondary piston.

4. Inspect the master cylinder bore. If it is corroded, replace the master cylinder. Never use abrasives on the bore.

NOTE: Always lubricate parts with clean, fresh brake fluid before assembly.

Assembly

1. Install new seals on the secondary piston.

2. Install the spring and secondary piston into the cylinder.

3. Install the primary piston, depress and install the snap-ring.

BENDIX MINI-MASTER

Diassembly

1. Remove the reservoir cover and diaphragm, and drain the fluid from the reservoir.

2. Remove the four bolts that secure the body to the reservoir using Chevrolet special socket number J-25085 or equivalent.

NOTE: Do not remove the two small filters from the inside of the reservoir unless they are damaged and are to be replaced.

3. Remove the small O-ring and the two compensating valve seals from the recessed areas on the bottom side of the reservoir.

4. Depress the primary piston using a tool with a smooth round end. Then remove the compensating valve poppets and the compensating valve springs from the compensating valve ports in the master cylinder body.

5. Remove the snap-ring at the end of the master cylinder bore. Then release the piston and remove the primary and secondary piston assemblies from the cylinder bore. It may be necessary to plug the front compensating valve port to remove the secondary piston assembly.

Assembly

1. Lubricate the secondary piston assembly and the master cylinder bore with clean brake fluid.

2. Assemble the secondary spring (shorter of the two springs) in the open end of the secondary piston actuator, and assemble the piston return spring (longer spring) on the projection at the rear of the secondary piston.

3. Insert the secondary piston assembly, actuator end first, into the master cylinder bore and press the assembly to the bottom of the bore.

4. Lubricate the primary piston assembly with clean brake fluid. Insert the primary piston assembly, actuator end first, into the bore.

5. Place the snap-ring over a smooth round ended tool and depress the pistons in the bore.

6. Assemble the retaining ring in the groove in the cylinder bore.

7. Assemble the compensating valve seals and the small O-ring seal in the recesses on the bottom of the reservoir. Be sure that all seals are fully seated.

8. While holding the pistons depressed, assemble the compensating valve springs and the compensating valve poppets in the compensating valve ports.

9. Holding the pistons compressed, position the reservoir on the master cylinder body and secure it with the four mounting bolts. Torque the bolts to 12–15 ft. lbs. (16–20 Nm).

Wheel Cylinders

Disassembly

1. In case of a leak, remove brake shoes (replace if soaked with grease or brake fluid), boots, piston wheel cylinder cups and wheel cylinder cup expansion spring.

NOTE: A slight amount of fluid on boot may not be a leak, but may be preservative oil used on assembly.

2. Wash wheel cylinder bore with clean brake fluid and inspect for scoring or pitting.

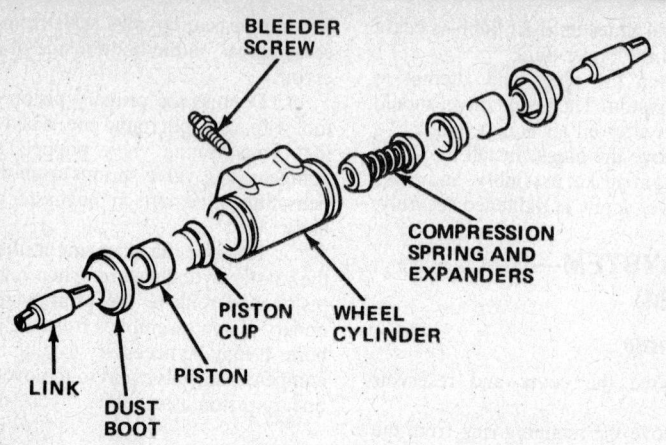

BLEEDER SCREW

COMPRESSION SPRING AND EXPANDERS

PISTON CUP

WHEEL CYLINDER

LINK

DUST BOOT

PISTON

Typical wheel cylinder

Use extreme care in cleaning the wheel cylinder after reconditioning. Remove all dust or grit by flushing the cylinder with clean brake fluid; wipe dry with a clean lintless cloth and clean a second time with brake fluid. Dry the wheel cylinder with air pressure, then flush with clean brake fluid. (Be sure the bleeder screw port and the bleeder screw are clean and open.)

Wheel cylinder bores or pistons that are badly scored or corroded should be replaced. The old piston cups should be discarded when reconditioning wheel cylinders.

Cylinder walls that have light scratches, or show signs of corrosion, can usually be cleaned with crocus cloth, using a circular motion. However, cylinders that have deep scratches or scoring may be honed, providing the diameter of the cylinder bore is not increased more than .002". A cylinder *that does not clean up at .002" should be discarded and a new cylinder installed. (Black stains on the cylinder walls are caused by the piston cups and will do no harm.)*

Should inspection reveal the necessity of installing a new wheel cylinder proceed as follows:

1. Disconnect the brake tube from wheel cylinder.

2. Remove the wheel cylinder attaching bolts, then slide wheel cylinder out of backing plate.

Assembly

Before assembling pistons and new cups in wheel cylinder, dip them in brake fluid. If boots are deteriorated, cracked or do not fit tightly on brake shoe push rod, as well as wheel cylinder casting, new boots should be installed.

1. Wash wheel cylinder with clean brake fluid and wipe dry.

2. Install expansion spring in cylinder. Install wheel cylinder cups in each end of cylinder with open end of cups facing each other.

3. Install wheel cylinder pistons in each end of cylinder with recessed end of

pistons facing open ends of cylinder.

4. Install boots over ends of cylinder. Keep assembly compressed with aid of a brake cylinder clamp until brake shoes are assembled.

Brake Service

NON-SERVO TYPE

This brake is a non-servo, floating shoe type brake. Upper ends of shoes extend through wheel cylinder boots and contact inserts in wheel cylinder pistons. Shoe ends are held firmly against pistons by the brake shoe return spring. Lower ends of shoes are held against a fixed anchor plate by the anchor spring. Hold-down spring at center of each shoe holds shoes in alignment. Lining-to-drum clearance adjustment is made through eccentric cam type adjusting studs.

Brake Shoe Removal

1. Back off brake adjustment, then remove brake drum.

2. Remove brake shoe return spring. Spread upper end of shoes until they are clear of wheel cylinders and hold-down springs, then disengage shoes from anchor plate at bottom. Remove anchor spring from shoes.

3. Do not depress brake pedal while shoes are removed.

Cleaning and Inspection

1. Clean all dirt out of brake drum. Inspect drum for roughness, scoring, or out-of-round. Replace or recondition drum as necessary.

2. Carefully pull lower edge of each wheel cylinder boot away from cylinder and note whether interior is excessively wet with brake fluid. Excessive fluid indicates leakage past piston cups, requiring overhaul of wheel cylinder.

NOTE: A slight amount of fluid is nearly always present and acts as a lubricant for pistons.

3. Check backing plate attaching bolts to make sure they are tight. Clean all rust and dirt from ledges on backing plate where shoe rims make contact using fine emery cloth.

4. Inspect the shoe return and anchor springs and hold-down springs. If broken, cracked, or weakened by rust or corrosion, replace springs.

5. If brake linings are worn to the extent that replacement is necessary, replace linings.

Brake Shoe Installation

1. Inspect brake shoe lining assemblies and make sure there are no nicks or burrs on edges of shoes which contact backing plate.

2. Apply a light film of grease at the following points: where shoe webs contact

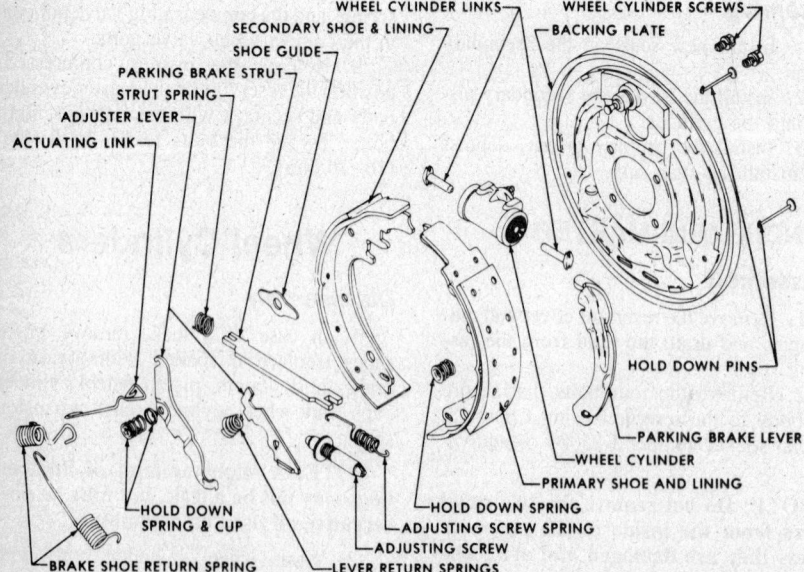

WHEEL CYLINDER LINKS

SECONDARY SHOE & LINING

SHOE GUIDE

PARKING BRAKE STRUT

STRUT SPRING

ADJUSTER LEVER

ACTUATING LINK

WHEEL CYLINDER SCREWS

BACKING PLATE

HOLD DOWN PINS

PARKING BRAKE LEVER

WHEEL CYLINDER

PRIMARY SHOE AND LINING

HOLD DOWN SPRING & CUP

HOLD DOWN SPRING

ADJUSTING SCREW SPRING

ADJUSTING SCREW

LEVER RETURN SPRINGS

BRAKE SHOE RETURN SPRING

Typical Bendix non-servo brake

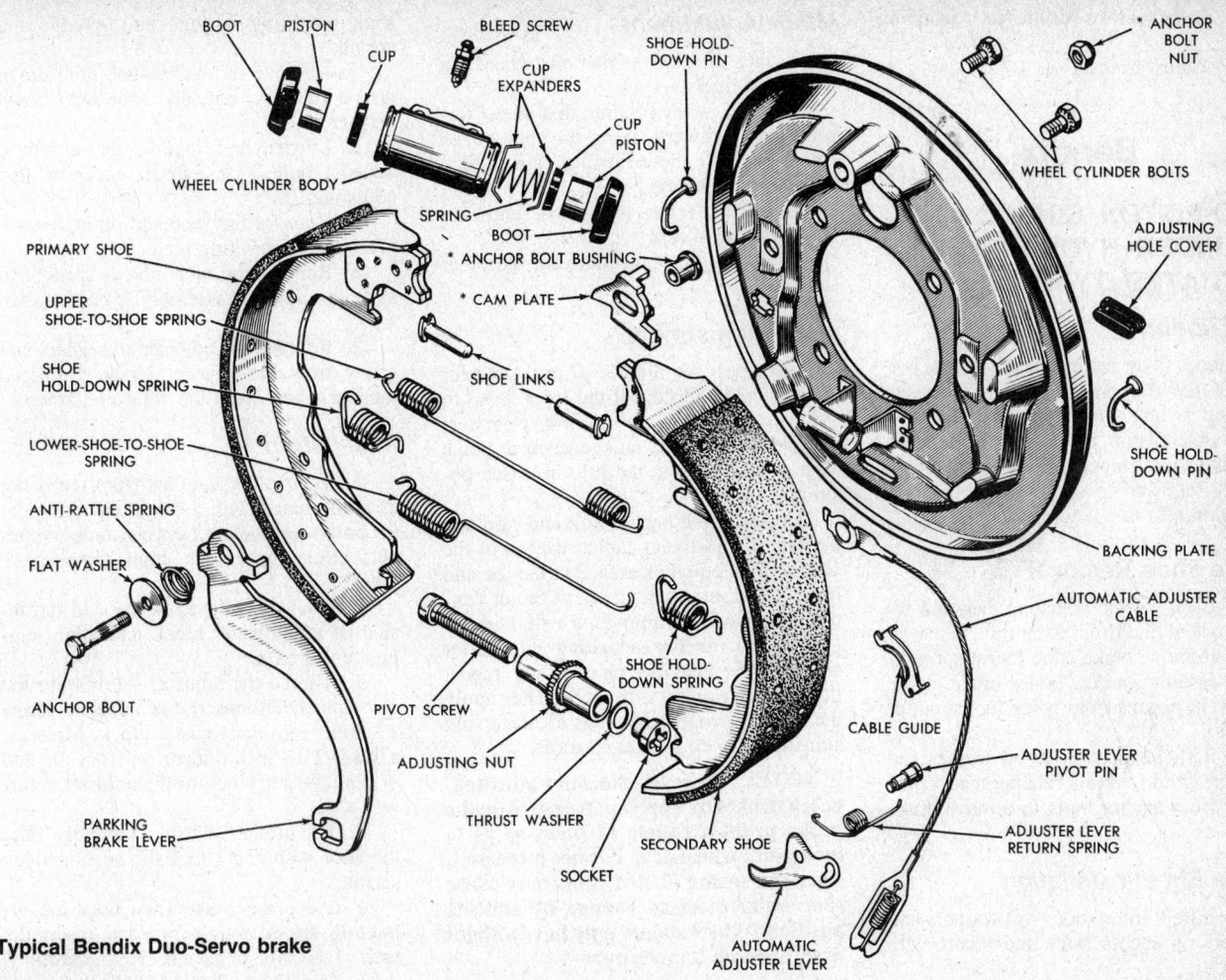

Typical Bendix Duo-Servo brake

Labels in figure:
BOOT, PISTON, CUP, BLEED SCREW, CUP EXPANDERS, SHOE HOLD-DOWN PIN, * ANCHOR BOLT NUT, WHEEL CYLINDER BODY, CUP PISTON, WHEEL CYLINDER BOLTS, SPRING, BOOT, * ANCHOR BOLT BUSHING, ADJUSTING HOLE COVER, PRIMARY SHOE, * CAM PLATE, UPPER SHOE-TO-SHOE SPRING, SHOE LINKS, SHOE HOLD-DOWN SPRING, LOWER-SHOE-TO-SHOE SPRING, SHOE HOLD-DOWN PIN, ANTI-RATTLE SPRING, BACKING PLATE, FLAT WASHER, AUTOMATIC ADJUSTER CABLE, ANCHOR BOLT, PIVOT SCREW, SHOE HOLD-DOWN SPRING, CABLE GUIDE, ADJUSTER LEVER PIVOT PIN, ADJUSTING NUT, PARKING BRAKE LEVER, THRUST WASHER, SECONDARY SHOE, ADJUSTER LEVER RETURN SPRING, SOCKET, AUTOMATIC ADJUSTER LEVER

hold-down springs; where anchor ends of shoe webs contact anchor plate; and at six places where shoe rims contact ledges on backing plate.

3. Install hold-down springs on backing plate. Hook anchor spring into slot at bottom of each shoe. Swing upper ends of shoes apart and position at backing plate, with lower ends of shoe webs engaging anchor plate and with anchor spring behind extension on anchor plate.

NOTE: The shoe with the shorter lining must be to the rear of the vehicle.

4. Swing shoes up into position with center of shoe webs engaging hold-down springs, and with upper ends inserted through wheel cylinder boots.

5. Install brake shoe return spring, being sure short end is hooked into slotted hole in rear shoe and long end in round hole in front shoe.

6. Install brake drum and wheel. Adjust brakes.

Bendix

DUO SERVO TYPE

Removing Rear Brake Shoes

1. With the vehicle elevated on a hoist, jack or suitable stand, loosen parking brake equalizer nut, remove rear wheel, and drum retaining clips. Remove drum.

2. Remove brake shoe return springs. (Note how secondary spring overlaps primary spring.)

3. Remove brake shoe retainers, springs and nails.

4. Slide eye of automatic adjuster cable off anchor and then unhook from lever. Remove cable, cable guide and anchor plate.

5. Disconnect lever spring from lever and disengage from shoe web. Remove spring and lever.

6. Spread anchor ends of the primary and secondary shoes and remove parking brake strut and spring.

7. Disengage parking brake cable from parking brake lever and remove brake assembly.

8. Remove the primary and secondary brake shoe assemblies and adjusting star wheel from support. Install wheel cylinder to hold pistons in cylinders.

Installing Rear Brake Shoes

1. Inspect the platforms of support for nicks or burrs. Apply a thin coat of lubricant to support platforms.

2. Attach parking brake lever to the back side of the secondary shoe.

3. Place the secondary and primary shoe in their relative position on a work bench.

4. Lubricate threads of adjusting screw and install it between the primary and secondary shoes with star wheel next to secondary shoe. The star adjusting wheels are stamped ''R'' (right side) and ''L'' (left side), and indicate their location on vehicle.

5. Overlap anchor ends of the primary and secondary brake shoes and install adjusting spring and lever.

6. Hold the brake shoes in their relative position and engage parking brake cable into parking brake lever.

7. Install parking brake strut and spring between the parking brake lever and primary shoe.

8. Place brake shoes on the support and install retainer nails, springs and retainers.

9. Install anchor pin plate.

10. Install ''eye'' of adjusting cable over anchor pin and install return spring between primary shoe and anchor pin.

11. Install cable guide in secondary shoe then install secondary return spring. (Be sure secondary spring overlaps primary.)

12. Place adjusting cable in groove of cable guide and engage hook of cable into adjusting lever.

13. Install brake drum and retaining clips.

14. Adjust brakes.

Bendix

TWO-PISTON SINGLE CYLINDER HYDRAULICALLY ACTUATED TYPE

Description

Both shoes pivot on anchor pins at the bottom of the support plate. The shoes are actuated by one wheel cylinder which is of the double piston type. Specification for heel and toe clearance of shoes should be strictly followed to obtain efficient brake operation.

Brake Shoe Removal

1. Back off the adjusting cam and remove wheel and drum assembly.

2. Remove brake shoe return spring.

3. Install wheel cylinder brake clamp to prevent pistons from being forced out of cylinder.

4. Remove C-washer, oil washer and retainer, guide spring retainer and guide spring from anchor bolts to remove brake shoes.

Brake Shoe Installation

1. Install brake shoes, oil washers and retainers on anchor bolts and secure with C-washers.

2. Install brake return spring.

3. Install wheel and drum assembly.

Adjustments

Since tapered brake lining is thicker at the center than at the ends, the adjustment procedures outlined in the paragraphs that follow must be performed in order to assure maximum braking efficiency.

Minor Adjustment

1. Jack up truck so that one wheel can be rotated freely.

2. Then, while rotating that wheel forward and backward, bring the shoe out to the drum with the adjusting cam until a light drag is obtained.

3. Back off the adjustment until the wheel is free to turn.

4. Repeat this procedure on the other shoe.

Major Adjustment

1. Inspect the fluid level in the master cylinder and add fluid if the level is ⅜" to ½" from the top of the reservoir or lower.

2. Loosen lock nuts and turn brake shoe anchor bolts to the fully released position.

3. Adjust the anchor bolt and cam and the minor adjustment cam at the top of the shoe to give equal clearance at the toe and heel. Make sure that sufficient center contact is maintained to produce a slight drag.

4. Lock anchor adjusting nut. After adjusting the clearance on one shoe, repeat the procedure on the other shoe. Then apply the brakes a couple of times to make sure adjustment is up to specifications.

NOTE: Whenever cams are adjusted, check brakes by applying pressure on the brake pedal a couple of times so as to make sure wheel drag has not increased, since the spring loaded cams may cause shoe adjustment to change by shifting position. Wheel should only have a slight drag at room temperature.

Kelsey Hayes

REAR BRAKE SHOES

Removal

1. Raise the truck until the wheel clears the floor.

2. Remove the wheel, hub and drum assembly.

3. Clamp the brake cylinder boots against the ends of the cylinder with brake piston clamps.

4. The two different types of brake shoe retracting springs and remove the springs.

5. Remove the brake shoe hold down post cotter key, nut, and shoe hold down washer.

6. Loosen and remove the eccentric adjuster bolt, lock washer, eccentric and adjusting link.

7. Remove the shoe and lining assembly from the backing plate.

8. Remove the anchor block spring and slide the adjuster assembly from the shoe web.

9. Remove the adjuster star wheel and screw from the adjuster block. Unthread the star wheel from the adjuster screw.

Installation

1. Wipe all brake dust from the brake assembly parts with a clean dry rag. Coat all points of contact between brake shoes and other parts with high temperature grease.

2. Coat the adjuster screw and the inside of the adjuster block with high temperature grease.

3. Thread the adjuster screw onto the star wheel and insert the adjuster screw assembly into the adjuster block. Maintain a 2.12–2.18 inch dimension from the end of the adjuster block to the adjuster screw web slot.

4. Install the adjuster assembly onto the shoe web and attach the anchor block spring.

5. Place the brake shoe over the retracting spring toggle pin and insert the ends of the shoe in the wheel cylinder links.

6. Install the shoe hold down washer and nut. Do not install the cotter pin.

7. Install the four brake shoe retracting springs. Make sure the retracting springs are installed. On 15 × 5" brakes the inner hook ends face the wheel cylinders. On 15 × 4" brakes the inner hook ends face the center of the axle.

8. Install the adjusting link, eccentric, lockwasher and adjuster bolt. Do not tighten.

9. Remove the brake piston clamps.

10. Tighten the shoe hold down nut until there is 0.015–0.025" clearance between the shoe and hold down washer with the shoe held against the backing plate. Install

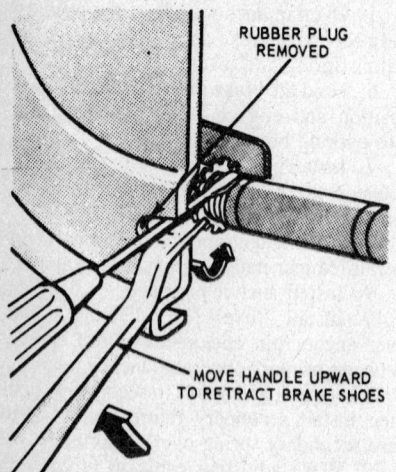

Typical brake adjustment procedure

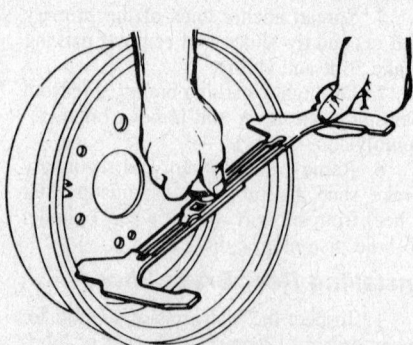

Measuring brake drum diameter

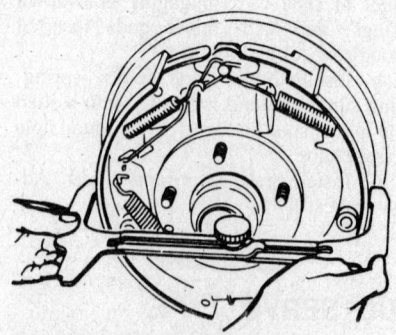

Measuring shoe mounted width

the cotter pin.

11. Center the shoes on the backing plate. Using a ½″ wrench, rotate the adjuster eccentric until the adjusting lever is at the index mark. Tighten the eccentric adjuster bolt to specification.

12. Install the wheel, hub and drum assembly.

13. Adjust the brake to obtain a slight drag. Subsequent adjustments will be automatic.

BRAKE SHOE ADJUSTMENT

The brake drums should be at normal room temperature, when the brake shoes are adjusted. If the shoes are adjusted when the shoes are hot and expanded, the shoes may drag as the drums cool and contract.

Self Adjusting Brakes

The brake shoes are automatically adjusted when the vehicle is driven in reverse and the brakes applied. A manual adjustment is required only after the brake shoes have been relined or replaced.

The two-cylinder brake assembly brake shoes are adjusted by turning adjusting wheels reached through slots in the backing plate.

Two types of two-cylinder brake assemblies are used on truck rear wheels. The assemblies differ primarily in the retracting spring hookup, and in the design of the adjusting screws and locks. However, the service procedures are the same for both assemblies.

The brake adjustment is made with the vehicle raised. Check the brake drag by rotating the drum in the direction of forward rotation as the adjustment is made.

1. Remove the adjusting slot covers from the backing plate.

2. Turn the rear (secondary shoe) adjusting screw inside the hole to expand the brake shoe until a slight drag is felt against the brake drum.

3. Repeat the above procedure on the front (primary) brake shoe.

4. Replace the adjusting hole covers.

5. Complete the adjustment by applying the brakes several times while backing the vehicle.

6. After the brake shoes have been properly adjusted, check the operation of the brakes by making several stops while operating in a forward direction.

Parking Brakes

Adjustment
Nine-Inch Diameter Drum

1. Release the parking brake lever in the cab.

2. From under the truck, remove the cotter pin from the parking brake linkage adjusting clevis pin. Remove the clevis pin.

3. Lengthen the parking brake adjusting link by turning the clevis. Continue to lengthen the adjusting link until the shoes seat against the drum when the clevis pin is installed.

4. Remove the clevis pin and shorten the linkage adjustment until there is 0.010″ clearance between the shoes and the drum. The measurement should be taken at all points around the drum with the clevis pin installed.

5. Install a new cotter pin in the clevis retaining pin and check the brake operation.

Twelve-Inch Diameter Drum

There is no internal adjustment on this brake. Adjustment is made on the linkage. Remove the clevis pin, loosen the nuts on the adjusting rod, and turn the clevis on the rod until a ¼–⅜″ free play is obtained at the brake lever. Tighten the nuts, and connect the clevis to the bellcrank with the clevis pin.

DISC BRAKES

Floating Caliper Disc Brakes

This disc brake is a floating caliper design with one or two pistons on one side of the rotor. It is a two piece unit consisting of the caliper and cylinder housing. The caliper is mounted to the anchor plate on two mounting pins which travel in bushings in the anchor plate. The bushings and pins are protected by toot type seals.

Two brake shoe and lining assemblies are used in each caliper, one on each side of the rotor. The shoes are identical and are attached to the caliper with two mounting pins.

The cylinder housing contains the two pistons. The pistons are fitted with an insulator on the front and a seal on the back lip. A friction ring is attached to the back of the piston with a shouldered cap screw. The pistons and cylinder bores are protected by boot seals which are fitted to a groove in the piston and attached to the cylinder housing with retainers. The cylinder assembly is attached to the caliper with two cap screws and washers.

The anchor plate is bolted directly to the spindle. It positions the caliper assembly over the rotor forward of the spindle.

DISC BRAKE SHOE ADJUSTMENT

The front disc brake assembly is designed so that it is inherently self-adjusting and requires no manual adjustment.

Automatic adjustment for lining wear is achieved by the piston and friction ring sliding outward in the cylinder bore. The piston assumes a new position in the cylinder and maintains the correct adjustment.

FRONT DISC BRAKE SHOE AND LINING

Replace shoe and lining assemblies when lining is worn to a minimum of ¹⁄₁₆″ in thickness (combined thickness of shoe and lining ¼″ minimum).

Removal

1. Remove the shoe and lining mounting pins, anti-rattle springs and old shoe and lining assemblies.

Installation

1. Remove the master cylinder cover.

2. Loosen the piston housing-to-caliper mounting bolts sufficiently to permit the installation of new shoe and lining assemblies. Do not move pistons.

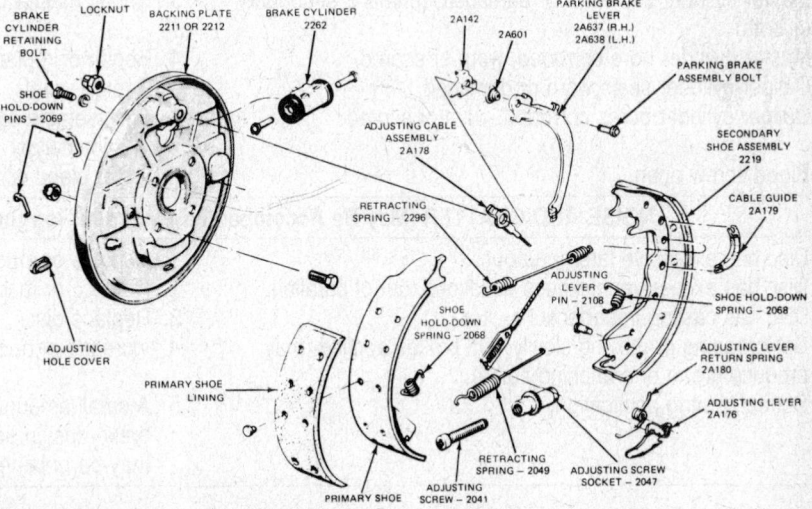

Kelsey-Hayes heavy duty brake

DISC BRAKES
FLOATING CALIPER

DISC BRAKES—TROUBLE DIAGNOSIS

Cause	Correction
1. Master cylinder fluid level low.	1. Fill to proper level with approved fluid. (Fluid level drops as disc brake linings wear.)
2. Poor quality brake fluid (low boiling point) in system.	2. Drain hydraulic system and fill with approved.
3. Air in hydraulic system.	3. Bleed hydraulic system and refill with approved fluid.
4. Hoses soft or weak (expanding under pressure).	4. Replace defective hoses. Combination valve and all cups and seals in complete brakes.
1. Power brake malfunctioning.	1. Check and repair power unit.
2. Linings soiled with brake fluid, oil or grease.	2. Replace shoes and linings.
3. Lines, hoses or connections dented, kinked, collapsed, clogged or disconnected.	3. Repair or replace defective parts.
4. Master cylinder cups swollen.	4. Drain hydraulic system, flush system with brake fluid and replace combination valve and all cups and seals in complete brake system.
5. Master cylinder bore corroded or rough.	5. Repair or replace master cylinder.
6. Caliper pistons frozen or seized.	6. Disassemble caliper and free pistons (replace if necessary).
7. Caliper cylinder bores corroded or rough.	7. Disassemble caliper and remove corrosion or roughness, or replace caliper.
8. Pedal push rod and linkage binding.	8. Free and lubricate.
9. Metering valve not working.	9. Replace combination valve.

GRABBING OR PULLING (Severe Reaction To Pedal Pressure and Out of Line Stops)

Cause	Correction
1. Linings soiled with brake fluid, oil or grease.	1. Replace shoes and linings.
2. Caliper loose.	2. Tighten caliper mounting bolts to specified torque.
3. Lines, hoses or connection dented, kinked, collapsed or clogged.	3. Repair or replace defective parts.
4. Master cylinder bore corroded or rough.	4. Repair or replace master cylinder.
5. Caliper pistons frozen or seized.	5. Disassemble caliper and free pistons (replace if necessary).
6. Caliper cylinder seals soft or swollen.	6. Drain hydraulic system, flush system with brake fluid and replace all cups and seals in complete brake system.
7. Caliper cylinder bores corroded or rough.	7. Disassemble caliper and remove corrosion or roughness, or replace caliper.
8. Pedal linkage binding (and suddenly releasing).	8. Free and lubricate linkage.
9. Metering valve not functioning properly.	9. Replace combination valve.

FADING PEDAL (Pedal Falling Away Under Steady Pressure)

Cause	Correction
1. Poor quality brake fluid (low boiling point) in system.	1. Drain hydraulic system and fill with approved fluid.
2. Hydraulic connections loose; lines or hoses ruptured (causing leakage).	2. Tighten or replace defective parts.
3. Master cylinder cup worn or damaged. (primary, secondary or both).	3. Repair master cylinder.
4. Master cylinder bore corroded, worn or scored.	4. Repair or replace master cylinder.
5. Caliper cylinder seals worn or damaged.	5. Replace seals.
6. Caliper cylinder bores corroded, worn or scored.	6. Disassemble caliper and remove corrosion or scoring, or replace caliper.
7. Bleed screw open.	7. Close bleed screw and bleed hydraulic system.

NOISE AND CHATTER (May Be Accompanied By Brake Roughness and Pedal Pumping)

Cause	Correction
1. Disc has excessive lateral runout.	1. Replace or machine disc.
2. Disc has excessive thickness variations (out of parallel).	2. Replace or machine disc.
3. Disc has casting imperfections.	3. Replace disc.
4. Car creeping or moving slowly with brakes applied (may produce groan or crunching noise).	4. Increase or decrease pedal effort slightly.
5. Squeal, during application.	5. A small amount of high-pitched squeal is inherent in disc brake design and must be considered normal. Some relief may be obtained with service package backing.

DISC BRAKES—TROUBLE DIAGNOSIS

Cause	Correction

DRAGGING BRAKES (Slow or Incomplete Release of Brakes)

1. Lines, hoses or connections dented, kinked, collapsed or clogged.
2. Master cylinder compensating port restricted by swollen primary cup.

3. Residual pressure check valve in lines to front wheels.
4. Caliper pistons frozen or seized.
5. Caliper cylinder seals swollen.

6. Caliper cylinder bores corroded or rough.

7. Hydraulic push rod on power brake out of adjustment or binding (causing primary cup to restrict master cylinder compensating port).

---

1. Repair or replace defective parts.

2. Drain hydraulic system, flush system with brake fluid and replace combination valve and all cups and seals in complete brake system.
3. Remove check valve.
4. Disassemble caliper and free pistons (replace if necessary).
5. Drain hydraulic system, flush system with clean brake fluid and replace combination valve and all cups and seals in complete brake system.
6. Disassemble caliper and remove corrosion or roughness, or replace caliper.
7. Adjust or free and lubricate.

---

3. Install new shoe and lining assemblies. Install the brake shoe mounting pins and anti-rattle springs. Be sure that the spring tangs are located in the holes provided in the shoe plates.

4. Torque the brake shoe mounting pins to 17–23 ft. lbs.

5. Reset the pistons to the correct location in the cylinders by placing shims or feeler gauges of .023 to .035" thickness between the shoe plate of the outboard shoe and lining assembly and the caliper; then, retighten the piston housing-to-caliper mounting bolts. Keep the cylinder housing square with the caliper.

6. Loosen the piston housing-to-caliper mounting bolts and remove the shims.

7. Torque the piston housing-to-caliper mounting bolts to 155 to 185 ft. lbs.

8. Check the master cylinder reservoirs.

9. Install the master cylinder cover.

DISC BRAKE CALIPER

Removal

1. Remove the wheel and tire assembly.

2. Remove the pins and nuts retaining the caliper assembly to the anchor plate.

3. Disconnect the brake hose from the caliper and remove the caliper.

Installation

1. Connect the brake hose to the caliper.

2. Position the caliper assembly to the anchor plate and install the retaining pins and nuts. Torque the nuts to specifications.

3. Install drum and wheel and bleed brake system.

If the caliper assembly is leaking, the piston assemblies must be removed from

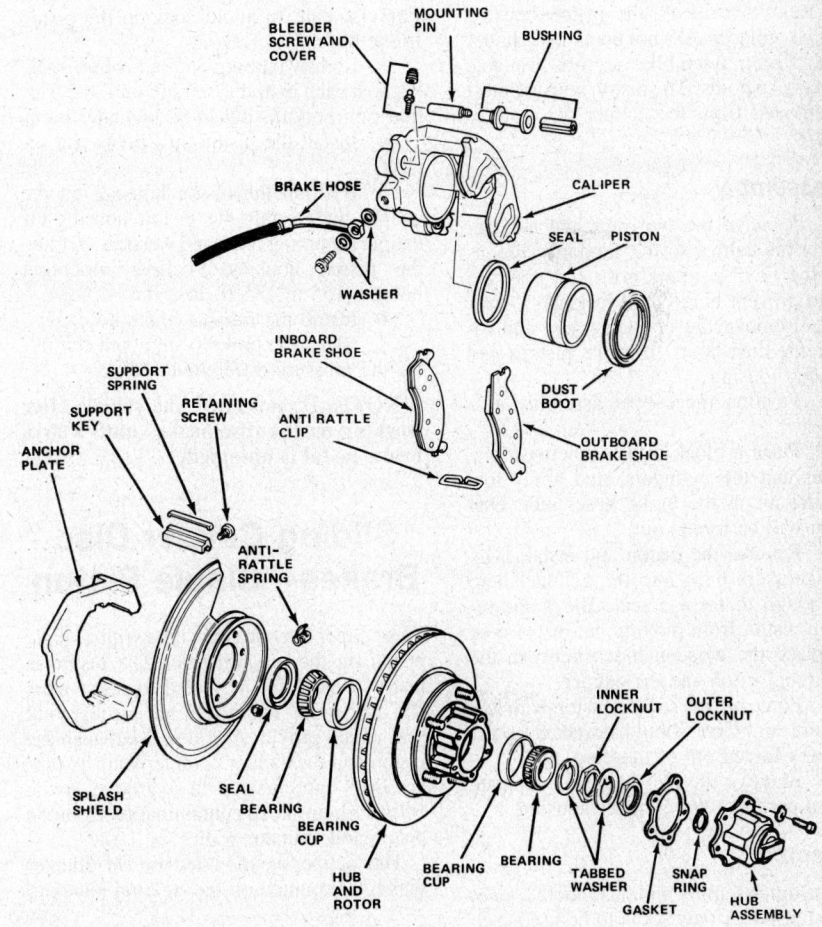

Typical floating caliper disc brake

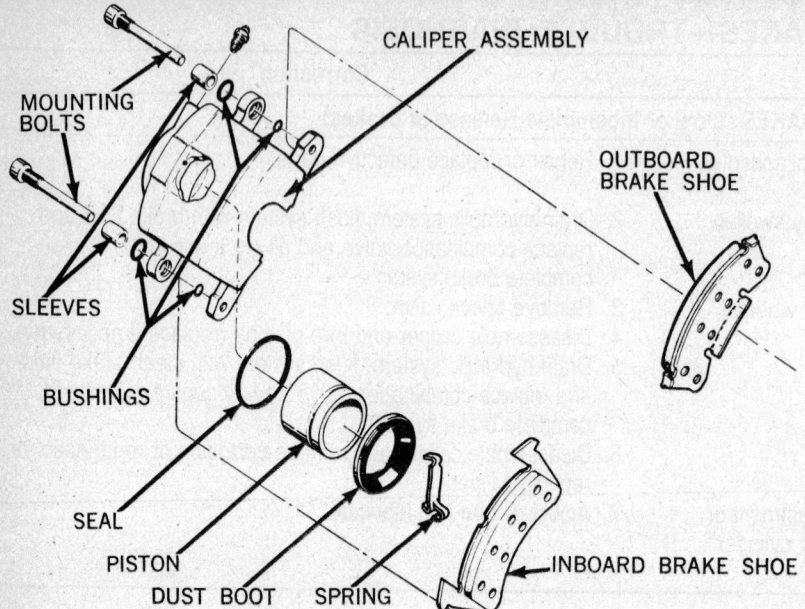

MOUNTING BOLTS

CALIPER ASSEMBLY

OUTBOARD BRAKE SHOE

SLEEVES

BUSHINGS

SEAL

PISTON

DUST BOOT   SPRING

INBOARD BRAKE SHOE

Typical single piston sliding caliper disc brake

the piston housing and replaced. If the cylinder bores are scored, corroded or excessive wear is evident, the piston housing must be replaced. Do not hone the cylinder bores. Piston assemblies are not available for oversize bores. The piston housing must be removed from the caliper for replacement.

Disassembly

1. Remove the two pins and nuts retaining the caliper to the support. Disconnect the flexible brake hose and plug the end to prevent brake fluid leakage.
2. Remove the boot retainers and remove the dust boots from the pistons and cylinder housing.
3. Position the caliper assembly in a vise.
4. Place a block of wood between the caliper and the cylinders, and apply low pressure air to the brake hose inlet. One piston will be forced out.
5. Reverse the piston and install it by hand pressure back into the cylinder bore far enough to form a seal. Block the reversed piston from moving out of the bore and place the wooden block between the remaining piston and the caliper.
6. Force out the second piston with low pressure air. Care should be taken as the piston is forced out of the bore.
7. Remove the two bolts and separate the caliper from the cylinder housing.

Assembly

The piston assembly and dust boots are not to be reused. A new set is to be used each time the caliper is assembled.

1. Apply a film of clean brake fluid in the cylinder bores and on the piston assemblies. Do not apply brake fluid on the insulators.

2. Start the piston assemblies into the cylinder bores using firm hand pressure. Exercise care to avoid cocking the piston in the bore.
3. Lightly tapping with a rawhide mallet, seat each piston assembly until the friction ring bottoms out in the cylinder bore.
4. Install the piston dust boots and retainers.
5. Position the piston housing on the caliper and install the piston housing-to-caliper mounting bolts and washers. Torque the piston housing-to-caliper mounting bolts to 155 to 185 ft. lbs.
6. Install the flexible brake hose.
7. Bleed the brake system and centralize the pressure differential valve.

NOTE: Do not move the vehicle after working on the disc brakes until a firm brake pedal is obtained.

Sliding Caliper Disc Brakes—Single Piston

This caliper is a one piece type with a single piston on the inboard side. The piston is made of steel and is plated to resist wear and corrosion. The piston has a square cut seal which provides for a seal between the piston and the caliper cylinder wall. A rubber dust boot located in a groove in the cylinder helps keep contamination from the piston and cylinder wall.

The caliper is mounted on an adapter which is mounted on the steering knuckle.

DISC BRAKE ADJUSTMENT

No adjustment is required on this unit other than applying the pedal several times after the unit has been worked on. This is to seat

the shoes and after this is done the hydraulic pressure maintains the proper clearance between the brake shoes and the rotor.

BRAKE SHOE REMOVAL

Replace the brake shoes when the linings are worn within 1/16" of the shoe or the rivets.

Removal

1. Remove the master cylinder cover and if the cylinder is more than 1/3 full remove the fluid necessary to make the cylinder only 1/3 full. This is done to prevent any overflow from the cylinder when the piston is pushed into the bore of the caliper.
2. Raise vehicle on hoist and remove the front wheels.
3. Compress the piston back into the bore by using a large C-clamp and compressing the unit until the piston bottoms in the bore.
4. Remove the two retaining bolts that hold the caliper into the support. If the caliper has retaining clips remove the retaining clips and anti-rattle springs. If the caliper has key type retainers, remove the key retaining screws, and using a hammer and drift, punch drive the key out of the caliper.
5. Slide the caliper off the rotor disc. Be careful not to damage the dust boot on the piston when removing the caliper.

NOTE: Do not let the caliper hang with the brake hose supporting the weight. This can cause damage to the hose which could result in a loss of brakes. Set the caliper on the front suspension arm or tie rod.

6. Remove the outer shoe from the caliper. It may be necessary to tap the shoe to loosen it from the caliper. Remove the inner shoe from the caliper or spindle assembly depending on where the shoe stays.
7. Remove the shoe support spring from the piston.

Cleaning and Inspection

Clean the sliding surfaces of the caliper and clean any dirt from the mounting bolts, clips or keys.

Inspect the boot on the piston for signs of cracks, cuts or other damage. Check to see if there is signs of fluid leaking around the seal on the piston. This will show up in the boot. If there is an indication of a fluid leak, the entire caliper has to be disassembled and the seal replaced.

Installation

1. Make sure that the piston is fully bottomed in the cylinder bore and install the outboard shoe in the recess of the caliper.

NOTE: On shoes with anti-rattle springs be sure to install the spring before installing the shoe in the caliper.

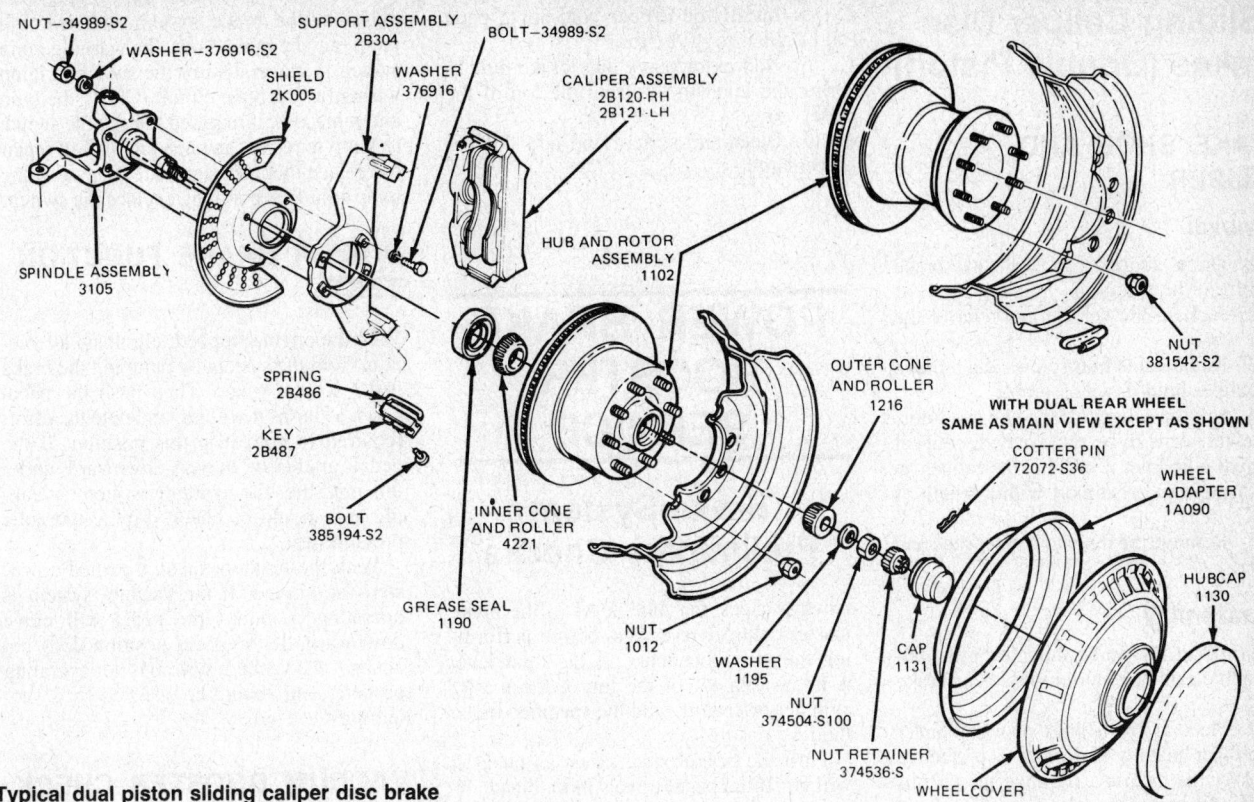

Typical dual piston sliding caliper disc brake

2. Place the outer shoe on the caliper and press it into place with finger pressure.

3. Position the caliper on the rotor and carefully slide it down into position over the rotor.

4. Install the caliper mounting bolts and torque them to 35 ft. lbs. On models with retaining clips install the anti-rattle springs and the retaining clips and torque the retaining screws to 200 in. lbs. On models with key type retainers press down the caliper and install the key in its slot and drive it in place with a hammer and drift. Install the retaining screw and torque to 12–18 ft. lbs.

5. Install the wheels and lower the vehicle. Check the master cylinder fluid level and add any fluid necessary to bring it up to the proper level.

6. Pump the brake pedal several times until a firm brake pedal is established. Road test the vehicle to check for proper operation.

DISC CALIPER

Removal

1. Remove the cover on the master cylinder and check if the fluid level is ⅓ full. If it is more than ⅓ full remove the necessary amount to bring the level down. This step is necessary to avoid overflow from the master cylinder when the piston is compressed into the cylinder bore.

2. Raise the vehicle and remove the wheel.

3. Compress the piston into the caliper bore and remove the brake hose from the caliper. Tape the end of the hose to prevent dirt from entering the line.

4. Remove the caliper retaining bolts, clips or wedges and remove the caliper from the vehicle.

Disassembly

1. Clean the outside of the caliper with clean brake fluid and drain any fluid from the caliper.

2. Remove the piston from the caliper by connecting the hydraulic line to the caliper and gently stroking the brake pedal. This will push the piston from the caliper bore.

3. With care remove the boot from the caliper piston bore.

4. Remove the piston seal from the caliper bore using a piece of wood or plastic.

NOTE: DO NOT use a metal tool to remove the seal. This can damage the bore or burr the edges of the seal groove.

5. Remove the bleeder valve.

Cleaning and Inspection

1. Clean all the parts with clean brake fluid and blow out all the passages in the caliper.

NOTE: When ever the caliper is dis-

assembled discard the boot and piston seal. These parts must not be reused.

2. Inspect the outside of the piston for signs of wear, corrosion, scores or any other defects. If any defects are detected replace the piston.

3. Check the caliper bore for the same defects as the piston. However, the bore can be cleaned up to a point with crocus cloth. If there are any marks that will not clean up with the cloth the caliper must be replaced.

Assembly and Installation

1. Lube the caliper bore and the piston with clean brake fluid and position the seal for the piston in the cylinder bore groove.

2. Install the dust boot into the groove in the piston with the fold faces toward the open end of the piston.

3. Install the piston in the bore being careful not to unseat the piston seal in the bore.

4. With the piston bottomed in the cylinder position the boot in the groove in the caliper. Make sure that the retaining ring in the seal is pressed down evenly around the cylinder.

5. Install the bleeder screw in the caliper and install the caliper back on the vehicle.

6. Connect the brake hoses and bleed the calipers of air. When bleeding is done pump the pedal several times to develop a firm brake pedal.

Sliding Caliper Disc Brakes (Double Piston)

BRAKE SHOE AND CALIPER

Removal

1. Drain about ⅔ of the total brake fluid from the reservoir.
2. Jack up the vehicle and remove the front wheels.
3. Remove the four screws and remove the caliper hold-down assembly.
4. Lift the caliper off the hub and rotor. If the caliper is to be removed, disconnect the hydraulic line; if not, lay the caliper on the suspension or support with a length of wire.
5. Remove the inner and outer shoe and lining.

Disassembly

1. Drain the brake fluid from the caliper and clean the exterior with clean brake fluid.
2. Place a small block of wood under the caliper pistons and place a protective pad over the exterior. Remove the pistons by directing compressed air into the caliper fluid outlet.
3. Remove and discard piston boots.
4. Remove the piston seals from the groove in the caliper bore.

Assembly

1. Clean all parts in clean brake fluid and blow dry.
2. Dip the new piston seal in clean brake fluid and install it into the cylinder groove.

NOTE: Be sure that the seal is not rolled or twisted in the groove.

3. Install the dust boot in the cylinder groove.
4. Coat the outside diameter of the piston with clean brake fluid. Use something plastic or wood and gradually work the dust boot around the piston.
5. Press the piston straight into the caliper bore until it bottoms. Position the boot in the piston groove.

Installation

1. Install a new shoe and lining assembly into the anchor plate.
2. Push the pistons to the bottom of the piston bore. Place a small block of wood over both pistons and boots. Push the pistons to the bottom of the bores with a C-clamp.
3. Install the outer shoe and lining onto the caliper and install the shoe hold-down spring and pin.
4. Install the caliper assembly over the hub, rotor and inner shoe, and position into the inner grooves in the anchor plate.

5. Install the caliper hold-down parts and tighten to 40 ft. lbs.
6. Add extra heavy duty brake fluid to bring the level to ¼" from the top of the reservoir.
7. Bleed the system and add fluid as necessary.

POWER BRAKE BOOSTER SERVICE

Brake System Preliminary Checks

Always check the fluid level in the brake master cylinder reservoirs before performing the test procedures. If the fluid level is not within ¼" of the top of the master cylinder reservoirs, add the specified brake fluid.

Push the brake pedal down as far as it will go. If the pedal travels more than halfway between the released position and the floor, adjust the brakes. Several sharp brake applications while backing up may be necessary to adjust the brakes.

Road test the vehicle and apply the brakes at a speed of about 20 mph to see if the vehicle stops evenly. If not, the brakes should be adjusted. Perform the road test only when the brakes will apply and the vehicle can be safely stopped.

DUAL BRAKE WARNING LIGHT SYSTEM TESTS

1. Turn the ignition switch to the ACC or ON position. If the light on the brake warning lamp remains on, the condition may be caused by a shorted or broken switch, grounded switch wires or the differential pressure valve is not centered. Centralize the differential pressure valve. If the warning light remains on, check the switch connector and wire for a grounded condition and repair or replace the wire assembly. If the condition of the wire is good, replace the brake warning lamp switch.
2. Turn the ignition switch to the start position. If the brake warning lamp does not light, check the light and wiring and replace or repair wiring as necessary. When both brake systems are functioning normally, the equal pressure at the pressure differential valve during brake pedal application keeps the valve centered. The brake warning light will be on only when the ignition key is in the start position.
3. If the brake warning lamp does not light when a pressure differential condition

exists in the brake system, the warning lamp may be burned out, the warning lamp switch is inoperative or the switch to lamp wiring has an open circuit. Check the bulb and replace it, if required. Check the switch to lamp wires for an open circuit and repair or replace them, if required. If the warning lamp still does not light, replace the switch.

POWER BRAKE FUNCTION TEST

With the engine stopped, eliminate all vacuum from the system by pumping the brake pedal several times. Then push the pedal down as far as it will go, and note the effort required to hold it in this position. If the pedal gradually moves downward under this pressure, the hydraulic system is leaking and should be checked by a hydraulic pressure test.

With the brake pedal still pushed down, start the engine. If the vacuum system is operating properly, the pedal will move downward. If the pedal position does not change, the vacuum system is not operating properly and should be checked by a vacuum test.

VACUUM BOOSTER CHECK VALVE TEST

Disconnect the line from the bottom of the vacuum check valve, and connect a vacuum gauge to the valve. Start the engine, run it at idle speed, and check the reading on the vacuum gauge.

The gauge should register 17–19" with standard transmission and 14–15" in Drive range if equipped with an automatic transmission. Stop the engine and note the rate of vacuum drop. If the vacuum drops more than one inch in 15 seconds, the check valve is leaking. If the vacuum reading does not reach 18" or is unsteady, an engine tuneup is needed.

Remove the gauge and reconnect the vacuum line to the check valve.

VACUUM BOOSTER TEST

Bendix Piston Type

Disconnect the vacuum line from the booster end plate. Install a tee fitting in the end plate, and connect a vacuum gauge (no. 1) and vacuum line to the fitting. Install a second vacuum gauge (no. 2) in place of the pipe plug in the booster control valve body.

Start the engine, and note the vacuum reading on both gauges. If both gauges do not register manifold vacuum, air is leaking into the vacuum system. If both gauges register manifold vacuum, stop the engine and note the rate of vacuum drop on both gauges. If the drop exceeds one inch in 15 seconds on either gauge, air is leaking into the vacuum system. Tighten all vacuum connections and repeat the test. If leakage

POWER BOOSTER TROUBLE DIAGNOSIS

Condition	Possible Cause	Correction
Vacuum leak (booster in released position)	1. End plate, center plate or control valve body gaskets leak.	1. Recondition booster unit.
	2. Distortion of end plate.	2. Replace end plate.
	3. Misalignment of control valve poppet.	3. Disassemble, clean and correctly reassemble.
	4. Loose vacuum cylinder bolts.	4. Coat vacuum cylinder bolts lightly with a suitable sealing compound and tighten to specified torque.
	5. Loose control valve body screws.	5. Tighten control valve body screws to specified torque.
	6. Large control valve poppet spring not centered in spring retainer.	6. Disassemble unit and correctly reassemble.
Vacuum leak (booster in applied position)	1. Leak at control valve poppet and seat.	1. Clean and inspect poppet and seat for damage and repair as necessary.
	2. Dry or faulty piston leather packing.	2. Clean and lubricate piston leather or replace.
	3. Faulty control valve disphragm assembly.	3. Replace faulty parts.
External hydraulic leaks	1. Gasket (O-ring) leaking at hydraulic end plate joint.	1. Disassemble clean and replace (O-ring) gasket and reassemble.
	2. Fluid leaking at copper gasket under hydraulic cylinder end cap.	2. Remove end cap and inspect copper gasket and seat install new copper gasket.
Internal hydraulic leak at low pressures	1. Control valve hydraulic piston cup failure.	1. Recondition control valve unit.
	2. Faulty push rod seal.	2. Replace push rod seal.
Internal leaks at high pressure	1. Fluid passing copper gasket under hydraulic fitting in control valve.	1. Clean and inspect gasket and fitting, replace if faulty.
	2. Inspect cups and seals of master cylinder for cuts and scores.	2. Hone master cylinder and replace cups and seals.
	3. Inspect cups of the control valve hydraulic piston.	3. Replace faulty cups.
Hydraulic pressure buildup (without added input)	1. Check hydraulic piston check valve and slot for foreign material under valve.	1. Clean or replace valve and seats as condition indicates.
Failure to release	1. Weak vacuum cylinder piston return spring.	1. Replace vacuum cylinder piston return spring.
	2. Dry vacuum piston leather packing.	2. Lubricate vacuum piston leather packing.
	3. Swollen rubber cups due to inferior or contaminated brake fluid.	3. Flush hydraulic system and recondition or replace all cylinders.
	4. Damaged or dented vacuum cylinder shell.	4. Replace vacuum cylinder shell.
	5. Dirty or sticky control valve piston.	5. Recondition control valve assembly.
Failure of booster to operate within specified pressures	1. Rusty, dirty or distorted vacuum cylinder shell.	1. Clean or replace vacuum cylinder shell.
	2. Dry or worn vacuum cylinder leather packing.	2. Recondition and lubricate the vacuum booster.
	3. Swollen rubber cups due to inferior brake fluid.	3. Recondition the master cylinder. Replace brake fluid.
	4. Worn or scored hydraulic cups.	4. Recondition the master cylinder.
	5. Dirt, rust or foreign matter in any component of the system.	5. Recondition and lubricate the brake booster assembly.
Loss of fluid	1. Fluid leaking past cup in master cylinder.	1. Recondition master cylinder or replace.

POWER BOOSTER TROUBLE DIAGNOSIS

Condition	Possible Cause	Correction
	2. Brake wheel cylinders leaking.	2. Recondition or replace wheel cylinders.
	3. Loose hydraulic hose connectors.	3. Inspect and tighten all hydraulic connections.
	4. Leaking stop light switch.	4. Replace stop light switch.
Presence of brake fluid on hy-power vacuum cylinder	1. Piston cup or push rod seal leaking.	1. Recondition master cylinder.
Pedal kicks back against foot when brakes are applied	1. Vacuum leakage.	1. Inspect and correct vacuum leak.
	2. Dirt under control valve or damaged seat.	2. Clean and recondition booster assembly.
	3. Weak or broken spring.	3. Replace spring.
Brakes are slow to release ①	1. Incorrect pedal linkage adjustment.	1. Adjust and lubricate pedal linkage.
	2. Compensating port of master cylinder plugged.	2. Clean master cylinder with compressed air.
	3. Brake shoes sticking.	3. Free up and lubricate brake shoes.
	4. Weak brake shoe return spring.	4. Replace brake shoe return spring.
	5. Booster control valve piston sticking.	5. Clean booster control valve piston and lubricate.
	6. Booster air filter clogged.	6. Clean air filter in mineral spirits.
	7. Control valve diaphragm return spring missing.	7. Install new control valve return spring.
	8. Defective check valve in slave cylinder piston.	8. Recondition slave cylinder pistons.
	9. Dirt under atmospheric valve disc.	9. Clean atmospheric valve.
Engine runs unevenly at idle with brakes released	1. Vacuum leakage.	1. Inspect and tighten all vacuum fittings.
	2. Dirt under control valve disc or damaged seat.	2. Clean control valve or replace.
	3. Defective spring.	3. Replace defective spring.
Engine runs evenly and pedal is hard with brakes applied	1. Control valve piston assembly not seating on vacuum disc.	1. Clean or replace control valve piston assembly.
	2. Defective control valve plate and diaphragm.	2. Replace control valve plate and diaphragm.
	3. Defective pressure plate and diaphragm.	3. Replace pressure plate and diaphragm.
Brake pedal is hard at different intervals	1. Defective manifold check valve.	1. Clean or replace manifold check valve.
	2. Slave cylinder piston sticking due to dirt or inferior brake fluid.	2. Clean and recondition slave cylinder.
	3. Brake booster air cleaner clogged.	3. Clean air cleaner in mineral spirits and blow dry with compressed air.

① Jack up truck and determine whether or not the brakes are dragging before further testing is done.

still exists, the leak may be localized as follows:

1. Disconnect the vacuum line and gauge no. 1 from the booster.

2. Connect vacuum gauge no. 1 directly to the vacuum line. Start the engine and note the gauge reading. Stop the engine and check the rate of vacuum drop. If gauge no. 1 does not register manifold vacuum, or if the vacuum drop exceeds 1″ in 15 seconds, the leak is in the vacuum line or check valve connections.

3. Reconnect vacuum gauge no. 1 and the vacuum line to the tee fitting. Start the engine, and run it at idle speed for one minute. Depress the brake pedal sufficiently to cause vacuum gauge no. 2 to read

from zero to 1 inch of vacuum. Gauge no. 1 should register manifold vacuum of 17–19″ with standard transmission and 14–16″ in Drive range if equipped with an automatic transmission. If the drop of vacuum on gauge no. 2 is slow, the air cleaner, or air cleaner line, may be plugged. Inspect and if necessary, clean the air cleaner.

4. Release the brake pedal and observe the action of gauge no. 2. Upon releasing the pedal, the vacuum gauge must register increasing vacuum until manifold vacuum is reached. The rate of increase must be smooth, with no lag or slowness in the return to manifold vacuum. If the gauge readings are not as outlined, the booster is not operating properly and should be removed

and overhauled.

VACUUM BOOSTER TEST

Diaphragm Type

This procedure can be used to test all diaphragm boosters which are equipped with a pipe thread outlet on the atmosphere portion of the diaphragm chamber.

Remove the pipe plug from the rear half of the booster chamber, and install a vacuum gauge. Start the engine and run it at idle speed. The gauge should register 18–21″ of vacuum.

1. With the engine running, depress the brake pedal with enough pressure to show

a zero reading on the vacuum gauge. Hold the pedal in the applied position for one minute. Any downward movement of the pedal during this time indicates a brake fluid leak. Any kickback (upward movement) of the pedal indicates brake fluid is leaking past the hydraulic piston check valve.

2. With the engine running, push down on the brake pedal with sufficient pressure to show a zero reading on the vacuum gauge. Hold the pedal down, and shut the engine off. Maintain pedal position for one minute. A kickback of the pedal indicates a vacuum leak in the vacuum check valve, in the vacuum line connections, or in the booster.

BLEEDING VACUUM-HYDRAULIC BOOSTER SYSTEMS

1. Eliminate vacuum in the booster by depressing the brake pedal several times while the engine is not running.

2. On trucks not equipped with reservoir tanks, disconnect the manifold tube at the booster side of the manifold check valve (engine not running).

3. Alternately loosen the brake tube at each unit until all air is expelled. Booster slave-cylinder is bled first.

— CAUTION —
Where air pressure brake bleeding equipment is used to bleed brakes, do not use more than 25–30 psi.

NOTE: A piston stop is provided in the slave cylinder to eliminate the possibility of damaging the return spring while bleeding the system. This damage occurs only when bleeding the brakes with a vacuum present in the booster system.

Bendix Hydro-Boost

The Bendix Hydro-Boost uses the hydraulic pressure supplied by the power steering pump to provide a power assist to brake application.

Disassembly

1. Place the booster in a vise with the bracket end up. Using a hammer and chisel, cut the bracket nut that holds the linkage bracket to the booster assembly. The nut should be cut at the open slot in the booster cover threads. Care must be exercised to avoid damage to the threads. Spread the nut and remove the bracket.

2. Remove the pedal boot by pulling if off over the pedal rod eyelet.

3. Position pedal rod removing tool around the pedal rod. The tool should be resting on the booster cover. Insert a punch through the pedal rod from the lower side

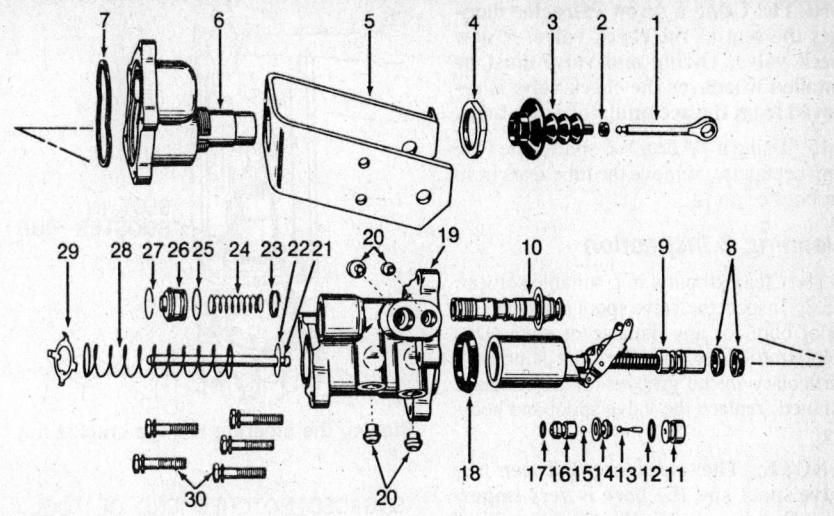

Bendix Hydro-Boost

1. Pedal push rod
2. Pedal push rod grommet
3. Pedal push rod boot
4. Bracket nut
5. Linkage bracket
6. Booster cover
7. Cover to housing seal
8. Input rod seals
9. Input rod and piston assy
10. Spool assembly
11. Plunger seat
12. O-ring
13. Spacer
14. Spacer
15. Check valve ball
16. Accumulator check valve
17. O-ring
18. Piston seal
19. Booster housing
20. Tube seat inserts
21. Output push rod
22. Push rod retainer
23. Spiral snapring
24. Spool spring
25. Plug O-ring
26. Spool plug
27. Snapring
28. Piston return spring
29. Spring retainer
30. Housing to cover bolts

of the special tool. Push the punch through until it rests on the higher side of the tool. Push up on the punch to shear the pedal rod retainer; remove the pedal rod.

4. Remove the grommet from the groove near the end of the pedal rod and from the groove in the input rod.

5. Disengage the tabs of the spring retainer from the ledge inside the opening near the master cylinder mounting flange of the booster. Remove the retainer and piston return spring from the opening.

6. Pull straight out on the output push rod to remove the push rod and push rod retainer from inside the booster piston.

7. Press in on the spool plug, and insert a small punch into the hole on top of the housing. This unseats one side of the spool plug snap-ring from the groove in the bore. Remove the snap-ring.

8. Remove the spool plug from the bore with a pair of pliers. Remove the O-ring from the plug and discard. Remove the spool spring from the bore.

9. Place the booster cover in a soft-faced vise and remove the cover retaining bolts. Remove the booster assembly from the vise and separate the booster cover from the housing. Remove the large seal ring and discard.

10. Press in on the end of the spool assembly, and use a spiral snap-ring removing tool to remove the snap-ring from the forward groove in the spool. Discard snap-ring.

11. Remove the input rod and piston

assembly, and the spool assembly from the booster housing.

12. Remove the input rod seals from the input rod end, and the piston seal from the piston bore in the housing. Discard the seals.

13. Remove the plunger, seat, spacer and ball from the accumulator valve bore in the flange of the booster housing. Remove the O-ring from the seat and discard.

14. Thread a screw extractor into the opening in the check valve in the bottom of the accumulator valve bore, and remove the check valve from the bottom of the bore. Discard the check valve and O-ring.

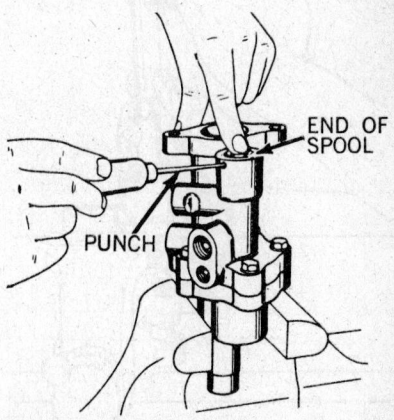

Removing the spool plug from the Hydro-Boost unit

NOTE: Using a screw extractor damages the seat in the check valve. A new check valve, O-ring and valve must be installed whenever the check valve is removed from the accumulator valve bore.

15. Using a ¼" or a ⁵⁄₁₆" spiral flute type screw extractor, remove the tube seats from the booster ports.

Cleaning & Inspection

1. Clean all parts in a suitable solvent.

2. Inspect the valve spool and the valve spool bore for any damage or ware. Discoloration of the spool or bore is normal, particulary in the grooves. If any damage is noted, replace the valve spool and housing.

NOTE: The clearance between the valve spool and the bore is very important. Because of this, the valve spool and housing are to be replaced only as an assembly.

3. Inspect the input rod and piston assembly for any damage or ware. Replace any defective components.

4. Inspect the piston bore in the housing for any damage or ware. If defective, replace the booster housing and spool valve assembly.

Assembly

—————— **CAUTION** ——————

Parts must be kept VERY clean. If there is any reason to doubt the cleanliness of the components, re-wash before assembly.

Lubricate all seals and metal friction points with power steering fluid before assembly. Whenever the booster is disassembled, be sure that seals, tube inserts, spiral snap-ring, check valve and ball are replaced.

1. Position a tube seat in each booster port and screw a spare tube nut in each port to press the seat down into the port. Do not

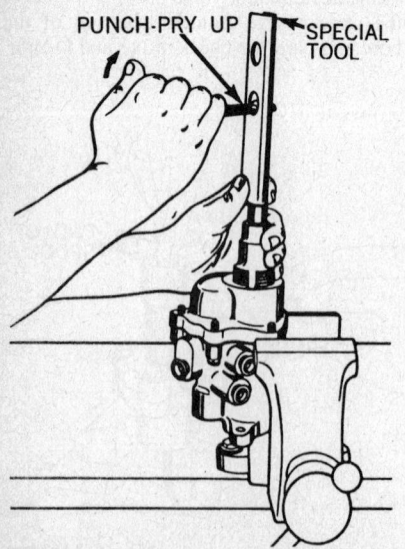

Removing the booster pedal rod

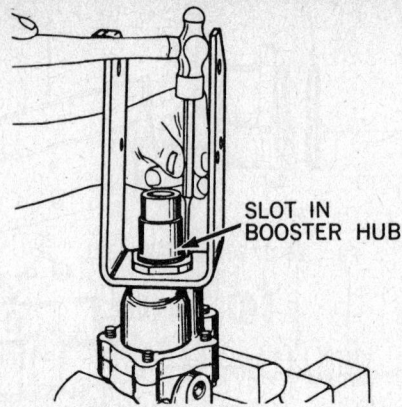

Staking the steering linkage bracket nut

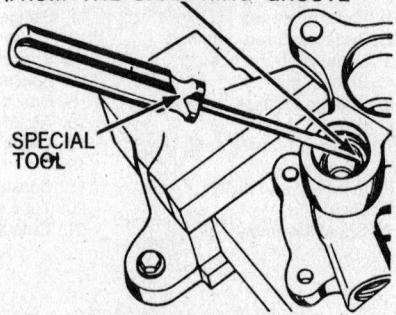

Removing the spiral snap-ring

tighten the tube nuts in the port as this may deface the seats. Remove the spare tube nuts and check for aluminium chips in the ports. Be sure that there is no foreign matter in the ports.

2. Coat the piston bore and piston seal with clean power steering fluid. Assemble the seal in the piston bore. The lip of the seal must be towards the rear (away from the master cylinder mounting flange). Be sure that the seal is fully seated in the housing.

3. Lubricate the input rod end, input rod seals and the seal installer tool with clean power steering fluid. Slide the seals on the tool with the lip of the cups towards the open end of the tool. Slide the tool over the input rod end end down to the second groove; then slide the forward seal off the tool and into the groove. Assemble the other seal in the first groove. Be sure, that both seals are fully seated.

4. Lubricate the piston and piston installing tool with clean power steering fluid. Insert the large end of the tool into the piston and the tool and piston into the piston bore, through the seal.

5. Position the O-ring on the accumulator check valve and coat the assembly with clean power steering fluid. Insert the check valve in the accumulator valve recess in the housing flange. Place the ball and spacer in the same recess.

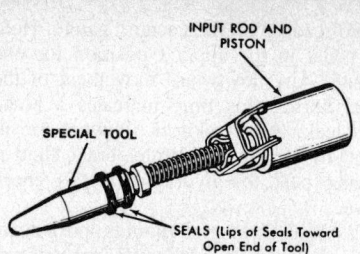

Installing the pushrod seals

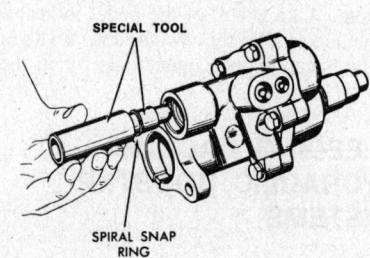

Installing the spiral snap-ring

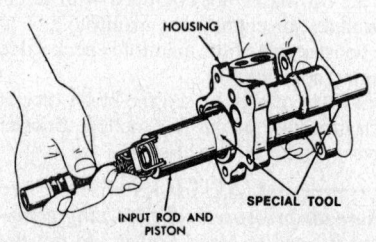

Installing the input rod and piston assembly in the booster

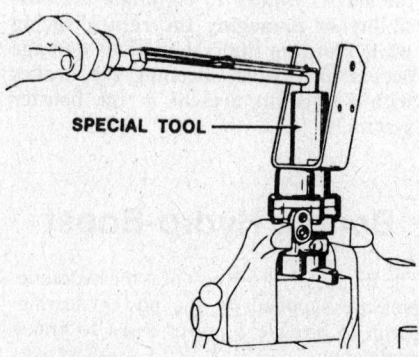

Installing the linkage braket nut

6. Place the O-ring on the changing valve plunger seat and insert the plunger into the seat. Dip the assembly in clean power steering fluid and insert it into the changing valve recess.

7. Coat the spool assembly with clean power steering fluid and insert in the spool bore. Be sure that the pivot pins on the upper end of the input rod lever assembly are engaged in the groove in the sleeve. Remove piston installing tool.

8. Separate the two components of the snap-ring installation tool and place the spiral snap-ring on the tool. Insert the rounded

end of the installer into the spool bore. While pressing on the rear of the spool, slide the snap-ring off the tool and into the groove near the forward end of the spool by pressing in on the tool sleeve. Check to be sure that the retaining ring is fully seated.

9. Place the housing seal in the groove in the housing cover. Join the booster housing and cover and secure with five attaching bolts. Tighten the bolts to 18–26 ft. lbs.

— CAUTION —

It is very important that the same cover attaching bolts are used as they are designed for the booster only. If they are damaged replace with the same part numbers.

10. Place an O-ring on the spool plug. Insert the spool spring and the spool plug in the forward end of the spool bore. Press in on the plug and position the snap-ring in its groove in the spool valve bore.

11. Place the linkage bracket on the booster assembly. The tab on the inside of the large hole in the bracket should fit into the slot in the threaded portion of the booster cover.

12. Install the bracket nut with a staking groove outward on the threaded portion to the booster cover. Use special tool and tighten to 95–120 ft. lbs.

13. Insert a small punch into the staking groove of the nut, at the slot in the booster cover, and with a hammer stake the nut in place. Be sure that the threads on the nut are deformed so the nut will not loosen.

14. Position a new boot and grommet on the pedal rod. Moisten the grommet and insert the grommet end of the pedal rod into the input rod of the booster. When the grommet is fully seated, the pedal rod will rotate freely.

15. Install the boot on the booster cover.

Bendix Master Vac

Removal

1. Disconnect clevis at brake pedal to push rod.
2. Remove vacuum hoses from power cylinder.
3. Disconnect hydraulic line from master cylinder.
4. Remove the four attaching nuts and lock washers that hold the unit to the firewall. Remove the power brake unit.

Disassembly

1. Remove four master cylinder to vacuum cylinder attaching nuts and washers.
2. Separate master cylinder from vacuum cylinder, then remove the rubber seal from the outer groove at end of master cylinder.
3. Remove the push rod from the power section. (Do not disturb adjusting screw.)

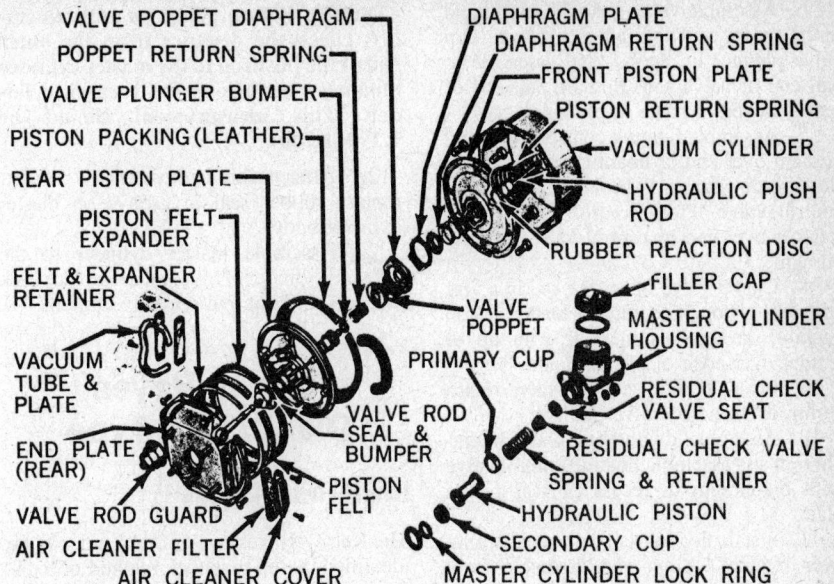

Bendix Master Vac

4. Remove push rod boot and valve operating rod.
5. Scribe alignment marks across the rear shell and vacuum cylinder. Remove all but two of the end plate attaching screws (opposite each other). Hold down on the rear shell while removing the two remaining screws to prevent the piston return spring from expanding.
6. Scribe a mark across the face of the piston, to index the mark on the rear shell, and remove rear shell with vacuum piston and piston return spring.
7. Remove vacuum hose from vacuum piston and from vacuum tube on inside of rear shell. Separate rear shell from vacuum piston.
8. Remove air cleaner and vacuum tube assembly, and air filter from the rear shell.
9. Spring the felt retaining ring enough to disengage ring from grooves in bosses on rear piston plate.
10. Remove piston felt and expander ring from piston assembly.
11. Remove six piston plate attaching screws and separate front piston plate and piston packing from piston plate.
12. Remove valve return spring, floating control valve and diaphragm assembly, valve spring and diaphragm plate. Separate floating control valve spring-retainer and control valve diaphragm from control valve.
13. Remove rubber reaction disc and shim (if present) from front piston plate.

NOTE: Do not remove the valve operating rod and valve plunger from the rear piston plate unless it is necessary to replace defective parts. Normally, the next two steps can be omitted.

14. When it is necessary to replace the valve operating rod or valve plunger, re-

move valve rod seal from groove in piston plate and pull seal over end of rod.

15. Hold piston with valve plunger side down and inject alcohol into valve plunger through opening around valve rod. This will wet the rubber lock in the plunger. Then drive or pry valve plunger off the valve rod.

NOTE: If master cylinder is not to be rebuilt, omit steps 16–19.

16. Remove snap-ring from groove in base at end of master cylinder.
17. Remove piston assembly, primary cup, retainer spring, and check-valve from master cylinder.
18. Remove filler cap and gasket from master cylinder body.
19. Remove secondary cup from master cylinder piston.

Cleaning Note

After disassembly, cleaning of all metal parts in satisfactory commercial cleaner solvent is recommended. Use only alcohol or Declene on rubber parts or parts containing rubber. After cleaning and drying, metal parts should be rewashed in clean alcohol or Declene before assembly.

Assembly

Steps 1–5 apply to a completely disassembled master cylinder. Otherwise, omit steps 1–5.

1. Coat bore of master cylinder with brake fluid.
2. Dip secondary cup in brake fluid and install on master cylinder piston.
3. Dip other piston parts in brake fluid and assemble the piston. Install piston.
4. Install snap-ring into groove of cylinder.
5. Use new gasket and install filler cap.

6. Assemble valve rod seal on rod and insert valve rod through the piston. Dip valve plunger in alcohol and assemble to ball end of valve rod. Be sure ball end of rod is locked in place in plunger.

7. Assemble floating control valve diaphragm over end of floating control valve. Be sure disphragm is in recess of floating control valve. Press control valve spring retainer over end of control valve and diaphragm.

8. Clamp valve operating rod in a vise with rear piston plate up. Lay leather piston packing on rear piston plate with lip of leather over edge of piston plate.

9. Install floating control valve return spring over end of valve plunger.

10. Assemble diaphragm plate to diaphragm and assemble floating control valve with diaphragm in recess of rear piston plate.

11. Install floating control valve spring over retainer. Align and assemble front piston plate with rear piston plate. Center the floating control valve spring on front piston plate and center valve plunger stem in hole of piston.

12. Holding front and rear piston plates together, loosely install six piston plate cap screws.

13. Install shim and rubber reaction disc in recess at center of front piston plate.

NOTE: A piston assembling ring is handy in assembling the piston.

14. Place the assembling tool over piston packing, turn piston assembly upside down and assemble the expander ring against inside lip of leather packing. Saturate felt with vacuum cylinder oil or shock absorber fluid—type A. Then assemble in expander ring. Assemble retainer ring over bosses on rear piston plate. Be sure retainer is anchored in grooves of piston plate.

15. Assemble air cleaner filter over vacuum tube of air cleaner and attach air cleaner shell in position with screws.

16. Slide vacuum hose onto vacuum inlet tube of piston and align hose to lay flat against piston.

17. Wipe a coat of vacuum cylinder oil on bore of cylinder. Remove assembling ring from vacuum piston and coat leather piston packing with vacuum cylinder oil.

18. Install rear shell over end of valve operating rod and attach vacuum hose to tube end on each side of end plate.

19. Center small diameter end of piston return spring in vacuum cylinder. Center large diameter of spring on piston. Check alignment mark on piston with marks on vacuum cylinder and rear shell, compress spring and install two attaching screws at opposite sides to hold rear shell and cylinder together. Now, install balance of screws and tighten evenly.

20. Dip small end of pushrod boot in alcohol and assemble guard over end of valve operating rod and over flange of shell.

21. Insert large end of pushrod through hole in end of vacuum cylinder and guide into hole of front piston plate.

NOTE: Before going on with assembly, check the distance from the outer end of the pushrod to the master cylinder mounting surface on the vacuum cylinder. This measurement should be 1.195–1.200″.

22. After pushrod adjustment is correct, replace rubber seal in groove on master cylinder body.

23. Assemble master cylinder to the vacuum cylinder at four studs. Replace lock washers and nut and securely tighten.

Kelsey-Hayes Diaphragm Type

IDENTIFICATION

The Kelsey-Hayes power brake unit can be identified by the twistlock method of locking the housing and cover together, plus the white-colored vacuum check valve assembly.

Removal

1. With engine off, apply brakes several times to equalize internal brake pressure.

2. Disconnect hydraulic line from master cylinder.

3. Disconnect vacuum hose from power brake check valve.

4. Disconnect power brake from brake pedal (under instrument panel).

5. Disconnect power brake unit from dash panel.

6. Remove power brake and master cylinder assembly from the vehicle.

Disassembly

1. Separate master cylinder from power brake unit.

2. Remove master cylinder pushrod and air cleaner plate.

3. Mount the power unit in a vise with the master cylinder attaching-studs up.

4. Scribe an index line across the housing and cover for reassembly reference.

5. Pry out the housing lock. Do not damage the lock, as it must be used at assembly.

6. Remove check valve from cover by prying out of rubber grommet.

7. Place parking brake flange holding tool over the master cylinder mounting studs.

8. Rotate the tool and cover in a counterclockwise direction. Then, separate the cover from the housing. This will expose the power piston return spring and diaphragm.

9. Lift out the power piston return spring. Remove the brake unit from the vise.

10. Remove power piston by slowly lifting the piston straight up.

11. Remove air cleaner, guide seal and seal retainer from the cover.

12. Remove the block seal from the center hole of the housing, using a blunt drift. (Don't scratch the bore of the housing, it could cause a vacuum leak.)

Power Piston Disassembly

1. Remove power piston diaphragm from the power piston. Keep it clean.

2. Remove screws that attach the plastic guide to the power piston. Remove guide and place to one side.

3. Remove the power piston square seal ring, reaction ring insert, reaction ring and reaction plate.

4. Depress operating rod slightly, then remove the Truarc snap-ring.

5. Remove control piston by pulling the operating rod.

6. Remove the O-ring seal from the end of the control piston.

7. Remove the filter elements and dust felt from the control piston rod.

Cleaning and Inspection

Thoroughly wash all metal parts in a suitable solvent and dry with compressed air. The power diaphragm, plastic power piston and guide should be washed in a mild soap and water solution. Blow dust and all cleaning material out of internal passages. All rubber parts should be replaced, regardless of condition. Install new air filters at assembly. Inspect all parts for scoring, pits, dents or nicks. Small imperfections can be smoothed out with crocus cloth. Replace all badly damaged parts.

Assembly

When assembling, be sure that all rubber parts, except the diaphragm and the reaction ring are lubricated with silicone grease.

1. Install control piston O-ring onto the piston.

2. Lubricate and install the control piston into the power piston. Install the Truarc snap-ring into its groove. Wipe all lubricant off the end of the control piston.

3. Install air filter elements and felt seal over the pushrod and down past the retaining shoulder on the rod. Install the power piston square seal ring into its groove.

4. Install the reaction plate in the power piston. Align the three holes with those in the power piston.

5. Install the rubber reaction ring in the reaction plate. Do not lubricate this ring.

6. Lubricate outer diameter of the reaction insert and install in the reaction ring.

7. Install reaction insert bumper into the guide.

8. Place guide on the power piston, align the holes with the aligning points on the power piston. Install retaining screws and torque to 80–100 in. lbs.

9. Install diaphragm on power piston; be sure that the diaphragm is correctly seated in the power piston groove.

10. With the housing blocked to prevent damage, install the block seal in the housing.

11. Install a new cover seal on the retainer and lubricate thoroughly, inside and out, with silicone grease, then install in the cover bore. Install new air filter.

12. Lubricate check valve grommet and install the vacuum check valve.

13. Mount the power unit in a vise, with master cylinder attaching studs up.

14. Apply a light coating of silicone grease to the bead, outer edge only, of the power piston diaphragm.

15. Install the power piston assembly in the housing with the operating rod down.

16. Install the power piston return spring into the flange of the guide.

17. Place the cover over the return spring and press down on the cover. At the same time, pilot the guide through the seal.

18. Rotate the cover to lock it to the housing. Be sure the scribe lines are in correct index and that the diaphragm is not pinched during assembly.

19. Install the housing lock on one of the long tangs of the housing.

20. Remove the power unit from the vise.

21. Install the master cylinder push-rod and air cleaner plate, then install the master cylinder on the studs. Install attaching nuts and washers. Torque to 200 in. lbs.

Installation

1. Install the power brake seal to the firewall.

2. Install power brake unit onto firewall and torque the attaching nuts to 200 in. lbs.

3. Install pushrod to brake pedal attaching bolt. Torque to 30 ft. lbs.

4. Install vacuum hose onto the power brake unit.

5. Attach the hydraulic tube and fill the master cylinder. Bleed hydraulic system.

6. Adjust stop-light switch if necessary.

Delco Single Diaphragm Booster

Disassembly

1. Scribe a mark on the bottom center of front and rear housings for reassembly.

2. Attach a base tool to the front housing and clamp the base in a vise with the power section up.

3. Separate the front and rear housings by securing a spanner wrench to the bracket. Press down on the wrench and rotate rear housing counterclockwise to the unlocked position. Loosen the housing carefully as it is spring loaded.

4. Remove the spanner wrench, then lift the rear housing and power piston assembly from the unit. Remove the return spring.

5. Remove the silencer by removing the retaining ring on the push rod.

6. Remove the seal, vacuum check valve and grommet from the front housing.

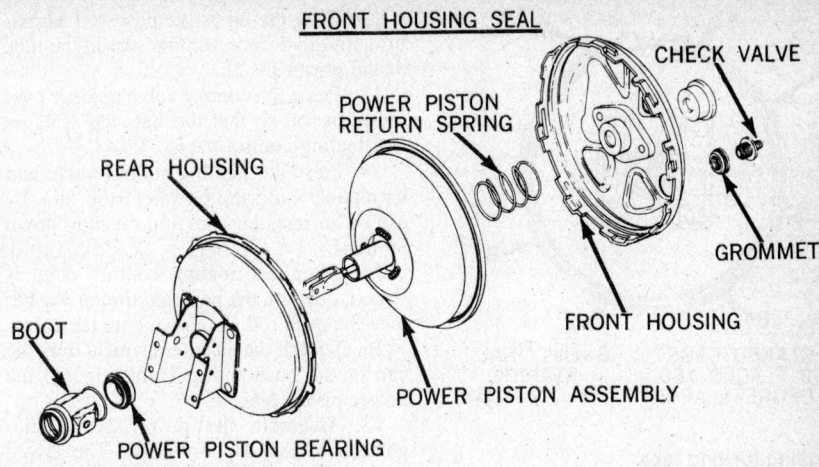

Delco single diaphragm booster

7. Remove the power piston assembly from the rear housing.

8. Remove the silencer from the neck of the power piston tube.

9. Remove the lock ring from the power piston.

10. Remove the reaction retainer, piston, plate, levers, bumper and spring.

11. Place a power piston wrench in a vise and position the assembly so that the three lugs on the tool fit into the three notches in the piston.

12. Press down on the support plate and rotate it counterclockwise until it separates from the power piston.

13. Remove the diaphragm from the support plate.

14. Position the power piston, tube down, in a tool fabricated from a piece of wood 2″ × 4″ × 8″ long with a 1⅜″ hole in the center clamped in a vise.

15. Remove the snap-ring on the air valve.

16. Using the power pump and press plate insert the power piston, tube down, in a press plate and remove the air valve assembly using a ⅜″ drive extension as a remover.

17. Remove the floating control valve assembly from the push rod. Use a new one when rebuilding.

18. Push the master cylinder push rod from the center of the reaction retainer.

19. Remove the O-ring from the groove in the master cylinder piston rod.

Assembly

1. Use clean brake fluid and thoroughly clean all resuable brake parts.

2. Inspect all rubber parts and replace if nicked, cut or damaged.

3. When rebuilding make sure that no grease or mineral oil comes in contact with any of the rubber parts.

4. Install a new vacuum check valve

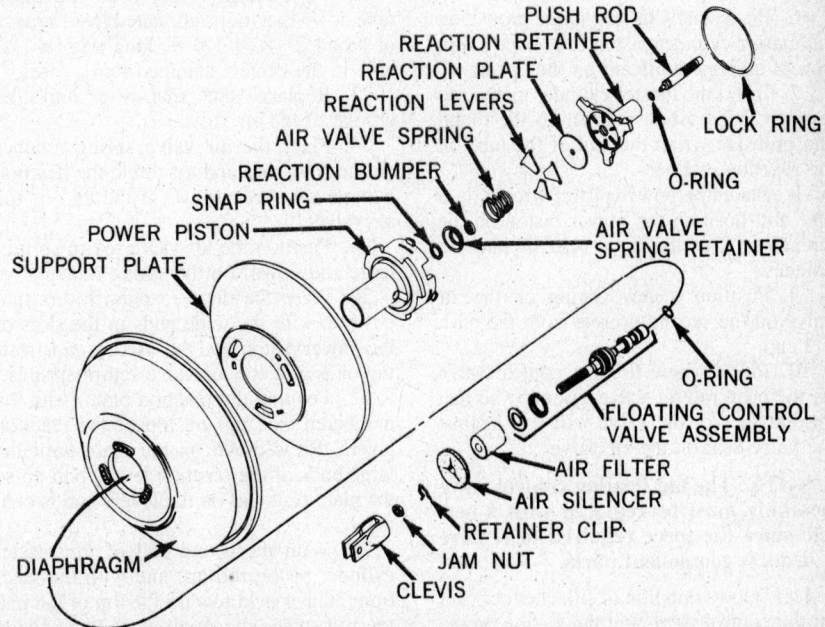

Power piston assembly

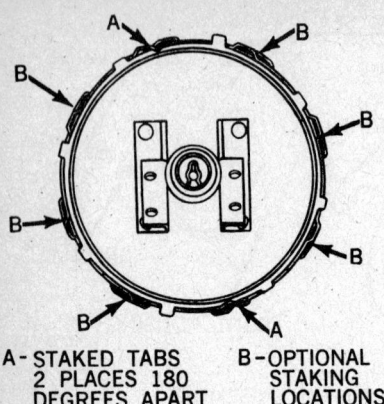

A - STAKED TABS
2 PLACES 180
DEGREES APART

B - OPTIONAL
STAKING
LOCATIONS

Housing locking tabs

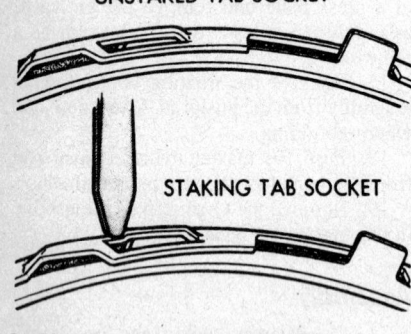

UNSTAKED TAB SOCKET

STAKING TAB SOCKET

Staking the housing locking tabs

using a new grommet.

5. Position a new front housing seal so that the flat surface of the cup lies against the bottom depression in the housing.

6. Place a new O-ring in the groove on the master cylinder piston rod, wipe a thin film of silicone lubricant on the O-ring.

7. Insert the master cylinder piston rod through the reaction retainer so the round end protrudes from the end of the tube on the reaction retainer.

8. Place the power piston wrench in a vise and position the power piston on the wrench so that the three lugs fit into the notches.

9. Position a new O-ring on the air valve on the second groove from the push rod end.

10. Place a new floating control valve on the push rod-air valve assembly so that the flat face of the valve will seat against the valve seat on the air valve.

NOTE: The old floating control valve assembly must be replaced with a new one since the force required to remove it distorts component parts.

11. Wipe a thin film of silicone lubricant on the control valve and the O-ring on the air valve.

12. Push the air valve push rod assembly, air valve first, onto its seat in the tube of the power piston.

13. Place the control valve retainer over the push rod so that the flat side seats on the floating control valve.

14. Press the floating control valve and its retainer onto the power piston tube by use of an installer tool and pushing down by hand.

15. After the floating control valve is seated, position the push rod limiter washer over the push rod and down onto the valve.

16. Stretch the air filter element over the end of the push rod and press it into the power piston tube.

17. Assemble the power piston diaphragm to the support plate. The raised flange of the diaphragm is pressed through the hole in the center of the support plate.

NOTE: Be sure that the edge of the center hole fits into the groove in the flange of the diaphragm.

18. Pull the diaphragm away from the outside diameter of the support plate so that the support plate can be gripped with both hands.

19. With the power piston still positioned on the holding tool in a vise, coat the bead of the diaphragm that contacts the power piston with silicone lubricant.

20. Place the support plate and diaphragm assembly over the tube of the power piston with the locking tangs facing downward.

NOTE: The flange of the power piston will fit into the groove on the power piston.

21. Press down and rotate the support plate clockwise, until the lugs on the power piston come against the stops on the support plate.

22. Turn the assembly over and place tube down in a tool, fabricated from a piece of wood 2" × 4" × 8" long with a 1⅜" hole in the center, clamped into a vise.

23. Replace the snap-ring into the groove of the air valve.

24. Place the air valve spring retainer on the snap-ring and assemble the reaction bumper into the groove in the end of the air valve.

25. Position the air valve return spring, large end down, on the spring retainer.

26. Place the three reaction levers into position with the wide ends in the slots of the power piston and the narrow ends resting on top of the air valve return springs.

27. Position the reaction plate (with the numbered side up) on top of the reaction levers. Press down on the plate until the large ends of the reaction levers pop up so the plate rests flat on the levers and is centered.

28. With the round end of the master cylinder piston rod up, and with the reaction retainer held toward the top of the piston rod, place the small end of the piston rod in the hole in the center of the reaction

plate. Line up the ears on the reaction retainer with the notches in the power piston and push the reaction retainer down until the ears seat in the notches.

29. With pressure on the reaction retainer, position the large lock ring down over the master cylinder push rod.

30. There is a lug on the power piston which has a raised divider in the center. One end of the lock ring goes under the lug and on one side of the divider.

31. As you work your way around the power piston, the lockring goes over the ear of the reaction retainer and under a lug on the power piston until the other end of the lock ring is seated under the lug with the raised divider.

NOTE: Make certain both ends of the lock ring are securely under the large lug.

32. Place a new power piston bearing in the center of the rear housing so the flange on the center hole of the housing fits into the groove of the power piston bearing. The large flange on the power piston bearing will be on the stud side of the housing. Coat the inside of the bearing with silicone lubricant.

33. Place the air silencer over the holes on the tube of the power piston. Wipe the tube with silicone lubricant.

34. Attach the holding fixture to the front housing and clamp the base in a vise.

35. Place the power piston return spring over the insert in the front housing.

36. Lubricate the inside diameter of the support plate seal, the reaction retainer tube, and the beaded edge of the diaphragm with silicone lubricant.

37. Place the rear housing assembly over the front housing assembly and align the scribe marks of the two housings so they will match when in the locked position.

38. Place a spanner wrench on the rear housing and tighten the nuts and washers to the bolts.

39. Press down on the spanner wrench and twist the rear housing clockwise until fully locked.

NOTE: Do not break the studs loose in the rear housing or put pressure on the power piston tube when locking the housings.

40. Remove the spanner wrench and the holding fixture from the front housing.

41. Push the felt silencer over the push-rod and seat it against the end of the power piston tube.

42. Push the plastic boot and seat it against the rear housing. The raised tabs on the side of the boot will locate in the holes in the center of the brackets.

43. Stake the front and rear housing in two places: 180° apart.

NOTE: The interlock tabs should not be used for staking a second time. When all tabs have been staked once, the housing must be replaced.

Delco Tandem Dual Diaphragm Type

Disassembly

1. Scribe a line across the front and rear housing for reassembly.

2. Attach the base of a special holding fixture or equivalent to the front housing with nuts and washers and draw down tight to eliminate damage to the studs. Clamp the base in a vise with the power section up.

3. On vehicles with a straight mounting bracket place a spanner wrench over the studs on the rear housing and attach with nuts and washers.

4. On vehicles with a tilted mounting bracket there is a special tool placed inside the mounting bracket with the spanner wrench placed on top.

5. Press down on the spanner wrench and rotate the rear housing counterclockwise to separate the two housings. Remove the special tools.

6. Remove the power piston return spring, and remove and discard the vacuum check valve and grommet from the front housing.

7. Remove the front housing seal.

8. Remove the boot retainer and boot from the rear housing and remove the felt silencer from inside the boot.

9. Remove the power piston group from the rear housing and remove the primary power piston bearing from the center opening of the rear housing.

10. Remove piston rod retainer and piston rod from the secondary piston.

11. Mount a special double ended tool with the large diameter end up in a vise. Position the secondary power piston so that the two radial slots in the piston fit over the ears of the tool.

NOTE: Due to an optional construction design on the primary and secondary power pistons the special tool used in step 11 will have to be reworked.

12. Fold back the primary diaphragm from the outside diameter of the primary support plate. Grip the edge of the support plate and rotate it counterclockwise to unscrew the primary power piston from the secondary power piston.

13. Remove the housing divider from the secondary power piston bearing from the housing divider.

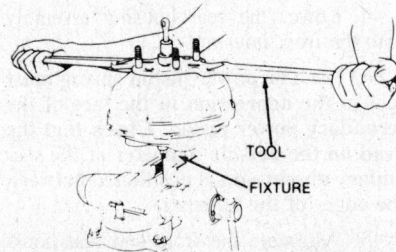

Unlocking the front and rear housings

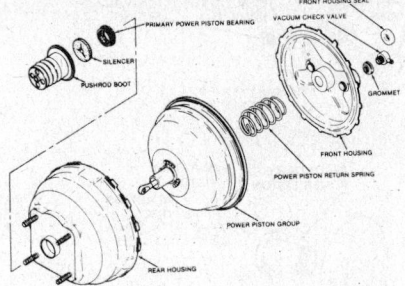

Delco tandem dual diaphragm booster

14. The secondary power piston should still be positioned on the special double ended tool. Fold back the secondary diaphragm from the outside diameter of the secondary support plate. Rotate the support plate clockwise to unlock the secondary power piston.

15. Remove the secondary diaphragm from the secondary support plate.

16. Remove the reaction piston and disc from the center of the secondary power piston by pushing down on the end of the piston.

17. Remove the air valve spring from the end of the valve, if not removed earlier.

18. Remove the primary diaphragm and piston using the same procedure as the secondary with the exception of turning the support plate counterclockwise to unlock it.

19. Remove the air filter from the tubular section of the primary power piston.

20. Remove the power head silencer from the neck of the power piston tube.

21. Remove the rubber reaction bumper from the end of the air valve.

22. Using snap-ring pliers, remove the retaining ring from the air valve.

23. Remove the air valve push rod assembly.

   a. The recommended method would be to place the primary power piston in an arbor press and press the air valve push rod assembly out the bottom of the power piston tube using a rod not larger than ½" in diameter.

   b. An alternate method would be to insert a heavy, round shanked screwdriver on both sides of the pushrod and pull the air valve-push rod assembly straight out.

24. Remove the O-ring seal from the air valve.

Assembly

1. Use clean brake fluid and thoroughly clean all reusable brake parts.

2. Inspect all rubber parts and replace if nicked, cut or damaged.

3. When rebuilding, make sure that no grease or mineral oil comes in contact with any of the rubber parts.

4. Install a new vacuum check valve and a new grommet in the front housing.

5. Place a new seal in the front housing

so that the flat surface lies against the bottom of the depression in the housing.

6. Reassemble the power piston group.

7. Lubricate the inside and outside diameter of the O-ring seal with silicone lubricant and place on the air valve.

8. Wipe a thin film of silicone lubricant on the large and small outside diameter of the floating control valve. If the floating control valve needs replacement, it will be necessary to replace the complete air valve-push rod assembly.

9. Place the air valve end of the air valve push rod assembly into the tube of the primary power piston. Manually press the air valve push rod assembly so that the floating control valve bottoms on the tube section of the primary power piston.

10. Place the inside diameter of the floating control valve retainer on the outside diameter of the special installer. Place it over the pushrod so that the closed side of the retainer seats on the floating control valve. Using the installer manually press

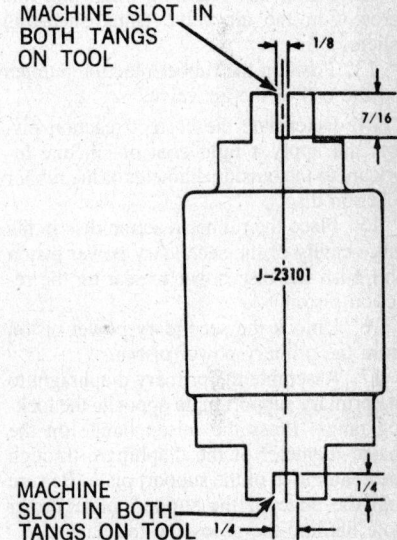

Reworking the tool for optional power piston design

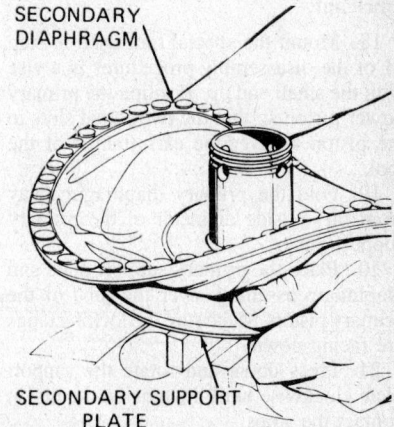

Locking or unlocking the secondary support plate and secondary power piston

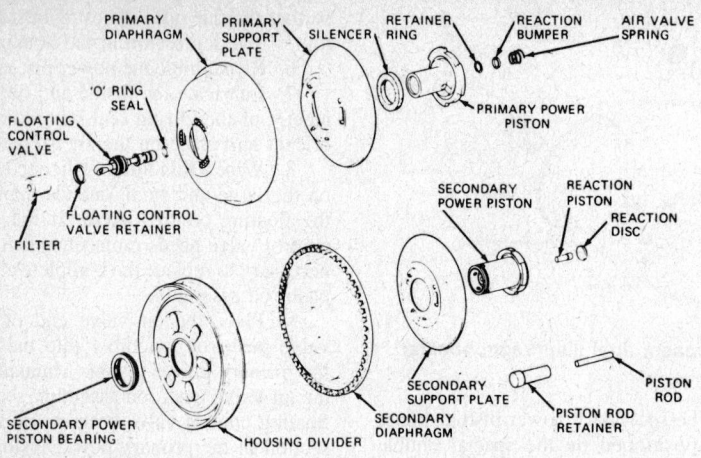

Power piston group

the retainer and floating control valve to seat in the tube.

11. Stretch the filter element over the pushrod and press it into the piston tube.

12. Place the retaining ring into the groove in the air valve using snap-ring pliers.

13. Position the rubber reaction bumper on the end of the air valve.

14. Determine the correct reaction piston and apply a light coat of silicone lubricant to the outside diameter of the rubber reaction disc.

15. Place the rubber reaction disc in the large cavity of the secondary power piston and push the disc down to seat on the reaction piston.

16. Unlock the secondary power piston from the primary power piston.

17. Assemble the primary diaphragm to the primary support plate opposite the locking tangs. Press the raised flange on the inside diameter of the diaphragm through the center hole of the support plate. Be sure that the edge of the support plate center hole fits into the groove of the flange.

NOTE: Lubricate the inside diameter of the diaphragm and the raised surface of the flange with a light coat of silicone lubricant.

18. Mount the special tool used in step 11 of the disassembly procedures in a vise with the small end up. Position the primary power piston so that the two radial slots in the piston fit over the ears (tangs) of the tool.

19. Fold the primary diaphragm away from the outside diameter of the primary support plate.

20. Place the primary support plate and diaphragm assembly over the tube of the primary piston. Make sure the locking tangs are facing down.

21. Press down and rotate the support plate clockwise until the tabs on the piston contact the stops.

22. Place the power head silencer on the tube of the piston so that the holes at the base of the tube are covered.

23. Coat the outside of the tube with silicone lubricant.

24. Remove the primary piston assembly from the special tool and lay it aside.

25. Assemble the secondary diaphragm to the secondary support plate following the same steps for assembling the primary support plate except mount the special tool with the large diameter up, and press down and turn the plate counterclockwise until the piston contacts the stops.

26. Leave the secondary power piston on the tool and in the vise.

27. Apply a light coat of talcum powder or silicone lubricant to the bead on the outside diameter of the secondary diaphragm. This will make it easier for reassembly of the front and rear housing.

28. Place the secondary bearing in the inside diameter of the housing divider so that the extended lip of the bearing faces up.

29. Lubricate the inside diameter of the bearing with silicone lubricant.

30. Using a special protector tool or equivalent, position the secondary bearing on the threaded end of the secondary power piston.

31. Hold the housing divider so that the six oblong protrusions on the middle of the divider are facing up. Press the divider down over the tool and onto the piston tube so it rests against the support ring. Remove the bearing protector tool.

32. Pick up the primary power piston

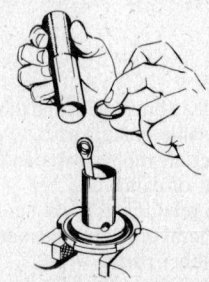

Installing the floating control valve retainer

Seating the floating control valve assembly

assembly and fold the primary diaphragm away from the outside diameter of the support plate.

33. Place the small end of the air valve return spring on the air valve so that it contacts the air valve retaining ring.

34. Position the primary power piston. Make sure that the air valve return spring seats down over the raised center section of the secondary piston.

35. Rotate the secondary power piston clockwise into the threaded portion of the primary piston. Tighten to 5–15 ft. lbs.

36. Fold the primary diaphragm back into position.

37. Cover the outside diameter of the piston rod retainer with a light coat of silicone lubricant.

38. Insert the master cylinder piston rod retainer into the secondary power piston so that the flat end bottoms against the rubber reaction disc.

39. Place the new primary piston bearing in the rear housing center hole. The thin lip of the bearing will protrude to the outside of the housing. Coat the inside diameter of the bearing with silicone lubricant.

40. Mount the holding fixture in a vise and position the front housing so that the housing studs fit in the holes provided in the tool.

41. Place the power piston return spring over the inset in the front housing.

42. Assemble the power piston assembly to the rear housing by pressing the tube of the primary piston through the rear housing bearing until the housing divider seats in the rear housing and the primary piston bottoms against the housing.

43. Hold the rear housing with the mounting studs up and position it so that the tangs on the edge of the front housing are locked in the slots on the edge of the rear housing. The scribe marks on the top of the housings will be in line.

44. Lower the rear housing assembly onto the front housing.

NOTE: The power piston spring must seat in the depression in the face of the secondary power piston. Check that the bead on the outside diameter of the secondary diaphragm is positioned between the edges of the housing.

45. Assemble the front and rear housings with the spanner wrench.

46. Replace the silencer and boot.

Steering

INDEX

Manual Steering

Power Steering

BEFORE SERVICING, SEE THE SAFETY NOTICE AT THE FRONT OF THE BOOK

MANUAL STEERING GEAR

STEERING GEAR ALIGNMENT

Before any steering gear adjustments are made, it is recommended that the front end of the truck be raised and a thorough inspection be made for stiffness or lost motion in the steering gear, steering linkage and front suspension. Worn or damaged parts should be replaced, since a satisfactory adjustment of the steering gear cannot be obtained if bent or badly worn parts exist.

It is also very important that the steering gear be properly aligned in the truck. Misalignment of the gear places a stress on the steering worm shaft, therefore a proper adjustment is impossible. To align the steering gear, loosen the steering gear-to-frame mounting bolts to permit the gear to align itself. Check the steering gear to frame mounting seat. If there is a gap at any of the mounting bolts, proper alignment may be obtained by placing shims where excessive gap appears. Tighten the steering gear-to-frame bolts. Alignment of the gear in the truck is very important and should be done carefully so that a satisfactory, trouble-free gear adjustment may be obtained.

Gemmer Worm and Double Roller Tooth Type

With Screw Adjusted Mesh

The steering gear is of the worm and roller type with a 24 to 1 gear ratio. The cross shaft is straddle mounted with a bearing surface at the top and bottom points of the shaft mounting areas. The three tooth cross

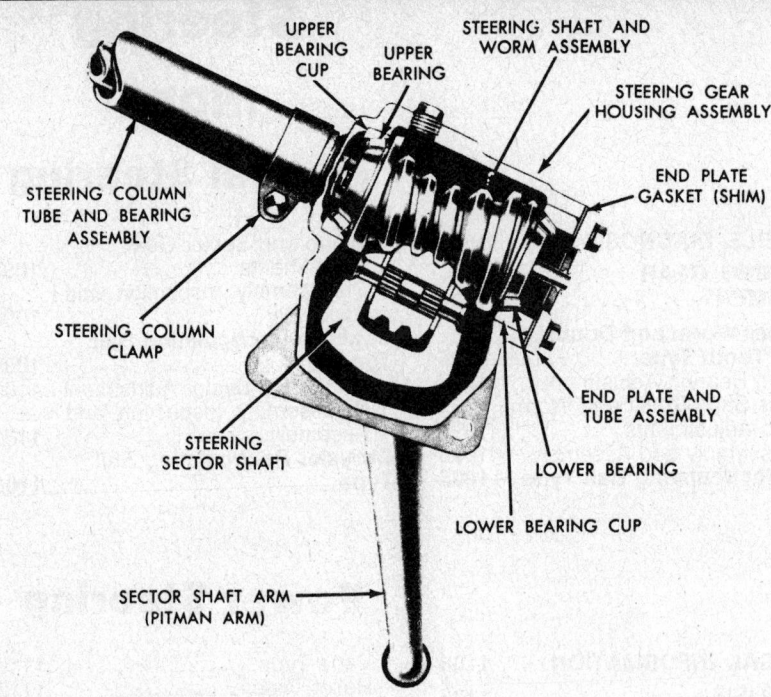

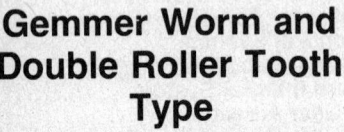

Worm and roller type steering gear

shaft roller is mounted in ball bearings. The proper lubricant used in the gear box is S.A.E. 90 Extreme Pressure Lubricant.

The external adjustments given below will properly adjust the steering gear.

WORM BEARING ADJUSTMENT

1. Turn the steering wheel about one full turn from straight ahead and secure it so it doesn't move.
2. Determine if there is any worm gear end-play by shaking the front wheel sideways and noting if there is any end movement that may be felt between the steering wheel hub and the steering jacket tube. (Be

sure any movement noted is not looseness in the steering jacket tube.)

3. If end play is present, adjust the worm bearings by loosening the four cover cap screws about ⅛″. Separate the top shim, using a knife blade, and remove it. Do not damage the remaining shims or gaskets.

4. Replace the cover and recheck the end-play again. If necessary, repeat steps 2 and 3 until the end-play movement is as small as possible without tightening the steering gear too much.

NOTE: Adjustment may be done with the Pitman arm disconnected. With the steering wheel turned about one full turn from straight ahead and using a spring scale tool, adjust with the shims as given above until the spring scale pull is between ¼ and ⅝ ft. lbs.

CROSS SHAFT ROLLER AND WORM MESH ADJUSTMENT

1. Turn the steering wheel to the middle of its turning limits with the Pitman arm disconnected. The steering gear roller should be on the worm high spot.

2. Shake the Pitman arm sideways to determine the amount of clearance between the worm cross shaft roller. Movement of more than 1/32″ indicates that the roller and worm mesh must be adjusted.

3. Loosen the adjusting screw lock nut and tighten the external cross shaft adjusting screw a small amount. Recheck the clearance by shaking the Pitman arm. Re-

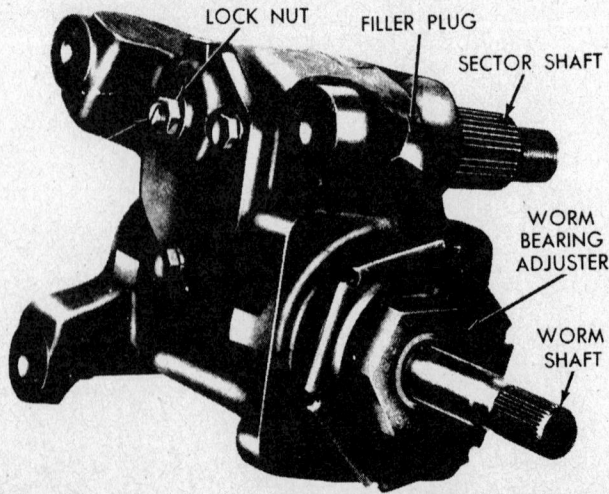

Steering gear adjustments

STEERING TROUBLE DIAGNOSIS

Condition	Possible Cause	Correction
Excessive Play or Looseness in the Steering	1. Steering gear shaft adjusted too loose or shaft and/or bushing badly worn. 2. Excessive steering gear worm end play due to bearing adjustment. 3. Steering linkage loose or worn. 4. Front wheel bearings improperly adjusted. 5. Steering arm loose on steering gear shaft. 6. Steering gear housing attaching bolts loose. 7. Steering arms loose at steering knuckles. 8. Working pins or bushings. 9. Loose spring shackles.	1. Replace worn parts and adjust according to instructions. 2. Adjust according to instructions. 3. Replace worn parts. 4. Adjust wheel bearings. 5. Inspect for damage to the gear shaft and steering arm, replace parts as necessary. 6. Tighten the attaching bolts to specifications. 7. Tighten according to specifications. 8. Replace king pins and bushings. 9. Adjust or replace parts as necessary.
Hard Steering	1. Low or uneven tire pressure. 2. Insufficient lubricant in the steering gear housing or in steering linkage. 3. Steering gear shaft adjusted too tight. 4. Improper caster or toe-in. 5. Steering column misaligned.	1. Inflate the tires to recommended pressures. 2. Lubricate as necessary. 3. Adjust according to instructions. 4. Align the wheels. 5. See "Steering Gear Alignment."
Wheel Tramp (Excessive Vertical Motion of Wheels)	1. Incorrect tire pressure. 2. Improper balance of wheels, tires and brake drums. 3. Loose tie rod ends or steering connections. 4. Worn or inoperative shock absorbers. 5. Excessive run-out of brake drums, wheels or tires.	1. Inflate the tires to recommended pressures. 2. Balance as necessary. 3. Inspect and repair as necessary. 4. Replace the shock absorbers. 5. Repair or replace as required.
Shimmy	1. Badly worn and/or unevenly worn tires. 2. Wheels and tires out of balance. 3. Worn or loose steering linkage parts. 4. Worn king pins and bushings. 5. Loose steering gear adjustments. 6. Loose wheel bearings. 7. Improper caster setting. 8. Weak or broken springs. 9. Incorrect tire pressure or tire sizes not uniform. 10. Faulty shock absorbers.	1. Rotate tires or replace if necessary. 2. Balance wheel and tire assemblies. 3. Replace parts are required. 4. Replace king pins and bushings. 5. Adjust steering gear as necessary. 6. Adjust wheel bearings. 7. Adjust caster to specifications. 8. Replace as required. 9. Check tire sizes and inflate tires to recommended pressure 10. Replace as necessary.
Pull to One Side (Tendency of the Vehicle to Veer in one Direction Only)	1. Incorrect tire pressure or tires not uniform. 2. Wheel bearings improperly adjusted. 3. Dragging brakes. 4. Improper caster, camber or toe-in. 5. Grease, dirt, oil or brake fluid on brake linings. 6. Broken or sagging rear springs. 7. Bent front axle, linkage or steering knuckle. 8. Worn or tight king pin bushings.	1. Check tire sizes and inflate the tires to recommended pressures. 2. Adjust wheel bearings. 3. Inspect for weak, or broken brake shoe spring, binding pedal. 4. Adjust to specifications. 5. Inspect, replace and adjust as necessary. 6. Replace the rear springs. 7. Replace the parts as necessary. 8. Lubricate or replace as necessary.
Wander or Weave	1. Improper caster, camber or toe-in. 2. Worn king pin and bushings. 3. Worn or improperly adjusted front wheel bearings. 4. Loose spring shackles. 5. Incorrect tire pressure or tire sizes not uniform. 6. Loose steering gear mounting bolts. 7. Tight king pin bushings. 8. Tight king pin thrust bearings.	1. Adjust to specifications. 2. Replace parts as required. 3. Adjust or replace parts as necessary. 4. Adjust or replace parts as necessary. 5. Check tire sizes and inflate tires to recommended pressure. 6. Tight to specifications. 7. Lubricate or ream to proper fit. 8. Adjust to .001 to .005 inch cleareance.

peat until the clearance is correct. (Do not overtighten.)

NOTE: The cross shaft roller and worm mesh adjustment may be done, using a spring scale tool, by measuring the amount of wheel pull as the external cross shaft adjusting screw is tightened. When the spring scale pull is between ⅞ and 1⅛ ft. lbs., the adjustment is correct.

4. Tighten the Pitman arm attaching nut to 100–125 ft. lbs. The steering wheel nut (if loosened) should be tightened to 15–20 ft. lbs. torque.

Disassembly

1. Remove steering gear oil seal, using a suitable puller.
2. Remove cross shaft, using an arbor to prevent bearings from dropping out.
3. Remove cover, shims and cover gasket.
4. Remove worm gear, thrust bearings and bearing cups.

Assembly

1. Clean and inspect all parts, replace as necessary.

NOTE: If either thrust bearing is excessively worn, replace them both.

2. Reassemble steering gear, using new oil seal.
3. Perform worm bearing and cross shaft roller and worm mesh adjustments.
4. Lubricate to specifications.

Ford Steering Gear—Recirculating Ball Type

STEERING WORM AND SECTOR GEAR ADJUSTMENTS

The ball nut assembly and the sector gear must be adjusted properly to maintain a minimum amount of steering shaft end play and a minimum amount of backlash between the sector gear and the ball nut. There are only two adjustments that may be done on this steering gear and they should be done as given below:
1. Remove the steering gear from the vehicle.
2. Loosen the locknut on the sector shaft adjustment screw and turn the adjusting screw counterclockwise about three turns.
3. Measure the worm bearing preload by attaching an in. lbs. torque wrench to the input shaft. Note the reading required to rotate input shaft about 1½ turns either side of center. If the torque reading is not about 4–5 in. lbs., adjust the gear as given in the next step.

4. Loosen the steering shaft bearing adjuster lock nut and tighten or back off the bearing adjusting screw until the preload is within the specified limits.
5. Tighten the steering shaft bearing adjuster lock nut, and recheck the preload torque.
6. Turn the input shaft slowly to either stop. Turn gently against the stop to avoid possible damage to the ball return guides. Then rotate the shaft three turns to center the ball nut.
7. Turn the sector adjusting screw clockwise until the proper torque (9–10 in. lbs.) is obtained that is necessary to rotate the worm gear past its center (high spot).
8. With the input shaft centered, hold the sector shaft and check the lash between the ball nuts, balls, and worm shaft by applying 15 lbs. torque to the steering input shaft in both right and left turn directions. The total travel of the wrench should not exceed 1¼".
9. Tighten the sector adjusting screw locknut, and recheck the backlash. Install the steering gear.

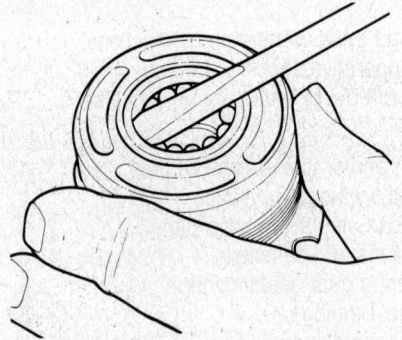

Removing bearing retainer from the adjuster plug

Disassembly

1. Rotate the steering shaft three turns from either stop.
2. Remove the sector shaft adjusting screw locknut and loosen the screw one turn. Remove the steering shaft bearing adjuster, and the housing cover bolts and remove the sector shaft. Remove the shaft by turning the screw clockwise. Keep the shim with the screw.
3. Remove the sector shaft from the housing.
4. Carefully pull the steering shaft and ball nut from the housing, and remove the steering shaft lower bearing. Do not run the ball nut to either end of the worm gear to prevent damaging the ball return guides. Disassemble the ball nut only if there are signs of binding or tightness.
5. To disassemble the ball nut, remove the ball return guide clamp and the ball return guides from the ball nut. Keep ball nut clamp side up until ready to remove the ball bearings.

6. Turn the ball nut over and rotate the worm shaft from side to side until all 50 balls have dropped out into a clean pan. With all balls removed, the nut will slide off the wormshaft.
7. Remove the upper bearing cup from the bearing adjuster and the lower cup from the housing. It may be necessary to tap the housing or the adjuster on a wooden block to jar the bearing cups loose.

Inspection

1. Carefully clean and inspect all parts. If the inspection shows bearing damage, the sector shaft bearing and the oil seal should be pressed out.
2. If the sector shaft bearing and oil seals were removed, press new bearings and oil seals into the housing. Do not clean, wash, or soak seals in cleaning solvent.
3. Apply the recommended steering gear lubricant to the housing and seals, filling the pocket between sector shaft bearings.

Assembly

1. Install the bearing cup in the lower end of the housing and a bearing cup in the adjuster nut. Install a new seal in the bearing adjuster if the old seal was removed.
2. Apply gear lube to the outside of the worm shaft and the inside of the ball nut. Lay the steering shaft down, and position the ball nut on the shaft with the guide holes upward and the shallow end of the teeth to the left of the steering wheel position. Align the grooves in worm and ball nut by sighting through the guide holes.
3. Insert the ball guides into the holes in the ball nut, lightly tapping them, if necessary, to seat them.
4. Insert 25 balls into the hole in the top of each ball guide. If necessary, rotate the shaft slightly to distribute the balls evenly in the circuit.
5. Install the ball guide clamp, tightening the screws to the proper torque. Check that the worm shaft rotates freely.
6. Coat the threads of the steering shaft bearing adjuster, the housing cover bolts, and the sector adjusting screw with a suitable oil-resistant sealing compound. Do not apply sealer to female threads and do not get sealer on the steering shaft bearings.
7. Coat the worm bearings, sector shaft bearings, and gear teeth with steering gear lubricant.
8. Clamp the housing in a vise, with the sector shaft axis horizontal, and place the steering shaft lower bearing in its cup. Place the steering shaft and ball nut assemblies in the housing.
9. Position the steering shaft upper bearing on top of the worm gear and install the steering shaft bearing adjuster, adjuster nut, and the bearing cup. Leave the nut loose.
10. Adjust the worm bearing preload according to the instructions given earlier.
11. Position the sector adjusting screw

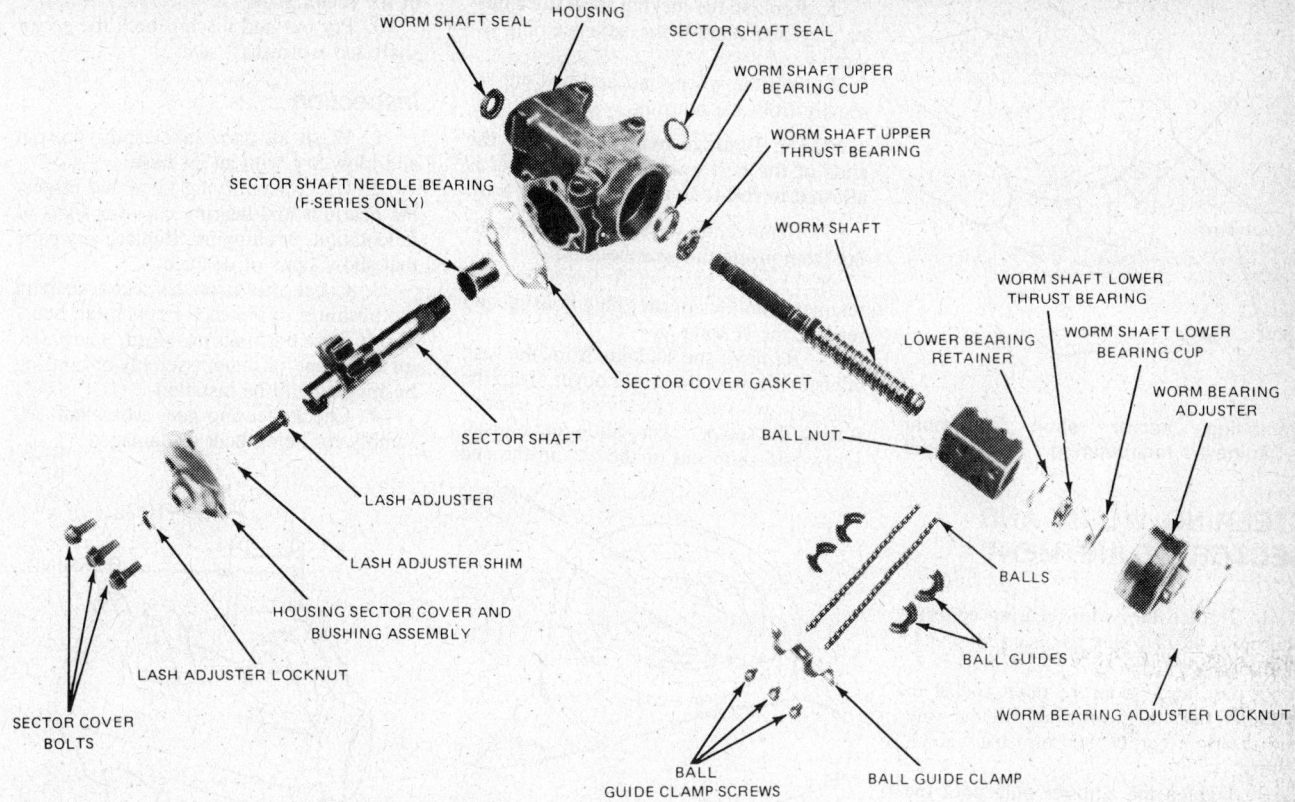

WORM SHAFT SEAL   HOUSING   SECTOR SHAFT SEAL

WORM SHAFT UPPER BEARING CUP

WORM SHAFT UPPER THRUST BEARING

SECTOR SHAFT NEEDLE BEARING (F-SERIES ONLY)

WORM SHAFT

WORM SHAFT LOWER THRUST BEARING

WORM SHAFT LOWER BEARING CUP

LOWER BEARING RETAINER

WORM BEARING ADJUSTER

SECTOR COVER GASKET

SECTOR SHAFT

BALL NUT

LASH ADJUSTER

BALLS

LASH ADJUSTER SHIM

HOUSING SECTOR COVER AND BUSHING ASSEMBLY

BALL GUIDES

LASH ADJUSTER LOCKNUT

WORM BEARING ADJUSTER LOCKNUT

SECTOR COVER BOLTS

BALL GUIDE CLAMP SCREWS

BALL GUIDE CLAMP

Exploded view of Saginaw recirculating ball model

and adjuster shim, and check for a clearance of not more than 0.002″ between the screw head and the end of the sector shaft. If the clearance exceeds 0.002″, add enough shims to reduce the clearance to under 0.002″ clearance.

12. Start the sector shaft adjusting screw into the housing cover. Install a new gasket on the cover.

13. Rotate the steering shaft until the ball nut teeth mesh with the sector gear teeth, tilting the housing so the ball will tip toward the housing cover opening.

14. Lubricate the sector shaft journal and install the sector shaft and cover. With the cover moved to one side, fill the gear with lubricant (about 0.97 lb.). Push the cover and the sector shaft into place, and install the two top housing bolts. Do not tighten the bolts until checking to see that there is some lash between the ball nut and the sector gear teeth. Hold or push the cover away from the ball nut and tighten the bolts to the proper torque (30–40 ft. lbs.).

15. Loosely install the sector shaft adjusting screw lock nut and adjust the sector shaft mesh load as given earlier. Tighten the adjusting screw lock nut.

Saginaw Recirculating Ball Type

The steering gear is of the recirculating ball nut type. the ball nut, mounted on the worm

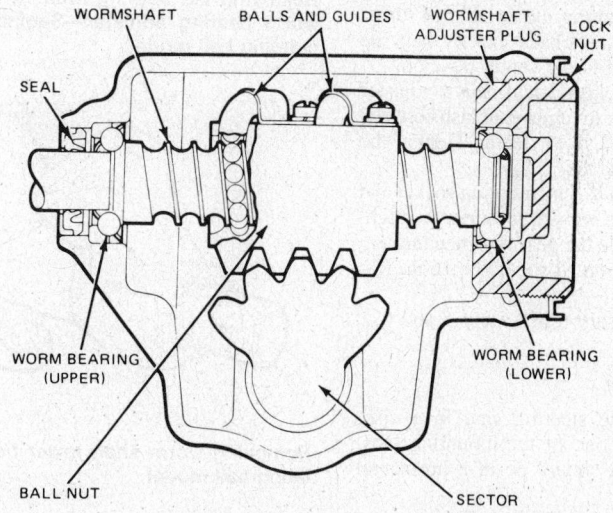

WORMSHAFT   BALLS AND GUIDES   WORMSHAFT ADJUSTER PLUG   LOCK NUT

SEAL

WORM BEARING (UPPER)

WORM BEARING (LOWER)

BALL NUT

SECTOR

Cross section of Saginaw recirculating ball model

gear, is driven by means of steel balls which circulate in helical grooves in both the worm and nut. Ball return guides attached to the nut serve to recirculate the two sets of balls in the grooves. As the steering wheel is turned to the right, the ball nut moves upward. When the wheel is turned to the left, the ball nut moves downward.

The sector teeth on the pinion shaft and the ball nut are designed so that they fit the tightest when the steering wheel is straight

ahead. This mesh action is adjusted by an adjusting screw which moves the pinion shaft endwise until the teeth mesh properly. The worm bearing adjuster provides proper preloading of the upper and lower bearings.

Before doing the adjustment procedures given below, ensure that the steering problem is not caused by faulty suspension components, bad front end alignment, etc. Then, proceed with the following adjustments.

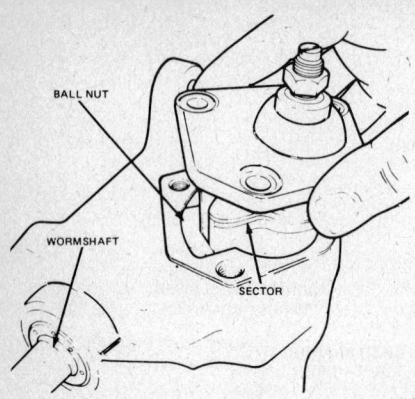

Removing sector shaft assembly —Saginaw recirculating ball model

STEERING WORM AND SECTOR ADJUSTMENT

1. Tighten the worm bearing adjuster plug until all end play has been removed, then loosen ¼ turn.

2. Use an $^{11}/_{16}$ in. 12 point socket to carefully turn the wormshaft all the way into the right corner then turn back about ½ turn.

3. Tighten the adjuster plug until the proper thrust bearing preload is obtained (5–8 in. lbs.). Tighten the adjuster plug locknut to 85 ft. lbs.

4. Turn the wormshaft from one stop to the other counting the number of turns. Then turn the shaft back exactly half the number of turns to the center position.

5. Turn the lash (sector shaft) adjuster screw clockwise to remove all lash between the ball nut and sector teeth. Tighten the locknut to 25 ft. lbs.

6. Using an $^{11}/_{16}$ in. 12 point socket and an in. lb. torque wrench, observe the highest reading while the gear is turned through the center position. It should be 16 in. lbs. or less. If necessary repeat steps 5 and 6.

7. If necessary repeat steps 5 and 6.

Disassembly

1. Place the steering gear in a vise, clamping onto one of the mounting tabs. The wormshaft should be in a horizontal position.

2. Rotate the wormshaft from stop to stop and count the total number of turns. Turn back exactly halfway, placing the gear on center.

3. Remove the three self locking bolts which attach the sector cover to the housing.

4. Using a plastic hammer, tap lightly on the end of the sector shaft and lift the sector cover and sector shaft assembly from the gear housing.

NOTE: It may be necessary to turn the wormshaft by hand until the sector will pass through the opening in the housing.

5. Remove the locknut from the adjuster plug and remove the adjuster plug assembly.

6. Pull the wormshaft and ball nut assembly from the housing.

NOTE: Damage may be done to the ends of the ball guides if the ball nut is allowed to rotate to the end of the worm.

7. Remove the worm shaft upper bearing from inside the gear housing.

8. Pry the wormshaft lower bearing retainer from the adjuster plug housing and remove the bearing.

9. Remove the locknut from the lash adjuster screw in the sector cover. Turn the lash adjuster screw clockwise and remove it from the sector cover. Slide the adjuster screw and shim out of the slot in the end of the sector shaft.

10. Pry out and discard both the sector shaft and wormshaft seals.

Inspection

1. Wash all parts in cleaning solvent and blow dry with an air hose.

2. Use a magnifying glass and inspect the bearings and bearing caps for signs of indentation, or chipping. Replace any parts that show signs of damage.

3. Check the fit of the sector shaft in the bushings in the sector cover and housing. If these bushings are worn, a new sector cover and bushing assembly or housing bushing should be installed.

4. Check steering gear wormshaft assembly for being bent or damaged.

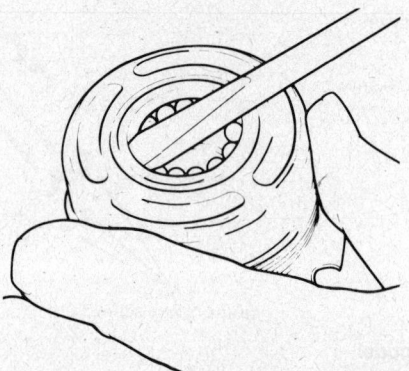

Removing the bearing retainer from the worm bearing adjuster—Saginaw recirculating ball model

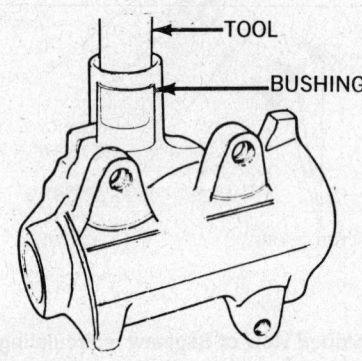

Removing sector shaft bushing—Saginaw recirculating ball model

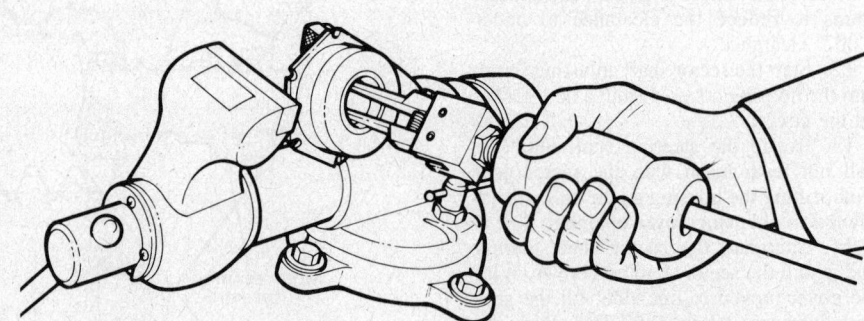

Removing worm shaft lower bearing cup from the adjuster plug—Saginaw recirculating ball model

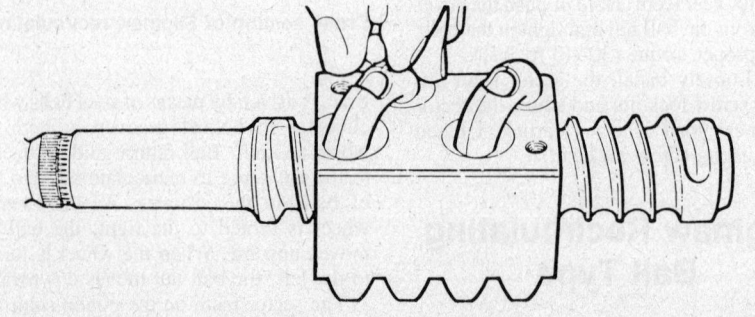

Filling the ball circuits—Saginaw recirculating ball model

SHAFT SEAL REPLACEMENT

1. Remove the old seal from the pump body.
2. Install the new seal by pressing the outer diameter of the seal with a suitable size socket.

NOTE: Make sure the socket is large enough to avoid damaging the external lip of the seal.

SECTOR SHAFT BUSHING REPLACEMENT

1. Place the steering gear housing in an arbor press.
2. Press the sector shaft bushing from the housing.

NOTE: Service bushings are bored to size and require no further reaming.

SECTOR COVER BUSHING REPLACEMENT

1. The sector cover bushing is not serviced separately. The entire sector cover assembly including the bushing must be replaced as a unit.

BALL NUT SERVICE

If there is any indication of binding or tightness when the ball nut is rotated on the worm the unit should be disassembled, cleaned and inspected as follows:

Ball Nut Disassembly

1. Remove the screws and clamp retaining the ball guides in the ball nut. Pull the guides out of the ball nut.
2. Turn the ball nut upside down and rotate the wormshaft back and forth until all the balls have dropped out of the ball nut. The ball nut can now be pulled endwise off the worm.
3. Wash all parts in solvent and dry them with air. Use a magnifying glass and inspect the worm and nut grooves and the surface of all balls for signs of indentation. Check all ball guides for damage at the ends. Replace any damaged parts.

Ball Nut Assembly

1. Slip the ball nut over the worm with the ball guide holes up and the shallow end of the ball nut teeth to the left from the steering wheel position. Sight through the ball guide to align the grooves in the worm.
2. Place two ball guide halves together and insert them in the upper circuit in the ball nut. Place the two remaining guides together and insert them in the lower circuit.
3. Count out 25 balls and place them in a suitable container. This is the proper number of balls for one circuit.

4. Load the 25 balls into one of the guide holes while turning the wormshaft gradually away from that hole.
5. Fill the remaining ball circuit in the same manner.
6. Assemble the ball guide clamp to the ball nut and tighten the screws to 18–24 in. lbs.
7. Check the assembly by rotating the ball nut on the worm to see that it moves freely.

NOTE: Do not rotate the ball nut to the end of the worm threads as this may damage the ball guides.

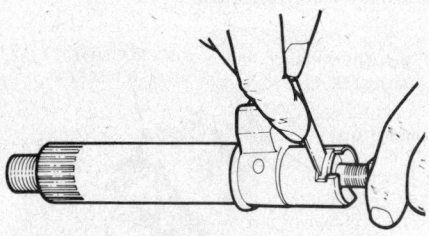

Checking lash adjuster end clearance —Saginaw recirculating ball model

Assembly

1. Coat the threads of the adjuster plug, sector cover bolts and lash adjuster with a non-drying oil resistant sealing compound.

NOTE: Do not apply compound to the female threads. Use extreme care when applying compound to the bearing adjuster so that it does not come in contact with the wormshaft bearing.

2. Place the steering gear housing in a vise with the wormshaft bore horizontal and the sector cover opening up.
3. Make sure that all seals, bushings and bearing cups are installed in the gear housing and that the ball nut is installed on the wormshaft.

4. Slip the wormshaft upper bearing assembly over the wormshaft and insert the wormshaft and ball nut assembly into the housing, feeding the end of the shaft through the upper ball bearing cup and seal.
5. Place the wormshaft lower bearing assembly in the adjuster plug bearing cup and press the stamped retainer into place with a suitable size socket.
6. Install the adjuster plug and locknut into the lower end of the housing while carefully guiding the end of the wormshaft into the bearing until nearly all end play has been removed from the wormshaft.
7. Position the lash adjuster including the shim in the slotted end of the sector shaft.

NOTE: End clearance should not be greater than .002. If the end clearance is greater than .002 a shim package is available with thicknesses of .063, .065, .067, .069.

8. Lubricate the steering gear with 11 oz. of steering gear grease. Rotate the wormshaft until the ball nut is at the other end of its travel and then pack as much new lubricant into the housing as possible without losing out the sector shaft opening. Rotate the wormshaft until the ball nut is at the other end of its travel and pack as much lubricant into the opposite end as possible.
9. Rotate the wormshaft until the ball nut is in the center of travel. This is to make sure that the sector shaft and ball nut will engage properly with the center tooth of the sector entering the center tooth space in the ball nut.
10. Insert the sector shaft assembly including lash adjuster screw and shim into the housing so that the center tooth of the sector enters the center tooth space in the ball nut.
11. Pack the remaining portion of the lubricant into the housing and also place

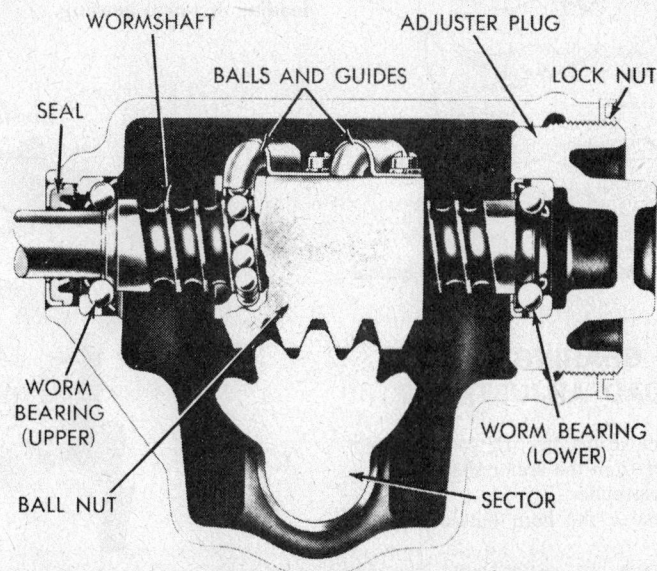

Chrysler recirculating ball type steering gear

some in the sector cover bushing hole.

12. Place the sector cover gasket on the housing.

13. Install the sector cover onto the sector shaft by reaching through the sector cover with a screwdriver and turning the lash adjuster screw counterclockwise until the screw bottoms, then back the screw off one-half turn. Loosely install a new lock nut onto the adjuster screw.

14. Install and tighten the sector cover bolt to 30 ft. lbs.

Chrysler Recirculating Ball Type

The steering gear is of the recirculating ball nut type. The ball nut, mounted on the worm gear, is driven by means of steel balls which circulate in helical grooves in both the worm and nut. Ball return guides attached to the nut serve to recirculate the two sets of balls in the grooves. As the steering wheel is turned to the right, the ball nut moves upward. When the wheel is turned to the left, the ball nut moves downward.

The sector teeth on the pinion shaft and the ball nut are designed so that they fit the tightest when the steering wheel is straight ahead. This mesh action is adjusted by an adjusting screw which moves the pinion shaft endwise until the teeth mesh properly. The worm bearing adjuster provides proper preloading of the upper and lower bearings.

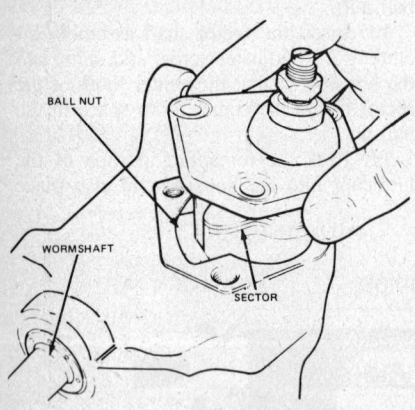

Removing sector shaft assembly—typical

WORM BEARING PRE-LOAD ADJUSTMENT

1. Remove the steering gear arm and lockwasher from the sector shaft, using a suitable gear puller.

2. Remove the horn button or horn ring.

3. Loosen the sector-shaft adjusting screw locknut, and back out the adjusting screw about two turns.

4. Turn the steering wheel two complete turns from the straight ahead position, and place an in. lb. torque wrench on the steering shaft nut.

5. Rotate the steering shaft at least one turn toward the straight ahead position while measuring the torque on the torque wrench. The torque should be between $1\frac{1}{8}$ and $4\frac{1}{2}$ in. lbs. to move the steering wheel. If torque is not within these limits, loosen the worm shaft bearing adjuster locknut and turn the adjuster clockwise to increase the preload or counterclockwise to decrease the preload. When the preload is correct, hold the adjuster screw steady and tighten the locknut. Recheck preload.

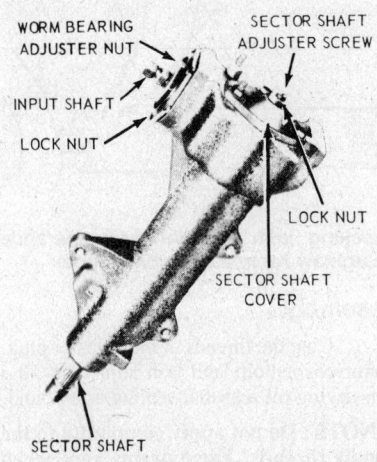

Steering gear adjustment locations

BALL NUT RACK AND SECTOR MESH ADJUSTMENT

NOTE: This adjustment can be accurately made only after proper preloading of worm bearing.

1. Turn steering wheel gently from one stop to the other, counting the number of turns. Turn the steering wheel back exactly half way, to the center position.

2. Turn the sector-shaft adjusting screw clockwise to remove all lash between ball nut rack and the sector gear teeth, then tighten adjusting screw locknut to 35 ft. lbs.

3. Turn the steering wheel about ¼ turn away from the center or high spot position. With the torque wrench on the steering wheel nut measure the torque required to turn the steering wheel through the high spot at the center position. The reading should be between 8 and 11 in. lbs. This is the total of the worm shaft bearing preload and the ball nut rack and sector gear mesh load. Readjust the sector-shaft adjustment screw if necessary to obtain a correct torque reading.

4. After completing the adjustments, place the front wheels in a straight ahead position, and with the steering wheel and steering gear centered, install the steering arm on sector-shaft. Tighten the steering arm retaining nut to 180 ft. lbs.

STEERING GEAR

Disassembly and Assembly

1. Attach the steering gear assembly to a holding fixture and put the holding fixture in a bench vise. Thoroughly clean the outside surface before disassembly.

2. Loosen the sector-shaft adjusting screw locknut, and back out the adjusting screw about two turns to relieve the mesh load between the ball nut rack and the sector gear teeth.

3. Position the steering gear worm shaft in a straight ahead position.

4. Remove the attaching bolts from the sector-shaft cover and slowly remove the sector-shaft while sliding an arbor tool into the housing. Remove the locknut from the

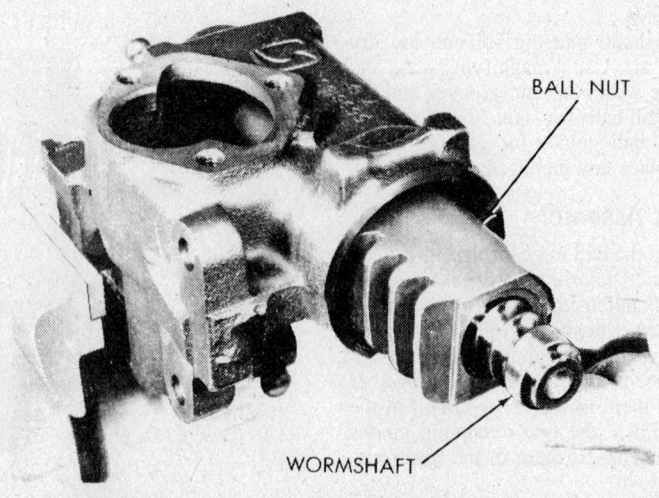

Removing the wormshaft and ballnut assembly

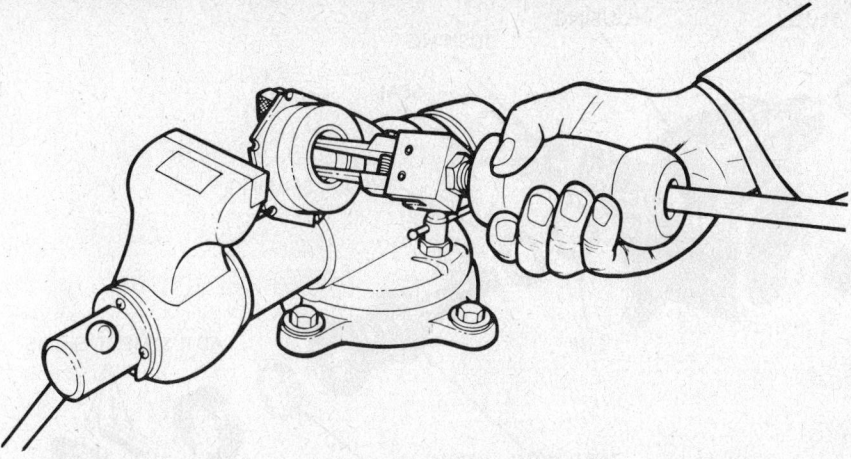

Removing wormshaft lower bearing cup using special tool

adjusting screw and remove the screw from the cover by turning it clockwise. Slide the adjustment screw and its shim out of the slot in the end of the sector-shaft.

5. Loosen the worm shaft bearing adjuster locknut with a brass drift (punch) and remove the locknut. Hold the worm shaft steady while unscrewing the adjuster. Slide the worm adjuster off the shaft.

─────── **CAUTION** ───────

Handle the adjuster carefully to avoid damaging the aluminum threads. Also, do not run the ball nut down to either end of the worm shaft to avoid damaging the ball guides.

6. Carefully remove the worm and ball nut assembly. This assembly is serviced as a complete assembly only and is not to be disassembled or the ball return guides removed or disturbed.

7. Remove the sector-shaft needle bearing by placing the gear housing in an arbor press; insert a tool in the lower end of the housing and press both bearings through the housing.
The sector-shaft cover assembly, including a needle bearing or bushing, is serviced as an assembly.

8. Remove the worm shaft oil seal from the worm shaft bearing adjuster by inserting a blunt punch behind the seal and tapping alternately on each side of the seal until it is driven out of the adjuster.

9. Remove the worm shaft in the same manner as that given in step 8. *Be careful not to cock the bearing cup and distort the adjuster counter bore.*

10. Remove the lower cup if necessary. Pull the bearing cup out.

11. Wash all parts in clean solvent and dry thoroughly. Inspect all parts for wear, scoring, pitting, etc. Test operation of the worm shaft and ball nut assembly. If ball nut does not travel smoothly and freely on the worm shaft or if there is binding, replace the assembly.

NOTE: Extreme care must be taken when handling the aluminum worm

bearing adjuster to avoid thread damage. Also, be careful not to damage the threads in the gear housing. Always lubricate the worm bearing adjuster before screwing it into the housing.

12. Inspect the sector-shaft for wear and check the fit of the shaft in the housing bearings. Inspect the fit of the shaft pilot bearing in the housing. Be sure the worm shaft is not bent or damaged.

13. Install the sector-shaft lower needle bearing. Press the bearing into the housing about $7/16$ in. below the end of the bore to leave space for the new oil seal.

14. Install the upper needle bearing in the same manner and press it into the inside end of the housing bore flush with the inside end of the bore surface.

15. Install the worm shaft bearing cups (upper and lower) by placing them and their spacers in the adjuster nut and press them into place.

16. Install the worm shaft oil seal by placing the seal in the worm shaft adjuster with the metal seal retainer up. Drive the seal into place with a suitable sleeve until it is just below the end of the bore in the adjuster.

NOTE: Apply a coating of steering gear lubricant to all moving parts during assembly. Also, put lubricant on and around oil seal lips.

17. Clamp the holding fixture and housing in a bench vise with the bearing adjuster opening upward. Place a thrust bearing in the lower cup in the housing.

18. Hold the ball nut from turning and insert the worm shaft and ball nut assembly into the housing with the end of the worm shaft resting in the thrust bearing. Place the upper thrust bearing on the worm shaft. Thoroughly lubricate the threads on the adjuster and the threads in the housing.

19. Place a protective sleeve of tape over the splines on the worm shaft to avoid damaging the seal. Slide the adjuster assembly over the shaft.

20. Thread the adjuster into the housing and tighten the adjuster to 50 ft. lbs. while rotating the worm shaft to seat the bearings.

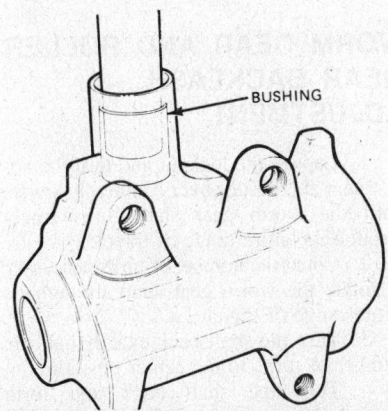

Removing sector shaft bushing

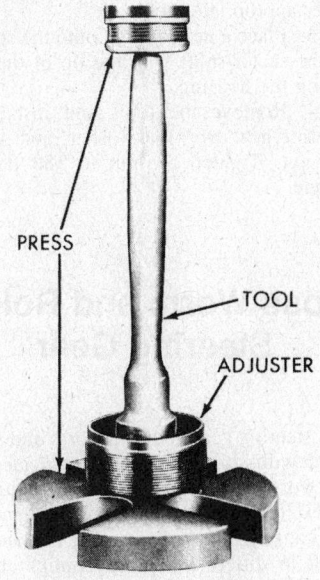

Installing the wormshaft upper bearing cup

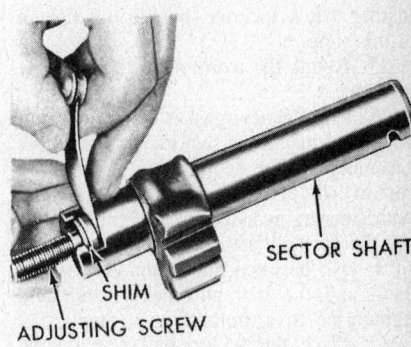

Measuring the sector shaft adjusting screw end clearance

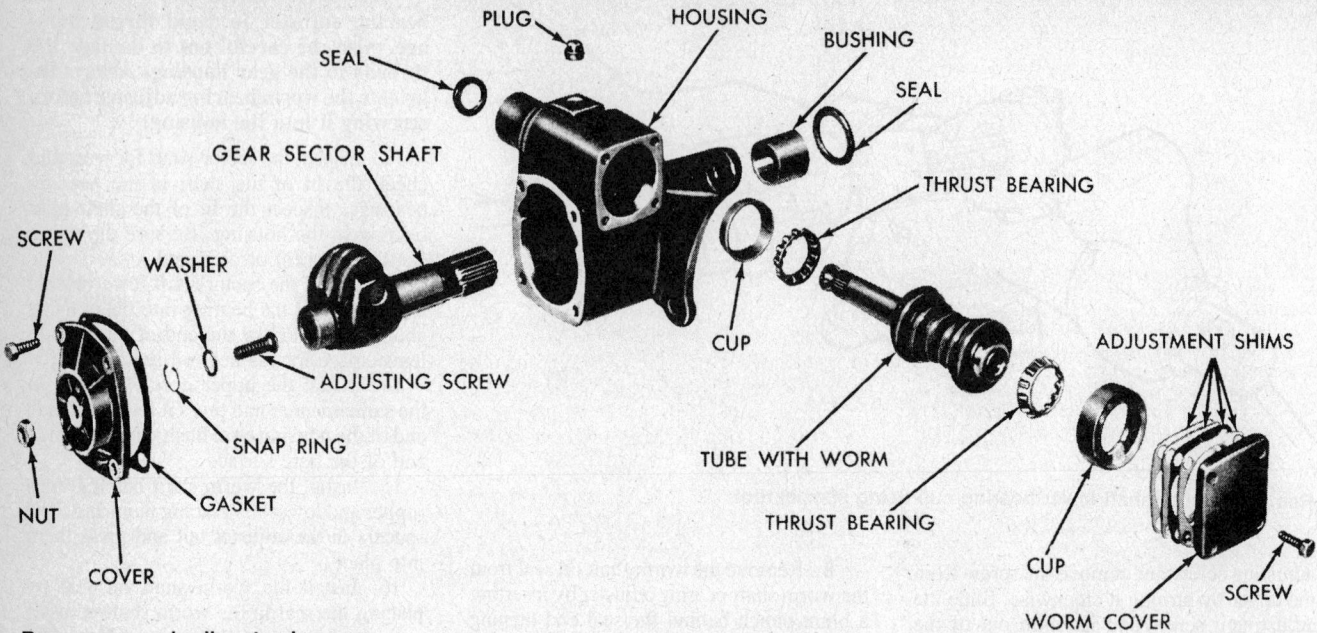

PLUG HOUSING BUSHING
SEAL SEAL
GEAR SECTOR SHAFT THRUST BEARING
SCREW
WASHER
ADJUSTING SCREW
SNAP RING CUP ADJUSTMENT SHIMS
NUT
GASKET TUBE WITH WORM
COVER THRUST BEARING
CUP SCREW
WORM COVER

Ross worm and roller steering gear

21. Loosen the adjuster so no bearing preload exists. Tighten the adjuster for a worm shaft bearing preload of 1⅛ to 4½ in. lbs. Tighten the bearing adjuster locknut and recheck the preload.

22. Before installing the sector-shaft, pack the worm shaft cavities in the housing above and below the ball nut with steering gear lubricant. A good grade of multi-purpose lubricant may be used if steering gear lubricant is not available. *Do not use gear oil.* Pack enough lubricant into the worm cavities to cover the worm.

23. Slide the sector-shaft adjusting screw and shim into the slot in the end of the shaft. Check the end clearance for no more than 0.004 in. clearance. If the clearance is not within the limit, remove old shim and install a new shim, available in three different thicknesses, to get the proper clearance.

24. Start the sector-shaft and adjuster screw into the bearing in the housing cover. Using a screwdriver through the hole in the cover, turn the screw counterclockwise to pull the shaft into the cover. Install the adjusting screw locknut, but do not tighten at this time.

25. Rotate the worm shaft to center the ball nut.

26. Place a new gasket on the housing cover and install the sector-shaft and cover aasembly into the steering gear housing. Be sure to coat the sector-shaft and sector teeth with steering gear lubricant before installing the sector-shaft in the housing. Allow some lash between the sector-shaft sector teeth and the ball nut rack. Install and tighten the cover bolts to 25 ft. lbs.

27. Place the sector-shaft seal on the cross-shaft with the lip of the seal facing the housing. Press the seal in place.

28. Turn the worm shaft about ¼ turn away from the center of the high spot po-

sition. Using a torque wrench and a ¾ in. socket on the worm shaft spline, check the torque needed to rotate the shaft through the high spot. The reading should be between 8 and 11 in. lbs. Readjust the sector-shaft adjusting screw until the proper reading is obtained. Tighten the locknut to 35 ft. lbs. and recheck sector-shaft torque.

SECTOR-SHAFT OIL SEAL

Replacement

1. Remove the steering gear arm retaining nut and lockwasher.

2. Remove seal with a seal puller or other appropriate tool.

3. Place a new oil seal onto the splines of the sector-shaft with the lip of the seal facing the housing.

4. Remove the tool, and install the steering gear arm, lockwasher, and retaining nut. Tighten the nut to 180 ft. lbs. torque.

Ross Worm and Roller Steering Gear

The steering gear is of the worm and roller type, with shim adjustments provided for the worm gear bearings and an adjusting screw for the sector shaft adjustment.

This steering gear assembly is manufactured in different housing configurations, but the disassembly, assembly and adjustments are basically the same. The different models are identified by the size of the sector shaft.

Models	Sector Shaft Diameter
254, 301	1¼ inch
376, 378	1⅜ inch
408	1½ inch
504	1¾ inch

BEARING PRELOAD ADJUSTMENT

1. Loosen the four capscrews which fasten the end cover to the steering gear housing.

2. Alternately tighten the capscrews evenly and rotate the worm gear shaft. Tighten the screws to 18 to 22 ft. lbs.

3. If necessary, remove the end cover and either add or subtract from the number of shims, and repeat steps 1 and 2 to obtain the correct bearing preload.

WORM GEAR AND ROLLER GEAR BACKLASH ADJUSTMENT

1. Loosen the locknut and turn the adjustment at the side cover counterclockwise until the worm gear shaft turns freely through its entire range of travel.

2. Count the number of turns necessary to rotate the worm gear shaft through its entire range of travel.

3. Turn the shaft back exactly half the number of turns to the center position.

4. Turn the shaft back and forth through its center of travel and tighten the adjustment screw to obtain a rolling torque requirement of 7 to 12 inch lbs.

5. Hold the adjustment screw in position and torque the locknut to 16–20 ft. lbs.

6. Recheck the rolling torque and repeat the above procedure if necessary.

Disassembly

1. Drain the lubricant from the gear.

2. Make index marks on the roller gear and shaft assembly and on the steering arm to assure correct alignment during reassembly.

3. Remove the nut and lockwasher from the shaft.

4. Using a puller remove the arm from the shaft.

NOTE: Do not use a hammer or wedge to remove the steering arm or damage to the gear and shaft assembly may result.

5. Remove the four side cover attaching screws and remove the cover and roller gear and shaft assembly as a unit.

6. Remove the locknut from the adjustment screw and turn the screw clockwise until it is completely unthreaded from the side cover, then remove the roller gear and shaft assembly from the cover.

7. Remove the four end cover attaching screws and remove the cover from the housing.

8. Withdraw the worm gear and shaft assembly from the housing.

9. Remove the lower and upper bearing cups and ball bearings from the shaft.

10. Remove and discard both the worm gear shaft and roller gear shaft housing oil seals.

Inspection

1. Clean all parts with a suitable cleaning solvent and blow dry with an air hose.

2. Check the steering gear housing for cracks, leaks or breaks and replace if damaged.

3. Examine the roller gear to assure that it has proper freedom of movement and does not have excessive lash or roughness. Replace if necessary.

4. Check the adjustment screw of the roller gear and shaft assembly for excessive end play. If end play exceeds 0.015 inch, remove the retaining ring, thrust washer and screw from the gear and shaft assembly and replace with new parts.

5. Inspect the roller gear and shaft needle bearings for wear or damage. Insert a shaft through each bearing and check for clearance. If clearance exceeds 0.010 inch, replace the bearings. Either needle bearing may be removed by pressing out with a piloted mandrel. When pressing in a new bearing make sure that the face of the bearing is flush with the bearing boss of the cover or housing.

6. Inspect the worm gear and shaft assembly for wear, scoring or pitting. Polish the assembly with a fine abrasive cloth or replace if necessary.

7. Check the upper and lower ball bearings and cups of the worm gear and shaft assembly for wear and damage. Replace the ball bearings as a full set if worn or damaged.

Assembly

1. Press new oil seals into the worm gear shaft and roller gear shaft oil seal bores of the housing with the longer lip of each seal facing into the housing.

2. Lubricate the worm gear and shaft assembly and upper ball bearing and cup with SAE 80 gear lubricant.

3. Install the bearing and cup on the shaft.

4. Carefully install the shaft assembly into the steering gear housing.

5. Lubricate the lower end of the worm gear and shaft assembly and lower ball bearing and cup with SAE 80 gear lubricant.

6. Install the bearing, cups and spacer on the shaft.

7. Position the shims and end cover on the steering gear housing and install the four capscrews loosely.

8. Adjust the bearing preload.

9. Position the tapped hole of the side cover to the adjustment screw of the roller gear and shaft assembly and thread the adjustment screw counterclockwise into the cover until the end of the shaft just touches the inner face of the cover.

10. Install a locknut loosely on the adjustment screw.

11. Install a new side cover gasket.

12. Lubricate the roller gear with SAE 80 gear lubricant.

13. Carefully insert the gear and shaft assembly into the steering gear housing. The roller gear and worm gear must mesh to seat the side cover to the housing.

14. Tighten the side cover capscrews to 18–22 ft. lbs.

15. Make a worm gear and roller gear backlash adjustment.

16. Clamp the exposed section of the roller gear and shaft assembly firmly into a soft jaw vise.

17. Align the index marks made during disassembly and position the steering arm to the splined end of the shaft.

18. Install the lockwasher and nut on the shaft threads and tighten the nut to draw the arm into position on the splines.

19. Fill the steering gear housing to the required level with SAE 80 gear lubricant.

STEERING TROUBLE DIAGNOSIS
Power Steering

Condition	Possible Cause	Correction
Hard Steering	1. Low or uneven tire pressure.	1. Inflate the tires to recommended pressures.
	2. Insufficient lubricant in the steering gear housing or in steering linkage.	2. Lubricate as necessary.
	3. Steering gear shaft adjusted too tight.	3. Adjust according to instructions.
	4. Improper caster or toe-in.	4. Align the wheels.
	5. Steering column misaligned.	5. See "Steering Gear Alignment."
	6. Loose, worn or broken pump belt.	6. Adjust or replace belt.
	7. Air in system.	7. Bleed air from system.
	8. Low fluid level in the pump reservoir.	8. Fill to correct level.
	9. Pump output pressure low.	9. See "Pressure Test."
	10. Leakage at power cylinder piston rings. (Linkage type).	10. Replace piston rings and repair as required.
	11. Binding or bent cylinder linkage. (Linkage type).	11. Replace or repair as required.
	12. Valve spool and/or sleeve sticking. (Linkage type).	12. Free-up or replace as required.

STEERING TROUBLE DIAGNOSIS
Power Steering

Condition	Possible Cause	Correction
Intermittent or No Power Assist	1. Belt slipping and/or low fluid level.	1. Adjust or replace belt. Add fluid as necessary.
	2. Piston or rod binding in power cylinder. (Linkage type).	2. Repair or replace piston and rod.
	3. Sliding sleeve stuck in control valve. (Linkage type).	3. Free-up or replace sleeve.
	4. Improper pump operation.	4. Refer to "Power Steering Pump."
Poor or No Recovery from Turns	1. Improper caster setting.	1. Adjust to specifications.
	2. Steering gear adjustments too tight.	2. Adjust according to instructions.
	3. Improper spool nut adjustment. (Linkage type).	3. Adjust according to instructions.
	4. Valve spool installed backwards. (Linkage type).	4. Install valve spool correctly.
	5. Low tire pressure.	5. Inflate tires to recommended pressure.
	6. Tight steering linkage.	6. Lubricate as necessary.
	7. King pins frozen.	7. Lubricate as necessary.
Lack of Effort (Both Turns)	1. Improper sector shaft adjustment.	1. Adjust Sector Shaft.
	2. Pressure plates on wrong side of reactions rings.	2. Gear Recondition.
Lack of Effort (Left Turn Only)	1. Left turn reaction seal "O" ring worn, damaged or missing.	1. Gear Recondition.
	2. Left turn reaction oil passageway not drilled in housing or cylinder head.	2. Replace parts as required.
	3. Left turn reaction ring sticking in cylinder head.	3. Replace parts as required.
Lack of Effort (Right Turn Only)	1. Right turn U-shaped reaction seal worn, damaged, or missing.	1. Gear Recondition.
	2. Right turn reaction oil passageway not drilled in housing head, or ferrule pin.	2. Replace parts as required.
	3. Right turn reaction ring sticking in housing head.	3. Replace parts as required.
Lack of Assist (Left Turn Only)	1. Left turn reaction seal "O" ring worn, damaged, or missing.	1. Gear Recondition.
Lack of Assist (Right Turn Only)	1. Right turn U-shaped reaction seal worn, damaged, or missing.	1. Gear Recondition.
	2. Worm sealing ring (teflon) worm sleeve seal, ferrule pin "O" ring damaged or worn.	2. Gear Recondition.
	3. Excessive internal leakage thru piston end plug and/or side plugs.	3. Replace worm-piston assembly.
Lack of Assist (Both Turns)	1. Low oil level in pump reservoir (usually accompanied by pump noise).	1. Fill to proper level.
	2. Loose pump belt.	2. Adjust belts.
	3. Pump output low.	3. Pressure test pump.
	4. Engine idle too low.	4. Adjust engine idle.
	5. Excessive internal leakage thru piston end plug and/or side plugs.	5. Replace worm-piston assembly.

STEERING TROUBLE DIAGNOSIS
Power Steering Noise

Condition	Possible Cause	Correction
Objectionable "Hiss"	1. Noisy valve	1. Do not replace valve unless "hiss" is extremely objectionable. A replacement valve will also exhibit sight noise and is not always a cure for the objection.
Rattle or Chuckle Noise in Steering Gear	1. Gear loose on frame.	1. Check gear mounting bolts. Torque bolts to specifications.
	2. Steering linkages looseness.	2. Check linkage pivot points for wear. Replace if necessary.
	3. Pressure hose touching other parts of truck.	3. Adjust hose position. Do not bend tubing by hand.
	4. Loose Pitman shaft over center adjustment. **NOTE:** A slight rattle may occur on turns because of increased clearance off the "high point". This is normal and clearance must not be reduced below specified limits to eliminate this slight rattle.	4. Adjust
	5. Loose Pitman arm.	5. Torque Pitman arm pinch bolt.
Squawk Noise in Steering Gear When Turning or Recovering From a Turn	1. Dampener O-ring on valve spool cut.	1. Replace dampener O-Ring.
	2. Loose or worn valve.	2. Replace valve.
Chirp Noise in Steering Gear	1. Gear relief valve.	1. Replace relief valve.
Chirp Noise in Steering Pump	1. Loose belt.	1. Adjust belt tension.
Belt Squeal (Particularly Noticeable at Full Wheel Travel and Standstill Parking)	1. Loose belt.	1. Adjust belt tension.
Growl Noise in Steering Pump	1. Excessive back pressure in hoses or steering gear caused by restriction.	1. Locate restriction and correct. Replace part if necessary.
Growl Noise in Steering Pump (Particularly Noticeable at Standstill Parking)	1. Scored pressure plates, thrust plate or rotor.	1. Replace parts and flush system.
	2. Extreme wear of cam ring.	2. Replace parts.
Groan Noise in Steering Pump	1. Low oil level.	1. Fill reservoir to proper level.
	2. Air in the oil. Poor pressure hose connection.	2. Torque connector. Bleed system.
Rattle or Knock Noise in Steering Pump	1. Loose pump pulley nut.	1. Torque nut.
Rattle Noise in Steering Pump	1. Vanes not installed properly.	1. Install properly.
	2. Vanes sticking in rotor slots.	2. Repair or replace.
Swish Noise in Steering Pump	1. Defective flow control valve.	1. Replace part.
Whine Noise in Steering Pump	1. Pump Shaft bearing scored.	1. Replace housing and shaft. Flush and bleed system.

POWER STEERING

GENERAL INFORMATION

The procedures for maintaining, adjusting, and repairing the power steering systems and components discussed in this chapter are to be done only after determining that the steering linkages and front suspension systems are correctly aligned and in good condition. All worn or damaged parts should be replaced before attempting to service the power steering system. After correcting any condition that could affect the power steering, do the preliminary tests of the steering system components.

PRELIMINARY TESTS

Lubrication

Proper lubrication of the steering linkage and the front suspension components is very important for the proper operation of the steering systems of trucks equipped with power steering. Most all power steering systems use the same lubricant in the steering gear box as in the power steering pump reservoir, and the fluid level is maintained at the pump reservoir.

With power cylinder-assist power steering, the steering gear is of the standard mechanical type and the lubricating oil is self contained within the gear box and the level is maintained by the removal of a filler plug on the gear box housing. The control valve assembly is mounted on the gear box and is lubricated by power steering oil from the power steering pump reservoir, where the level is maintained.

Air Bleeding

Air bubbles in the power steering system must be removed from the fluid. Be sure the reservoir is filled to the proper level and the fluid is warmed up to operating temperature. Then, turn the steering wheel through its full travel three or four times until all the air bubbles are removed. Do not hold the steering wheel against its stops. Recheck the fluid level.

Fluid Leaks

Check all possible leakage points (hoses, power steering pump, or steering gear) for loss of fluid. Turn engine on and rotate the steering wheel from stop to stop several times. Tighten all loose fittings and replace any defective lines or valve seats.

Turning Effort

Check the turning effort required to turn the steering wheel after aligning the front wheels and inflating the tires to the proper pressure.

1. With the vehicle on dry pavement and the front wheel straight ahead, set the parking brake and turn the engine on.

2. After a short warm-up period for the engine, turn the steering wheel back and forth several times to warm the steering fluid.

3. Attach a spring scale to the steering wheel rim and measure the pull required to turn the steering wheel one complete revolution in each direction. The effort needed to turn the steering wheel should not exceed the limits specified.

NOTE: This test may be done with the steering wheel removed and a torque wrench applied on the steering wheel nut.

Fluid Level Check

1. Run the engine until the fluid is at the normal operating temperature. Then, turn the steering wheel through its full

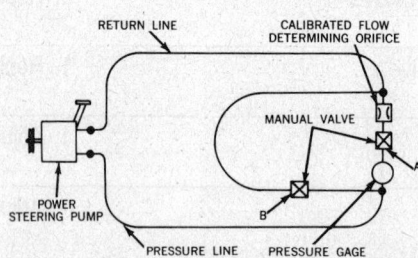

Power steering pump test circuit diagram

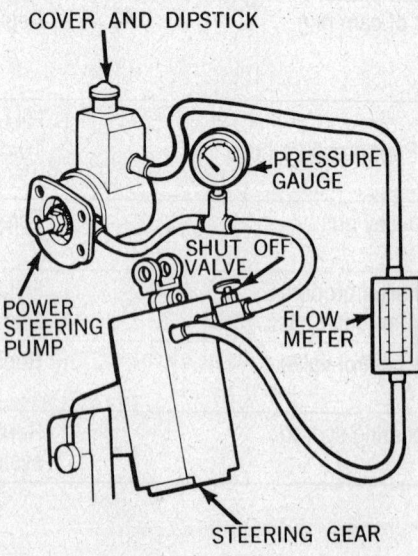

Testing power steering hydraulic system for internal leakage using a pressure gauge, shut off valve and flow meter —typical

travel three or four times, and shut off the engine.

2. Check the fluid level in the steering reservoir. If the fluid level is low, add enough fluid to raise the level to the Full mark on the dipstick or filler tube.

Pump Belt Check

1. Inspect the pump belt for cracks, glazing, or worn places. Using a belt tension gauge, check the belt tension for the proper range of adjustment. The amount of tension varies with the make of truck and the condition of the belt. New belts (those belts used less than 15 minutes) require a higher figure. The belt deflection method of adjustment may be used only if a belt tension gauge is not available. The belt should be adjusted for a deflection of ¼" to ⅜".

Power Steering Pump Flow

Since the power steering pump provides all the power assist in a power steering system, the pump must operate properly at all times for the system to work. After performing all the checks given above, the power steering pump may be tested for proper flow by the following procedures:

Two Gauges and Flow Meter

1. Disconnect the pressure and return lines at the power steering pump and connect the test pressure and return lines. The test lines are connected to a pressure gauge and two manual valves.

2. Open the two manual valves, connect a tachometer to the engine, and start the engine. Run the engine at idle speed until the reservoir fluid temperature reaches about 165–175 degrees Fahrenheit. This temperature must be maintained during the test. Manual valve B may be partially opened to create a back pressure of no more than 350 psi to aid the temperature rise. Reservoir fluid must be at the proper level.

3. After the engine and the reservoir fluid are sufficiently warmed up, close the manual valve B. Note the pressure gauge reading. It must be a minimum of 620 psi.

4. If the pressure reading is below the minimum acceptable pressure, the pump is defective and must be repaired. If the pressure reading is at or above the minimum value, the pump is normal. Open manual valve B and proceed to the pump fluid pressure test.

Power Steering Pump Fluid Pressure Test

1. Keep the lines and pressure gauge connected as in the Pump Flow Test.

2. With manual valve A and B opened fully, run the engine at the proper idle speed. Then, close manual valve A and manual valve B, in that order.

——— CAUTION ———
Do not keep both valves closed for more than 5 seconds since the fluid temperature

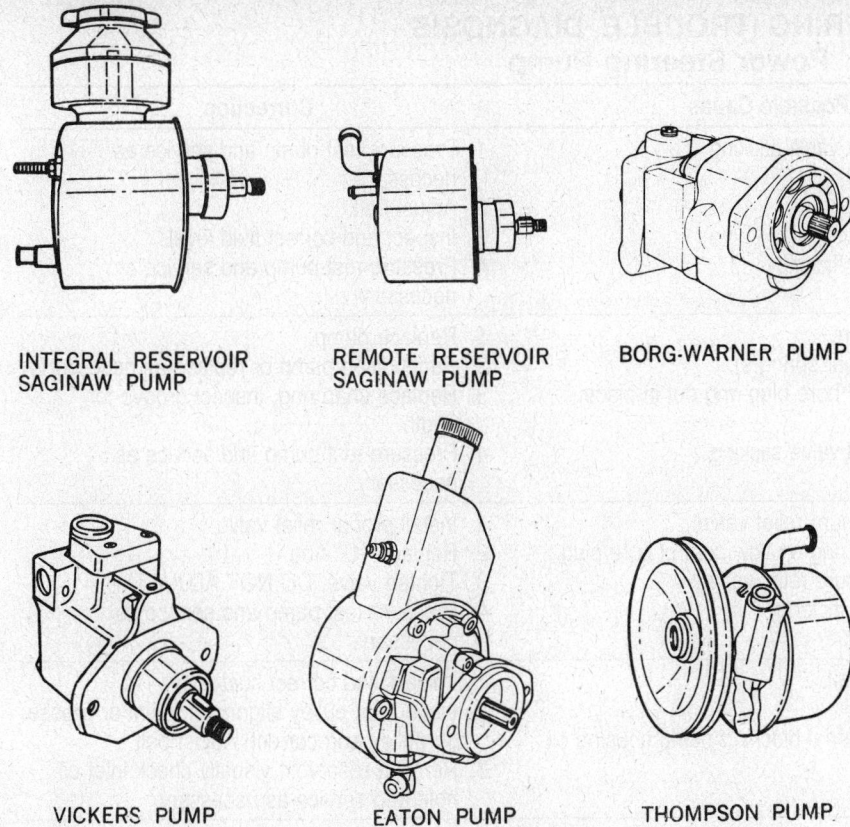

INTEGRAL RESERVOIR SAGINAW PUMP

REMOTE RESERVOIR SAGINAW PUMP

BORG-WARNER PUMP

VICKERS PUMP

EATON PUMP

THOMPSON PUMP

Identification of power steering pumps used on General Motors Trucks—typical

will increase abnormally and cause unnecessary wear to the pump.

3. With both manual valves closed, the pressure reading should be as given in the specifications. If the pressure is below the minimum reading, the pump is defective and must be repaired. If the pressure reading is at or above the minimum reading, the pump is normal and the power steering gear or power assist control valve must be checked.

Checking the Oil Flow and Pressure Relief Valve in the Pump Assembly

When the wheels are turned hard right, or hard left, against the stops, the oil flow and pressure relief valves come into action. If these valves are working and are not stuck there should be a slight buzzing noise.

—————— CAUTION ——————
Do not hold the wheels in the extreme position for over three or four seconds because, if the pressure relief valve is not working, the pressure could get high enough to damage the system.

Single Gauge

1. Install the test pressure gauge (O-2000 psi) between the power steering pump and the control valve.

2. With the fluid at a temperature of 170 to 190°F, the engine running above idle and the shut-off valve open, observe the pressure reading while moving the wheels to the end of their right and left travel.

3. If the gauge registers the correct relief valve pressure, the hydraulic system should be satisfactory. If pressure cannot be built up on either side of the gear, internal pump or gear problems exist.

NOTE: A shuttle valve equipped power cylinder may register a sharp drop-off in pressure at the end of the wheel travel and is considered normal.

4. To check the pump, close the shut-off valve and observe the pressure gauge. The pressure reading should be at relief valve pressure.

NOTE: Do not keep the shut-off valve closed longer than 15 seconds as damage to the pump could occur.

5. Repeat the closing of the shut-off valve twice more and record the highest pressure reading each time.

6. If the pressure readings are within 50 lbs. of each other and with-in the pump relief valve specifications, the pump operation is normal.
Example: Pump specifications—900 to 1500 psi.
Readings: 1st—1310 psi
2nd—1290 psi
3rd—1320 psi

7. If the readings are high but do not repeat within-in 50 lbs. of each other, the flow control valve can be sticking. If 100 lbs. difference is noted below the low listed specification, replace the flow valve and recheck the system.

Relief Valve Pressure

Relief valve pressures normally range between 800 to 2000 psi, depending upon the requirements of the power steering system and the axle application used on the vehicle. The lighter the truck, the less pressure is needed to operate the steering system, while the opposite is true of the heavier vehicles.

The minimum pressures with the wheels straight ahead and at engine idle should be in the 80 to 120 psi range.

Power Steering Hose Inspection

1. Inspect both the input and output hoses of the power steering pump for worn spots, cracks, or signs of leakage. Replace hose if defective, being sure to reconnect the replacement hose properly. Many power steering hoses are identified as to where they are to be connected by special means, such as fittings that will only fit on the correct pump fitting, or hoses of special lengths.

Test Driving Truck to Check the Power Steering

When test driving to check power steering, drive at a speed between 15 and 20 mph. Make several turns in each direction. When a turn is completed, the front wheels should return to the straight ahead position with very little help from the driver.

If the front wheels fail to return as they should and yet the steering linkage is free, well oiled and properly adjusted, the trouble is probably due to misalignment of the power cylinder or improper adjustment of the spool valve.

The power steering pump supplies all the power assist used in power steering systems of all designs. There are various designs of pumps used by the truck manufacturers but all pumps supply power to operate the steering systems with the least effort. All power steering pumps have a reservoir tank built onto the oil pump. These pumps are driven by belt turned by pulleys on the engine, normally on the front of the crankshaft.

During operation of the engine at idle speed, there is provision for the power steering pump to supply more fluid pressure. During driving speeds or when the truck is moving straight ahead, less pressure is needed and the excess is relieved through a pressure relief and flow control valve. The pressure relief part of the valve is inside the flow control and is basically the same for all pumps. The flow control valve regulates, or controls, the constant flow of fluid from the pump as it varies with the demands of the steering gear. The

STEERING TROUBLE DIAGNOSIS
Power Steering Pump

Condition	Possible Cause	Correction
Intermittent Assist	1. Flow control valve sticking. 2. Slipping belt. 3. Low fluid level. 4. Low pump efficiency.	1. Pressure test pump and service as necessary. 2. Adjust belt. 3. Inspect and correct fluid level. 4. Pressure test pump and service as necessary.
No Assist	1. Pump seizure. 2. Broken slipper spring(s). 3. Flow control bore plug ring not in place. 4. Flow control valve sticking.	1. Replace pump. 2. Recondition pump or replace as necessary. 3. Replace snap ring. Inspect groove for depth. 4. Pressure test pump and service as necessary.
No Assist When Parking Only	1. Wrong pressure relief valve. 2. Broken "O" ring on flow control bore plug. 3. Loose pressure relief valve. 4. Low pump efficiency	1. Install proper relief valve. 2. Replace "O" ring. 3. Tighten valve. DO NOT ADJUST. 4. Pressure test pump and service as necessary.
Noisy Pump	1. Low fluid level. 2. Belt noise. 3. Foreign material blocking pump housing oil inlet hole.	1. Inspect and correct fluid level. 2. Inspect for pulley alignment, paint or grease on pulley and correct. Adjust belt. 3. Remove reservoir, visually check inlet oil hole and service as necessary.
Pump Vibration	1. Pump hose interference with sheet metal or brake lines. 2. Belt loose. 3. Pulley loose or out of round. 4. Crankshaft pulley loose or damaged. 5. Bracket pivot bolts loose.	1. Reroute hoses. 2. Adjust belt. 3. Replace pulley. 4. Replace crankshaft pulley. 5. If unable to tighten, replace bracket.
Pump Leaks	1. Cap or filler neck leaks. 2. Reservoir solder joints leak. 3. Reservoir "O" ring leaking. 4. Shaft seal leaking. 5. Loose rear bracket bolts. 6. Loose or faulty high pressure ferrule. 7. Rear bolt holes stripped or casting cracked.	1. Correct fluid level. 2. Resolder or replace reservoir as necessary. 3. Inspect sealing area of reservoir. Replace "O" ring or reservoir as necessary. 4. Replace seal. 5. Tighten bolts. 6. Tighten fitting to 24 foot-pounds or replace as necessary. 7. Repair, if possible, or replace pump.

pressure relief valve limits the hydraulic pressure built up when the steering gear is turned against its stops.

During pump disassembly, make sure all work is done on a clean surface. Clean the outside of the pump thoroughly and do not allow dirt of any kind to get inside. Do not immerse the shaft oil seal in solvent.

If replacing the rotor shaft seal, be extremely careful not to scratch sealing surfaces with tools.

Pump Overhaul

VANE TYPE POWER STEERING PUMP

The vane type power steering pump is used in Saginaw steering systems. The operation is basically the same as that of the roller type pumps. Centrifugal force moves a number of vanes outward against the pump ring, causing a pumping action of the fluid to the control valve.

Removal

1. Disconnect hoses at the pump, securing them in a raised position to prevent oil drainage. Cap or cover the ends of the hoses to keep dirt out.
2. Install two caps on the pump fittings to prevent oil drainage.
3. Loosen the bracket-to-pump mounting nuts, move pump toward engine slightly, and remove the pump drive belt.
4. Remove the bracket-to-pump bolts and remove the pump from the truck.
5. While holding the drive pulley steady, loosen and remove the pulley attaching nut. Slide the pulley off the shaft.

NOTE: Do not hammer the pulley off the shaft.

Installation

1. To install the pump on the truck, reverse the removal procedure. Always use a new pulley nut, tightening it to 35–45 ft. lbs. torque.
2. After reconnecting the hoses to the pump, fill the reservoir with fluid and bleed the pump of air by turning the drive pulley counterclockwise (as viewed from the front) until air bubbles do not appear.
3. Install the pump drive belt over the pulley, move the pump against the belt until tight enough, then tighten the mounting bolts and nuts.

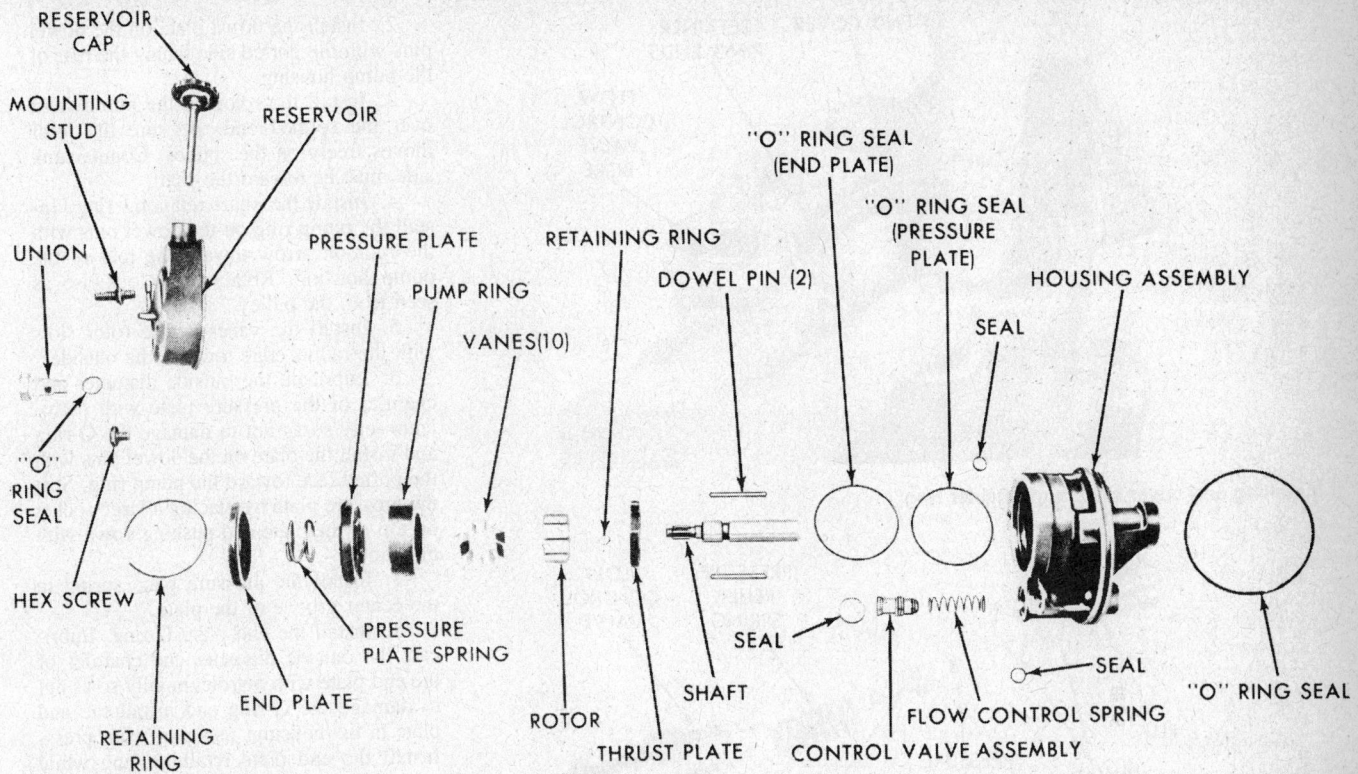

Exploded view of vane type pump

Labels in figure: RESERVOIR CAP, MOUNTING STUD, RESERVOIR, UNION, "O" RING SEAL, HEX SCREW, RETAINING RING, END PLATE, PRESSURE PLATE SPRING, PRESSURE PLATE, PUMP RING, VANES(10), ROTOR, THRUST PLATE, RETAINING RING, DOWEL PIN (2), SHAFT, SEAL, CONTROL VALVE ASSEMBLY, FLOW CONTROL SPRING, "O" RING SEAL (END PLATE), "O" RING SEAL (PRESSURE PLATE), SEAL, HOUSING ASSEMBLY, SEAL, "O" RING SEAL

4. Bleed the air from the system.

Disassembly

1. Clean the outside of the pump in a non-toxic solvent before disassembling.

2. Mount the pump in a vise, being careful not to squeeze the front hub too tight.

3. Remove the union and seal.

4. Remove the reservoir retaining studs and separate the reservoir from the housing.

5. Remove the mounting bolt and union O-rings.

6. Remove the filter and filter cage; discard the element.

7. Remove the end plate retaining ring by compressing the retaining ring and then prying it out with a removal tool. The retaining ring may be compressed by inserting a small punch in the 1/8" diameter hole in the housing and pushing in until the ring clears the groove.

8. Remove the end plate. The end plate is spring-loaded and should rise above the housing level. If it is stuck inside the housing, a slight rocking or gentle tapping should free the plate.

9. Remove the shaft woodruff key and tap the end of the shaft gently to free the pressure plate, pump ring, rotor assembly, and thrust plate. Remove these parts as one unit.

10. Remove the end plate O-ring. Separate the pressure plate, pump ring, rotor assembly, and thrust plate.

Inspection

Clean all metal parts in a non-toxic solvent

and inspect them as given below:

1. Check the flow control valve for free movement in the housing bore. If the valve is sticking, see if there is dirt or a rough spot in the bore.

2. Check the cap screw in the end of the flow control valve for looseness. Tighten if necessary being careful not to damage the machined surfaces.

3. Inspect the pressure plate and the pump plate surfaces for flatness and check that there are no cracks or scores in the parts. Do not mistake the normal wear marks for scoring.

4. Check the vanes in the rotor assembly for free movement and that they were installed with the radiused edge toward the pump ring.

5. If the flow control valve plunger is defective, install a new part. The valve is factory calibrated and supplied as a unit.

6. Check the drive shaft for worn splines, breaks, bushing material pick-up, etc.

7. Replace all rubber seals and O-rings removed from the pump.

8. Check the reservoir, studs, casting, etc. for burrs and other defects that would impair operation.

Assembly

1. Install a new shaft seal in the housing and insert the shaft at the hub end of housing, splined end entering mounting face side.

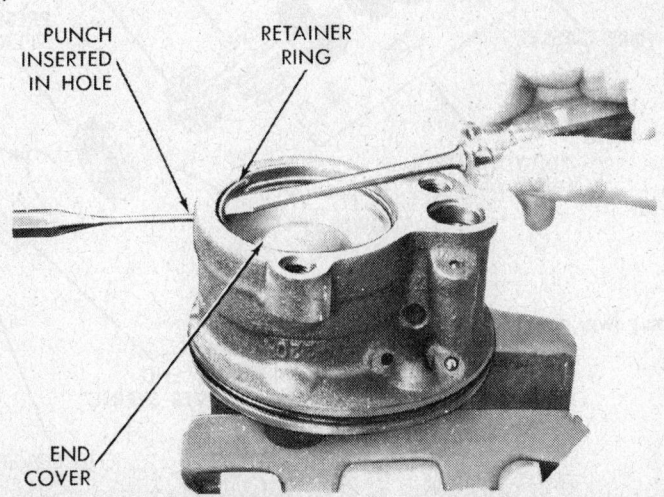

Labels in figure: PUNCH INSERTED IN HOLE, RETAINER RING, END COVER

Removing end cover retaining ring

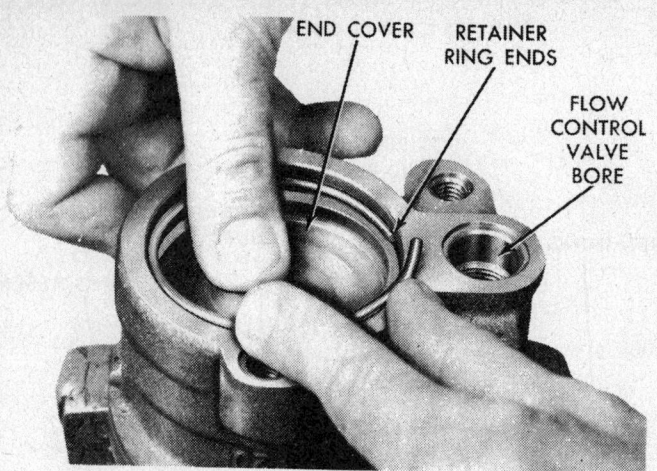

Installing end cover plate and retainer ring

END COVER — RETAINER RING ENDS — FLOW CONTROL VALVE BORE

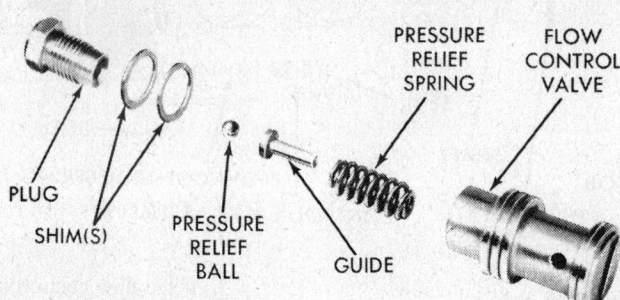

PLUG — SHIM(S) — PRESSURE RELIEF BALL — GUIDE — PRESSURE RELIEF SPRING — FLOW CONTROL VALVE

Flow control valve, vane type pump

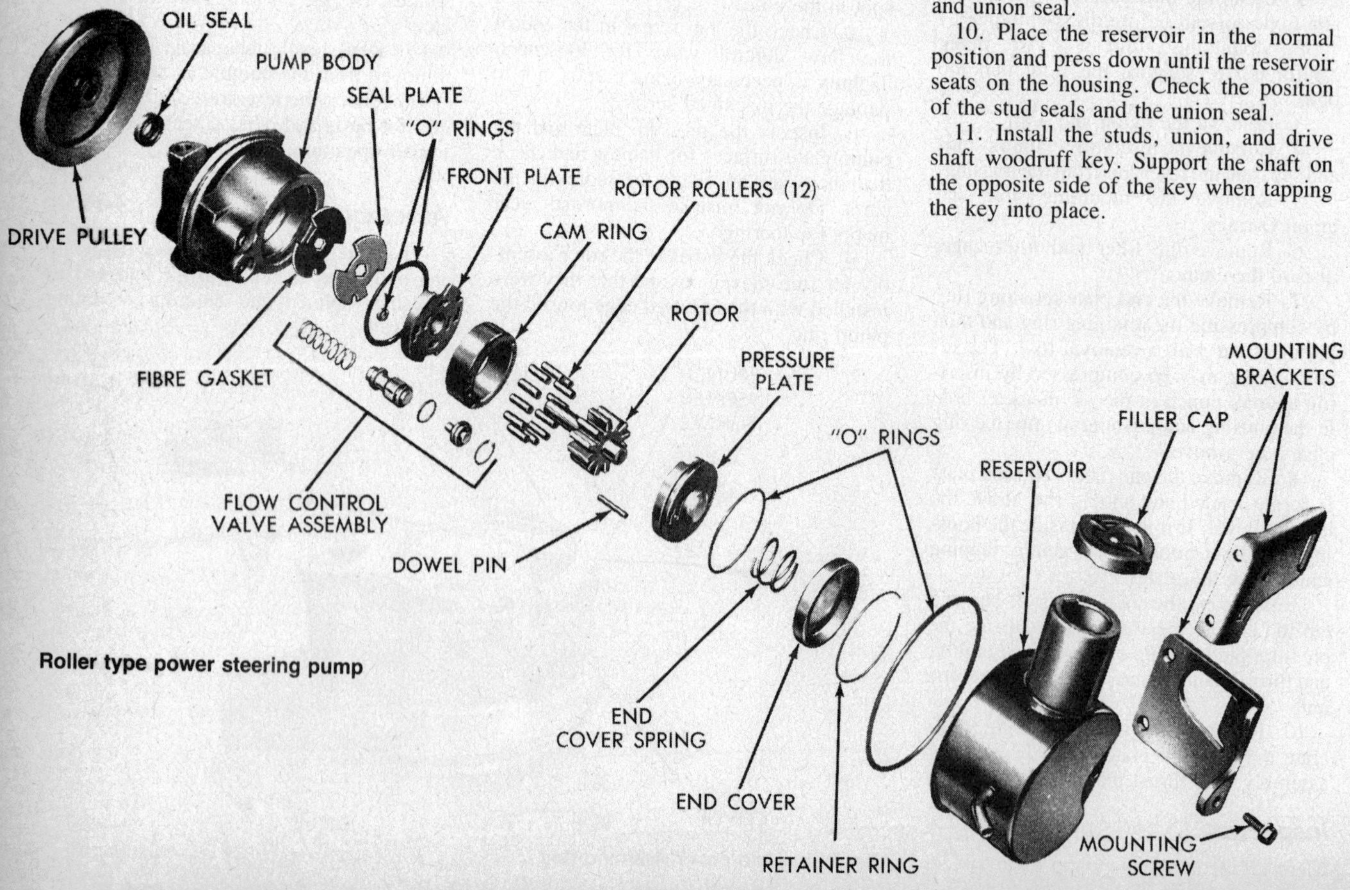

OIL SEAL — PUMP BODY — SEAL PLATE — "O" RINGS — FRONT PLATE — ROTOR ROLLERS (12) — CAM RING — ROTOR — PRESSURE PLATE — "O" RINGS — RESERVOIR — FILLER CAP — MOUNTING BRACKETS — DRIVE PULLEY — FIBRE GASKET — FLOW CONTROL VALVE ASSEMBLY — DOWEL PIN — END COVER SPRING — END COVER — RETAINER RING — MOUNTING SCREW

Roller type power steering pump

2. Install the thrust plate on the dowel pins with the ported side facing the rear of the pump housing.

3. Install the rotor on the pump shaft over the splined end. Be sure the rotor moves freely on the splines. Countersunk side must be toward the shaft.

4. Install the shaft retaining ring. Install the pump ring on the dowel pins with the rotation arrow toward the rear of the pump housing. Rotation is clockwise as seen from the pulley.

5. Install the vanes in the rotor slots with the radius edge towards the outside.

6. Lubricate the outside diameter and chamfer of the pressure plate with petroleum jelly so as not to damage the O-ring and install the plate on the dowel pins with the ported face toward the pump ring. Seat the pressure plate by placing a large socket on top of the plate and pushing down with the hand.

7. Install the pressure plate spring in the center groove of the plate.

8. Install the end plate O-ring. Lubricate the outside diameter and chamfer of the end plate with petroleum jelly so as not to damage the O-ring and install the end plate in the housing, using an arbor press. Install the end plate retaining ring while pump is in the arbor press. Be sure the ring is in the groove and the ring gap is positioned properly.

9. Install the flow control spring and plunger, hex head screw end in bore first. Install the filter cage, new filter stud seals and union seal.

10. Place the reservoir in the normal position and press down until the reservoir seats on the housing. Check the position of the stud seals and the union seal.

11. Install the studs, union, and drive shaft woodruff key. Support the shaft on the opposite side of the key when tapping the key into place.

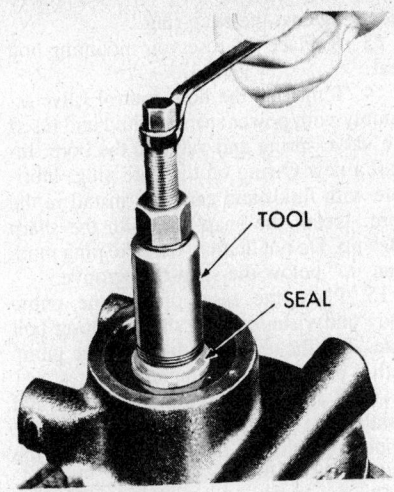

Removing shaft seal

ROLLER TYPE POWER STEERING PUMP

The roller type power steering pump is designed similar to other constant flow centrifugal force pumps. A star-shaped rotor forces 12 steel rollers against the inside surface of a cam ring. As the rollers follow the eccentric pattern of the cam ring, oil is drawn into the inlet ports and exhausted through the discharge ports while the rollers are moved into vee shaped cavities of the rotor, forcing oil into the high pressure circuit. A flow control valve permits a regulated amount of fluid to return to the intake side of the pump when excess output is produced during high speed operation. This reduces the power needs to drive the pump and minimizes temperature build-up.

The flow control valve used in one make of pump is a two-stage valve. Fluid under high pressure passes through two holes into a metering circuit located in a sealed passage. At low speed, about 2.7 gpm. passes to the gear. As speed increases and the valve moves, excess fluid is bypassed to the inlet and the valve blocks flow through one hole. This drops the flow to about 1.6 gpm. at high speeds.

When steering conditions produce excessive pressure needs (such as turning the wheels against the stops), the pressure built up in the steering gear exerts force on the spring end of the flow control valve.

This end of the valve contains the pressure relief valve. High pressure lifts the relief valve ball from its seat, allowing fluid to flow through a trigger orifice located in the front land of the flow control valve. This reduces pressure on the spring end of the valve which then opens and allows the fluid to return to the intake side of the pump. This action limits the maximum pressure output of the pump to a safe level. Normally, the pressure needs of the pump are below the maximum limits, causing the pressure relief ball and the flow control valve to remain closed.

Removal

1. Loosen the pump mounting and locking bolts and remove the belt.
2. Disconnect both hoses at the pump. Cap and tie the hoses out of the way. Cap the hose fittings on the pump.
3. Remove the mounting and locking bolts, the pump and brackets from the truck.

Installation

1. Position the pump and brackets on the engine and install the mounting and locking bolts.
2. Install the drive belt and adjust for the proper tension.
3. Connect the pressure and return hoses, using a new pressure hose O-ring.
4. Fill the pump reservoir to the top of the filler neck with power steering fluid.
5. Start the engine and turn the steering wheel several times from stop to stop to bleed the pump of air. Check the level and add fluid if necessary.

NOTE: When checking the level, see that the level is as follows: engine cold—bottom of filler tube; engine hot—half way up filler tube.

Disassembly

1. Remove pump from engine, drain reservoir, and clean outside of pump. Clamp the pump in a vise at the mounting bracket.
2. Remove the drive pulley.
3. Remove the shaft seal by installing the seal remover adapter over the end of the drive shaft with the large end toward the pump. Place the seal remover tool over the shaft and through the adapter. Then, screw the tapered thread well into the metal portion of the seal. Tighten the large drive nut and remove the seal.
4. Remove the pump from the vise and remove the bracket mounting bolts. Remove the bracket.

5. Remove the reservoir and place the pump in a soft-faced vise with the shaft down. Discard the mounting bolt and the reservoir O-rings.
6. Move the end cover retaining ring around until one end of the ring lines up with the hole in the pump body. Insert a small punch in the hole and push it in far enough to bend the ring so a screwdriver can be inserted between the ring and the housing. Remove the ring.
7. Remove the end cover and spring from the housing. It may be necessary to tap the cover gently to loosen it in the housing.
8. Remove the pump from the vise and turn the pump over so the rotating pump may come out of the housing. Tap the end of the drive shaft to loosen these parts. Lift the pump body off the rotating group. Check that the seal plate is removed from the bottom of the housing bore.
9. Discard the O-rings from the pressure plate and end cover.
10. Remove the snap-ring, bore plug, flow control valve and spring from the housing. Discard the O-ring. If necessary to dismantle the flow control valve for cleaning, see the procedure for disassembly.

Inspection

1. Remove the clean out plug with an Allen wrench.
2. Wash all metal parts in clean, nontoxic solvent. Blow out all passages with compressed air and air dry all cleaned parts.
3. Inspect the drive shaft for excessive wear and the seal area for nicks or scoring. Replace if necessary.
4. Inspect the end plates, rollers, rotor and cam ring for nicks, burrs, or scratches. If any of the components are damaged enough to cause poor operation of the pump, all the interior parts may have to be replaced to prevent later failures.

Installing pressure plate

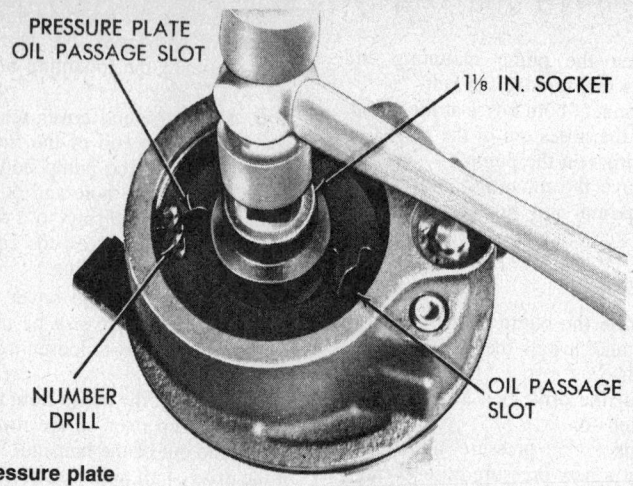

Seating pressure plate

5. Inspect the pump body drive shaft bushing for excessive wear. Replace the pump body and bushing as one assembly.

Assembly

1. Install the 1/8" pipe clean out plug, tightening it to 80 in. lbs. torque.
2. Place the pump body on a clean flat surface and install a new shaft seal into the bore.
3. Install a new end cover O-ring into the groove in the pump bore. Be sure to lubricate the O-ring with power steering fluid before installing it.
4. Lubricate and install a new O-ring in the groove on the pump body where the reservoir fits snugly.
5. Install the brass seal plate to the bottom of the housing bore. Align the notch in the seal plate with the dowel pin hole in the housing.
6. Carefully install the front plate with the chamfered edge down in the pump bore. Align the index notch in the plate with the dowel pin hole in the housing.

CAUTION
Be extremely careful to align the dowel pin hole properly. Pump can be completely assembled with the dowel pin not seated properly in the hole.

---

7. Place the dowel pin in the cam ring and position the cam ring inside the pump bore. Notch in the cam ring must be facing up (away from the pulley end of pump housing). If the cam ring has two notches, one machined and one cast, install the cam ring with the machined notch up. Check the amount of dowel pin extending above the cam ring surface. If more than 3/16" is showing, the dowel pin is not seated in the index hole in the housing.
8. Install the rotor and shaft in the cam ring and carefully install the 12 steel rollers in the cavities of the rotor. Lubricate the rotor, rollers, and the inside surface of the cam ring with power steering fluid. Rotate the shaft by hand to be sure all the rollers are seated parallel with the shaft and are not sticking or binding.

9. Position the pressure plate by carefully aligning the index notch on the plate with the dowel pin and inserting a clean drill (number 13 to 16) in the cam ring oil hole next to the dowel pin notch until it bottoms on the housing floor.
10. Lubricate and install a new O-ring on the pressure plate. Position the pressure plate in the pump bore so that the dowel pin is in the index notch on the plate and the drill extends through the oil passage in the pressure plate. Seat the pressure plate on the cam ring using a clean 1 1/8" socket and a soft-faced hammer to tap it gently. Remove the drill and inspect the plate at both oil passage slots to be sure that the plate is squarely seated on the cam ring.
11. Place the large coil spring over the raised portion of the installed pressure plate.
12. Place the end cover, lip edge facing up, over the spring. Press the end cover down below the retaining ring groove. Install the retaining ring in the groove. Be sure the end cover chamfer is squarely

seated against the snap-ring.
13. Replace the reservoir mounting bolt seal.
14. Lubricate the flow control valve assembly with power steering fluid and insert the valve spring and valve in the bore. Install a new O-ring on the bore plug, lubricate with fluid, and carefully install in the bore. Install the snap-ring with the sharp edge up. Do not depress the bore plug more than 1/16" below the snap-ring groove.
15. Place the reservoir on the pump body and visually align the mounting bolt hole. Tap the reservoir down on the pump with a plastic-faced hammer.
16. Remove the pump from the vise and install the mounting brackets with the mounting bolts on the pump. Tighten the bolts to 18 ft. lbs. torque.
17. Install the drive pulley by using the installer tool as follows: place the pulley on the end of the shaft and thread the installer tool into the 3/8" threaded hole in the end of the shaft. Put the installer shaft in a vise and tighten the drive nut against the thrust bearing, pressing the pulley on the shaft until it is flush. Do not try to press the pulley on the shaft without the special installer tool since the pump interior will be damaged by any other installation procedure. A small amount of drive shaft end play will be seen when the pulley is installed. This end play is necessary and will be minimized by a thin coat of oil between the rotor and the end plates when the pump is operating.
18. Install the pump assembly on the engine, install the drive belt and hoses (use new O-ring on pressure hose), and check for leaks.

FLOW CONTROL VALVE

Disassembly

1. After removing the pump from the engine and the reservoir from the pump,

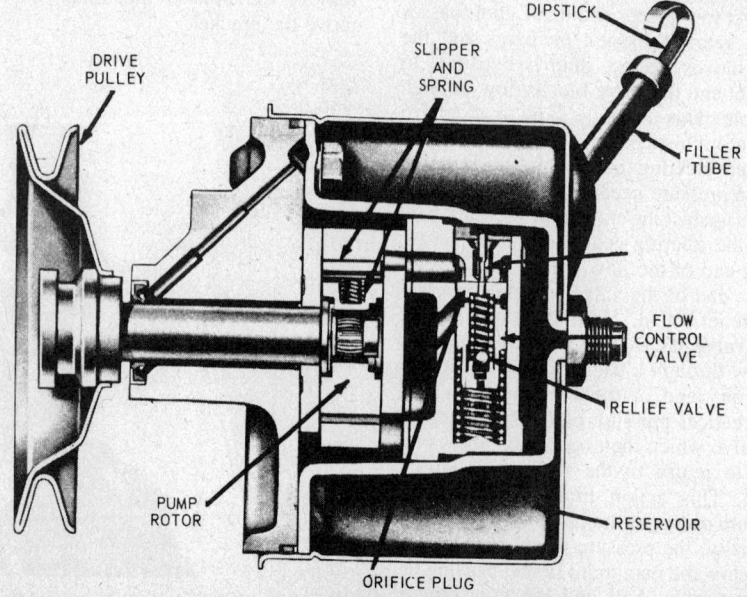

Ford Thompson power steering pump—sectional view

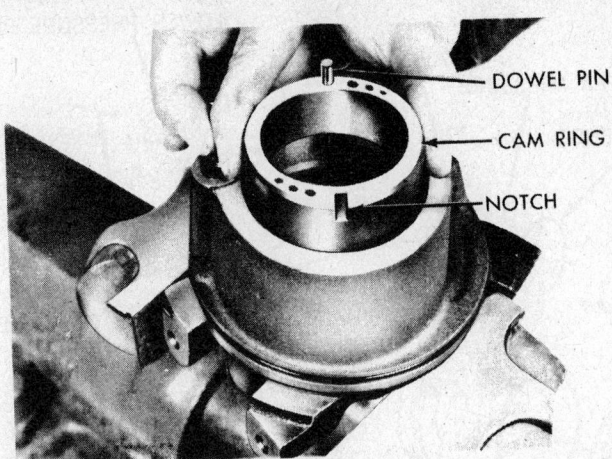

Installing cam ring

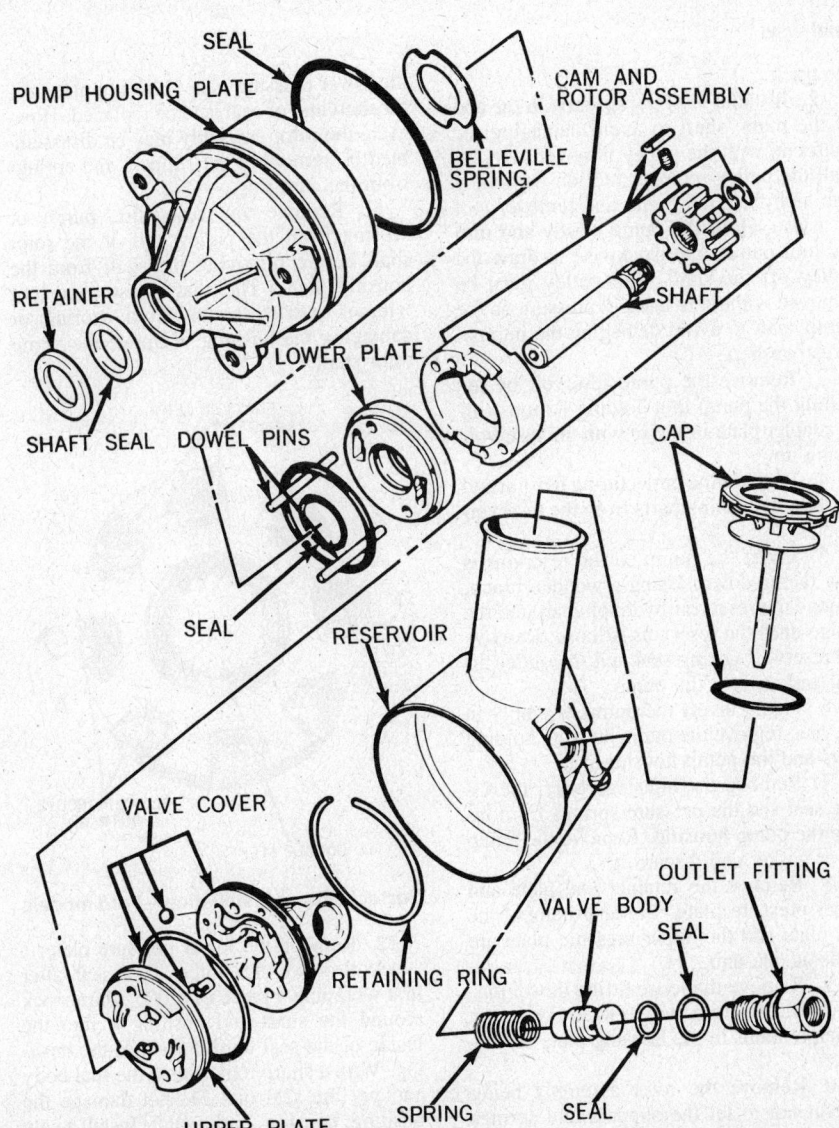

Exploded view of model C-11 slipper type pump

remove the snap-ring and plug from the flow bore. Discard the O-ring.

2. Depress the control valve against the spring pressure and allow the valve to spring out of the bore. If the valve is stuck in the bore or it did not come out of the bore far enough, it may be necessary to tap the housing lightly to remove it.

3. If the valve has dirt or foreign particles on it or in its bore, the rest of the pump needs cleaning. The hoses should be flushed and the steering gear valve body reconditioned. If the valve bore is badly scored, replace the pump body and the flow control valve.

4. Remove any nicks or burrs by gently rubbing the valve with crocus cloth. Clamp the valve land in a vise with soft-jaws and remove the hex head ball seat and shims. Note the number and gauge (thickness) of the shims on the ball seat. They must be re-installed for the same shim thickness to keep the same value of relief pressure.

5. Remove the valve from the vise and remove the pressure relief ball, guide, and spring.

Assembly

1. Insert the spring, guide and pressure relief ball in the end of the flow control valve.

2. Install the hex head plug using the exact number and thickness shims that were removed. Tighten the plug to 80 in. lbs. torque.

3. Lubricate the valve with power steering fluid and insert the flow control valve spring and valve in the housing bore. Install a new O-ring on the bore plug, lubricate with fluid and carefully install into the bore. Install the snap-ring. Do not depress the bore plug more than 1/16" beyond the snap-ring groove.

Slipper Type Power Steering Pump

The slipper type power steering pump is a belt-driven constant displacement assembly that uses a number of spring-loaded slippers in the pump rotor to force fluid from the inlet side to the flow control valve. Openings in the metering pin allow a flow of about two gpm. of fluid to the steering gear before the flow control valve directs the excess fluid to the inlet side of the pump again. Maximum pressure in the pump is limited by the pressure relief valve which opens when the pressure exceeds the maximum limits.

The slipper type power steering pump discussed in this section is used on Ford trucks and is called the Ford-Thompson power steering pump.

Removal

1. Drain the fluid from the pump reservoir by disconnecting the fluid return hose

STEERING GEAR
POWER

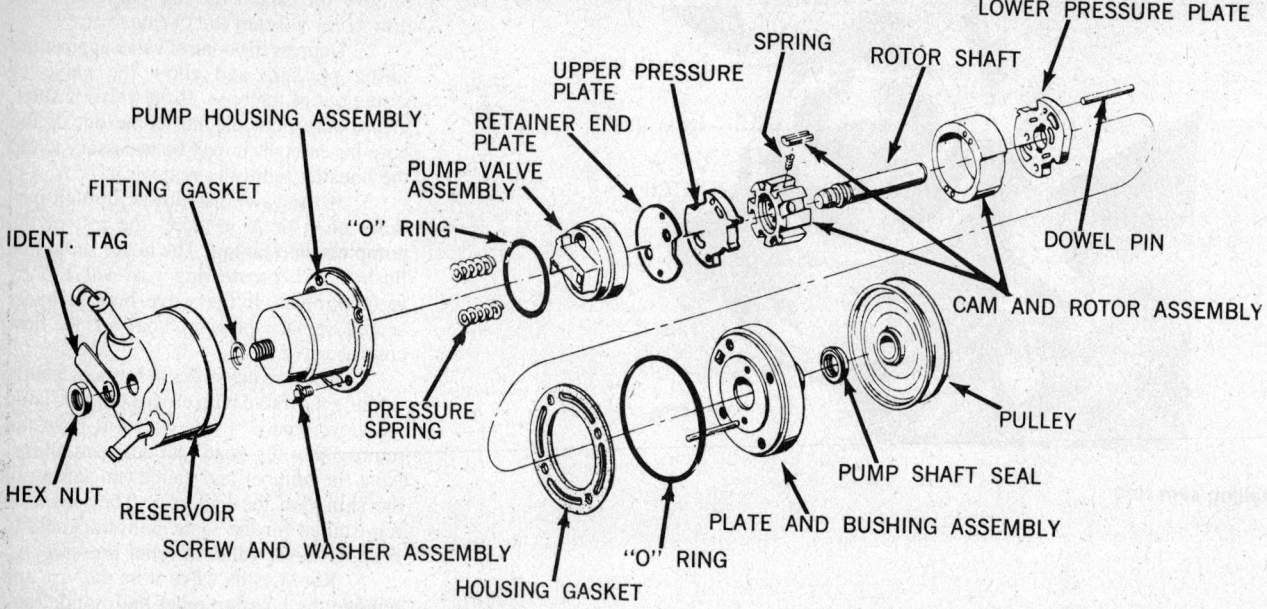

Ford Thompson power steering pump—sectional view

at the pump. Then, disconnect the pressure hose from the pump.

2. Remove the mounting bolts from the front of the pump. On eight cylinder engines, there is a nut on the rear of the pump that must be removed. After removing all the mounting bolts and nuts from the pump, move the unit inward to loosen the belt tension and remove the belt from the pulley. Then remove the pump from the engine.

Installation

1. Position the pump on the mounting bracket and loosely install the mounting bolts and nuts. Put the drive belt over the pulley and move the pump outward against the belt until the proper belt tension is obtained. Measure the belt tension with a gauge for the proper adjustment. Only in cases where a belt tension gauge is not available should the belt deflection method be used. If the belt deflection method is used, be sure to check the belt with a tension gauge at the earliest time since the deflection method is not accurate.

2. Tighten the mounting bolts and nuts to the specified torque limits.

3. Tighten the pressure hose fitting hex nut to the proper torque. Then connect the pressure hose to the pump and tighten the hose nut to the proper torque.

4. Connect the fluid return hose to the pump and tighten the clamp.

5. Fill the pump reservoir with power steering fluid and bleed the air bubbles from the system.

6. Check for leaks and recheck the fluid level. If necessary, add fluid to raise the level properly.

Disassembly

1. Drain as much fluid from the pump as possible after removing the pump from the truck.

2. Install a 3/8–16″ capscrew in the end of the pump shaft to avoid damaging the shaft end with the pulley remover tool. Install the pulley remover tool on the pulley hub and place the pump and remover tool in a vise. Hold the pump steady and turn the tool nut counterclockwise to draw the pulley off the shaft. The pulley must be removed without in and out pressure on the pump shaft to avoid damaging the internal thrust washers.

3. Remove the pump reservoir by installing the pump in a holding fixture with an adapter plate in a vise with the reservoir facing up.

4. Remove the outlet fitting hex nut and any other attaching parts from the reservoir case.

5. Invert the pump so the reservoir is now facing down. Using a wooden block, remove the reservoir by tapping around the flange until the reservoir is loose. Remove the reservoir O-ring seal and the outlet fitting gasket from the pump.

6. Again invert the pump assembly in the vise, remove the pump housing holding bolts and the pump housing.

7. Remove the housing cover, the O-ring seal and the pressure springs from inside the pump housing. Remove the pump cover gasket and discard it.

8. Remove the retainer end plate and upper pressure plate. In some pumps, the end plate and the upper pressure plate are made as one unit.

9. Remove the loose fitting dowel pin. Be careful not to bend the fixed dowel pin which remains in the housing plate assembly.

10. Remove the rotor assembly being careful not to let the slippers and springs fall out of the rotor. It may not be necessary to disassemble the rotor assembly unless

the lower pressure plate, housing plate, rotor shaft and/or seal is to be replaced. However, the rotor assembly may be disassembled by removing the slippers and springs from the cam ring.

11. Remove any rust, dirt, burrs, or scoring from the pulley end of the rotor shaft before removing the shaft from the housing plate. The shaft must come out without restrictions to avoid scoring or damaging the bushing. Remove the pump rotor shaft.

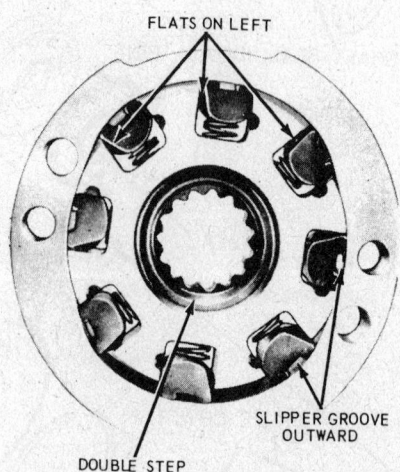

Correct slipper installation—Ford models

12. Remove the lower pressure plate.

13. Remove the rotor shaft seal after first wrapping a piece of 0.005″ shim stock around the shaft and pushing it into the inside of the seal until it touches the bushing. With a sharp tool, pierce the seal body and pry the seal out. Do not damage the bushing, housing, or the shaft. Install a new seal using a soft-faced hammer.

14. If the pump has a flow control valve,

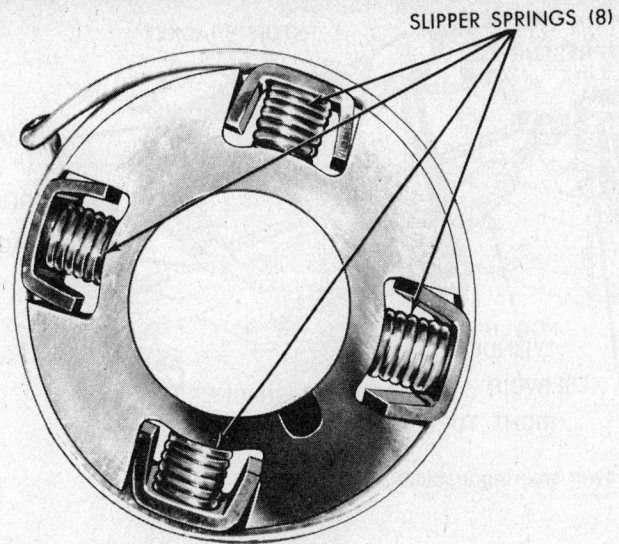

SLIPPER SPRINGS (8)

Correct slipper installation—Chrysler models

disassemble according to instructions given in the section on the roller type power steering pump.

Inspection

1. Wash all metal parts in clean, non-toxic solvent. Blow out all oil passages with compressed air and air dry all cleaned parts.

2. Inspect the drive shaft for excessive wear and seal area for nicks or scoring. Replace if necessary.

3. Inspect the pressure plates, slippers, rotor, and cam ring for nicks, burrs, or scratches. If any of the parts are damaged enough to cause poor operation or binding of the pump, replace the defective part.

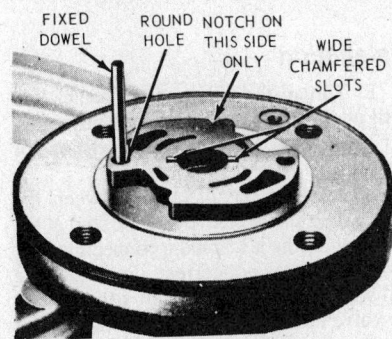

FIXED DOWEL ROUND HOLE NOTCH ON THIS SIDE ONLY WIDE CHAMFERED SLOTS

Lower pressure plate installed

4. Inspect the pump body drive shaft bushing for excessive wear. Replace if necessary.

Assembly

1. With the pump assembly positioned on the adapter plate in the holding fixture, install the lower pressure plate on the anchor pin with the chamfered slots at the center hole facing up.

2. Lubricate the rotor shaft with power steering fluid and insert the shaft into the lower pressure and housing plates.

3. Assemble the rotor, slippers, and springs by wrapping a piece of wire around the rotor, installing the springs, and sliding a slipper in each groove of the rotor over the springs. Then, insert the assembly into

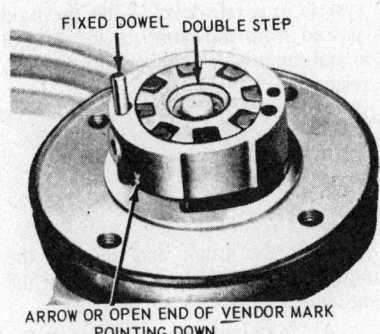

FIXED DOWEL   DOUBLE STEP

ARROW OR OPEN END OF VENDOR MARK POINTING DOWN

Cam and rotor installation

the cam ring. Be sure the flat side of the slippers are toward the left side. Be sure that the springs are installed straight and are not cocked to one side under the slippers.

4. Install the cam ring and rotor assembly on the drive shaft with the fixed dowel passing through the first hole to the left of the cam notch when the arrow on the cam outside diameter is pointing toward the lower pressure plate. If the cam and rotor assembly does not seat properly, turn the rotor shaft slightly until the spline teeth mesh, allowing the cam and rotor to drop into position.

5. Insert the loose fitting dowel through the cam insert and lower pressure plate into the hole in the housing plate assembly. When both dowels are installed properly, they will be the same height.

6. Install the upper pressure plate so the tapered notch is facing down against the cam insert. The fixed dowel should pass through the round dowel hole and the loose

dowel through the long hole. The slot between the ears on the outside of the pressure plate should match the notch on the cam insert.

7. Install the retainer end plate so the slot on the end plate matches the notches on the upper pressure plate and the cam insert.

FIXED DOWEL   EARS

Upper pressure plate installation

8. Install the pump valve assembly O-ring seal on the pump valve assembly. Do not twist the seal.

9. Place the pump valve assembly on top of the retainer end plate with the large exhaust slot on the pump valve in line with the outside notches of the cam, upper pressure plate, and retainer end plate. All parts must be fully seated. If correctly installed, the relief valve stem will be in line with the lube return hole in the pump housing plate.

10. Put small amounts of vaseline on the pump housing plate to hold the cover gasket in place. Install the cover gasket in place.

11. Insert the pressure plate springs into the pockets in the pump valve assembly.

12. Plug the intake hole in the housing.

13. Lubricate the inside of the housing and the housing cover seal with power steering fluid. Install two studs for use as positioning guides, one in the bolt hole nearest the drain hole and the other in the bolt hole on the opposite side of the housing plate.

14. Align the small lube hole in the housing rim and the lube hole in the housing plate. Install the housing, using a steady, even, downward pressure. Do not jar the pressure spring out of position. Remove the

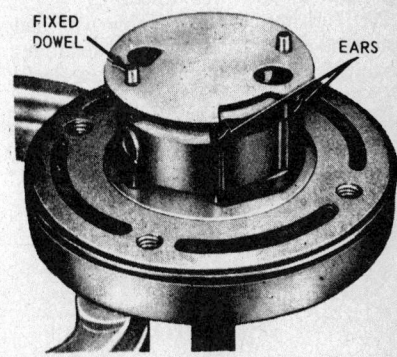

FIXED DOWEL   EARS

Retainer end plate installation

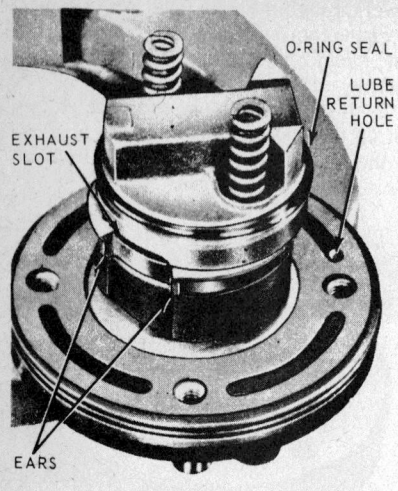

Valve and pressure spring installation

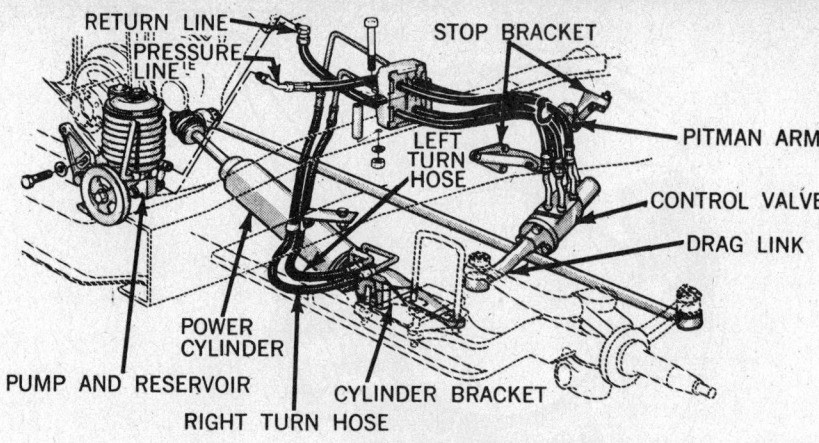

Linkage type power steering installation—typical

guide studs and loosely install the housing retaining bolts finger tight.

15. Tighten the retaining bolts evenly to 28–32 ft. lbs. until the housing flange contacts the gasket.

16. Install a ⅜–16 hex head screw into the end of the rotor shaft and put a torque wrench on it. Check the amount of torque needed to rotate the rotor shaft. If the torque is more than 15 in. lbs., loosen the retaining bolts slightly and rotate the rotor shaft. Then, retighten the retaining bolts evenly. Do not use the pump if the shaft torque exceeds 15 in. lbs.

17. Release the pin in the bench holding fixture and shake the pump assembly back and forth. If there is a rattle, the pressure springs have fallen out of their seats and must be reinstalled.

18. Install the reservoir O-ring seal on the housing plate without twisting it. Lubricate the seal and install the reservoir, aligning the notch in the reservoir flange with the notch in the outside edge of the pump housing plate and bushing assembly. Using only a soft-faced hammer, tap at the rear outer corners of the reservoir. Inspect the assembly to be sure the reservoir is fully seated on the housing plate.

19. Install the identification tag (if one was removed) on the outlet valve fitting. Install the outlet valve fitting nut and tighten to 48–45 ft. lbs. torque.

20. Turn the pump assembly over and install the pulley using the tool used to remove the pulley. Turn the tool nut clockwise to draw the pulley on the shaft until it is flush with the shaft end. Do not exert inward and outward pressures on the shaft to avoid damaging the internal thrust areas. Remove the tool.

Bendix Linkage–Type Power Steering System

The Bendix linkage-type power steering is a hydraulically controlled system composed of an integral pump and fluid reservoir, a control valve, a power cylinder, connecting fluid lines, and the steering linkage. The hydraulic pump, which is driven by a belt turned by the engine, draws fluid from the reservoir and provides pressure through hoses to the control valve and the power cylinder. There is a pressure relief valve to limit the pressures within the steering system to a safe level. After the fluid has passed from the pump to the control valve and the power cylinder, it returns to the reservoir.

CONTROL VALVE CENTERING SPRING

Adjustment

1. Raise the truck and remove the spring cap attaching screws and remove the spring cap.

— **CAUTION** —

Be very careful not to position the hoist adapters of two post hoists under the suspension and/or steering components. Place the hoist adapters under the front suspension lower arms.

2. Tighten the adjusting nut snug (about 90–100 in. lbs.); then, loosen the nut ¼ turn (90 degrees). Do not turn the adjusting nut too tight.

3. Place the spring cap on the valve housing. Lubricate and install the attaching screws and washers. Tighten the screws to 72–100 in. lbs. torque.

4. Lower the truck and start the engine. Check the steering effort using a spring scale attached to the steering wheel rim for a pull of no more than 12 lbs.

POWER STEERING CONTROL VALVE

Removal

1. Raise the truck. If a two post hoist is used, be sure to place the hoist adapters under the front suspension steering arms. Do not allow the hoist adapters to contact the steering linkage.

2. Disconnect the four fluid line fittings at the control valve and drain the fluid from the lines. Turn the front wheels back and forth to force all the fluid from the system.

3. Loosen the clamping nut and bolt at the right end of the sleeve.

4. Remove the roll pin from the steering arm-to-idler arm rod through the slot in the sleeve.

5. Remove the control valve ball stud nut.

6. Remove the ball stud from the sector shaft arm.

7. After turning the front wheels fully to the left, unthread the control valve from the center link steering arm-to-idler arm rod.

Installation

1. Thread the valve on the center link until about four threads are still visible.

2. Position the ball stud in the sector shaft arm.

3. Measure the distance between the grease plug in the sleeve and the stud at the inner end of the left spindle connecting rod. If the distance is not correct, disconnect the ball stud from the sector shaft arm and turn the valve on the center link until the correct distance is obtained.

4. When the distance is correct and the ball stud is positioned in the sector shaft arm, align the hole in the steering arm-to-idler arm rod with the slot near the end of the valve sleeve. Install the roll pin in the rod hole to lock the valve in place on the rod.

5. Tighten the valve sleeve clamp bolt to the proper torque.

6. Install the ball stud nut and tighten to the proper torque. Install a new cotter pin.

7. Connect all fluid lines to the control valve and tighten all fittings securely. Do not over-tighten.

8. Fill the fluid reservoir with power steering fluid to the full mark on the dipstick.

9. Start the engine and run it for a few minutes to warm the fluid in the power steering system. Turn the steering wheel back and forth to the stops and check the system for leaks.

10. Increase the engine idle speed to about 1000 rpm. Turn the steering wheel back and forth several times, then stop the engine. Check the control valve and hose connections for leaks.

11. Recheck the fluid level and add fluid if necessary.

12. Start the engine again, and check the position of the steering wheel when the front wheels are straight ahead. Do not make any adjustments until toe-in is checked.

13. With engine running, check front wheel toe-in.

14. Check steering wheel turning effort which should be equal in both directions.

POWER STEERING POWER CYLINDER

Removal and Installation

1. Disconnect the two fluid lines from the power cylinder and drain the fluid.

2. Remove the pal nut, attaching nut, washer and the insulator from the end of the power cylinder rod. Remove the cotter pin and castellated nut holding the power cylinder stud to the center link.

3. Disconnect the power cylinder stud from the center link.

4. Remove the insulator sleeve and washer from the end of the power cylinder.

5. Inspect the tube fittings and seats in the power cylinder for nicks, burrs, or other damage. Replace the seats or tubes if damaged.

6. Install the washer, sleeve and the insulator on the end of the power cylinder rod.

7. While extending the rod as far as possible, insert the rod in the bracket on the frame and then, compress the rod so the stud may be inserted in the center link. Secure the stud with the castellated nut and a new cotter pin.

8. Install the insulator, washer, nut, and a pal nut on the power cylinder rod.

9. Connect the two fluid lines to their proper ports on the power cylinder.

10. Fill the reservoir with power steering fluid to the full mark on the dipstick. Start the engine and run for a few minutes to warm the fluid. Turn the steering wheel back and forth to the stops to fill the system. Stop the engine.

11. Recheck the fluid level and add fluid if necessary. Check for fluid leaks.

12. Start the engine again, turn the steering wheel back and forth, and check for leaks while the engine is running.

CONTROL VALVE

Disassembly

1. Clean the outside of the control valve of dirt and fluid.

2. Remove the centering spring cap from the valve housing. The control valve should be put in a soft-faced bench vise during disassembly. Clamp the control valve around the sleeve flange only to avoid damaging the valve housing, spool, or sleeve.

3. Remove the nut from the end of the valve spool bolt. Remove the washers, spacer, centering spring, adapter, and the bushing from the bolt and valve housing.

4. Remove the two bolts holding the valve housing and the sleeve together. Separate the valve housing and the sleeve.

5. Remove the plug from the sleeve. Push the valve spool out of the centering spring end of the valve housing, and remove the seal from the spool.

6. Remove the spacer, bushing and valve housing.

7. Drive the pin out of the travel regulator stop with a punch and hammer. Pull the head of the valve spool bolt tightly against the travel regulator stop before driving the pin out of the stop.

8. Turn the travel regulator stop counterclockwise in the valve sleeve to remove the stop from the sleeve.

9. Remove the valve spool bolt, spacer, and rubber washer from the travel regulator stop.

10. Remove the rubber boot and clamp from the valve sleeve. Slide the bumper, spring, and ball stud seat out of the valve sleeve and remove the ball stud socket from the sleeve.

11. Remove the return port hose seat and the return port relief valve.

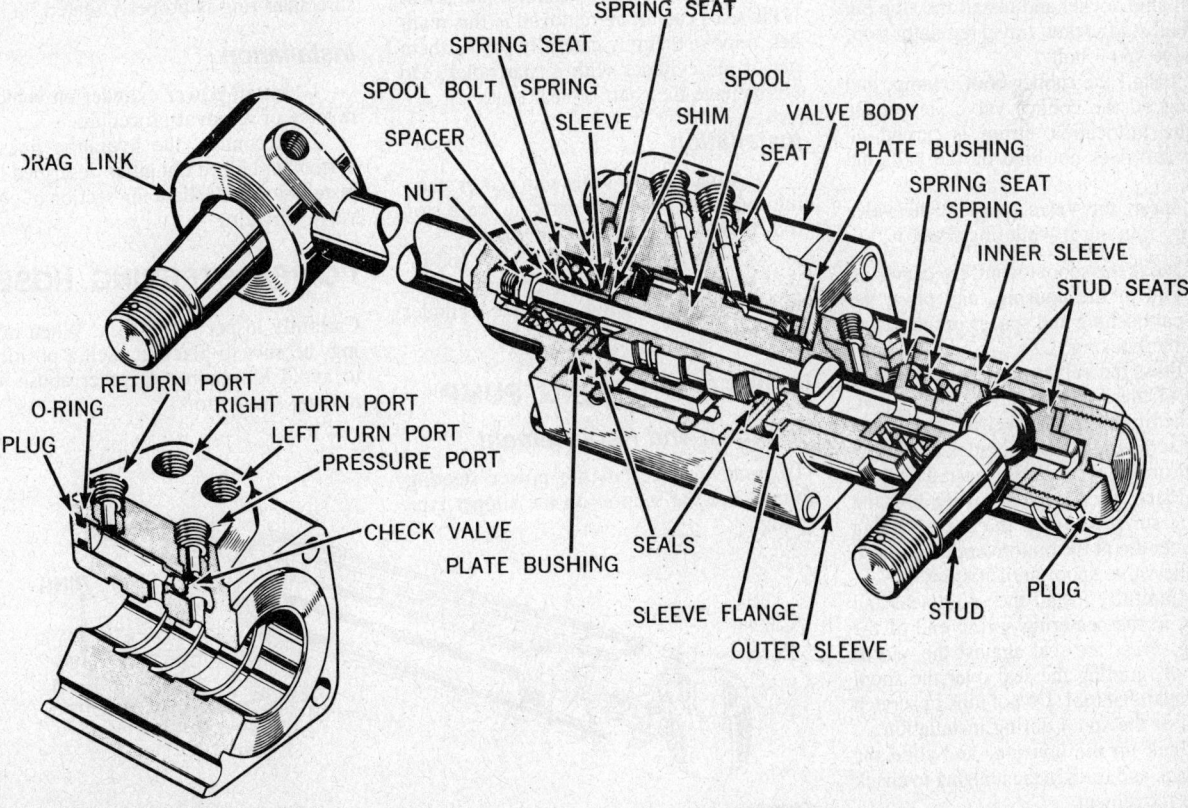

Control valve cross section—typical

12. Remove the spring plug and O-ring. Then remove the reaction limiting valve.

13. Replace all worn or damaged hose seats by using an Easy-Out screw extractor or a bolt of proper size as a puller. Tap the existing hole in the hose seat, using a starting tap of the correct size. Remove all metal chips from the hose seat after tapping. Place a nut and washer on a bolt of the same size as the tapped hole. The washer must be large enough to cover the hose seat port. Insert the bolt in the tapped hole and remove the hose seat by turning the nut clockwise and drawing the bolt out. Install a new hose seal in the port, and thread a bolt of the correct size in the port. Tighten the bolt enough to bottom the seal in the port.

Assembly

1. Coat all parts of the control valve assembly with power steering fluid. Seals should be coated with lubricant before installation.

2. Install the reaction limiting valve, spring and plug. Install the return port relief valve and the hose seat.

3. Insert one of the ball stud seats (flat end first) into the ball stud socket, and insert the threaded end of the ball stud into the socket.

4. Place the socket in the control valve sleeve so that the threaded end of the ball stud can be pulled out through the slot.

5. Place the other ball stud seat, spring, and bumper in the socket. Install and securely tighten the travel regulator stop.

6. Loosen the stop just enough to align the nearest hole in the stop with the slot in the ball stud socket and install the stop pin in the ball stud socket, travel regulator stop, and valve spool bolt.

7. Install the rubber boot, clamp, and the plug on the control valve sleeve. Be sure the lubrication fitting is turned on tightly and does not bind on the ball stud socket.

8. Insert the valve spool in the valve housing, rotating it while installing it.

9. Move the spool toward the centering spring end of the housing, and place the small seal bushing and spacer in the sleeve end of the housing.

10. Press the valve spool against the inner lip of the seal and, at the same time, guide the lip of the seal over the spool with a small screwdriver. Do not nick or scratch the seal or the spool during installation.

11. Place the sleeve end of the housing on a flat surface so that the seal, bushing and spacer are at the bottom end; then push down the valve spool until it stops.

12. Carefully install the spool seal and bushing in the centering spring end of the housing. Press the seal against the end of the spool, guiding the seal over the spool with a small flat tool. Do not nick or scratch the seal or the spool during installation.

13. Pick up the housing, and slide the spool back and forth in the housing to check for free movement.

14. Place the valve sleeve on the housing so that the ball stud is on the same side of the housing as the ports for the two power cylinder lines. Install the two bolts in the sleeve, and torque them to the proper torque.

15. Place the adapter on the centering spring end of the housing, and install the bushing, washers, spacers and centering spring on the valve spool bolt.

16. Compress the centering spring and install the nut on the bolt. Tighten the nut snug (about 90–100 in. lbs.); then, loosen it not more than ¼ turn. Do not overtighten to avoid breaking the stop pin at the travel regulator stop.

17. Move the ball stud back and forth to check for free movement.

18. Lubricate the two cap attaching bolts. Install the centering spring cap on the valve housing, and tighten the two cap bolts to the proper torque.

19. Install the nut on the ball stud so that the valve can be put in a vise. Then, push forward on the cap end of the valve to check the valve spool for free movement.

20. Turn the valve around in the vise, and push forward on the sleeve end to check for free movement.

POWER CYLINDER SEAL

Removal

1. Clamp the power cylinder in a vise and remove the snap-ring from the end of the cylinder. Do not distort or crack the cylinder in the vise.

2. Pull the piston rod out all the way to remove the scraper, bushing, and seals. If the seals cannot be removed in this manner, remove them by carefully prying them out of the cylinder with a sharp pick. Do not damage the shaft or seal seat.

Installation

1. Coat the new seals with power steering fluid and place the parts on the piston rod. Coat with grease or lubricant.

2. Push the rod in all the way, and install the parts in the cylinder with a deep socket slightly smaller than the cylinder opening.

POWER STEERING PUMP

Removal and Replacement

To remove or install the power steering pump, see the section on the slipper type pump.

Saginaw Linkage-Type Power Cylinder

Removal

1. Remove the two hoses which are connected to the cylinder and drain fluid into a container.

2. Remove power cylinder from frame bracket.

3. Remove cotter pin and nut and pull stud out of relay rod.

4. Remove cylinder from vehicle.

Inspection

1. Check seals for leaks around cylinder rod. If leaks are found, replace seals.

2. Check hose connection seats for damage and replace if necessary.

3. For service other than seat or seal replacement, it is necessary to replace the power cylinder.

4. The ball stud may be replaced by removing snap-ring.

Disassembly and Assembly

1. To remove piston rod seal, remove snap-ring and pull out on rod. Remove back-up washer, piston rod scraper and piston rod seal from rod.

2. To remove the ball stud, depress the end plug and remove the snap-ring. Push on the end of the ball stud and the end plug, spring, spring seat, ball stud and seal may be removed. If the ball seat is to be replaced, it must be pressed out.

3. Reverse disassembly procedure. Be sure snap-ring is properly seated.

Installation

1. Install power cylinder on vehicle in reverse of removal procedure.

2. Reconnect the hydraulic lines, fill system and bleed out air as described in the installation and balancing section of control valve servicing.

POWER STEERING HOSES

Carefully inspect the hoses. When installing, be sure to place in such a position as to avoid all chafing or other abuse when making sharp turns.

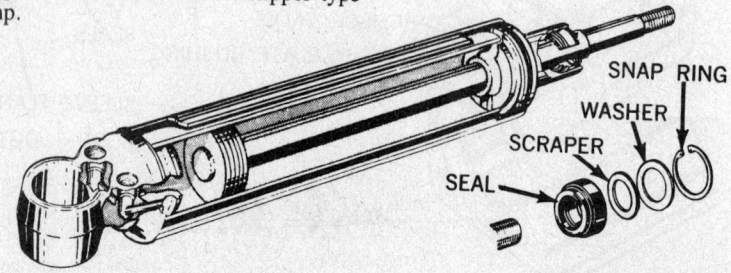

Phantom view of power cylinder—typical

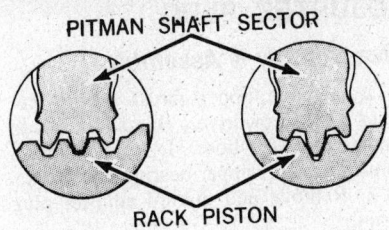

CONSTANT RATIO VARIABLE RATIO

Comparison of constant ratio and variable ratio steering shaft teeth

Saginaw Rotary-Type Power Steering

The rotary-type power steering gear is designed with all components in one housing.

The power cylinder is an integral part of the gear housing. A double-acting type piston allows oil pressure to be applied to either side of the piston. The one-piece piston and power rack is meshed to the sector shaft.

The hydraulic control valve is composed of a sleeve and valve spool. The spool is held in the neutral position by the torsion bar and spool actuator. Twisting of the torsion bar moves the valve spool, allowing oil pressure to be directed to either side of

the power piston, depending upon the directional rotation of the steering wheel, to give power assist.

On many trucks of the General Motors Corporation, a modified version of the rotary valve power steering system provides variable ratio steering to assist the driver to steer the truck easier and safer. The steering gear ratio will vary from a high ratio of about 16:1 while steering straight ahead to a lower gear ratio of about 12.1:1 while making a full turn to either side.

ROLLER PUMP

Removal

Remove the reservoir cover and use a suction gun to empty the reservoir. Disconnect the hoses from the pump and tie them in a raised position to prevent oil drainage. Loosen the pump adjusting screw and remove the pump belt, then take out the retaining bolts and remove the pump and reservoir.

Installation

Position the pump assembly and install the retaining bolts. Be sure there is clearance between the pump bracket and the engine front support bracket. Install the hoses and place the pump belt on the pulley. Adjust the belt to ½" deflection, then tighten the adjusting screw.

Connect the hoses to the pump assembly.

Fill the reservoir to within ½" of the top with automatic transmission fluid type A.

Start the engine and rotate the steering wheel several times to the right and left to expel air from the system, then recheck the oil level and install the reservoir cover.

POWER STEERING UNIT

Fluid Used

This unit uses automatic transmission fluid type A. The fluid capacity is 4½ pints.

Bleeding the System

Fill the pump reservoir to within ½" of the top. Start and run the engine to attain normal operating temperatures. Now, turn the steering wheel through its entire travel three or four times to expel air from the system, then recheck the fluid level.

Checking Steering Effort

Run the engine to attain normal operating temperatures. With the wheels on a dry floor, hook a pull scale to the spoke of the steering wheel at the outer edge. The effort required to turn the steering wheel should be 3½–5 lbs. If the pull is not within these limits, check the hydraulic pressure.

Pressure Test

To check the hydraulic pressure, disconnect the pressure hose from the gear. Now con-

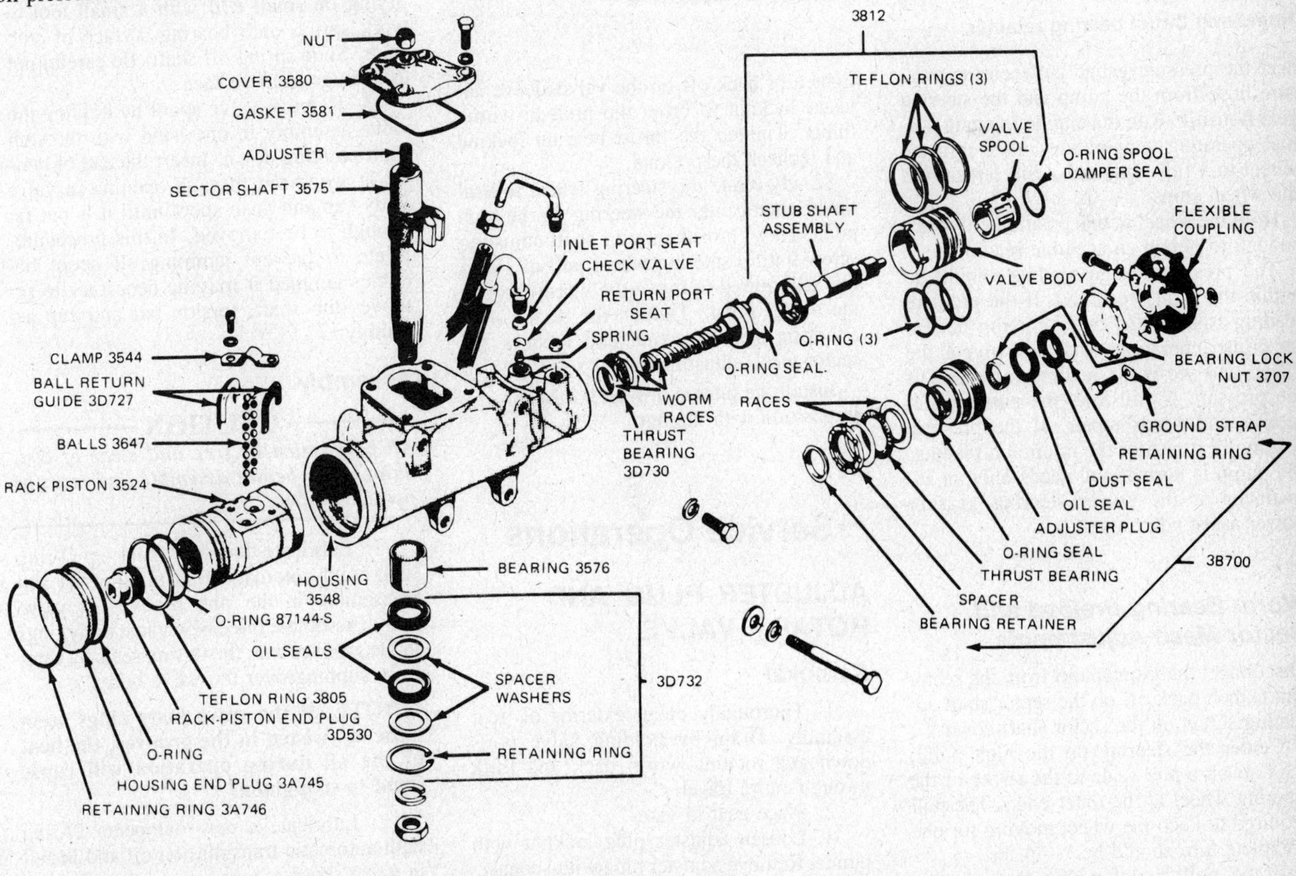

Exploded view of Saginaw power steering gear used on light trucks

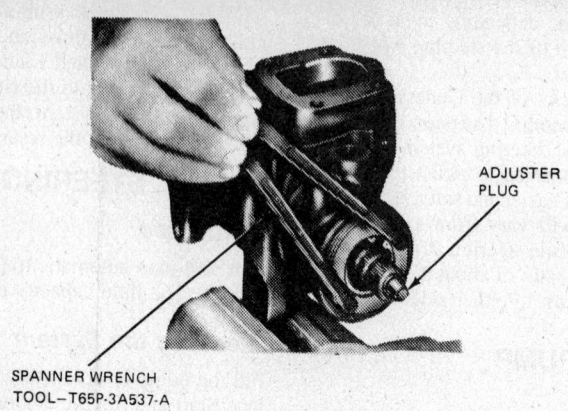

SPANNER WRENCH
TOOL—T65P-3A537-A

Removing adjuster plug

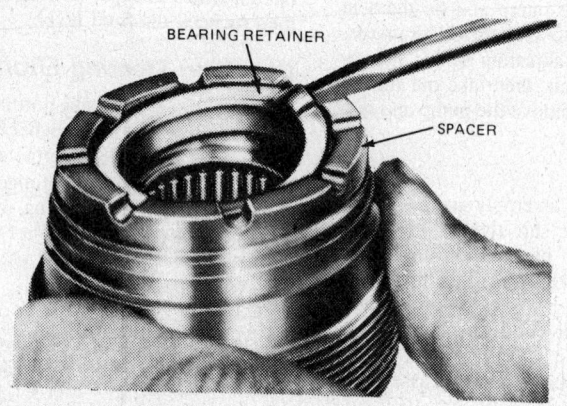

BEARING RETAINER

SPACER

Removing thrust bearing retainer

nect the pressure gauge between the pressure hose from the pump and the steering gear housing. Run the engine to attain normal operating temperatures, then turn the wheel to a full right and a full left turn to the wheel stops.

Hold the wheel in this position only long enough to obtain an accurate reading.

The pressure gauge reading should be within the limits specified. If the pressure reading is less than the minimum needed for proper operation, close the valve at the gauge and see if the reading increases. If the pressure is still low, the pump is defective and needs repair. If the pressure reading is at or near the minimum reading, the pump is normal and needs only an adjustment of the power steering gear or power assist control valve.

Worm Bearing Preload and Sector Mesh Adjustments

Disconnect the pitman arm from the sector shaft, then back off on the sector shaft adjusting screw on the sector shaft cover.

Center the steering on the high point, then attach a pull scale to the spoke of the steering wheel at the outer edge. The pull required to keep the wheel moving for one complete turn should be ½–⅔ lbs.

If the pull is not within these limits, loosen the thrust bearing locknut and

tighten or back off on the valve sleeve adjuster locknut to bring the preload within limits. Tighten the thrust bearing locknut and recheck the preload.

Slowly rotate the steering wheel several times, then center the steering on the high point. Now, turn the sector shaft adjusting screw until a steering wheel pull of 1–1½ lbs. is required to move the worm through the center point. Tighten the sector shaft adjusting screw locknut and recheck the sector mesh adjustment.

Install the pitman arm and draw the arm in position with the nut.

Service Operations

ADJUSTER PLUG AND ROTARY VALVE

Removal

1. Thoroughly clean exterior of gear assembly. Drain by holding valve ports down and rotating worm back and forth through entire travel.
2. Place gear in vise.
3. Loosen adjuster plug locknut with punch. Remove adjuster plug with spanner.
4. Remove rotary valve assembly by grasping stub shaft and pulling it out.

ADJUSTER PLUG

Disassembly & Assembly

1. Remove upper thrust bearing retainer with screwdriver. Be careful not to damage bearing bore. Discard retainer. Remove spacer, upper bearing and races.
2. Remove and discard adjuster plug O-ring.
3. Remove stub shaft seal retaining ring (Truarc pliers will help) and remove and discard dust seal.
4. Remove stub shaft seal by prying out and discard.
5. Examine needle bearing and, if required, remove same by pressing from thrust bearing end.
6. Inspect thrust bearing spacer, bearing rollers and races.
7. Reassemble in reverse of above.

ROTARY VALVE

Disassembly

Repairs are seldom needed. Do not disassemble unless absolutely necessary. If the O-ring seal on valve spool dampener needs replacement, perform this portion of operation only.

1. Remove cap-to-worm O-ring seal and discard.
2. Remove valve spool spring by prying on small coil with a small tool to work spring onto bearing surface of stub shaft. Slide spring off shaft. Be careful not to damage shaft surface.
3. Remove valve spool by holding the valve assembly in one hand with the stub shaft pointing down. Insert the end of pencil or wood rod through opening in valve body cap and push spool until it is out far enough to be removed. In this procedure, rotate to prevent jamming. If spool becomes jammed it may be necessary to remove stub shaft, torsion bar and cap assembly.

Assembly

——— CAUTION ———

All parts must be free and clear of dirt, chips, etc., before assembly and must be protected after.

1. Lubricate three new back-up O-ring seals with automatic transmission oil and reassemble in the ring grooves of valve body. Assemble three new valve body rings in the grooves over the O-ring seals by carefully slipping over the valve body.

NOTE: If the valve body rings seem loose or twisted in the grooves, the heat of the oil during operation will cause them to straighten.

2. Lubricate a new dampener O-ring with automatic transmission oil and install in valve spool groove.
3. Assemble stub shaft torsion bar and cap assembly in the valve body, aligning

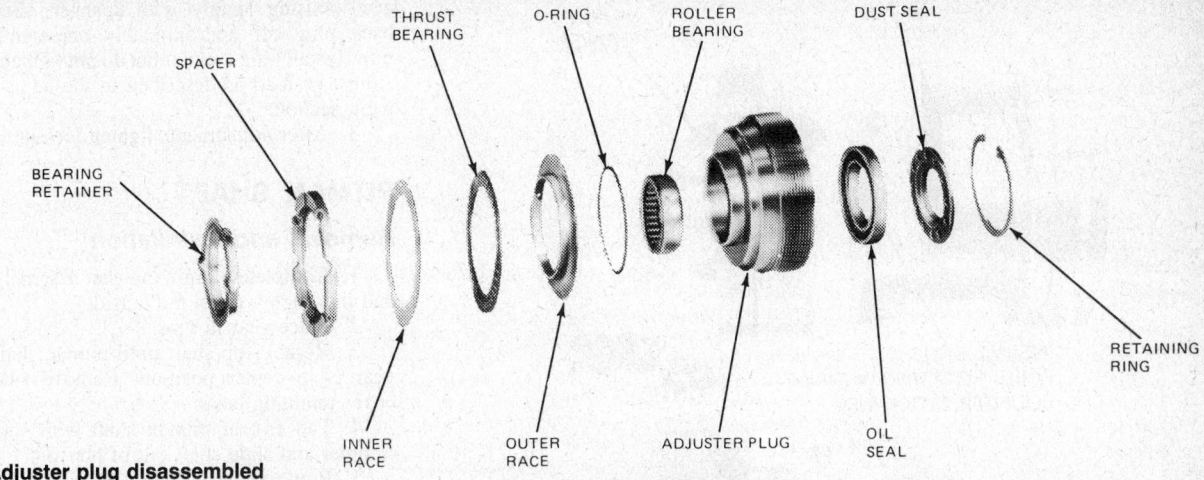

Adjuster plug disassembled

BEARING RETAINER · SPACER · THRUST BEARING · O-RING · ROLLER BEARING · DUST SEAL · INNER RACE · OUTER RACE · ADJUSTER PLUG · OIL SEAL · RETAINING RING

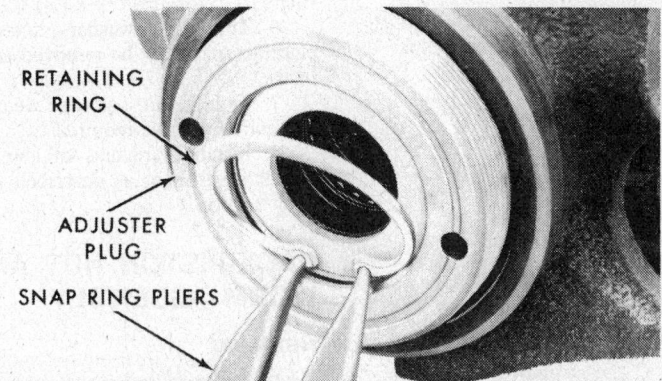

RETAINING RING · ADJUSTER PLUG · SNAP RING PLIERS

Removing adjuster plug retaining seal ring

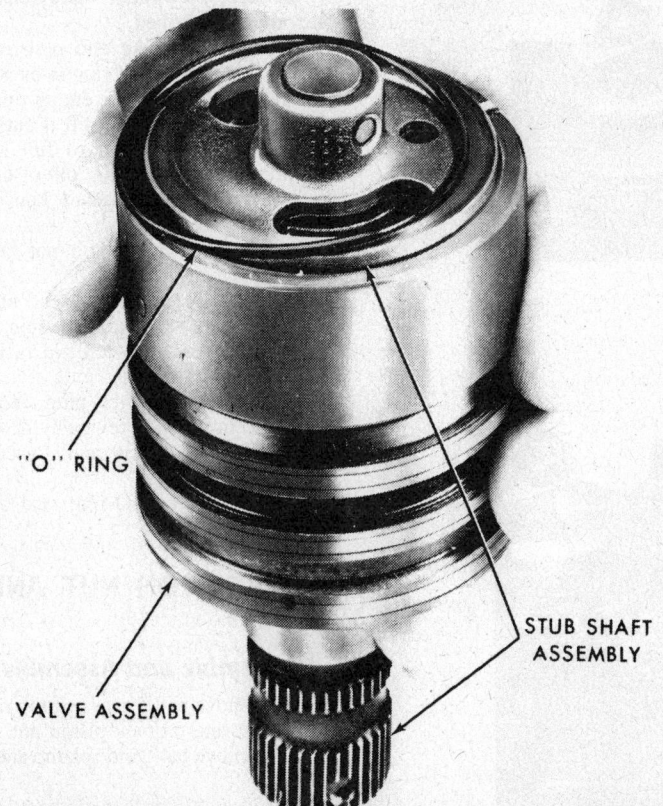

"O" RING · VALVE ASSEMBLY · STUB SHAFT ASSEMBLY

Separating valve spool (center) from valve body

the groove in the valve cap with the pin in the valve body. Tap lightly with soft remainder of assembly. Valve body pin must be in the cap groove. Hold parts together during the remainder of assembly.

4. Lubricate spool. With notch in spool toward valve body, slide the spool over the stub shaft. Align the notch on the spool with the spool drive pin on stub shaft and carefully engage spool in valve body bore. Push spool evenly and with slight rotating motion until it reaches the drive pin. Rotate slowly, with some pressure, until notch engages pin. Be sure dampener O-ring seal is evenly distributed in the spool groove.

— **CAUTION** —

Use extreme care because spool to valve body clearance is very small. Damage is easily caused.

5. With seal protector over stub shaft, slide valve spool spring over shaft, with small diameter of spring going over shaft last. Work spring onto shaft until small coil is located in stub shaft groove.

6. Lubricate a new cap to O-ring seal and install in valve body.

ADJUSTER PLUG AND ROTARY VALVE

Installation

1. Align narrow pin slot on valve body with valve body drive pin on the worm. Insert the valve assembly into gear housing by pressing against valve body with finger tips. Do not press on stub shaft or torsion bar. The return hole in the gear housing should be fully visible when properly assembled.

— **CAUTION** —

Do not press on stub shaft as this may cause shaft and cap to pull out of valve body, allowing the spool dampener O-ring seal to slip into valve body oil grooves.

2. With seal protector over end of stub shaft, install adjuster plug assembly into

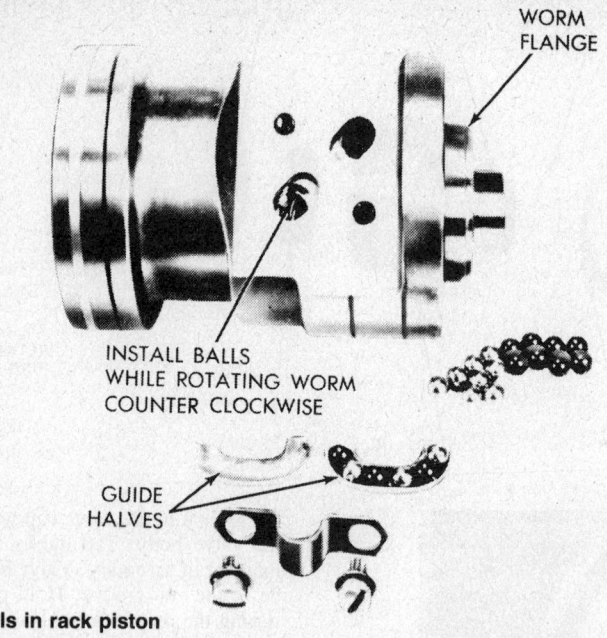

Installing balls in rack piston

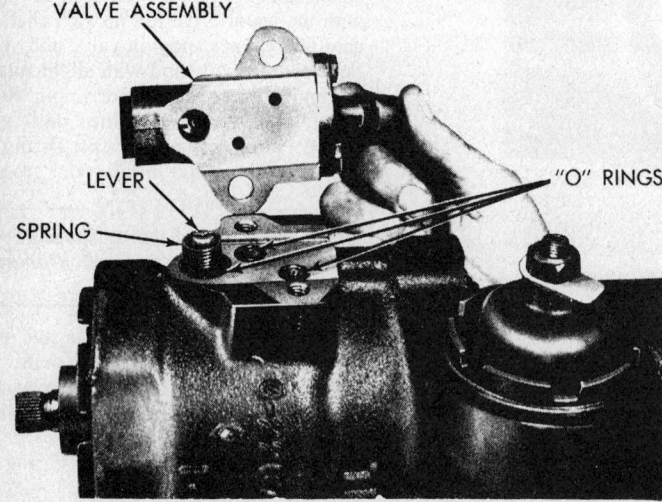

Removing valve body assembly

Removing pilot lever

gear housing snugly with spanner, then back plug off approximately one-eighth turn. Install plug locknut but do not tighten. Adjust preload as described in the adjustment section.

3. After adjustment, tighten locknut.

PITMAN SHAFT

Removal and Installation

1. Completely drain the gear assembly and thoroughly clean the outside.

2. Place gear in vise.

3. Rotate stub shaft until pitman shaft gear is in center position. Remove side cover retaining bolts.

4. Tap end of pitman shaft with soft hammer and slide shaft out of housing.

5. Remove and discard side cover O-ring seal.

6. The seals, washers, retainers and bearings may now be removed and examined.

7. Examine all parts for wear or damage and replace as required.

8. Install in reverse of above. Make proper adjustment as described in adjustment section.

RACK-PISTON NUT AND WORM ASSEMBLY

Removal

1. Completely drain the gear assembly and thoroughly clean the outside.

2. Remove pitman shaft assembly as previously described.

3. Rotate housing end plug retaining ring so that one end of ring is over hole in gear housing. Spring one end of ring so pin punch can be inserted to lift it out.

4. Rotate stub shaft to full left turn position to force end plug out of housing.

5. Remove and discard housing end plug O-ring seal.

6. Remove rack-piston nut end plug with ½" square drive.

7. Insert special tool in end of worm. Turn stub shaft so that rack-piston nut will go into tool and then remove rack-piston nut from gear housing.

8. Remove adjuster plug and rotary valve assemblies as previously described.

9. Remove worm and lower thrust bearing and races.

10. Remove cap O-ring seal and discard.

RACK-PISTON NUT AND WORM

Disassembly and Assembly

1. Remove and discard piston ring and back-up O-ring on rack piston nut.

2. Remove ball guide clamp and return guide.

3. Place nut on clean cloth and remove ball retaining tool. Make sure all balls are removed.

4. Inspect all parts for wear, nicks, scoring or burrs. If worm or rack-pinion nut need replacing, both must be replaced as a matched pair.

5. In reassembling reverse the above.

NOTE: When assembling, alternate black and white balls, and install guide and clamp. Packing with grease helps in holding during assembly. When new balls are used, various sizes are available and a selection must be made to secure proper torque when making the high point adjustment.

RACK-PISTON NUT AND WORM ASSEMBLY

Installation

1. Install in reverse of removal procedure.

2. In all cases use new O-ring seals.

3. Make adjustments as previously described.

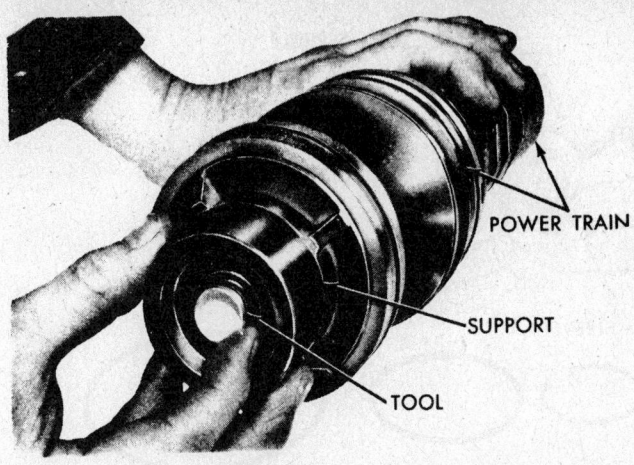

Retaining bearing rollers with arbor tool

Chrysler Full-Time Power Steering (Constant Control Type)

The Chrysler Corporation Constant Control Type Power Steering Gear System consists of a hydraulic pressure pump, a power steering gear and connecting hoses.

The power steering gear housing contains a gear shaft and sector gear, a power piston with gear teeth milled into the side of the piston which is in constant mesh with the gear shaft sector teeth, a worm shaft which connects the steering wheel to the power piston through a coupling. The worm shaft is geared to the piston through recirculating ball contact.

A pivot lever is fitted into the spool valve at the upper end and into a drilled hole in the center thrust bearing race at the lower end. The center thrust bearing race is held firmly against the shoulder of the worm shaft by two thrust bearings, bearing races and an adjusting nut. The pivot lever pivots in the spacer which is held in place by the pressure plate.

When the steering wheel is turned to the left the worm shaft moves out of the power piston a few thousandths of an inch, the center thrust bearing race moves the same distance since it is clamped to the worm shaft. The race thus tips the pivot lever and moves the spool valve down, allowing oil under pressure to flow into the left-turn power chamber and force the power piston down. As the power piston moves, it rotates the cross-shaft sector gear and, through the steering linkage, turns the front wheels.

On a right turn the worm shaft moves into the power piston, the center thrust bearing race thus tips the pivot lever and

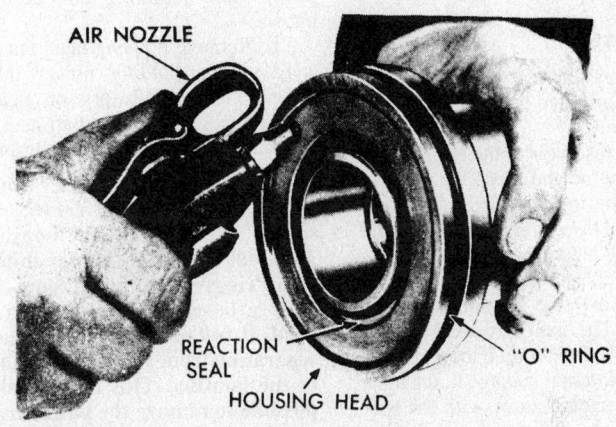

Removing reaction seal from wormshaft support

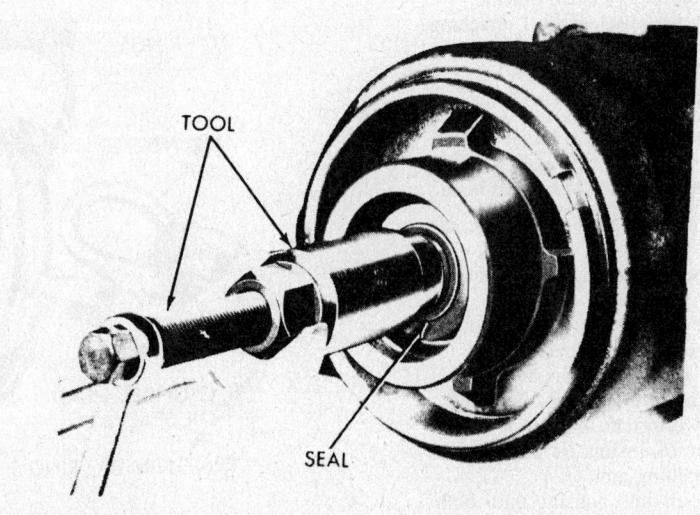

Removing worm shaft oil seal

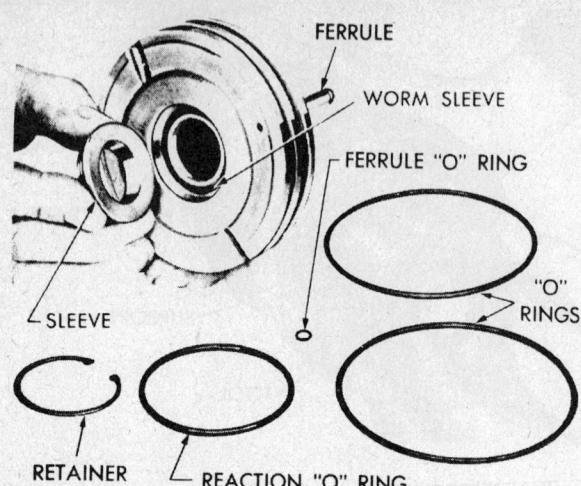

Removing cylinder head oil seal

moves the spool valve up, allowing oil under pressure to flow into the right power chamber and force the power piston up.

Pressure Test

Connect the pressure test hoses with the pressure gauge installed between the pump and steering gear.

Now, fill the reservoir to the level mark, then start the engine and bleed the system. Allow the engine to idle until the fluid in the reservoir is between 150° F. and 170° F. Now turn the steering wheel to the extreme right and check the pressure reading, then turn to the extreme left and check the reading again. The gauge reading should be equal in each direction. If not, it indicates excessive internal leakage in the unit.

The pressure should agree with the specifications in Pump section for satisfactory power steering operation.

Reconditioning

1. Drain gear by turning worm shaft from limit to limit with oil connections held downward. Thoroughly clean outside.

2. Remove valve body attaching screws, body and three O-rings.

3. Remove pivot lever and spring. Pry under spherical head with a small bar.

NOTE: Use care not to collapse slotted end of valve lever as this will destroy bearing tolerances of the spherical head.

4. Remove steering gear arm from sector shaft.

5. Remove snap-ring and seal back-up washer.

6. Remove seal, using proper tool to prevent damage to relative parts.

7. Loosen gear shaft adjusting screw locknut and remove gear shaft cover nut.

8. Rotate wormshaft to position sector teeth at center of piston travel. Loosen power train retaining nut.

9. Insert tools into housing until both tool and shaft are engaged with bearings.

10. Turn worm shaft either to full left

or full right (depending on car application) to compress power train parts. Then remove power train retaining nut as mentioned above.

11. Remove housing head tang washer.

12. While holding power train completely compressed, pry on piston teeth with a small bar, using shaft as a fulcrum, and remove complete power train.

NOTE: Maintain close contact between cylinder head, center race and spacer assembly and the housing head. This will eliminate the possibility of reactor rings becoming disengaged from their grooves in cylinder and housing head. It will prohibit center spacer from separating from center race and cocking in the housing. This could make it impossible to remove the power train without damaging involved parts.

13. Place power train in soft-jawed vise in vertical position. The worm bearing rollers will fall out. Use of arbor tool will hold

roller when the housing is removed.

14. Raising housing head until wormshaft oil shaft just clears the top of wormshaft and position arbor tool on top of shaft and into seal. With arbor in position, pull up on housing head until arbor is positioned in bearing. Remove when the housing is removed.

15. Remove large O-ring from housing head groove.

16. Remove reaction seal from groove in face of head with air pressure directed into ferrule chamber.

17. Remove reactor spring, reactor ring, worm balancing ring and spacer.

18. While holding wormshaft from turning, turn nut with enough force to release staked portions from knurled section and remove nut.

NOTE: Pay strict attention to cleanliness.

19. Remove upper thrust bearing race (thin) and upper thrust bearing.

20. Remove center bearing race.

21. Remove lower thrust bearing and lower thrust bearing race (thick).

22. Remove lower reaction ring and reaction spring.

23. Remove cylinder head assembly.

24. Remove O-rings from outer grooves in head.

25. Remove reaction O-ring from groove in face of cylinder head. Use air pressure in oil hole located between O-ring grooves.

26. Remove snap-ring, sleeve and rectangular oil seal from cylinder head counterbore.

27. Test wormshaft operation. Not more than 2 in. lbs. should be required to turn it through its entire travel, and with a 15 ft. lb. side load.

NOTE: The worm and piston is serviced as a complete assembly and should not be disassembled.

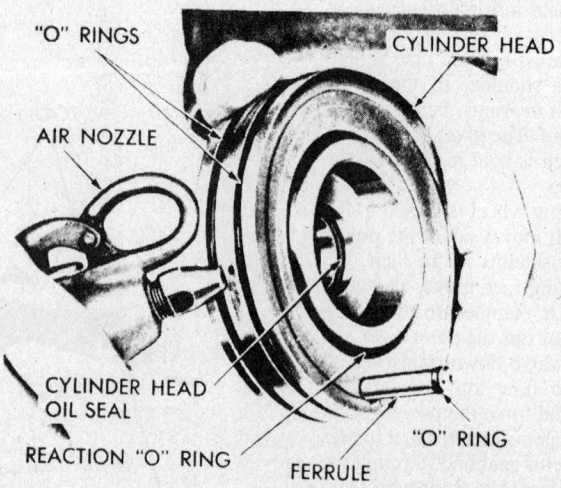

Removing reaction seal from cylinder head

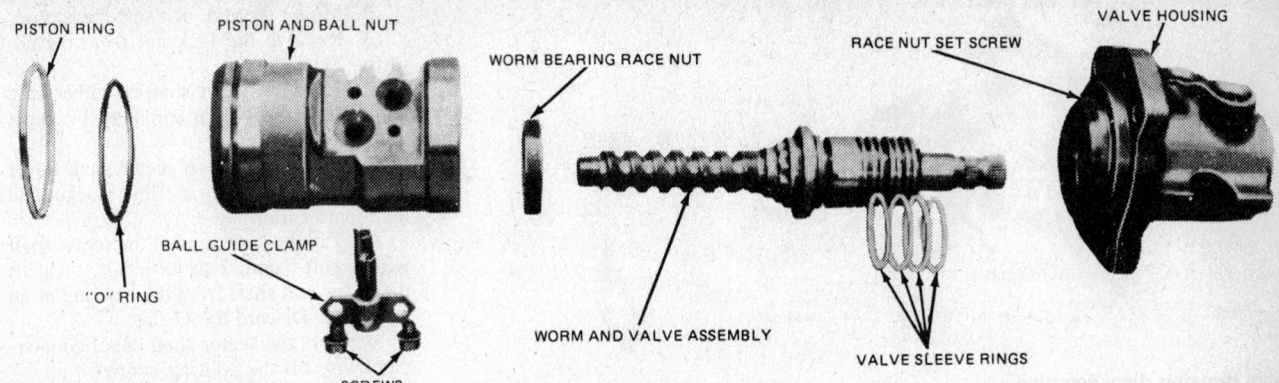

PISTON RING   PISTON AND BALL NUT   WORM BEARING RACE NUT   RACE NUT SET SCREW   VALVE HOUSING

"O" RING   BALL GUIDE CLAMP   SCREWS   WORM AND VALVE ASSEMBLY   VALVE SLEEVE RINGS

Ball nut and valve housing

28. Shaft side play should not exceed 0.008 in. under light pull applied 2⁵⁄₁₆ in. from piston flange.

29. Assemble in reverse of above, noting proper adjustments and preload requirements following.

30. When cover nut is installed, tighten to 20 ft. lbs. torque.

31. Valve mounting screws should be tightened to 200 in. lbs. torque.

32. With hoses connected, system bled, and engine idling roughly, center valve unit until not self-steering. Tap on head of valve body attaching screws to move valve body up, and tap on end plug to move valve body down.

33. With steering gear on center, tighten gear shaft adjusting screw until lash just disappears.

34. Continue to tighten ³⁄₈ to ¹⁄₂ turn and tighten locknut to 50 ft. lbs.

Ford Integral Power Steering Gear

The Ford integral power steering unit is a torsion-bar type.

The torsion bar power steering unit includes a worm and one-piece rack piston, which is meshed to the gear teeth on the steering sector shaft. The unit also includes a hydraulic valve, valve actuator, input shaft and torsion bar assembly which are mounted on the end of the worm shaft and operated by the twisting action of the torsion bar.

The torsion-bar type of power steering gear is designed with the one piece rack-piston, worm and sector shaft in one housing and the valve spool in an attaching housing. This makes possible internal fluid passages between the valve and cylinder, thus eliminating all external lines and hoses, except the pressure and return hoses between the pump and gear assembly.

The power cylinder is an integral part of the gear housing. The piston is double acting, in that fluid pressure may be applied to either side of the piston.

A selective metal shim, located in the valve housing of the gear is for the purpose of tailoring steering gear efforts. If efforts are not within specifications they can be changed by increasing or decreasing shim thickness as follows:

1. Efforts heavy to the left—increase shim thickness.

2. Efforts light to the left—decrease shim thickness.

Adjustments

The only adjustment which can be performed is the total over center position load, to eliminate excessive lash between the sector and rack teeth.

1. Disconnect the Pitman arm from the sector shaft.

2. Disconnect the fluid return line at the reservoir, at the same time cap the reservoir return line pipe.

3. Place the end of the return line in a clean container and cycle the steering wheel in both directions as required, to discharge the fluid from the gear.

4. Turn the steering wheel to 45 degrees from the left stop.

5. Using an in. lb. torque wrench on the steering wheel nut, determine the torque required to rotate the shaft slowly through an approximately ¹⁄₈ turn from the 45 degree position.

6. Turn the steering gear back to center, then determine the torque required to rotate the shaft back and forth across the center position. Loosen the adjuster nut, and turn the adjuster screw until the reading is 11–12 in. lbs. greater than the torque 45 degrees from the stop. Tighten the lock nut while holding the screw in place.

7. Recheck the readings and replace the Pitman arm and the steering wheel hub cover.

8. Correct the fluid return line to the reservoir and fill the reservoir with specified lubricant to the proper level.

VALVE CENTERING SHIM

Removal and Installation

1. Hold the steering gear over a drain pan in an inverted position and cycle the input shaft several times to drain the remaining fluid from the gear.

2. Mount the gear in a soft-jawed vise.

3. Turn the input shaft to either stop then, turn it back approximately 1¾ turns to center the gear.

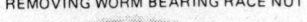

REMOVING WORM BEARING RACE NUT

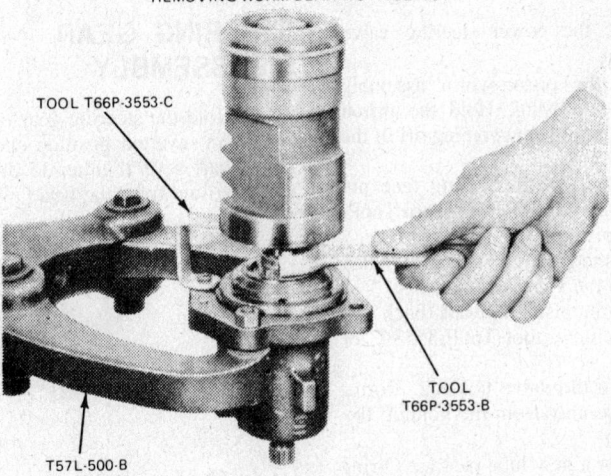

TOOL T66P-3553-C   TOOL T66P-3553-B   T57L-500-B

Removing worm bearing race nut

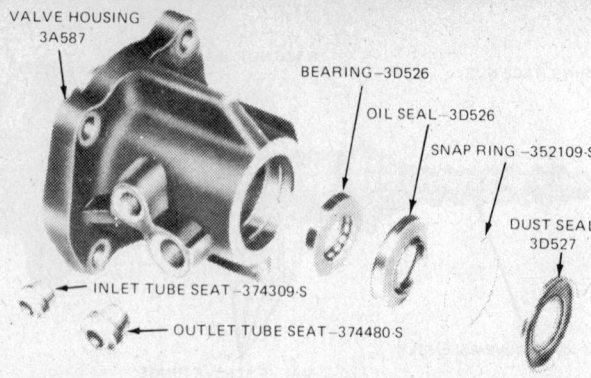

Valve housing disassembled

4. Remove the two sector shaft attaching screws, the brake line bracket and the identification tag.

5. Tap the lower end of the sector shaft with a soft-faced hammer to loosen it, then lift the cover and shaft from the housing as an assembly. Discard the O-ring.

6. Remove the four valve housing attaching bolts. Lift the valve housing from the steering gear housing while holding the piston to prevent it from rotating off the worm shaft.

7. Remove the valve housing and the lube passage O-rings and discard them.

8. Place the valve housing, worm and piston assembly in the bench mounted holding fixture with the piston on the top.

9. Rotate the piston upward (back off) 3½ turns.

10. Insert tool T66P-3553-C or equivalent (with the arm facing away from the piston) into a bolt hole in the valve housing. Rotate the arm into position under the piston.

11. Loosen the Allen head race nut set screw from the valve housing.

12. Using tool T66P-3553-B or equivalent, loosen the worm bearing race nut.

13. Lift the piston-worm assembly from the valve housing. During removal hold the piston to prevent it from spinning off at the shaft.

14. Change the power steering valve centering shim.

15. Install the piston-worm assembly into the valve housing. Hold the piston worm to prevent it from spinning off of the shaft.

16. Install the worm bearing race nut and torque to 2–8 in. lbs. using tool T66P-3553-B or equivalent.

17. Install the race nut set screw (Allen head) through the valve housing.

18. Rotate the piston upward (back off) ½ turn and remove tool T66P-3553-C or equivalent.

19. Remove the valve housing, worm, and piston assembly from the holding fixture.

20. Position a new lube passage O-ring in the counterbore of the gear housing.

21. Apply vaseline to the teflon seal on the piston.

22. Place a new O-ring on the valve housing.

23. Slide the piston and valve into the gear housing being careful not to damage the teflon seal.

24. Align the lube passage in the valve housing with the one in the gear housing, and install but do not tighten the attaching bolts.

25. Rotate the ball nut so that the teeth are in the same place as the sector teeth. Tighten the four valve housing attaching bolts to 35–45 ft. lbs.

26. Position the sector shaft cover O-ring in the steering gear housing. Turn the input shaft as required to center the piston.

27. Apply vaseline to the sector shaft journal; then, position the sector shaft and cover assembly in the gear housing. Install the brake line bracket, steering gear identification tag and the two sector shaft cover attaching studs.

28. Position an in. lb. torque wrench on the gear input shaft and adjust the meshload to approximately 4 in. lbs. Then, torque the sector shaft cover attaching studs to 55–70 ft. lbs.

29. After the cover attaching bolts have been tightened to specification, adjust the mesh load to 17 in. lbs. with an in. lb. torque wrench.

STEERING GEAR DISASSEMBLY

1. Hold the steering gear over a drain pan in an inverted position and cycle the input shaft several times to drain the remaining fluid from the gear.

2. Mount the gear in a soft-jawed vise.

3. Remove the lock nut from the adjusting screw.

4. Turn the input shaft to either stop then, turn it back approximately 1¾ turns to center the gear.

5. Remove the two sector shaft cover attaching studs, the brake line bracket and the identification tag.

6. Tap the lower end of the sector shaft with a soft-hammer to loosen it, then lift the cover and shaft from the housing as an assembly. Discard the O-ring.

7. Turn the sector shaft cover counterclockwise off the adjuster screw.

8. Remove the four valve housing attaching bolts. Lift the valve housing from the steering gear housing while holding the piston to prevent it from rotating off the worm shaft. Remove the valve housing and the lube passage O-rings and discard them.

9. Stand the valve body and piston on end with the piston end down. Rotate the input shaft counterclockwise out of the piston allowing the ball bearings to drop into the piston.

10. Place a cloth over the open end of the piston and turn it upside down to remove the balls.

11. Remove the two screws that attach the ball guide clamp to the ball nut and remove the clamp and the guides.

12. Install the valve body assembly in the holding fixture (do not clamp in a vise) and loosen the race nut screw (Allen head) from the valve housing and remove the worm bearing race nut.

13. Carefully slide the input shaft, worm and valve assembly out of the valve housing. Due to the close diametrical clearance between the spool and housing, the slightest cocking of the spool may cause it to jam in the housing.

14. Remove the shim from the valve housing bore.

Valve Housing

1. Remove the dust seal from the rear of the valve housing and discard the seal.

2. Remove the snap-ring from the valve housing.

3. Turn the fixture to place the valve housing in an inverted position.

4. Insert special tool in the valve body assembly opposite the seal end and gently tap the bearing and seal out of the housing. Discard the seal. Caution must be exercised

Removing bearing and oil seal

when inserting and removing the tool to prevent damage to the valve bore in the housing.

5. Remove the fluid inlet and outlet tube seats with an EZ-out if they are damaged.

6. Coat the fluid inlet and outlet tube seats with vaseline and position them in the housing. Install and tighten the tube nuts to press the seats to the proper location.

7. Coat the bearing and seal surface of the housing with a film of vaseline.

8. Seat the bearing in the valve housing. Make sure that the bearing is free to rotate.

9. Dip the new oil seal in gear lubricant; then, place it in the housing with the metal side of the seal facing outward. Drive the seal into the housing until the outer edge of seal does not quite clear the snap-ring groove.

10. Place the snap-ring in the housing; then, drive on the ring until the snap-ring seats in its groove to properly locate the seal.

11. Place the dust seal in the housing with the dished side (rubber side) facing out. Drive the dust seal into place. The seal must be located behind the undercut in the input shaft when it is installed.

Worm and Valve

1. Remove the snap-ring from the end of the actuator.

2. Slide the control valve spool off the actuator.

3. Install the valve spool evenly and slowly with a slight oscillating motion into the flanged end of valve housing with the valve identification groove between the valve spool lands outward, checking for freedom of valve movement within the housing working area. The valve spool should enter the housing bore freely and fall by its own weight.

4. If the valve spool is not free, check for burrs at the outward edges of the working lands in the housing and remove with a hard stone.

5. Check the valve for burrs and if burrs are found, stone the valve in a radial direction only. Check for freedom of the valve again.

6. Remove the valve spool from the housing.

7. Slide the spool onto the actuator making sure that the groove in the spool annulus is toward the worm.

8. Install the snap-ring to retain the spool. The beveled ID of the snap-ring must be assembled toward the spool.

9. Check the clearance between the spool and the snap-ring. The clearance should be between .0005–.035 inch. If the clearance is not within these limits, select a snap-ring that will allow a clearance of .002 inch.

Piston and Ball Nut

1. Remove the teflon ring and the O-ring from the piston and ball nut.

2. Dip a new O-ring in gear lubricant and install it on the piston and ball nut.

3. Install a new teflon ring on the piston and ball nut being careful not to stretch it any more than necessary.

Steering Gear Housing

1. Remove the snap-ring and the spacer washer from the lower end of the steering gear housing.

2. Remove the lower seal from the housing. Lift the spacer washer from the housing.

3. Remove the upper seal in the same manner as the lower seal. Some housings require only one seal and one spacer.

4. Dip both sector shaft seals in gear lubricant.

5. Apply lubricant to the sector shaft seal bore of the housing and position the sector shaft inner seal into the housing with the lip facing inward. Press the seal into place. Place a spacer washer (0.090 inch) on top of the seal and apply more lubricant to the housing bore.

6. Place the outer seal in the housing with the lip facing inward and press it into place. Then, place a 0.090 inch spacer washer on top of the seal.

7. Position the snap-ring in the housing. Press the snap-ring into the housing to properly locate the seals and engage the snap-ring in the groove.

STEERING GEAR ASSEMBLY

Do not clean, wash, or soak seals in cleaning solvent.

1. Mount the valve housing in the holding fixture with the flanged end up.

2. Place the required thickness valve spool centering shim in the housing.

3. Carefully install the worm and valve in the housing.

4. Install the race nut in the housing and torque it to 42 ft. lbs.

5. Install the race nut set screw (Allen head) through the valve housing and torque to 20–25 in. lbs.

6. Place the piston on the bench with the ball guide holes facing up. Insert the worm shaft into the piston so that the first groove is in alignment with the hole nearest to the center of the piston.

7. Place the ball guide in the piston. Place the 27 to 29 balls, depending on the piston design, in the ball guide turning the worm in a clockwise direction as viewed from the input end of the shaft. If all of the balls have not been fed into the guide upon reaching the right stop, rotate the input shaft in one direction and then in the other while installing the balls. After the balls have been installed, do not rotate the input shaft or the piston more than 3½ turns off the right stop to prevent the balls from falling out of the circuit.

8. Secure the guides in the ball nut with the clamp.

9. Position a new lub passage O-ring in the counterbore of the gear housing.

10. Apply petroleum jelly to the teflon seal on the piston.

11. Place a new O-ring on the valve housing.

12. Slide the piston and valve into the gear housing being careful not to damage the teflon seal.

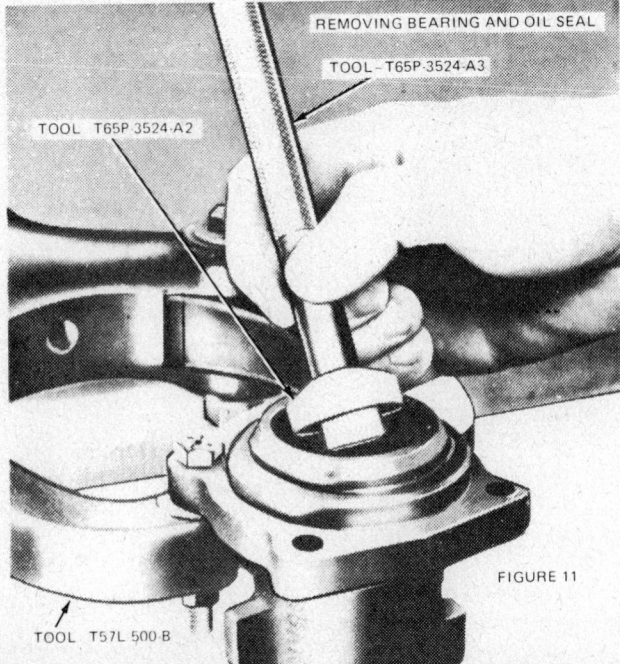

TOOL-T65P-3524-A3

REMOVING BEARING AND OIL SEAL

TOOL T65P-3524-A2

TOOL T57L-500-B

FIGURE 11

Steering gear housing and sector shaft seal assembly

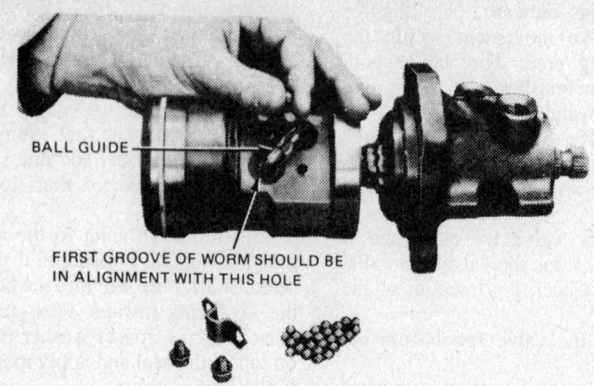

BALL GUIDE

FIRST GROOVE OF WORM SHOULD BE
IN ALIGNMENT WITH THIS HOLE

Loading balls into the ball guide

13. Align the lube passage in the valve housing with the one in the gear housing and install but do not tighten the attaching bolts.

14. Rotate the ball nut so that the teeth are in the same plane as the sector teeth. Tighten the four valve housing attaching bolts to 35–45 ft. lbs.

15. Position the sector shaft cover O-ring in the steering gear housing. Turn the input shaft as required to center the piston.

16. Apply vaseline to the sector shaft journal then position the sector shaft and cover assembly in the gear housing. Install the brake line bracket, the steering identification tag and two sector shaft cover attaching bolts. Torque the bolts to 55–70 ft. lbs.

17. Attach an in. lb. torque wrench to the input shaft. Adjust the mesh load to 17 in. lbs.

Manual Transmission

INDEX

MANUAL TRANSMISSION

Jumping out of High Gear

1. Misalignment of transmission case or clutch housing.
2. Worn pilot bearing in crankshaft.
3. Bent transmission shaft.
4. Worn high speed sliding gear.
5. Worn teeth in clutch shaft.
6. Insufficient spring tension on shifter rail plunger.
7. Bent or loose shifter fork.
8. End-play in clutch shaft.
9. Gears not engaging completely.
10. Loose or worn bearings on clutch shaft or mainshaft.

Sticking in High Gear

1. Clutch not releasing fully.
2. Burred or battered teeth on clutch shaft.
3. Burred or battered transmission mainshaft.
4. Frozen synchronizing clutch.
5. Stuck shifter rail plunger.
6. Gearshift lever twisting and binding shifter rail.
7. Battered teeth on high speed sliding gear or on sleeve.
8. Lack of lubrication.
9. Improper lubrication.
10. Corroded transmission parts.
11. Defective mainshaft pilot bearing.

Jumping out of Second Gear

1. Insufficient spring tension on shifter rail plunger.
2. Bent or loose shifter fork.
3. Gears not engaging completely.
4. End-play in transmission mainshaft.
5. Loose transmission gear bearing.
6. Defective mainshaft pilot bearing.
7. Bent transmission shaft.
8. Worn teeth on second speed sliding gear or sleeve.
9. Loose or worn bearings on transmission mainshaft.
10. End-play in countershaft.

Sticking in Second Gear

1. Clutch not releasing fully.

2. Burred or battered teeth on sliding sleeve.
3. Burred or battered transmission mainshaft.
4. Frozen synchronizing clutch.
5. Stuck shifter rail plunger.
6. Gearshift lever twisting and binding shifter rail.
7. Lack of lubrication.
8. Second speed transmission gear bearings locked will give same effect as gears stuck in second.
9. Improper lubrication.
10. Corroded transmission parts.

Jumping out of Low Gear

1. Gears not engaging completely.
2. Bent or loose shifter fork.
3. End-play in transmission mainshaft.
4. End-play countershaft.
5. Loose or worn bearings on transmission mainshaft.
6. Loose or worn bearings in countershaft.
7. Defective mainshaft pilot bearing.

Sticking in Low Gear

1. Clutch not releasing fully.
2. Burred or battered transmission mainshaft.
3. Stuck shifter rail plunger.
4. Gearshift lever twisting and binding shifter rail.
5. Lack of lubrication.
6. Improper lubrication.
7. Corroded transmission parts.

Jumping out of Reverse Gear

1. Insufficient spring tension on shifter rail plunger.
2. Bent or loose shifter fork.
3. Badly worn gear teeth.
4. Gears not engaging completely.
5. End-play in transmission mainshaft.
6. Idler gear bushings loose or worn.
7. Loose or worn bearings on transmission mainshaft.
8. Defective mainshaft pilot bearing.

Sticking in Reverse Gear

1. Clutch not releasing fully.
2. Burred or battered transmission mainshaft.
3. Stuck shifter rail plunger.
4. Gearshift lever twisting and binding shifter rail.
5. Lack of lubrication.
6. Improper lubrication.
7. Corroded transmission parts.

Failure of Gears to Synchronize

1. Binding pilot bearing on mainshaft, will synchronize in high gear only.
2. Clutch not releasing fully.
3. Detent springs weak or broken.
4. Weak or broken springs under balls in sliding gear sleeve.
5. Binding bearing on clutch shaft.
6. Binding countershaft.
7. Binding pilot bearing in crankshaft.
8. Badly worn gear teeth.
9. Scored or worn cones.
10. Improper lubrication.
11. Constant mesh gear not turning freely on transmission mainshaft. Will synchronize in that gear only.

Gears Spinning When Shifting into Gear from Neutral

1. Clutch not releasing fully.
2. In some cases an extremely light lubricant in transmission will cause gears to continue to spin for a short time after clutch is released.
3. Binding pilot bearing in crankshaft.

--- CAUTION ---

Care must be exercised during the disassembly and assembly of manual transmission due to the usage of metric nuts and bolts. The proper wrenches and sockets should be used to avoid damage to the transmission and fasteners. Do not attempt to interchange metric threaded fasteners with U.S. Fine or Standard fasteners as damage can result.

MANUAL TRANSMISSION SERVICE

CLEANING OF TRANSMISSION COMPONENTS

Cleanliness of parts, tools, and work area is of the utmost importance. All transmission components (except bearing assemblies) should be cleaned in cleaning solvent and dried with compressed air before any inspection or work is begun. Great care

should be taken when cleaning bearings. Bearings should always be cleaned separately from other parts in clean cleaning solvent and not gasoline. They must never be cleaned in a hot solution tank. It is advisable that they be soaked in cleaning fluid and then tapped against a block of wood in order to free any solidified lubricant that may be trapped inside. Rinse bearings thoroughly in clean solvent and then dry them with moisture-free compressed air being careful not to spin the bearings with the air stream. Rotate each bearing slowly and inspect rollers or balls for any signs of excessive wear, roughness, or damage. Those bearings not in excellent condition must be replaced. If they pass this inspection, they should be dipped in clean oil and wrapped in clean lintless cloth to protect them until installation.

INSPECTION OF TRANSMISSION COMPONENTS

All parts must be completely and carefully inspected and replaced for any signs of wear, stress, discoloration or warpage due to excessive heat. Whenever available, the magna flux process should be used on all parts except roller and ball bearings, to detect small cracks unseen by the eye. Inspect the breather assembly to see that it is not clogged or damaged and check all threaded parts for stripped or cross threads. Oil passages must be cleared of obstructions by the use of air pressure or brass rods and all gaskets, oil seals, lock wires, cotter pins, and snap rings are to be replaced. Small nicks or burrs in gears or splines can be removed with a fine abrasive stone. It is important that any housings or covers having cracks or other damage should be replaced and not welded. Synchronizers, not in excellent condition, must be replaced. The bronze synchronizer cone should be checked for wear or for any steel chips that may have become imbedded in it. Springs must be inspected for free length, compressed length, distortion, or collapsed coils.

NOTE: The splines on many clutch gears, mainshafts, etc., are equipped with a machined relief called a "hopping guard". With the clutch gear engaged, the mating gear is free to slip into this notch, preventing the two gears from separating or "walking out of gear" under various load conditions. This is not a worn or chipped gear. Do not grind or discard the gear.

Check all shafts for spline wear or damage. If the mainshaft 1st and reverse sliding gear or clutch hub have worn into the sides of the splines, the shaft should be replaced. Shift forks, shift rods, interlock balls and pins must be replaced if scored, worn, distorted or damaged.

Dodge/Plymouth A-230 3-Speed

The Dodge A-230 is a three-speed transmission equipped with two synchronizer units to assist in the engagement of all forward gears. Lubricant capacity is 5 pints.

Disassembly

SHIFT HOUSING AND MECHANISM

1. Shift to second gear.
2. Remove side cover. If shaft O-ring seals need replacement:
   a. Pull shift-forks out of shafts.
   b. Remove nuts and operating levers from shafts.
   c. Deburr shafts. Remove shafts.

DRIVE PINION RETAINER AND EXTENSION HOUSING

1. Remove pinion bearing retainer from front of transmission case. Pry off retainer oil seal. For clearance:
   a. With a brass drift, tap drive pinion as far forward as possible. Rotate cut away part of second gear next to countershaft gear. Shift second–third synchronizer sleeve forward.
   b. Remove speedometer pinion adapter retainer. Work adapter and pinion out of extension housing.
   c. Unbolt extension housing. Break housing loose with plastic hammer and carefully remove.

IDLER GEAR AND MAINSHAFT

1. Insert dummy shaft in case to push reverse idler shaft and key out of case.

2. Remove dummy shaft and idler rollers.
3. Remove both tanged idler gear thrust washers.
4. Remove mainshaft assembly through rear of case.

COUNTERSHAFT GEAR AND DRIVE PINION

1. Using a mallet and dummy shaft, tap the countershaft rearward enough to remove key. Drive countershaft out of case, being careful not to drop the washers.
2. Lower countershaft gear to bottom of case.
3. Remove snap-ring from pinion bearing outer race (outside front of case).
4. Drive pinion shaft into case with plastic hammer. Remove assembly through rear of case.
5. If bearing is to be replaced, remove snap-ring and press off bearing.
6. Lift counter shaft gear and dummy shaft out through rear of case.

MAINSHAFT

1. Remove snap-ring from front end of mainshaft along with second gear stop ring and second gear.
2. Spread snap-ring in mainshaft bearing retainer. Slide retainer back off the bearing race.
3. Remove snap-ring at rear of mainshaft. Support front side of reverse gear. Press bearing off mainshaft.
4. Remove from press. Remove mainshaft bearing and reverse gear from shaft.
5. Remove snap-ring and first-reverse synchronizer assembly from shaft. Remove stop ring and first gear rearward.

Cleaning and Inspection

See Cleaning and Inspection instructions at the beginning of the Transmission section.

Assembly

COUNTERSHAFT GEAR

1. Slide dummy shaft into countershaft gear.
2. Slide one roller thrust washer over dummy shaft and into gear, followed by 22 greased rollers.
3. Repeat Step 2, adding one roller thrust washer on end.
4. Repeat steps 2 and 3 at other end of countershaft gear. There is a total of 88 rollers and 6 thrust washers.
5. Place greased front thrust washer on dummy shaft against gear with tangs forward.
6. Grease rear thrust washer and stick it in place in the case, with tangs rearward. Place countershaft gear assembly in bottom of transmission case until drive pinion is installed.

PINION GEAR

1. Press new bearing on pinion shaft with snap-ring groove forward. Install new

snap-ring.
2. Install 15 rollers and retaining ring in drive pinion gear.
3. Install drive pinion and bearing assembly into case.
4. Position countershaft gear assembly by positioning it and thrust washers so countershaft can be tapped into position. Be careful to keep the countershaft against the dummy shaft to keep parts from falling between them. Install key in countershaft.
5. Tap drive pinion forward for clearance.

MAINSHAFT

1. Place a stop ring flat on the bench. Place a clutch gear and a sleeve on top. Drop the struts in their slots and insert a strut spring with the tang inside on strut. Turn the assembly over and install second strut spring, tang in a different strut.
2. Slide first gear and stop ring over rear of mainshaft and against thrust flange between assembly over rear of mainshaft, first and second gears on shaft.
3. Slide first–reverse synchronizer indexing hub slots to first gear stop ring lugs.
4. Install first–reverse synchronizer clutch gear snap-ring on mainshaft.
5. Slide reverse gear and mainshaft bearing on shaft, supporting inner race of bearing. Be sure snap-ring groove on outer race is forward.
6. Install bearing retaining snap-ring on mainshaft. Slide snap-ring over the bearing and seat it in groove.
7. Place second gear over front of mainshaft with thrust surface against flange.
8. Install stop ring and second–third synchronizer assembly against second gear. Install second–third synchronizer clutch gear snap-ring on shaft.
9. Move second–third synchronizer sleeve forward as far as possible. Install front stop ring inside sleeve with lugs indexed to struts.
10. Rotate cut out on second gear toward countershaft gear for clearance.
11. Insert mainshaft assembly into case. Tilt assembly to clear cluster gears and insert pilot rollers in drive pinion gear. If assembly is correct, the bearing retainer will bottom to the case without force. If not, check for a misplaced strut, pinion roller, or stop ring.

REVERSE IDLER GEAR

1. Place dummy shaft into idler gear. Insert 22 greased rollers.
2. Position reverse idler thrust washers in case with grease.
3. Position idler gear and dummy shaft in case. Install idler shaft and key.

EXTENSION HOUSING

1. Remove extension housing yoke seal. Drive bushing out from inside housing.
2. Align oil hole in bushing with oil slot in housing. Drive bushing into place.

Drive new seal into housing.

3. Install extension housing and gasket to hold mainshaft and bearing retainer in place.

DRIVE PINION BEARING RETAINER

1. Install outer snap-ring on drive pinion bearing. Tap assembly back until snap-ring contacts case.

2. Using seal installer tool or equivalent, install a new seal in retainer bore.

3. Position main drive pinion bearing retainer and gasket on front of case. Coat threads with sealing compound, install bolts, torque to 30 ft. lbs.

GEARSHAFT MECHANISM AND HOUSING

1. If removed, place two interlock levers in pivot pin with spring hangers offset toward each other, so that spring installs in a straight line. Place E-clip on pivot pin.

2. Grease and install new O-ring seals

on both shift shafts. Grease housing bores and insert shafts.

3. Install spring on interlock lever hangers.

4. Rotate each shift shaft fork bore to straight up position. Install shift forks through bores and under both interlock levers.

5. Position second–third synchronizer sleeve to rear, in second gear position. Position first–reverse synchronizer sleeve to middle of travel, in neutral position. Place

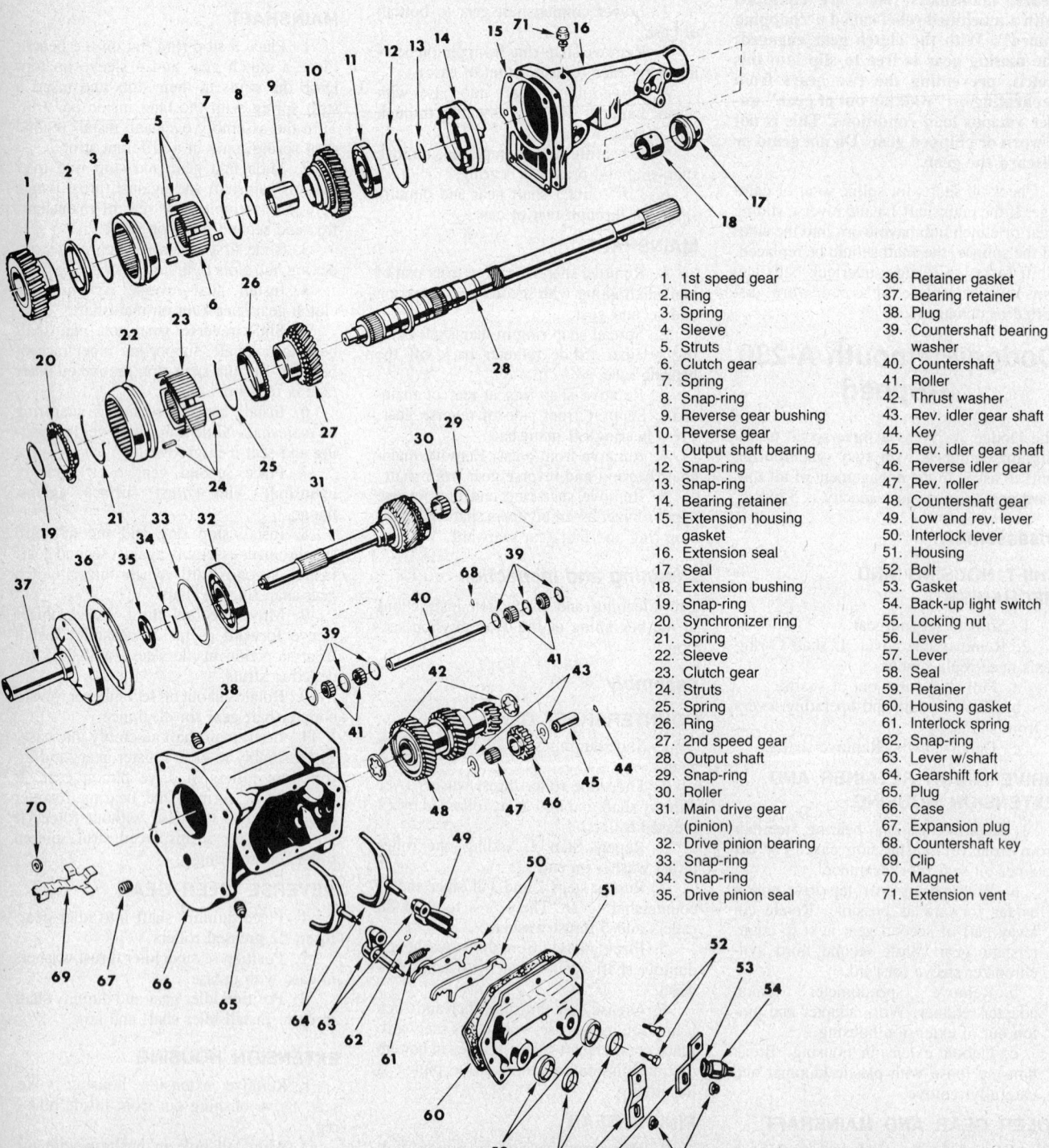

1. 1st speed gear
2. Ring
3. Spring
4. Sleeve
5. Struts
6. Clutch gear
7. Spring
8. Snap-ring
9. Reverse gear bushing
10. Reverse gear
11. Output shaft bearing
12. Snap-ring
13. Snap-ring
14. Bearing retainer
15. Extension housing gasket
16. Extension seal
17. Seal
18. Extension bushing
19. Snap-ring
20. Synchronizer ring
21. Spring
22. Sleeve
23. Clutch gear
24. Struts
25. Spring
26. Ring
27. 2nd speed gear
28. Output shaft
29. Snap-ring
30. Roller
31. Main drive gear (pinion)
32. Drive pinion bearing
33. Snap-ring
34. Snap-ring
35. Drive pinion seal
36. Retainer gasket
37. Bearing retainer
38. Plug
39. Countershaft bearing washer
40. Countershaft
41. Roller
42. Thrust washer
43. Rev. idler gear shaft
44. Key
45. Rev. idler gear shaft
46. Reverse idler gear
47. Rev. roller
48. Countershaft gear
49. Low and rev. lever
50. Interlock lever
51. Housing
52. Bolt
53. Gasket
54. Back-up light switch
55. Locking nut
56. Lever
57. Lever
58. Seal
59. Retainer
60. Housing gasket
61. Interlock spring
62. Snap-ring
63. Lever w/shaft
64. Gearshift fork
65. Plug
66. Case
67. Expansion plug
68. Countershaft key
69. Clip
70. Magnet
71. Extension vent

shift forks in the same positions.

6. Install gasket and gearshift mechanism. The bolt with the extra long shoulder must be installed at the center rear of the case. Torque bolts to 15 ft. lbs.

7. Install speedometer drive pinion gear and adapter. Range number on adapter, which represents the number of teeth on the gear, should be in 6 o'clock position.

TORQUE SPECIFICATIONS

Manual A-203 3-Speed	ft. lbs.
Back up light switch	15
Extension housing bolts	50
Drive pinion bearing retainer bolts	30
Gearshift operating lever nuts	18
Transmission to clutch housing bolts	50
Transmission cover retaining bolts	12
Transmission drain plug	25

Dodge/Plymouth A-390 3-Speed

The A-390 is a three speed synchromesh transmission. Lubricant capacity is 4½ pints.

Disassembly

1. Remove the bolts that attach the cover to the case. Remove the cover and gasket.

2. Remove the long spring that retains the detent plug in the case. Remove the detent plug with a small magnet.

3. Remove the bolt and retainer securing the speedometer pinion adapter to the transmission case. Carefully work the adapter and pinion out of the extension housing.

4. Remove the bolts that attach the extension housing to the transmission case. Slide the extension housing off the output shaft.

5. Remove the bolts that attach the input shaft bearing retainer to the case. Slide the retainer off the shaft. Using a suitable tool, pry the seal out of the retainer. Be careful not to nick or scratch the bore in which the seal is pressed or the surface on which the seal is bottomed.

6. Remove the lubricant fill plug from the right side of the case. Working through the fill plug opening, drive the roll pin out of the countershaft with a ¼ inch punch.

7. Working with the countershaft bearing arbor and a soft faced hammer, tap the countershaft toward the front of the case with the arbor tool to remove the expansion plug from the countershaft bore at the front of the case. The countershaft is a loose fit in the case and will slide easily.

8. Insert the arbor tool through the front of the case and push the countershaft out of the rear of the case so the roll pin hole in the countershaft does not travel through the roller bearings. The countershaft gear will drop to the bottom of the case. Remove the countershaft from the rear of the case.

9. Place both shift levers in neutral (center) position.

10. Remove the input shaft assembly and stop ring from the front of the case.

11. Remove the set screw that secures the first–reverse shift fork to the shift rail. Slide the first–reverse shift rail out through the rear of the case.

12. Move the second–third shift fork rearward for access to the set screw. Remove the set screw from the fork. Using a suitable tool, rotate the shift rail one quarter (¼) turn.

13. Lift the interlock plug from the case with a magnet.

14. Tap on the inner end of the second–third shift rail to remove the expansion plug from the front of the case. Remove the shift rail through the front of the case.

15. Remove the second–third shift rail detent plug and spring from the detent bore with a magnet.

16. Tap the output shaft assembly rearward until the output shaft bearing clears the case. Remove both shift forks. Remove the snap-ring that retains the output shaft bearing to the output shaft.

17. Assemble the output shaft bearing removal tool over the output shaft and bearing. Remove the output shaft bearing.

18. Remove the output shaft assembly through top of the case.

19. Using a suitable drift, drive the reverse idler gear shaft toward the rear, and out of the transmission case.

20. Lift the reverse idler gear and thrust washer out of the case.

21. Remove the countershaft gear, arbor assembly, and thrust washers from the bottom of the case.

22. Remove the countershaft roll pin from the bottom of the case.

23. Remove the snap-ring that retains the second–third synchronizer clutch gear and sleeve assembly on the output shaft. Slide the second–third synchronizer assembly off the end of the output shaft.

NOTE: Do not separate the second-third synchronizer clutch gear, sleeve, struts, or spring unless inspection reveals that a replacement is necessary.

24. Slide the second gear and stop ring off the output shaft.

25. Remove the snap-ring and thrust washer retaining the first gear. Slide the first gear and stop ring off the output shaft.

26. Remove the snap-ring that retains the first–reverse synchronizer hub on the output shaft. The first–reverse synchronizer hub is a press fit on the output shaft. To avoid damage to the synchronizer, remove the synchronizer hub using an arbor press. Do not attempt to remove or install the hub by hammering or prying.

Overhaul

SHIFT LEVERS AND SEALS

1. Remove the operating levers from their respective shafts. Remove any burrs from the shafts to avoid damage to the case.

2. Push the shift levers out of the transmission case. Remove and discard the O-ring seal from each shaft.

3. Lubricate the new seals with transmission oil and install them on the shafts.

4. Install the shift levers in the case.

5. Install the operating levers and tighten the retaining nuts to 18 ft. lbs.

INPUT SHAFT BEARING AND ROLLERS

1. Remove the snap-ring securing the bearing on the input shaft. Carefully press the input shaft out of the bearing with an arbor press.

2. Remove the fifteen bearing rollers from the cavity in the end of the input shaft.

3. Install the 15 bearing rollers in the cavity of the input shaft. Coat the rollers with a thin film of grease to retain them during installation.

4. Slide the input shaft bearing over the input shaft, snap-ring groove away from the gear end. Seat the bearing assembly on the input shaft with an arbor press.

5. Secure the bearing with the snap-ring. Be sure the snap-ring is properly seated. If a large snap-ring around the bearing was removed, be sure to install it at this time.

SYNCHRONIZERS

NOTE: If either synchronizer is to be disassembled, mark all parts so that they will be reassembled in the same position. Do not mix parts from the two synchronizers.

1. Push the synchronizer hub off each synchronizer sleeve.

2. Separate the struts and springs from the hubs.

3. Install the spring on the front side of the first–reverse synchronizer hub, making sure that all three strut slots are fully covered. Hang the three struts on the spring and in the slots with the wide end of the strut inside the hub.

4. With the alignment marks on the hub and sleeve aligned, push the sleeve down on the hub until the struts are in the neutral detent. Place the stop ring on top of the

synchronizer assembly.

5. With the alignment marks on the second–third synchronizer sleeve and hub aligned, slide the sleeve on the hub. Drop in the three struts in the strut slots. Install the spring with the hump in the center, into the hollow of the strut. Turn the assembly over and install the other spring so that the hump in the center of the spring is inserted in the same strut. Place the stop ring on each end of the synchronizer assembly.

COUNTERSHAFT GEAR AND BEARING

1. Remove the countershaft bearing arbor, the roller bearings and the two bearing retainers from the countershaft gear.

2. Coat the bore in each end of the countershaft gear with grease.

3. Insert the countershaft arbor and install twenty five roller bearings and the retainer washer in each end of the countershaft gear.

4. Position the countershaft gear and arbor assembly in the transmission case. Align the gear bore and the thrust washers with the bores in the case and install the countershaft.

5. Using a feeler gauge, check the countershaft gear end play. The end play should be within 0.004–0.018 inch. If the clearance is not within limits, replace the thrust washers.

6. After establishing the correct end play, install the arbor tool in the countershaft gear and lower the gear and tool out of the bottom of the transmission case.

Assembly

1. Coat the countershaft gear thrust surfaces in the case with a thin film of grease and position the two thrust washers in place. Place the countershaft gear and arbor assembly in the proper position in the bottom of the transmission case. The countershaft gear will remain in the bottom of the case until the output and input shafts are installed.

2. Coat the reverse idler gear thrust surfaces in the case with a thin film of

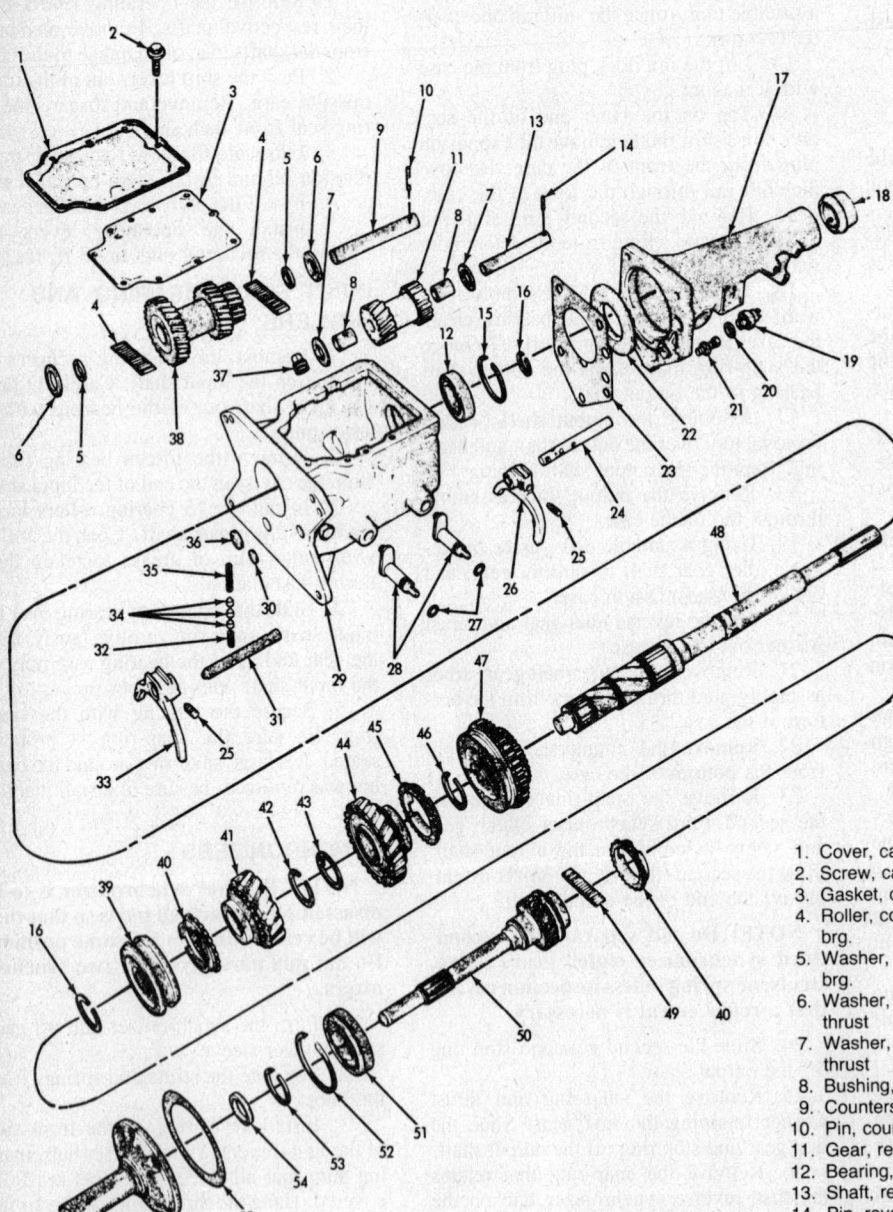

1. Cover, case
2. Screw, case cover
3. Gasket, case cover
4. Roller, countershaft brg.
5. Washer, countershaft brg.
6. Washer, countershaft thrust
7. Washer, reverse idler thrust
8. Bushing, reverse idler
9. Countershaft
10. Pin, countershaft roll
11. Gear, reverse idler
12. Bearing, output shaft
13. Shaft, reverse idler
14. Pin, reverse idler stop
15. Snap-ring, output shaft brg. outer
16. Snap-ring, output shaft, inner
17. Extension
18. Seal, extension
19. Switch, back-up lamp
20. Gasket, back-up lamp switch
21. Screw, extension lockwasher, extension screw
22. Retainer, output shaft brg.
23. Gasket, extension
24. Rail, gearshift first and reverse
25. Screw, fork set
26. Fork, gearshift first and reverse
27. Seal, gearshift lever shaft oil
28. Lever, gearshift
29. Case
30. Plug
31. Rail, gearshift second and third
32. Spring, gearshift detent pin
33. Fork, gearshift second and third
34. Pin, gearshift detent
35. Spring, gearshift detent pin
36. Plug
37. Plug, case filler
38. Gear, countershaft
39. Synchronizer assy., second and third
40. Ring, synchronizer second and third stop
41. Gear, second speed
42. Snap-ring, low speed gear thrust washer
43. Washer, low speed gear thrust
44. Gear, Low Speed
45. Ring, synchronizer low stop
46. Snap-ring, synchronizer low and reverse clutch gear
47. Synchronizer assy., low and reverse
48. Shaft, output
49. Roller, output shaft pilot
50. Shaft, input
51. Bearing, input shaft
52. Snap-ring, bearing, outer
53. Snap-ring, bearing, inner
54. Seal, bearing retainer oil
55. Gasket, bearing retainer
56. Retainer, bearing
57. Screw, bearing retainer

grease and position the two thrust washers in place. Install the reverse idler gear in the case and align the gear bore with the thrust washers in the case bore. Install the reverse idler shaft.

3. Measure the reverse idler gear end play with a feeler gauge. End play should be 0.004–0.018 inch. If the clearance is not within limits, replace the thrust washers. If the end-play is correct, leave the reverse idler gear in place.

4. Lubricate the output shaft splines and the machined surfaces with transmission oil.

5. Slide the first reverse synchronizer onto the output shaft with the fork groove toward the front. The first–reverse synchronizer hub is a press fit on the output shaft. To eliminate the possibility of damage to the hub, install the hub using an arbor press.

NOTE: Do not attempt to install the hub by hammering or driving.

Secure the hub on the output shaft with the snap-ring.

6. Slide the first gear and stop ring onto the output shaft, aligning the slots in the stop ring with the struts. Install the thrust washer and snap-ring.

7. Slide the second gear and stop ring on the output shaft.

8. Install the second–third synchronizer assembly on the output shaft. Rotate the second gear to index the struts with the slots in the stop ring. Secure the synchronizer with a snap-ring.

9. Position the output shaft assembly in the transmission case. Place the transmission in a vertical position with the front of the case flat on the work bench. Place a 1¼ inch block of wood under the end of the output shaft. The block of wood will hold the output shaft assembly up during installation of the output shaft bearing.

10. Install the large snap-ring on the output shaft bearing. Place the bearing on the output shaft with the large snap-ring up. Drive the bearing on the shaft until it is seated on the shaft. Secure the bearing on the output shaft with the snap-ring. Return the transmission to a horizontal position.

11. Insert both shift forks in the case and in their proper sleeves. Push the output shaft assembly into position and tap it forward until the output shaft bearing is seated in the transmission case.

12. Install the *shortest* detent spring followed by a detent plug into the case. Place the second–third synchronizer assembly in the second gear position.

13. Align the second–third shift fork and install the second–third shift rail. The second–third shift rail is the shortest of the two shift rails. It will be necessary to depress the detent plug to enter the shift rail in the bore. Move the rail inward until the detent plug engages the forward notch (second gear position).

14. Secure the fork to the rail with the set screw. Move the synchronizer to the neutral position.

15. Install a new expansion plug in the transmission case.

16. Install the interlock plug in the transmission case with a magnet. If the second–third shift rail is in the neutral position, the top of the interlock plug will be slightly lower than the surface of the first–reverse shift rail bore.

17. Align the first–reverse fork and install the first–reverse shift rail. Move the rail inward until the center notch (neutral) is aligned with the detent bore. Secure the fork to the rail with the set screw.

18. Using a suitable tool, install a new oil seal in the input shaft bearing retainer bore.

19. Coat the bore of the input shaft gear with a thin film of grease.

Install the fifteen roller bearings in the bore.

NOTE: A thick, heavy grease will plug the lubricant holes and prevent lubrication of the roller bearings.

20. Place the stop ring, slots aligned with the struts, into the second–third synchronizer. Tap the input shaft assembly into place in the case while holding the output shaft to prevent the roller bearings from dropping.

21. Roll the transmission over so that it rests on both the top edge and the shift levers. The countershaft gear will drop into place. Using a screwdriver, align the countershaft gear and thrust washers with the bore in the transmission case.

22. Working from the rear of the case, slide the countershaft into position being careful to keep the countershaft in contact with the arbor to avoid dropping parts out of position. Be sure that the roll pin hole in the countershaft aligns with the roll pin hole in the case.

23. Install the roll pin. Install a new expansion plug in the countershaft bore at the front of the case. Install the plug flush or below the face of the case to prevent interference with the clutch housing.

24. Slide the extension housing, with a new gasket, over the output shaft and against the case. Coat the attaching bolt threads with a sealing compound. Install and tighten the attaching bolts to 50 ft. lbs.

25. Install the input shaft bearing retainer and a new gasket. Make sure that the oil return slot is at the bottom. Coat the threads with a sealing compound, install the attaching bolts and tighten to 30 ft. lbs.

26. Install the remaining detent plug into the case followed by the detent spring.

27. Install the filler plug and the back-up light switch. Pour lubricant over the entire gear train while rotating the input shaft and the output shaft.

28. Place the cover and a new gasket on the transmission. Coat the attaching screw threads with a sealing compound. Install and tighten the attaching screws to 22 ft. lbs.

Dodge/Plymouth Overdrive-4

The overdrive-4 transmission is a four speed unit with all forward gears synchronized. Third gear is direct, while the fourth gear is the overdrive ratio. Lubricant capacity is 7 pints.

Disassembly

GEARSHIFT HOUSING AND MECHANISM

1. If available, mount transmission in a repair stand.

2. Disconnect gearshift control rods from the shift control levers and the transmission operating levers.

3. Remove the two gearshift control housing mounting bolts.

4. Remove gearshift control housing from the transmission extension housing or mounting bracket (if so equipped).

5. Remove the gearshift control housing mounting bracket bolts, then remove the bracket (if so equipped).

6. Remove back-up light switch (if so equipped).

7. Remove output companion flange nut and washer, if used, then pull the flange from the mainshaft (output shaft).

8. Remove gearshift housing-to-transmission case attaching bolts.

9. With all levers in the neutral detent position, pull housing out and away from the case.

TORQUE SPECIFICATIONS

	ft. lbs.
Cover to case screws	22
Back-up light switch	15
Extension housing to case bolts	50
Extension housing to cross member bolts	50
Gearshift lever nuts	18
Input shaft bearing retainer bolts	30
Shift fork to shift rail set screw	10
Transmission to clutch housing bolts	50
Transmission drain plug	25
Transmission filler plug	15

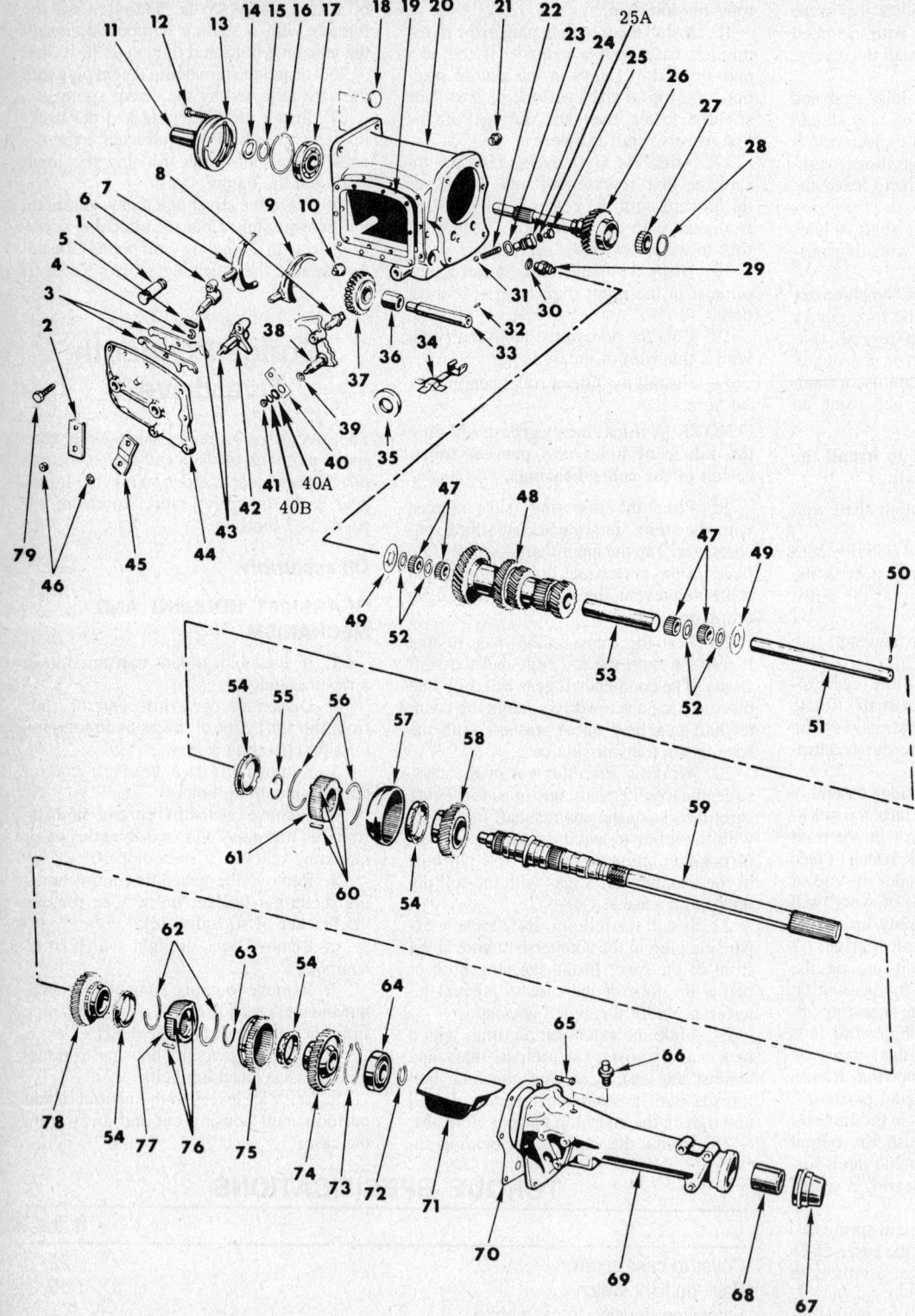

8. Reverse fork
9. 1st and 2nd fork
10. Drain plug
11. Retainer
12. Screw
13. Retainer gasket
14. Drive pinion seal
15. Snap-ring
16. Snap-ring
17. Drive pinion bearing
18. Plug
19. Housing gasket
20. Transmission case
21. Filler plug
22. Rev. detent ball spring
23. Gasket
24. Retainer
25. Plug
25a. Gasket
26. Main drive gear (pinion)
27. Roller
28. Snap-ring
29. Back-up light switch
30. Gasket
31. Rev. Lever detent ball
32. Rev. idler shaft key
33. Rev. idler gear shaft
34. Magnet clip
35. Magnet
36. Bushing
37. Reverse idler gear
38. Reverse lever w/shaft
39. Seal
40. Reverse lever
41. Nut
42. 1st and 2nd lever w/shaft
43. Seal
44. Housing
45. 1st and 2nd lever
46. Nut
47. Rollers
48. Countershaft gear
49. Countershaft washer
50. Countershaft key
51. Countershaft
52. Washer
53. Spacer
54. Stop ring
55. Snap-ring
56. Spring
57. Sleeve
58. Overdrive gear
59. Main or output shaft
60. Struts
61. 3rd and direct gear
62. Spring
63. Snap-ring
64. Front bearing
65. Extension bolt
66. Extension vent
67. Output shaft seal
68. Extension bushing
69. Extension
70. Extension gasket
71. Vent baffle
72. Snap-ring
73. Snap-ring
74. 1st speed gear
75. 1st and 2nd clutch sleeve gear
76. Synchronizer struts
77. Clutch gear
78. 2nd speed gear
79. Case housing bolt

1. Interlock pin
2. Direct and overdrive lever (3rd/4th)
3. Interlock lever
4. Snap-ring
5. Interlock spring
6. 3rd and overdrive (4th) lever
7. 3rd and overdrive (4th) fork

A-833 4-speed

NOTE: If first and second, or third and fourth shift forks remain in engagement with the synchronizer sleeves, move the sleeves and remove forks from the case.

10. Remove nuts, lock washers and flat washers that hold first–second, and third–fourth speed shift operating levers to the shafts.

11. Disengage shift levers from the flats on the shafts and remove levers. Remove the E-ring on the overdrive four speed.

EXTENSION HOUSING, MAINSHAFT AND MAIN DRIVE PINION

1. Remove the bolt and retainer holding the speedometer pinion adapter in the extension housing, then remove the pinion adapter.

2. Remove the bolts attaching the extension housing to the transmission case.

3. Rotate the extension housing on the output shaft to expose the rear of the countershaft. Install one bolt to hold the extension in place.

4. Drill a hole in the countershaft extension plug at the front of the case.

5. Reaching through this hole, push the countershaft to the rear to expose the Woodruff key; when exposed, remove it. Push the countershaft forward against the expansion plug, and using a brass drift, tap the countershaft forward until the expansion plug is removed.

6. Using a countershaft arbor, push the countershaft out the rear of the case, but don't let the countershaft washers fall out of position. Lower the cluster gear to the bottom of the transmission case.

7. Remove the bolt and rotate the extension back to the normal position.

8. Remove the drive pinion attaching bolts and slide the retainer and gasket from the pinion shaft, then pry the pinion or seal from the retainer. When installing the new seal, don't nick or scratch the seal bore in the retainer or the surface on which the seal bottoms.

9. Using a brass drift, tap the pinion and bearing assembly forward and remove through the front of the case.

10. Slide the third and overdrive synchronizer sleeve slightly forward, slide the reverse idler gear to the center of its shaft, and tap the extension housing rearward. Slide the housing and mainshaft assembly out and away from the case.

11. Remove the snap-ring holding the third and overdrive synchronizer clutch gear and sleeve assembly to the mainshaft, then remove the synchronizer assembly.

12. Slide the overdrive gear and stop ring off the mainshaft. Using pair of long nose pliers, compress the snap ring holding the mainshaft bearing in the extension housing. With it compressed, pull the mainshaft assembly and bearing out of the extension housing.

13. Remove the snap-ring holding the

mainshaft on the shaft. The bearing is removed by inserting steel plates on the front side of the first speed gear, then pressing the mainshaft through the bearing being careful not to damage the gear teeth.

14. Remove the bearing, retainer ring, first speed gear and stop ring from the shaft.

15. Remove the snap-ring. Remove the first and second clutch gear and sleeve assembly from the mainshaft.

16. Remove the drive pinion bearing inner snap-ring, then using an arbor press, remove the bearing. Remove the snap-ring and bearing rollers from the cavity in the drive pinion.

17. Remove the countershaft gear from the bottom of the case, then remove the arbor, needle bearings, thrust washers and spacers from the center of the countershaft gear.

18. Remove the reverse gearshift lever detent spring retainer, gasket, plug, and detent ball spring from the rear of the case.

19. The reverse idler gear shaft is a tight fit in the case and will have to be pressed out.

20. If there is oil leakage visible around the reverse gearshift lever shaft, push the lever shaft in and remove it from the case. Remove the detent ball from the bottom of the transmission case and remove the shift fork from the shaft and detent plate.

Assembly

REVERSE SHAFT

Follow the first four steps only if you removed the reverse shaft in the disassembly procedure.

1. Install a new oil seal O-ring on the lever shaft and coat the shaft with grease; insert it into its bore and install the reverse fork in the lever.

2. Install the reverse detent spring and gasket; insert the ball and spring and install the plug and gasket.

3. Place the reverse idler gear shaft in position in the end of the case and drive it in far enough to position the reverse idler gear on the protruding end of the shaft with the fork slot toward the rear. While doing this, engage the slot with the reverse shift fork.

4. With the reverse idler gear correctly positioned, drive the reverse gear shaft into the case far enough to install the Woodruff key. Drive the shaft in flush with the end of the transmission case. Install the back-up light switch and gasket.

COUNTERSHAFT GEAR AND DRIVE PINION

1. Coat the inside bore of the countershaft gear with a thin film of grease and install the roller bearing spacer with an arbor, into the gear; center the spacer and arbor.

2. Install the roller bearings and a spacer ring on each end.

3. Replace worn thrust washers; coat the new ones with grease and install them

over the arbor with the tang side toward the case boss.

4. Install the countershaft assembly into the case and allow the gear assembly to sit on the bottom of the case so that the thrust washers won't come out of position.

5. Press the drive pinion bearing on the pinion shaft. Make sure the outer snap ring groove is toward the front end and the bearing is seated against the shoulder on the gear.

6. Install a new snap-ring on the shaft to hold the bearing in place; make sure the snap-ring is seated and that there is minimum end play. There are several snap-ring thicknesses available for adjustment.

7. Place the pinion shaft in a soft-jawed vise and install the roller bearings in the cavity of the shaft. Coat them with grease and install the bearing retaining snap-ring.

8. Install a new oil seal in the bore.

EXTENSION HOUSING BUSHING

1. Remove the yoke seal from the extension housing.

2. Drive out the old bushing and drive in a new one, aligning the oil hole in the bushing with the slot in the housing.

3. Place a new seal in the opening of the extension housing and then drive it into place.

MAINSHAFT

Assemble the synchronizer as follows:

1. Place a stop ring flat on a bench followed by the clutch gear and sleeve; drop the struts in their slots and snap in a strut spring placing the tang inside one strut. Install the second strut spring tang in a different strut after turning the assembly over.

2. Slide the second speed gear over the mainshaft with the synchronizer cone toward the rear and down against the shoulder on the shaft.

3. Slide the first and second gear synchronizer assembly including stop rings with lugs indexed in the hub slots, over the mainshaft down against the second gear cone and hold it there with a new snap-ring. Slide the next snap-ring over the shaft and index the lugs into the clutch hub slots.

4. Slide the first speed gear with the synchronizer cone toward the clutch sleeve just installed over the mainshaft and into position against the clutch sleeve gear.

5. Install the mainshaft bearing retaining ring followed by the mainshaft rear bearing; press the bearing down into position and install a new snap ring to secure it. There are several snap-ring thicknesses available for minimum end play.

6. Install the partially assembled mainshaft into the extension housing far enough to engage the bearing retaining ring in the slot in the extension housing. Compress the ring with pliers so that the mainshaft ball bearing can move in and bottom against its thrust shoulder in the extension housing. Release the ring and make sure that it is seated.

7. Slide the overdrive gear over the

mainshaft with the synchronizer cone toward the front followed by the gear's snap-ring.

8. Install the third–overdrive gear synchronizer clutch gear assembly on the mainshaft against the overdrive gear. Make sure to index the rear stop ring with the clutch gear struts.

9. Install the snap-ring and position the front stop ring over the clutch gear again lining up the ring lugs with the struts; coat a new extension gasket with grease and place it in position.

10. Slide the reverse idler gear to the center of its shaft and move the third–overdrive synchronizer as far forward as possible without losing the struts.

11. Insert the mainshaft assembly in the case tilting it as necessary. Place the third–overdrive sleeve in the neutral detent.

12. Rotate the extension on the mainshaft to expose the rear of the countershaft and install one bolt to hold it in position.

13. Install the drive pinion and bearing assembly through the front of the case and position it in the front bore. Install the outer snap-ring in the bearing groove and tap lightly into place. If it doesn't bottom easily, check to see if a strut, pinion roller or stop ring is out of position.

14. Turn the transmission upside down while holding the countershaft gear to prevent damage. Then lower the countershaft gear assembly into position making sure that the teeth mesh with the drive pinion gear.

15. Start the countershaft into the bore at the rear of the case and push until it is in about halfway; then install the Woodruff key and push it in until it is flush with the rear of the case.

16. Rotate the extension back to normal position and install the bolts; turn the transmission upright and install the drive pinion bearing retainer and gasket. Coat the threads with sealing compound and tighten the attaching bolts to 30 ft. lbs.

17. Install a new expansion plug in its bore.

GEARSHIFT HOUSING AND MECHANISM

1. Install the interlock levers on the pivot pin and secure with the E-ring. Install the spring with a pair of pliers.

2. Grease and install new O-ring seals on both shift shafts; grease the housing bores and push the shafts through.

3. Install the operating levers and tighten the retaining nuts to 18 ft. lbs.; make sure the third-overdrive lever points down.

4. Rotate each shift shaft fork bore straight up and install the third–overdrive shift fork in its bore and under both interlock levers.

5. Position both synchronizer sleeves in neutral and place the first and second gear shift fork in the groove of the first and second gear synchronizer sleeve. Slide the reverse idler gear to neutral. Turn the trans-

TORQUE SPECIFICATIONS

	ft. lbs.
Back up light switch	15
Drive pinion bearing, retainer bolts	30
Extension housing to case bolts	50
Gearshift to mounting plate	24
Gearshift mounting plate to extension	12
Shift lever nuts	18
Transmission to clutch housing bolts	50
Transmission drain plug	25

mission on its right side and place the gearshift housing gasket in place holding it there with grease. Install the reverse detent ball and spring into the case bore.

6. As the shift housing is lowered in place, guide the third–overdrive shift fork into its synchronizer groove then lead the shaft of the first and second shift lever.

7. Raise the interlock lever with a screwdriver to allow the first and second shift fork to slip under the levers. The shift housing will now seat against the case.

8. Install the bolts lightly and shift through all the gears to check for proper operation.

9. The reverse shift lever and the first and second gear shift lever have cam surfaces which mate in reverse position to lock the first and second lever, the fork and synchronizer in the neutral position.

10. To check for proper operation, put the transmission in reverse, and, while turning the input shaft, move the first and second lever in each direction. If it locks up or becomes harder to turn, select a new shift lever size with more or less clearance. If there is too little cam clearance, it will be difficult or impossible to shift into reverse.

11. Grease the reverse shaft, install the operating lever and nut, and install the speedometer drive pinion gear and adapter, making sure the range number is in the straight down position.

Ford 3.03 3-Speed

The Ford 3.03 is a fully synchronized three speed transmission. All gears except reverse are in constant mesh. Forward speed gear changes are accomplished with synchronizer sleeves.

Disassembly

1. Drain the lubricant by removing the lower extension housing bolt.

2. Remove the case cover and gasket.

3. Remove the long spring that holds the detent plug in the case and remove the detent plug with a small magnet.

4. Remove the extension housing and gasket.

5. Remove the front bearing retainer and gasket.

6. Remove the filler plug on the right

side of the transmission case. Working through the plug opening, drive the roll pin out of the case and countershaft with a ¼ inch punch.

7. Hold the countershaft gear with a hook. Install dummy shaft and push the countershaft out of the rear of the case. As the countershaft comes out, lower the gear cluster to the bottom of the case. Remove the countershaft.

8. Remove the snap-ring that holds the speedometer drive gear on the output shaft. Slip the gear off the shaft and remove the gear lock ball.

9. Remove the snap-ring that holds the output shaft bearing. Using a special bearing puller, remove the output shaft bearing.

10. Place both shift levers in the neutral (center) position.

11. Remove the set screw that holds the first–reverse shift fork to the shift rail. Slip the first–reverse shift rail out through the rear of the case.

12. Move the first–reverse synchronizer forward as far as possible. Rotate the first–reverse shift fork upwards and lift it out of the case.

13. Place the second–third shift fork in the second position. Remove the set screw. Rotate the shift rail 90 degrees.

14. Lift the interlock plug out of the case with a magnet.

15. Remove the expansion plug from the second–third shift rail by lightly tapping the end of the rail. Remove the second–third shift rail.

16. Remove the second–third shift rail detent plug and spring from detent bore.

17. Remove the input gear and shaft from the case.

18. Rotate the second–third shift fork upwards and remove from case.

19. Using caution, lift the output shaft assembly out through top of case.

20. Lift the reverse idler gear and thrust washers out of case. Remove the countershaft gear, thrust washer and dummy shaft from case.

21. Remove the snap-ring from the front of the output shaft. Slip the synchronizer and second gear off shaft.

22. Remove the second snap-ring from output shaft and remove the thrust washer, first gear and blocking ring.

23. Remove the third snap-ring from the output shaft. The first–reverse synchronizer hub is a press fit on the output shaft. Re-

move the synchronizer hub with an arbor press.

— CAUTION —

Do not attempt to remove or install the synchronizer hub by prying or hammering.

Disassembly and Assembly of Sub-Assemblies

SHIFT LEVERS AND SEALS

1. Remove shift levers from the shafts. Slip the levers out of case. Discard shaft sealing O-rings.

2. Lubricate and install new O-rings on shift shafts.

3. Install the shift shafts in the case and secure shift levers.

INPUT SHAFT BEARINGS

1. Remove the snap-ring securing the input shaft bearing. Using an arbor press, remove the bearing.

2. Press the input shaft bearing onto shaft using correct tool.

SYNCHRONIZERS

1. Scribe alignment marks on synchronizer hubs before disassembly. Remove each synchronizer hub from the synchronizer sleeves.

2. Separate the inserts and insert springs from the hubs.

— CAUTION —

Do not mix parts from the separate synchronizer assemblies.

3. Install the insert spring in the hub of the first–reverse synchronizer. Be sure that the spring covers all the insert grooves.

Start the hub on the sleeve making certain that the scribed marks are properly aligned. Place the three inserts in the hub, small ends on the inside. Slide the sleeve and reverse gear onto hub.

4. Install one insert spring into a groove on the second–third synchronizer hub. Be sure that all three insert slots are covered. Align the scribed marks on the hub and sleeve and start the hub into the sleeve. Position the three inserts on the top of the retaining spring and push the assembly together. Install the remaining retainer spring so that the spring ends cover the same slots as the first spring. Do not stagger the springs. Place a synchronizer blocking ring on the ends of the synchronizer sleeve.

COUNTERSHAFT GEAR BEARINGS

1. Remove the dummy shaft, needle bearings and bearing retainers from the countershaft gear.

2. Coat the bore in each end of the countershaft gear with grease.

3. Hold the dummy shaft in the gear and install the needle bearings in the case.

4. Place the countershaft gear, dummy shaft, and needle bearings in the case.

5. Place the case in a vertical position. Align the gear bore and the thrust washers with the bores in the case and install the countershaft.

6. Place the case in a horizontal position. Check the countershaft gear end play with a feeler gauge. Clearance should be between 0.004–0.018 inch. If clearance does not come within specifications, replace the thrust washers.

7. Install the dummy shaft in the countershaft gear and leave the gear at the bot-

tom of the transmission case.

Assembly

1. Cover the reverse idler gear thrust surfaces in the case with a thin film of lubricant, and install the two thrust washers in the case.

2. Install the reverse idler gear and shaft in the case. Align the case bore and thrust washers with gear bore and install the reverse idler shaft.

3. Measure the reverse idler gear end play with a feeler gauge; clearance should be between 0.004–0.018 inch. If end play is not within specifications, replace the thrust washers. If clearance is correct, leave the reverse idler gear in case.

4. Lubricate the output shaft splines and machined surfaces with transmission oil.

5. The first–reverse synchronizer hub is a press fit on the output shaft. Hub must be installed in an arbor press. Install the synchronizer hub with the teeth-end of the gear facing towards the rear of the shaft.

— CAUTION —

Do not attempt to install the first–reverse synchronizer with a hammer.

6. Place the blocking ring on the tapered surface of the first gear.

7. Slide the first gear on the output shaft with the blocking ring toward the rear of the shaft. Rotate the gear as necessary to engage the three notches in the blocking ring with the synchronizer inserts. Install the thrust washer and snap-ring.

8. Slide the blocking ring onto the tapered surface of the second gear. Slide the second gear with blocking ring and the sec-

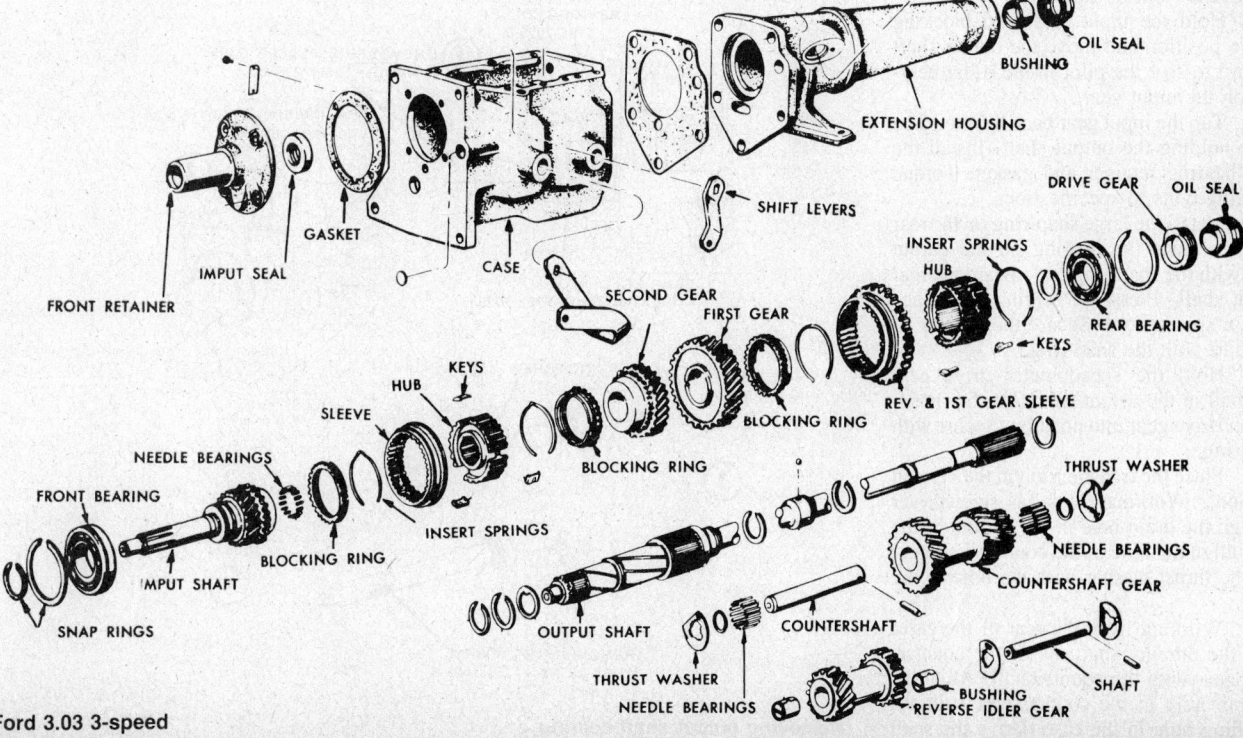

FRONT RETAINER — IMPUT SEAL — GASKET — CASE — SHIFT LEVERS — EXTENSION HOUSING — BUSHING — OIL SEAL

SECOND GEAR — FIRST GEAR — BLOCKING RING — DRIVE GEAR — OIL SEAL — INSERT SPRINGS — HUB — KEYS — REAR BEARING — REV. & 1ST GEAR SLEEVE

NEEDLE BEARINGS — HUB — KEYS — SLEEVE — BLOCKING RING — BLOCKING RING — INSERT SPRINGS

FRONT BEARING — IMPUT SHAFT — SNAP RINGS — OUTPUT SHAFT — THRUST WASHER — NEEDLE BEARINGS — COUNTERSHAFT — BUSHING — REVERSE IDLER GEAR — NEEDLE BEARINGS — COUNTERSHAFT GEAR — THRUST WASHER — SHAFT

Ford 3.03 3-speed

ond–third synchronizer on the mainshaft. Be sure that the tapered surface of second gear is facing the front of the shaft and that the notches in the blocking ring engage the synchronizer inserts. Install the snap-ring and secure assembly.

9. Cover the core of the input shaft with a thin coat of grease.

─────── CAUTION ───────
A thick film of grease will plug lubricant holes and cause damage to bearings.

Install bearings.

10. Install the input shaft through the front of the case and insert snap-ring in the bearing groove.

11. Install the output shaft assembly in the case. Position the second–third shift fork on the second–third synchronizer.

12. Place a detent plug spring and a plug in the case. Place the second–third synchronizer in the second gear position (toward the rear of the case). Align the fork and install the second–third shift rail. It will be necessary to depress the detent plug to install the shift rail in the bore. Move the rail forward until the detent plug enters the forward notch (second gear).

13. Secure the fork to the shift rail with a set screw and place the synchronizer in neutral.

14. Install the interlock plug in the case.

15. Place the first–reverse synchronizer in the first gear position (towards the front of the case). Place the shift fork in the groove of the synchronizer. Rotate the fork into position and install the shift rail. Move the shift rail inward until the center notch (neutral) is aligned with the detent bore. Secure shift fork with set screw.

16. Install a new shift rail expansion plug in the front of the case.

17. Hold the input shaft and blocking ring in position and move the output shaft forward to seat the pilot in the roller bearings on the input gear.

18. Tap the input gear bearing into place while holding the output shaft. Install the front bearing retainer and gasket. Torque attaching bolts to specifications.

19. Install the large snap-ring on the rear bearing. Place the bearing on the output shaft with the snap-ring end toward the rear of the shaft. Press the bearing into place using a special tool. Secure the bearing to the shaft with the snap-ring.

20. Hold the speedometer drive gear lock ball in the detent and slide the speedometer drive gear into position. Secure with snap-ring.

21. Place the transmission in the vertical position. Working with a screwdriver through the drain hole in the bottom of the case, align the bore of the countershaft gear and the thrust washer with the bore in the case.

22. Working from the rear of the case, push the dummy shaft out of the countershaft gear with the countershaft. Align the roll pin hole in the countershaft with the matching hole in the case. Drive the shaft

into place and install the roll pin.

23. Position the new extension housing gasket on the case with sealer. Install the extension housing and torque to specification.

24. Place the transmission in gear and pour gear oil over entire gear train while rotating the input shaft.

25. Install the remaining detent plug and long spring in case.

26. Position cover gasket on case with sealer and install cover. Torque cover bolts to specifications.

27. Check operation of transmission in all gear positions.

TORQUE SPECIFICATIONS

	ft. lbs.
Input shaft gear bearing retainer to transmission case	30–36
Transmission to flywheel housing	37–42
Transmission cover to transmission case	14–19
Speedometer cable retainer to transmission extension	3–4.5
Transmission extension to transmission case	42–50
Flywheel housing to engine	40–50
Gear shift lever to cam and shaft assembly lock nuts	18–23
U-Joint flange to output shaft	60–80
Filler plug	10–20
Shifter fork set screws	10–18
T.R.S. switch to case	15–20

Lubricant Refill Capacity

	U.S. Pints	Imp. Pints
Ford Type 3.03	3.5	3.0

Ford 4-Speed Overdrive Transmission

The Ford 4-speed overdrive transmission is fully synchronized in all forward gears. The 4-speed shift control is serviced as a unit and should not be disassembled. The lubricant capacity is 4.5 pints.

Disassembly

1. Remove retaining clips and flat washers from the shift rods at the levers.

2. Remove shift linkage control bracket attaching screws and remove shift linkage and control brackets.

3. Remove cover attaching screws. Then lift cover and gasket from the case. Remove the long spring that holds the detent plug in the case. Remove the plug with a magnet.

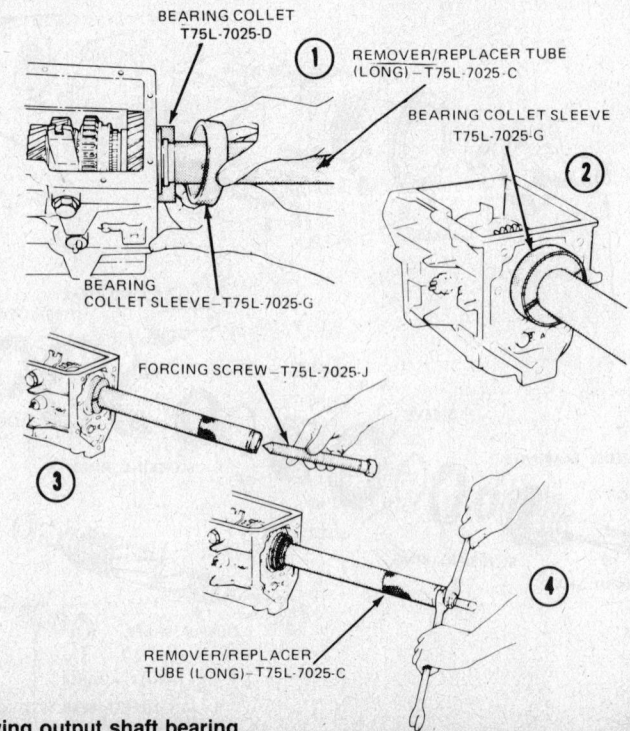

Removing output shaft bearing

4. Remove extension housing attaching screws. Then, remove extension housing and gasket.

5. Remove input shaft bearing retainer attaching screws. Then, slide retainer from the input shaft.

6. Working a dummy shaft in from the front of the case, drive the countershaft out the rear of the case. Let the countergear assembly lie in the bottom of the case. Remove the set screw from the first–second shift fork. Slide the first–second shift rail out of the rear of the case. Use a magnet to remove the interlock detent from between the first–second and third–fourth shift rails.

7. Locate first–second speed gear shift lever in neutral. Locate third–fourth speed gear shift lever in third speed position.

NOTE: On overdrive transmissions, locate third–fourth speed gear shift-lever in the fourth speed position.

8. Remove the lockbolt that holds the third–fourth speed shift rail detent spring and plug in the left side of the case. Remove spring and plug with a magnet.

9. Remove the detent mechanism set screw from top of case. Then, remove the detent spring and plug with a small magnet.

10. Remove attaching screw from the third–fourth speed shift fork. Tap lightly on the inner end of the shift rail to remove the expansion plug from front of case. Then, withdraw the third–fourth speed shift rail from the front. Do not lose the interlock pin from rail.

11. Remove attaching screw from the first and second speed shift fork. Slide the first–second shift rail from the rear of case.

12. Remove the interlock and detent plugs from the top of the case with a magnet.

13. Remove the snap-ring or disengage retainer that holds the speedometer drive gear to the output shaft, then remove speedometer gear drive ball.

14. Remove the snap-ring used to hold the output shaft bearing to the shaft. Pull out the output shaft bearing.

15. Remove the input shaft bearing snap-rings. Use a press to remove the input shaft bearing. Remove the input shaft and blocking ring from the front of the case.

16. Move output shaft to the right side of the case. Then, maneuver the forks to permit lifting them from the case.

17. Support the thrust washer and first-speed gear to prevent sliding from the shaft, then lift output shaft from the case.

18. Remove reverse gear shift fork attaching screw. Rotate the reverse shift rail 90°, then, slide the shift rail out the rear of the case. Lift out the reverse shift fork.

19. Remove the reverse detent plug and spring from the case with a magnet.

20. Using a dummy shaft, remove the reverse idler shaft from the case.

21. Lift reverse idler gear and thrust washers from the case. Be careful not to drop the bearing rollers or the dummy shaft from the gear.

22. Lift the countergear, thrust washers, rollers and dummy shaft assembly from the case.

23. Remove the next snap-ring from the front of the output shaft. Then, slide the

third–fourth synchronizer blocking ring and the third speed gear from the shaft.

24. Remove the next snap-ring and the second speed gear thrust washer from the shaft. Slide the second speed gear and the blocking ring from the shaft.

25. Remove the snap-ring, then slide the first–second synchronizer, blocking ring and the first speed gear from the shaft.

26. Remove the thrust washer from rear of the shaft.

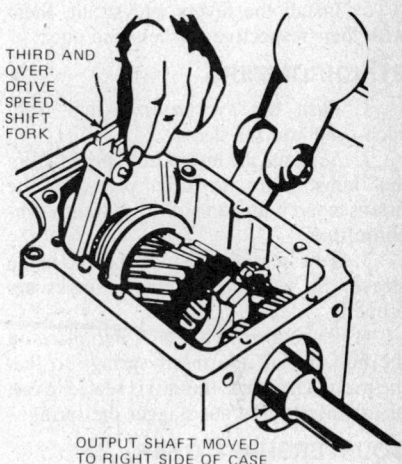

Removing shift fork from case

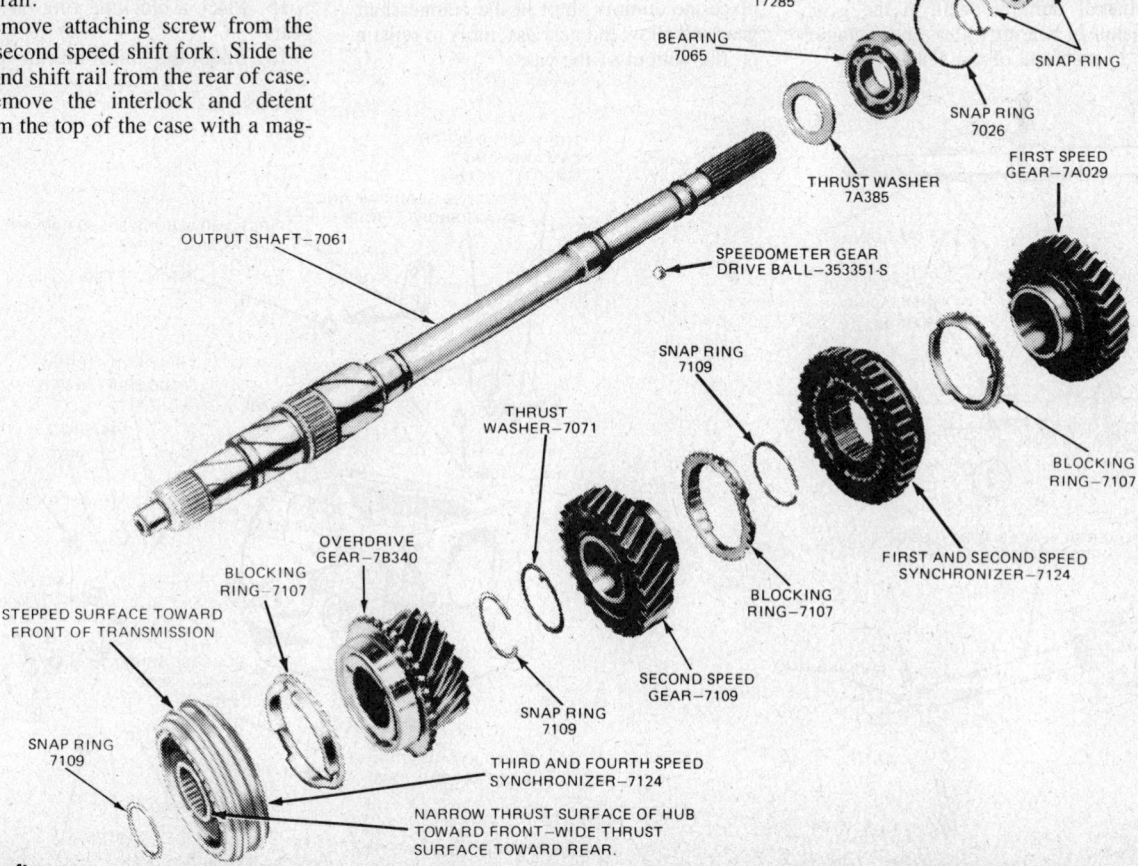

Output shaft

Unit Repairs

CAM AND SHAFT SEALS

1. Remove attaching nut and washers from each shift lever, then remove the three levers.
2. Remove the three cams and shafts from inside the case.
3. Replace the old O-rings with new ones that have been well-lubricated.
4. Slide each cam and shaft into its respective bore in the transmission.
5. Install the levers and secure them with their respective washers and nuts.

SYNCHRONIZERS

1. Push the synchronizer hub from each synchronizer sleeve.
2. Separate the inserts and springs from the hubs. Do not mix parts of the first–second with parts of third–fourth synchronizers.
3. To assemble, position the hub in the sleeve. Be sure the alignment marks are properly indexed.
4. Place the three inserts into place on the hub. Install the insert springs so that the irregular surface (hump) is seated in one of the inserts. Do not stagger the springs.

COUNTERSHAFT GEAR

1. Dismantle the countershaft gear assembly.
2. Assemble the gear by coating each end of the countershaft gear bore with grease.
3. Install dummy shaft in the gear. Then install 21 bearing rollers and a retainer washer in each end of the gear.

REVERSE IDLER GEAR

1. Dismantle reverse idler gear.
2. Assemble reverse idler gear by coating the bore in each end of reverse idler gear with grease.
3. Hold the dummy shaft in the gear and install the 22 bearing rollers and the retainer washer into each end of the gear.
4. Install the reverse idler sliding gear on the splines of the reverse idler gear. Be sure the shift fork groove is toward the front.

INPUT SHAFT SEAL

1. Remove the seal from the input shaft bearing retainer.
2. Coat the sealing surface of a new seal with lubricant, then press the new seal into the input shaft bearing retainer.

Assembly

1. Grease the countershaft gear thrust surfaces in the case. Then, position a thrust washer at each end of the case.
2. Position the countershaft gear, dummy shaft, and roller bearings in the case.
3. Align the gear bore and thrust washers with the bores in the case. Install the countershaft.
4. With the case in a horizontal position, countershaft gear end-play should be from .004–.018 in. Use thrust washers to obtain play within these limits.
5. After establishing correct endplay, place the dummy shaft in the countershaft gear and allow the gear assembly to remain on the bottom of the case.

6. Grease the reverse idler gear thrust surfaces in the case, and position the two thrust washers.
7. Position the reverse idler gear, sliding gear, dummy, etc., in place. Make sure that the shift fork groove in the sliding gear is toward the front.
8. Align the gear bore and thrust washers with the case bores and install the reverse idler shaft.
9. Reverse idler gear end-play should be 0.004–0.018 in. Use selective thrust washers to obtain play within these limits.
10. Position reverse gear shift rail detent spring and detent plug in the case. Hold the reverse shift fork in place on the reverse idler sliding gear and install the shift rail from the rear of the case. Lock the fork to the rail with the Allen head set screws.
11. Install the first–second synchronizer onto the output shaft. The first and reverse synchronizer hub are a press fit and should be installed with gear teeth facing the rear of the shaft.

NOTE: On overdrive transmissions, first and reverse synchronizer hub is a slip fit.

12. Place the blocking ring on second gear. Slide second speed gear onto the front of the shaft with the synchronizer coned surface toward the rear.
13. Install the second speed gear thrust washer and snap-ring.
14. Slide the fourth gear onto the shaft with the synchronizer coned surface front.
15. Place a blocking ring on the fourth gear.
16. Slide the third–fourth speed gear

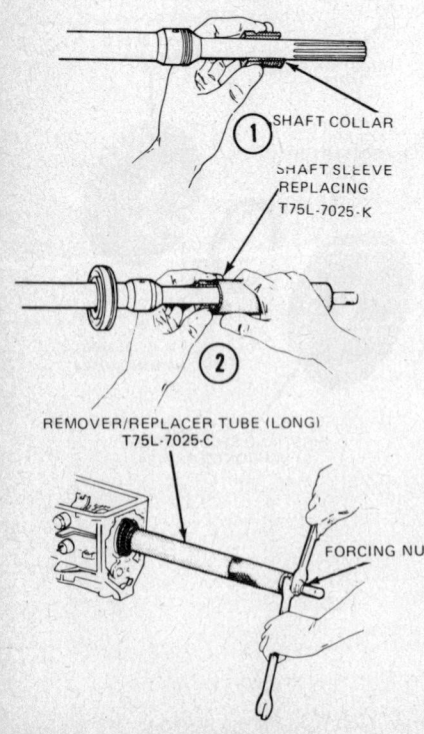

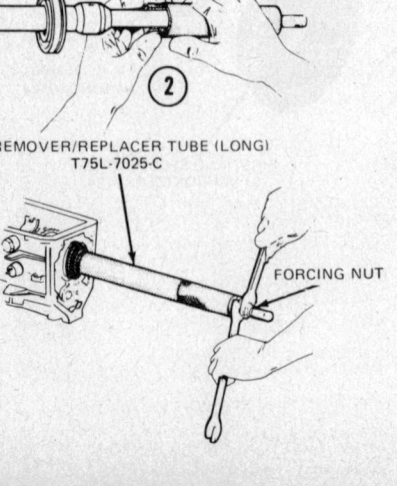

Installing output shaft bearing

Cams, shafts and shift levers

synchronizer onto the shaft. Be sure that the inserts in the synchronizer engage the notches in the blocking ring. Install the snap-ring onto the front of the output shaft.

17. Put the blocking ring on the first gear.

18. Slide the first gear onto the rear of the output shaft. Be sure that the inserts engage the notches in the blocking ring and that the shift fork groove is toward the rear.

19. Install heavy thrust washer onto the rear of the output shaft.

20. Lower the output shaft assembly into the case.

21. Position the first–second speed shift fork and the third–fourth speed shift fork in place on their respective gears. Rotate them into place.

22. Place a spring and detent plug in the detent bore. Place the reverse shift rail into neutral position.

23. Coat the third–fourth speed shift rail interlock pin (tapered ends) with grease, then position it in the shift rail.

24. Align the third–fourth speed shift fork with the shift rail bores and slide the shift rail into place. Be sure that the three detents are facing the outside of the case. Place the front synchronizer into fourth-speed position and install the set screw into the third–fourth speed shift fork. Move the synchronizer to neutral position. Install the third–fourth speed shift rail detent plug, spring and bolt into the left side of the transmission case. Place the detent plug (tapered ends) in the detent bore.

25. Align first–second speed shift fork with the case bores and slide the shift rail into place. Lock the fork with the set screw.

26. Coat the input gear bore with a small amount of grease. Then install the 15 bearing rollers.

27. Put the blocking ring in the third–fourth synchronizer. Place the input shaft gear in the case. Be sure that the output shaft pilot enters the roller bearing of the input shaft gear.

28. With a new gasket on the input bearing retainer, dip attaching bolts in sealer, install bolts and torque to 30–36 ft. lbs.

29. Press on the output shaft bearing, then install the snap-ring to hold the bearing.

30. Position the speedometer gear drive ball in the output shaft and slide the speedometer drive gear into place. Secure gear with snap-ring.

31. Align the countershaft gear bore and thrust washers with the bore in the case. Install the countershaft.

32. With a new gasket in place, install and secure the extension housing. Dip the extension housing screws in sealer, then torque screws to 42–50 ft. lbs.

33. Install the filler plug and the drain plug.

34. Pour E.P. gear oil over the entire gear train while rotating the input shaft.

35. Place each shift fork in all positions to make sure they function properly. Install the remaining detent plug in the case, followed by the spring.

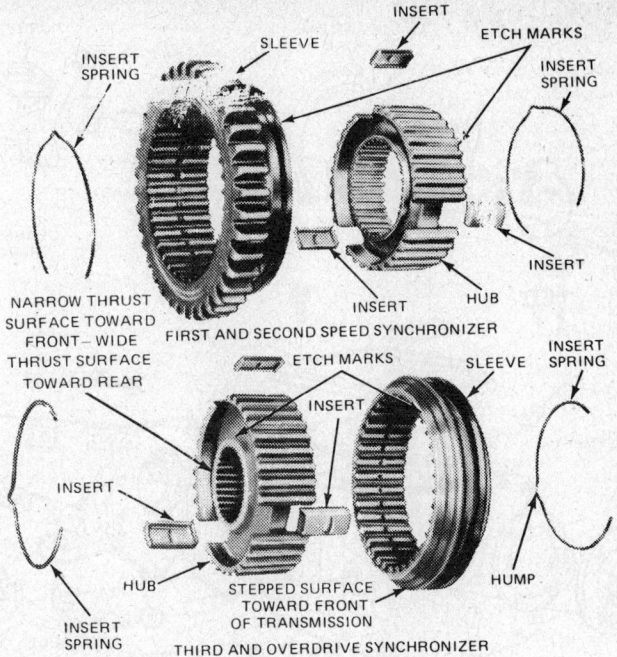

Synchronizers disassembled

36. With a new cover gasket in place, install the cover. Dip attaching screws in sealer, then torque screws to 14–19 ft. lbs.

37. Coat the third–fourth speed shift rail plug bore with sealer. Install a new plug.

38. Secure each shift rod to its respective lever with a spring washer, flat washer and retaining pin.

39. Position the shift linkage control bracket to the extension housing. Install and torque the attaching screws to 12–15 ft. lbs.

Ford Single Rail 4-Speed, Overdrive Transmission

The Single Rail Overdrive (SROD) transmission is a 4-speed unit that has all forward speeds synchronized. A single control rod (rail) connects the shift lever to the transmission shift lever rails. The lubricant capacity is 4.5 pints.

Disassembly

1. Remove the lower extension housing bolt to drain the transmission.

2. Remove the cover screws; remove the cover and discard the gasket.

3. Remove the screw, detent spring and plug from the case; a magnetized rod will aid in removal.

4. Drive the roll pin from the shifter shaft.

5. Remove the backup lamp switch, snap-ring, and the dust cover from the rear of the extension housing.

6. Remove the shifter shaft from the turret assembly.

7. Remove the extension housing bolts and housing; discard the gasket.

8. Remove the speedometer gear snapring; slide the gear from the shaft and remove the drive ball.

9. Remove the output shaft bearing snap-ring. Remove the bearing.

10. Use a dummy shaft to push the countershaft out of the rear of the case. Lower the countershaft gear to the bottom of the case.

11. Remove the input shaft bearing retainer attaching bolts and slide the retainer and gasket from the input shaft; discard gasket.

12. Remove the input shaft bearing snap-ring; remove the bearing.

13. Remove the input shaft and blocking ring (including roller bearings) from the case.

14. Remove the overdrive shift pawl, gear selector and interlock plate. Remove the 1–2 gearshift selector arm plate. Remove the roll pin from the 3rd–overdrive shift fork.

15. Drive the 3rd–overdrive shift rail and expansion plug from the rear of the case. Remove the mainshaft.

16. Remove the 1st and 2nd gear shift fork; remove the 3rd–overdrive shift fork.

17. Remove the countershaft gear and thrust washers from the case.

18. Remove the snap-ring from the front of the output shaft. Slide the 3rd gear and O.D. synchronizer, blocking ring, and gear from the shaft.

19. Remove the next snap-ring and washer; remove second gear. Remove next snap-ring and remove the 1st–2nd synchronizer. Slide the 1st gear and blocking ring from the rear of the shaft.

20. Remove the roll pin from the reverse

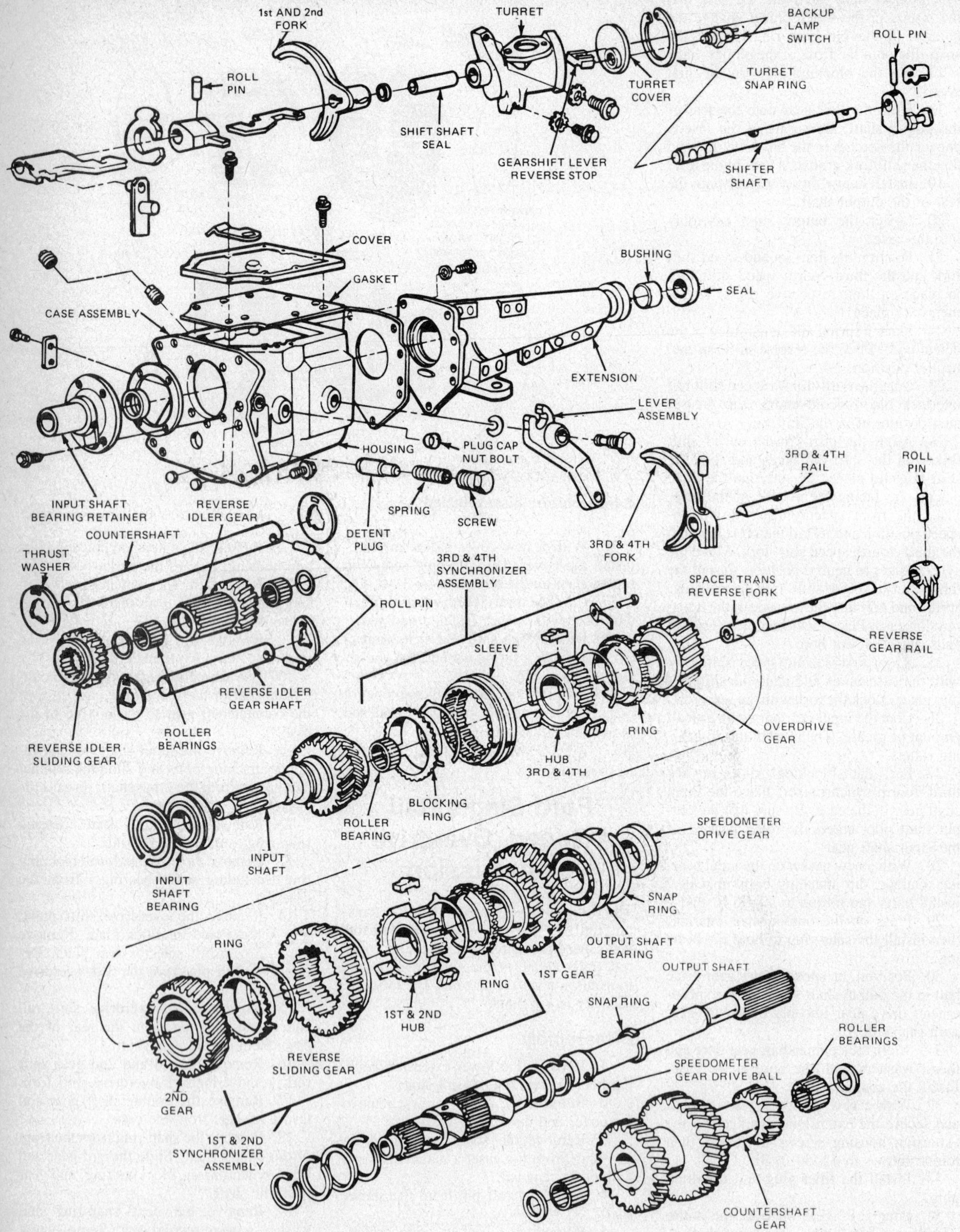

1st AND 2nd FORK

ROLL PIN

TURRET

BACKUP LAMP SWITCH

ROLL PIN

SHIFT SHAFT SEAL

TURRET COVER

TURRET SNAP RING

GEARSHIFT LEVER REVERSE STOP

SHIFTER SHAFT

COVER

BUSHING

SEAL

GASKET

CASE ASSEMBLY

EXTENSION

LEVER ASSEMBLY

PLUG CAP NUT BOLT

HOUSING

3RD & 4TH RAIL

ROLL PIN

INPUT SHAFT BEARING RETAINER

REVERSE IDLER GEAR

SPRING

DETENT PLUG

SCREW

3RD & 4TH FORK

COUNTERSHAFT

3RD & 4TH SYNCHRONIZER ASSEMBLY

SPACER TRANS REVERSE FORK

THRUST WASHER

ROLL PIN

REVERSE GEAR RAIL

SLEEVE

REVERSE IDLER GEAR SHAFT

REVERSE IDLER SLIDING GEAR

ROLLER BEARINGS

RING

OVERDRIVE GEAR

HUB 3RD & 4TH

ROLLER BEARING

BLOCKING RING

SPEEDOMETER DRIVE GEAR

INPUT SHAFT

INPUT SHAFT BEARING

SNAP RING

OUTPUT SHAFT BEARING

RING

1ST GEAR

OUTPUT SHAFT

RING

SNAP RING

1ST & 2ND HUB

ROLLER BEARINGS

REVERSE SLIDING GEAR

SPEEDOMETER GEAR DRIVE BALL

2ND GEAR

1ST & 2ND SYNCHRONIZER ASSEMBLY

COUNTERSHAFT GEAR

Single rail overdrive transmission

fork, slide the reverse shifter rail through the rear of the case, and remove the reverse gearshift fork and spacer.

21. Drive the reverse gear shaft out the rear of the case.

22. Remove the reverse idler gear, thrust washers and roller bearings.

23. Remove the retaining clip, reverse gearshift relay lever and reverse gear selector fork pivot pin. Remove the O.D. shift control link assembly. Remove the shift shaft seal from the rear of the case; remove the expansion plug from the front of the case.

Assembly

Assembly is the reverse. Tighten the extension housing bolts in a criss-cross pattern to 42–50 ft. lbs. The bearing rollers, extension housing bushing, shifter shaft and gear shift damper bushing are to be lubricated with grease before assembly (Ford #ESW-M1C109-A or the equivalent). The gear shift shaft sleeve and the turret cover assembly should be coated with sealer prior to installation. The intermediate and high

rail welch plug must be seated firmly; it must not protrude above the front face of the case, nor seat below 0.6 in. below the front face.

With the 1st gear thrust washer clamped tightly against the output shaft shoulder, 1st gear endplay must be 0.005–0.024 in. 2nd gear endplay must be 0.003–0.021 in. O.D. endplay must be 0.009–0.023 in. Countershaft gear endplay, checked after installation between the thrust washers, must be 0.004–0.018 in.

When the gearshift selector arm plate is seated in the 1st–2nd shift fork plate slot, the shifter shaft must pass freely through the bore without binding.

Muncie Model SM330 3-Speed (83MM)

The G.M. Corporation Model SM 330 (83MM) (Muncie) is a three-speed transmission using helical constant mesh gears. The engagement of all gears except reverse is assisted by synchronizers.

GENERAL DATA

Type	3-Speed
Synchromesh gears	1st, 2nd, and 3rd
Model	SM330 (83MM)
Gear ratios	
1st speed	3.03:1
2nd speed	1.75:1
3rd speed	1.00:1
Reverse	3.02:1

TRANSMISSION UNIT

Disassembly

1. Remove side cover and shift forks.

2. Unbolt extension and rotate to line up groove in extension flange with reverse idler shaft. Drive reverse idler shaft and key out of case with a brass drift.

3. Move second-third synchronizer sleeve forward. Remove extension housing and mainshaft assembly.

4. Remove reverse idler gear from case.

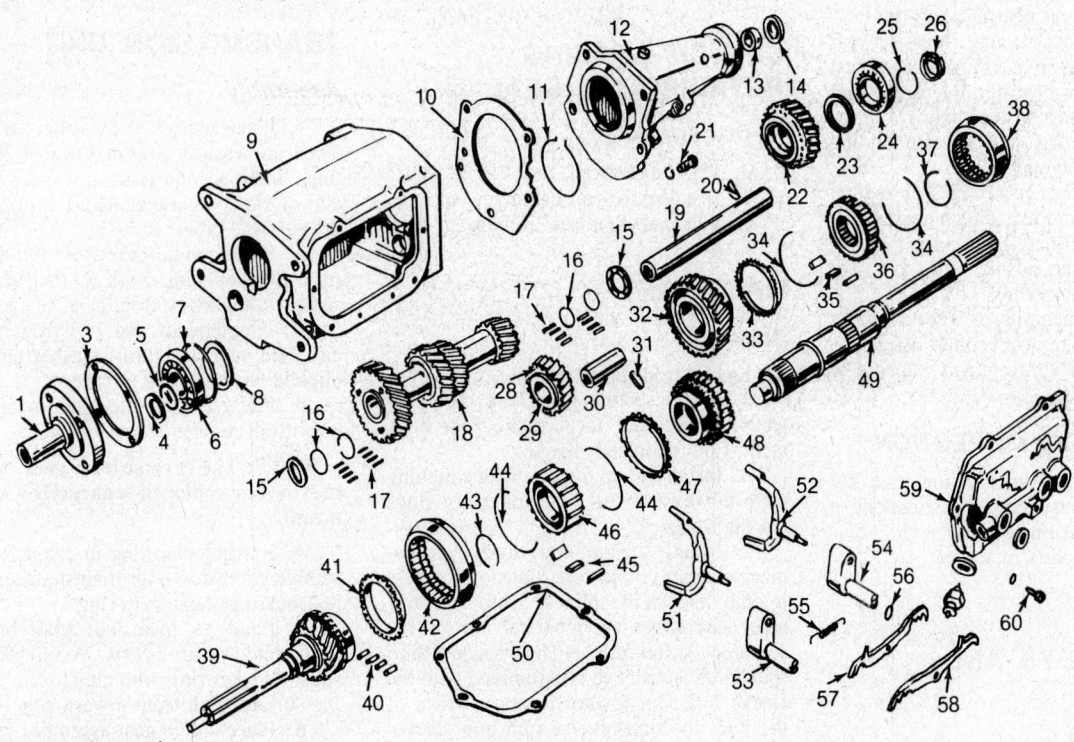

Muncie 83 mm 3-speed

1. Bearing retainer
2. Bolt and lock washer
3. Gasket
4. Oil seal
5. Snap-ring (bearing-to-main drive gear)
6. Main drive gear bearing
7. Snap-ring bearing
8. Oil slinger
9. Case
10. Gasket
11. Snap-ring (rear bearing-to-extension)
12. Extension
13. Extension bushing
14. Oil seal
15. Thrust washer
16. Bearing washer
17. Needle bearings
18. Countergear
19. Countershaft
20. Woodruff key
21. Bolt (extension-to-case)
22. Reverse gear
23. Thrust washer
24. Rear bearing
25. Snap-ring
26. Speedometer drive gear
27. Retainer clip
28. Reverse idler gear
29. Reverse idler bushing
30. Reverse idler shaft
31. Woodruff key
32. 1st speed gear
33. 1st speed blocker ring
34. Synchronizer key spring
35. Synchronizer keys
36. 1st and reverse synchronizer hub assembly
37. Snap-ring
38. 1st and reverse synchronizer collar
39. Main drive gear
40. Pilot bearings
41. 3rd speed blocker ring
42. 2nd and 3rd synchronizer collar
43. Snap-ring
44. Synchronizer key spring
45. Synchronizer keys
46. 2nd and 3rd synchronizer hub
47. 2nd speed blocker ring
48. 2nd speed gear
49. Mainshaft
50. Gasket
51. 2nd and 3rd shifter fork
52. 1st and reverse shifter fork
53. 2-3 shifter shaft assembly
54. 1st and reverse shifter shaft assembly
55. Spring
56. O-ring seal
57. 1st and reverse detent cam
58. 2nd and 3rd detent cam
59. Side cover
60. Bolt and lock washer

5. Remove third speed blocker ring from clutch gear.

6. Expand snap-ring which holds mainshaft rear bearing. Tap gently on end of mainshaft to remove extension.

7. Remove clutch gear bearing retainer and gasket.

8. Remove snap-ring. Remove clutch gear from inside case by gently tapping on end of clutch gear.

9. Remove oil slinger and 16 mainshaft pilot bearings from clutch gear cavity.

10. Slip clutch gear bearing out front of case. Aid removal with a screwdriver between case and bearing outer snap-ring.

11. Drive countershaft and key out to rear.

12. Remove countergear and two tanged thrust washers.

MAINSHAFT

Disassembly

1. Remove speedometer drive gear. Some speedometer drive gears, made of metal, must be pulled off.

2. Remove rear bearing snap-ring.

3. Support reverse gear. Press on rear of mainshaft to remove reverse gear, thrust washer, and rear bearing. Be careful not to cock the bearing on the shaft.

4. Remove first and reverse sliding clutch hub snap-ring.

5. Support first gear. Press on rear of mainshaft to remove clutch assembly, blocker ring, and first gear.

6. Remove second and third speed sliding clutch hub snap-ring.

7. Support second gear. Press on front of mainshaft to remove clutch assembly, second speed blocker ring, and second gear from shaft.

CLEANING AND INSPECTION

For more detailed information, see the "Cleaning and Inspection" instructions at front of transmission section.

1. Wash all parts in solvent.

2. Air dry.

CLUTCH KEYS AND SPRINGS

Replacement

Keys and springs may be replaced if worn or broken, but the hubs and sleeves must be kept together as originally assembled.

1. Mark hub and sleeve for reassembly.

2. Push hub from sleeve. Remove keys and springs.

3. Place three keys and two springs, one on each side of hub, so all three keys are engaged by both springs. The tanged end of the springs should not be installed into the same key.

4. Slide the sleeve onto the hub, aligning the marks.

TORQUE SPECIFICATIONS
Muncie-83MM

	ft. lbs.
Extension to case attaching	45
Drain plug	30
Filler plug	15
Side cover attaching bolts	22
Main drive gear retainer bolts	22
Transmission case to clutch housing bolts	45

EXTENSION OIL SEAL AND BUSHING

Replacement

1. Remove seal.

2. Using bushing remover and installer, or other suitable tool, drive bushing into extension housing.

3. Drive new bushing in from rear. Lubricate inside of bushing and seal. Install new oil seal with extension seal installer or suitable tool.

CLUTCH BEARING RETAINER OIL SEAL

Replacement

1. Pry old seal out.

2. Install new seal using seal installer or suitable tool. Seat seal in bore.

MAINSHAFT

Assembly

1. Lift front of mainshaft.

2. Install second gear with clutching teeth up; the rear face of the gear butts against the mainshaft flange.

3. Install a blocking ring with clutching teeth downward. All three blocking rings are the same.

4. Install second and third synchronizer assembly with fork slot down. Press it onto mainshaft splines. Both synchronizer assemblies are identical but are assembled differently. The second-third speed hub and sleeve is assembled with the sleeve fork slot toward the thrust face of the hub; the first-reverse hub and sleeve, with the fork slot opposite the thrust face. Be sure that the blocker ring notches align with the synchronizer assembly keys.

5. Install synchronizer snap-ring. Both synchronizer snap-rings are the same.

6. Turn rear of shaft up.

7. Install first gear with clutching teeth upward; the front face of the gear butts against the flange on the mainshaft.

8. Install a blocker ring with clutching teeth down.

9. Install first and reverse synchronizer assembly with fork slot down. Press it onto mainshaft splines. Be sure blocker ring notches align with synchronizer assembly

keys and synchronizer sleeves face front of mainshaft.

10. Install snap-ring.

11. Install reverse gear with clutching teeth down.

12. Install steel reverse gear thrust washer with flats aligned.

13. Press rear ball bearing onto shaft with snap-ring slot down.

14. Install snap-ring.

15. Install speedometer drive gear and retaining clip.

TRANSMISSION UNIT

Assembly

1. Place a row of 29 roller bearings, a bearing washer, a second row of 29 bearings, and a second bearing washer at each end of the countergear. Hold in place with grease.

2. Place countergear assembly through rear case opening with a tanged thrust washer, tang away from gear, at each end. Install countershaft and key from rear of case. Be sure that thrust washer tangs are aligned with notches in case.

3. Place reverse idler gear in case. Do not install reverse idler shaft yet.

NOTE: The reverse idler gear bushing may not be replaced separately—only as a unit.

4. Expand snap-ring in extension. Assemble extension over mainshaft and onto rear bearing. Seat snap-ring.

5. Load 16 mainshaft pilot bearings into clutch gear cavity. Assemble third speed blocker ring onto clutch gear clutching surface with teeth toward gear.

6. Place clutch gear assembly, without front bearing, over front of mainshaft. Make sure that blocker ring notches align with keys in second-third synchronizer assembly.

7. Stick gasket onto extension housing with grease. Assemble clutch gear, mainshaft, and extension to case together. Make sure that clutch gear teeth engage teeth of countergear anti-lash plate.

8. Rotate extension housing. Install reverse idler shaft and key.

9. Torque extension bolts to 45 ft. lbs.

10. Install oil slinger with inner lip facing forward. Install front bearing outer snap-ring and slide bearing into case bore.

11. Install snap-ring to clutch gear stem. Install bearing retainer and gasket and torque to 20 ft. lbs. Retainer oil return hole must be at 6 o'clock.

12. Shift both synchronizer sleeves to neutral positions. Install side cover, inserting shifter forks in synchronizer sleeve grooves.

13. Torque side cover bolts to 20 ft. lbs.

Muncie Model SM465 4-Speed (117MM)

Muncie model CH-465-SM-465 transmission is a four speed transmission using helical gears. The action of all gears except reverse is aided by synchronizers.

TRANSMISSION UNIT

Disassembly

1. Remove transmission cover assembly.

NOTE: Move reverse shifter fork so that reverse idler gear is partially engaged before attempting to remove cover. Forks must be positioned so rear edge of the slot in the reverse fork is in line with the front edge of the slot in the forward forks as viewed through tower opening.

2. Lock transmission into two gears. Remove the universal joint flange nut, universal joint front flange and brake drum assembly.

NOTE: On 4-wheel drive models, use a special tool to remove mainshaft rear lock nut.

3. Remove parking brake and brake flange plate assembly on those vehicles having a drive-shaft parking brake.

4. Remove rear bearing retainer and gasket.

5. Slide speedometer drive gear off mainshaft.

6. Remove clutch gear bearing retainers and gasket.

7. Remove countergear front bearing cap and gasket.

8. Using a prybar, pry off countershaft front bearing.

9. Remove countergear rear bearing snap-rings from shaft and bearing. Using special tool, remove countergear rear bearings.

10. Remove clutch gear bearing outer race to case retaining ring.

11. Remove clutch gear and bearing by tapping gently on bottom side of clutch gear shaft and prying directly opposite against the case and bearing snap-ring groove at the same time. Remove fourth gear synchronizer ring.

— **CAUTION** —

Index cut out section of clutch gear in down position with countergear to obtain clearance for removing clutch gear.

---

12. Remove rear mainshaft bearing snap-ring and, using special tools, remove bearing from case. Slide 1st speed gear thrust washer off mainshaft.

13. Lift mainshaft assembly from case. Remove synchronizer cone from shaft.

14. Slide reverse idler gear rearward and move countergear rearward, then lift to remove from case.

15. To remove reverse idler gear, drive reverse idler gear shaft out of case from front to rear using a drift. Remove reverse idler gear from case.

SUBASSEMBLIES TRANSMISSION COVER

Disassembly

1. Remove shifter fork retaining pins and drive out expansion plugs.

NOTE: The third and fourth shifter fork must be removed before the reverse shifter head pin can be removed.

2. With shifter shafts in neutral position, remove shafts.

— **CAUTION** —

Care should be taken when removing the detent balls and springs since removal of the shifter shafts will cause these parts to be forcibly ejected.

---

3. Remove retaining pin and drive out reverse shifter shaft.

Assembly

1. In reassembling the cover, care should be taken to install the shifter shafts in order—reverse, 3rd–4th, and 1st–2nd.

2. Place fork detent ball springs and balls in cover.

3. Start shifter shafts into cover and, while depressing the detent balls, push the shafts over the balls. Push reverse shaft through the yoke.

4. With the 3rd–4th shaft in neutral, line up the retaining holes in the fork and shaft.

NOTE: Detent balls should line up with detents in shaft.

5. After 1st and 2nd fork is installed, place two inner-lock balls between the low speed shifter shaft and the high speed shifter shaft in the crossbore of the front support boss. Grease the interlock pin and insert it in the 3rd–4th shifter shaft hole. Continue pushing this shaft through cover bore and fork until retainer hole in fork lines up with hole in shaft.

6. Place two interlock balls in crossbore in front support boss between reverse, and 3rd and 4th shifter shaft. Then push remaining shaft through fork and cover bore, keeping both balls in position between shafts until retaining holes line up in fork and shaft. Install retaining pin.

7. Install 1st/2nd fork and reverse fork retaining pins. Install new shifter shaft hole expansion plugs.

CLUTCH GEAR AND SHAFT

Disassembly

1. Remove mainshaft pilot bearing rollers from clutch gear if not already re-

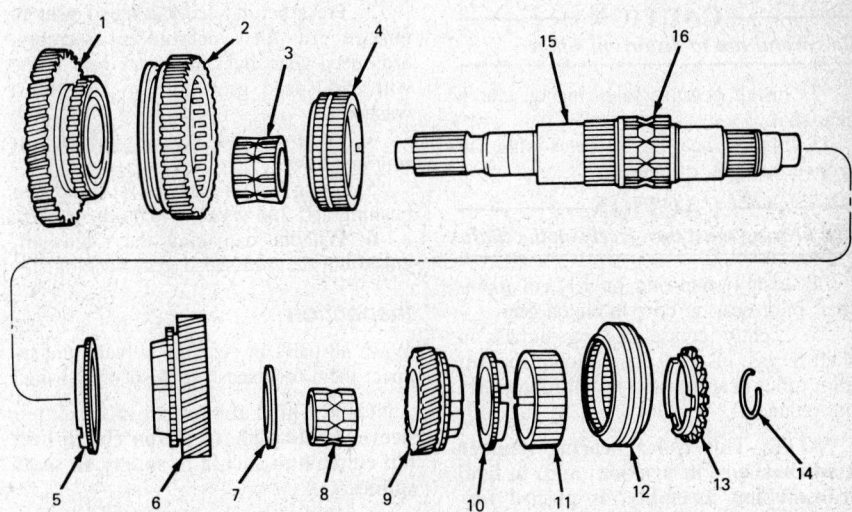

Muncie 117 mm 4-speed mainshaft

1. 1st speed gear	10. 3rd speed blocker ring
2. Reverse driven gear	11. 3rd-4th speed synchronizer hub assembly
3. 1st gear bushing	
4. 1st-2nd gear synchronizer hub assembly	12. 3rd-4th speed synchronizer sleeve
5. 2nd speed blocker ring	13. 4th speed blocker ring
6. 2nd speed gear	14. Snap-ring
7. Thrust washer	15. Mainshaft
8. 3rd speed bushing	16. 2nd speed gear bushing
9. 3rd speed gear	

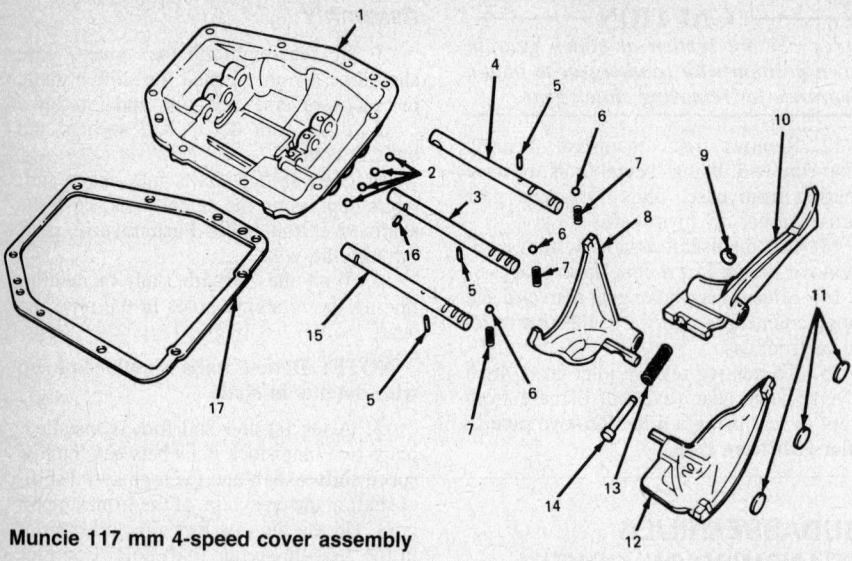

Muncie 117 mm 4-speed cover assembly

1. Transmission cover
2. Interlock balls
3. 3rd–4th shifter shaft
4. Reverse shifter shaft
5. Fork retaining pin
6. Detent ball
7. Detent spring
8. 3rd–4th shifter fork
9. C-ring lock clip
10. Reverse shifter fork
11. Shifter shaft hole plugs
12. 1st–2nd shifter fork
13. Interlock plunger spring
14. Reverse interlock plunger
15. 1st–2nd shifter shaft
16. Interlock pin
17. Cover gasket

moved, and remove roller retainer. Do not remove snap-ring on inside of clutch gear.

2. Remove snap-ring securing bearing on steam of clutch gear.

3. To remove bearing, position a special tool to the bearing and, with an arbor press, press gear and shaft out of bearing.

Assembly

1. Press bearing and new oil slinger onto clutch gear shaft using a special tool. Slinger should be located flush with bearing shoulder on clutch gear.

— CAUTION —
Be careful not to distort oil slinger.

2. Install bearing snap-ring on clutch gear shaft.

3. Install bearing retainer ring in groove on O.D. of bearing.

— CAUTION —
The bearing must turn freely on the shaft.

4. Install snap-ring on I.D. of mainshaft pilot bearing bore in clutch gear.

5. Lightly grease bearing surface in shaft recess, install transmission mainshaft pilot roller bearings and install roller bearing retainer.

NOTE: This roller bearing retainer holds bearings in position, and, in final transmission assembly, is pushed forward into recess by mainshaft pilot.

BEARING RETAINER OIL SEAL

Replacement

1. Remove retainer and oil seal assem-

bly and gasket.

2. Pry out oil seal.

3. Install new seal with lip of seal toward flange of tool.

4. Support front surface of retainer in press and drive seal into retainer.

5. Install retainer and gasket on case.

MAINSHAFT

Disassembly

1. Remove first speed gear.
2. Remove reverse driven gear.
3. Press behind second speed gear to remove 3rd–4th synchronizer assembly, 3rd speed gear and 2nd speed gear along with 3rd speed gear bushing and thrust washer.
4. Remove 2nd speed synchronizer ring and keys.
5. Using a press, remove 1st speed gear bushing and 2nd speed synchronizer hub.
6. Without damaging the mainshaft, chisel out the 2nd speed gear bushing.

Inspection

Wash all parts in cleaning solvent and inspect them for excessive wear or scoring.

NOTE: Third and fourth speed clutch sleeve should slide freely on clutch hub but clutch hub should fit snugly on shaft splines.

Third speed gear must be running fit on mainshaft bushing and mainshaft bushing should be press fit on shaft.

First and reverse sliding gear must be sliding fit on synchronizer hub and must not have excessive radial or circumferential play. If sliding gear is not free on hub, inspect for burrs which may have rolled up

on front end of half-tooth internal splines and remove by honing as necessary.

Assembly

1. Lubricate with E.P. oil and press onto mainshaft.

— CAUTION —
1st, 2nd and 3rd speed gear bushings are sintered iron, exercise care when installing.

2. Press 1st and 2nd speed synchronizer hub onto mainshaft with annulus toward rear of shaft.

3. Install 1st and 2nd synchronizer keys and springs.

4. Press 1st speed gear bushing onto mainshaft until it bottoms against hub.

NOTE: Lubricate all bushings with E.P. oil before installation of gears.

5. Install synchronizer blocker ring and 2nd speed gear onto mainshaft and against synchronize hub. Align synchronizer key slots with keys in synchronizer hub.

6. Install 3rd speed gear thrust washer onto mainshaft inserting washer tang in slotted shaft. Then press 3rd speed gear bushing onto mainshaft against thrust washer.

7. Install 3rd speed gear and synchronizer blocker ring against 3rd speed gear thrust washer.

8. Align synchronizer key ring slots with synchronizer assembly keys and drive 3rd and 4th synchronizer assembly onto mainshaft. Secure assembly with snapring.

9. Install reverse driven gear with fork groove toward rear.

10. Install 1st speed gear against 1st and 2nd synchronizer hub. Install 1st speed gear thrust washer.

COUNTERSHAFT

Disassembly

1. Remove front countergear retaining ring and thrust washer. Do not re-use this snap-ring or any others.

2. Press countershaft out of clutch countergear assembly.

3. Remove clutch countergear and 3rd speed countergear retaining rings.

4. Press shift from 3rd speed countergear.

COUNTERSHAFT

Assembly

1. Press the 3rd speed countergear onto the shaft.

NOTE: Install gear with marked surface toward front of shaft.

2. Using snap-ring pliers, install new 3rd speed countergear retaining ring.

3. Install new clutch countergear rear retaining ring.

4. Press countergear onto shaft against snap-ring.

5. Install clutch countergear thrust washer and front retaining ring.

TRANSMISSION UNIT

Assembly

1. Lower the countergear into the case.

2. Place reverse idler gear in transmission case with gear teeth toward the front. Install idler gear shaft from rear to front, being careful to have slot in end of shaft facing down and flush with case.

3. Install mainshaft assembly into case with rear of shaft protruding out rear bearing hole in case. Rotate case onto front end.

NOTE: Install 1st speed gear thrust washer on shaft, if not previously installed.

4. Install snap-ring on bearing O.D. and place rear mainshaft bearing on shaft. Drive bearing onto shaft and into case.

5. Install synchronizer cone on mainshaft and slide rearward to clutch hub.

6. Install snap-ring on clutch gear bearing O.D. Index cut out portion of clutch gear teeth to obtain clearance over countershaft drive gear teeth, and install into case.

7. Install clutch gear bearing retainer and gasket and torque to 15–18 ft. lbs.

8. Rotate case onto front end.

9. Install snap-ring on countergear rear bearing O.D., and drive bearing into place. Install snap-ring on countershaft at rear bearing.

10. Tap countergear front bearing assembly into case.

11. Install countergear front bearing cap and new gasket and torque to 20–30 in. lbs.

12. Slide speedometer drive gear over mainshaft to bearing.

13. Install rear bearing retainer with new gasket. Be sure snap-ring ends are in lube slot and cut out in bearing retainer. Install bolts and tighten to 15–18 ft. lbs. Install brake backing plate assembly on those models having driveshaft brake.

NOTE: On models equipped with 4-wheel drive, install rear lock nut and washer and torque to 120 ft. lbs. and bend washer tangs to fit slots in nut.

14. Install parking brake drum and/or universal joint flange.

NOTE: Lightly oil seal surface.

15. Lock transmission in two gears at once. Install universal joint flange locknut and tighten to 90–120 ft. lbs.

16. Move all transmission gears to neutral except the reverse idler gear which should be engaged approximately 3/8 of an inch (leading edge of reverse idler gear taper lines up with the front edge of the 1st speed gear). Install cover assembly and gasket. Shifting forks must slide into their proper positions on clutch sleeves and reverse idler gear. Forks must be positioned as in removal.

17. Install cover attaching bolts and gearshift lever and check operation of transmission.

New Process 435 Four Speed Transmission

TRANSMISSION UNIT

Disassembly

1. Mount the transmission in a holding fixture. Remove the parking brake assembly, if one is installed.

2. Shift the gears into neutral by replacing the gear shift lever temporarily, or by using a bar or screw driver.

3. Remove the cover screws, the second screw from the front on each side is shouldered with a split washer for installation alignment.

4. While lifting the cover, rotate slightly counterclockwise to provide clearance for the shift levers. Remove the cover.

5. Lock the transmission in two gears and remove the output flange nut, the yoke, and the parking brake drum as a unit assembly.

NOTE: The drum and yoke are balanced and unless replacement of parts are required, it is recommended that the drum and yoke be removed as a assembly.

6. Remove the speedometer drive gear pinion and the mainshaft rear bearing retainer.

7. Before removal and disassembly of the drive pinion and mainshaft, measure the end play between the synchronizer stop ring and the third gear.

NOTE: Record this reading for reference during assembly.

Clearance should be within 0.050–0.070 inch. If necessary, add corrective shims during assembly.

8. Remove the drive pinion bearing retainer.

9. Rotate the drive pinion gear to align the space in the pinion gear clutch teeth with the countershaft drive gear teeth. Remove the drive pinion gear and the tapered roller bearing from the transmission by pulling on the pinion shaft, and rapping the face of the case lightly with a brass hammer.

10. Remove the snap-ring, washer, and the pilot roller bearings from the recess in the drive pinion gear.

11. Place a brass drift in the front center of the mainshaft and drive the shaft rearward.

12. When the mainshaft rear bearing has cleared the case, remove the rear bearing and the speedometer drive gear with a suitable gear puller.

13. Move the mainshaft assembly to the rear of the case and tilt the front of the mainshaft upward.

14. Remove the roller type thrust washer.

15. Remove the synchronizer and stop rings separately.

16. Remove the mainshaft assembly.

17. Remove the reverse idler lock screw and lock plate.

18. Using a brass drift held at an angle, drive the idler shaft to the rear while pulling.

19. Lift the reverse idler gear out of the case.

NOTE: If the countershaft gear does not show signs of excessive side play or end play and the teeth are not badly worn or chipped, it may not be necessary to replace the countershaft gear.

20. Remove the bearing retainer at the rear end of the countershaft. The bearing assembly will remain with the retainer.

TORQUE SPECIFICATIONS
Muncie-117MM

	ft. lbs.
Rear bearing retainer	18
Cover bolts	25
Filler plug	35
Drain plug	35
Clutch gear bearing retainer bolts	18
Universal joint front flange nut	95
Power take off cover bolts	18
Parking brake	22
Countergear front cover screws	25
Rear mainshaft lock nut (4 wheel drive models)	95

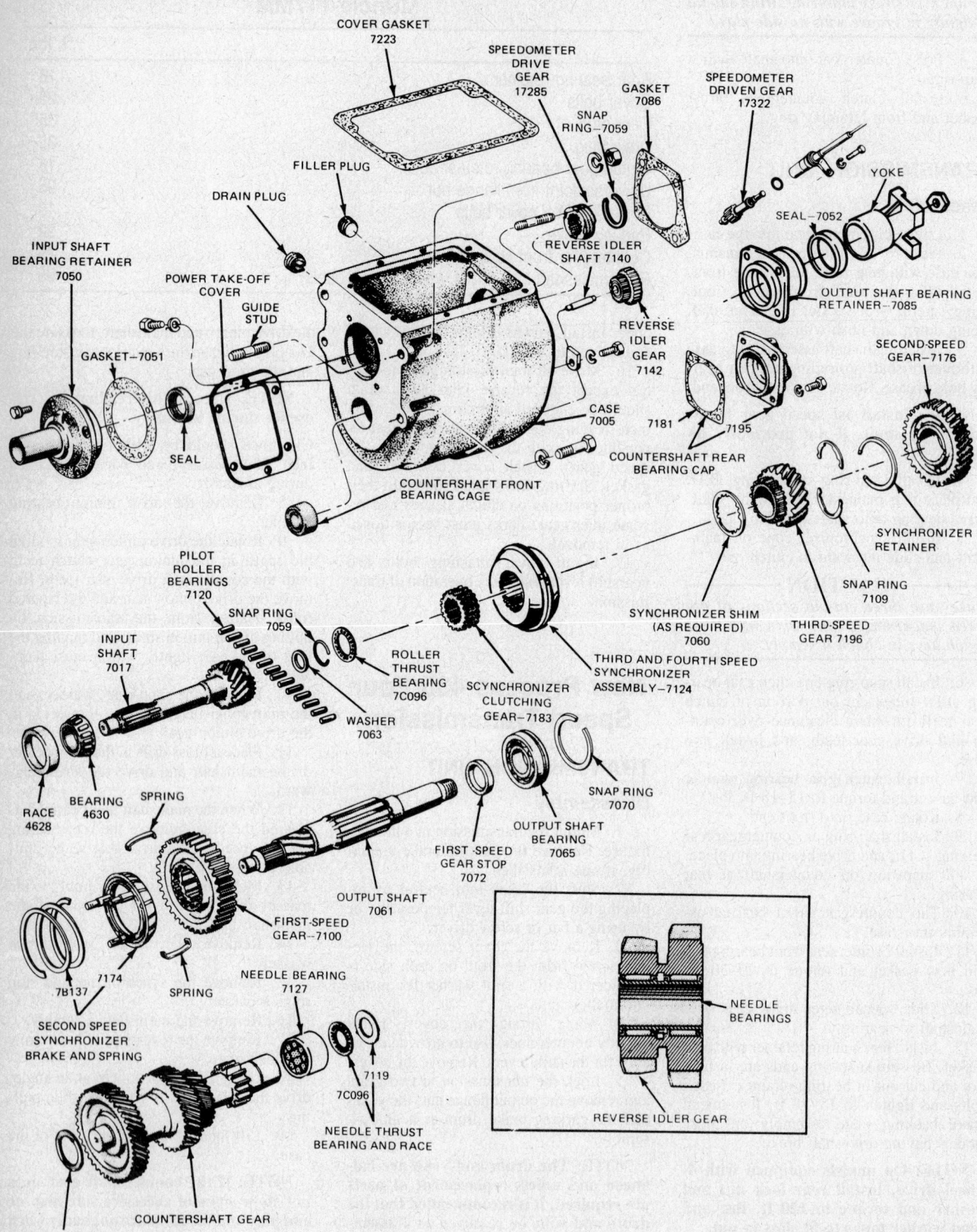

COVER GASKET
7223

SPEEDOMETER
DRIVE GEAR
17285

GASKET
7086

SPEEDOMETER
DRIVEN GEAR
17322

SNAP
RING—7059

YOKE

FILLER PLUG

SEAL—7052

DRAIN PLUG

REVERSE IDLER
SHAFT 7140

OUTPUT SHAFT BEARING
RETAINER—7085

INPUT SHAFT
BEARING RETAINER
7050

POWER TAKE-OFF
COVER

GUIDE
STUD

REVERSE
IDLER
GEAR
7142

SECOND-SPEED
GEAR—7176

GASKET—7051

COUNTERSHAFT REAR
BEARING CAP

7181

7195

SYNCHRONIZER
RETAINER

SEAL

CASE
7005

SNAP RING
7109

COUNTERSHAFT FRONT
BEARING CAGE

THIRD-SPEED
GEAR 7196

SYNCHRONIZER SHIM
(AS REQUIRED)
7060

PILOT
ROLLER
BEARINGS
7120

SNAP RING
7059

ROLLER
THRUST
BEARING
7C096

SCYNCHRONIZER
CLUTCHING
GEAR—7183

THIRD AND FOURTH SPEED
SYNCHRONIZER
ASSEMBLY—7124

INPUT
SHAFT
7017

SNAP RING
7070

WASHER
7063

OUTPUT SHAFT
BEARING
7065

RACE
4628

BEARING
4630

SPRING

FIRST-SPEED
GEAR STOP
7072

OUTPUT SHAFT
7061

FIRST-SPEED
GEAR—7100

7174

7B137

SPRING

NEEDLE BEARING
7127

SECOND SPEED
SYNCHRONIZER
BRAKE AND SPRING

7119

7C096

NEEDLE
BEARINGS

COUNTERSHAFT GEAR

NEEDLE THRUST
BEARING AND RACE

REVERSE IDLER GEAR

THRUST WASHER

New Process 435 4-speed

21. Tilt the cluster gear assembly and work it out of the transmission case.

22. Remove the front bearings from the case with a suitable driver.

SUB-ASSEMBLIES
MAINSHAFT

Disassembly

1. Remove the clutch gear snap-ring.

2. Remove the clutch gear, the synchronizer outer stop ring to third gear shim, and the third gear.

3. Remove the special split lock ring with two screw drivers. Remove the second gear and synchronizer.

4. Remove the first-reverse sliding gear.

5. Drive the old seal out of the bearing retainer.

Assembly

1. Place the mainshaft in a soft-jawed vise with the rear end up.

2. Install the first-reverse gear. Be sure the two spline springs, if used, are in place inside the gear as the gear is installed on the shaft.

3. Place the mainshaft in a soft-jawed vise with the front end up.

4. Assemble the second speed synchronizer spring and synchronizer brake on the second gear. Secure the brake with a snap-ring making sure that the snap-ring tangs are away from the gear.

5. Slide the second gear on the front of the mainshaft. Make sure that the synchronizer brake is toward the rear. Secure the gear to the shaft with the two piece lock ring. Install the third gear.

6. Install the shim between the third gear and the third-fourth synchronizer stop ring. Refer to the measurements of end play made during disassembly to determine if additional shims are needed.

NOTE: The exact determination of end-play must be made after the complete assembly of the mainshaft and the main drive pinion is installed in the transmission case.

REVERSE IDLER GEAR

─────── CAUTION ───────

Do not disassemble the reverse idler gear. If it is no longer serviceable, replace the assembly complete with the integral bearings.

COVER AND SHIFT FORK UNIT

NOTE: The cover and shift fork assembly should be disassembled only if inspection shows worn or damaged parts, or if the assembly is not working properly.

Disassembly

1. Remove the roll pin from the first-second shift fork and the shift gate with an "easy out".

NOTE: A square type or a closely wound spiral "easy out" mounted in a tap is preferable for this operation.

2. Move the first-second shift rail forward and force the expansion plug out of the cover. Cover the detent ball access hole in the cover with a cloth to prevent it from flying out. Remove the rail, fork, and gate from the cover.

3. Remove the third-fourth shift rail, then the reverse rail in the manner outlined in steps 1 and 2 above.

4. Compress the reverse gear plunger and remove the retaining clip. Remove the plunger and spring from the gate.

Assembly

1. Install the spring on the reverse gear plunger and hold it in the reverse shift gate. Compress the spring in the shift gate and install the retaining clip.

2. Insert the reverse shift rail in the cover and place the detent ball and spring in position. Depress the ball and slide the shift rail over it.

3. Install the shift gate and fork on the reverse shift rail. Install a new roll pin in the gate and the fork.

4. Place the reverse fork in the neutral position.

5. Install the two interlock plungers in their bores.

6. Insert the interlock pin in the third-fourth shift rail. Install the shift rail in the same manner as the reverse shift rail.

7. Install the first-second shift rail in the same manner as outlined above. Make sure the interlock plunger is in place.

8. Check the interlocks by shifting the reverse shift rail into the Reverse position. It should be impossible to shift the other rails with the reverse rail in this position.

9. If the shift lever is to be installed at this point, lubricate the spherical ball seat and place the cap in place.

10. Install the back-up light switch.

11. Install new expansion plugs in the bores of the shift rail holes in the cover. Install the rail interlock hole plug.

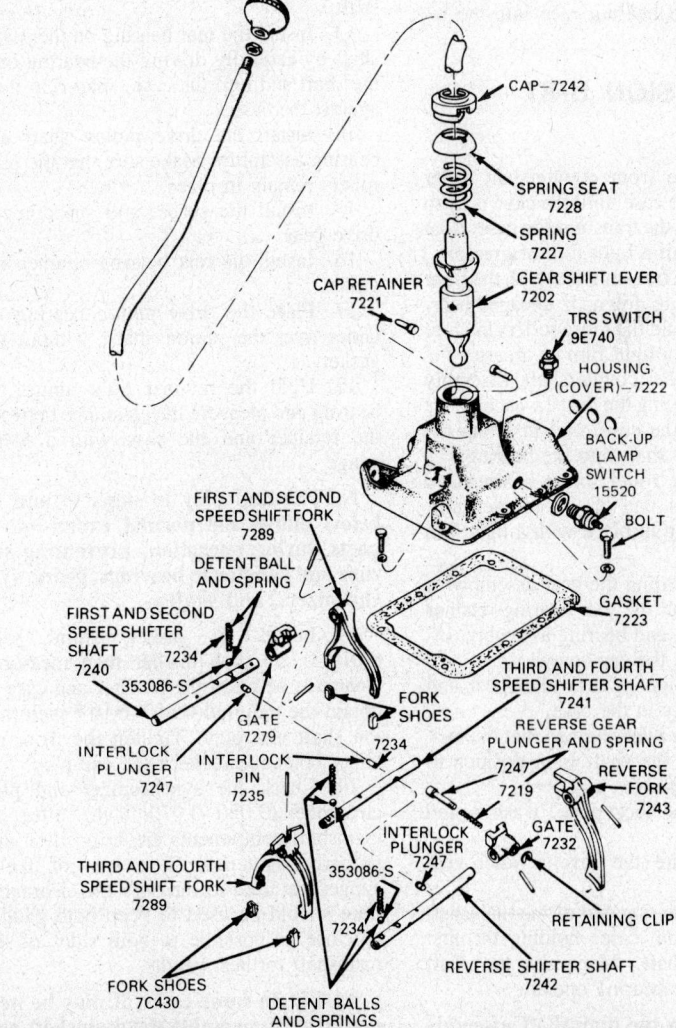

NP 435 gearshift housing

DRIVE PINION AND BEARING RETAINER

Disassembly

1. Remove the tapered roller bearing from the pinion shaft with a suitable tool.
2. Remove the snap-ring, washer, and the pilot rollers from the gear bore, if they have not been previously removed.
3. Pull the bearing race from the front bearing retainer with a suitable puller.
4. Remove the pinion shaft seal with a suitable tool.

Assembly

1. Position the drive pinion in an arbor press.
2. Place a wood block on the pinion gear and press it into the bearing until it contacts the bearing inner race.
3. Coat the roller bearings with a light film of grease to hold the bearings in place, and insert them in the pocket of the drive pinion gear.
4. Install the washer and snap-ring.
5. Press a new seal into the bearing retainer. Make sure that the lip of the seal is toward the mounting surface.
6. Press the bearing race into the retainer.

TRANSMISSION UNIT

Assembly

1. Press the front countershaft roller bearings into the case until the cage is flush with the front of the transmission case. Coat the bearings with a light film of grease.
2. Place the transmission with the front of the case facing down. If uncaged bearings are used, hold the loose rollers in place in the cap with a light film of grease.
3. Lower the countershaft assembly into the case placing the thrust washer tangs in the slots in the case, and inserting the front end of the shaft into the bearing.
4. Place the roller thrust bearing and race on the rear end of the countershaft. Hold the bearing in place with a light film of grease.
5. While holding the gear assembly in alignment, install the rear bearing retainer gasket, retainer, and bearing assembly. Install and tighten the cap screws.
6. Position the reverse idler gear and bearing assembly in the case.
7. Align the idler shaft so that the lock plate groove in the shaft is in position to install the lock plate.
8. Install the lock plate, washer, and cap screw.
9. Make sure the reverse idler gear turns freely.
10. Lower the rear end of the mainshaft assembly into the case, holding the first gear on the shaft. Maneuver the shaft through the rear bearing opening.

NOTE: With the mainshaft assembly moved to the rear of the case, be sure

TORQUE SPECIFICATIONS
New Process 435

	ft. lbs.
Cover screws	20–40
Drive gear retaining screw	15–25
Front countershaft retainer screw	15–25
Front countershaft bearing washer screw	12–22
Flange nut	125
Mainshaft rear retainer screw	15–25
Rear countershaft retainer screw	15–25
PTO cover screws	8–12
Filler and drain plugs	25–45
Reverse idler shaft lock screw	20–40
Brake link shoulder screw	20–40

LUBRICANT CAPACITY

New Process 435	7 pt.

the third-fourth synchronizer and shims remain in position.

11. Install the roller type thrust bearing.
12. Place a wood block between the front of the case and the front of the mainshaft.
13. Install the rear bearing on the mainshaft by carefully driving the bearing onto the shaft and into the case, snap-ring flush against the case.
14. Install the drive pinion shaft and bearing assembly. Make sure that the pilot rollers remain in place.
15. Install the spacer and speedometer drive gear.
16. Install the rear bearing retainer and gasket.
17. Place the drive pinion bearing retainer over the pinion shaft, without the gasket.
18. Hold the retainer tight aginst the bearing and measure the clearance between the retainer and the case with a feeler gauge.

NOTE: End play in steps 19 and 20 below allows for normal expansion of parts during operation, preventing seizure and damage to bearings, gears, synchronizers, and shafts.

19. Install a gasket shim pack 0.010–0.015 inch thicker than measured clearance between the retainer and case to obtain the required 0.007–0.017 inch pinion shaft end play. Tighten the front retainer bolts and recheck the end play.
20. Check the synchronizer end play clearance (0.050–0.070 inch) after all mainshaft components are in position and properly tightened. Two sets of feeler gauges are used to measure the clearance. Care should be used to keep both gauges as close as possible to both sides of the mainshaft for best results.

NOTE: In some cases, it may be necessary to disassemble the mainshaft and change the thickness of the shims to keep

the end play clearance within the specified limits, 0.050–0.070 inch. Shims are available in two thicknesses.

21. Install the speedometer drive pinion.
22. Install the yoke flange, drum, and drum assembly.
23. Place the transmission in two gears at once, and tighten the yoke flange nut.
24. Shift the gears and/or synchronizers into all gear positions and check for free rotation.
25. Cover all transmissions components with a film of transmission oil to prevent damage during start up after initial lubricant fill-up.
26. Move the gears to the neutral position.
27. Place a new cover gasket on the transmission case, and lower the cover over the transmission.
28. Carefully engage the shift forks into their proper gears. Align the cover.
29. Install a shouldered alignment screw with split washer in the screw hole second from the front of the cover. Try out gear operation by shifting through all ranges. Make sure everything moves freely.
30. Install the remaining cover screws.

New Process Model 445 4-Speed Transmission

TRANSMISSION UNIT

Disassembly

1. Place the transmission in a holding fixture and drain the lubricant.
2. Shift the transmission gears into neutral. Remove the gearshift cover attaching bolts. Note that the two bolts opposite the tower are shouldered to properly position the cover. Lift the cover straight up and remove.
3. Lock the transmission in two gears at once and remove the mainshaft nut and yoke.
4. Loosen and remove the extension housing bolts. Remove the mainshaft ex-

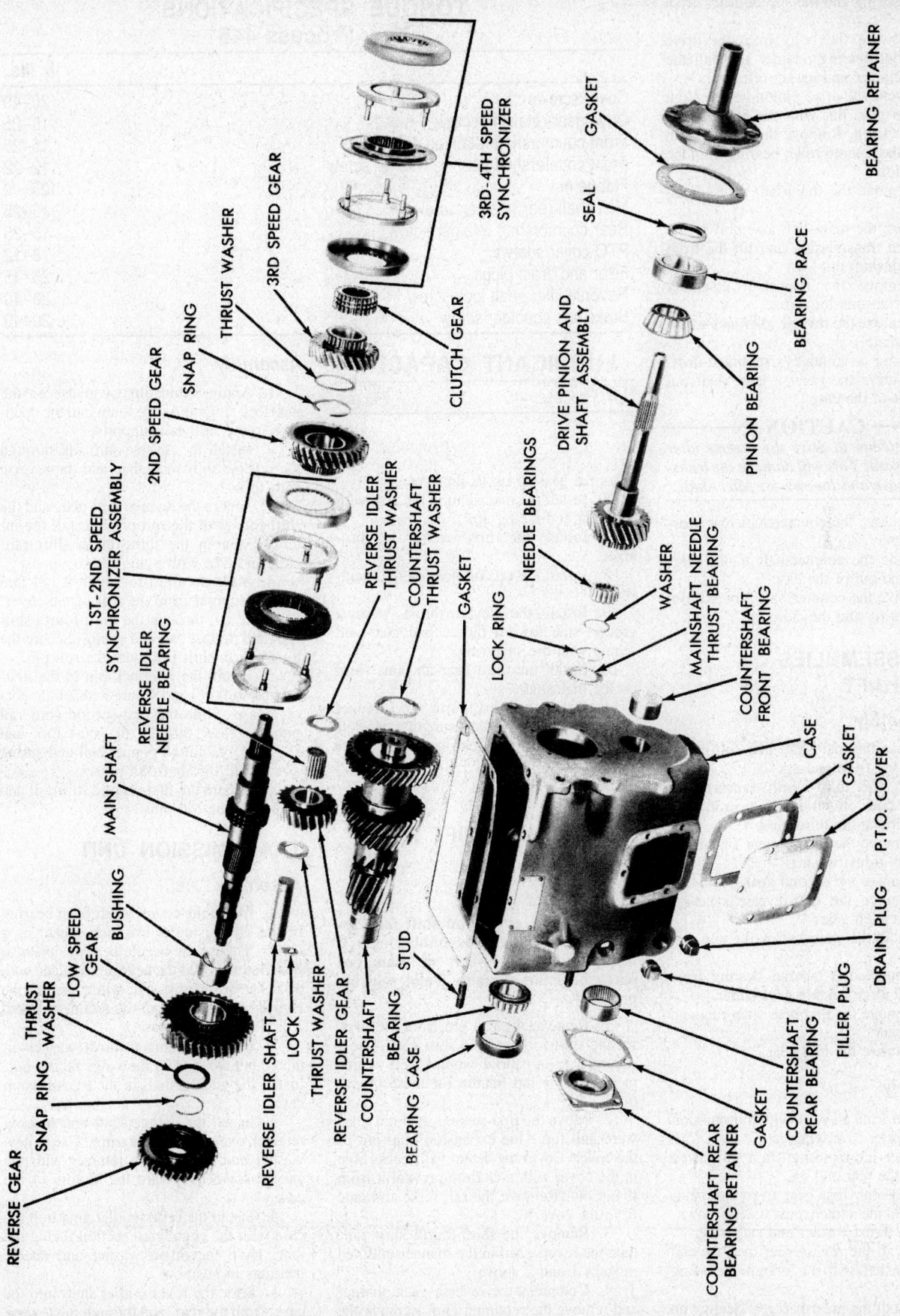

BEARING RETAINER

GASKET

SEAL

BEARING RACE

PINION BEARING

3RD-4TH SPEED SYNCHRONIZER

3RD SPEED GEAR

CLUTCH GEAR

THRUST WASHER

SNAP RING

2ND SPEED GEAR

DRIVE PINION AND SHAFT ASSEMBLY

NEEDLE BEARINGS

WASHER

LOCK RING

MAINSHAFT NEEDLE THRUST BEARING

COUNTERSHAFT FRONT BEARING

1ST-2ND SPEED SYNCHRONIZER ASSEMBLY

REVERSE IDLER THRUST WASHER

COUNTERSHAFT THRUST WASHER

GASKET

REVERSE IDLER NEEDLE BEARING

CASE

GASKET

P.T.O. COVER

MAIN SHAFT

BUSHING

LOW SPEED GEAR

THRUST WASHER

SNAP RING

REVERSE GEAR

REVERSE IDLER SHAFT

LOCK

THRUST WASHER

REVERSE IDLER GEAR

COUNTERSHAFT

STUD

BEARING

BEARING CASE

FILLER PLUG

DRAIN PLUG

COUNTERSHAFT REAR BEARING RETAINER

GASKET

COUNTERSHAFT REAR BEARING

tension housing and the speedometer drive pinion.

5. Remove the bolts from the drive pinion front bearing retainer and pull the bearing retainer and gasket off.

6. Rotate the drive pinion gear to align the pinion gear flat with the countershaft drive gear teeth. Remove the drive pinion gear and the tapered roller bearing from the transmission.

7. Remove the mainshaft thrust bearing.

8. Push the mainshaft assembly to the rear of the transmission and tilt the front of the mainshaft up.

9. Remove the mainshaft assembly from the transmission case.

10. Remove the reverse idler lock screw and lock plate.

11. Using a suitable size brass drift, carefully drive the reverse idler shaft out the REAR of the case.

——————— CAUTION ———————

Do not attempt to drive the reverse idler shaft forward! This will damage the transmission case and the reverse idler shaft.

12. Remove the countershaft rear bearing retainer.

13. Slide the countershaft to the rear, then up and out of the case.

14. Drive the countershaft forward, out of the bearing and the case.

SUB-ASSEMBLIES
MAINSHAFT

Disassembly

1. Place the mainshaft in a soft-jawed vise with the front end up.

2. Lift the third-fourth synchronizer and high speed clutch off the mainshaft.

3. Remove the third gear.

4. Remove the second gear snap-ring. Lift off the thrust washer.

5. Remove the second gear.

6. Remove the first-reverse synchronizer and clutch gear.

7. Install the mainshaft in the vise rear end up.

8. Remove the tapered bearing from the shaft with a suitable gear puller.

9. Remove the first gear snap-ring and thrust washer.

10. Remove the first gear.

Assembly

1. Lubricate all parts with transmission lubricant prior to assembly.

2. Place the mainshaft in a soft-jawed vise with the rear end up.

3. Slide the first gear over the mainshaft, with the clutch gear facing down. Install the thrust washer and snap-ring.

4. Install the revese gear over the end of the mainshaft with the fork groove facing down.

5. Install the mainshaft rear bearing on the mainshaft with a sleeve of suitable size.

TORQUE SPECIFICATIONS
New Process 445

	ft. lbs.
Cover screws	20–40
Drive gear retaining screw	15–25
Front countershaft retaining screw	15–25
Front countershaft bearing washer screw	12–22
Flange nut	125
Mainshaft rear retainer screw	15–25
Rear countershaft retainer screw	15–25
PTO cover screws	8–12
Filler and drain plugs	25–45
Reverse idler shaft lock screw	20–40
Brake link shoulder screw	20–40

LUBRICANT CAPACITY

New Process 445	7½ pts.

Press the bearing on its inner race.

6. Install the mainshaft in the vise with the front end facing up.

7. Install the first-reverse synchronizer.

8. Install the second gear on the mainshaft.

9. Install the keyed thrust washer, ground side toward the second gear and secure with the snap-ring.

10. Install the third gear and one shim on the mainshaft.

11. Install the third fourth synchronizer over the mainshaft. Make sure that the slotted end of the clutch gear is positioned toward the third gear.

COVER AND SHIFT FORK UNIT

Disassembly

NOTE: The cover and shift fork assembly should be disassembled only if inspection shows worn or damaged parts, or if the assembly is not working properly.

1. Remove the roll pin from the first-second shift fork and the shift gate. Use a square-type or spirial wound "easy-out" mounted in a tap handle for these operations.

2. Move the first-second shift rail rearward and force the expansion plug out of the cover. Cover the detent ball access hole in the cover with a cloth to prevent it from flying out. Remove the rail fork, and gate from the cover.

3. Remove the third-fourth shift rail, then the reverse rail in the manner outlined in steps 1 and 2 above.

4. Compress the reverse gear plunger and remove the retaining clip. Remove the plunger and spring from the gate.

Assembly

1. Apply a thin film of grease on the interlock slugs and slide them into the openings in the shift rail supports.

2. Install the reverse shift rail through the reverse shift fork plate and the reverse shift fork.

3. Secure the reverse shift plate and the shift fork with the roll pins. Install the interlock pin in the third-fourth shift rail. Hold in place with a thin film of grease.

4. Slide the third-fourth shift rail into the rail support from the rear of the cover. Slide the rail through the third-fourth shift fork and poppet ball and spring. Secure the third-fourth shift fork with the roll pin.

5. Install the interlock pin in the first-second shift rail and secure with a light coat of grease. Slide the first-second shift rail into the case, through the shift fork and shift gate. Hold the poppet ball and spring down until the shaft rail passes.

6. Secure the first-second shift rail and gate with the roll pins.

TRANSMISSION UNIT

Assembly

1. Install the countershaft front bearing in the case using a 1⅜ inch socket as a driver. Grease the needle bearings prior to installation. Hold the bearings in place with a socket of suitable size while seating the bearing retainer. Drive the retainer in until it is flush with the case.

2. Install the tanged thrust washer on the countershaft with the tangs facing out. Install the countershaft in the transmission case.

3. Install the countershaft rear bearing retainer over the rear bearing. Use a new washer and position the retainer with the curved segment toward the bottom of the case.

4. Install the reverse idler gear into the case with the chamfered section facing the rear. Hold the thrust washer and needle bearings in position.

5. Slide the reverse idler shaft into the case, from the rear, and through the reverse idler gear. Make sure that the lock notch

is down and at the rear of the case.

6. Install the reverse idler shaft lock and bolt.

7. Place the mainshaft in a soft-jawed vise with the front end facing up.

8. Install the drive gear on top of the mainshaft.

9. Measure the clearance between the high-speed synchronizer and the drive gear with two feeler gauges.

If the clearance is greater than 0.043–0.053 inch, install synchronizer shims between the third gear and the synchronizer brake drum. After the required shims have been installed, remove the drive gear from the mainshaft.

10. Install the mainshaft into the transmission case. Place the thrust washer over the pilot end of the mainshaft.

11. Position the drive gear so that the cutaway portion of the gear is facing down. Slide the drive gear into the front of the case and engage the mainshaft pilot in the pocket of the drive gear.

12. Slip the drive gear front bearing retainer over the shaft on gasket, and do not secure with bolts.

13. Install the mainshaft rear bearing retainer. Tighten the screws to specifications.

14. Hold the retainer against the front of the transmission case and measure the clearance between the front bearing retainer and the front of the case with a feeler gauge. Record the measurement and remove the bearing retainer.

15. Install a gasket pack on the front bearing retainer which is 0.010–0.015 inch thicker than the clearance measured in step 14. Install the front bearing retainer and torque attaching screws to specification.

16. The end play float of the front synchronizer must be checked before installation of the transmission cover assembly. Measure the end play ''float'' by inserting two feeler gauges opposite one another between the third gear and the synchronizer stop ring. Accurate measurement can be made only after all mainshaft parts are in place and torqued to specification.

17. If the front synchronizer end play ''float'' does not fall between 0.050–0.070 inch, shims should be added or removed as required, from between the third gear and the synchronizer stop ring.

18. Install the yoke retaining nut on the rear of the mainshaft. Shift the transmission into two gears at the same time and torque the yoke nut to 125 ft. lbs.

19. Shift the transmission into neutral.

20. Install the cover gasket.

21. Shift the transmission into second gear. Shift the cover into second.

22. Carefully lower the cover into position. It may be necessary to position the reverse gear to permit the fork to engage its groove.

23. Install the cover aligning screws (shouldered) and tighten with fingers only.

24. Install the remaining cover screws and tighten to specifications.

Saginaw 3-Speed (GM–SM326–76MM)

The G.M. Corporation Model SM326 (Saginaw) is a synchromesh three-speed transmission using helical constant mesh gears. The engagement of all gears except reverse is assisted by synchronizers.

GENERAL DATA

Type	3-Speed
Synchromesh gears	1st, 2nd, and 3rd
Models SM326 and SM326 w/Overdrive	
Gear ratios	
1st speed	2.85:1
2nd speed	1.68:1
3rd speed	1.00:1
Reverse	2.95:1

TRANSMISSION UNIT

Disassembly

1. Remove side cover assembly and shift forks.

2. Remove clutch gear bearing retainer.

3. Remove clutch gear bearing to gear stem snap-ring. Pull clutch gear outward until a screwdriver can be inserted between bearing and case. Remove clutch gear bearing.

4. Remove speedometer driven gear and extension bolts.

5. Remove reverse idler shaft snap-ring. Slide reverse idler gear forward on shaft.

6. Remove mainshaft and extension assembly.

7. Remove clutch gear and third-speed blocker ring from inside case. Remove 14 roller bearings from clutch gear.

8. Expand the snap-ring which retains the mainshaft rear bearing. Remove the extension.

9. Using a dummy shaft, drive the countershaft and key out the rear of the case. Remove the gear, two tanged thrust washers, and dummy shaft. Remove bearing washer and 27 roller bearings from each end of countergear.

10. Use a long drift to drive the reverse idler shaft and key through the rear of the case.

11. Remove reverse idler gear and tanged steel thrust washer.

MAINSHAFT

Disassembly

1. Remove second and third speed sliding clutch hug snap-ring from mainshaft. Remove clutch assembly, second speed blocker ring, and second speed gear from front of mainshaft.

2. Depress speedometer drive gear retaining clip. Remove gear. Some units have a metal speedometer drive gear which must be pulled off.

3. Remove rear bearing snap-ring.

4. Support reverse gear. Press on rear of mainshaft. Remove reverse gear, thrust washer, spring washer, rear bearing, and snap-ring. When pressing off the rear bearing, be careful not to cock the bearing on the shaft.

5. Remove first and reverse sliding clutch hub snap-ring. Remove clutch assembly, first speed blocker ring, and first gear.

Cleaning and Inspection

See Cleaning and Inspection instructions at the beginning of Transmission section.

CLUTCH KEYS AND SPRINGS

Replacement

Keys and springs may be replaced if worn or broken, but the hubs and sleeves are matched pairs and must be kept together.

1. Mark hub and sleeve for reassembly.

2. Push hub from sleeve. Remove keys and springs.

3. Place three keys and two springs, one on each side of hub, in position, so all three keys are engaged by both springs. The tanged end of the springs should not be installed into the same key.

4. Slide the sleeve onto the hub, aligning the marks.

NOTE: A groove around the outside of the synchronizer hub marks the end that must be opposite the fork slot in the sleeve when assembled.

EXTENSION OIL SEAL AND BUSHING

Replacement

1. Remove seal.

2. Using bushing remover and installer tool, or other suitable tool, drive bushing into extension housing.

3. Drive new bushing in from the rear. Lubricate inside of bushing and seal. Install new oil seal with extension seal installer tool or other suitable tool.

CLUTCH BEARING RETAINER OIL SEAL

Replacement

1. Pry old seal out.

2. Install new seal using seal installer or suitable tool. Seat seal in bore.

MAINSHAFT

Assembly

1. Turn front of mainshaft up.

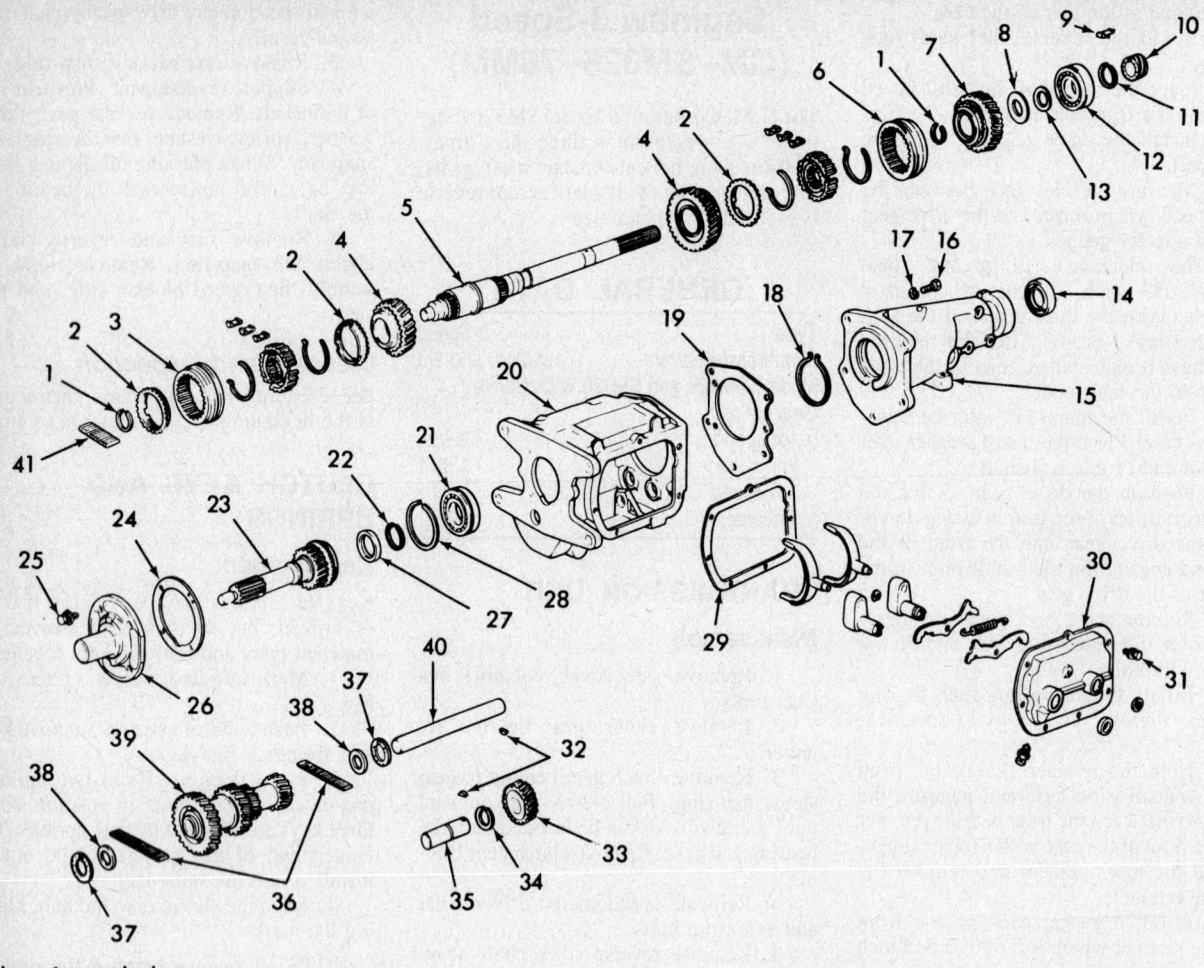

Saginaw transmission

1. Synchronizer retainer ring	7. Gear assembly	16. Bolt	25. Bolt and lockwasher	34. Retaining ring
2. Synchronizer blocking ring	8. Thrust washer	17. Washer	26. Retainer assembly	35. Shaft
3. Synchronizer assembly	9. Retainer clip	18. Rear bearing location ring	27. Ring	36. Roller
4. Second speed gear	10. Speedometer drive gear	19. Gasket	28. Clutch gear bearing locating ring	37. Washer
5. Main shaft	11. Ring	20. Case	29. Cover gasket	38. Washer
6. Synchronizer assembly	12. Mainshaft bearing	21. Bearing assembly	30. Cover assembly	39. Gear assembly
	13. Washer	22. Ring	31. Bolt and lockwasher	40. Counter gear shaft
	14. Seal	23. Clutch gear	32. Woodruff keys	41. Mainshaft bearing roller
	15. Extension housing	24. Gasket	33. Gear assembly	

2. Install second gear with clutching teeth up; the rear face of the gear butts against the flange on the mainshaft.

3. Install a blocker ring with clutching teeth down. All three blocker rings are the same.

4. Install second and third speed synchronizer assembly with fork slot down. Press it onto mainshaft splines. Both synchronizer assemblies are the same. Be sure that blocker ring notches align with synchronizer assembly keys.

5. Install synchronizer snap-ring. Both synchronizer snap-rings are the same.

6. Turn rear of shaft up.

7. Install first gear with clutching teeth up; the front face of the gear butts against the flange on the mainshaft.

8. Install a blocker ring with clutching teeth down.

9. Install first and reverse synchronizer assembly with fork slot down. Press it onto mainshaft splines. Be sure blocker ring notches align with synchronizer assembly keys.

10. Install snap-ring.

11. Install reverse gear with clutching teeth down.

12. Install steel reverse gear thrust washer and spring washer.

13. Press rear ball bearing onto shaft with snap-ring slot down.

14. Install snap-ring.

15. Install speedometer drive gear and retaining clip. Press on metal speedometer drive gear.

TRANSMISSION UNIT

Assembly

1. Using dummy shaft load a row of 27 roller bearings and a thrust washer at each end of countergear. Hold in place with grease.

2. Place countergear assembly into case through rear. Place a tanged thrust washer, tang away from gear at each end. Install countershaft and key, making sure that tangs align with notches in case.

3. Install reverse idler gear thrust washer, gear, and shaft with key from rear of case. Be sure thrust washer is between gear and rear of case with tang toward notch in case.

TORQUE SPECIFICATIONS
Saginaw-76mm

	ft. lbs.
Extension to case attaching bolts	35–55
Drain and filler plugs	10–15
Side cover attaching bolts	18–24
Clutch gear retainer bolts	18–24

NOTE: The reverse idler gear bushing may not be replaced separately—only as a unit with the gear.

4. Expand snap-ring in extension. Assemble extension over rear of mainshaft and onto rear bearing. Seat snap-ring in rear bearing groove.

5. Install 14 mainshaft pilot bearings into clutch gear cavity. Assemble third speed blocker ring onto clutch gear clutching surface with teeth toward gear.

6. Place clutch gear, pilot bearings, and third speed blocker ring assembly over front of mainshaft assembly. Be sure blocker rings align with keys in second-third synchronizer assembly.

7. Stick extension gasket to case with grease. Install clutch gear, mainshaft, and extension together. Be sure clutch gear engages teeth of countergear anti-lash plate. Torque extension bolts to 45 ft. lbs.

8. Place bearing over stem of clutch gear and into front case bore. Install front bearing to clutch gear snap-ring.

9. Install clutch gear bearing retainer and gasket. The retainer oil return hole must be at the bottom. Torque to 10 ft. lbs.

10. Install reverse idler gear shaft E-ring.

11. Shift synchronizer sleeves to neutral positions. Install cover, gasket, and forks, aligning forks with synchronizer sleeve grooves. Torque side cover bolts to 10 ft. lbs.

12. Install speedometer driven gear.

Tremec T-150 3-Speed Transmission (77 mm)

The Tremec T-150 (77 mm) transmission is used in varied vehicle applications, with or without transfer cases. The gear selection is controlled by either a top shift housing or by a remote control shift lever assembly. Although some of the gears and case applications are not interchangeable, the gear arrangement is basically the same.

Disassembly

1. Remove the bolts securing the transfer case to the transmission. Remove the transfer case.

2. Remove the transfer case drive gear locknut, flat washer, and drive gear. Remove the large fiber washer from the rear

bearing adapter. Move the second-third clutch sleeve forward and the first-reverse sleeve to the rear before removing the locknut.

3. Remove the transmission oil plug and drive the countershaft out of the case with a suitable size drift. Do not lose the countershaft access plug when removing the countershaft. With the countershaft removed the countershaft gear will lie at the

bottom of the case, leave it there until the mainshaft is removed.

4. Punch alignment marks in the front bearing cap and the transmission case for assembly reference.

5. Remove the front bearing cap and gasket.

6. Remove the large lock ring from the front bearing.

7. Remove the clutch shaft, front bearing, and the second-third synchronizer assembly. A special tool is required for this operation.

8. Remove the rear bearing and adapter assembly with a brass drift and hammer. Drive the adapter out the rear of the case with light blows from the hammer.

9. Remove the mainshaft assembly. Tilt the spline end of the shaft downward and lift the front end up and out of the case.

10. Remove the countershaft tool and

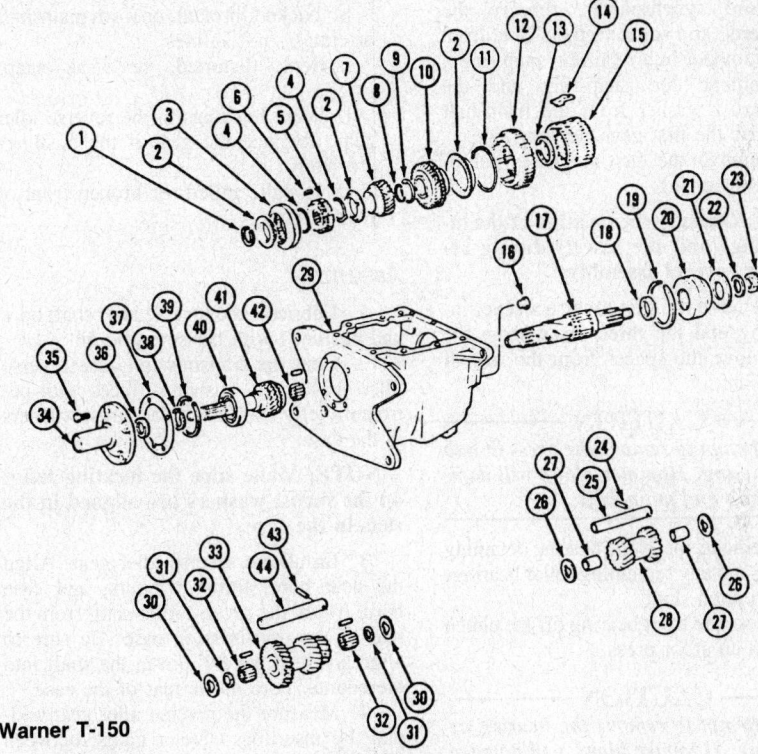

Warner T-150

1. Mainshaft retaining snap-ring
2. Synchronizer blocking rings (3)
3. Second-third synchronizer sleeve
4. Second-third synchronizer insert spring (2)
5. Second-third hub
6. Second-third synchronizer insert (3)
7. Second gear
8. First gear retaining snap-ring
9. First gear tabbed thrust washer
10. First gear
11. First-reverse synchronizer insert spring
12. First-reverse sleeve
13. First-reverse hub retaining snap-ring
14. First-reverse synchronizer insert (3)
15. First-reverse hub
16. Countershaft access plug
17. Mainshaft
18. Mainshaft spacer
19. Rear bearing adapter lock ring
20. Rear bearing and adapter assembly
21. Fiber washer
22. Flat washer
23. Locknut
24. Roll pin
25. Reverse idler gear shaft
26. Thrust washer
27. Bushing (part of idler

gear)
28. Reverse idler gear
29. Transmissioncase
30. Thrust washer (2)
31. Bearing retainer (2)
32. Countershaft needle bearings (50)
33. Countershaft gear
34. Front bearing cap
35. Bolt (4)
36. Front bearing cap oil seal
37. Gasket
38. Front bearing retainer snap-ring
39. Front bearing lockring
40. Front bearing
41. Clutch shaft
42. Mainshaft pilot roller bearings
43. Roll pin
44. Countershaft

arbor as an assembly. Remove the countershaft thrust washers, countershaft roll pin, and any pilot roller bearings that may have fallen into the case.

11. Remove the reverse idler shaft. Insert a brass drift through the clutch shaft bore in the front of the case and tap the shaft until the end with the roll pin clears the counter bore in the rear of the case. Remove the shaft.

12. Remove the reverse idler gear and thrust washers from the case.

13. Remove the retaining snap-ring from the front of the mainshaft. Remove the second-third synchronizer assembly and second gear. Mark the hub and sleeve for reference during assembly.

NOTE: Observe the position of the insert springs and the inserts during removal for correct assembly.

14. Remove the insert springs from the second-third synchronizer, remove the three inserts, and separate the sleeve from the synchronizer hub retaining snap-ring.

15. Remove the snap-ring and the tabbed thrust washer from the mainshaft and remove the first gear blocking ring.

16. Remove the first-reverse synchronizer hub snap-ring.

NOTE: Observe the position of the insert springs and the inserts during removal for correct assembly.

17. Remove the first-reverse sleeve, insert spring and the three insert from the hub. Remove the spacer from the rear of the mainshaft.

CAUTION
Do not attempt to remove the press fit hub by hammering. Hammer blows will damage the hub and mainshaft.

18. Remove the front bearing retaining snap-ring and any remaining roller bearings from the clutch shaft.

19. Press the front bearing off the clutch shaft with an arbor press.

CAUTION
Do not attempt to remove the bearing by hammering. Hammer blows will damage the bearing and the clutch shaft.

20. Clamp the rear bearing adapter in a soft-jawed vise. Do not over-tighten.

21. Remove the rear bearing retaining snap-ring. Remove the bearing adapter from the vise.

22. Press the rear bearing out of the adapter with an arbor press.

Cleaning and Inspection

1. Thoroughly wash all parts in clean solvent and dry with compressed air.

NOTE: Do not dry the bearings with compressed air, use a clean shop cloth.

2. Clean the needle and clutch shaft bearings by placing them in a shallow parts cleaning tray and covering them with sol-

vent. Allow the bearings to air dry on a clean shop cloth.

3. Check the case for the following:
   a. Cracks in the bores, bosses, or bolt holes.
   b. Stripped threads in bolt holes.
   c. Nicks, burrs, rough surfaces in the shaft bores or on the gasket surfaces.

4. Check the gear and synchronizer assemblies for the following:
   a. Broken, chipped, or worn gear teeth.
   b. Damaged splines on the synchronizer hubs or sleeves.
   c. Bent or damaged inserts.
   d. Damaged needle bearings or bearing bores in the countershaft gear.
   e. Broken or worn teeth or excessive wear of the blocking rings.
   f. Wear of galling of the countershaft, clutch shaft, or reverse idler shaft.
   g. Worn thrust washers.
   h. Nicked, broken, or worn mainshaft or clutch shaft splines.
   i. Bent, distorted, or weak snap-rings.
   j. Worn bushings in the reverse idler gear. Replace the gear if the bushings are worn.
   k. Rough, galled, or broken front or rear bearings.

Assembly

1. Lubricate the reverse idler shaft bore and bushings with transmission oil.

2. Coat the transmission case reverse idler gear thrust washer surfaces with petroleum jelly and install the thrust washers in the case.

NOTE: Make sure the locating tangs on the thrust washers are aligned in the slots in the case.

3. Install the reverse idler gear. Align the gear bore, thrust washers, and case bore. Install the reverse idler shaft from the rear of the transmission case. Be sure to align and seat the roll pin in the shaft into the counter bore in the rear of the case.

4. Measure the reverse idler gear end-play by inserting a feeler gauge between the thrust washer and the gear. End-play should be 0.004–0.018 inch. If end play exceeds 0.018 inch, remove the reverse idler gear and replace the thrust washers.

5. Coat the needle bearing bores in the countershaft gear with petroleum jelly. Insert the arbor tool in the bore of the gear and install the (25) needle bearings and the retainer washers at each end of the countershaft gear.

6. Coat the countershaft gear thrust washer surface with petroleum jelly and position the thrust washers in the case.

NOTE: Make sure the locating tangs on the thrust washers are aligned in the slots in the case.

7. Insert the countershaft into the bore at the rear of the case just far enough to hold the thrust washer in place.

8. Install the countershaft gear in the case. Do not install the roll pin at this time. Align the gear bore, thrust washers, the bores in the case, and install the countershaft.

NOTE: Do not remove the arbor tool completely.

9. Measure the countershaft gear end-play by inserting a feeler gauge between the washer and the countershaft gear. End-play should be 0.004–0.018 inch. If the end-play exceeds 0.018 inch, remove the gear and replace the thrust washer.

10. When the correct countershaft gear end-play has been obtained, install the countershaft arbor and remove the countershaft. Allow the countershaft gear to remain at the bottom of the case, leave the countershaft in the case enough to hold the thrust washer in place.

11. Coat the splines and machined surfaces on the mainshaft with transmission oil. Install the first-reverse synchronizer on the output shaft splines by hand. The end of the hub with the slots should face the front of the shaft. Use an arbor press to complete the hub installation. Install the retaining snap-ring in the groove farthest to the rear.

CAUTION
Do not attempt to drive the hub on the shaft with a hammer.

12. Coat the splines of the first-reverse hub with transmission oil and install the first reverse sleeve and gear halfway onto the hub, with the gear end of the sleeve facing the rear of the shaft. Align the marks made during disassembly.

13. Install the insert spring in the first-reverse hub. Make sure the spring bottoms in the hub and covers all three insert slots. Position the three "T" shaped inserts in the hub with the small ends in the hub slots and the large ends inside the hub. Push the inserts fully into the hub so they seat on the insert spring, slide the first-reverse sleeve and gear over the inserts until the inserts engage in the sleeve.

14. Coat the bore and the blocking ring surface of first gear with transmission oil and place blocking ring on the tapered surface of the gear.

15. Install the first gear on the output shaft. Rotate the gear until the notches in the blocking ring engage the inserts in the first-reverse synchronizer assembly. Install the tanged thrust washer, sharp end facing out, and retaining snap-ring on the mainshaft.

16. Coat the bore and blocking ring surface of the second gear with transmission oil. Place the second gear blocking ring on the tapered surface of second gear.

17. Install the second gear on the output shaft with the tapered surface of the gear facing the front of the mainshaft.

18. Install one insert spring into the second-third synchronizer hub. Be sure that the spring covers all three insert slots in the

hub. Align the second-third sleeve with the hub using the marks made during disassembly. Start the sleeve onto the hub.

19. Place the three inserts into the hub slots and on top of the insert spring. Push the sleeve fully onto the hub to engage the inserts in the sleeve. Install the remaining insert spring in the exact position as the first spring. The ends of both springs must cover the same slot in the hub and not be staggered.

NOTE: The inserts have a small lip on each end. When they are correctly installed, this lip will fit over the insert spring.

20. Install the second-third synchronizer assembly on the mainshaft. Rotate the second gear until the notches in the blocking ring engage the inserts in the second-third synchronizer assembly.

21. Install the retaining snap-ring on the mainshaft and measure the end-play between the snap-ring and the second-third synchronizer hub. The end-play should be 0.040–0.014 inch. If the end-play exceeds the limit, replace the thrust washer and all the snap-rings on the mainshaft assembly. Install the spacer on the rear of the mainshaft.

22. Install the mainshaft assembly in the case. Be sure that the first-reverse sleeve and gear is in the neutral (centered) position.

23. Press the rear bearing into the rear bearing adapter with an arbor press. Install the rear bearing retaining ring and the bearing adapter lockring.

24. Support the mainshaft assembly and install the rear bearing and adapter assembly in the case. Use a soft faced hammer to seat the adapter in the case.

25. Install the large fiber washer in the rear bearing adapter. Install the transfer drive gear, flat washer, and locknut. Tighten the locknut to 150 ft. lbs. torque.

26. Press the front bearing onto the clutch shaft. Install the bearing retaining snap-ring on the clutch shaft and the lockring into its groove.

27. Coat the bore of the clutch shaft assembly with petroleum jelly and install the (15) roller bearings in the clutch shaft bore.

------------ CAUTION ------------
Do not use chassis grease or a similar heavy grease in the clutch shaft bore. Heavy grease will plug the lubricant holes in the shaft and prevent proper lubrication of the roller bearings.

28. Coat the blocking ring surface of the clutch shaft with transmission oil. Position the blocking ring on the clutch shaft.

29. Support the mainshaft assembly and insert the clutch shaft through the front bearing bore in the case. Seat the mainshaft pilot in the clutch shaft roller bearings. Tap the bearings into place with a soft faced hammer.

30. Apply a thin film of sealer to the front bearing cap gasket and position the gasket on the case. Be sure the cutout in the gasket is aligned with the oil return hole in the case.

31. Remove the front bearing cap oil seal with a suitable tool. Install a new seal with a suitable driver.

32. Install the front bearing cap and tighten the bolts to 33 ft. lbs. Be sure that the marks on the cap and the transmission case are aligned and the oil return slot in the cap lines up with the oil return hole in the case.

33. Make a wire loop about 18–20 inches long and pass the wire under the countershaft gear assembly. The wire loop should raise and support the countershaft gear assembly when it is pulled upward.

34. Raise the countershaft gear with the wire. Align the bore in the countershaft gear with the front thrust washer and the countershaft. Start the countershaft into the gear with a soft faced hammer.

35. Align the roll pin hole in the countershaft with the roll pin holes in the case and complete the installation of the countershaft. Install the countershaft access plug in the rear of the case and seat with a soft faced hammer.

36. Install the countershaft roll pin in the case. Use a magnet or needle nose pliers to insert and start the pin in the case. Use a ½ inch punch to seat the pin. Install the transmission filler plug.

37. Shift the synchronizer sleeves through all gear ranges and check their operation. If the clutch shaft and mainshaft appear to bind in the neutral position, check for blocking rings sticking on the first or second gear tapers.

38. Install the transfer case on the transmission. Tighten the attaching bolts to 30 ft. lbs.

SHIFT CONTROL HOUSING

Disassembly

1. Remove the back-up light switch and the transmission controlled spark switch (TCS) if so equipped.

2. Remove the shift control housing cap, gasket, spring retainer, and the shift lever spring as an assembly.

3. Invert the housing and mount in a soft-jawed vise.

4. Move the second-third shift rail to the rear of the housing, rotate the shift fork toward the first-reverse rail until the roll pin is accessible. Drive the roll pin out of the fork and rail with a pin punch. Remove the shift fork and the roll pin.

NOTE: The roll pin hole in the shift fork is offset. Mark the position of the shift fork for assembly reference.

5. Remove the second-third shift rail using a brass drift or hammer. Catch the shift rail plug as the rail drives it out of the housing. Cover the shift and poppet ball holes in the cover to prevent the poppet ball from flying out. Mark the location of the shift rail for assembly reference.

TORQUE SPECIFICATIONS Tremec T-150

	ft. lbs.
Back-up light switch	15–20
Fill and drain plugs	10–20
Front bearing cap bolt	30–36
Shift control housing bolts	20–25
Transfer case drive gear locknut	150
Transfer case to transmission bolts	30
TCS switch	18

LUBRICANT CAPACITY

SAE 80–90 gear lube	3 pts.

6. Rotate the first-reverse shift fork away from the notch in the housing until the roll pin is accessible. Drive the roll pin out of the fork and rail using a pin punch. Remove the shift fork and roll pin.

NOTE: The roll pin hole in the shift fork is offset. Mark the position of the shift fork for assembly reference.

7. Remove the first-reverse shift rail using a brass drift or hammer. Catch the shift rail plug as the rail drives it out of the housing. Cover the shift and poppet ball holes in the cover to prevent the poppet ball from flying out. Mark the location of the shift rail for assembly reference.

8. Remove the poppet balls, springs, and the interlock plunger from the housing.

Assembly

1. Install the poppet springs and the detent plug in the housing.

2. Insert the first-reverse shift rail into the housing, and install the shift fork on the shift rail.

3. Install the poppet ball on the top of the spring in the first-reverse rail.

4. Using a punch or wooden dowel, push the poppet ball and spring downward into the housing bore and install the first-reverse shift rail.

5. Align the roll pin holes in the first-reverse shift fork and install the roll pin. Move the shift rail to the neutral (center) detent.

6. Insert the second-third shift rail into the housing and install the poppet ball on top of the spring in the shift rail bore.

7. Using a punch or wooden dowel, push the poppet ball and spring downward into the housing bore and install the second-third shift rail.

8. Align the roll pin holes in the second-third shift rail and the shift fork and install the roll pin. Move the shift rail to the neutral (center) position.

9. Install the shift rail plugs in the housing, and remove the shift control cover from the vise.

10. Install the shift lever, shift lever spring, spring retainer, gasket, and the shift control housing cap as an assembly. Tighten the cap securely.

11. Install the back-up light switch and the TCS switch if so equipped.

Warner T-14A, T-15A 3-Speed

The Warner T-14A, T-15A are fully synchronized three-speed transmissions having helical drive gears throughout. Lubricant capacity is 2½ pints.

TRANSMISSION UNIT

Disassembly

1. Separate transfer case from transmission by removing five capscrews.

2. Remove gearshift housing and disassembly by removing shift rails, poppet balls, springs, and shift forks.

3. Remove nut, flat washer, transfer case drive gear, adapter, and spacer.

4. Remove main drive gear bearing retainer gasket.

5. Remove main drive gear and mainshaft bearing snap-rings and bearings.

6. Remove main drive gear and mainshaft assembly.

NOTE: The T-15A transmission must be shifted into second gear to allow removal of the mainshaft and gear assembly.

7. On remote shift models, remove roll pins from lever shafts and housing. From inside case, slide levers and interlock assembly out. Remove forks and lever assemblies.

8. Remove lock plate from reverse idler shaft and countershaft.

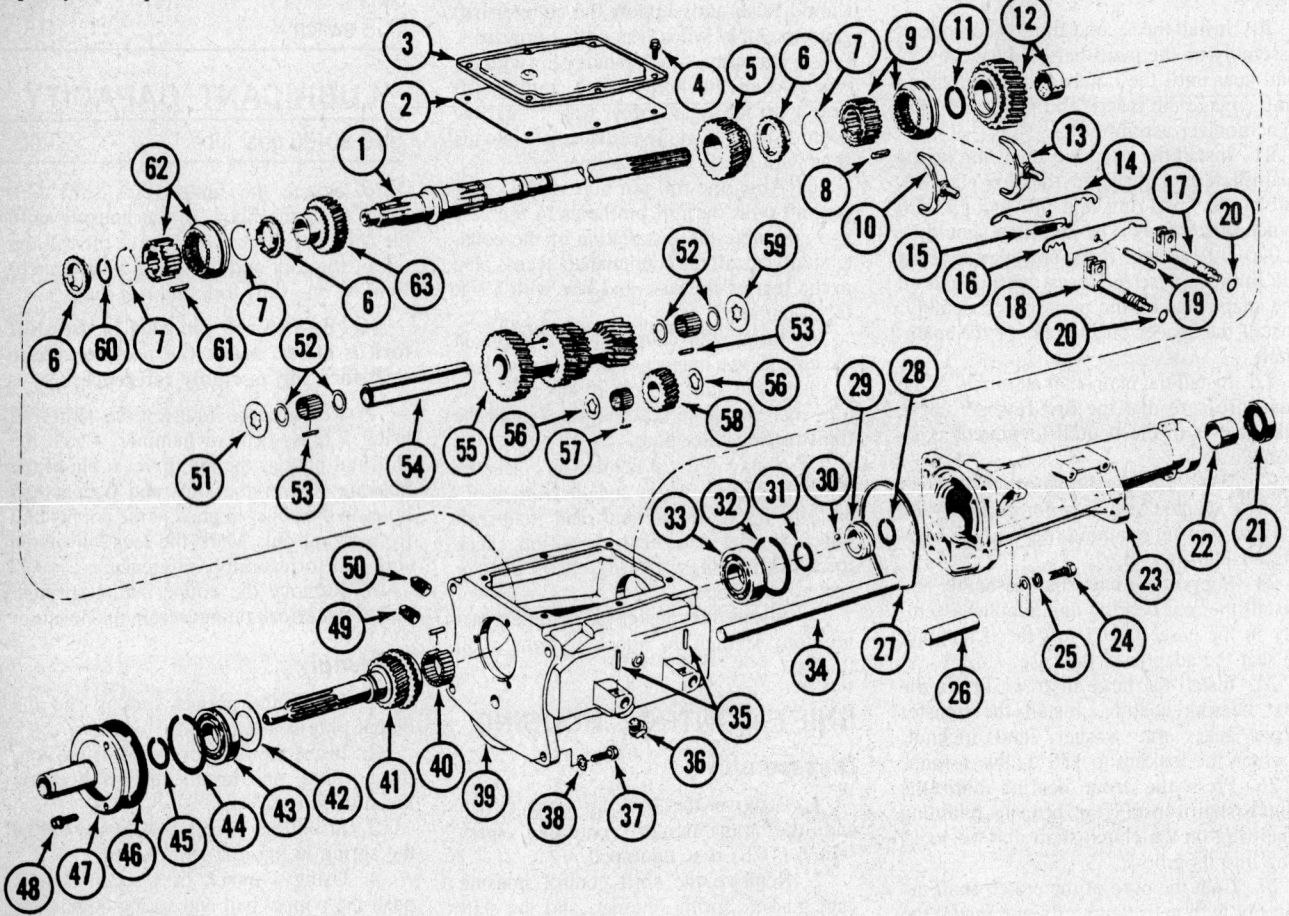

Warner T-14 or T-15

1. Spline shaft	14. Shifter interlock first and reverse lever	26. Idler gear shaft	38. Lock washer
2. Gasket		27. Rear bearing cap gasket	39. Case
3. Case cover	15. Speed finder interlock poppet spring	28. Speedometer drive gear ring	40. Spline shaft pilot bearing roller
4. Bolt	16. Shifter interlock second and third lever	29. Speedometer drive gear	41. Clutch shaft
5. First gear		30. Speedometer drive gear ball	42. Front ball bearing washer
6. Clutch friction ring set	17. Shifter fork first and reverse shaft		43. Front ball bearing
7. Shaft plate retaining spring	18. Shifter fork second and third shaft	31. Rear ball bearing lockring	44. Front ball bearing lockring
8. Clutch shaft first and reverse plate	19. Shifter fork interlock lever pivot pin	32. Rear ball bearing lockring	45. Front ball bearing snap-ring
9. First and reverse clutch assembly	20. Shifter fork shaft seal	33. Rear ball bearing	46. Gasket
10. Shifter second and high fork	21. Rear bearing cap oil seal	34. Countershaft	47. Front bearing cap
11. Clutch first and reverse gear snap-ring	22. Rear bearing cap bushing	35. Shifter fork retaining pin	48. Bolt
12. Reverse gear	23. Rear bearing cap	36. Solenoid control switch	49. Drain plug
13. Shifter first and reverse R fork	24. Bolt	37. Bolt	50. Filler pipe plug
	25. Lock washer		51. Front countershaft gear thrust washer
			52. Countershaft gear

bearing roller washer
53. Countershaft gear bearing roller
54. Countershaft gear roller bearing spacer
55. Countershaft gear
56. Reverse idler gear bearing roller washer
57. Reverse idler gear bearing roller
58. Reverse idler gear
59. Rear countershaft thrust washer (less lip)
60. Clutch second and third snap-ring
61. Clutch shaft second and third plate
62. Second and third clutch assembly
63. Second gear

9. Drive countershaft out to rear with dummy shaft. Remove countergear and two thrust washers. Remove spacer washers, rollers, and spacer from gear.

10. Drive reverse idler shaft out to rear. Remove gear, washers, and roller bearings.

11. Remove clutch hub snap-ring and second-third synchronizer assembly.

12. Remove second and reverse gears.

13. Remove clutch hub snap-ring and low synchronizer assembly.

14. Remove low gear.

SYNCHRONIZER

Disassembly and Assembly

1. Remove springs. Low synchronizer has only one spring; second-third, two.

2. Mark sleeve and hub before separating.

3. Remove hub.

4. Remove three shifter plates from hub.

5. Inspect all parts for wear.

6. Assembly in reverse order of disassembly. On second-third unit, make sure that spring openings are 120 degrees from each other, with spring tension opposed.

NOTE: If a synchronized assembly is replaced on a floor shift unit, the shift fork operating the synchronizer being replaced must have the letter A just under the shaft hole on the side opposite the pin.

Inspection

1. Wash all parts in solvent.

2. Air dry but do not spin bearings with air pressure.

3. Check case bearing and shaft bores for cracks or burrs.

4. Check all gears and bronze blocking rings for cracks, and chipped, worn, or cracked teeth. If any gears are replaced, also replace the meshing gears.

5. Check all bearings and bushings for wear or damage.

6. Check that synchronizer sleeves slide freely on clutch hubs.

TRANSMISSION UNIT

Assembly

1. Place reverse idler gear with dummy shaft, roller bearing, and thrust washers in case. Install reverse idler shaft.

2. Assemble countershaft center spacer, four bearing spacers, and bearing rollers in countershaft gear.

3. Install large countergear thrust washer in front of case. Position small thrust washer on countergear hub with lip facing groove in case. Holding countergear in position, push in countershaft from rear.

4. Install lock plate in slots of reverse idler shaft and countershaft.

5. Install to mainshaft:
   a. Low gear
   b. Bronze blocking ring

c. Low synchronizer assembly
d. Largest snap-ring that fits in groove
e. Second gear
f. Bronze blocking ring
g. Second-third synchronizer assembly
h. Largest snap-ring that fits in groove
i. Reverse gear

6. Install mainshaft assembly through top of case.

7. Install bronze blocking ring to second-third synchronizer assembly.

8. On remote shift units, install shifter shafts, with new O-rings, into case.

NOTE: T-15 interlock levers are marked as to location. T-14 levers have no marks and are interchangeab.

9. Depress interlock lever while installing shift fork into shift lever and synchronizer clutch sleeve. Install poppet spring. Install tapered pins securing shafts in case.

10. Install main drive gear roller bearings.

11. Install main drive gear and oil slinger into case with cutaway portion of gear toward countergear. Install main drive gear to mainshaft.

12. Using bearing installer and thrust yoke tool, install main drive gear and mainshaft bearings and drive into position. The thrust yoke is needed to prevent damage to the synchronizer clutch.

13. Install main drive gear and mainshaft bearing snap-rings. The mainshaft bearing snap-ring is 0.010 thicker than main drive gear bearing snap-ring.

14. Install mainshaft rear bearing adapter, spacer, transfer case drive gear, flat washer, and nut. Torque nut to 130–170 ft. lbs.

15. Install main drive gear bearing retainer (with new oil seal) and gasket. Align oil drain holes in retainer and gasket.

16. Install case cover gasket. On remote shift units, install cover gasket with vent holes to left side.

17. Position gear train and floor-shift assembly in neutral. Insert shifter forks into clutch sleeves and torque to 8–15 ft. lbs.

Warner T-18, T-18A and T-19 Series 4-Speed

The Warner T-18, T-18A and T-19 trans-

missions have four forward speeds and one reverse. A power take-off opening is provided on certain transmissions, depending upon the models and applications and can be located on either the right or left sides of the case. The T-18 and T-18A transmissions are synchronized in second, third and fourth speeds only, while the T-19 transmission is synchronized in all forward gears. The disassembly and assembly remains basically the same for the transmission models.

TRANSMISSION UNIT

Disassembly

1. After draining the transmission and removing the parking brake drum (or shoe assembly), lock the transmission in two gears and remove the U-joint flange, oil seal, speedometer driven gear and bearing assembly. Lubricant capacity is 6½ pints.

2. Remove the output shaft bearing retainer and the speedometer drive gear and spacer.

3. Remove the output shaft bearing snap-ring, and remove the bearing.

4. Remove the countershaft and idler shaft retainer and the power take-off cover.

5. After removing the input shaft bearing retainer, remove the snap-rings from the bearing and the shaft.

6. Remove the input shaft bearing and oil baffle.

7. Drive out the countershaft (from front). Keep the dummy shaft in contact with the countershaft to avoid dropping any rollers.

8. After removing the input shaft and the synchronizer blocking ring, pull the idler shaft.

9. Remove the reverse gear shifter arm, the output shaft assembly, the idler gear, and the cluster gear. When removing the cluster, do not lose any of the rollers.

SUB-ASSEMBLIES

Disassemblies

OUTPUT SHAFT

1. Remove the third- and high-speed synchronizer hub snap-ring from the output shaft, and slide the third- and high-speed synchronizer assembly and the third-speed gear off the shaft. Remove the synchronizer sleeve and the inserts from the hub. Before removing the two snap-rings from the ends

TORQUE SPECIFICATIONS

Location	N.m.	ft. lbs.
Front bearing retainer to case	14–20	10–15
Cover to case	14–24	10–18
Control levers to lever shafts	20–34	15–25
Rear bearing retainer to case	31–37	23–27
Companion flange to mainshaft	122–163	90–120
Control lever housing bolt	14–20	10–15

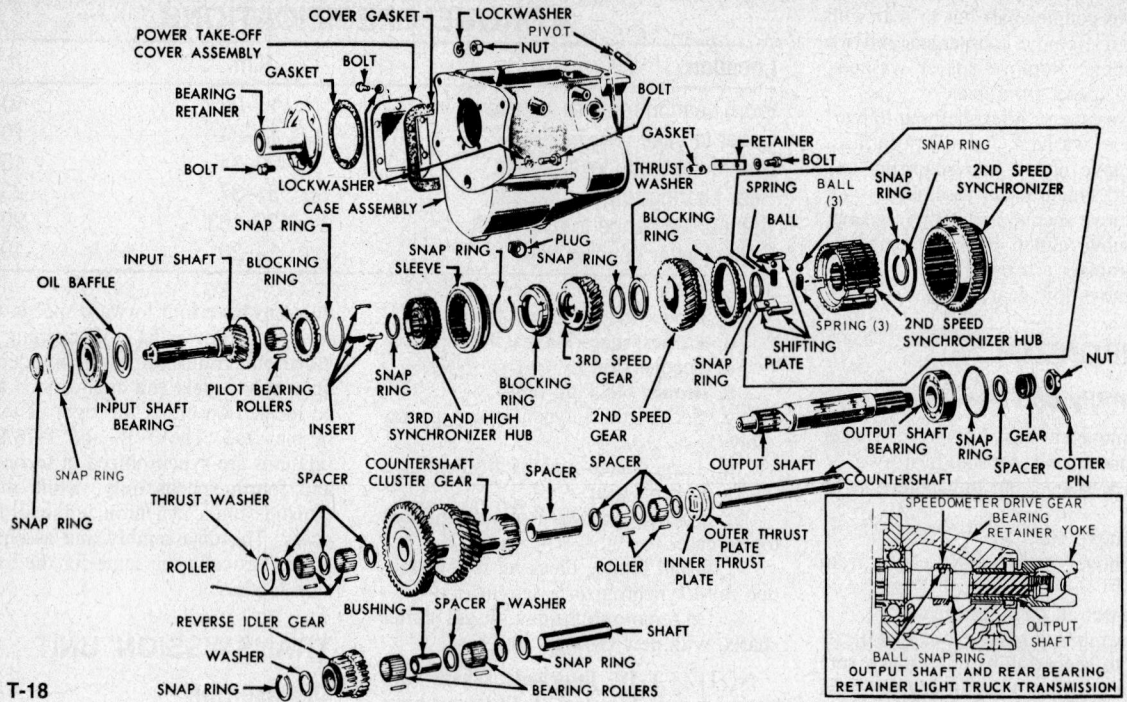

POWER TAKE-OFF COVER ASSEMBLY — COVER GASKET — LOCKWASHER — PIVOT — NUT — BEARING RETAINER — GASKET — BOLT — BOLT — BOLT — CASE ASSEMBLY — GASKET — RETAINER — BOLT — SNAP RING — 2ND SPEED SYNCHRONIZER — SPRING — BALL (3) — SNAP RING — THRUST WASHER — BLOCKING RING — BALL — LOCKWASHER — OIL BAFFLE — INPUT SHAFT — BLOCKING RING — SNAP RING — SLEEVE — PLUG — SNAP RING — 3RD SPEED GEAR — SHIFTING PLATE — SPRING (3) — 2ND SPEED SYNCHRONIZER HUB — INPUT SHAFT BEARING — PILOT BEARING ROLLERS — SNAP RING — INSERT — BLOCKING RING — 3RD AND HIGH SYNCHRONIZER HUB — 2ND SPEED GEAR — SNAP RING — NUT — SNAP RING — THRUST WASHER — SPACER — COUNTERSHAFT CLUSTER GEAR — SPACER — SPACER — OUTPUT SHAFT — OUTPUT SHAFT BEARING — SNAP RING — GEAR — COTTER PIN — SPACER — ROLLER — ROLLER — OUTER THRUST PLATE — INNER THRUST PLATE — COUNTERSHAFT — SNAP RING — REVERSE IDLER GEAR — BUSHING — SPACER — WASHER — SHAFT — WASHER — SNAP RING — SNAP RING — BEARING ROLLERS

SPEEDOMETER DRIVE GEAR — BEARING RETAINER YOKE — BALL SNAP RING — OUTPUT SHAFT
OUTPUT SHAFT AND REAR BEARING RETAINER LIGHT TRUCK TRANSMISSION

Warner T-18

of the hub, check the end play of the second-speed gear (0.005–0.024 inch).

2. Remove the second-speed synchronizer snap-ring. Slide the second-speed synchronizer hub gear off the hub. Do not lose any of the balls, springs, or plates. Pull the hub off the shaft, and remove the second-speed synchronizer from the second-speed gear. Remove the snap-ring from the rear of the second-speed gear, and remove the gear, spacer, roller bearings, and thrust washer from the output shaft. Remove the remaining snap-ring from the shaft.

CLUSTER GEAR

Remove the dummy shaft, pilot bearing rollers, bearing spacers, and center spacer from the cluster gear.

REVERSE IDLER GEAR

Rotate the reverse idler gear on the shaft, and if it turns freely and smoothly, disassembly of the unit is not necessary. If any roughness is noticed, disassemble the unit.

GEAR SHIFT HOUSING

1. Remove the housing cap and lever. Be sure all shafts are in neutral before disassembly.

2. Tap the shifter shafts out of the housing while holding one hand over the holes in the housing to prevent loss of the springs and balls. Remove the two shaft lock plungers from the housing.

SUB-ASSEMBLIES
Assembly

CLUSTER GEAR ASSEMBLY

Slide the long bearing spacer into the cluster gear bore, and insert the dummy shaft in the spacer. Hold the cluster gear in a vertical position, and install one of the bearing spacers. Position the 22 pilot bearing rollers in the cluster gear bore. Place a spacer on the rollers, and install 22 more rollers and another spacer. Hold a large thrust washer against the end of cluster gear and turn the assembly over. Install the rollers and spacers in the other end of the gear.

REVERSE IDLER GEAR ASSEMBLY

1. Install a snap-ring in one end of the idler gear, and set the gear on end, with the snap-ring at the bottom.

2. Position a thrust washer in the gear on top of the snap-ring. Install the bushing on top of the washer, insert the 37 bearing rollers, and then a spacer followed by 37 more rollers. Place the remaining thrust washer on the rollers, and install the other snap-ring.

OUTPUT SHAFT ASSEMBLY

1. Install the second speed gear thrust washer and snap-ring on the output shaft. Hold the shaft vertically, and slide on the second speed gear. Insert the bearing rollers in the second-speed gear, and slide the spacer into the gear. (The T-18 model does not contain second speed gear rollers or spacer). Install the snap-ring on the output shaft at the rear of the second-speed gear. Position the blocking ring on the second-speed gear. Do not invert the shaft because the bearing rollers will slide out of the gear.

2. Press the second-speed synchronizer hub onto the shaft, and install the snap-ring. Position the shaft vertically in a soft-jawed vise. Position the springs and plates in the second-speed synchronizer hub, and place the hub gear on the hub.

3. With the T-19 model, press the first and second speed synchronizer onto the shaft and install the snap-ring. Install the first speed gear and snap-ring on the shaft and press on the reverse gear. For the T-19, ignore steps 2 and 4.

4. Hold the gear above the hub spring and ball holes, and position one ball at a time in the hub, and slide the hub gear downward to hold the ball in place. Push the plate upward, and insert a small block to hold the plate in position, thereby holding the ball in the hub. Follow these procedures for the remaining balls.

5. Install the third speed gear and synchronizer blocking ring on the shaft.

6. Install the snap-rings at both ends of the third and high-speed synchronizer hub. Stagger the openings of the snap-rings so that they are not aligned. Place the inserts in the synchronizer sleeve, and position the sleeve on the hub.

7. Slide the synchronizer assembly onto the output shaft. The slots in the blocking ring must be in line with the synchronizer inserts. Install the snap-ring at the front of the synchronizer assembly.

GEAR SHIFT HOUSING

1. Place the spring on the reverse gear shifter shaft gate plunger, and install the spring and plunger in the reverse gate. Press the plunger through the gate, and fasten it with the clip. Place the spring and ball in the reverse gate poppet hole. Compress the spring and install the cotter pin.

2. Place the spring and ball in the reverse shifter shaft hole in the gear shift housing. Press down on the ball, and position the reverse shifter shaft so that the reverse shifter arm notch does not slide over the ball. Insert the shaft part way into the

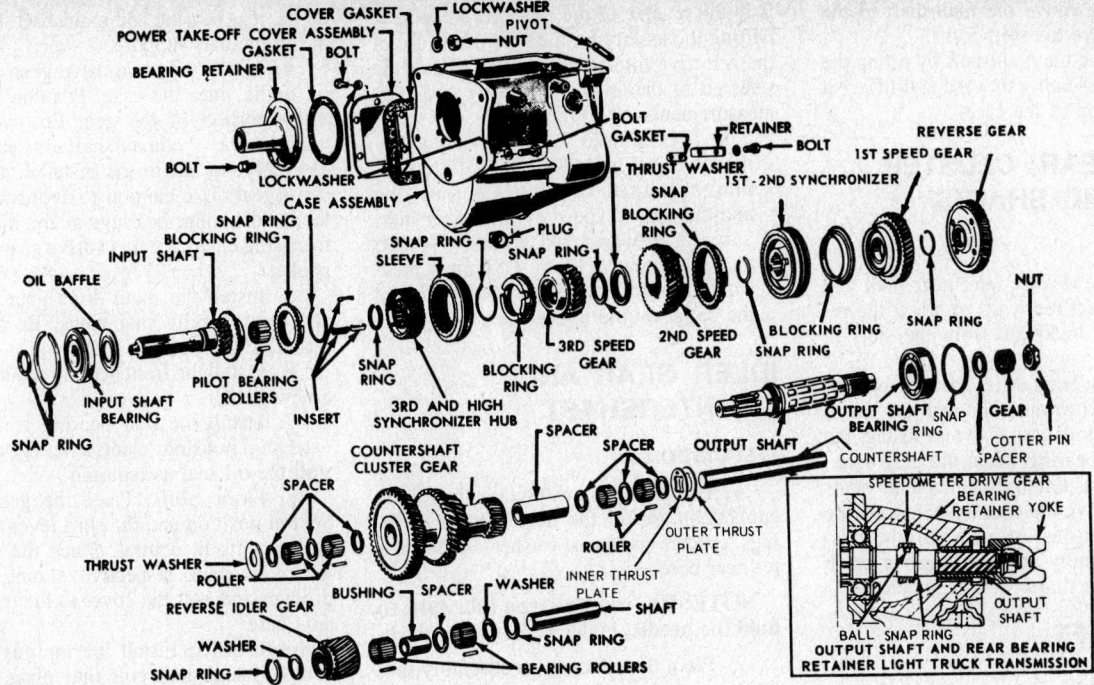

Warner T-19

housing.

3. Slide the reverse gate onto the shaft, and drive the shaft into the housing until the ball snaps into the groove of the shaft. Install the lock screw lock wire to the gate.

4. Insert the two interlocking plungers in the pockets between the shifter shaft holes. Place the spring and ball in the low and second shifter shaft hole. Press down on the ball, and insert the shifter shaft part way into the housing.

5. Slide the low and second shifter shaft gate onto the shaft, and install the corresponding shifter fork on the shaft so that the offset of the fork is toward the rear of the housing. Push the shaft all the way into the housing until the ball engages the shaft groove. Install the lock screw and wire that fastens the fork to the shaft. Install the third and high shifter shaft in the same manner. Check the interlocking system. Install new expansion plugs in the shaft bores.

TRANSMISSION UNIT

Assembly

1. Coat all parts, especially the bearings, with transmission lubricant to prevent scoring during initial operation.

2. Position the cluster gear assembly in the case. Do not lose any rollers.

3. Place the idler gear assembly in the case, and install the idler shaft. Position the slot in the rear of the shaft so that it can engage the retainer. Install the reverse shifter arm.

4. Drive out the cluster gear dummy shaft by installing the countershaft from the

rear. Position the slot in the rear of the shaft so that it can engage the retainer. Use thrust washers as required to get 0.006 to 0.020 inch cluster gear end play. Install the countershaft and idler shaft retainer.

5. Position the input shaft pilot rollers and the oil baffle, so that the baffle will not rub the bearing race. Install the input shaft and the blocking ring in the case.

6. Install the output shaft assembly in the case, and use a special tool to prevent jamming the blocking ring when the input shaft bearing is installed.

7. Drive the input shaft bearing onto the shaft. Install the thickest select-fit snapring that will fit on the bearing. Install the input shaft snap-ring.

8. Install the output shaft bearing.

9. Install the input shaft bearing without a gasket, and tighten the bolts only enough to bottom the retainer on the bearing snap-ring. Measure the clearance between the retainer and the case, and select a gasket (or gaskets) that will seal in the oil and prevent end play between the retainer and the snap-ring. Torque the bolts to specification.

10. Position the speedometer drive gear and spacer, and install a new output shaft bearing retainer seal.

11. Install the output shaft bearing retainer. Torque the bolts to specification, and install safety wire.

12. Install the brake shoe (or drum), and torque the bolts to specification. Install the U-joint flange. Lock the transmission in two gears and torque the nut to specification.

13. Install the power take-off cover plates with new gaskets. Fill the transmission according to specifications.

Warner T-15-D 3-Speed

The Warner T-15-D transmission has three synchronized forward speeds and one reverse. The transmission has either a remote controlled shift lever on the steering column or a top cover shift lever assembly. This transmission can be used with or without a transfer case in the drive line with the use of different extension housing or bearing retainer designs.

MAINSHAFT

Removal

1. Drain the transmission of its lubricant and remove either the top cover or the shift lever assembly from the top of the transmission. Remove the front bearing retainer.

2. Remove the front main drive gear bearing snap-rings and remove the bearing from the shaft and transmission case with the aid of a bearing puller or its equivalent.

3. Remove the main drive gear from the transmission case by having the cutaway portion of the gear teeth positioned downward towards the cluster gear. As the gear is removed from the mainshaft, do not lose the needle roller bearing from the bearing pocket.

4. Remove the rear extension housing or the bearing retainer from the rear of the transmission case.

5. Remove the mainshaft rear bearing snap-rings and remove the bearing from the mainshaft and transmission case with a bearing puller or its equivalent.

6. *Column shift:* Position the gears in

second speed, move the mainshaft to the left and remove the shift forks.

7. Remove the mainshaft by tilting the front of the assembly upward and lifting it through the top of the case.

IDLER GEAR, CLUSTER GEAR AND SHAFTS

Removal

1. Tap the reverse idler gear shaft and the countershaft rearward to allow the removal of the lockplate from the slots in both shafts.

2. Using a brass drift, drive the reverse idler gear shaft towards the rear and out of the transmission case. Avoid losing the needle roller bearings from the gear bore.

3. Using a dummy countershaft or its equivalent, drive the countershaft from the rear of the transmission case. Lift the cluster gear assembly from the transmission case. Mark the thrust washer locations.

MAINSHAFT

Disassembly

1. Remove the second/third speed synchronizer snap-ring from the front of the mainshaft. Remove the synchronizer from the mainshaft, after matchmarking the sleeve and hub.

2. Remove the second speed gear from the mainshaft.

3. Remove the reverse gear from the rear of the mainshaft. Remove the rear synchronizer (first/reverse) hub snap-ring.

4. Remove the first/reverse synchronizer unit from the rear of the mainshaft.

NOTE: Only one blocker ring is used with the first/reverse synchronizer assembly as the reverse speed gear is not a synchromesh unit.

5. Remove the first speed gear from the mainshaft.

Cleaning and Inspection

1. Clean the transmission case with solvent and inspect for cracks, worn bearing bores or other damages.

2. Clean and inspect all gears and bronze blocking rings for cracks, chipped or cracked teeth or excessive wear on the teeth. Should a gear require replacement, the meshing gear should be replaced also.

3. Inspect all bearings and bushings for wear or damage. The thrust washers should be renewed upon transmission assembly, if grooved or distorted.

4. Inspect the synchronizer clutch sleeves for abnormal wear and ease of operation.

5. Lubricate all internal transmission components before installation.

MAINSHAFT

Assembly

1. The assembly of the mainshaft gears

is in the reverse of the removal procedure. During the assembly, the snap-rings are of the selective thickness type and should be selected to obtain the following end play measurements.

    a. Second/third speed synchronizer—0.004 to 0.020 inch (0.10 to 0.51 mm) measured between the snap-ring and the second speed synchronizer hub.

    b. First/reverse synchronizer—0.005 to 0.020 inch (0.13 to 0.51 mm) measured between the first speed gear and the collar on the mainshaft.

IDLER GEAR AND COUNTERSHAFT

Installation

1. Using the dummy countershaft or its equivalent, install the needle roller bearings, spacers and thrust washers in the cluster gear bore.

NOTE: Use vaseline type lubricant to hold the needle, roller bearings in place.

2. Place the cluster gear assembly into the transmission case and install the countershaft from the rear to the front of the case, through the cluster gear, forcing the dummy shaft out the front shaft bore of the case.

3. During the installation of the countershaft, be sure to maintain alignment of the spacers and thrust washers.

4. Install the needle roller bearings into the bore of the reverse idler gear and hold in place with a vaseline type lubricant.

5. Position the thrust washers on the gear and place the assembly between the transmission case web and the rear inner surface of the case.

6. Carefully drive the reverse idler gear shaft through the case bore and into the reverse idler gear assembly. Be sure to keep the thrust washers aligned to avoid damage to them.

7. With both the countershaft and the reverse idler gear shaft in Place, install the lock plate with the tabs on the top side, into the slots of each shaft. Drive the shafts forward until the lock plate is flush against the case surface.

MAINSHAFT

Installation

1. Tilt the mainshaft assembly and install the rear of the shaft assembly into the case. Lower the mainshaft assembly into the case. If the transmission is controlled by a steering column shift lever, move the mainshaft and install the shifting forks into place on the clutch sleeves and shift mechanism.

2. Using a mainshaft support or equivalent, block and support the front of the mainshaft. Install the rear mainshaft bearing with a bearing installer tool or equivalent.

3. Install the large and small snap-rings

on the rear bearing and mainshaft. Remove the front shaft support.

4. Install the main drive gear with the oil baffle, into the case. Position the cutaway portion of the gear downward towards the countershaft/cluster gear assembly, to aid in the installation of the drive gear. Use caution to avoid dropping the needle roller bearings as the mainshaft front stub enters the main drive gear bearing pocket.

5. Install the main drive gear bearing and the retaining snap-rings. Be sure the oil baffle is in place.

6. Install the front bearing retainer with a new gasket.

7. Install the rear bearing retainer or extension housing, using a new gasket. Install the oil seal as required.

8. **Floor Shift:** Place the gears in a neutral position and the shift lever housing components in neutral. Place the shifting levers in their respective sliding sleeve grooves and bolt the cover to the transmission case.

Column Shift: Install the top cover with a new gasket and bolt into place on the transmission.

9. Fill the transmission with lubricant to its proper level (3 pints) and move the gear shifting mechanism by hand to be assured of proper gear selection before installation of the transmission into the vehicle.

Warner SR-4 4-Speed

The Warner SR-4 transmission is a four speed, constant mesh unit, providing synchromesh engagement in all forward gears.

TRANSMISSION UNIT

Disassembly

1. Separate the transmission from the transfer case, if attached.

2. Drain the lubricant from the transmission by removing the lower adapter housing bolt.

3. If the shift lever housing has not been removed, place the shift lever in the neutral position, remove the retaining bolts and lift the shift lever housing from the transmission.

4. Remove the flanged nut holding the offset lever to the shift rail. Remove the offset lever.

5. Remove the adapter housing retaining bolts and the housing from the transmission case.

6. Remove the shift control housing retaining bolts and remove the cover and gasket. Mark the location of the two dowel bolts to reinstall in their original position.

7. Remove the spring clip holding the reverse lever to the reverse lever pivot bolt. Remove the reverse lever pivot bolt, allowing the removal of the reverse lever and

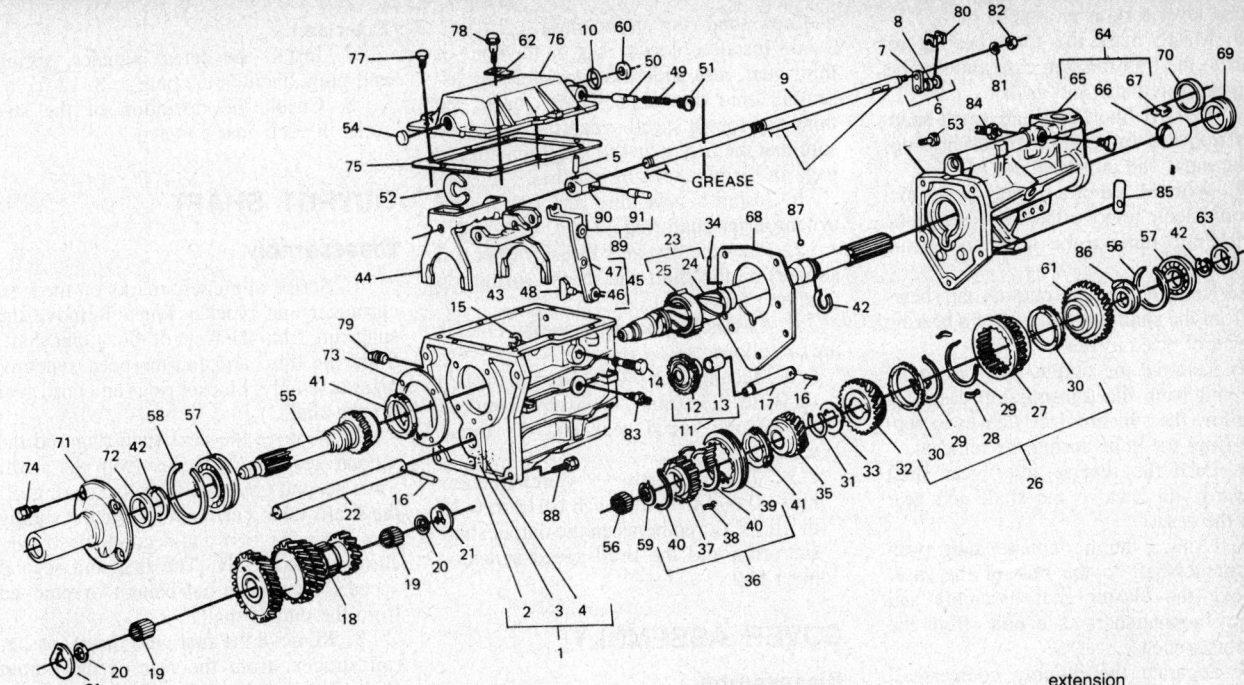

GREASE

Warner SR-4

1. Case assembly—
   transmission
2. Case—transmission
3. Magnet—transmission
   case chip
4. Nut spring $^9/_{64}$
5. Pin—$^3/_{16}$ diameter ×
   $^{13}/_{16}$ rolled spring
6. Lever assembly—
   transmission gearshift
   shaft offset
7. Lever transmission
   gearshift shaft offset
8. Pin—transmission
   gearshift shaft offset
   lever
9. Shaft—transmission
   shifter
10. Seal—O-ring
11. Gear and bush
    assembly—
    transmission reverse
    idler sliding
12. Gear—transmission
    reverse idler sliding
13. Bushing—
    transmission reverse
    idler gear
14. Pin—transmission
    reverse gear selector
    fork pivot
15. Ring—$^7/_{16}$ retaining
16. Pin—$^1/_4$ x 1 spring
17. Shaft—transmission
    reverse idler gear
18. Gear—transmission
    countershaft
19. Roller—transmission
    countershaft bearing
20. Washer—208/.918 flat
21. Washer—
    transmission
    countershaft gear
    thrust
22. Countershaft—
    transmission
23. Shaft assembly—
    transmission output
24. Shaft—transmission

output
25. Hub—transmission
    synchronizer 1st and
    2nd gear cluster
26. Shaft and gear
    assembly—
    transmission output
27. Gear—transmission
    reverse sliding
28. Insert—transmission
    synchronizer hub
29. Spring—transmission
    synchronizer retaining
30. Ring—transmission
    synchronizer blocking
31. Ring—transmission
    2nd speed gear
    retaining snap
32. Gear—transmission
    2nd speed
33. Washer—
    transmission 2nd
    speed gear thrust
34. Pin—$^1/_8$ × $^1/_4$ rolled
    spring
35. Gear—transmission
    3rd speed
36. Synchronizer
    assembly—3rd and
    4th speed
37. Hub—transmission
    synchronizer
38. Insert—transmission
    synchronizer hub
39. Sleeve—transmission
    3rd and 4th gear
    clutch hub
40. Spring—transmission
    synchronizer retaining
41. Ring—transmission
    synchronizer blocking
42. Ring—transmission
    m/d gear bearing
    shaft snap
43. Fork—transmission
    1st & 2nd gear shift
44. Fork—transmission
    3rd & 4th gear shift
45. Lever assembly—
    transmission reverse
    gear shaft relay

46. Retaining—
    transmission reverse
    gear shaft relay lever
47. Lever—transmission
    reverse gear shaft
    relay
48. Fork—transmission
    reverse gear shift
49. Spring—transmission
    shifter interlock
50. Plunger—
    transmission
    meshlock
51. Screw—m12 x 10
    round head flat
52. Plate—transmission
    gear selector interlock
53. Screw & washer
    assembly—m10 x 30
    hex head
54. Plug—$^3/_4$ diameter
    welch type
55. Shaft—transmission
    input
56. Roller—transmission
    mainshaft bearing
57. Bearing assembly—
    transmission m/d gear
    ball
58. Ring—m/d gear
    bearing retaining snap
59. Ring—1.00 retaining
60. Seal—transmission
    shift shaft
61. Gear—transmission
    1st speed
62. Clip—spark control
    switch wire retaining
63. Gear—speedometer
    drive
64. Extension assembly—
    transmission
65. Extension—
    transmission
66. Bushing—
    transmission
    extension
67. Stop—transmission
    gear shift lever
    reverse
68. Gasket—transmission

extension
69. Seal assembly—
    transmission
    extension oil
70. Plug—transmission
    extension
71. Retainer—
    transmission input
    shaft gear bearing
72. Seal assembly—
    transmission input
    shaft oil
73. Gasket—transmission
    input shaft bearing
    retainer
74. Bolt—M8 x 20 hex
    head-lock
75. Gasket—transmission
    case cover
76. Cover—transmission
    case
77. Screw—m6 x 20 hex
    head
78. Bolt—m6 x 32 hex
    washer HD shoulder
79. Plug—$^1/_2$-14 pipe
    (filler)
80. Bushing—
    transmission gear
    shift damper
81. Washer—spring lock
82. Nut—hexagon
83. Switch assembly—
    back-up lamp
84. Switch assembly—
    transmission seat belt
    warning sensor
85. Tag—transmission
    service identification
86. Washer—
    transmission 1st gear
    thrust
87. Ball—.25 diameter
88. Screw and
    lockwasher
    assembly—m12 x 40
89. Arm assembly—
    transmission control
    selector
90. Arm—transmission
    control selector
91. Pin—transmission
    gear shift

reverse lever fork as an assembly.

8. Match mark the front bearing retainer to the transmission case and remove the bearing retainer and gasket.

9. Remove the large and small snaprings from the front and rear ball bearings on the input and output shafts.

10. With the aid of a bearing puller tool or equivalent, remove the input shaft ball bearing and remove the input shaft from the case.

11. Remove the rear (output shaft) bearing from the shaft with the aid of a bearing puller tool or equivalent.

12. Remove the output shaft assembly as a unit from the transmission case. Do not allow the synchronizer sleeves to separate from the hubs during the removal.

13. Push the reverse idler gear shaft rearward and remove the shaft and gear from the case.

14. Using a dummy countershaft, push the countershaft to the rear of the case. Remove the cluster gear assembly and dummy countershaft as a unit, from the transmission case.

15. Separate the dummy countershaft and remove the 50 needle roller bearings, spacers and thrust washers from the cluster gear.

NOTE: The cluster gear front thrust washer is of a plastic material, while the rear thrust washer is metal.

COUNTERSHAFT GEAR BEARING

Replacement

1. Remove the dummy shaft, bearing retainer washers and needle bearings from the countershaft gear. Clean and inspect the parts.

2. Coat the bore at each end of the countershaft gear with grease to retain the needle bearings.

3. While holding the dummy shaft in the gear, install the needle bearings and retainer washers in each end of the gear.

4. Slide first gear off the output shaft, and remove the first speed blocker ring. Take care not to lose the sliding gear from the first and second speed synchronizer assembly.

5. Clean and inspect all parts.

Assembly

1. Place a blocker ring on the cone of first gear, and slide the gear and ring assembly onto the output shaft. Make sure that the inserts in the synchronizer engage in the blocker ring notches.

2. Install the spring pin retaining first gear to the output shaft.

3. Install a blocker ring on the cone of second gear, and slide the gear and ring assembly onto the output shaft. Make sure that the inserts in the synchronizer engage in the blocker ring notches.

4. Install the second gear thrust washer

and new snap-ring on the shaft.

5. Install a blocker ring on the cone of third gear, and slide the gear and ring assembly onto the output shaft. Install the third and fourth speed synchronizer. Make sure that the inserts in the synchronizer engage in the blocker ring notches.

6. Install a new third and fourth gear synchronizer snap-ring.

7. Place the first gear thrust washer (oil slinger) on the shaft and on the spring pin retaining first gear.

8. Assembly end play measurements are as follows:

    a. Second gear—0.004 to 0.014 inch (0.10 to 0.35 mm), measured between the second speed gear and the thrust washer.

    b. Third/fourth synchronizer hub—0.004 to 0.014 inch (0.10 to 0.35 mm), measured between the output shaft snap-ring and the third speed synchronizer hub.

COVER ASSEMBLY

Disassembly

1. Remove the detent screw, spring and plunger.

2. Pull the shifter shaft rod rearward, rotating it counterclockwise.

3. Remove the spring pin retaining the manual selector and interlock to the shifter shaft.

4. Remove the shifter shaft from the cover taking care not to damage the seal.

5. Remove the manual selector and interlock plate.

6. Remove the first and second speed shifter fork. Remove the third and fourth speed shifter fork.

7. Clean and inspect all parts. Replace the shifter shaft seal and welch plug, if damaged.

Assembly

1. Assemble the two plastic inserts to each shift fork; the two projections on the inside of the inserts fit into the blind holes in the ends of the shift forks. Insert the selector arm plates into the shift forks.

2. Install the third and fourth speed shifter fork into the cover.

3. Install the first and second speed shifter fork into the cover. Lubricate the shifter shaft bore with grease.

4. Install the manual selector arm through the interlock plate, and position the two pieces into the cover, with the wide leg of the interlock plate towards the inside of the transmission case.

5. Align the shifter shaft in the cover, and insert the shaft through the shifter forks and manual selector. Coat the shifter shaft with a light coating of grease. Make sure the detent grooves face the plunger side of the cover.

6. Align the pin holes in the manual selector arm and shifter shaft. Install the spring pin flush with the surface of the se-

lector arm.

7. Install the detent plunger, spring, and plug. Tighten the plug to 8–12 ft. lbs.

8. Check the operation of the shift forks in each gear position.

OUTPUT SHAFT

Disassembly

1. Scribe alignment marks on the synchronizer and blocker rings. Remove the snap-ring from the front of the output shaft. Slide the third and fourth speed synchronizer assembly, blocker rings and third gear off the shaft.

2. Remove the next snap-ring and the second gear thrust washer from the shaft. Slide second gear and the blocker ring off the shaft, taking care not to lose the sliding gear from the first and second speed synchronizer assembly. The first and second speed synchronizer hub cannot be removed from the output shaft.

3. Remove the first gear thrust washer (oil slinger) from the rear of the output shaft. Remove the spring pin retaining first gear onto the shaft.

SYNCHRONIZER

Disassembly and Assembly

1. Scribe reference marks on the hub and sleeve of the synchronizer.

2. Push the sleeve from the hub of each synchronizer.

3. Separate the inserts and insert springs from the hubs. Do not mix the parts between the first/second speed synchronizer and the third/fourth speed synchronizer. Clean and inspect all parts.

NOTE: The first/second speed synchronizer hub is not to be removed from the shaft. They have been assembled and machined as a matched unit during manufacturing to assure concentricity.

4. To assemble, position the sleeve on the hub, aligning the previously marked reference points.

5. Position the three inserts per hub and install the insert springs, being sure that the bent end of the springs are seated in one of the inserts. The springs on each side of the hubs must face in opposite directions and the openings be 180 degrees apart.

TRANSMISSION UNIT

Assembly

1. Coat the countershaft thrust washers with a vaseline type lubricant and position the plastic type washer at the front of the case and the metal washer at the rear of the case.

2. With the 50 needle roller bearings in place in the cluster gear and the dummy countershaft in place, install the countershaft/cluster gear assembly into the case.

TORQUE SPECIFICATIONS①

	ft. lbs.	N.m.
Backup lamp switch	10	14
Adapter housing bolt	23	31
Detent plug (in housing)	10	14
Fill plug	20	27
Front bearing cap bolt	13	18
Offset lever nut	10	14
Reverse lever pivot bolt	20	27
Shift control housing bolt	10	14
Transmission-to-clutch housing bolt	55	75
Universal joint clamp strap bolt	14	19

① All torque values given in foot-pounds and newton-meters with dry fits unless otherwise specified.

--- CAUTION ---

Be sure the thrust washers are not displaced during the gear installation.

3. Align the cluster gear bore with the case bores and install the countershaft from the rear to the front of the case, pushing the dummy countershaft from the gear and case.

4. Position the reverse idler gear with the shift lever groove facing to the front and install the shaft from the rear of the case.

5. Being careful not to disturb the synchronizers, install the output shaft assembly into the transmission case. Install the fourth gear blocking ring in the third speed synchronizer sleeve, engaging the inserts on the hub with the grooves of the blocking ring.

6. Install the 15 roller bearings in the input shaft pocket and retain with a vaseline type lubricant. Install the input shaft into the case and engage the shaft in the third/fourth synchronizer, while the stub of the output shaft is installed in the pocket of the input shaft.

--- CAUTION ---

Do not jam or drop the 15 roller bearings during the input shaft installation.

7. Install the input shaft front bearing. Block the first speed gear against the rear of the case, align the bearing with the bearing bore in the case and drive the bearing completely onto the input shaft and into the transmission case.

NOTE: To identify the front and rear bearings, look for a notch in the front bearing race. The rear bearing has no notch.

8. Install the front bearing retaining and locating snap-rings.

9. Install the front bearing cap oil seal and install the cap (bearing retainer) with a new gasket to the transmission case. Install the retaining bolts.

10. Install the first speed thrust washer on the output shaft with the oil grooves facing the first speed gear. Install the rear bearing onto the output shaft and into the case bearing bore.

NOTE: Be sure the first gear thrust washer is engaged on the first gear roll pin before installing the rear bearing.

11. Install the retaining and locating snap-rings on the rear bearing and output shaft.

12. Position the reverse lever in the case, on the pivot bolt and install the retaining clip. Tighten the pivot bolt. Be sure the reverse lever fork is engaged in the reverse idler gear.

13. Rotate the input shaft and output shaft gears and blocking rings to insure freeness of movement. Blocking ring to gear clutch tooth face should have a clearance of 0.030 inch (0.001 mm).

14. Place the reverse lever in the neutral position and install the cover assembly on the transmission case. Place the two dowel bolts in their original positions and install the remaining retaining bolts.

15. Install a new oil seal in the adapter housing and, using a new gasket, install the adapter housing to the transmission case.

16. Install 3 pints of lubricant into the transmission.

17. Install the offset lever and retain with the flanged nut.

18. Depending upon the installation of the transmission into a vehicle, the shift lever housing can be installed and the transmission attached to the transfer case.

Warner T-176 4-Speed

The Warner T-176 transmission is a constant mesh unit, synchronized in all forward gears and with one reverse gear.

TRANSMISSION UNIT

Disassembly

1. Remove the transfer case from the rear of the transmission.

2. Remove the shift control housing. Mark the location of the two dowel bolts in the housing.

3. Drain the lubricant from the transmission, if not previously done. Remove the rear adapter housing.

4. With a dummy countershaft tool, remove the countershaft from the transmission, front to rear. Allow the cluster gear to lay on the bottom of the case.

5. Remove the rear bearing locating and retaining snap-rings. Remove the rear bearing with a bearing remover tool or equivalent.

6. Match mark the front bearing retainer to the case for easier installation, remove the retaining bolts and the retainer.

7. Remove the locating and retaining snap-rings from the front bearing. Remove the front bearing and the input shaft using a puller tool or equivalent.

8. Remove the mainshaft pilot bearing rollers from the input shaft pocket. Engage the third speed synchronizer.

9. Remove the mainshaft assembly by lifting the front of the shaft upward and out.

10. Remove the cluster gear assembly from the case. Locate and remove any thrust washers and needle roller bearings from the case.

11. Tap the reverse idler gear shaft from the case and remove the reverse idler gear and thrust washers.

12. Separate the reverse idler gear from the sliding gear. Do not lose the needle roller bearings.

MAINSHAFT

Disassembly

1. Remove the third/fourth speed synchronizer snap-ring from the front of the mainshaft.

2. Remove the third/fourth synchronizer from the mainshaft and slide the hub from the sleeve. Remove the inserts and springs. Inspect the blocking rings for wear and damage.

3. Remove the third speed gear and the second speed gear snap-ring. Remove the second speed gear and the blocking ring. Remove the tabbed thrust washer.

4. Remove the snap-ring from the first/second synchronizer hub. Remove the hub and the reverse gear with sleeve as an assembly. Match mark the hub and sleeve for assembly references. Remove the inserts and springs as the sleeve is removed.

5. Remove the first speed gear thrust washer from the rear of the shaft and remove the first speed gear and the blocking ring.

Inspection of Transmission Components

CASE

1. Cracks in the bores, sides, bosses or at bolt holes.

2. Stripped bolt hole threads.

3. Nicks, burrs, roughness on gasket or shaft bore surfaces.

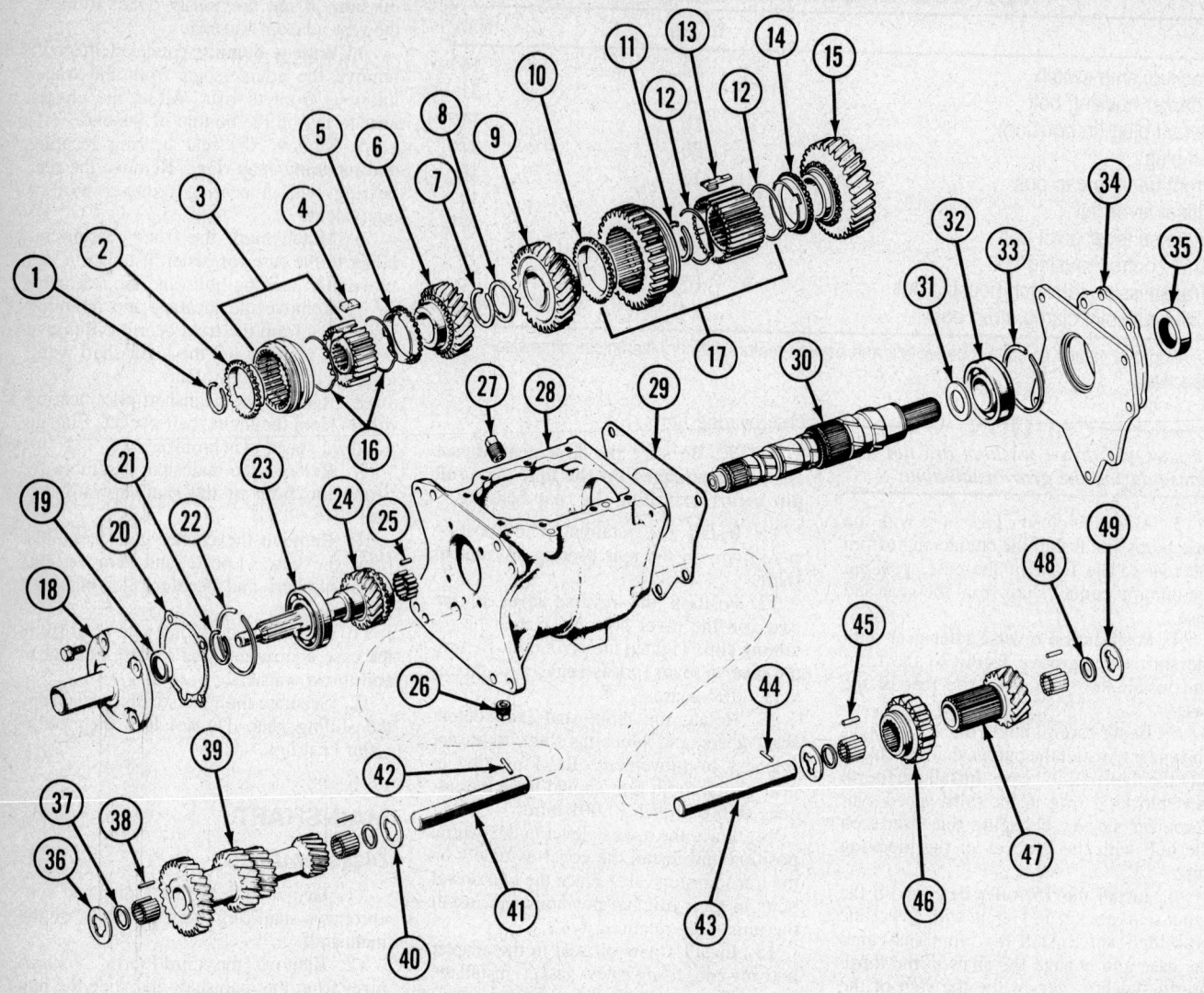

Warner T-176

1. Third-fourth gear snap-ring
2. Fourth gear synchronizer ring
3. Third-fourth gear clutch assembly
4. Third-fourth gear plate
5. Third gear synchronizer ring
6. Third speed gear
7. Second gear snap-ring
8. Second gear thrust washer
9. Second speed gear
10. Second gear synchronizer ring
11. Main shaft snap-ring
12. First-second synchronizer spring
13. Low-second plate
14. First gear
15. First gear
16. Third-fourth synchronizer spring
17. First-second gear clutch assembly
18. Front bearing cap
19. Oil seal
20. Gasket
21. Snap-ring
22. Lock ring
23. Front ball bearing
24. Clutch shaft
25. Roller bearing
26. Drain plug
27. Fill plug
28. Case
29. Gasket
30. Spline shaft
31. First gear thrust washer
32. Rear ball bearing
33. Snap-ring
34. Adapter plate
35. Adapter seal
36. Front countershaft gear thrust washer
37. Roller washer
38. Rear roller bearing
39. Countershaft gear
40. Rear countershaft thrust washer
41. Countershaft
42. Pin
43. Idler gear shaft
44. Pin
45. Idler gear roller bearing
46. Reverse idler sliding gear
47. Reverse idler gear
48. Idler gear washer
49. Idler gear thrust washer

GEARS, SHAFTS AND SYNCHRONIZER UNITS

1. Chipped, broken or worn gear teeth.
2. Damaged splines.
3. Worn or broken teeth or blocking rings.
4. Bent or broken synchronizer inserts or springs.
5. Damaged needle bearings or operating surfaces.
6. Wear or galling of the mainshaft, countershaft, clutch shaft or idler gear shaft.
7. Worn or broken thrust washers.
8. Bent, distorted, broken or weak snap-rings.
9. Rough, galled, worn or broken front or rear bearing.

MAINSHAFT

Assembly

1. Assemble the first/second synchronizer hub, inserts and springs. Install the clutch sleeve. Be sure to position the spring ends 180 degrees apart.
2. Install the assembled first/second speed synchronizer hub and the reverse gear with sleeve, on the mainshaft. Secure with a new snap-ring.
3. Install the first speed gear and blocking ring on the rear of the mainshaft and install the first gear thrust washer.
4. Install a new tabbed thrust washer on the mainshaft with the tab seated in the mainshaft tab bore.
5. Install the second speed gear and the blocking ring on the mainshaft and secure with a new snap-ring.
6. Install the third speed gear and blocking ring on the mainshaft.
7. Assemble the third/fourth speed synchronizer hub, inserts, and springs. Be sure the spring ends are 180 degrees apart.
8. Install the assembled third/fourth speed synchronizer on the mainshaft and secure with a new snap-ring.
9. The measured end play between the snap-ring and the third/fourth speed synchronizer should be 0.004 to 0.014 inch (0.10 to 0.35 mm).

TRANSMISSION UNIT

Assembly

1. Load the reverse idler gear with the 44 needle roller bearings and a bearing retainer on each end of the gear. Install the sliding gear on the reverse idler gear. Install lubricated thrust washers into the case.
2. Install the reverse idler assembly into the case and install the reverse idler gear shaft.
3. Engage the thrust washer locating tabs in the case locating slots.
4. Seat the reverse idler gear shaft roll pin into the counterbore in the case. The

reverse idler gear end play should be 0.004 to 0.018 inch (0.10 to 0.45 mm).
5. Install the 42 needle roller bearings in the cluster gear, using the dummy countershaft as a bearing holder. Use of a vaseline type lubricant is suggested to hold the bearings in place.
6. Position the lubricated thrust washers in place on the inside of the transmission case. Position the thrust washer tabs in the tab slots of the case.
7. Insert the countershaft into the rear case bore, just far enough to hold the rear thrust washer. Lower the cluster gear assembly into the case and align the gear bore with the case bore. Push the countershaft into the cluster gear, displacing the dummy countershaft out the front case bore hole. Do not completely remove the dummy countershaft.
8. Measure the cluster gear end play which should be 0.004 to 0.018 inch (0.10 to 0.45 mm). Correct as required and reinstall the dummy countershaft into the cluster gear, pushing the countershaft from the gear.
9. Allow the cluster gear to remain at the bottom of the case until the input and mainshaft has been installed to provide the necessary assembly clearance.
10. With the synchronizers in the neutral position, install the mainshaft assembly into the case.
11. Install the front bearing part way on the input shaft and install the 15 roller bearing in the shaft pocket.

NOTE: Do not use a heavy grease to hold the bearings in the pocket as the grease can plug the lubrication holes. Use only a vaseline type lubricant.

12. Position the blocking ring on the third/fourth synchronizer. Support the

mainshaft assembly and insert the input shaft through the front bearing bore of the case. Seat the mainshaft pilot hub into the bearing pocket of the input shaft and tap the front bearing and input shaft into the case, using a soft faced hammer.
13. When the bearing is fully seated, install the bearing retainer housing, but not the snap-rings at this time.
14. Install the rear bearing on the mainshaft and the bearing bore of the case. It will be necessary to seat the rear bearing further than the locating snap-ring would allow, so do not install the locating snap-ring until after the retaining snap-ring is installed.
15. Remove the front bearing retainer housing and fully seat the front bearing on the input shaft. Install the retaining and locating snap-rings. Install a new oil seal in the retainer housing and install on the transmission case.
16. Install the locating snap-ring on the rear bearing, if not previously done.
17. To install the cluster gear and countershaft, turn the transmission case on end with the input shaft down. Align the cluster gear bore and thrust washers with the case bores. Tap the countershaft into place and displace the dummy countershaft out the front of the case. Do not allow the dummy shaft to drop to the floor.
18. Level the transmission case and install the extension adapter housing with a new gasket.
19. Shift the synchronizer sleeves by hand to insure correct operation. Install 3.5 pints of lubricant into the case and install a new gasket on the shift housing flange. With the gears in the neutral position and the shift lever forks in their neutral position, install the shift lever housing in place on the transmission case.

TORQUE SPECIFICATIONS①

	ft. lbs.	N.m.
Backup lamp switch	15	20
Drain and fill plugs	15	20
Front bearing cap bolts	13	18
Shift housing-to-transmission case bolts	13	18
Support plate bolts	18	24

①All torque values given in foot-pounds and newton-meters with dry fits unless otherwise specified.

T-176 SPECIFICATIONS
Lubricant Capacity and End-Play Tolerances

End-Play Tolerances:
Countershaft Gear to Case	0.004 to 0.018 inch (0.10 to 0.45 mm)
Reverse Idler Gear to Case	0.004 to 0.018 inch (0.10 to 0.45 mm)
Mainshaft Gear Train	0.004 to 0.018 inch (0.10 to 0.45 mm)
Lubricant Capacity	3.5 pints (1.7 liters)
Lubricant Type	SAE 85W-90, APJ GL5

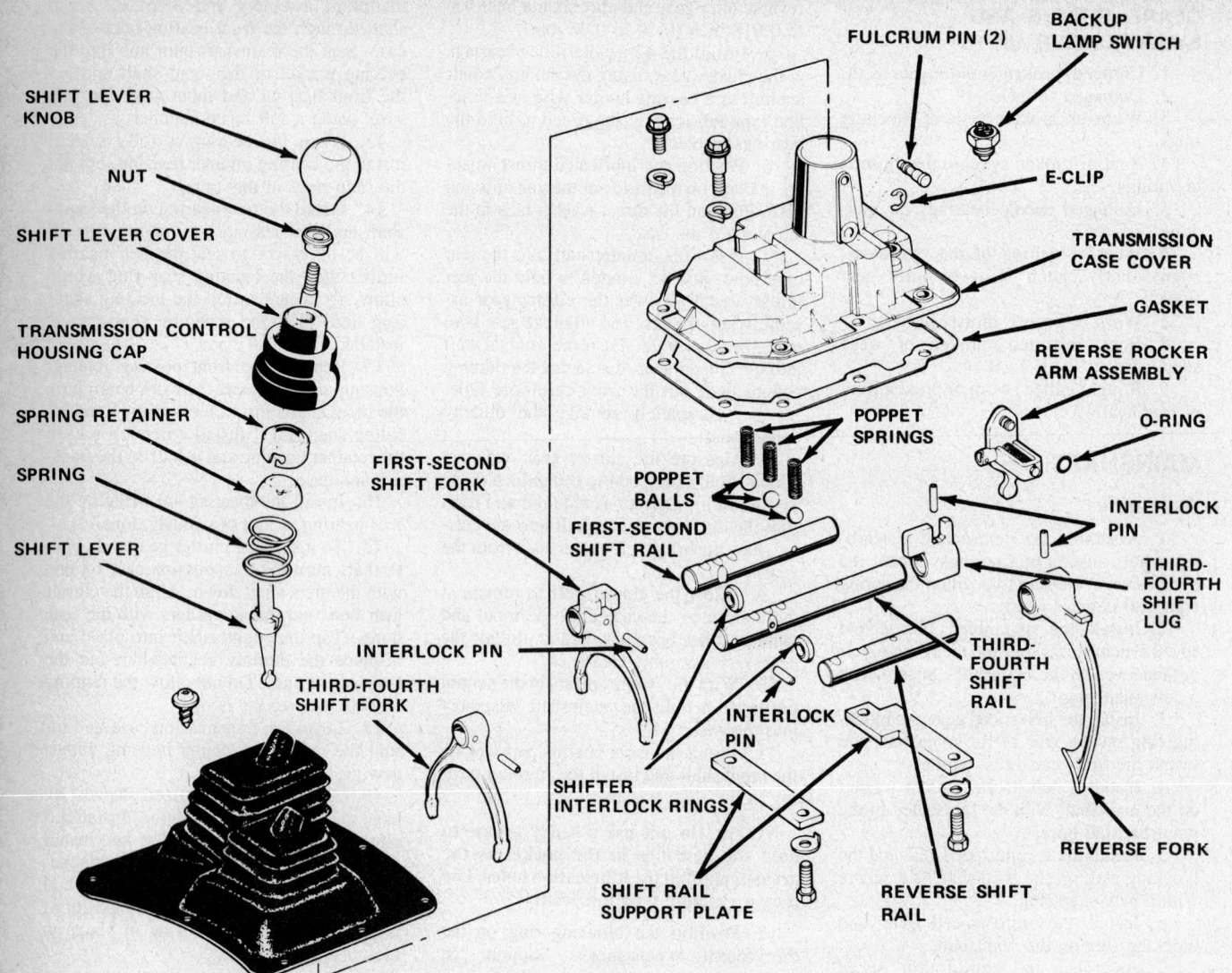

SHIFT LEVER KNOB

NUT

SHIFT LEVER COVER

TRANSMISSION CONTROL HOUSING CAP

SPRING RETAINER

SPRING

SHIFT LEVER

FULCRUM PIN (2)

BACKUP LAMP SWITCH

E-CLIP

TRANSMISSION CASE COVER

GASKET

REVERSE ROCKER ARM ASSEMBLY

O-RING

INTERLOCK PIN

THIRD-FOURTH SHIFT LUG

POPPET SPRINGS

POPPET BALLS

FIRST-SECOND SHIFT FORK

FIRST-SECOND SHIFT RAIL

INTERLOCK PIN

THIRD-FOURTH SHIFT FORK

INTERLOCK PIN

THIRD-FOURTH SHIFT RAIL

SHIFTER INTERLOCK RINGS

SHIFT RAIL SUPPORT PLATE

REVERSE SHIFT RAIL

REVERSE FORK

T-176 Shift Control Housing

Transfer Cases

INDEX

TRANSFER CASE APPLICATION CHART

	Chev./GMC	Dodge/Plymouth	Ford	International	Jeep
Dana 20			X	X	X
Dana 21			X		
Dana 24			X		
Dana 300				X	X
International TC-143				X	
New Process 201		X			
New Process 202				X	
New Process 203	X	X	X		
New Process 205	X		X	X	
New Process 208	X	X	X		X
New Process 219					X
Rockwell T223		X	X	X	
Spicer 20				X	X
Warner Quadra-Trac					X
Warner 1345			X		

TRANSFER CASE

Trouble Analysis

SLIPS OUT OF GEAR (HIGH–LOW)

1. Shifting poppet spring weak.
2. Bearing broken or worn.
3. Shifting fork bent.
4. Improper control rod adjustment.

SLIPS OUT OF FRONT WHEEL DRIVE

1. Shifting poppet spring weak or broken.
2. Bearing worn or broken.
3. Excessive shaft end-play.
4. Shifting fork bent.

HARD SHIFTING

1. Lack of lubricant.
2. Shift lever binding on shaft.
3. Shifting poppet ball scored.
4. Shifting fork bent.
5. Low tire pressure.

BACKLASH

1. Companion yoke loose.
2. Transfer case loose on mounts.
3. Internal parts excessively worn.

NOISY

1. Low lubricant level.
2. Bearings improperly adjusted or excessively worn.
3. Gears worn or damaged.
4. Improper alignment of driveshafts or U-joints.

OIL LEAKAGE

1. Excessive amount of lubricant in case.
2. Vent clogged.
3. Gaskets or seals leaking.
4. Bearings loose or damaged.
5. Driveshaft yoke mating surfaces scored.

OVERHEATING

1. Excessive or insufficient amount of lubricant.
2. Bearing adjustment too tight.

CLEANING AND INSPECTION

CLEANING

During overhaul, all components of the transfer case (except bearing assemblies) should be thoroughly cleaned with solvent and dried with air pressure prior to inspection and reassembly.

1. Clean the bearing assemblies as follows.

NOTE: Proper cleaning of bearings is of utmost importance. Bearings should always be cleaned separately from other parts.

a. Soak all bearing assemblies in clean solvent or fuel oil. Bearings should never be cleaned in a hot solution tank.

b. Slush bearings in solvent until all old lubricant is loosened. Hold races so that bearings will not rotate; then clean bearings with a soft bristled brush until all dirt has been removed. Remove loose particles of dirt by tapping bearing flat against a block of wood.

c. Rinse bearings in clean solvent; then blow bearings dry with air pressure.

CAUTION
Do not spin bearings while drying.

d. After drying, rotate each bearing slowly while examining balls or rollers for roughness, damage, or excessive wear. Replace all bearings that are not in first class condition.

NOTE: After cleaning and inspecting bearings lubricate generously with recommended lubricant, then wrap each bearing in clean paper until ready for reassembly.

2. Remove all portions of old gaskets from parts, using a stiff brush or scraper.

INSPECTION

1. Inspect all parts for discoloration or warpage.
2. Examine all gears and splines for chipped, worn, broken or nicked teeth. Small nicks or burrs may be removed with a fine abrasive stone.
3. Inspect the breather assembly to make sure that it is open and not damaged.
4. Check all threaded parts for damaged, stripped, or crossed threads.
5. Replace all gaskets, oil seals and snap-rings.
6. Inspect housings, retainers and covers for cracks or other damage. Replace the damaged parts.
7. Inspect keys and keyways for condition and fit.
8. Inspect shift forks for wear, distortion or any other damage.
9. Check detent ball springs for free length, compressed length, distortion or collapsed coils.
10. Check bearing fit on their respective

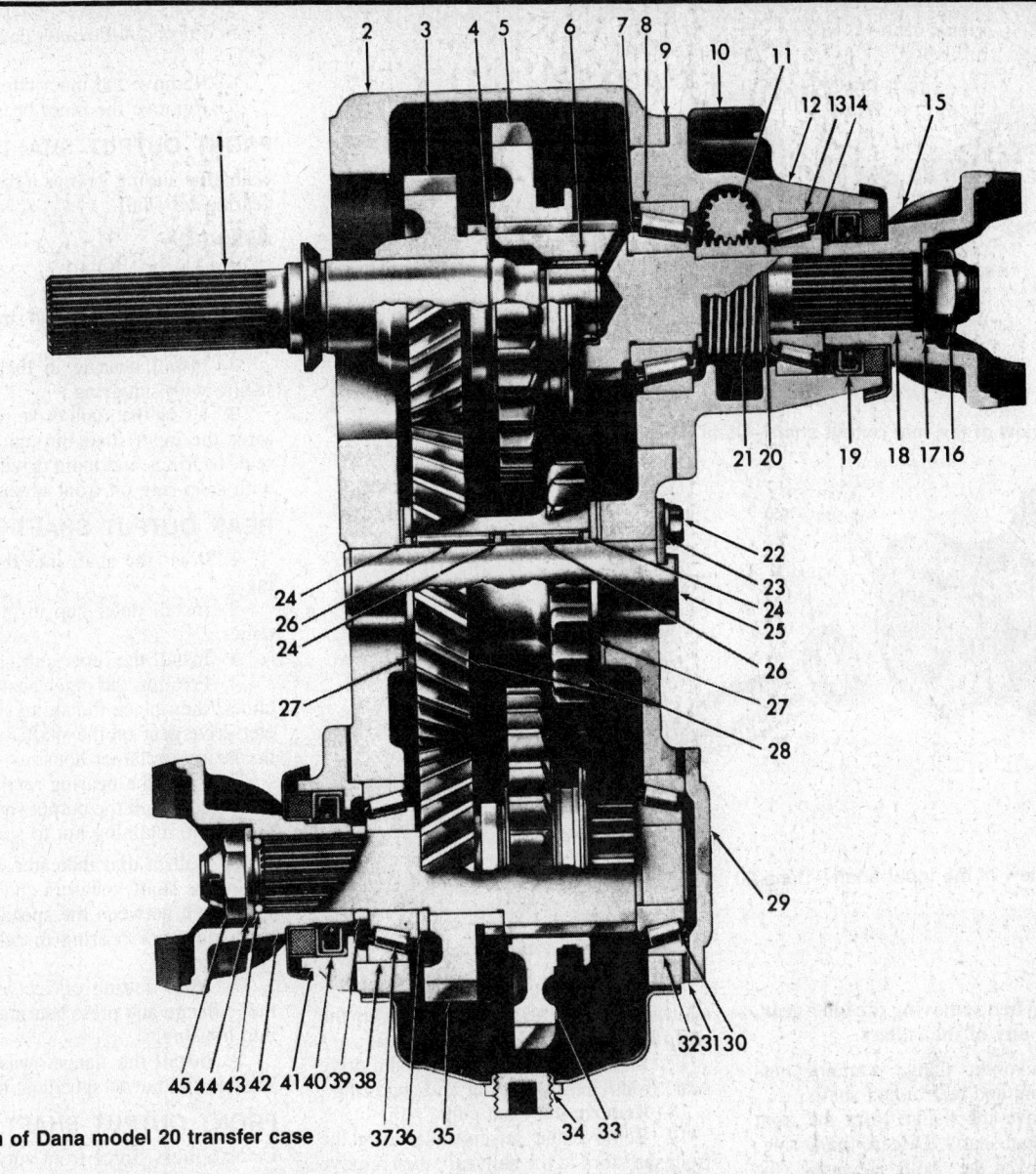

Cross section of Dana model 20 transfer case

1. Input shaft
2. Transfer case
3. Input gear
4. Snap-ring
5. Sliding clutch gear
6. Rear input shaft needle bearing
7. Rear output shaft front bearing
8. Rear output shaft front bearing cup
9. Rear output shaft housing gasket
10. Rear output shaft housing breather
11. Speedometer driven gear
12. Rear output shaft housing
13. Rear output shaft rear bearing cup
14. Rear output shaft rear bearing
15. Rear output shaft yoke
16. Rear output shaft locknut
17. Washer
18. Rear output shaft
19. Rear output shaft seal
20. Shims
21. Speedometer drive gear
22. Intermediate shaft lock plate bolt
23. Intermediate shaft lock plate
24. Intermediate shaft bearing spacer
25. Intermediate shaft
26. Intermediate shaft needle bearings
27. Intermediate shaft
28. Intermediate gear
29. Front output shaft rear cover
30. Front output shaft rear bearing
31. Front output shaft rear cover shim pack
32. Front output shaft
33. Front output shaft sliding clutch gear
34. Drain plug
35. Front output shaft drive gear
36. Spacer
37. Front output shaft front bearing
38. Front output shaft front bearing cup
39. Spacer
40. Front output shaft seal
41. Front output shaft bearing
42. Front output shaft yoke
43. Rubber O-ring
44. Washer
45. Front output shaft locknut

Also labeled: tanged thrust washer, rear bearing cup.

shafts and in their bores or cups. Inspect bearings, shafts and cups for wear.

NOTE: If either bearings or cups are worn or damaged, it is advisable to replace both parts.

11. Inspect all bearing rollers or balls for pitting or galling.

12. Examine detent balls for corrosion or brinneling. If shift bar detents show wear, replace them.

13. Replace all worn or damaged parts. When assembling the transfer case, coat all moving parts with recommended lubricant.

Dana Model 20

The Dana Model 20 is a two-speed gearbox that controls the power from the transmission to the front and rear driving axles. Positions of the transfer case are: four-wheel-drive low (4L), neutral (N), two-wheel-drive high (2H) and four-wheel-drive high (4H).

Disassembly
TRANSFER CASE

1. Clean any dirt from the transfer case and remove the bottom cover plate.

2. Remove the retaining plug, flat washer, detent spring and ball which engages the front drive shift rail detent rod. Then, remove plug from front drive detent rod access hole.

3. Remove the retaining plug, detent spring and ball which engages the rear drive shift rail detent rod.

4. Remove the idler shaft lockplate.

5. Using a hammer and soft drift, drive the idler shaft rearward and out of the case; then lift out the thrust washers and idler gear.

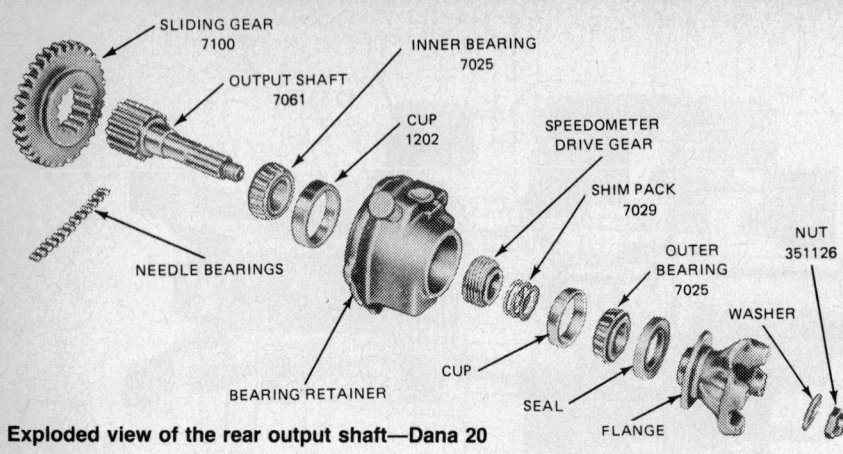

Exploded view of the rear output shaft—Dana 20

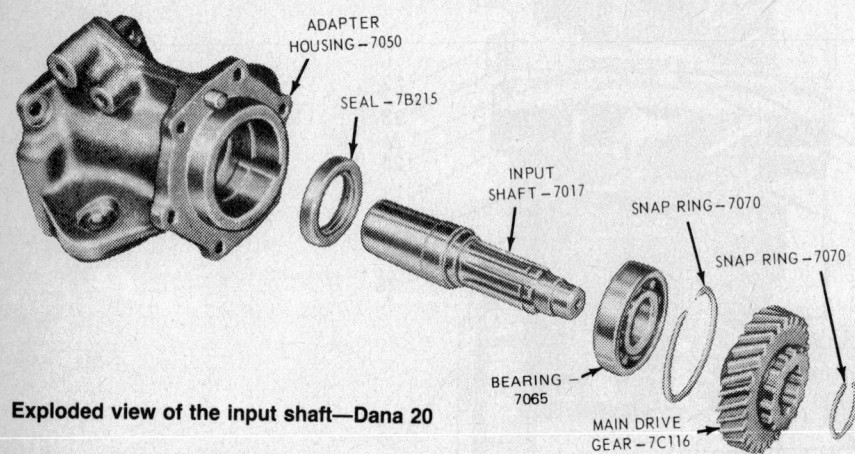

Exploded view of the input shaft—Dana 20

NOTE: When removing the idler gear, do not lose any of the rollers.

6. Remove the flange retaining nuts from the front and rear output shafts.

7. Remove the flange from the front and rear output shafts. Discard the O-ring.

8. Remove the bolts securing the adapter housing to the case; then remove the adapter as an assembly.

9. Remove the bolts which attach the rear output shaft bearing retainer to the case; then remove the retainer and output shaft as an assembly.

NOTE: Be sure not to lose any of the rollers.

10. Disconnect the shift rail link from the two shift rails.

11. Lift out the rear output shaft sliding gear.

12. Remove the setscrew securing the rear fork to the shift rail; then remove the rear drive shift rail and fork.

13. Remove the front output shaft rear cover and shims. Fasten the shims together.

14. Remove the front output shaft bearing retainer and gasket.

15. Tap the threaded end of the front output shaft; then remove the rear cup.

16. Angle the front output shaft front bearing away from the main drive gear to allow removal of the snap-ring; then tap the shaft and rear bearing out of the case.

17. Lift out the sliding gear, main drive gear, front bearing, spacer and snap-ring.

18. Remove the front cup.

19. Remove the setscrew securing the front shift fork to the shift rail; then remove the rail and fork.

20. Remove the detent rods.

21. Remove shift rail oil seal.

INPUT SHAFT

1. Remove the snap-ring from the front of the shaft.

2. Place the adapter housing and input shaft on a press and force the shaft out of the main drive gear and housing.

3. Remove the bearing retaining snap-ring; then remove bearing.

4. Remove the seal in the adapter housing.

REAR OUTPUT SHAFT

1. Remove needle bearings from bore of shaft.

2. Remove speedometer driven gear.

3. Place bearing retainer and shaft assembly in a press; then force shaft out of retainer.

4. Lift off speedometer drive gear and shims. Tag shims for reassembly.

5. Press out the outer cup, bearing and seal.

6. Remove the inner cup.

7. Remove the inner bearing.

FRONT OUTPUT SHAFT

Using the sliding gear as a base, press rear bearing off shaft.

Assembly

INPUT SHAFT

1. Install a new seal in the adapter housing.

2. Install bearing in the housing and secure with snap-ring.

3. Using the main drive gear as a base, force the input shaft through the housing, seal, bearings and main drive gear. Secure with snap-ring on front of shaft.

REAR OUTPUT SHAFT

1. Press the shaft into the inner bearing.

2. Install outer cup in the bearing retainer.

3. Install the inner cup.

4. Position the outer bearing in the retainer; then place the shims and speedometer drive gear on the shaft. Install shaft in the bearing retainer housing.

5. Place the bearing retainer and shaft in a vise. Install the output shaft flange and torque the retaining nut to specifications.

6. With a dial indicator on the flange end of the shaft, measure end-play. Adjust shim pack between the speedometer drive gear and outer bearing to achieve correct clearance.

7. After setting correct end-play, remove flange and press bearing retainer seal into housing.

8. Install the flange, washer and nut. Tighten the nut to specifications.

FRONT OUTPUT SHAFT

Using a press, force front output rear bearing on shaft.

SHIFT RAIL OIL SEALS

Install the two shift rail oil seals with appropriate tools.

TRANSFER CASE

1. Install the front detent rod in the case.

2. Slide the front drive shift rail all the way into the case and place the shift fork on the rail as it enters the case. Secure the fork to the rail with the setscrew.

3. Position the front output shaft sliding gear in the shift fork.

4. Install the rear detent rod.

5. Slide the rear drive shift rail into the case and position the shift fork on the rail as the rail enters the case. Secure the fork to the rail with the setscrew.

NOTE: The shift rails should be inserted so that the detents are positioned as shown in illustration.

6. While holding the sliding gear and

main drive gear in position, install the front output shaft and rear bearing assembly through the two gears.

7. Install the main drive gear spacer and secure with the snap-ring.

8. Install the front output shaft rear bearing cup.

9. Place the front output shaft rear cover and shims on the case and install the attaching bolts.

10. Install the front output shaft front bearing on the shaft. Install the front bearing cup.

11. If the front bearing retainer oil seal was removed, install a new seal. Position the bearing retainer and gasket to the case and install the attaching bolts.

12. Place the rear output shaft rear bearing retainer on a work bench and install 13 needle bearings in the splined hub of the output shaft, using vaseline or grease.

13. Position the rear output shaft rear bearing retainer assembly to the case and install the attaching bolts.

14. Install the rear output shaft sliding gear in the shifting fork and on the splines of the output shaft.

15. Position the adapter housing assembly on the rear output shaft and case. Install the attaching bolts.

16. Install the roller bearings in the bore of the idler shaft gear with vaseline or grease.

17. Position the idler gear and thrust washers in the case; then drive the idler shaft into the rear of the case through the idler gear and thrust washers.

SPECIFICATIONS

END PLAY (IN.)

Front output shaft	0.001–0.005
Rear output shaft	0.001–0.005

TORQUE LIMITS (FT. LBS.)

Transfer case to transmission extension bolts	20–30
Transfer case to transmission output shaft nut	60–80
Front output shaft rear cover bolts	25–32
Front output shaft bearing retainer bolts	25–32
Idler shaft cover bolts	25–32
Front and rear output flanges	80–85

NOTE: After installing the idler shaft, tap the sides of the case to relieve any possible binding.

18. Install the idler shaft lock plate.

19. Secure the shift rail link to the two shift rails.

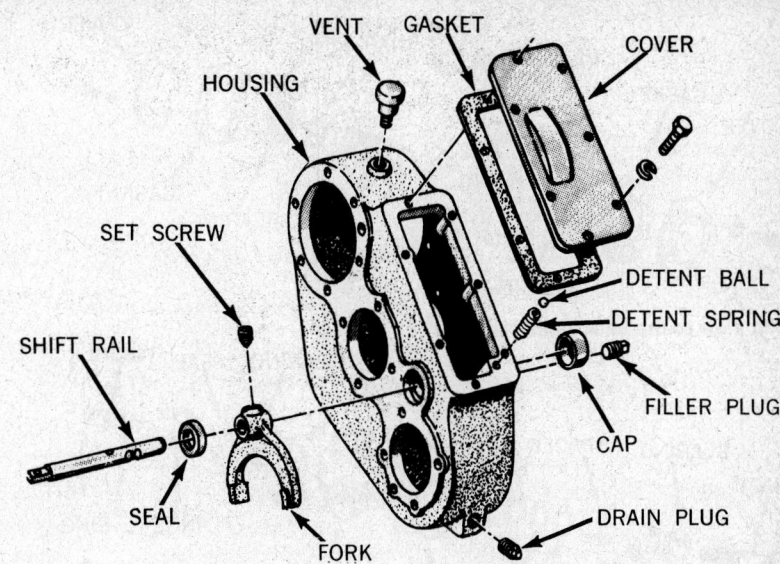

Exploded view of the case housing and shift mechanism—Dana 21

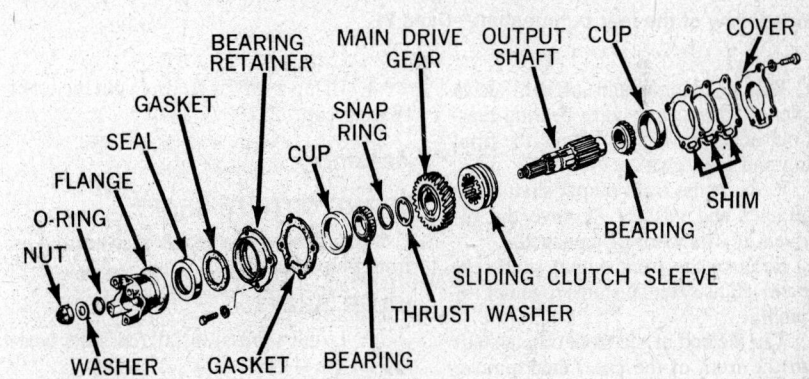

Exploded view of the front output shaft—Dana 21

20. Install the front and rear drive shift rail detent balls, springs and retaining plugs.

NOTE: Be sure that the heavier loaded spring and flat washer are installed in the front drive shift rail.

21. Install the rod access hole plug.

22. Install the flange, washer and retaining nut on each of the output shafts. Be sure to install a new O-ring in the front output shaft flange. Torque the attaching nuts to specifications.

23. With a dial indicator on the front drive output shaft, check the end-play. If not within specifications, adjust the shim pack at the front output shaft rear cover.

24. Place the cover plate on the case and install the attaching bolts.

Dana Model 21

The Dana Model 21 is a single-speed gearbox that transmits power to the front driving axle. There are two positions of the transfer case; front drive axle engaged and front drive axle disengaged.

Disassembly
TRANSFER CASE

1. Clean all dirt from transfer case and drain lubricant.

2. Remove bolts that attach the cover to the top of the case; then remove the cover.

3. Remove the setscrew securing the shift fork to the rail. Tap the shift rail rearward; then remove the rail cap from the rear of the case.

4. Remove the shift rail and fork.

5. Remove the detent spring and ball which engages the front drive shift rail.

6. Remove the flange attaching nuts, flat washer and O-ring from the front and rear output shafts. Discard the O-rings.

7. Remove the flange from the front and rear output shafts.

8. Remove the bolts that attach the rear output shaft bearing retainer to the case; then remove the retainer and output shaft as an assembly.

9. Remove the front and rear idler shaft covers.

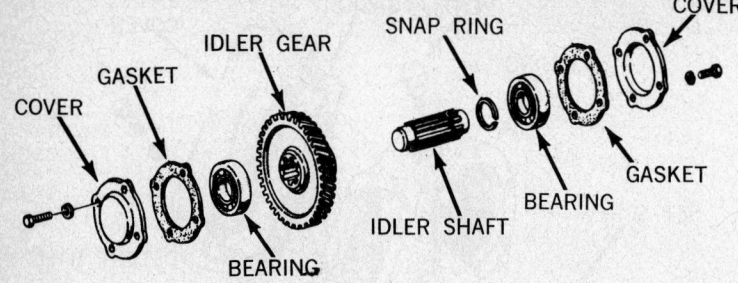

COVER GASKET IDLER GEAR SNAP RING COVER

BEARING IDLER SHAFT GASKET

BEARING

Exploded view of the idler shaft—Dana 21

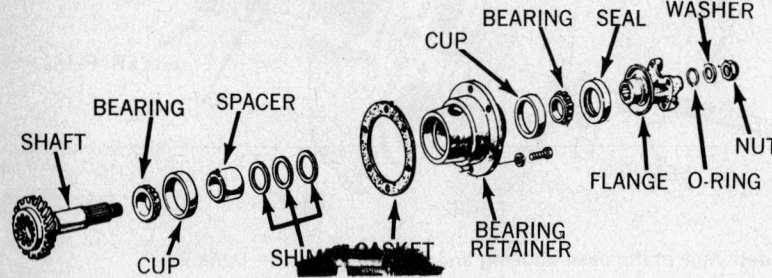

CUP BEARING SEAL WASHER

SHAFT BEARING SPACER

NUT

CUP FLANGE O-RING

SHIMS GASKET BEARING RETAINER

Exploded view of the rear output shaft—Dana 21

10. Using a hammer and soft drift, drive the idler shaft and rear idler bearing rearward out of the case; then lift out the front bearing and idler gear.

11. Remove the front output shaft bearing retainer and gasket. Remove the retainer seal if it is worn or damaged.

12. Remove the front output shaft rear cover and shims. Tie the shims together for reassembly.

13. Tap the end of the front output shaft toward the front of the case; then remove the front bearing cup. Remove the rear bearing cup by tapping the shaft rearward.

14. Angle the front output shaft front bearing away from the main drive gear to remove the snap-ring from its groove in the shaft. Drive the output shaft and rear bearing out of the case.

15. Remove the sliding gear, main drive gear, front bearing, thrust washer and snap-ring from the case.

16. Remove the shift rail seal.

FRONT OUTPUT SHAFT BEARING

To remove the front output shaft rear bearing, use the sliding gear as a base and press off the bearing.

IDLER SHAFT

1. Remove the snap-ring from the idler shaft.

2. Using the idler gear as a base, press the idler shaft out of the rear bearing.

REAR OUTPUT SHAFT

1. To remove the output shaft from the bearing retainer tap shaft rearward. Remove the shims and spacer.

2. Remove the inner bearing from the output shaft.

3. Place the bearing retainer on a press and force out the outer cup, outer bearing and oil seal.

4. Using a soft drift, drive out the inner bearing cup.

Assembly

FRONT OUTPUT SHAFT

Using an arbor press, force rear bearing on front output shaft.

IDLER SHAFT

1. Using a press, install rear idler bearing on the shaft.

2. Install snap-ring.

REAR OUTPUT SHAFT

1. Press the inner bearing on the output shaft.

2. Using a soft-faced hammer, tap the inner bearing cup into the retainer.

3. Install the outer cup.

4. Place spacer and shims on the output shaft; then install the shaft in the bearing retainer housing.

5. Install the outer bearing on the shaft.

6. Place the bearing retainer and output shaft in a vise. Measure end-play with a dial indicator on end of the shaft. If not within specifications, adjust shim pack between the spacer and the front and rear bearing cones.

7. After setting correct end-play, install the bearing retainer seal.

TRANSFER CASE

1. While holding the drive gear, sliding gear and thrust washer in the case, install the front output shaft, from the rear, through the gears and washer. Install the snap-ring.

2. Install the front output shaft rear bearing cup.

3. Place the front output shaft rear cover and shims on the case. After removing old sealant from all mating surfaces with thinner, apply gasket sealer to the attaching bolts and torque to specifications. With the cover installed, apply sealer to the outside edge of the adjusting shims, case and cover joints.

4. Install the front output shaft rear bearing on the shaft. Install the front bearing.

5. If the front bearing retainer oil seal was removed, install a new seal. Position the bearing retainer and gasket to the case and install attaching bolts.

6. Install the flange, new O-ring, washer and attaching nut on the front output shaft.

7. With a dial indicator on the front drive output shaft, check the end-play. If not within specified limits, increase or decrease the shim pack thickness at the front output shaft rear cover.

8. Place the idler gear in the case; then install the idler shaft through the gear. Install the front bearing.

9. Place the front and rear idler covers and gaskets on the case; then install attaching bolts.

10. Install a new shift rail seal.

11. Install the shift rail detent ball and spring in the top of the case.

12. Slide the shift rail into the case and position the fork on the rail as the rail enters the case. Depressing the detent ball and spring will allow the rail to pass. Secure the fork to the rail with the setscrew. Install the shift rail cap.

13. Position the rear output shaft and bearing retainer assembly to the case, then install the attaching bolts.

14. Install the flange, new O-ring, washer and attaching nut on the rear output shaft.

15. Place the top cover and gasket on the case, then install attaching bolts.

16. Fill the transfer case to the proper level with the recommended lubricant.

SPECIFICATIONS

END PLAY (IN.)

Front output shaft	0.001–0.005
Rear output shaft	0.001–0.005

TORQUE LIMITS (FT. LBS.)

Transfer case to transmission extension bolts	20–30
Transfer case to transmission output shaft nut	125–150
Front output shaft rear cover bolts	25–32
Front output shaft bearing retainer bolts	25–32
Idler shaft cover bolts	25–32

Dana Model 24

The Dana Model 24 is a two-speed gearbox

that is manually controlled by a shift lever in the cab. The transfer case positions are: four-wheel-drive low (4L), neutral (N), two-wheel-drive high (2H) and four-wheel-drive high (4H).

Disassembly

1. Clean any dirt from the transfer case and remove the power take-off cover plate.
2. Remove both idler shaft bearing retainers.
3. Using a soft-faced hammer, tap the idler shaft and bearing to the rear until the bearing is free of the case.
4. Remove the idler shaft, two gears and spacer.
5. Remove the idler shaft front bearing.
6. Remove the flange retaining nuts from the front output shaft, the input shaft and the rear output shaft.
7. Remove the flanges and washers.
8. Remove the front output shaft front and rear bearing retainers.
9. Tap the front output shaft and rear bearing through the gears and case. Remove the high speed gear.
10. Remove the front output shaft front bearing and washer.
11. Remove the setscrew that retains the front drive shaft fork to the shift rail.
12. Remove the front output shaft sliding gear.
13. If the input shaft oil seal is to be replaced, remove it with a four-jaw puller and slide hammer.
14. Remove the input shaft bearing retainer.
15. If the output shaft bearing retainer oil seal is to be replaced, remove it with a puller and slide hammer.
16. Remove the rear output shaft bearing retainer; then remove the speedometer drive assembly.
17. Loosen the rear output shaft assembly from the case by driving on the front end of the input shaft with a soft-faced hammer.
18. Remove the rear output shaft and bearing retainer as an assembly.
19. Tap the input shaft through the front bearing, through the main drive gear, through the sliding gear and out of the case.
20. Lift the main drive gear out of the case and then drive out the input shaft front bearing.
21. Remove the setscrew that retains the rear drive shift fork to the shift rail.
22. Remove the rear output shaft sliding gear.
23. Remove the shift rail link from the two shift rails.
24. Remove the retaining plug, detent spring and ball which engage the front drive shift rail detent rod.
25. Remove the retaining plug detent spring and ball which engages the rear drive shift rail detent rod. Remove the front drive detent rod access hole plug.
26. Pull the front drive shift rail to the furthest outward position.

27. Pull the rear drive shift rail far enough to allow the two detent rods to slide out.
28. Remove the rear drive shift rail and fork.
29. Remove the shift rail seals.

Assembly

1. Slide the front drive shift rail all the way into the case and position the shift fork on the rail as the rail enters the case.
2. Install the two detent rods in the case.
3. Install the rear drive shift fork and hold the detent rods and the fork in place as the rear drive shift rail is pushed in as far as possible.

NOTE: In steps 2 and 3, the shift rails should be inserted so that the detents are positioned as shown in illustration.

4. Pull the front drive shift rail out to its next detent. This will permit the rear drive shift rail to be pushed in to the full extent of its travel. After pushing the rear drive shift rail all the way in, push the front drive shift rail back to its extreme inward position.
5. Install the rear drive shift detent ball, spring and retaining plug; then install the access hole plug.
6. Install the front drive shift rail detent ball, spring and retaining plug.
7. Secure the shift rail link in the two shift rails.
8. Place the rear output sliding gear in the shift fork and secure the fork to the rear drive shift rail with the setscrew.
9. Install the input shaft front bearing and retainer assembly. Coat retainer and bolts with sealer.
10. Place the main drive gear in the case; then slide the input shaft into the rear of the case through the main drive gear and through the front bearing and retainer.
11. Install the roller bearings in the splined hub of the rear output shaft assembly with petrolatum jelly or grease. Then install the shaft and bearing retainer assembly, making sure that the output shaft is aligned correctly with the input shaft. Coat the case, bearing retainer and bolts with sealer.
12. Position the front output sliding gear in the shift fork and secure the folk to the front drive shift rail with the setscrew.
13. While holding the sliding gear and high speed gear in position, install the front output shaft and rear bearing assembly through the two gears from the rear of the case.
14. After coating with sealer, install the front output shaft rear bearing retainer and gasket.
15. Install the washer and bearing over the front output shaft at the front of the case and then install the front bearing retainer and gasket. Coat retainer with sealer.
16. Install the flange, washer, flange retaining nut and cotter key on each of the three shafts. Torque to specifications.

17. Place the idler shaft gears in the case and install the shaft and rear bearing assembly from the rear. After applying sealer to the plate and bolts, install the rear bearing retainer.
18. Position the spacer on the front end of the idler shaft and install the front bearing. Tap the bearing lightly with a mallet or soft-faced hammer.
19. Install the washer, retaining nut and cotter pin on the front end of the idler shaft.
20. After applying sealer to the plates and bolts, install the idler shaft front bearing retainer and the power take-off cover plate.

SPECIFICATIONS

END PLAY (IN.)

Front Output Shaft	0.003–0.007
Rear Output Shaft	0.003–0.007

TORQUE LIMITS (FT. LBS.)

Transfer case to transmission extension bolts	20–30
Transfer case to transmission output shaft nut	60–80
Front output shaft rear cover bolts	25–32
Front output shaft bearing retainer bolts	25–32
Idler shaft cover bolts	25–32

Dana 300

The 300 is used in Jeep® CJ models only. It has a cast iron case, four gear positions and employs an external floor mounted gearshift linkage for range control. It is a part time, 2 speed unit with undifferentiated high and low ranges. It is used with both manual and automatic transmission. Low range reduction is 2.6:1.

Disassembly

1. Drain the unit and remove the shift lever assembly.
2. Remove the bottom cover.

NOTE: The bottom cover has been coated with a sealant. Use a putty knife to break the seal and work the knife around the bottom of the cover to break it loose. Don't try to wedge the cover off.

3. With a puller, remove the front and rear yokes.
4. Unbolt and remove the input shaft support from the case. The rear output shaft gear and input shaft will come with it as an assembly.

NOTE: The support has been coated with sealant, remove it as you did the bottom cover.

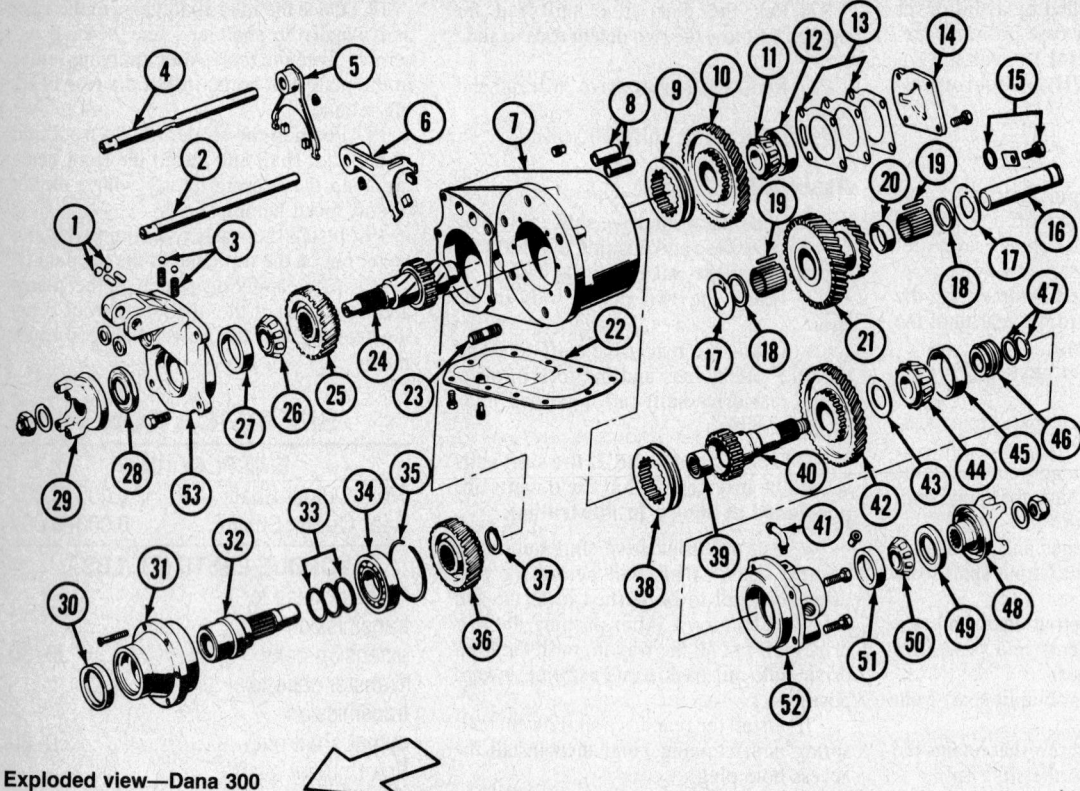

Exploded view—Dana 300

1. Interlock plugs and interlocks
2. Shift rod—rear output shaft fork
3. Poppet balls and springs
4. Shift rod—front output shaft fork
5. Front output shaft shift fork
6. Rear output shaft shift fork
7. Transfer case
8. Thimble covers
9. Clutch sleeve—front output shaft
10. Clutch gear—front output shaft
11. Bearing—front output shaft rear
12. Race—front output shaft

13. End-play shims—front output shaft
14. Cover plate
15. Lock plate, bolt and washer
16. Intermediate gear shaft
17. Thrust washer
18. Bearing spacer (thin)
19. Intermediate gear shaft needle bearings
20. Bearing spacer (thick)
21. Intermediate gear
22. Bottom cover
23. Stud (case-to-trans.)
24. Front output shaft
25. Front output shaft

bearing
26. Front output shaft bearing (front)
27. Front output shaft bearing race
28. Oil seal
29. Front yoke
30. Seal
31. Support—input shaft
32. Input shaft
33. Shims
34. Input shaft bearing
35. Input shaft bearing snap-ring
36. Rear output shaft gear
37. Snap-ring
38. Clutch sleeve—rear output shaft
39. Input shaft rear

gear
40. Rear output shaft
41. Vent
42. Clutch gear—rear output shaft
43. Thrustwasher
44. Bearing—rear output shaft front
45. Race—rear output shaft bearing
46. Speedometer drive gear
47. End-play shims
48. Rear yoke
49. Rear output shaft oil seal
50. Bearing—rear output shaft rear
51. Bearing race
52. Rear bearing cap
53. Front bearing cap

bearing (needle) (or pilot bearing)
40. Rear output shaft

5. Remove the rear output shaft clutch sleeve from the case.

6. Remove and discard the snap ring retaining the rear output shaft gear on the input shaft and remove the gear.

7. Remove and discard the input bearing snapring.

8. Remove the input shaft bearing from the support. Tap the end of the shaft with a soft mallet to aid removal.

9. Remove the input shaft bearing and end-play shims from the shaft with an arbor press.

10. Remove the input shaft oil seal from the support.

11. Unbolt and remove the intermediate shaft lockplate.

12. Remove the intermediate shaft. Tap

the shaft out of the case using a brass punch and plastic mallet.

13. Remove and discard the intermediate shaft O-ring seal.

14. Remove the intermediate gear assembly and thrust washers.

NOTE: The thrust washers have locating tabs which must fit into notches in the case at assembly.

15. Remove the needle bearings and spacers from the intermediate gear. There are 48 needle bearings and three spacers.

16. Remove the rear bearing cap attaching bolts and remove the cap. A plastic mallet will aid in removal.

NOTE: The rear bearing cap has been coated with sealant.

17. Remove the end play shims and speedometer drive gear from the rear output shaft.

18. Remove and discard the rear output shaft oil seal. Remove the bearings and races from the rear cap.

19. Unbolt and remove the front and rear output shaft shift forks from the shift rods.

20. Remove the shift rods. Insert a punch through the clevis pin holes in the rods and rotate the rods while pulling them out of the case.

NOTE: When the shift rods are free of the case, take care to avoid losing the shift rod poppet balls and springs.

21. Remove the shift forks from the case.

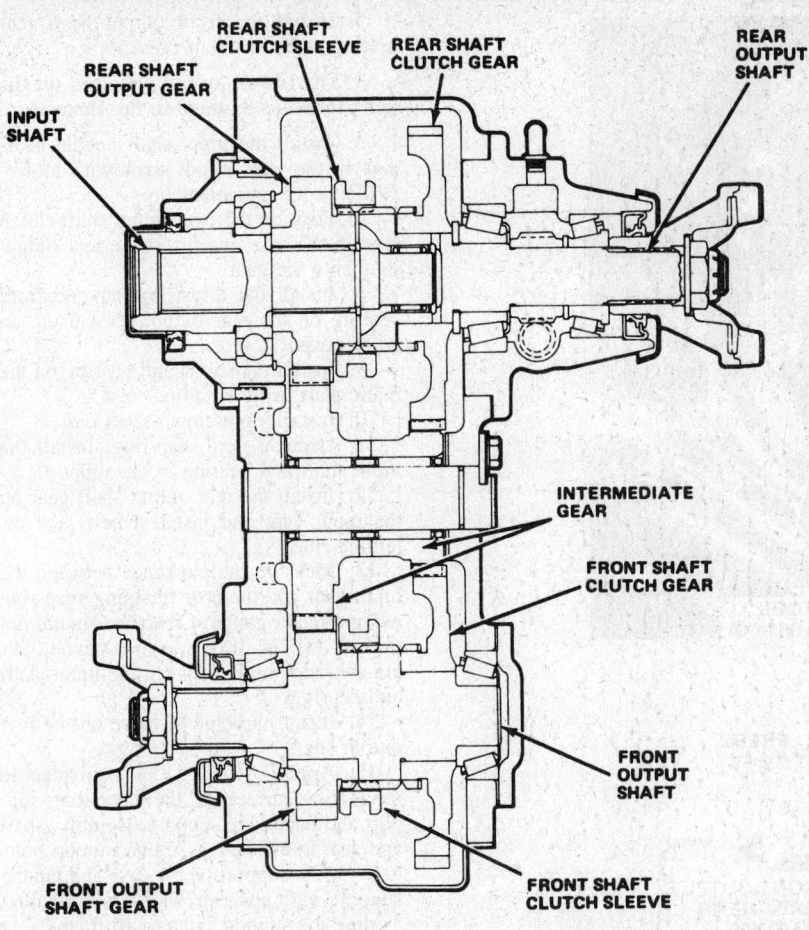

INPUT SHAFT

REAR SHAFT OUTPUT GEAR

REAR SHAFT CLUTCH SLEEVE

REAR SHAFT CLUTCH GEAR

REAR OUTPUT SHAFT

INTERMEDIATE GEAR

FRONT SHAFT CLUTCH GEAR

FRONT OUTPUT SHAFT

FRONT OUTPUT SHAFT GEAR

FRONT SHAFT CLUTCH SLEEVE

Dana 300 power flow

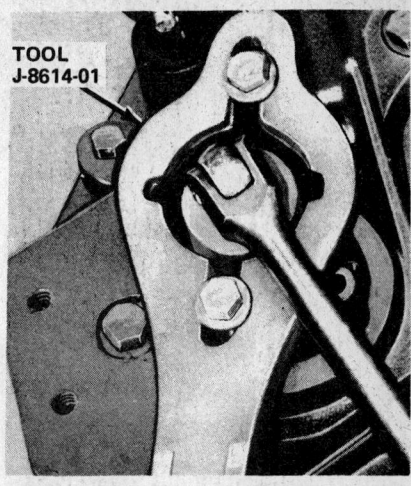

TOOL J-8614-01

Output shaft yoke nut removal

22. Remove the bolts attaching the front cap to the case and remove the cap.

NOTE: The front cap has been coated with sealant.

23. Remove the front output shaft and shift rod oil seals from the front cap.

24. Remove the bearing race from the front cap.

25. Remove the cover plate bolts and remove the plate and end play shims from the case. Keep the shims together for assembly.

26. Move the front output shaft toward the front of the case.

27. Remove the front output shaft rear bearing race.

28. Remove the rear output shaft front bearing. Position the case on wood blocks. Seat the clutch gear on the case interior surface and tap the shaft out of the bearing with a soft mallet.

NOTE: If the bearing is difficult to remove, an arbor press may have to be used.

29. Remove the rear output shaft front bearing, thrust washer, clutch gear and output shaft from the case.

30. Remove the front output shaft rear bearing with an arbor press.

CAUTION

Be sure to support the case with wood blocks positioned on either side of the case bore.

31. Remove the case from the press and remove the output shaft, clutch gear and sleeve and the shaft rear bearing.

32. Remove the front output shaft front bearing with an arbor press and tool J-22912-01 or its equivalent.

33. Remove the front output shaft from the gear.

34. Remove the input shaft rear needle bearing from the rear output shaft using tool J-29369-1 or its equivalent. Support the shaft in a vise during removal.

35. Using a ⅜″ drive, ⁷⁄₁₆″ socket, remove the shift rod thimbles from the case.

Assembly

Coat all parts with SAE 85W-90 oil before assembly.

FRONT YOKE OIL SEAL

TOOL J-25180

Yoke oil seal removal

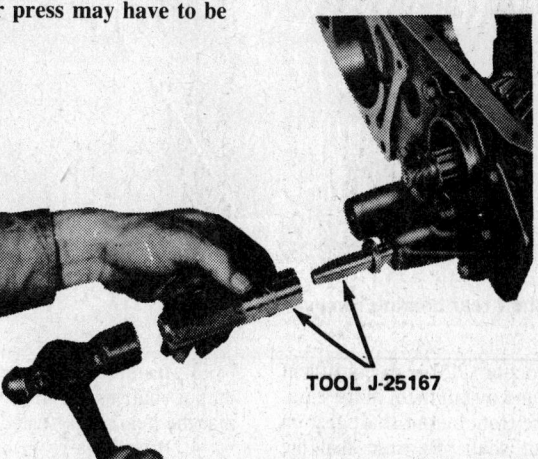

TOOL J-25167

Shift rod oil seal installation

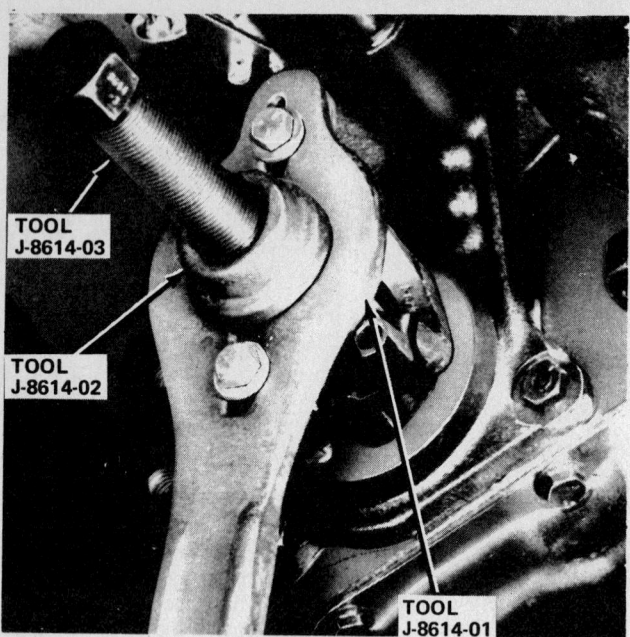

Yoke removal

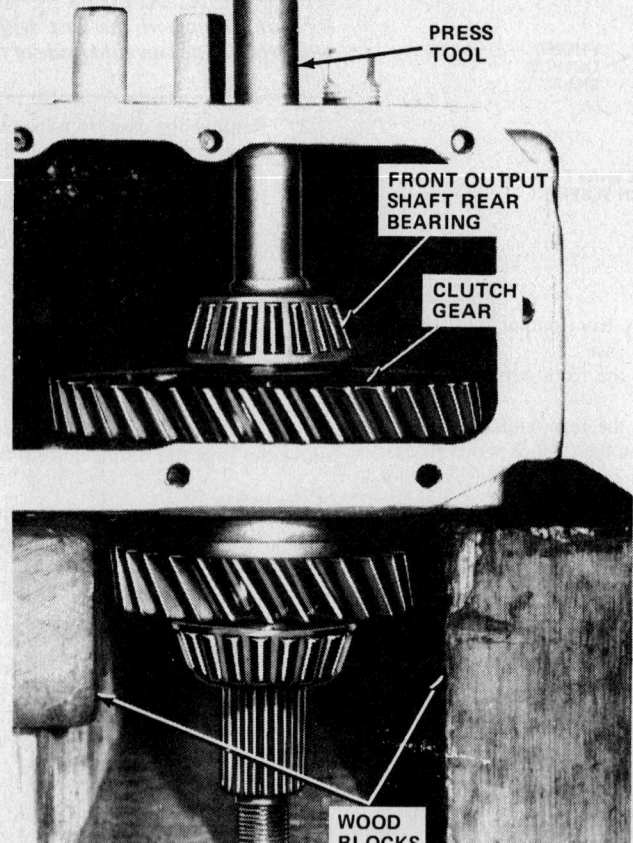

Front output shaft rear bearing removal

1. Apply Loctite® 220 or its equivalent to the thimbles and install them in the case.

2. Install the front output shaft gear on the front output shaft. Be sure that the clutch teeth on the gear face the shaft gear teeth.

3. Install the front bearing on the front output shaft using an arbor press. Be sure that the bearing is seated against the gear.

4. Install the front output shaft in the case and install the clutch sleeve and gear on the shaft.

5. Install the front output shaft rear bearing using an arbor press.

NOTE: Install an old yoke nut on the shaft to avoid damage to the threads.

6. Install the input shaft needle bearings in the rear output shaft with tool J-29179 or its equivalent.

7. Position the rear output shaft clutch gear in the case and insert the rear output shaft into the gear.

8. Install the thrust washer and front bearing on the rear output shaft using an arbor press.

9. Install the shims and bearing on the input shaft using an arbor press.

10. Install a new input shaft seal.

11. Using a new snap-ring, install the input shaft and bearing in the support.

12. Install the rear output shaft gear on the input gear and install a new gear retaining ring.

13. Measure the clearance between the input gear and the gear retaining snap-ring using a feeler gauge. Clearance should not exceed .003 in. If clearance is beyond tolerance, add shims between the input shaft and bearing.

14. Install the clutch sleeve on the rear output shaft.

15. Apply Loctite® 515 or equivalent to the mating surfaces of the input shaft support and install the support assembly, shaft and gear in the case. Use two support bolts to align the support on the case and tap the support into position with a soft mallet. Torque the support bolts to 10 ft. lbs.

16. Install the rear bearing cap front bearing race.

17. Install the rear bearing cap rear bearing race.

18. Position the rear output shaft rear bearing in the rear bearing cap.

19. Install the rear output shaft yoke oil seal.

20. Install the speedometer gear and end-play shims on the rear output shaft.

21. Apply Loctite® 515 or equivalent to the mating surfaces of the cap and install the rear bearing cap. Use two cap bolts to align the cap and tap it into place with a soft mallet.

22. Tighten the cap bolts to 35 ft. lbs.

23. Install the rear output shaft yoke. Torque a new locknut to 120 ft. lbs.

24. Clamp a dial indicator on the rear output shaft bearing cap. Position the indicator stylus so that it contacts the end of the shaft.

25. Pry the shaft back and forth to check end-play. End-play should be .001–.005 in. If play is not correct, remove or add shims between the speedometer drive gear and the output shaft rear bearing.

26. Install the front output shaft rear bearing race.

27. Install the front output shaft end play shims and cover plate. Tighten the cover plate bolts to 35 ft. lbs.

NOTE: Apply Loctite® 220 to the bolts before installation.

14. After the shafts are removed, remove the oil seals and the bearing snap rings, and press or tap out the two ball bearings.

15. Pry and remove the thrust washer from the boss for the front output shaft roller bearing in the other half of the case.

16. Press the roller bearing cage from the inside and out of the cover.

17. Press the ball bearing on the outer race from the outside and out of the cover.

Cleaning and Inspection

1. Clean all parts in solvent, removing all traces of old gaskets, sealants and lubricants, and dry the parts with compressed air.

2. Examine all the ball and roller bearings for wear or damage and replace as necessary.

3. Inspect the sprocket teeth and bores for damage and wear. Check the internal splines and clutch teeth for chipped surfaces. Small nicks or burrs can be removed with a file.

4. Check the smooth and splined surfaces of the shafts for wear or damage. The sliding clutch must move freely on the output shaft, but excessive clearance is remedied by replacement of parts.

5. Examine the chain for bent or broken lines. If either condition exists, replace the chain.

Assembly

1. Install the two snap rings in the outer grooves of both bearing bores in the front half of the case.

2. Coat both bearing bores with lubricant and press or tap with a soft hammer both ball bearing assemblies into the case.

3. Install the two snap rings in the inner grooves of the two bearing bores in the front case half.

4. Install the shaft oil seals from the outside of the front case half. They are best installed with a press.

5. On a frame mounted transfer case, position the lightly lubricated shafts in the bearings, then, pull the shafts into the bearings by tightening the flange attaching nuts with the flanges installed. The input shaft is installed with the identification groove toward the rear of the transfer case. Tighten the flange attaching nut on the front output shaft to 200–250 ft. lbs., and the flange attaching nut on the input shaft until it bottoms, then back off two turns and retighten to 140–150 ft. lbs.

6. The output shaft in transmission mounted transfer case is installed in the same manner as outlined for frame mounted units in step 5.

7. The input shaft in transmission mounted transfer cases has a snap-ring to be installed on the front end of the shaft prior to installation in the bearing. The shaft is then pressed or tapped into the bearing with a soft hammer until the snap-ring is

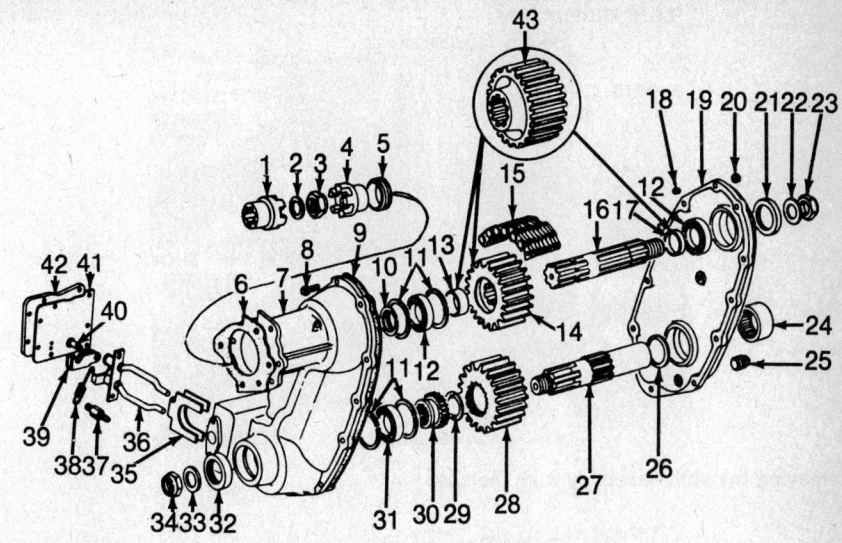

Exploded view of a transmission mounted TC143 transfer case

1. Transmission shaft coupling	9. Gasket	20. Flange nut	33. Washer
2. Washer	10. Snap input shaft ring	21. Seal	34. Output shaft end nut
3. Transmission shaft end nut	11. Bearing snap-ring	22. Washer	35. Shift shoe
4. Input shaft coupling	12. Ball bearing	23. End nut	36. Assembly shifter
5. Speedometer gear	13. Long spacer	24. Roller bearing	37. Spring stud
6. Gasket	14. Upper sprocket (old style)	25. Drain plug	38. Shift spring
7. Transmission mounted type case	15. Chain	26. Thrust washer	39. Shift clevis
8. Flange bolt	16. Input shaft	27. Output shaft	40. Clevis pin
	17. Short spacer	28. Lower sprocket	41. Shift cover gasket
	18. Dowel ring	29. Thrust washer	42. Shift cover
	19. Cover	30. Sliding clutch	43. Upper sprocket (new style)
		31. Ball bearing	
		32. Seal	

Removing the shift cover

bottomed against the bearing.

8. Assemble the shift shoe to the sliding clutch and install the sliding clutch to the front output shaft.

9. Insert the shifter assembly into the transfer case so the shift cranks of the shifter pass through the shift shoe before being guided into the shift bosses. Make sure the shifter operates the sliding clutch and then secure the assembly with the bolt and spring stud.

NOTE: The flange bolt must be installed before the spring stud because the

position of the spring stud when installed prevents the installation of the flange bolts.

10. Install the thrust washer to the front output shaft and the long spacer to the input shaft, if so equipped with a long spacer.

NOTE: Be sure the thrust washer tangs fit down into the splines on the shaft.

11. Lightly lubricate the bores of both sprockets and secure the case in a soft jawed vise by the end of the input shaft.

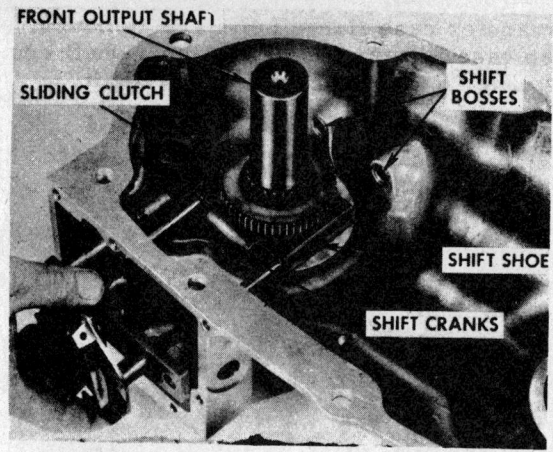

Removing the shift assembly from the case

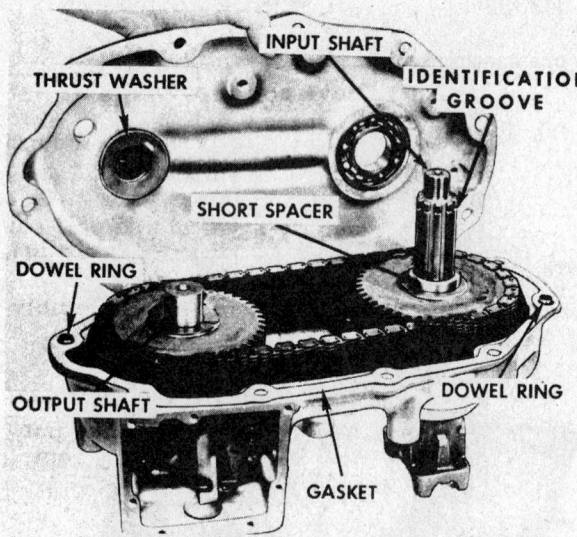

Removing the cover from the case

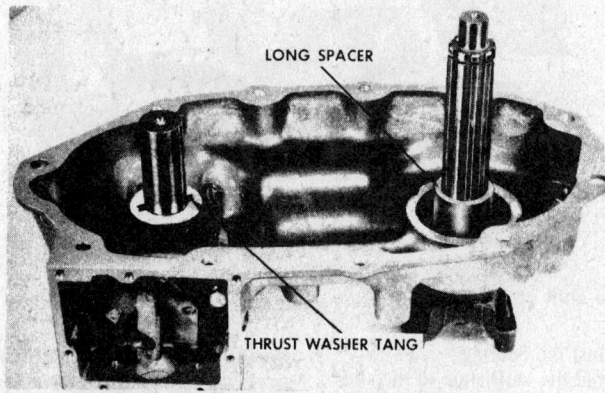

Installing the thrust washer and long spacer

12. Install the upper sprocket to the outer end of the input shaft. Do not slide the sprocket completely into the case.

13. Position the chain over the sprocket and place the lower sprocket inside the chain.

14. Pull down on the lower sprocket enough to slide the lower sprocket onto the output shaft.

15. Slide both sprockets and chain onto the sprockets as far as they will go.

16. Install the short spacer on the input shaft (not required on later models).

17. Install the shift spring between the spring post and the shifter assembly.

18. Press the ball bearing into the input

shaft bore of the rear cover from the inside surface.

19. Press the roller bearing into the output shaft bore of the rear cover from the outside surface until it is flush with the bearing bore.

20. Press the seal for the rear of the input shaft (rear output) into the cover until it is flush.

21. Place the cover on a bench, inside facing up. Coat the back side of the thrust washer with a thin coat of sealant and position it on the roller bearing boss with the tang on the washer mated with the oil passage in the boss.

NOTE: Use the sealant sparingly and make sure none of it enters the bearing or blocks the two oil passages.

22. Position a new gasket and two dowel rings on the mating surface of the case.

23. Position the cover onto the case, guiding the two shafts into their respective bearings. Secure the cover to the case with the attaching nuts and bolts, tightening them to 29–38 ft. lbs.

24. Install the indicator light switch to the case and check its operation with a test light.

25. Install the shift cover gasket and cover on the case and secure it with bolts and lockwashers tightened to 4–6 ft. lbs. *Do not overtighten.*

26. Install the rear output flange on the rear of the input shaft so both the input flange and the output flange are on the same plane. The flanges must be assembled in this manner to prevent vibration.

27. Install the washer and a nylon insert locknut on the shaft tightened to 140–150 ft. lbs. to secure the flange.

New Process Model 201

The New Process Model 201 transfer case is a 2-speed gearbox which provides speed reduction and couples power to the front and rear driving axles.

--- CAUTION ---

Do not engage front driving axle when operating truck on hard surfaced roads at high speeds.

DE-CLUTCH AND SHIFT ROD

Adjustment

NOTE: All adjustments must be made with the front axle engaged and the transfer case in low range.

1. Disconnect de-clutch and shift rods at shift levers.

2. Adjust de-clutch rod length until lever clears rear end of slot in cab underbody by ⅝ in. Secure adjusting yoke with locknut.

3. Adjust shift rod length until distance between protusions on shift and de-clutch

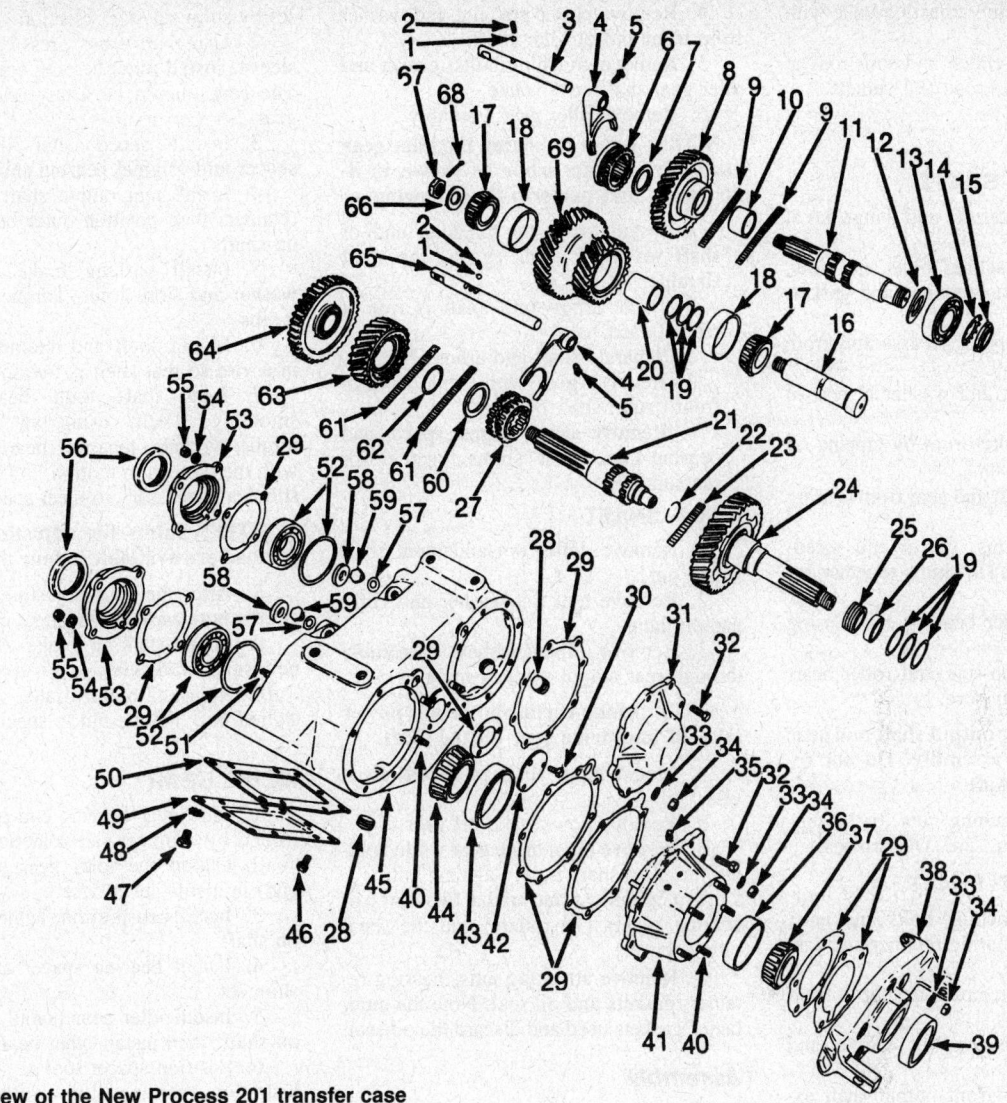

Exploded view of the New Process 201 transfer case

1. Ball, shift bar poppet
2. Spring, shift bar poppet ball
3. Bar, front output shaft
4. Fork, shift
5. Screw, set
6. Clutch, front output sliding
7. Fork, shift
8. Gear, front output drive
9. Bearing, roller (70 req'd)
10. Spacer, bearing
11. Shaft, front output front gear
12. Washer, thrust
13. Bearing, ball
14. Retainer, lock
15. Nut, bearing retaining
16. Shaft, idler gear
17. Cone, idler gear bearing
18. Cup, idler gear bearing
19. Shim, set

20. Spacer, bearing
21. Shaft input
22. Ring, snap
23. Bearing, roller (15 req'd)
24. Gear, rear output drive w/shaft
25. Gear, speedometer drive
26. Spacer, speedometer drive gear
27. Clutch, two-speed sliding
28. Plug, pipe
29. Gasket, set
30. Bolt, hex head, w/lock washer
31. Retainer, front output shaft rear bearing
32. Bolt, hex head, w/lock washer
33. Washer, lock
34. Nut, hex
35. Breather
36. Cup, rear output shaft outer bearing

37. Cone, rear output shaft outer bearing
38. Support, hand brake
39. Seal, rear output shaft outer bearing oil
40. Stud
41. Retainer, rear output drive gear bearing
42. Plate, idler shaft cover
43. Cup, rear output shaft inner bearing
44. Cone, rear output shaft inner bearing
45. Case, transfer
46. Bolt w/washer
47. Bolt, hex head
48. Washer, lock
49. Cover, power take-off opening
50. Gasket, power take-off cover
51. Stud

52. Bearing, input and front output ball
53. Retainer, input and front output bearing
54. Washer, lock
55. Nut, hex
56. Seal, input and front output bearing retainer oil
57. Gasket
58. Seal, front and rear output shift bar oil
59. Screw, poppet ball retainer
60. Washer, thrust
61. Bearing, roller (70 req'd)
62. Spacer, bearing
63. Gear, input drive
64. Gear, power take-off
65. Bar, two-speed shift
66. Washer
67. Nut, hex
68. Pin, cotter
69. Gear, idler

levers is ¼ in. Secure adjusting yoke with locknut.

4. Connect de-clutch and shift rods at shift levers and then road test vehicle.

Disassembly

REAR OUTPUT SHAFT

1. Remove cotter pin and flange nut at rear output shaft.

2. Remove attaching bolts and nuts, then remove bearing retainer and gasket. Discard gasket.

3. Remove output shaft assembly from case.

4. Remove nut and washer at rear of shaft.

5. Remove brake drum by tapping on it lightly (if necessary).

6. Remove shaft and gear from bearing retainer.

7. Remove shims, spacer and speedometer drive gear. Tie shims together for reassembly.

8. Remove inner bearing cone, using a suitable puller.

9. Remove snap-ring and roller bearings from shaft gear bore.

NOTE: The rear output shaft and gear is serviced as an assembly. Do not remove gear from shaft.

10. Remove attaching nuts, brake support, bearing and oil seal. Discard seal.

FRONT OUTPUT SHAFT

1. Remove attaching bolts and nuts, then remove rear bearing retainer and gasket. Discard gasket.

2. Remove cotter pin and nut at front output shaft.

3. Remove attaching nut, washer and companion flange.

4. Remove the front output shaft assembly through the rear of the case.

5. Remove sliding clutch gear.

6. Position front output shaft assembly in a soft-jawed vise.

7. Remove lock retainer and bearing nut.

8. Using a suitable puller, remove bearing.

9. Remove front output shaft drive gear by lifting upward and holding the thrust washers against the hub to retain bearing rollers.

10. Carefully set aside thrust washers, then remove the two rows of bearing rollers (70 rollers) and the spacer separating them.

11. Remove attaching nuts and bearing retainer with gaskets. Note number of gaskets used.

IDLER GEAR, SHIFT BAR AND FORK

1. Remove safety wire and setscrews securing shift forks to shift bars.

2. Remove poppet ball retaining plugs, gaskets and poppet ball springs.

3. Pull shift bars out of the case, then remove shift forks and poppet balls.

4. Remove cotter pin, nut and washer from front end of idler shaft.

5. Remove attaching bolts, gasket and idler gear shaft cover plate.

6. Remove idler gear assembly.

NOTE: When removing the idler gear assembly, use an arbor as shown in illustration and perform the following:

a. Install arbor on threaded end of shaft so that it seats against the shaft shoulder.

b. Drive arbor until shaft is free at rear of case.

c. Separate shaft and arbor.

d. Remove gear with arbor through front output shaft opening.

e. Remove arbor, shims, spacer and bearing cones. Tie shims together for reassembly.

INPUT SHAFT

1. Remove cotter pin and input shaft flange nut.

2. Remove nut, flat washer and companion flange.

3. Remove input shaft assembly through rear output shaft opening in case.

NOTE: Make certain to retain power take-off and drive gear on the shaft.

4. Mount input shaft in a soft-jawed vise.

5. Remove power take-off gear.

6. Remove input drive gear while holding thrust washers tightly against hub.

7. Carefully remove the two rows of bearing rollers (70 rollers) and the separating spacer.

8. Remove attaching nuts, bearing retainer, gaskets and oil seal. Note the number of gaskets used and discard the oil seal.

Assembly

The transfer case is assembled in the reverse order of disassembly. The following procedures concerning preloading bearings and bearing adjustment however, must all be completed before (or in some cases, during) installation of shaft and gear assemblies.

INPUT SHAFT

1. The input shaft drive gear bearing consists of 70 rollers divided into two rows by a spacer.

2. Coat gear bore with grease, then position rollers and spacer.

3. Hold thrust washers against hub to retain rollers, then install gear on shaft.

4. Input shaft end-play is controlled by gasket thickness between case and bearing retainer.

5. Position retainer on case, then measure, clearance with a feeler gauge.

6. Select gasket(s) with a thickness .005 in. more than measured clearance.

7. Remove retainer and install selected gasket(s), then reinstall retainer.

REAR OUTPUT SHAFT

1. Rear output shaft bearing preload is

set by shim set size selection.

2. Using an arbor press and suitable sleeve, install inner bearing cone on shaft. The cone should be firmly seated against gear.

3. Install speedometer drive gear, spacer and original bearing shim set.

4. Install rear output shaft in bearing retainer, then position outer bearing cone on shaft.

5. Install parking brake drum, flat washer and slotted nut. Torque nut to 125 ft. lbs.

6. Mount shaft and retainer assembly in a vise so that shaft is free to rotate.

7. Turn shaft until bearing rolls smoothly. Then, using an inch-pound torque wrench, measure bearing preload with the wrench in motion. Subtract or add shims as necessary to meet specifications.

NOTE: Shims for adjusting bearing preload are available in four thicknesses.

8. After the final adjustment, remove slotted nut, washer and brake drum.

9. Install parking brake support and new support oil seal.

10. Reinstall brake drum, washer and slotted nut. Torque nut to specifications.

IDLER GEAR

1. Idler gear bearing end-play is controlled by shim set size selection.

2. Clamp the idler gear shaft (large end) in a soft-jawed vise.

3. Install bearing cone against shoulder on shaft.

4. Install bearing spacer and original shim set.

5. Install idler gear (small end down) on shaft, then install other bearing cone.

6. Position spacer tool as shown in illustration, then install flat washer and nut. Torque nut to specifications.

7. Rotate gear until bearing rolls smoothly. Then using a dial indicator, measure idler gear bearing end-play. Add or subtract shims as necessary to meet specifications.

8. Disassemble idler gear shaft assembly. Tie newly selected shims together.

9. To install gear assembly in the case, position bearing cone in in the large end of the gear, then place gear (small end up) on a bench.

10. Install the same arbor used to remove idler gear shaft, a spacer, new shims and other bearing cone in the idler gear.

11. Hold the idler gear assembly in the case with the small diameter gear facing rearward, then insert the shaft through the case (from rear) and thread it into the previously installed arbor.

12. Tap on the shaft until arbor extends through opposite side of case.

13. Remove arbor.

TWO-SPEED CLUTCH

When installing the two-speed clutch on the input shaft, make certain that the recessed

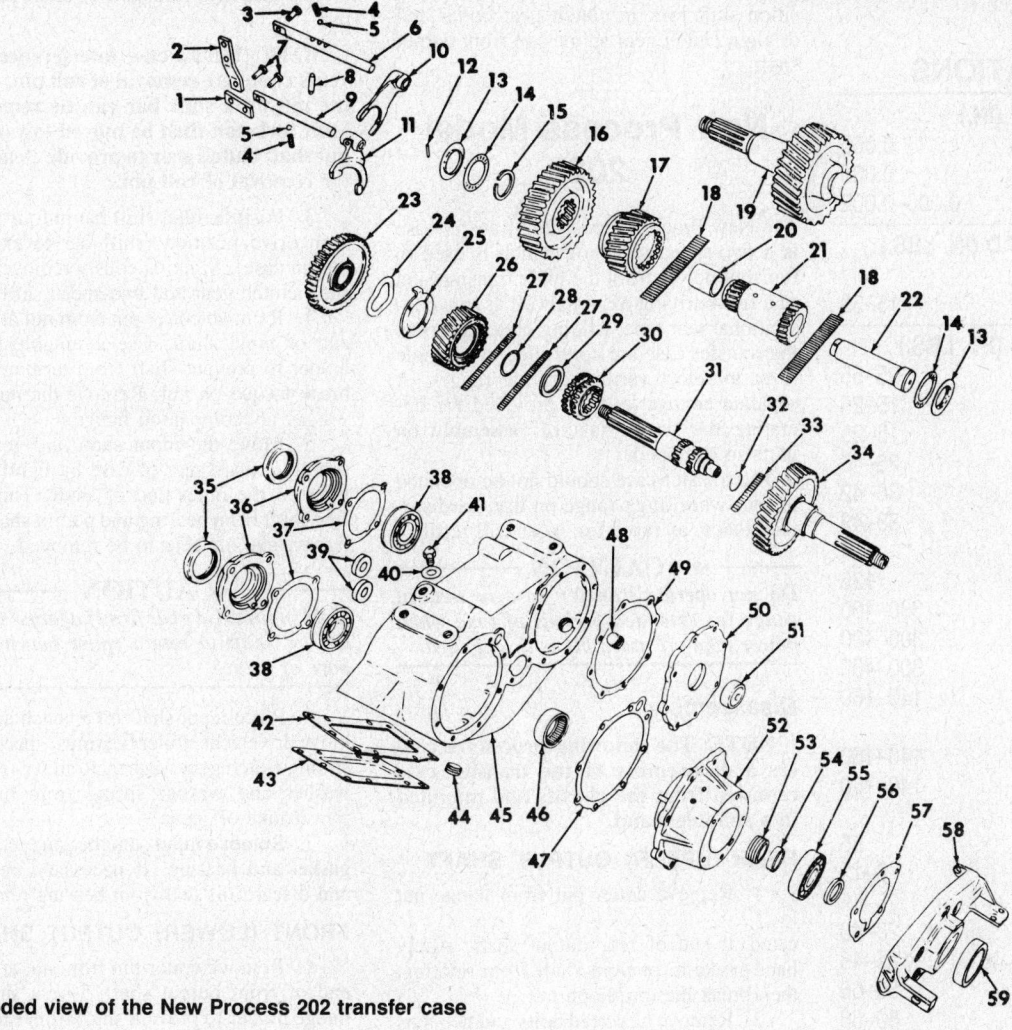

Exploded view of the New Process 202 transfer case

1. Link, shift lever
2. Lever, shift
3. Pin, rod
4. Spring, shift bar poppet
5. Ball, shift bar poppet
6. Bar, shift, two-speed
7. Pin, rod
8. Plunger, shift bar interlock
9. Bar, shift idler
10. Fork, shift, two-speed
11. Fork, shift, idler
12. Pin, idler shaft
13. Bearing, thrust, race
14. Bearing, thrust, needle
15. Ring, snap, idler
16. Gear, idler drive
17. Gear, sliding, idler
18. Bearing, roller, idler, shaft
19. Gear, lower shaft (front output)

20. Spacer, rotating shaft
21. Shaft, idler gear, rotating
22. Shaft, idler gear, stationary
23. Gear, PTO, input shaft, upper
24. Spring, friction washer, input shaft
25. Washer, friction, input shaft
26. Gear, drive, input shaft, upper
27. Bearing, roller, input shaft, front
28. Spacer, input shaft drive gear bearing
29. Washer, input shaft sliding clutch
30. Gear, clutch, input shaft, upper
31. Shaft, input
32. Ring, snap
33. Bearing, roller, drive gear

34. Gear, shaft, output drive
35. Seal, oil, input and output shaft, front
36. Retainer, bearing, input and output shaft, front
37. Gasket, bearing retainer
38. Bearing, input and output shaft, front
39. Seal, oil, shift bar
40. Gasket, shift bar poppet screw
41. Screw, shift bar poppet
42. Gasket, PTO cover
43. Cover, PTO opening
44. Plug, pipe
45. Case, transfer
46. Bearing, gear, output shaft, inner
47. Gasket, rear bearing retainer, upper

48. Plug, pipe
49. Gasket, rear bearing retainer, lower
50. Retainer, lower rear bearing (front output shaft)
51. Bearing, lower shaft, rear
52. Retainer, upper rear (output shaft) bearing
53. Gear, speedometer drive gear
54. Spacer, speedometer drive gear
55. Bearing, output shaft drive gear, outer
56. Spacer, brake drum flange
57. Gasket, brake drum support
58. Support, hand brake
59. Seal, oil, output shaft bearing, rear

side of the gear is toward the front of the case.

SPECIFICATIONS

END PLAY (IN.)

Input shaft	0.005
Front output shaft	0.005
Idler gear	0.000–0.002

BEARING PRELOAD (IN. LBS.)

Rear output shaft bearings	15–30

TORQUE LIMITS (FT. LBS.)

Front retainer nut	35–55
Poppet screw	15–25
Idler cover screw	15–25
Drain and filler plugs	25–45
Top cover	38–42
All bearing caps	38–42
Flange and idler shaft nut	125
Input shaft	300–400
Front output shaft	300–400
Rear output shaft	300–400
Idler shaft nut	140–160
Front output shaft flange nut	140–160
Input shaft flange nut	140–160
Driveshaft mating flange nuts	35
Breather	8–12
Brake support nut	25–45
Brake retaining screw	20–40
Brake retainer nut	25–45
Brake drum	60–66
Brake mounting	60–66
Brake drum nut	140–160
P.T.O. screw	8–12
P.T.O. to case	38–42
P.T.O. bearing cap	38–42
P.T.O. top cover	38–42
P.T.O. shaft	300–400

FRONT OUTPUT SHAFT

1. The front output shaft drive gear bearing consists of 70 bearing rollers divided into two rows by a spacer.

2. Coat gear bore with grease, then position rollers and spacer.

3. Hold thrust washers against each hub to retain rollers, then install gear on shaft.

4. Shaft end-play is controlled by gasket thickness between case and bearing retainer.

5. Position retainer on case, then measure clearance with a feeler gauge.

6. Select gasket(s) with a thickness .005 in. more than measured clearance.

7. Remove retainer and install selected gasket(s), then reinstall retainer.

8. When installing the front output shaft assembly in the case, locate front output shift bar as far toward rear of case as possible. This will make it possible to position shift fork in clutch gear collar and to align clutch gear splines on front output shaft.

New Process Model 202

The New Process Model 202 transfer case is a two-speed gear box which is used to transmit power from the main transmission to a front driving axle, as well as to a conventional rear axle. Sliding clutch gears in the transfer case are controlled by a single lever to select various driving ranges. A separate control lever is provided for operating the power take-off assembly on units so equipped.

The transfer case should not be operated in four-wheel high range on dry, hard surface roads, as rapid tire wear will result.

---CAUTION---
Do not operate transfer case in neutral range for extended periods of time when power take-off assembly is disengaged.

Disassembly

NOTE: The following procedure covers a disassembly of the transfer case removed from the chassis and mounted in a suitable stand.

REAR (UPPER) OUTPUT SHAFT

1. Remove cotter pin from flange nut located at end of rear output shaft. Apply hand brake to prevent shaft from rotating; then break the torque on nut.

2. Remove hex head bolts and two nuts securing bearing retainer to case. Remove the rear output shaft assembly. Remove and discard gasket.

3. Place the output shaft assembly on a bench.

4. Remove the nut and flat washer at rear of shaft. Tap brake drum lightly and remove drum from shaft. Slide off brake drum flange spacer.

5. Remove output shaft with drive gear from upper rear bearing retainer. Slide off speedometer drive gear, spacer and drive gear inner bearing. Remove snap-ring and fifteen roller bearings.

6. Remove hex nuts and lock washers securing hand brake support to upper rear bearing retainer. Remove brake support and drive gear outer bearing. Remove oil seal and discard.

INPUT SHAFT

1. Remove ten capscrews and lock washers attaching power take-off cover or assembly (if so equipped). Remove and discard gasket.

2. Remove shift bar poppet screw, spring and ball. Through the rear output shaft opening in case, remove roll pin securing two-speed shift fork on bar. Use a 5/32 in. diameter steel rod to drive out roll pin.

NOTE: Where case interference prevents complete removal of roll pin, drive the pin until shift bar can be removed. Shift fork can then be moved toward input shaft clutch gear to provide clearance for removal of roll pin.

3. Position idler shift bar in four-wheel high drive position (shift bar to extreme rear in case). Simultaneously remove input shaft clutch gear and two-speed shift fork.

4. Remove cotter pin from nut at outer end of input shaft. Use a suitable flange holder to prevent shaft from turning; then break torque on nut. Remove the nut, flat washer and companion flange.

5. Move the input shaft and gear assembly toward rear of case by lightly tapping on the outer end of shaft. This will free shaft from bearing and permit shaft and power take-off gear to be removed.

---CAUTION---
Hold input drive gear firmly against shoulder on shaft to retain roller bearings in bore of gear.

6. Place input shaft on a bench and remove drive gear, roller bearings, spacer and sliding clutch gear washer. Remove friction washer and washer spring from hub of power take-off gear.

7. Remove input shaft bearing retainer, gasket and bearing. If necessary, remove and discard oil seal from bearing retainer.

FRONT (LOWER) OUTPUT SHAFT

1. Remove cotter pin from nut at outer end of front output shaft. Use a suitable flange holder to prevent shaft from turning; then break torque on nut. Remove nut, flat washer and flange.

2. Remove hex head bolts and nuts attaching input shaft rear bearing retainer to case. Lightly tap on end of shaft, moving it toward rear of case to displace shoulder on rear bearing retainer. Remove drive gear and shaft.

3. Press drive gear rear bearing from retainer. Remove front bearing retainer and bearing. If lubricant leakage is evident at the retainer, remove oil seal and discard.

IDLER SHIFT BAR AND GEAR

1. Remove roll pin securing fork to idler shift bar. Use a 5/32" diameter steel rod to drive out pin. Withdraw shift bar and fork.

NOTE: Spring tension on poppet ball will displace ball from case upon removing shift bar.

2. Remove shift bar interlock plunger and spring.

3. Remove roll pin from outer end of idler gear stationary shaft. Using a brass drift, drive the idler shaft toward rear of case. Remove shaft.

4. Remove idler gear rotating shaft assembly through the opening from which the

rear output shaft assembly was removed. Place the gear assembly on a bench.

5. Remove thrust bearing and thrust bearing race at each end of rotating shaft. Remove individual roller bearing and spacer.

6. Remove snap-ring; then separate idler drive gear and shaft. Remove sliding clutch gear.

Assembly

Lubricate all bearings, bushings, spline shafts and shift bar forks at their contact surfaces during assembly. This will provide initial lubrication and avoid possible damage when the transfer case is first operated.

IDLER SHIFT BAR AND GEAR

1. Place the idler gear rotating shaft in a vertical position with the large splined gear end resting on bench.

2. Position sliding clutch gear on shaft with the groove which receives idler shift fork, facing upward.

3. Position drive gear on shaft so that gear internal splines engage splines on shaft.

——————— CAUTION ———————

The long shoulder side of drive gear must face slid-clutch gear to provide clearance with the inside face of case.

4. Install snap-ring and check for proper side clearance with drive gear. This is accomplished by inserting a feeler gauge between the ring and gear. Three different thicknesses of snap-rings are available for obtaining proper clearance. Select and install proper size. Refer to Specifications for recommended snap-ring side clearance.

NOTE: Snap-ring side clearance must be maintained to prevent possible ring breakage.

5. Coat the bore of idler gear rotating shaft with Lubriplate No. 110; then assemble roller bearings and spacer. Apply Lubriplate to thrust bearing and bearing race; then assemble at each end of idler rotating shaft. Carefully place rotating shaft assembly in case. Align shaft with opening in front and rear of case for installing the stationary shaft. Install stationary shaft, making certain not to disturb roller bearing arrangement in bore of rotating shaft. Tap the shaft lightly until seated. Install roll pin in shaft at front of case.

6. Position poppet spring and ball in case. Hold the spring and ball in a compressed position and insert idler shift bar at front side of case. Place idler shift fork in position on sliding gear (shoulder on fork toward front of case) and install on shift bar. Secure fork to shift bar with roll pin.

NOTE: Side of shift bar employing only one detent must be facing upwards.

INPUT SHAFT

1. Place the input drive gear on a bench and assemble roller bearings and spacer.

Coat the gear bore with Lubriplate No. 110 to retain bearing rollers.

2. Install sliding clutch washer; then carefully position drive gear with bearings on shaft. Place friction washer on shaft next to drive gear, with the tang opposite gear.

3. Assemble friction washer spring on hub of power take-off gear.

NOTE: Install spring on recess side of gear.

4. Assemble input shaft with drive gear and power take-off gear in case. Hold the drive gear firmly to clutch gear washer to keep roller bearings in place.

NOTE: Rotate friction washer until tang engages blind hole in power take-off gear.

5. With the idler shift bar in four-wheel high drive position (shift bar to extreme rear of case), insert interlock plunger in case.

6. Install two-speed shift bar in case so that side of bar with the single detent is facing the idler shift bar. Install sliding clutch gear and two-speed shift bar fork. Install rod pin to secure fork to shift bar.

7. Install input shaft bearing.

——————— CAUTION ———————

Movement of input shaft toward rear of case while installing bearing will permit rollers to become displaced from bore of drive gear.

8. Position bearing retainer to case and install hex head bolts finger tight. Do not torque bolts at this time since gasket thickness must be determined following installation of rear output shaft assembly.

FRONT (LOWER) OUTPUT SHAFT

1. Install front output shaft bearing in face of case.

2. Install front output shaft and drive gear.

3. Press drive gear rear bearing in retainer. Install bearing with stamped end of bearing resting on press. Position gasket and retainer at rear face of case. Install hex head bolts with lock washers and tighten securely.

4. Install new oil seal in bearing retainer. Assemble retainer to front face of case and install hex head bolts finger tight. Do not torque bolts at this time.

REAR (UPPER) OUTPUT SHAFT

1. Support rear output shaft bearing retainer in a press; then install shaft inner bearing flush with outer surface of retainer.

2. Place bearing retainer on a bench and assemble drive gear and shaft. Position speedometer drive gear and spacer on shaft. Assemble outer bearing on shaft and install in upper rear bearing retainer. Install hand brake drum spacer.

3. Install new oil seal in hand brake support. Install gasket and brake support to upper rear bearing retainer.

4. Position gasket to bearing retainer

and install the rear output assembly on case.

INPUT AND FRONT OUTPUT SHAFT

Bearing Adjustment

The fit of the input and front output shaft bearing retainer to their respective bearings is controlled by gasket thickness. To determine the correct thickness or number of gaskets required, measure the clearance between retainer and case with a feeler gauge. Select gasket(s) which will give a bearing retainer fit within specified limits. See Specifications. Remove the retainer; then install selected gasket(s) and retainer.

SPECIFICATIONS

BEARING CLEARANCE (IN.)

Input and front output shaft bearings	0.003–0.006
Gasket thickness available	0.009–0.011
	0.0135–0.0165

SNAP RING (IN.)

Side clearance	0.007–0.013
Thickness available	0.092–0.094
	0.095–0.097
	0.098–0.100

POPPET BALL SPRING

Free length	1.0 in.
Pressure @ $^{21}/_{32}$"	30 lbs.

TORQUE LIMITS (FT. LBS.)

Flange nut	Minimum 125

New Process Model 203 (Full Time Four Wheel Drive)

The New Process Model 203 transfer case is a full-time 4WD unit that operates in 4WD at all times. The unit incorporates a differential similar to axle differentials; compensating for different speeds of the front and rear axles resulting from varying speeds while turning and operating over different surfaces.

There are five shift positions with this transfer case; Neutral, High and High Lock, and Low and Low Lock. The Lock positions are used under low traction conditions. In the Lock position, the differential action of the transfer case is eliminated, by locking the front and rear output shafts together. In this mode, neither the front or rear axle can rotate independently of the other.

Disassembly

1. Loosen rear output shaft flange retaining nut and remove front output shaft

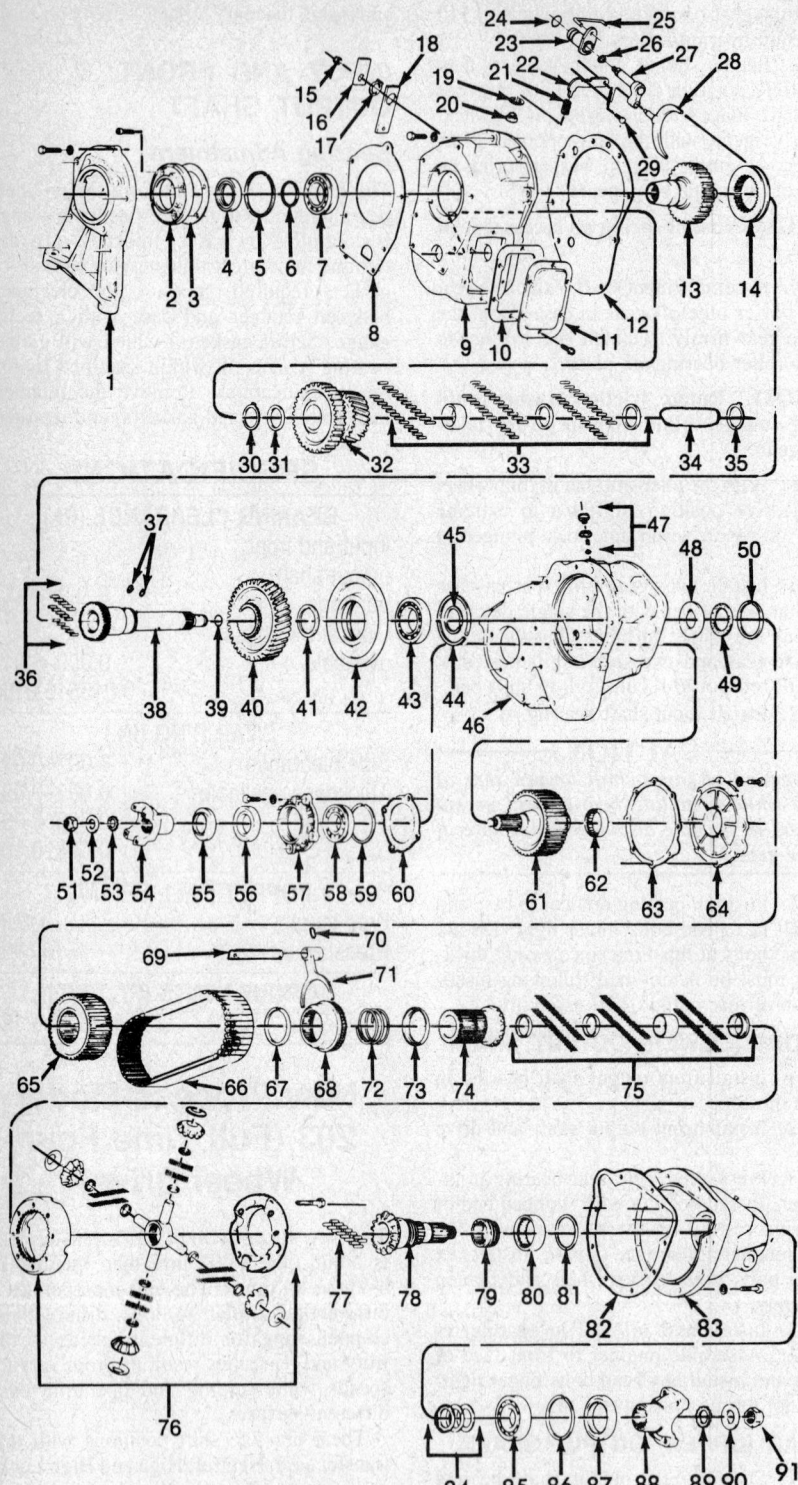

Exploded view of the New Process 203 full time transfer case

1. Adapter
2. Input gear bearing retainer
3. Input gear bearing retainer gasket
4. Input gear bearing retainer seals
5. Bearing outer ring
6. Bearing to shaft retaining ring
7. Input gear bearing
8. Adapter to selector housing gasket
9. Range selector housing (range box)
10. P.T.O. cover gasket
11. P.T.O. cover
12. Selector housing to chain housing gasket
13. Main drive input gear
14. Range selector sliding clutch
15. Shift lever lock nut
16. Range selector shift lever
17. Shift lever retaining ring
18. Lockout shift lever
19. Detent plate spring plug
20. Detent plate spring plug gasket
21. Detent plate spring
22. Detent plate
23. Lockout shifter shaft
24. O-ring seal
25. Lockout shaft connector link
26. O-ring seal
27. Range selector shifter shaft
28. Range selector shift fork
29. Detent plate pivot pin
30. Thrust washer
31. Spacer (short)
32. Range selector counter gear
33. Counter roller bearings and spacers (72 bearings req'd.)
34. Countergear shaft
35. Thrust washer
36. Input shaft roller bearings (15 req'd.)
37. Thrust washer pins (2 req'd.)
38. Input shaft
39. O-ring seal
40. Low speed and bushing
41. Thrust washer
42. Input shaft bearing retainer
43. Input shaft bearing
44. Input shaft bearing retaining ring (large)
45. Input shaft bearing retaining ring
46. Chain drive housing
47. Lockout shift rail poppet plug, gasket, spring and ball
48. Thrust washer
49. Lubricating thrust washer
50. Retaining ring
51. Flange lock nut
52. Washer
53. Seal
54. Front output yoke
55. Dust shield
56. Front output shaft bearing retainer seal
57. Front output shaft bearing retainer
58. Front output shaft bearing
59. Bearing outer ring
60. Bearing retainer gasket
61. Front output shaft
62. Front output shaft rear bearing
63. Front output rear bearing retainer cover gasket
64. Front output rear bearing retainer
65. Drive shaft sprocket
66. Drive chain
67. Retaining ring
68. Sliding lock clutch
69. Lockout shift rail
70. Shift fork retaining pin
71. Lockout shift fork
72. Lockout clutch spring
73. Spring washer cup
74. Front side gear
75. Front side gear bearing and spaces (123 bearings req'd.)
76. Differential carrier assembly (132 bearings req'd.)
77. Rear output shaft roller bearings (15 req'd.)
78. Rear output shaft
79. Speedometer drive gear
80. Rear output shaft front roller bearing
81. Oil pump O-ring seal
82. Rear output housing gasket
83. Rear output housing
84. Shim pack
85. Rear output rear bearing
86. Bearing retainer
87. Rear output shaft seal
88. Rear output flanger
89. Rear output shaft rubber seal
90. Washer
91. Flange nut

flange and washer.

2. Tap the front output shaft dust seal away from case assembly. Remove front output shaft bearing retainer and gasket.

3. Position transfer case assembly on blocks with input shaft facing downward.

4. Remove rear output shaft assembly from transfer case. Slide the differential carrier off the shaft.

5. Place a 1½ in. to 2 in. band type hose clamp on input shaft to retain bearings.

6. Lift shift rail and driveout pin retaining shift fork.

7. Remove shift rail poppet ball plug, gasket and ball from case. Use a magnet to remove poppet ball.

8. Push shift rail down, lift up on lockout clutch and remove shift fork from clutch assembly.

9. Remove front output shaft rear bearing retainer. It may be necessary to gently tap front of shaft or cautiously pry retainer from case. Make certain that no roller bearings are lost from rear cover.

10. When necessary, remove rear bearing by pressing.

11. Pry front output shaft front bearing from lower side of case.

12. Remove front output shaft assembly from case.

13. Lift intermediate housing from range box, after removing bolts.

14. Remove chain from intermediate housing.

15. Remove lockout clutch, drive gear and input shaft from range box.

16. Install a 1½" to 2" band type hose clamp on end of input shaft to retain roller bearings.

17. Pull up on shift rail and remove rail from link.

18. Lift input shaft assembly from range box.

Assembly

1. Position range box with input gear side down, on wood blocks.

2. Place gasket on input housing.

3. Install lockout clutch and drive sprocket on input shaft assembly. Install a 2″ band type hose clamp on end of input shaft to prevent loss of bearings during installation.

4. Place input shaft, lockout clutch and drive sprocket in range box. Align tab on bearing retainer with notch in gasket.

5. Engage lockout clutch shift rail to the connector link. Position rail in housing bore and turn shifter shaft lowering rail into the housing. This will prevent the link and rail from becoming disconnected.

6. Place the drive chain in housing with the chain around the outer wall.

7. Secure the chain housing to the range box. Be sure that the shift rail engages the channel of the housing. Place the chain on the input drive sprocket.

8. Place the front output sprocket in transfer case. Turn the clutch drive gear to assist in positioning chain on sprocket.

9. Position the shift fork and rail on the clutch assembly. Install the clutch assembly completely into the drive sprocket. Insert retaining pin in shift fork and rail.

10. Install front output bearing, gasket, retainer, bolts, flange, gasket, seal, washer and retaining nut.

11. If rear bearing was removed from front output shaft, press a new bearing into the outside face of cover until bearing is flush with opening.

12. Install front output shaft, rear bearing, retainer, gasket and bolts.

13. Slip differential carrier assembly on the input shaft. Bolts on carrier must face rear of shaft.

14. Load bearings in pinion shaft, install rear output housing assembly, gasket and bolts.

15. Install a dial indicator on the rear housing. The indicator must contact the end of the output shaft. While holding the rear flange, rotate the front output shaft and find the highest point of gear hop. Reset indicator and with rear output shaft at high point, pull up on the end of the shaft to determine end-play. Remove indicator and install shim pack to control end-play to between 0 and .005″. The shim pack is positioned on the shaft in front of the rear bearing. Check for binding of rear output shaft.

16. Insert lockout clutch shift rail poppet ball, spring and screw plug in transfer case.

17. Install poppet plate spring, gasket and plug, if they were not previously installed.

18. Install shift levers on the range box, if these were not left on vehicle.

19. Torque all bolts, locknuts and plugs to specifications.

20. Fill transfer case with specified lubricant until the proper level is reached. Secure filler plug.

TRANSFER CASE SUBASSEMBLIES OVERHAUL

LOCKOUT CLUTCH ASSEMBLY

Disassembly

1. Remove front side gear from input shaft assembly.

2. Remove thrust washer, roller bearings and spacers from front side gear bore. The position of the spacers must be noted.

3. Remove the snap-ring which holds the drive sprocket to clutch assembly. Slip the drive sprocket from the front side gear.

4. Remove the lower snap-ring.

5. Remove sliding gear, spring and spring cup washer from the front side gear.

6. Thoroughly clean and inspect all component parts. Replace any component that is worn or defective.

Assembly

1. Place spring cup washer, spring and sliding clutch gear on front side gear.

2. Secure sliding clutch to front side gear with a snap-ring.

3. Spread petroleum jelly on front side gear and install roller bearings and spacers.

4. Place thrust washer in gear end of front side gear.

5. Slide drive sprocket on clutch splines and secure with snap-ring.

DIFFERENTIAL CARRIER ASSEMBLY

Disassembly

1. Separate differential carrier sections and lift out pinion gear and spider assembly.

2. Note that undercut side of pinion gear spider faces toward front of side gear.

3. Remove pinion thrust washers, pinion roller washer gears and roller bearings from spider unit.

4. Thoroughly clean and inspect all component parts. Replace any component that is worn or damaged.

Assembly

1. Spread petroleum jelly on pinion gears and install roller bearings.

2. Position on the leg of each spider, pinion roller washer, pinion gear and thrust washer.

3. Position the spider assembly in front half of the carrier. The undercut surface of the spider thrust surface face downward or toward teeth.

4. Secure carrier halves together. Make certain the marks are aligned. Torque all bolts to specifications.

INPUT SHAFT ASSEMBLY

Disassembly

1. Remove thrust washer and spacer from shaft.

2. Remove bearing retainer assembly from input shaft.

3. Hold low speed gear and lightly tap shaft from gear. Note the position of the thrust washer pins in input shaft.

4. Remove snap-ring holding input bearing in retainer using a screw driver. Lightly tap rear bearing out of retainer.

5. Remove pilot roller bearing and O-ring from end of input shaft.

6. Thoroughly clean and inspect all component parts. Replace any component that is worn or damaged.

Assembly

1. Tap or press input bearing into retainer. Be sure that ball loading slots are toward concave side of retainer. Install securing snap ring. Make certain that selective snap-ring of proper thickness is used to provide tightest fit.

2. Position low speed gear on shaft, clutch end facing gear end of input shaft.

3. Place thrust washers on input shaft, align slot in washer with pin in shaft. Slide

or tap washers into position.

4. Place input bearing retainer on shaft and secure with snap-ring. Snap-rings are selective. Use snap-ring that provides tightest fit.

5. Slip spacer and thrust washer on shaft and align with locating pin.

6. Spread heavy grease on end of shaft and install roller bearings.

7. Install rubber O-ring at end of shaft.

RANGE BOX

Disassembly

1. Remove poppet plate spring, plug and gasket.

2. Remove clutch fork and sliding gear by disengaging sliding clutch gear from input gear.

3. Remove upper shift lever from shifter shaft.

4. Remove snap-ring and lower shift lever.

5. Push shifter shaft assembly down and remove lockout clutch connector link. The long end of connector link engages poppet plate.

6. Remove shifter shaft assembly and separate shafts. Remove O-rings.

7. When necessary to remove poppet plate, drive pivot shaft out and remove plate and spring from bottom of case.

8. Remove input gear bearing retainer and seal assembly. Release snap-ring from retainer and tap bearing out of assembly.

9. Release snap-ring holding input shaft bearing to shaft and remove bearing.

10. Remove countershaft from cluster gear and case assembly from intermediate case side. Remove cluster gear assembly from range box.

11. Remove cluster gear thrust washers from case.

12. Thoroughly clean and inspect all component parts. Replace any component that is worn or damaged.

Assembly

1. Spread heavy grease in cluster bore and using proper tool install roller bearings and spacers.

2. Spread heavy grease on case and install thrust washers. Engage tab on thrust washers with slot in case.

3. Place cluster gear assembly in case and install countershaft through front of range box and into gear assembly. Flat face of countershaft must be aligned with case gasket.

4. Place bearing on input gear shaft with snap-ring groove facing out, install a new retaining ring. Insert input gear and bearing in housing. The retaining ring used in this operation is a select fit. Use ring that provides the tightest fit.

5. Secure input gear and bearing with a snap-ring.

6. Match up oil slot in retainer with drain hole in case and insert input gear bearing retainer and gaskets. Install bolts and

torque to specifications.

7. Spread sealant on pin and install poppet pin and pivot pin in housing.

8. Lubricate and install new O-rings on inner and outer shifter shafts.

9. Insert shifter shafts in housing and engage long end of lockout clutch connector link with outer shifter shaft. Complete this operation before assembly bottoms out.

10. Install lower shift lever and retaining ring.

11. Install upper shift lever and shaft retaining nut.

12. Install shift fork and sliding clutch gear. Push fork up into shifter shaft and engage poppet plate. Move sliding clutch gear onto input shaft gear.

13. Insert poppet plate spring, gasket and plug in housing top. Make certain that spring engages poppet plate.

INPUT GEAR BEARING

Replacement

1. Remove bearing retainer and gasket from housing.

2. Remove and discard snap-ring holding bearing in retainer.

3. Pry bearing from case and remove from shaft.

4. Inspect input gear and bearing retainer for damage or wear. Replace if necessary.

5. Place new bearing and snap-ring on input gear. Using a soft hammer, tap bearing into position. Secure snap-ring.

6. Insert bearing retainer into housing and secure with attaching bolts. Tighten bolts to specifications.

INPUT GEAR RETAINER SEAL

Replacement

1. Remove bearing retainer from housing.

2. Remove seal from retainer by prying.

3. Place new seal on retainer and install with proper seal driver.

4. Install bearing retainer in housing and secure with attaching bolts. Tighten bolts to specifications.

REAR OUTPUT SHAFT HOUSING ASSEMBLY

Disassembly

1. Remove speedometer driven gear from housing.

2. Remove rear output flange and washer, if they have not been removed previously.

3. Using a soft hammer tap on flange end of pinion and remove the pinion. If speedometer drive gear does not come off with pinion reach into case and remove.

4. Remove old seal from bore with

suitable prying tool.

5. Remove snap ring retaining rear output rear bearing.

6. Tap bearing out of housing.

7. Install a long drift into rear opening of housing and drive out front output bearing. Remove seal and discard.

Assembly

1. Spread grease on front bearing seal and place in bore. Place bearing in bore and press until it bottoms in housing.

2. Using a soft hammer tap rear bearing into place. Secure with proper snap-ring. Snap-rings are selective, use the one that provides the tightest fit.

3. Place rear seal in bore and drive into position with suitable tool. When seal is in position it should be approximately ⅛" to 3/16" below housing face.

4. Place speedometer drive gear on output shaft with shims of approximately .050" thickness. Insert output shaft into carrier through housing front opening.

5. Install flange and washer on output shaft. Leave retaining nut loose until shim requirements are known.

6. Install speedometer driven gear.

SPECIFICATIONS

TORQUE (FT. LBS.)

Adapter to transfer case bolts	38
Adapter to transmission bolts	40
Transfer case to frame nuts (upper)	50
Transfer case to frame nuts (lower)	65
Shift lever attaching nuts	25
Shift lever rod swivel locknuts	50
Shift lever locking arm nut	150 in. lbs.
Skid plate bolt retaining nuts	45
Crossmember bolt retaining nuts	45
Adapter mount bolts	25
Intermediate case to range box bolts	30
Front output bearing retainer bolts	30
Output shaft yoke nuts	150
Front output rear bearing retainer bolts	30
Differential assembly screws	45
Rear output shaft housing	30
Poppet ball retainer nut	15
PTO cover bolts	15
Front input bearing retainer bolts	20
Filler plug	25

FRONT OUTPUT SHAFT BEARING RETAINER SEAL

Replacement

1. Remove old seal from retainer bore.
2. Inspect and clean retainer.
3. Spread sealer on outer edge of new seal.
4. Place new seal in retainer bore and drive into position with proper tool.

FRONT OUTPUT BEARING

Replacement

1. Remove rear cover from case assembly and discard gasket.
2. Press old bearing from cover.
3. Place new bearing on outside face of cover. Cover bearing with a wood block and press into cover until bearing is flush with opening.
4. Place gasket on transfer case and tap cover into position using a soft hammer. Secure cover with attaching bolts and tighten to specifications.

New Process Model 205

The New Process Model 205 transfer case is a two-speed gearbox mounted between the main transmission and the rear axle. The gearbox transmits power from the transmission and engine to the front and rear driving axles.

Disassembly

TRANSFER CASE

1. Clean the exterior of the case.
2. Remove the nuts from the universal joint flanges.
3. Remove the front output shaft rear bearing retainer, front bearing retainer and drive flange.
4. Tap the front output shaft assembly from the case with a soft hammer. Remove the sliding clutch, front output high gear, washer and bearing from the case.
5. Remove the rear output shaft housing attaching bolts and remove the housing, output shaft, bearing retainer and speedometer gear.
6. Slide the rear output shaft from the housing.

NOTE: Be careful not to lose the 15 needle bearings that will be loose when the rear output shaft is removed.

7. Drive the two ¼ in. shift rail pin access hole plugs into the transfer case with a punch and hammer.
8. Remove the two shift rail detent nuts and springs from the case. Use a magnet to remove the two detent balls.
9. Position both shift rails in neutral and remove the shift fork retaining roll pins with a long punch.
10. Remove the clevis pin from one shift rail and rail link.
11. Remove the range shift rail first, then the 4WD shift rail.
12. Remove the shift forks and sliding clutch from the case. Remove the input shaft bearing retainer, bearing and shaft.
13. Remove the cup plugs and rail pins, if they were driven out, from the case.
14. Remove the locknut from the idler gear shaft.
15. Remove the idler gear shaft rear cover.
16. Remove the idler gear shaft, using a soft hammer and a drift.
17. Roll the idler gear assembly to the front output shaft hole and remove the assembly from the case.

REAR OUTPUT SHAFT AND YOKE

1. Loosen rear output shaft yoke nut.
2. Remove shaft housing bolts, then remove the housing and retainer assembly.
3. Remove retaining nut and yoke from the shaft, then remove the shaft assembly.
4. Remove the discard snap ring.
5. Remove thrust washer and pin.
6. Remove tanged bronze washer. Re-

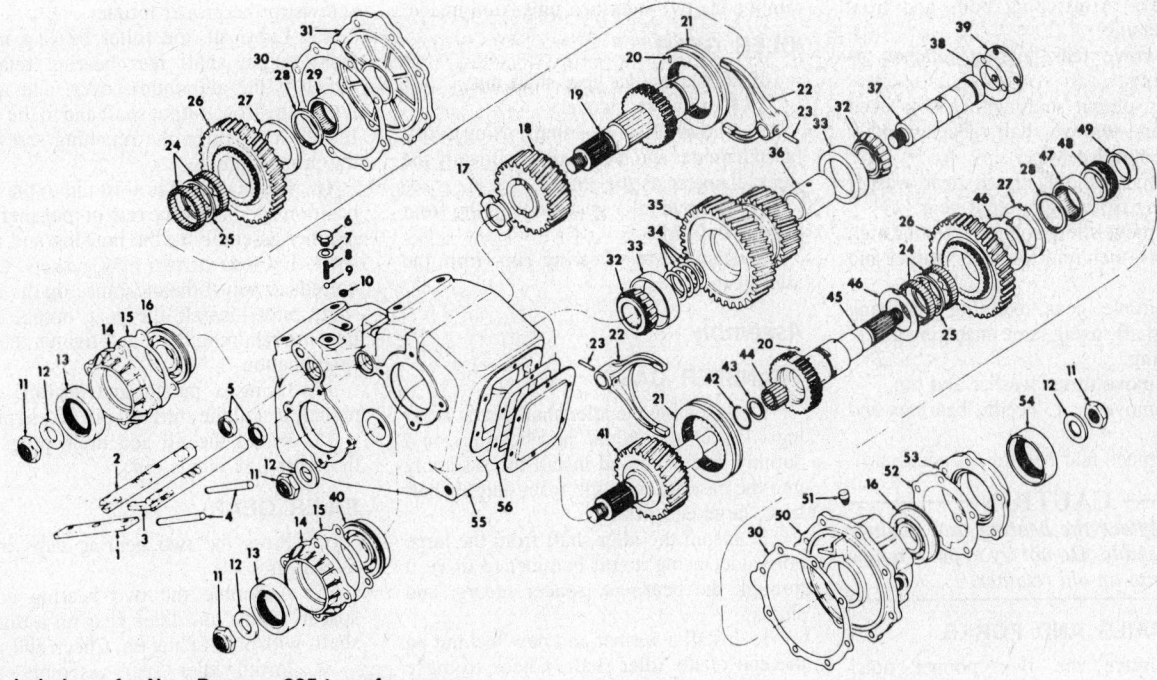

Exploded view of a New Process 205 transfer case

1. Shift lever link	8. Spring	15. Gasket	22. Fork	29. Bearing	36. Spacer	43. Washer	50. Retainer
2. Bar	9. Ball	16. Bearing	23. Pin	30. Gasket	37. Shaft	44. Bearing	51. Breather
3. Bar	10. Plug	17. Washer	24. Bearing	31. Retainer	38. Gasket	45. Gear	52. Gasket
4. Plunger	11. Nut	18. Gear	25. Spacer	32. Cone	39. Cover	46. Washer	53. Retainer
5. Seal	12. Washer	19. Shaft	26. Gear	33. Cup	40. Bearing	47. Bearing	54. Seal
6. Screw	13. Seal	20. Pin	27. Washer	34. Shim set	41. Shaft	48. Gear	55. Case
7. Gasket	14. Retainer	21. Clutch	28. Ring	35. Gear	42. Ring	49. Spacer	56. Gasket

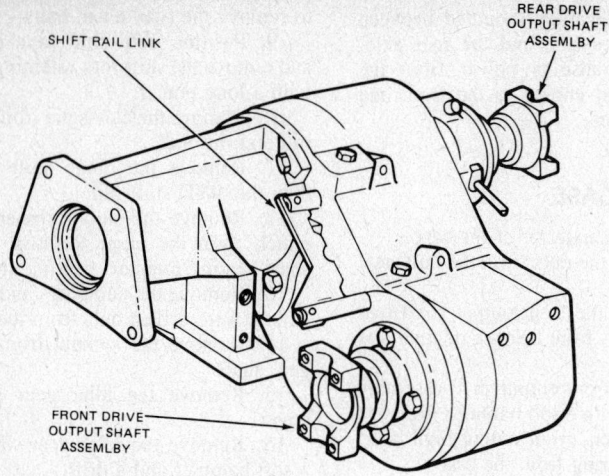

SHIFT RAIL LINK

REAR DRIVE
OUTPUT SHAFT
ASSEMLBY

FRONT DRIVE
OUTPUT SHAFT
ASSEMLBY

Front view of a model 205 transfer case

move gear needle bearings, spacer and second row of needle bearings.

7. Remove tanged bronze thrust washer.

8. Remove pilot rollers, retainer ring and washer.

9. Remove oil seal retainer, ball bearing, speedometer gear and spacer. Discard gaskets.

10. Press out bearing.

11. Remove oil seal from the retainer.

FRONT OUTPUT SHAFT

1. Remove lock nut, washer and yoke.

2. Remove attaching bolts and front bearing retainer.

3. Remove rear bearing retainer attaching bolts.

4. Tap output shaft with a soft-faced hammer and remove shaft, gear assembly and rear bearing retainer.

5. Remove sliding clutch, gear, washer and bearing from high output gear.

6. Remove sliding clutch from the high output gear; then remove gear, washer and bearing.

7. Remove gear retaining snap-ring from the shaft, using large snap-ring picks. Discard ring.

8. Remove thrust washer and pin.

9. Remove gear, needle bearings and spacer.

10. Replace rear bearing, if necessary.

— CAUTION —
Always replace the bearing and retainer as an assembly. Do not try to press a new bearing into an old retainer.

SHIFT RAILS AND FORKS

1. Remove the two poppet nuts, springs, and using a magnet, the poppet balls.

2. Remove cup plugs on top of case, using a ¼" punch.

3. Position both shift rails in neutral, then remove fork pins with a long handled screw extractor.

4. Remove clevis pins and shift rail link.

5. Lower shift rails; upper rail first and then lower.

6. Remove shift forks and sliding clutch.

7. Remove the front output high gear, washer and bearing. Remove the shift rail cup plugs.

INPUT SHAFT

1. Remove snap-ring in front of bearing. Tap shaft out rear of case and bearing out front of case, using a soft-faced hammer or mallet.

2. Tilt case up on power take-off and remove the two interlock pins from inside.

IDLER GEAR

1. Remove idler gear shaft nut.

2. Remove rear cover.

3. Tap out idler gear shaft, using a soft-faced hammer and a drift approximately the same diameter as the shaft.

4. Remove idler gear through the front output shaft hole.

5. Remove two bearing cups from the idler gear.

Assembly

TRANSFER CASE

1. Assemble the idler shaft gears, bearings, spacer and shims, and bearings on a dummy shaft tool and install the assembly into the case through the front output shaft bore, large end first.

2. Install the idler shaft from the large bore side, using a soft hammer to drive it through the bearings, spacer, gears, and shims.

3. Install a washer and new locknut on the end of the idler shaft. Check to make sure the idler gear rotates freely. Tighten the locknut to specification.

4. Install the idler shaft cover with a new gasket so the flat side faces the rear bearing retainer of the front output shaft. Install and tighten the two retaining screws to the proper torque.

5. Install the interlock pins into the interlock bore through the front of the output

shaft opening.

6. Start the 4WD shift rail into the front of the case, solid end of the rail first, with the detent notches facing up.

7. Position the shift fork onto the shift rail with the long end facing inward. Push the rail through the fork and into the Neutral position.

8. Position the input shaft and bearing in the case.

9. Start the range shift rail into the case from the front, with the detent notches facing up.

10. Position the sliding clutch to the shift fork. Place the sliding clutch on the input shaft and align the fork with the shift rail. Push the rail through the fork into the Neutral position.

11. Install the roll pins that lock the shift forks to the shift rails with a long punch.

12. Position the front wheel drive high gear and its thrust washer in the case. Position the sliding clutch in the shift fork. Shift the rail and fork into the front wheel drive (4WD-Hi) position, while at the same time, meashing the clutch with the mating teeth on the front wheel drive high gear.

13. Align the thrust washer, high gear and sliding clutch with the bearing bore in the case and insert the front output shaft and low gear into the high gear assembly.

14. Install a new seal in the front bearing retainer of the front output shaft, and install the bearing and retainer and new gasket in the case. Tighten the bearing retainer cap screws to the proper torque.

15. Lubricate the roller bearing in the front output shaft rear bearing retainer, which is the aluminum cover, and install it over the front output shaft and to the case. Install and tighten the retaining screws to the proper torque.

16. Move the range shift rail to the High position and install the rear output shaft and retainer assembly to the housing and input shaft. Use one or two new gaskets, as required, to adjust the clearance on the input shaft pilot. Install the rear output shaft housing retaining bolts and tighten them to specification.

17. Using a punch and sealing compound, install the shift rail pin access plugs.

18. Install the fill and drain plugs and the cross-link clevis pin.

IDLER GEAR

1. Press the two bearing cups in the idler gear.

2. Assemble the two bearing cones, spacer, shims and idler gear on a dummy shaft, with bore facing up. Check end-play.

3. Install idler gear assembly (with dummy shaft) into the case, large end first, through the front output shaft bore.

4. Install idler shaft from large bore side, driving it through with a soft-faced hammer or mallet.

5. Install washer and new locknut. Check for free rotation and meausre end-play. Torque locknut to specifications.

6. Install idler shaft cover and new gas-

ket. Torque cover bolts to specifications.

NOTE: Flat side of cover must be positioned towards front output shaft rear cover.

SHIFT RAILS AND FORKS

1. Press the two rail seals into the case.

NOTE: Install seals with metal lip outward.

2. Install interlock pins from inside case.

3. Insert slotted end of front output drive shift rail (with poppet notches up) into back of case.

4. While pushing rail through to neutral position, install shift fork (long end inward).

5. Install input shaft and bearing into case.

6. Install end of range rail (with poppet notches up) into front of case.

7. Install sliding clutch on fork, then place over input shaft in case.

8. Push range rail, while engaging sliding clutch and fork, through to neutral position.

9. Drive new lockpins into forks through holes at top of case.

NOTE: Tilt case on power take-off opening to install range rail lockpin.

FRONT OUTPUT SHAFT AND GEAR

1. Install two rows of needle bearings in the front low output gear and retain with grease.

NOTE: Each row consists of 32 needle bearings and the two rows are separated by a spacer.

2. Position front output shaft in a soft-jaw vise, with spline end down. Place front low gear over shaft with clutch gear facing down; then install thrust washer pin, thrust washer and new snap-ring.

NOTE: Position snap ring gap opposite the thrust washer pin.

3. Place front drive high gear and washer in case. Install sliding clutch in the shift fork, then put fork and rail into 4-High position, meshing front drive high gear and clutch teeth.

4. Align washer, high gear and sliding clutch and bearing bore. Insert front output shaft and low gear assembly through the high gear assembly.

5. Install front output bearing and retainer with a new seal in the case.

6. Clean and grease rollers in front output rear bearing retainer. Install on case with one gasket and bolts coated with sealant. Torque bolts to specifications.

7. Install front output yoke, washer and locknut. Torque locknut to specifications.

REAR OUTPUT SHAFT

1. Install two rows of needle bearings into the output low gear, retaining them with grease.

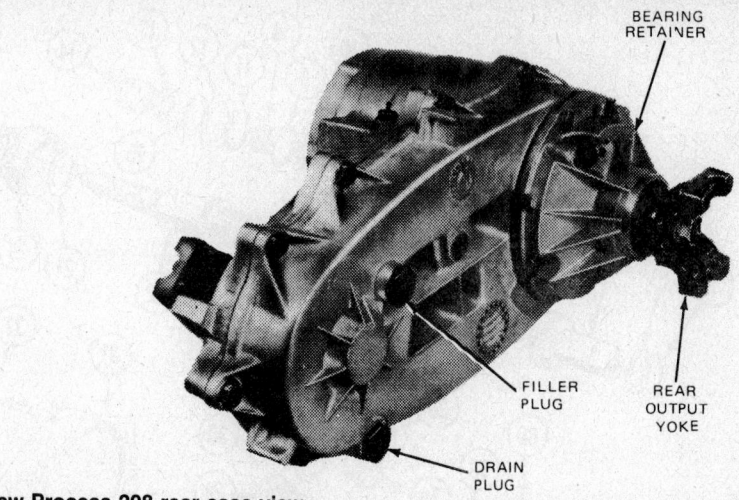

New Process 208 rear case view

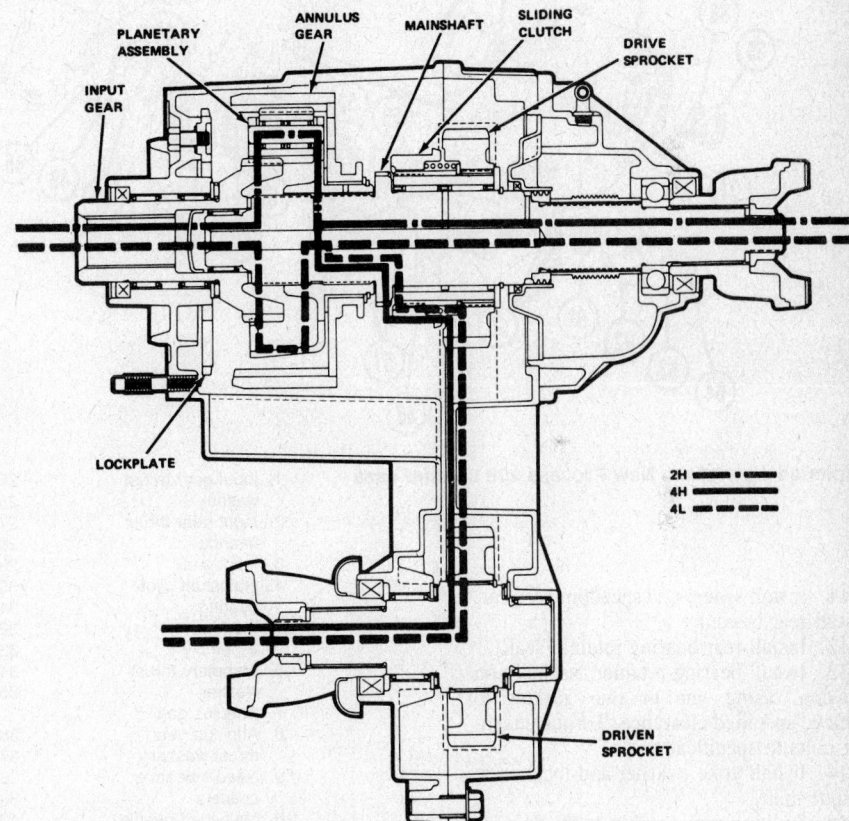

Power flow New Process 208 transfer case

NOTE: Each row consists of 32 needle bearings and the two rows are separated by a spacer.

2. Install thrust washer (with tang down in clutch gear groove) onto the rear output shaft.

3. Install output low gear onto shaft with clutch teeth facing downward.

4. Install thrust washer over gear with tab pointing up and away. Install washer pin.

5. Install large thrust washer over shaft and pin. Turn washer until tab fits into slot

located approximately 90° away from pin.

6. Install snap-ring and measure shaft end-play.

7. Grease pilot bore and install needle bearings.

NOTE: There are 15 pilot needle bearings.

8. Install thrust washer and new snapring in pilot bore.

9. Press new bearing into retainer housing.

10. Install housing on output shaft assembly.

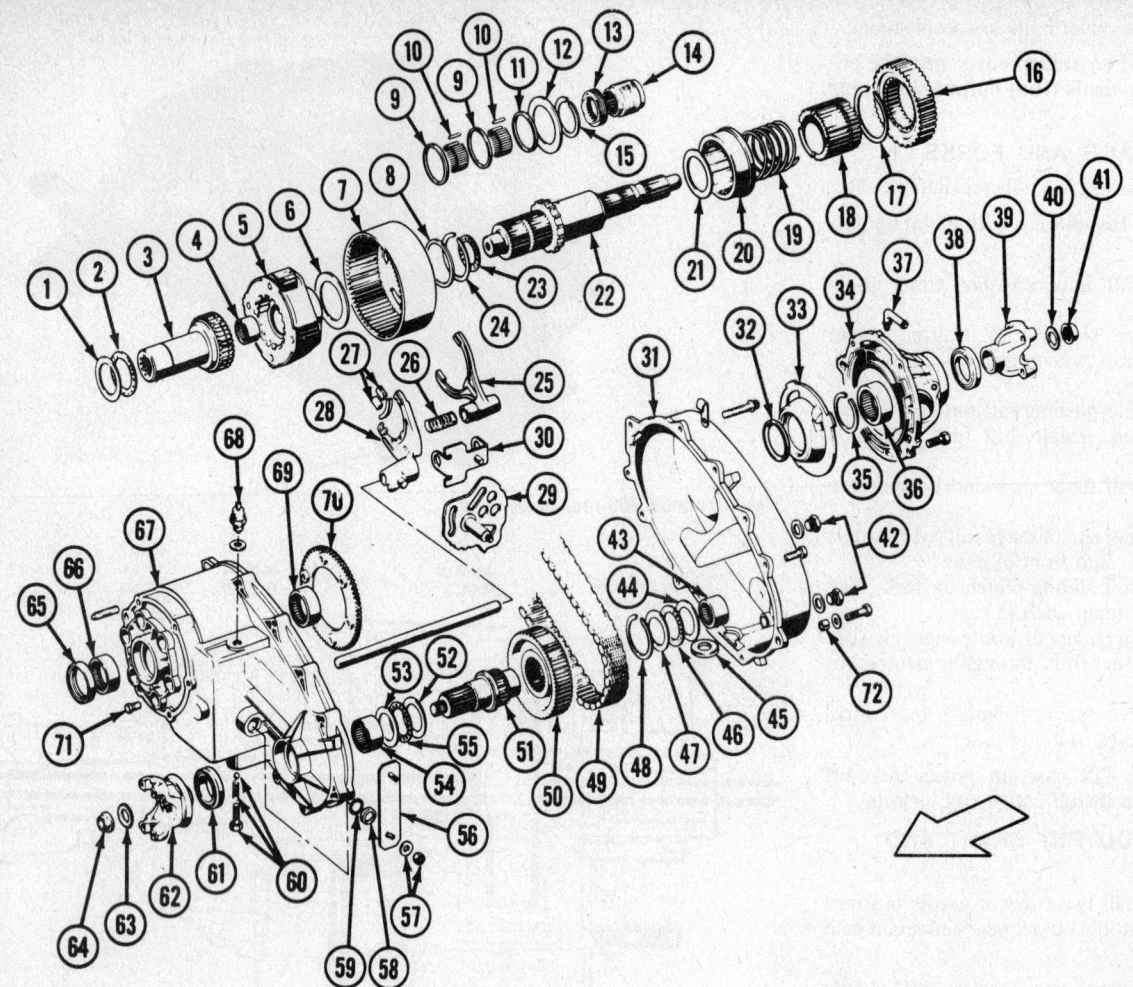

Exploded view of the New Process 208 transfer case

1. Input gear thrust washer
2. Input gear thrust bearing
3. Input gear
4. Mainshaft pilot bearing
5. Planetary assembly
6. Planetary thrust washer
7. Annulus gear
8. Annulus gear thrust washer
9. Needle bearing spacers
10. Mainshaft needle bearings (120)
11. Needle bearing spacer
12. Thrust washer
13. Oil pump
14. Speedometer gear
15. Drive sprocket retaining ring
16. Drive sprocket
17. Sprocket carrier stop ring
18. Sprocket carrier
19. Clutch spring
20. Sliding clutch
21. Thrust washer
22. Mainshaft
23. Mainshaft thrust bearing
24. Annulus gear retaining ring

25. Mode fork
26. Mode fork spring
27. Range fork inserts
28. Range fork
29. Range sector
30. Mode fork bracket
31. Rear case
32. Seal
33. Pump housing
34. Rear retainer
35. Rear output bearing
36. Bearing snap-ring
37. Vent tube
38. Rear seal
39. Rear yoke
40. Yoke seal washer
41. Yoke nut
42. Drain and fill plugs
43. Front output shaft rear bearing
44. Front output shaft rear thrust bearing race (thick)
45. Case magnet
46. Front output shaft rear thrust bearing
47. Front output shaft rear thrust bearing race (thin)
48. Driven sprocket retaining ring
49. Drive chain
50. Driven sprocket
51. Front output shaft
52. Front output shaft

front thrust bearing race (thin)
53. Front output shaft front thrust bearing race (thick)
54. Front output shaft front bearing
55. Front output shaft front thrust bearing
56. Operating lever
57. Washer and locknut
58. Range sector shaft seal retainer
59. Range sector shaft seal
60. Detent ball, spring and retainer bolt
61. Front seal
62. Front yoke
63. Yoke seal washer
64. Yoke nut
65. Input gear oil seal
66. Input gear front bearing
67. Front case
68. Lock mode indicator switch and washer
69. Input gear rear bearing
70. Lockplate
71. Lockplate bolts
72. Case alignment dowels

11. Install spacer and speedometer gear. Install rear bearing.

12. Install rear bearing retainer seal.

13. Install bearing retainer assembly on housing, using one or two gaskets to achieve specified clearance. Torque attaching bolts to specifications.

14. Install yoke, washer and locknut on output shaft.

15. Position range rail in high, then install output shaft and retainer assembly on case. Torque housing bolts to specifications.

CASE

1. Install power take-off cover and gasket. Torque attaching bolts to specifications.

2. Install cup plugs at rail pin holes.

NOTE: After installing, seal the cup plugs.

3. Install drain and filler plugs. Torque to specifications.

4. Install shift rail cross link, clevis pins and lock pins.

SPECIFICATIONS

END PLAY (IN.)

Idler Gear	0.000–0.002 in.
Rear Output Shaft	0.002–0.027 in.

TORQUE LIMITS (FT. LBS.)

Idler Shaft Locknut	150
Idler Shaft Cover	20
Front Output Shaft Front Bearing Retainer	30–35
Front Output Shaft Yoke Locknut	130–150
Rear Output Shaft Bearing Retainer and Housing	30–35
Rear Output Shaft Yoke Locknut	130–150
P.T.O. Cover	15
Front Output Shaft Rear Bearing Retainer	30–35
Filler and Drain Plugs	30
Case to Frame	130
Case to Adapter	25
Adapter Mount	75
Case Bracket to Frame	
Upper	30
Lower	65
Adapter to Transmission	
Manual Transmission	30–35
Automatic Transmission	30–35

New Process Model 208

Assembly

1. Slide the thrust washer against the gear on the rear output shaft.

2. Place the three space rings in position on the rear output shaft. Liberally coat the shaft with petroleum jelly and install the two rows (60 each) of needle bearings in position on the rear output shaft.

3. Carefully slide the sprocket gear carrier over the needle bearings. Be careful not to dislodge any of the needles.

4. Install the retaining ring on the sprocket gear.

5. Slide the chain drive sprocket onto the sprocket carrier gear.

The 208 is a part-time unit with a two piece aluminum housing. On the front case half, the front output shaft, front input shaft, four wheel drive indicator switch and shift lever assembly are located. On the rear case half, the rear output shaft, bearing retainer and drain and fill plugs are located.

Disassembly

1. Drain the fluid from the case.

2. Remove the attaching nuts from the front and rear output yokes. Remove the yokes and sealing washers.

3. Remove the four bolts and separate the rear bearing retainer from the rear case half.

4. Remove the retaining ring, speedometer drive gear nylon oil pump housing,

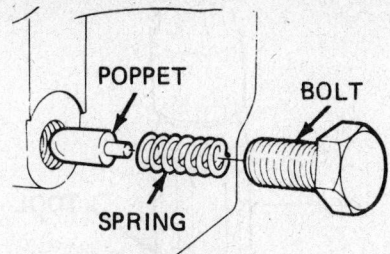

Poppet, spring and bolt

and oil pump gear from the rear output shaft.

5. Remove the eleven bolts and separate the case halves by inserting a screwdriver in the pry slots on the case.

6. Remove the magnetic chip collector from the bottom of the rear case half.

7. Remove the thick thrust washer, thrust bearing and thin thrust washer from the front output shaft assembly.

8. Remove the drive chain by pushing the front input shaft inward and by angling the gear slightly to obtain adequate clearance to remove the chain.

9. Remove the output shaft from the front case half and slide the thick thrust washer, thrust bearing and thin thrust washer off the output side of the front output shaft.

10. Remove the screw, poppet spring and check ball from the front case half.

11. Remove the four wheel drive indicator switch and washer from the front case half.

12. Position the front case half on its face and lift out the rear output shaft, sliding clutch and clutch shift fork and spring.

13. Place a shop towel on the shift rail. Clamp the rail with a vise grip pliers so that they lay between the rail and the case edge. Position a pry bar under the pliers and pry out the shift rail.

14. Remove the snap ring and thrust washer from the planetary gear set assembly in the front case half.

15. Remove the annulus gear assembly and thrust washer from the front case half.

16. Lift the planetary gear assembly from the front case half.

17. Lift out the thrust bearing, sun gear, thrust bearing and thrust washer.

18. Remove the six bolts and lift the gear locking plate from the front case half.

19. Remove the nut retaining the external shift lever and washer. Press the shift control shaft inward and remove the shift selector plate and washer from the case.

20. From the rear output shaft, remove the snap-ring and thrust washer retaining the chain drive sprocket and slide the sprocket from the drive gear.

21. Remove the retaining ring from the sprocket carrier gear.

22. Carefully slide the sprocket carrier gear from the rear output shaft. Remove the two rows of 60 loose needle bearings. Remove the three separator rings from the output shaft.

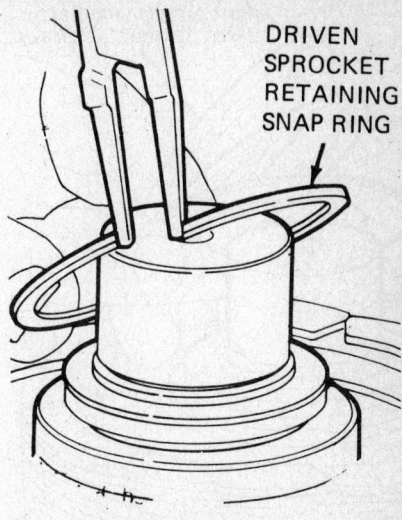

Driven sprocket retaining snap-ring

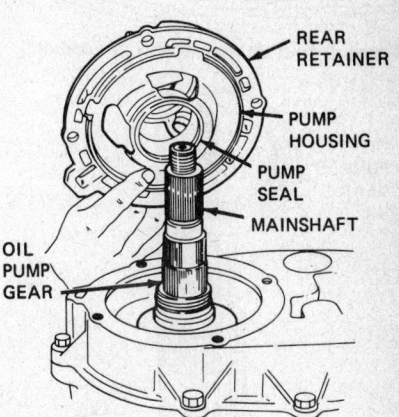

Rear retainer

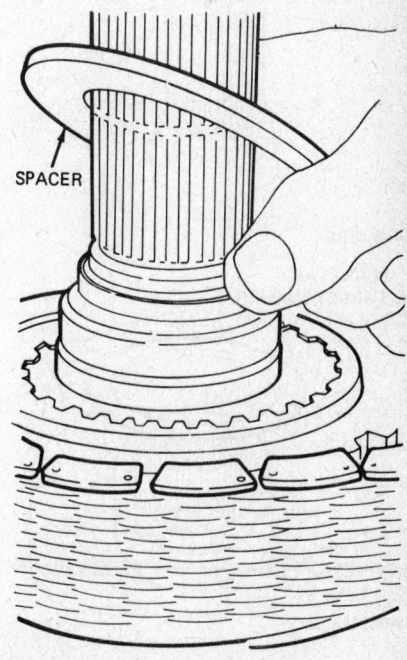

Drive sprocket thrust washer

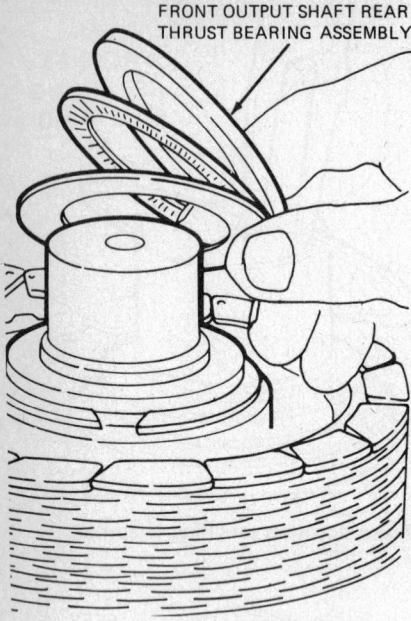

FRONT OUTPUT SHAFT REAR
THRUST BEARING ASSEMBLY

Front output shaft rear thrust washer

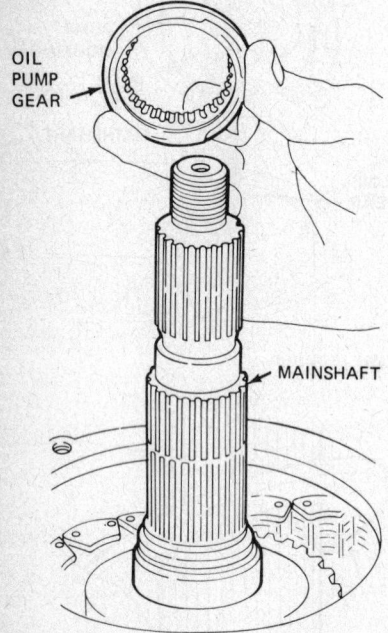

OIL
PUMP
GEAR

MAINSHAFT

Oil pump

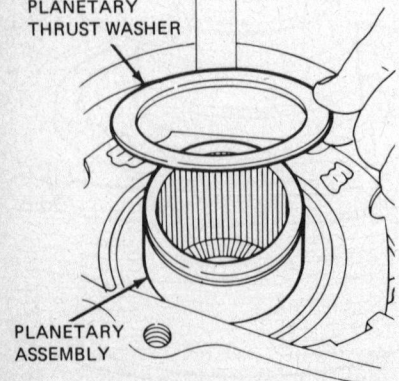

PLANETARY
THRUST WASHER

PLANETARY
ASSEMBLY

Planetary thrust washer and planetary assembly

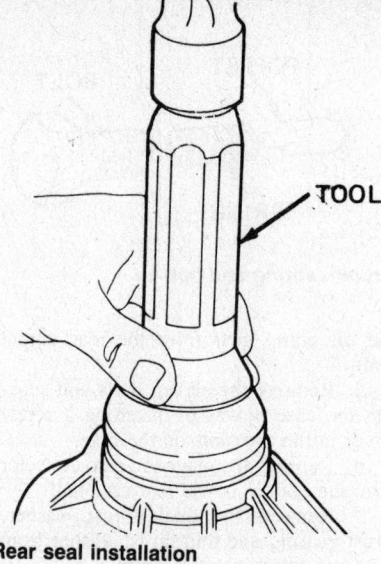

TOOL

Rear seal installation

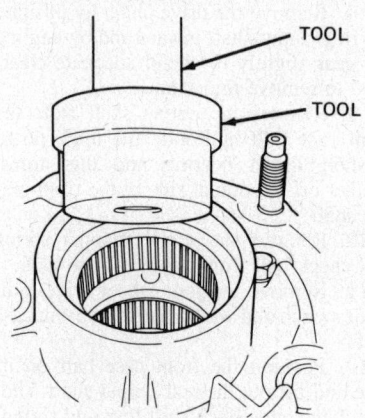

TOOL

TOOL

Input gear bearing removal

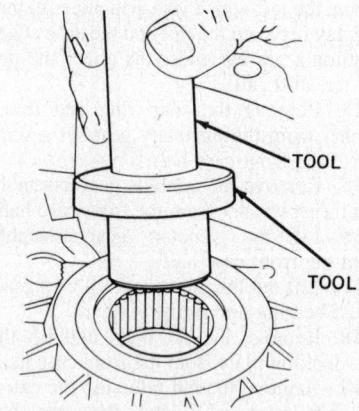

TOOL

TOOL

Front output shaft rear bearing installation

6. Install the thrust washer and snap ring on the rear output shaft.

7. Install the shift selector plate and washer through the front of the case.

8. Place the shift lever assembly on the shift control shaft and torque the nut to 14–20 ft. lbs.

9. Place the locking plate in the front case half and torque the bolts to 25–35 ft. lbs.

10. Place the thrust bearing and washer over the input shaft of the sun gear. Insert the input shaft through the front case half from the inside and insert the thrust bearing.

11. Install the planetary gear assembly so the fixed plate and planetary gears engage the sun gear.

12. Slide the annulus gear and clutch assembly with the shift fork assembly engaged, over the hub of the planetary gear assembly. The shift fork pin must engage the slot in the shift selector plate. Install the thrust washer and snap ring.

13. Position the shift rail through the shift fork hub in the front case. Tap lightly with a soft hammer to seat the rail in the hole.

14. Position the sliding clutch shift fork on the shift rail and place the sliding clutch and clutch shift spring into the front case half. Slide the rear output shaft into the case.

15. On the output side of the front output shaft, assemble the thin thrust washer, thrust bearing, and thick thrust washer and partially insert the front output shaft into the case.

16. Place the drive chain on the rear output shaft drive gear. Insert the rear output shaft into the front case half and engage the drive chain on the front output shaft drive gear. Push the front output shaft into position in the case.

17. Assemble the thin thrust washer, thrust bearing and thick thrust washer on the inside of the front output shaft drive gear.

18. Position the magnetic chip collector into position in the front case half.

19. Place a bead of RTV sealant completely around the face of the front case half and assemble the case halves being careful that the shift rail and forward output shafts are properly retained.

20. Alternately tighten the bolts to 20–25 ft. lbs.

21. Slide the oil pump gear over the input shaft and slide the spacer collar into position.

22. Engage the speedometer drive gear onto the rear output shaft and slide the retaining ring into position.

23. Use petroleum jelly to hold the nylon oil pump housing in position at the rear bearing retainer. Apply a bead of RTV sealant around the mounting surface of the retainer and carefully position the retainer assembly over the output shaft and onto the rear case half. The retainer must be installed so that the vent hole is vertical when the case is installed.

24. Torque the retainer bolts alternately to 20–25 ft. lbs.

25. Place a new thrust washer under each yoke and install the yokes on their respective shafts. Place the oil slinger under the front yoke. Torque the nuts to 90–130 ft. lbs.

26. Install the poppet ball, spring and screw in the front case half. Torque the

screw to 20–25 ft. lbs.

27. Install the 4WD indicator switch and washer and tighten to 15–20 ft. lbs.

28. Fill the unit with 6 pints of Ford CJ fluid or Dexron® II.

New Process 219

Introduced in the 1980 model year of Jeep® vehicles as the Quadra-Trac®, this is a full-time unit. The 4WD mode is fully differentiated in 4H only. The 4L and Lock ranges are undifferentiated. The 4H differentiation is accomplished by a torque biasing viscous coupling and an open differential connected to the coupling. Two drive sprockets and an interconnecting drive chain are used to distribute input torque.

Disassembly

1. Drain the lubricant from the case.

2. Remove the front and rear output shaft yokes and discard the yoke seal washers and yoke nuts.

3. Mark the rear retainer and rear case for an alignment reference.

4. Unbolt and remove the rear retainer. If necessary, use a soft mallet to loosen the retainer. Under no circumstances should the retainer be pried off.

5. Remove the differential shims and speedometer drive gear from the rear output shaft. Mark the shims for reference.

6. Remove the rear output bearing snap-ring and remove the bearing from the retainer using a soft mallet.

NOTE: The rear output bearing has one side shielded. Note this for reassembly.

7. Remove the rear output shaft seal from the retainer using a screwdriver or punch.

8. Position the front case assembly on wood blocks. The blocks should have V cuts made in them for more positive support of the case.

9. Remove the case halve bolts. The case halves may be pried apart using a screwdriver in the notches provided at the case ends.

NOTE: The two case end bolts have flat washers and alignment dowels. Note their location for assembly.

10. Remove the rear output shaft and viscous coupling as an assembly. Tap the shaft with a plastic mallet if necessary.

11. Remove the O-ring seal and pilot roller bearings from the mainshaft.

12. Remove the rear output shaft from the viscous coupling.

13. Remove the shift rail spring from the rail.

14. Remove the plastic oil pump from the shaft bore in the rear case. Note the pump position for assembly reference. The end with the recess must face the shaft bore when installed.

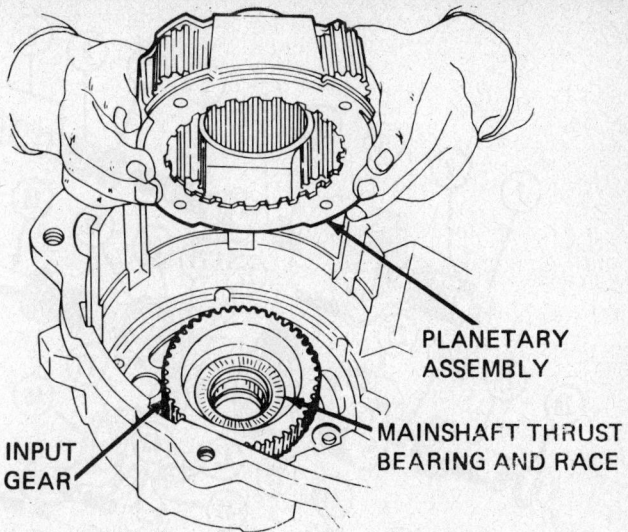

Input gear, mainshaft thrust bearing and planetary installation

15. Remove the rear output shaft bearing seal from the case. A screwdriver may be used to pry it out.

16. Remove the front output shaft thrust bearing assembly. Remove the thick washer, bearing and thin washer.

17. Remove the driven sprocket retaining snap-ring.

18. Remove the drive sprocket, drive chain, driven sprocket, side gear clutch and clutch gear as an assembly. Place the assembly on a workbench and mark the components for assembly.

19. Remove the needle bearings and spacers from the mainshaft and side gear bore. A total of 82 bearings and three spacers is used.

20. Remove the side gear/clutch gear assembly from the drive sprocket. Remove two snap-rings and remove the clutch gear from the side gear.

21. Remove the side gear clutch, mainshaft thrust washer and remaining mainshaft needle bearing spacer.

22. Remove the front output shaft and shaft thrust bearing assembly. Note the installation sequence of the bearing assembly.

23. Remove the front output shaft seal from the front case using a screwdriver or punch.

24. Remove the shift rail spring from the shift rail.

25. Remove the clutch sleeve, mode fork and spring as an assembly.

26. Remove the mainshaft thrust washer and mainshaft. Grasp the shaft and pull it straight up and out.

27. Move the range operating lever downward to the last detent position.

28. Disengage the range fork lug from the range sector slot.

29. Remove the annulus gear retaining snap-ring and thrust washer.

30. Remove the annulus gear and range fork.

31. Remove the planetary thrust washer from the hub.

32. Remove the planetary assembly.

33. Remove the mainshaft thrust bearing from the input gear.

34. Remove the input gear and remove the input gear thrust bearing and race.

35. Remove the range selector detent ball and spring retaining bolt and remove the detent ball and spring.

36. Remove the range selector and operating lever attaching nut and lockwasher, and remove the lever.

37. Remove the range selector.

38. Remove the range selector O-ring and retainer.

39. Remove the input gear oil seal from the front case with a screwdriver.

Assembly

Lubricate all parts before assembly with 10W-30 motor oil. Petroleum jelly will be indicated for some assemblies. Do not use chassis lube or other heavy lubricants.

1. Install new input gear and rear output shaft bearing oil seals. Seat the seals flush with the edge of the seal bore or with the seal groove in the case. Coat the seal lips with petroleum jelly after installation.

2. Install the input gear thrust bearing race in the case counterbore.

3. Install the input gear thrust bearing on the input gear and install the gear and bearing in the case.

4. Install the mainshaft thrust bearing in the bearing recess in the input gear.

5. Install the planetary assembly on the input gear. Make sure that the planetary pinion teeth mesh fully with the input gear.

6. Install the planetary thrust washer on the planetary hub.

7. Install a new sector shaft O-ring and retainer in the shaft bore in the case.

8. Install the range selector in the front case. Install the operating lever on the sector shaft and install the lever attaching washer and locknut on the shaft. Tighten the locknut to 17 ft. lbs.

9. Install the detent spring, ball and

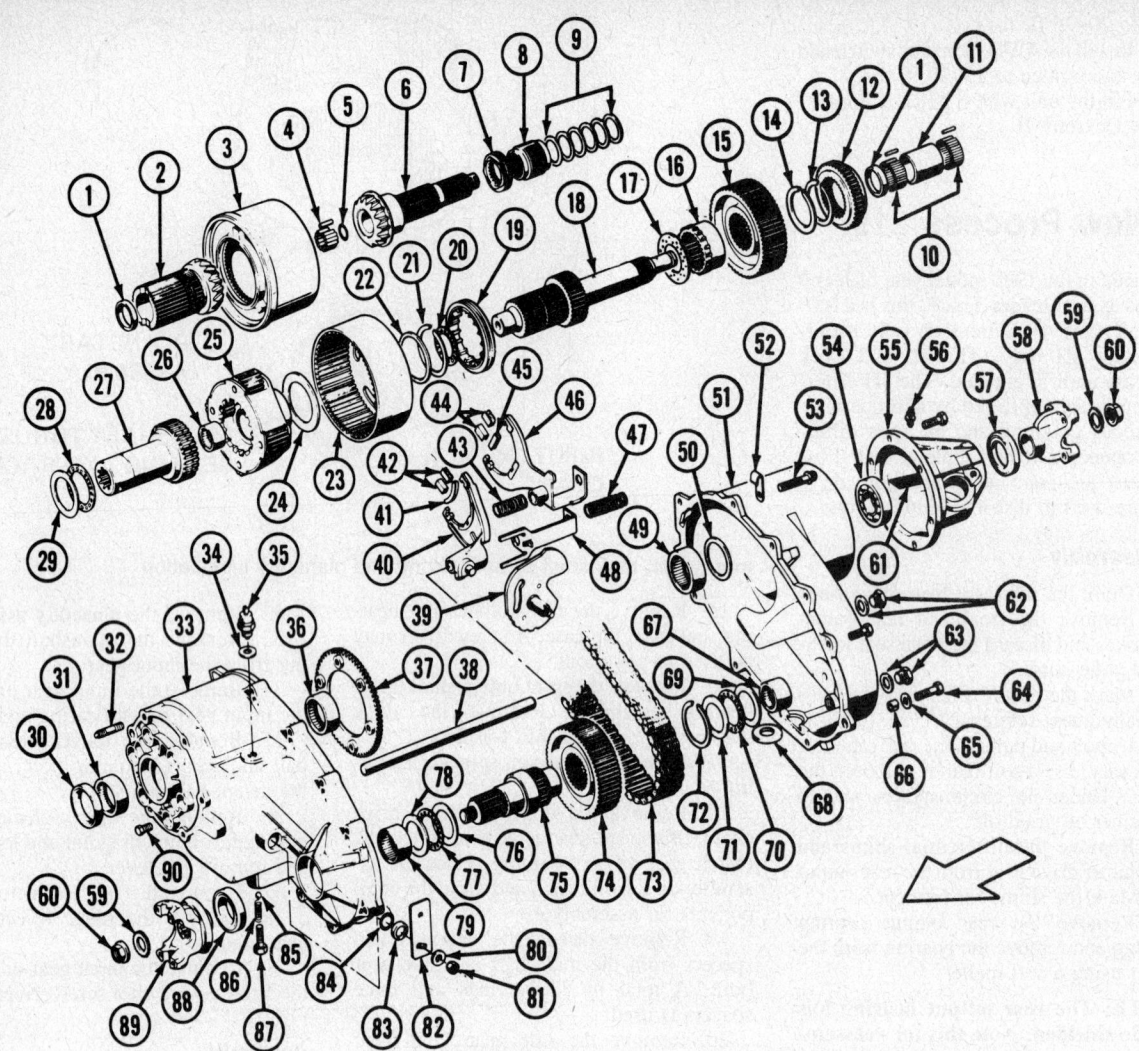

Exploded view of the New Process 219 transfer case

1. Mainshaft rear bearing spacer— short (2)
2. Side gear
3. Viscous coupling and differential assembly
4. Mainshaft rear pilot roller bearings (15)
5. Mainshaft O-ring
6. Rear output shaft
7. Oil pump
8. Speedometer gear
9. Differential end play shims (selective)
10. Mainshaft needle bearings (82)
11. Mainshaft rear bearing spacer
12. Clutch gear
13. Clutch gear locating ring
14. Drive sprocket locating ring
15. Drive sprocket
16. Side gear clutch
17. Mainshaft thrust

washer
18. Mainshaft
19. Clutch sleeve
20. Mainshaft thrust bearing
21. Annulus gear retaining ring
22. Annulus gear thrust washer
23. Annulus gear
24. Planetary thrust washer
25. Planetary assembly
26. Mainshaft front pilot bearing
27. Input gear
28. Input gear thrust bearing
29. Input gear thrust bearing race
30. Input gear oil seal
31. Input gear front bearing
32. Front case mounting stud (6)
33. Front case
34. Lock mode indicator switch

gasket
35. Lock mode indicator switch
36. Input gear rear bearing
37. Low range lockplate
38. Shift rail
39. Range sector
40. Range fork
41. Range fork insert
42. Range fork pads
43. Mode fork pads
44. Mode fork pads
45. Mode fork insert
46. Mode fork
47. Shift rail spring
48. Mode fork bracket
49. Rear output shaft bearing
50. Rear output shaft bearing seal
51. Rear case
52. Wiring clip
53. Spline bolt
54. Rear output bearing
55. Rear retainer
56. Vent

57. Output shaft oil seal
58. Rear yoke
59. Yoke seal washer
60. Yoke locknut
61. Vent chamber seal
62. Fill plug and gasket
63. Drain plug and gasket
64. Rear case bolt
65. Washer (2)
66. Case alignment dowel
67. Front output shaft rear bearing
68. Magnet
69. Front output shaft rear thrust bearing race (thick)
70. Front output shaft rear thrust bearing
71. Front output shaft rear thrust bearing race (thin)
72. Driven sprocket retaining snap-ring
73. Drive chain

74. Driven sprocket
75. Front output shaft
76. Front output shaft front thrust bearing race (thin)
77. Front output shaft front thrust bearing
78. Front output shaft front thrust bearing race (thick)
79. Front output shaft front bearing
80. Washer
81. Locknut
82. Operating lever
83. Range sector shaft seal retainer
84. Range sector shaft seal
85. Detent ball
86. Detent spring
87. Detent retaining bolt
88. Front output shaft seal
89. Front yoke
90. Lockplate bolts

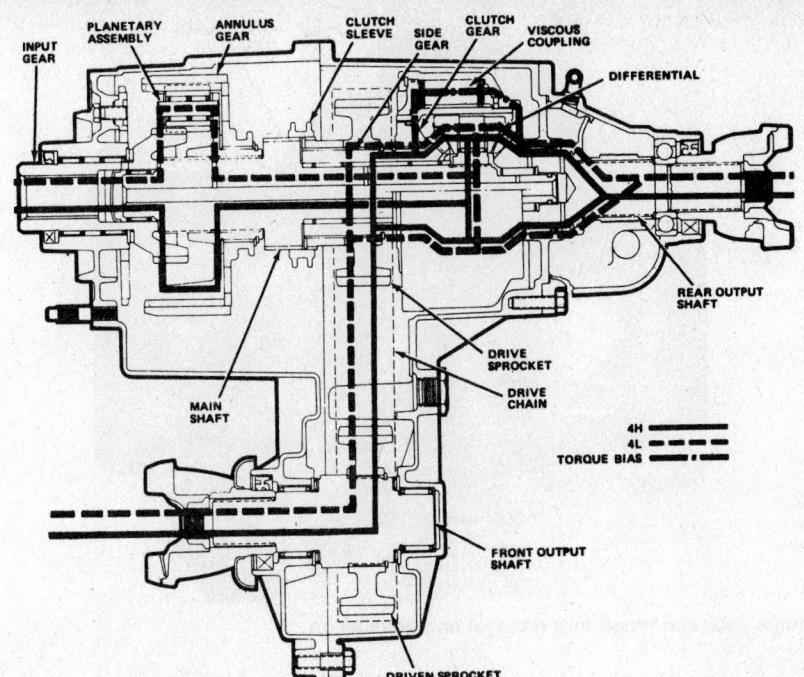

Differential shim, speedometer gear and oil pump

Power flow New Process 219 transfer case

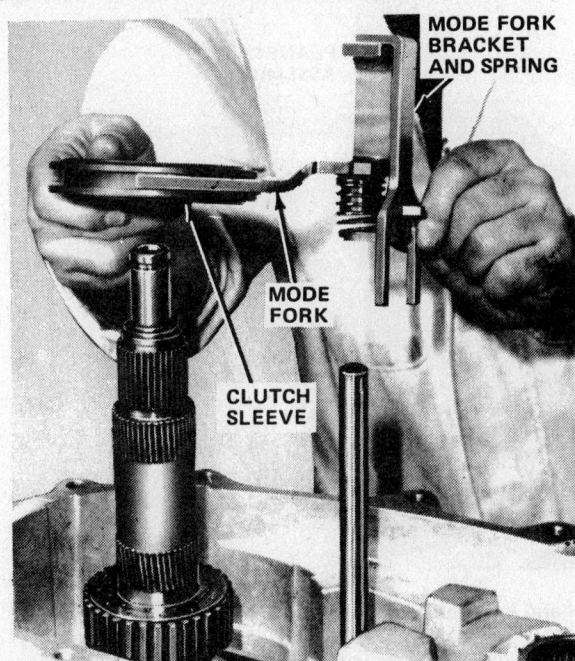

Clutch sleeve and mode fork removal and installation

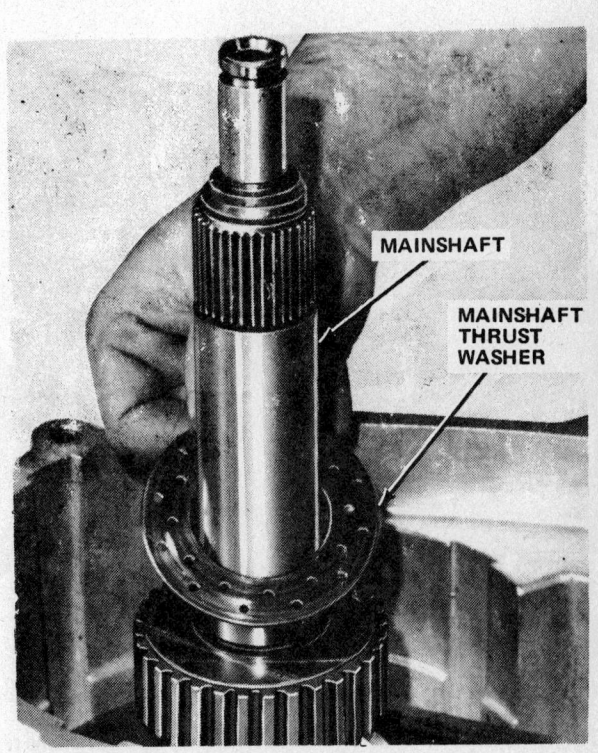

Mainshaft and thrust washer

retaining bolt in the front case detent bore. Tighten the bolt to 22 ft. lbs.

10. Move the range selector to the last detent position.

11. Assemble the annulus gear and range fork. Install the assembled fork and gear over the planetary assembly. Be sure that the annulus gear is fully meshed with the planetary pinions.

12. Insert the range fork lug in the range detent slot.

13. Install the annulus thrust washer and retaining ring on the annulus gear hub.

14. Align the mainshaft thrust washer in the input gear, if necessary.

15. Install the mainshaft. Be sure the shaft is fully seated in the input gear.

16. Install the mainshaft thrust washer on the mainshaft.

17. Install the short mainshaft needle bearing spacer on the shaft.

18. Apply a liberal coating of petroleum jelly to the mainshaft needle bearing surface and install 41 of the 82 needle bearings on the shaft. Be sure the bearings seat on the short spacer.

19. Install the long needle bearing spacer on the shaft. Lower the spacer onto the previously installed needle bearings carefully to avoid displacing them.

20. Align the shift rail bore in the case with the bore in the range fork and install the shift rail.

NOTE: Remove all traces of oil from the case shift rail bore before installing the rail. Oil in the case bore may prevent the rail from seating completely and prevent rear case installation.

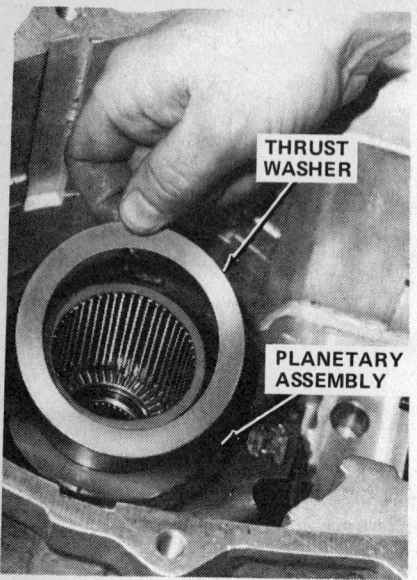

Planetary thrust washer removal and installation

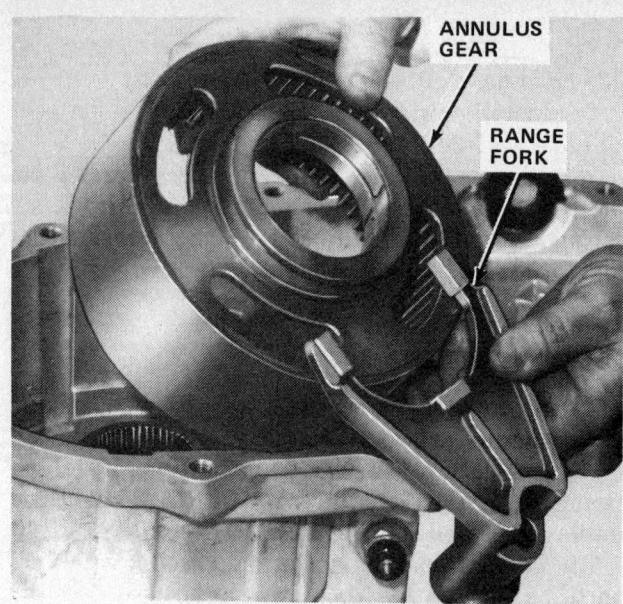

Annulus gear and range fork removal and installation

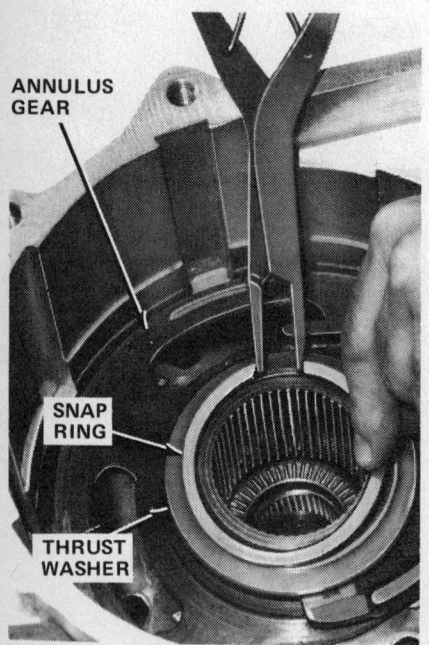

Annulus gear snap-ring and thrust washer

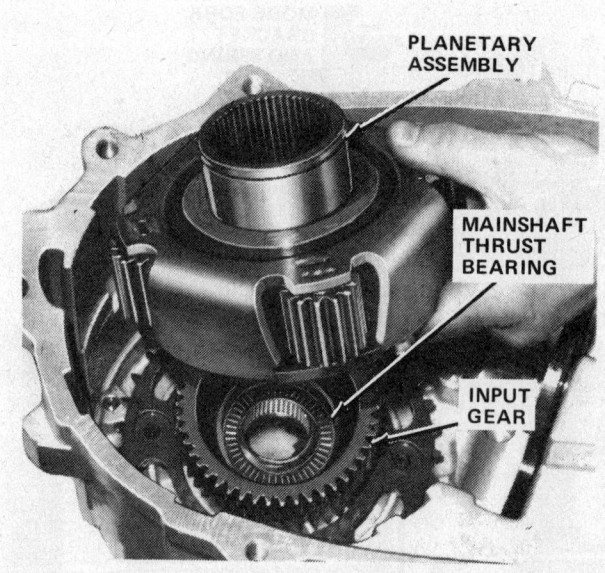

Planetary assembly removal and installation

21. Assemble the mode fork, mode fork spring and mode fork bracket.

22. Install the clutch sleeve in the mode fork. Be sure the sleeve is positioned so that the ID numbers on the sleeve face upward when the sleeve is installed.

23. Align the clutch sleeve and mode fork assembly with the shift rail and install the assembly on the shift rail and mainshaft. Be sure that the clutch sleeve is meshed with the mainshaft gear.

24. Lubricate the remaining 41 needle bearings and place them on the mainshaft.

25. Install the side gear clutch on the mainshaft with the teeth facing downward. Be sure the gear teeth mesh with the clutch sleeve.

26. Install the remaining short mainshaft needle bearing spacer. Install the spacer carefully to avoid displacing previously installed bearings.

27. Install the front output shaft front thrust bearing in the front case. Correct sequence is thick race, bearing, thin race.

28. Install the front output shaft in the front case.

29. Install the clutch gear on the side gear. The tapered side of the clutch gear teeth must face the side gear teeth.

30. Install the clutch gear and drive sprocket locating snap-rings on the side gear. Install the snap-rings so that they face each other.

31. Position the drive and driven sprock-

ets in the drive chain and install the assembled side and clutch gears in the drive sprocket.

32. Install the assembled drive chain, sprockets and side gear on the mainshaft and front output shaft. Align the sprockets with the shaft, keeping the assembly level and carefully lower the assembly onto both shafts simultaneously. Do not displace any of the needle bearings.

33. Install the driven sprocket retaining snap-ring.

34. Install the front output shaft rear thrust bearing assembly on the front output shaft. Correct installation sequence is thin race, thrust bearing, thick race.

35. Install the shift rail spring on the

shift rail.

36. Install a new O-ring on the mainshaft pilot bearing hub.

37. Coat the mainshaft pilot roller bearing hub and bearings with a liberal amount of petroleum jelly and install the rollers on the shaft.

38. Install the rear output shaft in the viscous coupling. Be sure it is fully seated.

39. Install the assembled viscous coupling and rear output shaft on the mainshaft. Align the mainshaft pilot hub with the pilot bearing bore in the rear output shaft and carefully lower the assembly onto the mainshaft. Take care to avoid displacing the roller bearings.

40. Align the clutch gear teeth with the viscous coupling teeth and seat the coupling fully onto the clutch gear.

NOTE: When correctly installed, the clutch gear teeth will not be visible or extend out of the coupling.

41. Install the magnet in the front case, if removed.

42. Clean the mating surfaces of the case halves thoroughly.

43. Apply Loctite® 515 or equivalent to the mating surfaces and all attaching bolts.

44. Join the case halves, aligning the dowels and install the bolts. Torque the bolts to 22 ft. lbs.

NOTE: The two end bolts require flat washers.

45. Install the oil pump on the rear output shaft and seat it in the case. The side with the recess should face the inside of the case.

46. Install the speedometer drive gear and differential shift, on the output shaft.

47. Install the vent chamber seal in the rear retainer.

48. Align and install the rear retainer on the case. Make the retainer finger tight only.

49. Install the yoke on the rear output shaft. Make the yoke finger tight only.

50. Mount a dial indicator on the rear retainer. Position the indicator stylus so that it contacts the top of the yoke nut.

51. Install the yoke on the front output shaft and rotate the shaft ten complete revolutions.

52. Rotate the front output shaft again and note the play indicated on the dial. End play should be .002–.010 inch. If the end play must be adjusted, remove the rear retainer and add or subtract shims as required.

53. Remove both output shaft yokes and discard the nuts.

54. Install the front and rear yoke seals.

55. Remove the rear retainer bolts, apply Loctite® 515 or equivalent to the mating surface of the retainer and to the bolts and install the bolts. Torque them to 22 ft. lbs.

56. Install new yoke seal washers on the output shafts, install yokes on the shafts and install new yoke nuts. Tighten the nuts to 110 ft. lbs.

57. Install the drain plug and tighten to

18 ft. lbs.

58. Pour 4 pints of 10W-30 motor oil into the case and install the fill plug. Tighten it to 18 ft. lbs.

Warner Quadra-Trac®

The Quadra-Trac® transfer case provides full-time, four-wheel drive under all driving conditions. The front and rear driveshafts are driven by a limited slip differential in the transfer case. The limited slip differential is connected to the input shaft by a link-belt type chain. In operation, if the rear axle loses traction, then the engine torque will be transfered through the transfer case differential to the front axle.

The transfer case contains a manually actuated lockout system that locks the front and rear driveshafts together, cancelling the differential action. This feature is used under extreme marginal traction situations.

NOTE: In order to spare the transfer case differential side gears and brake cones from excessive and possibly damaging wear, do not spin the wheels excessively when the vehicle is stuck or bogged down.

An optional gear reduction unit mounted at the rear of the input shaft is available for the Quadra-Trac® unit, making it a two-speed transfer case.

PERFORMANCE CHECKS TRANSFER CASE DIFFERENTIAL TORQUE BIAS CHECK

1. With the lock-out feature *not* engaged and the transmission in Park, raise the vehicle until the front wheels are free of the ground.

2. Disconnect the rear driveshaft from the transfer case.

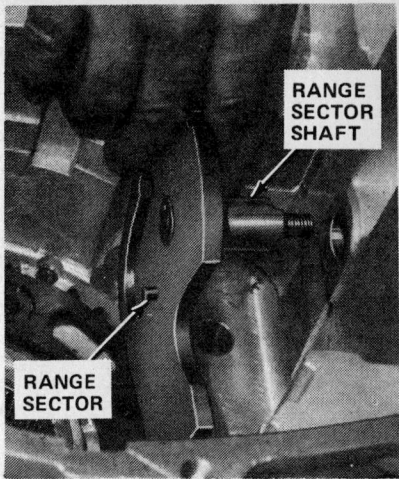

Range sector installation

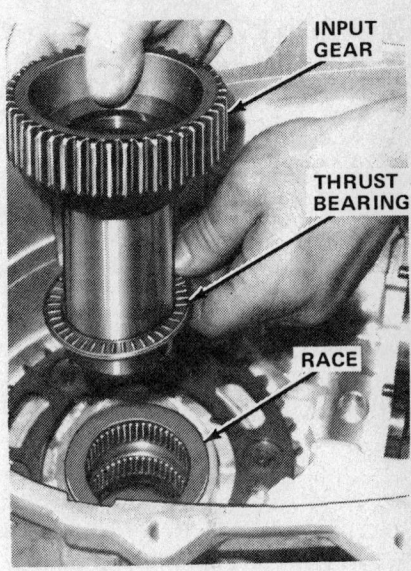

Input gear and thrust bearing removal and installation

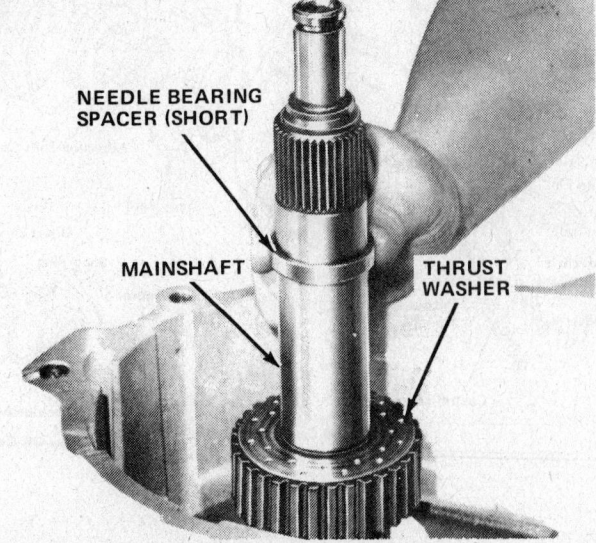

Mainshaft and thrust bearing installation

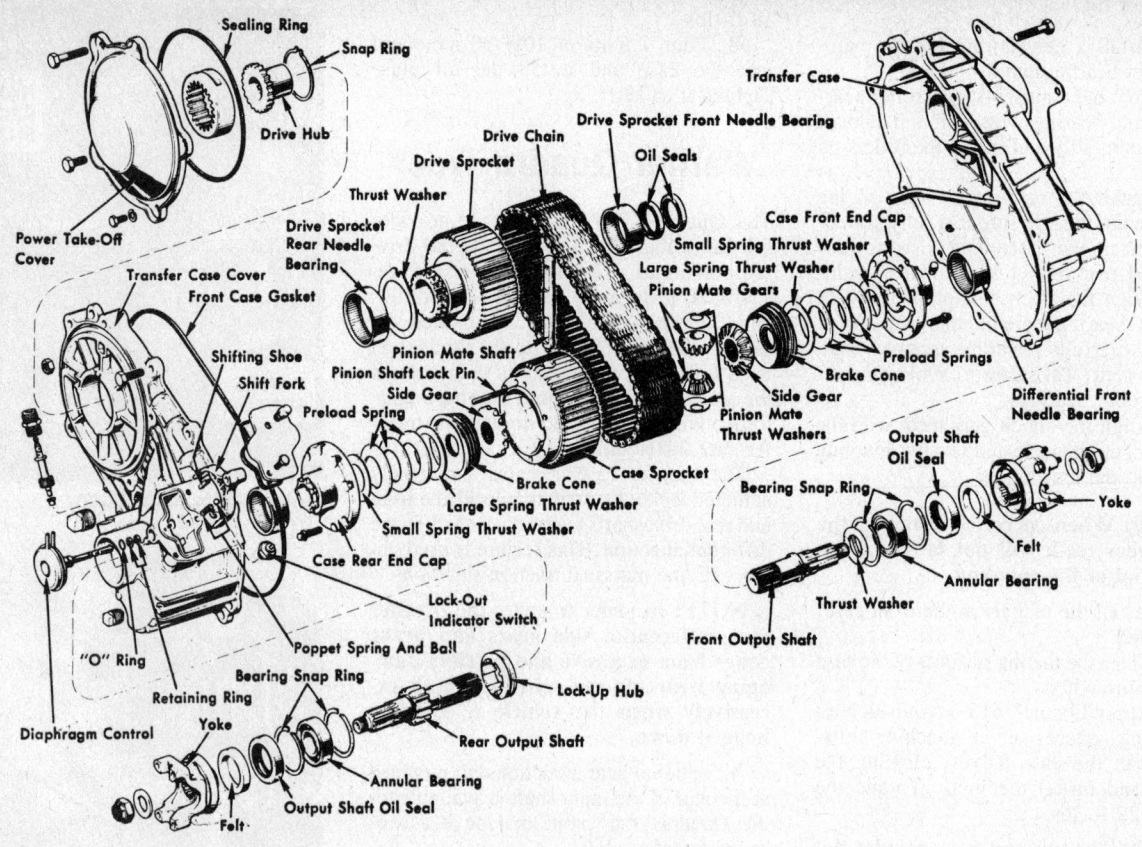

Exploded view of the Warner Quadra-Trac® without the optional reduction unit

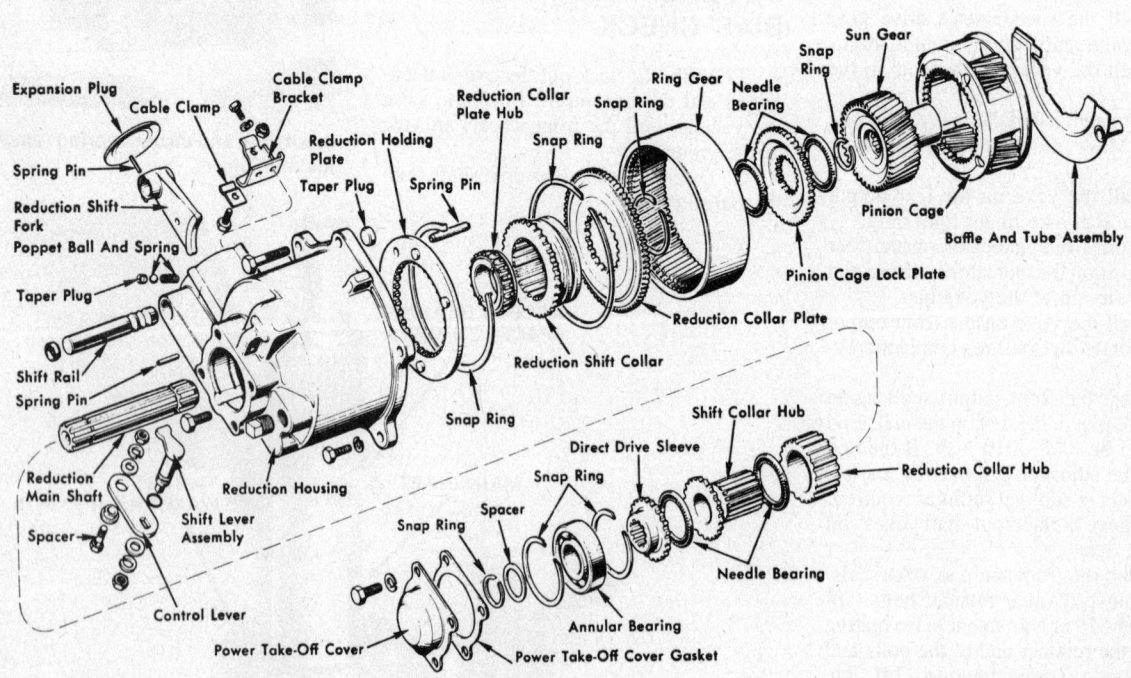

Exploded view of the Warner Quadra-Trac® optional reduction unit

3. Turn the rear yoke retaining nut with a torque wrench and socket, taking note of how much torque is required to force the cone clutches to slip. They should slip when 110 to 270 ft. lbs. are applied.

Slippage below 10 ft. lbs. indicates replacement of the differential is needed. If no slippage occurs at 270 ft. lbs., improper lubrication is indicated. Drain and refill the transfer case and reduction unit, if so equippped, with the proper lubricant mixture.

DRIVE CHAIN TENSION CHECK

1. Drain the lubricant from the transfer case.
2. Remove the chain inspection plug and insert a steel rule into the hole.
3. A new chain will be 1.575 in. from the outer edge of the plug hole. When the slack in the chain reaches ½–¾ in., the chain should be replaced. No adjustment is possible.
4. Reinstall the drain and chain inspection plugs, and refill the unit with the proper lubricant mixture.

REAR CASE COVER

Removal

Most Quadra-Trac® components can be serviced without removing the complete unit from the vehicle. To gain access to the rear output shaft, drive sprocket and thrust washer, chain, differential and needle bearing, or the diaphragm control system, just the rear cover has to be removed.

1. Lift and support the vehicle.
2. If the vehicle is equipped with a reduction unit, continue on to the next step for the reduction unit removal procedure. If the vehicle is not equipped with a reduction unit, proceed to step 7.
3. Loosen all the bolts that attach the reduction unit to the transfer case cover.
4. Move the reduction unit backward just enough to allow the oil to drain from the unit.
5. Loosen the cable retaining bolt at the shift control lever. Loosen the cable clamp bolt and remove the control cable from the clamp bracket and control lever.
6. When the oil has drained, remove the bolts which hold the reduction unit to the transfer case cover. Move the reduction unit rearward to clear the transmission output shaft and pinion cage which is attached to the transfer case drive sprocket. The pinion cage will remain with the transfer case assembly.

NOTE: The pinion cage should not be removed if the transfer case cover assembly is to be removed, but may be removed for inspection or replacement if the transfer case cover assembly is to remain in the vehicle. Removal of the pinion cage involves only removing the

Case sprocket and end caps marked for assembly reference

BLOCK

Transfer case cover positioned for disassembly

snap-ring which holds the cage to the sprocket and sliding the cage backward.

7. Remove the transfer case drain plug and allow the unit to drain.
8. Mark the rear output shaft yoke and universal joint to provide an alignment reference during reassembly. Disconnect the rear drive shaft front universal joint from the transfer case rear yoke.
9. Mark the diaphragm control vacuum hoses for identification during reassembly, then disconnect them. Also remove the lock-up indicator switch wire and the speedometer cable. Remove the indicator switch.
10. Disconnect the parking brake cable guide from the pivot on the right frame side.
11. Remove the bolts which attach the case cover assembly to the case (front housing). Carefully slide the cover assembly backward off the front output shaft and the transmission output shaft.

Disassembly

1. To disassemble the unit, remove the rear output shaft yoke.
2. If the unit is *not* equipped with a reduction unit, remove the power take-off cover from the rear of the transfer case cover. Remove the sealing ring from the transfer case cover.
3. Using a piece of wood 2 in. × 4 in. and 6 in. long, support the cover and drive sprocket.
4. If *not* equipped with a reduction unit, remove the drive hub and sleeve from the drive sprocket rear splines by expanding the internal snap-ring. The ring expanding tabs are accessible through a slot in the outside edge of the drive sleeve.
5. If equipped with a reduction unit, remove the pinion cage snap-ring and carrier.
6. Lift the case cover from the drive sprocket and differential. The cover, rear output shaft, bearings and seal, drive sprocket rear needle bearing, and lock-up hub can now be serviced without any fur-

WOOD BLOCK

Differential and drive sprocket positioned for chain installation

ther disassembly of other components.

7. Slide the drive sprocket toward the differential unit and remove the chain. The differential unit may now be serviced without any further disassembly of other components.

Assembly

1. Position the drive sprocket on a block of wood 2 in. × 4 in. and 6 in. long.

2. Place the differential assembly about 2 in. from the drive sprocket and with the front end of the differential on the bench.

3. Position the drive chain around the drive sprocket and the differential assembly. Be sure that the chain is properly engaged with the sprocket and differential teeth and that the slack is removed from the chain.

4. Insert the rear output shaft into the differential.

5. Shift the lock-up hub rearward in the case cover. Lubricate the drive sprocket thrust washer and insert it in position on the case cover.

6. Carefully align the case cover and position it onto the drive sprocket and differential. The output shaft may have to be slightly rotated to align it with the lock-up hub. Be sure that the drive sprocket thrust washer stays positioned correctly.

7. If equipped with a reduction unit, install the pinion cage onto the drive sprocket rear splines. Install the snap-ring. Be sure that the snap-ring seats properly in the groove.

8. If the vehicle is *not* equipped with a reduction unit, assemble the drive hub,

drive sleeve, and snap-ring, then install them onto the drive sprocket rear splines. Be sure the snap-ring seats properly.

9. Turn the drive sleeve or pinion cage to make sure the drive sprocket thrust washer did not come out of position. No binding should be present.

10. If *not* equipped with a reduction unit, install the power take-off sealing ring and cover and tighten the attaching screws.

11. Install the speedometer gear on the rear output shaft.

12. Install the rear output shaft oil seal and the rear yoke and nut. Tighten the nut to specification.

Installation

13. Clean the groove which the front oil seal gasket fits into and install the seal.

14. Install two ⅜ in. 16 × 2 in. long pilot studs into the transfer case front cover housing.

15. Move the cover assembly forward to mesh with the front output shaft and transmission output shaft. It may be necessary to rotate the rear output shaft slightly to allow the two sets of splines to engage.

16. After the cover assembly has been moved forward and is evenly touching the front half of the case, remove the pilot studs and install the rear cover attaching bolts. Tighten the bolts alternately and evenly to specifications.

17. Install the lock out indicator switch and connect the lock out switch wire, diaphragm control vacuum hoses, and the speedometer cable.

18. Install the rear drive shaft.

19. Install the parking brake cable guide to the pivot on the right frame side.

20. Install the reduction unit, if so equipped, as follows:

21. Position the reduction unit to the transfer case and mesh the caged pinions with the sun gear and ring gear, and align the sun gear inner splines with the transmission output shaft splines.

22. Move the reudction unit forward until it touches the sealing ring.

23. Install the attaching screws loosely, then tighten them alternately to specification.

24. Connect the shift control cable and adjust it by first removing the swivel block from the control lever. Move the control lever to the most forward position. Thread the swivel block in or out on the cable end to obtain the correct length to fit the swivel block in the control lever.

25. Install the proper type and amount of lubricant and lower the vehicle.

NOTE: Use 8 oz. of Jeep Lubricant Concentrate Part No. 8123004 or 5356068 or Lubrizol® 762 (there is no substitute) mixed with SAE 30 non-detergent motor oil. 3.5 pints of the mixture is required to fill the transfer case without a reduction unit, 4.5 pints with a reduction unit.

DIFFERENTIAL ASSEMBLY

Disassembly

1. Mark end caps and case sprocket with paint. Marks must be used to identify front end cap, rear end cap and proper orientation of caps to case sprocket.

2. Remove front end cap. If necessary, tap gently with a soft hammer.

3. Remove thrust washer, preload springs, brake cone and side gears from case sprocket. Care must be taken to keep the various pieces together as they must be installed as a unit.

4. Invert the case sprocket and remove rear cap. If necessary, tap gently with a soft hammer.

5. Remove the thrust washers, preload springs, brake cone and side gears. Care must be taken to keep the various pieces together as they must be installed as a unit.

6. Raise the case sprocket. The pinion shaft lock pin should fall out. If the pin does not fall, drive the pin out with a ¼ in. pin punch.

7. Drive the pinion mate shaft out of case sprocket, using a brass drift and hammer. Care must be taken to avoid damaging the pinion mate thrust washers.

8. Thoroughly clean and inspect all component parts. Replace any damaged or worn parts with a complete matched set.

Assembly

Prelubricate all bearings and thrust surfaces with Jeep Lubricant Concentrate Part No. 8123004 or 5356068 or Lubrizol® 762 (there is no substitute) prior to installation.

1. Slide the pinion mate shaft in the case sprocket three inches.

2. Install the pinion mate thrust washers and gears on shaft in the proper order.

3. Align the pinion mate shaft lockpin hole with hole in case sprocket. Lightly drive the pinion mate shaft into case sprocket until lockpin holes are exactly aligned.

4. Move the pinion mate gears apart until the gears are pressing the washers against the case sprocket.

5. Engage the pinion mate gear with the front side gears. Insert the brake cone over the gear and in case sprocket. Install the large thrust washer and preload springs, concave side of springs facing toward brake cone.

6. Lubricate the small thrust washer and place it on the front end cap. Install the front end cap, secure with attaching screws and alternately tighten to proper torque. Make certain that alignment marks are in order.

7. Invert the case sprocket and end cap and install the pinion shaft lock pin.

8. Mesh remaining side gear with pinion mate gears.

9. Insert the remaining brake cone over the side gear. Install the large thrust washer and preload spring, concave side of springs facing toward brake cone.

10. Lubricate the small thrust washer and place it on the rear end cap. Install the rear cap, tighten attaching screws finger tight.

11. Insert the front and rear output shafts in the differential and rotate until both shafts have aligned with the splines on the brake cones and side gears. Alternately tighten the retaining screws to proper torque.

SPECIFICATIONS

TORQUE (FT. LBS.)

Transfer case breather	6–10
Chain measuring access hole plug	6–14
Drain plug	15–25
Fill plug	15–25
Lock-up cover to transfer case	8–10
Lock-out indicator switch	10–15
Output Shaft Nut	90–150
PTO cover to transfer case bolts: 3/8 in.-16	15–25
5/16 in.-18	10–20
Speedometer adapter	20–30
Transfer case cover to transfer case	15–25
Transfer case to transmission extension bolt	30–50
Reduction unit cable housing clamp nut	7–12
Fill plug	15–25
Shift lever cable clamp nut	10–20
Shift lever to shift nut	15–25
Reduction PTO cover to case	15–25
Reduction unit to transfer case bolts: 3/8 in.-16	15–25
5/16 in.-18	8–10

DIAPHRAGM CONTROL, SHIFT FORK AND LOCK-UP HUB

Disassembly

1. Remove the vent cover and seal ring.

2. Remove the retaining rings positioning the shift fork on diaphragm. Carefully pry the shift fork forward to gain access to the retaining rings. Remove the spring with a magnet.

3. Caution must be exercised in removal of the diaphragm control rod as it is retained by a spring loaded detent ball. Insert a magnet into the hole to hold the detent ball. Slip the diaphragm control rod out of case. Remove detent ball and spring.

4. Remove shifting fork, plastic shifting shoes and lock-up hub.

Assembly

1. Lubricate the shifting shoes and place them in the shift fork.

2. Install the shift fork and lock-up hub assembly in the case cover, long end of shift fork first (toward rear). Make certain that the shift fork does not separate from the lock-up hub by reaching through the needle bearings.

REDUCTION UNIT

Disassembly

1. Remove PTO cover and gasket.

2. Remove snap-ring from reduction main shaft rear end, slide the reduction main shaft and sun gear assembly forward and out. Remove needle bearings.

3. Remove as an assembly, the ring gear, reduction collar plate, pinion cage lock plate, shift collar hub and reduction collar hub. Using a soft hammer, remove the shift collar hub from the pinion cage lock plate.

4. Remove the pinion cage lock plate,

3. Insert the diaphragm control rod in the case and shifting fork, stopping before the detent ball hole is reached.

4. Install the detent ball and spring. Depress the detent ball with a 1/4 in. pin punch and slide the diaphragm control rod into place.

5. Install the shift fork retaining pin, (clips) and the diaphragm retaining spring, the spring should be below the surface of the bore.

6. Install the vent cover and seal ring. needle bearing, ring gear, reduction collar plate and shift collar hub. Separate the reduction collar hub and needle bearing from shift collar hub.

5. When necessary, separate the reduction collar plate and ring gear by removing retaining snap-ring.

6. Remove needle bearing and direct drive sleeve from the reduction shift collar.

7. Shift the reduction shift collar to the neutral (center) detent with the control lever. Disengage the shift fork. Place the shift in the direct drive detent position (rear), align the collar outer teeth with the inner teeth in the reduction holding plate. Place the fork and collar in the reduction position (front) detent, and remove the reduction shift collar.

8. Remove the annular bearing rear snap-ring and bearing.

9. Remove the shift fork locating spring pin, large expansion plug, shift rail taper plug, and control lever.

10. Drive the spring pin out of the shift fork and rail with a 3/16 in. pin punch. Slide the shift rail forward out of the shift fork, and remove the shift fork. Remove the spring shift fork poppet ball. Drive the poppet taper plug into the shift rail bore and remove the plug and spring.

11. Remove the shift lever retaining pin and the shift lever assembly.

12. Remove the reduction holding plate snap-ring and reduction holding plate.

Assembly

1. Align the shift fork locating spring holes in the reduction holding plate and housing. Install the reduction holding plate. Locating pins should index the plate in the case. Secure the plate with a snap-ring, tabs facing forward.

2. Install the shift lever assembly into the housing, lever towards the rear. Position seal ring on groove in shift lever shaft.

3. Move the shift lever assembly inward and install taper pin.

4. Install the shift rail in the shift rail rear bore, grooved end first. Position the shift rail with flat side towards the poppet spring. Engage the shift rail with the shift lever assembly and position the rail so it is flush with the edge of the poppet bore. Place the poppet ball on the end of spring and insert the assembly in the poppet bore, using a spring pin as an installation tool. Depress the poppet ball and slide the shift rail over the poppet ball as far as the spring pin will allow. Remove the spring pin and place the shift rail in the first detent position.

5. Position the shift rail so the flat side is facing the shift lever assembly and the spring pin bore is aligned with the spring pin bore in the shift fork. Once the spring pin holes are aligned, install the spring pin so that it is flush with the outside surface of the shift fork.

6. Install the shift rail taper plug, poppet bore taper plug, shift rail cover expansion plug, shift fork spring locating pin and the control lever.

7. Place the shift fork in the neutral position (center) detent. Install the reduction shift collar so that the outer teeth engage with the reduction holding plate inner teeth, and the shift collar fork groove forward of the shift fork. Place the shift fork in the direct drive (rear) detent. Move the shift collar away and to the rear of the shift fork until the groove aligns with the shift fork. Engage the collar groove with the shift fork.

8. Place the direct drive sleeve in the reduction shift collar, needle bearing surface facing toward the front. Lubricate and install the needle bearing, against the direct drive sleeve.

9. Assemble the reduction collar plate hub and ring gear. Make certain that snap-rings are seated in their grooves.

10. Install the needle bearing and reduction collar hub on the shift collar hub.

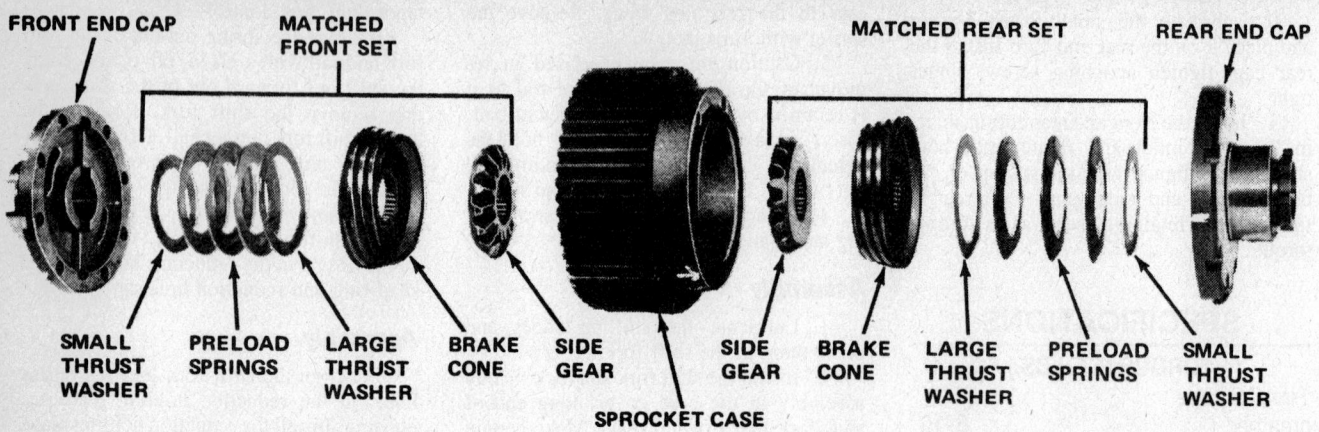

FRONT END CAP • MATCHED FRONT SET • MATCHED REAR SET • REAR END CAP

SMALL THRUST WASHER • PRELOAD SPRINGS • LARGE THRUST WASHER • BRAKE CONE • SIDE GEAR • SPROCKET CASE • SIDE GEAR • BRAKE CONE • LARGE THRUST WASHER • PRELOAD SPRINGS • SMALL THRUST WASHER

Differential sprocket assembly sequence

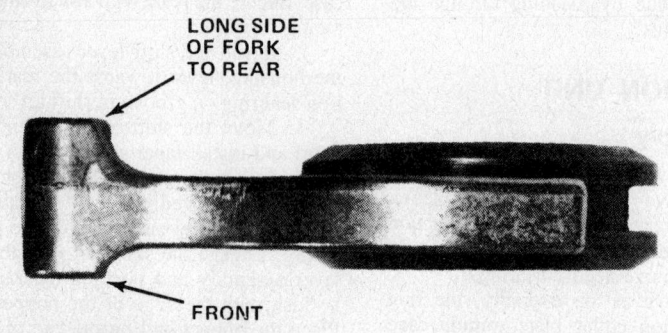

LONG SIDE OF FORK TO REAR

FRONT

Shift fork and lockup hub assembly

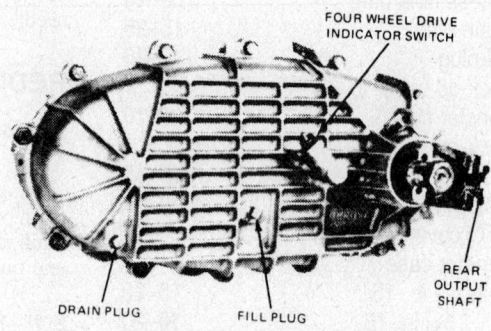

FOUR WHEEL DRIVE INDICATOR SWITCH

DRAIN PLUG • FILL PLUG • REAR OUTPUT SHAFT

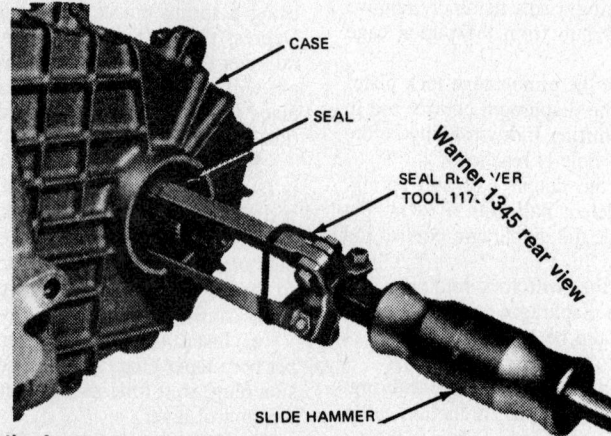

CASE

SEAL

SEAL REMOVER TOOL 117...

Warner 1345 rear view

SLIDE HAMMER

Removing the front output shaft seal from the case

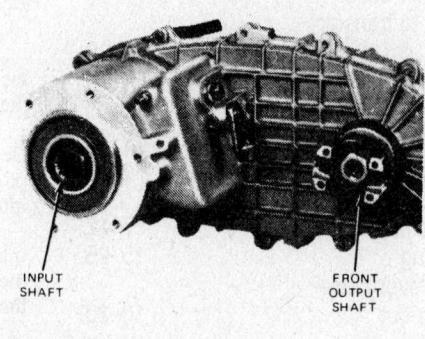

INPUT SHAFT • FRONT OUTPUT SHAFT

Warner 1345 front view

11. Install the ring gear, reduction collar plate and hub on the shift collar hub.

12. Place a needle bearing on the shift collar hub and the reduction collar hub.

13. Tap the pinion cage lock into place on the shift collar hub with a soft hammer and install assembly in housing. Place needle bearings on the shift collar hub and the pinion cage lock plate.

14. Install the reduction main shaft and sun gear into shift collar hub and through the direct drive sleeve and annular bearing. With a brass drift gently tap the assembly as far to the rear as possible. Place the rear spacer on the main shaft and secure with the selective snap-ring which gives the tightest fit, between .004 in. and .009 in. clearance. Snap rings are available in thicknesses ranging from 0.089 in. to 0.105 in.

15. Install PTO cover and gasket, tighten attaching bolts to proper torque.

Warner 1345

The 1345 is a two piece all aluminum part time unit, lubricated by a positive displacement oil pump that channels oil through drilled holes in the rear output shaft. The pump turns with the output shaft and allows towing of the vehicle for extended distances.

Disassembly

1. Drain the fluid from the case.

2. Remove both output shaft yokes.

3. Remove the 4WD indicator switch.

4. Unbolt and remove the case cover. The cover may be pried off using a screwdriver in the pry bosses.

5. Remove the magnetic chip collector from the bottom of the case.

6. Slide the shift collar hub off the rear output shaft.

7. Compress the shift fork spring and remove the upper and lower spring retainers from the shaft.

8. Lift the four wheel drive lockup fork and lockup shift collar assembly from the case.

9. Remove the thrust washer being careful not to lose the nylon wear pads on the lockup fork.

10. Remove the snap ring and thrust washer from the front output shaft.

11. Grip the chain and both sprockets

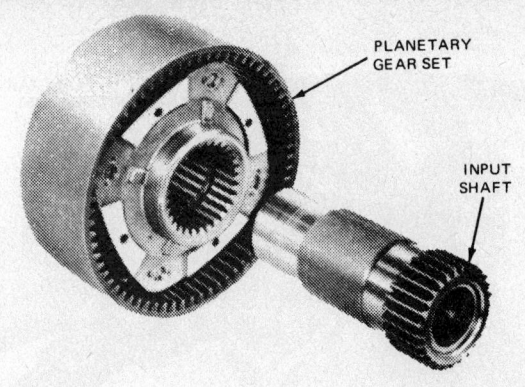

Removing the input shaft from the planetary gear set

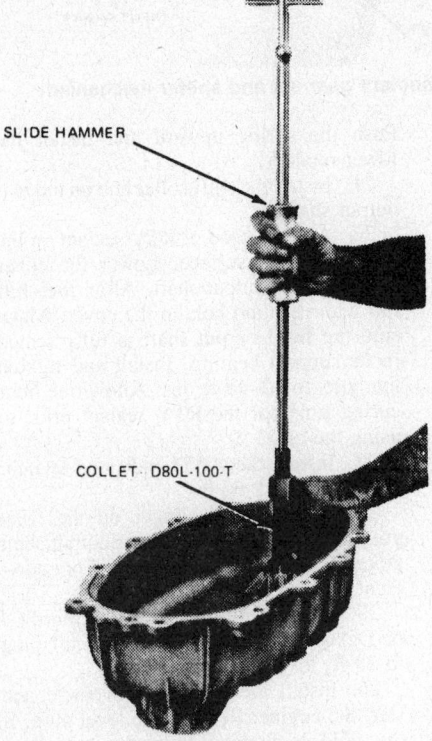

Removing the needle bearing

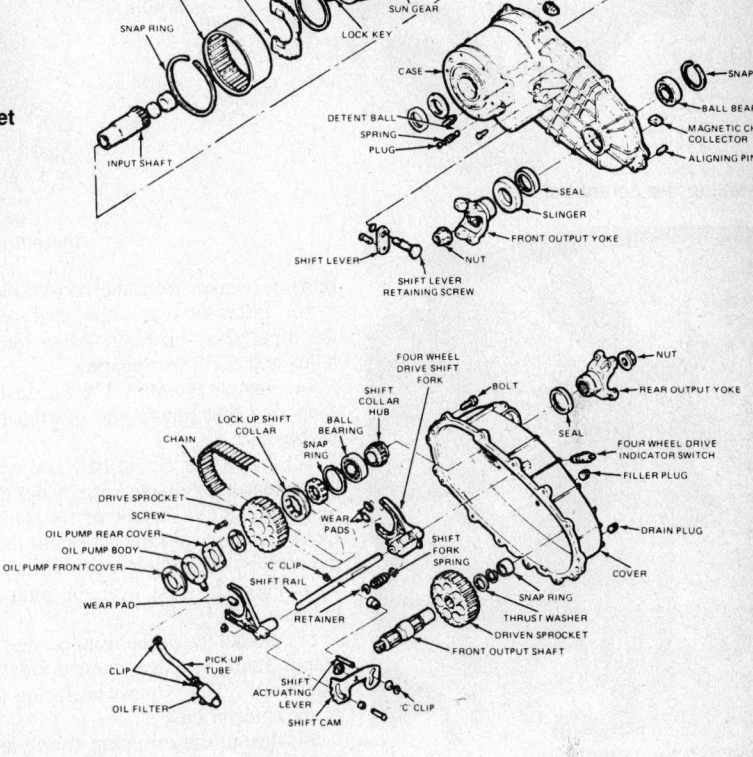

Exploded view of the Warner 1345 transfer case

and lift them straight up to remove the drive sprocket, driven sprocket and chain from the output shafts.

12. Lift the front output shaft from the case.

13. Remove the four oil pump attaching screws and remove the oil pump rear cover, pickup tube, filter and pump body, two pump pins, pump spring and oil pump front cover from the rear output shaft.

14. Remove the snap ring that holds the bearing retainer inside the case. Lift the rear output shaft while tapping on the bearing retainer with a plastic hammer.

NOTE: Two dowel pins will fall into the case when the retainer is removed.

Lift the rear output shaft and bearing retainer from the case.

15. Remove the rear output shaft from the bearing retainer. If necessary, press the

needle bearing assembly out of the retainer.

16. Remove the C-clip that holds the shift cam to the actuating lever inside the case.

17. Remove the retaining screw and lift the shift lever from the case.

NOTE: When removing the lever, the shift cam will disengage from the shift lever shaft and may release the detent ball and spring from the case.

18. Remove the planetary gear set, shift rail, shift cam, input shaft and shift forks, as an assembly, from the case. Be careful not to lose the two nylon wear pads on the shift fork.

19. Remove the spacer washer from the bottom of the case.

20. Drive the plug from the detent spring bore.

Assembly

Before assembly, lubricate all parts with clean automatic transmission fluid; either Ford CJ or Dexron® II.

1. Assemble the planetary gear set, shift rail, shift cam, input shaft and shift

fork together as a unit. Make sure that the boss on the shift cam is installed toward the case. Install the spacer washer on the input shaft.

2. Place the rear output shaft in the planetary gear set, making sure that the shift cam engages the shift fork actuating pin.

3. Lay the case on its side. Insert the rear output shaft and planetary gear set into the case. Make sure the spacer washer remains on the input shaft.

4. Install the shift rail into the hole in the case. Install the outer roller bushing into the guide in the case.

5. Remove the rear output shaft and position the shift fork in neutral.

6. Place the shift control lever shaft through the cam, and install the clip ring. Make sure that the shift control lever is pointed downward and is parallel to the front face of the case.

7. Check the shift fork and planetary gear engagement.

8. If removed, press a new needle bearing assembly into the bearing retainer.

9. Insert the output shaft through the

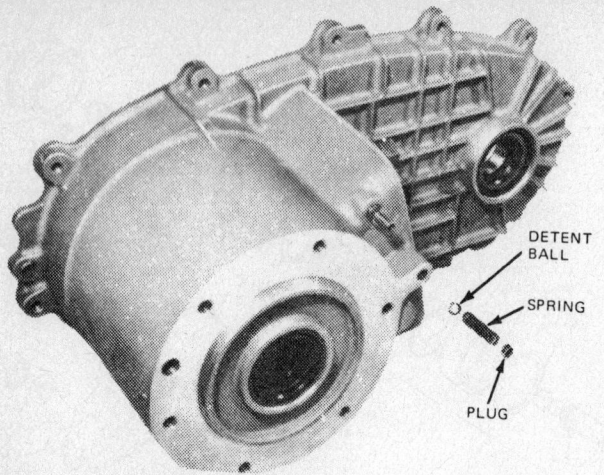

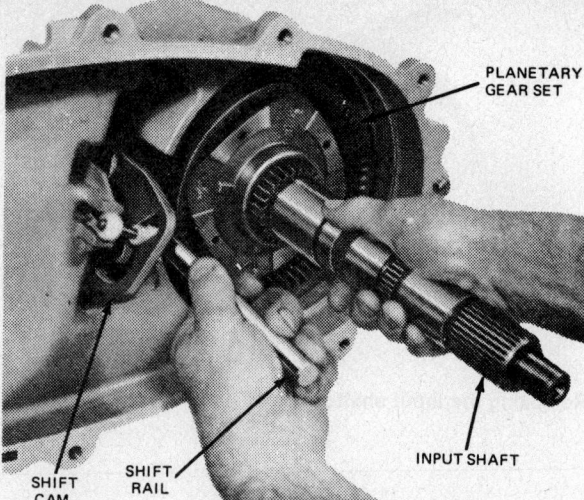

Installing the detent ball

Installing the planetary gear set and shifter mechanism

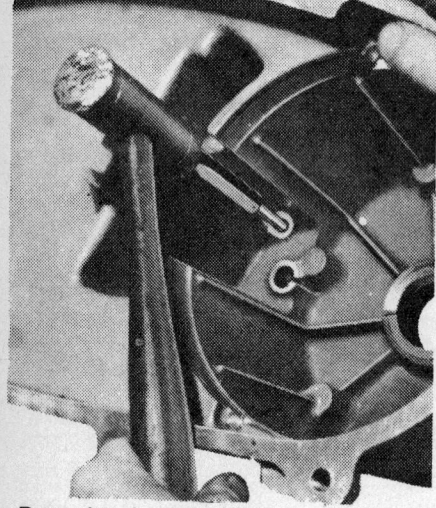

Removing the detent ball

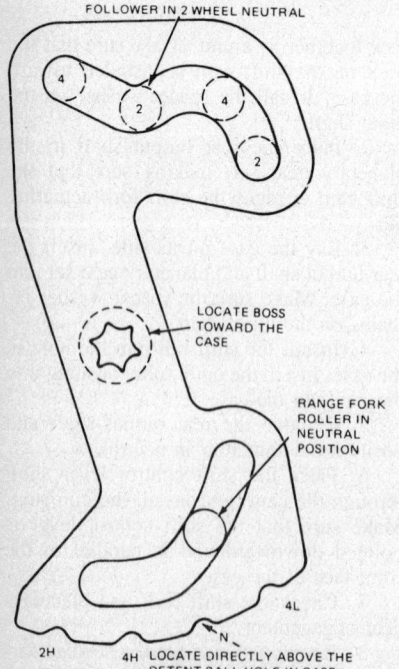

Connect the shift cam engagement

bearing retainer from the bottom outward.

10. Insert the rear output shaft pilot into the input shaft bushing. Align the dowel holes and the lower bearing.

11. Install the dowel pins. Install the snap ring that retains the bearing retainer in the case.

12. Insert the detent ball and spring in the detent bore in the case. Coat the seal plug with RTV sealant or its equivalent. Drive the plug into the case until the lip of the plug is 1/32 in. below the surface of the case. Peen the case over the plug in two places.

13. Install the pump front cover over the output shaft with the flanged side down. The word "TOP" must be facing the top of the transfer case.

14. Install the oil pump spring and two pump pins with the flat side outward in the hole in the output shaft. Push both pins in to install the oil pump body, pickup tube and filter.

15. Place the oil pump rear cover on the output shaft with the flanged side outward. The word "TOP" must be positioned toward the top of the case. Apply Loctite® or its equivalent to the oil pump bolts and torque them to 36–40 in. lbs.

16. Install the thrust washer on the rear output shaft nest to the oil pump.

17. Place the drive sprocket on the front output shaft. Install the snap ring and thrust washer.

18. Install the chain on the drive sprocket and driven sprocket. Lower the chain into position in the case. The driven sprocket is installed through the front output shaft bearing and the drive sprocket is installed in the rear output shaft.

19. Engage the 4WD shift fork on the shift collar. Slide the shift fork over the shift shaft and the shift collar over the rear output shaft. Make sure the nylon wear pads are installed on the shift fork tips and the necked-down part of the shift collar is facing downward.

20. Push the 4WD shift spring downward and install the upper spring retainer.

Push the spring upward and install the lower retainer.

21. Install the shift collar hub on the rear output shaft.

22. Apply a bead of RTV sealant on the case mounting surface. Lower the cover over the rear output shaft. Align the shift rail with its blind hole in the cover. Make sure the front output shaft is fully seated in its support bearing. Install and tighten the bolts to 40–45 ft. lbs. Allow one hour curing time for the RTV sealant prior to using the case.

23. Install the 4WD indicator switch. Torque to 8–12 ft. lbs.

24. Press the oil slinger on the front yoke. Install the front and rear output shaft yokes. Coat the nuts with Loctite® or equivalent and torque to 100–130 ft. lbs.

25. Fill the unit with 6 pints of Ford CJ or Dexron® II ATF. Tighten the fill plug to 18 ft. lbs.

26. Install the unit in the vehicle and start the engine. Remove the level plug. If the fluid is flowing from the hole in a stream, the pump is not operating properly. The fluid should drip slowly from the hole.

Drive Axles

INDEX

DRIVE AXLES

The rear axle must transmit power through 90°. To accomplish this, straight cut bevel gears or spiral bevel gears were used. This type of gear is satisfactory for differential side gears, but since the centerline of the gears must intersect, they rapidly became unsuited for ring and pinion gears. The lowering of the driveshaft brought about a variation of the bevel gear, which is called the hypoid gear. This type of gear does not require a metting of the gear centerlines and can therefore be underslung, relative to the centerline of the ring gear.

Gear Ratios

The drive axle of a vehicle is said to have a certain axle ratio. This number (usually a whole number and a decimal fraction) is actually a comparison of the number of gear teeth on the ring gear and the pinion gear. For example, a 4.11 rear means that theoretically, there are 4.11 teeth on the ring gear and one tooth on the pinion. Actually, on a 4.11 rear, there are 37 teeth on the ring gear and nine teeth on the pinion gear. By dividing the number of teeth on the pinion gear into the number of teeth on the ring gear, the numerical axle ratio (4.11) is obtained. This also provides a good method of ascertaining exactly which axle ratio one is dealing with.

Differential Operation

The differential is an arrangement of gears that permits the rear wheels to turn at different speeds when cornering and divides the torque between the axle shafts. The differential gears are mounted on a pinion shaft and the gears are free to rotate on this shaft. The pinion shaft is fitted in a bore in the differential case and is at right angles to the axle shafts.

Power flow through the differential is as follows. The drive pinion, which is turned by the driveshaft, turns the ring gear. The ring gear, which is bolted to the differential case, rotates the case. The differential pinion forces the pinion gears against the side gears. In cases where both wheels have equal traction, the pinion gears do not rotate on the pinion shaft, because the input force of the pinion gear is divided equally between the two side gears. Consequently the pinion gears revolve with the pinion shaft, although they do not revolve on the pinion shaft itself. The side gears, which are splined to the axle shafts, and meshed with the pinion gears, rotate the axle shafts.

When it becomes necessary to turn a corner, the differential becomes effective and allows the axle shafts to rotate at different speeds. As the inner wheel slows down, the side gear splined to the inner wheel axle shaft also slows down. The pinion gears act as balancing levers by maintaining equal tooth loads to both gears while allowing unequal speeds of rotation at the axle shafts. If the vehicle speed remains constant, and the inner wheel slows down to 90 percent of vehicle speeds, the outer wheel will speed up to 110 percent.

Limited-Slip Differential Operation

Limited-slip differentials provide driving force to the wheel with the best traction before the other wheel begins to spin. This is accomplished through clutch plates or cones. The clutch plates or cones are located between the side gears and inner wall of the differential case. When they are squeezed together through spring tension and outward force from the side gears, three reactions occur. Resistance on the side gears causes more torque to be exerted on the clutch packs or clutch cones. Rapid one-wheel spin cannot occur, because the side gear is forced to turn at the same speed as the case. Most important, with the side gear and the differential case turning at the same speed, the other wheel is forced to rotate in the same direction and at the same speed as the differential case. Thus driving force is applied to the wheel with the better traction.

DIFFERENTIAL DIAGNOSIS

The most essential part of rear axle service is proper diagnosis of the problem. Bent or broken axle shafts or broken gears pose little problem, but isolating an axle noise and correctly interpreting the problem can be extremely difficult, even for an experienced mechanic.

Any gear driven unit will produce a certain amount of noise, therefore, a specific diagnosis for each individual unit is the best practice. Acceptable or normal noise can be classified as a slight noise heard only at certain speeds or under unusual conditions. This noise tends to reach a peak at 40–60 mph, depending on the road condition, load, gear ratio and tire size. Frequently, other noises are mistakenly diagnosed as coming from the rear axle. Vehicle noises from tires, transmission, driveshaft, U-joints and front and rear wheel bearings will often be mistaken as emanating from the rear axle. Raising the tire pressure to eliminate tire noise (although this will not silence mud or snow treads), listening for noise at varying speeds and road conditions and listening for noise at drive and coast conditions will aid in diagnosing alleged rear axle noises.

External Noise Elimination

It is advisable to make a thorough road test to determine whether the noise originates in the rear axle or whether it originates from the tires, engine transmission, wheel bearings or road surface. Noise originating from other places cannot be corrected by overhauling the rear axle.

Road Noise

Brick roads or rough surfaced concrete, may cause a noise which can be mistaken as coming from the rear axle. Driving on a different type of road (smooth asphalt or dirt) will determine whether the road is the cause

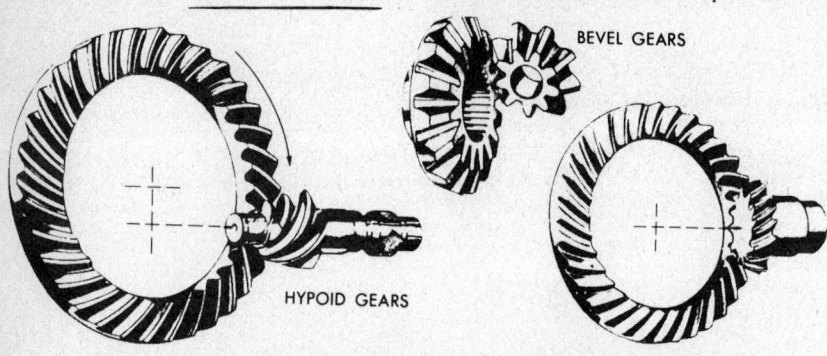

BEVEL GEARS

HYPOID GEARS

SPIRAL BEVEL GEARS

Hypoid gear application
(© Chevrolet Div., G.M. Corp)

Bevel gear application
(© Chevrolet Div., G.M. Corp)

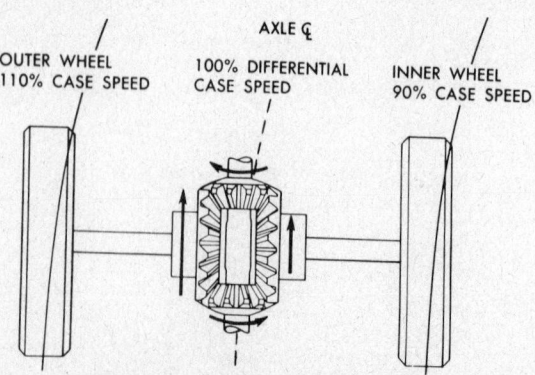

AXLE ℄

OUTER WHEEL 110% CASE SPEED

100% DIFFERENTIAL CASE SPEED

INNER WHEEL 90% CASE SPEED

Differential action during cornering
(© Chevrolet Div., G.M. Corp)

of the noise. Road noise is usually the same on drive or coast conditions.

Tire Noise

Tire noise can be mistaken as rear axle noises, even though the tires on the front are at fault. Snow tread and mud tread tires or tires worn unevenly will frequently cause vibrations which seem to originate elsewhere; *temporarily, and for test purposes only,* inflate the tires to 40–50 lbs. This will significantly alter the noise produced by the tires, but will not alter noise from the rear axle. Noises from the rear axle will normally cease at speeds below 30 mph on coast, while tire noise will continue at lower tone as car speed is decreased. The rear axle noise will usually change from drive conditions to coast conditions, while tire noise will not. Do not forget to lower the tire pressure to normal after the test is complete.

Engine and Transmission Noise

Engine and transmission noises also seem to originate in the rear axle. Road test the vehicle and determine at which speeds the noise is most pronounced. Stop the car in a quiet place to avoid interfering noises. With the transmission in neutral, run the engine slowly through the engine speeds corresponding to the car speed at which the noise was most noticeable. If a similar noise was produced with the car standing still, the noise is not in the rear axle, but somewhere in the engine or transmission.

Front Wheel Bearing Noise

Front wheel bearing noises, sometimes confused with rear axle noises, will not change when comparing drive and coast conditions. While holding the car speed steady, lightly apply the footbrake. This will often cause wheel bearing noise to lessen, as some of the weight is taken off the bearing. Front wheel bearings are easily checked by jacking up the wheels and spinning the wheels. Shaking the wheels will also determine if the wheel bearings are excessively loose.

Rear Axle Noises

If a logical test of the vehicle shows that the noise is not caused by external items, it can be assumed that the noise originates from the rear axle. The rear axle should be tested on a smooth level road to avoid road noise. It is not advisable to test the axle by jacking up the rear wheels and running the car.

True rear axle noises generally fall into two classes—gear noise and bearing noises, and can be caused by a faulty driveshaft, faulty wheel bearings, worn differential or pinion shaft bearings, U-joint misalignment, worn differential side gears and pinions, or mismatched, improperly adjusted, or scored ring and pinion gears.

REAR WHEEL BEARING NOISE

A rough rear wheel bearing causes a vibration or growl which will continue with the car coasting or in neutral. A brinelled rear wheel bearing will also cause a knock or click approximately every two revolutions of the rear wheel, due to the fact that the bearing

rollers do not travel at the same speed as the rear wheel and axle. Jack up the rear wheels and spin the wheel slowly, listening for signs of a rough or brinelled wheel bearing.

DIFFERENTIAL SIDE GEAR AND PINION NOISE

Differential side gears and pinions seldom cause noise since their movement is relatively slight on straight ahead driving. Noise produced by these gears will be more noticeable on turns.

PINION BEARING NOISE

Pinion bearing failures can be distinguished by their speed of rotation, which is higher than side bearings or axle bearings. Rough or brinelled pinion bearings cause a continuous low pitch whirring or scraping noise beginning at low speeds.

SIDE BEARING NOISE

Side bearings produce a constant rough noise, which is slower than the pinion bearing noise. Side bearing noise may also fluctuate in the above rear wheel bearing test.

GEAR NOISE

Two basic types of gear noise exist. First is the type produced by bent or broken gear teeth which have been forcibly damaged. The noise from this type of damage is audible over the entire speed range. Scoring or damage to the hypoid gear teeth generally results from insufficient lubricant, improper lubricant, improper breakin, insufficient gear backlash, improper ring and pinion gear alignment or loss of torque on the drive pinion nut. If not corrected, the scoring will lead to eventual erosion or fracture of the gear teeth. Hypoid gear tooth fracture can also be caused by extended overloading of the gear set (fatigue fracture) or by shock overloading (sudden failure). Differential and side gears rarely give trouble, but common causes of differential failure are shock loading, extended overloading and differential pinion seizure at the cross-shaft, resulting from excessive wheel spin and consequent lubricant breakdown.

The second type of gear noise pertains to the mesh pattern between the ring and pinion

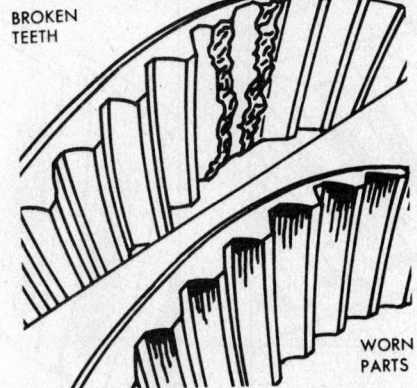

BROKEN TEETH

WORN PARTS

Two types of damage which cause gear noise
(© Chevrolet Div., G.M. Corp)

gears. This type of abnormal gear noise can be recognized as a cycling pitch or whine audible in either drive, float or coast conditions. Gear noises can be recognized as they tend to peak out in a narrow speed range and remain constant in pitch, whereas bearing noises tend to vary in pitch with vehicle speeds. Noises produced by the ring and pinion gears will generally follow the pattern below.

A. Drive Noise: Produced under vehicle acceleration.

B. Coast Noise: Produced while the car coasts with a closed throttle.

C. Float Noise: Occurs while maintaining constant car speed (just enough to keep speed constant) on a level road.

D. Drive, Coast and Float Noise: These noises will vary in tone with speed and be very rough or irregular if the differential or pinion shaft bearings are worn.

Bearing Diagnosis

This section will help in the diagnosis of bearing failure and the causes. Bearing diagnosis can be very helpful in determining the cause of rear axle failure.

When disassembling a rear axle, the general condition of all bearings should be noted and classified where possible. Proper recognition of the cause will help in correcting the problem and avoiding a repetition of the failure.

Some of the common causes of bearing failure are:

    a. Abuse during assembly or disassembly.

    b. Improper assembly methods.

    c. Improper or inadequate lubrication.

    d. Bearing contact with dirt or water.

    e. Wear caused by dirt or metal chips.

    f. Corrosion or rust.

    g. Seizing due to overloading.

    h. Overheating.

    i. Frettage of the bearing seats.

    j. Brinelling from impact or shock loading.

    k. Manufacturing defects.

    l. Pitting due to fatigue.

To avoid damage to the bearing from improper handling, it is best to treat a used bearing the same as a new bearing. Always work in a clean area with clean tools. Remove all outside dirt from the housing before exposing a bearing and clean all bearing seats before installing a bearing.

—— CAUTION ——
Never spin a bearing, either by hand or with compressed air, as this will lead to almost certain bearing failure.

LIMITED-SLIP DIFFERENTIAL DIAGNOSIS

Lubrication

The use of proper lubricant is very important in limited-slip type drive axles. The

DRIVE AXLES

forces applied when cornering tend to apply the clutch pack or clutch cones. The use of the wrong lubricant can cause the clutch surfaces to grab and chatter while turning. Always follow the manufacturer's recommendations regarding drive axle lubrication. When chatter is encountered, the differential lubricant should be drained and refilled with the specified lubricant.

Testing

The clutch operation on all limited-slip type axles can be tested as follows. Refer to the manufacturer in question.

AMERICAN MOTORS "TWIN-GRIP"

1. With the engine off and the transmission in neutral, jack up one rear wheel.
2. Block the other wheel to prevent it from moving.
3. With a socket and torque wrench on the axle shaft nut, turn the raised wheel forward.
4. The torque required to move the wheel should be 70–100 ft lbs for 8⅞ in. axles or 80–120 ft lbs for 7⁹⁄₁₆ in. axles.
5. A breakaway torque which is less than the specified figure, indicates a need for repair or replacement.

CADILLAC CONTROLLED DIFFERENTIAL

This unit should not be serviced. If a malfunction exists that cannot be cured by changing the fluid, remove the unit and install a new one.

CHRYSLER CORP. SURE-GRIP

1. Place the vehicle on a hoist with the engine off and the automatic transmission in Park (manual transmission in low gear).
2. Attempt to rotate the wheel by hand, by gripping the tire.
3. If it is extremely difficult, if not impossible, to rotate either wheel the Sure-Grip differential can be assumed to be performing satisfactorily.
4. If it is relatively easy to continuously turn either rear wheel, the unit should be removed and replaced.

CAUTION

The Sure-Grip differential is serviced as a unit only. Under no circumstances should the unit be disassembled and reinstalled.

FORD MOTOR COMPANY EQUA-LOK

1. Jack up one rear wheel and remove the wheel cover.
2. Block the other wheel front and rear to prevent the car from moving.
3. Using a 200 ft lbs capacity torque wrench on one of the wheel lug nuts, measure the torque required to continuously rotate the wheel. The breakaway torque reading can be disregarded. The minimum torque to continuously rotate the wheel should be as follows.

All axles except integral carrier type: 75 ft lbs.

Integral carrier type axles: 50 ft lbs.

4. If the minimum torque is not as specified, the differential should be checked for improper assembly.

FORD MOTOR COMPANY TRACTION-LOK

1. Follow the procedure for the Ford Motor Company Equa-Lok rear. The minimum torque to continuously rotate the wheel (disregarding the breakaway torque) should be at least 40 ft lbs through 1979 and 30 ft lbs for 1980 and later.

GENERAL MOTORS CORP. (EXCEPT CADILLAC) POSITRACTION

1. Place the transmission in neutral.
2. Raise one rear wheel off the floor and block the other rear wheel (front and rear) to prevent the car from moving.
3. Install a torque wrench and extension on the lug nut and note the torque required to continuously rotate one rear wheel. Disregard the breakaway torque figure, as this may be a great deal higher.
4. The minimum torque to continuously rotate the rear wheel should be at least 35 ft lbs. If it is not, the rear axle is in need of service.

General Diagnosis

Improper operation of a limited-slip type rear axle is generally indicated by clutch slippage or grabbing, which will sometimes produce a whirring or chatter sound. Occasionally, this condition is induced by improper lubrication. Check the unit for the wrong type of lubricant or lubricant which has broken down or become contaminated. Replace the lubricant with the type specified by the manufacturer.

During normal operation, i.e., straight-ahead driving, both wheels are rotating at equal speeds, and the driving force is distributed equally between both wheels. When cornering, the inside wheel delivers extra driving force, causing slippage in both clutch packs. Therefore, if the wheel rotation of both rear wheels is not equal, the unit will constantly be functioning as if the car were cornering. This will cause constant slippage and lead to eventual failure of the unit. It is important that there be no excessive differences in wheel and tire size, wear pattern, or tire pressures between both rear wheels. Swerving on acceleration is an indication of one or more of the above conditions. Before attempting an overhaul or replacement operation, check both rear wheels for identical tire sizes, tire pressure, tire tread depth, and wear pattern.

DRIVE AXLE DISASSEMBLY ANALYSIS

Testing the Gear Tooth Contact Pattern

Once it has been established that the differential is indeed in need of service, the worst procedure is to simply plunge ahead and remove the differential and disassemble the parts. Prior to disassembly, a tooth contact pattern test should be made. However, it is worthwhile to first know the nomenclature associated with hypoid gear teeth.

The thick end of the tooth is called the heel and the thin end of the tooth is called the toe. The base half of the tooth is called the flank

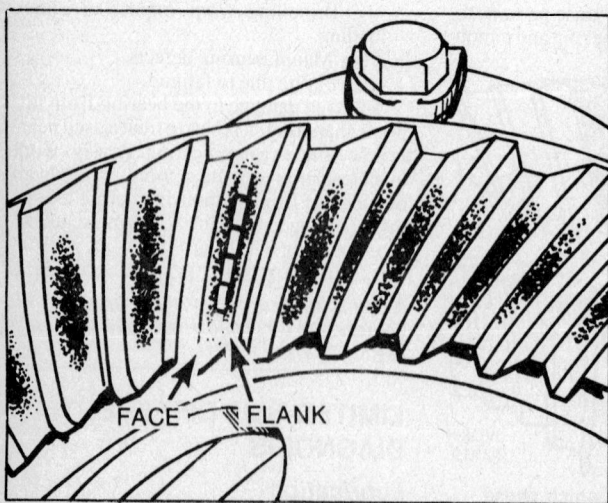

Gear tooth face and flank showing oval gear tooth contact pattern

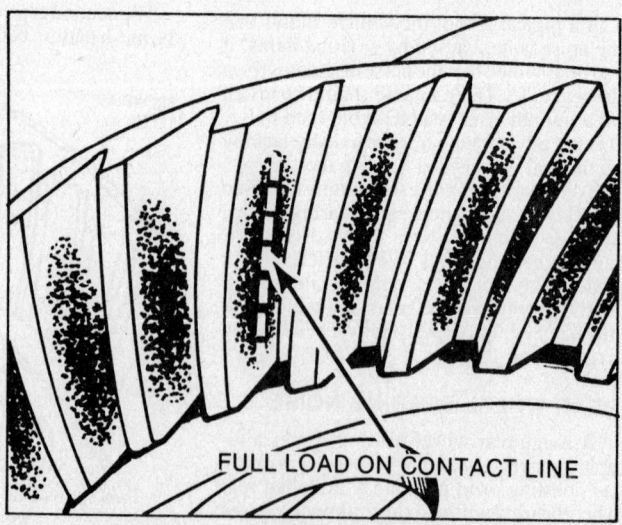

Gear tooth contact pattern showing load centered on gear tooth

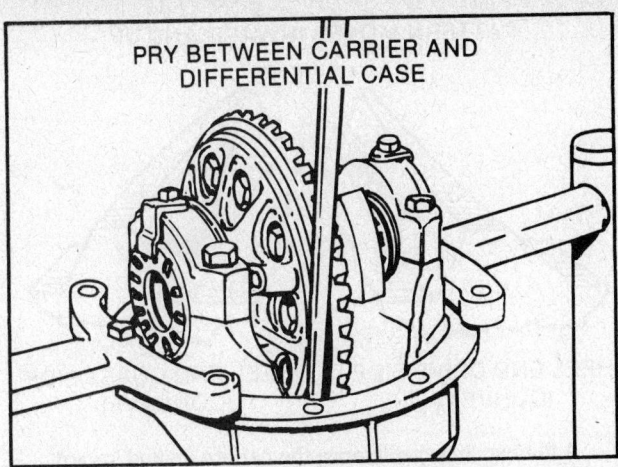

PRY BETWEEN CARRIER AND DIFFERENTIAL CASE

Applying a load to the differential case

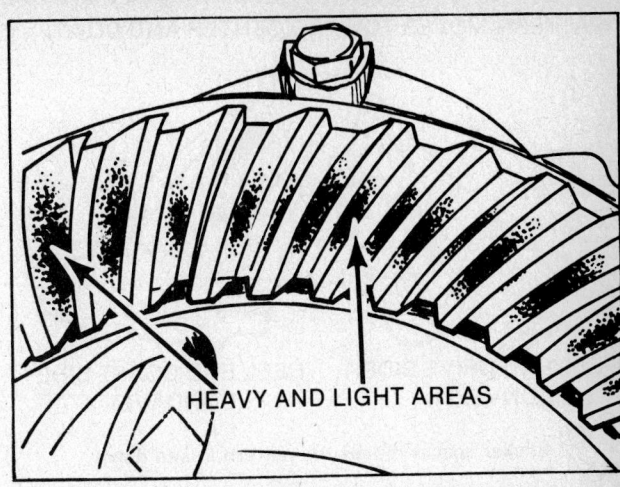

HEAVY AND LIGHT AREAS

Excessive run-out will cause an uneven pattern

and the other end of the tooth is known as the face. The imaginary line at the halfway point between the face and flank is known as the pitch line. The space between the meshed pinion and ring gear tooth is known as back-lash.

A gear tooth contact pattern can be made with the carrier in or out of the housing depending on the type of carrier. On integral carrier models, the lubricant must be drained and the rear cover removed. The ring gear will now be exposed and the test can be made with the carrier still in the housing. On re-movable carrier models, drain the lubricant and remove the carrier from the housing. The test can be made on the bench.

Unlike simple spur gears, hypoid gear teeth leave a complex pattern on the ring gear. When hypoid gears turn, the line con-tact between pinion and ring gear teeth has the same wiping motion as with spur gear teeth. Because of the complicated movement of hypoid gear teeth, the contact area takes an oval shape as opposed to the rectangular shape left by spur gear teeth. Actually, the tooth contact test shows where each gear tooth has been wiped by the movement of the contact line, so that you can tell whether the gears are set correctly. With a properly ad-justed ring and pinion (with properly ad-justed pinion depth and backlash) the tooth contact will be close to center. In this case,

the load is borne by the strongest part of the tooth. If the gear setting is off, the contact line may reach any part of the edge of a tooth, and the metal will be overloaded at that point. When overload occurs, rapid deterioration of the gears will follow.

PREPARING THE TEST

Coat the drive gear teeth with a metallic base artists' oil color such as zinc white or titanium white. The tooth coating material must be smooth and firm enough to spread without running. A consistency somewhat like toothpaste works well. If it is necessary to thicken the material, add a small amount of cup grease.

NOTE: Prussian blue dye does not work well, since the blue tends to smear the pattern.

Thoroughly clean the ring gear and pinion before applying the testing material. Any gear lube left on the teeth will make the pat-tern quite unreadable. Coat the drive and coast sides of all the ring gear teeth, but leave the pinion gear teeth clean. Do not apply the coating too thickly as the pattern will be smeared.

Because the axle gears are normally easy to rotate, turning resistance must be applied to produce pressure between the pinion and ring gear teeth to make a legible pattern. On a removable carrier type axle, insert a large

screwdriver between the carrier housing and the differential case rim. Apply the load squarely against the case rim while prying out against the upper or lower section of the carrier housing. On integral carrier models, apply the parking brake to a point where it requires approximately 50 ft lbs to turn the pinion with a torque wrench. Since the shape and position of the contact pattern will vary, depending on the load, try to use the same load for each test or the results can be mis-leading. This is especially true when testing after an overhaul.

Once the gears have a load applied, obtain a tooth contact pattern by rotating the ring gear and pinion one complete turn in each direction. This will produce a constant pat-tern on the coast and drive side of each tooth. Do not rotate the ring gear more than one rev-olution in each direction as this will tend to obscure the pattern.

NOTE: If the pattern does not look right on the first try, try again.

Making a good gear tooth test takes a little practice; so if it is not right, try again.

INTERPRETING GEAR TOOTH CONTACT PATTERNS

The tooth contact pattern should be the same on every tooth. If the pattern shows

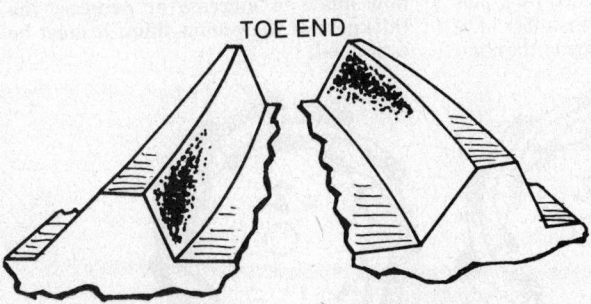

THICKER SPACER NEEDED

TOE END

HEEL END-DRIVE SIDE (CONVEX)

HEEL END-COAST SIDE (CONCAVE)

Tooth contact patterns high on the tooth side

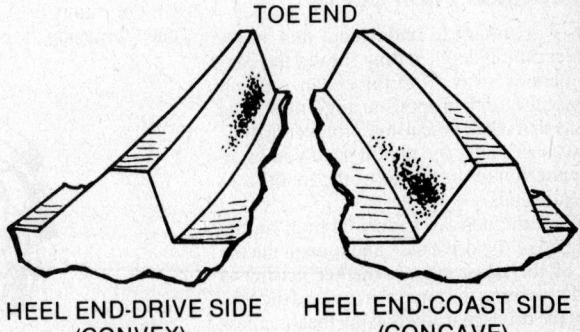

THINNER SPACER NEEDED

TOE END

HEEL END-DRIVE SIDE (CONVEX)

HEEL END-COAST SIDE (CONCAVE)

Gear contact pattern low on tooth side

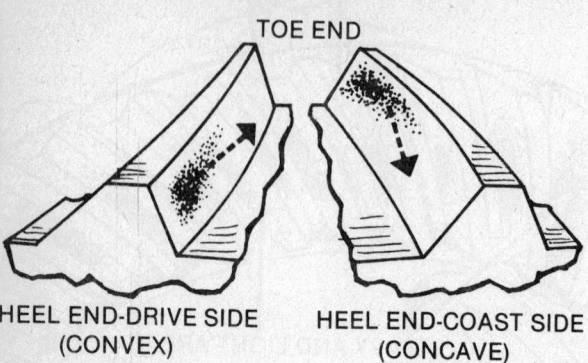

PATTERN MOVES TOWARD CENTER AND DOWN

TOE END

HEEL END-DRIVE SIDE (CONVEX)   HEEL END-COAST SIDE (CONCAVE)

A thicker spacer moves the pattern in and down

PATTERN MOVES INWARD AND UP

TOE END

HEEL END-DRIVE SIDE (CONVEX)   HEEL END-COAST SIDE (CONCAVE)

A thinner spacer will move the pattern up and inward

heavy and light areas on different teeth, check the ring gear and differential case for excessive run-out.

NOTE: Run-out can be cured in many cases by removing the ring gear from the case, rotating it 90° or 180°, and remounting it.

Since you can only apply test load pressure to the gears, the contact pattern will be less distinct toward the tooth ends. But, when the ring gear and pinion are under operating loads in the vehicle, the tooth contact area spreads out, especially towards the heel end of the tooth. For this reason, do not try to "get by" with a tooth contact pattern that is centered, but favors the heel end of the teeth. This will only lead to overloading at the heel ends of the gear teeth. On the other hand, a contact pattern which is reasonably centered, but favors the toe end of the teeth, is acceptable.

Assuming that the tooth contact pattern is even on all teeth, the main problems is to get the most distinct part of the pattern centered on both the teeth. The contact patterns should be nearly opposite each other on both sides of each tooth. In some cases, the pattern will be centered on the drive side and off center on the coast side, or vice versa. The off center pattern can be moved to a more acceptable position by slightly altering the backlash. This procedure will not seriously affect the other pattern. More often, however, the pattern will be off center on both sides of the teeth. The basic cause of this condition is an improperly adjusted pinion.

ADJUSTING PINION DEPTH

It is necessary to understand that an incorrect pinion depth setting moves the contact pattern away from the center on both sides of the tooth in opposite directions. This means that when you install a thicker or thinner washer under the pinion head you bring the pattern into the center of the tooth from opposite ends.

When the contact pattern is high on the heel end of the drive side and low on the toe end of the coast side, a thicker washer is needed to bring the pinion in, toward the center of the drive gear. Increasing the thickness of the spacer washer will bring the pattern in, toward the center of the drive gear teeth, and also will move the pattern down from the

tooth face. However, this movement is less than the in-or-out movement.

When tooth contact is low on the toe end of the drive side and high on the heel end of the coast side, the pinion must be moved out, by installing a thinner washer under the pinion head. This will move the pattern inward toward the center, and will also result in slight movement of the pattern up from the tooth flank.

A factory service facility will use special tools and gauge blocks to determine the thickness of the spacer under the pinion head. In the absence of such specialized equipment, the following procedure may be used. Bear in mind that with the "hit-or-miss" method, each time you are wrong with the pinion depth, the unit must be disassembled, the spacer thickness changed, and the unit must be completely set up again.

Gather a handful of spacers to cover any thickness and several collapsible pinion spacers (if the unit uses them). Assemble the unit. If the original gear set is being reused, and the tooth contact pattern is reasonably correct, install a new spacer of the same thickness as the old one. This will provide a reasonable starting point. If the gear contact pattern test indicates a need for movement of the pinion, use a new spacer 0.001–0.002 in. thicker or thinner, depending on the direction the pinion must go. If a new gear set is being used, the thickness of the spacer will have to be determined in the following manner. Compare the markings on the old and new pinion. It will usually be marked with a number preceded by a plus (+) or minus (−) sign. This number indicates the production deviation from the nom-

inal pinion, which are known as "zero pinions." In service, zero pinions are rare. Assume that the old pinion is marked with a plus two (+2). Assume that the new pinion is marked with a +3. By comparing the pinion markings, find the numerical difference between the two pinions, in this case +1. With a micrometer, measure the thickness of the original spacer. We will assume that the old spacer is 0.030 in. thick. If the numerical difference between pinions is a positive number (+1) the spacer should be 0.001 in. thinner than the original spacer, or 0.029 in. total. If the numerical difference is a negative number (say, −1) then the spacer should be increased by 0.001 in., to 0.031 in. total. This will only provide a reasonable beginning point.

It is rare that this method works out the first time. Assemble the pinion, differential, and ring gear with the spacer of calculated thickness. The side bearing preload, backlash, pinion nut torque, and pinion rotating torque must all be set correctly. Obtain a gear tooth pattern on the ring gear teeth and analyze the results. Small deviations from the acceptable pattern can usually be made by varying the backlash within the limits of specifications. If the gear tooth contact pattern is off, the unit must be disassembled and another spacer installed. This spacer must be of suitable thickness to compensate for the contact pattern test.

NOTE: Without special tools, there is absolutely no way of determining exactly how much to increase or decrease the thickness of the pinion shim; it must be estimated.

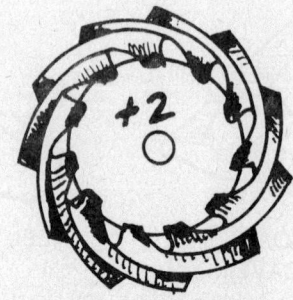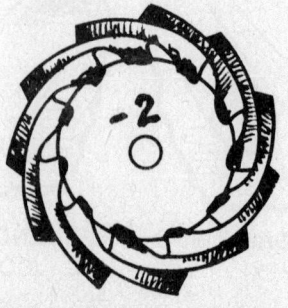

One example of pinion markings

After estimating the thickness of the new shim, assemble the unit again, setting all pre-loads and backlash. Check the contact pattern again and act accordingly. If the unit uses a collapsible spacer, be sure a new one is installed each time it is disassembled. Crushed spacers can not be used again. It is well to note that the unit may have to be assembled and disassembled several times before an acceptable contact pattern is obtained.

Adjusting Backlash

The tooth contact pattern can be altered slightly, by varying the backlash adjustment within the limits of the specifications. The backlash adjustment can be used to alter a pattern which is slightly off center on either side of the tooth, but should not be used as a substitute for pinion depth adjustment. This adjustment must always be made after the pinion depth has been adjusted.

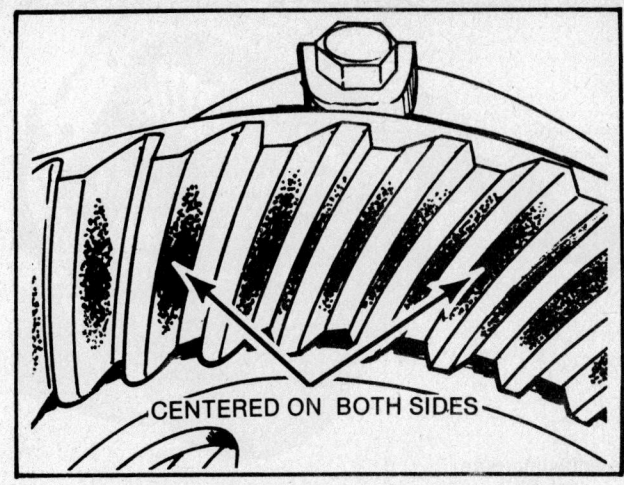

Gear tooth contact pattern showing load centered on gear tooth

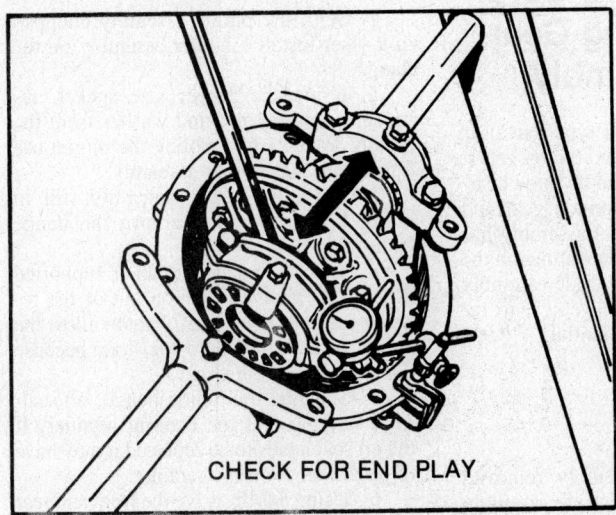

Checking differential bearing end-play

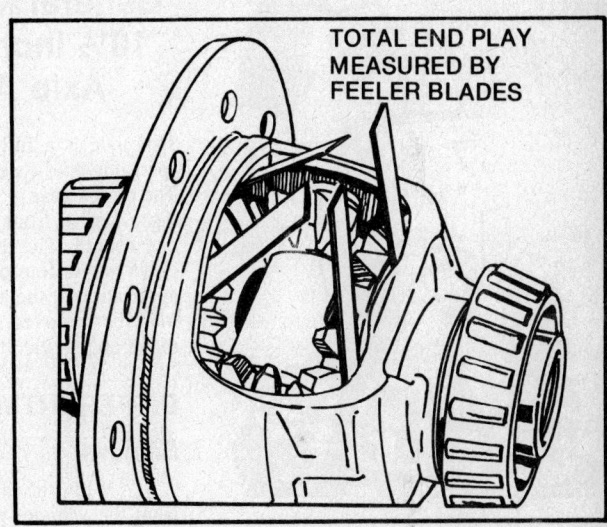

Checking total differential end-play

Front Wheel Drive Halfshaft Troubleshooting

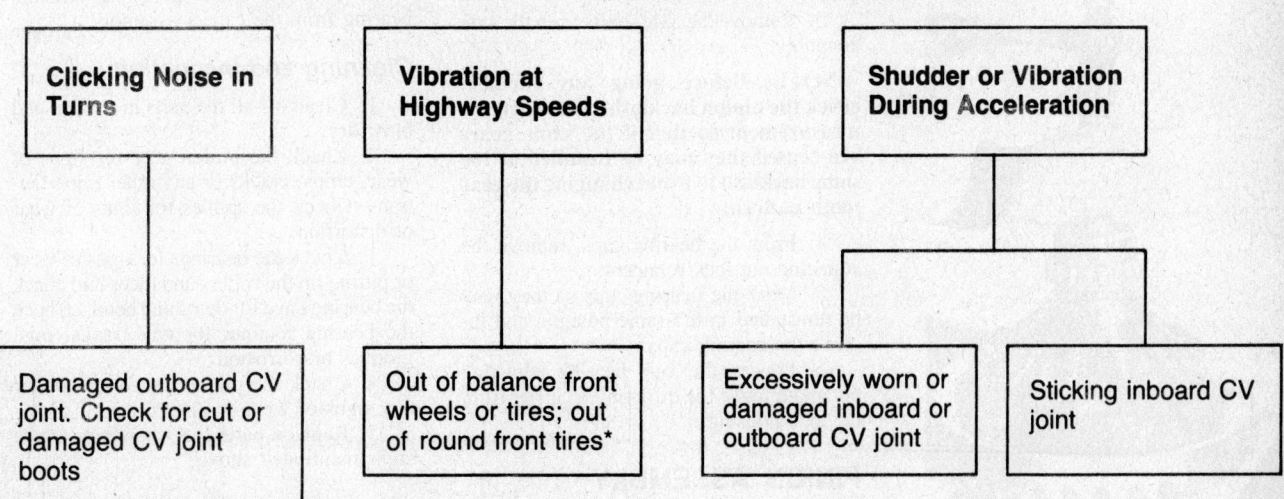

Clicking Noise in Turns	Vibration at Highway Speeds	Shudder or Vibration During Acceleration	
Damaged outboard CV joint. Check for cut or damaged CV joint boots	Out of balance front wheels or tires; out of round front tires*	Excessively worn or damaged inboard or outboard CV joint	Sticking inboard CV joint

*Halfshafts do not usually contribute to rotational vibrations.

Loosening the adjusting nuts

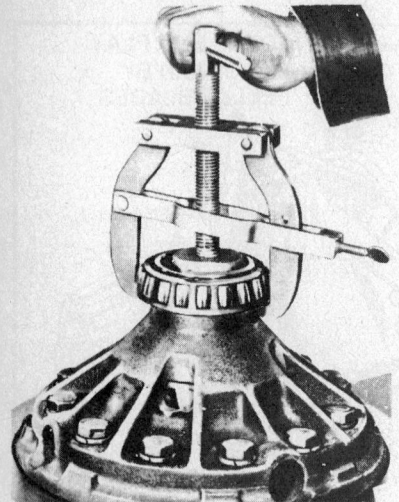

Differential bearing removal

Differential bearing installation

General Motors Corp. 10½ Inch Ring Gear Axle Assembly

This axle is a full floating type that uses special hypoid type drive and pinion gears. The pinion gear is supported by three bearings, two in front of the pinion gear and one behind. The differential assembly has either two or four pinions depending on the application of the axle. This axle assembly must be removed from the vehicle to remove and service the differential.

DIFFERENTIAL

Removal

1. With the axle assembly removed from the vehicle, place the axle assembly in a vise or holding fixture.
2. Remove the bolts that retain the cover assembly and remove the cover, allowing the gear lubricant to drain into a pan.
3. Remove the axle shafts from the axle assembly.

NOTE: Before going any further, check the pinion backlash and record the measurement so that if the same gears are reused they may be installed at the same backlash to avoid changing the gear tooth pattern.

4. From the bearing caps, remove the adjusting nut lock retainers.
5. Mark the bearing caps so they may be reinstalled in the same position and remove the bearing caps.
6. Loosen the side bearing adjusting nut and remove the differential carrier from the axle housing.

PINION ASSEMBLY

Removal

1. Remove the differential assembly from the axle.

2. Check the pinion bearing for the proper preload. The force required to turn the pinion should be 25-35 in. lbs. for used bearings. If there is no reading, shake the companion flange to check for any looseness in the bearing. If there is any looseness present the bearing should be replaced.
3. Remove the retaining bolts for the pinion bearing from the axle housing.
4. Remove the bearing retainer and pinion assembly from the axle housing. It may be necessary to tap the pilot end of the pinion shaft to help remove the pinion assembly from the carrier.
5. Record the thickness of the shims that are removed from between the carrier assembly and the bearing retainer assembly.

DRIVE PINION

Disassembly

1. With the pinion assembly clamped in a vise, install a holder assembly on the flange.
2. Using the proper size socket, remove the pinion nut and washer from the pinion. When reassembling the pinion use a new nut and washer assembly.
3. With the holder assembly still in place, use a puller to remove the flange from the pinion.
4. With the bearing retainer supported in a press, press the pinion out of the retainer assembly. Be careful not to allow the pinion gear to fall onto the floor because this can damage the gear.
5. Separate the pinion flange, oil seal, front bearing and the bearing retainer. If the oil seal needs to be replaced it may have to be driven from the retainer.
6. Using a drift, drive the front and rear bearing cups from the bearing retainer.
7. Support the pinion assembly in a press, with the bearing supported. Press the bearing from the pinion gear.
8. Using a drift, drive the straddle bearing from the carrier assembly.

Cleaning and Inspection

1. Clean off all the parts in solvent and blow dry.
2. Check the pinion gear for signs of wear, chips, cracks or any other imperfections. Check the splines for signs of wear or distortion.
3. Check the bearings for signs of wear or pitting on the rollers and races and check the bearing cage for dents and bends. Check the bearing retainer for any cracks, pits, grooves or corrosion.
4. Check the pinion flange splines for any signs of wear or distortion.
5. Replace parts that show any of the signs mentioned above.

DIFFERENTIAL CASE

Disassembly

1. Scribe a line across the two halves

of the differential case so they may be reassembled in the same position, and with the ring gear removed, separate the two halves. To remove the ring gear, remove the ring gear bolts and washers, and using a soft hammer tap the ring gear from the case.

2. Remove the internal parts from the inside of the case and set them aside in order that they may be reassembled in the same position.

Cleaning and Inspection

1. Check the differential gears, pinions, thrust washers and spider for any signs of unusual wear, chips, cracks or pitting.

2. Check all mating surfaces for signs of wear.

3. Replace parts that show any of the signs mentioned above.

DIFFERENTIAL CASE

Assembly

1. Using a good quality gear lubricant coat all of the parts.

2. Assemble the differential pinions and thrust washers onto the spider and install the assembly into the differential case.

3. Line up the scribe marks on the two halves of the differential case and install the ring gear. Install the ring gear washers and bolts and torque the bolts to approx. 10 ft. lbs.

SIDE BEARING

Replacement

1. Install a bearing puller on the bearing and remove the bearing assembly from the differential case.

2. Check the bearings for any signs of wear on distortion.

3. Install the new bearing by setting it in place on the differential case and, using a bearing driver, drive the bearing onto the case assembly until it seats against the shoulder on the case.

DRIVE PINION

Assembly and Adjustment

1. Coat all of the parts with a good quality gear lubricant.

2. With the pinion gear in a press, press the rear bearings onto the pinion assembly.

3. In the bearing retainer, install the front and rear bearing cups using a driver of the proper size.

4. In the axle housing, install the straddle bearing assembly using the proper size driver.

5. Install the bearing retainer with the bearing cups in place on the pinion gear and install a new collapsible spacer.

6. Press the front bearing onto the pinion gear.

7. Lubricate the oil seal with a good quality high pressure grease and install the

Measuring backlash

Removing retainer bolts

seal into the retainer bore. Be sure to press the seal down until it rests against the internal shoulder.

8. Install the pinion flange and oil deflector onto the splines of the pinion gear and install a new lock washer and pinion nut.

9. With the pinion flange clamped in a vise and a holder assembly installed on the flange, tighten the nut to obtain the proper preload. Measure the amount of torque required to turn the pinion gear. For a new bearing the torque required is 25–35 in. lbs. and for an old bearing it is 5–15 in. lbs. To preload the bearing, tighten the pinion nut to approx. 350 ft. lbs. and take a reading of the torque required to turn the pinion. Continue tightening the nut until the proper preload is obtained.

———— CAUTION ————
Do not tighten the nut too tightly because it will collapse the spacer too much. This will make replacement necessary.

Removing pinion nut

DRIVE PINION ASSEMBLY

Installation

1. If installing a new pinion gear, check the top of the new gear for the depth code number.

2. Compare the new number with the

Removing flange

Removing pinion rear bearing

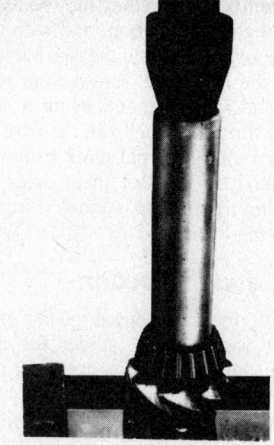

Installing pinion rear bearing

Pressing drive pinion from bearing retainer

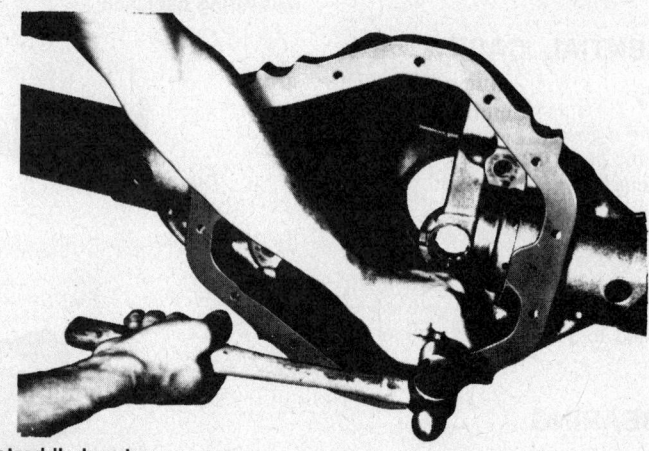

Removing straddle bearing

Installing straddle bearing

old number on top of the old pinion and check the pinion depth chart for preliminary setting of the pinion depth.

3. Check the thickness of the original shims removed from the pinion and either add or subtract from the shims according to the chart.

4. Place the shim on the carrier assembly dnd line the holes up with those in the axle housing. Make sure the surfaces are

clean of all dirt and grease.

5. Install the retainer and pinion assembly in the housing making sure the holes line up and install the retaining bolts. Torque the bolts to approx. 45 ft. lbs.

DIFFERENTIAL CASE

Installation and Adjustments

1. Place the bearing cups over the side bearings on the differential assembly and place the unit into the carrier in the axle housing.

2. Install the bearing caps making sure the marks are lined up and install the bolts. Tighten the bearing retaining bolts.

3. Loosen the right side nut and tighten the left side nut until the ring gear comes in contact with the pinion gear. Do not force the gears together. This brings the gears to zero lash.

4. Back off the left side adjusting nut about two slots and install the lock fingers into the nut.

5. In this order tighten the right side adjusting nut firmly to force the case assembly into tight contact with the left side adjusting nut and then loosen the right side nut until it is free from the bearing.

6. Again retighten the right side ad-

justing nut until it comes in contact with the bearing. Tighten the right adjusting nut about two slots if it is an old bearing or three slots if it is a new bearing.

7. Install the lock retainers into the slots and torque the bearing cap bolts to 100 ft. lbs. This procedure now insures that the bearings are preloaded properly. If more adjustments are made, make sure the preload stays the same. To do this, one adjusting nut must be loosened the same amount the other nuts is tightened.

8. Install a dial indicator on the housing and measure the amount of backlash between the ring and pinion gear. The backlash should measure between 0.003 to 0.012 of an inch with the best figure being between 0.005 to 0.008 of an inch.

9. If the bakclash is more than 0.012 of an inch, loosen the right side adjusting nut one slot and tighten the left side one slot. If the backlash is less than 0.003 of an inch, loosen the left side nut one slot and tighten the right side one slot. These adjustments should bring the backlash measurement into an acceptable range.

Pattern Check

1. Clean all the oil off the ring gear and using a gear marking compound, coat all of the teeth of the ring gear.

2. Make sure the bearing caps are torqued to 110 ft. lbs. and apply load to the gears while rotating the pinion. Rotate the ring gear one full turn in both directions.

NOTE: Load must be applied to the assembly while rotating or the pattern will not show completely.

3. Check the pattern on the ring gear and following the chart, adjust the assembly to get the contact pattern located centrally on the face of the ring gear teeth.

General Motors Corp. 8½ and 8⅞ Inch Ring Gear Axle Assembly

This axle assembly is the semi-floating type with Hypoid type drive pinion and ring gears. The drive pinion gear is supported by two bearings. The differential case contains two pinion gears. The carrier assembly is not removable since it is part of the axle assembly but the design allows for the differential assembly to be serviced while the axle is still in the vehicle. The ring gear is bolted to a one piece differential case that is supported by two preloaded roller bearings.

DIFFERENTIAL CASE

Removal

1. Remove the inspection cover from the axle housing and drain the gear lubricant into a pan.
2. Remove the screw or pin that holds the pinion shaft in place and remove the shaft.
3. Push the axle shaft s in a little and remove the "C" locks from the ends of the shafts. Remove the axle shafts from the housing.
4. Before going any further, the backlash should be measured and recorded. This will allow the old gears to be reassembled at the same amount of lash to avoid changing the gear tooth pattern. It also helps to indicate if there is gear or bearing wear, and if there is any error in the original backlash setting.
5. Roll the differential pinions and thrust washers out of the case and also remove the side gears and thrust washers. Make sure to mark the pinions and side gears so they can be reassembled in their original position.
6. Mark the bearing caps and housing and loosen the retaining bolts. Tap the caps lightly to loosen them. When the caps are loose, take the bolts all the way out and then reinstall the bolts just a few turns. This will keep the case from falling out of the housing when it is pried loose.
7. With a pry bar, very carefully pry the case assembly loose. Be careful not to damage the gasket surface on the housing when prying. The case assembly may suddenly come free if the bearings were preloaded, so pry very slowly.
8. When the case assembly is loose, remove the bolts for the bearing caps and remove the caps. Place the caps so they may be reinstalled in the same position. Place any shims that are removed with the cap they were removed from.

DRIVE PINION

Removal

1. With the differential removed, check the pinion preload. Do this by checking the amount of torque needed to turn the pinion gear. For a new bearing, it should be 20–25 in. lbs., and for a used bearing it should be 10–15 in. lbs. If there is no preload reading check the pinion for looseness. If there is any looseness the bearing should be replaced.
2. With a holder assembly installed on the flange, use a socket of the proper size and remove the flange nut and washer.
3. Remove the flange by using a puller assembly and drawing the flange off the pinion splines.

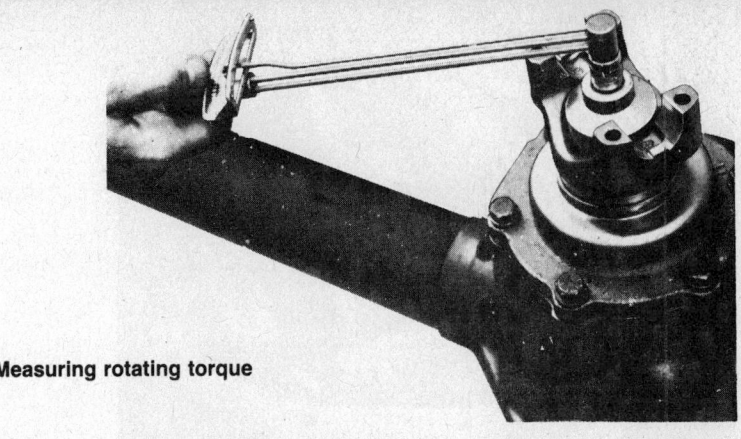

Measuring rotating torque

		CODE NUMBER ON ORIGINAL PINION				
		+2	+1	0	-1	-2
CODE NUMBER ON SERVICE PINION	+2	—	ADD .001	ADD .002	ADD .003	ADD .004
	+1	SUBT. .001	—	ADD .001	ADD .002	ADD .003
	0	SUBT. .002	SUBT. .001	—	ADD .001	ADD .002
	-1	SUBT. .003	SUBT. .002	SUBT. .001	—	ADD .001
	-2	SUBT. .004	SUBT. .003	SUBT. .002	SUBT. .001	—

Pinion depth codes

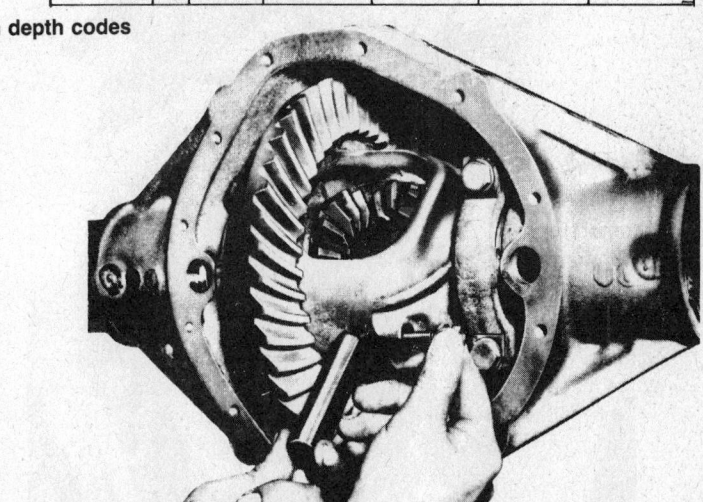

Differential pinion shaft removal

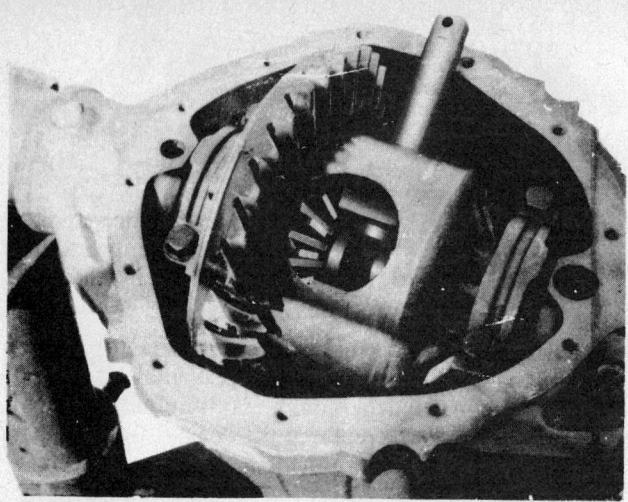

Positioning case for best clearance

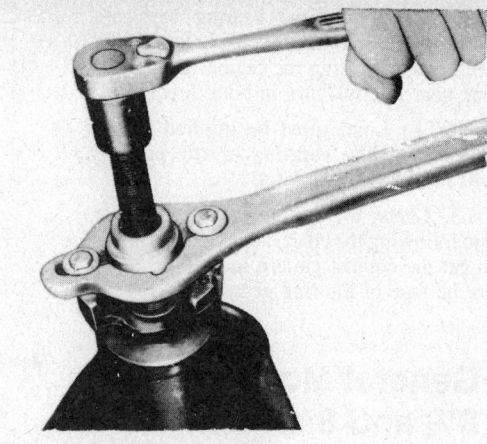

Drive pinion flange removal

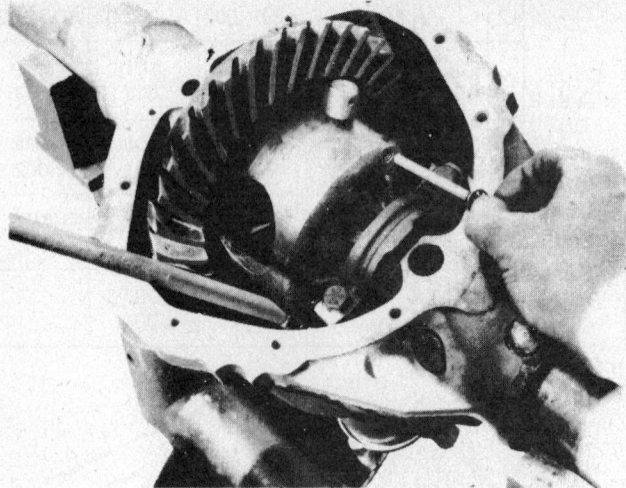

Removing lock screw

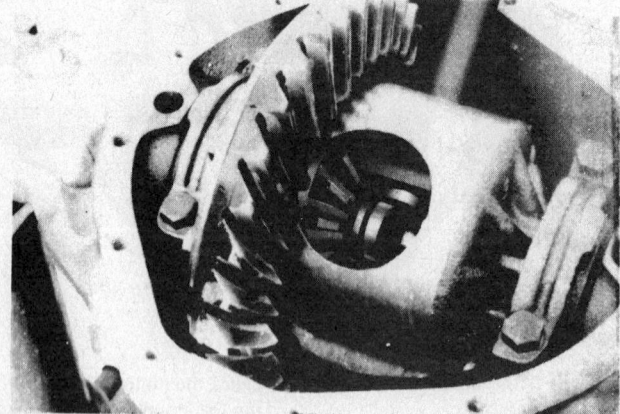

Pushing the axle shaft inward

4. Thread the pinion nut a few turns onto the pinion shaft. Using a brass drift and hammer, lightly tap the end of the pinion shaft to remove the pinion from the carrier. Be careful not to allow the pinion to fall out of the carrier after it breaks loose.

5. With the pinion removed from the carrier, discard the old seal pinion nut and collapsible spacer and install new ones

when reassembling.

Cleaning and Inspection

1. Clean all parts in solvent and blow dry.

2. Check all of the parts for any signs of wear, chips, cracks or distortion. Replace any parts that are defective.

3. Check the fit of the differential side

DIFFERENTIAL BEARING

Replacement

1. With a bearing puller attached to the bearing, pull the bearing from the case.

2. Place the new bearing on the case hub with the thick side of the inner race toward the case. Using a bearing driver, drive the bearing onto the case until it seats against the shoulder on the case.

DRIVE PINION BEARING

Replacement and Adjustment

1. Depending on the bearing that is being replaced, remove the front or rear bearing cup from the carrier assembly.

2. With the pinion gear mounted in a press, press the rear bearing from the pinion shaft. Be sure to record the thickness of the shims that are removed from between the bearing and the gear.

3. Using a bearing driver of the proper size, install a new bearing cup for each one that was removed. Make sure the cups are seated fully against the shoulder in the housing.

4. The pinion depth must now be checked to determine the nominal setting. This allows for machining variations in the housing and enables you to select the proper shim so that the pinion depth can be set for the best bear tooth contact.

5. Clean the housing and carrier assemblies to insure accurate measurement of the pinion depth.

6. Lubricate the front and rear pinion bearings with gear lubricant and install them in their races in the carrier assembly.

7. Using a pinion setting gauge, select the proper clover leaf plate, and install it on the preload stud.

8. Insert the stud through the rear bearing, with the proper size pilot on the stud, and through the front bearing using the proper pilot. Install the hex nut and tighten it until it is just snug.

9. Holding the preload stud with a

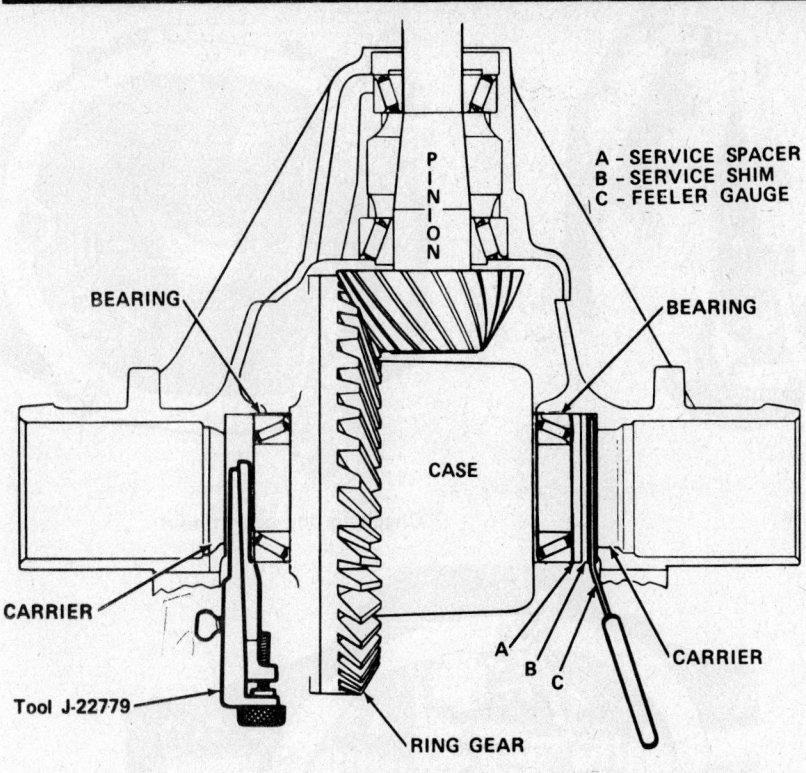

A — SERVICE SPACER
B — SERVICE SHIM
C — FEELER GAUGE

EXAMPLE

RING GEAR SIDE		OPPOSITE SIDE	
.250″	Thickness of Tool J-22779 required to force ring gear into contact with pinion	Combined total of: Service Spacer (A) Service Shim (B) Feeler Gauge (C)	.265″
$-.010″$ .240″	TO MAINTAIN PROPER BACKLASH (.005″ - .008″), ring gear is moved away from pinion by subtracting .010″ shims from ring gear side and adding .010″ shims to other side		$+.010″$ .275″
$+.004″$	TO OBTAIN PROPER PRELOAD on side bearings, add .004″ shims to each side.		$+.004″$
.244″	Shim dimension required for ring gear side	Shim dimension required for opposite side	.279″

Determining side bearing shim requirements

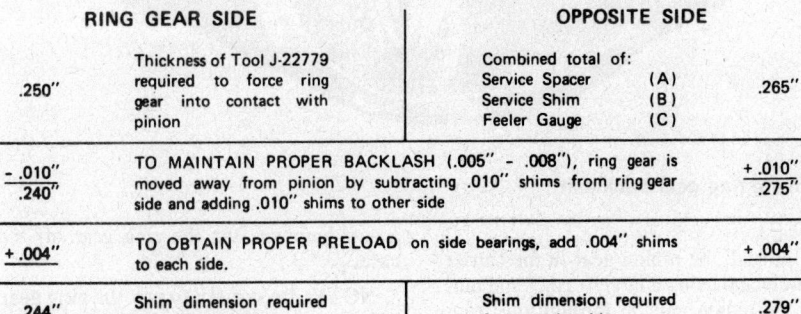

Wheel bearing removal

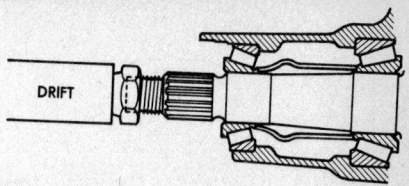

Removing drive pinion

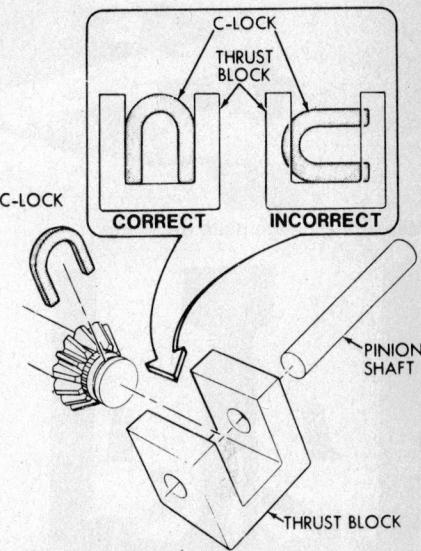

Correct C-lock position

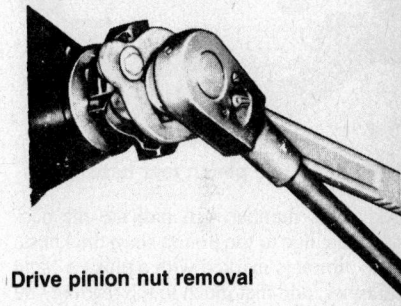

Drive pinion nut removal

gears in the case and the fit of the side gear and axle shaft splines.

wrench, tighten the hex nut until 20 in. lbs. of torque are required to rotate the bearings.

10. Install the side bearing discs on the ends of the arbor assembly, using the step of the disc that fits the bore of the carrier.

11. Install the arbor and plunger assembly into the carrier. Make sure the side bearing discs fit properly.

12. Install the bearing caps in the carrier assembly finger tight to make sure the discs do not move.

13. Mount a dial indicator on the mounting post of the arbor. Have the contact button resting on the top surface of the plunger.

14. Preload the dial indicator by turning it one-half revolution and tightening it in this position.

15. Use the button on the gauge plate that corresponds to the ring gear size and turn the plate so the plunger rests on top of it.

16. Rock the plunger rod back and forth across the top of the button until the dial indicator reads the greatest amount of variation. Set the dial indicator to zero at the point of most variation. Repeat the rocking of the plunger several times to check the setting.

17. Turn the plunger until it is removed from the gauging plate button. The dial indicator will now read the pinion shim thickness required to set the nominal pinion depth. Make a note of the reading.

18. Check for the pinion code number on the rear face of the pinion gear being

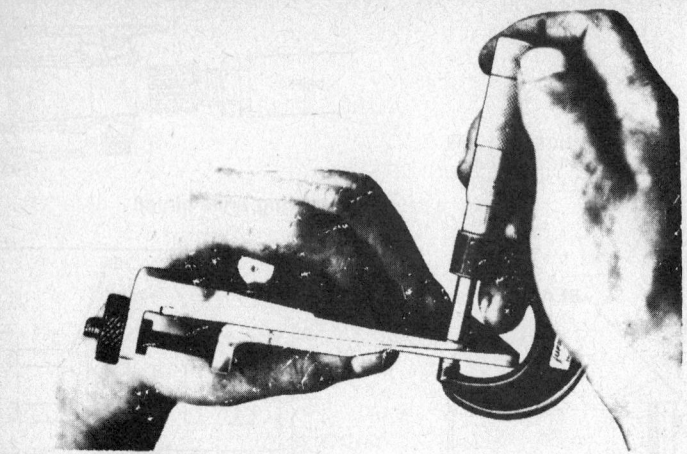

Measuring gauge plate thickness

Checking ring gear runout

Removing drive pinion rear bearing

Checking ring gear backlash

used. This number will indicate the necessary change to the pinion shim thickness. If the pinion is marked with a plus (+) and a number, add that much to the reading you got from the dial indicator. If the pinion has no mark, use the reading from the dial indicator as the correct shim thickness. If the pinion is marked with a minus (−) and a number, subtract that much from the reading on the dial indicator.

19. Remove the depth gauging tools from the carrier assembly and install the proper size shim on the pinion gear.

20. Lubricate the bearing with gear lubricant and using a press, press the bearing into place on the pinion shaft.

PINION GEAR

Installation and Adjustment

1. Lubricate the front bearing with gear lubricant and install it in the front cup.

2. Install the pinion seal in the bore. Using a seal driver and the proper size gauge plate, drive the seal in until the gauge plate is flush with the shoulder of the carrier.

3. Coat the seal lips with gear lubricant and install a new bearing spacer on the pin-

ion gear.

4. Install the pinion gear in the carrier assembly and using a large washer and nut, draw the pinion gear in through the front bearing far enough to get companion flange in place.

5. With the companion flange installed on the pinion shaft, use a holder assembly and tighten the pinion nut until all of the end play is removed from the drive pinion.

6. When there is no more end play the preload should be checked. The preload of the bearing is the amount of torque required to turn the pinion gear. The preload should be 20–25 in. lbs. on new bearings and 10–15 in. lbs. on reused bearings. Tighten the pinion nut until these figures are reached. Do Not over tighten the pinion. This will collapse the spacer too much and make it necessary to replace it.

7. Turn the pinion gear several times to make sure the bearings are seated and recheck the preload.

RING GEAR

Replacement

1. Remove all of the bolts that hold the ring gear to the differential case and with

a soft hammer, tap the ring gear off the case.

NOTE: Do not try to pry the ring gear off the case. This will damage the machined surfaces.

2. Clean all dirt from the case assembly and lubricate the case with gear lube. Align the ring gear bolt holes with the holes in the carrier and lightly press the ring gear onto the case assembly. Install all of the bolts and tighten them all evenly, using a criss-cross pattern to avoid cocking the ring gear.

3. When the ring gear is firmly seated against the case, tighten the bolts to 60 ft. lbs.

DIFFERENTIAL CASE ASSEMBLY

Installation and Adjustment

1. Install the thrust washers and side gears into the case assembly. If the original parts are being used, be sure to place them in their original position.

2. Place the pinions in the case so they are 180 degrees apart as they engage the side gears.

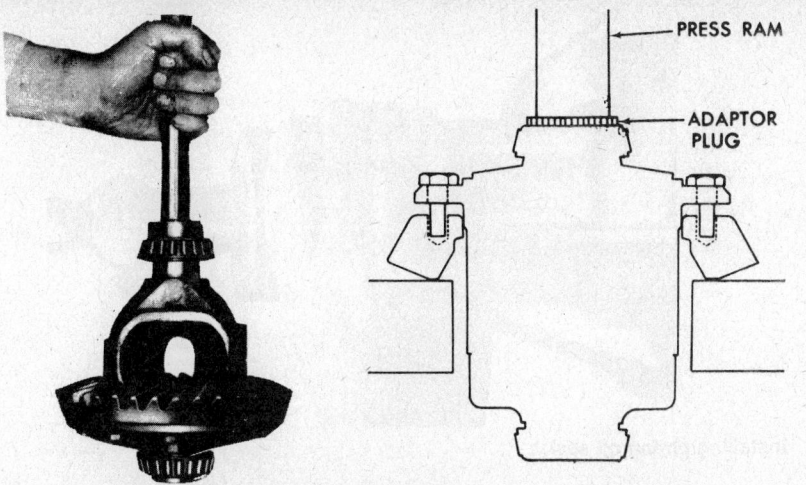

Differential bearing installation

Ring gear-to-case installation

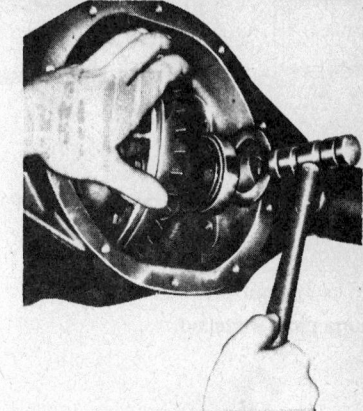

Installing differential shims

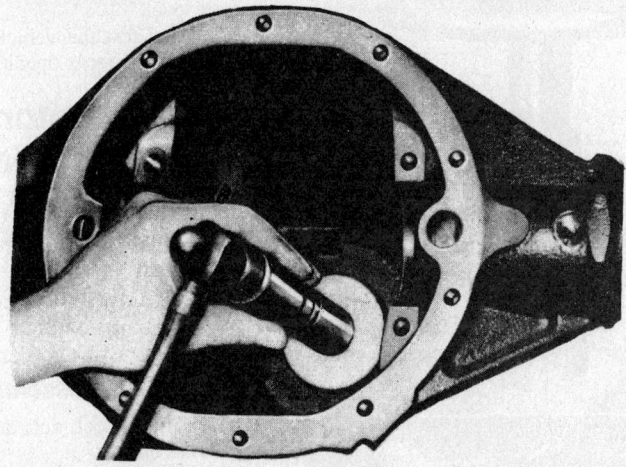

Installing pinion rear bearing cup

Installing rear bearing

3. Turn the pinion gears so the hole in the case lines up with the holes in the gears. When the holes are aligned, install the pinion shaft and lock screw. Do not tighten the lock screw too tightly at this time.

4. Check the bearings, bearing cups, cup seat and carrier caps to make sure they are in good condition.

5. Lubricate the bearings with gear lube. Install the cups on the proper bearings and install the differential assembly in the carrier. Support the carrier assembly to keep it from falling.

6. Install a support strap on the left side bearing and tighten the bearing bolts to an even, snug fit.

7. With the ring gear tight against the pinion gear, insert a gauging tool between the left side bearing cup and the carrier housing.

8. While lightly shaking the tool back and forth, turn the adjusting wheel until a slight drag is felt. Tighten the lock nut.

9. Between the right side bearing and carrier, install a service spacer, 0.170 of an inch thick, a service shim and a feeler gauge. The feeler gauge must be thick enough so a light drag is felt when it is moved between the carrier and the shim.

10. Add the total of the service spacer,

service shim and the feeler gauge. Remove the gauging tool from the left side of the carrier and using a micrometer, measure the thickness in at least three places. Average the readings and record the result.

11. Refer to the chart to determine the proper thickness of the shim packs.

12. Install the left side shim first, then install the right side shim between the bearing cup and spacer. Position the shim so the chamfered side is outward or next to the spacer. If there is not enough chamfer around the outside of the shim, file or grind the chamfer a little to allow for easy installation.

13. If there is difficulty in installing the shim, partially remove the case from the carrier and slide both the shim and case back into place.

14. Install the bearing caps and torque them to 60 ft. lbs. Tighten the pinion shaft lock screw.

NOTE: The differential side bearings are now preloaded. If any adjustments are made in later procedures, make sure not to change the preload. Do Not change the total thickness of the shim packs.

15. Mount a dial indicator on the carrier assembly with the indicator button perpen-

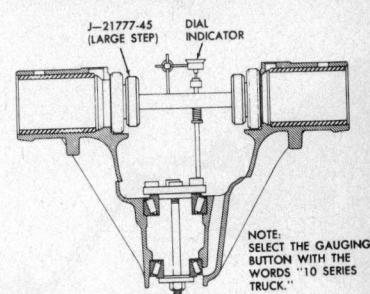

Gauging tools installed in carrier

dicular to the tooth angle and in line with the gear rotation.

16. Measure the amount of backlash between the ring and pinion gears. The backlash should be between 0.005–0.008 of an inch. Take readings at four different spots on the gear. There should not be variations greater than 0.002 of an inch.

17. If there are variations greater than 0.002 of an inch between the readings, check the runout between the case and ring gear. The gear runout should not be greater than 0.003 in. If the runout does exceed 0.003 in. check the case and ring gear for the deformation or dirt between the case

1227

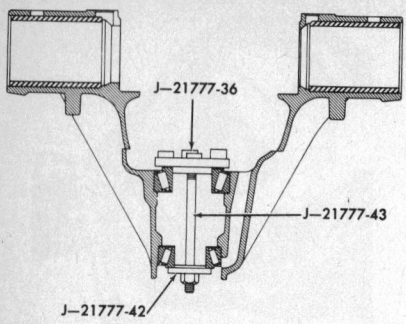

Gauge plate installed

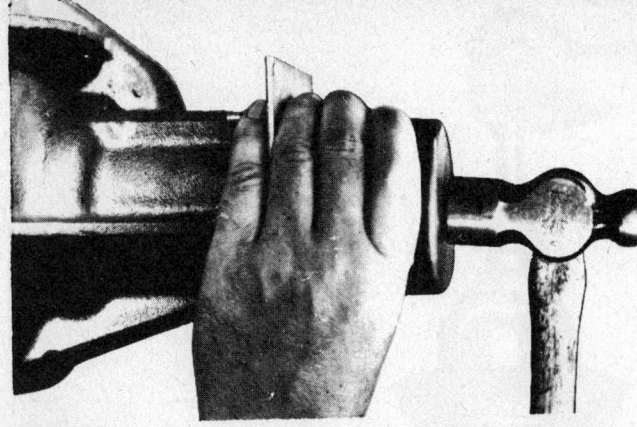

Installing pinion oil seal

Installing pinion front bearing cup

Pinion rear bearing removal

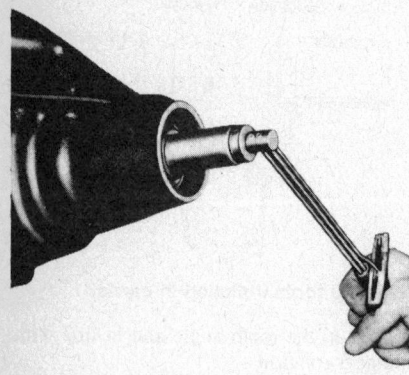

Measuring rotating torque

and gear.

18. If the gear backlash exceeds 0.008 in., increase the thickness of the shims on the ring gear side and decrease the thickness of the shims on the opposite side, an equal amount.

19. If the backlash is less than 0.005 in., decrease the shim thickness on the ring gear side and increase the shim thickness on the opposite side an equal amount.

Gear Pattern Check

Before final assembly of the differential, a pattern check of the gear teeth must be made. This determines if the teeth of the ring and pinion gears are meshing properly, for low noise level and long life of the gear teeth. The most important thing to note is if the pattern is located centrally up and down on the face of the ring gear.

1. Wipe any oil out of the carrier and wipe all dirt and oil from the teeth of the ring gear.

2. Coat the teeth of the ring gear with a gear marking compound.

3. With the bearing caps torqued to 55 ft. lbs., expand the brake shoes until it takes 20–30 ft. lbs. of torque to turn the pinion gear.

4. Turn the companion flange so the ring gear makes one full rotation in one direction, then turn it one full rotation in the opposite direction.

5. Check the pattern on the teeth and refer to the chart for any adjustments necessary.

6. With the gear tooth pattern checked and properly adjusted, install the axle hous-ing cover gasket and cover and tighten securely. Fill the axle with gear lube to the correct level.

7. Road test the vehicle to check for any noise and proper operation of the rear.

General Motors Corp. 12¼ Inch Rear Axle Models H110, H135, H150 and H170

DISASSEMBLY OF SUBASSEMBLIES

Differential Disassembly

1. Remove lock nut, adjusting screw, and thrust block.

2. Remove two adjuster lock cap screws and locks.

3. Punch-mark bearing caps and carrier to help in locating caps for assembly. Remove bearing adjusters and bearing caps.

NOTE: Do not pry caps free with a screwdriver or distort locating dowels.

4. Carefully remove differential assembly from carrier.

5. Use differential side bearing remover to pull bearing cones off each side of case.

6. Make sure that differential case halves are punch-marked so that they can be reassembled in same position.

7. Remove drive gear, and separate case halves.

8. Remove two side gears; differential spider, and four differential pinions.

9. Remove pinion and side gear thrust washers to complete differential disassembly.

Drive Pinion Disassembly

1. Remove seal retainer and gasket from carrier.

2. Use brass drift against inner end of pinion to drive out pinion and bearings assembly.

3. Remove shim pack from carrier from those models having tapered roller

Drive pinion front bearing removal

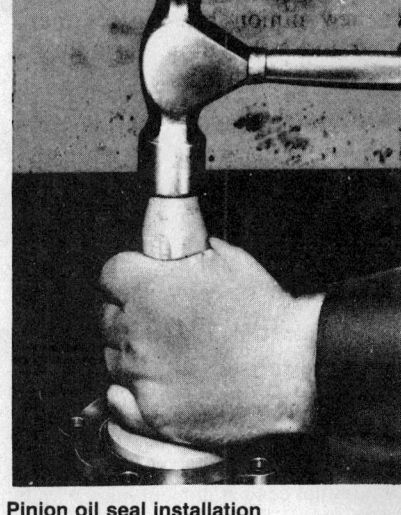

Pinion oil seal installation

outer bearings.

4. According to the model, it may be necessary to use a drift to remove the pinion rear bearing.

5. Clamp yoke in soft-jawed vise. Remove yoke nut and washer and separate drive pinion from yoke.

6. Separate yoke from oil seal retainer.

7. Place retainer in a soft-jawed vise and, using a hammer and chisel, remove oil seal and then the felt oil seal.

8. On models with tapered roller outer bearing, remove bearing cup, outer tapered bearing cone, and bearing spacer from drive pinion.

9. Using bearing remover press plate with press, separate bearing cone (some models) or roller bearing (on all other models) from drive pinion.

10. On models H110 and H135, remove bearing lock ring, and use press plates with arbor press to remove roller bearing from inner end of drive pinion. This completes drive pinion disassembly.

ASSEMBLY OF SUBASSEMBLIES

NOTE: Thoroughly clean and lubricate all components with axle lubricant before reassembling.

Drive Pinion Assembly

1. Clean counterbore of oil seal retainer. Saturate felt seal in oil and install evenly in retainer. Soak oil seal in light engine oil for about one hour before installing. Coat outer surface of seal lightly with sealing compound to prevent oil leaks between seal and retainer.

2. Install oil seal into retainer with lip of seal toward inner side of retainer. Using a seal installer, press oil seal into retainer with face of seal flush with retainer face.

3. Retainer surface must be clean and smooth to prevent oil leaks between retainer and carrier.

4. On models H150 and H170, press

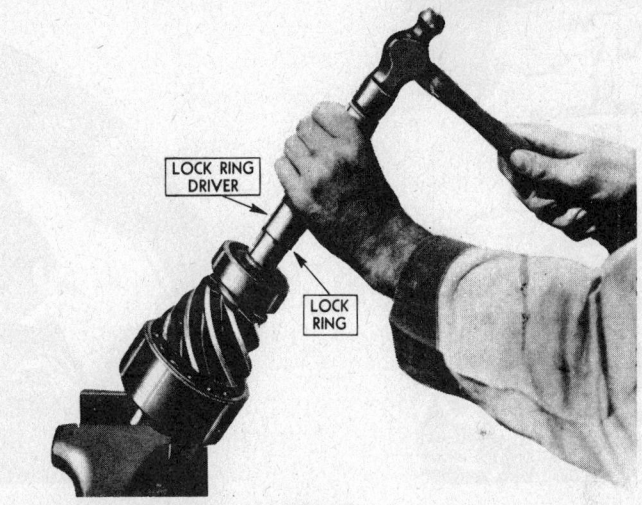

Pinion rear bearing lock ring installation

bearing into place into carrier bore.

5. On models H110 and H135, press roller bearing into position on drive pinion with chamfered side of inner race facing toward pinion shoulder. Position bearing lock ring to secure bearing on drive pinion.

NOTE: Opposed tapered roller bearing cones, two bearing cups, and spacer used on some models are serviced and replaced as a unit. The spacer is a preselected one to provide proper bearing adjustment.

6. Models with tapered roller bearings:

a. Press inner bearing cone into place with largest side of cone facing pinion gear end.

b. Install original shim pack in carrier. If original ring gear and pinion are reinstalled, use shims that were removed. Shims are available in five thicknesses: 0.012, 0.015, 0.018, 0.021 and 0.024 inch. When using new gears, start with one 0.021 inch shim and refer to General Axle Service section for details on checking pinion depth.

c. Insert pinion assembly into carrier (on models H150 and H170), align roller

bearing with carrier boss. Install bearing spacer, bearing cup and bearing cone with wide side facing pinion splines.

7. Models with double-row ball bearing: Using a 2-inch pipe or tubing, drive bearing unit into proper seating position.

8. With pinion assembly properly positioned in carrier, install new gasket. Install seal retainer onto yoke, and assemble yoke and retainer assembly onto splined end of drive pinion.

9. Secure retainer to carrier with lock washers and cap screws and torque to specifications.

10. Secure pinion assembly with yoke washer and nut and torque to 220 ft. lbs. This completes drive pinion assembly.

Differential Assembly

1. To facilitate installation of drive gear, install two guide pins (cut ½"–20 × 2" bolts) in gear. Start guide pins through case flange holes and tap drive gear onto case. If one differential gear is bad, the complete set should be replaced.

2. Lubricate differential case inner walls and all component parts with axle

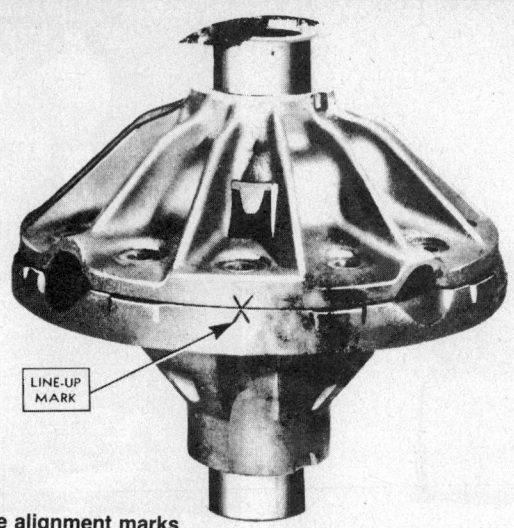

Differential case alignment marks

LINE-UP MARK

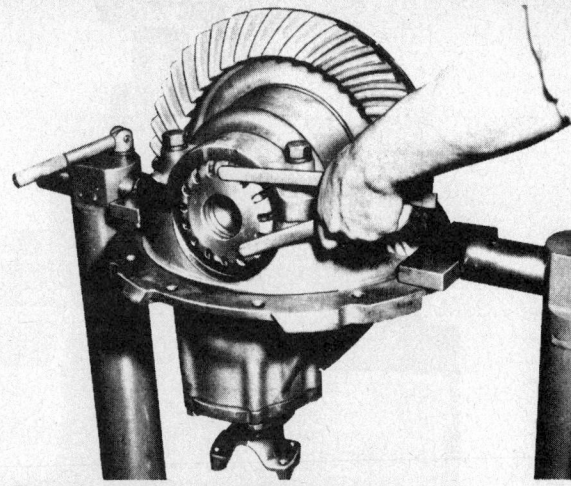

Backlash and preload adjustment

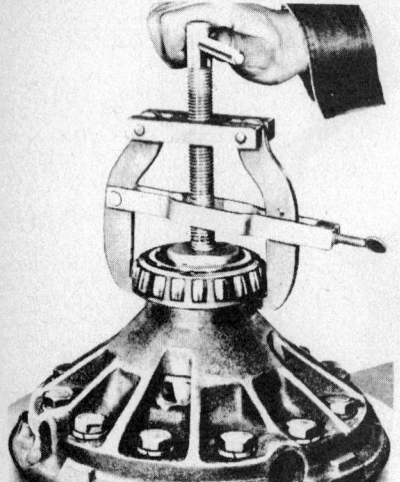

Differential bearing removal

Checking backlash

Differential bearing installation

lubricant. Place differential pinions and thrust washers on spider.

3. Assemble side gears, pinions and side gear and pinion thrust washers to left half of differential.

4. Assemble drive gear half (right half of differential, being sure to line up marks on the two halves.

5. Install differential-to-drive gear cap screw and lock washers and tighten evenly until drive gear is flush with case flange. Remove guide pins and install cap screws and torque to specifications.

6. Differential side bearing cones can be installed with special installer tool.

INSTALLATION OF SUBASSEMBLIES

Differential Installation

1. Install bearing cap locating dowels in caps. Lubricate side bearings and place bearing cups on bearings.

2. Install differential assembly into carrier. Carefully install bearing adjusters into carrier.

3. Install bearing caps, aligning punch marks previously made. Be sure that bearing adjuster threads are engaged with carrier and caps. Tighten adjusters alternately and evenly. Tighten bearing cap screws until lock washers are flat.

Drive Gear and Pinion Adjustment

1. Loosen bearing cap screws just enough to loosen right-hand bearing adjuster (pinion side) and tighten left-hand bearing adjuster (opposite pinion side.) Using adjuster, remove all backlash between drive gear and pinion.

2. Back off left-hand bearing adjuster about two notches to point where notch in adjuster is aligned with lock. Tighten right-hand bearing adjuster solidly to seat bearing. Again loosen right-hand adjuster enough to free bearing; then retighten snugly against bearing. Draw up right-hand adjuster one or two more notches until adjuster notch aligns with lock.

3. With dial indicator on carrier adjuster, slowly oscillate drive gear and take backlash reading. Backlash should be 0.005 to 0.008-inch.

4. If backlash exceeds 0.008-inch, loosen right-hand adjuster one notch; then tighten left-hand adjuster one notch. If less than 0.005 inch, loosen left-hand adjuster one notch and tighten right-hand adjuster one notch.

12¼ INCH REAR AXLE SPECIFICATIONS
Models H110, H135, H150 and H170

TYPE:	Hypoid
ADJUSTMENTS AND CLEARANCES:	
Backlash—Ring Gear To Pinion	0.005"–0.008"
Adjustment Method	See text
Pinion Depth Adjustment:	
Models With Tapered Bearings: Adjustment Method	Shims
Shim Pack Thickness:	
Initial	0.021"
Available	0.012", 0.015", 0.018", 0.021", 0.024"
Models With Ball Bearings: Adjustment Method	None
Backlash-Side Gear to Pinion Gear	0.007"–0.009"
Thurst Block To Gear Clearance	0.005"–0.007"
TOLERANCES:	
Ring Gear Run-out (Max. when mounted to case)	
H110	0.005"
H135, H150, H170	0.0065"
Differential Case Run-out At Flange (Max.): All Models	0.002"
Axle Shaft Run-out At Center of Shaft (Max.): All Models	0.016"
DIMENSIONS:	
Differential Case Diameter At Side Gear	
H110	2.193"–2.195"
H135, H150, H170	2.409"–2.411"
Side Gear Hub Diameter	
H110	2.189"–2.191"
H135, H150, H170	2.405"–2.407"
Pinion Gear (Inside Diameter)	
H110	0.879"–0.882"
H135, H150, H170	0.9415"–0.9445"
Thrust Washer Thickness: All Models	0.058"–0.062"
Diameter Of Spider Arms	
H110	0.874"–0.875"
H135, H150, H170	0.9365"–0.9375"
Thrust Block Thickness: All Models	0.1845"–0.1885"
Diameter of Axle Shaft Splines	
H110	0.874"–0.875"
H135, H150, H170	0.9365"–0.9375"
TORQUE VALUES:	
Ring Gear Bolts	
H110	118 ft. lbs.
H135, H150, H170	165 ft. lbs.
Differential Bearing Cap Bolts: All Models	205 ft. lbs.
Pinion Yoke Nut: All Models	220 ft. lbs.
Differential Bearing Adjuster Nut Lock Bolt: All Models	15 ft. lbs.
Differential Carrier To Housing Bolts: All Models	83 ft. lbs.
Thrust Block Lock Nut: All Models	128 ft. lbs.

12¼ INCH REAR AXLE SPECIFICATIONS
Models H110, H135, H150 and H170

TYPE:	Hypoid
Pinion Bearing Retainer Bolts	
H110	95 ft. lbs.
H135	98 ft. lbs.
H150	93 ft. lbs.
H170	165 ft. lbs.

Ring gear thrust pad adjustment

Spreading the gear carrier

Separating the case halves

Dana Corporation

9¾ AND 10½ INCH RING GEAR AXLE ASSEMBLIES

The Dana Corporation's 9¾ and 10½ inch ring gear axle assemblies are basically the same, but with certain exceptions. The differential side bearing shims are located between the side bearing cup assembly and the differential case on the 9¾ inch ring gear axle assembly, while on the 10½ inch ring gear axle assembly, the side bearing shims are located between the side bearing cup and the axle housing. Both axles use inner and outer shims on the pinion gear. The inner shims are used to control the pinion depth in the housing, while the outer shims are used to preload the pinion bearings. The 9¾ inch ring gear axle uses a solid differential carrier with a removable side and pinion gear shaft. The 10½ inch ring gear axle uses a split differential carrier with the side and pinion gears mounted on a cross shaft.

DIFFERENTIAL CASE
Removal
9¾ AND 10½ INCH

1. The axle assembly can be overhauled either in or out of the vehicle, depending on the repairman's discretion. Either way, the free-floating axles and

5. After backlash has been adjusted, again tighten bearing cap screws until their respective lock washers flatten out.

6. Check drive gear run-out.

7. Install side bearing adjusting nut lock and secure with cap screws and lock washers.

Checking Pinion Depth (Models with Tapered Roller Bearings Only)

NOTE: Refer to tooth contact chart in the General Axle Service section.

1. Coat drive gear with red lead. Turn pinion shaft several revolutions in both directions while applying considerable drag on drive gear.

2. Pinion depth is determined by shim pack selection. Shim packs are available in thicknesses of: 0.012, 0.015, 0.018, 0.021, and 0.024-inch.

3. Changing pinion depth will again require adjusting backlash. After pinion depth and backlash have been adjusted, torque bearing caps to specifications.

Thrust Block Installation

1. Install thrust block and lock nut to adjusting screw. Thread screw and block into carrier until block contacts drive gear. Rotate gear and note change of drag. Adjust these parts until point of greatest drag is reached. Back screw off about a 30 degree turn to provide 0.005 to 0.007-inch clearance between block and gear. Make certain screw does not turn at all when tightening lock nut to 135 foot-pounds torque.

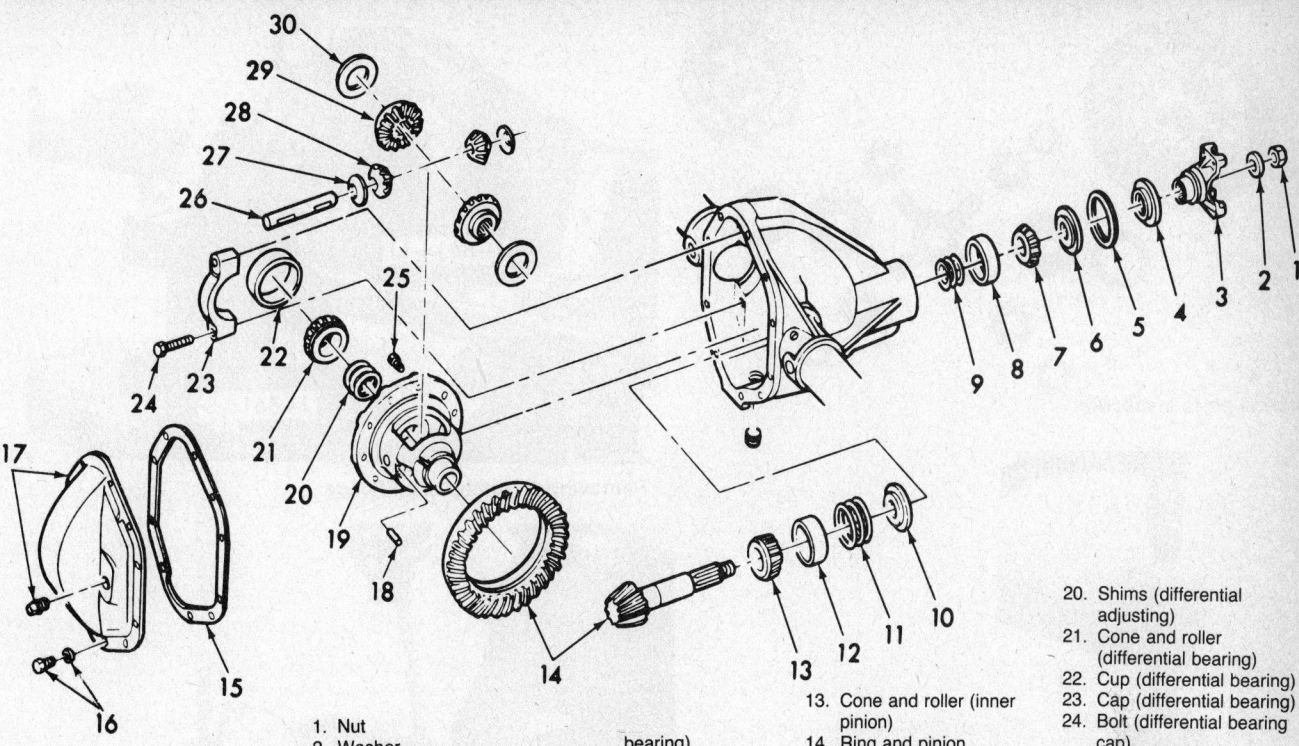

Dana 9¾ inch ring gear axle

1. Nut
2. Washer
3. Companion flange
4. Pinion oil seal
5. Gasket
6. Outer pinion oil slinger
7 and 8. Cone and roller (outer pinion bearing)
9. Shims (outer pinion bearing)
10. Inner pinion oil slinger
11. Shims (inner pinion bearing)
12. Cup (inner pinion bearing)
13. Cone and roller (inner pinion)
14. Ring and pinion
15. Gasket (housing cover)
16. Screw and washer (cover)
17. Cover and plug
18. Lock pin (pinion shaft)
19. Differential case
20. Shims (differential adjusting)
21. Cone and roller (differential bearing)
22. Cup (differential bearing)
23. Cap (differential bearing)
24. Bolt (differential bearing cap)
25. Bolt (ring gear)
26. Pinion shaft
27. Thrust washer (pinion)
28. Pinion
29. Side gear
30. Thrust washer (side gear)

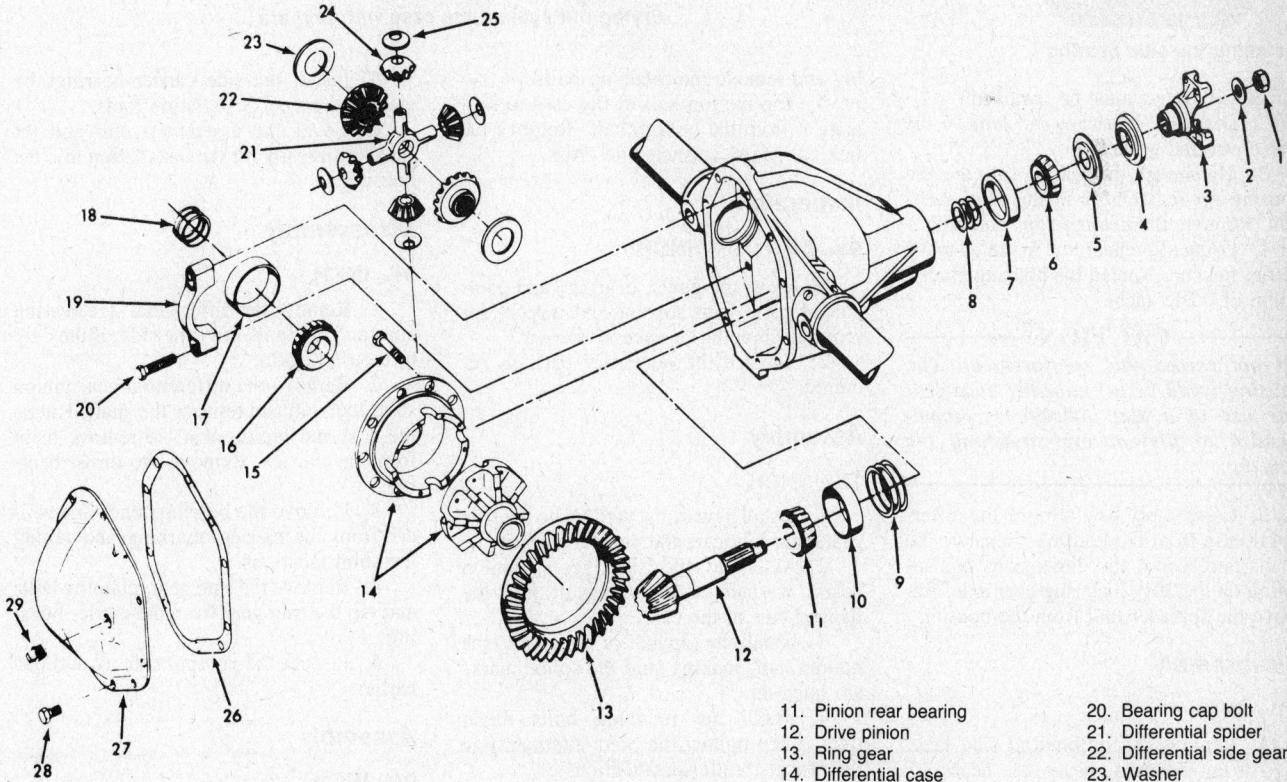

Dana 10½ inch ring gear axle

1. Pinion nut
2. Washer
3. Companion flange
4. Oil seal
5. Oil slinger
6. Pinion front bearing
7. Front bearing cup
8. Preload shim pack
9. Pinion depth shim pack
10. Rear bearing cup
11. Pinion rear bearing
12. Drive pinion
13. Ring gear
14. Differential case
15. Ring gear bolt
16. Differential side bearing
17. Side bearing cup
18. Side bearing adjusting shims
19. Bearing cap
20. Bearing cap bolt
21. Differential spider
22. Differential side gear
23. Washer
24. Pinion gear
25. Washer
26. Gasket
27. Cover
28. Cover screw
29. Drain plug

Internal parts inspection

Removing the companion flange

Installing the side bearing

Prying out against the case with prybars

wheel assemblies must be removed.

2. Drain the lubricant and remove the rear cover and gasket.

3. Matchmark the bearing caps and the housing for reassembly in the same position. Remove the bearing caps and bolts.

4. Using a spreader tool mounted to the carrier housing, spread the housing a maximum of 0.015 inch.

——— CAUTION ———
Do not exceed this measurement. The housing could be permanently damaged. The use of a dial indicator is recommended to prevent over-stretching the housing.

5. Using a pry bar, remove the differential case from the housing. Separate the shims and record the dimensions and location on the 10½ inch ring gear axle. Remove the spreader tool from the housing.

Disassembly

10½ INCH

1. Remove the differential side bearings from the case, using the necessary puller tools.

2. Remove the ring gear bolts and tap the ring gear from the case with a soft-faced hammer.

3. Scribe the case halves for reassem-

bly and remove the retaining bolts.

4. Tap the top half of the case to separate it from the bottom half. Remove the internal gears, washers and cross.

Inspection

9¾ AND 10½ INCH

1. Clean the gears, bearings and component parts with solvent and inspect for scoring, chipping or excessive wear.

2. Replace the necessary parts as required.

Assembly

10½ INCH

1. Install new thrust washers to the side gears and lubricate the contact surfaces.

2. Assemble the side gears, pinion bears, washers and cross shaft into the flanged half of the case.

3. Install the top half of the case to the bottom half, making sure the scribe marks are lined up.

4. Install the retaining bolts finger tight. Then tighten the bolts alternately to the proper torque specifications.

5. If a new ring gear is to be installed or the old one used, install it to the differential case and align the bolt holes. Tighten the bolts aternately to the proper torque specifications.

6. Install the side carrier bearings by using the proper installation tools.

7. Cover the assembled unit and set aside until ready for the installation into the housing.

Disassembly

9¾ INCH

1. Remove the differential side bearing cups and tag to identify the side, if they are to be used again.

2. Remove the differential gear pinion shaft lock pin and remove the shaft. Rotate the side and pinion gears to remove them from the carrier. Remove the thrust bearings.

3. Remove the bearing cones and rollers from the carrier, marking and noting the shim locations.

4. Remove the ring gear retaining bolts and tap the ring gear from the carrier housing.

5. Inspect the components as outlined earlier.

Assembly

9¾ INCH

1. Install the differential side gears, the differential pinion gears and new thrust washers into the differential carrier.

2. Align the pinion gear shaft holes and

install the pinion shaft into the carrier. Align the lock pin hole in the shaft and carrier. Install the lock pin and peen the hole to avoid having the pin drop from the carrier.

3. Install the differential case side bearings with the proper installation tools. Do not install the shims at this time.

4. Place the carrier assembly into the axle housing with the bearing cups on the bearing cones. Install the bearing caps in their original position and tighten the bearing cap bolts enough to keep the bearing caps in place.

5. Install a dial indicator on the housing so that the indicator button contacts the carrier flange. Press the differential carrier to prevent side play and center the dial indicator. Rotate the carrier and check the flange for run-out. If the run-out is greater than 0.002 inch, the defect is probably due to the bearings or to the carrier and should be corrected.

6. Remove the assembly and install the ring gear. Torque the retaining bolts to specifications and reinstall the assembly into the housing and again install the bearing caps in their original position and tighten the cap bolts enough to keep the bearings caps in place.

7. Again, install the dial indicator and position the indicator button to contact the ring gear back surface. Rotate the assembly and the run-out should be less than 0.002 inch. If over 0.002 inch, remove the assembly and relocate the ring gear 180 degrees. Reinstall the assembly and recheck. If the run-out remains over the 0.002 inch tolerance, the ring gear is defective. If the measurement is within tolerances, continue on with the assembly.

8. Position two pry bars between the bearing cap and the housing on the side opposite the ring gear. Pull on the pry bars and force the differential carrier as far as possible towards the dial indicator. Rock the assembly to seat the bearings and reset the dial indicator to "O".

9. Reposition the prybars to the opposite side of the carrier and force the carrier assembly as far towards the center of the housing. Read the dial indicator scale. This will be the total amount of shims required for setting the backlash during the reassembly, less the bearing preload. Record the measurement.

10. Remove the differential carrier from the housing and set aside.

SIDE BEARING SHIM SELECTION FOR THE 10½ INCH

1. With the pinion gear not in the axle housing, place the bearing cups over the side bearings and install the differential carrier into the axle housing.

2. Place the shim that was originally installed on the ring gear side back into its original position.

Pinion code location

Old Pinion Marking	New Pinion Marking								
	- 4	- 3	- 2	- 1	0	+ 1	+ 2	+ 3	+ 4
+ 4	+ 0.008	+ 0.007	+ 0.006	+ 0.005	+ 0.004	+ 0.003	+ 0.002	+ 0.001	0
+ 3	+ 0.007	+ 0.006	+ 0.005	+ 0.004	+ 0.003	+ 0.002	+ 0.001	0	- 0.001
+ 2	+ 0.006	+ 0.005	+ 0.004	+ 0.003	+ 0.002	+ 0.001	0	- 0.001	- 0.002
+ 1	+ 0.005	+ 0.004	+ 0.003	+ 0.002	+ 0.001	0	- 0.001	- 0.002	- 0.003
0	+ 0.004	+ 0.003	+ 0.002	+ 0.001	0	- 0.001	- 0.002	- 0.003	- 0.004
- 1	+ 0.003	+ 0.002	+ 0.001	0	- 0.001	- 0.002	- 0.003	- 0.004	- 0.005
- 2	+ 0.002	+ 0.001	0	- 0.001	- 0.002	- 0.003	- 0.004	- 0.005	- 0.006
- 3	+ 0.001	0	- 0.001	- 0.002	- 0.003	- 0.004	- 0.005	- 0.006	- 0.007
- 4	0	- 0.001	- 0.002	- 0.003	- 0.004	- 0.005	- 0.006	- 0.007	- 0.008

Pinion code chart

3. Install the bearing caps in their proper positions and tighten the bolts enough to keep the bearings in place.

4. Mount a dial indicator on the axle housing with the indicator button contacting the back of the ring gear.

5. Position two prybars between the bearing shim and the housing on the ring gear side of the differential carrier. Force the differential carrier away from the dial indicator and set the indicator to "0".

6. Reposition the prybars to the opposite side of the differential carrier and force the carrier back towards the dial indicator. Repeat several times until the same reading is obtained each time.

7. To the dial indicator reading, add the thickness of the shim and record the results to be used later in the assembly.

DRIVE PINION

Removal

10½ AND 10½ INCH

1. Remove the pinion nut and flange from the pinion gear, using the proper removing tools.

2. Remove the pinion gear assembly from the housing. It may be necessary to tap the pinion from the housing with a soft faced hammer. Catch the pinion so as not to allow it to drop on the floor.

3. With a long drift, remove the inner bearing cup, pinion seal, slinger, gasket, outer pinion bearing and the shim pack. Tag the shim pack for reassembly.

4. Remove the rear pinion bearing cup and shim pack from the housing. Tag the shims for reassembly.

5. Remove the rear pinion bearing from the pinion gear with an arbor press and special plates.

Inspection of the Components

1. Clean all components in a solvent and inspect the the bearings, cups and rollers for scoring, chipping or excessive wear. Inspect the flanges and splines for excessive wear. Inspect all gear surfaces for excessive wear or chipping.

2. Replace the necessary bearing assemblies, gears and thrustwashers as required.

PINION SHIM SELECTION

Ring gears and pinions are supplied in matched sets only. The matched numbers are etched on both gears for verification. On the rear face of the pinion, a + (plus) or a − (minus) number will be etched, indicating the best running position for each particular gear set. This dimension is controlled by the shimming behind the inner bearing cup. Whenever baffles or oil slingers are used, they become part of the adjusting shim pack. An example: If a pinion is etched + 3, this pinion would require 0.003 inch less shims than a pinion etched 0. This means by removing shims, the mounting distance of the pinion is increased by 0.003 inch, which is just what a + (plus) etching indicates. If a pinion is etched −3, it would be necessary to add 0.003 inch more shims than would be required if the pinion was etched 0. By adding the 0.003 inch shims, the mounting distance of the pinion is decreased 0.003 inch, which is just what the − (minus) etching indicates. Pinion adjusting shims are available in thicknesses of 0.003, 0.005 and 0.010 inch. An example: If a new gear set is used and the old pinion reads +2 and the new pinion reads −2, add 0.004 inch shims to the original shim pack.

Assembly

9¾ AND 10½ INCH

1. Select the correct pinion depth shims and install in the rear pinion bearing cup bore.

2. Install the rear bearing cup in the axle housing with the proper tool.

3. Add or subtract an equal amount of shim thickness to or from the preload or outer shim pack, as was added or subtracted from the inner shim pack.

4. Install the front pinion bearing cup into its bore in the axle housing.

5. Press the rear pinion bearing onto the pinion gear shaft and install the pinion gear with bearing into the axle housing.

6. Install the preload shims and the front pinion bearing. Do not install the oil seal at this time.

7. Install the flange with the holding bar tool attached, the washer and the nut on the pinion shaft end. Torque the nut to 250 ft. lbs. for the 10½ inch and 255 ft. lbs. for the 9¾ inch.

8. Remove the holding bar from the flange and with an inch pound torque wrench, measure the rotating torque of the pinion gear. The rotating torque should be 10 to 20 in. lbs. with the original bearings and 20 to 40 in. lbs. with new bearings. Disregard the torque reading necessary to start the shaft to turn.

9. If the preload torque is not in specifications, adjust the shim pack as required.

   a. To increase preload, decrease the thickness of the preload shim pack.

   b. To decrease preload, increase the thickness of the preload shim pack.

10. When the proper preload is obtained, remove the nut, washer and flange from the pinion shaft.

11. Install a new pinion seal into the housing and reinstall the flange, washer and nut. Using the holder tool, torque the nut to 250 ft. lbs. for the 10½ inch and 255 ft. lbs. for the 9¾ inch.

Assembly of Differential Carrier Into Axle Housing

9¾ INCH

1. As outlined in the Differential Carrier Assembly procedure, the amount of shims required for setting the backlash less bearing preload had been selected and the measurement recorded.

2. With the pinion gear installed and properly set, position the differential carrier assembly into the axle housing and install the bearing caps in their proper positions. Tighten the cap bolts just enough to hold the bearing cups in place.

3. Install a dial indicator on the axle housing with the indicator button contacting the back of the ring gear.

4. Position two prybars between the bearing cup and the axle housing on the ring gear side of the case and pry the ring gear into mesh with the pinion gear teeth, as far as possible. Rock the ring gear to allow the teeth to mesh and the bearings to seat. With the pressure still applied by the prybars, set the dial indicator to "0".

5. Reposition the prybars on the opposite side of ring gear and pry the gear as far as it will go. Take the dial indicator reading. Repeat this procedure until the same reading is obtained each time. This reading represents the necessary amount of shims between the differential carrier and the bearing on the ring gear side.

6. Remove the bearing from the differential carrier on the ring gear side and install the proper amount of shims. Reinstall the bearing.

7. Remove the differential carrier bearing from the opposite side of the ring gear. To determine the amount of shims needed, use the following method.

   a. Subtract the size of the shim pack just installed on the ring gear side of the carrier from the reading obtained and recorded when measurement was taken without the pinion gear in place during the Differential Carrier Assembly procedure. To this figure, add an additional 0.015 inch to compensate for preload and backlash. An example: If the first reading was 0.085 inch and the shims installed on the ring gear side of the carrier were 0.055 inch, the correct amount of shims whould be 0.085 − 0.055 + 0.015 = 0.045 inch.

8. Install the required shims as determined under step 7 and install the differential side bearing. The installation of the shims should give the proper preload to the bearings and the proper backlash to the ring and pinion gears.

10½ INCH

1. Install the differential carrier, with the side bearings and cups installed, in place in the axle housing.

2. Select the smallest of the original shims as a gauging shim and place it between the bearing cup and the housing on the ring gear side.

3. Install the bearing caps and tighten the bolts enough to hold the cups in place.

4. Mount a dial indicator on the ring gear side of the axle housing and position the indicator button on the rear side of the ring gear.

5. Position two prybars between the bearing cup and the housing on the side opposite the ring gear. With the prybars, force the differential carrier towards the dial indicator and set the indicator dial to "0".

6. Reposition the prybars on the ring gear side of the carrier and force the ring gear into mesh with the pinion gear while observing the dial indicator reading. Repeat this operation until the same reading is obtained each time.

7. Add this indicator reading to the gauging shim thickness to determine the correct shim dimension for installation on the ring gear side of the differential carrier.

8. An example: If the gauging shim was 0.115 inch and the indicator reading was 0.017 inch, the correct shim would be 0.115 + 0.017 = 0.172 inch.

9. Remove the gauging shim and install the correct shim into position between the bearing cup and the axle housing on the ring gear side of the housing.

10. To determine the correct dimension for the remaining shim, refer to the Side Bearing Shim Selection for the 10½ inch and obtain the recorded shim size. From that figure, subtract the size of the shim installed in step 9 and then add 0.006 inch for the bearing preload and backlash.

11. An example: If the reading of the shim just installed on the ring gear side of the carrier was 0.172 inch and the reading obtained during the checking of clearance without the pinion installed was 0.329, the correct shim dimension would be as follows: 0.329 − 0.172 = 0.157 + 0.006 = 0.163 inch.

Installation of Differential Carrier Into Axle Housing

9¾ INCH

1. Spread the axle housing with the spreader tool no more than 0.015 inch. Install the differential bearing outer cups in their correct locations and install the cups in their respective locations.

2. Install the bolts and tighten finger-tight. Rotate the differential carrier and ring gear and tap with a soft-faced hammer to insure proper seating of the assembly in the axle housing.

3. Remove the spreader tool and torque the cap bolts to specifications.

4. Install a dial indicator and check the ring gear backlash at four equally spaced points of the ring gear circle. The backlash must be within a range of 0.004 to 0.009 inch and must not vary more than 0.002 inch between the points checked.

5. If the backlash is not within specifications, the shim packs must be corrected to bring the backlash within limits.

6. Check the tooth contact pattern and verify.

7. Complete the assembly, fill to proper level with lubricant and operate to verify proper assembly.

10½ INCH

1. Spread the axle housing with a spreader tool, no more than 0.015 inch.

The carrier assembly is in place in the housing.

2. Assemble the shim, as determined previously, into place between the bearing cup and the housing. Remove the spreader tool.

3. Install the bearing caps in their marked positions and torque the bolts to specifications.

4. Install a dial indicator and check the ring gear backlash at four equally spaced points around the ring gear.

5. The backlash must be within 0.004 to 0.009 inch and must not vary more than 0.002 inch between the positions checked.

6. Whenever the backlash is not within the allowable limits, it must be corrected. Changing of the shim packs is required.

   a. Low backlash is corrected by decreasing the shim on the ring gear side and increasing the opposite side shim an equal amount.

   b. High backlash is corrected by increasing the shim on the ring gear side and decreasing the opposite side shim an equal amount.

7. Check the tooth contact pattern and correct as required.

8. Complete the assembly, fill to the correct level and operate to verify correct repairs.

Dana-Spicer Single Reduction Models 30, 44, 44-1, 60-1,2, 70

DIFFERENTIAL

Removal

1. Drain lubricant.
2. Remove cover and gasket.

NOTE: Attached to a cover bolt is a metal tag which shows the number of teeth on pinion and ring (drive) gear.

3. Remove bearing cap screws. Note the matching marks on cap and carrier and make sure caps are reassembled to correct markings.

4. Using a spreader tool, spread carrier a maximum of 0.020 inch and measure amount of spread with a dial indicator.

------ CAUTION ------

Carrier may be permanently damaged if spread more than 0.020 inch. Do not attempt differential removal without using a spreader.

5. Carefully lift differential assembly out of carrier.

6. Remove the spreader assembly after removing the differential assembly from the housing.

DRIVE PINION

Disassembly

1. Pull flange (yoke) from shaft splines

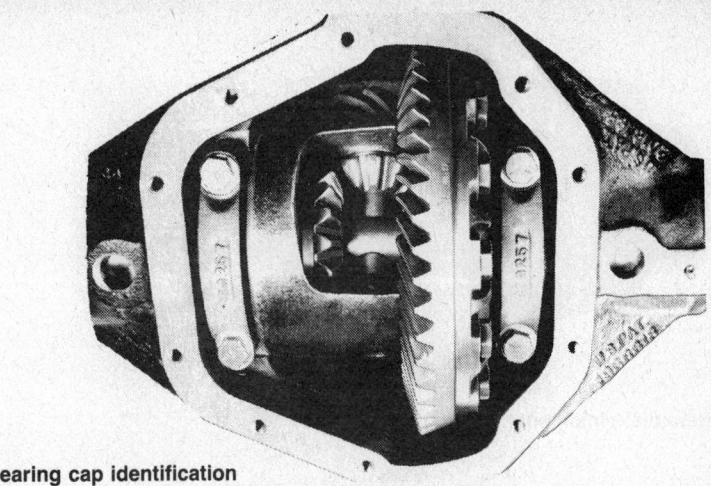

Bearing cap identification

Spreading rear axle housing

Measuring differential case drive gear mounting flange runout

of drive pinion.

2. Using a press or soft hammer, drive pinion and inner bearing cone assembly out of carrier.

3. Remove and tag shim pack from splined end of pinion.

NOTE: If either ring (drive) gear or pinion are to be replaced, write down markings (+), (−), or (0) located at face end of pinion for reassembly reference.

4. Remove oil seal assembly from carrier bore. This frees oil seal gasket, oil slinger, and bearing cone.

5. If replacement of the pinion tapered bearings is necessary, the bearing cups should be removed from carrier as follows:

   a. Use remover with a driver or slide hammer to remove inner bearing cup from carrier. This frees shim pack. Remove and tag shims for reassembly.

DRIVE AXLES
DANA-SPICER

Removing differential pinion shaft lock pin

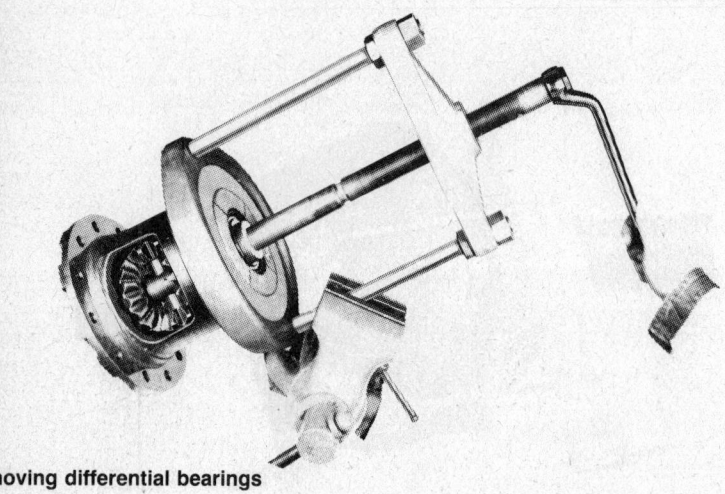

Removing differential bearings

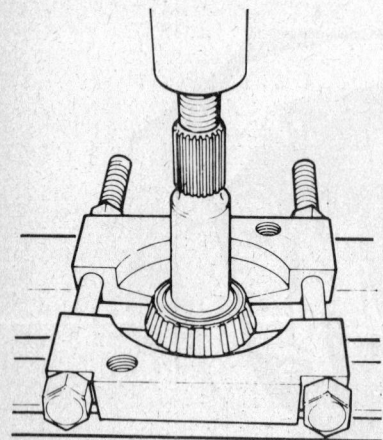

Pinion rear bearing removal

   b. Remove outer bearing cup.

6. Use remover set to separate bearing cone from drive pinion.

7. Separate oil slinger from pinion.

NOTE: This oil slinger is only found on some axle models.

DIFFERENTIAL
Disassembly

1. Remove and label the two bearing cups.

2. Use a suitable type puller to remove the bearing cones. Remove and label adjusting shims.

3. Drive out pinion shaft lock pin.

NOTE: On the Spicer Model 70 rear axle, punch-mark the differential case halves (for reassembly reference) and separate. Remove the differential spider, pinion gears, side gears and thrust washers.

4. Separate ring gear from case.

5. Remove pinion shaft, two pinions, two side gears, and four thrust washers from case.

Assembly

1. Place side gears with new thrust washers in position inside case.

2. Place pinions and thrust washers in position in case.

3. Install the differential pinion shaft in position in case between two pinions. Align shaft lock pin hole with lock pin hole in case and install pinion shaft lock pin. Peen hole to prevent pin from falling out.

NOTE: On the Spicer Model 70 rear axle, install the differential spider along with its pinion gears, side gears and thrust washers into the differential case

halves. Bolt the two halves together making sure the punch-marks line up.

4. Place ring (drive) gear in proper position against flange of case and bolt ring gear to case. Alternately tighten these bolts until all bolts are tightened to proper torque.

NOTE: Do not install differential cones or shim packs until pinion depth and bearing preload have been checked out. Differential bearing adjustment is a part of axle assembly procedure.

DIFFERENTIAL BEARING
Adjustment

1. Press fit bearing cones tightly against shoulders on case.

NOTE: Do not install shims at this time.

2. Install bearing cups.

3. Install spreader tool and dial indicator, and spread carrier as described in Differential Removal.

4. Place differential assembly into carrier.

5. Install bearing caps using their respective cap screws. Make sure caps are assembled to their correct markings. Hand tighten bearing cap screws.

6. Install dial indicator at carrier with indicator button contacting back of ring (drive) gear. Rotate ring gear and check run-out.

7. If run-out exceeds 0.002-inch, remove the differential assembly and remove the ring gear from the case.

8. Reinstall differential assembly without ring gear and check run-out of differential case flange. If run-out still exceeds 0.002-inch, the defect is probably due to bearings or case, and should be corrected before proceeding.

9. Remove differential from carrier.

NOTE: Do not install shims behind the bearings until final installation.

DRIVE PINION
Installation

1. If either drive pinion or ring (drive) gear must be replaced, they must be installed as a set. (These parts are matched and lapped at time of manufacture to obtain the correct gear tooth contact.)

2. Whenever it is necessary to install a new drive pinion, the plus (+) or minus (−) marking on face of rear end of pinion must be considered. Select a new pinion and ring gear set with markings as near as possible to those on old pinion. If marking on both old and new pinion is the same, do not change thickness of shim pack.

3. The approximate difference between markings on old and new drive pinion is the adjustment that will have to be made in the shim packs.

4. Once proper adjustment in shim packs has been made, place oil slinger, if

PINION SETTING CHARTS (U.S. AND METRIC)
By utilizing these specifications, proper gear contact should be established.

Old Pinion Marking	New Pinion Marking (U.S. Standards)								
	−4	−3	−2	−1	0	+1	+2	+3	+4
+4	+0.008	+0.007	+0.006	+0.005	+0.004	+0.003	+0.002	+0.001	0
+3	+0.007	+0.006	+0.005	+0.004	+0.003	+0.002	+0.001	0	−0.001
+2	+0.006	+0.005	+0.004	+0.003	+0.002	+0.001	0	−0.001	−0.002
+1	+0.005	+0.004	+0.003	+0.002	+0.001	0	−0.001	−0.002	−0.002
0	+0.004	+0.003	+0.002	+0.001	0	−0.001	−0.002	−0.003	−0.004
−1	+0.003	+0.002	+0.001	0	−0.001	−0.002	−0.003	−0.004	−0.005
−2	+0.002	+0.001	0	−0.001	−0.003	−0.003	−0.004	−0.005	−0.005
−3	+0.001	0	−0.001	−0.002	−0.003	−0.004	−0.005	−0.006	−0.007
−4	0	−0.001	−0.002	−0.003	−0.004	−0.005	−0.006	−0.007	−0.008

Old Pinion Marking	New Pinion Marking (Metric)								
	−10	−8	−5	−3	0	+3	+5	+8	+10
+10	+.20	+.18	+.15	+.13	+.10	+.08	+.05	+.03	0
+8	+.18	+.15	+.13	+.10	+.08	+.05	+.03	0	−.03
+5	+.15	+.13	+.10	+.08	+.05	+.03	0	−.03	−.05
+3	+.13	+.10	+.08	+.05	+.03	0	−.03	−.05	−.08
0	+.10	+.08	+.05	+.03	0	−.03	−.05	−.08	−.10
−3	+.08	+.05	+.03	0	−.03	−.05	−.08	−.10	−.13
−5	+.05	+.03	0	−.03	−.05	−.08	−.10	−.13	−.15
−8	+.03	0	−.03	−.05	−.08	−.10	−.13	−.15	−.18
−10	0	−.03	−.05	−.08	−.10	−.13	−.15	−.18	−.20

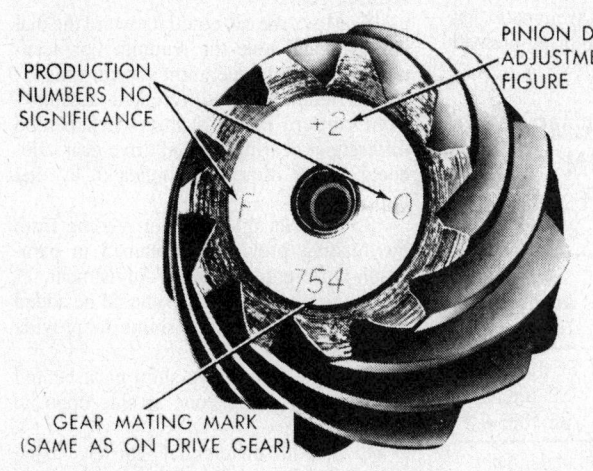

Drive pinion markings

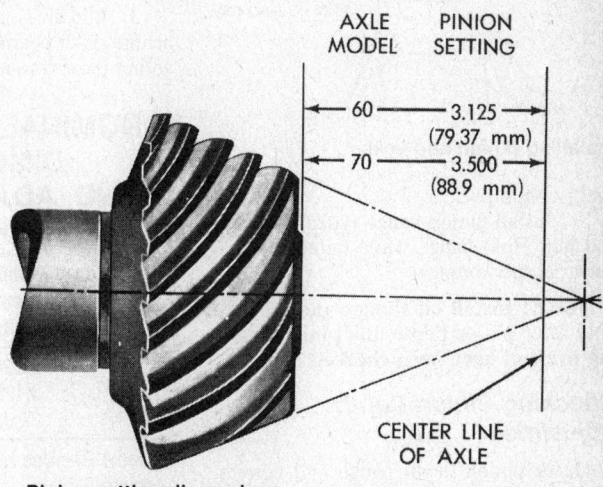

Pinion setting dimensions

so equipped, over pinion shaft. Install pinion inner bearing cone over shaft, and use bearing installer and an arbor press to press bearing onto pinion shaft. Bearing must be seated tightly against shoulder or oil slinger.

5. Use pinion front bearing cup installer to install outer bearing cup into carrier bore.

6. Install the selected inner shim pack in carrier. Then use pinion rear bearing cup installer to install inner bearing cup.

7. Insert pinion, oil slinger (when used) and inner bearing cone assembly into carrier and place the selected shim pack into position on outer end of pinion shaft.

8. Place outer bearing cone over pinion shaft, then use installer to seat bearing tight

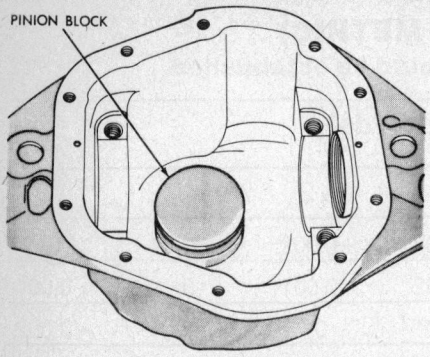

Master pinion block installed in the pinion bore

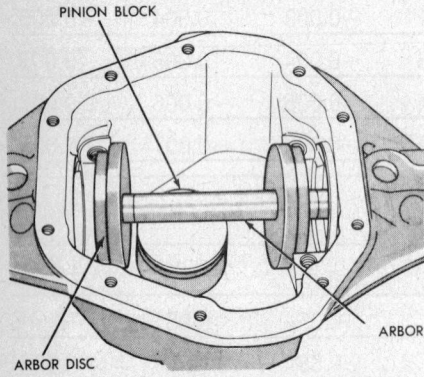

Arbor discs and arbor in position

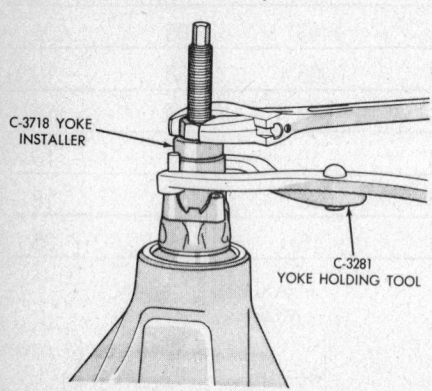

Installing pinion and yoke

against shim pack.

9. Install pinion flange (yoke), washer and nut. Hold flange while tightening the nut to proper torque.

NOTE: Install oil slinger and oil seal only after pinion depth and pinion bearing preload have been checked out.

Checking Pinion Depth Adjustment

1. A pinion depth gauge and correct adapter, which gives a micrometer reading, should be used to determine pinion depth. The actual pinion depth setting can be determined by adding gauge reading to thickness of step plate and comparing result with the nominal dimension of 2.625-inch (models 44/60) or 3.125-inch (model 60), or 3.500 inch (model 70).

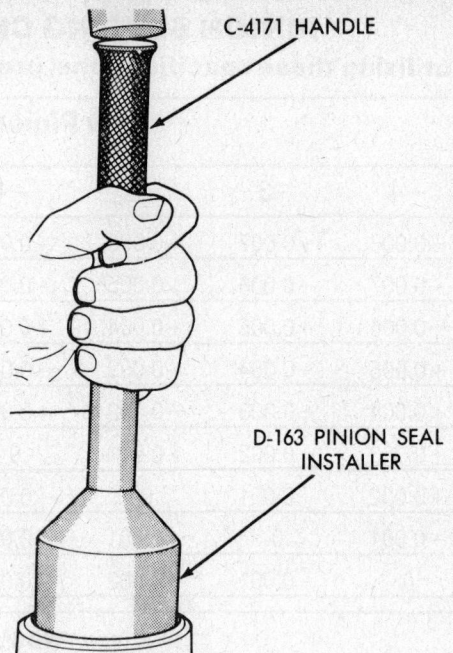

Installing pinion seal

2. If the pinion setting is within minus (−) 0.001-inch to plus (+) 0.003-inch of this nominal dimension, the pinion position can be considered satisfactory.

3. If pinion setting exceeds these limits, it must be corrected by adjusting thickness of shim pack behind the pinion inner bearing cup.

Pinion Bearing Preload Adjustment

1. Use a torque wrench to check pinion bearing preload.
2. Rotating torque of pinion should be from 15 to 30 in. lbs.
3. Add or remove shims from pack just behind outer bearing cone to bring preload within these torque limits.

NOMINAL ASSEMBLY DIMENSION AND ADAPTOR DISC CHART

Axle Model	Nominal Assembly Dimension	Adapter Disc Tool Number
44	2.625″	SE-1065-9-SS
60	3.125″	SE-1065-9-Y
70①	3.500″	SE-1065-9-Y

① Model 70—Use a 0.375 shim under dial pointer

DIFFERENTIAL

Installation

1. Use dial indicator and spreader tool as described in Differential Removal, to spread carrier a maximum of 0.020-inch.

2. Install bearing cups and place differential assembly in carrier. Rotate differential and, with a soft hammer, tap ring (drive) gear to assure a proper bearing seating.

3. Reinstall bearing caps in their proper locations as indicated by marks made during the removal procedure. Finger tighten cap screws. Relieve the spreader tool pressure, and tighten cap screws to 70–90 ft. lbs.

4. Move differential assembly tightly against drive pinion.

5. Install dial indicator securely to carrier, then set button at zero and against back of drive gear.

6. Move the differential toward the dial indicator and note the reading. For accuracy, repeat this operation several times.

7. Remove the differential assembly from carrier. Install a shim pack behind differential bearing cone at drive gear side, equal to the dimension indicated by dial indicator.

8. Subtract the indicator reading from the reading previously obtained in paragraph Differential Bearing Adjustment.

9. To the above result should be added 0.015 to 0.020-inch in shims to provide bearing preload.

10. Install the above shim pack behind differential bearing cone at side opposite to drive gear.

11. Spread differential carrier, using spreader tool.

12. Install differential bearing cups then locate differential assembly in carrier.

13. Rotate differential assembly, tapping gear to seat bearings.

14. Install differential bearing caps in their correct location as indicated by marks made upon disassembly. Finger tighten cap screws.

15. Remove differential carrier spreader tool. Tighten differential bearing cap screws to proper torque.

16. Install dial indicator and check drive gear to drive pinion backlash at four equally spaced points around the drive gear. Backlash must be held to 0.003 to 0.006-inch and must not vary more than 0.002-inch between positions checked.

17. Whenever backlash is not within limits, differential bearing shim pack should be corrected.

Dodge/Plymouth 8⅜ and 9¼ in. Integral Carrier Axle

See the Dodge/Plymouth truck section for external identification and axle shaft service.

DIFFERENTIAL

Removal

1. Raise the rear of the vehicle and support safely.

2. Remove the wheels, drums and the housing cover screws. Drain the lubricant from the axle housing by removing the cover.

3. Turn the differential carrier case to make the differential pinion shaft lock screw accessible and remove it from the case. Slide the pinion shaft from the case.

4. Push both axle shafts towards the center of the axle assembly and remove the C-washer clips from the recessed grooves of the axle shafts. Withdraw the axle shafts carefully to avoid damaging the axle shaft bearings in the axle tubes.

5. Clean the inside of the differential case with solvent and blow dry with compressed air.

6. Check for differential side-play by inserting a prybar between the left side of the axle housing and the differential case flange. Using a prying motion, determine whether side-play exists. There should be no side-play.

7. Paint the ring gear teeth and make a gear tooth contact pattern. Determine if proper depth of mesh can be obtained.

8. If side-play was found in step six, proceed to step nine. If no side-play was found in step six, check the drive gear run-out. Mount a dial indicator and index the indicator stem at right angles in the rear face of the ring gear. Rotate the ring gear and mark the ring gear and case at the point of greatest run-out. Total indicator reading should not exceed 0.005 in. If it does, the possibility exists that the case must be replaced.

9. Measure and record the pinion bearing preload. Use an in. lb. torque wrench to measure the preload.

10. Remove the pinion nut, washer and pinion flange.

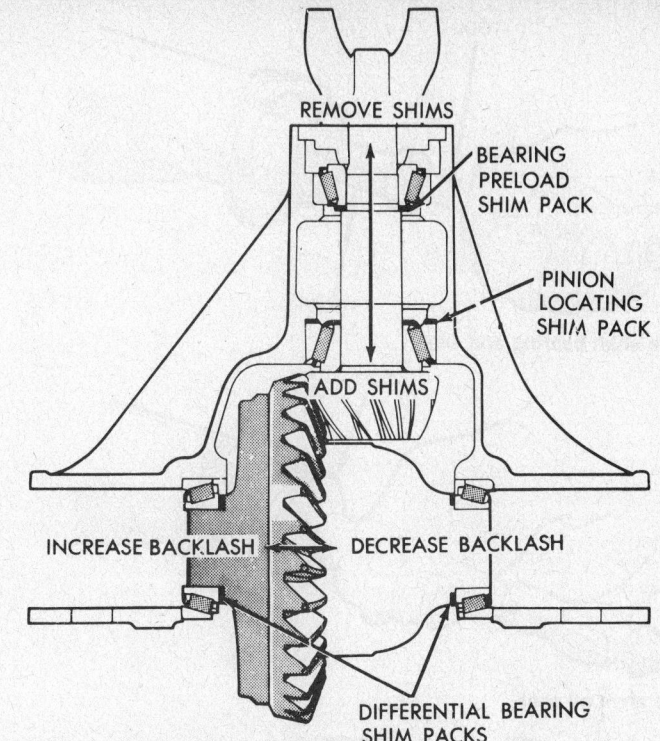

Using shims to adjust gear tooth contact

Removing differential pinion shaft lock pin

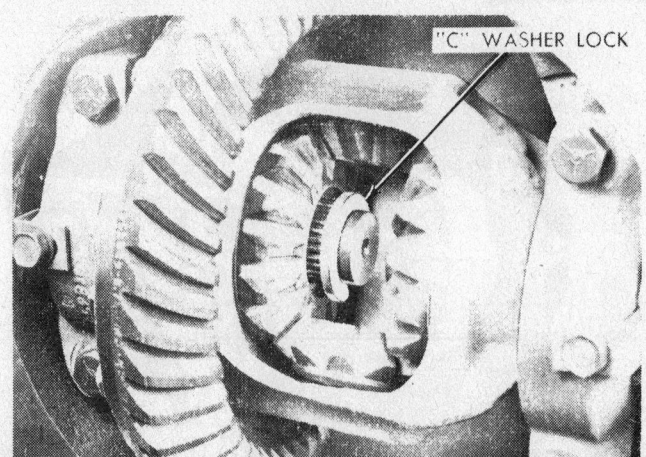

Removing axle shaft C-locks

1241

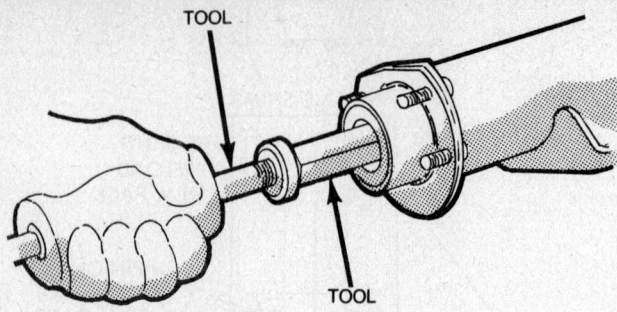

Removing axle shaft bearing and seal

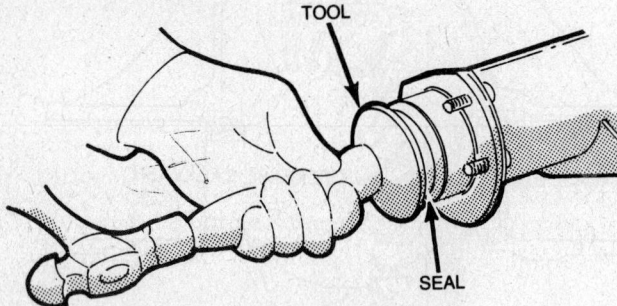

Installing axle shaft oil seal

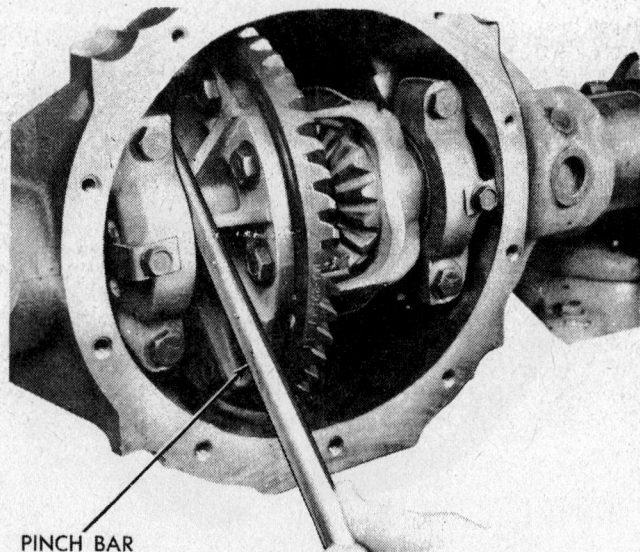

Checking differential side play

Measuring drive gear runout

11. Remove and discard the pinion oil seal.

12. Match-mark the axle housing and the differential bearing caps.

13. Remove the threaded adjusters and the differential bearing caps. There is a special wrench to do this through the axle tube.

14. Remove the differential case from the housing. The differential bearing cups and threaded adjuster must be kept together so they can be installed in their original position.

Disassembly

1. To remove the drive pinion or front bearing cone, drive the pinion rearward out of the bearing. This will result in damage to the bearing and cup. The bearing cone and cup must be replaced with new parts. Discard the collapsible spacer.

2. Drive the front and rear bearing cups from the housing with a brass drift. Remove the shim from behind the rear bearing cup and record the thickness.

3. Remove the rear bearing cone from the pinion stem with a puller.

4. Clamp the differential case and ring gear in a vise with soft jaws.

5. Remove the ring gear bolts (left-hand thread). Tap the ring gear loose with a soft-faced mallet.

6. If the ring gear run-out exceeded 0.005 in., recheck the case as follows. Install the differential case, cups, caps, and adjusters in the housing. Turn the adjusters to eliminate all side-play and tighten the differential cap bolts snugly. Measure the run-out at the ring gear flange face. Total indicator reading should not exceed 0.003 in. It is often possible to reduce run-out by removing the ring gear and remounting 180° from its original position. Remove the differential case from the housing.

7. Remove the pinion shaft lock-screw and remove the pinion shaft.

8. Rotate the differential side gears until the differential pinion shafts can be removed through the opening in the case.

9. Remove the differential side gears and thrust washers.

10. Using a puller or a press and press plates, remove the differential side bearings.

Assembly

1. Lubricate all parts, before assembly, with rear axle lubricant.

2. Install the thrust washers on the differential side gears and install the side gears into the case.

3. Place thrust washers on both differential pinions and, working through the opening in the case, mesh the pinion gears with the side gears. The pinions should be exactly 180° apart.

4. Rotate the side gears 90° to align the pinions and thrust washers with the pinion shaft holes.

5. From the pinion shaft lockpin hole side of the case, insert the slotted end of

the pinion shaft through the case, conical thrust washer and just through one of the pinion gears.

6. Install a thrust block through the side gear hub, so that the slot is centered between the side gears.

7. Hold all these parts in alignment, and align the lockpin holes in the pinion shaft and case. Install the lockpin from the pinion shaft side of the ring gear flange, temporarily.

8. With a stone, relieve the edge of the chamfer on the inside diameter of the ring gear.

9. Heat the ring gear (fluid bath or heat lamp) to a temperature not exceeding 300°F.

NOTE: Do not heat ring gear with a torch.

10. Align the ring gear with the case. Insert the ring gear screws through the case flange and into the ring gear.

11. Alternately tighten each cap screw to 70 ft. lbs.

12. Position each differential bearing cone on the hub of the differential case (taper away from ring gear) and install the bearing cones. An arbor press may be helpful.

Pinion Depth of Mesh

1. The proper pinion setting (relative to the ring gear) is determined by a shim which has been selected before the pinion is to be installed in the carrier. Pinion bearing shims are available in 0.001 in. increments.

2. The head of the pinion is marked with a "plus" (+) or a "minus" (−) mark that is followed by a number ranging from zero to four. If the old and new pinions have the same marking and the old bearing is being installed, use a shim of the original thickness. If the old pinion is marked zero (0), however, and the new pinion is marked plus two (+2), try a shim that is 0.002 in. thinner. If the new pinion is marked axle housing cup bore and install minus two (−2), try a shim that is 0.002 in. thicker.

3. Position the selected shim in the bore of the rear bearing cup. Install the cup.

NOTE: Special pinion depth measuring tools are available for both the 8⅜ and 9¼ inch axles. When using the special tools, follow the manufacturer's recommended procedures. Without the special tools, complete the following procedure and check the pinion depth by examining the pinion to ring gear tooth contact pattern. Correct as required by adding or subtracting shims controlling the pinion depth.

4. Place the rear pinion bearing cone on the pinion stem (small side away from pinion head).

5. Lubricate the front and rear bearing cones and install the rear pinion bearing cone onto the pinion stem with an arbor press.

Putting identification marks on bearing caps and housing

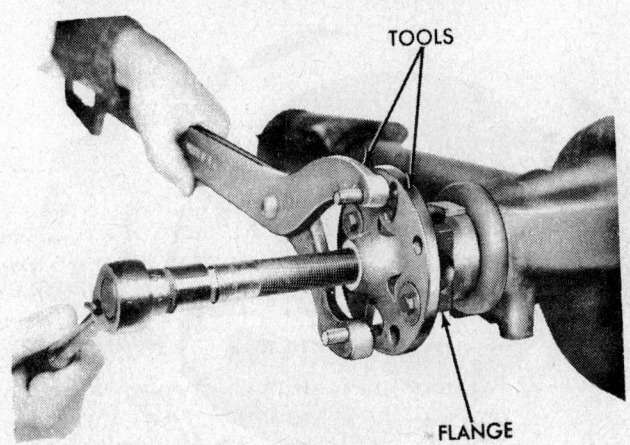

Loosening or tightening hex adjuster

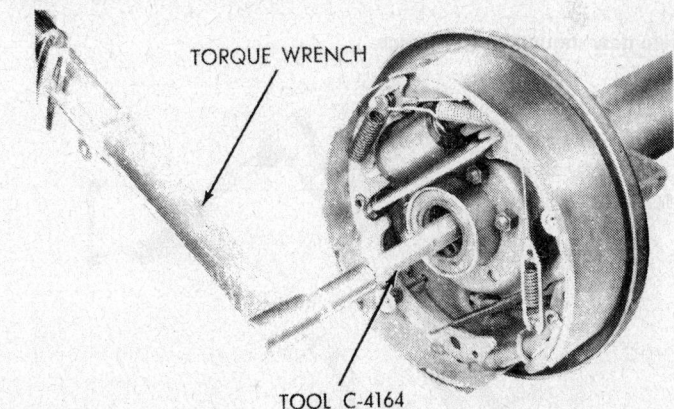

Removing drive pinion companion flange

6. Insert the pinion bearing and collapsible spacer assembly through the carrier and install the front bearing cone. Install the companion flange.

NOTE: During installation of the pinion bearing do not collapse the spacer.

7. Install the drive pinion oil seal into the carrier. Be sure to properly seat the seal.

8. Support the pinion in the carrier.

9. Install the Belleville washer (convex side up) and pinion nut.

10. Hold the companion flange and tighten the pinion nut to remove all endplay, while rotating the pinion to ensure proper bearing seating. Remove the tools and rotate the pinion several revolutions.

11. Torque the pinion nut to 210 ft. lbs. With an in. lbs. torque wrench, measure the pinion bearing preload, which would be 20–35 in. lbs. for new bearings or 10 in. lbs. over the original figure if the old

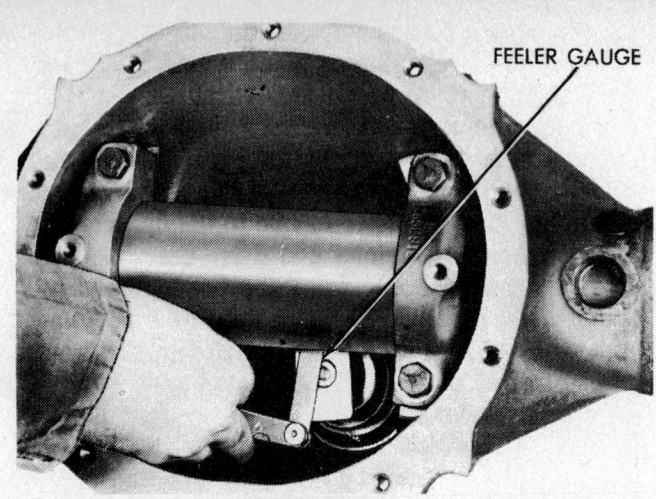

Determining drive pinion depth mesh shim pack thickness

Checking drive gear mounting flange face

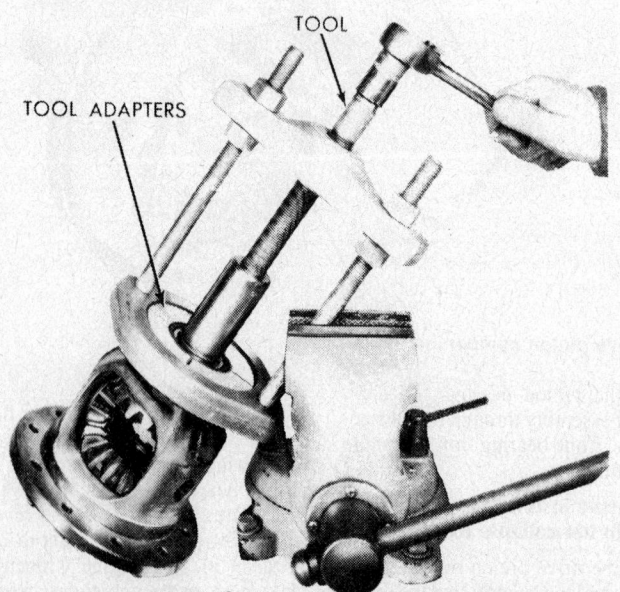

Removing differential bearing cone

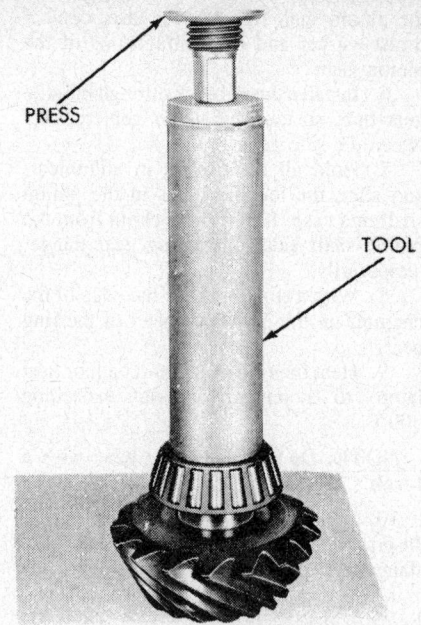

Installing drive pinion rear bearing cone

pinion bearing is used.

NOTE: The correct preload reading can only be obtained with the carrier nose upright. The final assembly is incorrect if the final pinion nut torque is below 210 ft. lbs. or if the pinion bearing preload is not within specifications. Under no circumstances should the pinion nut be backed off to reduce the pinion bearing preload; if this is done, a new collapsible spacer will have to be installed and the unit adjusted again until proper preload is obtained.

DIFFERENTIAL BEARING PRELOAD AND RING GEAR-TO-PINION BACKLASH

The threaded adjuster uses a hex drive hole, and requires special tool C-4164 to adjust the side bearing preload through the axle tube. An adjuster lock with two pointed teeth which engage in the exposed adjuster thread when the lock is tightened is provided. The shims will range from 0.020–0.038 in. and will be equipped with internal centering tabs. The shims, marked with a number which represents its thickness in thousandths of an inch, can be installed with either side against the pinion head.

1. Index the gears so that the same gear teeth are in contact throughout the adjustment.

2. The differential bearing cups will not always move with the adjusters. It is important to seat the bearings by rotating them 5–10 times in each direction, each time the adjusters are moved.

3. With the pinion bearings installed and the preload set, install the differential

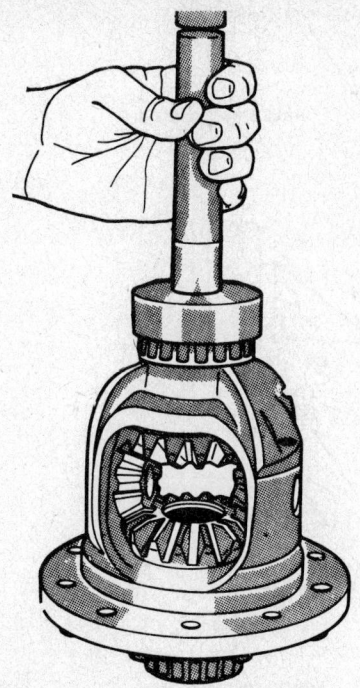

Installing differential bearing cone

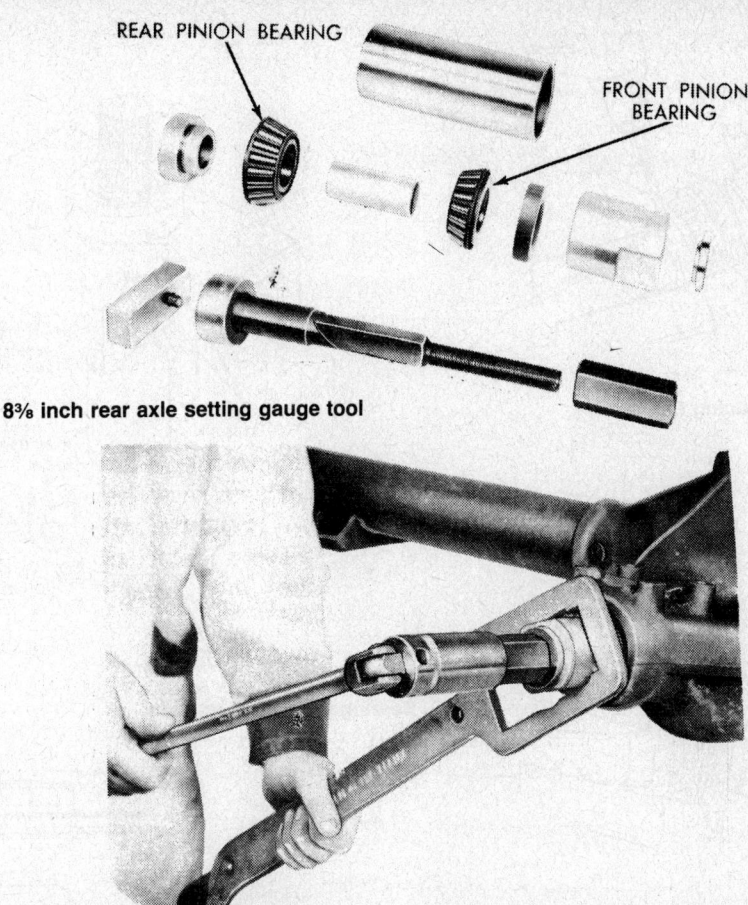

8⅜ inch rear axle setting gauge tool

with adjusters, caps and bearings. Lubricate the bearings and adjuster threads. Check to be sure that there are no crossed threads. Tighten the top cap screws on the right and left to 10 ft. lbs. Tighten the bottom cap screws fingertight until the head is just seated on the bearing cap.

4. Using the tool, check to be sure that the adjuster rotates freely. Turn both adjusters in until bearing play is eliminated with some drive gear backlash (0.010 in.). Seat the bearing rollers.

5. Install and register a dial indicator against the drive side of a gear tooth. Check the backlash at four positions to find the point of minimum backlash. Rotate the gear to the position of least backlash and mark the tooth so that all readings will be taken at the same point.

6. Loosen the right adjuster and turn the right adjuster until the backlash is 0.003–0.004 in. with each adjuster tightened to 10 ft. lbs. Seat the bearings rollers.

7. Tighten the differential bearing cap screws to 100 ft. lbs.

8. Tighten the right adjuster to 70 ft. lbs. and seat the rollers, until the torque remains constant at 70 ft. lbs. Measure the backlash. If the backlash is not 0.006–0.008 in. increase the torque on the right adjusters and seat the rollers until the correct backlash is obtained. Tighten the left adjuster to 70 ft. lbs. and seat the bearings until the torque remains constant.

9. If the assembly is properly done, the initial reading on the left adjuster will be approximately 70 ft. lbs. If it is substantially less, the entire procedure should be repeated.

10. After adjustments are complete, install the adjuster locks. Be sure the teeth are engaged in the adjuster threads. Torque

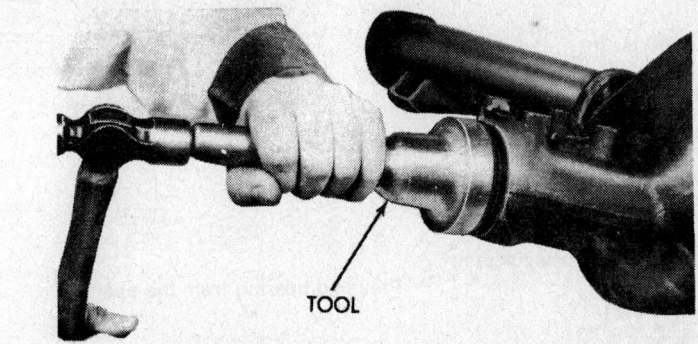

Seating bearing caps in axle housing

Installing drive pinion oil seal

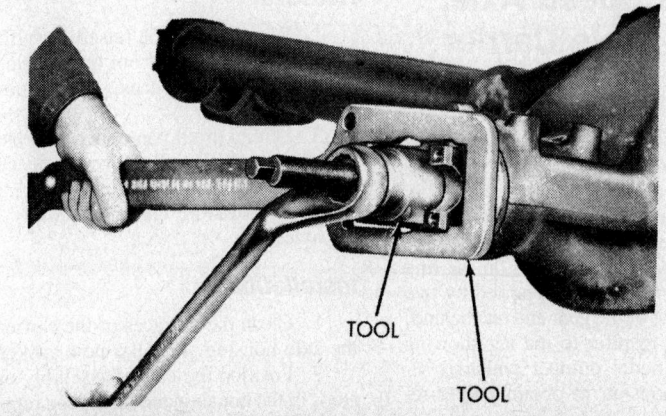

Installing drive pinion companion flange

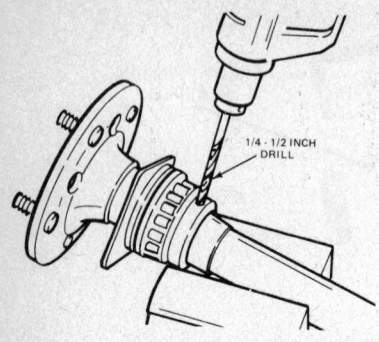

Drilling retaining ring

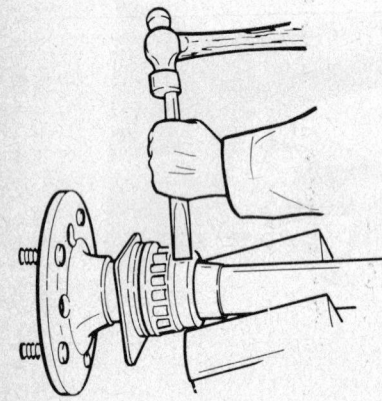

Removing rear wheel bearing retaining ring

the lockscrews to 90 in. lbs.

Final Assembly

1. Install the axle shafts, C-clips, reinstall the pinion shaft and lock screw and tighten securely.

2. Install the cover on the differential housing, using a new gasket.

3. Refill the rear axle housing with lubricant.

Ford Semi-Floating Single Speed Axle, Removable Carrier Type

This is a conventional type axle used on light duty Ford trucks. The axle design uses a removable carrier with the assembly bolted to the axle housing. The axle uses hypoid type gears and has the pinion gear mounted below the center line on the ring gear. The pinion gear is supported by two bearings in front of the gear and one behind. It is important to refer to the tag showing the axle and model number which is secured to the housing to obtain proper replacement parts.

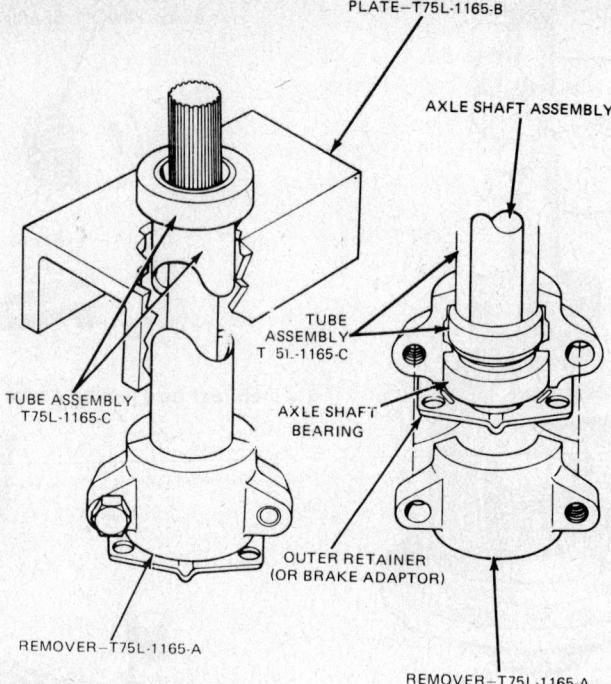

Bearing remover installed

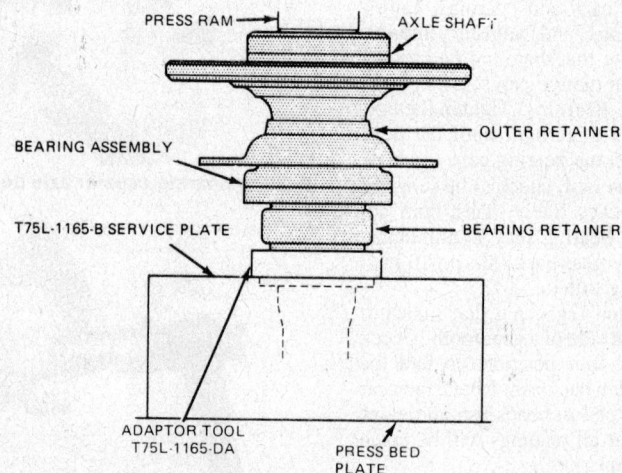

Pressing bearing from the shaft

CARRIER ASSEMBLY

Removal

1. With the vehicle raised on a lift, remove the axle shafts from the housing.

2. Remove the drive shaft from the carrier assembly.

3. With a drain pan under the axle, remove the retaining bolts from the carrier and drain the gear lube.

4. Remove the carrier assembly from the axle.

Installation

1. Clean the surfaces of the carrier and the axle housing. Install a new gasket.

2. Position the carrier assembly on the studs in the housing and install the retaining nuts. Torque the nuts to 30–40 ft. lbs.

3. Install the drive shaft and torque the bolts to 13–17 ft. lbs.

4. Install the axles in the housing and secure.

5. Fill the axle housing to the proper level with gear lube and road test for proper operation.

DIFFERENTIAL CASE

Removal and Disassembly

1. Remove the carrier assembly from the axle housing and mount the carrier in a holding fixture.

2. Mark the bearing caps and adjusting nuts so they may be installed in their original positions when assembling.

3. Remove the adjusting nut locks, bearing caps and adjusting nuts.

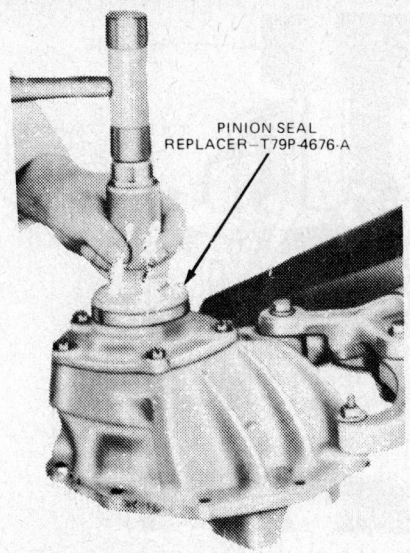

Installing the pinion seal

4. Lift the differential assembly out of the carrier. Using a bearing puller, remove the side bearings from the differential case.

5. Mark the side of the case, the ring gear and the cover so they can be installed in their original positions.

6. Remove the bolts that retain the ring gear to the case and using a soft hammer, tap the ring gear from the case.

7. Using a drift, drive the lock pin from the pinion shaft and separate the halves of the differential case.

8. Drive the pinion shaft out of the case using a brass drift and remove the thrust washers and gears.

DRIVE PINION AND BEARING RETAINER

Removal and Disassembly

1. With a holding fixture installed on the flange, remove the pinion nut and washer. Leave the holding fixture on the flange and using a puller, remove the flange from the pinion shaft.

2. Using a seal puller, remove the pinion seal from the retainer assembly.

3. Remove the bolts from the retainer assembly and lift the retainer from the carrier. Measure the thickness of the shim that was between the retainer and the carrier assembly. Record the result.

4. Install a piece of hose on the pinion pilot bearing surface in front of the pinion gear. Mount the retainer assembly in a press and press the pinion gear out of the retainer.

5. Mount the pinion shaft in a press and press the rear bearing from the pinion shaft.

PINION BEARING CUP

Replacement

1. With the retainer assembly mounted in a press, using the proper tool, press the

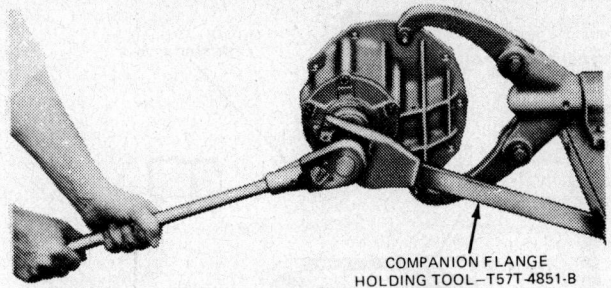

Removing the pinion shaft nut

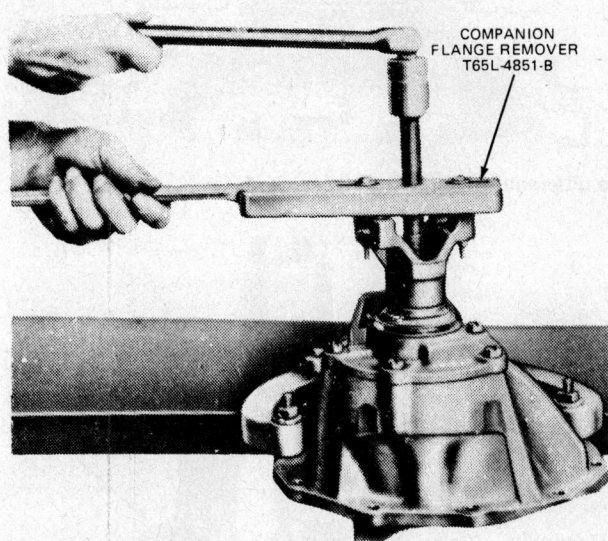

Removing the companion flange

Removing the pinion seal

front and rear bearing cups from the assembly.

2. Check the inside surfaces of the retainer for any nicks, dirt or distortion.

3. Install the new cups by pressing them into place with the proper tool. When the cups are installed, make sure they are seated in the retainer by trying to fit a .0015 in. feeler gauge, between the cup and the bottom of the bore.

PILOT BEARING

Replacement

1. Using a bearing driver, drive the bearing and retainer out of the carrier assembly.

2. Using the same tool, drive the new bearing into place until the driver bottoms against the case.

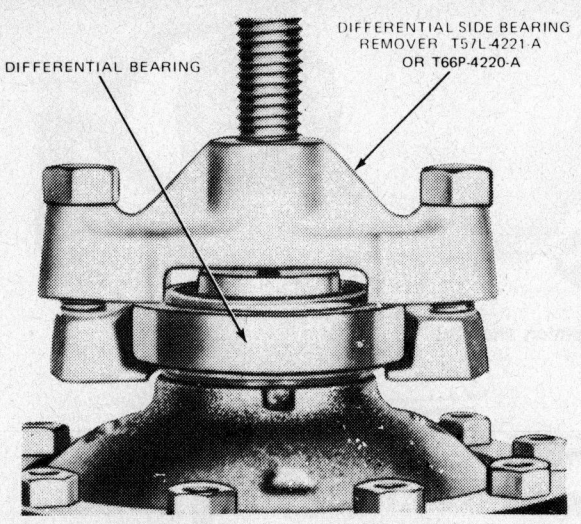

DIFFERENTIAL BEARING

DIFFERENTIAL SIDE BEARING REMOVER T57L-4221-A OR T66P-4220-A

Removing the differential bearing

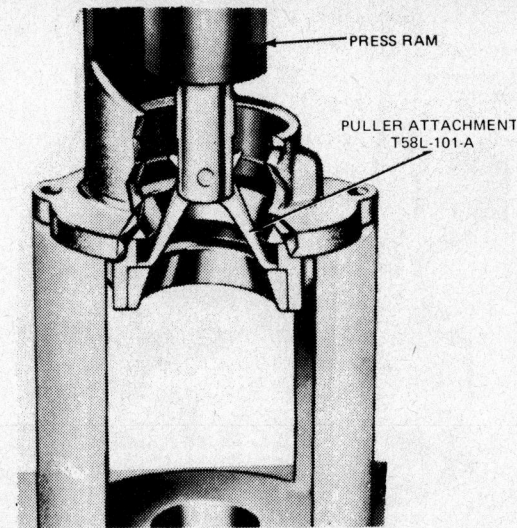

PRESS RAM

PULLER ATTACHMENT T58L-101-A

Removing the pinion rear bearing cup

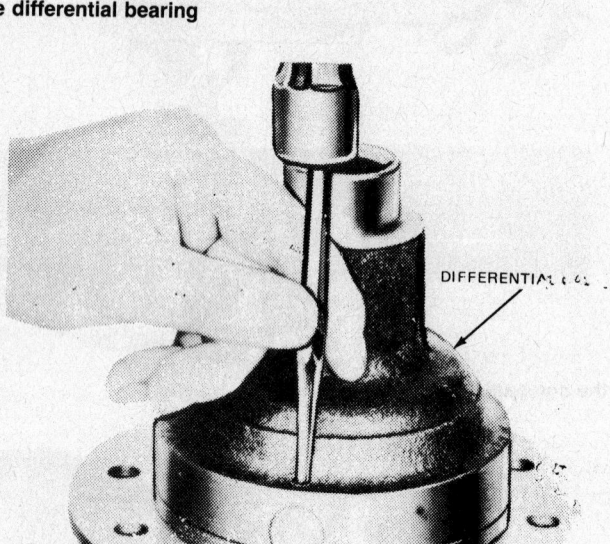

DIFFERENTIAL CASE

DIFFERENTIAL PINION SHAFT

Removing the differential pinion shaft lock pin

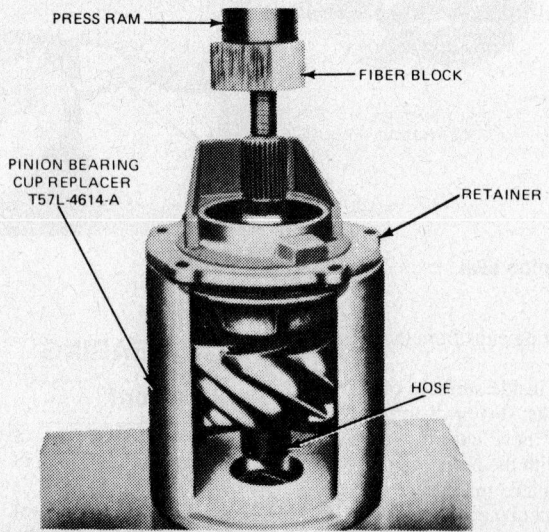

PRESS RAM

FIBER BLOCK

PINION BEARING CUP REPLACER T57L-4614-A

RETAINER

HOSE

Removing the pinion front bearing cone

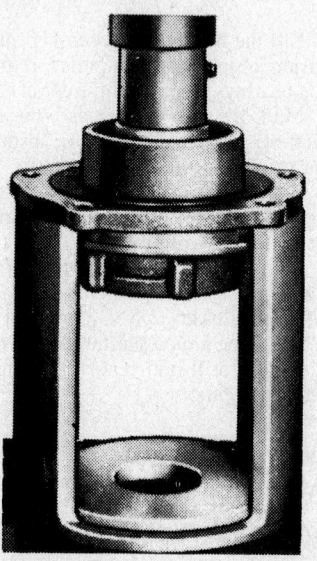

Installing the pinion front bearing cup

3. Drive a new retainer into place with the concave side up.

DRIVE PINION AND BEARING RETAINER

Assembly and Installation

1. Mount the pinion gear in a press and press the rear bearing into place.

2. Install the bearing spacer, bearing retainer and front bearing on the pinion shaft and press them into place. Be careful not to crush the bearing spacer.

3. Install a new O-ring in the groove in the retainer assembly. Do not twist the O-ring when fitting it into place.

4. Lubricate both pinion bearings.

5. Check the thickness of the original shim that was recorded earlier. Located on the head of the pinion gear is the shim adjustment number. Compare the number on the old pinion with the one on the new

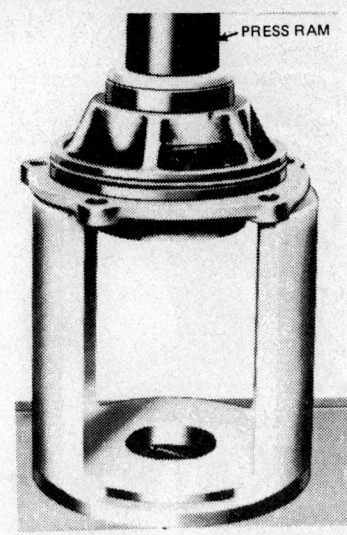

Installing the pinion rear bearing cup

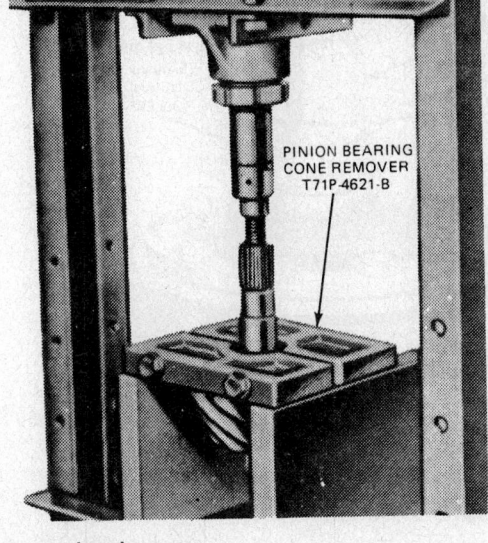

Removing the pinion rear bearing cone

PINION BEARING
CONE REMOVER
T71P-4621-B

Removing the pinion retainer assembly

PINION GEAR
LOCATING SHIM

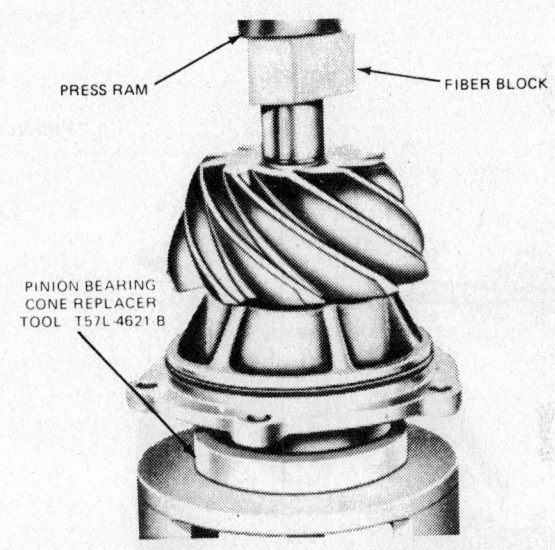

Installing the pinion front bearing

PRESS RAM — FIBER BLOCK

PINION BEARING
CONE REPLACER
TOOL T57L-4621 B

pinion. Refer to the table which indicates the amount of change to the original shim thickness for proper operation.

6. Install the new shim on the housing and install the pinion and retainer assembly, being careful not to damage the O-ring.

7. Install the bearing retainer bolts and torque them to 30–40 ft. lbs.

8. Using a seal driver, install a new pinion seal in the retainer assembly.

9. Position a holding tool on the flange and install the flange on the pinion shaft. With the holding tool still in place, install the washer and nut on the pinion shaft and torque the nut to 175 ft. lbs. Check the pinion bearing preload. The preload should be 8–14 in. lbs. for used bearings and 22–32 in. lbs. for new bearings. *Do not* overtighten the nut. *Do not* back off the nut to obtain the proper preload. If the 175 ft. lbs. initial torque was too much, the collapsible spacer must be replaced. Tighten

the pinion only enough to obtain the right preload torque.

DIFFERENTIAL CASE

Assembly and Installation

1. Lubricate all of the differential parts with gear lube before assembling.

2. Install a side gear and thrust washer in the case bore. Using a soft hammer, drive the pinion shaft into the case far enough to hold a pinion thrust washer and gear. Place the second pinion thrust washer and gear in position and carefully tap the pinion shaft into place. Be sure to line up the holes for the lock pin in the pinion shaft.

3. With the second side gear and thrust washer in place, install the cover on the differential case. Drive the pinion lock pin into place. Insert an axle shaft spline into the side gear and check for free rotation of

the gears.

4. Install two, two inch long 7/16 (N.F.) bolts through the differential case and thread them a little way into the ring gear. These will act as a guide when installing the ring gear on the case. Tap the ring gear into place.

5. Remove the guide pins and install the ring gear bolts. Tighten the bolts evenly to 65–85 ft. lbs.

6. If the differential bearings were removed, install the assembly in a press and press the new bearings into place.

7. Coat the bearing bores in the carrier with gear lube and install the bearing cups on the bearings. Place the differential assembly in the carrier.

8. Slide the differential case in the carrier bore until there is a slight amount of backlash between the gears.

9. Install the adjusting nuts in the carrier so that they just contact the bearing

1249

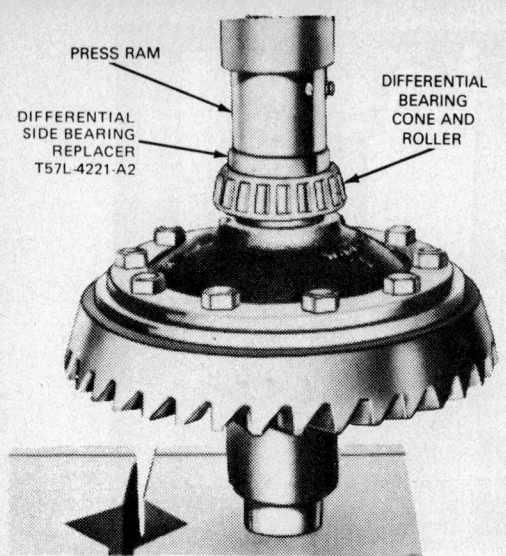

Installing the differential bearing

PAINT MARKING INDICATES POSITION IN WHICH GEARS WERE LAPPED

Pinion and ring mesh timing

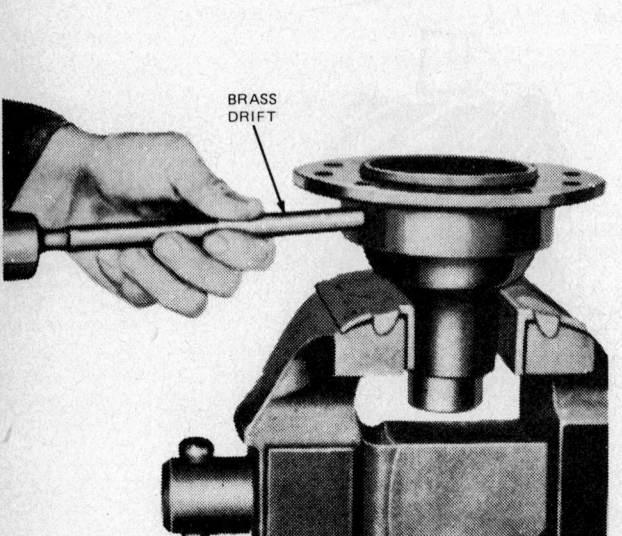

Driving out the differential pinion shaft

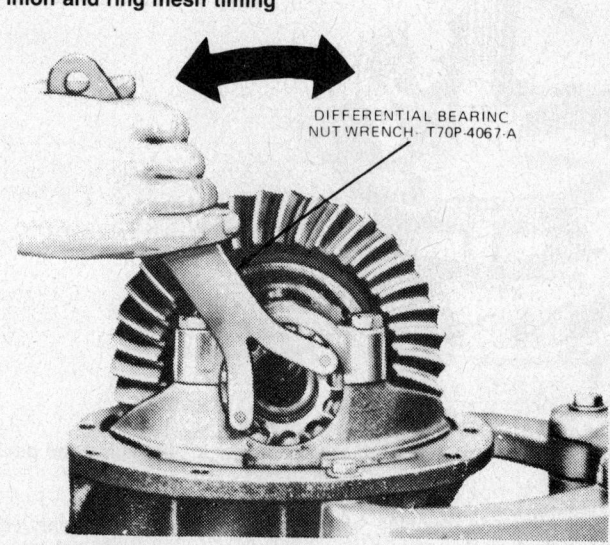

Backlash adjustment

cups. The nuts should be engaged about the same number of threads on each side.

10. Position the bearing caps in the carrier. Be careful to line up the marks. Install the cap bolts and torque them to 70–80 ft. lbs. Make sure the adjusting nuts turn freely as the bolts are being tightened.

11. Adjust the backlash and bearing preload as follows:

a. Loosen the bearing cap bolts then retighten them to 35 ft. lbs.

b. Loosen the adjusting nut on the pinion side so that it is away from the bearing cup. Tighten the nut on the opposite side so that the ring gear is forced into the pinion with no backlash.

c. Recheck the nut on the pinion side to make sure it is still loose. Now tighten this nut until it contacts the bearing cup. After it contacts the cup, turn it two more notches.

d. Rotate the ring gear several times in each direction. This helps to seat the bearings in the cups.

e. Again loosen the nut on the pinion side. If there is any backlash between the gears, tighten the nut on the ring gear side until the backlash is removed.

f. Install a dial indicator on the carrier assembly. Tighten the nut on the pinion side until it just contacts the cup. With the dial indicator set at zero, tighten the pinion side nut until the case is spread 0.008–0.012 in. with new bearings and 0.005–0.008 in. with old bearings. As this preload is applied the ring gear is forced away from the pinion and usually results in the correct backlash.

g. Mount the dial indicator on the ring gear and check the gear for backlash. Make sure the bearing caps are torqued to 75–85 ft. lbs.

h. The backlash should be between 0.008–0.012 in. If the backlash is not correct, loosen one nut and tighten the other an equal amount to move the ring gear in or out to correct the measurement. When making final adjustments, always move the adjusting nuts in a tightening direction. To do this, if a nut had to be loosened one notch, loosen it two notches and tighten it one. This makes certain the nut is in contact with the cup and will not shift when the vehicle is in

Checking backlash

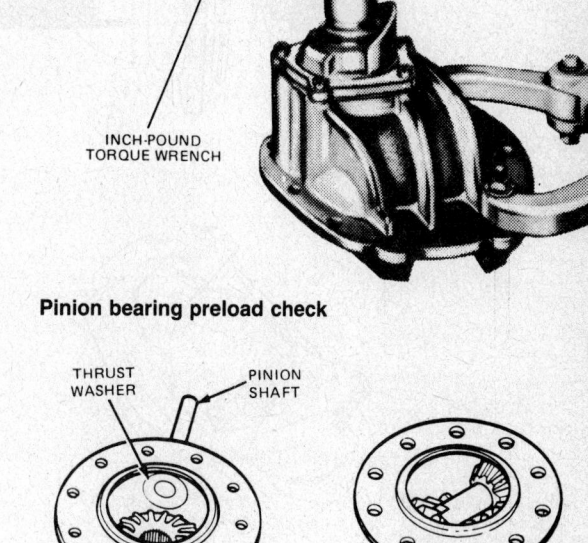

INCH-POUND
TORQUE WRENCH

Pinion bearing preload check

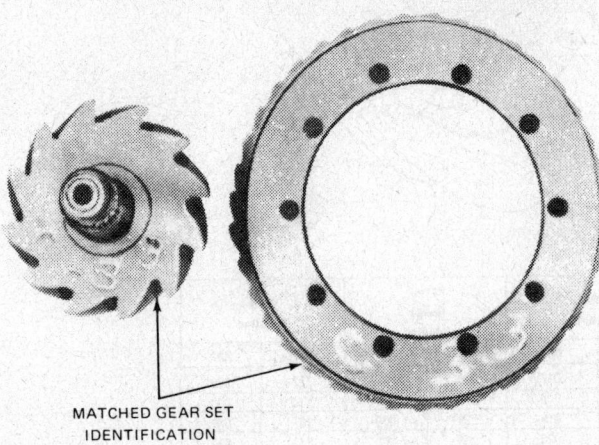

MATCHED GEAR SET
IDENTIFICATION

Pinion and ring markings

THRUST
WASHER

PINION
SHAFT

PINION SHAFT
LOCK PIN

PINION SHAFT

THRUST
WASHER

Differential case assembly

operation.

i. Coat the ring gear teeth with a marking compound and check the tooth pattern. If the pattern is not correct make the necessary changes to bring it into adjustment.

12. Install the carrier assembly in the vehicle and road test for proper operation.

Rockwell-Standard 12 Inch Ring Gear

This rear axle is a full-floating type, used primarily in one-ton Chevy and GMC trucks, with a hypoid drive gear and pinion. It uses a four-pinion differential assembly. The straddle mounted pinion has two tapered roller bearings in front of the pinion teeth and a straight roller bearing behind the pinion teeth. The differential carrier assembly can be removed while the axle remains in the truck.

DIFFERENTIAL BEARING
NUT WRENCH—T70P-4067-A

Side bearing preload adjustment

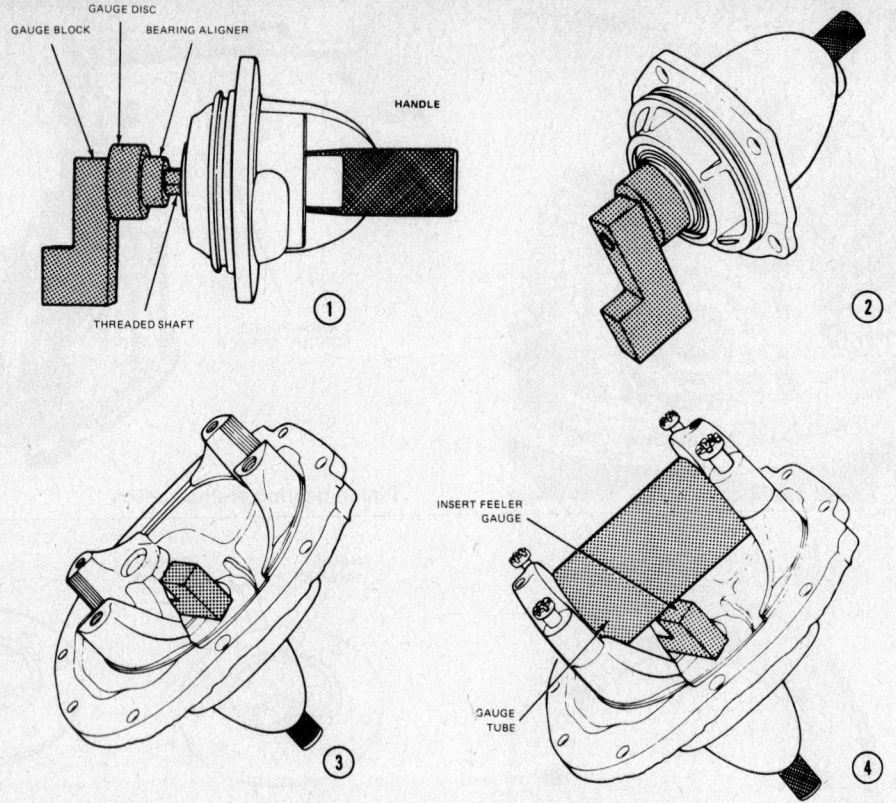

Using the pinion depth gauge tool

Feeler Gauge Reading		Shim Required		Feeler Gauge Reading		Shim Required		Feeler Gauge Reading		Shim Required	
(mm)	(in)	(mm)	(in)	(mm)	(in)	(mm)	(in)	(mm)	(in)	(mm)	(in)
.889	.035	.127	.005	.584	.023	432	.017	.279	.011	.737	.029
.864	.034	.152	.006	.559	.022	451	.018	.254	.010	0762	.030
.838	.033	.178	.007	.533	.021	483	.019	.229	.009	.787	.031
.813	.032	.203	.008	.508	.020	508	.020	.203	.008	.813	.032
.787	.031	.229	.009	.483	.019	533	.021	.178	.007	.838	.033
.762	.030	.254	.010	.457	.018	559	.022	.152	.006	.864	.034
.737	.029	.279	.011	.432	.017	.584	.023	.127	.005	.889	.035
.711	.028	.305	.012	.406	.016	610	.024	.102	.004	914	.036
.686	.027	.330	.013	.381	.015	635	.025	.076	.003	940	.037
.660	.026	.356	.014	.356	.014	660	.026	.051	.002	965	.038
.635	.025	.381	.015	.330	.013	686	.027				
.610	.024	.406	.016	.305	.012	.711	.028				

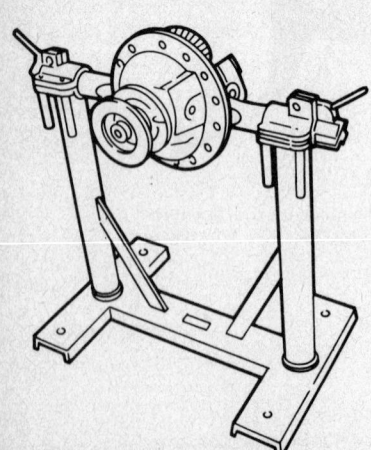

Carrier mounted in the repair stand

Thrust adjusting screw

DIFFERENTIAL CARRIER ASSEMBLY

Removal

1. Remove axle shafts.

2. Drain lubricant. Disconnect propeller shaft at pinion shaft yoke.

3. Remove carrier from axle housing and clean thoroughly.

Disassembly

1. Punch mark carrier leg, bearing cap, and bearing adjusting nut to assist in reassembly.

2. Remove screws, adjusting nut locks, bearing caps and adjusting nuts.

3. Loosen lock nut and back off drive gear thrust block adjusting screw.

4. Lift differential out of carrier and remove thrust block from end of adjusting screw inside of carrier.

5. Punch mark differential case halves for correct reassembly alignment and separate case halves.

6. Remove pinion shaft, pinions, side gears, thrust washers and differential bearing cones.

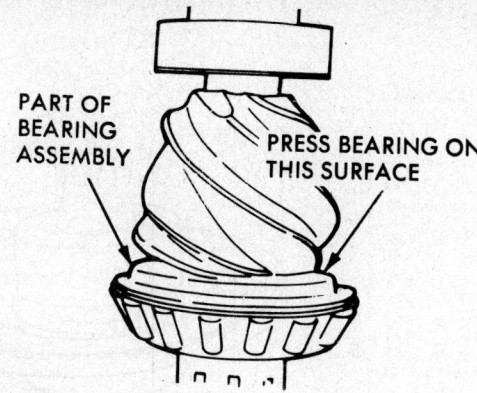

Bearing installation

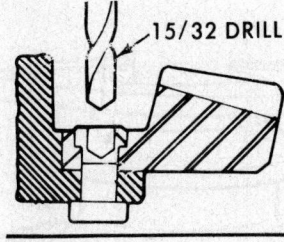

15/32 DRILL

RIGHT

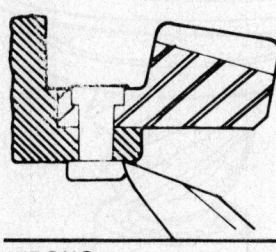

WRONG

Removing the rivets

7. To remove drive gear, carefully center punch each rivet in center of rivet head. Use a drill 1/32 inch smaller than the body of rivet to drill through the rivet head. Press out rivets.

8. Remove pinion shaft nut, washer and yoke. Driving yoke off will cause run-out.

9. Remove pinion bearing cover and oil seal assembly and, using puller screws, remove bearing cage. Using a pinch bar to remove cage will damage shims. Driving pinion from inner end with a drift will damage bearing lock ring groove.

10. Wire bearing cage shim pack together to facilitate adjustment when reassembling.

11. Tap pinion shaft out of cage with soft mallet or press shaft from cage. Remove bearing from cage.

12. Remove spacers and inner bearing from shaft.

13. Remove pinion shaft rear pilot bearing lock ring, and then bearing.

14. Remove oil seal assembly from bearing cover.

15. Clean all parts thoroughly in a suitable solvent and blow dry with compressed

Punch-marking the carrier leg

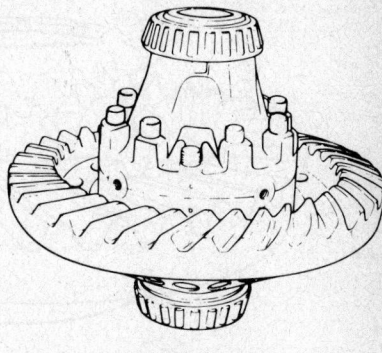

Carrier identification marks

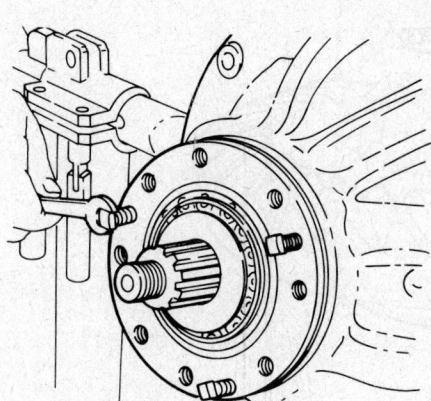

Removing the bearing cage

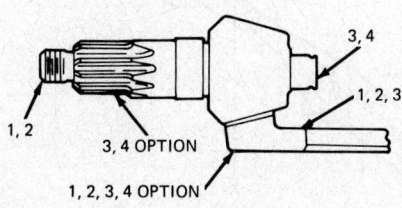

STRADDLE MOUNTED PINION
(Shown with parallel sided splines)

Gear set identification

air. Do not spin bearings with air pressure as they might score due to absence of any lubrication.

Inspect all parts for wear or roughness and replace if necessary. (For details, see Cleaning and Inspection in General Axle Service section).

Inspect all machined surfaces for nicks, burrs or scratches.

Assembly

1. Press drive pinion inner bearing cone firmly against pinion shoulder.

2. Press rear pilot bearings firmly

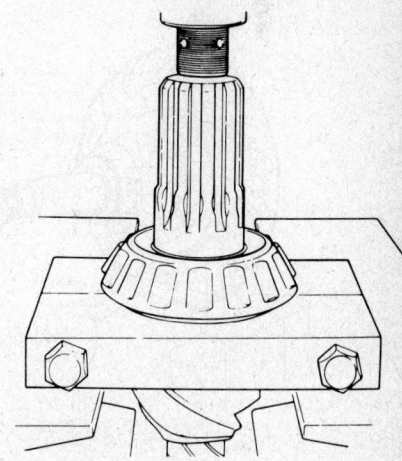

Removing the inner bearing

against pinion shoulder and install lock ring into pinion shaft groove.

3. Press bearing cups firmly against bearing cage shoulders.

4. Lubricate pinion bearings with SAE 90 oil and insert pinion and bearing assembly into pinion cage.

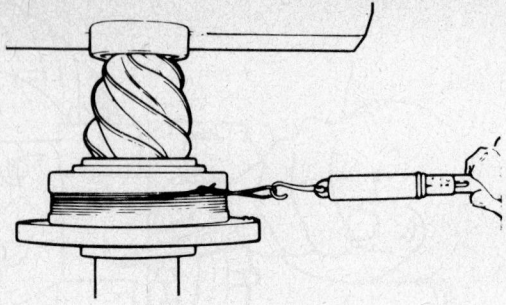

Measuring preload torque

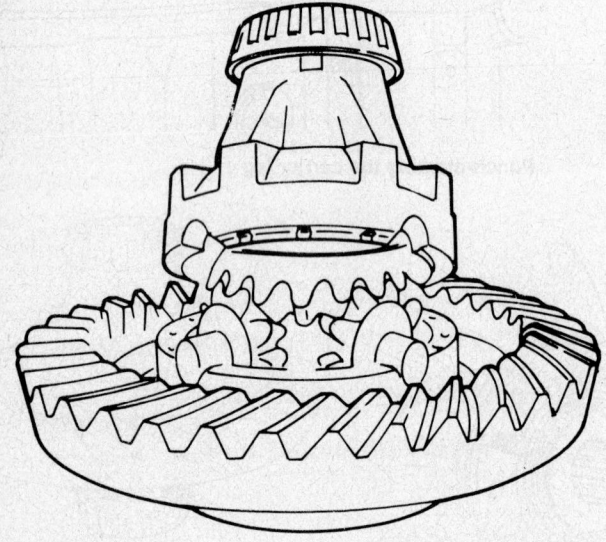

Aligning the mating marks

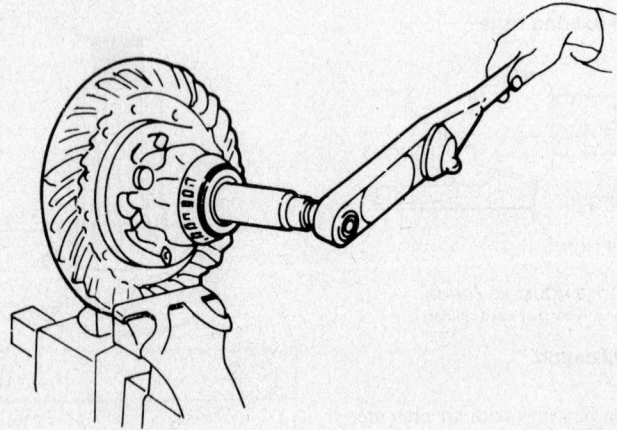

Checking the rotating torque

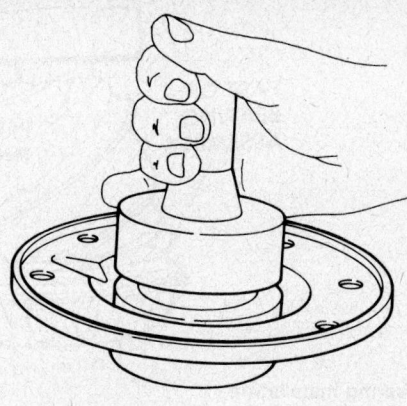

Installing the seal

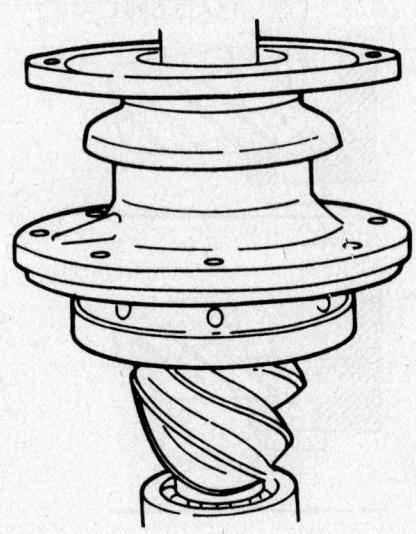

Installing the flange

5. Place original spacers on pinion shaft, and install front bearing and press firmly against spacers. Rotate cage several revolutions to assure normal bearing contact. If a press is not available, install pinion yoke and nut and torque to specifications.

6. While the assembly is in the press under pressure or pinion nut torques to specifications, check pinion bearing pre-load. The correct pressures and torque for checking pre-load are:

7. Wrap a soft wire around cage and pull on horizontal line with pound scale when determining pinion bearing pre-load, first measure diameter of the pinion cage. Assuming cage diameter is 6 inches, the pulling radius would be 3 inches; therefore, 5 pounds pull on the scale would equal 15 inch-pounds pre-load.

8. Use rotating torque, not starting torque. If rotating torque is not within 5 to 15 inch-pounds, use thinner spacer to increase pre-load or thicker spacer to decrease pre-load. Torque must be near low limit inch-pounds with original pinion bearings and near high limit when using new bearings. Remove yoke and install new oil seal.

9. Lubricate pinion shaft oil seal and lightly coat outer edge of seal body with

Pinion Shaft Thread Size and Number of Threads Per Inch	Required Pressure to Obtain Correct Pre-Load lbs.	Required Torque to Obtain Correct Pre-Load ft. lbs.
1 in. × 20	12,000	300–400
1¼ in. × 18	22,000	700–900
1½ in. × 12	28,000	800–1100
1½ in. × 18	28,000	800–1100
1¾ in. × 12	28,000	800–1100

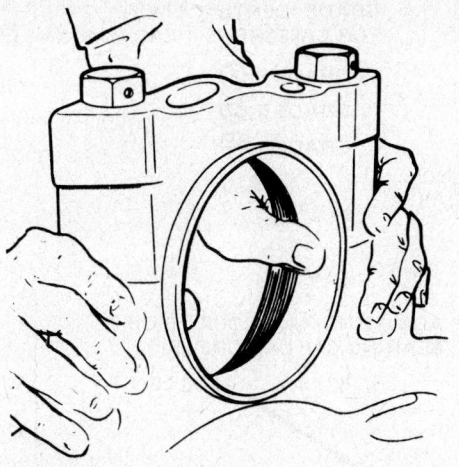

Fitting the bearing caps

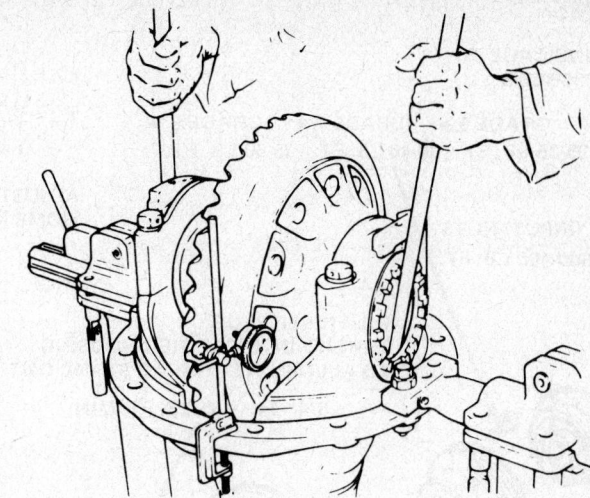

Adjusting the bearing preload

Checking backlash

Installing the bearing caps

non-hardening sealing compound. Press seal against cover shoulder. Install new gasket and bearing cover.

10. Install pinion yoke, washer and nut. Place pinion and cage assembly over carrier studs, hold hoke and tighten nut to specified torque. Install cotter key without backing off nut to align cotter key holes.

11. Place original shim pack on carrier studs with thin shims on both sides to create maximum sealing. Position pinion and cage assembly over studs and tap into position with soft mallet. Install lock washers and nuts. Tighten nuts to specified torque. If a new pinion is being installed, consult the General Axle Service section for correct procedure.

12. Rivet drive gear to differential case using new rivets. Rivets should not be heated, but always upset cold. When correct rivet is used, head being formed will be at least ⅛ inch larger in diameter than

rivet hole and approximately the same height as performed head. Avoid excessive pressure as it might distort case holes and cause gear eccentricity. Unless shops are equipped to do cold upsetting of rivets properly, replacement bolts should be used.

13. Lubricate differential case inner walls and all component parts with rear axle gear lubricant during assembly.

14. Install thrust washer and side gear in drive gear half of case. Assemble pinions and thrust washers on pinion shaft and position this assembly in the case. Place other side gear and thrust washer in position on the four pinions.

15. Install other case half with mating marks aligned. Draw case down evenly

with four bolts. Check for free rotation of differential gears and correct if necessary. Install and torque remining bolts and then lock wire.

16. Press differential bearings squarely and firmly on differential case halves. Differential bearing cup fit in the pedestal bores should be checked before installing assembly in carrier.

17. Temporarily install bearing cups, threaded adjusting nuts or split ring and bearing caps. Tighten cap bolts to specified torque. Bearing cups must be of a hand push fit in the bores; if not, the bores must be enlarged with a scraper or emery cloth. Use a blued bearing cup as a gauge to check each fit.

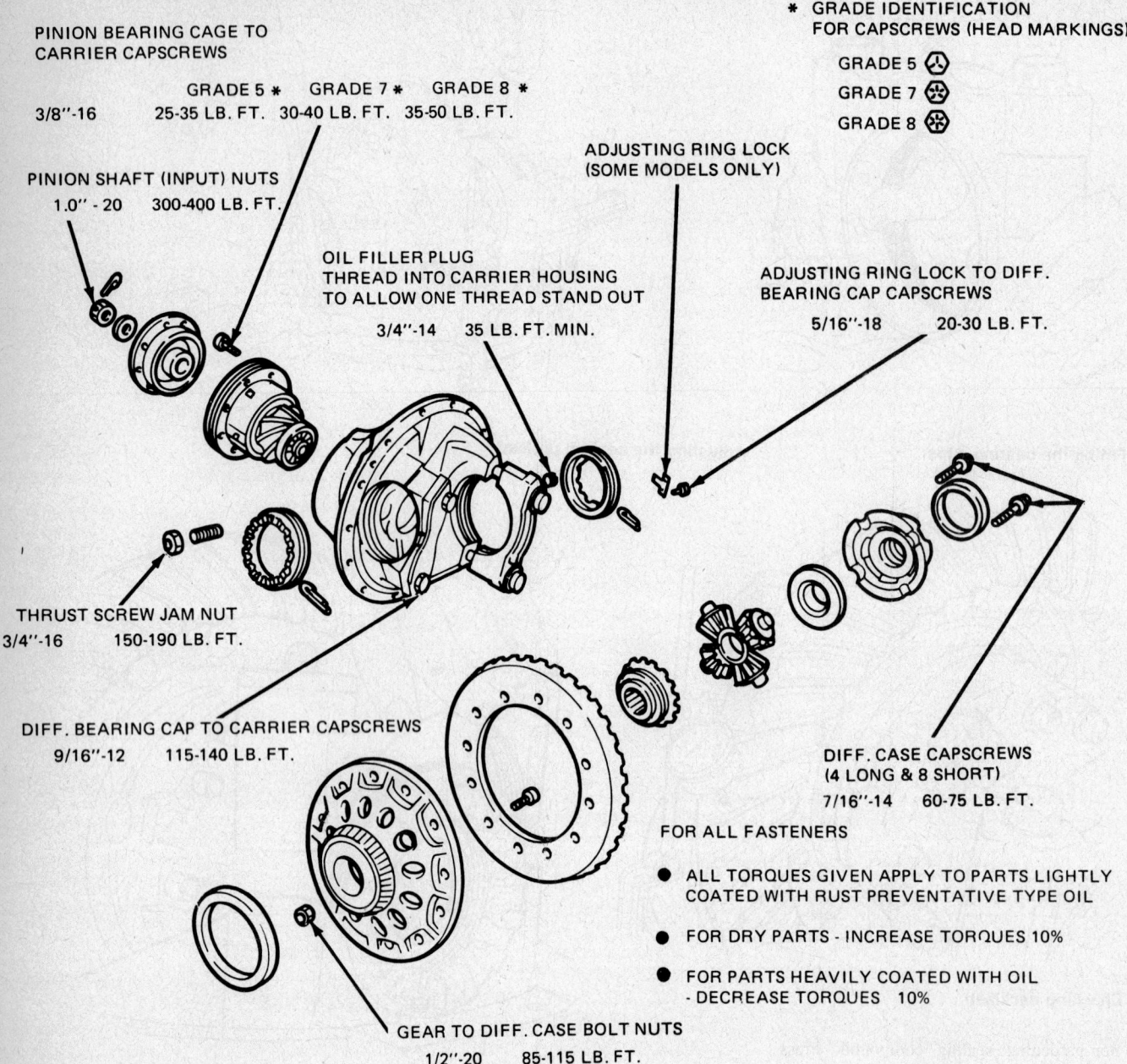

PINION BEARING CAGE TO
CARRIER CAPSCREWS

GRADE 5 *   GRADE 7 *   GRADE 8 *

3/8''-16   25-35 LB. FT.   30-40 LB. FT.   35-50 LB. FT.

* GRADE IDENTIFICATION
FOR CAPSCREWS (HEAD MARKINGS)

GRADE 5

GRADE 7

GRADE 8

PINION SHAFT (INPUT) NUTS

1.0'' - 20   300-400 LB. FT.

ADJUSTING RING LOCK
(SOME MODELS ONLY)

OIL FILLER PLUG
THREAD INTO CARRIER HOUSING
TO ALLOW ONE THREAD STAND OUT

3/4''-14   35 LB. FT. MIN.

ADJUSTING RING LOCK TO DIFF.
BEARING CAP CAPSCREWS

5/16''-18   20-30 LB. FT.

THRUST SCREW JAM NUT
3/4''-16   150-190 LB. FT.

DIFF. BEARING CAP TO CARRIER CAPSCREWS
9/16''-12   115-140 LB. FT.

DIFF. CASE CAPSCREWS
(4 LONG & 8 SHORT)
7/16''-14   60-75 LB. FT.

FOR ALL FASTENERS

- ALL TORQUES GIVEN APPLY TO PARTS LIGHTLY
  COATED WITH RUST PREVENTATIVE TYPE OIL

- FOR DRY PARTS - INCREASE TORQUES 10%

- FOR PARTS HEAVILY COATED WITH OIL
  - DECREASE TORQUES 10%

GEAR TO DIFF. CASE BOLT NUTS
1/2''-20   85-115 LB. FT.

Fastener torques

18. Lubricate differential bearings and cups with axle lubricant. Place cups over bearings and position assembly in carrier housing. Turn adjusting nuts hand tight against bearing cups.

19. Install bearing caps in correct location as marked, and tap lightly into position. Be sure caps fit over adjusting nuts properly and are not cross-threaded. Some backlash must be present between drive gear and pinion. Install and torque bearing cap bolts.

20. Attach a dial indicator to the carrier with the pointer resting against back face of drive gear. Eliminate all end play by turning right adjusting nut clockwise. Ro-

tate drive gear and check runout. If runout exceeds 0.008 inch, remove differential and check the cause.

21. Tighten adjusting nuts, one notch each, to pre-load differential bearings.

22. Position dial indicator so the pointer rests against face of one of the drive gear teeth. Check backlash between drive gear and pinion at 90 degree intervals of rotation.

23. Adjust backlash to 0.006–0.012 inch (0.006 preferred, especially on new gears). When adjusting backlash, back off one adjusting nut and advance opposite nut the same amount to maintain bearing pre-load.

depth (see General Axle Service section) was not used, adjust gears using the tooth contact method. Then proceed to step 25. If depth gauge method was used, go directly to step 25.

25. Torque bearing cap bolts and install and torque adjusting nut locks and cap screws and lock wire.

26. Hold drive gear thrust block on rear face of gear with heavy grease, rotate gear until hole in thrust block aligns with adjusting screw hole in carrier. Install adjusting screw and lock nut, tighten screw enough to locate thrust block firmly against

24. If the Pinion Setting Procedures (depth gauge method) for adjusting pinion

ROCKWELL–STANDARD BEARING PRELOAD

Axle Model	Pinion Shaft Nut–Thread Size and Torque Limits (ft. lbs.)		Press Ram Pressure for Preload Check (Tons)	Pinion and Cross Shaft Bearing Preload (in. lbs.)	Backlash Limits (in.)	Differential Bearing Preload Adjusting Nut Notches Tighten from Zero End Play (each Adjusting Nut)
Single–speed	1–20	300–400	6	5–15	0.005–0.015	1
Single reduction	1¼ × 18	700–900	11	5–15	0.005–0.015	1
	1¼ × 18	800–1100	14	5–15	0.005–0.015	1
	1½ × 12	800–1100	14	5–15	0.005–0.015	1
	1½ × 18	800–1100	14	5–15	0.005–0.015	1

back face of gear. Back off adjusting screw ¼ turn to create 0.010–0.015 inch clearance and lock securely with nut. Recheck to assure minimum clearance of 0.010 inch during full rotation of drive gear.

Installation

1. Install a new gasket on axle housing flange. Start carrier into clean housing and hold in place with four equally spaced washers and nut. Tighten nuts alternately to draw carrier evenly into housing. Install and torque carrier flange lock washers and nuts.

2. Install axle drive shafts and connect universal joint at pinion flange.

3. Fill axle housing to proper level and road test vehicle.

TORQUE SPECIFICATIONS

Carrier to housing	½–20	94–102
screw or	⅝–18	186–205
stud nut	¾–16	325–360
Differential	½–20	94–102
case bolt	9⁄16–18	132–145
	⅝–18	186–205
	¾–16	325–360
Differential	⅝–11–18	127–140
bearing cap	¾–10–16	230–250
bolt	⅞–9	345–370
	⅞–14	375–415
	1–12	555–615
Differential	5⁄16–18	15–17
bearing	½–13	85–91
adjuster	9⁄16–12	120–129
lock bolt	⅝–11	168–180
Pinion shaft	1–20	300–400
yoke nut	1–¼–18	700–900
	1–½–18	800–1100
	1–½–12	800–1100
	1–¾–12	800–1100
Shaft flange stud	7⁄16–20	52–58

International Harvester Co. Single Speed, Light

CARRIER ASSEMBLY

Disassembly

1. Mount the carrier assembly in a suitable fixture.

2. Remove the cotter pins from the bearing adjuster locks and remove the locks from the bearing caps.

3. Match mark the carrier legs to the bearing caps to identify properly upon reassembly.

4. Remove the ring gear thrust block and adjusting screw from the carrier housing.

5. Cut and remove the lock wire. Remove the bearing cap stud nuts or cap screws. Remove the bearing cap stud nuts or cap screws. Remove the bearing caps and adjusting nuts.

NOTE: Bearing cap pilot rings may be used on some axle models. Do not lose or damage.

6. Tip the differential assembly away from the pinion and lift the assembly from the housing.

NOTE: Due to the weight of the differential assembly, a lifting device may be used to assist in the removal.

DIFFERENTIAL CASE AND GEAR ASSEMBLY

Disassembly

1. Match mark the differential case halves for the proper reassembly.

2. Cut the lock wire and remove the cap screws or stud nuts and separate the case halves.

3. Remove the spider, pinions, side gears and thrust washers from the case

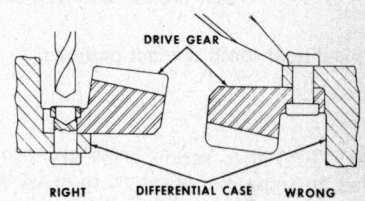

Removing the rivets

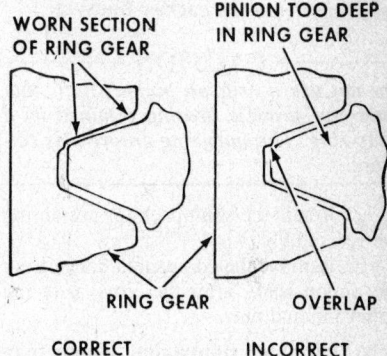

Correct and incorrect backlash using worn gears

halves.

4. Remove the ring gear rivets by center punching each rivet head and using a drill, 1⁄32 inch smaller than the rivet body, drill through the rivet head. Use a punch to press out the remaining part of the rivet.

— CAUTION —
Never use a chisel to cut off the head of the rivets or damage to the differential case can result.

PINION AND CAGE ASSEMBLY

Removal

1. Remove the pinion cage cap screws and remove the pinion cage assembly from the differential carrier.

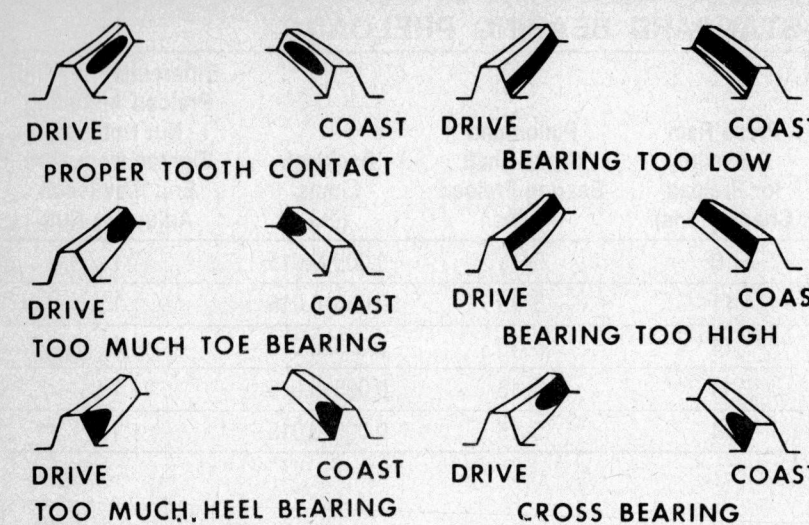

DRIVE   COAST
PROPER TOOTH CONTACT

DRIVE   COAST
TOO MUCH TOE BEARING

DRIVE   COAST
TOO MUCH HEEL BEARING

DRIVE   COAST
BEARING TOO LOW

DRIVE   COAST
BEARING TOO HIGH

DRIVE   COAST
CROSS BEARING

Typical gear tooth contact patterns

NOTE: Puller screw holes are provided on some pinion cages, to assist in the removal of the cage from the housing. If no puller screw holes are present, a brass drift can be used on the inner end of the pinion to force the pinion and cage assembly from the carrier housing.

--------- CAUTION ---------
Do not use a drift on pinion shafts that have the straddle bearing retained by a snap-ring. The snap-ring groove may collapse.

2. Retain the shim pack for use during the reassembly.

3. Remove the companion flange from the pinion shaft, after the removal of the cotter pin and nut.

NOTE: The companion flange may have to be tapped of the pinion shaft with a soft hammer.

4. Remove the outer bearing from the cage by holding the cage in a vise and tapping on the pinion shaft end, and forcing the shaft through the cage.

--------- CAUTION ---------
Do not allow the component parts to fall.

5. Remove the spacer or spacer combination from the pinion shaft.

6. Remove the rear tapered thrust bearing from the pinion with the aid of a suitable puller.

7. Remove the straddle bearing retainer, if equipped, and remove the bearing with the aid of a suitable puller.

NOTE: The straddle bearing may be retained by staking of the pinion shaft end, by a snap-ring, or by a cap screw and washer.

8. Remove the cork seal, and oil seal from the pinion cage.

DIFFERENTIAL CARRIER ASSEMBLY

Precautions to be Observed During the Reassembly

1. Before assembly, lubricate the bearings and cups and rewrap to maintain cleanliness.

2. Use correct rivet pressure when installing the ring gear to the differential case, or if bolts are available, be assured that the proper torque is applied in tightening.

3. Be sure that the bearing caps and adjusting nuts are correctly aligned and that the bearing cups fit properly. Irreparable damage can result to the differential carrier or bearing caps if the alignment is off.

4. Observe the proper torque settings when tightening any nuts or bolts.

Five Steps in the Reassembly of the Differential Assembly

1. **Pinion bearing preload:** This is determined by the thickness of the spacer between the two pinion thrust bearings, when tightened in the pinion cage.

2. **Establish pinion nominal dimension:** Use the manufacturers pinion setting gauge (SE-1065), or use an equivalent tool. Changes to this dimension can be made by adding or removing shims to move the pinion in or out of the carrier housing.

3. **Set the ring gear lash:** Move the ring gear to or from the pinion by means of the differential bearing adjusters.

4. **Preload the differential bearings:** This is accomplished by tightening the bearing adjusting nuts after zero end play has been obtained on the bearings.

5. **Check the gear tooth contact:** Use the paint impression method for this operation.

DIFFERENTIAL CARRIER

Assembly

1. Install the ring gear on the differential case with either the rivet method or by bolts.

2. When installing rivets, observe the pressures needed to upset the rivets.

NOTE: Hold the pressure force for one minute to assure that the rivet will fill the hole.

3. Install the side gear and thrust washer in the ring gear half of the differential case.

4. Place the spider, the pinion gears and thrust washers in position and install the component side gear and thrust washer.

5. Align the previously made match marks and position the component case half to the ring gear case half.

6. Install the cap screws or stud nuts and torque to specifications.

7. Check the gears for freedom of movement and install the lock wire.

8. Install the differential bearings on the differential case.

Rivet Size	Pressure Tons
7/16	18–20
1/2	20–25
9/16	36
5/8	45–50
3/4	50

PINION AND CAGE ASSEMBLY

Installation

1. Install the rear thrust tapered bearing and the straddle bearing on the pinion shaft.

2. Install the straddle bearing retainer.

NOTE: If the straddle bearing is of the type to be staked, use a blunt pin punch and stake in at least four to six equidistant places, approximately 1/8 inch in from the pinion circumference. The size of the pinion will dictate the number of staked points on the pinion end.

3. Renew the bearing cups in the pinion cage, as necessary.

4. Lubricate the bearings and cups and install the pinion shaft through the pinion cage.

5. Install the spacer or spacer combination on the pinion shaft, followed by the outer pinion tapered bearing.

6. Temporarily assemble the companion flange and the washer and nut onto the pinion shaft, tightening the nut to specifications while holding the flange in a vise.

7. To measure the pinion bearing preload, wrap a strong cord or soft wire around the pinion cage and attach the other end to

BOLT TORQUE SPECIFICATIONS

SAE Grade Number	1 or 2	5	6 or 7	8

Capscrew Head Markings

Manufacturer's marks may vary. Three-line markings on heads shown below, for example, indicate SAE Grade 5.

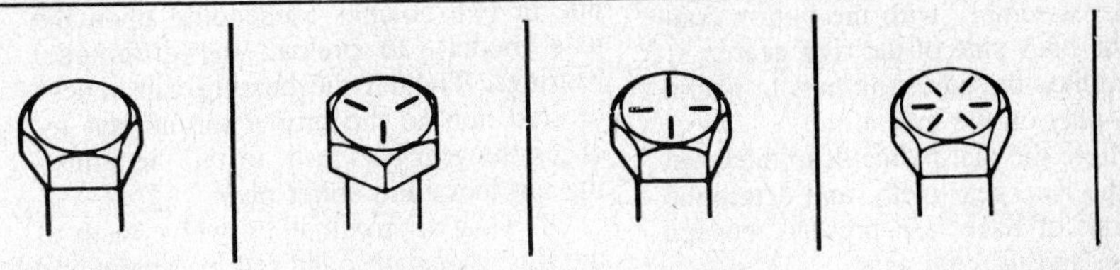

Usage	Used Frequently	Used Frequently	Used at Times	Used at Times
Capscrew Diameter and Minimum Tensile Strength psi (Kg/sq cm)	To ½-69,000 (4850.7000)	To ¾-120,000 (8436.0000)	To ⅝-140,000 (9842.0000)	150,000 (10545.0000)
	To ¾-64,000 (4499.2000)	To 1 -115,000 (8084.5000)	To ¾-133,000 (9349.9000)	
	To 1 -55,000 (3866.5000)			

Quality of Material	Indeterminate		Minimum Commercial		Medium Commercial		Best Commercial	
Capscrew Body Size (Inches) — (Thread)	Torque Ft-Lb	kg m	Torque Ft-Lb	kg m	Torque Ft-Lb	kg m	Torque Ft-Lb	kg m
¼-20	5	0.6915	8	1.1064	10	1.3830	12	1.6596
-28	6	0.8298	10	1.3830			14	1.9362
5/16-18	11	1.5213	17	2.3511	19	2.6277	24	3.3192
-24	13	1.7979	19	2.6277			27	3.7341
⅜-16	18	2.4894	31	4.2873	34	4.7022	44	6.0852
-24	20	2.7660	35	4.8405			49	6.7767
7/16-14	28	3.8132	49	6.7767	55	7.6065	70	9.6810
-20	30	4.1490	55	7.6065			78	10.7874
½-13	39	5.3937	75	10.3725	85	11.7555	105	14.5215
-20	41	5.6703	85	11.7555			120	16.5960
9/16-12	51	7.0533	110	15.2130	120	16.5960	155	21.4365
-18	55	7.6065	120	16.5960			170	23.5110
⅝-11	83	11.4789	150	20.7450	167	23.0961	210	29.0430
-18	95	13.1385	170	23.5110			240	33.1920
¾-10	105	14.5215	270	37.3410	280	38.7240	375	51.8625
-16	115	15.9045	295	40.7985			420	58.0860
⅞- 9	160	22.1280	395	54.6285	440	60.8520	605	83.6715
-14	175	24.2025	435	60.1605			675	93.3525
1- 8	235	32.5005	590	81.5970	660	91.2780	910	125.8530
-14	250	34.5750	660	91.2780			990	136.9170

a inch-pound scale. Rotate the pinion cage by pulling on the spring scale and reading the scale while the cage is rotating. Refer to the specifications listed within this chapter.

8. If the preload does not agree with the specifications, a thicker or thinner spacer or spacer combination must be used.

9. When the proper preload is obtained, assemble the pinion bearing cage by removing the companion flange, install the oil seal, cork gasket, reinstall the companion flange, washer and nut. Torque the nut to specifications and install the cotter pin.

PINION NOMINAL DIMENSION

To locate the pinion nominal dimension, refer to the specifications listed within this chapter. Some pinions will have the dimension stamped or etched on the gear end of the shaft. Refer and compare to the specifications. The pinion variation, noted in thousands of an inch, will be etched on the gear end of the pinion shaft. This figure will be used in determining the amount of shims needed to locate the pinion gear in the proper relationship to the ring gear centerline.

NOTE: Refer to the beginning of the Rear Axle Drive section for the procedure to follow in the use of the pinion setting gauge tool. If the pinion setting gauge tools are not available, the pinion depth will have to be adjusted by assembling the carrier assembly, installing the pinion cage assembly and the differential assembly into the carrier housing, and observing the tooth contact pattern on the ring gear. This is a trial and error method and very time consuming.

DIFFERENTIAL ASSEMBLY

Installation, Preload, Backlash

1. Install the differential assembly with the bearing cups on the differential bearings into the legs of the carrier housing.

2. Install the bearing adjusting nuts and the bearing caps. Install the cap screws or stud nuts and turn the adjusting nuts while tightening the bearing caps to assure freedom of movement of the adjusting nuts.

— CAUTION —

If the bearing caps are not positioned properly, the adjusting nuts may be crossthreaded, and irreparable damage to the carrier housing or to the bearing cups may result.

3. With the side bearing caps loosened to permit the bearing cup movement, loosen the adjusting nuts only enough to notice end play on a dial indicator, mounted on the carrier assembly with the button contacting the back side of the ring gear.

4. Tighten the adjusting nuts to obtain zero end-play on the indicator.

5. Move the dial indicator to the coast side of the ring gear teeth, and determine the amount of back lash present between the pinion and the ring gear.

6. To adjust the back lash, move the ring gear towards or away from the pinion by means of the differential bearing adjusting nuts. Move the adjusting nuts the same distance, either in or out to maintain the differential bearing zero end-play.

7. When the correct backlash clearance is established, tighten each adjusting nut one or two notches (depending upon the axle model), to preload the differential bearings. Tighten the bearing cap screws or stud nuts to the proper torque and recheck the gear backlash. Install the adjusting nut locks and cotter pins.

8. Coat approximately twelve teeth of the ring gear with oiled red lead paint and rotate the pinion in its normal rotation and check the drive side of the ring gear teeth for the tooth contact impression.

NOTE: A sharper tooth contact impression may be obtained by applying a small amount of resistance to the gear with a flat steel bar and using a wrench to turn the pinion.

9. If the area of contact starts near the toe end of the ring gear and extends about ⅔ of the tooth length, the tooth contact is satisfactory.

10. Install the ring gear thrust block, if equipped. Adjust the block firmly against the back face of the ring gear and back off the screw ¼ turn and lock the jam nut.

11. Install the carrier assembly into the housing, following the reverse procedure of the removal operation.

ENGINE

Gasoline Engine Troubleshooting

See applicable Car or Unit Repair section for specific service procedures

INDEX TO SYSTEMS

System	To Test	Group
Battery	Engine need not be running	1
Starting system	Engine need not be running	2
Primary electrical system	Engine need not be running	3
Secondary electrical system	Engine need not be running	4
Fuel system	Engine need not be running	5
Engine compression	Engine need not be running	6
Engine vacuum	Engine must be running	7
Secondary electrical system	Engine must be running	8
Valve train	Engine must be running	9
Exhaust system	Engine must be running	10
Cooling system	Engine must be running	11
Engine lubrication	Engine must be running	12

INDEX TO PROBLEMS

Problem Symptom	Begin at Specific Diagnosis, Number
Engine Won't Start	
Starter doesn't turn	1.1, 2.1
Starter turns, engine doesn't	2.1
Starter turns engine very slowly	1.1, 2.4
Starter turns engine normally	3.1, 4.1
Starter turns engine very quickly	6.1
Engine fires intermittently	4.1
Engine fires consistently	5.1, 6.1
Engine Runs Poorly	
Hard starting	3.1, 4.1, 5.1, 8.1
Rough idle	4.1, 5.1, 8.1
Stalling	3.1, 4.1, 5.1, 8.1
Engine dies at high speeds	4.1, 5.1
Hesitation (on acceleration from standing stop)	5.1, 8.1
Poor pickup	4.1, 5.1, 8.1
Lack of power	3.1, 4.1, 5.1, 8.1
Backfire through the carburetor	4.1, 8.1, 9.1
Backfire through the exhaust	4.1, 8.1, 9.1
Blue exhaust gases	6.1, 7.1
Black exhaust gases	5.1
Running on (after the ignition is shut off)	3.1, 8.1
Susceptible to moisture	4.1
Engine misfires under load	4.1, 7.1, 8.4, 9.1
Engine misfires at speed	4.1, 8.4
Engine misfires at idle	3.1, 4.1, 5.1, 7.1, 8.4

SAMPLE SECTION

Test and Procedure	Results and Indications	Proceed to
4.1 Check for spark: Hold each spark plug wire approximately $\frac{1}{4}''$ from ground with gloves or a heavy, dry rag. Crank the engine and observe the spark.	If no spark is evident	4.2
	If spark is good in some cases	4.3
	If spark is good in all cases	4.6

SPECIFIC DIAGNOSIS

This section is arranged so that following each test, instructions are given to proceed to another, until a problem is diagnosed.

SECTION 1—BATTERY

Test and Procedure	Results and Indications	Proceed to
1.1 Inspect the battery visually for case condition (corrosion, cracks) and water level.	If case is cracked, replace battery.	1.4
	If the case is intact, remove corrosion with a solution of baking soda and water. **(CAUTION: Do not get the solution into the battery).** Fill with water.	1.2

DIRT ON TOP OF BATTERY
CORROSION
PLUGGED VENT
LOOSE CABLE OR POSTS
CRACKS
LOW WATER LEVEL

Inspect the battery case

1.2 Check the battery cable connections: Insert a screwdriver between the battery post and the cable clamp. Turn the headlights on high beam, and observe them as the screwdriver is gently twisted to ensure good metal to metal contact.	If the lights brighten, remove and clean the clamp and post; coat the post with petroleum jelly, install and tighten the clamp.	1.4
	If no improvement is noted	1.3

TESTING BATTERY CABLE CONNECTIONS USING A SCREWDRIVER

1.3 Test the state of charge of the battery using an individual cell tester or hydrometer.	If indicated, charge the battery. **NOTE: If no obvious reason exists for the low state of charge (i.e., battery age, prolonged storage), proceed to:**	1.4

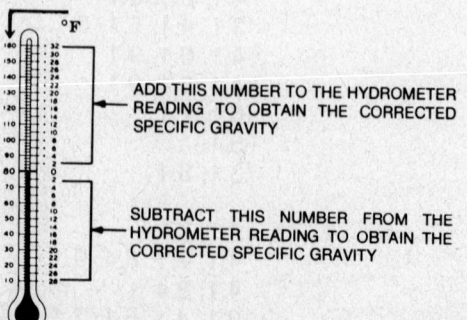

°F

ADD THIS NUMBER TO THE HYDROMETER READING TO OBTAIN THE CORRECTED SPECIFIC GRAVITY

SUBTRACT THIS NUMBER FROM THE HYDROMETER READING TO OBTAIN THE CORRECTED SPECIFIC GRAVITY

Specific Gravity (@ 80° F.)

Minimum	Battery Charge
1.260	100% Charged
1.230	75% Charged
1.200	50% Charged
1.170	25% Charged
1.140	Very Little Power Left
1.110	Completely Discharged

The effects of temperature on battery specific gravity (left) and amount of battery charge in relation to specific gravity (right)

Test and Procedure	Results and Indications	Proceed To
1.4 Visually inspect battery cables for cracking, bad connection to ground, or bad connection to starter.	If necessary, tighten connections or replace the cables.	2.1

SECTION 2—STARTING SYSTEM

Test and Procedure	Results and Indications	Proceed to
Note: Tests in Group 2 are performed with coil high tension lead disconnected to prevent accidental starting.		
2.1 Test the starter motor and solenoid: Connect a jumper from the battery post of the solenoid (or relay) to the starter post of the solenoid (or relay).	If starter turns the engine normally	2.2
	If the starter buzzes, or turns the engine very slowly	2.4
	If no response, replace the solenoid (or relay).	3.1
	If the starter turns, but the engine doesn't, ensure that the flywheel ring gear is intact. If the gear is undamaged, replace the starter drive.	3.1
2.2 Determine whether ignition override switches are functioning properly (clutch start switch, neutral safety switch), by connecting a jumper across the switch(es), and turning the ignition switch to "start".	If starter operates, adjust or replace switch.	3.1
	If the starter doesn't operate	2.3
2.3 Check the ignition switch "start" position: Connect a 12V test lamp or voltmeter between the starter post of the solenoid (or relay) and ground. Turn the ignition switch to the "start" position, and jiggle the key.	If the lamp doesn't light or the meter needle doesn't move when the switch is turned, check the ignition switch for loose connections, cracked insulation, or broken wires. Repair or replace as necessary.	3.1
	If the lamp flickers or needle moves when the key is jiggled, replace the ignition switch.	3.3

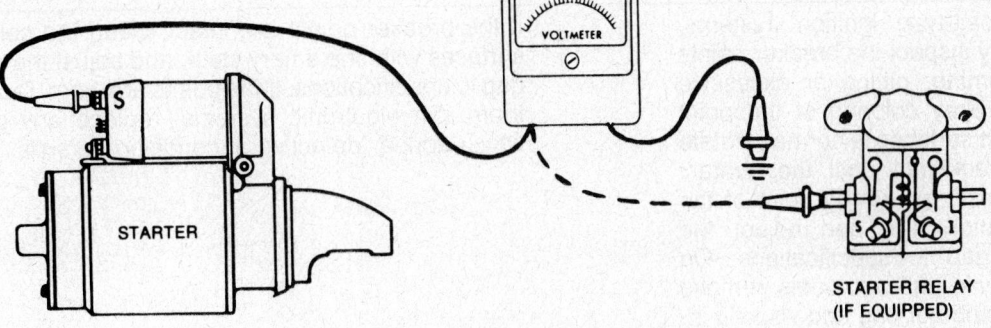

Checking the ignition switch "start" position

Test and Procedure	Results and Indications	Proceed to
2.4 Remove and bench test the starter, according to specifications in the car section.	If the starter does not meet specifications, repair or replace as needed	3.1
	If the starter is operating properly	2.5

Test and Procedure	Results and Indications	Proceed To
2.5 Determine whether the engine can turn freely: Remove the spark plugs, and check for water in the cylinders. Check for water on the dipstick, or oil in the radiator. Attempt to turn the engine using an 18″ flex drive and socket on the crankshaft pulley nut or bolt.	If the engine will turn freely only with the spark plugs out, and hydrostatic lock (water in the cylinders) is ruled out, check valve timing.	9.2
	If engine will not turn freely, and it is known that the clutch and transmission are free, the engine must be disassembled for further evaluation.	See Car Section

SECTION 3—PRIMARY ELECTRICAL SYSTEM

Test and Procedure	Results and Indications	Proceed to
3.1 Check the ignition switch "on" position: Connect a jumper wire between the distributor side of the coil and ground, and a 12V test lamp between the switch side of the coil and ground. Remove the high tension lead from the coil. Turn the ignition switch on and jiggle the key.	If the lamp lights	3.2
	If the lamp flickers when the key is jiggled, replace the ignition switch.	3.3
	If the lamp doesn't light, check for loose or open connections. If none are found, remove the ignition switch and check for continuity. If the switch is faulty, replace it.	3.3

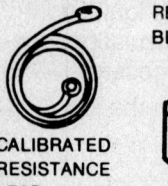

Checking the ignition switch "on" position

Test and Procedure	Results and Indications	Proceed to
3.2 Check the ballast resistor or resistance wire for an open circuit, using an ohmmeter.	Replace the resistor or resistance wire if the resistance is zero. **NOTE: Some ignition systems have no ballast resistor.**	3.3

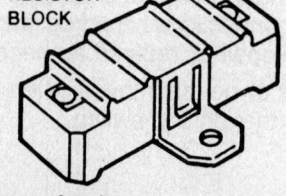

RESISTOR BLOCK

CALIBRATED RESISTANCE LEAD

Two types of resistors

Test and Procedure	Results and Indications	Proceed to
3.3 On point-type ignition systems, visually inspect the breaker points for burning, pitting or excessive wear. Gray coloring of the point contact surfaces is normal. Rotate the crankshaft until the contact heel rests on a high point of the distributor cam and adjust the point gap to specifications. On electronic ignition models, remove the distributor cap and visually inspect the armature. Ensure that the armature pin is in place, and that the armature is on tight and rotates when the engine is cranked. Make sure there are no cracks, chips or rounded edges on the armature.	If the breaker points are intact, clean the contact surfaces with fine emery cloth, and adjust the point gap to specifications. If the points are worn, replace them. On electronic systems, replace any parts which appear defective. If condition persists	3.4

Test and Procedure	Results and Indications	Proceed To
3.4 On point-type ignition systems, connect a dwell-meter between the distributor primary lead and ground. Crank the engine and observe the point dwell angle. On electronic ignition systems, conduct a stator (magnetic pickup assembly) test. See Electronic Ignition Unit Repair Section.	On point-type systems, adjust the dwell angle if necessary. **NOTE: Increasing the point gap decreases the dwell angle and vice-versa.** If the dwell meter shows little or no reading On electronic ignition systems, if the stator is bad, replace the stator. If the stator is good, proceed to the other tests in The Electronic Ignition Unit Repair Section.	**3.6** **3.5**

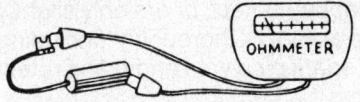

Dwell is a function of point gap

3.5 On the point-type ignition systems, check the condenser for short: connect an ohmeter across the condenser body and the pigtail lead.	If any reading other than infinite is noted, replace the condenser	**3.6**

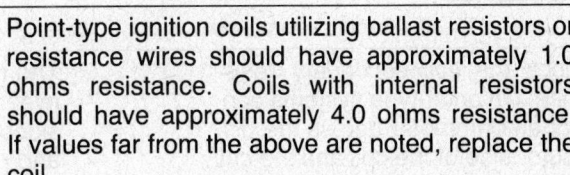

Checking the condenser for short

3.6 Test the coil primary resistance: On point-type ignition systems, connect an ohmmeter across the coil primary terminals, and read the resistance on the low scale. Note whether an external ballast resistor or resistance wire is used. On electronic ignition systems, test the coil primary resistance.	Point-type ignition coils utilizing ballast resistors or resistance wires should have approximately 1.0 ohms resistance. Coils with internal resistors should have approximately 4.0 ohms resistance. If values far from the above are noted, replace the coil.	**4.1**

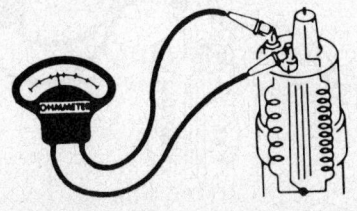

Checking the coil primary resistance

SECTION 4—SECONDARY ELECTRICAL SYSTEM

Test and Procedure	Results and Indications	Proceed to
4.1 Check for spark: Hold each spark plug wire approximately ¼" from ground with gloves or heavy, dry rag. Crank the engine, and observe the spark.	If no spark is evident	**4.2**
	If spark is good in some cylinders	**4.3**
	If spark is good in all cylinders	**4.6**

Check for spark at the plugs

4.2 Check for spark at the coil high tension lead: Remove the coil high tension lead from the distributor and position it approximately ¼" from ground. Crank the engine and observe spark. **CAUTION: This test should not be performed on engines equipped with electronic ignition.**	If the spark is good and consistent	**4.3**
	If the spark is good but intermittent, test the primary electrical system starting at 3.3.	**3.3**
	If the spark is weak or non-existent, replace the coil high tension lead, clean and tighten all connections and retest. If no improvement is noted	**4.4**

4.3 Visually inspect the distributor cap and rotor for burned or corroded contacts, cracks, carbon tracks, or moisture. Also check the fit of the rotor on the distributor shaft (where applicable).	If moisture is present, dry thoroughly, and retest per 4.1.	**4.1**
	If burned or excessively corroded contacts, cracks, or carbon tracks are noted, replace the defective part(s) and retest per 4.1.	**4.1**
	If the rotor and cap appear intact, or are only slightly corroded, clean the contacts thoroughly (including the cap towers and spark plug wire ends) and retest per 4.1.	
	If the spark is good in all cases	**4.6**
	If the spark is poor in all cases	**4.5**

CORRODED OR LOOSE WIRE — HIGH RESISTANCE CARBON — EXCESSIVE WEAR OF BUTTON — ROTOR TIP BURNED AWAY

Inspect the distributor cap and rotor

4.4 Check the coil secondary resistance: On point-type systems connect an ohmmeter across the distributor side of the coil and the coil tower. Read the resistance on the high scale of the ohmmeter. On electronic ignition systems, see The Electronic Ignition Unit Repair Section for specific tests.	The resistance of a satisfactory coil should be between 4,000 and 10,000 ohms. If resistance is considerably higher (i.e., 40,000 ohms) replace the coil and retest per 4.1. **NOTE: This does not apply to high performance coils.**	

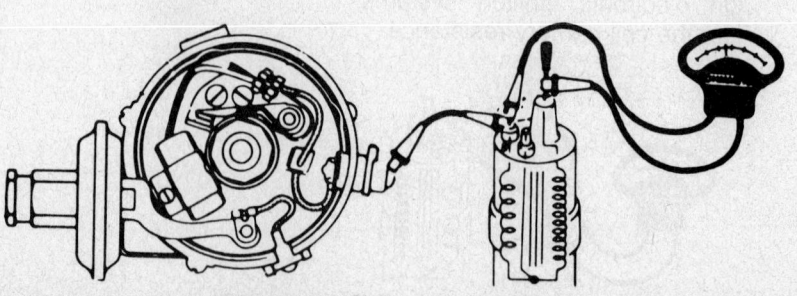

Testing the coil secondary resistance

Spark Plug Analysis

Normal

APPEARANCE

This plug is typical of one operating normally. The insulator nose varies from a light tan to grayish color with slight electrode wear. The presence of slight deposits is normal on used plugs and will have no adverse effect on engine performance. The spark plug heat range is correct for the engine and the engine is running normally.

CAUSE

Properly running engine

RECOMMENDATION

Before reinstalling this plug, the electrodes should be cleaned and filed square. Set the gap to specifications. If the plug has been in service for more than 10–12,000 miles, the entire set should probably be replaced with a fresh set of the same heat range.

Incorrect Heat Range

APPEARANCE

The effects of high temperature on a spark plug are indicated by clean white, often blistered insulator. This can also be accompanied by excessive wear of the electrode, and the absence of deposits.

CAUSE

Check for the correct spark plug heat range. A plug which is too hot for the engine can result in overheating. A car operated mostly at high speeds may require a colder plug. Also check ignition timing, cooling system level, fuel mixture and leaking intake manifold.

RECOMMENDATION

If all ignition and engine adjustments are known to be correct, and no other malfunction exists, install spark plugs one heat range colder.

Oil Deposits

APPEARANCE

The firing end of the plug is covered with a wet, oily coating.

CAUSE

The problem is poor oil control. On high mileage engines, oil is leaking past the rings or valve guides into the combustion chamber. A common cause is also a plugged PCV valve, and a ruptured fuel pump diaphragm can also cause this condition. Oil fouled plugs such as these are often found in new or recently overhauled engines, before normal oil control is achieved, and can be cleaned and reinstalled.

RECOMMENDATION

A hotter spark plug may temporarily relieve the problem, but the engine is probably in need of engine work.

Carbon Deposits

APPEARANCE

Carbon fouling is easily identified by the presence of dry, soft, black, sooty deposits.

CAUSE

Changing the heat range can often lead to carbon fouling, as can prolonged slow, stop-and-start driving. If the heat range is correct, carbon fouling can be attributed to a rich fuel mixture, sticking choke, clogged air cleaner, worn breaker points, retarded timing or low compression. If only one or two plugs are carbon fouled, check for corroded or cracked wires on the affected plugs. Also look for cracks in the distributor cap between the towers of affected cylinders.

RECOMMENDATION

After the problem is corrected, these plugs can be cleaned and reinstalled if not worn severely.

Ash Deposits

APPEARANCE

Ash deposits are characterized by light brown or white colored deposits crusted on the side or center electrodes. In some cases it may give the plug a rusty appearance.

CAUSE

Ash deposits are normally derived from oil or fuel additives burned during normal combustion. Normally they are harmless, though excessive amounts can cause misfiring. If deposits are excessive in short mileage, the valve guides may be worn. Reddish or rusty deposits are caused by manganese, an anti-knock compound replacing lead in unleaded gas. No engine malfunction is indicated.

RECOMMENDATION

Ash-fouled plugs can be cleaned, gapped and reinstalled.

Splash Deposits

APPEARANCE

Splash deposits occur in varying degrees as spotty deposits on the insulator.

CAUSE

These usually occur after a long delayed tune-up. By-products of combustion have accumulated on pistons and valves because of a delayed tune-up. Following tune-up or during hard acceleration, the deposits loosen and are thrown against the hot surface of the plug. If the deposits accumulate sufficiently, misfiring can occur.

RECOMMENDATION

These plugs can be cleaned, gapped and reinstalled.

High Speed Glazing

APPEARANCE

Glazing appears as shiny coating on the plug, either yellow or tan in color.

CAUSE

During hard, fast acceleration, plug temperatures rise suddenly. Deposits from normal combustion have no chance to fluff-off; instead, they melt on the insulator forming an electrically conductive coating which causes misfiring.

RECOMMENDATION

Glazed plugs are not easily cleaned. They should be replaced with a fresh set of plugs of the correct heat range. If the condition recurs, using plugs with a heat range one step colder may cure the problem.

Detonation

APPEARANCE

Detonation is usually characterized by a broken plug insulator.

CAUSE

A portion of the fuel charge will begin to burn spontaneously, from the increased heat following ignition. The explosion that results applies extreme pressure to engine components, frequently damaging spark plugs and pistons.

Detonation can result by over-advanced ignition timing, inferior gasoline (low octane) lean air fuel mixture, poor carburetion, engine lugging or an increase in compression ratio due to combustion chamber deposits or engine modification.

RECOMMENDATION

Replace the plugs after correcting the problem.

Test and Procedure	Results and Indications	Proceed To
4.5 Visually inspect the spark plug wires for cracking or brittleness. Ensure that no two wires are positioned so as to cause induction firing (adjacent and parallel). Remove each wire, one by one, and check resistance with an ohmmeter.	Replace any cracked or brittle wires. If any of the wires are defective, replace the entire set. Replace any wires with excessive resistance (over 8000 Ω per foot for suppression wire), and separate any wires that might cause induction firing.	**4.6**

Misfiring can be the result of spark plug leads to adjacent, consecutively firing cylinders running parallel and too close together

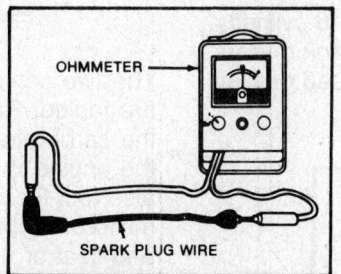

On point-type ignition systems, check the spark plug wires as shown. On electronic ignitions, do not remove the wire from the distributor cap terminal; instead, test through the cap

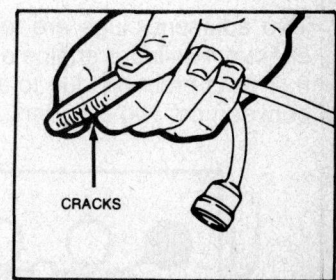

Spark plugs wires can be checked visually by bending them in a loop over your finger. This will reveal any cracks, burned or broken insulation. Any wire with cracked insulation should be replaced

Test and Procedure	Results and Indications	Proceed To
4.6 Remove the spark plugs, noting the cylinders from which they were removed, and evaluate according to the chart in this section.	See chart.	**See Chart**
4.7 Reinstall the spark plugs.		**4.8**

4.7 Reinstall the spark plugs.

NOTE: Modern electronic ignition systems generate extremely high voltages and high heats. The spark plug boots can soften and actually fuse to the ceramic insulator of the spark plugs after long exposures to high temperature and voltage. If this happens, the boot (and possibly the wire) must be replaced.

To help alleviate this condition, many manufacturers are recommending new silicone compounds to slow the deterioration. The compounds are generally nonconductive, protective lubricants that will not dry out, harden, or melt away. They form a weather-tight seal between rubber or plastic and metal and are found in several typical locations: Inside the insulating boots of spark plug wires, inside primary ignition circuit cable connectors, on distributor and rotor cap electrodes, and under the GM HEI control module.

Application Point	Silicone Compound
GENERAL MOTORS: Under HEI module	Supplied with new module, or use GE-642 or DC-340
FORD MOTOR COMPANY: Inside spark plug boots, on end of cable when installing new boot, and on rotor and cap electrodes	Ford part number D7AZ-19A331-A or use GE-627 or DC-111
CHRYSLER CORPORATION: ¼″ deep within spark control computer connector cavity coating rotor electrode	Use Mopar part number 2932524 or NLGI Grade 2 EP (not a silicone) supplied with new rotor, or use GE-628 or DC-111
AMERICAN MOTORS (Prestolite system): Distributor primary connector—coat male terminal, fill female ¼ full	AMC part number 8127445 or GE-623

GE: General Electric
DC: Dow Corning

Test and Procedure	Results and Indications	Proceed To

4.8 Examine the location of all the plugs.

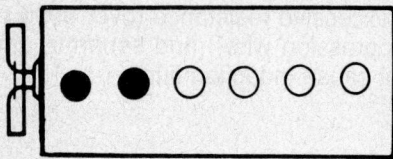

Two adjacent plugs are fouled in a 6-cylinder engine, 4-cylinder engine or either bank of a V-8. This is probably due to a blown head gasket between the two cylinders.

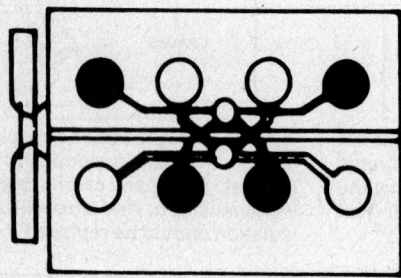

An unbalanced carburetor is indicated. Following the fuel flow on this particular design shows that the cylinders fed by the right-hand barrel are fouled from overly rich mixture, while the cylinders fed by the left-hand barrel are normal.

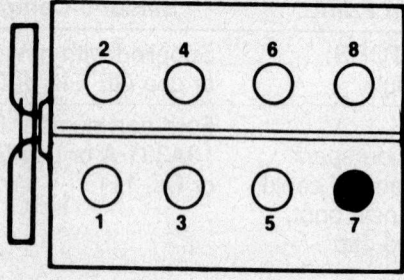

Finding one plug overheated may indicate an intake manifold leak near the affected cylinder. If the overheated plug is the second of two adjacent, consecutively firing plugs, it could be the result of ignition cross-firing. Separating the leads to these two plugs will eliminate cross-fire.

The following diagrams illustrate some of the conditions that the location of plugs will reveal.

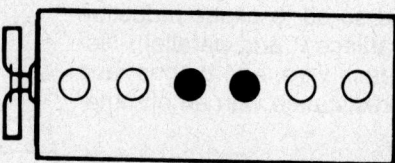

The two center plugs in a 6-cylinder engine are fouled. Raw fuel may be "boiled" out of the carburetor into the intake manifold after the engine is shut-off. Stop-start driving can also foul the center plugs, due to overly rich mixture. Proper float level, a new float needle and seat or use of an insulating spacer may help this problem.

If the four rear plugs are overheated, a cooling system problem is suggested. A thorough cleaning of the cooling system may restore coolant circulation and cure the problem.

Occasionally, the two rear plugs in large, lightly used V-8's will become oil fouled. High oil consumption and smoky exhaust may also be noticed. It is probably due to plugged oil drain holes in the rear of the cylinder head, causing oil to be sucked in around the valve stems. This usually occurs in the rear cylinders first, because the engine slants that way.

4.9

Test and Procedure	Results and Indications	Proceed To
4.9 Determine the static ignition timing. Using the crankshaft pulley timing marks as a guide, locate top dead center on the compression stroke of the number one cylinder.	The rotor should be pointing toward the No. 1 tower in the distributor cap, and, on electronic ignitions, the armature spoke for that cylinder should be lined up with the stator.	4.10
4.10 Check coil polarity: Connect a voltmeter negative lead to the coil high tension lead, and the positive lead to ground. **NOTE: Reverse the hook-up for positive ground systems.** Crank the engine momentarily. *Checking coil polarity*	If the voltmeter reads up-scale, the polarity is correct.	5.1
	If the voltmeter reads down-scale, reverse the coil polarity (switch the primary leads).	5.1

SECTION 5—FUEL SYSTEM

Test and Procedure	Results and Indications	Proceed to
5.1 Determine that the air filter is functioning efficiently: Hold paper elements up to a strong light, and attempt to see light through the filter.	Clean permanent air filters in solvent (or manufacturer's recommendation), and allow to dry. Replace paper elements through which light cannot be seen.	5.2
5.2 Determine whether a flooding condition exists: Flooding is identified by a strong gasoline odor, and excessive gasoline present in the throttle bore(s) of the carburetor. *If the engine floods repeatedly, check the choke butterfly flap*	If flooding is not evident	5.3
	If flooding is evident, permit the gasoline to dry for a few moments and restart.	
	If flooding doesn't recur	5.7
	If flooding is persistent	5.5
5.3 Check that fuel is reaching the carburetor: Detach the fuel line at the carburetor inlet. Hold the end of the line in a cup (not styrofoam), and crank the engine.	If fuel flows smoothly	5.7
	If fuel doesn't flow	5.4
	If fuel flows erratically.	
	NOTE: Make sure that there is fuel in the tank	

Check the fuel pump by disconnecting the output line (fuel pump-to-carburetor) at the carburetor and operating the starter briefly

Test and Procedure	Results and Indications	Proceed To
5.4 Test the fuel pump: Disconnect all fuel lines from the fuel pump. Hold a finger over the input fitting, crank the engine (with electric pump, turn the ignition or pump on); and feel for suction.	If suction is evident, blow out the fuel line to the tank with low pressure compressed air until bubbling is heard from the fuel filler neck. Also blow out the carburetor fuel line (both ends disconnected).	5.7
	If no suction is evident, replace or repair the fuel pump. **NOTE: Repeated oil fouling of the spark plugs, or a no-start condition, could be the result of a ruptured vacuum booster pump diaphragm, through which oil or gasoline is being drawn into the intake manifold (where applicable).**	5.7
5.5 Occasionally, small specks of dirt will clog the small jets and orifices in the carburetor. With the engine cold, hold a flat piece of wood or similar material over the carburetor, where possible, and crank the engine.	If the engine starts, but runs roughly the engine is probably not run enough. If the engine won't start.	5.9
5.6 Check the needle and seat: Tap the carburetor in the area of the needle and seat.	If flooding stops, a gasoline additive (e.g., Gumout) will often cure the problem.	5.7
	If flooding continues, check the fuel pump for excessive pressure at the carburetor (according to specifications). If the pressure is normal, the needle and seat must be removed and checked, and/or the float level adjusted.	5.7
5.7 Test the accelerator pump by looking into the throttle bores while operating the throttle.	If the accelerator pump appears to be operating normally	5.8
	If the accelerator pump is not operating, the pump must be reconditioned. Where possible, service the pump with the carburetor(s) installed on the engine. If necessary, remove the carburetor. Prior to removal	5.8

Check for gas at the carburetor by looking down the carburetor throat while someone moves the accelerator

Test and Procedure	Results and Indications	Proceed To
5.8 Determine whether the carburetor main fuel system is functioning: Spray a commercial starting fluid into the carburetor while attempting to start the engine.	If the engine starts, runs for a few seconds, and dies	5.9
	If the engine doesn't start	6.1
5.9 Uncommon fuel system malfunctions: See below:	If the problem is solved	6.1
	If the problem remains, remove and recondition the carburetor.	

Condition	Indication	Test	Prevailing Weather Conditions	Remedy
Vapor lock	Engine will not re-start shortly after running.	Cool the components of the fuel system until the engine starts. Vapor lock can be cured faster by draping a wet cloth over a mechanical fuel pump.	Hot to very hot	Ensure that the exhaust manifold heat control valve is operating. Check with the vehicle manufacturer for the recommended solution to vapor lock on the model in question.
Carburetor icing	Engine will not idle, stalls at low speeds.	Visually inspect the throttle plate area of the throttle bores for frost.	High humidity, 32–40° F.	Ensure that the exhaust manifold heat control valve is operating, and that the intake manifold heat riser is not blocked.
Water in the fuel	Engine sputters and stalls; may not start.	Pump a small amount of fuel into a glass jar. Allow to stand, and inspect for droplets of a layer of water.	High humidity, extreme temperature changes.	For droplets, use one or two cans of commercial gas line anti-freeze. For a layer of water, the tank must be drained, and the fuel lines blown out with compressed air.

SECTION 6—ENGINE COMPRESSION

Test and Procedure	Results and Indications	Proceed to
6.1 Test engine compression: Remove all spark plugs. Block the throttle wide open. Insert a compression gauge into a spark plug port, crank the engine to obtain the maximum reading, and record.	If compression is within limits on all cylinders	7.1
	If gauge reading is extremely low on all cylinders	6.2
	If gauge reading is low on one or two cylinders: (If gauge readings are identical and low on two or more adjacent cylinders, the head gasket must be replaced.)	6.2

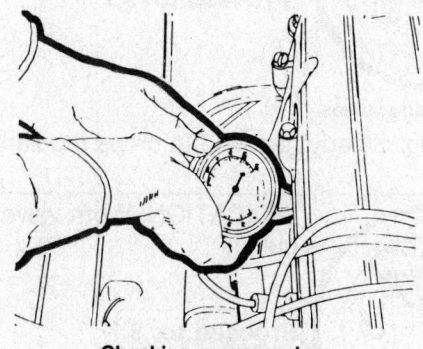

Checking compression

6.2 Test engine compression (wet): Squirt approximately 30 cc. of engine oil into each cylinder, and retest per 6.1.	If the readings improve, worn or cracked rings or broken pistons are indicated:	**See Car Section 7.1**
	If the readings do not improve, burned or excessively carboned valves or a jumped timing chain are indicated.	
	NOTE: A jumped timing chain is often indicated by difficult cranking.	

GENERAL TROUBLESHOOTING AND DIAGNOSIS

SECTION 7—ENGINE VACUUM

Test and Procedure	Results and Indications	Proceed to
7.1 Attach a vacuum gauge to the intake manifold beyond the throttle plate. Start the engine, and observe the action of the needle over the range of engine speeds.	See below.	**See below**

INDICATION: Normal engine in good condition

Proceed to: 8.1

Normal engine

Gauge reading: Steady, from 17–22 in./Hg.

INDICATION: Sticking valves or ignition miss

Proceed to: 9.1, 8.3

Sticking valves

Gauge reading: Intermittent fluctuation at idle

INDICATION: Late ignition or valve timing, low compression, stuck throttle valve, leaking carburetor or manifold gasket

Proceed to: 6.1

Incorrect valve timing

Gauge reading: Low (10–15 in./Hg) but steady

INDICATION: Improper carburetor adjustment or minor intake leak.

Proceed to: 7.2

Carburetor requires adjustment

Gauge reading: Drifting needle

INDICATION: Ignition miss, blown cylinder head gasket, leaking valve or weak valve spring

Proceed to: 8.3, 6.1

Blown head gasket

Gauge reading: Needle fluctuates as engine speed increases

INDICATION: Burnt valve or faulty valve clearance: Needle will fall when defective valve operates

Proceed to: 9.1

Burnt or leaking valves

Gauge reading: Steady needle, but drops regularly

INDICATION: Choked muffler, excessive back pressure in system

Proceed to: 10.1

Clogged exhaust system

Gauge reading: Gradual drop in reading at idle

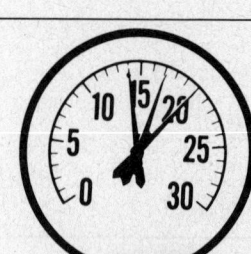

INDICATION: Worn valve guides

Proceed to: 9.1

Worn valve guides

Gauge reading: Needle vibrates excessively at idle, but steadies as engine speed increases

---

White pointer = steady gauge hand | Black pointer = fluctuating gauge hand

Test and Procedure	Results and Indications	Proceed To
7.2 Attach a vacuum gauge per 7.1, and test for an intake manifold leak. Squirt a small amount of oil around the intake manifold gaskets, carburetor gaskets, plugs and fittings. Observe the action of the vacuum gauge.	If the reading improves, replace the indicated gasket, or seal the indicated fitting or plug:	8.1
	If the reading remains low:	7.3
7.3 Test all vacuum hoses and accessories for leaks as described in 7.2. Also check the carburetor body (dashpots, automatic choke mechanism, throttle shafts) for leaks in the same manner.	If the reading improves, service or replace the offending part(s):	8.1
	If the reading remains low:	6.1

SECTION 8—SECONDARY ELECTRICAL SYSTEM

Test and Procedure	Results and Indications	Proceed to
8.1 Remove the distributor cap and check to make sure that the rotor turns when the engine is cranked. Visually inspect the distributor components.	Clean, tighten or replace any components which appear defective.	8.2
8.2 Connect a timing light (per manufacturer's recommendation) and check the dynamic ignition timing. Disconnect and plug the vacuum hose(s) to the distributor if specified, start the engine, and observe the timing marks at the specified engine speed.	If the timing is not correct, adjust to specifications by rotating the distributor in the engine: (Advance timing by rotating distributor opposite normal direction of rotor rotation, retard timing by rotating distributor in same direction as rotor rotation.)	8.3
8.3 Check the operation of the distributor advance mechanism(s): To test the mechanical advance, disconnect the vacuum lines from the distributor advance unit and observe the timing marks with a timing light as the engine speed is increased from idle. If the mark moves smoothly, without hesitation, it may be assumed that the mechanical advance is functioning properly. To test vacuum advance and/or retard systems, alternately crimp and release the vacuum line, and observe the timing mark for movement. If movement is noted, the system is operating.	If the systems are functioning	8.4
	If the systems are not functioning, remove the distributor, and test on a distributor tester.	8.4
8.4 Locate an ignition miss: With the engine running, remove each spark plug wire, one at a time, until one is found that doesn't cause the engine to roughen and slow down. **CAUTION: Do not pull on the wire to remove the boot from the plug. Be sure your hand is insulated from the wire.**	When the missing cylinder is identified	4.1

GENERAL TROUBLESHOOTING AND DIAGNOSIS

SECTION 9—VALVE TRAIN

Test and Procedure	Results and Indications	Proceed to
9.1 Evaluate the valve train: Remove the valve cover, and ensure that the valves are adjusted to specifications. A mechanic's stethoscope may be used to aid in the diagnosis of the valve train. By pushing the probe on or near push rods or rockers, valve noise often can be isolated. A timing light also may be used to diagnose valve problems. Connect the light according to manufacturer's recommendations, and start the engine. Vary the firing moment of the light by increasing the engine speed (and therefore the ignition advance), and moving the trigger from cylinder to cylinder. Observe the movement of each valve.	Sticking valves or erratic valve train motion can be observed with the timing light. The cylinder head must be disassembled for repairs.	See Car Section
9.2 Check the valve timing: Locate top dead center of the No. 1 piston, and install a degree wheel or tape on the crankshaft pulley or damper with zero corresponding to an index mark on the engine. Rotate the crankshaft in its direction of rotation, and observe the opening of the No. 1 cylinder intake valve. The opening should correspond with the correct mark on the degree wheel according to specifications.	If the timing is not correct, the timing cover must be removed for further investigation.	See Car Section

SECTION 10—EXHAUST SYSTEM

Test and Procedure	Results and Indications	Proceed to
10.1 Determine whether the exhaust manifold heat control valve is operating: Operate the valve by hand to determine whether it is free to move. If the valve is free, run the engine to operating temperature and observe the action of the valve, to ensure that it is opening.	If the valve sticks, spray it with a suitable solvent, open and close the valve to free it, and retest. If the valve functions properly	10.2
	If the valve does not free, or does not operate, replace the valve.	10.2
10.2 Ensure that there are no exhaust restrictions: Visually inspect the exhaust system for kinks, dents, or crushing. Also note that gases are flowing freely from the tailpipe at all engine speeds, indicating no restriction in the muffler or resonator.	Replace any damaged portion of the system.	11.1

SECTION 11—COOLING SYSTEM

Test and Procedure	Results and Indications	Proceed to
11.1 Visually inspect the fan belt for glazing, cracks, and fraying, and replace if necessary. Tighten the belt so that the longest span has approximately ½″ play at its mid-point under thumb pressure (see Maintenance Section).	Replace or tighten the fan belt as necessary.	**11.2**

Checking belt tension

Test and Procedure	Results and Indications	Proceed to
11.2 Check the fluid level of the cooling system.	If full or slightly low, fill as necessary.	**11.5**
	If extremely low	**11.3**
11.3 Visually inspect the external portions of the cooling system (radiator, radiator hoses, thermostat elbow, water pump seals, heater hoses, etc.) for leaks. If none are found, pressurize the cooling system to 14–15 psi.	If cooling system holds the pressure	**11.5**
	If cooling system loses pressure rapidly, reinspect external parts of the system for leaks under pressure. If none are found, check dipstick for coolant in crankcase. If no coolant is present, but pressure loss continues	**11.4**
	If coolant is evident in crankcase, remove cylinder head(s), and check gasket(s). If gaskets are intact, block and cylinder head(s) should be checked for cracks or holes.	
	If the gasket(s) is blown, replace, and purge the crankcase of coolant.	**12.6**
	NOTE: Occasionally, due to atmospheric and driving conditions, condensation of water can occur in the crankcase. This causes the oil to appear milky white. To remedy, run the engine until hot, and change the oil and oil filter.	
11.4 Check for combustion leaks into the cooling system: Pressurize the cooling system as above. Start the engine, and observe the pressure gauge. If the needle fluctuates, remove each spark plug wire, one at a time, noting which cylinder(s) reduce or eliminate the fluctuation.	Cylinders which reduce or eliminate the fluctuation, when the spark plug wire is removed, are leaking into the cooling system. Replace the head gasket on the affected cylinder bank(s).	**See Car Section**

Pressurizing the cooling system

Test and Procedure	Results and Indications	Proceed To
11.5 Check the radiator pressure cap: Attach a radiator pressure tester to the radiator cap (wet the seal prior to installation). Quickly pump up the pressure, noting the point at which the cap releases.	If the cap releases within ±1 psi of the specified rating, it is operating properly.	**11.6**
	If the cap releases at more than ±1 psi of the specified rating, it should be replaced.	**11.6**

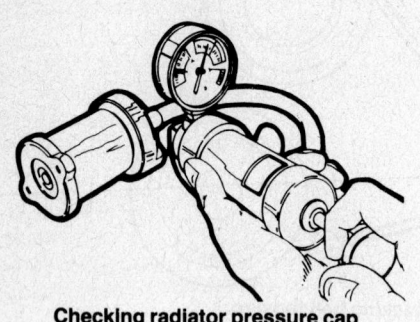

Checking radiator pressure cap

Test and Procedure	Results and Indications	Proceed To
11.6 Test the thermostat: Start the engine cold, remove the radiator cap, and insert a thermometer into the radiator. Allow the engine to idle. After a short while, there will be a sudden, rapid increase in coolant temperature. The temperature at which this sharp rise stops is the thermostat opening temperature.	If the thermostat opens at or about the specified temperature	**11.7**
	If the temperature doesn't increase (If the temperature increases slowly and gradually, replace the thermostat.)	**11.7**
11.7 Check the water pump: Remove the thermostat elbow and the thermostat, disconnect the coil high tension lead (to prevent starting), and crank the engine momentarily.	If coolant flows, replace the thermostat and retest per 11.6.	**11.6**
	If coolant doesn't flow, reverse flush the cooling system to alleviate any blockage that might exist. If system is not blocked, and coolant will not flow, replace the water pump.	**See Car Section**

SECTION 12—LUBRICATION

Test and Procedure	Results and Indications	Proceed to
12.1 Check the oil pressure gauge or warning light: If the gauge shows low pressure, or the light is on for no obvious reason, remove the oil pressure sender. Install an accurate oil pressure gauge and run the engine momentarily.	If oil pressure builds normally, run engine for a few moments to determine that it is functioning normally, and replace the sender.	—
	If the pressure remains low	**12.2**
	If the pressure surges	**12.3**
	If the oil pressure is zero	**12.3**
12.2 Visually inspect the oil: If the oil is watery or very thin, milky, or foamy, replace the oil and oil filter.	If the oil is normal	**12.3**
	If after replacing oil the pressure remains low	**12.3**
	If after replacing oil the pressure becomes normal	—
12.3 Inspect the oil pressure relief valve and spring, to ensure that it is not sticking or stuck. Remove and thoroughly clean the valve, spring, and the valve body.	If the oil pressure improves	—
	If no improvement is noted	**12.4**

Test and Procedure	Results and Indications	Proceed To
12.4 Check to ensure that the oil pump is not cavitating (sucking air instead of oil): See that the crankcase is neither over nor underfull, and that the pickup in the sump is in the proper position and free from sludge.	Fill or drain the crankcase to the proper capacity, and clean the pickup screen in solvent if necessary. If no improvement is noted	**12.5**
12.5 Inspect the oil pump drive and the oil pump:	If the pump drive or the oil pump appear to be defective, service as necessary and retest per 12.1.	**12.1**
	If the pump drive and pump appear to be operating normally, the engine should be disassembled to determine where blockage exists.	
12.6 Purge the engine of ethylene glycol coolant: Competely drain the crankcase and the oil filter. Obtain a commercial butyl cellosolve base solvent, designated for this purpose, and follow the instructions precisely. Following this, install a new oil filter and refill the crankcase with the proper weight oil. The next oil and filter change should follow shortly thereafter (1000 miles).		

GENERAL TROUBLESHOOTING AND DIAGNOSIS

Diesel Engine Troubleshooting

NOTE: The following troubleshooting procedures cover problems usually associated with diesel engines. Those problems common to both gasoline and diesel engines are covered in the gasoline engine troubleshooting procedures.

INDEX TO PROBLEMS

SECTION 1—Fuel System

Test and Procedure		Results and Indication	Proceed To
1.1a	Check for pressure at the outlet of the feed pump	If pressure exists, there is a clog in the supply line. Clean or replace it. If there is little or no pressure at the outlet, the filter is clogged. Clean or replace the filter. If the filter is clear, the feed pump piston is inoperative. Relace it.	1.1b
1.1b	Check the feed pump valves	If the inlet and outlet valves do not operate, the check valve or spring is broken. Replace it.	1.2a
1.2a	Check for fuel leakage at the overflow or return line	A clogged filter can result in high pressure causing leakage. Replace the filter.	1.2b
1.2b	Check for fuel in the filter leaking at the overflow valve	If leakage is found, the overflow valve is damaged. Replace it.	1.2c
1.2c	Check for leakage at the injection pump overflow valve	If leakage is found, it is caused by: damaged overflow valve, sticking plunger, or sticking delivery valve. Replace the defective part(s).	1.2d
1.2d	Check the injection pump plunger feed pressures.	If pressure at the plungers is low, replace the plunger(s).	1.2e

Test and Procedure		Results and Indication	Proceed To
1.2e	Check to make sure the injection pump is operating	An inoperative pump is caused by: a damaged or missing shaft key, or a damaged drive gear train.	1.3a
1.3a	Check that the pump timing marks are correctly aligned in the gear train	Incorrect timing marks alignment must be corrected.	1.3b
1.3b	Check that the injection pump is properly mounted	Remove and install the pump correctly	1.4a
1.4a	Install an injection nozzle on a tester and make sure that fuel is continuously ejected	A broken or intermittent stream is caused by a damaged spring or a sticking nozzle needle	1.4b
1.4b	With the nozzle on the tester as in 1.4a, check that shutoff is clean with no dribble or afterdrip	Dribble is caused by a defective nozzle valve seat. Replace the nozzle.	1.4c
1.4c	Using a tester, check injection pressure	Low pressure is a result of a weak spring. Replace the spring or adjust the initial injection pressure.	1.5a
1.5a	See 1.2a	Proceed as in 1.2a	1.5b
1.5b	Check for water in the fuel	Drain and clean the tank	1.5c
1.5c	Check for air in the fuel lines	Air can be introduced through a damaged fuel inlet line, a loose inlet line connector or a damaged gasket	1.5d
1.5d	Check for insufficient fuel feed	Insufficient fuel feed is caused by: a damaged feed pump, a clogged tank vent, or a clogged filter. Replace or repair as necessary.	1.6a
1.6a	Check the control rack action for smooth operation	Uneven control rack operation is caused by: a sticking plunger, improper meshing of the rack and pinion, poor seating of the plunger spring, insufficient clearance between the plunger and lower spring seat, or an overly tight delivery valve holder. Replace or adjust as necessary.	1.6b
1.6b	Check that the injection pump discharge is uniform	If the output is uneven, adjust as necessary	1.6c
1.6c	Check that the injection pump discharge volume is adequate	An inadequate discharge volume is caused by a worn plunger or a broken spring	1.6d
1.6d	Check for even low speed engine performance	If the engine performs unevenly or erratically at low speed only, a worn feed pump piston or defective feed pump valve is the cause.	1.6e
1.6e	Check for smooth engine operation throughout the operating range	This problem is usually caused by mechanical governor defects such as: a defective low speed spring, defective damper spring, or excessive friction among moving parts. Replace the defective parts.	1.6f
1.6f	Check the injectors on a tester	Improper nozzle operation should be corrected accordingly	1.7a
1.7a	Check the operating governor	A broken or weak spring in the governor will prevent full speed operation.	1.7b
1.7b	Check the injectors on a tester for a drop in injector output	A drop in output is caused by a sticking needle or a dirty nozzle. Replace or clean as necessary.	1.8a

GENERAL TROUBLESHOOTING AND DIAGNOSIS

Test and Procedure		Results and Indications	Proceed To
1.8a	Check the injection pump for proper rack and pinion action	A catching or dirty rack and pinion will cause overspeeding.	1.8b
1.8b	Check the governor adjustment	An improperly adjusted governor will cause overspeeding. Adjust.	1.9a
1.9a	Check the injection pump output	Low output can be caused by: Incorrect adjustment—Adjust Loose delivery valve—Tighten Broken delivery valve seal—Replace Poor valve seat contact—Replace Broken/weak delivery valve spring—Replace	1.9b
1.9b	Check for unusual noise at the injection pump	A noisy pump is an indication of a broken plunger spring	1.9c
1.9c	Check plunger operation	A sticking injection pump plunger will cause power loss. Replace.	1.9d
1.9d	Check the injection timer	A lag in injection timing is caused by large clearances in the timer due to wear. Replace.	1.9e
1.9e	Check for air or water in the fuel	Bleed the air or drain the fuel and clean the tank and lines	1.9f
1.9f	Check the injection timing	Readjust timing if necessary	1.10a
1.10a	Check the initial injection timing	Adjust if necessary	1.10b
1.10b	Check the injection pressure	High pressure will cause knock. Adjust as necessary	1.10c
1.10c	Check the injector nozzle	A clogged nozzle causes knock. Clean or replace the nozzle.	1.11a
1.11a	Check the injection pump output and timing	Excessive output, coupled with incorrect timing causes knock. Adjust as necessary	1.11b
1.11b	Check the delivery valve seat	Replace a defective seat	1.11c
1.11c	Check the pump plungers	Replace badly worn plungers	1.11d
1.11d	Check injector opening pressure on a tester	Adjust as necessary	1.11e
1.11e	Check the injector	Replace a broken nozzle spring or sticking needle.	

SECTION 2—ENGINE MECHANICAL

Test and Procedure		Results and Indications	Proceed To
2.1a	Check for piston seizing	Seized pistons are caused by low oil pressure, oil breakdown, or overheating. Replace the pistons and liners.	2.1b
2.1b	Check for a damaged flywheel ring gear	A damaged ring gear will cause poor meshing with the starter. Replace the ring gear.	2.1c
2.1c	Make a compression check	Low compression can be caused by: sticking rings, worn rings, worn liners. Replace the rings or liners.	2.2a
2.2a	A knocking noise at idle or during acceleration can be caused by a variety of wear problems.	Use a stethoscope or similar listening device to try to pinpoint the source of the noise. Among other reasons for knocking are: piston pins, rod bearings, loose rod caps, crankshaft journals and/or bearings, crankshaft thrust washer. Replace any worn parts.	2.2b
2.2b	An infrequently encountered noise is a continuous growl during acceleration	This problem is usually caused by problems in the engine timing gears. Poor contact, excessive backlash or loose gears are usually at fault.	2.2c
2.2c	Intermittent noises are the hardest to find. They are usually caused by broken moving parts.	Check the gear train for a chipped or cracked gear; the oil pan for broken parts or foreign objects or the cylinder head for a broken valve or valve spring.	2.3
2.3	Check for oil in the combustion chambers	Oil entering the combustion chambers will cause the engine to overspeed if the amount of oil is too great, or run unevenly. Check for broken or sticking rings, bad head gasket(s) or worn valve guides.	2.4
2.4	Check the compression	Low compression is the main cause of power loss. The main causes for low compression are: worn rings or liners, cracked valves, warped head or block, and bad head gasket.	2.5
2.5	A large amount of black exhaust is caused by low compression	See 2.4 above	2.6
2.6	If the engine stops suddenly during operation, the cause is usually sudden damage	Check the pistons, main bearings or rod bearings for lack of lubrication. A seized camshaft is also a result of low or no lubrication. Check the timing gears for damage.	2.7
2.7	Check for excessive clearance between the bearings and journals on both the mains and rod bearings. Check the oil pressure.	Replace as necessary. Replace the pump as necessary.	2.8
2.8	Aside from the usual leaking gasket problems, check the condition of the combustion chamber O-rings.	Replace as necessary	2.9
2.9	Compression leakage is usually caused by a seal defect between the head and the block	Check the head gasket; check for loose head bolts; check for head or block warpage. Replace or repair as necessary.	

Engine Overheating Troubleshooting

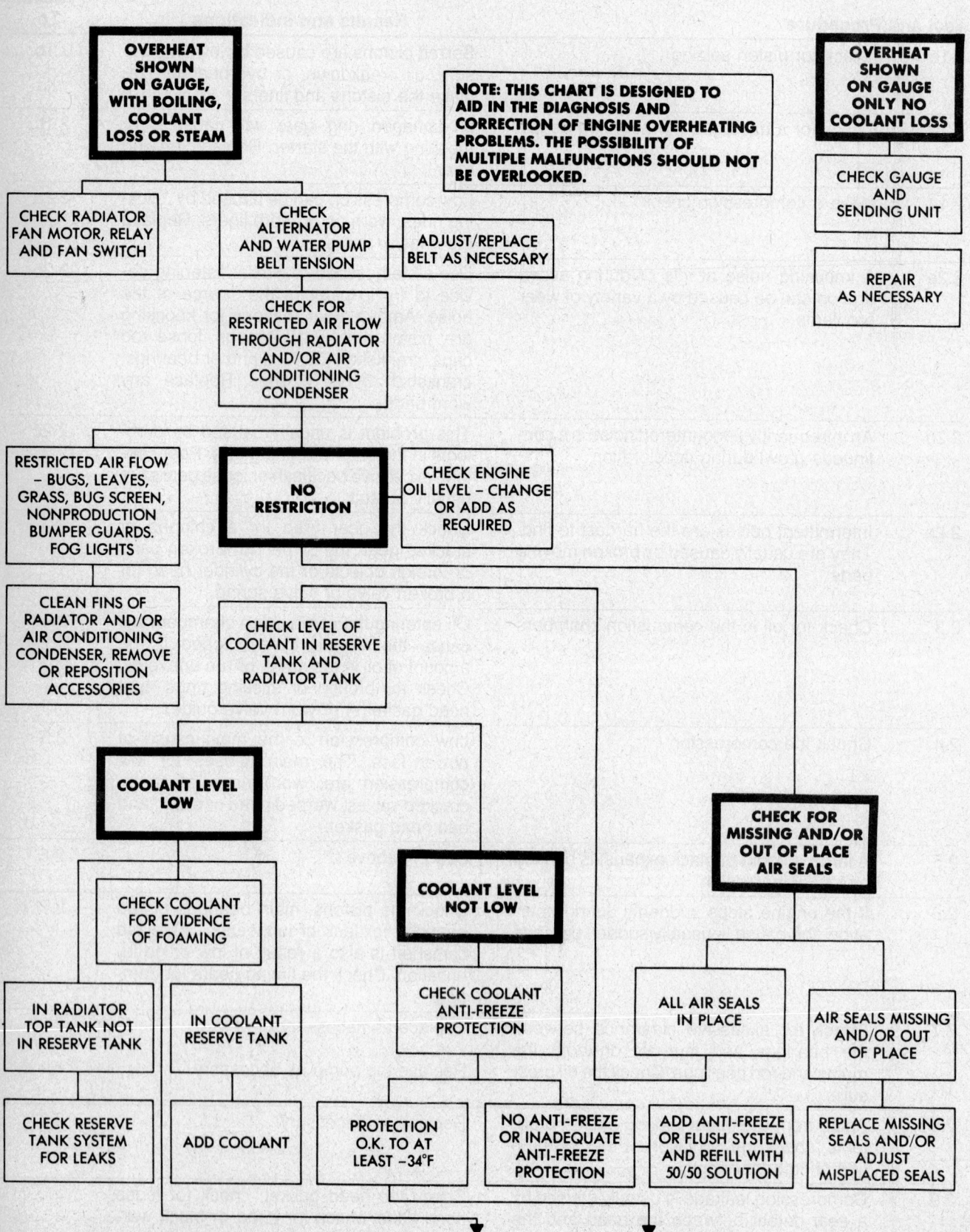

OVERHEAT SHOWN ON GAUGE, WITH BOILING, COOLANT LOSS OR STEAM

NOTE: THIS CHART IS DESIGNED TO AID IN THE DIAGNOSIS AND CORRECTION OF ENGINE OVERHEATING PROBLEMS. THE POSSIBILITY OF MULTIPLE MALFUNCTIONS SHOULD NOT BE OVERLOOKED.

OVERHEAT SHOWN ON GAUGE ONLY NO COOLANT LOSS

CHECK RADIATOR FAN MOTOR, RELAY AND FAN SWITCH

CHECK ALTERNATOR AND WATER PUMP BELT TENSION

ADJUST/REPLACE BELT AS NECESSARY

CHECK GAUGE AND SENDING UNIT

REPAIR AS NECESSARY

CHECK FOR RESTRICTED AIR FLOW THROUGH RADIATOR AND/OR AIR CONDITIONING CONDENSER

RESTRICTED AIR FLOW – BUGS, LEAVES, GRASS, BUG SCREEN, NONPRODUCTION BUMPER GUARDS. FOG LIGHTS

NO RESTRICTION

CHECK ENGINE OIL LEVEL – CHANGE OR ADD AS REQUIRED

CLEAN FINS OF RADIATOR AND/OR AIR CONDITIONING CONDENSER, REMOVE OR REPOSITION ACCESSORIES

CHECK LEVEL OF COOLANT IN RESERVE TANK AND RADIATOR TANK

COOLANT LEVEL LOW

CHECK COOLANT FOR EVIDENCE OF FOAMING

COOLANT LEVEL NOT LOW

CHECK FOR MISSING AND/OR OUT OF PLACE AIR SEALS

IN RADIATOR TOP TANK NOT IN RESERVE TANK

IN COOLANT RESERVE TANK

CHECK COOLANT ANTI-FREEZE PROTECTION

ALL AIR SEALS IN PLACE

AIR SEALS MISSING AND/OR OUT OF PLACE

CHECK RESERVE TANK SYSTEM FOR LEAKS

ADD COOLANT

PROTECTION O.K. TO AT LEAST –34°F

NO ANTI-FREEZE OR INADEQUATE ANTI-FREEZE PROTECTION

ADD ANTI-FREEZE OR FLUSH SYSTEM AND REFILL WITH 50/50 SOLUTION

REPLACE MISSING SEALS AND/OR ADJUST MISPLACED SEALS

Engine Overheating Troubleshooting

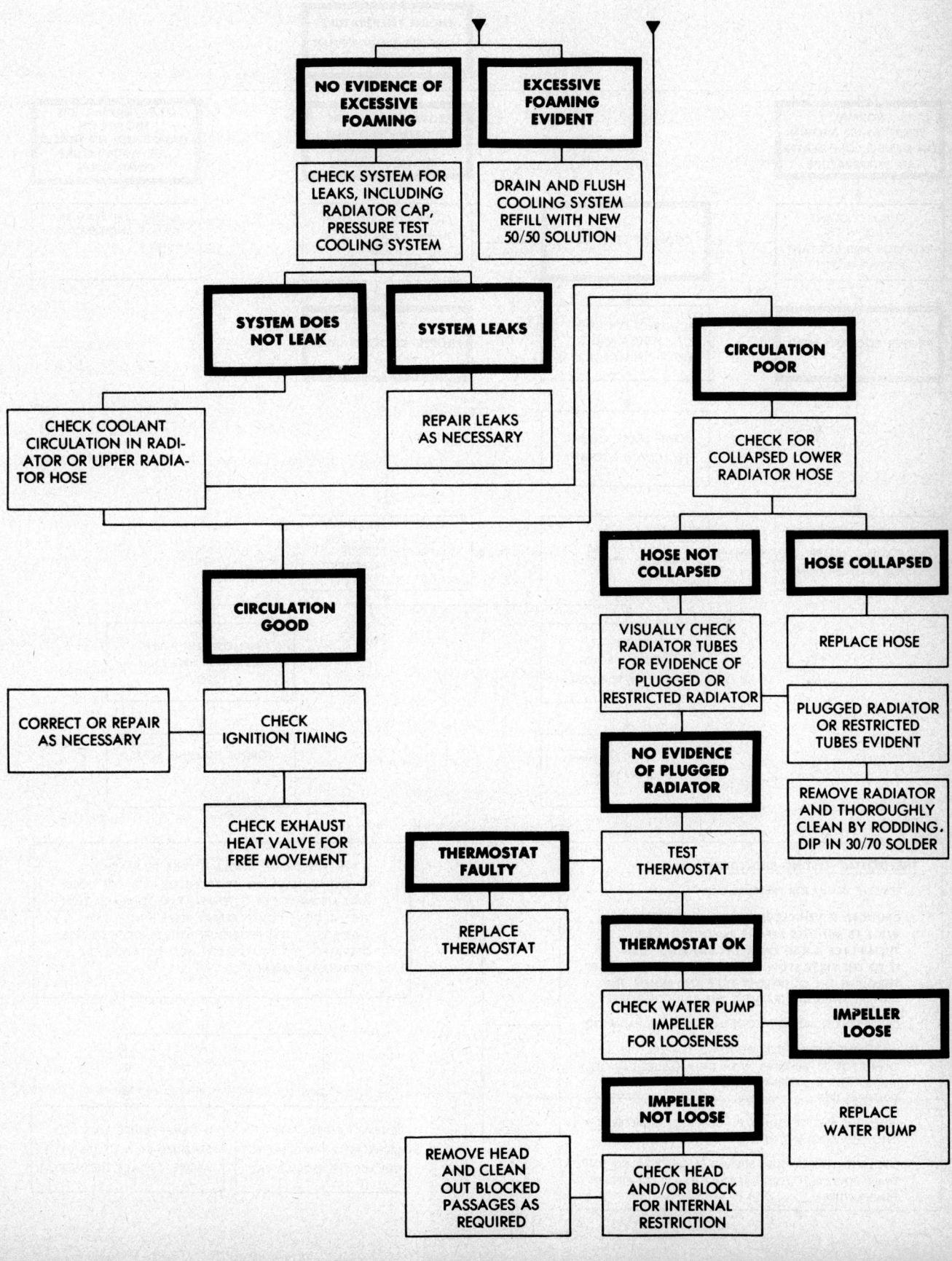

GENERAL TROUBLESHOOTING AND DIAGNOSIS

Low Engine Temperature Troubleshooting

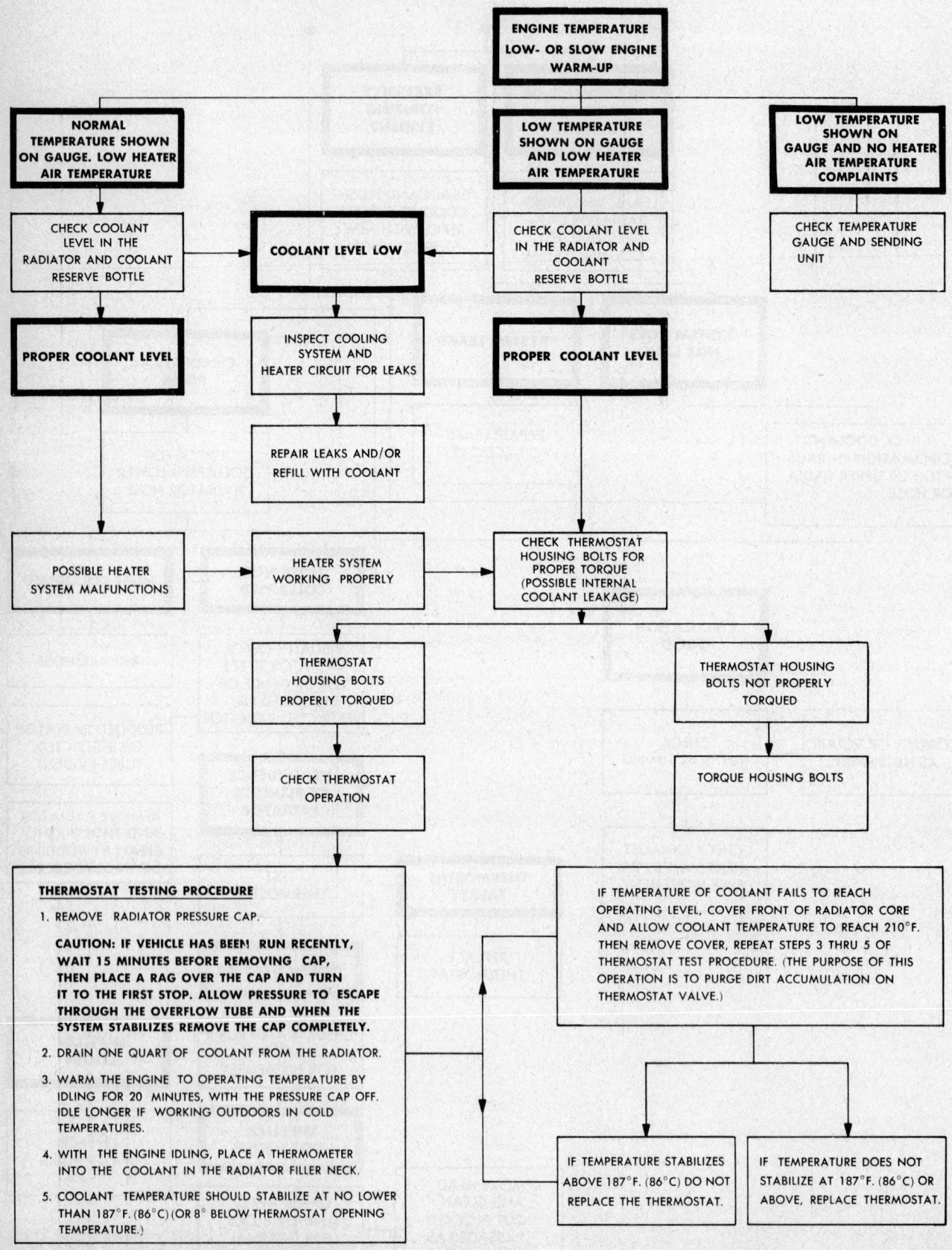

ENGINE TEMPERATURE LOW- OR SLOW ENGINE WARM-UP

NORMAL TEMPERATURE SHOWN ON GAUGE. LOW HEATER AIR TEMPERATURE

LOW TEMPERATURE SHOWN ON GAUGE AND LOW HEATER AIR TEMPERATURE

LOW TEMPERATURE SHOWN ON GAUGE AND NO HEATER AIR TEMPERATURE COMPLAINTS

CHECK COOLANT LEVEL IN THE RADIATOR AND COOLANT RESERVE BOTTLE

COOLANT LEVEL LOW

CHECK COOLANT LEVEL IN THE RADIATOR AND COOLANT RESERVE BOTTLE

CHECK TEMPERATURE GAUGE AND SENDING UNIT

PROPER COOLANT LEVEL

INSPECT COOLING SYSTEM AND HEATER CIRCUIT FOR LEAKS

PROPER COOLANT LEVEL

REPAIR LEAKS AND/OR REFILL WITH COOLANT

POSSIBLE HEATER SYSTEM MALFUNCTIONS

HEATER SYSTEM WORKING PROPERLY

CHECK THERMOSTAT HOUSING BOLTS FOR PROPER TORQUE (POSSIBLE INTERNAL COOLANT LEAKAGE)

THERMOSTAT HOUSING BOLTS PROPERLY TORQUED

THERMOSTAT HOUSING BOLTS NOT PROPERLY TORQUED

CHECK THERMOSTAT OPERATION

TORQUE HOUSING BOLTS

THERMOSTAT TESTING PROCEDURE

1. REMOVE RADIATOR PRESSURE CAP.

   CAUTION: IF VEHICLE HAS BEEN RUN RECENTLY, WAIT 15 MINUTES BEFORE REMOVING CAP, THEN PLACE A RAG OVER THE CAP AND TURN IT TO THE FIRST STOP. ALLOW PRESSURE TO ESCAPE THROUGH THE OVERFLOW TUBE AND WHEN THE SYSTEM STABILIZES REMOVE THE CAP COMPLETELY.

2. DRAIN ONE QUART OF COOLANT FROM THE RADIATOR.

3. WARM THE ENGINE TO OPERATING TEMPERATURE BY IDLING FOR 20 MINUTES, WITH THE PRESSURE CAP OFF. IDLE LONGER IF WORKING OUTDOORS IN COLD TEMPERATURES.

4. WITH THE ENGINE IDLING, PLACE A THERMOMETER INTO THE COOLANT IN THE RADIATOR FILLER NECK.

5. COOLANT TEMPERATURE SHOULD STABILIZE AT NO LOWER THAN 187°F. (86°C) (OR 8° BELOW THERMOSTAT OPENING TEMPERATURE.)

IF TEMPERATURE OF COOLANT FAILS TO REACH OPERATING LEVEL, COVER FRONT OF RADIATOR CORE AND ALLOW COOLANT TEMPERATURE TO REACH 210°F. THEN REMOVE COVER, REPEAT STEPS 3 THRU 5 OF THERMOSTAT TEST PROCEDURE. (THE PURPOSE OF THIS OPERATION IS TO PURGE DIRT ACCUMULATION ON THERMOSTAT VALVE.)

IF TEMPERATURE STABILIZES ABOVE 187°F. (86°C) DO NOT REPLACE THE THERMOSTAT.

IF TEMPERATURE DOES NOT STABILIZE AT 187°F. (86°C) OR ABOVE, REPLACE THERMOSTAT.

DRIVELINE
Clutch System Troubleshooting

Condition	Possible Cause	Corrective Action
Clutch chatter	1. Grease on driven plate (disc) facing. 2. Binding clutch linkage. 3. Loose, damaged facings on driven plate (disc). 4. Engine mounts loose. 5. Incorrect height adjustment of pressure plate release levers. 6. Clutch housing or housing to transmission adapter misalignment. 7. Loose driven plate hub.	1. Replace plate. 2. Check for worn, bent, broken parts. Replace as required. Lube linkage. 3. Replace driven plate. 4. Tighten mounts. Replace if damaged. 5. Adjust release lever height. 6. Check bore and face run out. Correct as required. 7. Replace driven plate.
Clutch grabbing	1. Oil, grease on driven plate (disc) facing. 2. Broken pressure plate. 3. Warped or binding driven plate. Driven plate binding on clutch shaft.	1. Replace driven plate. 2. Replace pressure plate. 3. Replace warped driven plate. Replace clutch shaft if defective, scored, worn.
Clutch slips	1. Lack of lubrication in clutch linkage (linkage binds, causes incomplete engagement. 2. Incorrect pedal, or linkage adjustment. 3. Broken pressure plate springs. 4. Weak pressure plate springs. 5. Grease on driven plate facings (disc).	1. Lubricate linkage. 2. Adjust as required. 3. Replace pressure plate. 4. Replace pressure plate. 5. Replace driven plate.
Incomplete clutch release	1. Incorrect pedal or linkage adjustment or linkage binding. 2. Incorrect height adjustment on pressure plate release levers. 3. Loose, broken facings on driven plate (disc). 4. Bent, dished, warped driven plate caused by overheating.	1. Adjust as required. Lubricate linkage. 2. Adjust release lever height. 3. Replace driven plate. 4. Replace driven plate.
Grinding, whirring grating noise when pedal is depressed	1. Worn or defective throwout bearing. 2. Starter drive teeth contacting flywheel ring gear teeth.	1. Replace throwout bearing. 2. Look for milled or polished teeth on ring gear. Align clutch housing, replace starter drive or drive spring as required.
Squeal, howl, trumpeting noise when pedal is being released (occurs during first inch to inch and one-half of pedal travel)	1. Pilot bushing worn or lack of lubricant.	1. Replace worn bushing. If bushing appears OK, polish bushing with emery, soak lube wick in oil, lube bushing with oil, apply film of chassis grease to clutch shaft pilot hub, reassemble. **NOTE:** Bushing wear may be due to misalignment of clutch housing or housing to transmission adapter.
Vibration or clutch pedal pulsation with clutch disengaged (pedal fully depressed)	1. Worn or defective engine transmission mounts. 2. Flywheel run out, or damaged or defective clutch components.	1. Inspect and replace as required. 2. Replace components as required. (Flywheel run out at face not to exceed 0.005″).

Manual Transmission Troubleshooting

Condition	Probable Cause
Jumping out of high gear	1. Misalignment of transmission case or clutch housing. 2. Worn pilot bearing in crankshaft. 3. Bent transmission shaft. 4. Worn high speed sliding gear. 5. Worn teeth in clutch shaft. 6. Insufficient spring tension on shifter rail plunger. 7. Bent or loose shifter fork. 8. End-play in clutch shaft. 9. Gears not engaging completely. 10. Loose or worn bearings on clutch shaft or mainshaft.
Sticking in high gear	1. Clutch not releasing fully. 2. Burred or battered teeth on clutch shaft. 3. Burred or battered transmission mainshaft. 4. Frozen synchronizing clutch. 5. Stuck shifter rail plunger. 6. Gearshift lever twisting and binding shifter rail. 7. Battered teeth on high speed sliding gear or on sleeve. 8. Lack of lubrication. 9. Improper lubrication. 10. Corroded transmission parts. 11. Defective mainshaft pilot bearing.
Jumping out of second gear	1. Insufficient spring tension on shifter rail plunger. 2. Bent or loose shifter fork. 3. Gears not engaging completely. 4. End-play in transmission mainshaft. 5. Loose transmission gear bearing. 6. Defective mainshaft pilot bearing. 7. Bent transmission shaft. 8. Worn teeth on second speed sliding gear or sleeve. 9. Loose or worn bearings on transmission mainshaft. 10. End-play in countershaft.
Sticking in second gear	1. Clutch not releasing fully. 2. Burred or battered teeth on sliding sleeve. 3. Burred or battered transmission mainshaft. 4. Frozen synchronizing clutch. 5. Stuck shifter rail plunger. 6. Gearshift lever twisting and binding shifter rail. 7. Lack of lubrication. 8. Second speed transmission gear bearings locked will give same effect as gears stuck in second. 9. Improper lubrication. 10. Corroded transmission parts.
Jumping out of low gear	1. Gears not engaging completely. 2. Bent or loose shifter fork. 3. End-play in transmission mainshaft. 4. End-play in countershaft. 5. Loose or worn bearings on transmission mainshaft. 6. Loose or worn bearings in countershaft. 7. Defective mainshaft pilot bearing.
Sticking in low gear	1. Clutch not releasing fully. 2. Burred or battered transmission mainshaft. 3. Stuck shifter rail plunger. 4. Gearshift lever twisting and binding shifter rail. 5. Lack of lubrication. 6. Improper lubrication. 7. Corroded transmission parts.

GENERAL TROUBLESHOOTING AND DIAGNOSIS

Condition	Probable Cause
Jumping out of reverse gear	1. Insufficient spring tension on shifter rail plunger. 2. Bent or loose shifter fork. 3. Badly worn gear teeth. 4. Gears not engaging completely. 5. End-play in transmission mainshaft. 6. Idler gear bushings loose or worn. 7. Loose or worn bearings on transmission mainshaft. 8. Defective mainshaft pilot bearing.
Sticking in reverse gear	1. Clutch not releasing fully. 2. Burred or battered transmission mainshaft. 3. Stuck shifter rail plunger. 4. Gearshift lever twisting and binding shifter rail. 5. Lack of lubrication. 6. Improper lubrication. 7. Corroded transmission parts.
Failure of gears to synchronize	1. Binding pilot bearing on mainshaft, will synchronize in high gear only. 2. Clutch not releasing fully. 3. Detent spring weak or broken. 4. Weak or broken springs under balls in sliding gear sleeve. 5. Binding bearing on clutch shaft. 6. Binding countershaft. 7. Binding pilot bearing in crankshaft 8. Badly worn gear teeth. 9. Scored or worn cones. 10. Improper lubrication. 11. Constant mesh gear not turning freely on transmission mainshaft. Will synchronize in that gear only.
Gears spinning when shifting into gear from neutral	1. Clutch not releasing fully. 2. In some cases an extremely light lubricant in transmission will cause gears to continue to spin for a short time after clutch is released. 3. Binding pilot bearing in crankshaft.
Noisy in all gears	1. Insufficient lubricant. 2. Worn countergear bearings. 3. Worn or damaged main drive gear or countergear. 4. Damaged main drive gear or mainshaft bearings. 5. Worn or damaged countergear anti-lash plate.
Noisy in high gear	1. Damaged main drive gear bearing. 2. Damaged mainshaft bearing. 3. Damaged high speed gear synchronizer.
Noisy in neutral	1. Damaged main drive gear bearing. 2. Damaged or loose mainshaft pilot bearing. 3. Worn or damaged countergear anti-lash plate. 4. Worn countergear bearings.
Noisy in all reduction gears	1. Insufficient lubricant. 2. Worn or damaged drive gear or countergear.
Noisy in second only	1. Damaged or worn second gear constant mesh gears. 2. Worn or damaged countergear rear bearings. 3. Damaged or worn second gear synchronizer.
Noisy in second only	1. Damaged or worn second gear constant mesh gears. 2. Worn or damaged countergear rear bearings. 3. Damaged or worn second gear synchronizer.
Noisy in third only (four speed)	1. Damaged or worn third gear constant mesh gears. 2. Worn or damaged countergear bearings.

GENERAL TROUBLESHOOTING AND DIAGNOSIS

Condition	Probable Cause
Noisy in reverse only	1. Worn or damaged reverse idler gear or idler bushing. 2. Worn or damaged mainshaft reverse gear. 3. Worn or damaged reverse countergear. 4. Damaged shift mechanism.
Excessive backlash in all reduction gears	1. Worn countergear bearings. 2. Excessive end–play in countergear.

Automatic Transmission Troubleshooting

Keeping alert to changes in the operating characteristics of the transmission (changing shift points, noises, etc.) can prevent small problems from becoming large ones. If the problem cannot be traced to loose bolts, fluid level, misadjusted linkage, clogged filters or similar problems, you should probably seek professional service.

TRANSMISSION FLUID INDICATIONS

The appearance and odor of the transmission fluid can give valuable clues to the overall condition of the transmission. Always note the appearance of the fluid when you check the fluid level or change the fluid. Rub a small amount of fluid between your fingers to feel for grit and smell the fluid on the dipstick.

If The Fluid Appears	It Indicates
Clear and red colored	Normal operation
Discolored (extremely dark red or brownish) or smells burned	Band or clutch pack failure, usually caused by an overheated transmission. Hauling very heavy loads with insufficient power or failure to change the fluid often results in overheating. Do not confuse this appearance with newer fluids that have a darker red color and a strong odor (though not a burned odor).
Foamy or aerated (light in color and full of bubbles)	The level is too high (gear train is churning oil) An internal air leak (air is mixing with the fluid). Have the transmission checked professionally.
Solid residue in the fluid	Defective bands, clutch pack or bearings. Bits of band material or metal abrasives are clinging to the dipstick. Have the transmission checked professionally.
Varnish coating on the dipstick	The transmission fluid is overheating

Problem	Possible Cause	Correction
Slow initial engagement	1. Improper fluid level. 2. Damaged or improperly adjusted linkage. 3. Contaminated fluid. 4. Faulty clutch and band application, or oil control pressure system.	1. Add fluid as required. 2. Repair or adjust linkage. 3. Perform fluid level check. 4. Perform control pressure test.
Rough initial engagement in either forward or reverse	1. Improper fluid level. 2. High engine idle. 3. Looseness in the driveshaft, U-joints or engine mounts. 4. Incorrect linkage adjustment. 5. Faulty clutch or band application, or oil control pressure system. 6. Sticking or dirty valve body.	1. Perform fluid level check. 2. Adjust idle to specifications. 3. Repair as required. 4. Repair or adjust linkage. 5. Perform control pressure test. 6. Clean, repair or replace valve body.

Problem	Possible Cause	Correction
No drive, slips or chatters in first gear in D. All other gears normal.	1. Faulty one-way clutch.	1. Repair or replace one-way clutch.
No drive, slips or chatters in second gear.	1. Improper fluid level. 2. Damaged or improperly adjusted linkage. 3. Intermediate band out of adjustment. 4. Faulty band or clutch application, or oil pressure control system. 5. Faulty servo and/or internal leaks. 6. Dirty or sticking valve body. 7. Polished, glazed intermediate band or drum.	1. Perform fluid level check. 2. Repair or adjust linkage. 3. Adjust intermediate band. 4. Perform control pressure test. 5. Perform air pressure test. 6. Clean, repair or replace valve body. 7. Replace or repair as required.
No drive in any gear.	1. Improper fluid level. 2. Damaged or improperly adjusted linkage. 3. Faulty clutch or band application, or oil control pressure system. 4. Internal leakage. 5. Valve body loose. 6. Faulty clutches. 7. Sticking or dirty valve body.	1. Perform fluid level check. 2. Repair or adjust linkage. 3. Perform control pressure test. 4. Check and repair as required. 5. Tighten to specification. 6. Perform air pressure test. 7. Clean, repair or replace valve body.
No drive forward—reverse OK.	1. Improper fluid level 2. Damaged or improperly adjusted linkage. 3. Faulty clutch or band application, or oil pressure control system. 4. Faulty forward clutch or governor. 5. Valve body loose 6. Dirty or sticking valve body.	1. Perform fluid level check. 2. Repair or adjust linkage. 3. Perform control pressure test. 4. Perform air pressure test. 5. Tighten to specification. 6. Clean, repair or replace valve body.
No drive, slips or chatters in reverse—forward OK.	1. Improper fluid level 2. Damaged or improperly adjusted linkage. 3. Looseness in the drivehsaft, U-joints or engine mounts. 4. Bands or clutches out of adjustment. 5. Faulty oil pressure control system. 6. Faulty reverse clutch or servo. 7. Valve body loose. 8. Dirty or sticking valve body.	1. Perform fluid level check. 2. Repair or adjust linkage. 3. Repair as required. 4. Adjust as necessary. 5. Perform control pressure test. 6. Perform air pressure test. 7. Tighten to specifications. 8. Clean, repair or replace valve body.
Starts in high—in D drag or lockup at 1–2 shift point or in 2 or 1.	1. Improper fluid level. 2. Damaged or improperly adjusted linkage. 3. Faulty governor. 4. Faulty clutches and/or internal leaks. 5. Valve body loose. 6. Dirty, sticking valve body. 7. Poor mating of valve body to case mounting surfaces.	1. Perform fluid level check. 2. Repair or adjust linkage. 3. Repair or replace governor, clean screen. 4. Perform air pressure test. 5. Tighten to specifications. 6. Clean, repair or replace valve body. 7. Replace valve body or case.

GENERAL TROUBLESHOOTING AND DIAGNOSIS

Problem	Possible Cause	Correction
Starts up in 2nd or 3rd but no lockup at 1-2 shift points.	1. Improper fluid level. 2. Damaged or improperly adjusted linkage. 3. Improper band and/or clutch application, or oil pressure control system. 4. Faulty governor. 5. Valve body loose. 6. Dirty or sticking valve body. 7. Cross leaks between valve body and case mating surface.	1. Perform fluid level check. 2. Repair or adjust linkage. 3. Perform control pressure test. 4. Perform governor check. Replace or repair governor, clean screen. 5. Tighten to specification. 6. Clean, repair or replace valve body. 7. Replace valve body and/or case as required.
Shift points incorrect.	1. Improper fluid level. 2. Improper vacuum hose routing or leaks. 3. Improper operation of EGR system. 4. Linkage out of adjustment. 5. Improper speedometer gear installed. 6. Improper clutch or band application, or oil pressure control system. 7. Faulty governor. 8. Dirty or sticking valve body.	1. Perform fluid level check. 2. Correct hose routing. 3. Repair or replace as required. 4. Repair or adjust linkage. 5. Replace gear. 6. Perform shift test and control pressure test. 7. Repair or replace governor—clean screen. 8. Clean, repair or replace valve body.
No upshift at any speed in D.	1. Improper fluid level. 2. Vacuum leak to diaphragm unit. 3. Linkage out of adjustment. 4. Improper band or clutch application, or oil pressure control system. 5. Faulty governor. 6. Dirty or sticking valve bdy.	1. Perform fluid level check. 2. Repair vacuum line or hose. 3. Repair or adjust linkage. 4. Perform control pressure test. 5. Repair or replace governor, clean screen. 6. Clean, repair or replace valve body.
Shifts 1-3 in D.	1. Improper fluid level. 2. Intermediate band out of adjustment. 3. Faulty front servo and/or internal leaks. 4. Polished, glazed band or drum. 5. Improper band or clutch application, or oil pressure control system. 6. Dirty or sticking valve body.	1. Perform fluid level check. 2. Adjust band. 3. Perform air pressure test. Repair front servo and/or internal leaks. 4. Repair or replace band or drum. 5. Perform control pressure test. 6. Clean, repair or replace valve body.
Engine over-speeds on 2-3 shift.	1. Improper fluid level. 2. Linkage out of adjustment. 3. Improper band or clutch application, or oil pressure control system. 4. Faulty high clutch and/or intermediate servo. 5. Dirty or sticking valve body.	1. Perform fluid level check. 2. Repair or adjust linkage. 3. Perform control pressure test. 4. Perform air pressure test. Repair as required. 5. Clean repair or replace valve body.
Mushy 1-2 shift.	1. Improper fluid level 2. Incorrect engine idle and/or performance. 3. Improper linkage adjustment. 4. Intermediate band out of adjustment.	1. Perform fluid level check. 2. Tune, adjust engine idle as required. 3. Repair or adjust linkage. 4. Adjust intermediate band. 5. Perform control pressure test.

Problem	Possible Cause	Correction
Mushy 1-2 shift.	5. Improper band or clutch application, or oil pressure control system. 6. Faulty high clutch and/or intermediate servo release. 7. Polished, glazed band or drum. 8. Dirty or sticking valve body.	6. Perform air pressure test. Repair as required. 7. Repair or replace as required. 8. Clean, repair or replace valve body.
Rough 1-2 shift.	1. Improper fluid level. 2. Incorrect engine idle or performance. 3. Intermediate band out of adjustment. 4. Improper band or clutch application, or oil pressure control system. 5. Faulty intermediate servo. 6. Dirty or sticking valve body.	1. Perform fluid level check. 2. Tune, and adjust engine idle. 3. Adjust intermediate band. 4. Perform control pressure test. 5. Air pressure check intermediate servo. 6. Clean, repair or replace valve body.
Rough 2-3 shift	1. Improper fluid level. 2. Incorrect engine idle or performance. 3. Improper band or clutch application, or oil control pressure system. 4. Faulty intermediate servo apply and release and high clutch piston check ball. 5. Dirty or sticking valve body.	1. Perform fluid level check. 2. Tune and adjust engine idle. 3. Perform control pressure test. 4. Air pressure test the intermediate servo apply and release and the high clutch piston check ball. Repair as required. 5. Clean, repair or replace valve body.
Rough 3-1 shift at closed throttle in D.	1. Improper fluid level. 2. Incorrect engine idle or performance. 3. Improper linkage adjustment. 4. Improper clutch or band application or oil pressure control system. 5. Faulty governor operation. 6. Dirty or sticking valve body.	1. Perform fluid level check. 2. Tune, and adjust engine idle. 3. Repair or adjust linkage. 4. Perform control pressure test. 5. Perform governor test. Repair as required. 6. Clean, repair or replace valve body.
No forced downshifts.	1. Improper fluid level. 2. Linkage out of adjustment. 3. Improper clutch or band application, or oil pressure control system. 4. Faulty internal kickdown linkage. 5. Dirty or sticking valve body.	1. Perform fluid level check. 2. Repair or adjust linkage. 3. Perform control pressure test. 4. Repair internal kickdown linkage. 5. Clean, repair or replace valve body.
No 3-1 shift in D.	1. Improper fluid level. 2. Incorrect engine idle, or performance. 3. Faulty governor. 4. Dirty or sticking valve body.	1. Perform fluid level check. 2. Tune, and adjust engine idle. 3. Perform govenor check. Repair as required. 4. Clean, repair or replace valve body.
Runaway engine on 3-2 downshift.	1. Improper fluid level. 2. Linkage out of adjustment. 3. Intermediate band out of adjustment. 4. Improper band or clutch application, or oil pressure control system.	1. Perform fluid level check. 2. Repair or adjust linkage. 3. Adjust intermediate band. 4. Perform control pressure test. 5. Air pressure test check the intermediate servo. Repair servo and/or seals.

GENERAL TROUBLESHOOTING AND DIAGNOSIS

Problem	Possible Cause	Correction
Runaway engine on 3-2 downshift.	5. Faulty intermediate servo. 6. Polished, glazed band or drum. 7. Dirty or sticking valve body.	6. Repair or replace as required. 7. Clean, repair or replace valve body.
No engine braking in manual first gear.	1. Improper fluid level. 2. Linkage out of adjustment. 3. Bands or clutches out of adjustment. 4. Faulty oil pressure control system. 5. Faulty reverse servo. 6. Polished, glazed band or drum.	1. Perform fluid level check. 2. Repair or adjust linkage. 3. Adjust as necessary. 4. Perform control pressure test. 5. Perform air pressure test of reverse servo. Repair reverse clutch or rear servo as required. 6. Repair or replace as required.
No engine braking in manual second gear.	1. Improper fluid level. 2. Linkage out of adjustment. 3. Intermediate band out of adjustment. 4. Improper band or clutch application, or oil pressure control system. 5. Intermediate servo leaking. 6. Polished or glazed band or drum.	1. Perform fluid level check. 2. Repair or adjust linkage. 3. Adjust intermediate band. 4. Perform control pressure test. 5. Perform air pressure test of intermediate servo for leakage. Repair as required. 6. Repair or replace as required.
Transmission noisy—valve resonance.	1. Improper fluid level. 2. Linkage out of adjustment. 3. Improper band or clutch application, or oil pressure control system. 4. Cooler lines grounding. 5. Dirty sticking valve body. 6. Internal leakage or pump cavitation.	1. Perform fluid level check. 2. Repair or adjust linkage. 3. Perform control pressure test. 4. Free up cooler lines. 5. Clean, repair or replace valve body. 6. Repair as required.
Transmission overheats.	1. Improper fluid level. 2. Incorrect engine idle, or performance. 3. Improper clutch or band application, or oil pressure control system. 4. Restriction in cooler or lines. 5. Seized one-way clutch. 6. Dirty or sticking valve body.	1. Perform fluid level check. 2. Tune, or adjust engine idle. 3. Perform control pressure test. 4. Repair restriction. 5. Replace one-way clutch. 6. Clean, repair or replace valve body.
Transmission fluid leaks.	1. Improper fluid level. 2. Leakage at gasket, seals, etc. 3. Vacuum diaphragm unit leaking.	1. Perform fluid level check. 2. Remove all traces of lube on exposed surfaces of transmission. Check the vent for free breathing. Operate transmission at normal temperatures and inspect for leakage. Repair as required. 3. Replace diaphragm.

Automatic Transmission Troubleshooting

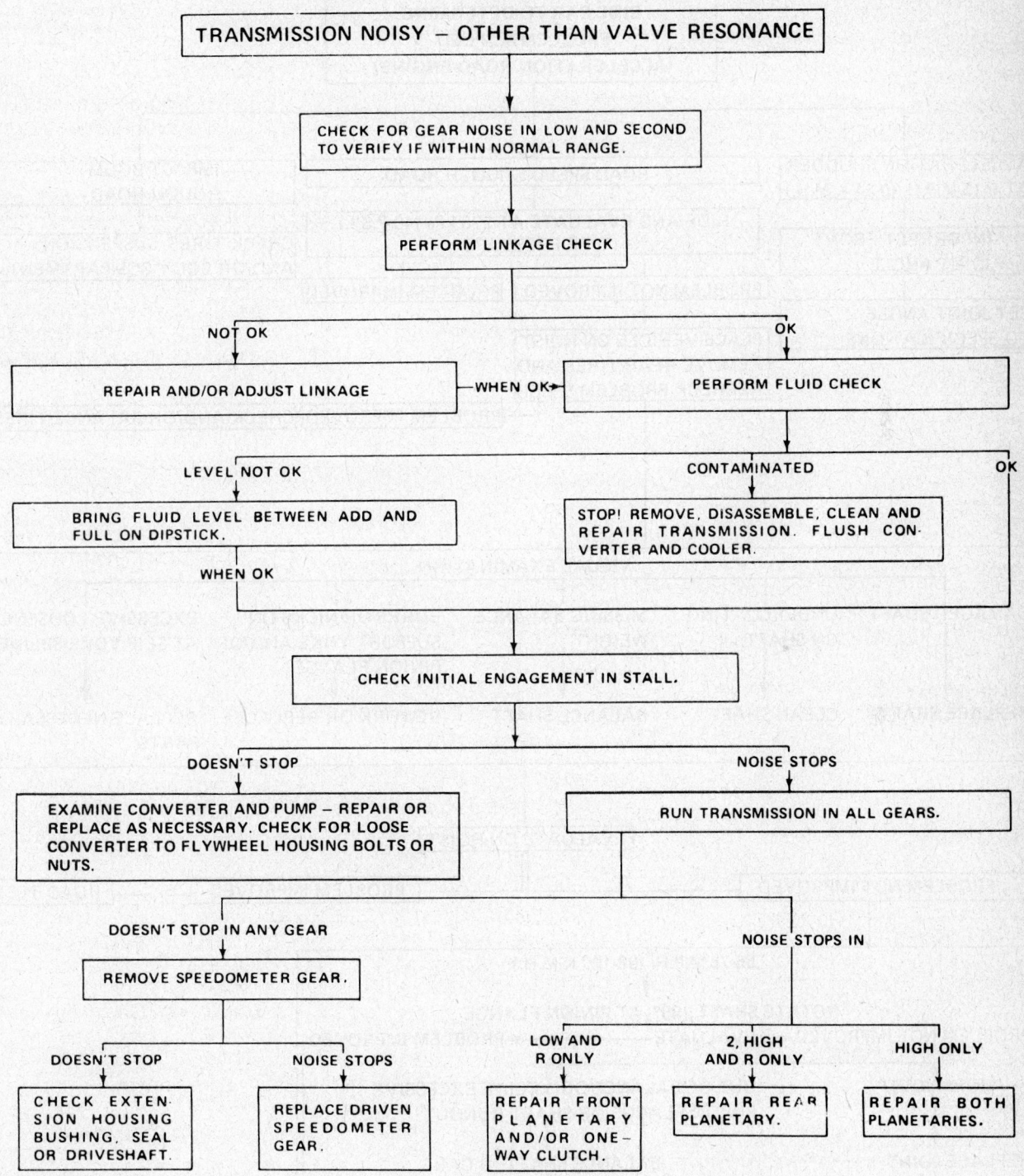

TRANSMISSION NOISY — OTHER THAN VALVE RESONANCE

CHECK FOR GEAR NOISE IN LOW AND SECOND TO VERIFY IF WITHIN NORMAL RANGE.

PERFORM LINKAGE CHECK

NOT OK — REPAIR AND/OR ADJUST LINKAGE — WHEN OK

OK — PERFORM FLUID CHECK

LEVEL NOT OK — BRING FLUID LEVEL BETWEEN ADD AND FULL ON DIPSTICK.

CONTAMINATED — STOP! REMOVE, DISASSEMBLE, CLEAN AND REPAIR TRANSMISSION. FLUSH CONVERTER AND COOLER.

OK

WHEN OK

CHECK INITIAL ENGAGEMENT IN STALL.

DOESN'T STOP — EXAMINE CONVERTER AND PUMP — REPAIR OR REPLACE AS NECESSARY. CHECK FOR LOOSE CONVERTER TO FLYWHEEL HOUSING BOLTS OR NUTS.

NOISE STOPS — RUN TRANSMISSION IN ALL GEARS.

DOESN'T STOP IN ANY GEAR — REMOVE SPEEDOMETER GEAR.

NOISE STOPS IN

DOESN'T STOP — CHECK EXTENSION HOUSING BUSHING, SEAL OR DRIVESHAFT.

NOISE STOPS — REPLACE DRIVEN SPEEDOMETER GEAR.

LOW AND R ONLY — REPAIR FRONT PLANETARY AND/OR ONE-WAY CLUTCH.

2, HIGH AND R ONLY — REPAIR REAR PLANETARY.

HIGH ONLY — REPAIR BOTH PLANETARIES.

Driveshaft Troubleshooting
Vibration, Roughness, Rumble and/or Boom

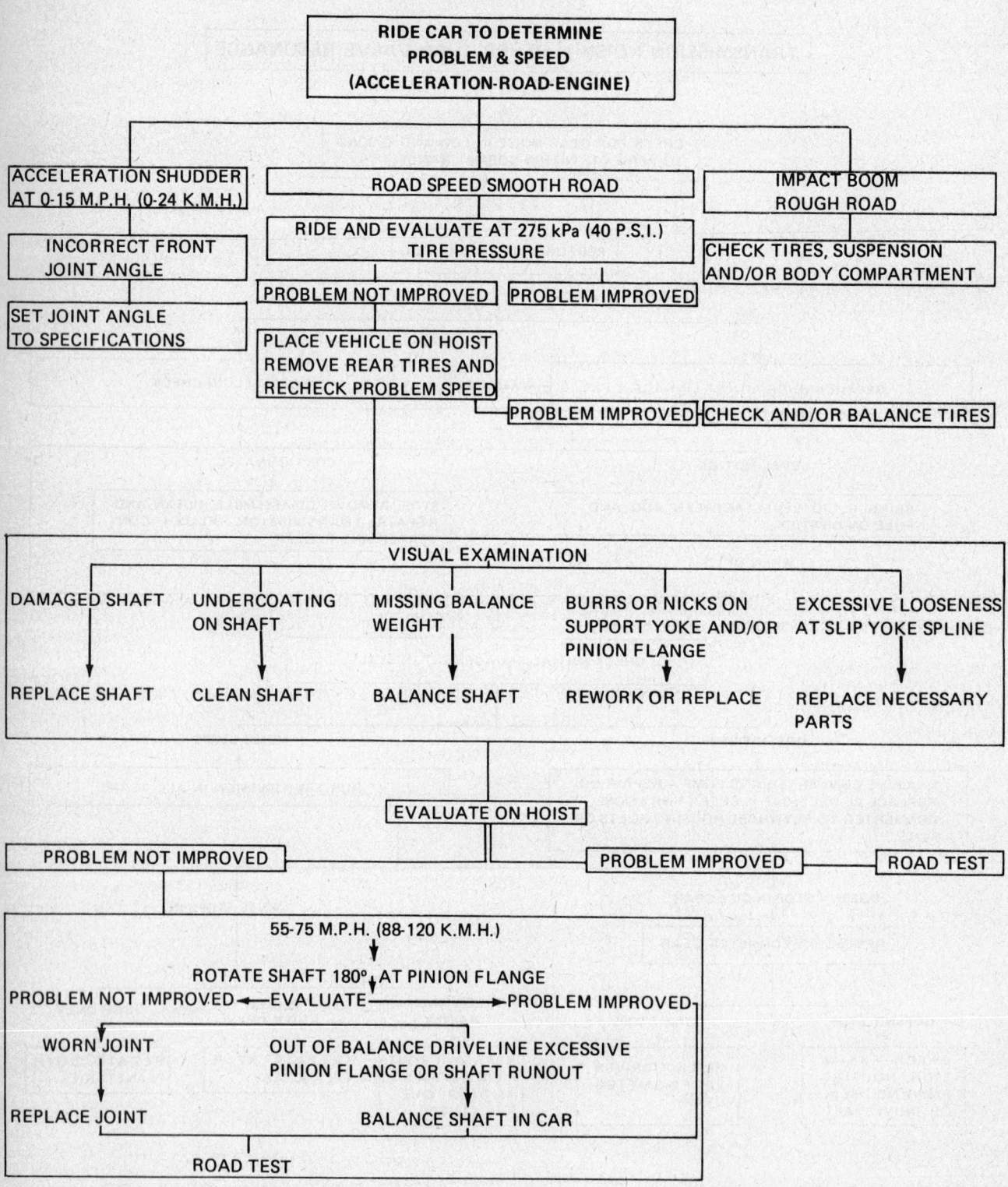

GENERAL TROUBLESHOOTING AND DIAGNOSIS

Universal Joint Troubleshooting

Problem	Possible Cause	Correction
Leak at front slip yoke. **NOTE:** An occasional drop of lubricant leaking from splined yoke is normal and requires no attention.	1. Rough outside surface on splined yoke. 2. Defective transmission rear oil seal.	1. Replace seal if cut by burrs on yoke. Minor burrs can be smoothed by careful use of crocus cloth or honing with a fine stone. Replace yoke if outside surface is rough or burred badly. 2. Replace transmission rear oil seal. 3. Bring transmission oil up to proper level after correction.
Knock in drive line, clunking noise when car is operated under floating condition at 10 mph in high gear or neutral.	1. Worn or damaged universal joints. 2. Side gear hub counterbore in differential worn oversize.	1. Disassemble universal joints, inspect and replace worn or damaged parts. 2. Replace differential case and/ or side gears as required.
Ping, snap or click in drive line. **NOTE:** Usually occurs on initial load application after transmission has been put into gear, either forward or reverse.	1. Loose upper or lower control arm bushing bolts. 2. Loose companion flange.	1. Tighten bolts to specified torque. 2. Remove companion flange, turn 180° from its original position, apply white lead to splines and reinstall. Tighten pinion nut to specified torque.

Front Wheel Drive Halfshaft Troubleshooting

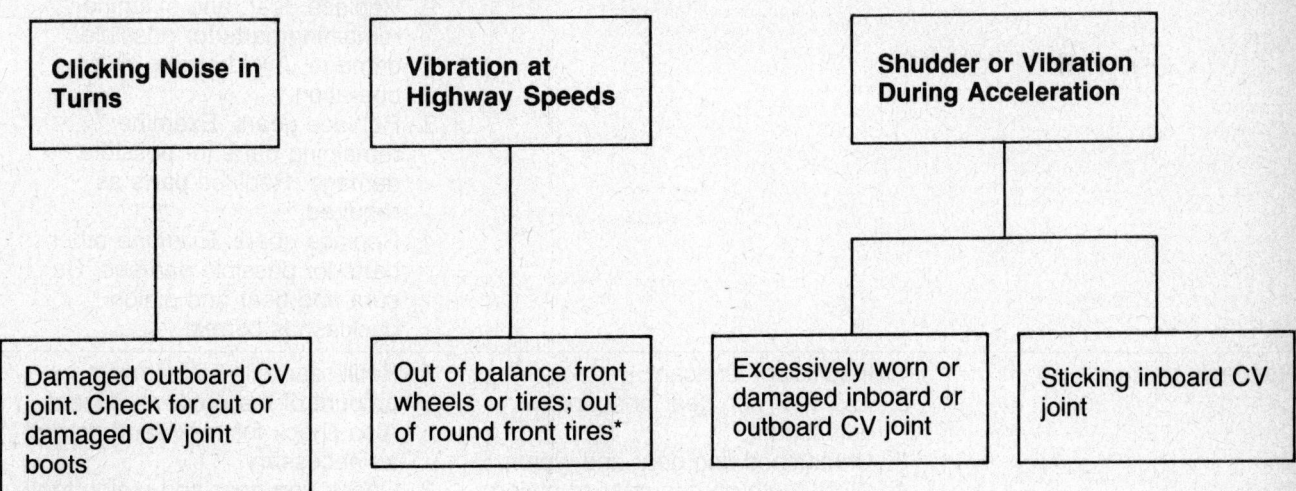

*Halfshafts do not usually contribute to rotational vibrations.

1297

Drive Axle Troubleshooting

Condition	Possible Cause	Correction
Rear wheel noise	1. Loose wheel. 2. Spalled wheel bearing cup or cone. 3. Defective or brinelled wheel bearing. 4. Excessive axle shaft endplay. 5. Bent or sprng axle shaft flange.	1. Tighten loose wheel nuts. 2. Check rear wheel bearings. If spalled or worn, replace. 3. Defective or brinelled bearings must be replaced. Check rear axle shaft end play. 4. Readjust axle shaft end play. 5. Replace bent or sprung axle shaft.
Scoring of differential gears and pinions	1. Insufficient lubrication. 2. Improper grade of lubricant. 3. Excessive spinning of one wheel.	1. Replace scored gears. Scoring marks on the pressure face of gear teeth or in the bore are caused by instantaneous fusing of the mating surfaces. Scored gears should be replaced. Fill rear axle to required capacity with proper lubricant. 2. Replace scored gears. Inspect all gears and bearings for possible damage. Clean and refill axle to required capacity with proper lubricant. 3. Replace scored gears. Inspect all gears, pinion bores and shaft for scoring, or bearings for possible damage.
Tooth breakage (ring gear and pinion)	1. Overloading. 2. Erratic clutch operation. 3. Ice-spotted pavements. 4. Improper adjustments.	1. Replace gear. Examine other gears and bearings for possible damage. Avoid future overloading. 2. Replace gear, and examine remaining parts for possible damage. Avoid erratic clutch operation. 3. Replace gears. Examine remaining parts for possible damage. Replace parts as required. 4. Replace gears. Examine other parts for possible damage. Be sure ring gear and pinion backlash is correct.
Rear axle noise	1. Insufficient lubricant. 2. Improper ring gear and pinion adjustment. 3. Unmatched ring gear and pinion. 4. Worn teeth on ring gear or pinion. 5. End-play in drive pinion bearings. 6. Side play in differential bearings. 7. Incorrect drive gearlash. 8. Limited-slip differential—moan and chatter.	1. Refill rear axle with correct amount of the proper lubricant. Also check for leaks and correct as necessary. 2. Check ring gear and pinion tooth contact. 3. Remove unmatched ring gear and pinion. Replace with a new matched gear and pinion set. 4. Check teeth on ring gear and pinion for contact. If necessary, replace with new matched set. 5. Adjust drive pinion bearing preload.

Problem	Possible Cause	Correction
Rear axle noise		6. Adjust differential bearing preload. 7. Correct drive gear lash. 8. Drain and flush lubricant. Refill with proper lubricant.
Loss of lubricant	1. Lubricant level too high. 2. Worn axle shaft oil seals. 3. Cracked rear axle housing. 4. Worn drive pinion oil seal. 5. Scored and worn companion flange. 6. Clogged vent. 7. Loose carrier housing bolts or housing cover screws.	1. Drain excess lubricant. 2. Replace worn oil seals with new ones. Prepare new seals before replacement. 3. Repair or replace housing as required. 4. Replace worn drive pinion oil seal with a new one. 5. Replace worn or scored companion flange and oil seal. 6. Remove obstructions. 7. Tighten bolts or cover screws to specifications and fill to correct level with proper lubricant.
Overheating of unit	1. Lubricant level too low. 2. Incorrect grade of lubricant. 3. Bearing adjusted too tightly. 4. Excessive wear in gears. 5. Insufficient ring gear-to-pinion clearance.	1. Refill rear axle. 2. Drain, flush and refill rear axle with correct amount of the proper lubricant. 3. Readjust bearings. 4. Check gears for excessive wear or scoring. Replace as necessary. 5. Readjust ring gear and pinion backlash and check gears for possible scoring.

CHASSIS

Shock Absorber and Rear Spring Troubleshooting

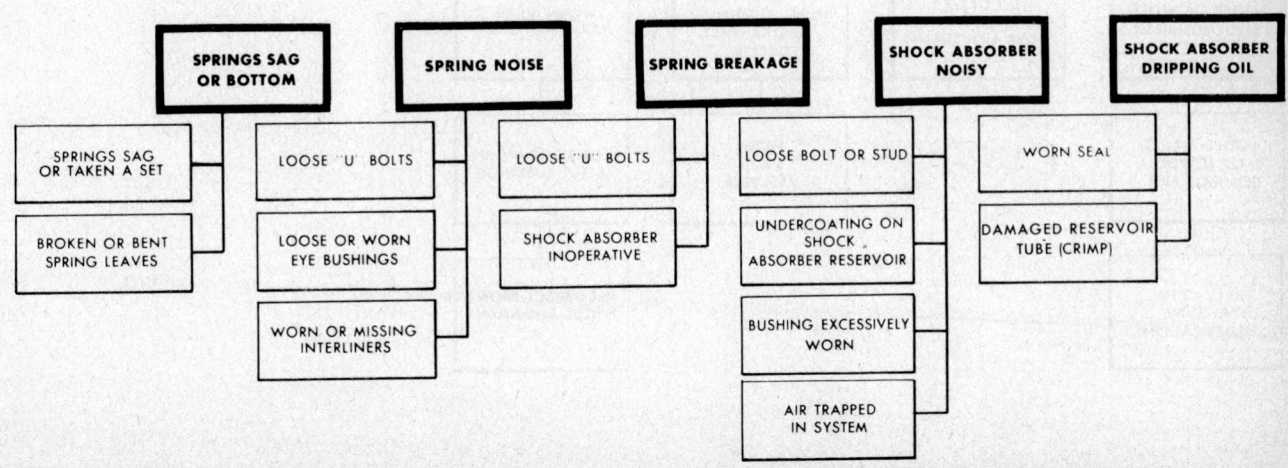

Front Suspension and Steering Linkage
Troubleshooting—Rear Wheel Drive

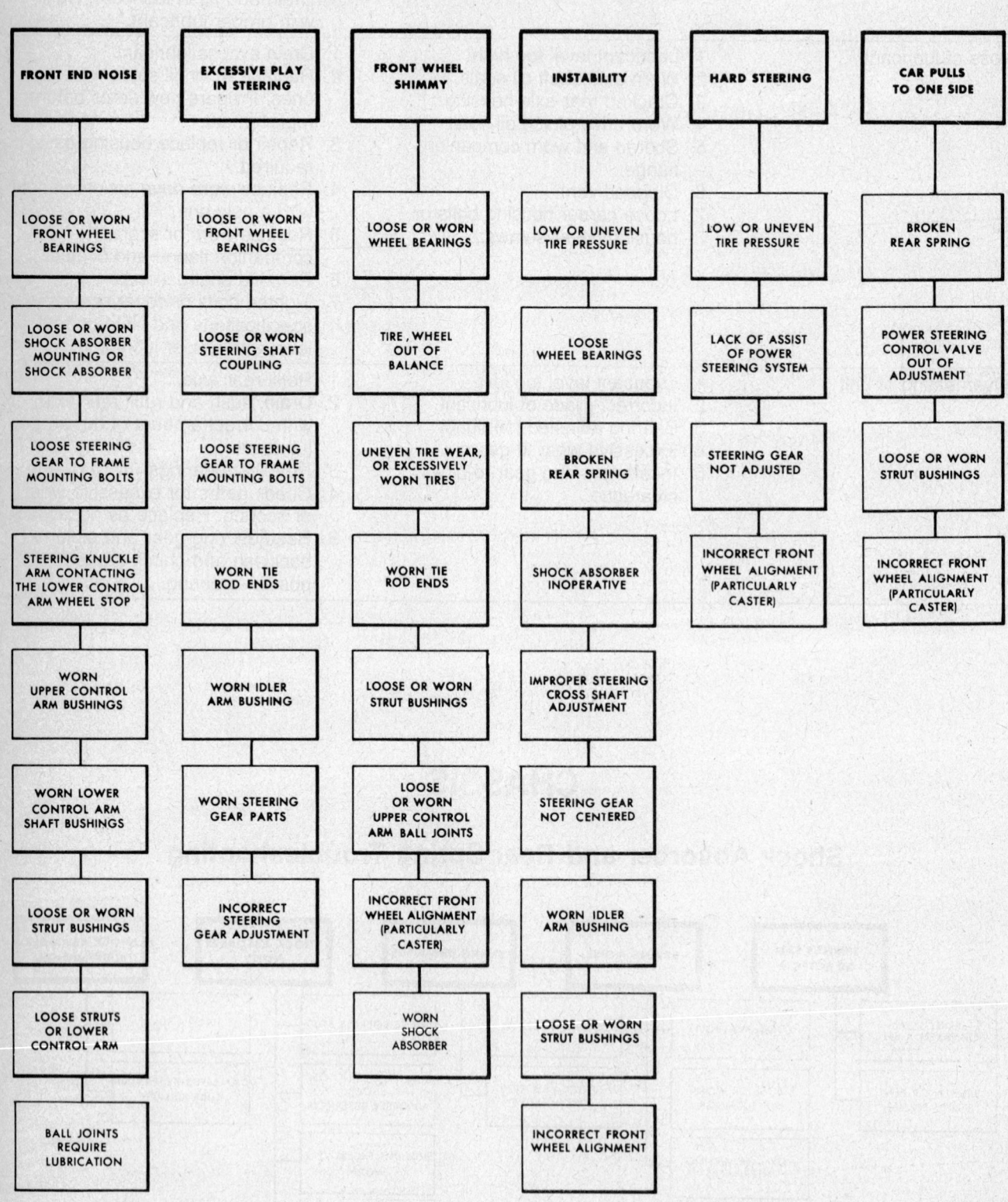

FRONT END NOISE	EXCESSIVE PLAY IN STEERING	FRONT WHEEL SHIMMY	INSTABILITY	HARD STEERING	CAR PULLS TO ONE SIDE
LOOSE OR WORN FRONT WHEEL BEARINGS	LOOSE OR WORN FRONT WHEEL BEARINGS	LOOSE OR WORN WHEEL BEARINGS	LOW OR UNEVEN TIRE PRESSURE	LOW OR UNEVEN TIRE PRESSURE	BROKEN REAR SPRING
LOOSE OR WORN SHOCK ABSORBER MOUNTING OR SHOCK ABSORBER	LOOSE OR WORN STEERING SHAFT COUPLING	TIRE, WHEEL OUT OF BALANCE	LOOSE WHEEL BEARINGS	LACK OF ASSIST OF POWER STEERING SYSTEM	POWER STEERING CONTROL VALVE OUT OF ADJUSTMENT
LOOSE STEERING GEAR TO FRAME MOUNTING BOLTS	LOOSE STEERING GEAR TO FRAME MOUNTING BOLTS	UNEVEN TIRE WEAR, OR EXCESSIVELY WORN TIRES	BROKEN REAR SPRING	STEERING GEAR NOT ADJUSTED	LOOSE OR WORN STRUT BUSHINGS
STEERING KNUCKLE ARM CONTACTING THE LOWER CONTROL ARM WHEEL STOP	WORN TIE ROD ENDS	WORN TIE ROD ENDS	SHOCK ABSORBER INOPERATIVE	INCORRECT FRONT WHEEL ALIGNMENT (PARTICULARLY CASTER)	INCORRECT FRONT WHEEL ALIGNMENT (PARTICULARLY CASTER)
WORN UPPER CONTROL ARM BUSHINGS	WORN IDLER ARM BUSHING	LOOSE OR WORN STRUT BUSHINGS	IMPROPER STEERING CROSS SHAFT ADJUSTMENT		
WORN LOWER CONTROL ARM SHAFT BUSHINGS	WORN STEERING GEAR PARTS	LOOSE OR WORN UPPER CONTROL ARM BALL JOINTS	STEERING GEAR NOT CENTERED		
LOOSE OR WORN STRUT BUSHINGS	INCORRECT STEERING GEAR ADJUSTMENT	INCORRECT FRONT WHEEL ALIGNMENT (PARTICULARLY CASTER)	WORN IDLER ARM BUSHING		
LOOSE STRUTS OR LOWER CONTROL ARM		WORN SHOCK ABSORBER	LOOSE OR WORN STRUT BUSHINGS		
BALL JOINTS REQUIRE LUBRICATION			INCORRECT FRONT WHEEL ALIGNMENT		

Suspension and Steering Linkage
Troubleshooting— Front Wheel Drive

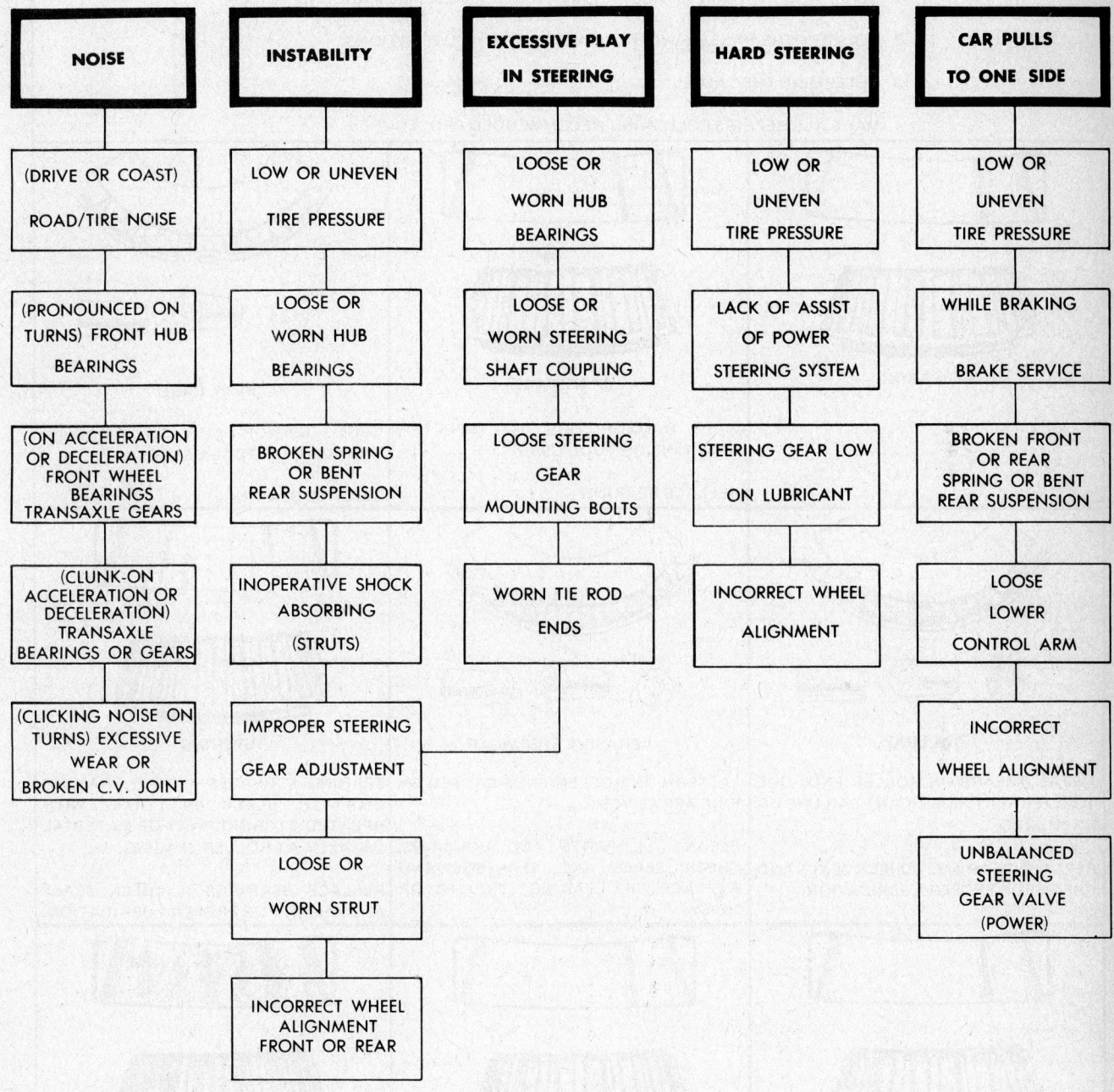

NOISE

- (DRIVE OR COAST) ROAD/TIRE NOISE
- (PRONOUNCED ON TURNS) FRONT HUB BEARINGS
- (ON ACCELERATION OR DECELERATION) FRONT WHEEL BEARINGS TRANSAXLE GEARS
- (CLUNK-ON ACCELERATION OR DECELERATION) TRANSAXLE BEARINGS OR GEARS
- (CLICKING NOISE ON TURNS) EXCESSIVE WEAR OR BROKEN C.V. JOINT

INSTABILITY

- LOW OR UNEVEN TIRE PRESSURE
- LOOSE OR WORN HUB BEARINGS
- BROKEN SPRING OR BENT REAR SUSPENSION
- INOPERATIVE SHOCK ABSORBING (STRUTS)
- IMPROPER STEERING GEAR ADJUSTMENT
- LOOSE OR WORN STRUT
- INCORRECT WHEEL ALIGNMENT FRONT OR REAR

EXCESSIVE PLAY IN STEERING

- LOOSE OR WORN HUB BEARINGS
- LOOSE OR WORN STEERING SHAFT COUPLING
- LOOSE STEERING GEAR MOUNTING BOLTS
- WORN TIE ROD ENDS

HARD STEERING

- LOW OR UNEVEN TIRE PRESSURE
- LACK OF ASSIST OF POWER STEERING SYSTEM
- STEERING GEAR LOW ON LUBRICANT
- INCORRECT WHEEL ALIGNMENT

CAR PULLS TO ONE SIDE

- LOW OR UNEVEN TIRE PRESSURE
- WHILE BRAKING BRAKE SERVICE
- BROKEN FRONT OR REAR SPRING OR BENT REAR SUSPENSION
- LOOSE LOWER CONTROL ARM
- INCORRECT WHEEL ALIGNMENT
- UNBALANCED STEERING GEAR VALVE (POWER)

Tapered Wheel Bearing Troubleshooting

CONSIDER THE FOLLOWING FACTORS WHEN DIAGNOSING BEARING CONDITION:

1. GENERAL CONDITION OF ALL PARTS DURING DISASSEMBLY AND INSPECTION.

2. CLASSIFY THE FAILURE WITH THE AID OF THE ILLUSTRATIONS.

3. DETERMINE THE CAUSE.

4. MAKE ALL REPAIRS FOLLOWING RECOMMENDED PROCEDURES.

GOOD BEARING

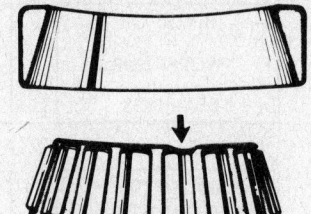

BENT CAGE

CAGE DAMAGE DUE TO IMPROPER HANDLING OR TOOL USAGE.

REPLACE BEARING.

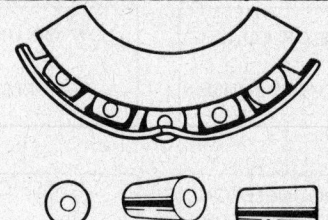

BENT CAGE

CAGE DAMAGE DUE TO IMPROPER HANDLING OR TOOL USAGE.

REPLACE BEARING.

GALLING

METAL SMEARS ON ROLLER ENDS DUE TO OVERHEAT, LUBRICANT FAILURE OR OVERLOAD.

REPLACE BEARING — CHECK SEALS AND CHECK FOR PROPER LUBRICATION.

ABRASIVE STEP WEAR

PATTERN ON ROLLER ENDS CAUSED BY FINE ABRASIVES.

CLEAN ALL PARTS AND HOUSINGS, CHECK SEALS AND BEARINGS AND REPLACE IF LEAKING, ROUGH OR NOISY.

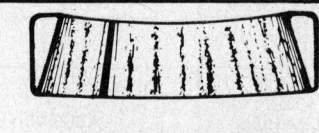

ETCHING

BEARING SURFACES APPEAR GRAY OR GRAYISH BLACK IN COLOR WITH RELATED ETCHING AWAY OF MATERIAL USUALLY AT ROLLER SPACING.

REPLACE BEARINGS — CHECK SEALS AND CHECK FOR PROPER LUBRICATION.

MISALIGNMENT

OUTER RACE MISALIGNMENT DUE TO FOREIGN OBJECT.

CLEAN RELATED PARTS AND REPLACE BEARING. MAKE SURE RACES ARE PROPERLY SEATED.

INDENTATIONS

SURFACE DEPRESSIONS ON RACE AND ROLLERS CAUSED BY HARD PARTICLES OF FOREIGN MATERIAL.

CLEAN ALL PARTS AND HOUSINGS, CHECK SEALS AND REPLACE BEARINGS IF ROUGH OR NOISY.

FATIGUE SPALLING

FLAKING OF SURFACE METAL RESULTING FROM FATIGUE.

REPLACE BEARING — CLEAN ALL RELATED PARTS.

Tapered Wheel Bearing Troubleshooting

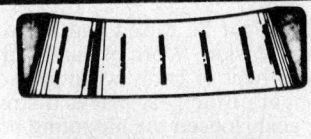

BRINELLING

SURFACE INDENTATIONS IN RACEWAY CAUSED BY ROLLERS EITHER UNDER IMPACT LOADING OR VIBRATION WHILE THE BEARING IS NOT ROTATING.

REPLACE BEARING IF ROUGH OR NOISY.

CAGE WEAR

WEAR AROUND OUTSIDE DIAMETER OF CAGE AND ROLLER POCKETS CAUSED BY ABRASIVE MATERIAL AND INEFFICIENT LUBRICATION. CHECK SEALS AND REPLACE BEARINGS.

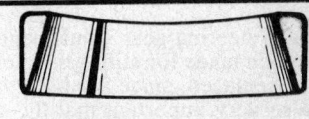

ABRASIVE ROLLER WEAR

PATTERN ON RACES AND ROLLERS CAUSED BY FINE ABRASIVES.

CLEAN ALL PARTS AND HOUSINGS, CHECK SEALS AND BEARINGS AND REPLACE IF LEAKING, ROUGH OR NOISY.

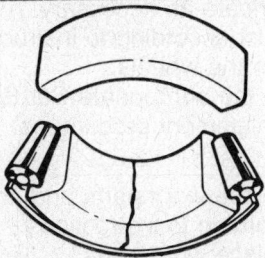

CRACKED INNER RACE

RACE CRACKED DUE TO IMPROPER FIT, COCKING, OR POOR BEARING SEATS.

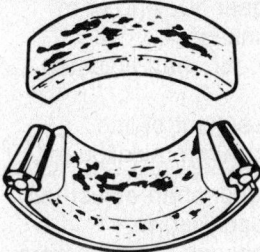

SMEARS

SMEARING OF METAL DUE TO SLIPPAGE, SLIPPAGE CAN BE CAUSED BY POOR FITS, LUBRICATION, OVERHEATING, OVERLOADS OR HANDLING DAMAGE.

REPLACE BEARINGS, CLEAN RELATED PARTS AND CHECK FOR PROPER FIT AND LUBRICATION.

REPLACE SHAFT IF DAMAGED.

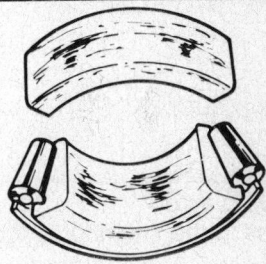

FRETTAGE

CORROSION SET UP BY SMALL RELATIVE MOVEMENT OF PARTS WITH NO LUBRICATION.

REPLACE BEARING. CLEAN RELATED PARTS. CHECK SEALS AND CHECK FOR PROPER LUBRICATION.

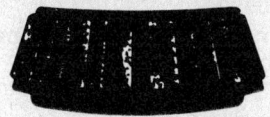

HEAT DISCOLORATION

HEAT DISCOLORATION CAN RANGE FROM FAINT YELLOW TO DARK BLUE RESULTING FROM OVERLOAD OR INCORRECT LUBRICANT.

EXCESSIVE HEAT CAN CAUSE SOFTENING OF RACES OR ROLLERS.

TO CHECK FOR LOSS OF TEMPER ON RACES OR ROLLERS A SIMPLE FILE TEST MAY BE MADE. A FILE DRAWN OVER A TEMPERED PART WILL GRAB AND CUT META, WHEREAS, A FILE DRAWN OVER A HARD PART WILL GLIDE READILY WITH NO METAL CUTTING.

REPLACE BEARINGS IF OVER HEATING DAMAGE IS INDICATED. CHECK SEALS AND OTHER PARTS.

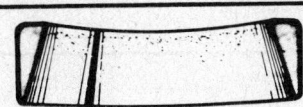

STAIN DISCOLORATION

DISCOLORATION CAN RANGE FROM LIGHT BROWN TO BLACK CAUSED BY INCORRECT LUBRICANT OR MOISTURE.

RE-USE BEARINGS IF STAINS CAN BE REMOVED BY LIGHT POLISHING OR IF NO EVIDENCE OF OVERHEATING IS OBSERVED.

CHECK SEALS AND RELATED PARTS FOR DAMAGE.

GENERAL TROUBLESHOOTING AND DIAGNOSIS

Manual Steering Troubleshooting

INSPECTION AND ALIGNMENT

Before any steering gear adjustments are made, it is recommended that the front end of the car be raised and a thorough inspection be made for stiffness or lost motion in steering gear, steering linkage and front suspension. Worn or damaged parts should be replaced, since a satisfactory adjustment of the steering gear cannot be obtained if bent or badly worn parts exist.

It is also very important that the steering gear be properly aligned in the car. Misalignment of the gear places a stress on the steering worm shaft, therefore a proper adjustment is impossible. To align the steering gear, loosen the mounting bolts to permit the gear to align itself. Check the steering gear mounting seat, and if there is a gap at any of the mounting bolts, proper alignment may be obtained by placing shims where excessive gap appears. Tighten the steering gear bolts. Alignment of the gear in the car is very important and should be done carefully so that a satisfactory, trouble-free gear adjustment may be obtained.

Condition	Possible Cause	Corrective Action
Hard steering	1. Low or uneven tire pressure. 2. Insufficient lubricant in the steering gear housing or in steering linkage. 3. Steering gear shaft adjusted too tight. 4. Front wheels out of line. 5. Steering column misaligned.	1. Inflate tires to recommended pressures. 2. Lubricate as necessary. 3. Adjust according to instructions. 4. Align the wheels. 5. See the appropriate Car Section for alignment procedures.
Excessive play or looseness in the steering wheel	1. Steering gear shaft adjust too loose or badly worn. 2. Steering linkage loose or worn. 3. Front wheel bearings improperly adjusted. 4. Steering arm loose on steering gear shaft. 5. Steering gear housing attaching bolts loose. 6. Steering arms loose at steering knuckles. 7. Worn ball joints. 8. Worm shaft bearing adjustment too loose.	1. Replace worn parts and adjust according to instructions. 2. Replace worn parts. 3. Adjust according to instructions. 4. Inspect for damage to the gear shaft and steering arm, replace parts as necessary. 5. Tighten attaching bolts to specifications. 6. Tighten according to specifications. 7. Replace the ball joints as necessary. 8. Adjust worm bearing preload according to instructions.

Power Steering Systems Troubleshooting

Condition	Possible Cause	Corrective Action
Hard steering	1. Improper tire pressure. 2. Loose pump drive belt. 3. Low or incorrect fluid. 4. Loose, bent or poorly lubricated front end parts. 5. Improper front end alignment. 6. Bind in steering column or linkage.	1. Inflate tires to recommended pressures. 2. Tighten or replace belt. 3. Refill reservoir with proper fluid; check for leaks; 4. Tighten or replace parts; lubricate at all fittings. 5. Align front end.

Condition	Possible Cause	Correction Action
Hard steering	7. Air in hydraulic system. 8. Low pump output or leaks in system. 9. Obstruction in lines. 10. Pump valves sticking or out of adjustment.	6. Disassemble and inspect component parts. Repair or replace as necessary. 7. Bleed system, refill and check for leaks. 8. Disassemble pump, check for worn or damaged parts. Check for leaks in the system. 9. Clean or replace lines. 10. Replace or adjust valves.
Loose steering	1. Loose wheel bearings 2. Faulty shocks. 3. Worn linkage components. 4. Loose steering gear mounting or linkage points. 5. Steering mechanism worn or improperly adjusted. 6. Valve spool improperly adjusted	1. Adjust wheel bearings. 2. Relace shocks. 3. Replace worn components. 4. Tighten mountings or linkage. 5. Replace and/or adjust mechanism. 6. Adjust valve spool.
Veer or wander	1. Improper tire pressure. 2. Improper front end alignment. 3. Dragging brakes. 4. Bent frame. 5. Improper rear end alignment. 6. Faulty shocks or springs. 7. Loose or bent front end components. 8. Play in Pitman arm. 9. Loose wheel bearings. 10. Binding Pitman arm. 11. Spool valve sticking or improperly adjusted.	1. Inflate tires to recommended pressures. 2. Align front end. 3. Inspect, replace and/or adjust brakes. 4. Straighten frame. 5. Inspect shocks and control arm torque. Replace and/or adjust as necessary. 6. Replace as necessary. 7. Replace as necessary. 8. Inspect bushings and arm. Replace as necessary. 9. Adjust to specifications. 10. Replace arm. 11. Adjust or replace as necessary.
Wheel oscillation	1. Improper tire pressure. 2. Loose wheel bearings. 3. Improper front end alignment. 4. Bent spindle. 5. Worn, bent or broken front end components. 6. Tires out of round or out of balance. 7. Excessive lateral runout in disc brake rotor.	1. Inflate tires to recommended pressures. 2. Adjust to specifications. 3. Align front end. 4. Replace spindle. 5. Inspect, repair or replace as necessary. 6. Replace or balance tires. 7. Reface or replace rotor.
Noises	1. Loose belts. 2. Low fluid, air in system. 3. Foreign matter in system. 4. Improper lubrication. 5. Interference or chafing in linkage. 6. Steering gear mountings loose. 7. Incorrect adjustment or wear in gear box. 8. Faulty valves or wear in pump.	1. Replace and/or adjust belts. 2. Refill and check for leaks. 3. Disassemble and clean system. 4. Lubricate all fittings. 5. Disassemble, inspect, replace or adjust components. 6. Tighten mountings. 7. Disassemble, inspect, repair, replace and/or adjust parts. 8. Replace parts as necessary.

How To Read Tire Wear

The way your tires wear is a good indicator of other parts of the suspension. Abnormal wear patterns are often caused by the need for simple tire maintenance, or for front end alignment.

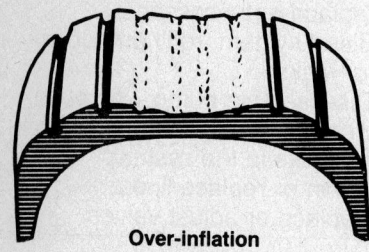

Over-inflation

Excessive wear at the center of the tread indicates that the air pressure in the tire is consistently too high. The tire is riding on the center of the tread and wearing it prematurely. Occasionally, this wear pattern can result from outrageously wide tires on narrow rims. The cure for this is to replace either the tires or the wheels.

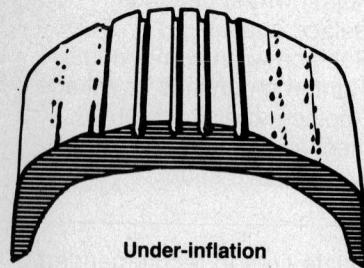

Under-inflation

This type of wear usually results from consistent under-inflation. When a tire is under-inflated, there is too much contact with the road by the outer treads, which wear prematurely. When this type of wear occurs, and the tire pressure is known to be consistently correct, a bent or worn steering component or the need for wheel alignment could be indicated.

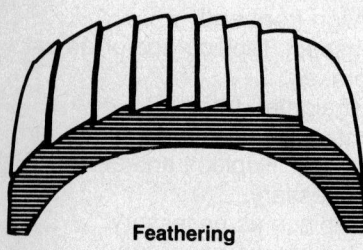

Feathering

Feathering is a condition when the edge of each tread rib develops a slightly rounded edge on one side and a sharp edge on the other. By running your hand over the tire, you can usually feel the sharper edges before you'll be able to see them. The most common causes of feathering are incorrect toe-in setting or deteriorated bushings in the front suspension.

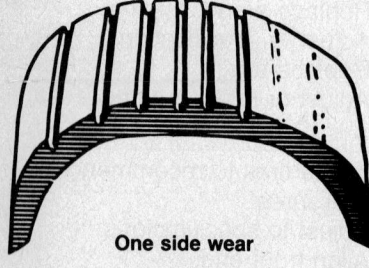

One side wear

When an inner or outer rib wears faster than the rest of the tire, the need for wheel alignment is indicated. There is excessive camber in the front suspension, causing the wheel to lean too much putting excessive load on one side of the tire. Misalignment could also be due to sagging springs, worn ball joints, or worn control arm bushings. Be sure the vehicle is loaded the way it's normally driven when you have the wheels aligned.

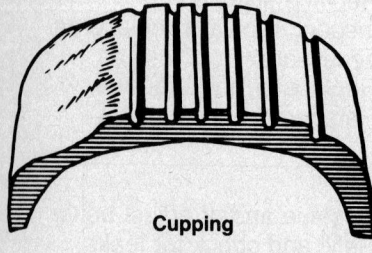

Cupping

Cups or scalloped dips appearing around the edge of the tread almost always indicate worn (sometimes bent) suspension parts. Adjustment of wheel alignment alone will seldom cure the problem. Any worn component that connects the wheel to the suspension can cause this type of wear. Occasionally, wheels that are out of balance will wear like this, but wheel imbalance usually shows up as bald spots between the outside edges and center of the tread.

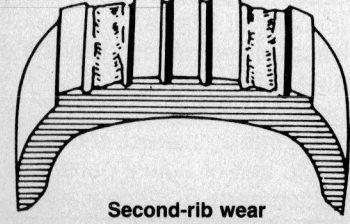

Second-rib wear

Second-rib wear is usually found only in radial tires, and appears where the steel belts end in relation to the tread. It can be kept to a minimum by paying careful attention to tire pressure and frequently rotating the tires. This is often considered normal wear but excessive amounts indicate that the tires are too wide for the wheels.

Drum Brake Troubleshooting

Condition	Possible Cause	Correction Action
Pedal goes to floor	1. Fluid low in reservoir. 2. Air in hydraulic brake system. 3. Improperly adjusted brake. 4. Leaking wheel cylinders. 5. Loose or broken brake lines. 6. Leaking or worn master cylinder. 7. Excessively worn brake lining.	1. Fill and bleed master cylinder. 2. Fill and bleed hydraulic brake system. 3. Repair or replace self-adjuster as required. 4. Recondition or replace wheel cylinder and replace both brake shoes. 5. Tighten all brake fittings or replace brake line. 6. Recondition or replace master cylinder and bleed hydraulic system. 7. Reline and adjust brakes.
Spongy brake pedal	1. Air in hydraulic system. 2. Improper brake fluid (low boiling point). 3. Excessively worn or cracked brake drums. 4. Broken pedal pivot bushing.	1. Fill master cylinder and bleed hydraulic system. 2. Drain, flush and refill with brake fluid. 3. Replace all faulty brake drums. 4. Replace nylon pivot bushing.
Brakes pulling	1. Contaminated lining. 2. Front end out of alignment. 3. Incorrect brake adjustment. 4. Unmatched brake lining. 5. Brake drums out of round. 6. Brake shoes distorted. 7. Restricted brake hose or line. 8. Broken rear spring.	1. Replace contaminated brake lining. 2. Align front end. 3. Adjust brakes and check fluid. 4. Match primary, secondary with same type of lining on all wheels. 5. Grind or replace brake drums. 6. Replace faulty brake shoes. 7. Replace plugged hose or brake line. 8. Replace broken spring.
Squealing brakes	1. Glazed brake lining. 2. Saturated brake lining. 3. Weak or broken brake shoe retaining spring. 4. Broken or weak brake shoe return spring. 5. Incorrect brake lining. 6. Distorted brake shoes. 7. Bent support plate. 8. Dust in brakes or scored brake drums.	1. Cam grind or replace brake lining. 2. Replace saturated lining. 3. Replace retaining spring. 4. Replace return spring. 5. Install matched brake lining. 6. Replace brake shoes. 7. Replace support plate. 8. Blow out brake assembly with compressed air and grind brake drums.
Chirping brakes	1. Out of round drum or eccentric axle flange pilot.	1. Repair as necessary, and lubricate support plate contact areas (6 places).
Dragging brakes	1. Incorrect wheel or parking brake adjustment. 2. Parking brakes engaged. 3. Weak or broken brake shoe return spring. 4. Brake pedal binding. 5. Master cylinder cup sticking. 6. Obstructed master cylinder relief port. 7. Saturated brake lining. 8. Bent or out of round brake drum.	1. Adjust brake and check fluid. 2. Release parking brakes. 3. Replace brake shoe return spring. 4. Free up and lubricate brake pedal and linkage. 5. Recondition master cylinder. 6. Use compressed air and blow out relief port. 7. Replace brake lining. 8. Grind or replace faulty brake drum.

GENERAL TROUBLESHOOTING AND DIAGNOSIS

Condition	Possible Cause	Corrective Action
Hard pedal	1. Brake booster inoperative. 2. Incorrect brake lining. 3. Restricted brake line or hose. 4. Frozen brake pedal linkage.	1. Replace brake booster. 2. Install matched brake lining. 3. Clean out or replace brake line or hose. 4. Free up and lubricate brake linkage.
Wheel locks	1. Contaminated brake lining. 2. Loose or torn brake lining. 3. Wheel cylinder cups sticking. 4. Incorrect wheel bearing adjustment.	1. Reline both front or rear of all four brakes. 2. Replace brake lining. 3. Recondition or replace wheel cylinder. 4. Clean, pack and adjust wheel bearings.
Brakes fade (high speed)	1. Incorrect lining. 2. Overheated brake drums. 3. Incorrect brake fluid (low boiling temperature) 4. Saturated brake lining.	1. Replace lining. 2. Inspect for dragging brakes. 3. Drain, flush, refill and bleed hydraulic brake system. 4. Reline both front or rear or all four brakes.
Pedal pulsates	1. Bent or out of round brake drum.	1. Grind or replace brake drums.
Brake chatter and shoe knock	1. Out of round brake drum. 2. Loose support plate. 3. Bent support plate. 4. Distorted brake shoes. 5. Machine grooves in contact face of brake drum. (Shoe Knock). 6. Contaminated brake lining.	1. Grind or replace brake drums. 2. Tighten support plate bolts to proper specifications. 3. Replace support plate. 4. Replace brake shoes. 5. Grind or replace brake drum. 6. Replace either front or rear or all four linings.
Brakes do not self adjust	1. Adjuster screw frozen in thread. 2. Adjuster screw corroded at thrust washer. 3. Adjuster level does not engage star wheel. 4. Adjuster installed on wrong wheel.	1. Clean and free-up all thread areas. 2. Clean threads and replace thrust washer if necessary. 3. Repair, free up or replace adjusters as required. 4. Install correct adjuster parts.

Disc Brake Troubleshooting

Condition	Possible Cause	Correction Action
Noise—Groan—Brake noise emanating when slowly releasing brakes (creep-groan).	1. Not detrimental to function of disc brakes—no corrective action required. (Indicate to operator this noise may be eliminated by slightly increasing or decreasing brake pedal efforts.)	
Rattle—Brake noise or rattle emanating at low speeds on rough roads, (front wheels only).	1. Shoe anti-rattle spring missing or not properly positioned. 2. Excessive clearance between shoe and caliper.	1. Install new anti-rattle spring or position properly. 2. Install new shoe and lining assemblies.

Condition	Possible Cause	Corrective Action
Scraping	1. Mounting bolts too long. 2. Loose wheel bearings.	1. Install mounting bolts of correct length. 2. Readjust wheel bearings to correct specifications.
Front brakes heat up during driving and fail to release	1. Operator riding brake pedal. 2. Stop light switch improperly adjusted. 3. Sticking pedal linkage. 4. Frozen or seized piston. 5. Residual pressure valve in master cylinder. 6. Power brake malfunction.	1. Instruct owner how to drive with disc brakes. 2. Adjust stop light to allow full return of pedal. 3. Free up sticking pedal linkage. 4. Disassemble caliper and free up piston. 5. Remove valve. 6. Replace.
Leaky wheel cylinder	1. Damaged or worn caliper piston seal. 2. Scores or corrosion on surface of cylinder bore.	1. Disassemble caliper and install new seal. 2. Disassemble caliper and hone cylinder bore. Install new seal.
Grabbing or uneven brake action	1. Causes listed under "Pull." 2. Power brake malfunction.	1. Corrections listed under "Pull". 2. Replace.
Brake pedal can be depressed without braking effect	1. Air in hydraulic system or improper bleeding procedure. 2. Leak past primary cup in master cylinder. 3. Leak in system. 4. Rear brakes out of adjustment. 5. Bleeder screw open.	1. Bleed system. 2. Recondition master cylinder. 3. Check for leak and repair as required. 4. Adjust rear brakes. 5. Close bleeder screw and bleed entire system.
Excessive pedal travel	1. Air, leak, or insufficient fluid in system or caliper. 2. Warped or excessively tapered shoe and lining assembly. 3. Excessive disc runout. 4. Rear brake adjustment required. 5. Loose wheel bearing adjustment. 6. Damaged caliper piston seal. 7. Improper brake fluid (boil). 8. Power brake malfunction.	1. Check system for leaks and bleed. 2. Install new shoe and linings. 3. Check disc for runout with dial indicator. Install new or refinished disc. 4. Check and adjust rear brakes. 5. Readjust wheel bearing to specified torque. 6. Install new piston seal. 7. Drain and install correct fluid. 8. Replace.
Brake roughness or chatter (pedal pumping)	1. Excessive thickness variation of braking disc. 2. Excessive lateral runout of braking disc. 3. Rear brake drums out-of-round. 4. Excessive front bearing clearance.	1. Check disc for thickness variation using a micrometer. 2. Check disc for lateral runout with dial indicator. Install new or refinished disc. 3. Reface rear drums and check for out-of-round. 4. Readjust wheel bearings to specified torque.
Excessive pedal effort	1. Brake fluid, oil or grease on linings. 2. Incorrect lining. 3. Frozen or seized pistons. 4. Power brake malfunction.	1. Install new shoe linings as required. 2. Remove lining and install correct lining. 3. Disassemble caliper and free up pistons. 4. Replace.

GENERAL TROUBLESHOOTING AND DIAGNOSIS

Condition	Possible Cause	Corrective Action
Pull	1. Brake fluid, oil or grease on linings. 2. Unmatched linings. 3. Distorted brake shoes. 4. Frozen or seized pistons. 5. Incorrect tire pressure. 6. Front end out of alignment. 7. Broken rear spring. 8. Rear brake pistons sticking. 9. Restricted hose or line. 10. Caliper not in proper alignment to braking disc.	1. Install new shoe and linings. 2. Install correct lining. 3. Install new brake shoes. 4. Disassemble caliper and free up pistons. 5. Inflate tires to recommended pressures. 6. Align front end and check. 7. Install new rear spring. 8. Free up rear brake pistons. 9. Check hoses and lines and correct as necessary. 10. Remove caliper and reinstall. Check alignment.

ELECTRICAL

Turn Signal and Flasher Troubleshooting

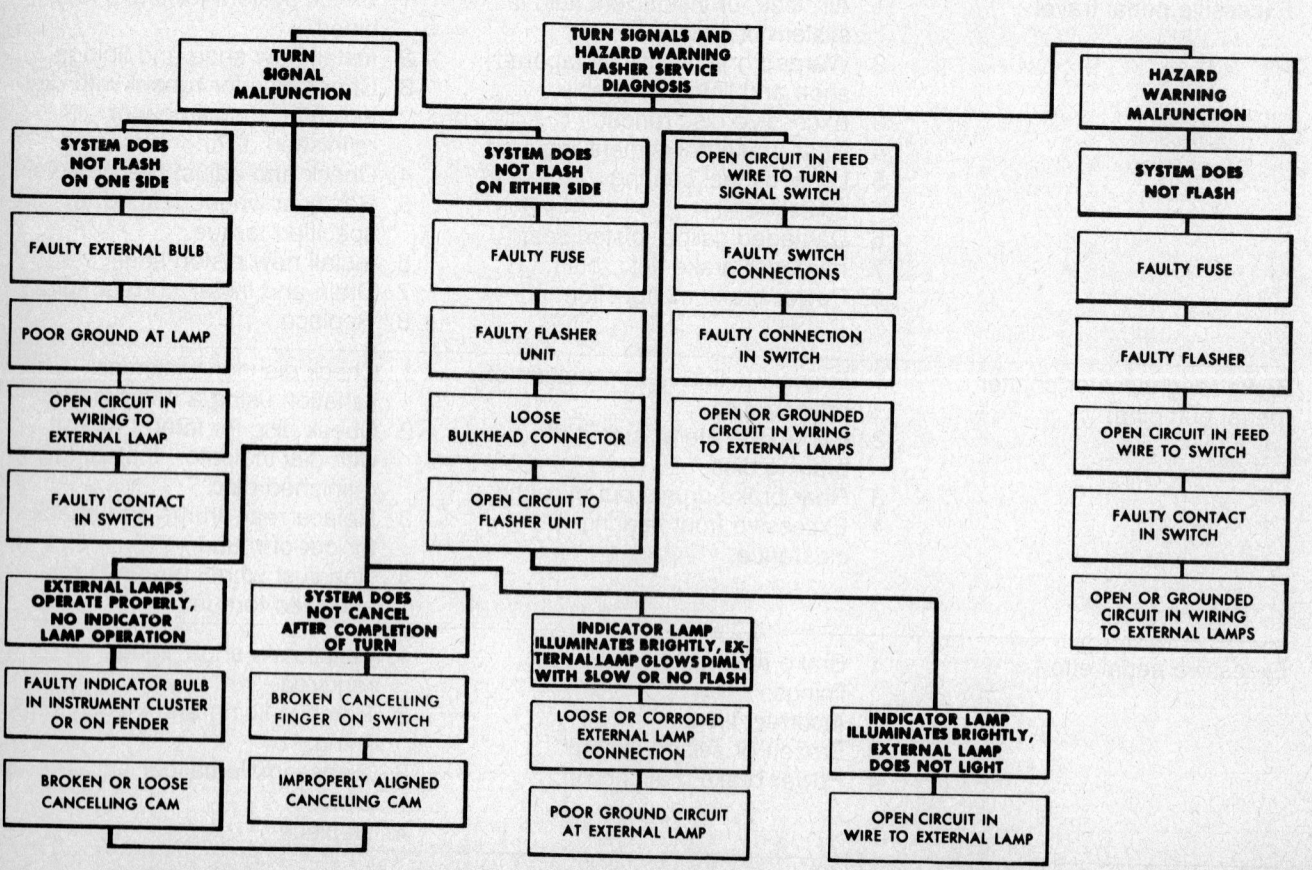

Windshield Wiper Troubleshooting

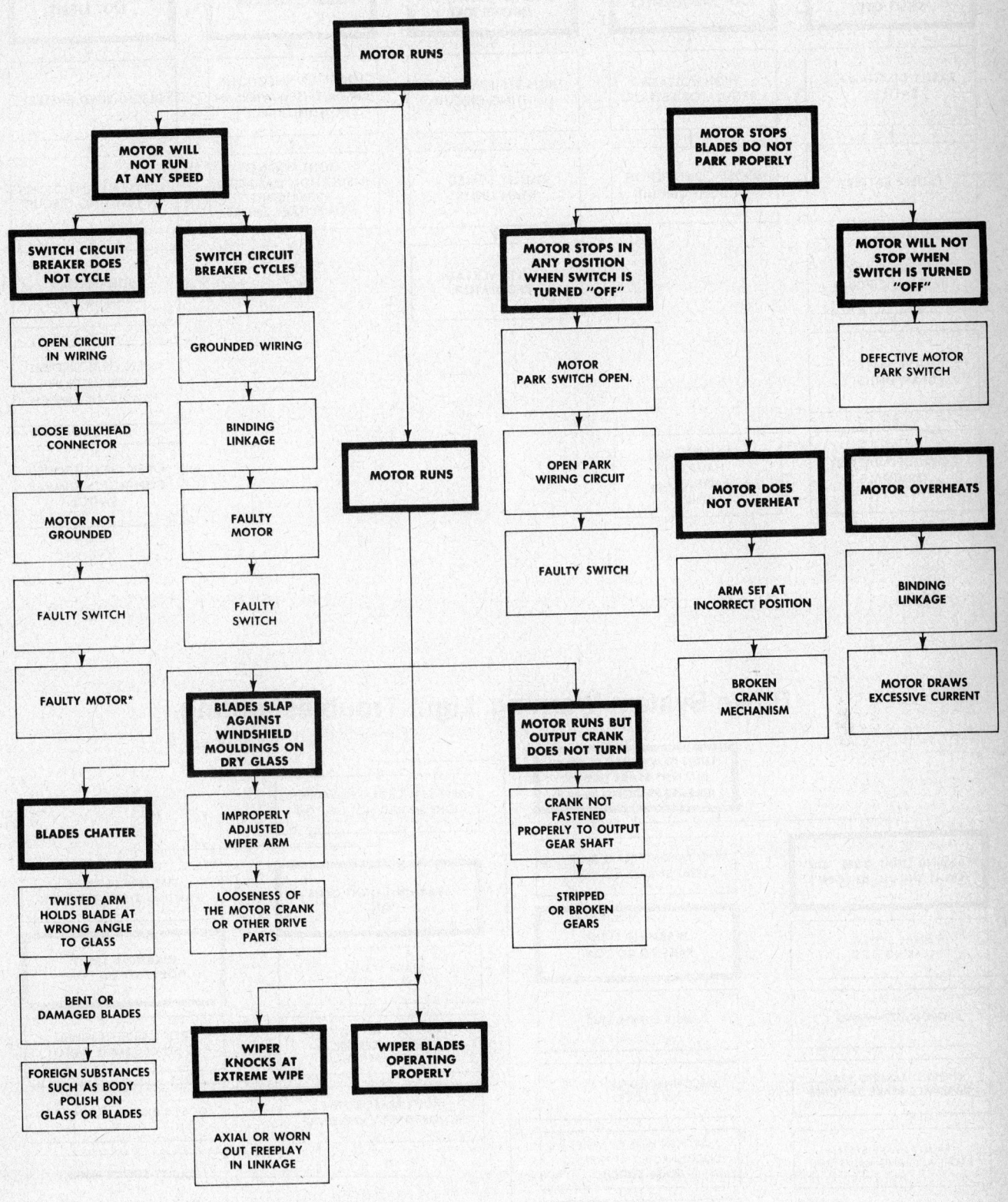

Headlamp Troubleshooting

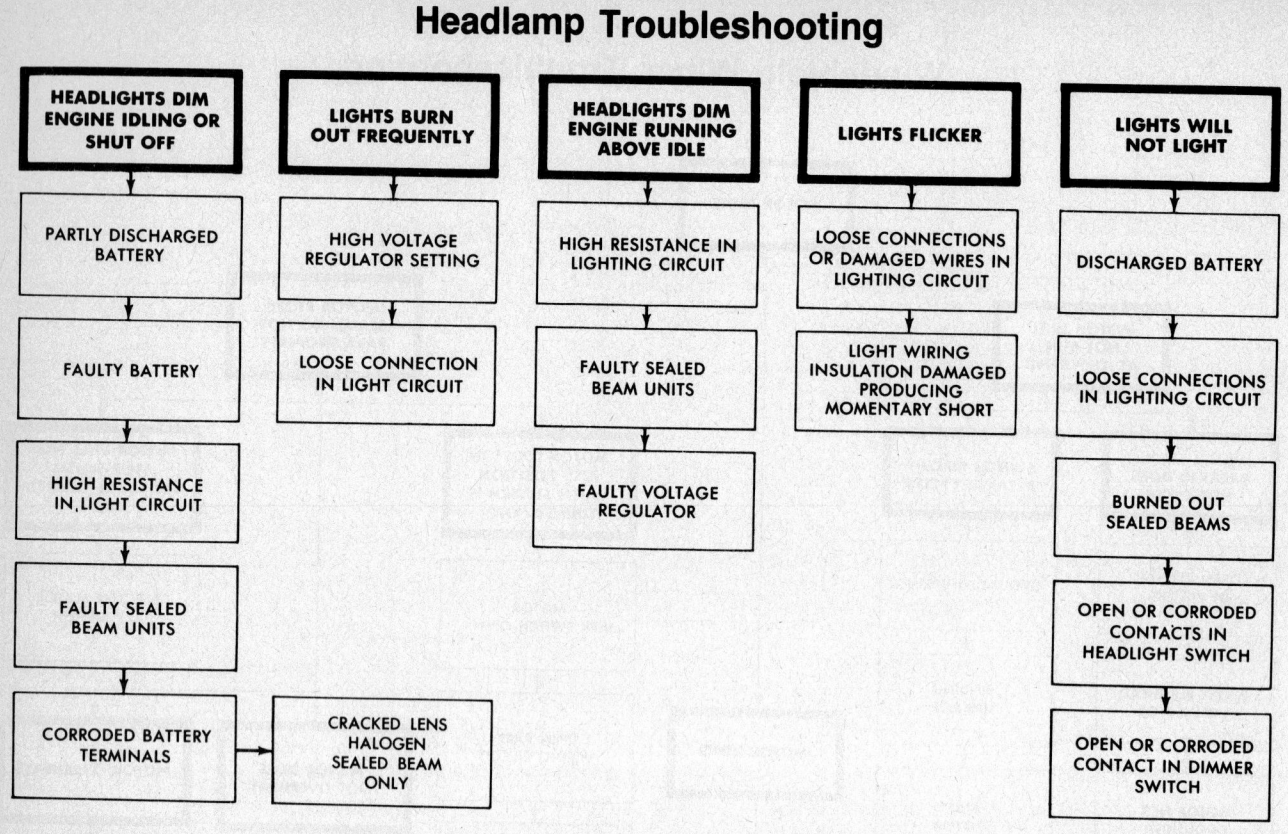

Brake System Warning Light Troubleshooting

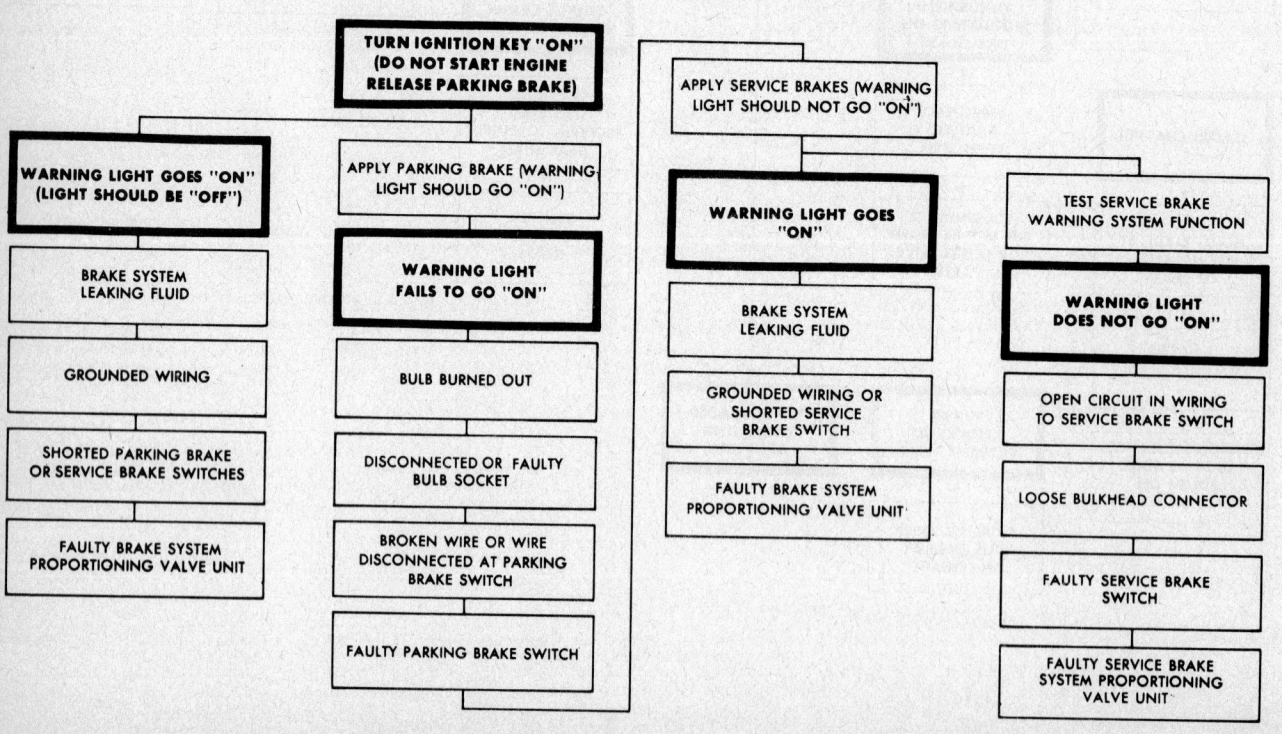

Fuel Gauge System Troubleshooting

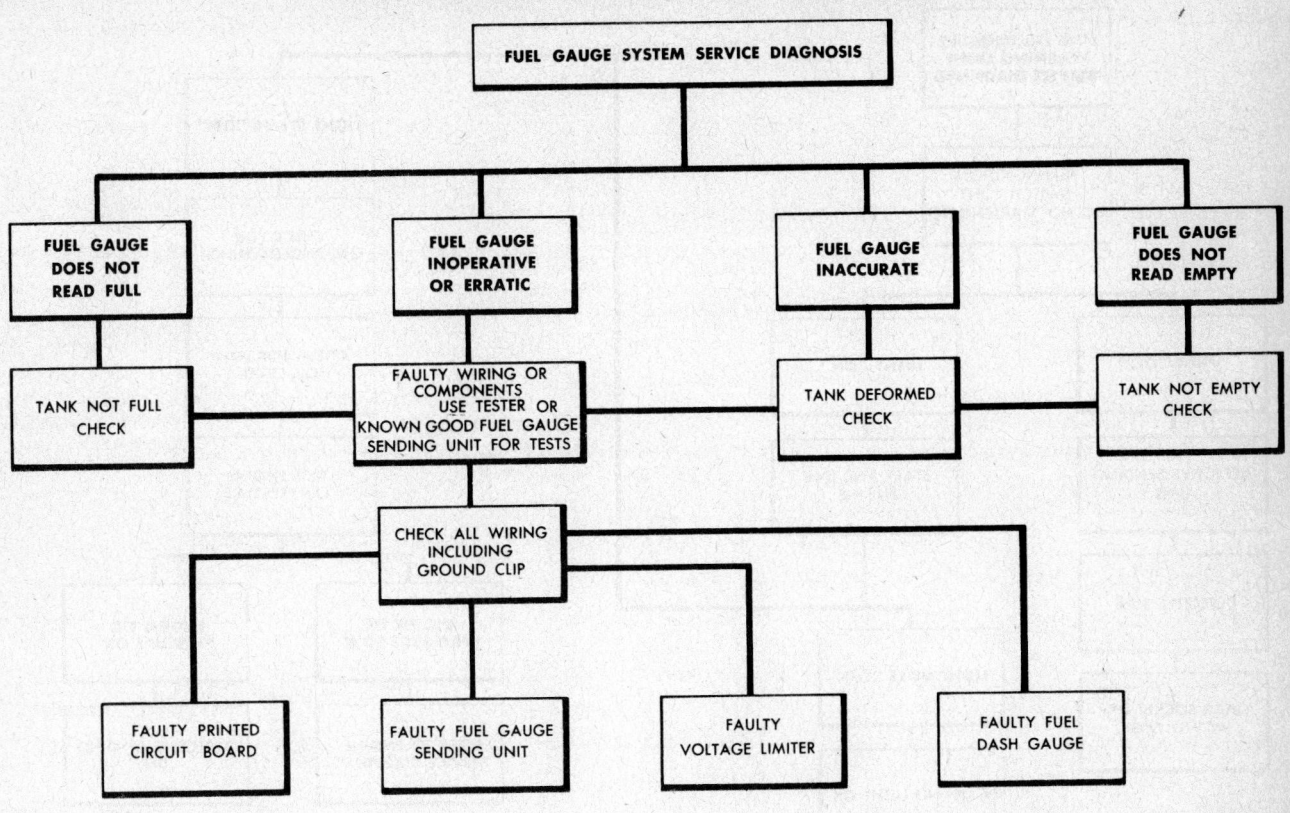

Voltage Limiter Troubleshooting

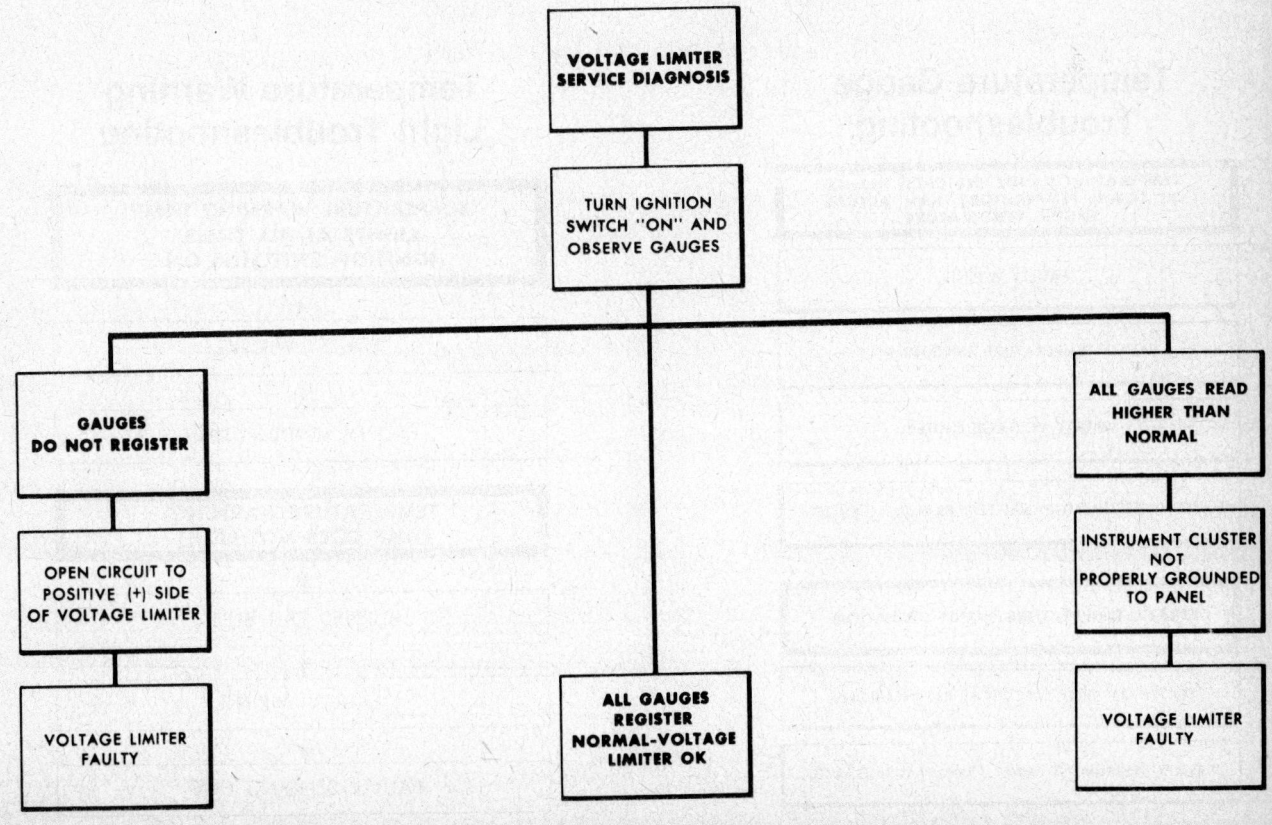

GENERAL TROUBLESHOOTING AND DIAGNOSIS

Low Oil Pressure Warning Light Troubleshooting

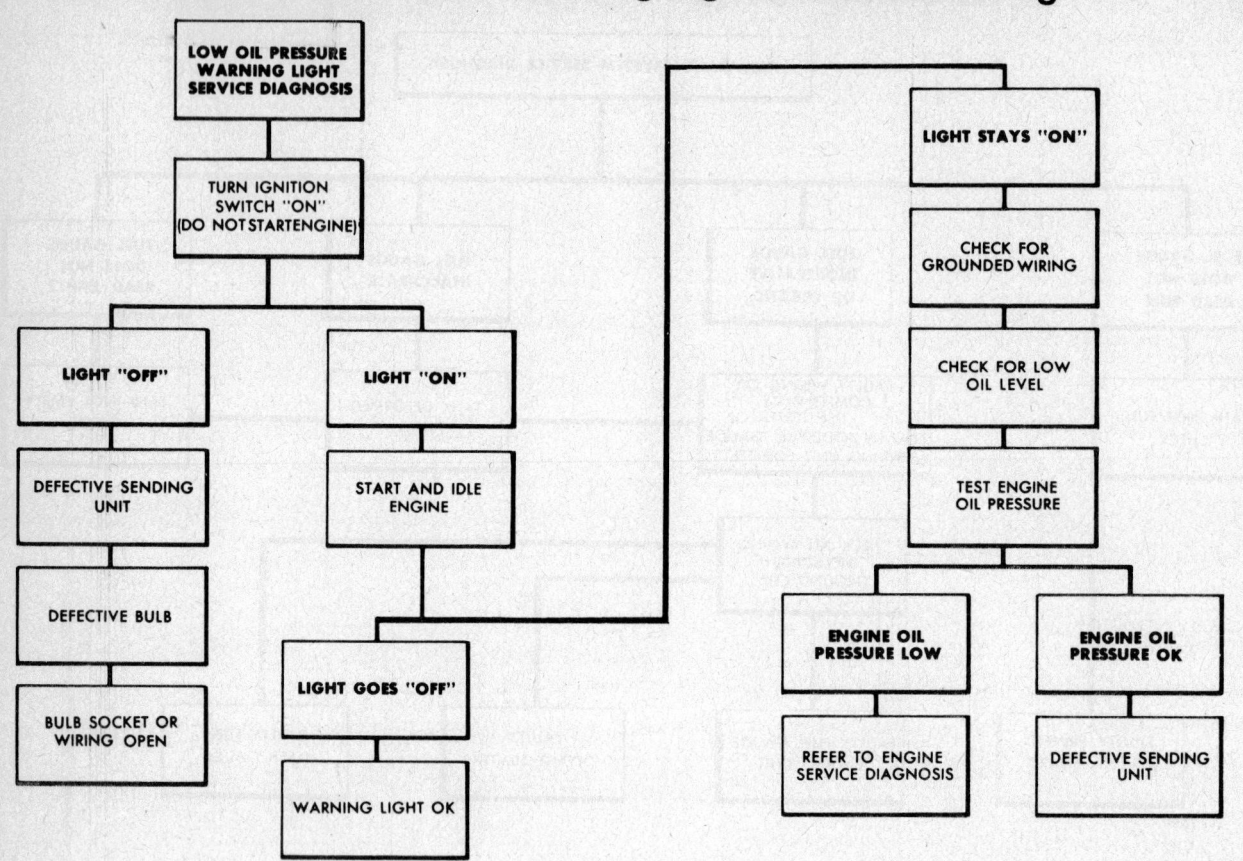

Temperature Gauge Troubleshooting

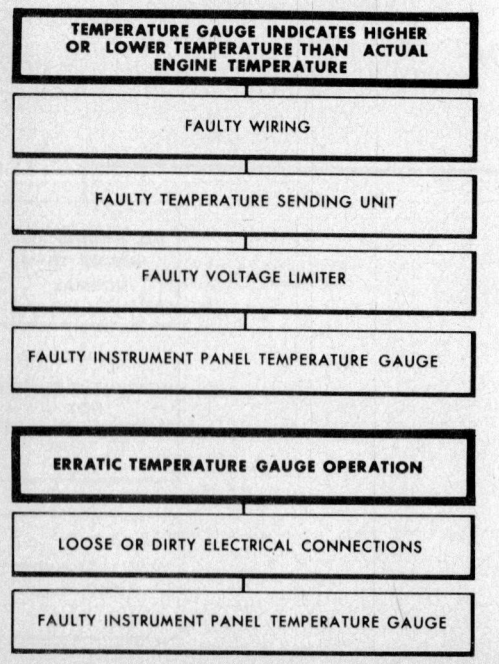

Temperature Warning Light Troubleshooting

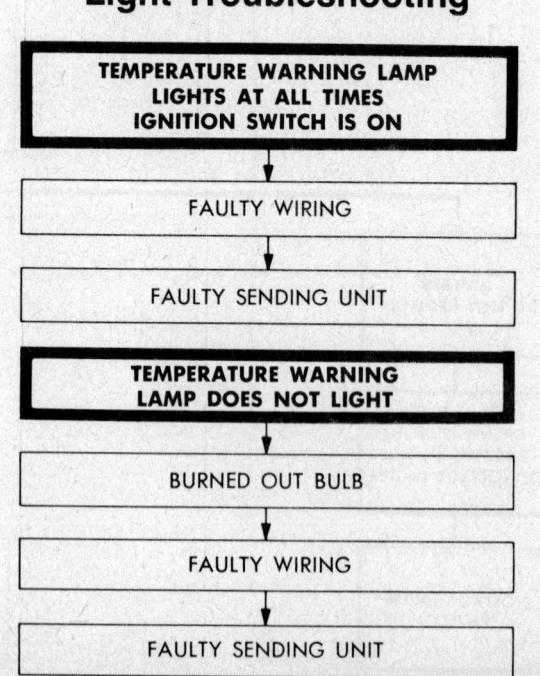

GENERAL TROUBLESHOOTING AND DIAGNOSIS

Automotive Air Conditioning System Troubleshooting

CAUTION: Every automotive air conditioner refrigeration system contains fluid under high pressure—even when the system is at rest. Leakage can cause fracture of metal parts in a high pressure explosion. Such accidental explosions often result in the escape of liquid refrigerant that is at −25°F. At this temperature accidental contact with human skin can cause severe frostbite. NEVER ATTEMPT TO WORK ON AN AUTOMOTIVE AIR CONDITIONING SYSTEM WITHOUT THE PROPER TOOLS OR A THOROUGH KNOWLEDGE OF HOW THIS SYSTEM OPERATES. Any attempt to tighten a loose fitting can be dangerous unless the proper techniques, tools and safety precautions are used.

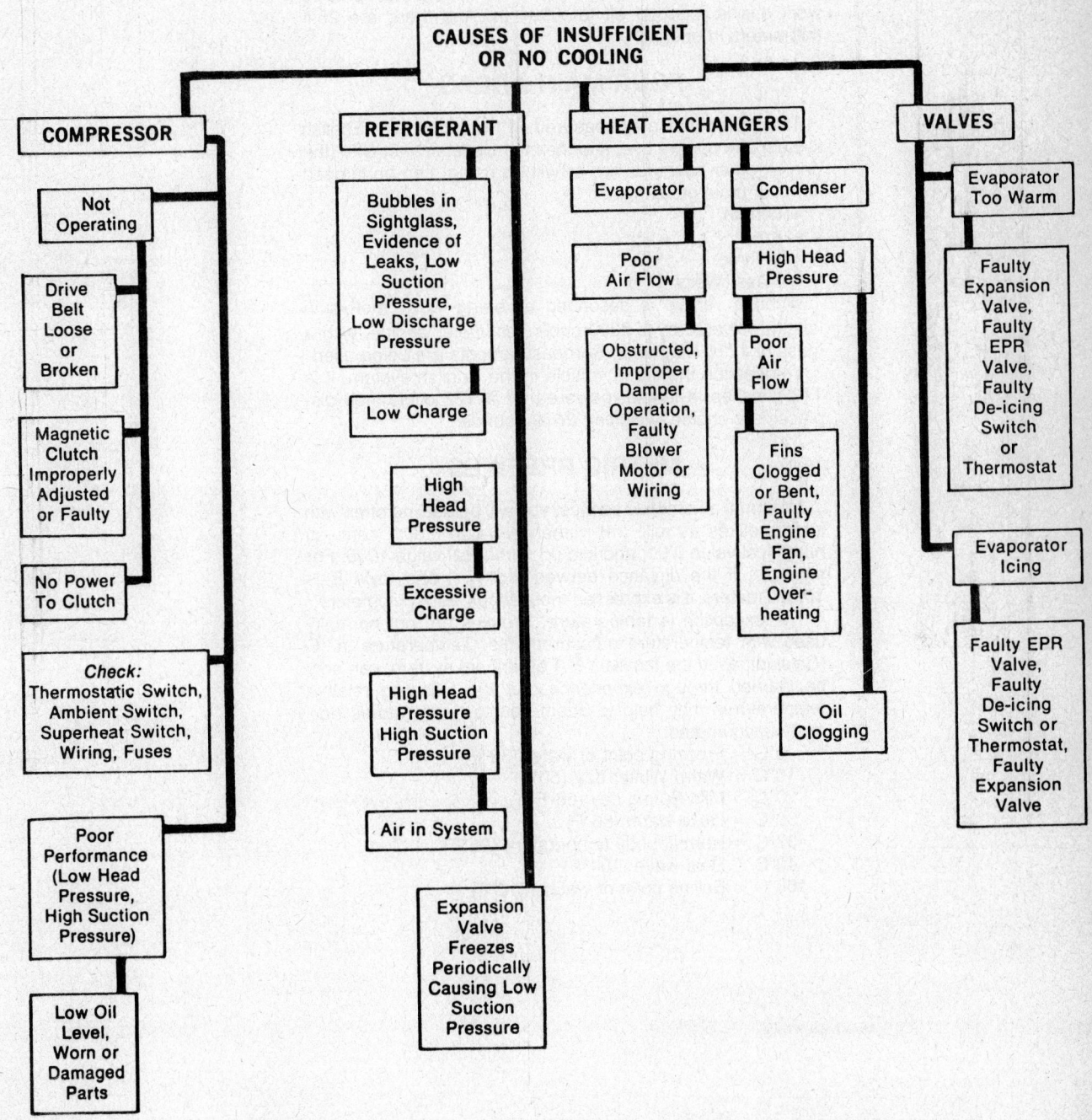

HOW IT WORKS

The metric system is based on multiples of 10, like our money (100 cents = $1; or 10 pennies = 1 dime, 10 dimes = $1). The foundation of the metric system is the meter (which is a little more than 39 inches in length).

This meter is divided into 1000 parts, each part called a millimeter. Do not confuse the millimeter with a millionth of a meter just because it sounds like a million. One millimeter is 1/1000th of a meter.

Since one meter is actually 39.37 inches, a millimeter (mm) is .03937 inches (39.37 ÷ 1000). For all but the most precise work this is rounded off to .0394 in. And there are 25.4 millimeters in one inch.

FOUR MAIN AREAS

The things that are measured in the customary English system (the one we use) and the metric system—or SI—(the one all other countries are or will be using) can be lumped into four main groupings:

- Length
- Area
- Volume
- Mass (Weight)

When a vehicle is described as being 4.557 meters in length, powered by a 2000 cubic centimeter engine, with a mass of 1210 kilograms, SI measurements are being used.

To describe the same vehicle in the English system, it is 179.4 inches in length, powered by a 122 cubic inch displacement engine, weighing 2679 pounds.

METRIC PREFIXES

In normal automotive service, you will be dealing often with such prefixes as milli (m) numerical value 0.001; centi (c) numerical value 0.01; and kilo (k) numerical value 1000. For example, if the distance between town A and town B is 10,000 meters, it is expressed more simply as 10 kilometers.

The exception is temperature. Prefixes are not normally used with temperature measurements. Temperature in °C (Celsius), as in the familiar °F (Fahrenheit) system, can only be learned through experience, but the following relative temperatures may help to orient you to temperatures normally encountered.

    0°C = Freezing point of water (32°F)
  10°C = Warm Winter day (50°F)
  20°C = Mild Spring day (68°F)
  30°C = Quite warm (86°F)
  37°C = Normal body temperature (98°F)
  40°C = Heat wave (104°F)
100°C = Boiling point of water (212°F)

BASIC UNITS IN METRIC MEASUREMENT

Measurement	Metric Unit	Replaces Customary English Unit	Approximate Size
Length	Millimeter (mm)	Inch (in.)	Diameter of a paper clip wire
	Centimeter (cm)	Inch (in.)	Width of paper clip
	Meter (m)	Yard	Little longer than a yard (about 1.1 yards)
	Kilometer (km)	Mile	Little more than ½ mile (about .6 mile)
Weight (Mass)	Gram (g)	Ounce (oz)	Little more than weight of a paper clip
	Kilogram (kg)	Pound (lb)	Little more than 2 pounds (about 2.2 pounds)
	Metric Ton	Ton	Little more than a short ton (about 2200 pounds)
Volume	Milliliter (ml)	Ounce (liquid) (oz)	Five of these equal 1 teaspoon
	Liter (l)	Quart (qt)	Little larger than a quart (about 1.06 quarts). 4 liters is slightly more than 1 gallon
	Cubic centimeter (cm³)	Cubic inch (cu. in.)	There are about 60 cm³ in 1 cubic inch
Pressure	Kilopascal (Kpa)	Psi	Atmospheric pressure (14.7 psi) is about 100 kilopascals. 1 psi = 6.89 Kpa
Torque	Newton-Meter (Nm)	Foot-pound (ft lb)	A newton-meter (Nm) is about ⅓ larger than a foot-pound
Temperature	Degree Celcius (°C)	Degree Fahrenheit (°F)	See scale
Force	Newton (N)	Pounds force (lbs)	1 pound of force equals approximately 4½ newtons
Power	Kilowatt (kW)	Horsepower (hp)	1 kilowatt equals approximately 1¼ horsepower

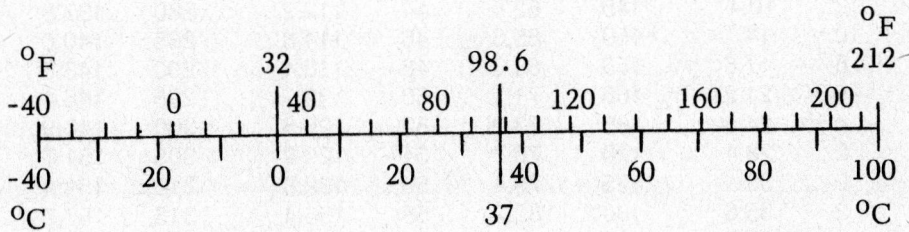

METRIC TABLES

ENGLISH TO METRIC CONVERSION: MASS (WEIGHT)

Current mass measurement in pounds and ounces (lbs. & ozs.). The metric unit of mass (or weight) is the kilogram (kg). Even though this table does not show conversion of masses (weights) larger than 15 lbs, it is easy to calculate larger units by following the data immediately below.

To convert ounces (oz.) to grams (g): multiply the number of ozs. by 28
To convert grams (g) to ounces (oz.): multiply the number of grams by .035

To convert pounds (lbs.) to kilograms (kg): multiply the number of lbs. by .45
To convert kilograms (kg) to pounds (lbs): multiply the number of kilograms by 2.2

lbs	kg	lbs	kg	oz	kg	oz	kg
0.1	0.04	0.9	0.41	0.1	0.003	0.9	0.024
0.2	0.09	1	0.4	0.2	0.005	1	0.03
0.3	0.14	2	0.9	0.3	0.008	2	0.06
0.4	0.18	3	1.4	0.4	0.011	3	0.08
0.5	0.23	4	1.8	0.5	0.014	4	0.11
0.6	0.27	5	2.3	0.6	0.017	5	0.14
0.7	0.32	10	4.5	0.7	0.020	10	0.28
0.8	0.36	15	6.8	0.8	0.023	15	0.42

ENGLISH TO METRIC CONVERSION: TEMPERATURE

To convert Fahrenheit (°F) to Celsius (°C): take number of °F and subtract 32; multiply result by 5; divide result by 9
To convert Celsius (°C) to Fahrenheit (°F): take number of °C and multiply by 9; divide result by 5; add 32 to total

Fahrenheit (F)		Celsius (C)		Fahrenheit (F)		Celsius (C)		Fahrenheit (F)		Celsius (C)	
°F	°C	°C	°F	°F	°C	°C	°F	°F	°C	°C	°F
−40	−40	−38	−36.4	80	26.7	18	64.4	215	101.7	80	176
−35	−37.2	−36	−32.8	85	29.4	20	68	220	104.4	85	185
−30	−34.4	−34	−29.2	90	32.2	22	71.6	225	107.2	90	194
−25	−31.7	−32	−25.6	95	35.0	24	75.2	230	110.0	95	202
−20	−28.9	−30	−22	100	37.8	26	78.8	235	112.8	100	212
−15	−26.1	−28	−18.4	105	40.6	28	82.4	240	115.6	105	221
−10	−23.3	−26	−14.8	110	43.3	30	86	245	118.3	110	230
− 5	−20.6	−24	−11.2	115	46.1	32	89.6	250	121.1	115	239
0	−17.8	−22	− 7.6	120	48.9	34	93.2	255	123.9	120	248
1	−17.2	−20	− 4	125	51.7	36	96.8	260	126.6	125	257
2	−16.7	−18	− 0.4	130	54.4	38	100.4	265	129.4	130	266
3	−16.1	−16	3.2	135	57.2	40	104	270	132.2	135	275
4	−15.6	−14	6.8	140	60.0	42	107.6	275	135.0	140	284
5	−15.0	−12	10.4	145	62.8	44	112.2	280	137.8	145	293
10	−12.2	−10	14	150	65.6	46	114.8	285	140.6	150	302
15	− 9.4	− 8	17.6	155	68.3	48	118.4	290	143.3	155	311
20	− 6.7	− 6	21.2	160	71.1	50	122	295	146.1	160	320
25	− 3.9	− 4	24.8	165	73.9	52	125.6	300	148.9	165	329
30	− 1.1	− 2	28.4	170	76.7	54	129.2	305	151.7	170	338
35	1.7	0	32	175	79.4	56	132.8	310	154.4	175	347
40	4.4	2	35.6	180	82.2	58	136.4	315	157.2	180	356
45	7.2	4	39.2	185	85.0	60	140	320	160.0	185	365
50	10.0	6	42.8	190	87.8	62	143.6	325	162.8	190	374
55	12.8	8	46.4	195	90.6	64	147.2	330	165.6	195	383
60	15.6	10	50	200	93.3	66	150.8	335	168.3	200	392
65	18.3	12	53.6	205	96.1	68	154.4	340	171.1	205	401
70	21.1	14	57.2	210	98.9	70	158	345	173.9	210	410
75	23.9	16	60.8	212	100.0	75	167	350	176.7	215	414

ENGLISH TO METRIC CONVERSION: TORQUE FT./LBS.

Torque is expressed as either foot-pounds (ft./lbs.) or inch-pounds (in./lbs.). The metric measurement unit for torque is the Newton-meter (Nm). This unit—the Nm—will be used for all SI metric torque references, both the present ft./lbs. and in./lbs.

To convert foot-pounds (ft./lbs.) to Newton-meters: multiply ft./lbs. by 1.3
To convert inch-pounds (in./lbs.) to Newton-meters: multiply in./lbs. by .11

ft./lbs.	N-m	ft./lbs	N-m	ft./lbs.	N-m	ft./lbs.	N-m
0.1	0.1	33	44.7	74	100.3	115	155.9
0.2	0.3	34	46.1	75	101.7	116	157.3
0.3	0.4	35	47.4	76	103.0	117	158.6
0.4	0.5	36	48.8	77	104.4	118	160.0
0.5	0.7	37	50.7	78	105.8	119	161.3
0.6	0.8	38	51.5	79	107.1	120	162.7
0.7	1.0	39	52.9	80	108.5	121	164.0
0.8	1.1	40	54.2	81	109.8	122	165.4
0.9	1.2	41	55.6	82	111.2	123	166.8
1	1.3	42	56.9	83	112.5	124	168.1
2	2.7	43	58.3	84	113.9	125	169.5
3	4.1	44	59.7	85	115.2	126	170.8
4	5.4	45	61.0	86	116.6	127	172.2
5	6.8	46	62.4	87	118.0	128	173.5
6	8.1	47	63.7	88	119.3	129	174.9
7	9.5	48	65.1	89	120.7	130	176.2
8	10.8	49	66.4	90	122.0	131	177.6
9	12.2	50	67.8	91	123.4	132	179.0
10	13.6	51	69.2	92	124.7	133	180.3
11	14.9	52	70.5	93	126.1	134	181.7
12	16.3	53	71.9	94	127.4	135	183.0
13	17.6	54	73.2	95	128.8	136	184.4
14	18.9	55	74.6	96	130.2	137	185.7
15	20.3	56	75.9	97	131.5	138	187.1
16	21.7	57	77.3	98	132.9	139	188.5
17	23.0	58	78.6	99	134.2	140	189.8
18	24.4	59	80.0	100	135.6	141	191.2
19	25.8	60	81.4	101	136.9	142	192.5
20	27.1	61	82.7	102	138.3	143	193.9
21	28.5	62	84.1	103	139.6	144	195.2
22	29.8	63	85.4	104	141.0	145	196.6
23	31.2	64	86.8	105	142.4	146	198.0
24	32.5	65	88.1	106	143.7	147	199.3
25	33.9	66	89.5	107	145.1	148	200.7
26	35.2	67	90.8	108	146.4	149	202.0
27	36.6	68	92.2	109	147.8	150	203.4
28	38.0	69	93.6	110	149.1	151	204.7
29	39.3	70	94.9	111	150.5	152	206.1
30	40.7	71	96.3	112	151.8	153	207.4
31	42.0	72	97.6	113	153.2	154	208.8
32	43.4	73	99.0	114	154.6	155	210.2

METRIC TABLES

ENGLISH TO METRIC CONVERSION: LIQUID CAPACITY

Liquid or fluid capacity is presently expressed as pints, quarts or gallons, or a combination of all of these. In the metric system the liter (l) will become the basic unit. Fractions of a liter would be expressed as deciliters, centiliters, or most frequently (and commonly) as milliliters.

To convert pints (pts.) to liters (l): multiply the number of pints by .47
To convert liters (l) to pints (pts.): multiply the number of liters by 2.1
To convert quarts (qts.) to liters (l): multiply the number of quarts by .95

To convert liters (l) to quarts (qts.): multiply the number of liters by 1.06
To convert gallons (gals). to liters (l): multiply the number of gallons by 3.8
To convert liters (l) to gallons (gals.): multiply the number of liters by .26

gals	liters	qts	liters	pts	liters
0.1	0.38	0.1	0.10	0.1	0.05
0.2	0.76	0.2	0.19	0.2	0.10
0.3	1.1	0.3	0.28	0.3	0.14
0.4	1.5	0.4	0.38	0.4	0.19
0.5	1.9	0.5	0.47	0.5	0.24
0.6	2.3	0.6	0.57	0.6	0.28
0.7	2.6	0.7	0.66	0.7	0.33
0.8	3.0	0.8	0.76	0.8	0.38
0.9	3.4	0.9	0.85	0.9	0.43
1	3.8	1	1.0	1	0.5
2	7.6	2	1.9	2	1.0
3	11.4	3	2.8	3	1.4
4	15.1	4	3.8	4	1.9
5	18.9	5	4.7	5	2.4
6	22.7	6	5.7	6	2.8
7	26.5	7	6.6	7	3.3
8	30.3	8	7.6	8	3.8
9	34.1	9	8.5	9	4.3
10	37.8	10	9.5	10	4.7
11	41.6	11	10.4	11	5.2
12	45.4	12	11.4	12	5.7
13	49.2	13	12.3	13	6.2
14	53.0	14	13.2	14	6.6
15	56.8	15	14.2	15	7.1
16	60.6	16	15.1	16	7.6
17	64.3	17	16.1	17	8.0
18	68.1	18	17.0	18	8.5
19	71.9	19	18.0	19	9.0
20	75.7	20	18.9	20	9.5
21	79.5	21	19.9	21	9.9
22	83.2	22	20.8	22	10.4
23	87.0	23	21.8	23	10.9
24	90.8	24	22.7	24	11.4
25	94.6	25	23.6	25	11.8
26	98.4	26	24.6	26	12.3
27	102.2	27	25.5	27	12.8
28	106.0	28	26.5	28	13.2
29	110.0	29	27.4	29	13.7
30	113.5	30	28.4	30	14.2

ENGLISH TO METRIC CONVERSION: FORCE

Force is presently measured in pounds (lbs). This type of measurement is used to measure spring pressure, specifically how many pounds it takes to compress a spring. Our present force unit (the pound) will be replaced in SI metric measurements by the Newton (N). This term will eventually see use in specifications for electric motor brush spring pressures, valve spring pressures, etc.

To convert pounds (lbs.) to Newton (N): multiply the number of lbs. by 4.45

lbs.	N	lbs.	N	lbs.	N	oz.	N
0.01	0.04	21	93.4	59	262.4	1	0.3
0.02	0.09	22	97.9	60	266.9	2	0.6
0.03	0.13	23	102.3	61	271.3	3	0.8
0.04	0.18	24	106.8	62	275.8	4	1.1
0.05	0.22	25	111.2	63	280.2	5	1.4
0.06	0.27	26	115.6	64	284.6	6	1.7
0.07	0.31	27	120.1	65	289.1	7	2.0
0.08	0.36	28	124.6	66	293.6	8	2.2
0.09	0.40	29	129.0	67	298.0	9	2.5
0.1	0.4	30	133.4	68	302.5	10	2.8
0.2	0.9	31	137.9	69	306.9	11	3.1
0.3	1.3	32	142.3	70	311.4	12	3.3
0.4	1.8	33	146.8	71	315.8	13	3.6
0.5	2.2	34	151.2	72	320.3	14	3.9
0.6	2.7	35	155.7	73	324.7	15	4.2
0.7	3.1	36	160.1	74	329.2	16	4.4
0.8	3.6	37	164.6	75	333.6	17	4.7
0.9	4.0	38	169.0	76	338.1	18	5.0
1	4.4	39	173.5	77	342.5	19	5.3
2	8.9	40	177.9	78	347.0	20	5.6
3	13.4	41	182.4	79	351.4	21	5.8
4	17.8	42	186.8	80	355.9	22	6.1
5	22.2	43	191.3	81	360.3	23	6.4
6	26.7	44	195.7	82	364.8	24	6.7
7	31.1	45	200.2	83	369.2	25	7.0
8	35.6	46	204.6	84	373.6	26	7.2
9	40.0	47	209.1	85	378.1	27	7.5
10	44.5	48	213.5	86	382.6	28	7.8
11	48.9	49	218.0	87	387.0	29	8.1
12	53.4	50	224.4	88	391.4	30	8.3
13	57.8	51	226.9	89	395.9	31	8.6
14	62.3	52	231.3	90	400.3	32	8.9
15	66.7	53	235.8	91	404.8	33	9.2
16	71.2	54	240.2	92	409.2	34	9.4
17	75.6	55	244.6	93	413.7	35	9.7
18	80.1	56	249.1	94	418.1	36	10.0
19	84.5	57	253.6	95	422.6	37	10.3
20	89.0	58	258.0	96	427.0	38	10.6

METRIC TABLES

ENGLISH TO METRIC CONVERSION: PRESSURE

The basic unit of pressure measurement used today is expressed as pounds per square inch (psi). The metric unit for psi will be the kilopascal (kPa). This will apply to either fluid pressure or air pressure, and will be frequently seen in tire pressure readings, oil pressure specifications, fuel pump pressure, etc.

To convert pounds per square inch (psi) to kilopascals (kPa): multiply the number of psi by 6.89

Psi	kPa	Psi	kPa	Psi	kPa	Psi	kPa
0.1	0.7	37	255.1	82	565.4	127	875.6
0.2	1.4	38	262.0	83	572.3	128	882.5
0.3	2.1	39	268.9	84	579.2	129	889.4
0.4	2.8	40	275.8	85	586.0	130	896.3
0.5	3.4	41	282.7	86	592.9	131	903.2
0.6	4.1	42	289.6	87	599.8	132	910.1
0.7	4.8	43	296.5	88	606.7	133	917.0
0.8	5.5	44	303.4	89	613.6	134	923.9
0.9	6.2	45	310.3	90	620.5	135	930.8
1	6.9	46	317.2	91	627.4	136	937.7
2	13.8	47	324.0	92	634.3	137	944.6
3	20.7	48	331.0	93	641.2	138	951.5
4	27.6	49	337.8	94	648.1	139	958.4
5	34.5	50	344.7	95	655.0	140	965.2
6	41.4	51	351.6	96	661.9	141	972.2
7	48.3	52	358.5	97	668.8	142	979.0
8	55.2	53	365.4	98	675.7	143	985.9
9	62.1	54	372.3	99	682.6	144	992.8
10	69.0	55	379.2	100	689.5	145	999.7
11	75.8	56	386.1	101	696.4	146	1006.6
12	82.7	57	393.0	102	703.3	147	1013.5
13	89.6	58	399.9	103	710.2	148	1020.4
14	96.5	59	406.8	104	717.0	149	1027.3
15	103.4	60	413.7	105	723.9	150	1034.2
16	110.3	61	420.6	106	730.8	155	1068.7
17	117.2	62	427.5	107	737.7	160	1103.2
18	124.1	63	434.4	108	744.6	165	1137.6
19	131.0	64	441.3	109	751.5	170	1172.1
20	137.9	65	448.2	110	758.4	175	1206.6
21	144.8	66	455.0	111	765.3	180	1241.0
22	151.7	67	461.9	112	772.2	185	1275.5
23	158.6	68	468.8	113	779.1	190	1310.0
24	165.5	69	475.7	114	786.0	195	1344.5
25	172.4	70	482.6	115	792.9	200	1378.9
26	179.3	71	489.5	116	799.8	250	1723.7
27	186.2	72	496.4	117	806.7	300	2068.4
28	193.0	73	503.3	118	813.6	350	2411.5
29	200.0	74	510.2	119	820.5	400	2756.0
30	206.8	75	517.1	120	827.4	450	3100.5
31	213.7	76	524.0	121	834.3	500	3445.0
32	220.6	77	530.9	122	841.2	600	4134.0
33	227.5	78	537.8	123	848.0	700	4823.0
34	234.4	79	544.7	124	854.9	800	5512.0
35	241.3	80	551.6	125	861.8	900	6201.0
36	248.2	81	558.5	126	868.7	1000	6890.0

GENERAL CONVERSION TABLE

Multiply By	To Convert	To	—
Length			**—**
2.54	Inches	Centimeters	.3937
25.4	Inches	Millimeters	.03937
30.48	Feet	Centimeters	.0328
.304	Feet	Meters	3.28
.914	Yards	Meters	1.094
1.609	Miles	Kilometers	.621
Volume			
.473	Pints	Liters	2.11
.946	Quarts	Liters	1.06
3.785	Gallons	Liters	.264
.016	Cubic inches	Liters	61.02
16.39	Cubic inches	Cubic cms.	.061
28.3	Cubic feet	Liters	.0353
Mass (Weight)			
28.35	Ounces	Grams	.035
.4536	Pounds	Kilograms	2.20
Area			
6.45	Square inches	Square cms.	.155
.836	Square yds.	Square meters	1.196
Force			
4.448	Pounds	Newtons	.225
.138	Ft./lbs.	Kilogram/meters	7.23
1.36	Ft./lbs.	Newton-meters	.737
.112	In./lbs.	Newton-meters	8.844
Pressure			
.068	Psi	Atmospheres	14.7
6.89	Psi	Kilopascals	.145
Other			
1.104	Horsepower (DIN)	Horsepower (SAE)	.9861
.746	Horsepower (SAE)	Kilowatts (KW)	1.34
1.60	Mph	Km/h	.625
.425	Mpg	Km/1	2.35
—	**To obtain**	**From**	**Multiply by**

TAP DRILL SIZES

NATIONAL COARSE OR U.S.S.						NATIONAL FINE OR S.A.E.					
Screw & Tap Size	Threads Per Inch	Use Drill Number	Screw & Tap Size	Threads Per Inch	Use Drill Number	Screw & Tap Size	Threads Per Inch	Use Drill Number	Screw & Tap Size	Threads Per Inch	Use Drill Number
No. 5	40	39	1/2	13	27/64	No. 5	44	37	1/2	20	29/64
No. 6	32	36	9/16	12	31/64	No. 6	40	33	9/16	18	33/64
No. 8	32	29	5/8	11	17/32	No. 8	36	29	5/8	18	37/64
No. 10	24	25	3/4	10	21/32	No. 10	32	21	3/4	16	11/16
No. 12	24	17	7/8	9	49/64	No. 12	28	15	7/8	14	13/16
1/4	20	8	1	8	7/8	1/4	28	3	1 1/8	12	1 3/64
5/16	18	F	1 1/8	7	63/64	5/16	24	1	1 1/4	12	1 11/64
3/8	16	5/16	1 1/4	7	1 7/64	3/8	24	Q	1 1/2	12	1 27/64
7/16	14	U	1 1/2	6	1 11/32	7/16	20	W			

DRILL SIZES IN DECIMAL EQUIVALENTS

Inch	Decimal	Wire	mm	Inch	Decimal	Wire	mm	Inch	Decimal	Wire	mm	Inch	Decimal	Wire & Letter	mm	Inch	Decimal	Letter	mm	Inch	Decimal	mm
1/64	.0156		.39		.0610		1.55		.1285	30			.2090	4			.3160	O			.5315	13.5
	.0157		.4	1/16	.0625		1.59		.1299		3.3		.2126		5.4		.3189		8.1	35/64	.5469	13.89
	.0160	78			.0630		1.6		.1339		3.4		.2130	3			.3228		8.2		.5512	14.0
	.0165		.42		.0635	52			.1360	29			.2165		5.5		.3230	P		9/16	.5625	14.28
	.0173		.44		.0650		1.65		.1378		3.5	7/32	.2188		5.55		.3248		8.25		.5709	14.5
	.0177		.45		.0669		1.7		.1405	28			.2205		5.6		.3268		8.3	37/64	.5781	14.68
	.0180	77			.0670	51		9/64	.1406		3.57		.2210	2		21/64	.3281		8.33		.5906	15.0
	.0181		.46		.0689		1.75		.1417		3.6		.2244		5.7		.3307		8.4	19/32	.5938	15.08
	.0189		.48		.0700	50			.1440	27			.2264		5.75		.3320	Q		39/64	.6094	15.47
	.0197		.5		.0709		1.8		.1457		3.7		.2280	1			.3346		8.5		.6102	15.5
	.0200	76			.0728		1.85		.1470	26			.2283		5.8		.3386		8.6	5/8	.6250	15.87
	.0210	75			.0730	49			.1476		3.75		.2323		5.9		.3390	R			.6299	16.0
	.0217		.55		.0748		1.9		.1495	25			.2340	A			.3425		8.7	41/64	.6406	16.27
	.0225	74			.0760	48			.1496		3.8	15/64	.2344		5.95	11/32	.3438		8.73		.6496	16.5
	.0236		.6		.0768		1.95		.1520	24			.2362		6.0		.3445		8.75	21/32	.6562	16.66
	.0240	73		5/64	.0781		1.98		.1535		3.9		.2380	B			.3465		8.8		.6693	17.0
	.0250	72			.0785	47			.1540	23			.2402		6.1		.3480	S		43/64	.6719	17.06
	.0256		.65		.0787		2.0	5/32	.1562		3.96		.2420	C			.3504		8.9	11/16	.6875	17.46
	.0260	71			.0807		2.05		.1570	22			.2441		6.2		.3543		9.0		.6890	17.5
	.0276		.7		.0810	46			.1575		4.0		.2460	D			.3580	T		45/64	.7031	17.85
	.0280	70			.0820	45			.1590	21			.2461		6.25		.3583		9.1		.7087	18.0
	.0292	69			.0827		2.1		.1610	20			.2480		6.3	23/64	.3594		9.12	23/32	.7188	18.25
	.0295		.75		.0846		2.15		.1614		4.1	1/4	.2500	E	6.35		.3622		9.2		.7283	18.5
	.0310	68			.0860	44			.1654		4.2		.2520		6.4		.3642		9.25	47/64	.7344	18.65
1/32	.0312		.79		.0866		2.2		.1660	19			.2559		6.5		.3661		9.3		.7480	19.0
	.0315		.8		.0886		2.25		.1673		4.25		.2570	F			.3680	U		3/4	.7500	19.05
	.0320	67			.0890	43			.1693		4.3		.2598		6.6		.3701		9.4	49/64	.7656	19.44
	.0330	66			.0906		2.3		.1695	18			.2610	G			.3740		9.5		.7677	19.5
	.0335		.85		.0925		2.35	11/64	.1719		4.36		.2638		6.7	3/8	.3750		9.52	25/32	.7812	19.84
	.0350	65			.0935	42			.1730	17		17/64	.2656		6.74		.3770	V			.7874	20.0
	.0354		.9	3/32	.0938		2.38		.1732		4.4		.2657		6.75		.3780		9.6	51/64	.7969	20.24
	.0360	64			.0945		2.4		.1770	16			.2660	H			.3819		9.7		.8071	20.5
	.0370	63			.0960	41			.1772		4.5		.2677		6.8		.3839		9.75	13/16	.8125	20.63
	.0374		.95		.0965		2.45		.1800	15			.2717		6.9		.3858		9.8		.8268	21.0
	.0380	62			.0980	40			.1811		4.6		.2720	I			.3860	W		53/64	.8281	21.03
	.0390	61			.0981		2.5		.1820	14			.2756		7.0		.3898		9.9	27/32	.8438	21.43
	.0394		1.0		.0995	39			.1850	13			.2770	J		25/64	.3906		9.92		.8465	21.5
	.0400	60			.1015	38			.1850		4.7		.2795		7.1		.3937		10.0	55/64	.8594	21.82
	.0410	59			.1024		2.6		.1870		4.75		.2810	K			.3970	X			.8661	22.0
	.0413		1.05		.1040	37		3/16	.1875		4.76	9/32	.2812		7.14		.4040	Y		7/8	.8750	22.22
	.0420	58			.1063		2.7		.1890		4.8		.2835		7.2	13/32	.4062		10.31		.8858	22.5
	.0430	57			.1065	36			.1890	12			.2854		7.25		.4130	Z		57/64	.8906	22.62
	.0433		1.1		.1083		2.75		.1910	11			.2874		7.3		.4134		10.5		.9055	23.0
	.0453		1.15	7/64	.1094		2.77		.1929		4.9		.2900	L		27/64	.4219		10.71	29/32	.9062	23.01
	.0465	56			.1100	35			.1935	10			.2913		7.4		.4331		11.0	59/64	.9219	23.41
3/64	.0469		1.19		.1102		2.8		.1960	9			.2950	M		7/16	.4375		11.11		.9252	23.5
	.0472		1.2		.1110	34			.1969		5.0		.2953		7.5		.4528		11.5	15/16	.9375	23.81
	.0492		1.25		.1130	33			.1990	8		19/64	.2969		7.54	29/64	.4531		11.51		.9449	24.0
	.0512		1.3		.1142		2.9		.2008		5.1		.2992		7.6	15/32	.4688		11.90	61/64	.9531	24.2
	.0520	55			.1160	32			.2010	7			.3020	N			.4724		12.0		.9646	24.5
	.0531		1.35		.1181		3.0	13/64	.2031		5.16		.3031		7.7	31/64	.4844		12.30	31/32	.9688	24.6
	.0550	54			.1200	31			.2040	6			.3051		7.75		.4921		12.5		.9843	25.0
	.0551		1.4		.1220		3.1		.2047		5.2		.3071		7.8	1/2	.5000		12.70	63/64	.9844	25.0
	.0571		1.45	1/8	.1250		3.17		.2055	5			.3110		7.9		.5118		13.0	1	1.0000	25.4
	.0591		1.5		.1260		3.2		.2067		5.25	5/16	.3125		7.93	33/64	.5156		13.09			
	.0595	53			.1280		3.25		.2087		5.3		.3150		8.0	17/32	.5312		13.49			

FREEZING AND BOILING POINTS OF SOLUTIONS ACCORDING TO PERCENTAGE OF ALCOHOL OR ETHYLENE GLYCOL

Freezing Point of Solution	Alcohol Volume %	Alcohol Solution Boils at	Ethylene Glycol Volume %	Ethylene Glycol Solution Boils at
20°F.	12	196°F.	16	216°F.
10°F.	20	189°F.	25	218°F.
0°F.	27	184°F.	33	220°F.
−10°F.	32	181°F.	39	222°F.
−20°F.	38	178°F.	44	224°F.
−30°F.	42	176°F.	48	225°F.

NOTE: Boiling points are at sea level. For every 1,000 feet of altitude, boiling points are approximately 2°F. lower than shown. For every pound of pressure exerted by the pressure cap, boiling points are approximately 3°F. higher than shown.

TO INCREASE THE FREEZING PROTECTION OF ANTI-FREEZE SOLUTIONS ALREADY INSTALLED

Cooling System Capacity Quarts	Number of Quarts of ETHYLENE GLYCOL Anti-Freeze Required to Increase Protection													
	From +20°F. to					From +10°F. to					From 0°F. to			
	0°	−10°	−20°	−30°	−40°	0°	−10°	−20°	−30°	−40°	−10°	−20°	−30°	−40°
10	1¾	2¼	3	3½	3¾	¾	1½	2¼	2¾	3¼	¾	1½	2	2½
12	2	2¾	3½	4	4½	1	1¾	2½	3¼	3¾	1	1¾	2½	3¼
14	2¼	3¼	4	4¾	5½	1¼	2	3	3¾	4½	1	2	3	3½
16	2½	3½	4½	5¼	6	1¼	2½	3½	4¼	5¼	1¼	2¼	3¼	4
18	3	4	5	6	7	1½	2¾	4	5	5¾	1½	2½	3¾	4¾
20	3¼	4½	5¾	6¾	7½	1¾	3	4¼	5½	6½	1½	2¾	4¼	5¼
22	3½	5	6¼	7¼	8¼	1¾	3¼	4¾	6	7¼	1¾	3¼	4½	5½
24	4	5½	7	8	9	2	3½	5	6½	7½	1¾	3½	5	6
26	4¼	6	7½	8¾	10	2	4	5½	7	8¼	2	3¾	5½	6¾
28	4½	6¼	8	9½	10½	2¼	4¼	6	7½	9	2	4	5¾	7¼
30	5	6¾	8½	10	11½	2½	4½	6½	8	9½	2¼	4¼	6¼	7¾

Test radiator solution with proper hydrometer. Determine the number of quarts of solution to be drawn off from a full cooling system and replace with undiluted anti-freeze, to give the desired increased protection. For example, to increase protection of a 22-quart cooling system containing Ethylene Glycol (permanent type) anti-freeze, from +20°F. to −20°F. will require the replacement of 6¼ quarts of solution with undiluted anti-freeze.

QUARTS OF ETHYLENE GLYCOL REQUIRED FOR PROTECTION TO TEMPERATURES SHOWN

Cooling System Capacity Quarts	Number of Quarts of ETHYLENE GLYCOL Required for Protection													
	1	2	3	4	5	6	7	8	9	10	11	12	13	14
10	+24°F.	+16°F.	+ 4°F.	−12°F.	−34°F.	−62°F.								
11	+25	+18	+ 8	− 6	−23	−47								
12	+26	+19	+10	0	−15	−34	−57°F.							
13	+27	+21	+13	+ 3	− 9	−25	−45							
14			+15	+ 6	− 5	−18	−34							
15			+16	+ 8	0	−12	−26							
16			+17	+10	+ 2	− 8	−19	−34°F.	−52°F.					
17			+18	+12	+ 5	− 4	−14	−27	−42					
18			+19	+14	+ 7	0	−10	−21	−34	−50°F.				
19			+20	+15	+ 9	+ 2	− 7	−16	−28	−42				
20				+16	+10	+ 4	− 3	−12	−22	−34	−48°F.			
21				+17	+12	+ 6	0	− 9	−17	−28	−41			
22				+18	+13	+ 8	+ 2	− 6	−14	−23	−34	−47°F.		
23				+19	+14	+ 9	+ 4	− 3	−10	−19	−29	−40		
24				+19	+15	+10	+ 5	0	− 8	−15	−23	−34	−46°F.	
25				+20	+16	+12	+ 7	+ 1	− 5	−12	−20	−29	−40	−50°F.
26					+17	+13	+ 8	+ 3	− 3	− 9	−16	−25	−34	−44
27					+18	+14	+ 9	+ 5	− 1	− 7	−13	−21	−29	−39
28					+18	+15	+10	+ 6	+ 1	− 5	−11	−18	−25	−34
29					+19	+16	+12	+ 7	+ 2	− 3	− 8	−15	−22	−29
30					+20	+17	+13	+ 8	+ 4	− 1	− 6	−12	−18	−25

NOTE: +32° is freezing. For capacities under 10 quarts multiply true capacity by 3, find quarts of anti-freeze for the tripled volume, divide by 3 for the number of quarts to add. For capacities over 30 quarts divide true capacity by 3, finds quarts of anti-freeze for the ⅓ of volume, multiply by 3 for the number of quarts to add.

GENERAL MAINTENANCE

INTRODUCTION

Routine maintenance is probably the most important part of automobile care and the easiest to neglect. A regular program aimed at monitoring essential systems ensures that all components are in good and safe working order, and can prevent small problems from developing into major headaches. Routine maintenance also pays off big dividends in keeping major repair costs at a minimum and extending the life of the car.

The owner's manual that came with your car includes a maintenance schedule, indicating service intervals in numbers of months or thousands of miles. This schedule should always be followed, if possible. We have provided, in each section, a guide to service intervals based on an averaging of manufacturer's recommendations. In most cases, the suggested interval offered here will be close to that given by the manufacturer of your car, but the manufacturer's schedule should always take precedence.

We have divided the maintenance work to be done into three categories: Under Hood, Under Car, and Exterior. The checks in each section require only a few minutes of attention every few weeks; the services to be performed can be easily accomplished in a morning. The most important part of any maintenance program is regularity. The few minutes or occasional morning spent on these seemingly trivial tasks will forestall or eliminate major problems later.

UNDER HOOD

Automatic Transmission, Automatic Transaxle

The fluid level in the automatic transmission or transaxle should be checked every three months or 6000 miles. All automatic transmissions have a dipstick for fluid level checks.

1. Drive the car until it is at normal operating temperature. The level should not be checked immediately after the car has been driven for a long time at high speed, or in city traffic in hot weather; in those cases, the transmission should be given a half hour to cool down.

2. Stop the car, apply the parking brake, then shift slowly through all gear positions, ending in Park. Leave the engine running.

3. Remove the dipstick, wipe it clean, then reinsert it, pushing it fully home.

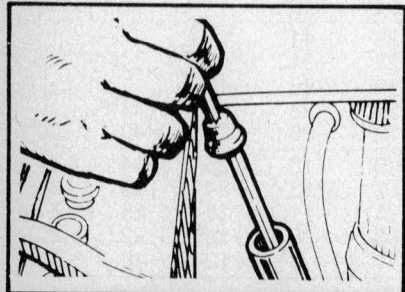

Check the automatic transmission fluid level with the dipstick provided

4. Pull the dipstick again and, holding it horizontally, read the fluid level.

5. Cautiously feel the end of the dipstick to determine the temperature. Most dipsticks are marked with both cool and hot levels. If the fluid is not up to the correct level, more will have to be added.

NOTE: On 1980 and later Citation, Omega, Phoenix, Skylark, Cavalier, Cimarron, J2000, Celebrity, Cierra and A6000, the "Cold" level marks (dimples) are above the "Hot" level area.

6. Fluid is added through the dipstick tube. You will probably need the aid of a spout or a long-necked funnel. Be sure that whatever you pour through is perfectly clean and dry. Fluid recommendations can be found in the owner's manual or the Automatic Transmission Unit Repair Section in this book.

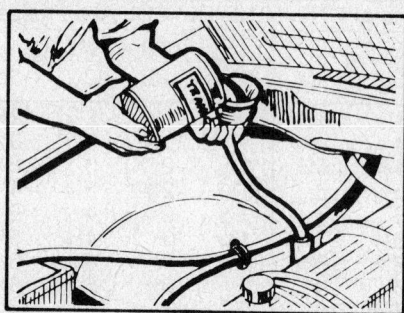

Fill the automatic transmission through the dipstick tube

Add fluid slowly, and in small amounts, checking the level frequently between additions. Do not overfill, which will cause foaming, fluid loss, slippage, and possible transmission damage.

Battery
FLUID LEVEL (EXCEPT "MAINTENANCE FREE" BATTERIES)

Check the battery electrolyte level at least once a month, or more often in hot weather or during periods of extended car operation. The level can be checked through the case on translucent polypropylene batteries; the cell caps must be removed on other models. The electrolyte level in each cell should be kept filled to the split ring inside, or the line marked on the outside of the case.

If the level is low, add only distilled water,

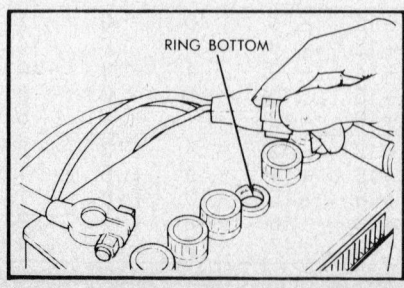

Fill the battery cell to the bottom of the split ring

or colorless, odorless drinking water, through the opening until the level is correct. Each cell is completely separate from the others, so each must be checked and filled individually.

If water is added in freezing weather, the car should be driven several miles to allow the water to mix with the electrolyte. Otherwise, the battery could freeze.

SPECIFIC GRAVITY (EXCEPT "MAINTENANCE FREE" BATTERIES)

At least once a year, check the specific gravity of the battery. It should be between 1.20 and 1.26 at room temperature. See the "Charging and Starting Systems" Section in this book for details.

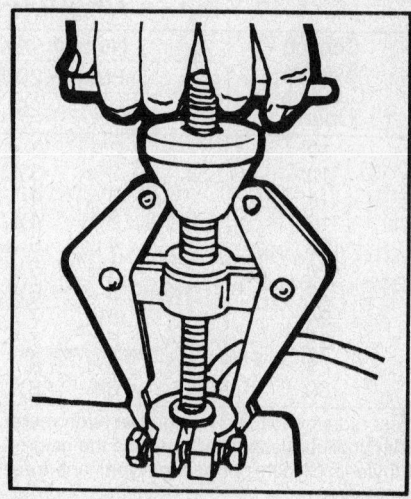

Use a puller to remove the clamp on post-type batteries

CABLES AND CLAMPS

Once a year, the battery terminals and the cable clamps should be cleaned. Loosen the clamps and remove the cables, negative cable first. On batteries with posts on top, the use of a puller specially made for the purpose is recommended. These are inexpensive, and available in auto parts stores. Side terminal battery cables are secured with a bolt.

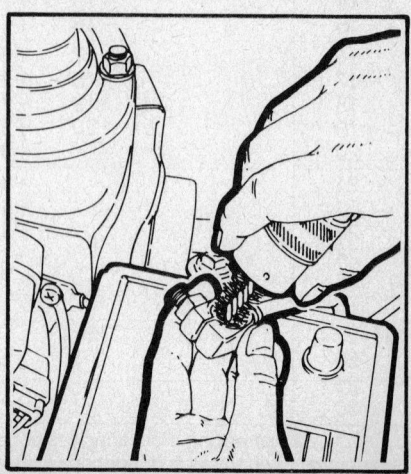

Clean the clamp with a wire brush

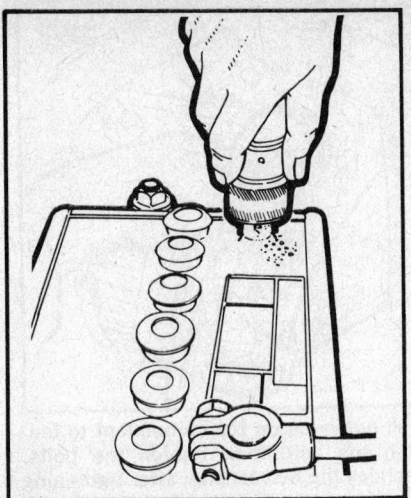

The posts are easily cleaned with a wire brush, or the battery post tool shown

Clean the cable clamps and the battery terminal with a wire brush, until all corrosion, grease, etc. is removed and the metal is shiny. It is especially important to clean the inside of the clamp thoroughly, since a small deposit of foreign material or oxidation there will prevent a sound electrical connection and inhibit either starting or charging. Special tools are available for cleaning these parts, one type for conventional batteries and another type for side terminal batteries.

Before installing the cables, loosen the battery hold-down clamp or strap, remove the battery and check the battery tray. Clear it of any debris, and check it for soundness. Rust should be wire brushed away, and the metal given a coat of anti-rust paint. Replace the battery and tighten the hold-down clamp or strap securely, but be careful not to overtighten, which will crack the battery case.

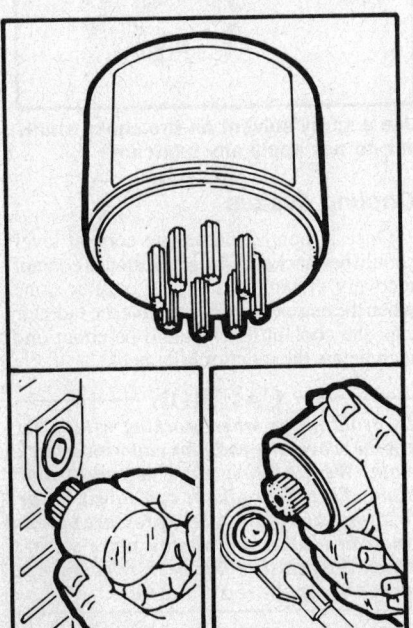

A special tool is required to clean the terminals and clamps on side terminal batteries

After the clamps and terminals are clean, reinstall the cables, negative cable last; do not hammer on the clamps to install. Tighten the clamps securely, but do not distort them. Give the clamps and terminals a thin external coat of grease after installation, to retard corrosion.

Check the cables at the same time that the terminals are cleaned. If the cable insulation is cracked or broken, or if the ends are frayed, the cable should be replaced with a new cable of the same length and gauge.

NOTE: Keep flame or sparks away from the battery; it gives off explosive hydrogen gas. Battery electrolyte contains sulphuric acid. If you should splash any on your skin or in your eyes, flush the affected area with plenty of clear water; if it lands in your eyes, get medical help immediately.

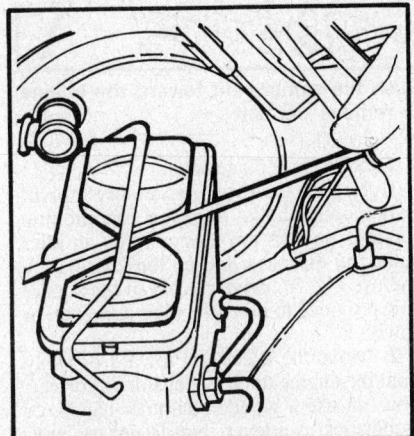

Lever the bail off the master cylinder cap with a screwdriver

Brake Fluid

Once a month, the fluid level in the brake master cylinder should be checked.

1. Park the car on a level surface.
2. Clean off the master cylinder cover before removal. Most covers are held on by a wire bail, which can be pushed aside with thumb pressure, or levered off with a screwdriver. Some covers are retained by a bolt. Some of the newer master cylinders with plastic reservoirs have screw caps. Remove the cover, being careful not to drop or tear the rubber diaphragm which will probably be underneath. Be careful also not to drip any brake fluid on painted surfaces; the stuff eats paint.

NOTE: Brake fluid absorbs moisture from the air, which reduces effectiveness and will corrode brake parts once in the system. Never leave the master cylinder or the brake fluid container uncovered for any longer than necessary.

3. The fluid level should be about ¼ inch below the lip of the master cylinder well.
4. If fluid addition is necessary, use only extra heavy duty disc brake fluid meeting DOT 3 specifications. The fluid should be reasonably fresh, because brake fluid deteriorates with age.

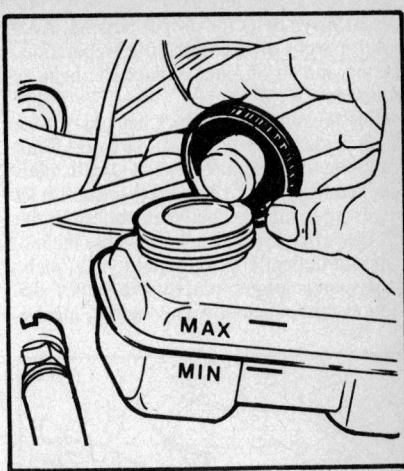

Screw caps are used on some master cylinders

5. Replace the cover, making sure that the diaphragm is correctly seated.

If the brake fluid level is constantly low, the system should be checked for leaks. However, it is normal for the fluid level to fall gradually as the disc brake pads wear; expect the fluid level to drop about ⅛ inch for every 10,000 miles of wear.

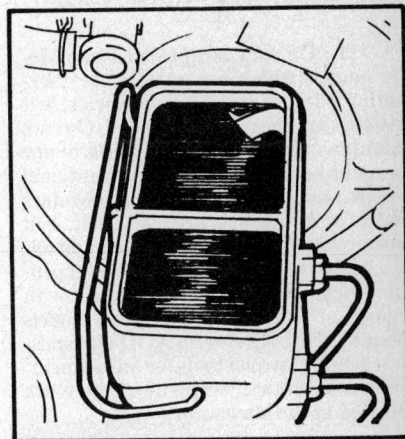

Proper brake fluid level

Belt Tension

Every six months or 12,000 miles, check the water pump, alternator, power steering pump, air pump, and air conditioning com-

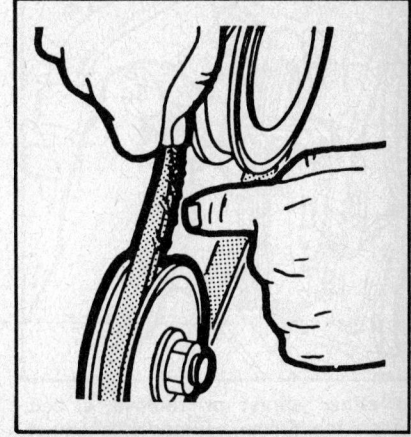

Check the belts for wear

pressor drive belts for proper tension. Also look for signs of wear, fraying, separation, glazing and so on, and replace the belts as required.

Belt tension should be checked with a gauge made for the purpose. If a gauge is not available, tension can be checked with moderate thumb pressure applied to the belt at its longest span midway between pulleys. If the belt has a free span less than twelve inches, it should deflect approximately 1/8–1/4 inch. If the span is longer than twelve inches, deflection can range between 1/8 and 3/8 inches.

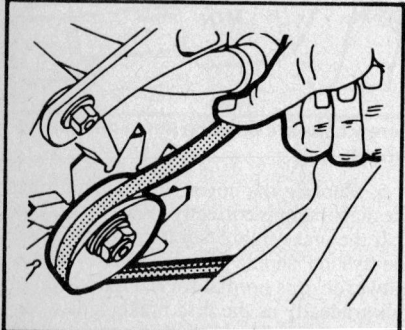

Check the belt tension at the middle of the longest span between pulleys

NOTE: On cars except American Motors models which use a one-piece "serpentine" belt to drive all accessories, belt tension is automatically adjusted. On cars which have two "serpentine" belts, or one "serpentine" belt as well as conventional V-belts, and on all American Motors models with the "serpentine" belt, belt tensions usually must be checked and adjusted. Belt tension is higher on "serpentine" belts and cannot be tested with thumb pressure. Some Ford models (Thunderbird/XR-7 with AOD transmission) require special tools for adjustment. American Motors "serpentine" belts are adjusted at the alternator.

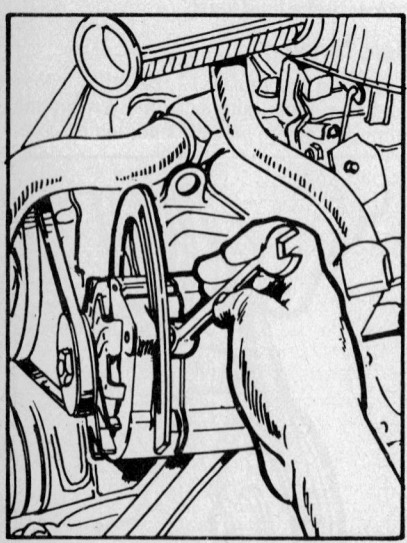

To either adjust or remove a belt, loosen the driven component's adjusting bolt

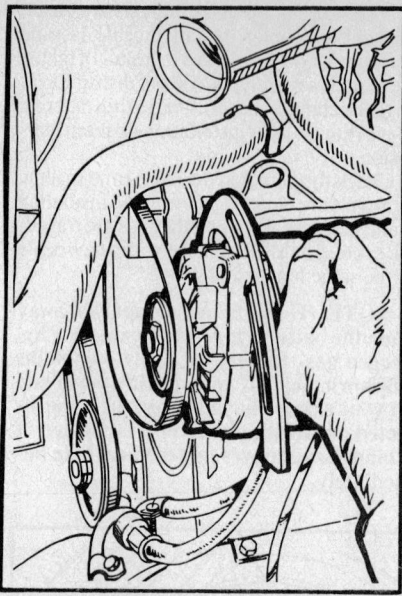

Push the component toward the engine to remove the belt

To adjust or replace belts:

1. Loosen the driven accessory's pivot and mounting bolts. Some air conditioning compressor belts are tensioned by an idler pulley; in this case, loosen the idler pulley and use a 1/2 in. drive ratchet in the square hole provided to lever the idler pulley up or down.

2. Move the accessory toward or away from the engine until the tension is correct. You can use a wooden hammer handle or broomstick as a lever, but do not use anything metallic.

3. Tighten the bolts and recheck the tension. If new belts have been installed, run the engine for a few minutes, then recheck and readjust as necessary.

NOTE: If the driven component has two drive belts, the belts should be replaced in pairs to maintain proper tension.

It is better to have belts too loose than too tight, because overtight belts will lead to bearing failure, particularly in the water pump and alternator. However, loose belts place an extremely high impact load on the

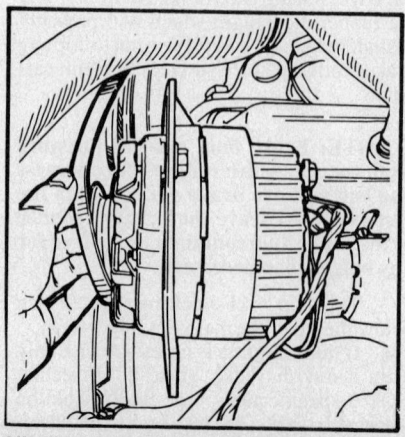

Slip the replacement belt over the pulley

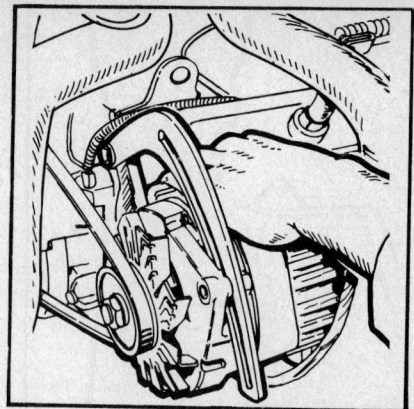

Pull outwards on the component to tension the belt, then tighten the bolts; recheck the belt tension after tightening

driven component due to the whipping action of the belt.

Carburetor and Choke Linkage

Every 12 months or 6000 miles, examine the carburetor linkage and choke plate for free movement. The choke plate action can generally be freed, if necessary, with the application of a solvent made for the purpose to the ends of the choke shaft. This solvent will also clean grease and dirt from the throttle linkage.

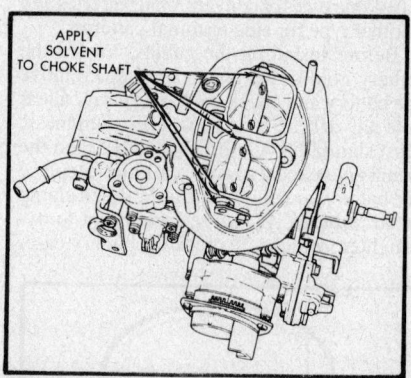

Use a spray solvent on the choke shaft, but do not apply any lubricants

Cooling System

Once a month, the engine coolant level should be checked. On cars without a coolant recovery system, this should only be done when the engine is cold. Remove the radiator cap; the coolant level should be about one inch below the radiator filler neck.

--- CAUTION ---
To avoid injury when working with a hot engine, cover the radiator cap with a thick cloth. Wear a heavy glove to protect your hand. Turn the radiator cap slowly to the first stop, and allow all the pressure to vent (indicated when the hissing noise stops). When the pressure has been released, remove the cap the rest of the way.

On cars with a coolant recovery tank, coolant should be visible within the tank; as long as the coolant is between the markings on the tank, the level is correct.

Fill level mark on crossflow radiator.

Hot and cold level fill marks, constant-full system.

Proper coolant level is about one inch below the radiator neck, or between the lines on the recovery tank

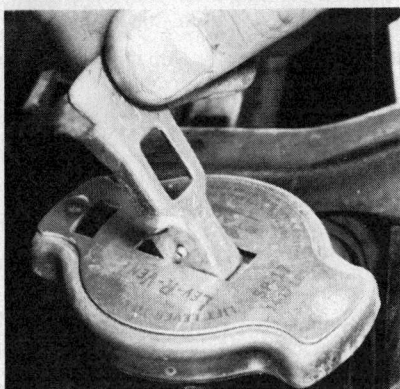

Some caps have a lever to vent pressure. The lever must be pulled up before unscrewing the cap

If coolant is needed, a 50/50 mix of ethylene glycol-based antifreeze and water should always be used, both winter and summer. This is imperative on cars with air conditioning; without the antifreeze, the heater core could freeze when the air conditioning is used. Add coolant to the radiator if the car does not have a coolant recovery system. Add coolant to the recovery tank on cars so equipped.

The radiator hoses and clamps and the radiator cap should be checked at the same time as the coolant level. Hoses which are brittle, cracked, or swollen should be replaced. Clamps should be checked for tightness

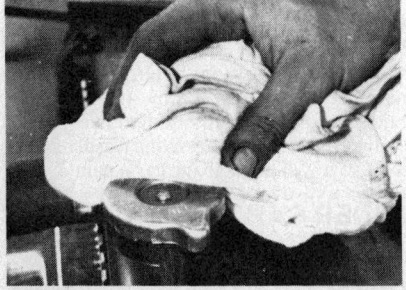

If the engine is hot, place a rag over the radiator cap

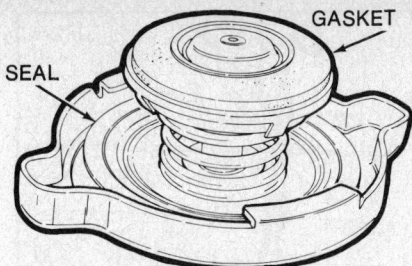

Check the radiator cap gasket and sealing surface

(screwdriver tight only—do not allow the clamp to cut into the hose or crush the fitting). The radiator cap gasket should be checked for any obvious tears, cracks or swelling, or any signs of incorrect seating in the radiator neck.

The cooling system should be drained, flushed and refilled after the first 24 months or 24,000 miles, and every year thereafter.

1. Drain the radiator by opening the drain cock at the bottom. Some radiators do not have these; the lower radiator hose must be disconnected at the radiator instead. If the engine block has drain plugs, they should be opened to speed draining.

Most radiators have a drain cock at the bottom; unscrew to drain

2. Close the drain cocks and fill the system with clear water. A cooling system flushing additive can be used, if desired.
3. Run the engine until it is hot. The heater should be turned on to its maximum heat position so that the core is flushed out.
4. Drain the system, then flush with water until it runs clear.
5. Clean out the coolant recovery tank, if equipped.
6. Fill the system with a 50/50 mix of ethylene glycol-based antifreeze and water. Fill the coolant recovery tank midway between the marks with this mixture also (except G.M. cars, which should be filled to the "Full Cold" mark).
7. Run the engine until it is hot, then let it cool and top up the radiator or coolant recovery tank as necessary with the antifreeze/water mixture.

Heat Riser

The heat riser is a thermostatically or vac-

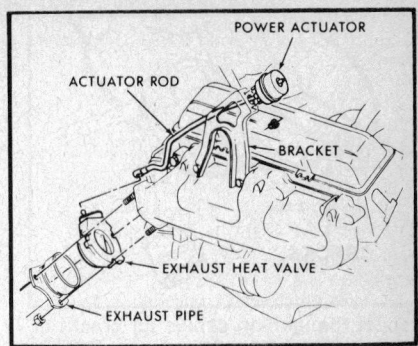

Exploded view of a vacuum-operated heat riser

uum operated valve in the exhaust manifold. (Not all cars have one.) it closes when the engine is warming up, to direct hot exhaust gases to the intake manifold, in order to preheat the incoming fuel/air mixture. If it sticks open, the result will be frequent stalling during warmup, especially in cold and damp weather. If it sticks shut, the result will be a rough idle after the engine is warm.

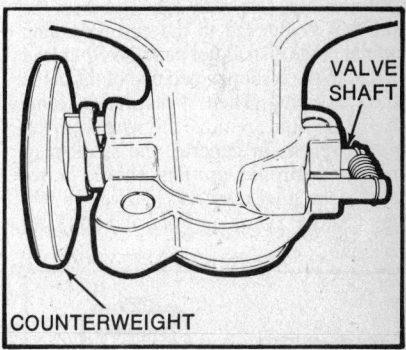

Thermostatically-operated heat control valve

NOTE: Some 1981 and later GM engines are equipped with an electrically heated ceramic grid mounted below the carburetor which takes the place of a heat riser.

The heat riser should move freely. It can be checked easily when the engine is cold by giving the counterweight on the valve shaft a twirl, or pulling the vacuum rod to open and shut the valve. If the valve is sticking or binding, a quick shot of solvent made for the purpose will free it up. This solvent should be applied every six months or 6000 miles to keep the valve free. If the valve is still stuck after application of the solvent, sometimes rapping the end of the shaft lightly with a hammer will break it loose. Otherwise, the components will have to be removed for further repairs.

Ignition Cables

The ignition system (points, condenser, rotor, spark plugs, etc.) receives regular attention in the form of a tune-up, and thus is not covered here. But one of the most commonly overlooked components is the ignition cable, or spark plug wire.

Although they rarely show any visible signs of deterioration, the ignition cables should be checked at every tune-up, and re-

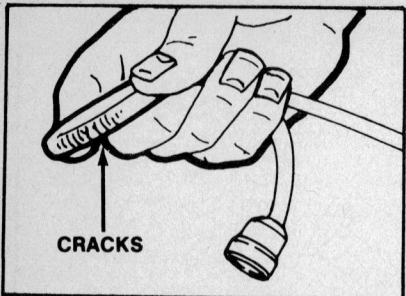

Inspect the ignition cables for cracks or breaks in the insulation

placed every 50,000 miles. Cracking and embrittlement are of course obvious signs of wear, but most newer cables have silicone insulation and thus are not prone to display these conditions.

The most reliable way to check the cables is with an ohmmeter. On conventional ignitions, the resistance should be less than 7,000 ohms per foot (wire removed). On cars with electronic ignitions, it is generally recommended to leave the wire attached to the distributor cap; test with one lead from the ohmmeter connected to the corresponding terminal in the distributor cap, the other lead touched to the disconnected end of the cable at the spark plug. Then, if resistance seems close to the limit, remove the wire from the cap and retest. In general, the spark plug wires on electronic ignitions should be replaced if the total resistance is over 36,000 ohms (50,000 ohms on Ford and Chrysler products).

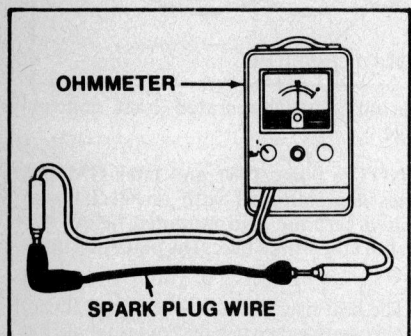

Test the ignition cables with an ohmmeter. Conventional ignition cables should be removed from the distributor cap, but electronic ignition wires should first be tested through the cap

Always replace the cables with new ones of the same type. Replace the wires one at a time, working from the longest to the shortest.

Oil Level

The engine oil should be checked on a regular basis, ideally at each fuel stop, or once a week. It is best to check when the engine is at operating temperature, but checking the level immediately after shutting off the engine will give a false reading, because all of the oil will not yet have drained back into the crankcase. The car should be parked on a level surface to obtain an accurate reading.

1. Remove the oil dipstick. Wipe it clean, then replace it, seating it firmly.

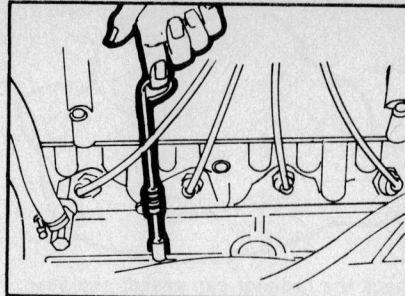

Check the engine oil level with the dipstick

2. Remove the dipstick again and hold it horizontally to prevent the oil from running. The level should be between the "Add" and "Full" marks on the dipstick. The dipstick may be marked "Add" and "Full", "Add" and "Safe", or may have lines scribed on it; in any case, the oil level should be above the lower marking.

3. If the oil is below the lower mark, enough oil should be added to the engine to raise the level to the upper mark. The markings are usually spaced so that one-half to one quart of oil will raise the level from the "Add" mark to the "Full" mark. Oil is added through the capped opening in the valve cover. Only oils labeled SE or SF should be used; select a viscosity that will be compatible with the temperatures expected until the next drain interval.

Add oil through the valve cover

NOTE: The diesel engines used in G.M. cars require the use of SF/CC or SF/CD type oils only. Do not use oil which is rated for SE or SF use only, or which is rated for CD use. Do not use the oil if the rating CD appears anywhere on the can, either alone or in combination with ratings other than SF, such as SE/CD. The use of CD type oil will void the manufacturer's warranty, and may cause expensive engine damage and leakage.

4. Replace the dipstick, then check the level again after any additions of oil. Be careful not to overfill, which will lead to leakage and seal damage.

Power Steering

The power steering fluid level is checked with a dipstick inserted into the pump reservoir. The dipstick may be attached to the reservoir cap, or inserted into a tube on the pump body. The level should be checked at every oil change. On all cars except Ford products, the level can be checked with the fluid either warm or cold; on Fords, the engine must be at operating temperature.

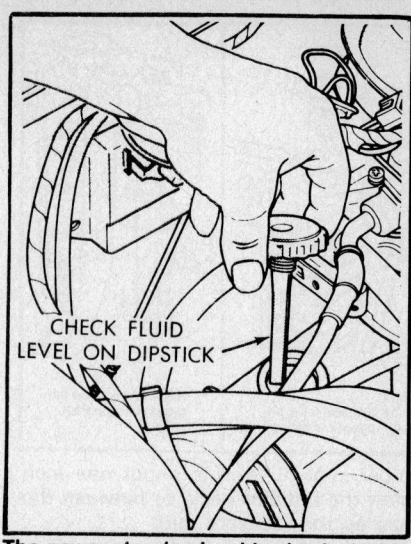

The power steering level is checked with the dipstick installed in the reservoir

1. On Ford products, with the engine hot and idling, turn the steering wheel back and forth to the full right and full left stops several times, then center the wheels and shut off the engine.

2. On all cars, with the engine off, pull or unscrew the dipstick and check the level. If the engine is warm, the level should be between the "Hot" and "Cold" marks on the dipstick; on Fords, the level should be between the "Cold Full" and "Hot Full" marks. If the engine is cold, the fluid should be between the "Add" and "Cold" marks; this does not apply to Ford products.

3. If the level is low, add power steering fluid until correct. Be careful not to overfill, which will cause fluid loss and seal damage.

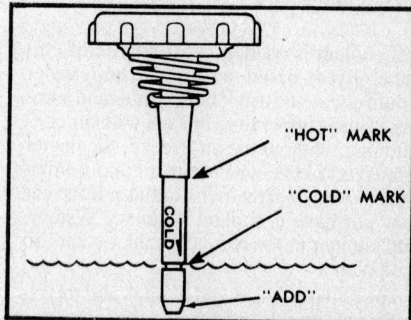

Power steering dipstick markings, typical of all types except Ford

Windshield Washer Fluid

Check the fluid level in the windshield washer tank at every oil level check. The fluid can be mixed in a 50% solution with water, if desired, as long as temperatures remain above freezing. Below freezing, the fluid should be used full strength. Never add engine coolant antifreeze to the washer fluid, because it will damage the car's paint.

UNDER CAR

Axle

The fluid level in the drive axle should be checked every 12 months or 12,000 miles. On the front wheel drive Omni, Horizon,

Aries and Reliant with automatic transmission, the drive axle lubricant is separate from the automatic fluid and must be checked separately. The level can be checked through the fill plug in the drive axle housing.

On the American Motors Eagle, SX/4 and Kammback, both drive axles should be checked. Both assemblies have fill plugs for this purpose.

1. With the car parked on a level surface, remove the filler plug. The plug can be found either in the rear cover of the differential, or on the front of the pinion housing.

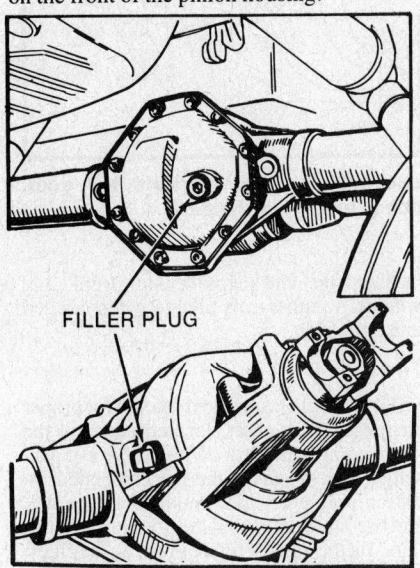

FILLER PLUG

Rear axle filler plug locations

2. If lubricant dribbles out when the plug is removed, the level is correct. Otherwise, stick in your finger (watch out for sharp threads); the fluid should be even with or just a little below the filler hole.

3. If lubricant is needed, use SAE 80W-90 GL-5 gear oil (SAE 80W GL-5 in very cold climates) to fill standard axles. Limited slip axles require a special lubricant, available in auto parts stores. The Omni, Horizon, Aries, Reliant drive axles should be filled with DEXRON® II ATF fluid.

4. When the level is correct, install the plug and tighten until snug. Do not overtighten.

Drive axles should be drained and refilled according to the manufacturer's maintenance schedule, usually found in the owner's manual. If the unit is used in severe driving conditions (trailer towing, etc.) the lubricant should be changed more often. Some later model drive axles do not require regular draining and refilling. Refer to the owner's manual for information on this subject. The axle may be drained by removing the drain plug at the bottom of the axle housing, if present. Otherwise the rear cover (if equipped) must be removed or a suction gun used through the filler hole. Always use silicone sealer or a gasket when re-installing the rear cover. Run sealer around the insides of the bolt holes. Tighten the bolts a few turns at a time in a crisscross pattern.

Exhaust System

The exhaust system should be checked twice a year for general soundness. Inspect

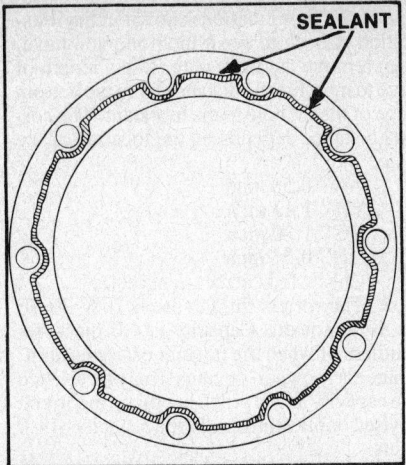

SEALANT

Apply a bead of silicone sealer to the rear cover if no gasket is used

the pipes for holes, broken welds, leaking seams, or loose connections. Leaks at connections can sometimes be successfully repaired with the use of a commercial exhaust pipe sealer, but holes or breaks warrant replacement of the part. The exhaust pipe hangers and straps should be examined for any breaks or cracks; replace these as necessary. Some slight cracking of rubber hangers is normal, but deep cracks or cuts are cause for replacement.

— CAUTION —
Check the exhaust system only when it is cold. The temperature on an exhaust system using a catalytic converter can reach 1000°F after only a short period of engine operation.

Manual Transmission, Manual Transaxle

The fluid level in the manual transmission (or transaxle on front wheel drive cars) should be checked twice a year, or every 6000 miles.

1. Park the car on a level surface. The transmission should be cool to the touch.

2. Remove the filler plug from the side of the transmission or transaxle. If lubricant trickles out as the plug is removed, the fluid level is correct. If not, stick in your finger

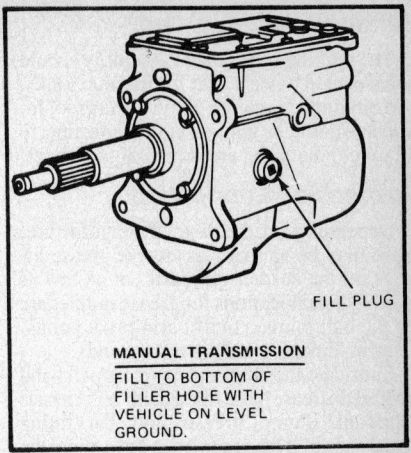

FILL PLUG

MANUAL TRANSMISSION
FILL TO BOTTOM OF FILLER HOLE WITH VEHICLE ON LEVEL GROUND.

Typical manual transmission filler plug location

(watch out for sharp threads); the lubricant should be right up to the edge of the filler hole.

3. If lubricant is needed, use SAE 80W-90 GL-5 gear lubricant (SAE 80W GL-5 in extremely cold climates) in manual transmissions.

Front wheel drive transaxles use different lubricants. The Omni and Horizon with the A412 transaxle (starter on the radiator side of the engine) require GL-4 hypoid gear lubricant; the same SAE viscosities apply (80W-90 or 80W; 75W in temperatures below −30°F). GL-5 classification lubricants are specifically *not* recommended. Omnis and Horizons with the A460 transaxle (starter on the firewall side of the engine), and all Aires and Reliant models use DEXRON® II automatic transmission fluid.

The front wheel drive Citation, Omega, Phoenix, Skylark, Cavalier, J2000, Cimarron, Celebrity, Cierra and A6000 require DEXRON® II automatic transmission fluid. The use of a manual transmission lubricant is specifically *not* recommended.

The Ford Escort, EXP, and Mercury Lynx and LN-7 use Ford Type F automatic transmission fluid. The use of a manual transmission lubricant is specifically *not* recommended.

4. When the level is correct, install the filler plug and tighten until snug.

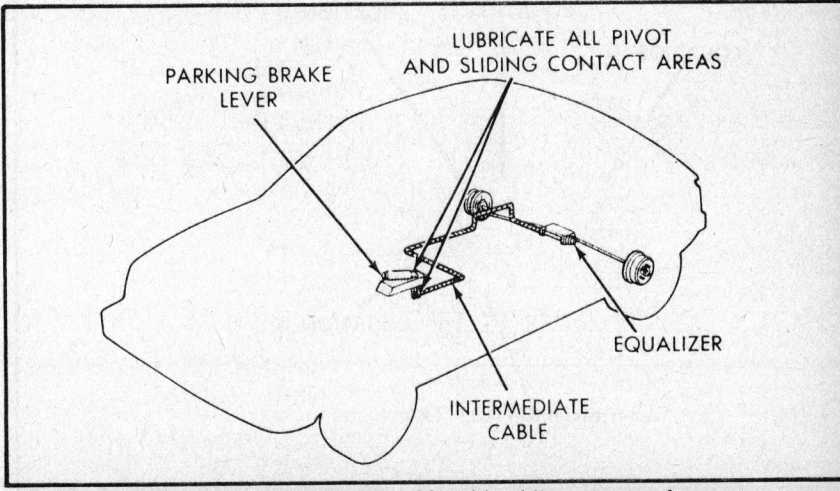

LUBRICATE ALL PIVOT AND SLIDING CONTACT AREAS

PARKING BRAKE LEVER

EQUALIZER

INTERMEDIATE CABLE

Lubricate the parking brake cable with white waterproof grease

GENERAL MAINTENANCE

Parking Brake Linkage

The parking brake cable assembly should be inspected twice a year for fraying, kinks, and binding. A smooth white waterproof lubricant should be applied at the same time to all pivot points and areas in sliding contact.

Suspension Lubrication

Depending on the year of manufacture, there may be as many as twelve grease fittings on the suspension parts, or as few as two. Typical locations for grease nipples are on the ball joints, control arm pivot points, steering linkage, and the tie-rod ends.

Lubricate these fittings with a small hand operated grease gun filled with EP chassis lubricant. Pump grease into the fitting slowly, until it begins to ooze out around the joint, or until the grease begins to expand the rubber boot around the fitting. Be extremely careful not to rupture any seals or boots, as this will lead to lubricant loss and contamination of the parts involved.

Occasionally, the grease nipples may become clogged with dirt or hardened grease. If so, unscrew them with a wrench of the proper size and clean them out with solvent. When reinstalled, they may be covered with plastic caps made for the purpose, or a piece of aluminum foil.

The chassis and suspension parts should be lubricated once a year, or every 7500 miles, whichever comes first.

Transfer Case

If you have a four-wheel drive AMC car, you should check the transfer case lubricant level every 5000 miles.

1. Park the car on a level surface.
2. Check the build date tag on the rear of the transfer case.
3. If the transfer case was built after March 1980, the fill plug will be at location "A" in the illustration. Remove the fill plug. The lubricant should be right up to the edge of the filler hole. Check and correct as necessary.
4. If the transfer case was built before March, 1980, the filler plug may be in any one of the four locations shown in the illustration. Check to see which one you have, then remove the filler plug. Use a length of wire to measure the distance from the bottom edge of the fill hole to the lubricant. The correct distance depends on the location of the hole:

> "A" 0.56 inch
> "B" 1.13 inch
> "C" 1.20 inch
> "D" 0.56 inch
> Check and correct as necessary.

5. The correct fluid to use is 10W-30 SE or SF motor oil. Capacity is 4.0 pints, regardless of when the transfer case was built. Some early owner's manuals may have listed the capacity as 3.0 pints, but this is incorrect; revised publications call for a capacity of 4.0 pints.

The transfer case should be drained and refilled every 15,000 miles. The drain plug is located at the lower edge of the rear face of the case. Installation torque for the plugs is 18 ft. lbs. The case is made from aluminum, so this figure should not be exceeded.

EXTERIOR

Drain Holes and Underbody

Most cars have drain holes spaced along the lower edge of the rocker panels and doors. These holes should be cleared of any debris or rust twice a year. A small screwdriver can be used to open plugged drain holes.

Every spring, the underbody should be flushed with clear water to remove deposits of mud, road salt, and debris. It is advisable to loosen any packed-in sediment before flushing to assure a more thorough cleaning.

Hinges and Locks

Once a year, the door, hood, and trunk hinges, and all locks should be lubricated to ensure smooth operation. The hinge points should be lightly oiled. Lock cylinders may be easily lubricated with a shot of silicone spray directed into the keyhole. Silicone lubricant also works well on the door latch

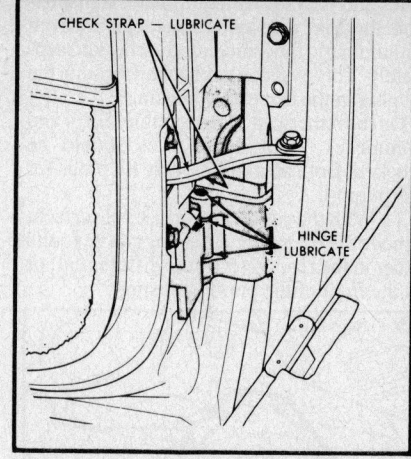

Use engine oil to lubricate the door, hood, and trunk hinges

mechanisms, and keeps the door, trunk, and window weatherseals pliable when applied in a light film.

Tires

Tires should be checked weekly for proper air pressure. A chart, located either in the glove compartment or on the driver's or passenger's door, gives the recommended inflation pressures. Maximum fuel economy and tire life will result if the pressure is maintained at the highest figure given on the chart. Pressures should be checked before driving since pressure can increase as much as six pounds per square inch (psi) due to heat buildup. It is a good idea to have your own accurate pressure gauge, because not all gauges on service station air pumps can be trusted. When checking pressures, do not neglect the spare tire. Note that some spare tires require pressures considerably higher than those used in the other tires.

While you are about the task of checking air pressure, inspect the tire treads for cuts, bruises and other damage. Check the air valves to be sure that they are tight. Replace any missing valve caps.

Check the tires for uneven wear that might indicate the need for front end alignment or tire rotation. Tires should be replaced when a tread wear indicator appears as a solid band across the tread.

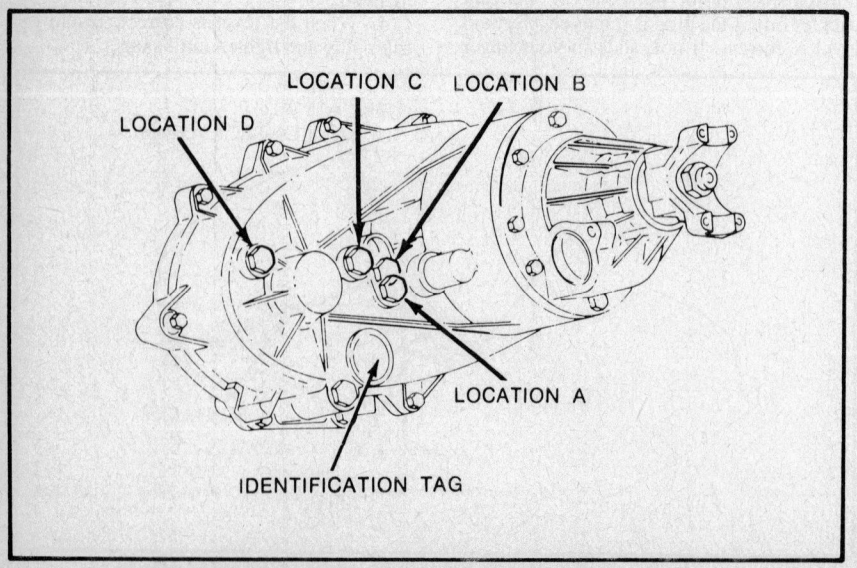

AMC transfer case fill plug locations (© AMC)

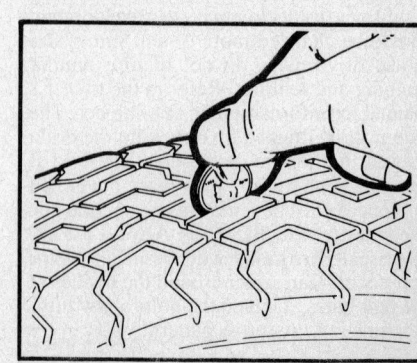

Tire tread depth can be checked with a penny. If the top of Lincoln's head is visible, the tires are due for replacement

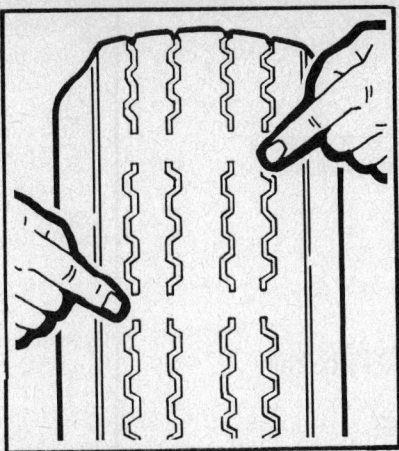

Tread wear indicators will appear as a band across the tire when the tread has worn out.

When buying new tires, give some thought to the following points, especially if you are considering a switch to larger tires or a different profile series:

1. All four tires must be of the same construction type. This rule cannot be violated. Radial, bias, and bias-belted tires must not be mixed.

2. The wheels should be the correct width for the tire. Tire dealers have charts of tire and rim compatibility. A mismatch will cause sloppy handling and rapid tire wear. The tread width should match the rim width (inside bead to inside bead) within an inch. For radial tires, the rim width should be 80% or less of the tire (not tread) width.

3. The height (mounted diameter) of the new tires can change speedometer accuracy, engine speed at a given road speed, fuel mileage, acceleration, and ground clearance. Tire manufacturers furnish full measurement specifications.

4. The spare tire should be usable, at least for short distance and low speed operation, with the new tires.

5. There shouldn't be any body interference when loaded, on bumps, or in turns.

TIRE ROTATION

Tire rotation is recommended every 6000 miles or so, to obtain maximum tire wear. The pattern you use depends on whether or not your car has a usable spare. Radial tires should not be cross-switched (from one side of the car to the other); they last longer if their direction of rotation is not changed. Snow tires sometimes have directional arrows molded into the side of the carcass; the arrow shows the direction of rotation. They will wear very rapidly if the rotation is reversed. Studded tires will lose their studs if their rotational direction is reversed.

NOTE: Mark the wheel position or direction of rotation on radial tires or studded snow tires before removing them.

STORAGE

Store the tires at the proper inflation pressure if they are mounted on wheels. Keep them in a cool dry place, laid on their sides. If the tires are stored in the garage or basement, do not let them stand on a concrete floor; set them on strips of wood.

Windshield Wipers and Washers

For maximum effectiveness and longest element life, the windshield and wiper blades should be kept clean. Dirt, tree sap, road tar and so on will cause streaking, smearing and blade deterioration if left on the glass. It is advisable to wash the windshield carefully with a commercial glass cleaner at least once a month. Wipe off the rubber blades with the wet rag afterwards. For access to the blades on wiper systems which park below the hood line, turn the ignition key to "On" and run the wipers to the center of the windshield. Shut the wipers off with the ignition key, not the wiper switch. Do not attempt to move the wipers by hand; damage to the motor and drive mechanism will result.

If the blades are found to be cracked, broken or torn, they should be replaced immediately. Replacement intervals will vary with usage, although ozone deterioration usually limits blade life to about one year. If the wiper pattern is smeared or streaked, or if the blade chatters across the glass, the elements should be replaced. It is easiest and most sensible to replace the elements in pairs.

There are basically three different types of refills, which differ in their method of replacement. One type has two release buttons, approximately one-third of the way up from the ends of the blade frame. Pushing the buttons down releases a lock and allows the rubber filler to be removed from the frame. The new filler slides back into the frame and locks in place.

The second type of refill has two metal tabs which are unlocked by squeezing them together. The rubber filler can then be withdrawn from the frame jaws. A new refill is installed by inserting the refill into the front frame jaws and sliding it rearward to engage the remaining frame jaws. There are usually four jaws; be certain when installing that the

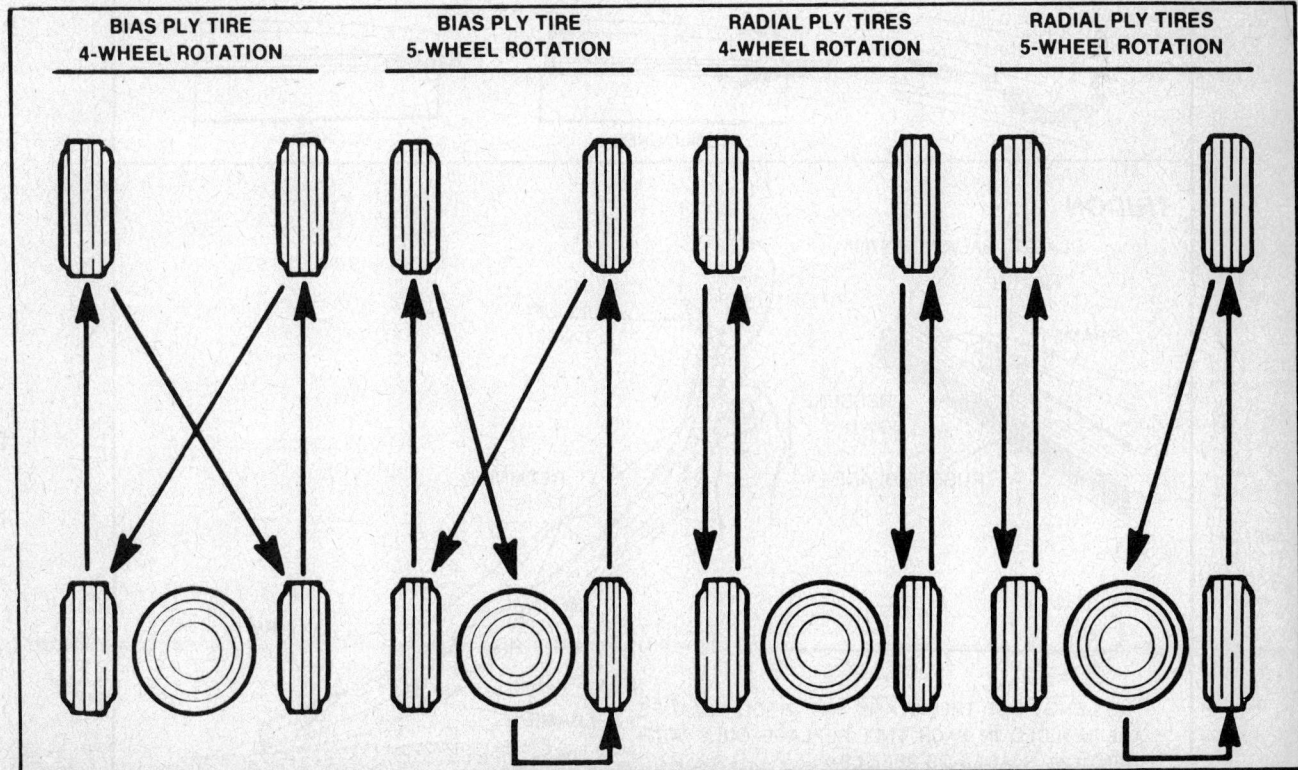

| BIAS PLY TIRE 4-WHEEL ROTATION | BIAS PLY TIRE 5-WHEEL ROTATION | RADIAL PLY TIRES 4-WHEEL ROTATION | RADIAL PLY TIRES 5-WHEEL ROTATION |

Tire rotation diagrams

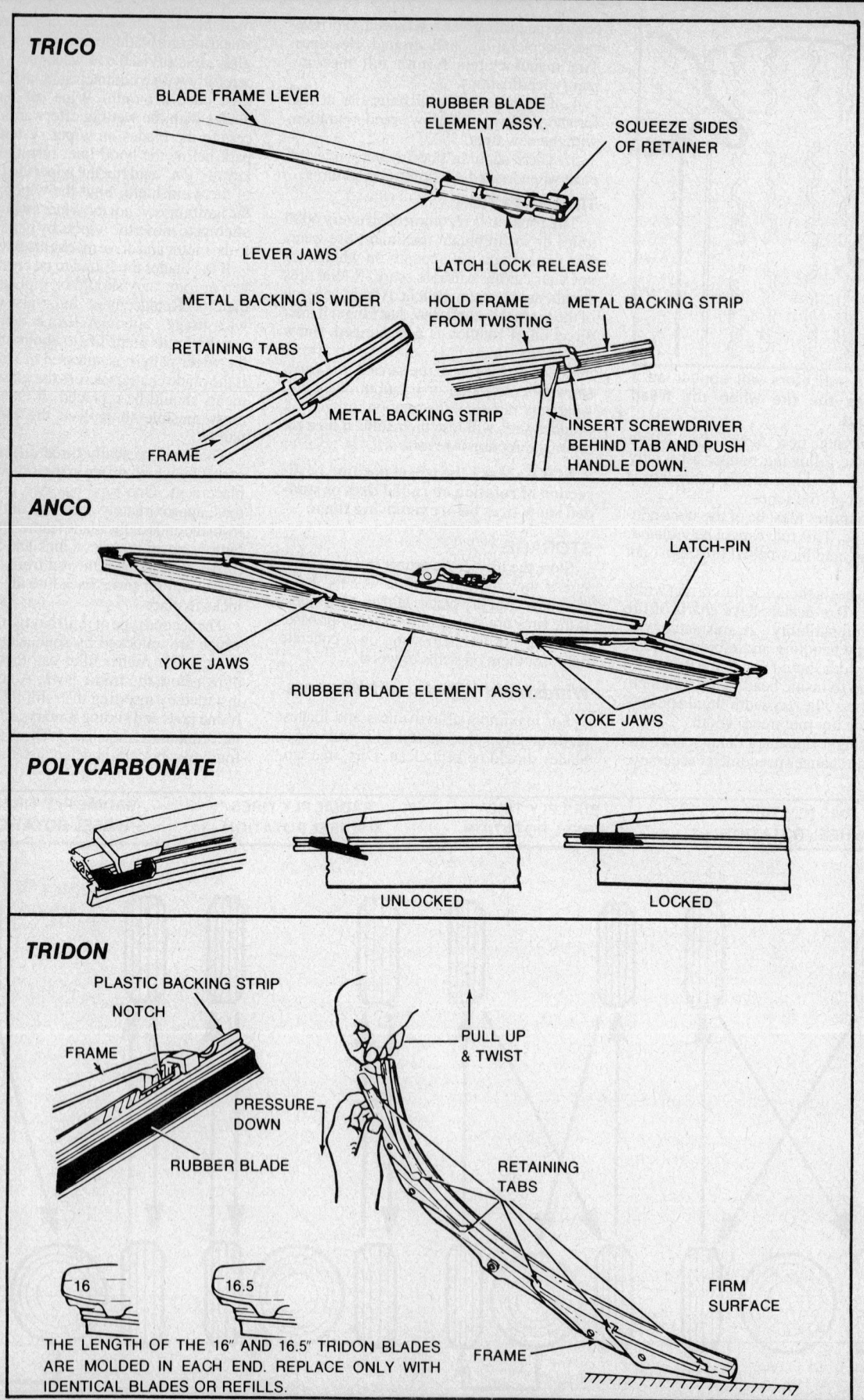

TRICO

BLADE FRAME LEVER

RUBBER BLADE ELEMENT ASSY.

SQUEEZE SIDES OF RETAINER

LEVER JAWS

LATCH LOCK RELEASE

METAL BACKING IS WIDER

RETAINING TABS

FRAME

METAL BACKING STRIP

HOLD FRAME FROM TWISTING

METAL BACKING STRIP

INSERT SCREWDRIVER BEHIND TAB AND PUSH HANDLE DOWN.

ANCO

LATCH-PIN

YOKE JAWS

RUBBER BLADE ELEMENT ASSY.

YOKE JAWS

POLYCARBONATE

UNLOCKED

LOCKED

TRIDON

PLASTIC BACKING STRIP

NOTCH

FRAME

PRESSURE DOWN

RUBBER BLADE

PULL UP & TWIST

RETAINING TABS

FIRM SURFACE

FRAME

16

16.5

THE LENGTH OF THE 16" AND 16.5" TRIDON BLADES ARE MOLDED IN EACH END. REPLACE ONLY WITH IDENTICAL BLADES OR REFILLS.

Windshield wiper blade replacement methods

refill is engaged in all of them. At the end of its travel, the tabs will lock into place on the front jaws of the wiper blade frame.

The third type is a refill made from polycarbonate. The refill has a simple locking device at one end which flexes downward out of the groove into which the jaws of the holder fit, allowing easy release. By sliding the new refill through all the jaws and pushing through the slight resistance when it reaches the end of its travel, the refill will lock into position.

Regardless of the type of refill used, make sure that all of the frame jaws are engaged as the refill is pushed into place and locked. The metal blade holder and frame will scratch the glass if allowed to touch it.

Washer Nozzle Adjustment
CENTERED SINGLE POST—NON-ADJUSTABLE NOZZLES

This type is usually located on the rear center of the hood panel, directly in front of the windshield. By loosening the body retaining nut from under the hood, the nozzle body can be turned to provide the best spray discharge to cover the windshield. Tighten the retaining nut while holding the nozzle body in position.

CENTERED SINGLE POST—ADJUSTABLE NOZZLES

This nozzle is adjusted with a wrench, screwdriver, or pliers. If the nozzle has no gripping area, the adjustment is made by inserting a stiff wire into the nozzle opening and moving the nozzle in the direction desired. When using the wire as an adjuster tool, do not force the nozzle; the wire can be broken within the nozzle opening.

INDIVIDUAL NOZZLES

A tab is usually fastened to the nozzle stem to assist in turning the nozzle in the desired direction. If a tab is not present, use a pair of pliers to gently move the nozzle.

WIPER ARM NOZZLES

No adjustment is necessary on this type of nozzle, because the opening is centered on the wiper arm and moves along with the arm.

TOOLS AND EQUIPMENT

The service procedures in this book presuppose a familiarity with hand tools and their proper use. However, it is possible that you may have a limited amount of experience with the sort of equipment needed to work on an automobile. This section is designed to help you assemble a basic set of tools that will handle the majority of jobs you may undertake.

In addition to the normal assortment of screwdrivers and pliers, automotive service work requires an investment in wrenches, sockets and the handles needed to drive them, and various measuring tools such as torque wrenches and feeler gauges.

The best approach to gathering the required equipment is to proceed slowly, buying high-quality tools as they are needed. An initial investment should be made in a set of quality wrenches, ranging in size from 1/4 inch to one inch, if your car has standard bolts, or from 5 mm to 19 mm if your car has metric fasteners. High quality forged wrenches are available in three styles: open end, box end, and combination open/box end. The combination tools are generally the most desirable as a starter set; the wrenches shown in the illustration are of the combination type.

NOTE: Many later model American cars use both metric and standard nuts and bolts.

The other set of tools inevitably required is a ratchet handle and socket set. This set should have the same size range as your wrench set. The ratchet, extension, and flex drives for the sockets are available in many sizes; it is advisable to choose a 3/8 inch drive set initially. One break in the inch/metric sizing war is that metric-sized sockets sold in the U.S. have inch-sized drive (1/4, 3/8, 1/2, etc.). Sockets are available in six and twelve point versions: six point types are generally cheaper and are a good choice for a first set. The choice of a drive handle for the sockets should be made with some care. If this is your first set, take the plunge and invest in a flex-head ratchet; it will get into many places otherwise accessible only through a long chain of universal joints, extensions and adapters. An alternative is a flex handle; such a tool is shown in the illustration, below the ratchet handle. In addition to the range of sockets mentioned, a rubber-lined spark plug socket should be purchased. Spark plugs have either a 13/16 or a 5/8 inch hex; get the correct socket for the plugs in your car.

The most important thing to consider when purchasing hand tools is quality. Don't be misled by the low cost of "bargain" tools. Forged wrenches, tempered screwdriver blades, and fine tooth ratchets are a much better investment than their less expensive counterparts. The skinned knuckles and frustration inflicted by poor quality tools make any job an unhappy chore. Another consideration is that quality tools sold by reputable firms come with an on-the-spot replacement guarantee—if the tool breaks, you get a new one, no questions asked.

The tools needed for basic maintenance jobs, in addition to those just mentioned, include:

1. Jackstands, for support;
2. Oil filter wrench;
3. Oil filler spout or funnel;
4. Grease gun;
5. Battery hydrometer;
6. Battery post and clamp cleaner;
7. Container for draining oil
8. Many rags for the inevitable spills.

In addition to these items there are several others which are not absolutely necessary, but handy to have around. These include a transmission funnel and filler tube, a drop (trouble) light on a long cord, an adjustable wrench (crescent wrench), and slip joint pliers.

A more extensive list of tools, suitable for tune-up work, can be drawn up easily. While the tools involved are slightly more sophisticated, they need not be outrageously expensive. For example, there are several inexpensive tach/dwell meters on the market that are every bit as good for the average mechanic as a $100.00 professional model. The key to these purchases is to make them with an eye towards adaptability and wide range. Using the tach/dwell meter example again, if the model you buy runs up to at least 1,500 rpm on the tachometer scale, the dwell meter works on 4, 6, or 8 cylinder engines, and the tachometer unit is adaptable to both conventional and electronic ignitions, it will serve for a long time on a variety of automobiles. A basic list of tune-up tools could include:

1. A tach/dwell meter;
2. Spark plug gauge and gapping tool;
3. Feeler blades;
4. Timing light.

In this list, the choice of a timing light should be made carefully. A light which works on the DC current supplied by the car battery is the best choice; it should have a xenon tube for brightness. If your car has electronic ignition, the light should have an inductive pick-up (the timing light illustrated has one of these), and since nearly all cars will have electronic ignition in the future, this feature is a reasonable one to look for.

In addition to these basic tools, there are several other tools and gauges you may find useful. These include:

1. A compression gauge. The screw-in type is slower to use, but eliminates the possibility of a faulty reading due to escaping pressure.
2. A manifold vacuum gauge.
3. A test light.
4. An induction meter. This is used to determine whether or not there is current flowing in a wire, and thus is extremely helpful in electrical troubleshooting.

Finally, you will probably find a torque wrench necessary for all but the most basic of work. The beam type models are perfectly adequate, although the newer click (breakaway) type are more precise. Whichever type you choose, plan on having it recalibrated every once in a while.

SPECIAL TOOLS

Several procedures in this manual refer to special tools needed to make repairs or adjustments. These tools can be purchased from the following companies:

AMC, GM	Special Tool Division Kent-Moore Corp. 1501 South Jackson St. Jackson, MI 49203
Ford	Owatonna Tool Co. Owatonna, MN 55060
Chrysler	Miller Special Tools A Division of Utica Tool Co. 32615 Park Lane Garden City, MI 48135

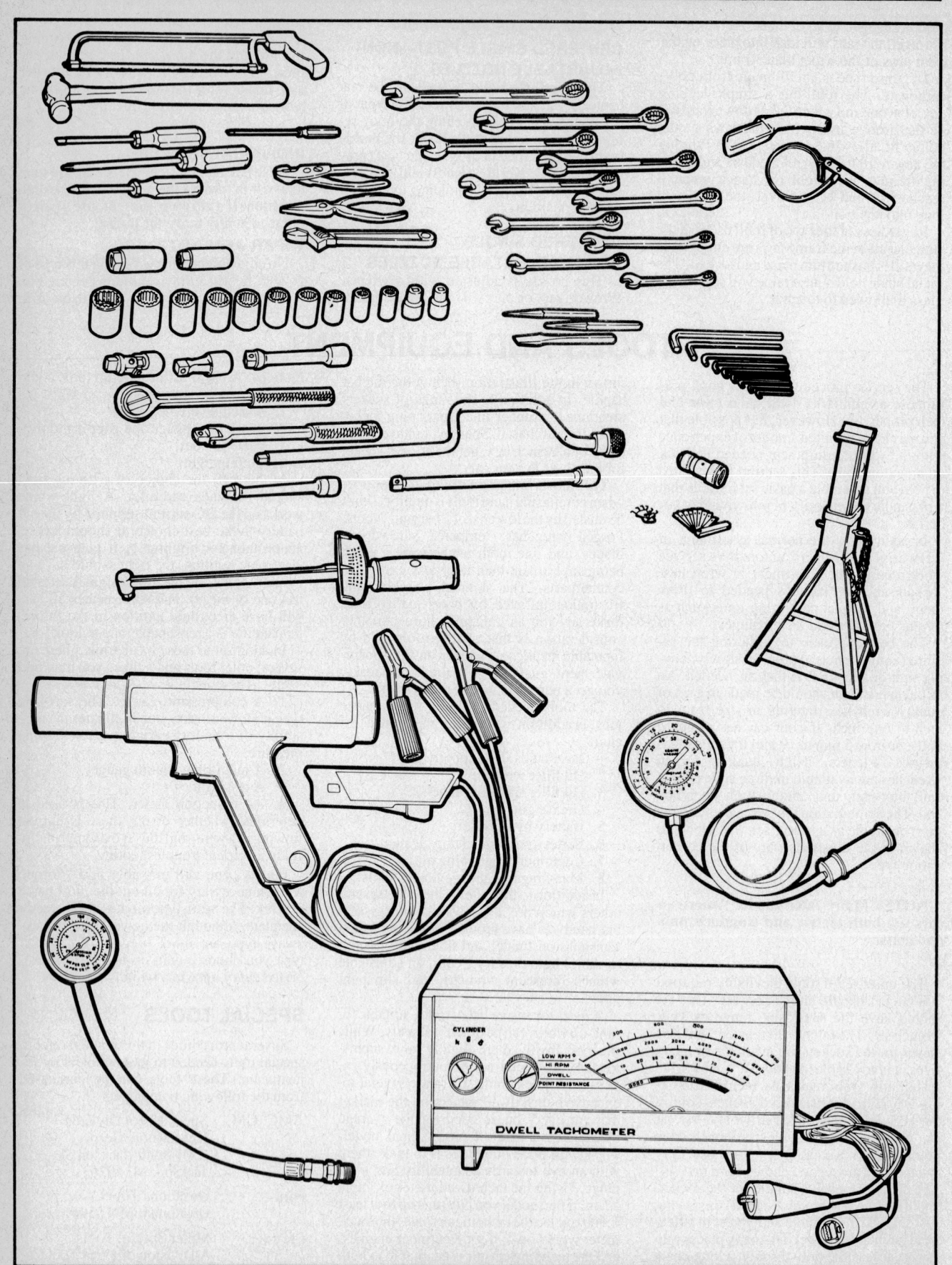

A basic tool collection will handle almost any automotive repair work

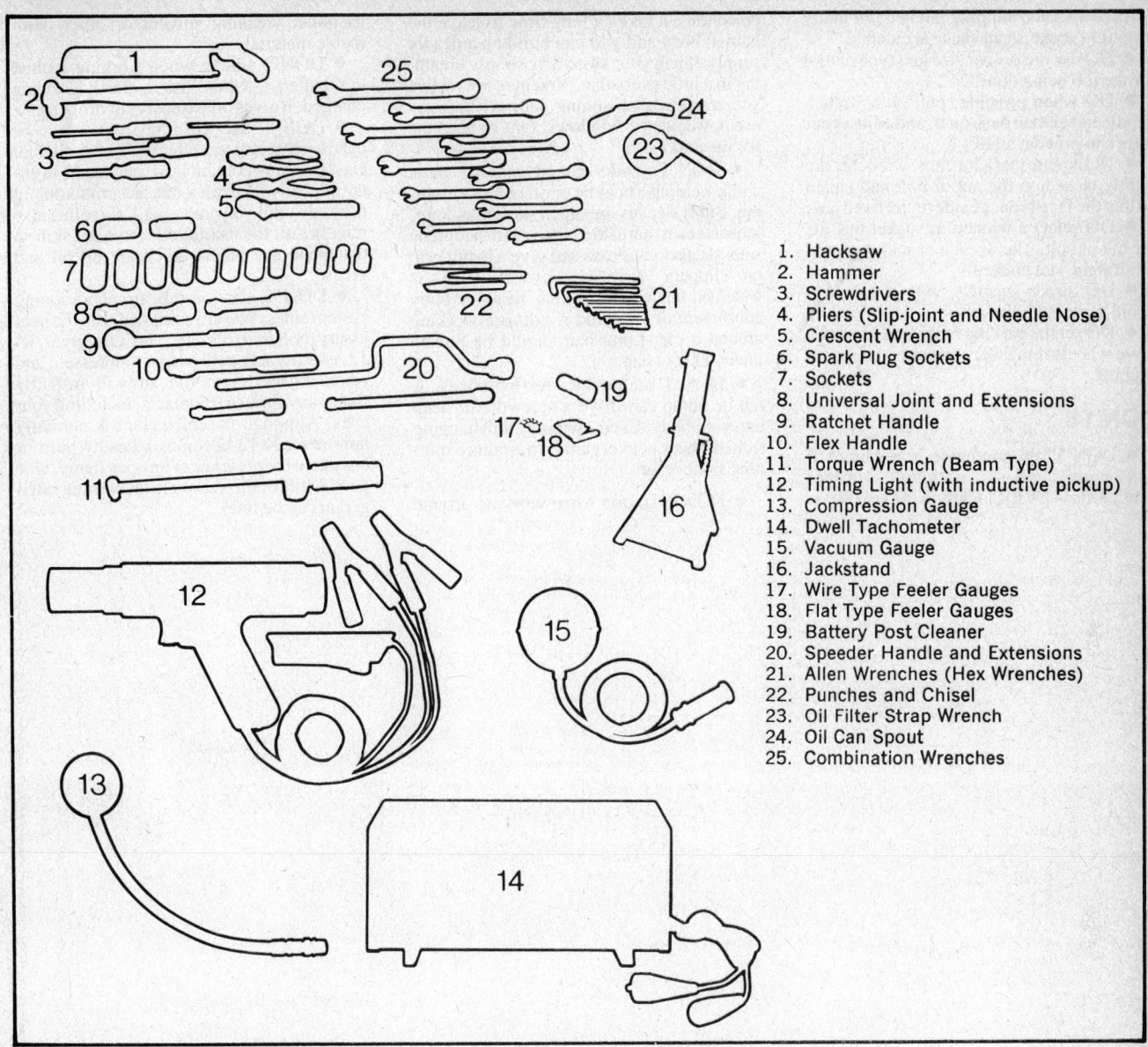

1. Hacksaw
2. Hammer
3. Screwdrivers
4. Pliers (Slip-joint and Needle Nose)
5. Crescent Wrench
6. Spark Plug Sockets
7. Sockets
8. Universal Joint and Extensions
9. Ratchet Handle
10. Flex Handle
11. Torque Wrench (Beam Type)
12. Timing Light (with inductive pickup)
13. Compression Gauge
14. Dwell Tachometer
15. Vacuum Gauge
16. Jackstand
17. Wire Type Feeler Gauges
18. Flat Type Feeler Gauges
19. Battery Post Cleaner
20. Speeder Handle and Extensions
21. Allen Wrenches (Hex Wrenches)
22. Punches and Chisel
23. Oil Filter Strap Wrench
24. Oil Can Spout
25. Combination Wrenches

SERVICING YOUR CAR SAFELY

It is virtually impossible to anticipate all of the hazards involved with automotive maintenance and service, but care and common sense will prevent most accidents.

The rules of safety for mechanics range from "don't smoke around gasoline," to "use the proper tool for the job." The trick to avoiding injuries is to develop safe work habits and take every possible precaution.

DO'S

● DO keep a fire extinguisher and first aid kit within easy reach.

● DO wear safety glasses or goggles when cutting, drilling, grinding or prying, even if you have 20-20 vision. If you wear glasses for the sake of vision, they should be made of hardened glass that can serve also as safety glasses, or wear safety goggles over your regular glasses.

● DO shield your eyes whenever you work around the battery. Batteries contain sulphuric acid. In case of contact with the eyes or skin, flush the area with water or a mixture of water and baking soda and get medical attention immediately.

● DO use safety stands for any undercar service. Jacks are for raising vehicles; safety stands are for making sure the vehicle stays raised until you want it to come down. Whenever the car is raised, block the wheels remaining on the ground and set the parking brake.

● DO use adequate ventilation when working with any chemicals or hazardous materials. Follow the manufacturer's directions for usage. Brake fluid, anti-freeze, sol-vents, paints, etc. are all deadly poisons if taken internally. Seal the containers tightly after use and store them safely, out of the reach of children.

● DO use caution when working on clutches or brakes. The asbestos used in the friction material will cause lung cancer if inhaled. Wipe the component with a damp rag to remove dust, and dispose of the rag after use.

● DO disconnect the negative battery cable when working on the electrical system. The secondary ignition system can contain up to 40,000 volts.

● DO properly maintain your tools. Loose hammberheads, mushroomed punches and chisels, frayed or poorly grounded electrical cords, excessively worn screwdrivers, spread open-end wrenches, cracked sockets, slipping ratchets, or faulty droplight sockets can cause accidents.

- DO use the proper size and type of tool for the job being done.
- DO when possible, pull on a wrench handle rather than push on it, and adjust your stance to prevent a fall.
- DO be sure that adjustable wrenches are tightly closed on the nut or bolt and pulled so that the face is on the side of the fixed jaw.
- DO select a wrench or socket that fits the nut or bolt. The wrench or socket should sit straight, not cocked.
- DO strike squarely with a hammer; avoid glancing blows.
- DO set the parking brake and block the drive wheels if the work requires the engine running.

DON'TS

- DON'T run an engine in a garage or anywhere else without proper ventilation—EVER! Carbon monoxide is poisonous; it takes a long time to leave the human body and you can build up a deadly supply of it in your system by simply breathing in a little every day. You may not realize you are slowly poisoning yourself. Always use power vents, windows, fans or open the garage doors.
- DON'T work around moving parts while wearing a necktie or other loose clothing. Short sleeves are much safer than long, loose sleeves; hard-toed shoes with neoprene soles protect your toes and give a better grip on slippery surfaces. Jewelry such as watches, fancy belt buckles, beads or body adornment of any kind is not safe working around a car. Long hair should be hidden under a hat or cap.
- DON'T use pockets for toolboxes. A fall or bump can drive a screwdriver deep into your body. Even a wiping cloth hanging from the back pocket can wrap around a spinning shaft or fan.
- DON'T smoke when working around gasoline, cleaning solvent or other flammable material.
- DON'T smoke when working around the battery. When the battery is being charged, it gives off explosive hydrogen gas.
- DON'T use gasoline to wash your hands; there are excellent soaps available. Gasoline may contain lead, and lead can enter the body through a cut, accumulating in the body until you are very ill. Gasoline also removes all the natural oils from the skin so that bone dry hands will suck up oil and grease.
- DON'T service the air conditioning system unless you are equipped with the necessary tools and training. The refrigerant, R-12, is extremely cold when compressed, and when released into the air will instantly freeze any surface it contacts, including your eyes. Although the refrigerant is normally non-toxic, R-12 becomes a deadly poisonous gas in the presence of an open flame. One good whiff of the vapors from burning refrigerant can be fatal.